THE EDITORS

Keith Johnson, F.R.A.H.S., F.S.A.G. has been a Councillor of the Society of Australian Genealogists since 1970, was President between 1978-1985, and Vice President in 1975-77 and 1985-1986. He has been Vice President, 1988-1991 of the Royal Australian Historical Society and was a Councillor between 1975-1985.

Malcolm Sainty, F.S.A.G. has been a Councillor of the Society of Australian Genealogists since 1970 and was Vice President between 1973-1976. He has been President of the Australasian Federation of Family History Organizations (AFFHO) since 1990.

Messrs Johnson and Sainty recognise that many genealogists require to undertake investigations internationally as well as within the regions where particular families originated. They have for many years encouraged the widest dissemination of research data and reference material for family historians. They are Directors of the Library of Australian History, Publishers of North Sydney, Australia, which has published over 80 titles of a local and family history nature since 1977. They are Executive Committee members of the Australian Biographical and Genealogical Record and in an honorary capacity have supervised the A.B.G.R. publishing programme since its inception in 1982. This Project has to date published nine volumes, with two more in preparation.

Published works which they have jointly compiled and edited include – *Genealogical Research Directories* (1981-1990). *Index of Births, Deaths and Marriages, Sydney Morning Herald 1831-1853* (1969-1975), *Gravestone Inscriptions – Sydney Burial Ground* (1973), *Census of New South Wales – November 1828* (1980 & 1985). Mr Johnson was co-editor with Richard Reid of *The Irish Australians: Selected Articles for Australian and Irish Family Historians* (1984). He has contributed biographies to the *Australian Dictionary of Biography*.

Genealogical Research Directory

National & International

Keith A. Johnson & Malcolm R. Sainty

1991

PUBLISHED BY (THE EDITORS OF THE)
GENEALOGICAL RESEARCH DIRECTORY

Typeset by Photoset Computer Service, Sydney, NSW. 2000
Printed by The Book Printer, Melbourne.
Published 1991
ISBN 0 908120 79 6

REPRESENTATIVES:

AUSTRALIA:
K.A. Johnson,
17 Mitchell Street (P.O. Box 795),
NORTH SYDNEY, NSW. 2060.

BELGIUM:
Dr Luc Vander Avort,
XII Apostelenstraat 12,
B-2800 MECHELEN.

BRITAIN:
Mrs Elizabeth Simpson,
2 Stella Grove,
TOLLERTON, NTT NG12 4EY. ENG.

CANADA:
Mrs J. Tyson,
94 Binswood Ave.,
TORONTO, ONT. M4C 3N9.

FRANCE:
M. Xavier Guyot,
21 rue Notre Dame de Recouvrance,
F-45006 ORLEANS.

GERMANY & GERMAN LANGUAGE:
Friedrich R. Wollmershäuser,
Herrengasse 8-10,
D-7938 OBERDISCHINGEN BRD.

IRELAND:
Paul Gorry,
16 Hume St, St. Stephen's Green,
DUBLIN 2.

NETHERLANDS:
Ms H.J. Witte,
Spaakstede 35-06,
NL-4421 ES KAPELLE (ZLD).

NEW ZEALAND:
Mrs A. Lewis,
76A Washington Ave.,
BROOKLYN, Wellington.

SCANDINAVIA:
Sveriges Slaktforskatforbund,
Box 15222,
S-161 15 BROMMA, Sweden.

SOUTH AND CENTRAL AFRICA:
Mr J. Goldsmith,
P.O. Box 5155,
WALMER, Pt. Elizabeth 6065 RSA.

U.S.A.:
Mrs Jan Jennings,
3324 Crail Way,
GLENDALE, CA 91206.

CONTENTS

TABLE DES MATIERES

INHALT

FEATURES OF THE GRD

PUBLICATION:

The **Genealogical Research Directory** is published between mid April and early May each year. The closing date for entries for the following year is 31 October to 15 December depending on local circumstances, each year.

DISTRIBUTION

The **Directories** are released in several countries simultaneously and copies posted surface mail to nearby countries. All contributors should receive their copy by the end of May.

A paperback copy of the **Directory** in which a contributor's entries appear, is sent automatically to the contributor free of charge (except for postage). Contributors may also pay an additional fee to receive a fully hardbound copy. Additional copies both paperback and hardbound are available for purchase by individuals, organizations and libraries from our agents listed on page 4.

ENTRY FORMS

Forms may be obtained from any of our agents. They are available in English, French, German, Dutch & Swedish from the relevant agents. Forms are normally available from July each year for the following year's **Directory**. Many genealogical societies distribute the forms from August to October and the Agents post forms to all contributors recorded in past **Directories**.

It is recommended that if you require an entry form and have not received one through the above methods by mid October, you should request one from your nearest Agent as listed on page 4.

SOCIETY LISTING:

Genealogical Societies and Historical Societies with Genealogy Groups, may be listed FREE of charge in the Society section of the **Directory**. See the first page of that section for further particulars.

CALENDAR OF GENEALOGICAL EVENTS

This section of the **Directory** (pages 26 & 27) is a list of major events of Provincial, National or International importance. Please advise the Editors via our Agents of any such events planned for the future.

RESEARCH ARTICLES

Each edition of the **Directory** in recent years has contained a concise article of International research interest. A modest payment is made for writing a published article and the Editors invite competent people to submit appropriate articles.

DISPLAY NOTICES

Private researchers, professional genealogists and persons offering goods and services associated with genealogy may lodge display advertisements with our agents who will advise the cost.

IMPROVE THE NEXT DIRECTORY

The Editors welcome suggestions from contributors and readers as to how the **Directory** or the entry forms may be improved in future. A number of people have made suggestions, some of these are discussed in the Introduction.

NEW FEATURES IN THIS DIRECTORY

1. A ONE NAME SOCIETY section has been enlarged. See that section.
2. Improved SUBJECT ENTRIES. See that section for details.
3. New GEOGRAPHIC division in the main Surname listing.

INTRODUCTION

The 1991 GRD marks the eleventh year of publication during which period the **Directory** has become the largest surname queries listing in the World. For several years, each edition has contained over 100,000 references, all newly submitted by the contributors. It has been said that the **Directory** has become one of the most important and useful genealogical tools ever published.

The Editors have received many letters from contributors advising of their great success in linking their family with that of another person in a different country to the family's country of origin. Others have informed us that they found a distant cousin living nearby, with whom they had not previously made contact.

Again, we have undertaken all the data entry in-house, over 4 million key strokes in the surname listing section alone. It is impossible to meticulously proof read every word but the Editors have proof read every surname, 100,000 of them. The other items in the listing, such as the time period, place, province and country, are sorted on the computer, and the listings are then checked for inconsistencies in spelling, particularly of place names. Judging from the very few instances of errors which contributors draw to our attention, the data entry and proof reading methods used appear to be satisfactory. If an error is reported to us, and we feel that the error rendered the entry useless for the contributor, then we publish the correct information in the following **Directory** at no charge. Less than 20 such problems have been notified to us for each of the last five editions.

The 1991 edition contains a much enlarged SUBJECT ENTRIES section which is explained more fully in the following article **Tips — Does & Don'ts : How to make the most out of the GRD** .

We again record out thanks to our Agents: Amy Lewis (NEW ZEALAND), Jan Jennings (USA), Elizabeth and Philip Simpson (UK), Jeannette Tyson (CANADA), John Goldsmith (AFRICA), Mr A. J. Witte (NETHERLANDS), Friedrich Wollmerhauser (GERMANY), Luc Vander Avort (BELGIUM), Elizabeth Thorsell (SCANDINAVIA), Paul Gorry (IRELAND) and to Margaret Audin of Paris, who continued to assist us. They not only received entry forms and sorted out various problems but assisted with promotion and gave us useful advice which has been greatly appreciated.

Thanks also to those who assisted in the production of the **Directory** . Allison Allen and Jill Weaver, who did the bulk of the data entry; Philip Graham who assisted with computer technical advice, typesetting and who prepared the display advertisements and notices, Colin Chapman for his Chapman Codes; John Pickett and John Spurway for language translation; Ron Scott of British Columbia for supplying material used for this **Directory** . Thanks also to our typesetters and printers listed on page 4.

We gratefully acknowledge the assistance of many genealogical societies which sent out entry forms to their members. As a service to these Societies and to genealogists worldwide we list societies free of charge in a section of this book. Many thanks also to many individuals who helped to promote the **Directory** and to others who offered advice for its improvement.

K. A. Johnson & M. R. Sainty
26 February 1991

IMPORTANT NOTICE – POSTAGE

In the past the Editors have recommended that when writing to a contributor in another country the writer should include International Reply Coupons (I.R.C's.) to cover the cost of their reply postage.

It is now evident that postal authorities worldwide are making an excessive profit on the I.R.C's and we now recommend that they NOT be used.

We believe that a person writing to a contributor in another country, will get a response if the contributor believes there is a family connection. In the event that the contributor does reply, then it is assumed that a continuing two way correspondence may result and that both parties should pay their own postage.

When writing to a contributor in your own country it is suggested that the practice of enclosing a self addressed stamped envelope should be continued.

WRITING INTERNATIONALLY

Some people may be reluctant to write to a contributor in a "New World" country such as America or Australia about a family based in the "Old World". Indeed a person living in Canada may think that a contributor living in New Zealand could not possibly assist with their German ancestry. Not so.

As an example, one of the Editors recently discovered a book privately published in New York by an American in 1935 who had researched his Buckinghamshire, English ancestry, a collateral branch of his family. The American researcher had substantially corrected and enlarged the family pedigree from 1413 to 1650 and disproved a pedigree published in England in 1880. Only 25 copies of the book were published in 1935 yet it contains more accurate and extensive material about that English family than any known extant collection of material in England today.

Remember, it is important when considering writing to a contributor that you do so on the basis of their area of research, and not where the contributor lives.

TIPS – DOES & DON'TS
HOW TO MAKE THE MOST OUT OF THE *GRD*

Understanding the entries:

Page 32 contains a simple explanation of the entries in the main SURNAME listing. The SUBJECT entries are explained on the page preceding the subject entries.

SURNAME (or Family Name):

These have been listed in strict alphabetical order ignoring spaces and punctuation. They all appear in upper case (capital letters). Examples are as follows:

De Lange will not appear with all the other names with the prefix of De but will appear as DE LANGE between DELANEY and DELANNOY. Names with punctuation such as O'Connor will appear as O'CONNOR after OCONNOR followed by OCTERLONIE etc. and not by O'D etc.

One exception to the strict alphabetical listing are names prefixed by Mc and Mac. These have always been a problem to indexers and we have taken the policy to list them in the same sequence although separately. Therefore MACLEOD will be followed by MCLEOD. The computer program which sorts the names reads Mc and Mac as MC although they are printed with their proper prefix. It would appear that the computer sort gives preference in sorting to MAC over MC but when sorting them with other names starting with M it placed the MAC/MC names between MAZ and MEA rather than between MAB and MAD. As this has been noted on the relevant pages, it is a simple matter to locate the MAC/MC entries.

Names with the prefix VAN or VAN DER etc. have been entered according to the way in which they were submitted by the contributor. Different countries and families have different preferences when indexing such names. A name such as VAN DER AVORT may therefore be listed by a Belgium contributor as VAN DER AVORT and will be listed with "V" entries whilst an American may submit the name as AVORT, VAN DER and it will be listed with "A". Some contributors have listed the name in both ways.

Brackets () in surnames are NOT ALLOWED. If the name M(A)CLA(O)UGHL(L)A(O)(I)N were submitted where do you expect the computer should place it. In small name listings this form of expressing alternative names is permissable in that only a few McLaughlan names and variations may be found. But in a major listing such as the **GRD** it would be hopelessly lost. All brackets and the letters within them, have therefore been deleted and in many cases such as Clark(e) the reader should know that when searching the name Clarke one should also look under Clark and Clerk etc. The same applies to slash marks MAYER/MEYER. If a name is to appear under ME then it will have to be listed separately to MA. They are over 20 pages apart in the **GRD** . Additionally, a double entry such as this would be sorted as a separate name and risks being widely separated from the main name intended.

NEW GEOGRAPHIC ORDER

Following several suggestions for improving the readability of the **GRD** we have changed the computer program so that entries for the same Surname are sub listed together according to Country. All the Smith's of Australia should be followed by the Smith's of Canada, Denmark, etc. to USA. We are sure that this has improved the readability of the **GRD**.

If this change proves successful we may be able to further break down the entries into State or Provincial areas within countries.

FIRST NAMES

The practice of placing first names in the **GRD** is discouraged because the Editors feel that it restricts the possibility of the contributor receiving contact from others. If a particular person is recorded, the reader may not be descended from that person nor even be aware that the recorded person was a member of their family and would not bother to write to the contributor.

A clue to a particular missing ancestor is more likely to come from a wider research for the family name rather than a search for a particular person.

We do permit the inclusion of first names for very common surnames because some people are searching for a particular person who has moved from their ancestral village and cannot be located. Also in the case of Scandinavian names, the first name often assists to trace the family. However, in most cases the Editors recommend that only family names be recorded and reserve the right to delete first names unless the family name is a common one or the contributor gives good reason as to why it should be included.

DATES

For consistency of data entry, checking and reading the **Directory** , the Editors insist that only whole years be submitted. 1850-80 is permissable and also the addition of S e.g. 1880S. Other acceptable additions are PRE meaning any time before e.g. PRE 1880; C meaning Circa (approximately) e.g. C1880; and + meaning after e.g. 1880+.

Terms such as 18th cent.; 1700 to date; before; approx.; and "sorry I don't know" are not acceptable.

For people searching a name throughout the past the word ALL may be inserted in the time period. However, contributors should only use this if they are in fact searching every instance of the name throughout recorded history. Otherwise they risk having a poor response to their entry. It is the Editors opinion that only in the case of an unusual name should "ALL" be used or in the case of one name study experts gathering material for a data base. To assist people in this latter category we commenced a new section in the 1990 **Directory** for One Name Studies or single family name associations and further details are given in that section. It is intended that this section will be enlarged in the next edition and details will be included in the entry form.

PLACE NAMES

On the entry form, contributors are asked to record the town or parish, or local area (such as a USA county) followed by a state or province or large district such as a UK county, followed by a country or nation. There are towns, counties and cities with the same or very similar names within a nation and in other nations. In some instances a place name is given but no larger area indicating that the contributor is not sure which town it is. In other cases the town is not given indicating that the contributor either does not know the town in which the family resided or is interested in all branches of the family within the larger geographic area.

The Editors have checked many place names given by contributors because the spelling of the name appeared incorrect or unusual. In thousands of instances the Editors have corrected the place names. In some cases the place name given was not able to be identified by the Editors in place name gazetteers or geographical dictionaries and these have been left as submitted. It is possible that contributors have recorded names of properties or old versions of place names.

It would appear however, that many contributors record place names as they appear on documents such as birth and death certificates and shipping lists without checking gazetteers to determine the correct spelling of the name.

NATIONAL NAMES

Abbreviations used refer basically to historic borders in Europe and to modern borders elsewhere. Thus a person searching for their German ancestors from Prussia are more likely to find them recorded in pre 1918 records under the German Empire geographic name rather than under the present name of the district in Poland or the Soviet Union. Likewise the pre 1974 county borders of the United Kingdom have been used as the old records refer only to them.

Because the **GRD** is used by many people from different countries we have listed places in the UK according to the different countries in the UK: England, Scotland, Ireland, Wales, Channel Islands and Isle of Man. Because the UK county names are coded, it assists the reader to identify the county more readily if the above are recorded also. e.g. LAN, UK could well be taken for Lanarkshire in Scotland by many readers rather then Lancashire in England even though the list of abbreviations will reveal that the correct abbreviation for Lanarkshire is LKS. Conversely, a place formerly in the colony of Virginia would be recorded in its present day state which could be Kentucky, USA.

A full list of abbreviations used in this **Directory** are printed on pp.28-31 and maps showing regions within several countries are at the end of the **Directory**.

REFERENCE NUMBER

The number in bold type in square brackets represents the END of the reference and refers the reader to the address of the contributor of that entry. These are listed between the black lines following the SUBJECT section.

OTHER WORDS, PHRASES AND SIGNS

We regret that due to the nature of the layout, data entry and checking of the **GRD** the main surname or family name section of the **Directory** cannot contain other words and symbols such as "born on". Contributors wishing to personalise an entry should place it in the I: category of the SUBJECT entry section of the **Directory** as detailed in that section.

CONTACTING CONTRIBUTORS

The letter to the Editors read "...I was so excited to find the name Bloggs in the 1989 GRD, I got the contributors name from telephone directory assistance and phoned them right away ... I was so disappointed to be told that they had not contributed the name Bloggs... could you please tell me who did."

It was the THIRD almost identical letter received within a few weeks of publication, each dealing with a different surname. With alarm we searched through the original entry forms to see why we had made such serious mistakes. In every case the forms revealed that the contributor had indeed recorded the name they had denied submitting. The letter writers had contacted the correct persons, they confirmed their addresses. Are our contributors so forgetful of their ancestors or were they caught under the shower and didn't want to talk about it right then. We suspect the latter is the case. Lesson number 1, DON'T make your initial contact with a contributor by telephone — write first.

We have received a number of complaints from people who have received letters from users who have written asking about families from time periods and places which have no relevance to the entry placed by the contributor. The writers complain that often such letters contain no return postage.

The Editors must admit that they file such letters, unless there is a very good explanation as to why the person is writing about an entry not recorded. A reader may have reasons to write to a contributor not because of the surname they submitted but because they were researching in a particular place and hoped that they may be able to assist with a local contact name. In such cases ensure that return postage has been included or offer reimbursement.

If a contributor records that they are searching a particular name in the time period: 1750-1780 it should not be assumed that they have an interest in that name AFTER that time period. It is likely that they have discovered the name as that of a female ancestor's maiden name and will only be interested in that name in the time period recorded and not even earlier because they may not be interested in following female lines further back, other than recording her parents or know that the family were only temporarily of the particular place.

Likewise it is important to write to a contributor only if you feel that your query has some relevance to the place recorded. It is important to note that the place recorded is the main or central place of interest and it is quite proper to write to the contributor if the place in which you are interested is close to that recorded in the **GRD**. It is important therefore to consult maps to ascertain just how close the places are to each other.

It is acceptable that you write to a person who has recorded a particular place, about your own research in a far distant place provided you explain that you feel there may be some connection because of particular circumstances.

It is also acceptable to write to a contributor about a name which is slightly different from that which you are searching, e.g. Editor — Sainty has written to a person researching the name Sanctuary and asked that he keep an eye out for any references to the name Sankey which he is researching because the two names have been known to appear in the same parishes in central Norfolk, England and on occasions have been intermixed by the clerks misuse of one name for the other in church records. Although not related, the Sanctuary researcher was able to provide details of a baptism which confirmed Sankey/Sainty relationships and linked research back from 1740 to 1540. However it is important to establish such contact with other contributors on the basis that there is some probability that you can assist one another. As **GRD** Editors we are more than a little concerned at the number of contributors who record names such as Jones or Wilson with no town recorded and often no county, province or state and a wide time period. Some people must like receiving letters. We would not write to the contributor of such a vague entry.

DON'T write to a contributor because you are interested in the surname of the contributor. We have received many letters over the years "... please list the contributors in alphabetical order as well as numerical because it will save me reading through all of them to find a name I am interested in..." The Editors would like to shoot such people only we appreciate their custom !!

If a contributor wishes to be written to about their own surname, they will record it in the main queries listing. There are many reasons a person is not interested in tracing their own surname not the least of which is the fact that most women acquire their husband's surname and have only secondary interest in his ancestry, not even for the sake of children in some instances as they may be fathered by a previous husband. A man may not be tracing his own surname because his father may have been adopted by foster parents whose name he was given. So please do not write to contributors because you have found a name in the Contributors list. The Editors will NOT ever publish the list in alphabetical order.

DON'T send money to people who write to you stating that they have a considerable amount of material on the name Bloggs and will give you a copy of it all for "X" payment, sight unseen. By all means pay for photocopies sent to you by a contact you make, after you have established that they can indeed supply you with material of interest. We are not suggesting that you ask or expect to pay for photocopies of every item exchanged. However, if a person offers you a large quantity of material, which you have established is of interest to you, we suggest you offer to pay for the copying.

POSTAGE

It is strongly suggested that when a reader writes for the first time to a contributor you enclose a self addressed stamped envelope within your own country. If writing internationally, refer to our new policy on page 9. After the initial contact both parties should pay their own postage. Some societies sell foreign postage stamps.

CHANGE OF ADDRESS

We have been asked to introduce a change of address section so that users can note such changes from past **Directories**. Experience has shown that this does not work in that a person consulting an older edition will not look through all later editions to check if the contributor has recorded a change.

We do however encourage contributors to record changes of address with our agents so that our master mail list can be updated and in the event of users enquiring for an up to date address we can advise them, or pass their letter on.

The best way to ensure that you receive follow up mail is to repeat your entries in the latest edition.

SUBJECT ENTRIES

The 1991 **GRD** contains a much improved section of Subject entries. For ease of reading and for consistency, we have developed eight basic categories and prefixed each with the following codes:

G:	General.	O:	Occupations.
I:	Individuals.	P:	Places.
M:	Migration.	R:	Religion.
MY:	Military.	S:	Shipping & Ships.

The Editors have divided the entries submitted into these categories. In future, the entry forms will allow the contributor to nominate the category. For various reasons a contributor may wish to enter "Battle of Waterloo" under P: (for Place) or MY: (for Military) or both.

Not all contributors make a thoughtful attempt to write down their subject entries following traditional principles for alphabetical indexing. "The Rose & Crown Inn, Saffron Walden, Ess, Eng − 1750S" should not be indexed under "T". It would best be recorded as a P: entry "Saffron Walden, Ess, Eng − Rose & Crown Inn − 1750S." or by placing Eng first. Alternatively if the main interest was in Inns it should be recorded as a G: entry "Inns − Eng, The Rose & Crown, Saffron Walden, Ess − 1750S". Contributors may wish to record an item in several different categories. Change the order of the entry accordingly.

Some contributors attempt to connect a Subject entry to a Surname entry. This cannot be done and such subject entries become meaningless and have been deleted. Other contributors have submitted very wide or vague Subject entries − "Migration Germany to USA − all − 1600+" Rather a big subject! If you are indeed accepting all information perhaps the following "M: Germany to USA − Data base in preparation − 1600+".

Size of Entries

We set length limits for subject entries and these are recorded on the entry form. The Editors reserve the right to change any entry considered to be too long or meaningless in its original form. We urge contributors to give thought when submitting subject entries. This section of the **Directory** could be of considerable assistance to persons engaged in particular local studies or tracing a particular individual as well as broader based historical research.

FRANCE

EXPLICATION Le *Genealogical Research Directory* (GRD) est publié chaque année depuis 1981. Parmi les publications de recherches de son genre, il est devenu le plus grand du monde. Dans les éditions récentes, plus de 100 000 entrées ont été publiées. Elles n'ont pas été transmises d'une édition à l'autre mais plutôt soumises de nouveau par les collaborateurs, qui sont disposés à partager les fruits de leurs recherches avec les autres.

Une explication visuelle des méthodes utilisées par le GRD se trouve à la page 32. A part de la liste principale de noms de famille, il y a plusieurs autres sections dans le GRD. Quelques points à noter:-

LISTE DE NOMS DE FAMILLE La liste principale de noms de famille commence à la page 33. Les noms sont énumérés par ordre alphabétique stricte sans reférence ni aux espaces ni à la ponctuation. Par conséquent, tous les noms de familles préfixés avec *la* ou *von* ne sont pas énumérés ensemble mais suivant la lettre qui suit *la* ou *von* .

ORDRE GEOGRAPHIQUE Sous un nom de famille particulier, les entrées sont énumérés par ordre PAYS.

NOMBRE DE REFERENCE Le nombre entre crochets indique la fin de l'entrée et aussi se réfère au collaborateur dont le nom et l'adresse sont énumérés vers la fin de l'annuaire. Cette section est indiquée par un bord noir.

DATES Les dates publiées indiquent la période recherchée. Des symboles variés sont employés ainsi: *PRE 1880* veut dire avant 1880. *1880+* veut dire de 1880 à une date ultérieure non spécifiée. *1880S* veut dire de 1880 à 1889. *C1880* veut dire circa (vers) 1880. *All* (tout) veut dire à n'importe quelle période jusqu'aujourd'hui. Tout autre terme est exclus. **ENDROITS** En général, le nom d'une ville ou d'un village est indiqué, à moins que le collaborateur cherche une famille dans une région géographique plus grande. Ce nom est en général suivi de celui d'une province, d'un comté ou d'un état et puis de celui de la nation. Ces derniers noms sont toujours abrégés et leurs codes sont énumérés aux pages 28 à 31.

SUJETS Beaucoup de collaborateurs sont en train de faire des recherches sur un endroit particulier ou bien ils ont un(e) ancêtre qu'on peut identifier par son association avec un endroit ou un emploi particulier. Ces entrées se trouvent dans la section intitulée SUBJECTS qui suit la section principale de noms de famille. Les sujets sont classés par les huit catégories suivantes:

G: General; I: Individuals (Individus); M: Migration; MY: Military (Militaire); O: Occupations (Emplois); P: Place names (noms de lieu); R: Religion; S: Shipping and Ships (Navires et leurs passagers).

Les feuilles d'inscription pour tous les annuaires futurs permettront au collaborateur d'indiquer la catégorie dans laquelle son entrée apparaîtra. Les entrées dans la section intitulée SUBJECT (Suject) n'ont aucun rapport avec les noms de famille énumérés dans la section principale du GRD.

ONE NAME SOCIETY Le GRD de 1990 présente une nouvelle section qui donne aux organisations ou aux collaborateurs la possibilité d'enregistrer leurs recherches sur un nom de famille particulier ou sur les descendants d'une seule personne. On demande une somme modique pour ces entrées, si l'annuaire n'est pas exigé. Ecrivez au représentant le plus proche pour demander une feuille d'inscription particulière. Les représentants sont énumérés à la page 4.

LISTES DES ASSOCIATIONS Ces listes sont insérées gratuitement pour rendre service aux associations et aux collaborateurs. Vous êtes priés d'informer les Editeurs d'un changement quelconque.

ANNONCES PUBLICITAIRES Les chercheurs privés, généalogistes professionels et personnes qui offrent des services associés à la généalogie peuvent insérer des annonces publicitaires dans la dernière section du GRD. Ecrivez à nos représentants pour vous informer des tarifs courants.

FRANCE REGIONS

Alphabetical listing of Departments in France cross-referenced to the main regional abbreviations — *Page Number* 28

Abréviations par ordre alphabétique du Département —

01 Ain	30 Gard
02 Aisne	31 Garonne (Haute)
03 Allier	32 Gers
04 Alpes de Hte Prov	33 Gironde
05 Alpes (Hautes)	34 Herault
06 Alpes Maritimes	35 Ille et Vilaine
07 Ardèche	36 Indre
08 Ardennes	37 Indre et Loire
09 Ariège	38 Isère
10 Aube	39 Jura
11 Aude	40 Landes
12 Aveyron	41 Loir et Cher
13 Bouches du Rhône	42 Loire
14 Calvados	43 Loire (Haute)
15 Cantal	44 Loire Atlantique
16 Charente	45 Loiret
17 Charente Maritime	46 Lot
18 Cher	47 Lot et Garonne
19 Corrèze	48 Lozère
2A Corse du Sud	49 Maine et Loire
2B Corse (Haute)	50 Manche
21 Côte d'Or	51 Marne
22 Côtes du Nord	52 Marne (Haute)
23 Creuse	53 Mayenne
24 Dordogne	54 Meurthe et Moselle
25 Doubs	55 Meuse
26 Drôme	56 Morbihan
27 Eure	57 Moselle
28 Eure et Lor	58 Nièvre
29 Finistère	59 Nord

60 Oise	
61 Orne	
62 Pas de Calais	
63 Puy de Dôme	
64 Pyrénées Atlantiques	
65 Pyrénées (Hautes)	
66 Pyrénées Orientales	
67 Rhin (Bas)	
68 Rhin (Haut)	
69 Rhône	
70 Saône (Haute)	
71 Saône et Loire	
72 Sarthe	
73 Savoie	
74 Savoie (Haute)	
75 Seine Maritime	
79 Sèvres (Deux)	
80 Somme	
81 Tarn	
82 Tarn et Garonne	
83 Var	
84 Vaucluse	
85 Vendée	
86 Vienne	
87 Vienne (Haute)	
88 Vosges	
89 Yonne	
90 Belfort (Terr de)	

75 PARIS	
77 Seine et Marne	
78 Yvelines	
91 Essonne	
92 Hauts de Seine	
93 Seine St Denis	
94 Val de Marne	
95 Val d'Oise	

RÉGION ILE-DE-FRANCE

15

DEUTSCHLAND

BEMERKUNGEN Seit der ersten Ausgabe im Jahre 1981 ist das jährliche Genealogical Research Directory (GRD) zur umfangreichsten Veröffentlichung seiner Art geworden. Neuere Ausgaben enthalten über 100 000 Eintragungen. Diese sind nicht etwa übertragungen aus älteren Ausgaben, sondern Neueintragungen von Einsendern, die bereit sind, ihre Entdeckungen auch anderen mitzuteilen.

Auf Seite 32 befindet sich eine graphische Erklärung der verschiedenen Abschnitte einer Eintragung. Ausser dem den grössten Buchteil bildenden Namensverzeichnis enthält das Directory auch andere, die Forschungsthemen und Vereine anführen. Zu merken sind:

NAMENSVERZEICHNIS Das Hauptverzeichnis beginnt auf S. 33. Namen erscheinen in einer streng alphabetischen Reihenfolge, die ein-bzw. mehrteilige Namen gleich behandelt. Namen mit la oder von kommen deshalb nicht zusammen vor, sondern sind nach dem darauffolgenden Buchstaben geordnet: so la Place, Lardner, la Rue, bzw. von Huben, Voniatis, von Knobelsdorf.

GEOGRAPHISCHE REIHENFOLGE Gleiche Namen erscheinen je nach Land, wobei die auf S. 28 angeführten Abkürzungen die Reihenfolge bestimmen. So erscheint Lesnard FRA vor Lesnard USA; Kluck WPR, GER vor Kluck USA.

EINSENDERNUMMER Die in eckigen Klammern stehende Nummer bezeichnet sowohl das Ende der Eintragung als auch den Einsender, dessen Name und Adresse man in jenem Buchteil findet, in dem die Seiten durch einen schwarzen Aussenrand bezeichnet sind.

ZEITRAUM Die angeführten Jahreszahlen geben den erforschten Zeitraum an. PRE 1880 bedeutet vor 1880. 1880+ bedeutet 1880 bis zu einem unbestimmten späteren Termin. 1880S bedeutet 1880 bis 1889. C1880 bedeutet circa 1880. Andere Abkürzungen sind nicht zulässig.

ORTSNAMEN Den Jahreszahlen folgt normalerweise der Orts-bzw. Gemeindename, es sei denn der Einsender interessiert sich für ein grösseres Gebiet. Es folgt der Name der Provinz bzw. des Bundeslandes, letztlich der des Landes. Abkürzungen auf Seiten 28 bis 31.

FORSCHUNGSTHEMEN Manche Einsender erforschen ein besonderes Thema bzw. einen Ahnen, der sich durch Verbindung zu einem Ort, einem Beruf usw. identifizieren lässt. Solche Eintragungen findet man im Kapitel SUBJECTS, das nach dem Namensverzeichnis steht. Themen sind zu einer der folgenden acht Gruppen gestellt. G: Allgemeine Themen; I: Individuen; M: Ein-bzw. Auswanderungen; MY: Militär; O: Berufe; P: Ortsnamen; R: Religion; S: Schiffswesen und Schiffe.

Beitragsformulare für zukünftigen Ausgaben sollen dem Einsender zu einer Wahl der Gruppe verhelfen. Eintragungen in diesem Kapitel stehen in keiner Beziehung zu solchen im Namensverzeichnis.

FAMILIENNAMENVEREINE Mit dieser 1990er Ausgabe führen wir ein neues Kapitel ein, das den Einsender, der sich für einen einzigen Familiennamen bzw. für die Nachkommen einer bestimmten Person interessiert, sein Interesse bekannt machen lässt. Bezieht der Einsender das Directory nicht, so erfolgt die Eintragung in dieses Kapitel gegen ein kleineres Gebühr. Bitte wenden Sie sich an unseren nächsten Repräsentanten, um das nötige Formular zu bekommen.

VEREINSVERZEICHNIS Um den Vereinen sowie unseren Lesern einen Dienst zu erweisen, erscheinen Eintragungen kostenlos. Wir bitten, uns über etwaige Änderungen zu informieren.

REKLAMEN Inserate für Waren bzw. Dienste genealogischer Art erscheinen im Schlussteil des Directory. Weiteres von unseren Repräsentanten.

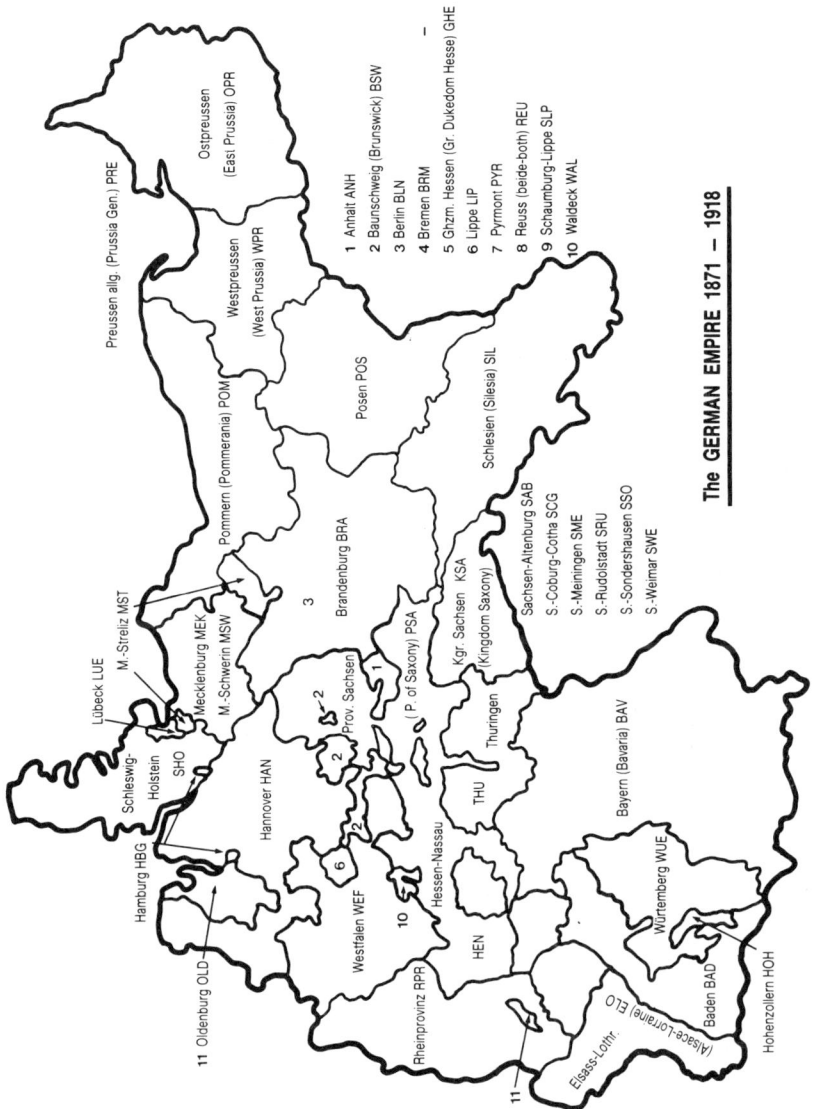

The GERMAN EMPIRE 1871 – 1918

Preussen allg. (Prussia Gen.) PRE

Ostpreussen (East Prussia) OPR

Westpreussen (West Prussia) WPR

Posen POS

Pommern (Pommerania) POM

Brandenburg BRA

Schlesien (Silesia) SIL

Prov. Sachsen

(P. of Saxony) PSA

Kgr. Sachsen KSA (Kingdom Saxony)

M.-Streliz MST

Mecklenburg MEK

M.-Schwerin MSW

Lübeck LUE

Schleswig-Holstein SHO

Hamburg HBG

Hannover HAN

Westfalen WEF

Oldenburg OLD

Rheinprovinz RPR

Hessen-Nassau

HEN

Thuringen

THU

Bayern (Bavaria) BAV

Würtemberg WUE

Baden BAD

Hohenzollern HOH

Elsass-Lothr. (Alsace-Lorraine) ELO

Sachsen-Altenburg SAB
S.-Coburg-Cotha SCG
S.-Meiningen SME
S.-Rudolstadt SRU
S.-Sondershausen SSO
S.-Weimar SWE

1 Anhalt ANH
2 Baunschweig (Brunswick) BSW
3 Berlin BLN
4 Bremen BRM
5 Ghzm. Hessen (Gr. Dukedom Hessel) GHE
6 Lippe LIP
7 Pyrmont PYR
8 Reuss (beide-both) REU
9 Schaumburg-Lippe SLP
10 Waldeck WAL

17

POLAND

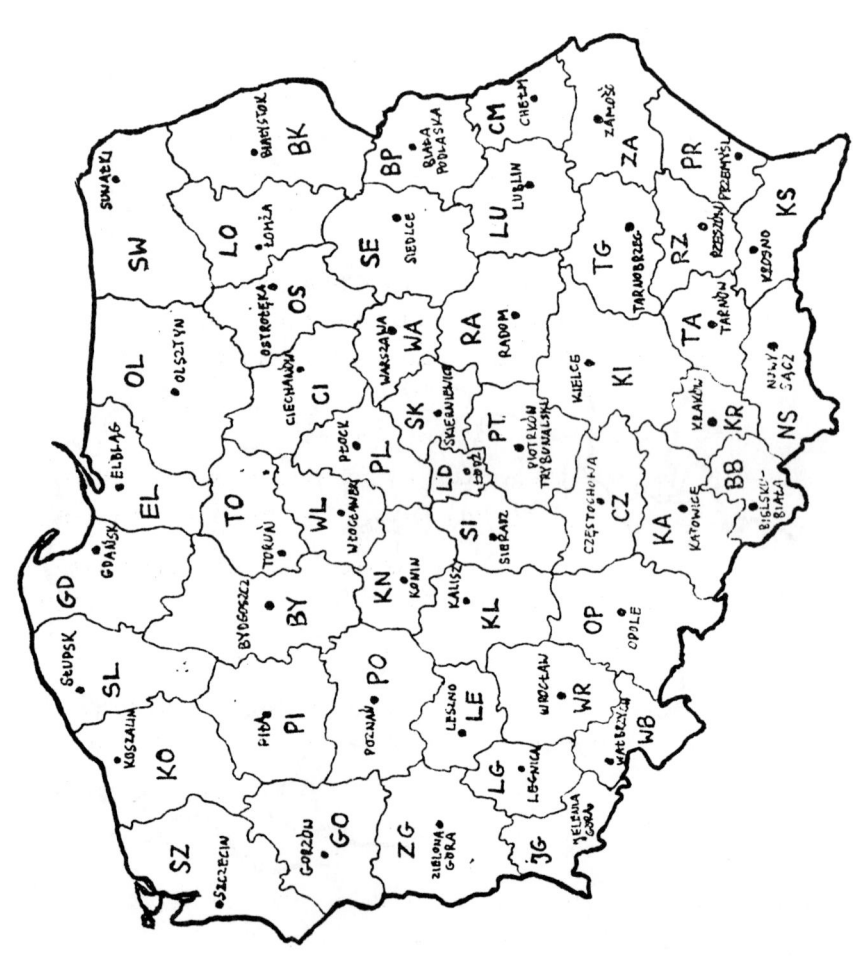

RESEARCH REPOSITORIES

Major Public Institutions of national and international importance.

AUSTRALIA

National Library of Australia, Canberra A.C.T. 2600
Hours: *Main Reading Room*
Mon.–Thurs. 9.30am–10.00pm. Fri.–Sat. 9.30am–4.45pm. Sun. 1.30pm–4.45pm.
Newspaper – Microcopy Reading Room
Mon., Wed. 9.30am–10.00pm. Tues., Thurs.–Sat. 9.30am–4.45pm. Sun. Closed.

Archives Office of New South Wales, 2 Globe St., Sydney. 2000.
Hours: Mon.–Fri. 9.00am–5.00pm. Sat. 10.00am–4.00pm:
Kingswood: Tues-Fri. 9am-5pm. Sat. 10am-4pm.

Mitchell Library, State Library of N.S.W., Macquarie St., Sydney. 2000.
Hours: Mon.–Fri. 9.00am–9.00pm. Sat. 9.00am–5.00pm. Sun. Closed.

LaTrobe Library, State Library of Victoria, 328 Swanston St., Melbourne. 3000.
Hours: Mon.–Sun. 10.00am–10.00pm.

Public Record Office of Victoria, 318 Little Bourke St., Melbourne 3000.

State Library of Queensland, Cultural Centre, Southbank, South Brisbane 4101.

Queensland State Archives, 162 Annerley Rd., Dutton Park 4102. Phone (07) 44 3215.

State Library of South Australia, GPO Box 386A, Adelaide 5001. Phone (08) 223 8414.

Public Record Office of South Australia, PO Box 713, N. Adelaide 5006. Phone (08) 267 8220.

State Library of Tasmania, 91 Murray St., Hobart 7000.

Archives Office of Tasmania, 91 Murray St., Hobart 7000. Phone (002) 302490.

State Library of Western Australia, 40 James St., Perth 6000. Phone (09) 328 7466.

Australian Archives Office, PO Box 34, Dickson, Canberra 2602. Phone (062) 433633.

CANADA

National Library of Canada, 395 Wellington St., Ottawa. Ontario K1A 0N4.

National Archives of Canada, 395 Wellington Street, Ottawa, Ont., K1A ON3. Phone (613) 995-5138.

Provincial Archives of Newfoundland and Labrador, Colonial Building, Military Road, St. John's, Nfld., A1C 2C9. Phone (709) 753-9390.

Public Archives of Nova Scotia, 6016 University Avenue, Halfax, N.S., B3H 1W4. Phone (902) 423-9115.

Public Archives of Prince Edward Island, P.O. Box 1000, Charlottetown, P.E.I., C1A 7M4. Phone (902) 368-4290.

Provincial Archives of New Brunswick, P.O. Box 6000, Fredericton, N.B., E3B 5H1. Phone (506) 453-2637 or 453-2122.

Archives nationales du Quebec, P.O. Box 10450, Sainte-Foy, Que., G1V 4N1. Phone (418) 644-4795.

Archives of Ontario, 77 Grenville Street West, Queen's Park, Toronto, Ont., M7A 2RD. Phone (416) 965-4030.

Provincial Archives of Manitoba, 200 Vaughan Street, Winnipeg, Man., R3C 1P5. Phone (204) 944-3971.

Saskatchewan Archives Board, Regina Office, University of Regina, Regina, Sask., S4S OA2. Phone (306) 787-4068; and Saskatoon Office, University of Saskatchewan, Saskatoon, Sask., S7N 0WO. Phone (306) 933-5832.

Provincial Archives of Alberta, 12845-102 Avenue, Edmonton, Alta., T5N 0M6. Phone (403) 427-1750.

Provincial Archives of British Columbia, 655 Belleville Street, Victoria, B.C., V8V 1X4. Phone (604) 387-5885 and 387-1952.

Yukon Archives, P.O. Box 2703, Whitehorse, Y.T., Y1A 2C6. Phone (403) 667-5321.

Archives of the Northwest Territories, Prince of Wales Northern Heritage Centre, Yellowknife, N.W.T., X1A 2L9. Phone (403) 873-7698.

BRITISH ISLES

ENGLAND

British Library

Main Reading Room, Great Russell St., London WC1B 3DG. Phone (01) 636 1544.
Hours: Mon., Fri., Sat. 9.00am–5.00pm. Tues., Wed., Thurs. 9.00am–9.00pm.

Newspaper Library, Colindale Ave., London NW9 5HE. Phone (01) 200 5515.
Hours: Mon.–Sat. 9.00am–5.00pm.

India Office Library and Record Office, 197 Blackfriars Rd., London SE1 8NG. Phone (01) 928 9531.
Hours: Mon.–Fri. 9.30am–6.00pm. Sat. 9.30am–12.45pm.

Oriental Department (Manuscripts & Books) 14 Store St., London WC1E 7DG. Phone (01) 636 7544 Ext. 259.
Hours: Mon.–Fri. 9.00am–4.45pm. Sat. 9.30am–12.45pm.

Public Record Office,

Census Office, Portugal St., London. WC2A. Hours: Mon.-Fri. 9.30am–4.50.
Chancery Lane, London. WC2A 1LR. Phone (01) 4050741.
Ruskin Avenue, Kew, Richmond. TW9 4DU. Phone (01) 8763444.

National Army Museum, Records Dept., Royal Hospital Rd., London. SW3 4HT. Phone (01) 7300717.

National Maritime Museum, Manuscripts, Greenwich, London, SE10 9NF. Phone (01) 8584422.

Birmingham Public Library & Archives, Chamberlain Sq., Birmingham B3 3HQ. Phone (021) 235 4217.
Hours: Mon.–Fri. 9.00am–6.00pm. Sat. 9.00am–5.00pm.

LONDON

Corporation of London R. O., PO Box 270, Guildhall, London. EC2P 2EJ. Phone (01) 6063030.

Greater London Record Office and Library, 40 Northampton Rd., London EC1R 0HB. Phone (01) 633 6851.
Hours: Tues.–Fri. 10.00am–4.45pm. (Closed late October).

IRELAND – NORTHERN

Public Record Office, 66 Balmoral Ave., Belfast. BT9 6NY. Ph. (0232) 661621 for appointment.

Linenhall Library, 17 Donegall Square North, Belfast.

ISLE OF MAN

Manx Museum Library, Kingswood Grove, Douglas. Phone (0624) 75522.

SCOTLAND

Scottish Record Office, General Register Hse., Princes St., Edinburgh. EH1 3YY. (031) 556 6585.

National Library of Scotland, Manuscripts: George IV Bridge, Edinburgh. EH1 1EW. (031) 226 4531.

WALES

National Library of Wales, Manuscripts & Records, Aberystwyth. SY23 3BU. Phone (0970) 3816.

Clwyd R. O., Hawarden Branch, The Old Rectory, Hawarden, Deeside. CH5 3NR. Ph. (0244) 532364.

Glamorgan Archives, County Hall, Cathays Park, Cardiff. CF1 3NE. Phone (0222) 820282.

Gwent County R. O., County Hall, Cwmbran. NP44 2XH. Phone (06333) 838838.

Gwynedd Archives, Victoria Dock, Caernarfon. LL55 1SH. Phone (0286) 4121.

Powys Archives, Cefnllys Road, Llandrindod Wells. LD1 5LD. (Phone (0597) 2212.

COUNTY ARCHIVE RESEARCH NETWORK

You will need a reader's ticket before you can use a number of county record offices. You MUST produce some official proof of identification when applying for a ticket

Before a visit to these or any other record offices you are advised to phone to enquire about opening hours, access provisions etc. Because of space shortages a number of offices now operate an appointments only service.

For a full list of repositories see *Record Repositories in Great Britain* H. M. Stationary Office, London.

COUNTY & CITY RECORD OFFICES (in COUNTY order) (see also under Sct, Wales & Ireland).

Avon — Bath City Record Office, Guildhall, Bath. BA1 5AW. Phone (0225) 61111.

Bristol R. O., The Council House, College Green, Bristol. BS1 5TR. Phone (0272) 266031.

Bedfordshire Record Office, County Hall, Bedford. MK42 9AP. Phone (0234) 228833.

Berkshire Record Office, Shire Hall, Shinfield Park, Reading. RG2 9XD. Phone (0734) 875444.

Buckinghamshire Record Office, County Hall, Aylesbury. HP20 1UA. Phone (0296) 395000.

Cambridgeshire Record Office, Shire Hall, Cambridge. CB3 0AP. Phone (0223) 317281.

Cambridgeshire R. O., Grammar School Walk, Huntingdon. PE18 6LF. Phone (0480) 425842.

Cheshire Record Office, Duke Street, Chester. CH1 1RL. Phone (0244) 602574.

Chester City Record Office, Town Hall, Chester. CH1 2HJ. Phone (0244) 40144.

Vleveland Archives Dept., 6 Marton Rd., Middlesbrough. TS1 1DB. Phone (0642) 248321.

Cornwall Record Office, County Hall, Truro. TR1 3AY. Phone (0872) 73698.

Cumbria Record Office, Carlisle, The Castle, Carlisle. CA3 8UR. Phone (0228) 23456.

Cumbria Record Office, Kendal, County Offices, Kendal. LA9 4RQ. Phone (0539) 21000.

Cumbria R. O., Barrow, 140 Duke St., Barrow-in-Furness. LA14 1XW. Phone (0229) 31269.

Derbyshire Record Office, County Offices, Matlock. DE4 3AG. Phone (0629) 3411.

Devon Record Office, Castle Street, Exeter. EX4 3PU. Phone (0392) 273509.

West Devon R. O., Unit 3, Clare Pl., Coxside, Plymouth. PL4 0JW. Phone (0752) 264685.

Dorset Record Office, County Hall, Dorchester. DT1 1XJ. Phone (0305) 204411.

Durham County Record Office, County Hall, Durham. DH1 5UL. Phone (0385) 64411.

Essex Record Office, County Hall, Chelmsford. CM1 1LX. Phone (0245) 267222.

Essex R. O., Colchester & N.E., Stanwell House, Stanwell St., CO2 7DL. Phone (0206) 572099.

Essex R. O., Southend, Library, Victoria Ave., Southend—on—Sea. SS2 6EX. Phone (0702) 612621.

Gloucestershire R. O., Clarence Row, Alvin St., Gloucester. GL1 3DW. Phone (0452) 425295.

Hampshire Record Office, 20 Southgate Street, Winchester. SO23 9EF. Phone (0962) 63153.

Portsmouth City Records Office, 3 Museum Road, Portsmouth. PO1 2LE. Phone (0705) 829765.

Southampton City Record Office, Civic Centre, Southampton. SO9 4XR. Phone (0703) 832251.

Hereford & Worcester R. O., County Hall, Spetchley Rd., Worcester. WR5 2NP. Phone (0905) 353366.

Hereford Record Office, The Old Barracks, Harold St., Hereford. HR1 2QX. Phone (0432) 265441.

Worcester (St Helen's) Record Office, Fish St., Worcester. WR1 2HW. Phone (0905) 353366.

Hertfordshire Record Office, County Hall, Hertford. SG13 8DE. Phone (0992) 555105.

Humberside County Record Office, County Hall, Beverley. HU17 9BA. Phone (0482) 867131.

South Humberside Record Office, Town Hall Square, Grimsby. DN31 1HX. Ph. (0472) 353481.

Kingston upon Hull City Record Office, 79 Lowgate, Hull. HU1 2AA. Phone (0482) 222015.

Kent Archives Office, County Hall, Maidstone. ME14 1XQ. Phone (0622) 671411.

West Kent Archives Office, Central Library, The Drive, Sevenoaks. Phone (0732) 452384.

Kent Archives Office, S.E. Kent, Library, Grace Hill, Folkestone. CT20 1HD. Ph. (0303) 57583.

Kent Archives Office, N.E. Kent, Library, Guildford Lawn, Ramsgate. CT11 9AI. (0843) 593532.

Lancashire Record Office, Bow Lane, Preston. PR1 8ND. Phone (0772) 54868.

Leicestershire Record Office, 57 New Walk, Leicester. LE1 7JB. Phone (0533) 544566.

Lincolnshire Archives Office, The Castle, Lincoln. LN1 3AB. Phone (0522) 25158.

Greater Manchester Co. R. O., 56 Marshall St, New Cross, Manchester. M4 5FU. (061) 2473383.

Merseyside Maritime Museum, Pier Head, Liverpool. L3 1DN. Phone (051) 7091551.

Liverpool R. O., City Library, William Brown St., Liverpool. L3 8EW. Phone (051) 2072147.

West Midlands-Birmingham Archives Dept., Chamberlain Sq., Birmingham. B3 3HQ. (021) 2354217.

Norfolk Record Office, Central Library, Norwich. NR2 1NJ. Phone (0603) 611277.

Northamptonshire R. O., Delapré Abbey, London Rd., Northampton. NN4 9AW. Ph. (0604) 762129.

Northumberland R. O., Melton Park, North Gosforth, Newcastle on Tyne. NE3 5QX. (091) 236 2680.

Nottinghamshire R. O., County House, High Pavement, Nottingham. NG1 1HR. Ph. (0602) 504524.

Oxfordshire R. O., County Hall, New Road, Oxford. OX1 1ND. Phone (0865) 815203.

Shropshire Record Office, Shirehall, Abbey Foregate, Shrewsbury. SY2 6ND. Ph. (0743) 25281.

Somerset Record Office, Obridge Road, Taunton. TA2 7PU. Phone (0823) 337600.

Staffordshire Record office, Eastgate Street, Stafford. ST16 2LZ. Phone (0785) 3121.

Lichfield Joint R. O., Lichfield Library, Bird St., Lichfield. WS13 6PN. Ph. (0543) 256787.

Suffolk Record Office, County Hall, Ipswich. IP4 2JS. Phone (0473) 230000.

Surrey R. O., County Hall, Penrhyn Road, Kingston upon Thames. KT1 2DN. Ph. (01) 5419065.

East Sussex R. O., The Maltings, Castle Precincts, Lewes. BN7 1YT. Phone (0273) 475400.

West Sussex Record Office, County Hall, Chichester. PO19 1RN. Phone (0243) 777983.

Tyne & Wear Archives, Blandford House, West Blandford St., Newcastle. NE1 4JA. (091) 2326789.

Warwick County Record Office, Priory Park, Cape Rd., Warwick. CV34 4JS. Phone (0926) 493431.

Isle of Wight County Record Office, 26 Hillside, Newport. PO30 2EB. Phone (0983) 524031.

Wiltshire Record Office, County Hall, Trowbridge. BA14 8JG. Phone (022) 143641.

North Yorkshire County Record Office, County Hall, Northallerton. DL7 8AD. Phone (0609) 3123.

York City Archives, Art Gallery Buildings, Exhibition Sq., York. YO1 2EW. Phone (0904) 51533.

Sheffield Record Office, Central Library, Surrey St., Sheffield. S1 1XZ. Phone (0742) 734756.

West Yorkshire Archives, Registry of Deeds, Newstead Rd., Wakefield. WF1 2DE. (0924) 367111.

FRANCE

Archives Nationales

60 rue des Francs—Bourgeois, F—75141 PARIS CEDEX 03. Phone: 42 77 11 30.
Hours: Mon.—Fri. 9—18h. Sat. or eve of holidays, documents ordered or reserved in advance before 15h. only. Closed second fortnight in July.

Minutier Central des Notaires Parisiens, 87 rue Vieille—du—Temple, F—75003 PARIS. Phone: 42 77 11 30.
Hours: Mon.—Sat. 9—18h. Sat. documents ordered or reserved in advance only. Closed second fortnight in July.

Centre Annexe d'Outre—Mer, 29 Chemin du Moulin de Testas, F—13090 AIX—EN—PROVENCE. Phone: 42 26 43 21.
Hours: Mon.—Fri. 9—17h. Closed second fortnight in July.

Cité des Archives Contemporaines, 2 rue des Archives, F—77300 FONTAINEBLEAU CEDEX. Phone: 60 72 59 00.
Hours: Mon.—Fri. 9—12, 13—17h. Documents ordered the eve at the latest.

Ministere de la Culture, Direction du Patrimoine, 3 rue de Valois, F—75001 PARIS. Phone: 42 69 10 40.
Hours: Mon.—Fri. 9—18h.

Ministere de la defense

Service Historique de l'Armée de Terre, Pavillion des Armes, Vieux Fort, Château de Vincennes, F—94300 VINCENNES CEDEX. Phone: 43 74 11 55.
Hours: Mon.—Thurs. 10—17.30, Fri. 10—16.30h. Closed Christmas week.

Service Historique de l'Armée de l'Air, Château de Vincennes, F—94304 VINCENNES CEDEX. Phone: 43 74 11 55.
Hours: Mon.—Thurs. 8.30—12, 13—17h., Fri. 8.30—12, 13—15h.

Service Historique de la Marine, Pavillion de la Reine, Château de Vincennes, F—94300 VINCENNES. Phone: 43 28 81 50.
Hours: Mon.—Fri. 9—17h. No annual closure.

Ministere des Finances, Service Hist. arch. économiques et financières, Centre des Affaires du Louvre, Bureau 6088, 151 rue Saint—Honoré, F—75056 PARIS RP. Phone 42 97 11 41.
Hours: Mon.—Fri. 9—11.45, 14—17h.

Ministere de la Justice, 13 Place Vendôme, F—75042 PARIS CEDEX 01. Phone: 42 61 80 22.
Consult documents in the *Archives Nationales*

Ministere des Affaires Etrangeres, Service Archives, 37 Quai d'Orsay, F—75007 PARIS. Phone: 45 55 95 40.
Hours: Mon., Tues., Thurs., Fri. 13.30—18.30h. Wed. 9.30—18.30h.

IRELAND

National Archives of Ireland, (incorporating former Public Record Office and State Paper Office), Bishop Street, Dublin 8.
Hours: Mon.-Fri. 10.00am-5.00pm.

National Library of Ireland, Kildare Street, Dublin 2.
Hours: Mon. 10.00am-9.00pm, Tues. & Wed. 2.00pm-9.00pm, Thurs. & Fri. 10.00am-5.00pm. Sat. 10.00am-1.00pm.

Genealogical Office, 2 Kildare Street, Dublin 2.
Hours: Consultancy Service Hours: Mon.-Fri. 10.00am-4.30pm.
Appointment necessary for viewing of manuscripts.

Registry of Deeds, King's Inn, Henrietta Street, Dublin 1.
Hours: Mon.-Fri. 10.00am-4.30pm.

Representative Church Body Library, Braemor Park, Churchtown, Dublin 14.
Hours: Mon.-Fri. 9.30am-1.00pm, 1.45pm-5.00pm.

For a full listing of repositories see *Directory of Irish Archives* edited by S. Helferty & R. Refausse, Irish Academic Press, Dublin, 1988.

NEW ZEALAND

National Archives, Air New Zealand Building, 141 Vivian St., Wellington 1.

Alexander Turnbull Library, National Library of New Zealand, 70 Molesworth St., Wellington 1. P.O. Box 12349, Wellington.

UNITED STATES OF AMERICA

National Archives and Records Service, Constitution Ave., Washington DC 20408.

Regional Archives Branches:
Boston — 380 Trapelo Road, Waltham, MA 02154.
    Serves: CT, ME, MA, NH, RI & VT.
New York — Building 22 — MOT Bayonne, Bayonne, NJ 07002.
    Serves: NJ, NY.
Philadelphia — 5000 Wissahickon Avenue, Philadelphia, PA 19144.
    Serves: DE, PA, MD, VA & WV.
Fort Worth — 4900 Hemphill Street (building address), PO Box 6216 (mailing address), Fort Worth, TX 76115.
    Serves: AR, LA, NM, OK & TX.
Denver — Building 48, Denver Federal Center, Denver, CO 80225.
    Serves: CO, MT, ND, SD, UT & WY.
Los Angeles — 24000 Avila Road, Laguna Niguel, CA 92677.
    Serves: AZ & Southern CA.
Atlanta — 1557 St Joseph Avenue, East Point, GA 30344.
    Serves: AL, GA, FL, KY, MS, NC, SC & TN.
Chicago — 7358 South Pulaski Road, Chicago, IL 60629.
    Serves: IL, IN, MI, MN, OH & WI.
Kansas City — 2306 East Bannister Road, Kansas City, MO 64131.
    Serves: IA, KS, MO & NE.
Seattle — 6125 Sand Point Way NE., Seattle, WA 98115.
    Serves: AK, ID, OR & WA.

Library of Congress, Genealogical Room, Thomas Jefferson Annex, Washington DC 20540.

New York Public Library, 5th Ave. and 42nd Sts., New York, N.Y. 10016.

Newberry Library, 60 West Walton St., Chicago, IL 60610.

Fort Worth Public Library, 300 Taylor Street, Fort Worth, Texas 76102. Phone (817) 870 7705.

NOTE: Please notify ADDITIONS & CORRECTIONS to:— The Editors of the GRD, C/— any of our Agents listed on page 4.

NOTE: Many repositories require readers to make an appointment. Phone first.

CALENDAR OF GENEALOGICAL EVENTS
EVENEMENTS D'INTERET GENEALOGIQUE
DATEN VON VERANSTALTUNGEN UND REISEN

Conferences

1991	**April 6**	**ENGLAND: BIRMINGHAM** *Annual General Meeting of Federation.* At: Birmingham & Midland Institute.
	Apr. 19-20	USA: San Francisco, California. *Annual Fair.* Host: California Genealogical Society.
	April 28	USA: Pasadena, California. *22nd Annual Genealogical Jamboree.* Host: Southern California Genealogical Society.
	April 26-28	CANADA: Fort McMurray, Alberta. *Annual Conference of Alberta Genealogical Society.* Host: Fort McMurray Branch. Contact: Bill Pacey, PO Box 6253, Ft. McMurray, Alberta.
	May 9-11	FRANCE: Bordeaux. *11th National Biennial Conference.* Contact: BSC, Palais des Congres, 33000 Bordeaux Lac.
	May 9-12	AUSTRALIA: Launceston, Tasmania. *6th Australasian Congress.* Host: Genealogical Society of Tasmania.
	May 17-20	NEW ZEALAND: Hastings. *Annual Conference of NZSOG.* Contact: PO Box 7194, Taradale.
	May 24-26	CANADA: Kingston, Ontario. *Annual OGS Seminar — Gateway to Upper Canada.* Host: Kingston Branch, OGS.
	May 29 -June 1	USA: Portland, Oregon. *National Genealogical Society Conference in the States.* *Come to the End of the Oregon Trail.* Host: Genealogical Forum of Oregon, Inc.
	June 21-25	IRELAND: Belfast, N. Irl. *Ulster Historical Foundation & FFHS (Federation) Conference.* Contact: Dr C. Kinealy, Ulster Historical Foundation.
	July 16-18	CANADA: Gaspe Bay, QUE. *Salute to the Pioneers of Gaspe Bay.* Contact: 54 Cutting Street, Coaticook, Que. J1A 2G3, Canada.
	July 8-12	USA: Washington DC. *National Archives.* Contact: Insttiute for Genealogical Research, PO Box 14274, Washington DC 20044
	Aug. 15-17	USA: Fort Wayne, Indianna. *Annual Federation of Genealogical Societies Conference.* Host: Allen County Pulic Library, Box 2270, Fort Wayne, IN, 46801.
	Sept. 6-8	ENGLAND: Sheffield. *Autumn Conference.* Host: Sheffield & District Family History Society.
	Sept. 9-13	ENGLAND: Oxford. Host: Heraldry Society.
	Sept. 19-25	IRELAND: Trinity College, Dublin. *First Irish Genealogical Congress.* Contact: Paul Gorry, 16 Hume Street, Dublin 2.

1992	Apr. 10-12	ENGLAND: Humberside. *Federation Council meeting & Conference.* Host: East Yorkshire Family History Society.
	Apr.	USA: San Francisco, California. *Annual Fair.* Host: California Genealogical Society.
	April	USA: Pasadina, California. *23rd Annual Jamboree.* Host: Southern California Genealogical Society.
	Apr. 29 -May 2	USA: Jacksonville, Florida. *National Genealogical Society Conference in the States.* Host: Jacksonville Genealogical Society.
	May 19-28	IRELAND: Kilkenny. *3rd Irish Origins Conference.* Contact: Patrick Nolan, College Rd., Kilkenny, Ireland.
	May 22-24	CANADA: Hamilton, Ontario. *Annual OGS Seminar.* Host: Hamilton Branch, Ontario Genealogical Society.
	Aug. ?	USA: *Annual Federation Conference.*
	Sept. 4-8	ENGLAND: Worcester. *6th British Family History Conference.* Host: Birmingham & Midland Society.
1993	Spring	ENGLAND: Norfolk. *25th Anniversary Conference.* Host: Norfolk & Norwich Family History Society.
	June 2-5	USA: Buffalo, NY. *National Genealogical Society Conference in the States.* Host: Western New York Genealogical Society.
	Sept. 3-5	ENGLAND: Suffolk. *Family History & Conservation.* Host: Suffolk Family History Society.
1994	**Spring**	**ENGLAND: Trent Park, London.** **Host: London & North Middlesex Family History Society.**
	June 1-4	**USA: Houston, Texas.** *National Genealogical Society Conference in the States.* Host: Clayton Library Friends.
	July	AUSTRALIA: Brisbane, QLD. *7th Australasian Congress.* Contact: PO Box 40, South Brisbane 4101, Australia.
	Autumn	ISLE OF MAN. *10th Anniversary Conference.* Host: Isle of Man Family History Society.
1995	**Mar. 31** **-April 4**	**ENGLAND: Isle of Wight.** *7th British Family History Conference.* Host: Isle of Wight Family History Society.

NOTE: ADDRESSES FOR THE ABOVE NAMED ORGANISATIONS ARE
LISTED IN THE SOCIETY SECTION OF THIS DIRECTORY.

ABBREVIATIONS — INTERNATIONAL

AUS	Australia	FLI	Liechtenstein	POL	Poland		
BEL	Belgium	FRA	France	PT	Portugal		
BRD	West Germany	FRG	(see BRD)	RO	Romania		
	(Bundesrepublik	GDR	(see DDR)	RSA	Rep. South Africa		
	Deutschland)	GER	[Old] German Empire	SCT	Scotland		
CAN	Canada	GR	Greece	SU	Soviet Union (USSR)		
CH	Switzerland	HU	Hungary	SWE	Sweden		
CS	Czechoslovakia	IOM	Isle of Man	UK	United Kingdom of		
DDR	East Germany	IRL	Ireland (Eire)		(see ENG SCT IRL &		
	(Deutsche Demokr.	ITL	Italy		WLS)		
	Republik)	LUX	Luxembourg (Land)	USA	United States of		
DEN	Denmark	NL	Netherlands		America		
ENG	England	NOR	Norway	WLS	Wales		
ESP	Spain (Espagñe)	NZ	New Zealand	YU	Yugolslavia		
FIN	Finland	OES	Austria				

More Abbreviations over Page ➡

ABBREVIATIONS — FRANCE REGIONS

Alphabetical listing of Departments in France cross-referenced to the
main regional abbreviations —

Abréviations par ordre alphabétique du Départment —

Ain	RHA	Gard	LGD	Meuse	LOR
Aisne	PIC	Gers	MP	Morbihan	BRT
Allier	AUV	Gironde	AQU	Moselle	LOR
Alpes-de-		Haut-Rhin	ALS	Nièvre	BRG
Haute-Provence	PCA	Haute-Corse	CR	Nord	NOR
Alpes-Maritimes	PCA	Haute-Garonne	MP	Oise	PIC
Ardèche	RHA	Haute-Loire	AUV	Orne	BN
Ardennes	CHA	Haute-Marne	CHA	Paris	RPA
Arège	MP	Haute-Saône	FC	Pas-de-Calais	NOR
Aube	CHA	Haute-Savoie	RHA	Puy-de-Dôme	AUV
Aude	LGD	Haute-Vienne	LMS	Pyrénées-Atlantiques	AQU
Aveyron	MP	Hautes-Alpes	PCA	Pyrénées-Orientales	LGD
Bas-Rhin	ALS	Hautes-Pyrénées	MP	Rhône	RHA
Bouches-du-Rhôn	PCA	Hauts-de-Seine	RPA	Saône-et-Loire	BRG
Calvados	BN	Hé rault	LGD	Sarthe	PL
Cantal	AUV	Ille-et-Vilaine	BRT	Savoie	RHA
Charente	PCH	Indre-et-Loire	CEN	Seine-et-Marne	RPA
Charente-Maritime	PCH	Isère	RPA	Seine-Maritime	HN
Cher	CEN	Jura	FC	Seine-St.-Denis	RPA
Corrèze	LMS	Landres	AQU	Somme	PIC
Core-du-Sud	CR	Loire	RHA	Tarn	MP
Côte-d'or	BRG	Loire-Atlantique	PL	Tarn-et-Gironne	MP
Côtes-du-Nord	BRT	Loiret	CEN	Territoire de Belfort	FC
Creuse	LMS	Loir-et-Cher	CEN	Val-de-Marne	RPA
Deux-Sèvres	PCH	Lot	MP	Val-d'Oise	RPA
Dorogne	AQU	Lot-et-Garonne	AQU	Var	PCA
Doubs	FC	Lozère	LGD	Vaucluse	PCA
Drôme	RHA	Maine-et-Loire	PL	Vendée	PL
Essone	RPA	Manche	BN	Vienne	PCH
Eure	HN	Marne	CHA	Vosges	LOR
Eure-et-Loir	CEN	Mayenne	PL	Yonne	BRG
Finistère	BRT	Meurthe-et-Moselle	LOR	Yvelines	RPA

ABBREVIATIONS – EUROPE

AUSTRIA – BELGIUM – FRANCE – GERMANY
– NETHERLANDS – SWITZERLAND

Österreich – Belgien – Frankreich – Deutschland – Niederlande – Schweiz
Autriche – Belgique – France – Allemagne – Pays-Bas – Suisse

AAR	Appenzell A.Rh., CH	HN	Normandie (Haute), FRA	PSA	Prov. Sachen (P. of Saxony), GER
AG	Aargau, CH				
AIR	Appenzell I.Rh., CH	HNT	Hainaut, BEL	PYR	Pyrmont, GER
ALS	Alsace, FRA	HOH	Hohenzollern, GER	REU	Reuss (beide), GER
ANH	Anhalt, GER	JU	Jura	RHA	Rhône-Alpes, FRA
AQU	Aquitaine, FRA	KAR	Kärnten (Carynthia), OES	RPA	Region Parisienne, FRA
ATW	Antwerpen, BEL				
AUV	Auvergne, FRA	KMS	Karl-Marx-Stadt, DDR	RPF	Rheinland-Pfatz (Rhineland
BAD	Baden, GER	KSA	Kgr. Sachsen (Kingdom Saxony), GER		Palatinale), BRD
BAV	Bayern (Bavaria), GER				
BAW	Baden-Württemberg, BRD	LBG	Limburg, BEL	RPR	Rheinprovinz, GER
		LGD	Languedoc, FRA	RST	Rostock, DDR
BAY	Bayern (Bavaria), BRD	LGE	Liège, BEL	SAA	Saarland, BRD
BBT	Brabant, BEL	LIP	Lippe, GER	SAB	Sachsen-Atenburg, GER
BE	Bern, CH	LMB	Limburg, NL		
BL	Basel-Landschaft, CH	LMS	Limousia, FRA	SCG	S. Coburg-Gotha, GER
BLN	Berlin, GER	LOR	Lorraine, FRA	SG	Sankt Gallen, CH
BLO	Berlin, DDR	LPZ	Leipzig, DDR	SH	Schaffhausen, CH
BLW	West-Berlin, BRD	LU	Luzern, CH	SHO	Schleswig-Holstein, BRD
BN	Normandie (Basse), FRA	LUE	Lübeck, GER		
		LXM	Luxembourg (Prov.), BEL	SIL	Schlesien (Silesia), GER
BRA	Brandenberg, GER				
BRG	Bourgogne, FRA	MAG	Magdeburg, DDR	SLP	Schaumburg-Lippe, GER
BRM	Bremen, BRD	MEK	Mecklenburg, GER		
BRT	Bretagne, FRA	MP	Midi-Pyrénées, FRA	SLZ	Salzburg, OES
BS	Basel-Stadt, CH	MST	M.-Streliz, GER	SME	S.-Meiningen, GER
BSW	Braunschweig (Brunswick, GER	MSW	M.-Schwerin, GER	SO	Solothurn, CH
		NBR	Neubrandenberg, DDR	SRU	S.-Rudostadt, GER
BUR	Burgenland, OES	NBT	Noord-Brabant, NL	SSO	S.-Sondershausen, GER
CEN	Centre, FRA	NEU	Nueuenburg, CH	STY	Steiermark (Styria), OES
CHA	Champagne, FRA	NMR	Namur, BEL		
COT	Cottbus, DDR	NOE	Neiderösterreich, OES	SUH	Suhl, DDR
CRS	Corse, FRA	NOH	Noord-Holland, NL	SWE	S.-Weimar, GER
DRE	Dresden, DDR	NOR	Nord, FRA	SWR	Schwerin, DDR
DRN	Drenthe, NL	NRW	Nordrhein-Westfalen (Nth Rhine Westphalia), BRD	SZ	Schwyz, CH
ELO	Elsass-Lothr. (Alsace-Lorraine), GER			TG	Thurgau, CH
				THU	Thuringen, GER
ERF	Erfurt, DDR	NSA	Niedersachsen, BRD	TI	Tessin, CH
FC	Franche-Conte, FRA	NW	Nidwalden, CH	TIR	Tirol (Tyrolia), OES
FFO	Frankfurt/Oder, DDR	OIJ	Overijssel, NL	UR	Uri, CH
FLE	Flevoland, NL	OLD	Oldenburg, GER	UTR	Utrecht, NL
FR	Freiburg, CH	OOE	Oberösterreich, OES	VD	Waad (Vaud), CH
FRI	Friesland, NL	OPR	Ostpreußen (East Prussia), GER	VOR	Vorarlberg, OES
GE	Genf, CH			VS	Wallis (Valais), CH
GEL	Gelderland, NL	OVL	Oost-Vlaanderen, BEL	WAL	Waldeck, GER
GHE	Ghzm. Hessen (Gr. Dukedom Hesse), GER	OW	Oberwalden, CH	WEF	Westfalen, GER
		PCA	Provence-Cote d'Azur, FRA	WIE	Wein (Vienna), OES
				WPR	Westpreußen (West Prussia), GER
GL	Glarus, CH	PCH	Poitou-Charentes, FRA		
GR	Graubunden, CH	PIC	Picardie, FRA	WUE	Württemberg, GER
GRA	Gera, DDR	PL	Pays de la Loire, FRA	WVL	West-Vlaanderen, BEL
GRO	Groningen, NL	POM	Pommern (Pommerania), GER	ZEL	Zeeland, NL
HAL	Halle, DDR			ZG	Zug, CH
HAN	Hannover, GER	POS	Posen, GER	ZH	Zürich, CH
HBG	Hamburg, GRD	POT	Potsdam, DDR	ZUH	Zuid-Holland, NL
HEN	Hessen-Nassau, GER	PRE	Preußen allg. (Prussia gen.), GER		
HES	Hessen (Hesse), BRD				

More Abbreviations over Page ➡

ABBREVIATIONS

ENGLAND — IRELAND — SCOTLAND — WALES
AUSTRALIA — CANADA — UNITED STATES OF AMERICA

ABD	Aberdeen, SCT	ESS	Essex, ENG	MO	Missouri, USA
ACT	Australian Capital Territory, AUS	FER	Fermanagh, IRL	MOG	Monaghan, IRL
		FIF	Fife, SCT	MON	Monmouthshire, WLS
AGY	Anglesey, WLS	FL	Florida, USA	MOR	Moray, SCT
AK	Alaska, USA	FLN	Flintshire, WLS	MS	Mississippi, USA
AL	Alabama, USA	GA	Georgia, USA	MT	Montana, USA
ALB	Alberta, CAN	GAL	Galway, IRL	NAI	Nairn, SCT
ALD	Alderney, CHI	GLA	Glamorgan, WLS	NB	New Brunswick, CAN
ANS	Angus, SCT	GLS	Gloucestershire, ENG	NBL	Northumberland, ENG
ANT	Antrim, IRL	GSY	Guernsey, CHI	NC	North Carolina, USA
AR	Arkansas, USA	HAM	Hampshire, ENG	ND	North Dakota, USA
ARL	Argyll, SCT	HEF	Herefordshire, ENG	NE	Nebraska, USA
ARM	Armagh, IRL	HI	Hawaii, USA	NFD	Newfoundland, CAN
AUS	Australia	HRT	Hertfordshire, ENG	NFK	Norfolk, ENG
AYR	Ayr, SCT	HUN	Huntingdonshire, ENG	NH	New Hampshire, USA
AZ	Arizona, USA	IA	Iowa, USA	NJ	New Jersey, USA
BAN	Banff, SCT	ID	Idaho, USA	NM	New Mexico, USA
BC	British Columbia, CAN	IL	Illinois, USA	NRY	North Riding, YKS
BDF	Bedfordshire, ENG	IN	Indiana, USA	NS	Nova Scotia, CAN
BEW	Berwick, SCT	INV	Inverness, SCT	NSW	New South Wales, AUS
BKM	Buckinghamshire, ENG	IOM	Isle of Man	NT	Northern Territory, AUS
BRE	Brecknockshire, WLS	IOW	Isle of Wight, UK	NTH	Northamptonshire, ENG
BRK	Berkshire, ENG	IRL	Ireland	NTT	Nottinghamshire, ENG
BUT	Bute, SCT	IRL	Ireland	NV	Nevada, USA
CA	California, USA	JSY	Jersey, CHI	NWT	North West Territories, CAN
CAE	Caernarvon, WLS	KCD	Kincardine, SCT		
CAI	Caithness, SCT	KEN	Kent, ENG	NY	New York, USA
CAM	Cambridgeshire, ENG	KER	Kerry, IRL	NZ	New Zealand
CAN	Canada	KID	Kildare, IRL	OFF	Offaly (Kings), IRL
CAR	Carlow, IRL	KIK	Kilkenny, IRL	OH	Ohio, USA
CAV	Cavan, IRL	KKD	Kirkcudbright, SCT	OK	Oklahoma, USA
CGN	Cardiganshire, WLS	KRS	Kinross, SCT	OKI	Orkney, SCT
CHI	Channel Islands	KS	Kansas, USA	ONT	Ontario, CAN
CHS	Cheshire, ENG	KY	Kentucky, USA	OR	Oregon, USA
CLA	Clare, IRL	LA	Louisiana, USA	OXF	Oxfordshire, ENG
CLK	Clackmannan, SCT	LAN	Lancashire, ENG	PA	Pennsylvania, USA
CMN	Carmarthen, WLS	LDY	Londonderry, IRL	PEE	Peebles, SCT
CO	Colorado, USA	LEI	Leicestershire, ENG	PEI	Prince Edward Is., CAN
CON	Cornwall, ENG	LET	Leitrim, IRL	PEM	Pembroke, WLS
COR	Cork, IRL	LEX	Leix (Queens), IRL	PER	Perth, SCT
CT	Connecticut, USA	LIM	Limerick, IRL	QLD	Queensland, AUS
CUL	Cumberland, ENG	LIN	Lincolnshire, ENG	QUE	Quebec, CAN
DBY	Derbyshire, ENG	LKS	Lanark, SCT	RAD	Radnorshire, WLS
DC	Dist. of Columbia, USA	LOG	Longford, IRL	RFW	Renfrew, SCT
DE	Delaware, USA	LND	London, ENG	RI	Rhode Island, USA
DEN	Denbighshire, WLS	LOU	Louth, IRL	ROC	Ross & Cromarty, SCT
DEV	Devon, ENG	MA	Massachusetts, USA	ROS	Roscommon, IRL
DFS	Dumfries, SCT	MAN	Manitoba, CAN	ROX	Roxburgh, SCT
DNB	Dunbarton, SCT	MAY	Mayo, IRL	RSA	Republic South Africa
DON	Donegal, IRL	MD	Maryland, USA	RUT	Rutland, ENG
DOR	Dorset, ENG	MDX	Middlesex, ENG	SA	South Australia, AUS
DOW	Down, IRL	ME	Maine, USA	SAL	Shropshire, ENG
DRY	Derry, IRL	MEA	Meath, IRL	SAS	Saskatchewan, CAN
DUB	Dublin, IRL	MER	Merioneth, WLS	SC	South Carolina, USA
DUR	Durham, ENG	MGY	Montgomeryshire, WLS	SCT	Scotland
ELN	East Lothian, SCT	MI	Michigan, USA	SD	South Dakota, USA
ENG	England	MLN	Midlothian, SCT	SEL	Selkirk, SCT
ERY	East Riding, YKS	MN	Minnesota, USA	SFK	Suffolk, ENG

← *More Abbreviations over page*

ABBREVIATIONS

SHI	Shetland, SCT	TYR	Tyrone, IRL	WEX	Wexford, IRL
SLI	Sligo, IRL	UK	United Kingdom	WI	Wisconsin, USA
SOM	Somerset, ENG	USA	United States	WIC	Wicklow, IRL
SRK	Sark, UK	UT	Utah, USA	WIG	Wigtown, SCT
SRY	Surrey, ENG	VA	Virginia, USA	WIL	Wiltshire, ENG
STS	Staffordshire, ENG	VIC	Victoria, AUS	WLN	West Lothian, SCT
STI	Stirling, SCT	VT	Vermont, USA	WLS	Wales
SSX	Sussex, ENG	WA	Washington, USA	WOR	Worcestershire, ENG
SUT	Sutherland, SCT	WA	Western Australia, AUS	WRY	West Riding, WKS
TAS	Tasmania, AUS	WAR	Warwickshire, ENG	WV	West Virginia, USA
TIP	Tipperary, IRL	WAT	Waterford, IRL	WY	Wyoming, USA
TN	Tennessee, USA	WEM	Westmeath, IRL	YKS	Yorkshire, ENG
TX	Texas, USA	WES	Westmorland, ENG		

← *More Abbreviations over Page*

THE CHAPMAN COUNTY CODES

Code **CHAPMAN** des comtés du Royaume Uni et de la République d'Irlande

A new set of County Codes has been developed in the UK. However, as the GRD and many other genealogical publications in English speaking countries have adopted the Chapman County Codes, we intend to retrain them in this and future editions. It must be noted that the counties referred to are those existing prior to 1974 when names and boundaries were changed.

ABBREVIATIONS FOR POLAND

The voievodships after 1975 administrative reform which are now within the borders of Poland:

BP	Biala Podlaska	KS	Krosno	SE	Siedlce
BK	Bialystok	LG	Legnica	SI	Sieradz
BB	Bielsko-Biala	LE	Leszno	SK	Skierniewice
BY	Bydgoszcz	LU	Lublin	SL	Slupsk
CM	Chelm	LO	Lomza	SW	Suwalki
CI	Ciechanow	LD	Lodz	SZ	Szczecin
CZ	Czestochowa	NS	Nowy Sacz	TG	Tarnobrzeg
El	Elblag	OL	Olsztyn	TA	Tarnow
GD	Gdansk	OP	Opole	TO	Torun
GO	Gorzow	OS	Ostroleka	WA	Warszawa
JG	Jelenia Gora	PI	Pila	WB	Walbrzych
KL	Kalisz	PT	Piotrkow	WL	Wloclawek
KA	Katowice	PL	Plock	WR	Wroclaw
KI	Kielce	PO	Poznan	ZA	Samosc
KN	Konin	PR	Przemysl	ZG	Zielona Gora
KO	Koszalin	RA	Radom		
KR	Krakow	RZ	Rzeszow		

The voievodships of the historical Eastern Lands of the Commonwealth of Poland and Lithuania which are now in the USSR:

BL	Brzesc Litewski	MS	Mscislaw	RS	Rus
BR	Braclaw	NG	Nowogrodek	SM	Smolensk
BZ	Blez	PC	Polock	TP	Tarnopol
IN	Inflanty	PD	Podole	TR	Troki
KJ	Kijow	PK	Prusy Ksiazece	WT	Witebsk
LW	Lwow		(the part now in	WN	Wolyn
MN	Minsk		the USSR)	ZD	Zmudi

The above particulars were kindly supplied by Rafal T. Prinke, President of the recently formed genealogical society in Poland (see under Society Listings).

EXPLANATION

1. FAMILY NAME
2. TIME PERIOD
3. TOWN, COUNTY or PROVINCE or STATE, COUNTRY or LAND
4. CONTRIBUTORS NUMBER (see page **665**

---

1. FAMILLE RECHERCHEE
2. PERIODE
3. VILLE, PROVINCE/REGION, PAYS
4. COLLABORATEURS (voir page **665**

---

1. FAMILIENNAME
2. ZEITRAUM
3. ORT, PROVINZ/BUNDESLAND. LAND
4. TEILNEHMER (siehe Seite **665**

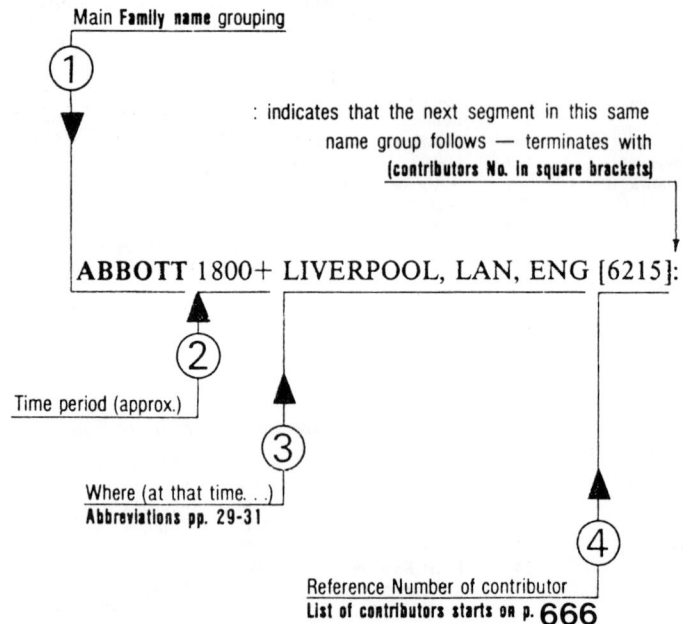

Main **Family name** grouping

①

: indicates that the next segment in this same
name group follows — terminates with
(contributors No. in square brackets)

ABBOTT 1800+ LIVERPOOL, LAN, ENG [6215]:

②

Time period (approx.)

③

Where (at that time. . .)
Abbreviations pp. 29-31

④

Reference Number of contributor
List of contributors starts on p. 666

DIRECTORY

AALTONEN 1889+ ORIMATTILA, UUSIMAA, FIN [38758]

AARONS PRE 1900 LND, ENG [36399]

AASEN 1700+ TUNHOVD, NUMEDAL, NOR [36905]

ABBER 1760-1777 NB & NS, CAN [33910]

ABBES 1820 LANDBEACH, CAM, ENG [34976]

ABBEY 1883 SYDNEY, NSW, AUS [37965] : 1790+ MILEHAM, NFK, ENG [37135] : 1876 DRIFFIELD, ERY, ENG [37965] : C1852 RICCALL, YKS, ENG [37965] : 1793+ CARNBEE, FIF, SCT [35090]

ABBIS 1820 LANDBEACH, CAM, ENG [34976]

ABBOT 1760+ FOLKESTONE, KEN, ENG [35560] : MARGARET 1800-1900 PENRITH, CUL, ENG [36180] : PRE 1820 SHOLDEN & DOVER, KEN, ENG [36532]

ABBOTT PRE 1900 BALLARAT, VIC, AUS [35435] : JOHN 1828-1906 PROTON TWP., ONT, CAN [34524] : CHARLES 1798-1878 CHATEAUGAY, QUE, CAN [34524] : 1800+ WOLLASTON, ENG [34511] : 1750+ CLAWTON, DEV, ENG [34804] : 1650 PINCHBECK, LIN, ENG [35369] : PRE 1900 ST PANCRAS, LND, ENG [35435] : PRE 1830 BECKINGTON, SOM, ENG [35709] : 1800+ NEWTON ABBOT, DEV, ENG [35998] : 1750-1900 LAUNCESTON & NORTH PETHERWIN, CON, ENG [37224] : PRE 1714 BELCHFORD, LIN, ENG [37318] : 1700-1950 ESS, ENG [37344] : 1840+ CARLISLE, WETHERAL, CUL, ENG [37635] : 1750-1850 REDBOURN, HRT, ENG [37885] : 1800-1900 HACKNEY & ISLINGTON, MDX, ENG [38471] : PRE 1900 KILLEEVAN, MOG, IRL [34569] : 1800 COR, IRL [38362] : 1850 LENAWEE CO., MI, USA [38192] : 1887+ WREXHAM, DEN, WLS [35598]

ABBOTTS 1790-1850 BANBURY, OXF, ENG [38265]

ABEL 1800S LONDON, ENG [34044] : ROBERT PRE 1820 NFK, ENG [34222] : 1680+ MARSH BALDON, OXF, ENG [34370] : 1830+ CHADDESLEY CORBETT, WOR, ENG [35919] : 1830+ BELBROUGHTON, WOR, ENG [35919] : PRE 1930 POTTERIES, STS, HRT & LAN, ENG [36502] : PRE 1800 HETHERSETT, NFK, ENG [37773] : 1750+ BLACKROD, LAN, ENG [38260] : PRE 1700 SEEBACH, RPF, GER [38681] : PRE 1830 INVERURIE, ABD, SCT [34613] : 1732+ NY, USA [38015] : 1750+ WLS [38260]

ABELE 1790+ WUE, GER [36343]

ABELL ALL YKS, ENG [34040] : 1630+ HATHERLEIGH, DEV, ENG [35587] : 1800S HOTON & THRINGSTONE, LEI, ENG [36511]

ABELVIK PRE 1900 ALESUND, NOR [37440]

ABERCOMBIE 1836-1925 HAGERSVILLE, ONT, CAN & ENG [34164]

ABERCROMBIE ALL FER, IRL [38226] : 1800-1820 GLASGOW, LKS, SCT [37071]

ABERDEEN ALL WORLDWIDE [35707]

ABERLINE 1800-1830 OSWESTRY, SAL, ENG [35798]

ABERNATHY C1794+ BERKELEY CO., WV, USA [38067]

ABERNETHY 1900S CAMPBELLFORD, ONT, CAN [34215] : ALL COLERIDGE & SHELBURNE, ONT, CAN [37518] : ALL ORANGEVILLE, ONT, CAN [37518] : ALL OFF, IRL [37518] : ALL TIP, IRL [37518] : C1900 DUBLIN, IRL [37518]

ABHAU 1700-1990 GHE & HEN, GER [35630]

ABLE PRE 1750 SFK, ENG [35642]

ABLETT PRE 1812 SFK, ENG [33813]

ABLITT PRE 1860 WESTMINSTER, MDX, ENG [37720]

ABORIGINAL CAROLINE 1860 ROMA, QLD, AUS [35870]

ABRAHAM PRE 1850 DDR [38616] : 1804+ LEEDS, WRY, ENG [34616] : 1775 WAINFLEET, LIN, ENG [35013] : PRE 1820 BARNETBY, LIN, ENG [35024] : PRE 1808 LONDON, ENG [36748] : 1700-1800 ASHBURTON, DEV, ENG [36988] : ALL ATHANASIENHOF, POS, GER [38372] : PRE 1850 RUSSIA [34318] : ALL VA, USA [38032]

ABRAHAMOWITCH ALL WORLDWIDE [38368]

ABRAHAMS C1900 WERRIBEE, VIC, AUS [37157] : C1880 PORT MELBOURNE, VIC, AUS [37157] : 1850+ WHITECHAPEL, LND, ENG [35390]

ABRAM PRE 1788 SOUTHPORT, LAN, ENG [37072]

ABRAMSON 1840-1852 PRE, GER [38236] : 1852-1923 NY, USA [38236] : 1920-40 NJ, USA [38236]

ABREU C1864 MARYBOROUGH, VIC, AUS [35384]

ABSALOM 1830-1850 NEWBURY, BRK, ENG [36623]

ABSOLOM 1820+ SYDNEY, NSW, AUS [37119]

ACETHORPE 1800+ BOSTON, LIN, ENG [36251]

ACHER 1765+ ATTLEBRIDGE, NFK, ENG [35458]

ACHTEN CATHARINA C1739 DIEPENBEEK, LBG, BEL [37430]

ACHTERKERKEN ALL WILFINGEN, NSA, GER [38637]

ACHY EPHRAIM 1822-1870 COLUMBIA CO., PA, USA [38732]

ACK PRE 1838 BAD, GER [34421]

ACKER ABRAHAM 1834+ WAINFLEET, ONT, CAN [34059] : PRE 1850 HARTLETON UNION CO., PA, USA [37528] : 1850-69 MEDINA CO., OH, USA [37528]

ACKERLEY PRE 1905 TIMPERLEY, CHS, ENG [36841] : 1905+ RICCARTON, CANTY, NZ [36841] : ALL WORLDWIDE [37350]

ACKERLY 1799+ NEW KINGSTON & MARGARETVILLE, NY, USA [37572] : ALL WORLDWIDE [37350]

ACKERMAN 1650+ SELZEN, RPF, BRD [37012] : RUDOLF PRE 1760 HENDSCHIKEN, AG, CH [34992] : 1820+ WEYMOUTH, DOR, ENG [34714] : 1500+ WORLDWIDE [37099]

ACKERMANS 1800+ S GRAVENHAGE, ZUH, NL [35338] : 1800+ GINNEKEN & BAVEL, NBT, NL [35338]

ACKFIELD 1800+ ENG [35762] : 1800+ IRL [35762]

ACKLAND 1900+ JUNG, VIC, AUS [36622] : 1799 CHATHAM, KEN, ENG [35369] : PRE 1875 ENG [36347] : C1770 LUPPITT, DEV, ENG [37264] : 1850+ PHILADELPHIA, PA, USA [36347]

ACKLEY RACHEL 1794-1876 COXSACKIEN CO., NY, USA [38140]

ACKROYD ALL CONISBOROUGH, YKS, ENG [34789] : 1800+ BRADFORD, WRY, ENG [36104]

ACOSTA 1550-1750 CABO ROJO, SAN JUAN, PUERTO RICO, USA [36340]

ACOURT ALL NORTH CADBURY, SOM, ENG [37332]

ACRED ALL UPWELL, NFK & CAM, ENG [37617]

ACRES PRE 1850 KEN, ENG [34593]

ACRET 1815+ WES, ENG [35465]

ACTON 1840S+ QUE & ONT, CAN [37438] : C1852 LONDON, ENG [34009] : ALL NTT & WAR, ENG [37412] : PRE 1850 MAY, IRL [34060] : 1800+ MAY, IRL [37438]

ADAIR C1818-1859 CLOUGHY, DOW, IRL [38402] : PRE 1904 PEVELY, MO, USA [36930] : 1830-1880 IN & IL, USA [38367]

ADAM 1870+ MORNINGTON, ONT, CAN [36716] :
PRE 1841 BAN, SCT [34357] : C1780 STI, SCT [35098]
: 1829 FALKIRK, STI, SCT [35259] : PRE 1875 STI,
SCT [35556] : JEAN C1800 KELLAS, MOR, SCT
[35848] : C1765 DALLAS, MOR, SCT [36431] : ALL
STIRLING, STI, SCT [38332]

ADAMEK 1870S ZDIAR, SLOVAKIA, CS [38223]

ADAMS 1800-1850 BERRIDALE & COOMA, NSW,
AUS [34307] : 1850+ LAUNCESTON, TAS, AUS
[34904] : ELIZA 1891+ GUNDY, NSW, AUS [35412] :
1846+ MAITLAND, NSW, AUS [35543] : 1855+
BEECHWORTH, VIC, AUS [35819] : 1880S
WOODEND, VIC, AUS [37497] : 1845 BULLEEN,
VIC, AUS [37497] : THOMAS 1854+ GLEBE, NSW,
AUS [37942] : 1880S MACKAY, QLD, AUS [37946] :
1868+ GLEN INNES, NSW, AUS [38069] :
RICHARD PRE 1851 ONTARIO CO., ONT, CAN
[34988] : 1820+ BIRMINGHAM, WAR, ENG [33946]
: 1850+ LONDON, ENG [34029] : 1890+
HALSTEAD, ESS, ENG [34029] : ALL FAREHAM,
HAM, ENG [34160] : THOMAS C1800 BRANDON,
SFK, ENG [34259] : 1867+ STAFFORD, STS, ENG
[34334] : 1835-1857 ADBASTON, STS, ENG [34334] :
1600+ HASTINGS, SSX, ENG [34747] : MARY 1800-
1850 BIRMINGHAM, WAR, ENG [34751] : JOHN
PRE 1700 BRADFORD ON AVON, WIL, ENG
[34908] : 1700+ TOTNES, DEV, ENG [34970] : PRE
1856 COVENTRY, WAR, ENG [35008] : PRE 1821
POLESWORTH, WAR, ENG [35090] : C1800-1850
DEV, ENG [35391] : 1800+ BOTOSHAM, CAM,
ENG [35465] : THOMAS C1817 BOW, MDX, ENG
[35955] : 1840-1910 ROMFORD, ESS, ENG [35955] :
PRE 1890 LEAMINGTON SPA, WAR, ENG [35962] :
PRE 1890 MORETON PINKNEY, NTH, ENG
[35962] : PRE 1830 OAKLEY, STS, ENG [36066] :
1800+ NOTTINGHAM, NTT, ENG [36105] : ALL
SOUTHGATE & CHELSEA, MDX, ENG [36171] :
ALL HARTING & WESTFIELD, SSX, ENG [36171] :
C1828 COTTENHAM, CAM, ENG [36185] : 1700-
1850 DOR, ENG [36222] : PRE 1881 ELLESMERE,
SAL, ENG [36230] : 1810+ BIRMINGHAM, WAR,
ENG [36239] : PRE 1850 EDMONTON, LND, ENG
[36247] : C1880 BRANDON, SFK, ENG [36307] : ALL
ESS, ENG [36500] : THOMAS PRE 1804
WOLVERHAMPTON, STS, ENG [36532] : PRE 1760
KINGSTONE, SOM, ENG [36581] : 1600S
CHEDWORTH & BIBURY, GLS, ENG [36585] :
1760-1800 COVENTRY, WAR, ENG [36649] : ALL
TOTNES, DEV, ENG [36744] : 1600+ WEM, SAL,
ENG [36756] : 1860-1950 CANNING TOWN, LND,
ENG [36990] : 1790 ALDERWASLEY, DBY, ENG
[37215] : PRE 1860 SAL, ENG [37273] : 1700+
CLANFIELD, OXF, ENG [37328] : PRE 1800
DOVER, KEN, ENG [37371] : ANN C1805
WIVELISCOMBE, SOM, ENG [37396] : 1800-1900
LITTLE HINTON, WIL, ENG [37763] : PRE 1800
DOR, ENG [37771] : C1780 ST ALBANS, HRT, ENG
[37898] : C1700 WEST COKER, SOM, ENG [37918] :
WILLIAM PRE 1830 KEN, ENG [38069] : 1750-1900
KIPPAX & HECK, YKS, ENG [38251] : HERBERT
C1900 BATTERSEA, SRY, ENG [38268] :
ANTHONY C1800 ENG [38268] : JOHN C1854
LAMBETH, SRY, ENG [38268] : 1800 THATCHAM,
BRK, ENG [38276] : 1800+ TIVERTON, DEV, ENG
[38396] : 1750-1800 EAST LONDON, MDX, ENG
[38516] : ALEX PRE 1850 MAGHERACROSS, FER,
IRL [33814] : PRE 1850 ENNISKILLEN, FER, IRL
[34201] : 1860+ CLADY, ANT, IRL [35372] :
WILLIAM 1830+ ARMAGH, ARM, IRL [36611] :
HENRY 1826-1926 LONDONDERRY, LDY, IRL &
AUS [34794] : ALL WELLINGTON, NZ [36744] : PRE
1830 OLD DEER, ABD, SCT [34197] : PRE 1853

NEWTON & SOUTH LEITH, MLN, SCT [34706] :
ALL MAYBOLE, AYR, SCT [34838] : 1750+
HAWICK, ROX, SCT [35038] : PRE 1895
ABERDEEN, ABD, SCT [36358] : 1857-1866
WHITBURN, SCT [37108] : ALL STIRLING, STI,
SCT [38332] : PRE 1880 CATTARAUGUS &
WYOMING COS., NY, USA [35270] : 1800S
BRUNSWICK CO., VA, USA [36896] : 1860-1960S
SUMMIT & STARK, OH, USA [36899] : RICHARD
1800-1910S LANCASTER & BERKS, PA, USA
[36899] : PRE 1800 BERKSHIRE CO., MA, NY & NJ,
USA [36917] : ALL BUTLER CO., PA, USA [36919] :
1700+ HALIFAX, VA & KY, USA [36931] : C1800
ULSTER CO., NY, USA [37017] : WILLIAM 1840+
VENANGO CO., PA, USA [37040] : HENRY PRE
1810 CARTER CO., TN, USA [37551] : 1700S
WILKES CO., NC, USA [37570] : 1630-1700
COLCHESTER, CT, USA [37783] : 1840-1870 ROME,
NY, USA [37783] : 1800-1870 OSWEGO CO., NY,
USA [37783] : PRE 1900 LANCASTER, BERKS CO.,
PA, USA [37804] : SARAH 1720-1780 DANBURY
NORFOLK, CT, USA [37806] : 1830-1900
VERMILION CO., IL & MO, USA [38025] :
GEORGE W. 1815 NEW YORK, NY, USA [38122] :
JOHN QUINCY 1863 GA, USA [38122] : JOHN
QUINCY 1845+ NEWBERRY PORT, MA, USA
[38122] : 1739-1761 WESTFORD, MA, USA [38139] :
1800+ DALE, PIKE, AL, USA [38326] : C1820
CLINTON, OH, USA [38527] : PRE 1876
RICHLAND CO., TN, USA [38531] : CHARLES
1850+ NEWHAVEN, CT, USA [38766]

ADAMSDOTTER LOTTA 1861-899 GRANNA
LANDSFORSAMLING, JONKOPINGS LAN, SWE
[38548]

ADAMSON PRE 1873 PERTH, TAS, AUS [33862] :
1849+ GEELONG, VIC, AUS [34922] : 1857+
MALDON, VIC, AUS [35379] : JOHN 1800+
PICKERING, NRY, ENG [34078] : PRE 1880
RIPON, NRY, ENG [36228] : PRE 1880
BALLYNURE, ANT, IRL [33993] : PRE 1857
EDINBURGH, MLN, SCT [35379] : 1800S
DOUGLAS, LKS, SCT [35391] : 1750+
ANSTRUTHERWESTER & PITTENWEEN, FIF,
SCT [35395] : PRE 1800 PITTENWEEM, FIF, SCT
[35627] : 1700+ DUMFRIES, SCT [35943] : PRE 1780
FIF, SCT [36679] : 1830+ FORFAR, ANS, SCT
[37167]

ADAY 1780-90 SCT [38151] : 1850-80 JASPER, AR, USA
[38151] : 1840+ TN, USA [38151]

ADCOCK 1852+ VIC, AUS [38771] : 1820-1840S
NOTTINGHAM, NTT, ENG [37308] : 1800+
MELBOURNE, DBY, ENG [37675] : PRE 1770
CARLTON, LEI, ENG [37675] : 1890S CRADOCK,
CAPE, RSA [37675] : 1700-1800 VA, USA [34749]

ADDEMS PRE 1893 IPSWICH, SFK, ENG [35114]

ADDERLEY PRE 1725 KINGSLEY, STS, ENG [36701]

ADDERTON 1720-1780 ST MARYS CO., MD, USA
[38119]

ADDINGTON 1700+ MAULDEN, BDF, ENG [34640] :
1830+ ALBANY, NY, USA [38530] : ALL
WORLDWIDE [37857]

ADDIS 1750+ GLS, ENG [33973] : 1850+ NY, USA
[33973] : PRE 1720 NORTHAMPTON, PA, USA
[36549] : ALL USA [36926] : 1750+ MON, WLS
[33973] : 1890S GLA, WLS [35084]

ADDISON 1840+ TAS, AUS [37128] : 1790-1900 ONT,
CAN [37461] : PRE 1900 NFK, ENG [36187] : 1690-
1850 WES, CUL & YKS, ENG [34970] : 1850+
WIGTON, CUL, ENG & CAN [34467] : 1859
COUROCK, SCT [33932] : 1803-1936 CAIRNIE,
ABD, SCT [34479] : PRE 1815 KINGSKETTLE, FIF,
SCT [35045] : 1750+ ANSTRUTHERWESTER &

PITTENWEEN, FIF, SCT [35395] : 1845+
MONTROSE, SCT & AUS [35056] : 1780-1820
ONTARIO CO., NY, USA [36968]
ADDLESEE ALL WORLDWIDE [34361]
ADDLETON PRE 1861+ MOONEE PONDS, VIC,
AUS [34423]
ADEN IDA M. 1850-1875 SWE [36331]
ADEY 1760S LANGLEY, STS, ENG [37898]
ADIE 1860-1920 LONDON, ENG [34230] : 1790-1870
LIMEHOUSE, MDX, ENG [37752] : 1800+
FRASERBURGH, ABD, SCT [36887] : ALL
WORLDWIDE [34831]
ADKIN 1700+ BURY ST EDMUNDS, SFK, ENG
[36088] : 1700+ BUNGAY, SFK, ENG [36088] : 1820S
MANCHESTER, LAN, ENG [36292]
ADKINS 1850-1950 SEVENOAKS, KEN, ENG [34946] :
ALL EDMONTON, LND, ENG [35631] : PRE 1755
KENILWORTH, WAR, ENG [37144] : PRE 1820
WARKWORTH, NTH, ENG [38424] : C1760
LUNENBURG CO., VA, USA [37536]
ADKINSON ALL ALLEGHENY CO., PA, USA [38036]
ADLAM ALL LONGBRIDGE DEVERILL, WIL, ENG
[34466] : ALL CROCKERTON, WIL, ENG [34466] :
PRE 1863 WESTBURY, WIL, ENG [34466] :
ROBERT 1700-1800 DILTON MARSH, WIL, ENG
[35361] : MATHEW 1828+ WIL, ENG [35361] : C1735
EBBESBOURNE WAKE, WIL, ENG [38489]
ADLASSNIG ALL KAERNTEN & MARGARETHEN,
OES [38369]
ADLEM C1765 TOLLARD ROYAL & ASHMORE,
DOR, ENG [34157]
ADLER 1800-1900 CS [36962] : 1700+
HAHNSTATTEN, HEN, GER [37042] : 1700-1900
BAV, GER [38128] : 1700+ FEUCHTWAGEN, BAY,
GER [38578] : PRE 1850 LINDELBACH, GER [38676]
: 1870-1900 BOLECHOWICE, KR, POL [35717] :
1860-1900 KARNIOWICE, KR, POL [35717] : 1830-
1860 KURDWANOW, KR, POL [35717] : C1860
RUDAWA CHRZANOW, KR, POL [35717]
ADLUM C1830 WEST HARNHAM, WIL, ENG [34281]
ADNER 1760-1790 HAVERSTRAW, NY, USA [36900]
ADNET PRE 1720 ASH, KEN, ENG [35462]
ADNUM PRE 1840 LEATHER MARKET, SRY, ENG
[34968]
ADOLPH 1750+ PRE, GER [33963] : ALL SIL, GER
[35310] : 1850+ SOMMEFELD, BLN, GER [38274]
ADORNATO PRE 1920 MESSINA, SICILY IS., ITL
[36271]
ADREON C1800-1900 BALTIMORE CO., MD, USA
[38030]
ADRIAENSE PRE 1701 BAARLE NASSAU, NBT, NL
[35008]
ADRIAENSEN PRE 1715 RAVELS, ATW, BEL [35008]
ADRIAN 1780+ PRE, GER [37532] : ALL
MARIENWEEDEN& RODAN, PRE, GER & NZ
[34645]
ADSETT ALL PETWORTH, SSX, ENG [37285]
ADSHEAD PRE 1853 MACCLESFIELD, CHS, ENG
[35872]
AERAY 1600-1720 ST BEES, CUL, ENG [37858]
AERNI 1825-1875 GOSREUTH, SG, CH [35283]
AERTS ANT 1730-1815 WERCHTER & ROTSELAAR,
BBT, BEL [38405]
AETHERD C1750 PER, SCT [37463]
AFFLECK 1700-1800 DALHAM, SFK, ENG [35706] :
PRE 1850 TYNEMOUTH, NBL & LAN, ENG [37846]
: 1800+ MAUCHLINE, AYR, SCT [33948] : PRE
1800 FIF, SCT [37693]
AFFRIAT PRE 1818 ENG [35743] : PRE 1818 ENG
[35743]
AGACE ALL ENG [37833]
AGANS ALL ONEIDA CO., NY & MI, USA [38287]

AGAR 1800S STILLINGFLEET, YKS, ENG [34309] :
ALL FARNDALE, YKS, ENG [35198] : PRE 1890
LONDON, ENG [36755] : DANIEL, THOM 1820-
1860 KIK, IRL [34143]
AGASSIZ 1910+ NEWTOWN, NSW, AUS [34967]
AGATE 1603+ HURSTPIERPOINT, SSX, ENG [36212]
AGER 1800-1900 ABBOTS RODING, ESS, ENG [34469]
AGNE 1700S LAMBSBORN PFALZ, BAV, GER [37516]
AGNEW 1800 IRL [34190] : PRE 1856
CARRICKFERGUS, ANT, IRL [35162] : 1800+
BALLYGAWLEY, TYR, IRL [36075] : 1845-1901
BALLYMACONNELL & GROOMSPORT, DOW,
IRL & AUS [33847] : C1807-1830 WIG, SCT [35820] :
PRE 1840 MD, USA [38017] : 1840S ATLANTA, GA,
USA [38017]
AGTERBERG 1680 UTRECHT, UTR, NL [38706]
AGUILA PRE 1850 SAN JOSE, BATANGAS,
PHILIPPINE [34891]
AGULLY 1700S PENTRIDGE, DOR, ENG [35297]
A'HARAH 1850+ BALLYAUTOGUE &
TEMPLEPATRICK, ANT, IRL [37425]
AHART 1845-60 COVE CREEK, WV, USA [37011]
AHEARN JOHN 1840 MAITLAND, NSW, AUS [37123]
: JOHN 1814 BANSHA, TIP, IRL [37123]
A'HEARN PRE 1800 COR, IRL [37984]
AHEARNE 1802-1818 DERWENT, TAS, AUS [37135] :
1818-1852 GEORGES RIVER, NSW, AUS [37135]
AHEIMER ALL BAW, BRD [37954]
AHERN 1800+ MELBOURNE, VIC, AUS [35734] :
1880+ TOWNSVILLE, QLD, AUS [36305] : PRE 1820
CAPWELL, COR, IRL [33766] : PRE 1800 COR, IRL
[35734] : 1750+ TIP, IRL [36602] : PRE 1800
CARRICK ON SUIR, WAT, IRL [37579]
AHERNE C1890 DEVONPORT, TAS, AUS [35748]
AHFELD PRE 1860 HAN, GER [34801]
AH-GEE PRE 1888 ESK, QLD, AUS [33832] : PRE 1888
CANTON, CHINA [33832]
AH GOOEY PRE 1900 REDESDALE, VIC, AUS
[35471]
AH KIN ALL BEGA, NSW, AUS [33769]
AHLERS 1800 KLEINNUCHEL, GER [37170]
AHOLIN PRE 1800 LARSMO, VAASA, FIN [34858]
AHPOO ALL WORLDWIDE [35875]
AHR 1560-1970S OTTENHAUSEN & ITTERSBACH,
BAW, GER [37021]
AHRENS 1820S GER [37024] : 1590+ HEMDINGEN,
SHO, GER [37542]
AH YING C1894 PERTH, WA, AUS [35348]
AH YUNG C1896 ROMA, QLD, AUS [35807]
AICHER ALL WORLDWIDE [38657]
AICKIN 1860S BELFAST, ANT, IRL [35123]
AID 1790+ ENG [34803]
AIKEN ALL BELFAST, ANT, IRL [34724] : 1750+
ANT, IRL [37099] : 1800+ ABERDEEN, SCT [33947]
: 1785 OLD MACHAR, ABD, SCT [34950] : ALL
WORLDWIDE [34724]
AIKEN (SEE AITKEN) [35855]
AIKENHEAD C1750-1800 ANS, SCT [36327]
AIKENS PRE 1820 IRL [38783]
AIKERLY ALL WORLDWIDE [37350]
AIKMAN 1850 MUSSELBURGH, MLN, SCT [35535] :
1700+ LANARK & CARLUKE, LKS, SCT & NZ
[36791] : 1700-1900 WORLDWIDE [36130]
AIMES PRE 1840 PARIS, RPA, FRA [36532]
AINGE 1820-1880 CAMBERWELL, LND, ENG [34621]
: PRE 1800 TYSOE, WAR, ENG [34621] : 1890S
BRITISH, GUIANA [34621]
AINGER 1770-1790 STEPNEY & ISLINGTON, LND,
ENG [37445] : PRE 1875 DOVERCOURT & GREAT
OAKLEY, ESS, ENG [38464] : PRE 1700 FRA [38464]

AINLEY 1880+ WATERLOO & SYDNEY, NSW, AUS [34979] : 1800+ HUDDERSFIELD, YKS, ENG [34863] : PRE 1880 YKS, ENG [34979]

AINSBURY C1830-40 ENG [33828]

AINSLEY PRE 1790 CAUNTON, NTT, ENG [34445] : 1830+ YKS & KEN, ENG [36574] : 1790-1900 WYOMING, NY, USA [38095]

AINSLIE 1750-1800 MLN, SCT [35624]

AINSWORTH PRE 1820 WAKEFIELD, YKS, ENG [34959]

AIR 1900+ SALTCOATS, SAS, CAN [36716] : PRE 1900 ANS, SCT & AUS [35512]

AIRAY PRE 1860 MANCHESTER, LAN, ENG [36019]

AIRD ALL LONDON, MDX, ENG [37950] : 1700-1850 KILMARNOCK, AYR, SCT [35151] : 1760+ ROSSKEEN, ROC, SCT [36509] : 1800+ ROSEMARKIE, ROC, SCT [36885]

AIREY 1890+ ROCHDALE, LAN, ENG [34790] : 1800+ STAINMORE, WES, ENG [35891] : PRE 1820 CLAUGHTON & LANCASTER, LAN, ENG [38248]

AIRNS 1750+ LKS, SCT [38279]

AIRY PRE 1800 WORLDWIDE [37280]

AISBETT 1830+ BIDDINGTON, DUR, ENG [37999]

AISBITT PRE 1840 NEWCASTLE ON TYNE, NBL, ENG [34795]

AISHE ALL WORLDWIDE [38252]

AISHEN 1780-1900 WORCESTER, WOR, ENG [37919]

AISTHORP PRE 1810 LIN, ENG [36143]

AISTHORPE 1888+ ROMA DISTRICT, QLD, AUS [37896] : PRE 1888 BUCKNALL, LIN, ENG [37896] : C1900S ARKSEY, YKS, ENG [37896] : C1800S CONINGSBY, LIN, ENG [37896]

AITCHESON 1800+ LARGO, FIF, SCT [37333]

AITCHISON 1850+ QLD, AUS [35882] : 1800-1837 HORNCLIFFE, NBL, ENG [38269] : PRE 1880 BEW, SCT [35400] : PRE 1834 DUDDINGSTON, MLN, SCT [35542] : 1830S GLASGOW, LKS, SCT [35730] : 1700+ ABBEY ST BATHANS, BEW, SCT [35882] : PRE 1839 WEST BARNS, ELN, SCT [36308] : 1829+ LARGO, FIF, SCT [37333] : SARAH 1865+ DENVER, CO, USA [37424] : 1600+ WORLDWIDE [38378]

AITKEN 1870+ PORT AUGUSTA, SA, AUS [37734] : 1800+ ALKBOROUGH, LIN, ENG [34681] : ALL MANCHESTER, LAN, ENG [34684] : 1840 LONDON, MDX, ENG [35067] : PRE 1840 CHADWELL, MDX, ENG [35354] : PRE 1900 MITCHAM, SRY, ENG [35577] : THOMAS 1881 FALLOWFIELD, LAN, ENG [36635] : 1870-1876 GEORGEHAM, DEV, ENG [37571] : 1700-1850 CLERKENWELL, MDX, ENG [37642] : 1820 BOMBAY, INDIA [35067] : 1834-1870 AIRDRIE, LKS, SCT [33991] : 1790S ABERCORN, MLN, SCT [34172] : 1790-1840 FALKIRK, STI, SCT [34359] : 1880+ SHOTTS, LKS, SCT [34404] : ALL ABERDEEN, ABD, SCT [34674] : 1790+ MIDHOPE BRIDGE, MLN, SCT [34681] : C1730 AUCHTERDERRAN, FIF, SCT [34768] : PRE 1889 CRIEFF, STI, SCT [35473] : 1830+ MONTROSE, ANS, SCT [35778] : 1770+ DUNROSSNESS, SHI, SCT [35855] : C1800 LARBERT, STI, SCT [35865] : 1800-1830 DUNFERMLINE, FIF, SCT [36268] : C1790 TARBOLTON, AYR, SCT [36431] : 1857+ GAUSTON, SCT [37572] : PRE 1838 ECCLES, BEW, SCT [37610] : 1700+ LKS, SCT [38476]

AITON PRE 1840 ABERDEEN, SCT [34519]

AKED C1700-1900 HALIFAX & WAKEFIELD, WRY, ENG [36037] : 1680-1800 HALIFAX, WRY, ENG [36049]

AKEHURST PRE 1800 HELLINGLY, SSX, ENG [35020]

AKELAND C1870 LAMBETH, LND, ENG [38276]

AKERAY ALL WORLDWIDE [37350]

AKERMAN PRE 1854 BKM, ENG [35384] : HELENA 1733-1794 SODERTALJE, SODERMANLAND, SWE [38550]

AKERS C1900 TOTTENHAM, MDX, ENG [35167] : 1800+ LEI & DBY, ENG [35169] : C1800 WASHINGTON CO., VA, USA [37824] : C1800 WYTHE CO., VA, USA [37824]

AKKERMAN C1850-1900 NOH, NL & RSA [38707]

AKKERMANS 1882 BREDA, NBT, NL [36307]

AKROYD 1857+ BIRMINGHAM, WAR, ENG & WLS [34653]

ALAND ALL ENG [33827]

ALBERD 1830+ VISBY, GOTTBERG, SWE & AUS [35056]

ALBERS 1835+ CINCINATTI, OH & IA, USA [36542]

ALBERT 1865+ HANGING GARDENS, VIC, AUS [37920] : 1830-1950S NB & QUE, CAN [34202] : 1840-1915 BLAIR CO., PA, USA [38106]

ALBERTS 1650-1750 NEW YORK, NY, USA [38113]

ALBOROUGH 1600-1850 NFK, ENG [34081]

ALBRATE PRE 1856 SOMMARIVA BOSCO, PIEDMONT, ITL [38085]

ALBRECHT 1700-1730S RPF, BRD [33755] : C1840-94 ST BRIDE & CLERKENWELL, LND, ENG [36425] : PRE 1850 KONIGSBERG, OPR, GER [36425] : PRE 1840 USA [38229]

ALBRESS 1915+ RYE, VIC, AUS [35220]

ALBRI 1788-1820 HORST, LMB, NL [37187]

ALBRIGHT 1800-1850 WEYBRIDGE, SRY, ENG [37618] : 1800+ MADISON CO., MO, USA [33755] : 1800+ MADISON CO., GA, USA [33755] : 1800+ TUSCALOOSA CO., AL, USA [33755] : 1800+ DARKE CO., OH, USA [33755] : 1820+ FAIRFIELD CO., OH, USA [33755] : 1800+ MONTGOMERY & KNOX COS., TN, USA [33755] : 1820+ RAPIDES PAR, LA, USA [33755] : 1760+ ORANGE CO., NC, USA [33755] : 1730+ BERKS CO., PA, USA [33755] : 1820+ HOUSTON CO., TX, USA [33755] : 1800+ CAMPBELL CO., TN, USA [33755] : PRE 1840 USA [38229]

ALBRISSON 1816 GA, USA [36358]

ALBRITTON 1850 AL, USA [36358]

ALBRO PRE 1850 NEWPORT, RI, USA [36941]

ALBROOK ALL WORLDWIDE [35326]

ALBURY PRE 1839 KEN, ENG [34886] : ALL CROYDON, SRY, ENG [37115] : ALL SRY, ENG [37115]

ALBUTT PRE 1820 BIRMINGHAM, WAR, ENG [37325]

ALCHIN 1838+ DALTON, NSW, AUS [35420] : PRE 1838 STAPLEHURST, KEN, ENG [35420]

ALCOCK 1815-1990 MITCHELL, PERTH CO., CAN & IRL [37499] : PRE 1850 CHEADLE, STS, ENG [33954] : 1800-1830 EYNSHAM, OXF, ENG [34274] : C1704 BURTON JOYCE & GEDLING, NTT, ENG [34836] : 1785-1808 ASTON LE WALLS, NTH, ENG [35990] : 1809-1853 ETTINGTON, WAR, ENG [35990] : 1800+ HANLEY, STS, ENG [35998] : 1870-80S HEACHAM, NFK, ENG [36301] : PRE 1800 STS, ENG [37389] : ALL GRIMSBY, LIN, ENG [37830] : PRE 1815 LONDON, ENG [37989] : 1836-70 PORTSMOUTH, HAM, ENG [37989] : PRE 1820 DUBLIN, IRL [34262] : 1865+ ABERDEEN, SCT [37989]

ALCORAN 1880S MACKAY, QLD, AUS [35823] : 1800+ NEWINGTON, MLN, SCT [35823]

ALCORN 1852+ ESSENDON & GISBORNE, VIC, AUS [34295] : 1857+ MILTON, NSW, AUS [38491] : 1840S-60S TYR, IRL [35243] : PRE 1852 SPROUSTON, ROX, SCT [34295] : 1700+ USA [36347]

ALDCROFT PRE 1857 CHORLTON ON MEDLOCK, LAN, ENG **[36230]**

ALDER ALL WANTAGE & WEST HENDRED, BRK, ENG **[34110]**

ALDERDICE 1700-1800 SANTRY, ANT, IRL **[36803]**

ALDERFER 1745+ MONTGOMERY CO., PA, USA **[36540]**

ALDERIDGE 1750+ BKM, ENG **[34416]**

ALDERMAN 1800S CONGRESBURY, SOM, ENG **[37729]** : 1880+ NTH, ENG **[37922]**

ALDERSLEY 1800+ KELBROOK, YKS, ENG **[34564]**

ALDERSON JOHN PRE 1800 RICHMOND, YKS, ENG **[34442]** : PRE 1900 HALIFAX, YKS, ENG **[34750]** : PRE 1869 HEIGHINGTON & AYCLIFFE, DUR, ENG **[35462]** : 1800+ BRADFORD, YKS, ENG **[36769]** : C1800 YKS, ENG **[36993]** : 1750-1890 DUR, ENG **[37137]**

ALDERTON JOHN 1846-1890 WILBERFORCE, NSW, AUS **[35831]** : 1750+ LITTLE & GREAT SAXHAM, SFK, ENG **[34416]** : ALL SFK, ENG **[34744]** : ALL INTWOOD, NFK, ENG **[36223]** : ALL IPSWICH, SFK, ENG **[36223]** : ALL BURY ST EDMUNDS, SFK, ENG **[36223]** : ALL GREAT CRESSINGHAM, NFK, ENG **[36223]** : ALL NORWICH, NFK, ENG **[36223]** : ALL NFK & SFK, ENG **[36223]** : 1793 INGHAM, SFK, ENG **[37106]** : 1790+ LEWES, SSX, ENG **[38209]** : ALL ANNAPOLIS, MD, USA **[36223]** : ALL ALLEGANY, MD, USA **[36223]** : ALL VA, USA **[36223]**

ALDHAM ALL NORWICH, NFK, ENG **[37689]**

ALDON C1870 MILTON, OXF, ENG **[35889]**

ALDRED JANE 1900+ RANDWICK, NSW, AUS **[35549]** : ALL YKS, ENG **[34040]** : C1860-1890S WANDSWORTH, SRY, ENG **[35347]** : PRE 1800 LAN, ENG **[38389]**

ALDRICH 18541990 BEAUFORT & RAGLAN, VIC, AUS **[33885]** : PRE 1855 CRANSTON PROVIDENCE, RI, USA **[33885]** : 1780 SHREWSBURY, VT, USA **[38131]**

ALDRIDGE 1791+ AUS **[35561]** : 1791+ SYDNEY, NSW, AUS **[35807]** : 1700S EAST WELLOW, HAM, ENG **[35597]** : C1772 MDX, ENG **[35807]** : PRE 1800 SHRAWLEY & HOLT, WOR, ENG **[36110]** : PRE 1650 MAPLE DURHAM, OXF, ENG **[36326]** : 1600-1700 MOTCOMBE, DOR, ENG **[36478]** : 1600-1700 BRATTON & ERLESTOKE, WIL, ENG **[36478]** : PRE 1800 AYLSHAM, NFK, ENG **[36593]** : PRE 1860 LONDON, ENG **[37392]** : ALL NFK & SFK, ENG **[37612]** : 1750-1810 WONSTON, HAM, ENG **[38003]** : 1800-1880 PANO AKIL, UPPER SIND, INDIA **[37203]**

ALDWELL 1843+ AUS & NZ **[35028]** : PRE 1843 AUCKLAND, NZ **[35028]** : PRE 1855 USA **[35028]**

ALEGOEDT ALL WORLDWIDE **[38358]**

ALEMANY 1700-1990 ALICANTE, ESP **[38346]**

ALEMOND 1820 STANTON ST JOHN, OXF, ENG **[35463]**

ALENSON PRE 1860 GRANTHAM & HORNCASTLE, LIN, ENG **[36022]**

ALEWOOD PRE 1843 GREENWICH, LND, ENG **[35559]**

ALEXANDER 1848-1862 GEELONG, VIC, AUS **[38207]** : PRE 1825 DEVIZES & POTTERNE, WIL, ENG **[34974]** : THOMAS C1719 RAMSBURY, WIL, ENG **[37002]** : 1900+ CHS, ENG **[37147]** : 1800+ HOLLINGBOURNE, KEN, ENG **[37405]** : ALL SFK, ENG **[37612]** : C1770+ HAM, ENG **[37868]** : 1796-1882 STEVENTON, HAM, ENG **[38761]** : 1800S TULLAMORE, OFF, IRL **[35398]** : 1700-1900 DON, IRL **[35600]** : ALL DOW, IRL **[35985]** : PRE 1850 IRL **[37923]** : 1800-1850S WATTEN, CAI, SCT **[34816]** : 1800S MAYBOLE, AYR, SCT **[35558]** : 1706+

CAMPBELL, SCT **[37564]** : 1840+ LKS, SCT **[37923]** : C1846 ALYTH, PER, SCT **[38207]** : 1800S ABERDEEN, SCT **[38281]** : PRE 1858 ELLON, ABD, SCT **[38412]** : 1820+ MUSSELBURGH, MLN, SCT & AUS **[33926]** : 1750-1800 ST HELENA **[38380]** : 1750-1850 UK **[36324]** : 1700-1800 CUMBERLAND, RI, USA **[36335]** : GEORGE M. 1828-1906 SOUTH FAYETTE TWP., PA, USA **[36576]** : JOSEPH S. 1820-1899 PGH, ALLEGHENY CO., PA, USA **[36576]** : JOHN R. 1854-1876 PGH, ALLEGHENY CITY, PA, USA **[36576]** : LUELLA B. 1861-1884 PGH, ALLEGHENY CITY, PA, USA **[36576]** : GEORGE B. 1856-1882 PGH, ALLEGHENY CITY, PA, USA **[36576]** : FLORENCE M. 1875-1905 PGH, ALLEGHENY CO., PA, USA **[36576]** : 1800S LEXINGTON & LOUISVILLE, KY & PA, USA **[37539]** : 1820 SC, USA **[38198]** : PRE 1900 CLARK, IL, USA **[38527]** : 1800+ WORLDWIDE **[37147]**

ALEXANDRE 1700-1800 ST HELIER, JSY, CHI **[35048]** : PRE 1875 CHI **[38286]** : 1780S JSY, CHI **[38396]** : 1875+ CANTERBURY, NZ **[38286]**

ALFLATT 1700-1850 NORFOLK, NFK, ENG **[37252]**

ALFORD 1800+ GEORGES RIVER, NSW, AUS **[34274]** : ALL WILLUNGA, SA, AUS **[36822]** : 1800+ BONAVENTURE, QUE, CAN **[34107]** : PRE 1810 DOR, ENG **[36496]** : PRE 1810 HAM, ENG **[36496]** : PRE 1810 WIL, ENG **[36496]** : 1761-1787 CHITTLEHAMPTON, DEV, ENG **[38761]**

ALFRED PRE 1884 MALLALA, SA, AUS & ENG **[35763]**

ALGAR 1800S GREAT YARMOUTH, NFK, ENG **[34086]** : ELLEN 1862+ BRENTFORD, MDX, ENG **[35805]**

ALGEO 1700+ ABBEY, RFW, SCT **[35395]**

ALGER PRE 1750 WATTISFIELD, SFK, ENG **[34707]** : 1600-1900 VT & MA, USA **[35292]** : 1700-1800 NY, USA **[35603]**

ALGUIRE PRE 1800 BERKS CO., PA, USA **[36702]**

ALI ALL SA, AUS **[35139]**

ALINSON PRE 1860 GRANTHAM & HORNCASTLE, LIN, ENG **[36022]**

ALISON 1700-1830 CHURCH LENCH, WOR, ENG **[37849]** : 1762 EDINBURGH, MLN, SCT **[37106]** : C1780 FIF, PER & KRS, SCT **[37463]**

ALKIN C1766-1777 DERBY, DBY, ENG **[35037]**

ALKINS PRE 1786 SHARDLOW ALTON, DBY, ENG **[33890]**

ALKIRE 1800+ VIGO CO., IN, USA **[38318]**

ALLABEN 1790-1850 DELAWARE, NY, USA **[38111]**

ALLAMAN 1700 GLOUCESTER, VA, USA **[38027]**

ALLAN C1888 CESSNOCK, NSW, AUS **[34009]** : 1830-1930 PORT FAIRY, VIC & WA, AUS **[34815]** : PRE 1860 MELBOURNE, VIC, AUS **[35339]** : 1870+ WILCANNIA, NSW, AUS **[36632]** : 1847+ STRATHALBYN, SA, AUS **[36632]** : 1860+ ALBURY, NSW, AUS **[37908]** : 1831-1844 ST JOHNS, NFD, CAN **[36550]** : PRE 1860 ENG **[34326]** : 1880S LIVERPOOL, SRY, ENG **[35156]** : PRE 1880 STOCKTON, DUR, ENG **[35212]** : PRE 1855 SOM, ENG **[35386]** : 1850-1875 BRADFORD, WRY, ENG **[36391]** : PRE 1900 BARROWFORD, LAN, ENG **[38464]** : PRE 1900 STRABAND, TYR, IRL **[33975]** : 1790-1870 AUGHATARRAGH, ARM, IRL **[38526]** : PRE 1876 N. IRL **[36878]** : 1895+ UPPER HUTT, NZ **[35386]** : PRE 1831 ROX, SCT **[33906]** : 1650-1900 PRESTONPANS, MLN, SCT **[33908]** : PRE 1683 BOTHWELL SHIELS, LKS, SCT **[33978]** : 1860+ GLASGOW, LKS, SCT **[34326]** : 1700-1800 ST MONANCE, FIF, SCT **[34637]** : 1600-1800 ST MONANCE, FIF, SCT **[35627]** : 1830S EDINBURGH, MLN, SCT **[35865]** : 1820S LKS, SCT **[35866]** : 1790-1828 BRECHIN & GLASGOW, ANS &

CLK, SCT [36550] : 1800+ BANCHORY
DEVENICK, KCD, SCT [36824] : 1900+ FINDON
PORTLETHEN, KCD, SCT [36824] : 1800S NEW
MONKLAND, LKS, SCT [36833] : 1750+
EDINBURGH, SCT [37134] : PRE 1637 TRANENT,
ELN, SCT [37852] : 1800+ EDINBURGH, MLN,
SCT [37908] : 1750-1850 KING, SCT [38100] : PRE
1880 ABERDEEN, SCT [38464] : ALEXANDER PRE
1903 LANDOWNER & FARMER, SCT [38477] :
PETER PRE 1860 STIRLING, STI, SCT [38477] :
1880-1920 ADDIWELL, MLN, SCT [38526] : 1845-
1930 MINNEAPOLIS, MN, USA [36550]

ALLARD PRE 1900 RICHMOND, TAS, AUS [34918] :
PRE 1865 CAMPBELLTOWN, TAS, AUS [35459] :
1850+ RIPPLE, WOR, ENG [34160] : PRE 1700 FRA
[38561] : MARY (POLLY) 1818+ MADISON CO., IL,
USA [37590] : HARDY 1830S WAYNE CO., MO,
USA [37590]

ALLART 1750+ SHREWSBURY, SAL, ENG [36058]

ALLASON 1845+ HOBART, TAS, AUS [34795]

ALLAWAY 1854+ VIC, AUS [35841] : PRE 1700
WINSLEY, WIL, ENG [34623] : C1850 GLS, ENG
[35841]

ALLBRIGHT PRE 1840 USA [38229]

ALLBROOK PRE 1900 LND, ENG [37731] : PRE 1900
LND, ENG [37731] : ALL WORLDWIDE [35326]

ALLCHIN PRE 1900 KEN, ENG [37377]

ALLCOCK C1880-1930S SG, CH [33971] : C1870-C1940
WALTHAMSTOW, ESS, ENG [33971] : ALL
LONDON, ENG [33971] : 1500-1700 STS, ENG
[36062] : 1750+ BETHNAL GREEN, MDX, ENG
[36872] : 1860 WATNALL CHAWORTH, NTT, ENG
[37215] : C1820 EASTBOURNE, SSX, ENG [37378]

ALLCORN ALL SSX, ENG [35063]

ALLCOTT ALL WAR, ENG [37621]

ALLDEN 1800-1850 BIRMINGHAM, WAR, ENG
[37084]

ALLDRIDGE PRE 1845 STRATFORD, LND, ENG
[35232] : 1810-1856 FLOORE, NTH, ENG [38275]

ALLEN HENRY 1800+ SYDNEY, NSW, AUS [33814] :
1906-1920 CASTLEMAINE, VIC, AUS [34191] :
1860+ MELBOURNE, VIC, AUS [34865] :
CHARLES 1850+ PORT ESPERANCE, TAS, AUS
[34888] : 1840S MELBOURNE, VIC, AUS [35039] :
1880+ PORT ARLINGTON, VIC, AUS [35140] :
1860+ LEXTON, VIC, AUS [35439] : THOMAS 1860-
1938 LORNE & COLAC, VIC, AUS [35477] : MARIA
C1903-48 COLAC, VIC, AUS [35477] : GEORGE
1894+ IPSWICH, QLD, AUS [35788] : JOHN PRE
1883 HAWTHORN, VIC, AUS [35867] : 1890+
ROCKHAMPTON, QLD, AUS [36305] : 1886-1890
MELBOURNE, VIC, AUS [36423] : 1855+ SYDNEY,
NSW, AUS [37909] : DENNIS 1830+ QUEBEC,
QUE, CAN [34168] : SOPHY 1910+ SALMON
ARMS, BC, CAN [34764] : 1910+ SALMON ARMS,
BC, CAN [34764] : 1895+ NS, CAN [35572] : 1842-
1844 CAN [36423] : PRE 1900 NB, CAN [36933] :
1900+ YARMOUTH, NS, CAN [37432] : PRE 1840
BURFORD, OXF, ENG [33997] : ALL KEN, ENG
[34110] : 1840S CHELTENHAM, GLS, ENG [34175] :
1850-1880 LAMBETH, LND, ENG [34175] : PRE 1810
BERMONDSEY, LND, ENG [34316] : 1800-1900
HECKMONDWIKE, WRY, ENG [34328] : 1770-1830
LONDON, ENG [34440] : 1750-1820 ST EWE, CON,
ENG [34448] : 1850-1900 LIVERPOOL, LAN & CHS,
ENG [34526] : 1750-1800 ROCHESTER, KEN, ENG
[34552] : ROBERT 1770+ WELLS, SOM, ENG
[34577] : 1700-1760 ILLMIRE & SAUNDERTON,
BKM, ENG [34687] : 1800S PORTSMOUTH, HAM,
ENG [34715] : 1830S WEST THURROCK, ESS, ENG
[34726] : 1820-1850 RAVENSDEN, BDF, ENG [34738]
: 1800S LONDON, MDX & ESS, ENG [34813] : PRE

1857 THURGARTON, NFK, ENG [34941] : C1818
SHEPTON BEAUCHAMP, SOM, ENG [34972] :
1800+ CRIPPLEGATE, LND, ENG [35125] : C1878
COLCHESTER, ESS, ENG [35348] : 1700+
READING, BRK, ENG [35355] : 1860+ BRISTOL,
GLS, ENG [35363] : PRE 1855 SOM, ENG [35386] :
RALPH PRE 1800+ HULL, YKS, ENG [35412] : PRE
1860 NORTHAMPTON, NTH, ENG [35439] : JOHN
WALTON 1850S CHATHAM, KEN, ENG [35472] :
ANN PRE 1826 N MANOR ST CHELSEA, LND,
ENG [35483] : THOMAS 1841+ POND PL
CHELSEA, LND, ENG [35483] : C1760
HANDSWORTH, STS, ENG [35552] : ALL MELTON
MOWBRAY, LEI, ENG [35572] : PRE 1900 RUT &
NTH, ENG [35637] : PRE 1750 ESS, ENG [35642] :
PRE 1860 BRADFORD, YKS, ENG [35758] : 1796
WHYBERTON, LIN, ENG [35835] : C1821
HEREFORD, HEF, ENG [35872] : PRE 1840 NBL,
ENG [35918] : PRE 1780 LOSTWITHIEL, CON, ENG
[35973] : 1800-1900 DBY, ENG [36005] : PRE 1850
DEDDINGTON, OXF, ENG [36183] : 1834+
DENVER, NFK, ENG [36276] : LAURA C1882
SPROWSTAN, NFK, ENG [36290] : ALL
PANGBOURNE, BRK, ENG [36326] : PRE 1840
SOUTH SHIELDS, DUR, ENG [36364] : 1790-1800
WROTHAM & SEAL, KEN, ENG [36423] : ALL
STAFFORD, STS, ENG [36537] : C1846
PERRANZABULOE, CON, ENG [36762] : C1800+
GRINTON, NRY, ENG [36810] : C1800+
WINDSOR, BRK, ENG [36810] : C1807 HIGH
WYCOMBE, BKM, ENG [36810] : JOHN 1790-1800
NUNEATON, WAR, ENG [36820] : PRE 1800
WILLERSEY, GLS, ENG [36998] : 1780+
CHALFONT ST PETER, BKM, ENG [37122] : 1800+
READING, BRK, ENG [37153] : 1740+
BURGHFIELD, BRK, ENG [37153] : JAMES 1790+
HAM, ENG [37168] : 1800-1900 BRISTOL, GLS, ENG
[37232] : 1800-1900 BATH, SOM, ENG [37232] : PRE
1800 DOVER, KEN, ENG [37371] : 1620
MANCHESTER, LAN, ENG [37531] : C1852
MARYLEBONE, MDX, ENG [37561] : PRE 1850
READING, BRK, ENG [37561] : 1800+ HERNE
BAY & WHITSTABLE, KEN, ENG [37707] : 1800-
1900 DEPTFORD, LND, ENG [37850] : PRE 1850
LONDON, ENG [37901] : PRE 1837
MARYLEBONE, LND, ENG [37909] : 1860-1900
MANCHESTER, LAN, ENG [38248] : 1840-1875
LONDON, MDX, ENG [38248] : 1700-1900 SWALE
MEDWAY, KEN, ENG [38249] : 1700+
FARNWORTH & BOLTON, LAN, ENG [38260] :
PRE 1700 KEN, ENG [38389] : FRANCIS 1750-1800
SHREWSBURY, SAL, ENG [38453] : ALL HUN &
VIC, ENG & AUS [34301] : 1850-1900 IOW, ENG &
CAN [38349] : JAMES C1800 FER & TYR, IRL
[33910] : ARTHUR 1795+ WIC, IRL [34168] :
DENNIS 1810-1830 WIC, IRL [34168] : 1800-1900
WEX & WEM, IRL [34496] : MARGARET 1850S
LOG, IRL [34515] : 1780-1900 MOUNTSHANNON,
CLA & GAL, IRL [34526] : PRE 1900
TULLYMULEN, ANT, IRL [35055] : PRE 1841
MONEYKEE, FER, IRL [35563] : 1800+ ANT, IRL
[36746] : 1700+ MAY & SLI, IRL [38725] : MONA
PRETORIA 1900 PATEA, NZ [36633] : PRE 1800
ABD, SCT [35113] : FRANK 1800-1900S MO & KS,
USA [35304] : 1895+ USA [35572] : 1635-1653
NORTHAMPTON CO., VA, USA [36354] : 1820+
JEFFERSON CO., NY, USA [36549] : 1600-1900 CT,
USA [36689] : 1700+ HALIFAX, VA & KY, USA
[36931] : ALL MA, USA [36933] : PRE 1880 JERSEY
CITY, NJ, USA [37003] : 1769-1774
WEATHERSFIELD, VT, USA [37005] : 1620-1730
MANCHESTER, MA, USA [37432] : JULIA 1913+

LANSING, MI, USA [37438] : 1885+ BUFFALO, NY, USA [37438] : 1816 ST LAWRENCE, NY, USA [37531] : 1775 MANCHESTER, VT, USA [37531] : 1630-1770 MANCHESTER, MA, USA [37531] : PRE 1865 WHITE & HABERSHAM CO., GA, USA [37587] : 1865+ WINDSOR, VT, USA [37592] : JOHN 1775+ SC, MS & NC, USA [37796] : MARY 1800 MONTGOMERY CO., NY, USA [38062] : 1800S MI & NY, USA [38098] : JACOB 1811-40 TRUMBULL CO., OH, USA [38138] : 1750-1850 HUDSON RIVER AREA, NY, USA [38153] : 1920+ LINCOLN, NE, USA [38552] : 1920+ MI, USA [38739] : PRE 1850 MARSHALL CO., TN, USA [38743] : JAMES 1760-1770 ROCKBRIDGE CO., VA, USA [38763] : 1750-1930 HUBBERSTON & MILFORD, PEM, WLS [34855] : 1750+ SWANSEA, GLA, WLS [37766] : 1800+ GLA & PEM, WLS [37827]

ALLENBY PRE 1850 WES, ENG & SCT [36297]

ALLENOR PRE 1800 CHOLLERTON, NBL, ENG [36110]

ALLERTNO 1860+ WEST AHM, MDX & LND, ENG [37284]

ALLERTON 1830-1860 CATALONIA, ESP [37284] : 1850 OH, USA [33910] : 1730-1820 PENLEY, FLN, WLS [37284] : 1800S WORLDWIDE [37500]

ALLESOP PRE 1875 FOSTON, DBY, ENG [34311]

ALLEWAY ALL WORLDWIDE [35893]

ALLEY 1800+ ELIZABETH TOWN & MT LUCAS, LEX & OFF, IRL [34486]

ALLEYNE 1840+ NZ [33798] : LOT PRE 1850 BARBADOS, W.INDIES [33798]

ALLEZ ALL JSY, ALD & GSY, CHI [35891]

ALLGAR C1600 ENG [34395]

ALLGEWAHR 1800-1900 EISLINGEN FILS & GOPPINGEN, STUTGART, GER [38374]

ALLIBONE C1780+ UK & USA [38533]

ALLICOOKE 1700S ENG [35706]

ALLIETTI 1840 LEVO, LOMBARDY, ITL [37163]

ALLIN PRE 1870 DEV, ENG [35473]

ALLING PRE 1670 LISKEARD & CALSTOCK, CON, ENG [36594] : 1630+ STRATFORD GUILFORD, CT, USA [34342]

ALLINGAME 1810-1840 LYTCHETT MINSTER, DOR, ENG [34016]`

ALLINGHAM 1800S GLENCAR, LET, IRL [36906] : 1850 SLIGO TOWN, SLI, IRL [36906]

ALLINGTON ALL SFK, ENG [34744] : 1825-1840 IN, USA [38105] : 1830-1850 MARINA, MADISON CO., IL, USA [38105]

ALLINSON PRE 1810 WORKINGTON, CUL, ENG [34795] : 1830S PENRITH, CUL, ENG [35914] : PRE 1779 LAN & WES, ENG [37706]

ALLIS ALL LIN, ENG [34301] : PRE 1852 OPR & PRE, GER & ENG [34753]

ALLISON 1840-1890 SYDNEY & GOULBURN, NSW, AUS [34294] : C1844 NEWCASTLE ON TYNE, NBL, ENG [34778] : PRE 1870 ALNWICK & SHILBOTTLE, NBL, ENG [34835] : ELEANOR 1800 ENG [35049] : 1818+ BARNARD CASTLE, DUR, ENG [35390] : PRE 1800 BARNARD CASTLE, DUR, ENG [35390] : PRE 1885 CAMBRIDGE, CAM, ENG [36430] : C1839 ROCHDALE, LAN, ENG [35807] : C1852 BATLEY, YKS, ENG [35807] : PRE 1779 LAN & WES, ENG [37706] : 1700-1830 CHURCH LENCH, WOR, ENG [37849] : PRE 1850+ SOUTH SHIELDS, DUR, ENG & AUS [35064] : C1830 NENAGH, TIP, IRL [35560] : 1800+ CASHEL, TIP, IRL [35874] : PRE 1874 DRY, IRL [36761] : ROBERT PRE 1858 DUBLIN, IRL [37481] : 1910+ RSA [34835] : 1840+ DUNDEE, ANS, SCT [33862] : 1800-1840 GREENOCK, RFW & ARL, SCT [34294] : PRE 1735 AYR, AYR, SCT [34501] : 1850+ BRIDGETON,

LKS, SCT [34559] : PRE 1860 PAISLEY, RFW, SCT [34706] : 1845-1855 OH, USA [37815]

ALLISTER ALL FERAGH, MOG & CAV, IRL [38391]

ALLISTON 1800 OCKENDON, SSX, ENG [35543]

ALLMAN PRE 1950 MANCHESTER, LAN, ENG [36201]

ALLMON WILLIAM 1779-1829 MONKEN HADLEY, MDX, ENG & AUS [34447]

ALLON C1700 GRINTON, NRY, ENG [36810]

ALLOTT 1809+ NSW, AUS [37993] : 1800-1850 RUT, ENG [38478]

ALLPORT ALL ENG [35552] : PRE 1860 ABBERLEY & HOLT, WOR, ENG [36110]

ALLPRESS ALL WORLDWIDE [37409]

ALLSOP 1900+ NSW, AUS [37115] : 1800-1850 CHELTENHAM, GLS, ENG [36512] : PRE 1850 SOUTHWARK, SRY, ENG [37321]

ALLSOPP C1800+ LINCOLN, LIN, ENG [34451]

ALLSUP C1800 WALTHAM ABBEY, ESS, ENG [37449]

ALLSWORTH 1840S MELBOURNE, VIC, AUS [35390] : 1800S MANCHESTER, LAN, ENG [35390]

ALLUM 1850+ WOLLONGONG, NSW, AUS [34979] : PRE 1850 BRK, ENG [34979] : PRE 1800 BUCKINGHAM, BKM, ENG [35232] : PRE 1810 MANCHESTER, LAN, ENG [37562] : PRE 1818 CHATHAM, KEN, ENG [37579] : PRE 1875 GREENE CO., PA, USA [37562]

ALLWARD PRE 1718 KINGSWEAR, DEV, ENG [34389]

ALLWEGE PRE 1850 KROSSEN, PRE, GER [35379]

ALLWOOD 1839+ SYDNEY, NSW, AUS [35141] : PRE 1840 SHEFFIELD, YKS, ENG [35946] : PRE 1840 CHESTERFIELD, DBY, ENG [35946] : PRE 1800 LOWDHAM, NTT, ENG [36196] : PRE 1750 FROME, SOM, ENG [38270] : 1774+ KINGSTON, JAMAICA, W.INDIES [35141]

ALLWRIGHT 1700-1800 OXF, ENG [37373]

ALMARI 1800 CURACAO [33751] : 1800 CURACAO, CARIBBEAN [38692]

ALMES 1700-1800 LND & SRY, ENG [34749]

ALMOND 1800-1860 DBY, ENG [33836] : PRE 1910 PINNER, MDX, ENG [37193] : 1800-64 WIGAN, LAN, ENG [37732] : 1800-1850 FARNWORTH WITH KEARSLEY, LAN, ENG [37934]

ALPE ALL ENG [37584]

ALPHEY C1800 LEWSON, KEN, ENG & AUS [35592]

ALPORT 1862+ MUSKOKA & ORILLIA, ONT, BC & NS, CAN [36326] : ALL OLD SWINFORD, WOR & WAR, ENG [36326] : 1849+ LYTTELTON, CANTY, NZ [36326] : ALL CAPE TOWN, RSA [36326]

ALSABROOK ALL WORLDWIDE [35326]

ALSBROOK ALL WORLDWIDE [35326]

ALSEBROOK ALL WORLDWIDE [35326]

ALSFORD PRE 1840 SRY & BKM, ENG [37078]

ALSOBROOK ALL WORLDWIDE [35326]

ALSOP 1800+ SYDNEY, NSW, AUS [37337] : 1700-1850 BRADLEY, STS, ENG [34783] : ALL IRON ACTON, GLS, ENG [37154] : 1935+ HARRINGAY, LND, ENG [37337] : 1750+ YORK & SHEFFIELD, WRY, ENG [37337] : 1800+ NOTTINGHAM, NTT, ENG [37337] : 1772-1807 CAROLINE CO., VA, USA [33761]

ALSTON PRE 1660 SFK, ENG [35142] : 1700+ LINGFIELD, SRY, ENG [36088] : ALL STONEHOUSE, LKS, SCT [35461] : PRE 1750 AYR, SCT [37434]

ALT PRE 1849 HES, BRD [35083]

ALTENBACH 1780-1833 ALS & LOR, FRA [38201]

ALTENKIRCH 1850-1900 VIENNA, WIEN, OES [36454] : 1900-1920S BUTTERWORTH & IBEKI,

TRANSKH, RSA **[36454]** : ALL WORLDWIDE **[36454]**

ALTENKIRK 1920+ RSA **[36454]** : ALL WORLDWIDE **[36454]**

ALTERATOR 1840 SCONE, NSW, AUS **[34182]**

ALTHAUS PRE 1821 MUNCHHAUSEN, HES, BRD **[34840]** : PRE 1850 LAUPERSWIL, BE, CH **[38747]**

ALTHER PRE 1840 IRL **[37428]**

ALTHOFFER ALL OFFENBURG, BAD, GER **[36078]**

ALTHOUSE 1725-1850 BERKS CO., PA, USA **[35318]** : 1750-90 NY, USA **[37454]**

ALTMOS PRE 1800 HEIMKIRCHEN, RPF, GER **[38681]**

ALTNOW PRE 1855 BRA, GER **[38016]**

ALTVATER 1700-1800 GER **[37823]** : ALL WUE, GER **[38572]**

ALTY PRE 1746 LYDIATE, LAN, ENG **[37072]**

ALVARICO ALL PHILIPPINE **[38730]**

ALVES PRE 1800 ABERDEEN, ABD, SCT **[37367]**

ALVEY 1850 KEGWORTH, LEI, ENG **[37215]**

ALVOS 1872+ TABULAM, NSW, AUS **[35544]**

ALWARD PRE 1800 BUTTERNUT RIDGE, NB & NJ, CAN & USA **[38225]** : 1700+ KINGSWEAR, DEV, ENG **[36000]**

ALWAY WM. H. & ANN 1829 CASTLEREAGH ST, SYDNEY, NSW, AUS **[36311]** : JOHN 1829 ST JAMES, SYDNEY, NSW, AUS **[36311]** : 1890S KEN, ENG **[35377]**

AMAND 1811-1946 ST-AMAND, BEAUJEU & CLUNY, CEN, RHA & BRG, FRA **[34136]**

AMANN ALL BAW, GER & BRD **[36656]** : ALL USA **[36656]**

AMATO PRE 1855 CALABRIA, ITL **[36679]**

AMBACH 1450-1650 MUEHLHAUSEN NECKAR, BAW, BRD **[38654]**

AMBIDGE ALL WORLDWIDE **[34712]**

AMBLER ALL YKS, ENG **[34550]**

AMBRIDGE ALL WORLDWIDE **[34712]**

AMBROSE 1800 ROTHERHITHE, KEN, ENG **[34204]** : 1830S DENHAM, SFK, ENG **[35409]** : 1800+ CAVENDISH, SFK, ENG **[38288]** : ALL LIM, IRL **[35950]** : ALL EDINBURGH, MLN, SCT **[35983]**

AMBROSIUS PRE 1700 ANKLAM, POM, DDR **[38561]**

AMBURY ALL ENG **[34659]** : 1810-1890 LONGHOPE, GLS, ENG **[34659]** : PRE 1834 USK, MON, WLS **[34445]**

AMELBERGER PRE 1730 BINGEN, RPF, GER **[38609]**

AMELUNG PRE 1700 GER **[38642]** : 1724 LEMGO, NSA, GER **[38748]** : 1724 BRAKE, NSA, GER **[38748]**

AMER 1820+ SOM, ENG **[35105]** : 1700-1800 WIL, ENG **[37232]**

AMERY 1700-1900 BERWICK & TWEEDMOUTH, NBL, ENG **[36461]** : 1600-1900 BORDER TOWNS, BEW, ROX & SEL, SCT **[36461]**

AMES PRE 1860 MDX, ENG **[34557]** : PRE 1780 ESS, ENG **[35642]** : SOPHIA 1823 HARTFORD CO., CT, USA **[38734]**

AMEY 1850S BERDEN, ESS, ENG **[37969]**

AMHERST 1066-1900S KEN, ENG **[35096]**

AMIDON PRE 1866 MASSACHUSETTS, CT, USA **[36748]**

AMIEL 1870-1925 DEAL, KEN, ENG **[33758]** : 1600-1900 VICDESSOS, ARIEGE, FRA **[33758]**

AMIOT (SEE AMYOT) **[36678]**

AMIS ALL GREAT YARMOUTH, NFK, ENG **[35647]**

AMLING PRE 1875+ GER **[34645]**

AMMERMANN ALL WORLDWIDE **[38666]**

AMMETT PRE 1830 STONEYFORD, ANT, IRL **[37927]**

AMMIDON PRE 1720S MA & CT, USA **[37522]**

AMMONS PRE 1940 TN & AR, USA **[37525]**

AMOR 1821+ PEWSEY, WIL, ENG **[34446]** : PRE 1840 BATH, SOM & WIL, ENG **[34865]**

AMOREY (SEE AMORY) **[36461]**

AMORY 1700-1900 BERWICK & TWEEDMOUTH, NBL, ENG **[36461]** : 1600-1900 BORDER TOWNS, BEW, ROX & SEL, SCT **[36461]**

AMOS 1880+ BOWEN, QLD, AUS **[35150]** : 1821+ SWANPORT, TAS, AUS **[36626]** : 1820+ AUS **[36626]** : C1915 ST JOHNS, NFD, CAN **[37777]** : PRE 1800 ARDLEY, OXF, ENG **[34112]** : 1830-1870 LIVERPOOL, LAN, ENG **[34762]** : PRE 1770 IRON ACTON, GLS, ENG **[35157]** : PRE 1800 OLNEY, BKM, ENG **[35397]** : C1800-1885 DOVER, KEN, ENG **[37777]** : C1725-1850 ISLINGTON, MDX, ENG **[37777]** : 1907+ REIGATE, SRY, ENG **[37777]** : 1750-1850 KEN, ENG **[37964]** : 1800-1850 IRL **[34762]** : ALL NZ **[35884]** : PRE 1860 SELKIRK, SCT **[34443]** : 1800-1850 CASTLETON & HOBKIRK, ROX, SCT **[34479]** : 1700+ MELROSE, ROX, SCT **[36626]**

AMOTT 1700+ MONMOUTH, GLS, ENG & AUS **[33790]**

AMOU ALL CANTON, CHINA **[34955]**

AMPHEA PRE 1850 ENG **[35386]**

AMPHLETT 1750-1800 CLAINES, WOR, ENG **[34552]** : PRE 1800 WOR, ENG **[37275]** : PRE 1800 GLS, ENG **[37275]**

AMSDEN PRE 1900 USA **[34419]**

AMUNDSEN PRE 1850 GULDBRANDSEN, BUS, NOR **[38066]**

AMY 1800+ ST MARTIN & GROUVILLE, JSY, CHI & AUS **[34882]** : PRE 1860 PA, USA **[38303]**

AMYOT PIERRE 1750+ ST AUGUSTIN, QUE, CAN **[36678]**

ANCELL 1500-1900 FALMOUTH, CON, ENG **[37680]** : 1500-1900 LAUNCESTON & PENZANCE, CON, ENG **[37680]**

ANCLIFFE PRE 1893 TODWICK & NORTON, WRY & DBY, ENG **[34116]**

ANDERS 1860+ BENDIGO, VIC, AUS **[35725]** : C1690-1860 BURTONWOOD, LAN, ENG **[34873]** : 1840-1860 ERNSDORF, PRE, GER **[35725]** : C1790 VALBY, SWE **[38172]** : HENSON 1820+ HENDERSON CO., NC, USA **[38141]** : WILLIAM 1600+ HOPEWELL CO., VA, USA **[38141]** : THOMAS PRE 1737 HENDERSON CO., NC, USA **[38141]** : PETER 1795-1860 HENDERSON CO., NC, USA **[38141]**

ANDERSDATTER 1819 SIROP, JUTLAND, DEN **[34654]**

ANDERSDOTTER C1820 JONSTORP & STROVELSTORP, MALMO, SWE **[34654]** : ANNA 1831 VENJAN, KOPPARBERGS, SWE **[38556]**

ANDERSDOTTER-DESAIX CRISTINA 1870+ USA **[38558]**

ANDERSEN 1874+ BUNDABERG, QLD, AUS **[34020]** : PETER C1870 CARCOAR, NSW, AUS **[35104]** : JENS ALL GRACEMERE, QLD, AUS & DEN **[35723]** : 1820+ COPENHAGAN, DEN **[34308]** : C1800 JYDERUP, SJELLAND, DEN **[35115]** : TONNES PRE 1870 VAMDRUP, RIBE, DEN **[37034]** : ALL CHRISTIANIA, NOR **[34938]** : PETER C1837 OSLO, NOR **[35104]** : 1838 DROUTHEIM, NOR **[35906]** : ANNA 1800-1850 NOR **[36331]** : ALL CHRISTIANA, NOR **[37558]** : 1880+ POLK CO.& BARRON CO, WI, USA **[34473]**

ANDERSON 1814-1900 LIVERPOOL, NSW, AUS **[33766]** : 1860-1892 PT ARTHUR & GLENORCHY, TAS, AUS **[33934]** : 1920+ CUNNAMULLA, QLD, AUS **[34270]** : 1880+ ALEXANDRIA, NSW, AUS **[34306]** : 1865+ GRAFTON, NSW, AUS **[34542]** : 1850+ AVOCA, TAS, AUS **[35116]** : 1800S SHOALHAVEN, NSW, AUS **[35134]** : 1844+

WATTLE FLAT, NSW, AUS [35504] : FOSTER 1835-1861 SYDNEY, NSW, AUS [35703] : 1850S + BOURKE, NSW, AUS [35831] : PRE 1914 AUS [36214] : 1852 + GEELONG, VIC, AUS [36276] : WILLIAM 1870 + SYDNEY, NSW, AUS [36295] : WILLIAM C1880 BRISBANE, QLD, AUS [36616] : KEITH 1980 + ALBANY, WA, AUS [36750] : PRE 1869 RICHMOND, NSW, AUS [37315] : 1849 + WOLLERT & YARRAWONGA, VIC, AUS [37962] : 1870 + COLLINGWOOD, VIC, AUS [37999] : 1877 + COLLENDINA, NSW, AUS [38069] : RICHARD PRE 1860 + PARKESBOURNE, NSW, AUS & SCT [36313] : 1809 + QUYON, QUE, CAN [34085] : 1880-1910 ONT, CAN [34401] : 1800 + BRUCE CO., ONT, CAN [37046] : CHRISTINE C1800 + DUFFERIN, ONT, CAN [37441] : VICTORIA E. 1890-1990 UXBRIDGE, ONT, CAN [37567] : JOSEPH 1852-1950 UXBRIDGE, ONT, CAN [37567] : WILLIAM HENRY 1879-1970 UXBRIDGE, ONT, CAN [37567] : C1800-1970 RENFREW CO., ONT, CAN [38464] : C1915-80 MOOSE JAW & PADDOCKWOOD, SAS, CAN [38464] : JESSE PRE 1835 VIENNA, ELGIN CO., ONT, CAN [38584] : EUNICE 1828S DEER ISLAND, NB, CAN [38785] : C1815 + SHERBORNE, DOR, ENG [34063] : C1850 + SHOREDITCH, LND, ENG [34063] : C1840 + NEWPORT, IOW, HAM, ENG [34063] : 1600-1800 HUTTON BUSCELL, YKS, ENG [34107] : PRE 1840 TUNBRIDGE WELLS, KEN, ENG [34269] : ANN 1697 ST BOTOLPH, LND, ENG [34539] : PRE 1860 PRESTON, LAN, ENG [34815] : 1800-1850 LEVERINGTON, CAM, ENG [34930] : PRE 1800 CAMBRIDGE, CAM, ENG [35032] : 1870S KENSINGTON, LND, ENG [35188] : PRE 1790 WHITEHAVEN, CUM, ENG [35242] : 1700 ECCLESHALL, STS, ENG [35288] : PRE 1866 ROYSTON, HRT, ENG [35504] : PRE 1850 LANCHESTER, CAM, ENG [35605] : PRE 1871 MARCH, CAM, ENG [35821] : 1750 + RAMSEY, HUN, ENG [35825] : 1800 GRISTON, NFK, ENG [35892] : 1800-1870 PLYMOUTH & PLYMPTON MAURICE, DEV, ENG [36214] : 1800 + NOTTINGHAM, NTT, ENG [36241] : PRE 1850 POTTERIES, STS, ENG [36502] : 1900 + EIGHTON BANKS, DUR, ENG [36503] : ALL SLOUGH, BKM, ENG [36616] : WILLIAM 1854-76 SLOUGH, BKM, ENG [36616] : 1820 HULME, LAN, ENG [36635] : SAMUEL SMITH 1860 + BISHOP AUCKLAND, DUR, ENG [36636] : ANDREW 1870S DURHAM, DUR, ENG [36636] : SMITH 1885 + DURHAM, DUR, ENG [36636] : PRE 1800 LEEDS, WRY, ENG [36636] : PRE 1858 SUNDERLAND, DUR, ENG [36777] : PRE 1858 FINCHLEY, MDX, ENG [36800] : C1855-1863 STOCKPORT, CHS, ENG [36984] : PRE 1910 LONDON, ENG [37062] : 1816 + DARTMOUTH, DEV, ENG [37231] : PRE 1885 LEICESTER, LEI, ENG [37346] : PRE 1900 LND, ENG [37385] : HENRY 1850S DUDDESTON, WAR, ENG [37476] : 1800S CHERTSEY & BURNHAM, SRY & BKM, ENG [37868] : PRE 1901 WHITBY, NRY, ENG [38580] : 1843 + ICELAND [37999] : PRE 1793 LETTERKENNY, DON, IRL [33766] : 1849 + GORTREIGHTY, ANT, IRL [33882] : JOHN G.R. PRE 1850 IRL [34254] : 1820 + MOG, IRL [34666] : REV. A.D. 1883 + INNISKEEL, DON, IRL [34934] : 1811 + WATERFORD, WAT, IRL [35427] : ROBERT C1830 KNOCKLOUGHRIE, DRY, IRL [35702] : FOSTER 1818-1833 MOG, IRL [35703] : PRE 1850 PORTADOWN, ARM, IRL [35918] : PRE 1853 SLIGO, SLI, IRL [36417] : PRE 1880 CALEDON, TYR, IRL [36750] : CHRISTINE C1800 + FER, IRL [37441] : PRE 1740 IRL [37589] : WILLIAM 1830-1850 SLIGO, SLI, IRL [38387] : MARGARET C1800 DOW,

IRL & AUS [35592] : 1860 + WAIKOUITI, OTAGO, NZ [34666] : JOSEPH 1865 + NZ [36750] : PRE 1914 RSA [36214] : 1780 + TYRIE, ABD, SCT [33783] : ANDREW ALL SHI, SCT [33872] : PRE 1892 SCT [33959] : PRE 1860 SCT [33959] : 1750 + COLDINGHAM, BEW, SCT [33963] : PRE 1900 SCT [33987] : 1828 BEITH, AYR & RFW, SCT [34021] : 1800 + FEARNAN, PER, SCT [34075] : C1760 DOUGLAS, LKS, SCT [34118] : 1861 + ALLOA, CLK, SCT [34260] : 1850 + PORTOBELLO, MLN, SCT [34260] : 1800S FORGUE, ABD, SCT [34336] : 1760-1860 KIRKINTILLOCH, DNB, SCT [34359] : C1770 OKI, SCT [34362] : PRE 1880 MLN & FIF, SCT [34383] : 1880-1900 FIF, SCT [34393] : C1810 BROXBURN, WLN, SCT [34542] : 1750-1850 CLK, SCT [34572] : PRE 1830 ANS, SCT [34590] : 1800S CORKERHILL, LKS, SCT [34598] : 1790 + CAWDOR, NAI, SCT [34666] : ALL BALMERINO, FIF, SCT [34758] : PRE 1846 BRECHIN, ANS, SCT [34840] : PRE 1860 STRICHEN, ABD, SCT [34870] : 1800S AIRDRIE, LKS, SCT [34961] : DAVID PRE 1857 FIF, SCT [35083] : 1730-1830 DUNFERMLINE, FIF, SCT [35094] : 1820-1840 DUNDEE, FORFAR, ANS, SCT [35102] : 1886 + LOGIE, FORFAR, ANS, SCT [35106] : 1800-1850 NEW CHANNELKIRK, BEW, SCT [35151] : 1790 + MOFFAT, DFS, SCT [35169] : PRE 1920 CLYDEBANK, DNB, SCT [35378] : C1855 + LEITH, MLN, SCT [35486] : WILLIAM 1833 CAMBUSLANG, LKS, SCT [35794] : PRE 1840 PETERHEAD, ABD, SCT [35877] : 1880S WALLS, SHI, SCT [35881] : 1830 + LKS, SCT [36276] : PRE 1800 GLASGOW, LKS, SCT [36295] : 1850 + KILSYTH, STI, SCT [36366] : C1790 ALVA, STI, SCT [36635] : 1739 CLACKMANNAN, CLK, SCT [36635] : 1761 ALLOA, CLK, SCT [36635] : PRE 1831 BISHOP MILLS, MOR, SCT [36673] : 1700 + CUNNINGSBURGH, SHI, SCT [36756] : 1774-1896 KIRKCALDY, FIF, SCT [36770] : 1700 + PAISLEY, RFW, SCT [36794] : 1800 + COLINTON, MLN, SCT [36871] : 1830 + EDINBURGH, MLN, SCT [36871] : 1800 + KIRKTON OF DESKFORD, BAN, SCT [36887] : C1810 STIRLING, STI, SCT [37263] : PRE 1850 LARGS, AYR, SCT [37434] : 1790-1890 OLD MONKLAND, LKS, SCT [37488] : 1740 + SHI, SCT [37527] : PRE 1762 DULL, PER, SCT [37852] : AGNES PRE 1775 KIRKCALDY, FIF, SCT [37906] : C1800 INCHTURE, PER, SCT [37918] : C1700 KENMORE, PER, SCT [37918] : PRE 1890 DNB, SCT [37923] : PRE 1890 LKS, SCT [37923] : 1810 TARVES, ABD, SCT [38192] : ALEXANDER 1820 + KENMORE, PER, SCT [38387] : 1750-1800S FYVIE, ABD, SCT [38422] : PRE 1830 PER, SCT [38464] : C1734 GREENOCK, RFW, SCT [38485] : 1820 + ABERDEEN, ABD, SCT [38539] : JOHN PRE 1797 + MUIRA LEE, TRINITY GASK, ANS, SCT [38567] : DAVID 1820 + KETTINS, ANS, SCT [38567] : JAMES 1809 + PAISLEY, RFW, SCT & USA [37040] : JOHN & CLAR 1869 JONKOPING, SMALAND, SWE [34395] : 1860S GOTHENBURG, SWE [35508] : JONAS 1846 + SWE [35641] : ANDERS PRE 1800 VENJAN & SOLLERON, KOPPARBERG, SWE [36672] : EMALINE 1822-1849 WAYNE CO., TN, USA [35301] : 1745-1800 ABBEVILLE, SC, USA [36354] : ARCHIBALD 1840-1860 COPHIAH CO., MS, USA [36573] : ARCHIBALD 1800-1850 RANKIN CO., MS, USA [36573] : 1900 SEATTLE & PALM SPRINGS, WA & CA, USA [37581] : 1825-1875 PHILADELPHIA, PA, USA [37740] : EZEKIEL 1775-1835 NY, USA [37810] : ISAAC 1835-1860 OAKLAND CO., MI, USA [37810] : 1812 OKMULGEE, OK, USA [38012] : JORDAN 1750 + CHESTERFIELD CO., VA, USA [38032] : NATHAN

1760+ CHESTERFIELD CO., VA, USA [38032] :
WILLIAM 1800S BALT, MD, USA [38182] :
GEORGE 1860+ CALHOUN, AL, USA [38187] :
1840 LENAWEE CO., MI, USA [38192] : 1800S
CRAWFORD CO., PA, USA [38522] : PRE 1825
KENT CO., DE, USA [38538] : PRE 1850 SCOTT CO.,
IL, USA [38538] : OSCAR 1877+ PHELPS CO., NE,
USA [38554] : MABEL 1887+ PHELPS CO., NE,
USA [38554] : SAM 1880+ PHELPS CO., NE, USA
[38554] : LINA 1880+ PHELPS CO., NE, USA [38554]
: 1869+ BEAR LAKE, MI, USA [38584]

ANDERSONS 1750-1850 KING EDWARD PARISH,
ABD, SCT [36712]

ANDERSSON ANDERS AUGUST 1911-1925 VIC,
AUS [34432] : ANDERS C1820-1900
HAGEBYHOGA, OSTERGOTLAND, SWE [35324] :
1800S OLAND, KALMAR, SWE [36966] : PRE 1900
GOTHENBURG, SWE [37062] : ALL OLAND, SWE
[38519] : ANDERS 1825 JARBO, GASTRIKLAND,
SWE [38556] : EDVARD 1888+ MINNIAPOLIS,
MN, USA [38557] : ADEL 1888+ MINNIAPOLIS,
MN, USA [38557] : ESKIL 1888+ MINNIAPOLIS,
MN, USA [38557] : INGRID 1888+ MINNIAPOLIS,
MN, USA [38557] : HELEN 1888+ MINNIAPOLIS,
MN, USA [38557] : ELLEN 1903+ JAMESTOWN,
NY, USA [38559] : GUNNAR 1903-1938
JAMESTOWN, NY, USA [38559] : OTTO 1906+
USA [38560] : JOHN 1911+ USA [38560] : ANNA
1894+ USA [38560] : MARIA 1899+ USA [38560] :
MARTHA 1899+ USA [38560]

ANDERTON 1855+ ARARAT, VIC, AUS [35239] :
1855+ ARARAT, VIC, AUS [38082] : 1800S
CHESTER, CHS, ENG [38082] : 1800S LIVERPOOL,
LAN, ENG [38082] : 1700-1850 GAWSWORTH, CHS,
ENG [38250] : ALL WORLDWIDE [38283]

ANDOVICK 1912-1919 C OLARADO SPGS, CO, USA
[35301]

ANDRADA 1874-1892 SAO MIGUEL, AZORES, PT
[37551] : PRE 1874 SAO MIGUEL, AZORES, PT
[37551]

ANDREA PRE 1800 KOBLENZ, RPR, GER [38437]

ANDREE PRE 1800 LAVINGTON, WIL, ENG [35857] :
PRE 1860 GER [37503]

ANDREEFF PRE 1860 GER [37503]

ANDREN 1800+ BURAGE, CON, ENG [35847]

ANDREOV 1866+ WARSAW, POL, GER & [37503]

ANDRES 1680-1920 SIL, GER [38634]

ANDRESAN 1800+ FLENSBURG, SHO, GER [37949]

ANDRESEN C1795 HORSBUELL, DEN [38671]

ANDRESON PRE 1852 ARENDAL, NOR [34270]

ANDREW EDWIN 1852+ MELBOURNE, VIC, AUS
[33797] : 1780-1840 RAWTENSTALL &
NEWCHURCH, LAN, ENG [34448] : 1810 ERY,
ENG [34731] : C1800 DUNCTON, SSX, ENG [34909]
: 1840+ WRAWBY, LIN, ENG [35223] : C1800
MANCHESTER, LAN, ENG [35871] : MOSES 1863+
SHERMANBURY, SSX, ENG [36212] : 1800+ ST
HILARY, CON, ENG [37426] : ARTHUR PRE 1825
ST HILARY, CON, ENG [37426] : 1750-1850
WESTON SUPER MARE, SOM, ENG [37747] : PRE
1850 STITHIANS, CON, ENG [38263] : PRE 1800
PLYMOUTH, DEV, ENG [38745] : PRE 1840 LKS,
SCT [33999] : C1790 CRAIGIE, AYR, SCT [36431] :
1800-1850 FALKIRK, STI, SCT [36763] : C1810
ABERDOUR, FIF, SCT [37982] : PRE 1830 ST
DAVID, FIF, SCT [37982] : 1700S SCT [38319] : 1700S
CENTER TWP., PA, USA [38319]

ANDREWS C1900 TOOWOOMBA, QLD, AUS [33870] :
1850-1916 NEWTOWN & ROOKWOOD, NSW, AUS
[34294] : WILLIAM 1844+ WARWICK, QLD, AUS
[34805] : 1870+ SOUTH CREEK (ST MARYS),
NSW, AUS [35101] : 1800+ NORTHDOWN

DISTRICT, TAS, AUS [35715] : PRE 1874 SOUTH
EAST, QLD, AUS [35854] : C1875
MUSWELLBROOK, NSW, AUS [37131] : 1860+
LONDON, ONT, CAN [37451] : C1820
AYLESBURY, BKM, ENG [33796] : EMMA C1790
ARKESDEN, ESS, ENG [34035] : 1790-1850
WORCESTER, WOR, ENG [34123] : 1760+
STEPNEY, MDX, ENG [34230] : 1750+ WINFRITH
& CHALDON, DOR, ENG [34283] : JOHN 1789-1843
FAREHAM, HAM, ENG [34314] : PRE 1860 SSX,
ENG [34376] : 1650-1750 SUDBURY, SFK, ENG
[34552] : PRE 1806 CON, ENG [34617] : 1840+
NEWMARKET, SFK, ENG [34650] : WILLIAM PRE
1817 WORCESTER, WOR, ENG [34805] : PRE 1829
BISHOPSTONE, WIL, ENG [34814] : 1800-1850 HRT,
ENG [34928] : RICHARD C1870 SAL, ENG [34935] :
1800S FITTLEWORTH, SSX, ENG [35024] : 1811+
SEAFORD, SSX, ENG [35101] : JOSHUA PRE 1750
NFK, ENG [35212] : 1830 PEWSEY, WIL, ENG
[35404] : WILLIAM C1825 DEV, ENG [35560] : 1800S
KEN, ENG [35715] : 1820-1840 HRT, ENG [35850] :
1800-1840 KENTON, DEV, ENG [35959] : 1800-1830S
PAIGNTON, DEV, ENG [36337] : PRE 1900
NEWBURY, BRK, ENG [36376] : PRE 1800
OVERTON, WIL, ENG [36376] : ALL LONDON,
ENG [36789] : 1780 ROSS ON WYE, HEF, ENG
[36798] : 1750+ BRAINTREE, ESS, ENG [36827] :
1900 GRIMSBY, LIN, ENG [36892] : C1720
SHAUGH PRIOR, DEV, ENG [36945] : 1700
RADWINTER, ESS, ENG [37125] : C1850 NEWTON
ST CYRES, DEV, ENG [37264] : PRE 1848 WIL,
ENG [37313] : 1841 HARDINGTON MANDEVILLE,
SOM, ENG [37378] : C1735 ALTON, HAM, ENG
[37420] : 1830+ MIDDLETON, LAN, ENG [37669] :
C1780 SADDLEWORTH, YKS, ENG [37669] : ALL
ENG [37739] : 1820S ST SAVIOURS, SRY, ENG
[37833] : 1600-1950 WASHWAY LIN, SUTTON
BRIDGE, LIN, ENG [38426] : PRE 1800 WOR, ENG
[38746] : PRE 1860 WIL, ENG & AUS [34463] : ALL
ANT, IRL [33842] : PRE 1870 MAGHERAFELT,
LDY, IRL [33977] : PRE 1850 NEWCASTLE, DOW,
IRL [34858] : 1816+ MANNING RIVER, LDY, IRL
& AUS [37130] : PRE 1920 TARANAKI, NZ [33985] :
1870+ WAIHOLA, OTG, NZ [34283] : 1830
KIRKCALDY, FIF, SCT [33848] : 1600+
HARTFORD, CT, USA [33989] : 1620+ CHEBACCO,
MA, USA [35276] : LEVI C1820-1871 NH, USA
[35324] : 1811 LANCASTER CO., PA, USA [37788] :
ELIZABETH 1825-1830 OGLETHORPE CO., GA,
USA [38155] : 1730+ IPSWICH, MA, USA [38308] :
JOHN 1850+ IN, USA [38324] : WILLIAM 1800-1900
BELMONT CO., OH, USA [38392] : 1874+
WELSHPOOL, MGY, WLS [35854] : 1840S MON,
WLS [38016] : ALL WORLDWIDE [34471]

ANEN 1800-1900 LUX, BEL [34255]

ANFINSON 1890+ SAN FRANCISCO, CA, USA
[38545]

ANGEL 1750+ STURSTON, NFK, ENG [33942] : 1800
SSX, ENG [34057] : PRE 1860 LONDON, ENG
[34428] : HENRY & WM. ALL ENG [34737] : PRE
1800 STOTTESDON, SAL, ENG [36488] : 1780-1800
HOO, KEN, ENG [36536] : 1833+ PUTNAM CO.,
IN, USA [36582] : ABRAHAM 1700-1850
SMITHFIELD PROVIDENCE, RI, USA [38130] :
1750-1800 NY & SUSSEX, NY & NJ, USA [38194] :
ALL WORLDWIDE [36488]

ANGELI C1500-C1850 PERGOLA, ITL [36139]

ANGELINI ALL PIZZOLI, AQUILA, ITL [33954]

ANGELL PRE 1860 ADELAIDE, SA, AUS & ENG
[35592] : PRE 1845 SOUTH WALSHAM, NFK, ENG
[36876] : ALL WORLDWIDE [36488]

ANGELS 1875 BDF, ENG [37448] : 1800+ MARCH, CAM, ENG [37448]

ANGER ALL NIEMEGK, DDR, GER [34938]

ANGHNEY DAVID 1750+ PA, USA [38241]

ANGIER PRE 1700 ESS, ENG [35642]

ANGLE 1800+ BELANGLO & MOSS VALE, NSW, AUS [35567]

ANGOVE C1900 SYDNEY, NSW, AUS [35034] : C1790 ILLOGAN, CON, ENG [35034] : 1700+ ILLOGAN & ST CLEER, CON, ENG [36961]

ANGUIN 1850-1875 KEWEENAW CO., MI, USA [38010]

ANGUS MARGARET 1781-1876 ST FOY, QUE, CAN [34489] : PRE 1860 ALSTON, CUL, ENG [34958] : PRE 1847 LIVERPOOL, LAN, CHS & FLN, ENG & WLS [37840] : THOMAS 1800-1895 MALTA [36634] : PRE 1900 ABD, SCT [34948] : 1700+ BANCHORY DEVENICK, KCD, SCT [36824] : ALL ANS, SCT [37480]

ANGWIN 1807+ SAINT BURYAN, CON, ENG [34627] : ALL LANDS END, CON, ENG [34627] : ALL ST JUST, CON, ENG & AUS [35712]

ANHOLT 1729+ GOEVORDEN SCHOONEBEEK, OIJ, NL [34398]

ANKIEWICZ JOHANN 1846 BOMST, POS, GER [36452] : ALL WORLDWIDE [36452]

ANKWICZ JOHANN 1846 BOMST, POS, GER [36452] : JOSEPH PRE 1794 WA, POL [36452] : ALL WORLDWIDE [36452]

ANNA HAGEDAN 1856-1900 GER [38090]

ANNABLE 1700S HORSLEY, DBY, ENG [38478]

ANNAL ALL WORLDWIDE [37413]

ANNAM 1800-1840 SHRAWLEY, WOR, ENG [37233]

ANNAN 1830 EDINBURGH, MLN, SCT [35865] : PRE 1750 DRUMMOCHIE, FIF, SCT [36436]

ANNAND 1846 BENDOCHY, PER, SCT [34224]

ANNEAR 1860+ CHARTERS TOWERS, QLD, AUS [36622] : 1800+ GWENNAP, CON, ENG & AUS [35712]

ANNENBERG 1850+ CHICAGO, IL, USA [36962]

ANNESLEY PRE 1900 DONNYBROOK, DUB, IRL [35521] : PRE 1900 BALLYSAX, KID, IRL [35521] : PRE 1854 MONAGHAN, MOG, IRL [38289]

ANNETT ALL WORLDWIDE [35944]

ANNEVELD 1700-1874 DOETINCHEM, GEL, NL [38712]

ANNIBAL 1700-1750 EAST HAMPTON, CT, USA [37591]

ANNING PRE 1860 DEV, ENG [35757] : PRE 1800 DEV, DOR & SOM, ENG [36166] : C1700-1800 DOR, ENG [36491] : 1800-1900 HONITON, DEV, ENG [37378]

ANNIS 1760S-1830S TORQUAY, DEV, ENG [35815] : PRE 1870 PEMBROKE DOCK, PEM, WLS [38718]

ANNIS-BROWN ALL WORLDWIDE [35331]

ANNISS 1750-1950 LONDON &, MDX, ENG [37344]

ANNON 1800-1900 WINNIFRED, ALB, CAN [34255]

ANNOP ALL WORLDWIDE [34312]

ANNUM 1800-1840 SHRAWLEY, WOR, ENG [37233]

ANNUP ALL WORLDWIDE [34312]

ANSALDO 1850+ BEECHWORTH, VIC, AUS [35147] : PRE 1850 GENOA, ITL [35147]

ANSCHUETZ 1772-1890 SCHLEUSINGEN, THURINGIA, GER [38148]

ANSCOMBE 1834+ SHERMANBURY, SSX, ENG [36212] : PRE 1820 SSX, ENG [37646]

ANSDELL C1800 HULL, YKS, ENG [35560] : C1780 WOODBURY, DEV, ENG [37757]

ANSEL PRE 1750 GER [38683]

ANSELL PRE 1800 HITCHIN, HRT, ENG [34450] : 1760S WIELD, HAM, ENG [34909]

ANSET ALL WORLDWIDE [37280]

ANSLEY 1780-1880 IRL [34290]

ANSLOW 1800-1900 FAIRFIELD, LAN, ENG [38521] : ALL WORLDWIDE [35068]

ANSMAN ALL USA [34419]

ANSON PRE 1830 KENNINGTON, SRY, ENG [36388] : PRE 1850 ENG &, INDIA [34603]

ANSTEY 1700-1800 KEWSTOKE, SOM, ENG [34158] : C1820 SOM, ENG [34972] : 1700S WASHFIELD, DEV, ENG [35131] : ALL DYRHAM & DOYNTON, GLS, ENG [36820]

ANSTEY-GODFREY ALL TAS, AUS [37127]

ANSTICE 1806 STH PETHERTON, SOM, ENG [35252]

ANSTY PRE 1670 SFK, ENG [38746]

ANTCLIFF PRE 1827 GRINGLEY ON THE HILL, NTT, ENG [37978]

ANTHONY 1820-1834 DIGBY, NS, CAN [35314] : PRE 1750 NFK, ENG [34660] : C1780 BAWDESWELL, NFK, ENG [35046] : 1769 BUCKLAND, HRT, ENG [35535] : PRE 1800 COGGESHALL, ESS, ENG [36379] : 1700-1800 BKM, ENG [36491] : EDWARD M. 1839 ENG [37025] : EDWARD M. 1866 EDEN, ERIE CO., NY, USA [37025] : MAY 1880+ ABERDARE, GLA, WLS [34954] : MAY 1900+ CARDIFF, GLA, WLS [34954] : ALL WORLDWIDE [38445]

ANTILL C1810-1870 KINGSTANLEY, GLS, ENG [35725]

ANTINGHAM 1700-1800 DUNTON, NFK, ENG [37845]

ANTON PRE 1900 FORGUE & MARNOCH, ABD, SCT [36245]

ANTONISSEN PRE 1775 STABROEK & ATW, OVL, BEL [38697]

ANTONY PRE 1820 NTT, ENG [38080] : 1770+ CRAIL, FIF, SCT [35822]

ANTRAM C1860 MELBOURNE, VIC, AUS [35877] : PRE 1846 HIGHLAND, OH, USA [34410]

ANYOP PRE 1600 ENG [34312]

APEL PRE 1700 BIRKUNGEN, PSA, GER [38048] : ALL GER [38664]

APELDOORN ALL NL [34478]

APELT PRE 1844 LANG HERMSDORF, SIL, GER [34766]

APLEN 1700S BROADWINSOR, DOR, ENG [38745] : 1700S THORNCOMBE, DEV, ENG [38745]

APLIN 1700+ SOM, ENG [36093] : 1800-50 WINDHAM & WINDSOR CO., VT, USA [37541]

APPEL PRE 1800 BRA, GER [38648]

APPERLEY 1650+ PAUNTLEY & KEMPLEY, GLS, ENG [34747] : 1800+ MORDIFORD, HEF, ENG [34747]

APPLEBY 1800S TAS, AUS [35531] : 1850 TAMWORTH, NSW, AUS [37907] : 1850 DUNGOG, NSW, AUS [37907] : C1861 LEEDS, YKS, ENG [34157] : PRE 1825 LAMBETH, LND, ENG [34450] : 1587+ COTHERSTONE, YKS, ENG [36961] : PRE 1800 BARNARD CASTLE, DUR, ENG [37663] : 1700+ LEEDS, ENG [37907] : 1700+ BARNARD CASTLE, DUR, ENG [38446] : PRE 1780 MA, USA [38363]

APPLEGARTH PRE 1650 STAINDROP, DUR, ENG [36499]

APPLER 1800S WORLDWIDE [37476]

APPLETON 1880+ SYDNEY, NSW, AUS [35259] : 1880+ ONT, CAN [38323] : C1800 LEICESTER, LEI, ENG [35032] : 1860S WESTOE, DUR, ENG [35259] : PRE 1820 FARNWORTH, LAN, ENG [35259] : PRE 1862 CUL, ENG [35389] : 1850-1860 LEEDS, YKS, ENG [35630] : 1790+ WINWICK NEWTON, LAN, ENG [38046] : PRE 1880 WAVERTREE, LAN, ENG [38512] : 1600+ WALDINGFIELD, SFK, ESS, MA, ENG & USA [36341]

APPLEWHITE ALL COVINGTON CO., MS, NC & SC, USA [37796]

APPLEYARD 1800+ TAS, VIC & WA, AUS [35836] : PRE 1800 YKS, ENG [34383] : 1860-1950 HALIFAX, YKS, ENG [34658] : 1700+ YKS, ENG [35836] : 1840-1890 SALFORD, LAN, ENG [37705] : PRE 1785 NEW BRENTFORD, MDX, ENG [38075] : PRE 1820 ALDENHAM, HRT, ENG [38075] : PRE 1820 ELSTREE, HRT, ENG [38075]

APPLING 1680-1800 YORK & AMELIA, VA, USA [38027]

APPS 1750 GOUDHURST, KEN, ENG [37215] : PRE 1900 WADHURST, SSX, ENG [37335]

APPULTON PRE 1820 FARNWORTH, LAN, ENG [35259]

APSEY PRE 1866 ROTHERHITHE, SRY, ENG & AUS [37948]

APT 1700-1770 PHILADELPHIA CO., PA, USA [38129]

APTHORP C1800+ GUMLEY, LEI, ENG [35477]

AQUILAQUA 1840 LEVO, LOMBARDY, ITL [37163]

AQUINO PRE 1873 NAIC, CAVITE, PHILIPPINE [34891]

ARABIN PRE 1800 LONDON, ENG [34314] : ALL WORLDWIDE [34778]

ARAM GERVAS PRE 1700 CLIFTON, NTT, ENG [36619] : PRE 1850 SRY & LND, ENG [37725] : C1800 ENG [38777]

ARAULT 1700 ALLONES, CEN, FRA [36418]

ARBEGUST 1650-1750 ENG [37784] : 1650-1750 GER [37784] : 1750-1816 PHILADELPHIA, PA, USA [37784]

ARBER 1800-1920 CREATON, NTH, ENG [35845]

ARBLASTER 1860+ BENDIGO, VIC, AUS [35205] : PRE 1860 BLOXWICH & BROWN HILLS, STS, ENG [35205]

ARBUCKLE 1796+ KILMARNOCK, AYR, SCT [34668]

ARCARI ALL ENG [37394]

ARCHABALD PRE 1900 GLASGOW, SCT [37443]

ARCHBELL PRE 1830 YKS, ENG [37923] : 1815+ RSA [37923]

ARCHBOLD 1700-1900 CHATTON, NBL, ENG [36776]

ARCHDALL 1870+ NSW, AUS [38211]

ARCHER 1855+ SYDNEY, NSW, AUS [34185] : PRE 1900S HOBART, TAS, AUS [34265] : PRE 1880 PYRMONT, NSW, AUS [34265] : 1857+ BALLARAT, VIC, AUS [34298] : 1830+ TUMUT, NSW, AUS [34978] : ALICE E. C1800S ENG [34133] : C1700-1810 LONDON, ENG [34339] : ALL KIRKBURTON, WRY, ENG [34822] : WILLIAM PRE 1860 TOTTENHAM, MDX, ENG [34935] : RICHARD PRE 1728+ ASHWELL, HRT, ENG [35072] : PRE 1900 HATFIELD, HRT, ENG [35433] : HARRIET PRE 1885 HAMMERSMITH, LND, ENG [35449] : 1765+ NFK, ENG [35458] : ANN PRE 1790 MDX, ENG [35541] : PRE 1716 SOUTH CROXTON, LEI, ENG [35572] : 1800+ DERBY, DBY, ENG [35632] : PRE 1750 EDWALTON, NTT, ENG [36619] : 1770-1850 MIDDLETON, LAN, ENG [36635] : 1630-1780 DENT, WRY, ENG [36635] : 1700-1850 ALNWICK, NBL, ENG [36879] : PRE 1887 SEACROFT, YKS, ENG [37346] : SAMUEL 1750+ BASILDON, ESS, ENG [37664] : 1700+ DOVENBY, CUL, ENG [37735] : PRE 1750 NTT, ENG [37739] : ALL DBY, ENG [38265] : PRE 1816 COVENTRY, WAR, ENG [38512] : PRE 1820 DUB, IRL [34265] : 1820+ KIK, IRL [36869] : 1800-1860 DUBLIN CITY, DUB, IRL [38301] : 1700-1800 CORK CITY, COR, IRL [38301] : PRE 1860 DUNDEE, PER, SCT [34014] : ALL SWANSEA, GLA, WLS [34298]

ARCHIBALD 1780+ NEW EDINBURGH, NS, CAN [34138] : SAMUEL 1860+ NORTH GWILLIMBURY, ONT, CAN [35648] : 1840S BENTINCK, ONT, CAN [38422] : C1880 LONDON, ENG [35014] : C1840 PLYMOUTH, DEV, ENG [36361] : 1800S DEPTFORD, KEN, ENG [36868] : C1800 EDINBURGH, MLN, SCT [33886] : 1700+ LIBERTON, MLN, SCT [34420] : 1841 NEWTOWN, MLN, SCT [35535] : 1700S MARKINCH, FIF, SCT [35558] : PRE 1810 TOUGH, ABD, SCT [36077] : PRE 1840 INVERESK, MLN, SCT [36884] : PRE 1741 INVERESK, MLN, SCT [37852] : 1830S DOWNLASIE, ABD, SCT [38422]

ARCHMAN PRE 1850S EDINBURGH, MLN, SCT [35433]

ARCUS 1790 DUNROSSNESS, SHI, SCT [35855]

ARDELL ROBERT 1874+ FRENCH, CAN [38216]

ARDEN PRE 1800 STOKE SUB HAMDON, SOM, ENG [34057] : 1800+ MANCHESTER, LAN, ENG [35586] : 1850+ LIN & CAM, ENG [37347]

ARDERN WILLIAM 1822+ ALTRINCHAM, CHS, ENG [35426]

ARDILL PRE 1823 BURRISOKANE, TIP, IRL [34781] : 1823+ FERBANE, OFF, IRL [34781] : ALL WORLDWIDE [34781]

ARDIN C1700 VANDOEUVRES, GE, CH [38348]

ARDING 1800-1840 WANTAGE, BRK, ENG [37877]

ARDREY ALL DUNGANNON, TYR & DOW, IRL & USA [36827]

ARDRON 1712-1748 TREETON & SHEFFIELD, YKS, ENG [35257]

ARELETT ALFRED LEAHY 1871+ GEELONG, VIC, AUS [35754] : ALFRED LEAHY 1871+ BIRREGURRA, VIC, AUS [35754]

ARENBURG JOHANN PRE 1750 GER [38453]

AREND PRE 1840 ZUSCH, GER [38033]

ARENSCHIELD 1827 HANOVER, GER [37605]

ARENSMEYER 1800+ EIDINGHAUSEN, WEF, GER [38023]

ARENTZ 1860+ TUMUT, NSW, AUS [37136] : 1880+ TINGHA, NSW, AUS [37889] : PRE 1855 WUE, GER [34886]

ARGENBRIGHT ALL WORLDWIDE [38576]

ARGENT C1815 CHINGFORD, ESS, ENG [34815] : 1820+ LONDON, ENG [36070] : 1700+ HALSTEAD, ESS, ENG [36070] : 1700+ ESS, ENG [36070] : PRE 1800 ESS & SFK, ENG [36399] : PRE 1900 SFK, ENG [37237] : 1730S GREAT SALING, ESS, ENG [37250]

ARGLES ALL AUS [35331]

ARGYLE 1880+ HAM, ENG [37861] : 1800+ SHEFFIELD, YKS & LAN, ENG [37861] : 1870+ LND, ENG [37861] : ALL ASHBURTON, NZ [36839]

ARIAS PRE 1800 ESP [38345]

ARIELL 1870+ REDFERN, NSW, AUS [38071] : C1870 WOLLOOMOOLOO, NSW, AUS [38071]

ARIS GEROGE C1860 SRY, ENG [35714]

ARISS ALL WORLDWIDE [34401]

ARKEY ALL WORLDWIDE [35161]

ARKLE 1790+ LONDON, ENG [37294]

ARKWELL 1700-1840 STROUD, GLS, ENG [38003]

ARKWRIGHT 1600+ LYTHAM & BLACKBURN, LAN, ENG [37218]

ARLER PRE 1850 NL [34478]

ARLISTON PRE 1825 GORTON, LAN, ENG [37546]

ARLOW PRE 1800 PEM, WLS [38461]

ARMATAG 1800-1836 ENG [35136]

ARMBRISTER 1837+ ST SALVADOR ISLAND, BAHAMAS, W.INDIES [36412]

ARMBURGH ALL MAHONE BAY, NS, CAN [34485]

ARMER PRE 1900 BELFAST, ANT & DOW, IRL [38481]

ARMES PRE 1855 EAST DEREHAM, NFK, ENG [35132] : ALL NORWICH, NFK, ENG [37612]

ARMETT PRE 1800 RUSHTON SPENCER, STS, ENG [37650]

ARMISHAW PRE 1833 UTTOXETER, STS, ENG [34955] : 1840+ ENG [38416] : ALL ENG & NZ [33975]

ARMISON PRE 1825 RADFORD, NTT, ENG [37000]

ARMITAG 1800-1836 ENG [35136]

ARMITAGE HENRY 1800+ LAUNCESTON, TAS, AUS [37999] : 1800+ HUDDERSFIELD, YKS, ENG [35636] : 1600-1750 KIRKBURTON, YKS, ENG [38342] : PRE 1700 MA, USA & ENG [38745]

ARMITT 1800-1820 NEITHROP, OXF, ENG [34842]

ARMOR 1800+ WHITEHAVEN, CUL, ENG [34680]

ARMOUR 1850+ LAUNCESTON, TAS, AUS [34421] : PRE 1850 NB, CAN [33904] : PRE 1900 LIM & COR, IRL [37807] : 1760+ KILMAURS, AYR, SCT [34110] : PRE 1850 NEILSTON, RFW, SCT [36583] : 1839-1862 EAST KILBRIDE, GLASGOW, SCT [36855] : 1750-1770 MAUCHLINE, AYR, SCT [38347] : 1850-1920 CO, USA [37807]

ARMSHEIMER 1650+ UNDENHEIM, RPF, BRD [37012]

ARMSTRONG 1877+ STRATHBOGIE, VIC, AUS [33837] : 1854+ WHITTLESEA, VIC, AUS [33837] : 1850+ VIC, AUS [34846] : 1850+ WA, AUS [34846] : ISABELLA 1866-84 QLD, AUS [35477] : THOMAS 1902-27 WANGARATTA, VIC, AUS [35477] : ALL VIC, AUS [35707] : 1939+ KIAMA, NSW, AUS [37154] : 1867 NEWTOWN, NSW, AUS [37965] : 1857 SYDNEY, NSW, AUS [37965] : C1870 TUDOR, ONT, CAN [34133] : 1810-1860 DURHAM CO., ONT, CAN [35602] : 1750+ ANNAPOLIS, NS, CAN [37049] : 1800-1920 ONT, CAN [37466] : 1730S BEWCASTLE, CUL, ENG [34688] : C1810 CARLISLE, CUL, ENG [34688] : 1850+ EVERTON, LAN, ENG [34688] : 1780-1880 NBL, ENG [34846] : PRE 1870 CROGLIN, CUL, NBL & DUR, ENG [34869] : PRE 1845 PENRITH, CUL, ENG [34911] : C1830 BIRMINGHAM, WAR, ENG [36302] : 1787+ HALTWHISTLE, NBL, ENG [36386] : C1725 THORNGRAFTON, NBL, ENG [36386] : JOHN PRE 1831 ROCHESTER, KEN, ENG [36767] : WM. & MARY 1800 HARBOTTLE, NBL, ENG [36767] : PRE 1840 WINGATE, DUR, ENG [37137] : PRE 1881 ST HELENS, LAN, ENG [37318] : PRE 1740 NORTH CLIFTON, NTT, ENG [37381] : 1700-1850 ALSTON, CUL, ENG [37457] : THOMAS 1750-1800 KENDAL & SELSIDE, WES, ENG [37779] : 1850-1950 SOUTH LONDON, ENG [38513] : PRE 1870 INDIA [35255] : 1800+ STRANAFELEY, FER, IRL [33837] : 1820+ GORTGARRON, FER, IRL [34455] : 1750-1820 DOW, IRL [34523] : 1700-1900 KESH, FER, IRL [34537] : C1840 GALLOON & DONAGH, FER, IRL [34688] : 1800+ WEX, IRL [34956] : SAMUEL 1800-1850 NEWTOWN BUTLER, FER, IRL [36728] : ALL ANT, IRL [37127] : ALL MAGHERACULMONEY, FER, IRL [37154] : WILLIAM C1808 BELFAST, ANT, IRL [37556] : 1860 KINGSCOURT, CAV, IRL [37791] : C1846 BALLYMOTE, SLI, IRL [37965] : ROBERT PRE 1842 MAGHERACULMONEY, FER, IRL [38291] : 1750-1850 DUB, IRL [38342] : JANE C1843-1920 LAINSBOROUGH LODGE, CAV, IRL & AUS [37146] : JANE C1829 AUGHNACLOY, TYR & NSW, IRL & AUS [37556] : PRE 1820 BALLYNAHINCH, DOW, IRL & NZ [36840] : ALL SOUTHDEAN, ROX, SCT [33833] : ALL CASTLETON, ROX, SCT [34254] : 1848+ GALASHIELS, ROX, SCT [34379] : PRE 1852 PER, SCT [34379] : PRE 1835 DUNDEE, ANS, SCT [34590] : PRE 1850 DALRY, KKD, SCT [34665] : 1700+ LANGHOLM, DFS, SCT [35038] : 1750+ HAWICK, ROX, SCT [35038] : PRE 1840 CASTLETON, ROX,

SCT [35215] : C1770-1805 DUNBAR, ELN, SCT [36327] : PRE 1750 DUNDEE, ANS, SCT [37049] : JOAN 1820-1845 SANQUHAR, DFS, SCT [37488] : PRE 1800 EWES & LANGHOLM, DFS, SCT [38461] : PRE 1920 GLASGOW, LKS, SCT & NZ [36840] : 1750-1890 ALBANY, NY, USA [35300] : 1850-1860 ROCK CO., WI, USA [37808] : PRE 1770 BERKS CO., PA, USA [38135] : PRE 1800 CLINTON & ROSS, OH, USA [38220] : 1700-1900 KY, VA & IN, USA [38328]

ARNABOLDI PRE 1880 ITL & ENG [38286] : ALL NZ [36773] : 1854+ NZ [38286]

ARNAP ALL WORLDWIDE [34312]

ARNAUT 1600-1990 MALDEGEN, OVL, BEL [38165]

ARNDELL PRE 1800 HEF, ENG [34886]

ARNDT 1800+ SEEMITZEL, POM, GER [37170] : KARL 1800-1900S ELMA, NY, USA [34059]

ARNEP ALL WORLDWIDE [34312]

ARNEST 1880-1930 SONOMA CO., CA, USA [38154] : 1850-1880 MIAME CO., IN, USA [38154]

ARNETT 1650-1850 KINGSTON UPON HULL, YKS, ENG [38745] : 1904-1950S YONKERS, NY, USA [37710]

ARNEYEP PRE 1600 ENG [34312]

ARNEYOPE PRE 1600 ENG [34312]

ARNHEIM 1843+ NEUTEICH, EL, POL [36254]

ARNHOP ALL WORLDWIDE [34312]

ARNHOUT 1750+ ALBANY CO., NY, USA [36962]

ARNIEL 1800-1850 PAISLEY, RFW, SCT [38276]

ARNIP ALL WORLDWIDE [34312]

ARNIPP ALL WORLDWIDE [34312]

ARNOLD 1855+ COOMA & BOMBALA, NSW, AUS [34273] : 1855+ BOMBALA, NSW, AUS [34977] : PRE 1841+ AUS [35064] : 1780+ DIGBY, NS, CAN [34138] : 1831+ DITCHEAT, SOM, ENG [33852] : 1800+ SAL, ENG [33855] : C1800 HRT, ENG [34258] : PRE 1820 MDX, ENG [34462] : 1750-1810 DATCHWORTH, HRT, ENG [34697] : PRE 1750 SAINT AUSTELL, CON, ENG [34974] : CATHERINE C1820 ENG [35049] : 1850+ POPLAR, LND, ENG [35125] : PRE 1815 SSX, ENG [35238] : PRE 1842 DENFORD, BRK, ENG [35530] : PRE 1867 LONDON, ENG [36888] : 1830-1900 BRISTOL, GLS, ENG [37232] : 1830-1900 BATH, SOM, ENG [37232] : 1800+ SHEERNESS & ROCHESTER, KEN, ENG [37405] : PRE 1620 ILCHESTER, SOM, ENG [38135] : PRE 1770 BRIGHSTONE, IOW, ENG [38420] : PRE 1854 LEIMEN, BAD, GER [34273] : PRE 1855 LEIMEN, BAD, GER [34977] : PRE 1835 KUSEL, BAV, GER [36972] : PRE 1827+ LET, IRL [37108] : C1812 NEWTONARDS, DOW, IRL [37890] : 1782 ZEELAND LIMBURG, ZEL & LMB, NL & BEL [38715] : 1836-1990 EDWARDSBURG & LANSING, MI, USA [36342] : WILLIE LEE 1899 LAUDERDALE, MS, USA [36448] : C1894 BOWLING GREEN, KY, USA [36448] : 1830-1870 BRADFORD CO., PA, USA [37013] : 1800S MACOUPIN CO., IL, USA [37562] : MARY C1786+ PA, USA [38067] : WILLIAM C1718 PROVIDENCE, RI, USA [38172] : 1800+ TN, USA [38195] : SAMUEL 1810-1814 MONTGOMERY CO., OH, USA [38330] : PRE 1862 KY, USA [38605] : ALL SPRINGFIELD, MO, USA [38605] : 1650+ BURLINGTON, NJ, USA [38605] : 1678+ PA, USA [38605] : 1800S WARRICK, IN, USA [38605]

ARNOLPH PRE 1650 NFK & SFK, ENG [34312]

ARNOP ALL WORLDWIDE [34312]

ARNOPP ALL WORLDWIDE [34312]

ARNOT 1766-1850 CRAIL, FIF, SCT [36320] : C1770-1820 DUNFERMLINE, FIF, SCT [36327] : 1720-1800 AUCHTERTOOL AREA, FIF, SCT [37842] : 1764-1779 ABERDOUR, FIF, SCT [37842] : JANET PRE

1794 ABBOTSHALL, FIF, SCT **[37906]** : FRANCIS C1800+ PAISLEY, RFW, SCT **[38593]**

ARNOTT 1880S HAMILTON, VIC, AUS **[37947]** : PRE C1860 ALLERTON, YKS, ENG **[35904]** : 1750-1830 LEEDS, WRY, ENG **[38047]** : 1800+ DYSART, FIF, SCT **[35524]** : C1770-1820 DUNFERMLINE, FIF, SCT **[36327]** : 1860-1900 DUNFERMLINE AREA, FIF, SCT **[37842]**

ARNOUP ALL WORLDWIDE **[34312]**

ARNSBY 1856+ THE CURRAGH, KID, IRL **[36287]**

ARNSPIGER 1750-1800 WASHINGTON CO., MD, USA **[38118]**

ARNUP ALL WORLDWIDE **[34312]**

ARNUPP ALL WORLDWIDE **[34312]**

ARNYAPE PRE 1600 ENG **[34312]**

ARNYOP PRE 1600 ENG **[34312]**

ARNYP PRE 1600 ENG **[34312]**

ARONSON 1900+ ST KILDA, VIC, AUS **[34455]**

ARPS C1884 ROCKHAMPTON, QLD, AUS **[33809]** : C1840 OES **[33809]**

ARRASCH 1800-1900 PUTZIG, WESTPREUβEN, POL **[38603]**

ARRINGTON 1800-1900 IA, USA **[38320]**

ARROWSMITH 1861+ PRICEVILLE, CAN **[34528]** : PRE 1800 DUR, ENG **[34383]** : PRE 1810 BARNARD CASTLE, DUR, ENG **[37663]**

ARSCOTT PRE 1700 DEV, ENG **[36389]** : ELIZABETH 1700+ HOLCOMBE BURNELL, DEV, ENG **[36813]** : PRE 1850 DEV, ENG **[36998]**

ARTERY 1860+ NSW, AUS **[33931]**

ARTEYS ALL SFK & NFK, ENG **[36203]**

ARTHUR 1850+ WARRNAMBOOL, VIC, AUS **[34755]** : 1840+ MT GAMBIER, SA, AUS **[36622]** : 1850+ MELBOURNE, VIC, AUS **[38082]** : 1855+ VIC, AUS **[38539]** : 1850+ VIC, AUS **[38539]** : 1860+ SA, AUS **[38539]** : 1880+ WA, AUS **[38539]** : C1800-1880 NEWCASTLE ON TYNE, NBL, ENG **[33862]** : PRE 1940 ENG **[34657]** : 1750-1820 BRISTOL, GLS, ENG **[34762]** : PRE 1900 BUTLEIGH & STREET, SOM, ENG **[34855]** : PRE 1819 DORKING, SRY, ENG **[35016]** : PRE 1833 GLS, ENG **[38077]** : 1775+ ST CLEMENTS, CON, ENG **[38539]** : 1700+ PADSTOW, CON, ENG **[38539]** : 1810+ SOM, ENG **[38539]** : 1820+ BRISTOL, GLS, ENG **[38539]** : 1834+ ST BLAZEY, CON, ENG **[38539]** : 1790+ BODMIN, CON, ENG **[38539]** : 1804+ REDRUTH, CON, ENG **[38539]** : 1730+ ILLOGAN, CON, ENG **[38539]** : 1800-1850 MACOSQUIN, LDY & MD, IRL & USA **[34244]** : 1800+ CERES, FIF, SCT **[34637]** : PRE 1850 COYLTON, AYR, SCT **[35406]** : C1823 BATHGATE, WLN, SCT **[36762]** : 1700-1800 OLD DEER, ABD, SCT **[36833]** : 1800S GREENOCK, RFW, SCT **[37566]** : 1800S PULASKI CO., KY, USA **[37570]** : 1860S RHINEBECK, DUTCHESS CO., NY, USA **[38223]** : 1880+ SWANSEA, GLA, WLS **[35248]** : C1835 PAMTEG, MON, WLS **[36185]** : ALL WORLDWIDE **[36363]**

ARTHURS 1700S CHILSON, OXF, ENG **[35186]** : 1600-1990 GLS, ENG **[36130]** : C1720 PLYMPTON ST MARY, DEV, ENG **[37264]** : ALL IRL **[37930]** : 1864+ BELFAST, ANT, IRL **[37930]** : 1900+ USA & CAN **[37930]**

ARTIS 1870+ SYDNEY, NSW, AUS **[36203]** : 1750+ MDX & SRY, ENG **[36203]** : ALL SFK & NFK, ENG **[36203]**

ARTLETT 1800+ DOVER, KEN, ENG **[36123]**

ARTRIDGE PRE 1850 CANEWDON, ESS, ENG **[34591]**

ARTT 1840 COOKSTOWN, TYR, IRL **[34546]**

ARTURS PRE 1700 CON, ENG **[35255]**

ARVIDSSON HAKAN PRE 1650 HAGERUD & SUNNE, VARMLAND, SWE **[38551]**

ARWINE PRE 1900 WORLDWIDE **[36932]**

ARY PRE 1800 WORLDWIDE **[37280]**

ASBELL 1810 BUTLER CO., OH, USA **[38143]**

ASBERRY 1830-1885 ENG **[35166]**

ASBRIDGE 1750-1800 SPALDING, LIN, ENG **[36112]**

ASBURY 1665 KENT CO., MD, USA **[37795]**

ASCAH 1650-1750 BE, CH **[38407]**

ASCHAM C1900 PORT ELIZABETH, RSA **[33917]**

ASCOTT (SEE ARSCOTT) **[36389]**

ASENDORF KURT 1900-1980S BEPPEN & THEDINGHAUSEN, DIEPHOLZ, GER **[34059]**

ASH 1850+ VIC, AUS **[37113]** : PRE 1837 CARBONEAR, NFD, CAN **[38412]** : 1869+ CONGLETON, CHS, ENG **[33920]** : PRE 1780 DITTISHAM, DEV, ENG **[33998]** : 1700-99 STOCKTON, WAR, ENG **[34315]** : 1720-1800 NORTH HILL, CON, ENG **[34793]** : PRE 1890 PLYMOUTH, DEV, ENG **[34892]** : ALL LIN, ENG **[35628]** : C1753 WADDINGTON, LIN, ENG **[35746]** : 1700-1900 PORTSEA, HAM, ENG **[36409]** : PRE 1830 BRIXHAM, DEV, ENG **[37393]** : 1700-1850 CALSTOCK, CON, ENG **[37761]** : 1600-1800 EAST, CON, ENG **[37761]** : PRE 1750 STONE & DILHORNE, STS, ENG **[37893]** : ALL LONDON, MDX, ENG **[38252]** : ALL WORLDWIDE **[38252]**

ASHAWE ALL THE HALL ON THE HHILL, LAN, ENG **[35824]**

ASHBERRY 1700-1800 LEI, ENG **[37665]**

ASHBRIDGE 1884+ TORPENHOW, CUL, ENG **[38067]**

ASHBURMER PRE 1850 DALTON IN FURNESS, LAN, ENG **[36259]**

ASHBURNER 1850+ KEN & MDX, ENG **[37128]**

ASHBY 18650+ SYDNEY, NSW, AUS **[34969]** : JAMES 1870 DUBBO, NSW, AUS **[35756]** : JAMES 1830+ GOSFORD, NSW, AUS **[35756]** : JAMES 1900 BALMAIN, NSW, AUS **[35756]** : C1800 HEYDON, ESS, ENG **[33886]** : 1750-1850 CLAPHAM, SRY, ENG **[34572]** : MILLER PRE 1770 SSX, ENG **[34847]** : PRE 1900 GREAT EASTON, RUT, ENG **[35637]** : JOSEPH 1775 GREAT ELLINGHAM, NFK, ENG **[35756]** : JOSEPH 1800+ COLCHESTER, ESS, ENG **[35756]** : 1800S LEI, ENG **[35970]** : 1850-1870 CLERKENWELL, LND, ENG **[36044]** : 1760-1880 LEI, ENG **[36320]** : 1780+ IGHTHAM, KEN, ENG **[36887]** : 1748+ RICKMANSWORTH, HRT, ENG **[36975]** : 1500+ HAREFIELD, MDX, ENG **[36975]** : 1700-1800 LEICESTER, LEI, ENG **[37665]** : 1800 HUNTINGTON, HUN, ENG **[38272]** : JOSEPH C1820+ ENG & AUS **[37951]** : ALL USA **[37558]**

ASHCROFT 1897+ TAMBELLUP, WA, AUS **[35455]** : 1872+ SANDHURST, VIC, AUS **[35455]** : 1830+ NEWBURGH, LAN, ENG **[34370]** : PRE 1800 LIVERPOOL, LAN, ENG **[34576]** : 1837+ CHILDWALL, LAN, ENG **[35455]** : PRE 1780 BRISTOL, GLS & SOM, ENG **[36388]** : 1833-1872+ MANCHESTER, LAN, ENG & AUS **[33847]**

ASHDOWN ALL LONDON, ENG **[34617]** : PRE 1840 CROWBOROUGH CROSS, SSX, ENG **[38755]** : ALL WORLDWIDE **[34617]**

ASHE ALL LONDON, MDX, ENG **[38252]** : PRE 1880 EAST MINARD, KER, IRL **[34187]** : ALL WORLDWIDE **[38252]**

ASHER PRE 1829 LEADENHAM, LIN, ENG **[35895]**

ASHFIELD PRE 1853 THELNETHAM, SFK, ENG **[33822]** : 1800+ ASHTON & BIRMINGHAM, WAR, ENG **[34749]**

ASHFORD 1770-1810 HODDESDON, HRT, ENG **[34834]** : 1810-1840 BETHNAL GREEN, LND, ENG **[34834]** : 1800 SHEPTON MALLET, SOM, ENG **[34890]** : PRE 1900 BIRMINGHAM, WAR, ENG **[35577]** : PRE 1850 BIRMINGHAM, WAR, ENG

[35785] : 1700-1930 BRISTOL, GLS, ENG [36894] :
PRE 1780 CRETINGHAM, SFK, ENG [37442] : ALL
STS, SAL & WAR, ENG [38754]

ASHFORTH C1800 SCAMPTON, LIN, ENG [36561]

ASHLEY 1750-1850 LITTLE BUDWORTH, CHS, ENG
[36983] : 1770+ LONDON, MDX, ENG [36987] :
1870+ GERALDINE, NZ [35993] : ALL ESS & SFK,
UK [37674] : PRE 1850 NC, USA [38536]

ASHLOCK 1830S NELSON CO., KY, USA [37527]

ASHMAN 1870+ GLADSTONE, QLD, AUS [37904]

ASHMORE ALL MUGGINTON, DBY, ENG [36846] :
PRE 1880 DBY, ENG [37353] : PRE 1880
ROTHERHAM, YKS, ENG [37353] : ALL
BIRMINGHAM, WAR, ENG [37959] : PRE 1850
DOVER, KEN, ENG & AUS [34865] : 1850-1900
BROWN, OH, USA [38054]

ASHPEY PRE 1826 NEWINGTON, KEN, ENG [34105]

ASHTON 1800+ NSW & QLD, AUS [33799] : 1860S
UARBRY, NSW, AUS [37106] : JANE 1800S NSW,
AUS & ENG [33895] : C1800 KIRBY MISPERTON,
YKS, ENG [35198] : 1620-1780 LITTLEBOROUGH,
NTT, ENG [36426] : 1820 YKS, ENG [37106] : 1850-
1900 CHERTSEY, SRY, ENG [37618] : PRE 1900
EDMONTON, MDX, ENG [37667] : 1800-1900 LIN,
ENG [37695] : PRE 1800 MANCHESTER, LAN,
ENG [37729] : 1840S WIGAN, LAN, ENG [38283] :
JOS. 1700+ HAUGHTON, LAN, ENG [38384] : JOS.
1788+ MANCHESTER, LAN, ENG [38384] : JOS.
ALL LONDON, ENG [38384] : JOHN P. 1810+
DENTON, LAN, ENG [38384] : WILLIAM 1816+
MANCHESTER, LAN, ENG [38384] : GEORGE
1814+ MANCHESTER, LAN, ENG [38384] : JOS.
1806+ HAUGHTON, LAN, ENG [38384] : JOHN B.
1812+ BISHOPWEARMOUTH, DUR, ENG [38384] :
THOMAS P. 1807+ DENTON, LAN, ENG [38384] :
WILLIAM C1810 PEWSEY, WIL, ENG [38489] :
1800+ BRIDGEND, GLA, WLS [34666]

ASHURST PRE 1744 STANDISH, LAN, ENG [37309]

ASHWELL PRE 1860 SA, AUS [34959] : ALL
ALLESLEY, WAR, ENG [34671] : C1850 HENLOW,
BDF, ENG [35585] : PRE 1840 NASH, MON, WLS
[36247]

ASHWIN PRE 1853 GEELONG, VIC, AUS [34587]

ASHWORTH PRE 1936 HUNTSVILLE, ONT, CAN
[38450] : 1859+ ROCHDALE, LAN, ENG [33942] :
1780-1830 RAWTENSTALL & NEWCHURCH, LAN,
ENG [34448] : ALL HASLINGDEN, LAN, ENG
[34564] : PRE 1850 BURNLEY, LAN, ENG [36187] :
1750-1800 HEPTONSTALL, WRY, ENG [36635] :
REUBEN PRE 1840 NEWCHURCH IN
ROSSENDALE, LAN, ENG [37414] : ANDERTON
PRE 1850 NEWCHURCH IN ROSSENDALE, LAN,
ENG [37414] : JOHN PRE 1860 WATERFOOT &
ROSSENDALE, LAN, ENG [37414] : 1850+
BAMFORD ROCHDALE, LAN, ENG [37626] : PRE
1860 HURST, CHS, ENG [37939] : 1811+ POSEY
CO., IN, USA [35286]

ASKEW 1833+ SYDNEY, NSW, AUS [35160] : PRE
1840 HALIFAX, YKS, ENG [35404] : 1750-1850
IPSWICH, SFK, ENG [37042] : PRE 1815
ALLENDALE, NBL, ENG [37663] : 1700-1750 LAN,
ENG [37858]

ASKEY 1820 LND, ENG [35828]

ASKHAM PRE 1770 THURLSTONE, WRY, ENG
[37754]

ASKIN 1800+ ANT, IRL [37116]

ASLETT ALL CHICHESTER & PORTSMOUTH, SSX
& HAM, ENG [36994]

ASON 1820 BDF, ENG [35377]

ASPERRY (SEE ASBERRY [35166]

ASPEY PRE 1910 LONDON, ENG [37062]

ASPINALL 1750+ DARWEN & IDLE, LAN, ENG
[36642]

ASPINDALE C1800 PRESTON, LAN, ENG [37066]

ASPREY PRE 1850 BDF, ENG [37062] : PRE 1900
MITCHAM, SRY, ENG [37987]

ASSAILLY PRE 1890 FRA [34084]

ASSELSTINE C1784+ LEN & ADD CO., ONT, CAN
[36651]

ASTBURY 1790+ GORSTAGE, CHS, ENG [34370] :
1800 WINTERLY MILLS, CHS, ENG [35023] : PRE
1890 LONDON, ENG [36486]

ASTICK PRE 1823 ARKHOLME, LAN, ENG [36227]

ASTILL 1830+ DERBY, DBY, ENG [37675] : ALL
WORLDWIDE [36500]

ASTIN PRE 1785 CREWKERNE, SOM, ENG [36581] :
PRE 1800 STS, ENG [37389] : MARY C1880
BURNLEY, LAN, ENG [38284] : PRE 1863
GLASGOW, LKS, SCT [37623]

ASTINGTON 1750-1850 CHEADLE, CHS, ENG [36416]

ASTLE 1700+ SMISBY, DBY, ENG [35874] : 1700+
MARSTON UPON DOVE, DBY, ENG [38745]

ASTLEY PRE 1775 HARBORNE, WAR, ENG [35517] :
RICHARD 1830+ SALFORD, LAN, ENG [37748] :
1750+ CHORLEY & HEAPEY, LAN, ENG [38260] :
1830-1870 LLANWNOG, MGY, WLS [35391]

ASTON PRE 1851 STUDLEY, WAR, ENG [34391] :
1700-1850 GLS, ENG [34739] : ALL IPSWICH, SFK,
ENG & AUS [33919]

ASTREY 1700-1800 GREAT MILTON, OXF, ENG
[34716]

ATACK ALL WORLDWIDE [37084]

ATCHESON PRE 1851 BALLANTAMPLE, CAV, IRL
[35225]

ATCHINSON 1675 HATFIELD, MA, USA [37740] :
1800-1850 MONROE CO., NY, USA [37740]

ATCHISON 1800-1837 HORNCLIFFE, NBL, ENG
[38269] : 1850 IL, USA [38320]

A'TEUILL ALL BRITTANY, FRA [34812]

ATHERALL 1700-1850 HARTFIELD, SSX, ENG
[37365]

ATHERFOLD 1770-1850 HARTFIELD, SSX, ENG
[34911]

ATHERSICH ALL BIRMINGHAM, WAR, ENG
[37265]

ATHERTON 1920S HILLSTON, NSW, AUS [38510] :
1910+ BRAZIL [37149] : 1860 LIVERPOOL, LAN,
ENG [35256] : 1900S LINCOLN, LIN, ENG [35256] :
PRE 1852 CARLISLE, CUL, ENG [35478] : 1800
MANCHESTER, LAN, ENG [35881] : 1800S
WIGAN, LAN, ENG [36253] : ALL LIVERPOOL,
ENG [36811] : PRE 1900 PRESTON, ALSTON, LAN,
ENG [36998] : 1840+ BOLTON, LAN, ENG [37626] :
1550-1650 ATHERTON LEIGH, LAN, ENG [37783] :
RICHARD 1770-1795 MANCHESTER, LAN, ENG
[37929] : ALL PRESTON, LAN & NSW, ENG & AUS
[35547]

ATHEY 1600S SEDGEFIELD, DUR, ENG [36527]

ATKIN C1790 NOTTINGHAM, NTT, ENG [34734] :
PRE 1715 METHERINGHAM, LIN, ENG [37318] :
C1800 MONKWEARMOUTH, DUR, ENG [37859]

ATKINS 1852+ GOULBURN & BOMBALA, NSW,
AUS [34273] : 1840+ BOMBALA, NSW, AUS [34977]
: PRE 1895 BALLARAT, VIC & CON, AUS & ENG
[37995] : 1800-1930 BIRMINGHAM, WAR, ENG
[33965] : 1850+ DOVER & CAPEL LE FERME,
KEN, ENG [34905] : 1700+ WAR, ENG [35458] :
JOHN 1700+ ABBOTS LANGLEY, HRT, ENG
[36291] : PRE 1830 SPILSBY, LIN, ENG [36748] :
PRE 1847 READING, BRK, ENG [37307] : 1750+
WOR, ENG [37323] : 1800-1900 KEN, ENG [37338] :
1780-1850 HRT, ENG [37829] : 1800 SOM, ENG
[38288] : PRE 1852 CAR, IRL [34273] : JAMES PRE

1840 CAR, IRL **[34979]** : HEZEKIAH 1830 BROOME CO., NY, USA **[38142]** : 1782+ ABBEVILLE, SC, USA **[38187]** : WYATT PRE 1846 FAYETTE CO., AL, USA **[38569]**

ATKINSON 1800+ ADELAIDE, SA, AUS **[34607]** : THOMAS C1900 GYMPIE, QLD, AUS **[34807]** : C1855 ADELAIDE, SA, AUS **[35744]** : 1800S TAS, AUS **[36796]** : 1914+ NSW, AUS **[37115]** : C1900 PERTH, WA, AUS **[37982]** : 1866 GEELONG, VIC, AUS **[37982]** : ISABELLA PRE 1840 LONDON, ENG **[33874]** : C1830 SANDHURST, KEN, ENG **[33917]** : CHARLES C1762+ IPSWICH, SFK, ENG **[33919]** : PRE 1893 GUISELEY, WRY, ENG **[33943]** : 1850 MORLAND S GATE, CUL, ENG **[34349]** : PRE 1881+ CHS, ENG **[34423]** : C1820 LONDON, ENG **[34581]** : 1800+ BDF, ENG **[34607]** : 1745 BOROUGHBRIDGE, NRY, ENG **[34731]** : 1762+ IPSWICH, SFK, ENG **[34777]** : WILLIAM PRE 1910 NORTH SHIELDS, NBL, ENG **[35200]** : 1700+ NFK, ENG **[35460]** : 1840+ BRADFORD, YKS, ENG **[35460]** : 1700+ LEEDS & BRADFORD, WRY, ENG **[36104]** : PRE 1770 CHOLLERTON & KIRKWHELANGTON, NBL, ENG **[36110]** : JESSE PRE 1881 CATCHGATE, DUR, ENG **[36164]** : PRE 1722 PENNINGTON IN FURNESS, CUL, ENG **[36204]** : 1700-1850 WESTERDALE, NRY, ENG **[36472]** : PRE 1820 BERWICK, NBL, ENG **[36588]** : PRE 1800 LEEDS, YKS, ENG **[36793]** : ALL YKS, ENG **[36796]** : 1880S RYTON ON TYNE, DUR, ENG **[36867]** : PRE 1910 HOLME ON SPALDING MOOR, YKS, ENG **[37094]** : ALL YKS, ENG **[37115]** : 1878+ CROYDON, SRY, ENG **[37115]** : ALL LIN, ENG **[37115]** : ALL LOUTH, LIN, ENG **[37115]** : PRE 1842 IDLE, YKS, ENG **[37174]** : PRE 1738 BELCHFORD, LIN, ENG **[37318]** : PRE 1820 YKS, ENG **[37491]** : 1606-1810 POULTON LE SANDS, LAN, ENG **[37524]** : 1800+ ERY, ENG **[37827]** : JOHN 1811-1871 HAMPSTHWAITE, LEEDS, NRY, ENG **[37887]** : PRE 1837 WIGAN, LAN, ENG **[37945]** : PRE 1860 LIVERPOOL, LAN, ENG **[37991]** : C1828 SAXILBY, LIN, ENG **[38272]** : 1790S INGLETON, YKS, ENG **[38283]** : 1700S APPLEBY, WES, ENG **[38440]** : PRE 1850 STS, ENG **[38461]** : THOMAS 1873+ PORTADOWN, ARM, IRL **[34807]** : 1860S ANT, IRL **[36831]** : 1800S BALLYMORE, ARM, IRL **[36857]** : JANE 1600+ KINGS CO., OFF, IRL **[36890]** : PRE 1849 KNOCKBRIDE, CAV, IRL **[37164]** : 1850+ DUNEDIN, OTAGO, NZ **[34607]** : 1900S WESTLAND, NZ **[36796]** : 1880+ CAMBRIDGE, NZ **[37115]** : ALL NZ **[37115]** : 1800-1850 KY, USA **[36346]** : 1850-1950 CO, USA **[36962]** : 1775-1800 WASHINGTON CO., PA, USA **[38137]** : GEORGE 1820-60 JUNIATA CO., PA, USA **[38138]** : 1790 OVERTON CO., TN, USA **[38143]**

ATLEY ALL SKERRIES, DUB, IRL **[36409]**

ATMORE ALL NFK, ENG **[37612]**

ATREE 1700-1800 RUDGEWICK, SSX, ENG **[38287]**

ATTEBERY 1750-1770 LOUDON, VA, USA **[36908]**

ATTENBOROUGH ALL NTT & DBY, ENG & AUS **[34040]**

ATTERBURY 1700+ KENILWORTH, WAR, ENG **[35496]** : ALL COSGROVE, NTH, ENG **[38358]**

ATTEWELL 1800 GOTHERINGTON, GLS, ENG **[34890]**

ATTFIELD 1840 LONDON, MDX, ENG **[35067]**

ATTKIN PRE 1850 ILKESTON, DBY, ENG **[36387]**

ATTON PRE 1740 BRAUNSTON, RUT, ENG **[36817]** : 1800-30 LIN, ENG **[37863]** : 1820-50 HULL, YKS, ENG **[37863]**

ATTREE 1820+ GREENWICH, KEN, ENG **[34017]**

ATTRIDGE C1860 ORF TWP. KENT CO., ONT, CAN **[34493]** : C1860 WENTWORTH, ONT, CAN **[34493]** :

1720+ FRYERNING, ESS, ENG **[38488]** : ALL COR, IRL **[34493]** : C1830 NY, USA **[34493]**

ATTRILL 1750+ PORTSEA, HAM, ENG **[33938]** : ALL ISLE OF WIGHT, HAM, ENG **[34812]** : 1800+ WHITWELL, IOW, ENG **[36623]**

ATTWELL ALL KEN, ENG **[35531]**

ATTWOOD 1854+ KYNETON, TYLDEN & ECHUCA, VIC, AUS **[36622]** : 1854+ SHEPPARTON & KYABRAM, VIC, AUS **[36622]** : 1750+ MAIDSTONE, KEN, ENG **[33973]** : 1850+ WANDSWORTH, SRY, ENG **[35078]** : PRE 1760 BURBAGE, WIL, ENG **[35346]** : PRE 1750 WAVENDON, BKM & BDF, ENG **[35701]** : PRE 1871 CRADLEY, WOR, ENG **[36613]** : PRE 1840 WOR, ENG **[36759]** : ALL BROMHAM, WIL, ENG **[37972]** : C1819 SHOREDITCH, MDX, ENG **[38441]** : PRE 1820 DUDLEY & ROWLEY REGIS, WOR, ENG & AUS **[35079]**

ATTWOOLL ALL WORLDWIDE **[36013]**

ATWELL C1832 READING, BRK, ENG **[35487]** : 1850 WOKINGHAM, BRK, ENG **[37690]**

ATWOOD 1750-1850 KEN, ENG **[37064]** : PRE 1840 KEN, ENG **[38033]** : C1760 VA, USA **[38323]** : 1770-1850 NY, USA **[38742]** : 1667-C1764 HARTFORD CO., CT, USA **[38764]**

ATWOOD (SEE ATTWOOD) **[36622]**

ATWOOL ALL WORLDWIDE **[36013]**

ATWOOLL ALL WORLDWIDE **[36013]** : ALL WORLDWIDE **[36013]**

AUBE 1800+ BEAUMONT, QUE, CAN **[34082]**

AUBIN PRE 1800 JSY, CHI **[34805]** : PRE 1900 LONDON, ENG **[34562]** : PRE 1619 TOUROUVRE, CEN, FRA **[38525]**

AUBREY 1800+ MERTHYR TYDFIL, GLA, WLS **[34568]**

AUBUSSON 1800+ LONDON, MDX, ENG **[35162]** : ALL WORLDWIDE **[35162]**

AUCKLAND PRE 1772 INGHAM, LIN, ENG **[34501]**

AUCOIN PRE 1850 INVERNESS CO., NS, CAN **[38447]**

AUDLEY PRE 1850 NANTWICH, CHS, ENG **[35229]** : 1700+ ENG **[35377]** : 1770-1890 LIVERPOOL, LAN, ENG **[35377]** : 1770-1800 CHS, ENG **[35377]** : ALL CAMBERWELL, SRY, LND & MDX, ENG **[35460]** : 1680-1700 BOSTON, MA, USA **[36737]** : 1680-1700 NEWPORT, RI, USA **[36737]**

AUER PRE 1855 AFFALTRACH, WUE, GER **[34886]** : PRE 1800 MARKDORF, BAW, GER **[38609]**

AUFDERHEIDE ALL WORLDWIDE **[36363]**

AUGE 1800S TSCHIEBSDORF, SIL, GER **[38623]**

AUGER 1800+ CHORLEY, LAN, ENG **[35614]** : PRE 1700 MINSTER, CON, ENG **[38214]**

AUGHY PRE 1855 LISBURN, DOW, IRL **[37925]**

AUGUSTIN 1730-1830 ZITTAU, KSA, GER **[38628]**

AUGUSTINE PRE 1800 MD, USA **[36702]**

AUKETT 1740+ HELLINGLY, SSX, ENG **[37560]**

AULD 1893+ BUNDAMBA, QLD, AUS **[35392]** : PRE 1875 KILLINCHY, DOW, IRL **[34895]** : PRE 1850 AYR, AYR, SCT & CAN **[34835]**

AULLS 1800-1850 LDY, IRL **[34687]**

AUNGER 1840+ SA, AUS **[38338]** : ALL CAN **[38338]** : ALL CON & DEV, ENG **[38338]** : ALL TRENEGLOS, CON, ENG **[38338]** : ALL LAUNCESTON, CON, ENG **[38338]** : ALL WARBSTOW, CON, ENG **[38338]** : ALL CALLINGTON, CON, ENG **[38338]** : 1890+ GRASS VALLEY & NEVEDA CITY, CA, USA **[38338]** : ALL USA **[38338]**

AURNHOUT 1750+ ALBANY CO., NY, USA **[36962]**

AUS DER SCHMITTEN ALL GER **[34861]**

AUSTEN 1840S+ CLARENCE RIVER, NSW, AUS **[35108]** : FRANCES C1790 BURWASH, SSX, ENG

[34011] : RICHARD 1780+ KEN, ENG [34181] : PRE 1900 WESTWELL & SUTTON, KEN, ENG [36118] : ALL TENTERDEN, KEN, ENG [36413] : 1730-1900 TENTERDEN, KEN, ENG [37326] : 1745-1850 LAMBERHURST, KEN, ENG [38265] : 1722 KING WILLIAM, VA, USA [38198]

AUSTERFIELD PRE 1860 WAKEFIELD, WRY, ENG [37708]

AUSTIN WILLIAM 1839+ MAITLAND, NSW, AUS [34030] : ELIZABETH 1839+ MAITLAND, NSW, AUS [34030] : HENRY 1857+ SYDNEY, NSW, AUS [34458] : 1840+ SYDNEY & MUDGEE, NSW, AUS [34977] : 1840+ MELBOURNE, VIC, AUS [35073] : PRE 1849 CHIPPENDALE, NSW, AUS [35419] : PRE 1850 SYDNEY, NSW, AUS [38730] : 1800-1900 ONT, CAN [37466] : PRE 1855 PINCHBECK, LIN, ENG [34043] : GEORGE 1835+ MDX, ENG [34363] : 1825-1900 BEXLEY HEATH, KEN, ENG [34458] : PRE 1870 LICHFIELD, STS, ENG [34463] : PRE 1800 BENENDEN, KEN, ENG [34858] : 1770+ LND, ENG [34977] : 1780+ BRIXHAM, DEV, ENG [35027] : 1810+ PRITTLEWELL, ESS, ENG [35157] : C1878 BURSLEM, STS, ENG [35348] : PRE 1855 UPPER HEYFORD, OXF, ENG [35386] : PRE 1850 ROYSTON, HRT, ENG [35865] : PRE 1863 BRISTOL, GLS, ENG [35985] : 1800-1950 LEEK WOOTTON, WAR, ENG [36012] : 1750-1900 BIRMINGHAM, WAR, ENG [36012] : JAMES EDWARD 1860+ LONDON, ENG [36378] : ALL TENTERDEN, KEN, ENG [36413] : C1760-1856 GODDINGTON & BLACKTHRON, OXF, ENG [36425] : C1860-1900 RYDE, IOW, ENG [36456] : ANN PRE 1606 KEN, ENG [36532] : PRE 1785 CREWKERNE, SOM, ENG [36581] : ALL NORTH TAWTON, DEV, ENG [36662] : PRE 1750 STAFFORD, STS, ENG [36701] : 1800S LONDON, ENG [36967] : 1605-1866 TADMARTON, OXF, ENG [37860] : ALL SAL, ENG [37884] : PRE 1818 KINGSLEY, STS, ENG [37893] : PRE 1809 TAPLOW, BKM, ENG [37909] : PRE 1840 ROLVENDEN, KEN, ENG [38730] : 1750-1820 TALLOW, WAT, IRL [38045] : 1863+ RANGIORA, NCY, NZ [35985] : 1800S SIMONSTOWN, RSA [35126] : C1745 SHEFFIELD, MA, USA [36319] : PRE 1850 CT, USA [36347] : 1860S SOLON, VA, USA [37169] : 1616-1678 DOVER, NH, USA [37803] : 1650+ RI, USA [38015] : PRE 1860 RI, USA [38037] : 1812-1872 DALLAS CO., MO, USA [38120] : 1700 NEW KENT, VA, USA [38198] : 1800 SC, USA [38198] : TABITHA 1790 PHILADELPHIA, PA, USA [38734] : CAIN 1791 CHESTER CO., PA, USA [38734] : PRE 1750 HADDONFIELD, NJ, USA & ENG [38746] : PRE 1833 WLS [34412] : 1700+ LLANRHIDIAN, GLA, WLS [35248]

AUSTWICK ALL BARNSLEY, WRY, ENG [36187]

AUTON C1850 YKS, ENG [33809] : C1872 YKS, ENG [35887] : ALL ARRATHORNE & HUNTON, NRY, ENG [36159] : 1790+ SANDY, BDF & HUN, ENG [37065]

AUTRIDGE 1818 FRA [37165]

AUVACHE ALL BETHNAL GREEN, LND, ENG & FRA [37261]

AUVRAY 1600+ ST AUBIN D'AUREMESNIL, HN, FRA [36678]

AUXIER (SEE OXYER) [38287]

AVANN C1700 KEN & SSX, ENG [34563]

AVARD PRE 1842 BRIGHTON & LONDON, SSX, ENG [34247] : 1730-1750 SALEHURST, SSX, ENG [35119] : 1729 BIDDENDEN, KEN, ENG [35119] : ALL WORLDWIDE [35643]

AVARGIN 1750+ KEN, ENG [34416]

AVENALL C1450 BLACKPOOL, LAN, ENG [34395]

AVENELL C1700-1880 RAMSBURY, WIL, ENG [35121] : 1784 LEIGH, KEN, ENG [35259] : PRE 1880 NR SWINDON, WIL, ENG [36882]

AVERILL 1600+ KEN, ENG [36093] : 1810 CHITTENDEN, VT, USA [36907] : 1790-1830 YORK CO., ME, USA [38201]

AVERY THOMAS 1880 QLD, AUS [36611] : 1700+ LISKEARD, CON, ENG [34742] : 1850S HILLINGDON & HAYES, MDX, ENG [34854] : ALL WEST BUCKLAND, DEV, ENG [35222] : 1600S-1900S STRATTON, CON, ENG [35424] : PRE 1849 BROMSGROVE, WOR, ENG [35507] : C1730-1900 SALFORD PRIORS, WAR, ENG [35883] : 1800+ MAIDSTONE, KEN, ENG [35915] : WILLIAM 1813+ BLEDLOW, BKM, ENG [36611] : PRE 1800 ST NEOT, CON, ENG [38214] : 1600+ NORTH & SOUTH MOLTON, DEV, ENG [38235] : PRE 1850 ERIE CO., NY, USA [37814]

AVES 1800S LONDON, ENG [34483]

AVEY PRE 1850 WEST, SFK, ENG [36479]

AVINS ALL ENG [38369] : ALL USA [38369]

AVIS 1800-1855 WLS, ENG [35287] : PRE 1900 LND, SSX & SRY, ENG [37195] : PRE 1810 WEST FIRLE & SELMESTON, SSX, ENG [37610]

AVISON ANN 1850+ DEWSBURY, WRY, ENG [34512]

AVON 1800+ FROME, SOM, ENG [34512] : 1880+ WESTBURY, WIL, ENG [34512]

AVRIL PRE 1824 GENEVA, CH [35189]

AWALT 1860-1950 PICKERING, MO, USA [38531]

AWDE ALL STARTFORTH, YKS, ENG [38446] : ALL WORLDWIDE [37663]

AWSITER 1600-1700 EALING, MDX, ENG [37077]

AXELBY 1910+ EAST END, LND, ENG [38581]

AXELL 1840 KEN, ENG [34594]

AXFORD C1600-1700 ERLESTOKE, WIL, ENG [36478] : PRE 1569 PLYMOUTH, CON, ENG [37939]

AXON 1700-1800 CHARLESTON CO., SC, USA [38129]

AXTELL C1820-1840 MENDHAM, NJ, USA [38112]

AXTEN ALL WORLDWIDE [36922]

AXWORTHY PRE 1830 STONEHOUSE, DEV, ENG [35739] : 1800-1840 PLYMOUTH, DEV, ENG [36536]

AYDON 1700-1990 NEWCASTLE, NBL, ENG [34249]

AYERS 1850S HUNGERFORD, BRK, ENG [34205] : 1828+ ISLINGTON, MDX, ENG [35903] : MARY PRE 1860 GLOUCESTER & BRISTOL, GLS, ENG [36590] : PRE 1850 DEV, ENG [38399] : 1860-1910 EDMORE, MI, USA [36738] : 1800-1870 CAYUGA CO., NY, USA [36738]

AYERST ALL ENG [33857] : PRE 1700 KEN, ENG [36589]

AYLETT 1775-1830 BISHOPS STORTFORD, HRT, ENG [36017] : 1775-1820 THORLEY, HRT, ENG [36017] : 1700S TAKELEY, ESS, ENG [37250]

AYLIFFE 1700-1900 LEI, ENG [37931]

AYLING 1800S NSW, AUS [36760] : 1700+ CHICHESTER, SSX, ENG [34681] : C1827 AMBERLEY, SSX, ENG [34936] : 1800+ SSX, ENG [35060] : C1850 SLINFORLD, SSX, ENG [36671] : PRE 1800 HEYSHOTT & WALBERTON, SSX, ENG [36760] : 1800S WANDSWORTH, SRY, ENG [36760] : PRE 1850 IOW, ENG [37214] : 1850+ PORTSMOUTH, HAM, ENG [37214] : 1800S HEYSHOTT, SSX, ENG [37833]

AYLMORE C1758 WEST WITTERING, SSX, ENG [34936] : PRE 1650 WEST WITTRING, SSX, ENG [37771]

AYMOND PRE 1830 NANCY, LOR, FRA [34159] : 1910+ EDMONDS, WA, USA [34159] : 1880+ ST CHARLES, MO, USA [34159]

AYNSLEY PRE 1900 POTTERIES, STS, ENG [36502] :
PRE 1770 KIRKWHELPINGTON & HARTBURN,
NBL, ENG & SCT [36502]

AYOTTE PRE 1880 ST TITE, QUE, CAN [35639]

AYRAULT C1600 ANGERS, ANJOU, FRA [35203] :
C1700 NEWPORT, RI, USA [35203]

AYRES 1860+ BALLARAT, VIC, AUS [37134] : PRE
1700 LEI, ENG [34258] : ALL CHESHAM, BKM,
ENG [36981] : 1650-1850 DOWNHAM, CAM, ENG
[37188] : 1700-1820 HORTON, BKM, ENG [37845] :
PRE 1800 FROME, SOM, ENG [38270] : 1800-1860
WAYNE CO., OH & PA, USA & ENG [37529]

AYTON 1700+ WEST HARRINGTON, DUR, ENG
[34505] : 1705+ KELSALE, SFK & LND, ENG
[36049]

AZURE 1830-1950 PEMBINA, ND, USA [36681] : 1840-
1950 BELCOURT, ROLETTE, ND, USA [36681]

AZUR-HAZEUR C1680+ LIEGE, LGE, BEL [36681]

BAALBERGEN 1585-1990 HAARLEM &
NOORDWYK, NOH & ZUH, NL [38713]

BAALHAM 1750-1850 SFK, ENG [35178]

BAAR 1700-1850 SHO, GER [35630]

BAARS ALL AMSTERDAM, NL [34801]

BABBAGE PRE 1750 BURRINGTON, DEV, ENG
[34214] : 1830 CHUDLEIGH, DEV, ENG [34546] :
ALL WAR, ENG [36886]

BABBINGTON 1700 SHERRINGTON, BKM, ENG
[34321] : 1800+ LND & MDX, ENG [37877] : PRE
1750 ALBANY CO., NY, USA [36917]

BABBS 1700 INWORTH, ESS, ENG [37928]

BABCOCK 1825+ NAPANEE, ONT, CAN [34140] :
1790-1900 LA CO.& KENT CO., ONT, CAN [34520] :
1810-1880 TIOGA CO., PA, USA [35317] : 1684-1727
BRISTOL, RI, USA [37499] : 1730-1800
STONINGTON, CT, USA [37783] : 1820-1850 ROME,
NY, USA [37783]

BABEL ALL NEISSE, SIL, GER [38685]

BABER 1860+ NSW, AUS [33768] : 1880S
MANDALAY, BURMA [35930] : 1800S
ROCHESTER, KEN, ENG [35930] : PRE 1861
BRISTOL, GLS, ENG [37318] : PRE 1880 MADRAS,
INDIA [35930] : ALL WORLDWIDE [36494]

BABITT 1750-1800 STEPNEY, LND, ENG [38516]

BABOT ALL ST HELIER, JSY, CHI, ENG [35474]

BACH PRE 1853 ENG [36775]

BACHELOR 1840+ RICHMOND, VIC, AUS [35731] :
1818+ RYE, SSX, ENG [35980]

BACHINSKI 1912+ WINNIPEG, MAN, CAN [34087]

BACK GEORGE PRE 1839 BRIGHTON, SSX, ENG
[34247] : PRE 1810 PLUCKLEY, KEN, ENG [34900] :
1849+ HYTHE, KEN, ENG [34900] : 1600+
SITTINGBOURNE, KEN, ENG [35355] : ALL SSX,
ENG [36510] : JACK 1914+ TRINIDAD [34247] :
ALL WORLDWIDE [38669]

BACKENS ALL WORLDWIDE [38669]

BACKHAUS JOHANN 1840-1900 ZELTEL, BRD, GER
[38781] : ANNA JOHANNAH 1860-1890 ZELTEL,
BRD, GER [38781]

BACKHOUSE JACOB 1870+ TAMWORTH &
GOULBURN, NSW, AUS [36600] : 1850+
MELBOURNE, VIC, AUS [38289] : 1700
LANCASTER, LAN, ENG [36151] : 1700 CARLISLE,
CUL, ENG [38379]

BACKLER 1700-1800 LND, ENG [35129]

BACKMAN ALL FIN [34164]

BACKOFEN C1800 STORKOW, BRA, GER [38626]

BACKUS 1800-1900 LMB, NL [36627]

BACON PRE 1718 CHAPEL, ESS, ENG [34142] : 1857
FINGRINGHOE, ESS, ENG [34358] : 1800+
HORNING, NFK, ENG [35824] : 1800+
SHOREDITCH & LND, MDX, ENG [36263] : 1800
WOODFORD, ESS, ENG [37928] : PRE 1600 ST

NICHOLAS, LND, ENG [38348] : PRE 1840 ESS,
ENG [38393] : ALL CAWSTON, NFK, ENG [38502] :
PRE 1830 NEWTON LIMAVADY, LDY, IRL [36806]
: C1660 MIDDLETOWN, CT, USA [34395] : JOHN
1750+ WELLESLEY, MA, USA [35276] : 1820-1850
JEFFERSON CO., NY, USA [37783] : 1750-1850
BUXTON, ME, USA [38045]

BACZKOWSKI 1890+ ST LOUIS, MO, USA [36912]

BADCOCK PRE 1760 WESTFIELD, SSX, ENG [35587]
: PRE 1820 SOUTHWARK, SRY, ENG [37362] : PRE
1860 HACKNEY, MDX, ENG [37362] : PRE 1860
SHOREDITCH, MDX, ENG [37362] : ALL ENG
[37833] : PRE 1750 SSX, ENG [37875] : PRE 1800
CON & DEV, ENG [38735]

BADDELEY 1835+ ASTBURY AREA, CHS, ENG
[36997] : ALL ENG [37113]

BADDER PRE 1770 BOLTON, LAN, ENG [34576]

BADDLEY 1700-1840 TONG & ALEVER, SAL, ENG
[36495] : 1840-1900 WOLVERHAMPTON, STS, ENG
[36495]

BADDOCK PRE 1860 SHOREDITCH, MDX, ENG
[37362] : PRE 1860 HACKNEY, MDX, ENG [37362]

BADE PRE 1860 GERSWALDE, PRE [38081]

BADEL 1600-1690 GENEVA, GE, CH [34514]

BADELL PRE 1820 LONDON, LND & MDX, ENG
[35940]

BADENOCH 1860S ADELAIDE, SA, AUS [34191]

BADER C1780 HAZERSWOUDE, ZUH, NL [38698]

BADGER PRE 1900 IRL [36481] : 1770+ VT, USA
[38116] : 1635+ MA, USA [38116] : 1790-1830
BARNWELL CO., SC, USA [38129]

BADGERY PRE 1855 NSW, AUS [35211]

BADGET ALL WORLDWIDE [38362]

BADGETT ALL WORLDWIDE [38362]

BADGETTE ALL WORLDWIDE [38362]

BADHAM WILLIAM 1700S LUGWARDINE, HEF,
ENG [36633] : PRE 1800 LEDBURY, HEF, ENG
[36633] : 1700S HEF, ENG [37221] : CHARLES WI N.
1900S WELLINGTON, NZ [36633] : 1900
CHRISTCHURCH, NZ [36633]

BADLEY 1800+ NSW, AUS [34418] : PRE 1884 LIN,
ENG [34418]

BADSEY ALL ENG [36045]

BAELBERGHE (VAN DE) 1357-1585 KORTRYK &
ROESELARE, WVL & OVL, BEL [38713]

BAENSCH 1855+ GERMANTOWN, VIC, AUS [35379]
: PRE 1850 KROSSEN, PRE, GER [35379]

BAER 1730-1830 TAEGERWILEN, TG, CH [35283] :
1800+ WUE, GER [35190] : 1800-1950
GREENVILLE, MERCER CO., PA, USA [36449]

BAERDGES PRE 1788 HOTTENBACH, RPF, GER
[38663]

BAERTGES PRE 1788 HOTTENBACH, RPF, GER
[38663]

BAEYER C1800-1840 BAV, GER [38325]

BAGBY PRE 1800 STS & WOR, ENG [36379]

BAGG PRE 1900 SWANAGE, DOR, ENG [34477] :
PRE 1790 WINTERBOURN ST MARTIN, DOR,
ENG [34828] : 1700-1850 DOR, ENG [38471]

BAGGALEY PRE 1920 CARLTON, LIN, ENG [34421] :
PRE 1920 LONDON, ENG [34421] : PRE 1800
STOKE ON TRENT, STS, ENG [37389]

BAGGALLAY ALL ENG [37959]

BAGGARLEY PRE 1850 LONDON, ENG [34610]

BAGGE C1750 DEWLISH, DOR, ENG [35203] : C1800-
1840 BIRMINGHAM, WAR, ENG [35883]

BAGGETT ALL WORLDWIDE [33921]

BAGGLEY C1630-83 HURST, BRK, ENG [36425]

BAGGOT 1800S WEST BROMWICH, WAR, ENG
[36666]

BAGGS 1848 SCT & IRL [36902]

BAGIER ALL LONDON, ENG **[36525]** : ALL EDINBURGH, SCT **[36525]**

BAGLEY 1800+ LIVERPOOL, LAN, ENG **[35970]** : PRE 1879 CAMBERWELL, SRY, ENG **[37452]** : PRE 1850 PATTINGHAM, STS, ENG **[37722]** : 1900+ LND, ENG & NZ **[36213]** : PRE 1840 TULLMAROE, OFF, IRL **[35013]** : 1940+ CHICAGO, IL, USA **[34132]** : SYLVESTER 1940 CHICAGO, IL, USA **[34132]** : PRE 1700 CT & MA, USA & ENG **[38745]**

BAGLIN PRE 1780 HORSLEY, GLS, ENG **[34995]**

BAGLOLE ALL TYNE VALLEY, PEI, CAN **[34987]**

BAGNALL 1842+ BOTANY, NSW, AUS **[35368]** : 1800-63 CHARLOTTETOWN, PEI, CAN **[36816]** : 1802+ ASHTON UNDER LYNE, LAN, ENG **[35368]** : PRE 1802 HYDE, CHS, ENG **[35368]** : 1700-1770 THORPE, DBY & STS, ENG **[36816]** : 1797+ CHS, ENG **[38212]**

BAGNELL PRE 1830 BLEDLOW, BKM, ENG **[35578]**

BAGNEY PRE 1700 NTT, ENG **[36126]**

BAGOT 1750-1850 COCKERHAM, LAN, ENG **[36983]**

BAGOTT ALL UK **[36062]**

BAGRA ALL SCT **[35415]**

BAGRIE ALL SCT **[35415]**

BAGS MARGARET ALL SCT & IRL **[36902]**

BAGS (SEE BAGGS) [36902]

BAGSHAW PRE 1800 CHAPEL EN-LE FRITH, DBY, ENG **[34588]**

BAGUE 1500-1700 STS, ENG **[36062]**

BAGULEY 1800+ CHS, ENG **[34132]** : PRE 1750 MANCHESTER, LAN, ENG **[37573]** : 1800S MACCLESFIELD, CHS, ENG **[38285]**

BAHL PRE 1865 BUFFALO, NY, USA **[38191]**

BAHNMAIER 1774+ OBERSTENFELD, WUE, GER **[38667]**

BAHNMUELLER C1720 WUE, GER **[38598]**

BAHOLE PRE 1855 FELLBACH, WUE, GER **[34886]**

BAHR 1848+ PORT LINCOLN, SA, AUS **[35040]** : 1880+ BENDIGO, VIC, AUS **[35040]** : PRE 1848 WILDEMANN, HAN, GER **[35040]**

BAHRENBURG 1850+ ST GEORGE IN EAST, LND, ENG **[37251]** : PRE 1850 GRASBERG, HAN, GER **[37251]**

BAHRINGER PRE 1850 BAW, BRD **[36542]**

BAHRLE 1870+ DARLING DOWNS, QLD, AUS **[34957]**

BAIER 1800S MALLMITZ, SIL, GER **[38623]**

BAIGENT ELI C1780+ FARNBOROUGH, HAM, ENG **[34017]**

BAIKIE 1875+ PIETERMARITZBURG, NATAL, RSA **[34688]** : 1750+ LONGHOPE, OKI, SCT **[34688]** : 1700+ CANISBAY, CAI, SCT **[34688]** : 1857+ EDINBURGH, MLN, SCT **[34688]** : 1885+ BERKELEY, CA, USA **[34688]**

BAILES 1840S STOKESLEY, YKS, ENG **[37525]**

BAILEY LUCY 1800+ NSW, AUS **[34902]** : WILLIAM 1800S O'CONNELL PLAINS & BATHURST, NSW, AUS **[35361]** : SAMUEL 1827+ HOBART & OATLANDS, TAS, AUS **[35394]** : CATHERINE 1829-1856 HOBART & TEA TREE, TAS, AUS **[35394]** : 1910+ AUS **[36996]** : GEORGE 1841+ OBERON, NSW, AUS **[37556]** : 1800S UK &, AUS & CAN **[34005]** : 1800S VANCOUVER IS, BC, CAN **[34005]** : 1913+ SIDMOUTH, DEV, ENG **[33920]** : 1750-1950 GRANTHAM & LINCOLN, LIN, ENG **[33952]** : WM.& THOMAS 1700-1800 ST KATHERINE CREE, LND, ENG **[34274]** : PRE 1822 WHAPLODE DROVE, LIN, ENG **[34285]** : PRE 1800 HUN, ENG **[34324]** : 1700+ WITTERSHAM, KEN, ENG **[34426]** : PRE 1900 SALFORD, LAN, ENG **[34604]** : 1750-1900 YKS, ENG **[34631]** : C1840 CHELMSFORD, HRT, ENG **[34654]** : 1750-1850 COBHAM, SSX, ENG **[34687]** : 1800 CAMBORNE, CON, ENG **[34890]** : ALL LND, SOM & GLS, ENG **[34951]** : PRE 1870 ENG **[34968]** : PRE 1795+ HAVERHILL, SFK, ENG **[35109]** : 1750-1850 HAVERHILL, SFK, ENG **[35151]** : 1830 RANSGATE, KEN, ENG **[35204]** : 1700S SWANTON ABBOT, NFK, ENG **[35322]** : PRE 1850 SOMERSHAM, HUN, ENG **[35323]** : 1600+ YALDING, KEN, ENG **[35355]** : PRE 1850 ROCKINGDOWN, ESS, ENG **[35389]** : C1840 MARYLEBONE, LND, ENG **[35485]** : PRE 1840 SFK, ENG **[35485]** : C1800S+ NEWCASTLE ON TYNE, NBL, ENG **[35537]** : WILLIAM PRE 1790 STS, ENG **[35541]** : 1799 GOSPORT, HAM, ENG **[35560]** : PRE 1775 SOUTH CROXTON, LEI, ENG **[35572]** : PRE 1856 NEWBURY, BRK, ENG **[35599]** : 1760-1792 BECCLES, SFK, ENG **[35749]** : 1800S WINSBURY, SAL, ENG **[35804]** : 1820S PERRANARWORTHAL, CON, ENG **[35815]** : 1750+ MELBOURNE, DBY, ENG **[35851]** : 1820+ GLOUCESTER, GLS, ENG **[35865]** : PRE 1850 BRIGSTOCK, NTH, ENG **[36046]** : 1765+ NORMANTON, WRY & LND, ENG **[36049]** : THOMAS 1820S BETHNAL GREEN, LND, ENG **[36068]** : LOUISA 1840S ISLINGTON, MDX, ENG **[36068]** : 1600-1800 WORKINGTON, LAN, ENG **[36106]** : C1865 FELIXKIRK, NRY, ENG **[36265]** : C1864 HERSHAM, SRY, ENG **[36265]** : PRE 1750 CAMBORNE, CON, ENG **[36277]** : C1799-1867 ST GEORGE WESTMINSTER, MDX, ENG **[36425]** : PRE 1960 STETCHWORTH, CAM, ENG **[36489]** : EMMA PRE 1884 COLNBROOK, BKM, ENG **[36510]** : EMMA 1884+ BETHNAL GREEN & CLERKENWELL, LND, ENG **[36510]** : C1770+ KINGS LYNN, NFK, ENG **[36753]** : 1800+ LONDON, MDX, ENG **[36769]** : MARY ANN 1838-1854 SHEPTON BEAUCHAMP, SOM, ENG **[36776]** : C1810 LOWESTOFT, SFK, ENG **[36860]** : 1900+ HAM, ENG **[36996]** : ALL EASTINGTON & WHITMINSTER, GLS, ENG **[36996]** : 1800-1900 PORTSMOUTH, HAM, ENG **[37084]** : PRE 1725 STS, ENG **[37098]** : 1600-1760 SOM, ENG **[37232]** : JAMES PRE 1900 FENTON, STS, ENG **[37319]** : C1780 FROME ST QUINTIN, DOR, ENG **[37378]** : C1950 BEXLEYHEATH, KEN, ENG **[37631]** : C1885 KENSAL GREEN, MDX, ENG **[37631]** : C1861 DEVIZES, WIL, ENG **[37631]** : C1800 STS, ENG **[37661]** : PRE 1860 LAMBETH, SRY, ENG **[37746]** : JEHU 1835-1899 LND, ENG **[37746]** : C1850 DAWLEY, SAL, ENG **[37883]** : PRE 1839 DINTON, WIL, ENG **[37909]** : 1700+ WIGAN, LAN, ENG **[38046]** : PRE 1850 BRIDFORD, DEV, ENG **[38079]** : 1600-1800 DENTON & HOMERSFIELD, NFK & SFK, ENG **[38194]** : 1800S SILEBY, LEI, ENG **[38285]** : 1800S ROMSEY, HAM, ENG **[38358]** : 1870+ NZ & AUS &, FIJI **[34005]** : PRE 1863 WEX, IRL **[33775]** : C1832 BELFAST, IRL **[34371]** : JOHN C1805-1841+ CLOGHER & AUGHNACLOY, TYR, IRL **[37556]** : GEORGE 1805-1841 CLOGHER & AUCHNACLOY, TYR, IRL **[37556]** : 1810S LISTOWEL, KER, IRL **[37947]** : 1840+ TRENTON, NJ, USA **[36326]** : 1800S GREENE & JEFFERSON CO., TN, USA **[37539]** : CHAMPION ALL LA, USA **[37801]** : LOUISA 1852 LA, USA **[37801]** : 1800-1900 MADISON CO., NC, USA **[38009]** : 1800-1900 YANCEY CO., NC, USA **[38009]** : 1800-1900 BUNCOMBE CO., NC, USA **[38009]** : ALL JEFFERSON CO., PA, USA **[38036]** : KATHERINE 1820 RUTHERFORD CO., NC, USA **[38109]** : PRE 1860 WORCESTER CO., MD, USA **[38135]** : C1917 SWANSEA, GLA, WLS **[37631]** : ALL WORLDWIDE **[38766]**

BAILEY (SEE BAYLEY) [36278]

BAILHACHE 1930+ CAMBERWELL, VIC, AUS **[34577]**

BAILLIE WILLIAM 1934 TAS, AUS [35427] : 1820+
LANARK, ONT, CAN [34102] : EBENEZER 1850+
IPSWICH, SFK, ENG [37191] : C1849
NEWTOWNARDS, DOW, IRL [34972] : 1775-1820
LKS, SCT [34102] : 1807 ABDIE, FIF, SCT [34529] :
WILLIAM 1836+ GLASGOW, SCT [35427] : C1795+
ROC & INV, SCT [35486] : C1850 GLASGOW, RFW
& LKS, SCT [36520] : 1800+ COATBRIDGE &
AIRDRIE, LKS, SCT [38260]

BAILY 1700-1800S LND, ENG [34086] : 1870-1920
CHIPPENHAM, WIL, ENG [34117] : 1800
CAMBORNE, CON, ENG [34844] : PRE 1850+
PHILADELPHIA, PA, USA [36578]

BAIN 1860+ YOUNG, NSW, AUS [35230] : 1856+
YASS, NSW, AUS [35230] : C1840 CORK CITY,
COR, IRL [35582] : PRE 1760 REISS, CAI, SCT
[33873] : PRE 1900 INVERESK & EDINBURGH,
ELN & MLN, SCT [33959] : PRE 1850 SCT [33999] :
PRE 1820 KNOCKBAIN, ROC, SCT [34613] : ALL
CROMARTY, ROC, SCT [34674] : C1835+ AVOCH,
ROC, SCT [35486] : C1800-1900 MONZIE &
DUNNING, PER, SCT [36128] : 1700+ FETLAR,
SHI, SCT [36266] : PRE 1861 FORRES, MOR, SCT
[36338] : 1780-1820 ECHOBANK, MLN, SCT [36392] :
1810-1830 WICK, CAI, SCT [36392] : PRE 1847
FODDERTY, ROC, SCT [36513] : 1790+
KILMADOCK, PER, SCT [36635] : ALL
ABERDEEN, ABD, SCT [36846] : 1800+ AVOCH,
ROC, SCT [36885] : ALL THURSO, CAI, SCT [37303]
: 1830+ LAUDER, BEW, SCT [37881] : PRE 1865
THURSO AREA, CAI, SCT [37896] : EDWARD PRE
1860 GREEN LAW, BEW, SCT [38483] : 1840+ DES
MOINES CO., IA, USA [35278] : 1800+
MUSKINGUM CO., OH, USA [35278] : C1715+
KINGSTON, NY, USA [36651] : 1860 FARILL, AL,
USA [38198]

BAINBRIDGE 1850 SAFFRON WALDEN, ESS, ENG
[34546] : PRE 1900 YORK & EASINGWOLD, NRY,
ENG [34588] : PRE 1800 COXWOLD &
ROMALDKIRK, NRY, ENG [34588] : 1500-1900
DUR, ENG [36689] : FRANCIS PRE 1800 NTT, DBY
& YKS, ENG [37679] : PRE 1850 NTT, ENG [37679] :
1810+ CARLISLE, CUL, ENG [37997] : 1900+
NORTHLAND, NZ [34588] : 1500-1900 MO, USA
[36689]

BAINE 1840 BETHNAL GREEN, MDX, ENG [37080] :
1860 GAL, IRL [35325]

BAINES 1840+ NSW, AUS [36295] : 1800S BRIERLEY
HILL, STS, ENG [35099] : PRE 1750 STAMFORD,
LIN, ENG [36295] : PRE 1830 LIVERPOOL, LAN,
ENG [37697] : ALL ORANGE CO. & GUILFORD
CO., NC, USA & SCT [38060]

BAIR 1740-1830 CHESTER, PA, USA [38054] : 1840
CHAMPAIGN, OH, USA [38054]

BAIRD ALL WENTWORTH, NSW, AUS [34838] :
1800S POPLAR, LND, ENG [33827] : 1890+
WARRINGTON, CHS, ENG [34109] : 1750-1850
TWEEDMOUTH, NBL, ENG [37395] : C1830
MOVILLE, DON, IRL [37007] : PRE 1850
GLENARM, ANT, IRL [37246] : ISABELLA 1800+
GARTSHERRIE, LKS, SCT [33784] : 1700+
JEDBURGH, ROX, SCT [34109] : PRE 1800 SORN,
AYR, SCT [34214] : 1820-1870S GLASGOW, LKS,
SCT [34359] : 1750-1850 INCH, AYR & WIG, SCT
[34523] : C1860 CAMBUSNETHAN, LKS, SCT
[34556] : C1830 CARNWATH, LKS, SCT [34556] :
AGNES C1850 GLASGOW, LKS, SCT [35033] : 1750-
1850 ST NINIANS, STI, SCT [35602] : 1833
GORBALS, LKS, SCT [35794] : 1800S FALKIRK,
STI, SCT [36846] : 1710+ MUIRAVONSIDE, STI,
SCT [37205] : PRE 1840 AUCHINLECK &
CUMNOCK, AYR, SCT [37374] : ANDREW BRUCE

1883 GRANGEMOUTH, STI, SCT [37444] : 1780-1850
MONTROSE, ANS, SCT [38483] : C1800 RFW, SCT
[38485] : ANDREW NEWTON 1806-1846
ASHEVILLE, NC, USA [35265] : 1700S
HUNTERDON CO., NJ, USA [35278] : ALL VA MIL
LDS, OH & VA, USA [38287] : C1800 PA, USA [38367]

BAIRNER 1800S CERES, FIF, SCT [37704]

BAIRSTOW 1750-1800 HALIFAX, WRY, ENG [33767]

BAISCH ALL ROTTINGEN, BRD, GER [34938]

BAITSON C1770 PORT MENTEITH, PER, SCT [35764]
: ALL WORLDWIDE [38429]

BAJETTO 1830-1880 FRANKFURT AD ODER, PRE,
GER [38691] : C1830-1880 FRANKFURT AM ODER,
PRE, GER [38711] : 1860-1950 DJAKARTA, JAVA,
INDONESIA [38691] : 1860-1950 DJAKARTA, JAVA,
INDONESIA [38711]

BAKE 1640-1720 ST TEATH, CON, ENG [34448]

BAKER 1922+ HORSHAM, VIC, AUS [33882] : 1881+
BRISBANE, QLD, AUS [34020] : THOMAS 1860+
HAMILTON, VIC, AUS [34287] : 1839+
MAITLAND, NSW, AUS [34685] : 1870S+
BOGGABRI, NEW ENGLAND, NSW, AUS [34902] :
1849+ ADELAIDE, SA, AUS [34976] : 1838+
GLEBE & BOTANY, NSW, AUS [35077] : 1870S
DIAMOND CREEK, VIC, AUS [35116] : 1845+
LAUNCESTON, TAS, AUS [35116] : THEOPHILUS
1826+ LAUNCESTON, TAS, AUS [35185] : 1850
LIVERPOOL, NSW, AUS [35508] : 1860+ JUNG,
VIC, AUS [35748] : 1900+ FREMANTLE, WA, AUS
[35847] : 1867+ WIMMERA & JUNG, VIC, AUS
[36622] : 1900+ PERTH, WA, AUS [36746] : PRE 1886
WARATAH, TAS, AUS [37106] : RUFUS 1860+
PORT CYGNET, HOBART, TAS, AUS [37159] :
1858+ CLARENCE RIVER, NSW, AUS [37349] :
C1830 LANE COVE, NSW, AUS [37500] : PRE 1850
HUNTER RIVER, NSW, AUS [38077] : PRE 1730
BRD [37428] : 1780-1990 OSNABRUCK, ONT, CAN
[34077] : 1773 QUEBEC CITY, QUE, CAN [34331] :
1825-1900 KENT CO., ONT, CAN [34520] : 1880S
MAITLAND, ONT, CAN [35078] : THOMAS PRE
1861 SOUTHAMPTON, ONT, CAN [38445] :
CHARLES SCOTT 1906+ CAN & ENG [37709] :
1800+ ST PETER PORT, GSY, CHI [35847] : PRE
1800 SRK, CHI [38293] : 1918+ ADDINGHAM,
LAN, ENG [33860] : PRE 1808 HEADLEY, HAM,
ENG [33860] : JOHN PRE 1838 HUNTON, KEN,
ENG [33944] : ALL SOM, ENG [34093] : PRE 1800
ROGATE, W SSX, ENG [34112] : EDWARD 1787+
ULCOMBE, KEN, ENG [34176] : 1910S
ROCHESTER, KEN, ENG [34218] : C1860 DOVER,
KEN, ENG [34273] : 1800-1900 LEIGHTON
BUZZARD, BKM, ENG [34337] : URIAH & ELIZA
C1800 SHEFFIELD, WRY, ENG [34369] : RACHEL
1841 SHEFFIELD, WRY, ENG [34369] : PRE 1843
MELBOURN, CAM, ENG [34582] : 1840 KEN, ENG
[34594] : 1810 NOTTINGHAM, NTT, ENG [34594] :
PRE 1839 ETCHINGHAM, SSX, ENG [34685] : PRE
1850 WATERINGBURY, KEN, ENG [34711] : PRE
1869 BDF, ENG [34757] : 1869+ BDF, ENG [34757] :
C1810 ST IVES, CON, ENG [34819] : C1800
DUDLEY, WOR, ENG [34822] : PRE 1850 CAM,
ENG [34858] : PRE 1858 RADSTOCK, SOM, ENG
[34858] : PRE 1790 NEWGATE, MDX, ENG [34892] :
SAMUEL PRE 1870 WOOLWICH, KEN, ENG
[34902] : SAMUEL PRE 1870 BURES, SFK, ENG
[34902] : 1800+ LEEDS, KEN, ENG [34956] :
THOMAS 1700-1850 GUESTLING & LEWES, SSX,
ENG [34970] : 1800-1840 TAUNTON, SOM, ENG
[34976] : 1750+ HANWELL, OXF, ENG [35015] :
1780+ BRADLEY & GNOSALL, STS, ENG [35019] :
1800+ NEWCASTLE, NBL, ENG [35038] : 1840
HOPTON, SFK, ENG [35067] : RICHARD PRE 1840

ENG [35077] : 1840+ SSX, ENG [35116] : PRE 1900
COLINDALE, LND, ENG [35175] : PRE 1790
CRUWYS MORCHARD, DEV, ENG [35185] : PRE
1850 WALCOT, SOM, ENG [35199] : ALL
HANWELL, MDX, ENG [35417] : C1850 CHUTE &
COLLINGBOURNE, WIL, ENG [35512] : PRE 1840
SOM, ENG [35556] : 1800+ BRISTOL, GLS, ENG
[35580] : 1840S WIL, ENG [35728] : PRE 1768
STREET, SOM, ENG [35728] : C1768 STREET, SOM,
ENG [35748] : JOHN WEAVER 1829+
BIRMINGHAM, WAR, ENG [35780] : C1859
SHERE, SRY, ENG [35860] : PRE 1874 MEOPHAM,
KEN, ENG [35970] : 1780S HOLLINGBOURNE,
KEN, ENG [36041] : PRE 1800 HARTLEY
WINTNEY, HAM, ENG [36047] : PRE 1800
LODDON, NFK, ENG [36073] : 1800+
GATESHEAD, DUR & NBL, ENG [36090] : 1800-
1840 SHOREDITCH, MDX, ENG [36099] : PRE 1830
BRIERLEY HILL & KINGSWINFORD, STS, ENG
[36110] : PRE 1800 THORNCOMBE, DOR, ENG
[36142] : ALL PRESTON, LAN & CON, ENG [36152]
: C1788 ROGATE, SSX, ENG [36185] : JOANE
1583+ HURSTPIERPOINT, SSX, ENG [36212] :
1803-1851 LAMBETH, SRY, ENG [36229] : C1800-
1860 CLERKENWELL, MDX, ENG [36229] : 1800-
1839 SALEHURST, SSX, ENG [36272] : GEORGE
1700+ LONDON, ENG [36291] : PRE 1630
ERLESTOKE, WIL, ENG [36478] : 1750-1850
EWHURST & IDEN, SSX, ENG [36485] : NELLIE
BRIGGS ALL HOUNSLOW, MDX, ENG [36646] :
CELIA ALL HOUNSLOW, MDX, ENG [36646] :
PRE 1909 BOURNEMOUTH, HAM, ENG [36650] :
PRE 1841 WOODCOTT, HAM, ENG [36650] : PRE
1860 STREET, SOM, ENG [36676] : 1850-1900
LIVERPOOL, LAN, ENG [36746] : 1800S
HERSTMONCEUX, SSX, ENG [36786] : 1800+
LONDON, MDX, ENG [36997] : PRE 1850
NOTTINGHAM, NTT, ENG [37179] : PRE 1853
HUNTINGDON, CAM, ENG [37181] : ROBERT
C1750 RUMBURGH, SFK, ENG [37191] : PRE 1850
BROADWOODKELLY & WINKLEIGH, DEV, ENG
[37195] : HANNAH PRE 1830 SSX, ENG [37210] :
1721 BROCKDISH, SFK, ENG [37250] : PRE 1850
PILTON, DEV, ENG [37264] : C1720 MALTON,
YKS, ENG [37288] : PRE 1900 NORTH
PETHERTON, SOM, ENG [37322] : PRE 1840
ROWLEY REGIS, STS, ENG [37331] : PRE 1900
SITTINGBOURNE, KEN, ENG [37339] : 1889+
LONDON, ENG [37592] : 1860+ KEN, ENG [37595] :
ALL DODDINTON, LIN, ENG [37673] : 1800-1844
ZEAL MONACHORUM, DEV, ENG [37709] : PRE
1830 EASTBOURNE & MAYFIELD, SSX, ENG
[37816] : PRE 1944 CHARLTON, LND, ENG [37853] :
C1800 BEKESBOURNE, KEN, ENG [37859] : C1800
FARNHAM, SRY, ENG [37898] : PRE 1841
BAMPTON, DEV, ENG [37899] : PRE 1820
RICKINGHALL SUPERIOR, SFK, ENG [37913] :
C1700 HALSTOCK, DOR, ENG [37918] : 1650
CHEDISTON, SFK, ENG [37928] : HAMLET PRE
1837 BURSLEM, STS, ENG [38248] : 1840S
ELTHAM, LND, ENG [38390] : WILLIAM 1838
ISLINGTON, LND, ENG [38397] : GEORGE W.
1750-1850 STANTON, SFK & NFK, ENG [38523] :
PRE 1850 BODIAM, SSX, ENG [38541] : PRE 1900
PENZANCE, ENG [38586] : JOHN 1786+
TILSHEAD, WIL, ENG & AUS [33919] : WILLIAM
C1772+ ENG & AUS [36639] : PRE 1860 BANTRY,
COR, IRL [33905] : C1832 CLA, IRL [35772] :
CORNELIUS 1830+ NANTINAN, LIM, IRL [35905]
: 1830S NORTH ISLAND, NZ [35516] : JOHN 1800S
NZ [36291] : LIONEL 1800S NZ [36291] : CHARLES
1900+ AUCKLAND, NZ [36818] : DANIEL PRE

1860 PAISLEY, RFW, SCT [34559] : PRE 1860
GLASGOW, LKS & MAY, SCT & IRL [36191] : 1614-
1990 LYNN, ESSEX CO., MA, USA [35316] : LOOE
C1780 PERTH AMBOY, NJ, USA [36572] : 1650-1850
READING, PA, USA [36924] : PRE 1800
PHILADELPHIA, PA, USA [36969] : 1860 BATH CO.,
KY, USA [37028] : RUFUS C1820 PLYMOUTH
ROCHESTER, MA, USA [37159] : C1800-1900S
FLINT, MI, USA [37351] : 1825 LAUREL CO., KY,
USA [37570] : PRE 1725 MD, USA [37587] :
BENJAMEN 1660-1750 KINGSTON, RI, USA
[37806] : C1813 BUFFALO, NY, USA [38173] : 1600-
1850 CLK & MON CO., IN & SC, USA [38287] :
1850+ PAWTUCKET, RI, USA [38454] : 1800+
NEWPORT, MON, WLS [35580]
BAKERINK 1900+ CO, USA [34510]
BAKER-YORK 1850-1935 EWHURST, SSX, ENG
[36485]
BAKES 1770 FEWTON, YKS, ENG [34793]
BAKEWELL 1850S+ NSW, AUS [33930] : 1800S+
NTT, ENG [33930] : 1200-1800 DBY & LEI, ENG
[35841] : 1815+ HIGHGATE, WOR, ENG [37534] :
1800+ BIRMINGHAM, WAR, ENG [37534] : ALL
NZ [33930]
BAKIE 1840-1863 LEATHERANWHEEL, CAI, SCT
[33955]
BAKKER 1835+ NIEUWEDIEP, NOH, NL [35141] :
1700S COLIJNSPLAAT, ZEL, NL [38358]
BAKLUND 1801+ PERNAJA, UUSIMAA, FIN [38758]
BALAAM PRE 1850 GREAT BENTLEY, ESS, ENG
[33937]
BALAKIN 1861+ HELSINKI, UUSIMAA, FIN [38758]
BALAM ALL WORLDWIDE [37882]
BALBACH ALL WORLDWIDE [38733]
BALCHIN 1740-1820 GODALMING, SRY, ENG
[37253] : C1830 KIRDFORD, SSX, ENG [37285]
BALCOMB 1800-1830 TICEHURST, SSX, ENG [36071]
BALCOMBE 1850+ VIC, AUS [34871] : 1820+ AUS
[38356] : 1800S HORNE, SRY, ENG [34871] : PRE
1820 ST HELENA [38356] : PRE 1820 UK [38356]
BALD 1800S WEST HOPES, ELN, SCT [35126] : 1800+
FIF, SCT [35994]
BALDAUF 1799S EDENKOBEN, PFALZ, GER [38184]
BALDERSTON 1800+ FALKIRK, STI, SCT [35244] :
PRE 1830 KIRKCALDY, FIF, SCT [35799]
BALDOCK PRE 1860 GAWLER, SA, AUS [34268] :
1890+ BLACKROCK & KEW, VIC, AUS [34919] :
1850+ LARGS, NSW, AUS [37136] : C1905-1950
SEVENOAKS, KEN, ENG [34101] : C1870-1910
EGERTON, KEN, ENG [34101] : PRE 1820 KEN,
ENG [34445] : C1760 WADHURST, SSX, ENG
[34939] : PRE 1849 BORTON, KEN, ENG [37136] :
C1800 BRIXTON, ENG [37239]
BALDOSER 1835-1860 OH, USA [36345] : PRE 1835
PA, USA [36345]
BALDREY PRE 1865 NORWICH, NFK, ENG [34648]
BALDRY 1700 KETTLEBURGH, SFK, ENG [35892] :
1700-1800 BURGATE & PALGRAVE, SFK, ENG
[35892] : 1800-1900 FLAMBROUGH, YKS, ENG
[35892] : 1700-1800 WORTHAN & BLONORTON,
SFK, ENG [35892] : PRE 1751 STRADBROKE, SFK,
ENG [37082]
BALDWIN 1852+ PORT ALBERT & MELBOURNE,
VIC, AUS [34177] : 1800+ DAPTO & MONARO,
NSW, AUS [35159] : ALL VIC, AUS [35386] : ALL
STRATFORD, VIC, AUS [35472] : C1847
MAITLAND, NSW, AUS [35807] : 1850+
VANCOUVER ISLAND, BC, CAN & ENG [37322] :
C1800 GLS, ENG [34258] : 1830+ CLITHEROE,
LAN, ENG [35214] : PRE 1855 OXF, ENG [35386] :
PRE 1786 KEN, ENG [35472] : PRE 1900 KEN, ENG
[35950] : 1860 MAIDSTONE, KEN, ENG [36250] :

FANNY 1840+ HASTINGS, SSX, ENG [36590] :
1850+ BEWDLEY, WOR, ENG [36614] : PRE 1750
KIRKBY IRELETH, LAN, ENG [36701] : PRE 1910
LONDON, ENG [37062] : 1760+ GIGGLESWICK &
SETTLE, YKS, ENG [37666] : PRE 1610 NORTH
CHURCH, BKM, ENG [38135] : PRE 1852
BANDON, COR, IRL [34177] : PRE 1850
WATERFORD, WAT, IRL [35496] : 1880 PATEA,
TARANAKI, NZ [36250] : ALL MAUI, HI, USA
[33756] : EDWARD 1850-1890 DRYDEN & ETNA,
NY, USA [35298] : 1700 NJ, USA [36730] : STEPHEN
1849+ CA, USA [37506] : PRE 1880 MO, USA [37562]
: 1862 VA, USA [38151]
BALDWINSON ALL AUS & NZ [34881]
BALE PRE 1800 LONDON, ENG [37587] : PRE 1900
ESS, ENG [37668] : 1900S NIAGARA CO., NY, USA
[37541] : 1825-1860 AL, USA [37587] : 1800-1845 SC,
USA [37587] : 1860-1865 ROME, GA, USA [37587] :
PRE 1900 PONTARDAWE, GLA, WLS [37062]
BALES JOHN C1775-1799 BUNWELL, NFK, ENG
[37052] : 1800S SOUTH, NFK, ENG [37052]
BALEY PRE 1850 NSW, AUS [35535]
BALFE 1750-1990 MEATH & LEEDS CO., MEA &
WIC, IRL & CAN [36669]
BALFOUR 1850+ ONT, CAN [37035] : C1800+
DUBLIN, IRL [35233] : PRE 1850 FER, IRL [37035] :
1700-1800 ROSSORRY & DEVENISH, FER, IRL
[37613] : 1700-1800 ANS, SCT [36081] : 1700+
PAISLEY, RFW, SCT [37073] : ALL WORLDWIDE
[35279]
BALGOWAN ALL ABD, SCT & AUS [35205]
BALICKI 1800+ POL [36096]
BALL JOHN 1840+ SA, AUS [35060] : THOMAS 1827-
1881 BENDIGO, VIC, AUS [35205] : 1870S SYDNEY,
NSW, AUS [35743] : 1853+ GEELONG &
INVERLEIGH, VIC, AUS [36622] : 1853+
WYCHEPROOF, VIC, AUS [36622] : 1844+
NEWCASTLE, NSW, AUS [37313] : 1890+
KAMERUKA, NSW, AUS [38491] : PRE 1882
MONCK TWP., ONT, CAN [36680] : 1800-1860
TRINITY, NFD, CAN [38045] : 1820+ PEI, CAN
[38460] : 1850+ PRESTON, LAN, ENG [38894] :
C1820+ BRIGHTON, SSX, ENG [34145] : PRE 1857
ISLINGTON, LND, ENG [34669] : 1830-1900 BURY,
SSX, ENG [34693] : DAVID PRE 1839
BAYSWATER, MDX, ENG [34753] : PRE 1891
BRISTOL, GLS, ENG [35339] : SARAH PRE 1860
SAL, ENG [35365] : PRE 1762 TETBURY, GLS, ENG
[35544] : 1800S LONDON, ENG [35743] : 1896+
KEN, ENG [35759] : PRE 1900 BDF, ENG [35954] :
1780+ ODELL, BDF & MDX, ENG [36123] : PRE
1900 ALDWARK & BAKEWELL, DBY, ENG [36189]
: PRE 1800 NOTTINGHAM, NTT, ENG [36619] :
1600-1800 DILWYN, HEF, ENG [36924] : 1850+
NEWTON, LAN, ENG [36997] : PRE 1775 STS, ENG
[37098] : PRE 1700 BODMIN, LANIVET &
WITHIEL, CON, ENG [37814] : 1800 GREASLEY,
NTT, ENG [37829] : THOMAS C1867 LIVERPOOL,
LAN, ENG [37865] : 1750-1840 WAREHAM, DOR,
ENG [38045] : PRE 1840 SALCOMBE, DEV, ENG
[38214] : 1800+ WEM, IRL [34149] : PRE 1856 ARM,
IRL [34545] : PRE 1880 MEA, IRL [36316] : 1870+
CHRISTCHURCH, NZ [34673] : 1870+
WELLINGTON, NZ [35235] : JAMES 1850+
CENTER DALE, IA, USA [36728] : 1790-1825
LOUDOUN CO., VA, USA [38088] : 1615S
GUILFORD, CT, USA [38184] : 1720+ BOLTON,
MA, USA [38520] : PRE 1880 CARDIFF, GLA, WLS
[36424]
BALLAGH 1860S+ COLAC, VIC, AUS [34937]
BALLAH AUGUSTUS 1790-1807 MONONGALIA,
WV, USA [37025]

BALLAM 1766+ WOOLPIT, SFK, ENG [37399]
BALLANTINE PRE 1833+ PERTH, PER, SCT [35414] :
PRE 1780 STEVENSTON, AYR, SCT [37630]
BALLANTYNE 1820+ HOLBORN & ST PANCRAS,
LND, ENG [35027] : 1840-1900 MELROSE, PEE, SCT
[33991] : ALL CASTLETON, ROX, SCT [34254] :
1790-1824 MAKERSTOUN, ROX, SCT [34525] :
1850+ EDINBURGH, MLN, SCT [35027] : 1836
HADDINGTON, ELN, SCT [37898]
BALLARD JAMES 1852 MAITLAND, NSW, AUS
[37123] : 1807+ PARRAMATTA, NSW, AUS [37309] :
RICHARD HENRY C1860 ALBURY, NSW, AUS
[37960] : RICHARD HENRY C1854 ECHUCA, VIC,
AUS [37960] : 1840S MARYLEBONE, LND, ENG
[34175] : ALL THATCHAM, BRK, ENG [35115] :
ALL DOVER, KEN, ENG [35258] : 1700S DUMMER,
HAM, ENG [36484] : ALL CRANBROOK, KEN,
ENG [37185] : PRE 1800 STAPLEHURST, KEN,
ENG [37185] : 1800-1930 CHICHESTER, SSX, ENG
[37185] : PRE 1700 SUTTON VALLENCE, KEN,
ENG [37185] : 1800-1900 SITTINGBOURNE, KEN,
ENG [37185] : PRE 1850 GOUDHURST, KEN, ENG
[37185] : 1500-1800 HAWKHURST, KEN, ENG
[37185] : PRE 1800 BENENDEN, KEN, ENG [37185]
: 1700-1850 HIGH HALDEN, KEN, ENG [37185] :
1800-1900 ROCHESTER, KEN, ENG [37185] : PRE
1800 BIDDENDEN, KEN, ENG [37185] : PRE 1807
HRT, ENG [37309] : PRE 1800 DOVER, KEN, ENG
[37652] : PRE 1800 SALEHURST & SEDLESCOMBE,
SSX, ENG [37875] : PRE 1850 HAWKHURST, KEN,
ENG [37945] : 1847-1899 WAYNE CO., TN, USA
[37029] : 1820-1875 KY, USA [37822] : ANNA 1826
CHILI, NY, USA [38062] : PRE 1862 BLAINA, MON
& GLA, WLS [36230]
BALLEINE PRE 1660 ST PIERRE, JERSEY, CHI
[36972]
BALLENBERGER 1600+ LEUTERSHAUSEN, BAV,
GER [37542]
BALLENGER 1650-1750 ENG [36898]
BALLENTINE 1840S CHARLOTTE CO., NB, CAN &
USA [38309] : 1850+ ST CLAIR CO., MI, USA &
CAN [38309] : ALL WORLDWIDE [38237]
BALLHAUSEN 1820+ CLAUSTHAL, HAN, GER
[35730]
BALLIEU ALL HARRISON CO., MO, USA [36916]
BALLINGALL PRE 1800 SCT [36538] : ANDREW
1820+ EDINBURGH, MLN, SCT [37444] : 1600+
ABERNETHY, PER, SCT [37734]
BALLINGER GEORGE C1812+ STREETSVILLE,
ONT, CAN [34524] : 1848+ TEWKESBURY, GLS,
ENG [33882] : 1650 CHEDWORTH, GLS, ENG
[35256] : PRE 1800 CIRENCESTER, GLS, ENG
[36092] : PRE 1800 LONDON, ENG [36092] : PRE
1880 GORT, GAL, IRL [34720] : ALL PA, NC & IL,
USA [38363]
BALLOUX 1772-1815 AUTUN, BRG, FRA [34136]
BALLS PRE 1870 NFK, ENG [34673] : PRE 1780 ESS,
ENG [35642] : PRE 1800 AYLSHAM, NFK, ENG
[36593] : PRE 1800 HALESWORTH, SFK, ENG
[36829] : 1800-1900 SW, NFK, ENG [37052] : MARY
1800S MEDWAY, KEN, ENG [37228]
BALMAIN 1700-1750 WEMYSS, FIF, SCT [33767]
BALMER 1860+ CLANE, KID, IRL [34171] : JAMES
1890+ BROOKLYN, NY, USA [34171]
BALMFORTH ALL HALIFAX, YKS, ENG [37959]
BALORY PRE 1751 LAXFIELD, SFK, ENG [37082]
BALOU 1920-1930S NYC, NY, USA [36936]
BALPH 1750-1900 BUTLER CO., PA, USA [37549]
BALRAME 1750+ BURNT ISLAND, FIF, SCT [34473]
BALSDON 1750-1850 SHEBBEAR, DEV, ENG [37339]

BALSHAW 1900+ SALE, CHS, ENG **[36818]** : 1800+ ORMSKIRK, LAN, ENG **[36818]** : PRE 1880 ORMSKIRK, LAN, ENG **[37708]**
BALSOM PRE 1850 TORQUAY, DEV, ENG **[34608]**
BALSTERS PRE 1846 HAN, GER **[38125]**
BALTUS PRE 1730 BEL **[38658]**
BALZER PRE 1816 HES, BRD **[35563]** : 1700-1850 SPRENDLINGEN, RPF, BRD **[38530]**
BAMBER PRE 1840 LIVERPOOL, LAN, ENG **[34370]** : ALL WORLDWIDE **[36152]**
BAMBERGER ALL SIGLISTORF, AG, CH **[38609]** : 1700+ KARLINDACK, BAY, GER **[38578]**
BAMBLING ALL ERSDEN, NBL, ENG **[34838]**
BAMBRICK 1850+ LONDON, MDX, ENG **[35172]** : 1700+ WINDSOR & CLEWER, BRK, ENG **[35172]** : ALL BANBRIDGE, DOW, IRL **[34223]**
BAMBRIDGE ALL WORLDWIDE **[34712]**
BAMBROOK ALL ESS, ENG **[36019]**
BAMFORD 1770+ DONNINGTON, ENG **[35465]** : PRE 1860 MACCLESFIELD, CHS, ENG **[35986]** : PRE 1800 YKS, ENG **[36754]** : 1800+ LITTLEBOROUGH, LAN, ENG **[37134]** : 1810 PINXTON, DBY, ENG **[37391]** : PRE 1875 LND, ENG **[37955]** : 1784+ RYEGATE, VT, USA **[37492]** : 1680-1750S ROCKINGHAM, NH, USA **[38054]** : 1730-1790 BARRINGTON, NH, USA **[38054]**
BAMKIN ALL WORLDWIDE **[36082]**
BAMLETT 1750-1830 BILLINGHAM, DUR, ENG **[36217]**
BAMPTON 1840+ NZ & AUS **[35555]**
BANAHAN 1800+ VT, USA **[38116]**
BANBROOK ALL ESS, ENG **[36019]**
BANCE 1750-1900 SOUTHAMPTON, HAM, ENG **[37077]** : 1800-1900 BRIGHTON, SSX, ENG **[37077]** : 1600-1850 NEWBURY, BRK, ENG **[37077]**
BANCROFT 1800S THEDDLETHORPE, LIN, ENG **[34380]** : 1783 BELCHFORD, LIN, ENG **[37039]** : PRE 1900 MIDDLESEX, READING, MA, USA **[37804]**
BAND ALL FIF, SCT **[37913]**
BANDY ALL HOUGHTON REGIS, BDF, ENG **[37647]** : 1700+ MILTON BRYAN, BDF, ENG **[37647]**
BANES 1650+ PITTENWEEM, FIF, SCT **[35627]**
BANES (SEE BAINES) **[38060]**
BANFIELD 1890+ LOCKHART, NSW, AUS **[34174]** : PRE 1846 STEYNING, SSX, ENG **[35872]**
BANFORD PRE 1790+ MONMOUTH, MON, WLS **[44423]**
BANG ALL FIN & SWE **[38547]**
BANGE ALL FIN & SWE **[38547]**
BANGERT 1617-1720 SUDECK, WAL, GER **[34912]**
BANGHART SHARLOTTA 1820+ JEFFERSON CO., OH, USA **[36322]** : JOHN PRE 1843 JEFFERSON CO., OH, USA **[36322]**
BANGS 1800+ ENFIELD, MDX, ENG **[35214]** : PRE 1850 LAKENHEATH, SFK, ENG **[35742]** : 1591 PANFIELD, ESS, ENG **[36944]** : ALL INGATESTONE, ESS, ENG **[37728]** : 1623+ EASTHAM, MA, USA **[36944]** : PRE 1700 MA, SSX & ESS, USA & ENG **[38745]**
BANHAM 1700+ THURLTON, NFK, ENG **[34420]** : 1750-1838 NEWTON FLOTMAN, NFK, ENG **[37477]**
BANISTER PRE 1850 DUDLEY & TIPTON, STS, ENG **[36808]** : PRE 1850 ETTINGSHALL & SEDGLEY, STS, ENG **[36808]**
BANKHEAD 1699+ KILMAURS, AYR, SCT **[34110]** : 1763-1820S KILWINNING & TARBOLTON, AYR, SCT **[34635]**
BANKIN PRE 1828 HORNCHURCH, ESS, ENG **[34758]** : PRE 1828 HORNCHURCH, ESS, ENG **[35090]** : 1700+ WORLDWIDE **[37500]**

BANKS 1812+ HOBART, TAS, AUS **[35137]** : 1800S+ GLENELG TWP., ONT, CAN **[37458]** : PRE 1815 MORETON VALENCE, GLS, ENG **[34795]** : C1800 HARBORNE, WOR, ENG **[34898]** : 1750+ NEWCASTLE, NBL, ENG **[35038]** : PRE 1850 FURNESS, LAN, ENG **[35165]** : PRE 1760 WHEPSTEAD, SFK, ENG **[35391]** : PRE 1800 MARSKE BY RICHMOND, YKS, ENG **[35448]** : 1700+ ASTON, BIRMINGHAM, WAR, ENG **[35494]** : FRANCIS 1698+ BIRMINGHAM, WAR, ENG **[35494]** : 1870+ WIMBLEDON, SRY, ENG **[35725]** : 1840-1850 QUENDON, ESS, ENG **[35725]** : 1810-1870 RICKLING, ESS, ENG **[35725]** : 1750 STONE, STS, ENG **[36062]** : PRE 1842 CITY & EAST, LND, ENG **[36076]** : 1770S-1840S LEDBURY, HEF, ENG **[36541]** : 1800+ BOLTON, LAN, ENG **[36662]** : PRE 1885 LAN, ENG **[36886]** : ALL DEVONPORT, DEV, ENG **[37158]** : RALPH ALL STOKE DAMEREL, DEV, ENG **[37158]** : PRE 1800 NFK, ENG **[37416]** : PRE 1850 WOR, HEF & STS, ENG **[37703]** : 1800S ST GILES, MDX, ENG **[37833]** : PRE 1850 LONDON, MDX, ENG **[38376]** : PRE 1800 BOUGHTON MONCHELSEA, KEN, ENG **[38376]** : ANN 1769-1825 LONDON & PARRAMATTA, NSW, ENG & AUS **[36311]** : PRE 1864 DUBLIN, IRL **[37991]** : ALL LOG, IRL **[38346]** : 1850 DUNDEE, ANS, SCT **[34149]** : 1850+ ST MARGARET'S HOPE, OKI, SCT **[34688]** : ALL CAI, SCT **[34981]** : PRE 1850 EDINBURGH, MLN, SCT **[38364]** : 1800S KY, USA **[37028]** : PRE 1686 HENRICO CO., VA, USA **[38120]** : 1600-1800 USA & ENG **[35289]**
BANLOCK ALL SFK, ENG **[35933]**
BANN ALL POYNTON, WORTH, CHS, ENG **[33765]**
BANNAM 1855+ LONGFORD, TAS, AUS **[35525]**
BANNER 1790S ILKESTON, DBY, ENG **[36032]**
BANNERMAN ALL VIC, AUS **[34674]** : 1750-1850 WEST GWILLIMBURY, ONT, CAN **[35269]** : 1850+ GREY & BRUCE, ONT, CAN **[37484]** : ROSE 1800+ LATHERON, CAI, SCT **[34606]** : PRE 1800 LOTH, SUT, SCT **[34606]** : ALL LOTHBEG, SUT, SCT **[34674]** : PRE 1800 HALKIRK, CAI, SCT **[37484]** : 1700 HALKIRK, LKS, SCT **[37484]** : PRE 1850 KILDONAN, SUT, SCT **[37484]**
BANNING PRE 1800 CAN & SCT **[38386]** : 1700 LAYCOCK, WIL, ENG **[34466]** : PRE 1850 CHIPPENHAM, WIL, ENG **[34466]** : 1700 CHARLTON, WIL, ENG **[34466]** : PRE 1875 BIGGIN HILL, KEN, ENG **[36468]** : 1860-1880 STEPNEY, MDX, ENG **[37336]** : 1840-1875 WOKINGHAM, BRK, ENG **[37336]** : 1790-1840 EVERLEY, WIL, ENG **[37336]**
BANNISTER 1900+ CHINCHILLA, QLD, AUS **[35807]** : C1830 BEDINGFIELD, SFK, ENG **[33910]** : 1800 BRIGHTON, SSX, ENG **[34057]** : PRE 1800 KIDDERMINSTER, WOR, ENG **[34711]** : PRE 1827 BASINGSTOKE, HAM, ENG **[34753]** : 1904 EDMONTON, MDX, ENG **[35575]** : C1650-1850 IOW, ENG **[36478]** : 1800+ EXETER, DEV & WAR, ENG **[38261]** : C1700 IOW, ENG **[38700]** : PRE 1850 DUDLEY & TIPTON, STS, ENG & NZ **[36808]** : PRE 1850 ETTINGSHALL & SEDGLEY, STS, ENG & NZ **[36808]**
BANNON 1850 WHITEHAVEN, CUL, ENG **[36798]** : ALL TIPPERARY, TIP, IRL **[35514]**
BANTIN PRE 1856 CAMDEN TOWN, LND, ENG **[34305]**
BANTOCK ALL SFK, ENG **[35933]**
BANTON PRE 1830 MAIDENHEAD, BRK, ENG **[38681]**
BANYARD 1880+ PARRAMATTA, NSW, AUS **[34979]** : 1750+ FORDHAM, CAM, ENG **[35706]**
BANZIGER ALL GR, CH **[36982]**

BAPTISTA PRE 1898 NEWCASTLE ON TYNE, NBL, ENG **[36475]**

BAPTY 1840+ LEEDS, YKS, ENG **[38091]**

BARA PRE 1725 JOUY LES REIMS, CHA, FRA **[36964]** : ALL WORLDWIDE **[37193]**

BARAGER 1840+ THURLOW TWP., ONT, CAN **[34510]**

BARASS 1790+ NEWCASTLE ON TYNE, NBL, ENG **[34415]**

BARBAR 1696-1770 MIDHURST, SSX, ENG **[36091]** : 1670-1750 ALRESFORD, HAM, ENG **[36091]** : 1777-1935 CATHERINGTON, HAM, ENG **[36091]**

BARBARY ALL ELO, GER **[38742]**

BARBEAU 1850-1880 CAN **[35298]**

BARBEE C1665-1679 ESSEX CO., VA, USA **[35284]** : C1690-1752 STAFFORD CO., VA, USA **[35284]**

BARBER PRE 1863 PARRAMATTA, NSW, AUS **[35583]** : 1800-1900 PARRAMATTA, NSW, AUS **[37895]** : C1832 CAMPBELLTOWN, NSW, AUS **[37947]** : HENRY 1890+ NARRANDERA, NSW, AUS **[38071]** : 1850+ SHANNONVILLE, ONT, CAN **[34466]** : 1860+ ONT, CAN **[38323]** : BENJAMIN C1868 NTH SHEFFIELD, YKS, ENG **[34193]** : 1840+ PORTSEA, HAM, ENG **[34237]** : 1700S AUSTONLEY, WRY, ENG **[35126]** : C1800 BOSSALL, YKS, ENG **[35198]** : C1862 TUNSTALL, STS, ENG **[35348]** : PRE 1840 SOUTHWARK, LND, ENG **[35544]** : 1670-1750 ALRESFORD, HAM, ENG **[36091]** : 1696-1770 MIDHURST, SSX, ENG **[36091]** : 1777-1935 CATHERINGTON, HAM, ENG **[36091]** : C1800 LOWER NEWTON, LAN & NFK, ENG **[37246]** : 1800+ CUL, ENG **[37274]** : ALL WAR, ENG **[37404]** : 1600-1920 HUDDERSFIELD, WRY, ENG **[37736]** : PRE 1800 HEPWORTH, WRY, ENG **[37893]** : 1700-1800 MANCHESTER, LAN, ENG **[37895]** : PRE 1800 YKS, ENG **[38080]** : 1780+ SIBTON, SFK, ENG **[38291]** : PRE 1830 HENNOCK, DEV, ENG **[38377]** : 1830S BUNGAY, SFK, ENG **[38390]** : 1800-1900 HAYLING & PORTSMOUTH, HAM, ENG **[38471]** : 1860+ BRIGHTON & HOVE, SSX, ENG **[38539]** : PRE 1900 ANT, IRL **[34466]** : PRE 1830 DUBLIN, IRL **[35556]** : PERCY C1909 CAPETOWN, RSA **[34193]** : 1790-1830 CT & NY, USA **[35307]** : 1830-1860 HALL CO., GA, USA **[35307]** : PRE 1800 BUCKS CO., PA, USA **[36917]** : 1644+ HARTFORD CO., CT, USA **[37802]** : DORRENCE W. 1832-1886 ERIE, PA, WI & NY, USA **[37813]** : 1680-1730 DORCHESTER CO., MA, USA **[38764]**

BARBIEUR 1725-1800 MONS, HNT, BEL **[38405]**

BARBIN SALLY 1806-1820 FRANKLIN CO., GA, USA **[38155]**

BARBOR 1696-1770 MIDHURST, SSX, ENG **[36091]** : 1777-1935 CATHERINGTON, HAM, ENG **[36091]** : 1670-1750 ALRESFORD, HAM, ENG **[36091]** : C1785 AMHERST, VA, USA **[37819]**

BARBOT 1700S ST ANNES SOHO, MDX, ENG **[37890]** : 1700S ST GILES IN THE FIELDS, MDX, ENG **[37890]**

BARBOUR 1800+ ARDROSSAN, AYR, SCT **[37949]**

BARBY 1850+ DUNGOG, NSW, AUS **[35374]** : PRE 1850 TODDINGTON, BDF, ENG **[35374]**

BARCAS ALL WORLDWIDE **[37742]**

BARCINI ALL WORLDWIDE **[37742]**

BARCLAY 1830-1850 YASS, NSW, AUS **[34175]** : 1850-1900 ALBURY, NSW, AUS **[34175]** : C1895 HOBART, TAS, AUS **[36836]** : C1849 NORTH EASTERN, LND, ENG **[36836]** : PRE 1865 TIP, IRL **[36631]** : 1874-1946 WAITARA, NEW PLYMOUTH, NZ **[36836]** : ALL EDINBURGH, MLN, SCT **[34093]** : 1810-1840 EDINBURGH, MLN, SCT **[34175]** : 1800+ FIF, SCT **[34226]** : ANDREW PRE 1851 PER, FIF & KRS, SCT **[34447]** : C1720+ CADDER, LKS, SCT **[35051]** : PRE

1833+ PERTH, PER, SCT **[35414]** : 1700-1800 MARYKIRK, KCD, SCT **[37485]** : 1740+ DORNOCH, SUT, SCT **[38385]**

BARCROFT 1800S ROSSENDALE, LAN, ENG **[36194]** : 1900+ HASLINGDEN, LAN, ENG **[36271]** : 1800+ WHALLEY, LAN, ENG **[36271]**

BARCZYKOWSKI ALL POL **[37041]** : 1880+ BALTIMORE, MD, USA **[37041]**

BARDEN PRE 1837 CATSFIELD, SSX, ENG **[34806]** : C1871 BATTERSEA, LND, ENG **[36759]** : PRE 1840 WEX, IRL **[34984]**

BARDILL PRE 1850 DBY, ENG **[37739]**

BARDIN PRE 1750 SOHO, LND, ENG & FRA **[36396]**

BARDO ALL WORLDWIDE **[36292]**

BARDSLEY SAM 1780-1850 OLDHAM, LAN, ENG **[35320]** : PRE 1850 OLDHAM, LAN, ENG **[36380]** : JOHN 1865-1900 PHILADELPHIA, PA, USA **[35320]**

BARDWELL 1700-1800 SFK, ENG **[34081]** : 1700-1900 NORWICH, NFK, ENG **[34081]**

BARDY 1880+ CA, USA **[37041]** : 1880+ TACOMA, WA, USA **[37041]**

BARDYKOSKI 1880+ TACOMA, WA, USA **[37041]** : 1880+ BALTIMORE, MD, USA **[37041]**

BARDYKOWSKI ALL LOMZA, POL **[37041]**

BARDZIKOWSKI ALL LOMZA, POL **[37041]**

BARE 1800S SHAHJAHAUPUR, INDIA **[38319]** : ALL AUGUSTA, VA, USA **[38319]**

BAREFIELD ALL PA, USA **[37505]**

BAREHAM SUSAN 1828+ CORNARD, SFK, ENG **[35634]**

BARENGO ALL OZEGNA, TORINO, ITL **[37510]**

BARENS NANCY 1600-1700 BALLYGOSSONE, ARM, IRL **[36321]**

BARFF C1880 ADELAIDE, SA, AUS **[34898]** : C1913 IPSWICH, QLD, AUS **[34898]** : 1890+ EDGECLIFFE, NSW, AUS **[34898]**

BARFIELD ALL WORLDWIDE **[37759]**

BARFKNECHT ALL WORLDWIDE **[38687]**

BARFOOT WILLIAM PRE 1822 GUILDEN MORDEN, CAM, ENG **[35805]** : 1724 BISHOPS WALTHAM & BOTLEY, HAM, ENG **[36263]**

BARGERY ALL WEST CHINNOCK, SOM, ENG **[35854]** : ALL CREWKERNE, SOM, ENG **[36188]** : PRE 1900 SOUTH, WLS **[36188]**

BARHAM PRE 1860 LONDON &, KEN, ENG **[33957]** : PRE 1789 BATTLE, SSX, ENG **[35546]** : 1820S SHOREDITCH, LND, ENG **[35728]**

BARIL 1877 VILLERS SUR MER, BN, FRA **[38163]**

BARK 1945+ TX, USA **[37597]**

BARKEL PRE 1852 BLACKWATER, CON, ENG **[35441]**

BARKER THOMAS C1860+ TICKERA, SA, AUS **[34035]** : DAVID 1857+ ALBANY CREEK, QLD, AUS **[35462]** : 1857+ NW COAST, TAS, AUS **[38492]** : 1827-1904 CLEVELAND, TAS, AUS & ENG **[35195]** : WILLIAM PRE 1885 WEST ZORA, ONT, CAN **[34216]** : PRE 1900 LONDON, ENG **[33883]** : 1700-1900S HANLEY & STOKE ON TRENT, STS, ENG **[33958]** : ARTHUR 1900 BURTON STATHER, LIN, ENG **[34091]** : ROBERT 1614 HAXEY, LIN, ENG **[34091]** : MARGARET 1765+ MARSKE IN CLEVELAND, NRY, ENG **[34181]** : JOSEPH 1740+ NRY, ENG **[34181]** : C1917 KEMPSTON & BEDFORD, BDF, ENG **[34372]** : JOHN C1800 BATH, SOM, ENG **[34475]** : PRE 1800 CAENBY & MUCKTON, LIN, ENG **[34745]** : PRE 1840 ABERFORD, WRY, ENG **[34776]** : 1799+ MARSTON MORTAINE, BDF, ENG **[34781]** : 1750+ LONDON, ENG **[34813]** : JAMES 1770+ DUNMOW, ESS, ENG **[34884]** : PRE 1865 SILSDEN, YKS, ENG **[35091]** : PRE 1840 SOUTH ELMHAM, SFK, ENG **[35212]** : PRE 1857 WESTHORPE &

FINNINGHAM, SFK, ENG **[35462]** : 1800-1844 LND, ENG **[35485]** : PRE 1850 SWAFFHAM, NFK, ENG **[35729]** : PRE 1860 ASTBURY, CHS, ENG **[36051]** : 1800+ NOTTINGHAM, NTT, ENG **[36219]** : 1798-1852 BISHOP STORTFORD, HRT, ENG **[36229]** : PRE 1840 FODDINGTON, BDF, ENG **[36293]** : ALL LONGTON, STS, ENG **[36492]** : ALL COLLEORTON, LEI, ENG **[36492]** : PRE 1850 LONDON, ESS, ENG **[36709]** : 1750-1850 APPLETON & STRETTON, CHS, ENG **[36740]** : 1850+ LND & ESS, ENG **[36794]** : 1750-1850 FARNHAM, SFK, ENG **[36833]** : C1768-1845 STERNFIELD, SFK, ENG **[36836]** : 1700+ STEPNEY, MDX, ENG **[37099]** : PRE 1760 FINGHALL, YKS, ENG **[37288]** : MRS SARAH PRE 1801 ERY, ENG **[37352]** : PRE 1850 NEWCHURCH IN ROSSENDALE, LAN, ENG **[37414]** : C1770 TUNSTALL, SFK, ENG **[37420]** : PRE 1800 BARWICK IN ELMET, WRY, ENG **[37426]** : 1830+ MADELEY DIST, SAL, ENG **[37443]** : PRE 1900 OLD KENT ROAD, LND, ENG **[37622]** : 1870+ WEMBLEY, MDX, ENG **[37622]** : PRE 1880 SPALDING, LIN, ENG **[37622]** : MARTHA 1820+ GAINSBOROUGH, LIN, ENG **[37775]** : PRE 1843 BRAUGHING, HRT, ENG **[37896]** : PRE 1860 STALYBRIDGE, CHS, ENG **[37939]** : 1700+ LARLING, NFK, ENG **[38492]** : JOHN 1870-1930 WALTHAMSTOW, LND, ENG **[38549]** : 1700-1800 TIP & WAT, IRL **[34514]** : PRE 1853 DUNFERMLINE, FIF, SCT **[33770]** : 1740+ WESTFIELD, MA & NY, USA **[36319]**

BARKERS 1910+ MOOSE JAW, SAS, CAN **[34521]** : 1880-1890 GLOSSOP, DBY, ENG **[34521]**

BARKHAUSEN ALL GER **[36694]**

BARKLA 1800+ ST AUSTELL, CON, ENG **[35152]**

BARKLEY 1853+ ALBURY, NSW, AUS **[33820]**

BARKMEYER 1780+ SLOCHTEREN & ROTTERDAM, GR & ZH, NL **[38712]**

BARLAND ALL WORLDWIDE **[37095]**

BARLING PRE 1830 ROMNEY MARSH, KEN, ENG **[34022]** : ALL WORLDWIDE **[37979]**

BARLOW 1840S ADELAIDE, SA, AUS **[34979]** : 1820+ VIC, AUS & UK **[35056]** : 1830+ WENTWORTH CO., ONT, CAN **[34051]** : 1800-1850 SUTTON YORK, ONT, CAN **[38407]** : PRE 1860 KINGSWINFORD, STS, ENG **[33776]** : ALL REDDISH, LAN, ENG **[34674]** : ALL NORWICH, NFK, ENG **[34822]** : 1750-1850 MDX, ENG **[34846]** : 1800-1850 YKS, ENG **[34846]** : PRE 1840 NTT, ENG **[35246]** : PRE 1850 LONDON, MDX, ENG **[35413]** : 1700-1850 NORTHWICH, CHS, ENG **[36410]** : 1875-1900 ALDERSHOT, HAM, ENG **[36527]** : THOMAS 1800S ASHTON UNDER LYNE, LAN, ENG **[36527]** : RICHARD 1840S ECCLES & PENDLETON, LAN, ENG **[36585]** : 1795 DARWEN, LAN, ENG **[36679]** : 1700-1850 BIRMINGHAM, WAR, ENG **[37068]** : PRE 1800 NEWCASTLE UNDER LYME, STS, ENG **[37389]** : 1840-1888 BLACKFRIARS & MARYLEBONE, LND, ENG **[37445]** : JOHN PRE 1830 MANCHESTER, LAN, ENG **[37961]** : C1700-1800 WOLSTANTON, STS, ENG **[38055]** : 1750+ LEI, KEN & LND, ENG & CAN **[34467]** : 1730 STRATFORD, NH, USA **[38131]** : PRE 1850 PEM, WLS **[35413]**

BARLUND 1803+ PERNAJA, UUSIMAA, FIN **[38758]**

BARMBY 1799 BIRSTALL, WRY, ENG **[34352]**

BARNABY 1820-1830 CAN **[38099]** : 1855 NFK, ENG **[35870]**

BARNACLE ALL LEI, ENG **[35716]** : 1790+ STONEY STANTON, LEI, ENG **[35716]** : 1807+ NAILSTONE, LEI, ENG **[35716]** : 1805+ ASHBY DE-LA ZOUCH, LEI, ENG **[35716]** : 1880+ GRANTHAM, LIN, ENG

[35716] : 1765+ AYLESTONE, LEI, ENG **[35716]** : 1800-1900 BIRMINGHAM, WAR, ENG **[36012]** : ALL WAR, ENG **[37404]**

BARNARD PRE 1830 LOW HAM, SOM, ENG **[34197]** : C1700 BRAINTREE, ESS, ENG **[37321]** : C1800 SHEERNESS, KEN, ENG **[37715]** : C1700-1850 HODDESDON, HRT, ENG **[37770]** : 1600S ENG **[37803]** : 1800-1900 LONDON, ENG **[37844]** : C1730 WASHINGTON, SSX, ENG **[37859]** : C1690 KEULEN, GER **[36459]** : 1800S SARATOGA CO., NY, USA **[38019]**

BARNARDISTON 1680S LONDON, ENG **[34296]**

BARNCASTLE 1831-1884 GLEBE & SYDNEY, NSW, AUS **[33933]**

BARNDEN PRE 1840 PORTSEA, HAM, ENG **[35810]** : PRE 1829 WEST TARRING, SSX, ENG **[37892]**

BARNELL C1870 SAUNDERS CO., NE, USA **[38173]** : C1810-60 CUYAHOGA CO., OH, USA **[38173]**

BARNES 1840+ RAYMOND TERRACE, NSW, AUS **[35117]** : JAMES H. 1900+ PARRAMATTA, NSW, AUS **[35410]** : 1830+ PARRAMATTA, NSW, AUS **[35410]** : 1820+ SYDNEY & BATHURST, NSW, AUS **[35557]** : PRE 1896 SYDNEY, NSW, AUS **[35843]** : 1793 SYDNEY, NSW, AUS **[35920]** : 1850+ CARLTON, VIC, AUS **[36605]** : 1860+ MOYSTON, VIC, AUS **[36825]** : 1660+ ST MICHAELS, BARBADOS **[38235]** : C1823 ENGLISH HARBOUR, NFD, CAN **[33852]** : THOMAS 1820-1850 BRUCE CO., ONT, CAN **[35602]** : C1765 MONTREAL, QUE, CAN **[37180]** : 1700-1850 EAST BARMING, KEN, ENG **[33785]** : 1750-1800 PORCHESTER, HAM, ENG **[33787]** : C1770-1884 ALL SAINTS, HUN, ENG **[33862]** : 1780+ HIGHWORTH, WIL, ENG **[34190]** : 1820S LONDON &, WIL, ENG **[34191]** : PRE 1792 LONDON, ENG **[34275]** : C1830 SOUTH CADBURY, SOM, ENG **[34393]** : PRE 1840 BECKLEY & RYE, SSX, ENG **[35117]** : PRE 1782 KEMPSFORD, GLS, ENG **[35236]** : MARY 1804 ALDERBURY, WIL, ENG **[35369]** : 1800 HENDON, MDX, ENG **[35410]** : PRE 1830 NEWCHURCH IOW, HAM, ENG **[35527]** : 1790S BENENDEN, KEN, ENG **[35557]** : 1840 WARMINSTER, WIL, ENG **[35566]** : 1700+ ASHTON KEYNES, GLS, ENG **[35824]** : 1800S HOLKHAM, NFK, ENG **[35872]** : 1824+ SOMERSTOWN, MDX, ENG **[35921]** : PRE 1850 ACCRINGTON, LAN, ENG **[36095]** : ALL LAN, ENG **[36152]** : PRE 1813 PORTSEA, HAM, ENG **[36255]** : 1890+ CHEADLE, CHS, ENG **[36349]** : 1800+ GREENWICH, LND, ENG **[36402]** : 1700+ LONDON & BURTON ON TRENT, MDX, ENG **[36462]** : PRE 1850 SELSEY, SSX, ENG **[36605]** : PRE 1850 STREET, SOM, ENG **[36676]** : 1700+ LEXDEN & BRIGHTLINGSEA, ESS, ENG **[36794]** : 1750+ EAST STOKE, DOR, ENG **[36825]** : 1760+ MARYPORT, CUL, ENG **[37073]** : PRE 1810 LEI & NTT, ENG **[37078]** : C1800 SFK, ENG **[37180]** : 1800+ COLCHESTER, ESS, ENG **[37209]** : 1800+ BIRMINGHAM, WAR, ENG **[37209]** : MARY PRE 1830 SSX, ENG **[37210]** : C1800 WESTMINSTER, LND, ENG **[37239]** : 1800S SHEFFIELD, YKS, ENG **[37309]** : 1890 WORSBROUGH, YKS, ENG **[37309]** : PRE 1860 CON, ENG **[37394]** : PRE 1798 WICKHAM ST PAUL, ESS, ENG **[37568]** : PRE 1850 CHILTON FOLIAT, WIL, ENG **[37687]** : PRE 1764 DINTON, WIL, ENG **[37909]** : PRE 1806 EXETER, DEV, ENG **[38186]** : 1809+ NOTTINGHAM, NTT, ENG **[38186]** : PRE 1850 KELVEOON HATCH, ESS, ENG **[38205]** : PRE 1850 ROCHDALE, LAN, ENG **[38293]** : PRE 1800 WOR, ENG **[38746]** : 1896+ WELLINGTON, NZ **[35843]** : 1840+ WAIMEA SOUTH, NELSON, NZ **[36806]** : 1600+ HARTFORD, CT, USA **[33989]** : 1800S VENANGO CO., PA, USA **[35278]** : 1750-1825

VT, USA [36732] : 1825-1875 TRUMBULL, OH, USA
[36732] : BRINSLEY 1749 CHESTER CO., PA, USA
[36925] : MOSES 1774+ WILKES & ROWAN CO.,
NC, USA [36925] : 1630-1730 PLYMOUTH, MA, USA
[37432] : 1800+ SIMPSON, KY, USA [38027] : C1851
MO, USA [38184] : 1860S FULTON CO., IL, USA
[38223] : 1880-1920 ST LOUIS, MO, USA [38349] :
ALL WORLDWIDE [37180]

BARNET PRE 1857 MACCLESFIELD, CHS, ENG
[37318] : ALL WILSON CO., TN, USA [36351]

BARNETSON 1783+ DURRAN & WATTEN, CAI,
SCT [35013]

BARNETSONE PRE 1750 WALLS, OKI, SCT [36883]

BARNETT 1847+ ADELAIDE, SA, AUS [35039] :
1800+ ALB, CAN [35762] : 1930S TORONTO, ONT,
CAN [38038] : PRE 1980 LONDON, ENG [33960] :
1650-1820 GWENNAP, CON, ENG [34793] : PRE
1830 LND, ENG [34977] : 1700-1930 GRENDON
UNDERWOOD & SHALSTONE, BKM, ENG [35030]
: 1800-1810 PATTISHALL, NTH, ENG [35030] : PRE
1730 EVENLY, NTH, ENG [35030] : ALL
HAMMERSMITH, LND, ENG [35449] : PRE 1839
COVENTRY, WAR, ENG [35496] : JOSEPH 1840+
ENG [35762] : 1700-1850 HATTON & ROWINGTON,
WAR, ENG [35937] : ALL COVENTRY, WAR, ENG
[36005] : 1800S CHISWICK, MDX, ENG [36708] :
ALL HENLEY ON THAMES, OXF, ENG [36774] :
1830-1900 WHITECHAPEL, LND, ENG [37300] :
1820-90 SOUTHWARK, LND, ENG [37376] : 1820-
1900 TOTTENHAM, MDX, ENG [37376] : 1820+
LONDON, ENG [38204] : ALL PEASMARSH, SSX &
KEN, ENG [38230] : PRE 1838 ASHTON UNDER
HILL, GLS, ENG [38399] : 1807-1845 DUBLIN, IRL
[34002] : 1800+ PA, USA [35762] : 1909 CLARKE
CO., GA, USA [36903] : 1800-1900 ESTILL CO., KY,
USA [38089] : 1818-1891 POLK CO., MO, USA [38120]

BARNEWALL ALL IRL [36030]

BARNEY ALL BEAULIEU & SOUTHAMPTON,
HAM, ENG [36211] : 1600-1860 ALBRIGHTON, SAL,
ENG [37717]

BARNHARDT 1700+ RPR, GER [38765]

BARNHILL C1810-60 COLUMBIANA CO., OH, USA
[38173]

BARNICKLE 1712+ NARBOUROUGH, LEI, ENG
[35716] : ALL LEAMINGTON, WAR, ENG [35854]

BARNISH ALL ENG [37377]

BARNS PRE 1860 CON, ENG [37394] : PRE 1850 SFK,
ENG [38577]

BARNSDALL C1840 LEICESTER, LEI, ENG [37053] :
C1811 SAWLEY, DBY, ENG [37053]

BARNWELL 1800 WOLFHAMPCOTE, WAR, ENG
[34950] : THOMAS REEVE 1759-1839 BERBISE,
GUYANA [36103] : HENRY 1670-1725 IRL & BARB
[36103]

BARO ALL WORLDWIDE [37193]

BARON ALL BERMUDA [34378] : 1700-1870
HAMBRUCKEN, BAD, BRD [35300] : PRE 1880
WIGAN, LAN, ENG [38288] : PRE 1850
TANNYBROOK, ANT, IRL [36345]

BARONOWSKI 1600-1990 LOMZA, POL [38232]

BAROW ALL WORLDWIDE [37193]

BARR 1867+ DAYLESFORD, VIC, AUS [34787] :
C1853 FREMANTLE, WA, AUS [35135] : 1860
WINEHAM HURON CO., ONT, CAN [37442] :
ANNE 1800-1890 MDX, ENG [34722] : 1816
TWICKENHAM, MDX, ENG [35808] : 1700-1800S
LAN, ENG [36837] : ALL WAR, ENG [37672] : 1820-
1860 INDIA [34722] : 1800S LUCKNOW, INDIA
[35424] : MARTHA 1700+ IRL [34701] : PRE 1835
ANT, IRL [34758] : 1800S ARM, IRL [37443] : 1820
DOW, IRL [38362] : PRE 1855 KILMARNOCK,
AYR, SCT [34014] : 1800+ JOHNSTONE, RFW, SCT

[34049] : 1800 PAISLEY, RFW, SCT [34435] : 1834+
KILSYTH, STI, SCT [35347] : PRE 1834
BARRHEAD, RFW, SCT [35347] : PRE 1800
PAISLEY, RFW, SCT [35385] : 1800+ WISHAW,
LKS, SCT [35411] : 1849 BELLS HILL, LKS, SCT
[36599] : PRE 1900 WEST GREENOCK, RFW, SCT
[37745] : 1800S STAIR, AYR, SCT [37969] : PRE 1870
WASHINGTON CO., OH, USA [37505] : 1875-1885
KEWEENAW CO., MI, USA [38010]

BARRA ALL WORLDWIDE [37193] : C1780
WORLDWIDE [37698]

BARRABLE PRE 1800 PLYMOUTH, DEV, ENG
[36474] : PRE 1850 HOLSWORTHY, DEV, ENG
[37768]

BARRACLOUGH C1850 NEW MILL, YKS, ENG
[33912] : 1870S BRADFORD, WRY, ENG [36837]

BARRAR ALL WORLDWIDE [38279]

BARRAS ALL SOUTH SHIELDS, DUR, ENG [36010] :
1725+ LA, USA [36964]

BARRAT 1700-1750 STS, ENG [36911] : 1800+ NTH,
ENG [38488]

BARRATT 1919+ SA, AUS [35771] : PRE 1880
NEWPORT PAGNELL, BKM, ENG [33859] : 1800S
BIRMINGHAM, WAR, ENG [34715] : 1850S ST
PANCRAS, MDX, ENG [34953] : 1678 KING'S
CLIFFE, NTH, ENG [35369] : 1750+
BIRMINGHAM, WAR & STS, ENG [36435] : ALL
WIGSTON, LEI, ENG [37640] : 1830+ BKM & NTH,
ENG [38488]

BARREL 1800S+ GREAT ASHFIELD, SFK, ENG
[37262]

BARRELL 1700+ HEF, ENG [36209] : PRE 1880
IPSWICH, SFK, ENG [37768]

BARRENTS PRE 1700 FLATBUSH, NY, USA [38225]

BARRET 1750+ FEOCK, CON, ENG [36793] : PRE
1800 ANDOVER, HAM, ENG [37693] : C1820-1860
LIM, IRL [35206]

BARRETT 1855 MCLAREN VALE & NARACOORTE,
SA, AUS [34295] : 1840+ SYDNEY, NSW, AUS
[35027] : 1880+ EMMAVILLE, NSW, AUS [35428] :
1818+ LIVERPOOL & ADAMINABY, NSW, AUS
[35506] : 1836 SYDNEY, NSW, AUS [37106] : PRE
1813 GREAT WRATTING, SFK, ENG [33866] : PRE
1855 GREAT WRATTING, SFK, ENG [34295] : PRE
1856 GUILDFORD, SRY, ENG [34305] : 1700-1850
ALDBOURNE, WIL, ENG [34343] : 1704+
MERTHER, CON, ENG [34668] : 1797+
PLYMOUTH, DEV, ENG [34808] : PRE 1780
WESTACRE, NFK, ENG [35212] : 1782-1850
BURTON AGNES, NRY, ENG [35316] : PRE 1818
LEICESTER, LEI, ENG [35506] : 1790-1830
CHELSEA, LND, ENG [35850] : C1809 STS, ENG
[35887] : 1800+ DOR, ENG [35998] : 1850+ BRK,
ENG [36239] : 1700-1750 SAL, ENG [36911] : PRE
1850 OXF, ENG [37097] : ALL GREAT THURLOW,
SFK, ENG [37167] : ALL NEWCASTLE, NBL, ENG
[37366] : 1700-1900 CORSCOMBE, DOR, ENG [37378]
: C1860 ST CLEMENTS, OXF, ENG [37711] : 1800+
SWINDON, WIL, ENG [37877] : PRE 1855 LAN,
ENG [37885] : 1800 LITTLE TOTHAM, ESS, ENG
[37928] : 1750-1850 ROVENDEN, KEN, ENG [38287]
: GEORGE PRE 1860 LONDON, LND, ENG [38289]
: PRE 1857 ESS & NSW, ENG & AUS [34773] : 1800S
IRL [34102] : 1700+ COSHEDY, FER, IRL [34903] :
1900+ DUBLIN, IRL [35530] : PRE 1900 BALLINA,
MAY, IRL [35548] : 1775-1850 COR, IRL [36318] :
1800S SCT [34102] : C1850 ST WINDALL, MN, USA
[34395] : 1870-1900 BOSTON, MA, USA [34773] : ALL
PHILA & CHESTER CO., PA, USA [36318] : 1800+
WILSON CO., TN, USA [36351] : 1670+ KENT CO.,
DE, USA [36359] : 1670+ CECIL CO., MD, USA
[36359] : 1670+ KENT CO., MD, USA [36359] :

1670+ HARFORD CO., MD, USA [36359] : C1650
SALEM, MA, USA [37018] : 1840 CUTTINGSVILLE,
VT, USA [38131]

BARRIBAL C1741 ALTARNUN, CON, ENG [35335]

BARRIBALL 1698 NORTH HILL, CON, ENG [34793] :
C1774+ NORTH TAMERTON, CON, ENG [36875]

BARRICK C1700-1850 WHITBY, NRY, ENG [37423]

BARRIE 1700-1850 KIRRIEMUIR, ANS, SCT [34004] :
PRE 1840 GLASGOW, LKS, SCT [35929] : 1800+
ARNGASK, FIF, SCT [36195] : 1850S LADYBURN,
GLASGOW, SCT [36800] : PRE 1900 LKS & RFW,
SCT [36893] : C1825 LANARK, AYR, SCT [37143]

BARRIER ALL MELBOURNE & INGLEWOOD, VIC,
AUS [35888]

BARRINGER PRE 1800 LONDON, ENG [36092]

BARRINGTON 1860S NSW, AUS [33870] : 1700-1750
AYMESTREY, HEF, ENG [36229] : 1800-1950
ENNISTYMON, CLA, IRL [35308] : 1900-1960
DETROIT, MI, USA [34148]

BARRISKILL PRE 1860S PORTADOWN, ARM, IRL
[37909]

BARRITT 1800S WOODBRIDGE, SFK, ENG [36194] :
PRE 1900 TOTTINGTON, LAN, ENG [37443]

BARR LAIRD PRE 1900 WEST GREENOCK, RFW,
SCT [37745]

BARRO ALL WORLDWIDE [37193]

BARRON 1884+ ALLORA, QLD, AUS [36607] : 1800+
MARYLAND, LIN, ENG [33893] : 1860+
MANCHESTER, LAN, ENG [35404] : PRE 1850
MAIDSTONE, KEN, ENG [35722] : PRE 1864
STAINLAND, WRY, ENG [35733] : (NEE WELLER)
1895-1950 GILLINGHAM, KEN, ENG [36398] : PRE
1880 READING & ABINGDON, BRK, ENG [36607]
: PRE 1860 ABERDEEN, ABD, SCT &, INDIA
[33883] : CATHERINE 1800S DUBLIN, IRL [35361] :
PRE 1780 FORRES, MOR, SCT [35208]

BARROW 1853-1858 FITZROY, VIC, AUS [36606] :
PRE 1870 KEN, ENG [34105] : JOHN C1800
THORNTON IN LONSDALE, WRY, ENG [35955] :
PRE 1900 LONDON & CARLISLE, CUL, ENG
[36006] : PRE 1800 FYLDE, LAN, ENG [36073] :
1880+ KEN, ENG [37193] : PRE 1750
CRANBROOK & HAWKHURST, KEN, ENG
[37193] : 1750+ BURWASH & HEATHFIELD, SSX,
ENG [37193] : 1890+ PRESCOT, LAN, ENG [38274] :
1850 CONECUH CO., AL, USA [37792] : 1835
WREXHAM, DEN, WLS [36229] : ALL
WORLDWIDE [37193]

BARROWCLOUGH PRE 1815 ASTON UNDER
LYNE, LAN, ENG [37546] : PRE 1815 HEATON
NORRIS, LAN, ENG [37546]

BARROWMAN 1800S PORT CHALMERS, OTAGO,
NZ [35906]

BARROWS PRE 1880 LND, ENG [37057]

BARRY 1880+ ARGENTINA [37686] : 1850-1990
ADELAIDE, SA, AUS [35308] : 1850+ FRANKLIN,
TAS, AUS [35459] : 1900S MELBOURNE, VIC, AUS
[38760] : 1850+ BENDIGO & MELBOURNE, VIC &
LIM, AUS & IRL [35383] : 1880+ HALIFAX CO.,
NS, CAN [34253] : PRE 1860 LONDON, ENG [35393]
: 1840-1860S LONDON, MDX, ENG [36285] : 1860+
PLYMOUTH, DEV, ENG [37686] : 1850
KEELNAHULLA, COR, IRL [33929] : PRE 1874
BALLYHOOLY, COR, IRL [33957] : PRE 1850
BALLYMORE, ARM, IRL [34835] : MICHAEL PRE
1853 ANGLESBOROUGH, LIM, IRL [35065] : 1700-
1900 CLA, IRL [35308] : PRE 1855 LIMERICK, LIM,
IRL [35383] : PRE 1900 COBH & QUEENSTOWN,
COR, IRL [37686] : C1840 CORK, IRL [37718] : 1830S
COR, IRL [38270] : PRE 1850 GIRVAN, AYR, SCT
[34835] : 1780-1800 NORTH BERWICK, ELN, SCT

[35609] : 1870+ USA [34835] : C1750-1950 USA [35308]
: 1900+ SAN FRANCISCO, CA, USA [37686]

BARSCH C1846-1854 JOHANNISBERG &
DOEHLAU, OPR, GER [34083]

BARSHAM C1740 GRIMSTON, SFK, ENG [37321]

BARSTOW 1600-1750 YKS, ENG [34513] : 1840+
HELENA, WI, USA [34205]

BARTA PRE 1850 ZICI & ZITEC, JINDRICHUV,
HRADEC, CS [38461]

BARTEL C1820 PA, USA [38177]

BARTELL ALL DINGO, QLD, AUS [35118] : PRE 1880
GER [35118] : ALL KNICHHAGEN, HES, GER
[38237] : 1900+ NJ, USA [36320]

BARTELMEI ALL KAHOKA, MO, USA [35618]

BARTELS 1559-1652 HANNOVER, NSA, GER [38750] :
1700+ BEULAKE, OIJ, NL [35338]

BARTELT 1850S HAN, GER [36952] : 1866+ QUINCY,
ADAMS CO., IL, USA [36952]

BARTENS ALL EDDINGAUSEN, NSA, GER [38637] :
ALL WILFINGEN, NSA, GER [38637]

BARTENSCHLAG 1600 SCHWAIGERN, WUE, GER
[38574]

BARTER PRE 1850 KINGSKERSWELL, DEV, ENG
[34266] : PRE 1900 MDX, ENG [36893]

BARTH 1500S LIXHEIM, ALS & LOR, FRA [38659] :
1700-1800 ERFURT, PSA, GER [38643] : PRE 1800
SCHWIEBERDINGEN, WUE, GER [38681] :
C1835+ NEW YORK, NY, USA [38182] : 1830+
BUFFALO, NY, USA [38659] : 1830+ COLUMBUS,
OH, USA [38659]

BARTHLATE 1650-1750 FIF, SCT [35627]

BARTHOLEMEW C1821 BRISTOL, SOM, ENG [35336]

BARTHOLOMEW C1890+ OLD JUNEE, NSW, AUS
[35230] : 1850S+ ORANGE, NSW, AUS [35557] : PRE
1840 LONDON, ENG [34795] : C1837
ALVERSTOKE, HAM, ENG [35515] : 1800S
HIGHGATE, LND, ENG [36055] : 1880+
GRAVESEND, KEN, ENG [36704] : PRE 1900
GRAVESEND, KEN, ENG [37423] : 1840+
STEPNEY, MDX, ENG [37904] : 1800 PORTER CO.,
IN, USA [38240] : ALL WORLDWIDE [36235]

BARTLE 1860 HALIFAX, WRY, ENG [34957] : PRE
1800 COCKAYNE HATLEY, BDF, ENG [37729] :
1880+ STOCKTON ON TEES & KINGS LYNN,
NFK, ENG [38541] : 1880+ PETERBOROUGH,
CAM, ENG [38541] : 1830+ BLAENAVON, MON,
WLS [36614]

BARTLES 1790-1850 STEUBEN CO., NY, USA [38129]

BARTLESON C1815-80 ZARNGLAFF, POM, GER
[38309]

BARTLET PRE 1825 HARDINGTON, SOM, ENG
[37067] : PRE 1770 OXF, ENG [37739] : PRE 1888
GER [35280]

BARTLETON C1815-80 ZARNGLAFF, POM, GER
[38309]

BARTLETT 1850+ GEELONG, VIC, AUS [34542] :
1843+ LONGFORD, TAS, AUS [34910] : 1840-1900
HINTON & MORPETH, NSW, AUS [35395] :
JOSHUA 1800S ENFIELD, NSW, AUS [35513] :
1700+ ISLE OF WIGHT, HAM, ENG [33802] :
1850+ STOURBRIDGE, WOR, ENG [34323] : 1800+
YEOVIL, SOM, ENG [34597] : PRE 1816
FARNINGHAM, KEN, ENG [34911] : PRE 1850
BRACKNELL, BRK, ENG [34958] : ALL MDX,
ENG [35115] : ALICE 1874+ WOKINGHAM, BRK,
ENG [35154] : FREDERICK C1860 WOKINGHAM,
BRK, ENG [35154] : 1800S CHEDWORTH, GLS,
ENG [35256] : 1680S BRIGHTON, SSX, ENG [35259]
: 1800+ EAST CHINNOCK, SOM, ENG [35395] :
C1830 PLYMOUTH, DEV, ENG [35747] : ALL
BIGBURY, DEV, ENG [35989] : C1795 KYRE, WOR,
ENG [36109] : PRE 1900 KINGSTON & THAMES

DITTON, SRY, ENG [36245] : 1750-1800
WESTMINSTER, MDX, ENG [36388] : PRE 1850
ASKERSWELL, DOR, ENG [36424] : PRE 1823
PRESTON, HAM, ENG [36650] : 1814+ BRISTOL,
GLS, ENG [36995] : 1718+ BROADWINDSOR,
DOR, ENG [36995] : 1806+ KEYNSHAM, SOM,
ENG [36995] : PRE 1800 DOVER, KEN, ENG [37069]
: 1700-1800 BROADWINDSOR, DOR, ENG [37222] :
PRE 1850 NETHER HEYFORD, NTH, ENG [37357]
: ALL SUTTON NEXT DOVER, KEN, ENG [37714] :
ALL LITTLE MONGEHAM, KEN, ENG [37714] :
1600+ TAUNTON, SOM, ENG [37843] : PRE 1840
BUCKINGHAM, BKM, ENG [38002] : C1861
BIRMINGHAM, ENG [38450] : 1860+ ABD, SCT
[35847] : SILENCE 1760S-1839 HERKIMER CO., NY
& CT, USA [36319] : PRE 1750 ESSEX CO., MA, USA
[37808] : 1870+ JEFFERSON CO., CO, USA [38310] :
1850+ APPLE RIVER & GALENA, IL, USA [38343] :
1830-1853 PIKE, MO, USA [38576] : PRE 1830 VA,
USA [38576]

BARTLEY 1700S LONDON, ENG [34188] : 1700+
HAMBROOK, GLS, ENG [34908] : PRE 1841
LONDON, ENG & AUS [38585] : ALL TX, USA
[37933] : ROBERT 1776+ VA & NC, USA [37933] :
1700+ DEN, WLS [36009]

BARTO PRE 1900 CLEARFIELD CO., PA, USA [38218]

BARTOL PRE 1720 MARBLEHEAD, MA, USA [37049]

BARTOLD ADAM PRE 1635 ILSENBURG,
BRAUNSCHWEIG, GER [38563] : ADAM 1634-1672
SKULTUNA, VASTMAULAND, SWE [38563]

BARTON DANIEL 1858+ SYDNEY, NSW, AUS
[34449] : PRE 1870 LONDON, ENG [33957] : PRE
1870 BEXLEYHEATH & WILMINGTON, KEN,
ENG [33957] : 1800S LONDON, ENG [34937] :
GEORGE C1800+ LONG SUTTON, LIN, ENG
[35834] : GEORGE C1870+ SUTTON BRIDGE, LIN,
ENG [35834] : SAMUEL PRE 1810 HANDSWORTH,
STS, ENG [36374] : PRE 1800 KEN, ENG [36993] :
1830+ DEAL, KEN, ENG [36993] : PRE 1850
BLACKBURN & BURNLEY, LAN, ENG [37246] :
ALL KEN, ENG [38037] : 1790+ HADLOW, KEN,
ENG [38209] : 1700S WINCHESTER, HAM, ENG
[38358] : MARGARET 1820+ WISBECH, CAM &
NFK, ENG & AUS [33840] : 1750-1860 FER, IRL
[34392] : PRE 1858 ST JOHN'S, LIMERICK, LIM,
IRL [34449] : PRE 1625 KIK, IRL [37473] : WILLIAM
C1840 GLASGOW, SCT [35120] : 1830-40 ERIE CO.,
PA, USA [36582] : 1818+ CAYUGA, NY & IA, USA
[36582] : 1920-1930S NYC, NY, USA [36936] : DAVID
1850+ CALHOUN CO., MS, USA [37004] : PRICE
1890+ MO, USA [37004] : 1650-1750 SALEM, MA,
USA [37538] : 1800-1920 WAUSHARA CO., WI, USA
[38154] : 1800-1850 ZANESVILLE, OH, USA [38154] :
1850-1900 BERLIN, WI, USA [38154] : ABRAM 1822-
1919 LINCOLN CO., MO, USA [38187]

BARTOSZEWICZ 1895-1934 WARSAW, POL [34063]

BARTRAM 1810+ BUCKMINSTER, LEI, ENG [37360]

BARTSCH ALL WORLDWIDE [38666]

BARWICK 1700+ STEPNEY, LND, ENG [34747] :
PRE 1900 GREAT MONGEHAM, KEN, ENG
[35577] : PRE 1792 SUDBURY, SFK, ENG [35926] :
ALL LND, ENG [36288] : C1850 RIPON, YKS, ENG
[38168] : ALL NC, SC & GA, USA [38340] : 1600-1700
MD, USA [38340]

BARWISE PRE 1833 LIVERPOOL, LAN, ENG [34412]
: ALL CUL, ENG [35293]

BARZYKOWSKI ALL TACOMA, WA, USA [37041]

BASELEY C1832 BLETCHINGDON, OXF, ENG
[34281]

BASFORD PRE 1890 KIDDERMINSTER, WOR, ENG
[34605]

BASHAM 1855+ TAREE & YOUNG, NSW, AUS
[33763] : PRE 1855 POSLINGFORD, SFK, ENG
[33763]

BASHFORD 1794-1870S NUTFIELD & COULSDON,
SRY, ENG [33865] : PRE 1890 KIDDERMINSTER,
WOR, ENG [34605] : PRE 1923 MIDDLESBROUGH,
NRY, ENG [36028] : PRE 1842 REIGATE, SRY,
ENG [38568] : 1904+ SAN FRANCISCO, CA, USA
[38568]

BASKEN 1783+ IRL [35615]

BASKERFIELD 1600+ DEV, ENG [37356]

BASKERVILLE 1800-1900 CARLETON CO., ONT,
CAN [34199] : 1900+ OLDHAM, LAN, ENG [36568] :
1700 CHS, ENG [36568] : 1600+ DEV, ENG [37356]

BASKET 1700+ NORWICH, NFK, ENG [35403]

BASKETT ELLEN ANN PRE 1920 PORTSMOUTH &
LANDPORT, HAM, ENG [36646]

BASKIN 1817-50 STRABANE, TYR, IRL [35615] : PRE
1808 KILMACTHOMAS, WAT, IRL [35738] : PRE
1913 DUBLIN, DUB, LET & DOW, IRL [35738]

BASNETT 1780 DE, USA [36446] : 1795
MONONGALIA CO., VA, USA [36446] : 1793
ALLEGANY CO., MD, USA [36446]

BASON 1830-1873 BRILEY HILL, STS, ENG [37975] :
ALL WORLDWIDE [38429]

BASS C1800+ LUTON, BDF & HRT, ENG [34451] :
PRE 1800 EXETER, DEV, ENG [34809] : PRE 1800
WHEPSTEAD, SFK, ENG [35391] : 100S BDF, ENG
[36005] : 1800+ STANFORD LE HOPE, ESS, ENG
[37885] : ALL ESS, ENG [37973] : SAMUEL 1600S
BRAINTREE, MA, USA [37025] : 1800
LANCASTER, NH, USA [38131]

BASSEN C1680 GER [38598]

BASSETT 1836+ TAS, AUS [36299] : PRE 1822 DEV,
ENG [34417] : 1775-1840 TETCOTT, DEV, ENG
[34804] : 1737+ BRIDGERULE, DEV, ENG [34804] :
PRE 1819 MARGATE, KEN, ENG [34844] : 1750+
MAIDSTONE, KEN, ENG [35370] : 1873 ASTON,
WAR, ENG [35855] : 1800S LONDON, ENG [35984] :
1690+ OLD SWINFORD, WOR & WAR, ENG
[36326] : 1800-1910 LEICESTER, LEI, ENG [37858] :
1580-1632 GLOUCESTER, ENG [38151] : 1900
BROCKWORTH, GLS, ENG [38213] : PRE 1800
HINTS & DRAYTON, STS, ENG & IRL [38754] :
PRE 1730 INCH, DOW, IRL [34895] : PRE 1836 IRL
[36299] : C1700 LITTLE DUNKELD, PER, SCT
[37918]

BASSFORD PRE 1890 KIDDERMINSTER, WOR,
ENG [34605]

BASSINGTON C1800 SYDNEY, NSW, AUS [36225] :
C1690 BISHOPSGATE, LND, ENG [36225] : 1400-
1850 CAMBERWELL, SRY, ENG [36225] : C1700
WANDSWORTH, SRY, ENG [36225] : PRE 1850
PLUMSTEAD, KEN, ENG [36225] : PRE 1800
HOXTON, MDX, ENG [36225]

BASSTIAN 1823+ HOBART, TAS, AUS [36855] : PRE
1823 LONDON, ENG [36855]

BASTABLE 1875+ GILLINGHAM, DOR, ENG [34045]
: 1875+ MARNHULL & BRIDPORT, DOR, ENG
[34045] : PRE 1900 SOUTHWARK, SRY, ENG [34335]

BASTARD 1680-1740 LANTEGLOS BY
CAMELFORD, CON, ENG [34448] : PRE 1850
SHEERNESS, KEN, ENG [34725] : 1775
MICHAELSTOWE, CON, ENG [34950]

BASTIAN 1860+ FRYERS CREEK, VIC, AUS [34289] :
PRE 1800 NORDHAUSEN, ERF, DDR [38617] :
1750-1850 REIMERSWILLER, ALS, FRA [36898]

BASTIN 1900S SYDNEY, NSW, AUS [35752] : 1900+
MELBOURNE, VIC, AUS [35752] : 1790-1840 NEAR
BRISTOL, SOM, ENG [34123] : 1800-1860 GLS, ENG
[34123]

BASTINGS 1831+ ISLINGTON, LND, ENG [34668]

BASTOCK GEORGE 1780 ST MARYS, WAR, ENG [36782] : 1849-91 BIRMINGHAM, WAR, ENG [37860]

BATACLAN PRE 1873 NAIC, CAVITE, PHILIPPINE [34891]

BATARD C1700 DARDAGNY & GENEVA, GE, CH [38348]

BATCHELAR 1800+ LONDON, ENG [34547] : 1700+ SOUTH HACKNEY, MDX, ENG [34547]

BATCHELDER ANN 1600 HACKNEY, LND, ENG [35276] : 1800-1850S TROY & KINGFIELD, ME, USA [36944]

BATCHELDOR 1860+ OBERON, NSW, AUS [37556] : 1799-1860 RADFORD SEMELE & CUBBINGTON, WAR, ENG [37556] : 1770-1806+ MARTON & RADFORD SEMELE, WAR, ENG [37556]

BATCHELOR 1700-1800 TUDELEY & CAPEL, KEN, ENG [33785] : PRE 1900 TONBRIDGE, KEN, ENG [36021] : WILLIAM 1685+ TRING & WIGGINGTON, HRT, ENG [36068] : WILLIAM 1850S HESTON & ISLEWORTH, MDX, ENG [36068] : JOHN 1765-1774 REDBOURN & HARPENDEN, HRT, ENG [36068] : ELIZABETH 1765+ HARPENDEN, HRT, ENG [36068] : JOHN 1840S RICHMOND, SRY, ENG [36068] : HICKMAN 1857+ ISLEWORTH, MDX, ENG [36068] : ALL LND & SRY, ENG [36846] : 1700+ WARMINGTON, WAR, ENG [37304] : ALL KEN, ENG [37407] : PRE 1842 BRADFORD ON AVON, WIL, ENG & NZ [35940] : 1800S GA, USA [37004]

BATE WILLIAM ALL OLD SWINFORD, WOR, ENG [33892] : 1700+ HARBOROUGH MAGNA, WAR, ENG [34054] : 1600 HACKNEY, LND, ENG [35276] : 1865-1916 LIVERPOOL, LAN, ENG [35341] : 1830 CROFT, LAN, ENG [35341] : 1870+ ECCLESTON, LAN, ENG [35341] : C1700-50 GARBALDISHAM, NFK, ENG [35490] : 1695+ HELLAND, CON, ENG [35587] : ALL KEN & SSX, ENG [36413] : 1799+ ST AUSTELL & CARDINHAM, CON, ENG [36961] : THOMAS C1680 ENG [37168] : 1700-1900 BROMSGROVE, WOR, ENG [37257] : 1900+ BIRMINGHAM, AL, USA [35341]

BATEMAN 1852+ HASTINGS CO., ONT, CAN [34153] : PRE 1881 LEAMINGTON, WAR, ENG [34031] : MARY PRE 1788 MDX, ENG [35877] : 1750+ CON, WRY & SRY, ENG [36058] : WILLIAM 1800+ STEPNEY, LND, ENG [36068] : HARRIET 1820-1846 STEPNEY, LND, ENG [36068] : 1890+ NOTTINGHAM, NTT, ENG [36105] : 1880+ BRADFORD, WRY, ENG [36624] : C1850 WALSALL, STS, ENG [36649] : PRE 1780 ST BRIDGETS BECKERMET, CUL, ENG [36701] : 1830 BRISTOL, GLS, ENG [36860] : 1830-1900 STAPLETON, GLS, ENG [37058] : 1570-1830 BITTON & MANGOTSFIELD, GLS, ENG [37058] : PRE 1852 CORK, COR, IRL [34153] : ALL LOG, IRL [35628] : ROWLAND PRE 1700 KILLEEN, ARM, IRL [36880] : 1874+ CHRISTCHURCH & NELSON, NZ [33823] : 1650 CT, USA [36730]

BATES 1890+ MOONAMBEL, VIC, AUS [34174] : 1868+ KANGAROO VALLEY, NSW, AUS [34273] : PRE 1860 NSW, AUS [34880] : 1856+ MUDGEE & DUBBO, NSW, AUS [34978] : WILLIAM 1855+ BLACKTOWN, NSW, AUS [35874] : 1800-1900 QUE, CAN [33753] : C1829 HANDSWORTH, W MID, ENG [33880] : THOMAS 1853-1932 MANCHESTER, LAN, ENG [33892] : PRE 1830 WYCOMBE, BKM, ENG [34131] : PRE 1830 GRENDON, NTH, ENG [34197] : C1800 LIVERPOOL, LAN, ENG [34556] : PRE 1847 ALBURY, OXF, ENG [34815] : ALL BLOOMSBURY & HOLBORN, LND, ENG [34820] : PRE 1900 LND & KEN, ENG [34848] : PRE 1856 ENG [34978] : 1800+ ROCHDALE, LAN, ENG

[35342] : PRE 1812 HUDDERSFIELD, WRY, ENG [35733] : 1809 ALMONDBURY, WRY, ENG [35733] : 1776+ STAFFORD, STS, ENG [35737] : PRE 1800 WISBECH, CAM, ENG [35802] : 1700S SHIPDAM, NFK, ENG [35858] : 1700+ DRAYTON PARSLOW, BKM, ENG [35874] : ALL ENG [35901] : 1700-1800 ROTHWELL, NTH, ENG [36057] : PRE 1860 HEADCORN, KEN, ENG [36067] : ELIZABETH 1775-1825 CHESHAM, BKM, ENG [36100] : ALL KEN & SSX, ENG [36413] : THOMAS C1680 ENG [37168] : 1700-1800 NFK, ENG [37207] : 1800S LIVERPOOL, LAN, ENG [37221] : 1800-1900 ISLINGTON, MDX, ENG [37222] : PRE 1815 DOVER, KEN, ENG [37371] : PRE 1760 BKM, ENG [37498] : PRE 1760 LEEDS, YKS, ENG [37913] : 1840+ BALLYJAMESDUFF, CAV, IRL [34273] : ALL OMAGH, TYR, IRL [34645] : WILLIAM C. C1820-C1865 NJ, PA & DE, USA [37531] : C1755 SAYBROOK, CT & NY, USA [36319] : JULIA 1860-1870 SMITH CO., MS, USA [36330] : RICHARD 1850-1860 SMITH CO., MS, USA [36330] : 1720 RI, USA [37008] : 1800 ALBEMARLE CO., VA, USA [37027] : 1830S HICKMAN CO., TN, USA [37027] : WM. G.W. 1830-1891 HAMILTON CO., OH, USA [37797] : JOHN 1820+ HAMILTON CO., OH, USA [37797] : WM. G.W. 1800-1830 BUTLER CO., OH, USA [37797] : PRE 1814 NJ, USA [37797] : 1840-1870 KNOX CO., TN, USA [38144] : ALL WORLDWIDE [38429]

BATES-CROSS 1800+ BREEDON ON THE HILL, LEI, ENG [35851]

BATESON C1854 SALISBURY, VIC, AUS [35748] : 1893+ ROSEDALE, VIC, AUS [35748] : 1800S LEEDS, YKS, ENG [34845] : 1650-1800 CRAGG, LAN & YKS, ENG [35624] : C1712 FOXTON, CAM, ENG [35748] : ALL WORTLEY, WRY, ENG [36159] : ALL WORLDWIDE [38429]

BATEY PRE 1870 BLAYDON, DUR, ENG [34197]

BATH 1844 WALCHA, NSW, AUS [36640] : PRE 1600 WIL, ENG [34707] : WILLIAM 1825-1888 MORWELLHAM, DEV, ENG [34888] : 1800-1840 MYLOR, CON, ENG [35192] : 1800-1840 MADRON, CON, ENG [35192] : PRE 1840 KEN, ENG [36480] : ALL KEN, ENG [37371] : 1571+ WENDRON, CON, ENG [37975] : ALL KEN, ENG [38265] : ALL ANSTY, WIL, ENG [38489] : CHARLES C1830 EBBESBOURNE WAKE, WIL, ENG [38489]

BATHE PRE 1850 ADDERBURY, OXF, ENG [34611]

BATHER ALL SAL, ENG [34671] : PRE 1720 WALSALL & WOLVERHAMPTON, STS, ENG [36110]

BATHERIDGE PRE 1700 UK [36210]

BATHGATE 1837-1856 NEWTOWN & WARATAH, NSW, AUS [38761] : C1831 LONG GULLY, SCT [35384] : PRE 1700 ELN, SCT [36679] : 1797-1837 EDINBURGH, SCT [38761]

BATHIE PRE 1840 INDIA [36102]

BATHRIDGE PRE 1700 UK [36210]

BATINO PRE 1900 JANINA, CAIRO, GREECE [36455]

BATISTE 1870+ MOONTA, SA, AUS [35847] : PRE 1864 ST SAMPSONS, GSY, CHI [35575] : 1730+ ST PETER PORT, GSY, CHI [35847]

BATKIN 1830+ BATHURST & MURRINGO, NSW, AUS [33763] : PRE 1830 BIRMINGHAM, WAR, ENG [33763]

BATRIDGE PRE 1700 UK [36210]

BATSFORD 1700S GREAT HALLINGBURY, ESS, ENG [37250]

BATSON 1845+ ADELAIDE, SA, AUS [38209] : 1825 KETTERING, NTH, ENG [37151] : 1830 BUCKLAND, BRK, ENG [38209] : 1775-1800 COLUMBIA CO., GA, USA [38088]

BATT 1870+ MORUYA, NSW, AUS [34977] : 1850-1925 BETHNAL GREEN, MDX, ENG [34242] : 1800S HAM, ENG [35136] : 1850+ HAM, LND & SRY, ENG [35362] : 1760-1810 BENNINGTON, VT, USA [37591]

BATTARD PRE 1830 FRAULAUTERN, SAA, GER & FRA [38681]

BATTEN ALL LEFROY, TAS, AUS [34301] : C1860 MOGGILL & NERANG, QLD, AUS [34807] : ALL ENG [34301] : PRE 1850 BRISTOL, GLS, ENG [35215] : 1770+ STOKE DAMEREL, DEV, ENG [37317] : 1800 PENZANCE, CON, ENG [38756] : 1836 MI, USA [37531] : 1860 WAUPACA CO., WI, USA [37531] : 1842 WOOD CO., WI, USA [37531] : 1812 VT, USA [37531] : 1812 NY, USA [37531]

BATTERBY ALL BURNHAM THORPE, NFK, ENG [38411]

BATTERIDGE PRE 1700 UK [36210]

BATTERMANN 1700+ BREMEN, BRM, GER & BRD [35062]

BATTERSBY PRE 1840 LIMEHOUSE, LND, ENG [34612] : C1813 GREENWICH, KEN, ENG [35865] : 1800-1850 LND, ENG [37084] : 1700S IRL [34570] : ALL UK [36020]

BATTERSHELL 1750-1860 ENG [35136] : 1780-1880 BOURBON CO., KY & IL, USA [36901]

BATTERSON 1835-1860 MACLEAY RIVER, NSW, AUS [38007]

BATTESBY 1800-1900 ONT, CAN [34135]

BATTEY 1730-1885 WADWORTH, WRY, ENG [37860]

BATTIN 1775-1800 LAWHITTON, CON, ENG [34337]

BATTINGER 1700+ RPR, GER [38765]

BATTISHELL 1550+ SOUTH TAWTON, DEV, ENG [34747]

BATTISSON 1700+ BRAFIELD ON GREEN, NTH, ENG [34265]

BATTLE 1840+ LIVERPOOL, LAN, ENG [34566] : PRE 1820 SLIGO, SLI, IRL [34566]

BATTLEY 1800+ MENDLESHAM, SFK, ENG [34863] : 1730-1800 GAZELEY, SFK, ENG [35094] : PRE 1850 NFK, ENG [37773]

BATTLY PRE 1760 REDGRAVE, SFK, ENG [37420]

BATTRIDGE PRE 1700 UK [36210]

BATTS ALL HAMBLEDON, HAM, ENG [36405] : ALL WORLDWIDE [36023]

BATTY 1788-1800 SYDNEY, NSW, AUS [36293] : PRE 1865 ASTBURY, CHS, ENG [34578] : PRE 1850 HALIFAX, WRY, ENG [36037] : PRE 1800 MDX, ENG [36293] : PRE 1820 DONCASTER & SHEFFIELD, YKS, ENG [36589] : PRE 1840 SHIREOAKS, NTT, ENG [36854] : PRE 1730 SILKSTONE, WRY, ENG [37754]

BATY 1800+ CARLISLE, CUL, ENG [34243]

BAUDIN (SEE BEAUDIN) [36678]

BAUDRY PRE 1830 ANDERLECHT, BRUSSELS, BEL [33821]

BAUER 1854+ GRAFTON & GLEN INNES, NSW, AUS [34185] : 1865+ MARYBOROUGH, QLD, AUS [35878] : 1865+ BLACKALL, QLD, AUS [35878] : PRE 1710 AUERBACH, HES, BRD [35311] : C1850 ST MARYLEBONE, LND, ENG [35494] : PRE 1840 ALS, FRA [38029] : PRE 1860 WUE, GER [35297] : 1780-1850 WURTHEIM, BAD, GER [35494] : 1700+ NECKARSULM, BAD, GER [35566] : PRE 1865 BAV, GER [35878] : PRE 1840 HEPPENHEIM & KOLMBACH, HES, GER [38029] : PRE 1820 BAV, GER [38191] : C1800-1850 BAV, GER [38325] : 1815-1865 MEHLEM, RPR, GER [38528] : 1885+ SPOKANE, WA, USA [34159] : 1839+ HAMILTON CO., OH, USA [37797]

BAUERLE 1863+ CLINTON CO., MI, USA [35287]

BAUERLY 1830-1837 BAW, GER [35287] : 1837+ HILLSDALE CO., MI, USA [35287]

BAUERNFEIND PRE 1856 ALTEN-BUSECK, HES, GER [33824]

BAUERSOX 1730-1800 BERKS CO., PA, USA [35318]

BAUGH 1900+ JSY, CHI [38298] : PRE 1850 MADELEY, SAL, ENG [36188] : JOHN 1872+ DAWLEY, SAL, ENG & AUS [35794] : ALL USA [36896] : ALL WORLDWIDE [37382]

BAUGHAN 1800+ WOODSTOCK, OXF, ENG [37040] : 1789+ SALFORD, OXF, ENG [37380]

BAUGHMAN PRE 1850 BADEN BADEN, BAW, BRD [37565]

BAULAND C1796 RECKLINGHAUSEN, NRW, GER [38711]

BAULCH 1780+ MUCHELNEY, SOM, ENG [37905]

BAULD 1857+ LATROBE, TAS, AUS [36644] : PRE 1857 LEITH, MDL, SCT [36644]

BAULIG 1870+ ONEIDA, NY, USA [38111]

BAULLINGER 1800-1850S ALS, FRA [37548] : 1800-1850S ELO, GER [37548]

BAUM 1743-1900 WESTMORELAND CO., PA, OH & IN, USA [36901]

BAUMAN 1840+ ROSS CO., OH, USA [37565]

BAUMANN PRE 1840 OPR, PRE & WPR, GER [38176] : 1890 PA, USA [37605]

BAUMBACH EMMA AMELIA 1853-1891 PHILADELPHIA, PA, USA [38124]

BAUMEISTER PRE 1840 OPR, PRE & WPR, GER [38176]

BAUMER 1830+ LA & OH, USA [37532]

BAUMGARTEN PRE 1860 HAMBURG, HBG, GER [35818] : ALL GER [38037]

BAUMGARTNER 1800S OENSINGEN, SO, CH [36896] : PRE 1810 ROTHRIST, AG, CH [38029] : PRE 1870 ZURICH, ZH, CH [38125] : PRE 1750 SCHEPPACH, WUE, GER [35242] : 1790+ RPF, GER & CH [37534]

BAUMLE 1850-1895 WI, USA [36542]

BAUR PRE 1840 UNTERJESINGEN, WUE, GER [37587]

BAUST C1765 NUSSLOCH, BAD, GER [34239]

BAUTOVICH 1800S OES [38281] : PRE 1867 GUILIANAH, WIE, OES & AUS [33840]

BAUTSHER C1828-1882 QUE, CAN [35284] : C1829-1882 FRANKLIN CO., VT, USA [35284]

BAVERSTOCK 1800S WOOLVERTON, SOM, ENG [33958] : 1800-1864 WIMBOURNE, DOR, ENG [35407]

BAVINGTON 1813 MINSTER, KEN, ENG [34808]

BAVINS PRE 1820 HELIONS BUMPSTEAD, ESS, ENG [37913]

BAVINTON 1851+ CHEWTON, VIC, AUS [34808]

BAVISTER PRE 1800 CAM, ENG [34324]

BAVISTOCK ALL AUS [34961]

BAWCUTT 1780+ BURTON DASSETT, WAR, ENG [34677]

BAWDEN PRE 1900 COOLGARDIE, WA, AUS [37111] : PRE 1870 HELSTON, CON, ENG [34750] : 1750-1816 ST STITHIANS, CON, ENG [34343] : PRE 1840 CON, ENG [38004]

BAWDWEN PRE 1800 YKS, ENG [34383]

BAWER PRE 1890 NEW GROMEL, TAS, AUS [36775]

BAX C1800 DORKING, SRY, ENG [36071]

BAXE PRE 1700 OCKLEY, SRY, ENG [36179]

BAXENDALE ALL LAN, ENG [38514]

BAXTER 1800S DROUIN, VIC, AUS [35926] : 1843 GLASGOW, AUS & SCT [36608] : 1850 TRENTON, ONT, CAN [38395] : 1800 DENHOLME, WRY, ENG [34352] : C1800-1830 BIRMINGHAM, WAR, ENG [34548] : WILLIAM 1829 BROMSGROVE, WOR, ENG [34548] : 1750+ DISEWORTH, LEI, ENG [34921] : PRE 1835 SYDERSTONE, NFK, ENG

[35151] : PRE 1840 MORECAMBE, LAN, ENG
[35354] : 1800+ DONNINGTON, ENG [35465] :
1812-1880 BRANCEPETH, DUR, ENG [35706] : 1770-
1800S WOLSINGHAM, DUR, ENG [35706] : 1700-
1770 WRY, ENG [36126] : 1800+ SFK, ENG [36574] :
PRE 1870 LND, ENG [36843] : 1700+ HUN, ENG
[37099] : 1830+ LONDON, ENG [37341] : 1860S
CHELSEA, LND, ENG [37341] : PRE 1850
WISBECH, CAM, ENG [38386] : ALL DONCASTER,
YKS, STS & WAR, ENG [38754] : PRE 1860
KILDRESS, TYR, IRL [35612] : 1600-1800
BANBRIDGE, DOW, IRL [36556] : 1900+
PIETERMARITZBURG, RSA [34029] : 1826+
KILMARTIN, ARL, SCT [33811] : 1854-1903
GLASGOW, LKS, SCT [33811] : JOHN & JENNY
C1855-1880 GLASGOW, LKS, SCT [34369] : 1760+
KILBARCHAN, RFW, SCT [35503] : 1760+
LOCHWINNOCH, RFW, SCT [35503] : PRE 1861
ABERDEEN, ABD, SCT [37315] : JAMES 1808-1830
ADAIR, KY, USA [38157] : 1800S MERTHYR
TYDFIL, GLA, WLS [36961] : JOHN 1810+ (73
REGT), WORLDWIDE [34786]
BAY HUGH 1790-1810 BOURBON, KY, USA [38157]
BAYER C1700 NUSSLOCH, BAD, GER [34239]
BAYES PRE 1830 RAGLAN & MONMOUTH, MON,
WLS [35215]
BAYFORD 1700+ WELWYN, ESS, ENG [34678]
BAYLEE PRE 1760 BRAUNSTON, NTH, ENG [34258]
BAYLES PRE 1910 GORLESTON, NFK, ENG [36486] :
PRE 1900 WORLDWIDE [36933]
BAYLEY PRE 1860 BURNHAM, BKM, ENG [34588] :
PRE 1759 ASHWELL, HRT, ENG [35072] : 1751+
LONGNEY, GLS, ENG [36278] : PRE 1699
HARESFIELD, GLS, ENG [36278] : 1800S
MANCHESTER, LAN, ENG [36292] : 1750-1815
SMEETH & BRABOURNE, KEN, ENG [37069] :
1600-1760 SOM, ENG [37232] : PRE 1900
BIRMINGHAM, ENG [37245] : 1750 SHOBDEN,
HEF, ENG [37928] : 1700+ WIGAN, LAN, ENG
[38046] : 1840 HAWKHURST, KEN, ENG [38719] :
1820 SSX, ENG [38719] : 1835+ FLINT, FLN, WLS
[36761]
BAYLIE PRE 1608 KEN, ENG [36589]
BAYLIS 1750-1850 WOR, ENG [34615] : 1800+
TIBBERTON, WOR, ENG [34677] : 1700-1800
SOMERTON, OXF, ENG [37763] : PRE 1800 TYSOE,
WAR, ENG [37832] : PRE 1800 HRT, ENG [38746]
BAYLISS 1700-1900 OXF, ENG [34236] : 1700-1900
BRK, BKM & GLS, ENG [34236] : 1700-1900 LAN &
NTH, ENG [34236] : 1848-1870 BIRMINGHAM,
WAR, ENG [34355] : 1879+ MANCHESTER, LAN,
ENG [34355] : 1800S HRT, ENG [34684] : ALL
LONDON, ENG [36174] : PRE 1810 BIRMINGHAM,
WAR, ENG [36177] : PRE 1850 WORCESTER, WOR,
ENG [37067] : PRE 1800 MARTLEY, WOR, ENG
[38420]
BAYLOR PRE 1820 BALLYARTHUR & FERMOY,
COR, IRL [35713]
BAYLY 1866+ SOUTHAMPTON, HAM, ENG [33945] :
C1650-C1799 HURST & WOKINGHAM, BRK, ENG
[36425] : SEGATIA 1860S+ DEV, ENG [37317] :
1850+ ENG & NZ [34571] : 1850S TULLAMORE,
OFF, IRL [35398] : C1798+ NENAGH, TIP, IRL
[35995] : 1886+ TRANSVAAL, RSA [33945] : C1830+
EDINBURGH, MLN, SCT [35995] : 1800S
CANNOCK, STS, SCT [37898]
BAYNE PRE 1870 WAR, ENG [35639] : 1860 GAL, IRL
[35325] : C1800 MUTHILL, PER, SCT [37512]
BAYNES 1870+ MUNGINDI, NSW, AUS [35160] :
PRE 1860 EGTON CUM NEWLAND &
ULVERSTON, LAN & CUL, ENG [36082] : PRE 1700
ST ANDREWS, FIF, SCT [35227]

BAYNHAM 1810-1868 MDX & BKM, ENG [33822] :
ALL YATE, GLS, ENG [37154]
BAYSTON PRE 1790 CRAYKE, YKS, ENG [37288]
BAYTHROP PRE 1900 PRIEST HUTTON & BOLTON,
LAN, ENG [36508]
BAZELEY PRE 1890 MORETON PINKNEY, NTH,
ENG [35962]
BAZELY PRE 1855 GREAT YARMOUTH, NFK, ENG
[35956]
BAZIN PRE 1700 CHI, ENG [38021]
BAZLEY 1700+ DEV, ENG [37818] : 1900S PA, USA
[37818]
BEACH 1700-1850 GLS, ENG [37064] : PRE 1850
GOODRICH, HEF, ENG [37561] : MOSES C1710-
1790 MORRISTOWN, NJ, USA [37813] : PRE 1830
MENDHAM, NJ, USA [38112]
BEACHER PRE 1789 SELBORNE, HAM, ENG [35247]
BEACHING ALL WORLDWIDE [37880]
BEACHLER ALL WORLDWIDE [36540]
BEACOM PRE 1860 ENNISKILLEN, FER, IRL [34962]
: JOHN PRE 1847 WESTMORELAND CO., PA,
USA [36448]
BEADEN 1770-1840 PLYMOUTH, DEV, ENG [34747] :
1840+ LONDON, ENG [34747] : 1600-1800 PAUL &
MYLOR, CON, ENG [34747]
BEADLE C1800 SPITALFIELDS, LND, ENG [37053] :
1874 KA, USA [35325] : 1849 MI, USA [35325] : 1828
NY, USA [35325] : 1880 RINGGOLD CO., IA, USA
[35325]
BEADLES 1700-1780 VA, USA [36911]
BEADMAN WILLOUGHBY 1840+ SYDNEY &
PADDYS RIVER, NSW, AUS [38006] : PRE 1828
ENG [37131]
BEADON 1770+ SOM, ENG [34804]
BEADRY 1600+ PCH, FRA [37479]
BEAGLEY 1800+ KEN, SRY & HAM, ENG [36871] :
1870+ DUNEDIN, OTAGO, NZ [36871]
BEAHAN 1800S SOUTH CREEK, NSW, AUS [37500]
BEAK PRE 1858 SOM, ENG [38577]
BEAL PRE 1850 KEN & DUR, ENG [35620] : 1684+
SKIRPENBECK, ERY, ENG [35996] : MATILDA
C1807 SHEFFIELD, YKS, ENG [37383] : 1900+
WELLINGBOROUGH, NTH, ENG [37437] : 1677-
1700 HINGHAM, MA, USA [35314]
BEALE C1832 BLOXHAM, OXF, ENG [34806] : ALL
CON, ENG [35628] : 1700+ DEV, ENG [37356] :
1800+ MALMSBURY, WIL, ENG [37831] : 1818-
1854 SRY, ENG & AUS [35056]
BEALES PRE 1800 NORWICH, NFK, ENG [35915]
BEALEY PRE 1800 MERTON, DEV, ENG [36011]
BEALL PRE 1800 BRIGSTOCK, NTH, ENG [37392] :
PRE 1900 STAMFORD, LIN, ENG [37392] : 1850+
NEWCASTLE, YKS, ENG [37392] : PRE 1850
OAKHAM, RUT, NTH & LEI, ENG [37392] : 1920+
TYNEMOUTH, NBL & YKS, ENG [37392] : 1900-
1940 STAMFORD, LIN, ENG [37392] : PRE 1700
MD, USA [37587] : 1808 WASHINGTON CO., PA,
USA [37817] : 1680-1720 CHESTER CO., PA, USA
[38119]
BEAM 1790+ BEAMSVILLE, ONT, CAN [38323] :
1500+ ABBEVILLE, SC, AL & AR, USA [36970]
BEAMEN 1730 LANCASTER, MA, USA [38131]
BEAMES 1800S CHEDWORTH, GLS, ENG [35256]
BEAMISH PRE 1860 WARRNAMBOOL, VIC, AUS &
IRL [35758]
BEAMSLEY 1630+ BOSTON, MA, USA [36310]
BEAN 1799+ SYDNEY, NSW, AUS [35089] : C1860
SUNBURY, VIC, AUS [35233] : 1800+
PARRAMATTA, NSW, AUS [38208] : 1802-1843
ANNAPOLIS & DIGBY, NS, CAN [37490] : C1753
NORTH HAYLING, HAM, ENG [35089] : 1700+
YORK, YKS, ENG [35460] : PRE 1818+

BETHERSDEN, KEN, ENG **[35759]** : PRE 1840
BRIGHTON, SSX, ENG **[36361]** : 1700-1800S DEAL
AREA, KEN, ENG **[37714]** : PRE 1799 HAYLING,
HAM, ENG **[38208]** : 1800S WORLDWIDE **[36289]**

BEAR PRE 1850 CHATHAM, KEN, ENG **[36118]** :
1740-1830 CHESTER, PA, USA **[38054]**

BEARD PRE 1856 ESS, ENG **[34886]** : PRE 1750
WESTMINSTER, LND, ENG **[35181]** : C1810 KEN,
ENG **[35541]** : C1800 MINCHINHAMPTON, GLS,
ENG **[35791]** : PRE 1680 ST CLETHER, CON, ENG
[35973] : PRE 1800 GRANTCHESTER, CAM, ENG
[36073] : PRE 1900 EXETER, DEV, ENG **[36998]** :
1800S OH, USA **[38369]**

BEARDMORE ALL STS, ENG **[35994]** : C1820
LAMBETH, SRY, ENG **[38268]** : 1841-1878
GNOSALL & WEDNESBURY, STS, ENG & AUS
[33847]

BEARDSELL ALL LONDON, MDX & SRY, ENG &
CAN **[37452]**

BEARDSLEY 1750+ CRICH, DBY, ENG **[36218]**

BEARDWELL PRE 1845 CAVENDISH & NAYLAND,
SFK, ENG **[34612]**

BEARE 1800+ WEYMOUTH, DOR, ENG **[36435]**

BEARISTO 1800-1850 FRENCH RIVER, PEI, CAN
[34205]

BEARM PRE 1750 SHERIFFS LENCH, WOR, ENG
[38745]

BEARMAN PRE 1850 GREAT WALTHAM, ESS, ENG
[37753]

BEARN 1600-1800 ILSINGTON, DEV, ENG **[36106]**

BEART ALL WORLDWIDE **[35990]**

BEASLAND 1824 HELSTON, CON, ENG **[33929]** : 1856
LONDON, ENG **[33929]**

BEASLEY 1797+ WINDSOR, NSW, AUS **[35410]** :
1869-1877 MATLOCK & WOODSPOINT, VIC, AUS
[36836] : 1836 WALTON ON THE HILL, LAN, ENG
[35119] : 1770+ LEI, ENG **[35410]** : PRE 1900 COR &
SOM, ENG **[35750]** : JOHN PRE 1835 BRK, ENG
[35805] : PRE 1850 BRK, MDX & SRY, ENG **[35846]** :
C1870 BIRMINGHAM, WAR, ENG **[36649]** : 1849-
1860S STONELEIGH & LEMINGTON, WAR, ENG
[36836] : 1790+ LOUGHBOROUGH, LEI, ENG
[38494] : C1812 WILLIAMSON CO., TN, USA **[36354]**
: 1770-1810 WARREN, NC, USA **[37027]** : 1740-1770
AMELIA CO., VA, USA **[37027]** : 1760-1800 VA, USA
[37027] : PRE 1800 CAROLINE CO., VA, USA **[38044]**
: PRE 1850 RUTHERFORD CO., TN, USA **[38743]**

BEATON ALL EUROA, VIC, AUS **[34674]** : 1800S
COATES & WHITTLESEA, CAM, ENG **[35188]** :
PRE 1820 DBY, ENG **[35745]** : ALL EDINBURGH,
SCT **[34674]** : PRE 1880 FYVIE, ABD, SCT **[36792]** :
1780-1830 ROSSKEEN, ROC, SCT **[37628]** : 1830-1900
GLASGOW, LKS, SCT **[37628]** : DAVID 1745-1775
KINTYRE, ARL, SCT **[38123]** : DAVID 1774-1820
NC, USA **[38123]**

BEATSON THOMAS 1830+ ROCHDALE, LAN, ENG
[34247] : ALL WORLDWIDE **[38429]**

BEATTIE PRE 1868 BULLENBALONG, MONARO,
NSW, AUS **[37965]** : PETER & ANN 1879+ EPPING,
VIC, AUS **[38567]** : PRE 1880 BOLTONGATE, CUL,
ENG **[35764]** : 1880+ GOSPORT, HAM, ENG **[36417]**
: PRE 1870 TARMORE, CAV, IRL **[34442]** : 1780+
TYR, IRL **[34863]** : 1800-1850 TYR, IRL **[36240]** :
ELIZABETH J. 1820-75 ENNISKILLEN, FER, IRL
[36890] : PRE 1850 ARDROSSAN, AYR, SCT **[34835]**
: PRE 1853 DFS, SCT **[35035]** : JULIA 1815+ DUN,
ANS, SCT **[36308]** : 1850+ LOCHMABEN &
HODDAM, DFS, SCT **[37175]** : 1850+ ST MUNGO
& DRYFESDALE, DFS, SCT **[37175]** : C1850
GLASGOW, SCT **[37965]** : ALL SCT **[38100]** : ALL
ANS, SCT **[38100]** : PETER PRE 1830+ ERROL,
PER, SCT **[38567]** : 1750-1850 WASHINGTON &

ORANGE CO., NY, USA **[38287]** : PRE 1830
PASSAIC CO., NJ, USA **[38783]** : ALL
WORLDWIDE **[33858]**

BEATTIE (SEE BEATTY) **[37556]**

BEATTY C1860-1940+ OBERON & COWRA, NSW,
AUS **[37556]** : C1750-1880+ KILSKERRY &
TRILLICK, TYR & FER, IRL, AUS & USA **[37556]** :
C1870+ NEW YORK, NY, USA & CAN & IRL
[37556] : C1870+ BOBCAYGEON, ONT & SAS,
CAN & USA **[37556]** : 1800-1830 TYR, IRL **[34476]** :
PRE 1846 IRL **[36417]** : 1870S SLIGO, SLI, IRL
[36417] : PRE 1846 SLIGO & COLLOONEY, SLI, IRL
[36417] : PRE 1800 ARM, IRL **[36417]** : PRE 1911
MAGHERALIN, DOW, IRL **[37892]** : 1700S
LISMOY, LET, IRL **[38054]** : 1900+ YOKOHAMA,
JAPAN **[37556]** : 1874+ GLASGOW, DNB, SCT
[36417] : 1716-1741 YARROW, SEL, SCT **[38117]** :
PRE 1860 USA **[36417]**

BEAUBEIN 1865-1875 KEWEENAW CO., MI, USA
[38010]

BEAUBIER 1850-1980 WALLACEBURG, ONT, CAN
[34257] : 1860-1900 THAMESVILLE, ONT, CAN
[34257]

BEAUCHAMP 1825+ KELSO, NSW, AUS **[35504]** :
PRE 1860 MONTREAL, QUE, CAN **[38033]** : PRE
1850 JSY, CHI **[34117]** : PRE 1817 CHERTSEY, SRY,
ENG **[35090]** : 1780-1850 WESTMINSTER, LND,
ENG **[35495]** : PRE 1817 CHERTSEY, SRY, ENG
[35504] : PRE 1890 HOVE & STANMER, SSX, ENG
[37768] : WILLIAM 1700S LONDON, ENG **[38374]** :
1860+ MI, USA **[38033]** : 1676+ SOMERSET, MO,
USA **[38187]** : WILLIAM 1760-1790 EASTERN
SHORE, MD, USA **[38374]** : WILLIAM 1811-1840
WAYNE CO., IN, USA **[38374]** : WILLIAM 1840+
HUNTINGTON CO., IN, USA **[38374]** : WILLIAM
1790-1810 GUILFORD CO., NC, USA **[38374]**

BEAUCHAMPS (SEE BOSH) **[38287]**

BEAUCHEMIN 1700 CAN **[38493]**

BEAUCLERE ALL WORLDWIDE **[35137]**

BEAUDIN PAUL 1830+ ST EDOUARD, QUE, CAN
[36678] : RENE 1660+ POITIER, PCH, FRA **[36678]**

BEAUDRY 1580-1660 CHEMIRE EN CHARNIE, FRA
[34514] : 1600+ PCH, FRA **[37479]**

BEAUFORD DANIEL 1720 NC, USA **[38122]**

BEAUFORT JOHN 1665 VA, USA **[38122]** : JOHN 1642
VA, USA **[38122]**

BEAUFOU 1000+ BEAUFOUR, NOR, FRA **[35608]**

BEAUFOY ALL ENG **[35608]** : ALL WAR, ENG **[38514]**

BEAUMONT C1855 LIVERPOOL, NSW, AUS **[33898]** :
1865-1880 BLACKWOOD, VIC, AUS **[35793]** : 1750-
1850 WARMFIELD, WRY, ENG **[33916]** : C1750-1850
ALMONDBURY, WRY, ENG **[35151]** : 1800-1840
LEWES & LONDON, SSX, ENG **[35793]** : 1800+
ALMONDBURY, WRY, ENG **[36104]** : 1760-1830
ALMONDBURY, WRY, ENG **[36147]** : 1775-1800
HOLMFIRTH, YKS, ENG **[36345]** : PRE 1790
STONE EASTON, SOM, ENG **[36779]** : GEORGE
C1700-1800 MARSDEN & ALMONBURY, WRY,
ENG **[37372]** : 1800+ WELTON, LIN, ENG **[37448]** :
C1870 HULL, ERY, ENG **[37856]** : PRE 1890
HARTSHEAD, YKS, ENG & NZ **[36840]** : 1700-1800
HEF, SAL & RAD, ENG & WLS **[36003]** : 1850-1900
BALLYMENA, ANT, IRL **[35187]**

BEAUNE 1600-1680 MONTLUCON, FRA **[34514]**

BEAUTRON 1750-1802 QUE, CAN **[34482]**

BEAUVAIS 1560-1640 MORTAGNE & PERCHE, BN,
FRA **[34514]** : 1800 LORIENT, FRA **[36596]** : ALL
WORLDWIDE **[36596]**

BEAVAN 1800-1900 WEOBLEY, HEF, ENG **[37074]**

BEAVER 1880+ WEST MELBOURNE, VIC, AUS
[34430] : C1841 NORTH, ENG **[35120]** : 1800+

BOLTON & CHORLEY, LAN, ENG [36198] : C1700-1800 DOWNHAM, LAN, ENG [36198]

BEAVERS 1700-1899 SHANMOY, TYR, IRL [36080]

BEAVES 1700-1800 SOUTHAMPTON, HAM, ENG [36025]

BEAVIN 1700-1850 ALDBOURNE, WIL, ENG [34343]

BEAVINGTON 1800-1900 CHIPPING NORTON, GLS, ENG [35166]

BEAVIS 1857 SMITHFIELD, NSW, AUS [34595] : 1840-1860 BULLEEN, VIC, AUS [35717] : 1850 TEXAS, QLD, AUS [35756] : 1850 MAITLAND, NSW, AUS [35756] : 1830+ CLARENCETOWN, TAS, AUS [35756] : 1750+ BROADHEMPSTON, DEV, ENG [34700] : ALL BEDMINSTER & BRISTOL, GLS, ENG [35391] : 1800-1850 COWLINGE, SFK, ENG [35717] : PRE 1800 GODSHILL, IOW, ENG [38700]

BEAZLEY 1900+ MELBOURNE, VIC, AUS [34568] : PRE 1850 RYDE, HAM, ENG [33799] : ALL SOUTHAMPTON, HAM, ENG [36536]

BEBB 1840+ LONDON, ENG [34810]

BEBBINGTON ALL STS, ENG [35218] : 1733 OVER ST CHAD, CHS, ENG [35282]

BECHER 1500+ LND, KEN & BDF, ENG [34109] : 1700+ BENGAL ARMY & EICS, INDIA [34109] : PRE 1823 KOVEL, OES [35002]

BECHTEL PRE 1840 BREMEN, BRM, GER [37986] : AMELIA C1820 BERKS CO., PA, USA [34126]

BECK PRE 1900 BLANKENBACH, HES, BRD [38636] : C1800 CAP D'ESPOIR, QUE, CAN [35612] : PRE 1751 KIRCHBERG, AG, CH [37103] : 1820+ DOEBELN, SAX, DDR [34803] : 1850-1900 DEN [38451] : PRE 1889 LANDPORT & SOUTHAMPTON, HAM, ENG [33890] : C1830 STROUD, GLS, ENG [33918] : PRE 1900 BLACK HILL AREA, DUR, ENG [34333] : PRE 1820 LYNSTED, KEN, ENG [34445] : C1820 WORCESTER, WOR, ENG [34760] : PRE 1869 BRISTOL, ENG [34797] : C1700 LEA, KEN, ENG [35053] : PRE 1810 BRANTINGHAM & HULL, ERY, ENG [35940] : ALL LONDON, ENG [36326] : ALL SSX, ENG [36510] : PRE 1725 STS, ENG [37098] : PRE 1850 WUE, GER [38675] : 1763 BRAUNSDORF, GER [38748] : 1821-1824 WEISSENFELS, KSA, GER [38748] : C1840 DUBLIN, IRL [34395] : PRE 1850 BELFAST & NEWTOWNARDS, DOW & ANT, IRL [34733] : PRE 1860 PORTARLINGTON, OFF, IRL [38272] : PRE 1900 ANON, DFS, SCT [38434] : 1810+ WAYNE CO., KY, USA [34203] : 1850+ MILWAUKEE CO., WI, USA [36962] : PRE 1865 PHILADELPHIA, PA, USA [37587]

BECKEL ALL LIESBERG, HES, GER [36571]

BECKENSALE 1776+ BAMPTON, OXF, ENG [36975]

BECKER 1805+ LORCH, RUEBOFRIM, BRD [34308] : PRE 1900 ROSENBECK, NRW, BRD [35004] : PRE 1850 BAW, BRD [35269] : 1986 KIEL, SHO, BRD [38748] : 1984-1987 HEIDE, SHO, BRD [38748] : 1950 KASSEL, HES, BRD [38748] : PRE 1856 OESTRICH, PPF, GER [33824] : 1602-1683 SUDECK, WAL, GER [34912] : 1850S LUCKA, SAB, GER [35050] : 1860 MANNHEIN, GER [35808] : 1726-1839 BARNTRUP, LIP, GER [38748] : 1718-1861 BLOMBERG, LIP, GER [38748] : 1650-1829 DETMARSEN, LIP, GER [38748] : 1658-1813 GROSSALMERODE, GHE, GER [38748] : 1788-1986 ELBRINXEN, LIP, GER [38748] : 1903-1980 ESCHENBRUCH, LIP, GER [38748] : 1846-1868 HOLZHAUSEN, PYR, GER [38748] : 1661-1735 WICKENRODE, GHE, GER [38748] : 1890 NIEHEIM, GER [38748] : 1824-1840 RHODEN, WAL, GER [38748] : 1870-1948 BAD PYRMONT, LIP & PYR, GER [38748] : 1793 GESEKE, LIP, GER [38748] : 1919 KOELN, RPR, GER [38748] : 1844 DECKBERGEN, LIP, GER [38748] : 1744 IKENHAUSEN, GER [38748] : 1850-1870

BROOKLYN, NY, USA [35269] : 1860+ CHICAGO, IL, USA [35269] : 1780 LEHIGH, PA, USA [35325] : 1869 NEW YORK, NY, USA [38748]

BECKERLEG 1825+ GERMOE, CON, ENG [36885]

BECKER-LIPHARD 1726 BLOMBERG, LIP, GER [38748] : 1709 WICKENRODE, GHE, GER [38748] : 1654-1698 GROSSALMERODE, GHE, GER [38748]

BECKER-LIPHARDT 1630 WICKENRODE, GHE, GER [38748] : 1657-1672 GROSSALMERODE, GHE, GER [38748]

BECKETT 1800-1850 DURAL, NSW, AUS [34307] : PRE 1910 FOOTSCRAY, VIC, AUS [35047] : 1800S ELMSLEY & LANARK, ONT, CAN [36727] : C1800 OLD PERLICAN, NFD, CAN [37513] : PRE 1810 CAMBRIDGE, CAM, ENG [34795] : C1864 BETHNAL GREEN, MDX, ENG [34926] : PRE 1846 LIVERPOOL, LAN, ENG [35047] : C1850-1870 BIRMINGHAM, WAR, ENG [35791] : 1700-1880 STEEPLE CLAYDON, BKM, ENG [37194] : 1800-1900 BASCHURCH, SAL, ENG [37508] : C1770 POOLE, DOR, DEV & SOM, ENG [37513] : WILLIAM 1855-1870 GREAT YARMOUTH, NFK, ENG [38255] : 1760-1990 KENDAL, WES, ENG [38511] : 1850 BALLINDERRY, ANT, IRL [35024] : 1740-1860 BETTISFIELD, FLN, WLS [37508]

BECKHAM PRE 1850 LIM & COR, IRL [37807]

BECKINGHAM 1849+ AUS [35561] : PRE 1849 OVERTON, WIL, ENG [35561]

BECKINGTON 1800+ NEWCASTLE, NBL, ENG [33837]

BECKLEY 1500-1600 SOUTHWARK, SRY, ENG [37783] : PRE 1832 CHESHAM, BKM, ENG [37899]

BECKMAN ALL ENG [37416] : PRE 1850 LND, ENG [38777] : PRE 1864 GER [36935] : 1840-1950 CLARKSTON, MI, USA [36935]

BECKMANN 1700-1800 ANGERMUNDE, UCKERMARK, BRA [38603] : PRE 1840 SCHEDMER, LIP, GER [37416] : PRE 1753 HEIDE, SHO, GER [38671] : ALL WORLDWIDE [38666]

BECKSTEAD 1790-1840 OSNABRUCK, ONT, CAN [35603]

BECKWAY ALL ESS & CAM, ENG [36955] : ALL LINTON & HORSEHEATH, CAM, ENG [36955] : 1784+ GREAT CHESTERFORD & HADSTOCK, ESS, ENG [36955]

BECKWITH PRE 1830 MASHAM, NRY, ENG [34588] : PRE 1860 RIPON & WATH, YKS, ENG [35533] : 1870+ LEEDS, YKS, ENG [36797] : 1700-50 LONDON &, ESS, ENG [37670]

BECQUET PRE 1725 VITRIVAL, NMR, BEL [38234] : PRE 1725 PEISSANT, HAINAULT, BEL [38234] : PRE 1725 DIEST, LBG, BEL [38234] : PRE 1725 SOLRE SUR SAMBRE, NOR, FRA [38234]

BECX 1575-1650 COLOGNE, BRD [36317]

BEDALL PRE 1800 EDGMOND, SAL, ENG [38420]

BEDDALL 1800+ NEWCASTLE, ENG [35015]

BEDDINGTON 1819+ HULLAVINGTON, WIL, ENG [36975]

BEDDOWS 1800S SAL, ENG [36038]

BEDELL 1783-1802 NB, CAN [34073] : 1802-1840 WENTWORTH CO., ONT, CAN [34073] : PRE 1640 ESS, ENG [34073] : PRE 1640 CAM, ENG [34073] : 1650-1783 STATEN ISLAND, NY, USA [34073] : 1640-1783 HEMPSTEAD, NY, USA [34073]

BEDELLA 1700+ MERTHER & PROBUS, CON, ENG [35208]

BEDESCHI ALL GUIBIASCO, TI, CH [38672]

BEDFORD 1850-1900 NSW, AUS [34422] : 1864+ GEELONG, VIC, AUS [37920] : 1880+ VIC, AUS [38539] : 1847+ LONGFORD, TAS, AUS [38539] : 1800S HRT, ENG [34684] : PRE 1774 YATELEY, HAM, ENG [34689] : C1840 LONDON, ENG [36092] :

PRE 1850 LONGFORD, MDX, ENG [36160] : PRE
1850 LONDON, MDX, ENG [36160] : PRE 1820
WRY, ENG [37402] : PRE 1803 LEEDS, YKS, ENG
[37610] : PRE 1810 ARDSLEY EAST, WRY, ENG
[37708] : PRE 1850 YKS, ENG [38293] : 1840+
BIRMINGHAM, WAR, ENG [38539] : ALL MD,
USA [38735] : ALL BEDFORD & FULTON CO., PA,
USA [38735] : 1750+ NY, USA & CAN [34988] :
1820+ WREXHAM, DEN, WLS [38539]

BEDKOBER ALL COLOGNE, GER & ENG [35518]

BEDSON 1892+ MITCHAM, VIC, AUS [34430]

BEDWELL PRE 1900 BETHNAL GREEN, LND, ENG
[34048] : PRE 1700 ESS, ENG [35642]

BEE 1750+ HOUGHTON LE SPRING, DUR, ENG
[34456] : PRE 1715 METHERINGHAM, LIN, ENG
[37318] : PRE 1880 HAMBLETON &, LAN, ENG
[38254] : 1700-1800 CHARLESTON CO., SC, USA
[38129]

BEEBAR ALL WORLDWIDE [38445]

BEEBE PRE 1756 HOUGHTON, HUN, ENG [34734] :
1860S MI, USA [38451]

BEEBY 1854+ AUS [35111] : C1800 BULKINGTON,
WAR, ENG [33796] : PRE 1854 BDF, ENG [35111]

BEEBY (SEE BEEBE) [34734]

BEECH ANN PRE 1800 WOLVERHAMPTON, STS,
ENG [36532] : PRE 1850 BIRMINGHAM, WAR,
ENG [36765] : PRE 1830 MENDHAM, NJ, USA
[38112]

BEECHAM 1850S+ NEWCASTLE, NSW, AUS [35239]
: 1600+ OXF, ENG [34980] : MARY PRE 1722
THORNEY & WISBECH, CAM, ENG [36149]

BEECHELL PRE 1850 DUKINFIELD, CHS, ENG
[37150]

BEECHER C1820 MD, USA [36116] : 1840-1890
WASHINGTON, MO, USA [36116]

BEECHER (SEE BECHER) [34109]

BEECHEY PRE 1830 BIDFORD ON AVON &
BROOM, WAR, ENG [37840] : PRE 1840
WORLDWIDE [37991]

BEECHING 1760+ SMARDEN, KEN, ENG [35444] :
1780+ CHARING, KEN, ENG [35444] : PRE 1850
SSX, ENG [37371] : C1770 KEN, ENG [38389] : 1800-
1900 UK [38070] : ALL WORLDWIDE [37880]

BEECROFT 1867+ SYDNEY, NSW, AUS [38208] :
PRE 1866 LONDON, ENG [38208]

BEEDIE ALL FRASERBURG, ABD, SCT [36743]

BEEDLE JOHN C1800-1880 PLYMOUTH, DEV, ENG
[34007]

BEEDON PRE 1770 HACHESTON, SFK, ENG [37420]

BEEHAG 1750-1900 SOUTHMINSTER, ESS, ENG
[36485]

BEEL 1900+ BEECHWORTH, VIC, AUS [36622] :
1700+ LADOCK, CON, ENG [35804]

BEEMAN C1900 NEWBURGH, ONT, CAN [34251]

BEEMER 1925 IA, USA [38751]

BEENHAM 1867 SLOUGH, BKM, ENG [34120]

BEENY ALL ENG [38369]

BEER PRE 1878 SYDNEY, NSW, AUS [34898] : C1850-
1874 SYDNEY, NSW, AUS [38208] : 1700+ DEAN
PRIOR, DEV, ENG [33820] : C1800 KEN, ENG
[34273] : 1800+ SOM, ENG [34455] : 1650+
CHULMLEIGH, DEV, ENG [34747] : PRE 1848
BLOOMSBURY, MDX, ENG [35016] : PRE 1820
HIGH BRAY, DEV, ENG [35523] : PRE 1820
ELHAM, KEN, ENG [35728] : 1804-1830 GORRAN,
CON, ENG [35922] : 1855 FALMOUTH, CON, ENG
[35922] : 1800+ WEYMOUTH, DOR, ENG [36435] :
1820-1840S BUCKFASTLEIGH, DEV, ENG [37308] :
1864-1910 WELLINGTON, NZ [35922]

BEERE C1643-1792 TWYWARD REATH, CON, ENG
[35922]

BEERS 1670+ FAIRFIELD, CT, USA [38066]

BEESLEY PRE 1830 OXF, ENG [35030] : ALL
PRESCOT, LAN, ENG [37846]

BEESON PRE 1880 SHARDLOW, DBY, ENG [34261] :
1718-1783 HOBY, LEI, ENG [37053] : C1800
LEICESTER, LEI, ENG [37053] : PRE 1825
CHENIES, BKM, ENG [37249]

BEESTON 1800-1840 CHELSEA, LND, ENG [35850]

BEETHAM PRE 1800 SCARCROFT, ERY & YKS,
ENG [34487] : PRE 1774 SHERBURN IN ELMET,
YKS, ENG [37144] : 1700-1850 FARLAM, CUL, ENG
[37457]

BEEVERS PRE 1700 KIRKBURTON, WRY, ENG
[37372]

BEEZEMER PRE 1850 GOUDA, ZUH, NL [38646]

BEEZLEY 1850S ARMIDALE, NSW, AUS [34902]

BEEZLY ALL STANFORD IN THE VALE, BRK,
ENG [36076]

BEGBIE 1850+ SYDNEY, QLD, AUS [34015] : 1750+
LONDON, ENG [37260]

BEGEMANN 1670 IN DER LUTTE, WEF, GER [38748]

BEGG PRE 1900 KILWAUGHTER, ANT, IRL [35967] :
1910+ DUNEDIN, NZ [35479]

BEGGIN 1800-1860 FER, IRL [35093]

BEGGS 1860+ KEWELL, VIC, AUS [34685] : 1850+
ENG [38059] : PRE 1840 BALLYMENA, ANT, IRL
[34262] : PRE 1860 ANT, IRL [34685] : PRE 1860
CARRICKFERGUS, ANT, IRL [37636] : PRE 1850
BALLYCLARE, ANT, IRL [38411] : 1820 ANT, IRL
[38434] : 1822-1880 GUERNSEY CO., OH, USA
[37781]

BEGIN 1750+ QUE, CAN [37482] : 1840+ ONT, CAN
[37482]

BEGLEY 1860S+ VIC, AUS [34937]

BEH 1850S MITCHELL'S FLAT, NSW, AUS [34940] :
1800 GROSSBOTTWAR, WUE, GER [34940]

BEHA PRE 1800 BAW, GER [38669]

BEHAM C1820-70 PA, USA [38590]

BEHAN 1855+ BEECHWORTH, VIC, AUS [35160] :
PRE 1857 OATLANDS, TAS, AUS [35217] : PRE 1855
WIC, ENG [35160] : 1845 KILDARE, KID, IRL [37163]

BEHM 1700S BERKHOLZ, BRA, GER [35968]

BEHN 1900+ HAMBURG STADT, HBG, GER [38603]

BEHNEMAN PRE 1882 VISSELHOUEDE, HAN, GER
[37563]

BEHRENS GESINE 1840-1900 GER [38781]

BEHSMAN 1800 HBG & BRD, GER [35873]

BEICHERT C1800-1850 NARAMAWITZ, POS, GER
[35725]

BEIER 1800S LANGHEINERSDORF, SIL, GER
[38623]

BEIGHTON REV. THOMAS 1790+ EDNASTON,
DBY, ENG [35217] : PRE 1820 DBY, ENG [38080]

BEIJER C1700 EEMNES, UTR, NL [38698]

BEILBY RICHARD 1842+ SYDNEY & KEMPSEY,
NSW, AUS [36600] : 1842+ SYDNEY, NSW, AUS
[37119] : JONOTHAN 1800+ HULL, YKS, ENG
[36600]

BEILSTEIN PRE 1833 BILLINGS, GHE, GER [36726]

BEIMER 1850+ KENDSHA CO., WI & IL, USA &
GER [37796]

BEINE PRE 1840 IRL [35246]

BEIR 1740-1830S COVENTRY TWP., CHESTER CO.,
PA, USA [38054]

BEIRNE 1780-1990 ELFIN, ROS, IRL [33818] : 1790+
CASTLEPLUNKET, TULSK, ROS, IRL [33927] :
1800S CAARON, ROS, IRL [38281]

BEISSENHIRTZ 1730 LEMGO, WEF, GER [38748]

BEIT 1750-1850 OVERTON CO., TN & PA, USA [38392]

BEITH 1840S+ VIC, NSW, AUS [33930] : 1910+ NSW,
AUS [33930] : 1830S ARL, SCT [33930] : 1800+
GLASGOW, RFW, SCT [36768] : 1870S GLASGOW,

LKS, SCT [36788] : 1800+ PAISLEY, RFW, SCT [37879]

BELAM ALL WORLDWIDE [37882]

BELBEN PRE 1780 DOR, ENG [36417]

BELBIN C1791 + AUS [34444]

BELBONE PRE 1780 DOR, ENG [36417]

BELCHAMBER ALL SSX, ENG [37922]

BELCHAMBERS ALL SSX, ENG [37922]

BELCHER C1831 WARMINSTER, WIL, ENG [35091] : ALL MDX, ENG [35115] : PRE 1800 SPARSHOLT, BRK, ENG [35523] : 1700-1800 WESTBURY ON SEVERN, GLS, ENG [35968] : 1800-1850 WARMINSTER, WIL, ENG [36130] : ALL LONDON, ENG [37743] : PRE 1882 STRATFORD, TARANAKI, NZ [34270] : 1790-1810 FRANKLIN CO., VA, USA [38144] : ALLEN 1883 WV, USA [38450] : ALL WORLDWIDE [38450]

BELCONGER 1600-1700 MASS, FRA [38216]

BELDON PRE 1829 WRY, ENG [36459] : C1700 WESTFIELD, MA, USA [34395]

BELFIELD PRE 1890 BRADFORD, WRY, ENG [35378] : PRE 1900 NTT & DBY, ENG [37412] : 1782-1789 CLAREMONT, NH, USA [37005]

BELFIT PRE 1900 NTT & DBY, ENG [37412]

BELFITT PRE 1900 NTT & DBY, ENG [37412]

BELFORD PRE 1900 WESTMINSTER, LND, ENG [34562] : 1770-1790 DOW, IRL [36908] : ALL SCT [36497]

BELFORE 1730-1770 KNOCKBRIDE, CAV, IRL [33771]

BELFRAGE 1902+ FOOTSCRAY, VIC, AUS [34430]

BELGRAVE 1869+ ADELAIDE, SA & VIC, AUS [34530]

BELGROVE 1700+ CASSINGTON, OXF, ENG [34121]

BELICARD 1792-1943 MONTCEAUX & BEAUJEU, BRG & RHA, FRA [34136]

BELIEU ALL HARRISON CO., MO, USA [36916]

BELITHER 1860S PLUMSTEAD, SSX & LND, ENG [37853]

BELITZER 1833-1899 BADEN, BAW, BRD [38738]

BELK PRE 1700 HARTHILL, WRY, ENG [36147] : 1750-1850 OVERTON CO., TN & PA, USA [38392]

BELL 1865-1880S CASTLEMAINE, VIC, AUS [33806] : WILLIAM PRE 1856 MCLAREN VALE, SA, AUS [33941] : 1865+ DUROA, VIC, AUS [34798] : 1865+ TOOWOOMBA & WARWICK, QLD, AUS [34937] : 1900S MACKAY, QLD, AUS [34957] : PRE 1871+ INVERELL, NSW, AUS [35088] : JAMES C1840-1853 MAITLAND & DUNGOG, NSW, AUS [35108] : 1840-1870 IPSWICH, QLD, AUS [35138] : PRE 1842+ DUNGOG, NSW, AUS [35237] : 1860+ MACKAY, QLD, AUS [35392] : 1920+ BRISBANE, QLD, AUS [35392] : 1930+ IPSWICH, QLD, AUS [35392] : 1839-1860 RICHMOND, NSW, AUS [36595] : WILLIAM R. 1830+ HOBART, TAS, AUS [37312] : ALFRED R. 1859+ GUNNEDAH, NSW, AUS [37312] : ROBERT 1881-1887+ BRISBANE, QLD & WA, AUS [37781] : 1850+ MT LEY, QLD, AUS [37949] : 1830+ SA, AUS [38484] : 1880+ BIRDSVILLE, QLD, AUS [38484] : 1830S-1860S CHATHAM, ONT, CAN [34088] : 1830+ LAMBTON CO., ONT, CAN [34138] : 1820+ PEEL, ONT, CAN [34982] : ROBERT JAMES C1890 TODMORDEN MILLS, TORONTO, ONT, CAN [38452] : C1800 LOCKERLY, HAM, ENG [33841] : 1750+ STRENSHAM, WOR, ENG [34160] : PRE 1800 GOSBERTON, LIN, ENG [34311] : PRE 1830 LONDON, ENG [34571] : PRE 1800 LONDON, ENG [34576] : 1800 ALLENDALE, NBL, ENG [34890] : C1750 PRESTON, LAN, ENG [34993] : 1714+ ROTHBURY, NBL, ENG [35026] : MARY 1800S CROSSCANONBY, CUL, ENG [35409] : 1700S KIRKBY MOORSIDE, NRY, ENG [35460] :

EDWARD 1840+ BIRKENHEAD, CHS, ENG [35712] : ALCE (SIC) 1646 WORFIELD, SAL, ENG [35794] : 1820-1840 BEDLINGTON, NBL, ENG [35813] : 1750+ RAGNALL, NTT, ENG [35847] : MATTHEW 1800+ HOXTON, MDX, ENG [35905] : 1800+ LEEDS, DURHAM & BRADFORD, YKS, ENG [35947] : PRE 1880 YKS, ENG [35983] : SETH PRE 1750 FULFORD, YKS, ENG [35983] : PRE 1850 RICHMOND, YKS, ENG [36085] : 1800+ BRADFORD & LEEDS, WRY, ENG [36104] : PRE 1890 BELFORD & NEWCASTLE ON TYNE, NBL, ENG [36110] : C1860 LANCASTER, LAN, ENG [36227] : ROBERT C1829 WHITTINGTON, NBL, ENG [36270] : WILLIAM PRE 1850 GREAT WHITTINGTON, NBL, ENG [36270] : THOMAS 1816+ NEWCASTLE UPON TYNE, NBL, ENG [36270] : WILLIAM PRE 1850 CORBRIDGE, NBL, ENG [36270] : ISAAC PRE 1800 WREAY BY CARLISLE, CUL, ENG [36270] : ROBERT PRE 1851 NEWCASTLE UPON TYNE, NBL, ENG [36270] : WILLIAM C1906 WEST HARTLEPOOL, DUR, ENG [36270] : THOMAS PRE 1800 WREAY BY CARLISLE, CUL, ENG [36270] : WILLIAM C1788 WREAY BY CARLISLE, CUL, ENG [36270] : PRE 1854 ST GILES, DUR, ENG [36604] : R. 1815-1860 NEWCASTLE UPON TYNE, NBL, ENG [36717] : 1700-1850 WARBURTON, CHS, ENG [36740] : JAMES 1728+ ALLENDALE, NBL, ENG [37019] : ALL ALRESFORD, HAM, ENG [37044] : C1800 CARTMEL, LAN, ENG [37246] : PRE 1730 DALTON IN FURNESS, LAN, ENG [37353] : PRE 1750 SOUTHERY & METHWOLD, NFK, ENG [37402] : 1760S MARKET RASEN, LIN, ENG [37445] : 1650-1800 FARLAM, CUL, ENG [37457] : 1700-1800 IPSWICH & KELSALE, SFK, ENG [37642] : PRE 1838 LONDON, MDX, ENG [37840] : 1700-1868 WHITEHAVEN, CUL, ENG [37858] : 1800+ CARLISLE, CUL, ENG [37907] : 1820+ NEWCASTLE ON TYNE, NBL, ENG [37997] : 1820 MEPAL, CAM, ENG [38209] : 1780S-1850 FANGDALEBECK, NRY, ENG [38269] : ROBERT C1814 GATESHEAD FELL, DUR, ENG [38269] : FRANCIS 1720S-1750S GREAT BROUGHTON, NRY, ENG [38269] : C1811 HORNSEY, MDX, ENG [38441] : PRE 1840 CARLISLE, CUL, ENG [38722] : 1750+ ALLENDALE, NBL & VIC, ENG & AUS [35186] : ARCHIBALD C1750 CHESHUNT, HRT, ENG & SCT [34303] : PRE 1870 CREIGHTONS GRANGE, TIP, IRL [34254] : 1800+ IRL [34367] : PRE 1820 FER, IRL [34982] : JOHN 1865+ BENRAW, DOW, IRL [35219] : ALL LOG, IRL [35628] : PRE 1815 ANT, IRL [36552] : 1750+ HOLLYMOUNT, MAY, IRL [37110] : JANE 1760S TUBERINEAN, WEX, IRL [37454] : PRE 1840 LOCKBRIDE, CAV, IRL [38004] : GEORGE PRE 1820 FER, IRL [38435] : GEORGE PRE 1770 DON, IRL [38769] : 1860+ GLASGOW, SCT [33795] : C1670 KELSO, ROX, SCT [34118] : 1740-1772 CASTLETON, ROX, SCT [34408] : PRE 1820 KIRKOSWALD, AYR, SCT [34713] : ALL STRACHAN, KCD, SCT [34838] : PRE 1850 DUNBLANE, PER, SCT [34937] : PRE 1866 GREENLOANING, PER, SCT [34937] : C1780 KIRKCOLM, WIG, SCT [34993] : PRE 1600 ARKINHOLME, DFS, SCT [35165] : PRE 1850 DFS, SCT [35199] : 1800+ DFS, SCT [35293] : PRE 1860 OLD MONKLAND, LKS, SCT [35392] : 1870S GLASGOW, SCT [35508] : 1800+ CHIRNSIDE, BEW, SCT [35611] : 1700+ ST CUTHBERTS, MLN, SCT [35825] : 1750+ OLD MONKLAND, LKS, SCT [35979] : 1800-1850 DUMFRIES, DFS, SCT [36205] : 1820S ST ANDREWS, FIF, SCT [36292] : C1840 PORT GLASGOW, RFW, SCT [36806] : 1800-1910

GLASGOW, LKS, SCT [37432] : WILLIAM 1744+ HODDOM, DFS, SCT [37443] : PRE 1900 LONGFORGAN & ERROL, PER, SCT [37496] : PRE 1803 INVERESK & EDINBURGH, MLN, SCT [37852] : 1800+ CUPAR, FIF, SCT [37946] : WILLIAM 1820S MONIMAIL, FIF, SCT & NZ [36862] : PRE 1836 MONTGOMERY CO. & FRANKLIN CO., OH & PA, USA [35270] : 1825-1849 PICKENS CO., SC, USA [37029] : JOSEPH 1850-1870 GREENE CO. & MADISON CO., OH, USA [37781] : 1832 OKMULGEE, OK, USA [38012] : THOMAS 1834-1850 PA, USA [38130] : PRE 1800 BOTETOURT CO., VA, USA [38311] : GEORGE PRE 1850 PA, USA [38769]

BELLAGAMBA C1500-C1780 CASTELLEONE DI SUASA, ITL [36139] : C1500-C1780 CORINALDO, ITL [36139]

BELLAMY 1800+ PENNANT HILLS, NSW, AUS [35360] : WILLIAM 1839+ MORPETH, NSW, AUS [38291] : 1820+ SOUTHWARK, SRY, ENG [34092] : PRE 1900 OLD SWINFORD, WOR, ENG [34314] : PRE 1945 LONDON, ENG [34892] : 1800+ WALSOKEN & OUTWELL, NFK & CAM, ENG [35342] : PRE 1800 HOLBORN, LND, ENG [35360] : JAMES 1783-1810S TAUNTON, SOM, ENG [36880] : 1715+ WESTBURY ON SEVERN, GLS, ENG [37051] : PRE 1789 KETTLETHORPE, LIN, ENG [37318] : 1700+ NOTTINGHAM, NTT, ENG [37375] : PRE 1825 EXETER, DEV, ENG [38291]

BELLAS ALL LONG MARTIN, WES, ENG [37939]

BELLCHAMBERS PRE 1825 DEPTFORD, KEN, ENG [36154] : 1800+ LND, ENG [36869]

BELLEMAN 1600S COLIJNSPLAAT, ZEL, NL [38358]

BELLER 1800 WERBERLOW, POM, GER [37170]

BELLERT PRE 1800 WERBELOW, POM, GER [35448] : 1800 STETTIN, POM, GER [37170]

BELLETT 1840+ GEELONG, VIC, AUS [38289] : 1760S LONDON, ENG [35151] : PRE 1880 CLA, IRL [35956]

BELLEVILLE 1860+ QUEBEC, CAN [34098]

BELLINGER 1880+ LISDILLON, TAS, AUS [34910] : PRE 1800 LONDON, ENG [36092] : EDMUND 1730 SAVANNAH, GA, USA [35328] : EDMUND 1740S SAVANNAH, GA, USA [37585]

BELLINGHAM 1840+ SYDNEY, NSW, AUS [36846] : 1800+ DUDLEY, WOR, ENG [35125] : 1700+ LILLESHALL, SAL, ENG [35125]

BELLIS ALL HANLEY, ENG [36656] : ALL WHITFORD, FLN, WLS [37667] : ALL AGY, WLS & CAN [36656]

BELLOWS PRE 1871 SOUTHAMPTON, HAM, ENG [36993]

BELSER 1800+ HIGHLAND CO., OH, USA [38764]

BELSEY ALL KEN, ENG [36532] : PRE 1806 GOODNESTONE, KEN, ENG [36804]

BELSHAM PRE 1840 MALDON, ESS, ENG [35374]

BELSTEAD 1750 TOLLESHUNT MAJOR, ESS, ENG [37928]

BELT PRE 1834 WINLATON, DUR, ENG [36459]

BELTON C1846 CHIPPING, HRT, ENG [34229] : C1800+ HORNCASTLE & LINCOLN, LIN, ENG [34451] : 1775+ EDMONTON, MDX, ENG [36434]

BELTRAMI PRE 1850 CAVERGNO, TI, CH [35718]

BEMENT PRE 1880 CARDIFF, WLS [37459]

BEMIS 1780-1820 ROYALSTON, MA, USA [37086]

BEMISS 1800-40 LORAIN CO., OH, USA [37007]

BEMOND PRE 1830 MGY, WLS [37137]

BEMROSE C1880-1930 COTGRAVE, NTT, ENG [38401]

BENAVIDES 1500-1630 SANTO DOMINGO, STO DOMING [36340]

BENAZET 1600-1900 VICDESSOS ARCONAC, ARIEGE, FRA [33758]

BENBOW 1870+ CARHARRACK, CON, ENG [35151] : 1800+ DUNSTAN GREEN, KEN, ENG [37166] : 1700-1850 NC & IN, USA [36319] : C1700 MGY, WLS [36319]

BENCE 1830 SOUTHAMPTON, HAM, ENG [37122] : 1800-1850 SOM & NSW, ENG & AUS [35422]

BENCH 1820+ ASHMORE, DOR, ENG [35297] : 1700S PENTRIDGE, DOR, ENG [35297] : PRE 1820 TOLLARD ROYAL, WIL, ENG [35297]

BENDALL PRE 1860 CAM, ENG [34883] : C1850 BRIDPORT, DOR, ENG [37264]

BENDEL PRE 1750 BIBERACH, GER [38661]

BENDELOW C1800 WELL, NRY, ENG [36147]

BENDEN 1700+ ADELAIDE, SA, AUS & ENG [36303]

BENDER 1790-1830 SOUTHWARK, LND, ENG [37376] : PRE 1855 MOSBACH, BAD, GER [34886] : PRE 1830 LANCASTER & SOMERSET CO., PA, USA [37565] : 1726+ ROCKINGHAM, VA, USA [38054] : JACOB WILLIAM 1874-1937 KEWANEE & HENRY CO., IL & AN, USA [38124] : 1750-1800 LANCASTER CO., PA, USA [38770] : ALL WORLDWIDE [37785]

BENDILY PRE 1890 DENHAM SPRINGS, LA, USA [36543]

BENDING 1865+ BEAUFORT, VIC, AUS [35193] : PRE 1600 EAST BUDLEIGH, DEV, ENG [36389]

BENDINGE PRE 1600 PAY HEMBURY, DEV, ENG [36389]

BENDIX PRE 1875 ZWICKAU, GER [34645]

BENDLE PRE 1800 CARLISLE, CUL, ENG [35722] : 1800+ NORTH MOLTON, DEV, ENG [35825]

BENDYNGE PRE 1600 HONITON, DEV, ENG [36389]

BENEDICT 1820-1850 LEEDS, ONT, CAN [38097] : 1850-1900 LEE, IA, USA [38097] : 1750-1813 CORNWALL, CT, USA [38098] : 1813 HAMILTON MADISON, NY, USA [38098] : 1870-90 IN, USA [38533] : 1617+ CT & NY, USA & ENG [37522]

BENEGHAN HANNAH 1839 BLACKHEATH, ENG [36316]

BENES JAMES 1826 WIMBLEDON, SRY & LND, ENG [34924] : 1940+ PHILADELPHIA, PA, USA [36578] : PRE 1940 BROOKLYN & QUEENS, NY, USA [36578]

BENETOT ALL WORLDWIDE [37093]

BENFIELD PRE 1900 SWANAGE, DOR, ENG [34477] : PRE 1830 DOR, ENG [35866] : PRE 1840 BRIGHTON, SSX, ENG [35925] : 1700+ OXFORD, OXF, ENG [36685] : 1750+ LND, ENG [38375]

BENGE 1800 ROTHERHITHE, KEN, ENG [34204]

BENGEL PRE 1750 GER [38640]

BENGER 1849+ SA, AUS [34775] : PRE 1849 DOR, ENG [34775]

BENGREE ALL WORLDWIDE [37688]

BENGREY ALL WORLDWIDE [37688]

BENGRY ALL WORLDWIDE [37688]

BENGTSSON JONES 1861+ ARE, JAMTLAND, SWE [38566] : JOHAN 1886+ ARE, JAMTLAND, SWE [38566] : LILLY 1909+ ROCHESTER, NY, USA [38546] : BERTA 1906+ IRWIN, PA, USA [38546] : VIKTOR 1896+ MI, USA [38566]

BENHAM C1850 BATHURST, NSW, AUS [35028] : PRE 1850 ESS, ENG [35028] : 1850-1950 ALDERSHOT & FARNHAM, SRY, ENG [36662] : C1794 NEW ALRESFORD, HAM, ENG [37235] : 1800+ BINSTED NEAR ALTON, HAM, ENG [38425] : 1800+ BRANSTON & LEICESTER, LEI, ENG [38425] : 1790-1820 FRANKLIN, KY, USA [38373]

BENISH 1800 VIENNA, OES [37582]

BENJAMIN ANSON PRE 1898 ONT, CAN [35641] : 1830-1880 LONDON, ENG [36658] : PRE 1630

HEATHFIELD, SSX, ENG [37529] : 1632
HEATHFIELD, SSX, ENG [37531] : 1830-1880 NEW
YORK, NY, USA [36658] : 1632 CAMBRIDGE, MA,
USA [37531] : ALL FLINT, FLN, WLS [37667]

BENN C1784+ LEN & ADD CO., ONT, CAN [36651] :
1750 PERLEBERG, BRA, GER [37509] : 1740+
ALBANY, NY, USA [34408] : C1715+ KINGSTON,
NY, USA [36651]

BENNEKERS ALL WORLDWIDE [38710]

BENNER C1650 CON, ENG [34258] : 1767+
JAGODNAJA, SU [38590]

BENNET ANDREW B. PRE 1858 QUE, CAN [34993] :
C1650 CON, ENG [34258] : 1800+ TILLICOULTRY,
CLK, SCT [33996] : 1700S DUNDEE, ANS, SCT
[34172] : 1760-1900 GLENCAIRN, DFS & FIF, SCT
[36877] : 1740 NJ, USA [37008] : 1830-1870S
CAERNARVON, CAE, WLS [36522]

BENNETOT ALL WORLDWIDE [37093]

BENNETT 1860+ GUMERACHA, SA, AUS [33920] :
C1880+ ARMIDALE, NSW, AUS [34426] : 1844+
SURRY HILLS, NSW, AUS [34685] : C1860
ADELAIDE & PT AUGUSTA, SA, AUS [35401] :
1844 BURWOOD, VIC, AUS [35531] : 1838+
MUSWELLBROOK, NSW, AUS [35740] : 1860+
GEELONG, VIC, AUS [36484] : SAMUEL SMITH
ALL SYDNEY, NSW, AUS [36643] : STEPHEN N.
1862+ NORTH SHORE & SYDNEY, NSW, AUS
[36643] : 1896 MAITLAND, NSW, AUS [37172] : PRE
1868 GYMPIE, QLD, AUS [37315] : CHARLES
1884+ ADELAIDE, SA, AUS [37954] : 1890+
SYDNEY, NSW, AUS [38277] : 1800 WENTWORTH
CO., ONT, CAN [34231] : 1860S CHATHAM, ONT,
CAN [38390] : CAROLINE 1866+ SOUTHWARK,
LND, ENG [33797] : DANIEL 1870+
SOUTHWARK, LND, ENG [33797] : ALL
ORPINGTON, KEN & LND, ENG [33919] : 1800S
SUNDERLAND, DUR, ENG [33982] : ALL
ALCESTER, GLS, ENG [33985] : ALL STUDLEY,
WAR, ENG [33985] : 1600-1800 MEOPHAM, KEN,
ENG [34107] : PRE 1810 SEVENOAKS, KEN, ENG
[34115] : C1600 STREET, DUR, ENG [34157] : 1850+
BRADFORD, YKS, ENG [34323] : C1800 TOLLARD
ROYAL, WIL, ENG [34426] : C1800 TOLLARD
FARNHAM, DOR, ENG [34426] : THOMAS 1850S
MANCHESTER, LAN, ENG [34452] : THOMAS PRE
1812 ROTHERMAN, YKS, ENG [34452] : 1870
LONDON, ENG [34565] : 1800+ HRT, ENG [34571] :
1831+ DUNSTABLE, BDF, ENG [34700] : 1750+
ASPLEY GUISE, BDF, ENG [34700] : THOMAS 1846
LEEDS, YKS, ENG [34751] : THOMAS 1847-1856
MANCHESTER, LAN, ENG [34751] : THOMAS 1815
ROTHERHAM, YKS, ENG [34751] : 1800-1870
LIVERPOOL, LAN, ENG [34762] : JOHN C1670 ST
MELLION, CON & DEV, ENG [34836] : PRE 1800
SOUTH HILL, CON & DEV, ENG [34836] : PRE
1920 DEV, ENG [34844] : PRE 1900 SAL, ENG
[34861] : 1800S CAMBORNE, CON, ENG [34881] :
PRE 1890 PLYMOUTH, DEV, ENG [34892] : PRE
1800 DARTON, WRY, ENG [34974] : 1700+ ST
MERRYN, CON, ENG [35007] : 1800+ SHIFNAL,
SAL, HEF & STS, ENG [35019] : PRE 1770 YATE,
GLS, ENG [35157] : 1820+ ST MARYLEBONE,
LND, ENG [35244] : PRE 1860 ENG [35255] : C1800-
1850 CHS, ENG [35391] : 1500-1700 PHILLEIGH &
GERRANS, CON, ENG [35576] : PRE 1838
TOLLARD, WIL, ENG [35740] : PRE 1850
LONDON, ENG [35823] : PRE 1830 DOR, ENG
[35866] : MARGARET 1855-1900 WEST HAM, ESS,
ENG [36101] : ALL LAN, ENG [36152] : ALL
MIDDLETON, LAN, ENG [36187] : 1750-1850
CANTERBURY, KEN, ENG [36261] : PRE 1850
GWINEAR, CON, ENG [36416] : C1750-1850

SHAFTESBURY, DOR, ENG [36478] : PRE 1750
BURBAGE, LEI, ENG [36528] : PRE 1840
TAVISTOCK & PLYMOUTH, DEV, ENG [36594] :
ALL DEV & CON, ENG [36594] : SAMUEL SMITH
C1830 NBL & LIN, ENG [36643] : PRE 1860
MANCHESTER, LAN, ENG [36765] : 1850S
CRICKLADE, WIL, ENG [36799] : 1800+
IGHTHAM & BOROGREEN, KEN, ENG [36887] :
THOMAS PRE 1765 HARBORNE, STS, ENG [37103]
: PRE 1832 MACCLESFIELD, CHS, ENG [37138] :
1800-1850 HAM, ENG [37172] : 1700S NORWICH &
REDENHALL, NFK, ENG [37250] : 1750+
STRATFORD, MDX, ENG [37284] : PRE 1836
ASTLEY ABBOTTS & WORFIELD, SAL, ENG
[37406] : C1820 DIDSBURY, LAN, ENG [37573] :
PRE 1738 STROUD, GLS, ENG [37610] : PRE 1777
LEEDS, WRY, ENG [37610] : 1700+
DEDDINGTON, OXF, ENG [37625] : 1800+
HIGHWORTH, WIL, ENG [37625] : 1850-5
HEADLEY, HAM, ENG [37709] : 1855-1960
LYMINGTON, HAM, ENG [37709] : PRE 1837
SKELMERSDALE, LAN, ENG [37732] : 1700-1800
BIRMINGHAM, WAR, ENG [37924] : CHARLES
PRE 1884 ENG [37954] : 1800+ CRADLEY, HEF,
ENG [38020] : 1800-1860 HORBURY, WRY, ENG
[38028] : 1800+ LAMBETH, SRY, ENG [38488] :
C1828 PIMLICO, LND, ENG [38721] : 1785+
EXETER, DEV, ENG & AUS [33926] : 1800+
BALLYCOPELAND, DOW, IRL [34190] : C1837
DUB, IRL [34685] : 1780-1848 CLONAKILTY, COR,
IRL [34693] : C1850S BALLYMURPHY, DOW, IRL
[34788] : 1852 TANDRAGEE, ARM, IRL [34788] :
ALL TANDRAGEE, ARM, IRL [35531] : PRE 1880
ATHBOY, MEA, IRL [35574] : 1820S SKULL, COR,
IRL [36831] : 1750+ WEX, IRL [37026] : 1790 COR,
IRL [38362] : 1849-1880 AUCKLAND, NZ [34693] :
1920+ WESTPORT, BULLER, NZ [38277] : 1860
DUNBLAIN, PER, SCT [35912] : 1816-1871
EDINBURGH, SCT [37469] : PRE 1870
EDINBURGH, MLN, SCT [38600] : 1800-1830 IOM,
UK [34016] : RALPH PRE 1750 UK [37703] : 1789-
1900 ESSEX, OH, USA [35316] : SAMUEL SMITH
C1830 NEW YORK, NY, USA [36643] : 1895-1915
BUTTE, MT, USA [36909] : PRE 1800 WARREN CO.,
NY & RI, USA [36917] : 1860-1880 KEWEENAW
CO., MI, USA [38010] : 1800-1860 YORK CO., SC,
USA [38129] : SAMUEL 1812 HAMILTON CO., OH,
USA [38152] : SAMUEL 1747 NJ, USA [38152] : 1770-
1840 BLAIR CO., PA, USA [38310] : 1870+
JEFFERSON CO., CO, USA [38310] : THOMAS
1855+ JAMAICA, W.INDIES [35220] : ALL
WORLDWIDE [35832]

BENNETT-ROBINS PRE 1830 LONDON, ENG [35061]

BENNETTS 1878+ MOONTA, SA, AUS [35012] : PRE
1850 ST JUST, CON, ENG [33884] : PRE 1860 CON,
ENG [34684] : PRE 1878 REDRUTH, CON, ENG
[35012] : 1800+ CAMBORNE, CON, ENG [36909] :
PRE 1840 PENWITH, CON, ENG [37379]

BENNEY C1823 ST COLUMB MAJOR, CON, ENG
[35251]

BENNIE PRE 1870 GLASGOW, SCT [35255] : ALL
GLASGOW, LKS, SCT [35924]

BENNINGER 1845+ WELLINGTON CO., ONT, CAN
[34231] : 1835 CARRICK TWP., ONT, CAN [34503] :
1800S USA [38369]

BENNINGTON PRE 1900 ENG [37061]

BENNION PRE 1833 WENDOVER, BKM, ENG
[37896]

BENNT 1750 ONGAR, ESS, ENG [37683]

BENNY 1861+ CANTERBURY, NZ [35584] : 1860-1870
KEWEENAW CO., MI, USA [38010]

BENOIT PRE 1908 FRANKFURT, FFO, BRD [37369] :
C1800 CAPE BRETON, NS, CAN [36694] : 1840-1875
STANBRIDGE, QUE, CAN [37547]

BENSEMANN 1840+ NELSON, NZ [35058]

BENSETTE 1870+ WINDSOR, ONT, CAN [34983]

BENSINGER PRE 1743 WUE, GER [36972]

BENSKIN C1834 THURCASTON, LEI, ENG [34661] :
1500+ LEI & NTT, ENG [37266]

BENSLEY 1700-1800 NFK, ENG [37207]

BENSON 1820+ RICHMOND, NSW, AUS [33996] :
PRE 1900 BLACKWOOD, VIC, AUS [35055] : 1840+
ONT & NY, CAN & USA [36539] : 1700S COLTON,
LAN, ENG [34053] : PRE 1825 MDX, ENG [34428] :
1800-1870 BROMFIELD, CUL, ENG [34515] : ALL
PICKERING, YKS, ENG [34629] : 1800+
ISLINGTON, MDX, ENG [34882] : C1830 ALL
SAINTS, WAR, ENG [35152] : 1700+ KINGSWEAR,
DEV, ENG [36000] : 1700S COLTON, LAN, ENG
[36868] : C1814 ABERFORD, YKS, ENG [37144] :
PRE 1764 BELCHFORD, LIN, ENG [37318] : 1800+
NOTTINGHAM, NTT, ENG [37839] : 1600-1700
CUL, ENG [37858] : 1800S CARLISLE, CUL, ENG
[38422] : PRE 1750 HAMPSTHWAITE, YKS, ENG
[38690] : PRE 1830 WORKINGTON, CUL, ENG
[38722] : 1780+ ENG & AUS [34803] : C1700-1832
MOG, IRL [34246] : 1800 WISHAW, DON, IRL
[37125] : 1840-1863 FAIRFAX CO., VA, USA [38030] :
1860-1870 BALTIMORE CITY, MD, USA [38030] :
1865-1869 ADAMS CO., PA, USA [38030] : 1860-1865
FREDERICK CO., MD, USA [38030] : WALTER
1900+ BERKELEY, CA, USA [38555] : LINDEMAN
M. 1900+ KANSAS CITY, KS, USA [38555] :
ANDREW 1900-1960 BERKELEY, CA, USA [38555] :
CHARLIE 1890+ RED OAK, IA, USA [38555] :
RAYMOND 1900+ BERKELEY, CA, USA [38555] :
EDWARD 1900+ BERKELEY, CA, USA [38555]

BENSTEAD 1880-1901 UK [36654]

BENT 1780+ YARMOUTH, NS, CAN [35291] : 1700+
MANCHESTER, LAN, ENG [34303] : 1840-1870 ST
LUKES, MDX, ENG [34693] : 1800S
MANCHESTER, LAN, ENG [36194] : 1780
LITTLEPORT, CAM, ENG [38209] : PRE 1853
SLIGO, SLI, IRL [36417] : 1750+ WEX, IRL [37026] :
PRE 1880 MLN & FIF, SCT [34383]

BENTLEY ALL TAS, AUS [35258] : 1850+ ONT, CAN
[35603] : 1790+ NIAGARA DISTRICT, ONT, CAN
[38323] : SARAH C1780 HIGHGATE, LND, ENG
[34539] : PHOEBE & JANE 1810+ HUN, ENG
[35164] : MARTHA 1820-1850 FENDRAYTON,
HUN, ENG [35164] : ELIZABETH 1808-1813 HUN,
ENG [35164] : 1770-1810 SOM, ENG [35603] : PRE
1750 LONDON, MDX, ENG [36379] : 1800-1900
WINTRINGHAM, ERY, ENG [36394] : 1800 EAST
STOKE & NEWARK, NTT, ENG [37829] : PRE 1825
SWARKESTONE, DBY, ENG [37961] : THOMAS
C1840 WIMBLEDON & CLAPHAM, SRY, ENG
[38268] : PRE 1790 HIGHGATE, LND, ENG [38730] :
1750+ MANCHESTER, LAN, ENG & AUS [34008] :
C1820-1860 GLASGOW, LKS, SCT & FIJI [34008] :
1800-1860 MEA, IRL [35603] : ALL WELLINGTON,
NZ [36839]

BENTLY 1700-1850 LOWER PEOVER, CHS, ENG
[34163] : PRE 1865 LONDON, ENG [35976]

BENTON ALL ESS, ENG [36500] : PRE 1877 KEN,
MDX & SRY, ENG [37358] : ALL INVERNESS, FL,
USA [35302]

BENTOT ALL WORLDWIDE [37093]

BENTOTE ALL WORLDWIDE [37093]

BENVIE 1780+ LIFF, ANS, SCT [35644]

BENWELL PRE 1850 LONDON, MDX, ENG [37716]

BENWICK 1810 LONDON, MDX, ENG [35067]

BENYA PRE 1880 FARRELL, SLOVAKIA &
MERCER, PA, USA &, SLOVAKIA [38063]

BENYON PRE 1820 GOULBURN, NSW, AUS [37133] :
PRE 1820 SAL, ENG [37133] : PRE 1833
WENDOVER, BKM, ENG [37896] : ALL
ECCLESTON, CHS, ENG [38074]

BEQUET PRE 1725 SOLRE SUR SAMBRE, NOR,
FRA [38234]

BEQUETTE 1700+ ST GENEVIEVE, MO & IL, USA
[36917] : 1850-1900 PRAIRIE DU ROCHER, IL, USA
[38234] : 1800-1900 FREDERICKTOWN, MO, USA
[38234] : ALL WORLDWIDE [38234]

BERCHTOL 1655+ KONKEN, RPF, BRD [37004]

BERCINI PRE 1860 STAZZONA, LOMBARDY, ITL
[35519]

BERDEU 1819-1835 SRY, ENG & AUS [34267]

BEREMAN ALL GRAFFHAM, SSX, ENG [35146]

BERENDSEN ALL WEHL, GEL, NL [38358]

BERENMEISTER ANNE E. 1801 STROMBERG, PRE,
GER [38780]

BERENTROTH ALL GER [38690]

BERESFORD PRE 1820 HOBART, TAS, AUS [35217] :
PRE 1840S RIPLEY, DBY, ENG [33780] : 1750-1900
UTTOXETER, STS, ENG [34714] : 1850S HANLEY,
STS, ENG [37945] : PRE 1827 NANTWICH, CHS,
ENG [37945]

BERG 1877 NOR [37493] : 1865 CHORTITZA, SU
[38434] : PRE 1850 GREBBESTAD, STKM, SWE
[35232] : 1850+ ST LOUIS, MO, USA [36912]

BERGEN PRE 1870 BALLACOLLA, LEX, IRL [37521]

BERGER PRE 1830 LEIHGESTERN, HES, BRD
[34753] : C1850 SCHWEIDNITZ, SIL, GER [34083] :
PRE 1827 RIEMERTSHEIDE & BORKENDORF,
SIL, GER [34083] : PRE 1812 LUEBEN, SIL, GER
[36954] : PRE 1675 DIERDORF, RPF, GER [36972] :
LOUIS C1860 BLN, GER [37819] : PRE 1800
BERNSTADT, PSA, GER [38675]

BERGH 1850-1900 NOR [34135]

BERGIN C1814 CORDERRY, TIP, IRL [33936] : 1800+
THREE CASTLES, KIK, IRL [37534] : 1800+
KILKENNY, KIK, IRL & AUS [34864]

BERGMAN 1830-1870 BALTIMORE CITY, BAY &
MD, BRD & USA [38895] : ERNEST 1900+
BROOKLYN, NY, USA [38668] : ARTHUR 1900+
BROOKLYN, NY, USA [38668]

BERGMANN C1840 RATHSKIRCHEN, RPF, BRD
[36961] : PRE 1850 ZIESAR, MAG, DDR [34462] :
PRE 1800 WEISSTEIN & WALDENBURG, SIL,
GER [33901] : 1830S HBG, GER [35402]

BERGNE CHARLES 1872-90 LONDON, ENG [37926]

BERGSTRASSER 1650-1750 WORMS, RHL-PFALZ,
GER [38662]

BERGSTROM 1875+ PERNAJA, UUSIMAA, FIN
[38758] : 1800-1900 HAWKES BAY, NZ [38273] :
1800+ OHAKUNE, NZ [38273] : PRE 1870
VERMILLAN, SWE [38273]

BERIMAN ALL GRAFFHAM, SSX, ENG [35146]

BERJAY ALL ROSCH, BUKOVINA, RO [37045]

BERKETT PRE 1950 HOPE, NLN, NZ [36249]

BERKHUIZEN C1819 VOORSCHOTEN, ZUH, NL
[34390]

BERKOWITZ 1700+ RIGA, SU [34943]

BERKS 1800+ HANDSWORTH, STS, ENG [38481]

BERLAYMONT (SEE BERL [38169]

BERLEMANN 1650-1790 PARTENHEIM, RPF, BRD
[37011]

BERLEMONT ALL BRA, BEL [38169]

BERMAN 1600S NIEUWERKERK, ZEL, NL [38358]

BERNARD 1854+ BATHURST, NSW, AUS [34446] :
1400+ DUBLIN, WIC, IRL [33989] : 1800-1900
NEWMARKET, COR, IRL [37844] : 1700-1770 NEW

YORK, NY, USA **[34205]** : 1800+ MONROE, MI, USA **[38517]**

BERNDROD PRE 1790 HOLZAPPEL, LAHNKREIS, GER **[38690]**

BERNDROTH PRE 1780 SCHEIDT, LAHNKREIS, GER **[38690]**

BERNDT 1870 WULFLATZKE, POM, GER **[38018]**

BERNER PRE 1850 BRD **[38238]**

BERNHARDT PRE 1700 GER **[38669]** : PRE 1900 HEILIGENSTADT, HES, GER **[38674]** : 1700-1850 DARMSTADT, HES, GER **[38740]** : 1800-1960 HAMILTON, OH, USA **[38740]** : 1800-1900 CINCINNATI, OH, USA **[38740]**

BERNHART PRE 1955 RANKWEIL, OES **[34175]**

BERNITT PRE 1850 DDR **[38616]**

BERNONVILLE 1650-1750 LONDON, ENG **[34828]** : 1650-1750 BLOIS, FRA **[34828]**

BERNTSEN 1700+ ZEDDAM, NL **[37016]**

BEROVITCH ALL WORLDWIDE **[36030]**

BERQUIST 1870+ PALMERSTON NTH, NZ **[36892]**

BERRELL PRE 1800 CASTLE BELLINGHAM, LOU, IRL **[35727]**

BERREMAN ALL GRAFFHAM, SSX, ENG **[35146]**

BERRIDGE 1600+ MARKET OVERTON, RUT & LEI, ENG **[36827]** : 1780+ SUTTON BONINGTON, NTT, ENG **[37258]** : 1770+ ISLINGTON & SYDNEY, LND & NSW, ENG & AUS **[35155]**

BERRIGAN 1880+ BATHURST & LITHGOW, NSW, AUS **[35155]** : PRE 1870 NFD, CAN **[38537]**

BERRIMAN 1880 GAWLER, SA, AUS **[36371]** : 1840+ HUNTER REGION, NSW, AUS **[36632]** : ALL GRAFFHAM, SSX, ENG **[35146]** : PRE 1800 GULVAL, CON, ENG **[35500]** : 1731 LUDGVAN & HALSE TOWN, CON, ENG **[36371]** : 1800+ NUNHEAD, LND, ENG **[37206]** : ALL USA **[33984]**

BERRINGTON 1700+ LONDON, ENG **[36470]** : 1850+ HEREFORD, HEF, ENG **[37070]**

BERRISFORD PRE 1900 STOKE ON TRENT, STS, ENG **[34548]** : 1800+ RADFORD, NTT, ENG **[34790]**

BERRJERI ALL ROSCH, BUKOVINA, RO **[37045]**

BERROW 1700-1800 WORCESTER, WOR, ENG **[35305]**

BERRY 1853+ SA, AUS **[34883]** : 1880+ BALLARAT, VIC, AUS **[35493]** : 1860+ SYDNEY, NSW, AUS **[35509]** : 1870+ FITZROY, VIC, AUS **[35841]** : 1880S HILL END, BRISBANE, QLD, AUS **[35854]** : 1823+ NSW, AUS **[36608]** : 1800S GRAVENHURST, ONT, CAN **[34103]** : EDMUND 1861 GUELPH, ONT, CAN **[34392]** : 1800+ ST HELIER, JSY, CHI **[34508]** : 1770+ SOUTHLEIGH & WITNEY, OXF, ENG **[33861]** : EMMA 1868-1880S LIVERPOOL ST HELEN'S, ENG **[34103]** : 1800 CAMBERWELL, SRY, ENG **[34204]** : THEODIUS PRE 1803 STEVENAGE, HRT, ENG **[34447]** : 1800S WALTHAMSTOW, LND, ENG **[34483]** : 1700-1800S WISBECH, CAM, ENG **[34483]** : PRE 1800 TURLANGTON, LEI, ENG **[34508]** : 1800+ MARKET HARBOROUGH, LEI, ENG **[34508]** : 1650-1750 HUSBORN CRAWLEY, BDF, ENG **[34552]** : 1753-1831 NEWARK, NTT, ENG **[34672]** : C1830 WIL, ENG **[35841]** : C1886 LEAMINGTON, WAR, ENG **[35854]** : PRE 1760 GLS & BKM, ENG **[36002]** : PRE 1760 NTH & WAR, ENG **[36002]** : 1865+ SRY, ENG **[36002]** : 1830-1866 MARTON, WAR, ENG **[36002]** : 1840+ FRINDSBURY & HIGHAM, KEN, ENG **[36002]** : 1760+ CHIPPING WARDEN, NTH, ENG **[36002]** : C1820-1840 LND & MDX, ENG **[36002]** : 1897+ STROOD, KEN, ENG **[36002]** : PRE 1760 LEI & DBY, ENG **[36002]** : PRE 1760 STS & WOR, ENG **[36002]** : 1750+ SFK & NFK, ENG **[36058]** : PRE 1900 SHOREDITCH, LND, ENG **[36584]** : 1797-1823 ENG **[36608]** : PRE 1820 SOUTH

MALLING, SSX, ENG **[36752]** : 1750+ NATLAND, WES, ENG **[36821]** : WILLIAM PRE 1840 SSX, ENG **[37210]** : 1800+ BRIDPORT, DOR, ENG **[37378]** : EMILY PRE 1896 KINGSTON ON THAMES, SRY, ENG **[37481]** : PRE 1634 DEV, ENG **[37529]** : 1755-1790 CREDITON, DEV, ENG **[37657]** : PRE 1848 MDX, ENG **[38437]** : HENRY J. 1870 CHRISTCHURCH, DEV, ENG **[38540]** : HENRY 1820-1882 LEI & NSW, ENG & AUS **[34942]** : PRE 1862 ARM, IRL **[34571]** : ALL FIF, SCT **[34758]** : PRE 1750 FIF, SCT **[36679]** : 1819+ MADISON, NY, USA **[35616]** : 1851+ USA **[36002]** : 1680-1830 KENT CO., DE, PA & MD, USA **[37529]** : 1800+ SHEFFIELD, VT, USA **[38411]** : 1887-1914 WREXHAM, WLS **[34408]**

BERRYER ALL ELO, GER **[37045]**

BERRYERE ALL ROSCH, BUKOVINA, RO **[37045]**

BERRYMAN GEORGE C1851-1892 GRENFELL, NSW, AUS **[34449]** : 1700-1800 ST AGNES, CON, ENG **[34697]** : ALL GRAFFHAM, SSX, ENG **[35146]** : 1850S CON, ENG **[35509]** : ALL PENWITH, CON, ENG **[37379]** : PRE 1875 SRY, ENG **[37745]** : 1914+ BIRMINGHAM, WAR, ENG & AUS **[34351]** : ALL USA **[33984]**

BERST PRE 1823 ELO, GER **[36726]**

BERT ALL HOLLAND, ZUH, NL **[38702]**

BERTEELE 1800+ WEVELGEM, WF, BEL **[34163]**

BERTEL PRE 1850 WUERTTENBURG, GER **[34914]**

BERTELSON 1806+ SANDUIKEN, BERGEN, NOR & AUS **[38204]**

BERTGES PRE 1788 HOTTENBACH, RPF, GER **[38663]**

BERTHELSEN C1850 DEN **[33809]** : PRE 1888 OSTERILD THISTED, DEN **[34442]**

BERTHET 1700+ LORIOL, DROME, FRA **[36637]**

BERTHILLER PRE 1670 STY, OES **[38669]**

BERTHOLD 1700+ GER **[35566]**

BERTHON 1830+ AVOCA, TAS, AUS **[35929]** : PRE 1830 LEYTON, ESS, ENG **[35929]**

BERTIKEN PRE 1850 VJELE, DEN **[35953]**

BERTRAM 1820 BAV, GER **[36730]** : 1800-1890 PER, SCT **[35981]** : 1760+ ROWAN CO., NC & KY, USA **[34203]**

BERTRAND C1866 BORBECK, NRW, FRG **[38717]** : PRE 1900 VENLO, LMB, NL **[38717]**

BERTWELL 1776-1990 OSSIPEE, NH, USA **[35294]**

BERY 1800S LAN, ENG **[37442]**

BERZDORF PRE 1900 NIEVENHEIM, BRD **[38615]**

BESANT 1800S MELCOMBE REGIS, DOR, ENG **[34116]**

BESFOOT 1750+ PORTSMOUTH, HAM, ENG **[34747]**

BESFORD 1850+ BELFAST, ANT, DOW & ARM, IRL **[35636]** : ALL WORLDWIDE **[33940]**

BESNARD PRE 1660 PARIS, RPA, FRA **[38756]** : 1720+ CORK, COR, IRL **[38756]**

BESSANT PRE 1850 ELING, HAM, ENG **[38420]**

BESSELINKS PRE 1700 ZUTPHEN, NL **[36630]**

BESSELL PRE 1870 CHELSEA, LND, ENG & AUS **[35739]** : C1700 BARBADOES, W.INDIES **[37032]**

BESSEN 1860 PORT GERMEIN, SA, AUS **[37186]**

BESSER PRE 1890 ISLINGTON, LND, ENG **[34454]**

BESSERER PRE 1900 SINSHEIM & ELSENZ, BAW, GER **[38609]**

BEST PRE 1862 WEST MAITLAND, NSW, AUS **[37899]** : 1745 BEMERTON, WIL, ENG **[34120]** : 1700-1900 HEIGHINGTON, DUR, ENG **[34211]** : 1770-1800 EAST COWTON, NRY, ENG **[34211]** : 1800S STOKESLEY, NRY, ENG **[34211]** : 1700S GREAT AYTON, NRY, ENG **[34211]** : 1800S RADFORD SNENTON, NTT, ENG **[34342]** : PRE 1852 ENG **[34661]** : 1700-180S FOVANT, WIL, ENG **[34791]** : PRE 1854 SHEPTON BEAUCHAMP, SOM, ENG

[34886] : PRE 1849 HEIGHINGTON & RYCLIFFE, DUR, ENG [35462] : PRE 1800 BEMERTON, WIL, ENG [36474] : PRE 1840 HAMMERSMITH, LND & MDX, ENG [36478] : GEORGE 1710-LANDULPH & ST IVE, CON, ENG [36734] : 1750-1850 RUAN LANIHORN, CON, ENG [37224] : 1800-1880 CANTERBURY, KEN, ENG [37783] : 1850 FRECKENHAM, SSX, ENG [37829] : PRE 1850 SSX, ENG [37875] : GEORGE 1758-1790 EAST PECKHAM, KEN, ENG [37891] : 1600-1800 ARMAGH, ARM, IRL [33851] : 1820S KILLEVY, ARM, IRL [37106] : SAMUEL 1840-1860 MONROE CO., OH, USA [36734] : NAOMI 1860-1867 OLNEY, RICHLAND CO., IL, USA [36734] : PRE 1840 SC, USA [38576] : 1851-1864 ITAWAMBA, MS, USA [38576]

BESTFORD ALL WORLDWIDE [33940]

BESTING 1700+ KRUBERG, GER [34988]

BESTON 1881+ SYDNEY, NSW, AUS [38213]

BESTWICK 1850+ BATHURST, NSW, AUS [38596] : 1800S FLASH, STS, ENG [36670] : 1790+ LEEK, STS, ENG [37666] : PRE 1820S DEVONPORT, DEV, ENG [38596]

BESWICK 1823+ TAS, AUS [35531] : PRE 1870 SCARBOROUGH, NRY, ENG [34612] : PRE 1875 BASFORD, NTT, ENG [34612] : C1848 ROCHDALE, LAN, ENG [35514] : C1870 ROCHDALE, LAN, ENG [35955] : 1776+ KNUTSFORD, CHS, ENG [36132] : PRE 1850 MANCHESTER, LAN, ENG [36768] : 1720+ SUTTON BONINGTON, NTT, ENG [37258]

BETCHLEY 1840-1860 LEWISHAM, KEN, ENG [35630]

BETHEL 1832+ SAL, ENG [37178] : 1800S ROSCREA, TIP, IRL [37129] : 1690-1740 DARBY CO., PA, USA [38310] : 1730-1790 LOUDOUN CO., VA, USA [38310]

BETHELL 1800-1850 BATTERSEA, SRY, ENG [37495] : 1820+ SALFORD, LAN, ENG [38410]

BETHERIDGE PRE 1700 UK [36210]

BETHRIDGE PRE 1700 UK [36210]

BETHUNE 1780-1830 ROSSKEEN, ROC, SCT [37628] : 1830-1900 GLASGOW, LKS, SCT [37628] : C1819 SALTBURN & KINCARDINE, ROC & SUT, SCT [38592] : DAVID 1774-1820 NC, USA [38123]

BETRIDGE PRE 1700 UK [36210]

BETSCHART 1837 SZ, CH [33754]

BETSEY PRE 1800S PORT LOUIS, MAURITIUS [35161]

BETSON 1600+ MILWICH, STS, ENG [36701]

BETT 1600-1750 ST MONANCE, FIF, SCT [35627]

BETTEL PRE 1900 MILLHILL, MDX, ENG [33830]

BETTERIDGE PRE 1850 STOW IN THE WOLD, GLS, ENG [36385] : PRE 1800 OAKTHORPE, LEI, ENG [36976] : PRE 1700 UK [36210]

BETTERTON 1700+ STOW ON THE WOLD, GLS, ENG [34236] : 1700+ USA [34236]

BETTIS PRE 1852 MILE END RD, LND, ENG [34305]

BETTLES ALL WORLDWIDE [37922]

BETTLEY 1800+ ROTHERHITHE, SRY, ENG [36263]

BETTON PRE 1900 WESTBURY & PONTESBURY, SAL, ENG [37681]

BETTRIDGE PRE 1700 UK [36210]

BETTS 1860+ BALLARAT, VIC, AUS [33850] : PRE 1850 STOKE HAMMOND, BKM, ENG [33850] : 1730+ FELTHORPE, NFK, ENG [34092] : C1800 NORWICH, NFK, ENG [35720] : THOMAS 1800+ LONDON, ENG [36000] : C1730-1900 STIFFKEY & TIBBENHAM, NFK, ENG [36128] : C1700 PATTISWICK, ESS, ENG [37053] : PRE 1800 SOUTH WILLINGHAM, LIN, ENG [37692] : PRE 1799 NORTH TUDDENHAM, NFK, ENG [37726] : 1700+ MAULDON, BDF, ENG [38241] : 1698+

LONG ISLAND, NY, USA [34130] : PRE 1820 VA, USA [38576]

BETTY PRE 1900 TAUNTON, SOM, ENG [35232]

BEUCK ALL GER [35884]

BEUGELSDIJK C1750 ALKEMADE, ZUH, NL [38698]

BEUKE 1865+ BOMBALA & COOMA, NSW, AUS [34421] : PRE 1837 HORNBURG, PRE [34421]

BEUSCHEL PRE 1700 GEMMHAGEN, WUE, GER [37510]

BEUTINS 1700-1900 GER [34624]

BEVAN 1800+ PENNANT HILLS, NSW, AUS [35360] : PRE 1900 COLEFORD, GLS, ENG [33966] : 1850S-1879 WORCESTER & WHITTINGTON, WOR, ENG [36190] : PRE 1900 SOUTHAMPTON, HAM, ENG [36496] : 1750-1900 LIVERPOOL, LAN, ENG [37880] : 1800+ LLANGYNIDR, BRE, WLS [34082] : PRE 1850 NANTYGLO, MON, WLS [34569] : PRE 1851 PYLE, GLA, WLS [36636] : 1800+ ABERGAVENNY, MON, WLS & ENG [34236]

BEVANS HARVEY C1865+ CALGARY, ALB, CAN [34524] : PRE 1700 LLANGENNY, BRE, WLS [36432]

BEVEN 1800+ DARENTH, KEN, ENG [37213]

BEVERDAM 1860 ALMELO, OIJ, NL [35338]

BEVERIDGE 1920+ PERTH, WA, AUS & SCT [38181] : PRE 1800 COCKAIRNIE, FIF, SCT [34809] : 1800+ DALGETY, FIF, SCT [35969] : 1800S MLN, SCT [38490]

BEVERLEY 1750+ HOWDEN, YKS, ENG [36793]

BEVERLY WILLIAM 1790+ PICKERING, NRY, ENG [34078]

BEVERN C1880+ SA, AUS [34591] : C1850 CAPE TOWN, RSA [34591]

BEVIN 1700-1850 ALDBOURNE, WIL, ENG [34343] : PRE 1850 HEF, ENG [36159]

BEVING ALL LUX [35591]

BEVINGTON PRE 1842 HOBART, TAS, AUS [35218] : PRE 1900 ENG [34268] : ALL STS, ENG [35218] : 1810+ LEIGHTON, SAL, ENG [35218] : PRE 1850 WESTON SUBEDGE, GLS & WOR, ENG [37299]

BEVIS 1770+ CARISBROOK, IOW, ENG [35342] : PRE 1810 ALVERSTOKE, HAM, ENG [35483] : 1767 FAREHAM, HAM, ENG [35903]

BEVITT 1700-1800 LONDON, ENG [34701]

BEWICK 1830+ FLIMBY, CUL, ENG [35293]

BEWLEY 1728+ MORLAND, WES, ENG [36132]

BEWS PRE 1860 WARRNAMBOOL, VIC, AUS [35758] : 1770S KIRKWALL, OKI, SCT [34688]

BEWSEY 1846+ ST PANCRAS, MDX, ENG [37611]

BEWSHER 1750-1800 PATTERDALE, WES, ENG [37779]

BEYER 1600-1800 ERFURT, THU, GER [36463] : 1700+ OBERWEISSBACH, THU, GER [37582] : 1750-1800 WUE, GER [37593] : PRE 1740 PA, USA [37587] : 1875-1920 AL, USA [37593] : ALL WORLDWIDE [34961]

BEYRAND ALL SAARBRUCKEN, GER [38063] : 1868-1955 HERMINIE & WESTMORELAND, PA, USA & GER [38063]

BEZANSON ISIAH PRE 1847 STORMONT, NS, CAN [33807] : PRE 1850 NS, CAN [33904]

BEZER ALL GABELA, BOSNIA & HERC, YU [36775]

BEZONA 1785 ALESSANDRIA, PIEDMONT, ITL [38022]

BEZZANT ALL WORLDWIDE [36746]

BIANCHI 1800-1900 DOMEGGE CADORE, BELLUNO, ITL [38337]

BIBB 1860+ VIC & NSW, AUS [35073] : ALL STOURPORT, WOR, ENG [36525]

BIBBINS PRE 1760 BILSTON & WEDNESBURY, STS, ENG [36110]

BIBBY C1850 HABERGAM, LAN, ENG [36649] : PRE 1693 LAN, ENG [37706]

BICCARD 1775-1884 CAPE TOWN, CAPE, RSA [34947]
BICE 1868+ BENDIGO, VIC, AUS [34798]
BICHARD 1720S JSY, CHI [38396]
BICHRIDGE PRE 1830 SONNING, BRK, ENG [35200]
BICK 1800-1860 GLOUCESTER, GLS, ENG [34084]
BICKELL PRE 1840 DEV, ENG [38393]
BICKELMAIER PRE 1856 OESTRICH, PPF, GER [33824]
BICKER 1738-1815 ALVERDISSEN, WEF, GER [38750] : 1714 ULLENHAUSEN, WEF, GER [38750]
BICKERDIKE PRE 1743 GREAT OUSEBURN & BRAFFERTON, WRY & NRY, ENG [37852]
BICKERS C1800 WALPOLE, SFK, ENG [37191] : PRE 1840 THIRSK, YKS, ENG [37991] : ALL WORLDWIDE [36832]
BICKERSTAFF PRE 1860 LAN, ENG [36019] : C1835-1885 ENG & CAN [38182] : C1875-1900 NEW YORK, NY, USA [38182]
BICKERTON 1740+ DAWLEY, SAL, ENG [37266]
BICKFORD JOHN 1775-1851 ANGASTON, SA, AUS [37146] : 1832-1870 ASHPRINGTON, DEV, ENG [34658] : STEPHEN 1698+ LODDISWELL, DEV, ENG [37146] : 1750-1850 ST MARYS, CON, ENG [37615]
BICKLE 1800 KELLY, DEV, ENG [37080]
BICKLEY ALL WROXETER, SAL, ENG [34263] : PRE 1845 BRISTOL, SOM, ENG [36121] : 1700+ GREAT NESS & BASCHURCH, SAL, ENG [37508]
BICKNALL 1800S NOTTINGHAM, NTT, ENG [36506]
BICKNELL 1855-1900 CENTRAL, VIC, AUS [37996] : PRE 1840 LND, ENG [34819] : C1875 WOOLWICH, KEN, ENG [37144] : 1800-1850 GODALMING, SRY, ENG [37996]
BIDDICK 1800-1850 TRURO, CON, ENG [36966]
BIDDIX 1740+ NC, USA [36974]
BIDDLE 1800-1900 LONDON, ENG [35285] : 1800-1870 BRISTOL, GLS, ENG [36795] : 1700+ WHISSENDINE, RUT, ENG [36863] : PRE 1800 HAM, ENG [37588] : C1820-1880S NJ, PA & DE, USA [36319] : WILLIAM 1812+ WV, USA [37453]
BIDDLECOMB 1830+ WIMBORNE, DOR, ENG [37360]
BIDDLECOMBE ALL LODERS, DOR, ENG [36492] : 1790+ LND, ENG [37712]
BIDDULPH PRE 1908 WEST BROMWICH, STS, ENG [34982] : PRE 1611 SEDGLEY, STS, ENG [36954]
BIDEN PRE 1845 PORTSMOUTH, HAM, ENG [34494]
BIDMEAD 1750-1950 COVENTRY, WAR, ENG [37058] : 1800+ ENG [37560] : 1810+ DUNGANNON, TYR, IRL [36827]
BIDWELL ALL WORLDWIDE [37588] : ALL WORLDWIDE [37637]
BIEBER 1650-1860 STRASBURG, ELO, GER [38026] : 1850+ CHEMNITZ, KSA, GER [38651]
BIEGLER 1750-1770 PHILADELPHIA CO., PA, USA [38763]
BIELA PRE 1860 GOTHA, GER [34588]
BIELSKY 1700+ SU [34943]
BIENVENU ALL CAN & USA [35640] : ALL WORLDWIDE [36310]
BIER 1800S SHO, GER [34553] : 1850 SCT [34553]
BIERBAUER ALL GER [38319]
BIERBOWER ALL GER [38319] : 1900+ FANNIN & LEE CO., TX, USA [36947]
BIERBRAUER ALL GER [38319]
BIERER ALL GREENSBURG, PA & NY, USA [33756]
BIERI 1825-1875 GOSREUTH, SG, CH [35283]
BIERLY 1725+ NORTH ELMHAM, NFK, ENG [35824]
BIERMAN ALL GER [34861]
BIFFIN 1840S CAMDEN, NSW, AUS [34791] : 1700-1800S FOVANT, WIL, ENG [34791]

BIFSELL PRE 1870 CHELSEA, LND, ENG & AUS [35739]
BIGBY C1750-1800 LONDON, ENG [37260]
BIGELOW 1800-1900 MN, USA [37464]
BIGGAR 1840+ NSW & VIC, AUS [37128] : 1750+ YKS, ENG [36749]
BIGGART 1810-1890 BEITH, AYR, SCT [35391]
BIGGEMANN PRE 1900 LANGENHOLTHAUSEN, NRW, BRD [35004] : PRE 1900 DEKEN BEI BALVE, NRW, BRD [35004] : 1900+ WESTLOCK, ALB, CAN [35004]
BIGGER PRE 1700 ANT, IRL & SCT [37795]
BIGGERSTAFF 1600+ ENG [37099]
BIGGERSTAFFE ALL LONDON, ENG [37237]
BIGGIN PRE 1849+ CASTLE CARY, SOM, ENG & AUS [35664]
BIGGINGTON PRE 1900 LONDON, ENG [36107]
BIGGINS PRE 1830 WITHAM, ESS, ENG [33869]
BIGGS 1863+ ST KILDA, VIC, AUS [35746] : SAMUEL 1800S EXETER, DEV, ENG [33928] : PRE 1850 STOKENCHURCH, OXF, ENG [34727] : CHARLES 1826-1893 BRISTOL, GLS, ENG [35271] : PRE 1863 BRISTOL, GLS, ENG [35746] : 1500+ OXF & BKM, ENG [37099] : ALL CUBLINGTON, BKM, ENG [37249] : 1750+ PILTON, SOM, ENG [37328] : PRE 1860 LND, ENG [37941] : CHARLES 1826-1893 BURLINGTON FLATS & NORWICH, NY, USA [35271] : 1800-1835 MONTGOMERY CO., VA, USA [38330]
BIGHAM PRE 1874 DOW, IRL [35985]
BIGLIN TOM 1889-1965 GRIMSBY, LIN & YKS, ENG [36443]
BIGMORE ALL AUS [35840]
BIGNIL C1666 QUENINGTON, GLS, ENG [35259]
BIGNILL 1840 WESTON, NTH, ENG [35808]
BIGNY PRE 1835 LONDON, LND & NFK, ENG [35576]
BIGRAVE PRE 1800 ENG [38754]
BIJL 1800-1900 NIJMEGEN, GEL, NL [38337]
BIJLO 1660-1690S BIEZELINGE, ZEL, NL [38358]
BILGER ALL LOR, FRA [38431] : ALL ALS, FRA [38431] : 1850+ USA [37457] : 1860+ JEFFERSON CO., NY, USA [38431]
BILKENROTH 1750-1850 DESSAU, ANH, GER [38565]
BILKEY FANNY 1860-1900 MANCHESTER, LAN, ENG [38409] : JOHN HENRY 1860-1920 MANCHESTER, LAN, ENG [38409] : JOHN 1820-1875 MANCHESTER, LAN, ENG [38409]
BILL 1840+ CAVE HILL, ANT, IRL [34484]
BILLANY 1750 ERY, ENG [34731]
BILLARD 1819-1909 AUTUN, BRG, FRA [34136]
BILLE ALL CAN [38664] : ALL GER [38664] : ALL USA [38664]
BILLEN 1800 ORENHOFEN, RPF, GER [36907]
BILLENS PRE 1818 LONDON, MDX, ENG [35542]
BILLET 1900S WA, AUS [35706]
BILLING C1800 BRIXWORTH, NTH, ENG [35377] : PRE 1845 GRIMSTONE AREA, NFK, ENG [36265] : C1800 ENG & DEN [34041]
BILLINGHAM 1820-1850 DUDLEY ST THOMAS, WOR, ENG [34399] : 1700+ MAULDEN, BDF, ENG [34640] : 1817-1838 WOR, ENG [35436]
BILLINGHURST 1750-1850 DEV, ENG [36430]
BILLINGS 1750-1850 MISSISQUOI, QUE, CAN [37486] : 1850 BLAKENEY, NFK, ENG [34546] : ALL LEI, ENG [36005] : 1819-1850S HACKNEY & STEPNEY, MDX, ENG [36836] : ALL LONDON, ENG [37728] : PRE 1826 BRIGHTON, SSX, ENG [37856] : JOHN 1775 ENG [38156] : 1806+ NORWICH, USA [35391] : 1700-1850 NEWPORT, RI, USA [36335] : CHARLES 1817-1901 TIOGA CO., PA, USA [38156]

BILLINGTON ALL SOMERTON, OXF, ENG [35901] :
PRE 1870 RED STREET, STS, ENG [36504] : 1760-
1780 ESSEX CO., NJ, USA [36328] : 1780-1820
MARSHALL CO., TN, USA [36328] : JOHN 1620-
1700 PLYMOUTH, MA, USA [36555]

BILLIOU 1600-1700 STATEN ISLAND, NY, USA &
FRA [38225]

BILLS 1760-1800 EGMANTON, NTT, ENG [36561] :
1600-1700 BOURNE, LIN, ENG [38287]

BILNEY ALL NFK & SFK, ENG [34938] : 1700-1800
STRADBROKE, SFK, ENG [35069]

BILO (SEE BIJLO) [38358]

BILSBOROUGH 1700-1850 GARGRAVE, WRY, ENG
[37859]

BILSON PRE 1860 BRILEY HILL, STS, ENG [37975]

BILTON PRE 1800 HALTON HOLGATE, LIN, ENG
[35255] : 1700+ LONGHORSLEY & HEBRON, NBL,
ENG [36609]

BIMSON C1700-1760 ENG [36289]

BINDER 1750 RAYLEIGH, ESS, ENG [37928] : PRE
1860 DEARBORN CO., IN, USA [37797] : 1850+
HAMILTON CO., OH, USA [37797]

BINDING 1854+ CRANBOURNE, VIC, AUS [34796] :
1757+ BROMPTON RALPH, SOM, ENG [34796] :
1787+ COMBEFLOREY, SOM, ENG [34796] : C1700
LND & MDX, ENG [35034]

BINDON C1775-1850 DRAYTON, SOM, ENG [37544] :
ALL WORLDWIDE [34929]

BINDSCHADLER ALL ERLENBACH, ZH, CH [38665]
: ALL MANNEDORF, ZH, CH [38665] : ALL
ZURICH, ZH, CH [38665]

BINDSCHEDLER ALL ZURICH, ZH, CH [38665] :
ALL MANNEDORF, ZH, CH [38665] : ALL
ERLENBACH, ZH, CH [38665]

BINE PRE 1820 LONDON, ENG [34105]

BINES 1700+ ESS, ENG [36093]

BINFIELD PRE 1880 KEN, ENG [36841]

BINGHAM 1850+ YAMBUK, VIC, AUS [35835] :
1750+ NORTON, DBY, ENG [34762] : PRE 1813
BIRMINGHAM, WAR, ENG [35223] : 1750-1880
KIDDERMINSTER, WOR, ENG [35835] : 1800+
MARYLEBONE, MDX, ENG [37718] : PRE 1860
BOYLE, ROS, IRL [33876] : PRE 1865 LURGAN,
ARM, IRL [35128] : THOMAS C1814 SCT [37718]

BINGLEY 1820-1920 GRIMSBY, LIN, ENG [37645]

BINKS 1900+ AUS [36295] : ELLIOT C1851-1915
BISHOP AUCKLAND, DUR, ENG [34721] : ALL
LAN, ENG [36119] : PRE 1900 YKS, ENG [36295] :
ALL ESS, ENG [36500] : ALL FINGHALL, NRY,
ENG [37627] : 1700-1800 NRY, ENG [38269]

BINLEY BENJAMIN 1868 IROQUOIS CO., IL, USA
[36736] : 1888 WRIGHT CO., MO, USA [36736]

BINNELL 1500S-1700S WROCKWARDINE, SAL,
ENG [35126]

BINNEY PRE 1860 ARBROATH, ANS, SCT [36963]

BINNIE 1850+ ONT, CAN [37492] : 1750+ PEE, SCT
[37492]

BINNS 1800S WOLSTANTON, STS, ENG [33949] :
1700-1780 MARYLEBONE, LND, ENG [34143] : 1867
STILLINGFLEET, YKS, ENG [34309] : 1823
WAKEFIELD, YKS, ENG [35369] : PRE 1900
SKIPTON, WRY, ENG [36126] : ALL YKS, ENG
[37379] : 1820S LEEDS, WRY, ENG [37754] : PRE
1820 ADWALTON PAR BIRSTALL, WRY, ENG
[37754]

BINNY ALL FORFAR, ANS, SCT [37767]

BINSKY PRE 1880S BERLIN, BLN, GER [37529]

BINSTEAD C1850 NZ [35836]

BINSTED 1750-1873 PORTSEA, HAM, ENG [33995]

BINYON ALL WORLDWIDE [37696]

BIOLETTI 1777-1869 PORTSEA, HAM, ENG & ITL
[36207]

BIOLEY ALL WORLDWIDE [38633]

BIONARD PRE 1840 LONDON, ENG [37743]

BIONDI C1500-C1850 PERGOLA, ITL [36139]

BIRBECK 1760 KIRKLAND, WES, ENG [34731] :
1870-1980 FLAXTON, YKS, ENG [34834] : 1800-1900
NORTH LONDON, ENG [38244] : 1700-1850
WORCESTER, WOR, ENG [38244] : 1600-1900
WORLDWIDE [38244]

BIRCH PRE 1900 ADELONG & WAGGA, NSW, AUS
[35087] : 1808+ HOBART, TAS, AUS [35877] : PRE
1850 DEAL, KEN, ENG [33804] : PRE 1822
MAIDSTONE, KEN, ENG [34043] : PRE 1900
STOKE ON TRENT, STS, ENG [34548] : 1700+
BINSTED, SSX, ENG [34747] : PRE 1850 ST
LEONARDS, SSX, ENG [35173] : ALL
MANCHESTER, LAN, ENG [36242] : 1800+
BIRMINGHAM, WAR, ENG [36532] : C1890 BIRMINGHAM,
WAR, ENG [36679] : 1800+ LIVERPOOL, LAN,
ENG [36746] : 1850S DISEWORTH, LEI, ENG
[36847] : 1800-1875 WEST LONDON, MDX, ENG
[37222] : PRE 1800 NTT & DBY, ENG [37412] : 1800-
41 NESTON, CHS, ENG [37732] : 1841+
WALLASEY, CHS, ENG [37732] : PRE 1830
SHEFFIELD, YKS, ENG [38248] : PRE 1860
LIMERICK, LIM, IRL [34454] : 1780-1900
CORRAGHDUFF & EMYVALE, MOG, IRL [36075] :
1906-1926 THAMES WAIHI, WKT, NZ [36746] :
1895-1906 JOHANNUSBURG, RSA [36746] : 1815+
DENBIGH, DEN, WLS [38539]

BIRCHALL 1850-1950 ST HELENS, LAN, ENG [34552]

BIRCHELLS C1500 ENG [34395]

BIRCHENOUGH WILLIAM 1800-1860 ENG [38337] :
1800-1910 PASSAIC CO., NJ, USA [38337]

BIRCHETT ALL WORLDWIDE [37293]

BIRCHLER 1900+ WORLDWIDE [33974]

BIRCHLEY 1700-1800S GLS & WOR, ENG [37221]

BIRD 1885 TAS, AUS [34775] : C1876 HAMILTON,
VIC, AUS [37177] : C1883+ TAS, AUS [37177] :
1879+ BIRREGURRA, VIC, AUS [37177] : 1650+
CAN [33903] : 1700-1860 ENG [33753] : 1830-1865
LONDON, ENG [33960] : 1787-1823 IBSTONE,
BKM, ENG [33995] : 1920+ SOUTHALL, MDX,
ENG [33997] : PRE 1800 SAFFRON WALDEN &
LITTLEBURY, ESS, ENG [34099] : PRE 1850
GUISBOROUGH & PICKERING, YKS, ENG
[34099] : 1940-1970 WESTERHAM, KEN, ENG
[34099] : 1850-1925 YORK, YKS, ENG [34099] : 1750-
1900 LUPPITT, DEV, ENG [34632] : PRE 1825
EYTON ON THE WEALDS MOORS, SAL, ENG
[34711] : ALL SFK, ENG [34744] : 1831-1851 GLS,
ENG [35092] : ALL BOVEY TRACEY, DEV, ENG
[35345] : PRE 1765 NORTHIAM, SSX, ENG [35587] :
1815+ WOR & WAR, ENG [35827] : 1800+
MAIDEN NEWTON, DOR, ENG [35964] : PRE 1900
WALSHAM LE WILLOWS, SFK, ENG [35978] :
1700-1900 MDX & LND, ENG [36007] : 1700-1800
ANCASTER, LIN, ENG [36057] : PRE 1850
BRIERLEY HILL & KINGSWINFORD, STS, ENG
[36110] : PRE 1790 MIDDLEZOY, SOM, ENG [36278]
: 1600-1850 DAWLEYMAGNA, SAL, ENG [36556] :
1600-1850 PITCHFORD, SAL, ENG [36556] : PRE
1750 AYLSHAM, NFK, ENG [36593] : 1800S
BETHNAL GREEN, LND, ENG [36764] : C1791
BILLESDON, LEI, ENG [36803] : PRE 1800
HALESWORTH, SFK, ENG [36829] : PRE 1836
BADBY, NTH, ENG [37068] : 1730S TAKELEY, ESS,
ENG [37250] : 1830-1900 BIRKENHEAD, CHS, ENG
[37734] : 1830-1900 CHESTER, CHS, ENG [37734] :
1860-1920 LIVERPOOL, LAN, ENG [37734] : JOHN
EDMUND 1800+ ST PANCRAS, LND, ENG [37775]
: 1880S HANDSWORTH, STS, ENG [37827] : C1700

FARNHAM, HAM, ENG **[37898]** : 1800-1900 LIVERPOOL, LAN, ENG **[37931]** : ELIZABETH PRE 1860 LAMBOURNE, ESS, ENG **[38755]** : 1800S SHARNBROOK, BDF, ENG & AUS **[35558]** : PRE 1840 BELFAST, IRL **[34775]** : 1800 KINGS, OFF, IRL **[35342]** : PRE 1847 BALLYCUMBER, OFF, IRL **[37177]** : PRE 1770 ABERLADY & PRESTONPANS, ELN, SCT **[37852]** : C1600 MA, USA **[34395]** : 1630-1700 HARTFORD, CT, USA **[37783]** : PRE 1890 WORLDWIDE **[36249]** : ALL WORLDWIDE **[37099]**

BIRDSALL 1800-1900 ONT, CAN **[37466]** : C1863 HAZLEWOOD, WRY, ENG **[37726]**

BIRDSELL ALL MDX & SRY, ENG **[37452]**

BIRDSEYE 1600S READING, DBY, ENG **[34342]** : 1630+ CT, USA **[34342]**

BIRDWOOD C1832 BELGAUM, INDIA **[36259]**

BIRDZELL 1780-1810 CAYUGA CO., NY, USA **[36334]**

BIREBENT 1600-1900 VICDESSOS ARCONAC, ARIEGE, FRA **[33758]**

BIRGAN 1850+ CLEVELAND, QLD, AUS **[34015]**

BIRGUM 1865-90 GER **[37605]**

BIRKBECK 1700-1900 ASKRIGG, NRY, ENG **[38244]** : ALL WORLDWIDE **[38244]**

BIRKBY ALL KIPPAX & LEEDS, YKS, ENG **[36763]**

BIRKENBEIL PRE 1850 SINSHEIM & ELSENZ, BAW, GER **[38609]**

BIRKENHEAD C1800 KINGSLEY, CHS, ENG **[34333]** : ALL ENG **[35552]**

BIRKENSHAW 1700-1820 LEDSTONE, WRY, ENG **[38381]**

BIRKETT PRE 1825 OWERSBY, LIN, ENG **[34240]** : 1795-1900 BRK, LND & MDX, ENG **[34467]** : 1800-1850 KIRKBY LONSDALE, WES, ENG **[35006]** : PRE 1840 MORECAMBE, LAN, ENG **[35354]** : PRE 1750 HAWKSHEAD, LAN, ENG **[36701]** : 1833 LAN, ENG **[36859]** : C1808 WINDERMERE, WES, ENG **[37144]** : 1700-1800 HAWKSHEAD & KESWICK, WES & CUL, ENG **[37460]** : PRE 1950 HOPE, NLN, NZ **[36249]** : 1878 AUCKLAND, NZ **[36859]**

BIRKHEAD 1650-1750 ANNE ARUNDEL CO., MD, USA **[38119]**

BIRKIN C1890 BORROWASH, DBY, ENG **[34734]** : 1700+ NOTTINGHAM, NTT, ENG **[37248]**

BIRKITT PRE 1900 WOOLWICH, KEN, ENG **[33965]**

BIRKLEY 1822+ YEOVIL, SOM, ENG **[34926]**

BIRKMIRE 1700-1855 DFS, KKD & WIG, SCT **[36108]** : 1840-1900 PHILADELPHIA, PA, USA **[36108]** : 1800-1920 NEW YORK, NY, USA **[36108]**

BIRKMYER 1790-1890 LIVERPOOL, LAN, ENG **[36108]** : 1700-1855 DFS, KKD & WIG, SCT **[36108]**

BIRKMYRE 1790-1890 LIVERPOOL, LAN, ENG **[36108]** : 1850 PORT GLASGOW, SCT &, INDIA **[34708]** : ALL ANT, DOW & LDY, IRL **[36108]** : 1600-1855 GLASGOW, LKS, RFW & DNB, SCT **[36108]** : 1700-1855 DFS, KKD & WIG, SCT **[36108]**

BIRKS 1888+ PARRAMATTA, NSW, AUS **[35022]** : PRE 1850 KIDDERMINSTER, WOR, ENG **[34711]** : PRE 1850 STOKE ON TRENT, STS, ENG **[35022]** : C1750 BRAMPTON LE MORTHEN, WRY, ENG **[36147]**

BIRMINGHAM PRE 1845 WANDSWORTH, LND, ENG **[36475]** : PRE 1850 CARRA, GAL, IRL **[34621]**

BIRNEY 1800 SLAVEBARN, TIP, IRL **[33848]** : 1700+ CASTLEREA, ROS, IRL **[35355]**

BIRNIE C1700-1800 STRICHEN, ABD, SCT **[34400]**

BIRRELL PRE 1820 WETHERAL, CUL, ENG & SCT **[35592]** : PRE 1828 KILRENNY, FIF, SCT **[35525]**

BIRRI 1650+ BOURGOGNE, FRA **[38598]**

BIRT PRE 1850 SWANAGE, DOR, ENG **[36517]**

BIRTLES 1700+ KNUTSFORD, CHS, ENG **[35183]** : 1850+ MANCHESTER, LAN, ENG **[35183]** : 1800-1900 SANDBACH & ODDROOE, CHS, ENG **[38250]**

BIRTWHISTLE PRE 1900 DELPH & HALIFAX, WRY, ENG **[36037]** : PRE 1820 HALIFAX, YKS, ENG **[38512]**

BIRTWISLE 1600-1800 TARWIN, CHS, ENG **[36218]**

BISBINGS 1600S MMASTRICHT, LMB, NL **[38358]**

BISCHOFF C1830 SCHIMBORN, GER **[38527]**

BISCO ALL WORLDWIDE **[37051]**

BISCOE 1750+ NEWENT, GLS, ENG **[36825]**

BISH ALL SSX, ENG **[37922]**

BISHCHOFF C1700-50 WORMS & HANAU, RPF, GER **[38348]**

BISHOP ALL WA, AUS **[34562]** : 1855+ FINGAL, TAS, AUS **[34853]** : 1830+ NSW, AUS **[35520]** : 1832 SYDNEY, NSW, AUS **[35557]** : 1855+ MOONTA, SA, AUS **[35776]** : 1750-1900 U IS COVE & BRADLEY'S COVE, NFD, CAN **[34250]** : 1870-1909 DUNDAS, ONT, CAN **[34251]** : PRE 1860 TORONTO, ONT, CAN **[36652]** : PRE 1678 JSY, CHI **[34104]** : ANTOINE 1700-1755 ST BRELADE, JSY, CHI **[38396]** : 1800+ WYKE REGIS, DOR, ENG **[33774]** : C1850S NOTTINGHAM, NTT, ENG **[33928]** : 1722 FORDINGTON, DOR, ENG **[33967]** : MARY 1823 UP OTTERY, DEV, ENG **[34195]** : 1812-1858 BRACKLEY, NTH, ENG **[34251]** : PRE 1750 ISLEHAM, CAM, ENG **[34445]** : 1760+ SHERBORNE, DOR, ENG **[34777]** : PRE 1855 SOM, ENG **[34853]** : PRE 1914 SHOREDITCH, MDX, ENG **[35031]** : PRE 1834 HULL, YKS, ENG **[35061]** : C1845 PRIDDY, SOM, ENG **[35391]** : PRE 1831 LEDBURY, HEF, ENG **[35557]** : 1780+ GOUDHURST, KEN, ENG **[35776]** : C1825 WOOTTON, OXF, ENG **[35910]** : 1800S LONDON, ENG **[35933]** : 1700-1800 SAL & HEF, ENG **[36003]** : PRE 1700 BDF, BKM & HRT, ENG **[36042]** : 1801-1900 GLOUCESTER, GLS, ENG **[36248]** : 1900-1990 GLOUCESTER, GLS, ENG **[36248]** : ALL MAIDSTONE & EAST MALLING, KEN, ENG **[36326]** : C1750-1850 BURTON BRADSTOCK, DOR, ENG **[36478]** : 1800-1820 DEVONPORT, DEV, ENG **[36536]** : PRE 1860 READING, BRK, ENG **[36761]** : 1800-1900 BRENTFORD, MDX, ENG **[37222]** : 1840-1870 WEYMOUTH, DOR, ENG **[37233]** : PRE 1850 BRIGHTON, SSX, ENG **[37279]** : 1800+ READING, BRK, ENG **[37638]** : C1775 LEI, ENG **[37661]** : PRE 1816 BIRMINGHAM, WAR, ENG **[37662]** : 1850+ TAUNTON, SOM, ENG **[37719]** : 1800-1850 HOLBORN, MDX, ENG **[37765]** : 1660-1900 WESTERLEIGH, GLS, ENG **[37870]** : C1700 EAST COKER, SOM, ENG **[37918]** : 1800S SSX, ENG & NZ **[36607]** : PRE 1854 IRL **[34696]** : 1750+ IRL **[37306]** : 1850+ CHRISTCHURCH, CANTY, NZ **[36326]** : 1800S WHITBURN, WLN, SCT **[34367]** : 1720+ CURRIE, MLN, SCT **[37666]** : 1810-1850 HANCOCK CO., TN, USA **[36731]** : 1750-1820 SPARTENBURG, SC, USA **[36737]** : 1749 NJ, USA **[37008]** : C1770-1840 OH, USA **[38112]** : 1660S GUILFORD, CT, USA **[38184]**

BISHOPRICK 1800+ BEVERLEY, YKS, ENG **[38471]**

BISHTON 1800S SAL, ENG **[33958]**

BISS 1800+ KIEL, SHO, BRD **[34459]** : 1800+ HEF, ENG **[34459]** : 1800+ BOURNEMOUTH, HAM, ENG **[34459]** : PRE 1770 SOM & WIL, ENG **[36478]**

BISSE PRE 1770 SOM & WIL, ENG **[36478]** : 1700+ LONDON, MDX, ENG **[36700]**

BISSEGER 1814 NIEDERHELFENSCHWIL, SG, CH **[33754]**

BISSELL 1790-1850 LEEDS, ONT, CAN **[38097]** : PRE 1738 NEEDINGWORTH, HUN, ENG **[36425]** : 1591-1840 WATERBURY, CT, USA **[37803]**

BISSET PRE 1860 OLD MACHAR, ABD, SCT **[34816]** : PRE 1850 PER, SCT **[36993]** : 1800+ NEWBURGH,

FIF, SCT **[37167]** : ALL EAST NEUK, FIF, SCT **[37704]**

BISSETT 1857+ FOREST, TAS, AUS **[36644]** : 1840+ WARWICK, CUL, ENG **[37635]** : C1770+ KIRKLISTON, MLN, SCT **[35629]** : 1818 PETERHEAD, ABD, SCT **[35855]** : C1793 BOTHWELL, LKS, SCT **[36644]**

BISSILL PRE 1870 CHELSEA, LND, ENG & AUS **[35739]**

BISSINGER 1700-1800 WUE, GER **[38652]**

BISSLAND 1882+ SOUTH MELBOURNE, VIC, AUS **[34798]**

BISSON 1600+ JSY, CHI **[34532]**

BISSOT 1700-1800 ST MONANCE, FIF, SCT **[35627]**

BISWELL PRE 1900 LONDON, ENG & CAN **[34164]**

BITHELL 1855 ROPETT, DEN, WLS **[38022]**

BITOL ALL WORLDWIDE **[37453]**

BITSCH PRE 1855 SCHRIESHEIM, BAD, GER **[34886]**

BITTEL 1600+ SELZEN, RPF, BRD **[37012]**

BITTER C1850 UTRECHT, UTR, NL **[38702]**

BITTICK 1800+ MO, USA **[36974]** : 1800+ TN, USA **[36974]** : 1815+ AR, USA **[36974]**

BIVINS PRE 1850 KINGSCLERE, HAM & WIL, ENG **[37687]**

BIZET 1800 JARNAC, FRA **[36596]**

BIZOT PRE 1900 ALKEMADE, ZUH, NL **[34613]**

BJERCK 1820S TRONDHEIM, NOR **[35906]**

BJORK ALBERT S. PRE 1900 STOCKHOLM, SWE **[38049]**

BJORNDAHL ALL KOKKOLA, FIN **[33873]** : 1875+ WORLDWIDE **[33873]**

BJORNERUD 1700+ TINN, TELEMARK, NOR **[36905]**

BJORNVIK PRE 1780 LARSMO, VAASA, FIN **[34858]**

BJORSTROM ALL JEMTLAND & UPPSALA, SWE **[34508]**

BLACHFORD PRE 1850 HAM, DOR & IOW, ENG & CAN **[38021]**

BLACK 1850+ SOUTH PRESTON, VIC, AUS **[35157]** : 1853+ ALLORA, QLD, AUS **[36607]** : 1864+ BLAYNEY, NSW, AUS **[36641]** : 1860S YACKANDANDAH, VIC, AUS **[37908]** : 1850+ GREY CO., ONT, CAN **[34051]** : ALL ST STEPHEN, NB, CAN **[36713]** : ANN 1814-1852 ONTARIO CO., ONT, CAN & IRL **[38396]** : 1700+ YARMOUTH, NFK, ENG **[34303]** : PRE 1800 KIRK MERRINGTON, DUR, ENG **[34316]** : CECELIA 1958+ GRAYSHOTT, HAM, ENG **[34341]** : PRE 1900 CARLISLE, CUL, ENG **[35470]** : PRE 1700 AYLSHAM, NFK, ENG **[36593]** : PRE 1830 OMAGH, TYR, IRL **[34113]** : 1798 DOW, IRL **[34474]** : PRE 1840 LURGAN, ARM, IRL **[35128]** : 1810+ SCARVA, ARM, IRL **[35157]** : 1600+ BOYLE, ROS, IRL **[35355]** : 1700+ BELFAST, ANT, DOW & ARM, IRL **[35636]** : 1750-1900 BALLYCASTLE, ANT, IRL **[36115]** : PRE 1853 DRUMCREE, ARM, IRL **[36607]** : PRE 1850 BALLYMOTE, SLI, IRL **[36760]** : PRE 1800 LETTERKENNY, DON, IRL **[38056]** : C1840 TYR, IRL **[38253]** : 1850+ IRL **[38481]** : 1840 AUCKLAND, NZ **[34878]** : 1675 WEMYSS, FIF, SCT **[33767]** : C1860 MAYBOLE, AYR, SCT **[33880]** : WILLIAM C1730 PAISLEY, RFW, SCT **[33910]** : 1800+ ABERDEEN, SCT **[33947]** : 1800+ DUNDEE, ANS, SCT **[34049]** : 1730-1740 KNOCKANDO, MOR, SCT **[34205]** : JAMES 1800 DUMFRIES, DFS, SCT **[34621]** : 1800S DALRY, KKD, SCT **[35126]** : C1800+ ST NINIANS, STI, SCT **[35629]** : 1850-1900S DUNDEE, ANS, SCT **[35938]** : PRE 1870 SHOTTS, LKS & ARL, SCT **[36191]** : 1800S INVERURIE, ABD, SCT **[36843]** : 1800+ ST CYRUS, KCD, SCT **[36971]** : PRE 1700 CARNWATH & LANARK, LKS, SCT **[37374]** : PRE 1780 AYR, SCT **[37434]** : JEAN 1850+ OCHILTREE,

AYR, SCT **[37444]** : PRE 1811 TEMPLE, MLN, SCT **[37852]** : C1820 PETERHEAD, ABD, SCT **[37908]** : C1850 EDINBURGH, MLN, SCT **[38253]** : 1800+ LANARK, LKS, SCT & NZ **[36791]** : ALL UK **[37674]** : 1830-1850 BOLIVAR, PA, USA **[36444]** : 1870 SALTSBURG, PA, USA **[36444]** : 1804-1838 CHESTER DISTRICT, SC, USA **[36553]** : 1800S HUTCHISON & TOPEKA, KS, USA **[36918]** : 1900+ MI, USA **[38481]** : 1600-1800 USA & ENG **[35289]**

BLACKALL PRE 1800 APPLEFORD, BRK, ENG **[35595]** : 1800+ EXETER, DEV, ENG **[37166]** : 1860-1867 NZ **[37156]**

BLACKALLER C1781 ILSLEY, BRK, ENG **[36276]**

BLACKBERRY 1843+ TAS, AUS **[37177]** : ALL ENG **[37177]** : PRE 1842 WHITECHAPEL, LND, ENG **[37177]**

BLACKBOURN C1813+ ROWSTON, LIN, ENG **[35746]** : ALL TATHWELL, LIN, ENG **[35746]** : C1803+ ASHBY DE LA LAUNDE, LIN, ENG **[35746]** : C1793+ BRAUNCEWELL (TEMPLE BREWER), LIN, ENG **[35746]** : C1802 DIGBY, LIN, ENG **[35746]** : 1770+ TIMBERLAND, LIN, ENG **[35746]**

BLACKBURN 1863+ SYDNEY, NSW, AUS **[35160]** : 1700-1850 YKS & LAN, ENG **[34067]** : WILLIAM 1800S BORDLEY MOOR, YKS, ENG **[34499]** : PRE 1825 YKS, ENG **[34712]** : 1600-1700 GREYSTOKE, CUL, ENG **[36098]** : JOSHUA PRE 1685 ENG **[37052]** : ALL NFK, ENG **[37052]** : 1800 NEWINGTON, LND, ENG **[37192]** : 1860+ LEEDS, WRY, ENG **[37202]** : 1875-1900 LIVERPOOL, LAN, ENG **[37255]** : 1790+ ASHTON UNDER LYNE, LAN, ENG **[37255]** : 1790+ MANCHESTER, LAN, ENG **[37255]** : 1700-1800 COLNE VALLEY, WRY, ENG **[37372]** : 1720-1840 LONDON, MDX, ENG **[37734]** : 1700-1900 STOCKTON ON TEES, DUR, ENG **[37854]** : 1700-1900 THORNABY ON TEES, NRY, ENG **[37854]** : 1900+ LIVERPOOL, LAN, ENG **[38274]** : 1800-1850 CARROWCLARE, LDY, IRL **[35845]** : PRE 1860 GLASGOW, SCT **[35705]** : ISABELLA 1831+ AYR, SCT & AUS **[35477]** : PRE 1800 BEDFORD CO., PA, USA **[35312]**

BLACKBURNE 1875-1900 LIVERPOOL, LAN, ENG **[37255]** : 1790+ MANCHESTER, LAN, ENG **[37255]** : 1790+ ASHTON UNDER LYNE, LAN, ENG **[37255]**

BLACKER 1841+ NSW, AUS **[33794]** : PRE 1900 NSW, AUS **[34968]** : 1856+ SALE, VIC, AUS **[35725]** : PRE 1856 BOLTON, YKS, ENG **[35725]** : 1777-1835 SHEFFIELD, YKS, ENG **[35849]** : PRE 1800 ARM, IRL **[37087]**

BLACKETT 1839-1900 ST JOHNS WOOD, LND, ENG **[34829]**

BLACKFORD PRE 1825+ SYDNEY, NSW, AUS **[34423]** : 1750+ BURWASH & MAYFIELD, SSX, ENG **[34473]** : 1750-1800 BURNHAM & SHIPSTON, BKM & WAR, ENG **[34552]** : 1800-1840 HIGHCLERE, HAM, ENG **[36150]**

BLACKHALL C1800+ ARBOUGH, TYR & DRY, IRL **[34568]** : 1783+ FRAZERBURGH, ABD, SCT **[35462]** : 1790S EDINBURGH, SCT **[37134]**

BLACKHAM JOSIAH 1773+ LONDON, ENG **[34091]** : OBADIAH 1700+ BIRMINGHAM, WAR, ENG **[34091]** : 1780+ BIRMINGHAM, WAR, ENG **[37258]** : ALL HINSTOCK, SAL, ENG **[38005]** : PRE 1850 WOLVERHAMPTON, STS, ENG **[38420]** : 1700+ IRL **[33887]**

BLACKHURST 1800+ BARROW IN FURNESS, CUL & LKS, ENG & SCT **[34718]**

BLACKIE C1700 LITTLE DUNKELD, PER, SCT **[37918]** : 1800S PITTENDRUM, ABD, SCT **[38422]**

BLACKLAW 1700S+ LAURENCEKIRK, KCD, SCT **[37485]** : PRE 1900 ABERDEEN, ABD, SCT **[38412]**

BLACKLEDGE PRE 1668 LAN, ENG **[37706]** : 1630+ CAMBRIDGE ARMS, MA & CT, USA **[36931]**

BLACKLER ALL BRIXHAM, DEV, ENG **[34298]** : PRE 1830 KINGSTON, SRY, ENG **[37107]**

BLACKLEY 1913+ CORRIMAL, NSW, AUS **[36615]** : 1780-1860 CAMBRIDGE, CAM, ENG **[33960]** : C1852-1868 GAL, IRL **[35446]** : 1868+ SOUTHLAND, NZ **[35446]** : ALL DFS, SCT **[34617]** : PRE 1852 DFS, SCT **[35446]**

BLACKLOCK 1972+ DRUMMOYNE, NSW, AUS **[34423]** : C1800-1850 DERBY, DBY, ENG **[36053]** : PRE 1800 STANWIX, CUL, ENG **[38708]** : C1800+ ARL, SCT & NZ **[36258]**

BLACKMAN PRE 1880 WILMINGTON & BEXLEYHEATH, KEN, ENG **[33957]** : WILLIAM C1847+ LONDON & NORTH WEST, KEN, ENG **[33957]** : PRE 1856 KEN, ENG **[34412]** : 1790S MAIDSTONE, KEN, ENG **[37106]** : C1800 HAM, ENG **[37172]** : PRE 1800 HOOE, SSX, ENG **[37875]** : 1900-1920 STODDARD CO., MO & TN, USA **[38532]** : MARY PRE 1790 NC, USA **[38536]**

BLACKMOORE PRE 1910 SOUTHAMPTON, HAM, ENG **[36761]**

BLACKMORE 1800+ TIVERTON, DEV, ENG **[36785]**

BLACK-NICOL 1750+ EDINBURGH, MLN, SCT **[35025]**

BLACKSLEY ALL HOLBORN, LND, ENG **[34723]**

BLACKSTOCK 1760-1820S CAV, IRL **[34088]** : 1820S-1830S NEW YORK, NY, USA **[34088]**

BLACKSTONE 1545-1650 ENG **[38040]** : 1630-1800 VA, USA **[38040]** : 1787-1850 TN, USA **[38040]**

BLACKTON 1800+ NORMANTON, DBY, ENG **[36887]**

BLACKWELL 1860S BULLI, NSW, AUS **[34793]** : 1857+ SOFALA & HUNTER REGION, NSW, AUS **[35239]** : C1855-1880 GOLDFIELDS & CASTLEMAINE, VIC, AUS **[38541]** : 1820-1950 MIDDLESBROUGH, YKS, ENG **[34234]** : 1829 CROWAN, CON, ENG **[34793]** : MARY 1782-1854 GREAT HUCKLOW, DBY, ENG **[36576]** : SUSAN 1860 UXBRIDGE, MDX, ENG **[36634]** : 1840+ BIRMINGHAM, WAR, ENG **[36649]** : 1700-1800 BISLEY & MISERDEN, GLS, ENG **[36649]** : PRE 1850 GREYTOWN, KEN, ENG & NZ **[36255]** : ALL MS, USA **[36540]** : PRE 1850 VA, USA **[38576]**

BLACKWOOD 1790-1830 ARTREA & DESERTCREAT, TYR, IRL **[36184]** : PRE 1833 MORNINGSIDES, EDINBURGH, SCT **[34797]** : PRE 1820 SCT **[35829]** : 1700-1800 NC, USA **[36324]**

BLACOE ALL LYTHAM, LAN, ENG **[36822]**

BLADDERWICK ALL NTT, ENG **[36532]**

BLADEN 1700+ HRT, ENG **[37829]**

BLADES PRE 1750 GRINTON, YKS, ENG **[36704]** : 1780-1860 NTH, ENG **[38003]**

BLADON 1800-1910 BIRMINGHAM, WAR, ENG **[37074]**

BLAGBROUGH PRE 1840 HALIFAX, WRY, ENG **[38028]**

BLAGG PRE 1900 NTT, ENG **[36126]**

BLAIKIE PRE 1833 DUNOON, ARL, SCT **[35148]**

BLAIN 1700-1850 VARENNES, QUE, CAN **[34242]** : 1700-1850 QUE, CAN **[34242]** : 1800+ NICHOL FOREST, CUL, ENG **[33774]** : 1850-1880S FRANKLIN CO., NY, USA **[34729]**

BLAIR PRE 1900-11 ARMIDALE, NSW, AUS **[33807]** : PRE 1900 VIC, AUS **[34268]** : ALEXANDER PRE 1839 LAUNCESTON, TAS, AUS **[38075]** : 1865+ NSW, AUS & ENG **[35547]** : 1830+ HUNTINGDON CO., QUE, CAN **[36664]** : C1825-1870 NEWCASTLE ON TYNE, NBL, ENG **[34372]** : C1850 BRISTOL, SOM, ENG **[35860]** : ALEXANDER PRE 1840 ENG **[38075]** : PRE 1840 LDY, IRL **[34228]** : PRE 1840

MOG, IRL **[34268]** : 1800S OMAGH & CROSH, TYR, IRL **[34598]** : PRE 1850 ARM, IRL **[36664]** : ALL BELFAST, IRL **[36878]** : 1730-1780 IRL **[38107]** : 1770-1830 STRABANE, TYR, IRL **[38216]** : 1700S ANT, IRL **[38522]** : JOHN PRE 1797 DALRY, AYR, SCT **[33807]** : 1775-1910 BOTHKENNAR, STI, SCT **[34039]** : PRE 1850 EDINBURGH, MLN, SCT **[34097]** : 1800-1900 PITLOCHRY, PER, SCT **[34135]** : 1800 KIRKCALDY, FIF, SCT **[34529]** : 1770 CAMPSIE, STI, SCT **[35252]** : 1720-50 AYR, SCT **[35266]** : 1680-1820 SCT **[35300]** : 1650-1800 ST MONANCE, FIF, SCT **[35627]** : 1781 STRACHLACHLAN, ARL, SCT **[35854]** : GRACE C1827+ DALRY, AYR, SCT **[35995]** : PRE 1858 NEW MONKLAND, LKS, SCT **[36288]** : PRE 1850 FORFAR, ANS, SCT **[36361]** : PRE 1869 EDINBURGH, SCT **[36632]** : 1750+ EDINBURGH, SCT **[37134]** : PRE 1880 RFW & LKS, SCT **[37554]** : 1650 EDINBURGH, MLN, SCT **[37570]** : ALEXANDER PRE 1840 SCT **[38075]** : 1750-1900 TARBERT, ARL, SCT **[38355]** : 1720+ YORK CO., PA, USA **[35266]** : 1870+ RUSSELL, KY, USA **[36567]** : PRE 1870 BURKE, NC, USA **[36567]** : 1800-1850 BEDFORD, PA, USA **[36908]** : 1890-1989 BOSTON, MA, USA **[36915]** : 1860 BURLINGTON, VT, USA **[38131]** : 1790-1820 KNOX CO., TN, USA **[38227]**

BLAISE PRE 1675 MIDDLESEX, VA, USA **[38044]**

BLAIZDELL PRE 1820 LONDON, ENG **[33821]**

BLAKE 1850+ ALEXANDRIA, NSW, AUS **[35360]** : C1850 BENDIGO, VIC, AUS **[35377]** : ANN 1830+ SYDNEY, NSW, AUS **[35527]** : 1880+ BRISBANE, QLD, AUS **[35743]** : 1860+ MELBOURNE, VIC, AUS **[36245]** : WILLIAM 1890+ WA, AUS **[37149]** : PRE 1850 ORANGE & BATHURST, NSW, AUS **[38568]** : PATRICK 1846+ LA CO., ONT, CAN **[34154]** : 1761+ SAINT JOHN, NB, CAN **[34470]** : ALL SOUTHAMPTON, HAM, ENG **[33802]** : PRE 1900 SOUTHWARK, SRY, ENG **[34335]** : PRE 1900 DOR, ENG **[34364]** : 1839 PORT ISAAC, CON, ENG **[34565]** : 1800+ ROMSEY, HAM, ENG **[34880]** : PRE 1850 CHELSEA, LND, ENG **[35360]** : 1700+ SALISBURY, WIL, ENG **[35475]** : 1720+ HURSTBORNE TARRANT, HAM, ENG **[35587]** : 1750-1850 SOM, ENG **[35720]** : 1800+ LONDON, ENG **[35785]** : PRE 1820 YEOVIL, SOM, ENG **[35961]** : 1600-1700 BURY ST EDMUNDS, SFK, ENG **[36438]** : C1808 GRIMSTONE, NFK, ENG **[37131]** : PRE 1900 ANDOVER, HAM, ENG **[37226]** : PRE 1860 CHELSEA, MDX, ENG **[37729]** : PRE 1800 WEST TYTHERLEY, HAM, ENG **[38700]** : PRE 1854 RATHFARNHAM, DUB, IRL **[35162]** : JOHN ISIDORE 1780+ DUBLIN, IRL **[35429]** : WM. JOS 1840+ KINSALE, COR, IRL **[35429]** : 1840S COR, IRL **[35516]** : PRE 1840 DRUMBANE, TIP, IRL **[35818]** : PRE 1860 KILRAORAN, TIP, IRL **[35818]** : PRE 1800 CLOONMORE, MAY, IRL **[36652]** : PRE 1900 CAR, IRL & AUS **[35512]** : PRE 1890 CHRISTCHURCH, NZ **[35727]** : 1881 LYTTELTON, NZ **[35727]** : 1740-1772 ROX, SCT **[34408]** : ELIZABETH PRE 1791 WESTERKIRK, DFS, SCT **[34501]** : PRE 1900 FORGUE, ABD, SCT **[36245]** : 1700+ SYMINGTON, LKS, SCT **[36815]** : PRE 1761 MA, USA **[34470]** : C1835 BUTLER, OH, USA **[38527]**

BLAKEBOROUGH ALL RAINTON, NRY, ENG **[36492]**

BLAKEBROUGH 1840+ MELBOURNE, VIC, AUS **[36360]** : PRE 1840 YKS, ENG **[36360]**

BLAKELEY C1789 COLD NORTON, ESS, ENG **[33899]** : 1820+ HAWKWELL, ESS, ENG **[33899]** : PRE 1870 HUNSLET, YKS, ENG **[37442]**

BLAKELY 1850+ BEECHWORTH, VIC, AUS **[35785]** : PRE 1918 MAGNETEWAN, ONT, CAN **[38450]** :

1770+ MUNDON, ESS, ENG **[35042]** : PRE 1850 WI, USA **[38052]**

BLAKEMORE ROBERT 1750+ SAL, ENG **[35429]** : 1800S SHREWSBURY, SAL & LND, ENG **[35560]** : PRE 1720 WALSALL & WILLENHALL, STS, ENG **[36110]** : C1810 WEST BROMWICH, STS, ENG **[37298]** : ALL STS, SAL & WAR, ENG **[38754]**

BLAKENEY PRE 1808 GALWAY, GAL, IRL **[34254]**

BLAKESLEE 1750-1900 LEROY & PLEASANT GROVE, MN, PA & NY, USA **[38392]**

BLAKESLEY 1750-1900 LEROY & PLEASANT GROVE, MN, PA & NY, USA **[38392]**

BLAKEY 1800+ NEWCASTLE, NBL, ENG **[36135]** : 1850+ SUNDERLAND, DUR, ENG **[36614]** : PRE 1860 SUNDERLAND, DUR, ENG **[36765]** : 1700S WRY, ENG **[38577]**

BLAKIE PRE 1950 DUR & NBL, ENG **[38594]**

BLAMEY 1650-1800 GWENNAP, CON, ENG **[35395]** : 1790+ GWENNAP, CON, ENG **[35749]**

BLAMIRE 1850-1914 MARRICKVILLE, NSW, AUS **[35570]** : PRE 1850 PRESTON, LAN, ENG **[35570]** : 1700 ORTON, WES, ENG **[36151]** : 1700-1850 KENDAL, WES, ENG **[36320]**

BLAMPIED 1600+ JSY, CHI **[34532]** : PRE 1880 TRINITY, JSY, CHI, UK **[36200]**

BLANC 1850+ NS, CAN **[36404]**

BLANCE ALL WORLDWIDE **[37340]**

BLANCH ALL CAN & IRL **[36539]**

BLANCHARD 1840+ WINDSOR, NSW, AUS **[35088]** : PRE 1838 PARRAMATTA, NSW, AUS **[35088]** : PRE 1800 BOLDRE, HAM, ENG **[38420]** : 1780+ PLYMOUTH, DEV, ENG **[38499]** : 1590-1660 ROUEN, HN, FRA **[34514]**

BLANCHET ALL QUE & ONT, CAN **[37502]** : 1630-1990 CAN & USA **[34124]**

BLANCHETT ALL WOOTTON BASSETT, WIL, ENG **[35899]**

BLANCHFIELD 1890+ BEGA, NSW, AUS **[36615]** : 1800-1850 BLOOMSBURY, LND, ENG **[36410]**

BLANCHFLOWER PRE 1850 SWAFFHAM, NFK, ENG **[36061]** : 1800-1850 NFK, ENG **[36873]**

BLANCK (SEE BLANC) [36404]

BLAND PRE 1860 CARCOAR, NSW, AUS **[35232]** : PRE 1800 SALKELD, CUL, ENG **[34148]** : CATHERINE C1833 BULBY & HAWTHORPE, LIN, ENG **[34302]** : C1815 NBL & DUR, ENG **[35646]** : RICHARD 1840-75 LIVERPOOL, LAN, ENG **[38246]** : JOHN 1840-1912 LIVERPOOL, LAN, ENG **[38246]** : 1830-1900 LIVERPOOL, LAN, ENG **[38246]** : 1800S LND, ENG & AUS **[35422]** : 1800+ EDINBURGH, MLN, SCT **[34008]**

BLANDFORD C1797-1874 STEPNEY & BOW COMMON, MDX, ENG **[36836]** : 1730-1844 FONTMELL MAGNA, DOR, ENG **[37709]** : 1874+ INVERCARGILL WELLINGTON, NZ **[36836]** : 1800+ TREVETHIN, MON, WLS **[36614]**

BLANEY 1800-1900 DOR, ENG **[34477]** : C1828+ KIRKFIELD BANK & LARKHALL, LKS, SCT **[35995]**

BLANKENSHIP 1790-1900 BLOUNT CO., TN, USA **[37586]**

BLANKLEY C1700 HOBY, LEI, ENG **[37053]**

BLANKS 1815 BALSHAM, CAM, ENG **[35770]** : C1860S STEPNEY, MDX, ENG **[36876]** : C1860S SHADWELL, MDX, ENG **[36876]**

BLANKSBY 1880+ WANDIN & WANGARATTA, VIC, AUS **[36622]**

BLANN ALL WORLDWIDE **[34737]**

BLANSHARD PRE 1775 LIN & YKS, ENG **[33998]**

BLANTON ALL USA **[36545]**

BLASER 1700-1900 GER **[35630]**

BLASSON 1700+ HIGHAM FERRERS, NTH, ENG **[36477]**

BLATCH 1800-1835 LONDON, ENG **[34022]**

BLATCHFORD 1825 PLYMOUTH, DEV, ENG **[35332]**

BLAXTER ALL EDEN, NSW, AUS **[35901]**

BLAY 1880+ AUS **[36674]** : 1845+ MARRABEL, SA, AUS **[37984]** : 1845 ADELAIDE, SA, AUS **[37984]** : PRE 1901 ETON, BKM, ENG **[36674]** : PRE 1892 COOKHAM, BRK, ENG **[36674]** : GEORGE 1832-1881 PINCHBECK INN, LIN, ENG **[36674]** : PRE 1906 KENSINGTON, LND, ENG **[36674]** : PRE 1903 ST OLAVE, LND, ENG **[36674]** : PRE 1895 ST SAVIOUR, LND, ENG **[36674]** : THOMAS 1800-1847 THURLBY BY BOURNE, LIN, ENG **[36674]** : PRE 1901 OXFORD, HRT, ENG **[36674]** : PRE 1906 ISLINGTON, LND, ENG **[36674]** : 1880+ NZ **[36674]** : 1880+ RSA **[36674]** : ALL WORLDWIDE **[36674]**

BLAYLOCK ALL CUL, ENG **[36089]** : 1810+ KKD, SCT & ENG **[34467]**

BLAYNEY PRE 1830 WORCESTER, WOR, ENG **[34784]** : PRE 1830 DUB & KID, IRL **[35117]** : PRE 1860 BALLINA, MAY, IRL **[35546]** : 1700-1855 LLANDIHAM, MGY, WLS **[35445]**

BLAZE ALL ENG **[38265]**

BLAZEBY 1700-1800 NORWICH, NFK, ENG **[37052]**

BLAZER 1800+ NFK, ENG **[37347]**

BLAZEY 1750+ WYMONDHAM, NFK, ENG **[34710]**

BLEAKLEY 1830+ MAKENNY, TYR, IRL **[36615]**

BLEASDALE 1820-1860 PRESTON, LAN, ENG **[35860]**

BLECHSCHMIDT ALL HOF, BAV, GER **[38176]**

BLEDSOE ALL WORLDWIDE **[36521]**

BLEE 1889+ TOWNSVILLE, QLD, AUS **[35335]** : 1844+ ST AUSTELL, CON, ENG **[35335]** : C1841 LOSTWITHIEL, CON, ENG **[35335]**

BLEIJCK 1636-1688 BROOKLYN, NY, USA **[36317]**

BLEIMEISTER ALL MEK, GER **[38037]**

BLENCOWE ALL UK **[37421]**

BLENK PRE 1760 STANHOPE, DUR, ENG **[36202]**

BLENKARNE PRE 1830 ASHBY DE LA ZOUCH, LEI, ENG **[34725]**

BLENKIN PRE 1900 GATESHEAD, DUR, ENG **[37711]**

BLENKINSOP 1860+ BURRAWANG, NSW, AUS **[35511]** : 1750+ DUR, ENG **[35511]**

BLENKINSOPP 1800+ WES & DUR, ENG **[34680]** : PRE 1840 CHESTER LE STREET, DUR, ENG **[37137]** : 1850+ WEST COAST, NZ **[34680]**

BLENNERHASSET PRE 1770 KER, IRL **[36880]**

BLETHPEN PRE 1650 CON, ENG **[35255]**

BLETSHO ALL WORLDWIDE **[36521]**

BLETSO ALL WORLDWIDE **[36521]**

BLETSOE ALL WORLDWIDE **[36521]**

BLETSOR ALL WORLDWIDE **[36521]**

BLEWETT ALL VIC & NSW, AUS **[33872]** : PRE 1850 LONGHOPE, GLS, ENG **[34739]** : PRE 1800 MOUSEHOLE, CON, ENG **[37832]**

BLEWITT 1800+ PENZANCE & SPENNYMOOR, CON, ENG **[34680]** : 1850+ GREYMOUTH, NZ **[34680]**

BLEY 1750-1850 LAMPORSCHLOCH, ALS, FRA **[36898]**

BLICK PRE 1849 WIL, ENG **[34412]** : 1750+ STROUD, GLS, ENG **[35970]**

BLIEMENTSRIEDER PRE 1900 ROSENHEIM, BAY, BRD **[36963]**

BLIGH 1850+ BRIGHTON, SSX, ENG **[34057]** : PRE 1750 DRAYTON PARSLOW, BKM, ENG **[35701]** : 1820S DOW, IRL **[36292]** : 1830 USA **[34057]**

BLIGHT 1740-1850 ILLOGAN, CON, ENG **[34697]** : C1830 CON, ENG **[35384]** : 1800+ ILLOGAN, CON, ENG **[35493]** : ALL LANGTREE & NEWTON ST PETROCK, DEV, ENG **[36516]** : C1780 ST HILARY, CON, ENG **[36961]** : PRE 1816 PLYMOUTH, DEV,

ENG [37998] : 1805-1885 ILLOGAN, CON, ENG & AUS [33926]

BLIJENBERG PRE 1800 CLINGE, OVL, BEL [38697]

BLINCO PRE 1800 TEVERSHAM, CAM, ENG [34445]

BLINCOE 1800S WINDSOR & CLEWER, BRK, ENG [35899]

BLIND PRE 1680 SIEGELSBERG, WUE, GER [38661]

BLINKMANN 1819-1881 WULFSDORF, HBG, GER [38750]

BLINMAN 1840+ BLINMAN, SA, AUS [34777]

BLINN 1695+ KASHOFEN PFALZ, BAV, GER [37516]

BLINTACH ALL WORLDWIDE [36992]

BLISHEN 1800+ LONDON, ENG & AUS [37132]

BLISS 1700S NAUNTON, GLS, ENG [35186] : 1900+ PONDERS END, MDX, ENG [35403] : 1854+ HAYTON, CUL, ENG [38469] : 1783+ POTTERSPURY, NTH, ENG [38469] : PRE 1800 GLS, MA & CT, ENG & USA [38746] : MARY 1810 ONTARIO CO., NY, USA [36575]

BLISSARD ALL DRAYCOT CERNE, WIL, ENG [36424]

BLITH PRE 1790 BKM, ENG [35701]

BLITHE 1780+ TETCOTT, DEV, ENG [34804]

BLITSO ALL WORLDWIDE [36521]

BLITSOE ALL WORLDWIDE [36521]

BLOCH PRE 1875 POS, GER [37009] : ALL WORLDWIDE [34318]

BLOCKLEY PRE 1868 CARLTON, LIN, ENG [34421]

BLOCKSIDGE 1800S SAL, ENG [36194]

BLODGETT 1820+ CENTRETON, ONT, CAN [38418] : LEVI 1770-1850 TOWNSEND, VT, USA [36335] : LEVI 1770-1850 WENDELL, MA, USA [36335] : 1600-1850 STRATFORD, NH, USA [38131] : PRE 1820 SAILSBURG, CT, NY & VT, USA [38418] : ALL WORLDWIDE [38418]

BLODORN 1650+ NEVENGORNITZ, SHO, GER [37170]

BLOEDORN PRE 1900 WI, USA [38684]

BLOEMKER PRE 1830 LIENEN, PRE, GER [37034]

BLOESCH ALL WORLDWIDE [38747]

BLOGG HENRY 1840+ CROMER, NFK, ENG [37775]

BLOICE PRE 1850 SFK, ENG [36124] : PRE 1850 ESS, ENG [36124]

BLOIS 1700+ STRATFORD, SFK, ENG [36256]

BLOM 1885+ CAMPERDOWN & COLAC, VIC, AUS [36622] : PRE 1752 RHINE RIVER, BAW, BRD [37574] : PRE 1752 RHINE RIVER, WUE, GER [37574] : ALL UTR, NL [33769] : ALL BADHOEVEDORP, AMSTERDAM, NL [36894] : C1700 ALPHEN RIETVELD, ZUH, NL [38160]

BLOMEFIELD 1800-1900 LICHFIELD, STS, ENG [36986] : ALL WORLDWIDE [37737]

BLOMFIELD 1820+ AUS [33768] : PRE 1750 STOKE FERRY, NFK, ENG [34139] : ALL ENG [36800] : 1567+ NORTON & WOOLPIT, SFK, ENG [37399] : ALL WORLDWIDE [37737]

BLONG ALL IRL [37122] : ALL WORLDWIDE [37122]

BLOOD 1600S ROTON, MA, USA [36944] : 1617-1900S GROTON, MA, USA [38308]

BLOODWORTH 1852+ MARYBOROUGH, VIC, AUS [35223] : C1842+ HINDMARSH, SA, AUS [35223] : C1720+ DURSLEY & ULEY, GLS, ENG [35223] : ALL RUT, ENG [36005]

BLOOM PRE 1840 STOWMARKET, SFK, ENG [36396] : 1800-1845 YARMOUTH, NFK, ENG [37996] : 1850S WORLDWIDE [36831] : 1822+ WORLDWIDE [37317]

BLOOMBERG ALL UK [34665]

BLOOMFIELD PERCY 1940-1950 THE PATCH, VIC, AUS [35391] : C1840 BRANT CO., ONT, CAN [34251] : PRE 1830 SFK, ENG [34090] : PRE 1850 WEST HAM, LND, ENG [34608] : 1690-1820 ASSINGTON,

SFK, ENG [34672] : 1850 LIVERPOOL, ENG [34844] : ALL ESS, ENG [35113] : PRE 1875 BURY ST EDMUNDS, SFK, ENG [37753] : C1823 ESS, ENG [37912] : ALL WORLDWIDE [37737]

BLOOR C1833 TUNSTALL, STS, ENG [35348] : PRE 1800 STS, ENG [37650] : PRE 1851 DALE ABBEY, DBY, ENG [38248]

BLOORE ALL STS & WOR, ENG [36062]

BLORE PRE 1811 CHELSEA, LND, ENG [35037] : PRE 1850 IBSTONE, OXF & BKM, ENG [37948]

BLOSS ALL FRAMLINGHAM, SFK, ENG [34263]

BLOW ALL LONDON, SRY & KEN, ENG [35630] : PRE 1860 MARKETHILL, ARM, IRL [37510]

BLOWER 1860-1990 CA & PA, USA [38203] : 1800-1860 FLN, WLS [38203]

BLOWS 1840S MANEA, CAM, ENG [35959]

BLOXHAM PRE 1900 IRL [37776]

BLOXIDGE 1787-1873 BIRMINGHAM, WAR, ENG [37860]

BLOXSIDGE 1900+ HIGH WYCOMBE, BKM, ENG [38213]

BLOYCE 1700+ GREAR BROMLEY, ESS, ENG [36256]

BLUCHER 1879-1891 WITTENBURG, MSW, GER [35820] : C1857 BRESEGARD, MSW, GER [35820]

BLUCKE 1800S WATERLESS, WILLOUGHBY, LEI, ENG [35424]

BLUE 1800+ BALLYMENA, ANT, IRL [35489] : WILLIAM 1820+ AYR & SYDNEY, AYR & NSW, SCT & AUS [35155]

BLUETT ALL VIC & NSW, AUS [33872] : ALL AUS [34741] : 1700-1800 FALMOUTH, CON, ENG [34741] : ALL LAUNCESTON & NORTH PETHERWIN, CON, ENG [37224] : ALL NZ [34741] : ALL RSA [34741]

BLUFORD PRE 1810 BRISTOL, SOM, ENG [38263]

BLUM 1835 GL, CH [38518] : 1780-1840 HEINZENHAUSEN, BAY, GER [36966] : C1748 RUDESBURG, SHO, GER [37819]

BLUMCKE PRE 1940 STETTIN, POM, GER [36306] : PRE 1940 DEUTSCH KRONE, POM, GER [36306]

BLUME 1876+ SYDNEY, NSW, AUS [37139] : 1833 HUSUM AUST NISMBURG, HAN, BRD [38327] : 1860+ APLERBECK, WEF, GER [34563] : ALL LIEBENBURG, HAN, GER [37154]

BLUMENSHINE 1700+ RPR, GER [38765]

BLUMFIELD ALL WORLDWIDE [37737]

BLUMKE PRE 1900 TUTZ, POM, GER [36306] : PRE 1900 DEUTSCH KRONE, POM, GER [36306] : PRE 1940 USA [36306]

BLUMSOM PRE 1930 EAST END & WALTHAMSTOW, LND, ENG [35167]

BLUNDELL 1908+ MELBOURNE, VIC, AUS [34794] : PRE 1800 CHELSFIELD, KEN, ENG [34314] : PRE 1836 NORTH MEOLS, LAN, ENG [34432] : 1700+ LUTON, BDF, ENG [34650] : 1800S LIVERPOOL, LAN, ENG [36665] : PRE 1861 KEN, ENG [38293] : 1790+ SALTHURST, SALTHOUSE, NFK, ENG & AUS [34803] : PRE 1750 MANOSTERORIS & EDENDERRY, OFF, IRL [38084]

BLUNDEN 1857-1870 SINGLETON & WARATAH, NSW, AUS [38761] : 1857-1870 MURRURUNDI, NSW, AUS [38761] : 1818-1850 STEVENTON & BASINGSTOKE, HAM, ENG [38761] : 1600+ SSX, ENG & AUS [36827] : ALL WORLDWIDE [38014]

BLUNDONE C1875-1950 BRENTWOOD, ESS, ENG [34508]

BLUNT 1870+ MUSWELLBROOK, NSW, AUS [35740] : 1855+ VIC, AUS [36304] : THOS LAMBKIN PRE 1823+ GOUDHURST, KEN, ENG [34592] : 1840S BIRMINGHAM, WAR, ENG [36011] : 1770-1830 GOUDHURST, KEN, ENG [36304] : 1750+

MAIDSTONE, KEN, ENG **[38075]** : 1750+
ROLVENDEN, KEN, ENG **[38075]** : 1750+
QUEENBOROUGH, KEN, ENG **[38075]**
BLUNTACH ALL WORLDWIDE **[36992]**
BLUNTISH ALL WORLDWIDE **[36992]**
BLUNTO ALL WORLDWIDE **[36992]**
BLUNTOCH ALL WORLDWIDE **[36992]**
BLUNTOEG ALL WORLDWIDE **[36992]**
BLY 1860-85 LINCOLN CO., AR, USA **[38314]**
BLYDE PRE 1820 PONTEFRACT, YKS, ENG **[35946]** :
PRE 1840 BEXHILL, SSX, ENG **[36752]**
BLYTH PRE 1850 ST FAITHS, NFK, ENG **[37737]** :
PRE 1900 NEW KILPATRICK, DNB, SCT **[33966]** :
PRE 1900 GLASGOW, DNB, SCT **[33966]** : PRE 1900
BURNT ISLAND, FIF, SCT **[33966]**
BLYTHE JOHN C1870-1930 TORONTO, ONT, CAN
[34354] : 1804+ GLOUCESTER, GLS, ENG **[33880]** :
C1870 NORTH LONDON, ENG **[34655]** : 1820+
NORTH SHIELDS, NBL, ENG **[35396]** : PRE 1880
WAR, ENG **[36429]** : 1700+ HILLSBOROUGH,
DOW, IRL **[37625]** : 1800+ DUNDEE, ANS, SCT
[35343]
BOADLE ALL ST BEES, CUL, ENG **[34173]**
BOAG PRE 1930 LAUNCESTON, TAS, AUS **[34050]** :
ALL NEWCASTLE UPON TYNE, NBL, ENG
[36878] : C1800 PEEBLES, PEE, SCT **[35057]** : 1820S
HUSTON & KILLELLAN, RFW, SCT **[35135]** : ALL
DUNDEE, ANS, SCT **[36509]** : 1750 DUNNING,
PER, SCT **[37106]** : 1850+ LAUDERDALE, SC, USA
[35135]
BOALER PRE 1700 DBY, ENG **[36196]**
BOARD PRE 1800 WINCHESTER, HAM, ENG **[33802]**
: 1750-1820 BUCKLAND ST MARY, SOM, ENG
[35813] : 1800+ WV, USA **[38235]** : 1740+ PA, USA
[38235]
BOARDALL 1860 HALIFAX, WRY, ENG **[34957]**
BOARDMAN 1800-1900 CAMDEN, NSW, AUS **[34537]**
: 1855-1900 SYDNEY, NSW, AUS **[35782]** : 1847
OLDHAM, LAN, ENG **[33936]** : 1700-1900
PINCHBECK, LIN, ENG **[34537]** : PRE 1841
LIVERPOOL, LAN, ENG **[34942]** : PRE 1855
LONDON, ENG **[35782]** : 1800S+ BLACKLEY,
LAN, ENG **[37313]** : PRE 1858 BLAKELY &
OLDHAM, LAN, ENG **[37972]** : 1700-1900
MANCHESTER, LAN, ENG **[38745]** : PRE 1930
NEW BEDFORD, MA, USA **[37223]**
BOARLAND ALL WORLDWIDE **[37095]**
BOASE 1850+ SA, AUS **[33887]** : 1840+ VIC, AUS
[35055] : 1850+ BALLARAT, VIC, AUS **[35986]** :
1750+ PENZANCE, CON, ENG **[33887]** : ALL
PENZANCE & NEWLYN, CON, ENG **[34724]** : PRE
1860 ST IVES, CON, ENG **[35055]** : 1726+ ISLES OF
SCILLY, CON, ENG **[36000]** : ALL LUDGVAN &
PENZANCE, CON, ENG **[36145]**
BOATE 1840-1940 NSW, AUS **[34438]** : 1800-1840 WAT,
IRL **[34438]**
BOATWRIGHT PRE 1870 SFK, ENG **[34883]**
BOBALJIK ALL WORLDWIDE **[38021]**
BOBBINS 1700-1800 BURNHAM THORPE, NFK,
ENG **[37845]**
BOBIER 1860-1914 CHATHAM, ONT, CAN **[34257]** :
1860-1900 THAMESVILLE, ONT, CAN **[34257]** :
1850-1980 WALLACEBURG, ONT, CAN **[34257]**
BOBO 1790-1850 UNION CO., SC, USA **[38188]**
BOCCALATTE 1946+ PUNCHBOWL, NSW, AUS
[36600]
BOCH 1800-1855 ABENHAHN SIERSHAN, GER
[37597]
BOCHMANN ALL HOHENSTEIN, KMS, DDR **[36552]**
BOCK 1600S KUNZENDORF & OPPAU, SIL, GER
[33901] : PRE 1860S BRUNSWICK, GER **[37139]**
BOCKETT 1750+ HAMPSTEAD, LND, ENG **[37327]**

BOCKMANN 1760-1860 HARKENSEE, KLUTZ,
MSW, DDR **[36783]**
BODAAN ALL DEN HAAG, ZUH, NL **[38705]**
BODDY 1856+ YARRAM, VIC, AUS **[35708]** : PRE
1800 SCALBY, NRY, ENG **[34333]** : 1704+
CREDITON, DEV, ENG **[36995]** : 1847+ BRISTOL,
ENG **[36995]** : 1800-1850 AXBRIDGE, SOM, ENG
[37278] : 1830-1900 BINGLEY, WRY, ENG **[37278]** :
1800-1850 SOUTH BRENT, SOM, ENG **[37278]** :
C1816 EAST BEDFONT, MDX, ENG **[38441]** : 1850-
1960 NORWICH, NFK, ENG **[38471]**
BODE 1750-1825 WULFTEN, HAN, GER **[37798]**
BODEKER ALL FAVERSHAM, KEN & LND, ENG
[34093]
BODEN 1700-1900 BIRMINGHAM, WAR, ENG
[37058] : ALL EYSTRUP, HAN, GER **[36571]** : MARY
1824 CALCUTTA, INDIA **[35788]** : PRE 1880 SCT &
CAN **[38463]**
BODEN (SEE BOWDEN) **[34276]**
BODFISH ALL WORLDWIDE **[37860]**
BODGER 1750+ EDMONTON, MDX, ENG **[37885]**
BODIELLA 1700+ MERTHER & PROBUS, CON,
ENG **[35208]**
BODILY PRE 1818 GREENS NORTON, NTH, ENG
[36748]
BODIMEAD ALL HARROW, MDX, ENG **[36981]**
BODINEAU PRE 1850 CAN & FRA **[38386]**
BODINNAR ALL PENZANCE & NEWLYN, CON,
ENG **[34724]** : PRE 1830 PAUL, CON, ENG **[35437]** :
1600-1900 PAUL, CON, ENG **[37680]**
BODKIN 1700-1900 LONDON, MDX, ENG **[36438]** :
PRE 1900 GILLINGHAM, KEN, ENG **[37405]** : 1700-
1800 GALWAY, GAL, IRL **[36438]**
BODMIN PRE 1800 GLS, ENG **[34837]**
BODY PRE 1800 ST MEWAN, CON, ENG **[34753]** :
PRE 1850 SOM, ENG **[37695]**
BOECKS PRE 1700 ANTWERPEN, OVL, BEL **[38697]**
BOEG PRE 1670 BLAUFELDEN, WUE, GER **[37510]**
BOEGEHOLD ALL WORLDWIDE **[37572]**
BOEHI 1730-1830 TAEGERWILEN, TG, CH **[35283]**
BOEHM PRE 1900 ROSENHEIM, BAY, BRD **[36963]** :
C1720 LONDON, ENG **[35990]** : PRE 1850 WI, USA
[38052] : ALL WORLDWIDE **[36930]**
BOELLER PRE 1770 NECKARREMS, WUE, GER
[38661]
BOERKAMP 1738+ EMLICHHEIM, NSA, BRD
[34398]
BOES ALL NL & CAN **[34396]**
BOESE 1864+ KIDDERMINSTER, WOR, ENG
[35905] : 1800+ SCHLAWE, POM, GER **[35905]** :
1883+ NZ **[35905]** : ALL WORLDWIDE **[35905]**
BOESHORE PRE 1807 LEBANON CO., PA, USA &
GER **[37529]**
BOESLER 1881-1951 VALLEY CO., NE & WI, USA &
GER **[38309]** : 1800-1940 WORLDWIDE **[38309]**
BOEUF C1650 VENDOEUVRES, GE, CH **[38348]**
BOFINGER PRE 1856 WUE, GER **[34463]**
BOGAERT PRE 1800 OVL, BEL **[38697]**
BOGAN ALL OTTAWA VALLEY, ONT, CAN **[35833]**
BOGART ALL USA **[37787]**
BOGENSCHNEIDER ALL WORLDWIDE **[38065]**
BOGG 1800+ LONDON, ENG **[34416]**
BOGGESS 1810-25 MADISON CO., AL, USA **[38314]**
BOGGETT PRE 1830 LONDON, ENG **[35238]**
BOGGIS PRE 1800 LONDON, ENG **[34013]** : ALL
HUMPHREYS GULLY, NZ **[37162]** : ALL
TEMUKA, NZ **[37162]**
BOGGS 1800S CARNAMOYLE, LDY, IRL **[33880]** :
PRE 1900 PORTSTEWART, ANT, IRL **[35976]**
BOGIE 1880-1990 FIF, SCT **[34393]**
BOGOFF ALL WORLDWIDE **[37549]**

BOGUE JOHN PRE 1840 ENG [35404] : 1800+ FER, IRL [38189] : 1750 DUNNING, PER, SCT [37106]

BOGUST 1850+ STEPNEY, LONDON, MDX, ENG [36989] : 1900+ CUSTON HOUSE, LONDON, ESS, ENG [36989]

BOHANNON 1818-1880S PLESHEY, ESS, ENG [33865]

BOHEIM 1840-1900 MILWAUKEE, WI, USA [36542]

BOHL 1800+ VIC, AUS [35352] : 1800+ HOLLAND, NL & DEN [35352]

BOHLEN 1850-70 PA, USA [38100]

BOHME OSCAR 1877+ DERMSDORF, SAX, GER [35641]

BOHN PRE 1850 BRA, GER [38648]

BOHNE PRE 1900 HANNOVER, HAN, GER [38674]

BOHNHOF 1750-1840 WISMAR, MEK, GER [38565]

BOHNSTEDT PRE 1850 MEK, GER [38675]

BOHRINGER PRE 1855 ERLENBACH, WUE, GER [34886]

BOHUN LOUISA ANN 1770-1790 BECCLES, SFK, ENG [36678]

BOILEAU ALL BOURDONNAY, LOR, FRA [36078]

BOILES 1800+ SHIPSTON ON STOUR, WAR & BDF, ENG [36123]

BOISEN PRE 1876 ADELAIDE, SA, AUS & DEN [33890]

BOISVERT 1750+ QUE, CAN [38360] : 1790+ KANKAKEE CO., IL, USA [38360] : 1860+ CLOUD CO., KS, USA [38360]

BOKENHEUER 1849+ LAASE, MEK, GER [38572]

BOKSTAL 1700S ZUID BEVELAND, ZEL, NL [38358]

BOL PRE 1800 WINSCHOTEN, GRO, NL [35916]

BOLAM 1740+ CHESTER LE STREET, DUR, ENG [36961]

BOLAND C1840 OFF, IRL [33796] : 1800+ THE BAWN, OFF, IRL [34574] : PRE 1840 IRL [37133]

BOLBERGE (VON) 1373-1391 BAALBERGE, MAG, DDR [38713]

BOLDEN 1885+ MIDDLESEX CO., ONT, CAN [36323] : C1820 LONDON, ENG [33937] : ALL SOLLINDGE, KEN, ENG [36822]

BOLDT ALL GER [35945]

BOLE PRE 1860 KILDRESS, TYR, IRL [35612]

BOLEYN GEORGE 1850+ AUS [34610]

BOLGER 1850+ GEELONG, VIC, AUS [38289] : 1860+ VIC, AUS [38539] : 1830+ LEX, IRL [38539]

BOLICEK PRE 1890 MORAVIA, OES [35290]

BOLICK 1850-1920 DES MOINES CO., IA, USA [38154] : 1750-1830 LINCOLN CO., NC, USA [38154]

BOLIEU 1830-1880 SHIAWASSEE CO., MI, USA [38009]

BOLIN 1830 YEOVIL, SOM, ENG [34844]

BOLINGBROKE 1750-1900 BRK, ENG [36007]

BOLITHO 1500-1800 WENDRON, MORVAH & ST JUST, CON, ENG [37680]

BOLL 1840-1870 TEMPLIN, BRA, GER [37973]

BOLLARD 1700-1900 NORTHFIELD & BIRMINGHAM, WOR, ENG [37257] : 1700-1900 BIRMINGHAM, WAR, ENG [37257]

BOLLE ALL BROUWERSHAVEN, ZEL, NL [38694]

BOLLENHAGEN ALL WORLDWIDE [38666]

BOLLES ALL SUSQUEHANNA CO., PA, USA [36356] : 1633+ USA [37592]

BOLLIER ALL WORLDWIDE [36540]

BOLLING PRE 1600 YKS, ENG [37570]

BOLLINGER 1702+ LANCASTER, PA, USA [38067]

BOLLOKE ALL GLS, ENG [37742]

BOLOTIN 1800-1990 NEW HAVEN CO., CT, USA [38096]

BOLSHAW 1760+ HOLMES CHAPEL, CHS, ENG [38221]

BOLSRUD 1800-90 OSLO, NOR [38533]

BOLSTRIDGE 1850+ STANTHORPE, QLD, AUS [35428] : PRE 1850 BEDWORTH, WAR, ENG [35428]

BOLT 1800+ TAVISTOCK, DEV, ENG [35076] : 1838 FALMOUTH, CON, ENG [36804]

BOLTE 1700-1800 BLINDOW, BRA, GER [38599]

BOLTER 1700-1800 MA, USA [35502]

BOLTON 1876+ YOUNG, NSW, AUS [34772] : PRE 1865 SYDNEY & QUEANBEYAN, NSW, AUS [35087] : 1850+ MICHELAGO, NSW, AUS [35562] : 1850+ CHEWTON, VIC, AUS [36439] : ANN 1835 SOUTH CREEK, NSW, AUS [37123] : ALL REDLINGFIELD, SFK, ENG [34772] : ALL WILBURTON, ESS, ENG [34772] : PRE 1830 NORWICH, NFK, ENG [34850] : 1830-1860 DUDLEY, WOR, ENG [34850] : 1740+ KEMBLE, WIL, ENG [35511] : PRE 1849 TOTTENHAM, MDX, ENG [35530] : 1750+ LONDON, ENG [36004] : PRE 1700 COCKERMOUTH, CUL, ENG [36032] : PRE 1875 WEST BROMWICH, WAR, ENG [36116] : 1691-1811 PRESTON & HESKET, LAN, ENG [36618] : C1800 MEYSEY HAMPTON, WIL, ENG [36975] : 1600-1780 WILMSLOW, CHS, ENG [36983] : C1800 RAMSGATE, KEN, ENG [37053] : C1740 WITNEY, OXF, ENG [37053] : 1817 COLESHILL, WAR, ENG [37106] : C1790 LANCASTER, LAN, ENG [37144] : PRE 1800 DILHORNE, STS, ENG [37893] : 1700+ WIGAN, LAN, ENG [38046] : PRE 1850 CLOYDAGH, CAR, IRL [35512] : PRE 1850S WEX, IRL [36659] : 1800-1850 NEW YORK, USA [35916] : PRE 1830 COLUMBIA CO., GA, USA [37587] : 1800-1990 NEW HAVEN CO., CT, USA [38096]

BOLYTOUT PRE 1821 MARTHAM, NFK, ENG [34539]

BOMAN 1866+ PORVOO, UUSIMAA, FIN [38758]

BONAR 1860-1880 KILBIRNIE, AYR, SCT [37485] : PRE 1830 SCT [37957]

BONARIUS 1855+ NUNDLE, NSW, AUS [34977] : PRE 1855 WHITECHAPEL, MDX, ENG [34977]

BONAS 1830+ MDX, ENG & AUS [33790]

BONAWITZ 1800S BERKS CO., PA, USA [35165]

BOND C1890 PANMURE, VIC, AUS [35137] : 1930+ SOUTH GIPPSLAND, VIC, AUS [35774] : 1880+ BENALLA, VIC, AUS [35774] : 1900+ BALLARAT, VIC, AUS [35774] : 1860 IPSWICH, QLD, AUS [35808] : CHARLES PRE 1862 PAYNEHAM, SA, AUS & ENG [33890] : PRE 1930 PORT PERRY, ONT, CAN [36707] : 1781 LOOSE, KEN, ENG [34142] : 1800-1890 SHEPTON MONTAGUE, SOM, ENG [34306] : PRE 1840 DEV, ENG [34445] : 1800-1850 HOLSWORTHY, DEV, ENG [34525] : PRE 1821 WHITEHURCH, DOR, ENG [34689] : 1788+ GLASTONBURY, SOM, ENG [34777] : 1800-1880 DEV, ENG [35402] : PRE 1750 PRESTON, LAN & CUL, ENG [35624] : WILLIAM C1820 WIGGENHOE & KINGS LYNN, NFK, ENG [35729] : PRE 1800 BARRINGTON, SOM, ENG [35758] : 1820+ MILVERTON, SOM, ENG [35774] : PRE 1900 BOOTHSTOWN, LAN, ENG [35986] : 1800-1900 HEF, LAN & NFK, ENG [36042] : PRE 1875 ESS, ENG [36050] : 1800S CORNWOOD & PLYMOUTH, DEV, ENG [36205] : PRE 1850 DISS, NFK, ENG [36530] : 1350S BRIXTON, SRY, ENG [36530] : 1800-1900 READING, BRK, ENG [36653] : C1700 LADOCK, CON, ENG [36899] : PRE 1850 GLASTONBURY & YEOVIL, SOM, ENG [37067] : 1820+ BLACKBURN, LAN, ENG [37132] : PRE 1730 CALSTOCK & PLYMOUTH, CON, ENG [37320] : 1800S LIN, ENG [37352] : PRE 1850 EAST, NFK, ENG [37718] : C1600+ SLAIDBURN, YKS, ENG [37888] : C1816 EAST BEDFONT, MDX, ENG [38441] : 1750-1850 SCO, ME, USA [38045] : 1876+ RICHLAND CO., TN, USA [38531]

BOND-HUGES PRE 1820 SOUTHWARK, SRY, ENG [36072]

BONDS 1700-1850 TRURO & FALMOUTH, CON, ENG [37224] : 1800-1850 SC, USA [35307] : 1850-1910 MARSHALL CO., MS, USA [35307]

BONE ALL CYGNET, TAS, AUS [33786] : PRE 1850S LONDON & ENFIELD, ENG [34240] : PRE 1900 DEVONPORT & PLYMOUTH, DEV, ENG [34439] : 1760S WIELD, HAM, ENG [34909] : PRE 1800 REDRUTH, CON, ENG [35496] : ALL GOSPORT, HAM, ENG [35936] : 1800+ NBL, ENG [35998] : 1800+ LONDON, ENG [36004] : 1700-1850 LISS, HAM, ENG [36727] : PRE 1780 EAST WORLDHAM, HAM, ENG [37420] : C1760 COSTESSEY, NFK, ENG [37726] : 1800 ELSING, NFK, ENG [37733] : ALL TERRYGLASS, TIP, IRL [34441]

BONELL 1800+ DBY, ENG [38261]

BONES 1800+ ESS, ENG [34818]

BONESS 1800+ SEEMITZEL, POM, GER [37170]

BONETTO PRE 1800 CON, ENG [34686]

BONEY 1800+ MARIETTA, TX, USA [38746]

BONFIELD 1850+ VIC, AUS [36361] : PRE 1900 SWANAGE, DOR, ENG [34477] : PRE 1850 HRT, ENG [36361] : C1800 CITY OF LONDON, ENG [36874] : 1700+ DOR, ENG [38215]

BONG ALL FIN & SWE [38547]

BONGERS 1700S UTRECHT, UTR, NL [38358]

BONHAM EZRA 1846+ NAIRNE, SA, AUS [36611] : 1853+ PENSHURST & SYDNEY, NSW, AUS [38541] : 1844 BKM, ENG [34193] : 1854 TOWCESTER, NTH, ENG [38282] : ALL WORLDWIDE [35854]

BONIAK PRE 1900 PO, POL [36355]

BONIFACE PRE 1800 BEEDING & UPPER BEEDING, SSX, ENG [33858] : 1908+ PLYMOUTH, DEV, ENG [36771] : C1760S SSX, ENG [37745] : 1800S LONDON, MDX & SRY, ENG [38258]

BONIWELL C1669 SHEFFIELD, YKS, ENG [35257]

BONNARD C1675 ONEX, GE, CH [38348]

BONNE 1600+ WINGENE, WF, BEL [34163]

BONNELL 1800S LAKE MACQUARIE, NSW, AUS & ENG [33895] : PRE 1870 WARRINGTON, LAN, ENG [35967]

BONNER CON 1850+ MELBOURNE, VIC, AUS [34871] : 1860+ SA, AUS [34871] : 1840+ AUS [37113] : PRE 1830 LND, ENG [36538] : PRE 1859 BRISTOL, GLS, ENG [38718] : 1876 GLOUCESTER, GLS, ENG [38719] : CON 1800-1850 DON, IRL [34871] : PRE 1850 EDINBURGH, MLN, SCT [36664] : 1636-1760 SUSSEX CO., VA, USA [36354]

BONNET C1600 GENEVA, GE, CH [38348]

BONNETT 1850-1888 WARRNAMBOOL, VIC, AUS [35136] : PRE 1742 NFK, ENG [34222]

BONNEY C1855 TAS, AUS [35887] : C1840+ SOUTHAMPTON, HAM, ENG [37063] : C1780+ PORTSEA, HAM, ENG [37063] : 1800 MANUDEN, ESS, ENG [37250] : PRE 1850 LND, ENG & IRL [37091] : C1734 PEMBROKE, MA, USA [37820]

BONNICK ALL WAR, ENG [38514]

BONNY THOMAS 1800S ROCHESTER, KEN, ENG [34499] : PRE 1900 KEN, ENG [37517] : 1850+ POPLAR & HACKNEY, MDX, ENG [37677] : 1890+ ROMFORD & WESTHAM, ESS, SRY & BRK, ENG [37677] : PRE 1800S BREDHURST & RAINHAM, KEN, ENG [37677] : 1840-75 SITTINGBOURNE & MURSTON, KEN, ENG [37677] : 1800-60 BREDGAR & HARTLIP, KEN, ENG [37677] : 1870+ EDMONTON & ISLINGTON, MDX, ENG [37677]

BONO C1830 HAMPSTEAD, MDX, ENG [34700]

BONSER ALL WORLDWIDE [38439]

BONTEMS PRE 1834 ENG & FRA [37760]

BONTZ C1700 NUSSLOCH, BAD, GER [34239] : PRE 1700 GEISLINGEN, WUE, GER [38683]

BONUS 1880+ WINDSOR, NSW, AUS [35497] : 1800S RICHMOND & WINDSOR, NSW, AUS [35926]

BOOBIER C1838 LONDON, ENG [35827]

BOOBY PRE 1850+ TAUNTON, SOM, ENG [37518]

BOOBYER ALL ENG [37269]

BOOCOCK 1700+ WAKEFIELD, YKS, ENG [35445]

BOODTS PRE 1850 VRASENE, OVL, BEL [38697]

BOOK 1750S GER [34130] : 1885+ KNOWLTON TWP., NJ, USA [34130]

BOOKER 1842 BRIGHTON, VIC, AUS [38282] : PRE 1835 PAINSWICK, GLS, ENG [37913] : 1800S LONDON, MDX & SRY, ENG [38034] : 1800S BIRMINGHAM, WAR, ENG [38034] : PRE 1700 LODSWORTH, SSX, ENG [38499] : 1850-1990 SHEFFIELD, YKS & LAN, ENG & NZ [37990] : PRE 1890 TN, USA [38217]

BOOKLESS 1830-1832 ARGENTEUIL CO., QUE, CAN [34365] : 1850+ NEWCASTLE, NBL, ENG [37853] : PRE 1830 BEW, SCT [34365] : 1847+ KIRKCALDY, FIF, SCT [35525] : PRE 1700 COCKBURNSPATH, BEW, SCT [37853]

BOOKS PRE 1900 WORLDWIDE [35577]

BOOL JOHN PRE 1880 BATH, SOM, ENG [38776]

BOOLE PRE 1900 BIRMINGHAM, WAR, ENG [37460]

BOOLES PRE 1820 LINCOLN, LIN, ENG [35934] : PRE 1700 AYLSHAM, NFK, ENG [36593]

BOOLEY C1864 BALLARAT, VIC, AUS [35777]

BOOMER 1800+ ONT, CAN [38421] : 1730S+ ST OSWALDS, DUR, ENG [38269]

BOOMHOWER 1790-1900 ONT & QUE, CAN [34520]

BOON PRE 1900 ONT & QUE, CAN & ENG [38391] : 1750+ DEV, ENG [34456] : 1900+ TOTTENHAM, MDX, ENG [35167] : 1900+ WALTHAMSTOW, LND, ENG [35167] : ALL DOWNHAM, NFK, ENG [35167] : ALL WALPOLE ST ANDREW, NFK, ENG [35177] : 1700+ DEV, ENG [36209] : 1800+ SHERINGTON, BKM, ENG [37070] : PRE 1600 SAXMUNDHAM, SFK, ENG [37420] : 1700-1800 N & S LEITH, MLN, SCT [36327]

BOONE C1764 LINCOLNS INN, LND, ENG [35013] : PRE 1900 RI, USA & CAN [36933] : ALL WORLDWIDE [37785]

BOONHAM C1820+ BADDESLEY ENSOR, WAR, ENG [36753] : C1784+ RATCLIFFE CULEY, LEI, ENG [36753]

BOONSTRA ELIZ. 1850+ MELBOURNE, VIC, AUS [35803]

BOORMAN 1720+ SSX, ENG [37260] : PRE 1850 HEADCORN, KEN, ENG [37663]

BOOS PRE 1816 ISERLOHN, WEF, GER [38647]

BOOSEY 1640+ WETHERSFIELD, CT, USA [38066]

BOOT MARY PRE 1874 SHEFFIELD, WRY, ENG [37960]

BOOTE PRE 1840 LIVERPOOL, LAN, ENG [35423] : PRE 1876 MANCHESTER, LAN, ENG [37235]

BOOTH 1849+ VIC, AUS [34412] : 1850+ NSW, AUS [34424] : C1860-1900 MUCKLEFORD, VIC, AUS [35221] : C1900 BOULDER, WA, AUS [35221] : JOHN SMITH 1862+ FORTITUDE VALLEY, QLD, AUS [35462] : PRE 1890 NEWTOWN, NSW, AUS [35781] : ALL LAUNCESTON, TAS, AUS [35913] : 1879+ WIMMERA, VIC, AUS [36622] : 1915+ DRUMMOYNE, NSW, AUS [37906] : 1850+ OTTAWA, ONT, CAN [36662] : C1800 SOWERBY, WRY, ENG [33796] : 1840+ NORTH BIERLEY, WRY, ENG [34355] : 1800+ HEPWORTH, WRY, ENG [34355] : 1870+ BRADFORD, WRY, ENG [34355] : PRE 1900 MANCHESTER, LAN, ENG [34360] : PRE 1856 YKS, ENG [34412] : PRE 1900

CUL, ENG [34424] : 1780-1850 ACCRINGTON, LAN, ENG [34440] : PRE 1870 BASFORD, NTT, ENG [34612] : PRE 1830 WARBLETON, SSX, ENG [34725] : WILLIAM 1793 + SSX & KEN, ENG [34954] : PRE 1770 ECCLESFIELD, WRY, ENG [34974] : PRE 1850S HUDDERSFIELD, YKS, ENG [35061] : 1820S BATTLE, SSX, ENG [35151] : C1832 TINTWHISTLE, LAN, ENG [35221] : 1800 + ROCHDALE, LAN, ENG [35342] : PRE 1786 DUFFIELD, DBY, ENG [35462] : ABRAHAM PRE 1862 NOTTINGHAM & NEWARK, NTT, ENG [35462] : PRE 1780 WADDINGHAM, LIN, ENG [35587] : 1765 MACCLESFIELD, CHS, ENG [35872] : 1700 + ROUSBY, YKS, ENG [35908] : 1700 WARTON, LAN, ENG [36151] : PRE 1837 BARWELL, LEI, ENG [36429] : C1880 CASTLETON, LAN, ENG [36649] : 1700-1750 BRADFORD, WRY, ENG [36682] : PRE 1805 TONGE WITH HAULGH, LAN, ENG [36742] : PRE 1860 WAKEFIELD, YKS, ENG [37094] : PRE 1620 SAXMUNDHAM, SFK, ENG [37420] : PRE 1750 LEEDS, WRY, ENG [37643] : PRE 1930 ROMFORD, ESS, ENG [37685] : WILLIAM 1750-1800 CANTERBURY, KEN, ENG [37740] : EDWARD 1810 + MANCHESTER, LAN, ENG [37748] : 1800 + APPERLEY, GLS, ENG [38020] : MATTHEW PRE 1820 SHEFFIELD, YKS, ENG [38248] : LAVINIA 1810-1830 NBL, ENG [38761] : C1850 BALLYNABARNY, WIC, IRL [33899] : 1800S TOOMYVARA, TIP, IRL [34015] : PRE 1850 KILBEGGAN, WEM, IRL [35897] : PRE 1850 SOUTHERN, IRL [35897] : 1800-1850 ABD, SCT [38253]

BOOTHBY 1857 + ROMSEY, VIC, AUS [36360]
BOOTHE 1860 + MOOREFIELD, ONT, CAN [34231]
BOOTHEY PRE 1860 CHERRY GARDENS, SA, AUS [34815]
BOOTHROYD 1860 + TAS, AUS [35059] : 1860-1900 DARLINGTON, DUR, ENG [34211]
BOOTON PRE 1915 STOCKTON ON TEES, DUR, ENG [38596] : 1830-1850 GALLIO CO., OH, USA [36731]
BOOTS PRE 1837 ICKLESHAM, BREDE & UDIMORE, KEN & SSX, ENG [34780]
BOOTTEN JAMES 1850 BURFORD, SAL, ENG [33956] : JAMES 1826 + WOR, ENG [33956]
BOOTY EBENEZER C1825 CLAIBORNE, MS, USA [37801] : ABNER C1780 GREENE, NC, USA [37801]
BOOZER PRE 1865 MONTGOMERY CO., PA, USA [36359]
BORAS ALL GABELA, BOSNIA & HERC, YU [36775]
BORASTON PRE 1780 WAR & WOR, ENG [34873]
BORCHARDT PRE 1864 GERSWALDE, PRE, GER [34840]
BORCHERS 1870-1920 COOK CO., IL, USA [35298]
BORDEAU 1850 + TILBURY, ONT, CAN [34983]
BORDEN 1665 + ENG [38195]
BORDLAND ALL WORLDWIDE [37095]
BORDOLLO PRE 1800 GRUENSTADT, RPF, GER & ITL [34815]
BORE PRE 1729 RADFORD, NTT, ENG [37000]
BOREHAM ALL ESS, ENG [34493] : PRE 1900 LONDON, ENG [34671] : C1800-1880 REDE, SFK, ENG [37752]
BOREHARD PRE 1877 GER [36621]
BOREN 1830 + CAPE GIRARDEAU CO., MO, KY & TN, USA [37796] : 1830 + JEFFERSON CO., MO, KY & TN, USA [37796] : ALL IL & TN, USA [38230] : 1700-1900 KY, VA, SC, IN, USA [38328]
BORGE GENEROSA 1800-1895 SINGLA, MALTA [36634]
BORGER ALL ST CLAIR CO., IL, USA [36930]

BORGOS ALL RORAS, S TRNDLG, NOR [36326] : ALL MN, USA [36326]
BORJESSON ALL HAARNOSAND, SWE [38175]
BORLAND PRE 1840 TYR, IRL [34489] : PRE 1860S STRABANE, TYR, IRL [34937] : 1750-1800 IRL [38115] : 1800S KILWINNING, AYR, SCT [33779] : 1760 CRAIGIE, AYR, SCT [35773] : ALL WORLDWIDE [37095]
BORLASE STEVENS 1800 + WORLDWIDE [35032]
BORN 1700-1800 ERFURT, PSA, GER [38643] : PRE 1750 WEINHEIM & ALZEY, RPF, GER [38681]
BORNE PRE 1900 NTT & MDX, ENG [36893]
BORNHOLDT 1480-1970S BILSEN & RENZEL, SHO, GER [37021] : 1850 + NEW YORK & VARIOUS, NY & IA, USA [37021]
BORNSTEIN 1850 + SYDNEY, NSW, AUS [34969]
BORNTREGER 1700S RPF, BRD [38184]
BOROMEO 1850 + BENDIGO, VIC, AUS [35040]
BOROUGHS PRE 1860 ELMDON, ESS, ENG [34869]
BOROWSKI ALL KRAKOW, POL [37041]
BORRI C1500 + SAN LORENZO IN CAMPO, ITL & USA [36139]
BORRMANN ALL WORLDWIDE [38666]
BORROUGH PRE 1850 CALVERLEY & GUISELEY, WRY, ENG [36159]
BORROW 1790 + TATHAM, LAN, ENG [36227]
BORSLEY 1800 + DUNCHURCH, WAR, ENG [34315]
BORTEL 1863-1892 WOOD CO., OH, USA [38092]
BORTHWICK JOHN 1660 + HERIOT, MLN, SCT [36254] : GEORGE 1780 + DUMFRIES, DFS, SCT [36254]
BORTMAN 1792-1808 VA, KY & OH, USA [33761]
BORWELL PRE 1860 YORK, NRY, ENG [36022]
BORWICK PRE 1820 EGTON CUM NEWLAND, LAN & CUL, ENG [36082]
BOS PRE 1820 EESVEEN, OIJ, NL [36283]
BOSANKO 1900 + SHEPPARTON, VIC, AUS [35453] : 1800 CROWAN, CON, ENG [35023] : PRE 1859 + CAMBORNE, CON, ENG [35453]
BOSCH MARTIN 1750-1810 KAPSWEYER, RPF & BAV, GER [38528]
BOSCHEN 1800 + HAN, GER [34421]
BOSCOMBE PRE 1850 CORSHAM, WIL, ENG [37855]
BOSE 1800S TARMSTEDT, BRM, BRD [38019]
BOSELEY ALL VIC, AUS [35746]
BOSHAW ALL L'ASSOMPTION & SANDWICH, ONT, CAN & USA [38287]
BOSHER PRE 1870 BETHNAL GREEN, MDX, ENG [36866] : PRE 1920 LEICESTER, LEI, ENG [36866]
BOSHOFF PRE 1800 BAYONNE, FRA [34948] : PRE 1800 HBG, GER [34948] : PRE 1800 NL [34948]
BOSIN PRE 1643 HOLSTEIN, GER [38544]
BOSLEY 1780 + EASTHAMPSTEAD, BRK, ENG [33938] : PRE 1854 THATHCHAM, BRK, ENG [35578] : ALL GLOUCESTER, GLS, ENG [36743]
BOSMA PRE 1910 KOLLUMERLAND, FRI, NL [34218]
BOSMAN PRE 1850 ALKEMADE, ZUH, NL [34613]
BOSS 1845 + CARCOAR AREA, NSW, AUS [36316] : 1700-1850 WASHINGTON CO., RI, USA [38287]
BOSSAU PRE 1800 BAYONNE, FRA [34948] : PRE 1800 HBG, GER [34948]
BOSSE 1900 + ECHUCA, VIC, AUS [36622] : 1850 + BEECHWORTH, VIC, AUS [37154] : PRE 1850 LIBENBURG, HAN, GER [37154]
BOSSELMAN ALL WORLDWIDE [34634]
BOSSELMANN ALL WORLDWIDE [34634]
BOSSERT JAKOB PRE 1751 BIRR, AG, CH [34992]
BOSSOM ALL ENG [35819]
BOSSON 1800 + SANDBACH AREA, CHS, ENG [36997] : 1830-34 STOKE RIVERS, DEV, ENG [37863]

BOSTOCK C1780 WREXHAM, CHS, ENG [34222] :
PRE 1836 ASHBY DE LA ZOUCH, LEI, DBY &
RUT, ENG [37840] : C1825 DUBLIN, IRL [35456]

BOSUSTOW 1700-1800 CON, ENG [35424]

BOSVILE PRE 1752 SELBY, CARLTON, JUXTA,
SNAITH, YKS, ENG [36039]

BOSWELL PRE 1843 PARRAMATTA, NSW, AUS
[34780] : 1600+ NORTHWICH KELSALL, CHS,
ENG [36218] : PRE 1842 ENG & SCT [36747]

BOSWORTH ALL KETTERING, NTH, ENG [36830] :
ALL CASTLE DONNINGTON, LEI & DBY, ENG
[37078] : 1770+ SHOREDITCH, LND, ENG [37552] :
ALL PORT ELIZABETH, RSA [36830]

BOTEL 1700-1900 SEEMUHLEN, SHO, BRD [35638] :
1700 GLUSING, GER [35638]

BOTELER 1850-1890 MONTGOMERY CO., MD, USA
[36737]

BOTEREL PRE 1740 CON, ENG [34644]

BOTHA C1754 SWELLENDAM, CAPE, RSA [36459]

BOTHMANN PRE 1871 GER [38112] : 1871+ NY, IL &
MN, USA [38112]

BOTHROYD 1860-1900 DARLINGTON, DUR, ENG
[34211] : 1850-1881 FERRYHILL, DUR, ENG [34211]

BOTICA ALL GABELA, BOSNIA & HERC, YU [36775]

BOTLEY 1750+ DEPTFORD, KEN, SRY & LND,
ENG [37065]

BOTO ALL GABELA, BOSNIA & HERC, YU [36775]

BOTSCH PRE 1750 GER [38640]

BOTT 1850+ TAS, AUS [34186] : ALL GSY, CHI
[36826] : ALL JSY, CHI [36826] : PRE 1792
LONDON, ENG [34275] : ALL SPITALFIELDS,
LND, ENG [34820] : PRE 1750 STAFFORD, STS,
ENG [36701] : PRE 1860 BIRMINGHAM, WAR,
ENG [36775] : 1800+ UPWELL, NFK, ENG [37152]

BOTTCHER 1750-1870 WULFTEN, HAN, GER [37798]

BOTTER 1657+ ZWARTSLUIS, OIJ, NL [34398] :
1690+ HOOGEVEEN, DRN, NL [34398]

BOTTERELL 1700-1800 WOR & SAL, ENG [36003]

BOTTERILE PRE 1863 PLUMSTEAD, SSX & LND,
ENG [37853]

BOTTERING PRE 1790 BDF & HRT, ENG [35701]

BOTTERWECK 1680 BOEMIGHAUSEN, WAL, GER
[34912]

BOTTING 1700-1900 SSX, ENG [35069] : 1650-1750
NUTHURST, SSX, ENG [35288] : 1730-1830 WEST
GRINSTEAD, SSX, ENG [35643] : C1840
LAMBETH, SRY, ENG [35768] : 1700-1900
CUXTON, SHORNE & RAINHAM, KEN, ENG
[38354]

BOTTLE PRE 1900 HACKNEY, LND, ENG [33965] :
C1700-1800 NOTTINGHAM, NTT, ENG [37977]

BOTTOMLEY PRE 1880 HOLMFIRTH, WRY, ENG
[33850] : PRE 1850 NORLAND & BARKISLAND,
WRY, ENG [37372] : 1700-1850 RIPPONDEN, WRY,
ENG [37736] : 1860-1902 KEWEENAW CO., MI,
USA [38010]

BOTTRALL ALL ST JUST, CON, ENG [36506]

BOTTRELL 1850+ WITNEY, OXF, ENG [36802]

BOTTRILL PRE 1800 WAR, ENG [37245] : 1800+
MDX, ENG [37836]

BOTTS ISAAC PRE 1650 ENG [37784]

BOTWRIGHT 1800+ LONDON, ENG [34258] : PRE
1800 SFK, ENG [34258] : 1800 MDX & SFK, ENG
[38039]

BOUCHARD 1740-1800 SURAT, INDIA [37056]

BOUCHER 1900+ GIPPSLAND, VIC, AUS [37149] :
1874 DARWIN, NT, AUS [37952] : ALL QUE, CAN
[34517] : 1740-1800 BOUCHERVILLE, QUE, CAN
[36737] : PRE 1792 BOX, WIL, ENG [34858] :
JOSEPH PRE 1830 WIL, ENG [35713] : C1850
COKER, SOM, ENG [37233] : 1760-1852 ENG & AUS
[34189] : PRE 1870 LIM, IRL [34555] : 1750-1800

CERES, FIF, SCT [37779] : 1780-1830
CUMBERNAULD, DNB, SCT [37779]

BOUCHERE ALL AMBOISE, PL, FRA [36492] : ALL
METZ, ALS, FRA [36492]

BOUCHIER C1750-1890 LEEDS, YKS, ENG [37842] :
1790+ MT SHANNON, GAL, IRL [33927] : 1780-
1900 CLA & GAL, IRL [34526]

BOUCK 1850+ WALSINGHAM TWP., ONT, CAN
[34129]

BOUCLET PRE 1849 CALAIS, FRA [34886]

BOUDREAULT PRE 1890 LA MALBAIE, QUE, CAN
[37442]

BOUDRIE 1860+ DARTFORD, KEN, ENG [33821]

BOUET 1620-1660 MARANS, PCH, FRA [34514]

BOUFFIER 1849-1863 PATERSON, NSW, AUS [36267]
: 1880-1910 SINGLETON, NSW, AUS [36267] : 1863-
1920 CESSNOCK, NSW, AUS [36267] : PRE 1849
NEUDORF, HES, BRD [36267]

BOUG 1750 DUNNING, PER, SCT [37106]

BOUGHEN C1812 ASHILL, NFK, ENG [34518] : C1840
SAHAM TONEY, NFK, ENG [34518]

BOUGHEY ALL WORLDWIDE [36997]

BOUGHNER 1820 NORFOLK CO., ONT, CAN [37490]

BOUGHTON PRE 1700 CRANBROOK, KEN, ENG
[37185] : 1630-1850 FAIRFIELD CO., CT, USA [36335]

BOUGOURD PRE 1880 ST SAMPSONS, GSY, CHI
[35575]

BOUILLANE PRE 1730 BERNE, BE, CH [38408]

BOUIS PRE 1780 FRA [35270] : 1780+ HARFORD &
BALTIMORE CO.S, MD, USA [35270]

BOUK 1850+ WALSINGHAM TWP., ONT, CAN
[34129]

BOULANGER ALEXANDRE PRE 1855 VILLERS LE
SEX AISNE, PIC, FRA [38408]

BOULCA 1900+ LONDON, ENG [35783] : PRE 1900
BARCELONA, ESP [35783] : 1900+ GLASGOW,
LKS, SCT [35783] : ALL WORLDWIDE [35783]

BOULD WILLIAM 1845+ MORNINGTON, VIC,
AUS [34915] : C1880S ROSEDALE, VIC, AUS [35748]
: WILLIAM 1845+ HUDDERSFIELD, WRY, ENG
[34915]

BOULDEN PRE 1797 GRADE, CON, ENG [34752] :
PRE 1800 MAIDSTONE, KEN, ENG [38254]

BOULDING PRE 1800 SHEFFIELD, WRY, ENG
[36480]

BOULDS ALL WHITECHURCH, GLA, WLS [37950]

BOULER PRE 1797 BRAMPTON, YKS, ENG [34893]

BOULT 1600-1700 BOSTON, LIN, ENG [34505] : C1750
DEV & CON, ENG [36594]

BOULTED PRE 1820 ESS, ENG [35902]

BOULTER PRE 1875 BURFORD, OXF, ENG [33997] :
PRE 1875 UPTON, OXF, ENG [33997] : 1800-1860
BRISTOL, SOM, ENG [37964] : 1900+ TEMUKA,
CANT, NZ [33997]

BOULTING PRE 1828 BLOOMSBURY, MDX, ENG
[33860]

BOULTON MILLICENT ALL SYDNEY, NSW, AUS
[35122] : C1840 LEWISHAM, KEN, ENG [34205] :
PRE 1860 BROOMWICH, STS, ENG [35061] : PRE
1804 CORSE, GLS, ENG [36177] : 1800+
LEICESTER, LEI, ENG [36414] : 1803+
KEMPSFORD, GLS, ENG [36975] : PRE 1812
KEMBLE, WIL, ENG [37510] : PRE 1800
BIDDULPH & ENDON, STS, ENG [37893] : 1800+
HULL, ERY, ENG [37907] : 1850+ ENG & AUS
[33881]

BOURACIER ALL PARIS, RPA, FRA [36193]

BOURCHIER 1780-1900 CLA & GAL, IRL [34526]

BOUREN 1863 BULLI, NSW, AUS [34793]

BOURGERY 1620-1700 TROIS RIVIERES, QUE, CAN
[34514] : 1580-1640 LA ROCHELLE, PCH, FRA
[34514]

BOURGUIGNON 1770-1859 FOSSES LA VILLE, NMR, BEL **[38158]**

BOURKE PRE 1920 NSW & VIC, AUS **[34424]** : 1860+ AUS **[34960]** : PRE 1900 HORSHAM, VIC, AUS **[35752]** : PRE 1850 PORT PHILLIP DIST., VIC, AUS **[35752]** : JOHN CONWAY 1800+ VIC, AUS **[36602]** : JOHN 1866+ RUTHERGLEN, VIC, AUS **[37555]** : ALL ST HELIER, JSY, CHI **[36763]** : PRE 1850 WANDSWORTH, SRY, ENG **[36153]** : PRE 1866 CASTLECONNELL, LIM, IRL **[33775]** : 1800S HOLLYFORD, TIP, IRL **[34015]** : 1870 DOON, LIM, IRL **[34015]** : ALL ARM, IRL **[34040]** : ALL MAY, IRL **[34189]** : 1800-1850 COR, IRL **[34307]** : 1798 BALLYCASTLE, MAY, IRL **[34708]** : 1700-1900 KILLALA, MAY, IRL **[34717]** : 1780+ 'CORK ESTATES', COR, IRL **[34800]** : PRE 1830 LIM, IRL **[34903]** : 1850+ DERRYHASNA & CASTLECONNELL, LIM, IRL **[34960]** : C1800-1860 TIP, IRL **[35206]** : 1750-1800 BRUFF, LIM, IRL **[35228]** : PRE 1800 LIM, IRL **[35589]** : 1800+ RATHKEALE, LIM, IRL **[36602]** : JANE 1842+ LIM, IRL & AUS **[37161]**

BOURMAN 1812-1865 STROUD, GLS, ENG **[34658]**

BOURNE 1838+ WOLLOMBI, NSW, AUS **[33939]** : 1890S OLD JUNEE, NSW, AUS **[35230]** : JOSEPH C1850-1900 TORONTO, ONT, CAN **[34354]** : PRE 1838 RODE, SOM, ENG **[33939]** : ALL SOUTHWARK, SRY, ENG **[34308]** : PRE 1860S APPLEDORE, KEN, ENG **[34458]** : 1790+ COLEFORD, GLS, ENG **[34609]** : 1600+ HASTINGS, SSX, ENG **[34747]** : 1835 KEN, ENG **[34793]** : 1860S LIVERPOOL, LAN, ENG **[35331]** : ALL WOLVERHAMPTON, STS, ENG **[36537]** : ALL WEST BROMWICH, STS, ENG **[36537]** : HENRY PRE 1600 EAST HADDON, NTH, ENG **[36619]** : PRE 1700 HASTINGS, SSX, ENG **[36883]** : 1847+ REDDITCH, WOR, ENG **[37230]** : PRE 1800 WAREHORN, KEN, ENG **[38033]** : PRE 1700 KEN, ENG **[38389]** : 1600+ NEW KENT CO., VA, USA **[34350]** : 1670+ KY, USA **[37592]**

BOURNER 1860+ EAST GRINSTEAD & HORSHAM, SSX, ENG **[36967]** : 1800 SSX, ENG **[38320]**

BOURNES ALL GLS & SOM, ENG **[37672]**

BOURNOUVEAU C1820 HAMMILLE, BEL **[34521]**

BOURS C1700 NEWPORT, RI, USA **[35203]**

BOURSANT C1732 GENEVA, GE, CH **[38348]**

BOURTON 1700S SOM, DOR & WIL, ENG **[34739]** : 1800+ BECKINGTON, SOM, ENG **[36195]**

BOUSFIELD 1800+ MAROKE BY SEA, YKS, ENG **[35908]** : 1700+ KIRKBY STEPHEN, WES, ENG **[35908]** : 1650 GREAT MUSGRAVE, WES, ENG **[35908]**

BOUSIE 1700-1800 FIF, SCT **[35627]**

BOUTALL 1500-1650 ENG **[38061]**

BOUTELL 1500-1650 ENG **[38061]** : 1635-1900 USA **[38061]**

BOUTELLE 1635-1900 USA **[38061]**

BOUTILIER 1400+ ETOBON, FRA **[34500]**

BOUTIN 1600-1690 LA ROCHELLE, PCH, FRA **[34514]**

BOUTON PRE 1716 NEUHANAU, HES, GER **[38348]** : 1630-1850 FAIRFIELD CO., CT, USA **[36335]**

BOUTRON 1750-1802 QUE, CAN **[34482]**

BOUTWELL 1635-1900 USA **[38061]**

BOUVEYRON 1600-1900 AU CABANNES, ARIEGE, FRA **[33758]**

BOUVIER PRE 1700 CHOUGNI, GE, CH **[38348]**

BOUWER 1724+ STELLENBOSCH, CAPE, RSA **[34947]**

BOVAIRD PRE 1820 DON, IRL **[38056]**

BOVARD PRE 1910 HAMILTON, ONT, CAN **[34365]**

BOVAY C1700 GENEVA, GE, CH **[38348]**

BOVEY PRE 1789 IPPLEPEN, DEV, ENG **[35157]** : PRE 1890 MDX & LND, ENG **[35701]** : C1800 ST BLAZEY, CON, ENG **[37641]**

BOVIS ALL WORLDWIDE **[36118]**

BOW 1800+ DOR, ENG **[35998]** : 1791+ BERRY POMEROY, DEV, ENG **[38291]** : 1700+ AIRTH, STI, SCT **[34977]**

BOWATER PRE 1660 WOR, ENG **[36319]** : ALL WORLDWIDE **[35984]**

BOWCETT 1732-1841 EASTHAM, WOR, ENG **[36513]**

BOWCHER ALL CON, ENG **[35063]** : 1850-1920S CAMBERWELL, LND, ENG **[37780]**

BOWCOCK 1850S ETRURIA & TUNSTALL, STS, ENG **[36504]** : 1770-1800 SWATON, LIN, ENG **[36682]**

BOWDEN 1849+ AUBURN RIVER, QLD, AUS **[34276]** : 1850+ ROMA, QLD, AUS **[34276]** : 1870+ LAIDLEY, QLD, AUS **[34276]** : 1835+ CENTRAL, QLD, AUS **[34276]** : 1855+ COLINTON, QLD, AUS **[34276]** : 1860+ ESK, QLD, AUS **[34276]** : 1840 PENOLA, SA, AUS **[34456]** : C1900 PERTH, WA, AUS **[34456]** : ALL AUS **[35389]** : C1815 CHS, ENG **[34276]** : PRE 1840 STOCKPORT, CHS, ENG **[34285]** : 1750+ HOUGHTON LE SPRING, DUR, ENG **[34456]** : 1600+ UPLOWMAN, DEV, ENG **[34747]** : PRE 1870 STOCKPORT, CHS, ENG **[34870]** : 1800S PENZANCE, CON, ENG **[35187]** : WILLIAM 1858 STOCKPORT, CHS, ENG **[35343]** : PRE 1840 SHAPWICK, SOM, ENG **[35346]** : PRE 1840 STARESTON, DEV, ENG **[35389]** : 1780+ WEST BUCKLAND, DEV, ENG **[35526]** : PRE 1790 ATTLEBOROUGH, NFK, ENG **[35587]** : PRE 1801 LODDISWELL, DEV, ENG **[35895]** : 1600-1800 ILSINGTON, DEV, ENG **[36106]** : 1700+ ST ENODER, CON, ENG **[37088]** : PRE 1815 CANTERBURY, KEN, ENG **[37142]** : PRE 1850 BIRMINGHAM, ENG **[37245]** : PRE 1800 MEVAGISSEY & ST AUSTELL, CON, ENG **[37319]** : MARTHA 1810+ SHURLACH & WINGHAM, CHS, ENG **[37546]** : PRE 1800 SOUTH MOLTON, DEV, ENG **[37725]** : THOMAS C1871 ECCLES, LAN, ENG **[37934]** : 1810-1850 MARPLE, CHS, ENG **[37934]** : 1870-1900 CHORLEY, LAN, ENG **[37934]** : THOMAS C1857 PENDLETON, LAN, ENG **[37934]** : ALL KILDARE, KID, IRL **[35514]** : 1840 FRESHFORD, KIK, IRL **[37521]** : C1832 ISLAND OF HERM, CHI, UK **[35569]** : 1821-1851 SNOW HILL, MD, USA **[37803]** : 1855-1865 KEWEENAW CO., MI, USA **[38010]**

BOWDITCH 1850S CLAPHAM, SRY, ENG **[35156]** : 1830 UPWAY, DOR, ENG **[37691]**

BOWDLE 1800-1850 WALPOLE ST PETER, NFK, ENG **[36394]**

BOWE 1858 HEATHCOTE, VIC, AUS **[35801]** : 1852 MELBOURNE, VIC, AUS **[35801]** : 1913+ SYDNEY, NSW, AUS **[36366]** : 1830+ RIO DE JANEIRO, BRAZIL **[35801]** : 1795+ LONDON, ENG **[35801]** : 1827+ NEWCASTLE ON TYNE, NBL, ENG **[35801]** : 1800+ NRY, ENG **[36193]** : 1850+ TULLAROAN, KIK, IRL **[36366]** : ALL WORLDWIDE **[36472]**

BOWELL 1700+ BROMLEY, ESS, ENG **[36256]**

BOWELS ALL ASH & CANTERBURY, KEN, ENG **[34564]**

BOWEN 1852+ MELBOURNE, VIC, AUS **[38213]** : 1856+ GEELONG & DROUIN, VIC, AUS **[38213]** : 1800+ ST PETER PORT, GSY, CHI **[35847]** : PRE 1851 LONDON, ENG **[35893]** : EDWARD 1877+ ST GILES, LND, MDX, ENG **[36519]** : JOSEPH C1905 ST GILES, LND, MDX, ENG **[36519]** : MARGARET 1880+ ST GILES, LND, MDX, ENG **[36519]** : EDWARD 1848+ ST MARGARET WEST, LND, MDX, ENG **[36519]** : JOHN 1873+ ST GILES, LND,

MDX, ENG [36519] : PRE 1800 YARDLEY, WOR, ENG [36530] : PRE 1865 WEST BROMWICH, STS, ENG [36766] : 1700+ BURGHILL & HEREFORD, HEF, ENG [37625] : 1800+ WOLVERHAMPTON, STS, ENG [38046] : PRE 1840 MALLOW, COR, IRL [33808] : 1800S TIP, IRL [35768] : JOHN C1840 KCD, SCT [37200] : GEORGE C1820 KCD, SCT [37200] : ALL KCD, SCT [37200] : 1730-1800 SMITHFIELD, RI, USA [37806] : 1750+ ORANGE & ULSTER COS., NY, USA [38015] : JAMES C1800 VA, USA [38044] : EDWARD DEWITT C1860 CLEVELAND, OH, USA [38397] : PRE 1850 PEM, WLS [34319] : ALL DOWLAIS, GLA, WLS [37154]

BOWER 1820-1850 BREMEN, BRD [33835] : JOHN 1800+ YKS, ENG [34078] : SARAH 1800-1990 NFK, ENG [34249] : PRE 1775 TITCHFIELD, HAM, ENG [35483] : 1550-1620 TINGEWICK, BKM, ENG [36010] : 1600 MANBY, LIN, ENG [36944] : SAMUEL 1830+ YKS, ENG [37153] : PRE 1850 BLANTYRE, LKS, SCT [36705]

BOWERLY C1800+ KEN & WOR, ENG [33812]

BOWERMAN PRE 1850 BRACKLEY, NTH, ENG [36502] : PRE 1870 BICESTER & MIDDLETON STONEY, OXF, ENG [36502] : 1700S CHARLBURY, OXF, ENG [37083]

BOWERS 1860+ NABIAC, NSW, AUS [35157] : 1800+ ONT & QUE, CAN [34500] : 1745+ ECCLES, NOR, ENG [34374] : ALL BLACKHEATH, LND, ENG [34663] : ALL SFK, ENG [34744] : 1800+ ROCHDALE, LAN, ENG [35342] : PRE 1840 BARKING, ESS & NFK, ENG [36178] : 1700+ CHEDDLETON, STS, ENG [36701] : 1740+ HILDERSTONE, STS, ENG [36701] : FRANCIS 1850S GREAT YARMOUTH, NFK, ENG & AUS [35498] : 1800S WATERFORD, WAT, IRL [35464] : PRE 1830 ST HELENA [36468] : 1800-1950 WORCESTER, MA, USA [38154] : PRE 1800 YORK, PA, USA [38220] : ALL WORLDWIDE [37785]

BOWES 1850+ BALLARAT, VIC, AUS [35986] : 1870+ PARRAMATTA, NSW, AUS [37353] : PRE 1710 KIDDERMINSTER, WOR, ENG [34711] : PRE 1760 FURNESS, LAN, ENG [37353] : 1800-80 LIVERPOOL, LAN, ENG [37353] : 1750-1850 STANHOPE, DUR, ENG [38516] : 1790-1850 DUBLIN & ROSCREA, TIP, IRL [34672] : 1800+ FER, IRL [38189]

BOWES (SEE BOWE) [35801]

BOWGIN PRE 1850 SOMERLEYTON, SFK & NFK, ENG [36037]

BOWIE 1780-1900 MAN, CAN [34126] : PRE 1871 EDINBURGH, SCT [33906] : 1730-1900 STRAITON, AYR, SCT [34126] : PRE 1800 CARNOCK, FIF, SCT [34861] : 1820S NERABUS, ARL, SCT [34911] : 1800+ EDINBURGH, MLN, SCT [35395] : 1805+ FALKIRK, STI, SCT [35921]

BOWINKELMANN 1691 WEWER, GER [38748]

BOWKER ALL OLDHAM, LAN, ENG [34443] : JAMES PRE 1840 THORNTON IN LONSDALE, WRY, ENG [35955]

BOWLE 1800-1840 SOM, ENG [38742]

BOWLER 1840+ SCONE, NSW, AUS [34277] : C1844 MAITLAND, NSW, AUS [36284] : ALL CAN & ENG [34140] : C1780 WITLEY, SRY, ENG [34277] : 1750-1800 DARLEY, DBY, ENG [36084] : PRE 1800 NTT, ENG [36196] : C1790 SHOREDITCH, MDX, ENG [36276] : PRE 1880 CHELSEA, LND, ENG [36377] : PRE 1820 CHS & LAN, ENG [37085]

BOWLES 1850+ WARREN, NSW, AUS [34901] : 1780+ FELTHORPE, NFK, ENG [34092] : PRE 1858 DEAL, KEN, ENG [34648] : 1800+ CAPEL & LAMBERHURST, KEN, ENG [36219] : PRE 1840 MALDON, ESS & LND, ENG [36396] : PRE 1857

MACCLESFIELD, CHS, ENG [37318] : GEORIANA 1832 TUDELY & TONBRIDGE, KEN, ENG [37614] : PRE 1850 SILVERMINES, TIP, IRL [36298] : 1750+ WLS [36470]

BOWLEY 1900+ BRISTOL & YATE, GLS, ENG [37322]

BOWLING ALL BOLTON, LAN, ENG [36774] : GEORGE W. 1866-1886 FAYETTE CO., WV, USA [38109]

BOWLS PRE 1700 AYLSHAM, NFK, ENG [36593]

BOWLT C1800 HEWORTH, DUR, ENG [36364]

BOWMAN 1890+ BOTANY, NSW, AUS [35149] : C1855 PLEASANT CREEK, VIC, AUS [35391] : 1798+ RICHMOND & HUNTER VALLEY, NSW, AUS [38211] : 1880+ BIRDSVILLE, QLD, AUS [38484] : 1830+ SA, AUS [38484] : 1820+ ENG [33788] : PRE 1858 MDX, ENG [35213] : MARY C1720 STANHOPE, DUR, ENG [35972] : 1800 NRY, ENG [36680] : 1800+ ISLINGTON, MDX & LND, ENG [37065] : PRE 1860 PAMBER & TADLEY, HAM, ENG [37261] : 1800+ KENDAL, WES, ENG [37443] : PRE 1900 IPSWICH, SFK, ENG [37941] : PRE 1870 DUBLIN, IRL [34652] : 1800+ DFS, SCT [35293] : 1800S EDINBURGH, MLN, SCT & AUS [35422] : ADAM 1820 PA, USA [33910] : GEORGE 1767 NJ, USA [34129] : PRE 1850 MA & NH, USA [34504] : 1800S NEWBURGH & YONKERS, NY, USA [36918] : 1863+ DODGE CO., NE, USA [36919] : MARY C1793 SC, USA [37801] : 1830+ OH, USA [38058] : 1840+ MONTGOMERY CO., NY, USA [38176] : GEORGE 1731-1770 FREDERICK, VA, USA [38187] : PRE 1870 USA [38303]

BOWMER 1730S+ ST OSWALDS, DUR, ENG [38269]

BOWN 1800S HOLWELL, DOR, ENG [34188] : 1800+ DUNCHURCH, WAR, ENG [34315] : 1700-1850 WIL, ENG [35069]

BOWNAS PRE 1785 BARBON & KIRKBY LONSDALE, WES, ENG [38248]

BOWNES 1850-1950 WINSFORD, CHS, ENG [36983] : 1800-1900 RILEY, DBY, ENG [36983]

BOWNESS C1768 CUL, ENG [35646]

BOWRING 1820+ PECKHAM, SRY, ENG [35461] : 1800+ STOCKWELL, SRY, ENG [35461]

BOWRON 1800+ LONDON, ENG [33946]

BOWSHER 1820S CHIPPENHAM, WIL, ENG [34191] : 1834-48 LONDON, ENG [37863]

BOWSKILL GEORGE PRE 1750 STANTON, NTT, ENG [36619] : REV SIDNEY 1900+ HEMEL HEMPSTEAD, HRT, ENG [37191]

BOWTELL 1829+ NSW, AUS [34976] : 1829 HALSTEAD, ESS, ENG [34976] : ALL ESS, ENG [37741] : 1500-1650 ENG [38061] : PRE 1830 LINSDELL, ESS, ENG [38755] : 1635-1900 USA [38061]

BOWY PRE 1710 RIBBESFORD, WOR, ENG [34711]

BOWYER ALL YORK & HURON CO., ONT, CAN [38419] : 1795 BRAY, BRK, ENG [34120] : PRE 1850 CHS, ENG [35945] : PRE 1815 WOR, ENG [36793] : ALL HASTINGS, SSX, ENG [36830] : ALL LONDON, ENG [38419]

BOX 1844+ VIC, AUS [35233] : 1844+ NSW, AUS [35233] : JAMES 1850S+ VIC, AUS [35477] : PRE 1852 MALMESBURY, WIL, ENG [33806] : 1750+ HOLSWORTHY, DEV, ENG [34108] : C1820+ LONDON, ENG [35233] : WILLIAM 1795+ STOKE DAMEREL, DEV, ENG [35477] : DANIEL 1781+ BRADFORD, YKS, ENG [36638] : PRE 1880 WESTMINSTER, MDX, ENG [37834]

BOXALL 1800-1900 CAMDEN TOWN & FULHAM, MDX, ENG [34187] : 1800+ SRY, MDX & BKM, ENG [36574]

BOXER PRE 1850 LND & SRY, ENG [37091]

BOXSELL 1840+ KANGAROO VALLEY, NSW, AUS [35360]

BOY PRE 1850 QUE, CAN [34102]

BOYACK PRE 1839 LAURENCEKIRK, KCD, SCT [36308] : ANNE PRE 1856 SCT [37481]

BOYCE 1870-1880 BENDIGO, VIC, AUS [35725] : RICHARD C1880S SYDNEY, NSW, AUS [35843] : PRE 1790 WHITTLESEY, CAM, ENG [35186] : ALL HEREFORD & STEPNEY, HEF & SRY, ENG [36997] : AMELIA 1818+ FINCHLEY, LND, ENG [37055] : EMMA 1824+ FINCHLEY, LND, ENG [37055] : JOHN 1786-1872 LND, ENG [37055] : JOHN 1786+ STIFFKEY, NFK, ENG [37055] : DAVID PRE 1852 HASTINGS, SSX, ENG [38509] : 1800+ TULLYISH, DOW, IRL [34808] : 1820-1850 BELFAST, ANT, IRL [35725] : 1720-1800 HUNTERDON, NJ, USA [36908]

BOYD SARAH PRE 1800 TAS, AUS [33878] : 1890-1910 WAAIA, VIC, AUS [35136] : PRE 1900 BLACKHEATH, NSW, AUS [35245] : 1842+ GEELONG, VIC, AUS [35439] : 1840S EVANDALE, TAS, AUS [35501] : C1870 ANGORICHINA, SA, AUS [35744] : 1830-1950 AVOCA, VIC, AUS [38272] : 1830+ SYDNEY, NSW, AUS [38288] : THOMAS 1826+ TURRAMURRA & SYDNEY, NSW, AUS [38597] : 1800+ JARVIS, ONT, CAN [34497] : 1840+ UXBRIDGE, ONT, CAN [35622] : PETER 1850+ CAN [38071] : C1850+ MONTREAL, QUE, CAN [38406] : PRE 1852 SLI, IRL [34014] : 1800+ ENNISKILLEN, FER, IRL [34408] : 1830S FER, IRL [35136] : 1760-1850 MOG, IRL [35600] : PRE 1840 BAILIEBOROUGH, CAV, IRL [35842] : 1800S ANT, IRL [36289] : C1823 NEWRY, DOW, IRL [36599] : 1750-1850 ATHLONE, ROS, IRL [36724] : 1780S DONAGHADEE, DOW, IRL [36862] : 1750-1822 DOW, IRL [38100] : PRE 1850 KINGSCOURT, CAV, IRL [38272] : PRE 1850 KILLYBEGS, DON, IRL [38597] : JAMES PRE 1792 KILLARNEY, KER, IRL [38597] : 1700-1760 ULSTER, N IRL [36352] : 1851-1856 NEW PLYMOUTH, NZ [36770] : 1870+ HAVELOCK, NZ [36818] : 1800-1900 ST ANDREWS, FIF, SCT [33800] : PRE 1840 SLAMANNAN, STI, SCT [33999] : 1770+ ORCHILL, PER, SCT [34075] : PRE 1848 LINLITHGOW, WLN, SCT [35439] : C1830 KCD, SCT [35515] : 1790+ ARL, SCT [35622] : JAMES 1797 ERROL, PER, SCT [35773] : ALL AYR, SCT [36002] : 1780-1850 SLAMANNAN, STI, SCT [36763] : 1750+ PAISLEY, RFW, SCT [36793] : 1800+ CUMBERNAULD, DNB, SCT [36875] : 1360 SCT [37008] : ALL FORT WILLIAM, INV, SCT [37127] : PRE 1820 WIGTOWN, WIG, SCT [37663] : C1700 CRIEFF, PER, SCT [37918] : 1770-1800 JEDBURGH, ROX, SCT [38465] : 1700+ NORTH UIST, INV, SCT [38476] : 1700+ FRANKLIN CO., VA, USA [34350] : 1790-1850 WEST SPRINGFIELD, MA, USA [36352] : JOHN 1740-1760 UPTON, MA, USA [36352] : 1760-1820 SHELBURNE, MA, USA [36352] : 1900-1990 PERU, IN, USA [36352] : 1790-1890 WILTON, NH, USA [36352] : 1820-1990 CENTRAL OHIO, OH, USA [36352] : 1800-1950 BRATTLEBORO, VT, USA [36352] : 1770-1950 WHITTINGHAM, VT, USA [36352] : 1740-1800 WORCESTER, MA, USA [36352] : 1822-1990 COLUMBUS, OH, USA [36352] : 1900-1953 ALLEN & COLDWATER, MI, USA [36352] : 1740-1800 HOPKINTON, MA, USA [36352] : 1773-1990 WILMINGTON, VT, USA [36352] : 1822-1990 DELAWARE, OH, USA [36352] : 1700+ CHESTER CO., PA, USA [36917] : 1850+ NOBLE CO., OH, USA [36956] : WILLIAM 1832 TN, USA [37801] : WILSON 1852 TYLER, SMITH, TX, USA [37801] : 1790-1850 ELBERT CO., GA, USA [38129] : 1790-1807 SHELBY CO., KY, USA [38763] : ALL

WORLDWIDE [37785] : 1200+ WORLDWIDE [38597]

BOYDELL 1800S LONDON & SAL, ENG [36967]

BOYDEN PRE 1820 STS, ENG [37722]

BOYELL PRE 1855 ENG [36068] : RICHARD 1855+ MARYLEBONE, MDX, ENG [36068]

BOYENTON (SEE BOYNTO [36550]

BOYER 1850+ KYNETON, VIC, AUS [35798] : SUZANNE 1880+ ST EDOUARD, QUE, CAN [36678] : PRE 1860 THORNTON, LEI, ENG [34370] : 1800-1850 LOUGHBOROUGH, LEI, ENG [35798] : 1800-1900 GREAT BUDWORTH, CHS, ENG [37211] : ALL LAN, ENG [38514] : PRE 1850 TITUSVILLE, PA, USA [33804] : C1775+ NY & PA, USA [37764]

BOYES THOMAS 1750+ CAN [35429] : 1800+ HAMBLETON, HAM, ENG [34140] : 1790 ENG [34149] : 1878+ SALFORD, LAN, ENG [35565] : ALL HAMBLEDON, HAM, ENG [36405] : C1820 RADFORD SEMELE & CUBBINGTON, WAR, ENG [37556] : THOMAS 1700+ DFS, SCT [35429] : 1800 LOCHMABEN, DFS, SCT [36667] : PRE 1846 APPLEGARTH, DFS, SCT [37238] : 1800+ SAN FRANCISCO, CA, USA [34140]

BOYES (SEE BOYS) [35399]

BOYLAN 1880-1900S LEADVILLE, CO, USA [38324] : 1850+ NEW YORK, NY, USA [38324]

BOYLE THOMAS 1890+ BALMAIN, NSW, AUS [34427] : 1861+ CONJOLA, NSW, AUS [35842] : MICHAEL 1834+ PARRAMATTA & WINDSOR, NSW, AUS [36600] : 1840+ NSW, AUS [37900] : JAMES PRE 1851 EXETER, DEV, ENG [34539] : ANN 1851 EXETER, DEV, ENG [34539] : 1800-1940 PRESTON, LAN, ENG [38251] : 1830+ RATHMELTON, DON, IRL [33921] : PRE 1850 KILKENNY, IRL [34551] : PRE 1830 LISHEENANDRAN, GAL, IRL [34652] : DORRINGTON 1800+ DERRYGARVE, LDY, IRL [34882] : 1750-1930 DUNLOY, ANT, IRL [36115] : PRE 1930 DON, IRL [36165] : 1750-1830 CLONEEN & CLONMEL, TIP, IRL [36769] : 1800+ DUNGLOE, DON, IRL [37900] : 1830+ DUBLIN, IRL [38539] : PRE 1840 SCT [36272] : PRE 1860 RAGLAN, GLASGOW, LKS, SCT [36848]

BOYLES 1800+ SHARNBROOK, BDF & WAR, ENG [36123]

BOYNE 1700+ DON, IRL [37826]

BOYNTON 1778-1850 SUDBURY, MA, USA [36550] : 1762-1765 DUNSTABLE, NH, USA [37005] : 1787-1813 WEATHERSFIELD & MORETOWN, VT, USA [37005]

BOYS 1917+ MELBOURNE, VIC, AUS [35399] : 1841+ CIRCULAR HEAD, TAS, AUS [35399] : 1843-1852 MELBOURNE, VIC, AUS [35399] : PRE 1850S ST MARGARETS & DARTFORD, KEN, ENG [34458] : PRE 1841 BRIDGWATER, SOM, ENG [35399] : 1700S ESS, ENG [37494] : 1852 HASTINGS, SSX, ENG [38509]

BOYSEN PRE 1876 ADELAIDE, SA, AUS & DEN [33890]

BOYSINGER PRE 1820 BENTON CO., TN, PA & KY, USA & GER [37529]

BOYSON 1820-1880 LONDON, ENG [36780] : 1800+ HAMBURG, HBG, GER [36780]

BOYT PRE 1805 WELLINGTON, SOM, ENG [36828] : PRE 1847 MONMOUTH, MON, WLS [36828]

BOYTE ALL STURMINSTER MARSHALL, DOR, ENG [34261]

BOYTON C1900-1950 LONDON, ENG [34007]

BOZ C1850 ADELAIDE, SA, AUS [34035]

BOZE JOHN PRE 1830 VA & KY, USA [33757]

BRAAMS 1876 EVERMEER FRIESLAND, NSA, GER [38750]

BRAATHU LARS PRE 1900 AAKLUNGEN, TELEMARK, NOR [34481] : ELISE 1879+ AAKLUNGEN, TELEMARK, NOR & CAN [34481]

BRABANDT PRE 1800 PERVER, PSA, GER [38648]

BRABAZON ALL WORLDWIDE [34299]

BRABBIN ANN 1800+ LAN, ENG [38204]

BRABENDER C1830 HELENSBURGH, DNB, SCT [35502]

BRABIN 1857+ JUNEE, NSW, AUS [33763] : PRE 1857 BOLTON, LAN, ENG [33763]

BRABNER C1865 SMYTHSDALE, VIC, AUS [35777] : 1900-1916 LIVERPOOL & LONDON, LAN, ENG [37773] : PRE 1800 CHS, ENG [37773] : PRE 1834 EDINBURGH, MLN, SCT [35542]

BRABYEN 1700-1900 CON, ENG [36170] : 1800-1900 GLA, WLS [36170]

BRABYN 1700-1900 CON, ENG [36170] : 1800-1900 GLA, WLS [36170]

BRACE THOMAS 1820-1840S CHEMUNG CO., NY, USA [37001] : PRE 1880 LIVINGSTON CO., NY, USA [38222]

BRACEBRIDGE PRE 1640 LEI, ENG [37706]

BRACEFIELD 1819+ HASTINGS, SSX, ENG [34668]

BRACEGIRDLE PRE 1876 BOLTON, LAN, ENG [35137] : 1600S MOBBERLEY, CHS, ENG [37039]

BRACEWELL JANE 1847+ KEIGHLEY, YKS, ENG [35343] : C1800 BURNLEY, LAN, ENG [35871]

BRACEY 1700-1900 NFK, ENG [37884]

BRACHE 1860+ CAPETOWN, RSA [38274]

BRACHER 1852+ RICHMOND, VIC, AUS [35188] : PRE 1852 DEV & SOM, ENG [35188] : 1800S KIDDERMINSTER, WOR, ENG [35188]

BRACK PRE 1716 LANCHESTER, DUR, ENG [37635] : ALL WORLDWIDE [37476]

BRACKE 1800+ BRD [36602]

BRACKEN 1840-1860 TAS, AUS [33928] : 1850+ ARMIDALE, NSW, AUS [35194] : 1920+ WINNIPEG, MAN, CAN [35194] : 1800+ ELLISVILLE, ONT, CAN [35194] : 1637-1770 LANCASTER, SKERTON, LAN, ENG [37524] : PRE 1860S MOUNTMELLICK, LEX, IRL [34431] : PRE 1900 TULLAMORE, OFF, IRL [34536] : OWEN 1728-1776 TULLAMORE, OFF, IRL [34792] : 1847 CARROLLTON, OH, USA [35194] : 1800+ UTICA, NY, USA [35194]

BRACKER 1750+ ODELL, BDF, ENG [36123] : 1800+ MECKLENBURG, GER [37907]

BRACKLEY C1740 DRAYTON BEAUCHAMP, BKM, ENG [35095]

BRACKNELL 1750+ BETHNAL GREEN, MDX, ENG [36872]

BRACKS PRE 1840 COCKPEN & LASSWADE, MLN, SCT & NZ [36884]

BRADBEER C1839 CORFE TAUNTON, SOM, ENG [37518] : 1750+ NORTH CURRY, SOM, ENG [37766]

BRADBURN 1820+ DURHAM CO., ONT, CAN [34075]

BRADBURY 1870-1920 WARWICK, QLD, AUS [35158] : PRE 1880 ROCHDALE, LAN, ENG [34429] : 1900S CAMBERWELL, LND, ENG [34496] : C1850S THANE, OXF, ENG [35158] : 1856 HARROW, MDX, ENG [36253] : C1832 WHITCHURCH, BKM, ENG [36253] : 1800-1870 SHABBINGTON, BKM, ENG [36795] : PRE 1870 DENTON, LAN & CHS, ENG [36980] : PRE 1881 ST HELENS, LAN, ENG [37318] : 1700-1850 WYCOMBE, BKM, ENG [37761]

BRADDEN ALL BDF, ENG [33984]

BRADDOCK 1680+ CHEDDLETON, STS, ENG [36701] : 1800+ SANDBACH & MACCLESFIELD AREA, CHS, ENG [36997]

BRADDON ALL WORLDWIDE [33984]

BRADEN 1882-1900 ASOTIN, WA, USA [34064] : PRE 1882 MO, USA [34064]

BRADFIELD 1850+ IPSWICH, QLD, AUS [36300] : PRE 1846 MONKTON FARLEIGH, WIL, ENG [35223] : ALL CHIPPENHAM, WIL, ENG [36300] : PRE 1712 ENG [36972] : 1649+ NTT, ENG [38382] : 1870+ PLYMOUTH, DEV, ENG & AUS [34703] : 1820+ CAPE, RSA [38382] : ALL WORLDWIDE [36300]

BRADFORD 1854+ RUSHWORTH, VIC, AUS [35801] : 1852 SYDNEY, NSW, AUS [35801] : 1840-1980 NSW, AUS [35862] : 1800S MARYLEBONE & READING, LND & BRK, ENG [33981] : 1718 GREAT BROMLEY, ESS, ENG [34204] : PRE 1800 LIDLINGTON, BDF, ENG [34588] : C1789+ EDENHAM, LIN, ENG [35233] : PRE 1885 CAMBRIDGE, CAM, ENG [35430] : 1826+ CLAPHAM, LND, ENG [35801] : PRE 1850 SOHO, LND, ENG [35925] : 1800+ LIDLINGTON, BDF, ENG [35947] : PRE 1830 BRIERLEY HILL & SEDGLEY, STS, ENG [36110] : PRE 1800 KINGSBURY EPISCOPI, SOM, ENG [36581] : PRE 1770 EXFORD, SOM, ENG [37622] : 1829-1900 LEOMINSTER, HEF, ENG & AUS [33847] : PRE 1840 BELFAST, ANT, IRL [35862] : PRE 1850 DUB, IRL & RSA [38772] : ELIZABETH 1770S AUGUSTA CO., VA, USA [36321] : SAMUEL 1700S AUGUSTA CO., VA, USA [36321]

BRADGATE PRE 1631 LEI, ENG [37706]

BRADIN 1831-1870 INDEPENDENCE, MO, USA [38187]

BRADLEY C1790 SYDNEY, NSW, AUS [35089] : 1814+ CASTLEREAGH, NSW, AUS [35090] : 1858+ NTH ADELAIDE, SA, AUS [35785] : 1788 SYDNEY, NSW, AUS [35920] : WILLIAM C1835 MANVERS TWP., ONT, CAN [34064] : 1835-1900 DURHAM & LAMBTON COS., ONT, CAN [34250] : PRE 1850 NB, CAN [36702] : ALL ELGIN CO., ONT, CAN [36702] : 1800-1850 DURHAM, DUR, ENG [33908] : 1883-1910 LONDON, ENG [34331] : 1800+ OTTRINGHAM, YKS, ENG [34341] : 1760-1800 WELL, NRY, ENG [34352] : C1840 PEMBRIDGE, HEF, ENG [34358] : 1800+ PRESTON, LAN, ENG [34512] : PRE 1830 BOLTON, LAN, ENG [34576] : 1750-1850 LIVERPOOL, LAN, ENG [34762] : PRE 1850 RIGTON & FEWSTON, WRY, ENG [34776] : PRE 1824 PENDLETON, LAN, ENG [34959] : 1844+ STOCKPORT, CHS, ENG [35039] : PRE 1800 HUDDERSFIELD, YKS, ENG [35061] : JOHN 1770+ WHITBY, ENG [35484] : CHARLOTTE 1792-1812 WHITBY, ENG [35484] : 1780+ ELLESBOROUGH, BKM, ENG [35899] : 1655+ SHIPSTON ON STOUR, WOR, ENG [35990] : PRE 1804 SELBY & BRAYTON, WRY, ENG [36039] : 1700-1800 KETTERING, NTH, ENG [36057] : 1750-1850 EPSOM, SRY, ENG [36261] : HANNAH PRE 1850 MANCHESTER, LAN, ENG [36297] : 1600-1850 DAWLEYMAGNA, SAL, ENG [36556] : PRE 1838 HANDLEY, DOR, ENG [36629] : PRE 1820 LAN, ENG [36747] : 1800+ WARNDON, WOR, ENG [36825] : 1825+ LONDON, MDX & SRY, ENG [36997] : PRE 1850 LAN & WES, ENG [37246] : PRE 1780 GREASLEY, NTT, ENG [37381] : 1750+ LOUTH, LIN, ENG [37487] : 1869+ DERBY, DBY, ENG [37662] : PRE 1858 ETTINGSHALL, STS, ENG [37662] : 1850-80 LANGCLIFFE, YKS, ENG [37711] : FRANCIS PRE 1871 LEICESTER & MATLOCK, DBY, ENG [38031] : 1700-1900 SAL, ENG [38073] : PRE 1855 GORTON, LAN, ENG [38288] : PRE 1850 BATH, SOM, ENG & SCT [34733] : PRE 1840 DRAPERSTOWN, DRY, IRL [33869] : 1800S ROCKSWALLACE, MOG, IRL [34250] : 1840-1901

DOW, IRL **[34331]** : PRE 1900 INISHRUSH, LDY, IRL **[36529]** : 1830+ SCARTAGLEN, KER, IRL **[36809]** : 1700+ DON, IRL **[37826]** : DAVID 1800+ NEWRY, DOW, IRL **[37942]** : ALL GULLADUFF, LDY, IRL **[38275]** : ALL HUTON, SCT & IRL **[33959]** : 1630+ NEW ENGLAND, CT, USA **[34342]** : MILO 1800+ JANEAU, WI, USA **[34511]** : C1734 HANOVER CO., VA, USA **[36354]** : PRE 1820 FAIRFIELD, CT, USA **[36702]** : 1750+ FAIRFIELD CO., CT & NY, USA **[36917]** : 1630 SALEM, MA, USA **[37531]** : 1840-1990 KENT, DE, USA **[38136]** : JAMES C1805 HARDIN CO., KY, NC & VA, USA **[38535]** : MONROE 1822-1883 JOHNSON CO., AR, USA **[38569]** : HOBBS 1750-1840 KERSHAW CO., SC & AL, USA **[38569]** : MONROE 1822-1883 PICKENS CO., AL, USA **[38569]** : HOBBS 1750-1835 ANSON CO., NC & SC, USA **[38569]**

BRADLY PRE 1841 LND, ENG **[35910]**

BRADMAN C1890+ YASS & HARDEN, NSW, AUS **[35230]**

BRADNEY PRE 1870 NEWTOWN, NSW, AUS **[35781]** : 1796 BIRMINGHAM, WAR, ENG **[35560]**

BRADSHAW C1840 TAS, AUS **[34456]** : 1890+ PERTH, WA, AUS **[35595]** : 1880+ BRISBANE, QLD, AUS **[36616]** : 1780+ STORMONT CO., ONT, CAN **[38411]** : 1880-1913 BURNLEY, LAN, ENG **[34050]** : 1750+ ROTHWELL, NTH, ENG **[34416]** : 1845 PORT ISAAC, CON, ENG **[34565]** : 1800 CROOKESMOOR, SHEFFIELD, YKS, ENG **[34940]** : 1820+ BOSTON, LIN, ENG **[35054]** : 1834 NEWTON, LAN, ENG **[35369]** : 1880S CHELMSFORD, ESS, ENG **[35595]** : 1700+ DARCY LEVER, LAN, ENG **[35824]** : 1800-1900 MANCHESTER, LAN, ENG **[36098]** : PRE 1800 YKS, ENG **[36098]** : 1824 WESTMILL, HRT, ENG **[36640]** : 1750-1850 DBY, ENG **[37188]** : EDWARD 1816 BALLINTRA, DON, IRL **[34176]** : 1814 COLERAINE, ANT, IRL **[34468]** : PRE 1770 CONCORD, MA, USA **[34225]** : PRE 1730 BUCKS CO., PA, USA **[35620]**

BRADWELL 1850S BOTTISHAM, CAM, ENG **[34574]** : 1785-1841 HOPE & BRADWELL, DBY, ENG **[36345]**

BRADY JAMES & MARY 1880+ SYDNEY, NSW, AUS **[34449]** : 1880+ COOKTOWN, QLD, AUS **[37133]** : 1880+ BRISBANE, QLD, AUS **[38484]** : 1830S+ MONO MILLS, ONT, CAN **[34259]** : PRE 1860 MANCHESTER, LAN, ENG **[34268]** : PRE 1830 LONDON, ENG **[35050]** : C1810 NORWICH, NFK, ENG **[35259]** : PRE 1840 BARKING SIDE, ESS, ENG **[35866]** : ALL HURLEY & REMENHAM, BRK, ENG **[36407]** : ALL LAMBETH, SRY, ENG **[36407]** : ALL HENLEY ON THAMES, OXF, ENG **[36407]** : 1800-1880 IRL **[34290]** : PRE 1830 KESH, FER, IRL **[35430]** : ALL SKERRIES, DUB, IRL **[36409]** : 1800 CAVAN, CAV, IRL **[36493]** : PRE 1880 ENNIS, CLA, IRL **[38484]** : PRE 1880 GLASGOW, SCT **[37133]** : 1800+ DOUGLAS, IOM, UK & NZ **[34632]** : 1870+ STEELE CO., MN, USA **[34259]** : 1880-1900 DEKALB, IL, USA **[36561]** : 1770-1800 PA, USA **[37808]**

BRAECKEL 1575-1645 ZOELEN, NL **[36317]**

BRAEKELAERE ALL OLSENE, BEL **[38162]**

BRAES 1850S LKS, SCT **[33810]**

BRAET 1300-1990 NEVELE, OVL, BEL **[38165]**

BRAETTIG PRE 1840 BRAETZ, BRA, GER **[34840]**

BRAGG 1856-1918 BOWRAL & COOTAMUNDRA, NSW, AUS **[38761]** : PRE 1760 FINSTHWAITE, LAN, ENG **[34053]** : 1740+ CREDITON, DEV, ENG **[35027]** : PRE 1870 BELFORD, NBL, ENG **[36110]** : PRE 1860 CROYDON & MITCHAM, SRY, ENG **[37913]** : 1820-1856 CHAFFCOMBE &

CREWKERNE, SOM, ENG **[38761]** : PRE 1800 MA, USA **[38017]**

BRAGLIN PRE 1957 CAN **[34055]**

BRAHAM 1800+ IPSWICH, SFK, ENG **[35342]** : PRE 1750 GREAT HALE, LIN, ENG **[36148]**

BRAID 1840+ BLENHEIM & WELLINGTON, NZ **[36836]** : 1750-1850 FIF, SCT **[34229]** : 1840S ARBROATH, ANS, SCT **[36836]** : PRE 1855 CUMBERNAULD, DNB, SCT **[37925]**

BRAILSFORD 1750-1850 PILHAM, LIN, ENG **[37038]** : 1750-1850 ATTERCLIFFE, YKS, ENG **[37038]**

BRAIN 1850S+ NEWCASTLE, NSW & TAS, AUS **[35239]** : 1833+ LAUNCESTON, TAS, AUS **[35531]** : 1700-1800 BARTON ON-THE HEATH, WAR, ENG **[34872]** : 1800S OXF, ENG **[35017]** : C1890+ BATH, SOM, ENG **[35223]** : ALL BANBURY, OXF, ENG **[37937]** : ALL OXF, ENG **[37937]** : C1870 DOWOAIF, SOUTH, WLS **[35223]**

BRAINE PRE 1850 NEW YORK, NY, USA **[37473]**

BRAISGIRDLE C1873 BOLTON, LAN, ENG **[35137]**

BRAITHWAITE C1840+ VIC, AUS **[37888]** : 1857+ COOKSTON PLACE, CUL, ENG **[34452]** : PRE 1759 ESKDALE, CUL, ENG **[34452]** : 1759-1851 EGREMONT, CUL, ENG **[35085]** : ROBERT 1700-1880 BATH, SOM, ENG **[36890]** : 1850-1978 BRUSH PRAIRIE, WA, USA **[35085]**

BRAKE 1928+ HAMILTON, ONT, CAN **[35553]** : PRE 1820 YETMINSTER, DOR, ENG **[36581]** : 1880+ MARINE CITY, MI, USA **[33908]**

BRAMBLE 1900S SYDNEY, NSW, AUS **[38582]** : 1760-1850 HEYDON, NFK, ENG **[35524]** : ALL PENZANCE, CON, ENG **[37160]** : PRE 1850 CRAWLEY, HAM, ENG **[37855]**

BRAMBLES 1700+ BRIDLINGTON, YKS, ENG **[35892]**

BRAMBLEY PRE 1850 BENTWORTH ALTON, HAM, ENG **[35016]**

BRAME C1710+ KIRBY LE SOKEN, ESS, ENG **[37063]**

BRAMES PRE 1800 KEN, ENG **[34707]**

BRAMFITT 1850+ WHEATLEY HILL, DUR, ENG **[36056]** : 1800-1900 LUMLEY, DUR, ENG **[36056]** : PRE 1800 YKS, ENG **[36056]** : 1750-1820 DURHAM, DUR, ENG **[36056]** : 1850-1900 HOUGHTON LE SPRING, DUR, ENG **[36056]** : 1850+ WINGATE, DUR, ENG **[36056]** : 1800-1900 CHESTER LE STREET, DUR, ENG **[36056]** : ALL WORLDWIDE **[36056]**

BRAMFOOT ALL WORLDWIDE **[36056]**

BRAMHALL 1870S SHEFFIELD, YKS, ENG **[34937]** : ALL LANG, ENG **[38514]**

BRAMLAGE 1600+ OLD, GER **[37532]** : 1820+ USA **[37532]**

BRAMLEY PRE 1832 CLAYPOLE, LIN, ENG **[34442]** : 1700+ SHEPSHED, LEI, ENG **[35538]** : ALL GRIMSBY, LIN, ENG **[37355]** : 1700+ WORLDWIDE **[35538]**

BRAMMER 1700-1800 NTT, ENG **[37829]**

BRAMON 1853 HERKIMER CO., NY, USA **[35295]**

BRAMPTON 1918+ CAN **[37864]** : PRE 1900 EALING, LND, ENG **[37864]**

BRAMSTOM PRE 1750 ESS, ENG **[35642]**

BRAMWELL 1802+ NOTTINGHAM, NTT, ENG **[34238]** : 1800+ PERTH, PER, SCT **[37659]** : PRE 1800 INVERKEITHING, FIF, SCT **[37659]** : ALL SCT & ENG **[37659]** : 1851-1859 KEWEENAW CO., MI, USA **[38010]**

BRANCH 1650+ WITHINGTON, GLS, ENG **[34747]** : 1800-1860 SOUTH WEST COS., MO, USA **[38737]** : 1850-1880 VA, USA **[38737]**

BRANCHETT 1750-1850 KEN, ENG **[34337]** : PRE 1880 BOUGHTON, KEN, ENG **[36584]**

BRANCHI 1900+ VA, USA [37593]
BRANCHU C1650 CARTIGNY, GE, CH [38348]
BRAND 1830+ WATERLOO CO., CAN [34090] : PRE 1650 SOHAM, CAM, ENG [34445] : PRE 1845 WILLINGORE, LIN, ENG [35074] : PRE 1850 YAXHAM, NFK, ENG [35212] : 1730 BENGEO, HRT, ENG [35980] : ALL NTT, ENG [36174] : LOUIS C1872 ST CLEMENT DANES, MDX, ENG [36519] : PRE 1830 GER [34090] : PRE 1855 LEUTERHAUSEN, BAD, GER [34886] : PRE 1305 BREMEN, BRM, GER [37819] : 1840-1880 PIERSHIL & BRIELLE, ZUH, NL [37187] : 1650-1820 DUNDEE, PER, SCT [35283] : PRE 1790 DUNFERMLINE, FIF & KRS, SCT [36509] : 1800 LOCHMABEN, DFS, SCT [36667] : 1800-1950 MONTGOMERY CO., NY, USA [35318] : 1800-1950 SYRACUSE, NY, USA [35318]
BRANDENBURG 1750-1800 SOMERSET CO., PA, USA [38108]
BRANDES 1800+ BASSE HANOVER, NSA, BRD [37012]
BRANDEY PRE 1830 MDX, ENG [37150]
BRANDHAM PRE 1800 RADLEY, BRK, ENG [38745]
BRANDIS 1750-1850 WIL & LND, ENG [34194] : THOMAS PRE 1850 ESS, ENG [34583] : PRE 1839 ST PANCRAS & TOTTENHAM, MDX, ENG [34691] : PRE 1800 WAR, ENG [35846] : C1800+ MDX, ENG [35846] : 1840+ BUTLERS MARSTON, WAR, ENG [35846] : C1800+ COMBROOK, WAR, ENG [35846]
BRANDLING 1400+ NBL, ENG [35723]
BRANDON 1656+ AYLESBURY, BKM, ENG [35578] : PRE 1871 LEIGHTON BUZZARD, BDF, ENG [35778] : C1848 DUBLIN, IRL [35133] : PRE 1850 FER, TYR & ANT, IRL [37246] : 1804 VA, USA [38121]
BRANDS PRE 1750 PETERHEAD, ABD, SCT [36792]
BRANDS (SEE BRANS) [38358]
BRANDSEN 1800-1900 ERMELO, GEL, NL [34069]
BRANDT 1850+ SHANGHAI, CHINA [35568] : 1800-1829 RAICHARTSHAUSEN, BAD, GER [34238] : ALL MSW, GER [34488] : PRE 1850 HAMBURG, GER [35568] : 1750-1800 MORRIS, NJ, USA [38366]
BRANGWIN PRE 1840 OXF, ENG [37500]
BRANIGAN 1800-1900 MAY, IRL [36344] : 1800+ PHILADELPHIA CO., PA, USA [36344]
BRANKIN PRE 1870 PORTADOWN, ARM, IRL [35911]
BRANNIGAN PRE 1900 BELFAST, ANT, IRL [34018]
BRANS 1700S TIEL, GEL, NL [38358] : ALL WORLDWIDE [34814]
BRANSCOMBE 1850S STEPNEY, MDX, ENG [34628] : 1800-1850 OXFORD, OXF, ENG [36530]
BRANSON C1860 OLNEY & NEWPORT PAGNAL, BKM, ENG [35387] : ALL IRL & ENG [37930]
BRANT 1830+ MONTGOMERY CO., OH & MO, USA [38050]
BRANTHWAITE PRE 1850 WHITE HAVEN, CUL, ENG [34755]
BRANTSMA 1879+ SNEEK, FRI, NL [34990]
BRAODMEAD C1780 EGG BUCKLAND, DEV, ENG [34456]
BRASEE (SEE BRAZIE) [38369]
BRASH 1790S MID CALDER, MLN, SCT [33945] : PRE 1790 GLASGOW, LKS, SCT [35406] : 1788 SCT [37795]
BRASHEAR PRE 1850 IN & PA, USA [38023]
BRASIE (SEE BRAZIE) [38369]
BRASIER 1760+ CHOLSEY, OXF, ENG [35822] : PRE 1750 ENBOURNE, CHIEVELEY, BRK, ENG [35866]
BRASK 1860S NUESTED, DEN [38017]
BRASSETT 1800S SCT [36796]
BRASSINGTON 1850+ ULLADULLA & WOLLONGONG, NSW, AUS [36600] : C1880 MELBOURNE, VIC, AUS [37302] : 1840+ BEESTON RYLANDS, NTT, ENG [35712]
BRATBY PRE 1800 KIRK IRETON, DBY, ENG [36281]
BRATFIELD 1840+ WILLIAMS RIVER, NSW, AUS [36284]
BRATLEY PRE 1900 LIN, ENG [35949] : ALL WORLDWIDE [37487]
BRATT ALL LND, ENG [36037]
BRATTEN 1900S ENG [35161]
BRATTLE ALL ENG [35884]
BRAUER JOHANNES ALL CAPETOWN, CAPE, RSA & AUS [35122] : GERTRUD ALL CAPETOWN & BRISBANE, CAPE & QLD, RSA & AUS [35122]
BRAUN PRE 1900 HUNTSVILLE, ONT, CAN [36677] : PRE 1880 TRECHTINGSHAUSEN, RPF, GER [35147] : PRE 1700 DETWANG, BAV, GER [35242] : 1800S HOCHDORF, WUE, GER [37814] : PRE 1840 BAD, GER [38190] : PRE 1860 DESSAU, ANH, GER [38190] : PRE 1825 DINGELFINGEN, BAV, GER [38191] : PRE 1850 BADEN, GER [38218] : 1860+ SAN ANTONIO, TX, USA [38190]
BRAUN (SEE BROWNE) [37920]
BRAUNE C1880 STETTIN, GER [36779]
BRAWN 1830 ST MARTINS, SAL, ENG [34890]
BRAXTON 1853+ TAS, AUS [35776] : 1677 LAN, ENG [36358] : PRE 1820 LONDON, ENG & AUS [35776]
BRAY 1850+ SYDNEY, NSW, AUS [34298] : 1880+ NORTHCOTE, VIC, AUS [34298] : 1862+ DAYLESFORD, VIC, AUS [34787] : 1887+ MELBOURNE, VIC, AUS [35379] : PRE 1887 MARYBOROUGH, VIC, AUS [35379] : 1860S WINCHELSEA, VIC, AUS [35390] : 1880S BENDIGO, VIC, AUS [35390] : BESSIE 1880-1971 AUS [36180] : 1870+ CASTLEMAINE, VIC, AUS [36622] : 1878-1900 LUDDENHAM & SYDNEY, NSW, AUS [38761] : 1800+ EXETER, ONT, CAN [34085] : JOHN H.G. 1880+ MEDICINE HAT, ALB, CAN [37426] : ALL PORTSEA, HAM, ENG [34298] : PRE 1800 DEV & CON, ENG [34319] : PRE 1850 ST TEATH & CAMBORNE, CON, ENG [34360] : PRE 1800 BUCKLAND DINHAM, SOM, ENG [34739] : 1800S SOM, ENG [34791] : 1650 REDRUTH, CON, ENG [34793] : PRE 1850 CON, ENG [34929] : 1800-1850 LISKEARD, CON, ENG [35006] : 1770+ ST HILARY, CON, ENG [35342] : C1790 LANDRAKE, CON, ENG [35349] : 1840S ASTON, WAR, ENG [35390] : NICHOLAS PRE 1803 ALTARNUN, CON, ENG [35471] : 1890S BARNSTAPLE & ILFRACOMBE, DEV, ENG [35557] : PRE 1807 GWENNAP & ST BLAZEY, CON, ENG [35588] : 1820S ST GENNYS, CON, ENG [35612] : PRE 1899 ROCHE & TRURO, CON, ENG [36039] : PRE 1800 ENG [37133] : JOHN 1840 BEWDLEY, WOR, ENG [37426] : PRE 1830 WIL, ENG [37617] : PRE 1836 LONDON, MDX, ENG [37647] : 1550-1650 PLYMOUTH, DEV, ENG [37783] : PRE 1850 HOXTON, LND, ENG [37832] : 1810+ REDRUTH, CON, ENG [37921] : 1800+ LAUNCESTON, CON, ENG [37997] : PRE 1800 CAMBORNE, CON, ENG [38214] : PRE 1799 BODMIN, CON, ENG [38389] : 1843-1879 ST BREWARDS, CON, ENG [38761] : 1851+ CURRAGHAKIMKEEN & DOON, LIM, IRL [35900] : 1890-1990 MIRAMAR, WTN, NZ [36249] : PRE 1890 HOPE, NLN, NZ [36249] : 1910+ WELLINGTON, NZ [37149] : PRE 1880 WORLDWIDE [36180]
BRAYLEY 1770+ TETCOTT, DEV, ENG [37317]
BRAYS 1700+ TUNSTALL AREA, KEN, ENG [37411]
BRAYSHAW 1700-1841 IDLE, YKS, ENG [34793] : 1800+ IDLE & THACKLEY, WRY, ENG [36617]
BRAZEE (SEE BRAZIE) [38369]
BRAZEL ALL WORLDWIDE [37130]

BRAZENALL PRE 1830 ENG **[38217]**
BRAZIE ALL LORAIN CO., OH & NY, USA **[38369]**
BRAZIER 1880TEROWIE, SA, AUS **[33935]** : 1850+
WARE, HRT, ENG **[33935]** : PRE 1850 GREAT
BADDOW, ESS, ENG **[33935]** : PRE 1850 BURY ST
EDMUNDS, SRY, ENG **[34725]** : 1850+ MUCH
WENLOCK, SAL, ENG **[34782]** : 1820S CLAINES,
WOR, ENG **[36011]** : 1800+ SRY, ENG **[36871]** : ALL
ALRESFORD, HAM, ENG **[37044]** : C1789
CHIEVELY, BRK, ENG **[37235]** : 1800+
EVERSHOLT, BDF, ENG **[37647]** : 1800+
WANSTEAD, LND, ENG **[37839]** : 1800+ BOW,
LND, ENG **[37839]**
BRAZIL PRE 1880 WAT, IRL & NZ **[36840]**
BRAZNEAL 1850+ GATESHEAD, DUR, ENG **[33982]**
BREACH PRE 1879 COORANBONG, NSW, AUS
[35097] : PRE 1900 ARBORFIELD, BRK, ENG
[35958] : 1855-1877 CHISLEHURST, KEN, ENG
[35958]
BREADMORE 1860+ ALLENDALE, VIC, AUS **[36610]**
: PRE 1850 KENSINGTON, LND, ENG **[38288]** :
ALL WORLDWIDE **[36610]**
BREALEY PRE 1826 NOTTINGHAM, NTT, ENG
[37866]
BREAR 1896-1935 HALIFAX, YKS, ENG **[34658]**
BREAU 1873-1912 NORFOLK CO., ONT, CAN **[34114]**
BREAUX C1945 HOUSTON, TX, USA **[38166]**
BRECHT 1800 RHEINSHEIM, BAW, BRD **[37028]**
BRECKELL PRE 1879 PRESTWICH, LAN, ENG
[35097]
BRECKENRIDGE 1840+ WESTBURY, TAS, AUS
[34871] : 1765 DALGAIN, AYR, SCT **[34214]** : 1700+
TEMPLE, SCT **[34871]** : 1770-1870 DUMFRIES, DFS,
SCT **[37779]** : ALL WORLDWIDE **[34028]**
BRECKINRIDGE 1800+ EDINBURGH, SCT **[34871]**
BRECKON 1865-1957 WARRNAMBOOL, VIC, AUS
[33891] : 1500-1900 NRY, ENG **[36472]**
BREDE PRE 1800 DAMEROW, POM, GER **[35448]** :
1800 DAMEROW, POM, GER **[37170]**
BREDIUS PRE 1759 DELFSHAVEN, ZUH, NL **[38706]**
BREE 1800-1860 ENG **[37858]** : PRE 1860 DEAL, KEN,
ENG **[37871]**
BREED 1850+ YERONG CREEK, NSW, AUS **[35203]**
: C1850 BIGGLESWADE, BDF, ENG **[34372]** : C1800
MALDON, ESS, ENG **[35203]** : C1800
BEKESBOURNE, KEN, ENG **[37859]** : PRE 1700
LYNN, MA, USA **[33804]**
BREEDING 1800 NOTTINGHAM, NTT, ENG **[37391]**
BREEN ALL ARM, IRL **[35139]** : 1800-1900
KILLARNEY, KER, IRL **[36565]** : 1820-1850S
CAPPAGH WHITE, TIP, IRL **[37540]** : 1750-1800
DERRYLIN, FER, IRL **[37613]** : 1850+ BLACK
BROOK, CLINTON, NY, USA **[37540]**
BREEZE C1836-1850S NORWICH & CAWSTON,
NFK, ENG **[35133]** : PRE 1900 STS & CHS, ENG
[37098] : JANE 1770 SFK & NFK, ENG **[37250]** : PRE
1850 CHARITON CO., MO & VA, USA **[36927]** : PRE
1778 MGY, WLS **[36613]**
BREHAM PRE 1836 ALTENHEIM, GER **[37797]** :
1836+ HAMILTON CO., OH, USA **[37797]**
BREHM PRE 1840 NORKA, VOLGA, SU **[36543]** :
C1876 BUFFALO, NY, USA **[38650]** : C1876
DEFIANCE, USA **[38650]**
BREI 1870-1900 WAUSHARA CO., WI, USA **[36546]**
BREILMAYER 1497+ MUNDINGEN, WUE, GER
[38667]
BREIMAIER ALL WORLDWIDE **[38667]**
BREITBART 1800-1900 COLOGNE, GER **[37064]**
BREITENSTEIN PRE 1770 BEBERSTEDT, PSA, GER
[38048]
BREITMAYER PRE 1755 BREITENHOLZ, GER
[37587]

BREKSER ALL WORLDWIDE **[34010]**
BREM 1920+ WACO, TX, USA **[38609]**
BREMER 1800+ SYDNEY, NSW, AUS **[35031]** : 1700-
1800 MELLINGHAUSEN, NSA, GER **[38643]**
BREMNER 1800+ HALIFAX, NS, CAN **[35970]** : 1830-
1860 GLASGOW, SCT **[34028]** : C1795 GREENOCK,
RFW, SCT **[34371]** : PRE 1827 GLASGOW, LKS, SCT
[34598] : PRE 1800 LAURENCEKIRK, KCD, SCT
[34753] : PRE 1860 CLYTHMAIN, CAI, SCT **[34797]** :
C1780 FOCHABERS, MOR, SCT **[35848]** : 1800S
ABD, SCT **[36292]** : 1820-1855 SAN FRANCISCO,
CA, USA **[35970]**
BREMSON ALL WORLDWIDE **[36015]**
BREN 1850+ BRK, ENG **[36239]**
BRENAN PRE 1810 WRY, ENG **[37402]**
BRENCH 1700+ MDX, ENG **[35377]** : 1700-1890
RUGBY, WAR, ENG **[35377]** : 1700-1890 SLOUGH,
BKM, ENG **[35377]**
BRENCHLEY ALL SITTINGBOURNE, KEN, ENG
[36326] : 1700-1900 SWALE MEDWAY, KEN, ENG
[38249]
BREND 1800-1880 BIDEFORD, DEV, ENG **[38224]**
BRENELL C1650 KINGSWEAR, DEV, ENG **[36000]**
BRENNAN RICHARD ALL TAS, AUS **[33984]** :
RICHARD 1790+ VIC, AUS **[33984]** : 1850+
MELBOURNE, VIC, AUS **[34871]** : CATHERINE
1832+ PARRAMATTA, NSW, AUS **[34885]** : JOHN
1860+ MELBOURNE, VIC, AUS **[35404]** : 1840+
FRANKLIN, TAS, AUS **[35459]** : C1905 ONT, CAN
[34521] : 1877+ LIVERPOOL, LAN, ENG **[34566]** :
PRE 1834 BIRMINGHAM, WAR, ENG **[34900]** :
1820-1850 LURGAN, ANT, IRL **[34022]** : ALL
CASTLECOMER, KIK, IRL **[34593]** : PRE 1860
JENKINSTOWN, KIK, IRL **[34811]** : 1850+
COREY, WEX, IRL **[34852]** : 1700-1850 TULLA,
CLA, IRL **[34871]** : PRE 1821 KILKENNY, KIK, IRL
[34900] : 1800-1830 CASTLECOMER, KIK, IRL
[36566] : PRE 1900 DOWNPATRICK, DOW, IRL
[37405] : 1800-1850 IRL **[38039]** : C1820 GALEY &
KNOCKCROCHERY, ROS, IRL **[38592]** : 1850+ IL,
USA **[38039]** : ALL WORLDWIDE **[33773]**
BRENNER GEORGE 1820 PA, USA **[38142]**
BRENT 1800+ ENG **[36470]** : 1650 LARKSTOKE, GLS,
ENG **[37462]** : C1864 LORAIN CO., OH, USA **[38369]**
BRENTON PRE 1897 WANDSWORTH, LND, ENG
[35020]
BRENTZELL PRE 1836+ LAVENBURG, GER **[35110]**
: 1788+ SCHLESWIG HOLSTEIN, GER **[35110]**
BRERETON 1857+ MALMSBURY & EDGECOMBE,
VIC, AUS **[37962]** : PRE 1849 HAMMERSMITH,
LND, ENG **[33992]** : PRE 1900 STOKE ON TRENT,
STS, ENG **[34548]** : 1800-1930 CHURCH
MINSHULL, CHS, ENG **[36983]** : PRE 1857
HARTHILL, CHS, ENG **[37962]**
BRESEE 1700+ VT, USA **[35611]**
BRESLIN 1800S CASTLEDERMOT, KID, IRL **[35535]** :
C1700-1890 MONASEED & GOREY, WEX, IRL
[37415]
BRESSOW 1780+ BAD FRIEIEMUWALDE, PRE,
GER **[35429]**
BRETHERTON PRE 1800 LIVERPOOL, LAN, ENG
[36822]
BRETHETT 1560+ ENG **[35164]**
BRETIN 1700-1850 RADZYMIN, WA, POL **[38652]**
BRETNEY ALL ENG **[36414]** : ALL IRL **[36414]**
BRETT 1840 PARRAMATTA, NSW, AUS **[36596]** : ALL
AUS **[38270]** : 1850+ VIC, AUS **[38771]** : PRE 1700
WESTWELL, KEN, ENG **[34445]** : PRE 1840
POSLINGFORD, SFK, ENG **[34533]** : 1760-1860
LEAMINGTON, WAR, ENG **[34589]** : 1760-1880 ST
NICHOLAS AT WADE, KEN, ENG **[34589]** : 1757-
1822 BASSINGBOURNE, CAM, ENG **[35368]** : PRE

1800 ESS & SFK, ENG **[36399]** : 1618-1681 KEN,
ENG **[36560]** : C1800 BERDEN, ESS, ENG **[36978]** :
C1840 PATTISWICK, ESS, ENG **[37449]** : 1700-1900
HOLBORN & LONDON, MDX, ENG **[38745]** : PRE
1810 ENG & AUS **[35397]** : C1806-1829 DUBLIN, IRL
[34704] : 1700-1800 DUBLIN, IRL **[37381]** : 1840
BANDON, COR, IRL **[38270]** : PRE 1850 WEX, IRL
[38771]

BRETTELL 1500-1700 STS, ENG **[36062]**

BRETTSCHNEIDER C1840 OES **[38618]**

BREUNIG 1750-1890 WURZBERG, HES, BRD **[35340]**

BREUNINGER PRE 1750 WALDBACH, WUE, GER
[35242] : ALL WUE, GER **[38683]**

BREW 1860 + BUNINYONG, VIC, AUS & IRL **[34864]**

BREWER 1885 + BOMBALA, NSW, AUS **[34966]** :
1920 + RANDWICK, NSW, AUS **[35843]** : 1870 +
RICHMOND, VIC, AUS **[36605]** : 1870 + QLD, AUS
[36605] : 1870-1900 WEST MAITLAND, NSW, AUS
[36682] : PRE 1900 CARNBOURN, DOR, ENG
[33966] : PRE 1720 ST ERVAN, CON, ENG **[33992]** :
1832 PADSTOW, CON, ENG **[34565]** : 1700-1900
BERE REGIS, DOR, ENG **[34714]** : 1800 + ESS,
ENG **[34818]** : 1665 + ST COLUMB MAJOR, CON,
ENG **[35587]** : 1800 + OWMBY BY SPITAL, LIN,
ENG **[35990]** : 1850 + DOVER, KEN, ENG **[36123]** :
1700-1900 LAN, ENG **[36261]** : PRE 1870 SOUTH
MOLTON, DEV, ENG **[36605]** : 1750 + WALSALL,
STS, ENG **[36821]** : PRE 1910 ESS, ENG **[37668]** :
PRE 1820 + DAGGONS DAMERHAM, WIL, ENG
[37912] : PHILLIP C1740 EDMONSHAM, DOR,
ENG **[38489]** : JOHN C1800 VERWOOD, DOR, ENG
[38489] : 1800 + BRIGHTON, SSX, ENG & NZ
[36257] : 1800-1840 TN, USA **[38088]** : 1700S VA, USA
[38108] : JONAS 1773 + BERKSHIRE CO., MA, USA
[38569] : PRE 1810 TN, USA **[38576]**

BREWERTON 1800S READING, BRK, ENG **[35899]** :
PRE 1843 READING, BRK, ENG **[36841]** : 1843 +
NELSON, NZ **[36841]**

BREWIN 1800-1900 CUL & YKS, ENG **[37858]**

BREWITT 1830 + RSA **[34946]**

BREWSTER 1840 + SYDNEY, NSW, AUS **[34977]** :
1750 + MDX & SRY, ENG **[36203]** : 1570 +
SCROOBY, NTT, ENG **[36944]** : 1700 + LONG
MELFORD, SFK, ENG **[37638]** : PRE 1800
GRANTHAM, LIN, ENG **[37712]** : C1800 ERROL,
PER, SCT **[34974]** : 1620 PLYMOUTH, MA, USA
[36944] : PRE 1762 CT, USA **[37037]**

BREWTON ALL HEF, ENG **[36889]**

BREYMAIER ALL WORLDWIDE **[38667]**

BREYMAYER 1497 + MUNDINGEN, WUE, GER
[38667] : ALL WORLDWIDE **[38667]**

BREYMEYER ALL WORLDWIDE **[38667]**

BREYNARD PRE 1819 + PRESCOTT, ONT, CAN
[34553]

BRIAN PRE 1820 WESTMINSTER, LND, ENG **[35544]**
: 1850S AVOCA, WIC, IRL **[36032]**

BRIAND 1686 + POUGHILL, DEV, ENG **[35027]** :
1750-1800 BRT, FRA **[34459]**

BRIANT 1400 + LUXULYAN, CON, ENG **[33989]** :
1700-1800S CHERTSEY, SRY, ENG **[34032]** : C1750-
1850 MINSTER IN SHEPPEY, KEN, ENG **[34718]** :
1680-1720 CURY, CON, ENG **[34793]** : 1746 +
BRADFORD ON AVON, WIL, ENG **[36276]** : 1816
WASHINGTON CO., TN, USA **[37570]**

BRICE 1855 + INVERELL, NSW, AUS **[38077]** : ALL
ST SAMPSONS, GSY, CHI **[35433]** : PRE 1850
GRANTHAM, LIN, ENG **[37245]** : 1700S ANT, IRL
[33886]

BRICHENO ALL HUN & CAM, ENG & AUS **[34705]**

BRICKEL C1700-1850 MOTCOMBE, DOR, ENG
[36478]

BRICKELL PRE 1540 NORTHENDEN, CHS, ENG
[35097] : C1700-1850 MOTCOMBE, DOR, ENG
[36478] : C1880 SYRACUSE, NY, USA **[38263]**

BRICKER 1750-1990 MD, PA & OH, USA **[38203]**

BRICKNELL 1750 KINGSTON & PORTSMOUTH,
HAM, ENG **[35847]** : PRE 1850 EXETER &
AYLESBEARE, DEV, ENG **[37321]**

BRIDDON PRE 1850 GREASLEY, NTT, ENG **[36516]**

BRIDE PRE 1850 KELZE, HES, BRD **[38636]**

BRIDEL 1770S-1870 LONDON, ENG **[33971]**

BRIDEN PRE 1843 HRT, ENG **[37442]** : ALL LAN,
ENG **[38514]**

BRIDER 1700 + WISBOROUGH GREEN &
KIRDFORD, SSX, ENG **[34747]**

BRIDGE 1846 + FAIRY MEADOW, NSW, AUS **[35863]**
: PRE 1840 MAIDSTONE, KEN, ENG **[34816]** :
MARIAH 1780 + BURY, LAN, ENG **[35484]** : 1800-
1860 PAWLETT & WINSCOMBE, SOM, ENG
[35725] : ALL EDENSOR & GREAT LONGSTONE,
DBY, ENG **[36189]** : ADMIRAL 1805-1863 ENG
[36576] : 1873 + BALLINGTON, CHS, ENG **[36847]** :
PRE 1900 DEVONPORT, DEV, ENG **[37979]** :
MARY 1829-1907 PGH, ALLEGHENY CO., PA,
USA **[36576]**

BRIDGEFOOT ELIZ 1734 NTH, ENG **[35119]**

BRIDGEFORD ALL SCT **[37857]**

BRIDGELAND PRE 1857 BOLTON, LAN, ENG **[33763]**

BRIDGEMAN ALL LIM, IRL **[35950]** : PRE 1844
WAIMEA PLAINS, NELSON, NZ **[35008]**

BRIDGEMAN-WILTON 1848 + MORPHETT VALE,
SA, AUS **[35025]**

BRIDGEN 1790 + WHITTINGTON, STS, ENG **[36045]**

BRIDGENS PRE 1830 DBY, ENG **[33776]**

BRIDGER PRE 1800 WOOLBEDING, W SSX, ENG
[34112] : 1700-1900 SSX, ENG **[36007]** : ALL SRY,
ENG **[36811]** : ALL ENG **[37214]**

BRIDGES 1853 + BRUNSWICK, VIC, AUS **[35425]** :
1870-74 ROCKHAMPTON & BRISBANE, QLD,
AUS **[37994]** : 1874-82 NSW, AUS **[37994]** : 1820 +
KIRBY CANE, NFK, ENG **[34015]** : PRE 1853
NEWNHAM, HRT, ENG **[35425]** : 1800 +
NEWNHAM & BALDOCK, HRT, ENG **[35524]** :
1800 + DERBY, DBY, ENG **[36257]** : 1600 +
LONDON, ENG **[36756]** : PRE 1750 ALCESTER,
WAR, ENG **[37103]** : 1800 + SWAFFHAM, NFK,
ENG **[37160]** : ALL NORWICH, NFK, ENG **[37612]** :
PRE 1820 FARINGDON AREA, BRK, ENG **[37720]** :
PRE 1854 HARTFORD, HUN, ENG **[37945]** : 1821
BOCKING, ESS, ENG **[37994]** : RUTH 1700
IPSWICH, MA, USA **[35273]** : 1700-1800 ME, USA
[37808] : ALL WORLDWIDE **[38753]**

BRIDGFOOT 1845 RAMSEY, HUN, ENG **[33936]**

BRIDGMAN 1820 + KENSINGTON, LND, ENG
[37134] : ALL LIM, IRL **[35950]**

BRIDGMAN-WILTON PRE 1848 LANIVET, CON,
ENG **[35025]**

BRIDGWATER 1700-1900 PULBOROUGH &
BILLINGSHURST, SSX, ENG **[34749]** : 1800 +
WORCESTER, WOR, ENG & AUS **[36835]**

BRIDLE PRE 1800 SYDLING ST NICHOLAS, DOR,
ENG **[34347]**

BRIDSON 1700 + CASTLETOWN, IOM **[35964]**

BRIEDE PRE 1900 KELZE, HES, BRD **[38636]**

BRIELLAT 1800S ENG **[35586]**

BRIEN 1854 + NEWCASTLE, NSW, AUS **[34965]** :
1820S KEN, ENG **[35799]** : 1800 + CLONMEL, TIP,
IRL **[34556]** : PRE 1860 MAGHERACROSS, FER,
IRL **[34965]** : ELLEN 1790-1880 KILLARNEY, KER,
IRL **[35003]** : PRE 1876 TIP & OFF, IRL **[34886]** :
1779-1830 LOGAN CO., KY, USA **[38118]**

BRIENINGER C1840-1926 HAGERSTOWN, MD, USA
& GER **[37813]**

BRIERLEY ALL OLDHAM, LAN, ENG **[34443]** : 1846-1900 HALIFAX, YKS, ENG **[34658]** : PRE 1790 MARSDEN & COLNE VALLEY, WRY, ENG **[37372]** : C1750-1830 BILSTON & SEDGELEY, STS, ENG **[37642]**

BRIERLY 1846-1900 HALIFAX, YKS, ENG **[34658]**

BRIESCHKE PRE 1875 WPR, GER **[36839]**

BRIESE 1878+ SA & VIC, AUS **[38293]** : PRE 1878 WALCA, WPR, GER **[38293]**

BRIFFS 1800+ KENNINGHALL, NFK, ENG **[34639]**

BRIGGES C1860 DALTON LE DALE, DUR, ENG **[35715]** : 1600-1800 LEI, ENG **[36146]**

BRIGGS 1850+ VIC, AUS **[34412]** : 1820-1900 ALBION TWP., ONT, CAN **[37011]** : 1750+ LND, ENG **[33963]** : 1820+ TRANMERE PK, CHS, ENG **[34326]** : C1870 SHEERNESS, KEN, ENG **[34395]** : PRE 1860 KEN, ENG **[34412]** : PRE 1820 WALPOLE, SFK, ENG **[34504]** : 1800+ KENNINGHALL, NFK, ENG **[34639]** : PRE 1880 ACCRINGTON, LAN, ENG **[34675]** : 1700S FARNHAM, NRY, ENG **[34776]** : PRE 1820S NTT, ENG **[34873]** : 1897+ BOURNEMOUTH, DOR, ENG **[35114]** : 1800+ PECKHAM, MDX, ENG **[35169]** : 1800+ LAMBETT, MDX, ENG **[35169]** : 1774 BETHNAL GREEN, LND, ENG **[35560]** : C1804+ GREAT CHART, KEN, ENG **[35759]** : C1911+ ALDINGTON, KEN, ENG **[35759]** : 1700S FELTHORPE & NORWICH, NFK, ENG **[35780]** : 1830-1900 CLACTON ON SEA & IPSWICH, SFK, ENG **[36146]** : 1600-1800 LEI, ENG **[36146]** : DAISY MARIA PRE 1920 SHEERNESS, KEN, ENG **[36646]** : FRANK PRE 1940 HOUNSLOW, MDX, ENG **[36646]** : FRANK PRE 1940 BORDEN, HAM, ENG **[36646]** : FRANK PRE 1940 PORTSEA, HAM, ENG **[36646]** : ELLEN ANN PRE 1900 PORTSMOUTH & LANDPORT, HAM, ENG **[36646]** : CHARLES E.F. PRE 1940 PORTSMOUTH, HAM, ENG **[36646]** : FRANK PRE 1940 SWINDON, WIL, ENG **[36646]** : FRANK PRE 1940 STEPHENFIELD & KINGSLEY, HAM, ENG **[36646]** : 1770-1820 NORTH FRODINGHAM, YKS, ENG **[37011]** : 1750-1800 BOLTON, LAN, ENG **[37613]** : 1730-1840 ACTON, MDX, ENG **[37657]** : PRE 1635 HALIFAX, WRY, ENG **[37806]** : 1700-1850 CUL, ENG **[37858]** : 1700-1900 WAKEFIELD, YKS, ENG **[38579]** : PRE 1850 ANT, IRL **[34412]** : PRE 1824 KKD, SCT **[33959]** : 1800+ GLASGOW, LKS, SCT **[34326]** : 1767+ HADDINGTON, ELN, SCT **[35921]** : DANIEL 1665-1730 E GREENWICH, RI, USA **[35271]** : 1780-1810 DUTCHESS CO., NY, USA **[36710]** : 1800 WESTMORELAND CO., PA, USA **[37005]** : 1800-1850 YANCEY CO., NC, USA **[38009]** : 1770-1800 RUTHERFORD CO., NC, USA **[38009]** : 1850-1900 MADISON CO., NC, USA **[38009]**

BRIGHT PRE 1714 LYNEHAM, WIL, ENG **[35163]** : C1700S+ COVENTRY, WAR, ENG **[35163]** : PRE 1725 ESS, ENG **[35642]** : GEORGE WM. PRE 1857 LONDON, SRY, ENG **[36371]** : 1880+ PECKHAM, LND, ENG **[36378]** : 1700+ DEV, ENG **[36516]** : PRE 1800 LAMBETH, LND, ENG **[36891]** : PRE 1800 WOOLWICH, LND, ENG **[36891]** : ALL LUTON, BDF, ENG **[36891]** : 1800S COLCHESTER, ESS, ENG **[37186]** : PRE 1850 ZEAL MONACHORUM, DEV, ENG **[37617]** : PRE 1875 BLACKFRIARS, LND, ENG **[37890]** : ALL CAM, ENG **[38257]** : 1750-1900 BANDON, COR, IRL **[37859]**

BRIGHTING 1830S PIMLICO, LND, ENG **[36797]**

BRIGHTMAN C1800 KEN, ENG **[37715]**

BRIGHTON ALL NFK, ENG **[35628]**

BRIGHTWELL PRE 1853 EYDON, NTH, ENG **[35544]** : PRE 1822 BROUGHTON, OXF, ENG **[35544]** : PRE 1880 LONDON, MDX, ENG **[37768]**

BRIGNALL PRE 1800 PATRICK BROMPTON, NRY, ENG **[37621]**

BRILL 1860-1880S USA **[37600]**

BRIMAGE 1790-1900 ST PETER PORT, GSY, CHI **[37435]**

BRIMBLE 1850+ NEWCASTLE, NSW, AUS **[35800]** : C1726 KINGSTON DEVERILL, WIL, ENG **[34972]** : PRE 1809 KELSTON, SOM, ENG **[35223]** : PRE 1800 KINGSTON DEVERILL, WIL, ENG **[35800]** : PRE 1800 KINGSTON DEVERILL, WIL, ENG **[38214]** : 1890+ GREYMOUTH, NZ **[37443]**

BRIMBLECOMBE 1800+ DEV, ENG & AUS **[35137]**

BRIMFIELD PRE 1830S HER, ENG **[34873]** : PRE 1850 WOODSTOCK, OXF, ENG **[37855]** : PRE 1850 LEOMINSTER, HEF, ENG **[37855]**

BRIMICOMBE ALL DEV, ENG **[36078]**

BRIMMACOMBE 1700-1850 HOLSWORTHY, DEV, ENG **[34525]**

BRIMNER 1800-1850 GLASGOW, LKS, SCT **[36824]**

BRIMS WILLIAM 1837-1846 QUEANBEYAN, NSW, AUS **[34699]** : DANIEL 1837-1846 BROULEE, NSW, AUS **[34699]** : 1925+ EDINBURGH, MLN, SCT **[35021]** : DANIEL 1820+ SUFFOLK CO., MA, USA **[34699]**

BRIMSON ALL WORLDWIDE **[36015]**

BRIMYARD 1700-1850 EVESHAM, WOR, ENG **[35621]**

BRIN 1850+ CHICAGO, IL, USA **[36962]**

BRINDLE 1800+ BLACKBURN, LAN, ENG **[38481]**

BRINDLEY PRE 1790 WATERHOUSE TANEMILL, ENG **[33890]** : 1800+ WEST BROMWICH, STS, ENG **[35235]** : C1800 SHOTTLE, DBY, ENG **[36790]** : 1700-1800 NEWCASTLE, STS, ENG **[38474]**

BRINE 1750+ WINFRITH & CHALDON, DOR, ENG **[34283]** : PRE 1890 FROME, SOM, ENG **[35650]** : 1800+ CHANDLERS FORD, HAM, ENG **[35650]** : GABRIEL C1736 PEWSEY, WIL, ENG **[38489]** : ALL WORLDWIDE **[37201]**

BRINEGAR 1850-1870 BREMER CO., IA, USA **[36940]** : ALL SURREY CO., NC, USA **[36940]** : 1830-1850 CARROLL CO., IN, USA **[36940]** : ALL USA & UK **[36357]**

BRINGHAM ALL LAFAYETTE, IN, IA & CA, USA **[38570]** : PRE 1860 NEBRASKA CITY, NE, MO & IN, USA **[38570]**

BRINGSRUD 1650+ UVDAL, NUMEDAL, NOR **[36905]**

BRINK 1800-1860S PIKE CO., PA, USA **[35298]**

BRINKE 1600-1700 REICHENBACH, WB, POL **[38495]**

BRINKER 1820+ OH, USA **[38587]**

BRINKHOF 1775+ AMSTERDAM, NOH, NL **[35753]**

BRINKHOFF 1750-1860S SCHNATHORST, GER **[38524]**

BRINKHURST PRE 1890 SSX, ENG **[34376]**

BRINKLEY PRE 1600 SOUTH EAST, SFK, ENG **[37420]** : PRE 1840 TN & KY, USA **[36570]**

BRINKWELL 1700+ CHICHESTER & UPMARDEN, SSX, ENG **[34747]**

BRINKWORTH GEORGE 1824+ HORSLEY, GLS, ENG **[34475]** : MARY ANN 1850+ HORSLEY, GLS, ENG **[34475]** : JAMES 1781+ HORSLEY, GLS, ENG **[34475]** : ISAAC ALL HORSLEY, GLS, ENG **[34475]**

BRINNING 1800-1900 LITTLEHAM, DEV, ENG **[37757]**

BRINSON ALL WORLDWIDE **[36015]**

BRINT ERNEST 1850-1940 STRATFORD UPON AVON, GLS, ENG **[37567]**

BRISAC 1750-1800 LONDON & ST HELIER, JSY, CHI **[34552]**

BRISBANE 1840+ MELBOURNE & BERWICK, VIC, AUS **[36276]** : PRE 1793 EDINBURGH, MLN, SCT **[36276]** : 1793-1840 PERTH & BLAIRGOWRIE, PER, SCT **[36276]** : PRE 1840 AYR, SCT **[37169]**

BRISCOE 1650+ BENGAL ARMY &, LND, ENG
[34109] : C1800 WARRINGTON, LAN, ENG [34333] :
1820 BRILL, BKM, ENG [36649] : PRE 1640 LITTLE
MISSENDEN, BKM, ENG [38135]

BRISSINGHAM 1700 YOXFORD, SFK, ENG [37928]

BRISSON 1633 LA ROCHELLE, AUNIS, FRA [38364]

BRISTOE 1840+ CEDAR CO., MO, USA [36942]

BRISTOL 1730-1800 RENSSELAER CO., NY, USA
[36688]

BRISTOW 1870+ BAIRNSDALE, VIC, AUS [37989] :
ISAAC PRE 1850 GRITTLETON, GLS, ENG [34908]
: 1600-1650 ENG [36688] : PRE 1800 WIL, ENG
[37695] : 1850+ BERMONDSEY, LND, ENG [37989]
: PRE 1850 ORPINGTON, KEN, ENG [37989] :
C1550 GREAT LEIGHS, ESS, ENG [38348] : 1640-
1800 NEW HAVEN, CT, USA [36688]

BRITAIN PRE 1775 NEWTON, NJ, USA [37473]

BRITNELL ALL WORLDWIDE [35707]

BRITT PRE 1860 DENILIQUIN, NSW, AUS [34901] :
ROBERTA 1935+ GOREHILL, NSW, AUS [36600] :
1880S LIVERPOOL, SRY, ENG [35156] : PRE 1850
DUNMORE, KIK, IRL [37300] : CAROLINE C1830
MARION, MS, USA [37801]

BRITTAIN 1850 GEELONG, VIC, AUS [34038] :
JAMES 1827+ COLMSWORTH, BDF, ENG [35343] :
1900 BRISTOL, PA, USA [35279]

BRITTEN PRE 1850 CHATTERIS, CAM, ENG [34931] :
PRE 1850 WOODFORDCUM & THRAPSTON, NTH
& LND, ENG [37321]

BRITTENHAM 1800-1830 ROSS CO., OH & IL, USA
[36546]

BRITTIN SAMUEL 1850-1900 C OF L, ENG [37614]

BRITTINGHAM 1750-1800 SUSSEX CO., DE & OH,
USA [36546] : 1750-1800 SOMERSET CO., MD, USA
[38091]

BRITTON C1860S MT KEIRA, NSW, AUS [35105] :
1840+ BERRY, NSW, AUS [35856] : 1700+ WAGGA
& SYDNEY, NSW, AUS & IRL [36303] : PRE 1900
CON, ENG [34046] : MARY PRE 1750 GEORGE
NYMPTON, DEV, ENG [34963] : 1890-1925
PRESTWICH, LAN, ENG [35565] : PRE 1835 DEV,
ENG [35621] : PRE 1730 ULLESKELF, YKS, ENG
[35983] : ALL ASHTON & MIDDLETON, LAN,
ENG [36187] : 1700+ DEV, ENG [36209] : 1800+
BUTTSBURY, ESS, ENG [36662] : PRE 1895 SELBY,
YKS, ENG [37094] : PRE 1900 ENG [37443] : 1750S
WYTHE CO., VA, USA [36672]

BRITTYN ALL LEIDEN, ZUH, NL [38705]

BRITZ ALL USA [36661] : ALL WORLDWIDE [36661]

BRIZARD 1700+ MASKINONGE, QUE, CAN & FRA
[38727]

BRIZZEE ALL CH [37787] : ALL USA [37787]

BROAD 1830+ NSW, AUS [37554] : PRE 1850 ST
MAWGAN IN PYDAY, CON, ENG [35810] : 1850+
HOO, KEN, ENG [37328] : 1700+ EAST MALLING,
KEN, ENG [37328] : PRE 1830 LONDON & SRY,
ENG [37554] : C1750-1850 BERMONDSEY, SRY,
ENG [37718]

BROADBENT ALL SOWERBY BRIDGE, YKS, ENG
[34732] : JAS 1600+ SADDLEWORTH, WRY, ENG
[36291] : 1800-1900 BRADFORD, YKS, ENG [38471] :
THOMAS PRE 1800+ SEDGEBROOK, LIN, ENG
& CAN [35778]

BROADBRIDGE 1850+ SRY & ESS, ENG [35182] :
ALL CHICHESTER, SSX & HAM, ENG [35182]

BROADFOOT 1850+ PRESTONPANS, NBL, ENG
[34614]

BROADFUTE 1800+ HAMILTON, LKS, SCT [34918]

BROADHEAD 1800-1900 SHEPPARTON, VIC, AUS
[38070] : C1870 SHEPPARTON, MDX, ENG [35121] :
1740+ BIRMINGHAM, WAR, ENG [36558] : PRE
1700 WOOLDALE, WRY, ENG [37893]

BROADHURST PRE 1840 NEWCASTLE UNDER
LYME, STS, ENG [34880] : MARTHA PRE 1825
MACCLESFIELD, CHS, ENG [36192] : 1840+
ASHTON, WAR, ENG [36885]

BROADLEY HENRY PRE 1775 LUND, ERY, ENG
[36192] : 1820-1844 HUTTON CRANSWICK, ERY,
ENG [36391]

BROADRIBB ALL SOM & WIL, ENG [34801]

BROADWATER ALL CHESTERTON, OXF, ENG
[34110]

BROADWAY ALL WOR, ENG [37722] : 1700-99
YEOVIL, SOM, ENG [37756]

BROADY ALL WORLDWIDE [35945]

BROCAS 1700S-1800S SHREWSBURY, SAL, ENG
[35126]

BROCK PRE 1839 ANDOVER, HAM, ENG [34166] :
1800+ WOR, ENG [35812] : 1500-1650
STRADBROKE AREA, SFK, ENG [36335] : PRE
1820 LONDON, MDX, ENG [36379] : 1700-1850
LOPHAM, NFK & SFK, ENG [36491] : PRE 1845
ALSAGER, CHS, ENG [37298] : ALL DUNHAM &
FRANSHAM, NFK, ENG [37712] : 1830+
MARIENWERDER, PRE, GER [36945] : PRE 1730
OLD KILPATRICK, DNB, SCT [35227] : 1770-1820S
OLD KILPATRICK, DNB, SCT [35848] : 1800-1900
OWEN CO., KY, USA [36939]

BROCKBANK C1760 EGREMONT, CUL, ENG [36431]
: 1700-1800 CUL, ENG [37858]

BROCKBANK (SEE BROCK [37290])

BROCKESBY JOSEPH 1850S HULL, YKS, ENG
[37383]

BROCKHOUSE 1850 ST PANCRAS, LND, ENG
[37445]

BROCKHURST PRE 1770 DUNCTON, SSX, ENG
[34725]

BROCKIE ALL BORDERS, SCT [33886] : PRE 1850
MERTOUN, BEW, SCT [35823]

BROCKLEBANK 1800+ AUS & ENG [33769] : 1750-
1850 ERY & SFK, ENG [37290] : 1700-1900 BOOTLE,
CUL, CHS & LAN, ENG [37858]

BROCKLEHURST 1680 WIRKSWORTH, DBY, ENG
[37215]

BROCKLEY ANN 1850S HULL, YKS, ENG [37383]

BROCKMAN PRE 1800 LND & KEN, ENG [37644]

BROCKMANN PRE 1877 CATERNBERG, WEF, GER
[35864] : PRE 1852 CUXHAVEN, NSA, GER [38632]

BROCKSHIRE PRE 1800 ENG [36143]

BROCKSOP PRE 1800 ENG [36143]

BROCKWAY GEORGE 1837+ LABRADOR, NFD,
CAN &, ECUADOR [37161] : C1820 LEYTON, ESS,
ENG [33937] : GEORGE 1825+ POOLE, DOR, ENG
& AUS [37161] : 1850-1900 KEWEENAW CO., MI,
USA [38010] : JAMES 1850+ CA, USA & ENG
[37161]

BROCKWELL PRE 1829 LAMBETH, SRY & LND,
ENG [37452]

BRODBECK 1760-1800 TUBINGEN, WUE, GER
[38689] : PRE 1840 TUSCARAWAS, OH, USA [38220]
: PRE 1832 BALTIMORE, MD, USA [38335]

BRODBRIDGE PRE 1800 BOXGROVE &
CHICHESTER, SSX, ENG [35182]

BRODER 1750-1830 BECHELN, PRE, GER [38405]

BRODERICK 1785-1845 COR, IRL [34183]

BRODERIDGE 1650+ KINGSWEAR, DEV, ENG
[36000]

BRODETSKY ALL WORLDWIDE [37750]

BRODIE 1885+ BRISBANE, QLD, AUS [36290] : 1820
ERY, ENG [34731] : C1740 TURRIFF, ABD, SCT
[34713] : PRE 1832 DUNDEE, ANS, SCT [34979] :
1750-1850 CULLEN, ABD, SCT [35283] : 1740-1840
KILMICHAEL & KILMARTIN, ARL, SCT [35813] :
C1800-1900 EDINBURGH, MLN & FIF, SCT [36128]

: PRE 1885 OLRIG & THURSO, CAI, SCT [36290] :
1825-1850 SPOTT, ELN, SCT [36308] : PRE 1707
DYKE, MOR, SCT [37772] : C1775+
BLAIRGOWRIE, PER & ALB, SCT & CAN [34203]

BROECKAERT ALL ATW, BEL [38169]

BROEKMAN NICOLAAS PRE 1769 HANOVER,
HAN, GER [36453]

BROER 1700-1890 HOORN, NOH, NL [34069] : 1820-
1900 BAARN, UTR, NL [34069]

BROERZE 1825-1900 BAARN, UTR, NL [34069]

BROGAN 1850S GOULBURN, NSW, AUS [35557] :
C1840 LIVERPOOL & PARR, LAN, ENG [36874] :
PRE 1860 WEM, IRL [34557] : 1830S THURLES, TIP,
IRL [35557]

BROICH PRE 1820 NRW & RPF, BRD [38616]

BROMAN 1800+ EMSWORTH AREA, HAM, ENG
[36997] : CATH J. PRE 1723 GAVLE, FIN & SWE
[38564]

BROMANN PRE 1800 PERVER, PSA, GER [38648]

BROMBY 1860S CRESSY, TAS, AUS [34875]

BROMFIELD PRE 1845 TATTENHALL, CHS, ENG
[34262] : 1800+ LIVERPOOL, LAN & HAM, ENG
[37625] : 1860 IRL [35246]

BROMHAM 1750-1775 CALNE & CORSHAM, WIL,
ENG [37263]

BROMLEY 1930+ PERTH, WA, AUS [34230] : 1819+
RICHMOND, NSW, AUS [34966] : THOMAS PRE
1890 BROMLEY, KEN, ENG [34779] : 1700+ MDX,
ENG [35445] : PRE 1700 ESS, ENG [35642] : PRE
1860 MANCHESTER, LAN, ENG [36019] :
PERCIVAL J.G. 1850-1950 HOLBORN &
CLERKENWELL, MDX, ENG [36398] : PRE 1810
SHEFFIELD, YKS, ENG [36589] : ALL
STRATFORD TO WARWICK, WAR, ENG [37090]

BROMSGROVE ALL WORLDWIDE [35965]

BROMWELL PRE 1730 BKM, BDF & NTH, ENG
[35701]

BRONBECK ALL NSW, AUS [37182] : ALL
PORTSMOUTH, HAM & NFK, ENG [37182]

BRONDGEEST C1780-1830 LND, ENG [34345]

BROOF PRE 1850 UTTOXETER, STS, ENG [36976]

BROOK 1857+ VIC, AUS [35807] : 1800+ CEYLON
[37306] : PRE 1880 HOLMFIRTH, WRY, ENG [33850]
: PRE 1800 BATLEY & WAKEFIELD, YKS, ENG
[34952] : PRE 1913 GILDERSOME & LEEDS, WRY,
ENG [35031] : 1800+ GOLCAR & LONGWOOD,
YKS, ENG [35214] : 1800+ BINGLEY, YKS, ENG
[35734] : C1852 BATLEY, YKS, ENG [35807] : 1700-
1800 SSX, ENG [36589] : E. 1840-1880S
KIMBERWORTH & THORPE HESLEY, YKS, ENG
[36884] : 1790-1840 RASTRICK, WRY, ENG [36900] :
PRE 1840 DEWSBURY, WRY, ENG [37708] : PRE
1850 HUDDERSFIELD, YKS, ENG [38675]

BROOKBANK MARGARET 1851 IN, USA [38086]

BROOKBANKS PRE 1800 WOR, ENG [37832] : 1800+
LND, ENG [37832]

BROOKE C1800 SARAWAK, BORNEO [38383] : 1780-
1800 NORWICH, NFK, ENG [34088] : C1770
HASLEY, SSX, ENG [34806] : 1803 WORBLETON,
SSX, ENG [36281] : PRE 1866 NOTTINGHILL,
LND, ENG [36632] : 1820+ MANCHESTER, LAN,
ENG [36818] : ALL WARLINGHAM, SRY, ENG
[37627] : C1700 CIRENCESTER, GLS, ENG [38383] :
C1500 BROMSBERROW, HEF & GLS, ENG [38383] :
C1700 BATH, SOM, ENG [38383] : 1760-1900
KINAWLEY, CAV & FER, IRL [34094]

BROOKER 1840+ LINCOLN CO., ONT, CAN [38448]
: PRE 1837 FRANT, SSX, ENG [33944] : 1800S
CHATHAM, KEN, ENG [35377] : PRE 1780
ROTHERFIELD, SSX, ENG [35406] : PRE 1872
DEPTFORD & GREENWICH, LND, ENG [35956] :
1616+ HURSTPIERPOINT, SSX, ENG [36212] :

1800+ STOCKCROSS & NEWBURY, BRK, ENG
[37705] : C1800 ISLINGTON, MDX, ENG [37885] :
1830S CHERTSEY, SRY, ENG [37989] : 1750-1850
EAST GRINSTEAD, SSX, ENG [38003] : 1800+
COOKHAM & MAIDENHEAD, BRK & LND, ENG
& AUS [37065]

BROOKES JOHN 1650-1700 EASTON, SFK, ENG
[34143] : PRE 1894 BIRMINGHAM, WAR, ENG
[34269] : ELISHA 1799-1869 OLD SWINFORD,
WOR, ENG [34314] : 1870-1920 BILSTON, STS, ENG
[34399] : 1800+ HARDWICKE, GLS, ENG [34681] :
JOSEPH 1824+ LEI, ENG [37153] : 1880S RYTON,
SAL, ENG [37230] : PRE 1810 MARYLEBONE,
LND, ENG [37361] : PRE 1820 SAVERNAKE, WIL,
ENG [37687] : JOHN 1856+ LEI, ENG & AUS
[37153]

BROOKFIELD 1853+ MELBOURNE, VIC, AUS
[34808] : 18181 SHOREDITCH, MDX, ENG [34808]

BROOKING 1700-1750 WOLBOROUGH, DEV, ENG
[34552] : 1750-1850 LONDON, ENG [37038] : 1820+
NORTHLEW, DEV, ENG [37092]

BROOKING (SEE BROOKL [34552]

BROOKLING 1700-1750 WOLBOROUGH, DEV, ENG
[34552]

BROOKMAN 1840-1860 TALLYGAROOPNA, VIC,
AUS [33934] : BENJAMIN 1794+ BRISTOL, ENG
[35867] : ANN PRE 1834 BRISTOL, ENG [35867] :
1870+ EDINBURGH, MLN, SCT [36705]

BROOKMYRE 1840-1910 ELMIRA, NY, USA [36108]

BROOKS C1883 TAMWORTH, NSW, AUS [34277] :
1850+ HURTLE VALE, SA, AUS [34883] : PRE 1880
GOULBURN, NSW, AUS [34968] : ALL EMERALD,
QLD, AUS [35118] : ALL ROCKHAMPTON, QLD,
AUS [35118] : 1880+ HEYWOOD, VIC, AUS [35233] :
1840+ MT FROME & MUDGEE, NSW, AUS [35567]
: 1860+ GULGONG, NSW, AUS [35567] : 1875+
COONAMBLE, NSW, AUS [35567] : 1840+
ADELAIDE & JAMESTOWN, SA, AUS [38494] :
1820S-1850S CARLETON CO., ONT, CAN [34094] :
1830+ WELLESBOURNE, WAR, ENG [34113] :
ELISHA 1799-1869 OLD SWINFORD, WOR, ENG
[34314] : 1840-1870 LOUGHBOROUGH, LEI, ENG
[34337] : PRE 1886 OLDHAM, LAN, ENG [34443] :
1700-1800 MERRIOTT, SOM, ENG [34665] : C1860
HOLLINWOOD, LAN, ENG [34734] : 1850S
HAMPSTEAD, MDX, ENG [34738] : 1850
CAMBERWELL, SRY, ENG [34738] : 1820S
CANTERBURY, KEN, ENG [34738] : PRE 1810
CAMBRIDGE, CAM, ENG [34795] : 1852 SOM, ENG
[34878] : PRE 1885 NORTH TAWTON, DEV, ENG
[35118] : 1780+ BLEDLOW, BKM, ENG [35169] :
PRE 1870 CHELMONDISTON, SFK, ENG [35406] :
1800S CHS, ENG [35567] : PRE 1800 GRANTHAM,
LIN, ENG [35724] : 1813 ISLINGTON, MDX, ENG
[35903] : PRE 1854 GREAT YARMOUTH, NFK,
ENG [35956] : PRE 1820 YEOVIL, SOM, ENG [35961]
: PRE 1720 AINSWORTH, LAN, ENG [36032] :
C1810 SHOREDITCH, MDX, ENG [36099] :
WILLIAM M. 1800+ DEPTFORD, KEN, ENG
[36263] : 1700S CHATHAM, KEN, ENG [36527] :
1650-1750 ROCHESTER, KEN, ENG [36527] : 1600S
MAIDSTONE, KEN, ENG [36527] : 1600+ LEI,
ENG [36603] : 1750+ KEDLESTON, DBY, ENG
[36603] : 1600+ BREEDON ON THE HILL, LEI,
ENG [36603] : 1800+ MANCHESTER, LAN, ENG
[36603] : JOHN 1750S WAINFLEET, LIN, ENG
[36880] : 1850+ WIL, ENG [36885] : 1750-1850
ROYTON, LAN, ENG [36898] : 1844+ LONDON,
ENG [36959] : JOSEPH 1824+ LEI, ENG [37153] :
1800-1860 COTE & WITNEY, OXF, ENG [37194] :
1700+ WORKSOP, NTT, ENG [37241] : 1850+
SHEFFIELD, YKS, ENG [37241] : 1870+

HULBERRY, KEN, ENG **[37262]** : 1800S+
SHOREHAM, KEN, ENG **[37262]** : C1770 CALNE &
CORSHAM, WIL, ENG **[37263]** : ALL
CLAYBROOK, LEI, ENG **[37291]** : 1800S
TIVERTON, DEV, ENG **[37497]** : 1890S UPTON
PARK, ESS, ENG **[37677]** : C1770 RUNCORN, CHS,
ENG **[37697]** : C1820-1867 TATTERSHALL, LIN,
ENG **[37896]** : PRE 1860 NETHERSEAL, LEI, ENG
[37975] : 1820+ KENYON CLOUGH, LAN, ENG
[38266] : 1831-1876 TEWKESBURY, GLS, ENG
[38275] : ALL THORNBOROUGH, BKM, ENG
[38358] : PRE 1845 LONDON, ENG **[38390]** : JOHN
1856+ LEI, ENG & AUS **[37153]** : 1760-1900
KINAWLEY, CAV & FER, IRL **[34094]** : 1826+
ROSCREA, TIP, IRL **[35233]** : PRE 1790
LUNENBURG, VA, USA **[33757]** : 1630-1820
HADDAM, CT, USA **[36335]** : 1850-1910 BEDFORD
CO., TN, USA **[36912]** : C1835-1900 MN & WI, USA
[38112] : JONATHAN 1700-1800 WOODBRIDGE
MIDDLESEX, NJ, USA **[38130]** : 1600+ HADDON,
MA, USA **[38241]**

BROOKSHIRE 1750-1800 WILKES CO., VA, USA
[36737]

BROOKSON ALL SRY & ALL, UK **[37674]** : ALL UK
[37674]

BROOM 1880+ LIVERPOOL, LAN, ENG **[34341]** :
ALL WORCESTER, WOR, ENG **[35417]** : 1830-1900
LND, ENG **[35916]** : PRE 1842 AYR, SCT **[34859]**

BROOMAN 1700+ PLYMOUTH & PEMBROKE,
DEV, ENG **[37735]** : C1835 DUBLIN, IRL & SCT
[37263]

BROOME 1800S STOCKPORT, CHS, ENG **[33982]**

BROOMFIELD PRE 1821 WOLVERHAMPTON, STS,
ENG **[35061]** : ALL MONKWEARMOUTH, DUR,
ENG **[36046]** : 1774+ LYNDHURST, HAM, ENG
[36860]

BROOMHALL PRE 1920 BIRMINGHAM, WAR,
ENG **[34736]** : 1802 NANTWICH, CHS, ENG **[35282]**

BROOMHEAD 1800 MANCHESTER, LAN, ENG
[35881] : 1700S WRY, ENG **[37570]**

BROOMHEW ALL CAN & USA **[34133]**

BROPHEY 1800-1900 LEEDS & LONDON, SRY &
YKS, ENG & IRL **[35630]**

BROPHY C1865 CASTLE EDEN, DUR, ENG **[35507]**

BROSNAN PRE 1860 BALLYBRICKEN, LIM, IRL
[35189] : 1750-1880 CASTLEISLAND, KER, IRL
[36776] : ALL KER, IRL **[36854]** : PRE 1890 KER, IRL
[38177]

BROSSEAU ALL CASSOMPTIN, QUE, CAN **[35327]** :
1750-1850 L'ACADIE, QUE, CAN **[38047]**

BROSTER PRE 1800 BOLLINGTON, CHS, ENG
[36032] : 1800-1900 NESTON, CHS, ENG **[36983]**

BROTHERS 1820S ENG **[34216]** : 1900+ LAMAR
CO., TX, USA **[36947]** : 1800+ RUTHERFORD CO.,
TN, USA **[36947]** : 1820+ WORLDWIDE **[34216]**

BROTHERTON PRE 1860 LIVERPOOL & GREAT
SANKEY, LAN, ENG **[36849]** : 1700-1800
MANCHESTER & SHEFFIELD, LAN & WRY,
ENG **[37203]** : ALL NY, USA **[37584]** : ALL CT, USA
[37584]

BROTHERWOOD 1829-1929 TUDELY &
TONBRIDGE, KEN, ENG **[37614]** : ELIZABETH
1787-1850 TUDELY & TONBRIDGE, KEN, ENG
[37614] : THOMAS 1780-1880 TUDELY &
TONBRIDGE, KEN, ENG **[37614]**

BROTZMANN PRE 1876 RUDERSDORF, B BURG,
GER **[35465]**

BROUGH 1850+ BALLARAT, VIC, AUS **[36240]** :
1800-1850 BELPER & CRICH, DBY, ENG **[33916]** :
PRE 1836 STS, ENG **[34859]** : PRE 1840
LIVERPOOL, LAN, ENG **[35354]** : THOMAS 1880-
1900 MACCLESFIELD, CHS, ENG **[36018]** : 1750-

1850 LASTINGHAM, NRY, ENG **[36240]** : PRE 1700
STS, ENG **[37389]** : 1800 ALFORD, LIN, ENG **[37487]**
: PRE 1820 BIRMINGHAM, WAR, ENG **[37662]** :
PRE 1800 NOTTINGHAM, NTT, ENG **[37692]** :
1800+ ARNGASK, FIF, SCT **[36195]** : PRE 1830
ERROL, PER, SCT **[37146]**

BROUGHAM JOHN 1860+ VIC, NSW & SA, AUS
[36243] : JOHN C1842-1860+ MOTUEKA, NELSON,
NZ **[36243]** : ALL WORLDWIDE **[36490]**

BROUGHAN PRE 1900 CLONMORE, CAR, IRL
[38300]

BROUGHTON 1700+ STANSTED
MOUNTFITCHET, ESS, ENG **[34939]** : PRE 1850
LONDON, ENG **[35925]** : C1739 LINTON IN
CRAVEN, WRY, ENG **[37002]** : PRE 1850 PENDLE,
LAN, ENG **[37379]** : 1721-1816 BARNOLDSWICK,
WRY, ENG **[37988]** : TRUMAN 1833-1903 PA & MN,
USA **[38124]**

BROUILLET MICHEL 1640-1670 QUE, CAN **[37479]**

BROUN ANDERS C1837 STOCKHOLM, SWE **[34898]**

BROUSE 1800S CARLETON CO., ONT, CAN **[36666]**

BROUST 1570-1654 MORTAGNE, BN, FRA **[34514]**

BROW ELIZABETH 1800-1830 STIRLING, STI, SCT
[35865]

BROWER JEREMIAH 1750-1786 HALFMOON, NY,
USA **[37809]** : JEREMIAH 1786+ HIGHGATE, VT,
USA **[37809]**

BROWETT 1890-1990 WENTWORTH CO., ONT, CAN
[34124] : 1800-1990 PECKHAM, LND & SRY, ENG
[34124] : PRE 1850 LEICESTER, LEI, ENG **[35530]**

BROWN WILLIAM 1840+ MELBOURNE, VIC, AUS
[33846] : THOMAS 1863 WAGGA WAGGA, NSW,
AUS **[33891]** : MARY 1858-1935 TUENA, NSW, AUS
[33891] : 1806+ CATTAI, NSW, AUS **[33939]** : 1832+
JERRYS PLAINS, NSW, AUS **[33939]** : NAOMI
1820+ MT PROSPECT & PENTRIDGE, VIC, AUS
[33996] : 1850+ SYDNEY, NSW, AUS **[34428]** :
EBEN 1860+ LAUNCESTON, TAS, AUS **[34542]** :
JAMES 1865-1924 PICTON, NSW, AUS **[34698]** :
FRANCES 187601930 NSW, AUS **[34699]** : DAVID
1840+ SA, AUS **[34775]** : WILLAIM 1858+
CLUNES, VIC, AUS **[34881]** : 1857+ NATIMUK,
VIC, AUS **[35057]** : MELONA PRE 1854 SYDNEY,
NSW, AUS **[35084]** : EMMA 1840S HOBART & ST
LEONARDS, TAS, AUS **[35136]** : PRE 1836
HOBART, TAS, AUS **[35344]** : RICHARD PRE 1836
HOBART, TAS, AUS **[35344]** : LOUIS 1859
MAITLAND, NSW, AUS **[35409]** : 1840-1880
BUNGAY & WINGHAM, NSW, AUS **[35546]** : 1821-
1840 SYDNEY, NSW, AUS **[35782]** : C1856 DALBY,
QLD, AUS **[35807]** : ADA 1883+ SURRY HILLS,
NSW, AUS **[35827]** : WILLIAM 1850+
FREMANTLE, WA, AUS **[35847]** : FRANCES 1892
GRAFTON, NSW, AUS **[36311]** : ALEXANDER 1914
NARRANDERA, NSW, AUS **[36313]** : ESTER 1835+
PARRAMATTA & QUEANBEYAN, NSW, AUS
[36600] : ROBERT C1855 ALBURY, NSW, AUS
[36638] : THOMAS NOBLE 1890+ SYDNEY, NSW,
AUS **[36749]** : JOHN 1850+ LAUNCESTON, TAS,
AUS **[37134]** : WILLIAM 1854-1880 GEELONG, VIC,
AUS **[37155]** : FRANCIS 1856+ ERINA, NSW, AUS
[37312] : SAMUEL WM. 1839-1913 THE GLEBE,
SYDNEY, NSW, AUS **[37556]** : EUPHEMIA PRE
1878 MYRTLEFORD, VIC, AUS **[37901]** : THOMAS
JOSEPH PRE 1873 BRAIDWOOD, NSW, AUS
[37954] : 1850+ ST KILDA, VIC, AUS **[38281]** :
WILLIAM PRE 1851 SYDNEY, NSW, AUS **[38288]** :
1850+ CORRYONG, VIC, AUS **[38539]** : 1850+
YACKANDANDAH, VIC, AUS **[38539]** : 1850+
TALLANGATTA, VIC, AUS **[38539]** : 1850+
ALBURY, NSW, AUS **[38539]** : PETER PRE 1880 MT
GAMBIER, SA, AUS **[38755]** : JAMES C1856-1925

LAUNCESTON, TAS, AUS & USA [33806] : DAVID 1840S MONTREAL, QUE, CAN [34392] : 1830+ BARRIE, ONT, CAN [34466] : 1800S VAL CARTIER, QUE, CAN [34937] : WILLIAM 1800+ KING'S COVE, NF, CAN [34998] : 1750+ BONAVISTA BAY, NF, CAN [34998] : 1800+ SALVAGE, NF, CAN [34998] : 1800-1900 PLACENTIA BAY, NFD, CAN [35103] : C1845-1920 CULROSS & TEESWATER, ONT & SAS, CAN [36693] : WILLIAM 1837+ WASKADA, SAS, CAN [36716] : JAMES 1841+ OWEN SOUND, ONT, CAN [36716] : PRE 1870 BC, CAN [36729] : PETER C1820 ST JOHNS, NFD, CAN [37155] : 1850+ CLIFFORD, ONT, CAN [37484] : HARRIET 1850+ HAMIOTA, MAN & ONT, CAN & ENG [34519] : 1820+ WHITTINGTON, DBY, ENG [33916] : C1830 STROUD, GLS, ENG [33918] : 1800+ CHS, ENG [33927] : PRE 1851 UPPINGHAM, RUT, ENG [34006] : JOHN PRE 1849 NFK, ENG [34009] : 1800+ BEDFORD, ENG [34049] : PRE 1843 WEST MALLING, KEN, ENG [34055] : GEORGE 1890 WINDSOR, BRK, ENG [34120] : ANN 1790 NEWINGTON, SRY, ENG [34204] : 1850+ LEICESTER, LEI, ENG [34260] : PRE 1880 SEAHAM, DUR, ENG [34293] : PRE 1880 SOUTH SHIELDS, DUR, ENG [34293] : 1760-1800 WEYMOUTH, DOR, ENG [34337] : 1800-1870 MANCHESTER, LAN, ENG [34440] : PRE 1820 ISLEHAM, CAM, ENG [34445] : PRE 1670 PILHAM, LIN, ENG [34445] : PRE 1900 NORTH LEIGH, OXF, ENG [34466] : CLARINDA 1700+ SCOULTON, NFK, ENG [34572] : 1700-1900 MAIDSTONE, KEN, ENG [34624] : JONATHON 1844+ OUGHTERSIDE, CUL, ENG [34627] : RICHD FERROW 1848+ OUGHTERSIDE, CUL, ENG [34627] : JOHATHON 1782+ ASPATRIA, CUL, ENG [34627] : RICHARD 1805+ BOLTON, CUL, ENG [34627] : WILLIAM 1750+ STEVINGTON, BDF, ENG [34640] : PRE 1800 SAL, ENG [34647] : PRE 1900 HEF, ENG [34647] : ELIZABETH 1700-1800 BLEDLOW, BKM, ENG [34687] : 1800+ CHITHURST, SSX, ENG [34700] : 1880+ HEIGHAM, NFK, ENG [34710] : 1750-1950 LONDON, ENG [34714] : 1700-1900 OXFORD, OXF, ENG [34739] : 1670-1750 GWENNAP, CON, ENG [34793] : 1790+ DUR, ENG [34803] : JOHN 1801+ STONE, STS, ENG [34844] : GEORGINA 1700+ OVINGTON, ENG [34943] : 1800+ LEWISHAM, KEN, ENG [34980] : 1600+ WAR, ENG [34980] : 1836+ CHELMSFORD, ESS, ENG [35026] : 1820+ MARGATE, KEN, ENG [35054] : 1800 HERNE HILL, KEN, ENG [35054] : 1800 BOUGHTON UNDER BLEAN, KEN, ENG [35054] : GEORGE 1820 HOPTON, SFK, ENG [35067] : 1818 CAVENDISH, SFK, ENG [35119] : C1840 MICHELMARSH & TIMSBURY, HAM, ENG [35127] : JOHN C1855 POOLE, DOR, ENG [35131] : ISABELLA 1790-1806 NEWCASTLE ON TYNE, NBL, ENG [35232] : C1770-1835 STRETHAM, CAM, ENG [35238] : C1750-1820 BURTON COGGLES, LIN, ENG [35238] : PRE 1720 CON, ENG [35255] : PRE 1650 HIGH WYCOMBE, BKM, ENG [35292] : MARGARET E. C1870 SOUTH SHIELDS, DUR, ENG [35337] : ALICE PETITE PRE 1846 KEN, ENG [35346] : 1700+ READING, BRK, ENG [35355] : 1840+ NORTH SHIELDS, NBL, ENG [35396] : 1800S RINGSFIELD, SFK, ENG [35398] : 1852+ CROYDON, SRY, ENG [35468] : PRE 1800 WITNEY, OXF, ENG [35503] : HEPZIBAH C1827 NORWICH, NFK, ENG [35507] : PRE 1843 NFK, ENG [35546] : JOHN 1770S STEPNEY, LND, ENG [35560] : PATMOS 1770S STEPNEY, LND, ENG [35560] : WILLIAM 1837-1855 SOUTHAMPTON, HAM, ENG [35566] : ALL GATESHEAD, DUR,

ENG [35579] : PRE 1780 EPPING, ESS, ENG [35587] : FRANK 1880-1907 SRY, ENG [35604] : PRE 1750 ESS, ENG [35642] : WILLIAM 1800+ BINGLEY, YKS, ENG [35734] : C1826+ SOUTH BERSTED, SSX, ENG [35746] : THOMAS PRE 1848 MDX, ENG [35863] : MARY C1749 THURLESTON, DEV, ENG [35895] : PRE 1749 THURLESTON, DEV, ENG [35895] : 1750+ LOFTUS, YKS, ENG [35908] : PRE 1878 NORTHAMPTON, NTH, ENG [35956] : PRE 1768 BISHOP AUCKLAND, DUR, ENG [36046] : ALL GARSTON, LIVERPOOL, LAN, ENG [36063] : JOSEPH PRE 1820 WEYMOUTH, DOR, ENG [36100] : THOMAS 1790-1850 SRY & MDX, ENG [36100] : PRE 1860 GLOUCESTER, GLS, ENG [36113] : ALL OAKSEY, WIL, ENG [36118] : 1820-1870 HERTFORD, HRT, ENG [36136] : JAMES 1840 READING, BRK, ENG [36147] : JOSEPH C1825 ROCHDALE, LAN, ENG [36149] : PRE 1815 HORNCASTLE, LIN, ENG [36168] : PRE 1805 MELLING, LAN, ENG [36180] : ELIZABETH 1816-1840 LND & WORSLEY, LAN, ENG [36255] : C1800 WESTMINSTER, LND, ENG [36271] : HENRY 1811+ HOPTON, SFK, ENG [36296] : C1842 CHICHELEY, BKM, ENG [36302] : C1671-1753 RAMSGATE & BROADSTAIRS, KEN, ENG [36311] : SYDNEY 1890+ AVON, ENG [36359] : SYDNEY PRE 1880 COLEFORD, GLS, ENG [36359] : HERBERT PRE 1880 COLEFORD, GLS, ENG [36359] : JOHN PRE 1900 COLEFORD, GLS, ENG [36359] : MARTIN PRE 1880 COLEFORD, GLS, ENG [36359] : HERBERT 1890+ LANGFORD, AVON, ENG [36359] : HENRY PRE 1880 COLEFORD, GLS, ENG [36359] : HANNAH 1840+ SALE, CHS, ENG [36363] : PRE 1890 ISLINGTON, LND, ENG [36377] : ALL LEEMING, NRY, ENG [36492] : PRE 1850 ESS, ENG [36500] : PRE 1800 TWEEDMOUTH, NBL, ENG [36588] : ELIZABETH 1832+ BEDLINGTON, NBL, ENG [36609] : PRE 1800 IDLE & THACKLEY, WRY, ENG [36617] : THOMAS 1860+ CHACEWATER, REDRUTH, CON, ENG [36617] : 1830+ FAILSWORTH, MANCHESTER, LAN, ENG [36617] : 1650-1800 CHATTON, NBL, ENG [36776] : MICHAEL 1793+ PINCHBECK, LIN, ENG [36823] : JOHN 1838+ HULL, YKS, ENG [36855] : WILLIAM HENRY 1819 ROTHERHITHE, LND, ENG [36880] : PRE 1780 THETFORD, NFK, ENG [36883] : 1655 FRILLENDEN, KEN, ENG [36944] : 1800+ PLYMOUTH, DEV, ENG [36971] : 1800+ STRATTON, CON, ENG [36971] : 1765+ OAKSEY, WIL, ENG [36997] : THOMAS C1670+ QUEQUET WATER, CUL, ENG [37019] : BETSY C1670+ QUEQUET WATER, CUL, ENG [37019] : 1780+ CLIPSTON, NTH, ENG [37070] : PRE 1840 DEV, ENG [37107] : 1700 COLCHESTER, ESS, ENG [37125] : C1802 BRIGHTON, SSX, ENG [37144] : HARRIETT 1802+ OLDHAM, LAN, ENG [37175] : WILLIAM 1790+ OWTHORNE, ERY, ENG [37175] : 1850+ BRIDLINGTON, NRY, ENG [37202] : ROBERT 1913+ LEEDS, WRY, ENG [37202] : 1848 STOKE DAMEREL, DEV, ENG [37204] : 1840-1900 DOCKHEAD, SRY, ENG [37213] : 1800-1850 WIVELISCOMBE, SOM, ENG [37222] : PRE 1880 STEPNEY, LND, ENG [37237] : JOHN 1780+ CROYDON, SRY, ENG [37250] : ALL LEWES, SSX, ENG [37285] : 1800+ LONDON, ENG [37306] : PRE 1840 MANCHESTER, LAN, ENG [37309] : JAMES C1790S UPPER SWELL, GLS, ENG [37320] : 1830-1900 WINCHCOMB & LEIGH, GLS, ENG [37320] : 1800-1830 STOW ON THE WOLD & STANWAY, GLS, ENG [37320] : ALICE 1877 BURTON UPON TRENT, DBY, ENG [37334] : ALL BURTON UPON

TRENT, DBY, ENG [37334] : 1750-1811 REDRUTH, CON, ENG [37343] : PRE 1900 BACUP, LAN, ENG [37414] : PRE 1850 CLIFFORD, WRY, ENG [37484] : 1700-1800 TEALBY, LIN, ENG [37487] : SAMUEL WM. C1822-1839 TOTTENHAM COURT, LND, ENG [37556] : ALL NORWICH, NFK, ENG [37612] : SOPHIA PRE 1900 NEWMARKET, SFK, ENG [37619] : 1700+ EARITH, HUN, ENG [37637] : POTTO 1800+ HOUGHTON AND WYTON, HUN, ENG [37637] : 1600-1850 BAUGHHURST, HAM, ENG [37651] : JAMES PRE 1864 LONDON, ENG [37703] : PRE 1880 LND, ENG [37739] : C1800 WHITTLESEY, CAM, ENG [37770] : PRE 1750 ALMONDBURY, WRY, ENG [37893] : 1800 WESTLETON, SFK, ENG [37928] : ALL LUTON, BDF, ENG [37937] : PRE 1814 WHITCHURCH, SAL, ENG [37946] : PRE 1900 MORPETH, NBL, ENG [37979] : 1730+ WIGAN, LAN, ENG [38046] : 1750-1800 LEEDS, WRY, ENG [38047] : AGNES 1762+ WORKINGTON, CUL, ENG [38067] : PRE 1850 EARLS COLNE, ESS, ENG [38205] : 1600-1750 RYE, SSX, ENG [38224] : C1850 GAINSBOROUGH, LIN, ENG [38272] : WILLIAM 1825 RUTLAND, LEI, ENG [38288] : ANNE 1784+ BRUTON, SOM, ENG [38291] : 1850S TANFIELD, DUR, ENG [38329] : JOS. PRE 1806 SOUTHWARK, SRY, ENG [38384] : ELLEN 1800+ DUR, ENG [38454] : 1700-1900 EAST LONDON, MDX, ENG [38516] : 1820+ STEPNEY, LND & MDX, ENG [38539] : PRE 1830 BELGAUM, INDIA [36259] : ROBERT 1880-1911 LONDONDERRY, LDY, IRL [34101] : JAMES 1800+ IRL [34161] : PRE 1850 DOW, IRL [34617] : 1800-1900 DOW, IRL [34846] : PRE 1840 BALLILAW, TYR, IRL [34941] : ALL COR, IRL [34985] : MARIA PRE 1845 WIC & DUB, IRL [35488] : C1822 KILLINCHY, DOW, IRL [35552] : 1800+ LIM, IRL [35951] : MARY C1800 ANT, IRL [36860] : MARY PRE 1856 LISBURN, DOW, IRL [37138] : ROBERT PRE 1853 ATHLONE, WEM, IRL [37915] : 1870S DUNEDIN, NZ [34603] : 1896+ WELLINGTON, NZ [35843] : JOHN PRE 1915 CHRISTCHURCH, NZ [36359] : ALEXANDER 1855-1911 GREEN ISLAND, OTAGO, NZ [36766] : ALFRED 1879+ SPRINGSTON & LINCOLN, CANTY, NZ [36823] : ROBERT ALL BLUE SPUR, NZ [37162] : PRE 1879 CHRISTCHURCH, CANTY, NZ & ENG [35953] : JOHN PRE 1798 EDINBURGH, MLN, SCT [33774] : PRE 1825 SCT [33777] : WILLIAM PRE 1824 MELROSE, ROX, SCT [33806] : 1850 LINLITHGOW, WLN, SCT [33810] : 1790-1851 EASDALE, ARL, SCT [33811] : PRE 1820 MAUCHLINE, AYR, SCT [33845] : PRE 1800 GLADSMUIR, ELN & MLN, SCT [33959] : ALL LKS, SCT [33975] : 1750+ PAISLEY, RFW, SCT [33986] : PRE 1740 SORN, AYR, SCT [34214] : 1820+ BURNT ISLAND & KINGHORN, FIF, SCT [34260] : 1851+ DUMBARTON, DNB, SCT [34260] : WILLIAM C1800 DUNFERMLINE, FIF, SCT [34345] : JAMES C1825 RAW YARDS, AIRDRIE, LKS, SCT [34369] : ELIZABETH PRE 1764 WESTERKIRK, DFS, SCT [34501] : JAMES 1870 SCT [34511] : WILLIAM ALL PENNINGHAM, WIG, SCT [34564] : JAMES 1810 THANKERTON, LKS, SCT [34618] : 1700+ COLLACE, PER, SCT [34637] : ALEXANDER 1800S EDINBURGH, MLN, SCT [34698] : ROBERT 1849 BOTHWELL, DNB, SCT [34761] : C1837 GOREBRIDGE, MLN, SCT [35057] : ELIZABETH 1814 OLD MONKLAND, LKS, SCT [35259] : LOIS 1790 KILMARNOCK, AYR, SCT [35259] : 1800 LINN MILL, DFS, SCT [35350] : PRE 1800 FALKIRK, STI, SCT [35377] : ROBERT 1835+ GLENLUCE, WIG, SCT [35411] : CATHERINE 1845+ GLENLUCE, WIG, SCT [35411] : ALL STONEHOUSE, LKS, SCT [35461] : SARAH PRE 1852 GLASGOW, LKS, SCT [35473] : 1780+ DYSART, FIF, SCT [35524] : MARY 1797 ERROL, PER, SCT [35773] : C1830 PORT GLASGOW, RFW, SCT [35854] : C1811 EDINBURGH, MLN, SCT [35854] : JOHN PRE 1900 ANS, SCT [35950] : ALEXANDER PRE 1900 ANS, SCT [35950] : AGNES 1800-1840 AIRDRIE, LKS, SCT [36032] : ANDREW 1800-1840 AIRDRIE, LKS, SCT [36032] : JAMES 1800-1840 AIRDRIE, LKS, SCT [36032] : EUPHEMIA PRE 1824 PER, SCT [36276] : 1800S BANFF, BAN, SCT [36277] : JESSIE PRE 1867 EDINBURGH, MLN, SCT [36308] : PRE 1803 INVERKEITHING, FIF, SCT [36308] : C1730-1860 BO'NESS, WLN, SCT [36509] : PRE 1824 AIRDRIE, LKS, SCT [36509] : 1800S DUNDEE, ANS, SCT [36706] : ALEXANDER 1830-1860 DURISDEER, DFS, SCT [36766] : BARBARA C1786 STEWARTON, AYR, SCT [36802] : AGNES C1803 SLAMANNAN, STI, SCT [36875] : FRED 1800-1900 EDINBURGH, MLN, SCT [37338] : PRE 1800 LARBERT, STI, SCT [37374] : JOHN 1800+ KILMARNOCK, AYR, SCT [37443] : DAVID 1830+ KILMARNOCK, AYR, SCT [37443] : ROBERT 1860+ DALRY, AYR, SCT [37443] : WILLIAM C1780 LEITH, MLN, SCT [37449] : ALEXANDER 1860-1870 AYR, AYR, SCT [37485] : 1890-1978 EDINBURGH, MLN, SCT [37835] : PRE 1890 ABD, SCT [37835] : 1770S EDINBURGH, MLN, SCT [37869] : 1680-1760 KINNELL, ANS, SCT [37869] : 1800S LANGLOAN, STI, SCT [37898] : 1800S NEWBURGH, ABD, SCT [38402] : ALEXANDER 1858+ DNB, SCT & AUS [36313] : STEPHEN 1810-1840 LONDON, UK [37956] : MARTHA 1800-1900 KEITHBURG, IL, USA [34749] : PHOEBE C1752+ SMITHFIELD, RI, USA [35271] : ELIZ PRE 1900 TN, USA [35312] : 1910+ THERMOPOLIS, WY, USA [36077] : 1890+ ROUNDUP, MT, USA [36077] : ANN C1790-1856 CHESTER CO., PA, USA [36319] : 1632-1920 EDWARDSBURG & BANGOR, MI, USA [36342] : 1808 NYC, NY, USA [36358] : MARTIN 1870+ LACKAWANNA CO., PA, USA [36359] : SYDNEY 1870+ LACKAWANNA CO., PA, USA [36359] : HENRY 1870+ LACKAWANNA CO., PA, USA [36359] : HERBERT 1870+ LACKAWANNA CO., PA, USA [36359] : 1800 IL, USA [36548] : A.S. PRE 1817 VA, USA [36570] : WILLIAM S. PRE 1817 TRIGG CO., KY, USA [36570] : 1775-1850 WILKES CO., VA, USA [36737] : DAVID 1750-1810 WASHINGTON CO., TN, USA [36901] : 1682 EASTHAM, MA, USA [36944] : THOMAS PRE 1770 VA, USA [36973] : PRE 1850 OGLETHORPE CO., GA, USA [37003] : BENJAMIN 1825 NEW YORK, NY, USA [37038] : 1830-1900 INYO, CA, USA [37038] : JOHN BENTON C1800 DAVIDSON CO., TN, USA [37536] : 1800S OH, USA [37562] : NATHAN 1820 ERIE CO., PA, USA [37586] : LEWIS 1850+ PEEKSKILL, NY, USA [37796] : PRE 1840 POULTNEY, RUTLAND, VT, USA [37804] : 1719-1730 KENT CO., MD, USA [38009] : 1850-1900 BUNCOMBE CO., NC, USA [38009] : 1850-1900 MADISON CO., NC, USA [38009] : 1680-1700 BRUNSWICK CO., VA, USA [38009] : 1800-1850 WASHINGTON CO., TN, USA [38009] : 1680-1770 PRINCE GEORGE CO., VA, USA [38009] : 1727-1790 LUNENBURG CO., VA, USA [38009] : 1770-1800 BURKE CO., NC, USA [38009] : THOMAS 1700-1800 LYNN, MA, USA [38051] : NICHOLAS 1630-1730 LYNN, MA, USA [38051] : 1810-1820 NEWPORT, NH, USA [38009] : 1798-1860 LANCASTER CO., SC, USA [38107] : PRE 1794 MECKLENBURG CO., VA, USA [38120] : 1805-23 TN, USA [38151] : 1830-40 CARROLLTON, IL, USA [38151] : 1770-1850

CAYUGA CO., NY, USA **[38153]** : MATHIAS C1815 YORK CO., PA, USA **[38172]** : MAHLON 1755 TRENTON, NJ, USA **[38180]** : GEORGE W. 1900 LOS ANGELES, CA, USA **[38187]** : 1850 DETROIT, MI, USA **[38287]** : FRANK 1850-1870 IL, USA **[38312]** : RUREY 1850-1870 IL, USA **[38312]** : PETER 1650S WINDSOR, CT, USA **[38331]** : MARY ANN 1834-1912 HARRISON CO., OH, USA **[38371]** : JOSEPH 1820-63 LYNCHBURG, VA, USA **[38518]** : C1650-1775 FAIRFIELD CO., CT, USA **[38767]** : 1800-1850 FRANKLIN CO., NC, USA **[38770]** : PRE 1900 BARRY & CARDIFF, GLA, WLS **[36178]** : PRE 1900 NEWPORT, MON, WLS **[36178]** : JOSEPH PRE 1800 TINTERN, MON, WLS **[37085]**

BROWNE WILLIAM 1865-1876 COSTERFIELD, VIC, AUS **[34171]** : SUSAN 1865+ BALLARAT, VIC, AUS **[34430]** : 1910 LISMORE, NSW, AUS **[35066]** : JOSEPH 1850+ MELBOURNE, VIC, AUS **[36301]** : JOSEPH 1830-50S SYDNEY, NSW, AUS **[36301]** : 1816+ NSW, AUS **[37554]** : 1830+ BRUSSELS, BEL **[36030]** : 1833+ MIDDLESEX, ONT, CAN **[34080]** : PRE 1830 NORWICH, NFK, ENG **[34287]** : HUGH 1949+ STANSTED, ESS, ENG **[34341]** : HENRY PRE 1840 NORWICH, NFK, ENG **[35042]** : ARTHUR 1500-1600 HIGH WYCOMBE, BKM, ENG **[35292]** : PRE 1875 ISLINGTON, MDX, ENG **[35532]** : 1600-1800 SOUTH WEALD, ESS, ENG **[36588]** : 1835 EAST DEREHAM, NFK, ENG **[36781]** : SARAH PRE 1840 HEF, ENG **[37210]** : 1750-1800 DISS, NFK, ENG **[37246]** : PRE 1585 REPTON, DBY, ENG **[37554]** : ISABELLA C1800 MARYPORT, CUL, ENG **[37735]** : PRE 1640 HIGH WYCOMBE, BKM, ENG **[38135]** : JOHN 1820+ HOCKERING, NFK, ENG & AUS **[38204]** : 1832 PSA, GER **[37920]** : 1755-1816 LUCKNOW & CALCUTTA, INDIA **[37554]** : WILLIAM PRE 1770 BENGAL, INDIA **[37644]** : PRE 1810 TULLAMORE, OFF, IRL **[34080]** : J.G. 1800+ IRL **[34161]** : WILLIAM 1845+ WESTPORT, MAY, IRL **[34430]** : JAMES 1830 GLENDERMONT, LDY, IRL **[34461]** : MARY KATHLEEN PRE 1818 NEWMARKET & MEELIN, COR, IRL **[35217]** : 1800+ LIM, IRL **[35951]** : 1700+ SHRULE, GAL, IRL **[37554]** : 1600+ DOW, IRL **[37554]** : C1800 INNISHANNON, COR, IRL **[37859]** : WILLIAM 1805-85 DUMFRIES, DFS, SCT **[36999]**

BROWNFIELD C1850 GRAVESEND, KEN, ENG **[35863]** : C1823 GREENWICH, KEN, ENG **[35863]** : 1850S CINCINATTI, OH, USA **[36355]** : 1860-1900 LAWRENCE CO., MO, USA **[36355]**

BROWNIE PRE 1841 ABD, SCT **[37313]**

BROWNING 1875+ CARLTON, VIC, AUS **[33915]** : 1861+ URALLA, NSW, AUS **[34304]** : 1855-1900 NEVILLE, NSW, AUS **[34493]** : PRE 1842 GOULBURN, NSW, AUS **[38288]** : 1890+ CALGARY, ALB, CAN **[36523]** : 1802+ KEN, ENG **[34142]** : 1816-1900 SOM, ENG **[34658]** : 1848 AXBRIDGE, SOM, ENG **[34668]** : 1800-1855 RAMSEY, HUN, ENG **[34693]** : PRE 1850 LONGNEY, GLS, ENG **[34716]** : 1790+ EXETER, DEV, ENG **[34956]** : 1800S TORQUAY, DEV, ENG **[35438]** : C1850-1880 BATTERSEA PARK, LND, ENG **[35725]** : RICHARD 1791 ST GEORGE, MDX, ENG **[36320]** : C1813 FROME, SOM, ENG **[36364]** : PRE 1850 MALLING, KEN, ENG **[36517]** : 1700-1800 GLS, ENG **[37829]** : PRE 1840 ELHAM, KEN, ENG **[38389]** : ALL GLS, ENG **[38419]** : C1850 TIP, IRL **[33915]** : PRE 1930 LISMORE, WAT, IRL **[35639]** : 1600-1715 SCT & IRL **[37740]** : 1890S TALLADEGA, AL, USA **[37792]** : PRE 1715 JAMES CITY CO., VA, USA **[38311]** : LORENZO D. 1832-1898 LICKING, UNION CO., OH, USA **[38569]**

BROWNLEE PRE 1820 IRL **[33905]** : C1870 LADHOPE, ROX, SCT **[35486]**

BROWNLIE PRE 1860 LKS, SCT **[37923]**

BROWNLOW 1840+ OBERON & BATHURST, NSW, AUS **[35395]** : C1830 BURTON JOYCE, NTT, ENG **[34734]** : 1840-1900 SWINDERBY, LIN, ENG **[37495]**

BROWNSCOMBE C1800 CADBURY, DEV, ENG **[35050]**

BROWSTER 1700+ KILRENNY, FIF, SCT **[34637]**

BRUBAKER 1790+ BOTETOURT CO., VA & OH, USA **[36540]**

BRUCCIANI PRE 1842 GREENWICH, KEN, ENG **[34452]** : PRE 1824 FLORENCE, ITL **[34452]** : 1800+ FLORANCE, ITL **[36621]**

BRUCE 1800-1840 WALLERAWANG & HARTLEY, NSW, AUS **[34307]** : 1840+ SYDNEY, NSW, AUS **[35505]** : 1900 CAMBERWELL, VIC, AUS **[35755]** : 1860 LINDENOW, VIC, AUS **[35755]** : ELIZABETH PRE 1800 CUL, ENG **[34164]** : PRE 1854 PADDINGTON, LND, ENG **[34669]** : PRE 1700 DEDHAM, ESS, ENG **[36121]** : PRE 1773 LONG CRENDON, BKM, ENG **[36866]** : ALL SOUTH SHIELDS, DUR, ENG **[37704]** : PRE 1860 KIMMAGE, DUB, IRL **[34581]** : PRE 1600 AIRTH, STI, SCT **[33886]** : 1200+ CLK, SCT **[33986]** : JANE KIDD PRE 1835 ST ANDREWS, FIF, SCT **[34310]** : 1750+ BRAEHUNGIE & DUNBEATH, CAI, SCT **[34591]** : 1750+ LATHERON, CAI, SCT **[34606]** : 1845+ LONGHOPE, OKI, SCT **[34688]** : C1830 CARNBEE, FIF, SCT **[35207]** : 1800+ UNST, SHI, SCT **[35505]** : 1600-1700 FIF, SCT **[35627]** : 1817 PETERHEAD, ABD, SCT **[35855]** : C1800-1942 DUNKELD & FORGANDENNY, PER & FIF, SCT **[36128]** : 1780+ SCT **[36239]** : C1750-1800 N & S LEITH, MLN, SCT **[36327]** : JANET 1800S RENFREW, RFW, SCT **[37106]** : JEAN 1700S DUNNING, PER, SCT **[37106]** : PRE 1840 CAI, SCT **[37913]**

BRUCK 1600+ HANAU, HEN, GER **[38667]**

BRUCKIN 1750-1850 LONDON, ENG **[37038]**

BRUCKSHAW PRE 1860 STOCKPORT, CHS, ENG **[34865]**

BRUDE C1792 ENG **[36594]**

BRUDENELL PRE 1800 SOM & WIL, ENG **[37225]**

BRUDER 1840+ LAURENBURG & DETROIT, PRE & MI, GER & USA **[34983]**

BRUECKMANN PRE 1740 AUERBACH, HES, BRD **[35311]**

BRUEN ISAAC H. 1798-1890 CHATHAM TWP, MORRIS CO., NJ, USA **[37023]** : 1650-1700 NEWARK, NJ, USA **[38523]**

BRUENE 1616-1654 REHENGGE, WAL, GER **[34912]**

BRUENING 1741+ GER **[36638]**

BRUERE 1700-1800 WORLDWIDE **[37381]**

BRUERTON REUBEN PRE 1840 DARLASTON, STS, ENG **[36374]**

BRUETON SARAH 1850S ASTON, WAR, ENG **[37476]**

BRUFORD 1765-1865 TAUNTON, SOM, ENG **[35720]** : 1800S BRISTOL, SOM, ENG **[35720]** : PRE 1810 BROOMFIELD, SOM, ENG **[38263]**

BRUGGY 1860 MELBOURNE, VIC, AUS **[37984]**

BRUGOTTI 1800S LONDON, ENG **[36789]**

BRUHN 1700+ BUSUM, SHO, GER **[37542]** : PRE 1800 BOERZOW, MEK, GER **[38632]**

BRUICK PRE 1870 HARTON, DUR, ENG **[34869]**

BRUIN MARY PRE 1764 GREENWICH, KEN, ENG **[36810]**

BRUINSMA PRE 1880 APPELSCHA, FRI, NL **[36283]**

BRULE ALL ST GERMAIN AMIENS, PIC, FRA **[34985]**

BRUMBY PRE 1810 LINCOLN, LIN, ENG **[34240]** : PRE 1770 PILHAM, LIN, ENG **[34445]**

BRUMFITT C1868 SKIPTON, WRY, ENG [34675]

BRUMLEY 1820-1853 FAYETTE & SHELBY CO., TN, USA [38092] : 1820-1853 HARDEMAN CO., TN, USA [38092]

BRUMMER 1700+ HERBOLZHEIM, BAV, GER [37542]

BRUMMIT 1780-1830 BOSTON, LIN, ENG [37342]

BRUMMITT 1800+ KIRTON & ALGARKIRK, LIN, ENG [34916] : 1810+ IPSWICH, SFK, ENG [37284] : 1840+ STRATFORD, MDX, ENG [37284] : 1700+ LINCOLN, LIN, ENG [37284]

BRUMWELL 1800+ NEWCASTLE UPON TYNE, NBL, ENG [36717]

BRUN RENEE 1550+ PCH, FRA [37429] : VINCENT 1550+ PCH, FRA [37429]

BRUNDAGE 1800+ NS, CAN [38460] : 1800+ PEI, CAN [38460]

BRUNDELL SOPHIA PRE 1785 BISHOPS GATE, LND, ENG [34461] : 1700-1850 SFK, ENG [36816] : 1860+ DUNEDIN, OTAGO, NZ [36816]

BRUNDISH PRE 1833 MENDLESHAM & STOWMARKET, SFK, ENG [35459]

BRUNEEL 1600-1700 ARDOOIE, WF, BEL [34163]

BRUNER 1850+ VA, USA [36956] : 1850+ PA, USA [36956] : 1850+ BROOKE CO., WV, USA [36956]

BRUNET ALL STE AGATHE, QUE, CAN [35327] : FRANCOIS 1700-1765 QUE, CAN [37479] : 1565-1645 TOUROUVRE & L'AIGLE, BN, FRA [34514] : 1590-1660 BARDAIS & BARLIEU, FRA [38779]

BRUNET DE ROCHEBRUNE C1730 NL [35883]

BRUNGARDT 1876+ ELLIS CO., KS, USA [38057]

BRUNGER 1840+ SMARDEN, KEN, ENG [36892] : C1783 TENTERDEN, KEN, ENG [38389]

BRUNKE 1700 GER [35873]

BRUNKHORST 1860-1930 JACKSON CO., IL, USA [36912]

BRUNNER PRE 1886+ TOOWOOMBA, QLD, AUS [37174] : PRE 1800 AARAU, AG, CH [37103] : 1700+ NECKARSULM, BAD, GER [35566] : PRE 1860 HEDDESHEIM, BAD, GER [37174] : PRE 1875 CLEVELAND, OH, USA [37034] : 1820-1900 NIAGARA, NY, USA [37535]

BRUNNERUS C1650 ALEM, SWE [38544]

BRUNNING SARAH 1808-1887 SUDBURY, SFK, ENG [35634] : ALL WORLDWIDE [34737]

BRUNO 1780-1817 KAMPEN, OY, NL [38691] : 1780-1817 KAMPEN, OY, NL [38711]

BRUNS PRE 1760 RINTELN, LIP, GER [38669] : PRE 1800 PRY & LIP, GER [38669] : HERMANN 1773+ PEINE, USA [38668] : GEORG 1773+ PEINE, USA [38668]

BRUNSDON 1880S RICHMOND, VIC, AUS [35390] : 1850S BRK, ENG [35390] : 1880S CHRISTCHURCH, NZ [35390]

BRUNSKILL PRE 1850 CROOK, DUR, ENG [38457]

BRUNSON PRE 1760 BARROW, LEI, ENG [38512] : 1810-1820 AL, USA [37815]

BRUNT PRE 1850 DBY, ENG [34686] : C1784 HARTSHORNE, DBY, ENG [35144] : PRE 1850 WIGMORE, HEF, ENG [37681] : 1780S DBY & STS, ENG [37751]

BRUNTLETT 1876-1990 WANGANUI, NZ [36832]

BRUNTON 1800+ DRURY LANE, LND, ENG [34367] : PRE 1860 SELKIRK, SCT [34443] : PRE 1783 NEWBATTLE, MLN, SCT [37852] : PRE 1772 NEWBATTLE, MLN, SCT [37852]

BRUNWIN ALL ESS, ENG [34204]

BRUSCH ALL WORLDWIDE [37696]

BRUSH ALL WORLDWIDE [37696]

BRUSHABER ALL WORLDWIDE [37803]

BRUSHE ALL WORLDWIDE [37696]

BRUSO 1848-1950 WORCESTER, MA, USA [38047]

BRUTON 1750-1850 EDGEWARE, MDX, ENG [36165] : 1840-1850 LND, ENG [36165] : 1700-1799 HRT, ENG [36165] : 1850-1900 HASTINGS, SSX, ENG [36165] : 1800-1870 BRISTOL, GLS, ENG [36292] : ALL DEV, ENG [36469] : 1800-1900 WATFORD, HRT, ENG [36977]

BRUTY PRE 1800 ESS & SFK, ENG [36399] : 1815 STUTTON, SFK, ENG [36798]

BRUYERE 1800-1850 USA & CAN [37502]

BRYAN 1861+ GLOUCESTER; GLS, ENG [34823] : 1710 ST AGNES NEAR TRURO, CON, ENG [35208] : C1797+ ALFRETON, DBY, ENG [35249] : ALL DENTON, LIN, ENG [35515] : ALL ROCHESTER, KEN, ENG [36756] : ALL BATTLE, SSX, ENG [36756] : C1750 LONDON, MDX, ENG [36978] : PRE 1800 STEPNEY & SPITALFIELDS, MDX, ENG [36986] : PRE 1800 STEPNEY, MDX, ENG [36986] : PRE 1800 LND, ENG [36986] : PRE 1800 MORCOTT, RUT, ENG [37381] : C1650 MARCHAM, BRK, ENG [37420] : WILLIAM 1841-1871+ LIMEHOUSE & POPLAR, MDX, ENG [37546] : 1870-90 ENG [37701] : 1780S LONDON, ENG [37947] : PRE 1861 COR, IRL [34823] : PRE 1793 WEX, IRL [35037] : PRE 1840 KIK, IRL [35404] : ROGER C1814 COR, IRL [37546] : 1847-1856 MALTA [36986] : SARAH 1753-1782 HARRISONBURG, VA, USA [36321] : FANNIE CLAY C1894 BOWLING GREEN, KY, USA [36448] : THOMAS 1710 RICHMOND CO., VA, USA [38066] : 1675-1775 CUMBERLAND CO., PA, USA [38118] : 1775-1780 ORANGE CO., NC, USA [38118] : 1790-1810 WATERBURY, CT, USA [38137]

BRYANS 1858-1931 LISNASKEA, FER, IRL [34233] : 1800+ LURGAN & ARMAGH, ARM, IRL [34970] : 1800S ARMAGH, ARM, IRL [35186] : 1800S BONHILL, DNB, SCT [35186]

BRYANT 1850+ LUCKNOW, NSW, AUS [34459] : HENRY L. PRE 1870+ LAUNCESTON, TAS, AUS [34592] : HENRY LEWIS PRE 1870+ TAS, AUS [34592] : 1850-1900 MONARO AREA, NSW, AUS [34842] : AMBROSE 1840-1900 GOULBURN, NSW, AUS [34842] : PRE 1860S HOBART, TAS, AUS [35746] : 1884+ GLASS, TAS, AUS [35869] : 1860S PORT GAWLER & ADELAIDE, SA, AUS [37981] : 1850+ MONARO, NSW, AUS [38596] : C1850-1900 MIDDLESEX CO., ONT, CAN [35605] : 1800+ PEI, CAN [38460] : 1800+ KENT CO., NB, CAN [38460] : PRE 1850 BITTON, GLS, ENG [33850] : C1840 BATH, SOM, ENG [33918] : PRE 1864 HAM, ENG [33959] : 1750+ BRISTOL, SOM, ENG [34100] : MARY 1816 DEVONPORT, DEV, ENG [34195] : ANNIE JANE 1862 ENG [34511] : PRE 1800 BENENDEN, KEN, ENG [34858] : PRE 1850 NEWBURY, BRK, ENG [34869] : CHARLES 1700+ BRADFORD ON AVON, WIL, ENG [34908] : 1850-1900 STS, ENG [35094] : PRE 1820 SOM & DEV, ENG [35098] : PRE 1849 LONG SUTTON, SOM, ENG [35117] : PRE 1900 BRISTOL, GLS, ENG [35339] : PRE 1866 ESS, ENG [35515] : ALL BROADWAY, SOM, ENG [36529] : CATHERINE 1820S KEN, ENG [36634] : PRE 1870 LND, ENG [36645] : 1750+ OLD WARDEN, BDF, ENG [37223] : C1805 KENSINGTON, LND, ENG [37321] : 1830+ WIMBORNE, DOR, ENG [37360] : ALL ST ERTH, CON, ENG [37558] : PETER PRE 1850 HAMSEY & DITCHLING, SSX, ENG [38483] : 1832-1890 WASHINGTON CO., IN, USA [36553] : 1810-1832 KY, USA [36553] : THOMAS PRE 1850 NC, USA [37551] : THOMAS 1880 DECATUR CO., IA, USA [37551] : ENOCH 1857 MO, USA [37551] : 1800+ GLA & MON, WLS [34459]

BRYCE 1850S+ CLARENCE RIVER, NSW, AUS [35108] : 1850+ SOUTH COAST, NSW, AUS [36637] :

1843-1850S PORT ELIZABETH, RSA [35108] : C1750-1850 MAYBOLE, AYR, SCT [33845] : ALL LKS, SCT [33975] : PRE 1900 WHITBURN, WLN, SCT [34784] : C1816 LEITH, SCT [35108] : 1780+ DYSART, FIF, SCT [35977] : 1780-1840 GLASGOW, STI, SCT [36763] : 1860 EDINBURGH, MLN, SCT [36871] : PRE 1900 SCT [37517]

BRYDE FLORA 1745-1775 KINTYRE, ARL, SCT [38123]

BRYDEN 1840-1900 BALMAIN, NSW, AUS [35857] : PRE 1825 GLENHOLM, PEE, SCT [34365] : 1820+ IRVINE, AYR, SCT [36749] : 1800+ CUMNOCK, AYR, SCT [37480] : ALL DAILLY, AYR, SCT [37480]

BRYDIE ALL EAST NEUK, FIF, SCT [37704]

BRYDON PRE 1650 NFK & SFK, ENG [34312] : PRE 1838 ECCLES, BEW, SCT [37610]

BRYER C1800 HILL FARRANCE, SOM, ENG [37053]

BRYLL 1825-1890 W UKRAINE, SU [36331]

BRYN 1700-1900 WLS [38278]

BRYSON 1700+ BOLDON, DUR, ENG [38587] : 1800-1870 CUMBERNAULD, DNB, SCT [37767] : PRE 1720 DFS, SCT [38587] : 1700+ LAUDER, BEW, SCT [38587] : 1700+ COLDINGHAM, BEW, SCT [38587]

BUATTE 1700 IL, USA [38320]

BUBB C1800 AVENING, GLS, ENG [34952]

BUBBINGS ALL NFK, ENG [37612]

BUBNA ALL WIE, OES [34135]

BUCH C1830 PRE, GER [37536]

BUCHAN 1700-1800 PER, SCT [34937] : ALL FRASERBURGH, ABD, SCT [36061] : PRE 1900 PETERHEAD, ABD, SCT [36433] : PRE 1800 COCKENZIE, ELN, SCT [37852]

BUCHANAN 1850+ VIC, AUS [34685] : 1867+ SYDNEY, NSW, AUS [34979] : C1862 PYRMONT & SYDNEY, NSW, AUS [37556] : 1800-1870 DUNHAM, QUE, CAN [36738] : 1867+ WAIKATO & THAMES, NZ [35584] : 1750+ JOHNSTONE & KILBARCHEN, RFW, SCT [34049] : 1850+ SHETTLESTON, LKS, SCT [34049] : HELEN 1763-1830 GLASGOW, LKS, SCT [34557] : MARGARET 1831 WICK, CAI, SCT [34580] : PRE 1841 KILMARTIN, ARL, SCT [34911] : PRE 1867 GLASGOW, LKS, SCT [34979] : C1770+ CADDER, LKS, SCT [35051] : 1839 BISHOPBRIGGS, LKS, SCT [35119] : 1780S BORLAND PARK, PER, SCT [35259] : PRE 1910 SOUTH LEITH, MLN, SCT [35051] : ALL GLASGOW, SCT [36094] : PRE 1849 KIRKINTILLOCH, DNB, SCT [36282] : 1850-1856 GLASGOW, SCT [36282] : 1800+ KILMARTIN & KNAPDALE, ARL, SCT [36827] : 1200 SCT [37008] : MARY 1805+ KILMARNOCK, AYR, SCT [37424] : PRE 1900 EAST KILBRIDE, LKS, SCT & AUS [34603] : 1800+ RYEGATE, VT, USA [37492] : 1900S ENID, OK, USA [38531]

BUCHANON MARY 1770-1848 ISLE OF MULL, ARL, SCT [36712] : 1750-1900 FAYETTE CO., PA, USA [38344]

BUCHER 1700S TOLLER PORCORUM, DOR, ENG [35964]

BUCHNER 1800 ECHING, BAV, GER [37483]

BUCHS PRE 1881 STETTIN, POM, GER [38112] : 1881+ MN, USA [38112]

BUCHWALD PRE 1910 BUCZYCZ, LVOV, RUSSIA [34127]

BUCK 1700S FRONTENAC, ONT, CAN [34353] : 1939-1945 TORONTO, ONT, CAN [36420] : PRE 1800 LONDON, ENG [33968] : 1780 RADFORD, NTT, ENG [34120] : 1800+ BRIGHTON & SOUTHWICK, SSX, ENG [34749] : 1800S ELLINGHAM, NFK, ENG [35046] : PRE 1850 EDMONTON, LND, ENG [36247] : 1700-1800 KEN, ENG [36491] : C1800 LEEDS, WRY, ENG [37246] : PRE 1850 HINDLEY, LAN,

ENG [37573] : 1700S-1800S LONDON, MDX & SRY, ENG [38034] : 1740+ GER [34408] : 1800+ GREBIN, SHO, GER [37170] : 1738-1812 KARBY ECKERNFOERDE, SHO, GER [38750] : 1760+ SUSQUEHANNA, PA, USA [34408] : 1770-1800 PA, USA [36666] : 1700-1900 MO, USA [36689] : JOHAN C. C1770+ PA & VA, USA [37604] : DANIEL C1790-1840 JEFFERSON CO., PA & NY, USA [38055]

BUCKBY 1786-1850 CRAWFORD, NTH, ENG [35119] : 1724+ LITTLE BOWDEN, NTH, ENG [35921]

BUCKEL PRE 1820 WALSHAM LE WILLOWS, SFK, ENG [37287] : PRE 1850 GUEMAR, ALS, FRA [35635]

BUCKELS 1800+ OSGOODE, ONT, CAN [34514]

BUCKENHAM 1600+ SFK, ENG [36093]

BUCKERFIELD PRE 1829 WROUGHTON, WIL, ENG [35016]

BUCKHAM C1750 KELSO, ROX, SCT [34118] : 1790+ ROX, SCT & CAN [35611]

BUCKINGHAM 1876-1899 AUS [37443] : 1890+ BRANTFORD, ONT, CAN [37443] : PRE 1800 OXF, ENG [35030] : PRE 1800 SSX, ENG [35500] : PRE 1852 WEEK ST MARY, CON, ENG [35744] : PRE 1850 EYNSHAM, OXF, ENG [36379] : 1814 FADMOOR, YKS, ENG [36907] : 1830-1865 LND, ENG [37443] : ALL LUTON & DUNSTABLE, BDF, ENG [37937] : PRE 1700 GWENNAP, CON, ENG [38540]

BUCKLAND ALL PORTSEA, HAM, ENG [34298] : JOHN PRE 1820 SOHO, LND, ENG [34461] : PRE 1650 WEST HARPTREE, DEV, ENG [34741] : 1820-1840 WIL & HRT, ENG [35850] : 1800+ GLOUCESTER, GLS, ENG [35989] : PRE 1846 POTTERNE, WIL, ENG [36079] : 1600-1760 WIL, ENG [37232] : SARAH PRE 1861 WROUGHTON, WIL, ENG [37481] : PRE 1883 PONTYPOOL, MON, WLS [37911]

BUCKLE 1850+ WOLLONGONG, NSW, AUS [35105] : 1800S STILLINGFLEET, YKS, ENG [34309] : PRE 1880 BRIGHTON, SRY, ENG [35174] : 1700S ST CLEMENT DANES, LND, ENG [35858] : ANNIE 1868-1906 HUNSINGORE & LEEDS, WRY, ENG [37887]

BUCKLER PRE 1862 SRY, ENG [38568]

BUCKLES 1750-1870 IRL [38779]

BUCKLEY 1880+ MELBOURNE & SYDNEY, AUS [33957] : JOSEPH C1900 VIC & NSW, AUS [33957] : JAMES 1900+ GUNNEDAH, NSW, AUS [35084] : ALICE 1815+ PARRAMATTA, NSW, AUS [35513] : 1870+ COLERAINE, VIC, AUS [35587] : 1830+ THE OAKS, NSW, AUS [37115] : 1900+ CASTLE HILL, NSW, AUS [37115] : 1830+ NSW, AUS [37115] : 1870+ HARWOOD, NSW, AUS [37116] : CATHERINE PRE 1830 SYDNEY, NSW, AUS [37982] : 1850-1900 KEN CO. & NBL CO., NB, CAN [36662] : 1850+ ST JOHN, NB, CAN [37450] : C1885 SADDLEWORTH, LAN & YKS, ENG [36028] : ALL SADDLEWORTH, WRY, ENG [36999] : PRE 1890 LEEDS, YKS, ENG [37094] : PRE 1830 LONDON, ENG [37115] : 1790 SEIGHFORD, STS, ENG [37209] : PRE 1824 CUL, ENG [37450] : C1800 OLDHAM, LAN, ENG [37807] : JOSEPH C1900 FRA [33957] : 1760-1840 INCHIGEELAGH, COR, IRL [34672] : 1800+ COR, IRL [35448] : 1780+ BANTEER, COR, IRL [36343] : PRE 1824 HILLSBOROUGH & BELFAST, DOW, IRL [37450] : 1820-1850 CAPPAGH WHITE, TIP, IRL [37540] : PRE 1850 KINNIEGH, COR, IRL [37540] : PRE 1814 OOLA, LIM, IRL [37540] : 1900+ NZ [37115] : 1880+ NATICK, MA, USA [37450] : 1850+ ESSEX CO., NY, USA [37540] : 1850+ BLACK BROOK, CLINTON, NY, USA [37540]

BUCKMAN PRE 1861 KEN, ENG [34412] : 1820 BRIGHTON, SSX, ENG [34565] : PRE 1750 SSX, ENG [37589]

BUCKMASTER 1820+ YASS, NSW, AUS [36610] : ALL WORLDWIDE [36610]

BUCKNELL 1886 MELBOURNE, VIC, AUS [34594] : 1841 CULWORTH & CROUGHTON, NTH, ENG [36423] : PRE 1860 TEIGNMOUTH & BUDLEIGH, DEV, ENG [37393]

BUCKNER 1819+ MANNING RIVER, NSW, AUS & ENG [37130]

BUCKNEY PRE 1816 BATTERSEA, LND, ENG [33774]

BUCKRELL ALL SOM, ENG [34057] : ALL WORLDWIDE [34057]

BUCKRIDGE 1850-1900 WELLINGTON, NZ [38278]

BUCKTHORP 1750-1850 HRT, ENG [35178]

BUCKTON PRE 1860 LEEDS, WRY, ENG [33968] : ALL REDCAR, YKS, ENG [37433] : 1861+ TAUHOA, NORTHLAND, NZ [33968]

BUCKWELL 1700-1750 BECKLEY, SSX, ENG [35157] : 1850 LAMBETH, MDX, ENG [35256] : 1890 ORPINGTON, KEN, ENG [36887] : ALL WORLDWIDE [37698]

BUDD 1816-1833 WOLLOMBI, NSW, AUS [35422] : PRE 1871 READING, BRK, ENG [34116] : 1690S MEDSTEAD, HAM, ENG [34909] : PRE 1758 CANDOVER, KEN, ENG [35016] : H. HAYWARD 1780+ GREAT MISSENDEN, BKM, ENG [36880] : HOPEWELL H. 1780+ MDX, ENG [36880] : 1800-1850 KENSINGTON, LND, ENG [37321] : ALL CON & DEV, ENG [38735] : 1790-1830 CASHEL, TIP & LND, IRL & ENG [35422] : PRE 1777 RYE, NY, USA [37473]

BUDDE ALL RHODEN, SLP, GER [38637] : 1700+ BREMEN, BRM, GER & BRD [35062]

BUDDEN 1838+ MUSWELLBROOK, NSW, AUS [34426] : PRE 1839 PORTSMOUTH, HAM, ENG [34166] : ALL WORLDWIDE [37084]

BUDDENDORFF ALL BERLIN, BLN, GER [38637]

BUDDLE DORATHY PRE 1910 MONTGOMERY CO., NY, USA [36950]

BUDDON 1838+ MUSWELLBROOK, NSW, AUS [35740] : PRE 1838 TOLLARD, WIL, ENG [35740]

BUDDS 1852+ BUNINYONG, VIC, AUS [35498] : 1837+ MELBOURNE, VIC, AUS & IRL [35498] : 1830+ LAUNCESTON, TAS, AUS & IRL [35498] : 1820S CARLOW, CAR, IRL & AUS [35498]

BUDEN SARAH 1800 BERE FERRERS, DEV, ENG [35471]

BUDGE 1860-1890 ORANGE, NSW, AUS [34422] : PRE 1890 CHARTERS TOWERS, QLD, AUS [35339] : ALL NSW, AUS [37308] : 1800 SKYE, INV, SCT [33918] : 1800-1900 GLASGOW, LKS, SCT [34557]

BUDGEL ALL NFD, CAN [35619] : 1820S SOUTH BARROW, SOM, ENG [35815]

BUDGEN PRE 1900 SOUTH WEST, ENG [38594]

BUDREY ALL SFK, ENG [37629]

BUELL 1550-1650 CHESTERTON, HUN, ENG [37783] : C1700 FARNHAM, HAM, ENG [37898] : 1630-1781 HARTFORD CO., CT, USA [36310]

BUER PRE 1876 KINGSTON, LND, ENG [35827]

BUETER ANNA ANGELA PRE 1850 HASELUNNE, NSA, BRD [34481]

BUETTEL ALL WORLDWIDE [35115]

BUFFAM PRE 1881 ONT, CAN [38434]

BUFFETT 1600+ NFD, CAN [34490] : ALL CAN [34490] : MARTHA PRE 1825 DUNCHIDEOCK, DEV, ENG [35788] : 1750+ HOLCOMBE BURNELL, DEV, ENG [36813] : ALL UK [34490] : ALL USA [34490]

BUFFEY PRE 1821 BATH, SOM, ENG [35824]

BUFFINGTON 1800-1850 MARSHALL CO., GA & MS, USA [35307]

BUGBEE C1800S ASHTABULA CO., OH, USA [37562] : 1800-1900 MADISON CO., NY, USA [37586]

BUGDEN 1852-1900 CAMDEN, NSW, AUS [33766] : 1750-1870 DONHEAD ST MARY, WIL, ENG [33766]

BUGG PRE 1760 WHELNETHAM, SFK, ENG [37253] : PRE 1860 DRINKSTONE & HESSETT, SFK, ENG [38077]

BUGGE 1700 VITZDORF, FEHMARN, BRD [35873]

BUGGINS PRE 1799 LONDON, MDX, ENG [35895]

BUGLAR ALL WORLDWIDE [37244]

BUGLER ALL WORLDWIDE [37244]

BUHLER ALL ENG [35177]

BUHMANN C1738 BELDORF, SHO, GER [38671]

BUIE (SEE BOWIE) [34126]

BUIRNS 1856+ WILLIAMSTOWN, VIC, AUS [34037] : PRE 1856 EGLISH, OFF, IRL [34037]

BUISSARD PRE 1844 FRA [38605] : 1800S NY, USA [38605]

BUIST C1850 N OTTAWA, ONT, CAN [34527] : 1820S LAN, ENG [38281]

BUKOWSKI 1750-1870 GDANSK AREA, POL [35153] : ALL WORLDWIDE [35153]

BULCOCK 1855 DARWEN, LAN, ENG [36679]

BULFORD ALL WORLDWIDE [36671]

BULGER PRE 1900 LIVERPOOL, LAN, ENG [34999] : PRE 1900 WEST LONDON, ENG [37062] : RICHARD 1830+ MANCHESTER, LAN, ENG [37083] : RICHARD PRE 1810 DUBLIN, IRL [37083]

BULGIN ALL DOWLISH WAKE, SOM, ENG [34428] : 1795+ BRADFORD ON AVON, WIL, ENG [36276]

BULICEK PRE 1890 MORAVIA, OES [35290]

BULKA ALL WORLDWIDE [35783]

BULL GEORGE 1820+ MT PROSPECT & PENTRIDGE, VIC, AUS [33996] : 1900+ JUNEE, NSW, AUS [34446] : 1910-1939 WEST BRUNSWICK, VIC, AUS [35047] : 1882-1902 HAMILTON, VIC, AUS [35047] : 1800S-1900S NIMBI, NSW, AUS [35117] : PRE 1700 LUE, BRD [38561] : PRE 1850 KILMERSDON, SOM, ENG [34314] : 1858 WOOLWICH, KEN, ENG [34446] : PRE 1800 PADBURY, BKM, ENG [34588] : PRE 1776 HOUGHTON, HUN, ENG [34734] : ALL KETTLESTONE, NFK, ENG [34758] : C1840 NORTHWOOD, HAM, ENG [34812] : PRE 1758 CANDOVER, KEN, ENG [35016] : PRE 1870 NEWBURY, BRK, ENG [35031] : PRE 1850 BREMHILL, WIL, ENG [35045] : PRE 1837 BIRMINGHAM, WAR, ENG [35047] : 1820S EXETER, DEV, ENG [35259] : 1840S PARR, LAN, ENG [35259] : 1785+ BECKLEY, SSX, ENG [35587] : PRE 1819 SOUTHAMPTON, HAM, ENG [36079] : PRE 1842 NORTH CRAWLEY, BKM, ENG [36302] : 1750+ NORTH ASTON, OXF & BRK, ENG [36329] : MARY PRE 1730 GLOUCESTER & BRISTOL, GLS, ENG [36590] : C1820 LIDLINGTON, BDF, ENG [36803] : ALL EYDON, NTH, ENG [36922] : ALL OXFORD, OXF, ENG [36922] : C1824 HITCHAM, SFK, ENG [37302] : PRE 1862 MDX, ENG [37358] : C1728-1760 EASTCHEAP, LND, ENG [37494] : 1800S NTT, ENG [37570] : ALL DBY & STS, ENG [37661] : C1750-1850 ENG [37790] : 1740-1840 CREWKERNE, SOM, ENG [38028] : 1600-1700 DONNINGTON, GLS, ENG [38342] : 1820-1860 MEK, GER [35317] : 1700+ STUBBENDORF, SHO, GER [37542] : 1846+ NOR & AUS [38212] : 1837-1849 CHRISTCHURCH, NZ [35047] : 1855-1893 ZILWAUKEE, MI, USA [35317] : C1760 FREDERICK CO., VA, USA [37788]

BULLAMORE PRE 1865 WAKEFIELD, YKS, ENG [34384]

BULLARD 1790-1850 LEEDS, ONT, CAN [38097] : 1740 SPALDING, LIN, ENG [35369] : 1850-1990 DECATUR, IA, USA [38097]

BULLEN 1840+ MELBOURNE, VIC, AUS [34174] : PRE 1888 BRIGHTON, SSX, ENG [33832] : C1834 WIMPOLE, CAM, ENG [35202] : ALL WEYMOUTH, DOR, ENG [35259] : 1770-1850 BICKERSTAFFE, LAN, ENG [36112] : 1900S KEN, ENG [36222] : PRE 1840 CON, ENG [37107] : ALL SFK, ENG [37629] : 1850+ ISLINGTON, MDX, ENG [37677] : ALL DALSTON, LAN, ENG [38502] : JONATHON 1812 THOMPSON & ROCKY RIVER, NFK & NSW, ENG & AUS [36371]

BULLENT PRE 1850 NFK, ENG [36067]

BULLER 1700-1800 HALESWORTH, SFK, ENG [34469] : ALL SOM, ENG [34730] : 1750-1850 HADDENHAM, CAM, ENG [35595] : PRE 1792 LEWANNICK, CON, DEV & SOM, ENG [36039]

BULLERING ALL GER [34861]

BULLETT 1700+ BUXHALL, SFK, ENG [35475]

BULLEY 1820 ENG [34565]

BULLIANS PRE 1850 NS, CAN [34610] : PRE 1800 LITTLE DUNKELD, PER, SCT [34610]

BULLING 1800S LONDON, ENG [33982]

BULLINGER 1700-1800 SPEIER, RPR, GER [38765] : 1800+ LANDAU, ODESSA, SU [38765]

BULLIONS PRE 1800 LITTLE DUNKELD, PER, SCT [34610]

BULLIVANT PRE 1838 OAKHAM, RUT, ENG [37892]

BULLOCH C1900+ MAN, CAN [34213] : 1800+ CUMBERNAULD, DNB, SCT [36875] : 1600-1780 DNB & LKS, SCT [37456] : C1850-1910 MO, USA [34213]

BULLOCK JOSEPH 1834+ BATHURST & DUBBO, NSW, AUS [34019] : JOSEPH 1834+ MELBOURNE, VIC, AUS [34019] : BENJAMIN 1834+ BATHURST, NSW, AUS [34019] : WILLIAM 1860+ BENDIGO, MELBOURNE, VIC, AUS [35059] : 1860+ HOMEBUSH, VIC, AUS [35529] : 1856+ MT FROME & MUDGEE, NSW, AUS [35567] : 1850+ NEW ENGLAND, NSW, AUS [37889] : PRE 1800 SRY & KEN, ENG [34383] : JOHN 1836 BIRMINGHAM, WAR, ENG [34586] : PRE 1900 CANNOCK, STS, ENG [34711] : SAMUEL 1837+ ST ENODER, CON, ENG [35059] : PRE 1842 LANHYDROCK & ST WINNOW, CON, ENG [35459] : GEORGE PRE 1700 DBY, ENG [35897] : PRE 1845 MANCHESTER, LAN, ENG [36513] : ALL LONDON, ENG [36834] : 1700+ WOBURN, BDF, ENG [36987] : PRE 1750 STS, ENG [37098] : 1841 HARDINGTON MANDEVILLE, SOM, ENG [37378] : 1600S+ CHEADLE, STS, ENG [37413] : ALL WESTBURY ON SEVERN, GLS, ENG [37742] : PRE 1750 BLAISDON, GLS, ENG [37763] : PRE 1630 ESS, ENG [38135]

BULLOT EUGENE 1817 FRA [37165] : 1841 NEW PLYMOUTH, NZ [37165]

BULLOWS 1800+ MDX & ESS, ENG [35975]

BULMAN 1850-1910 NEWCASTLE ON TYNE, NBL, ENG [34551]

BULMER 1850+ TAREE, NSW, AUS [34690] : RICHARD 1750+ YKS, ENG [36291] : C1811 SKILTON, NRY, ENG [37627] : 1890+ EGGLESCLIFFE, NRY, ENG [37627] : 1730S+ ST OSWALDS, DUR, ENG [38269] : ALL HOVINGHAM & LEAVENING, YKS, ENG [38421] : ALL WORLDWIDE [38329]

BULMERINGK PRE 1700 LUE, BRD [38561]

BULPIN 1800+ BRIDGEWATER, SOM, ENG [34815]

BULPIT C1800 LOCKERLEY, HAM, ENG [38700]

BULPITT PRE 1800 ANDOVER, HAM, ENG [37693]

BULSON PRE 1804 HULL, YKS, ENG [37383] : 1800S CASTLE CARY, SOM, ENG [37818]

BULT C1780 KINGSTON ST MARY, SOM, ENG [34926] : 1800 FALMOUTH, CON, ENG [37186]

BULTER 1860-1870 KEWEENAW CO., MI, USA [38010]

BULTITUDE 1821 MARTHAM, NFK, ENG [34539]

BUMANN PRE 1800 OLDENBURG, SHO, GER [38648]

BUMBA PRE 1867 SUCHDOL, TREBON, CS [36338]

BUMBY ALL ESS, ENG [36136]

BUMFORD PRE 1677 ILMINGTON, GLS, ENG [37909]

BUNBY PRE 1830 BAWTRY, YKS, ENG [33959]

BUNCE 1800S LONDON, ENG [34472] : WALTER 1850+ ISLINGTON, LND, ENG [34915] : 1700+ WOOTTON RIVERS, WIL, ENG [35874] : PRE 1800 BURBAGE, WIL, ENG [38700] : JAMES 1800-1850 FALLS VILLAGE, CT, USA [33752] : LOUIS 1880S GROVELAND, MA, USA [33752] : TOM 1612-1682 HARTFORD, CT, USA [33752] : LOUIS 1900S DES MOINES, IA, USA [33752]

BUNCH PRE 1751 YATELEY, HAM, ENG [34689] : ALL USA [34981] : C1790 BEDFORD CO., VA, USA [37527]

BUNCIS PRE 1910 ESTRAPOLIA, KIEV, RUSSIA [34127]

BUNCLARKE 1810+ BUCKFASTLEIGH, DEV, ENG [34700] : ALL STAVERTON, DEV, ENG [34700]

BUNDEY 1800+ AUS [34194] : 1750-1850 LONDON, ENG [34194] : 1750-1850 BEAULIEU & NEW FOREST, HAM, ENG [34194]

BUNDOCK 1855+ KOORALBYN, BEAUDESERT, QLD, AUS [36617] : 1820S TURNHAM GREEN, MDX, ENG [34709] : 1760S ESS, ENG [34709] : ALL ENG [34709] : 1820S SOUTHWARK, SRY, ENG [34709] : 1836-1913 EXTON, HAM & LND, ENG [36049] : PRE 1835 PAIGNTON, DEV, ENG [36617]

BUNDWICK 1760S ESS, ENG [34709]

BUNDY 1825-1860 WAYNE CO., TN, USA [38088]

BUNESS PRE 1900 WOOLWICH, KEN, ENG [35548]

BUNGAY ALL ALDERBURY, WIL, ENG [38357] : ALL WORLDWIDE [37855] : ALL WORLDWIDE [38357]

BUNGEY 1773 ALDERBURY, WIL, ENG [35369] : ALL ALDERBURY, WIL, ENG [38357] : ALL WORLDWIDE [37855] : ALL WORLDWIDE [38357]

BUNGY ALL WORLDWIDE [37855]

BUNING ALL ENG [38229]

BUNK ALL OSTERIESLAND, NDS, BRD [38685] : ALL WORLDWIDE [38599]

BUNKE 1700-1800 RODENSLEBEN, PSA, GER [38643]

BUNKER 1700+ AMERSHAM, BKM, ENG [34416] : ALL NORTHAMPTON CO., VA, USA [36557]

BUNKIN PRE 1839 MDX, ENG [34876]

BUNKWORTH PRE 1803 ENG & AUS [34873]

BUNN PRE 1800 ORMESBY NR FILBY, NFK, ENG [35173] : 1800S BETHNAL GREEN, LND, ENG [36055] : PRE 1815 BKM, ENG [36086] : MARY 1755-1826 NORWICH, NFK, ENG [37052] : C1800-1850 CHERTSEY, SRY, ENG [37618] : 1819 KENDLESTONE, WIC, IRL [35369]

BUNNEG 1841-1872 SALZWEDEL, SAXONY, DDR [36317]

BUNNETT PRE 1820 BRECKLES, NFK, ENG [35587]

BUNNIG 1700+ GREBIN, SHO, GER [37170]

BUNNING 1800+ STAMFORD, LIN, ENG [37202] : ALL ENG [38229] : 1800+ GREBIN, SHO, GER [37170]

BUNNY 1650-1700 ST TEATH, CON, ENG [34448]

BUNNYNGE ALL ENG [38229]

BUNSTER 1830+ HOBART, TAS, AUS [36622]

BUNSTONE ALL SOUTH PETHERTON, SOM, ENG [37558]

BUNT 1843+ SYDNEY, NSW, AUS [35452] : 1891+ BARCALDINE, QLD, AUS [35452] : C1840 CAMDEN, NSW, AUS [37968] : 1862+ WOODBRIDGE, ONT, CAN [38187]

BUNTING PRE 1800 SOHAM, CAM, ENG [34445] : ALL THURNING, NFK, ENG [37050] : 1810 HEACHAM, NFK, ENG [37452] : 1800+ NEWINGTON, SRY, ENG [38247] : 1740-1890 BARONY, LKS, SCT [37872] : 1900S NM, USA [37050] : 1900S CO, USA [37050] : 1900S AZ, USA [37050] : 1900S UT, USA [37050] : 1700-1900 WORLDWIDE [36977]

BUNWORTH ALL WORLDWIDE [38721]

BUNYAN ALL WORLDWIDE [36135]

BUNYARD 1800+ COOKHAM, BRK, ENG [34642] : 1800+ PAINGTON, DEV, ENG [34642] : 1800-1820 OH, USA [38137]

BUNYNG ALL ENG [38229]

BUNYNGE ALL ENG [38229]

BUNYON ALL LND, ENG & INDI [35997]

BUPELL 1800+ SAMPFORD PEVERELL, DEV, ENG [36069]

BURBAGE PRE 1715 ST CLEMENTS, TRURO, CON, ENG [35587] : ALL YEOVIL, SOM & DOR, ENG [37269] : PRE 1860 WORCESTER CO., MD, USA [38135]

BURBANK 1830+ COOLGARDIE, WA, AUS [37665]

BURBECK ALL WORLDWIDE [38244]

BURBERY 1808-1850 LONDON, ENG [36762]

BURBIDGE 1840-1859 CAMBERWELL, SRY, ENG [34860] : ALL EAST KNOYLE, WIL, ENG [34955] : WILLIAM 1700 LOUGHBOROUGH, LEI, ENG [36619] : 1700-1900 KEEVIL, WIL, ENG [37056] : PRE 1860 WIL, ENG [37320]

BURBRIDGE 1873 WINCHCOMBE, GLS, ENG [35761] : PRE 1828 KEW, SRY, ENG [36167] : 1850+ TOTTENHAM, MDX, ENG [36167] : 1700-1860 KEN, ENG [37015]

BURC PIERRE PRE 1760 MANTOU LIMOGE, LMS, FRA [38408]

BURCHALL PRE 1900 WORTHING & WEST TARRING, SSX, ENG [35978]

BURCHAN 1781 BOSTON, MA, USA [36358]

BURCHAT ALL WORLDWIDE [37293]

BURCHELL 1800S READING, BRK, ENG [34715] : PRE 1820 MDX, ENG [35255] : C1750 CITY OF LONDON, ENG [36010] : 1730S HUNTON, KEN, ENG [37909]

BURCHETT 1830+ TAS, AUS [33798] : 1758-1851 HURSTMONCEAUX, SSX, ENG [36280] : ALL WORLDWIDE [37293]

BURD ALL BOVEY TRACEY, DEV, ENG [35345] : ALL CREDITON, DEV, ENG [38411]

BURD (BIRD) [36278]

BURDA PRE 1867 BUDE JOVICE, TREBON, CS [36338]

BURDEKIN 1870+ HUNTER REGION, NSW, AUS [36632]

BURDEN JOHANNA 1820+ AUS [38075] : 1862-1864 ST PETER PORT, GSY, CHI [36301] : 1850+ KIDDERMINSTER, WOR, ENG [34113] : 1750+ KIDDERMINSTER, WOR, ENG [34711] : C1878 BIRMINGHAM, WAR, ENG [35807] : PRE 1790 PORTSEA, HAM, ENG [35973] : C1841 EBONY, KEN, ENG [35980] : 1824+ TENTERDEN, KEN, ENG [35980] : C1700-1850 CHALDON HERRING, DOR, ENG [36435] : C1700 SEMLEY, WIL, ENG [37691] : DANIEL 1821 BATHFORD, SOM, ENG [37800] : 1750+ MAIDSTONE, KEN, ENG [38075] : 1750+ ROLVENDEN, KEN, ENG [38075] : 1750+

QUEENBOROUGH, KEN, ENG [38075] : PRE 1770 DOR, ENG [38399] : ALL CON & DEV, ENG [38735] : 1800+ DEANSTON, PER, SCT [38726] : ELLEN 1848-1906 BATHFORD, WA, USA & ENG [37800]

BURDETT PRE 1900 EARLS BARTON, NTH, ENG [35637] : 1904+ LONDON, ENG [35939]

BURDEU 1819-1835 SRY, ENG & AUS [34267]

BURDG ALL BIBURY, GLS, ENG [35259]

BURDGE ALL SOM, ENG [38742]

BURDICK 1790-1890 ADELAIDE & MIDDLESEX CO., ONT, CAN [34375] : 1800-1850 CHATAUQUA CO., NY, USA [34375] : 1600-1800 WORLDWIDE [35289]

BURDIN C1850 TN, USA [38044]

BURDITT PRE 1900 EARLS BARTON, NTH, ENG [35637]

BURDOCK 1760+ LONDON, ENG [34230]

BURDON PRE 1960 WADEBRIDGE, CON, ENG [34657]

BURDT 1886-1990 CHARLEVOIX CO., MI, USA & DDR [38062]

BURDUS 1800+ ORANGE, NSW, AUS [37839] : 1800+ PARRAMATTA, NSW, AUS [37839] : 1700+ NTT, ENG [37839]

BURES PRE 1870 SAUNDERS CO., NE, USA [35290]

BURFIELD PRE 1800 SOMPTING, SSX, ENG [34112] : PRE 1880 BRIGHTON & HOVE, SSX, ENG [37768] : ALL CENTRE CO., PA, USA [37505]

BURFOOT ALL WORLDWIDE [37254]

BURFOOTE ALL WORLDWIDE [37254]

BURFORD 1860 GLS, ENG [36264] : 1830-50 STOURBRIDGE, WOR, ENG [37271]

BURFURD 1850+ CASTLEMAINE, VIC, AUS [37997]

BURG PRE 1700 ARLINGTON, GLS, ENG [35259] : 1700-1850 RHEIN BAVARIA, BAV, GER [38154] : 1850-1990 DES MOINES, IA, USA [38154] : 1890-1990 DALLAS CITY, IL, USA [38154]

BURGAR PRE 1810 PAPA WESTRAY, OKI, SCT [35346] : PRE 1780 HARDYSTON, NJ, USA [38480]

BURGE 1873 CASTLEMAINE, VIC, AUS [35479] : SIMON 1836+ SPAXTON, SOM, ENG [34630] : SAMUEL 1836+ SPAXTON, SOM, ENG [34630] : GEORGE PRE 1816 SPAXTON, SOM, ENG [34630] : CAROLINE 1806+ BRISTOL, ENG [34683] : PRE 1780 BENENDEN, KEN, ENG [35227] : 1790S NORTHLEACH, GLS, ENG [35259] : PRE 1872 CAMBORNE, CON, ENG [35479]

BURGER ALL FREIENWIL, AG, CH [38609] : C1828 PRE, GER [37022]

BURGES 1760S TONBRIDGE, KEN, ENG [35259]

BURGESS C1862+ ADELAIDE, SA, AUS [34035] : JOHN 1872+ COSTERFIELD, VIC, AUS [34171] : PRE 1850 BRIGHTON, VIC, AUS [34961] : 1860+ PARRAMATTA, NSW, AUS [34979] : 1850+ SOUTH CREEK (ST MARYS), NSW, AUS [35101] : MARY ANNE PRE 1820 HOBART, TAS, AUS [35217] : C1840 MAITLAND & BOLWARRA, NSW, AUS [38077] : 1850+ GREY CO., ONT, CAN [34051] : ALL ONT, CAN & ENG [35302] : 1700+ PORTSMOUTH, HAM, ENG [34006] : PRE 1860 CAMBRIDGE, CAM, ENG [34021] : ALL SUNDRIDGE & SEVENOAKS, KEN, ENG [34110] : ANN 1780-1840 STOKE ON TRENT, STS, ENG [34143] : 1800+ DUNCHURCH, WAR, ENG [34315] : 1800S SFK, ENG [34813] : 1600+ BATTLE & WESTFIELD, SSX, ENG [34939] : 1800+ SOUTHAMPTON, DOR, ENG [34970] : 1730+ POUGHILL, DEV, ENG [35027] : 1700-1900 SFK, ENG [35069] : PRE 1801 STOKE CHARITY, HAM, ENG [35247] : C1760 WESTFIELD, SSX, ENG [35259] : PRE 1824 TONBRIDGE, KEN, ENG [35259] : 1800+ BIRMINGHAM, WAR, ENG [35862] : PRE 1795 DACRE, WRY, ENG [36011] : PRE 1850

LEICESTER, LEI, ENG [36086] : PRE 1800 KINGS LYNN, NFK, ENG [36264] : PRE 1850 NANTWICH, CHS, ENG [36385] : 1800+ HAM, ENG [36662] : PRE 1800 EWHURST, SSX, ENG [36752] : PRE 1840 EAST GULDEFORD, SSX, ENG [36752] : PRE 1785 SRY, ENG [36811] : ALL LONDON, ENG [36834] : 1800+ SANDBACH & CONGLETON AREA, CHS, ENG [36997] : PRE 1816 RADFORD, NTT, ENG [37000] : PRE 1725 SHINFIELD & WOKINGHAM, BRK, ENG [37420] : 1834-38 HIGHBRAY, DEV, ENG [37863] : PRE 1830 BRISTOL, ENG [38289] : PRE 1833 SRY, ENG & AUS [34463] : C1840-1868 CAR, IRL [34035] : ALL MOG, IRL [34226] : PRE 1900 TULLOW, CAR, IRL [34784] : PRE 1866 TULLAMORE, OFF, IRL [35530] : PRE 1841 DFS, SCT [35090] : C1855+ LEITH, MLN, SCT [35486] : ALL BAN & MOR, SCT [37767] : PRE 1800 NEW YORK CITY, NY, USA [38435] : 1700-1850 FLOYD CO., KY, USA [38524] : PRE 1750 LOUISA CO., VA, USA [38538]

BURGESS SALSBURY ALL KETTERING, NTH, ENG [36830]

BURGETT C1778-1837 HAMPSHIRE CO., WV, USA [35284]

BURGHER 1800-1825 PA, USA [38201]

BURGIN PRE 1900 DBY, ENG [36216] : 1924 HASLAND, DBY & HUN, ENG [37723] : PHILIP ALL LONDON & MELBOURNE, MDX & VIC, ENG & AUS [35467]

BURGIS 1550+ UFFCULM, OAKFORD & N MOLTON, DEV, ENG [34747] : 1780-1860 LONDON, MDX, ENG [38396]

BURGISS 1700+ CRUDWELL, WIL, ENG [35248]

BURGOYNE 1900S MOSS VALE, NSW, AUS [35567] : C1788 KINGTON, HEF, ENG [34553] : 1900+ DEVONPORT, DEV, ENG [35989] : 1700+ OXFORD, OXF, ENG [36685]

BURHENNE 1697 WICKENRODE, GHE, GER [38748]

BURK 1870+ UNION CO., TN, USA [37004]

BURKART 1806+ GER [35465]

BURKE 1840-1990 QUEANBEYAN, NSW, AUS [33818] : JOHN 1864-1898 CHARTERS TOWERS, QLD, AUS [33933] : 1860+ VIC & SA, AUS [35190] : ALL VIC, AUS [35707] : C1850 MT ALEXANDER, VIC, AUS [35899] : 1850S KEILOR, VIC, AUS [36268] : JOHN 1830S BRAIDWOOD, NSW, AUS [37954] : 1860+ ABERDEEN & TAMWORTH, NSW, AUS [38760] : C1835+ MONTREAL, QUE, CAN [38406] : THOMAS 1828-1838 ST HELIER, JER, CHI [35494] : EDMOND F. 1827+ ST HELIER, JER, CHI [35494] : PRE 1856 GSY, CHI [38760] : 1848+ ASTON, WAR, ENG [34668] : PRE 1850 WANDSWORTH, SRY, ENG [36153] : 1800-1900 LAN, ENG [37761] : JOHN 1847-1864 KILRUSH & TULLABRACK, CLA, IRL [33933] : 1850+ LONDONDERRY, LDY, IRL [34256] : 1800+ GALWAY, GAL, IRL [34933] : 1850+ DERRY HASNA & CASTLECONNELL, LIM, IRL [34960] : 1750-1800 BRUFF, LIM, IRL [35228] : PATRICK C1800-1840 GAL, IRL [35389] : PRE 1824 GAL, IRL [35424] : THOMAS 1750-1825 DUBLIN, DUB, IRL [35494] : 1800-1950 BALLYMACARBERRY & CLONMEL, WAT, IRL [36565] : 1840+ BREDAGH, GAL, IRL [36815] : 1800S RATHNURE, WEX, IRL [36874] : 1700-1840 LETTERKENNY, DON, IRL [37118] : PRE 1840 KILTARTAN, GAL, IRL [37169] : 1814 OOLA, LIM, IRL [37540] : PRE 1870 ANTRIM, ANT, IRL [37636] : THOMAS C1840 KILLARNEY, KER, IRL [37664] : 1700-1850 IRL [37761] : C1830 SLI, IRL [38292] : PRE 1900 ENNIS, CLA, IRL [38484] : 1800+ MO & IL, USA [36574] : 1840-1900 SCHUYLKILL CO., PA, USA [38106] : ALL WORLDWIDE [34944]

BURKE (SEE BOURKE) [34424]

BURKENSHAW PRE 1842 GOULBURN, NSW, AUS [38008]

BURKERT 1871 WURBEN, SCHLESIEN, GER [38641] : 1726 MARKAUSCH, BOHMEN, OES [38641]

BURKET PRE 1790 NFK, ENG [34222]

BURKETT 1830 ST LUKES, MDX, ENG [34731]

BURKEY 1800-1870 ALBISHEIM, KIRKHEIM BOLANDEN, RHEIN-BEIREN, GER [38374]

BURKHARD 1840 REUCHELHEIM, STADT-ARNSTEIN, BRD [38327]

BURKHARDT PRE 1855 BAW, BRD [37545] : PRE 1854 ZWICKAU, SAX & PSA, GER [35251] : 1855+ JEFFERSON CO., IA, USA [37545]

BURKHART 1800+ GER [36342] : 1800+ EDWARDSVILLE, IL, USA [36342] : 1800+ ST LOUIS, MO, USA [36342]

BURKHEAD 1814 NC, USA [36908] : 1840-1860 TN, USA [36908]

BURKHERR PRE 1813 ELO, GER [38437]

BURKITT 1750-1850 SCREDINGTON & THREEKINGHAM, LIN, ENG [37096]

BURKMYRE C1900 RENTON, DNB, SCT [36835]

BURKS C1850 TN & GA, USA [36899] : PRE 1900 CHRISTIAN & GREEN, MD, USA [36899]

BURL C1700 FARNHAM, HAM, ENG [37898]

BURLAND ALL IRL [38769] : ALL WORLDWIDE [35627]

BURLEIGH 1800+ CASTLETON, ONT, CAN [34121] : PRE 1900 FLORENCE COURT, FER, IRL [35433]

BURLEY 1800+ OXF, ENG [35712] : PRE 1680 NOTTINGHAM, NTT, ENG [36532] : 1700+ LOWER GRAVENHURST, BDF, ENG [37304] : ALL TREGONY, CON, ENG [37730] : 1949+ CANTERBURY, NZ [35928]

BURLIGH 1800-1900 GLASGOW, SCT [36977]

BURLING 1801-1841 STRATFORD, ESS, ENG [33950] : PRE 1820 EASTRY, KEN, ENG [34281] : ALL CROYDON, SRY, ENG [34308]

BURLINGAME WILLIAM 1812-1900 CHARLESTOWN & SCRANTON, RI & PA, USA [36948]

BURMAN C1870 MELBOURNE, VIC, AUS [35089] : ALL GREAT YARMOUTH, NFK, ENG [34086] : C1806 LONDON, ENG [35089]

BURMESTER PRE 1746 HAMBURG, HBG, BRD [38659]

BURN PRE 1810 COAL PIT BANK, SAL, ENG [34711] : 1795 WES, ENG [34731] : PRE 1887 SEACROFT, YKS, ENG [37346] : PRE 1770 ST ANDREWS, FIF, SCT [35496]

BURNAND PRE 1920 TAUMARUNUI, NZ [33964]

BURNARD 1780-20 CON, ENG [38151] : ALL CON & DEV, ENG [38735]

BURNE 1750+ ENG [35060] : 1800+ BODMIN, CON, ENG [37457]

BURNELL C190 GREENBUSHES, WA, AUS [34223] : PRE 1850 CHUDLEIGH, DEV & LND, ENG [36396] : 1780S LONDON, ENG [37106]

BURNET 1800S BIDEFORD, DEV, ENG [34457] : 1500-1600 ERYHOLME, NRY, ENG [37633] : 1800-1855 HADDINGTON, ELN, SCT [35499] : C1750-1880 SC & TN, USA [38242]

BURNETT JOHN PRE 1875 SYDNEY, NSW, AUS [33807] : JOHN PRE 1875 BRIGHTON, SSX, ENG [33807] : 1775+ SFK, ENG [34416] : 1850+ PRESTONPANS, NBL, ENG [34614] : PRE 1850 LONDON, ENG [34671] : PRE 1680 KINGSWINFORD, STS, ENG [36110] : PRE 1850 LND, ENG [37057] : 1750-1820 CUL, ENG [37613] : PRE 1901 KNOTTINGLEY & HULL, WRY & ERY, ENG [38580] : 1850+ TODLEHILLS, ABD, SCT

[34374] : PRE 1850 ABD, SCT [35386] : ALL FRASERBURGH, ABD, SCT [36061] : JOSEPH C1802 COYLTON, AYR, SCT [37153] : 1820 + WAYNE CO., KY, USA [34203] : 1607 + NASHVILLE, TN & VA, USA [38743]

BURNEY C1850 ROCHESTER, NBL, ENG [35350]

BURNFIELD PRE 1820 PA, USA [34410]

BURNFORD 1700-1850 WALDSGRAVE, WAR, ENG [34004]

BURNHAM 1750 + CHARWELTON, NTH, ENG [34747] : C1806 ALFRETON, DBY, ENG [35249] : 1600 + NORWICH, NFK, ENG [35276] : 1750-1850 ROTHWELL, NTH, ENG [36057] : PRE 1581 NORWICH, NFK, ENG [36721] : C1760 CRIPPLEGATE, LND, ENG [37420] : PRE 1630 NORWICH, NFK, ENG [38135] : 1770 SHREWSBURY, VT, USA [38131]

BURNINGHAM 1865-1900 ALB, CAN [37402]

BURNISH ALL ENG [37377]

BURNITT PRE 1901 KNOTTINGLEY & HULL, WRY & ERY, ENG [38580]

BURNS 1870-1880 PATERSON, NSW, AUS [34182] : 1897 CUAN, NSW, AUS [34182] : 1880 + BAIRNSDALE, VIC, AUS [34563] : 1860 BRUNSWICK, VIC, AUS [34793] : 1850 + MAITLAND & SYDNEY, NSW, AUS [35237] : 1800-1900 SHOALHAVEN, NSW, AUS [35742] : 1865 + NSW, AUS [35807] : 1860 TALBOT, VIC, AUS [36640] : GEORGE 1850 SURRY HILLS, NSW, AUS [36640] : 1846 + DAWN TWP., ONT, CAN [34154] : PRE 1830 COLTON, LAN, ENG [34053] : PRE 1880 LAN, ENG [34958] : 1800 + DBY & STS, ENG [35019] : ALL NBL, ENG [35540] : PRE 1850 KIRBY IRELETH & ALL, CUL & LAN, ENG [36082] : 1870 + GREENWICH, LND, ENG [36237] : 1700 + COLTON, LAN & WES, ENG [36868] : 1770-1900 ST PANCRAS & MARYLEBONE, LND, ENG [37861] : ROBERT 1770 + LND, ENG [37861] : PRE 1841 TIP, IRL [34022] : ALL DOONBEG, CLA, IRL [34154] : PRE 1860 BELEEK, FER, IRL [34473] : 1820S CAV, IRL [34793] : C1800S BUNCRANA, DON, IRL [34887] : NORMAN 1850 + BELFAST, ANT, IRL [35084] : PRE 1853 + IRL [35237] : 1600 + BOYLE, ROS, IRL [35355] : C1800 CORK, COR, IRL [35512] : 1808-1831 GALLOON, FER, IRL [36281] : ROSE PRE 1841 + CARLOW, CAR, IRL [36314] : 1700-1900S LONDONDERRY, LDY, IRL [36796] : 1850 + CARRIGENAGH & KILKEEL, DOW, IRL [37405] : ROBERT PRE 1830 CAV & MOG, IRL [38391] : 1600-1850 KIRRIEMUIR, ANS, SCT [34004] : PRE 1750 ARBROATH, ANS, SCT [34053] : C1800 LKS, SCT [34127] : 1830-1850 STRAITON, AYR, SCT [34345] : MARTHA 1866 + LANARK, LKS, SCT [34627] : C1866 LKS, SCT [34756] : MARG 1850 AYR, SCT [34843] : 1850S DUNDEE, ANS, SCT [35007] : PRE 1850 GLASGOW, LKS, SCT [35863] : C1830 EDINBURGH, SCT [35906] : C1825 PER, SCT [36276] : 1800S GLASGOW & TOLCROSS, SCT [36706] : PRE 1750 CUPAR, FIF, SCT [37242] : C1725 ARBROATH, ANS, SCT [37242] : 1830-1875 EIKHART CO., IN, USA [36738] : ANNA 1835 + DEARBORN CO., IN, USA [37797] : JANE 1843 WEST HARRISON, DEARBORN CO., IN, USA [37797] : JAMES TURNER 1835 + HAMILTON CO., OH, USA [37797] : JAMES TURNER 1835 + DEARBORN CO., IN, USA [37797] : ANNA 1835 + HAMILTON CO., OH, USA [37797] : ROBERT 1770 + WORLDWIDE [37861]

BURNSIDE 1813-1884 EVANDALE, TAS, AUS [35195] : PRE 1900 LAN & YKS, ENG [38512]

BURNSIDES 1500-1630 IRL [37784]

BURR 1800 + COPLE, BDF, ENG [34315] : 1750 + ASHWELL, HRT, ENG [35592] : 1800 ST LEONARD, MDX, ENG [35756] : 1700S TUNBRIDGE WELLS, KEN, ENG [36665] : 1870 + NAVESTOCK, ESS, ENG & CAN [36050] : 1860 + FYFIELD, ESS, ENG & CAN [36050] : 1870 + NAVESTOCK, ESS, ENG & CAN [36050] : 1860 + FYFIELD, ESS, ENG & CAN [36050] : PRE 1840 NENAGH, TIP, IRL [35112] : C1900 OMAHA & LINCOLN, NE, USA [37467] : PRE 1885 + SANDUSKY, OH, USA [37467] : 1650-1750 MA, USA [38529] : 1620 + MA, USA [38746]

BURRAGE PRE 1800 HORSHAM, W SSX, ENG [34112] : C1810 GUNTON, SFK, ENG [35725] : 1847 + GREAT YARMOUTH, NFK, ENG [35725] : 1820 + CORTON, SFK, ENG [35725] : C1780-1820 LOUND, SFK, ENG [35725]

BURRAS 1750 + LEEDS, YKS, ENG [36087]

BURRELL MARTHA 1870 + COLEBROOK, TAS, AUS [35725] : 1880-1890 SOUTH MELBOURNE, VIC, AUS [35725] : 1857 + BENDIGO, VIC, AUS [35725] : 1869-1877 MATLOCK & WOODSPOINT, VIC, AUS [36836] : 1850 + BENDIGO, VIC, AUS [37497] : PRE 1800 LONDON, ENG [33869] : 1720-1785 STERNFIELD, SFK, ENG [34205] : PRE 1713 NORWICH, NFK, ENG [34222] : 1650-1720 SEDGEFIELD, DUR, ENG [34552] : 1790 ERY, ENG [34731] : PRE 1850 SMALLBURGH & SLOLEY, NFK, ENG [36048] : 1865 MDX, ENG [36287] : CATH 1800 + WEEDON, BKM, ENG [36471] : 1500-1900 STRATFORD, LND, ENG [36689] : 1750-1880 STERNFIELD, SFK, ENG [36833] : 1764 + STERNFIELD & SAXMUNDHAM, SFK, ENG [36836] : 1800 + COLCHESTER, ESS, ENG [38293] : 1915 + DANNEVIRKE, HAWKES BAY, NZ [35889] : 1878 + MANGAROA & WHITEMANS VALLEY, NZ [36836] : C1830-1860 JAMAICA, W.INDIES [35725]

BURRETT 1840 + YOUNG, NSW, AUS [36269]

BURRIDGE C1838 GREAT TORRINGTON, DEV, ENG [34898] : C1870 ACTON, MDX, ENG [35211] : PRE 1850 TEIGNMOUTH, DEV, ENG [35211] : PRE 1850 EXETER, DEV, ENG [36037] : ALL EATON BRAY, BDF, ENG [37746]

BURROUGHS 1780 + BENGAL ARMY &, GLS & LND, ENG [34109] : PRE 1740 SOHAM, CAM, ENG [34445] : 1800S BURNLEY, LAN, ENG [35638] : 1700 + BENGAL ARMY &, CAV, IRL &, INDIA [34109] : 1700 + BAGENALSTOWN, CAR, IRL [38498] : 1740S NEWTOWN, NY, USA [38038] : PRE 1850 JACKSON CO., MI, USA [38231] : PRE 1850 WHITEHALL, NY, USA [38231]

BURROW 1750-1850 WORKINGTON, CUL, ENG [34762] : C1824 MANCHESTER, LAN, ENG [35478]

BURROWES ALL GUYANA [35933] : PRE 1833 CORK, COR, IRL & AUS [34845] : ALL BARBADOS, W.INDIES [35933]

BURROWS JOSEPH 1901 + MELBOURNE, VIC, AUS [33797] : 1800 + BRISBANE, QLD, AUS [34271] : 1900 + DEE WHY, NSW, AUS [34271] : 1810 + TAS & VIC, AUS [36312] : ALL MILTON BRYAN, BDF, ENG [33797] : PRE 1860 TODDINGTON, BDF, ENG [33830] : PRE 1900 HODDESDON, HRT, ENG [33830] : PRE 1800 OLDHAM, LAN, ENG [33912] : PRE 1800 DEDDINGTON, OXF, ENG [34112] : PRE 1880 HOXTON, LND, ENG [34376] : 1760 EAST TISTED, HAM, ENG [34909] : C1863 CLERKENWELL, MDX, ENG [34926] : C1843 CAMBERWELL, SRY, ENG [35460] : MARTHA PRE 1851 WELLESLEY GVE CHELSEA, LND, ENG [35483] : 1800 + HAM, ENG [35566] : 1870S DEPTFORD, SRY, ENG [35727] : GEORGE 1736 +

HOUGHTON CONQUEST, BDF, ENG **[35805]** : PRE 1849 PURFLEET, ESS, ENG **[35863]** : PRE 1835 WAVENDON, BKM, ENG **[35955]** : PRE 1850 GRAPPENHALL, CHS, ENG **[35967]** : 1700-1850 TODDINGTON, BDF, ENG **[37306]** : 1800-1860 PINNER, MDX, ENG **[37376]** : 1850-1880 HOXTON, LND, ENG **[37376]** : 1840+ WETHERAL, CUL, ENG **[37635]** : 1800S DEVONPORT, DEV, ENG **[37833]** : 1800S BARDWELL, SFK, ENG **[37833]** : 1840+ WITHAM, ESS, ENG **[38244]** : 1834 GEORGETOWN, DEMERARA, GUIANA **[35130]** : ALL GUYANA **[35933]** : 1820S SLI, IRL **[34788]** : C1850 SLIGO, SLI, IRL **[36875]** : 1800+ KILMARNOCK, AYR, SCT **[34271]** : ALL SUSQUEHANNA CO., PA, USA **[36356]** : ALL BARBADOS, W.INDIES **[35933]**

BURRUP 1800S GLS, ENG **[35723]** : ALL WORLDWIDE **[38020]**

BURSLEM PRE 1901 GOONERY BORE, NSW, AUS **[34011]** : 1902+ BOURKE, NSW, AUS **[34011]** : 1850S+ PT CYGNET, TAS, AUS **[34011]** : PRE 1888 WOOLLAHRA, NSW, AUS **[34011]** : PRE 1765 STANTON, DBY, ENG **[34011]** : 1600-1700 WOOLSTANTON, STS, ENG **[38474]**

BURSNALL PRE 1851 GRANTHAM & HORNCASTLE, LIN, ENG **[36022]**

BURSON ALL WANTAGE, BRK, ENG **[38279]** : C1790 VA, USA **[38590]**

BURSTON PRE 1622 MILVERTON, SOM, ENG **[36604]** : ALL WIVERLIPSCOMBE, SOM, ENG **[37950]** : 1700+ SOM & LND, ENG & WLS **[37322]**

BURT 1850+ NSW, AUS **[33794]** : PRE 1870S COLAC, VIC, AUS **[34937]** : 1800+ WELLINGTON CO., ONT, CAN **[34215]** : GEORGE PRE 1816 LANGPORT, SOM, ENG **[34204]** : PRE 1880 CREWKERNE, SOM, ENG **[34730]** : 1810S+ KEN, ENG **[35108]** : PRE 1850 CHIPPING SODBURY, GLS, ENG **[35229]** : PRE 1800 NEWCASTLE ON TYNE, NBL, ENG **[35348]** : 1800S READING, BRK, ENG **[35899]** : C1700 BATCOMBE, SOM, ENG **[35899]** : 1700S LONDON, ENG **[35899]** : PRE 1890 FALMOUTH, CON, ENG **[35962]** : PRE 1890 PENRYN, CON, ENG **[35962]** : ALL LONDON, ENG **[36834]** : PRE 1882 EAST GRINSTEAD, SSX, ENG **[36967]** : 1800+ HARBLEDOWN, KEN, ENG **[36987]** : PRE 1845 ENG & USA **[36748]** : PRE 1825 FALKIRK, STI, SCT **[33906]** : C1830 CARNWATH, LKS, SCT **[34556]** : PRE 1920 EAST WEMYSS, FIF, SCT **[34605]** : 1830S DUNFERMLINE, FIF, SCT **[34618]** : C1780 EDINBURGH, MLN, SCT **[34713]** : 1845 HOLYTOWN, RFW, SCT **[34761]** : ALL COCKPEN, MLN, SCT **[35854]** : 1750-1768 DIGHTON, MA, USA **[35314]**

BURTENSHAW PRE 1829+ BRIGHTON, SSX, ENG **[34423]**

BURTENSHAW COX 1800S ENG **[35024]**

BURTON GEORGE 1857+ O'CONNELL, NSW, AUS **[34030]** : 1700+ DELORAINE, TAS, AUS **[35355]** : JAMES 1800S+ NSW, AUS **[35831]** : 1830+ LYNDHURST, NSW, AUS **[36316]** : 1850 BLAYNEY, NSW, AUS **[36641]** : RALPH PRE 1876 ONT, CAN **[35641]** : MAUDE 1876+ ONT, CAN **[35641]** : EDWARD 1809-1876 VICTORIA CO., ONT, CAN **[37441]** : ALL ROSSENDALE, LAN, ENG **[34564]** : 1700S SOM, DOR & WIL, ENG **[34739]** : WILLIAM 1800-1900 AMERSHAM VALE & DEPTFORD, LND, ENG **[34749]** : ALL SNITTERFIELD, WAR, ENG **[34823]** : JOSEPH 1780S WAR, ENG **[34823]** : ALL DYNCHURCH & COVENTRY, WAR, ENG **[34823]** : PRE 1795 WESTMINSTER, MDX, ENG **[35114]** : PRE 1600 ESS, ENG **[35642]** : PRE 1820 MUNDON & MALDON, ESS, ENG **[35902]** : 1800+ ELTHAM,

KEN, ENG **[35947]** : 1800+ N W KENT, KEN, ENG **[36104]** : 1800+ BRIGHTON, SSX, ENG **[36219]** : 1800+ LOUTH, LIN, ENG **[36241]** : 1838 LEI, ENG **[36287]** : 1800+ STS & WAR, ENG **[36587]** : 1839+ MEDWAY, KEN, ENG **[37051]** : 1800 AYLSHAM, NFK, ENG **[37170]** : PRE 1800 COVENTRY, WAR, ENG **[37225]** : PRE 1900 YKS, ENG **[37377]** : PRE 1850 GREAT YARMOUTH, NFK, ENG **[37385]** : PRE 1844 GOLBORNE, LAN, ENG **[37573]** : C1800 EASTWICK, HRT, ENG **[37718]** : PRE 1780 HAGLEY, WOR, ENG **[37736]** : PRE 1800 NTT, ENG **[37739]** : PRE 1800 BRINDLE & GORTON, LAN, ENG **[37893]** : 1700-1899 CLONFEACLE AREA, TYR, IRL **[36080]** : WILLIAM 1870-1898 TIPPERARY, TIP, IRL **[37135]** : MARGARET C1864 GLEN AHERLOWE, TIP, IRL **[37135]** : THOMAS C1860 TIP, IRL & ENG **[37135]** : 1800+ BEATH & MARKINCH, FIF, SCT **[33970]** : ALL COCKPEN, MLN, SCT **[35854]** : 1780-1850 FRANKLIN CO., GA, USA **[38107]** : ALL GRANVILLE CO., NC, USA **[38190]** : ALL WI, USA **[38230]** : 1800+ GREENUP, IL, USA **[38343]**

BURTON-PYE 1750+ SOUTHREPPS, NFK, ENG **[37276]**

BURTROYD 1800 EAST FERRY, LIN, ENG **[37448]**

BURVILL 1750-1850 KINGSTON, KEN, ENG **[37880]**

BURWELL WILLIAM HENRY 1835 ONT, CAN **[37788]** : C1794 FREDERICK, VA, USA **[34573]** : ALL WORLDWIDE **[36651]**

BURY 1800 BURNLEY, LAN, ENG **[35638]** : 1600-1800 FIF, SCT **[35627]** : ANN 1850S KIRKCALDY, FIF, SCT **[35752]**

BUSBY 1848+ QUE, CAN **[34528]** : 1900S CAMBERWELL, SRY, ENG **[36633]**

BUSCALL 1780-1840 NORWICH, NFK, ENG **[34307]**

BUSCH 1800-1900 HOPSTEN & ROTTERDAM, WEF & ZH, FRG & NL **[38712]** : PRE 1855 RUDESHEIM, HEN, GER **[35864]** : LEWIS 1710-1737 GER **[37784]**

BUSCHE ALL LIEKWEGEN, SLP, GER **[38637]**

BUSELMAYER PRE 1865 OSTERBURKEN, BAD, GER **[37819]**

BUSENIUS 1800+ PRE, GER **[36683]** : 1850 RENSTI OR JOSEPHIN, POL **[36683]**

BUSER 1870-1880 CINCINNATI, OH, USA **[38238]**

BUSH C1854+ BALLARAT, VIC, AUS **[34591]** : 1853+ GEELONG, VIC, AUS **[35379]** : HESTER C1760 SOM, ENG **[34065]** : PRE 1800 ORSETT & EASTWOOD, ESS, ENG **[34204]** : ALL GREAT WALTHAM, ESS, ENG **[34460]** : PRE 1850 BRISTOL, GLS, ENG **[34591]** : 1800+ SEAHAM HARBOUR, DUR, ENG **[35364]** : PRE 1850 WEST HARPTREE, SOM, ENG **[35378]** : PRE 1853 ENGLISHCOMB, SOM, ENG **[35379]** : PRE 1852 BRISTOL, GLS, ENG **[35379]** : PRE 1825 HACKFORD, NFK, ENG **[35411]** : 1825+ HACKNEY, LND, ENG **[35411]** : PRE 1750 ESS, ENG **[35642]** : C1874 ULVERSTON, LAN, ENG **[35887]** : PRE 1750 ALFORD, LIN, ENG **[36148]** : 1750-1850 ROCKBOURNE, HAM, ENG **[36155]** : PRE 1840 WORMEGAY, NFK, ENG **[36363]** : 1700 HAPTON, NFK, ENG **[36483]** : PRE 1800 SAFFRON WALDEN, ESS, ENG **[37749]** : 1845 LAUREN CO., KY, USA **[38103]**

BUSHBY 1750+ MUKER, NRY, ENG **[35891]** : PRE 1820 LONDON, ENG **[36469]**

BUSHELL PRE 1860 LIVERPOOL, LAN, ENG **[35114]** : 1790+ PIMLICO, MDX, ENG **[35114]** : PRE 1840 LND, ENG **[35902]** : PRE 1780 SHALBOURNE, WIL, ENG **[37687]** : ALL WOTTON UNDER EDGE, GLS, ENG **[37746]**

BUSHER ALL LONDON, ENG **[37728]**

BUSHILL 1800-62 WESTMINSTER, LND, ENG
[37863]
BUSHING PRE 1850 BRD [38238]
BUSHNELL PRE 1776 LONG CRENDON, BKM,
ENG [36866] : PRE 1810 READING, BRK, ENG
[37300] : ALL OXF & BRK, ENG [37373]
BUSICK 1750-1850 DORCHESTER CO., MD, NC &
IN, USA [36901]
BUSIKO 1800+ STERLITSCH, MEK, GER [35465]
BUSKILL 1715 YORK, YKS, ENG [34939]
BUSLEN ALL WORLDWIDE [36006]
BUSS PRE 1700 KEN, ENG [36588] : 1800-1840
ARDLEIGH, ESS, ENG [36987] : 1750-1800 SRY,
ENG [37340]
BUSSELL WILLIAM G. C1800-1840 EAST
STONEHOUSE, DEV, ENG [35955] : 1795+
BAMPTON, DEV, ENG [37902] : C1840 BURSTOCK,
DOR, ENG [37983]
BUSSELMAJOR PRE 1865 OSTERBURKEN, BAD,
GER [37819]
BUSSER PRE 1750 CAMBERG, RPF, GER [38681]
BUSSEY 1650-1775 EAST RUDHAM, NFK, ENG
[37222]
BUSSLER 1700-1850 GUNDERSHEIM, RPF, BRD
[38530]
BUSSWELL PRE 1785 EVINGTON, LEI, ENG [34501]
BUST 1891 NOTTINGHAM, NTT, ENG [35391] :
1866+ CHRISTCHURCH, NZ [34653]
BUSUTTIL 1700-1900 ZEITUN, MALTA [38070]
BUSWELL C1833 WOOTTON, OXF, ENG [35910]
BUT 1730-1750 BRISSEL, BEZIERS, LGD, FRA [38681]
BUTCHARD C1808 PRESCOT, LAN, ENG [36112] :
PRE 1775 INCHTURE, PER, SCT [33873]
BUTCHER 1911 COBRAM, VIC, AUS [36279] : C1900
MILDURA, VIC, AUS [36279] : 1884+ ADELAIDE,
SA, AUS [36309] : PRE 1850 HASELBURY
PLUCKNETT, SOM, ENG [33850] : PRE 1825
HOLLINGBOURNE, KEN, ENG [34105] : PRE 1890
LEE, LND, KEN & SRY, ENG [34325] : C1800+
SAFFRON WALDEN, ESS, ENG [34451] : ALL IOW,
HAM, ENG [34724] : 1819 SHOREDITCH, MDX,
ENG [34726] : 1800+ ESS, ENG [34818] : PRE 1750
SFK, ENG [35642] : PRE 1750 ESS, ENG [35642] :
1785+ LONGBRIDGE DEVERILL, DEV, ENG
[36771] : 1809+ WARMINSTER, WIL, ENG [36771] :
C1850 SOUTHAMPTON, HAM, ENG [37063] : 1830S
TILTY, ESS, ENG [37151] : SARAH 1753 SFK, ENG
[37250] : 1800-1900 KEN, ENG [37403] : 1800-1900
SSX, ENG [37403] : C1850 PETERBOROUGH, CAM,
ENG [37847] : 1700-1850 RUDGEWICK, SSX, ENG
[38287] : 1800+ WHEELY & COLCHESTER, ESS,
ENG [38395] : 1800+ NORWICH, NFK, ENG &
AUS [34591] : 1640+ RI, USA [38015]
BUTIN JEAN 1750 PARIS, FRA [37801]
BUTLER 1820+ NSW, AUS [34996] : C1810 SYDNEY,
NSW, AUS [35089] : 1860+ BROOKFIELD, QLD,
AUS [36286] : 1855+ IPSWICH, QLD, AUS [36865] :
NATHANIEL PRE 1850 ONONDAGA TWP.
BRANT CO., ONT, CAN [34347] : 1832-1900
HASTINGS CO., ONT, CAN [34996] : 1910+ ELM
CREEK, MAN, CAN [34996] : 1889-1910 LONDON,
ONT, CAN [34996] : 1832-1850 COLBORNE, ONT,
CAN [34996] : 1810-1850 CAN [35317] : CHRISTINA
1900+ WINDSOR, ONT, CAN [36678] : PRE 1900
NB, CAN & IRL [36933] : 1800S BEDWORTH, WAR,
ENG [33934] : PRE 1822 CANTERBURY, KEN,
ENG [34043] : 1840S CHELTENHAM, GLS, ENG
[34191] : 1800+ BARROWFORD, LAN, ENG [34564]
: PRE 1900 GATESHEAD, DUR, ENG [34858] : 1780-
1840 FROME, SOM, ENG [34996] : PRE 1850
NANTWICH, CHS, ENG [35229] : THOMAS 1700+
LND, ENG [35429] : 1880 HEBBURN QUAY, NBL,

ENG [35756] : 1850 ST GEORGE IN EAST, MDX,
ENG [35756] : C1835 BRIXTON, SRY, ENG [35764] :
1797-1887 CAMBERWELL, SRY, ENG [36049] : PRE
1800 WEDNESBURY & BILSTON, STS, ENG
[36110] : 1720-1830 RAMPTON, NTT, ENG [36426] :
1850-1880 CAMBERWELL, SRY, ENG [36586] : 1600-
1700 POULTON, LAN, ENG [36618] : 1750-1850
HIGH WYCOMBE, BKM, ENG [36708] : PRE 1610
WORCESTER, WOR, ENG [36976] : PRE 1610
KINGS NORTON, WAR, ENG [36976] : C1800
LONDON, MDX, ENG [36978] : ROBERT PRE 1799
BURGH ST MARGARET, NFK, ENG [37052] : PRE
1850 GLASTONBURY, SOM, ENG [37067] : 1800
CHRISTCHURCH, HAM, ENG [37173] : 1800S LIN,
ENG [37352] : PRE 1860 SHRIVENHAM, BRK, ENG
[37357] : 1800+ CHETTON, SAL, ENG [37406] : PRE
1900 ESS, ENG [37668] : PRE 1830 SHEFFIELD,
WRY, ENG [37875] : 1764+ DINTON, WIL, ENG
[37909] : 1850+ HACKNEY, LND, ENG [37983] :
PRE 1710 NORTH FAWLEY, BRK, ENG [38375] :
1800+ STANTON ST JOHN, OXF, ENG [38375] :
PRE 1870 CAMBRIDGE & GRANTCHESTER,
CAM, ENG [38403] : ALL LIN & VIC, ENG & AUS
[34301] : 1800+ THURLES, TIP, IRL [33963] : 1800+
INISTOIGE, KIK, IRL [34415] : 1750-1840 KIK, IRL
[34753] : ALL IRL [34938] : 1830-1860 ATHLONE,
WEM, IRL [35151] : PRE 1870 DUBLIN, IRL [35400] :
ALL GOREY, WEX, IRL [35474] : MARY ALL IRL
[35529] : 1720+ KILKINNEY, WIC, IRL [37802] :
1805-1830 EAST CLONEA, WAT, IRL [38117] : PRE
1901 HAMILTON CO. & RICHMOND, OH, TN &
VA, USA [35270] : 1830-1870 MI, USA [35317] : 1800-
1920 WESTCHESTER, NY, USA [36445] : 1752-1765
CHARLOTTE CO., VA, USA [36554] : 1752-1765
LUNENBURG CO., VA, USA [36554] : 1770+ GA,
USA [36974] : 1791 GREENVILLE, NY, USA [37086] :
RUTH J. 1828-1918 BATH, NY & IL, USA [37596] :
JOHN 1800-1870 MAYNARD, MA, USA [37806] :
1695-1946 AL & TX, USA [37812] : 1695-1946 ME, VA
& KY, USA [37812] : PRE 1800 MD, USA [38196] :
1700-1899 VA, USA [38366] : DEMA IRENE C1817
LEWIS CO., NY, USA [38431] : SOLWEIG 1986+
BELLINGHAM, WA, USA [38560] : ABIGAIL 1767
MA & CT, USA [38734] : PRE 1850 ANTIGUA,
W.INDIES [35413] : PRE 1850 PEM, WLS [35413] :
WILLIAM C1780 PEM, WLS [36452] : ELIZABETH
C1780 PEM, WLS [36452] : THOMAS C1805 PEM,
WLS [36452]
BUTROID 1800+ STOCKWITH, LIN, ENG [37448]
BUTROYD 1800+ OWSTON FERRY, LIN, ENG
[37448]
BUTT 1837+ CAMDEN & ALBURY, NSW, AUS
[33763] : 1867+ HEYWOOD & AVOCA, VIC, AUS
[34681] : PRE 1837 STICKLAND, DOR, ENG [33763]
: 1728+ DOR & SOM, ENG [34045] : PRE 1875 ENG
[34543] : 1750+ MATSON, GLS, ENG [34681] :
1860+ MINSTERWORTH, GLS, ENG [34681] : PRE
1700 NORTON, GLS, ENG [34716] : 1850+ YKS,
ENG [35403] : PRE 1845 BRISTOL, SOM, ENG
[36121] : 1700-1900S GLS, WOR & LAN, ENG [37221]
: 1600-1750 SOM, ENG [37232] : PRE 1900
CARISBROOKE, IOW, ENG [37949]
BUTTANSHAW ALL WORLDWIDE [37715]
BUTTEL 1600+ SELZEN, RPF, BRD [37012]
BUTTENSHAW ALL WEST PECKHAM, KEN, ENG
[34558] : ALL WORLDWIDE [37715]
BUTTER PRE 1856 DUNDEE, ANS, SCT [33845] : PRE
1900 PER, CAI & LKS, SCT [37987]
BUTTERFIELD 1800-50 ORONO, DURHAM CO.,
ONT, CAN [37528] : 1700 BRISTOL, ENG [34321] :
PRE 1810 HITCHIN, HRT, ENG [34450] : 1750+
HITCHIN, HRT, ENG [35908] : ALL YKS, ENG

[36157] : C1790 BOLTON LE SANDS, LAN, ENG
[36227] : ALL SD, USA **[34264]** : PRE 1950 IN, USA
[38768] : PRE 1950 IL & MO, USA **[38768]** : PRE 1845
ME, USA **[38768]**

BUTTERS PRE 1850 AUCHTERMUCHTY, FIF, SCT
[37693]

BUTTERTON 1700+ STOKE & TRENTHAM, STS,
ENG **[37908]**

BUTTERWORTH 1854+ VIC, AUS **[34261]** : WILLIAM
1829+ HOBART, TAS & NSW, AUS **[35250]** : JOHN
1880+ ADELAIDE, SA, AUS **[36611]** : 1780-1870
SALFORD, LAN, ENG **[34440]** : 1700S-1800S
CARTWORTH, WRY, ENG **[35126]** : 1700S SOUTH
MUSKHAM, NTT, ENG **[35186]** : 1830+ HYDE,
CHS, ENG **[37828]** : 1850-1910 OLDHAM, LAN,
ENG **[38370]** : ALL ENG & AUS **[35345]** : 1770+
HEYWOOD, LAN & NSW, ENG & AUS **[38204]**

BUTTERY ALL LEI, LIN & NTT, ENG **[34361]** : 1800+
BOTHAMSALL, NTT, ENG **[35970]** : PRE 1860 LKS,
SCT **[37354]** : ALL WORLDWIDE **[33903]**

BUTTFIELD 1855+ SA, AUS **[36267]** : PRE 1855 BDF,
ENG **[36267]**

BUTTIMER 1800+ THOMASTON, ME & LIM, USA &
IRL **[38225]**

BUTTON ALL ESS, ENG **[34436]** : PRE 1855
CLAVERING, ESS, ENG **[34463]** : 1830+
BIDENDEN, KEN, ENG **[34467]** : PRE 1860
LITTLEBURY, ESS, ENG **[34869]** : PRE 1850
SOTHERTON & YOXFORD, SFK, ENG **[35222]** :
JAMES 1820+ WAKEFIELD, WRY, ENG **[38031]** :
THOMAS 1849-1932 LEICESTER & WAKEFIELD,
WRY, ENG **[38031]** : 1700-1900 CON, ENG **[38278]**

BUTTONSHAW ALL WORLDWIDE **[37715]**

BUTTREE PRE 1860 LKS, SCT **[37354]**

BUTTREY PRE 1760 FARNLEY BY LEEDS &
BATLEY, YKS, ENG **[36668]**

BUTTROSE ALL WORLDWIDE **[37987]**

BUTTS 1800+ LAMBETH, SRY, ENG **[37443]** : 1840+
DUR, ENG **[37443]** : 1780-1795 DUTCHESS CO., NY,
USA **[38763]**

BUTTWEILER JOHN 1840-1860 PORT CLINTON,
OH, USA **[38482]**

BUTZ ALL USA **[36930]**

BUUREN VAN PRE 1725 S'GRAVENLAND, NOH,
NL **[38706]**

BUWALDA C1800 ELL, LMB, NL **[38064]**

BUXTON PRE 1700 HEATON, STS, ENG **[34384]** :
PRE 1840 CHESTERFIELD, DBY, ENG **[35946]** :
1800+ DBY, ENG **[35951]** : 1820+ MIDDLETON,
NFK, ENG **[35974]** : PRE 1858 SPARHAM, NFK,
ENG **[36828]** : 1785-9 TISSINGTON, DBY, ENG
[37863] : ALL NBL & DUR, ENG **[38754]** : 1790-1830
ROANE & MORGAN CO.S, TN, USA **[36566]** :
1630+ MA, NH & VT, USA **[36896]** : ALL TN, USA
[38519] : ALL MD, USA **[38519]** : ALL VA, USA
[38519] : ALL MO, USA **[38519]**

BUYERS 1770S GLASGOW, LKS, SCT **[37879]**

BUZENUS 1800+ PRE, GER **[36683]** : 1850+ RENSTI
OR JOSEPHIN, POL **[36683]**

BUZZARD PRE 1880 LONDON, ENG **[35219]** : 1750-
1855 LEICESTER, LEI, ENG **[35320]** : 1720-1780
MONTGOMERY CO., PA, USA **[36738]**

BUZZEY 1800+ BARNARD CASTLE, DUR, ENG
[35633]

BYAM 1840+ LAUNCESTON, TAS, AUS **[34904]** :
PRE 1820 BARDWELL, SFK, ENG **[33992]**

BYARD ALL YKS, ENG **[34550]** : ALL DEV, ENG
[34550] : ALL STS, ENG **[34550]**

BYARS PRE 1750 GRANVILLE DISTRICT, NC, USA
[38538]

BYASS PRE 1900 ENG **[35978]**

BYATT 1900 MANCHESTER, LAN, ENG **[35881]**

BYCROFT PRE 1790 FRIESTON, LIN, ENG **[35212]** :
1810+ KINGS LYNN, NFK, ENG **[35212]** : 1800+
WRANGLE, LIN, ENG **[36791]** : CLAUDE 1890+
PATTERSON PASSIAC CO., NJ, USA **[35212]**

BYE C1836 OLVESTON, GLS, ENG **[34281]** : 1700-1850
HARTLEY WINTNEY, HAM, ENG **[37838]**

BYERLEY 1843+ AUS **[38540]** : PRE 1839 STROUD,
GLS, ENG **[35720]** : JOSEPH 1830+ BRISTOL,
LONDON, & SFK, ENG **[38540]** : SIR JOHN 1800S
FARMHILL & STROUD, GLS, ENG **[38540]** : 1820S
PARIS, FRA **[35720]**

BYERS 1853+ DARK CORNER, NSW, AUS **[35504]** :
1750-1900 CLIBURN & BOLTON, WES & YKS,
ENG **[34855]** : 1810+ GUISBOROUGH, NRY, ENG
[36412] : 1750-1860 MANCHESTER, LAN, ENG &
IRL **[35592]** : C1855 BALLYJAMESDUFF, CAV, IRL
[34273] : 1800-1870 CORLEA, TULLY CORBETT,
MOG, IRL **[34440]** : PRE 1853 ANNAN, DFS, SCT
[35504] : 1800 ECCLESMANCHIOX, MLN, SCT
[35755]

BYFIELD C1800 FOLKSWORTH MORBONE, HUN,
ENG **[38078]**

BYFORD ALL ENG **[37006]**

BYGOTT 1850-1920 HASTINGS CO., ONT, CAN
[34996]

BYGRAVES 1860 BIGGLESWADE, BDF, ENG **[35024]**

BYNION C1650 NEWPORT PAGNELL, BKM, ENG
[34041]

BYRAM PRE 1800 EARSDON, NBL, ENG **[37505]**

BYRD 1780-1880 YANCEY CO., NC, USA **[38009]**

BYRIDEN PRE 1843 HRT, ENG **[37442]**

BYRNE 1863+ BRISBANE & MARYBOROUGH,
QLD, AUS **[34588]** : PRE 1840 SYDNEY, NSW, AUS
[35400] : 1850+ BACCHUS MARSH, VIC, AUS
[35793] : PRE 1890 ENMORE, NSW, AUS **[37315]** :
1850-1900 CHILTERN, VIC, AUS **[37996]** : 1850-1890
PARRAMATTA, NSW, AUS **[37996]** : 1770-1850 WIC,
IRL **[34071]** : PRE 1860 DUBLIN, IRL **[34557]** : PRE
1863 CORK, COR, IRL **[34588]** : C1820-1870 WAT,
IRL **[34618]** : 1780-1840 JOHNSWELL, KIK, IRL
[34687] : 1750-1840 KIK, IRL **[34753]** : PRE 1865
BARAVORE FORD, WIC, IRL **[34959]** : C1870 CAR
& LEX, IRL **[35034]** : 1800+ DUBLIN, IRL **[35352]** :
1750-1800 DUBLIN, IRL **[35494]** : PRE 1860 TIP, IRL
[35750] : PATRICK PRE 1850 RATHDRUM, WIC,
IRL **[36297]** : 1830-1855 TIP, IRL **[37150]** : 1800-1850
CLONOVLTY, TIP, IRL **[37996]** : PRE 1900
VICARSTOWN, LEX, IRL **[38300]** : 1863-1900
GLASSAN, WEM, IRL **[38301]** : PRE 1900 CAR, IRL
[38769] : JOHN 1810-1883 PETERSHAM, CAR &
NSW, IRL & AUS **[36311]** : DANIEL 1876
PETERSHAM, CAR & NSW, IRL & AUS **[36311]** :
JOHN 1808-1883 ARDRISTAN, CAR & NSW, IRL &
AUS **[36311]**

BYRNES MICHAEL 1860+ MUDGEE, NSW, AUS
[34978] : C1870 SOUTHGATE, NSW, AUS **[35515]** :
1863+ GLEBE, NSW, AUS **[36316]** : 1840+
GOULBURN, NSW, AUS **[37314]** : 1801+ SYDNEY,
NSW, AUS **[38208]** : 1800-1815 DUNGAUNNIA, IRL
[34182] : MARTIN PRE 1856 CLA, IRL **[34701]** : PRE
1860 LIM, IRL **[34978]** : DAVID PRE 1800 IRL
[35066] : PRE 1800 MAGHERAFELT, LDY, IRL
[38208] : JAMES C1840-1918 DUB, IRL & AUS
[35356]

BYRNES (SEE BURNS) [36314]

BYRNS C1848 CAMPERDOWN, NSW, AUS **[35515]**

BYROM 1860+ QLD & NSW, AUS **[34955]** : PRE 1860
BLACKBURN, LAN, ENG **[34955]**

BYRON 1820S-1860S TIPPERARY & BANSHA, TIP,
IRL **[35044]** : 1800S OFF, IRL **[35398]** : 1800+
SEAGERTON, PA, USA **[38295]**

BYSH 1700-1850 EAST GRINSTEAD, SSX, ENG **[34697]** : 1840+ HARTFIELD, SSX, ENG **[36759]**

BYSHOP C1782 WINFRITH NEWBURGH, DOR, ENG **[34586]**

BYWATER ALL BANBURY, OXF, ENG **[36713]** : 1800+ HEF, ENG **[37323]** : PRE 1800 RAD, WLS **[37323]**

BZOTOKOSKI ANNA 1800S IL, USA **[36678]**

CABANNE 1700-1850 BORDEAUX, FRA **[35283]**

CABBAN ALL WORLDWIDE **[36383]**

CABBLE C1782 STOCKTON, WIL, ENG **[37002]** : ALL DUNDEE, ANS, SCT **[37619]**

CABLE 1870+ GREY BRUCE CO., ONT, CAN **[34407]** : 1830-1860S FRONTENAC CO., ONT, CAN **[34407]** : PRE 1740 SOUTH EAST, SFK, ENG **[37420]** : WILLIAM 1700-1766 LITCHFIELD, CT, USA **[38130]**

CABOURN PRE 1770 LIN, ENG **[36143]**

CACCIA PRE 1829 EXETER, DEV, ENG **[34452]**

CACI PRE 1819 PENZANCE, CON, ENG **[34452]** : 1780-1830 CON, ENG **[34751]** : 1820+ EDINBURGH, MLN, SCT **[34452]**

CACKETT PRE 1810 CHATHAM, KEN, ENG **[36741]**

CADD 1750-1840 HILLESDEN, BKM, ENG **[34016]**

CADDALL PRE 1712 CLUNIE, PER, SCT **[37852]**

CADDAYE ALL DEN, WLS **[34593]**

CADDEY ALL WORLDWIDE **[34457]**

CADDICK 1700-1900 TIPTON, STS, ENG **[34711]** : PRE 1880 BERMONDSEY, SRY, ENG **[34978]** : C1810 SEDGLEY, STS, ENG **[37883]**

CADDY 1840-1860 CON, ENG **[33928]** : PRE 1836 ST HILARY, CON, ENG **[35425]** : 1700+ WENDRON, CON, ENG **[35587]** : ALL MARAZION, CON, ENG **[36774]** : PRE 1860 WENDRON, CON, ENG **[37729]** : 1808+ BODMIN & MORPETH, CON & NSW, ENG & AUS **[35155]** : ALL RSA **[34683]**

CADE PRE 1780 GLENTHAM, LIN, ENG **[35587]**

CADER ALL WORLDWIDE **[35526]**

CADGE 1700+ LONG MELFORD, SFK, ENG **[37638]**

CADIL C1759 WHITFIELD, NTH, ENG **[36945]**

CADMAN 1840 MARYLEBONE, MDX, ENG **[34940]** : 1800-1900 AUDLEM, CHS, ENG **[35203]** : 1800+ WEST HAM, LND & ESS, ENG **[36111]** : PRE 1860 SAL, ENG **[36116]** : C1860 WASHINGTON, DC, USA **[36116]** : PRE 1850 CT & NY, USA **[38746]**

CADRON PRE 1770 LAVALTERIE, QUE, CAN **[37537]**

CADWALADER CHRISTIAN 1750 SAVANNAH, GA, USA **[35328]**

CADWALLADER 1854 WISTANSTOW, SAL, ENG **[34878]** : 1800+ BISHOPS CASTLE, SAL, ENG **[35880]** : 1836 HIGHLAND CO., OH, USA **[35295]** : 1750+ MGY, WLS **[35880]**

CADWALLENDER 1850+ WOLVERHAMPTON, STS, ENG **[38247]**

CADWELL ALL WORLDWIDE **[33858]**

CADY C1600 GENEVA, GE, CH **[38348]**

CADZOW PRE 1878 MYRTLEFORD, VIC, AUS **[37901]**

CAESAR 1890+ BRISBANE, QLD, AUS **[35105]** : 1890+ MT GRAVATT, QLD, AUS **[35105]** : ALL TIP, IRL **[37133]** : 1550-1990 WORLDWIDE **[37867]**

CAFFELL JAMES C1818 POPLAR, MDX, ENG **[35955]** : 1800S STEPNEY, MDX, ENG **[36633]** : JAMES 1700S BUCKATON, SOM, ENG **[36633]**

CAFFERY 1900-1990 GULGONG, NSW, AUS **[33778]**

CAFING 1700 COWFOLD, SSX, ENG **[35288]**

CAGGETT 1700-1850 GSY, CHI **[35494]** : 1700-1850 ENG **[35494]**

CAGNIE PRE 1860 COR, IRL **[34977]**

CAHER 1850S ENNIS, CLA, IRL & AUS **[36862]**

CAHILL 1890+ DARWIN, NT, AUS **[34868]** : 1857+ QLD, AUS **[34868]** : 1880+ NT, AUS **[34868]** : 1860S BALLARAT, VIC, AUS **[35390]** : 1880+ SYDNEY,

NSW, AUS **[37997]** : PRE 1920 BRISTOL, SOM & VIC, ENG & AUS **[37995]** : 1800-1870 THOMASTOWN, KIK, IRL **[34018]** : RICHARD 1858+ DUNNAMRY, KIK, IRL **[34781]** : PRE 1855 GORT, GAL, IRL **[34868]** : PRE 1857 BROADFORD, CLA, IRL **[34911]** : 1800-1950 RATHMORE, KER, IRL **[35308]** : 1850S KILKENNY, KIK, IRL **[35390]** : 1700+ CLONLISMULLEN & THURLES, TIP, IRL **[37415]**

CAHOON THOMAS HENRY 1885 LISBURN, ANT, IRL **[34395]** : 1750+ DOW, IRL **[35060]** : 1790-1850 NY & OH, USA **[36541]**

CAIGOU 1880+ NELSON, NZ **[36818]**

CAIL GEORGE H. 1845-1890 MARION CO., FL, USA **[38144]**

CAILLE JEANNE 1600+ FRA **[37429]**

CAILLEAUX ALL WORLDWIDE **[37815]**

CAIN MARTIN 1840S NEUREA, NSW, AUS **[33939]** : C1855 SYDNEY, NSW, AUS **[35089]** : PRE 1870 LONDON, ENG **[33957]** : PRE 1814 ST PAULS WALDEN, HRT, ENG **[35840]** : C1716-54 BURNHOPE, CUL, ENG **[37019]** : PRE 1871 NEWPORT, SAL, ENG **[37396]** : PRE 1839 LIVERPOOL, LAN, ENG **[37991]** : PRE 1820 BALLAUGH, IOM **[34137]** : ALL CLA, IRL **[33773]** : PRE 1870 CAHERAGH, SKIBBEREEN, COR, IRL **[33957]** : PRE 1900 BANBRIDGE, DOW, IRL **[35962]** : 1800+ DOW, IRL **[37170]** : 1881 CINCINNATI, OH, USA **[34498]** : 1630-1750 PLYMOUTH & YARMOUTH, MA, USA **[37432]** : PRE 1840 SARATOGA, NY, USA **[38052]**

CAINE 1890-1990 CAROLINE, MD, USA **[38136]**

CAINES 1841 HARDINGTON MANDEVILLE, SOM, ENG **[37378]**

CAINS PRE 1800 HANHAM & OLDLAND, GLS, ENG **[33771]**

CAIRNCROSS 1750-1880 MARYKIRK & MONTROSE, ANS, SCT **[35813]** : PRE 1867 PER, SCT **[35863]** : 1800+ EDINBURGH, MLN, SCT &, ST HELENA **[35032]**

CAIRNDUF 1798 KILMARNOCK, AYR, SCT **[35903]**

CAIRNEY 1800+ BANBRIDGE, DOW, IRL **[35644]** : 1800+ CRIEFF, PER, SCT **[35644]** : PRE 1880 SHOTTS, LKS, SCT & ENG **[36191]**

CAIRNS PRE 1900 BALLARAT, VIC, AUS **[34593]** : 1850+ BALLARAT, VIC, AUS **[35384]** : 1900+ THORNLEIGH, NSW, AUS **[36509]** : PRE 1860 SAINTFIELD, DOW, IRL **[34895]** : PRE 1874 DOW, IRL **[35985]** : PRE 1886 KILMOODS & NEWTONARDS, DOW, IRL **[36509]** : PRE 1898 TURAKINA, WANGANUI, NZ **[34616]** : 1874+ PAPANUI, CBY, NZ **[35985]** : 1820 CARRIDEN, WLN, SCT **[33810]** : PRE 1835 CHIRNSIDES, BEW, SCT **[34797]** : PRE 1860 SCT **[35384]** : 1700S HAWICK, ROX, SCT **[35635]** : 1820-1840 WEST BARNS, ELN, SCT **[36308]** : 1800S RENFREW, RFW, SCT **[36633]** : PRE 1860 CHIRNSIDE, BEW, SCT **[36848]** : 1800+ WIGTOWN & KNIGHTSWOOD, WIG & DNB, SCT & IRL **[35579]**

CAISH PRE 1810 SHERFIELD ENGLISH, HAM, ENG **[36478]**

CAISSY PRE 1890 CARLETON, QUE, CAN **[37442]**

CAISTER PRE 1900 LIN & NTT, ENG **[34335]** : 1700-1850 DOVER AREA, KEN, ENG **[37720]**

CAITHNESS C1825 FORFAR, CAI, SCT & AUS **[35079]** : ALL WORLDWIDE **[36469]**

CAKE 1700-1900 DOR, ENG **[36012]**

CAKEBREAD 1800S MDX, ENG **[37423]**

CALABY 1850+ HOMEBUSH, AVOCA, VIC, AUS **[33915]** : C1850+ ADELAIDE, SA, AUS **[33915]** : PRE 1850 NFK, ENG **[33915]**

CALAGE PIERRE PRE 1850 ST-JEAN, VADASEE, MONTPELLIER, MP, FRA [34061] : ALL FRA [34061]

CALBO 1700-1820 LA CORUNA, GALICIA, ESP [36937]

CALCADA ALL WORLDWIDE [38256]

CALDECUTT PRE 1807 BIRMINGHAM, WAR, ENG [36259]

CALDER 1880+ HOBART, TAS, AUS [34670] : 1700-1850 OKENBURY, WOR, ENG [36653] : 1850+ INNISHANNON, COR, IRL [35765] : 1850+ DESERTSERGES, COR, IRL [35765] : PRE 1844 TEMPO, TYR, IRL [37556] : 1820-1850 INNISHANNON, COR, IRL [37859] : PRE 1800 INVERNESS CITY, INV, SCT [35911] : PRE 1880 THURSO, CAI, SCT [36201] : PRE 1805 PITFORIE & MOULIN, PER, SCT [37852]

CALDERBANK 1800+ WIGAN, LAN, ENG [38260] : 1800+ CHORLEY & WHITTLE LE WOODS, LAN, ENG [38260]

CALDERWOOD PRE 1850 AYR, SCT [38039]

CALDICOTT 1842 YKS, ENG [35120] : JAMES 1800S HEF, ENG [36633]

CALDRON C1770 TIMBERLAND, LIN, ENG [35746]

CALDWELL JOHN JNR. 1853+ MONARO, NSW, AUS [33815] : DAVID 1853+ MONARO, NSW, AUS [33815] : ROBERT 1853+ MONARO, NSW, AUS [33815] : C1881 YOUNG, NSW, AUS [35391] : C1868 JAMIESON, VIC, AUS [35391] : PRE 1854+ GOULBURN, NSW, AUS [35759] : PRE 1900 WAGGA WAGGA, NSW, AUS [35781] : 1820+ SIMCOE CO., ONT, CAN [34465] : 1830+ BELLEVILLE, ONT, CAN [34510] : PRE 1850 ENG [34465] : PRE 1710 GNOSALL, STS, ENG [36701] : PRE 1900 WARRINGTON, LAN, ENG [37561] : PRE 1850 HEYWOOD, LAN, ENG [37561] : PRE 1900 MCHENAGHE KILLEGAR, LET, IRL [34466] : PRE 1850 DRUMCLAMPH, TYR, IRL [35897] : 1700-1800 DRY, IRL [36939] : HENRY PRE 1820 ANT, IRL [38222] : 1700-1850 STEVENSTON, AYR, SCT [37985] : 1760+ NJ, USA [34510] : WILLIAM PRE 1825 MONTGOMERY, NYS, USA [36447] : 1800-1840 BOTETOURT CO., VA, USA [36738] : 1700-1800S HARDY CO., WV, USA [37562] : 1800-1900 TRUMBULL CO., OH, USA [38344]

CALEY 1870S-1890S BERRIEDALE, ONT, CAN [34103] : ALL SHIMPLING, NFK, ENG [36402] : ALL SKINNINGROVE, NRY, ENG [36402] : 1650-1700 FRITTON, NFK, ENG [36483] : 1700+ BERGH APTON, NFK, ENG [36483] : THOMAS 1854-1870S DOUGLAS, IOM, UK [34103] : 1870S CLEVELAND, OH, USA [34103]

CALHOUN 1810-1840 PRESTON, VA, USA [36908] : PRE 1900 SALT LAKE CITY, UT, USA [38538] : 1800-1900 ERIE CO., PA, USA [38588]

CALKINS 1820-1850 OTSEGO CO., NY, USA [36334] : PRE 1860 CT & NY, USA [37808] : PRE 1700 MON, WLS [38746]

CALKWELL PRE 1860 HARBROUGH, LIN, ENG [38111]

CALLABY 1750-1800 BAGTHORPE, NFK, ENG [38453]

CALLACHAN PRE 1855 DUBBO, NSW, AUS [33932]

CALLAGHAN 1800-1900 IRL, SCT & ENG, AUS [34227] : 1860+ MULBRING CREEK, NSW, AUS [34942] : 1814+ WINDSOR & PORT MACQUARIE, NSW, AUS [35420] : JEREMIAH 1860S CONCORD, NSW, AUS [36316] : PRE 1910 POONAKIRKEE, MAHARASHTRA, INDIA [37101] : PRE 1850 KILLARNEY, KER, IRL [35224] : 1817+ COR, IRL [35253] : PRE 1814 DOW, IRL [35420] : 1806+ CARRIGALINE, COR, IRL [35921] : C1845

ENNISTYMON, CLA, IRL [36302] : 1700-1900 SLIGO, COR, IRL [36977] : PRE 1900 CORK, COR, IRL [37101] : PRE 1880 DRUMBEG, ANT & DOW, IRL [37927] : MARGARET C1833 CAV, IRL [37960] : 1820+ WORLDWIDE [35224]

CALLAHAN 1840-1900 ONT, CAN [37456] : 1750-1850 KANTURK, COR, IRL [37456] : 1820-40 ANT, IRL [38202]

CALLAN 1800+ ADLINGTON & BLACKROD, LAN, ENG [38260]

CALLANAN ALL CLA, IRL [33773] : 1800+ KINVARA, GAL, IRL [35201] : 1830-1860 LOUGHREA, GAL, IRL [38117]

CALLANDER PRE 1841 BALFRON, STI, SCT [37138]

CALLARD PRE 1700 DEV, ENG [34610]

CALLAWAY 1800+ IRL & AUS [33769] : 1650-1700 SOMERSET CO., MD, USA [36354] : C1820 ASHE CO., NC, USA [38044] : C1820 GRAYSON CO., VA, USA [38044]

CALLEN PRE 1860 DON, IRL [33931] : PRE 1900 ANT, IRL [37708]

CALLENDAR ANNE 1932+ LONDON, ENG [34341] : ALL UPPER WAIWERA, NZ [34638]

CALLERY 1700+ LET, IRL [35080]

CALLEY 1875+ NEWCASTLE, NSW, AUS [37132] : 1800S WIL, ENG [35723] : 1670+ CHURSTON FERRERS & BRIXHAM, DEV, ENG [37132]

CALLINAN PRE 1856 BORRISOLEIGH, TIP, IRL [35028] : 1820+ NEWMARKET, CLA, IRL [37902] : PRE 1860 KELLS, CLA, IRL [37982] : 1800+ KILSHANNY & KILFENORA, CLA, IRL [38295] : 1800+ IRL & NZ [36850]

CALLINGHAM PRE 1690 GODALMING, SRY, ENG [37420]

CALLIS 1840+ WILLUNGA, SA, AUS [34600] : PRE 1907 LEICESTER, LEI, ENG [36496]

CALLOW C1795 DBY, ENG [34645] : 1600-1700 MAUGHOLD, IOM, ENG [34872] : PRE 1800 MAUGHOLD, IOM, UK [35866]

CALLOWAY PRE 1860 ALD, CHI [33984]

CALLOWHILL 1700-1850 LONDON, ENG [34258]

CALLSEN 1863-1900 CHICAGO, IL, USA [38451]

CALOE JOHN 1840S LIVERPOOL, LAN, ENG [37692]

CALOW C1825 TANSLEY, DBY, ENG [34661]

CALTHORPE PRE 1840 BROOME, NFK, ENG [36079] : 1600-1800 NFK, ENG [36205]

CALTON 1773 LAMBETH, LND, ENG [35259] : 1855 LND, ENG [35575] : PRE 1800 BASLOW, DBY, ENG [37875]

CALVER HENRY 1864+ BURNHAM, NFK, ENG [34916] : 1750-1870 ROTHERHITHE, LND, ENG [36053] : 1750-1870 YARMOUTH, NFK, ENG [36053] : 1750 PEASENHALL, SFK, ENG [37928]

CALVERLEY 1700-1800S LEEDS, WAKEFIELD, WRY, ENG [36837]

CALVERT 1915 BRANTFORD, ONT, CAN [33853] : PRE 1760 YKS, ENG [33998] : PRE 1800 KIRK MERRINGTON, DUR, ENG [34316] : 1700S BROMFIELD, CUL, ENG [34392] : 1800+ SUNDERLAND, DUR, ENG [35719] : 1864+ GUISBOROUGH, NRY, ENG [36412] : C1840 PATELEY BRIDGE, WRY, ENG [37378] : PRE 1900 LND & SRY, ENG [37731] : PRE 1830 YKS, ENG [37760] : PRE 1900 CROOK, DUR, ENG [38013] : PRE 1900 DUR, ENG [38457] : JOHN & JACK 1970 CA, USA [33853] : JIM 1950+ CA, USA [33853] : HERBERT 1902 PONTYPRIDD, GLA, WLS [33853]

CALVIN 1885-1925 SAN FRANCISCO, CA, USA [33754]

CALWELL 1842 PT PHILLIP, VIC, AUS [37112]

CALWILL 1860+ LONDON, ONT, CAN [37451]

CALZADA ALL WORLDWIDE [38256]

CAMBELL PRE 1700 DBY, ENG [37875] : 1750-1900 BALLYMENA, ANT, IRL [38024]

CAMBERS 1800+ COPLE, BDF, ENG [34315]

CAMBORN PRE 1750 WINTERBOURNE, GLS, ENG [34908]

CAMBREY 1890-1913 MELBOURNE, VIC, AUS [34767]

CAMBRIDGE ALL HARTLEPOOL, DUR, ENG [36473] : 1750+ FILEY, YKS, ENG [36473] : PRE 1700 ENG [36700] : 1850-1871 UK [36654]

CAMENISCH ALL GR, CH [36982] : 1800+ KY, USA [36982] : ALL WORLDWIDE [36982]

CAMERON 1850 HOBART, TAS, AUS [34421] : ROBERT 1893+ QUORN, SA, AUS [34583] : ALL NSW, AUS [34695] : JOHN 1850+ SYDNEY, NSW, AUS [34695] : C1850 VIC, AUS [34874] : PETER 1840-1900 GEELONG & ORBOST, VIC, AUS [35053] : 1841+ PORTLAND, VIC, AUS [35748] : 1852+ NORTHERN RIVERS, NSW, AUS [36272] : 1860+ NORTHERN RIVERS, NSW, AUS [36299] : 1850+ SHOALHAVEN, NSW, AUS [36299] : PRE 1886 YULGILBAR, NSW, AUS [37315] : 1900 PAKENHAM, VIC, AUS [38213] : 1855+ KINCARDINE, ONT, CAN [34235] : 1840+ VAN KLEEK HILLS, ONT, CAN [34408] : C1880 N OTTAWA, ONT, CAN [34527] : C1880 CUMBERLAND, ONT, CAN [36350] : C1870 LONDON, ENG [33914] : 1860 NEEDLES, IOW, ENG [35152] : 1800-1850 MANCHESTER, LAN, ENG [36635] : PRE 1850 GLENELG, INV, SCT [33993] : C1816 KINGUSSIE, INV, SCT [34058] : 1800-1855 FORTINGALL, PER, SCT [34235] : 1700+ LOCHBROOM & DINGWALL, ROC, SCT [34403] : PRE 1850 LOCHABER, INV, SCT [34419] : PRE 1714 GREENOCK, DNB, SCT [34501] : C1780 KENMORE, PER, SCT [34527] : 1750-1850 INV & ARL, SCT [34572] : ROBERT PRE 1850 PERTH, PER, SCT [34583] : ALEXANDER PRE 1830 PETTY, INV, SCT [34613] : JAMES 1770+ PER, SCT [35053] : PETER 1815-1840 LOGIE ALMOND, PER, SCT [35053] : 1700-1900 ISLE OF SKYE, INV, SCT [35179] : 1700S+ KILMALLIE, ARL, SCT [35331] : PRE 1910 SOUTH LEITH, MLN, SCT [35380] : 1800-1860 ROC, SCT [35382] : 1700-1800S EDINBURGH, SCT [35424] : 1700+ KNOCKANDOO & ELGIN, MOR, SCT [35460] : 1810 MORVERN, ARL, SCT [35509] : 1750+ GLEN URQUHART, INV, SCT [35524] : ANNE PRE 1854 MORVERN, ARL, SCT [35553] : PRE 1830 EDINBURGH, MLN, SCT [35748] : PRE 1830 HALKIRK, CAI, SCT [35799] : PRE 1850 PAISLEY, RFW, SCT [35806] : 1730+ FORT WILLIAM, ARL, SCT [35909] : 1750 DINGWALL, ROC, SCT [35937] : 1770-1850S MULL, ARL, SCT [35938] : PRE 1836 KIRKMICHAEL, BAN, SCT [35955] : ALL INV, SCT [35993] : PRE 1860 SKYE, INV, SCT [36272] : SARAH 1785 FORTINGALL, PER, SCT [36314] : DUNCAN 1785 FORTINGALL, PER, SCT [36314] : C1800 KIRKMICHAEL, BAN, SCT [36607] : 1840+ STRATHDON, ABD, SCT [36607] : 1780+ LOGIE COLDSTONE, ABD, SCT [36620] : 1800-1820 LOCHEIL, ARL, SCT [36635] : 1790-1840 LKS, SCT [36913] : C1819 OBAN, ARL, SCT [37143] : SAMUEL PRE 1860S MORVERN, ARL, SCT [37164] : 1840-1900 FALKIRK, STI, SCT [37213] : 1800-1900 ABERDEEN, ABD, SCT [37367] : PRE 1850 ISLAY, ARL, SCT [38403] : 1800-1853 KILMONIVAIG, INV, SCT [38486] : C1800-1860 MORVEN & BALLACHOULISH, ARL, SCT [38541] : ROBERT C1825 CRIEFF, PER, SCT & AUS [33840] : DOCTOR C1850+ USA [35053] : C1930 KALISPELL, MT, USA [36350] : 1825-1920 MILLERSBURG, OH, USA [36561] : 1810-1820 STARK CO., OH, USA [36561] :

1780-1810 BEAVER CO., PA, USA [36561] : 1890+ MI, USA [37451] : 1800-1900 DES MOINES, IA, USA [38025]

CAMFIELD 1700-1900 SSX, ENG [37338]

CAMM C1819 HOBART, TAS, AUS [35748] : PRE 1820 SOWERBY, WRY, ENG [33796]

CAMMACK PRE 1800 NEWBERRY CO., SC, USA & IRL [36969]

CAMMERELL PRE 1770 NECKARREMS, WUE, GER [38661]

CAMP 1780 NB, CAN [34231] : PRE 1840 CHARLETON, DEV, ENG [34025] : PRE 1900 LONDON, ENG [34617] : 1808 BARKWAY, HRT, ENG [36640] : PRE 1620 HUNSDON, HRT, ENG [38135]

CAMPAIGN 1824+ DUFFERIN CO., ONT, CAN [34407]

CAMPAIGNE 1650+ CAV, IRL [34407] : ALL SOUTHERN, IRL [37366]

CAMPANY ALL WORLDWIDE [36233]

CAMPBELL 1845+ LARRAS LAKE, NSW, AUS [33930] : 1800+ TAS, AUS [34846] : LEWIS 1817 SYDNEY, NSW, AUS [34939] : 1834-1843 NORFOLK ISLAND, NSW, AUS [34966] : 1845+ BOMBALA, NSW, AUS [34966] : 1800S BATHURST, NSW, AUS [34979] : 1853+ CAMPERDOWN, VIC, AUS [35057] : C1880+ COONAMBLE, NSW, AUS [35090] : JAMES 1860+ YASS & BURROWA, NSW, AUS [35159] : BRADSHAW 1840+ AUS [35224] : 1840 CHIPPENDALE, NSW, AUS [35419] : 1866+ FITZROY, VIC, AUS [35708] : SUSAN 1840+ SYDNEY, NSW, AUS [35803] : PRE 1924 LISMORE, VIC, AUS [36276] : 1835+ MONARO, NSW, AUS [36295] : JOHN 1842+ HARGREAVES, NSW, AUS [37106] : 1850+ PORT LINCOLN, SA, AUS [37115] : C1830-1850 MOLONG, NSW, AUS [37141] : 1862-1886 NEWCASTLE, NSW, AUS [37911] : SAMUEL 1841+ CLARENCETOWN, NSW, AUS [38006] : CHARLES WM. 1850+ PADDINGTON, NSW, AUS [38582] : ALL CARADOC, MIDDLESEX, ONT, CAN [33854] : 1880+ PERTH CO., ONT, CAN [34066] : 1800S FRONTENAC, ONT, CAN [34353] : ARCHIBALD C1850 PEI, CAN [34515] : ALL NS, CAN [36713] : 1783+ SHELBURNE, NS, CAN [36713] : 1800+ WEYMOUTH, NS, CAN [36713] : 1837-1852 BRANTFORD, ONT, CAN [37490] : 1800+ PICTOU, NS, CAN [37821] : ALL BRADFORD, ONT, CAN [38432] : BRIDGET 1700+ ENG [34571] : PRE 1870 SUNDERLAND, DUR, ENG [34588] : ALL CUL, ENG [35293] : 1853 CARLISLE, CUL, ENG [35391] : THOMAS DUNCAN 1899 LEICESTER, LEI, ENG [35391] : PRE 1899 HUDDERSFIELD, WRY, ENG [35733] : PRE 1814 SOUTHAMPTON, HAM, ENG [36588] : C1820-1838 LONDON, ENG [38208] : PRE 1850 INDIA & IR [37339] : ALL COOTEHILL, CAV, IRL [33823] : 1700-1830S MOG, IRL [34246] : ALL BALLYMONEY, ANT, IRL [34441] : ALL DUBLIN, IRL [34765] : LEWIS 1783 GALWAY, GAL, IRL [34939] : PRE 1857 CULLUMONY, TYR, IRL [34941] : JOHN PRE 1850 DUNDALK, LOU, IRL [35216] : BRADSHAW PRE 1835 LET, IRL [35224] : ALL BELFAST, ANT, IRL [35474] : JAMES C1855 GAL, IRL [35541] : PRE 1826+ ROCKCORRY, MOG, IRL [35759] : ELIZABETH 1808-1895 ARMOY, ANT, IRL [35815] : PRE 1842 SLI, IRL [35824] : HENRY C1830 TAMNYASKEY, LDY, IRL [35848] : 1838+ BOYLE & WOODFIELD, ROS, IRL [36276] : C1800-1900 RATHFRILAND, DOW, IRL [36821] : ALL BELFAST, DOW, IRL [37303] : 1800-1850 MACOSQUIN, LDY & ONT, IRL & CAN [34244] : 1870+ AUCKLAND & MANGANUI, NZ [34588] :

1840-1870S GLASGOW, SCT **[33835]** : JAMES 1750+
ST NINIANS, STI, SCT **[33956]** : JAMES 1800+
BARONY, LKS, SCT **[33956]** : ALL TYNEDRUM,
SCT **[33975]** : ALL PT GLASGOW, RFW, SCT **[34002]**
: 1800+ PAISLEY, RFW, SCT **[34049]** : 1829-1894
EARUSH NEAR UIG, SKYE, INV, SCT **[34122]** :
C1786 PAISLEY, RFW, SCT **[34122]** : 1851+
PENICUIK, MLN, SCT **[34122]** : PRE 1935
GLASGOW, LKS, SCT **[34122]** : 1795+ PAISLEY,
RFW, SCT **[34122]** : WILLIAM 1760S
CAMPBELTOWN, ARL, SCT **[34156]** : 1800-1910
DRUMLEMBLE, ARL, SCT **[34156]** : C1780+
DALNOE, PER, SCT **[34203]** : ROBERT C1821
KIRKOSWALD, AYR, SCT **[34300]** : 1700+ ISLE OF
COLL, ARL, SCT **[34309]** : CATHERINE 1800-1850
MULL, ARL, SCT **[34345]** : 1750+ KEITH, BAN,
SCT **[34387]** : PRE 1900 ARL, SCT **[34419]** : PRE 1850
AYR, SCT **[34575]** : 1800+ HALKIRK, CAI, SCT
[34606] : 1859+ EDINBURGH, SCT **[34609]** :
DONALD PRE 1820 KNOCKBAIN, ROC, SCT
[34613] : 1850+ ROTHESAY, BUT, SCT **[34614]** :
JOHN PRE 1800 ABERDEEN, ABD, SCT **[34618]** :
C1790 ISLAY, ARL, SCT **[34644]** : JOHN C1780-1850
LATHERON, CAI, SCT **[34646]** : PRE 1860
TWYNHOLM, KKD, SCT **[34665]** : 1847+
GREENOCK, RFW, SCT **[34668]** : 1874 NEW
KILPATRICK, DNB, SCT **[34751]** : 1800+ ASSYNT,
SUT, SCT **[34764]** : 1880+ URQUHART & LOGIE
WESTER, ROC, SCT **[34764]** : PRE 1835
ARROCHAR, DNB, SCT **[34816]** : C1830
GLASGOW, SCT **[34903]** : JOHN 1830-1850
LANDBERWICK, WIG, SCT **[34924]** : C1825
DALRY, AYR, SCT **[34972]** : C1835 IONA, ARL, SCT
[35057] : 1750+ DUNFERMLINE, FIF, SCT **[35059]** :
C1810 MOTHERWELL, LKS, SCT **[35089]** : 1789
KILCONQUHAR, FIF, SCT **[35090]** : 1840S
CLIFTON, PER, SCT **[35123]** : ALL AYR, SCT
[35139] : 1700+ KILMARNOCK, AYR, SCT **[35151]** :
1780-1840 CANONBIE, DFS, SCT **[35151]** : ALL
ISLE OF TIREE, ARL, SCT **[35198]** : PRE 1856
TARBOT & INVERARAY, ARL, SCT **[35222]** :
NORMAN C1804 BRACADALE SKYE, INV, SCT
[35259] : 1850 GLASGOW, SCT **[35325]** : ELIZABETH
1800 KILMICHAEL, ARL, SCT **[35377]** : PRE 1860
GLASGOW, SCT **[35378]** : C1845+ GLASGOW,
LKS, SCT **[35486]** : 1830S ARL, SCT **[35516]** : JANET
1806+ LOUDON, AYR, SCT **[35560]** : ALLAN
1800+ CRAIGIE, AYR, SCT **[35560]** : PRE 1790
PAISLEY, RFW, SCT **[35587]** : WILLIAM PRE 1850
DUDDINGSTON, MLN, SCT **[35713]** : 1980
EDINBURGH, MLN, SCT **[35733]** : 1869
DUMFRIES, DFS, SCT **[35733]** : 1760-1780
MACKAIRN, ARL, SCT **[35813]** : 1800-1860 ISLE OF
MULL, ARL, SCT **[35952]** : 1790S PORT GLASGOW,
RFW, SCT **[35959]** : 1800-70 TOBERMORY, ARL,
SCT **[36262]** : PRE 1790S ISLE OF SKYE, SCT **[36358]**
: 1815-1855 ALVA, CLK, SCT **[36392]** : 1800-60
KILNINVER, ARL, SCT **[36583]** : PRE 1850 ABD,
SCT **[36792]** : 1240 SCT **[37008]** : PRE 1685 FALKIRK,
STI, SCT **[37029]** : ROBERT 1717 DUNNING, PER,
SCT **[37106]** : JOHN 1808 DUNNING, PER, SCT
[37106] : C1850 ARROCHAR, DNB, SCT **[37131]** :
C1800 GLASGOW, LKS, SCT **[37141]** : C1820
DOLLAR, CLK, SCT **[37148]** : 1820S AYR, SCT
[37263] : PRE 1850 DUMBARTON, DNB, SCT **[37434]**
: 1790-1890 OLD MONKLAND, LKS, SCT **[37488]** :
PRE 1900 STORNAWAY, ROC, SCT **[37496]** :
ROBERT PRE 1800 WATTEN, CAI & SUT, SCT
[37727] : 1700+ INV, SCT **[37949]** : PRE 1857 LKS,
SCT **[37991]** : 1800-1930 TARBERT, ARL, SCT **[38355]**
: C1850 ISLAY, SCT **[38418]** : 1840S+ OLD
MONKLAND, LKS, SCT **[38423]** : 1800-1853

KILMONIVAIG, INV, SCT **[38486]** : 1750-1850
INVEROY, INV, SCT **[38486]** : CHARLES C1800
CRAIGNISH, ARL, SCT **[38504]** : 1800+ LITTLE
DUNKELD, PER, SCT & NZ **[36869]** : 1890S
DETROIT, MI, USA **[33902]** : MARY 1700S
AUGUSTA CO., VA, USA **[36321]** : 1805 NC, USA
[36358] : 1850-1870 LASALLE CO., IL, USA **[36731]** :
1810-1850 FAYETTE CO., PA, USA **[36731]** : 1750-
1850 BRADFORD CO., PA, USA **[37018]** : JOHN
PRE 1860S IL & NY, USA **[37522]** : 1700-1810
LOUDOUN CO., VA, USA **[37577]** : LAUGHLIN
1755-1791 ORANGE CO. & RANDOLPH CO., NC,
USA **[37586]** : CHARLES 1884+ HAMILTON CO.,
OH, USA **[37797]** : WM. F. 1867+ HAMILTON CO.,
OH, USA **[37797]** : 1800-1860 FAYETTE CO., TN,
USA **[38092]** : 1830+ POTTSVILLE, PA, USA **[38324]**
: 1870-1883 TAMAQUA, PA, USA **[38324]** :
MATTHEW 1781-1835 HUNTINGDON CO., PA,
USA **[38371]** : PRE 1810 MADISON, KY, USA **[38576]**
: 1859 WORLDWIDE **[33932]**
CAMPBELL **NORTH** SUSAN 1876 PETERSHAM, NB
& NSW, CAN & AUS **[36311]**
CAMPE PRE 1720 DEV, ENG **[35866]**
CAMPIN 1760+ APPLETON WITH EATON, OXF,
ENG **[35822]** : 1800+ GLS, ENG **[35880]**
CAMPION 1850S PONTON FARM, LIN, ENG **[36848]**
: PRE 1850 DUB, IRL **[34429]** : PRE 1860 LEX, IRL
[34678] : 1860 HOKITIKA, NZ **[34678]** : 1900+
SEATTLE, WA, USA **[36752]**
CAMPSIE PRE 1800 FALKIRK, STI, SCT **[35377]**
CAMPTON PRE 1800 SUTTON, BDF, ENG **[38494]** :
1811-1820 ADAMS CO., OH, USA **[33761]** : ALL
WORLDWIDE **[36429]**
CAMYRE 1826 MONTREAL, QUE, CAN **[37490]**
CANAL 1600-1900 MERCUS GARRBET, ARIEGE,
FRA **[33758]**
CANARD 1800-1850 WAYNE CO., TN, USA **[38088]**
CANAVAN 1857+ GIPPSLAND, VIC, AUS **[35399]** :
PRE 1857 WIC, IRL **[35399]**
CANDELORO PRE 1830 CASALBORDINO, CHIETI,
ITL **[34127]**
CANDISH ALL SYDNEY, NSW, AUS **[36365]**
CANDLER 1800S+ MDX, ENG **[37868]**
CANDY PRE 1840 CLOFORD, SOM, ENG **[37179]**
CANE 1735 CHRISHALL, ESS, ENG **[35808]** : 1840+
BEITH, AYR, SCT **[37575]**
CANFIELD 1840 BLENHEIM, ONT, CAN **[36444]**
CANHAM 1780+ FORDHAM, NFK, ENG **[34710]** :
1850+ NORWICH, NFK, ENG **[34710]** : PRE 1850
NFK, ENG **[36702]** : ALL LITTLEPORT, CAM, ENG
[37274]
CANINS 1750-1830 BARTON STACEY, HAM, ENG
[36286]
CANMANN 1850+ IL, USA **[36962]**
CANN 1875-1914 SYDNEY, NSW, AUS **[34073]** : PRE
1850S WINGHAM AREA, NSW, AUS **[35544]** : 1874
ADELAIDE, SA, AUS **[35722]** : 1760-1850
WYMONDHAM, NFK, ENG **[34073]** : PRE 1650
BRISTOL, GLS, ENG **[34162]** : ALL
BRADWORTHY, DEV, ENG **[34471]** : 1765-1837
WILTON, SOM, ENG **[35815]** : PRE 1800 NORTH,
DEV, ENG **[36389]** : 1650-1750 SALEM, MA, USA
[34162] : PRE 1863 MACHEN, GLA, WLS **[34726]**
CANNAN 1841+ BALMAIN, NSW, AUS **[34009]** : PRE
1841 LONDON, ENG **[34009]**
CANNANE C1840 O'CALLAGHAN'S MILLS, CLA,
IRL **[38079]** : C1840 DERRYNAVEAGH &
OATFIELD, CLA, IRL **[38079]**
CANNELL 1770+ CRINGLEFORD, NFK, ENG
[34710]
CANNEY 1700+ DOVER NECK & HAMPTON, NH,
USA **[38520]**

CANNING 1855+ BALLARAT & CRESWICK, VIC, AUS [34039] : 1700-1900 WAR, ENG [36349] : 1800+ WIL, ENG [36785] : 1845-7 ESS, ENG [37863] : C1800 GARVAGH, DRY, IRL [34395] : ALL CASTLE TOWN ROCHE, COR, IRL [34460] : 1750+ BEITH, AYR, SCT [37110] : 1800-1840 ERIE CO., PA, USA [38373]

CANNINGS 1600-1700 WIL, ENG [36438]

CANNON 1850+ SYDNEY, NSW, AUS [38011] : 1824+ CAMPBELLTOWN, TAS, AUS [38492] : 1810+ DONCASTER, WRY, ENG [33916] : PRE 1925 DUDLEY, WOR, ENG [34427] : 1890+ CANNING TOWN, LND, ENG [34460] : PRE 1848 BLOOMSBURY, MDX, ENG [35016] : 1800-1850 KINGSCLERE, HAM, ENG [35055] : 1850+ WOOLWICH, KEN, ENG [37274] : 1800+ CHELMSFORD, ESS, ENG [37274] : 1700+ LAMPORT & OLDHAM, NTH, ENG [37735] : ALL CASTLETOWNROCHE, COR, IRL [34460] : PRE 1870 GAL, IRL [34797] : 1850+ FALCARRAGH, DON, IRL [38011] : PRE 1784 FEDERALSBURG, CAROLINE CO., MD, USA [34992] : 1880+ BOSTON, MA, USA [38011] : 1880+ BUTTE, MT, USA [38011] : 1880+ SEATTLE, WA, USA [38011]

CANNONE PRE 1850 ITL [34984]

CANNOVAN FELIX 1700+ IRL [34701]

CANSICK 1665+ MARRICK, YKS, ENG [35462]

CANSLER 1741-1804 LINCOLN CO., NC, USA [38120]

CANT 1863+ CENTRAL, QLD, AUS [34021] : 1821 DUNFERMLINE, FIF, SCT [34021] : ALL ANS, KCD & PER, SCT [36089]

CANTELIUS PRE 1650 GER [38544]

CANTERBURY ALL BATH, SOM, ENG [35474]

CANTEY TIEGUE 1640S CHARLESTON, SC, USA [35328] : TIEGE 1740S CHARLESTON, SC, USA [37585]

CANTILLON ALL BALLYHEIGUE, KER, IRL [36232] : ALL BALLYORGAN, LIM, IRL [36232] : ALL IRL [36232]

CANTLE PRE 1790 BEDMINSTER, SOM, ENG [34723]

CANTON C1780+ REYNALTON, PEM, WLS [36753]

CANTRELL ALL YKS, ENG [36399]

CANTSTAETTER PRE 1750 WUE, GER [38661]

CANTWELL 1826+ TAS, AUS [35148] : MICHAEL 1839+ BOOROWA, HOVELLS CREEK, NSW, AUS [36314] : 1800-1826 OXF, ENG [35148] : 1840 DOVER, KEN, ENG [36781] : 1800+ BALLINGARRY, TIP, IRL [33825] : MICHAEL C1800-1830S KILLENAULE, TIP, IRL [36314] : 1835 DUBLIN, IRL [36781]

CANTY PRE 1865 LIMERICK, LIM, IRL [33805] : PRE 1833 TIP, IRL [34959] : 1815 LIM, IRL [35837]

CANVIN 1850+ SCT [38481]

CAPALDO PRE 1950 CAMPO DI GIOVE, ABR, ITL [37519]

CAPE JOHN 1750-1850 BUDVILLE, SOM, ENG [36555]

CAPEL PRE 1828 LONG BUCKBY, NTH, ENG [34584] : PRE 1840 MOULTON, NTT, ENG [35404] : 1700+ ENG [36291]

CAPELIN PRE 1800 GODALMING, SRY, ENG [37253]

CAPELING ALL WORLDWIDE [37359]

CAPENER 1900+ LONDON, ENG [34496]

CAPENTER 1830+ ECHUCA, VIC, AUS [36622]

CAPLAN PRE 1900 BIERSS, KOVNA, LITHUANIA [36455]

CAPLE 1858-1896 SYDNEY, NSW, AUS [37110] : 1700+ WINSCOMBE, SOM, ENG [37110] : 1830+ STRATFORD, MDX, ENG [37284] : 1800+ BRISTOL, GLS, ENG [37284]

CAPLEMAN 1815+ GER [35507]

CAPLEN PRE 1800+ BURITON & NEWPORT, HAM & IOW, ENG [35824]

CAPNER C1830 SOLIHULL, WAR, ENG [37518]

CAPON 1870+ BAIRNSDALE, VIC, AUS [34896] : PRE 1870 NFK, ENG [34896] : 1860 BIGGLESWADE, BDF, ENG [35024] : PRE 1850 LONDON, ENG [35556] : 1600-1900 DENNINGTON, SFK, ENG [38579]

CAPPS 1870+ FREMANTLE, WA, AUS [34530] : PRE 1800 GREAT HALE, LIN, ENG [36148] : C1780 LONDON, MDX & SRY, ENG [37239]

CAPRON 1870+ BRISTOL, GLS, ENG [34542]

CAPSTICKS 1790S EAST RETFORD, NTT, ENG [33917]

CAPTEIN PRE 1850 ROTTERDAM, ZUH, NL [38646]

CARADICE 1700+ MIDDLETON IN LONSDALE, WES, ENG [37196] : 1600+ CLAPHAM, YKS, ENG [37196]

CARADINE 1700-1800 SAL & HEF, ENG [36003]

CARAPEZZA ANGELE 1924-60 BARBOUR CO., WV, USA [38109]

CARBERRY ALL JAMBEROO, NSW, AUS [33838] : 1800-1860 ARM, IRL [34846]

CARBIS PRE 1857 ST JUST, CON, ENG [34043] : 1800+ MARAZION, CON, ENG [36885]

CARBUHN 1800 BRD [35873] : 1700 GER [35873]

CARD ALL LENNOX & ADDINGTON CO., ONT, CAN [35608] : ALL WESTBURY, SOM, ENG [35391] : 1750-1870 SSX, ENG [37338] : 1700-1800 ROTHERFIELD, SSX, ENG [37365] : 1700-1800S CHEDDAR, SOM, ENG [37544] : ALL MOUNTAIN ASH, GLA, WLS [35391]

CARDEN 1700+ SPELDHURST, KEN, ENG [34110] : ALL BRIGHTON, SSX, ENG [34247] : ALL VA & WV, USA & ENG [38060] : 1700+ ORANGE CO., NC, USA & ENG [38175] : ALL WORLDWIDE [36097]

CARDER 1880 MARION'S LEIGH, DEV, ENG [35943]

CARDIFF 1820+ KILDEN, KID, IRL & AUS [34971]

CARDING 1700-1800 SAL & HEF, ENG [36003]

CARDNO 1800-1830 ABERDEEN, ABD, SCT [33767]

CARDON SUSANNAH C1820-1860 LONDON, ENG [34007]

CARDONA PRE 1800 MENORCA, ESP [36353]

CARDONNE PRE 1800 GERS, FRA [35620]

CARDWELL PRE 1905 BRIGHT, VIC, AUS [37901] : ALL HEYWOOD, LAN, ENG [35417] : 1750+ STANZIKER, LAN, ENG [38285] : PRE 1845 ARM, IRL [37901]

CARE PRE 1888 SMETHWICK, STS & WAR, ENG [34391] : ALL ENG [36201] : JEANNE 1600+ FRA [37429]

CAREFOOT PRE 1800 WORLDWIDE [34746]

CAREFORD ALL ENG [34323]

CAREW 1800+ SOUTH MONAGHAN, ONT, CAN [34507] : PRE 1800 IRL [34507] : 1800+ KILKENNY, KIK, IRL [37110]

CAREY 1870+ BAIRNSDALE, VIC, AUS [35222] : 1855+ MT GAMBIER, SA, AUS [35222] : 1852+ PARRAMATTA, NSW, AUS [36267] : FLURENCE 1850+ MORPETH, NSW, AUS [36598] : 1880+ BRISBANE, QLD, AUS [38484] : PRE 1855 JSY, CHI [35222] : C1827 STREET & GLASTONBURY, SOM, ENG [34157] : PRE 1900 CON, ENG [34634] : PRE 1914 CAMBERWELL, LND, ENG [34723] : ALL SOM, ENG [37176] : 1750-1800 LAMBETH, LND, ENG [37246] : 1800+ TOTTENHAM, MDX, ENG [37437] : PRE 1880 BETHNAL GREEN, LND, ENG [37871] : PRE 1735 SSX, ENG [37875] : C1806 DOOLOUGH, MAY, IRL [34752] : C1812 CORK, COR, IRL [35854] : BRIDGET C1843+ LIM, IRL [36601] : 1830S CORK, COR, IRL [36691] : ALL

DROGHEDA, LOU, IRL [36784] : C1814+ GALWAY, GAL, IRL [36875] : PRE 1890 FAHY, GAL, IRL [38484] : 1750-1900 EASTON & NORTHUMBERLAND CO., PA, USA [37021]

CARFIELD 1800+ ENG & AUS [38005]

CARFORT ALL ENG [34323]

CARFRAE ALL CURRIE & EDINBURGH, SCT & AUS [33959]

CARGILL 1800+ CRAIG, ANS, SCT [36971]

CARIGE 1850+ BRISTOL, AVON, ENG [36469]

CARIUS ALL BRISBANE, QLD, AUS [36616]

CARJEL PRE 1700 RHOEDA & BREUNA, HES, GER [38642]

CARKEEK 1700+ REDRUTH, CON, ENG [35125]

CARLAN 1800+ LND, ENG [37420] : PRE 1815 IRL [37420]

CARLAW C1776 BATHGATE, WLN, SCT [34118]

CARLE 1850+ GLENLUCE, WIG, SCT [35411]

CARLEE PRE 1850 AMSTERDAM, NOH, NL [38303]

CARLESS HENRY 1851-1876+ LIMEHOUSE & POPLAR, MDX, ENG [37546] : EDMOND 1859-1881+ POPLAR, MDX, ENG [37546] : GEORGE 1846-1871+ LIMEHOUSE & POPLAR, MDX, ENG [37546] : C1840 KILCOMMON, MAY, IRL [36649]

CARLETON ALL WORLDWIDE [34944]

CARLEY 1740+ GSY, CHI [34532] : ALL SSX, ENG [36378] : PRE 1795 BRIGHTLING, SSX, ENG [38397]

CARLILE 1840 ERY, ENG [34731] : PRE 1820 CALVERLEY, WRY, ENG [36583] : C1850+ PAISLEY, RFW, VIC & WA, SCT & AUS [37888] : WILLIAM 1843-1870 IL, USA [38732] : WILLIAM 1890-1902 PERKINS, OK, USA [38732]

CARLING 1875+ NEWCASTLE, NSW, AUS [34783] : 1800-1875 WILLINGTON, DUR, ENG [34783]

CARLINGTON ALL WORLDWIDE [35331]

CARLISLE 1885+ GEELONG, VIC, AUS [37964] : PRE 1900 CROYDON, SRY, ENG [37692] : PRE 1850 SHEFFIELD, WRY, ENG [37846] : 1750-1850 KENDAL, WES, ENG [38511] : 1800-1850 BANDON, COR, IRL [34693] : C1850+ PAISLEY, RFW, VIC & WA, SCT & AUS [37888] : 1800-1900 HIGHLAND CO., OH, USA [35266] : 1700-1800 LOUDOUN CO., VA, USA [35266]

CARLON ANNIE 1868+ MAITLAND, NSW, AUS [35104] : 1730+ ALBRIGHTON, SAL, ENG [37717]

CARLOUGH DAVID 1906-1910 HIGHLAND MILLS, NY, USA [38233]

CARLOW 1800-1940 BIRMINGHAM, WAR, ENG [37717] : ALL WORLDWIDE [37717]

CARLSDOTTER LOVISA PRE 1884 BEXHEDA JONKOPING, SWE [38543]

CARLSEN 1872+ HOBART & COLLINSVALE, TAS, AUS [33786] : ARNEL 1870+ STOCKHOLM, SWE [36138]

CARLSON CARL 1850+ STOCKHOLM, SWE [36138] : 1825-1875 SWE [36331]

CARLSSDOTTER LOVISA 1884 NEW YORK, NY, USA [38543]

CARLSSON LOVISA 1884 NEW YORK, NY, USA [38543]

CARLSTROM ALL LONDON, ENG [36234]

CARLTON 1870-85 MUSKOKA, ONT, CAN [36722] : 1800S APPLEBY, WES, ENG [37134] : 1600-1800 TILMANSTONE, KEN, ENG [38502] : 1800S LONDON, ENG [38502] : PRE 1870 ENNISKILLEN, ARM, IRL [34006] : PRE 1870 DRY, IRL [34060] : RICHARD 1700+ STAFFORD, MA, USA [38241] : 1850-1880 DENTON CO., TX, USA [38367]

CARLY ALL SSX, ENG [36378]

CARLYLE ALL SCT [35414] : 1812 GLASGOW, LKS, SCT [35809] : 1800 RFW, SCT [38320] : C1850+ PAISLEY, RFW, VIC & WA, SCT & AUS [37888]

CARMALT 1730-1760 COVENT GARDEN, LND, ENG [36595]

CARMAN 1840 CAWSTON, NFK, ENG [34546] : 1860 MAIDSTONE, KEN, ENG [36250] : 1630-1783 HEMPSTEAD, FISHKILL, NY, USA [34366] : 1600-1820 NY, USA [37522] .

CARMEAN 1860+ ROSS CO., OH, USA [38323]

CARMER PRE 1900 PUTNAM CO., MO, USA [36672]

CARMICHAEL 1700+ IRL & SCT [38336] : PRE 1818 COMRIE, PER, SCT [34339] : C1780 EDINBURGH, MLN, SCT [34713] : PRE 1880S GLASGOW, LKS, SCT [34873] : PRE 1800 ST ANDREWS, FIF, SCT [35126] : C1808 MUTHILL, PER, SCT [35249] : 1780S ABBEY MADDERTY, PER, SCT [35259] : PRE 1882 EDINBURGH, SCT [36841] : C1810 STIRLING, STI, SCT [37263]

CARMO PRE 1861 SAO MIGUEL, AZORES, PT [37551] : 1861-1890 SAE MIGUEL, AZORES, PT [37551]

CARMODY 1854+ IPSWICH, QLD, AUS [34763] : 1840-1900 VIC, AUS [36780] : 1800+ CHARLOTTETOWN, PEI, CAN [37431] : 1850-1900 MONTREAL, QUE, CAN [38442] : PRE 1854 ENNISTYMON, CLA, IRL [34763] : 1700-1800 CLA, IRL [36780] : ALL WORLDWIDE [37431]

CARN 1855+ LISDILLON, TAS, AUS [34910]

CARNAHAN PRE 1820 OH, USA [34410]

CARNDUFF 1800+ IRL & SCT [34229] : C1850 AYR, SCT [33914]

CARNE C1740+ REDRUTH, CON, ENG [35746]

CARNEAL ALL VA MIL LDS, OH & VA, USA [38287]

CARNEGIE 1700S INVERKEILLOR, ANS, SCT & AUS [35422]

CARNELL AUCHER ALL NSW, AUS [34558] : 1750-1900 OCHRE PIT COVE, NFD, CAN [34250] : ALL HADLOW, KEN, ENG [34558] : PRE 1853 CON, ENG [35709] : PRE 1849 ST IVES, CON, ENG [38288]

CARNEY 1848+ GANNONS CREEK, NSW, AUS [35157] : 1850+ HOBART, TAS, AUS [35459] : 1840+ BATHURST, NSW, AUS [36305] : ALL ISLE OF WIGHT, HAM, ENG [33802] : PRE 1850 FRENCHPARK, ROS, IRL [38777] : 1800-40 ROCHESTER, NY, USA [37007]

CARNIEAL 1800+ LONDON, ENG [34542]

CARNLEY 1850-1930 AL, USA [36449]

CARNOCHAN PRE 1813 KIRKGUNZEON, KKD, SCT [35021]

CARNT C1800 SHEERNES, KEN, ENG [34296]

CAROLAN PRE 1850 EASKEY, SLI, IRL [38178] : PRE 1820 IRL [38178] : ALL WORLDWIDE [38178]

CAROLIN PRE 1866 NJ, USA & IRL [38733]

CAROLINE PRE 1850 SRY & KEN, ENG [34383] : 1900+ RSA [34760]

CAROLUS MAGNUS ALL AACHEN, EUROPA [38644]

CARON ALL QUE, CAN [34517] : 1800+ ABBEVILLE & AMIENS, NOR, FRA [37294] : PRE 1700 AMIENS, PIC, FRA [38167]

CARPENTER ALL AUS [34574] : ALL MELBOURNE, VIC, AUS [34674] : 1876+ SA & WA, AUS [34861] : 1835+ NEWCASTLE, NSW, AUS [35156] : PRE 1850 BRISTOL, GLS, ENG [33765] : 1760 CHILMARK, WIL, ENG [34204] : 1700-1750 WOLBOROUGH, DEV, ENG [34552] : 1800 DEV, ENG [34574] : PRE 1829 BRIGHTON, SSX, ENG [34696] : 1800S NEWENT, GLS, ENG [34823] : ALL WINCANTON & SHEPTON MALLET, SOM, ENG [34861] : PRE 1854 TROWBRIDGE, WIL, ENG [34999] : UNNI 1800S PADDINGTON, LND, ENG [35234] : 1720S HAWLING, GLS, ENG [35259] : 1770+ CARISBROOK, IOW, ENG [35342] : 1800+ ACTON, MDX, ENG [35433] : 1800+ HOLBORN, LND, ENG

[35524] : C1850 ENG [35532] : 1780+ LEWES, SSX, ENG [35560] : ALL BRISTOL, GLS & LAN, ENG [36152] : ALL WAR, ENG [36861] : C1756 MILDENHALL, SFK, ENG [36955] : PRE 1800 EXETER, DEV, ENG [37085] : 1650-1770 BATH, SOM, ENG [37232] : C1780 MORDEN, SRY, ENG [38268] : PRE 1700 FROME, SOM, ENG [38270] : ALL NEW YORK, USA [34674] : LYMAN 1800 MA, USA [37509] : JAMES W. 1889 ADAMS CO., IN, USA [37788] : JAMES W. 1862 OH, USA [37788] : 1650+ RI, USA [38015] : 1789 POMFRET, VT, USA [38362] : 1780-1830 WAKE CO., NC, USA [38770] : 1780-1830 CUMBERLAND CO., NC, USA [38770] : 1861-1920S GLA, WLS [34861]

CARPENTER (SEE CAPEN [36622]

CARPENTIER PRE 1800 ST EDOUARD GENTILLY, QUE, CAN & FRA [37443]

CARR 1846+ SYDNEY, NSW, AUS [34979] : 1850-1922 BALLARAT, VIC, AUS [35384] : 1860+ BRISBANE, QLD, AUS [35853] : 1850+ VIC, AUS [35853] : 1851+ MELBOURNE & BARNAWATHA, VIC, AUS [36597] : C1890+ SYDNEY, NSW, AUS [36597] : 1870-1920 DUBBO, NSW, AUS [36648] : 1776 DEAL, KEN, ENG [33929] : 1800 BETHNAL GREEN, MDX, ENG [34204] : 1837 ALNWICK, NBL, ENG [34540] : 1820+ LONG HOUGHTON, NBL, ENG [34614] : PRE 1867 TODDINGTON, BDF, ENG [34757] : 1747 FEWTON, YKS, ENG [34793] : 1800+ NORTH SHIELDS, NBL, ENG [34852] : JOHN 1800+ BURNHAM, NFK, ENG [34916] : PRE 1846 LND, ENG [34979] : JOHN PRE 1790 NEWCASTLE, NBL, ENG [35212] : C1900 ALDERSHOT, HAM, ENG [35387] : 1850+ HANSLOPE & HAVERSHAM, BRK, ENG [35387] : PRE 1830 SSX, ENG [35556] : ALL LIN, ENG [35628] : PRE 1850 MANCHESTER, LAN, ENG [35853] : JOHN 1860-1915 WEST HAM, ESS, ENG [36101] : WILLIAM 1820-1900 BETHNAL GREEN & WEST HAM, MDX & ESS, ENG [36101] : GEORGE 1931-1941 WEST HAM & LEWISHAM, ESS & KEN, ENG [36101] : 1700-1750 ARKSEY, WRY, ENG [36112] : JOHN T. 1816 MORPETH, NBL, ENG [36367] : PRE 1840 LONG CRENDON, BKM, ENG [36866] : PRE 1830 BUCKTON, NBL, ENG [37357] : ALL EAST LONDON, MDX, ENG [37700] : PRE 1832 MANCHESTER, LAN, CHS & WRY, ENG [37840] : 1834 NORTH MEOLS, LAN, ENG [37911] : 1800+ DUR, ENG [38454] : EDWARD PRE 1870 MAIDSTONE, KEN, ENG [38585] : ALL MANCHESTER, LAN, ENG & NZ [33981] : PRE 1865 GAL & ROS, IRL [34911] : PRE 1850 KIK, IRL [35199] : PRE 1829 KER, IRL [35340] : 1820-1880 MAYNOOTH, KID, IRL [38301] : 1820-1920 NEWRY, DOW, IRL [38511] : 1820-1860 BENNINGTON CO., VT, USA [35301] : 1700-1800 NY, USA [35603] : 1700-1795 LOUDOUN CO., VA, USA [37577] : 1800-1920 BROOKLYN, NY, USA [37783] : 1750-1850 SUFFOLK CO., NY, USA [37783] : PRE 1789 COLUMBIA CO., NY, USA [38055] : PRE 1890 OH, USA [38303] : 1880+ KNIGHTSVILLE, IN, USA [38454]

CARRADICE 1800+ KENDAL, WES, ENG [37196] : 1700+ NATLAND, WES, ENG [37196] : 1600+ CLAPHAM, YKS, ENG [37196] : 1700+ MIDDLETON IN LONSDALE, WES, ENG [37196]

CARRADUS 1700+ NATLAND, WES, ENG [37196] : 1800+ KENDAL, WES, ENG [37196]

CARRAGHER 1860+ SISLANEY, MOG, IRL [37079]

CARRAHER 1865+ KINSALE, COR, IRL [37079]

CARRATT 1850-1900S BALMAIN, NSW, AUS [34265] : PRE 1820 HAYDOR, LIN, ENG [34265]

CARRE 1600-1690 LA GUERCHE, PL, FRA [34514]

CARREAL (SEE CARNEAL [38287]

CARREL PRE 1880 ST OUEN & ST LAWRENCE, JSY, CHI, UK [36200]

CARRICK 1850+ LAMBTON CO., ONT, CAN [34375] : 1820-1860 FREDERICTON, NB, CAN [36934] : PRE 1850 HALTWHISTLE, NBL, ENG [34375] : 1750-1880 CUL & NBL, ENG [37338] : PRE 1900 HULL, YKS, ENG [37433] : 1700-1800 DALSTON, CUL, ENG [37654] : 1700+ SSX, ENG & NZ [35555] : C1850 LIMERICK, IRL [35959] : JANE 1825+ ARBUCKLE & NEW MONKLAND, LKS, SCT [34369] : C1832 ISLAY, ARL, SCT [36820]

CARRIER PRE 1822 LES CAYES, STE DOMING [37819] : PRE 1900 AR, USA [38217]

CARRINGTON PRE 1800 HUN, ENG [34660] : PRE 1725 ESS, ENG [35642] : JAMES 1600S LONDON, MDX, ENG [36211] : 1600+ BREWOOD, STS, ENG [36701] : 1650-1900 NORTHEAST, ESS, ENG [37042] : 1750-1900 CHELMONDISTON, SFK, ENG [37042] : 1650-1700 CT, USA [34123] : 1810 CIRCLEVILLE, OH, USA [35295] : 1750-1800 WASHINGTON CO., NY, USA [38523] : 1200-1900 WORLDWIDE [36169]

CARRION C1697 CARTAGENA, ESP [37819]

CARROL 1800+ GLENGARRY, ONT, CAN [35614] : 1840-1860 GLASGOW, LKS, SCT [36663]

CARROLL 1850-1990 BRAIDWOOD, NSW, AUS [33818] : C1850 ADELAIDE, SA, AUS [34025] : ALL VIC, AUS [34042] : 1850+ NSW, AUS [34526] : MARY PRE 1865 SOUTH GRAFTON, NSW, AUS [34539] : 1872+ HARVEY, HAMELIN, WA, AUS [35132] : 1867 WARWICK, QLD, AUS [35560] : 1854+ SYDNEY, NSW, AUS [35843] : 1890S+ BOGAN GATE, NSW, AUS [35843] : ALL BOMBALA, NSW, AUS [35843] : ALL CONDOBOLIN, NSW, AUS [35843] : JAMES C1865 WICKLIFFE, VIC, AUS [35848] : JAMES C1860 MELBOURNE, VIC, AUS [35848] : MARG MCGREGOR 1920S-1980S BAIRNSDALE, VIC, AUS [36311] : C1850 MELBOURNE, VIC, AUS [36612] : 1800+ YASS & GUNDAGAI, NSW, AUS [37993] : 1823+ PEI, CAN [38460] : 1850+ ISLINGTON, LND, ENG [33894] : 1850+ BERMONDSEY, SRY & LND, ENG [35495] : 1780-1810 LONDON, ENG [35609] : 1840S CORK CITY, COR, IRL [34204] : JOHN PRE 1816 TIPPERARY, TIP, IRL [34539] : 1830+ OFF, IRL [34702] : PRE 1800 CLA, IRL [35032] : 1800S MAY, IRL [35134] : OWEN PRE 1820 IRL [35426] : RICHARD 1820+ IRL [35426] : C1822 KILLINCHY, DOW, IRL [35552] : PRE 1857 FERBANE, OFF, IRL [35843] : JAMES C1840 DUB, IRL [35848] : PRE 1850 TULLAMORE, OFF, IRL [36612] : PRE 1870 CASTLEREAGH, ROS, IRL [37510] : PATRICK PRE 1800 TIPPERARY, TIP, IRL [37579] : 1700+ KIK, IRL [37826] : CATHERINE C1811 WEX, IRL [37992] : 1830S ATHY, KID, IRL & AUS [34845] : ELLEN 1806-1826 CORK, COR & NSW, IRL & AUS [37556] : NORA C1878-1969 WITCHITAW, KS, USA [34997]

CARRON 1890+ MELBOURNE, VIC, AUS [34798]

CARROTT C1780 CLAYPOLE, LIN, ENG [37007]

CARROWDICE 1700+ MIDDLETON IN LONSDALE, WES, ENG [37196] : 1600+ CLAPHAM, YKS, ENG [37196]

CARRUCAN 1890+ CRESWICK, VIC, AUS [34174]

CARRUTH PRE 1832 CRAIGAROGAN, ANT, IRL [35545]

CARRUTHERS ALL CAYUGA, ONT, CAN [34155] : 1880-1950 LONDON, ONT, CAN [34498] : PRE 1850 CUL, ENG [35165] : 1860+ YKS, ENG [35293] : PRE 1900 SANDFORD, OXF, ENG [36893] : PRE 1850 ARVAGH, CAV, IRL [33905] : PRE 1840 DRY, IRL [34809] : 1800+ DFS, SCT [35293] : 1740 LINN MILL,

DFS, SCT **[35350]** : 1830S LANGHOLM, DFS, SCT
[37999] : 1908+ CHICAGO, MI, USA **[34498]**

CARSCADDEN 1830+ FER, IRL **[33951]** : 1841+ IRL
& SCT **[33951]**

CARSCALLEN 1725-1753 LIM, IRL **[34408]** : ALL
ATHLONE, ROS, IRL **[38172]** : 1756 NEW YORK,
NY, USA **[38172]**

CARSON PRE 1886 VIC, NSW & QLD, AUS **[34170]** :
RICHARD 1802+ WETHERAL, CUL, ENG **[35805]** :
CAROLINE 1840+ CHS, ENG **[36641]** : PRE 1930
SOUTH OCKENDON, ESS, ENG **[37685]** : PRE 1850
DEVENISH, FER, IRL **[34201]** : 1818 FER, IRL
[35295] : PRE 1900 KILREA, LDY & ANT, IRL
[36529] : DANIEL 1800-1830 TYR, IRL **[37784]** : PRE
1865 DONAGHCLONEY, DOW, IRL **[37976]** :
ROBERT ALL DONAGHCLONEY, DOW, IRL
[37976] : PRE 1840 ARM, IRL **[38424]** : PRE 1840
MOG, IRL **[38424]** : PRE 1840 FER, IRL **[38424]** :
ROBERT PRE 1860 DONAGHCLONEY, DOW, IRL
[38776] : 1836+ ANNAGHANOON, DOW, IRL &
AUS **[35150]** : WILLIAM C1848 ST QUIVOX, AYR,
SCT **[34300]** : 1800+ ROSENEATH, DNB, SCT
[34550] : C1890 CARLUKE, LKS, SCT **[34556]** : ALL
SCT **[34758]** : 1750+ WHITTINGHAM, ELN, SCT
[35475] : 1800S WYTHE CO., VA, USA **[36896]** : 1825-
1900 NEWPORT & CINCINNATI, KY & OH, USA
[37539] : ORVILLE 1889 FILLMORE CO., NE, USA
[38132]

CARSTAIRS PRE 1900 EDINBURGH, MLN, SCT
[34784] : 1600-1800 FIF, SCT **[35627]** : MITCHELL
1825+ CRAIL, FIF, SCT **[35822]**

CARSTENS C1876 DALBY, QLD, AUS **[35807]**

CARSWELL PRE 1800 ELN, SCT **[36272]**

CART 1800S LEICESTER, LEI, ENG **[37818]**

CARTER 1860-1940 SYDNEY, NSW, AUS **[34438]** :
1855+ MAITLAND, NSW, AUS **[34786]** : PRE 1856
HOBART, TAS, AUS **[34798]** : 1857+ EMERALD
HILL, VIC, AUS **[34798]** : HENRY C1840 DAPTO,
NSW, AUS **[34807]** : MATTHEW 1834+
GOULBURN, NSW, AUS **[34807]** : 1840+ HOBART,
TAS, AUS **[34904]** : 1816+ WARKWORTH, NSW,
AUS **[35197]** : 1850+ NSW & VIC, AUS **[36608]** :
WILLIAM 1870+ HAY, NSW, AUS **[36637]** : 1820+
RICHMOND, NSW, AUS **[37130]** : 1870+ SYDNEY,
NSW, AUS **[38490]** : 1850+ ADAMINABY, NSW,
AUS **[38491]** : 1870+ VIC, AUS **[38539]** : MILES
1853+ GOLDFIELDS, VIC & NSW, AUS **[38541]** :
PRE 1841 NS, CAN **[34904]** : 1800-1950 PRINCE
EDWARD CO., ONT, CAN **[36688]** : ALL
SOUTHAMPTON, HAM, ENG **[33802]** : GEORGE
C1800S SOM, ENG **[33812]** : HENRY PRE 1885
BIRMINGHAM, ENG **[33890]** : 1840+ BINFIELD,
BRK, ENG **[34008]** : ROBERT 1794-1818
SOUTHAMPTON, HAM, ENG **[34065]** : CAROLINE
E. 1841+ SOUTHAMPTON, HAM, ENG **[34065]** :
1800+ LEWISHAM, KEN, ENG **[34163]** : 1800S
UPWELL, ISLE OF ELY, CAM, ENG **[34172]** : C1840
LONDON, ENG **[34258]** : 1850-1880 STEPNEY &
BROMLEY, LND, ENG **[34469]** : 1770-1820
ARDELEY, HRT, ENG **[34697]** : 1630-1870
BENGEO, HRT, ENG **[34697]** : 1700S PAULTON,
SOM, ENG **[34739]** : MATTHEW PRE 1834 ISLE OF
ELY, CAM, ENG **[34807]** : 1800+ BETHNAL
GREEN, MDX, ENG **[34818]** : PRE 1830 WEST
EXETER, DEV, ENG **[34904]** : HAROLD 1700+
LND, ENG **[34943]** : 1800+ LEWISHAM, KEN,
ENG **[34980]** : PRE 1790 WROXTON, OXF, ENG
[34995] : PRE 1806 SHABBINGTON, BKM, ENG
[34995] : 1850 LEWKNOR, OXF, ENG **[34995]** :
FLOWER PRE 1800 MDX, ENG **[35232]** : 1780+
LEMBOURN, BRK, ENG **[35379]** : C1754
LICHFIELD, STS, ENG **[35552]** : 1820-1850

THURLOW, SFK, ENG **[35717]** : THOMAS 1830-
1880 WELNEY, NFK & HAM, ENG **[35737]** :
ELIZABETH 1830-1880 WELNEY, NFK & HAM,
ENG **[35737]** : C1700-1900 FINSBURY, LND, ENG
[35892] : PRE 1840 SPEEN & NEWBURY, BRK,
ENG **[35902]** : 1880 MARION'S LEIGH, DEV, ENG
[35943] : PRE 1863 STOKESLEY, YKS, ENG **[35985]** :
PRE 1856 TIVERTON, DEV, ENG **[36015]** : PRE
1900 SOUTHAMPTON, HAM, ENG **[36021]** : 1750+
BISHOPS STORTFORD, HRT & ESS, ENG **[36123]** :
GEORGE 1850-1860 LIN, ENG **[36143]** : PRE 1800
BREAGE & GERMOE, CON, ENG **[36145]** : PRE
1750 BROMPTON ON SWALE, NRY, ENG **[36159]** :
PRE 1890 BIRMINGHAM, WAR, ENG **[36288]** :
1800-1880 BREDE & ICKLESHAM, SSX, ENG
[36485] : WILLIAM 1870+ PADDINGTON &
WESTMINSTER, LND, ENG **[36510]** : 1700-1850
DEV, ENG **[36688]** : 1700-1840S EWHURST, SRY,
ENG **[36879]** : 1600-1898 LONDON, ENG **[36894]** :
1776-1783 BREAGE, CON, ENG **[37108]** : PRE 1880
LONDON, ENG **[37237]** : 1750+ WALPOLE ST
ANDREWS, NFK, ENG **[37304]** : C1780 BILSDALE,
NRY, ENG **[37388]** : 1826+ HOLWAY TAUNTON,
SOM, ENG **[37518]** : C1829 BRISTOL, GLS & SOM,
ENG **[37556]** : PRE 1729 LANCASTER, LAN, ENG
[37706] : PRE 1800 ILKESTON, DBY, ENG **[37739]** :
PRE 1860 ST THOMAS, OXFORD, OXF, ENG
[37771] : PRE 1875 LEE, KEN, ENG **[37816]** : C1800
BATH, SOM, ENG **[37918]** : PRE 1800 ST MARYS
HOO, KEN, ENG **[38027]** : 1820+ STS, ENG **[38488]** :
C1811 CHOLDERTON, WIL, ENG **[38489]** : 1800S
LONG ASHTON, SOM, ENG **[38490]** : 1840+ KEN,
ENG **[38539]** : 1850+ WAVERTREE & LIVERPOOL,
LAN, ENG **[38539]** : PRE 1840 ENG **[38730]** : 1800-
1900 MILDENHALL, SFK & QLD, ENG & AUS
[35422] : PRE 1863 WEX, IRL **[34412]** : 1800-1860
WIC, IRL **[34438]** : 1800S COR, IRL **[35617]** : 1800-
1850 LIM, IRL **[36608]** : PRE 1853 RATHKEALE,
LIM, IRL **[38541]** : 1850+ ARM, IRL & NZ **[35953]** :
1863+ CHRISTCHURCH, CBY, NZ **[35985]** : 1798
OHIO CO., VA, USA **[35295]** : 1663 COROTOMON,
LANCASTER CO., VA, USA **[36358]** : HATTIE M.
C1875+ SERGEANT BLUFF, IA, USA **[37530]** :
WILLIAM W. C1840+ NY, USA **[37530]** : WILLIAM
W. C1875+ SERGEANT BLUFF, IA, USA **[37530]** :
1700-1825 NJ & TN, USA **[37539]** : PRE 1845
KNOXVILLE, TN, USA **[37817]** : 1855-1870
KEWEENAW CO., MI, USA **[38010]** : 1750-1825 NY,
USA **[38113]** : 1750-1850 OVERTON CO., TN, PA &
MA, USA **[38392]** : HONOR C1910 HERKIMER, NY,
USA **[38584]** : 1750+ LOUP CO., NE, USA **[38745]** :
1800-1830 WAKE CO., NC, USA **[38770]** : 1800-1830
CUMBERLAND CO., NC, USA **[38770]**

CARTER-GIBBS 1850S CAMBERWELL, SRY, ENG
[34204]

CARTHER WILLIAM 1900+ GLENGARRY CO.,
ONT, CAN **[36678]**

CARTHEW PRE 1800 GWITHIAN, CON, ENG **[33972]**
: ELLEN PRE 1876 CON, ENG **[34310]** : C1790
DEVONPORT, DEV, ENG **[35457]** : 1795+
GWITHIAN, CON, ENG **[38539]**

CARTHY ALL SLIGO, SLI, IRL **[36822]** : ALL GAL,
IRL & AUS **[35213]**

CARTIER ALL WORLDWIDE **[38237]**

CARTLEDGE C1810 STS & DBY, ENG **[34581]** : C1837
MANCHESTER, LAN, ENG **[34581]** : PRE 1857
CAMELEY, SOM, ENG **[34978]** : JOHN 1813+ STS
& DBY, ENG **[36294]** : CHARLES 1809+
HOLBORN, LND, ENG **[36294]** : JAMES 1837
MANCHESTER, ENG **[36294]** : WILLIAM MICH
C1775 HOLBORN, LND, ENG **[36294]** : JAMES

117

1810+ STS & DBY, ENG [36294] : HENRY 1804+ HOLBORN, LND, ENG [36294]

CARTON PRE 1860 KEN, ENG [35523] : C1825 IRL [35225]

CARTWRIGHT 1836+ WINDSOR & KURRAJONG, NSW, AUS [36600] : JOHN C1845 SYDNEY, NSW, AUS [36767] : 1700+ WAGGA & WOLLONGONG, NSW, AUS & UK [36303] : 1700-1900 BEWDLEY, WOR, ENG [34004] : 1700-1850 COVENTRY, WAR, ENG [34004] : 1700-1850 ASHBOURNE, DBY, ENG [34004] : PRE 1800 HOLMFIRTH, YKS, ENG [34613] : 1740 SEDGLEY, STS, ENG [34950] : PRE 1820 DUDLEY, WOR, ENG [35125] : PRE 1770 WOMBOURNE, STS, ENG [36110] : 1700-1770 COLESHILL, WAR, ENG [36635] : PRE 1812 WOOLDALE, WRY, ENG [36742] : 1700-1900 HOLMFIRTH, YKS, ENG [36844] : 1850-1880S OAKHILL, STS, ENG [36884] : PRE 1800 DRAYCOTT IN THE MOORS, STS, ENG [37722] : PRE 1850 MANCHESTER, LAN, ENG [38428] : PRE 1855 FER, IRL [35332] : PRE 1842 DRUNG, CAV, IRL [36629] : C1900 HECTOR, POPE CO., AR, USA [36899] : 1790-1810 PASQUOTANK CO., NC, USA [38518]

CARTY 1800+ ANTRIM, ANT, IRL [34933] : 1824-1840 DUBLIN CITY, DUB, IRL [35132] : C1800-1848 OFF, IRL [35389] : 1830-1920 NEW CASTLE, DE, USA [38136]

CARUANA 1700-1900 MALTA [38070]

CARUTH PRE 1832 HYDE PARK, ANT, IRL [35545]

CARVELL 1750-1850 BADBY, NTH, ENG [36150] : 1750-1850 NEWNHAM, NTH, ENG [36150]

CARVER 1860S GYMPIE, QLD, AUS [34015] : 1400-1700 DONCASTER, YKS, ENG [33952] : ISAAC 1570-1670 BOSTON, LIN, ENG [33952] : SIMON 1735-1825 NORTHALLERTON, YKS, ENG [33952] : PRE 1850 NORWICH, NFK, ENG [34611] : 1760 PETWORTH, SSX, ENG [34909] : C1820 SUTTON, SSX, ENG [36215] : JOHN PRE 1700 NORTHALLERTON, YKS, ENG [36619] : 1840 BROMPTON, MDX, ENG [37080] : 1700+ CLIFFORD, HEF, ENG [38020] : 1650-1900 JAMAICA [33952] : 1682-1900 PA, USA [33952] : 1630-1900 BOSTON, USA [33952]

CARVETH ALL CON, ENG [34139] : PRE 1800 SIBREOCK AREA, CON, ENG [36272] : C1720 PROBUS, CON, ENG [36899] : 1700+ LADOCK, CON, ENG [36961]

CARVIL ELIZABETH 1714+ HOLCOT, NTH, ENG [36068]

CARVILL ALL MD, USA [38068]

CARWARDINE 1750-1800 BOSBURY, HEF, ENG [35813] : 1760+ WELLAND & HANLEY CASTLE, WOR, ENG [35813] : C1700-1850 GLS & WIL, ENG [37642]

CARYESFORD 1800+ LONDON, ENG [34323]

CARYSFORTH ALL WORLDWIDE [34323]

CAS 1876 ROOSENDAAL EN NISPEN, NBT, NL [36307]

CASASOLA 1880+ MANCHESTER, LAN, ENG [35586]

CASBOLT ALL CAM, ENG & AUS [35776]

CASBURN 1834+ BURWELL, CAM, ENG [37131]

CASE PRE 1900 MAITLAND, NSW, AUS [34536] : 1800+ BATHURST, NSW, AUS [34692] : 1750-1870 ELSTOW & KEMPSTON, BDF, ENG [34520] : 1700-1900 WHISTON & LIVERPOOL, LAN, ENG [34591] : PRE 1850 LITTON CHENEY, DOR, ENG [35407] : PRE 1900 NFK, ENG [36122] : C1700-1800 MOTCOMBE, DOR, ENG [36478] : 1700-1800 CUL, ENG [37858] : C1847 AYR, SCT [34432] : 1700+ NJ,

USA [34408] : 1828-1864 SEARCY CO., AR, USA [38120] : 1760+ MORRIS CO., NJ, USA [38531]

CASEBEER 1830S TUSCARAWAS CO., OH, USA [38339]

CASELY PRE 1830 DUNSFORD, DEV, ENG [37643]

CASEMENT 1799 WHITEHAVEN, CUL, ENG [37960] : PRE 1812 ANDREAS, IOM [35185] : PRE 1770 MAUGHOLD, IOM [35185] : PRE 1800 BRIDE, IOM [35185] : C1777 INCH, DOW, IRL [37772]

CASEMORE 1850+ WATERLOO & HURON CO., ONT, CAN [34075]

CASEY 1830-1850 SYDNEY, NSW, AUS [34545] : 1871+ COOMA & ADAMINABY, NSW, AUS [34781] : C1850S SMYTHDALE, VIC, AUS [35136] : 1770 ADOLPHUSTOWN & COLBORNE, ONT, CAN [34109] : PRE 1850 TIP, IRL [34060] : PRE 1880 ST LAWRENCE PARISH, LIM, IRL [35440] : C1800 TIP, IRL [35625] : 1800+ SLI, IRL [35998] : 1800-1860 LIM, IRL [36824] : 1827 ROTH, CLA, IRL [37178] : PRE 1900 DUNGARVAN, WAT, IRL [37197] : PRE 1886 BALLYHEARNEY, VALENTIA ISL., KER, IRL [37537] : 1900+ NZ [37115] : 1700+ N & S KINGSTON, RI, USA [34109] : JOHN 1860+ BUFFALO, NY, USA [37438] : PRE 1881 CHICAGO, IL, USA [38042]

CASH PRE 1810 SHERFIELD ENGLISH, HAM, ENG [36478] : 1700-1850 ALFORD, LIN, ENG [37843] : ALL LOUTH, LIN & SRY, ENG [37972] : C1880 KNUTSFORD, CHS, ENG [38292]

CASHEL PRE 1880 LIM, IRL [36773]

CASHEN 1800-1890 CASHEL, TIP, IRL [33778]

CASHIN 1700-1850 COR, IRL [38299] : 1700-1850 TIP, IRL [38299] : PRE 1870 TIP, IRL [38299]

CASHION 1800S TAS, AUS [35340]

CASHLEY AGNES PRE 1839 EDINBURGH, SCT [34310]

CASHMAN THOMAS C1840+ EXETER, NH, USA [38593] : JAMES 1897+ ST LOUIS, MO, USA [38593]

CASHMORE ESTHER PRE 1790 HANDSWORTH, STS, ENG [36374] : 1800-1920 BIRMINGHAM, WAR, ENG [37074]

CASKIE PRE 1820 LIMAVADY, LDY, IRL [37450] : 1840 STEWARTON, AYR, SCT [35903]

CASLER JOHN 1860 SHIAWASSEE CO., MI, USA [38142]

CASLEY ALL VIC, AUS [35500]

CASPAR C1800 PETERZELL TRIBERG, BAW, BRD [38509] : PHILLIP HEIN C1820 SCHILTACH, SH, CH [38509] : C1815 LOWENWIRTH, SH, CH [38509] : C1830 NICE, PCA, FRA [38711]

CASPER PRE 1842 BRD [36020]

CASS ALL SOUTH SHIELDS, DUR, ENG [35337] : C1700-1800 MOTCOMBE, DOR, ENG [36478] : 1750-1870 MARYPORT, CUL, ENG [36983] : PRE 1877 KIK, IRL [35872] : 1813+ VT, USA [37592] : HENRY C1800-1880 NH & OH, USA [37813]

CASSADY 1780 LONDON, ENG & AUS [34008] : PRE 1850 LAWRENCEVILLE, AL, USA [37010] : 1802-1810 KNOX CO., TN, USA [38144]

CASSE PRE 1750 CANN & SHAFTESBURY, DOR, ENG [36478]

CASSEL 1800-1840 FRANKLIN, PA, USA [38095] : 1840-1910 RICHLAND, OH, USA [38095] : 1750-1815 DAUPHIN, PA, USA [38095]

CASSELL 1850+ ROTHERHITHE, LND, ENG [37206] : PRE 1850 SCT [35720] : 1920-1930 SYRACUSE & ONONDAGA, NY, USA [36654]

CASSELLS (SEE CHASSE [37923]

CASSELS ALL WORLDWIDE [37103]

CASSEY PRE 1835 EXETER, DEV, ENG [33812] : ALL GLS & ALL, ENG [37674] : ALL LONDON &, ALL, ENG [37674] : ALL UK & IOM [37674]

CASSIDY 1810-1840 SYDNEY, NSW, AUS [33826] :
THOMAS C1850 GAWLER, SA, AUS [35223] : 1871
BEALIBA, VIC, AUS [35529] : 1861-1880S LONDON,
ENG [34027] : 1800S REDHILL, CAV, IRL [34367] :
1800S DERRYGONNELLY, FER, IRL [34367] : 1850
TULLINTEANE, DON, IRL [34890] : PRE 1814
MONAGHAN, MOG, IRL [34917] : 1810-1829 CAV,
IRL [36281] : 1800S SCT [37474] : 1900+ CA, USA
[37474] : 1800-1910 BLAIR CO., PA, USA [38106] :
PRE 1900 NEW HAVEN, CT, USA [38537]

CASSILLS 1800-1870 BISHOPWORTH, DUR, ENG
[34748]

CASSIN 1820S DUBLIN, IRL [35509] : JOHN 1826-
1855 KIK, IRL [38104] : JOHN 1855-1910
MILWAUKEE, WI, USA [38104] : MARY HICKEY
1847-1857 OH, USA [38104] : JOHN 1880-1940
BUFFALO, ERIE, NY, USA [38104] : MARY
HICKEY 1855-1914 MILWAUKEE, WI, USA [38104]
: JOHN 1847-1857 OH, USA [38104] : JOHN 1900-
1980 BUFFALO, ERIE, NY, USA [38104]

CASSITY PRE 1832 MONTGOMERY CO., KY, USA
[36929]

CASSON PRE 1800 HEYSHAM, LAN, ENG [38248]

CASSWILL PRE 1850 BRISTOL & WATCHET, SOM,
ENG [34730]

CASTAN 1600-1700 PARIS, RPA, FRA [34514]

CASTEEL JOSEPH 1775-1810 TN, USA [37786] :
JOSEPH 1800-1830 MONROE CO., KY, USA [37786]

CASTELL (SEE CASTLE) [34677]

CASTER PRE 1880 CHICAGO, IL, USA [38042]

CASTERTON 1830S KETTERING & ALL, NTH, ENG
[37151]

CASTILLO PRE 1850 WALWORTH, LND, ENG
[35548] : PRE 1750 DUBLIN, IRL [38017] : PRE 1794
CHRISTIANBURG, VA, USA [38017]

CASTLE 1850+ COLAC, VIC, AUS [34871] : 1660-1750
SOUTHAM, WAR, ENG [34677] : PRE 1825
HAMMERSMITH, LND, ENG [34814] : FRED
1800+ LONDON, ENG [34871] : 1800+ KEN, ENG
[36609] : PRE 1780 LENTON, NTT, ENG [37000] :
PRE 1800 NTT, ENG [37739] : 1820S
CAMBERWELL, SRY, ENG [37833] : C1760-1815
DURHAM, DUR, ENG [37834] : 1750S MILE END
NEW TOWN, MDX, ENG [37834] : 1800S MDX &
LND, ENG [37868] : PRE 1770 HEPWORTH, WRY,
ENG [37893] : PRE 1786 KEN, ENG [38389] : 1810-
1850 PARMA, NY, USA [37810] : 1790+ NY, USA
[38522]

CASTLEDINE PRE 1800 DERBY, DBY, ENG [33796] :
1670+ SYSTON, LEI, ENG [36827] : PRE 1685 NTH,
ENG [37706]

CASTLES ALL BINALONG, NSW, AUS [35561]

CASTLETINE 1850+ MAITLAND, NSW, AUS [34424]

CASTLEY 1853+ ADELAIDE, SA, AUS [35801] :
1853+ LEYTON, VIC, AUS [35801] : 1850+
ROSSGIL, CUL, ENG [35801] : C1550-1882
ROSGILL, SHAP, WES, ENG [37890]

CASTLING 1800-1900 ANNFIELD PLAIN, DUR,
ENG [34135]

CASTNER 1700-1800 BASKING RIDGE, NJ, USA
[38524]

CASTREE 1800+ HEF, ENG [38020]

CASTRIOTTI C1200-1500 DIBA, ALBANIA [34672]

CASWELL PRE 1784 NETHERBURY, DOR, ENG
[34275] : 1400-1800 DEV, SOM & WAR, ENG [36169] :
1700S MA, USA [35322]

CASY 1820-1875 MS, USA [37822]

CATCHINGS 1840-1863 TALLAPOOSA, AL, USA
[36735] : 1863-1990 COOSA, AL, USA [36735] : 1823-
1840 HENRY, GA, USA [36735] : 1790-1823
GREENE, GA, USA [36735] : 1775-1800 WILKES,
GA, USA [36735]

CATCHPOLE PRE 1830 BANHAM, SFK, ENG [33932]
: 1750+ LONDON, ENG [37898]

CATER 1700-1800 SYMONDS INN, LND, ENG [34828]
: 1817+ BIRMINGHAM, WAR, ENG [35584]

CATES 1890+ VANCOUVER, BC, CAN [37048] :
1860+ CUMBERLAND CO., NS, CAN [37048] :
1800S LONDON & SOUTHERN COUNTIES &,
KEN, ENG [35106] : 1750+ WASHINGTON CO.,
ME, USA [37048]

CATHCART C1800+ LOCHGELLY, FIF, SCT [35629] :
1810-1820 CHESTER, SC, USA [38347]

CATHER ALL WORLDWIDE [37036]

CATHERLOUGH 1702-1772 BARRELLS, WAR, ENG
[36097]

CATHERWOOD PRE 1889 COLERAINE, ANT, IRL &
CAN [34164]

CATHERY PRE 1825 EMSWROTH & HAVANT,
HAM, ENG [34382]

CATHEY 1780-1880 ROWAN CO., NC, USA [38119] :
1810-40 NC, USA [38314]

CATHRO 1880S MELBOURNE, VIC, AUS [35089] :
1880S WELLINGTON, NZ [35089] : PRE 1780
DUNDEE, ANS, SCT [34979] : 1800S DUNDEE,
FORFAR, ANS, SCT [36842]

CATION PRE 1766 TORRYBURN, FIF, SCT [36308]

CATLEUCH PRE 1850 ELN, SCT [37353]

CATLEY 1868+ CLARE, SA, AUS [38209] : PRE 1766
BILTON IN HINSTY, ERY, ENG [37852] : 1750+
BARLEY, HRT, ENG [38209]

CATLING 1700-1800 KENNINGHALL, NFK, ENG
[38269]

CATO C1824 HOBART, TAS, AUS [34011] : 1870-1920
VIC, AUS [34844] : 1845+ VIC, AUS [37145] : ALL
TRING, HRT, ENG [37692] : PRE 1760
OCHILTREE, AYR, SCT [35406]

CATON SAMUEL 1853 CAMPBELLS CRK, VIC, AUS
[35242] : 1851 ERNESTOWN, ONT, CAN [36680] :
PRE 1790 EGREMONT, CUL, ENG [35085] : PRE
1840 ESS, ENG [35242] : PRE 1850 ESS, ENG [37749]

CATT 1870-1990 CAMPERDOWN, NSW, AUS [33818] :
1838+ DUNDAS, NSW, AUS [34685] : PRE 1838
NORTHIAM, SSX, ENG [34685] : 1715+ BECKLEY,
SSX, ENG [35587] : 1730-1850S ETCHINGHAM &
SALEHURST, SSX, ENG [37541]

CATTANACH PRE 1820 KINGUSSIE, INV, SCT
[34058] : PRE 1880 BADENOCH, INV, SCT [34268] :
ANN 1820-1870 BALLATER, SCT [36316]

CATTELL PRE 1854 LONG SUTTON, SOM, ENG
[36629] : C1780 HILL FARRANCE, SOM, ENG
[37053]

CATTERSON 1850+ STREATHAM, SRY, ENG
[35595]

CATTO PRE 1850 FOVERAN, ABD, SCT [36061] :
1800S ABERDEEN, ABD, SCT [36660]

CATTON PRE 1830 BURY ST EDMUNDS, SFK, ENG
[38270]

CAUBROATH 1660+ KILBARCHAN, RFW, SCT
[35395]

CAUDEL PRE 1800 MILDENHALL, SFK, ENG
[36955]

CAUDELL 1720+ FRANKLIN CO., STEPHENS CO.,
GA, USA [36914]

CAUDWELL ALL EGMANTON, NTT, ENG [36174]

CAUFIELD 1840S-60S ULSTER, IRL [35243]

CAUGHTREY 1900 LONDON, ENG [35705]

CAULFIELD ALL DONALD & MELBOURNE, VIC,
NSW & SA, AUS & IRL [35383] : PRE 1900 KELLS,
ANT, IRL [37708] : ALL ANNACURRA, WIC, IRL
[38300]

CAULIER ELIZ 1800+ LND, ENG [33875]

CAULKINGS PRE 1860 CT & NY, USA [37808]

CAUNCE 1786-1965 MANCHESTER, LAN, ENG [36513]

CAUSBY 1870+ BELFAST, ANT & DOW, IRL [37425]

CAUSE JANE 1810-1840 PLYMPTON, DEV, ENG [36634] : PRE 1670 BRIGHSTONE, IOW, ENG [36668]

CAUSER 1884+ BIRMINGHAM, WAR, ENG [36847]

CAUSTON 1800S CAM, ENG [35500] : ALL ENG [37677]

CAUSWAY 1790 ST GILES IN FIELDS, LND, ENG [37080]

CAVALIER EVELYN 1872 DUNEDIN, SOUTH IS., NZ [35471]

CAVALLO 1895+ CINCINNATI, OH & NY, USA [38743]

CAVANAGH PRE 1855 MOUNT ALEXANDER, VIC, AUS [35211] : ALL KEN, ENG [37595] : PRE 1830 MANCHESTER, LAN, ENG [38248] : 1750-1850 BALLINGARRY, TIP, IRL [33908] : 1840+ DUB, IRL [34174] : PRE 1841 ENNISCORTHY, WEX, IRL [35088] : ELIZA 1838+ DUBLIN, IRL [36598] : 1850+ BALLINABOY & CLIFDEN, GAL, IRL [36884] : PRE 1880 BALLINASLOE, GAL, IRL & USA [34454]

CAVANAUGH C1840 ROS, IRL [34145] : 1770S-1920 CLINTON & CARROLL, IA, USA & IRL [37529]

CAVE ALL LONDON, ONT, CAN [38480] : 1700 LEICESTER, LEI, ENG [34321] : 1820+ BRISTOL, GLS, ENG [34628] : PRE 1700 ROTHWELL & WAKEFIELD, YKS, ENG [34939] : MARY 1801 BIRMINGHAM, LEI, ENG [35343] : PRE 1875 ISLINGTON, MDX, ENG [35532] : 1800S WIGAN, LAN, ENG [35964] : 1881+ ST HELENS, LAN & MDX, ENG [37147] : C1805 SKELMERSDALE, LAN, ENG [38283] : 1880+ NE, USA [38323]

CAVELL 1700-1900 PENZANCE AREA, CON, ENG [35166]

CAVENAGH 1874+ BENDIGO, VIC, AUS [34174] : PRE 1866 KAPUNDA, SA, AUS [34174]

CAVENDISH ALL SYDNEY, NSW, AUS [36365]

CAVENEE WILLIAM W. 1850 HOLMES CO., OH, USA [38086]

CAVERS PRE 1833 ECCLES, BEW, SCT [37610]

CAVILL (SEE CAVELL) [35166]

CAW 1860-1900 LIVERPOOL, ENG [34413] : 1901-1913 NZ [34413]

CAWARDINE 1700-1800 SAL & HEF, ENG [36003]

CAWKWELL PRE 1820 YKS, ENG [35983]

CAWLEY C1947 ADELAIDE, SA, AUS [34694] : C1800 ISLINGTON, MDX, ENG [37885]

CAWOOD PRE 1750 WOODBRIDGE, NJ, USA [38225]

CAWT PRE 1830 LONDON, ENG [35335]

CAWTE 1770+ MEONSTOKE, HAM, ENG [35760] : ALL ENG [37044]

CAWTHORNE 1750-1800 CHESTER LE STREET, DUR, ENG [36056] : 1784 TERRINGTON, NFK, ENG [36253] : 1890S ROTHERHAM, YKS, ENG [37309]

CAYFORD C1835+ WOLLONGONG, NSW, AUS [35249]

CAYGIL 1680-1814 ASKRIGG & BEDALE, NRY, ENG [34352]

CAYGILL ALL WORLDWIDE [35994]

CAYON ALL WORLDWIDE [37815]

CAYOU ALL WORLDWIDE [37815]

CAYZER 1700S ST MAWGAN, CON, ENG [36961]

CEASAR 1844+ ENG [34528] : 1700-1860 BRAMLEY & SILCHESTER, HAM, ENG [37118] : 1805+ LONGSWAMP, PA, USA [38335] : 1863+ HENRY CO., OH, USA [38335] : PRE 1805 MONTGOMERY CO., PA, USA [38335] : 1550-1990 WORLDWIDE [37867]

CEASER 1940+ LUCAS CO., OH, USA [38335] : 1914+ DECATUR, IN, USA [38335] : 1914+ MECOSTA CO., MI, USA [38335] : 1916+ EMMET CO., MI, USA [38335] : 1914+ ROSCOMMON CO., MI, USA [38335]

CECIL 1800-1910 LONDON, ENG [36766]

CEDAR 1850+ PELHAM, NY, USA [35489]

CEDERHOLM 1885+ USA [36320]

CEENEY PRE 1819 CLERKENWELL, MDX, ENG [35083]

CELEY C1770 SOM, ENG [35926]

CELY 1730+ WELLINGTON, HEF, ENG [37833]

CERINI 1880+ NAIRNE, SA, AUS [36611] : 1842 GIUMAGLIO, TICINO, CH [35903]

CERVENKA PRE 1850 BLATNA, BOHEMIA, CS [37569]

CERVENY PRE 1900 PLZEN, BOH & MI, CS & USA [37446]

CESAR 1550-1990 WORLDWIDE [37867]

CEULEMANS PIETER PRE 1865 LBG, BEL [37430]

CEUNEWEELS ALL WORLDWIDE [38161]

CHABOT 1600+ FRA [37479]

CHAD PRE 1763 SHEPTON BEAUCHAMP, SOM, ENG [34270]

CHADBURN 1900-1940 ST PANCRAS, LND, ENG [37719]

CHADD ALL AUS [34554]

CHADDERTON PRE 1880 OLDHAM, LAN, ENG [38370] : ALL WORLDWIDE [37286]

CHADWICK 1870+ STRATFORD, VIC, AUS [35708] : 1830+ BURY, LAN, ENG [33942] : MARY 1784-1861 ROCHDALE, LAN, ENG [34721] : JOHN C1760+ ROCHDALE & BROOKSIDE, LAN, ENG [34721] : C1860 HOLLINWOOD, LAN, ENG [34734] : C1832 LIVERPOOL, LAN, ENG [35131] : 1750-1836 ENG [35136] : 1822 BOLTON LE MOORS, LAN, ENG [35560] : 1780-1860 SOYLAND & RIPPONDEN, WRY, ENG [38003] : 1750-90 NEW LONDON, CT, USA [38054]

CHAFFE 1850+ DUCKINFIELD, NSW, AUS [35157] : PRE 1800 BUCKFASTLEIGH, DEV, ENG [35157]

CHAILLE ALL WORLDWIDE [37890]

CHALCRAFT PRE 1900 HAM, ENG [34850]

CHALIFOUX PRE 1900 MONT LAURIER, QUE, CAN [34245] : 1800S QUE, CAN [36942] : 1840+ WA, USA [36942]

CHALK 1700+ HALE, HAM, ENG [34121] : C1812 ENG [34553] : 1800+ ISLINGTON, MDX, ENG [34882] : PRE 1735 DOWNTON & WHITEPARISH, WIL, ENG [36478] : 1750 WITHAM, ESS, ENG [37928]

CHALKE 1860 WINTERSLOW, WIL, ENG [35376]

CHALKER 1900S THIRLMERE, NSW, AUS [35567]

CHALLEN 1700-1950 SSX, ENG [36007]

CHALLENOR 1700-1900 STS, ENG [37703]

CHALLICE 1750+ SSX & ESS, ENG [36574] : 1700+ ESS, ENG [37620] : 1900+ EXMINSTER, BDF, ENG [37647] : PRE 1900 CON & DEV, ENG [37749]

CHALLIES 1800S LEEDS CO., ONT, CAN [36666]

CHALLINOR C1800S AUS & IRL [33794]

CHALLIS 1855+ TAS, AUS [33786] : PRE 1900 LONDON, ENG [34545] : C1800 ELMDON, ESS, ENG [34936] : 1800+ WIMBISH, ESS, ENG [35776] : 1700+ ESS, ENG [37620] : 1740+ MT NESSING & ELMDON, ESS, ENG & AUS [35056]

CHALLONER 1805 MARDEN, KEN, ENG [34540] : ALL LINCOLN & NORTHAMPTON, LIN & NTH, ENG [37078]

CHALMERS 1870-1915 BALLARAT, VIC, AUS [34191] : 1853+ NEWCASTLE, NSW, AUS [34275] : 1860+ TALBOT, VIC, AUS [37908] : 1800+ LONDON, ENG [37908] : 1860S SHOREDITCH, LND, ENG &

AUS **[34845]** : C1800S SCT **[34133]** : 1800S MARKINCH, FIF, SCT **[34144]** : 1780+ GLASGOW, LKS, SCT **[34260]** : 1866+ DUMBARTON, DNB, SCT **[34260]** : ALL FIF, SCT **[34758]** : 1810S BRECHIN, ANS, SCT **[36497]** : 1786+ ALYTH, PER, SCT **[37684]** : 1841+ INVERARITY, FORFAR, ANS, SCT **[37684]** : PRE 1860 ABD, SCT **[37708]** : PRE 1802 NEWBATTLE, MLN, SCT **[37852]**

CHALTON PRE 1850 OLD SWINFORD, WOR, ENG **[34711]** : PRE 1800 SSX & HAM, ENG **[35222]** : PRE 1850 CHS, ENG **[35945]**

CHALWELL 1864+ GEELONG, VIC, AUS **[37920]** : 1640-1816 TREGONY & LAMORRAN, CON, ENG **[35576]**

CHAMARD-BOIS 1834-1887 ST-GEOIRE & BEAUJEU, BRT, FRA **[34136]**

CHAMBERLAIN 1840-1900 EVANDALE, TAS, AUS **[35195]** : 1844+ MELBOURNE, VIC, AUS **[35219]** : 1829+ RICHMOND, NSW, AUS **[35419]** : ALL LENNOX & ADDINGTON CO., ONT, CAN **[35608]** : C1750 WHITTINGTON, STS, ENG **[33796]** : 1700+ BDF, ENG **[34416]** : 1750-1900 MANCHESTER, LAN, ENG **[34855]** : PRE 1850 CAM, ENG **[34858]** : PRE 1830 LIN, ENG **[34982]** : PRE 1860 BEDWORTH, WAR, ENG **[35533]** : PRE 1800 MANSFIELD, NTT, ENG **[36493]** : C1748 RICKMANSWORTH, HRT, ENG **[36975]** : PRE 1870 ISLINGTON, MDX, ENG **[37362]** : CHARLOTTE C1700 ESS, ENG **[37683]** : HUGH C1670 ESS, ENG **[37683]** : ALL NFK, ENG **[37973]** : 1690-1900 OVERTON, HAM, ENG **[38265]** : 1740+ ROSCREA, TIP, IRL **[33862]** : 1790-1820 SUSSEX CO., NJ, USA **[38139]** : JACOB 1830+ HILLSBORO, PETERBOROUGH, NH, USA **[38183]** : WALDO 1882-1969 SUDBURY, MIDDLESEX, MA, USA **[38183]** : PRE 1750 PA, USA **[38605]**

CHAMBERLEYN PRE 1815 SOUTHWARK, SRY, ENG **[36810]**

CHAMBERLIN PRE 1800 NEWBURY, VT, USA **[34113]** : REBECCA 1806-1860 MONROE CO., OH, USA **[36734]** : JOHN D. 1800-1825 ALLEGANY CO., MD, USA **[36734]**

CHAMBERS 1880+ NSW, AUS **[34424]** : 1769+ HOLDERNESS, YKS, ENG **[34063]** : PRE 1800 HORSHAM, W SSX, ENG **[34112]** : 1890+ MIDDLESBROUGH, YKS, ENG **[34710]** : 1820+ ELSING, NFK, ENG **[34710]** : PRE 1870 CIRENCESTER, GLS, ENG **[35525]** : PRE 1820 HEANOR, DBY, ENG **[35830]** : 1800+ COVENTRY, WAR, ENG **[35951]** : 1850S BIRMINGHAM, WAR, ENG **[35965]** : 1800-1900 ULCOMBE, KEN, ENG **[36071]** : 1740-1860 KIMPTON, HRT & BDF, ENG **[37194]** : 1800S BIRMINGHAM, WAR, ENG **[37331]** : PRE 1900 HULL, YKS, ENG **[37433]** : 1700-1850 NTT, ENG **[37858]** : 1700-1900 SWALE MEDWAY, KEN, ENG **[38249]** : 1799-1860 LINCOLN, LIN, ENG **[38511]** : 1832 EASKY, SLI, IRL **[35809]** : PRE 1900 BANBRIDGE, DOW, IRL **[36428]** : 1800S TYR, IRL **[36710]** : C1800 DOW, IRL **[37180]** : BENJAMIN 1709+ ANT, IRL **[38533]** : 1700+ AIRTH, STI, SCT **[34977]** : AZIKIEL PRE 1800 IA, USA **[33941]** : SCOTT 1800-1875 IA, USA **[33941]** : 1820S MORRISTOWN, NJ, USA **[34088]** : 1720 CULPEPER, VA, USA **[36907]** : 1800-1900 PA & IA, USA **[38025]** : 1885+ CLEVELAND, OH, USA **[38415]** : PRE 1865 OGDENSBURG, ST LAWRENCE, NY, USA **[38415]**

CHAMBLEY 1700-1920 ENG **[37736]**

CHAMNEY PRE 1840 BALLYGANNON, WIC, IRL **[37179]**

CHAMP C1829+ TAS & VIC, AUS **[36276]** : C1775 WEYBRIDGE, SRY, ESS & DEV, ENG **[36276]** : PRE 1861 LEAMINGTON, WAR, ENG **[36276]** : 1879 HEIGHAM, NFK, ENG **[36287]** : 1860+ SFK, ENG **[37341]** : PRE 1875 ST GILES, MDX & LND, ENG **[37452]** : 1650+ PORTARLINGTON, LEX & KID, IRL **[36087]**

CHAMPAGNE 1835+ TICONDEROGA, NY, USA **[34408]**

CHAMPION ISAAC 1802-1810 SYDNEY, NSW, AUS **[33764]** : 1860+ NSW, AUS **[37176]** : PRE 1771 SHEFFIELD, YKS, ENG **[33764]** : 1812+ DITCHEAT & WRAXHALL, SOM, ENG **[33852]** : 1837+ LAMBOURN, BRK, ENG **[33882]** : 1840S REDRUTH, CON, ENG **[33934]** : 1750-1850 SOM, ENG **[34535]** : PRE 1824 DURSLEY, GLS, ENG **[34696]** : ALL WAR, ENG **[35066]** : PRE 1850 PROBUS, CON, ENG **[35930]** : 1800+ ST HELENS, CON, ENG **[35993]** : 1650-1850 SOM, ENG **[37232]** : HARRIET 1800-1840 CON, ENG **[37434]** : PRE 1900 BATTERSEA, LND, ENG **[38276]** : PRE 1890 PLUMSTEAD, LND, ENG **[38390]** : C1880 GREENE CO., GA, USA **[36903]** : PRE 1760 NORTHUMBERLAND, VA, USA **[36973]**

CHANCE ALL KEN, ENG **[34831]** : ALL LONDON, ENG **[34831]** : 1800S LYE, WOR, ENG **[36670]** : PRE 1785 BROMSGROVE, WOR, ENG **[37103]**

CHANCELLOR ALL SOM, ENG **[34299]**

CHANDLER 1849+ SYDNEY, NSW, AUS **[34979]** : 1860+ HEALESVILLE, VIC, AUS **[35136]** : JAMES 1860+ DARLINGTON, NSW, AUS **[37904]** : 1840S SYDNEY, NSW, AUS **[38211]** : 1850+ CHILTERN, VIC, AUS **[38213]** : 1801-1843 STANSTEAD CO., PQ, CAN **[37577]** : 1839-1911 LND & MDX, ENG **[33976]** : C1800 SONNING & READING, BRK, ENG **[34152]** : 1819 SHOREDITCH ST LEONARDS, LND, ENG **[34761]** : C1789 DEVIZES, WIL, ENG **[34858]** : PRE 1827 EDENBRIDGE, KEN, ENG **[34906]** : PRE 1849 MANNINGFOLD, WIL, ENG **[34979]** : THOMAS PRE 1840 CRONDALL, HAM, ENG **[35042]** : 1800+ HUN & CAM, ENG **[35069]** : PRE 1820 BIRCHINGTON & ASH, KEN, ENG **[35462]** : PRE 1780 SSX, ENG **[37069]** : C1800 STEPNEY, MDX, ENG **[37885]** : 1800+ ALDBOURNE, WIL, ENG **[38213]** : 1700+ LONDON, ENG & AUS **[36266]** : PRE 1820 VA, USA **[36570]** : PRE 1800 VA, USA **[36926]** : 1770-1800 WILKES DISTRICT, NC, USA **[38009]** : 1830-1900 MADISON CO., NC, USA **[38009]** : 1800-1830 EDGEFIELD CO., SC, USA **[38009]** : WILLIAM 1744 CHESTER CO., PA, USA **[38152]**

CHANEY PRE 1850 LONDON, ENG **[37216]** : PRE 1840 DOVER, KEN, ENG **[37634]** : 1525-1600 LONG BENNINGTON, LIN, ENG **[38216]** : 1755-1780 TN, VA, AL, NC, USA **[37812]**

CHANNING 1840-75 CULLUMPTON, DEV, ENG **[35889]** : 1840-75 TIVERTON, DEV, ENG **[35889]**

CHANT 1700+ MONTACUTE, SOM, ENG **[34426]** : PRE 1815 FISHERTON ANGER, WIL, ENG **[35211]** : PRE 1820 WEST CHINNOCK, SOM, ENG **[35211]** : 1750-1850 MARTOCK, SOM, ENG **[36688]** : 1770+ BRIXHAM, DEV, ENG **[37132]** : 1901+ USA **[35085]**

CHANTER ALL SANDFORD, DEV, ENG **[34671]**

CHANTLER 1560-1860 SANDHURST, KEN & SSX, ENG **[35394]**

CHAPADOS JOANNIS C1700 FRA **[37429]**

CHAPIN 1890+ FORT SCOTT, KS, USA **[38361]**

CHAPLAIN 1750-1850 RUTHERGLEN, LKS, SCT **[37872]**

CHAPLES 1800 FROYLE, HAM, ENG **[37448]**

CHAPLIN 1850-1920 MOUNT BARKER, SA & VIC, AUS **[35384]** : PRE 1800 ENG **[34209]** : PRE 1850 NFK, ENG **[34317]** : 1700S ELLINGHAM, NFK, ENG **[35322]** : 1830-1900 LND, ENG **[35402]** : PRE 1850 RUGBY, WAR, ENG **[35838]** : 1810

KELVEDON, ESS, ENG [36798] : JAMES 1830 +
BROMPTON RALPH, SOM, ENG [37986] :
CHARLES 1860-1880 WLS [33900] : JAMES PRE
1856 CARDIFF, WLS [37986]

CHAPMAN ALL NEW ANGLEDOOL, NSW, AUS
[34938] : 1840 MAITLAND & ARMIDALE, NSW,
AUS [34976] : ALL VIC, AUS [35707] : 1906 +
WILCANNIA, NSW, AUS [35771] : PRE 1896
BRUNSWICK, VIC, AUS [35796] : 1867 +
MELBOURNE, VIC, AUS [37178] : 1854 + NAIRNE,
SA, AUS [37189] : LUDOVICK 1890S-1948
BRISBANE, QLD, AUS [37982] : SARAH PRE 1850
SA & WIL, AUS & ENG [37995] : 1600-1700
BARBADOS [36393] : 1840 + KENT, ONT, CAN
[37484] : PRE 1850 ST ISSEY, CON, ENG [33799] :
PRE 1780 RADWINTER, ESS, ENG [33821] : 1700S
CHERTSEY, SRY, ENG [34032] : 1820 +
HORSFORD, NFK, ENG [34092] : ALL SNEINTON,
NTT, ENG [34241] : PRE 1860 SALFORD, LAN,
ENG [34370] : 1840 ST IVES, ENG [34498] : PRE 1836
CON, ENG [34617] : ALL PICKERING, YKS, ENG
[34629] : 1795 + WETHERINGSETT, SFK, ENG
[34710] : PRE 1805 WICKFORD, ESS, ENG [34837] :
PRE 1800 HARTFIELD, SSX, ENG [34911] : C1850
STOKE DAMEREL, DEV, ENG [34952] : 1830 +
SKIPTON, YKS, ENG [35169] : PRE 1850 WEST
LAVINGTON, WIL, ENG [35346] : GEORGE 1833
TONBRIDGE, KEN, ENG [35560] : PRE 1870
HAWKHURST, KEN, ENG [35742] : 1750-1850
ALTARNUN, CON, ENG [35823] : PRE 1820 ESS &
MDX, ENG [35866] : 1900 MANCHESTER, LAN,
ENG [35881] : PRE 1892 CON, ENG [35893] : 1827
CLERKENWELL, MDX, ENG [35922] : PRE 1850
ESS, ENG [36019] : 1800S NTT, ENG [36038] : C1800
TURNHAM GREEN, MDX, ENG [36051] : 1700-
1800 ROTHWELL, NTH, ENG [36057] : C1790-1825
PITSEA & DAGENHAM, ESS, ENG [36090] : PRE
1850 HORNCASTLE, LIN, ENG [36168] :
ELIZABETH 1800 + SHOREDITCH, LND, ENG
[36378] : ALL FROME, SOM, ENG [36393] : 1820S
LANGFORD, ESS, ENG [36393] : 1800-1865
BERMONDSEY, SRY, ENG [36627] : ALL
CLERKENWELL, LND, ENG [36846] : SUSANNAH
C1805 NFK, ENG [36873] : PRE 1854 HISTON,
CAM, ENG [37189] : C1700 COTTENHAM, CAM,
ENG [37189] : 1845-1900 MANSFIELD, NTT, ENG
[37208] : PRE 1840 THURGARTON, NFK, ENG
[37385] : 1880 + CAMBERWELL, LND, ENG [37385]
: PRE 1825 PURLEY, BRK, ENG [37416] : 1840-1900
LODDON, NORWICH & ST FAITHS, NFK, ENG
[37737] : 1550-1650 SOUTHWARK, SRY, ENG [37783]
: 1750-1800 FINCHINGFIELD, ESS, ENG [37859] :
1816-23 DEV, ENG [37863] : 1780-1840 GREAT
MONGEHAM, KEN, ENG [37880] : PRE 1740
FROME, SOM, ENG [38270] : 1800 WHITTLESEA,
CAM, ENG [38272] : C1845 STAMFORD, LIN, ENG
[38272] : PRE 1890 SAWSTON, CAM, ENG [38364] :
SAMUEL C1830 ULCOMBE, KEN, ENG [38487] :
PRE 1850 HATFIELD, HRT, ENG [38722] : 1800
FRISKNEY, LIN, ENG [38756] : 1811 + DOUGLAS,
IOM [36476] : 1800-1910 KILLYDONAGH &
EMYVALE, MOG, IRL [36075] : PRE 1800 DUBLIN,
IRL [36476] : ALL CHRISTCHURCH, NZ [38487] :
ISA C1740-1820 BAN, SCT [34646] : 1700-1800 ST
MONANCE, FIF, SCT [35627] : 1800 + POLMONT,
STI, SCT [36869] : PRE 1860 ARBROATH, ANS &
CAI, SCT [36963] : LUDOVICK 1871-1890S
BONNEYTONHILL, ABD, SCT [37982] : PRE 1840
HOUSTON, RFW, SCT [38056] : 1945 BLUE ASH
CINCINNATI, OH, USA [34498] : 1940 OMAHA,
NE, USA [34498] : WILLIAM 1910 + USA [36075] :
1800 + MEDINA, OH, USA [36338] : 1850 +

JOHNSON CO., IL, USA [36956] : 1925 +
MCCRACKEN CO., KY, USA [36956] : 1750-1800
GENESEO, NY, USA [37435] : 1850-1870
KEWEENAW CO., MI, USA [38010] : PRE 1865
TREFEGLWYS, MGY, WLS [34050] : 1600S MGY,
WLS [37331] : 1790-1900 LLANWNOG, MGY, WLS
[37934] : GEORGE 1800-1846 MGY, WLS [37934] :
1830-1870 NEWTOWN, MGY, WLS [37934]

CHAPPEL ADELIA L. 1839-1923 SEATTLE, WA, AUS
[37951] : 1800 + CON, ENG [35306] : 1900 +
BEDFORD, BDF, ENG [35306] : PRE 1825 GULVAL,
CON, ENG [35709] : 1917 + SUNDERLAND, DUR,
ENG [37878]

CHAPPELL 1700 + DEV, ENG [34271] : C1800
MASBROUGH & RAWMARSH, WRY, ENG [34974]
: 1500-1700 STS, ENG [36062] : ALL SFK & NFK,
ENG [37250] : 1700-1890 MANCHESTER &
CHORLTON, LAN, ENG [38745] : PRE 1860 LND,
ENG & FRA [36741] : 1810 + PIKE CO., IN, USA
[36310] : ALL PERQUIMANS CO., NC, USA [36557]

CHAPPELLS PRE 1820 STS & CHS, ENG [36089]

CHAPPERLIN 1600-1750 WIL, ENG [37232]

CHAPPLE 1850 + EXETER, DEV, ENG [34702] : PRE
1860 WILLITON, SOM, ENG [34780] : PRE 1770
ALPHINGTON, DEV, ENG [35211] : C1690-1773
BATTLESDEN & CARDINGTON, BDF, ENG
[36068] : 1700S-1800S CHITTLEHAMPTON, DEV,
ENG [36211] : 1800 + WILLITON, SOM, ENG [36610]
: 1840 + LYTTELTON, CHCH, NZ & IRL [33926]

CHAPPLEMAN 1600 + DEV, ENG [38235]

CHARBONNEAU 1775-1850 GRAND CALUMETTE
IS, QUE, CAN [36703]

CHARBONNIER ALL WORLDWIDE [38169]

CHARD 1850 + CASTLEMAINE, VIC, AUS [37997] :
1865 + SRY, ENG [34457] : PRE 1870
CREWKERNE, SOM, ENG [36180] : 1600-1890
BRISTOL, GLS, ENG [36894]

CHARDAVOYNE C1685-C1781 PLYMOUTH, DEV,
ENG [37890]

CHARGE PRE 1910 WATFORD, HRT, ENG [35458]

CHARIE ALL WORLDWIDE [35778]

CHARITY ALL HARRINGWORTH, NTH, ENG
[33916]

CHARKER ALL ENG [35458]

CHARLAND 1820 NAPIERVILLE, QUE, CAN [36907]

CHARLEBOIS 1050 + QUE, CAN [36568]

CHARLES 1740-1760 OTTERY ST MARY, DEV, ENG
[34552] : 1900 + WANSTEAD, ENG [35701] : 1900 +
BRISTOL, GLS, ENG [35701] : 1640-1950
MEMBURY & AXMINSTER, DEV, ENG [35701] :
1790-1870 MEMBURY, DEV, ENG [36439] : SARAH
1870-85 WORCESTER, WOR, ENG [37919] : 1800-
1857 NEWTOWN, KID, IRL [34183] : C1839
CLAREMORRIS, MAY, IRL [36762] : 1800-1900
DRAPERSTOWN & COOKSTOWN, LDY, IRL
[37227] : 1820-1840S KILDRESS & COOKTOWN,
TYR, IRL [37308] : ANDREW 1832-1910
DRAPERSTOWN, LDY & WOR, IRL & ENG [37227
: SARAH 1858-70 CRUMLIN, MON, IRL & ENG
[37919] : PRE 1786 NEWBATTLE, MLN, SCT [37852]
: 1890-1990 NEW YORK, NY, USA [34552] : JAMES
1862-1942 DRAPERSTOWN & DESERTMARTIN,
TX, USA & IRL [37227] : ALL MON & GLA, WLS
[37269]

CHARLESTON NELSON PRE 1917 MONROE, NY,
USA [38233]

CHARLESWORTH 1850 + WALHALLA & SALE, VIC
AUS [34421] : 1841 + SA, AUS [34775] : PRE 1840
LONDON, ENG [34421] : PRE 1850 HEF, ENG
[34421] : PRE 1840 KEN, ENG [34775] : ALL
BUCKMINSTER, LIN, ENG [36174] : PRE 1780

THURLSTONE, PENISTONE, WRY, ENG [37754] : 1857S ENG [38184]

CHARLETON THOMAS C1714-1788 ELSDON, NBL, ENG [36244] : ALL WORLDWIDE [37272]

CHARLEY 1860S KAMLOOPS, BC, CAN [36729] : ALL ENG [35460] : ALL MARYLEBONE, LND & MDX, ENG [35460]

CHARLICK JANE 1800 NEWTON FERRERS, DEV, ENG [36309]

CHARLTON PRE 1807 SYDNEY, NSW, AUS [37982] : 1800 BETHNAL GREEN, MDX, ENG [34204] : 1870-1900 DENTON, DUR, ENG [34211] : ALL GILLINGHAM, DOR, ENG [34595] : PRE 1850 OLD SWINFORD, WOR, ENG [34711] : 1780+ NBL, ENG [35579] : PRE 1900 BRISTOL, GLS, ENG [37272] : PRE 1900 WALLSEND, NBL, ENG [37704] : 1750+ EXETER & CREWKERNE, DEV, ENG [37735] : PRE 1800 NTT, ENG [37739] : 1700-1800 STOURTON, WIL, ENG [37747] : PRE 1900 HIGH SPEN, DUR, ENG [38457] : ALL GORTIN & ROUSKY, TYR, IRL [34772] : 1850S MONEYMORE, LDY, IRL [37879]

CHARLWOOD ALL SRY, ENG [35727] : ALL SSX, ENG [35727] : 1865+ PADDINGTON, MDX, ENG [35727]

CHARMAN 1770-1810 EPSOM, SRY, ENG [34687] : PRE 1893 WARNHAM, SSX, ENG [36215]

CHARNLEY PRE 1800 TATHAM, LAN, ENG [36701] : 1800-1840 LIVERPOOL, LAN, ENG [37869]

CHARRON-DUCHARME PRE 1640 MEAUX, CHA, FRA [34106]

CHARTER 1852+ PORTLAND & WARRACKNABEAL, VIC, AUS [35205] : 1850-1920 CHINA [37220] : PRE 1852 CAM, ENG [35205]

CHARTERIS 1725+ CHARTRES, FRA [34408]

CHARTERS 1700-1900 CHATTON, NBL, ENG [36776] : 1800S ST HELENS, LAN, ENG & CEYL [37220] : 1800+ DFS, SCT [35719]

CHARTIER 1750 LONDON, ENG [34149] : PRE 1756 SPITALFIELDS, LND, ENG & FRA [37261] : 1700 BLOIS, FRA [34149] : PRE 1650 LAFLECHE, PL, FRA [38525]

CHARTRAN PRE 1666 ECTOT LES BANS, HN, FRA [35005]

CHARTRAND PRE 1666 ECTOT LES BANS, HN, FRA [35005]

CHASE 1800-1850 HULL, QUE, CAN [34113] : 1800 KINGS LYNN, NFK, ENG [33848] : 1790+ PRIVETT, HAM, ENG [35905] : 1829+ BRAMDEAN, HAM, ENG [35905] : 1720-1730 EASTHAM, MA, USA [38099]

CHASELING 1850+ NSW, AUS [33768]

CHASEMORE 1700S HORSHAM, SSX, ENG [34117]

CHASNEY 1700-1800 BURNHAM THORPE, NFK, ENG [37845]

CHASSE 1940+ QUE, CAN [36678]

CHASSELLS PRE 1860 LKS, SCT [37923]

CHASTAIN 1083-1990 CHAROST, FRA [35316]

CHATAGUIER 1830+ FRA [34029]

CHATER C1816 BURTON DASSETT, WAR, ENG [35746] : ALL WOR & STS, ENG [37373]

CHATFIELD 1800S BRIGHTON, SSX, ENG [34223] : 1800+ MDX, ENG [34739] : PRE 1800 SSX, ENG [34739] : PRE 1800 UTTOXETER & CHEADLE, STS, ENG [34955] : 1780+ HAILSHAM, SSX, ENG [35436] : 1750 ARDINGLY, SSX, ENG [38209]

CHATHAM ALL USA [38312]

CHATLEY ALL GREAT LEIGHS, ESS, ENG [34151] : 1700S LONDON, ENG [34151]

CHATTAWAY C1800-1875 KINGS COUGHTON, WAR, ENG [35883]

CHATTEN 1900+ THREE HILLS, ALB, CAN [34477] : 1800+ ONT, CAN [34477]

CHATTERLEY 1750-1850 MUCCLESTONE, STS, ENG [38005]

CHATTERSON ADELINE S. 1800+ ONT, CAN [34511]

CHATTERTON PRE 1869 MELBOURNE, VIC, AUS [35736] : PRE 1900 HECK, WRY, ENG [36187] : 1781+ WEST HALTON, LIN, ENG [36421] : PRE 1850 WRY, ENG [37731] : PRE 1845 WORLDWIDE [37428]

CHATWICK C1790 COLCHESTER, ESS, ENG [33796]

CHATWIN PRE 1819 BIRMINGHAM, WAR, ENG [36177]

CHATWORTH PRE 1815 DUNSTER, SOM, ENG [37144]

CHAUNCEY PRE 1900 ME, USA [36933]

CHAUSSE 1600-1670 BOURG DE MAILLE, FRA [34514]

CHAUVIN 1862 BOLLEVILLE, HN, FRA [38163]

CHAVE 1963 CHICAGO, MI, USA [34498] : 1963 BETHLEHEM, MI, USA [34498] : 1963 DETROIT, MI, USA [34498]

CHAVIS PRE 1700 ESS, ENG [38745]

CHAWNER 1800S KEN, ENG [35994]

CHEATHAM PRE 1800 ENG [38196]

CHEATLE 1830+ ASHBY DE LA ZOUTH, LEI, ENG [37911]

CHECKETTS 1700-1850 ASTON CANTLOW, WAR, ENG [36065] : 1847+ WHITTINGTON, WOR, ENG [37230]

CHECKLAND C1874 WESTMINSTER, MDX, ENG [37148]

CHECKLEY 1650+ SAPCOTE & NEWBOLD VERNON, LEI, ENG [36827]

CHECKSFIELD PRE 1840 TENTERDEN, KEN, ENG [37541]

CHEEK C1750 COGGESHALL, ESS, ENG [37053]

CHEESEMAN 1700+ PORTSMOUTH, HAM, ENG [33814] : PRE 1880 MDX, ENG [34848] : PRE 1826 CAMBERWELL, LND, ENG [35948] : ALL LIN, ENG [35983] : 1800+ WROTHAM & SEVENOAKS, KEN, ENG [36887]

CHEESMAN 1970+ NIAGARA FALLS, ONT, CAN [34510] : 1800+ SOUTHWICK, SSX, ENG [35482] : ALL KEN, ENG [36157] : ALL SSX, ENG [36157] : ALL EAST PECKHAM, KEN, ENG [36157] : C1770 HAMBLEDON, SRY, ENG [36860]

CHEETHAM 1830-1890S CONGLETON, CHS, ENG [34605] : 1790+ OLDHAM, LAN, ENG [36568] : 1860S BINGHAM, NTT, ENG [36831] : 1830S+ BINGHAM, NTT, ENG [37317] : PRE 1850 NTT, ENG [37739]

CHEEVER 1500-1650 ST ANDREW HUBBARD, LND, ENG [37783]

CHEFFINGS PRE 1900 ENG [35901]

CHEGWIDDEN PRE 1880+ SA, AUS [35453] : PRE 1736 WENDRON, CON, ENG [33992]

CHELFORD PRE 1820 LITTLE CHEVERALL, WIL, ENG [35853]

CHELLEW PRE 1850 LUDGVAN, CON, ENG [36145] : 1860-1875 KEWEENAW CO., MI, USA [38010] : ALL WORLDWIDE [35747]

CHELLINGWORTH 1800-1910 BIRMINGHAM, WAR, ENG [37074]

CHELMAN 1840S GOTHENBURG, SWE [38079]

CHENEY 1848+ BATHURST, NSW, AUS [35412] : 1890S HUMULA, NSW, AUS [37947] : 1600-1750 YAXLEY, SFK, ENG [37457]

CHENIER 1760-1800 POINTE CLAIRE, QUE, CAN [35283]

CHENOWETH PRE 1854 LONDON &, ENG [35035]

CHERITON PRE 1900 TIVERTON, DEV, ENG **[33965]**

CHERRETT C1895-1917 BOURNEMOUTH, DOR & HAM, ENG **[34794]**

CHERRY 1847+ WILBERFORCE, NSW, AUS **[35393]** : C1848 HAM & WIL, ENG **[34836]** : PRE 1777 GREAT HASELEY, OXF, ENG **[35046]** : PRE 1650 HRT, ENG **[35642]** : 1800+ CHRISTCHURCH & NEWGATE, LND, ENG **[36863]** : ALL BKM, ENG **[37139]** : PRE 1850 HULL, ERY, ENG **[37459]** : 1800-1900 GRINTON, NRY, ENG **[38244]** : 1700+ MOG, IRL **[34572]**

CHESBOROUGH 1860S SYRACUSE, NY, USA **[37541]**

CHESEBROUGH 1500+ BOSTON, LIN, ENG **[38745]**

CHESHAM 1800+ NORTHILL & OLDWARDEN, BDF, ENG **[37151]** : 1700S GREAT HALLINGBURY, ESS, ENG **[37250]**

CHESHIRE PRE 1750 SHIFNAL, SAL, ENG **[35181]** : 1800S PORTSEA, HAM, ENG **[36409]** : PRE 1870 BIRMINGHAM, WAR, ENG **[37325]** : 1800-1900 BIRMINGHAM, WAR, ENG **[37924]**

CHESNEL PRE 1820 LE NEUFBOURG, BN, FRA **[36704]**

CHESNEY ALL ANT, IRL **[33985]** : ALL AHOGHILL, ANT, IRL **[38288]**

CHESSELLS 1848+ VIC, AUS **[35379]** : PRE 1848 GREAT SHEFFORD, BRK, ENG **[35379]**

CHESSUM 1800+ BIGGLESWADE & HITCHIN, BDF, ENG **[37151]**

CHESTER 1860 NEW RICHMOND, QUE, CAN **[38131]** : C1850 NOTTINGHAM, NTT, ENG **[34734]** : 1800+ SOM, ENG **[34933]** : PRE 1842 MELTON MOWBRAY, LEI, ENG **[35572]** : ALL LND, ENG **[37668]**

CHESTERFIELD 1750+ CON, ENG **[35060]**

CHESTERMAN PRE 1835 CHELTENHAM, GLS, ENG **[35773]**

CHESTERTON PRE 1750 HUNGERTON, LEI, ENG **[34370]** : 1500-1650 STS, ENG **[36062]**

CHESTLE PRE 1800 IOW, ENG **[38700]**

CHESTNUT ALL ANT, IRL **[35706]** : ALL USA **[35706]**

CHESTNUTWOOD 1800S BERKS CO., PA, USA **[35165]**

CHESWORTH 1900S LAN, ENG **[37221]** : PRE 1750 CHS & STS, ENG **[38055]**

CHETWIN PRE 1800 BOSBURY, HEF, ENG **[36633]**

CHETWYND C1870 BADDESLEY ENSON, WAR, ENG **[37669]**

CHEVALIER PRE 1800 JSY, CHI **[37256]** : ALL COWES, IOW, ENG **[37256]**

CHEVALLEY PRE 1900 VD, CH **[37910]**

CHEVALLIER PRE 1700 LOTHBURY, LND, ENG **[34828]** : ALL ASPALL, SFK & CHI, ENG **[37735]**

CHEVELAN PRE 1800 FRA **[36503]**

CHEVELEY 1500+ ESS, ENG **[35403]**

CHEVIN PRE 1860 LND, ENG **[36645]**

CHEW 1840+ BATHURST, NSW, AUS **[34693]** : PRE 1840 SYDNEY, NSW, AUS **[35548]** : PRE 1840 LIVERPOOL, LAN, ENG **[34693]** : PRE 1671 ANNE ARUNDEL CO., MD, USA **[37551]**

CHEWINGS 1840+ SA, AUS **[36267]** : PRE 1840 NTH PETHERTON, SOM, ENG **[36267]**

CHEYNE ALL TANGWICK, SHI, SCT **[36756]** : C1800 ABD, SCT **[36856]**

CHIASSON PRE 1910 INVERNESS CO., NS, CAN **[38447]**

CHIBI ALL WORLDWIDE **[37453]**

CHICK GEORGE 1833 MAITLAND, NSW, AUS **[37106]** : PRE 1850 LONDON, ENG **[34287]** : C1800 WEST CHINNOCK, SOM, ENG **[35502]** : 1830-1860 BATH, SOM, ENG **[35798]** : PRE 1900 ILMINSTER, SOM, ENG **[36529]** : C1850 GUERNSEY, CHI, ENG

[36671] : GEORGE 1810 LONDON, ENG **[37106]** : 1612-1742 BERWICK, ME, USA **[35294]**

CHIDGEY PRE 1830 EXFORD, SOM, ENG **[37622]**

CHIDLOW PRE 1806 MANCHESTER, LAN, ENG **[38248]**

CHIKI ALL WORLDWIDE **[37453]**

CHILCOT 1700-1800 PITMINSTER, SOM, ENG **[37381]**

CHILCOTT C1821 KILTON, SOM, ENG **[37144]**

CHILD 1850+ MELBOURNE, VIC, AUS **[34414]** : 1800S SWAFFHAM, NFK, ENG **[34151]** : 1700+ BOLTON, LAN, ENG **[34414]** : RICHARD PRE 1833 MANCHESTER, ENG **[35250]** : C1835 BRIXTON, SRY, ENG **[35764]** : PRE 1830 READING, BRK, ENG **[35946]** : 1600-1900 BRISTOL, GLS, ENG **[36130]** : 1780-1810 FELMINGHAM, NFK, ENG **[38453]**

CHILDERS 1660 HENRICO, VA, USA **[38198]**

CHILDERSON 1751 BRAMHAM, YKS, ENG **[34939]**

CHILDES PRE 1830 READING, BRK, ENG **[35946]**

CHILDREN C1800 BARRINGTON, TAS, AUS **[35089]**

CHILDS WILLIAM 1804-1888+ LIVERPOOL, NSW, AUS **[35497]** : PRE 1910 HAMPTON, LND, ENG **[34968]** : PRE 1838 MELBURY OSMOND, DOR, ENG **[35895]** : PRE 1830 READING, BRK, ENG **[35946]** : PRE 1650 THURSLEY, SRY, ENG **[37420]** : 1850+ ROWLEY GREEN, HRT, ENG & AUS **[33926]** : 1850+ CHRISTCHURCH, CANTERBURY, NZ **[36750]** : 1700-1850 NH, USA **[33753]** : ALL OH & NY, USA **[36571]** : 1600+ MA, CT & ME, USA **[38021]**

CHILLINGSWORTH 1800-1900 LONDON, ENG **[35174]** : 1750-1900 CHELTENHAM, GLS, ENG **[35174]**

CHILLINGWORTH PRE 1849 HAMMERSMITH, LND, ENG **[33992]** : 1750-1900 CHELTENHAM, GLS, ENG **[35174]** : 1800-1900 LONDON, ENG **[35174]** : 1750+ OXFORD, OXF, ENG **[38375]** : 1750+ SEVENHAMPTON, WIL, ENG **[38375]**

CHILVER PRE 1820 POTTER HEIGHAM, NFK, ENG **[37716]** : PRE 1850 LONDON, MDX, ENG **[37716]**

CHILVERS 1830+ TOTTINGTON, NFK, ENG **[33942]** : PRE 1815 SFK, ENG **[35162]** : 1825+ CASTLEACRE, NFK, ENG **[37483]**

CHINDBLOM 1870+ CHICAGO, IL, USA **[37821]**

CHINERY PRE 1800 GARBOLDISHAM, NFK, ENG **[35571]**

CHING PRE 1850 CON & DEV, ENG **[35058]** : 1750-1860 COMBE & VERNHAM DEAN, HAM, ENG **[36485]** : ALL ENG **[37738]** : 1840+ NELSON, NZ **[35058]**

CHINN 1750-1810 ST MARY HINTON, DOR, ENG **[37602]**

CHINNICK PRE 1860 DEV, ENG **[35378]**

CHIPMAN PRE 1750 ST ENODER, CON, ENG **[34573]** : PRE 1834 BLISLAND, CON, ENG **[37446]** : 1780+ GUILFORD, NC, USA **[38517]** : 1830+ SCHUYLER, IL, USA **[38517]**

CHIPPERFIELD PRE 1842 CHIGWELL ROW, ESS, ENG **[34278]** : PRE 1749 LONDON, ENG **[34278]**

CHIPPETT 1799-1876 LEADING TICKLES, NFD, CAN **[34208]**

CHIPPING 1800-1830 BRIGHTON, SSX, ENG **[36035]** : PRE 1847 NORWOOD, SRY, ENG **[36035]**

CHISHOLM 1850+ BRANT, ONT, CAN **[35627]** : 1860+ DUNEDIN, OTAGO, NZ **[36871]** : 1900+ NZ & SCT **[33800]** : 1750+ ST ANDREWS, FIF, SCT **[33800]** : C1780 KILLEARNAN, ROC, SCT **[34713]** : 1800+ LEMPETLAW, ROX, SCT **[35627]** : PRE 1802 NEW DEER, ABD, SCT **[36673]** : 1830+ HADDINGTON, ELN, SCT **[36871]** : 1860+ EDINBURGH, MLN, SCT **[36871]** : 1790S INV &

ROC, SCT [37263] : HELEN PRE 1860 GREEN LAW, BEW, SCT [38483] : 1780+ FIF, SCT & AUS [35056]

CHISLETT 1800+ HERMITAGE BAY, NFD, CAN [36684] : C1772 HORSINGTON, SOM, ENG [34581]

CHISNALL 1725-1800 RAYDON, SFK, ENG [36717]

CHISNELL 1870S CHESHUNT, HRT, ENG [37151] : 1870S NOTTINGHAM, NTT, ENG [37151] : 1800-1840S ALDGATE & STEPNEY, LND, ENG [37151]

CHISOLM 1820 NC, USA [38198]

CHISWELL C1840 CON, ENG [35838]

CHITAYAT ALL BAGDAD, IRAQ [38481]

CHITHAM PRE 1870 ESS, ENG [36765]

CHITTAM PRE 1800 ESS, ENG [36019]

CHITTENDEN JAMES 1800+ DOVER, KEN, ENG [36621] : 1650-1860 STAPLEHURST, KEN, ENG & AUS [36874]

CHITTICK 1840-1880 WOOLWICH, KEN, ENG [36349]

CHITTLE PRE 1830 KINGSCLERE & BURGHCLERE, HAM, ENG [37687]

CHITTLEBURGH 1840-1900 KIRBY LE SOKEN, ESS, ENG [37376]

CHITTY C1850 TAS, AUS [34853] : 1841+ LAUNCESTON, TAS, AUS [35801] : 1846+ MELBOURNE, VIC, AUS [35801] : 1841+ FARNHAM, SRY, ENG [35801] : PRE 1902 CAMBERWELL, LND, ENG [35948] : PRE 1685 GODALMING, SRY, ENG [37420] : 1750+ SRY, ENG [38075]

CHITWOOD PRE 1800 NC, USA [33907]

CHIUPKA ALL GALICIA, POL & SU [34146]

CHIVAS C1800 PETERHEAD, ABD, SCT [38253]

CHIVERS 1838+ MUSWELLBROOK, NSW, AUS [35740] : 1800S BRIGHTON, SSX, ENG [34621] : C1850 SHOREDITCH, MDX, ENG [35872] : 1825+ SOUTHWARK, SRY, ENG [35921] : 1830+ BECKINGTON, SOM, ENG [36195] : PRE 1842 WIL, ENG [36841] : ALL LAMBETH, LND & MDX, ENG [37452]

CHIVERTON PRE 1744 HEADLEY & SELBORNE, HAM, ENG [35247] : ALL HAM, SRY & SSX, ENG [35247]

CHLAP PRE 1800 LANDSBERG, OPR, GER [38648]

CHOAT ALL COLCHESTER, ESS, ENG [34663]

CHOATE PRE 1660 IPSWICH, MA, USA [38348]

CHOLLAGE 1775-1830 ROSENKOPF PFALZ, BAV, GER [37516]

CHOMPION PRE 1699 PAUL, CON, ENG [37319]

CHONG 1870-1920 RUSHWORTH, VIC, AUS [34191]

CHOREA ALL WORLDWIDE [37244]

CHOULERTON PRE 1850 DBY & NTT, ENG [36140]

CHOULS PRE 1830 GREAT BEDWYN, WIL, ENG [35346]

CHOVIN (SEE CHUVIN) [38237]

CHOWN 1800+ KENTISBEARE, DEV, ENG [33950] : 1700-1900 LYMPSTONE, DEV, ENG [38579]

CHOYCE 1727+ PONSONBY, CUL, ENG [38067]

CHRAUN PRE 1800 IRL [33869]

CHRIMES 1700-1850 BIRKENHEAD, CHS, ENG [37306]

CHRINGHALL ALL WORLDWIDE [37193]

CHRISFORD 1550-1850 SANDHURST & HAWKHURST, KEN, ENG [35394]

CHRISKER HENRY 1770-1790 GETTYSBURG, ADAMS, PA, USA [38780]

CHRISMAN 1830S WAYNE CO., KY, USA [38017]

CHRIST ALL HEN & WEF, GER [34861] : PRE 1750 WALDBACH, WUE, GER [35242]

CHRISTENSEN 1880+ HERVEY BAY, QLD, AUS [33887] : 1870+ VIC, AUS [34550] : 1800+ VREILA, DEN [33887] : 1820+ COPENHAGAN, DEN [34308] : PRE 1850 HJORRING, DEN [34442] : 1834+

HAASUM, VIBORG, DEN [34926] : PRE 1856 FREDERICK SANDS, DEN [35113] : PRE 1888 VARDE, DEN [35451] : 1840+ HELSINGOR, DEN [35489] : 1850-1870S JEGINDA & LEMVIG, SJELLAND, DEN [36285] : PRE 1876 DEN [36878] : 1800S ALS, SHO, DEN [38019] : 1700+ RORAS, S TRNDLG, NOR [36326] : ALL OSLO, NAES, NOR [36881]

CHRISTER PRE 1850 STANLEY, DUR, ENG [36499]

CHRISTERSEN PRE 1870 ALLER, DEN [35339]

CHRISTESEN 1800-1850 HEJLES, VEJLE, DEN [34753]

CHRISTIAANS C1914 WOENSEL, NBT, NL [35557]

CHRISTIAENS 1845 BEVEREN LEIE, OVL, BEL [38162]

CHRISTIAN 1840+ MACLEAY RV, NSW, AUS [34306] : 1740+ LIVERPOOL, LAN, ENG [34174] : 1750-1850 BOURNE, LIN, ENG [37018] : 1600+ CON, ENG [38725] : 1800+ WITHYHAM, SSX, ENG [38725] : 1700+ WATERFORD, WAT, IRL [38725] : PRE 1840 KRISTIANSUND, NOR [35525] : 1760+ DURRAN & WATTEN, CAI & DUB, SCT & IRL [35013] : ALL IOM, UK [35746] : PRE 1700 MAUGHOLD & LEZAYRE, IOM, UK [35866] : GILBERT 1770S AUGUSTA CO., VA, USA [37585] : MARY JOICE 1816 MADISON CO., GA, USA [38155] : DAVID PRE 1820 TUSCARAWAS, OH, USA [38348] : ALL OH, USA & GER [38369]

CHRISTIANE M. ANNE 1660+ COLAR, NY, USA [36678]

CHRISTIANSEN PRE 1873 YDING, JUTLAND, DEN [34003] : PRE 1864 CARLOW, SHO, DEN [37978]

CHRISTIANSON 1825-1880 KRISTIANNA, NOR [36331]

CHRISTIE PRE 1927 BLACKHEATH, NSW, AUS [35245] : PRE 1900 BALLARAT, VIC, AUS [35245] : PRE 1800 NS, CAN [34403] : PRE 1800 NS, CAN & ENG [34403] : 1840+ NS, CAN & SCT [34500] : PRE 1900 LONDON, ENG [35245] : 1726+ ISLES OF SCILLY, CON, ENG [36000] : LOUISA 1802-1829 HALLIFORD, MDX, ENG [36678] : PRE 1860 ABD, SCT [33808] : 1809+ BALQUHIDDER, CLK, SCT [33996] : 1700S MENMUIR, ANS, SCT [34032] : PRE 1790 BRECHIN, ANS, SCT [34053] : C1800-1900 ABERDOUR, ABD, SCT [34400] : 1700+ CLK, SCT [34572] : PRE 1832 ALVAH, BAN, SCT [34840] : PRE 1841 GLASGOW, LKS, SCT [35572] : C1800 ST NINIANS, STI, SCT [35602] : 1700+ FIF, SCT [35627] : C1750-1840 FORDYCE, BAN, SCT [36652] : 1770+ HUNTLY, ABD, SCT [36652] : 1780-1850 ARBUTHNOT, KCD, SCT [37129] : C1775 CARNBEE, FIF, SCT [37704] : PRE 1855 PAISLEY, RFW, SCT [37925] : PRE 1860 GLASGOW, SCT [38057] : PRE 1800 SCT & ENG [34403]

CHRISTIN 1700+ LONDON, LND, ENG [36637]

CHRISTINEZ C1856 WORLDWIDE [35887]

CHRISTLE 1788+ ICKLETON, CAM, ENG [35537]

CHRISTMAN C1830 RUTHERFORD CO., NC, USA [37032]

CHRISTMANN C1705 EDENKOBEN, PFALZ, GER [38184] : PRE 1800 WATTENHEIM, RPF, GER [38681]

CHRISTMAS 1860+ SYDNEY, NSW, AUS [34979] : ALL STEEPLE MORDEN & HAWTHORN, CAM & VIC, AUS [35467] : PRE 1840 MDX, ENG [34865] : PRE 1842 MDX, ENG [34979] : 1800+ KENSINGTON, LND, ENG [36493] : DANIEL PRE 1854 SOUTH, WLS [34992]

CHRISTOFFER 1800-1900 EAST LONDON, MDX, ENG [38516] : 1750-1850 OSTERHOLZ SCHARMBECK, HAN, GER [38516]

CHRISTOFFERSON ALL MANISTEE, MI, USA [36325]

CHRISTOPHER 1840-1900 YORK TWP., ONT, CAN [34346] : PRE 1850 ZENNOR, CON, ENG [33972] : PRE 1845 WANDSWORTH, LND, ENG [36475] : 1780-1900 WEYMOUTH, DOR, ENG [37211] : 1890-1920 LACONIA, NH, USA [37211] : MELINDA 1828-1919 HAYWOOD CO., NC, USA [38141]

CHRISTOPHERSON 1600+ COLTON & ULVERSTON, LAN, ENG [35306]

CHRISTY C1865 SYDNEY, NSW, AUS [35582] : PRE 1800 ASHWELL, HRT, ENG [35229] : 1720-1800 DOW, IRL [35283] : 1700+ LECROPT, PER, SCT [38726] : ALL USA [37592] : 1860S CUMING CO., NE, USA [38323]

CHRYSTAL 1800S ST BOSWELLS & COCKBURNSPATH, BEW & ROX, SCT [37853]

CHUBB PRE 1880 AXBRIDGE, SOM, ENG [34713] : 1750+ ST EDMONDS, WIL, ENG [35475]

CHUN 1720-1850 SILCHESTER, HAM, ENG [37118]

CHUNN 1850-1900 LONDON, ENG [34399]

CHURCH 1850-1925 BETHNAL GREEN, MDX, ENG [34242] : PRE 1800 THANET, KEN, ENG [34269] : 1800S SOM, ENG [34979] : 1840S KENTISH TOWN, LND, ENG [35728] : PRE 1850 WELWYN, HRT, ENG [37067] : 1550-1650 ASHTON, NTH, ENG [37783] : 1800 LEISTON, SFK, ENG [37928] : PRE 1838 IVER, BKM, ENG & AUS [34463] : 1800-1930 NEW ROMNEY, KEN & QLD, ENG & AUS [35422] : G.R. 1962 KER, IRL [34111] : 1836 LDY, IRL [37605] : PRE 1850 LDY, IRL [38457] : 1786 KENNEBEC CO., ME, USA [38243] : 1850+ PLEASINGTON, CA, USA [38454] : 1620+ PLYMOUTH, MA, USA [38454] : ALL WORLDWIDE [36498]

CHURCHES 1856+ KELSO, NSW, AUS [35504] : PRE 1855 MEARE, SOM, ENG [35504]

CHURCHILL 1850+ GOULBURN DISTRICT, NSW, AUS [35854] : 1800+ WOODSTOCK, NB, CAN [34163] : ALL MOOREPARK, MAN, CAN [34629] : 1750+ WOODSTOCK, OXF, ENG [34455] : PRE 1842 HARDINGTON MANDEVILLE, SOM, ENG [35854] : ALL ILMINSTER & ILTON, SOM, ENG [36529] : ELLEN C. PRE 1843 DOVER & BUCKLAND, KEN, ENG [36532] : 1700+ MORCHARD BISHOP, DEV, ENG [37088] : MARTHA 1820+ POOLE, DOR & HAM, ENG [37161] : ALL DEDDINGTON & BLADON, OXF, ENG [38079]

CHURCHILL (SEE CHURC [34250]

CHURCHMAN PRE 1800 SAWSTON, CAM, ENG [33764]

CHURCHWARD ALL WORLDWIDE [36009]

CHURCHWILL 1700S DARTMOUTH, DEV, ENG [34250]

CHURCHWOOD 1825 CROYDON, SRY, ENG [36640]

CHURCHYARD 1700S WICKHAM MARKET, SFK, ENG [34172] : C1899 BANHAM, NFK, ENG [36307]

CHUVIN ALL WORLDWIDE [38237]

CIELOUZYK PRE 1900 PO, POL [36355]

CINA PRE 1910 SALO, ITL [37510] : 1910+ IL, USA [37510]

CIROU 1870-1900 ST HELIER, JSY, CHI [38178] : ALL BN, FRA [38178] : ALL FRA [38178] : ALL WORLDWIDE [38178]

CISCO PRE 1840 PASSAIC CO., NJ, USA [38783]

CIVELL 1600S LONDON, ENG [33918]

CIVIL PRE 1840 HEXHAM, NBL, ENG [35918]

CIZMAR PRE 1875 CS [35310]

CLAASSEN ALL GER [38610]

CLACHER ALL STI, SCT & AUS [34686]

CLACK 1852+ HOBART, TAS, AUS [35877] : 1854+ BRIGHTON, VIC, AUS [35877] : 1880-1920 LONDON & SWINDON, LND & WIL, ENG [37243] : 1700+ LITTLEPORT, CAM, ENG [37839]

CLAES JEAN JOSEPH PRE 1900 BRUSSELS, BEL [38776]

CLAIBORNE 1690-1784 KING WILLIAM CO., VA, USA [36973]

CLAMMER C1850 DRESDEN, IA, USA [36899]

CLAMPETT 1864+ BOOROWA & GRENFELL, NSW, AUS [37555]

CLAMPIN ALL UK [37674]

CLAMPITT PRE 1850 HEAVITREE, DEV, ENG [37855] : 1850+ CALCUTTA, W.BENGAL, INDIA [37855]

CLANCY 1850+ MELBOURNE, VIC, AUS [35379] : 1870S MELBOURNE, VIC, AUS [35508] : 1841+ MELBOURNE, VIC, AUS [35793] : 1860+ BRAYBROOK & FOOTSCRAY, VIC, AUS [38539] : PRE 1850 DUBLIN, IRL [35379] : PRE 1841 TIP, IRL [35793] : 1830S KIK, IRL [37139] : C1820 BALLYNAMONEY, COR, IRL [37944] : 1850+ GAL, IRL [38539]

CLANDENNING 1864 GANANOQUE, ONT, CAN [34521]

CLANFIELD 1800-1840 CUDDESDON, OXF, ENG [37757]

CLAOUE ALL LGD & MP, FRA [36078]

CLAP (SEE CLAPP) [36550]

CLAPHAM 1800-1990 STANNINGTON, ERY, ENG [34552] : PRE 1820 BATLEY & WAKEFIELD, YKS, ENG [34952] : 1724-1830 FINEDON, NTH, ENG [35119] : PRE 1820 LEEDS, YKS, ENG [36752]

CLAPP 1887 BRACEBRIDGE, ONT, CAN [37493] : PRE 1900 BEAMINSTER, WIL, ENG [34089] : PRE 1900 YATTON, SOM, ENG [34089] : 1633-1679 DORCHESTER, MA, USA [36550] : 1850-1870 ALBANY, NY, USA [37013] : ALL WORLDWIDE [37757]

CLAPPER 1800-1860 WAYNE CO., OH & PA, USA [37529]

CLAPPERTON PRE 1810 SCT [35371]

CLAPSHAW PRE 1830+ FARNHAM, SRY, ENG [35928] : PRE 1800+ YEOVIL, SOM, ENG [35928]

CLAPSON ALL SSX, ENG [36501]

CLARANCE 1400-1950 ESS, ENG [34717]

CLARE 1858+ WALCHA, NSW, AUS [35147] : 1800+ ADELAIDE, SA, AUS [36756] : GEORGE 1850 COCKFIGHTERS CREEK, NSW, AUS [38500] : 1820+ LONDON, ENG [34092] : 1900+ KEN & SOM, ENG [34848] : PRE 1900 LND, MDX & SFK, ENG [34848] : 1800+ CLERKENWELL & BETHNAL GREEN, MDX, ENG [37877] : PRE 1860 TIP, IRL [34686] : PRE 1858 RATHDRUM, WIC, IRL [35147]

CLARET 1600-1900 VICDESSOS ARCONAC, ARIEGE, FRA [33758]

CLARGO PRE 1848 NETTLEBED, OXF, ENG [35578]

CLARIDGE 1590-1670 DRAYTON & BANBURY, OXF, ENG [35030] : 1801+ SWANBOURNE, BKM, ENG [38291]

CLARIUS PRE 1855 HOCHST, HEN, GER [37894]

CLARK 1830-1880S VIC, AUS [33984] : 1830+ HOBART, TAS, AUS [34456] : 1838+ CARCOAR, NSW, AUS [34900] : 1840S CARCOAR, NSW, AUS [35134] : WILLIAM JAMES 1860+ GLENELG, SA, AUS [35208] : THOMAS HENRY 1840-1886 WILLOUGHBY, NSW, AUS [35373] : PRE 1845 WANGARATTA, VIC, AUS [35441] : 1859+ STAWELL, VIC, AUS [35487] : 1864-1876 BOMBALA, NSW, AUS [35506] : ELIZA ISABELL 1857+ ALBERT PARK, VIC, AUS [35590] : JOHN 1857+ COLLINGWOOD, VIC, AUS [35590] : 1900-1990 WA, AUS [35718] : SYDNEY 1872+

SEYMOUR, VIC, AUS [35792] : PRE 1860
NEWCASTLE, NSW, AUS [36270] : 1840-1900
TUMUT, NSW, AUS [38073] : ROBERT 1855+
PERTH CO., ONT, CAN [34066] : ANNE 1848+
MANITOULIN ISLAND, ONT, CAN [36712] :
DUNCAN 1848+ MANITOULIN ISLAND, ONT,
CAN [36712] : JAMES 1820+ ST BRELADE, JSY,
CHI [38396] : MARY JANE 1820-1851 ST HELIER,
JSY, CHI [38396] : PRE 1825 WOTTON UNDER
EDGE, GLS, ENG [37765] : 1851+ SUTTON, ISLE
OF ELY, CAM, ENG [33920] : 1770-1841 GREAT
MARLOW, BKM, ENG [33945] : PRE 1914
YATTON, SOM, ENG [34089] : C1812 GRANTLEY,
YKS, ENG [34157] : PRE 1800 SUNDERLAND,
DUR, ENG [34316] : PRE 1770 ISLEHAM, CAM,
ENG [34445] : MARY 1700-1800 LIVERPOOL, LAN,
ENG [34514] : ANN 1729 WATFORD, HRT, ENG
[34539] : PRE 1872 LIDLINGTON, BDF, ENG [34588]
: PRE 1810 MOULOSE, BKM, ENG [34588] : 1770+
BISHOP WILTON, ERY, ENG [34854] : C1800S
SOUTHWARK, SRY, ENG [34887] : PRE 1840
LAMBERHURST & GOUDHURST, KEN, ENG
[34897] : CHARLOTTE 1840+ KIRTON, LIN, ENG
[34916] : ANN 1840+ KIRTON, LIN, ENG [34916] :
HENRY C1842 DEDDINGTON, OXF, ENG [35104]
: 1665-1740 BURTON LATIMER, NTH, ENG [35119]
: 1800S HAVERSHAM, BKM, ENG [35256] : PRE
1879 RAINHAM, ESS, ENG [35368] : 1800+
GREATHAM, DUR, ENG [35487] : GEORGE 1790-
1846 BASILDON, ESS, ENG [35488] : PRE 1863
CON, ENG [35506] : JOHN PRE 1857 ISLINGTON,
LND, ENG [35590] : WM. THOMAS 1860-80
DOWNEND MANGOTSFIELD, GLS & DBY, ENG
[35624] : PRE 1725 ESS, ENG [35642] : 1887
BALHAM, SRY, ENG [35720] : PRE 1800 BELPER,
DBY, ENG [35745] : SYDNEY 1827+ WIL, ENG
[35792] : 1700+ TREGAVETHAN, CON, ENG
[35804] : JOHN 1840S ADDINGTON, KEN, ENG
[35876] : PRE 1860 ENG [35884] : 1830+ NORTH
CRAY, KEN, ENG [35915] : PRE 1850 PRESTON,
LAN, ENG [35918] : 1850-1950 ROYSTON, HRT,
ENG [35992] : 1750-1820 DORCHESTER, DOR, ENG
[36051] : PRE 1880 BASSINGBOURN, CAM & HRT,
ENG [36061] : 1757-1827 DORKING, SRY, ENG
[36071] : PRE 1750 PYRTON, OXF, ENG [36073] :
PRE 1790 SHERSTON MAGNA, WIL, ENG [36113] :
PRE 1795 WESTERN ON THE GREEN, OXF, ENG
[36281] : MARY ANN PRE 1830 SOUTHWARK,
SRY, ENG [36388] : JOHN PRE 1830 LIMEHOUSE,
MDX, ENG [36388] : 1600-1900 NRY, ENG [36472] :
1600-1800 WHICKHAM, DUR, ENG [36556] :
GEORGE 1860+ WALTHAM ABBEY, MDX, ENG
[36564] : GEORGE 1832-1902 SUDBURY, SSX, ENG
[36564] : SPENCER 1867+ WALTHAM ABBEY,
MDX, ENG [36564] : 1810+ E STRATTON, HAM,
ENG [36650] : 1800+ RODBOROUGH, GLS, ENG
[36868] : DAVID 1800+ CAMBRIDGE, CAM &
BDF, ENG [37065] : MARY 1777 COLD ASHBY,
NTH, ENG [37106] : PRE 1830 GLOUCESTER, ENG
[37179] : 1800-1850 GREENWICH, KEN, ENG
[37340] : 1750-1800 CROMER, NFK, ENG [37456] :
JOHN PRE 1830 MILTON BRYAN, BDF, ENG
[37647] : 1700+ HARRINGTON, CUL, ENG [37735] :
PRE 1870 LONDON, ENG [37743] : 1750-1810 DRY,
ENG [37829] : C1900 DONCASTER, WRY, ENG
[37831] : C1725-C1825 BROOK, NORTHBOURNE,
KEN, ENG [37890] : C1824 ST GEORGE, MDX,
ENG [37972] : PRE 1700 ENG [38043] : PRE 1730
COCKERHAM, LAN, ENG [38248] : PRE 1800
KIRKHAM & GARSTANG, LAN, ENG [38254] :
C1850 WILBY, SFK, ENG [38288] : C1800
WYVERSTON, SFK, ENG [38288] : 1780+ LONG

SUTTON, LIN, ENG [38494] : 1810-1990 DEV, ENG
& VIC [35718] : WILLIAM PRE 1874 CAV, IRL
[33951] : C1848 CAV, IRL [36599] : C1700 ULSTER,
IRL [37795] : ALL TIP, IRL & AUS [35213] : PRE
1860 GLASGOW, SCT [33838] : PRE 1800
LATHERON, CAI, SCT [33873] : C1800
ROSEHARTY, ABD, SCT [34006] : ANDREW 1830
PAISLEY ABBEY, RFW, SCT [34075] : 1850
DUNDEE, ANS, SCT [34149] : 1800+
CAMPBELTOWN, ARL, SCT [34326] : 1835+
GLASGOW, LKS & AYR, SCT [34373] : PRE 1900
LESMAHAGOW, LKS, SCT [34373] : 1750+ WICK,
CAI, SCT [34456] : PRE 1900 DFS, SCT [34617] : PRE
1850 BALLACHULISH, ARL, SCT [34719] : PRE
1857 DUNDEE, ANS, SCT [34758] : PRE 1900
EDINBURGH, MLN, SCT [34784] : 1800+
GLENMUICK, ABD, SCT [34916] : 1780+ PAISLEY,
RFW, SCT [35027] : ALEXANDER PRE 1809
PAISLEY, RFW, SCT [35258] : 1761 THORNHILL
MADDERTY, PER, SCT [35259] : PRE 1857
KILMARNOCK, AYR, SCT [35379] : CHARLES
PRE 1870S LOGIE, FIF, SCT [35433] : PRE 1860
ABERFOYLE, PER, SCT [35601] : ALL KIRKWALL,
OKI, SCT [35612] : 1800+ BARONY, LKS, SCT
[35785] : JOHN C1820 GOVAN, LKS, SCT [35848] :
PRE 1850 PER, SCT [36025] : 1500-1850 SCT [36222] :
PRE 1850 DFS, SCT [36429] : ALL ABD, SCT [36429] :
PRE 1800 EDINBURGH, SCT [36514] : PRE 1811
KINLOSS, MOR, SCT [36673] : ALEXANDER C1830
GLASGOW, SCT [36878] : ISOBELLA PRE 1850
LKS, SCT [37287] : PRE 1763 NEWTYLE, ANS, SCT
[37772] : PRE 1807 BURNTISLAND, FIF, SCT
[37982] : 1700-1850 NH, USA [33753] : OLIVER 1800
WINDSOR, CT, USA [35273] : WELCOME S. 1860-
1876 STEPHENSON CO., IL, USA [35329] :
HARRIET C1845 TRUMBULL CO., OH, USA [36319]
: MARTHA C1845 TRUMBULL CO., OH, USA
[36319] : PRE 1700 HADLEY, MA, USA [36319] : PRE
1744 DUTCHESS CO., NY, USA [36680] : 1800-1850
NY, USA [36732] : 1892 CLARKE CO., GA, USA
[36903] : 1838+ PHILADELPHIA, PA, USA [36965] :
1814 OH, USA [37008] : JOHN PRE 1840
SCHENECTADY CO., NY, USA [37009] : PRE 1850
BURLINGTON CO., PA, USA [37018] : 1930+
CLEVELAND, OH, USA [37451] : 1668
YARMOUTH, MA, USA [37531] : 1837+ LAVACA
CO., TX, USA [37533] : 1780-1797 MERCER CO., KY,
USA [37533] : 1797-1837 ST LOUIS CO., MO, USA
[37533] : 1798-1866 BEDFORD CO., PA, USA [37577] :
COL. JESSE C1810 BENNINGTON, VT, USA [37810]
: JOHN 1640 NEW HAVEN, CT, USA [38066] :
SUSAN PRE 1813 HARTFORD, CT & NY, USA
[38181] : 1790-1825 AMHERST CO., VA, USA [38201]
: C1700 RICHMOND, VA, USA [38348] : 1770+ NY,
USA [38529] : DAVID PRE 1800 NC, USA [38536] :
1790-1810 LITTLE FALLS, NY, USA [38537] : 1750-
1800 EDGEFIELD, NC, USA [38576] : C1840-80
HOWARD CO., IN, USA [38590] : 1650+
CHAUTAUQUA CO., NY, MA & CT, USA & ENG
[36970] : ELIZA 1860+ WLS & ENG [34048]

CLARKE 1844 BATHURST, NSW, AUS [34288] : 1830-
1900 BOX HILL, NSW, AUS [34438] : WILLIAM
1841+ NSW, AUS [34449] : RICHARD 1841+
REDFERN, SYDNEY, NSW, AUS [34449] : 1869+
GUNDAGAI, NSW, AUS [34534] : ROBERT 1857+
GUNDAROO, NSW, AUS [34534] : 1806+
WINDSOR, NSW, AUS [34534] : 1827-1900 SUTTON
FOREST, NSW, AUS [34534] : EDWARD JOHN
1833+ INVERARY PARK, NSW, AUS [34806] :
MICHAEL 1840-1860 JAMBEROO, NSW, AUS
[34842] : 1860S LANDSBOROUGH, VIC, AUS [34845]
: RICHARD 1870+ REDFERN & PETERSHAM,

NSW, AUS [34887] : WILLIAM 1841+ SYDNEY, NSW, AUS [34887] : 1830S PARRAMATTA, NSW, AUS [35011] : PRE 1865 CAMPBELLTOWN, TAS, AUS [35459] : 1820+ NEPEAN, NSW, AUS [35511] : JOHN C1860 BRIGHTON, SA, AUS [35525] : RICHARD C1857 MELBOURNE, VIC, AUS [35573] : ELIZA 1887+ ALBERT PARK, VIC, AUS [35590] : 1850+ PENGUIN, TAS, AUS [35800] : PRE 1860 NEWCASTLE, NSW, AUS [36270] : WILLIAM 1860+ MUDGEE, NSW, AUS [36273] : 1875+ NSW, AUS [36608] : 1880+ LOCHEIL, NSW, AUS [38491] : 1700-1850 BARBADOS [38355] : 1840-1900 BROCKVILLE, ONT, CAN [34402] : 1855+ EMBRO & BRAEMAR, ONT, CAN [34528] : 1820S+ ST THOMAS, ONT, CAN [34588] : WILLIAM 1910+ VANCOUVER, BC, CAN [36075] : JOSEPH 1900+ ALB, CAN [36075] : 1800-1950 PRINCE EDWARD CO., ONT, CAN [36688] : 1800+ ONT & MI, CAN & USA [34062] : PRE 1820 FORD, NBL, ENG [33776] : AMELIA PRE 1881 STOKE NEWINGTON, MDX, ENG [34031] : PRE 1914 YATTON, SOM, ENG [34089] : PRE 1880 HEYBRIDGE, ESS, ENG [34261] : PRE 1800 BIRMINGHAM, WAR, ENG [34275] : PRE 1765 NUNEHAM COURTNAY, OXF, ENG [34370] : PRE 1841 LIVERPOOL, LAN, ENG [34449] : PRE 1851 ESS, ENG [34593] : 1700+ KIDDERMINSTER, WOR, ENG [34711] : 1600S FARWAY, DEV, ENG [34715] : PRE 1800 HALTON, CON, ENG [34741] : 1650+ NEWENT, GLS, ENG [34747] : EDWARD JOHN 1807+ WOLVERHAMPTON, STS, ENG [34806] : CLEMENT 1815-1852 ISLINGTON & HACKNEY, LND, ENG [34829] : ROBERT 1725-1850 ACLE & GREAT YARMOUTH, NFK, ENG [34829] : GEO WALTON 1780-1847 ACLE & UPTON, NFK, ENG [34829] : GEO WALTON 1810-1847 ISLINGTON, LND, ENG [34829] : CLEMENT 1725-1850 GREAT YARMOUTH & ACLE, NFK, ENG [34829] : 1800+ BRISTOL, ENG [34880] : PRE 1841 LIVERPOOL, LAN, ENG [34887] : PRE 1820 SOM, ENG [34904] : PRE 1845 PECKHAM, LND, ENG [34968] : RICHARD 1820+ NORTHAMPTON, NTH, ENG [35027] : THOMAS PRE 1874 WITHAM, ESS, ENG [35042] : JEMIMA C1842 HEYBRIDGE, ESS, ENG [35042] : PRE 1769 HEADLEY, HAM, ENG [35247] : PRE 1760 TONBRIDGE, KEN, ENG [35259] : PRE 1853 CHURCHOVER, WAR, ENG [35344] : PRE 1820 PLUMLEY, CHS, ENG [35354] : SOPHIA PRE 1825 DEOPHAM, NFK, ENG [35411] : 1900+ DULWICH & STANMORE, LND & MDX, ENG [35495] : PRE 1871 ICKLESHAM, ESS, ENG [35517] : PRE 1828 BRISTOL, SOM, ENG [35573] : PRE 1725 ESS, ENG [35642] : 1820+ ST MELLION, CON, ENG [35706] : PRE 1771 WESTLEY WATERLESS, CAM, ENG [35770] : 1840S WARKLEIGH, DEV, ENG [35799] : PRE 1800 GREAT ELLINGHAM, NFK, ENG [35800] : MARY ELIZ. 1850S ADDINGTON, KEN, ENG [35876] : PRE 1860 HIGHBROOK & EAST GRINSTEAD, SSX, ENG [36053] : 1800+ ROYSTON, HRT & MDX, ENG [36061] : WILLIAM 1730-1800 MARNHULL, DOR & SOM, ENG [36100] : PRE 1900 KINGSWINFORD & SEDGLEY, STS, ENG [36110] : PRE 1821 SFK, ENG [36124] : C1820 ELLINGTON, HUN, ENG [36147] : ALL THURSFORD, NFK, ENG [36171] : 1869+ PYECOMBE, SSX, ENG [36212] : 1700-1850 DEBENHAM, SFK, ENG [36213] : 1700-1796 FARNHAM, ESS, ENG [36229] : PRE 1900 LEI, ENG [36387] : 1939-1945 WOLVERHAMPTON, STS, ENG [36420] : 1542-1923 HOLT, WOR, ENG [36513] : 1760+ SSX, ENG [36605] : 1853+ LONDON, ENG [36608] : ELIZABETH PRE 1830 PADDINGTON,

LND, ENG [36619] : ELIZ C1800-1880 SHEPTON BEAUCHAMP, SOM, ENG [36776] : C1820 LIDLINGTON, BDF, ENG [36803] : PRE 1900 EASTBOURNE, LND, ENG [36805] : 1843 LEI, ENG [36859] : WILLIAM C1800 BURWASH, SSX, ENG [37140] : 1750-1850 BATH, SOM, ENG [37232] : ALL HASTINGS & EAST GULDEFORD, SSX, ENG [37236] : 1850-99 EASTBOURNE, SSX, ENG [37243] : PRE 1850 LONG SUTTON, LIN, ENG [37371] : 1700-1848 WITNEY, OXF, ENG [37380] : 1800+ NFK, ENG [37409] : 1800S LND, ENG [37442] : PRE 1900 BLOCKLEY, WOR, ENG [37443] : 1850+ SOUTHWARK, LND, ENG [37718] : 1800 METHWOLD, NFK, ENG [37733] : 1800+ BRISTOL, SOM, ENG [37847] : PRE 1850 FRANT & BURWASH, SSX, ENG [37871] : 1700+ ICKBURGH, NFK, ENG [38745] : C1764 TUAM, MAY, IRL [33880] : WILLIAM PRE 1874 CAV, IRL [33951] : 1400+ DUBLIN, WIC, IRL [33989] : 1800+ IRL [34098] : 1830-1800 LISBELLAW, FER, IRL [34402] : PRE 1850 BELFAST, IRL [34797] : 1836-1900 CORK CITY, COR, IRL [35044] : MICHAEL C1830 MEA, IRL [35560] : 1800-1870 BELLABAY, MOG, IRL [35600] : HENRY 1822+ MAGHERA, LDY, IRL [35702] : 1840+ BALLINASLOE, GAL, IRL [35765] : 1780-1860 CURR, KILLADRORY & SESKINORE, TYR, IRL [36075] : PRE 1900 BELFAST, IRL [36360] : CATHERINE C1851 BELFAST, ANT, IRL [37135] : 1700-1820 NEW ROSS, WEX, IRL [38299] : 1800+ CRIEFF, PER, SCT [34098] : PRE 1830 PAISLEY, RFW, SCT [34113] : PRE 1900 LESMAHAGOW, LKS, SCT [34373] : 1800S GLASGOW, LKS & AYR, SCT [34373] : PETER C1850+ PERTH, PER, SCT [35629] : PRE 1815 DALKEITH, MLN, SCT [36224] : PRE 1855 WEYMILLS, SCT [37948] : 1700+ ANNAN, DFS, SCT [38336] : 1900+ RI, USA [34734]

CLARKIN ALL IRL [36830] : ALL CAVAN, CAV, IRL [38174]

CLARKSON 1806+ SYDNEY, NSW, AUS [37119] : 1800-1900 UTTOXETER, STS, ENG [34714] : PRE 1890 DEWSBURY, YKS, ENG [35379] : ISABELLA PRE 1808 LONDON, ENG [35431] : PRE 1783 OULTON, YKS, ENG [37144] : PRE 1634 GARSTANG, ENG [37706] : PRE 1860 YKS, ENG [37760] : 1750+ DOUGLAS, LKS, SCT [33956] : 1830+ AIRDRIE, LKS, SCT [33956] : 1800-1900 MENDOTA, MN, USA [34714] : THOMAS 1810-1870 WARREN CO., KY, USA [36734]

CLARRIS 1855+ QLD, AUS [37894]

CLARRY 1880+ BUNDABERG, QLD, AUS [34893] : C1856 COGGESHALL, ESS, ENG [34893] : 1870S LITTLE COGGESHALL, ESS, ENG [36797]

CLARY 1800+ GALLATIN CO., IL, USA [36565] : 1800-1813 DARKE CO., OH, USA [37005] : SAMUEL 1824 LAPORTE, IN, USA & IRL [37481]

CLASEN 1700-1900 WEDDINGSTEDT, SHO, GER [38750]

CLASING 1873 HOLZHAUSEN, PYR, GER [38748] : 1804 ALVERDISSEN, WEF, GER [38748] : 1742 STEINBERGEN, SLP, GER [38750]

CLASON PRE 1855 LOGIE & DUNBLANE, PER, SCT [37512]

CLASPAR ALL WORLDWIDE [36033]

CLASPER PRE 1900 ENG [34478] : ALL WORLDWIDE [36033]

CLASSEN ALL USA [38610]

CLATER 1780+ EAST RETFORD, NTT, ENG [36426] : PRE 1760 WHATTON, NTT, ENG [36426]

CLATWORTHY 1680-1770 TAUNTON, SOM, ENG [38028]

CLAUE ALL LGD & MP, FRA [36078]

CLAUGHTON 1788+ HORSFORTH, WRY, ENG [38469]

CLAUS 1700-1765 BAW, GER [34408]

CLAUSON 1800+ WORLDWIDE [34662]

CLAUSSE PRE 1700 BOURDONNAY, LOR, FRA [36078]

CLAUSSEN 1700-1900 WITTENWURT, SHO, GER [38750]

CLAVE ALL LGD & MP, FRA [36078]

CLAVERING 1858 BRANTON, NBL, ENG [37703]

CLAXSON ALL WORLDWIDE [36029]

CLAXTON 1800+ ONT, CAN [34252] : PRE 1873 ENG [34252] : JOSEPH 1800+ BURNHAM, NFK, ENG [34916] : PRE 1800 GARBOLDISHAM, NFK, ENG [35571]

CLAY ALL ESS, ENG [36136] : THOMAS C1800 ROTHERHITHE, LND, ENG [37143] : C1650 NTT, ENG [37698] : 1750+ NEWCASTLE UNDER LYME, STS, ENG [37705] : PRE 1835 LAN, ENG [37739] : 1748+ PETROCKSTOWE, DEV, ENG & AUS [35422] : KATEY PRE 1760 ROTTERDAM, HOLLAND, NL [34992] : ALL FLN, WLS [34593]

CLAYBAN ALL WORLDWIDE [36033]

CLAYBER ALL WORLDWIDE [36033]

CLAYBERT ALL WORLDWIDE [36033]

CLAYBIN ALL WORLDWIDE [36033]

CLAYBON ALL WORLDWIDE [36033]

CLAYBORN ALL WORLDWIDE [36033]

CLAYBORNE ALL WORLDWIDE [36033]

CLAYBOURN ALL WORLDWIDE [36033]

CLAYBOURNE ALL WORLDWIDE [36033]

CLAYBUARN ALL WORLDWIDE [36033]

CLAYBURN ALL WORLDWIDE [36033]

CLAYBURNE ALL WORLDWIDE [36033]

CLAYBYN ALL WORLDWIDE [36033]

CLAYDEN 1800+ ESSEX, ESS, ENG [36872]

CLAYDON 1854+ ARTHUR RIVER, WA, AUS [37894] : PRE 1900 STEBBING, ESS, ENG [36589] : PRE 1860 SRY, ENG [37358] : PRE 1790 ESS, ENG [37668]

CLAYFIELD PRE 1887 PARRAMATTA, NSW, AUS [34691] : PRE 1845 NEWCASTLE, NSW, AUS [34691]

CLAYTON 1880+ QLD, AUS [34550] : 1845+ BATHURST, NSW, AUS [38568] : PRE 1860 CLAVERING, ESS, ENG [33822] : 1829+ LIN & NTT, ENG [34238] : JACK 1935+ WILLESDEN, MDX, ENG [34341] : C1809 EARDISLAND, HEF, ENG [34358] : C1800+ LINCOLN, LIN, ENG [34451] : ALL SOUTHWARK, LND, ENG [34564] : ALL SEVENOAKS, KEN, ENG [34564] : 1850S GRIMSBY, ERY, ENG [34854] : C1800-1850 LONDON, ENG [34952] : PRE 1870 BRADFORD, YKS, ENG [35285] : 1800-1900 YORK, YKS, ENG [35394] : 1800S DBY, ENG [35727] : 1750+ SELSEY, SSX, ENG [36085] : ALL WAKEFIELD, WRY, ENG [36159] : PRE 1750 COLLINGHAM & HAREWOOD, WRY, ENG [36159] : JOHN 1800S SOUTHWARK, SRY, ENG [36211] : C1840+ ASHTON, LAN, ENG [36414] : 1790+ OLDHAM, LAN, ENG [36568] : 1770 HALIFAX, WRY, ENG [36635] : PRE 1880 BARTON ON HUMBER, LIN, ENG [36664] : C1861-1863 STOCKPORT, CHS, ENG [36984] : C1880-1890 ASHTON UNDER LYNE, LAN, ENG [36984] : C1890-1902 BOLTON, LAN, ENG [36984] : ALL HAM & SSX, ENG [37195] : 1750-1800 HORSLEY, DBY, ENG [38478] : PRE 1840 ROTIDALE, YKS, ENG [38568] : JOSEPH 1790-1836 DONCASTER, YKS, ENG & AUS [34447] : 1800-1850 WARREN & EDMUNSON CO., KY, USA [36573] : AUGUSTINE 1755-1810 SPARTENBURG, SC, USA [36573] :

1902+ USA [36984] : 1650+ SALEM, NJ & DE, USA [37826]

CLEAR 1902 MONARO, NSW, AUS [34966]

CLEARWATER 1700+ NJ & NY, USA [35963]

CLEARY 1870+ LYONVILLE, VIC, AUS [35040] : 1840+ MELBOURNE, VIC, AUS [37157] : 1840+ WANDONG & KILMORE, VIC, AUS [37157] : 1850 QUE & ONT, CAN [34095] : 1860 ST CATHERINE, QUE, CAN [38131] : 1820 BRISTOL, SOM, ENG [37841] : PRE 1830 WAT, IRL [34858] : C1850+ TIP, IRL [35249] : ALL BUNMAHON & BALLYMARID, WAT, IRL [36043] : 1800+ CLEANISH, FER, IRL & AUS [33769] : PRE 1900 TRINITY WITHOUT, WAT, IRL & NZ [36840]

CLEASBY 1500-1600 GREAT AYTON, NRY, ENG [37633]

CLEATON 1790+ OLDHAM, LAN, ENG [36568]

CLEAVE 1700+ ST CLEARS, CON, ENG [35355] : 1840-1880 ST MINVER, CON, ENG [35860] : 1830-1850 BRIDERULE, DEV, ENG [36771] : 1791+ HOLSWORTHY, DEV, ENG [36771] : ELIZABETH 1830+ CON, ENG [37153] : 1500+ EGLOSHAYLE & ST KEW, CON, ENG [37749] : 800-1800 WORLDWIDE [36169]

CLEAVER 1842+ PERTH, WA, AUS [35589] : 1820+ KIDDERMINSTER, WOR, ENG [35041] : PRE 1820+ COVENTRY, WAR, ENG [35453] : PRE 1840 HRT, ENG [35589] : 1700-1900 LEAMINGTON HASTINGS, WAR, ENG [36786] : 1600-1700 HARBOROUGH MAGNA, WAR, ENG [36786] : C1803 GUILSBOROUGH, NTH, ENG [36803]

CLEAVES 800-1800 WORLDWIDE [36169]

CLEETON PRE 1800 SAL, ENG [37941]

CLEETS PRE 1860 WESTMINSTER, MDX, ENG [37834]

CLEEVE 800-1800 WORLDWIDE [36169]

CLEEVES 800-1800 WORLDWIDE [36169]

CLEGG 1856-1904 WANDIN, VIC, AUS [37892] : PRE 1800+ CHURCH & OSWALDTWISTLE, LAN, ENG [36955] : JOHN PRE 1792 LONDON, ENG [37052] : PRE 1800 STS, ENG [37098] : PRE 1856 BIRSTALL, YKS, ENG [37892]

CLEGGETT 1820+ KEN, ENG [33788]

CLEGHORN PRE 1880 LONDON, ENG [35953] : 1850-1950 MANCHESTER, LAN, ENG [36098] : PRE 1850 TRANENT, ELN, SCT [33881] : 1700-1850 HADDINGTON, ELN, SCT [36098]

CLELAND 1840-1990 CAN [35630] : 1850+ NOTTINGHAM, NTT, ENG [36105] : 1750-1900 ANT & DOW, IRL [35630] : ALL KILLYLEAGH, DOW, IRL [38411] : 1400+ CLELAND, LKS, SCT [33989] : 1800+ SCT [36105]

CLELLAND PRE 1850 STONEHOUSE, LKS, SCT [34245]

CLEMENS 1881 BOXTEL, NBT, NL [36307]

CLEMENT 1880S ROCKHAMPTON, QLD, AUS [35259] : C1840 ST JAMES CLERKENWELL, MDX, ENG [35259] : CHARLES ROBT. 1790-1856 WESTMINSTER, LND, ENG [35780] : PRE 1830 GUISBOROUGH, NRY, ENG [37204] : 1750-1850 DBY, ENG [37207] : 1600-1750 ESSEX CO., MA, USA [37538] : 1731-1800 NH, USA [37538] : PRE 1863 NY, USA [37787]

CLEMENT-LALLEMAND 1830+ MASKINONGE, QUE, CAN [36678]

CLEMENTS 1855-1880 BELLEVILLE, ONT, CAN [35638] : 1800+ STEPNEY, LND, ENG [34029] : 1800+ CIRENCESTER, GLS, ENG [34029] : 1790+ CIRENCESTER, GLS, ENG [34029] : 1830+ HALSTEAD, ESS, ENG [34029] : 1700+ RODBOROUGH, GLS, ENG [34664] : C1830 GLOUCESTER, GLS, ENG [35391] : 1800+ LND &

MDX, ENG [35760] : C1780-1820 SALFORD PRIORS, WAR, ENG [35883] : 1700S WOKINGHAM, BRK, ENG [36425] : 1750-1841 CHADLINGTON, OXF, ENG [36653] : PRE 1816 RADFORD, NTT, ENG [37000] : PRE 1835 WOR & LND, ENG [37057] : PRE 1790 BETHNAL GREEN, LND, ENG [37261] : C1800 WICKHAM BISHOPS, ESS, ENG [37312] : 1800+ BETHNAL GREEN, LND, ENG [37827] : PRE 1850 POPLAR, MDX, ENG [37833] : 1850-1875 DUNBOYNE, MEA, IRL [33962] : 1800-1860 TYR, IRL [36666] : EVA (ACTRESS) 1870-1900S LND & DUR, ENG, RSA & AUS [36311] : C1851 CA, USA [35391] : PRE 1800 BOURBON CO., KY, USA [36929] : NELSON 1800 SC, USA [38536]

CLEMENTSON PRE 1850 SWALWELL, DUR, ENG [37693]

CLEMMA C1750 ST DENNIS, CON, ENG [36945]

CLEMMER 1934 YAKIMA, WA, USA [38095] : 1918-1939 RIO GRANDE, CO, USA [38095] : 1885-1925 BUTLER, NE, USA [38095] : 1940-1962 MULTNOMAH, OR, USA [38095] : 1933 CLARK, WA, USA [38095]

CLEMMINGS ALL WORLDWIDE [37724]

CLEMMONS 1790-1850 HARRISON CO., KY, USA [36566] : WILLIAM 1820-1827 SANGAMON, IL, USA [38157]

CLEMO C1500 CRANTOCK, CON, ENG [35563]

CLEMONS EUGENE PRE 1864 FULTON CO., NY, USA [36950]

CLEMOW 1805-1880 CLUNES, VIC, AUS [34530]

CLEMSON PRE 1760 ALBERBURY, MGY, WLS [35719] : 1760+ ALBERBURY, MGY, WLS [35719]

CLENDENIN 1830-1930 IL, USA [36733]

CLENDENNEN 1700-1860 LANCASTER, PA, USA [35300]

CLENNAN PRE 1890 CARLISLE, CUL, ENG [37925]

CLENNELL 1870 STANLEY, DUR, ENG [36499]

CLENT 1600-1700 ROCHFORD, WOR, ENG [34930]

CLERIHEW PRE 1900 ABERDEEN, ABD, SCT [33883]

CLERK 1880+ INVERLOCH, VIC, AUS [34550] : 1750-1900 SOM, ENG [34550] : 1800-1900 WIL, ENG [34550] : PRE 1830 SOM, ENG [35523] : 1726 THORNHILL MADDERTY, PER, SCT [35259]

CLERKIN ALL CAVAN, CAV, IRL [38174]

CLERMONT JEAN C1790+ ST BENOIT, DEUX MONTAGNES, QUE, CAN [34506] : PRE 1800 QUE, CAN [34506] : JEAN C1790+ QUE, CAN [34506]

CLERMONT DIT MANUBY C1790+ ST BENOIT, DEUX MONTAGNES, QUE, CAN [34506] : PRE 1800 QUE, CAN [34506] : C1790+ QUE, CAN [34506]

CLEVE 1700-80 SOUTH DOWN, SSX, ENG [38472] : 800-1800 WORLDWIDE [36169]

CLEVELAND 1853+ VIC, AUS [34021] : PRE 1800 ENG [34207] : PRE 1820 UK [37804] : 1790-1850 ELBERT CO., GA, USA [38129] : 1830-1880 FLOYD CO., IN, USA [38367]

CLEVERLEY C1880 ISLE OF WIGHT, HAM, ENG [35365] : PRE 1895+ SOUTHEND ON SEA, ESS, ENG [35928] : 1800+ MELKSHAM, WIL, ENG [37617] : 1770 LONDON, ENG [38472]

CLEVES 800-1800 WORLDWIDE [36169]

CLEVETTE 1740-1990 CLAPHAM, SSX, ENG [38472]

CLEWES 1784-1788 WHITECHAPEL, MDX, ENG [38441]

CLEWS 1900S MOSS VALE, NSW, AUS [35567] : C1797-1873 BIRMINGHAM, WAR, ENG [33847] : 1840 SHREWSBURY, SAL, ENG [33982] : 1838+ SHELTON, STS, ENG [34668]

CLIBBORN 1820+ LIVERPOOL, LAN, ENG [38443] : 1650-1840 MOATE, WEM, IRL [38443]

CLIFF PRE 1700 MARSTON ON DOVE, DBY, ENG [34311] : PRE 1850 ARNOLD, NTT, ENG [36387] :

PRE 1800 CHEADLE, STS, ENG [37389] : PRE 1850 BARDON HILL, LEI, ENG [38390]

CLIFFARD 1720S ALL CANNINGS, WIL, ENG [35259]

CLIFFE 1775-1835 HUDDERSFIELD, WRY, ENG [36900] : PRE 1786 YKS, ENG [38080] : 1100-1900 WORLDWIDE [36169]

CLIFFORD C1850 MT ALEXANDER, VIC, AUS [35899] : 1830-1850 CAMPBELLTOWN, NSW, AUS [36315] : 1850-1920 STANTHORPE, QLD, AUS [36315] : C1843 NSW, AUS [38485] : C1860 DRAYTON, QLD, AUS [38485] : 1691+ BLEEDON ON HILL, LEI, ENG [34577] : ALL LND, ENG [35628] : JAMES PRE 1805 MAIDSTONE, KEN, ENG [36309] : ALL CASTLEMAINE, KER, IRL [34643] : 1780+ VT, USA [38116] : 1800-1858 KEENE, NY, USA [38741]

CLIFT PRE 1840 BIRMINGHAM, WAR & WIL, ENG [33953] : PRE 1875 ENG [34519] : 1750+ BIRMINGHAM, WAR & STS, ENG [36435] : C1800-1880 OXF, ENG [38242] : PRE 1880 KNIGHTON, RAD, WLS [38730]

CLIFTON 1825+ HUNTER VY, NSW, AUS [33939] : C1856 SEAHAM, NSW, AUS [35515] : PRE 1825 GRENDON, NTH, ENG [33939] : 1800-1850 GROOMBRIDGE, KEN, ENG [34205] : PRE 1850 HASTINGS, SSX, ENG [34431] : 1800+ SPITALFIELDS, LND, ENG [34791] : 1600-1800 TICEHURST, SSX, ENG [35394] : C1830 WEEK ST MARY, CON, ENG [35744] : 1750-1900 BROMYARD, HEF, ENG [36109] : 1500-1550 DBY, ENG [36802] : PRE 1600 NTT & LND, ENG [36802] : PRE 1800 BOSTON, LIN, ENG [37381] : 1661-1800 HEYSHAM, LAN, ENG [37524] : 1700+ GEDNEY, LIN, ENG [38280] : PRE 1731 PRINCE GEORGE CO., VA, USA [37029] : 1830-1889 HARDIN CO., TN, USA [37029] : PRE 1800 KENT CO., DE, USA [38538]

CLIMPSON 1750+ GREAT MISSENDEN, BKM, ENG [34416]

CLINCE ALL WORLDWIDE [35941]

CLINCH 1700S NTH, ENG [36038] : 1830+ BOLTON MANOR, KEN, ENG [37206] : 1700 WITNEY, OXF, ENG [37277]

CLINE 1850 PERTH, ONT, CAN [35638] : ALL GER [36498] : ALL DDR &, GER [36498] : ALL BRD, GER [36498] : ELIZABETH 1820-1860 PA, OH & MO, USA [36321] : 1802 PA, USA [38121]

CLINETOB ALL WORLDWIDE [36548]

CLINGAN 1700-1780 DON & CAV, IRL [37589]

CLINGE PRE 1800 WAR, ENG [37085]

CLINGLER PRE 1930 HAMILTON CO., OH, USA [36973]

CLINK ALL SCT [36509]

CLINKARD 1700+ GARSINGTON, OXF, ENG [33963] : PRE 1900 GARSINGTON & OXFOD, OXF, ENG [35940]

CLINKER PRE 1665 CHAWTON, HAM, ENG [37420] : 1600+ CHAWTON, HAM, ENG [37448] : ALL WORLDWIDE [37448]

CLINKSCALES ALL WORLDWIDE [38237]

CLINTON 1845+ VIC & NSW, AUS [35073] : PRE 1810 ENG [38777] : 1800S BRACKLIN, FER, IRL & AUS [36313] : 1816-1827 TRUMBULL CO., OH, USA [36553] : 1810-1816 FRANKLIN CO., KY, USA [36553] : 1837-1950 WARRICK CO., IN, USA [36553]

CLISBY 1750+ LONDON, ENG [34314] : ALL WORLDWIDE [34600]

CLIST PRE 1850 COSSINGTON, SOM & NTT, ENG [36082]

CLITHEROW 1650-1750 NTH, ENG [36415]

CLIUE 800-1700 ENG [36169]

CLIVE 800-1900 WORLDWIDE [36169]

CLIVES 800-1980 WORLDWIDE [36169]

CLOCKNER 1800S FRA [38605]

CLOETE PRE 1880 SIMONSTOWN, CAPE, RSA [36468]

CLOGG 1800+ MORVAL, CON, ENG [37905]

CLOHESY PRE 1853 CASTLECOMER, KIK, IRL [34039] : 1830+ KILBEHINY, COR, IRL [38299] : 1810+ LIM, IRL [38299]

CLOIREC PRE 1890 ENNIS, CLA, IRL [38484] : ALL WORLDWIDE [38484]

CLOKE 1850+ SANDWICH, KEN, ENG [36137]

CLONEY ALL WORLDWIDE [36028]

CLONON 1800+ EASTON, MA, USA & IRL [38175]

CLOPTON 1700-1800 STAFFORD CO., NH, USA [34749]

CLORE 1750-1900 GEMMINGEN, BADEN, GER [38574] : PRE 1900 CULPEPER, VA, USA [38574]

CLOSE MARY 1800S FREDERICTON & BEAR RIVER, NB & NS, CAN [37499] : 1800+ NEWCASTLE, NBL, ENG [35644] : ALL BRK, ENG [35868] : ALL BALTONSBOROUGH, SOM, ENG [35899] : PRE 1750 WINSTON, DUR, ENG [36159]

CLOSSON 1780-1900 KITLEY TWP., ONT, CAN [36938] : PRE 1820 HARWICH, ESS, ENG [35758]

CLOST ALL OTTAWA, ONT, CAN [34095]

CLOTHIER 1780S KILMINGTON, SOM, ENG [35815] : PRE 1878 YEOVIL, SOM, ENG [36180]

CLOTHWORTHY PRE 1850 BELFAST & NEWTOWNARDS, DOW & ANT, IRL [34733]

CLOTWORTHY 1875-1914 EAST BUDLEIGH, DEV, ENG [37709]

CLOTZ 1872+ BALLARAT, VIC, AUS [36278]

CLOUGH PRE 1900 MARYBOROUGH, VIC, AUS [33997] : 1916+ REGINA, SAS, CAN [36412] : 1920-90 VANCOUVER, BC, ALB & SAS, CAN [37486] : 1660-1800 WINWICK & CULCHETH, LAN, ENG [34352] : 1900+ ILFORD, ESS, ENG [35460] : 1800+ WILLOUGHBY WITH SLOOTHBY, LIN, ENG [35524] : C1850 LONDON, ENG [35860] : ALL MONKWEARMOUTH, DUR, ENG [36046] : PRE 1819 ST GILES, DUR, ENG [36604] : PRE 1910 GREYMOUTH, WLD, NZ [33997]

CLOURIC PRE 1890 ENNIS, CLA, IRL [38484]

CLOUSE 1780-1870 WASHINGTON CO., TN, USA [38009]

CLOUSEN 1800S SHO, GER [35797]

CLOUSTON 1800 SANDWICK, OKI, SCT [37170] : ALL OKI, SCT &, WORLDWIDE [34705]

CLOUT 1776 BOXLEY, KEN, ENG [34176] : 1820S ELHAM, KEN, ENG [35728] : ALL WORLDWIDE [34874]

CLOUTEN 1849+ NSW, AUS [34977] : 1849+ MAITLAND, NSW, AUS [35073] : PRE 1849 FOLKESTONE, KEN, ENG [34977] : PRE 1815 FOLKESTONE, KEN, ENG [37104]

CLOUTING PRE 1750 SOUTH EAST, SFK, ENG [37420]

CLOUTMAN 1700+ SOUTH HACKNEY, MDX, ENG [34547]

CLOVER 1700-1880 BOYTON, SFK, ENG [34846] : 1750+ BATTISFORD, SFK, ENG [35475]

CLOW 1800+ CAN [35450] : 1795+ KILMUIR, INV, SCT [35450] : 1860+ MULL, ARL, SCT [35450] : ALL DUNBLANE, PER, SCT [35450] : 1700+ SCT [35880] : 1800+ USA [35450]

CLOWSER ARTHUR PRE 1848+ HRT, ENG [34592] : 1700-1900 LONDON, MDX, ENG [36438]

CLUB 1750-1890 MACDUFF, BAN, SCT [36877]

CLUBB PRE 1850 SOUTHWOLD, SFK, ENG [36829]

CLUBBE ALL UK [37240]

CLUDERAY ALL PANNAL & LEEDS, WRY, ENG [37988]

CLUER PRE 1862+ LONDON, LND, ENG [37912]

CLUES 1900+ SALE & JOHNSONVILLE, VIC, AUS [36622]

CLUGSTON 1850-1885 MORUYA, NSW, AUS [38007] : 1700-1800S NEWTOWN HAMILTON, ARM, IRL [34483] : PRE 1810 SCT [36052]

CLULEE ALL WORLDWIDE [34949]

CLULEY 1770+ LAN, ENG [38020]

CLUNAN PRE 1830 GAL, IRL [35792]

CLUNE 1870+ MANNING RIVER, NSW, AUS [35089] : 1870S REDFERN & SYDNEY, NSW, AUS [35089] : 1863+ GLEBE, NSW, AUS [36316] : ANN 1850 TULLA, CLA, IRL [36316]

CLUNES JAMES C1864 NEWHILLS, ABD, SCT [38452] : WILLIAM PRE 1864 NEWHILLS, ABD, SCT [38452]

CLUTTER SAMUEL 1830-40 HOCKING CO., OH, USA [38086] : STEPHEN 1820 FAIRFIELD CO., OH, USA [38086]

CLUTTERBUCK PRE 1750 SAUL, GLS, ENG [34962] : ALL WORLDWIDE [36030]

CLUTTON PRE 1906 MELBOURNE, VIC, AUS [35136] : PRE 1906 SYDNEY, NSW, AUS [35136] : HARRIET C1813 BROOME & NORWICH, NFK, ENG [36590]

CLYDE PRE 1850 LAUNCESTON, TAS, AUS [38306]

CLYDESDALE 1800 GLASGOW, LKS, SCT [35879]

CLYFTON PRE 1600 NTT & LND, ENG [36802]

CLYNE C1790 ABD, SCT [33914] : 1786+ BOWER, CAI, SCT [35013]

CLYNE (SEE CLINE) [35638]

CLYVE 800-1700 WORLDWIDE [36169]

CMOLIK C1932 WINNIPEG, MAN, CAN [34251] : ALL ROZMITAL, CS [34251]

COAD PRE 1870 NEW NORFOLK, TAS, AUS [35055] : PRE 1940 RUTHERGLEN, VIC, AUS [35055] : C1800S CON & DEV, ENG [35381] : PRE 1822 WIC, IRL [34502]

COADIC 1898-1990 BAYE, BRT, FRA [34136]

COADY 1814 MAGHERA, CLA, IRL [34176]

COAKER ALL WORLDWIDE [37882]

COAKLEY ALL WIDNES, LAN, ENG [36525] : ALL SALFORD, LAN, ENG [36525]

COALE JOHN PRE 1650 ENG [37551]

COARD PRE 1862+ MANCHESTER, LAN, ENG [35928]

COASTGUARDS 1800-1900 PAUL, SENNEN COVE, ST MAWES, CON, ENG [36398]

COAT 1852 BRISTOL, SOM, ENG [34540]

COATEN 1655-1700 FINEDON, NTH, ENG [35119]

COATES PRE 1897 ARALUEN & GLEN INNES, NSW, AUS [35757] : C1830 ONTARIO CO., ONT, CAN [34988] : 1400+ BOSHAM, SSX, ENG [33989] : PRE 1834 BEMPTON, ERY, ENG [34285] : 1775+ BULMER, NRY, ENG [34333] : PRE 1775 GANTHORPE, NRY, ENG [34333] : PRE 1775 TERRINGTON, NRY, ENG [34333] : C1780-1830 SINNINGTON, NRY, ENG [34380] : PRE 1770 THIRSK, YKS, ENG [34494] : ALL WIRKSWORTH, DBY, ENG [35346] : PRE 1800 BRIGNALL, YKS, ENG [36704] : PRE 1691 ENG [36972] : 1700-1830 NORTH FRODINGHAM, YKS, ENG [37011] : 1800+ LONDON, ENG [37160] : 1800-1832 ROTHERHITHE, SRY, ENG [37345] : ALL YKS, ENG [37407] : PRE 1900 CLITHEROE, LAN, ENG [37774] : PRE 1708 COXWOLD, NRY, ENG [37852] : C1806-1829 DUBLIN, IRL [34704]

COATS PRE 1858 YKS, ENG [34587] : 1700+ PAISLEY, RFW, SCT [34263] : PRE 1840 BLANTYRE, LKS, SCT [34618]

COBAUGH ALL USA [37804]

COBB C1850 POOLE, DOR, ENG [35131] : 1700-1900 HECKINGTON, LIN, ENG [35643] : 1750+ EAST STOKE, DOR, ENG [36825] : 1850+ YORK, YKS, ENG [36975] : 1900+ LEI, ENG [37291] : PRE 1900 HECKINGTON, LIN, ENG [37291] : RICHARD C1818 ISLINGTON, LND, ENG [38397] : CHARLES 1800+ CAM, ENG [38413] : 1800 KINGS COURT, IRL [35543] : 1650-1780 TAUNTON, MA, USA [37013] : 1755-1839 TAUNTON, MA, USA [38151] : 1840-1870 CLIFTON HILL, MO, USA [38373]

COBBAN PRE 1850S MILLBANK, ABD, SCT [34431] : C1860 BURGHEAD, MOR, SCT [35994]

COBBETT 1750+ FARNHAM, SRY, ENG [34532] : PRE 1870 WOKING, SRY, ENG [36142]

COBBHAM C1800 SSX, ENG [33841]

COBBIN C1800 MOUNTNESSING, ESS, ENG [33841]

COBBING 1800+ LONDON, ENG [36686]

COBBLEDICK PRE 1830 BOSCASTLE, CON, ENG [36309] : ALL WORLDWIDE [36762]

COBBY PRE 1850 DOR, ENG [34317] : 1830+ LONDON, ENG & AUS [37134]

COBCROFT C1800+ NSW, AUS [33930] : C1814 SYDNEY, NSW, AUS [35089]

COBDEN PRE 1800 CHICHESTER, SSX, ENG [37765]

COBELDICK ALL WORLDWIDE [36762]

COBER PRE 1900 SOMERSET CO., PA, USA [34115]

COBLEIGH C1600-1650 SOUTH MOLTON, DEV, ENG [36949]

COBLEY ALL LND, ENG [35707] : PRE 1860 COVENTRY, WAR, ENG [37964]

COBURN 1837+ HARVEY, NB, CAN [34163] : ALL ASHBY DE-LA ZOUCHE, LEI, ENG & NZ [33981]

COCHRAN 1800+ TYR, IRL [35137] : PRE 1852 PAISLEY, RFW, SCT [35806] : 1700+ PAISLEY, RFW, SCT [36794] : ROBERT 1850S PAISLEY, RFW, SCT [37879] : 1850+ STATION IS, NY, USA [36794] : 1830-1840S MARION CO., IN, USA [36940] : 1840-1860 APPANOOSE CO. & VAN BUREN CO., IA, USA [36940] : PRE 1774 CHESTER CO., PA, USA [36972] : ANN PRE 1851 GUERNSEY, OH, USA [37481] : PRE 1870 JOHNSON CO., IL, USA [38017] : 1795-1850 NORTH HERO, VT, USA [38133]

COCHRANE 1856+ BRISBANE, QLD, AUS [33845] : 1848 SNOWY RIVER SHIRE, NSW, AUS [35414] : JOHN 1875+ ARMIDALE, NSW, AUS [37310] : 1788-1900 AUS [37964] : 1800S FRONTENAC, ONT, CAN [34353] : 1885+ WINNIPEG, MAN, CAN [38584] : PRE 1854 WEST DERBY, DBY, ENG [35091] : 1800S BAILIEBOROUGH, CAV, IRL [34973] : 1700+ FINTONA, TYR, IRL [35080] : 1850+ BELFAST, ANT, DOW & ARM, IRL [35636] : 1800+ MONKSTOWN, DUB, IRL [37306] : MARY PRE 1846 STI, SCT [33951] : PRE 1831 RFW, SCT [35091] : PRE 1825 LESMAHAGOW, LKS, SCT [35406] : PRE 1848 SCT [35414] : PRE 1838 STI & CLK, SCT [35525] : 1796+ BEITH, AYR, SCT [35780] : C1800-1860 DUNFERMLINE, FIF, SCT [37964] : PRE 1900 GLASGOW, LKS, SCT [38298] : ALL WORLDWIDE [38739]

COCK 1860+ NEVILLE, NSW, AUS [33870] : 1859+ CLUNES, VIC, AUS [34530] : 1863-1911 BROADMEADOWS, VIC, AUS [35594] : PRE 1914 AUS [36214] : 1600-1990 GENAARDS BERGEN, OVL, BEL [38165] : PRE 1860 ST KEVERNE, CON, ENG [33870] : 1700-1900 GWITHIAN, CON, ENG [33972] : PRE 1800 WEST WYCOMBE, BKM, ENG [34104] : PRE 1800 HIGH WYCOMBE, BKM, ENG [34104] : C1840 BROADSTAIRS, KEN, ENG [34395] : PRE 1800 LYNG, NFK, ENG [34858] : PRE 1820 CHULMLEIGH, DEV, ENG [34963] : C1770 DRAYTON BEAUCHAMP, BKM, ENG [35095] : PRE 1760 BREAGE, CON, ENG [35587] : 1843-1863

SPALDING, LIN, ENG [35594] : PRE 1725 ESS, ENG [35642] : 1600+ ESS, ENG [36093] : 1809-1880 LND, ENG [36117] : 1770-1860 TRURO & ST DENNIS, CON, ENG [36214] : C1750 TRURO, CON, ENG [36945] : PRE 1830 PLYMOUTH, DEV, ENG [37579] : PRE 1914 RSA [36214] : C1686 HENRICO CO., VA, USA [36354]

COCKAYNE C1770 NOTTINGHAM, NTT, ENG [34734]

COCKBAINE 1700S THRELKELD, CUL, ENG [33917]

COCKBURN SAMUEL 1859+ MELBOURNE, VIC, AUS [35574] : 1820+ QUE, CAN [36272] : C1790 NORTH LONDON, MDX, ENG [36803] : 1840S SCT [33856] : PRE 1850 ABBEY ST BATHANS, SCT [33959] : PRE 1850 LINLITHGOW, STI, SCT [34097] : 1700+ COLDSTREAM, ROX, SCT [34163] : SAMUEL PRE 1839 BEW, SCT [35574] : 1800+ AUCHTERMUCHTY, FIF, SCT [35644] : PRE 1820 ELN, SCT [36272] : DAVID 1860S DUNS, BEW, SCT & AUS [35498]

COCKE 1550-1700 NORWICH, NFK, ENG [38287] : 1800+ DFS, SCT [35293]

COCKELL PRE 1820 STRETHAM & WITCHFORD, CAM, ENG [35391]

COCKER ALBERT H. 1882+ ADELAIDE, SA, AUS [36309] : PRE 1850 MIDDLETON, LAN, ENG [36187] : JOHN PRE 1800 YEALMPTON, DEV, ENG [36309] : PRE 1820 INVERURIE, ABD, SCT [34613]

COCKERELL C1813 STOW UPLAND, SFK, ENG [33899] : 1700-1820 SFK, ENG [35701] : ALL ENG [37739] : 1750 KENTON, SFK, ENG [37928]

COCKERILL WILLIAM ALL SHELBORNE, ONT, CAN [37440] : 1750-1900 PETERBOROUGH, HUN, ENG [33908]

COCKERTON ALL PORT OF SPAIN, TRINIDAD, W.INDIES [36805]

COCKIN PRE 1800 SPALDING, LIN, ENG [36107] : 1830S TUTBURY, STS, ENG [37230] : 1800+ TIPTON, STS, ENG [37230] : 1830+ REDDITCH, WOR, ENG [37230]

COCKING 1790+ MAN, CAN [37426] : ALL YKS, ENG [36399] : 1750-1850 NORTH MUSKHAM, NTT, ENG [36561] : 1700S BASSINGHAM, LIN, ENG [37039] : 1780-1890 ILLOGAN, CON, ENG [37488]

COCKLIN 1854-1874 STEPNEY, LND, ENG [38417]

COCKRAM 1700+ KNOWSTONE, DEV & SOM, ENG [37322]

COCKS 1938+ MOSS VALE & BOWRAL, NSW, AUS [34780] : 1839+ ADELAIDE, SA, AUS [35349] : 1905+ WIMMERA, VIC, AUS [36622] : 1880+ CHS, ENG [34526] : JOHN PRE 1900 TRURO, CON, ENG [36290] : 1850+ ENG [36470] : 1800S HITCHIN, HRT, ENG [36764] : 1800S OLD WINDSOR, BRK, ENG [36764] : 1800+ NFK, ENG [36658] : ELIJAH 1853 PAKENHAM, SFK, ENG [37106] : C1600-1700 CHERTSEY, SRY, ENG [37618]

COCKSEDGE ELIJAH 1826 ERISWELL, SFK, ENG [37106]

COCKSHAW ALL ST LAWRENCE, YKS, ENG [36557]

COCKSHOTT 1400-1800 SABDEN, LAN, ENG [34928]

COCKSING 1800+ WALSALL, STS, ENG [36821]

COCKTON (SEE CROCKTO [35471]

CODD 1700+ SHILLELAGH, WIC, IRL [38385]

CODDING PRE 1850 OH, USA [38303]

CODDINGTON ALL KEN, ENG [37015] : 1700+ OLDBRIDGE, MEA, IRL [34299]

CODE 1820+ LANARK CO., ONT, CAN [34502]

CODLIN PRE 1840 HACKNEY, LND, ENG [36377]

CODRINGTON PRE 1837 IRON ACTON, GLS, ENG [37878] : 1803+ WESTERLEIGH, GLS, ENG [37878]

CODY 1820+ WOLLOMBI, NSW, AUS [33963] : 1750+ KIK, IRL [33963] : PRE 1828 SHORTLES,

CRAIG, KILMANAGH, KIK, IRL [34013] : C1810 WEXFORD, WEX, IRL [34016] : PRE 1820 COR, IRL [34984] : C1835 CASTLEGAR, GAL, IRL [35900] : PRE 1830 KIK, IRL [36372]

COE 1806+ CAMBERWELL, SRY, ENG [33899] : PRE 1825 WATERBEACH, CAM, ENG [35238] : 1802 LONG SUTTON, LIN, ENG [35369] : PRE 1800 NTH, ENG [36006] : 1800-1820 MIAMI CO., OH, USA [38741]

COEHOORN 1550-1990 FRI, NL [33983] : 1550-1990 NBT, NL [33983] : 1550-1950 GRO, FRI & BRA, NL [38704]

COEHORN 1450-1900 ALS, FRA [33983]

COELHO ALL SURINAME [33751] : ALL SURINAME [38692]

COEN ALL GALWAY, GAL, IRL [34684] : PRE 1730 FRANEKER, FRI, NL [35008]

COEVERT 1700-1750 LONG ISLAND, NY, USA [36943]

COFFEE JANE 1700+ CHURCHTOWN, WEM, IRL [35093] : PRE 1840 IRL [35532]

COFFEY 1810-1832 SYDNEY, NSW, AUS [34659] : 1856 SYDNEY, NSW, AUS [34764] : 1882+ BALLARAT, VIC, AUS [35185] : 1800-1850 DOVER, KEN, ENG [33834] : 1837-1858 KID, IRL [34035] : ELLEN 1830S COR, IRL [34764] : PRE 1840 CAPPAGHWHITE, TIP, IRL [35406] : PRE 1890 FETHARD, TIP, IRL [35521] : PRE 1840 IRL [35532] : 1600-1700 IRL [36898]

COFFIELD 1800-50 IRL [36431]

COFFILL ALL UK [37674]

COFFIN C1794 STRAFFORD CO., NH, USA [35263] : PRE 1840 USA [36969] : ALL WORLDWIDE [35804]

COGAN C1745 KINGSTON ST MARY, SOM, ENG [34926] : 1755 FLETCHING, SSX, ENG [38209] : PRE 1700 SOM, ENG [38745]

COGGAN PRE 1849 LONG SUTTON, SOM, ENG [35117] : 1650-1700 HAXEY, LIN, ENG [36635] : 1700+ SOM, ENG [38209] : 1600S LANCASTER, MA, USA [36944]

COGGER PRE 1849 LUDSDOWN, KEN, ENG [33821] : THOMAS 1770S LONDON, MDX, ENG [35471] : 1800 LONDON, ENG [38719]

COGGINS 1790+ SOULDERN, OXF, ENG [33956]

COGHELAN 1800-1870 SYDNEY, NSW, AUS [36293]

COGHILL PRE 1800 LONDON, MDX & HRT, ENG [34743]

COGHLAN 1860-1880 BRISTOL, GLS, ENG [34187] : 1850 ADARE, LIM, IRL [34546] : C1813 CLONES, MOG, IRL [34806] : 1795-1825 BANTRY, COR, IRL [36666] : 1830-1850 CARDIFF, GLA, WLS [34187] : 1800S WORLDWIDE [37500]

COGMAN ALL NORWICH, NFK, ENG [37612]

COGRAVE ALL HESSLE, YKS, ENG [35814]

COGSWELL 1600 WESTBURY & LEIGH, ENG [35276] : ALL WORLDWIDE [38259]

COHEN PRE 1850 LONDON, ENG [35556] : SOLOMON 1850+ COVENTRY, WAR, ENG [36254] : PRE 1800 LND, ENG [36399] : 1700-1990 ENG [38096] : 1840-1856 GER [38236] : ALL FORDON, PRE, GER & AUS [33799] : 1885 GREYSTONES, WIC, IRL [37791] : 1880 DUBLIN, IRL [37791] : 1700-1990 NEW YORK, NY, USA [38096] : 1856-1940 NEW YORK, NY, USA [38236]

COHN C1800-1900 HAMBURG, GER [35591]

COHOON 1650-1800 NEW MILFORD, CT, USA [38588]

COHORN 1000-1500 SWE [33983]

COHORNE 1450-1950 PCA, FRA [33983]

COITTE 1825-1854 NANTES, FRA [36601]

COKER 1600-1900 BDF & BKM, ENG [36007] : C1800 ESS, ENG [36978] : ALL WORLDWIDE [37882]

COLBORNE JAMES PRE 1870 BRISTOL, ENG [38776]

COLBOURNE ALL NFD, CAN [35619] : 1800+ DOR, ENG [33875] : 1600+ ROWLEY REGIS, STS, ENG [36701]

COLBRAN 1800+ ROTHERFIELD, SSX, ENG [34785] : 1800S BRIGHTON & HURSTNONCEUX, SSX, ENG [36786]

COLBY 1850 LAMBETH, SRY, ENG [34940] : C1856 KIRKLEY, SFK, ENG [35131] : PRE 1650 MA, USA [38746]

COLCHIN ALL ENG [34343]

COLCLOUGH PRE 1860 WEX, IRL [36581] : PRE 1860 KIK, IRL [36581]

COLCORD 1730+ CHESTER, NH, USA [35276]

COLDCLOTH PRE 1750 CAM, ENG [35642]

COLDICUTT 1870S THAMES, NZ [35988]

COLDING 1770-1830 BARNWELL CO., SC, USA [38129]

COLDRAKE ALL IRL [34131]

COLDS 1810S MON, WLS [35516]

COLDSTREAM PRE 1854+ CUPAR, FIF, SCT [35553]

COLDWELL CHARLOTTE C1845 SYDNEY, NSW, AUS [36767] : PRE 1820 HOLMFIRTH, YKS, ENG [34613] : 1700-1850 YKS, ENG [36844] : ALL YKS, ENG [37078]

COLE 1919+ LIDCOMBE, NSW, AUS [33817] : 1859-1910 LITHGOW, NSW, AUS [33817] : 1859-1890 BRAIDWOOD, NSW, AUS [33817] : 1910-1920 NEWTOWN, NSW, AUS [33817] : 1870-1890 SURRY HILLS, NSW, AUS [33817] : 1850+ GRAFTON & GLEN INNES, NSW, AUS [34185] : PRE 1900 VIC, AUS [34657] : GEORGE 1848-1900 GOULBURN, NSW, AUS [34842] : 1852+ SYDNEY, NSW, AUS [34856] : 1830+ MUSWELLBROOK, NSW, AUS [35740] : 1836-7 SYDNEY, NSW, AUS [35854] : PRE 1820 QUE, CAN [34383] : 1825+ HALTON & PEEL COS., ONT, CAN [34407] : 1777-1890 NB, CAN [36718] : 1820+ SOPHIASBURGH, PEI, CAN [38387] : PRE 1850 SELBORNE, HAM, ENG [34201] : 1700+ SHORNE, KEN, ENG [34263] : PRE 1890 LND, KEN & SRY, ENG [34325] : 1790+ HAVERHILL, SFK, ENG [34334] : PRE 1820 SRY & KEN, ENG [34383] : SAMUEL 1790S COLCHESTER, ESS, ENG [34499] : SAMUEL 1820S CHATHAM, KEN, ENG [34499] : 1849 SRY, ENG [34540] : 1700-1800 NORTH CRAWLEY, BKM, ENG [34552] : 1800+ SOUTHSEA & PORTSMOUTH, HAM, ENG [34639] : PRE 1800 ST ENODER, CON, ENG [34684] : 1800+ GLS, ENG [34684] : 1700+ NEWLYN, CON, ENG [34684] : 1820S UXBRIDGE, MDX, ENG [34738] : 1820S WHITECHAPEL, MDX, ENG [34738] : PRE 1850 BRISTOL, GLS, ENG [34776] : 1830-1852 EXETER, DEV, ENG [34856] : C1820-1850 WEST HACKNEY, MDX & LND, ENG [35037] : BENJAMIN C1780 MATTISHALL, NFK, ENG [35046] : 1849+ GODMANCHESTER, HUN, ENG [35185] : PRE 1820+ COVENTRY, WAR, ENG [35453] : 1800S LAMBETH, SRY, ENG [35804] : ALL LONDON, ENG [35807] : PRE 1835 STOKE DAMEREL, DEV, ENG [35854] : PRE 1830 EAST STRATTON, HAM, ENG [35902] : 1892+ CROYDON, LND & SRY, ENG [36002] : PRE 1847 NORWOOD, SRY, ENG [36035] : 1800-1900 LAYER BRETON, ESS, ENG [36136] : 1750-1850 HILPERTON, WIL, ENG [36226] : PRE 1800 LONDON, MDX & SRY, ENG [36379] : JOHN PRE 1715 ENG [36527] : EDWARD 1695-1705 ENG [36527] : MARG. & JAMES 1700S COLWALL, HEF, ENG [36633] : ANDREW C1810 ENG [36873] : 1724 BISHOPS NYMPTON, DEV, ENG [36995] : PRE 1663 HESTON, MDX, ENG [37029] : C1800 BOW, LND, ENG [37053] : PRE 1849 PLYMOUTH, DEV,

ENG [37174] : ALL SSX, ENG [37210] : ALL WIL,
ENG [37232] : PRE 1700 WOODBRIDGE, SFK, ENG
[37250] : ALL DOWNHAM, CAM, ENG [37494] :
PRE 1860 MAIDSTONE, KEN, ENG [37494] : PRE
1800 CHIPPENHAM, WIL, ENG [37695] : 1910
HASLAND, DBY, ENG [37723] : PRE 1900
PAILTON & COVENTRY, WAR, ENG [37750] : ALL
MARYLEBONE, LND, ENG [37937] : EDITH C1889
CHISWICK, MDX, ENG [37992] : 1750-1850
MICHELDEVER, HAM, ENG [38003] : PRE 1850
BRIXHAM, CON, ENG [38276] : PRE 1900
LONDON, SRY, SFK & NFK, ENG [38512] : ALL
WAR, ENG [38514] : ALL DEV, ENG & NZ [36850] :
1868 INDIA [35865] : 1710+ TIP, IRL [34407] : PRE
1850 DUBLIN, IRL [38457] : 1800S JEFFERSON
CO., OH, USA [35278] : 1880 MO & IL, USA [35279] :
1784-1900 PROVIDENCE, RI, USA [36915] : 1653+
ST MARY'S CO., MD, USA [37029] : WILLIAM
1650+ ANNE ARUNDEL CO., MD, USA [37551] :
C1850 MORGAN CO., IL, USA [37782] : WILLIAM
1804-1880 SULLIVAN CO., NY, USA [38053] :
WILLIAM PRE 1800 PA, USA [38053] : 1790-1860
RUTLAND, VT, USA [38054] : 1790-1860 MT
HOLLY, VT, USA [38054] : 1800 OTSEGO CO., NY,
USA [38188] : 1800+ NEW YORK, NY, USA [38587]

COLECHIN ALL ENG [34343]

COLECLOUGH 1840S WIGAN, LAN, ENG [38266]

COLEMAN 1888+ SYDNEY, NSW, AUS [34533] :
1800+ APPIN & CAMPBELLTOWN, NSW, AUS
[38006] : 1840-90 AIMA, VIC, AUS [38275] : 1820-48
ADELAIDE, SA, AUS [38275] : 1800+ ONT, CAN
[34490] : 1930+ MONTREAL, QUE, CAN [37753] :
1770-1910 TRINITY, NFD, CAN [38045] : 1842-1865
CAN [38144] : 1800+ NFK, ENG [34049] : PRE 1888
MARKET HARBOROUGH, LEI, ENG [34533] : ALL
WINFARTHING, NFK, ENG [34597] : PRE 1838
WALMER, KEN, ENG [34689] : 1819+ BRIGHTON,
SSX, ENG [34781] : PRE 1750 BEXHILL, SSX, ENG
[34806] : PRE 1800 WESTFIELD, SSX, ENG [35128] :
PRE 1820 BURWASH, SSX, ENG [35397] : PRE 1900
LAKENHEATH, SFK, ENG [35742] : PRE 1839
RAMSBURY, WIL, ENG [35792] : PRE 1840 KINGS
STANLEY, GLS, ENG [35930] : 1800+
MANCHESTER, LAN, ENG [35990] : PRE 1860
CHILWORTH, SRY, ENG [36095] : PRE 1810
BIRMINGHAM, WAR, ENG [36177] : 1850-1860
BKM, ENG [36526] : C1834 LITTLE STRETTON,
LEI, ENG [36803] : 1829+ BROAD BLUNSDON,
WIL, ENG [36975] : PRE 1850 CON, ENG [37061] :
1780-1810 QUEINBOROUGH, LEI, ENG [37129] :
ALL PORTSMOUTH, HAM, ENG [37214] : 1800S
YKS, ENG [37910] : 1800-30 MAIDSTONE, KEN,
ENG [38275] : 1700+ LANIVET, CON, ENG [38446] :
PRE 1650 WOR & WIL, ENG [38746] : 1837
STEPNEY, LND, ENG & AUS [34845] : 1750-1820
WAT & COR, IRL [38045] : 1877-1880 SCT [36526] :
1820-1865 LAWRENCE & DAVIESS CO., IN, USA
[33760] : 1800+ USA [34490] : 1870-80 BEAVER,
BEAVER CO., PA, USA [38087] : 1830-1880
JEFFERSON CO., KY, USA [38091] : 1750-1830
DINWIDDIE CO., VA, USA [38091] : 1820-1900
WYOMING, NY, USA [38095] : 1865-1900 DES
MOINES, IA, USA [38105] : 1885-1910 MCCOOK,
NE, USA [38105] : 1840-1860 IN, USA [38105] : 1830-
1850 SC, USA [38105] : PRE 1850 WESTERN, PA,
USA [38218] : 1750-1904 CUMBERLAND &
FRANKLIN CO., VA, USA [38315]

COLES WILLIAM C1889 GLADSTONE, QLD, AUS
[35501] : 1860-1870 BENDIGO, VIC, AUS [35725] :
1850-1920 EVERCREECH &WESTON SUPER
MARE, SOM, ENG [34458] : PRE 1850S DEVERILL
& SALISBURY, WIL, ENG [34458] : PRE 1820

PLYMTREE & MEMBURY, DEV, ENG [35701] :
1700+ BOXGROVE & CHICHESTER, SSX, ENG
[35987] : 1846 BATH, SOM, ENG [36860] : C1800
KEN, ENG [36860] : 1841 HARDINGTON
MANDEVILLE, SOM, ENG [37378] : ALL
EVERCREECH, SOM, ENG [37672] : PRE 1800
CLIFTON REYNES, BKM, ENG [37712] : 1800+
KILCOOLY, LIM, IRL [37422]

COLESBY 1700-1800 BIRMINGHAM, WAR, ENG
[37924]

COLEY PRE 1840 GRANVILLE CO., NC, USA [38311]

COLGAN C1880 BAGENALSTOWN (NOW MAIN
BHEAG), CAR, IRL [35046] : 1840 OFF, IRL [37558] :
PRE 1907 ANT, IRL [37601] : ALL NY, USA [37558] :
JOHN 1907-1917 EUREKA, CA, USA [37601]

COLGATE ALL KEN, ENG [37595] : ALL IRL [35618]

COLGRAVE ALL WORLDWIDE [35501]

COLIN PRE 1900 WAR, ENG [36508]

COLING C1880 ROMA, QLD, AUS [35807] : C1870
TAROOM, QLD, AUS [35807] : PRE 1870
KENILWORTH, WAR, ENG [35807]

COLLAMORE 1800S BARNSTAPLE, DEV, ENG
[33958]

COLLARD 1780+ LIVERPOOL, LAN, ENG [33927] :
1500+ SOM, ENG [34610] : MATILDA 1800+
YEOVIL, SOM, ENG [34610] : WILLIAM 1700+
BRISTOL, GLS, ENG [34610] : 1805
RODBOROUGH, GLS, ENG [35560] : PRE 1900
EXETER, DEV, ENG [37214] : PRE 1850 LONDON,
MDX, ENG [38376] : 1800S BATH, SOM, ENG &
AUS [35422]

COLLECT 1750 RUAN LANIHORN, CON, ENG
[37224]

COLLEDGE 1750 WIRKSWORTH, DBY, ENG [35970]

COLLEGE 1800S WAR, ENG [33934]

COLLET 1720S NOTGROVE, GLS, ENG [35259] : ALL
WENDOVER, BKM, ENG [37988] : JOSEPH
PIERRE 1630-1660 ST JACQUES AMIENS, PIC,
FRA [36681]

COLLETH ALL WORLDWIDE [35918]

COLLETT 1821 CHELTENHAM, GLS, ENG [34176] :
1800-1860 PENDOWER, CON, ENG [36214] : ALL
WEDNESBURY, STS, ENG [36537] : PRE 1840
LEONARD STANLEY, GLS, ENG [36800] : PRE
1900 NTH & OXF, ENG [36893] : 1839 RIPTON
REGIS, HUN, ENG [37723] : 1780-1850 STROUD,
GLS, ENG [38407] : ALL WORLDWIDE [36498]

COLLEY 1830+ DEWSBURY, WRY, ENG [34512] :
PRE 1839 COTTISFORD, OXF & BKM, ENG [34753]
: 1800+ CHELSEA & LONDON, MDX, ENG [35342]
: ALL BRISTOL & CASTLE CARY, SOM, ENG
[36995] : 1880+ NZ [36871]

COLLIA PRE 1850 CALABRIA, ITL [36679]

COLLICK ALL ASHTON, CON, ENG [36145]

COLLICOTT C1785 WHITCHURCH, DEV, ENG
[36945] : 1760+ LND, ENG & AUS [33790]

COLLIE ALL VIC, AUS [37115] : PRE 1830 ST
ANDREWS, LLANBRYDE, MOR, SCT [34192] :
1800-1880 BANFF, BAN, SCT [36663]

COLLIER PRE 1916 RICHMOND RIVER, NSW, AUS
[35236] : 1855+ BALMAIN, NSW, AUS [35573] :
1800+ KEN, ENG [33921] : 1800+ FENTON, NBL,
ENG [34085] : 1700 SUTTON VENY, WIL, ENG
[34466] : ALL REDDISH, LAN, ENG [34674] : C1790
WESTBURY, WIL, ENG [35076] : 1700S HANLEY,
STS, ENG [35322] : 1784-1847 LOWTON, LAN, ENG
[35341] : PRE 1850 OWERMOIGNE, DOR, ENG
[35407] : PRE 1804 LND, ENG [35493] : PRE 1876
WALWORTH, SRY, ENG [35573] : PRE 1795+
READING, BRK & LND, ENG [35573] : ALL STS,
ENG [35628] : ALL BIRMINGHAM, WAR, ENG
[35628] : 1850+ MORTON, YKS, ENG [35734] : ALL

FULHAM, LND, ENG [36031] : PRE 1807 LONDON, MDX, ENG [36204] : PRE 1820 LONDON, MDX & SRY, ENG [36379] : C1600-1700 SUTTON VENY & UPTON LOVELL, WIL, ENG [36478] : ALL HOOK, YKS, ENG [36704] : PRE 1800 LONDON, ENG [37069] : 1730 + BRIXHAM, DEV, ENG [37132] : 1800S MDX, ENG [37423] : PRE 1850 FULFORD, STS, ENG [37617] : PRE 1830 SMITHSTOWN & FASIDININ, KIK, IRL [33775] : 1770-1870 ANT, IRL [37461] : C1750-1850 DUNFERMLINE, FIF, SCT [37964] : 1900 + NEW YORK, NY, USA [35628] : 1860-85 LINCOLN CO., AR, USA [38314]

COLLIGNAN ALL ALLEGHENY CO., PA, USA [38036]

COLLIN 1785 WEST STOW, SFK, ENG [38209]

COLLING 1800 SUNDERLAND, DUR, ENG [35912]

COLLINGBOURNE 1700-1770 BADGWORTH, GLS, ENG [35166]

COLLINGE 1925-90 VANCOUVER, BC, CAN [37486]

COLLINGHAM PRE 1730 SSX, ENG [37875]

COLLINGRIDGE PRE 1915 BATTERSEA, LND, ENG [37102]

COLLINGS 1840-1990 AMHERST, VIC, AUS [33885] : 1899-1959 AUBURN, NSW, AUS [35445] : PRE 1841 POWEY, CON, ENG [33885] : C1840 HASTINGS, SSX, ENG [33918] : PRE 1840 KEWSTOKE, SOM, ENG [35360] : 1600-1899 BRISTOL, ENG [36894] : ALL STOKE DAMEREL & DEVONPORT, DEV, ENG [37158] : 1835 EAST STONEHOUSE, DEV, ENG [37770]

COLLINGTON 1820 + CROYDON, SRY, ENG [35343]

COLLINGWOOD PRE 1870 + VIC, AUS [33890] : PRE 1850 NSW, AUS [34812] : 1850 + ROSEWOOD, QLD, AUS [34812] : PRE 1870 YKS, ENG [33890] : 1740 + NEWCASTLE UPON TYNE, NBL, ENG [33979] : PRE 1850 LIN, ENG [34812] : PRE 1800 GRANTHAM, LIN, ENG [37726] : WILLIAM 1812-1902 IRL [36576] : FANNIE 1866 PGH, ALLEGHENY CO., PA, USA [36576] : LEWIS 1865 PGH, ALLEGHENY CO., PA, USA [36576] : LOY H. 1878 PGH, ALLEGHENY CO., PA, USA [36576] : ANNA 1875-1896 PGH, ALLEGHENY CO., PA, USA [36576] : CLEMENS 1870 PGH, ALLEGHENY CITY, PA, USA [36576] : ELIZA 1850-1921 PA, USA [36576] : HOWARD 1878 PGH, ALLEGHENY CO., PA, USA [36576] : SARAH E. 1852-1899 PGH, ALLEGHENY CO., PA, USA [36576] : DAVID 1862 PGH, ALLEGHENY CO., PA, USA [36576] : BERT 1868 PGH, ALLEGHENY CO., PA, USA [36576] : GEORGE J. 1872-1910 PGH, ALLEGHENY CO., PA, USA [36576] : 1890 + NEW YORK, NY, USA [37726]

COLLINS BRIDGET PRE 1843 SUTTON FOREST & BERRIMA, NSW, AUS [33812] : PRE 1826 + PUNCHBOWL & OATLEY, NSW, AUS [34423] : HENRY PRE 1867 PIPER'S RV., TAS, AUS [35578] : 1870-1885 LITTLE OYSTER COVE, TAS, AUS [35584] : PRE 1850 AUS [35743] : JAMES 1800 + SYDNEY, NSW, AUS [35843] : 1990 + CANBERRA, ACT, AUS [35895] : WILLIAM 1804 HOBART, TAS, AUS [37106] : 1860 + SYDNEY, NSW, AUS [37128] : PRE 1880 MANSFIELD, VIC, AUS [37497] : C1856 WOLLONGONG, NSW, AUS [37891] : PRE 1743 WRESTLINGWORTH, BDF & CAM, ENG [33866] : 1800 + SUDBURY, SFK, ENG [33982] : 1623 + STITHIANS, CON, ENG [33995] : 1740-1880 STYTHIANS, CON, ENG [34016] : C1780-1920S NTT & DBY, ENG [34040] : 1700 + BETHNAL GREEN, LND, ENG [34062] : 1750-1850 PYWORTHY, DEV, ENG [34108] : ALL ENG [34131] : ROSEMARY C1713 NFK, ENG [34222] : 1800 + COTTESBROOKE, NTH, ENG [34315] : PRE 1820 CHRISTCHURCH, SRY, ENG [34316] : ALL

CRANBROOK, KEN, ENG [34325] : 1822 + HAM, ENG [34327] : PRE 1900 MARLOW & WYCOMBE, BKM, MDX & HRT, ENG [34382] : ALL CHITHURST, SSX, ENG [34700] : ALL ROGATE, SSX, ENG [34700] : 1840-1890 NORTH LONDON, ENG [34719] : 1600 + MADRON, CON, ENG [34747] : 1780 + BEXHILL, SSX, ENG [34806] : PRE 1900 SHOREDITCH, LND, ENG [34825] : 1820 + ABBOTS LEIGH, SOM, ENG [35157] : PRE 1800 PRESHUTE, WIL, ENG [35346] : C1875 BINSTED, HAM, ENG [35457] : PRE 1870 ENG [35546] : GEORGE 1860 LND, ENG [35870] : 1800 + ROCHESTER, KEN, ENG [35972] : PRE 1730 PATTINGHAM & SEDGLEY, STS, ENG [36110] : PRE 1850 GLOUCESTER, GLS, ENG [36113] : PRE 1860 BATTERSEA, LND, ENG [36377] : 1732-1764 SHRAWLEY, WOR, ENG [36513] : 1750-1870 WARBURTON, CHS, ENG [36740] : WILLIAM 1860 + HACKNEY, MDX, ENG [36871] : GEORGE C1840 LONDON, ENG [36877] : PRE 1857 + WOODGREEN & LONDON, MDX, ENG [36955] : WILLIAM PRE 1783 GREENWICH, SRY, ENG [37106] : C1774 SHERBURN IN ELMET, YKS, ENG [37144] : ALL STOKE DAMEREL & DEVONPORT, DEV, ENG [37158] : 1600-1700 SOM, ENG [37232] : PRE 1750 CUXTON, KEN, ENG [37325] : 1700-1930 SRY, ENG [37348] : C1860 DORCHESTER, DOR, ENG [37378] : 1750-1850 WELLS, SOM, ENG [37508] : 1300-1400 + SSX, ENG [37648] : 1825 + ESS, ENG [37656] : 1700-99 YEOVIL, SOM, ENG [37756] : 1650-1750 STEPNEY, MDX, ENG [37783] : 1800S BURSLEM & WOLSTANTON, STS, ENG [37908] : WILLIAM 1800-1850 CON, ENG [37945] : 1860 + TRURO, CON, ENG [38050] : PRE 1615 BRAMFORD, SFK, ENG [38135] : 1800S WOOLWICH, KEN, ENG [38215] : PRE 1735 RUT, ENG [38229] : PRE 1800 RICHMOND & WINDLESHAM, SRY, ENG [38248] : 1400 + SNAILS CROFT, DOR, ENG [38745] : 1750-1820 LONDON, ENG [38774] : 1870 + INDIA [37274] : EDWARD PRE 1773 IRL [34161] : PRE 1870 CORK CITY, COR, IRL [34272] : 1830 + DOW, IRL [34956] : C1830 TULLA, CLA, IRL [35332] : PRE 1900 BALLYDEHOB, COR, IRL [35814] : PRE 1850 DUNMANWAY, COR, IRL [35829] : EMILY HELEN C1895-1900 CORK CITY, COR & TIP, IRL [36498] : ALL LIMERICK, LIM & WIC, IRL [36498] : 1800 + LIM, IRL [36746] : ELIZABETH 1810-1820 TUAM, GAL, IRL [38780] : 1860 + PICTON, MBH, NZ [36746] : PRE 1850 DUNBAR, ELN, SCT [34804] : HOPE PRE 1806 CULPEPER, VA, USA [34573] : ANTHONY PRE 1900 USA [36725] : 1600-1700 VA, USA [36934] : PRE 1840 VA, USA [37565] : ALL ALLEGHENY CO., PA, USA [38036] : 1876-1890 LYON, KS, USA [38095] : 1890-1910 PLACER, CA, USA [38095] : PRE 1865 NARBERTH, PEM, WLS [34665]

COLLINSON 1800 + BRADFORD, WRY, ENG [34401] : 1753 PRESTWICH, LAN, ENG [35369]

COLLIS 1835 + WATERLOO CO., ONT, CAN [38463] : 1800 + CAMBRIDGE, CAM, ENG [35172] : PRE 1840 BARKING & LONDON, ESS, ENG [36178] : 1800S BRISTOL, GLS, ENG [37122] : PRE 1835 LIN, ENG [38463] : ALL WORLDWIDE [37060]

COLLISON ALL MAIDSTONE, KEN, ENG [37359] : ALL PRESTON, LAN, ENG [38415] : 1835-1870S SOUTH CREAKE, NFK, ENG & NZ [36803]

COLLISTER WILLIAM 1856-1858 LIVERPOOL, LAN, ENG [34125] : PRE 1820S DENBIGH, DEN, WLS [35483]

COLLITT C1850 MORTON ON SWALE, YKS, ENG [34936]

COLLIVER PRE 1849 KINGSTON, DEV, ENG [34570]

COLLOCOTT 1852+ KING WILLIAMS TOWN, CAPE, RSA [34947]

COLLS 1700-1800S STAMFORD, LIN, ENG [34032] : 1760+ STAMFORD, LIN, ENG [35768]

COLLUM C1885-1905+ ARARAT, VIC, AUS [34289]

COLLYER PRE 1855 ISLE OF WIGHT, HAM, ENG [34014] : 1830-1900 KENNINGTON, SRY, ENG [37964] : PRE 1830 SHEERNESS, KEN, ENG [37964]

COLMAN 1800+ MARSHAM, NFK, ENG [37276] : 1832-1990 SWANSEA, GLA, WLS [34777]

COLMER 1700S BALTONSBOROUGH, SOM, ENG [35899]

COLONEL 1837-1850 DEV, ENG [34774]

COLPOYS 1820+ NEWMARKET, CLA, IRL [37902]

COLQUHOUN 1765 CADDER, LKS, SCT [35252] : 1760-1780S GLASGOW, LKS, SCT [35483] : PRE 1810 MUCKAIRN, ARL, SCT [36583] : 1800+ CUMBERNAULD, DNB, SCT [36875] : PRE 1900 LKS, SCT [36893] : 1190 SCT [37008] : C1832 GLASGOW, LKS, SCT [37106] : C1743 GREENOCK, RFW, SCT [38485] : 1500+ REHOBOTH, MA & CT, USA & SCT [36970]

COLSON RRE 1780 NORWICH, NFK, ENG [34716] : PRE 1820 NEEDHAM MARKET, SFK, ENG [34716] : C1798 HURSLEY, HAM, ENG [35457]

COLSTON 1460+ BISHOPRIGGS, LKS, SCT [36256]

COLT 1700S DOWNPATRICK, DOW, IRL [38373] : PRE 1773 HARTFORD, CT, USA [34410] : 1635+ USA [35263]

COLTER 1825-1830 NB, CAN [36672] : 1800S DERRYHILLAUGH, FER, IRL [35395] : PRE 1880 OH, USA [35601] : PRE 1860 TUSCARAWAS CO., OH, USA [36672]

COLTMAN PRE 1860 OLD BRENTFORD, MDX, ENG [34187] : 1880-1900 BRISTOL, SOM, ENG [36586] : 1750-1800 STEPNEY, LND, ENG [38516]

COLTON 1850 DRIFFIELD, ERY, ENG [34111] : ALL NTT, ENG [36174]

COLUMBUS 1700-1900 ENG [38096] : 1800-1990 CLINTON CO., PA, USA [38096]

COLVIL C1870 GLASGOW, LKS, SCT [34122]

COLVILL 1800S CHATHAM, KEN, ENG [37885]

COLVILLE ARCHIBALD 1920+ EMMAVILLE, NSW, AUS [38071] : PRE 1791+ LEUCHARS, FIF, SCT [35072] : 1830+ KIRKCALDY, FIF, SCT & CAN [37486]

COLVIN ALL IRL & UK [36333] : PRE 1861 APPLEGARTH, DFS, SCT [35330] : PRE 1900 STONEHAVEN & FETTERESSO, KCD, SCT [36061] : 1820+ PETERHEAD & FRASERBURGH, ABD, SCT [36061]

COLWELL 1842 PT PHILLIP, VIC, AUS [37112] : C1830 CON & DEV, ENG [35744] : 1700-1876 SOUTHAMPTON, HAM, ENG [36751] : JOHN 1820+ GAINSBOROUGH, LIN, ENG [37775] : 1700S-1900S LONDON, MDX & SRY, ENG [38034] : PRE 1830 BARNSTAPLE, DEV, ENG [38596]

COLYER HENRY 1800 BULLS CREEK, SA, AUS [35361] : C1830 BEXLEY & DARTFORD, KEN, ENG [36479] : 1791-1850 SEVENOAKS, KEN, ENG [37453] : C1800-1900 WESTMINSTER, KEN, ENG [37453] : C1870+ WESTFORD, GRANITEVILLE, MA, USA [34432]

COMANS 1800-1840 BOHERLAHAN, TIP, IRL [34183]

COMB ALL AUS [33975] : 1853 BALLARAT & BENDIGO, VIC, AUS [35828] : C1816 GUILDFORD, SRY, ENG [35828]

COMBELLACK 1750+ TREGUNSTIS & SEVORGAN, CON, ENG [33829] : 1750+ WENDRON, CON, ENG [33829]

COMBEN C1802 NORTHWOOD, IOW, ENG [35131] : PRE 1835 PORTLAND, DOR, ENG [35211] : 1880+ NEWHAVEN, SSX, ENG [37293]

COMBER C1815 SLAUGHAM, SSX, ENG [35764] : ALL LONDON, ENG [36627] : 1800-1880 BERMONDSEY, SRY, ENG [36627]

COMBS 1750 MAPERTON, SOM, ENG [38209]

COMER PRE 1850 EXFORD & WITHYPOOL, SOM, ENG [37322] : 1700+ CAROLINE CO., VA, USA [34350] : JOHN PRE 1804 SHENANDOAH CO., VA, USA [37590] : 1840-1990 USA [38768] : 1840-1990 MORGAN, MO, USA [38768] : 1800-1850 ROSS & VINTON, OH, USA [38768] : PRE 1850 PA & NC, USA [38768]

COMERFORD 1854+ FITZROY, VIC, AUS [35384] : C1815 PORTSMOUTH, HAM, ENG [37904] : C1818 GOLDEN, TIP, IRL [33775] : 1750+ CLONMORE, IRL [33963] : PRE 1860 KIK, IRL [34682]

COMES 1800 ORENHOFEN, RPF, GER [36907]

COMFORD PRE 1725 WORLDWIDE [34094]

COMFORT 1786+ LINCOLN CO., ONT, CAN [34094] : PRE 1725 WORLDWIDE [34094]

COMINI PRE 1850 BRUSIO, GR, CH [34010]

COMISKEY PRE 1850 MEA, IRL [36702]

COMMANDER 1800 ENG [34565]

COMMINS PRE 1795 EXETER, DEV, ENG [35259] : 1870S NORWICH, NFK, ENG [35259] : ALL WEYMOUTH, DOR, ENG [35259] : 1828 LONDON, ENG [35855] : 1800+ ABBEY, CLA, IRL [33898]

COMMON PRE 1850 DFS, SCT [35199]

COMMONS 1860+ WINSTER, DBY, ENG [34329] : PRE 1860 MOUNT JENNINGS, MAY, IRL [34329]

COMPORT PRE 1725 WORLDWIDE [34094]

COMPTON 1650+ WAR, ENG [34054] : 1750+ ALDWYNS, GLS, ENG [34421] : PRE 1818 BARNWOOD & GLOUCESTER, GLS, ENG [34823] : 1500+ WIL & HAM, ENG [36213] : 1700+ CARHAM, DUR, ENG [36685] : 1840S BENTON CO., AL, USA [36926] : WILLIAM 1845 MADISON CO., IA, USA [38086] : ALL WORLDWIDE [36429]

COMSTOCK PRE 1770 DEV & SOM, ENG [34589] : 1590S-1780S NORFOLK, NEW LONDON, CT, USA & ENG [38532]

COMYNS 1807+ BELFAST, DOW, IRL [37921]

CONCALVES C1910-1920 REVERE CITY, MA, USA [36337]

CONCANNON PRE 1847 GAL, IRL [34250] : DOMINIC PRE 1900 CHARLESTOWN, MA, USA [36563]

CONDELL PRE 1852 COTTENHAM, CAM, ENG [35132] : 1840S WIC, IRL [38339]

CONDIE PRE 1845 ADELAIDE, SA, AUS & SCT [36768] : PRE 1820 DUNFERMLINE, FIF, SCT [35457]

CONDON 1870 DAYLESFORD, VIC, AUS [35204] : 1859+ ULLADULLA & WOLLONGONG, NSW, AUS [36600] : 1855+ GLEBE, NSW, AUS [37944] : PRE 1820 SILEBY, LEI, ENG [38512] : 1800-1850 CORK CITY, COR, IRL [34274] : C1820 MITCHELLSTOWN, COR, IRL [37944] : 1800+ LIM, IRL & AUS [36642] : ALL WORLDWIDE [35875]

CONDRAM SARAH PRE 1817 IRL [34539]

CONDREN 1860+ TAMWORTH, NSW, AUS [35765] : PRE 1856 DUBLIN, IRL [35765]

CONDRICK PRE 1882 TIP, IRL [34779]

CONDUCT 1770-1870 BISHOPS WALTHAM, HAM, ENG [35760]

CONDUIT 1760-1830 DURNFORD, WIL, ENG [35464] : 1830+ MEONSTOKE, HAM, ENG [35760]

CONE 1880+ CLEVELAND, OH, USA [38369]

CONEY PRE 1800 LOUTH, LIN, ENG [37692] : 1550-1650 BASINGTHORPE, LIN, ENG [38216]

CONEYBEARE 1800-1990 HOLBETON, DEV, ENG [36398]

CONGALTON 1800-1820 DUNBLANE, PER, SCT [36635]

CONGDON 1800+ ST PINNOCK, CON, ENG [36254] : 1834 LAUNCESTON, CON, ENG [36860] : PRE 1870 PHILLEIGH, CON, ENG [36877] : JANE 1832-1900 MANCHESTER, LAN, ENG [37543] : SAM 1870-1900 MANCHESTER, LAN, ENG [37543]

CONGER PRE 1750 WOODBRIDGE, NJ, USA [38225]

CONGRESS 1855-1890 AMHERST, VIC, AUS [37996] : 1810-1850 NY, USA [37996]

CONGREVE 1800-1900 PER, SCT [35981]

CONIGLAND ALL NY & PA, USA [36578]

CONIL PRE 1750 CAT, ESP [36353]

CONINGSBY 1600 NORTH LEIGH, OXF, ENG [34466] : PRE 1822 ENG [37897]

CONISTON PRE 1830 ERY, ENG [37617]

CONKLIN 1780+ ERNESTOWN & ADDINGTON CO., ONT, CAN [34486] : PRE 1850 JEFFERSON CO., NY, USA [36702]

CONLAN 1853+ NEW ENGLAND, NSW, AUS [36629]

CONLEY C1900 BETHNAL GREEN, MDX, ENG [38441] : PRE 1900 IOM [34384] : 1700-1850 IRL [34081] : PRE 1850 ANT, IRL [34739] : PRE 1840 TYR, IRL [36338] : 1860+ SANDUSKY, ERIE, OH [36338] : C1855 LEWIS CO., WV, USA [37003] : PRE 1850 COSHOCTON, OH, USA [38708]

CONLON PRE 1900 SYDNEY, NSW, AUS [34593] : PRE 1857 CLA, IRL [34911] : 1870+ LURGANCULLENBOY, ARM, IRL [37678] : 1800-1870 FAUGHART, LOU, IRL [37678] : PRE 1820 IRL [38435]

CONN 1840S LANARK CO., ONT, CAN [37568] : PRE 1820 DROITWICH, WOR, ENG [34576] : PRE 1861 SUNDERLAND, DUR, ENG [37878] : PRE 1830 FORGUE, ABD, SCT [34861] : 1855-1870 KEWEENAW CO., MI, USA [38010]

CONNAGHAN PRE 1898 DON, IRL [33862]

CONNALE 1843+ CLA, IRL [37111]

CONNATTY PRE 1900 ENG [36893]

CONNAUGHTY 1840+ ORANGE, NSW, AUS [35105]

CONNELL 1874+ DAYLESFORD, VIC, AUS [34039] : JOHN 1802+ SYDNEY, NSW, AUS [36284] : 1869 FORBES, NSW, AUS [36804] : 1810+ SHEERNESS, KEN, ENG [34290] : PRE 1903 CASTLEFORD, YKS, ENG [36839] : 1840 DUBLIN, IRL [34015] : 1800+ CORK CITY, COR, IRL [34850] : PRE 1870 CAV, IRL [35005] : PRE 1860 WEM, IRL [35382] : 1800+ CLA, IRL [35407] : 1800-1900 NAVAN & BOYERSTOWN, MEA, IRL [35845] : 1775-1850 COR, IRL [36318] : PRE 1900 VICARSTOWN, LEX, IRL [38300] : 1750-1900 GLASGOW, LKS, RFW & DNB, SCT [34229] : 1780+ IRVINE, AYR, SCT [36254] : 1800-1880 KILMARNOCK & GALSTON, AYR, SCT [37446] : PRE 1918 KILMARNOCK, AYR, SCT [37556] : PRE 1740 SPARTANBERG, SC, USA [38783]

CONNELLAN C1900+ BARCALDINE, QLD, AUS [35723] : 1800 DUBLIN, IRL [34805] : MARY PRE 1860 CLA, IRL [35488] : 1800S KILCOLUM, CLA, IRL [35723]

CONNELLEY CHARLES PRE 1825 FEDERALSBURG, CAROLINE CO., MD, USA [34992]

CONNELLY CHRISTINA 1850+ VIC, AUS [33849] : 1830+ GREENDALE, NSW, AUS [34758] : 1796+ WILBERFORCE, NSW, AUS [35431] : ALL HILLGROVE & ARMIDALE, NSW, AUS & IRL [34599] : MARY PRE 1895 LIVERPOOL, LAN, ENG [36164] : PRE 1850 TUAM, GAL, IRL [34433] : PRE

1830 HOLYWOOD, DOW, IRL [34758] : C1810 GAL, IRL [35203] : 1834-1898 CARABROWN, GAL, IRL [35900] : PRE 1900 CLONAKILTY, COR, IRL [36963] : 1810 DUBLIN, DUB, IRL [38272] : PRE 1860 DALKEITH, MLN, SCT & IRL [36191] : PRE 1860 OSWEGO, NY, USA [34958]

CONNELY C1820 CHATHAM, KEN, ENG [33914]

CONNER 1800-1930 NORTHUMBERLAND CO., NB, CAN [34404] : 1814 CANAGH CASTLE, ROS, IRL [37911] : 1750-1814 ALLEGANY CO., MD, USA [38026] : 1830-1900 CLINTON CO., OH, USA [38026] : 1750-1850 EZRA, ID & MO, USA [38287]

CONNERTY 1840+ ORANGE, NSW, AUS [35105]

CONNETT PRE 1800 DUNSFORD, DEV, ENG [36662]

CONNIBEARE C1800 BROMPTON RALPH, SOM, ENG [36610]

CONNOCK 1796 YEOVIL, SOM, ENG [36599]

CONNOLE PRE 1900 CLA, IRL &, WORLDWIDE [38305]

CONNOLLY 1840-1990 QUEANBEYAN, NSW, AUS [33818] : 1895-1900 ARCADIA, VIC, AUS [35191] : 1880-1890 KIALLA, VIC, AUS [35191] : 1890-1895 WHROO (WHOOREL ?), VIC, AUS [35191] : 1870-1880 REDESDALE, VIC, AUS [35191] : 1900-1940 RUSHWORTH, VIC, AUS [35191] : 1850-1870 MARYBOROUGH, VIC, AUS [35191] : 1810-1910 MILLES ROCHES & WALES, ONT, CAN & IRL [34514] : C1892+ KIAMA, NSW, ENG [35249] : C1856 BRISTOL, ENG [35249] : PRE 1827 GAL, IRL [35088] : PRE 1840 KID, IRL [35088] : 1830-1855 MOG, IRL [35191] : 1800+ DRONAHAIR, LET, IRL [35248] : MICHAEL PRE 1880 LIMERICK, LIM, IRL [35462] : 1820 TULLAMORE, OFF, IRL [35865] : 1800+ EMATRIS, CAV, IRL [37181] : SUSAN PRE 1836 DUBLIN, IRL [37913] : EDWARD C1845 NAVAN, MEA, IRL [38205] : MARY 1863-1867 WAIKATO & AUCKLAND, NZ [35729] : PRE 1874 HAMILTON, LKS, SCT [35021]

CONNOP 1800-1850 HRT, ENG [36165]

CONNOP (SEE CONNOR) [37323]

CONNOR 1847-1990 GOULBURN, NSW, AUS [33818] : MICHAEL 1850+ IPSWICH, NSW, AUS [33929] : 1830-1885 GOULBURN, NSW, AUS [35559] : 1830S PARRAMATTA & RICHMOND, NSW, AUS [35586] : 1844+ PAMBULA, NSW, AUS [35825] : 1860+ LOWER CLARENCE RIVER, NSW, AUS [38006] : PRE 1850 SHOREDITCH & STEPNEY, LND, ENG [34450] : 1800+ DEPTFORD, KEN, ENG [35972] : CATHERINE 1821+ MANCHESTER, LAN, ENG [37165] : 1800+ HEF, ENG [37323] : PRE 1808 STOKE DAMEREL, DEV, ENG [37361] : PRE 1860 LIM, IRL [34588] : MARY PRE 1830 DUBLIN, IRL [35232] : 1851+ CURRAGHAKIMKEEN & DOON, LIM, IRL [35900] : PRE 1850 SHANKILL & LURGAN, ARM, IRL [36259] : 1800S COLUMBIA CO., NY, USA [37544]

CONNORS 1840-1990 QUEANBEYAN, NSW, AUS [33818] : 1850+ NSW, AUS [34614] : 1830+ LONDON, ENG [34614] : 1870 DOON, LIM, IRL [34015] : PRE 1900 LIMERICK, LIM, IRL [34097] : C1830 KILMALEY, CLA, IRL [34426] : ALL WIC, IRL [34938] : 1800+ COR, IRL [35410] : 1800+ BANTRY, COR, IRL [35710] : 1832 DUNLAVIN, WIC, IRL [37558] : C1830 BALLYHALE, KIK, IRL [37944] : 1850+ WORCESTER, MA, USA [38047] : 1800+ WORLDWIDE [35159]

CONOLLY ALL HANWELL, MDX, ENG [35989] : ALL CASTLETOWN, ANT, IRL [35989]

CONOVER 1800-1885 WARREN CO., NJ, USA [38201]

CONQUERGOOD 1781+ ORMISTON, ROX, SCT [34474]

CONQUEST PRE 1800 WHITTLESEY, CAM, ENG [34581] : PRE 1880 NFK & CAM, ENG [36363]

CONRAD 1880S SOUTH MELBOURNE, VIC, AUS [35136] : ALL LUNENBURG, NS, CAN [36713] : 1800S SILBER, SIL, GER [38623] : PRE 1860 PA, USA [37587] : 1800-1850 PA, USA [38741]

CONRAN 1860+ NSW, AUS [37176] : PRE 1829 DUBLIN, IRL [35483]

CONROY 1800+ BEHAGH, CLA, IRL [33898] : 1800+ FINAVARA, CLA, IRL [33898] : 1820+ PORTARLINGTON, OFF, IRL [34781] : 1830-1850 BALLYFIN, LEX, IRL [34827] : 1800S WAT, IRL [35986]

CONSIDINE 1800+ CASTLE CONNELL, LIM, IRL [35986]

CONSINDINE 1808 CLA, IRL [36860]

CONSTABLE 1838-1990 ADELAIDE, SA, AUS [33885] : PRE 1839 KEN, ENG [33885] : 1700S WESTON ON THE GREEN, OXF, ENG [34032] : 1829 STRETHAM, CAM, ENG [35535] : PRE 1700 ESS, ENG [35642] : PRE 1800 CAM, ENG [36183] : 1650-1750 ANS, SCT [36081] : PRE 1800 KENT, MD, USA [37010]

CONSTANT 1790-1850 BALTIMORE CITY, MD, USA [36911]

CONSTANTINE 1880+ SYDNEY, NSW, AUS [34544] : 1800S COR, IRL [35617]

CONVERSE PRE 1850 AMHERST, NH, USA [36949]

CONWAY PRE 1900 NSW, AUS [34968] : 1880+ TOWNSVILLE, QLD, AUS [35548] : PRE 1900 BENDIGO, VIC & DEV, AUS & ENG [37995] : C1820+ MANCHESTER, LAN, ENG [33812] : 1800S BILSTON, STS, ENG [36253] : PRE 1870 LEADGATE, DUR, ENG [36499] : C1860 SHERBORNE, DOR, ENG [37200] : TERRENCE ALL MOG, IRL [33844] : C1892 BANGOR, DOW, IRL [34972] : ALL BALLINA, MAY, IRL [35548] : ALL CORK, IRL [36744] : 1820+ COR, IRL [36869] : 1715-50 FER & LOG, IRL [38054] : ELLEN C1790+ TIP, IRL [38593] : 1780-1880 IRL [38779] : 1855+ AUCKLAND, NZ [33823] : ALL AUCKLAND, NZ [36744] : ALL COROMANDEL, NZ [36744] : 1600S HAWARDEN, FLN, WLS [35899] : 1800S DOWLAIS, GLA, WLS [36961] : C1800 CILYCWM, CMN, WLS [36961]

CONYERS 1600+ LONDON, ENG [36572] : 1500-1590S DUR, ENG [37780] : 1564 CARLETON, NTH, ENG [37780] : ALL NANESAND CO., VA, USA [36572]

COOBAN C1820-1920 ST LOUIS, MO, USA [37249]

COOGAN CATHERINE 1850S BALLARAT & HAMILTON, VIC, AUS [34045] : 1830-1872 IRL [36895]

COOK ROSA 1898+ CARLTON, VIC, AUS [34174] : 1860-1920 FOOTSCRAY, VIC, AUS [34191] : 1857+ BENDIGO, VIC, AUS [34435] : WILLIAM JAMES C1840+ LANE COVE, SYDNEY, NSW, AUS [34449] : 1843+ SYDNEY, NSW, AUS [35157] : 1853+ COSTERFIELD, VIC, AUS [35379] : JOHN 1880S MIDDLE PARK, VIC, AUS [35471] : FRANCIS 1872 CARCTON, VIC, AUS [35471] : DR A.C. PRE 1839+ SYDNEY, NSW, AUS [35506] : ALL TAMWORTH AREA, NSW, AUS [35534] : JAMES C1850 BERRY PARK MORPETH, NSW, AUS [35583] : ESTER 1800S COMBO CRK, WOLLAR, NSW, AUS [36314] : 1870-1920 DUBBO, NSW, AUS [36648] : 1817 SYDNEY, NSW, AUS [37119] : 1840+ MACLEAY RIVER, NSW, AUS [37119] : 1830+ GOSFORD, NSW, AUS [37119] : 1858 ODESSA, ONT, CAN [36680] : WILLIAM H. 1790+ MAN, CAN [37426] : ALL CAN [37466] : 1700-1990 ONT, CAN [37466] : ROSANNA 1800S DEER ISLAND, NB, CAN [38785]

: DOROTHY 1800S DEER ISLAND, NB, CAN [38785] : C1853 LOWESTOFT, SFK, ENG [33820] : ALL WALTHAM, ENG [33823] : 1800S CAMBRIDGE, CAM, ENG [33898] : CHRISTOPHER 1835+ NEW WINDSOR, BRK, ENG [33938] : PRE 1830 ARDINGLEY, SSX, ENG [33998] : PRE 1860 SFK, ENG [34258] : 1800+ COPLE, BDF, ENG [34315] : 1830+ PORTSEA, HAM, ENG [34435] : PRE 1810 KINGSTON SEYMOUR, CUL, ENG [34442] : JAMES PRE 1814 OLDHAM, LAN, ENG [34487] : GEORGE 1850-1860 NORTHLEACH, GLS, ENG [34567] : CHARLES PRE 1850 NORTHLEACH, GLS, ENG [34567] : ELIZA 1850-1860 NORTHLEACH, GLS, ENG [34567] : C1770 HASLEY, SSX, ENG [34806] : PRE 1830 SALEHURST, SSX, ENG [34816] : ALL BETHNAL GREEN, LND, ENG [34820] : ALL LOWESTOFT, SFK, ENG [34822] : 1876+ COVENTRY, WAR, ENG [34839] : 1780-1832 FROME, SOM, ENG [34996] : PRE 1750 BKM, ENG [35030] : 1819+ WOOLWICH, KEN, ENG [35039] : CLEAR PRE 1845 BOXTED & GLEMSFORD, SFK, ENG [35070] : 1800-1826 BETHNAL GREEN, LND, ENG [35148] : WILLIAM C1687 HAWLING, GLS, ENG [35259] : C1719 BRIGHTON, SSX, ENG [35259] : PRE 1840 CHIPPING BARNETT, HRT, ENG [35379] : PRE 1853 KEN, ENG [35379] : C1840 HURSLEY & BENTLEY, HAM, ENG [35457] : FRANCIS S. 1800S LONDON, MDX, ENG [35471] : JAMES C1830 LONDON, MDX, ENG [35471] : DANIEL 1860S HAM, ENG [35565] : C1828+ COLEBY, LIN, ENG [35746] : C1842+ NAVENBY, LIN, ENG [35746] : 1850S OXFORD, OXF, ENG [35804] : EDITH 1701-1773 STOURTON, WIL, ENG [35815] : 1800S WALTHAM ON THE WOLDS, LEI, ENG [35899] : 1800+ HALSTEAD & COGGESHALL, ESS, ENG [35987] : 1700-1800 STS, ENG [36062] : PRE 1740 DUDLEY, WOR, ENG [36110] : ALL CALBOURNE, IOW, ENG [36142] : 1800-1900 APPLETON LE STREET, ERY, ENG [36394] : 1800-1850 BARTON LE STREET, ERY, ENG [36394] : 1850-1900 HULL, ERY, ENG [36394] : PRE 1900 EAST, LND, ENG [36479] : 1700+ POPLAR, MDX, ENG [36571] : JOHN HENRY 1800 SFK, ENG [36596] : 1700+ EXETER, DEV, ENG [36664] : PRE 1610 BIDDULPH, STS, ENG [36701] : 1840-1870 AYLESBY, LIN, ENG [36762] : 1700+ BOCKING, ESS, ENG [36871] : C1750 LAYSTON & BRAUGHING, HRT, ENG [36978] : PRE 1830 MDX, ENG [37150] : PRE 1755 SEATON ROSS, YKS, ENG [37288] : PRE 1702 POTTERHANWORTH, LIN, ENG [37318] : 1895 HALSTEAD, ESS, ENG [37346] : PRE 1880S BIRMINGHAM, WAR, ENG [37384] : WILLIAM H. 1768 ST ANDREWS, HOLBORN, LND, ENG [37426] : 1810 WALMER, KEN, ENG [37520] : PRE 1900 FAVERSHAM, KEN, ENG [37561] : 1835+ SPITALFIELDS, MDX, ENG [38247] : PRE 1800 CLUTTON, SOM, ENG [38745] : MARION 1919 ARUNDEL & LITTLEHAMPTON, SSX, ENG & AUS [36311] : THOMAS 1919 ARUNDEL & LITTLEHAMPTON, SSX, ENG & AUS [36311] : JOHN PRE 1795 ARM, IRL [34993] : 1700+ CASTLEREA, ROS, IRL [35355] : 1800+ LEX, IRL [35847] : 1800-1832 CORK CITY, COR, IRL [35903] : PRE 1800 MUFF, DON, IRL [36958] : C1820-1890 FER & LKS, IRL & SCT [34635] : 1800-1850 TILLICOULTRY, CLK, SCT [33822] : ALL DUNDEE, ANS, SCT [34226] : PRE 1800 ARRAN, BUT, SCT [34419] : C1820 FARNELL, ANS, SCT [34713] : C1863 WIG, SCT [34756] : 1795+ GALSTON, AYR, SCT [34993] : C1750-1942 DUNFERMLINE & BEATH, FIF, SCT [36128] : PRE

1838 KILWINNING, AYR, SCT **[36314]** : 1700-1900
KENNOWAY, FIF, SCT **[36394]** : 1800S+ ISLE OF
ARRAN, BUT, SCT **[36648]** : 1860-1900
BRIDGETON, LKS, SCT **[37872]** : 1700-1800
CAMBUSLANG, LKS, SCT **[37872]** : 1880-1930
RUTHERGLEN, LKS, SCT **[37872]** : 1820-1880
CALTON, LKS, SCT **[37872]** : PRE 1890 LKS, SCT
[37923] : PRE 1890 DNB, SCT **[37923]** : ARCHIBALD
PRE 1840 SCT **[38585]** : 1960+ PHILADELPHIA, PA,
USA **[34510]** : 1900+ SPRINGFIELD, MO, USA
[34993] : 1780+ ONEIDA, NY, USA **[35322]** : JULIA
PRE 1893 WESTMORELAND CO., PA, USA **[36448]**
: WILLIAM PRE 1893 WESTMORELAND CO., PA,
USA **[36448]** : 1850+ PHILADELPHIA, PA, USA
[36578] : PRE 1820 SALEM, MA, USA **[36949]** : 1850-
1990 WI, USA **[37466]** : 1855 CO, USA **[37466]** : 1700-
1800 PA, USA **[37466]** : NANCY 1800+ ORANGE
CO. & GUILFORD CO., NC, USA **[38060]** : PRE 1850
BRADFORD CO., PA & NY, USA **[38309]** : 1850+
SMITHFIELD, PA, IA & NE, USA **[38309]**

COOK (SEE COOKE) [36717]

COOKE 1852+ PORTLAND, VIC, AUS **[34685]** :
1885+ COOMA, NSW, AUS **[35117]** : 1800S
NEWCASTLE, NSW, AUS **[35117]** : ALL CALOOLA,
NSW, AUS **[35259]** : C1885+ ESSENDON, VIC, AUS
[35526] : C1842 NSW, AUS **[38485]** : 1800+
LANARK, ONT, CAN **[34167]** : RICHARD 1840+
LEEDS CO., ONT, CAN **[38431]** : C1700-1800
WAKEFIELD, WRY, ENG **[33862]** : 1910+
CONGLETON, CHS, ENG **[33920]** : PRE 1830
EATON, LEI, ENG **[34197]** : 1800+
SWANBOURNE, BKM, ENG **[34550]** : PRE 1852
ALDERBURY, WIL, ENG **[34685]** : C1830
BRIGHTLEY, NTH, ENG **[34942]** : 1690-1840
HAWLING, GLS, ENG **[35259]** : ALL LITTLE
MILTON, OXF, ENG **[35259]** : PRE 1600
GARBOLDISHAM, NFK, ENG **[35571]** : 1750
LOFTUS, YKS, ENG **[35908]** : 1700+ STROUD,
GLS, ENG **[36266]** : 1730+ RAYDON, SFK, ENG
[36717] : 1835+ BURSLEM, STS, ENG **[36997]** : PRE
1800 LEATHERHEAD, SRY, ENG **[37062]** : PRE
1900 CREWE, CHS, ENG **[37237]** : PRE 1800 WEST
MERSEA, ESS, ENG **[37718]** : 1700S WOR, ENG
[37765] : 1700S+ HUN & MDX, ENG **[37868]** : PRE
1600 DRONFIELD, DBY, ENG **[37875]** : PRE 1860
ST AUSTELL, CON, ENG **[37913]** : PRE 1830
WORKINGTON, CUL, ENG **[38722]** : 1800+ COR,
IRL **[34167]** : JOHN ALL ARM, IRL **[34993]** : PRE
1849 DUBLIN, IRL **[35189]** : C1880 PORTADOWN,
ARM, IRL **[35507]** : PRE 1860 ANT, ARM & DON,
IRL **[35897]** : PRE 1800 MUFF, DON, IRL **[36958]** :
C1822 ANT, IRL **[38485]** : C1792 ARM, IRL **[38485]** :
1795+ GALSTON, AYR, SCT **[34993]** : PRE 1830
FIF, SCT **[36877]** : 1763+ EDINBURGH, SCT **[37662]**
: 1790-1840 DUNDEE, ANS, SCT **[38511]** : C1828 UK
[35772] : AMY C1767 UK **[37321]** : PRE 1815
MUSKINGHAM CO., OH, USA **[34410]** : 1800-1900
CUYAHOGA FALLS, OH, USA **[34537]** : 1698
PRESTON, CT, USA **[37531]**

COOKINGHAM PRE 1910 PROVIDENCE, RI, USA
[38537]

COOK-LODWICK 1820 DEARBORN CO., IN, USA
[36925]

COOKSEY PRE 1920 HOUNSLOW, LND, ENG
[38205] : ALL PRINCE GEORGE CO., CHAS CO.,
MD, USA **[36914]**

COOKSLEY JANE C1860 BRK, ENG **[35154]** : PRE
1800 CHURSTON FERRERS, DEV, ENG **[38507]**

COOKSON 1800+ KIRKHAM, LAN, ENG **[34092]** :
1755 TARVIN, CHS, ENG **[35282]**

COOLE EMILY 1868+ BRISTOL, GLS, ENG **[36149]** :
1700-1820 ROCKBOURNE, HAM, ENG **[36213]** :

ALFRED PRE 1890 BRISTOL, ENG & WLS **[36149]** :
MARIE ANNE PRE 1900 WLS **[36149]**

COOLEY ALL LND, ENG **[35707]** : PRE 1838 CLA,
IRL **[37912]** : 1800-1990 MACON CO., MO, USA
[35313]

COOLING 1700+ ROWSTON, LIN, ENG **[34221]** :
PRE 1792 YKS, ENG **[35037]**

COOM 1800+ FINCHLEY, LND, ENG **[35800]**

COOMBE ALL NSW, AUS **[35901]** : PRE 1830 NORTH
BOVEY, DEV, ENG **[35959]** : 1830+ KENN, DEV,
ENG **[35959]** : PRE 1800 DARTMOUTH &
DITTISHAM, DEV, ENG **[37393]** : C1835 BRISTOL,
GLS, ENG & AUS **[35079]** : 1890+ RSA **[35224]**

COOMBE (SEE COOMBS) [36289]

COOMBER 1700-1850 MAIDSTONE, KEN & SRY,
ENG **[34343]** : 1750-1837 WITHYHAM, SSX & KEN,
ENG **[34687]** : 1700-1900 STREAT & NEWTIMBER,
SSX, ENG **[34749]** : 1800-1880 SRY, ENG **[36627]** :
ALL LONDON, ENG **[36627]** : 1700-1850
TONBRIDGE, KEN, ENG **[37365]** : 1700-1800 KEN,
SSX & SRY, ENG **[37725]** : PRE 1840
WOODSCHURCH, KEN, ENG **[38033]**

COOMBES 1860S DUBBO, NSW, AUS **[33934]** : PRE
1893 LONDON, ENG **[35472]** : SUSANNAH 1800+
ST SWITHINS, WOR, ENG **[35549]** : 1800 LAN &
STS, ENG **[36683]** : 1800-1900 CON, ENG **[36844]** :
1840-1990 UK & AUS **[35421]**

COOMBS PRE 1850S NAILSEA, SOM, ENG **[34673]** :
PRE 1912 BIRMINGHAM, WAR, ENG **[34914]** :
ALL HAM & WIL, ENG **[35058]** : PRE 1832 HAM,
ENG **[35895]** : C1650-1730 WIL, ENG **[36289]** : 1700-
1800 CANN & SHAFTESBURY, DOR, ENG **[36478]** :
PRE 1780 HANBOROUGH, OXF, ENG **[36883]** :
1840S+ DUNEDIN & THAMES, NZ **[34673]** : 1840+
NELSON, NZ **[35058]** : 1865-1875 KEWEENAW CO.,
MI, USA **[38010]** : C1860 MONMOUTH, MON, WLS
[34914] : 1825-1900 BRE, WLS & ENG **[36703]**

COOMER ALL ENG **[34485]** : 1720+ PLIMPTON,
MA, USA **[38766]**

COON C1820-1860 WELLINGTON CO., ONT, CAN
[35277] : 1780+ ST HILARY, CON, ENG **[35342]** :
1850-1900 PORT ELIZABETH, RSA **[37914]** : C1795-
C1820 NY, USA **[35277]** : 1860+ SANILAC CO., MI,
USA **[35277]** : PRE 1900 MI, USA **[35371]** : 1850+
KENOSHA CO., WI, USA **[36962]** : CATHERINE
1823 ULSTER CO., NY, USA **[38062]**

COONAN C1823 LOWER ORMOND, TIP, IRL **[35872]**

COONE 1831 AYMESTREY, HEF, ENG **[36229]** : 1810
BERRIEW, MGY, WLS **[36229]**

COONEY PRE 1940 MELBOURNE, VIC, AUS **[34547]**
: 1863+ LONDON, ENG **[36995]** : JANE C1809+
IRL **[38067]** : 1850-1900 NY, USA & NL **[37502]** : ALL
WORLDWIDE **[38766]**

COOP WINIFRED 1884+ WOODEND, VIC, AUS
[35484]

COOPER JOHN 1854+ TAWONGA, VIC, AUS **[33877]**
: 1862+ TAWONGA, VIC, AUS **[33877]** : ED.
THORNHILL 1874+ MELBOURNE, VIC & WA,
AUS **[34178]** : ROBERT 1813+ SYDNEY, NSW,
AUS **[34695]** : PRE 1890 ANGASTON, SA, AUS
[34816] : JOHN 1825+ GUNNING, NSW, AUS
[35155] : SAMUEL 1840S SYDNEY, NSW, AUS
[35158] : C1850-1920 WARWICK DISTRICT, QLD,
AUS **[35158]** : 1870+ SHEPPARTON, VIC, AUS
[35379] : PRE 1875 BRIDGEWATER, TAS, AUS
[35379] : 1823+ HOBART TOWN, TAS, AUS **[35384]** :
1850+ PATERSON, NSW, AUS **[35395]** : 1860+
MELBOURNE, VIC, AUS **[35734]** : 1880+ QLD,
AUS **[35743]** : 1870+ MELBOURNE, VIC, AUS
[36360] : 1870+ GLENORCHY, VIC, AUS **[36362]** :
THOMAS 1800S MARKHAM TWP., ONT, CAN
[34378] : 1850+ KENT CO., ONT, CAN **[34520]** :

1880+ HALDIMAND CO., ONT, CAN [38323] :
JOHN 1800+ COMBE, OXF, ENG [33877] : JOHN
1800+ HORSPATH, OXF, ENG [33877] : 1822+
WARWICK, WAR, ENG [33880] : 1818+
WARWICK, WAR, ENG [33880] : C1772 DEV, ENG
[33880] : 1830S LAN, ENG [33934] : PRE 1826 ISLE
OF WIGHT, HAM, ENG [33995] : ROBERT 1800-
1940 EAST GRINSTEAD, SSX, ENG [33998] :
ROBERT 1800-1930 ENG [33998] : PRE 1855 ISLE
OF WIGHT, HAM, ENG [34014] : ALL
FARRINGTON, ENG [34046] : 1800S WEST HAM,
ESS, ENG [34086] : PRE 1800 HIGH WYCOMBE,
BKM, ENG [34104] : PRE 1800 WEST WYCOMBE,
BKM, ENG [34104] : 1700+ BRAMSHA, HAM, ENG
[34121] : 1700+ DOWNTON, WIL, ENG [34121] :
1810+ DONCASTER & SHEFFIELD, YKS, ENG
[34178] : 1700 ROWLEY REGIS, STS, ENG [34210] :
PRE 1700 SFK, ENG [34258] : 1800+ SHIFNAL,
SAL, ENG [34315] : 1700 LEI, ENG [34321] : JAMES
C1800-1840 WEST CHILTINGTON, SSX, ENG
[34432] : C1770-1870 WATTISHAM & KESGRAVE,
SFK, ENG [34508] : 1700-1870 BDF & HUN, ENG
[34520] : 1750-1900 LONDON, ENG [34714] : C1844
BERMONDSEY, LND, ENG [34972] : C1820
LILLESHALL & NEWTOWN BY WEM., SAL, ENG
[35158] : C1801 SHEFFIELD, YKS, ENG [35257] :
1832 ST MARTINS IN THE FIELDS, LND, ENG
[35259] : C1874 COLCHESTER, ESS, ENG [35348] :
ELIZA 1828+ FULLWICK, WIL, ENG [35361] :
PHILIP 1700 FULLWICK, WIL, ENG [35361] : PRE
1860 ENG [35379] : PRE 1823 SALFORD, LAN, ENG
[35384] : PRE 1798 LONDON, ENG [35397] : C1830
WESTMINSTER, MDX, ENG [35438] : PRE 1854
THATCHAM, BRK, ENG [35578] : 1811+ ENG
[35631] : JOHN 1794-1877 SUDBURY, SFK, ENG
[35634] : HENRIETTA 1816-1855 MAIDSTONE,
KEN, ENG [35634] : ALL NTH, ENG [35637] : 1810
NEWHAVEN, SSX, ENG [35710] : 1800+ STS, ENG
[35785] : C1795 REARSBY, LEI, ENG [35807] : 1500-
1990 STONEY STANTON & LEICESTER, LEI,
ENG [35944] : 1800 RYE, SSX, ENG [35970] : 1800+
MANCHESTER & CLAYTON BRIDGE, LAN, ENG
[36066] : PRE 1850 CARLTON & BREWELL, NFK,
ENG [36082] : 1790-1870 HORNCHURCH, ESS,
ENG [36090] : PRE 1840 BILSTON &
WOLVERHAMPTON, STS, ENG [36110] : 1750+
PODBURY, BKM & CAM, ENG [36123] : PRE 1860
CITY OF WESTMINSTER, LND, ENG [36377] :
1750-1850 LIVERPOOL, LAN, ENG [36390] : ALL
BEVERLEY, ERY, ENG [36405] : PRE 1880
OKEHAMPTON, DEV, ENG [36424] : 1700-1850
NRY, ENG [36472] : 1800+ DUDLEY, ENG [36488] :
PRE 1837 SHEFFIELD, YKS, ENG [36589] : JAMES
1850-1930 LEISTON CUM SIZEWELL, SFK, ENG
[36590] : 1750+ WHITBY, YKS, ENG [36609] :
1700+ LITTLE LONDON, WRY, ENG [36743] :
1830-50 BARTON UPON HUMBER, LIN, ENG
[36831] : ALL LASHAM, HAM, ENG [37044] : PRE
1850 OLD BASING, WIL, ENG [37067] : PRE 1800
ULVERSTONE, CUL, ENG [37085] : 1800
AYLSHAM, NFK, ENG [37170] : SUSAN 1700S
ASHWELLTHORPE, NFK, ENG [37191] : ARNOLD
C1750 BRANDESTON, SFK, ENG [37191] : C1860
BLANDFORD, DOR, ENG [37200] : 1750+
RENHOLD, BDF, ENG [37304] : 1870S CHERTSEY,
LND, ENG [37369] : 1841 HARDINGTON
MANDEVILLE, SOM, ENG [37378] : 1773 ORSTON,
DBY, ENG [37391] : 1859 TAMWORTH, STS, ENG
[37594] : PRE 1900 WHITBY & EGTON, NRY, ENG
[37616] : 1855+ TENTERDEN, KEN, ENG [37675] :
PRE 1750 WILSON, LEI, ENG [37675] : 1819-1907
LEEDS, YKS, ENG [37803] : PRE 1800 CASTLE

CARY, SOM, ENG [37818] : 1700-1850 SOUTHAM,
WAR, ENG [37858] : 1800+ THAXTED, ESS, ENG
[37889] : PRE 1828 WOKING, SRY, ENG [37909] :
PRE 1850 ST MARYLEBONE, MDX, ENG [37945] :
1816 DARTFORD, KEN, ENG [38282] : 1810S
WIGAN, LAN, ENG [38283] : C1900 MELBOURNE,
DBY, ENG [38471] : 1800+ STERT, WIL, ENG
[38494] : 1700+ ALLINGTON, DOR, ENG [38745] :
THORNHILL 1840+ YKS, ENG & NZ [34178] :
1800-1890 DUNGIVEN, LDY, IRL [33991] : 1800+
EDERNY, FER, IRL [34075] : PRE 1900 ISLAND
BRIDGE, LEX, IRL [35339] : JOSEPH 1815-1840
WIC, IRL [35714] : 1850 BANSHA, TIP, IRL [35847] :
1800S ARM, IRL [35964] : ALL IRL [36030] : 1770
IRL [37531] : ROBERT PRE 1850 MLN, SCT [35375] :
1700+ ST MONANCE, FIF, SCT [35627] : ROBERT
1844+ LEITH, SCT [37165] : 1800-1850 PITSLIGO,
ABD, SCT [38422] : 1830-1836 CHI, UK [35569] : PRE
1785 NC, USA [36324] : 1840-1860 TALLAPOOSA,
AL, USA [36735] : JOHN PRE 1793 NC, USA [36939] :
1815 STILLWATER, NY, USA [37531] : 1650+ RI,
USA [38015] : 1760+ RENSSELAER CO., NY, USA
[38016] : BENJAMIN 1889 WAYNE, NE, USA [38156]
: ISRAEL 1860 MURRAY, IA, USA [38156] :
ROBERT 1820 OH, USA [38180] : 1795+
JEFFERSON CO., OH, USA [38531] : SUSAN 1880S
ABERGAVENNY, MON, WLS [35498] : 1800+
CHEPSTOWE, MON, WLS [35710] : AUSTIN ALL
WORLDWIDE [36030]

COOPER-SMITH 1800+ EAST LONDON, ENG
[37699]

COOR PRE 1825 NC, USA [38340]

COOSE 1770+ WEST TIEGNMOUTH, DEV, ENG
[36271]

COOTE 1870-1910 BULMER, ESS, HAM & WIL, ENG
[36213] : PRE 1840 CAV, IRL [34273]

COOTES 1900S MALVERN & KEW, VIC, AUS [34919]

COOZENS PRE 1885 BATH, SOM, ENG [37830]

COPCUTT 1752+ WADDESDON, BKM, ENG [35578]

COPE C1809 SPONDON, DBY, ENG [34661] : PRE
1840 POLESWORTH, WAR, ENG [34665] : PRE 1850
BALHAM STOCKWELL LONDON, LND, ENG
[36204] : PRE 1762 LEIGH WITH BRANSFORD,
WOR, ENG [36847] : PRE 1820 BOURNE, LIN, ENG
[37379] : PRE 1840 STOURPORT, WOR, ENG [37722]
: PRE 1750 UPPER ARLEY, STS, ENG [38420] : 1876
GLS, ENG [38719] : ALL OXF, ARM & MOG, ENG
& IRL [38754] : PRE 1854 DUBLIN, IRL [33812]

COPELAND ALL DOLPHIN LEIGH, YKS, ENG
[36557] : 1780S CHINNOR, OXF, ENG [36966] :
ANNE 1766+ DFS & BAN, SCT [34161] : ALL KKD,
SCT [37728] : SINGLETON 1800-1855 AR, TN & NC,
USA [37525] : 1820+ CLAY & GREENE, AR, USA
[37525] : ALL WORLDWIDE [38739]

COPELDYK ALL WORLDWIDE [36762]

COPENGER 1700+ CUMBERLAND CO., PA, USA
[37004]

COPENHAVER 1700-1800S VA, USA [36579]

COPHER 1800S BATH CO., KY, USA [37028]

COPLAN WILLIAM PRE 1700 BAN & DFS, SCT
[34161]

COPLAND 1890+ MELBOURNE, VIC, AUS [38582] :
PRE 1900 ABD, SCT [34053] : 1600-1800
KIRKGUNZEON, KKD, SCT [34107] : ANNE
1766+ DFS & BAN, SCT [34161] : 1800+
KIRKMICHAEL, DFS, SCT [37329] : ALL SHI, SCT
[37340] : 1800-1830 INVERURIE, ABD, SCT [37485] :
1750-1860 EDINBURGH, MLN, SCT & NZ [35961]

COPLEY STEPHEN 1800+ SHEFFIELD, YKS, ENG
[33956] : 1500S ENG [34395] : PRE 1835 BRISTOL,
GLS, ENG [35215] : ROBERT PRE 1877 BLEAN,
KEN, ENG [35788]

COPP 1810 AXMINSTER, DEV, ENG [35252] : 1800S TORRINGTON, DEV, ENG [36842] : DAVID 1805 NEW ORLEANS, LA, USA [37585]

COPPARD CHARLES 1870-1930 LND, ENG [38549]

COPPENS 1730-1830 OORDEGEM, OVL, BEL [38405]

COPPER ABEL 1840 OGLE, IL, USA [38784]

COPPERTHWAIGHT ALL SOUTHAMPTON, HAM, ENG [33802]

COPPES 1870S LA SALLE CO., IL, USA [38339]

COPPIN C1850 ADELAIDE, SA, AUS [35722] : 1800+ ADDINGTON, SRY, ENG [35343] : C1850 ADELHEID, GER [35722]

COPPING PRE 1726 HARTEST, SFK, ENG [37655] : JOSEPH 1830S MALDON, ESS, ENG [37692]

COPPINS 1850+ VICTORIA CO., ONT, CAN [34485] : PRE 1800 KEN, ENG [34445] : 1800+ EGERTON, KEN, ENG [34485] : 1800+ IVOR, KEN, ENG [34485] : 1868 CHARING & RAINHAM, KEN, ENG [36423] : 1800+ PA, USA [34485]

COPPLESTONE 1700-1850 DEV, ENG [33814]

COPSEY 1750-1847 BRENTWOOD, ESS, ENG [33787] : 1800 GLEMSFORD, SFK, ENG [34976] : C1857 CHELMSFORD, ESS, ENG [35337] : 1700-1770 TOSTOCK, SFK, ENG [36213] : 1797 LAWSHALL, SFK, ENG [38518]

COPUS ALL WORLDWIDE [37091]

CORAM PRE 1900 NEWTON ABBOT & CULLOMPTON, DEV, ENG [35730]

CORBALLY PRE 1850 DUNDALK, LOU, IRL [35216]

CORBERT 1800S TAS, AUS [35531]

CORBET 1800+ BRINKSTY COMMON, WOR, ENG [37632] : PRE 1780S DFS, SCT [34873] : PRE 1850 BLANTYRE, LKS, SCT [36705] : ALEX 1800+ WICK, CAI, SCT [36813] : ALL BOTHWELL & UDDINGSTON, LKS, SCT [37684]

CORBETT 1800S TAS, AUS [35531] : 1850+ BRAIDWOOD, NSW, AUS [37942] : LAWRENCE 1840-1899+ WAGGA WAGGA, NSW, AUS & IRL [37559] : C1876 WOLVERHAMPTON, STS, ENG [34189] : PRE 1800 NRY, ENG [37103] : PRE 1830 CRADLEY, HEF, ENG [37320] : C1810 SEDGLEY, STS, ENG [37883] : PRE 1640 MARKET BOSWORTH, LEI, ENG [38245] : 1640+ DESFORD, LEI, ENG [38245] : PRE 1875 TUNSTEAD, NFK, ENG [38435] : PRE 1861 TIP, IRL [35088] : PRE 1875 WAT, IRL [35986] : PRE 1850 DROMARA, DOW, IRL [37238] : 1824+ KINGSCOURT, CAV, IRL [37911] : JOHN 1884 INV, SCT [37444] : ROBERT 1678 WEYMOUTH, MA, USA [38110] : NATHANIEL 1742-1812 ROWE, MA, USA [38110] : MOSES 1767-1853 HARTSVILLE, NY, USA [38110]

CORBIN 1700+ MARGATE, KEN, ENG [34602] : C1870 STOKEWAKE, DOR, ENG [35252] : PRE 1850 FORDINGBRIDGE, HAM & DOR, ENG [37335] : 1790 VA, USA [37028]

CORBIT PRE 1870 DROMARA, DOW, IRL [37238]

CORBOY PRE 1880 MONEYGALL, TIP, IRL [35398]

CORBRIDGE ALL WORLDWIDE [34040]

CORBY PRE 1857 MEDBOURNE, LEI, ENG [35378] : 1780-1900 EASTON MAUDIT, NTH, ENG [37495] : JOHN 1790+ DRAUGHTON, NTH, ENG [38396] : 1754+ ENFIELD, MDX, ENG [38441] : PRE 1880 MONEYGALL, TIP, IRL [35398]

CORBYN PRE 1850 DEAL, KEN, ENG [33804]

CORCORAN 1890-1930 BOOROWA, NSW, AUS [36624] : 1851+ TAS, AUS [38485] : C1857-1944 CARABROWN, GAL, IRL [35900] : PRE 1900 ROS, IRL [38303] : C1829 COR & LIM, IRL [38485] : 1850+ GORE, NZ [35900] : PRE 1852 SAN FRANCISCO, CA, USA [34433] : 1840+ WI, USA [36942] : C1850 USA [38485]

CORDAROY 1815-1835 MARYLEBONE, MDX, ENG [37336] : 1860-1900 ST LUKES, MDX, ENG [37336] : 1850-1855 BETHNAL GREEN, MDX, ENG [37336]

CORDEAUX 1700-1800 SYDNEY, NSW, AUS & ENG [37670]

CORDELL 1817-1851 LAUNCESTON, TAS, AUS [34794] : 1851+ MELBOURNE, VIC, AUS [34794] : 1800-1817 BERMONDSEY, SRY, ENG [34794] : C1700 WILKES CO., NC, USA [36914]

CORDEN C1800 EASTWOOD, NTT, ENG [37869]

CORDER ALL VA, KY, TN, MO, USA [38363]

CORDERY GEORGE C1860-80 UPTON, BRK, ENG [36880]

CORDES 1800-1860 HANKENSBEUTTLE, GER [38199]

CORDINER C1800 PETERHEAD, ABD, SCT [37245] : 1700-1900 PETERHEAD, MOR, SCT [37290]

CORDING PRE 1840 LONDON, ENG [35205] : 1800-1900 LONDON, ENG [38278] : 1840+ WELLINGTON, NZ [35205] : 1800-1900 WELLINGTON, NZ [38278]

CORDINGLEY PRE 1830 ENG [37085]

CORDON PRE 1750 LONDON, MDX, ENG [36379]

CORDRAY C1625 CHUTE, WIL, ENG [38348]

CORDUKES 1800-1841 DALBY & HUTTON RUDBY, NRY, ENG [36783]

CORDY 1700+ WESTERLEIGH, GLS, ENG [35798] : PRE 1700 CHIPPING SODBURY, GLS, ENG [35798] : 1700+ HOLM HELE, NFK, ENG [36743] : PRE 1800 GLOUCESTER & COALEY, GLS, ENG [37320]

CORE 1860-1880 RICHLAND CO., WI, USA [36444]

COREE 1850S KILCORCORAN, CLA, IRL [36307]

COREY 1800S GSY, CHI [35137] : 1870+ PLYMOUTH, DEV, ENG [36771] : 1800S+ CLA, IRL [38510] : 1600-1800 EDINBURG & SARATOGA CO., NY, USA [38153]

CORFIELD PRE 1900 LIVERPOOL, LAN, ENG [35199] : PRE 1900 BIRKENHEAD, CHS, ENG [35199] : PRE 1880 TIPTON, STS, ENG [37357] : 1150+ WORLDWIDE [38005]

CORFMAT ALL WORLDWIDE [35193]

CORIN 1804+ GULVAL, CON, ENG [34627] : ALL PENZANCE & MADRON, CON, ENG [34724]

CORKE PRE 1864 OATLANDS, TAS, AUS [34170] : JANE PRE 1800 HANLEY WILLIAM, WOR, ENG [36619]

CORKER PRE 1825 YKS, ENG [34383]

CORKERY PRE 1880 IRL [37987] : C1848-1900 NZ [37987]

CORKFIELD PRE 1700 DARLASTON, STS, ENG [36110]

CORKHILL ALL WORLDWIDE [35884]

CORKILL C1800 MANCHESTER, LAN, ENG [34559] : PRE 1750 MAUGHOLD, IOM [38185] : PRE 1850 GREBA & KIRK GERMAN, IOM [36260] : PRE 1730 MAUGHOLD, IOM, UK [35866] : ALL WORLDWIDE [35884]

CORKIN 1800-1980 SOUTH SHIELDS, DUR, ENG [38513]

CORLE PRE 1850 LYCOMING CO., PA, USA [37914]

CORLES PRE 1700 COCKERHAM, LAN, ENG [38248]

CORLESS 1864-1910S LEWISHAM, LND, ENG [35815] : 1830S-1864 TORQUAY, DEV, ENG [35815] : 1814-1830S GAL, IRL [35815]

CORLETT 1880+ WALLASEY, CHS, ENG [36790] : 1850+ DUBLIN, IRL [34256]

CORLIS 1700+ TUAM, GAL, IRL [34263] : PRE 1655 HAVERHILL, MA, USA [36560]

CORMACK PRE 1851 KIK, IRL [35389] : 1750+ WICK, CAI, SCT [34456] : 1800-1920 INVERURIE, ABD, SCT [35981]

CORMICAN C1830 ANT, IRL [35057]

CORMIE 1860+ TAREENA, SA, AUS [33824]

CORNEAU 1580-1660 FONTENAY LE COMTE, PCH, FRA [38779]

CORNEILL 1850+ KINGSTOW, NY, USA [38066]

CORNELISSE 1700S KRUININGEN, ZEL, NL [38358]

CORNELIOUS ALL MULLINGAR, WEM, IRL [37701]

CORNELIUS 1800-1840 PHILLEIGH, CON, ENG [34191] : 1700-1850 DEVONPORT, DEV & CON, ENG [37740] : PRE 1840 INDIA [36102]

CORNELL PRE 1866 GAWLER, SA, AUS [36622] : 1852+ CASTERTON, WIMMERA & HORSHAM, VIC, AUS [36622] : 1852+ DOOEN, EUROA & DIMBOOLA, VIC, AUS [36622] : 1815+ LONDON, MDX, ENG [35459] : 1750+ LONDON &, ESS, ENG [37294] : PRE 1820 LITTLE DUNMOW, ESS, ENG [37726]

CORNER 1850+ PATERSON, NSW, AUS [35395] : 1825+ SYDNEY, NSW, AUS [35929] : PRE 1812 KELLOE & EASINGTON, DUR, ENG [36202] : 1800+ LAN, ENG [36363] : PRE 1825 EDINBURGH, MLN, SCT [35929]

CORNEWALL C1815 ACOMB, ERY, ENG [37627]

CORNEY 1800+ HOUGHTON, CUL & HRT, ENG [36123]

CORNFOOT 1750+ FIF, SCT [38463]

CORNFORD 1600+ EWHURST, SSX, ENG [34747] : PRE 1809 WARTLING, SSX, ENG [35020] : 1820S WARBLETON, SSX, ENG [35135] : 1750-1850 MAIDSTONE, KEN, ENG [37880]

CORNFORTH PRE 1880 BROMPTON, YKS, ENG [36800] : 1740-1780 LIVERTON, NRY, ENG [37859] : ALL WORLDWIDE [37404]

CORNING ALL USA [38421]

CORNISH C1825 WELLINGTON, SOM, ENG [33936] : 1770+ ALVERSTOKE, HAM, ENG [33938] : 1700S CHIVELSTONE, DEV, ENG [34570] : PRE 1860 CON, ENG [35011] : 1780+ ST HILARY, CON, ENG [35342] : C1800 ST HILARY, CON, ENG [35349] : C1800 EXETER, DEV, ENG [35381] : C1897 BRENTFORD, MDX, ENG [35418] : 1900+ SCARBOROUGH, YKS, ENG [35418] : 1800+ LONDON, ENG [36004] : ALL COLEBROOKE & CREDITON, DEV & LND, ENG [37195] : PRE 1900 ENG [37731] : PRE 1759 DINTON, WIL, ENG [37909] : 1875-1892 RUSSELL, NZ [35709] : ALL WORLDWIDE [37195]

CORNOCK 1890-1910 CHELTENHAM, GLS, ENG [36486] : 1800-1900 SLIMBRIDGE, GLS, ENG [37192]

CORNWALL 1860S TOOMUC VALLEY, VIC, AUS [35774] : 1866+ GEMBROOK, VIC, AUS [35774] : 1852+ MELBOURNE, VIC, AUS [35774] : 1700-1890 LAMBETH & CAMBERWELL, SRY, ENG [34204] : MARY 1837-1850 DEV, ENG [34774] : PRE 1900 BOTTISHAM, CAM, ENG [36489] : PRE 1840 BELFAST, ANT, IRL [35774] : PRE 1850 OLDCASTLE & HOWTH, MEA & DUB, IRL & RSA [38772]

CORNWELL C1797+ RICHMOND, NSW, AUS [35537] : PRE 1754 FULBOURN, CAM, ENG [35070] : 1600-1750 SFK, ENG [35178] : PRE 1900 NEWMARKET, SFK, ENG [37619] : PRE 1850 ESS, TIP & DUB, ENG & IRL [38772] : PRE 1728 TRANENT, ELN, SCT [37852] : PRE 1850 NY, USA [35290]

CORORCAN 1855+ MELBOURNE, VIC, AUS [35379] : PRE 1855 KIK, IRL [35379]

COROUGH ALL DOW, IRL [38084] : ALL WORLDWIDE [38084]

CORP PRE 1877 SA, AUS [35709] : C1810 YEOVIL, SOM, ENG [34063] : PRE 1850 ENG [35709]

CORPE ALL SOM, ENG [36242] : PRE 1810 ROTHERHITHE, KEN, ENG [37906]

CORPS 1700-1750 CRAYTHORNE, NRY, ENG [34552]

CORR 1800+ LOU, IRL [34918]

CORRIE PRE 1850 IOW, ENG [38270]

CORRIGALL PRE 1808 HARRAY, OKI, SCT [35021]

CORRIGAN PRE 1832 YORK & AGHADE, YKS & CAR, ENG & IRL [33812] : 1800+ DONAGHMOYNE, MOG, IRL [33829] : 1800+ DUNAREE & DRUMBERAGH, MOG, IRL [33829] : 1790-1840 TIP, IRL [34175] : 1860S FER, IRL [35156] : 1700-1900 ROS, IRL [37031] : 1780-1830 KIK, IRL [38404]

CORRIGIN ALL DUR, ENG [34293]

CORRINGTON 1810 CIRCLEVILLE, OH, USA [35295] : 1600+ USA [35295]

CORRISS 1839+ KIRK GERMAN, IOM [34288]

CORRIVEAU PRE 1643 FONTCLAIREAU, ANGOULEME, FRA [34106]

CORRY C1824 CLA, IRL [35249]

CORSALITZ PRE 1860 WPR, GER [37427]

CORSAN 1795+ LND, ENG [36254]

CORSE PRE 1800 LKS, SCT [36955]

CORSON 1700+ NJ, USA [34121]

CORSTON 1700+ WYMONDHAM, NFK, ENG [36483]

CORT C1830 BLACKBURN, LAN, ENG [37169]

CORTIS 1560+ GORING, SSX, ENG [36827] : ALL WORLDWIDE [36283]

CORWIN MATTHIAS 1590-1633 WAR, ENG [37453]

CORY 1850-1990 ADELAIDE, SA, AUS [36025] : 1823+ VACY, NSW, AUS [36241] : 1500-1850 STRATTON, CON, ENG [36025] : 1806+ TAVISTOCK, DEV, ENG [36771] : 1853+ PLYMOUTH, DEV, ENG [36771] : 1830+ BRIDGERULE, DEV, ENG [36771]

CORYELL 1750+ CAN [34490] : 1750+ USA [34490]

COSAR ALL SCT [37354]

COSBURN ALL WORLDWIDE [35540]

COSBY 1800+ WELLAND CO., ONT, CAN [34114] : PRE 1812 ENG [34114] : 1780+ WAR, ENG [34823]

COSE C1760-1820 DEV, ENG [36289]

COSER ALL SCT [37354]

COSGRAVE C1830 BUTLER'S BRIDGE, CAV, IRL [35922] : 1849-1906 AUCKLAND, NZ [35922]

COSGROVE 1840+ NSW, AUS [35854] : PRE 1841 CLAREMORRIS, MAY, IRL [34305] : PRE 1858 AVOCA, WIC, IRL [35147] : ALL NEWBRIDGE, WIC, IRL [35854] : C1820-1850 FOHARTY, PARISH DOON, GAL, IRL [36337] : C1856-1900 BELTURBET, CAV, IRL [36632] : 1800S AVOCA, WIC, IRL [36642] : C184-1884 WGTN, NZ & IRL [34651] : PETER PRE 1850 LANARK, LKS, SCT [36192]

COSIER PRE 1841 LOCKERLEY, HAM, ENG [34295] : PRE 1800 WENDOVER, BKM, ENG [37729]

COSMAN C1800+ KINGS CO., NB, CAN [34366] : C1780 DIGBY, NS, CAN [34366]

COSNAHAN 1700+ IOM [37646]

COSS PRE 1822 CAVETOWN, MD, USA [35289] : JACOB 1820S ROSS CO., OH, USA [37001]

COSSAR C1732 COLDINGHAM, BEW, SCT [34491] : ALL SCT [37354]

COSSENEAU ALL WORLDWIDE [37768]

COSSENS PRE 1800 KINGOLDRUM, ANS, SCT [36401] : PRE 1800 CORTACHY & GLAMIS, ANS, SCT [36401]

COSSENTINE 1800S ST AUSTELL, CON, ENG [37913]

COSSER ALL SCT [37354]

COSSTICK ALL SSX, ENG [37875]

COSTAIN PRE 1790 MAUGHOLD, IOM, UK [37579]

COSTANZO ALL APRIGLIANO (VICO), COSENZA, ITL [34047]

COSTE CALDE 1700S PRESCOT, LANGUEDOC, FRA [33856]

COSTELLO C1940 DARLINGHURST, NSW, AUS [34694] : C1867+ PIRRON YALLOCK, VIC, AUS [35746] : C1866+ GEELONG, VIC, AUS [35746] : 1840+ BURRAWA & ALBURY, NSW, AUS [38008] : 1820-1920 MIDDLESBROUGH & DUBLIN, YKS, ENG & IRL [35767] : C1840 GAL, IRL [33812] : C1854 GORMANSFIELD, TIP, IRL [34281] : PRE 1866 LIM, IRL [35746] : ALL IRL [36545] : 1750-1816 KER, IRL [36618] : PRE 1840+ IRL [38008] : ALL USA [36545]

COSTER PRE 1840 BRINKWORTH, WIL, ENG [34612] : 1750+ EALING & OLD BRENTFORD, MDX, ENG [37251] : 1853-1856 READING, BRK, ENG [37251] : 1854+ KINGSTON, SRY, ENG [37251]

COSTICK 1848+ YAPTON, SSX, ENG [36959]

COSTIDELL 1800+ WESTERHAM, KEN, ENG [36088]

COSTIGAN PRE 1852 BANTRY BAY, COR, IRL [35649] : PRE 1852 YOUGHAL, COR, IRL [35649]

COSTLEY 1840-1850 COPIAH CO., MS, USA [36573]

COSWAY JOHN 1683 TIVERTON, DEV, ENG [34091]

COSWELL 1840-1900 TUMUT, NSW, AUS [38073]

COTHAM 1800+ MERRICKVILLE, ONT, CAN [34466] : PRE 1850 KILCROW, MOG, IRL [34466]

COTHER ALL WORLDWIDE [37715]

COTHRON 1790+ NC, USA [38058]

COTMAN 1700-1900 NORWICH, NFK, ENG [34303]

COTON ALL ASTON & BIRMINGHAM, WAR, ENG [36234]

COTTAIRE 1800-1850 LILLE, NOR, FRA [35151]

COTTAM PRE 1870 MANCHESTER, LAN, ENG [38377]

COTTEE MARIA PRE 1820 SOHO, LND, ENG [34461] : PRE 1860 WITHAM, ESS, ENG [35374] : PRE 1820 ESS, ENG [35902]

COTTER 1850+ RATCLIFFE, LND, ENG [37902] : 1750-1850 INCHIGEELAGH, COR, IRL [36618]

COTTEREL 1740-1800 SIDBURY, DEV, ENG [34834] : 1800+ LND, ENG [36088]

COTTERELL PRE 1840 ASHBRITTLE, SOM, ENG [36538] : LT. E. C1914-1919 LONDON (WW1), ESS, ENG [37756]

COTTERILL 1650-1750 GUISBOROUGH, NRY, ENG [34181] : PRE 1886 DEV, ENG [35384] : C1800 BARKING, ESS, ENG [35434] : C1800 BLACKWALL, LND, ENG [35434] : C1820+ LONDON, ENG [36838] : C1850 CROYDON, SRY, ENG [36838] : PRE 1861 PINXTON, DBY & NTT, ENG [37267]

COTTINGHAM PRE 1750 AYLSHAM, NFK, ENG [36593]

COTTLE C1857+ SYDNEY, NSW, AUS [38541] : PRE 1840 SWAINWICK, BATH, SOM, ENG [34003]

COTTOM 1800S VIC, AUS [33793]

COTTON 1200-1800 WAR & STS, ENG [34067] : 1200-1800 CAM & NFK, ENG [34067] : 1800S BIRMINGHAM, WAR, ENG [34309] : ALL SOTHERTON & YOXFORD, SFK, ENG [35222] : 1800-1900 ELLENHALL, STS, ENG [36512] : 1852+ BROMLEY, LND, ENG [38539] : 1800-1830 SCT [33767] : 1700-1770 HALIFAX CO., NC, USA [38129]

COTTON-BLUNTISH ALL WORLDWIDE [36992]

COTTREL 1791 HARBURY, WAR, ENG [34677]

COTTRELL 1840S PENRITH, NSW, AUS [35373] : PRE 1860 FRIMLEY, SRY, ENG [34428] : C1837 MANCHESTER, LAN, ENG [35373] : ALL MO, USA [34220]

COUANE 1800+ CTE VAUDREUIL, QUE, CAN [36657]

COUCH RICHARD 1716+ NORTH HILL, CON, ENG [35471] : ALL ST IVES, CON, ENG [36506] : PRE 1850 CON, ENG [37020] : PRE 1900 DEV, ENG [37020] : 1720-1750 BRUNSWICK CO., VA, USA [36737]

COUCHMAN PRE 1880 EWELL, KEN, ENG [36613]

COUCTAS 1750-1850 LND, ENG [36143]

COUDEL 1841 NOTTINGHAM, NTT, ENG [34540]

COUETTE 1824-1854 NANTES, FRA [36601]

COUGER PRE 1850 NJ, USA [35312]

COUGHENHOUR CHRISTIAN 1760S ROWAN CO., NC, USA [37585]

COUGHLAN 1800+ NORTHUMBERLAND CO., NB, CAN [38460] : 1786+ PEI, CAN [38460]

COUGHLIN 1860S IRL [37568]

COUGHRAN 1700+ FINTONA, TYR, IRL [35080]

COUGHTREY 1900 LONDON, ENG [35705] : 1860+ BERKHAMPSTEAD, HRT, ENG [36981] : 1760+ CHESHAM, BKM, ENG [36981]

COUL 1800+ SPANAY, MOR, SCT [34852]

COULDWELL ALL PENISTONE, WRY, ENG [34116]

COULES 1800S LONDON, ENG [35342]

COULL 1867+ SYDNEY & NARARA, NSW, AUS [35159] : PRE 1860 KEN, ENG [35159] : 1800+ FERRYDEN, KCD, SCT [36971]

COULLES 1845-1920 PLYMOUTH, DEV, ENG [36771]

COULLING PRE 1770 OXF, ENG [37739]

COULLIS ALL ENG [34652]

COULL-JAMES ALL AUS [35159]

COULOMB PRE 1880 TRINITY & ST LAWRENCE, JSY, CHI, UK [36200]

COULSON PRE 1836 LAUNCESTON, TAS, AUS [34548] : JOHN C1805 LND, ENG [34548] : 1853+ LONDON, ENG [34548] : 1800S NBL, ENG [35165] : PRE 1850 LONG STANTON, CAM, ENG [35323] : PRE 1860 SWAVESEY, CAM, ENG [35323] : PRE 1850 HEMINGFOLD GREY, HUN, ENG [35323] : PRE 1860 HOLYWELL CUM NEDINGWORTH, HUN, ENG [35323] : PRE 1791 BELLINGHAM, NBL, ENG [35779] : PRE 1857 LIN, ENG [35904] : 1798+ NORTHAMPTON, NTH, ENG [35921] : PRE 1800 CAM, ENG [36183] : 1750+ WHITBY, YKS, ENG [36609] : PRE 1768 GLENTHAM, LIN, ENG [37318] : PRE 1800 SUNDERLAND, DUR, ENG [37693] : 1790+ DURHAM, DUR, ENG & AUS [34803] : ALL NZ [36839]

COULSTOCK PRE 1750 SSX, ENG [37875]

COULTAS PRE 1831 ENG [34502]

COULTER PRE 1898 GLEBE, NSW, AUS [34968] : ALL BOWRAVILLE, NSW, AUS [35546] : PRE 1858 CLOGHBOY, TYR, IRL [35247] : PRE 1870 KILLEGGAN, ANT, IRL [35546] : 1939-1945 LISBURN, ANT, IRL [36420] : 1850+ KALAMAZOO, MI, USA [34148] : JOSEPHUS 1800+ GOSHEN, PERRY TWP, CHOSOCTON, OH, USA [34511] : 1840+ CEDAR CO., MO & TN, USA [36942]

COULTES PRE 1861 HALTON CO., ONT, CAN [34502]

COULTHARD 1700-1800 NETHER WASDALE, CUL, ENG [34872] : 1800-1850 ALTON, HAM, ENG [36025] : 1500-1700 CARLISLE, CUL, ENG [36025] : 1851+ WEARDALE, DUR, ENG [38277] : 1700-1800 DFS, SCT [37858]

COULTON 1830S WINDSOR, NSW, AUS [37971] : 1700+ HARBERTON, DEV, ENG [34970] : 1800S BUCKS CO., PA, USA [36926]

COUMBS C1690 ALTARNUM, CON, ENG [35335]

COUNDLEY PRE 1820 ROCK, WOR, ENG [36110]

COUNT PRE 1819+ RAYLEIGH, ESS, ENG [37108]

COUNTRYMAN 1780-1990 OSNABRUCK, ONT, CAN [34077]

COUPE 1790-1870 LAN, ENG [34175] : PRE 1790 BOLDOVER, DBY, ENG [35029]

COUPER 1810+ STRICHEN, ABD, SCT **[33783]** : 1910+ WICK, CAI, SCT **[33920]** : 1800+ GLASGOW, LKS, SCT **[34918]** : 1800S EASTWOOD & CATHCART, RFW, SCT **[35395]** : 1800S FIF, SCT **[35715]**

COUPERTHWAITE 1841 TYNEMOUTH, NBL, ENG **[37443]**

COUPLAND 1810+ CAWKWELL, LIN, ENG **[35587]** : ANNE 1766+ DFS & BAN, SCT **[34161]** : 1800+ HUTTON CORBIE, DFS, SCT **[37175]**

COURCHA C1890 BROMLEY & ALL, LND, ENG **[37151]**

COUREUL 1570+ FRA **[34068]**

COURNOYER 1816+ QUE & ONT, CAN **[34068]**

COURONNE C1800 MAURITIUS, FRA **[34843]**

COURRONNE 1824 PORT LOUIS, MAURITIUS **[37106]**

COURSE C1827 FOWLMERE, CAM, ENG **[35202]**

COURT 1840+ SYDNEY, NSW, AUS **[34533]** : 1840+ NSW, AUS **[36305]** : 1850 NEWCASTLE, NSW, AUS **[38214]** : C1800 EYNSHAM, OXF, ENG **[34274]** : PRE 1840 MANCHESTER, LAN, ENG **[34533]** : C1829 SOM, ENG **[34972]** : PRE 1850 STRATFORD ON AVON, WAR, ENG **[36385]** : 1800+ ESS, ENG **[36756]** : ALL COTHELSTONE, SOM, ENG **[36834]** : PRE 1830 STANWAY, GLS, ENG **[37320]**

COURTAULD PRE 1750 SOHO, LND, ENG & FRA **[36396]**

COURTENAY PRE 1720 RACKENFORD, DEV, ENG **[35866]** : 1700S IRL **[38325]**

COURTICE PRE 1800 BUCKLAND BREWER, DEV, ENG **[35032]**

COURTIER 1840+ STS, ENG **[36683]** : 1800+ RPA, FRA **[36683]**

COURTIN PRE 1750 PREVILLY, CEN, FRA **[36353]**

COURTNAGE ALL WORLDWIDE **[38323]**

COURTNEY PRE 1800 LADOCK, CON, ENG **[36899]** : 1800+ CUL, ENG **[37274]** : PRE 1845 TEMPLEPATRICK, ANT, IRL **[34115]** : WILLIAM 1836-1907 PISECO, NY, USA **[38140]** : 1810-1830 ORANGEBURG CO., SC, USA **[38188]** : PRE 1700 VA, USA **[38311]**

COURTNEY (SEE COURTE [35866]

COURTOIS PRE 1870 ARTHABASKA, QUE, CAN **[38033]**

COURTRAYE 1780 BOMBAY, INDIA **[33783]**

COUSEN PRE 1887 FRODINGHAM, LIN, ENG **[35439]** : PRE 1900 MANCHESTER, LAN, ENG **[35439]**

COUSENS 1855+ KILMORE & DUNEDIN, VIC, AUS & NZ **[35467]** : PRE 1900 STOKE ON TRENT, STS, ENG **[37389]**

COUSIJN JACOB 1775 S'GRAVENLAND, NOH, NL **[38706]**

COUSINEAU C1850-1870 STE ROSE, QUE, CAN **[34047]** : 1870+ OTTAWA, ONT & QUE, CAN **[34047]** : PRE 1690 GRAND MILLAR, LMS, FRA **[34047]** : PRE 1690 JUMILHAC LE GRAND, PERIGORD, FRA **[34047]** : PRE 1690 GRAND MILLAR, PERIGORD, FRA **[34047]** : PRE 1690 JUMILHAC LE GRAND, LMS, FRA **[34047]**

COUSINER C1760 DILTON, WIL, ENG **[35076]**

COUSINS JEAN C1903 FREMANTLE, WA, AUS **[35729]** : PRE 1880 HAM, ENG **[34102]** : 1600-1750 CREWKERNE, SOM, ENG **[35178]** : 1550-1750 ESS, ENG **[35178]** : 1550-1850 SFK, ENG **[35178]** : 1650-1750 LND, ENG **[35178]** : 1800-1840 WOTTON UNDER EDGE, GLS, ENG **[35860]** : 1800-1990 WALPOLE ST PETER, NFK, ENG **[36394]** : PRE 1850 FUGGLESTONE, WIL, ENG **[37287]** : C1800 FIVEHEAD, SOM, ENG **[37952]** : 1750+ NH, USA **[34256]**

COUSINTINE PRE 1929 EMSDALE, ONT, CAN **[37439]**

COUTANCHE PRE 1830 ST CLEMENT, JSY, CHI **[35440]**

COUTENAY C1600 ENG **[34395]**

COUTIN C1740 VILLE DE BRANGE, BN, FRA **[37819]**

COUTS 1800+ ABD, SCT **[36971]**

COUTTS C1890+ DONNYBROOK, WA, AUS **[35249]** : C1860+ STEPNEY, MDX, ENG **[35249]** : 1850+ NZ **[36750]** : PRE 1850 GLENMUICK, ABD, SCT **[35819]** : PRE 1830 KCD, SCT **[36077]** : PRE 1830 ABD, SCT **[36077]** : 1700-1890S HUNTLY, ABD, SCT **[37442]** : PRE 1845 KINCARDINE ON FORTH AREA, FIF & PER, SCT **[37842]** : ALL WORLDWIDE **[33868]**

COUTURE PRE 1890 DULUTH, MN & WA, USA **[38746]**

COUVES C1852 GEELONG, VIC, AUS **[35748]**

COUZENS 1906+ KANGAROO VALLEY, NSW, AUS **[34874]** : PRE 1880 EMSWORTH & HAVANT, HAM & SSX, ENG **[34382]** : ALL BERWICK BASSETT & AVEBURY, WIL, ENG **[34874]** : C1800 BATH, SOM, ENG **[37952]**

COVARRUBIA 1500-1630 MEXICO CITY, MEXICO **[36340]**

COVE PRE 1860 YKS, ENG **[37018]** : PRE 1800 SEEND, WIL, ENG **[37371]** : PRE 1800 STOCKBURY, KEN, ENG **[37602]**

COVELL PRE 1830 HADDENHAM, CAM, ENG **[35391]** : 1844 WYANDOTTE CO., OH, USA **[38192]**

COVENTRY ALL ECCLESTON, CHS, ENG **[38074]** : 1700-1900 PER, SCT **[35179]**

COVER PRE 1760 SRY, ENG **[37420]**

COVERLEY CHARLOTTE 1870+ BARROWBY, LIN, ENG **[34916]**

COVEY 1820+ ONT, CAN **[34129]** : 1750+ ONT, CAN **[34490]**

COVILL C1630 NORWICH, NFK, ENG **[34573]** : PRE 1900 CAM, ENG **[36122]**

COVILLE PRE 1900 CAM, ENG **[36122]**

COW 1770+ SCT **[38274]**

COWAN 1860+ PERTH, WA, AUS **[33795]** : 1858+ TAREE DISTRICT, NSW, AUS **[37145]** : 1838+ FIREFLY CREEK, NSW, AUS **[37451]** : 1858+ HOBART, TAS, AUS **[37954]** : C1830 SOUTH MONAGHAN, ONT, CAN **[34507]** : 1860+ QUEBEC, QUE, CAN **[36654]** : 1800S TORONTO, ONT, CAN **[36670]** : ALEX. 1870+ PRINCETON, ONT, CAN **[37438]** : 1801-1869 UPPER, CAN **[37470]** : 1858-1869 DURHAM & HOPE TWP., ONT, CAN **[37470]** : 1770-1820 PERTH, ONT, CAN **[37470]** : 1860+ SUNDERLAND, DUR, ENG **[33795]** : PRE 1775 BOTHAL & MORPETH, NBL, ENG **[36110]** : C1900 TRIMDON GRANGE, DUR, ENG **[36408]** : JOHN 1800-1836 MEA, IRL **[34200]** : 1700-1800S KILSKEERY, TYR, IRL **[34483]** : PRE 1830 IRL **[34507]** : ALL CAV, IRL **[37584]** : 1796 KILBRANDON, ARL, SCT **[33811]** : PRE 1850 LARBERT, STI, SCT **[34097]** : 1750-1850 WIG, SCT **[34229]** : 1870S PORT GLASGOW, RFW, SCT **[35625]** : C1880 ROBERTON, ROX, SCT **[36408]** : 1890+ MELROSE, ROX, SCT **[36408]** : PRE 1860 DORNOCH, DFS, SCT **[36408]** : 1728-1770 FALKIRK, STI, SCT **[37205]** : 1800-1850 JEDBURGH, ROX, SCT **[37628]** : PRE 1858 AIRTH, STI, SCT **[37954]** : 1600+ SCT **[38388]** : 1800S+ MOFFAT, DFS, SCT **[38436]** : 1700+ INV, SCT & AUS **[37970]** : 1820+ COLMONELL, AYR, SCT & NZ **[36803]** : 1801-1869 SCT & USA **[37470]** : C1757 LANCASTER CO., PA, USA **[36354]** : GEORGE 1880+ FL, USA & CAN **[37438]**

COWANS 1850+ SELBY, YKS, ENG **[35038]**

COWARD 1887+ CHARTERS TOWERS, QLD, AUS [34852] : JOHN 1875+ QUIRINDI, NSW, AUS [34942] : CHARLES 1900+ QUIRINDI, NSW, AUS [34942] : JOHN 1875+ MERIGALA, NSW, AUS [34942] : 1800+ KIRBY, LAN, ENG [34852] : DANIEL C1832 BRADFORD ON AVON, WIL, ENG [34942] : (ARMY) PRE 1882 ENG [35792] : 1700-1900 DOR, ENG [36012] : 1475+ KIRKBY IRELETH, LAN, ENG [36701] : 1880+ TELLISFORD, SOM, ENG [37088] : PRE 1743 LAN, ENG [37706] : 1700-1900 ALDINGHAM, LAN, ENG [37858] : JAMES 1801 RUTHERFORD CO., NC, USA [38109] : THOMAS PRE 1892 GLEN FALLS, WARREN CO., NY, USA [38140] : ALL WORLDWIDE [35875]

COWDREY 1850+ SYDNEY, NSW, AUS [34977]

COWDROY PRE 1920 WALWORTH, MDX, ENG [37685]

COWELL 1855+ BOMBALA, NSW, AUS [34977] : PRE 1855 PECKHAM, SRY, ENG [34750] : PRE 1822 ESS, ENG [35083] : 1800+ STOCKPORT, CHS, ENG [37907] : 1750 THEBERTON, SFK, ENG [37928] : 1750+ DOUGLAS, IOM [37306] : 1700-1800 BALLAUGH, IOM, UK [36618]

COWEN 1830+ CYGNET, TAS, AUS [33786] : 1600-1800 WORKINGTON, LAN, ENG [36106] : PRE 1850 NBL, ENG [37646] : PRE 1850 DUR, ENG [37646]

COWENS 1700-1850 ALNWICK, NBL, ENG [36879]

COWFIELD PRE 1864 EDINBURGH, MLN, SCT [37852]

COWGILL 1800-1840 LEEDS, YKS, ENG [33861] : ALL WRY, ENG [35470] : PRE 1682 SETTLE, WRY, ENG [36972] : 1880+ ST LOUIS, MO, CT & NJ, USA & ENG [37796]

COWIE GENERAL C1849 STEWKLEY, OXF, ENG [34667] : 1800+ PADDINGTON, LND, ENG [36768] : PRE 1881 ENG [37787] : PRE 1881 ENG [37787] : 1860+ DUNEDIN, OTAGO, NZ [36816] : PRE 1880 PORTESSIE, BAN, SCT [34192] : ALL ANS, SCT [34226] : 1800+ CURRIE, MLN, SCT [34916] : 1800+ MONTROSE, ANS, SCT [35127] : PRE 1800 FALKIRK, STI, SCT [35377] : 1830-60 BANFF, BAN, SCT [36816]

COWIN 1800S IOM [34979]

COWLAND 1875+ CARLTON, VIC, AUS [34978] : PRE 1875 ESS, ENG [34978] : 1800-1900 BUSHEY, HRT, ENG [36977]

COWLE PRE 1820 CHULMLEIGH, DEV, ENG [35128] : 1700-1900 BRADDAN, IOM [37306]

COWLER 1775 STANDON, HRT, ENG [35980] : PRE 1900 CUL, ENG [38434]

COWLES 1800 CAMBRIDGE, CAM, ENG [35027] : PRE 1890 HAMPDEN CO., MA, USA [38365]

COWLEY 1840-1900 SUTTON, SRY, ENG [34514] : PRE 1800 KEMPTON & ELSTOW, BDF, ENG [34588] : 1700+ FAIRFORD, GLS, ENG [34591] : 1720 LAMBOURNE, BRK, ENG [34731] : 1700-1900 ENG [35292] : 1850S-1890S WHITECHAPEL, LND, ENG [35815] : 1870S LONGCOMPTON, WAR, ENG [35889] : PRE 1920 LONDON, LND, ENG [36363] : C1813 LIDLINGTON, BDF, ENG [36803] : ALL BALLAUGH, IOM [35776] : C1800+ DUNBOYNE, MEA, IRL [33792] : 1915+ DANNEVIRKE, HAWKES BAY, NZ [35889]

COWLING 1650-1680 ST TEATH, CON, ENG [34448] : 1600+ MADRON, CON, ENG [34747] : PRE 1792 YKS, ENG [35037] : 1800+ MIDDLETON ST GEORGE, DUR, ENG [35891] : PETER PRE 1790 NORWICH & LEICESTER, ENG [37640] : ALL LND, ENG [37750] : C1874 WIMBLINGTON, CAM, ENG [37830]

COWLISHAW PRE 1850 GRINDON, WAR, ENG [36188]

COWMAN C1811 CLONSKILTY, COR, IRL [35454] : ALL WORLDWIDE [34553]

COWNEY PRE 1775 BOTHAL & MORPETH, NBL, ENG [36110]

COWNLEY 1850S WOR & STS, ENG [36194]

COWPER 1870+ DUNDAS, ONT, CAN [34251] : 1760+ LASTINGHAM, NRY, ENG [34078] : WILLIAM 1800S LIN, ENG [34378] : PRE 1650 NTT, ENG [36126] : PRE 1750 CUNDALL, NRY, ENG [37754]

COWPERTHWAITE 1750-1850 STELLA, DUR, ENG [35153] : PRE 1883 DUNDEE, ANS, SCT [37442]

COWRIE GENERAL C1849 STEWKLEY, OXF, ENG [34667]

COX 1803+ HOBART & SOUTH MELBOURNE, TAS & VIC, AUS [33864] : 1890+ NAMBUCCA RV, NSW, AUS [34306] : 1890+ CLARENCE RV, NSW, AUS [34306] : 1840+ PATTERSON, NSW, AUS [34306] : CHRISTIANA 1841+ MULGOA & CAWDOR, NSW, AUS [34418] : JOHN 1841+ MULGOA & CAWDOR, NSW, AUS [34418] : 1878+ MUDGEE, NSW, AUS [34534] : 1860-1920 TALBOT, VIC, AUS [34551] : 1850+ CRYSTAL BROOK, SA, AUS [34600] : ALL EUROA, VIC, AUS [34674] : 1900+ WELLINGTON, NSW, AUS [34843] : 1850+ BATHURST, NSW, AUS [34969] : WILLIAM 1850+ BALMAIN, NSW, AUS [35033] : PRE 1859 EPPING FOREST, TAS, AUS [35091] : 1842+ SHEFFIELD, TAS, AUS [35095] : 1873+ ROCKHAMPTON, QLD, AUS [35121] : WILLIAM 1835+ NEW NORFOLK, TAS, AUS [36290] : WILLIAM 1858+ QLD, AUS [36290] : 1850+ GAWLER, SA, AUS [37186] : 1864 BATAVIA [37952] : 1870+ LAKEFIELD, ONT, CAN [34485] : 1875+ ONT, CAN [38059] : BETTY 1770-1800 YATE, GLS, ENG [33771] : PRE 1790 LONDON, ENG [33864] : PRE 1900 ANDOVER, HAM, ENG [33959] : 1800+ FLINSTOCK, ENG [33963] : PRE 1900 MELCOMBE REGIS, DOR & HAM, ENG [34116] : 1860+ HIGH WYCOMBE, BKM, ENG [34190] : 1800 LAMBETH, SRY, ENG [34210] : PRE 1850S NTT & LIN, ENG [34240] : 1800+ BRISTOL, ENG [34485] : 1830S RODBOROUGH, GLS, ENG [34605] : PRE 1766 CHESTERFIELD, DBY, ENG [34623] : ALL LONG SUTTON, SOM, ENG [34674] : PRE 1850 LEWES, SSX, ENG [34686] : PRE 1850 CLAINES, WOR, ENG [34739] : JONATHAN 1790+ WISBECH, CAM, ENG [35033] : C1850 BRIXTON, LND, ENG [35038] : PRE 1840 CRONDALL, HAM, ENG [35042] : 1800+ SSX, ENG [35060] : C1800 TRING, HRT, ENG [35095] : 1850-1950 LAN & HAM, ENG [35292] : 1800S JESSE, ENG [35367] : 1800S AYLESBURY, ENG [35367] : PRE 1870 NORTHAMPTON, ENG [35367] : 1800S WADDESDON, ENG [35367] : PRE 1850 NFK, ENG [35556] : 1700-1900 TREGONY & LAMORRAN, CON, ENG [35576] : 1700+ BATTLE, SSX, ENG [35587] : 1800+ HUISH EPISCOPI, SOM, ENG [35734] : PRE 1840 LND, ENG [35902] : PRE 1860 FINSTOCK & CHARLBURY, OXF & BKM, ENG [35940] : PRE 1824 WOOLWICH, KEN, ENG [36010] : PRE 1800 CITY OF LONDON, ENG [36035] : 1700+ KEN, ENG [36093] : PRE 1800 NEWINGTON BAGPATH, GLS, ENG [36113] : ALL CAM, ENG [36183] : THOMAS PRE 1711 WIL, ENG [36211] : 1834-1874 HARROW, MDX, ENG [36253] : C1835 GRANTHAM, LIN, ENG [36253] : WILLIAM PRE 1826 UXBRIDGE, MDX, ENG [36290] : 1800+ SOM, ENG [36326] : 1870-1900 BEXHILL, SSX, ENG [36439] : 1750+ SHERRINGTON, BKM, ENG [36439] : 1800-1900 LONDON, MDX, ENG [36439] :

1750+ OLNEY, BKM, ENG [36439] : PRE 1800 SAL, ENG [36480] : 1750-1900 SEDGLEY, STS, ENG [36495] : 1804-1918 EASTHAM, WOR, ENG [36513] : 1800S OLD WINDSOR, BRK, ENG [36764] : 1800S HITCHIN, HRT, ENG [36764] : 1830+ BRIGHTON, SSX, ENG [36815] : 1836-1899 WHATLEY, SOM, ENG [36816] : 1850 WHITNEY, OXF, ENG [36851] : PRE 1850 CAM, COALEY, GLS, ENG [37101] : 1770+ ISLEWORTH, MDX, ENG [37251] : ELIZA 1820+ WOODMINSTERNE, SRY, ENG [37310] : GEORGE PRE 1837 READING, BRK, ENG [37321] : 1788+ SLIMBRIDGE, GLS, ENG [37343] : 1750-1850 AXMINSTER, DEV, ENG [37378] : C1600-1700 CHERTSEY, SRY, ENG [37618] : PRE 1850 LIN, ENG [37771] : 1800+ STEPNEY, MDX, ENG [37885] : PRE 1880 SALFORD, LAN, ENG [37925] : ALL LONDON, MDX, ENG [37950] : C1895+ SCARBOROUGH, NRY, ENG [38401] : 1850+ WALSALL, STS & QLD, ENG & AUS [34768] : PRE 1840 FER, IRL [35129] : 1796 CORK, COR, IRL [35770] : 1750+ MONASTEREVAN, KID & LEX, IRL [36087] : PRE 1840 LIM, IRL [37991] : PRE 1870 BLANTYRE, LKS, SCT [37242] : JOHN PRE 1883 SAN FRANCISCO, CA, USA [36678] : PRE 1885 PA, USA [36729] : 1800-1900 CASS CO., MI, USA [36924] : SOLOMON C1743+ YORK, BUCKS & MONTGOMERY CO., PA, NC & VA, USA [37003] : JOHN PRE 1810 NEW CASTLE CO., DE, USA [37003] : 1836+ TN, USA [38058] : THOMAS 1827-1850 AL, FL & GA, USA [38340]

COXE 1650-1750 TETBURY, GLS, ENG [34012]

COXEN C1840 LONDON, ENG [36092]

COXHEAD PRE 1749 WESTERN ON THE GREEN, OXF, ENG [36281] : 1800+ KINTBURY, BRK, ENG [36975]

COXON 1842 OXFORD CO., ONT, CAN [34106] : PRE 1842 ENG [34106] : 1830 ALNWICK, NBL, ENG [34614] : 1820+ DBY & STS, ENG [35019] : 1774+ GATESHEAD, DUR, ENG [36961]

COY 1750+ HARBY, LEI, ENG [37258] : PRE 1800 WORLDWIDE [37450]

COYLE PRE 1844 SYDNEY, NSW, AUS [34816] : 1875 BRISTOL, GLS, ENG [34836] : 1850+ MILFORD, DON, IRL [33902] : 1830-1872 IRL [36895] : 1800-1900 HARTFORD, CT, USA [38297] : EDDIE 1860+ HARTFORD, CT, USA [38297] : CHARLES 1860+ HARTFORD, CT, USA [38297] : JAMES 1860+ HARTFORD, CT, USA [38297] : PATRICK 1830+ HARTFORD, CT, USA [38297] : MARY 1860+ HARTFORD, CT, USA [38297] : 1800-1900 CT, USA [38297]

COYNE 1878-1990 MACKAY, QLD, AUS [35100] : 1840-1900 WELLINGTON, NSW, AUS [35523] : 1800+ IRL [33963] : JOHN J. 1790-1840 NEWPORT, MAY, IRL [34514] : 1814 CLIFDEN, GAL, IRL [35100] : 1861-69 BALLYLANDERS, LIM, IRL [35100] : 1870-76 MITCHELSTOWN, COR, IRL [35100] : 1855 CLONMEL, TIP, IRL [35100]

COYTE JAMES & MARY 1800S PLYMOUTH, DEV, ENG [34889]

COZART ALL WORLDWIDE [36965]

COZENS 1700-1850 SOM, ENG [36242] : 1890 SHOLING, HAM, ENG [38210]

CRAAY 1855-1870 KEWEENAW CO., MI, USA [38010]

CRAB PRE 1700 NORTH HILL, CON, ENG [35973]

CRABB ALL KADINA, SA, AUS [35012] : 1840+ ADELAIDE, SA, AUS [38209] : PRE 1895 BODMIN LAND, CON, ENG [36249] : PRE 1730 BOBBINGWORTH, ESS, ENG [37568] : 1720+ LISKEARD, CON, ENG [38209] : 1881 ABERDEEN, SCT [38470] : PRE 1820 WHITE CO., TN, USA [38314]

CRABBE 1820S+ SYDNEY, NSW, AUS [34791] : PRE 1830 LND & MDX, ENG [34791]

CRABER 1880S+ SYDNEY, NSW, AUS [35735] : 1876+ ADELAIDE, SA, AUS [35735]

CRABLE 1800-1870 FAYETTE, PA, USA [37589]

CRABTREE 1880+ BOWLING, BRADFORD, YKS, ENG [35460] : PRE 1829 WAKEFIELD, YKS, ENG [36954] : PRE 1820 LANGFIELD & HEPTONSTALL, WRY, ENG [37372] : 1700+ ORANGE CO., NC, USA & ENG [38175]

CRACE PRE 1900 LONDON, MDX & SRY, ENG [34743]

CRACK ALL EAST HARLING, NFK, ENG [35819] : WILLIAM 1850S+ PENZANCE, CON, ENG [35876] : PRE 1860 BURNLEY, LAN, ENG [37866]

CRACKBONE ALL ENG [37803]

CRACKLAND 1750-1850 HAVERHILL, SFK, ENG [35151]

CRACKNELL 1860-190 PICTON, NSW, AUS [33766] : 1750-1870 FINCHINGFIELD, ESS, ENG [33766] : ALL ESS, ENG [34493] : PRE 1793+ HAVERHILL, SFK, ENG [35109] : 1750-1850 HAVERHILL, SFK, ENG [35151] : PRE 1841 BAPCHILD, KEN, ENG [35898] : ALL ENG [36639] : 1800+ HOLLINGBOURNE & STROOD, KEN, ENG [37405]

CRADDECK 1800+ KEN, ENG [34884]

CRADDICK 1800+ SHEPPY, KEN, ENG [35947]

CRADDOCK PRE 1850 NRY, ENG [35620] : 1800 KEN, ENG [36239] : PRE 1865 WIDEMOUTH, CON, ENG [37144] : PRE 1600S NEWTON, WLS [35096] : ALL WORLDWIDE [37397]

CRADDUCK PRE 1822 BOUGHTON MONCHELSEA, KEN, ENG [34325]

CRADOCK 1855+ PARRAMATTA, NSW, AUS [35513] : 1800+ BIRMINGHAM, WAR, ENG [36980] : ALL WORLDWIDE [37397]

CRADOCKE ALL WORLDWIDE [37397]

CRADY 1827-1884 HARDIN CO., KY, USA [35301]

CRAFFORD PRE 1650 UK [34746]

CRAFT 1650-1850 ENG [37515] : 1740+ MD, USA [36956] : 1800+ NOBLE CO., OH, USA [36956] : 1740+ FAYETTE CO., PA, USA [36956] : PRE 1777 WASHINGTON CO., PA, USA [37529]

CRAFTER 1750-1860 ERITH, KEN, ENG [34829]

CRAFTS 1600S ROXBURY, SUFFOLK CO., MA, USA [38745]

CRAGG 1769 RUDGEWICK & BOLNEY, SSX, ENG [36384]

CRAGGS 1700-1750 CHESTER LE STREET, DUR, ENG [34552]

CRAGHEAD PRE 1710 ABD, SCT [34053]

CRAIB 1874+ DUNEDIN, OTAGO, NZ [36877] : PRE 1880 MACDUFF, BAN & ABD, SCT [36877]

CRAIG 1870+ BRISBANE, QLD, AUS [33845] : 1857-1900 SYDNEY & GOULBURN, NSW, AUS [34294] : 1840S MELBOURNE, VIC, AUS [35136] : PRE 1890 ENMORE, NSW, AUS [37315] : 1840+ MERIVALE, ONT, CAN [33851] : C1800 CANTERBURY, KEN, ENG [35502] : 1810+ SOUTHWARK, SRY, ENG [36772] : PRE 1665+ MELMERBY, CUL, ENG [37019] : ALL NBL, ENG [37704] : PRE 1828 CLOUGH, DOW, IRL [33924] : C1830 ANT, IRL [34668] : CATHERINE C1858 GLENTIES, DON, IRL [35104] : 1800+ DUNGANNON, TYR, IRL [36135] : 1840+ BELFAST, ANT, IRL [36827] : PRE 1867 BELFAST, ANT, IRL [36848] : PRE 1860 MONEYMORE, DRY, IRL [37981] : 1775-1825 DRY, IRL [38342] : ISABELLA 1760S OMAGH, TYR, IRL [38537] : PRE 1785 EAST KILBRIDE, DNB, SCT [34127] : 1800 NIGG, KCD, SCT [34210] : C1716 CADDER, LKS, SCT [35252] : PRE 1800 PAISLEY,

RFW, SCT [35385] : 1768 DUNBARTON, SCT [35906]
: PRE 1850 PER, ARL & INV, SCT [37105] : C1801
AUCHTERGAVEN, PER, SCT [37144] : PRE 1830
GLASGOW, LKS, SCT [37179] : ALL WICK, CAI,
SCT [37627] : PRE 1850 PAISLEY, RFW, SCT [38276]
: ALL NORFOLK CITY, VA, USA [36557] : ALL
WORLDWIDE [36333]

CRAIGIE 1860S WENTWORTH, NSW, AUS [37178] :
PRE 1850 CALDBECK, CUL, ENG [34442] : ALL
DUMBARNIE, PER, SCT [37673] : 1700+
WORLDWIDE [36004]

CRAIGIE-HALKETT ALL HALL HILL OR LA HILL,
FIF, SCT [37673]

CRAIGMILES ALEXANDER 1774-1807 TYR, IRL
[38150] : 1807-1859 BUTLER CO., OH, USA [38150]

CRAIGS ALL NBL, ENG [37704]

CRAIK 1900+ ONT, CAN [34215] : WM. SAMUEL
1900S DUNEDIN, NZ [36633] : 1800S MONTROSE,
ANS, SCT [34028] : 1800S DUMFRIES, DFS, SCT
[36633]

CRAIKE C1784 WATH MILLS, NRY, ENG [34281]

CRAIN 1795 TUGBY, LEI, ENG [36817]

CRAINE 1854 ONT, CAN [37788] : 1750-1850 PEEL,
IOM, UK [36003]

CRALLE ALL USA [38735]

CRALLEY ALL USA [38735]

CRAMER C1750-1800 PA, USA [37790] : C1835+ NEW
YORK, NY, USA [38182]

CRAMMER C1850 LONDON, ENG [36092]

CRAMOND 1890S+ JAMBEROO, NSW, AUS [33930] :
1870S+ MURRUMBURRAH, NSW, AUS [33930] :
1834+ ESS, ENG [34653] : PRE 1820 NEWCASTLE
ON TYNE, NBL, ENG [35722] : PRE 1860 ENG &
SCT [36747] : ALL SCT [33930]

CRAMP PRE 1847 SOM, ENG [35097]

CRAMPHORN ALL ESS, ENG [37741]

CRAMPTON ALL ORANGE, NSW & VIC, AUS &
IRL [35547] : 1820+ BLYTH, CAM, ENG [36772] :
1700-1860 CRANBROOK, KEN, ENG [37252] : ALL
NTT & DBY, ENG [37412]

CRANAGE PRE 1800 BARTON UNDER
NEEDWOOD, STS, ENG [33796]

CRANBROOK 1820-1900 ROYSTON, HRT, ENG
[35992] : C1790 LONDON, ENG [37106]

CRANCHER C1840-1870 GREAT YARMOUTH, NFK,
ENG [35725]

CRANDALL 1810+ ALBION OSWEGO CO., NY,
USA [36549] : 1810+ CAMDEN ONEIDA CO., NY,
USA [36549] : 1880 MA, USA [38187]

CRANE 1870+ BUNDABERG, QLD, AUS [36286] :
SARAH 1700-1798 IPSWICH, SFK, ENG [34143] :
1800S SPRATTON, NTH, ENG [34309] : C1790 KEN,
ENG [34815] : 1800-1850 HEVINGHAM, NFK, ENG
[36057] : 1700-1850 CORRINGHAM, LIN, ENG
[36057] : C1780 SFK, ENG [37167] : 1835+
PORTSMOUTH, HAM, ENG [37360] : ALL
LYTCHETT MATRAVERS, DOR, ENG [37360] :
1870+ LEICESTER, LEI, ENG [37360] : ALL NFK,
ENG [38462] : PRE 1920 BRISTOL, SOM & VIC,
ENG & AUS [37995] : PRE 1840 COR, IRL [36518] :
C1725 WEYMOUTH, MA, USA [36319]

CRANFIELD 1800+ ESS, ENG [34818] : PRE 1864
SHOREDITCH, MDX, ENG [37259]

CRANFORD PRE 1900 DARTMOUTH &
DITTISHAM, DEV, ENG [37393]

CRANKE 1750-1850 WHICHAM & WHITBECK, CUL,
ENG [35624]

CRANMERE PRE 1715 DENNINGTON, SFK, ENG
[37420]

CRANNEY PRE 1900 KIK, IRL [38589] : 1870+ USA
[38589] : ALL WORLDWIDE [38589]

CRANNY PRE 1854 LONDON, ENG [34901]

CRANOR 1650-1750 LONDON, MDX, ENG [38041] :
1650-1700 BETHNAL GREEN & STEPNEY, MDX,
ENG [38041] : 1650-1700 WOR, ENG [38041] : 1650-
1733 DORCHESTER CO., MD, USA [38041]

CRANSTON 1700-1900 INDIA [36977] : PRE 1831
VIRGINIA, CAV, IRL [34270] : 1793
CASTLECOMER, KIK, IRL [35369] : 1700-1900
ROX, SCT [36977] : 1800+ BIGGER, LKS, SCT
[37422] : 1780S CRAWFORD, LKS, SCT [37751]

CRANSTONE C1830 KILMARNOCK, AYR, SCT
[35866]

CRANSTOUN C1880-1954 EDENDALE, SLD, NZ
[36853] : ALL LKS, SCT [36853]

CRANWELL PRE 1850 GREAT HORMEAD, HRT,
ENG [37832]

CRAPP ALL WORLDWIDE [36639]

CRAPPER 1800S HALIFAX, YKS, ENG [36851]

CRAPPS 1800 VA, USA [37792]

CRART PRE 1800 TYWARDREATH & FOWEY, CON,
ENG [34139]

CRASE 1800+ CON & DEV, ENG [38338] : 1840+
GRASS VALLEY & NEVEDA CITY, CA, USA
[38338]

CRASK C1830 TERRINGTON, NFK, ENG [35717]

CRATE 1720-1900 WONSTON, HAM, ENG [38003]

CRATES 1851+ HADLOW, KEN, ENG [34711] : PRE
1851 BRISTOL, GLS, ENG [34711]

CRATHERS ALL CAN & ENG [34133]

CRAUAN MARY 1820+ WAKEFIELD, WRY, ENG
[38031]

CRAUN 1800+ TAS, AUS [34283]

CRAVEN JOSHUA 1800S BRADFORD, YKS, ENG
[34499] : 1750-1800 S YKS, ENG [36084] : THOMAS
1880 SALFORD, LAN, ENG [37184] : C1800 LEEDS,
WRY, ENG [37643] : 1820+ WORCESTER, WOR,
ENG [37889] : PRE 1800 BUCKS CO., PA, USA
[36729] : 1774+ ALBEMARLE CO., VA, USA [36895]

CRAW 1700+ HAMILTON, LKS, SCT [34670] : 1700+
MILLHEUGH & LARKHALL, LKS, SCT [34670] :
1750-1860 LARKHALL, LKS, SCT [35937] : PRE 1730
BOLTON, CT, USA [37510]

CRAWFIELD 1880+ BALLARAT, VIC, AUS [36278]

CRAWFORD PRE 1860 VIC, AUS [34433] : GRACE
C1880 KAPUNDA, SA, AUS [34583] : 1856-1912
FRANKLIN, TAS, AUS [34698] : 1855+ BOMBALA,
NSW, AUS [34977] : C1850+ YEA, VIC, AUS [35249]
: 1839+ ADELAIDE, SA, AUS [35444] : 1839+
CASTLEMAINE, VIC, AUS [35731] : PRE 1892
MUSWELLBROOK, NSW, AUS [35781] : 1850+
TOOWOOMBA, QLD, AUS [36538] : 1850+
CAMLACHIE & LAMBTON CO., ONT, ALB & BC,
CAN [34375] : 1700-1900S MONTREAL, QUE, CAN
[35327] : 1770-1850 WILFESMOREFEN &
KIRKTON, LIN, ENG [34769] : C1847 FELLING,
DUR, ENG [35332] : C1876 EAST BRIXTON, LND,
ENG [36290] : PRE 1881 BELFAST & DONEGORE,
ANT, IRL [34389] : PRE 1850 ANTRIM, ANT, IRL
[34784] : PRE 1718 LONDONDERRY, LDY, IRL
[35616] : ALL ENNISKILLEN, FER, IRL [35739] :
PRE 1840 DRY, IRL [35782] : PRE 1830
COOKSTOWN, TYR, IRL [36538] : CHARLES
GORE 1820-75 ENNISKILLEN, FER, IRL [36890] :
PRE 1810 MAGHERAGALL, ANT, IRL [37927] :
1720-1860 NEWTON FORBES, LOG, IRL [38054] :
1820S CLOONE, LET, IRL [38054] : 1690-1725 FER,
IRL [38054] : JANET 1870+ DUNEDIN, NZ [36611] :
C1840 AUCKLAND, NZ [36860] : 1787+ PAISLEY,
RFW, SCT [33882] : PRE 1850 LILLIESLEAF &
MINTO, ROX, SCT [34375] : PRE 1923 GLASGOW,
LKS, SCT [34391] : 1840+ PAISLEY, RFW, SCT
[34871] : PRE 1855 CUPAR, FIF, SCT [34977] : PRE
1815 KIRKGUNZEON, KKD, SCT [35021] : C1890-

1970 DUNFERMLINE, FIF, SCT **[35078]** : AGNES PRE 1825 DOLPHINTON, LKS, SCT **[35184]** : PRE 1850 PORT GLASGOW & GREENOCK, RFW, SCT **[35229]** : JAMES C1840-1893 STRAITON & DALMELLINGTON, AYR, SCT **[35739]** : 1800 + KALRYE, KKD, SCT **[35993]** : 1800 + DFS, SCT **[35993]** : C1827 + DALRY, AYR, SCT **[35995]** : ALL PAISLEY, RFW, SCT **[36789]** : ALL KILBIRNIE, AYR, SCT **[36890]** : JOHN C1825 LANARK, AYR, SCT **[37143]** : 1780-1860 GLASSFORD, LKS, SCT **[37488]** : 1800S ARL, SCT **[37566]** : 1700-1800 PERTH & DUNDEE, ANS & PER, SCT **[37702]** : PRE 1859 KILBIRNIE, AYR, SCT **[37925]** : ALL GLASGOW & RICHMOND, LKS & VIC, SCT & AUS **[35467]** : ALIAS PSEUDO PRE 1800 UK **[34746]** : PRE 1800 PA, USA **[34895]** : 1718 + PELHAM, MA, USA **[35616]** : 1848 + RANDOLPH CO., IL, USA **[36538]** : 1850 + NY, USA **[36538]** : CLAIRBORNE 1850 BENTON CO., MO, USA **[37501]** : WILLIAM 1860-1880 EATONVILLE, IL, USA **[37501]** : 1865-1875 KEWEENAW CO., MI, USA **[38010]** : 1850-90 FAYETTE, IA, USA **[38054]** : 1753-1775 AUGUSTA CO., VA, USA **[38144]** : C1780-1880 TN, USA **[38242]** : 1700 + GREENE CO., VA, USA **[38765]**

CRAWFORD-LINDSAY 1690-1860 IRL **[38054]**

CRAWLEY 1830 + SCONE, NSW, AUS **[34421]** : 1800S LEFROY, TAS, AUS **[35116]** : 1865 + LIVERPOOL, LAN, ENG **[34566]** : 1800 + TODDINGTON & HENLOW, BDF, ENG **[36797]** : 1850 + MDX, ENG **[37868]** : PRE 1846 DROGHEDA, LOU, IRL **[34566]** : PRE 1920 COR, IRL **[34844]** : PRE 1853 CARRICKFERGUS, ANT, IRL **[35820]** : 1850 + BRIDGETON, LKS, SCT **[34559]** : ALL USA **[38735]**

CRAWSHAW PRE 1832 MANCHESTER, LAN, ENG **[33813]**

CRAY ALL OH & IN, USA **[35321]** : ALL NC, IL & PA, USA **[35321]**

CRAYE 1855-1870 KEWEENAW CO., MI, USA **[38010]**

CRAYFORD PRE 1650 UK **[34746]**

CRAYMER ALL UK & AUS **[37717]**

CRAYS ALL MERCER & LAWRENCE, PA, USA **[35321]** : ALL ONSLOW, NC, USA **[35321]** : ALL TRUMBULL, OH, USA **[35321]** : ALL WOOD, OH, USA **[35321]** : ALL AUGUSTA, GA, USA **[35321]** : ALL TRUMBULL, OH, USA **[35321]** : ALL VERMILLION, IL, USA **[35321]** : ALL DE KALB, IN, USA **[35321]**

CRAYTHORNE PRE 1850 WHARMINGTON & CREIGHTON, NTH, ENG **[36082]**

CREAGER ALL MORGAN & RENMARK, SA, NSW & HRG, AUS & BRD **[35383]**

CREAKE ALL NFK, ENG **[37973]**

CREAM JOHN 1798 EDINBURGH, MLN, SCT **[34539]**

CREAMER PRE 1850 NRW, BRD **[38616]** : PRE 1874 NFK, ENG **[34603]** : C1750-1800 PA, USA **[37790]**

CREAR C1750-1900 THURSO, CAI & OKI, SCT **[37987]**

CREARY 1800S NOTTINGHAM, NTT, ENG **[36842]**

CREASEY 1800 + IPSWICH, SFK, ENG **[35342]**

CREASSER 1790 + YKS, ENG **[37443]**

CREASY C1870 CROYDON, SRY, ENG **[35418]**

CREBBIN 1930S TEA GARDENS, NSW, AUS **[38582]**

CREBER 1760S STOKE DAMEREL, DEV, ENG **[34296]** : 1800-1850 PLYMPTON, DEV, ENG **[34337]** : 1800-1870 PLYMOUTH, DEV, ENG **[37845]**

CREECH 1790 + USA & UK **[36357]**

CREED PRE 1820 SSX, ENG **[35546]** : PRE 1800 KEN & SSX, ENG **[36272]** : PRE 1855 TEMPLEMORE & LONDONDERRY, DRY, IRL **[34593]** : PRE 1855 LIM, IRL **[35206]** : ALL WORLDWIDE **[37084]**

CREEDAN PRE 1910 HOPKINTON, MA, USA **[38537]**

CREEDY ALL INAGH, CLA, IRL & AUS **[34588]**

CREEGAN MRS CRELLIE 1870-1915 DORMAN PARK, E GRINSTEAD, SSX, ENG **[35124]** : 1860 POCKLINGTON, WRY, ENG **[37694]** : 1921 GOLDERS GREEN, LND, ENG **[37694]** : C1833 RELAGH & CORNULLA, LET, IRL **[35900]** : C1860-1960 WREYS BUSH, NZ **[35900]**

CREEK C1860 KYNETON, VIC, AUS **[35203]** : 1800-1860 GREAT BADDOW, ESS, ENG **[35203]**

CREER PRE 1860 WESTMINSTER, MDX, ENG **[37729]** : 1790 + DOUGLAS, IOM **[36967]**

CREESE PRE 1865 WOR, ENG **[35841]**

CREGHAN 1860 LISNAWESNAGH, FER, IRL **[35085]**

CREIGHTON 1800 + KINGSTON & ADDINGTON CO., ONT, CAN **[34486]** : 1800 + BRANT, ONT, CAN **[35627]** : 1800-1850 LND, ENG **[36304]** : CHARLES PRE 1880 ULDALE, CUL, ENG **[38567]** : THOMAS C1843 + ULDALE, CUL, ENG **[38567]** : CHARLES C1805 GOSFORTH, CUL, ENG **[38567]** : WILLIAM PRE 1887 HARRAS DYKE & GOSFORTH, CUL, ENG **[38567]** : 1800 + NBL & DUR, ENG **[38754]** : 1840 LDY, IRL **[34565]** : CHARLES 1786 + DON, IRL **[38567]** : 1700 + SCT **[35627]** : PRE 1750 WORLDWIDE **[38345]**

CRELLIN 1870 + FITZROY, VIC, AUS **[35455]**

CREMER PRE 1850 NRW, BRD **[38616]** : ALL WELLS & NORWICH, NFK, ENG **[35989]**

CREPIN ALL ENG **[37652]**

CRERAR 1800 + INVER, SCT **[34149]**

CRESDEE PRE 1910 SOUTHERN PARK, HAM, ENG **[36265]**

CRESPIN 1750 LONDON, ENG **[34149]**

CRESSEY 1700-1800 HEMINGBOROUGH, YKS, ENG **[37011]**

CRESSWELL 1850 + VIC, AUS **[37923]** : ALL ASHTON, LAN, ENG **[34778]** : C1800 NOTTINGHAM, NTT, ENG **[35595]** : PRE 1810 COPFORD, ESS, ENG **[36388]** : 1800-1900 ELMSTONE HARDICK, GLS, ENG **[37278]** : 1700 + WOR, ENG **[37923]** : PRE 1725 HEF, ENG **[37923]** : 1849 LONGTON, STS, ENG **[37952]** : 1800 + ST HELENS, LAN, ENG **[38011]** : 1800 + STOCKPORT, CHS, ENG **[38011]** : PRE 1850 WOLVERHAMPTON, STS, ENG **[38420]** : PRE 1860 PORT LOUIS, MAURITIUS **[34958]**

CRESWELL PRE 1810 WILKES CO., GA, USA **[38126]**

CRESWICK 1840 + GLEBE, NSW, AUS **[34788]** : 1700 + ASHMANSWORTH, HAM, ENG **[34788]**

CRETELLI 1880 + ONT, CAN **[36679]** : PRE 1880 CATANZARO, ITL **[36679]**

CREUGER ALL ECHUCA & SWANHILL, VIC, SA & HBG, AUS & BRD **[35383]**

CREVESON 1800S OH & IN, USA **[37028]**

CREVISTON 1750 + BEDFORD, PA, USA **[38587]**

CREW ABRAHAM 1850-1860S NETHERTON & DUDLEY, STS, ENG **[34764]** : 1700S GREAT COXWELL, BRK, ENG **[38206]** : PRE 1800 BANDON, COR, IRL **[36652]**

CREWDSON PRE 1880 TORVER, LAN, ENG **[34958]**

CREWE 1860 + BRISBANE & MARYBOROUGH, QLD, AUS **[34588]** : 1858 IPSWICH, QLD, AUS **[38592]** : PRE 1860 LIVERPOOL, LAN, ENG **[34588]** : 1750 + CHS, ENG **[36242]** : C1820 NEWCASTLE UNDER LYME, STS, ENG **[37846]** : C1850 WREXHAM, WLS **[34015]**

CREWS PRE 1742 STOKE CLIMSLAND, CON, ENG **[37610]** : 1700-1800 STOKE CLIMSLAND, CON, ENG **[38516]**

CREY 1830-1850S LEX, IRL **[34027]**

CRIBB 1812 + NSW, AUS **[34534]** : PRE 1800 POOLE & WAREHAM, DOR, ENG **[36401]** : 1800 + GRAYS, ESS, ENG & AUS **[35712]**

CRIBBES PRE 1850 GORDON, BEW, SCT **[35823]**

CRIBBIN PRE 1820 ENG **[38258]**
CRIBBINS PRE 1850 RAMSGATE, KEN, ENG **[35211]**
CRICHTON GEORGE C1890 WALHALLA, VIC, AUS **[34266]** : ALL BOTHERWELL, LKS, SCT **[34266]** : THOMAS C1800 BOTHWELL, LKS, SCT **[34266]** : THOMAS 1750+ BLAIRGOWRIE & ALYTH, PER, SCT **[34486]** : ALL DUNDEE, ANS, SCT **[36999]**
CRICK 1855+ HADDON, VIC, AUS **[35487]** : 1800+ CAROLTON CUM WILLINGHAM, CAM, ENG **[35487]** : ALL ENG **[35933]** : C1858 CLINTON CO., OH, USA **[38367]** : C1850 WASHINGTON CO., PA, USA **[38367]**
CRICKENBERGER ALL USA **[36545]**
CRICKMORE 1700S FRESSINGFIELD, SFK, ENG **[37250]**
CRIDDLE 1700 WIVELISCOMBE, SOM, ENG **[34204]** : 1740-1870 TAUNTON, SOM, ENG **[38028]**
CRIDER PRE 1820 PENDLETON DISTRICT, SC, USA **[37029]**
CRIDGE PRE 1852 SOM, ENG **[37144]**
CRIDLAND C1820 SHOREDITCH, LND, ENG **[35259]** : PRE 1830 BRADFORD ABBAS, DOR, ENG **[36424]**
CRIEDLAND C1820 SHOREDITCH, LND, ENG **[35259]**
CRIEF 1700+ ALT WIED, GER **[34130]**
CRIGER 1805-1845 ERIE CO., NY, USA **[38139]**
CRIGHTON 1820+ CAPETOWN, RSA **[38377]**
CRILLY 1840-1900 SCT **[37870]**
CRIMSTON 1850+ SYDNEY, NSW, AUS **[35358]**
CRINGAL ALL WORLDWIDE **[37193]**
CRINGHALL ALL WORLDWIDE **[37193]**
CRINGLE ALL WORLDWIDE **[37193]**
CRIPPS 1835-1991 HOBART, TAS, AUS **[36280]** : 1888+ MELBOURNE, VIC, AUS **[36280]** : C1847 KINTBURY, BRK, ENG **[35391]** : 1750+ ST JAMES, HANOVER SQ., LND, ENG **[36123]** : 1828-1851 BRIGHTON, SSX, ENG **[36280]** : 1837 LONDON, MDX, ENG **[36280]** : 1851-1900+ WORTHING, SSX, ENG **[36280]** : 1865+ CHADDLEWORTH, BRK, ENG **[36975]** : C1855-1890 ROOT, NY, USA **[36280]** : C1850-1913 SCHENECTADY, NY, USA **[36280]**
CRISBY C1750 GOSPORT, HAM, ENG **[34456]**
CRISFIELD 1852+ CHILTERN, VIC, AUS **[35731]**
CRISFORD 1700S EWHURST, SSX, ENG **[35501]** : PRE 1800 SSX, ENG **[37741]**
CRISP 1740-1860 LOWESTOFT, SFK, ENG **[34440]** : 1800+ SOHAM, CAM, ENG **[36257]** : PRE 1850 MANNINGTREE & MISTLEY, ESS, ENG **[36409]** : PRE 1865 DOWNHAM MARKET & BURNHAM, NFK, ENG **[36425]** : PRE 1900 ILMINSTER & KINGSTONE, SOM, ENG **[36529]** : PRE 1914 AMPTHILL, BDF, ENG **[36980]** : 1820+ LICHFIELD, STS, ENG **[36980]** : 1700-1820 NOTTINGHAM, NTT, ENG **[37058]** : 1750-1950 LONDON & MDX, ENG **[37344]** : 1750+ NFK & CAM, ENG **[37347]** : PRE 1850 BRADFORD ON AVON, WIL, ENG **[37695]** : ALL NFK, ENG **[37973]**
CRISPIN 1860+ GRAFTON, NSW, AUS **[38597]** : PRE 1834 EXETER, DEV, ENG **[38597]**
CRISPY ALL CLONAKILTY, COR, IRL **[36076]**
CRIST 1790+ BOTETOURT CO., VA & OH, USA **[36540]**
CRISTALL ALL DUNDEE, ANS, SCT **[37619]**
CRISTWELL 1800S OH, USA **[36709]**
CRISWELL 1850+ WARRICK CO., IN, USA **[38234]**
CRITCHLEY 1830+ MAITLAND, NSW, AUS **[34596]** : PRE 1831 MAITLAND, NSW, AUS **[36632]** : PRE 1858 BOLTON, LAN, ENG **[36522]** : PRE 1858 LIVERPOOL, LAN, ENG **[36522]** : 1815+ TARBOCK, LAN, ENG **[37560]**
CRITCHLOW PRE 1830 BAKEWELL, DBY, ENG **[35047]**

CRITTALL 1800+ IGHTHAM, KEN, ENG **[37181]**
CRITTELL ALL WORLDWIDE **[34313]**
CRITTENDEN 1855+ PETERSHAM, NSW, AUS **[35567]** : 1750+ VT, USA **[34485]** : ALL WORLDWIDE **[36222]**
CROAD PRE 1871 PRESTON, DOR, ENG **[37876]**
CROAKE 1870-1900 TORONTO, ONT, CAN **[37808]** : PRE 1900 KIK, IRL **[37808]**
CROARKIN C1800 DUNRAYMON, MOG, IRL **[34356]** : C1800 BALLYBAY, MOG, IRL **[34356]**
CROASDALE 1750-1800 WALTON LE DALE, LAN, ENG **[37613]** : ALL WORLDWIDE **[34053]**
CROCE 1800+ PORT SAID, EGYPT **[34271]**
CROCHET 1750+ KINFAUNS, PER, SCT **[35644]**
CROCKER PRE 1890 LATROBE, TAS, AUS **[33878]** : 1890+ PERTH, WA, AUS **[36825]** : 1800 ST JOHNS, NFD, CAN **[38193]** : 1700-1800 SHEBBEAR, DEV, ENG **[34469]** : 1860-1880 STEPNEY & BROMLEY, LND, ENG **[34469]** : C1805 REVELSTOKE, DEV, ENG **[36803]** : 1800-1850 YETMINSTER, DOR, ENG **[37021]** : 1814 BOYTON, CON, ENG **[37080]** : ALL LOOE, CON, ENG **[37224]** : 1860+ BRISTOL, SOM, ENG **[37622]** : PRE 1788 EXFORD, SOM & DEV, ENG **[37622]** : 1800 NEW LEBANON, NY, USA **[38047]** : 1500+ BUTLER CO., PA, MA & CT, USA & ENG **[36970]**
CROCKETT 1800+ MDX, ENG **[36978]** : 1779+ KNOX CO., ME, USA **[37802]** : 1800+ PONTYPOOL, MON, WLS **[37597]**
CROCKFORD C1760-1887+ SYDNEY, NSW, AUS **[37556]** : C1760-1887+ CUTCOMBE & WHEDDON CROSS, SOM, ENG **[37556]**
CROCKTON PRE 1851 LONDON, MDX, ENG **[35471]**
CROCOMBE PRE 1866 TAVISTOCK, DEV, ENG **[35132]**
CROFFORD PRE 1700 ENG **[34746]**
CROFS SARAH 1855+ SYDNEY, NSW, AUS **[35567]**
CROFT 1870+ NEW ENGLAND, NSW, AUS **[36295]** : PRE 1860 ADELAIDE, SA, AUS **[36858]** : 1850+ MARYS COVE, LAB, CAN **[34349]** : JOHN 1808-1811 (49TH REGT) MONTREAL, QUE, CAN **[35527]** : 1808+ MONTREAL, QUE, CAN **[35527]** : THOMAS 1834-1850 DEV, ENG **[34349]** : 1800-1850 POPLAR, MDX, ENG **[35422]** : ALL LEI & NTH, ENG **[36006]** : PRE 1800 ASHBY PUERORUM, LIN, ENG **[36168]** : 1775+ BISHOPTHORPE, YKS, ENG **[37443]** : 1800+ LOUTH, LIN, ENG **[37487]** : 1650-1850 ENG **[37515]** : 1810-1900S WOODPLUMPTON & FYLDE, LAN, ENG **[37710]** : PRE 1922 BAWTRY & CONISBROUGH, YKS, ENG & NZ **[33959]** : 1860+ CANTERBURY, NZ **[36858]** : 1920+ PEMBROKE, VA, USA **[34498]**
CROFTON 1860-1900 KIMBLESWORTH, DUR, ENG **[36217]** : PRE 1792 ST DAVIDS, PEM, WLS **[37146]**
CROFTS ALFRED 1800 LAUNCESTON, TAS, AUS **[35049]** : C1862 WANDILIGONG, VIC, AUS **[37302]** : PRE 1850 NEWBOLD ON AVON, WAR, ENG **[36380]** : C1846 LIVERPOOL, LAN, ENG **[37302]** : 1750-1860 BROUGHTON, FLN, WLS **[38028]**
CROFUT 1650-1850 USA **[34746]**
CROKE 1840S CAMDEN, NSW, AUS **[34044]** : 1870+ COR, IRL **[35358]**
CROKEN ALL PEI, CAN **[34356]**
CROKER 1800-1840 UGBOROUGH, DEV, ENG **[35861]** : 1840+ BRISTOL, SOM, ENG **[37622]**
CROLE 1794 ISLINGTON, MDX, ENG **[37080]**
CROLL PRE 1844 GLASGOW, LKS, SCT **[37238]**
CROLLY PRE 1830 DUB, IRL **[34421]**
CROM 1831-1880 WOOD CO., OH, USA **[38092]** : 1800-1831 HARRISON, OH, USA **[38092]** : 1700-1806 LANCASTER & CHESTER CO., PA, USA **[38092]**

CROMACK PRE 1863 MANCHESTER & SALFORD, LAN, ENG [33771]
CROMARTIE 1700+ OKI, SCT [33903]
CROMB 1700-1800S COLLACE, PER, SCT [36837]
CROMBIE 1700-1920 KEMNAY & INVERURIE, ABD, SCT [35981] : ALL DUMFRIES, DFS, SCT [37176] : PRE 1800 ST ANDREWS, FIF, SCT [37179]
CROME PRE 1903 LONDON, ENG [36249] : PRE 1850 ST FAITHS, NFK, ENG [37737] : ALL WORLDWIDE [38612]
CROMER 1600-1800 MAURSMUNSTER, ALS & LOR, FRA [36328] : JOHN 1820+ FULTON CO., NY, USA [36950] : 1800-1920 LA & TX, USA [38746]
CROMERTIE PRE 1700 WALLS, OKI, SCT [36883]
CROMIE 1800+ ONT, CAN & IRL [34500] : PRE 1900 DOW, IRL [37807]
CROMMELIN ALL CH [36197] : ALL ENG [36197]
CROMPTON 1849-65 ST ARNAUD, VIC, AUS [35259] : 1870+ ROCKHAMPTON, QLD, AUS [35259] : C1800 SOWERBY, WRY, ENG [33796] : C1850 HOLLINWOOD, LAN, ENG [34734] : PRE 1830 PRESTON, LAN, ENG [35259] : 1780+ BRADFORD & HUNSWORTH, WRY, ENG [36263] : EMMA 1835-1886 PANCRAS, MDX & LND, ENG [36443] : PRE 1880 BOLTON, LAN, ENG [36508] : 1810+ BOLTON, LAN, ENG [37175]
CROMWELL THOMAS 1830-1860 ST SYLVESTER, QUE, CAN [34200] : PRE 1700 STANTON ST BERNARD, WIL, ENG [36158] : THOMAS 1820-1840 DUB, IRL [34200] : 1850-1900 BALTIMORE, MD, USA [38770]
CRONAN 1868 MITCHAM, VIC, AUS [34761] : PRE 1850 QUEANBEYAN, NSW, AUS [37901]
CRONE C1800 MONKWEARMOUTH, DUR, ENG [37859]
CRONIMUS 1600+ OFFWILLER, ELO, GER [37012]
CRONIN PRE 1850 QUEANBEYAN, NSW, AUS [37901] : 1800-1900 RATHMORE, KER, IRL [35308] : C1848 RATHMORE, KER, IRL [35920] : 1780+ KILLARNEY, KER, IRL [36343] : PRE 1845 IRL [36358]
CRONJE 1790-1900 BAARN, UTR, NL [34069]
CRONK ALL ENG [34938]
CRONKHITE PRE 1800 NY, USA [34130]
CRONKWRITE 1800+ HULL, QUE, CAN [34130]
CRONSHAW 1800-1880 BLACKBURN, LAN, ENG [37547]
CROOK 1860+ ECHUCA, VIC, AUS [35387] : 1750-1830 ALVERSTOKE, HAM, ENG [33787] : 1800S GLS, ENG [34000] : 1805 DEV, ENG [35272] : PRE 1770 URCHFONT, WIL, ENG [35387] : PRE 1875 ASHFORD, KEN, ENG [35970] : PRE 1812 TURTON, LAN, ENG [36742] : PRE 1860 CRAWSHAWBOOTH, LAN, ENG [37414] : 1807 YORK, YKS, ENG [37859] : 1775-1850 GREENE CO., VA & TN, USA [37539]
CROOKENDEN ALL ADELAIDE, SA, AUS [37998] : ALL LONDON, ENG [37998]
CROOKER 1630-1990 MA, USA [34377]
CROOKES 1774+ ARKSEY, WRY, ENG [38469]
CROOKS 1872+ VIC, AUS [34412] : PRE 1780 NEWCASTLE, NBL, ENG [35973] : 1700-1800 ECCLESTON, CHS, ENG [38074] : PRE 1800 MOUNTSORREL, LEI & NTH, ENG [38512] : PRE 1800 NELSON CO., KY, USA [38135] : 1828-1923 WAYNE CO., KY & OR, USA [38741]
CROOM 1850+ BRIDPORT, DOR, ENG [37902] : PRE 1872 MANCHESTER, LAN, ENG [38288] : PRE 1700 BRIDPORT, DOR, ENG [38745]
CROOMS PRE 1850 SOM, ENG [36364]
CROPLEY 1860 GLEBE, NSW, AUS [35141] : PRE 1870 BRUNSWICK, VIC, AUS [35796] : CLARKE 1850S+

DERRIMUT, VIC, AUS [35876] : 1820+ ELY, CAM, ENG [35141] : PRE 1900 HOLBORN, LND, ENG [37617]
CROPP 1882+ SOUTH MELBOURNE, VIC, AUS [34798]
CROPPER C1850 NEWCHURCH, LAN, ENG [36649]
CROSAR ALL SCT [37354]
CROSBEY C1850 MDX, ENG [35033]
CROSBIE 1800S NORHAM, NBL, ENG [38414] : 1800S OLD MELROSE, ROX, SCT [38414] : PRE 1900 CLK, TAS & VIC, SCT & AUS [34301]
CROSBY 1900+ VANCOUVER, BC, CAN [35341] : 1888+ RUNCORN, CHS, ENG [35341] : 1600+ CLIBURN, WES, ENG [36256] : PRE 1835 WICKLOW, WIC, IRL [35578] : 1750-1860 GAL, IRL [36440]
CROSER ALL YKS, ENG & AUS [34705] : ALL SCT [37354]
CROSIER ALL WORLDWIDE [36573]
CROSLEY 1796 THORNTON, YKS, ENG [34793]
CROSS 1901 SCOTTS DISCOVERY EXPEDITION, ANTARCTICA [37952] : 1813+ HUNTER VY, NSW, AUS [33939] : 1850+ SYDNEY, NSW, AUS [35073] : ALL BOOLBURRA, QLD, AUS [35452] : 1894+ TEMORA, NSW, AUS [35536] : C1850 DINGO CREEK, NSW, AUS [35826] : ROBERT 1814-1864 SYDNEY & MAITLAND, NSW, AUS [37556] : 1852+ AMHERST, VIC, AUS [37999] : 1849-1852 SA, AUS [37999] : 1800-1850 SUTTON, QUE, CAN [36738] : ALBERT 1900-1917 ENG &, CAN & FRA [35362] : PRE 1813 SPROATLEY, YKS, ENG [33939] : 1830+ STANFORD, NOR, ENG [34374] : 1881 ELY, CAM, ENG [34540] : 1700-1711 BOW BRICKHILL, BKM, ENG [34552] : PRE 1750 EASTHAMPSTEAD & WARFIELD, BRK, ENG [34588] : PRE 1883 WINKFIELD & BRAY, BRK, ENG [34588] : JESSE 1780-1860 ENG [34722] : WILLIAM WELLS 1800+ ENG [35362] : 1790S BABCARY, SOM, ENG [35780] : C1836 WINCANTON, SOM, ENG [35826] : 1750+ BREEDON ON THE HILL, LEI, ENG [35851] : 1700+ BRIDLINGTON, YKS, ENG [35892] : 1820+ ROTHERHITHE, SRY, ENG [35914] : PRE 1862 UPPER NORWOOD, SRY, ENG [36035] : ALL LEI, ENG [36179] : 1800+ ICKFORD, BKM, ENG [36239] : PRE 1780 KILMINGTON, SOM & WIL, ENG [36478] : PRE 1762 BILLINGE, LAN, ENG [36742] : C1700 HALBERTON, DEV, ENG [37264] : 1800+ LONDON &, DEV, ENG [37294] : 1850+ CHS, ENG [37482] : ROBERT C1786-1814 HUMBLETON & HULL, ERY, ENG [37556] : JOHN C1770 SOUTH HANNINGFIELD, ESS, ENG [37664] : ALL ESS, SFK & KEN, ENG [37664] : C1800 LITTLE CLACTON, ESS, ENG [37952] : 1820+ WIL, ENG [37999] : C1871 BURTON ON TRENT, HEF & HRT, ENG [38450] : 1700-1900 GREAT HOLLAND, ESS, ENG [38579] : 1883+ WELLINGTON, NZ [34588] : PRE 1870 LKS, SCT [35830] : 1735+ MANSFIELD, CT, USA [36582] : 1823-50 ONEIDA CO., NY, USA [36582] : 1870-1900 FRANKLIN CO., VT, USA [36738] : ALL MI & NY, USA [37787] : 1634-1700 CA & PA, USA [38203] : PRE 1850 GA, USA [38536] : ALL WORLDWIDE [35518]
CROSSAN ALL AUGHNISH, DON, IRL [35833]
CROSSAR PRE 1840 LKS & MLN, SCT [37354] : PRE 1840 SCT [37354] : ALL SCT [37354]
CROSSE ALL ESS, ENG [37664]
CROSSER PRE 1840 LKS & MLN, SCT [37354] : ALL SCT [37354] : PRE 1840 SCT [37354]
CROSSET 1850+ VIC, AUS [34186]
CROSSFIELD PRE 1820 SOWERBY, LAN & WRY, ENG [34382]

CROSSLAND 1700-1900 ENG [37228] : 1780-1850 PORTSEA, HAM, ENG [37228]

CROSSLANDS 1890-1940 WYKE, WRY, ENG [36624]

CROSSLEY PRE 1860 BIRMINGHAM, WAR, ENG [35095] : 1800-1850 TODMORDEN, LAN, ENG [38370] : C1750 BUCKS CO., PA, USA [36572]

CROSSMAN 1860+ NSW, AUS [37176] : C1850 PRINCES, PEI, CAN [35646] : ALL ST JOHNS, NFD, CAN [37386] : PRE 1850 WALTON, SOM, ENG [36676] : 1800S DEV, ENG [36679] : ALL BUCKFASTLEIGH, DEV, ENG [37386] : ALL SOM, ENG [37386]

CROSSON 1850-1910 VINE PRAIRIE, CRAWFORD CO., AR, USA [38737]

CROSSWELL 1812+ TAS, AUS [34283] : PRE 1820 SOM, ENG [33869] : 1790+ SOM, ENG [34283] : ALL ENG [36289] : ALL HAM, ENG [36289]

CROSTON ALL WORLDWIDE [34703] : ALL WORLDWIDE [34907]

CROTAZ 1700S ST BATHELEMY, VD, CH [34518]

CROTHERS 1600+ ANNAHILT, DOW, IRL [33851] : 1790 CABRAGH, DOW, IRL [35085] : PRE 1839 POYNTYPASSE, ARM, IRL [37915]

CROTOSHINSKY ALL WORLDWIDE [37239]

CROTTENDEN ALL WORLDWIDE [36222]

CROTTY 1860-1900 NSW, AUS [36780] : PRE 1841 TIP, IRL [34804] : 1700-1850 CLA, IRL [36780] : 1850-1880 USA [36780]

CROUCH HARRIET 1886+ SYDNEY, NSW, AUS [34302] : ALL WOKURNA, SA, AUS [35012] : HARRIET PRE 1886 ST HELIER, JSY, CHI & UK [34302] : JAMES RICHARD PRE 1886 ST HELIER, JSY, CHI & UK [34302] : JOHN & MARY C1847 BDF, ENG [35164] : 1800+ RAMSAY, HUN, ENG [35396] : 1800+ WHITTLESEA, CAM, ENG [35396] : 1823-1880 SOUTHWARK, LND, ENG [36117] : 1800+ WEYMOUTH, DOR & LND, ENG [36868] : C1790 BILLINGSGATE, LND, ENG [37670] : 1688+ CT, USA [37592] : JONATHAN 1850-1870 SANGAMON, IL, USA [38157] : 1837-1960 WARREN, TN, USA [38588]

CROUCHER JOSEPH C1857 GOULBURN, NSW, AUS [36638] : ALL NFD, CAN [34207] : 1800+ HALIFAX, NS, CAN [34207] : PRE 1800 ENG [34207] : PRE 1800 KEN, ENG [34252] : PRE 1842 ALTON, HAM, ENG [34911] : 1870S PANCRAS, LND, ENG [35188] : 1764-1850 DORKING, SRY, ENG [36071] : PRE 1850 BINSTED, HAM, ENG [37743] : 1840-1920 RICHMOND, WAIMEA, NZ [38458] : 1840-1900 RIWAKA, NELSON, NZ [38458] : 1840-1900 WELLINGTON, NZ [38458] : 1840-1900 OAMARU, TARANAKI, NZ [38458]

CROUCHLEY PRE 1900 CHS, ENG [37098]

CROUCHMAN 1800-1900 HARLOW, ESS, ENG [37657] : 1890-1920 ENFIELD, MDX, ENG [37657] : 1800-1900 CITY OF LONDON, ENG [37657]

CROUDACE 1700-1800 NEWCASTLE, NBL, ENG [35094]

CROUGH 1840+ GEELONG, VIC, AUS [34456]

CROUTCH 1700-1850 ROTHERFIELD, SSX, ENG [37365]

CROW 1853+ BALLARAT, VIC, AUS [33774] : 1855+ HOBART, TAS, AUS [34670] : 1800S BIRMINGHAM, WAR, ENG [34931] : PRE 1840 HUNSDON, HRT, ENG [35098] : PRE 1830 MILDENHALL & LAKENHEATH, SFK, ENG [36179] : PRE 1850 BALDERTON, NTT, ENG [36411] : 1830+ REDDITCH, WOR, ENG [37230] : THOMAS 1785 COR, IRL [37614] : ALL LISBURN, ANT, IRL [37621] : 1782-1820 EYEMOUTH, BEW, SCT [35341] : PRE 1870 PAISLEY, RFW, SCT [36793]

: CARL DAVID PRE 1885 GRANDVIEW, IA, USA [36672]

CROWDEN 1850+ DELORAINE, TAS, AUS [34186] : 1850S CLERKENWELL, MDX, ENG [34187]

CROWDER 1800S CORNWALL, ONT, CAN [34150] : 1800S STORMONT, ONT, CAN [34150] : C1880 LIVERPOOL, LAN, ENG [38437] : WILLIAM 1818-1826 KY, USA [38145] : REBECCA 1826-1845 MACOUPIN CO., IL, USA [38145] : REBECCA 1818-1826 KY, USA [38145] : APELLONAR PRE 1876 WORLDWIDE [37235]

CROWE 1800-1850 ADAMINABY, NSW, AUS [34307] : C1920S DUNKELD, VIC, AUS [35233] : 1800S FRONTENAC, ONT, CAN [34353] : C1800+ LIVERPOOL, LAN, ENG [34451] : 1650-1863 POLESWORTH, WAR, ENG [34649] : 1880+ DEBENHAM, SFK, ENG [34710] : PRE 1830 CASTLE FENNELL, DON, IRL [35719] : PRE 1830 FER, IRL [35719] : PRE 1820 DERRIAGHY, ANT, IRL [37927] : ALL LIM, LDY & TIP, IRL [38176] : 1800-1850 MACOSQUIN, LDY & PA, IRL & USA [34244] : 1800+ SCHOHARIE CO., NY, USA [38176]

CROWELL PRE 1800 MA, USA & ENG [38745]

CROWFOOT 1840+ HUNTER REGION, NSW, AUS [36632] : PRE 1725 SFK, ENG [35642] : PRE 1800 WORLDWIDE [34746]

CROWFORD PRE 1800 WORLDWIDE [34746]

CROWFORTHE PRE 1650 UK [34746]

CROWHURST ALL SSX, ENG [37236] : C1735 MEOPHAM, KEN, ENG [37536] : 1800S CUXTON, KEN, ENG [37773] : 1750-1900 IGHTHAM & BRENCHLEY, KEN, ENG [38354]

CROWLE 1800-1860 TRURO, CON, ENG [36439]

CROWLEY 1880+ KALGOORLIE, WA, AUS [34023] : 1875+ ROCKHAMPTON, QLD, AUS [34270] : 1800+ WEST BROMWICH, STS, ENG [35235] : 1880+ HUNSLET, YKS, ENG [35235] : C1856 BRISTOL, ENG [35249] : C1820 WEST BROMWICH, STS, ENG [37827] : PRE 1900 DUNMANWAY, COR, IRL [34023] : PRE 1875 KER, IRL [34270] : PRE 1849 CORK CITY, COR, IRL [35258] : C1830 CLONAKILTY, COR, IRL [36076] : 1800-50 BANDON & CORK, COR, IRL [36652] : 1750-1850 CASTLEISLAND, KER, IRL [36776] : C1830 GARRAN, KIK, IRL [37106]

CROWNA 1862 BELFAST, ANT, IRL [34761]

CROWSTON 1800+ SCAMBLESBY, LIN, ENG [37487]

CROWTHER 1800+ SAL & STS, ENG [35019] : PRE 1810 HALIFAX, YKS, ENG [35225] : C1892 LIVERPOOL, LAN, ENG [37865] : PRE 1848 BRADFORD, WRY, ENG [37948]

CROWTHERS 1790 CABRAGH, DOW, IRL [35085]

CROYDEN ALL ENG [35246]

CROZIER ALL BATHURST, NSW, AUS [38730] : 1875+ CANTERBURY, NZ [38286] : ALL WORLDWIDE [36573]

CRUBB 1800S KEN, ENG [35377]

CRUDDAS C1847 DURHAM, DUR, ENG [36102]

CRUDEN PRE 1900 DUNDEE, ANS, SCT [38412]

CRUICKSHANK ALL PORTSMOUTH, HAM, ENG [36409] : PRE 1885 CHRISTCHURCH, CANTY, NZ & SCT [35953] : C1750 ABD, SCT [33914] : 1780+ TARVES & OLD MACHAR, ABD, SCT [34326] : 1800S GAMRIE, BAN, SCT [34336] : 1760-1840 ABD, SCT [34615] : C1740-1860 CUMMINSTOWN, ABD, SCT [34771] : 1740-1840 MONQUHITTER, ABD, SCT [34771] : 1880-1936 ROTHIEMAY, BAN, SCT [34771] : 1700-1990 TURRIFF, ABD, SCT [34771] : ALL KNOCKANDOO & ELGIN, MOR, SCT [35460] : C1813 KEITH, BAN, SCT [35585] : 1760-1840 ROTHES, MOR, SCT [37767]

CRUICKSHANKS 1890+ NEWTOWN, NSW, AUS [38582]

CRUIKBOOM MARIE ALL NEUFCHATEAU, LBG, BEL [34924]

CRUIKSHANK 1800+ KIRKMAIDEN, WIG, SCT [34602]

CRUIKSHANKS PRE 1850 BRECHIN, ANS, SCT [36705]

CRUISE 1850-1890 O'BRIENS BRIDGE, CLA, IRL [38007]

CRUM PRE 1860 DURHAM, ONT, CAN [35601] : PRE 1861 MON, WLS [35895]

CRUMB 1800-1900 MD, USA [34749] : ALL WORLDWIDE [34471]

CRUMP 1850+ MELBOURNE, VIC, AUS [37920] : 1700+ KINGSTONE & WELLINGTON, GLS, ENG [34747] : PRE 1880 DEV, ENG [34847] : 1840+ PENRITH, CUL, ENG [36620] : 1800 HESKET IN THE FOREST, CUL, ENG [36620] : 1806 HUTTON IN THE FOREST, CUL, ENG [36620] : 1800S CREDITON, DEV, ENG [36762] : PRE 1820 DUDLEY, WOR, ENG [38755] : PRE 1820 KER, IRL [36325]

CRUMPLER ALL LYTCHETT MATRAVERS, DOR, ENG & USA [35723]

CRUMPTON ALL HARTLEPOOL, DUR, ENG [34619]

CRUNDELL ALL YALDING, KEN, ENG [37627]

CRUNDEN ALL WORLDWIDE [36222]

CRUNDWELL PRE 1849 LONDON, ENG [35770]

CRUSE JAMES PRE 1850 MELBOURNE, VIC, AUS [34879] : 1700+ ASHBURTON, DEV, ENG [38398] : 1700-1800 STOKE CLIMSLAND, CON, ENG [38516]

CRUTCHLEY 1732+ STOWE BY CHARTLEY & KINGSTON, STS, ENG [37762]

CRUTTENDEN 1700-1900 HOLLINGTON, SSX, ENG [34975] : PRE 1725 BECKLEY & UDIMORE, SSX, ENG [36272] : WILLIAM 1770S+ KEN & SSX, ENG [36298] : 1750-1900 SALEHURST & BEXHILL, SSX, ENG [37207] : PRE 1782 ETCHINGHAM, SSX, ENG [37541] : ALL WORLDWIDE [36222] : ALL WORLDWIDE [36298]

CRUWYS 1755+ EXETER, DEV, ENG [35972] : PRE 1870 KNOWSTONE, DEV & SOM, ENG [37322]

CRUX PRE 1850 BENDIGO, VIC & CON, AUS & ENG [37995] : 1800S BETHUNE & KEARNEY, ONT, CAN [36727]

CRYBBACE 1800-1830S EDINBURGH, MLN, SCT [34875]

CRYDERMAN 1800-1900 ONT, CAN [34135]

CRYER C1847 SPRATTON, NTH, ENG [34586] : 1870-1890 ROCHDALE, LAN, ENG [35955]

CSEPE ALL CABANY, HAVES, HU [36695]

CSIBI ALL WORLDWIDE [37453]

CSIKI ALL WORLDWIDE [37453]

CUBBAGE 1700+ KINGSFEY, BKM, ENG [34640]

CUBBIN PRE 1740 ARBORY, IOM, UK [35866]

CUBBITT PRE 1870 IRL [35192]

CUBBON (SEE CUBBIN) [35866]

CUBIS 1855+ SYDNEY, NSW, AUS [35160] : PRE 1855 HEF, ENG [35160]

CUBITT C1835+ GREAT YARMOUTH, NFK, ENG [35725] : 1750-1800 NFK, ENG [37246]

CUCKOW 1850+ HOO, KEN, ENG [37328] : 1700+ GILLINGHAM, KEN, ENG [37328]

CUDBETH PRISCILLA 1754-1849 STANFORD, DUTCHESS CO., NY, USA [38031]

CUDDIHY 1860S CLONMEL, TIP, IRL [35560]

CUDLIPP ALL WORLDWIDE [37091]

CUDMORE PRE 1820 KINGS NYMPTON, DEV, ENG [37104]

CUERDALE PRE 1772 BURNLEY & BLACKBURN, LAN, ENG [37002]

CUEREL ALL WORLDWIDE [34678]

CUFF PRE 1900 LONDON, ENG [34825] : ALL ENG & IRL [33921]

CUFFE PRE 1850 ROS, IRL [37893]

CUILLERIER 1600-1700 CLERMONT CREANS, PIC, FRA [34514]

CULBERT 1890+ CAN [38072] : C1840 DUNGANNON, TYR, IRL [34661] : 1700-1860 LETTERKENNY, DON, IRL [37118]

CULBERTSON 1790+ LANCASTER CO., PA, USA [37564]

CULBREATH 1700+ IRL [33826]

CULEY (SEE CULY) [38280]

CULL 1840+ KENOSHA CO., WI, USA [36962] : 1800-1850 CENTRE, PA, USA [38529]

CULLAR C1800-1900 PA, USA [35305]

CULLEN 1839 KINGS PLAINS, NSW, AUS [34038] : 1850+ COLO & HOWES VALLEY, NSW, AUS [35159] : PRE 1830 SYDNEY, NSW, AUS [35159] : 1822+ PICTON, NSW, AUS [35203] : 1860+ KYNETON, VIC, AUS [35203] : 1840+ MAITLAND & BURRAWANG, NSW, AUS [35511] : 1850+ BALLARAT, VIC, AUS [35986] : C1840+ JAMBEROO, NSW, AUS & IRL [36313] : 1860+ NTT, ENG [34614] : PRE 1850 KEN, ENG [35949] : PRE 1850 KEN, ENG [36584] : 1700-1900 HUISH EPISCOPI, SOM, ENG [36776] : PRE 1822 KILLINKERE, CAV, IRL [35203] : C1840 ENNISCORTHY, WEX, IRL [35203] : 1780+ EDARNEY, FER, IRL [35511] : 1600-1900 GAL, IRL [35944] : PRE 1860 ABBEYLEIX, LEX, IRL [37521] : PRE 1850 ROS, IRL [38365] : MAURICE 1800-1854 LIM, IRL & AUS [35093] : PRE 1800+ BRACKLIN, FER, IRL & AUS [36313] : ALL MON & NOBLE CO., OH, USA & IRL [38287]

CULLEY 1818+ AYLESBURY, BKM, ENG [34237] : ALL BINGHAM, NTT, ENG [35177] : PRE 1840 BRK, ENG [35902] : 1800S MDX & SRY, ENG [37868]

CULLIFORD 1600-1750 SOM, ENG [36170]

CULLIN ALL NFD & NS, CAN [38391] : PRE 1850 KEN, ENG [36584]

CULLINAN PRE 1910 FOOTSCRAY, VIC, AUS [35796] : 1800S INAGH, CLA, IRL [35398] : C1865 COR & LIM, IRL [35848] : 1800-1868 KNOCKAVILLA, COR, IRL [37156] : 1800+ GALWAY, GAL, IRL & NZ [36257]

CULLING PRE 1850 KEN, ENG [36584] : 1830+ KEINTON & MANDEVILLE, SOM, ENG [36761]

CULLIVER PRE 1770 WEST COKER, SOM, ENG [38483]

CULLODEN 1815 BELLARY, MADRAS, INDIA [36862]

CULLUM 1600-1700 KENTON, SFK, ENG [36213] : C1740-1760S BRAMPTON, SFK, ENG [37191] : 1800+ LONDON, LND & SSX, ENG [38288]

CULLY C1700 ALTON PRIORS, WIL, ENG [37918]

CULMBACH ALL GNOIEN, MEK, DDR [34812]

CULP 1786+ CAN [38448] : 1870+ SCIOTO & CHAMPAIGN CO., OH, USA [37565] : PRE 1870 GREENUP CO., KY, USA [37565] : PRE 1810 PA, USA [38448]

CULPEPER 1730 CHOWAN, NC, USA [38198]

CULPEPPER 1740 NORFOLK, VA, USA [38198]

CULVER 1616+ USA [37592]

CULVERHOUSE ALL FROME, SOM, ENG [36393]

CULVERSON 1799 DEPTFORD, SRY, ENG [34309]

CULVERWELL 1892 DEPTFORD, LND, ENG [37418]

CULY ALL WORLDWIDE [38280]

CUMBEN 1700-1890 PORTLAND, DOR, ENG [36988]

CUMBS 1770+ HILLINGTON, MDX, ENG [36326]

CUMING 1912+ PERTH, WA, AUS [34435] : 1845
TRURO, CON, ENG [34435]
CUMMARD 1870+ LIVERPOOL, LAN, ENG [37669]
CUMMIN 1721+ ALLOA, CLK, SCT [36635] : ALL
SCT & USA [36348]
CUMMING 1870+ DAVIS CK, NSW, AUS [34843] :
PRE 1800 TORQUAY, DEV, ENG [34576] : 1840-90
LIVERPOOL, LAN, ENG [36508] : 1860+ GREAT
BEDWYN, WIL, ENG [36637] : 1850+ BALHAM,
SRY, ENG [36637] : 1870+ HALLIFORD, SRY,
ENG [36637] : PRE 1900 SOUTHWARK, LND, ENG
[38581] : PRE 1780 EAST KILBRIDE, DNB, SCT
[34127] : 1780+ ROSENEATH, DNB, SCT [34550] :
1850 INV, SCT [34843] : 1800 URQUHART, INV,
SCT [34843] : 1650+ ABBEY & KILBARCHAN,
RFW, SCT [35395] : 1700+ SHI, SCT [36857] : 1800+
ABD, SCT [37443] : ALEXANDER 1690+ SLUIE,
MOR, SCT [37794] : JAMES 1720+ SLUIE, MOR,
SCT [37794] : ALEXANDER PRE 1700 SLUIE, MOR,
SCT [37794] : JAMES 1720+ SLUIE, MOR, SCT
[37794]
CUMMINGS 1830+ SYDNEY, NSW, AUS [34977] :
1800-1900 QLD, AUS [38070] : JOHN 1785-1862
COLCHESTER CO., NS, CAN [38421] : ALL BOW,
MDX, ENG [34938] : PRE 1829 DEVON, DEV, ENG
[36679] : 1700+ AIRTH, STI, SCT [34977] : C1862
LKS, SCT [36877] : PRE 1840 ISLE SKYE, INV, SCT
[36882] : ALL AYR, SCT [37805] : 1800S GREENE,
CHENANGO CO., NY, USA [36319] : 1793
ALLEGANY CO., MD, USA [36446] : 1869-1939 ST
CLAIR, OXFORD, MI, USA [36910] : 1775-1820
FREDERICK CO., MD, USA [36953] : 1820-1900
HARRISON CO., OH, USA [36953] : LENORA ALL
WI, USA [38124]
CUMMINS 1857+ SYDNEY, NSW, AUS [38208] :
WILLIAM PRE 1852 LIVERPOOL &
MANCHESTER, LAN, ENG [34701] : PRE 1820
HAM, ENG [35902] : 1840S LND, ENG [37692] : PRE
1710 LUEBECK, LUE, GER [38632] : 1800+ ABBEY,
CLA, IRL [33898] : 1750-1820 DONAGHEADY, TYR,
IRL [34074] : 1845 MALLOW, COR, IRL [35332] :
1750-1850 BALLYWACKAN, CLA, IRL [36240] :
JOHN 1800 BALLYVAUGHAN, CLA, IRL [36274] :
PRE 1856 BELFAST, IRL [38208] : 1800+ MO, USA
[37030] : 1880+ PLATTE CO., NE, USA [38323] :
1850+ LLANELLI, CMN, WLS [35566]
CUMPSTON 1790-1850 SOUTHAMPTON, HAM, ENG
[37129]
CUMSTIE 1800-1900 ARL & LKS, SCT [35044]
CUMYN ALL SCT & USA [36348]
CUNCLIFFE 1650-1700 BLACKBURN, LAN, ENG
[37166]
CUNDA 1855-1870 KEWEENAW CO., MI, USA [38010]
CUNDIFF PRE 1800 ENG [38196]
CUNDIT PRE 1802 MELTON MOWBRAY, LEI, ENG
[35572]
CUNDY 1835+ LAUNCESTON, TAS, AUS [35865] :
1844+ ADELAIDE, SA, AUS [37913] : ALL CON,
ENG & AUS [34929] : ALL SWANSEA, GLA, WLS
[36501]
CUNION 1800S MIDDLESBROUGH, ERY, ENG
[36636] : 1830S BURTON CONSTABLE, NRY, ENG
[36636] : 1800+ GUISBRO, NRY, ENG [36636]
CUNNABEL 1750-1850 HALIFAX & WINDSOR, NS,
CAN [36763] : 1675-1750 BOSTON, MA, USA [36763]
CUNNEEN 1900+ CARLTON, VIC, AUS [34702]
CUNNING PRE 1700 NORTH HILL, CON, ENG
[35973] : PRE 1805 NJ & OH, USA & IRL [35270]
CUNNINGHAM 1880+ TEROWIE, SA, AUS [33935] :
1919 CROOKWELL, NSW, AUS [34421] : 1875+
DERBY, TAS, AUS [35116] : EDWARD 1818+
SOUTHERN DISTS., TAS, AUS [35816] : 1800-1830

HOBART, TAS, AUS [37150] : 1800+
GUYSBOROUGH, NS, CAN [35627] : JOE PRE 1827
DARTFORD, ONT, CAN [36677] : PRE 1860
MANCHESTER, LAN, ENG [33835] : PRE 1850
COLCHESTER, ESS, ENG [36154] : PRE 1850
PRINCETOWN, DEV, ENG [36800] : ALL
PORTSMOUTH, HAM, ENG [36846] : ALL
PRINCETON, DEV, ENG [36846] : ALL LONDON,
ENG [36846] : 1880-88 HASTINGS, SSX, ENG [37380]
: PRE 1786 GORING, SSX, ENG [37380] : 1807-80
PORTSEA, HAM, ENG [37380] : 1888-1938
TUNBRIDGE WELLS, KEN, ENG [37380] : 1850-
1875 CASTLEISLAND, KER, IRL [33962] : PRE 1855
RATHCAHILL, LIM, IRL [34039] : PRE 1840 DRY,
IRL [34809] : PRE 1795 ARM, IRL [34993] : C1800
CLA, IRL [35203] : PRE 1829+ DOW, IRL [35453] :
1840+ DRY, IRL [35712] : EDWARD PRE 1818
KILROSS, TYR, IRL [35816] : SAMUEL C1830 ANT,
IRL [35894] : JAMES 1849-1914 ANT, IRL [35894] :
ALL BALLYSHANNON, DON, IRL [36774] : JOHN
1745 IRL [37514] : 1870-1890 BUTTEVANT, COR,
IRL [38188] : 1840+ MEA, IRL [38539] : PRE 1850
KILLYBEGS, DON, IRL [38597] : 1750+ ST
ANDREWS, FIF, SCT [33800] : PRE 1856
MAYBOLE, AYR, SCT [33845] : PRE 1850 BEITH,
AYR, SCT [33905] : 1820-1860 KILPATRICK, DNB,
SCT [34751] : 1795+ GALSTON, AYR, SCT [34993] :
1800S CROMARTY, ROC, SCT [35116] : PRE 1859+
RENFREW, RFW, SCT [35453] : PRE 1880 FORTH,
LKS, SCT [35457] : 1750-1800 CORSTORPHIN,
MLN, SCT [35582] : PRE 1750 ANSTRUTHER, FIF,
SCT [35745] : C1750-1830 DOONHOLM, AYR, SCT
[35883] : 1820-1850 WEMYSS, FIF, SCT [36268] :
1780-1830 MENSTRIE, CLK, SCT [36392] : 1810-1840
INVERKEILLOR, ANS, SCT [36392] : 1800+
CARLUKE, LKS, SCT [36692] : ALL LEITH, MLN,
SCT [36774] : PRE 1817 SCT [37130] : PRE 1780
WHITBURN, WLN, SCT [37374] : PRE 1864
EDINBURGH, MLN, SCT [37852] : ELIZABETH
PRE 1862 EDINBURGH, MLN, SCT [38597] : PRE
1760 GLASGOW, LKS, SCT [38597] : SOPHIA 1823-
1898 RUSH CO., IN, USA [37014] : JOHN 1765 NY,
USA [37514] : JOHN 1782 NEWBURGH, NY, USA
[37514] : JOHN 1820 ONONDAGA CO., NY, USA
[37514] : 1800-40 BLAIRSVILLE INDIANA, PA, USA
[38087] : 1800+ MUSKINGUM CO., OH, USA
[38330] : 1835+ MIAMI CO., IN, USA [38330]
CUNNINGTON 1828+ CHESTERTON, HUN, ENG
[35112] : 1850-1910 BRENTFORD, MDX, ENG
[37657] : 1700+ KINGSCLIFFE, NTH & LND, ENG
[37735]
CUNY PRE 1818 REMERVILLE, LOR, FRA [34159]
CUPER C1780 ESS, ENG [36010]
CUPPAGE 1800S TOMAREY HILL, ARM, IRL [37977]
CUPPLEDITCH ALL WORLDWIDE [36762]
CURCHAIN ALL BDF, ENG [34416]
CURCHIN ALL BDF, ENG [34416]
CURD PRE 1900 CAMBERWELL, LND, ENG [36067] :
1871+ MEDWAY, KEN, ENG [37051]
CURDT C1850+ GREY & WATERLOO, ONT, CAN
[36714] : PRE 1829+ FRITZLAR & WALDECK,
WAL, GER [36714]
CURE 1800S STEEPLE, DOR, ENG [35723]
CURL 1800S LONG SUTTON, SOM, ENG [35464] :
1800+ CURRY RIVEL, SOM, ENG [35734]
CURLE PRE 1850 EDINBURGH, ELN, SCT [34611] :
PRE 1800 SCT [36538]
CURLEY 1850+ HOBART, TAS, AUS [34853] : PRE
1880 ATHLONE, WEX, IRL [34287] : THOMAS PRE
1841 GAL, IRL [35042]
CURLING 1850+ TORONTO, ONT, CAN [37761] :
1700-1850 KEN, ENG [37064] : 1700-1800 KEN, ENG

[37761] : 1800-1900 MILTON BY GRAVESEND, KEN, ENG [37761]

CURNICK 1795+ BATTERSEA, LND, ENG [33774]

CURNOCK PRE 1815 BRENTFORD, MDX, ENG [34959]

CURNOW 1600-1750 ST IVES, CON, ENG [34214] : 1650-1720 GWENNAP, CON, ENG [34793] : PRE 1840 CON, ENG [35709] : ALL WORLDWIDE [36339]

CURR C1813 HAVERSHAM, BKM, ENG [35104]

CURRALL PRE 1760 BKM, ENG [37498]

CURRAN PRE 1850 SYDNEY, NSW, AUS [34287] : 1848-1887 BOMBALA, NSW, AUS [34966] : 1860S PORT GAWLER & ADELAIDE, SA, AUS [37981] : 1870+ AMHERST ISLAND, ONT, CAN [37035] : C1800+ DUBLIN, IRL [33792] : PRE 1860 BAILIEBOROUGH, CAV, IRL [34039] : PRE 1940 DUBLIN, IRL [34547] : 1857+ BANBRIDGE, DOW, IRL [34808] : C1788 KER, IRL [35336] : PRE 1864 KILMACKMORE, ROS, IRL [35392] : 1860S DON, IRL [35415] : 1825 WIC, IRL [35837] : FRANCIS 1820-1840 ARM, IRL [36634] : PRE 1870 BALLYHALBERT, DOW, IRL [37035] : JOHN C1830 CONWAL, DON, IRL [37143] : 1700+ TIP & LEX, IRL [37826] : 1700+ DON, IRL [37826] : JAMES PRE 1750 NEWMARKET, COR, IRL [38174] : 1824+ CAPE TOWN, CAPE, RSA [34947] : ALL RSA & IRL [34945] : 1864+ GLASGOW, SCT [34808] : MARY 1900+ MALDEN, MA, USA [36563]

CURREN C1800+ DUBLIN, IRL [33792] : PRE 1860 SLI, IRL [38365]

CURRENT ALL HOUGHTON REGIS, BDF, ENG [34838]

CURRER MOLLY C1760-1784 BURGHFIELD, BRK, ENG [36068] : 1753-1778 SELKIRK, SEL, SCT [38117]

CURREY 1850+ NEWCASTLE, NSW, AUS [35598] : 1848+ BATHURST, NSW, AUS [38596]

CURRIE 1800+ AUS [33769] : 1880+ COLLINGWOOD, VIC, AUS [35059] : 1860S LAUNCESTON, TAS, AUS [35116] : HUGH PRE 1910 ONT, CAN [36725] : 1780+ SHEET HARBOUR, NS, CAN [37821] : 1800+ ST JOHN, NB & NS, CAN [38225] : JOHN J. 1926+ CAN & USA [36725] : 1850+ NOTTINGHAM, NTT, ENG [36105] : PRE 1848 WIC, IRL [34412] : 1830+ BELTURBET, FER, IRL [35372] : 1800+ BALLYMENA, ANT, IRL [35489] : PRE 1860 STONEHOUSE, LKS, SCT [34598] : PRE 1848 LEITH, MLN, SCT [35185] : 1700+ DFS, SCT [35293] : 1855+ SALINE, FIF, SCT [35372] : 1845+ LEITH & EDINBURGH, MLN, SCT [35486] : C1837 HAWICK, ROX, SCT [35486] : 1856 CAMBUSNETHAN, LKS, SCT [35761] : PRE 1849 GLASGOW, LKS, SCT [35761] : 1780+ EDINBURGH, MLN, SCT [35921] : 1600-1900 EDINBURGH, MLN, SCT [35944] : ALL SCT [36105] : PRE 1800 ANNAN, DFS, SCT [36209] : PRE 1850 PER, SCT [36361] : 1750+ DUNLOP, AYR, SCT [36802] : 1750-1825 COLONSAY, ARL, SCT [37460] : PRE 1833 GALSTON, AYR, SCT [37575] : PRE 1770 FORDYCE, BAN, SCT [37835] : REV J. 1800+ PORTOBELLO, MLN, SCT [38492] : 1853-1930 DUMFRIES, DFS, SCT & AUS [35469] : PRE 1865 FAIRIBAULT CO., MN, USA [36356] : ARCHIE 1910+ PHILADELPHIA, PA, USA [36725] : ARCHIE 1910+ PITTSBURGH, PA, USA [36725]

CURRIN 1700+ NTH, ENG [33973] : 1700+ ENG [36470]

CURROR 1790-1870 LARGO, FIF, SCT [38511]

CURRY 1840+ REGENTVILLE, NSW, AUS [36273] : 1800-1900 SINGLETON, NSW, AUS [36293] : 1900+ CROYDON, NSW, AUS [37136] : 1848+ BATHURST, NSW, AUS [38596] : 1750-1850 SHOREDITCH & ST GILES, LND, ENG [35576] :

MICHAEL C1725 YKS, ENG [35996] : 1500S+ YORK CITY, YKS, ENG [35996] : ALL KNARESBOROUGH, WRY, ENG [35996] : WILLIAM C1800 NORTH SHIELDS, NBL, ENG [36585] : PRE 1880 WINGATE, DUR, ENG [37136] : C1800 KNARESBOROUGH, YKS, ENG [37148] : PRE 1815 BAKEWELL, DBY, ENG [38596] : PRE 1840 TYR, IRL [34463] : 1850 ARM, IRL [34666] : PRE 1840 OMAGH, TYR, IRL [36273] : 1870 AKAROA, CANTY, NZ [34666] : 1725-1800 KENT CO., DE, USA [36953] : 1650+ SALEM, NJ & DE, USA [37826] : 1800+ NEATH, GLA, WLS [36209]

CURSON 1856-1951 ADELAIDE, SA, AUS [33950] : 1700+ DEPTFORD, MDX, ENG [33950] : PRE 1850 MID, NFK, ENG [37718]

CURT C1850+ GREY & WATERLOO, ONT, CAN [36714] : PRE 1829+ FRITZLAR & WALDECK, WAL, GER [36714]

CURTAIN 1856+ BENDIGO, VIC, AUS [35332] : P.J. PRE 1840 LIM, IRL [34161]

CURTAYNE P.J. PRE 1840 LIM, IRL [34161]

CURTICE ALL SSX, ENG [37922]

CURTIN C1840 CARCOAR, NSW, AUS [35217] : DAVID DONALD C1857 BOTHWELL & ELDERSLIE, TAS, AUS [35217] : 1750-1810 TOURMAFULLA, LIM, IRL [34071] : P.J. PRE 1840 LIM, IRL [34161] : 1800-1850 COR, IRL [34307] : PRE 1830+ CORK CITY, COR, IRL [34423] : DAVID PRE 1841 GLOUNAKEEL & MEELIN, COR, IRL [35217] : PRE 1856 MOY, CLA, IRL [35332] : 1830 MIDDLETON, COR, IRL [36907]

CURTIS 1841+ SUNBURY, VIC, AUS [35399] : MARGARET 1873 RICHMOND, MELBOURNE, VIC, AUS [35593] : GEORGE 1869+ RICHMOND, MELBOURNE, VIC, AUS [35593] : 1835+ LAUNCESTON, TAS, AUS [35865] : 1800-1820 ONT, CAN [36334] : PRE 1800 SRY & KEN, ENG [34383] : PRE 1800 BRISTOL, ENG [34428] : 1700-1850 TROWBRIDGE, WIL, ENG [34975] : C1880 LONDON, ENG [35014] : PRE 1700 MARSH GIBBON, BKM, ENG [35030] : PRE 1685 WESTERN, SSX, ENG [35216] : 1800S DEV, ENG [35377] : 1700-1800 CON, ENG [35424] : RICHARD G. 1800S LND, ENG [35593] : C1790 MILTON ABBOT, DEV, ENG [35938] : ALL BEEDON, BRK, ENG [36144] : ALL MILDENHALL, SFK, ENG [36179] : 1770S-1884 ST SAMPSON & FLUSHING, CON, ENG [36190] : 1850+ HELPSTON, NTH, ENG [36421] : 1850S NOTTINGHAM, NTT, ENG [36506] : 1700-1950 NORTON & SANDHURST, GLS, ENG [36556] : 1680+ TADLEY, HAM, ENG [36981] : PRE 1850 LND & SRY, ENG [37091] : 1830 CHRISTCHURCH, HAM, ENG [37173] : 1800-1860 MARYLEBONE, LND, ENG [37253] : 1800S NFK, ENG [37922] : PRE 1876 TEWKESBURY, GLS, ENG [38275] : 1811 BEDFIELD, SFK, ENG [38282] : 1800+ STROUD, GLS, ENG [38324] : 1800-1875 YEOVIL, SOM, ENG [38421] : PRE 1841 OFF, IRL [35399] : ALL WESTPORT, NZ [38275] : 1635-1740 WETHERSFIELD & FARMINGTON, CT, USA [33905] : JOSHUA 1797 NC, USA [35286] : NANCY 1813 POSEY CO., IN, USA [35286] : 1600-1670 SOMERSET CO., MD, USA [36566] : 1823-1896 WI & CT, USA [37577] : 1790 STRATFORD, NH, USA [38131]

CURTISS 1860+ ST KILDA, VIC, AUS [38008]

CURWEN C1700 WORKINGTON, CUL, ENG [35573] : C1802 BARTON PRESTON, LAN, ENG [35573]

CURWOOD 1850 RICHMOND, SRY, ENG [34890]

CURZON 1700S CRICH, DBY, ENG [36018] : PRE 1810 CROYDON & MITCHAM, SRY, ENG [37913]

CUSACK C1900 NORTH SYDNEY, NSW, AUS [36490]

CUSH 1800+ GUM FLAT, NSW, AUS [35101]
CUSHEN PRE 1820 LIM, IRL [35830]
CUSHIN 1850 CLONMEL, TIP, IRL [33783]
CUSHING 1800+ NORWICH, NFK, ENG [36815]
CUSHMAN 1820S DUXBURY, MA, USA [38223]
CUSHWAY 1750 BETHNAL GREEN, MDX, ENG [34204]
CUSICK PRE 1880 IRL [36542]
CUSS PRE 1900 ASHTON KEYNES, WIL & GLS, ENG [37387] : 1900+ ASHTON KEYNES, WIL & GLS, ENG [37387]
CUSTERSON PRE 1800 CROYDON, CAM, ENG [36489] : 1828+ KINGSTON, CAM, ENG [36489] : PRE 1800 GAMLINGAY, CAM, ENG [36489] : 1870+ COMBERTON, CAM, ENG [36489]
CUSTIS 1700+ VA, USA [35739]
CUSTUS 1860-1870 KEWEENAW CO., MI, USA [38010]
CUSWORTH PRE 1880 SHEFFIELD, WRY, ENG [36403] : PRE 1825 ROTHERHAM, WRY, ENG [36403]
CUTBUSH C1821-1840S BREDE, SSX, ENG [33950]
CUTCLIFFE PRE 1850 DEV, ENG [34741]
CUTHBERT 1833-1900 FRANKLIN & HOBART, TAS, AUS [38761] : PRE 1880 HINDERWELL, YKS, ENG [37094] : PRE 1813 HACKNEY, LND, ENG [37703] : ALL SFK, ENG [37728] : PRE 1950 BAN, SCT [37835]
CUTHBERTON 1800-1880 GALSTON, AYR, SCT [37446]
CUTHBERTSON C1800 LONDON, ENG [34291] : 1750-1870 PETTIGO, FER, IRL [35918] : 1830 PAISLEY, RFW, SCT [33848] : 1852+ PENICUIK, MLN, SCT [34122] : PRE 1821 EDINBURGH, MLN, SCT [34281]
CUTHILL 1800-1896 STOW, PEE, SCT [33991]
CUTLER 1833+ NSW, AUS [38485] : 1750+ ONT, CAN [38241] : PRE 1833 LONDON, ENG [38485] : 1860+ CA, USA [36962]
CUTMORE 1750-1850 BASSINGBOURNE, CAM, ENG [37118]
CUTRER LEWIS 1799 SC, USA [37801] : EDWARD 1845 WASHINGTON, LA, USA [37801] : ISAAC C1814 MS, USA [37801] : JOSEPH C1805 SC, USA [37801]
CUTRONE PRE 1920 MARTONE, CALABRIA, ITL [36271]
CUTTANCE ALL CON, ENG & NZ [34603]
CUTTEN JAMES 1755+ ENG [34314] : ALL WORLDWIDE [34314]
CUTTING PRE 1851 MENDLESHAM, SFK, ENG [37700] : 1860-1880S CAPE TOWN, CAPE, RSA & AUS [37559] : ALL WORLDWIDE [37127]
CUTTLE ALL WORLDWIDE [35596]
CUTTS 1868+ REDCLIFFE, QLD, AUS [36284]
CUVELIER C1820 JANDRAIN JANDRENOILLE, BBT, BEL [38160]
CUZNER ALL WORLDWIDE [37695]
CYMUTKOWKI 1732-1874 DREISSIGHUFEN & DOEHLAU, OPR, GER [34083]
CZAJKOWSKI 1400-1990 LOMZA BIALYSTOK, POL [38232]
CZUBOKA 1800+ RADYMNO, GALICIA, POL [36686]
DABAKAUSEN ALL WORLDWIDE [38670]
DABBS 1750-1800 CITY OF LONDON, ENG [38516]
DABELL 1700-1900 NTT, ENG [36242]
DABERKAUSEN ALL WORLDWIDE [38670]
DABILL PRE 1650 NTT, ENG [37829]
DABINETT 1843+ ATHERSTONE, SOM, ENG [34856]
DABNEY PRE 1720 VA, USA [38311]
DABURGER ALL RIEDERING & ROSENHEIM, BAV, BRD [38567]

DACARE ALL LEICESTER, ENG [34838]
DACEY 1850+ SUSQUEHANNA CO., PA & NY, USA [35299]
DACH 1700+ WALDLAUBERSHEIM, RPR, GER [37042]
DACK PRE 1800 NFK, ENG [38288]
DACKOMBE PRE 1850 LND, ENG [37832]
DA COSTA C1680-1800 LONDON, ENG [36630]
DA COSTA-BAROA 1800-1900 SANTE MARIA, AZORES [34378]
DACRE ALL WORLDWIDE [36136]
D'ACRE 1800S DUBLIN, IRL [35738]
DACRES ALL WORLDWIDE [36136]
DADD ALL KEN, ENG [33925]
DADDOW 1700-1800 ST AGNES, CON, ENG [34697]
DADE 1840+ SFK, ENG [37341]
DADSON 1880+ LAUNCESTON, TAS, AUS [34770] : ALL TORONTO, ONT, MAN & BC, CAN [34348] : 1800+ CRANBROOK, KEN, ENG [34348] : PRE 1828 EAST MALLING, KEN, ENG [35016]
DADSWELL ALL NFK, ENG [37409] : 1300-1400+ SSX, ENG [37648]
DAELEMANS ALL WORLDWIDE [38169]
DAELMAN 1600-1990 HALST, OVL, BEL [38165]
DAELMANS (SEE DAELEM [38169]
DAEMMER ALL WAL & WEF, GER [34861]
DAFF PRE 1800 WAKEFIELD & ROTHWELL, WRY, ENG [38540]
DAFT 1830 ATHERSTONE, WAR, ENG [37546]
DAGG PRE 1880 TIP & OFF, IRL [36886]
DAGGETT 1750-1790 BOLTON, LEBANON, COVENTRY, CT, USA [37808]
DAGLASS C1836 NORWICH, NFK, ENG [35133]
DAGLISH 1880S CHIRTON, NBL, ENG [36867]
DAGNALL C1850 WARRINGTON, LAN, ENG [36092]
DAGNEAUX 1760-1844 AMSTERDAM, NOH, NL [38691] : 1760-1844 AMSTERDAM, NOH, NL [38711]
DAGWORTHY 1794-1850S BRIDFORD, DEV, ENG [38079]
DAHIA C1825 SCT [37513]
DAHL PRE 1856 KALLUNBORG, DEN [34633] : WUBKE M. 1770-1900 GER [38781]
DAHLHAEUSER 1880+ OH & PA, USA [38728]
DAHLIN PRE 1900 VARMLAND, SWE [35270] : PRE 1900 WOODBURY CO., IA, USA [35270]
DAHLSTROM 1600-1739S LARBRO, GOTLAND, SWE [38346]
DAHM 1860-1954 QLD, AUS [37973]
DAHMS PRE 1876 RUDERSDORF, B BURG, GER [35465]
DA HORA ALL WORLDWIDE [37653]
DAILLOTT 1800-1900 DUNLOY, ANT, IRL [36115]
DAILLY HELEN PRE 1827 EXETER, DEV, ENG [34539]
DAILY 1850+ MARYLEBONE, MDX, ENG [37902] : 1790+ LONDON CO., VA, USA [38064] : 1760+ WASHINGTON CO., MD, USA [38064] : 1840-1900 DUPAGE CO., IL, USA [38133]
DAINES ALL NFK, ENG [37612] : 1800-1900 NFK, ENG [37884]
DAINTY PRE 1840 WELLINGTON, SAL & WOR, ENG [37736]
DAIROLLES PIERRE 1800S FRA [36633] : ADRIENNE 1864 FRA [36633]
DAISH C1700 ALTON PRIORS, WIL, ENG [37918]
DAISLEY 1849+ ONSLOW, QUE, CAN [35615] : MARGARET PRE 1849 SLI, IRL [35615]
DAIX C1867-1990 DEPERE, WI, USA [35002]
DAKE PRE 1875 MEDINA CO., OH, USA [37034]
DAKER ALL WORLDWIDE [36136]
DAKERS 1790-1810 KIRKBY OVERBLOW & STAINBURN, WRY, ENG [37650] : ALL SCT [38100]

: ALL ANS, SCT **[38100]** : ALL WORLDWIDE **[36136]**

DAKIN PRE 1900 LONDON, ENG **[34772]** : 1600-1850 ENG **[36169]** : C1883 STEPNEY, MDX, ENG **[37204]** : PRE 1730 PENISTONE, WRY, ENG **[37754]**

DAKINS PRE 1850 RAD, WLS **[37323]**

DALBY PRE 1800 ESS, ENG **[37668]**

DALCK 1800+ KONITZ, WPR, GER **[34932]**

DALE 1840S+ ORANGE, NSW, AUS **[34937]** : C1850 DALBY, QLD, AUS **[35807]** : 1860+ BOLERO, NSW, AUS **[36648]** : 1860+ NARRANDERA, NSW, AUS **[36648]** : 1860-1900 ARDLETHAN, NSW, AUS **[36648]** : 1850-60 DANDENONG, VIC, AUS **[36648]** : 1850-60 PYALONG, VIC, AUS **[36648]** : 1840-60 GIPPSLAND, VIC, AUS **[36648]** : 1850S MELBOURNE, VIC, AUS **[36648]** : PRE 1820 BRAMHAM, WRY, ENG **[33910]** : EMILY 1860S LOUGHTON, STS, ENG **[33949]** : 1800+ LIVERPOOL, LAN, ENG **[34326]** : 1800+ DARTFORD, KEN, ENG **[34670]** : 1810+ WEST HESLERTON, ERY, ENG **[34854]** : PRE 1850S DULVERTON, SOM, ENG **[34937]** : C1826 THRUSSINGTON, LEI, ENG **[35807]** : PRE 1878 LIN, ENG **[35895]** : ALL LEADENHAM, LIN, ENG **[35901]** : PRE 1820 OXF, ENG **[36183]** : 1800+ WISTON & HENFIELD, SSX, ENG **[36219]** : PRE 1850 NEWTON, CHS, ENG **[36385]** : 1886+ LIVERPOOL, LAN, ENG **[37255]** : PRE 1750 ORFORD, SFK, ENG **[37420]** : PRE 1840 SANDBACH, CHS, ENG **[37722]** : 1740-1840 MALPAS, CHS, ENG **[37975]** : PRE 1860 CONGLETON, CHS, ENG **[38289]** : ALL DULVERTON, SOM, ENG & AUS **[35213]** : PRE 1880 BREIM, NORDFJORD, NOR **[37821]** : C1878 TARANAKI, NZ **[35895]** : MARGERY PRE 1820 TIONESTA OR BELDENVILLE, PA & WI, USA **[38394]**

DALEMANS (SEE DAELEM [38169]

DALES PRE 1857 LIN, ENG **[35895]** : 1800-1900 SAINTFIELD, DOW, IRL **[36884]**

DALETHORPE 1775+ NEWARK ON TRENT, NTT, ENG **[35194]**

DALEY 1843+ MUSWELLBROOK, NSW, AUS **[34942]** : 1817+ LAUNCESTON, TAS, AUS **[35185]** : PRE 1800+ PARRAMATTA, NSW, AUS **[35237]** : 1900+ MACKAY, QLD, AUS **[35241]** : 1840+ COWRA & FORBES, NSW, AUS **[35241]** : 1828+ SYDNEY, NSW, AUS **[35510]** : 1850+ MARYLEBONE, MDX, ENG **[37902]** : PRE 1860 BANTRY, COR, IRL **[33905]** : PRE 1850 ST LAWRENCE PARISH, LIM, IRL **[35440]** : 1800S DRUMKILROOSK & KILLASHANDRA, CAV, IRL **[38490]**

DALEY (SEE DEELY) [34424]

DALGARNO 1750+ ABD, SCT **[35060]**

DALGLEISH 1800+ LESMAHAGOW, LKS, SCT **[33948]** : 1853-1890 KKD & AYR, SCT **[33971]** : PRE 1810 SELKIRK, SEL, SCT **[35430]**

DALGLIESH PRE 1923 GLASGOW, LKS & STI, SCT **[34706]** : ALL WORLDWIDE **[35832]**

DALGLISH C1860+ CARLTON & MELBOURNE, VIC, AUS **[37447]** : C1770-1850 ANNAN & DORNOCK, DFS, SCT **[37447]** : C1770-1850 LANGHOLM, DFS, SCT **[37447]** : C1837+ GORBALS, LKS, SCT **[37447]** : 1750+ CAMPSIE, STI, SCT **[38476]**

DALITZ ALL WORLDWIDE **[35519]**

DALKIN PRE 1881 ENG **[37787]** : PRE 1881 SCT **[37787]** : ALL WORLDWIDE **[37787]**

DALL 1750+ FALKLAND & BURNT ISLAND, FIF, SCT **[34473]**

DALLAS C1852 SYDNEY, NSW, AUS **[37919]** : C1865 MERRIWA, NSW, AUS **[37919]** : C1830+ EDINBURGH, MLN, SCT **[35995]**

DALLEY C1750 DOLBY, LEI, ENG **[34400]** : ALL GREAT MALVERN, WOR, ENG **[36031]** : 1770-1820 WESTMINSTER, MDX, ENG **[36031]** : PRE 1820 STRABANE, TYR, IRL **[34804]**

DALLIMORE ALL IOW, GLS & SOM, ENG **[37279]**

DALLOWAY 1800-1900 PRESTON, LAN, ENG **[37850]**

DALLY 1910+ SA, AUS **[37149]** : FREDERICK 1890+ WA, AUS **[37149]** : THOMAS 1910+ THE ROCK, NSW, AUS **[37149]** : 1800+ SHEPTON BEAUCHAMP, SOM, ENG **[36195]** : 1840+ SITHNEY, CON, ENG **[37149]** : 1700+ WENDRON, SITHNEY, CON, ENG **[37149]** : BENNETT 1800+ HELSTON DISTRICT, CON, ENG **[37149]**

DALMAYR PRE 1850 AUGSBURG, BAY, BRD **[36963]**

DALRYMPHE 1700+ SCT **[34240]**

DALRYMPLE 1900 MACKAY, QLD, AUS **[35450]** : CHARLOTTE 1905 DUBLIN, IRL **[37518]** : PRE 1825 KIRKINTILLOCK, DNB, SCT **[34127]** : 1670-1822 WIGTON, WIG, SCT **[34649]** : 1800S GLASGOW, LKS, SCT **[35767]** : 1800+ CHAUTAUQUA, NY & IA, USA **[36931]**

DALTON 1800+ NSW, AUS **[34424]** : 1850+ GEELONG, VIC, AUS **[34550]** : PRE 1850 TAS, AUS **[34978]** : 1884+ GUNNEDAH, NSW, AUS **[35254]** : 1870 MELBOURNE, VIC, AUS **[35755]** : 1900+ FITZROY & GEELONG, VIC, AUS **[36268]** : 1803+ PARRAMATTA & PITT TOWN, NSW, AUS **[36600]** : 1824+ GRENVILLE & LEEDS, ONT, CAN **[37467]** : SUSANNA 1760-1860 CROWLAND, LIN, ENG **[33952]** : 1800+ CARLISLE, CUL, ENG **[34550]** : 1800 SOUTHEND, ESS, ENG **[35943]** : PRE 1840 NTH, ENG **[36183]** : PRE 1850 STRATFORD ON AVON, WAR, ENG **[36385]** : PRE 1800 FAWKHAM & HORTON KIRBY, KEN, ENG **[37325]** : PRE 1850 HORNCASTLE, LIN, ENG **[37392]** : PRE 1824 LIN, ENG **[37467]** : REV. PETER 1678-1708 BRAMLEY, HAM, ENG **[38084]** : PRE 1870 GRIMSBY, HULL, ERY, ENG **[38580]** : MARY 1800+ KIK, IRL **[35093]** : PRE 1890 KIK, IRL **[35750]** : 1850 CORK, IRL **[35755]** : (BROTHERS) PRE 1900 TINAHELY, WIC, IRL **[38305]** : C1800-1880 CAPETOWN, RSA & IRL **[36874]** : 1811+ TN, USA **[38058]** : PRE 1900+ BOSTON, MA & LA, USA **[38305]**

DALY 1844+ MELBOURNE, VIC, AUS **[34767]** : C1800 HAMILTON, VIC, AUS **[34767]** : 1887-1914 FOOTSCRAY, VIC, AUS **[34767]** : 1860-1890 BACCHUS MARSH, VIC, AUS **[34767]** : 1848+ YUROKE, VIC, AUS **[34767]** : 1852-88 SYDNEY, NSW, AUS **[35406]** : 1850+ MARYLEBONE, MDX, ENG **[37902]** : PRE 1866 BALLYVAUGHAN, CLA, IRL **[33813]** : 1800+ GAL, IRL **[35201]** : C1810-1855 KER, IRL **[35389]** : PRE 1840 ENNISTYMON, CLA, IRL **[35406]** : PRE 1830 OFF, IRL **[35533]** : 1800+ CLA, IRL **[35847]** : PRE 1900 CLARA, OFF, IRL **[36596]** : PRE 1827+ LET, IRL **[37108]** : WILLIAM 1825-1929 REALLEN KISKEAM, COR, IRL **[37800]** : ALL DRUMKILROOSK, CAV & NSW, IRL & AUS **[35547]** : 1844+ NZ **[34767]** : 1849-1850 WHITBURN, SCT **[37108]** : 1852-1901 HARTHILL, LKS, SCT **[37108]**

DALZELL C1788 KKD, SCT **[36254]**

DALZIEL 1870+ BELFAST, ANT, DOW & ARM, IRL **[35636]** : PRE 1760 WIGTOWN, WIG, SCT **[35242]** : 1850S AYR, SCT **[35970]** : 1800+ DUMFRIES, DFS, SCT **[36085]** : PRE 1813 WIG, SCT **[37890]** : 1800+ NEW CUMNOCK, AYR, SCT **[38726]**

DAM 1766+ SCARBOROUGH, CUMBERLAND, ME, USA **[38571]**

DAMAL ALL BIETINGEN, BAW, FRG **[38657]**

DAMAN JOHN 1700+ LEBANON, CT, USA [38766]
DAMBOURGES J.B. 1700-1780 FRA [37479]
DAMER MARY 1752-1820 KIMPTON, HRT, ENG [35634]
DAMERELL 1775+ DODBROOKE, DEV, ENG [38469]
D'AMICO PRE 1908 CAMPO DI GIOVE, ABR, ITL [37519]
DAMMANN PRE 1828 GROSFIEL, MEK, GER [36726] : 1799+ RIDDERS, SHO, GER [37542]
DAMOUR 1833 QUE, CAN [38583]
DAMUDE 1790-1800S BUCK CO., PA, USA [34059]
DANBY 1500-1600 SWINTON, NRY, ENG [37342] : 1500-1600 CHESTERTON, CAM, ENG [37342]
DANCE PRE 1874 HUNGERFORD, BRK, ENG [35932] : 1750+ CROWLE, WOR, ENG [37462] : 1800+ CANNING TOWN, LND, ENG [37660]
DANCEY ALL GREAT SOMERFORD, WIL, ENG [36424]
DANCKAERT ALL EXKLOO, OVL, BEL [38694]
DANDENO 1850-1900 ONT, CAN [38774] : 1700-1780 QUE, CAN [38774]
DANDIE PRE 1850S FERRY PORT ON CRAIG, FIF, SCT [35544]
DANDRIDGE PRE 1873 DRAYTON, OXF, ENG [35463] : 1700+ VA, USA [35739]
DANE 1700 NUTHURST, SSX, ENG [35288] : PRE 1950 INDIA [34186]
DANECH 1800S TAS, AUS [35137]
DANECKER 1600-1800 WUE, GER [37015]
DANES 1800+ GOSPORT, HAM, ENG [37378] : PRE 1800 DALLINGTON & KINGSTHORPE, NTH, ENG [37650]
DANFORD C1805 OH, USA [37788]
DANFORTH 1800+ YKS, ENG [34762] : C1600 FRAMLINGHAM, SFK, ENG [35857] : PHILIP C1759-1841 NH & ME, USA [35324]
DANGERFIELD 1800+ DEVIZES, WIL, ENG [34119] : 1750+ STROUD, GLS, ENG [34119] : 1850+ LONDON, ENG [34119] : PRE 1820 BIRMINGHAM, WAR & STS, ENG [37331]
D'ANGIBAU ALL ENG [37378]
DANGUELL 1600-1800 FIF, SCT [35627]
DANIEL 1850+ MELBOURNE, VIC, AUS [34683] : 1750+ SANDHURST, GLS, ENG [34160] : C1854 BRISTOL, GLS, ENG [34805] : 1825+ BRISTOL & CLIFTON, GLS, ENG [35172] : ALL HASTINGS, SSX, ENG [36796] : 1800S NORWICH, NFK, ENG [36796] : PRE 1860 HASTINGS, SSX, ENG [36883] : MARY 1788 LONDON, ENG [37106] : PRE 1790 BRISTOL, GLS, ENG [37146] : PRE 1830 STEPNEY, MDX, ENG [37279] : C1800-1870 LAMBETH & SOUTHWARK, SRY, ENG [37279] : JOHN 1750+ BATH, SOM, ENG [38241] : 1840S BIDEFORD, DEV, ENG [38270] : PRE 1650 NFK, ENG [38746] : 1800-1900S NZ [36796] : 1790+ AYR, SCT & AUS [34705] : JAMES PRE 1750 MIDDLESEX, VA, USA [33757] : 1820+ MONROE CO., AL, USA [37792] : 1800-1930 BATH CO., KY, USA [38089] : NICHOLAS PRE 1720 MONSERRAT, W.INDIES [36180] : 1830+ LLANSAMLET, GLA, WLS [37116]
DANIELL 1775+ BIGGLESWADE, BDF, ENG [34416] : 1600-1700 WIL, ENG [36226] : 1820-1850 MONROE CO., MS, USA [38088] : 1870+ LYMAN, NH, USA [38116]
DANIELLS 1790-1840 SIDBURY, DEV, ENG [34834]
DANIELS C1847 WINDSOR, NSW, AUS [34806] : GEORGE H. PRE 1890 GOULBURN, NSW, AUS [34806] : 1849+ DAPTO & BOTANY, NSW, AUS [35574] : ROBT. & SARAH ALL WALCHA, NSW, AUS [35854] : MARY 1804 SYDNEY, NSW, AUS [37106] : 1800+ ILLOGAN, CON, ENG [34666] : PRE

1849 FECKENHAM, WOR, ENG [35574] : 1800-1850 LIVERPOOL, LAN, ENG [36112] : 1800-1920 LEI, ENG [36688] : PRE 1920 STOKES CROFT, AVON, ENG [36996] : 1850+ NFK, ENG [37360] : 1800-1820 NORTH CREAKE, NFK, ENG [37845] : ANN 1765+ SPOFFORTH, WETHERBY, NRY, ENG [37887] : PRE 1834 RODBOROUGH, GLS, ENG [37978] : 1750-1850 COR, IRL [35494] : 1800-1900 NEW YORK CO., NY, USA [38045] : C1870 BENTON CO., IA, USA [38173] : 1800 NC, USA [38197] : 1830S ADDISON CO., VT, USA [38221] : 1800+ WHEELOCK, VT, USA [38520] : C1840 CAE, WLS [35034] : C1800 SWANSEA, GLA, WLS [35131]
DANIELSEN 1800S NOR [38182] : C1885-1953 BRONX CO., NY, USA [38182]
DANIELSON ALL NOR [38470] : 1700+ SHI, SCT [36266]
DANIELSSON OLOF DANIEL PRE 1900 JUNSELE, VASTERNORRLAND, SWE [34481]
DANKS PRE 1850 MADELEY, SAL, ENG [34569]
DANN PRE 1860 HAWTHORN, VIC, AUS [35200] : FRANCIS PRE 1660 BARBADOS [38016] : 1797 SHIPBOURNE, KEN, ENG [34142] : FRANCIS 1660+ STAMFORD, CT, USA [38016]
DANNATT ALL LIN, ENG [34221] : 1800S WALESBY, LIN, ENG [36851]
DANNECKER PRE 1800 LEIDRINGEN, WUE, GER [38667]
DANNEGER 1600-1800 WUE, GER [37015]
DANNEL PRE 1750 WOR, ENG [38745]
DANNER 1800+ WELLAND CO., ONT, CAN [34138] : 1700+ USA [38065]
DANNOR 1756-1792 FREDERICK CO., MD, PA & KY, USA [36901]
DANSON 1850+ NSW, AUS [37113]
DANTHER 1905+ MELBOURNE, VIC, AUS [35479]
DANTSEY ALL DRAYCOT CERNE, WIL, ENG [36424]
DANVERS 1800+ TAS, AUS [36312] : 1800+ NSW & VIC, AUS [36312]
DARABY ALL CAN [34212]
DARBEY 1800+ SEDGLEY, STS, ENG [34092]
DARBON 1800+ LITTLE LINFORD, BKM, ENG [38241]
DARBY PRE 1800 NOR, ENG [34383] : 1780+ SOHO, LND, ENG [34550] : 1700-1800 HELMINGHAM & KENTON, SFK, ENG [36213] : 1620+ ROWLEY REGIS, STS, ENG [36701] : 1789 ROWLEY REGIS, STS, ENG [37369] : 1800+ BRECON, WLS [37827]
DARCH PRE 1880 SOUTHWARK, SRY, ENG [36072]
DARCY C1860 CASTLE FORBES BAY, TAS, AUS [34853] : 1800+ KILMOREY, CLA, IRL [33927] : PRE 1860 LEX, IRL [34853] : C1820-1860 TIP, IRL [35206]
D'ARCY PRE 1860 SYDNEY, NSW, AUS [35929] : PRE 1405 DURHAM, DUR, ENG [34573] : 1800+ CLA, IRL [33927] : 1800S KILLALOE, CLA, IRL [36851] : 1834 LEX, IRL [37984] : PRE 1850 DUB & TIP, IRL [38772] : PRE 1850 MEA, IRL & RSA [38772]
D'ARCY SEARLE PRE 1900 WORLDWIDE [38772]
DARDIS 1800-1875 TN, USA [37593]
DARE JOHN 1859+ MALDON, VIC, AUS [34011] : ALL AUS [35384] : 1892+ CHARLEVILLE & WINDORAH, QLD, AUS [37178] : ROBERT 1782+ STURMINSTER NEWTON, DOR, ENG [34011] : PRE 1880 CLATWORTHY, SOM & DEV, ENG [35384] : 1750-1850 ALBRIGHTON, SAL, ENG [38453]
DARGE 1800S CON & DEV, ENG [36290]
DARGIN 1795+ WINDSOR, NSW, AUS [34969] : C1792+ WINDSOR, NSW, AUS [35537]
DARIG 1600+ AAR, INNESHOLDEN, CH [36905]

DARK 1800S PORTSMOUTH, HAM, ENG [34881] : ALL WIL, ENG [36607] : PRE 1930 CON, ENG [36996]

DARKE 1855+ NSW, AUS [35746] : C1809+ STEPNEY, LND, ENG [35746]

DARKER ALL PLUMTREE, NTT, ENG [34838]

DARKINS (SEE DAWKINS [36314]

DARLEY 1850+ KEN & MDX, ENG [37128]

DARLING PRE 1900 KINGSTON, ENG [35055] : PRE 1819 ST GILES, DUR, ENG [36604] : 1750+ CARHAM, DUR, ENG [36685] : 1860+ INCH CLUTHA, OTAGO, NZ [36871] : 1700+ DUNBAR, ELN, SCT [36791] : PRE 1858 EDINBURGH, SCT [36855] : 1800+ GIFFORD, ELN, SCT [36871] : 1700 BOSTON, MA, USA [34466]

DARLINGTON 1800-80 BARRIE, ONT, CAN [38353] : C1866 STS, ENG [35414] : 1800-80 LIVERPOOL, LAN & CHS, ENG [38353] : 1830+ EDINBURGH, MLN, SCT [36276]

DARLOT 1800+ AUS & ENG [37670]

DARLOW PRE 1900 BIRMINGHAM, ENG [35505] : 1850+ SHEFFIELD, YKS, ENG [35505] : PRE 1900 NTH, ENG [35505] : 1850+ WORLDWIDE [37347]

DARNEL PRE 1810 WARREN CO., KY, USA [37529]

DARNES 1850+ SYDNEY, NSW, AUS [37904]

DA ROSA 1800-1900 MA, USA [34631]

DARR 1750-1850 LOUDOUN CO., VA, USA [38009]

DARRACH 1800+ COLONSAY, ARL, SCT [34256]

DARRAH 1800S HASTINGS CO., ONT, CAN [38445] : PRE 1825 USA [38445]

DARRAUGH PRE 1841 TYR, IRL [35615]

DARSY PRE 1859 TIP, IRL [35206]

DART HENRY C1800 EXBOURNE, DEV, ENG & CAN [38391] : 1680S NEW LONDON, CT, USA [34991] : 1820+ SCHENECTADY, NY, USA [36323]

DARTNALL 1780-1885 LANCASTER, WI, USA [36938]

DARUSMONT 1800+ CH [38238]

DARVIL 1780-1870 MONKS RISBOROUGH, BKM, ENG [34687]

DARWENT 1700+ GLOSSOP, DBY, ENG [34303]

DARWIN 1850 SA, AUS [38204]

DASH 1830+ KINGSTON UPON THAMES, SRY, ENG [34230] : 1840S BERWICK BASSETT, WIL, ENG [35156] : ALL ENG [35945]

DASHPER 1700-1900 SOUTH BANK LIVERPOOL, LAN, ENG [37931]

DASHWOOD PRE 1850 DOR, ENG [35433]

DA SILVA ALL VISEU, PT [38382]

DATE 1850+ AMPHITHEATRE & ST ARNAUD, VIC & WA, AUS [34045] : 1828+ TRURO, CON, ENG [34045] : PRE 1860 BRIDGEWATER, SOM, ENG [34780] : ALL SOM, ENG [36610]

DAU 1865+ KILMORE, VIC, AUS [35157] : 1650-1750 MUMMENDORF, MSW, GER [35157]

DAUBER 1700+ MAINHARDT, BAW, GER [35355]

DAUBLER 1790S NUSSDORF, BAW, BRD [34581]

D'AUBUSSON ALL WORLDWIDE [35162]

DAUERMAN 1500+ BURGSTEINFURT, WEF, GER [38065]

DAUGHERTY 1700S ANT, IRL [36558]

DAUL 1800+ HAN, BRD [37581]

DAULBY 1814+ BETHNAL GREEN, LND, ENG [34063] : 1783+ LIVERPOOL, LAN, ENG [37986] : ALL LIVERPOOL, LAN, ENG [38415] : 1800-1900 WLS [35954]

DAUM PRE 1875 OES [37009]

DAUN ELEANOR 1800-1810 ROSCOMMON, ROS & GAL, IRL [38780]

DAUNT PRE 1850 CORK, COR, IRL [37459] : PRE 1900 WORLDWIDE [37339]

DAUT C1800+ SIL, GER [37728]

DAUWELS 1660-1990 MALDEGEM, OVL, BEL [38165]

DAUX PRE 1658 ENG [37587] : PRE 1670 VA, USA [37587]

DA VARGA 1800+ PT [33948]

DAVENALL 1860 TEDDINGTON, MDX, ENG [34388]

DAVENPORT 1860-1900 BATHURST, NSW, AUS [33878] : 1900+ WA, AUS [33878] : 1863+ VIC, AUS [34550] : PRE 1860 LAN, ENG [33878] : 1700 LEICESTER, LEI, ENG [34321] : 1750+ MONKS KIRBY, WAR, ENG [34363] : 1800+ MANCHESTER, LAN, ENG [34550] : 1816+ RATHKEALE, LIM, IRL [35824]

DAVERKAUSEN ALL WORLDWIDE [38670]

DAVERKOSEN ALL WORLDWIDE [38670]

DAVERKUSEN ALL WORLDWIDE [38670]

DAVERON ALL ENNISTYMON, CLA, IRL & NZ [36854]

DAVEY 1850+ VIC, AUS [34550] : 1700+ DELORAINE, TAS, AUS [35355] : 1860+ CRESWICK, VIC, AUS [35797] : 1864+ DURHAM LEAD & FOOTSCRAY, VIC, AUS [36622] : 1900+ EMMAVILLE, NSW, AUS [37115] : C1860 NORTHUMBERLAND & DURHAM, ONT, CAN [34527] : C1830+ COBOURG, ONT, CAN [37434] : PRE 1820 MOUSEHOLE, CON, ENG [33912] : PRE 1760 BRADFIELD, SFK, ENG [33992] : PRE 1830 STH PETHERTON, SOM, ENG [34197] : 1800+ BATH, SOM, ENG [34550] : 1800S ST AUSTELL, CON, ENG [34634] : JOHN 1854 ALDERBURY, WIL, ENG [35369] : PRE 1725 ESS, ENG [35642] : 1720-1820 ROTTINGDEAN & BEEDING, SSX, ENG [35813] : PRE 1900 TIVERTON & BAMPTON, DEV, ENG [35978] : PRE 1820 CHITTLEHAMPTON, DEV, ENG [36514] : PRE 1819 MEVAGISSEY, CON, ENG [36538] : PRE 1840 LONDON, ENG [36755] : 1864+ BRISTOL, SOM, ENG [36995] : PRE 1864 BISHOPS NYMPTON, DEV, ENG [36995] : 1859+ SFK & NFK, ENG [37401] : 1550-1840 ST NEOT & CLEER, CON, ENG [37434] : 1600-1800 EAST, CON, ENG [37761] : 1700-1850 CALSTOCK, CON, ENG [37761] : 1700+ NORTH & SOUTH MOLTON, DEV, ENG [38235] : C1845-55 RATHDOWNEY, LEX, IRL [33828] : C1815-30 IRL [33828] : C1815-30 IRL [33828] : PRE 1820 DRAPERSTOWN, DRY, IRL [33869] : 1850+ DETROIT, MI, USA [37761]

DAVID RBT PROTHERDE PRE 1882 WARWICK, QLD, AUS [34567] : 1730-1990 BEVEREN OUDENAANDE, OVL, BEL [38165] : PRE 1800 SEVENOAKS, KEN, ENG [36396] : 1590-1660 BARDAIS & BARLIEU, FRA [34514] : 1850 ALTEN KIRSCHEN, GER [38379] : ELECTA 1826-1893 SUMMIT & MEDINA CO., OH, USA [37034] : JOHN PRE 1853 LAUGHARNE, CMN, WLS [34567] : PRE 1900 LLANHARAN, GLA, WLS [37339]

DAVIDGE PRE 1830 FROME, SOM, ENG [37056] : 1830+ BRISTOL, GLS, ENG [37056] : PRE 1850 LYCHETT MINSTER, DOR, ENG [37433]

DAVIDOWSKA 1940+ GDANSK, GD, POL [35315]

DAVIDSON ROSS 1845+ GEELONG, VIC, AUS [34171] : ALL GEELONG, VIC, AUS [35063] : 1825-1990 CAMPBELLTOWN, TAS, AUS & NZ [36850] : DAVID 1890+ PERTH CO., ONT, CAN [34066] : 1700-1850 STOCKPORT, CHS, ENG [33879] : PRE 1840 KIRKANDREWS, CUL, ENG [34201] : 1870 LONDON, ENG [34210] : GEORGE PRE 1850 CARLISLE, CUL, ENG [34583] : C1776 BELLINGHAM, NBL, ENG [36877] : 1860+ BLYTH & EARSDON, NBL, ENG [37889] : PRE 1800 LARNE, ANT, IRL [34575] : 1862 TANDRAGEE, ARM, IRL [34878] : PRE 1852 ARENDAL, NOR [34270] : 1793 INVERAVON, BAN, SCT [33783] : PRE 1880 BURGHEAD, MOR, SCT [33993] : 1800 NIGG, KCD, SCT [34210] : 1800 ABERDEEN, ABD, SCT

[34210] : 1700-1800 JOHNSTONE, DFS, SCT [34225] :
PRE 1879 NEILSTON & PAISLEY, RFW, SCT
[34706] : 1800+ PETERHEAD, ABD, SCT [34870] :
ALL GLASGOW, SCT [35063] : 1811 CRUDEN,
ABD, SCT [35369] : PRE 1850 MLN, SCT [35375] :
1700-1800 PITTENWEEM, FIF, SCT [35627] : PRE
1803 BRECHIN, ANS, SCT [35704] : PRE 1830 FIFE,
MOR, SCT [35758] : 1830-1852 GLASGOW, LKS, SCT
[35782] : JESSE 1800S ST ANDREWS, FIF, SCT
[35876] : JANET PRE 1900 PETERHEAD, ABD, SCT
[35917] : JAMES PRE 1900 PETERHEAD, ABD, SCT
[35917] : PRE 1800+ BRECHIN, ANS, SCT [35928] :
PRE 1800 FORFAR, ANS, SCT [35928] : DAVID PRE
1870 EDINBURGH, SCT [36575] : PRE 1900
MONTROSE, ANS, SCT [36773] : 1750+ BERVIE,
KCD, SCT [36971] : PRE 1847 GLASGOW, LKS, SCT
[37138] : 1700S+ DUNSE, BEW, SCT [37413] : PRE
1871 ARBIRLOT, ANS, SCT [37442] : 1790+
INVERKEITHING, FIF, SCT [37666] : 1800-1890
AIRDRIE, LKS, SCT & AUS [33991] : PRE 1750
YETHOLME, LKS, SCT & ENG [37361] : PRE 1900
ANS, SCT & NZ [34603] : 1826-1848 KANDY, SRI
LANKA [35044] : CLARENCE 1930+ IN, USA
[35164] : HELEN 1930+ IN, USA [35164] : ANNA
1860+ JODAVIESS CO. ELIZABETH, IL, USA
[36575] : C1795 ANNAPOLIS MD, WA, USA [37627] :
1840-1880 CALHOUN, AK, USA [38576] : 1820S
BUCKLEY, FLN, WLS [38281] : ALL WORLDWIDE
[36548]

DAVIE JOHN PRE 1850 ESS, ENG [34583] : 1550+
BARNSTAPLE & LANDKEY, DEV, ENG [34747] :
1720-1820 ROTTINGDEAN & BEEDING, SSX,
ENG [35813] : 1800+ KESSINGLAND, SFK, ENG
[36296] : 1650+ SCRAPTOFT, LEI, ENG [37266] :
1600-1750 CREEDY, DEV, ENG [37339] : 1790-1890S
GLASGOW, LKS, SCT [34359] : PRE 1828
CARDROSS, DNB, SCT [34598] : 1890+
GRANGEMOUTH, STI, SCT [34702]

DAVIES 1856-1900+ SYDNEY, NSW, AUS [34277] :
WILLIAM PRE 1899 NORTHCOTE, VIC, AUS
[34587] : C1891 NEWCASTLE, NSW, AUS [35014] :
BENJAMIN 1873+ SYDNEY, NSW, AUS [35162] :
1860 NEWCASTLE, NSW, AUS [35405] : C1857+
SYDNEY, NSW, AUS [35746] : 1862+ WALLSEND
& CESSNOCK, NSW, AUS [37920] : ELIZABETH
1871+ MOUNT EGERTON, VIC, AUS [37967] :
1870+ VIC & QLD, AUS [37974] : 1850-1870 CAN
[36624] : PRE 1900 SUNDERLAND, DUR, ENG
[33977] : ANN 1774-1820 AUDLEM, CHS, ENG
[34143] : PRE 1900 BEDFORD, BDF, ENG [34626] :
PRE 1880 LONDON, ENG [34626] : ARTHUR 1870-
1900 LIVERPOOL, LAN, ENG [34735] : PRE 1850
TETBURY, GLS & ESS, ENG [34958] : FRANCES
1807+ LONDON, MDX, ENG [35252] : PRE 1850S
AUDENSHAW & ASHTON UNDER LYNE, LAN,
ENG [35591] : PRE 1850 ST PANCRAS, MDX &
LND, ENG [35701] : C1850-1885 BIRMINGHAM,
WAR, ENG [35791] : 1738-1798 NORTON, GLS,
ENG [35813] : JOHN C1800-1863 PLYMOUTH, DEV,
ENG [35955] : PRE 1870 LONDON, ENG [36006] :
PRE 1800 TIVERTON, CHS, ENG [36066] : C1850
BREWOOD, STS, ENG [36370] : 1700S
SOUTHWARK, SRY, ENG [36484] : C1800-1900
LONDON, ENG [36632] : JOHN C1780+
OSWESTRY, SAL, ENG [36728] : C1857-1900 BOW,
MDX, ENG [36876] : 1800-1900 HEREFORD &
LEDBURY, HEF, ENG [36879] : 1750-1850
NANTWICH, CHS, ENG [36983] : ANDREW PRE
1789 DINDER, SOM, ENG [37103] : 1700
CHELMSFORD, ESS, ENG [37125] : MARY C1810
CLIFFORD, HEF, ENG [37320] : GEORGE 1841+
SHURLACK & WINCHAM, CHS, ENG [37546] :

ALFRED 1855-1929 WINCHAM & MOULTON,
CHS, ENG [37546] : EDWARD 1844+ SHURLACK
& WINCHAM, CHS, ENG [37546] : JOHN 1808+
SHURLACK & WINCHAM, CHS, ENG [37546] :
PRE 1840 CLAVERLEY & SHREWSBURY, SAL,
ENG [37710] : PRE 1850 READING, BRK, ENG
[37773] : EDWARD C1850 DAWLEY, SAL, ENG
[37883] : PRE 1828 STAFFORD, STS, ENG [37911] :
WILLIAM ALL MARYLEBONE, LND, ENG [37937]
: PRE 1890 GLS, ENG [37974] : C1788 LONDON,
ENG [38485] : PRE 1900 TOXTETH &
WAVERTREE, LAN, ENG [38586] : WINIFRED
1780+ LONDON, ENG & WLS [34662] : 1700-1900S
LAN, ENG & WLS [37221] : REV. 1800S CLONMEL,
TIP, IRL [37134] : 1880+ CAPE TOWN, RSA [35248]
: 1850-1900 CAMBUSLANG, LKS, SCT [35094] :
JOHN 1850+ CARBON CO., PA, USA [37545] :
1880+ ND, USA [37804] : PRE 1838 PEMBROKE,
PEM, WLS [33912] : C1840+ CMN, WLS [33922] :
PRE 1900 NEWPORT, MON, WLS [33982] : DAVID
1770+ LLANDEVALLEY, BRE, WLS [34134] :
ISAAC 1829-1900 GWENDDWR, BRE, WLS [34134] :
ROGER 1800+ GWENDDWR, BRE, WLS [34134] :
PRE 1832 KILCENNIN, CGN, WLS [34277] : JOHN
ALL NARBERTH, PEM, WLS [34564] : PRE 1900
MARDY, GLA, WLS [34611] : 1791-1885
LLANYCHAER & FISHGUARD, PEM & CGN,
WLS [34729] : ELIZABETH PRE 1814
HUBBERSTON, PEM, WLS [34855] : EDITH M.
1895+ GLA, WLS [34921] : PRE 1850 MERTHYR
TYDFIL, GLA, WLS [35127] : 1800+ LLANELLI,
CMN, WLS [35248] : PRE 1860 LLANDOVERY,
CMN, WLS [35540] : C1812 PENRYDD, PEM, WLS
[35854] : 1854 LAUGHARNE, CMN, WLS [35854] :
1865+ LLANIGON, BRE, WLS [35942] : 1810-1940
BRYNGWYN, RAD, WLS [36109] : GRIFFITH
1850+ TREFOR & LLITHFAEN, CAE, WLS [36590]
: PRE 1860 PORTHTYWIN (BURRY PORT), WLS
[36632] : PRE 1840 HAWARDEN & EWLOE, FLN,
WLS [36849] : DANIEL PRE 1860 GLA, WLS [36886]
: HANNAH PRE 1860 GLA, WLS [36886] : EINON
1779 BRONANT, CGN, WLS [37250] : PRE 1900
DISSERTH, LLANYRE, RAD, WLS [37300] : JOHN
C1815 HAY, BRE, WLS [37320] : 1870+ MERTHYR
TYDFIL, GLA, WLS [37343] : HANNAH 1867-1930S
BRECON, BRE, WLS [37399] : JOHN 1916+
KNIGHTON, RAD, WLS [37400] : MARTHA C1810-
1880 MGY, WLS [37681] : PRE 1900 CGN, WLS
[37804] : PRE 1870 BRE & CGN, WLS [37974] : 1700-
1800 GRESFORD, DEN, WLS [38074] : WILLIAM
PRE 1876 MER & CAE, WLS [38437] : 1850+
WREXHAM, WLS [38481] : ELIZABETH PRE 1870
NEWPORT, MON, WLS [38580]

DAVIL 1870-1920 MELBOURNE, VIC, AUS [34844]

DAVIN 1850+ VIC, AUS [34903]

DAVIS JOHN 1830+ O'CONNELL, NSW, AUS [34030]
: PRE 1910 COBURG, VIC, AUS [34037] : C1830
TAS, AUS [34170] : 1880-1920 FOOTSCRAY, VIC,
AUS [34191] : ROBERT 1889 BENDIGO, VIC, AUS
[34195] : LIANE 1966+ HAMILTON, QLD, AUS
[34341] : JOHN C1790+ AUS [34444] : 1859+
LISMORE, NSW, AUS [34449] : ALL MORTLAKE,
VIC, AUS [34838] : GEORGE PRE 1888 MOUNT
RANKIN & KELSO, NSW, AUS [35104] : ALL AUS
[35213] : PRE 1880 HAWKESBURY & SPRING
HILL, NSW, AUS [35396] : CHARLES C1886
SYDNEY, NSW, AUS [35585] : GEORGE 1850-1909
TAS & VIC, AUS [35841] : JAMES 1880 SYDNEY,
NSW, AUS [36610] : WILLIAM C1853+
BATHURST, NSW, AUS [36641] : C1853+
BLAYNEY, NSW, AUS [36641] : 1861 ADELONG,
NSW, AUS [36804] : ELEANOR C1810 SYDNEY,

NSW, AUS [37106] : HENRY C1900 BROKEN HILL, NSW, AUS [37106] : ALFRED 1900+ BRISBANE, QLD, AUS [37116] : DAVID 1834+ WOLLOMBI, NSW, AUS [37945] : 1860+ GEELONG, VIC, AUS [38288] : GEORGE E. C1896+ CROYDON & SYDNEY, NSW, AUS [38541] : HARRY B. 1860+ SINGLETON, NSW, AUS [38541] : PRE 1860 ORANGE, NSW, AUS [38568] : BENJAMIN 1800-1880 SMITHS FALLS, ONT, CAN [34143] : 1810-1880 MUSKOKA CO. & SIMCO CO., ONT, CAN [35602] : C1900-1954 TORONTO, ONT, CAN [36693] : 1800S WHITCHURCH & YORK, ONT, CAN [36727] : MARIA C1810 CAN [36949] : 1850S+ ELGIN CO., ONT, CAN [37490] : 1850+ OSHAWA, ONT, CAN [38395] : PRE 1900 BRISTOL, GLS, ENG [33958] : 1600-1700 BADMINTON, GLS, ENG [34012] : 1790-1870 HOO, KEN, ENG [34016] : 1780-1850 BISLEY SCRUBS, GLS, ENG [34084] : 1870S ESS, ENG [34117] : PRE 1839 ANDOVER, HAM, ENG [34166] : ELIZABETH C1813 BRISTOL, SOM, ENG [34195] : PRE 1725 BRISTOL, GLS, ENG [34445] : 1850+ ENG [34703] : 1770-1870 CASTLE CARY & LONG ASHTON, SOM, ENG [34729] : 1770-1870 WEST LAVINGTON, SOM, ENG [34729] : 1700+ NEWENT, GLS, ENG [34747] : PRE 1791 MDX, ENG [34758] : ELIZA PRE 1884 LONDON, ENG [34806] : PRE 1860 LND, ENG [34819] : ANN C1774-1790 GLS, ENG [34886] : PRE 1854 QUINTON, LEI, ENG [35008] : C1830-1866 WAR, ENG [35037] : WILLIAM 1780+ DEV, ENG [35060] : 1850S LONDON, ENG [35066] : C1770 CHOLESBURY, BKM, ENG [35095] : 1750+ WEDMORE, SOM, ENG [35112] : 1800-1816 EWHURST, SSX, ENG [35119] : PRE 1850 LONDON, ENG [35229] : PRE 1762 BARTON STACEY, HAM, ENG [35247] : PRE 1860 HALTON, CHS, ENG [35374] : JAMES C1806+ LONDON, ENG [35427] : JOSEPH 1850+ HAMPSTEAD, HRT, ENG [35461] : JOSEPH 1870+ BATH, SOM, ENG [35461] : 1800+ DOR, ENG [35465] : C1790-1945 ATTERCLIFFE & SHEFFIELD, WRY, ENG [35550] : REBECCA 1840-1860 SHERBORNE, DOR, ENG [35607] : 1800S BRISTOL, GLS, ENG [35715] : C1835 LONDON, ENG [35764] : 1832-1847 DOVER, KEN, ENG [35835] : 1822-1832 POPLAR, MDX, ENG [35835] : PRE 1850 OLDLAND COMMON, SOM, ENG [36121] : PRE 1850 HEF, ENG [36159] : PRE 1810 TACHBROOK, WAR, ENG [36177] : PRE 1820 STAUNTON, GLS, ENG [36177] : 1800-1900 PUTNEY, LND, ENG [36213] : MARY PRE 1818 BRENTWOOD, ESS, ENG [36263] : HARRIET 1843+ HAM, ENG [36332] : ALL LEE & WENDOVER, BKM, ENG [36407] : HARRIET 1800-1840 SILCHESTER, HAM, ENG [36407] : 1830+ TAVISTOCK, DEV, ENG [36641] : 1830-1880 LONDON, ENG [36658] : 1750-1850 WIL, ENG [36688] : WILLIAM C1810+ OSWESTRY, SAL, ENG [36728] : PRE 1840 BREDE, SSX, ENG [36752] : PRE 1860 LEDBURY, HEF, ENG [36803] : C1849 BIRMINGHAM, WAR, ENG [36876] : C1825-1847 HENLEY IN ARDEN, WAR, ENG [36876] : 1800-1840 SEVENOAKS, KEN, ENG [36879] : EDWARD 1809-1830S DEVONPORT, DEV, ENG [36880] : 1750+ HARTING, SSX, ENG [36997] : WILLIAM 1807-91 BIRMINGHAM, WAR, ENG [36998] : THOMAS 1825 BIRMINGHAM, WAR, ENG [37209] : PRE 1820 PORTSMOUTH, HAM, ENG [37214] : 1800-1900 BATH, SOM, ENG [37232] : ALL BROADWAY, WOR, ENG [37265] : ELIZA 1816+ EWELL, SRY, ENG [37310] : 1750+ ASTONINGHAM, HEF, ENG [37328] : PRE 1880 TIPTON, STS & WRY, ENG [37339] : 1829-32 POPLAR, LND, ENG [37863] : PRE 1845 GLS &

DEV, ENG [37882] : DAVID PRE 1830 ENG [37945] : HENRY HUGH C1840 LIVERPOOL, LAN, ENG [38003] : PRE 1830 CROPREDY, OXF & WAR, ENG [38176] : PRE 1881 LYDBROOK, GLS, ENG [38275] : 1850+ DUBLIN, IRL [34049] : 1700-1850 BIRR, KINGS, IRL [35860] : JOSEPH PRE 1800 DUBLIN CITY, IRL [35911] : C1795 OMEY ISLAND, IRL [35963] : PRE 1850S WEX, IRL [36659] : ALL MAGOUNASH, MAY, IRL & USA [36916] : CHARLES C1880 AUCKLAND, NZ [35585] : 1880-1925 WESTPORT, NZ [38275] : C1860 WASHINGTON CO., IN, USA [34395] : 1770 CULPEPPER CO., VA, USA [35275] : 1862 IN, USA [35325] : CHARLES C1851 NEW YORK, NY, USA [35585] : 1830+ SCHOHARIE, NY, USA [36549] : SUSAN L. 1889+ MACOUN, MO, USA [36723] : C1860 TERREHAUTE, IN, USA [36803] : 1650+ PRINCE GEORGE CO., CHAS CO., MD, USA [36914] : ALL FOUNTAIN, MN, USA [36916] : C1820 NY, USA [36923] : 1900+ AIKEN, SC, USA [36946] : PRE 1900 BARNWELL, SC, USA [36946] : 1850+ NOBLE CO., OH, USA [36956] : 1800+ HAMPSHIRE CO., VA, USA [36956] : WILLIAM PRE 1789 CHESTER CO. & WASHINGTON CO., PA, USA [37529] : JOHN 1727-1825 GREENE CO., PA, USA [37529] : 1750-1850 GREENE CO., TN, USA [37539] : JOHN 1871+ MAHASKA CO., IA, USA [37545] : 1796+ RI, USA [37592] : ALL BLADEN CO., NC, USA [37789] : PRE 1800 VA, USA [37795] : 1865-1875 KEWEENAW CO., MI, USA [38010] : 1680+ RI, USA [38015] : ALL JEFFERSON CO., PA, USA [38036] : 1854-70 MILO, IL, USA [38151] : OWEN 1804-1835 DAVIESS & OHIO COS., KY, USA [38157] : 1830+ SCHENECTADY CO., NY, USA [38176] : ALL OLDHAM, KY, USA [38319] : BENJAMIN 1740-1820 SC & GA, USA [38340] : JESSIE 1770+ OTSEGO CO., NY, USA [38431] : ALL ST LAWRENCE CO., NY, USA [38431] : ALL JEFFERSON CO., NY, USA [38431] : 1794+ HAVERHILL, GRAFTON, NH, USA [38571] : AMOS 1829 FAYETTE CO., OH, USA [38590] : JOSEPH 1770 NJ, USA [38590] : 1500+ POLK CO., AR & TN, USA & WLS [36970] : DAVID PRE 1668 PENCADER, CMN, WLS [34992] : 1700+ TINTERN, MON, WLS [36209] : 1850 CARDIFF, GLA, WLS [36803] : HENRY C1880 GLAMORGAN, GLA, WLS [37106] : 1800S PEMBROKE DOCK, PEM, WLS [37869]

DAVIS (SEE DAY) [35399]

DAVISON 1868+ MELBOURNE, VIC, AUS [33942] : 1900+ GUNNEDAH, NSW, AUS [35084] : 1862+ ADELAIDE, SA, AUS [37987] : PRE 1830 HEXHAM, NBL, ENG [33776] : 1810+ ADDERSTONE, NBL, ENG [33942] : C1827 WESTMINSTER, MDX, ENG [34898] : C1856 NEWCASTLE, NBL, ENG [35216] : 1700S+ HEDDON ON THE WALL, NBL, ENG [35706] : 1794+ WASHINGTON, NBL, ENG [35706] : 1825+ HOUGHTON LE SPRING, DUR, ENG [35706] : ALL OXTHORPE, LIN, ENG [35901] : PRE 1735 SCARBOROUGH, NRY, ENG [36184] : 1790-1882 HUTTON & RUDBY, NRY, ENG [36412] : 1832+ MIDDLESBROUGH, NRY, ENG [36412] : 1750-1950 LONDON &, MDX, ENG [37344] : 1800+ CONSETT, DUR, ENG [37663] : PRE 1832 SUNDERLAND & NEWCASTLE, DUR & NBL, ENG [37853] : 1772-1818 TANFIELD, DUR, ENG [38269] : 1820S-30S CHURTON, NBL, ENG [38269] : 1771 RYTON, DUR, ENG [38269] : 1830+ IOM [34857] : C1730 KIRKESWALD, LET, IRL [35152] : PRE 1880 ANT, IRL & SCT [37987] : ALL BALLYMENA, ANT, IRL & UK [36333] : BLYTH 1949+ MECHANICSBURG, PA, USA [36412]

DAVY 1550+ BARNSTAPLE, LANDKEY, N.MOLTON, DEV, ENG **[34747]** : PRE 1685 LYME REGIS, DOR, ENG **[36277]** : 1700S HEAVITREE & TOPSHAM, DEV, ENG **[36277]** : 1800+ TIVERTON, DEV, ENG **[36785]** : C1845-55 RATHDOWNEY, LEX, IRL **[33828]**

DAVYS C1550 MAIDENHEAD, BRK, ENG **[38348]**

DAW PRE 1830 DEV, ENG **[34696]** : PRE 1838 LONDON, ENG **[35064]** : PRE 1800 LONGHOPE, GLS, ENG **[35773]** : 1800-1850 WALWORTH, MDX, ENG **[36586]** : PRE 1830 MAKER, CON, ENG **[37630]** : 1800S WAT, IRL **[35882]**

DAWBER PRE 1848 SCOTTER, LIN, ENG **[33915]** : 1700+ UPHOLLAND, LAN, ENG **[38046]** : 1840S BALLYMENA, ANT, IRL **[35925]**

DAWE PRE 1863 GUNNISLAKE & CALSTOCK, CON, ENG **[35223]** : PRE 1856 BODMIN, CON, ENG **[35225]** : 1807+ BRATTON CLOVELLY, DEV, ENG **[37921]** : 1838+ TRESMEER, CON, ENG **[37921]**

DAWES 1820+ AUS **[35241]** : 1814 LONDON, ENG **[34761]** : PRE 1900 WALWORTH, SRY, ENG **[35020]** : 1750+ SRY, ENG **[35241]** : HENRY PRE 1859 TIVERTON, DEV, ENG **[35599]** : JAMES 1813-1888 KIMPTON, HRT, ENG **[35634]** : PRE 1900 ENG **[35639]** : C1760 BIRMINGHAM, WAR, ENG **[36779]** : C1700 TAMWORTH, STS, ENG **[36779]** : 1850S HANDSWORTH, STS, ENG **[36779]** : 1700+ LONDON, ENG, AUS & **[36266]** : 1800-1950 LA CROSS, WI, USA **[38154]**

DAWKING JOHN 1820-1860 HAMPSTEAD, ESS, ENG **[36634]**

DAWKINS PRE 1852 SHOREDITCH, LND, ENG **[34305]** : 1870-1900 POPLAR, MDX, ENG **[34693]** : 1700S BEVERLEY, YKS, ENG **[36314]** : 1750-1850 WOMENSWOLD, KEN, ENG **[37880]**

DAWN PRE 1860 MARSTON, LIN, ENG **[37062]** : 1790-1830 ROANE & MORGAN CO.S, TN, USA **[36566]**

DAWS 1720 FINEDON, NTH, ENG **[35119]**

DAWSON 1850-1880 GOULBURN, NSW, AUS **[33838]** : OCTAVIA 1800-1850 CLARENCE PLAINS, TAS, AUS **[35017]** : 1815+ SYDNEY, NSW, AUS **[35031]** : 1825 SYDNEY, NSW, AUS **[35082]** : JANE 1890S OLD JUNEE, NSW, AUS **[35230]** : 1838+ OBERON, NSW, AUS **[35245]** : 1900+ MELBOURNE, VIC, AUS **[36605]** : RALPH 1870+ NEW ENGLAND, NSW, AUS **[36632]** : 1850S SYDNEY, NSW, AUS **[37947]** : JOSEPH C1869 ROMA, QLD & NSW, AUS & IRL **[34447]** : ALL DENDERMONDE, OVL, BEL **[37171]** : JOHANNA 1839 NB, CAN **[37509]** : 1850+ CARLETON CO., ONT, CAN **[38431]** : 1850+ RUSSELL CO., ONT, CAN **[38431]** : ROSANNAH PRE 1850 DEPTFORD, KEN, ENG **[33765]** : C1775 SOUTH CREEKE, NFK, ENG **[33796]** : PRE 1840 BOROUGHBRIDGE, YKS, ENG **[34022]** : HENRY 1795 NORWICH, NFK, ENG **[34091]** : PRE 1820 HUNGERFORD, BRK, ENG **[34316]** : PRE 1820 WIL, ENG **[34316]** : PRE 1820 BKM, ENG **[34316]** : 1780+ CARSHALTON, SRY, ENG **[34710]** : PRE 1800 BIRCHINGTON, KEN, ENG **[35020]** : PRE 1800 HEDENHAM, NFK, ENG **[35173]** : 1700 OVERKILLET, LAN, ENG **[35288]** : 1880+ ASHBY & SCUNTHORPE, LIN, ENG **[35377]** : 1750+ CHS, ENG **[35377]** : 1750+ GRAPPENHALL, CHS, ENG **[35377]** : C1821 PICKHILL, YKS, ENG **[35708]** : THOMAS C1818 BARKBY, LEI, ENG **[35773]** : 1690S+ MARTON CUM GRAFTON, WRY, ENG **[35996]** : 1800S BDF, ENG **[36005]** : 1870+ SNEINTON & NOTTINGHAM, NTT, ENG **[36105]** : GEORGE 1800-1861 GILLING, RICHMOND, NRY, ENG **[36783]** : GEORGE 1780-1800 HEIGHINGTON,

DUR, ENG **[36783]** : 1800S ROTHERHITHE, SRY, ENG **[36851]** : 1800S FINSBURY & CLAPHAM, LND, ENG **[36868]** : C1891 MILE END OLD TOWN, MDX, ENG **[36876]** : C1891 ST GEORGE EAST, MDX, ENG **[36876]** : HENRY 1861 KENSINGTON, MDX, ENG **[36876]** : HENRY C1863-1864 WOOLWICH DOCKYARD, KEN, ENG **[36876]** : 1750-1800 BOLTON, LAN, ENG **[37166]** : 1770+ NTT, ENG **[37171]** : PRE 1900 KEN, ENG **[37377]** : PRE 1865 BETLEY, STS, ENG **[37406]** : PRE 1870 BERGH APTON, NFK, ENG **[37512]** : PRE 1750 MANCHESTER, LAN, ENG **[37573]** : ALL CHURWELL, WRY, ENG **[37621]** : C1850 LAN, ENG **[37661]** : ALL WARTON, LAN, ENG **[37706]** : PRE 1885 SHEFFIELD, WRY, ENG **[37831]** : 1700-1860 GREAT BARDFIELD, ESS, ENG **[37859]** : PRE 1856 GRAFTON REGIS, NTH, ENG **[37915]** : PRE 1890 CARLISLE, CUL, ENG **[37925]** : 1710+ ST BEES, CUL, ENG **[38067]** : PRE 1860 HARBROUGH, LIN, ENG **[38111]** : PRE 1900 DUR, ENG **[38457]** : WILLIAM 1800+ HAMMERSMITH, MDX, ENG & AUS **[34882]** : PRE 1810 LONDON, ENG & AUS **[35887]** : C1875 MANCHESTER, LAN, ENG & NZ **[35417]** : LETITIA 1839-1860 MOG, IRL **[33826]** : C1850 IRL **[37131]** : PRE 1800 TYR, IRL **[37984]** : FRANCIS PRE 1824 MONAGHAN, MOG, IRL **[38431]** : 1847 GLASGOW, LKS, SCT **[34224]** : 1750-1850 HUNTLY, ABD, SCT **[34615]** : 1850+ ALYA, STI, SCT **[34702]** : PRE 1820 EDINBURGH, MLN, SCT **[35245]** : PRE 1850 MONTROSE, ANS, SCT **[36168]** : 1825-1860 SCT **[36627]** : C1830 BOHARM, BAN, SCT **[36762]** : ALL INVERKEITHING, FIF, SCT **[36774]** : 1800S COATBRIDGE, LKS, SCT **[37898]** : 1780 MONONGALIA CO., VA, USA **[36446]**

DAY 1857+ AUBURN, SA, AUS **[33833]** : ANNA 1847-1925 GILBERTON, SA, AUS **[33892]** : PRE 1900 TUMUT, NSW, AUS **[34269]** : C1890-1895 GIPPSLAND, VIC, AUS **[35399]** : C1894-1917 CIRCULAR HEAD, TAS, AUS **[35399]** : PRE 1863 MOUNT GAMBIER, SA, AUS **[35399]** : 1867-1932 SINGLETON, NSW, AUS **[37310]** : 1838+ MAITLAND & JERRYS PLAINS, NSW, AUS **[38592]** : 1850-1900 ONT, CAN **[34373]** : 1900S GREY CO., ONT, CAN **[34991]** : 1800-1900 VERULAM, VICTORIA, ONT, CAN **[36483]** : 1850+ GRANDE PRAIRIE, ALB, CAN **[36483]** : ALL BROME & SUKLEY, QUE, CAN **[36938]** : PRE 1857 BRADNEY, SOM, ENG **[33833]** : HANNAH C1800+ FITZROY SQ, LND, ENG **[33892]** : SUSSANNAH C1800+ ENG **[33892]** : PRE 1839 SHOREDITCH, MDX, ENG **[34166]** : ALL MITCHAM, LND, ENG **[34595]** : PRE 1850 EYNESBURY & ST NEOTS, CAM, ENG **[34611]** : PRE 1850 EASTREY, KEN, ENG **[34648]** : PRE 1870 HACKNEY, MDX, ENG **[34691]** : PRE 1850 KINGS RIPTON, HUN, ENG **[34693]** : PRE 1850 BRIGHTON, SSX, ENG **[34763]** : 1870S KENSINGTON, LND, ENG **[35188]** : 1800S CHEDWORTH, GLS, ENG **[35256]** : 1785-1803 BURTON AGNES, NRY, ENG **[35316]** : PRE 1720 HAGBOURNE, BRK, ENG **[35866]** : ALL SFK, ENG **[35933]** : PRE 1800 WIL, ENG **[35994]** : ALL ECKINGTON, WOR, ENG **[36171]** : PRE 1800 WAR, ENG **[36183]** : 1750+ BIRSTALL, WRY, ENG **[36218]** : PRE 1870 IPSWICH, SFK, ENG **[36270]** : 1650-1750 LODDON, NFK, ENG **[36483]** : 1700 NORTON SUBCOURSE, NFK, ENG **[36483]** : 1750+ DEPWADE, NFK, ENG **[36483]** : 1650-1700 BROOKE, NFK, ENG **[36483]** : 1872 CLERKENWELL, MDX, ENG **[36640]** : 1850+ STOTFOLD, BDF, ENG **[36728]** : PRE 1880 REIGATE, SRY, ENG **[36741]** : 1800+ NTT, ENG

[36746] : PRE 1820 SFK, ENG [36866] : PRE 1700 HAMPNETT, GLS, ENG [36889] : 1900+ LANDPORT, HAM, ENG [37049] : PRE 1900 PORTSEA, HAM, ENG [37049] : ALL NTT & LEI, ENG [37078] : 1850 ST ALBANS, HRT, ENG [37082] : PRE 1806 SUDBURY, SFK, ENG [37082] : SUSANNAH 1806 GUILSBOROUGH, NTH, ENG [37106] : JOHN 1750S WELFORD, NTH, ENG [37106] : JOHN 1777 COLD ASHBY, NTH, ENG [37106] : 1600-1700 NFK, ENG [37207] : 1870+ HERTFORD, HRT, ENG [37398] : 1927+ BENNINGTON, HRT, ENG [37398] : PRE 1850 RAMSBURY, WIL, ENG [37687] : PRE 1807 BEDALE & WELL, NRY, ENG [37710] : 1700S LAVENHAM, SFK, ENG [37733] : 1770-1850 MARDEN, KEN, ENG [37880] : C1720 BOWERCHALKE, WIL, ENG [38489] : PRE 1800 SOM, ENG [38745] : 1850+ SSX, ENG & AUS [34763] : ALL CASTLEBAR, MAY, IRL [33823] : 1770S SOUTH AMBOY, NJ, USA [34991] : 1920S EUREKA, CA, USA [34991] : PRE 1820 GRAYSON, VA, USA [36567] : PRE 1870 BURKE, NC, USA [36567] : 1870+ RUSSELL, KY, USA [36567] : MAUD 1879-1912 SOUTH GRANVILLE, NY, USA [36902] : 1780-1840 NEW SALEM, MA, USA [36938] : 1700+ NY & MA, USA [37026] : ARTHUR 1921+ GARDEN CITY, NY, USA [37526] : 1850+ NEW ORLEANS, LA, USA [37583] : 1776-1910 PERSON CO., NC, USA [37583] : 1920+ WA, USA [37597] : 1800-1900 JEFFERSONVILLE, IN, USA [37597] : 1750-1850 OH, USA [37597] : 1775-1825 PHILADELPHIA, PA, USA [37740] : EZEKIAL 1800-1815 VA, USA [37815] : 1848-1855 KEWEENAW CO., MI, USA [38010] : JOHN 1802-45 BEAVER CO., PA, USA [38086] : 1800+ USA [38533] : 1850-1900 SOUTHERN COS., MO, USA [38737] : 1850-1910 CRAWFORD CO., AR, USA [38737] : 1790-1850 TN, USA [38737]

DAYE 1660S MOUNTFIELD, KEN, ENG [35259]

DAYMENT 1890+ BRENT, DEV, ENG [35943]

DAYSH PRE 1850 WICKHAM, HAM, ENG [34314]

DEACON 1855+ SYDNEY, NSW, AUS [34791] : 1855+ SYDNEY, NSW, AUS [38075] : ALL LONDON, ONT, CAN [35264] : 1820-1830S PLYMOUTH, DEV, ENG [33780] : 1800+ LONDON, ENG [33851] : 1800S SHOREDITCH, LND, ENG [34791] : 1750-1800 BRADFORD, WRY, ENG [36682] : 1600-1800 GOSPORT, HAM, ENG [37335] : 1700+ FORDINGRIDGE, HAM, DOR & WIL, ENG [37335] : 1600-1800 RAMSBURY & AMESBURY, WIL, ENG [37335] : PRE 1850 STOKE CLIMSLAND, CON, ENG [38075] : JOSEPH 1800-1820 CAR, WEX & TIP, IRL [35264] : PRE 1843 MOG, IRL [36923] : ALL COOK CO., IL, USA [35264] : MARTHA 1764-1851 BURLINGTON CO., NJ, USA [38127]

DE ACOSTA 1630-1730 OPORTO, PT [36937]

DEAKER (SEE D'ACRE) [35738]

DEAKIN PRE 1800 CHEADLE & LEIGH, STS, ENG [36196] : 1700-1800 ELMLEY CASTLE, WOR, ENG [37643]

DEAKINS 1800+ RAD, WLS [37400]

DEAL PRE 1832 CAVETOWN, MD, USA [35289] : 1740-1850 LANCASTER CO., PA, KY & IN, USA [36901]

DEAMEN 1789+ BENTLEY, WAR, ENG [37310]

DEAMER 1800+ ISLINGTON, MDX, LND & HRT, ENG [37065]

DEAN 1830+ LAUNCESTON, TAS, AUS [34542] : 1880+ SYDNEY, NSW, AUS [34979] : 1848+ SA, AUS [35451] : 1815+ SYDNEY, NSW, AUS [36647] : 1790S SYDNEY, NSW, AUS [37947] : 1790+ NSW, AUS [38212] : ALL NSW, AUS [38730] : 1849-77 TORONTO, ONT, CAN [36582] : PRE 1813 ST BRELADE, JSY, CHI [34254] : PRE 1847 WALTON ON THE HILL, SRY, ENG [33801] : PRE 1860 LEEDS, WRY, ENG [33968] : 1836+ KINTBURY, BRK, ENG [34011] : THOS & GEORGE C1790 FINSBURY SQUARE, LND, ENG [34274] : 1760-1800 MELCOMBE REGIS, DOR, ENG [34337] : 1800 WALTON ON THE HILL, SRY, ENG [34542] : ALL KIDSGROVE, STS, ENG [34933] : 1800 KIDSGROVE, CHS, ENG [35023] : PRE 1886 WEST DERBY, LAN, ENG [35036] : PRE 1830 HAM, ENG [35055] : PRE 1850 LONDON, ENG [35451] : 1800+ LAMBETH, SRY, ENG [35461] : C1700-1900 SHOREDITCH, LND, ENG [35892] : 1800-1900 HOLMER GREEN, BKM, ENG [36175] : C1750-1850 HACKNEY, LND. ENG [36289] : 1796-1830 DEPTFORD, KEN & MDX, ENG [36582] : 1750+ KEN, ENG [36647] : 1880S DERBY, DBY, ENG [36797] : 1750+ RICKMANSWORTH, HRT, ENG [36981] : PRE 1880 AYLESTONE PARK, LEI, ENG [37346] : 1700-1800 MANCHESTER, LAN, ENG [37602] : PRE 1860S ISLE OF ELY, CAM, ENG [37611] : GEORGE 1880S PENSHAW, DUR, ENG [37611] : ALL JARROW ON TYNE, DUR, ENG [37950] : 1820S WIGAN, LAN, ENG [38281] : PRE 1780 DORKING, SRY, ENG [38730] : PRE 1650 CHARD, SOM, ENG [38746] : DAVID C1800 IRL [36873] : 1800+ BOHARM, BAN, SCT [34075] : PRE 1872 INV, ROC & MOR, SCT [35496] : 1700-1990 UK & AUS [35421] : 1680-1990 NEW ENGLAND, USA [34124] : 1740+ FOXHILL, NJ, USA [34130] : 1800-1900 GRANT PARISH, LA, USA [36449] : PRE 1820S NY, USA [37522] : 1750-1850 CAIRO, NY & CT, USA [37591] : PRE 1860 DANRIDGE, TN, USA [38017] : SCHARLETT 1822-1856 USA [38124] : 1821 SILAS, KY, MO & AR, USA [38287] : 1620-1990 USA & CAN [34124] : 1790+ USA & UK [36357]

DEANE 1820-1836 HOBART, TAS, AUS [37943] : C1890 WOOLWICH, LND, ENG [35457] : ELLEN 1827+ WIGAN, LAN, ENG [35634] : 1800+ OXF, ENG [36239] : 1700+ RICHMOND, SRY, ENG [37943]

DEANER 1850+ PHILADELPHIA, PA, USA [36578]

DEANES GEORGE C1810 WOR, ENG [34222]

DEANS C1813 BRIDEKIRK, CUL, ENG [35990] : 1750+ HADDINGTON, ELN, SCT [33963] : 1860-1886 PAISLEY, RFW, SCT [35442] : PRE 1850 HORSLEYHILL & MINTO, ROX, SCT [38376]

DEAR ROGER C1739 PEWSEY, WIL, ENG [38489] : MARY 1759 PEWSEY, WIL, ENG [38489]

DEARBORN 1600 HANNAY & EXETER, DEV, ENG [35276] : 1800-1850 YORK CO., ME, USA [38129]

DEARDEN C1805 ROCHDALE, LAN, ENG [35560] : C1850 MANCHESTER, LAN, ENG [36635] : JOSEPH 1800+ LEEDS, WRY, ENG [36636]

DEARDORFF ALL WORLDWIDE [37785]

DEARING PRE 1870 LADBROKE & NEW BILTON, WAR, ENG [34629]

DEARINGER 1850-1900 CHEROKEE CO., IA, USA [38532]

DEARLING PRE 1840 SRY & KEN, ENG [34383]

DEARMAN PRE 1840 FINNINGLEY, NTT, ENG [33959] : ALL BENNINGTON, HRT, ENG [37777]

DEARN ALL BIRMINGHAM, WAR, ENG [37367]

DEARSLEY 1800-1850 CARBROOKE, NFK, ENG [36388]

DEARY ALL LIVERPOOL, LAN, ENG [37020] : ALL IRL [37020] : ALL BAY CO., MI, NY & QUE, USA & CAN [38287]

DEAS 1840+ NEWCASTLE, NSW, AUS [34905] : 1810+ BO'NESS, WLN, SCT [34905] : 1830S LEITH, MLN, SCT [35486] : ELI 1850 RICHMOND, GA, USA [36946] : 1600+ JAMESTOWN, VA, USA [36946] : PRE 1850 RICHMOND & ROBESON, NC, USA [36946]

DEASE ALL MAN, CAN [34362] : PRE 1830 BALLINDINE, MAY, IRL [36652]

DEATH PRE 1826 COLCHESTER, ESS, ENG [35147] : 1774-1852 BATTISFORD, SFK, ENG [36770] : 1750-1870 WHELNETHAM, SFK, ENG [37253] : PRE 1854 ALCONBURY, HUN, ENG [37308]

DEAVES PRE 1840 COR, IRL [38777]

DE BACKER 1600-1990 ST NIKLAAS, OVL, BEL [38165]

DEBACKERE 1500+ WORLDWIDE [38161]

DE BAER ALISON 1954-90 LONDON, ENG [37926]

DE BANK 1700S LONDON, MDX, ENG [35186] : 1771+ BATH, SOM, ENG [35186]

DEBANK ALL WORLDWIDE [36739]

DEBARTH C1835+ NEW YORK, NY, USA [38182]

DE BEAUMONT 1850-1870 CAN [36624] : 1852+ SOUTHPORT, LAN, ENG [36624] : 1700-1770 LONG ISLAND, NY, USA [36624]

DEBECK 1750-90 NY, USA [37454]

DE BEERS 1600S DREISCHOR, ZEL, NL [38358]

DEBENHAM 1840+ CLERKENWELL, MDX, ENG [38539] : 1600-1900 HARTEST, SFK, ENG [38579]

DEBEREWBY C1296 ENG [34041]

DEBEVOISE PRE 1740 GRAVESEND, NY, USA [38126]

DE BIGARE PRE 1890 CARLETON, QUE, CAN [37442]

DEBLANC 1683-1913 ST MARTINVILLE, LA, USA [34136]

DEBLEY C1820 FINSBURY, LND, ENG [35722]

DEBNAM 1840+ CLERKENWELL, MDX, ENG [38539]

DE BOARD 1800+ LEICESTER, LEI, ENG [34276] : PRE 1900 LAN & GLS, ENG [36508]

DEBONDI PRE 1880 LOMBARDY, ITL [37105]

DE BONDI ALL WORLDWIDE [33773]

DE BONTRIDDER C1780 NL [38711]

DE BOOS PRE 1860 LONDON, LND, ENG [38289]

DEBOOS ALL WORLDWIDE [36429]

DEBOUDRINGHIEN PRE 1800 MOESKROEN, HNT, BEL [38164]

DE BRAAK C1800 ELL, LMB, NL [38064]

DE BRAGA 1800-1900 AZORES, PT [36733]

DE BRETT 1854-1930 NEWINGTON & BROMLEY, SRY & KEN, ENG [36101]

DE BRUCK ALL WORLDWIDE [38169]

DE BRUIJN PRE 1791 MEER, ATW, BEL [35008]

DE BRUIN ALL OVL, BRA & ANT, BEL [38676]

DE BRUYN PRE 1850 AALST, BEL [38676] : 1800+ THE HAGUE, NL [36662]

DE BURGE PRE 1806 CHI [34683]

DEBUS ALL HAMBURG, GER [36773] : ALL LUBECK, GER [36773]

DE BUSK 1850+ WOLFE CO., KY, USA [38534]

DE BUSSARD C1770 WORLDWIDE [38605]

DECABOOTER 1890-1900 ANTWERP, ATW, BEL [38537]

DE CAREW ALL WORLDWIDE [36863]

DECELIS JOHN 1840-1899 PORT SAID, EGYPT [36634]

DECENT C1850-1990 MT GAMBIER & ADELAIDE, SA, AUS [34589] : C1850-1990 QLD, AUS [34589] : ALL WORLDWIDE [36480]

DECHANT PRE 1875 WITTMAN (SOLOTHUM), SU [37782]

DECK 1750S FRA & BRD [36964]

DECKER 1790-1830S LINCOLN CO., ONT, CAN [34094] : PRE 1860 AUERSTEDT, GER [38377] : 1650-1900 ME, NH & MA, USA [35263] : JOHN 1700-1800 COLUMBIA CO., NY, USA [36555] : C1820 ULSTER CO., NY, USA [37017]

DE COSTA FRANCISCO 1860S SAN MIGUEL, PT [37501]

DECOTTE ALL USA & CAN [37502]

DE COUAGNE 1650+ MONTREAL, QUE, CAN [36657]

DECOURCEY PAT 1850+ MELBOURNE, VIC, AUS [34864] : CATH 1850+ MELBOURNE, VIC, AUS [34864]

DE COURCY 1790-1850 PEI, CAN [38007] : ALL IRL [35554]

DE COURCY-IRELAND 1790-1850 PEI, CAN [38007]

DE CREMER 1630-1990 IDEGEM, OVL, BEL [38165]

DECROSS GONZALES ALL WORLDWIDE [37699]

DECROW 1842 FREEDOM, ME, USA [38193]

DEDDICOTT 1700-1800 WOR & SAL, ENG [36003]

DEDE 1700-1750 SPITALFIELDS, MDX, ENG [38516] : PRE 1720 FRA [38516]

DEDERT 1750-1827 AUGUSTDORF, LIP, GER [38671]

DEE 1863-1990 STONE HUT, SA, AUS [33778] : PRE 1822 SRY, ENG [35976] : PRE 1780 STOTESDEN, SAL, ENG [38420] : 1800S WAT, IRL [35398] : 1870+ ADDISON'S FLAT, NZ [35398] : 1848-1875 KEWEENAW CO., MI, USA [38010] : ALL CINCINNATI, OH, USA [38743]

DEEBLE PRE 1830 LISKEARD, CON, ENG [33953]

DEEDMAN PRE 1890 SRY, ENG [34848]

DEEGAN 1800+ CALCUTTA, INDIA [33933]

DEELEY PRE 1800 OLD SWINFORD, WOR, ENG [34314] : 1800+ DUDLEY, WOR, ENG [35125] : PRE 1850 BIRMINGHAM, WAR, ENG [35151] : ELY C1850 BIRMINGHAM, WAR, ENG [36572] : C1880 BATH, WIL, ENG [36572]

DEELY 1800+ AUS [34424] : 1849+ SYDNEY, NSW, AUS [35373] : ALL WEST BROMWICH, STS, ENG [36537] : PRE 1880 GAL, IRL [34424] : PRE 1849 LOUGHREA, GAL, IRL [35373]

DEEM 1760+ BRANSCOMBE, DEV, ENG [35027] : SARAH 1800S PA & OH, USA [36321]

DEEMING ALL STS, ENG [36183]

DEEN PRE 1860 KER, IRL [35160]

DEENEY 1859+ MONARO, NSW, AUS [34966]

DEER 1850-1900 NOTTINGHILL, MDX, ENG [35066] : PRE 1740 BURY ST EDMUNDS, SFK, ENG [37253] : 1900S SFK, ENG [37910]

DEERE PRE 1892 CAPPAMORE, LIM, IRL [35900]

DEERING 1800+ WHALSAY, SHI, SCT [35824]

DEES 1860-1950 HARTLEPOOL, DUR, ENG [37859] : 1850S NEWCASTLE UPON TYNE, NBL, ENG [37859]

DEES (SEE DEAS) [36946]

DEETER ALL PA, USA [38067]

DEETS C1909 STERLING, IL, USA [37022] : ABERN 1819-1898 USA [38124]

DE FEU PRE 1800 JSY, CHI [37760]

DEFIBAUGH C1775-1825 PA, USA [37790]

DE FLON 1858-1904 BULLI, NSW, AUS [35570] : 1858-1904 NEWCASTLE, NSW, AUS [35570] : PRE 1858 STOCKHOLM, SWE [35570]

DE FRAHS 1916 CAPETOWN, RSA [34193]

DE FRAINE 1858+ NSW, AUS [35379]

DE FRAITS 1916 CAPETOWN, RSA [34193]

DE FREITAS PRE 1803 FUNCHAL, IS. OF MADEIRA, PT [35223]

DEFTY PRE 1700 DUR, ENG [37693]

DE GANCE 1600-1800 FRA [37745]

DE GAND ALL FRA [36030]

DE GANS PRE 1750 WORLDWIDE [37745]

DE GARIS 1800S ST SAVIOUR, GSY, CHI [34880]

DEGAS PRE 1850 CEN, FRA [36073]

DE GAUDIA 1700-1800 ALICANTE, ESP [38346]

DEGEN PRE 1700 MARKOBEL & HANAU, HES, GER [38348]

DE GENNES ALL WORLDWIDE [37745]
DEGENS PRE 1850 WAGENINGEN, GEL, NL [38708]
DEGG PRE 1700 CON, ENG [35255]
DEGIDAN PRE 1864 CLA, IRL [34858]
DEGLASS (SEE DAGLASS [35133]
DE GOLIER PRE 1725 PARIS, FRA [38052]
DEGRANDPRE 1800+ BERTHIER & LAVALTRIE, QUE, CAN & FRA [34161]
DE GRAUWE ALL BREDA, NL [38676]
DE GREEF 1700-C1740S GEL, NL [38358]
DE GRIEK JACOBA 1870 DEN HELDER, NL [36782]
DE GROEN PRE 1850 NIJEGA, FRI, NL [38646]
DE GROFF 1650+ WINNEBAGO, IL & NY, USA [36931]
DE GROOT 1700S ZIERIKZEE, ZEL, NL [38358] : 1650-1880 ULSTER CO., NY, USA [37783]
DE GRUCHY GEORGE PRE 1886 ST HELIER, JSY, CHI & UK [34302] : PRE 1880 WHOLE ISLAND, JSY, CHI, UK [36200]
DE GRUSSA ALL WORLDWIDE [34850]
DEGUEHERY C1860-1880 MORNINGTON WATERLOO, PERTH CO, ONT, CAN [34103] : C1820-1850S DRESDEN, DRE, DDR [34103] : 1850S-1860S PHILADELPHIA, PA, USA [34103] : 1890S EBENEZER & WEST SENECA, NY, USA [34103]
DE HAAN 1800 HERTOGENBOSCH, NL [38379]
DE HART MATHIS 1749-1840 HANOVER TWP, MORRIS CO., NJ, USA [37023]
DEHNER ALL BAW, BRD & ENG [37750]
DE HORA ALL WORLDWIDE [37653]
DEIBERT 1750+ BERKS & SCHUYLKILL COS., PA, USA [37508]
DEIDERT 1938 BAD PYRMONT, PYR, GER [38748] : 1901 HUNFELD, WEF, GER [38748] : 1789-1902 GROSSENWIEDEN, SLP, GER [38750]
DEIGHTON C1686 DUR & YKS, ENG [33827] : 1795+ RUDSTON, YKS, ENG [34653] : PRE 1738 MAUNBY, KIRBY WISKE, NRY, ENG [37852]
DEISS 1650-1890 HERZNACH, AG, CH [36896] : ALL REICHENSACHSEN, BAD, GER [38748]
DEITERT 1743 HEMERINGEN, SLP, GER [38750]
DE JEAN ALL WORLDWIDE [37745]
DE JESUS PRE 1850 BULACAN, BULACAN, PHILIPPINE [34891]
DE JONG PRE 1900 ALKEMADE, ZUH, NL [34613]
DEJONG GRIETJE PRE 1866 OUDORP, ZUH, NL [38064]
DE JONG PRE 1800 HINDELOPEN & NIJEGA, FRI, NL [38646]
DE JONGE 1600S ELLEMEET, ZEL, NL [38358]
DE JUST C1710 LEIDEN, ZUH, NL [38698]
DE KEIJSER 1600S BIEZELINGE, ZEL, NL [38358]
DEKEN PRE 1700 ROMSEY, HAM, ENG [37335]
DEKEUSTER ALL GREEN BAY & DEPERE, IL & WI, USA [35002]
DEKKER 1700S HAAMSTEDE, ZEL, NL [38358] : PRE 1850 BUSSUM, NOH, NL [38694]
DE KNYFF ALL NL [38351]
DE KOEIJER 1700-C1740S OUDELANDE, ZEL, NL [38358]
DE KOK 1700-C1740S BIEZELINGE, ZEL, NL [38358]
DE KUIJER 1877 IJSSELSTEIN, UTR, NL [38716]
DELABAR ALL SCHELINGEN, BAD, GER [38534]
DE LA BERTAUCHE 1874 WORLDWIDE [38863]
DE LA BRUER C1400 DEV & CON, ENG [34395]
DE LACEY PRE 1850+ ST JOHN, NB, CAN [35454]
DE LA COUR 1700-1750 ST LAWRENCE, JSY, CHI [34552]
DE LA FLECHELLE 1800+ PARIS, RPA, FRA [34650]
DE LA HAYE PRE 1890 ST HELIER, JSY, CHI [35048] : JANE 1700S SMITHTOWN, LONG ISLAND, NY, USA [36321]

DELAHAYS 1877 VILLERS SUR MER, BN, FRA [38163]
DE LA HUNT 1800-1841 DROGHEDA, LOU & CAV, IRL [34693]
DELAHUNTY 1850+ KILMORE, VIC, AUS [35043] : 1835+ MICARKY, TIP, IRL [35043] : PRE 1850 TIP, IRL [35398]
DELAMONT 1860+ JSY, CHI [34688] : C1790 HASELBURY PLUCKNETT, SOM, ENG [34688] : ALL ENG [37269]
DE LA MOTE ALL ENG [34286]
DE LA MOTTE C1856 ROTTERDAM, ZUH, NL [38711]
DELANEY MARY E. PRE 1860 DAYLESFORD, VIC, AUS [35599] : PRE 1843 HOBART, TAS, AUS [36622] : 1890S GRANVILLE, NSW, AUS [37309] : 1813 WINDSOR, NSW, AUS [37309] : 1850+ GUYSBOROUGH, NS, CAN [35627] : BERNARD 1840 WAKEFIELD, WRY, ENG [35599] : PRE 1850 LND, ENG [36605] : PRE 1834 KIK, IRL [34183] : PRE 1900 COR, IRL [35199] : 1840S-60S CASTLECOMER, KIK, IRL [35243] : BERNARD 1851 DURROW, LEX, IRL [35599] : 1820-1840 KILKENNY, IRL [35850] : PRE 1800 DUB, IRL [37309] : 1700-20 IRL [38151]
DELANG 1680-1750 ULSTER CO., NY, USA [35318]
DELANY THOMAS 1833+ PARRAMATTA & TENNYSON, NSW, AUS [36600]
DE LA PITTE 1066+ ENG [35453] : PRE 1066+ FRA [35453]
DE LA PLAZA PRE 1832 VALPARAISO, USA &, CHILE [35109]
DE LA PORTE 1685+ LONDON, ENG [33946] : PRE 1685 GARD, LGD, FRA [33946]
DE LARBAR C1951 LOS ANGELES, CA, USA [38172]
DE LA SABLOMIERE 1824 PORT LOUIS, MAURITIUS [37106]
DE LA SOUDIERE PRE 1805 STRASBOURG, ALS, FRA [34582] : 1805-1826 OTTENSEN, SHO, GER [34582]
DELATOUR PRE 1850 BRISTOL, GLS, ENG [35215]
DELAUNAY 1700-1800 HAITI, W.INDIES [38523]
DELAVAL PRE 1580 NBL, ENG [36502] : 1500+ WORLDWIDE [38161]
DELAVILLE PRE 1800 KINGS, OFF, IRL [35342]
DE LEEUW 1850-1950 RANDWYCK, ZETTEN, BETHUWE, NL [34242] : 1900 ZWOLLE, OIJ, NL [35338]
DELEMERE PRE 1890 IRL [38303]
DE LEQ LEMONTAISE ALL WORLDWIDE [36890]
DELESTE ALL ENG [37199]
DELF EDWARD C1840 NORWICH & BIRKENHEAD, NFK & CHS, ENG [36590]
DELGENIESSE 1712-1844 BUZET, HEN, BEL [38158]
DELINE 1790+ ONT & QUE, CAN [34520]
DE LITTLE PRE 1820 CAV, IRL [34693]
DELL 1858 KENSINGTON, LND, ENG [34284] : 1858+ LEWISHAM, LND, ENG [34284] : 1575+ HRT, ENG [34672] : PRE 1620 THURSLEY, SRY, ENG [37420] : HENRY 1700 MORRIS CO., NJ, USA [34128] : RICHARD 1675-1724 BURLINGTON, NJ, USA [34128]
DELLA BOSCA PRE 1912 VERVIO, SONDRIO, ITL [33864]
DELLAR PRE 1833 STAMFORD RIVERS, ESS, ENG [33884]
DELLAWAY 1820+ CROYDON, SRY, ENG [37902]
DELLER 1850+ CARLTON, VIC, AUS [36605] : PRE 1791+ HEYDON, ESS, ENG [35453] : PRE 1850 BRK, ENG [36605] : C1810 TOTTENHAM, ENG [37239]

DELMASTRO PRE 1900 CAMPO DI GIOVE, ABR, ITL [37519]

DELONG 1725-1900 BERKS CO., PA, USA [35318] : 1680-1725 ULSTER CO., NY, USA [35318]

DE LOSA PRE 1920 CANNETO, LIPARI ISL., ITL [36271]

DELPRADO 1817-1900 SYDNEY, NSW, AUS [35782]

DEL PRADO ALL NSW, AUS & ESP [35498]

DELPRADO PRE 1820 LONDON, ENG [36372]

DELSAUX ALL WVL, BEL [38169]

DELVES ALL PERTH, WA, AUS [35136] : ALL LND, ENG [35136] : 1700-1900 SSX, ENG [36786]

DE MAEGT 1700 OOSTKAPELLE, ZEL, NL [38696]

DE-MANTON 1550-94 AUV, FRA [37217]

DEMARS ALL WORLDWIDE [35832]

DE MARTINIS PRE 1800 ITL [34984]

DEMAS ALL WORLDWIDE [35832]

DE MEERSMAN 1750-1990 BAARDEGEM, OVL, BEL [38165]

DEMERS ALL WORLDWIDE [35832]

DEMING 1600-1700 WETHERSFIELD, CT, USA [37783]

DEMOSS 1700-1770 FREDERICK CO., VA, USA [35661]

DE MOSS 1820+ RICHLAND CO., OH, USA [38066]

DEMOTT 1750+ NJ, USA [37578]

DEMPSEY 1815-1819 PARRAMATTA, NSW, AUS [35741] : 1878+ NEWCASTLE, NSW, AUS [37911] : 1830+ ASHTON, WAR, ENG [36885] : PRE 1839 KILDEN, KID, IRL [34971] : 1750-1860 ANT, IRL [37338] : 1840-1990 DALMELLINGTON, AYR, SCT [37338] : C1850S SCT [37474] : 1840-1870 DALRY, AYR, SCT [37485] : 1840-1990 NY, USA [37338]

DEMPSIE 1860-1990 DALMELLINGTON, AYR, SCT [37338] : 1840-1990 NY, USA [37338]

DEMPSON 1820+ ENNISKILLEN, FER, IRL [37982]

DEMPSTER 1830+ DUNTOCHER, DNB, SCT [34260] : PRE 1800 GREENOCK, RFW, SCT [36436] : 1800+ WORLDWIDE [34560]

DEMUTH PRE 1800 KAPPELRODECK, BAD, GER [36968]

DENAULT 1800-1950S QUE & MN, CAN & USA [34202]

DENBIGH PRE 1790 KEIGHLEY, WRY, ENG [38028]

DEN BLAAUWEN 1700S ZIERIKZEE, ZEL, NL [38358]

DENBY 1869+ MELBOURNE, VIC, AUS [37165] : 1846 CLUTTON, SOM, ENG [34757] : PRE 1895 PORT TALBOT, GLA, WLS [34757]

DENDY 1800+ HORSHAM, SSX, ENG [36967]

DENE 1700 NUTHURST, SSX, ENG [35288]

DENEAULT 1830-1950S QUE & MN, CAN & USA [34202]

DENEEN DENIS PRE 1826 CORK CITY, COR, IRL [38294]

DENGATE 1732+ TICEHURST, SSX, ENG [36071] : ALL SSX, ENG [36501]

DENGLER 1880+ ANTWERPEN, ATW, BEL [38163] : 1880+ CHENEE, LGE, BEL [38163] : 1500-1600 WILDBERG, BAD, DDR [38163] : 1674-1990 HOFFELT, LUX [38163] : 1880+ DETROIT, MI, USA [38163] : 1880+ DUNKIRK, NY, USA [38163]

DENHAM PRE 1840 LONDON, ENG [37743] : 1820-1875 MANCHESTER, LAN, ENG [38259] : ALL ENG [38494] : WM. EDWARD PRE 1904 BELFAST, ANT, IRL [38452] : C1780 AYR, AYR, SCT [36431] : C1800 EDINBURGH, MLN, SCT [38253]

DENHOLM 1850+ BALLAN, VIC, AUS [36297] : ALEXANDER PRE 1825 DEN [36297] : C1784 EDINBURGH, MLN, SCT [35714] : 1800-1900 MLN, SCT [36297] : 1880+ DUMFRIES, DFS, SCT [38253] : C1810-1870 EDINBURGH, MLN, SCT [38253]

DENICE 1750-1820 WEX, IRL [38774]

DENIEFFE 1750-1820 WEX, IRL [38774]

DE NIES ALL BRA, BEL [38169]

DENING 1842+ SYDNEY, NSW, AUS [37119] : 1850+ GOSFORD, NSW, AUS [37119]

DENISON PRE 1860 IRL [35546] : PRE 1842 SLI, IRL [35824] : PRE 1700 HARTFORD, CT, USA [33804]

DENITHORNE 1850-1950 AUS [34535] : 1750-1850 GULVAL, CON, ENG [34535]

DENJEAN 1600-1900 SUC-ET SENTENAC, ARIEGE, FRA [33758]

DENKER 1834 HANSFELD, DEN [37690]

DENLEY 1700-1900 ENG [37829] : C1815-1871+ EDGBASTON & BIRMINGHAM, WAR, ENG & IRL [33847]

DENMAN PRE 1830 STH PETHERTON, SOM, ENG [34197] : 1500-1900 SSX, ENG [35643] : 1841 SOM, ENG [35903] : 1837-1914 STH PETHERTON, SOM, ENG & AUS [35763] : ALL WORLDWIDE [37075]

DENMEAD PRE 1800 SOM & HAM, ENG [36166] : 1700+ SOM & LND, ENG [37735]

DENN 1800+ WEX, IRL [38189]

DENNARD 1827+ HOBART, TAS, AUS [35394]

DENNE 1730+ KEN, ENG [33790] : PRE 1800 BIRCHINGTON, KEN, ENG [37371]

DENNEEN 1850S+ PICTON, NSW, AUS [38294] : DENIS PRE 1826 CORK CITY, COR, IRL [38294]

DENNEHY PRE 1830 THOMAS TOWN, KIK, IRL [35533] : 1700-1830 KANTURK, COR, IRL [37456]

DENNERLEY 1800-1900 MACCLESFIELD, CHS, ENG [38250]

DENNET PRE 1800 DITTON, LAN, ENG [37697]

DENNETT 1800+ SSX, ENG [35829] : 1780-1940 STOGUMBER & BICKNOLLER, SOM, ENG [36373]

DENNEY 1780-1860 DEDHAM, ESS, ENG [33899] : PRE 1811 COBHAM, KEN, ENG [34720]

DENNIG 1650-1870 ELLMENDINGEN, BAW, GER [37021]

DENNING C1870-1890 WAGGA, NSW, AUS [38072] : ALL ENG [37679] : 1860+ LONDON, MDX, ENG [37994] : PRE 1812 LONGFORD, LOG, IRL [38072]

DENNIS 1850+ VIC, AUS [35836] : JOHN HENRY ALL BENDIGO, VIC, NSW & ARM, AUS & IRL [37995] : PRE 1860 LITTLEHAM, DEV, ENG [33780] : PRE 1850 SHOREDITCH, LND, ENG [33912] : PRE 1830 SFK, ENG [34445] : 1800+ DORCHESTER & WEYMOUTH, DOR, ENG [34714] : 1800-1900 LONDON, ENG [35228] : C1823 CON, ENG [35251] : 1650-1800 LND, ENG [35300] : 1500+ ESS, ENG [35403] : 1600-1900S WEEK ST MARY, CON, ENG [35424] : ALL TRURO, CON, ENG [35712] : 1700+ BARDNEY, LIN & MDX, ENG [35836] : PRE 1804 NORTH TAMERTON, DEV, ENG [36604] : 1790 KEA, CON, ENG [36640] : 1760+ HOLTON BECKERING, LIN, ENG [36827] : C1720 HOBY, LEI, ENG [37053] : ALL SCARBOROUGH, NRY, ENG [37209] : 1730S GREAT HALLINGBURY, ESS, ENG [37250] : 1800+ PAUL, CON, ENG [37426] : PRE 1838 PEASMARCH, SSX, ENG [38077] : PRE 1800 CAMBORNE, CON, ENG [38214] : C1850 ST JOSEPH CO., IN, USA [36957] : 1816-1876 GRUNDY CO., MO, USA [38094] : 1858-1931 HAZEVILLE, MO, USA [38094] : 1851-1862 JOILET, IL, USA [38094] : JOHN 1754 MONMOUTH, NJ, USA [38152]

DENNISON 1800+ COMBERMERE, ONT, CAN [34107] : C1630+ ALTOFTS & NORMANTON, WRY, ENG [34397] : PRE 1819 WOOLWICH, KEN, ENG [37174] : PRE 1840+ IDLE, YKS, ENG [37174] : C1824 IRL [37263] : 1800-1820 SOMERSET CO., PA, USA [38137] : C1770 MD & VA, USA [38177] : 1640+

ROXBURY, MA, USA [38520] : ALL WORLDWIDE [36844]

DENNISS ALL LIN, ENG [37487]

DENNISTON 1700-1800 LOG, IRL [36844] : ALL WORLDWIDE [36844]

DENNISTOUN ALL WORLDWIDE [36844]

DENNY D.F. 1854+ MALDON, VIC, AUS [34011] : D.F. 1824+ HOBART, TAS, AUS [34011] : FRANCIS PRE 1830 SYDNEY, NSW, AUS [34461] : 1860+ WEST MAITLAND, NSW, AUS [34685] : 1831+ SOUTH COAST & SYDNEY, NSW, AUS [36638] : 1865+ ORANGE, NSW, AUS [38568] : ALL NFD, CAN [35619] : 1700S CASTLETHORPE, BKM, ENG [35256] : HANNAH PRE 1822 GUILDEN MORDEN, CAM, ENG [35885] : PRE 1850 BUNGAY, SFK & NFK, ENG [36037] : 1800-1850 LOUND, SFK, ENG [37220] : 1850-1920 LOWESTOFT, SFK, ENG [37220] : ALL NORTHERN, BKM, ENG [38358] : C1831 DOUGLAS, IOM [36638] : 1800S DOW, IRL [38281] : PRE 1827 GLASGOW, LKS, SCT [35863]

DENNYS 1550+ LITTLEHAM BY BIDEFORD, DEV, ENG [34747]

DEN OUDEN ALL WORLDWIDE [34095]

DENOVAN ALL SCT & CAN [36705] : ALL WORLDWIDE [35554]

DENOVAN-DE COURCY 1834+ CORK CITY, COR, IRL [35554]

DENS 1732+ ARENDONK, ATW, BEL [38163]

DENSLOW 1500+ NETHERBURY, DOR, ENG [38745]

DENSTON 1700+ DOWNHAM, CAM, ENG [34221]

DENSUMBE C1795 LUSTLEIGH, DEV, ENG [35131]

DENT PRE 1900 MANCHESTER, LAN, ENG &, AUS & NZ [34705] : PRE 1820 SKELTON, YKS, ENG [33860] : PRE 1830 WES, ENG [34562] : PRE 1792 GUISBOROUGH, NRY, ENG [37204] : PRE 1790 HUTTON ROOF, WES, ENG [38248]

DENTON 1780-1820 BRADFIELD, WRY, ENG [33767] : 1850+ BARNSLEY, YKS, ENG [34323] : 1700+ SUNDERLAND, DUR, ENG [35306] : 1700+ BISHOPWEARMOUTH, DUR, ENG [35306] : ALL KEN, ENG [37127] : 1700-1750 GOSFORTH & EGREMONT, CUL, ENG [37246] : 1750+ TODDINGTON, BDF, ENG [37306] : 1850-1950 BALTIMORE CITY & CALVERT CO., MD, USA [37583] : MARTHA 1800+ VA, USA [38374]

DEN TOOM PRE 1850 NL [38769]

DEN TOONDER ALL WORLDWIDE [38358]

DENYER PRE 1800 GODALMING & THURSLEY, SRY, ENG [34382] : 1700+ SEND & MERROW, SRY, ENG [35229] : 1700+ SSX, ENG [35836] : 1700+ SSX, ENG [35987] : PRE 1900 HAM, IOW & SRY, ENG [37321] : ALL GODALMING & THURSLEY, SRY, ENG [37420]

DE ORELLI ALL LOCARNO, ITL [38672]

DEPAEPE 1700-1900 AVELGEM, WVL, BEL [38164]

DEPAPE PRE 1700 ANZEGEM, WVL, BEL [38164]

DEPAS 1800+ RHINE RIVER, ELO, GER [37012]

DEPASS 1800-1850 ENG [37593]

DEPELSENAIR ALL WORLDWIDE [35596]

DEPELSENAIRE ALL WORLDWIDE [35596]

DE PELSENAIRE ALL WORLDWIDE [35596]

DEPELSENER ALL WORLDWIDE [35596]

DEPELSENERE ALL WORLDWIDE [35596]

DEPENNA C1680 LA BASTIDE DE LEIRAN, LGD, FRA [38604]

DE PENNAT C1680 LA BASTIDE DE LEIRAN, LGD, FRA [38604]

DEPPE 1700-1800 HERZBERG, NSA, GER [38643]

DEPPER PRE 1860 LEI, ENG [35246]

DE PRAETERE ALL WORLDWIDE [38162]

DE PRINCE 1800 VEERE, ZEL, NL [38696]

DE PRINS ALL BRA, BEL [38672]

DEPUEY 1750 LITTLE FALLS, NY, USA [38038]

DE RAEYMAECKER PRE 1830 BRUSSELS, BEL [37203]

DE RAPHYLE 1600+ FLANDERS, BEL [37581]

DE RAPPARDE 1900+ BRUSSELS, BEL [35004] : 1900+ EDMONTON, ALB, CAN [35004]

DERBY ALL MONAGHAN & BALLYBAY, MOG, IRL & SCT [36016] : EDWARD 1832-1911 HOLTON, MI, USA [37014]

DERBYSHIRE ALL WORLDWIDE [38570]

DE RENZI PRE 1800 IRL [38771] : C1600-1820 DUBLIN & COLOGNE, IRL & GER [34672]

DE RENZY ALL BAGENALSTOWN, CAR & WEX, IRL [36532]

DERGES ALL CON & DEV, ENG [36290]

DERIFIELD 1500+ ENG & USA [37026]

DE RIJKE 1600S KAPELLE, ZEL, NL [38358] : ALL SCHERPENISSE, ZEL, NL [38694]

DERMAUX PRE 1800 MARKE, WVL, BEL [38164]

DERMODY 1800+ CALLAN, KIK, IRL [34933]

DERN 1800+ CHICAGO, IL, USA [37012]

DER NEDERLANDEN ALL NL [38351]

DE RODGERS 1850S HOBART, TAS, AUS [37989]

DE ROSA 1800-1900 MA, USA [34631]

DE ROZARIO PRE 1900 INDIA [37225]

DERRAUGH PRE 1841 TYR, IRL [35615]

DERRETT ALL LLANGEVIEW & UKS, MON & GLS, WLS & ENG [35961]

DERRICK C1798 SOM, ENG [36307] : 1780 TN, USA [38184]

DERRICOTT 1850S TINTAGEL, CON, ENG [34726] : 1700-1900 SAL & HEF, ENG [36003]

DERRY ALL NOTTINGHAM, NTT, ENG [36196] : PRE 1850 STRATFORD ON AVON, WAR, ENG [36385] : PRE 1800 ATTENBOROUGH, NTT, ENG [36493] : 1800-1900 VA, USA [36937]

DERSCH 1710-1790 WETTER, GHE, GER [38647]

DERUNGS ALL WORLDWIDE [38653]

DE RUSETT 1700+ WORLDWIDE [37240]

DERWIN ALL AUS [36631] : ALL WORLDWIDE [37521]

DESAIX 1870+ USA [38558]

DESBOROUGH ALL WORLDWIDE [34944]

DESBROUGH 1850+ EDWORTH, BDF, ENG [35908]

DESCHAMP 1850+ AUS [35224] : PRE 1850 CH [35224]

DESCHAMPS ALL WORLDWIDE [35291]

DESILLE 1500-1600 NMR, BEL [36943]

DE SILLE 1400-1600 BRG, FRA [36943]

DESJARDINS 1800+ ONT, CAN [37482]

DESLAURIERS-JEANSON 1830 QUE, CAN [38583]

DE SMIT 1700-C1740S TIEL, GEL, NL [38358]

DE SMITH 1800+ AMSTERDAM, NL [36987]

DESMOND CORNELIUS C1840S CLONMULT, COR, IRL [35522] : 1873 AUCKLAND, NZ [34609]

DES NOYERS ALL WORLDWIDE [38234]

DE SOUSA CARCEIRO ALL PT [35971]

DE SOUZA 1866+ PORT ADELAIDE, SA, AUS [34595] : ALL AZORE, ISLANDS [34595]

DESROCHES PRE 1920 KENT CO., NB, CAN [38447]

DESROSIERS PRE 1870 AROOSTOOK CO., ME, USA & CAN [38447]

DESSON PRE 1750+ ROTHIEMAY, BAN, SCT [34771]

DE STIRRUP PRE 1820 ROVEN, FRA [37370]

DESTRUWOLT ALL WORLDWIDE [38633]

DETALE PRE 1650 ONEX, GE, CH [38348]

DETERT C1838 RENDSBURG, SHO, DEN [35133] : C1856 EGESTORF, HAN, GER [35133]

DETLEFS PRE 1820 OLDENBURG, SHO, GER [38648]

DETLEFSEN 1872-1881 EAST ORANGE, NJ & NY, USA [37591]

DETLOR 1824-1850 TAMWORTH, ONT, CAN [34394] : 1770-1820 STATEN ISLAND, NY, USA [34394]

DETMER ALL BRD & USA [36933]

DETMERING ALL HAN, GER [38186]

DETMOLD ALL VIC, AUS [34554]

DE TOUFREVILLE 1700S LAURIENT, BRT, FRA [33886]

DETRICK 1821-1855 LOGON CO., OH, USA [35301]

DETTMAN 1790S ST PANCRAS, MDX, ENG [37106]

DETTMER ALL LND & MDX, ENG [36042] : 1780-1850S ST PANCRAS & MARYLEBONE, MDX, ENG [36095] : 1826 MITCHAM, SRY, ENG [37106]

DETTMERING ALL HAN, GER [38186]

DEUBEL 1700-1800 RANSWEILER, RHINELAND, GER [36561]

DEUCHAR 1750-1990 DUNNING, PER, SCT [38511]

DEUCHARS 1840+ DUNDEE, ANS, SCT [34637] : PRE 1763 NEWTYLE, ANS, SCT [37772]

DEUMER C1827 BURGKHAMMER, KSA, GER & AUS [35391]

DEUSA 1700-1990 ALICANTE, ESP [38346]

DEUTSCH C1600 BAUTZEN, OBERLAUSITZ, GER [38544]

DEVABAUGH C1775-1825 PA, USA [37790]

DEVANNEY ALL WORLDWIDE [34164]

DEVAURIEUX ALL FRA [36030]

DE VAUS 1860+ MELBOURNE, VIC, AUS [34178]

DE VEAR PRE 1840 WESTMINSTER, LND, ENG [36474]

DE VEKEY ALL TOKAJ, HU & ENG [37287]

DEVELING 1860-1865 HOBART, TAS, AUS [33778]

DEVENEUR ALL LBG, BEL [38169]

DEVENISH 1788-1849 WEM, IRL & AUS [37911]

DEVENPORT 1800+ EDGBASTON, WAR, ENG [34315] : 1700+ SAL, ENG [34370]

DEVENSHER PRE 1700 MEVAGISSEY, CON, ENG [37319]

DEVERAUX 1850S HOBART, TAS, AUS [33838]

DE VERDON PRE 1850 DUNDALK, LOU, IRL [35216]

DEVEREAU ALL WORLDWIDE [33921]

DEVERELL ROBERT 1850+ WARRNAMBOOL, VIC, AUS [33850] : PRE 1794 RODBOROUGH, GLS, ENG [37610] : GEORGE 1772 BATH, ENG [38595] : PRE 1850 MOUNTRATH, LEX, IRL [33850]

DEVEREUX 1800+ CAMPTON, BDF, ENG [34315] : 1750+ LITTLE & GREAT SAXHAM, SFK, ENG [34416] : 1750-1830 WEX, IRL [34071] : PRE 1830 IRL [36299]

DEVERILL 1595+ WILFORD, NTT, HRT & ESS, ENG [33970] : 1850+ USA [33970]

DEVERN 1790+ WLS [34803]

DEVERSON 1750+ LITTLE & GREAT SAXHAM, SFK, ENG [34416]

DEVEY 1854 ALDERBURY, WIL, ENG [35369] : PRE 1850 PATTINGHAM, STS, ENG [37722] : 1868-1933 ESSEX CO., NJ, USA [37810]

DEVILLIERS PRE 1900 CAPE TOWN, CAPE, RSA [36468]

DEVINE C1860 IPSWICH & TOOWOOMBA, QLD, AUS [35158] : 1750+ LND, ENG [33963] : 1600-1850 BETHNAL GREEN, LND, ENG [37223] : PRE 1850 BANAGHER, LDY, IRL [34707] : PRE 1870 KILRUSH, CLA, IRL [35147] : C1840S BELFAST, ANT, IRL [35158] : 1800-1900 BOYERSTOWN, MEA, IRL [35845] : 1700+ WATERFORD, WAT, IRL [36857]

DEVINS 1700-1800 ORANGE, NY, USA [37435]

DEVIS 1700-1800 WAR, ENG [37924]

DEVISSER ALL WAYNE CO., NY, USA & NL [37502]

DEVLIN 1840+ PORT MACQUARIE & GLEN INNES, NSW, AUS [34185] : 1800+ MOORTOWN & ARBOE, TYR, IRL [33829] : 1774-1798 BALLINDERRY, ANT, IRL [37524] : C1850-1900 GLASGOW, LKS, SCT [35730]

DEVOLLD 1850+ NOBLE CO., OH, USA [36956]

DEVOLON PRE 1800 NL [38159]

DEVONALD 1750-1860 HUBBERSTON & MILFORD, PEM, WLS [34855]

DEVONPORT 1800+ LONDON, ENG [36135] : PRE 1780 SUTTON BONNINGTON, NTT, ENG [37754]

DEVONSHIRE 1839+ EDMONTON, MDX, ENG [34616] : C1700 PRIORS MARSTON, WAR, ENG [36431]

DEVORE 1805+ KY, USA [37037] : LUKE 1810-1840 JEFFERSON CO., OH, USA [38573]

DE VOS BAUKE 1873+ FRI, NL [34990] : 1600S TERNEUZEN, ZEL, NL [38358]

DEVOULD 1790-1850 JEFFERSON CO., OH, USA [38108]

DE VREDE ALL OUDE TONGE, ZUH, NL [38358] : ALL SCHOUWEN DUIVELAND, ZEL, NL [38358]

DEVRIES JOHN & MARG. 1889+ CARLTON, VIC, AUS [37906]

DE VRIES PRE 1900 NIEUWENDAM, NL [36755]

DE VRIES LENTSCH ALL WORLDWIDE [36755]

DEW 1840+ SYDNEY, NSW, AUS [35240] : PRE 1790 CLEY NEXT THE SEA, NFK, ENG [34828] : PRE 1900 BRISTOL, ENG [35901] : 1840-1900 BIRMINGHAM, WAR, ENG [37850] : 1800+ LONDON, ENG [37898] : 1700S REEPHAM, NFK, ENG [37898] : 1850 BELMONT CO., OH, USA [38531]

DEWAR 1869+ LONGFORD, TAS, AUS [34770] : 1860+ WELLINGTON, NSW, AUS [36648] : 1863+ DUBBO, NSW, AUS [36648] : 1860+ GEURIE, NSW, AUS [36648] : PRE 1900 ENG [35053] : PRE 1800 MLN, SCT [34929] : PRE 1900 DUNDEE, PER, SCT [35053] : PRE 1900 MARKINCH, FIF, SCT [35823] : 1830+ DALMALLY, ARL, SCT [35886] : C1750-1800 FIF, SCT [36327] : 1700-1990 TULLIALLAN, PER, SCT [36394] : 1800+ DALRYMPLE, AYR, SCT [36648] : PRE 1860 DULL, PER, SCT [36761] : PRE 1900 DUNDEE, ANS, SCT [38412] : JAMES PRE 1840 DALRYMPLE, AYR, SCT [38585]

DE WARRIS JANET 1700S-1800S KINGSTON, JAMAICA, W.INDIES [36311]

DEWBERRY 1845+ ARMIDALE, NSW, AUS [34899]

DEWE 1800+ LND, ENG [33963]

DE WET JACOBUS 1500+ AMSTERDAM, NL [34949] : ALL WORLDWIDE [34949]

DEWEY 1700S DONHEADS & E. KNOYLE, WIL, ENG [36211] : 1600-1900 CT, USA [36689] : 1635+ MA, ME & CT, USA [38021]

DEWEZ PRE 1865 BEL [35841]

DEWHIRST ELIZ 1800+ SKIPTON, WRY, ENG [34915] : 1750+ BRADFORD, WRY, ENG [36263] : ALL LAN & WRY, ENG [36886]

DEWHURST PRE 1869 MANCHESTER, LAN, ENG [34539] : PRE 1841 ASHTON U LYNE, LAN, ENG [34539] : 1800+ SHAP & TEBAY, WES, ENG [34870] : 1700-1800 SSX, ENG [35094] : PRE 1850 CLITHEROE, LAN, ENG [37179] : C1855+ WHALLEY, LAN, ENG [37888]

DEWICK 1800+ NEWTON ON TRENT, NTT, ENG [35847] : 1750-1800 NTT & LIN, ENG [36084] : C1750-1850 NTH & NTT, ENG [37520] : 1800 NTT, ENG [37570]

DE WILD PRE 1815 NYKERK, GEL, NL [33751] : PRE 1815 NYKERK, GEL, NL [38692]

DEWING 1873 GREAT WALSINGHAM, NFK, ENG [36287]

DEWITT 1800+ IN, IA & WI, USA & ENG [38746]

DE WITTE ALL PEM, WLS [37682]

DEWLEY 1806+ EGHAM, SRY, ENG [35598]

DE WOUDELAD PRE 1800 PRE, GER [34944]

DEWS 1700-1840 GREAT TEW, OXF, ENG [37850] : 1800-1880 WELLSBOURNE, WAR, ENG [37850]

DE WULF 1500-1990 TIELT, WVL, BEL [38165]

DEXTER C1828 GATESHEAD, DUR, ENG [35332] : 1750-1850 LODDINGTON, NTH, ENG [36057] : 1860S HOXTON & SOHO, LND, ENG [37102]

DEY 1750+ CHUDLEIGH, DEV, ENG [36865] : ALL ABD & BAN, SCT [34861]

DEYE 1600+ OLD, GER [37532] : 1820+ IN, OH & KY, USA [37532]

DE ZEE 1846+ FRI, NL [34990]

DEZOETE ALL LEIDEN, ZUH, NL [38705]

DE ZWARTE 1700S ZIERIKZEE, ZEL, NL [38358]

D'HAESE 1560-1990 GUSLENANDE, OVL, BEL [38165]

DIAMOND PRE 1800 BATH, SOM, ENG [34003] : 1630-1650 DARTMOUTH, DEV, ENG [34162] : PRE 1740 BIDEFORD, DEV, ENG [34445] : 1750+ BRISTOL, SOM, ENG [35129] : 1800+ SRY, BRK & HAM, ENG [37351] : PRE 1880 WEM, IRL [35339] : 1650-1730 KITTERY, ME, USA [34162] : 1700-1800 NY, USA [35603]

DIBBLE 1850-1900 ADELAIDE, SA, AUS [34006] : 1700 BROMPTON RALPH, SOM, ENG [34204] : 1810+ DEV, ENG [37074] : C1818 ITHACA, NY, USA [35646] : 1600-1900 CT, USA [36689]

DIBDEN PRE 1720 DIBDEN, HAM, ENG [35252]

DI BIJARRI PRE 1960 CLERMONT FERRAND, PUY DE DOME, FRA [38305]

DIBLEY 1870+ LONDON, ENG [34152] : 1600+ BRK, ENG [34152] : ALL ENG [34726] : 1762 TICEHURST, SSX, ENG [34726] : PRE 1840 NEWBURY, BRK, ENG [36215] : ALL WORLDWIDE [38258]

DIBSDALL 1840+ SALISBURY, WIL, ENG [37556] : C1829 BRISTOL, GLS & SOM, ENG [37556] : C1864 TOTTENHAM COURT, LND, ENG [37556]

DIBSELL 1800-1860 LONDON, ENG [34464]

DICK 1800+ PORT MACQUARIE, NSW, AUS [34860] : 1898+ SYDNEY, NSW, AUS [34860] : 1855+ GEELONG, VIC, AUS [34922] : 1822+ LANARK CO., ONT, CAN [34052] : 1840-1880 LND & MDX, ENG [36430] : PRE 1854 KAFERTHAL, BAD, GER [35363] : 1800-1850 FORKHILL, ARM, IRL [35187] : MARY 1800 KILCOO, KID, IRL [38038] : 1775-1830 GLENDERMOTT, LDY, IRL [38216] : GODFREY 1882 DURBAN, NATAL, RSA [36367] : JAMES 1882 DURBAN, NATAL, RSA [36367] : PRE 1822 BATHGATE, WLN, SCT [34052] : ALL EDINBURGH, SCT [34674] : PRE 1855 DUNDEE, ANS, SCT [34922] : 1780+ HAMILTON, LKS, SCT [35977] : ANDREW 1833+ GLASGOW, LKS, SCT [36367] : C1750 BO'NESS, WLN, SCT [36431] : C1900 EDINBURGH, SCT [36856] : PRE 1850 ABD, SCT [36856] : MARGARET C1740 AYR, AYR, SCT [37106] : JANET C1770 EDINBURGH, MLN, SCT [37106] : 1800S OCHILTREE, AYR, SCT [37969] : 1800S DUNBLANE, PER, SCT [38281] : ALL ELGIN, MOR, SCT [38357] : 1750-1900 BERKS CO., PA, USA [35318]

DICKEN ALL ENG [34320] : 1700-1770 CULPEPPER CO., VA, USA [36566]

DICKENS PRE 1864+ GUYRA, NSW, AUS [35237] : PRE 1840 HIGH HOLBORN, MDX, ENG [33873] : 1780-1820 TWYWELL, NTH, ENG [35192] : 1700-1800 LONDON, HRT, ENG [36924] : 1848+ BRISTOL, SOM, ENG [37828] : JOHN 1860+ MIDDLETON & DEVONPORT, LAN & DEV, ENG [37828] : WINNIFRED PRE 1917 DEVONPORT, DEV, ENG [37828] : 1837+ MANCHESTER, LAN, ENG [37828] : WINNIFRED 1917+ NZ [37828] : 1900+ YONKERS, NY, USA [37828] : 1946+ RI, USA [37828] : MATTHEW 1870+ NJ & PA, USA [37828] : 1650+ RI, USA [38015]

DICKENSON PRE 1864 HOBART, TAS, AUS [34262] : 1780-1820 HALIFAX, WRY, ENG [33767] : 1700+ FRISKNEY, LIN, ENG [34221] : 1830+ TAMWORTH & DRAYTON BASSETT, STS, ENG [34243] : 1794-1820S FLINTHAM, NTT, ENG [34873] : PRE 1824 FOSDYKE, LIN, ENG [35029] : JOHN 1784+ GREAT CORBY, CUL, ENG [35805] : 1800-1900S ENG [36289] : 1800+ LEIGH, LAN, ENG [37147] : EDWARD 1830+ BUFFALO, NY, USA [37212]

DICKER 1690-1760 BAUGHURST, HAM, ENG [36229] : C1780 PORTSEA, HAM, ENG [37898]

DICKERSON SUSAN C1800 NJ, USA [37453] : SALLY C1770-1861 WILLIAMSON CO., IL, SC & VA, USA [37529]

DICKEY PRE 1870 AHOGHILL, ANT, IRL [33964] : PRE 1885 NORSEWOOD, HKY, NZ [33964] : 1800-1850 VENANGO CO., PA, USA [37011] : PRE 1855 MERCER CO., PA, USA [38125]

DICKFOSS PRE 1900 QLD, AUS [37973]

DICKIE 1830+ BRANTFORD, ONT, CAN [34521] : 1890-1900 KINGS LYNN, NFK, ENG [33779] : 1880-1899 LONGFORD, DBY, ENG [33779] : 1860-1879 CROSSMICHAEL, KKD, SCT [33779] : C1720-1860S TARBOLTON, AYR, SCT [34635] : 1750+ MONTROSE, ANS, SCT [35644] : WILLIAM 1785 MAUCHLINE, AYR, SCT [36728] : 1800+ IRVINE, AYR, SCT [38247]

DICKINSON PRE 1920 PERTH, WA, AUS [35722] : PRE 1850 COLTON, LAN, ENG [34053] : 1850 PENRITH, CUL, ENG [34349] : 1700-1800 WORKINGTON, CUL, ENG [34762] : 1789 HOGTHORPE, LIN, ENG [34808] : PRE 1860 ALSTON, CUL, ENG [34958] : 1700+ LAN, ENG [35364] : 1800-1850 ALTCAR, LAN, ENG [35595] : C1780 URSWICK IN FURNESS, LAN, ENG [35722] : C1780 URSWICK IN FURNESS, CUL, ENG [35722] : C1800 NETHERWHITTON, NBL, ENG [36102] : 1750-1850 MANCHESTER, LAN, ENG [36416] : 1650-1750 NORTH SOMERCOTES, LIN, ENG [37039] : PRE 1850 FURNESS, CUL, ENG [37379] : PRE 1688 LAN, ENG [37706] : PRE 1750 THURLSTONE, WRY, ENG [37893] : 1500-1800 YKS, ENG & USA [38021] : 1750-1950 WEXFORD & LEEDS CO., WEX & ONT, IRL & CAN [36669] : C1830 PIETERMARITZBURG, RSA [37140] : 1765-1805 RENSSELAER CO., NY, USA [36581]

DICKISON C1780 URSWICK IN FURNESS, CUL, ENG [35722] : C1780 URSWICK IN FURNESS, LAN, ENG [35722] : ALL WAR, ENG [37404]

DICKMAN PRE 1750 GREAT BEDWYN, WIL, ENG [35346]

DICKOB PRE 1840 SCHENKELBERG, HEN, GER [37856]

DICKON ALL ENG [34320]

DICKS 1760 BISLEY, GLS, ENG [36649] : ALL BICKENHALL, SOM, ENG [37269] : C1800 KEMERTON, WOR, ENG [37763]

DICKSON 1835 SYDNEY, NSW, AUS [35152] : 1863+ BULLAROOK, VIC, AUS [35487] : NORMAN 1940-1960 WILLIAMSFORD, TAS, AUS [36301] : ALL LIN & YKS, ENG [34320] : C1876-1912 MANCHESTER, LAN, ENG [36024] : JAMES PRE 1845 BELFAST, IRL [34270] : 1750-1881 ANS & FIF, SCT [34447] : PRE 1850 EDINBURGH, ELN, SCT [34611] : PRE 1845 INVERESK, MLN, SCT [34706] : C1836 SMEATON, MLN, SCT [35487] : 1700+ EDINBURGH DUNBAR, MLN, SCT [36791] : PRE

1864 EDINBURGH, MLN, SCT **[37852]** : PRE 1850 INVERNESS, SCT **[37956]** : PRE 1850 ABERDEEN, SCT **[37956]** : PRE 1860 EAGLESFIELD, DFS, SCT **[38411]** : PRE 1800 LKS, SCT **[38437]** : 1790+ BEW, SCT & CAN **[35611]** : 1800-1870 COLUMBIA & ONONDAGA COS., NY, USA **[37021]**

DIDCOCK 1750-1860 STOKE POGES, BKM, ENG **[36879]**

DIDDLE C1780-1814 KNOX CO., TN, USA **[37029]**

DIDHAM 1829-1857 WESTLEIGH, DEV, ENG **[33988]** : 1883+ WORLDWIDE **[33988]**

DIDSBURY ALL WORLDWIDE **[38279]**

DIDYCHUK ALL GALICIA, SU & POL **[34146]**

DIEBEL ALL ONT, CAN **[34378]** : JOHANN H. 1700S+ NIEDERJOSSA, HESSE, GER **[34378]** : ALL USA **[34378]**

DIEBOLD MICHAEL 1866S WINONA CO., MN, USA **[38785]**

DIECKHOFF 1790-1890 GUYSBOROUGH, NS, CAN **[34115]** : ALL WORLDWIDE **[34472]**

DIEDERICH 1855-1910 LORAIN CO., OH, USA **[38106]**

DIEDERRICH PRE 1850 HAMBURG, PRE, GER **[34931]**

DIEDRICHS PRE 1880 WEITZEN, HAN, GER **[38173]** : PRE 1910 JOHNSON CO., NE, USA **[38173]** : PRE 1900 OH, USA **[38173]** : PRE 1890 WHEATON, IL, USA **[38173]**

DIEDRICHSEN 1840+ MOGELTONER & JOJER, SHO, DEN **[34785]**

DIEFENBACH 1855+ FRANKLIN, TAS, AUS **[37954]** : PRE 1855 BERSTADT, HEN, GER **[37954]**

DIEFFENBACH PRE 1800 GER **[38196]** : PRE 1800 PA, USA **[38196]**

DIEFFENBAUGH C1775-1825 PA, USA **[37790]**

DIEHL CARL 1830S STUTTGART, BAW, BRD **[35471]** : EMILIE 1839 BAW, BRD **[35471]** : PRE 1875 MIDDLESEX CO., ENG & GER **[34519]** : 1920-1936 ROTTERDAM, ZUH, NL **[38166]** : PRE 1768 PHILADELPHIA, PA, USA **[37574]**

DIEHM PRE 1800 BETTINGEN, GER **[38676]**

DIEKMANN 1812-1893 KLEINENWIEDEN, SLP, GER **[38750]** : 1802 WESTENDORF, SLP, GER **[38750]**

DIEMERT 1828+ DEEMERTON, ONT, CAN **[35262]** : 1700+ STRASBOURG, ALS, FRA **[35262]**

DIEMES PRE 1854 WUERTTENBURG, GER **[34914]**

DIER 1800+ MARYBOROUGH, LEX, IRL **[34408]**

DIERCKENS 1600+ WINGENE, WF, BEL **[34163]**

DIERIKSE PRE 1800 DENDERLEEUW, BEL **[38676]**

DIERKING 1800 LANDESBERGEN, HAN, BRD **[38327]** : 1849 PROVISO LEYDEN TWP., COOK CO., IL, USA **[38327]**

DIERLAMM ALL WORLDWIDE **[38667]**

DIES C1784+ LEN & ADD CO., ONT, CAN **[36651]** : PRE 1800 NY, USA **[36355]** : ALL USA **[37812]**

DIETLE PRE 1800 WORLDWIDE **[38657]**

DIETRICH CHARLES 1857+ COLLINGWOOD, VIC, AUS **[33797]** : PRE 1820 ELTVILLE, BAW, BRD **[34581]**

DIETSCH 1690-1850 GRUSSENHEIM, FRA **[36907]**

DIETZ 1700+ BINGEN, GER **[37993]** : PRE 1650 OSTHEIM & HANAU, HES, GER **[38348]**

DIEZEMANN ALL WORLDWIDE **[36922]**

DIFENBAUGH C1775-1825 PA, USA **[37790]**

DIFFENBACH SUSANNAH 1750 LANCASTER, PA, USA **[38109]**

DIGANCE 1680-1840 HAM & SSX, ENG **[37745]** : ALL WORLDWIDE **[37745]**

DIGBY C1700-1850 WESTMINSTER, LND, ENG **[37642]** : PRE 1900 MINTERNE, DOR, ENG **[37979]**

DIGGES LA TOUCHE ALL WORLDWIDE **[33768]**

DIGGINS 1700+ TANGMERE, SSX, ENG **[34747]** : 1850+ LONDON, LND, ENG **[37437]** : 1850+ ALDERSHOT, HAM, ENG **[37437]**

DIGGLE C1850 BOLTON, LAN, ENG **[35514]** : 1800 PRESTWICH, LAN, ENG **[37669]** : ALL WORLDWIDE **[36419]**

DIGHTON FREDERICK 1845-1926 NSW & QLD, AUS **[38567]** : 1580-1630 GLOUCESTER, ENG **[38151]**

DIGNAM ALL DEVONPORT, DEV, ENG **[37979]** : 1820S MOORE, ROS, IRL & AUS **[36862]** : ELLEN C1824-1894 IRL & CAN **[36904]**

DIGNAN PRE 1840 BIRR, OFF, IRL **[34576]** : ELLEN C1824-1894 IRL & CAN **[36904]**

DIGNEY C1785 BARNYCARROL, MAY, IRL **[38322]** : ALL WORLDWIDE **[34399]** : ALL WORLDWIDE **[38322]**

DIGNUM 1820-1840 ADELAIDE, SA, AUS **[34976]** : 1820-1840 HAMPTON, SSX, ENG **[34976]**

DIGSBREY 1805 MARDEN, KEN, ENG **[34540]**

DI IORIO ALL CAMPO DI GIOVE, ABR, ITL **[37519]**

DIJKWEL 1700S ZUID BEVELAND, ZEL, NL **[38358]**

DIKE 1700+ HORNINGSHAM, WIL, ENG **[35076]**

DIKEMAN 1834+ ONT, CAN **[34231]** : 1651+ USA **[38767]**

DIKES 1770+ ESS, ENG **[36871]**

DILL PRE 1800 BAW & BAY, FRG **[38657]**

DILLENBURG 1855 RINGGOLD CO., IA, USA **[38243]**

DILLESTON 1700S BRUNDISH, SFK, ENG **[37191]**

DILLEY 1790+ ENG **[34261]** : ALL UK **[36131]**

DILLICATE PRE 1855 FREDERICTOWN, NB, CAN **[36164]** : ELIZABETH C1824-1855 FREDERICTOWN, NB, CAN **[36164]**

DILLIN PETER 1770-1820 COSHOCHTEN CO., PA & OH, USA **[38591]**

DILLING ALL NRW, BRD **[38636]**

DILLINGER PRE 1800 BERUS, SAA, GER **[38681]** : 1820-1850 BEDFORD CO., PA, USA **[38742]**

DILLINGHAM 1550-1625 MARKET HARBOROUGH, LEI, ENG **[38229]** : PRE 1800 LINCOLN CO., KY, USA **[38196]**

DILLION 1800+ WOLVERHAMPTON, STS, ENG **[35847]**

DILLMAN 1880+ HALIFAX CO., NS, CAN **[34253]**

DILLON 1860+ TAREENA, SA, AUS **[33824]** : 1850+ BERMONDSEY, SRY & LND, ENG **[35495]** : 1860+ MANCHESTER, LAN, ENG **[36818]** : PRE 1850 LONDON, MDX, ENG **[37561]** : PRE 1900 ASHTON UNDER LYNE, LAN, ENG **[37821]** : C1850 WICKHAM, HAM, ENG **[38276]** : PRE 1860 CLA, IRL **[33829]** : C1830 KILMALEY, CLA, IRL **[34426]** : 1830S THURLES, TIP, IRL **[35557]** : PRE 1840 IRL **[37133]** : WILLIAM JOHN 1740S ANT, IRL **[37501]** : PRE 1850 DUBLIN, IRL **[37821]** : 1700S BUCKS CO., PA, USA **[36926]** : JULIA E. 1860-1929 COUNCIL BLUFS & HESPERIA, IA & AZ, USA **[38591]** : MARY ELIZ 1870-1904+ HESPERIN VIDEL LA & SB COS., CA, USA **[38591]** : MARY ELIZ 1834-1868 SPRINGFIELD FRANKLIN KNOX CO., OH, USA **[38591]** : ISREAL 1800-1854 KNOX CO., MARENGO & SACTO, OH, IA & CA, USA **[38591]**

DILOSA PRE 1920 MESSINA, SICILY IS., ITL **[36271]**

DILWORTH 1840S+ NSW, AUS **[34902]** : JOSEPH PRE 1850 TYR, IRL **[34902]**

DI MAGGIO PRE 1900 SICILY, ITL **[37519]**

DIMENT 1825-1904 SOUTHSEA, HAM, ENG **[37351]** : 1800+ SRY, BRK & HAM, ENG **[37351]**

DI MEO ALL PIZZOLI, AQUILA, ITL **[33954]**

DIMITRESCU PRE 1880 RO **[37385]**

DIMMITT C1730-1775 NC, USA **[38325]**

DIMMOCK ALL KIMPTON, HRT, ENG **[36382]** : 1750-1850 HAMBRIDGE, SOM, ENG **[37544]**

DIMOCK 1801+ LIN & GLS, ENG [34387] : C1800 ST ALBANS, HRT, ENG [37898] : 1801+ VA, USA [34387]

DIMSDALE NANCY 1801 RUTHERFORD CO., NC, USA [38109]

DIN ALL SCT [37324]

DINE PRE 1786 KEN, ENG [38389]

DINEEN 1800+ PATRICKSWELL & KNOCKAINY, LIM, IRL [33829] : DENIS PRE 1826 CORK CITY, COR, IRL [38294] : 1895 LAWRENCE CO., SD, USA [38243]

DINES PRE 1730 BRK, ENG [35866]

DINGELDEIN ALL WORLDWIDE [37651]

DINGEMANS (SEE VAN D [38170]

DINGES PRE 1800 LANGMEIL, RPF, GER [38681]

DINGLE 1885+ IPSWICH, QLD, AUS [36305] : 1840+ CAMBORNE, KEHELLAND, CON, ENG [36819]

DINGMAN PETER 1888-1891 PALMERSTON, ONT, CAN [35303] : ISAAC PRE 1900 WELLINGTON CO., ONT, CAN [35303] : PETER 1887-1894 DRAYTON, ONT, CAN [35303]

DINGWALL 1880-1900 HAMILTON WENTWORTH, ONT, CAN [34482] : 1868+ GATESHEAD, DUR, ENG [34856] : C1800+ ABERDEEN, ABD, SCT [33792] : 1830S LERWICK, SHI, SCT [34856] : PRE 1837 CARGILL, PER, SCT [37136] : PRE 1850 GLASGOW, LKS, SCT [37832]

DINKINS PRE 1768 NC, USA [37786]

DINKLAGE 1643-1668 HARTUM, WEF, GER [38750]

DINN 1800+ NB, CAN [38189] : 1800+ NFD, CAN [38189] : 1800+ NEW ROSS, WEX, IRL [38189] : 1800+ BOSTON, MA, USA [38189]

DINNEEN DENIS PRE 1826 CORK CITY, COR, IRL [38294]

DINNIE 1770-1820S LIBERTON, MLN, SCT [34359]

DINNING PRE 1808 JSY, CHI [34452] : 1700-1750 CAMBUSLANG, LKS, SCT [37872]

DINNIS (SEE DENNIS) [35712]

DINSDALE PRE 1840 NEW MALTON, YKS, ENG [33831] : 1800+ KEIGHLEY, WRY, ENG [35970] : 1700+ STOCKTON ON TEES, DUR, ENG [37635] : 1700+ MIDDLETON TYAS, NRY, ENG [37635] : 1830+ RSA [34946]

DINSMORE 1800+ LONDONDERRY, LDY, IRL [35315]

DION 1830 QUE, CAN [38583]

DIONET 1620-1699 MONTALAMBERT, PCH, FRA [34514]

DIPAOLO PRE 1830 CASALBORDINO, CHIETI, ITL [34127]

DIPIETRO PRE 1830 CASALBORDINO, CHIETI, ITL [34127]

DIPLOCK PRE 1820 BRIGHTON, SSX, ENG [37142] : 1850+ BUXTED, SSX, ENG [37206] : 1830+ LITTLE HORSTEAD, SSX, ENG [37206] : 1800+ FRAMFIELD, SSX, ENG [37206]

DIPPELSMANN ALL WORLDWIDE [35253]

DIPROSE 1800-1989 LONGFORD, TAS, AUS [35089]

DIRCKES PRE 1750 DOSSEL, WARBURG, GER [37569]

DIRCKINCK-HOLMFELD C1800 WORLDWIDE [34041]

DIRISIO PRE 1830 CASALBORDINO, CHIETI, ITL [34127]

DIRSCHERL 1800+ STAMSRIED, BAV, GER [37483]

DISCHESEIT PRE 1830 TRAKEHNIN, PRE, GER [38191]

DISHAROON PRE 1850 WORCESTER CO., MD, USA [38135]

DISHER C1821 LIBERTON, MLN, SCT [36302] : PRE 1857 SCT [36888]

DISLEY 1800+ LAN, ENG [36363] : PRE 1820 HALSALL, LAN, ENG [37072] : 1800+ LEIGH, LAN, ENG [37147] : 1800+ WORLDWIDE [37147]

DISMORE 1700-1900 AUS [37077] : 1800-1900 CRANFORD, MDX, ENG [37077] : 1700-1850 HOLBORN, LND, ENG [37077] : 1800-1900 LIVERPOOL, LAN, ENG [37077] : 1750-1900 LONDON, MDX, ENG [37077] : 1700-1900 NZ [37077]

DISNEY 1700-1800 MONSEA, TIP, IRL [37844] : 1700-1900 GAL, IRL [37844] : 1700-1900 DOW, IRL [37844]

DISS 1700+ HALSTEAD, ESS & SRY, ENG [36871]

DISTENFELD ALL WORLDWIDE [37750]

DISTURNALL ALL BUSHBURY, STS, ENG [36537] : ALL BIRMINGHAM, WAR, ENG [36537]

DI TANA PRE 1880 CAMPO DI GIOVE, ABR, ITL [37519] : PRE 1920 MILFORD, MA, USA [37519]

DITCH 1830+ TICEHURST, SSX, ENG & CAN [34467]

DITCHFIELD C1818 WALSALL, STS, ENG [36649]

DITMARS 1780-1830 READINGTON, NJ, USA [38741]

DITTBRENNER ALL KLEIN TROMNAU, WPR, GER [37529]

DITTERICH 1850S MALDON, VIC, AUS [34793] : 1680-1750 BAMBERG, GER [34793]

DITTMER 1830S ST PANCRAS, MDX, ENG [37106]

DITTON C1875 THAME, MITCHAM & WIMBLEDON, LND, ENG [38483]

DIVALL ALL SRY, ENG [33925]

DIVANY 1800+ KILLARGA, LET, IRL [35248]

DIVE 1700-1850 IDEN, SSX, ENG [35829] : ALL SSX & KEN, ENG [37236]

DIVER 1850+ QUE & ONT, CAN [38171] : 1780+ NORWICH, NFK, ENG & AUS [34591] : C1880 BOMBAY, INDIA [38466] : 1800-1900 BALLYSHANNON, DON, IRL [38171]

DIVERDINE PRE 1750 LONDON, MDX, ENG [36379]

DIVES 1750+ LINGFIELD, SRY, ENG [36088] : 1600+ BROMHAM, BDF, ENG [36088]

DIVINE C1830 CAV, IRL [33812]

DIVINNIA PRE 1880 ROSS CO., OH, USA [37565]

DIVOT 1800+ DRUMARTON, DON, IRL [34785]

DIX PRE 1900 JSY, CHI [33966] : 1800-1850 MAIDENHEAD, BRK, ENG [38276] : PRE 1945 TETSCHEN, GER [38674] : PRE 1725 CT, USA [37510] : ALL WORLDWIDE [38674]

DIXEY 1850 AYLESBURY, BKM, ENG [34084] : 1880-1920 LONDON, ENG [34084]

DIXON 1853+ PORT ADELAIDE, SA, AUS [34595] : 1893+ WARRACKNABEAL, VIC, AUS [34685] : 1800+ COOKS RV, NSW, AUS [34860] : C1840S SYDNEY & GOULBURN, NSW, AUS [35158] : C1890 GIN GIN & BUNDABERG, QLD, AUS [35158] : 1870-1890S JUGIONG, NSW, AUS [35158] : 1860-1870S WARRELL CREEK, QLD, AUS [35158] : PRE 1858 GOOLWA, SA, AUS [35709] : 1850+ WILLIAMSTOWN, VIC, AUS [35802] : 1876-1911 OAKVALE, VIC, AUS [35835] : 1854-1876 SCOTCHMANS BUNINYONG, VIC, AUS [35835] : 1850S HURON, ONT, CAN [38475] : C1820 LONDON, ENG [34041] : 1700S MAIDSTONE, KEN, ENG [34205] : ALL LIN & YKS, ENG [34320] : C1700-1850S BURSTON, NFK, ENG [34339] : PRE 1840 SRY & KEN, ENG [34383] : PRE 1850 KESWICK, CUL, ENG [34442] : PRE 1811 WASDALE HEAD, CUL, ENG [34452] : 1800S CUL, ENG [34509] : 1800+ BARROWFORD, LAN, ENG [34564] : PRE 1849 ENG [34765] : 1848 BILSTON, STS, ENG [34851] : 1750+ WASHINGTON, DUR, ENG [34852] : 1828+ HEVERSHAM, WES, ENG [34926] : PRE 1800 ADEL, WRY, ENG [35079] : 1880+ NELSON, LAN, ENG [35169] : 1784

BROUGHTON IN FURNESS, LAN, ENG **[35243]** :
1631 KING'S CLIFFE, NTH, ENG **[35369]** : 1700-
1920 HARROW, MDX, ENG **[35403]** : ALL
WALSINGHAM, NFK, ENG **[35633]** : ALL
SOUTHAMPTON, HAM, ENG **[35802]** : PRE 1826
EYTHORNE, KEN, ENG **[35835]** : PRE 1860
ASHFORD, KEN, ENG **[36113]** : ALL BOLTON,
LAN, ENG **[36198]** : 1700+ LONDON, YKS & NTT,
ENG **[36266]** : 1840+ MARYPORT, CUL, ENG
[36439] : 1900+ SOUTH NORWOOD, SRY, ENG
[36439] : GEORGE PRE 1900 RETFORD, NTT, ENG
[36502] : 1700+ WEARDALE, DUR, ENG **[36961]** :
WILLIAM C1820 ALLENDALE, NBL, ENG **[37112]** :
JOHN 1870+ DONCASTER, YKS, ENG **[37112]** :
PRE 1785 KINGSCLIFFE, NTH, ENG **[37112]** : PRE
1820 THIXENDALE, ERY, ENG **[37357]** : ALL ST
BEES, CUL, ENG **[37484]** : C1870 BURY, LAN, ENG
[37669] : 1750-1820 OXWICK, NFK, ENG **[37845]** :
PRE 1803 NTT, ENG **[37893]** : 1851+ NEWCASTLE
ON TYNE, NBL, ENG **[37988]** : 1805-1940S
SPITALL, NBL, ENG **[38269]** : 1785 BRANXTON,
NBL, ENG **[38269]** : C1850 GAINSBOROUGH, LIN,
ENG **[38272]** : 1880S NORTON, ERY, ENG **[38356]** :
JOHN PRE 1885 NEWCASTLE UPON TYNE, NBL,
ENG **[38585]** : EMMERSON 1826+ DUR, ENG &
AUS **[37112]** : C1800 CLA, IRL **[35203]** : 1800+
DUBLIN, IRL **[37422]** : MARGARET C1815+
BARRAGH, CAR & QUE, IRL & CAN **[36904]** :
JOHN C1811-1872 BARRAGH, CAR & QUE, IRL &
CAN **[36904]** : 1800+ EDINBURGH, MLN, SCT
[36999] : 1740+ DFS, SCT **[38385]** : 1744+
BELMONT CO., OH, USA **[37564]** : 1824+ USA
[37592] : 1845+ JACKSON CO., MI, USA **[38231]** :
PRE 1800 HARTFORD, CT, USA **[38231]** : 1700+
CHATHAM CO., NC, USA **[38336]** : ROBERT PRE
1850 NC & GA, USA **[38536]** : JOSHUA COL. 1815-
1865+ FRED CO., MD, USA **[38591]** : 1800-1900
LOUISVILLE, KY, USA **[38770]** : 1800-1900
MUSCOGEE CO., GA, USA **[38770]** : PRE 1830 NY,
USA & IRL **[34741]** : 1870+ NEWPORT, MON, WLS
[36439] : ALL WORLDWIDE **[36548]**

DOAK 1863+ COLAC, VIC, AUS **[35437]** : 1800S
DROMORE, DOW, IRL **[35437]** : PRE 1880 IRVINE
& AYR, AYR, SCT **[33966]** : 1760-1810 AYR, SCT
[35813] : MARY POLLY C1800+ WYTHE CO., VA,
USA **[37604]**

DOAKES 1850-1950 BELFAST, ANT, IRL **[38024]**

DOANE 1800+ WELLAND CO., ONT, CAN **[37797]** :
1868+ GEORGETOWN, ONT, CAN **[37797]** : 1824-
1868 WALPOLE, HALDIMAND CO., ONT, CAN
[37797] : 1629-1980 USA **[35309]** : 1850-1949
BANGOR, ME, USA **[36915]** : 1770-1840 TOLLAND,
CT, USA **[36915]** : 1635-1758 EASTHAM, MA, USA
[36944]

DOBBERTEIN 1800+ SCHONHAUSEN, PRE, GER
[36240]

DOBBIE JOSEPH PRE 1820 YKS, ENG **[35541]** :
1800+ PAISLEY, RFW, SCT **[34049]** : 1800+
GLASGOW, SCT **[36835]** : 1800+ EDINBURGH,
SCT & AUS **[36257]**

DOBBIN 1818+ ARM, IRL **[36910]**

DOBBINSON 1800-1900 MDX, ENG **[34641]** : PRE
1841 SHOREDITCH, MDX, ENG **[35704]** : 1850-1900
AUCKLAND, NZ **[34641]** : 1891+ AUCKLAND, NI,
NZ **[35704]**

DOBBS 1800+ WOR, ENG **[37937]** : 1600S DOBBS
FERRY, NY, USA **[34353]** : 1925+ NEW YORK,
NY, USA **[34379]**

DOBBY WILLIAM 1860+ GOULBURN RIVER,
NSW, AUS **[35541]** : WILLIAM PRE 1860
RICHMOND, NSW, AUS **[35541]** : WILLIAM PRE

1820 YKS, ENG **[35541]** : JOSEPH PRE 1820 YKS,
ENG **[35541]**

DOBE 1840S CLA, IRL **[35259]**

DOBIE 1800-1880 DUNFERMLINE, FIF, SCT **[35094]** :
PRE 1840 DUNDEE, ANS, SCT **[35184]**

DOBIGNIE 1780-1830 BRUSSELS, BEL **[37203]**

DOBINS 1800S RATHKEALE, LIM, IRL **[38373]**

DOBIS 1910-30S FAYETTE CO., PA, USA **[38314]**

DOBNEY 1700-1800 TAUNTON, SOM, ENG **[37843]**

DOBOSCZ PRE 1900 WADOWICE, BB, POL **[38314]**

DOBSLAFF 1849+ GR. DOMBROWO, PRE, GER
[38614] : PRE 1808 GR. DOMBROWO, GER **[38614]** :
PRE 1808 GR. DOMBROWO, POL **[38614]**

DOBSON ALL ONT, CAN **[34465]** : 1900+
TORONTO, ONT, CAN **[34465]** : PRE 1950
NIAGARA FALLS, ONT, CAN **[34465]** : WILLIAM
1883+ MONTREAL, QUE, CAN **[35623]** : JOSEPH
1831+ ONTARIO CO., ONT, CAN **[35623]** : 1830-
1900 CARLETON CO., ONT, CAN **[36666]** :
THOMAS 1839-1860+ GREY CO., ONT, ALB & IL,
CAN & USA **[35623]** : PRE 1813 HIGH WYCOMBE,
BKM, ENG **[34104]** : PRE 1830 LONDON, ENG
[34197] : PRE 1840 KIRKANDREWS, CUL, ENG
[34201] : ALL YKS, ENG **[34465]** : PRE 1860 KEN,
ENG **[34465]** : 1750-1850 DUR, ENG **[34753]** : JOHN
1676+ FARLINGTON, YKS, ENG **[35623]** :
WILLIAM PRE 1666 WARBOROUGH, OXF, ENG
[35623] : 1800+ ORMSKIRK, LAN, ENG **[36112]** :
1859 LIVERPOOL, LAN, ENG **[36112]** : C1923
CLAYTON, LAN, ENG **[36171]** : C1840
NEWCHURCH, LAN, ENG **[36649]** : PRE 1850
SELBY, YKS, ENG **[37094]** : PRE 1800 YORK, YKS,
ENG **[37377]** : 1840-1900 SOUTH SHIELDS, DUR,
ENG **[37419]** : HENRY 1818-1870+ NEWCASTLE
ON TYNE, NBL & VIC, ENG & AUS **[35623]** :
WALTER 1822+ BRIDLINGTON, YKS, ENG &
CAN **[35623]** : 1800-1900 SCT **[34135]** : C1824 FORD,
MLN, SCT **[37333]** : 1756-1780 SELKIRK, SEL, SCT
[38117] : WILLIAM 1864+ INDIANAPOLIS, IN,
USA **[35623]** : FRANKLIN 1855+ MEIGS CO., OH
& CO, USA **[35623]** : RICHARD PRE 1850
LINCOLN, NE, USA **[35623]** : JOSEPH C. 1795-
1850+ FRANKLIN, TN, USA **[35623]** : JONATHAN
1659+ SCITUATE, MA, USA **[35623]** : DANIEL
1820+ LEE CO., IA, USA **[35623]** : GEORGE 1830+
PORT OF NOYES, MI, USA **[35623]** : THOMAS S.
1820-1902 LAMAR CO., SC & AL, USA **[35623]** : 1840
BUTLER, PA, USA **[38317]** : 1850 JEFFERSON, PA,
USA **[38317]**

DOCHE PRE 1700 HAVRE, HNT, BEL **[38167]**

DOCHERTY 1873-1877 GLASGOW, LKS, SCT **[33811]** :
1800+ WISHAW, LKS, SCT **[34934]** : 1940S
GLASGOW, SCT **[35843]** : 1820+ OLD & NEW
KILPATRICK, DNB, SCT & IRL **[35579]**

DOCHET PRE 1700 HAVRE, HNT, BEL **[38167]**

DOCHEZ 1700-1800 USA **[38167]**

DOCHOW 1700-1800 BERKHOLZ, BRA, GER **[35968]**

DOCKER 1750+ LIN & STS, ENG **[35525]**

DOCKRAY C1800 FOXBOROUGH, ROS, IRL **[35970]**

DOCKSEY 1850+ BALMAIN, NSW, AUS **[37117]** :
TOM PRE 1850 BRISTOL, GLS, ENG **[37117]** :
FRED PRE 1852 STEPNEY, LND, ENG **[37117]** :
1790S MARSTON ON DOVE, DBY, ENG **[37834]**

DOCWRA PRE 1850 GUILDEN MORDEN, CAM,
ENG **[37989]**

DOD DANIEL 1766-1831 AUDLEM, CHS, ENG
[34143]

DODD 1850S+ BEECHWORTH, VIC, AUS **[35522]** :
1833+ LEAMINGTON, WAR, ENG **[33882]** : PRE
1900 NBL, ENG **[33975]** : ROBERT WILSON 1880
DARLINGTON, DUR, ENG **[34512]** : PRE 1850 SAL,
ENG **[34861]** : PRE 1776 HIGHWORTH, WIL, ENG

[35236] : PRE 1858 TOPSHAM, DEV, ENG [35496] : PRE 1853 HOOLE, CHS, ENG [35504] : C1814 SEDBERGH, YKS, ENG [35920] : PRE 1860 LAN, ENG [35928] : PRE 1900 MANCHESTER, LAN, ENG [36019] : PRE 1828 BRIGHTON, SSX, ENG [36167] : PRE 1815 MILVERTON, WAR, ENG [36177] : 1800-1865 LIVERPOOL, LAN, ENG [36522] : PRE 1800 KEN, ENG [37180] : 1870+ NEW MILLS, DBY, ENG [37359] : C1839 TARVIN, CHS, ENG [37359] : PRE 1870 ROMILEY, CHS, ENG [37359] : 1800S WEST DERBY, LAN, ENG [37525] : 1795 MORLAND, WES, ENG [38209] : ALL CHESTER, CHS, ENG & SCT [34046] : PRE 1850 CASTLETOWNROCHE & MALLOW, COR, IRL [35522] : 1850+ SALEM, MA, USA [35522] : 1695 MD, USA [37795] : 1790-1870 UNION CO., SC, USA [38188] : 1830-1860 DENTON CO., TX, USA [38367]

DODDIN ALL ENG & SCT [36119]

DODDING ALL ENG & SCT [36119]

DODDINGE ALL ENG & SCT [36119]

DODDRELL 1830-1990 BRISTOL, GLS, ENG & SCT [37990]

DODDRIDGE 1850+ QUEBEC, QUE, CAN [34228]

DODDS 1860+ ROCKHAMPTON, QLD, AUS [38075] : 1870+ SYDNEY, NSW, AUS [38075] : C1800 NEWBURN, NBL, ENG [33886] : 1800+ WOOLER, NBL, ENG [34263] : PRE 1820 BRANCEPETH, DUR, ENG [34462] : MARGARET ANN C1851-1892 ROTHBURY, NBL, ENG [34721] : JANE C1825+ ROTHBURY, NBL, ENG [34721] : 1800+ CUL, ENG [37073] : PRE 1820 LONDON, ENG [38075] : 1750-1850 HADDINGTON, ELN, SCT [34615]

DODGE PRE 1810 MAIDSTONE, KEN, ENG [34816] : PRE 1850 DEV, ENG [36052] : PRE 1800 LONDON, ENG [37133] : 1800S CHISELBOROUGH, SOM, ENG [37544] : 1604-1813 BEVERLY, MA, USA [35294] : 1850-1870 KEWEENAW CO., MI, USA [38010] : 1857-1924 BRADFORD, WI, USA [38139] : NATHANIAL 1700S BLOCK ISLAND, CT, USA [38785]

DODGSON PRE 1850 PRESTON PATRICK, WES, ENG [37246] : 1820-40 ENG [38151] : 1660-1820 KENDAL, WES, ENG [38443] : 1800-1900 LIVERPOOL, LAN, ENG [38443] : 1820 ARKSEY, WRY, ENG [38469] : 1836-68 CARROLLTON, IL, USA [38151]

DODING ALL ENG & SCT [36119]

DODINGE ALL ENG & SCT [36119]

DODLEY 1800 MOBBERLEY, CHS, ENG [37598]

DODRELL 1830-1990 BRISTOL, GLS, ENG & SCT [37990]

DODRIDGE 1650+ POUGHILL, DEV, ENG [35027]

DODS C1873 ROX, SCT [36856]

DODSHON 1600-1640 BARBON, WMD, ENG [36635]

DODSLEY ALL NTT, ENG [36105]

DODSON PRE 1800 BRINKWORTH, WIL, ENG [34612] : PRE 1661 KINGSTON UPON THAMES, SRY, ENG [36030] : 1750-1900 BRIGHTON, SSX, ENG [37077] : 1700-1800 LONDON, MDX, ENG [37077] : 1700-1800 BROMLEY, KEN, ENG [37077] : 1700-1800 WINCHELSEA, SSX, ENG [37077] : 1700-1800 HURSTPIERPOINT, SSX, ENG [37077] : C1860 MECKLENBURG CO., VA, USA [36903] : 1760-1800 FREDERICK CO., MD, USA [38106]

DODT GUSTAVE 1800+ PRE, GER [35429]

DODWELL PRE 1755 LONG CRENDON, BKM, ENG [36866]

DODYINGE ALL ENG & SCT [36119]

DOEFFINGER PRE 1850 ENZWEIHINGEN, WUE, GER [38333]

DOEG 1800-1900 EXETER, DEV, ENG [34151] : 1760-1810 AYR, SCT [35813]

DOEL PRE 1793 BRADFORD ON AVON, WIL, ENG [33764] : PRE 1875 FROME, SOM, ENG [35764]

DOELEMAN 1600S DREISCHOR, ZEL, NL [38358]

DOEPNER C1846 DANZIG, WPR, GER [38626]

DOERING ALL GER [36719] : PRE 1770 BEBERSTEDT, PSA, GER [38048]

DOEVENDANS 1800+ VOLLENHOVE, OIJ, NL [35338]

DOGGETT 1750S CAMBRIDGE, CAM, ENG [34205] : 1800-1860 HRT & MDX, ENG [37829] : 1671-1767 LANCASTER CO., VA, USA [37029]

DOGUE 1856+ SYDNEY, NSW, AUS [36857]

DOHENY ALL BALLINALACKEN, KIK, IRL [38300]

DOHERNEY 1863+ SUNBURY, MDX, ENG [36326]

DOHERTY 1888+ MOONAMBEL, VIC, AUS [34174] : 1890+ WARWICK, QLD, AUS [35073] : 1800-1990 ST MALACHIE, QUE, CAN [36944] : MARY 1830-1889 STE CATHERINE, QUE, CAN [37809] : 1780+ CREE, KILRUSH, KILKEE, CLA, IRL [33927] : PRE 1853 LDY, IRL [34779] : PRE 1820+ RAPHOE, DON, IRL [35759] : ALL FER, IRL [36784] : 1800S PORTADOWN, ARM, IRL [36833] : 1700-1860 CLOUGHFIN & LIFFORD, DON, IRL [37118] : MARY 1812-1830 ANT, IRL [37809] : 1700+ DON, IRL [37826]

DOIDGE 1852+ VIC, AUS [35487] : 1797+ TAVISTOCK, DEV, ENG [35487] : 1700-1850 EAST, CON, ENG [37761]

DOIG 1800+ BIRKENHEAD, CHS, ENG [37306] : PRE 1850 DROMARA, DOW, IRL [37238] : PRE 1830 GLAMIS, ANS, SCT [34814] : PRE 1854 DUNDEE, TAY, SCT [35231] : 1780+ MONIMAIL, FIF, SCT [36509] : 1780-1810 GLAMIS, ANS, SCT [37172] : 1780-1810 DUNDEE, ANS, SCT [37172] : 1700+ FORFAR, ANS, SCT [37306]

DOLAN 1750+ WESTPORT, MAY, IRL [35611] : 1810-1980 SCT [37870]

DOLBAIR PRE 1700 COLYTON, DEV, ENG [38745]

DOLBEER 1900+ CASSOPOLIS, MI, USA [37597]

DOLD C1740 GLOTTERTAL, BAD, GER [33772] : C1750 OFINGEN, BAD, GER [34239]

DOLE 1819+ AUS [33764] : 1800-1900 OTTAWA, ONT, CAN [35605] : 1800-1819 BRISTOL, GLS, ENG [33764]

DOLING 1800+ MAPERTON, DOR, ENG [35201]

DOLL 1630-1790 RANSWEILER, RHINELAND, GER [36561]

DOLLACK PRE 1900 HU & YU [36709]

DOLLIDGE ALL SSX, ENG [35706]

DOLLING PRE 1745 LONDON, MDX, HRT & DOR, ENG [34743] : C1850 TOPSHAM, DEV, ENG [37378] : ALL WORLDWIDE [38258]

DOLLOUR 1850-1900 WILLENHALL, STS, ENG [36495]

DOLMAN ALL NFK, ENG [36790] : 1800S TATENHILL, STS, ENG [38502] : PRE 1800S TICKNALL, DBY, ENG [38502]

DOLMEGE PRE 1700 ELO, GER [36914] : 1700 LIM & TIP, IRL [36914]

DOLPHER GEORGE 1887+ HAMILTON CO., OH, USA [37797]

DOLPHIN 1790+ LIVERPOOL, LAN, ENG [34698] : 1840-1900 SCHUYLKILL CO., PA, USA [38106]

DOLTON 1700-1800 DODSBROOKE, DEV, ENG [36155]

DOLUETH 1870+ TEMESVAR, HU [34029]

DOMAILLE PRE 1867 GSY, CHI [34039]

DOMDEY PRE 1890 SCHWEDENHOHE, POS, GER [38618]

DOMINE ALL WORLDWIDE [36378]

DOMINGUEZ PRE 1856 LISBON, PT [33813]

DOMINICK PRE 1750 LND, ENG [38084]

DOMINY PRE 1853 SOM, ENG [36171] : 1841 HARDINGTON MANDEVILLE, SOM, ENG [37378]

DOMLEO ALL NTT & DBY, ENG [34319]

DOMMINNEY ALL WORLDWIDE [36378]

DOMSHY PRE 1900 L'VOV, GALICIA, UKRAINE [38438]

DOMVILLE 1500-1900 LIVERPOOL, LAN, ENG [34975]

DON 1800-1890 CUPAR, FIF, SCT [35524]

DONAGHIE PRE 1840 IRL [37428]

DONAGHUE 1820S LAN, ENG [38281] : C1830 KILMALEY, CLA, IRL [34426] : 1820S IRL [38281] : 1820S WLS [38281]

DONAGHY PRE 1857 BALLILAW, TYR, IRL [34941]

DONAHUE 1800+ LIM, IRL [35370] : 1700-1850 MAYO, KID & MAY, IRL [37068] : 1850-1870 PITTSBURGH, PA, USA [36900]

DONALD 1800+ SYDNEY, NSW, AUS [37976] : PRE 1850 WENTWORTH W FLAMB., ONT, CAN [37469] : PRE 1800 ANHORN, CUL, ENG [35440] : C1900 ENG [37469] : PRE 1870 DRY & DOW, IRL [38286] : 1869+ CANTERBURY, NZ [38286] : PRE 1821 MONIFEITH, ANS, SCT [33992] : 1809+ KINROSS, KRS, SCT [35708] : ALL DUNDONALD, AYR, SCT [36041] : JOHN 1814-1820 FORDOUN, KCD, SCT [36308] : PRE 1800 SCONE, PER, SCT [36436] : PRE 1831 ST VIGEANS, ANS, SCT [37442] : C1900 SCT [37469] : JOHN PRE 1850 FIF, SCT [37976] : PRE 1842 FIF, SCT [37976] : JOHN PRE 1850 ANS, SCT [37976] : PRE 1842 ANS, SCT [37976] : 1800+ HUNTLY, ABD, SCT [38355] : 1800-1850 OLD MELDRUM & ABERDEEN, ABD, SCT [38355]

DONALDSON 1850+ SURRY HILLS, NSW, AUS [34979] : C1859 TUDOR, ONT, CAN [34133] : 1857+ HARRISTON, ONT, CAN [38413] : 1700-1850 ALFORD & LINCOLN CITY, LIN, ENG [37843] : 1880-1935 LOCHGELLY, MLN, SCT [33891] : ADAM 1700 JOHNSTONE, DFS, SCT [34225] : C1800 FETTERESSO, KCD, SCT [34608] : PRE 1927 HAMILTON, LKS, SCT [35007] : 1780S FALKIRK, STI, SCT [35259] : CHRISTIAN PRE 1820 DUNNOTTAR, KCD, SCT [35462] : PRE 1800 FIF, SCT [35745] : C1800+ LARKHALL & KIRKFIELD BANK, LKS, SCT [35995] : 1800+ NEW KILPATRICK, RFW, SCT [36085] : 1800S FORFAR, ANS, SCT [36837] : 1750+ KINNEFF & CATTERLINE, KCD, SCT [36971] : WILLIAM 1818-1856 SHAPINSAY, OKI, SCT & AUS [37559]

DONALIES ALL KRS. GUMBINNEN, OPR, GER [38649]

DONANT 1700+ GER [35566]

DONARD 1800S PA, USA [36558]

DONATH C. GOTTLIB PRE 1857 LEUTERSDORF, GER [35641]

DONAVAN 1740+ NEWINGTON, KEN, ENG [36236] : 1863+ LONDON, ENG [36995]

DONAVON MATHEW PRE 1850 COR, IRL [34545]

DONCASTER PRE 1840 MARCH, CAM, ENG [37989]

DONDE C1700 ENFIELD, LND, ENG [35456] : PRE 1700 FRA [35456]

DONELLY 1850-1900 HEATHCOTE, VIC, AUS [35777] : 1850+ LIVERPOOL, LAN, ENG [34566] : PRE 1850 CORK, COR, IRL [34566] : PRE 1919 ROX & SEL, SCT [35934]

DONES C1890 BRISTOL, ENG [37131]

DONEVAN 1750+ CORK, COR, IRL [36236]

DONEY PRE 1853 ROS, IRL [34043] : 1800-1840 TIOGA CO., NY, USA [37782]

DONGES PRE 1810 MUNCHHAUSEN, HES, GER [34840]

DONITHORNE 1750-1850 GULVAL, CON, ENG [34535]

DONIVAN 1855-1890 KEWEENAW CO., MI, USA [38010]

DONJEE 1600+ ESP [35444]

DONKERS 1800+ S GRAVENHAGE, ZUH, NL [35338]

DONKERWOLKE ALL WORLDWIDE [38162]

DONN PRE 1875 LKS, SCT [35556]

DONNELL PRE 1870 DRY & DOW, IRL [38286] : 1869+ CANTERBURY, NZ [38286]

DONNELLY 1850+ KANGAROO VALLEY & BELLINGEN, NSW, AUS [35735] : 1860+ MELBOURNE, VIC, AUS [35857] : WILLIAM 1843+ DAPTO, NSW, AUS [37155] : CATHERINE PRE 1902 BERGALIA, NSW, AUS [37155] : JOHN PRE 1890 BALLYHEIFER, LDY, IRL [33871] : RICHARD PRE 1897 AGHAGASKIN, LDY, IRL [33871] : C1800+ ARMAGH, IRL [34672] : 1800+ BALLYCASTLE, ANT, IRL [35054] : PRE 1865 IRL [35424] : 1770-1830 DUBLIN, IRL [35777] : PRE 1889 IRL [35820] : PRE 1860 CLOONE, LET, IRL [35857] : PRE 1845 CASTLEBAR, MAY, IRL [38583] : CHARLES PRE 1860 LIM, IRL [38736] : 1889 OLD KILPATRICK, DNB, SCT [35820] : 1906+ BOSTON, MA, USA [37626] : PRE 1880 TREMPEALEW, WI, USA [38736]

DONNEMORROTH 1761+ SCT [38685]

DONNETT 1760-1850 DUNDEE, ANS, SCT [38511]

DONNITHORNE 1816S PENZANCE, CON, ENG [35593]

DONNY ALL WORLDWIDE [35517]

DONOGHOE 1840-1990 QUEANBEYAN, NSW, AUS [33818]

DONOGHUE 1800-1833 LONDON, ENG [37920] : 1820+ BALLYSTEEN & ASKEATON, LIM, IRL [34960] : PRE 1874 DRIMOLEAGUE, COR, IRL [35197] : PRE 1850 KILLARNEY, KER, IRL [35224] : 1800-1833 CLA, IRL [37920]

DONOHOE 1850+ HAY, NSW, AUS [34534] : PRE 1849 MIDDLEWICH, CHS, ENG [37886] : MICHAEL C1824 IRL [37886]

DONOVAN DANIEL 1860S-1870S WESBURY, TAS, AUS [34452] : 1860 SHOALHAVEN, NSW, AUS [34806] : ESTHER 1830-1840 PARRAMATTA, NSW, AUS [35484] : JOHN 1830+ PARRAMATTA, NSW, AUS [35484] : MATHEW 1840+ RICHMOND, VIC, AUS [35599] : MATHEW 1823+ FISH RV, NSW, AUS [35599] : 1793+ SYDNEY, NSW, AUS [36236] : 1852 KEILOR, VIC, AUS [37174] : 1800+ GLENGARRY, ONT, CAN [35614] : 1840+ HALIFAX, NS, CAN [37432] : 1740+ NEWINGTON, KEN, ENG [36236] : PRE 1940 LONDON, ENG [37062] : DANIEL PRE 1820 DUBLIN, IRL [34452] : THOMAS PRE 1850 TIPPERARY, IRL [34879] : 1750+ COR, IRL [34933] : JEREMIAH C1830S MIDLETON, COR, IRL [35522] : MATHEW PRE 1822 TRIM, MEA, IRL [35599] : 1750+ CORK, COR, IRL [36236] : PRE 1865 COR, IRL [36631] : PRE 1900 WEX, IRL [37750] : PATRICK 1870 BUTLERSTOWN, COR, IRL [38189] : 1840+ COR, IRL [38484] : 1820-1872 TRIM, MEA, IRL & AUS [34198] : 1800+ EASTON, MA, USA [38175] : 1850+ SHOSHONE, ID, USA [38189]

DOODING ALL ENG & SCT [36119]

DOODSON 1800 LAN, ENG & AUS [35079]

DOODY 1857 AVOCA, VIC, AUS [37174] : PRE 1827 WATERFORD, WAT, IRL [38291]

DOOLAN 1887+ ROCKHAMPTON, QLD, AUS [35900] : 1850-1931 LEX, IRL [34165] : MARY 1818+ LEIX (QUEENS), LEX, IRL [34925] : 1850+ COOLEYBROWN & ARDAGH, LIM, IRL [34960] : 1850S WEM, IRL [35332] : PRE 1892 CAPPAMORE,

LIM, IRL [35900] : 1700+ TIP, IRL [36602] : C1860-1920 LAWRENCE, NZ [35900]

DOOLE PRE 1840 IPSWICH, SFK, ENG [33992] : ALL IPSWICH, SFK, ENG [34616]

DOOLEY 1780-1840 JOHNSWELL, KIK, IRL [34687] : PRE 1740 IRL [37589] : 1800-1900 CLARA & AREA, OFF, IRL [38171] : 1850+ DURROW, LEX, IRL [38189] : PRE 1850 IRL [38196] : 1850-1900 TROY & AREA, NY, USA [38171] : PRE 1880 NY, USA [38196]

DOOLING 1700+ TIP, IRL [36602]

DOOLITTLE PRE 1820 WOR, ENG [34383]

DOONER MICHAEL 1856+ QLD & NSW, AUS [34699] : MICHAEL 1839-1856 MORETON BAY, NSW, AUS [34699]

DOOREY 1800S SRY, ENG [35161] : PRE 1820 SOUTHWARK, SRY, ENG [36072] : ALL WORLDWIDE [37116]

DOORNEKAMP 1800+ AMSTERDAM, NL [33802]

DOPLINGER PRE 1800 ZEHOLFING, BAV, GER [38191]

DORAM PRE 1880 AUS [37190]

DORAN ALL LONGFORD, TAS, AUS [34555] : 1830+ HUNTER RV, NSW, AUS [35034] : 1800-1850 STORMONT, ONT, CAN [35603] : 1813 NEW ROSS, WEX, IRL [36907] : PRE 1900 LDY, IRL & AUS [38585] : PRE 1850 PAISLEY, RFW, SCT [36765]

DORCY PRE 1900 YKS, ENG [35862]

DORE C1896 COONAMBLE, NSW, AUS [35725] : 1860-1880 BENDIGO & ECHUCA, VIC, AUS [35725] : 1850+ VIC, AUS [38539] : PRE 1850 QUE, CAN [34159] : 1800+ ISLE OF WIGHT, HAM, ENG [33802] : 1800S ENG [35161] : 1800+ ST PANCRAS, LND, ENG [35800] : ALL SHEFFIELD, YKS, ENG [37402] : 1900 IOW, ENG [38349] : 1750+ LIVERPOOL, LAN, ENG [38539] : PRE 1850 GODSHILL, IOW, ENG [38722] : 1830+ LIM, IRL [35725] : 1750+ GORTNAGLOGH, LIM, IRL [38539] : 1800+ OMAHA, USA [38539] : SUSANNA 1820-1870 CARDIFF, GLA, WLS [38409]

DOREY PRE 1800 JSY, CHI [36696] : 1800S ENG [35161] : PRE 1900 DOR, ENG [38076] : 1850+ LITTLE FALLS, MN, USA [34159]

DORGAN C1838 COR, IRL [37994]

DORGELOH 1611+ BUCHHOLZ, WEF, GER [38631]

DORIN 1900-1810 WILLENBURG, KRIES, OPR [38427] : 1900-1810 WILHELMSBURG, KRIES, OPR [38427] : 1900-1810 ORTELSBURG, KRIES, OPR [38427]

DORING PRE 1840 VELMEDEN, HES, GER [35232] : 1840-54 FRANKFURT AM MAIN, HES, GER [35232] : ALL WORLDWIDE [38666]

DORKS PRE 1850 HUN, ENG [37061]

DORMAN PRE 1838 BELFAST, ANT, IRL [34035] : 1796+ DOW, IRL [34698]

DORMEYER 1786+ LW, POL [38650]

DORNAN MICHAEL 1830S GASPE, NS, CAN [35607] : MICHAEL 1790 CUL, ENG [35607] : PRE 1830 CUL, ENG [38457]

DORNEY 1863+ SUNBURY, MDX, ENG [36326] : 1780 PA, USA [35325]

DORNSEIFFER ALL BAV, GER [35310]

DORON C1800-1835 WORKINGTON, CUL, ENG [34727]

DOROSULIC 1884-1969 DET & WAYNE, MI, USA [38063] : 1884-1969 SREMSKA MITROVICA, VOJVODINA, YU [38063]

DORR ALL KETTERING, NTH, ENG [37730]

DORREEN ALL CASTLE WILLIAM, ANT, IRL [35337] : ALL PAISLEY, RFW, SCT [36793]

DORRELL 1794 CLAINES, WOR, ENG [36606] : 1830 HALIFAX, WRY, ENG [36606]

DORRINGTON 1900+ COONABARABRAN, NSW, AUS [35567] : 1850+ MELBOURNE, VIC, AUS [35587] : 1840S SINGLETON, NSW, AUS [36862] : 1800S NS, CAN [38418] : 1850-1890 WINKFIELD, BRK, ENG [35375] : C1770+ LONDON, ENG [37312] : C1914+ HACKNEY, LND, ENG [38581]

DORSCH 1850+ COOK CO., IL, USA [38534]

DORSETT 1800+ LONDON, ENG [34167]

DORSEY ALL WARTER, ERY, ENG [36846] : ALL NAFFERTON, YKS, ENG [36846] : ALL GARTON ON THE WOLDS, ERY, ENG [36846] : ALL WALPOLE, NFK, ENG [36846] : ALL BISHOP WILTON, ERY, ENG [36846] : ALL TERRINGTON, NFK, ENG [36846] : 1780-1800 LINCOLN CO., NC, USA [37587] : 1800-1890 GA, USA [37587] : PRE 1780 MD, USA [37587] : JOHN T. 1808-1865+ FRED CO., BOLT & WINCH, PA, MD & VA, USA [38591]

DOSCHER ALL HIPSTEDT, HAN, GER [34421]

DOSS 1729+ PITTSYLVANIA CO., VA, USA [38044]

DOSSETTO 1876+ BRISBANE, QLD, AUS [34020]

DOSTER 1870S STOKE ST GREGORY, SOM, ENG [37692]

D'OSTERVALD ALL WORLDWIDE [38633]

DOTSON C1860 MECKLENBURG CO., VA, USA [36903]

DOTTIN 1780 STEPNEY, MDX, ENG [36871]

DOTY PRE 1700 WHITBY, YKS, ENG [33949] : 1830-1880 WINNEBAGO CO., IL & WI, USA [37017]

DOUB 1650-80 DOUBS, FRA [38202]

DOUBE C1800 CLA, IRL [35203] : 1840S CLA, IRL & SCT [35259] : C1860 PANMURE, NZ [35203]

DOUBELL 1800+ LINGFIELD, SRY, ENG [36088]

DOUBLE ALL TAS, AUS [37854] : 1750+ SFK, ENG [36093] : PRE 1800 ESS, ENG [36124] : PRE 1800 SFK, ENG [36124] : ALL SFK, ENG [37854] : 1500-1800 COPDOCK & IPSWICH, SFK, ENG [37854] : ALL WORLDWIDE [37854]

DOUBLEDAY PRE 1850 LONDON, ENG [35782]

DOUBT C1700 CON, ENG [34258]

DOUCET NICOLAS PRE 1785 LBG, BEL [37430] : ALL WORLDWIDE [36934]

DOUCH 1839+ BOMBALA, NSW, AUS [34976] : 1800-1839 DOR, ENG [34976]

DOUCHE PRE 1600 BASTOGNE, LXM, BEL [38167] : 1400 MIGNAULT, HNT, BEL [38167]

DOUCHET 1400 MIGNAULT, HNT, BEL [38167]

DOUD 1800-1850 NY, USA [36732]

DOUDS PRE 1850 CLOUGH, ANT, IRL [35546]

DOUGAL 1800S FALKIRK, STI, SCT [34381] : 1805 BLACKFORD, PER, SCT [35259] : PRE 1880 BEW, SCT [35400]

DOUGALL 1850+ ST KILDA, VIC, AUS [38281] : PRE 1890 DUNNING, PER, SCT [36607]

DOUGAN 1800+ PORTADOWN, ARM, IRL [34927]

DOUGANS PRE 1850S LISBURN, ANT & DOW, IRL [36659]

DOUGHARTY PRE 1700 WHITBY, YKS, ENG [33949]

DOUGHAUTY PRE 1860 TIPPERARY, TIP, IRL [34037]

DOUGHERTY PRE 1870 EDERNEY & IRVINESTOWN, FER, IRL [34018] : ALL FER, IRL [36784] : PRE 1850 BALLINA, SLI, IRL [37568] : 1800+ DOW, IRL [38473] : 1850-1950 LUZERNE, PA, USA [36733] : 1940S RENSSELAER CO., NY, USA [37568] : 1800+ BLUE RAPIDS & KAY CO., KS & OK, USA [38473]

DOUGHTE PRE 1750 BARNBY, YKS, ENG [33949]

DOUGHTIE PRE 1750 BARNBY, YKS, ENG [33949] : 1830S LEITH, MLN, SCT [35486]

DOUGHTY C1843-1929 NS, CAN & NZ [34651] : PRE 1700 BARNBY, YKS, ENG [33949] : PRE 1800 WHITBY, YKS, ENG [33949] : 1700S SOUTH

CREAKE, NFK, ENG [35322] : WILLIAM 1800 KIDDERMINSTER, ENG [35429] : 1800 + WARWICK, WAR, ENG [35992] : 1707 TOPHAM, WRY, ENG [37988] : 1900 + NZ [33949] : GORDON 1900S CHRISTCHURCH, NZ [33949]

DOUGHWAITE PRE 1800 BARNBY, YKS, ENG [33949]

DOUGLAS 1898 + DORA CREEK, NSW, AUS [34786] : PRE 1850 RICHMOND, NSW, AUS [35088] : 1850-1900S REDFERN, NSW, AUS [35785] : C1800S WALKERTON, ONT, CAN [34133] : 1800 CHELTENHAM, GLS, ENG [34109] : 1676-1709 SEDGEFIELD, DUR, ENG [34552] : 1863 CARLISLE, CUL, ENG [35906] : 1750-1880 CUL & NBL, ENG [37338] : PRE 1800 SUNDERLAND, DUR, ENG [37693] : PRE 1850 REDESDALE, NBL, ENG [37835] : 1800-1900S RATHMOYLAN, MEA, IRL [35785] : 1700-1890 KILLYMAN, DUNGANNON, TYR, IRL [36080] : PRE 1900 BELFAST, ANT, IRL [37708] : TINSLEY PRE 1900 BALLYNAHINCH, DOW, IRL [37755] : HENRY 1830 + STRAITON, AYR, SCT [34091] : ALL EDINBURGH, MLN, SCT [34093] : 1800 + JEDBURGH, ROX, SCT [34109] : 1770-1820 NISBET, CRAILING, ROX, SCT [34479] : 1780S FALKIRK, STI, SCT [35259] : EDWARD 1800S DALRY, AYR, SCT [35391] : WILLIAM 1790-1840 JEDBURGH, ROX, SCT [35602] : PRE 1850 ROGART, SUT, SCT [35819] : PRE 1920 HAWICK, ROX, SCT [35934] : PRE 1840 KILFINAN, ARL, SCT [35959] : PRE 1837 MUSSELBURGH, MLN, SCT [36513] : 1290 SCT [37008] : PRE 1800 GARVALD, ELN, SCT [37353] : PRE 1700 DNB, SCT [37562] : C1813 SOUTH LEITH, MLN, SCT [37834] : PRE 1900 SCT & ENG [33987] : 1750-1950 RENSSELAER, NY, USA [36733] : 1800-1700S KY, USA [37562] : PRE 1860 CHAMPAIGN CO., OH, USA [38135] : ALL WORLDWIDE [38675]

DOUGLAS-HAMILTON 1803 + ENG & AUS [33790]

DOUGLASS 1844 + PORTLAND, VIC, AUS [34278] : C1842 TAS, AUS [34278] : 1850 + MELBOURNE, VIC, AUS [36360] : 1880 + YORK, YKS, ENG [34754] : 1680-1800 CHATTON, NBL, ENG [34776] : 1750 + BARNARD CASTLE, DUR, ENG [38446] : 1844 + GLASGOW, SCT [34278] : 1850 + BROWN CO., IN, USA [38066] : WILLIAM C1710 MD & VA, USA [38177]

DOUHAN MARTEN PRE 1738 ULLFORS, TIERP, SWE [38550]

DOUHET 1400 DYON, BRT, FRA [38167]

DOULL 1886 + TAITA, NI, NZ [35704] : PRE 1760 REISS, CAI, SCT [33873] : PRE 1775 LATHERON, CAI, SCT [33873] : 1800 + EDINBURGH, MLN, SCT [34260] : PRE 1850 WICK, CAI, SCT [35635] : PRE 1843 THURSO, CAI, SCT [35704] : ALL WICK, CAI, SCT & AUS [35518]

DOULLE PRE 1750 CUA, FRA [36078]

DOULOVITCH ALL ENG & SU [37742]

DOULTREVAUL ALL WORLDWIDE [38633]

DOULTREWALD ALL WORLDWIDE [38633]

DOUP 1770 FREDERICK, MD, USA [38202]

DOUPE C1875 MELBOURNE, VIC, AUS [35203] : ALL AUS & NZ [35259] : C1800 CLA, IRL [35203] : 1840S CLA, IRL [35259]

DOUSE PRE 1845 REEDNESS, WRY, ENG [35440]

DOUST PRE 1853 + PATTERSON RIVER, NSW, AUS [35088] : ALL MAIDSTONE, KEN, ENG [37494]

DOUTHAIT PRE 1800 YKS, ENG [33949]

DOUTHATE PRE 1600 YKS, ENG [33949]

DOUTHEAITE PRE 1600 WHITBY, YKS, ENG [33949]

DOUTHWAITE PRE 1800 BARNBY, YKS, ENG [33949] : PRE 1700 WHITBY, YKS, ENG [33949] : 1840 WHITBY, NRY, ENG [37388]

DOUTTREY 1860-1870 ST PANCRAS, MDX, ENG [35725]

DOUTY PRE 1800 WHITBY, YKS, ENG [33949]

DOUWMA PRE 1850 JUTRIJP, FRI, NL [38646]

DOVE 1800-1850 DURHAM, DUR, ENG [33908] : PRE 1800 ENG [34870] : JASPER 1820 + BERMONDSEY, SRY, ENG [35013] : PRE 1880 CHESTER LE STREET, DUR, ENG [36514] : PRE 1800 REEPHAM, NFK, ENG [37082] : C1730 + BRESSINGHAM, NFK, ENG [38492] : ALL WORLDWIDE [37785]

DOVER 1755 + KESWICK, CUL, ENG [37460]

DOVEY 1765 CHRISHALL, CAM, ENG [38209] : 1886 + CARDIFF, GLA, WLS [34839]

DOW 1850 + BALLARAT, VIC, AUS [34435] : 1840 + PUOTON TWP., ONT, CAN [34937] : ROBERT C1880S PORT CHALMERS, NZ [37106] : 1750-1850 GASK, PER, SCT [34435] : C1720 EDINBURGH, MLN, SCT [34713] : 1650S + FOWLISWESTER, PER, SCT [34937] : PRE 1844 BRIDGEND, PER, SCT [35463] : 1788-1820 CALLENDAR, PER, SCT [36392] : JAMES C1780 MUTHILL, PER, SCT [37106] : 1800-1830 HUNTERDON CO., NJ, USA [37591]

DOWBER 1700 + WIGAN, LAN, ENG [38046]

DOWBIGGIN ALL WORLDWIDE [34833]

DOWD C1815 + KER, IRL [34145] : 1800 LONGFORD, LOG, IRL [35770] : 1815 WEX, IRL [36667] : 1800-70 SLI, IRL [37807]

DOWDE 1850 + ELPHIN, ROS, IRL & AUS [35372]

DOWDEN C1781 ASHCOTT, SOM, ENG [34157] : PRE 1850 ISLE OF WIGHT, HAM, ENG [35173] : 1810S WESTBURY, WIL, ENG [37947]

DOWELL PRE 1920 VIC, AUS [35055] : 1750-1800 CARLISLE, CUL, ENG [36431] : 1800-1900 WEYMOUTH, DOR, ENG [37233] : 1800 + EDINBURGH, MLN, SCT [34260] : 1875 CLINTON CO., IA, USA [36907]

DOWER 1900 + MELBOURNE, VIC, AUS [35771] : 1750 + LIM, IRL [38539]

DOWEY PRE 1856 MOIRA, DOW, IRL [35344]

DOWKER 1880S CHARTERS TOWERS, QLD, AUS [34266] : 1600-1650 SETTRINGTON, ERY, ENG [33767] : 1850 + BEETHAM & KENDAL, WES, ENG [34266] : PRE 1850 BEETHAM & KENDAL, WES, ENG [34266]

DOWLAND 1750-1850 KEN, ENG [37064] : ALL GLA, WLS [36886]

DOWLE 1854 + CAMDEN, NSW, AUS [34426] : C1817 DOVER, KEN, ENG [34273] : PRE 1838 KEN, ENG [34696] : 1800 + LYDD, KEN, ENG [34899]

DOWLER 1820-1990 BEAUHARNOIS DIST, QUE, CAN [34377] : PRE 1863 CLARK CO., MO, USA [36672]

DOWLING 1839 + MELBOURNE, VIC, AUS [34173] : 1830 + INGLEWOOD, QLD, AUS [34421] : PRE 1860 NSW, AUS [34880] : 1850S BACCHUS MARSH, VIC, AUS [35332] : 1850 + SINGLETON, NSW, AUS [35472] : 1900 + ORANGE, NSW, AUS [35771] : 1850 + BENDIGO, VIC, AUS [36602] : PRE 1879 SYDNEY, NSW, AUS [37899] : 1850 + MELBOURNE, VIC, AUS [38289] : PRE 1808 LONDON, ENG [34421] : PRE 1825 + BLACKBURN, LAN, ENG [36955] : 1660-1720 MARLBOROUGH, WIL, ENG [37233] : 1640-1700 NORTON ST PHILIP, SOM, ENG [37233] : PRE 1870 OXF, LIN & LND, ENG [37385] : 1780-1810 KIDDERMINSTER, WOR, ENG [37895] : 1750-1840 BURTON UPON TRENT, STS, ENG [37895] : ALL CASTLECONNELL, LIM, IRL [34173] : 1850 + COOLEYBROWN & ARDAGH, LIM, IRL [34960] : 1800-1840 DUB, IRL [35402] : 1700 + TIP, IRL [36602] : 1850 + NZ [36602] : BUCK 1850 + WORLDWIDE [36602]

DOWN C1880 NSW, AUS [34456] : ALL ENG [34254] : C1400 ENG [34395] : 1750 PLYMOUTH, HAM, ENG [34456] : C1700 YARNSCOMBE, DEV, ENG [34456] : C1780 EGG BUCKLAND, DEV, ENG [34456] : 1800+ ATHERINGTON, DEV, ENG [35362] : PRE 1800 DEV, DOR & SOM, ENG [36166] : 1840+ TAVISTOCK, DEV, ENG [36641] : 1852 MINEHEAD, SOM, ENG [36860] : PRE 1860 KENNINGTON & LAMBETH, SRY, ENG [37259] : C1765 CORSLEY, WIL, ENG [37536] : 1900+ NEWARK, NJ, USA [35362]

DOWNER PRE 1900 GREEN PONDS, TAS, AUS [36777] : 1800 WEST CHILTINGTON, SSX, ENG [37859]

DOWNES 1867+ RICHMOND, VIC, AUS [34577] : 1750+ LND, ENG [33963] : C1830 TWICKENHAM, MDX, ENG [34851] : PRE 1870 EDMONTON & ENFIELD, MDX, ENG [36061] : 1581-1704 EASTHAM, WOR, ENG [36513] : C1820 HEF, ENG [36860] : 1813+ BAUGHTON FIELDS, WOR, ENG [37181] : 1790+ MIDDLEHOPE, SAL, ENG [37181] : ALL WAR, ENG [37404] : PRE 1850 BIRMINGHAM, WAR, ENG [38002] : ALL STS, SAL & WAR, ENG [38754] : PRE 1827 CLA, IRL [35340]

DOWNEY 1844+ SYDNEY, NSW, AUS [35706] : 1844-1847 KIORA, NSW, AUS [35706] : PRE 1848 LAMBETH, SRY, ENG [37321] : 1800+ LAN, ENG [37482] : 1700-1800S TULLYVALLAN, ARM, IRL [34483] : PRE 1840 SHANAGOLDEN, LIM, IRL [35431] : ALL NEWTOWN BUTLER, FER, IRL [35706] : 1750+ FER, IRL [38476] : 1800S CRUMORD, DOW, IRL & AUS [35422] : 1885+ BUTTE CITY, MT, USA [37781] : 1860+ DUTCHESS CO., NY, USA [37781] : 1800+ MD, USA [38587]

DOWNEY (SEE DOWNIE) [35759]

DOWNHAM 1677 GLINTON, NTH, ENG [35369] : PRE 1780 MELLING, LAN, ENG [36180] : 1840+ BRIMPTON, BRK, ENG [36232]

DOWNIE 1800S WESTMINSTER, LND, ENG [36868] : PRE 1820+ RAPHOE, DON, IRL [35759] : C1800 AUCHTERMUCHTY, FIF, SCT [34527] : C1800 AYR, AYR, SCT [34713] : PRE 1837 BURNTISLAND, FIF, SCT [35223] : C1780 STRATHDON, ABD, SCT [36607] : 1760-1855 AIRDRIE, LKS, SCT [38053] : 1800+ WICK, CAI, SCT [38425]

DOWNING 1870 MELBOURNE, VIC, AUS [37307] : 1750-1800 S YKS, ENG [36084] : 1800-1850 DEVONPORT, DEV, ENG [36536] : PRE 1850 WERRINGTON & ALL, DEV, ENG [38772] : 1700+ NY, USA [37026] : 1651-1724 NORTHUMBERLAND CO., VA, USA [37029] : 1700+ NEW LONDON, CT, USA [38241] : C1776 CHESTER CO., SC, USA [38367]

DOWNS 1860S YORK CO., ONT, CAN [34407] : PRE 1835 WELLINGTON, SAL, ENG [34851] : C1880 CLIFTON, LAN, ENG [34851] : 1835-1860 BILSTON, STS, ENG [34851] : C1730 WORKSOP, NTT, ENG [36426] : PRE 1700 WHITEPARISH, WIL, ENG [36478] : PRE 1856 DUNGIVEN, DRY, IRL [34407] : 1800-1850 CLA, IRL [38039] : 1800 GLASGOW, SCT [34991] : 1800+ STILLWATER, MN, USA [34107] : 1850+ NY & IL, USA [38039] : C1830 ALBANY, NY, USA & CAN [38309] : 1850+ ST CLAIR CO., MI, USA & CAN [38309] : 1800-1880 POSEY CO., IN & NC, USA & IRL [38532]

DOWNTON C1824 DURNFORD, WIL, ENG [35464] : 1850+ BRIXHAM, DEV, ENG [36370] : ALL SOM, ENG [37233]

DOWNY 1800+ IRL [36830]

DOWRICK PRE 1842 TRURO, CON, ENG [35047] : 1650+ GORRAN, CON, ENG [35851]

DOWSE 1700+ LIN, ENG [34221] : 1775-1850 ENG [36708] : ALL UK [37421]

DOWTHAT PRE 1600 YKS, ENG [33949]

DOWTHWAT PRE 1600 WHITBY, YKS, ENG [33949]

DOWTHWATE PRE 1600 WHITBY, YKS, ENG [33949]

DOWTY PRE 1700 WHITBY, YKS, ENG [33949]

DOWZARD ALL WORLDWIDE [33857]

DOXON 1800+ GLOSSOP, DBY, ENG [36120]

DOYE ALL VIC, AUS [35082]

DOYLE EDWARD 1850+ GUNDAGAI & CARCOAR, NSW, AUS [35155] : 1855+ BEAUFORT, VIC, AUS [35193] : 1800+ VIC, AUS [35352] : ALL NYMAGEE, NSW, AUS [35843] : 1858+ WALCHA, NSW, AUS [35854] : 1890+ HILLGROVE, NSW, AUS [36632] : PRE 1930 NEWCASTLE, NSW, AUS [36632] : 1850S PORTLAND, VIC, AUS [37169] : 1803+ WINDSOR, NSW, AUS [37554] : ALL KING, YORK, ONT, CAN [35833] : C1830+ CHAFFEYS LOCK, ONT, CAN [36652] : PRE 1905 DERBY, DBY, ENG [34909] : PRE 1836 BANSHA, TIP, IRL [33936] : PRE 1837 TIP, IRL [34036] : PRE 1890 MAY, IRL [34293] : 1690-1750 BALLINCARRIG, CAR, IRL [34364] : 1690-1800 COOLADINE, WEX, IRL [34364] : PRE 1880 BALLINASLOE, GAL, IRL [34454] : PRE 1840 DUBLIN, IRL [34900] : 1807-1840 DAVIDTOWN, WEX, IRL [35132] : PRE 1870 DUBLIN, IRL [35400] : PRE 1858 NEWBRIDGE, WIC, IRL [35854] : PRE 1830 NEWTOWNBARRY, WEX, IRL [36652] : ALL TULLAMORE, OFF, IRL [36784] : 1790+ SWORDS, DUB, IRL [37169] : PRE 1803 DUBLIN, IRL [37554] : PRE 1818 WEX, IRL [38583] : PRE 1900 CAR, IRL [38769] : 1779 KIK, IRL [38778] : DIANE J. 1826-1894 HUNTINGDON CO., PA, USA [38371] : GARRETT ALL WORLDWIDE [35854] : 1879 IRL &, WORLDWIDE [37511]

DOYLY 1600-1850 NFK & SFK, ENG [37207]

DRACKE PRE 1770 LUEDE, PYR, GER [38632]

DRACOTT 1700-1900 LONDON, ENG [35229]

DRADDY PRE 1830 COR, IRL [38777]

DRAFFIN 1800S ENNISKILLEN, FER, IRL [38402] : 1800+ GIRVAN, AYR, SCT [34927]

DRAGE 1866+ NSW, AUS [35136] : 1850S SHOREDITCH, MDX, ENG [34953] : PRE 1866 LIN, ENG [35136] : PRE 1840 BOZEAT, NTH, ENG [35955]

DRAGER PRE 1700 BAV, GER [36353]

DRAGLAND 1893 GRAND FORKS, ND, USA [38470]

DRAIN 1910-1920 TUNSTALL, STS, ENG [36990] : 1850-1910 GODALMING, SRY, ENG [36990]

DRAKE 1850-1865 LAUNCESTON, TAS, AUS [34050] : 1850+ VIC & NSW, AUS [34274] : 1800-1870 ATTLEBOROUGH, NFK, ENG [34050] : PRUDENCE 1791 CHURCHSTANTON, SOM, ENG [34195] : 1760-1855 BIRMINGHAM, WAR, ENG [34274] : ALL ENG [34938] : PRE 1825 ALMONDBURY, WRY, ENG [35151] : WILLIAM PRE 1750 STOKEWAKE, DOR, ENG [35252] : 1755 WADDESON, BKM, ENG [35256] : ALL ENG [36430] : PRE 1800 DOR, ENG [36479] : ALL BARNSLEY, YKS, ENG [36704] : ELIAS 1835-1860 PLYMOUTH, DEV, ENG [36788] : SARAH PRE 1836 BUCKFASTLEIGH, DEV, ENG [37014] : PRE 1850 SHOREDITCH, MDX, ENG [37362] : PRE 1870 PADDINGTON, MDX, ENG [37362] : 1800+ NFK & SFK, ENG [37717] : ALL NFK & SFK, ENG [37737] : PRE 1770 LUEDE, PYR, GER [38632] : 1850+ NZ [34274] : 1800-1850 OH, USA [36732] : 1700-1800 MA, USA [36732] : 1750-1825 VT, USA [36732] : PRE 1668 PORTSMOUTH, NH, USA [37029] : WILLIAM 1800 JESSAMINE CO., KY, USA [38152] : WILLIAM 1766

DUTCHESS CO., NY, USA [38152] : 1850 IRL &, WORLDWIDE [37511]

DRAKEFORD 1650 BEDWORTH, WAR, ENG [34321] : PRE 1877 NEW MILLS, DBY, ENG [37359]

DRAMGOOL MARY PRE 1832 LOU, IRL [34310]

DRANE PRE 1870 TASMAN PENINSULAR, TAS, AUS [33886] : 1800-1940 FEOCK & CARDIFF, CON & GLA, ENG & WLS [36373]

DRANSFIELD ALL YKS, ENG [37084]

DRAPER 1800+ WA, AUS [34846] : 1834 HOBART, TAS, AUS [35152] : ALL ONT, CAN [34465] : 1820+ SIMCOE CO., ONT, CAN [34465] : ALL ALB, SAS & MAN, CAN [34485] : ALL COMPTON & BROME, QUE, CAN [34485] : 1800-1990 QUE & ONT, CAN [35630] : 1800-1880 YORK CO., ONT, CAN [37477] : 1846+ GOSBERTON & SPALDING, LIN, ENG [34528] : 1700-1800 DATCHWORTH, HRT, ENG [34697] : 1700-1830 BOLTON, LAN, ENG [34846] : PRE 1790 NEWGATE, MDX, ENG [34892] : 1800+ DEV, ENG [35057] : 1860+ SAWTRY, HUN, ENG [35594] : C1860 SURFLEET, LIN, ENG [35594] : 1870+ SNEINTON & NOTTINGHAM, NTT, ENG [36105] : PRE 1698 BRIGHSTONE, IOW, ENG [36668] : 1800+ LEIGH, LAN, ENG [37147] : CHARLES C1794 PEWSEY, WIL, ENG [38489] : 1778+ FALKIRK, STI, SCT [35921] : PRE 1855 STI, SCT [37354] : ALL PA, USA [34485] : ALL MA, USA [34485] : ALL VT, USA [34485] : ALL NY, USA [34485] : PRE 1900 MD, USA [38196]

DRAYTON PRE 1850S MONTACUTE, SOM, ENG [35433]

DREDGE ALL LONGBRIDGE DEVERILL, WIL, ENG [34466] : PRE 1830 OAKHILL & PYLLE, SOM, ENG [35215] : 1750+ SOUTHWARK, SRY, ENG [37251] : 1650-1750 LONGBRIDGE DEVERILL, WIL, ENG [37251] : PRE 1815 STEPNEY, MDX, ENG [37279] : 1800+ CANNING TOWN, LND, ENG [37660]

DREGGER 1957 KOENIGSTEIN, NRW, BRD [38748] : 1920 MUENSTER, WEF, GER [38748] : 1891 NIESIG FULDA, GHE, GER [38748] : 1857 BUEECKE, GER [38748] : 1921 KOELN, RPR, GER [38748]

DREHER PRE 1855 GER [33765] : 1770+ MULLHEIM, BAD, GER [37504] : ALL NY, USA [35618]

DREHMER ALL ONT, CAN [34488]

DREHWALD 1850+ NEW YORK CITY, NY, USA [37572]

DREIER PRE 1890 WITNAU, AG, CH [34719]

DREIJSSENAAR ALL WORLDWIDE [38358]

DRENCKHAN ALL MSW, GER [34488]

DRENNAN PRE 1760 TARBOLTON, AYR, SCT [36431]

DRENT C1850 FRI, NL [36283]

DRESSEL 1798-1890 SCHLEUSINGEN, THURINGIA, GER [38148]

DRESSER 1825+ LEAKE, YKS, ENG [37048] : 1810-1860 ORLEANS CO., NY, MI & IL, USA [36546] : 1800-1836 NH, USA [38529]

DREUX ALL WORLDWIDE [38303]

DREW STANDISH 1840+ SYDNEY, NSW, AUS [34973] : 1830+ CAMPBELLTOWN, TAS, AUS [35533] : HENRY 1930S QLD, AUS [36616] : 1850+ OSHAWA, ONT, CAN [38395] : 1800S LONDON, ENG [34472] : 1830+ HIGHWORTH, MDX, ENG [34614] : 1800-1900 WESTERHAM, KEN, ENG [34641] : PRE 1900 LND, ENG [36037] : 1700+ DUNCHIDEOCK, DEV, ENG [36813] : DANZEY 1800+ HEF, ENG [37323] : 1800S SRY, ENG [37868] : GEORGE 1790-1820 LIMERICK CITY, IRL [38084] : REV. THOMAS 1830-1870 BELFAST & SEAFORDE, DOW, IRL [38084] : 1850-1900 NELSON, NZ [34641] :

PRE 1830 PAISLEY, RFW, SCT [35533] : PRE 1875 BROOKLYN, NY, USA [38126]

DREWE PRE 1800 EXETER, DEV, ENG [35032]

DREWELL 1900-1920 LONDON, ENG [35001] : PRE 1900 WLS [35001]

DREWER 1750-1850 PRESTON PLUCKNETT, SOM, ENG [37378]

DREWERY 1750-1850 HULL, ENG [35228]

DREWETT ALL DEVIZES, WIL, ENG [37285] : PRE 1841 WIMBLEDON, SRY, ENG [38268]

DREWILL C1745-NFK, ENG [34222]

DREWITT 1700+ OXFORD & THAME, BKM, ENG [34662]

DREWS 1650-1850 ZARNEFANZ, POM, GER [38654]

DREYER ALL WORLDWIDE [38666]

DRIES ALL BAV, BAD & HEN, GER [38676]

DRIESTEN 1841+ FRI, NL [34990]

DRIFFIL 1750 YKS, ENG [35377]

DRIFFILL ALL BURTON ON STATHER, LIN, ENG [35377]

DRINAN ALL IRL [34068]

DRING PRE 1800 LIN & YKS, ENG [34886] : PRE 1784 KINGSTON UPON HULL, YKS, ENG [35578] : 1743-1852 WILTON, SOM, ENG [35815] : ALL NTT, ENG [36189] : ALL BOTTESFORD & MUSTON, LEI, ENG [36189] : 1800-1840 GRANTHAM, LIN, ENG [36189] : 1865+ CODNOR & HEANOR, DBY, ENG [36189] : 1760+ LONG SUTTON, LIN, ENG [36370]

DRINGELBERG 1500S LUND & MALMO, MAL, SWE [36320]

DRINKALL SARAH 1697 CROWLE, LIN, ENG [34091]

DRINKWATER 1800+ ISLIP, OXF, ENG [34681] : 1760+ APPLETON WITH EATON, OXF, ENG [35822] : 1739+ MELKSHAM, WIL, ENG [36276] : 1750-1850 MANCHESTER, LAN, ENG [36416] : 1850-90 HEYWOOD, LAN, ENG [36419] : PRE 1890 STILLINGTON, DUR, ENG [37204] : 1880S INGHAM CO., MI, USA [38339]

DRINNAN PRE 1760 TARBOLTON, AYR, SCT [36431]

DRINNANS C1855 MAUCHLINE, AYR, SCT [34521]

DRISCOLL 1870 LISMORE & SYDNEY, NSW, AUS [33765] : PRE 1850S CHARLTON, KEN, ENG [34873] : PRE 1844 LONDON, ENG [35035] : DINAS 1888 BATTERSEA & SOUTHWARK, SRY, ENG [37611] : DENNIS 1888 BATTERSEA & SOUTHWARK, SRY, ENG [37611] : PRE 1840 ST ANNS, COR, IRL [33780] : 1805+ GAL, IRL [35201] : PRE 1840 COR, IRL [37986] : 1855-1885 KEWEENAW CO., MI, USA [38010]

DRIVER 1801+ SYDNEY, NSW, AUS [35721] : 1750+ TUNBRIDGE WELLS, KEN, ENG [34416] : 1788 DURSLEY, GLS, ENG [35721] : 1750-1900 HOLBROOK, SFK, ENG [37042] : 1800+ BATTERSEA, SRY, ENG [37171] : 1800+ PUTNEY, SRY, ENG [37171] : 1800+ WANDSWORTH, SRY, ENG [37171] : PRE 1780 KETTLEBURGH & TUNSTALL, SFK, ENG [37420]

DRONFIELD PRE 1990 BROOKLYN, WTN, NZ [36249]

DROOGMANS JOSEPH PRE 1874 LBG, BEL [37430]

DROSTE 1863 HOLZHAUSEN, PYR, GER [38748] : 1696 LEMGO, WEF, GER [38748] : 1671-1748 LIEME, WEF, GER [38748] : 1817-1825 DETMARSEN, WEF, GER [38748] : 1770-1803 BRAKE, WEF, GER [38748]

DROTOS PRE 1830 SZENDROLAD, BORSOD, HU [37547]

DROUET PRE 1850 FRA [35727]

DROUGH 1870+ BALLARAT & CRESWICK, VIC, AUS [38277] : 1903+ WESTPORT & SEDDENVILLE, BULLER, NZ [38277]

DROUGHT PRE 1830 OFF & DUB, IRL [36095] : PRE 1870 DUBLIN, IRL & CAN [34733] : MARY 1837+ GLA, WLS & AUS [37161]

DROUITT C1800 WIMBLEDON, SRY, ENG [38268]

DROUN ALL WORLDWIDE [38277]

DROWER PRE 1800 COLYTON, DEV, ENG [33968] : 185+ WAIPUKURAU, HB, NZ [33968]

DROWN PRE 1850 STOWFORD, DEV, ENG [35959]

DRUATT 1700+ OXFORD & THAME, BKM, ENG [34662]

DRUCE ALL ENG [33872] : 1700-1800S SRY & HAM, ENG [34483]

DRUDGE PRE 1850 GUNVILLE, IOW, ENG [38722]

DRUERY ALL WORLDWIDE [36832]

DRUET 1700+ OXFORD & THAME, BKM, ENG [34662]

DRUETT PRE 1841 WIMBLEDON, SRY, ENG [38268] : C1800 ENG [38268]

DRUITT 1830-1926 RAWSONVILLE & SYDNEY, NSW, AUS [35103] : 1700+ OXFORD & THAME, BKM, ENG [34662] : C1800 COBHAM, SRY, ENG [38268]

DRULY PRE 1800 HAM, ENG [37693]

DRUM 1700-1840 ST WENDEL SAA, SAARLAND, BRD [35267] : 1880-1889 TOMBSTONE, AZ, USA [35148] : 1750-1850 WAYLAND, NY, USA [35267]

DRUMM 1860S ST LOUIS CO., MO, USA [38339]

DRUMMER PRE 1830 BAV, GER [38191]

DRUMMOND 1831+ INVERARY PARK, NSW, AUS [34174] : 1850+ BEECHWORTH, VIC, AUS [34174] : 1860+ BRIGHT, VIC, AUS [34174] : PETER 1852+ BALLARAT, VIC, AUS [37906] : 1840+ LAMBETH, SRY, ENG [37225] : PRE 1850 IRL [37225] : 1800+ AUCHTERARDER, PER, SCT [34098] : PRE 1731 CRIEFF, PER, SCT [34174] : 1800S PER, SCT [35379] : C1830S DUNDEE, ANS, SCT [35438] : 1750-1850 ST ANDREWS & DAIRSIE, FIF, SCT [35494] : C1851 PAISLEY, RFW, SCT [35826] : 1830+ MAYBOLE, AYR, SCT [35959] : 1800S EDINBURGH, MLN, SCT [36246] : PRE 1850 CRIEFF, PER, SCT [36361] : 1730-1750 KILLIN, PER, SCT [36635] : HELEN C1780 MARR. PETER MCGREGOR, SCT [36635] : ALL GALASHIELS, SCT [36878] : PRE 1860 GLASGOW, LKS, SCT [37179] : ARCHIBALD PRE 1855 DALGETY, FIF, SCT [37906] : ALL PER, SCT [38215]

DRURY 1880+ NELLIGEN, NSW, AUS [38491] : 1889+ MILTON, NSW, AUS [38491] : ALL LENNOX & ADDINGTON CO., ONT, CAN [35608] : PRE 1720 UTTERBY, LIN, ENG [34240] : 1870 PURTON, WIL, ENG [34273] : PRE 1900 MANCHESTER, LAN, ENG [34360] : 1800 ROLVENDEN, KEN, ENG [34940] : PRE 1840 ROLVENDEN, KEN, ENG [35546] : PRE 1900 ALVERSTOKE & GOSPORT, HAM, ENG [36037] : PRE 1815 SANDHURST, KEN, ENG [36272] : 1700-1900 EAGLE & HYKEHAM, LIN, ENG [36531] : 1800+ PORTSMOUTH, HAM, ENG [36756] : C1900-1920 PECKHAM, LND, ENG [37752] : 1750-1870 MELFORD, SFK, ENG [37752] : 1770-1810 TEMPLE, NH, USA [35317]

DRUSSEL ALL HATTMATT, ALS, FRA [36930]

DRY 1800-1840 WEX, IRL [35192]

DRYBURGH PRE 1800 KILCONQUHAR & ST MONANCE, FIF, SCT [37913]

DRYDEN 1800+ GWENNAP, CON, ENG [35712] : 1700+ DUR, ENG [35891] : PRE 1830 BUCKTON, NBL, ENG [37357] : PRE 1821 MONIFEITH, ANS, SCT [33992] : 1700S HAWICK, ROX, SCT [35635]

DRYHURST 1850+ SYDNEY, NSW, AUS [34977]

DRYSDALE CHARLES 1852+ COLLINGWOOD, VIC, AUS [34702] : 1820-1867 ORMSTOWN, QUE, CAN [34148] : 1820+ ONT, CAN [34465] : C1799 CLACKMANNAN, DNB, SCT [34127] : C1832 DOUNE, PER, SCT [35090] : 1830+ BATHGATE, WLN, SCT [35408] : 1820-1850 ALVA, CLK, SCT [36392]

DRYVER 1670-1840 BRABANT, BEL [38148]

DRYWA 1707-1890 SIERAKOWICE, GDANSK, POL [38148]

DUBB DAVID 1657-1739 VADSTENA, OSTERGOTLAND, SWE [38550]

DUBBLE ALL WORLDWIDE [37854]

DUBE 1900+ ONT, CAN [37482] : 1700+ QUE, CAN [37482]

DUBERRY 1850+ HACKNEY, LND, ENG [37983]

DUBLE ALL WORLDWIDE [37854]

DUBLER WILLIAM 1840-1859 BOURBON CO., KY, USA [35329] : ISAAC 1860-1877 EDGAR CO., IL, USA [35329]

DUBOCK 1790+ BETHNAL GREEN, LND, ENG [35560]

DUBOIS C1700 GENEVA, GE, CH [38348] : 1600-1700 STATEN ISLAND, NY, USA & FRA [38225]

DUBOSC ALL WORLDWIDE [38237]

DUBOULE C1775 GENEVA, GE, CH [38348]

DUBRELLE C1690 ATHLONE, WEM, IRL [35257]

DUBREUIL PRE 1730 AQU, FRA [37428]

DUCE ALL LEEDS, WRY, ENG [36636] : SMITH 1850+ RUABON, DEN, WLS [36636] : JOSEPH 1850+ RUABON, DEN, WLS [36636] : ALL CMN, WLS [36636] : JOHN 1850+ RUABON, DEN, WLS [36636]

DUCEY PRE 1900 GOREY, WEX, IRL [35184]

DU CHENE C1660 MANNHEIM, RPF, BRD [38677] : 1780-1830 DE, USA [35317]

DUCHESNE 1600-1690 GENEVA, GE, CH [34514]

DUCHOW PRE 1900 WI, USA [38684]

DUCK THOMAS 1848+ MYALL RIVER & MALLINSON, NSW, AUS [35394] : 1750S-1830S WHITBY, YKS, ENG [34094] : 1800+ SOM, ENG [36756] : 1800-1830 LONDON & ST LEONARDS, LND, ENG [37187] : 1750-1850 WHITBY, NRY, ENG [37435]

DUCKET 1800S DITTON, SAL, ENG [35233]

DUCKETT 1850-1900 NSW, AUS [34422] : C1700-1750 KINGSCLERE, HAM, ENG [36289]

DUCKHAM 1877+ GLADSTONE, QLD, AUS [35452] : 1860 HALBERTON, DEV, ENG [35452] : C1770 ERMINGTON, DEV, ENG [36945]

DUCKITT 1700+ YKS, ENG [37620]

DUCKLE PRE 1800 CORRINGHAM, LIN, ENG [37371]

DUCKWORTH PRE 1850 ALSTON, LAN, ENG [36998]

DUCOUDRAY 1750-1770 SHO, GER [36340] : 1750-1770 HAMBURG, HBG, GER [36340]

DUDDELL 1827+ NSW, AUS [38212]

DUDDY ALL KEN, ENG [37595]

DUDENHOFFER PRE 1868 PFALZ, BAY, GER [37504]

DUDGEN 1700+ KILMARNOCK, AYR, SCT [33989]

DUDGEON 1700-1990 SLI, IRL & AUS [35421]

DUDLEY C1778 SAL, ENG [33880] : 1782+ NEEN SAVAGE, SAL, ENG [33880] : C1850+ PETERBOROUGH, NTH, ENG [35163] : PRE 1810 YORK, YKS, ENG [36051] : 1500-1990 LEI, ENG [36130] : PRE 1930 SALE, CHS, ENG [36363] : PRE 1830 ST LUKES, OLD ST, MDX, ENG [36388] : PRE 1800 ESS, ENG [37832] : 1800+ BIRMINGHAM, WAR & LND, ENG [37868] : MARY PRE 1864 RAHEEN, TIP, IRL [37135] : THOMAS PRE 1870 WESTMORELAND CO., PA, USA [36448] : PRE 1797 WEAKLEY CO., TN, USA [36939] : 1780-1859 SURRY CO., NC, USA [38518]

DUDMAN 1700+ SRY & SSX, ENG [38323]

DUELL HARRIET 1843+ HAM, ENG [36332] :
ADELAIDE 1869+ SOM, ENG [36332] : ADELAIDE
1869+ HAM, ENG [36332] : CHARLES 1839+ NEW
FOREST, HAM, ENG [36332] : ADA ELSIE 1893+
STOCKBRIDGE, HAM, ENG [36332] : C1910
ISLINGTON, LND, ENG [36332] : ELLEN 1897+
STOCKBRIDGE, HAM, ENG [36332] : EMILY
ROSE 1895+ STOCKBRIDGE, HAM, ENG [36332] :
FRANK CHARLES 1869+ NEW FOREST, HAM,
ENG [36332] : 1850-1950 FONDULAC CO., WI, MN
& NY, USA [38392]

DUERDEN 1825-1900 BLACKBURN, LAN, ENG &
IRL [37547]

DUERKSEN 1840+ TAURIEN, SU [36543]

DUESE ALL WORLDWIDE [37739]

DUETSCH 1670+ MARNE, SHO, GER [37542]

DUFF ALL MEGALONG VALLEY, NSW, AUS [35259]
: 1800S MELBOURNE, VIC, AUS [37913] : 1850+
MELBOURNE, VIC, AUS [38213] : 1860+
BERWICK, VIC, AUS [38213] : 1840+ BECKWITH
TWP. LANARK CO., ONT, CAN [34375] : 1850+
LAMBTON CO., ONT, CAN [34375] : PRE 1800 ST
ALLEN, CON, ENG [34914] : 1857 DEWSBURY,
YKS, ENG [36319] : PRE 1870 INDIA [35255] : ALL
DROMARA, DOW, IRL [34627] : 1800+
LONGFORD, LOG, IRL [38213] : C1830-1860 IRL
[38325] : PRE 1845 MONEYDIE &
AUCHTERGAVEN, PER, SCT [34375] : GEORGE
C1740-1820 BAN, SCT [34646] : 1780+ WEST
TEMPAR & FORTINGALL, PER, SCT [34650] :
1860+ KIRKINTILLOCH, DNB, SCT [34650] : PRE
1940 DUNDEE, ANS, SCT [35255] : C1815 TYRIE,
ABD, SCT [35259] : PRE 1811 CLACKMARRAS &
ELGIN, MOR, SCT [35259] : 1800+ PITTENWEEN,
FIF, SCT [35822] : C1750+ BURNTYARDS, BANFF,
BAN, SCT [36258] : JANET PRE 1821 FIF, SCT
[37354] : PRE 1800 DORNOCH & CREICH, SUT,
SCT [37913] : DENNIS 1774-1808 SC, USA [37800] :
PHILLIP 1760-1840 GA, SC & IL, USA [37800] : PRE
1850 OH & VA, USA [38181]

DUFFEE C1840 PARR, LAN, ENG & IRL [36874]

DUFFELL PRE 1850 SSX, ENG [34610] : PRE 1888
SRY, ENG [37358]

DUFFETT 1775+ NFD, CAN [37479]

DUFFEY PRE 1908 DUBLIN, IRL [37701]

DUFFIELD 1826 NOTTINGHAM, NTT, ENG [34540] :
1784 NORWICH, NFK, ENG [34939] : 1816+
SANDFORD, OXF, ENG [35463] : PRE 1900 WRY,
ENG [36411] : PRE 1830 SCULCOATES, NRY, ENG
[37083] : 1800+ BALLYGOMARTIN, ANT, IRL
[37425] : ALL WEX, IRL & CAN [38391] : 1650+
SALEM, NJ & PA, USA [37826]

DUFFILL 1910-1915 REGINA, SAS, CAN [37548] :
1870-1910 NOTTINGHAM, NTT, ENG [37548] :
1915+ USA [37548]

DUFFIN ALL COOKSTOWN, TYR, IRL & USA
[36916]

DUFFUS C1890 BROKEN HILL, NSW, AUS [37159]

DUFFY 1890+ HENTY, NSW, AUS [34042] : 1890+
MELBOURNE, VIC, AUS [34042] : 1870+
MELBOURNE, VIC, AUS [35379] : PRE 1862+
BALLARAT, VIC, AUS [35746] : PRE 1838+
SYDNEY, NSW, AUS [35746] : C1850 NS, CAN
[36116] : PRE 1840 LARNE, ANT, IRL [34575] :
PATRICK PRE 1790 CALRY, SLI, IRL [35371] : PRE
1827 MOG, IRL [35724] : 1800-1900 TULLIMORE,
OFF, IRL [35923] : PRE 1858 MAY, IRL [36522] : PRE
1840 IRL [37428] : 1800S MEA, IRL [37969] : ALL
TRIM, MEA, IRL [38075] : C1790S CALRY, SLI, IRL
[38744] : 1870S-1920 DERRYGONNELLY, FER &
LKS, IRL & SCT [34635] : 1800+ NZ [38586] : ALL
GLASGOW, SCT [36094] : 1840-1880 GLASGOW,

LKS, SCT [37169] : 1850S SAN FRANCISCO, CA,
USA [36569]

DUFOUR 1680-1750 BEAUPRE, QUE, CAN [36703] :
PRE 1890 LA MALBAIE, QUE, CAN [37442]

DUFOURMONT PRE 1800 MARKE, WVL, BEL
[38164]

DUFTY PRE 1800 PERSHORE, WOR, ENG [35229] :
1800-1900 LONDON, ENG [35229]

DUGALD 1800-1840 KILMARNOCK, AYR, SCT
[34003]

DUGAN ALL AUS [38075] : 1750+ LISBURN, ANT,
IRL [35475] : 1800 GAL, IRL [36860] : 1835+
SUSQUEHANNA CO., PA & NY, USA [35299]

DUGARD 1750+ HARTLEBURY & BIRMINGHAM,
WOR, ENG [37058]

DUGARDE ALL WOODHAM FERRERS, ESS, ENG
[34460]

DUGAS 1800+ STE ELIZABETH, QUE, CAN [34082]

DUGDALE PRE 1767 GRESSINGHAM, LAN, ENG
[36227] : PRE 1839 MANCHESTER, LAN, ENG
[37072] : ALL TATHAM, LAN, ENG [37846]

DUGDALL PRE 1900 BRIXHAM, DEV, ENG [37393]

DUGGAN PRE 1883 ARMIDALE, NSW, AUS [33832] :
1850+ VIC, AUS [34578] : C1849 SYDNEY, NSW,
AUS [35233] : C1853 HARTLEY, NSW, AUS [37894] :
1884+ CHARLEVILLE, QLD, AUS [37894] : 1860+
NSW, AUS [38771] : 1800-1880 LIMERICK &
CONNAUGHT, ONT, CAN [34514] : PRE 1898
FARNHAM, ENG [37955] : PRE 1875 TIP, IRL
[34578] : 1843-1923 BORRISOLEIGH, TIP, IRL
[36293] : JOHN 1800+ FALCARRAGH, DON, IRL
[37942] : JOHN 1800+ GWEEDORE
LETTERKENNY, DON, IRL [37942] : 1860+
LYTTELTON, NZ [35986]

DUGGER ALL ENG [34460] : ALL WOR, ENG [34460]
: PRE 1750 CARTER CO., TN, USA [36929] : 1850-
1880 FULTON, AK, USA [38576]

DUGGIN C1840 WHITECHAPEL, LND, ENG [37053]

DUGGLE 1850+ ST KILDA, VIC, AUS [38281]

DUGHER ALL WOODHAM FERRERS, ESS, ENG
[34460]

DUGROS PRE 1725 SCHWARZENBACH, SAA, BRD
[36964]

DU HEAUME 1875+ MELBOURNE, VIC, AUS
[36761] : 1700+ JSY, CHI [34532] : PRE 1875 JSY,
CHI [36761]

DUHNE ALL BAD, GER & AUS [33919]

DUHON PRE 1800 RHA, FRA [36353]

DUIGNAN 1790+ WALSALL, STS, ENG [35749]

DUITT PRE 1900 LIMERICK, LIM, IRL [34097]

DUKE A.H. PRE 1718 WANGARATTA, VIC, AUS &
ENG [33840] : 1870+ ONT, CAN [38419] : ALL
ROTHERHAM, WRY, ENG [36492] : C1840+
PENSHURST, KEN, ENG [36880] : 1700-1800 ENG
[37207]

DUKER PRE 1855 LND, ENG [34977]

DUKES PRE 1800 WOLVERHAMPTON, STS, ENG
[36854] : 1800+ SHIREOAKS, NTT, ENG [36854] :
1780-1870 BIRMINGHAM, WAR, ENG [37074] :
FRANCES 1777-01832 DEV, ENG [38595]

DUKESON ALL WORLDWIDE [37281]

DULAKE PRE 1875 ENG [36828]

DULANTY ALL WORLDWIDE [37883]

DULEY 1848+ DAPTO, NSW, AUS [35598] : ALL ME,
USA [37803]

DULL 1700-1800 MCVEYTOWN, NJ, USA [38524]

DULLEY ALL WORLDWIDE [36099]

DULLION MARGARET PRE 1854 MONEYDIE &
PITLANDIE, PER, SCT [37769]

DULLOW 1780-1800 HOO, KEN, ENG [36536]

DULOV ALL ENG & SU [37742]

DULSON C1878 BURSLEM, STS, ENG [35348]

DULY 1760S NINFIELD, SSX, ENG **[3550l]**

DUMAS 1830 NEW RICHMOND, QUE, CAN **[38131]**

DUMAY 1811-1987 ST MARTINVILLE & PARIS, LA & RPA, USA & FRA **[34136]**

DUMBLETON 1800-1900 TAS, AUS **[37953]** : C1845 COVENTRY, WAR, ENG **[35746]** : 1800-1850 CAMDEN TOWN, MDX, ENG **[37495]** : PRE 1760 EAST HORSLEY, SRY, ENG **[37953]** : PRE 1760 HAWLEY, HAM, ENG **[37953]** : C1900 INDIA **[37953]**

DUMBRELL 1840+ SYDNEY, NSW, AUS **[37889]** : PRE 1800 HURSTPIERPOINT, SSX, ENG **[34112]** : 1800+ SSX, ENG **[37889]**

DUMBRILL 1780 FLETCHING, SSX, ENG **[38209]**

DUMETS ALL WORLDWIDE **[35832]**

DUMLING ALL MSW, GER **[34488]**

DUMMER ALL CAN & USA **[38782]**

DUMMETT 1859+ COBARGO, NSW, AUS **[34978]** : PRE 1859 SOM, ENG **[34978]**

DUMONT 1600-1900 QUE, CAN **[36568]** : 1900+ ATTLEBORO, MA, USA **[36568]**

DUMURIER DIT HAZUR 1680+ DAX, LANDES, MP, FRA **[36681]**

DUMVILLE 1850 MOBBERLEY, CHS, ENG **[37598]**

DUN ALL SCT **[37324]**

DUNBAR 1830+ NWT, ONT & BC, CAN **[36914]** : 1840 CORK CITY, COR, IRL **[34546]** : PRE 1864 TIP, IRL **[34886]** : 1700+ TIP, WIC & LIM, IRL **[36914]** : 1600+ TYR, DOW & ANT, IRL **[36914]** : MARY 1830S GLASGOW, LKS, SCT **[35794]** : PRE 1900 REAY & HALKIRK, CAI, SCT **[35961]** : 1700+ WICK, CAI, SCT **[35993]** : 1800-1890 KEITH, BAN, SCT **[36663]** : 1800+ AIKEN, SC, USA **[36946]**

DUNBAVIN 1830S-1856 DUBLIN, IRL **[34413]** : 1770-1830 NAAS, KID, IRL **[34413]**

DUNCAN 1850+ BENALLA, VIC, AUS **[33772]** : 1861 AUS **[35910]** : C1870 SURRY HILLS, NSW, AUS **[38077]** : ALL WHITEHEAD, NS, CAN **[34245]** : 1840+ GREY CO., ONT, CAN **[36690]** : JOHN (JACK) 1900+ CAN **[37210]** : 1860+ EDINBURGH & BOTHWELL, ONT, CAN & SCT **[34983]** : 1830 LONDON, ENG **[33772]** : JOHN 1815 LIVERPOOL, LAN, ENG **[37769]** : HENRY PRE 1849 ENG & AUS **[35713]** : 1840 ARM, IRL **[34421]** : 1830S ARMAGH, IRL **[35708]** : 1860S TYR, IRL **[36437]** : 1800S DUBLIN, IRL **[36585]** : PRE 1856 KILLYBEGS, DON, IRL **[38597]** : 1800+ WELLINGTON, NZ **[35776]** : 1840+ ST ANDREWS, FIF, SCT **[33800]** : 1808+ WEST KILBRIDE, AYR, SCT **[34284]** : 1821 RUTHVEN, BAN, SCT **[34336]** : PRE 1841 BAN, SCT **[34357]** : JOSEPH C1800-1900 ABERDOUR, ABD, SCT **[34400]** : PRE 1813 BARR HEAD, RFW, SCT **[34421]** : 1760-1860 DRYWELLS, CABRACH, BAN, SCT **[34479]** : 1750-1850 DUNDEE & FORAR, ANS, SCT **[34513]** : ALEX C1780-1860 SCT **[34646]** : C1700 ST MONANCE, FIF, SCT **[34768]** : ALL ABD & BAN, SCT **[34861]** : 1800+ PETERHEAD, ABD, SCT **[35027]** : MARGARET PRE 1715+ ELIE, FIF, SCT **[35072]** : DAVID C. 1800-1825 DUNNOTTAR, KCD, SCT **[35462]** : 1714-1853 MONTROSE, ANS, SCT **[35462]** : 1600-1800 FIF, SCT **[35627]** : 1851 FALKLAND, FIF, SCT **[35720]** : 1750-1870 DUNDONALD, AYR, SCT **[35790]** : 1979 CRARAE, ARL, SCT **[35826]** : 1920+ DUNOON, ARL, SCT **[35826]** : PRE 1830 GLASGOW, LKS, SCT **[36295]** : 1790S CARRIDEN, WLN, SCT **[36437]** : 1680-1750 KILLEARN, STI, SCT **[36585]** : 1750-1800 ALVA, STI, SCT **[36635]** : 1800+ OLD DEER, ABD, SCT **[36971]** : 1824+ ABD, SCT **[37443]** : PRE 1800 PETERHEAD, ABD, SCT **[37693]** : DAVID 1854 MONEYDIE & PITLANDIE, PER, SCT **[37769]** : DAVID 1871 FOULFORD & FOWLISWESTER,

PER, SCT **[37769]** : ANN 1874 CRIEFF, PER, SCT **[37769]** : MARY 1859 BLAIRGOWRIE, PER, SCT **[37769]** : ROBERT 1863 CLUNIE & AIKENHEAD, PER, SCT **[37769]** : ALEXANDER 1854 MONEYDIE, PER, SCT **[37769]** : JOHN 1860 CLUNIE & AIKENHEAD, PER, SCT **[37769]** : PRE 1780 BOTARY, ABD, SCT **[37835]** : PRE 1769 EASTHOUSES & NEWBATTLE, MLN, SCT **[37852]** : 1800-1830 PAISLEY, RFW, SCT **[38053]** : 1750-1860 CUMBERNAULD, SCT **[38199]** : C1820+ ABD, SCT **[38253]** : PRE 1821 LOSSIEMOUTH, MOR, SCT **[38390]** : 1830+ ABD, SCT **[38425]** : 1860S DEESIDE, FIF, SCT **[38475]** : PRE 1862 EDINBURGH, MLN, SCT **[38597]** : HENRY PRE 1849 SCT & AUS **[35713]** : 1800S DUNDEE, ANS, SCT & NZ **[36809]** : 1600-1900 COLUMBIA CO., NY, USA **[34472]** : 1760S CULPEPER CO., VA, USA **[37027]** : 1790 PULASKI CO., KY, USA **[37027]** : 1830S HICKMAN CO., TN, USA **[37027]** : 1735+ AUGUSTA CO., VA, USA **[37797]** : 1850-1900 SULLIVAN CO., NY, USA **[38053]** : ROLAND 1818-1910 HENDERSON CO., NC, USA **[38141]** : A.A. 1823-1910 HENDERSON CO., NC, USA **[38141]** : C1849 PATTERSON, NJ, USA **[38184]** : 1750-1793 FAUQUIER CO., VA, USA **[38763]**

DUNCANSON PRE 1800 FIF, SCT **[34861]** : 1670+ INVERKEITHING, FIF, SCT **[36268]** : 1750+ KINCARDINE ON FORTH, FIF, CLK & PER, SCT **[37842]** : 1750+ TULLIALLAN, FIF, CLK & PER, SCT **[37842]**

DUNCKER PRE 1750 TRARBACH & MOSEL, RPF, GER **[38663]** : 1749-1788 JESSEN ELSTER, KSA, GER **[38750]**

DUNCOMB PRE 1772 LND, ENG **[33777]** : PRE 1850 ENG **[36639]**

DUNCOMBE 1722+ TAS & VIC, AUS **[33777]** : PRE 1800 DUNTON, BKM, ENG **[35111]** : PRE 1850 ENG **[36639]** : PRE 1840 STAUTON LACEY, SAL, ENG **[36967]** : PRE 1897+ MI, USA **[35004]**

DUNDAS 1836+ KINTBURY, BRK, ENG **[34011]** : 1800S ENG **[36842]** : 1940+ HONG KONG **[37206]** : 1822+ LEGG, INNISHMACSAINT, FER, IRL **[38396]** : 1800+ THURSO, CAI, SCT **[34606]**

DUNDASS 1580-1630 SCT **[35317]**

DUNDEE ALL WORLDWIDE **[35456]**

DUNDERDALE 1800+ RAWCLIFFE, LAN, ENG **[34092]** : PRE 1830 FYLDE & HAMBLETON, LAN, ENG **[38254]**

DUNEMANN 1820+ CLAUSTHAL, HAN, GER **[35730]**

DUNFORD 1860S ENG **[36837]**

DUNGEY 1850+ NSW, AUS **[35444]** : 1850+ BALLARAT, VIC, AUS **[35444]** : 1846+ ONT, CAN **[35444]** : PRE 1840 CRANBROOK, KEN, ENG **[35444]** : 1841 HARDINGTON MANDEVILLE, SOM, ENG **[37378]** : 1860+ OTAGO, NZ **[35444]**

DUNHAM 1806-1855 HASLINGFIELD, CAM, ENG **[37314]** : 1700+ PENFIELD, NY, USA **[36342]** : 1700+ COLDWATER & QUINCY, MI, USA **[36342]** : ALL NY, USA **[38037]**

DUNHILL ALL UK **[37674]**

DUNHOFER ALL ALTHEIM, OOE, OES **[33814]**

DUNK 1700+ ZEDDAM, NL **[37016]**

DUNKER 1780+ OISTE, HAN, GER **[35865]**

DUNKERTON 1800+ SHEPTON MALLET, SOM, ENG **[34970]** : ALL WORLDWIDE **[33858]** : ALL WORLDWIDE **[37084]**

DUNKIN JOHN 1860+ ARMIDALE, NSW, AUS **[37139]** : WM. & ELIZ C1803+ HARBLEDOWN, KEN, ENG **[36767]** : MARY 1803+ HARBLEDOWN, KEN, ENG **[36767]** : ALL BKM, ENG **[37139]** : 1700+ USA **[34419]**

DUNKLE 1725-1900 BERKS CO., PA, USA **[35318]**

DUNKLEY ALL BDF & HUN, ENG [35359] : ALL NTH & BKM, ENG [36179] : PRE 1859 SHOREDITCH, LND, ENG [37647]

DUNLAP JOHN 1897-1925 COOK CO., IL, USA [38132] : 1770 BUCKS CO., PA, USA [38330] : 1740+ BURLINGTON CO., NJ, USA [38330]

DUNLEAVY PRE 1875 KER, IRL [36541]

DUNLEVY 1810+ DON, IRL [36691]

DUNLOP 1877+ WAGGA WAGGA, NSW, AUS [35708] : 1850+ BRISBANE, QLD, AUS [36305] : 1821+ LANARK, ONT, CAN [36974] : 1800+ CHUNDIKULI JAFNA, CEYLON [37306] : 1700-1850 LAMESLEY, DUR & NTH, ENG [35624] : PRE 1848 TULLYNAMULLAN, ANT, IRL [34598] : PRE 1870 ANT, IRL [35055] : JANE 1820+ BALLYSHIEL, ARM, IRL [35274] : 1850+ BELFAST, ANT, IRL [35625] : C1800 KERKINRIOLA, ANT, IRL [36271] : PRE 1800 BATHGATE, MLN, SCT [34491] : PRE 1855 DUNLOP, AYR, SCT [35970] : JAMES 1800+ FENWICK, AYR, SCT [36749] : AGNES C1800 FISHERROW, ELN, SCT [37168] : ANNIE C1823 EDINBURGH, MLN, SCT [37168] : ARCHIBALD C1800 FISHERROW, ELN, SCT [37168] : 1825+ JEFFERSON, NY, USA [36974]

DUNMIRE 1690-1810 CLARE, IRL [38095] : 1867-1930 DEFIANCE, OH, USA [38095] : 1880-1900 RICHLAND, OH, USA [38095] : 1830-1867 PA, USA [38095]

DUNMORE 1690-1810 CLARE, IRL [38095] : PRE 1840 GLASGOW, SCT [33954]

DUNMYER 1800-1900 CAMERIA CO., PA, USA [36897]

DUNN 1940+ AUSTINMER, NSW, AUS [33770] : THOMAS 1835-1856 NSW, AUS [33941] : 1842+ VIC, AUS [34657] : WILLIAM C1800 SA, AUS [35071] : JOHN 1835 HIGHERCOMBE, SA, AUS [35071] : 1799-1989 SYDNEY, NSW, AUS [35089] : 1828+ SACKVILLE REACH, NSW, AUS [35156] : PRE 1827 SACKVILLE REACH, NSW, AUS [35236] : 1860S+ GUNDAROO, NSW, AUS [35331] : C1860 SYDNEY, NSW, AUS [35336] : 1859+ BENDIGO, VIC, AUS [35857] : WILLIAM 1818 SYDNEY, NSW, AUS [35870] : THOMAS PRE 1885 TAS, AUS [36619] : PRE 1874 NSW, AUS [36645] : WILLIAM 1870+ BALLARAT, VIC, AUS [36763] : 1880S ADELONG, NSW, AUS [37145] : JOHN & ELIZ. 1854+ LANDSBORO, VIC, AUS [37557] : EDWARD & JANE 1870+ NSW & VIC, AUS [37949] : 1800+ SYDNEY, NSW, AUS [38208] : MICHAEL 1769-1829 75TH REGT PARRAMATTA & SYDNEY, NSW & ESS, AUS & ENG [36311] : C1890-1910 MIAMI, MAN, CAN [34101] : 1865-1890 PERTH CO., ONT, CAN [34101] : PRE 1850 SFK, ENG [34014] : 1660 MILVERTON, SOM, ENG [34204] : PRE 1850 OLD SWINFORD, WOR, ENG [34314] : PRE 1860 STIFFKEY, NFK, ENG [34570] : PRE 1800 TIVERTON, DEV, ENG [35050] : 1900+ MANCHESTER, LAN, ENG [35183] : C1782 NEWCASTLE ON TYNE, NBL, ENG [35221] : PRE 1850 PORTSEA & SOUTH HAMPTON, HAM, ENG [35221] : C1800 PLAITFORD, WIL, ENG [35456] : PRE 1800 GWINEAR, CON, ENG [35500] : PRE 1850 AUCKLAND, DUR, ENG [35857] : 1800 SOM, ENG [35873] : PRE 1900 KYO, DUR, ENG [36090] : 1750-1900 LAN, ENG [36130] : MARY PRE 1858 CATCHGATE, DUR, ENG [36164] : 1860+ SALOP, SAL, ENG [36523] : PRE 1800 STS & WOR, ENG [36547] : 1820-1860 PIMLICO, LND, ENG [36763] : 1830+ WALSALL, STS, ENG [36821] : 1790+ HRT, ENG [36872] : MICHAEL C1845 DURHAM, DUR, ENG [37112] : 1850 BRISTOL, ENG [37145] : C1780

PLYMPTON ST MARY, DEV, ENG [37264] : PRE 1830 BIRMINGHAM, WAR, ENG [37331] : PRE 1850 WIVELISCOMBE, SOM, ENG [37557] : ALL NFK, ENG [37612] : PRE 1860 NOTTINGHAM, NTT, ENG [37729] : PRE 1800 MUCKLESTONE, STS, ENG [37893] : PRE 1840 CON, ENG [38004] : PRE 1799 LND, ENG [38208] : 1774-1839 BERWICK ON TWEED, NBL, ENG & AUS [37988] : THOMAS 1809-1835 OFF, IRL [33941] : 1780-1900 BELFAST & DONAGHADEE, IRL [34672] : PRE 1815 DUBLIN, IRL [35090] : 1800S+ CLEARIESTOWN, KILMANNON, WEX, IRL [35106] : 1870S LIMERICK, IRL [35508] : 1800 CAR, IRL [35970] : PRE 1780 IRL [36547] : C1843 CAV, IRL [36599] : PRE 1850 LIM, IRL [36608] : 1700-1900S ST JOHNSTON, DON, IRL [36796] : 1800-1830 DUBLIN, IRL [36821] : C1800 PORTARLINGTON, OFF, IRL [38272] : PRE 1792 IRL [38596] : EDWARD 1844-1926 GREYTOWN, WAI, NZ [33961] : 1700-1900S RAKAIA, CANTERBURY, NZ [36796] : 1800+ GLASGOW, LKS, SCT [34260] : PRE 1900 ALLOA, CLK, SCT [34657] : C1870+ ST ANDREWS, FIF, SCT [34913] : 1870+ EDINBURGH, MLN, SCT [34913] : PRE 1840 GLASGOW, SCT [35331] : 1800 KRS, SCT [37170] : ALL SCT [37324] : PRE 1840 GLASGOW, LKS, SCT [38289] : PRE 1840 GLASGOW, LKS, SCT [38289] : ALBERT W. 1890+ SAN FRANCISCO, CA, USA [34770] : C1854 NEW YORK, NY, USA [35221] : PRE 1800 NC, USA [36570] : 1800-1900 IL, USA [36733] : 1740-1813 MD, USA [37795] : THOMAS 1830+ MA, USA & AUS [35093]

DUNNAGE 1790+ LONDON, ENG [33946]

DUNNE PRE 1830 ADELAIDE, SA, AUS [34575] : PRE 1874 NSW, AUS [36645] : REBECCA 1870-1930 SYDNEY, NSW, AUS [37904] : 1796+ SACKVILLE REACH, NSW, AUS [38596] : 1850+ MANCHESTER, LAN, ENG [35183] : PRE 1857 TYR, IRL [33812] : PRE 1860 ARDFINNAN, TIP & WAT, IRL [38541] : 1800S PER, SCT [34937]

DUNNETT ALL SFK, ENG [37042] : ALL NFK, ENG [37612] : PRE 1853 CASTLETOWN, CAI, SCT [34797]

DUNNEVAN 1740+ NEWINGTON, KEN, ENG [36236]

DUNNEVIN PRE 1890 PEI & NS, CAN [38746]

DUNNEY PRE 1900 KIK, IRL [38589] : 1850+ USA [38589] : ALL WORLDWIDE [38589]

DUNNIGAN C1845 KAMPTEE, NAGPORE, INDIA [35348]

DUNNILL 1840+ SHEFFIELD, WRY, ENG [34397] : 1650+ ALTOFTS & NORMANTON, WRY, ENG [34397] : 1750-1860 WAKEFIELD, WRY, ENG [34397]

DUNNING 1900+ NSW, AUS [34534] : 1800+ LONDON, ENG [33979] : PRE 1768 BRAFFERTON, NRY, ENG [37852]

DUNPHY 1875-1930 NB, CAN [36718] : C1830 ABBEYLEIX, LEX, IRL [34273] : PRE 1849 ABBEYLEIX, LEX, IRL [34977] : 1800-1950 BALLYMACARBERRY & CLONMEL, WAT, IRL [36565] : CATHERINE 1837+ TIP, IRL & AUS [35784]

DUNROE C1850 CAR & WEX, IRL [34395]

DUNROSE 1700+ UTTOXETER & NEWCASTLE, STS, ENG [34714] : C1890 BORROWASH, DBY, ENG [34734]

DUNSCOMBE PRE 1700 TOPSHAM & WOODBURY, DEV, ENG [36389] : 1790-1890 BRISTOL, GLS, ENG [38511]

DUNSHEA 1818+ AUS [35397] : PRE 1818 LISBURN, ANT & DOW, IRL [35397] : 1860+ NZ & AUS [35397]

DUNSMORE PRE 1840 DRY, IRL [34809] : PRE 1900 SCT [37456] : 1850S CAPE ANN, MA, USA [35156]

DUNSTALL ALL WORLDWIDE [35944]

DUNSTAN 1791+ WILBERFORCE, NSW, AUS
[34446] : C1850 CAMPBELLS CREEK, VIC, AUS
[37159] : 1698-1727 STITHIANS, CON, ENG [33995] :
THOMAS 1750-1800 FALMOUTH, CON, ENG
[35107] : THOMAS 1720-1750 STITHIANS, CON,
ENG [35107] : PRE 1836 REDRUTH, CON, ENG
[35711] : 1700S PERRANARWORTHAL, CON, ENG
[35780] : 1700-1900 CON, ENG [36170] : 1800S ENG
[37216] : SOPHIA 1880-1920 BRT, FRA [35107] :
CHARLES 1881-1882 DENVER, CO, USA [35107] :
1800-1900 GLA, WLS [36170]

DUNSTER PRE 1724 ILMINSTER, SOM, ENG [34270]
: 1800+ BERMONDSEY, SRY, ENG [36219] : 1800+
CHS & LAN, ENG [36363] : PRE 1890
TENTERDEN, KEN, ENG [38509] : PRE 1650 LAN,
ENG [38745]

DUNSTON 1850-1880 RICHLAND CO., WI, USA
[36444] : 1830 LOGAN CO., OH, USA [36444]

DUNSWORTH 1800 MCDONOUGH, IL, USA [34388]

DUNT 1750-1816 NEWTON FLOTMAN, NFK, ENG
[37477] : PRE 1800 BRK, ENG [37715]

DUNTHORNE ALL NORWICH, NFK, ENG [37612]

DUNTON 1875-1896 WELLS, SOM, ENG [35047] :
1912-1934 BROMSGROVE, WOR, ENG [35047] :
PRE 1904 NORTHAMPTON, NTH, ENG [35047]

DUNWOODY 1750-1820 BOARDMILLS, DOW, IRL
[38347]

DUON PRE 1800 RHA, FRA [36353]

DUPLOCK PRE 1850 BUXTED, SSX, ENG [37871]

DUPONT ISABELLE 1825-1840 BRUSSELS, BEL
[38724] : 1592+ HANAU, HEN, GER [38667]

DUPRES PRE 1780 LA, USA [36917]

DUPREZ PRE 1900 BOWRAL, NSW, AUS [38008] :
1830-1900 SRY & MDX, ENG [38008] : 1830-1900
HANSE, FRA [38008]

DUPUIS MOISE 1660+ COLAR, NY, USA [36678] :
1850+ BOUBONNAIS, IL, USA [36928]

DUQUETTE 1836 QUE, CAN [38583]

DURAN C1920 PISLEY, CA, USA [37159]

DURAND ALL ONEX & AVULLY, GE, CH [38348] :
1600+ PCH, FRA [37479] : 1746-1933 ST
MARTINVILLE & BEAUJEU, LA & RHA, USA &
FRA [34136]

DURANT PRE 1780 LA, USA [36917] : 1800+
WORLDWIDE [37147] : ALL WORLDWIDE [38237]

DURANT-CUMMING 1800 WORLDWIDE [36637]

DURBIN SIMEON PRE 1813 CHEWTON MENDUP,
SOM, ENG [34779] : C1856 BATH, SOM, ENG
[36860] : 1720-1750 BALTIMORE CO., MD, USA
[38137] : C1897 PONTYPOOL, MON, WLS [36860]

DURDEN PRE 1800 LONDON, ENG [37557] : 1800+
BIRMINGHAM, WAR, ENG [37557] : 1800-1900
BIRMINGHAM, WAR, ENG [38321] : PRE 1800
LONDON, MDX, ENG [38321]

DUREN 1790-1840 SUMMER CO., TN, USA [37533]

DURFEE 1840-1876 LEE CO., IL, USA [37538] : PRE
1850 MADISON CO., NY, USA [37538]

DURHAM 1854+ KOROIT, VIC, AUS [35057] : C1895
HOPETOUN, VIC, AUS [35057] : THOMAS P. 1865+
CAN [36838] : PRE 1800 PAINSWICK, GLS, ENG
[36441] : 1800+ LND, ENG [36603] : PRE 1840S
WRINGTON BRISTOL, SOM & GLS, ENG [36817] :
1774-1830S WESTMINSTER, LND, ENG [36838] :
1838-1850S BERMONDSEY, LND, ENG [36838] :
1600-1730 WESTMINSTER, MDX, ENG [36973] :
1809+ BATTERSEA, LND, ENG [37167] : ALL
KEN, ENG [37595] : PRE 1742 UXBRIDGE, MDX,
ENG [37811] : 1700+ DUNKIRK, FRA [36603] :
C1828 ANT, IRL [35057] : 1864+ AUCKLAND, NZ
[36838] : C1722-C1799 BATHGATE, WLN, SCT

[36838] : 1930-1988 CA, USA [36445] : THOMAS P.
1865+ USA [36838] : 1730-1830 VA, USA [36973]

DURIE-STARK 1840+ HUNTFIELD, LKS, SCT
[35025]

DURIEU 1795+ LONDON, ENG [38496]

DURKEE 1640-1990 IRL & ENG [38203] : 1640-1990
USA & CAN [38203]

DURKIN ALL SOUTHAMPTON, HAM, ENG [37658] :
ALL ROTHERHITHE, SRY, ENG [37658]

DURLICH PRE 1871 THRANA, UPPER LUSATIA,
GER [34766]

DURLING PRE 1778 ASH, KEN, ENG [33821]

DURMAN 1770-1885 NORTH PETHERTON, SOM,
ENG [38309]

DURNING 1800-1900 IRL, SCT & ENG, AUS [34227] :
1800S IRL [37515] : 1840-1900 BOSTON, MA, USA
[37515]

DURNO ALL ABD, SCT [37245]

DURNY 1850+ GUYSBOROUGH, NS, CAN [35627]

DURR 1880+ AUS [38176] : JOHANN PRE 1769
SCHWEIGEN, SW, GER [36453] : ALL
KIRCHHEIM TECH & NABURN, WUE, GER
[38176]

DURRAN ALL CAI, SCT [37658]

DURRAND ALL CAI, SCT [37658]

DURRANT C1780 CHESHAM, BKM, ENG [34041] :
1800+ NFK, ENG [34049] : 1780S HORSHAM, SSX,
ENG [35793] : 1870+ SWAFFHAM & CASTLE
ACRE, NFK, ENG [37332] : PRE 1870 BISHOPS
CAUNDLE & FOLKE, DOR, ENG [37332] : 1846-
1920 ST PANCRAS, LND, NFK & CAM, ENG
[37719] : 1750+ MILBORNE PORT, SOM & DOR,
ENG [37766] : 1850+ AMESBURY, WIL, ENG
[38288] : 1850+ FALKIRK, STI, SCT [34039] : 1650-
1700 MD, USA [37795] : 1740+ WORLDWIDE
[36981]

DURRELL ALL MISSISQUOI CO., QUE, CAN & USA
[38349]

DURRETT ALL TN, USA [35312]

DURRINGTON 1870+ HARWOOD, NSW, AUS
[37116]

DURROCH 1820+ ANSTRUTHER, FIF, SCT [35865]

DURSEY MICHAEL 1817-1838 BUTLER, OH, USA
[38157]

DURST PRE 1820 REICHWEILER, RPR, GER [34137]

DURTNALL ALL PYECOMBE, SSX, ENG [36938]

DURWARD PRE 1890 LIVERPOOL, LAN, ENG
[38424] : 1800-1870 ROME, ITL [37593]

DURYEA 1810+ LONG ISLAND, NY, USA [35508]

DUSKE PRE 1900 NZ & GER [34603]

DUSTIN 1770-1900 WEMBURY & PLYMOUTH, DEV,
ENG [36788]

DUSTOW ALL HEF, ENG [36889]

DUTCHER ALL CAN [34131]

DUTFIELD PRE 1800 PERSHORE, WOR, ENG [36190]

DUTHIE 1775-1780 IRL & SCT [34387] : 1750-1820
KCD, SCT [35813] : PRE 1800 ABD, SCT [36433]

DUTILHE 1750-1850 BORDEAUX, FRA [35283]

DUTSON 1780+ SUCKLEY, WOR, ENG [38020]

DUTT 1900S DALBY & BEAUDESERT, QLD, AUS &
GER [34957]

DUTTENHOEFER 1868+ CLERMONT CO., OH &
BAY, USA & GER [37504] : 1868+ HAMILTON CO.,
OH & BAY, USA & GER [37504]

DUTTON C1870 CARLTON, VIC, AUS [35708] : 1810-
1847 LEIGH, LAN, ENG [35341] : ALL
ALDERSHOT, HAM, ENG [36232] : C1796-1820S
BIRMINGHAM, WAR, ENG [36838] : C1820-1875+
LONDON, ENG [36838] : PRE 1729 ASTON SUB
EDGE, GLS, ENG [37909] : 1865+ AUCKLAND, NZ
[36838] : ASA 1803-1860 BELGRADE, ME & OH,

EAGLESFIELD ALL LEI, ENG [35177]

EAGLETON ALL BKM, ENG [35139] : ALL ASHENDON, BKM, ENG [35139] : PRE 1835 BESTHORPE, NFK, ENG [35151]

EAGLING 1821+ SYDNEY, NSW, AUS [35513] : PRE 1821 NORWICH, NFK, ENG [35513]

EAKINS PRE 1854 KILMORE, LOG, IRL [35779]

EALES 1700-1900 BERMONDSEY, SRY, ENG [34749] : ALL TOWCESTOR, NTH, ENG [35258]

EAMER PRE 1760 RPF, BRD [34246] : 1780-1990 OSNABRUCK, ONT, CAN [34077] : ALL BRK, ENG [37638]

EAMES 1800+ BILLINGSHURST & STEYNING, SSX, ENG [34749] : C1893 LUTON, HRT, ENG [35036] : PRE 1880 LIVERPOOL, LAN, ENG [35430] : 1822-1840 SOUTHAMPTON, HAM, ENG [37187] : 1700-1850 RICKMANSWORTH, HRT, ENG [37253] : 1750+ GARWAY, HEF, ENG [38020] : 1750-1850 BUTTEVANT, COR, IRL [37844] : 1600-1700 REHOBOTH, MA, USA & ENG [34749] : PRE 1890 LLANGWYLLOG, AGY, WLS [35430]

EARCHMAN ADAM 1800-1825 MOFFAT, DFS, SCT [35006]

EARDLEY 1820-1900 LONDON, ENG [35600] : EDWARD PRE 1775 UK [37703]

EAREA 1870+ SWAN BAY, NSW, AUS [37312]

EAREE 1843+ TOLLESHUNT MAJOR, ESS, ENG [37312]

EARHART 1760-1800 WASHINGTON CO., MD, USA [37603] : 1720-1760 PHILADELPHIA CO., PA, USA [37603]

EARL 185+ RICHMOND, VIC, AUS [34577] : 1803-1900 HOBART, TAS, AUS [34928] : PRE 1820 LIVERPOOL, NSW, AUS [35419] : 1850+ NORTH SYDNEY, NSW, AUS [38597] : C1827 TROWBRIDGE, WIL, ENG [35133] : PRE 1850 PENZANCE, CON, ENG [35589] : PRE 1840 CALLINGTON, CON, ENG [35589] : 1880-1910 LONDON, ENG [37219] : 1880+ LONGFIELD, KEN, ENG [37219] : 1850-1950 LYCOMING CO., PA, IA & MO, USA [38025]

EARLE 1750-1860 YKS, ENG [34846] : 1750-1840 SOUTHEASE, SSX, ENG [35643] : 1800-1900 GANTHORPE, YKS, ENG [35892] : 1600-1750 NORTON ST PHILIP, SOM, ENG [37232] : 1800+ HOUGHTON LE SPRING, DUR, ENG [38454]

EARLEY PRE 1811 CHELSEA, LND, ENG [35037] : THOMAS 1860 SALFORD, LAN, ENG [37184] : ALL WIL & HAM, ENG [37412] : THOMAS 1842 SCT [37184]

EARLL PRE 1856 LONDON &, ESS, ENG [35940]

EARNSHAW ALL ROCHDALE, LAN, ENG [34429] : C1870 BRISTOL, ENG [37131]

EARSDON PRE 1860 CLA, IRL [35488]

EARTHY 1800+ CLACTON, ESS, ENG [37046]

EARY ALL SFK, ENG [34744] : 1800+ WICKHAM BISHOPS, ESS, ENG [37312] : PRE 1800 WORLDWIDE [37280]

EASBY 1650-1750 CRAYTHORNE, ERY, ENG [34552]

EASENCY 1840-1860 WALDO CO., ME, USA [37576]

EASINGWOOD ALL ERY, ENG [37208] : 1850 MARKET WEIGHTON, ERY, ENG [37208] : 1850 GREAT DRIFFIELD, ERY, ENG [37208] : 1779+ SUTTON ON HULL, ERY, ENG [37208] : 1850 SWINE, ERY, ENG [37208] : 1821-1890S NORTH CAVE & ALTOFTS, YKS, ENG [37352]

EASLER ALL ALBERT CO., NB, CAN & USA [38447]

EASOM PRE 1800 WHITTLESEY, CAM, ENG [34581]

EASON C1830+ THROWLEY, KEN, ENG [34374] : 1850 MERRIOTT, SOM, ENG [34890] : C1700 YEOVIL, SOM, ENG [37918]

EASSIE 1870+ BROWNS CREEK, NSW, AUS [36641]

EASSON PRE 1850 ST MONANCE, FIF, SCT [37693]

EAST PRE 1830 STANWELL, MDX, ENG [34445] : ALL ENG [36221] : ALL LONDON, ENG [36789] : PRE 1840 OXF, ENG [37150] : ALL ENG & AUS [37199] : 1818-1835 CONECUH & MONROE, AL, USA [36911] : THOMAS 1843-1905 LIVINGSTON CO., IL, USA [38132]

EASTBURN 1850+ MELBOURNE, VIC, AUS [37967] : 1824+ BEESTON, WRY, ENG [37967]

EASTER PRE 1750 HARTBURN, NBL, ENG [36502]

EASTERBROOKS 1740+ BRATTLEBORO, VT, USA [38520]

EASTERBY 1850+ LONDON, ENG [34238]

EASTERLY ALL BATH, SOM, ENG [37950]

EASTGATE 1500-1800 WHEATACRE, NFK, ENG [34872]

EASTHAM 1750+ BURLINGTON CO., NJ, USA [36934]

EASTHOPE PRE 1839 PORTSEA, HAM, ENG [34166] : PRE 1860 WOLVERHAMPTON, STS, ENG [36249]

EASTICK 1895+ WIMMERA, VIC, AUS [36622] : 1800S GREAT YARMOUTH, NFK, ENG [34914]

EASTLAKE PRE 1820 DEV & CON, ENG [34319] : 1800-1900 ISLINGTON, MDX, ENG [35174] : 1750-1900 KENNINGTON, LND, ENG [35174]

EASTMAN 1880S NORTH GOWER, ONT, CAN [35078] : 1500S LANGFORD, WIL, ENG [36560] : 1850+ BIRKENHEAD, CHS, ENG [36769] : 1686-1770 HAMBURG, NJ, USA [36907] : LUCY C1817 MARCELIUS, NY, USA [38172]

EASTMENT PRE 1842 HARDINGTON MANDEVILLE, SOM, ENG [35854]

EASTNOPE ALL UK [37674]

EASTO 1871 DISS, NFK, ENG [37082]

EASTOE 1860+ HAGLEY, TAS, AUS [34770]

EASTON C1840 HASTINGS, SSX, ENG [33918] : 1675+ NRY, ENG [34181] : REGINALD 1807+ LONDON, ENG [34627] : 1834+ LEYTONSTONE, ESS, ENG [34627] : PRE 1811 BEXHILL, SSX, ENG [34806] : PRE 1900 CROYDON, SRY, ENG [35418] : ALL EXETER, DEV, ENG [36145] : 1800S HASTINGS, SSX, ENG [37714] : 1750-1860 ANT, IRL [37338] : 1770+ CARRIDEN, WLN, SCT [33810] : 1776 FORFAR, ANS, SCT [35560] : PRE 1800 LKS, SCT [38437]

EASTOR 1800 AYLSHAM, NFK, ENG [37170]

EASTTY C1800 IPSWICH, SFK, ENG [37449]

EASTWELL PRE 1854 GREAT GRANSDEN, HUN, ENG [35393]

EASTWOOD 1800-1900S LAN, ENG [34000] : 1700+ FISKERTON, LIN, ENG [34221] : PRE 1821 YKS, ENG [38080]

EATE 1820+ ALCUMBRY, HUN, ENG [36608]

EATINGER JACOB 1804-40 PORTAGE CO., OH, USA [38138]

EATON 1791+ RICHMOND, NSW, AUS [35537] : 1640+ NS, CAN [36800] : 1700-1800S LIVERPOOL & WEST DERBY, LAN, ENG [34032] : PRE 1857 TITTON BROOK, WOR, ENG [35247] : 1769+ BETHNAL GREEN, LND, ENG [35537] : 1840+ LIVERPOOL, LAN, ENG [35768] : 1820 LEICESTER, LEI & NTH, ENG [36414] : PRE 1880 KNUTSFORD, CHS, ENG [36522] : PRE 1842 MDX, ENG [36800] : PRE 1840 WAR, ENG [37200] : PRE 1750 BOBBINGWORTH, ESS, ENG [37568] : PRE 1900 ESS, ENG [37668] : 1573+ DOVER, KEN, ENG [37802] : 1790 GREASLEY, NTT, ENG [37829] : 1750-1800 NEW SALEM, MA, USA [36335] : JESSE 1820-1834 CATTARAUGUS CO., NY, USA [36345] : FRAZIER 1810-1850 ALLEGANY CO., NY, USA [36345] : JESSE 1820-1834 ALLEGANY CO., NY, USA [36345] : 1620S CT, USA [38184] : 1750

STAFFORD, MA, USA **[38241]** : 1800-1900
CUYAHOGA CO., OH, USA **[38764]** : PRE 1650
CHEPSTOW, MON, WLS **[38746]**

EATTS C1830 ST AGNES, CAM, ENG **[35401]**

EAVES PRE 1830 LEA MAYSTON, WAR, ENG **[34265]**
: PRE 1850 COVENTRY, WAR, ENG **[37225]** : 1800S
LEYLAND, LAN, ENG **[38444]** : C1790 NC, USA
[37536]

EBATHITE 1760+ RICKMANSWORTH, HRT, ENG
[36981]

EBBELS ALL DEV & LND, ENG **[36786]**

EBBERT C1750-1890 FREDERICK CO., MD, USA
[38030]

EBBINGHAUS ALL WEI, GER **[38607]**

EBDEN 1800-50 GREAT SNORING, NFK, ENG
[35524]

EBDON C1800 BUDLEIGH, DEV, ENG **[37452]**

EBENSEN ALL HEINDE, PRE, GER **[38637]**

EBERBACH PRE 1700 LAUFFEN, WUE, GER **[38683]**

EBERHARD PRE 1900 NOERDLINGEN, BAY, BRD
[36963]

EBERLE PRE 1735 PALATINATE, GER **[36972]**

EBERT 1779+ HEDDESHEIM, BAD, GER **[37894]** :
PRE 1779 MUNZFELDEN, GER **[37894]** : PRE 1750
GER **[38610]** : PRE 1800 GER **[38610]** : 1800-1900
ADAMS CO., PA, USA **[37013]** : 1860-1900
TOMPKINS CO., NY, USA **[37013]** : ALL
WORLDWIDE **[35577]**

EBERWEIN 1640-1700 MUSBERG, WUE, GER **[38599]**

EBOR PRE 1880 ENG **[35757]** : PRE 1880 LITHUANIA
[35757]

EBS PRE 1856 HAN, GER **[37811]**

EBSWORTHY ALL SYDNEY, NSW, AUS **[34287]**

EBURNE PRE 1850 WAR, ENG **[35962]**

EBY PRE 1800 MANHEIM, PA, USA & CH **[36969]**

EBZERY PRE 1835 ROBERTSTOWN, LIM, IRL
[37104]

ECCLES 1900+ NEWCASTLE, NSW, AUS **[37757]** :
ALL MANCHESTER, LAN, ENG **[34684]** : GEORGE
1810+ PRESTON, LAN, ENG **[35805]** : PRE 1800
WOR & WAR, ENG **[37703]** : C1730 DARWEN,
LAN, ENG **[38283]** : PRE 1840 DRUMBARNET
MIDDLE, DON, IRL **[35545]** : 1850S BELFAST,
ANT, IRL **[36848]** : C1850 DUBLIN, IRL **[37757]**

ECCLESTON 1827+ CAMPBELLTOWN, NSW, AUS
[35530] : 1819+ AUS **[36295]** : ALL WEST DERBY,
CHS, ENG **[35177]** : PRE 1800 EASTBOURNE, SSX,
ENG **[36295]** : PRE 1800 LAN, ENG **[36295]** : 1700-
1800 LOU, IRL **[37844]**

ECCLESTONE 1800 WARWICK, WAR, ENG **[35023]**

ECKARDT 1690-1709 KAISERLAUTERN, RPF, BRD
[34114] : 1709+ PALATINE BRIDGE, NY, USA
[34114]

ECKART PRE 1900 CHOLIN, CHOLNO, SU **[37510]**

ECKEL PRE 1800 GER **[35571]**

ECKER ABRAHAM 1834+ WAINFLEET, ONT, CAN
[34059] : 1709+ PALATINE BRIDGE, NY, USA
[34114]

ECKER (SEE ACKER) **[34059]**

ECKERMAN ALL FRANKLIN CO., PA, USA **[38287]**

ECKERT C1864 BREWARRINA, NSW, AUS **[34806]** :
1828+ EBERSTATT, WUE, GER **[34806]** : PRE 1750
SCHEPPACH, WUE, GER **[35242]** : ALL
REGENSBURG, GER **[36571]** : C1844 BRADFORD
CO., PA, USA **[36356]**

ECKFORD 1800+ BRANT, ONT, CAN **[35627]** : 1850S
AUCKLAND, NZ **[33934]** : 1800+ ROX, SCT **[35627]**
: 1700-1990 UK & AUS **[35421]**

ECKHARDT PRE 1800 FILDERN, WUE, GER **[38702]**
: ALL NEDERLANDEN, ZEL, NL **[38702]**

ECKLES PRE 1850 ROSS CO., OH, USA **[38538]**

ECKLEY PRE 1739 HANLEY WILLIAM, WOR, ENG
[36513] : ALL ENG & WLS **[37738]**

EDBROOK C1810 LND, ENG **[37239]**

EDDENS 1847+ NSW, AUS **[34534]**

EDDISFORD ALL ENG **[36363]**

EDDISON C1700-1750 ROC, SCT **[37790]**

EDDLEMAN ALL USA **[38312]**

EDDLEMON ALL USA **[38312]**

EDDLESTON ALL MELLOR, LAN, ENG **[34155]**

EDDOLLS PRE 1720 WIL, ENG **[35866]**

EDDY PRE 1850 ST JUST, CON, ENG **[33884]** : 1675
GWENNAP, CON, ENG **[34793]** : ALL
RUARDEAN, GLS, ENG **[36451]** : 1700-1870 CON,
ENG **[38005]** : 1845-1875 KEWEENAW CO., MI,
USA **[38010]** : C1880 SHELBY, IL, USA **[38263]** : ALL
WORLDWIDE **[38237]**

EDDYE 1616 CRANBROOKE, KEN, ENG **[37531]** :
PRE 1590 CRANBOOK, KEN, ENG **[38135]**

EDE 1863+ BALLARAT & RICHMOND, VIC, AUS
[35751] : 1700-1800S REIGATE, SRY, ENG **[33958]** :
1629+ ILLOGAN & ST MABYN, CON, ENG **[34726]**
: ALL CON, ENG **[35751]** : PRE 1863 OTAGO, NZ
[35751]

EDEL 1800+ GOWDALL & SNAITH, WRY & YKS,
ENG **[36772]**

EDELSVARD GUSTAF A. 1872-1908 MYSSJO
PERSASEN, JAMTLAND, SWE **[38566]** : CONRAD
1866+ MYSSJO PERSASEN, JAMTLAND, SWE
[38566] : ESTER H. 1879-1906 HARNOSAND,
JAMTLAND, SWE **[38566]** : PER ADOLF 1862-1897
OVIKEN, JAMTLAND, SWE **[38566]** : ALFRED E.
1901+ STOCKHOLM, SWE **[38566]**

EDEN 1700+ BOLNHURST, BDF, ENG **[34416]** :
C1878 ATWORTH, WIL, ENG **[34584]** : 1700S
WINSLOW, BKM, ENG **[38358]**

EDENFIELD 1723+ ENG **[38340]** : 1769+ SC & GA,
USA **[38340]**

EDENS PRE 1880 ST EBBS, OXF, ENG **[34750]**

EDEY ALL RUARDEAN, GLS, ENG **[36451]** : PRE
1800 RANDOLPH, VT, USA **[34113]**

EDGAR 1838+ PINE HILLS, VIC, AUS **[33833]** : 1877-
1950 ADELAIDE, SA, AUS **[34462]** : 1900+ TIBET,
CHINA **[37109]** : PRE 1750 ESS, ENG **[35642]** :
ABRAHAM PRE 1880 LANCHESTER, DUR, ENG
[36164] : 1690+ IPSWICH, SFK, ENG **[36203]** :
1800+ RANDALSTOWN, ANT, IRL **[35565]** : PRE
1850 DOW, IRL & SCT **[37180]** : 1800S TAPANUI,
NZ **[33833]** : 1876+ TAPANUI, NZ **[37109]** : 1600-
1800 MOFFAT, DFS, SCT **[33833]** : 1850+
BOTHWELL, LKS, SCT **[35565]** : 1830+ MAYBOLE,
AYR, SCT **[35959]** : PRE 1900 WEST GREENOCK,
RFW, SCT **[37745]**

EDGCOMB PRE 1854 IA, USA **[37574]**

EDGCOMBE PRE 1786 DEV, ENG **[35895]**

EDGE 1800-1900 DEPTFORD & BERMONDSEY,
LND, ENG **[34749]** : 1700+ BLOXWICH &
WALSALL, STS, ENG **[36256]** : 1800S
HARTINGTON, DBY, ENG **[36670]** : 1800-1900
WATERFALL, STS, ENG **[37375]** : HARRIET 1839
WATERFALL, STS, ENG **[37375]** : HARRIET 1851+
STS & LAN, ENG **[37375]** : PRE 1790 UK **[33864]**

EDGECOMBE PRE 1884 DEV, ENG **[35895]** : 1700+
THURLESTON, DEV, ENG **[35970]** : ALL DEV,
ENG **[37735]** : PRE 1750 CT, USA **[37570]**

EDGECUMBE ALL MALMESBURY, WIL, ENG
[34466] : ALL HULLAVINGTON, WIL, ENG **[34466]**
: ALL TEWKESBURY, GLS, ENG **[34466]** : ALL
EAST TYTHERTON, WIL, ENG **[34466]** : ALL
BRISTOL, SOM, ENG **[34466]**

EDGER PRE 1879 TIRRIL, WES, ENG **[34911]**

EDGERTON PRE 1830 IRONBRIDGE, SAL, ENG [33776] : 1700-1900 WEM & BASCHURCH, SAL, ENG [34411]

EDGHILL 1750-1850 BIRMINGHAM, WAR, ENG [37038]

EDGINGTON 1880 DARLINGTON, DUR, ENG [34512]

EDGLER 1700 PETWORTH, SSX, ENG [34909]

EDGLEY HANNAH 1786 MANCHESTER, LAN, ENG [34091]

EDGWORTH 1700+ GLS, ENG [37099]

EDICK JAMES 1840+ FULTON CO., NY, USA [36950]

EDIE C1835 ST ANDREWS, FIF, SCT [35963] : 1700-1860 PA, USA [37545]

EDIGER 1775-1835 MONTAUERWEIDE, DANZIG, W. PRE, GER [36543]

EDINGER ALL ENG [36585]

EDIS JOHN PRE 1800 GLOUCESTER, GLS, ENG [36590] : ALL ENG [36694]

EDISON 1845+ BAYHAM TWP., ONT, CAN [36323]

EDKIN ALL WORLDWIDE [38177]

EDKINS 1580-1700 WAR, ENG [35305] : ALL WORLDWIDE [38177]

EDMEADES 1800+ KEN, ENG [35806]

EDMISTON ALL UK & AUS [35056] : SAMUEL PRE 1770 VA, USA [35328] : WATSON 1770S ABINGDON, VA, USA [37585] : PRE 1744 WASHINGTON, VA, USA [38220]

EDMOND PRE 1800 BEMPTON, ERY, ENG [34285] : 1800-1820S KILRARY & RUTHERGLEN, LKS, SCT [34359] : 1800+ PER & STI, SCT [36705]

EDMONDS 1840 SYDNEY, NSW, AUS [33783] : 1750-1830 LONDON, ENG [34438] : PRE 1870 KIDDERMINSTER, WOR, STS & NTH, ENG [34745] : 1800-1850 CHELTENHAM, GLS, ENG [35556] : PRE 1890 LONDON, ENG [35556] : C1827 KEN, ENG [35786] : PRE 1800 HRT, ENG [35866] : PRE 1870 PENZANCE, CON, ENG [36870] : PRE 1700 RYE, SSX, ENG [38043] : PRE 1800 DUBLIN, IRL [34254] : ALICE 1785-1866 SCITUATE, RI, USA [35271] : 1850S MON, WLS [36867]

EDMONDSON C1800+ BURNLEY, LAN & YKS, ENG [34451] : 1800+ ROSSENDALE, LAN, ENG [36271] : 1750-1870 COCKERMOUTH, CUL, ENG [36983] : 1667-1875 HEYSHAM & POULTON LE SANDS, LAN, ENG [37524] : 1614-1642 MELLING, LAN, ENG [37524]

EDMONSON 1800-1900+ BROWN, OH, KY & PA, USA [38054]

EDMONSTONE PRE 1800 FIF, SCT [34576]

EDMUNDS 1850+ ADELAIDE, SA, AUS [34600] : ALL ASHLEWORTH, GLS, ENG [34823] : 1800+ BRISTOL, SOM, ENG [35489] : PRE 1900 HAMPSTEAD, MDX, ENG [35978] : PRE 1900 WORTHING, SSX, ENG [35978] : PRE 1900 BISHOPS WALTHAM AREA, HAM, ENG [36265] : 1700S ASTWELL PARK, NTH, ENG [37566] : C1740 ST ALBANS, HRT, ENG [37898] : C1740 ST ALBANS, HRT, ENG [37898] : PRE 1850 BEDWELLTY, MON, WLS [35540] : C1825 LLANGIBBY, MON, WLS [36185] : 1850S MON, WLS [36867]

EDNER 1850-1880 JEFFERSON CO., PA, USA [36900]

EDNEY PRE 1840 EAST DEAN, HAM, ENG [34570]

EDRICH PRE 1855 HAUTBOIS MAGNA, NFK, ENG [37512]

EDRIDGE ALL CROYDON, SRY, ENG [34669] : ALL LONDON, ENG [34669]

EDSALL ALL BREAMORE & FORDINGBRIDGE, HAM, ENG [33823]

EDSTER 1790-1810 GARRARD CO., KY, USA [36334]

EDVARDSEN ALL ADELAIDE & MORGAN, SA & NSW, AUS & NOR [35383]

EDWARD C1913 LEWISHAM, ONT, CAN [38450] : PRE 1790 FORTEVIOT, PER, SCT [33957] : ALL TANNADICE, ANS, SCT [36509] : CHARLOTTE 1804+ LLANGYFELACH, GLA, WLS [36636]

EDWARDS JOHN 1858 KANGAROO ISLAND, SA, AUS [34193] : 1849+ SA, AUS [34261] : 1840 PENOLA, SA, AUS [34456] : 1840S MELBOURNE, VIC, AUS [34563] : 1850S PORTLAND & PORT FAIRY, VIC, AUS [34563] : PRE 1880 WARKWORTH, NSW, AUS [34590] : 1848+ BACCHUS MARSH, VIC, AUS [34767] : 1858+ KOORINGA, SA, AUS [34778] : 1850S BALMAIN, NSW, AUS [34854] : JAMES 1840+ SYDNEY, NSW, AUS [34977] : JOSEPH 1850+ ALEXANDRIA, NSW, AUS [34977] : PRE 1896 WOOLLOOMOOLOO, NSW, AUS [34979] : 1800-1900 BATHURST & CALOOLA, NSW, AUS [35103] : 1850-1900 EVANDALE, TAS, AUS [35195] : FREDERICK PRE 1850 SYDNEY, NSW, AUS [35373] : PRE 1847 SINGLETON, NSW, AUS [35425] : 1850+ BRISBANE, QLD, AUS [35442] : WILLIAM 1858-1924+ MARSDEN, NSW, AUS [35497] : 1875+ OLDBURY & BERRIMA, NSW, AUS [35567] : 1867+ SUTTON FOREST, NSW, AUS [35567] : 1850+ IPSWICH, QLD, AUS [35814] : 1850+ NEWTOWN, NSW, AUS [35825] : C1903-1920S BALLANDRY, NSW, AUS [36313] : GEORGE 1871-1914 WOONONA, NSW, AUS [36598] : WILLIAM 1834-1902 DAYLESFORD, VIC, AUS [36598] : C1835-1896 GUNDAROO, NSW, AUS [37559] : ALL MENINDEE & WILCANNIA, NSW & SA, AUS & NOR [35383] : C1600 GUERNSEY, CHI [34342] : 1810 ASHLEY, HAM, ENG [33995] : PRE 1800 EAST GRINSTEAD, SSX, ENG [33998] : PRE 1800 SOM, ENG [34046] : PRE 1850 FARNHAM, SRY, ENG [34131] : 1800 CHILLINGTON, SOM, ENG [34172] : C1600-1800 UNY LELANT, CON, ENG [34214] : MARIA C1818 NFK, ENG [34222] : PRE 1870 HRT, ENG [34258] : 1840+ LONDON, ENG [34258] : 1700-1850 BRAUNSTON, NTH, ENG [34258] : ALL ASHENDON, BKM, ENG [34261] : ALL WITHAM FRIARY, SOM, ENG [34376] : PRE 1900 BIRMINGHAM & WORCESTER, WOR, ENG [34508] : C1809 ENG [34553] : ALL SOUTHWARK, LND, ENG [34564] : PRE 1800 LIVERPOOL, LAN, ENG [34576] : 1650+ KENNINGHALL, NFK, ENG [34639] : PRE 1884 MILE END, MDX, ENG [34689] : PRE 1890 BRETTENHAM, SFK, ENG [34719] : JOHN 1781-C1850 FORD & CORSHAM, WIL, ENG [34738] : JOHN C1850-1870 MARYLEBONE, MDX, ENG [34738] : JAMES 1854-C1920 HOUNSLOW & COWLEY, MDX, ENG [34738] : FRANCIS C1760-1790 FORD & CORSHAM, WIL, ENG [34738] : JAMES 1803-1867 WIL & MDX, ENG [34738] : JAMES 1800-1900 NEWINGTON & BERMONDSEY, LND, ENG [34749] : 1812 WOR, ENG [34777] : JOHN 1800S AXMINSTER, DEV, ENG [34930] : 1800+ SIDMOUTH, DEV, ENG [35027] : STEVEN 1850+ SOMERTON, SOM, ENG [35066] : PRE 1840 HASELBURY PLUCKNETT, SOM, ENG [35128] : 1800-1860 NORFOLK, NFK, ENG [35195] : THOMAS C1834 STS, ENG [35202] : JOSEPH PRE 1840 LIVERPOOL, LAN, ENG [35330] : PRE 1840 CON, ENG [35346] : 1700+ REDRUTH & TRURO, CON, ENG [35385] : C1800 OSWESTRY, SAL, ENG [35438] : JAMES 1823-1848 LONDON, ENG [35447] : 1800+ GREENWICH, KEN, ENG [35465] : PRE 1855 EVERLEIGH, WIL, ENG [35567] : PRE 1820 NORTHIAM, SSX, ENG [35587] : PRE 1820 LELANT, CON, ENG [35709] : GEO. RICHARD C1838 LONDON, ENG [35714] : JAMES

PRE 1851 NEWLYN EAST, CON, ENG **[35788]** :
1812+ WORKINGTON, CUL, ENG **[35921]** : PRE
1856 NORTHAMPTON, NTH, ENG **[35956]** : ANN
S. PRE 1870 LAMBETH, LND, ENG **[35958]** : 1800+
HAMMERSMITH, MDX, ENG **[35975]** : C1800
TRURO, CON, ENG **[36000]** : 1700-1900 WOOLTON,
LIVERPOOL, LAN, ENG **[36063]** : 1650-1750
BEDINGFIELD & KENTON, SFK, ENG **[36213]** :
1814-1843 LAMBETH, SRY, ENG **[36229]** : ROBERT
PRE 1829 LIVERPOOL, LAN, ENG **[36308]** : 1850-
1900 DARLASTON, STS, ENG **[36495]** : 1750-1850
LONGBRIDGE, WIL, ENG **[36688]** : R. 1800+
LONDON, ENG **[36717]** : 1770+ ALBURY, HRT,
ENG **[36978]** : PRE 1860 WOODFORD, ESS, ENG
[37097] : PRE 1856 REIGATE, SRY, ENG **[37138]** :
WILLIAM C1820S EPSOM, SRY, ENG **[37153]** :
1870+ EASTBOURNE, SSX, ENG **[37206]** : 1870+
NUNHEAD, LND, ENG **[37206]** : 1860+
SITTINGBOURNE, KEN, ENG **[37213]** : PRE 1900
GRAYS, ESS, ENG **[37237]** : 1800S WITLEY, SRY,
ENG **[37260]** : ALL BRINKWORTH & SWINDON,
WIL, ENG **[37468]** : 1750-1825 CHISLET, KEN, ENG
[37602] : ALL SFK, ENG **[37612]** : PRE 1910 ESS,
ENG **[37668]** : PRE 1840 ALSAGER, CHS, ENG
[37722] : PRE 1868 SOM, ENG **[37760]** : 1700-1900
BRISTOL, GLS, ENG **[37829]** : 1760-1840 GLS, ENG
[37870] : HENRY 1844 ST PANCRAS & CHELSEA,
LND, ENG **[37988]** : C1860S FINCHLEY, MDX,
ENG **[38002]** : CHARLES C1750-1840 ALSAGER,
CHS, ENG **[38055]** : 1600 ENG **[38131]** : WILLIAM
PRE 1880 PLYMOUTH, DEV, ENG **[38222]** : 1800-
1850 BANBURY, OXF, ENG **[38373]** : C1660+ EAST
HARLING, NFK, ENG **[38492]** : 1800+
BIRMINGHAM, WAR, ENG & AUS **[36257]** :
GEORGE C1780+ WOTTON UNDER EDGE, GLS
& NSW, ENG & AUS **[37988]** : PRE 1820 CAR, KIK
& WEX, IRL **[34376]** : MARGARET C1830 MOR,
SCT **[35848]** : 1810-1850 HANCOCK CO., TN, USA
[36731] : AARON 1700S SPRINGFIELD, NJ, USA
[36928] : ABRAHAM 1780-1800S FT WAYNE, IN,
USA **[36928]** : 1750-1850 CHATAUQUA CO., NY,
USA **[36957]** : PRE 1800 CAYUGA CO., NY, USA
[36957] : 1845-1875 KEWEENAW CO., MI, USA
[38010] : C1818 BERNARDSTON, MA, USA **[38052]** :
PRE 1806 FAIRFIELD, OH, USA **[38220]** : 1800 IL,
USA **[38531]** : 1890+ HARPIC CO., TX, USA **[38587]** :
C1840 MENEITH, MER, WLS **[33796]** : C1840+
PONTYPOOL, MON, WLS **[33922]** : PRE 1730
BANGOR, CAE, WLS **[34376]** : 1790 LLANOVER,
MON, WLS **[34546]** : 1800S LLANPUMPSAINT,
CMN, WLS **[34729]** : PRE 1850 MARCHWIEL, DEN,
WLS **[35925]** : PRE 1850 PENNAL, MER, WLS
[36388] : 1800-1870S MENAI, AGY, WLS **[36522]** :
PRE 1880 RUABON, DEN, WLS **[36849]** : 1830S
LOWER CHAPEL, BRE, WLS **[37320]** : ALL
YSCEIFIOG, FLN, WLS **[37667]** : 1650-1750
GRESFORD, DEN, WLS **[38074]**

EDWARDSON 1700+ WINWICK NEWTON, LAN,
ENG **[38046]** : 1800-1900 LIVERPOOL, LAN, ENG
[38074] : 1740+ SHI, SCT **[37527]**

EDWICK 1800+ WHEELY & COLCHESTER, ESS,
ENG **[38395]**

EDWICKER PRE 1830 TILLINGTON & PETWORTH,
SSX, ENG **[38254]**

EDWORTHY 1800+ DEV, ENG **[37766]** : C1818
SANDFORD, DEV, ENG **[37830]**

EDY ALL RUARDEAN & BRISTOL, GLS, ENG
[36451] : 1860+ PORT ELIZABETH, CAPE, RSA
[36451] : 1800+ NEATH, GLA, WLS **[36451]**

EELES 1700+ MONK SHERBORNE, HAM, ENG
[34309]

EENKHOORN 1840 GENEMUIDEN, OIJ, NL **[35338]**

EESEN VAN 1700-1830 AMSTERDAM, NH, NL
[38712]

EFEMEY PRE 1874 COLNBROOK, BRK, ENG **[36496]**

EFFERHEN C1495 KOELN, NRW, FRG **[38660]**

EFFORD PRE 1748 DEV, ENG **[34213]**

EGAN MILA 1970+ MURGON, QLD, AUS **[34341]** :
ALL AUS **[34759]** : 1850S KOROIT STATION, VIC,
AUS **[35259]** : 1840+ ADELAIDE, SA, AUS **[35385]** :
1840+ DIGBY, VIC, AUS **[35385]** : 1850+ GOLDEN
POINT, VIC, AUS **[36439]** : 1780+ NEWCASTLE
ON TYNE, NBL, ENG **[35221]** : 1820S ENNIS, CLA,
IRL **[35259]** : PRE 1840 CLA, IRL **[35385]** : MARY
PRE 1833 LIM, IRL **[35725]** : PRE 1870 OFF, IRL
[35745] : 1800-1858 OSSORY HILL & JOHNSWELL,
KIK, IRL **[36862]** : 1700-1990 IRL & AUS **[35421]** :
1842-1880 ALLEGHENY CO., PA, USA **[37605]**

EGBERS 1700S GEL, NL **[38358]**

EGEL 1821 GLOGAU, SIL, PRE **[35369]**

EGERTON PRE 1870 BICESTER, OXF, ENG **[36502]** :
PRE 1800 BENTHALL & BROSELEY, SAL, ENG
[37389]

EGGBEER ALL ENG **[38265]**

EGGBY PRE 1830 ALTON, HAM, ENG **[36147]**

EGGELING ALL HAN, GER & NZ **[34603]**

EGGERS 1720-1850 PINNEBERG, SHO, GER **[37021]**

EGGERSDORF 1890-1990 CHARLEVOIX CO., MI,
USA **[38062]**

EGGERT PRE 1839 GRUNBERG, UCKERMARK,
GER **[35465]** : 1800+ MECKLENBURG, GER **[37907]**

EGGINGTON 1800+ STS & WAR, ENG **[36587]**

EGGINS PRE 1863 SSX, ENG **[35031]** : 1700S+
EWHURST, SSX, ENG **[37910]**

EGGLESTON 1860S ASHTON, LAN, ENG **[35390]** :
C1800-1878 PICKAWAY CO., OH, USA **[35284]** :
SARAH 1687 WOBURN, MA, USA **[36944]** : 1900+
YONKERS, NY, USA **[37828]** : 1859-1931 LEIGH,
NE, USA **[38094]** : 1818-1877 NORTHEAST TWP.,
NY, USA **[38094]** : 1856-1925 DENNISON, IA, USA
[38094] : 1848-1861 WARREN, PA, USA **[38094]** :
1861-1925 GENEVA, NE, USA **[38094]**

EGGLESTONE PRE 1845 STANLEY, WRY, ENG
[34786]

EGGLETON 1788+ LIVERPOOL & PROSPECT,
NSW, AUS **[35511]** : PRE 1760 BURBAGE, WIL,
ENG **[35346]** : C1831 BROAD BLUNSDON, WIL,
ENG **[36307]** : C1895 ROSS ON WYE, HEF, ENG
[36816]

EGGO PRE 1850 CORTACHY, ANS, SCT **[37727]**

EGI ALL WORLDWIDE **[38693]**

EGLET ALL WORLDWIDE **[34313]**

EGLI 1650-1750 BAW, GER **[38219]** : 1700-1780
LANCASTER CO., PA, USA **[38219]**

EHAIN 1600-1800 RATSHAUSEN, WUE, GER **[37015]**

EHLER 1800+ GUYSBOROUGH, NS, CAN **[35627]**

EHLY ALL WORLDWIDE **[37600]**

EHRENREICH 1600-1950 BAV, GER **[38128]**

EHRHARD ANNA C. C1700+ YORK CO., PA, USA
[37604]

EHRHARDT 1700+ OBERWEISSBACH, THU, GER
[37582]

EHRLICH 1810+ BAD, GER **[37799]**

EIBENSTEIN PRE 1845 FRIEDRICHSHAIN, SIL,
GER **[38664]**

EICHBAUM PRE 1800 FREUSBURG, RPF, BRD
[38677] : PRE 1830 WOLFERODE, HAL, DDR **[38677]**
: PRE 1700 PLAU, SWR, DDR **[38677]** : C1533
RAPPOLTSWEILER, ELO, GER **[38677]** : PRE 1840
HAMELN, HAN, GER **[38677]**

EICHE ALL TOOTNAU, BAW, BRD **[38686]**

EICHER CHRISTIAN 1836-1912 NEWARK, WI, USA
[38156]

EICHLER 1800+ ZELLERFELD, HAN, GER & AUS [34882]

EICHSTEDT 1750-1840 STETTIN, POM, GER [38565]

EICKERET PRE 1894 GOORNONG, VIC, AUS [37497]

EICKSTEADT 1810-1870 GER [38199]

EIDELBERGER PRE 1900 AUGSBURG, BAY, BRD [36963]

EIJCK 1600S STAVENISSE, ZEL, NL [38358]

EIJKE 1746+ DREISCHOR, ZEL, NL [38358]

EILRICH ALL STOLP, POM, GER [36571]

EINSPORN 1850+ VIC, AUS [35379] : PRE 1850 LEHMOLLEN, PRE, GER [35379]

EINWECHTER PRE 1850 GHE, GER [36726]

EIPPER ALL WORLDWIDE [38533]

EISELE 1800-1850 GER [38089] : 1820-1950 BUTLER CO., OH, USA [38089]

EISENBEIS 1800-1860 BERKS CO., PA, USA [36552]

EISENHOWER ALL PA & KS, USA [35304]

EISENKRAMER PRE 1760 BAW, GER [38669]

EISENMANN 1500S MAINHARDT, WUE, GER [33901]

EISINKOLB PRE 1860 KARLSBAD AREA, BOHEMIA, CS [36963]

EITE PRE 1840 NTT, ENG [35246]

EITEL 1500S MAINHARDT, WUE, GER [33901]

EKENSTEEN ALL ENG & AUS [34303]

EKLUND 1880 SYDNEY, NSW, AUS [38214] : CARL JOHAN PRE 1870 RAMNAS VASTMANLAND, VASTMANLAND, SWE [38548]

EKMAN ALL LJUSNE, SWE [38175]

EKSTROM 1850+ SWE [38059]

ELAM PRE 1850 LIN, ENG [36143] : 1844+ TANEY CO., MO, USA [37003] : PRE 1844 TN, USA [37003]

ELAND ALL DRIBY, LIN, ENG [36477]

ELBOROUGH ALL WORLDWIDE [38252]

ELBRO ALL WORLDWIDE [38252]

ELCOCK 1700-1850 BARBADOS [38355] : PRE 1750 WHITEPARISH, WIL, ENG [36478] : 1850+ UK [34482]

ELDEN 1870+ MELBOURNE, VIC, AUS [37962] : PRE 1870 YARMOUTH, NFK, ENG [37962]

ELDER 1863+ VIC, AUS [35731] : 1850+ HAMILTON, ONT, CAN [38463] : ALL LONGHOUGHTON, NBL, ENG [34835] : 1830-1900 SOUTHWARK, SRY, ENG [37560] : 1810+ CON, ENG [37560] : WILLIAM C1890-4 GOREY, WEX, IRL [35184] : WILLIAM 1846 IRL [35184] : ALEXANDER C1847 PERTH, PER, SCT [33951] : 1815 KIRKCALDY, FIF, SCT [34529] : PRE 1810 CUPAR, FIF, SCT [34977] : ALEXANDER 1825 DOLPHINTON, LKS, SCT [35184] : WILLIAM 1846 SCT [35184] : 1600+ FIF, SCT [35627] : 1600-1700 KIRKCALDY, FIF, SCT [35627] : C1800+ NEWLANDS, PEE, SCT [35834] : C1860+ LKS, SCT [35834] : PRE 1850 FORFAR, ANS, SCT [36361] : C1800 GLASGOW, LKS, SCT [36431] : 1800+ ROSEMARKIE, ROC, SCT [36885] : PRE 1850 ANSTRUTHER, FIF, SCT [38463] : C1812 OH, USA [36923] : ALL WORLDWIDE [36333]

ELDERFIELD PRE 1880 BURY, LAN, ENG [37917]

ELDERKIN 1600S-1713 NEW LONDON, CT, USA & ENG [38532]

ELDERS 1750+ LAARWALD, NSA, BRD [34398]

ELDERSHAW 1894+ COOTAMUNDRA, NSW, AUS [35536] : PRE 1894 TEMORA, NSW, AUS [35536] : 1570+ BARLASTON, STS, ENG [36701]

ELDERT PRE 1805 BROOKLYN, NY, USA [38126]

ELDIN PRE 1812 KNOTTINGLY, YKS, ENG [37112]

ELDRED PRE 1800 SPALDING, LIN, ENG [36107] : 1650+ RI, USA [38015]

ELDRIDGE ALL BATTLE, SSX, ENG [35259] : PRE 1740 BATTLE, SSX, ENG [35587] : 1750+ NC, VA & TN, USA [38739]

ELEMENT PRE 1820 EDMONGTON & LONDON, MDX, ENG [36061] : 1700-1800 ROCHFORD, WOR & HEF, ENG [37762]

ELESMORE PRE 1875 WAR, ENG [35423]

ELEY 1700+ SFK, ENG [34943] : 1700S DALE ABBEY, DBY, ENG [36018] : JOSIAH 1783-1850 ROBERTSON CO., TN & VA, USA [38569]

ELFERS 1850+ KENOSHA CO., WI & IL, USA & GER [37796]

ELFICK PRE 1800 GRAVESEND, KEN, ENG [34707] : JOHN C1770 HASTINGS, SSX, ENG [37106]

ELFORD 1550+ WINTERBORNE HOUGHTON, DOR, ENG [34228] : 1730+ WINTERBORNE STICKLAND, DOR, ENG [34228] : 1800S HINKSEY, OXF, ENG [36670] : 1800S OXFORD, OXF, ENG [36670] : 1890+ MDX, ENG [36810]

ELGAR PRE 1760 KEN, ENG [38389]

ELGIE 1800+ NORTHALLERTON, YKS, ENG [36323]

ELGIN PRE 1840 VA, USA [38242]

ELHOR PRE 1704 WELDON, NTH, ENG [35597]

ELIAS PRE 1855 PISTYLL, CAE, WLS [35207]

ELIGH 1800-1830 ULSTER CO., NY, USA [37017]

ELIJAH 1855+ HAMILTON, VIC, AUS [35207]

ELIOT C1820 ABERDEEN, ABD, SCT [35747]

ELIS PRE 1800 BRYNSIENCYN, AGY, WLS [36168]

ELIZABETH AKIN/AIKEN 1849+ SINGLETON, NSW, AUS [35852]

ELKES PRE 1850 SHREWSBURY, SAL, ENG [36040] : 1835-1850 LIVERPOOL, LAN, ENG [36040] : 1845-1870 WESTMINSTER, LND, ENG [36040]

ELKINGTON 1860+ MT MORIAC, VIC, AUS [34011] : 1810+ BERMONDSEY, MDX, ENG [34011] : HENRY C1860 BANBURY, OXF, ENG [34935] : 1750-1950 LIVERPOOL, LAN, ENG [35403] : 1800-1950 COVENTRY, WAR, ENG [35403] : PRE 1830 WOLSTON, WAR, ENG [35962] : PRE 1900 LND, ENG [37256]

ELKINS PRE 1850 FARNHAM, SRY, ENG [34428] : 1770+ HAM, ENG [35760]

ELLACOMBE 1800+ CHUDLEIGH, DEV, ENG [37757]

ELLAM C1840-1850 YKS, ENG [35791]

ELLARD PRE 1900 RICHMOND, TAS, AUS [34918]

ELLEDGE 1900-1950 CA, USA [38100]

ELLENDEN PRE 1735 BOUGHTON ALUPH, KEN, ENG [34445]

ELLENWOOD 1630+ MA, USA [38015]

ELLER 1750+ JEFFERSON, TN & VA, USA [36931]

ELLERBECK PRE 1810 TADCASTER, NRY, ENG [37856]

ELLERBY PRE 1900 CHERTSEY, SRY, ENG [34105] : ALL NBL & NRY, ENG [36110] : 1700-1850 NARTOFT, NRY, ENG [37435] : ALL LIN, ENG [37929]

ELLERINGTON 1854-1874 ENG [36594]

ELLERY 1870S ABERDEEN, NSW, AUS [33810] : ALL ST COLUMB MINOR, CON, ENG [35500] : 1830+ MANCHESTER, LAN, ENG [37134]

ELLEY 1840+ HOBART, TAS, AUS [37989]

ELLICOMBE ALL WORLDWIDE [34833]

ELLIMAN PRE 1900 PRIORS MARSTON, WAR, ENG [34562]

ELLINGHAM 1700-1785 CLARE, SFK, ENG [35119]

ELLINGS 1840+ CON, ENG & NZ [36819]

ELLINGSWORTH C1880 WAGGA WAGGA, NSW, AUS [35203]

ELLINOOR PRE 1820 CARTMEL, LAN, ENG [34053]

ELLIOT C1700 BRIXHAM, DEV, ENG [34333] : 1700-1800 PLYMOUTH, DEV, ENG [34742] : 1650+ BRIXHAM, DEV, ENG [36000] : 1800+ CON, ENG & NZ [36850] : PRE 1879 DUBLIN, IRL [33777] :

1750-1850 LISNASKEA, FER, IRL [35151] : PRE 1899 CASTLETON, ROX, SCT [34665] : 1830+ STEWARTON, AYR, SCT [35914] : PRE 1840 MAUCHLINE, AYR, SCT [37144] : 1700S JEDBURGH, ROX, SCT & AUS [35422]

ELLIOTSON 1870+ OWEN SOUND, ONT, CAN [38396]

ELLIOTT ELVIRA C1900 SYDNEY, NSW, AUS [33765] : PRE 1876 WATERVALE, SA, AUS [33866] : 1848+ GUNDAGAI, NSW, AUS [34852] : C1870 BLACKWOOD, VIC, AUS [34963] : 1840+ BOMBALA, NSW, AUS [35240] : EDWARD 1861 MURRURUNDI, NSW, AUS [35498] : 1862+ SYDNEY, NSW, AUS [35843] : 1800+ FRANKLIN, TAS, AUS [38288] : 1848+ SYDNEY, NSW, AUS [38568] : WM. JAMES 1861-1906 MAITLAND & PRESCOTT, GRENVILLE, ONT, CAN [34103] : WM. CROZIER 1850S-1903 BROCKVILLE & MAITLAND, GRENVILLE, ONT, CAN [34103] : 1818-1821 ST JOHNS, NB, CAN [37015] : 1830+ PETERBOROUGH CO., ONT, CAN [37446] : 1800-1900 TICEHURST, SSX, ENG [33785] : NANCY PRE 1870 EATON BISHOP, HEF, ENG [33819] : PRISCILLA PRE 1840 LISSAN GROVES, ENG [33890] : 1800S MERTON, DEV, ENG [34075] : 1750-1850 CON, ENG [34078] : PRE 1830 MARTOCK, SOM, ENG [34197] : ALL LONGBRIDGE DEVERILL, WIL, ENG [34466] : 1810-1880 HOLBORN, LND, ENG [34469] : JAMES 1700+ ENG [34701] : ALL EMBLETON, NBL, ENG [34835] : 1750+ STAMFORDHAM, NBL, ENG [34852] : C1835 TRURO, CON, ENG [34963] : PRE 1858 ABBOTSKERSWELL, DEV, ENG [35035] : C1850 HORSLEY, GLS, ENG [35038] : PRE 1860 WESTHAM, ESS, ENG [35242] : PRE 1835 ALDGATE, LND, ENG [35485] : 1844-1877 STEPNEY, LND, ENG [35485] : ALL CAYTON, NRY, ENG [35633] : 1800+ GREAT LINFORD, BKM, ENG [35829] : PRE 1863 LIVERPOOL, LAN, ENG [35843] : PRE 1720 DEVA, ENG [35866] : PRE 1800 CHIDDINGLY, SSX, ENG [35898] : 1700-1850 LIN, ENG [36057] : PRE 1760 HALTWHISTLE, NBL, ENG [36110] : 1750+ MDX, ENG [36123] : PRE 1820 WYRLEY, STS, ENG [36177] : 1820+ HURSTPIERPOINT, SSX, ENG [36212] : 1870 STANLEY, DUR, ENG [36499] : 1840+ DARTFORD, KEN, ENG [37213] : 1850+ SUTTON AT HONE, KEN, ENG [37213] : 1850+ ERITH, KEN, ENG [37213] : 1800-1920 NEWCASTLE ON TYNE, NBL, ENG [37395] : 1870+ ESS, ENG [37677] : 1800+ WITHAM, ESS, ENG [37699] : ALL SOM, ENG [38288] : PRE 1846 RADFORD, NTT, ENG [38568] : 1890+ LND, ENG & AUS [35485] : EDWARD 1830S NOTTINGHAM, NTT, ENG & AUS [35498] : 1600+ GLS, ENG & AUS [35305] : JOSEPH PRE 1799 ONCHAN, IOM & ENG [34125] : PRE 1830 IRL [34060] : WM. CROZIER C1836 ENNISKILLEN DEVENISH, FER, IRL [34103] : 1700-1800S DORNAN, TYR, IRL [34483] : 1700-1800S BALLINA MALLARD, FER, IRL [34483] : PRE 1845 KILLIBEGS, DON, IRL [34494] : PRE 1850 CARRICKMACROSS, MOG, IRL [35750] : 1750-1820 IRL [37015] : 1800-50 ANNAGHMORE, ARM, IRL [37129] : PRE 1830 DON, IRL [37446] : 1770-1870 BALLINASLOE, GAL, IRL [38503] : JANE C1785-1861 FER & QUE, IRL & CAN [36904] : WILLIAM C1800-1879 FER & QUE, IRL & CAN [36904] : C1845 KILMARNOCK, AYR, SCT [34494] : C1700 LANGHOLM, DFS, SCT [35038] : PRE 1800 CHESTER, NH, USA [34113] : 1750-1800 LIBERTY CO., GA, USA [36737] : 1800-1900 FRANKLIN CO., NY, USA [37783] : PRE 1800 MD, USA [37795] : ALL

YORK, PA, USA [38319] : C1900+ KLAMATH FALLS, OR, USA [38584] : SAMUEL 1840S+ NEWPORT, MON, WLS [35876] : C1800S PORTLAND, WORLDWIDE [35381]

ELLIS 1890-1910 WEST WYALONG, NSW, AUS [33817] : 1857-1880 CASTLEMAINE & YERING, VIC, AUS [34035] : GEORGE 1865+ NYMBOIDA, NSW, AUS [34539] : PRE 1850 MT DUNEED, VIC, AUS [35224] : 1850+ MITTA MITTA, VIC, AUS [35719] : C1840 HARDEN, NSW, AUS [36271] : C1840 YASS, NSW, AUS [36271] : 1860+ WIMMERA, CRESWICK & UNION HL, VIC, AUS [36622] : 1750-1850 BARBADOS [38355] : 1880-1920 PETERBOROUGH, ONT, CAN [36675] : 1800+ PEI, CAN [38460] : PRE 1825 DONCASTER, ENG [33762] : 1860-1884 ST PANCRAS, LND, ENG [33817] : PRE 1860 BURNHAM MARKET, NFK, ENG [33817] : 1400+ MANCHESTER, LAN, ENG [33989] : PRE 1750 WRESSLE, YKS, ENG [33998] : C1820-1842 LIVERPOOL & WEST DERBY, LAN, ENG [34035] : 1800-1900 LEEDS, YKS, ENG [34074] : 1800+ WATSHEL, ENG [34082] : PRE 1840 PLYMOUTH, DEV, ENG [34197] : 1880+ MAIDSTONE, KEN, ENG [34218] : 1700 SWINESHEAD & SWABY, LIN, ENG [34221] : PRE 1810 HRT & ESS, ENG [34240] : PRE 1860 BATTERSEA, SRY, ENG [34463] : PRE 1880 MORPETH, NBL, ENG [34480] : 1780-1850 HANLEY, STS, ENG [34693] : 1800+ MIDHURST, SSX, ENG [34927] : C1740S WEST PACKHAM, KEN, ENG [35259] : 1800+ SHEFFIELD, YKS, ENG [35342] : ALL LAUGHTON, SSX, ENG [35588] : 1800S BIRMINGHAM, WAR, ENG [35965] : C1860 WARRINGTON, LAN, ENG [36092] : ALL EXETER, DEV, ENG [36145] : 1746 BOTTLEY, HAM, ENG [36263] : PRE 1900 ARNOLD, NTT, ENG [36387] : RICHARD 1800+ SFK, ENG [36572] : 1800 ELTHAM, LND, ENG [36805] : PRE 1880 YKS, ENG [36847] : 1850S HALIFAX, WRY, ENG [36867] : 1700-1850 KEN, ENG [37015] : WILLIAM 1824 BETHNAL GREEN, MDX, ENG [37080] : 1840 WICKHAM SKIETH, SFK, ENG [37080] : 1650+ CLOPHILL, BDF, ENG [37151] : 1700+ NOTTINGHAM, NTT, ENG [37248] : 1800+ BIRKENHEAD, CHS, ENG [37306] : PRE 1789 KETTLETHORPE, LIN, ENG [37318] : 1700-1790 ASHBURNHAM, SSX, ENG [37880] : PRE 1800 THURLSTONE, WRY, ENG [37893] : 1880+ EPSOM, SRY, ENG [37983] : PRE 1850 CAISTOR, LIN, ENG [38730] : 1700+ BALLYHEADY, CAV, IRL [34299] : PRE 1830 ANT, IRL [36271] : 1750-1900 LANARK, LKS, SCT [34404] : ARTHUR LEWIS 1910+ WASHINGTON, DC, USA [33762] : PRE 1800 SOMERSET, ME, USA [35323] : SAM 1900+ KANSAS CITY, KS, USA [36212] : 1750 MD & VA, USA [37795] : 1865-1880 KEWEENAW CO., MI, USA [38010] : 1650+ RI, USA [38015] : PRE 1900 USA & CAN [36933] : 1770+ ALBERBURY, MGY, WLS [35719] : 1700-1800 LLANDDEWI ABERARTH, CGN, WLS [37306] : HUGH C1650 DOLGELLEY, MER, WLS [37649] : 1000-1990 WORLDWIDE [36114]

ELLISDON 1800+ ST PANCRAS, LND, ENG [37775]

ELLISON PRE 1882 PARRAMATTA, NSW, AUS [34979] : C1800 LONDON, ENG [34367] : C1765 LND, ENG [34858] : 1770-1836 NEWCASTLE ON TYNE, NBL, ENG [35348] : C1800-1880S ERY, ENG [37236] : 1851+ GATESHEAD, DUR, ENG [37704] : PRE 1851 LONDON, ENG [37704] : 1700-1830 CHURCH LENCH, WOR, ENG [37849] : 1700-1830 WAR & WOR, ENG [37849] : 1700-1830 GREAT ALNE, WAR, ENG [37849] : 1722-1800S CARR IN ROSSENDALE, LAN, ENG [37988] : 1800-1880 WEST RIDING, YKS, ENG [38381] : C1850 FIVE

MILE TOWN, TYR, IRL **[35381]** : PRE 1850 FIVE MILE TOWN, TYR, IRL **[36271]** : 1900+ EDINBURGH, MLN, SCT **[33978]** : 1762+ KEENE, NH, USA **[34379]** : 1800-1900 MD, USA **[34749]**

ELLISTON 1800+ BULMER, ESS & SFK, ENG **[33970]** : PRE 1800 ESS, ENG **[36124]** : PRE 1800 SFK, ENG **[36124]** : ALL SFK, ENG **[37637]** : 1700-1830 CHURCH LENCH, WOR, ENG **[37849]** : 1700-1830 WAR & WOR, ENG **[37849]**

ELLITHORN 1760-1890S LANCASTER & PRESTON, LAN, ENG **[37710]**

ELLSON PRE 1800 CHS & SAL, ENG **[37936]** : 1850+ BIRMINGHAM, ENG **[37936]**

ELLSTON 1900 UK **[35508]**

ELLSWORTH C1680 MA, USA **[34395]** : CHRISTIANNE 1852-1870 STEPHENSON CO., IL, USA **[38145]** : WM. ORSEN 1820-1852 JEFFERSON CO., NY, USA **[38145]** : 1840-1863 SOUTH BEND, IN, USA **[38763]**

ELLWOOD ALL NS, NB & NJ, CAN & USA **[38349]** : PRE 1870 CROGLIN, CUL, ENG **[34869]** : PRE 1900 CUL & DUR, ENG **[36481]** : 1750-1950 WHITEHAVEN, CUL, ENG **[38377]**

ELLZEY JOHN 1550+ SOUTHAMPTON, HAM, ENG **[36572]**

ELMER 1855+ BEECHWORTH, VIC, AUS **[35819]** : 1800+ MDX & SRY, ENG **[37836]** : NATHANIEL 1700-1800 ORANGE CO., NY, USA **[38130]**

ELMQUIST 1870+ MINNEAPOLIS, MN, USA **[38545]** : 1884+ CHICAGO, IL, USA **[38545]**

ELMS 1810+ ARMIDALE, NSW, AUS **[37316]** : 1856+ BUNDABERG & DEGILBO, QLD, AUS **[37316]** : PRE 1870 DOR, SOM & DEV, ENG **[35735]** : PRE 1810 BARNSTAPLE, DEV, ENG **[37316]** : 1832 CORK CITY, COR, IRL **[35903]**

ELMSLIE 1750-1850 LOWLANDS, SCT **[34920]**

ELOLF ALL WORLDWIDE **[35310]**

ELPHICK 1860+ FORBES, NSW, AUS **[35529]** : 1875 PENSHURST & LEIGH; KEN, ENG **[34473]** : 1800+ MARESFIELD & WARNHAM, SSX, ENG **[34473]** : JOHN C1770 HASTINGS, SSX, ENG **[37106]**

ELPHINGSTONE C1800 SOWERBY, YKS, ENG **[35257]**

ELPHINSTONE PRE 1880 ENG & SCT **[37739]** : 1800-1850 NEW CHANNELKIRK, BEW, SCT **[35151]**

ELSEN 1700-1800 KOBLENZ, RPF, BRD **[38617]**

ELSER 1840 BLOCKINGEN, WUE, BRD **[38327]** : 1860 PHILADELPHIA, PA, USA **[38327]**

ELSEY PRE 1890 DORKING, SRY, ENG **[34021]** : ALL SSX, ENG **[34599]**

ELSLEY 1740-1870 BRAMLEY, SRY, ENG **[34258]** : 1800+ LONDON, ENG **[38204]**

ELSOM 1880+ WISBECH, CAM, ENG **[36636]**

ELSON 1820-1859 GODALMING, SRY, ENG **[36071]** : 1860+ GREAT BOOKHAM, SRY, ENG **[36071]** : PRE 1800 CHS & SAL, ENG **[37936]** : 1800-1900 USA **[38115]**

ELSON (SEE ELSTON) **[35726]**

ELSTON 1857+ SALE, VIC, AUS **[35725]** : C1800-1860 WINSCOMBE, SOM, ENG **[35725]**

ELSTONE 1700+ CHERTSEY, SRY, ENG **[36512]**

ELSWORTH 1830+ NORFOLK & ELGIN CO., ONT, CAN **[36323]**

ELSWORTHY MARY 1750+ SELWORTHY, SOM, ENG **[36813]**

ELTIS ALL WORLDWIDE **[35868]**

ELTON 1538-1820 LUTTERWORTH & SHAWELL, LEI, ENG **[36162]** : 1550-1800 CASTLE DONINGTON, LEI, ENG **[36162]** : ALL ASHBY DE LA ZOUCH, LEI, ENG **[36162]** : ALL APPLEBY MAGNA, LEI, ENG **[36162]** : ALL LEDBURY, HEF, ENG **[36162]** : ALL ELTON & STILTON, HUN, ENG **[36162]** : 1798 ENG **[38756]**

ELVER C1818 CHAPEL ALLERTON, SOM, ENG **[37148]**

ELVERS 1770-1850 LAMBETH, SRY, ENG **[34697]**

ELVEY MARY C1762 ATTLEBOROUGH, NFK, ENG **[35714]** : 1800+ LONDON, ENG **[37586]**

ELVIDGE 1850-1902 SCOTT CO., IL, USA **[36546]**

ELVIN 1810-1840 DON, IRL **[36691]**

ELVISH PRE 1725 ESS, ENG **[35642]**

ELWELL 1840S+ MAITLAND, NSW, AUS **[38211]** : 1750+ HAMMERSMITH, MDX, ENG **[34817]** : C1810 BIRMINGHAM, WAR, ENG **[37883]**

ELWIN 1700-1750 CLARE, SFK, ENG **[35119]** : 1800+ LONDON, ENG **[37699]**

ELWOOD 1800+ DUB, IRL **[37916]**

ELWORTHY 1880+ SOUTH YARRA, VIC, AUS **[35825]** : 1560+ DEV, ENG **[36096]** : 1750+ ENG **[36096]** : 1850+ WORLDWIDE **[36096]**

ELY ROBERT 1925+ LINTON, CAM, ENG **[33764]** : PRE 1800 ORSETT & MOUNTNESSING, ESS, ENG **[34204]** : PRE 1853 BALLINGDON, ESS, ENG **[35129]** : 1680+ MA, USA **[35322]** : JOUSHA 1683-1738 BURLINGTON CO., NJ, USA **[38330]** : JOUSHA 1738+ BUCKS CO., PA, USA **[38330]** : 1790+ USA & UK **[36357]**

ELZVIK 1736+ KOPPARBERG, SWE **[37036]**

EMANUEL C1820 FLN, WLS **[35153]** : 1893-1971 TREHERBERT & YSTALYFERA, GLA, WLS **[37399]**

EMBERSON 1750+ GREAT WALTHAM, ESS, ENG **[36827]** : ALL LONDON, ENG **[37237]** : PRE 1860 ESS, ENG **[37646]** : ALL INGATESTONE, ESS, ENG **[37728]** : ALL BRENTWOOD, ESS, ENG **[37728]**

EMBLIN 1800S CLIFTON, GLS, ENG **[34862]** : 1740-1850 CHEW MAGNA, SOM, ENG **[34862]** : 1800S BRISTOL, GLS, ENG **[34862]**

EMBREY 1800+ STS, ENG **[33855]**

EMBRY 1700-1900 BERWICK & TWEEDMOUTH, NBL, ENG **[36461]** : 1600-1900 BORDER TOWNS, BEW, ROX & SEL, SCT **[36461]**

EMDE 1640-1900 KORBACH, WAL, GER **[34912]**

EMERI C1700 GENEVA, GE, CH **[38348]**

EMERSON 1860+ BLACKBUTT, QLD, AUS **[35882]** : ALL CHIPPINGHAM, WIL, ENG **[34466]** : 1600 HAWKESBURY, GLS, ENG **[34466]** : ALL MALMESBURY, WIL, ENG **[34466]** : PRE 1750 HORTON, GLS, ENG **[34466]** : ARTHUR 1708+ GARRIGILL & ALSTON, CUL, ENG **[37019]** : 1700-1800 HOLKHAM, NFK, ENG **[38244]** : 1750-1850 STOWMARKET, SFK, ENG **[38290]** : 1700+ ARM, IRL **[35882]** : PRE 1870 DOW, IRL **[38286]** : 1869+ NZ **[38286]** : ALL WORLDWIDE **[35875]**

EMERY PRE 1900 BRISBANE, QLD, AUS **[36290]** : PRE 1900 PETERBOROUGH, ONT, CAN **[35604]** : 1800-1840 ST PANCRAS, LND, ENG **[34637]** : 1700S BOOTEN, STS, ENG **[35322]** : PRE 1815 ASHWICK, SOM, ENG **[35718]** : 1800+ SSX, ENG **[35943]** : 1837+ ENG **[35970]** : 1700-1900 BERWICK & TWEEDMOUTH, NBL, ENG **[36461]** : 1800S KINGS NORTON, WAR, ENG **[37299]** : PRE 1615 ROMSEY, HAM, ENG **[38135]** : PRE 1875 GER **[35604]** : JAMES 1813+ MAGHERACULMONEY, FER, IRL **[35343]** : 1600-1900 BORDER TOWNS, BEW, ROX & SEL, SCT **[36461]** : 1730+ PEMBROKE, NH, USA **[37492]**

EMIGH 1820+ OXFORD CO., ONT, CAN **[36710]** : 1700S DUTCHESS CO., NY, USA **[36710]**

EMINSON PRE 1800 ILKESTON, NTT, ENG **[38389]**

EMM PRE 1890 BISHOPSTONE, WIL, ENG **[37226]**

EMMERSON 1800S LONDON, ENG **[35907]** : 1800S DBY, ENG **[35907]** : 1700+ RAMSGATE, KEN, ENG **[37206]** : PRE 1900 ENG **[37739]** : PRE 1900 NORWICH, NFK, ENG **[37774]** : 1940+ HONG

KONG [37206] : PRE 1870 DOW, IRL [38286] : 1869 +
NZ [38286] : 1700-1900 KY, VA & IN, USA [38328]
EMMERTON 1840 + TAS, AUS [33786]
EMMETT ALL TAS, AUS [37127] : PRE 1800
KILLUCAN, WEM, IRL [33912]
EMMINES ALL UK [36020]
EMMONS URIAH 1847 HANCOCK CO., IN, USA
[38152]
EMMOTT 1600-1800 COWLING, NRY, ENG [37854]
EMMS 1740 + EATON, NFK, ENG [34710] : 1800 +
KENNINGHALL, NFK, ENG [37937]
EMO PRE 1856 ENNISKILLEN & CAVAN, FER &
CAV, IRL [37906]
EMOE ALL MAN, CAN [36672]
EMPSOM 1800S NEW RADFORD, NTT, ENG [34342]
EMPTAGE 1850 + BARBADOS [37294] : 1870 +
LONDON, ENG [37294] : ALL KEN, ENG [37929]
EMRICH PRE 1750 DOSSEL, WARBURG, GER
[37569]
EMSLEY 1800S LANARK CO., ONT, CAN [37458] :
CLARA C1911-1932 BRITISH INDIA, INDIA [35725]
EMSLIE C1750 ABERDEEN, ABD, SCT [35747] : PRE
1890 MONTROSE, ANS, SCT [36369]
EMTAGE ALL ENG [37386] : 1650-1750 MAIDSTONE,
KEN, ENG [37386] : ALL CANTERBURY, KEN,
ENG [37386] : ALL WORLDWIDE [37386]
ENDACOTT PRE 1850 CHAGFORD, DEV, ENG
[37060] : 1700 + THROWLEIGH, DEV, ENG [38745]
ENDALL PRE 1850 BANBURY, OXF, ENG [34025]
ENDERBY 1856-1920S SYDNEY & BATHURST, NSW,
AUS [35735] : C1870 LINCOLN, LIN, ENG [33772]
ENDERS 1700-1800 SITTERS, RHINELAND, GER
[36561]
ENDERSBY 1750 + WRESTLINGWORTH, BDF, ENG
[35214]
ENDYCOTT 1850 + SOUTHAMPTON, HAM, ENG
[37902] : 1850 + BRIDPORT, DOR, ENG [37902]
ENEVER 1800S ENG [36393]
ENFIELD 1858 + REDFERN & RANDWICK, NSW,
AUS [34899] : ALL UK & AUS [34899]
ENGEL ALL ALT FREUDENTAL, UKRAINE,
GROSSLIEBENTAL, SU [38372] : PRE 1870
LINKOPINGSLAN, OSTERGOTLAND, SWE
[37821]
ENGELBACK 1750-1830 LONDON, ENG [37122]
ENGELHARD PRE 1750 NECKARWEIHINGEN,
WUE, GER [38661] : 1800 + USA [38728]
ENGELHARDT 1800S BAD, GER [34102] : 1800S BAV,
GER [38153] : C1748 GUNZENHAUSEN, BAW,
GER [38626] : PRE 1850 WERBEN & ALTMART,
SAB, PRE [35795] : 1854 + OH & PA, USA [38728]
ENGELKEN 1650 + BREMEN, BRM, GER [35460]
ENGELS 1870-1971 KEWEENAW CO., MI, USA
[38010]
ENGELSMA 1805 + OLDEBOORN, FRI, NL [34990]
ENGELSSON 1870 + USA [38558]
ENGLAND 1880 + CHILTERN, VIC, AUS [35538] :
1880 + WATERLOO, VIC, AUS [35538] : 1800 +
WESTBURY, WIL, ENG [34817] : 1750-1870 LEEDS,
YKS, ENG [36983] : C1800 STOKE DAMEREL &
PLYMOUTH, DEV, ENG [37330] : PRE 1836
SAXTON IN ELMET, WRY, ENG [37726] : 1680 +
BURSTOCK & BROADWINSOR, DOR, ENG
[38745] : C1800 ABD, SCT [34400]
ENGLE 1800-1900 CS [36962] : 1850 + USA [36962]
ENGLEBACK 1750-1830 LONDON, ENG [37122]
ENGLEBREGHT 1850S AMSTERDAM, NL [33802]
ENGLEFIELD 1750-1825 BASINGSTOKE, HAM, ENG
[37222]
ENGLEHARDT 1854 + OH & PA, USA [38728]
ENGLEMANN 1900S BRISBANE, QLD, AUS [34015] :
1800 HALGARTEN, HEN, GER [34015]

ENGLISH 1880 + GOONDIWINDI, QLD, AUS [35335]
: 1911 + BRISBANE, QLD, AUS [38485] : THOMAS
1826-1870 REACH TWP., ONT, CAN [34064] : PRE
1800 FILBY, NFK, ENG [35173] : SUSANNA PRE
1900 NORTH SHIELDS, NBL, ENG [35200] : PRE
1840 MESSING, ESS, ENG [35406] : 1800 +
REDDITCH, WOR, ENG [35650] : PRE 1850
SWAFFHAM, NFK, ENG [35729] : PRE 1800 LND,
ENG [35746] : PRE 1850 LAMESLEY, DUR, ENG
[36481] : THOMAS 1700S NEWINGTON, SRY, ENG
[36633] : 1900 + ENG [37653] : PRE 1800 STROUD,
GLS, ENG [37700] : 1850-1950 LIVERPOOL, LAN,
ENG [38074] : 1883-1911 LONDON &, ESS, ENG
[38485] : PRE 1864 TIP, IRL [35088] : PRE 1866
PORTAFERRY, DOW, IRL [35335] : PRE 1860 COR,
IRL [37537] : PRE 1842 INCH, DOW, IRL [37772] :
1832-1909 TEMPLETON, CANT, NZ [34622] : 1860 +
PECK, MI, USA [34129] : 1860 + PECK, MI, USA
[34129]
ENGLISH EAST ALL ENG [37199]
ENGLUND ALL KALMAR, SWE [38519]
ENGOLHORN 1600-1800 BAD, BRD [35300]
ENLOW 1780-1810 MD & PA, USA [36913] : 1810-1860
RICHLAND, KNOX & HOLMES COS., OH, USA
[36913]
ENMAN PRE 1850 USA [37190]
ENNALS 1790 HARWICH, ESS, ENG [34204]
ENNER 1750 + TRURO, CON, ENG [36000]
ENNIS 1803-1840 SYDNEY, NSW, AUS [35782] : 1800S
FRONTENAC, ONT, CAN [34353] : 1700-1850 KEN,
ENG [37015] : 1770 + SYDNEY, ESS & NSW, ENG
& AUS [35155] : PRE 1875 VIRGINIA, CAV, IRL
[34044]
ENNOR 1816-1828 + TAVISTOCK, DEV, ENG [37108]
: 1851-1871 + CALSTOCK, CON, ENG [37108]
ENNOUF C1825 JERSEY, CHI, ENG [37062]
ENO 1850 CT, USA [35279]
ENOCK ALL WORLDWIDE [34949]
ENOS 1819 BERKSHIRE, MA, USA [35272] : C1820
BERKSHIRE, MA, USA [37030] : 1915 + SAN LUIS
OBISPO, CA, USA [38361]
ENOUF PRE 1830 FRA [37428]
ENRIGHT CHARLES 1800S BATHURST, NSW, AUS
[35361] : ALL WINDSOR, NSW, AUS [35431] : PRE
1870 LISTOWEL, KER, IRL [34262] : 1874
SHANAGOLDEN, LIM, IRL [35906] : C1840 LIM,
IRL [35922]
ENSAM PRE 1830 HERTINGFORDBURY, HRT,
ENG [37663]
ENSBY 1780 + STANDON & GREAT AWELL, HRT,
ENG [35214]
ENSING 1721 + LAARWALD, NSA, BRD [34398]
ENSMINGER 1600-1870 STRASBURG, ELO, GER
[38026]
ENSOM PRE 1900 KINGSTON UPON THAMES,
SRY, ENG [36245]
ENSOR 1849 BOTHWELL, TAS, AUS [36301] : 1700 +
BREEDON ON THE HILL, LEI, ENG [35851] : ALL
HILL HOOK, SUTTON COLDFIELD, WAR, ENG
[37068] : PRE 1850 SUTTON COLDFIELD, WAR,
ENG [37068]
ENSTEN ALL HARROW, MDX, ENG [37622]
ENSTON ALL WORLDWIDE [37271]
ENSTONE ALL WORLDWIDE [37271]
ENTENMANN 1800 BENNIGEN, WUE, GER [34940]
ENTICKNAP PRE 1900 OXFORD, ONT, CAN [38434] :
PRE 1700 LURGASHALL, SSX, ENG [37771]
ENTRICAN 1800 + WANGANUI, NZ [38273]
ENTRINGER 1443 + TUEBINGEN, BAW, FRG [38660]
ENTWHISTLE ROGER PRE 1900 LISBURN, ANT,
IRL [37755]

ENTWISLE C1750-1841 DARWEN & BANK TOP, LAN, ENG [35052]

ENTWISTLE C1750-1841 DARWEN & BANK TOP, LAN, ENG [35052] : PRE 1850 EDGEWORTH, LAN, ENG [37414] : 1790-1850 DARCY LEVER, LAN, ENG [37934] : 1830+ FARNWORTH & GREAT LEVER, LAN, ENG [37934] : 1800-1900 DEANE BY BOLTON, LAN, ENG [37934]

ENVARTSEN PRE 1870 REDDING, SHO, BRD [35330]

ENYON C1757 GREAT SHELFORD, CAM, ENG [36185]

EOFF ALL USA [36567]

EPLETT 1850+ MINERAL POINT, WI, USA [37343]

EPPERLEIN 1550-1900 LAUTER, KSA, GER [38628]

EPPERSON PRE 1900 JEFFERSON CO., IL & TN, USA [36544] : ROBERT 1800-1826 MONTGOMERY, KY, USA [38157]

EPPINGSTALL ALL WORLDWIDE [35799]

EPPLETT ALL TRURO, CON, ENG [36881]

EPTHORP ALL ENG [36872]

ERAUX 1700-1800 JER, CHI [35494]

ERB 1650-1800 BAW, GER [38219] : 1750-1850 LANCASTER CO., PA, USA [38219]

ERBER C1900 IL & MI, USA [38023]

ERDMANN 1770 PERLEBERG, BRA, GER [37509]

EREKSON PRE 1878 GOTTENBERG, SWE [37912]

ERHARDT PRE 1729 IGGLEHEIM & BOHL, RPF, BRD [37603] : ALL HARDEGSEN, NIEDERSACHSEN, FRG [38710] : ALL HANNOVERSCH MUNDEN, NIEDERSACHSEN, FRG [38710] : ALL TEMPLETON, IA, USA [38710] : ALL NEW YORK, NY, USA [38710]

ERHART 1855-1859 BRISBANE, NSW, AUS [34812] : 1859+ ALLORA, QLD, AUS [34812] : PRE 1900 GER [34812]

ERICHE PRE 1695 LOUVETOT, HN, FRA [34047]

ERICHSDOTTER 1600-1740S OTHEM, GOTLAND, SWE [38346]

ERICKSEN ERIC 1800-1875 LINAA, JUT, DEN [38194]

ERICKSON 1852+ MANNING RIVER, NSW, AUS & FIN [37130]

ERIKSDOTTER KERSIN 1662-1705 HJO, VASTERGOTLAND, SWE [38550]

ERIKSEN PRE 1850 FLENSBURG, DEN [33959] : 1750+ SOR ODAL, HEDMARK, NOR [34664] : 1740+ RORAS, S TRNDLG, NOR [36326]

ERIKSSON MATHILDA 1900+ MINNEAPOLIS, MN, USA [38559] : AUGUST PRE 1900 BOYCEVILLE, WI, USA [38559] : AUGUST 1900+ MINNEAPOLIS, MN, USA [38559] : AUGUST PRE 1900 SIOUX CITY, IA, USA [38559] : MATHILDA 1897-1900 NELSON, MO, USA [38559] : OLOF 1882+ SIOUX CITY, IA, USA [38559]

ERIN-FEINE PRE 1900 WORLDWIDE [36932]

ERLAM PRE 1750 OMBERSLEY, WOR, ENG [35181] : ALL ENG [35181]

ERLANDSON 1860+ COLAC, VIC, AUS [34937]

ERLENKOTTER ALL WORLDWIDE [38061]

ERNIP ALL WORLDWIDE [34312]

ERNST PRE 1859 WILLESDEN, MDX, ENG [35114] : ALL ENG [37279] : PRE 1750 WALDBACH, WUE, GER [35242] : PRE 1862 STERLOFF, PRE, GER [35393] : PRE 1750 BRA, GER [38627] : PRE 1760 ARMENHOF & FULDA, HES, GER [38663] : 1800+ MOKRIN, YU [38065]

ERNTSEN 1700+ HERBORN, LUX [37016]

ERNY 1750-1870 NEWVEILNOA, HEN, GER [38007]

ERNZEN 1700+ HERBORN, LUX [37016] : ALL USA [37016]

EROMANN ALL SIL, GER [38607]

ERP MARION 1932+ IN, USA [35164] : RUTH 1930+ IN, USA [35164]

ERPENBACH PRE 1750 NRW & RPF, BRD [38616]

ERREY ALL WORLDWIDE [34254]

ERRICKER ALL WORLDWIDE [36305]

ERRINGTON ALL YKS, ENG [33925] : 1800-1850 COUNDON & GATESHEAD, DUR, ENG [35624] : 1770+ MARSKE BY SEA, YKS, ENG [35908] : 1800-1816 GRINDON, DUR, ENG [38054] : 1700-1845 MARSKE IN CLEVELAND, NRY, ENG [38054]

ERSDOTTER KARIN 1823 JARBO, GASTRIKLAND, SWE [38556]

ERSDR MARIA MARGAR 1817-1900 VANNAS, VASTERBOTTEN, SWE [38104]

ERSKINE 1839+ AUS [37846] : C1808 BELFAST, ANT, IRL [37556] : JOHN C1770 CRAIGIE, AYR, SCT [34300] : CAMPBELL PRE 1806 DUNFERMLINE, FIF, SCT [36308] : 1190 SCT [37008] : PRE 1750 BEW, SCT [37069]

ERVIN PRE 1900 WORLDWIDE [36932]

ERVINE PRE 1900 WORLDWIDE [36932]

ERVING PRE 1900 WORLDWIDE [36932]

ERWIN PRE 1800 DUR, ENG [37693] : CATHERINE 1726-1781 CHARLESTON, SC, USA [35265] : PRE 1900 WORLDWIDE [36932]

ERWOOD JAMES 1755+ HENDON, WIL, ENG [34181] : ALL NETLEY, HAM, ENG [35525] : ALL WORLDWIDE [34181]

ERZBERGER 1800+ GER & USA [38065]

ESBENSEN PRE 1876 DEN [36878]

ESCHENBRENNER 1840+ USA [38650]

ESCHWEILER PRE 1801 ADENDORF, NRW, GER [35280]

ESCOTT PRE 1900 MANCHESTER, LAN, ENG [35439] : 1800-1860 PENDOWER, CON, ENG [36214]

ESCREET PRE 1800 HULL, ERY, ENG [36298]

ESDALE 1700-1840 ARM, IRL [36440]

ESDEN 1820+ SYDNEY, NSW, AUS [35557]

ESGATE C1915 WARDELL, NSW, AUS [36284]

ESLER ALL ALBERT CO., NB, CAN [38447] : 1800 BELFAST, ANT, IRL [36842]

ESLING PRE 1869 BURSTON, NFK, ENG & AUS [34339] : C1869+ DETROIT, MI, USA [34339]

ESMONDE C1882+ NARRANDERA, NSW, AUS [35746]

ESPELAND C1900 BERGEN, NOR [34058]

ESPIE JOHN 1826+ LESWALT, WIG, SCT [34627]

ESRY GEORGE H. 1841-1850 LONDON, ENG [38144]

ESSAM PRE 1910 WOODFORD, NTH, ENG [34269] : 1750-1850 ALL ST GEORGE'S, LND, ENG [34469] : 1850-1900 WHITECHAPEL, LND, ENG [34469]

ESSENBERG ALL GER [38037]

ESSERMAN ALL SYDNEY & MELBOURNE, AUS [34976]

ESSEX PRE 1800 LONG LONGFORD, WAR, ENG [35387] : ALL WORLDWIDE [35832]

ESSLINGER ALL CAN [36661] : ALL STUTTGART, WUE, GER [36661] : ALL USA [36661]

ESSMANN 1750 LANDESBERGEN, HAN, BRD [38327]

ESSON C1840 ABERDEEN, ABD, SCT [34579]

ESTE ALL ENG [36221] : ALL ENG [37199]

ESTEVAO PRE 1857 SAO MIGUEL, AZORES, PT [37551] : 1857-1887 SAO MIGUEL, AZORES, PT [37551]

ETCHELLS PRE 1849 ASHTON UNDER LYNE, LAN, ENG [34487]

ETCHINGHAM ALL WORLDWIDE [38196]

ETHERIDGE PRE 1800 HORSHAM, SSX, ENG [34112] : CHARLES C1819 LAMBETH, SRY, ENG [36873] : PRE 1850 BISHOPS CLEEVE, GLS, ENG [37339] : PRE 1880 WOODMANCOTE, BISHOPS CLEEVE, GLS, ENG [37510] : ALL MAISEMORE & ASHLEWORTH, GLS, ENG [37681]

ETHERINGTON 1848+ SYDNEY, NSW, AUS [34979] : PRE 1790 MUGGINTON, DBY, ENG [34311] : PRE 1848 WINDSOR, BRK, ENG [34979] : 1790S SUNNINGHILL, BRK, ENG [35557] : 1800+ SHOREDITCH & MILE END, MDX & LND, ENG [37065] : JOSHUA C1700-1768 YKS, ENG [37076] : 1800S KEN, ENG [37423] : ALL ENG [37833] : ALL WORLDWIDE [37076]

ETHIER 1590-1990 REPENTIGNY, QUE, CAN [38588]

ETTERY PRE 1870 MONKTON FARLEY & ALL, WIL, ENG [36082]

ETTY PRE 1750 BRANTINGHAM & HULL, ERY, ENG [35940]

EUART PRE 1900 MERRICKVILLE, ONT, CAN [34466] : PRE 1850 IRL [34466]

EUDEY 1820-1865 ILLOGAN, CON, ENG [35725]

EULENBURG PRE 1608 OBERMOSCHEL, RPF, BRD [36954]

EUREN ALL WORLDWIDE [37408]

EUREY 1800-1850 ADDLESTON, SRY, ENG [37618]

EURICH ALL WORLDWIDE [38657]

EUSTACE 1841+ SYDNEY, NSW, AUS [34695] : PRE 1750 GREAT MILTON, OXF, ENG [34716] : 1800+ PUSEY, BRK, ENG [36329]

EVA C1870 CLUNES, VIC, AUS [34683] : C1840 CON, ENG [34683] : 1800+ WENDRON, CON, ENG [36603] : 1800+ UK [36683]

EVAN PRE 1800 RUDBAXTON, PEM, WLS [34319] : 1780+ WLS [35060]

EVANS C1880 EAGLEHAWK, VIC, AUS [33918] : 1856+ ADELAIDE, SA, AUS [34777] : 1872-1890 CAULFIELD, VIC, AUS [34794] : 1840+ PARRAMATTA, NSW, AUS [34979] : 1861+ GRAFTON, NSW, AUS [35031] : C1806 SYDNEY, NSW, AUS [35089] : THOMAS WALTER 1861+ FORBES, NSW, AUS [35093] : THOMAS 1851+ PORT FAIRY, VIC, AUS [35209] : 1870+ COSTERFIELD, VIC, AUS [35476] : HARPER 1864+ WOODEND, VIC, AUS [35484] : 1900 FREMANTLE, WA, AUS [35800] : 1800 SA, AUS [35873] : JAMES 1860+ RYLSTONE, NSW, AUS [36269] : JAMES 1845+ MUDGEE, NSW, AUS [36269] : JAMES 1838-1845 VIC, AUS [36269] : 1860+ COOKTOWN, QLD, AUS [36288] : C1855 SA, AUS [36292] : 1832 SYDNEY, NSW, AUS [36292] : WILLIAM 1840S+ PATERSON, NSW, AUS [36637] : JOSEPH PRE 1900 QUEENSTOWN, TAS, AUS [37124] : 1792+ NSW, AUS [38212] : 1700-1900S REPENTIGNY, QUE, CAN [35327] : 1830-1900 CARLETON CO., ONT, CAN [36666] : JOHN 1800S BIDEFORD, DEV, ENG [34347] : CHARLOTTE 1824+ HORSLEY, GLS, ENG [34475] : JONATHAN 1800 HORSLEY, GLS, ENG [34475] : WILLIAM 1780+ NORTHAM, DEV & CON, ENG [34559] : 1800S ROSS ON WYE, HEF, ENG [34823] : PRE 1760 HORSLEY, GLS, ENG [34858] : 1820-1900 MANCHESTER, LAN, ENG [34865] : PRE 1839 HORSLEY, GLS, ENG [34979] : PRE 1862 CON, ENG [35031] : BENJAMIN 1790+ ST PETERS PARISH, HEF, ENG [35132] : PRE 1844 LOUGHTON, BKM, ENG [35462] : 1830+ CHESTER, CHS, ENG [35476] : JOHN H. PRE 1880 PECKHAM, KEN, ENG [35599] : 1810-1840 ST MARYLEBONE, LND, ENG [35720] : PRE 1830 WOLVERHAMPTON, STS, ENG [35824] : 1750+ SOM, ENG [35918] : 1750-1850 GRENDON & THORNBURY, HEF, ENG [36109] : 1838-1858 WORCESTER, WOR, ENG [36190] : PRE 1800 COGGESHALL, ESS, ENG [36379] : FRANCIS PRE 1840 WEOBLEY, HEF, ENG [36432] : PRE 1840 SAL, ENG [36480] : PRE 1800 THANET, KEN, ENG [36480] : 1750-1850 SARNESFIELD, HEF, ENG

[36552] : ELIZABETH 1700S LUGWARDINE, HEF, ENG [36633] : PRE 1720 RANTON, STS, ENG [36701] : PRE 1840 LONDON, ENG [36882] : PHILIP 1760+ WESTMINSTER, LND, ENG [37112] : ALL BIRMINGHAM, WAR, ENG [37265] : PRE 1879 LIVERPOOL, LAN, ENG [37318] : PRE 1834 OSWESTRY, SAL, ENG [37318] : PRE 1870 PADDINGTON, MDX, ENG [37720] : C1800+ SELBORNE, HAM, ENG [37778] : 1820+ HIGH WYCOMBE, BKM, ENG [37847] : THOMAS PRE 1860 CANNINGTON, SOM, ENG [37876] : PRE 1623 WEARE, SOM, ENG [37876] : WILLIAM PRE 1871 BRIDGWATER, SOM, ENG [37876] : ALL CLIFTON, BRS, ENG [37876] : C1825 DEVONPORT, CON, ENG [37981] : 1786 LANDBEACH, CAM, ENG [38209] : 1800S WEST BROMWICH, STS, ENG [38272] : PRE 1800 BURBAGE, WIL, ENG [38700] : C1705 COR, IRL [34521] : PRE 1835 DON, IRL [35719] : 1750-1850 CARRICKFERGUS, ANT, IRL [38588] : TOM 1846 CAPETOWN, RSA [36443] : 1770S KILMARNOCK, AYR, SCT [36741] : PRE 1849 KELSO, BEW, SCT [37925] : 1880-1901 UK [36654] : PRE 1780 PLAINFIELD, CT, USA [34113] : 1860-1950 MARSHALL CO., MS, USA [35307] : 1820-1840 UTICA, NY, USA [36968] : PRE 1755 HALIFAX CO., VA, USA [37587] : 1814 AL, USA [37799] : 1814 CINCINNATI, OH, USA [37799] : 1914+ WASHINGTON, DC, USA [38018] : 1780+ VT, USA [38520] : THOMAS 1880-1930 NEWBURG & CLEVELAND, OH, USA [38740] : MARIA 1825+ LLANBEDR, BRE, WLS [34134] : 1750-1850 LLANCAIACH FAWR, GLA, WLS [34234] : PRE 1850 TREDEGAR, MON, WLS [35127] : 1800+ CAERHUN, CAE, WLS [35377] : 1750+ CAE, WLS [35377] : 1780S ROWLAND & CAERHUN, CAE, WLS [35377] : NESTA C1820 MAESTY, GLA, WLS [35447] : JOHN C1820 MAESTY, GLA, WLS [35447] : C1824 BASSALLEG, MON, WLS [36185] : 1800S ABERYSTWYTH, CGN, WLS [36205] : 1750+ NEATH, GLA, WLS [36209] : PRE 1840 NASH, MON, WLS [36247] : 1700 WLS [36446] : PRE 1880 PONTYPOOL, MON, WLS [36849] : 1800-1835 RUABON, DEN, WLS [37172] : JANE 1751 LLANILAR, CGN, WLS [37250] : C1825 GRONANT & HOLYWELL, FLN, WLS [37330] : RACHEL C1830-1870 DEVYNOCK & BRECON, BRE, WLS [37399] : C1840 NEWCASTLE, MON, WLS [37561] : ALL WHITFORD, FLN, WLS [37667] : ALL CWM, FLN, WLS [37667] : 1750+ WREXHAM, DEN, WLS [37735] : C1817 CGN, WLS [37780] : C1818 RAD, WLS [37780] : 1854+ NANTYGLO, MON, WLS [37780] : PRE 1850 CGN, WLS [37804] : ALL MERTHYR TYDFIL, GLA, WLS [37950] : 1844+ NEWTOWN, MGY, WLS [38018] : PRE 1840 SOUTH, WLS [38217] : THOMAS 1800-1860 RHONDDA VALLEY, GLA, WLS [38740] : SARAH 1848 SWANSEA, GLA & STS, WLS & ENG [36443]

EVARY 1650+ UPLOWMAN, DEV, ENG [34747]

EVE C1830 KEN, ENG [33809] : 1800-1860 LONDON, ENG [34464] : PRE 1830 FRA [37428]

EVEES PRE 1850 ROCHESTER, KEN, ENG [36387]

EVELEIGH ALL WILLAND, DEV, ENG [35163] : C1900+ DERBY, DBY, ENG [35163] : C1750+ COVENTRY, WAR, ENG [35163] : 1800-1830S BRIXHAM, DEV, ENG [36337] : C1890 PARIS, FRA [35163]

EVELY ALL WHITBY, ONT, CAN [35601] : PRE 1855 DEV, ENG [35601] : 1780+ NORTHLEW, DEV, ENG [37224]

EVELYN 1800S BALLARAT, VIC, AUS [33838] : 1840S MT BARKER, SA, AUS [33838] : ALL NOWRA HILL, NSW, AUS [33838]

EVENDEN 1700+ LEWES, SSX, ENG [34970] : 1840-1917 CHATHAM, KEN, ENG [36803] : 1700S WOODCHURCH, KEN, ENG [37714]

EVENS 1800+ BISHOPSTEIGNTON, DEV, ENG [34602] : PRE 1760 PAULSON, ENG [36929] : PRE 1930 TALLULAH, LA, USA [36543] : 1680 MIDDLESEX, MA, USA [38022]

EVENSEN CHRISTEN 1840-1930 FILMORE CO., MN, USA [38392]

EVERALL 1910+ PERTH, WA, AUS [34230] : 1870-1927 SHANGHAI, CHINA [34230] : 1830-1870S LONDON, ENG [34230] : 1790-1850S RICHMOND & PUTNEY, SRY, ENG [34230] : 1868-1928 GUATEMALA [34230]

EVERARD PRE 1800 ASHWELL & WESTON, HRT, ENG [35229] : PRE 1900 SFK & NFK, ENG [35978] : PRE 1636 DEDHAM, ESS, ENG [37545] : 1800-1900 ROXWELL, ESS, ENG [38265] : ALL INDIA [37920]

EVERATT (SEE EVERETT [36622]

EVERDICK PRE 1820 OLDENBURG, SHO, GER [38648]

EVERED PRE 1650 SFK, ENG [38746]

EVEREST 1812+ HOBART, TAS, AUS [33780] : 1851+ VIC, AUS [35468] : PRE 1800 EAST GRINSTEAD, SSX, ENG [33780] : 1700S+ HEVER, KEN, ENG [35468] : 1825+ CROYDON, SRY, ENG [35468] : 1840+ NEWBERG, OR, USA [35468] : ALL WORLDWIDE [35468]

EVERET 1700-1800 ANCASTER, LIN, ENG [36057]

EVERETT 1855+ MORTLAKE, GEELONG & ROKEWOOD, VIC, AUS [36622] : 1855+ INVERLEIGH & POMBORNFIT, VIC, AUS [36622] : 1855+ HORSHAM & BREAD O'DAY, VIC, AUS [36622] : PRE 1900 LONDON, ENG [35556] : PRE 1900 SFK, NFK & MDX, ENG [35978] : PRE 1875 NFK, ENG [37256] : 1820+ SHOREDITCH, LND, ENG [37552] : 1800-1900 GREENE CO., TN, USA [37539] : 1636-1800 DEDHAM, MA, USA [37545] : 1855-1865 KEWEENAW CO., MI, USA [38010]

EVERILL 1800+ CLIFTON ON TEME, WOR, ENG [37632] : 1800+ BIRMINGHAM, WAR, ENG [37632]

EVERINGHAM ELVINA 1881 SACKVILLE REACH, NSW, AUS [35831] : 1840-1910 YORK CO., ONT, CAN [37477] : 1750-1840 LEEDS, WRY, ENG [37477]

EVERINGTON PRE 1810 LIN, ENG [36820] : ALL WORLDWIDE [34361]

EVERIST 1700S SOUTHFLEET, KEN, ENG [37019]

EVERITT 1820+ BURWOOD & SYDNEY, NSW, AUS [33996] : 1963+ HAMPSTEAD, LND, ENG [33858] : PRE 1902 TOTTENHAM, LND, ENG [33858] : PRE 1850 WILBURTON, CAM, ENG [34772] : ALL HILGAY, NFK, ENG [37689] : PRE 1800 WASHINGTON CO., PA, USA [34138] : 1700+ PA, USA [34408]

EVERITT (SEE EVERETT [36622]

EVERNDON 1700-1800 KEN, ENG [36924]

EVERS ALL MOUNT MORGAN, QLD, AUS [38361] : ALL ROCKHAMPTON, QLD, AUS [38361] : C1800 CHELMSFORD, ESS, ENG [35203] : PRE 1880 ZARPEN, SHO, GER [37563]

EVERSON 1800S CHIPPEWA, MIDDLESEX CO., ONT, CAN [38414]

EVERT 1750-1850 NY, USA [36962]

EVERWIJN 1500-1600 NMR OR ARNHEIM, BEL & GER [36943]

EVES 1800-1875 SIMCOE CO., ONT, CAN [34364] : 1800+ MORTLAKE, SRY, ENG [34272]

EVETT 1600+ HARGRAVE, SFK, ENG [36402]

EVIL 1700+ PELYNT & TALLAND, CON, ENG [35172]

EVISON 1850+ CAMBEWARRA, NSW, AUS [35134] : 1750 LIN, ENG [34321]

EWALD ALL AUS [34938] : PRE 1880+ PHILADELPHIA, PA, USA [36578]

EWAN 1800S AVOCA, TAS, AUS [35195] : C1780 LONGFORGAN, PER, SCT [35152] : 1830+ PERTH, PER, SCT [36892] : 1800S NEWBURGH, ABD, SCT [38402]

EWART RICHARD 1800S SOUTH SHIELDS, DUR, ENG [34889] : ALL CROSSBY, CUL, ENG [36144] : PRE 1800 HUDDERSFIELD, WRY, ENG [37385] : 1800+ DERRYGARVE, LDY, IRL [34882] : 1852 ABERDEEN, ABD, SCT [36358]

EWELL 1850+ SYDNEY, NSW, AUS [34864]

EWEN 1910+ SKEGNESS, LIN, ENG [36077] : PRE 1800 ABD, SCT [34053] : C1750-1850 GAMRIE, ABD, SCT [34400]

EWENS PRE 1940 BOGNOR REGIS, SSX, ENG [35386] : 1800+ HARTING, SSX, ENG [36987]

EWER PRE 1800 LONDON, ENG [34314]

EWERS PRE 1900 LONDON, ENG [33883] : 1800+ BURTON ON TRENT, STS, ENG [37337]

EWERT 1790+ ELLERWALD, DANZIG, W. PRE, GER [36543]

EWIN ROBERT 1800-1840 BALLEY GALLEY, TYR, IRL [36316]

EWING 1840-1900 CLEVELAND, TAS, AUS [35195] : PRE 1866 CON, ENG [36338] : 1700S AIRTH, STI, SCT [35186] : 1800+ GLASGOW, LKS, SCT [35989] : 1700+ CLACKMANNAN, CLK, SCT [35989] : PRE 1830 ABD, SCT [36077] : PRE 1830 KCD, SCT [36077] : PRE 1864 EDINBURGH, MLN, SCT [37852] : 1800+ WIGTOWN, WIG, SCT & IRL [35579] : 1874+ COUNCIL BLUFFS, IA, USA [36338] : PRE 1780 MA, USA [37541] : 1791-1800 CHRISTIAN CO., KY, USA [38118] : 1880-1817 LOGAN CO., KY, USA [38118] : PRE 1806 FAIRFIELD, OH, USA [38220] : WILLIAM 1700S CECIL CO., MD, USA [38536]

EWINGER 1850-1990 BURLINGTON, IA, USA [38154]

EWINS PRE 1854 QUINTON, LEI, ENG [35008]

EXCELL (SEE EXELL) [36622]

EXELL 1890+ WIMMERA, VIC, AUS [36622]

EXLER PRE 1900 MAIDENHEAD, BRK, ENG [35954]

EXTON MARY 1780-1880 SPALDING & CROWLAND, LIN, ENG [33952] : 1800+ GRANTHAM, LIN, ENG [35650] : C1550-1700 SUTTON VENY, WIL, ENG [36478]

EYCLESHYMER ALL WORLDWIDE [36962]

EYER 1750-1850 LAMPORSCHLOCH, ALS, FRA [36898]

EYERS PRE 1810 MANCHESTER, LAN, ENG [33771] : 1800-1870 SOM, ENG [34016] : 1830+ WIMBORNE, DOR, ENG [37360]

EYESDEN PRE 1830 EDMONTON, MDX, ENG [37137]

EYKELBOSCH 1800+ UK [34029]

EYLES 1801+ SYDNEY, NSW, AUS [34685] : 1800+ OXFORD, OXF, ENG [34805] : PRE 1850 TIDWORTH, HAM, ENG [35062] : PRE 1900 ENG [35901]

EYRE 1680+ LND & SRY, ENG [34109] : PRE 1870 BILLESDON & LEICESTER, LEI, ENG [34241] : PRE 1800 YKS, ENG [36399]

EYRES 1776 SHERBORNE, DOR, ENG [34777]

EYSENBERGER PRE 1633 BEDDELHAUSEN & ELSOFF, WEF, BRD [36954]

EYSTER 1700+ BERKS, PA, USA [38735]

EYTEL (SEE EITEL) [33901]

EYTON 1862+ WARRINGTON, LAN, ENG [33960] : 1800-1865 WARRINGTON, LAN, ENG [33960] : PRE 1800 FLN, WLS [38461]

FAAS PRE 1700 NL [38375]

FAASEN PRE 1700 NL [38375] : 1700+ RSA [38375]
FAASSEN 1800+ RSA [38375]
FABIAN C1850 PORTSMOUTH, HAM, ENG [34936]
FABRITZ 1872 ESSEN, RPR, GER [38750]
FACE PRE 1945 WAVERLEY, NSW, AUS [35386]
FACER PRE 1800 LONG BUCKBY, NTH, ENG [36518]
FACHINGER C1838 NEIDERHEIMBACH, PRE, GER [35515]
FACKRELL 1770-1840 NORTH PETHERTON, SOM, ENG [38309]
FACY 1710+ HATHERLEIGH, DEV, ENG [35587]
FADDIE 1834-1861 MONTROSE, ANS, SCT [33811]
FADLEY 1700-1820 MONTGOMERY CO., PA, USA [36953]
FAELL PRE 1740 CARNBEE, FIF, SCT [35227]
FAGAN PRE 1900 KEMPSEY, NSW, AUS [35425]
FAGEANCE 1700+ SEND & WEST HORSLEY, SRY, ENG [35229]
FAGEN (SEE FEEGAN) [34377]
FAGG PRE 1800 DOVER, KEN, ENG [36891]
FAGLIN ADELAIDE PRE 1855 VILLERS LE SEX AISNE, PIC, FRA [38408]
FAGUE PRE 1785 PA, USA [37587]
FAHEY 1800+ PORT MACQUARIE, NSW, AUS [34860] : 1840+ NSW, AUS [37900] : PRE 1840 GAL, IRL [37900]
FAHRMBACHER 1890-1960 HAM, ENG [36496] : 1890-1960 SRY, ENG [36496]
FAHY 1894 ORANGE, NSW, AUS [34965] : 1863 CLA, IRL [34965] : PRE 1900 GALWAY, GAL, IRL [38586] : ROGER C1790-1835 TIP, IRL [38593]
FAICHNEY PRE 1792 AUCHTERARDER, PER, SCT [34098]
FAIL 1800+ SRY, ENG [36871] : 1860+ AUCKLAND & OTAGO, NZ [36871]
FAILL 1800+ CALLANDER, PER & STI, SCT [36705]
FAIN 1800-1850 LEX, IRL [33879]
FAINT 1860+ TUMUT, NSW, AUS [37136]
FAIR 1750-1800 WHITBY, NRY, ENG [35813] : 1750-1850 TYNEMOUTH & NORTH SHIELDS, NBL, ENG [35813] : PRE 1825 BELTURBET, CAV, IRL [33854] : ALL DOW, IRL [36856] : PRE 1800 EDINBURGH, MLN, SCT [34713] : 1800S OLD MELROSE, ROX, SCT [38414] : 1650+ ALLEGANY CO., MD & PA, USA [36970]
FAIRBAIRN C1815 GLASGOW, LKS, SCT [34491] : 1700+ LILLIESLEAF, BEW, SCT [38476]
FAIRBARN 1820+ YORK CO., ONT, CAN [34465] : 1820+ QUEENSVILLE, ONT, CAN [34465] : PRE 1820 LEYBURN, YKS, ENG [34465]
FAIRBRASS 1890+ WESTHAM, LND, ENG [37757]
FAIRBROTHER 1800+ LAN, ENG [35505] : ALL OXF, ENG [36702] : ALL CHESTER, CHS, ENG [38074] : 1880+ USA [35505]
FAIRCHILD ELIJAH 1790-1860 MORRIS CO., NJ, USA [37453] : EPHRAIM 1827-1863 NJ, USA [37453] : EPHRAIM 1827-1863 IA, USA [37453]
FAIRCLOTH THOMAS 1827+ PULASKI CO., GA, USA [38340]
FAIRCLOUGH ALL KANMANTOO, SA, AUS [34561] : 1910 ARLTUNGA, NT, AUS [37952] : 1750-1900 WIGAN, LAN, ENG [34740] : PRE 1761 LAN, ENG [37706] : 1840 CHORLEY, LAN, ENG [37732] : ALL DRUTAMON, CAV, IRL [34561]
FAIREY PRE 1854 SOUTHWARK, SRY, ENG [34669] : 1800-1850 DEPTFORD, LND & SSX, ENG [36874]
FAIRFAX 1812+ HODDESDON, HRT, LND & WIL, ENG [33970] : PRE 1791 CLEEVE PRIOR, WOR, ENG [36011]
FAIRFIELD C1650 BEVERLY, MA, USA [34395] : 1845 VIGO, IN, USA [38518] : 1850 CLINTON CO., IN,

USA [38518] : 1819 HAMILTON CO., OH, USA [38518]
FAIRGRIEVE PRE 1850 LEITH, MLN, SCT [34929]
FAIRHALL 1900 SYDNEY, NSW, AUS [35881] : 1800S MORPETH, NSW, AUS [35881] : 1700S BREDE, SSX, ENG [35881]
FAIRHEAD 1750-1800S PRITTLEWELL & SOUTHEND, ESS, ENG [37677] : 1810 BROOME, NFK, ENG [37841]
FAIRHURST PRE 1850 LIVERPOOL, LAN, ENG [34545] : PRE 1880 BOLTON & ORMSKIRK, LAN, ENG [36508] : 1800-1900 LIVERPOOL, LAN, ENG [36983] : 1730+ WIGAN, LAN, ENG [38046]
FAIRLEY 1750+ BIGGAR, LKS, SCT [36085] : WILLIAM 1820+ BOTHWELL, LKS, SCT [37153]
FAIRLIE ALL ADELAIDE, SA, AUS [37189] : PRE 1863 MAYBOLE, AYR, SCT [37189] : 1740S LONG ISLAND, NY, USA [38038]
FAIRMAN ELIZABETH 1803-1821 HUNTINGDON CO., PA, USA [38371]
FAIRNINGTON PRE 1900 GATESHEAD, DUR, ENG [36113]
FAIRS 1700-1800 RAYDON, SFK, ENG [36717]
FAIRWEATHER 1820-1890 PARRAMATTA, NSW, AUS [37895] : PRE 1780 BRECHIN, ANS, SCT [34053] : PRE 1840 INVERBROTHICK, ANS, SCT [34691] : 1850-1900 DUNDEE, ANS, SCT [35717]
FAIST 1840-1900 SCHRAMBERG, WUE, GER [38679] : PRE 1840 WOLFACH, BAD, GER [38679]
FAITFEU 1600-1700 CLERMONT CREANS, PIC, FRA [34514]
FAITHFUL 1800S BIRMINGHAM, WAR, ENG [37299]
FAITHFULL PRE 1792 ENG [36310] : 1853+ REDHILL, SRY, ENG [36838]
FAIZEY PRE 1850 DEV, ENG [35872]
FAKE ALL WORLDWIDE [37637]
FAKES ALL WORLDWIDE [37637]
FALCK 1750-1850 GUNDERSHEIM, RPF, BRD [38530]
FALCONBRIDGE 1823+ HOBART TOWN, TAS, AUS [35384] : PRE 1823 ALLESLEY, WAR, ENG [35384]
FALCONER JAMES 1870+ DUNEDIN, NZ [36611] : ALL SOUTH LEITH, MLN, SCT [34619] : 1830+ CROY & DALCROSS, INV, SCT [36254] : PRE 1800 GLENSHEE & KIRKMICHAEL, PER, SCT [36401] : PRE 1800 ALYTH & DALNOID, PER, SCT [36401]
FALEMPIN PRE 1838 CALAIS, FRA [34886]
FALES PRE 1700 DUBLIN, IRL [37795] : PRE 1800 RI, USA [37804]
FALK 1600-1743S DALHAM, GOTLAND, SWE [38346] : 1890+ ALLEGENY, PA, USA [38185]
FALK (SEE FALCK) [38530]
FALKARD PRE 1812 SFK, ENG [33813]
FALKEROY C1400 ENG [34395]
FALKINER 1800S MELBOURNE, VIC, AUS [35945]
FALKINGHAM VAUGHAN 1900+ ST KILDA & ROSEBUD, VIC, AUS [36621] : C1580 ENG [34395]
FALKNER PRE 1865 DUBLIN, DUB, IRL [37443]
FALL 1911+ TABER, ALB, CAN [37426] : 1800+ WHITKIRK, WRY, ENG [37426] : PHILLIP 1500-1620 ENG [37784]
FALLA 1851+ CRESWICK, VIC, AUS [35709] : ALL GSY, CHI [37229] : PRE 1835 EDINBURGH, MLN, SCT [35709] : ALL WORLDWIDE [37229]
FALLE 1700-1800 ST HELIER, JSY, CHI [34552]
FALLEN 1840S-1850S GAL, IRL [36337]
FALLICK ALL ISLE OF WIGHT, HAM, ENG [33995]
FALLIS ALL VICTORIA, ONT, CAN [33854] : 1700-1735 NJ, USA [37795]
FALLON ALL NUNDLE, NSW, AUS [35534] : PRE 1800 KILLUCAN, WEM, IRL [33912] : PRE 1841 MAYO ABBEY, MAY, IRL [34305] : 1820-1860

MULLINGAR, WEM, IRL [35451] : ALL ATHLONE, ROS, IRL [35534]

FALLOON PRE 1860 LISBURN, ANT, IRL [36877]

FALLOWFIELD 1800-1920 LND, ENG [35916] : 1720-1750 ULVERSTON, LAN, ENG [36635]

FALLOWS 1710+ HAWKSHEAD, LAN, ENG [36701] : ALL LAN, ENG [37669] : ALL CHS, ENG [37669] : ALL STS, ENG [37669] : PRE 1900 BIRMINGHAM, WAR, ENG [38002]

FALLS 1760S VA, USA [38202] : 1800 BALTIMORE, MD, USA & AUS [35856]

FALSHAW PRE 1837 MANCHESTER, LAN, ENG [37072]

FALVY 1850+ MELBOURNE, VIC, AUS [33878]

FANCOURT ALL ENG [35914]

FANCY ALL NFD, CAN [35619]

FANDON 1865 MEMPHIS, TN, USA [34388]

FANDONI ALL ITL [35821]

FANE C1730 ONGAR, ESS, ENG [37683]

FANECO PRE 1860 SAN CHRISTORA DE OVAR, PT [34014]

FANNING 1820-1850 KID, IRL [34563] : PRE 1856 TIP, IRL [35713] : C1820 CORK CITY, COR, IRL [38322]

FANSHAW ROBERT 1740-1790 WIGAN, LAN, ENG [35849] : ALBERT BLACKE 1835-1855 SHEFFIELD, YKS, ENG [35849]

FANSHAWE ROBERT 1740-1790 WIGAN, LAN, ENG [35849]

FAN SICKLE 1830-1840 BUCKS CO., PA, USA [38201]

FANTHORPE 1880+ COTTINGHAM, YKS, ENG [36704]

FARAGHER PRE 1866 IOM, UK [35231]

FARAM 1800 THURLWOOD & STOCKPORT, CHS, ENG [35023]

FARBER C1800 HES, BRD [35563]

FARBROTHER 1600-1800 ASCOT UNDER WYCHWOOD, OXF, ENG [36653] : PRE 1830 OXF, ENG [37249]

FARBUSH 1500-1630 ENG [37784]

FARCKENS 1852+ THOMASTOWN & AMPITHEATRE, VIC, AUS [35205] : PRE 1852 NEUBUCKOW, MSW, GER [35205]

FARDY PRE 1880 VARMLAND, SWE [34169] : 1880+ DENVER, CO, USA [34169]

FAREY PRE 1900 PEY ROLLES, RHA, FRA [35448]

FARGHER 1800 DERBYHAVEN, MALEW, IOM [34890]

FARIMBELLA 1800+ ITL [35762]

FARINDON 1800S NEWDIGATE, SRY, ENG [33780]

FARKAS ALL BODOLO, ABAUY, HU [38438]

FARLAND 1800-1850 ROMSEY & HURSLEY, HAM, ENG [36783]

FARLEIGH 1800+ ENG [37306]

FARLEY 1844+ BEAUFORT, VIC, AUS [35436] : 1886-1919 NEWCASTLE, NSW, AUS [35570] : 1870-1886 COALCLIFF, NSW, AUS [35570] : 1863+ ROSEDALE, VIC, AUS [35748] : 1650+ COLDRIDGE, DEV, ENG [34747] : PRE 1800 TOTNES, DEV, ENG [35229] : PRE 1870 STAFFORD, STS, ENG [35570] : PRE 1850 MAIDSTONE, KEN, ENG [36298] : 1700-1850 KEN, ENG [36780] : PRE 1800 BISHOPS CLEEVE, GLS, ENG [36889] : PRE 1900 ALDERTON, GLS, ENG [36889] : C1750 ERMINGTON, DEV, ENG [36945] : PRE 1857 BRISTOL, GLS, ENG [38718] : C1860 CAV, IRL [35826] : KATH. 1841+ DUBLIN, IRL [37825] : PHILIP HEN. 1847+ DUBLIN, IRL [37825] : GEORGE 1843+ DUBLIN, IRL [37825] : PAT. WM. 1845+ DUBLIN, IRL [37825] : JAMES 1805+ DUBLIN, IRL [37825] : PETER 1848+ PHILADLEPHIA, PA, USA [37825] : MARIA 1855+ CAZENOVIA, MADISON, NY, USA [37825] :

JAMES 1851+ CAZENOVIA, MADISON, NY, USA [37825]

FARLINGER PRE 1770 RPF, BRD [34246] : 1784+ CORNWALL, ONT, CAN [34246]

FARLOW PRE 1860 ALBANY, NY, USA [37537]

FARMAN PRE 1850 NFK, ENG [36067]

FARMER C1858+ AUS [34444] : PRE 1850 ENG [34383] : C1790 HARTFIELD, SSX, ENG [34518] : C1817 BORO, SRY, ENG [34518] : 1820 OMBERSLEY, WOR, ENG [34677] : 1840+ LONDON, ENG [34768] : C1800-1850 DARLINGTON, DUR, ENG [36053] : C1800-1850 HAM, ENG [36289] : 1750+ TAMWORTH WIGGINTON, STS & WAR, ENG [36329] : 1800-1900 PLYMOUTH, DEV, ENG [37365] : 1852+ READING, BRK, ENG [37837] : PRE 1831 BERMONDSEY, SRY, ENG [37892] : C1847 PERTH, PER, SCT [33951] : PRE 1780 FIF, SCT [36679] : PRE 1838 BURKE, VT, USA [36923] : CRITTENDEN L. PRE 1850 YELL CO., AR, USA [36939] : 1838 OKMULGEE, OK, USA [38012]

FARMERY PRE 1720 SUTTON IN THE FOREST, NRY, ENG [36384] : PRE 1720 EASINGWOLD, NRY, ENG [36384]

FARNAGH ALL WORLDWIDE [37421]

FARNAPH ALL WORLDWIDE [37421]

FARNARTH ALL WORLDWIDE [37421]

FARNATH ALL WORLDWIDE [37421]

FARNELL 1700+ SUTTON COLDFIELD, WAR, ENG [34416] : 1900-1952 DARTFORD, KEN, ENG [36101] : 1800-1899 LAMBETH & LEWISHAM, SRY & KEN, ENG [36101] : 1700-1799 SRY & KEN, ENG [36101] : 1700+ AMPTHILL, BDF, ENG [37632]

FARNETH ALL WORLDWIDE [37421]

FARNHAM PRE 1635 CORNHILL, LND, ENG [36544] : PRE 1900 LONDON, ENG [37237] : PRE 1900 COOK CO., IL, USA [35371] : C1635 ESSEX CO., MA, USA [36544] : 1875-1910 ROCHESTER, NY, USA [38118]

FARNORTH ALL WORLDWIDE [37421]

FARNOTH ALL WORLDWIDE [37421]

FARNOUGH ALL WORLDWIDE [37421]

FARNSWORTH 1900S FOOTSCRAY, VIC, AUS [34430] : ALL ENG [33975] : PRE 1846 WAR, ENG [35035] : C1820-1870 SCARTHIN NICK, MATLOCK, DBY, ENG [36414]

FARNUM 1825-1850 SUTTON YORK, ONT, CAN [38407]

FARNWORTH 1700+ LAN, ENG [34062] : 1750-1800 CHS, ENG [36482]

FARQUAHARSON 1600-1800 TOUGH, ABD, SCT [36951]

FARQUHAR ALL KNOCKANDOO & ELGIN, MOR, SCT [35460] : 1800S KILMARNOCK, AYR, SCT [35501] : 1800 NEW CUMNOCK, AYR, SCT [36667]

FARQUHARSON 1700+ UDNY, ABD, SCT [34560] : ALL KNOCKANDOO & ELGIN, MOR, SCT [35460]

FARQUISON PRE 1838 TULLYMET, PER, SCT [38413]

FARR 1860+ SYDNEY, NSW, AUS [34978] : 1900+ OAKWOOD & FERGUS, ONT, CAN [36716] : PRE 1900+ TISDALE, SAS, CAN [37518] : PRE 1900 ISLINGTON, LND, ENG [34776] : 1811-1860 EDMONTON, MDX, ENG [35192] : PRE 1800 GRAVELEY & WESTON, HRT, ENG [35229] : 1880+ GRIMSBY, LIN, ENG [36511] : PRE 1880 HULL, YKS, ENG [36511] : PRE 1900 SOUTH WRAXALL, WIL, ENG [37248] : PRE 1900 CASTLE COMBE, WIL, ENG [37248] : PRE 1690 CROYDON, SRY, ENG [37361] : 1724+ CLODOCK, HEF, ENG [37827] : PRE 1802 SAL, ENG [37897] : 1850-1920 EDINBURGH, SCT [37469] : 1811-1873

EDINBURGH, SCT [37469] : PRE 1820 GA, USA
[37587] : EDWARD 1867+ GENESEE CO., MI, USA
[38146] : EPHRAIM 1831-1874 TUSCOLA CO., MI,
USA [38146]

FARRAHER 1800S IRL [38215]

FARRALL PRE 1880 STS, ENG [37231] : 1880S
ISLINGTON, MDX, ENG [37231]

FARRAN PRE 1900 HOWTH, DUB, IRL [38305]

FARRAN (SEE FARREN) [38305]

FARRANO PRE 1800 NTT, ENG [37829]

FARRANT 1890+ MELBOURNE, VIC, AUS [36632] :
PRE 1800 FRAMFIELD, SSX, ENG [36021] : ALL
HAVERHILL, SFK, ENG [36163]

FARRAR PRE 1900 LEEDS, WRY, ENG [36034] : 1850-
80 LEEDS, WRY, ENG [37711]

FARREL PRE 1814 DUBLIN, IRL [37316]

FARRELL 1910+ AUSTINMER, NSW, AUS [33770] :
JAMES C1850S NSW, AUS [33794] : 1880+
BOLWARRAH, VIC, AUS [34794] : PRE 1856 NSW,
AUS [35028] : 1830+ HUNTER RV, NSW, AUS
[35034] : 1815+ HOBART, TAS & NSW, AUS [35137]
: 1870+ BEMBOKA, NSW, AUS [35825] : ROBERT
PRE 1900 BURFORD, ONT, CAN [38445] :
ANDREW PRE 1881 BURFORD, ONT, CAN [38445]
: 1790+ ENG [34803] : MARY PRE 1841
SIDESTRAND, NFK, ENG [36532] : 1820-1849
KENSINGTON, LND, ENG [37050] : 1800+
BIRMINGHAM, WAR, ENG [37074] : ALL NJ, USA
&, ENG & IRL [38733] : C1800-1856 HAROLD'S
CROSS, DUB, IRL [34672] : PRE 1830 MEA, IRL
[34858] : PRE 1841 CRAIGAVOLE, LDY, IRL [35162]
: C1850 LISBURN, ANT, IRL [35502] : C1813
DUBLIN, IRL [36860] : PRE 1860 ROS, IRL [37521] :
PATRICK 1845+ DUBLIN, IRL [37825] : PRE 1854
STRABANE, TYR, IRL [37994] : ANDREW PRE
1881 IRL [38445] : 1811-1853 ENNISKILLEN, FER,
IRL [38761] : PRE 1900 DUNFERMLINE, FIF, SCT
[33770] : 1870-1900 NYC, NY, USA [36936] : PRE 1900
ST LOUIS, MO, USA [38538] : ANTHONY ALL
WORLDWIDE [35137]

FARRELL (SEE FERRELL) [34758]

FARRELLEY 1827+ CAV, IRL [37314] : ELIZABETH
PRE 1817 BLACK HILL, MEA & WEM, IRL [37314]

FARRELLY JAMES 1805+ DUBLIN, IRL [37825]

FARREN PRE 1900 TAS, AUS & USA [38305] : 1905
SHEERNESS, KEN, ENG [34575] : PRE 1900
HOWTH, DUB, IRL [38305]

FARRENDEN PRE 1750S SSX, ENG [37745]

FARRER 1758+ LONDON, ENG [36049] : 1880+
WINDERMERE, CUL, ENG [37853]

FARRIER ALL WORLDWIDE [37722]

FARRIN DINAH 1720-1725 NTH, ENG [35119]

FARRINGDON PRE 1830 CHISWICK & TURNHAM
GREEN, MDX, ENG [36051]

FARRINGTON ALL ENG [35011] : PRE 1830
CHISWICK & TURNHAM GREEN, MDX, ENG
[36051] : PRE 1855 WIC, IRL [38733] : ALL NJ, USA
[38733]

FARRIS 1750-1820 LISBURN, ANT, IRL [38100] :
JEREMIAH 1844-1890 HANCOCK CO., IL, USA
[36322] : LOUISA 1860-1885 FULTON CO., IL, USA
[36322] : JERRY 1844-1890 LA HARPE, IL, USA
[36322] : JOHNSON 1848-1885 FULTON CO.,
BCKHEART TWP., IL, USA [36322] : 1700-1900
WASHINGTON & HAWKINS CO., VA & TN, USA
[37539] : 1800-1950 KY & TN, USA [37539] : 1832
OKMULGEE, OK, USA [38012]

FARR-JONES 1890-1910 AUS [34394] : ALL UK [34394]
: 1850-1900 LLANFAIR CAEREINION, MGY, WLS
[34394]

FARRO ALL CHS & DBY, ENG [37617]

FARROW 1830+ WETHERINGSETT, SFK, ENG
[34710] : PRE 1825 WESTHORPE & FINNINGHAM,
SFK, ENG [35462] : C1800-1815 NFK, ENG [36478] :
PRE 1850 NORTHAMPTON, NTH, ENG [36748] :
C1809 MILDENHALL, SFK, ENG [36955] : 1700-
1800 SWANTON ABBOTT, NFK, ENG [37411] : PRE
1850 BURY ST EDMONDS AREA, SFK, ENG
[37720] : PRE 1850 WRY, ENG [38577] : 1850+
PUTNAM CO., IN, USA [36582] : 1853+ WAPELLO
CO., IA, USA [36582]

FARTHING 1814+ PARRAMATTA, NSW, AUS
[34967]

FARWELL 1865-1910 KEWEENAW CO., MI, USA
[38010]

FASANO ALL WORLDWIDE [35456]

FASNACHT 1700S LANCASTER, PA, USA [38108]

FASSEUR PRE 1910 ENGHIEN, HAINAUT, BEL
[35173]

FASTENRATH ALL WEI, GER [38607]

FASTNACHT 1520+ STRUEMPFELBACH, BAW,
FRG [38660]

FATHERS 1650-1830 CHARLETON HORETHORNE,
SOM, ENG [35445] : 1650-1830 HENSTRIDGE, SOM,
ENG [35445] : 1830-1930 BRIGHTON, SSX, ENG
[36167] : PRE 1750 NTH, ENG [36183]

FATHFULL 1700+ KINTBURY, BRK, ENG [35475]

FATIO PRE 1520 LA BURELLA, MONTECRISTESIA,
ITL [37381]

FAUCESWEAR ELIZA 1828 BORDEAUX, AQU, FRA
[35876]

FAUCETT 1860-1905 KEWEENAW CO., MI, USA
[38010]

FAUCONIER 1500-1800S MONT AUX MALADE,
NOR, FRA [35327]

FAUDREE MAJOR PRE 1830 HANOVER CO., VA,
USA [37580]

FAUGHT 1822-1860 GILES CO., TN, USA [37029]

FAULCONER 1766+ KY, USA [37592]

FAULDER 1800-1870 CUL & LAN, ENG [36098]

FAULDS MARGARET C1860 VIC, AUS [36853] :
GEORGE C1860 LUCKY WOMANS, VIC, AUS
[36853] : PRE 1902 RFW & LKS, SCT [34391] :
GEORGE C1830+ AYR, SCT [36853] : ALL
WORLDWIDE [36853]

FAULK C1825 OLD MARION, GA, USA [36354] :
1600+ USA [38326]

FAULKE 1770+ CRADLEY, HEF, ENG [38020]

FAULKENER 1880-1910 WEST BROMWICH, STS,
ENG [37068] : PRE 1860 LIOGITHALL, BKM, ENG
[37068]

FAULKES PRE 1820 SIBTHORPE, LIN, ENG [35725]

FAULKNER 1850+ NEW ENGLAND, NSW, AUS
[37889] : ALL SHOREDITCH, LND, ENG [34820] :
C1800 CRANFIELD, BDF, ENG [34853] : 1750+
BELBROUGHTON, WOR, ENG [35919] : PRE 1800
CITY OF LONDON, ENG [36035] : 1761-1833
AYMESTREY, HEF, ENG [36229] : 1800+
GLYMPTON, OXF, ENG [36892] : 1850S
SHEFFIELD, YKS, ENG [37692] : PRE 1900 LND,
ENG [37731] : ALL LAN, ENG [38514] : PRE 1870
DUBLIN, IRL [34268] : PRE 1865 IRL [34365] : 1830
OFF, IRL [37791] : 1830 DUBLIN, IRL [37791] : 1842
MGY, WLS [37694]

FAULKS PRE 1850 ASHWELL, RUT, ENG [33766]

FAULL 1800+ REDRUTH, CON, ENG [35355]

FAULSTICH PRE 1855 HOCHST, HEN, GER [37894]

FAUNCH PRE 1842 STRAND, MDX, ENG [34452]

FAURE C1700 GENEVA, GE, CH [38348]

FAURE D'ENTREMONT PRE 1748 CAUBONNE,
DAUPIN, FRA [38659]

FAUSET 1800-1850 REUERBACH, GER [36573]

FAUSSETT 1600+ DARTFORD, KEN, ENG [36756]

FAUST PRE 1740 ARGYLE, NS, CAN [35291] : C1800 MONTOUR & BERKS COS., PA, USA [37508]

FAUSZ PRE 1880 STETTIN & WRIEZEN, GER [36941]

FAUTLEY 1800+ BECKLEY, SSX, ENG [37560]

FAUX 1800S BRISTOL, SOM, ENG [34979]

FAVALORO 1800-1900 PALERMO, SICILY, ITL [38129]

FAVELL 1780+ MAN, CAN [37426]

FAVIER ALL LONDON, MDX & SRY, ENG [37225] : ALL IRL [37225]

FAVILL PRE 1760 DARLASTON, STS, ENG [36110]

FAVREAU J.B. 1840+ ST PHILIPPE, QUE, CAN [36678]

FAWCET PRE 1852 YKS, ENG [36841] : 1852+ NELSON, NZ [36841]

FAWCETT 1860 GEELONG, VIC, AUS [34038] : 1865+ DAYLESFORD, VIC, AUS [34039] : 1919+ FITZROY, VIC, AUS [34430] : 1860+ HOLBECK, YKS, ENG [34190] : 1800+ MUKER, NRY, ENG [35891] : ALL HALIFAX, WRY, ENG [36411] : PRE 1800 BRIDLINGTON, ERY, ENG [37630] : 1750-1850 ENNISKILLEN, FER, IRL [34513] : PRE 1850 ENNISKILLEN, FER, IRL [37035]

FAWCITT 1840S MANCHESTER, LAN, ENG [36024]

FAWKENER 1700+ SHREWSBURY, SAL, ENG [33887]

FAY MALCOLM F. 1910+ MAN, ALB & BC, CAN [38412] : 1710+ ASHWATER, DEV, ENG [34804]

FAYANT PRE 1900 BALCARRES, SAS, CAN [38438]

FAYERNO PRE 1600 GENEVA, GE, CH & ITL [38348]

FAYERS ROBERT 1791+ IPSWICH & BILDESTON, SFK, ENG [33919] : 1791+ IPSWICH, SFK, ENG [34777] : ALL BILDESTON & IPSWICH, SFK, ENG & AUS [33919]

FAYLE 1850 HAY, NSW, AUS [33848]

FAZAKERLEY C1850 WEST DERBY, LAN, ENG [35931]

FEAK ALL WORLDWIDE [37637]

FEAKE ALL WORLDWIDE [37637]

FEAKES 1800-1850 ST PANCRAS, LND, ENG [37765] : ALL WORLDWIDE [37637]

FEAKINS 1800-1900 MAIDSTONE, KEN, ENG [37365]

FEAR 1900+ EMMAVILLE, NSW, AUS [37115] : 1800S STANTON DEW, SOM, ENG [37969] : 1800-1902 VT & NE, USA [38764]

FEARBY GEORGE 1800+ DRINGHOUSES & TERRINGTON, YKS, ENG [34973] : ANN 1800+ DRINGHOUSES & TERRINGTON, YKS, ENG [34973]

FEARN 1810+ WALTHAM, KEN, ENG [33942] : 1730-1850 DERBY, DUFFIELD & BONSALL, DBY, ENG [34729] : 1840 DBY & STS, ENG [35019] : PRE 1900 SCT [37761] : 1750-1850 KING, SCT [38100]

FEARNS 1700+ YOXALL, STS, ENG [37266] : 1860+ MOTUEKA, NZ [36818]

FEARNSIDE 1830S WAKEFIELD, WRY, ENG [35599]

FEARON 1780+ BRIGHAM & WORKINGTON, CUL, ENG [37073] : 1650-1850 ASPATRIA, CUL, ENG [37654]

FEASTER 1786S MD, USA [38184]

FEATHER PRE 1842 NSW, AUS [34696] : 1810-1840 BIRMINGHAM, ENG [35850] : 1820+ BRADFORD, YKS, ENG [36769]

FEATHERBY PRE 1800 GILLINGHAM, KEN, ENG [35128] : 1780 CHATHAM, KEN, ENG [35350] : 1830+ TATHWELL, LIN, ENG [35587]

FEATHERINGILL ALL WORLDWIDE [38115]

FEATHERLY PRE 1825 GUILDERLAND, NY, USA [36935]

FEATHERSTONE C1865 ADELAIDE, SA, AUS [36283] : PRE 1890 LND, KEN & SRY, ENG [34325] : FRAN PRE 1883 NUNDALE, DUR, ENG [35867] : 1800+

MANCHESTER, LAN, ENG [35969] : 1780-1870 MANCHESTER, LAN, ENG [36130] : C1755 TROTTERSCLIFFE, KEN, ENG [37536] : PRE 1826 BRIGHTON, SSX, ENG [37856] : 1800-1870 MITCHELSTOWN, COR, IRL [36617]

FEAVER 1800+ WESTMINSTER, LND, ENG [36869] : ALL WORLDWIDE [34284]

FECHNER PRE 1844 FREISTADT, SIL, GER [34766] : 1800 GLOOEKZEN, B BURG, GER [35465]

FECKE ALL WORLDWIDE [37637]

FEDDER 1800+ PA, USA [37012]

FEDER ALL WORLDWIDE [38313]

FEDERLI 1885+ WOODEND, VIC, AUS [35915]

FEE PRE 1850 IRL [34377] : PRE 1870 LEITRIM, IRL [44443]

FEEBREY 1790+ GLS, ENG [34843]

FEEGAN PRE 1900 KKD, SCT [34377]

FEEHY 1850+ NZ [36602]

FEEK ALL WORLDWIDE [37637]

FEEKE ALL WORLDWIDE [37637]

FEEKES ALL WORLDWIDE [37637]

FEELY ALICE 1700+ ANERLEY, LND, ENG & IRL [34943] : PRE 1856 NENAGH, TIP, IRL [34452]

FEENAN 1830+ LOUGHGILLY, ARM, IRL [37560]

FEENARTY ALL ATHLONE, WEM, IRL [34002]

FEENEY 1866+ MOLONG, NSW, AUS [33867] : 1858+ WELLINGTON, NSW, AUS [35022] : 1820-1920 LONDON, LND & LET, ENG & IRL [35767] : 1827-1845 GAL, IRL [38150] : 1845-1887 CINCINNATI, OH, USA [38150]

FEEZ 1600+ ESCHAU, BAV, BRD [34303] : 1817-1905 SYRACUSE, NY, USA [34303]

FEGAN PRE 1800S CAV, IRL [36608]

FEGENT 1700-1900 SEND & GODALMING, SRY, ENG [35229]

FEHRMANN 1759 HOLZHAUSEN, PYR, GER [38748] : 1837 HAGEN, PYR, GER [38748]

FEICKERT 1750-1800 RANSWEILER, RHINELAND, GER [36561]

FEIGENBAUM 1850-1890 JASSI, ROM [38236] : 1884-1920 NEW YORK, NY, USA [38236]

FEINAUER ALL FORCHTENBERG, WUE, GER [35460] : 1600+ WUE, GER [35460]

FEIRON ALL WORLDWIDE [36728]

FEISER 1855-1865 KEWEENAW CO., MI, USA [38010]

FELBER 1700-1800 ILSENBURG, PSA, GER [38643]

FELDENBERGER C1798 ZEICHEN, GER [37022]

FELDENHEIMER 1700+ HENGSTFELD, BAW, GER [38578]

FELDKAMP PRE 1848 GER [37501] : 1848-1880 EDGAR CO., IL, USA [37501]

FELDMANN 1800+ RUGEN ISLAND, GER [37165]

FELIX 1750+ MDX & SRY, ENG [36203]

FELL ALL CASTLEMAINE, VIC, AUS [35707] : PRE 1897+ SALFORD, ONT, CAN [35004] : 1835+ LAMBETH, SRY, ENG [33893] : PRE 1801 ROUGHLEE & BURNLEY, LAN, ENG [34213] : PRE 1870 CHELMSFORD, ESS, ENG [34935] : MARSHALL 1700S WHITWELL, DBY, ENG [36018] : PRE 1837 PRESTON, LAN, ENG [37085] : PRE 1775 ESS, ENG [37885] : PRE 1850 WHITBURN, WLN, SCT [37463] : ROBERT 1740+ BALTIMORE, MD, USA [34143]

FELLINDER 1755 WINCHCOMBE, GLS, ENG [37827]

FELLINGHAM ALL BRIGHTON, SSX, ENG [37236]

FELLOW PRE 1750 SEDGLEY, STS, ENG [36110]

FELLOWES C1830-90 ICKLESHAM, SSX, ENG [35860] : 1800-1900 WESTMINSTER, MDX, ENG [36106] : 1750+ DUDLEY, WOR & STS, ENG [36435]

FELLOWS 1790-1900 DERBY, DBY, ENG [34729] : PRE 1831 CLAPHAM, SRY, ENG [35016] : ALL STS, ENG [35628] : ALL WHITCHURCH, OXF, ENG

[36326] : 1750+ DUDLEY, WOR & STS, ENG [36435] : PRE 1810 ISLINGTON, MDX, ENG [37885] : 1600-1750 MA, USA [37538] : 1750-1850 NH, USA [37538] : PRE 1800 OTSEGO CO., NY, USA [37541]

FELLS 1866-1936 NORTH KENSINGTON, LND, ENG [37079]

FELMINGHAM ALL WORLDWIDE [36521]

FELSCH 1800S WORLDWIDE [36291]

FELSNER ALL OES [37268]

FELSTEAD 1770+ ALBURY, HRT, ENG [36978]

FELTHAM 1890+ IANDRA, NSW, AUS [36269] : 1840+ MARULAN, NSW, AUS [36269] : 1750+ BISHOPSTONE, WIL, ENG [34899] : 1640+ STOURTON, WIL, ENG [35815] : C1881+ LONDON, ENG [35995] : 1750-1850 WHITSBURY, WIL, ENG [36213] : 1800+ BISHOPSTONE, WIL, ENG [36269]

FELTHOUSE 1800+ BURTON ON TRENT, STS, ENG & AUS [35019]

FELTIS PRE 1859 BOMBALA, NSW, AUS [35506] : 1880+ OWEN SOUND, ONT, CAN [38396]

FELTMATE ALL WORLDWIDE [34472]

FELTON ALL MCCLARENDALE, SA, AUS [36822] : 1750-1850 SAL, ENG [36108] : ALL SAL, ENG [37334] : ALL STOKE, STS, ENG [37334] : ALL WORLDWIDE [37334]

FELTWELL PRE 1870 SOUTHERY & DENVER, NFK, ENG [37402] : 1870+ SHEFFIELD, YKS, ENG [37402]

FENBY ALL WORLDWIDE [37352]

FENCOTT ALL WORLDWIDE [37619]

FENDEL 1870+ MELBOURNE, VIC, AUS [35515] : PRE 1838 NEIDERHEIMBACH, PRE, GER [35515]

FENDICK PRE 1860 NORTHWOLD, NFK, ENG [36425]

FENDLEY PRE 1830S NFK, ENG [33849]

FENDT PRE 1940 FARMINGTON, MI, USA [36551]

FENIMORE WILLIAM 1700+ NJ, USA [38127]

FENLON ALL ISLINGTON & ROTHERHITHE, LND, ENG [37321]

FENN 184 ELY, CAM, ENG [34540] : PRE 1780 HEDENHAM, NFK, ENG [35173] : 1700+ MDX, ENG [36165] : 1700+ HRT, ENG [36165] : 1800+ MDX, ENG [36179] : 1880 LND, ENG [36443] : ALL ENG [36500] : ALL MARYLEBONE, MDX, ENG [36636] : ALL PADDINGTON, MDX, ENG [36636] : SAMUEL 1800+ LONDON, MDX, ENG [36636] : C1950 LITTLE WALTHAM, ESS, ENG [36955] : ALL FOULSHAM & GREAT MELTON, NFK, ENG [36955] : ALL BARTON MILLS & MILDENHALL, SFK, ENG [36955] : 1900+ RICHMOND, SRY, ENG [36955] : ALL BAWDESWELL & BYLAUGH, NFK, ENG [36955] : 1900+ TWICKENHAM, MDX, ENG [36955] : 1820 SHOREDITCH, LND, ENG [37080] : 1830-1850 WALTON ON NAZE, ESS, ENG [37220] : ALL MURSLEY, BKM, ENG [37297] : 1600-1850 BKM, ENG [37297] : 1800+ MDX, ENG [37297] : 1800+ LONDON, ENG [37297] : ALL WORLDWIDE [37297]

FENNEL 1775+ LONDON, MDX, ENG [37923] : PRE 1850 ANT, IRL [37923]

FENNELL PRE 1880 BRISBANE, QLD & NSW, AUS [34170] : JOHN 1858+ HOTSPUR, VIC, AUS [37184] : 1800+ PANGBOURNE, BRK, OXF & MDX, ENG [36326] : THOMAS PRE 1848 LACOCK, WIL, ENG [37184]

FENNEN (SEE FOENNEN) [37024]

FENNER 1800+ ESS, ENG [34818] : ALL AYLESBURY, BKM, ENG [35196] : 1700+ BALHAM, LND, ENG [35377] : 1700+ MDX, ENG [35377] : PRE 1850 ROTHERFIELD, SSX, ENG

[35406] : PRE 1725 ESS, ENG [35642] : ALL WORLDWIDE [36216]

FENNESSY 1800+ COR, IRL [35201] : 1800+ LIMERICK, LIM, IRL [37218] : 1800+ CLONMEL, TIP, IRL [37218]

FENNIHOUSE ALL STS, SAL & WAR, ENG [38754]

FENSOM 1700-1833 HOLBORN, LND, ENG [33923] : 1800+ LONDON, ENG [34167]

FENSUM 1700-183 HOLBORN, LND, ENG [33923]

FENTER CHRISTIAN 1760+ NC, USA [38183]

FENTON 1845+ CORDILLERA, NSW, AUS [34917] : PRE 1870+ BRIGHTON & WAUBASHENE, ONT, CAN [37518] : PRE 1770 NEWCASTLE UNDER LYME, STS, ENG [33831] : PRE 1825 BIRMINGHAM, WAR, ENG [34778] : PRE 1840 NEW HUTTON, WES, ENG [34917] : C1800 OCKBROOK, DBY, ENG [35502] : PRE 1800 KENDAL, LAN, ENG [35722] : PRE 1730 STURTON LE STEEPLE, NTT, ENG [35983]

FENTRESS 1880-1900 MARTON SINNINGTON, NRY, ENG [36217]

FENWICK 1850+ BRISBANE, QLD, AUS [36305] : C1800+ SLEAFORD & HORNCASTLE, LIN, ENG [34451] : 1650-1710 STAMFORDHAM, NBL, ENG [34832] : 1650-1710 BELLS CLOSE & FELTON, NBL, ENG [34832] : 1640-1690 NEWCASTLE, NBL, ENG [34832] : PRE 1896 EASTBOURNE, SSX, ENG [37610] : C1830S DUNDEE, ANS, SCT [35438] : PRE 1880 PER, SCT [37987] : ALL WORLDWIDE [34832]

FENWICKE PRE 1570 KIRKWHELPINGTON, NBL, ENG [36502]

FERDAM 1800S ESS & SRY, ENG [37525]

FERDINANDO 1815+ HAWKESBURY RIVER, NSW, AUS [34273] : 1798+ PRE, GER [34273]

FEREDAY 1846+ GEORGETOWN, TAS, AUS [35477] : 1870S+ VIC, AUS [35477]

FERGSTAD PRE 1895 ROUND HILL, ALB, CAN [38736]

FERGUS PRE 1850 HAMILTON, LKS, SCT [34097] : PRE 1767 DOLLAR, CLK, SCT [34222] : PRE 1860 STIRLING, STI, SCT [35411]

FERGUSON 1940 CROYDON, NSW, AUS [34967] : 1867+ SYDNEY, NSW, AUS [34979] : C1843+ CIRCULAR HEAD, TAS, AUS [35399] : C1853+ HEATHCOTE, VIC, AUS [35477] : 1790-1850 DRUMMOND, ONT, CAN [35638] : ALEX 1811-1885 LANARK, ONT, CAN [37441] : 1800+ NS, CAN & SCT [34500] : FRANCES C1831 CON, ENG [34792] : PRE 1855 ALSWICK, NBL, ENG [34979] : 1885 BRAMPTON, CUL, ENG [38699] : 1820-1910 CLA, IRL [33947] : 1800+ MAGHERALIN, DOW, IRL [33970] : C1890 BELFAST, ANT, IRL [34385] : 1800+ CORK, IRL [34642] : 1800+ TAMLAGHT BY MONEYMORE, LDY, IRL [35218] : ALL BELFAST, ANT, IRL [35628] : 1700-1800 FER, CAV & ANT, IRL [35645] : 1814-1875 WEM, IRL [36560] : PRE 1820 TERRYHOOGAN, ARM, IRL [36692] : PRE 1800 LIM, IRL [37018] : ALL KILMORE, ARM, IRL [37154] : 1800+ KILKEEL, DOW, IRL [37405] : PRE 1873 PORTERDOWN, ARM, IRL [37894] : ROBERT 1870-1940 MAGHERALIN, DOW, IRL & NZ [33970] : JOHN PRE 1800 EDINBURGH, SCT [34487] : MAGGIE 1830+ PER, SCT [34620] : 1830S-1880S MUSSELBURGH, MLN, SCT [34635] : PRE 1900 SCT [34657] : C1760 DAILLY, AYR, SCT [34713] : 1800+ MOTHERWELL, LKS, SCT [34918] : 1780+ STI, SCT [34970] : 1700+ MUSSELBURGH & EDINBURGH, SCT [35015] : 1810+ INVERNESS, SCT [35331] : AGNES ALL EAST KILBRIDE, LKS, SCT [35957] : PRE 1840 DALMELINGTON, AYR, SCT [36191] : ROBERT 1800+ GLASGOW, LKS, SCT [36294] : JOHN ROBB 1833+ GLASGOW, LKS,

SCT [36294] : ADAM 1750-1780 ALYTH, PER, SCT [36320] : 1811-1853 INV, SCT [36608] : PRE 1840 BALQUHIDDER, PER, SCT [36788] : C1875 WEST GREENOCK, RFW, SCT [36835] : PRE 1850 AYR, SCT [37105] : ALEX 1811-1885 PER, SCT [37441] : ROBERT C1775+ CALLANDER, PER, SCT [37441] : PRE 1850 GLASGOW, SCT [37459] : ALL MULL, ARL, SCT [37441] : ANN PRE 1838 GLENISLA, ANS, SCT [37557] : 1810+ MOTHERWELL & HAMILTON, LKS, SCT [38253] : NELLIE 1770-1802 DALCATOIG, INV, SCT [38482] : 1803 + GLASGOW, SCT & AUS [36238] : 1910+ HAMILTON, LKS, SCT & NZ [38253] : PRE 1820 CHARITON CO., MO, USA [36927] : SUSAN PRE 1794 VA, USA [36939] : HUGH 1770-1810 BEDFORD CO., PA, USA [37529] : 1840-1910 CHENOA & MCLEAN, IL, USA [38043] : JAMES 1870 MO, USA [38156] : THOMAS J. 1866-1952 BLOOMFIELD, NE, USA [38156] : LEWIS 1827-1842 MENARD, IL, USA [38157] : 1750-1760 DUTCHESS CO., NY, USA [38188] : 1930S CA, USA [38451]

FERGUSSON DUNCAN 1800 SMITH FALLS, ONT, CAN [38451] : ALL DOW, IRL [34645] : ALL BALMERINO, FIF, SCT [34758] : C1800 ST NINIANS, STI, SCT [35602] : C1840-1880 GREENOCK, RFW, SCT [36835] : ALL MULL, ARL, SCT [37480] : PRE 1900 DFS, SCT & NZ [34617]

FERINO PRE 1720 LOCARNO, TI, CH & ITL [38681]

FERMOR 1650+ ROTHERFIELD & HASTINGS, SSX, ENG [34970]

FERN 1700+ INGLEBY & FOREMARK, DBY, ENG [35851]

FERNALD PRE 1900 WORLDWIDE [36933]

FERNIE 1860+ FERNIE & VANCOUVER, BC, CAN [36462] : 1780S+ LESLIE, FIF, SCT [34434]

FERNLEIGH C1700+ MAIDSTONE, KEN, ENG [33792]

FERNLEY C1800+ MAIDSTONE, KEN, ENG [33792]

FERNSIDE (SEE FEARNS [35599]

FERO 1800-1850 DELAWARE CO., NY, USA [38113]

FEROUS 1850-1890 SUSQUEHANNA CO., PA, USA [38113] : 1810-1850 DELAWARE CO., NY, USA [38113]

FERRABY PRE 1850 BURTON ON HUMBER, LIN, ENG [36382]

FERRAL 1800+ KENWYN & TRURO, CON, ENG [35712]

FERRALL C1800 HARBORNE, WOR, ENG [34898]

FERRARESE PRE 1900 ARARAQUARA, SAO PAULO, BRAZIL [36363] : PRE 1930 FONTE ALTO, TREVISO, ITL [36363]

FERRARI PRE 1850 LUDIANO, TI, CH [35718]

FERREL ALL TN, AR & CA, USA [38363]

FERRELL ROBERT PRE 1900 BURFORD, ONT, CAN [38445] : ALL HOLYWOOD, DOW, IRL [34758]

FERRETT C1800 JACOBSTOW, CON, ENG [38052]

FERRIER ALL TORONTO, ONT, CAN [38432] : 1750-1850 ARBROATH, ANS, SCT [34225] : ALL ABERLEMNO, ANS, SCT [34758] : PRE 1868 BRECHIN, ANS, SCT [34840] : 1790+ PERTH, PER, SCT [35042] : PRE 1781 PER, SCT [35729] : C1836 PER, SCT [35729] : 1800 ST VIGEANS, ANGUS, SCT [37170]

FERRIN PRE 1750 ONEX, GE, CH [38348]

FERRIROLI PRE 1850 MALVAGLIA, TI, CH [35718]

FERRIS 1880S-1930S BENAMBRA & MORASS CREEK, VIC, AUS [35777] : 1860-1880S MT GAMBIER & SANDY WATERHOLES, VIC, AUS [35777] : ALL WIL, ENG [37233] : PRE 1890 LIVERPOOL, LAN, ENG [38424] : 1820S TANDRAGEE, ARM, IRL [36301] : PRE 1881 CLOGHER, MAY, IRL [37955] : 1750-1820

LISBURN, ANT, IRL [38100] : C1830 SCT [37513] : 1700S CT, USA [35165] : 1830-1890 SARATOGA CO., NY, USA [36444] : 1800-1900 FRANKLIN CO., NY, USA [37783] : HENRY EDWARD 1870-1906 INDEPENDENCE OR HAMPTON, IA, USA [38031] : HENRY 1750-1807 STANFORD, DUTCHESS CO., NY, USA [38031]

FERRON ALL THREE RIVERS, QUE, CAN [35327] : 1700S IRL [36961]

FERROW 1800+ WOLLONGONG, NSW, AUS & ENG [33769]

FERRY 1636-1699 CANTERBURY, KEN, ENG [38098] : 1800S MADISON, NY, USA [38098]

FERRYMAN ALL WORLDWIDE [34723]

FERTADO 1885+ CONTRA COSTA CO., CA, USA [38323]

FESSENDEN C1730 CAMBRIDGE, MA, USA [36928]

FESTER 1620-1660 RUSTEN, SIL, GER [38689]

FETHERSTONE PRE 1830 COR, IRL [36271]

FETT PRE 1857 ANGELTHURN, BAD, GER [37819]

FETTER (SEE FEDDER) [37012]

FEUCHT ALL BAW, FRG [38657]

FEUERSTEIN 1860 NORKA, SU & WORLD [37511]

FEVER 1500+ KEN, ENG [33984] : PRE 1850 BRADFORD PEVERILL, DOR, ENG [33984] : ALL WORLDWIDE [34284]

FEVERHERDT PRE 1850 CAROW, POS, GER [34766]

FEVERS 1875-1900 BARNSLEY, YKS, ENG [38478]

FEW ALL ISLE OF ELY, CAM, ENG [37494]

FEWER 1800-1850 WATERFORD, WAT, IRL [38299]

FEWSTER PRE 1900 LND, ENG [35255] : 1750-1850 FAILSWORTH, LAN, ENG [35775] : 1800-1825 HEMINGBROUGH, YKS, ENG [38422]

FEZZEY 1700+ DEV & CON, ENG [36574] : 1865-1880 KEWEENAW CO., MI, USA [38010]

FFAROWE 1550+ LANEHAM, NTT, ENG [34408]

FIBBINS PRE 1900S MUSWELLBROOK, NSW, AUS [37910]

FICARRA PRE 1920 PERRINA, LIPARI ISL., ITL [36271]

FICHET 1665-1742 LAIZE & CORTAMBERT, BRG, FRA [34136]

FICK 1880+ CALLIGNEE, VIC, AUS [35725] : JOHANN 1740+ LUBECK, GER [35648] : PRE 1850 FEHMARN ISLAND, SHO, GER [35725] : JOHANN 1740+ IOM, UK [35648] : ROBERT 1860+ DOUGLAS, IOM, UK [35648]

FICKE PRE 1810 HARLINGEN, FRI, NL [38694]

FICKERT 1860-1950 BERLIN, GDR & FRG [38710]

FICKLING 1849+ MOREE, NSW & QLD, AUS [34261] : ALL SAHAM TONEY, NFK, ENG [36134]

FIDDES 1880+ SOUTH YARRA, VIC, AUS [35825] : C1775 CRAILING, ROX, SCT [34239] : 1750-1850 WESTRUTHER, BEW, SCT [34615] : C1800 ROX, SCT [36762]

FIDDLER 1843-1853 FINGAL, TAS, AUS [33879] : 1700-1850 STOCKPORT, CHS, ENG [33879] : 1829+ LONGHOPE, OKI, SCT [34688]

FIDDY 1724-1906 HAYNFORD, NFK, ENG [34649] : 1840S HAINFORD, NFK, ENG [36032]

FIDKIN URBAN 1817-1840 ISLINGTON, LND, ENG [36311] : URBAN 1817-1840 DENHAM CT & STANFIELD PK, LND & NSW, ENG & AUS [36311]

FIDLER 1849+ WISTOW, SA, AUS [33833] : 1853-1900 SALE, VIC, AUS [33879] : 1843-1853 FINGAL, TAS, AUS [33879] : 1840-1870 GLENORCHY, TAS, AUS [33934] : PRE 1849 OTTERBOURNE, HAM, ENG [33833] : 1700-1850 STOCKPORT, CHS, ENG [33833] : PRE 1850 EAST HAGBOURNE AND UPTON, BRK, ENG [37743] : ALL WORLDWIDE [37785]

FIEBIG ALL WORLDWIDE [37474]

FIEDLER 1877 DENILIQUIN, NSW, AUS [35065] :
1877+ EAST GIPPSLAND, VIC, AUS [35065]

FIELD 1895-1934 MELBOURNE, VIC, AUS [34794] :
1800+ BENDIGO, VIC, AUS [35080] : 1850-1900
WEST MAITLAND, NSW, AUS [35094] : GEORGE
C1812+ SALE, VIC, AUS [35527] : 1863+
BRIGHTON, VIC, AUS [35527] : 1844+ PAMBULA,
NSW, AUS [35825] : 1910+ SALE, VIC, AUS [36360] :
GEORGE C1720+ ONT, CAN & USA [35778] : PRE
1848 LONGSHAWS MILL, NBL, ENG [33863] :
1800+ HINTON AMPNER, HAM, ENG [33938] :
1785+ KEN, ENG [34181] : 1850-1900 LAMBETH,
LND, ENG [34469] : 1650-1750 WOLBOROUGH,
DEV, ENG [34552] : 1770-1800 BURNHAM, BKM,
ENG [34552] : 1835 LIMEHOUSE, LND, ENG [34731]
: 1800S E FARLEIGH & SNODLAND, KEN, ENG
[34738] : 1800S LOOSE & CHATHAM, KEN, ENG
[34738] : ALL LAINDON, ESS, ENG [34772] : PRE
1832 CHERTSEY, SRY, ENG [35037] : 1800-1900
CHERTSEY, SRY, ENG [35069] : 1700+ HULL,
YKS, ENG [35080] : PRE 1800 BIGHTON, HAM,
ENG [35247] : ALL KIRKBY MOORSIDE &
BRADFORD, YKS, ENG [35460] : HENRY ALL
BERMONDSEY, LND, ENG [35527] : 1855
MARDEN, KEN, ENG [35569] : C1850-1870
BIRMINGHAM, WAR, ENG [35791] : PRE 1880
WAKEFIELD, YKS, ENG [35898] : MARY C1808
POPLAR, MDX, ENG [35955] : 1790S OCKLEY,
SRY, ENG [36263] : 1750-1850 WINCHELSEA &
ICKLESHAM, SSX, ENG [36485] : MARY ANN
1800S LIMEHOUSE, MDX, ENG [36633] : 1800S
ENG [36837] : 1850+ REDDITCH, WOR, ENG
[37230] : 1750+ STRATFORD, MDX, ENG [37284] :
1840+ LONDON, ENG [37294] : PRE 1820 HEF &
SAL, ENG [37331] : C1845 READING, BRK, ENG
[37378] : C1860 ROUNTON, NRY, ENG [37378] :
1300-1400+ SSX, ENG [37648] : PRE 1700 LAN,
KEN & YKS, ENG [38021] : THOMAS PRE 1804
HARTLEY ROW, HAM, ENG [38248] : NAOMI
1847-1918 TICEHURST & WADHURST, SSX, ENG
& AUS [33847] : 1700+ GARFORD, BRK & SA,
ENG & AUS [35555] : 1800+ DUB, IRL [37598] :
1740S DUBLIN, IRL [37947] : 1848 EDINBURGH,
MLN, SCT [37263] : MARY 1701 MILTON, MA, USA
[35273] : ROBERT 1670-1700 MILTON, MA, USA
[35273] : 1750-1780 COLUMBIA, PA, USA [36703] :
PRE 1769 HUDSON VALLEY, NY, USA [37811] :
1620+ USA [38021] : 1820 OTSEGO CO., NY, USA
[38188] : JOHN 1750-1800S BEDFORD CO. &
ADAIR CO., VA & KY, USA [38315]

FIELDCAMP 1900S IL, TX & GA, USA [37501]

FIELDER PRE 1800 SSX, ENG [35546] : C1874
SOUTHAMPTON, HAM, ENG [35585]

FIELDHOUSE C1864 LAN, ENG [35414] : ALL
WORLDWIDE [36467]

FIELDING PRE 1830 LAN, ENG [35246] : C1851+
ASHTON & OLDHAM, LAN, ENG [36414] : C1900-
30 DARLEY DALE, DBY, ENG [36414] : 1700-1800
ROYTON, LAN, ENG [36844] : 1740-1840
STANHILL, LAN, ENG [38251] : 1720-1800 COR,
IRL [35813] : PRE 1900 KILMACOW, WAT, IRL
[36168] : ANN 1840 WEX, IRL [36316]

FIELDS 1800S KEARNEY & BETHUNE, ONT, CAN
[36727] : PRE 1940 LAWRENCE, MA, USA [33929] :
1790+ VA & KY, USA [36357] : PRE 1800 NC, USA
[37509] : PRE 1850 LAWRENCE CO., OH, USA
[37604] : 1820-1860 RUTHERFORD CO., TN, USA
[37798] : 1790+ USA & UK [36357]

FIELDWICK PRE 1880 LONDON, ENG [35956] :
C1884 MANCHESTER, LAN, ENG [35956]

FIENE 1900 ESCHENBRUCH, PYR, GER [38748] :
1843 MASPE, PYR, GER [38748]

FIFE C1783 CARRIDEN, WLN, SCT [37148] :
THOMAS C1838 SCT [38003] : 1800-1900 SCT [38278]

FIFIELD PRE 1900 BURNLEY, LAN, ENG [37644] :
PRE 1800 HAM, ENG [37773]

FIGG C1754 IPING, SSX, ENG [36185] : PRE 1900
LONDON, ENG [37078]

FIGGES 1775-1870 VERNHAMS DEAN, HAM, ENG
[38003]

FIGTREE 1889 SHEFFIELD, WRY, ENG [37136]

FIGURES C1800 GLS, ENG [33793] : PRE 1855 WAR,
ENG & IRL [38437]

FIKE 1835 SCHUYLKILL, PA, USA [34388]

FILBRICK PRE 1790 ESS, ENG [37668]

FILBURN ALL YKS, ENG [37407]

FILBY ALL NFK & WRY, ENG [36187]

FILCOCK 1800-1850 STS, ENG [33879]

FILDER 1670-1780 RODE, SOM, ENG [37233] : 1690-
1790 BRADFORD ON AVON, WIL, ENG [37233] :
1670-1730 TETBURY, GLS, ENG [37233]

FILER ALL CHEW MAGNA, SOM, ENG [34861]

FILES 1948+ BROKEN HILL, NSW, AUS [35771]

FILEWOOD 1640-1770 BECHINGLEY, SRY, ENG
[38540]

FILIATRAULT 1800-1900 MONTREAL & QUEBEC
CITY, QUE, CAN [35103]

FILIATREAU RENE 1650-1700 POITOV, FRA [37479]

FILIPCHUK C1860 STAWCHIN, BUKOVINA,
UKRAINE [34521]

FILKIN 1800-1850 LIVERPOOL, LAN, ENG [37460]

FILKINS C1760-1815 CAYUGA CO., NY, USA [38055]

FILL PRE 1900 YARMOUTH, NFK, ENG [36122]

FILLINGHAM PRE 1800 HAXEY, LIN, ENG [38383]

FILLION ANTOINE ALL ST HERMAS, QUE, CAN
[36723] : MATHAIS 1866+ ST HERMAS, ST JEAN
BAPTIST VG, QUE & MAN, CAN [36723]

FILMER ALL NSW, AUS [34534]

FILSCH 1700-1760 MANNHEIM, BAY, BRD [38178]

FILVOK 1800+ GER & SU [34087]

FILWOK 1800+ HES, BRD [34087] : 1939-1945 POL
[34087]

FIMMEL PRE 1845 SIL, PRE, GER [38490]

FINAN PRE 1870 ROS, IRL [37510]

FINCH 1870+ HILLSTON, NSW, AUS [38289] : ALL
SPROUGHTON, SFK, ENG [33823] : 1780+ WEST
SMITHFIELD, MDX, ENG [33889] : A.BAKER
1767+ WARWICK LANE, NEWGATE ST, LND,
ENG [33889] : 1700+ LONDON, MDX, ENG [33889]
: 1750-1820 EXETER, DEV, ENG [34809] : PRE 1760
ESS, ENG [35902] : 1800-1900 LONDON, ENG
[36531] : PRE 1800 BKM, ENG [36588] : PRE 1840
SOULDENE, OXF, ENG [37068] : 1700-50 EAST
GRINSTEAD, SSX, ENG [37340] : ALL LONDON,
MDX, ENG [37884] : ALL LIVERPOOL, LAN, ENG
[37884] : PRE 1820 ESS, ENG [37885] : PRE 1759
BIRDINBURY, WAR, ENG [37978] : 1790 SUTTON,
CAM, ENG [38209] : ALEXANDER PRE 1855
LONDON, ENG [38289] : PRE 1700 SSX, ENG
[38746] : 1850+ AUCKLAND & PIRONGIA, NZ
[33823] : ALL NZ [35058] : PRE 1855 COLUMBIANA
CO., OH, USA [37034]

FINCHAM 1850+ ENG [36470] : PRE 1800
THELNETHAM & DISS, NFK, ENG [37246]

FINCHER PRE 1862 SRY, ENG [38568]

FINCK C1820 FINSBURY, LND, ENG [35722] : JOHN
HERMAN PRE 1800 SPITALFIELDS, LND, ENG
[38483] : C1835 HAMBURG, HBG, GER [35791]

FINDELATOR PRE 1750 SCT [33914]

FINDEN 1780 MEDSTEAD, HAM, ENG [34909]

FINDLAY 1880+ MOOSEJAW, SAS, CAN [35627] :
1850+ ANT, IRL [35627] : 1788-1875 MONTROSE,
ANS, SCT [33811] : 1800+ ANGUS, ANS, SCT
[34408] : PRE 1850 GLASGOW, SCT [34835] : PRE

1842 EDINBURGH, MLN, SCT **[34886]** : 1800S
STRATHDON, ABD, SCT **[35411]** : PRE 1840
GLASGOW, SCT **[35913]** : 1840-1890 DALMENY,
WLN, SCT **[37329]** : C1847 SCT **[37474]** : 1800 +
MOR, SCT **[38425]**

FINDLEY 1800 UNION CO., SC, USA **[37792]**

FINDLOW 1650-1790 GAWSWORTH, CHS, ENG
[36983]

FINE ALL VA, MO, AR, CA, USA **[38363]**

FINEMAN 1800S ENG **[38369]**

FINEMORE 1800 + GREAT LINFORD, BKM, ENG
[35829]

FINGER C1820 CH **[37022]** : 1750-1803 LINCOLN CO.,
NC, USA **[38120]**

FINK PRE 1850 YELL CO., AR, USA **[36939]**

FINKS 1750-1900 SCHWAIGERN, WUE, GER & USA
[38574]

FINLAY MARIA PRE 1869 NEWFIELD, VIC, AUS
[35805] : PRE 1841 MEA & WEM, IRL **[35824]** : 1800-
1850 LARNE, ANT, IRL **[36682]** : PRE 1862
TULLYLISH, DOW, IRL **[36856]** : 1750 +
TRANENT, ELN, SCT **[34008]** : PRE 1853 DUNDEE,
ANS, SCT **[35134]** : PRE 1849 GLASGOW, LKS, SCT
[35761] : 1867 ST ANDREWS & ST LEONARDS,
FIF, SCT **[35811]** : 1867 + CUPAR, FIF, SCT **[35811]** :
PRE 1795 NAIRN, NAI, SCT **[36513]** : 1830-1840
CAMBUSNETHAN, LKS, SCT **[36848]**

FINLAYSON 1855 + SHOALHAVEN, NSW, AUS
[34979] : ROD 1850S GEELONG, VIC, AUS **[37117]** :
1857-1950 ULMARRA, NSW, AUS **[37349]** : ROD
1860S SOUTH ISLAND, NZ **[37117]** : 1860-1930S
INVERCARGILL, NZ **[37349]** : 1780 + DRUMBUIE,
ROC, SCT **[33993]** : C1800 LOCHALSH, ROC, SCT
[34362] : PRE 1855 INV, SCT **[34979]** : 1800S
DUNNET & THURSO, CAI, SCT **[36290]** : 1780 +
CARMICHAEL, LKS, SCT **[36749]** : 1800 + BOWER,
CAI, SCT **[36857]** : ROD PRE 1837 APPLECROSS &
PLOCKTON, ROC, SCT **[37117]** : 1800S
STRATHCARRON, ROC, SCT **[37349]** : MARY PRE
1811-27 ACHMORE KYLE OF LOCHALSH, ROC,
SCT **[37518]**

FINLEY CHARLES 1736 + IRL **[35302]** : 1800
STRANGFORD BAY, IRL **[38349]** : JOHN PRE 1783
ORANGE CO., NY, USA **[35302]** : NELSON PRE
1900 WAYNE CO., NY, USA **[35302]** : THERON
1838 + WALWORTH, NY, USA **[35302]** : 1790-1810
WARREN, KY, USA **[38373]**

FINLOW 1700-1840 STAFFORD, STS, ENG **[37252]**

FINN PRE 1884 + SUTHERLAND, NSW, AUS **[35143]**
: C1915 + DENILIQUIN, NSW, AUS **[35746]** : 1864 +
MELBOURNE, VIC, AUS **[35746]** : 1945 MANLY,
NSW, AUS **[35800]** : 1850 + VIC, AUS **[36305]** : PRE
1863 LND, ENG **[35746]** : 1830 + RAMSGATE, KEN,
ENG **[36865]** : PRE 1820 DOVER AREA, KEN, ENG
[37720] : C1848 KILBEHENNY, LIM, IRL **[34652]** :
C1850 + RATH LUIRC (CHARLEVILLE), COR,
IRL **[35143]** : C1850 + COR, IRL **[35143]** : C1800-1860
COR, IRL **[35206]** : EDWARD 1800 + CALLAN,
KIK, IRL **[35712]** : PRE 1920S BALLYHAUNIS,
MAY, IRL **[37831]** : 1800 + NEW ROSS, WEX, IRL
[38189] : 1700-1850 OFF, IRL **[38299]** : 1700-1850
WATERFORD, WAT, IRL **[38299]** : 1820S NENAGH,
TIP, IRL & AUS **[38862]** : 1850 + BALTIMORE, MD,
USA **[36895]**

FINNEGAN 1875 IRL **[34540]** : C1800 DUBLIN, IRL
[35773] : PRE 1781 ARDS PENINSULA, DOW, IRL
[38428] : ALL NJ, USA **[38733]**

FINNELL PRE 1836 + LOCHAIT, CLA, IRL **[35759]**

FINNERTY PRE 1850 STOKESTOWN, ROS, IRL
[34613] : PRE 1856 ST MARYS DUBLIN, IRL **[35162]**
: 1700-1850 STROKESTOWN, ROS, IRL **[36844]**

FINNEY 1810 + SHOREDITCH, LND, ENG **[34063]** :
1830 + RISCA, MON, WLS **[33955]**

FINNIE 1700-1800 COLINTON, MLN, SCT **[36652]**

FINNIGAN C1800 MEATH, MEA, IRL **[35859]** : 1875 +
MO, USA **[34368]** : 1885 + NE, USA **[34368]**

FINNIS 1750 + LAMBETH, MDX, ENG **[36872]**

FINNUCANE PRE 1830 MELOCK, CLA, IRL **[34978]**

FINSCHI ALL GR, CH **[36982]** `

FINTER HANS MICHAEL C1700 PALATINE, GER
[38183]

FINTZEL ALL WORLDWIDE **[38613]**

FINUCANE PRE 1814 CLA, IRL **[37866]**

FINZEL ALL WORLDWIDE **[38613]**

FIORENTI PRE 1800 ITL **[34984]**

FIORINANA ALL CAMPO DI GIOVE, ABR, ITL
[37519]

FIRDION PRE 1745 WETTOLSHEIM, ALS, FRA
[37504]

FIRESTONE 1740-1880 YORK CO., PA, OH & IN,
USA **[36901]**

FIRKINS C1893 ECKINGTON, WOR, ENG **[36171]**

FIRMAN PRE 1735 WEST STOWE, SFK, ENG **[34445]**
: 1640-1841 ASSINGTON, SFK, ENG **[34672]**

FIRMSTONE 1843 YKS, ENG **[35120]**

FIRTH PRE 1880 MELBOURNE, VIC, AUS **[36305]** :
1820 + SIMCOE CO., ONT, CAN **[34465]** : 1820
BRADFORD, YKS, ENG **[37174]** : 1700-1860
STROMNESS, OKI, SCT **[34498]**

FISCH PRE 1800 OGGERSHEIM, RPF, GER **[38681]**

FISCHBACH PRE 1820 OBERFISCHBACH, NRW,
BRD **[38636]**

FISCHER 1868 + SYDNEY, NSW, AUS **[34582]** :
SALIS 1850 + ST KILDA, VIC, AUS **[35822]** : EMMA
L. 1872 ADELAIDE, SA & VIC, AUS **[36311]** : PRE
1860 KOVEL, LGE, BEL **[35002]** : ALL BAV & RPF,
BRD **[35264]** : 1854 CARRICK TWP., ONT, CAN
[34503] : 1400-1850 AG, CH **[38035]** : PRE 1860
KARLSBAD AREA, BOHEMIA, CS **[36963]** : ALL
MARXHAGEN, RAMBOW, DDR **[34812]** : PRE 1890
ISLINGTON, LND, ENG **[34454]** : 1600S
SCHWEIDNITZ, SIL, GER **[33901]** : PRE 1860
POSEN, POS, GER **[34648]** : C1770 BERLIN, BLN,
GER **[37003]** : C1890 BRUNSWICK, HAN, GER
[37931] : 1700-1900 HILDESHEIM, GER **[37931]** :
ALL ZWICKAU & SAXONY, KSA, GER & NZ
[34645] : MARGRET PRE 1840 AMELAND, NL
[35371] : 1930 HOLLAND, NL **[37931]** : ALL
RENSSELAER CO., NY, USA **[35264]** : ALL
ALBANY CO., NY, USA **[35264]** : 1879 ST LOUIS,
MO, USA **[35279]** : SELMA 1900 + ST LOUIS, MO,
USA **[37003]** : 1880-1910S USA **[37600]** : 1865-1875
KEWEENAW CO., MI, USA **[38010]** : 1780-1819
DAUPHIN, PA, USA **[38095]** : 1750-1850 ROMNEY,
WV, USA **[38344]** : ALL USA **[38451]**

FISH PRE 1794 CARLTON COLVILLE, SFK, ENG
[33762] : 1800 + BEDFORD, ENG **[34049]** : PRE
1800S ESS, ENG **[34240]** : 1800-1850 WIGAN, LAN,
ENG **[35006]** : 1850-1900 LIVERPOOL, LAN, ENG
[35006] : 1750 + DARWEN, LAN, ENG **[37166]** :
C1881 MILE END, MDX, ENG **[37204]** : 1750S
GREAT HALLINGBURY, ESS, ENG **[37250]** :
C1801-1824 CUTCOMBE & WHEDDON CROSS,
SOM, ENG **[37556]** : LUKE 1760 CUL, ENG **[37788]** :
1820S ENG **[37947]** : PRE 1630 GREAT BOWDON,
LEI, ENG **[38135]** : PRE 1800 HALIFAX, VT, USA
[33804] : 1800-1900 TN, USA **[38040]** : PRE 1840 NC,
USA **[38040]** : PRE 1823 MEIGS CO., OH, USA
[38231]

FISHBACK C1850 OXFORD, ONT, CAN **[36671]**

FISHBOURNE 1700 + CAR, LEX & WIC, IRL **[34602]**

FISHER 1870-1900 MARYBOROUGH, VIC, AUS
[34191] : PRE 1930 BRIGHTON, VIC, AUS **[35055]** :

1800+ ORANGE, NSW, AUS [37839] : JOHN DUNCAN 1925+ SYDNEY, NSW, AUS [37906] : 1850+ GODERICH, ONT, CAN [35004] : 1800+ BRANDON, MAN, CAN [35004] : 1880+ DOUGLAS, MAN, CAN [35004] : 1917+ VANCOUVER, BC, CAN [35004] : 1800S LONDON & BKM, ENG &, CEYLON [36967] : 1820+ BIRMINGHAM, WAR, ENG [33946] : SARAH C1800-1850 LONDON, ENG [34007] : PRE 1840 UFTON NERVET, BRK, ENG [34628] : PRE 1850 STANDISH, LAN, ENG [34730] : 1800+ COLCHESTER, ESS, ENG [34916] : PRE 1800 ASHDON, ESS, ENG [35020] : 1800-1900 KINGS NORTON (BIRMINGHAM), WAR, ENG [35166] : C1756 ULEY, GLS, ENG [35223] : PRE 1750 ASHWELL, HRT, ENG [35229] : 1820+ NOTTINGHAM, NTT, ENG [35342] : C1808 LND, ENG [35552] : JOHN 1780S-1830S LONDON, ENG [35706] : DR ALDER 1806-1840S LONDON, ENG [35706] : THOMAS C1820-1850 KINGSTANLEY, GLS, ENG [35725] : 1700-1800+ LEI, ENG [36038] : PRE 1814 SHEFFIELD, WRY, ENG [36102] : 1830S NEWCASTLE UPON TYNE, NBL, ENG [36110] : PRE 1870 HITCHIN, HRT, ENG [36154] : 1680S BISHOPS WALTHAM, HAM, ENG [36263] : 1800+ PUSEY, MARCHAM, BRK & WIL, ENG [36329] : 1815+ NOTTINGHAM, NTT, ENG [36386] : WM. JAMES E. 1851 HASTINGS, SSX, ENG [36633] : GREEN 1700S NEWINGTON, SRY, ENG [36633] : EDWIN ARTHUR 1870 HOLBORN, MDX, ENG [36633] : JOHN & SARAH PRE 1800 NEWINGTON, SRY, ENG [36633] : WALTER 1753 CAMBERWELL, SRY, ENG [36633] : 1800+ NTT, ENG [36746] : C1750 THUNDRIDGE, HRT, ENG [36978] : 1650-1790 GAWSWORTH, CHS, ENG [36983] : 1800-1900 BRISTOL, GLS, ENG [37232] : 1800-1900 BATH, SOM, ENG [37232] : PRE 1700 DALTON IN FURNESS, LAN, ENG [37353] : PRE 1800 HUDDERSFIELD, WRY, ENG [37385] : 1700S GATELY, NFK, ENG [37498] : PRE 1850 SHOREDITCH & STEPNEY, MDX, ENG [37617] : WILLIAM C1800 CHEADLE HULME, CHS, ENG [37691] : PRE 1614 WINMARLEIGH, LAN, ENG [37706] : C1750-1850 MID, NFK, ENG [37718] : 1750+ WIL, HAM & MDX, ENG [37868] : 1750-1950 WONSTON, HAM, ENG [38003] : 1700+ WIGAN, LAN, ENG [38046] : 1800S BRADFORD, WIL, ENG & AUS [33919] : DANIEL 1812+ BRADFORD, WIL, ENG & AUS [33919] : PRE 1870 APPLEDORE & NORTHAM, DEV, ENG & AUS [38580] : PRE 1840 BAD, GER [38333] : BRITISH ARMY 1830S+ INDIA [36809] : ALL NZ [34155] : 1850+ CHRISTCHURCH, CBY, NZ [36746] : ALL DUNDRENNAN, KKD, SCT [34155] : 1800+ BALQUHIDDER, PER, SCT [34607] : DAVID 1790 AYR, AYR & LKS, SCT [35096] : PRE 1862 SCOTLANDWELL, KRS, SCT [35885] : 1720+ MUIRAVONSIDE, STI, SCT [37205] : 1700S PER, SCT [38215] : PRE 1800 LKS, SCT [38437] : 1879 ST LOUIS, MO, USA [35279] : 1646-1820 NORFOLK CO., MA, USA [35316] : 1800+ HIGHGATE, VT, USA [36323] : C1876 MI, USA [36923] : C1852 NY & MI, USA [36923] : FREDERICK 1770S CABARRUS CO., NC, USA [37585] : 1800+ BOURBON CO., KY, USA [38050] : 1790 WESTMORELAND CO., PA, USA [38143] : ANDREW 1850 PITTSBURG, PA, USA [38320] : 1820-1860 BEDFORD CO., PA, USA [38742] : WILLIAM 1816 USA & CAN [36677] : ALL WAYNE CO., NY, USA & NL [37502] : 1840-1880 MON, WLS [37232] : 1870+ NEWPORT, MON, WLS [38580]

FISHER-ROWE 1800-1850 REWE, DEV, ENG [37657]

FISHLOCK PRE 1833 STOCKLEY, WIL, ENG [34959] : PRE 1844 BISHOPS CANNINGS, WIL, ENG [37971]

FISHPOOL ALL WORLDWIDE [37707]

FISHWICK ALL NZ [36000]

FISK C1800 YEA, VIC & TAS, AUS [36312] : PRE 1840 HINDERCLAY, SFK, ENG [34911] : 1750+ ISLINGTON, MDX, ENG [35172] : 1750+ GRAVESEND, KEN, ENG [35172] : 1800+ NTH BRIXTON, SRY, ENG [35947] : 1800 CHITTENDEN CO., VT, USA [38362] : 1775 CT, USA [38362] : 1830-50 WASHINGTON CO., NY, USA [38751] : 1882+ STORM LAKE, IA, USA [38751] : 1860+ COLUMBIA CO., WI, USA [38751] : 1800 RUTLAND CO., VT, USA [38751]

FITCH 1844+ ADELAIDE, SA, AUS [37913] : PRE 1800 ASHDON, ESS, ENG [35020] : PRE 1700 ESS, ENG [35642] : PRE 1840 STEEPLE BUMPSTEAD, ESS, ENG [37913] : 1830+ MONROE, MI, USA [38517]

FITCHER PRE 1850 PENZANCE, CON, ENG [36297]

FITCHETT 1854 WOLVERHAMPTON, STS, ENG [34950] : 1680+ NORTHAMPTON CO., VA, USA [38032]

FITNESS PRE 1800 SSX, ENG [34847]

FITSCH PRE 1890 GLOWINSK, RYPIN, BY, POL [34246]

FITT 1810 SHOREDITCH, LND, ENG [37080] : PRE 1900 EAST LONDON, LND, ENG [37497] : 1860 PORT OF SPAIN, TRINIDAD, W.INDIES [35130] : ALL WORLDWIDE [37497]

FITTE PRE 1850 HAN, GER [37961]

FITTON C1700 WARRINGTON, CHS, ENG [36520] : PRE 1730 GAWSWORTH, CHS, ENG [36520] : PRE 1800 CHS, ENG [36520] : PRE 1750 ROSTHERNE, CHS, ENG [36520] : C1890 WHISTON, LAN, ENG [36520] : C1900 BUCKLEY, FLN, WLS [36520]

FITZ PRE 1843 GEELONG, VIC, AUS [34691]

FITZGERALD AGNES 1852+ BALLARAT & HAMILTON, VIC, AUS [34045] : 1912+ COLLINGWOOD, VIC, AUS [34549] : PRE 1869 MANLY, NSW, AUS [34691] : REBECCA 1869+ WINTON, QLD, AUS [34811] : MARY JANE 1885+ FITZROY, VIC, AUS [36279] : 1865+ URALLA, NSW, AUS [38208] : C1860S UARBRY, NSW, AUS & IRL [37106] : PRE 1791 MDX, ENG [35142] : WILLIAM PRE 1853 NTT, ENG & AUS [34811] : 1800+ CAMAS & BRUFF, LIM, IRL [33829] : 1800-1900 COR, IRL [34071] : 1700+ WATERFORD, WAT, IRL [34650] : 1862-1917 TIP, IRL [34844] : MARY PRE 1860 LIM, IRL [34902] : 1820+ COOLCAPPAGH & KILCOLEMAN, LIM, IRL [34960] : 1820+ ARDGOUL & RATHKEALE, LIM, IRL [34960] : 1800+ COR, IRL [35206] : JAMES PRE 1853 LIMERICK, LIM, IRL [36600] : C1830S CASTLECONNELL, LIM, IRL [37106] : 1800-1900 WAT, IRL [37661] : PRE 1864 ENNIS, CLA, IRL [38208] : 1830+ WATERFORD, IRL [38274] : PRE 1850 BALLYSIMON, LIM, IRL & NZ [36840] : ELIPHAL 1650-1730 KID, ENG & USA [37806] : 1850 HAVERHILL, MA, USA [34960] : PRE 1805 KY, USA [37037] : 1860-1910 COLUMBIANA CO., OH, USA [38106] : PRE 1896 NEWPORT, MON, WLS [33866] : PRE 1800 WORLDWIDE [36933]

FITZGIBBINS PRE 1850 PHILEDELPHIA, PA, USA [34036]

FITZGIBBON 1800-1850 TIP, IRL [37156] : PRE 1900 WORLDWIDE [37749]

FITZHENRY 1800+ OLD ROSS, WEX, IRL [38189]

FITZHERBERT PRE 1780 NORBURY & BEGBROKE, DBY & OXF, ENG [34012] : 1600S SSX, ENG [36679] : 1660-1780 SHERCOCK, CAV, IRL [34012]

FITZJOHN PRE 1850 WESTMILL, HRT, ENG [36061]

FITZMAURICE PRE 1890 ISLAND BRIDGE, LEX, IRL [35339] : PRE 1900 QUEENSTOWN, COR, IRL [35339]

FITZPATRICK 1830+ OBERON, NSW, AUS [35410] : 1780-1880 REEDS MILLS & KEMPTVILLE, ONT, CAN [34514] : MICHAEL C1830-1916 RICHIBUCTO, NB, CAN [36244] : 1800-1880 LIVERPOOL, LAN, ENG [34143] : CATHERINE PRE 1874 FER, IRL [33951] : 1780-1850 KID, IRL [34514] : C1860 BELFAST, ANT, IRL [34761] : CATHERINE 1824+ KIK, IRL [34877] : 1800+ KIK, IRL [34877] : C1880 BAGENALSTOWN (NOW MAIN BHEAG), CAR, IRL [35046] : PRE 1890 IRL [35184] : 1800 WIC, IRL [35410] : PRE 1840 BALLYCAHILL, TIP, IRL [35750] : PRE 1850 DOW, IRL [36073] : 1750-1850 TRIM, MEA, IRL [36618] : ALL MEATH, MEA, IRL [37115] : ALL KID, IRL [37115] : PRE 1855 IRL [37563] : BARTHOLOMEW PRE 1860 KELLS, CLA, IRL [37982] : DENIS 1860+ OSSORY TO DUBLIN, IRL [38302] : PRE 1890 SCT [35184] : 1818+ OLD RANDOLPH CO., GA, USA [36973] : PATRICK 1850-1870S LAFAYETTE CO., WI, USA [37001] : PRE 1800 PA, USA [38180]

FITZSIMMONS 1700-1800 CASTLETOWN, IOM, ENG [34872] : 1812-1885 ARM, IRL [36560] : C1860 GLASGOW & EDINBURGH, SCT [37512]

FITZSIMONDS 1845-1990 HINCHINBROOK TWP., QUE, CAN [34377] : PRE 1860 ULSTER, IRL [34377]

FITZSIMONS C1800 DUBLIN, IRL [34843] : C1840 WEM, IRL [35922] : 1830 WEM, IRL [36273] : ALL DOW, IRL [38228] : 1856-1926 AUCKLAND, NZ [35922]

FITZWILLIAM PRE 1840 GIRVAN, AYR, SCT [34197]

FIX ALL WORLDWIDE [38680]

FIXTER 1750+ LIN, ENG [35812]

FLACK 1858+ CASTLEREAGH & MUDGEE, NSW, AUS [34295] : 1900+ AUS [37168] : PRE 1858 BOTTISHAM, CAM, ENG [34295] : ALL CAM, ENG [34744] : 1700 RADWINTER, ESS, ENG [37125] : PRE 1850 CLERKENWELL, LND, ENG [38292]

FLACKNEY 1700+ DRAYTON PARSLOW, BKM, ENG [35874]

FLAD C1750 HAUSEN, HOH, GER [38604]

FLADUNG PRE 1834 RASDORF, KURHESSEN, GER [38618]

FLAHAVIN PRE 1861 LIM, IRL [34412]

FLAHERTY 1829+ WA, AUS [35139] : 1850+ BARNSLEY, YKS, ENG [36704] : ALL IRL [35139] : PRE 1870 SLI, IRL [36704] : 1800S CLA, IRL & AUS [35422]

FLAIG PRE 1830 BAW, BRD [38238]

FLAIN PRE 1930 EAST END, LND, ENG [38581]

FLAMANK PRE 1800 ST IVES & ST COLUMB, CON, ENG [35385] : ALL CON, ENG & AUS [35384]

FLAMM PRE 1600 BEMPILINGEN, BAW, BRD [38615] : ALL SCHWAIGERN, WUE, GER [38574]

FLANAGAN MARTIN C1907 IPSWICH, QLD, AUS [33819] : THOMAS 1863+ IPSWICH, QLD, AUS [33819] : MICHAEL C1907 IPSWICH, QLD, AUS [33819] : ELIZA 1856+ GUNDAROO, NSW, AUS [34885] : 1843+ GOULBURN, NSW, AUS [35335] : C1845-1894 GUNDAROO, NSW, AUS [37559] : 1840+ MONTREAL, QUE, CAN [34368] : 1846-1927 ERINSVILLE, ONT, CAN [38102] : 1834 BIRR, OFF, IRL [33793] : 1857+ DERRY CONNOLY, FER, IRL [35253] : C1818 HILSOCHLIGH (HILLSBOROUGH ?), DOW, IRL [35335] : 1750-1800 DERRYLIN, FER, IRL [37613] : 1775-1850 FER, IRL [37795] : 1846-1927 MAY, IRL [38102] : 1800S ARM, IRL [38422] : BRIDGET 1830-1840 TUAM, GAL, IRL [38780] :

JOHN 1810-1820 TUAM, GAL, IRL [38780] : 1846-1927 SAGINAW, MI, USA [38102]

FLANDERS PHILIP C1759-1841 NH & ME, USA [35324]

FLANN PRE 1700 PORTLAND, DOR, ENG [35211]

FLANNELLY 1840-1950 LEXINGTON & LOUISVILLE, KY, USA [37539]

FLANNERY 1900-1990 CAPTAINS FLAT, ACT, AUS [33778] : 1800S STS, ENG [36038] : 1700+ KILMACSHANE, KIK, IRL [34970]

FLANNIGAN PRE 1835 KILLIDAY, LIM, IRL [37142]

FLANSBURGH 1850-1930 WEST LONGWOOD, FL, USA [34004] : 1650-1900 CLARKSVILLE, ALBANY CO., NY, USA [34004] : 1850-1960 MARLBORO & BOSTON, MA, USA [34004]

FLAQUE PRE 1831 LGE, BEL [35002]

FLASHMAN PRE 1857 LONDON, MDX, ENG [35462]

FLATT 1750-1850 GAYWOOD, NFK, ENG [36394] : 1700S HEDSOR, BKM, ENG [36585] : JOSIAH 1830+ MENDHAM, SFK, ENG [37191]

FLAVELL 1750+ BIRMINGHAM, WAR, ENG [36087]

FLAVELLE ALL DRUMCREE, ARM, IRL [34805]

FLAXMAN 1836+ SA & VIC, AUS [34876] : PRE 1836 ENG [34876] : PRE 1752 TRING, HRT, ENG [35095]

FLEEGE PRE 1677 NL [38544]

FLEEMING PRE 1750 KILRENNY, FIF, SCT [37693]

FLEET C1800 WALPOLE, SFK, ENG [37191] : PRE 1850 PEASENHALL, SFK, ENG [38390]

FLEETWOOD PRE 1850 LIVERPOOL, LAN & LND, ENG [34686] : 1725+ BARNSLEY & DARTON, YKS, ENG [37686] : 1800+ LIVERPOOL, LAN, ENG [37986] : 1750-1820 LAN, ENG [38381] : ALL WORLDWIDE [36789]

FLEGG 1875+ BRIGHTON, VIC, AUS [36278] : 1750 DERSINGHAM, NFK, ENG [36278]

FLEISCHER PRE 1932 CAN [34055] : PRE 1932 WORLDWIDE [34055]

FLEISCHMAN 1800+ WHITMAN CO., WA, MN & WI, USA & GER [34988]

FLEISHER PRE 1942 ALB & BC, CAN [34055]

FLEMING C1878 TOOWOOMBA, QLD, AUS [35158] : 1870-1930S BUNDABERG, QLD, AUS [35158] : 1860+ VIC & SA, AUS [35190] : 1870+ HAWTHORN, VIC, AUS [35359] : 1900+ SYDNEY, NSW, AUS [35359] : 1848+ STRATHALBYN, SA, AUS [36632] : ALL YASS, NSW, AUS & SCT [35518] : 1800-1850 ST SAVIOURS, LND, ENG [33779] : 1800+ ENG [33948] : 1820-1830S ST HELENS, LAN, ENG [35158] : PRE 1800 WESTMINSTER, LND, ENG [35181] : JAMES PRE 1822 CARDINGTON, BDF, ENG [35805] : PRE 1850 LAN, ENG [35853] : C1350 BARTH, STRALSUND, GER [38544] : 1850-1880 INDIAN ARMY, INDIA [33779] : PRE 1860 DUBLIN, IRL [34014] : PRE 1866 ROSSINVER, SLI, IRL [35065] : C1779 CLONCORE, ARM, IRL [36259] : 1740-1800 DERRYMACROW, FER, IRL [37613] : 1800+ BUTLERSTOWN, COR, IRL [38189] : C1800 DRUMBESS, CAV, IRL [38292] : PRE 1880 PIERCESTOWN, WEX, IRL [38435] : 1870+ CHRISTCHURCH, NZ [35359] : PRE 1860 BOTHWELL 7 MOTHERWELL, LKS, SCT [35158] : 1780+ WISHAW, LKS, SCT [35411] : 1760+ KILBARCHAN, RFW, SCT [35503] : 1750+ GALSTON, AYR, SCT [35503] : PRE 1860 HAMILTON, LKS, SCT [35853] : C1750 WIGTON, SCT [36337] : PRE 1900 KILMARNOCK, AYR, SCT [36583] : 1850-1950 ST BERNARD PARISH NEW ORLEANS, LA, USA [37583] : 1791-1793 WARREN, NC, USA [38348]

FLEMMING 1851+ NSW, AUS & ENG [37130] : PRE 1825 BEDFORD, BDF, ENG [37067] : ALL EDINBURGH, SCT [34674]

FLENSBURG 1500-1800 MALMO, MAL, SWE [36320]
FLESCH ALL SCHELINGEN, BAD, GER [38534]
FLESHER PRE 1820 CALVERLEY, WRY, ENG [36583] : 1730-1850 WOOK CO., WV, USA [36450]
FLESSER PRE 1866 SCHMIEDEBERG & MELZOW, PRE, GER [34278]
FLETCHER 1850+ LAUNCESTON, TAS, AUS [34770] : 1850+ WERRIS CREEK, NSW, AUS [34903] : 1800+ WOLLOMBI, NSW, AUS [34903] : 1822 HOBART, TAS, AUS [35705] : WILLIAM 1876+ BINGARA, NSW, AUS [36600] : PRE 1830 HOBART, TAS, AUS & ENG [35758] : C1900+ RAVENSCRAG, SAS, CAN [34101] : 1700-1950 CROWLAND & SPALDING, LIN, ENG [33952] : PRE 1770 OWSTON, LIN, ENG [33992] : PRE 1850 LONDON, ENG [34317] : PRE 1750 HUNGERTON, LEI, ENG [34370] : C1800+ HORNCASTLE & LINCOLN, LIN, ENG [34451] : 1830S ST GILES, MDX, ENG [34518] : PRE 1850 LOOSE, KEN, ENG [34611] : C1810-1830 DROYLSDEN, LAN & CUL, ENG [34727] : 1844 BIRMINGHAM, WAR, ENG [35152] : PRE 1785 HUDDERSFIELD, YKS, ENG [35459] : SOPHIA 1835 KEN, ENG [35471] : ALL CUMBERLAND, CUL, ENG [35579] : JAMES 1800S EAST BARMING, KEN, ENG [35634] : PRE 1780 ESS, ENG [35642] : PRE 1822 BURSTON, NFK, ENG [35705] : PRE 1900 MIDDLESBROUGH, NRY, ENG [36046] : 1800+ GRAVESEND, KEN, ENG [36093] : PRE 1850 LYTHE & EGTON, NRY, ENG [36110] : ALL EXETER, DEV, ENG [36145] : ALL OXFORD, OXF, ENG [36145] : 1750+ EPSOM, SRY, ENG [36232] : 1800-1900 LONDON, MDX, ENG [36438] : 1850+ MICKLETON, GLS, ENG [36807] : 1871+ LADYWOOD, BIRMINGHAM, WAR, ENG [36807] : C1843-1850 WELLS, SOM, ENG [36848] : 1780+ BOTHEL & LORTON, CUL, ENG [37073] : 1700S SNODLAND, KEN, ENG [37921] : PRE 1872 BESWICK, LAN, ENG [38288] : PRE 1850 TIP, IRL [34797] : PRE 1800 LEX, IRL [37498] : 1750+ FER, IRL [38476] : 1830+ EDINBURGH, SCT [34785] : 1840S KILMODAN, ARL, SCT [35123] : 1830+ BALLACHULISH, ARL, SCT [36254] : PRE 1795 NAIRN, NAI, SCT [36513] : HUGH 1770-1848 ISLE OF MULL, ARL, SCT [36712]
FLETCHER-JONES ALL TAS & VIC, AUS [35063]
FLETT HARRY 1780-1860 WICK, CAI, SCT [34884] : PRE 1811 HARRAY, OKI, SCT [35021]
FLEURENT 1700 CAN [38493]
FLEURY 1600+ JSY, CHI [34532] : ALL CHI [36839] : C1500-1690 BN & PCH, FRA [35883] : 1700+ WATERFORD, WAT, IRL [35883] : ALL NZ [36839]
FLEUTY 1700S BE, LND & ESS, CH & ENG [37677] : 1800S WITHAM & HALSTEAD, ESS, ENG [37677]
FLEW C1860 AUS [37963]
FLEWIN PRE 1850 NORTH WEST, KEN, ENG & WLS [36104] : ALL WORLDWIDE [34412]
FLEXMAN C1676 MONKS RISBOROUGH, BKM, ENG [35095]
FLICHMAN 1840 GEBESHEIN HEPSEN, DARMSTADT, BRD [38327] : 1850 YORK TOWNSHIP, ADDISON, IL, USA [38327]
FLICK 1800S BUTLER, PA, USA [34353] : 1823-1883 HUSHVILLE, PA, USA [35316] : C1820-1900 MN & PA, USA [38112]
FLIETSTRA PETER 1826-1860 GRAND HAVEN, MI, USA [35271]
FLIGHT PRE 1800 YARMOUTH, NFK, ENG [36154] : C1800 DEPTFORD, KEN, ENG [36154] : 1850+ SLADES GREEN, ERITH, KEN, ENG [36807] : PRE 1870 POPLAR & BROMLEY, LND, ENG [37871]
FLIN PRE 1800 WHITEHAVEN, CUL, ENG [36822]

FLINDERS PRE 1800 CAM, ENG [35070] : PRE 1748 WARESLEY, HUN, ENG [35728]
FLINDT PRE 1750 OLDENBURG, SHO, GER [38648]
FLINN 1850+ VIC, AUS [35865] : 1900S SRY, ENG [34738] : 1800S MDX, ENG [34738] : C1830 LONDON, ENG [35865] : ALL CAR, IRL [35002]
FLINT 1835-1875 CANBERRA, ACT, AUS [34966] : 1700+ SHIPLEY & CUCKFIELD, SSX, ENG [34749] : 1792 SHIPLEY, SSX, ENG [36384] : PRE 1860 CHUDLEIGH, DEV, ENG [36408] : C1799 HACKNEY, MDX, ENG [37144] : PRE 1880 MADRAS, MADRAS, INDIA [36408] : 1830-1840S WEST GREENOCK, RFW, SCT [34359] : PRE 1880 LINLITHGOW, WLN, SCT [36408] : PRE 1860 WEST CALDER, MLN, SCT [36408] : PRE 1860 PAISLEY, RFW, SCT [36408] : PRE 1860 EDINBURGH, MLN, SCT [36408] : PRE 1800 ALLOA, CLK, SCT [36408] : PRE 1800 GLASGOW, LKS, SCT [36408] : PRE 1860 UPHALL, WLN, SCT [36408] : 1690+ WORCESTER CO., MA, USA [35322] : 1806+ AMESBURY, ESSEX, MA, USA [38571]
FLINTOFF 1800-1900 GANTHORPE, YKS, ENG [35892]
FLINTOFT PRE 1900 NRY, ENG [36048]
FLITCROFT 1800-1900 RICHMOND, SRY, ENG [35524]
FLITTER 1820+ OH, USA [38587]
FLOCK PRE 1910 NEWCASTLE, NSW, AUS [34979] : PRE 1845 ETELLE, BRITTANY, FRA [34858]
FLOCKE 1720-1816 NUEMBRECHT, RPR, GER [38647]
FLOCKHART PRE 1750 CLEISH, KRS, SCT [37242]
FLODL PRE 1890 GROSSTAXEN, OES [34131]
FLOOD 1870+ GRANVILLE, NSW, AUS [33893] : 1860 KINGS PLAINS, NSW, AUS [34038] : THOMAS JAMES 1880+ CAMPBELLTOWN, TAS, AUS [34770] : 1800+ SYDNEY, NSW, AUS [34770] : 1818+ SYDNEY, NSW, AUS [36236] : PRE 1899 BALLARAT, VIC, AUS [36372] : PRE 1860 LANARK CO., ONT, CAN [34376] : 1800-1850 MANCHESTER, ENG [37593] : 1800+ WATERFORD, WAT, IRL [33893] : PRE 1790 DUBLIN, IRL [34445] : JOSEPH PRE 1792 DUB, IRL [35353] : 1793+ CORK, COR, IRL [36236] : ALL MEA, IRL [36545] : 1800+ AVOCA, WIC, IRL [36772] : JOHN C1816 LIM, IRL [37155] : THOMAS 1777+ KID & WIC, IRL [38396] : 1800+ BALLYJAMESDUFF, CAV, IRL & AUS [33769]
FLOOKES PRE 1830 WESTMINSTER, LND, ENG [35495]
FLOOKS 1700+ DEERHURST, GLS, ENG [33802]
FLOR 1650-1850 HALSTED & TILLITSE, DEN [37515]
FLORACK EMMA 1855 BINGLEY, YKS, ENG [36633] : JACOB JOSEPH 1823 BOCHOLT, WEF, GER [36633] : JACOB JOSEPH 1909 DRESDEN, SAX, GER [36633]
FLORANCE 1803-1816 ONT, CAN [34849] : PRE 1803 CHICHESTER, SSX, ENG [34849] : C1800S CHICHESTER (AT ENVIRONS), SSX, ENG [37745] : 1834+ AUCKLAND, NZ [34849] : ALL WORLDWIDE [35080]
FLOREL 1600-1800 KRISTIANSTAD, KRIS, SWE [36320]
FLORENCE C1700-1800 FISHERFORD, BAN, SCT [36843] : PRE 1880 ABERDEEN, ABD, SCT & FRA [34003]
FLORES 1880S MELBOURNE, VIC, AUS [35471]
FLORY 1750-1900 IPSWICH AREA, SFK, ENG [37042] : 1700S PONDICHERY, INDIA [38659] : 1790+ FRANKLIN CO., VA & OH, USA [36540]
FLOURNOY 1800+ AL, USA [37010]

FLOWER 1800S DERBY TWP., ONT, CAN [37423] : 1760 SHOREDITCH, MDX, ENG [34204] : PRE 1850 KILMERSDON, SOM, ENG [34314] : PRE 1840 CAM, ENG [34445] : ALL TANFIELD & FRAMWELLGATE, DUR, ENG [34617] : C1800 LEICESTER, LEI, ENG [35032] : 1700+ NOTTINGHAM, NTT, ENG [35080] : PRE 1750 DOR, SOM & WIL, ENG [36166] : C1700-1800 ORSTON, NTT, ENG [37552] : ALL ROMSEY, HAM, ENG [38358] : ALL WORLDWIDE [34617]

FLOWERDAY 1800-1900S GREENWICH, KEN, ENG & NZ [36874] : PRE 1900 WORLDWIDE [37089]

FLOWERS ALL TANFIELD & FRAMWELLGATE, DUR, ENG [34617] : 1785+ LOWESTOFT & WORLINGHAM, SFK, ENG [35398] : EMMA 1840+ SHOREDITCH, LND, ENG [37775] : ALL WORLDWIDE [34617]

FLOYD 1880 WAVERLEY, NSW, AUS [36640] : PRE 1900 CON, ENG [36508] : PRE 1900 CUL, WES & LAN, ENG [36508] : 1600+ OXF & BKM, ENG [37099] : 1820 LEEDS, YKS, ENG [37112] : PRE 1800 STS, ENG [37389] : THOMAS 1886+ STONEHOUSE, GLS, ENG [37444] : MARGARET PRE 1883 BALLYCALLAN, DON, IRL [36678] : ROBERT PRE 1862 BALLYCALLAN, DON, IRL [36678] : THOMAS 1886+ ST ROLLEX, SCT [37444] : PRE 1770 CHARLESTOWN, MA, USA [34225] : 1840S BENTON CO., AL, USA [36926] : PRE 1900 WLS [36508]

FLUCK 1750+ ISLE OF WIGHT, HAM, ENG [33802] : 1720S HAWLING, GLS, ENG [35259] : 1820+ GLOUCESTER, GLS, ENG [35865] : 1750-1800 TIBBERTON, GLS, ENG [36663]

FLUDE 1750-1850 BETHNAL GREEN, LND, ENG [37223]

FLUDGER C1750+ ENG [37292]

FLUERTY ALL WORLDWIDE [35766]

FLUGGE 1860 PORT GERMEIN, SA, AUS [37186]

FLUISTER ALL WORLDWIDE [37249]

FLUKE 1760S WESTERLEIGH, GLS, ENG [35798]

FLUKS 1700+ ISLE OF WIGHT, HAM, ENG [33802]

FLUTTER ALL UK [34319]

FLUX 1700+ ISLE OF WIGHT, HAM, ENG [33802]

FLYNN ALL DELORAINE & LONGFORD, TAS, AUS [34555] : 1825+ SYDNEY & MAITLAND, NSW, AUS [34978] : 1850+ VIC, AUS [35865] : 1883-1968 CORAKI, NSW, AUS [36293] : PRE 1860 SYDNEY, NSW, AUS [37901] : 1909-1959 HOBART, TAS, AUS & CAN [36293] : 1800+ BLOOMSBURY, MDX, ENG [35914] : 1800+ PLYMOUTH, DEV, ENG [37924] : ALL CASTLEMAINE, KER, IRL [34643] : 1800-1853 CORK CITY, COR, IRL [35132] : 1840+ DUNGARVAN, WAT, IRL [35719] : PRE 1829 LISBURN, ANT & DOW, IRL [35724] : 1840 IRL [36579] : ARTHUR PRE 1845 ROS, IRL [37035] : PRE 1855 CORK, IRL [37957] : PRE 1855 KER, IRL [37957] : C1800-1960 ROS, IRL & SCT [37413] : 1851-1860S EDINBURGH, SCT [37086] : ARTHUR 1860-1872 ST LOUIS, MO, USA [37035] : 1830-1900 GIBSON CO., IN, USA [38234] : 1830-1900 WARRICK CO., IN, USA [38234] : 1875-1925 VANDERBURGH CO., IN, USA [38234]

FOALE 1777 DODBROOKE, DEV, ENG [38469]

FOAN PRE 1850 SOM, ENG [37127]

FOARD 1600-1800 LITTLEHAMPTON, SSX, ENG [34896]

FOARDER 1600-1800 LITTLEHAMPTON, SSX, ENG [34896]

FOAT PRE 1830 KEN, ENG [36143] : 1719-1820 ISLE OF THANET, KEN, ENG [36900]

FOCARD 1700-1800 BENACRE, SFK, ENG [34151]

FOCK 1872-1881 NEW YORK CITY, NY & NJ, USA [37591]

FODEN 1830-1860S WELLESLEY GVE CHELSEA, LND, ENG [35483] : 1770-C1830 ASTBURY HULME & WALFIELD, CHS, ENG [35483] : 1800S NEWCASTLE UNDER LYME, STS, ENG [36816] : PRE 1890 WOLSTANTON, STS, ENG & AUS [37671] : 1884-1910 HAWERA, NZ [36816]

FODER PRE 1870 AMSTERDAM, NL [33876]

FOE ALL ENG [36166]

FOEHN THERESIA 1861+ USA [38655] : 1861+ USA [38655]

FOENNEN 1860S WOHRDEN, SHO, GER [37024]

FOERSTER PRE 1750 GRUNSTADT & BISSERSH, RPF, GER [38681]

FOGAL 1850-1870 YORK CO., ONT, CAN [34482]

FOGARTY 1812+ HOBART, TAS, AUS [35042] : 1822+ MAITLAND, NSW, AUS [35197] : C1880 BATHURST, NSW, AUS [35570] : 1870+ QLD, AUS [36305] : 1880+ DUBBO, NSW, AUS [36648] : 1840-1855 ALYMER EAST, QUE, CAN [36935] : PRE 1840 LND, ENG [37273] : 1841+ CASHEL, TIP, IRL [34781] : PRE 1822 KILKENNY TOWN, KIK, IRL [35197] : PRE 1840 TIP, IRL [35745] : 1800S RORIDSTOWN, TIP, IRL [35768] : PRE 1850 CLOGHAN, OFF, IRL [36619] : 1750+ BALLINLONTY & THURLES, TIP, IRL [37415] : 1700-1830 URLINGFORD, KIK, IRL [38299] : 1840-1990 ROCHESTER, NY, USA [36935]

FOGARTY-CAHILL CORNELIUS C1900+ PORTAGE LA PRAIRIE, MAN, CAN [37415] : THOMAS C1810-1869 CLONLISMULLEN & DROM, TIP, IRL [37415]

FOGARTY-FEGEN C1920+ JERVIS BAY, NSW, AUS [37415] : C1800-1940 BALLINLONTY & THURLES, TIP, IRL [37415]

FOGDEN PRE 1900 DONNINGTON, SSX, ENG [35352]

FOGG C1813 COLCHESTER, ESS & NSW, ENG & AUS [35547]

FOGGETTY 1800 MAY, OFF, IRL [37170]

FOGGON PRE 1850 NBL, ENG [36481] : 1870 DUDLEY, NBL, ENG [36499]

FOGLIANI 1900S NOUMEA, NEW CALEDO [37910]

FOGO 1700-1900 KILLORN, STI, MLN & PER, SCT [34514]

FOINQUINOS ALL OUTER, MONGOLIA [38723] : ALL WORLDWIDE [38723]

FOLBIGG ALL WORLDWIDE [34416]

FOLDER PRE 1800 CUL, ENG [37089] : PRE 1800 LAN, ENG [37089]

FOLEY 1800+ SYDNEY, NSW, AUS [35843] : C1844 HALIFAX, NS, CAN [37305] : JOHN 1830+ LONDON, ENG [36600] : 1790-1837 SEDGLEY & TIPTON, STS, ENG [38248] : 1760 ARKSEY, WRY, ENG [38469] : PRE 1849 KILLALA, MAY, IRL [33822] : 1800-1840 COR, IRL [34183] : PRE 1840 KER, IRL [34368] : JOHN PRE 1833 (QUEENS), LEX, IRL [35232] : PRE 1880 BALLYFAUDEEN, CLA, IRL [35398] : C1850 IRL [35414] : C1840 DERRYNAVEAGH, CLA, IRL [38079] : C1840 O'CALLAGHAN'S MILLS, CLA, IRL [38079] : PRE 1850 COR, IRL [38435] : 1850-1900 NZ [35414] : 1745-1811 LEESBURG, VA, USA [35316] : 1845-1900 KEWEENAW CO., MI, USA [38010] : ELIZA THERESA 1750+ WORLDWIDE [36602]

FOLGER 1700-1900 MARYLEBONE, LND, ENG [37233] : PRE 1852 RATI BOR HAMMER, SIL, GER [38190]

FOLJAMBE 1600-1700 CHESTERFIELD, DBY & WRY, ENG [37339]

FOLKARD 1700-1800 BENACRE, SFK, ENG [34151]

FOLKERS PRE 1870 OSTFRIESLD, NSA, BRD [38435]

FOLKES 1824+ PARRAMATTA, NSW, AUS [34862] :
1780-1805 INDIA [34862] : 1806+ TRALEE, KER,
IRL [34862]

FOLKS 1850 BISHOPS STORTFORD, HRT, ENG
[34546]

FOLLAND 1818-1890 NORTH TAWTON, DEV, ENG
[37709]

FOLLER C1751-1800 NORTHAMPTON, PA, USA
[38348]

FOLLEY 1650+ CON, ENG [36209]

FOLLY 1750+ JACOBSTOW, CON, ENG [38446]

FOLSNER 1750+ GARCHING, BAV, GER [37483]

FOLSTER C1850 LANGEFELDE, SHO, GER & DEN
[34913]

FOLTZ 1790-1833 ALS & LOR, FRA [38201]

FOLWERK 1876+ ELLIS CO., KS, USA [38057]

FONTAIN PRE 1900 MANCHESTER, LAN, ENG
[34360]

FONTAINE ALL MONTMORENCY, QUE, CAN
[34985] : PRE 1845 ST HYACINTHE, QUE, CAN &
FRA [37443] : ALL CAN & USA [35640] : C1630
GENEVA, GE, CH [38348]

FOOD PRE 1840 BIRMINGHAM, WAR, ENG [38420]

FOOKS C1794 WEYHILL & APPLESHAW, HAM &
WIL, ENG [34836]

FOORD 1827+ NSW & VIC, AUS [37554] : 1600-1800
LITTLEHAMPTON, SSX, ENG [34896] : PRE 1827
BRIGHTON, SSX, ENG [37554]

FOORDER 1600-1800 LITTLEHAMPTON, SSX, ENG
[34896]

FOOT 1847-1873 BALLARAT, VIC, AUS [35436] :
1800+ QLD, AUS [38754] : JOB 1780+ OXF, ENG
[33963] : 1800+ BRIGHTON, SSX, ENG [35436] :
THOMAS 1738 BERE FERRERS, DEV, ENG [35471]
: WILLIAM 1776+ BERE FERRERS, DEV, ENG
[35471] : 1770+ WHITECHURCH, DEV, ENG
[35587] : PRE 1815 NORTH CADBURY, SOM, ENG
[35771] : PRE 1800 CHICHESTER, SSX, ENG [36154]

FOOTE C1850S NSW, AUS [33794] : 1819-1839
BOMBALA, NSW, AUS [34976] : 1900+ MAITLAND
& SINGLETON, NSW, AUS [37966] : 1800+ BURIN,
NFD, CAN [34349] : 1800S YARMOUTH, NS, CAN
[35291] : 1800+ HERMITAGE BAY, NFD, CAN
[36684] : 1800-1900 NS, CAN [38421] : PRE 1850
GREAT STAUGHTON, HUN, ENG [33870] : 1819-
1839 MANSTON, DOR, ENG [34976] : HARRIET
C1867-1960 PADDINGTON, LND, ENG [34997] :
1820+ MYTHE, DOR, ENG [35976] : PRE 1900
RAPHOE, DON, IRL [35270] : 1800-1850
MONKSTOWN, DUB, IRL [36390] : 1892+ PERTH,
PER, SCT [35450] : 1800+ KINCLAVEN, PER, SCT
[35450] : PRE 1900 DAUPHIN & CUMBERLAND,
PA, MD, OH, USA [35270] : 1600S SALEM, MA, USA
[35291]

FOOTIT 1800+ SWINDERBY, LIN, ENG [38395]

FOOTLITT PRE 1810 SALTWOOD, KEN, ENG [36645]

FOOTMAN 1860-1870 MALVERN, WOR, ENG [37233]

FOR PRE 1748 KENLEY, SAL, ENG [37897]

FORAN JOHN PRE 1811 LEX, IRL [34539]

FORBES 1860+ HEXHAM, VIC, AUS [36623] : PRE
1855+ LUDDESDOWN, KEN, ENG [34423] : PRE
1787 SOUTHWARK, LND, ENG [35578] : PRE 1800
ROCHESTER, KEN, ENG [38027] : PRE 1816
INDIA [37554] : 1820S DUBLIN, IRL [34260] : 1795-
1825 BANTRY, COR, IRL [36666] : 1800+
EDINBURGH & PORTOBELLO, MLN, SCT [34260]
: 1830+ INVERKEITHING, FIF, SCT [34260] :
1800+ METHLICK, ABD, SCT [34608] : 1700+
ABDIE, FIF, SCT [34637] : MASON 1700S-1800S
EDINBURGH, MLN, SCT [36314] : 1800-1840
LITTLE DUNKELD, PER, SCT [36623] : PRE 1850
ABYSONE, KCD, SCT [36696] : 1830-1890 BEITH,

AYR, SCT [37205] : 1842-1920 WELLINGTON, PER,
SCT & NZ [36255] : 1895+ NEW YORK, NY, USA
[34379] : JOHN PRE 1750 PATASQUATANK CO.,
NC, USA [35328] : AUTHOR 1770 PITT CO., NC,
USA [35328] : ANGELINE PRE 1854 NEW YORK
CITY, NY, USA [37504] : ARTHUR 1800 PITT CO.,
NC, USA [37585] : ALL WORLDWIDE [33868]

FORCE PRE 1827 CORK, COR, IRL [35563] : 1800S
WHIPPANEY, NJ, USA [38019]

FORCEILLE ALL LGE, BEL [35002]

FORD MARGARET 1850 IPSWICH, NSW, AUS
[33929] : 1850S ADELAIDE, SA, AUS [34025] : 1850+
QUEANBEYAN, NSW, AUS [34708] : JOHN 1828+
HOBART, TAS, AUS [34896] : 1860S MELBOURNE,
VIC, AUS [35136] : 1800S MUDGEE, NSW, AUS
[35359] : C1820 MAITLAND, NSW, AUS [35520] :
1860+ GRAFTON, NSW, AUS [35520] : SYDNEY G.
1896 ULTIMO, NSW, AUS [36311] : ARTHUR M.
1893 WEST KOGARAH, NSW, AUS [36311] : 1870+
CLUNES & DUNACH, VIC, AUS [36622] : 1800+
FRANKLIN, TAS, AUS [38288] : 1816+ NSW, AUS
[38389] : 1800+ CHAMPNEYS, NFD, CAN [33852] :
1800S NORBURY, CHS, ENG [33982] : 1750
LANGDON HILLS, ESS, ENG [34204] : ALL RODE,
SOM, ENG [34429] : ALL BURRINGTON, DEV,
ENG [34700] : ALL ROBOROUGH, DEV, ENG
[34700] : 1775 EAST HOATHLY, SSX, ENG [34708] :
1900+ OLDBURY, WOR, ENG [34782] : 1780+
LONDON, ENG [34896] : 1600-1800
LITTLEHAMPTON, SSX, ENG [34896] : 1800S
BERWICK PRIOR, OXF, ENG [35024] : ANN
1800+ CON, ENG [35060] : PRE 1797 SOM, ENG
[35142] : 1840+ CHELSEA, MDX, ENG [35458] :
PRE 1800 NINFIELD, SSX, ENG [35520] : MARY
1724 WORFIELD, SAL, ENG [35794] : 1760-1860
DOR, ENG [35916] : C1810 PORTSEA, ST MARYS,
HAM, ENG [35960] : C1750-1850 HAM, ENG [36289]
: PRE 1850 NINFIELD, SSX, ENG [36393] : 1750-
1880 BRADWELL ON SEA, ESS, ENG [36485] :
1850-1900 ASHBOURNE, DBY, ENG [36495] :
1800+ MONKTON DEVERILL, WIL, ENG [36521] :
1550S KEN, ENG [36560] : 1850 TICEHURST, SSX,
ENG [36584] : SARAH JANE C1871 ENG [36594] :
ALL NORBURY, CHS, ENG [36704] : 1800S
WANDSWORTH, SRY, ENG [36760] : 1825+
SANDBACH AREA, CHS, ENG [36997] : PRE 1850
CAM, COALEY, GLS, ENG [37101] : C1800 DEV,
ENG [37180] : PRE 1800 WOLVERHAMPTON, STS,
ENG [37389] : 1860+ SHOREDITCH & CHELSEA,
LND, ENG [37445] : PRE 1875 ENG [37739] : C1860
MANCHESTER, LAN, ENG [37856] : 1800-1850S
HOUGHTON LE SPRING, DUR, ENG [38269] :
1790S ISLINGTON, MDX, ENG [38269] : 1800S
NRY, ENG [38356] : C1815 DEV, ENG [38389] :
1700+ RICKINGHALL, SFK, ENG [38492] :
ARTHUR G. H. 1860S-1900S LONDON &
ASHFIELD, NSW, ENG & AUS [36311] : FRED J. G.
1860S-1940S LONDON, SYDNEY & BRISBANE,
NSW & QLD, ENG & AUS [36311] : PRE 1860
MILLSTREET, COR, IRL [33835] : PRE 1863 GAL,
IRL [35900] : PRE 1850 WIC, IRL [37313] : 1807
BALLINROBE, MAY, IRL [38069] : 1849+
CHRISTCHURCH, NZ [35960] : 1850 AUCKLAND,
NZ [38069] : REBECCA C1820 EDINBURGH, MLN,
SCT [35391] : PRE 1870 ANS, SCT [36361] : 1776
POLWARTH, BEW, SCT [38269] : PRE 1865
EDINBURGH, SCT & IRL [37852] : C1830
HAMMONDVILLE, USA [35906] : 1790-1900 NY,
USA [36733] : 1850-70 SHULLSBURG, WI, USA
[36909] : MARY VAUGHAN 1868-1914 CHICAGO,
COOK CO., IL, USA [37025] : THOMAS 1868-1918
CHICAGO, COOK CO., IL, USA [37025] : C1640-

C1775 ST MARY'S CO., MD, USA [37029] : 1800S COLUMBIA CO., NY, USA [37568] : 1730-1790 SMITHFIELD, RI, USA [37576] : 1806-1858 CASWELL CO., NC, USA [38120] : PRE 1800 USA [38389] : LABAN B. 1886-1910 MCDONALD CO., MO, USA [38732] : 1670-1860 WOODBRIDGE, NJ & NB, USA & CAN [38225]

FORDE 1864+ STAGEY CREEK, NSW, AUS [35101] : C1849 DERRINRAW, ARM, IRL [34385] : C1871 BELFAST, ANT, IRL [34385] : 1800S GAL, IRL [34607] : 1850+ WAIRO, SOUTHLAND, NZ [34607]

FORDEN 1845+ GEELONG, VIC, AUS [35043] : 1800+ DERBY, DBY, ENG [35043]

FORDER 1823+ MARLBOROUGH, WIL, ENG [35436]

FORDHAM 1750+ MELTON & HOLTON, SFK, ENG [34416] : PRE 1800 ESS, ENG [36379] : ALL WORLDWIDE [37366]

FORDYCE PRE 1860 SHOTTS, LKS, SCT & ENG [36191] : 1800-1820 STEUBENVILLE, OH, USA [38137]

FORECAST 1730 STEPNEY, MDX, ENG [34204]

FOREHEAD PRE 1800 MERE, WIL, ENG [38214]

FOREMAN 1700+ TARADALE, VIC & TIP, AUS & IRL [36303] : PRE 1880 LAXFIELD, SFK, ENG [37416] : 1920+ LOS ANGELES, CA, USA [36582] : ALL WORLDWIDE [36965]

FOREST 1700S ARTHURET, CUL, ENG [33774] : C1816 EDINBURGH, MLN, SCT [34972] : PRE 1750+ STOBO, PEE, SCT [35237]

FORESTER AARON 1700S HARLOWHILL, NBL, ENG [36244] : 1740-1800 WESTCHESTER CO., NY, USA [38227] : 1730-1783 DUTCHESS CO, NY, USA [38479]

FOREY RACHEL 1820+ LONDON, ENG [37748]

FORFAR PRE 1830 BANNOCKBURN & STIRLING, STI, SCT [36125]

FORGAN ALL FIF, SCT [37704]

FORGE 1850+ LONDON, ENG [34782]

FORGHAM 1500-1750 SAL & CHS, ENG [36062]

FORGIE PRE 1800 GLASGOW, SCT [35126]

FORGISON (SEE FERGUS [38188]

FORIS ALL WORLDWIDE [38682]

FORISCH ALL WORLDWIDE [38682]

FORISCHHIDVAR ALL WORLDWIDE [38682]

FORISCH VON FORISCHHIDVAR ALL WORLDWIDE [38682]

FORIS VON FORISCHHIDVAR ALL WORLDWIDE [38682] : SIEDBRUECKBRG ALL WORLDWIDE [38682]

FORKIN 1880 UTAM, GAL, IRL [35376]

FORMAN 1870+ RAVENSWOOD, QLD, AUS [35102] : ALL ENG [35751] : PRE 1800 NY, USA [36969]

FORNERET C1600 GENEVA, GE, CH [38348]

FORNES 1700-1990 ALICANTE, ESP [38346]

FORNO ALL LND, ENG & ITL [37655]

FORREST 1853+ GEELONG, VIC, AUS [33773] : 1840-1890 BURNER & MT BARKER, SA, AUS [34897] : SARAH 1775+ KIRKANDREW UPON ESK, CUL, ENG [33774] : ALL BOULTON, LAN, ENG [34938] : PRE 1820 CHERTSEY, SRY, ENG [35037] : 1700S HEXHAM, NBL, ENG [36851] : 1780+ LONDON, ENG [37341] : ALL BRIXTON & STREATHAM, SRY, ENG [37627] : 1800-1900 OAMARU, OTAGO, NZ [35923] : 1777+ UPHAL, MLN, SCT [33945] : 1790S MID CALDER, MLN, SCT [33945] : PRE 1834 GLASGOW, LKS, SCT [34897] : 1700S ELLON, ABD, SCT [35083] : 1700-1900 NEWARTHILL, LKS, SCT [35923] : ALL AVONSIDE, STI, SCT [37480] : ALL WORLDWIDE [33773]

FORRESTER ALL NEW ANGLEDOOL, NSW, AUS [34938] : 1788+ WINDSOR, NSW, AUS [35586] : 1830S EVANDALE, TAS, AUS [35586] : JOHN 1850-

1890 MELBOURNE, VIC, AUS [35803] : 1850+ MATILDA TWP., ONT, CAN [34051] : WILLIAM C1760-1838 LEEDS GRENVILLE CO., ONT & NB, CAN [38479] : C1770-1850S JOHNSTOWN, ONT, CAN [38479] : 1806-1865 WESTPORT, ONT, CAN [38479] : 1795-1886 SPENCERVILLE & SHANLY, ONT & NY, CAN & USA [38479] : 1800+ BEATH & ABERDOUR, FIF, SCT [33970] : ROBERT 1850+ CARNOCK, FIF, SCT [35803] : 1840 DUPAR, FIF, SCT [35912] : PRE 1800 CLACKMANNAN, CLK, SCT [36041] : 1870-1990 KIRKCALDY, FIF, SCT [36394] : 1700+ KINKELL, PER, SCT [38288] : 1740-1800 WESTCHESTER CO., NY, USA [38227] : 1811-1901 MONTROSE & EMERSON, IA & NE, USA [38479] : 1800-1890 AMSTERDAM, NY & ONT, USA & CAN [38479]

FORRETT ALL CUPAR & KILCONQUHAR, FIF, SCT [37972]

FORSAITH 1715+ BLOXHAM & LONDON, LIN, ENG [36827]

FORSAYETH PRE 1840 BALLINGARRY, TIP, IRL [34036]

FORSBERG C1856 FORS, ESKILTUNA, SWE [38228]

FORSCUE ALL SFK, ENG [35933]

FORSDICK 1800+ LONDON, ENG & NZ [36257]

FORSDYKE PRE 1800 SFK, ENG [37280]

FORSEY PRE 1808 SHOREDITCH, MDX, ENG [35553] : ALL DOR, ENG [36435]

FORSGREN MARIA J. 1870-1960 VANNAS, VASTERBOTTEN, SWE [38104] : KATARINA F. 1875-1965 VANNAS, VASTERBOTTEN, SWE [38104] : GRETA 1829 HAMRANGE, GASTRIKLAND, SWE [38556]

FORSHAW 1849+ VIC, AUS [35473] : 1850-1900 PRESTON, LAN, ENG [35473] : PRE 1850 TARLETON & HOLMES, LAN, ENG [35473] : 1800+ LIVERPOOL & SALFORD, LAN, ENG [35701] : 1940+ HAM, ENG [35701] : 1870+ LAMBETH, SRY & LND, ENG [35701] : PRE 1850 LND & SRY, ENG [37091]

FORSHAY 1800-1900 USA [38115]

FORSHEY ALL WORLDWIDE [37914]

FORST 1780S PLYMOUTH, DEV, ENG [36858]

FORSTER 1884+ NORTH MELBOURNE, VIC, AUS [34289] : 1880+ QUEENSTOWN, TAS, AUS [34289] : PRE 1870 NEWTOWN, NSW, AUS [35781] : ROBERT 1860S+ KEW, VIC, AUS [35876] : 1800S YORK CO., ONT, CAN [37458] : PRE 1830 HEXHAM, NBL, ENG [33940] : 1700-1911 GRAVESEND & SHEERNESS, KEN, ENG [34294] : 1822 BUNBURY, CHS, ENG [34358] : ALL SFK, ENG [35933] : 1800-1850 USWORTH, DUR, ENG [36056] : PRE 1900 NEWCASTLE & TYNEMOUTH, NBL, ENG [36110] : PRE 1800 DOR & HAM, ENG [36175] : PRE 1820 GATESHEAD, DUR, ENG [36202] : MATTHEW C1734-1799 HARLOWHILL, NBL, ENG [36244] : C1750-1850 STOKE DAMEREL, DEV, ENG [37361] : PRE 1700 PENSHAW, DUR, ENG [37635] : PRE 1800 CLIFTON REYNES & OLNEY, BKM, ENG [37712] : 1750+ DURHAM, DUR, ENG [37984] : PRE 1854 LIVERPOOL, LAN, ENG [38085] : PRE 1850 BLACKMORE, ESS, ENG [38205] : PRE 1700 EGGLESCLIFFE, DUR, ENG [38479] : 1730-1750 STANHOPE, DUR, ENG [38516] : 1750 SIEN, PRE, GER [36966] : 1730-1880 AYTON, BEW, SCT [35341] : WILLIAM C1690-1746 WESTCHESTER VILLAGE & CO., NY, USA [38479]

FORSYTH 1877 WARWICK, QLD, AUS [35808] : 1793+ QLD, AUS [37114] : C1800 LND, ENG [34853] : PRE 1780 LIMAVADY, DRY, IRL [37509] : PRE 1850 DERRIAGHY, ANT, IRL [37927] : PRE 1790 FER, IRL [38321] : 1874+ CHRISTCHURCH, NZ

[34673] : 1882+ RIVERTON, SI, NZ [36611] : PRE 1875 BALLINGRY, FIF, SCT [34001] : 1880-1925 GLASGOW, SCT [34867] : 1800+ WICK, CAI & ROX, SCT [35947] : 1900+ DRAINE, INV, SCT [35988] : PRE 1840 AIRDRIE, LKS, SCT [36191] : PRE 1825 FORRES & RAFFORD, MOR, SCT [36338] : PRE 1900 INV, SCT [36800] : PRE 1873 STI, SCT [37114] : 1692-1741 YARROW, SEL, SCT [38117] : PRE 1700 AYR, SCT [38321] : JOHN PRE 1870 CLACKMANNAN, CLK, SCT [38477] : FRANCIS C1830 CLACKMANNAN, CLK, SCT [38477] : CLEMENTINE PRE 1903 ALLOA, CLK, SCT [38477] : ALEXANDER PRE 1850 SCT [38477] : 1730S GROTON, CT, USA [34991] : 1790-1900 BALTIMORE, MD, USA [38321] : 1770-1790 YORK CO., PA, USA [38321]

FORSYTHE 1870S CUL, ENG [35865] : 1750+ BRONFIELD & CROSSCANONBY, CUL, ENG [36049] : PRE 1873 GORTIN, TYR, IRL [34673] : 1868 BALLYEDMOND, DOW, IRL [35865] : 1860-1914 KILLOUGH, DOW, IRL [37636] : 1845+ MAGHERA, DOW, IRL [37636] : 1770-1845 DRUMGOOLAND, DOW, IRL [37636] : 1880-1925 GLASGOW, SCT [34867] : 1826+ CAI, SCT [35880] : 1700+ BORDERS, SCT [35880]

FORTESCUE-ALAND ALL WORLDWIDE [33827]
FORTIER ALL CAN & USA [37515]
FORTNER C1790 NC, USA [37536]
FORTUNE PRE 1850 RATHILE, WEX, IRL [36773] : ALL NZ [36773] : 1800S EDINBURGH, MLN, SCT [34483] : 1850+ DIRLETON, ELN, SCT [35650] : 1780-1850 EDROM, BEW, SCT [36724] : PRE 1800 WLS [37562]

FORTY 1800+ LONDON, ENG [33948]
FORWARD 1700+ BEMERTON, WIL, ENG [34664] : 1800+ SALISBURY, WIL, ENG [34664] : PRE 1830 SSX & KEN, ENG [34816] : 1740-1800 SUTTON WALDRON, DOR, ENG [36987] : 1863 CUCKLINGTON, SOM, ENG [37691] : PRE 1800 MERE, WIL, ENG [38214] : 1860+ NZ [34664]

FORWEAR ELIZA 1828 BORDEAUX, AQU, FRA [35876]
FORWOOD 1700S PORTSMOUTH, HAM, ENG [34937] : 1760S 'MONACOMBE HOUSE', DEV, ENG [34937]

FORYSZ ALL WORLDWIDE [38682]
FOSBERG 1845+ MICHIGAMME, MI & CA, USA [33756]
FOSBERY C1875 LONDON, ENG [36490]
FOSBROOK 1911+ MITCHAM, VIC, AUS [34430]
FOSBURY C1875 LONDON, ENG [36490]
FOSCUE ALL SFK, ENG [35933]
FOSDICK PRE 1773 HARTFORD, CT, USA [34410] : MARIA 1800-1880 WOODSTOCK, IL, USA [37806]
FOSGATE MARSHALL ABEL 1856+ BERLIN, WORCESTER, MA, USA [38183]
FOSKER ALL SFK, ENG [35933]
FOSKETT 1846+ MDX, ENG [35345] : ALL BDF, HRT & BKM, ENG [37738]
FOSKEW ALL SFK, ENG [35933]
FOSS 1700S ARGYLE, NS, CAN [35291] : MARY 1780-1840 PENZANCE, CON, ENG [36297] : 1850+ WORCESTER, WOR, ENG [37384]
FOSSATI PRE 1850 GENOA, ITL [36982]
FOSSEY PRE 1800 SALFORD, BDF, ENG [34588] : C1813 LIDLINGTON, BDF, ENG [36803]
FOSSWAY ELIZA 1828 BORDEAUX, AQU, FRA [35876]
FOSTER 1800+ AUS [33769] : JAMES 1849+ PT ADELAIDE, SA, AUS [34437] : SYDNEY J. PRE 1892 HAY, NSW, AUS [34592] : 1850+ NSW, AUS [34614] : 1850+ TUMUT, NSW, AUS [34978] : 1850+

SOUTH CREEK (ST MARYS), NSW, AUS [35101] : ALF 1900+ SYDNEY, NSW, AUS [36600] : 1840+ PORTLAND, VIC, AUS [36648] : 1800+ GSY, CHI [33948] : 1850+ BRANDESBURTON, YKS, ENG [33861] : 1837-1857 BATH, SOM, ENG [33988] : PRE 1850 COVENTRY, WAR, ENG [34265] : EDWARD C1810+ LONDON, ENG [34486] : PRE 1790 CROWLE, LIN, ENG [34494] : 1830+ LONDON, ENG [34614] : PRE 1856 LIVERPOOL, LAN & YKS, ENG [34648] : STEPHEN C1827 STS, ENG [34792] : PRE 1870 GATESHEAD, DUR, ENG [34858] : PRE 1780 ATTENBOROUGH, NTT, ENG [34858] : 1700+ GUESTLING & LEWES, SSX, ENG [34970] : 1820+ BOVEY TRACEY, DEV, ENG [35114] : C1820 GATESHEAD, DUR, ENG [35153] : 1550+ LONDON &, ESS, ENG [35276] : 1770S BLACKROD, LAN, ENG [35560] : THOMAS PRE 1832 LIVERPOOL, LAN, ENG [35578] : ARTHUR ALFRED 1840+ LND, ENG [35762] : C1830 DODDINGTON, KEN, ENG [35860] : 1700+ ROXBY, YKS, ENG [35908] : ALL SFK, ENG [35933] : 1500-1800 SSX, ENG [35944] : PRE 1730 DARLASTON, STS, ENG [36110] : PRE 1900 YORK & HESLINGTON, YKS, ENG [36110] : 1830+ CARLISLE, CUL, ENG [36138] : ALL GREENS NORTON, NTH, ENG [36144] : 1870+ HAMPSTEAD & KILBURN, LND, ENG [36175] : PRE 1800 DOR & HAM, ENG [36175] : ISABEL C1777+ HARLOWHILL, NBL, ENG [36244] : C1851-52 MANCHESTER, LAN, ENG [36307] : 1800+ TAMWORTH, STS & WAR, ENG [36329] : C1750 OSBERTON, NTT, ENG [36426] : 1760-1800 CLIFTON CAMPVILLE, STA, ENG [36635] : PRE 1850 HANBURY, STS, ENG [36980] : PRE 1800 BILSTON, STS, ENG [36987] : 1880+ DARLASTON, STS, ENG [36991] : PRE 1750 STS & DBY, ENG [37098] : PRE 1822 UDIMORE, SSX, ENG [37104] : PRE 1780 LONDON, ENG [37133] : 1850 GREAT DRIFFIELD, ERY, ENG [37208] : PRE 1797 LISSINGTON, LIN, ENG [37318] : 1750-1880 BARKISLAND & SOYLAND, WRY, ENG [37372] : 1831 PICKERING, YKS, ENG [37442] : WILLIAM PRE 1832 STROUD, GLS, ENG [37454] : 1700+ RATTERY & TOTNES, DEV, ENG [37699] : 1800+ TRURO, CON, ENG [37699] : 1700S HINDERWELL, NRY, ENG [37859] : ALL PEASMARSH, SSX & KEN, ENG [38230] : 1750+ BOLTON, LAN, ENG [38260] : 1750+ BLACKROD & ASPULL, LAN, ENG [38260] : 1830+ HERTFORD, ENG [38274] : 1700+ FEN DISTRICT, LIN & CAM, ENG [38280] : 1750+ YKS, ENG [38440] : 1809-1850S BETHNAL GREEN, MDX, ENG [38441] : 1768-1789 BARNBY UPON DON, WRY, ENG [38469] : 1768-1789 WIL SICKHOUSE, WRY, ENG [38469] : PRE 1850 CAV, IRL [33905] : MICHAEL PRE 1851 DUBLIN, IRL [34437] : PRE 1830 WHITEHALL & KESH, FER, IRL [35430] : 1910+ DUBLIN, IRL [36075] : PRE 1880 RICHHILL, ARM, IRL [36877] : 1800S KIK, IRL [37910] : 1800+ TYR, IRL [37949] : PRE 1856 MONTEGO BAY, JAMAICA [34648] : 1890+ PAHIATUA, WAIRARAPA, NZ [36877] : 1800-1890 EDINBURGH, MLN, SCT [37338] : PRE 1840+ PHILADELPHIA, PA, USA [36578] : 1800+ ALBANY CO., NY, USA [36962] : 1800-1900 MAYVILLE, NY, USA [37464] : PRE 1830 SPARTANBURG, SC, USA [37587] : 1800-1900 FRANKLIN CO., NY, USA [37783] : COLISTA 1858-1890 ST CLAIR CO., MI, USA [38146] : 1700-1810 CT, USA [38342] : JOHN BLAIR 1819-1885 HUNTINGDON CO., PA, USA [38371] : 1800-1900 SOUTHINGTON, CT, USA [38531] : 1836 INDIANA

CO., PA, USA **[38590]** : 1881 SWANSEA, GLA, WLS **[37330]**

FOSTER-LYNAM 1926 STRATHFIELD, NSW, AUS **[34421]**

FOTH C1800-1900 GRAUDENZ, WPR, GER & USA **[38309]** : C1847-1938 MILWAUKEE, WI & NE, USA & GER **[38309]**

FOTHERBY 1800-1850 LIN, ENG **[36084]**

FOTHERGILL 1700+ KIRKBY LONSDALE, CUL, ENG **[36890]** : 1700+ REETH, YKS, ENG **[38034]** : 1700+ REDMIRE, YKS, ENG **[38034]** : 1700+ WEST WITTON, YKS, ENG **[38034]**

FOTHERINGHAM 1940+ NEWCASTLE, NSW, AUS **[33770]** : 1738-1791+ CLACKMANNAN, CLK, SCT **[37108]** : 1822-1865+ OLD MONKLAND, LKS, SCT **[37108]**

FOUCHER 1800-1900 MAREUIL SUR AY, CHA, FRA **[34842]**

FOULDS (SEE FOWLDS) [36436]

FOULGATE 1870+ INDIA **[37274]**

FOULGER C1860 AYLESBURY, BKM, ENG **[37233]** : 1700-1900 MARYLEBONE, LND, ENG **[37233]** : C1850 LIVERPOOL, LAN, ENG **[37233]**

FOULIS ALL EDINBURGH, MLN, SCT **[33946]** : PRE 1810 PAPA WESTRAY, OKI, SCT **[35346]**

FOULKES PRE 1880 GUNNING, NSW, AUS **[35022]** : 1860 BOLTON, LAN, ENG **[35622]** : C1845 STONY STRATFORD, BKM & NTH, ENG **[36668]** : 1750+ DAWLISH, DEV, ENG **[37088]** : 1700-1900 MARYLEBONE, LND, ENG **[37233]**

FOULKNER C1870+ LONDON, ENG **[34238]**

FOULSTON 1870S LITHGOW, NSW, AUS **[38541]**

FOUMIN PRE 1900 TORINO, ITL **[37510]**

FOUND 1700+ DEV, ENG **[36209]**

FOUNTAIN 1865+ BRISBANE, QLD, AUS **[34008]** : ALL CAN & USA **[35640]** : 1800+ WAKEFIELD, YKS, ENG **[34008]** : PRE 1900 MANCHESTER, LAN, ENG **[34360]** : C1832 HAVERSHAM, BKM, ENG **[35104]** : C1840-70 CHELSEA, MDX, ENG **[36153]** : PRE 1850 SOUTHWARK, SRY, ENG **[36153]** : PRE 1870 DOWNHAM, CAM, ESS & NBL, ENG **[36696]** : PRE 1900 NORMANTON, WRY, ENG **[36761]** : PRE 1700 MENTMORE, BKM, ENG **[37765]** : PRE 1690 TOTTERNHOE, BDF, ENG **[37885]** : 1850S LEEDS, YKS, ENG **[38082]** : 1760-1815 YKS, ENG **[38370]** : 1812+ OLDHAM, LAN, ENG **[38370]** : ALL YKS, ENG & AUS **[34189]** : 1900+ JOHNSONVILLE, WGTN, NZ **[36761]**

FOUNTAINE PRE 1840 G & L HALE, LIN, ENG **[35934]**

FOURIE PRE 1668 DAUPHINE, FRA **[36459]**

FOURNESS ALL WORLDWIDE **[33916]**

FOURNIER 1750+ QUE, CAN **[37482]**

FOUSHEE 1780-1790 LOUDON CO., VA, USA **[38763]**

FOWELL PRE 1870 CON, ENG **[37320]**

FOWKES PRE 1750 BYFIELD, NTH, ENG **[35181]**

FOWLDS PRE 1750 KILMARNOCK, AYR, SCT **[36436]**

FOWLER 1857+ CARISBROOK, VIC, AUS **[33896]** : HENRY 1826 CAMPBELLTOWN, NSW, AUS **[34539]** : 1839+ NARELLAN, NSW, AUS **[34791]** : PRE 1840 GOULBURN, NSW, AUS **[37133]** : PRE 1930 NORTH VANCOUVER, BC, CAN **[34519]** : ALL BIRMINGHAM, STS, ENG **[33823]** : 1700 LIN, ENG **[34504]** : JAMES PRE 1792 BRIGHTON, SSX, ENG **[34539]** : HENRY 1792 BRIGHTON, SSX, ENG **[34539]** : 1800-1830 BSM & OXF, ENG **[34667]** : EMMA PRE 1844 BEDMINSTER, SOM, ENG **[34701]** : 1800+ BATH, SOM, ENG **[34791]** : 1815 DACOMB, DEV, ENG **[35041]** : PRE 1770 DOR & SOM, ENG **[35098]** : 1700+ CHARFIELD, GLS, ENG **[35248]** : PRE 1820 LIN, ENG **[35255]** : PRE

1833 CHELTENHAM, GLS, ENG **[35904]** : 1700+ LIN, ENG **[36133]** : PRE 1820 KEN & SSX, ENG **[36272]** : 1800-1900 TAUNTON, SOM, ENG **[36531]** : PRE 1820 SOM, ENG **[37133]** : C1746 DERITEND & BOADESLEY, WAR, ENG **[37144]** : 1700+ TORTINGTON, SSX, ENG **[37206]** : PRE 1900 YKS, ENG **[37377]** : 1800+ STONEHOUSE, DEV, ENG **[37411]** : 1800+ COWFOLD, SSX, ENG **[37816]** : ALL TORRINGTON, DEV, ENG **[37922]** : PRE 1860 LONDON, MDX, ENG **[38760]** : PRE 1908 DUBLIN, IRL **[37701]** : 1858+ AUCKLAND, NZ **[33823]** : 1858+ DUNEDIN, NZ **[34673]** : 1860S TAIERI, OTO, NZ **[36799]** : PRE 1850 HADDINGTON, ELN, SCT **[33959]** : C1830-1858 SOUTH BELTON, ELN, SCT **[34673]** : 1700-1850 LOWLANDS, SCT **[34920]** : PRE 1780 FIF, SCT **[36679]** : 1800-1925 MARLBOROUGH UTICA, NY & WI, USA **[36542]** : SAMUEL 1860 MCCLEAN CO., IL, USA **[38132]** : 1795+ ST ISHMAELS, PEM, WLS **[36254]**

FOWLER (SEE FOLEY) [38079]

FOWLER-GUISE 1850+ WEST MAITLAND, NSW, AUS **[33923]**

FOWLES 1839+ CHIPPENDALE, NSW, AUS **[35419]** : PRE 1849 CROYDON, SRY, ENG **[33801]** : 1700+ TETBURY, GLS, ENG **[34662]** : 1814 BARROWFORD, LAN, ENG **[35282]** : 1800-1899 LAMBETH & LEWISHAM, SRY, ENG **[36101]**

FOWLIE C1819+ FYVIE, ABD, SCT **[36753]**

FOWNES 1500-1650 STAPLETON, DOR, ENG **[34012]** : 1750+ BIRMINGHAM, WAR, ENG **[36087]** : PRE 1780 BROUGHTON, WOR, ENG **[37361]**

FOX 1850+ WA, AUS **[35080]** : CHARLES P. PRE 1890 MELBOURNE, VIC, AUS **[35706]** : CHARLES P. PRE 1890 ADELAIDE, SA, AUS **[35706]** : CHARLES P. PRE 1890 BROKEN HILL, NSW, AUS **[35706]** : CHARLES P. PRE 1890 GEELONG, VIC, AUS **[35706]** : C1850 MAITLAND, NSW, AUS **[35753]** : JOHN 1818+ HOBART AREA, TAS, AUS **[35816]** : JOHN 1850S BRUNSWICK & BACCHUS MARSH, VIC, AUS **[35816]** : 1855 SANDHURST, VIC, AUS **[35855]** : PRE 1860S BERMUDA **[34458]** : 1797+ ONT, CAN **[34126]** : 1867+ HALTON CO., ONT, CAN **[36582]** : 1800S REDRUTH, CON, ENG **[33934]** : PRE 1850 CLAPHAM, SRY, ENG **[34003]** : 1700S PETERBOROUGH, NTH & HUN, ENG **[34032]** : 1750-1850 HOPE, DBY, ENG **[34822]** : MERCY PRE 1855 BURSLEM, STS, ENG **[34935]** : 1820+ BOSTON, LIN, ENG **[35141]** : PRE 1850 BRISTOL, GLS, ENG **[35215]** : 1700+ RINGSHALL, SFK, ENG **[35475]** : 1800-1870 HULL, ERY, ENG **[35706]** : WM. PEARSON 1800S LEEDS, WRY, ENG **[35706]** : GEORGE 1880S ALDERLEY EDGE, CHS, ENG **[35706]** : 1640-1890 SCALBY, ERY, ENG **[35706]** : PRE 1805 TAUNTON, SOM, ENG **[35727]** : C1600-1774 ELSTOW & CARDINGTON, BDF, ENG **[36068]** : ALL FRAMPTON, DOR, ENG **[36069]** : PRE 1820 ECCLESFIELD, WRY, ENG **[36102]** : PRE 1870S LONDON, ENG **[36146]** : JOHN 1830-1880 WOTTON UNDER EDGE, ENG **[36316]** : PRE 1670 SUTTON CUM LOUND, NTT, ENG **[36426]** : 1600-1700 LONDON, MDX, ENG **[36438]** : HANNAH 1761-1843 HOPE, DBY, ENG **[36576]** : 1845+ LEEDS, WRY, ENG **[37202]** : 1600-1720 WIL, ENG **[37232]** : 1600-1700 HAM, ENG **[37232]** : PRE 1800 THANET, KEN, ENG **[37371]** : PRE 1830 BRIXHAM, DEV, ENG **[37393]** : 1840-1900 LIN, ENG **[37495]** : 1800S SHOREDITCH & STOKE NEWINGTON, MDX, ENG **[37834]** : 1790S BETHNAL GREEN, MDX, ENG **[37834]** : 1600+ ST BEES, CUL, ENG **[37858]** : PRE 1824 YKS, ENG **[38080]** : 1750+ OUNDLE, NTH, ENG **[38279]** : PRE 1820 ILKESTON, NTT, ENG **[38389]** : 1739-1740

GRESHAM, NFK, ENG **[38465]** : 1600-1700
NEWCASTLE, STS, ENG **[38474]** : 1800+
FANTAGLEBE & LISDOONVARNA, CLA, IRL
[33829] : JOHN C1830 ASHFORD & KILEEDY, LIM,
IRL **[34070]** : ELLEN 1873 ASHFORD & KILEEDY,
LIM, IRL **[34070]** : JULIA 1878 ASHFORD &
KILEEDY, LIM, IRL **[34070]** : MAURICE 1896
GLANDUFF, BROADFORD NEWCASTLE, LIM,
IRL **[34070]** : JOHN PRE 1818 KILROSS, TYR, IRL
[35816] : 1800+ CLA, IRL **[37202]** : PRE 1862 LOG,
IRL **[37991]** : MICHAEL 1797+ TIP & ONT, IRL &
CAN **[34126]** : 1870S+ NELSON, NZ **[35706]** : PRE
1920S CHRISTCHURCH, NZ **[35706]** : PRE 1800
MELROSE, ROX, SCT **[37127]** : 1800S BUTLER, PA,
USA **[34353]** : 1900 JOPLIN, MO, USA **[36444]** : 1890
MONTGOMERY CO., KS, USA **[36444]** : 1890
RICHMOND, VA, USA **[36924]** : 1700-1800 MORRIS
CO., NJ, USA **[36924]** : PRE 1650 GLOUCESTER
CO., VA, USA **[36973]** : PRE 1830 OH, USA **[37018]** :
1700-1835 HARTFORD CO., CT, USA **[37782]** : PRE
1800 GLASTONBURY, CT, USA **[37808]** : PRE 1803
ONEIDA, NY, USA **[38220]**

FOXAL PRE 1830 LLANHILLETH & GILFACH,
MON, WLS **[37716]**

FOXALL 1700+ KIDDERMINISTER, WOR, ENG
[34711]

FOXCROFT ALL INGLETON, WRY, ENG **[36955]** :
ALL WESTHOUSE & MASONGILL, WRY, ENG
[36955] : C1750 TUNSTALL, LAN, ENG **[36955]** :
ALL THORNTON IN LONSDALE, WRY, ENG
[36955] : C1810 BURTON IN KENDAL, WES, ENG
[36955] : ALL BURTON, WRY, ENG **[36955]** : C1819
NEWCHURCH IN ROSSENDALE, LAN, ENG
[36955] : C1819 EDGESIDE, LAN, ENG **[36955]** :
C1800+ LANCASTER, LAN, ENG **[36955]**

FOXEN 1842 MADRAS, INDIA **[34609]**

FOXHALL 1840-1900 TREDEGAR, MON, WLS **[37716]**

FOXLEY PRE 1900 TODDINGTON, BDF, ENG
[33830] : 1650-1750 CHS, ENG **[36025]**

FOXON C1880 ISLINGTON, LND, ENG **[35014]**

FOXWELL 1813+ BERMONDSEY, SRY, ENG **[35013]**
: PRE 1903 SOM, ENG **[36841]**

FOY CATHERINE 1855-1857 SYDNEY, NSW, AUS
[34171] : C1800-1900 MARYLEBONE &
KENSINGTON, LND, ENG **[36478]** : C1840 CAV,
IRL **[34774]** : PRE 1800 IRL **[36682]** : C1847
MOUNTBELLOW NEAR TUAM, GAL, IRL **[36762]**

FOYSTER ALL CAM, ENG **[35500]** : THOMAS 1761-
1812 NORWICH, NFK, ENG **[37052]** : THOMAS
1800-1900 KENNINGHALL, NFK, ENG **[37052]** :
1700-1800 LITTLE BYTHAM, LIN, ENG **[38287]**

FRACIS PRE 1900 MAINSTONE, SAL, ENG **[37681]**

FRADD 1850+ BURRA, SA, AUS **[35810]** : PRE 1850
ST MAWGAN IN PYDAR, CON, ENG **[35810]** : PRE
1830 PLYMOUTH, DEV, ENG **[37630]**

FRADGLEIGH 1800S DUDLEY, WOR, ENG **[34427]**

FRADLEY (SEE FRADLEI **[34427]**

FRADSHAM 1750-1800 ATHERSTONE, WAR, ENG
[35320]

FRAGASSO PRE 1850 ITL **[34984]**

FRAGSTEIN ALL WORLDWIDE **[37728]**

FRAHER 1800+ DUNGARVAN, WAT, IRL **[35719]** :
1750+ TIP, IRL **[36602]**

FRAIN PRE 1840 IRL **[37094]** : 1840+ WORLDWIDE
[37094]

FRAIZER 1750+ PHILADELPHIA CO., PA, USA
[36580]

FRAMBOLD 1840-1890 REUTLINGEN, GER **[37296]**

FRAME PRE 1804 TULLIALLAN, PER, SCT **[34037]** :
1800+ BARONY, LKS, SCT **[35977]** : 1700+
STRATHAVEN, LKS, SCT **[37480]**

FRAMPTON ALL CHARLEVILLE, QLD, AUS **[35118]**
: 1800+ BLANDFORD FORUM, DOR, ENG **[34228]**
: 1700-1800 STAINES & GUSSAGE, MDX & DOR,
ENG **[34552]** : 1800-1900 PECKHAM RYE, SRY,
ENG **[36817]**

FRANC 1700+ BREMEN, NSA, GER **[38578]**

FRANCE 1880+ NSW, AUS **[37309]** : ALL
WAKEFIELD, WRY, ENG **[33916]** : PRE 1850 YKS,
ENG **[35745]** : 1700-1850 SHEFFIELD &
HANDSWORTH, WRY, ENG **[36727]** : ALL YKS,
ENG **[37115]** : ALL LIN, ENG **[37115]** : ALL LOUTH,
LIN, ENG **[37115]** : ALL YKS, ENG **[37115]** : 1700+
LAN, ENG **[37309]** : PRE 1780 WIGAN, LAN &
DBY, ENG **[38028]**

FRANCES 1200-1990 ENG & USA **[36114]**

FRANCIS 1860+ YINNAR, VIC, AUS **[34414]** : PRE
1900 NSW, AUS **[34536]** : PRE 1855 BARNSTAPLE,
DEV, ENG **[34582]** : 1650-1720 GWENNAP, CON,
ENG **[34793]** : PRE 1850 ROMFORD, ESS, ENG
[34825] : C1850 LONDON, ENG **[35050]** : PRE 1850
LND, ENG **[35055]** : PRE 1849+ SOM, ENG **[35064]** :
1813 HARLOW, ESS, ENG **[35251]** : 1850+
HACKNEY, MDX, ENG **[35458]** : PRE 1847+
MARYLEBONE, LND & MDX, ENG **[35460]** : PRE
1780 ESS, ENG **[35642]** : 1700-1900 SHIPLEY, SSX,
ENG **[35643]** : 1730S-1808 CHESTER, CHS, ENG
[35815] : C1900 STONEDON & REDHILL, BDF &
SRY, ENG **[36104]** : 1790+ ARDLEIGH, ESS, ENG
[36252] : 1930+ ASHFORD, MDX, ENG **[36252]** :
HENRY C1805 ARDLEIGH, ESS & SFK, ENG
[36252] : 1890+ WEST BROMPTON, LND, ENG
[36252] : 1860+ LITTLE BROMLEY, ESS, ENG
[36252] : 1875+ MARYLEBONE, LND, ENG **[36252]**
: 1850-1880 ALTON, HAM, ENG **[36292]** : 1700-1900
IOW & PORTSEA, HAM, ENG **[36409]** : 1840+
KEMPSTON, BDF, ENG **[36414]** : 1822+ CON,
ENG **[36608]** : JOHN 1707-1750 NFK, ENG **[36678]** :
1800+ LAMBETH, LND, ENG **[36785]** : PRE 1837
GREAT YARMOUTH, NFK, ENG **[36876]** : 1700S
ST ENODER, CON, ENG **[36961]** : C1778
ATTLEBOROUGH, NFK, ENG **[37053]** : PRE 1850
BKM, ENG **[37078]** : ALL CREDITON, DEV, ENG
[37195] : PRE 1800 INGHAM & TWYFORD, NFK,
ENG **[37246]** : PRE 1888 STAVELEY, DBY, ENG
[37267] : C1790-1840 FUGGLESTONE, WIL, ENG
[37287] : 1830-1859 OXF, ENG **[37301]** : PRE 1800
STOKE DAMEREL, DEV, ENG **[37410]** : C1880-1900
ALNWICK, NBL, ENG **[37447]** : 1872
BERMONDSEY, SRY, ENG **[37723]** : PRE 1811
SOM, ENG **[37957]** : 1800-1900 SNODLAND,
CUXTON & HALLING, KEN, ENG **[38354]** : 1750+
BRADWORTHY, DEV, ENG **[38446]** : 1780-1853 ST
AUSTELL & WILLIAMSTOWN, CON & SA, ENG &
AUS **[36371]** : 1200-1990 ENG & USA **[36114]** : C1828
MONKSTOWN & KINGSTON, DUB, IRL **[34157]** :
C1833-1912 MENLO, GAL, IRL **[35900]** : 1800-1900
MA, USA **[34631]** : ROBERT 1830-1879 BEAVER &
LAWRENCE CO., PA, USA **[37590]** : 1630-1700
WETHERSFIELD, CT, USA **[37783]** : 1700+
BRIDGEND, GLA, WLS **[34414]** : PRE 1850 MGY,
WLS **[37245]** : C1770+ ST CLEARS, CMN, WLS
[37447]

FRANCISCO ALL WORLDWIDE **[35579]**

FRANCKOMBE 1750-1850 SRY, ENG **[37137]**

FRANCOIS CHARLES C1575 MUCHEDENT, HN,
FRA **[36681]** : PRE 1600 VALENCIENES,
HAINAUT, FRA **[38696]** : C1650 AMSTERDAM,
NOH, NL **[38696]** : 1700 MIDDELBURG, ZEL, NL
[38696]

FRANCOMBE 1700-1800 BATH, SOM, ENG **[36155]**

FRANCOME 1830S FARRINGDON, BRK, ENG
[34172] : 1800+ FARRINGDON, BRK, ENG **[34681]** :

1800+ RODBOURNE & CHENEY, WIL, ENG
[34681] : 1700+ HADENWICK, WIL, ENG [34681]
FRANDSEN PRE 1910 VAMDRUP, RIBE, DEN [37034]
FRANK 1840+ BUTZBACK & FRANKFURT, HES,
GER [33882] : 1800+ NEUENDORF, WPR, GER
[37542] : 1700-1820 GOLS, BUR, OES [36957] : JOHN
PRE 1914 POTSDAM, NY, USA & IRL [38140]
FRANKCOM 1800+ BARRIE, ONT, CAN [34466] :
ALL HAWKESBURY, GLS, ENG [34466] : 1700
BAUTON, GLS, ENG [34466] : ALL WOTTON
UNDER EDGE, GLS, ENG [34466] : ALL LITTLE
BADMINTON, GLS, ENG [34466] : ALL TRESHAM,
GLS, ENG [34466] : ALL OLD SODBURY, GLS,
ENG [34466] : 1850+ WOTTON UNDER EDGE,
GLS, ENG [34484] : ALL HAWKESBURY, GLS,
ENG [34484] : 1830-1852 GLS, ENG & AUS [35592]
FRANKE PRE 1860 CAROW, MAG, DDR [34588]
FRANKENSTEIN 1830 BUETOW, POM, GER [34388] :
1800-1880 BERLIN, GER [38199]
FRANKFIELD C1850 GLOUCESTER, GLS, ENG
[34734]
FRANKING 1841 HARDINGTON MANDEVILLE,
SOM, ENG [37378]
FRANKISH 1780+ LIN, ENG [35377]
FRANKLAND 1850+ BARNARD CASTLE, DUR,
ENG [35806]
FRANKLIN 1850+ NSW, AUS [35352] : ALL
BRINDABELLA, NSW, AUS [35561] : 1853+
WAVERLEY, NSW, AUS [35574] : WILLIAM 1850+
CAMPBELLTOWN & ADELONG, NSW, AUS
[36600] : 1872 SANDHURST, VIC, AUS [37178] : ALL
LITTLE KIMBLE & WENDOVER, BKM, ENG
[34032] : 1725+ RUGELEY, STS, ENG [34639] :
1870S WHITTLESEA, CAM, ENG [35188] : 1840S ST
NEOTS, HUN, ENG [35188] : 1900S BIRMINGHAM,
WAR, ENG [35188] : PRE 1853 MDX, ENG [35574] :
1700-1850 AVEBURY, WIL, ENG [36158] : ALL
WAR, ENG [37404] : C1790+ WHITECHAPEL,
MDX, ENG [37494] : PRE 1850 BICKENHALL,
SOM, ENG [38018] : 1800S LIM, IRL [34845] : PRE
1880 LIM, IRL [36773] : 1800+ USA [34511] : PETER
1760 PHILADELPHIA, PA, USA [36925] : 1600-1750
BRISTOL CO., MA, USA [38108]
FRANKLYN 1850+ WA, AUS [33973] : 1500+ HRT &
MDX, ENG [33973]
FRANKS 1840+ CARLINGFORD, NSW, AUS [35360] :
1830+ SOUTH MONAGHAN, ONT, CAN [34507] :
PRE 1800 LONDON, MDX & SRY, ENG [34343] :
ALL GEDNEY, LIN, ENG [34362] : 1800S LND &
MDX, ENG [34791] : PRE 1853 LONDON, ENG
[35776] : 1600-1700 STS, ENG [36062] : PRE 1820
KEN, ENG [38755] : PRE 1830 ROSCREA, TIP, IRL
[34507]
FRANSE 1808+ KRUININGEN, ZEL, NL [38358]
FRANSEN 1772+ KLOETINGE, ZEL, NL [38358]
FRANSHAM 1700+ NORFOLK, NFK, ENG & NZ
[36257]
FRANSSEN PRE 1750 GOES, ZEL, NL [38358]
FRANTZ ALL WORLDWIDE [36540]
FRANZ 1762 RUETHEN, GER [38748]
FRANZEN 1800+ DUPAGE CO., IL, USA [37012]
FRARY 1635+ MA, USA [38021] : PRE 1750 MA, USA
& ENG [38746]
FRASCA PRE 1920 MARTONE, CALABRIA, ITL
[36271]
FRASE 1870-1880S LOGON & ELLICE, ONT, CAN
[37550] : 1700-1900 VANSBURG WITTUN, PRE,
GER [37550] : 1881-1897 EIMORE, MN, USA [37550]
FRASER PRE 1870 LAUNCESTON, TAS, AUS [33876]
: ALL AMHERST, VIC, AUS [34536] : 1857+
LIGHTS, SA, AUS [34685] : C1880 VIC, AUS [35826] :
ALL SYDNEY, NSW, AUS [36774] : 1900+

ZEEHAN, TAS, AUS [38729] : 1900+ BC, CAN
[34062] : DANIEL 1780+ ERNESTOWN &
ADDINGTON CO., ONT, CAN [34486] : ALL
STONEHAM, QUE, CAN [34489] : C1836 E
NISSOURI, ONT, CAN [34491] : SARAH 1800S
GREENHILL, PICTOU, NS, CAN [37499] : 1820-1850
LEEDS, ONT, CAN [38097] : 1847+
CAMBERWELL, LND, ENG [35710] : 1870-1890
LONDON, ENG [36116] : THOMAS PRE 1815
LAMBETH, SRY, ENG [37321] : 1810-1850S SLI, IRL
[34248] : PRE 1847 BANTRY, COR, IRL [35710] :
1880+ NZ [33921] : 1867+ DUNEDIN &
CHRISTCHURCH, NZ [35710] : C1870 DUNEDIN,
OTAGO, NZ [35826] : 1860+ LESMAHAGOW, LKS,
SCT [33795] : PRE 1800 ACHNAI'GAIRN, INV, SCT
[33884] : 1800-1854 BUCHANAN, STI, SCT [34156] :
C1820-1854 DRYMEN, STI, SCT [34156] : PRE 1808
AULDEARN, NAI, SCT [34391] : 1750-1850 LOGIE,
ROC, SCT [34523] : JAMES PRE 1900 GLASGOW,
SCT [34536] : JOHN PRE 1830 INVERURIE, ABD,
SCT [34613] : MARGARET C1770-1860 BAN, SCT
[34646] : 1800 URQUHART, INV, SCT [34843] : PRE
1851 CLYNE, SUT, SCT [35530] : PRE 1840 NIGG,
ROC, SCT [35710] : C1851+ PAISLEY, RFW, SCT
[35826] : PRE 1850 INVERNESS, INV, SCT [35925] :
PRE 1900 ANS, SCT [35950] : 1750-1850
DINGWALL, ROC, SCT [36240] : PRE 1900 NIGG,
ROC, SCT [36260] : 1800-1850 DORES, INV, SCT
[36724] : ALL KILMARNOCK, AYR, SCT [36774] :
JAMES 1780-1830 KIRKMICHAEL, BAN, SCT
[36783] : JAMES 1830-1875 KEITH, BAN, SCT [36783]
: 1847 FORTROSE, ROC, SCT [36804] : 1800+
URQUHART, ROC, SCT [36857] : 1750+
FRASERBURGH, ABD, SCT [36887] : 1818+
FERINTOSH, ROC, SCT [37329] : C1800-1860
DORES, INV, SCT [38541] : PRE 1880 KY & IL, USA
[38013]
FRASER-SUTHERLAND 1881+ NARACOORTE, SA,
AUS [35025]
FRATER PRE 1900 MANCHESTER, LAN, ENG
[34851] : 1922+ USA [34851]
FRATZKE ALL GRABIONNE, POS, GER [38372]
FRAUEN 1650+ NEUENKIRCHEN, SHO, GER
[38651]
FRAWLEY 1890+ ST ARNAUD & STAWELL, VIC,
AUS [36622] : 1800 CLA, IRL [35067] : C1824 CLA,
IRL [35249] : C1840 CROUGH, LIM, IRL [35365] :
ALL GREAT BEND, PA, USA & IRL [37503]
FRAYER C1800 HAVRE DE GRACE, FRA [37718]
FRAZER PRE 1860 SYDNEY, NSW, AUS [35008] :
JAMES 1774 NSW, AUS [35831] : PRE 1800+
SHANRAHAN & WATERFORD, TIP, IRL [35793] :
1700S+ LAURENCEKIRK, KCD, SCT [37485] :
PRE 1817 PERTH, PER, SCT [37496] : PRE 1800
TRANENT, ELN, SCT [37852]
FRAZIER 1750+ PHILADELPHIA CO., PA, USA
[36580] : 1860S CO, USA [36729] : 1830S RANDULPH
CO., IN, USA [36729] : 1780 GRANVILLE, NC, USA
[38198] : WM. HENRY 1850-1906 SPARTANBURG,
CHATAGUA, PA, USA [38780] : WM. HENRY 1850-
1906 LEON, ERIE, PA, USA [38780]
FREARSON 1820+ HOLBORN, LND, ENG [35027] :
1800+ IDLE & THACKLEY, WRY, ENG [36617]
FREAS 1730+ KNOWLTON TWP., NJ, USA [34130]
FREDERICK WILLIAM L. 1856-1929 PITTSBURG,
PA, USA & GER [37813]
FREDERICKSON PRE 1869 ISLAND OF
BORNHOLM, DEN [33959]
FREDRICKSEN 1870S LOLLAND, DEN [35638]
FREE PRE 1870 BKM, ENG [37692] : 1736+ PA, USA
[37578] : 1749-1830 SC, USA [37578] : 1830-1876

LAWRENCE CO., AL, USA [37578] : 1876-1910 BURNETT CO., TX, USA [37578]

FREEBORN PRE 1800 LND, ENG [34819] : PRE 1680 WONSTON, HAM, ENG [38003]

FREEBURY 1700+ MINCHINHAMPTON, GLS, ENG [34664] : PRE 1880 CHIRK & ALL, SAL, ENG [36082]

FREEDER ALL ENG & RSA [37742]

FREEDY 1780S QUE, CAN [38422] : ALL WORLDWIDE [38422]

FREEGARD 1800+ BREMHILL, WIL, ENG [36323]

FREEL 1800+ LIVERPOOL, LAN, ENG [36871] : PRE 1900 BELFAST, ANT & DOW, IRL [38481]

FREELAND C1880-1890 STAWELL, VIC, AUS [34748] : 1800+ CUMBERNAULD, DNB, SCT [36875]

FREEMAN WILLIAM 1842 GREENWICH, EBOR, NSW, AUS [34539] : THOMAS 1876+ WIRRIALPA, NSW, AUS [34539] : DONALD 1864+ NEW ENGLAND, NSW, AUS [35223] : 1888+ NHILL, VIC, AUS [35223] : 1840S SINGLETON, NSW, AUS [35331] : 1904+ QUEENSTOWN, TAS, AUS [35748] : C1875 DAYLESFORD, VIC, AUS [35748] : ALL NSW, AUS & ENG [34645] : 1850+ AUS & NZ [36088] : ALL BEL & NL [35924] : ORMAND 1890-1910 STETTLER, ALB, CAN [38409] : ORMAND 1800-1910 LETHBRIDGE, ALB, CAN [38409] : 1850S LOWESTOFT, SFK, ENG [33934] : 1800-1900S RUSHDEN, NTH, ENG [33958] : THOMAS 1674 ST BOTOLPH, LND, ENG [34539] : FRANCIS 1707 WATFORD, HRT, ENG [34539] : WILLIAM 1804 HEMEL HEMPSTEAD, HRT, ENG [34539] : FRANCIS 1749 GREAT GADDESDEN, HRT, ENG [34539] : THOMAS 1780 GREAT GADDESDEN, HRT, ENG [34539] : PRE 1810 GUNWALLOE, CON, ENG [34683] : 1900S SHEFFIELD, YKS, ENG [34937] : PRE 1748 BURWASH, SSX, ENG [35259] : C1687 HAWLING, GLS, ENG [35259] : 1830+ CORTON, SFK, ENG [35725] : 1700+ ROCHESTER, KEN, ENG [35924] : 1750+ CHILTON, BKM, ENG [36088] : 1700+ AYLESBURY, BKM, ENG [36093] : PRE 1858 HALIFAX, WRY, ENG [36766] : 1700+ LUTON, BDF, ENG [36922] : PRE 1620 BILLINGSHURST, SSX, ENG [36944] : PRE 1800 TREDINGTON, WOR, ENG [37371] : C1600-1810 KENSALE & MARLESFORD, SFK, ENG [37642] : C1820 UDIMORE & RYE, SSX, ENG [37915] : 1850-1920 SPALDING, LIN, ENG [38471] : 1800-1950 SPALDING, LIN, ENG [38471] : 1876+ MADRAS, INDIA [34667] : 1850+ CANTERBURY & NEW PLYMOUTH, NZ [34049] : 1857+ GREEN IS, DUNEDIN, OTAGO, NZ [36766] : 1630-1850 BOSTON, ATTLEBORO & DANA, MA, USA [36335] : 1691-1812 EASTHAM, MA, USA [36944] : 1680 SANDWICH, MA, USA [36944] : 1800S ANDREW CO., MO, USA [37562] : 1850S AL, USA [37792] : 1858 AL, USA [37792] : 1730-1830 MIDDLESEX, NJ, USA [38366] : 1830S CHATHAM, NJ, USA [38366] : PRE 1700 MA & SSX, USA & ENG [38746]

FREEMANTLE 1800+ LONDON, ENG [34341] : 1800 ENG [35873] : 1795+ LONDON, ENG [37132] : ALL HAM & WIL, ENG [38265]

FREEMON PRE 1900 TN & NC, USA [35312]

FREEN ALL HEF, ENG [37103]

FREER 1820-1840 ORLEANS CO., NY, USA [37576]

FREES 1857+ MELBOURNE, VIC, AUS [35096]

FREESE 1850-1900 NZ [34016]

FREESTONE 1800-1860 ISLINGTON, MDX, ENG [37207]

FREGGLETON C1706 CLAVERLEY, SAL, ENG [37710]

FREI JOHANN JAKOB PRE 1782 HENDSCHIKEN, AG, CH [34992] : ALL OBEREHRENDINGEN, AG,

CH [38609] : ALL AMINGEN, BRD, GER [34938] : ALL LINZ, OOE, OES [33814]

FREIDLANDER 1800S WHITECHAPEL, LND, ENG [38285]

FREITAS 1830S FLEURS, LISBON, PT [38204] : JOAO 1870 HONOKAU, HI, USA [37501] : 1890+ SAN JOAQUIN CO., CA, USA [38323]

FRELIGH 1790+ NEW YORK, NY, USA [34379]

FREMAUX 1700-1750 ST QUENTIN, PIC, FRA [36081]

FRENCH PRE 1858 TENTERFIELD, NSW, AUS [33807] : PRE 1890 LATROBE, TAS, AUS [33878] : 1840 LONGFORD, TAS, AUS [35089] : 1840+ LAMBOURNE, ESS, ENG [34272] : PRE 1930 HUNSLET & BRAMHALL, YKS, ENG [34382] : 1760-1820 LOOSE & ROCHESTER, KEN, ENG [34738] : ALL TAUNTON, SOM, ENG [34817] : ALL SOM, ENG [34817] : PRE 1848 WOR, ENG [35083] : PRE 1880 MERRINGTON, DUR, ENG [35212] : 1800+ GREENWICH, KEN, ENG [35465] : 1680-1753 ULEY, GLS, ENG [35960] : 1753-1872 LEONARD STANLEY, GLS, ENG [35960] : PRE 1885 CAMDEN TOWN, LND, ENG [36028] : 1815-1850 MESSING, ESS, ENG [36136] : PRE 1850 DEV, ENG [36765] : 1700-1800 NFK, ENG [37207] : 1780-1830 MERRIOTT, SOM, ENG [37533] : PRE 1900 ENG [37595] : ALL DUR, ENG [37704] : 1700-1800 WOLVERTON, BKM, ENG [37716] : 1720S DUNMOW, ESS, ENG [37721] : 1800S WHITE RHODING, ESS, ENG [37721] : 1800S HATFIELD BROAD OAK, ESS, ENG [37721] : 1820+ LIVERPOOL, LAN, ENG [37908] : 1600 SFK, ENG [38131] : PRE 1830 MAIDSTONE, KEN & SSX, ENG [38254] : PRE 1700 NETHER HEYFORD, NTH, ENG [38746] : 1800-1850 LOU, IRL [34200] : PRE 1860 DRY, IRL [34277] : 1850-1900 RICHARDSTOWN, LOU, IRL [37326] : 1800-1870 GAL, IRL [38041] : PRE 1848 ANT, IRL [38435] : 1860+ AUCKLAND, NZ [34588] : 1872+ AUCKLAND, NZ [35960] : 1700+ LKS, SCT [33980] : PRE 1780 LANARK, LKS, SCT [37374] : 1700 BOSTON, MA, USA [34466] : 1801-1875 NY, OH & MI, USA [36910] : 1720-1820 NH, USA [36913] : 1810-1850 LAWRENCE CO., AL, USA [37578] : 1900S OH, USA [37721] : PRE 1758 CULPEPER, VA, USA [37819] : HANNAH 1700-1745 WINDHAM, CT, USA [38130] : 1650S CT, USA [38184] : ALL COVINGTON, IN & NJ, USA [38287]

FRENDO ALL MALTA [37247]

FRENKEL 1909 JESSEN ELSTER, KSA, GER [38748] : 1837 ZEHBITZ, KSA, GER [38748] : 1837 ZEHBITZ, KSA, GER [38750]

FRESHWATER 1800S LITTLE PAXTON, HUN, ENG [35188] : PRE 1850 MELDRETH, CAM, ENG [37137]

FRETUS 1830+ SYDNEY, NSW, AUS [38204]

FRETZ ALL KENT CO., ONT, CAN [34154]

FREUD 1736 PERLEBERG, BRA, GER [37509]

FREUND PRE 1787 SCHLUCTERN, BAV, GER [36358]

FREW 1839 NS, CAN [37952] : 1800+ KILLINCHY, DOW, IRL [34190] : PRE 1840 KILMARNOCK, AYR, SCT [34003] : PRE 1800 KILWINNING, AYR, SCT [34112] : 1700+ AVONDALE, LKS, SCT [36764] : 1800+ GLASSFORD, LKS, SCT [36764] : 1721+ AVONDALE & STRATHAVEN, LKS, SCT [37399] : JAMES C1834 EDINBURGH, MLN, SCT & AUS [37143]

FREWETT 1750-1850 ENG [37137]

FREWIN ALL PYRTON, OXF, ENG [34429] : 1800-1814 STEPNEY, MDX, ENG [37251] : PRE 1799 STANFORD IN THE VALE, OXF, ENG [37655]

FREY PRE 1840 BAW, BRD [37565] : PRE 1848 WUTENBURG, BAW, BRD [38738] : C1814 NUSSLOCH, BAD, GER [34239] : ALL NUESS, WEF, GER [34861] : ALL MAGOLSHEIM, DDR,

GER [34938] : 1820-1850 SCHWARZWALD, BAD, GER [36896] : PRE 1675 KRAIGHAU, WUE, GER [36972] : PRE 1800 WEIDENTHAL, RPF, GER [38681] : PRE 1850 WAXHONANDER, PRE, GER [38768] : 1840+ ROSS CO., OH, USA [37565]

FRIAR PRE 1950 BANBRIDGE, DOW, IRL [38286] : 1860+ NZ [38286]

FRIDD PRE 1873 KEN, ENG [35351]

FRIDLEY 1850+ BLOOMINGTON, PA & IL, USA [37581]

FRIEBE C1850 LIEGNITZ, SIL, GER [34367]

FRIED 1830-1900 CINCINNATI, OH, USA [38149]

FRIEDA ALL ENG [37742]

FRIEDEWALD 1850+ SYDNEY, NSW, AUS [34544] : PRE 1850 KAFERTAL, BRD [34544]

FRIEDMAN 1700-1850 BAV, GER [38128]

FRIEDRICHS 1713-1733 PIVITSHEIDE, LIP, GER [38671]

FRIEDRICKS 1940-1977 OXFORD, MI, USA [33853]

FRIEL 1800-1880 KILMACRENAN, DON, IRL [35833]

FRIEND 1800-1900 WESTERHAM, KEN, ENG [34641] : PRE 1850 HYTHE, KEN, ENG [34725] : PRE 1820 BKM, ENG [34816] : 1850-1900 NELSON, NZ [34641]

FRIENDSHIP ALL LND, ENG [37279]

FRIER 1840-80 WALSALL, STS, ENG [36508] : PRE 1837 SCT [38437]

FRIES PRE 1810 PA, USA [37795] : 1830-1900 CINCINNATI, OH, USA [38149]

FRIETSCH 1860+ FIN & USA [38547]

FRIGAULT FRANCOIS PRE 1760 TEURTEVILLE, BN, FRA [38408]

FRIGEIRO 1800+ LONDON, ENG [35342]

FRIGGENS C1880 NATAL, RSA [38263] : ALL WORLDWIDE [38263]

FRIIS 1600+ KOPSHOLT & KLAUTOFT, DEN [35096]

FRINK DAVID C1800-1870 FREDERICKSBURG, ONT, CAN [37441]

FRISBEE 1883+ MELBOURNE, VIC, AUS [35746] : 1858-C1870 MELBOURNE, VIC, AUS [35746] : C1870-1883 ETON, BRK, ENG [35746] : C1822 LND, ENG [35746]

FRISBY 1800S ENG [35161] : 1700S PRESTLAND, RUT, ENG [36817] : PRE 1800 OAKHAM, RUT, ENG [37392]

FRISCHBIER PRE 1830S GUNTERBERG, UCKERMARK, GER [34766]

FRISK 1900S HAWERA, TARANAKI, NZ [36750] : 1860-1940 WAIMATE, CANTERBURY, NZ [36750] : 1900S WELLINGTON, NZ [36750]

FRISKE 1800+ GER [34087] : 1800+ AUTEMOFHA, POL [34087] : 1800+ AUTEMOFKA, SU [34087]

FRISKNEY ALL WORLDWIDE [34361]

FRISLEY C1890 LND & MDX, ENG [35418]

FRISTON PRE 1800 ENG [36298]

FRITTS 1780-1850 ROWAN, DAVIDSON CO., NC, USA [37782]

FRITZ C1850 STUTTGART, BAW, BRD [38509]

FRITZLEY 1700+ WORLDWIDE [34400]

FRIZZELL 1800-60 PORTADOWN, ARM, IRL [37129]

FRIZZI 1700-1900 ALS & LOR, FRA [36078]

FRODSHAM 1848 WARDLE, BUNBURY, CHS, ENG [35120]

FROEBIS PRE 1788 RHEINBROHL, RPF, GER [38663]

FROESCHLE PRE 1700 WORLDWIDE [38669]

FROGGATT 1836 DERBY, DBY, ENG [37391]

FROGGETT 1790-1850 LONDON, SRY, ENG [34601] : 1790-1850 LONDON, MDX, ENG [34601] : ALL SYDENHAM, KEN & LND, ENG [36477] : 1750-1850 FRA [34601]

FROHLICH 1824-1872 SALZWEDEL, SAXONY, DDR [36317]

FROHLING 1850+ BRISBANE, QLD, AUS [34020] : ALL POS, GER [34488]

FROHMMUELLER PRE 1854 WALLDORF & WISLO, BAD, BRD [35856]

FROHMULLER 1800+ BADEN, BAW, BRD [35856]

FROHWIRT PRE 1850 MSW, GER [35205]

FROLICH 1800 WORLDWIDE [35873]

FROMENT PRE 1820 WATERBEACH, CAM, ENG [35391]

FRONE 1790 MORRIS CO., NJ, USA [38330]

FRONK PRE 1900 DOMAZLICE, TAUS, CS [35290]

FROOMES ALL ENG [37833]

FROSGATE PRE 1800 ESS, ENG [35642]

FROSSELL PRE 1850 PERTENHALL, BDF, ENG [34665]

FROST 1849+ NSW, AUS [35807] : 1800S LAKE MACQUARIE, NSW, AUS & ENG [33895] : 1850-1873 SHEFFIELD, YKS, ENG [33811] : ROBERT 1796 EAST DEREHAM, NFK, ENG [34176] : C1800+ LUTON, BDF & LND, ENG [34451] : ALL WITTAGINTON, SOM, ENG [34534] : 1600-1800 WIRKSWORTH, DBY, ENG [34739] : PRE 1800 WELTON LE MARSH & WINTERTON, LIN, ENG [34745] : PRE 1800 BURY ST EDMUNDS, SFK, ENG [34745] : PRE 1800 HAGWORTHINGHAM, LIN, ENG [34745] : C1800 EASTHORPE, ESS, ENG [35406] : PRE 1900 MESSING, ESS, ENG [35406] : 1800+ THORNTON, BKM, ENG [35476] : C1750-1900 REEPHAM & HACKFORD, NFK, ENG [36128] : C1840 PADDINGTON, LND, ENG [36147] : 1700+ MDX & SRY, ENG [36203] : 1700+ SFK, ENG [36203] : PRE 1960 WILBRAHAM, CAM, ENG [36489] : 1850-65 DEV, ENG [36831] : PRE 1825 NOWTON, SFK, ENG [37253] : 1823-1864 BOUGHTON BLEAN & CANTY, KEN, ENG [37317] : 1720-1770S LOOE & ST GERMANS, CON, ENG [37320] : PRE 1820 NTT & DBY, ENG [37412] : C1750 STONEY MIDDLETON, DBY, ENG [37643] : 1800+ CHILHAM & SELLING, KEN, ENG [37707] : PRE 1800 WOLVERTON, BKM, ENG [37716] : ISAAC PRE 1840 BRISTOL, YKS, ENG [38049] : PRE 1882 HOYLAND, YKS & DBY, ENG & AUS [35365] : 1780-1840 ABD, SCT [38253] : BENJAMIN 1838-1898 FORT WAYNE, IN, USA [34745] : 1670S KITTERY, ME, USA [34991] : 1775-1820 CAMBRIDGE, MA, USA [38045]

FROSTICK PRE 1800 ESS, ENG [35642] : ALL WORLDWIDE [37932]

FROUD PRE 1850 ANDOVER, HAM, ENG [34311] : 1700-1850 WORLDWIDE [37348]

FROUDE C1800 BLACKAWTON, DEV, ENG [35938] : 1700-1850 WORLDWIDE [37348]

FROWD 1830-1851 MARSHFIELD, GLS, ENG [35594] : C1805 WEST KINGTON, WIL, ENG [35594] : 1872-1906 CHIPPENHAM & SWINDON, WIL, ENG [35594] : 1700-1930 WORLDWIDE [37348]

FROWDE 1700-1930 WORLDWIDE [37348]

FROYENHOVE PRE 1800 OVL & BRA, BEL [38676]

FRUDENDAHL C1850 HADERSLEV, SHO, BRD [36873]

FRUICHTEL PRE 1830 BAV, GER [38191]

FRUIT DAVID 1800-1825 BARTHOLOMEW CO., IN, USA [37551]

FRUM C1790 USA [38177]

FRUNCK SIMON PRE 1620 HESSEN, BSW, GER [38563] : SIMON 1620-1673 SKULTUNA, SWE [38563]

FRUNZ ALL ROLFSHAGEN, SLP, GER [38637]

FRUSHER 1820-1860 WISBECH, CAM, ENG [38207]

FRUWIRTH 1700-1820 GOLS, BUR, OES [36957]

FRY 1859+ QLD, AUS [35878] : ALL CARISBROOKE, ISLE OF WIGHT, HAM, ENG [33802] : C1880 NTH,

ENG [33809] : 1800+ BRISTOL, ENG [33963] : ALL KEN, ENG [34254] : ALL NEWTON ST PETROCK, DEV, ENG [34471] : PRE 1840 BREMHILL, WIL, ENG [34588] : 1750+ BRISTOL, GLS, ENG [34817] : C1813 NEWPORT, IOW, ENG [34972] : 1850+ LONDON, ENG [35038] : PRE 1860 EVERCREECH, SOM, ENG [35878] : 1600+ EAST PUTFORD, DEV, ENG [36254] : FRANCIS C1818+ HIGH WYCOMBE, BKM, ENG [36767] : 1627+ SUTTON BENGER, WIL, ENG [36767] : PRE 1825 GLASTONBURY, SOM, ENG [37067] : ALL WIL, ENG [37232] : PRE 1900 HEYTESBURY, WIL, ENG [37248] : PRE 1900 EAST LONDON, ENG [37416] : PRE 1900 MEREWORTH, KEN, ENG [37494] : 1891+ MANCHESTER, LAN, ENG [37831] : 1800S STROUD, GLS, ENG [37831] : 1820+ WESTMINSTER, LND, ENG [38292] : C1800 SOM, ENG [38488] : C1870 AUCKLAND, NZ [35974] : JOHN L. 1800+ PERRY TWP, COSHOCTON CO., OH, USA [34511] : 1700S BERKS CO., PA, USA [35165]

FRYATT 1812 COGGESHALL, ESS, ENG [35194]

FRYE 1750+ ESS, ENG [37494] : 1600+ BASING, ENG [37802] : 1800-1900S LANCASTER & BERKS, PA, USA [36899]

FRYER 1873+ STRATHFIELDSAYE, VIC, AUS & ENG [37161] : 1650+ NEWNHAM, GLS, ENG [34747] : 1700S BARWICK IN ELMET, WRY, ENG [34776] : PRE 1794 MANCHESTER, LAN, ENG [35459] : 1767 TITCHFIELD, HAM, ENG [35903] : PRE 1850 ESS, ENG [36019] : 1770-1850 KEN & BKM, ENG [36304] : 1780-1830 LONDON, MDX, ENG [37129] : ALL YORK, YKS, ENG [37433] : C1830 NURSTEAD, KEN, ENG [37536] : 1700S ROMSEY, HAM, ENG [38358] : PRE 1860 DUR & YKS, ENG [38768] : FREDERICK 1829+ HADDENHAM, BKM, ENG & AUS [37161]

FRYERS 1800-1875 LAN, ENG [37330]

FRYETT 1760+ RICKINGHALL, SFK, ENG [35475]

FUCE 1600-1850 KINGSCLERE, HAM, ENG [37651]

FUCHS PRE 1900 NEUERBURG, BRD [38615] : PRE 1584 SELBOLD, HEN, GER [36972] : PRE 1724 HEROLZ, FULDA, GER [38618] : ALL KRS. ASCH, SUDETENLAND, OES, CSR &, GER [38649]

FUCHSMANN 1700+ POL [34943] : 1700+ WORLDWIDE [34943]

FUDGE ALL DOR, ENG [37063]

FUDLORR 1650-1790 GAWSWORTH, CHS, ENG [36983]

FUELL PRE 1900 HAYES, MDX, ENG [33966]

FUELLING PRE 1670 OSTHEIM & LIEBENAU, HES, GER [38642]

FUGE ALL POUNDSTOCK, CON, ENG [34263] : PRE 1883 ST NEOT & POUNDSTOCK, CON, ENG [36039]

FUGGLE 1819+ TENTEREN, KEN, ENG [35033] : 1700S KENARDINGTON, KEN, ENG [37714]

FUHLROTH PRE 1885 FELDBERGEN, GER [36589]

FUHRHOP 1650+ BREMEN, BRM, GER [35460]

FUHRMANN PRE 1800 STOLP & SCHLAWE, POM, GER [38684]

FULBECK 1700-1740 OLD LEAKE, LIN, ENG [38453]

FULCHER PRE 1865 NORWICH, NFK, ENG [34648] : PRE 1900 LONDON, ENG [36469] : ALL NEW BARNET, HRT, ENG [36469] : ALL NFK, ENG [36469] : PRE 1900 BEEFORD, YKS, ENG [36676] : 1790-1850S NC, USA [36729] : C1755 AMHERST CO., VA, USA [38044]

FULFORD PRE 1800 IRL [35091] : PRE 1806 NC, USA [36324]

FULGHAM PRE 1801 MONTGOMERY CO., GA, USA [37029]

FULHAM 1828+ NSW, AUS [35406] : PRE 1828 DUBLIN, IRL [35406]

FULL 1800-60 STEPNEY, LND, ENG [37252]

FULLAGAR 1850-1900 QLD, AUS [38070] : PRE 1900 KEN, ENG [37377]

FULLALOVE RICHARD PRE 1874+ LONDON, ENG [34592]

FULLARD 1800S PORTSMOUTH, HAM, ENG [34188]

FULLARTON 1800+ CAMPBELTOWN, ARL, SCT [34326]

FULLER ALL MARYBOROUGH, VIC, AUS [34877] : 1870+ SYDNEY, NSW, AUS [34979] : 1800S PT ARTHUR, TAS, AUS [35068] : (ABORIGINAL) 1890+ AUBURN RIVER, QLD, AUS [35111] : 1838-1930 REDFERN, NSW, AUS [35187] : 1867+ VIC & NSW, AUS [35731] : ALL ONT, CAN [34133] : PRE 1900 ARDEN, BLOOMFIELD, ONT, CAN [35604] : 1900+ CAN & ENG [37525] : 1800S LONDON, ENG [33972] : ALL ENG [34131] : PRE 1780 WEST STOWE, SFK, ENG [34445] : PRE 1770 BREDE & WESTFIELD, SSX, ENG [34847] : PRE 1845 BOSTON, LIN, ENG [34850] : 1850+ SRY, ENG [34877] : THOMAS PRE 1870 NFK, ENG [34979] : PRE 1870 KEN, ENG [35022] : PRE 1773 MONTFIELD, SSX, ENG [35211] : 1830S NORTHILL, BDF, ENG [35728] : PRE 1860 LND, ENG [35746] : PRE 1700 COPMANTHORPE, YKS, ENG [35983] : 1709-1729 TICEHURST, SSX, ENG [36071] : 1823-1900 DORKING, SRY, ENG [36071] : PRE 1800 REIGATE, SRY, ENG [36216] : 1880 WEST WYMER, NFK, ENG [36287] : PRE 1860 HEMINGFORD ABBOTS, HUN, ENG [36486] : 1700-1900 CHELMONDISTON, SFK, ENG [37042] : 1810+ GREAT MASSINGHAM, NFK, ENG [37181] : 1800+ EASTBOURNE, SSX, ENG [37206] : 1840 STEPNEY, MDX, ENG [37690] : PRE 1900 BURWELL, CAM, ENG [38403] : PRE 1900 DUBLIN, IRL [34292] : JOHN 1837-1909 GREYTOWN, WAI, NZ [33961] : FRANCIS OSCAR 1859+ MOTUEKA, NELSON, NZ [36243] : 1700-1850 LOWLANDS, SCT [34920] : JOSEPH 1776-1790 WINDHAM, CT, USA [35273] : FLORENCE ALL JACKSON, MI, USA [35302] : FRANCIS OSCAR C1835-1859 BOSTON, MA, USA [36243] : EDNA 1811-1830 NY, USA [36345] : EDNA 1830-1840 GEAUGA CO., OH, USA [36345] : 1625-1700 SALEM, MA, USA [37783] : ALL NY & RI, USA [37787] : 1818-1846 DUTCHESS CO., NY, USA [38094] : 1600+ DEDHAM, NORFOLK CO., MA, USA [38745]

FULLERTON C1907 LIVERPOOL, LAN, ENG [35036] : 1700+ NBL, ENG [38476] : PRE 1850 LISBURN, DOW, IRL [34611] : 1750+ DOW, IRL [35060] : 1830+ DRY, IRL [35476]

FULLWOOD 1500-1700 WAR & WOR, ENG [35305]

FULMER PRE 1800 GER [37823] : 1800+ PA, USA [37823] : 1811 JEFFERSON CO., OH, USA [37823]

FULTON 1888+ SYDNEY, NSW, AUS [38208] : 1954+ VANCOUVER, BC, CAN [34244] : C1800 DEV, ENG [38391] : PRE 1820 BELFAST, ANT, IRL [34588] : 1791+ WINDY HILL, TYR, IRL [34941] : PRE 1850 BOGAY GLEBE, DON, IRL [35545] : PRE 1850 GORTINSLIEVE, DON, IRL [35545] : 1790+ BELFAST & TINLEY PARK, ANT & IL, IRI & USA [37581] : 1860+ HAWKES BAY, NAPIER, NZ [33889] : PRE 1870 BEW, SCT [35400] : PRE 1840 IRVINE, AYR, SCT [35545] : PRE 1840 DREGHORN, AYR, SCT [35545] : 1870S PAISLEY ABBEY, RFW, SCT [36788] : 1830-1855 SCT [37301] : PRE 1850 PAISLEY, RFW, SCT [37371] : PRE 1887 GREENOCK, RFW, SCT [38208] : 1835-1870 LOGAN, OH & MI, USA [36910] : MARGARET 1800-1900 BELMONT CO., OH & PA, USA [38392]

FULTZ 1750-1850 HALIFAX, NS, CAN [35151] : PRE 1800 GER & USA [38043]

FULWELL 1810-1860S DEFFORD, WOR, ENG [36190]

FUNCKE PRE 1850 GRUPPENBUHREN, OLD, GER [36363]

FUNDUS ALL BITTELBOURN & MOCKMUHL, WUE, GER [38176]

FUNGE ALL LONDON, ENG [37703]

FUNK PRE 1850 BAW, BRD [35269] : 1866+ LEER, NDS, BRD [38685] : PRE 1862 MUNCHHAUSEN, HES, GER [34840] : 1850+ BROOKLYN, NY, USA [35269] : 1760+ MONTGOMERY CO., PA, USA [36540] : 1893+ MN, USA [38685]

FUNKE 1804+ LEVERN, WEF, BRD [38685] : 1679+ WAGENFELD, NDS, BRD [38685] : PRE 1850 GRUPPENBUHREN, OLD, GER [36363]

FUNKIE PRE 1800 FIF, SCT [36679]

FUNNEL PRE 1760 RADWINTER, ESS, ENG [33821]

FUNNELL 1795+ HEATHFIELD, SSX, ENG [34563] : 1730+ MOUNTFIELD, SSX, ENG [35153] : 1800-1860 CHIDDINGLY, SSX, ENG [36485]

FUOCO PRE 1865 COSENZA, CALABRIA, ITL [36679]

FURBER ALL SAL, ENG [38005] : 1700+ LLANMYNECH & LLANYBLODWEL, MGY, WLS [37625]

FURBISHER 1732-1826 NORMANTON, WRY, ENG [36049]

FURBY ALL SA & NSW, AUS [33799] : 1865+ SOUTH EAST AREA, QLD, AUS [37896] : ALL LONDON, ENG [33799] : PRE 1865 SHOREDITCH, LND, ENG [37896]

FUREY 1842+ SYDNEY, NSW, AUS [36628] : ALL CASTLEDARGAN, SLI, IRL [34154] : PRE 1842 GAL, IRL [36628]

FURGASON PRE 1770 LANCASTER CO., PA, USA [38135]

FURGUSON 1880S GLASGOW, LKS, SCT [35728]

FURLONG 1870+ ST ALBANS, VIC, AUS [35822] : PRE 1860 LONDON, ENG [35393] : 1840-1860S LONDON, MDX, ENG [36285] : 1850+ LIVERPOOL, LAN, ENG [37865] : 1750-1830 WEX, IRL [34071] : ALL WATERFORD, WAT & WEX, IRL [36043] : 1850+ ANGLE, PEM, WLS [37384]

FURLONGER 1880+ HUNTERS HILL, NSW, AUS [33896]

FURLOTTE 1800S PORTAGE RIVER, NB, CAN [34991]

FURLOW 1800-1885 ULSTER CO., NY, USA [38113]

FURMENGER PRE 1800 BREDE, SSX, ENG [34467]

FURNEAUX 1800+ DEV, ENG [37178]

FURNELL PRE 1830 PORTSMOUTH, HAM, ENG [35866]

FURNER PRE 1840 BREDE, SSX, ENG [36752]

FURNESS 1880+ RAVENSWORTH, DUR, ENG [38436] : 1882+ JESMOND, NBL, ENG [38436] : 1847+ LEICESTER, LEI, ENG [38436] : 1800S+ RUGBY, WAR, ENG [38436] : 1847+ DINNINGTON, NBL, ENG [38436] : PRE 1804 NORWICH, NFK, ENG [38490]

FURNISH ALL REDLINGFIELD, SFK, ENG [34772]

FURNISS PRE 1900 HALIFAX, YKS, ENG [36685] : 1800 DERBY, DBY, ENG [37391] : 1828 TOWCESTER, NTH, ENG [38282]

FURNIVAL 1650-1750 CHURCH HULME, CHS, ENG [36983] : PRE 1850 AUDLEY, STS, ENG [37722]

FURPHY 1840+ MELBOURNE, VIC, AUS [34962] : PRE 1840 SEAGOE, ARM, IRL [34962]

FURRER PRE 1887 OBERHOFEN, BE, CH [37504] : PRE 1891 BASEL, BS, CH [37504]

FURRIAN 1600-1800 PIRTON, HRT, ENG [34411]

FURSE PRE 1900 NEWTON ABBOT, DEV, ENG [35730]

FURY 1780+ BATHGATE, WLN, SCT [38279]

FURZE PRE 1800 PAUL, CON, ENG [35375] : 1700-1800 RUAN LANIHORNE, CON, ENG [35712] : 1750+ RUAN LANIHORN, CON, ENG [37224]

FURZER C1800 MIDDLE CHINNOCK, SOM, ENG [35502]

FURZEY 1800-1870 DEV, ENG [33787]

FUSS 1850+ HEREROTE, HES, BRD [35631]

FUSSELL 1825-1860 SYDNEY, NSW, AUS [33817] : PRE 1825 BRISTOL, ENG [33817] : PRE 1800 NUNNEY, SOM, ENG [37179] : 1750-1850 TROWBRIDGE, WIL, ENG [37705]

FUTER 1800+ WANDSWORTH, SRY, ENG [37171] : 1800+ PUTNEY, SRY, ENG [37171]

FUTTER 1840+ ST PANCRAS, LND, ENG [35408]

FUTTON PRE 1800 CASTLEWELLAN, DOW, IRL [36793]

FUZZARD ALL VIC, AUS [37115]

FYALL 1620-1880 LEUCHARS, FIF, SCT [35937] : PRE 1825 WORLDWIDE [37428]

FYFE PRE 1880 BAN, SCT [36792] : C1792 PERTH, PER, SCT [37772]

FYFFE 1850+ VIC, AUS [35060] : PRE 1800 BRECHIN, ANS, SCT [36497]

FYLES PRE 1698 LAN, ENG [37706]

FYNCH 1832-1900S ENG & AUS [37153]

FYNN 1800+ CAMBRIDGE, CAM, ENG [35874] : 1800+ LEEDS, WRY, ENG [37379] : 1870S CLAREMORRIS, MAY, IRL [38267]

FYSH PRE 1750 MARSHLAND, ENG [35722]

FYSON ALL FOWLMERE, CAM, ENG [35554]

GAASTRA 1817+ OLDEBOORN, FRI, NL [34990]

GAB PRE 1850 CAM, COALEY, STONEHOUSE, GLS, ENG [37101]

GABB 1870+ SWINDON, WIL, ENG [37101] : PRE 1850 CAM, COALEY, STONEHOUSE, GLS, ENG [37101] : 1870+ BRISTOL, SOM, ENG [37101] : PRE 1770 DURSLEY & COALEY, GLS, ENG [37320]

GABBE PRE 1850 CAM, COALEY, STONEHOUSE, GLS, ENG [37101]

GABBEY 1780 KINTBURY, BRK, ENG [33783]

GABEL ALL KURHESSEN, BRD [35115]

GABLE 1831-1905 ENG & CAN [34164]

GABLIN 1700+ BERNSFELDEN, GER [35566]

GABOURY 1800-1950 MONTREAL, QUE, CAN [34257] : 1700-1940 ST JEAN BAPTISTE, QUE, CAN [34257]

GABRIEL 1800 STEPNEY, MDX, ENG [35965] : PRE 1840 BOUS, PRE, GER [38333] : 1880+ BUFFALO, NY, USA [38333]

GADBOIS CLEOPHAS 1840-1860 MALONE, NY, USA [38408] : CLEOPHAS 1840-1860 CA, USA [38408]

GADBURY 1833+ SYDNEY, NSW, AUS [35160]

GADD 1839+ HOBART, TAS, AUS [33786] : 1747+ FARNHAM, SRY, ENG [33786] : PRE 1826 SOM, ENG [34633] : C1800 WESTMINSTER, MDX, ENG [36975] : C1700S EASTERGATE AND AREA, SSX, ENG [37745]

GADDES PRE 1835 MILBURN, WES, ENG [36180]

GADDIE 1880+ RYLSTONE, NSW, AUS [34534]

GADDIS 1800+ CORNAKELLY, CAV, IRL [33977] : 1800+ USA [33977]

GADEN ALL WORLDWIDE [38356]

GADFIELD ALL ENG [35933]

GADSBURY PRE 1850 WORLDWIDE [34046]

GADSBY 1820+ SNELSTON, DBY & STS, ENG [35019] : ALL LITTLE LONDON, WRY, ENG [36743] : PRE 1800 LINCOLN, LIN, ENG [36812] : PRE 1900 LEICESTER, LEI, ENG [36812] : PRE 1800 CLAYPOLE & WASHINGBOROUGH, LIN, ENG

[36812] : 1780-1990 LINCOLN, LIN, ENG [38511] :
ALL WORLDWIDE [36812]

GAERTE ALL STARK CO., OH, IN & CA, USA [38230]

GAERTNER 1750 MEIMSHEIM, GER [36596]

GAETHJE 1600-1900 BORBY, SHO, GER [38748] :
1600-1900 HEMMELMARK, SHO, GER [38748]

GAETJE 1600-1900 BARKELSBY, SHO, GER [38748]

GAFFNEY C1829 MIDDLEWICH, CHS, ENG [37886] :
1840 DUBLIN, IRL [34844] : PRE 1830 DUBLIN,
IRL [35563] : ALL NEW ROSS, WEX, IRL [37796] :
FRANCIS C1792 IRL [37886] : CHARLES C1834 SLI,
IRL [37886] : PRE 1860 SLI, IRL [38365] : 1850+
DANE CO., WI & OH, USA [37796]

GAGE 1860+ ADELAIDE & JAMESTOWN, SA, AUS
[38494] : NELSON 1817-1893 HAMILTON, ONT,
CAN [38146] : ELIZABETH 1841+ ONT, CAN
[38146] : GEORGE 1852-1916 ONT, CAN [38146] :
SARAH JANE 1837+ ONT, CAN [38146] : (JOHN)
JAMES 1773-1854 ONT, CAN [38146] : EVALINE
1850-1920 SARNIA, ONT, CAN [38146] : 1800+
STEPNEY, MDX, ENG [37251] : 1750-1800
RUTHERFORD CO., NC, USA [38091] : 1700-1775
MIDDLESEX CO., NJ, USA [38091] : INA (IDA)
1860-1920 MI, USA [38146] : DESTMONEY 1823-
1900 ST CLAIR CO., MI, USA [38146] : ADELAIDE
1857+ ST CLAIR CO., MI, USA [38146] : ALL
SCHENECTADY CO., NY, USA [38176] : ROSANA
1823-1900 MICHIGAN & SUPERIOR, USA & CAN
[38146] : HORATIUS 1817-1893 ST CLAIR CO., MI,
USA & CAN [38146] : PRE 1890 WORLDWIDE
[36840]

GAGEN 1800-1900 GREAT MASSINGHAM, NFK,
ENG [37181]

GAGER MARY PRE 1817 LONDON, ENG [34701]

GAGNE 1700-1870 LA PRAIRIE, QUE, CAN [36907] :
PRE 1800 QUE, CAN & FRA [38386]

GAGNON PIERRE PRE 1635 TOUROUVRE, HN,
FRA [38408]

GAHAN 1850+ SYDNEY, NSW, AUS [34306] : 1800+
PEI, CAN [38460] : PRE 1840 DUBLIN, IRL [33813]

GAHEN ALL WEX, IRL [35579]

GAIGE PRE 1766 KEN, ENG [38389]

GAIGER PRE 1789 MARTYR WORTHY, HAM, ENG
[35247] : PRE 1762 BARTON STACEY, HAM, ENG
[35247]

GAIL 1830-1900 SYDNEY & MAITLAND, NSW, AUS
[37969] : 1800-1900 FRANKFURT, GER [37969]

GAIN 1800+ PEI, CAN [38460] : PRE 1830
PORTSMOUTH, HAM, ENG [34494] : PRE 1850
SOM, ENG [38077]

GAINER ALL WORLDWIDE [36441]

GAINGER 1900+ CLUNES, BEEAC & RUPANYUP,
VIC, AUS [36622]

GAINSFORD FREDERICK 1829-1840S MDX, ENG
[35366]

GAIR ALL NBL, ENG [37334] : 1841 TYNEMOUTH,
NBL, ENG [37442] : PRE 1730 DUNDEE, ANS, SCT
[36272] : ALL SCT [37334] : 1750-1845 ROC, SCT &
CAN [37499] : ALL WORLDWIDE [37334]

GAIRDNER 1800 HEWISON HALL, LKS, SCT [37879]

GAISFORD C1700-1800 WARMINSTER &
WESTBURY, WIL, ENG [36478]

GAIT PRE 1816 BRISTOL, SOM, ENG [34696] : PRE
1856 ENG [34968]

GAITSKELL PRE 1863 WHITEHAVEN, CUL, ENG
[33806]

GAITT 1800-1857 LONDON, ENG [34676] : ALL NZ
[34676]

GALAGHER 1841+ MELBOURNE, VIC, AUS [35238]
: PRE 1840 RAPHOE, DON, IRL [35238]

GALANTE PRE 1830 CASALBORDINO, CHIETI, ITL
[34127]

GALBRAITH 1650+ DOW & MOG, IRL [33826] :
1666+ DON, IRL [36895] : ALL INVERCARGILL,
NZ [36878] : PRE 1800 GIGHA, ARL, SCT [34156] :
C1810-1815 BUCHANAN, STI, SCT [34156] : PRE
1805 FALKIRK, STI, SCT [35259] : PRE 1800 SCT
[35910] : PRE 1830 GLASGOW, LKS, SCT [36431] :
ALL DNB, SCT [36878] : C1810 KIPPEN, STI, SCT
[36878] : C1850 DNB, SCT [36878] : JOHN PRE 1799
EDINBURGH, MLN & MDX, SCT & ENG [35723]

GALBREATH PRE 1805 CAMPBELTOWN, ARL, SCT
[38438]

GALDY 1800S CAVEIRAC, FRA [35968]

GALE LUCY 1850-1916 SA, VIC & NSW, AUS [34783] :
SHADRACK 1800+ MONTREAL, QUE, CAN
[37033] : GEORGE 1800-1900 TORONTO, ONT,
CAN [37033] : 1800-1900 BURBAGE, WIL, ENG
[34069] : 1850+ STEPNEY & LONDON, MDX, ENG
[34628] : PRE 1850 CROYDON, SRY, ENG [35604] :
PRE 1750 KEELBY, LIN, ENG [36059] : ALL
SCRUTON & ADDINGHAM, NRY & WRY, ENG
[36159] : PRE 1780 WINTERBOURNE KINGSTON,
DOR, ENG [36478] : 1780-1900 WARMINSTER,
WIL, ENG [37847] : 1845+ ST PANCRAS, MDX,
ENG [37847] : 1875+ WILLESDEN, MDX, ENG
[37847] : C1700 ALTON PRIORS, WIL, ENG [37918] :
1700+ SSX & WIL, ENG [38288] : 1865-1900
KEWEENAW CO., MI, USA [38010]

GALER 1850+ LONDON, LND & CAM, ENG [34905]
: ANDREW PRE 1796 PA, USA [37580]

GALIFORD PRE 1920 NEWPORT, MON, WLS [33866]

GALINAITIS PRE 1900 TAUROGGEN, LITHUANIA,
SU [38125]

GALIPEAU 1884+ RAINY RIVER, ONT, CAN [34159]

GALL ALL FORFAR, ANS, SCT [34226] : ALL
ABINGTON, LKS, SCT [34835] : 1600-1880
DUNFERMLINE, FIF, SCT [36894] : PRE 1854
CRUDEN BAY, ABD, SCT [38412] : ALL
WORLDWIDE [33858]

GALLACHER PRE 1898 DON, IRL [33862] : 1877-
1892+ PAISLEY, RFW, SCT [37108] : 1850-1871+
BARGEDDIE, LKS, SCT [37108]

GALLAGHER 1841+ SYDNEY, NSW, AUS [33794] :
MARY A. 1835 NEWCASTLE, NSW, AUS [36596] :
1850+ PARMES & MOLONG, NSW, AUS [37307] :
1851+ DUNMORE, NSW, AUS [37894] : 1867
SYDNEY, NSW, AUS [37965] : 1880+ SYDNEY,
NSW, AUS [38011] : PRE 1900 ENNISKILLEN, NB,
CAN & IRL [38447] : PRE 1860 KEN, ENG [34588] :
1840-1900 LIVERPOOL, LAN, ENG [34762] : 1826
LIVERPOOL, LAN, ENG [35824] : 1860+
MIDDLESBROUGH, NRY, ENG [37376] : PRE 1841
PETTIGO, TYR & DON, IRL [33794] : 1750-1850
GILLIN, OFF, IRL [34572] : PRE 1830 GAL, IRL
[35090] : 1800+ RAMELTON, DON, IRL [35970] :
1800 FALGARRAGH, DON, IRL [37125] : PRE 1860
RUSKY, DON, IRL [37537] : ALL IRL [37930] : 1846
TEMPLEHOUSE, SLI, IRL [37965] : 1846
BALLYMOTE, SLI, IRL [37965] : 1850+
FALCARRAGH, DON & LDY, IRL [38011] : PRE
1860 EDINBURGH, SCT [33813] : 1880+ SAN
FRANCISCO, CA, USA [38011]

GALLAGHLER 1800-1850 IRL [34762]

GALLAHER 1788+ BALTIMORE CO., MD, USA
[37564]

GALLANT C1755 KINGSCLERE, HAM, ENG [37168]

GALLE 1800+ PHILIPPINES &, GER [35239]

GALLEN PRE 1860 MEENREAGH, DON, IRL [37537]
: ALL YOUNGSTOWN, OH, USA [37537]

GALLEY C1850 GLOUCESTER, GLS, ENG [34734]

GALLIE 1850+ ELGIN, MOR, SCT [36885]

GALLIEN ROBERT C1600 FRA [37429]

GALLIGAN 1872+ QLD, AUS [37992] : PRE 1872 LIM, IRL [37992]

GALLIMORE PRE 1825 POTTERIES, STS, ENG [36502] : PRE 1775 STS, ENG [37098]

GALLINGER 1780-1990 OSNABRUCK, ONT, CAN [34077]

GALLION PRE 1880 PUTNAM CO., MO, USA [36672] : 1800S CAMPBELL, LUNENBURG CO., VA, USA [37782] : 1700+ HARTFORD CO., MD, USA [37782]

GALLIOTT 1700-1800 ENG [35494]

GALLIVEN 1850S LONDON, ENG [33967]

GALLOAY 1800+ DUNEDIN, OTAGO, NZ [36871]

GALLOGLY 1780-1880 CARRICKMACROSS, MOG, IRL [34346]

GALLON 1800-1900 ELGIN, MOR, SCT [34000]

GALLOP C1853+ VIC, AUS [36276] : 1700-1800 POYNINGS, SSX, ENG [34749] : 1813+ LYNCOMBE, SOM & DOR, ENG [36276] : PRE 1820 KEN, ENG [38755]

GALLOWAY 1900+ MELBOURNE, VIC, AUS [36632] : 1830S YORK MILLS, ONT, CAN [38422] : 1850S-1887 MDX & KEN, ENG [34413] : 1872+ WANDSWORTH, LND, ENG [37704] : PRE 1840 LIMEHOUSE, MDX, ENG & SCT [36099] : 1800S FER, IRL [38422] : 1859+ DUNEDIN, OTAGO, NZ [36877] : 1855+ NZ [37704] : PRE 1857 KIRKCUDBRIGHT, KKD, SCT [34036] : 1800-1850 MARKINCH, FIF, SCT [34816] : 1800+ DALRY, AYR, SCT [34916] : 1839 LOCHMABEN, DFS, SCT [35061] : 1800+ DYSART, FIF, SCT [35558] : PRE 1820 PAISLEY, RFW, SCT [35871] : 1800-1990 DYSART, FIF, SCT [36394] : PRE 1860 MADDISTON, STI, SCT [36877] : 1840+ GLASGOW, LKS, SCT [36885] : 1830-67 STORNOWAY, ROC, SCT [37704] : ALL FIF, SCT [37704] : 1800+ EDINBURGH, MLN, SCT [37704] : 1820+ GLASGOW, LKS, SCT [37704] : C1803 LARGS, FIF, SCT [38760] : PRE 1830 THANKERTON, LKS, SCT & CAN [34835] : 1750S+ FIF, SCT & IRL [34040] : ALL ST LOUIS, MO, USA [37704] : 1850+ MENDOCINO CO., CA, USA [37704] : ALL KEOKUK, IA, USA [37704] : ALL WORLDWIDE [38533]

GALLUS PRE 1700 HAUSEN A.D.W., WUE, GER [38681]

GALPIN C1790 PORTSEA, HAM, ENG [35401]

GALSTHARPE PRE 1900 JARROW, YKS, ENG [37392]

GALT 1800S MEARNS, RFW, SCT [35337] : 1800 AYR, AYR, SCT [35560] : PRE 1861 GLASGOW, LKS, SCT [37238] : PRE 1844 STEVENSTON, AYR, SCT [37575] : 1700+ WASHINGTON, DC & MD, USA [38336]

GALTON ALL POOLE, DOR, ENG [34119]

GALVIN 1870+ BENDIGO, VIC, AUS [34174] : C1850 FRANKLIN, TAS, AUS [34853] : C1830 KILMALEY, CLA, IRL [34426] : 1800-1860 ATHLONE, WEM, IRL [35382]

GALWITZ 1820S POL [37792]

GAMBELL 1871+ ULLADULLA, NSW, AUS [35368] : 1803+ WENDOVER, BKM, ENG [35368]

GAMBETTA C1967 NEWCASTLE, NSW, AUS [34694] : C1967 VIC, AUS [34694]

GAMBILL 1720-1777 CULPEPPER CO., VA, USA [38315]

GAMBLE 1800+ VIC, AUS [34446] : 1818+ FRINSTEAD, KEN, ENG [35824] : 1750-1860 BRADFORD, WRY, ENG [36228] : ALL LIN, ENG [36515] : ALL DBY, LEI & NTT, ENG [37078] : PRE 1869 ANT, IRL [34412] : C1860 MEENAGH HILL, TYR, IRL [35247]

GAMBLES 1800+ WHITEHAVEN, CUL, ENG [35992]

GAMBLING 1760 WHITEPARISH, WIL, ENG [35349]

GAMBRELL 1839+ WINDSOR, NSW, AUS [35394]

GAMBRIEL 1800+ CARDINGTON, BDF, ENG [35812]

GAMBRILL 1560-1860 WOODNESBOROUGH, KEN, ENG [35394]

GAMER PRE 1650 ESS & DEV, ENG [38746]

GAMES C1846 BRIGHTON, SSX, ENG [35807]

GAMLEN C1850 SOMERSET, KEN, ENG [35532]

GAMMA PRE 1600 WASSEN, UR, CH [38686]

GAMMAGE SAMUEL PRE 1800 BRISWORTH, NTH, ENG [38595]

GAMMIE 1660 ABD & BAN, SCT [35369] : 1700-1860 MONQUHITTER, ABD, SCT [35937]

GAMMON 1800-1900+ NS & BC, CAN [34403] : 1700-1750 WALLINGFORD, BRK, ENG [34552] : 1700S BRAUNTON, DEV, ENG [34931] : ALL WORLDWIDE [35159]

GAMMOND 1800-1850 POWICK & NORTON, WOR, ENG [37716]

GAMPTON 1800S PORTSMOUTH, HAM, ENG [34881]

GAMWELLS 1870+ ISLINGTON, LND, ENG [37775]

GANDAR C1560 THURSLEY, SRY, ENG [37420]

GANDER PRE 1835 SSX, ENG [35238] : WILLIAM 1789+ SSX, ENG [38549] : WILLIAM 1785+ CHIDDINGLY, SSX, ENG [38549]

GANE 1852-1863 GEELONG WEST, VIC, AUS [34796] : 1863+ MOUNT DORAN, VIC, AUS [34796] : 1780-1860 STEPNEY, LND, ENG [34440] : 1848-1852 (SHIPS NEREID & SUCCESS), ENG [34796] : C1800 ROAD, SOM, ENG [34796] : 1820-1840 (ROYAL MARINES), ENG [34796] : 1829 BRISTOL, SOM, ENG [35414] : PRE 1840 KEN, ENG [37370] : PRE 1826 ASHILL, SOM, ENG [38399]

GANEY 1880-1925 SOUTHWARK, LND, ENG [34242]

GANGE PRE 1852 WEST COKER, SOM, ENG [35045] : PRE 1830 SOM, ENG [35760]

GANGLEY ALL ENG [37407]

GANI PRE 1900 JANINA, CAIRO, GREECE [36455]

GANLEE ALL WORLDWIDE [37407]

GANLEY ALL WORLDWIDE [37407]

GANLY ALL WORLDWIDE [37407]

GANNAWAY 1760-1795 BUCKINGHAM CO., VA, USA [38763]

GANNON 1839-1990 MORUYA, NSW, AUS [33818] : ALL CORNWALL, ONT, CAN & IRL [37503] : 1780-1990 ELFIN, ROS, IRL [33818] : 1840 TULLAMORE, OFF, IRL & AUS [34845]

GANOR PRE 1853 CAMPBELLTOWN, TAS, AUS [35459]

GANSBERG ALL GER & DEN [34556]

GANT PRE 1900 HADLEIGH, SFK, ENG [37279] : 1750+ ROUGHTON, LIN, ENG [37487] : 1800-1950 BALTIMORE CITY & CALVERT CO., MD, USA [37583] : 1750-1800 ORANGE CO., NC, USA [37786]

GANTON PRE 1875 ONT, CAN [34222] : 1800+ MARKHAM, ONT, CAN [34465] : 1800+ CAN [34465] : 1800+ SIMCOE CO., ONT, CAN [34465] : PRE 1850 ROOS, YKS, ENG [34465]

GAODE 1840-1900 ORLEANS & JEFFERSON PAR., LA, USA [37599]

GAPPER PRE 1802 WOOTTON FITZPAINE, DOR, ENG [34689] : PRE 1800 SOM, ENG [37655] : PRE 1772 DOR, ENG [38399]

GARAWAY PRE 1787 DYRHAM, GLS & WIL, ENG [37144]

GARBADE 1680-1870 SCHARMBECK, HAN, GER [36896]

GARBE PRE 1900 STOLP & SCHLAWE, POM, GER [38684]

GARBER 1750-1840 LANCASTER CO., PA, USA [36738]

GARBETT PRE 1880 RETFORD, NTT, ENG [36502] : PRE 1900 HADLEIGH & DAWLEYMAGNA, SAL,

ENG [36502] : PRE 1900 MERTHYR TYDFIL, GLA, WLS [34241]

GARBUT 1860+ COOYAL, NSW, AUS [35807] : 1750-1850 SAL, ENG [34615]

GARBUTT 1860+ COOYAL, NSW, AUS [35807] : PRE 1918 WIMBLEDON, LND, ENG [37940] : 1700-1800 HAWNBY, NRY, ENG [38269] : 1820-1850 GAWBER, YKS, ENG [38478]

GARCAREK ALL KATHARINENHUETTE, SIL, GER [38678]

GARCIA PRE 1910 LONDON, ENG [37062] : DIEGO C1821 JEREZ DE LA FRONTERA, ESP [37819]

GARD 1841+ NSW, AUS [33808] : 1875+ QLD, AUS [33808] : 1800-1870 CON, ENG [33787] : 1800-1870 LONDON, ENG [33787] : 1730+ HAM, ENG [34181]

GARDE PRE 1855 BALLIBRANAGHAN, COR, IRL [33808]

GARDEN NORMAN 1875+ LONDON, ENG [35615] : PRE 1850 FOCHABERS, MOR, SCT [34809] : ALL WORLDWIDE [34373]

GARDENER 1867 SWINDON, WIL, ENG [34120] : 1700-1800 COCKERHAM, LAN, ENG [36983] : 1750-1850 HARKSTEAD, SFK, ENG [37042] : PRE 1860 WILLENHALL, STS, ENG [37068] : PRE 1820 NEWPORT, SAL, ENG [37068]

GARDINER 1900+ MELBOURNE, VIC, AUS [34798] : 1880+ PRESTON & MALVERN, VIC, AUS [34919] : 1890+ BOTANY, NSW, AUS [35149] : 1849+ MUSWELLBROOK, NSW, AUS [37316] : 1800+ SYDNEY, AUS [37907] : 1840-1900 GOULBURN, NSW, AUS [37914] : ALL CAVAN, ONT, CAN [33854] : 1880+ LAN, ENG [33923] : PRE 1850 OAKRIDGE LYNCH, GLS, ENG [34187] : PRE 1849 KINGSLEY, HAM, ENG [34587] : 1690 MEDSTEAD, HAM, ENG [34909] : 1800S WATCHFIELD, BRK, ENG [35525] : PRE 1750 ESS, ENG [35642] : ROBERT 1825+ PORTSEA, HAM, ENG [35780] : 1800+ WROTHAM, KEN, ENG [36092] : MARGERY C1770-1800 BOSBURY, HEF, ENG [36633] : C1765 SUDBURY, SFK, ENG [36949] : 1500-1700 BURY ST EDMUNDS, SFK, ENG [37342] : C1790 MEOPHAM, KEN, ENG [37536] : PRE 1880 IPSWICH, SFK, ENG [37768] : 1790-1830 LONDON, ENG & SCT [34769] : 1740-1800 TOOLINN & LISNASKEA, FER, IRL [37613] : PRE 1880 NITSHILL, RFW, SCT [34001] : PRE 1880 KILBIRNIE, STRATHCLYDE, SCT [34001] : 1700+ GLASGOW, LKS, SCT [34229] : PRE 1847 BRECHIN, ANS, SCT [34840] : PRE 1815 KENNOWAY, FIF, SCT [35045] : 1800S DUNBLANE, PER, SCT [35558] : 1870+ STIRLING, STI, SCT [35708] : 1780-1840 SHETLAND ISLAND, UK [36297]

GARDNER WILLIAM 1870-1874 COLLINGWOOD, VIC, AUS [34011] : 1841+ SHOALHAVEN, NSW, AUS [35117] : C1870 STONEYFORD, VIC, AUS [35203] : 1815+ WILBERFORCE, NSW, AUS [35331] : PRE 1863 MOUNT GAMBIER, SA, AUS [35399] : 1860 SYDNEY, NSW, AUS [35508] : 1848+ VIC, AUS [35797] : THOMAS 1880+ HILLGROVE, NSW, AUS [36629] : THOMAS 1826+ LONDON, ENG [34011] : 1800S OXFORD, OXF, ENG [34086] : C1875-1900 BIRMINGHAM, WAR, ENG [34086] : PRE 1500 SFK, ENG [34466] : 1700 WITNEY, OXF, ENG [34466] : 1841 CHELSFIELD, KEN, ENG [35117] : PRE 1769 TUNBRIDGE, KEN, ENG [35527] : C1878 TUDHOE, DUR, ENG [35715] : PRE 1869 READING, BRK, ENG [36475] : ALL POPLAR, MDX, ENG [36571] : ALL PRESTON, LAN, ENG [36774] : 1880S FALMOUTH, CON, ENG [37151] : PRE 1830 SHERBORNE, HAM, ENG [37579] : 1820+ WORCESTER, WOR, ENG [37889] : ALL

PILLING, LAN, ENG [38285] : MARG 1795-1852 MAGUIRESBRIDGE, FER, IRL [34524] : PRE 1832 ANT, IRL [37496] : C1841 ENNISKILLEN, FER, IRL & AUS [35365] : 1802+ HOPE TOWN, CAPE, RSA [34947] : 1800-1899 GLASGOW, LKS, SCT [33945] : 1700+ GLASGOW, LKS, SCT [34229] : C1846 GLASGOW, LKS, SCT [35203] : PRE 1815 GLASGOW, SCT [35331] : 1820S EDINBURGH, MLN, SCT [35865] : PRE 1800 WLN, SCT [37374] : 1720+ KILRENNY, FIF, SCT [37913] : C1920 CANTON, OH, USA [34086] : PRE 1790 RENSSELAER CO., NY & RI, USA [36917] : 1850+ ST JOSEPH, MO, USA [37037] : 1620-1750 MANCHESTER, MA, USA [37432] : 1870-1970 LEAVENWORTH CO., KS, USA [37798] : 1800-1890 BUCHANAN CO., MO, USA [37798] : 1680 HATFIELD, MA, USA [38066]

GARE 1700-1850 HIGH HAM, SOM, ENG [36776] : PRE 1850 GODNEY MERE, SOM, ENG [36875]

GARFIELD PRE 1821 LONDON, ENG [35842] : ALL BIRMINGHAM, WAR, ENG [37959]

GARFIELD-RICHARDS PRE 1850+ BINGHAM, NTT, ENG [38401]

GARFORTH ALL OLDHAM, LAN, ENG [35320]

GARGISS C1850 KLAIPEDIA, LITHUANIA [37132]

GARIBALDI 1840S GENOA, ITL [37390]

GARLAND 1860+ KADINA & MOONTA, SA, AUS [34783] : 1880+ MT EGERTON, CARLTON, VIC, AUS [35059] : 1880+ ADELAIDE, SA, AUS [37987] : 1800+ DOR, ENG [33875] : 1800-1820 CHALDON, SRY, ENG [34205] : 1700S LOVINGTON, SOM, ENG [34518] : 1700+ ST AUSTELL, CON, ENG [34783] : 1790S MANGOTSFIELD, GLS, ENG [35798] : PRE 1700 SHEFFIELD, WRY, ENG [36126] : 1800-1880 NFK, ENG [37140] : 1841 HARDINGTON MANDEVILLE, SOM, ENG [37378] : 1800-1990 CON, ENG [37549] : 1840-1990 ALLEGHENY CO., PA, USA [37549] : 1810-1870 FANNIN CO., GA, USA [38737] : 1810-1870 WESTERN COS., NC, USA [38737]

GARLICK ALL AUS [38215] : C1829 EWELME, OXF, ENG [35091] : PRE 1800 EWELME, OXF, ENG [35838] : ALL BRK, ENG [38215] : ALL WIL, ENG [38215] : ALL WORLDWIDE [38206]

GARLING 1815+ SYDNEY, NSW, AUS [35929] : 1860+ GULGONG, NSW, AUS [36632] : PRE 1800 UK [36406]

GARMENT 1700-1850 SRY, ENG [37880]

GARNER 1850S SYDNEY, NSW, AUS [34874] : 1900+ BURNIE, TAS, AUS [38729] : 1800S NORTH CAYUGA, ONT, CAN [37442] : ALL TARVIN, CHS, ENG [33916] : C1845 KING'S HEATH, WOR, ENG [34239] : PRE 1849 MARKET HARBOROUGH, LEI, ENG [34584] : HANNAH 1858 STOCKPORT, CHS, ENG [35343] : 1700+ BKM, NTH & BDF, ENG [36574] : C1800 LEI, ENG [36694] : PRE 1850 LIN, ENG [37105] : 1840S BOURNE, LIN, ENG [37129] : ALL GAINSBOROUGH, LIN, ENG [37195] : 1600-1750 SCALES, LAN, ENG [37858] : 1880-1900 THEDDLETHORPE, LIN, ENG [38478] : 1800S YKS & LAN, ENG & CAN [36710] : PRE 1850 MOATE, WEM, IRL [34003] : PRE 1880 PRINCE GEORGE CO., CHAS CO., MD, USA [36914] : 1750-1850 NY, USA [36962] : 1710-1850S ROWAN, NC, USA [38195]

GARNETT 1850+ LONDON, ENG [34747] : 1700-1800 SILKSTONE, YKS, ENG [34762] : PRE 1795 MANCHESTER, LAN, ENG [35097] : 1800+ LONDON, MDX, ENG [35169] : PRE 1800 MANCHESTER, LAN, ENG [36201] : 1600-1700 CASTERTON, WMD, ENG [36635] : 1870+ NRY, ENG [37733] : 1870+ DALSTON, LND, ENG [37733] : 1730-1860 HALIFAX, WRY, ENG [38028]

GARNHAM PRE 1840 LND, ENG [33830] : PRE 1847 ESS, ENG [36124] : C1600 STOWMARKET, SFK, ENG [37670] : 1750-1850 SHOREDITCH & STEPNEY, LND, ENG [38523]

GARNIER 1600S LONDON, ENG [33918]

GARNITZ ALL WORLDWIDE [33756]

GARNON C1800 LONDON, ENG [34556]

GARNSWORTHY ALL WORLDWIDE [35817]

GARRARD 1800S NEEDHAM MARKET, SFK, ENG [33982] : PRE 1775 NFK, ENG [34660] : PRE 1900 CHESTER, CHS, ENG [35055] : 1800-90 USA [38533]

GARRAT 1750+ EYEWORTH & CODICOTE, BDF & HRT, ENG [34416]

GARRATT PRE 1829 SYDNEY, NSW, AUS [34304] : PRE 1850 OLNEY, BKM, ENG [34311] : 1840+ BRUNTINGSTHORPE, LEI, ENG [35169] : C1840+ COTGRAVE, NTT, ENG [38401]

GARRATTY 1840S NSW, AUS [37947]

GARRELS ALL OSTFRIESLAND, NDS, BRD [38685]

GARRET PRE 1900 FRA [38218]

GARRETT PRE 1829 SYDNEY, NSW, AUS [34304] : 1874+ BARRIE, ONT, CAN [34466] : 1800S HACKNEY & ISLINGTON, MDX, ENG [34335] : 1843+ BATH, SOM, ENG [34466] : ALL LONDBRIDGE DEVERILL, WIL, ENG [34466] : C1815 SHEPTON BEAUCHAMP, SOM, ENG [34972] : PRE 1882+ IPSWICH, SFK, ENG [35536] : SOLOMON C1794 KINGSTON DEVERILL, WIL, ENG [35564] : PRE 1800 ASHWELL, HRT, ENG [35592] : PRE 1850 SHEPTON BEAUCHAMP, SOM, ENG [36529] : 1700-1850 WORCESTER, WOR, ENG [36653] : PRE 1815 LONDON, MDX, ENG [36673] : PRE 1800 BRADFORD ABBAS, DOR, ENG [37006] : PRE 1860 MOULTON, NTH, ENG [37708] : C1852 ST GEORGE & ST JAMES, MDX, ENG [37972] : 1700S TEST VALLEY, HAM, ENG [38358] : 1750-1800 BALLAGHMORE, LEX, IRL [33767] : ALL ANT, IRL [38084] : ALL IOM, UK [35746] : PRE 1830 RAMSAY, IOM, UK [37579] : 1800-1840 SC, USA [35307] : 1850-1900 MARSHALL CO., MS, USA [35307] : WILL 1914+ USA [35536] : PRE 1783 CHARLES CO., MD, USA [37029] : PRE 1820 SC, USA [38576] : 1875+ CARDIFF, GLA, WLS [34466]

GARRICK 1700-1800 SHETLAND, SHI, SCT [36585]

GARRIGA PRE 1820 SAN SEBASTIAN, GUIPUZCOA, ESP [36937]

GARRIOCH 1750S DUNROSSNESS, SHL, SCT [35855]

GARRISON 1900+ YORKTON, SAS, CAN [35601] : C1890 POLK CO., MN, USA [35601] : C1898 APPLETON CITY, MO, USA [35601]

GARRITY 1800-1900 TULLAMORE, OFF, IRL [35845]

GARROD PRE 1900 LND, ENG [34131] : 1870+ LEEDS, YKS, ENG [34710] : 1850-1900 ISLINGTON, LND, ENG [36990]

GARROW 1670+ BODMIN, CON, ENG [36434] : PRE 1720 ABD, SCT [36434]

GARROWAY PRE 1855 PINNER, MDX, ENG [35864]

GARRUD ALL SFK, ENG [38471]

GARRY PRE 1700 DETTENHEIM, GER [38681] : 1803 TUAM, GAL, IRL [36860]

GARSCADDEN 1841+ IRL & SCT [33951] : C1839 GLASGOW, LKS, SCT [33951]

GARSIDE PRE 1900 HALIFAX, WRY, ENG [36411] : 1700-1900 RISHWORTH & RIPPONDEN, WRY, ENG [38003]

GARSKE PRE 1846 STEBBE & STIBBE, POM, GER [34584]

GARST ALL WORLDWIDE [36540]

GARTELL PRE 1830 DOR, ENG [36271]

GARTELMANN 1847-1867 NEW YORK, NY, USA [38186]

GARTER PRE 1733 SANCREED, CON, ENG [33912] : 1790-1820 HERRIMER CO., NY, USA [36546]

GARTERELL 1770+ ST HILARY, CON, ENG [35342]

GARTH 1780-1860 GLASGOW, LKS, SCT [37329]

GARTHWAITE 1830S QUE, CAN [36710]

GARTNER PRE 1870 DEUTSCH SAGAR, KSA, PRE [34562]

GARTON PRE 1780 ATTENBOROUGH, NTT, ENG [34858] : PRE 1850 NTT, ENG [37739]

GARTRELL BEATRICE 1860-1880 CON, ENG [33900] : PRE 1860 ST HILARY, CON, ENG [34958]

GARTSHORE 1400+ KIRKINTILLOCH, DNB, SCT [33989]

GARTY PRE 1900 ST BATHANS & TARANAKI, NZ [38586]

GARTZAREK ALL SOSNOWITZ, SIL, GER [38678]

GARVEN ALL WORLDWIDE [35832]

GARVEY 1780-1880 CARRICKMACROSS, MOG, IRL [34346] : 1800+ CRATLOE, CLA, IRL [35248] : 1830-1850S GALWAY, GAL, IRL [36936] : 1830-1850S COR, IRL [36936]

GARVICK PRE 1900 PITSLIGO, ABD & BAN, SCT [36877]

GARVIN 1828-1910 ORANGE, NSW, AUS [34422] : 1900-1930 PEAK HILL, NSW, AUS [34422] : 1750-1830 IRL [34422]

GARVOCK PRE 1900 PITSLIGO, ABD & BAN, SCT [36877]

GARWOOD 1840+ BALLARAT, VIC, AUS [34533] : PRE 1840 POSLINGFORD, SFK, ENG [34533] : 1700 KETTLEBURGH, SFK, ENG [35892] : 1750-1850 SUDBURY, SFK, ENG [35916] : 1770+ BROCKLEY, SFK, ENG [36111] : C1833 NORWICH, NFK, ENG [37981] : C1803 BUNGAY, SFK, ENG [37981]

GASCOIGNE PRE 1850 KESWORTH, LEI, ENG [34611]

GASELTINE 1700-1850 SWALLOWFIELD, BRK, ENG [37365]

GASH MARY A. C1865+ SYDNEY & MANLY, NSW, AUS [36643] : PRE 1900 LINCOLN, LIN & YKS, ENG [35934]

GASKELL 1860-1890 KADINA, SA, AUS [35861] : C1856 MANCHESTER, LAN, ENG [33917] : PRE 1700 COLTON & ULVERSTON, LAN, ENG [34053] : PRE 1850 LAN, ENG [34730] : 1820-1860 ELTON, LAN, ENG [35861] : PRE 1863 LAN, ENG [38286] : 1500-1900 WORLDWIDE [36169]

GASKETT C1720 TREDINGTON, GLS, ENG [33793]

GASKILL 1800S PA, USA [38522] : 1500-1900 WORLDWIDE [36169]

GASKIN 1660+ ST MICHAELS, BARBADOS [38235] : C1820 MARY STRATFORD LE BOW, LND, ENG [33796] : PRE 1820 LND, ENG [34848] : 1750-1850 LIVERPOOL, LAN, ENG [36063] : PRE 1830 GOUDHURST, KEN, ENG [37652]

GASMIER C1844 GER [34193]

GASS 1850 DUMFRIES, DFS, SCT [34890]

GASSMAN 1865-1875 KEWEENAW CO., MI, USA [38010]

GASSON 1783+ STONE IN OXNEY, KEN, ENG [35980] : PRE 1840 TOTTENHAM, LND, ENG [37743]

GAST 1840+ SYDNEY, NSW, AUS [34550]

GASTER PRE 1828 GRANOW, BERNSTEIN, GER [35463]

GASTRELL ALL SHERSTON, WIL, ENG [37115] : ALL WIL, ENG [37115] : ALL GLS, ENG [37115]

GATCHELL 1600+ TRULL, SOM, ENG [35558]

GATECLIFFE 1800S KILHAM, YKS, ENG [34569]

GATELY PRE 1860 ROS, IRL [35750]

GATER 1550+ HILMORTON, WAR, ENG [35276]

GATES C1900 CROWS NEST, NSW, AUS [35434] :
PRE 1777 INGHAM, SFK, ENG [33992] : PRE 1860
FRIMLEY, SRY, ENG [34428] : PRE 1830
MIDHURST, SSX, ENG [35446] : C1830-1860
SOUTHAMPTON, HAM, ENG [35446] : JOSEPH
1804 POPWORTH EVERARD, CAM, ENG [35870] :
PRE 1914 KEN, ENG [35893] : PRE 1840
BRIGHTON, SSX, ENG [35925] : 1863 +
STEYNING, SSX, ENG [36761] : 1700-1800
TATTINGSTONE, SFK, ENG [37042] : 1841
HARDINGSTONE MANDEVILLE, SOM, ENG [37378]
: PRE 1814 BATTLE & NINFIELD, SSX, ENG
[37875] : 1800-1850 CAM & MDX, ENG [38021] :
1864 + ASHBURTON, NZ [35446] : RUSSELL 1810-
1853 BROOME & TOMPKINS CO., NY, USA [35271]
: JOHN C1769-1835 WALPOLE & LYNDON, NH &
VT, USA [35324] : PRISILLAH 1700 + MA, USA
[37784]
GATHERCOLE PRE 1820 ERISWELL, SFK, ENG
[34442] : 1835-1870S SOUTH CREAKE, NFK, ENG
[36803] : PRE 1920 NFK, ENG [37062] : SARAH
C1790 ERISWELL, SFK, ENG [37106]
GATIS 1780-1850 DARLINGTON, DUR, ENG [37615]
GATRELL C1847 EASTBOURNE, SSX, ENG [35772]
GATT PRE 1800 PENNAN, ABD, SCT [34192] : C1800
ABERDOUR, ABD, SCT [34840] : PRE 1850
PENNAN, BAN, SCT [37835]
GATTON ALL WORLDWIDE [37922]
GATTY ALL WORLDWIDE [37361]
GAUBERT 1820 LONDON, MDX, ENG [35067]
GAUCHWIN PRE 1870 GAL, IRL [34433]
GAUDIN 1846-1893 + SYDNEY, NSW, AUS [35497] :
1600-1800 LA ROCHELLE, QUE, CAN [34082]
GAUDION C1800 ALD, CHI [35998]
GAUDREAU 1910 SINTALUTA, SAS, CAN [33902]
GAUGHAN 1750 + KILMORE, MAY, IRL [34415]
GAUL C1880 MELBOURNE, VIC, AUS [35826]
GAULT PRE 1800 SCT [35336] : 1600-1700
ABERDEEN, SCT [38115]
GAUNSON PRE 1850 SYDNEY, NSW, AUS [34268]
GAUNT 1600 + ROWLEY REGIS, STS, ENG [36701] :
1750-1850 PENISTONE, YKS, ENG [36898] : PRE
1700 WOR, ENG [37097] : PRE 1700 STS, ENG
[37097]
GAUNTLETT 1600-1700 WIL, ENG [37232]
GAUTHIER FELIX PRE 1868 QUEBEC CITY, QUE,
CAN [37496] : 1647 + ST VIVIEN, HN, FRA [36678] :
PRE 1650 CELLES SUR BELLES, PCH, FRA [38525]
GAUWIN PRE 1880 MANCHESTER, ENG [34433]
GAVEN ALL WORLDWIDE [38733]
GAVEY 1800S CASTEL, GSY, CHI & NZ [36809]
GAVIN 1800S TRICHINOPOLY, MADRAS, INDIA
[36830] : ALL WORLDWIDE [38733]
GAW 1800 + KIRKCUDBRIGHT, DFS, SCT [34498]
GAWEN 1600 + HASTINGS, SSX, ENG [34747]
GAWKE PRE 1820 INDIA [36102]
GAWLER PRE 1800 WINCANTON, SOM, ENG
[35771]
GAWLEY 1830-1870 LURGAN, DOW, IRL [34346] :
1700 + IRL [34572]
GAWN PRE 1800 CASTLETOWN, MALEW, IOM
[34137]
GAWNE 1800S BRIDE, IOM [34288] : C1841-1905
GERMAN, IOM & NZ [34651]
GAWRON 1800 + NAWSIE, POL [35000]
GAWTHORN ALL LONDON, ENG [34558]
GAWTHORNE PRE 1880 WAR, ENG [35180]
GAWTHROP PRE 1800 ADDINGHAM &
BURNSALL, WRY, ENG [36159]
GAY 1841 + JAMBEROO, NSW, AUS [35597] : POLLY
1806-1886 POWNAL, PEI, CAN [37499] : PRE 1650
CARTIGNY, GE, CH [38348] : 1860 + LND, ENG

[34361] : ALL SOM, ENG [34361] : PRE 1857
THURGARTON, NFK, ENG [34941] : 1800-1880
BATH, SOM, ENG [35228] : 1800-1900 OLDLAND,
GLS, ENG [36512] : 1821-1847 + BERE FERRERS,
DEV, ENG [37108] : 1760 + BRADFORD ON AVON,
WIL & SOM, ENG [37552] : ALL MD, PA, KS, IL,
USA [37812] : MARTHA 1866 MADISON CO., KY,
USA [38109]
GAYLER 1787 + OTTERY, ST MARY, NFK, ENG
[33880] : ALL ESS, ENG [36500]
GAYLOR 1850 + HOBART, TAS, AUS [33880] : 1802 +
OTTERY, ST MARY, DEV, ENG [33880] : 1790 +
OTTERY, ST MARY, NFK, ENG [33880] : 1750-1880
ROYSTON, HRT, ENG [36485]
GAYLORD 1550-1600 PITMINSTER, SOM, ENG
[37783]
GAYTON 1748 + BRAFIELD ON-THE GREEN, NTH,
ENG [35921]
GAZARD 1770S MINCHINHAMPTON, GLS, ENG
[35560] : ALL HORSLEY & BERKELEY, GLS, ENG
[37988]
GAZZARD 1800S GLS, ENG [34845]
GEACH 1735 KENWYN, CON, ENG [34214]
GEAKE 1850-1900 LAUNCESTON, CON, ENG [35845]
: 1750-1900 SOUTH PETHERWIN, CON, ENG
[35845]
GEALE 1800 + ENG [35581]
GEANEY PRE 1860 KER, IRL [35406]
GEAR 1700S ENG [35516]
GEARING PRE 1858 BURNHAM, BKM, ENG [34720]
GEARMAN PRE 1900 USA [36336]
GEARON C1820-C1900 CAHER, TIP, IRL [34651]
GEARY 1850 + ADELAIDE, SA, AUS [35105] : 1860 +
WIMMERA, VIC, AUS [35848] : PRE 1850 LND,
ENG [34979] : C1820 LONDON, ENG [35848] : PRE
1810 MDX, ENG [37885] : ALL BUTTEVANT, COR,
IRL [34312] : PRE 1836 + QUEENSTOWN, COR,
IRL [37912] : 1800S MAINS OF BYNDALIE, ABD,
SCT [38422] : PRE 1775 PEM, WLS [38461]
GEARY (SEE GUIRY) [37305]
GEATON PRE 1830 PLYMOUTH, DEV, ENG [37630]
GEBBIE 1800 + KILMORE & BALLARAT, VIC, AUS
[35481] : 1800 + SA, AUS [35481] : 1800 + QLD, AUS
[35481] : 1800 + LETHBRIDGE, VIC, AUS [35481] :
1800 + MELBOURNE & GEELONG, VIC, AUS
[35481] : 1670 + KILMARNOCK, AYR, SCT [35481] :
1670 + RFW, SCT [35481] : 1670 + RICCARTON,
AYR, SCT [35481] : 1670 + AYR, SCT [35481] : 1670 +
DARVEL, AYR, SCT [35481] : 1670 + GLASTON,
AYR, SCT [35481] : 1670 + USA [35481] : 1800 +
WORLDWIDE [35481]
GEBECK 1813-1947 BSW, GER [38308]
GEBEKE 1813-1947 BSW, GER [38308]
GEBHARDT 1700S TRAISA, HERSEN-DARM, GER
[38038]
GEB MULLER ANNA ROSINA PRE 1857
SEIFHENNERSDORF, OBERDORF, GER [35641]
GECHTER 1625 + DITZINGEN, BAW, FRG [38660]
GECKS PRE 1800 WARSTEIN, PRE, GER [37856] :
1800 + SCHENKELBERG, HEN, GER [37856] :
1840 + CINCINATTI, OH, USA [37856]
GEDDES 1800 + CORNAKELLY, CAV, IRL [33977] :
1600-1900 ARM, IRL [35944] : 1800S PITTENWEEM,
FIF, SCT [34144] : 1800S MARKINCH, FIF, SCT
[34144] : C1771-1811 ROTHYMOON, INV, SCT
[35223] : C1775-1825 FIF, SCT [36327] : PRE 1880
BLAIRGOWRIE, PER, SCT [36612] : PRE 1800 PER,
SCT [37006] : 1750 + LKS, SCT [38020] : 1750-1900
CROMDALE, MOR, SCT [38355] : 1800 + USA
[33977]
GEDDIS 1820S ST THOMAS MOUNT, MADRAS,
INDIA [37808]

GEDGE 1800S NORWICH, NFK, ENG [35858]

GEDLING 1800+ AUS [34703] : C1800 VIC, AUS [34907] : C1850 ADELAIDE, SA, AUS [34907]

GEE PRE 1888 ESK, QLD, AUS [33832] : 1832+ WHITE HILLS, TAS, AUS [35578] : 1805-1820 DRUMMONDVILLE, QUE, CAN [33911] : 1800-1820 STANSTEAD CO., QUE, CAN [33911] : 1815-1860 WENTWORTH CO., ONT, CAN [33911] : 1815-1860 KENT CO., ONT, CAN [33911] : 1786+ WEST LINCOLN, ONT, CAN [34094] : PRE 1888 CANTON, CHINA [33832] : 1851 WILFORD, NTT, ENG [33999] : PRE 1829 LONGSTANTON, CAM, ENG [34010] : 1800-1900 POPLAR & STEPNEY, MDX, ENG [34135] : PRE 1900 ANSTEY & BIRSTALL, LEI, ENG [35175] : PRE 1900 HACKNEY, LND, ENG [35175] : PRE 1779 ASTBURY, CHS, ENG [35483] : 1890+ RADFORD, NTT, ENG [35529] : 1820-1890 WASHTENAW CO., MI, USA [33911] : 1820-1890 MONROE & MONTCALM CO., MI, USA [33911] : 1840-1890 ST JOSEPH & WAYNE CO., MI, USA [33911] : 1754-1800 MARLOW, CHESHIRE CO., NH, USA [33911] : 1840-1890 JACKSON & KENT CO., MI, USA [33911] : 1800-1805 ESSEX, VT, USA [33911] : 1790 LINCOLN CO., KY, USA [38143]

GEEHERN PRE 1870 SLI, IRL [38365]

GEEKIE 1700+ DUNDEE, SCT [35080]

GEEN PRE 1870 APPELDORE, DEV, ENG [34347] : 1820+ APPELDORE, KEN, ENG [34347] : 1600-1850 DEV, ENG [38216]

GEENRIETS C1700 AMSTERDAM, NL [38159]

GEENRITS ALL NL [38159]

GEER 1780+ ETCHINGTHAM, SSX, ENG [33867] : 1780-1850 IFORD, SSX, ENG [35643]

GEERTS 1790-1850 VRACENE, OVL, BEL [38405]

GEESON 1780+ ENG [37391]

GEEVES 1791 BASSINGBOURN, CAM, ENG [34761]

GEGG 1887+ HARESFIELD, GLS, ENG [37940] : PRE 1888 CHELSEA & POPLAR, MDX, ENG [37940] : ALL GLS, ENG [37940] : PRE 1920 CIRENCESTER, GLS, ENG [37940] : 1891+ PURTON, WIL, ENG [37940] : ALL LND, ENG [37940] : ALL SCT [37940] : PRE 1900 CHEPSTOW, MON, WLS [37940]

GEGGIE PRE 1800 CHIRNSIDE, BEW, SCT [34209]

GEH PRE 1860 HOBART, TAS, AUS & BRD [35758]

GEHERAN PRE 1870 SLI, IRL [38365]

GEHLHAUS PRE 1790 PA, USA & GER [38055]

GEHLING PRE 1850 PRE, GER [34766] : 1818 COTTBUS, BRA, PRE [35369]

GEHRICHEN PRE 1680 EISENACH, THU, GER [38606]

GEHRING ELIZABETH 1842-1864 STETTIN, MEK, GER [38104] : ELIZABETH 1864-1870 DENISON, CRAWFORD, IA, USA [38104] : ELIZABETH 1870-1911 CHICAGO, COOK, IL, USA [38104]

GEHRLEIN PRE 1870 PFALZ, BAY, GER [37504]

GEHRMANN PRE 1900 HEILSBERG, OPR, GER [38664]

GEIGER 1800-1840 BAV, GER [38374]

GEIL 1750+ BUSUM, SHO, GER [37542]

GEISBERGER ALL CH [38037]

GEISLER 1790-1820 FINKENBERG, TIROL, OES [35850] : 1900+ IN, USA [38328]

GEISMAR PRE 1750 DOSSEL, WARBURG, GER [37569]

GEISSLER 1727-1758 WURZEN, KSA, GER [38748]

GEIST 1840+ JOHNSTOWN, PA, USA [36343]

GELBACH CHRISTIAN PRE 1850 BALTIMORE, MD, USA [38049]

GELDER 1750+ LUDDINGTON, LIN, ENG [36793]

GELDERBLOM ALL DELFT, ZUH, NL [33751] : ALL DELFT, ZUH, NL [38692]

GELDERD PRE 1900 LAN, ENG [34406] : PRE 1900 YKS, ENG [34406]

GELL PRE 1650 HOPTON, DBY, ENG [36025] : 1790+ BRISTOL, GLS, ENG [37056] : PRE 1850 YKS, ENG [37731]

GELLER PRE 1850 FAYETTE CO., OH, USA [37565]

GELLEY PRE 1870 DALSTON, MDX, ENG [35390] : C1850 LANARK, LKS, SCT [35249]

GELLIE C1854+ MOORABBIN, VIC, AUS [35249]

GELLING WILLIAM 1830+ IOM, UK [35648]

GELLINGS 1700+ DUFFELWARD, GER [37016] : ALL USA [37016]

GELLY 1730-1770 INVERKEITHING, FIF, SCT [36268]

GEMMELL 1848 GLASGOW, LKS, SCT [35720] : 1800+ DUNDONALD, AYR, SCT [36749]

GENAU PRE 1788 DOSSEL, WARBURG, GER [37569]

GENDEL PRE 1863 DEVONPORT, DEV, ENG [35471]

GENDRE 1580-1660 SAINTONGE, SURGERES, PCH, FRA [34514]

GENDRON 1876-1900 ESSEX CO., ONT, CAN [36720] : PRE 1853 OSCADA CO., MI, USA [36720] : ALL ALPENA, MI, USA [36720] : 1906+ ONAWAY, MI, USA [36720] : ALL ONAWAY, MI, USA [36720] : 1900+ DETROIT, MI, USA [36720]

GENEVE PRE 1820 EAST LONDON, ENG [37062]

GENGE 1800S CORSCOMBE, DOR, ENG [35964] : ALL WORLDWIDE [35994]

GENN PRE 1850 BUTTSGROVE, YKS, ENG [38675] : ALL WORLDWIDE [34076]

GENOA PRE 1840 LND, ENG [33830]

GENRICH 1800-1866 POM, GER [38199]

GENSON 1600-99 STOCKTON, WAR, ENG [34315]

GENT C1877 INVERELL, NSW, AUS [38077] : 1910+ CONGLETON, CHS, ENG [33920] : PRE 1799 MACCLESFIELD, CHS, ENG [35872] : PRE 1800 EAST LONDON, MDX, ENG [36432] : ALL LAN, ENG [36508] : JOHN THOMAS C1840+ LEICESTER & HALIFAX, WRY, ENG [37311] : MARY C1840+ HALIFAX, WRY, ENG [37311] : ALL ENG [37416] : 1891+ TERRINGTON, NFK, ENG [37673] : ALL TILNEY ST LAWRENCE, NFK, ENG [37673] : ALL MANCHESTER, LAN, ENG [38426] : 1600-1950 BOSTON LIN, SUTTON BRIDGE, LIN, ENG [38426] : PRE 1689 CHARLES CITY CO., VA, USA [37786] : PRE 1717 ISLE OF WIGHT, VA, USA [37786]

GENTLE C1830 ASHWELL, HRT, ENG [35860]

GENTLEMAN 1800-1820 KETTLESTONE, NFK, ENG [34182] : 1800-1820 FAKENHAM, NFK, ENG [34182] : ALL WORLDWIDE [34182]

GENTLIHOLME ALL WORLDWIDE [34182]

GENTRY 1600+ ESS, ENG [36093] : 1700-1770 VA, USA [36566] : 1770+ ANDERSON CO., TN, USA [37004]

GENTZ 1850+ INVERELL, NSW, AUS [36628]

GEOFFRAY 1806-1979 ARDILLATS, RHA, FRA [34136]

GEOFFROY 1740-1851 JOLIETTE CO., QUE, CAN [34106] : PRE 1740 LANGRES, CHA, FRA [34106]

GEOGHAN C1840 MAITLAND, NSW, AUS [35431]

GEOGHEGAN PRE 1880 BALLYLEAGH, ROS, IRL [35926]

GEORGE 1827+ HOBART, TAS, AUS [34910] : HARVEY C1850 DENMAN, NSW, AUS [35541] : 1900S ROCKDALE, NSW, AUS [35567] : 1860+ NSW, AUS [38005] : 1860-1885 SHAKESPEARE, ONT, CAN [34099] : 1850+ CAN [34099] : ANDREW HENRY 1820-1920 EGANVILLE, ONT, CAN [34514] : ANDREW HENRY 1820-1920 QUE, CAN [34514] : 1800+ LONDON, ENG [33948] : 1700+ RISELEY, BDF, ENG [34416] : PRE 1905 SHEERNESS, KEN,

ENG **[34575]** : PRE 1910 LONDON, ENG **[34657]** :
PRE 1800 ST COLUMB MINOR, CON, ENG **[35500]**
: 1840S REDRUTH, CON, ENG **[35728]** : PRE 1790
SCALFORD, LEI, ENG **[35745]** : 1750+ EALING,
MDX, ENG **[35825]** : 1854+ BIRMINGHAM, WAR,
ENG **[35948]** : 1854+ BRISTOL, GLS, ENG **[35948]** :
1820S HERTFORD, HRT, ENG **[36136]** : PRE 1818
BATH, SOM, ENG **[36526]** : PRE 1750 AYLSHAM,
NFK, ENG **[36593]** : WILLIAM 1820-1840 LND,
ENG **[36634]** : PRE 1850 MDX, ENG **[36702]** : 1850+
TODDINGTON, BDF, ENG **[36797]** : 1800+
REDRUTH, CON, ENG **[36887]** : 1650-1750
MALMESBURY, WIL, ENG **[37232]** : ALL
SENNEN, CON, ENG **[37379]** : TITSI C1890+ ENG
[37453] : JAMES PRE 1801 WINCANTON, SOM,
ENG **[37655]** : 1750+ LECHLADE, GLS, ENG
[37763] : 1700-1900 CON, ENG **[38005]** : 1759+
WINSLOW, BKM, ENG **[38358]** : 1823
KINGSCLERE, YKS, ENG **[38518]** : FREDERICK
PRE 1900 WALTON & LIVERPOOL, LAN, ENG
[38586] : 1800+ MAXWELL'S BUSH, ACK, NZ
[35951] : PETER PRE 1693 BLOCK ISLAND, RI,
USA **[35271]** : PRE 1900 USA **[36933]** : 1855-1880
KEWEENAW CO., MI, USA **[38010]** : 1900-1950 CA,
USA **[38100]** : 1750-1800 NC, USA **[38108]** : C1850
PONTYPOOL, MON, WLS **[35045]**
GEORGENS C1800 LEISTADT, GER **[38064]**
GEORGESON 1800+ SKELMERSDALE, LAN, ENG
[37262]
GEORGHEGAN PRE 1800+ TRIM, MEA, IRL **[35237]**
GEORLETTE 1751-1831 FOSSES LA VILLE, NMR,
BEL **[38158]**
GERAGHTY 1800-1900 IRL, SCT & ENG, AUS **[34227]**
: 1837+ VIC, AUS **[35443]** : 1800-1900 TULLAMORE,
OFF, IRL **[35845]**
GERARD 1700+ BAYE, CHA, FRA **[36493]** : 1757-1990
NANCY, ALS & LOR, FRA **[38308]**
GERAUGHTY 1800S+ MDX, ENG **[37868]**
GERE 1780+ ETCHINGHAM, SSX, ENG **[33867]**
GEREHAN PRE 1870 SLI, IRL **[38365]**
GERHART 1897 ONT, CAN **[37493]**
GERIG ALL CH **[38238]**
GERKE ALL WORLDWIDE **[38666]**
GERLEIN PRE 1870 PFALZ, BAY, GER **[37504]**
GERLING CAROLINE PRE 1870 HILLE, NRW, BRD
[36575] : LENA PRE 1870 HILLE, NRW, BRD **[36575]**
GERLOFF PRE 1865 POM, GER **[38235]**
GERMAIN PRE 1840 QUE, CAN **[38033]** : 1500-1848
COXWOLD & EASINGWOLD, NRY, ENG **[34706]** :
ALL SAINT SAUVEUR RONLAY, FRA **[34985]**
GERMAINE 1700+ RATHVILLY, CAR, IRL **[34602]** :
1800+ CASTLEDERMOT, KID, IRL **[34602]**
GERMAN 1865-1900 BRAZIL **[36336]** : 1796 BREDE,
SSX, ENG **[35259]** : PRE 1850 ARNOLD, NTT, ENG
[36387] : 1810-1870 TN, USA **[36336]** : 1790+
CUMBERLAND CO., NC, USA **[36336]** : 1675-1730
CALVERT CO., MD, USA **[36336]** : 1775-1850
WILKES CO., VA, USA **[36737]**
GERMAN (SEE JARMAN) **[35259]**
GERMANY C1880 CHELMSFORD & BUTTSBURY,
ESS, ENG **[37151]**
GERMON PRE 1813+ MORETON HAMPSTEAD,
DEV, ENG **[37912]**
GEROCK 1850+ VIC, AUS **[34550]**
GEROCKH PRE 1700 LAUFFEN, WUE, GER **[38683]**
GEROMI PRE 1885 HAN, GER & ENG **[37138]**
GEROW ALL CAN **[35637]**
GERRANS PRE 1900 TREGONY & TRURO, CON,
ENG **[36455]**
GERRARD PRE 1900 POTTERIES, STS, ENG **[36502]**

GERRETT 1853+ GEELONG & BALLARAT, VIC,
AUS **[35564]** : SOLOMON C1819 FROME, SOM,
ENG **[35564]**
GERRISH 1830+ NEW YORK, USA **[35822]**
GERRITSEN 1700S WEHL, GEL, NL **[38358]**
GERRY 1897+ BRUSSELS, ONT, CAN **[34505]**
GERS ALL MERKSPLAS, ATW, BEL **[38170]**
GERST C1834 HORSTEIN, BAV, GER **[38527]** : ALL
WORLDWIDE **[36540]**
GERT PRE 1810 SAFENWIL, AG, CH **[38029]**
GERTONSSON C1820 ALMEBODA, SMALAND,
SWE **[34395]**
GERVERDINCK PRE 1900 NL **[36755]**
GERVES C1800 STANTON BY DALE, NTT, ENG
[34734]
GERVIN 1800+ REACH, OTTAWA, ONT, CAN
[35613] : 1850+ OTTAWA, ONT, CAN **[35613]** :
1800+ IRL **[35613]**
GERVINI PRE 1885 HAN, GER & ENG **[37138]**
GESELL 1735-1820 LANCASTER CO., PA, USA
[38342]
GESNER PRE 1700 CH **[33904]**
GESS PRE 1860 KROTOSHIN, POS, GER **[38052]**
GESSFORD PRE 1850 DEWITT CO., IL, USA **[38196]** :
PRE 1850 VA, USA **[38196]**
GETHIN AUBREY 1936-95 LONDON, ENG **[37926]**
GETHING 1800+ DUDLEY, WOR, ENG **[35342]**
GETTENS 1843-1921 SYDNEY, NSW, AUS **[35782]** :
PRE 1843 BRISTOL, SOM, ENG **[35782]**
GETTS C1797 PA, USA **[38177]**
GETTY PRE 1807 SYDNEY, NSW, AUS **[37982]**
GETZENDANNER ELIZABETH 1740-1826 FRED CO.,
MD, USA **[38591]** : ADAM 1742-1783 FRED CO.,
MD, USA **[38591]**
GFIFFIN PRE 1870 CORK, COR, IRL **[34566]**
GFROERER PRE 1780 WIESENSTETTEN, WUE &
HOH, GER **[38679]**
GHAST (SEE GHOST) **[34539]**
GHENT 1750-1950 DBY, ENG **[38471]**
GHENT (SEE GENT) **[35872]**
GHERARDIN ALL WORLDWIDE **[34751]**
GHOST JOHN 1728 WIGGINTON, HRT, ENG **[34539]**
: ANN 1778 TRING, HRT, ENG **[34539]**
GIACOMELLI PRE 1860 ENG **[34883]** : C1500-C1780
CASTELLEONE DI SUASA, ITL **[36139]**
GIBB 1860-1933 BALLARAT & WYCHEPROOF, VIC,
AUS **[35594]** : 1862+ OTAGO & KARTIGI, OTAGO,
NZ **[35885]** : PRE 1920 AYR, AYR, SCT **[33978]** :
1800+ FORFAR & DUNDEE, ANS, SCT **[34568]** :
PRE 1850 PETERHEAD, ABD, SCT **[34608]** : PRE
1877 FORFAR, ANS, SCT **[34758]** : C1765-1860
AUCHINLECK, AYR, SCT **[35594]** : PRE 1862
NEWARTHILL, LKS, SCT **[35885]** : 1720
DUMBERNAULD, MLN, SCT **[35937]** : 1800-1850
ABERDEEN, ABD, SCT **[36150]** : PRE 1800 ANS,
SCT **[36433]** : PRE 1820 PER, SCT **[36754]** : ALL
PAISLEY, RFW, SCT **[36789]**
GIBBARD PRE 1800 ARDLEY, OXF, ENG **[34112]** :
1750+ STEPNEY, MDX, ENG **[36879]** : PRE 1800
IVINGHOE, CHEDDINGTON, BKM, ENG **[37909]**
GIBBENS 1871+ FOOTSCRAY, VIC, AUS **[34039]**
GIBBIE (SEE GEBBIE) **[35481]**
GIBBINS PRE 1870 MILTON ERNEST & BEDFORD,
BDF, ENG **[34850]** : 1825-1860 YORK, YKS, ENG
[36051] : 1800-1850 ALVERSTOKE, HAM, ENG
[37214] : PRE 1850 PHILEDELPHIA, PA, USA **[34036]**
GIBBLING C1800-1850 COLCHESTER, ESS, ENG
[35725]
GIBBON PRE 1868 SOUTH SHIELDS, DUR, ENG
[36364] : C1790 BISHOPWEARMOUTH, DUR, ENG
[36961] : 1817-1850 LAMESLEY WALDRIDGE,
DUR, ENG **[36961]** : 1795+ LONDON & SSX, ENG

[36967] : 1800+ AUCKLAND, DUR, ENG [37598] : 1750 CHEDISTON, SFK, ENG [37928] : PRE 1750 GOUDA, ZUH, NL [35890] : ALL SCT & AUS [36348] : ALL USA & CAN [36348]

GIBBONS 1790+ SYDNEY, NSW, AUS [35397] : 1792+ ST JOHNS & BURNT ISLAND, NFD, CAN [33823] : PRE 1850 CAN & WLS [38386] : ALL EXETER, DEV, ENG [33823] : C1850 COVENTRY, WAR, ENG [34358] : 1798 OXFORD, OXF, ENG [34708] : PRE 1865 NEWTON BY TOFT, LIN, ENG [35129] : C1872+ BATH, SOM, ENG [35223] : PRE 1846 BOX, WIL, ENG [35223] : PRE 1790 LONDON, ENG [35397] : C1750 SEDGLEY, STS, ENG [35512] : 1751+ AYLESBURY, BKM, ENG [35578] : 1800+ OXF, ENG [35598] : 1800+ WOLVERHAMPTON, STS, ENG [36971] : C1770 MARTON & RADFORD SEMELE, WAR, ENG [37556] : 1853+ AUCKLAND, NZ [33823] : 1870+ CLEVELAND, OH, USA [36971] : 1775-1880 PA, USA [37011] : PRE 1750 MA, USA [37808] : PRE 1800 SC, USA [38783]

GIBBS 1840-1990 QUEANBEYAN, NSW, AUS [33818] : 1849+ PARRAMATTA, NSW, AUS [34979] : 1850+ GLENMAGGIE, VIC, AUS [36622] : 1850+ SALE, MAFFRA & HEYFIELD, VIC, AUS [36622] : PRE 1900 TRINITY BAY, NFD, CAN [33904] : 1832-1870 OSHAWA, ONT, CAN [34088] : 1800 BEAMINSTR, DOR, ENG [33967] : PRE 1835 MARYLEBONE, LND, ENG [34022] : ALL PETERBOROUGH, NTH & HUN, ENG [34032] : 1780-1820 KINGSBRIDGE, DEV, ENG [34088] : PRE 1800 TISSINGTON, DBY, ENG [34311] : ALL HORSLEY, GLS, ENG [34475] : 1700+ BRIDPORT, DOR, ENG [34532] : PRE 1800 GREAT MILTON, OXF, ENG [34716] : PRE 1829 BISHOPSTONE, WIL, ENG [34814] : 1700S DEV, ENG [34931] : 1840+ PLYMOUTH, DEV, ENG [35096] : C1780 BURSTOCK, DOR, ENG [35252] : 1700S PETERBOROUGH, NBL, ENG [35768] : PRE 1900 HEF, ENG [36069] : C1820 CITY OF LONDON, ENG [36076] : C1870 SOUTHWARK, LND, ENG [36076] : PRE 1840 BRIGHTHELMSTONE, SSX, ENG [36079] : 1800-1884 ALVINGTON, GLS, ENG [36293] : PRE 1850 BERKSWELL, WAR, ENG [36385] : ANNE 1800+ TUNBRIDGE WELLS, KEN, ENG [36471] : 1800-1840 BENTLEY HAY, STS, ENG [36536] : 1800 PORTLAND, ENG [36745] : 1800+ KINTBURY, BRK, ENG [36975] : 1800+ SAL, ENG [37705] : 1800 WIVELISCOMBE, SOM, ENG [37766] : PRE 1880 LONDON, ENG [38004] : C1700-1850 LONDON, MDX & SRY, ENG [38034] : 1840+ NELSON, NZ [36790] : ALL OH, CA & NJ, USA [38363]

GIBERSON 1822 FRANKLIN, OH, USA [37008]

GIBIRDI 1840S GENOA, ITL [37390]

GIBLER 1775-1800 SHENANDOAH CO., VA, USA [35301]

GIBLETT 1750+ CAMDEN TOWN, LND, ENG [35053] : ALL FROME, SOM, ENG [35198]

GIBLIN 1700 HEMPSTEAD, ESS, ENG [37125]

GIBNEY 1823+ YASS BINALONG, NSW, AUS [35159] : PRE 1850 CAV, IRL [33862]

GIBON 1860+ MALVERN, VIC, AUS [34037]

GIBSON THOMAS 1844+ SYDNEY, NSW, AUS [34449] : SUSANNA 1844+ SYDNEY, NSW, AUS [34449] : JOHN 1840+ MULGOA, NSW, AUS [36273] : 1830S TAS, AUS [36276] : 1860+ NEWCASTLE, NSW, AUS [37979] : PRE 1940 SYDNEY, NSW, AUS [38289] : C1875+ DUNGOG, NSW, AUS [38510] : 1835+ GUELPH, ONT, CAN [34231] : DOROTHY 1800-1900 NEWCASTLE UPON TYNE, DUR & NBL, ENG [34040] : 1764 NORMANTON, DBY, ENG [34120] : FRANK 1873 EAST SUTTON, KEN, ENG [34630] : CHARLES 1830+ ULCOMBE, KEN,

ENG [34630] : 1870+ RUNCORN, CHS, ENG [35341] : WILLIAM 1700-1800 QUEEN CAMEL, SOM, ENG [35361] : PRE 1840 LIVERPOOL, LAN, ENG [35423] : PRE 1880 BOLTON, LAN, ENG [36508] : 1700+ MALTON, NRY, ENG [36516] : 1650+ TOPCLIFFE BY THIRSK, NRY & YKS, ENG [36772] : PRE 1830 DANBURY, ESS, ENG [37137] : 1840+ WORKSOP, NTT, ENG [37241] : 1700+ STOCKTON ON TEES, DUR, ENG [37635] : 1800S LONDON, MDX, ENG [37833] : PRE 1900 SFK, ENG [37874] : PRE 1900 NFK, ENG [37874] : 1870-1900 ISLINGTON & EDMONTON, MDX, ENG [37877] : 1800-1880 MELTON MOWBRAY, LEI, ENG [37877] : PRE 1880 COWPEN VILLAGE, NBL, ENG [38218] : PRE 1850 LOW CONISCLIFFE, DUR, ENG [38473] : PRE 1850 BARNARD CASTLE, DUR, ENG [38473] : PRE 1912 HIGH WYCOMBE, BKM, ENG [38580] : 1822+ MARTHAM, NFK, ENG & AUS [33790] : PRE 1860 LE HAVRE, BN, FRA [34037] : C1800 DACCA, INDIA [38485] : 1800+ DONAGHADEE, DOW, IRL [33970] : PRE 1850 ARM, IRL [34866] : C1848 DUBLIN, DUB, IRL [35133] : JOHN PRE 1840 SEAGOE, ARM, IRL [36273] : 1780-1880 DONAGHADEE, DOW, IRL [36776] : PRE 1912 DROMORE, DOW, IRL [37439] : 1800-1850 ARDMORE, CAV, IRL [37956] : 1750-1850 BALMAGHIE, KKD, SCT [33779] : C1900 EDINBURGH, MLN, SCT [34792] : JAMES PRE 1849 EDINBURGH, SCT [35258] : CHARLES C1820 EDINBURGH, MLN, SCT [35391] : PRE 1858 BIGGAR, LKS, SCT [35441] : C1800+ ABERCORN, WLN, SCT [35629] : PRE 1820 PAISLEY, RFW, SCT [35829] : 1861 STIRLING, STI, SCT [35865] : PRE 1880 ABERDEEN, ABD, SCT [36201] : C1774 MONTROSE, ANS, SCT [36276] : ALL AYR, SCT [36497] : 1855 AUCHINLECK, AYR, SCT [36599] : 1750+ BEITH, AYR, SCT [37110] : 1750-1840 AYR, SCT [37338] : 1700-1850 KKD, SCT [37644] : 1790+ INVERKEITHING, FIF, SCT [37881] : 1800S+ LANARK, SCT [38436] : 1830+ CLIFTON BANK, ROX, SCT & CAN [34467] : 1920+ CHICAGO, IL, USA [33795] : 1830 THOMASTON, GA, USA [36946] : 1700+ WARREN CO., GA, USA [36946] : 1850+ ST LOUIS, MO, USA [37012] : LEVI PERRY C1860 BLACKFORD CO., IN, USA [37551] : LEVI PERRY 1820-1840 LEXINGTON, KY, USA [37551] : PRE 1820 LEXINGTON CO., KY, USA [37551] : PRE 1820 VA, USA [38196] : 1790-1950 ALLEGHENY CO., PA, USA [38344]

GIDDENS PRE 1870 NEW BILTON & RUGBY, WAR, ENG [34629] : MARY PRE 1825 HRT, ENG [36634]

GIDDINGS 1860-1950 SRY, ENG [35916] : PRE 1820 CAM, ENG [36095] : WILLIAM C1807+ KINGS CLIFFE, NTH, ENG [36643] : ALL WIL & LND, ENG [37057] : 1822-1901 HERKIMER, NY & MI, USA [36910]

GIDDINS 1800+ LAUNCESTON, TAS, AUS [34271] : WILLIAM ALL GROSE VALE & KURRAJONG, NSW, AUS [36643] : PRE 1817 WOLVERHAMPTON, STS, ENG [35061]

GIDEON 1900 MASON CO., IL, USA [38103] : 1850 KNOX CO., IN, USA [38103]

GIDLEY GRACE 1793+ WHITESTONE, DEV, ENG [35788] : PRE 1800 BRIXHAM, DEV, ENG [36143] : 1820-1850S BUCKFASTLEIGH, DEV, ENG [37308]

GIDMAN PRE 1664 NEWBOLD, ASTBURY & BIDDULPH, CHS & STS, ENG [36204]

GIDNEY C1844 PAGHAM, SSX, ENG [34893] : C1838 LAMBETH, SRY, ENG [34893] : C1879 BROMLEY, LND, ENG [34893]

GIEBELER 1720-1749 NIEDERSCHELDEN, NRW, BRD [35301]

GIEHR PRE 1800 SCHWARZENHOLZ, SAA, GER [38681]

GIERCKE HANS PRE 1625 WESTFALEN, GER [38563] : HANS 1625+ RISINGE, OSTERGOTLAND, SWE [38563]

GIERRIE 1800+ ABBEVILLE & AMIENS, NOR, FRA [37294]

GIERSBACH 1600-1750 EBERSBACH, BAV, GER [36966]

GIESCHEN 1810+ SOUTHWARK, LND, ENG [37552]

GIESEKE 1862+ AUS [35831] : 1800+ HAN, GER [35831]

GIESENKIRCHEN PRE 1800 NRW & RPF, BRD [38616]

GIESLER PRE 1870 ANH, GER [35340]

GIESZCZYK ALL WORLDWIDE [38687]

GIFFARD PRE 1820 ST MARTIN, JSY, CHI [36696] : PRE 1800 ENG [36166]

GIFFEN ALL ROYSTON, CAM, ENG [37922]

GIFFORD PRE 1850 SOM, ENG [35062] : C1745 COMPTON D, SOM, ENG [35252] : 1700S DUTCHESS CO., NY, USA [34392]

GIFT PRE 1750 FUSSGONHEIM, RPF, GER [38681] : 1750-1850 CUMBERLAND CO., PA, USA [38139] : 1760-1850 FRANKLIN CO., PA, USA [38139]

GIGG 1800-1880 NORTH LONDON, ENG [34719]

GIGGINS 1844+ RAYMOND TERRACE, NSW, AUS [35157]

GIGLER C1640 RAUCHENBERG, BAV, GER [38322] : 1857+ GREEN BAY, WI & CA, USA [38322]

GIGNAC ALL ST MAURICE, QUE, CAN [34985]

GIHON (SEE GIBSON) [35133]

GILABERT 1700-1990 ALICANTE, ESP [38346]

GILBAR 1840S SHOREDITCH, MDX, ENG [35464]

GILBERT CHARLES C1858 VIC, AUS [34815] : 1800-1900 VIC, AUS [34815] : 1850+ COLLINGWOOD & FRYERS CREEK, VIC, AUS [35214] : 1903-1930 NEWCASTLE, NSW, AUS [35570] : 1897-1903 KALGOORLIE, WA, AUS [35570] : 1853-1914 SA, AUS [35771] : GEORGE A. 1843+ PORT PHILLIP & NEWTOWN, VIC, AUS [38540] : C1834 HAMILTON, ONT, CAN [35357] : PRE 1828 ISLEWORTH, LND, ENG [33860] : PRE 1800 SOHAM, CAM, ENG [34316] : PRE 1850 SALISBURY, WIL, ENG [34317] : C1811 ST AUSTELL, CON, ENG [34374] : C1850-1855 WHITEHAVEN, CUL, ENG [34374] : C1857+ SWARTHMOOR & ULVERSTONE, LAN, ENG [34374] : PRE 1875 YKS, ENG [34654] : 1770-1840 LOUGHBOROUGH, LEI, ENG [34822] : 1800-1860 SHARDLOW, DBY, ENG [34822] : PRE 1800 KEN, ENG [34858] : C1870S SOUTH HUISH, DEV, ENG [35438] : 1800+ BREAGE, CON, ENG [35476] : 1850+ WORCESTER, WOR, ENG [35554] : PRE 1850 KENWYN & TRURO, CON, ENG [35570] : 1783-1800 CLERKENWELL, LND, ENG [35720] : 1800-1860 CHICHESTER, SSX, ENG [35720] : PRE 1800 ST JUST & ST BURYAN, CON, ENG [35736] : PRE 1820 CON, ENG [35830] : JAMES 1880+ KEN, ENG [35848] : 1700S GREAT BOWDEN, LEI, ENG [35858] : 1900-1950 EAST HAM, LND, ENG [36017] : 1850-1865 BISHOPS STORTFORD, HRT, ENG [36017] : 1840-1851 THORLEY, HRT, ENG [36017] : 1865-1900 MILE END & BETHNAL GREEN, MDX, ENG [36017] : 1865-1900 STEPNEY, MDX, ENG [36017] : JOHN PRE 1725 KEN & SSX, ENG [36272] : 1720-1839 BECKLEY & NORTHIAM, SSX, ENG [36272] : 1700-1800 LICHFIELD, STS, ENG [36438] : ALL MAIDSTONE, KEN, ENG [36743] : C1790-1900 GUNWALLOE, CON, ENG [36877] : PRE 1850 GEATT KIMBLE & ASHTON CLINTON, BKM, ENG [37084] : 1700-1800 DOWNHAM, CAM, ENG [37188] : 1800S DEV, ENG [37442] : PRE 1800 TENTERDEN, KEN, ENG [37736] : GEORGE C1876+ PONTIFRACT, YKS, ENG [37888] : C1700 ALTON PRIORS, WIL, ENG [37918] : ALL OXF & WAR, ENG [38176] : PRE 1760 BN, FRA [38408] : MARIE PRE 1760 TEURTHEVILLE, BN, FRA [38408] : PRE 1800 BAD, GER [37804] : 1860+ DUNEDIN, OTAGO, NZ [36877] : 1600-1900 EDINBURGH, MLN, SCT [35944] : PRE 1840 SCT [36017] : 1700+ TAUNTON, MA, USA [35314] : 1800-1850 STEUBEN CO., NY, USA [36334] : PRE 1800 BUCKS CO., PA, USA [36729] : 1860 GA, USA [37792] : 1845-1880 KEWEENAW CO., MI, USA [38010] : ALL LOGAN CO., OK, USA [38451] : 1700+ ORANGE CO., NC, USA & ENG [38175]

GILBERTS PRE 1750 KINGSWINFORD, STS, ENG [36110]

GILBOY 1860 IRL [37866]

GILCHREST 1760S+ CAMPBELTOWN, ARL, SCT [34156]

GILCHRIST 1850+ VIC, AUS [35731] : 1846+ SYDNEY, NSW, AUS [36312] : 1800+ CRAMAHE & COLBORNE, ONT, CAN [34109] : 1800+ ONT, CAN [34465] : LETITIA PRE 1933 ENG [34034] : FEDRICK C1800 ENG [34034] : STIRLING PRE 1933 ENG [34034] : 1870+ SOUTHAMPTON, HAM, ENG [35971] : 1800S IRL [36727] : 1840-50 NEWTOWNHAMILTON, ARM, IRL [38583] : PRE 1850 ISLE OF ISLAY, SCT [34465] : 1825+ THRONLEIBANK, RFW, SCT [36509] : ALL GLASGOW, LKS, SCT [36509] : PRE 1850 GLASGOW, LKS, SCT [37832] : ALL CUMBERNAULD, DNB, SCT & NZ [33981] : 1800+ CUMBERNAULD, DNB, SCT & NZ [36257]

GILDAY 1820+ LEEDS CO., ONT, CAN [34504]

GILDEA 1813+ SLIGO, IRL [37592]

GILDER 1880+ GIPPSLAND & SALE, VIC, AUS [36622]

GILDERSLEEVE 1750-1850 STUTTON, SFK, ENG [37042] : 1830-1900 DUTCHESS CO., NY, USA [37605]

GILDING C1810 WEST BRIDGFORD, NTT, ENG [34734]

GILDNER PRE 1890 RUDA PABIANIKA, POL [34519]

GILES EDWARD C1841 ADELAIDE, SA, AUS [34553] : CHARLES 1827+ HOBART, TAS, AUS [35394] : 1850+ VICTORIA, NS, CAN [37489] : 1750+ PORTSEA, HAM, ENG [33938] : 1800 LAMBETH, SRY, ENG [34210] : PRE 1857 CHELSEA, MDX, ENG [34458] : 1600+ NORTH MOLTON, DEV, ENG [34747] : C1854 BRISTOL, GLS, ENG [34805] : PRE 1840 WINCANTON, SOM, ENG [34897] : ELIZABETH PRE 1824 FROME, SOM, ENG [35583] : 1760-1840 GREAT YARMOUTH & NORWICH, NFK, ENG [35725] : 1800-1830 BRK, ENG [35850] : 1780+ CHADDESLEY CORBETT, WOR, ENG [35919] : 1700+ SELWORTHY, SOM, ENG [35972] : 1770S ST BLAZEY, CON, ENG [36190] : PRE 1850 PLYMOUTH, DEV, ENG [36474] : ALL HOTHFIELD, KEN, ENG [37015] : PRE 1800 CHEDZOY, SOM, ENG [37085] : 1800-1860 BROAD CLYST, DEV, ENG [37096] : BEATRICE 1870-1905 IPSWICH, SFK, ENG [37311] : HENRY WATSON C1840+ IPSWICH, SFK, ENG [37311] : ELIZABETH C1840+ IPSWICH, SFK, ENG [37311] : 1750+ WANTAGE, BRK, ENG [37328] : 1800-1900 YEOVIL, SOM, ENG [37435] : PRE 1817 PONTESBURY, SAL, ENG [38052] : 1847+ STEPNEY, LND, ENG [38417] : 1830S IRL [38417] : 1840+ GRAND FORKS, ND, USA [37422]

GILFILLAN 1700-1750 LONDONDERRY, IRL [34162]

GILGEN 1878+ SA, AUS [34839]

GILHAM 1827+ WESTBURY & HOBART, TAS, AUS
[35394] : ALL NFK, ENG [36014] : ALL SFK, ENG
[36014] : 1770+ ALTON & FARLINGTON, HAM,
ENG [37321]

GILHOOLEY 1845+ BOOROWA, NSW, AUS [37555] :
1876+ GRENFELL, NSW, AUS [37555] : PRE 1839
TIP, IRL [37555]

GILHOOLY 1851-1860S EDINBURGH, SCT [37086]

GILIS JOANNES PRE 1774 HASSELT & STEVOORT,
LBG, BEL [37430] : PRE 1774 LBG, BEL & NL [37430]

GILISEN PRE 1774 LBG, BEL & NL [37430]

GILISSEN PRE 1774 LBG, BEL & NL [37430]

GILKES PRE 1800 BKM, ENG [37498]

GILKESON 1840-55 OH, USA [38151] : 1864-1889
COVINGTON, KY, USA [38151]

GILKINSON 1820S ST CUTHBERTS, MLN, SCT
[33945]

GILL 1853-1920 MELBOURNE, VIC, AUS [33791] :
1840+ NSW, AUS [35073] : 1840+ FRYERSTOWN,
VIC, AUS [35391] : 1840-1900 WOODVILLE &
JONES ISLAND, NSW, AUS [35546] : THOMAS
1870+ BALLARAT, VIC, AUS [35803] : 1828+ NSW,
AUS [35878] : 1858+ SPRINGSURE, QLD, AUS
[35878] : 1854+ EDEN, NSW, AUS [35878] : PRE
1853 HACKNEY, LND, ENG [33791] : 1860+
PECKHAM, SRY, ENG [33899] : PRE 1840
NEWBANK, NORTHOWRAM, WRY, ENG [34003] :
1800+ SHERBURN, WRY, ENG [34020] : PRE 1850
WOOLWICH, KEN, ENG [34105] : ALL
AINDERBY, YKS, ENG [34619] : 1812+ CAXTON,
CAM, ENG [34777] : 1800-1900 TRURO, CON, ENG
[34872] : CHAS ATTWOOD 1800S LONDON, ENG
[34924] : 1800-1900 BURNLEY, LAN, ENG [35129] :
1800-1900 NORTHAMPTON, NTH, ENG [35177] :
1850 STAFFORD, STS, ENG [35256] : C1820 ST
BLAZEY, CON, ENG [35349] : 1700+ ST AGNES,
CON, ENG [35391] : C1820 PORTSEA, HAM, ENG
[35401] : 1700+ YORK, YKS, ENG [35460] : PRE
1840 BECKLEY, SSX, ENG [35546] : PRE 1828
MALDON, ESS, ENG [35724] : PRE 1828 LIN, ENG
[35878] : ALL KIRKBY LONSDALE, WES, ENG
[36063] : PRE 1750 KINGSWINFORD, STS, ENG
[36110] : PRE 1780 BECKLEY & UDIMORE, SSX,
ENG [36272] : WILLIAM 1820+ SADDLEWORTH,
WRY, ENG [36291] : JOHN 1787 LANGPORT, SOM,
ENG [36367] : 1770+ STOKE FERRY, NFK, ENG
[36846] : 1800-1850 WOR, ENG [37038] : 1700-1870
HELSTON, CON, ENG [37615] : PRE 1820
LEICESTER, LEI, ENG [38056] : C1890 KEIGHLEY,
YKS, ENG [38168] : PRE 1750 KEN, ENG [38389] :
PRE 1840 CON, ENG [38393] : PRE 1880
PAINSWICH, GLS, ENG [38435] : 1700+ RAMSAY,
IOM [34415] : 1800+ WATERFORD, WAT, IRL
[35627] : SOPHIA 1800+ TYR & ARM, IRL [36697] :
1800 NEWTOWN FORBES, LOG, IRL [38379] : PRE
1822 AUCHERTOOL, FIF, SCT [37946] : ALL PA,
USA [38359] : 1700+ LA SALLE CO., IL, USA [38765]
: ALL HERESAY, MI, USA & ENG [35302]

GILLAN ALL BALLYTAGGART, ANT, IRL [35480] :
C1795-1860S GLASGOW, LKS, SCT [34635] : PRE
1850 FIFE, MOR, SCT [35758]

GILLANDERS PRE 1840 LIRRAY, ROC, SCT [35925]

GILLARD 1880+ BOLTON, LAN, ENG [36198] : PRE
1880 CULMSTOCK, DEV & CON, ENG [36198] :
1800+ DRAYTON, SOM, ENG [37905]

GILLATT 1700+ CARLTON IN LINDRICK &
WORKSOP, NTT, ENG [36823] : 1600+ HATFIELD,
WRY, ENG [36823] : 1700+ HARTHILL, WRY,
ENG [36823] : ALL NORTON, DBY, ENG [38265] :
1879+ SPRINGSTON & LINCOLN, CANTY, NZ
[36823]

GILLBANKS ALL LAN, ENG [38514]

GILLBEE 1900+ VIC, AUS [34459]

GILLBERRY ALL WORLDWIDE [37735]

GILLBOY 1700-1900 HULL, ERY, ENG [37290]

GILLCHRIST 1782 LONDON, ENG [35720]

GILLELAND PRE 1850 IN, USA [35290]

GILLEN JOHN 1850S TORONTO, ONT, CAN [34997] :
JOHN 1850S LANARK, ONT, CAN [34997] : ALL
BALLYTAGGART, ANT, IRL [35480] : SAMUEL
C1894-1969 CANTON, SD, USA [34997]

GILLES C1790 BUCKINGHAM, BKM, ENG [36945]

GILLESPIE 1850+ TUENA, NSW, AUS [35736] :
ANDREW 1840+ SYDNEY, NSW, AUS [36295] :
1840+ NSW, AUS [37900] : ALEX 1795+
GLOUCESTER, GLS, ENG [34823] : PRE 1872
SHEERNESS, KEN, ENG [35956] : 1800-1845
LIVERPOOL, LAN, ENG [37040] : 1750-1850 ARM,
IRL [34513] : ALL BELFAST, IRL [34599] :
EDWARD 1800+ O'BRIENS BRIDGE, CLA & LIM,
IRL [35560] : PRE 1840 NEWRY, DOW, IRL [36295] :
1840+ BELFAST, ARM, IRL [36369] : PRE 1880 IRL
[36754] : 1800+ DUNGLOE, DON, IRL [37900] : PRE
1860 ENNISKILLEN, FER, IRL [38262] : PRE 1860
CLOGHER, TYR, IRL [38289] : PRE 1825
FIVEMILETOWN, TYR, IRL [38461] : ELIZA 1864+
NZ [35364] : 1750-1900 KINCAPLE, FIF, SCT [34004]
: 1820-1850S AIRTH, STI, SCT [34359] : ALEX PRE
1795 SCT [34823] : C1826 TILLICOULTRY, CLK,
SCT [35863] : PRE 1890 FINDHORN ELGIN, MOR,
SCT [36369] : HELEN C1831 DUMFRIES, DFS, SCT
[37424] : PRE 1850 ISLAY, ARL, SCT [38403] : ALL
SCT & AUS [38356]

GILLESPY 1860+ TONBRIDGE, KEN, ENG [34280]

GILLET 1800 DALLINGTON, SSX, ENG [35186]

GILLETT 1850+ GOULBURN AREA, NSW, AUS
[34185] : ALL NFD, CAN [34207] : PRE 1850
TINTINHULL, SOM, ENG [34185] : 1800
DALLINGTON, SSX, ENG [35186] : 1800-1900
LITTLEPORT & DOWNHAM, CAM, ENG [37227] :
1890+ MORRISON, IL, USA [35150] : 1570-1840 NY
& CT, USA & ENG [37522] : PRE 1700 CT & SOM,
USA & ENG [38746]

GILLETTE ALL NFD, CAN [34207] : 1800 CA, USA
[35313] : 1940+ ATLANTIC CO., NJ, USA [36580] :
1900-1950 PHILADELPHIA CO., PA, USA [36580]

GILLEY PRE 1850 SOUTHAMPTON, HAM, ENG
[36067]

GILLHAM PRE 1800 FLETCHING, SSX, ENG [34739]
: C1840 LIDDINGTON, RUT, ENG [35121] : 1800S
LONDON, ENG [36851]

GILLIAM C1760 BRUNSWICK CO., VA, USA [37536]

GILLIARD 1840-1890 HAMMILLE, BEL [34521] : 1860-
1900 CHARLEROI, HNT, BEL [34521] : 1880+ OAK
LAKE & VIRDEN, MAN, CAN [34521] : C1915
GRAND CLARIERE, MAN, CAN [34521] : C1875 ST
CLAUDE, CHA, FRA [34521] : C1900 ST CLAUDE,
JURA, FRA [34521] : 1870-1900 L'THIERNY, FRA
[34521]

GILLIBAN PRE 1806 LAN, ENG [35546]

GILLICK PRE 1840 CAV, IRL [34174] : ALL CAV, IRL
[35525]

GILLIE PRE 1820 NBL, ENG [36201] : PRE 1820 BEW,
SCT [36201] : 1700-1800 COLDINGHAM, BEW, SCT
[38407]

GILLIES PRE 1893 URANA, NSW, AUS [33770] :
1852+ GEELONG, VIC, AUS [33770] : PRE 1774
LBG, BEL & NL [37430] : C1814 YKS, ENG [34425] :
PRE 1852 PORTREE, ISLE OF SKYE, INV, SCT
[33770] : 1880+ PAISLEY, RFW, SCT [35018] : PRE
1840 SKYE, INV, SCT [36272]

GILLIGAN 1877+ GOULBURN, NSW, AUS & IRL
[34773]

GILLILAND PRE 1850 IN, USA [35290] : 1818 KT, USA [36337]

GILLIN 1750-1850 DUR, ENG [34753] : ALL BALLYTAGGART, ANT, IRL [35480]

GILLING 1820S ROTHERHAM, YKS, ENG [35509] : 1700+ NTT, ENG [37839] : MARTHA 1800-1840 NORTHAMPTON, NTH, ENG [38259]

GILLINGHAM PRE 1784 BRIGHSTONE, IOW, ENG [36668] : 1800-1900 ENG [37877]

GILLINGS 1850-1900 ENG [36828] : JASPER 1790-1850 TUNKHANNOCK & LEMON, PA, USA [36948]

GILLINGWATER 1600 CHEDISTON, SFK, ENG [37928]

GILLINS 1800 WESTMINSTER, LND, ENG [34204]

GILLION ALL PEI, CAN [35933]

GILLIS 1880+ JAMES, QLD, AUS [34425] : PRE 1774 LBG, BEL & NL [37430] : 1800+ BEUTHEN, SIL, GER [37196] : JANE PRE 1850 INNERLEITHEN, PEE, SCT [34935] : PRE 1790S ISLE OF SKYE, SCT [36358]

GILLISEN PRE 1774 LBG, BEL & NL [37430]

GILLISSEN PRE 1774 LBG, BEL & NL [37430]

GILLMAN C1800 OLNEY, BKM, ENG [34853] : 1800S GLS, ENG [35723]

GILLMORE PRE 1803 STOCKPORT, CHS, ENG [34213]

GILLON 1780+ EDINBURGH, WLN, SCT [34455] : 1750-1850 STI, WLN & MLN, SCT [34920] : 1800+ SKENE, ABD, SCT [36875]

GILLOTT 1800+ LONDON, MDX, ENG [35169] : 1850+ DUR, KEN & YKS, ENG [36574] : 1700+ CARLTON IN LINDRICK & WORKSOP, NTT, ENG [36823] : 1600+ HATFIELD, WRY, ENG [36823] : 1700+ HARTHILL, WRY, ENG [36823] : 1700-1900 GLS, ENG [37207]

GILLOWAY ALL LIMAVADY, LDY, IRL [35842]

GILLVOTT PRE 1800 HULL, ERY, ENG [36298]

GILMAN 1840+ LEIGH, LAN, ENG [34853] : 1870+ ASTON, BIRMINGHAM, WAR, ENG [35911] : PRE 1870 DBY, ENG [37377] : 1770-1850 YORK, ME, USA [33753] : 1700-1800 HENRICO CO., VA, USA [36554]

GILMARTIN PRE 1860 TIP, IRL [35750]

GILMARTIN (SEE KILMA [35546]

GILMER 1800S ARM, IRL [35964]

GILMORE 1800-1900 ISLINGTON, LND, ENG [37365] : PRE 1840 DRY, IRL [35024] : 1800-1900 LDY, IRL [35742] : 1800S ANT, IRL [36246] : 1800-1850 BALLINISLOE & FRENCHPARK, GAL, IRL [36297] : 1800S IRL [36842] : 1800+ DOW, IRL [37170] : SALLIE C1776 IRL [38340] : PRE 1830 PAISLEY, RFW, SCT [34113] : C1750 AYR, AYR, SCT [37106] : 1820-1865 LAWRENCE & DAVIESS CO., IN, USA [33760] : PRE 1800 VA, USA [38017]

GILMOUR PRE 1900 BALLYMENA, ANT, IRL [34792] : PRE 1900 DRY, IRL [36893] : PRE 1860 FIF, SCT [33966] : PRE 1820 RFW, SCT [33999] : PRE 1803 KETTLE, FIF, SCT [34285] : PRE 1830 DNB, SCT [34816] : 1750-1870 BLYTHSWOOD, GLASGOW, SCT [35790] : 1750+ BO'NESS, WLN, SCT [35979] : C1840 HOLYTOWN, LKS, SCT [38568]

GILPATRICK PRE 1800 DUR, ENG [36639] : 1800-1860 PORTLAND, ME, USA [38045] : 1719-1840 BIDDEFORD, ME, USA [38045]

GILPIN 1840+ CLEATOR MOOR, CUL, ENG [35396] : PRE 1792 HUDDERSFIELD, YKS, ENG [35459] : PRE 1850 LEEDS, WRY, ENG [37246] : 1700-1840 BEDFORD CO., VA, USA [38315]

GILROY 1860+ MOUNT FOREST, ONT, CAN [34466] : 1845+ MERRICKVILLE, ONT, CAN [34466] : PRE 1900 KILCROW, MOG, IRL [34466]

GILSON PRE 1800 WHITTLESEY, CAM, ENG [34884]

GILTNER ALL WORLDWIDE [38451]

GIMBER PRE 1860 MAIDSTONE, KEN, ENG [36870]

GIMBLETT PRE 1850 CORYTON, DEV, ENG [35959]

GIMBORN PRE 1850 NRW & RPF, BRD [38616]

GIMLIN PRE 1850 IL, USA [38013]

GIMMLER 1690-1710 WADERN AREA, SAA & RPR, GER [38528]

GIMSON 1750-1800 KEN & SRY, ENG [36081] : 1853 ROYSTON, CAM, ENG [38364]

GINGELL ALL GLS, ENG [37279] : PRE 1890 WIL, ENG & AUS [38746]

GINGERICH ALL PA, USA [38218]

GINGLE 1839 WROUGHTON, WIL, ENG [35120]

GINGREAU HILARIE 1670+ LA ROCHELLE, PCH, FRA [36678]

GINN 1860+ DALTON, NSW, AUS [35510] : 1700-1850 SOM, ENG [36222] : PRE 1765 SOHAM, CAM, ENG [37144]

GINNANE PRE 1896 BRUNSWICK, VIC, AUS [35796]

GINTY 1841+ REDFERN, NSW, AUS [34773] : PRE 1841 STOKESTOWN, ROS, IRL [34773]

GINTZ 1700-1900 OH & MO, USA [38328]

GIORDANI 1600+ PEDERSANO, TYROL, ITL [38322] : 1890+ LOS ANGELES, CA, USA [38322]

GIPPS PRE 1800 KEN & SAL, ENG [34671]

GIPSON C1770 RYHILL, YKS, ENG [34063]

GIR C1877 TICINO, TICINO, CH [37691]

GIRADDOT PRE 1860 SOYE, DOUBS, FRA [37537]

GIRARD 1700-1850 VARENNES, QUE, CAN [34242] : 1600-1681 PARIS, RPA, FRA [34514] : ALL FRA & AUS [35331]

GIRARDIN 1620-1740 BOUTE D'ILE, QUE, CAN & FRA [38779]

GIRAUD 1590-1670 FONTENAY LE COMTE, PCH, FRA [38779]

GIRAUDOIT (SEE GIROT [37429]

GIRDLER 1830+ NSW, AUS [34755] : ALL AUS [34961]

GIRDLESTONE PRE 1880 NFK, ENG [36514] : ALL WORLDWIDE [37234]

GIRIE 1740-60 BENDOCHY, PER, SCT [35152]

GIRLE 1789-1870S NORTH SHIELDS, NBL, ENG [36628] : 1800-1870S WEST AUCKLAND, DUR, ENG [36628] : 1773-1801 HACKNEY, MDX, ENG [36628] : PRE 1773 LONDON, MDX, ENG [36628] : 1878+ INVERCARGILL, SI, NZ [36628]

GIRLING PRE 1850 WOODBRIDGE, SFK, ENG [36086]

GIROERER PRE 1780 WIESENSTETTEN, WUE & HOH, GER [38679]

GIRON PRE 1700 ONEX, GE, CH [38348] : PRE 1870 ALSACE LORRAINE, FRA [38063] : 1870-1953 HERMINIE & WESTMORELAND, PA, USA [38063]

GIROTOIT ST JEAN 1660+ FRA [37429]

GIROUARD 1700-1860 MONTREAL, QUE, CAN [38033]

GIRT C1858 BILDERSTON, SFK, ENG [37302] : 1800+ TENDRING & COLCHESTER, ESS & SFK, ENG [38395]

GIRTON 1700+ VAN CAMP, COLUMBIA, VA, USA [38765]

GIRVAN PRE 1838 LOUDON, AYR, SCT [35407]

GISBORN 1800+ LEICESTER, LEI, ENG [34260]

GISBORNE 1840-1880 BIRKENHEAD, CHS, ENG [36624]

GISSESSON C1800 ALMEBODA, SMALAND, SWE [34395]

GITTINGS PRE 1900 NEWPORT, MON, WLS [37692]

GITTINS ALL BIRMINGHAM, WAR, ENG [37367] : 1800-1900 GREENWICH, LND, ENG [37850] : 1700-1800 PORTSMOUTH, HAM, ENG [37850]

GITTUS PRE 1880 PRESTEIGNE, RAD, WLS [37808]

GIVEN C1800+ MUCKENAGH, TYR, IRL [36838] :
1840+ LISNARABLE, TYR, IRL [38508] : 1760-1800
TATTRACONAUGHT, TYR, IRL [38537] : PRE 1820
CUPAR, FIF, SCT [35430]

GIVENS C1750-1820 ORANGE CO., NY & NJ, USA
[37529] : C1843 TN, USA [38184]

GJELSTROM ALL COPENHAGAN, DEN [34308]

GJERSON PRE 1870 VASTERVIK, KALMAR, SWE
[36800]

GLAB ALL GER [38527]

GLADDING 1700S CT, USA [35322]

GLADDLE ALL WORLDWIDE [36152]

GLADESTONES 1780+ GOSPORT, HAM, ENG
[38078]

GLADISH 1800+ WORLDWIDE [34256]

GLADMAN 1800S LAUGHTON, SSX, ENG [34223] :
PRE 1800 ENG [36688]

GLADSON (SEE GLADSTO [35819]

GLADSTONE 1855+ BEECHWORTH, VIC, AUS
[35819] : PRE 1850 BERWICK ON TWEED, NBL,
ENG [35819] : PRE 1800 NEWCASTLE, NBL &
DUR, ENG [38016] : C1816 HOLBORN, MDX, ENG
[38078] : 1700-1890 ROX, SCT [34615] : C1830
MOREBATTLE, ROX, SCT [36762]

GLADYZ ALL POL [38769]

GLAFLIN 1880+ AMESBURY, MA, USA [37450]

GLANAN ALL WORLDWIDE [37883]

GLANCY C1865 PORT GLASGOW, SCT [37536]

GLANFIELD 1750-1850 GRUNDISBURGH, SFK,
ENG [37042]

GLANTON 1849 ADELAIDE, SA, AUS [37986] : 1828+
COR, IRL [37986]

GLANVILL CAPT. C1800 PLYMOUTH, DEV, ENG
[38207]

GLANVILLE 1830+ COOMA, NSW, AUS [38596] :
1700+ ST NEWLYN EAST, CON, ENG [36205] :
1800+ PLYMOUTH, DEV, ENG [37046] : 1840
STOKE DAMEREL, DEV, ENG [37204] : PRE 1820
DEVONPORT, DEV, ENG [38596]

GLANZ C1830 HAMBURG, SHO, GER [36490]

GLASBY PRE 1800 ERY, ENG [34866] : 1700+
FINNINGLY & LOUND, NTT, ENG [37411] : ALL
WORLDWIDE [37904]

GLASGOW PRE 1895 PUKEKOHE, AKL, NZ [33964] :
PRE 1880 SHOTTS & AIRDRIE, LKS, SCT [36191] :
1880 MOUNTAIN VIEW, CA, USA [37501]

GLASHEEN 1800+ TIP, IRL [36602] : 1800+ NY, USA
[36602]

GLASS PRE 1900 ASHTON KEYNES, WIL & GLS,
ENG [37387] : 1900+ ASHTON KEYNES, WIL &
GLS, ENG [37387] : C1800 BALLINLEA, ANT, IRL
[35054] : 1700+ DUFFUS, MOR, SCT [34637] : 1840+
DUNDEE, ANS, SCT [34637] : PRE 1780
KILLEARNAN, ROC, SCT [34713] : 1700-1800
KINROSS, KRS, SCT [35885] : PRE 1791 TRANENT,
ELN, SCT [37852] : 1800+ GLASGOW, LKS, SCT &
IRL [34326] : 1791-1900S IN, IA & KS, USA [37812]

GLASSE PRE 1863 COLCHESTER, ESS, ENG [36876]

GLASSFORD ALL CHICAGO, IL, USA [35548]

GLASSINGTON 1871+ SYDNEY, NSW, AUS [34786]

GLASSON ALL CON, ENG [35063] : 1670+
WENDRON, CON, ENG [35587] : 1850+ CON,
ENG [35771]

GLASSUP PRE 1748 CALCUTTA, INDIA [38659]

GLATFELDER ALL CH [38197] : 1730S YORK CO.,
PA, USA & CH [38197]

GLATIGNY PRE 1800 LISDORF, SAA, GER & FRA
[38681]

GLAVES ALL SHEFFIELD, YKS, ENG [36994]

GLAZEBROOK 1800+ LONDON, ENG [33982] :
1750S RODMELL, SSX, ENG [35259]

GLAZIOR 1709+ BALLYORGAN, LIM, IRL [33862]

GLEADLE PRE 1700 HARTSHEAD, WRY, ENG
[37058]

GLEASON C1841 NEW MARLBORO, MA, USA
[35646] : 1820-1830 BUTLER CO., OH, USA [36328] :
1830-1850 HANCOCK CO., IL, USA [36328] : 1830+
WORCESTER CO., MA & RI, USA [38050]

GLEDHILL 1855 MELBOURNE, VIC, AUS [34600] :
1800+ HEBDON BRIDGE, YKS, ENG [33955] : PRE
1840 PENISTONE, WRY, ENG [34116] : PRE 1855
LONDON, ENG [34600] : 1800+ STAINLAND,
YKS, ENG [35214] : 1712+ BARKISLAND, WRY,
ENG [35815] : ALL BATLEY, WRY, ENG [37621]

GLEDSON JANE 1820+ BEDLINGTON, NBL, ENG
[36367]

GLEDSTANES 1810 GLENBRICK, LKS, SCT [34618]

GLEED 1750+ PURTON, WIL & BRK, ENG [36329]

GLEESON 1842-18148 QUEANBEYAN, NSW, AUS
[34966] : 1855+ NSW & VIC, AUS [35379] : 1840S
PORTLAND, VIC, AUS [35468] : 1840S
MELBOURNE, VIC, AUS [35468] : KATE 1884+
TORONTO & HAILEYVILLE, ONT, CAN [37526] :
JOHN 1886+ TORONTO & HAILEYVILLE, ONT,
CAN [37526] : KATE 1886+ MONTREAL, QUE,
CAN [37526] : 1800S WITHAM, CAM & SFK, ENG
& IRL [36874] : PRE 1837 CRUCKAWN &
KNOCKNADOGE, KIK, IRL [33775] : 1800S
TIPPERARY, IRL [34028] : PRE 1855 TIP, IRL
[35379] : 1820S THURLES, TIP, IRL [35516] : PRE
1870 COR, IRL [36486] : C1833 TIP, IRL [37912] :
VINCENT 1900-06 PITTSBURGH, PA, USA [37526] :
PATRICK 1844+ PA & OH, USA [37526] : JOHN
1855-85 PA & OH, USA [37526] : VINCENT 1888-99
KANSAS CITY, MO, USA [37526]

GLEIBERMAN ALL WORLDWIDE [34318]

GLEN 1853+ MELBOURNE, VIC, AUS [37465] :
1915+ JSY, CHI [37465] : 1880+ IPSWICH, NFK,
ENG [37465] : 1853+ MANCHESTER, LAN, ENG
[37465] : 1885+ BRISTOL, ENG [37465] : 1940+ RSA
[37465] : 1650+ LOCHWINNOCH, RFW, SCT
[34496] : C1834 NEW MONKLAND, LKS, SCT
[34752] : 1820 EDINBURGH, SCT [35067] : 1800+
RFW & ROX, SCT [35999] : 1769-1840
INVERKEITHING, FIF, SCT [37465] : ALL
DALMENY, MLN, SCT [37465] : ALL PRESTON
PANS, MLN, SCT [37465] : 1833-1909
COLDINGHAM, BEW, SCT [37465] : ALL
EDINBURGH, MLN, SCT [37465] : ALL
LINLITHGOW, WLN, SCT [37465] : ALL UPHALL,
WLN, SCT [37465]

GLENDENEN ALL DUR & NRY, ENG [36046] : 1800S
GUISBOROUGH, YKS, ENG [37765] : 1800S
MIDDLESBROUGH, YKS, ENG [37765]

GLENDENNING 1855+ FOOTSCRAY, SA, AUS
[36985] : 1855+ CASTLEMANE, SA, AUS [36985] :
1780+ HEXHAM, NBL, ENG [34606] : 1868+
NEWCASTLE UPON TYNE, NBL, ENG [36985] :
1820+ SUNDERLAND, DUR, ENG [36985] : 1850
DUMFRIES, DFS, SCT [34890] : PRE 1825 PARTON,
DFS, SCT [36985]

GLENDINNING PRE 1900 BELFAST, ANT, IRL
[36853] : C1847 EDINBURGH, SCT [34993] : ANN
ALL URFA, SYRIA [36853] : C1920+ USA [36853] :
WILLIAM C1890+ MISSIONARIES,
WORLDWIDE [36853]

GLENISTER 1800-1850 CHELTENHAM, GLS, ENG
[35595]

GLENN 1600-1700 BOURNE, LIN, ENG [38287] : ALL
DRUMNAGEE, ANT, IRL [34415] : 1780-1850 GA,
AL & SC, USA [36545] : 1792 CHESTER CO., SC,
USA [37817] : 1780-1890 JACKSON, IL, USA [38588]

GLENNON C1800 THE WARD, DUB, IRL [35152] :
C1775 NEW PARK, DUB, IRL [35152]

GLENNY PRE 1900 NEWRY & WARRENPOINT, DOW, ARM & DUB, IRL & NZ [35940]
GLENVILLE 1851 STOKE NEWINGTON, MDX, ENG [34761]
GLETNER C1800 WASHINGTON, MD, USA [38348]
GLEW PRE 1850 WISTOW, WRY, ENG [35925]
GLIDDEN ALL NEW ENGLAND, USA [36713]
GLIDDON 1886+ SYDNEY, NSW, AUS [38288]
GLISMANN PRE 1848 GLUCKSTADT, SHO, GER [37774]
GLOCK ALL FORCHTENBERG, WUE, GER [35460] : 1600+ WUE, GER [35460]
GLOCKNER C1800 WASHINGTON, MD, USA [38348]
GLOECKLER 1870-1920 VOLT & MT LAKE, MT & MN, USA [36675]
GLOISTEIN PRE 1900 UTHLEDE, HAN, GER [36852]
GLORIA ALL NOR, FRA [37385]
GLOS 1800 BRD [38327]
GLOSSOP 1700-1800 CHESTERFIELD, DBY, ENG [34623] : PRE 1900 NTT & DBY, ENG [37412]
GLOSTER ALL ENG [37279]
GLOVER PRE 1830 BOROUGHBRIDGE, YKS, ENG [34022] : C1845 BUSHBURY, STS, ENG [34239] : PRE 1819 EASTRY, KEN, ENG [34281] : 1700+ HARTSHORNE, DBY, ENG [34291] : PRE 1930 BIRMINGHAM, WAR, ENG [35055] : 1800S CHEDWORTH, GLS, ENG [35256] : 1600-1700 IPSWICH, SFK, ENG [35283] : 1800-1855 DEV, ENG [35402] : 1800+ WESTERHAM, KEN, ENG [36088] : PRE 1860 WROTHAM & OTLEY, KEN & WRY, ENG [36104] : C1800 LEEDS, WRY, ENG [36147] : 1800-1840 HYTHE, KEN, ENG [36272] : C1759 BADDESLEY ENSOR, WAR, ENG [36753] : 1790+ LONDON, ENG [37132] : PRE 1900 LONDON, ENG [37173] : 1640+ WYSALL, NTT & LEI, ENG [37266] : PRE 1864 ST MARGARETS, LEI, ENG [37346] : JOHN C1740 KENDAL, WES, ENG [37649] : 1800+ ENG [37993] : PRE 1750 MALVERN, WOR, ENG [38263] : PRE 1700 CON, ENG [38263] : PRE 1900 CLUTTON, SOM, ENG [38745] : 1750+ LISBURN, ANT, IRL [35475] : 1865+ AUCKLAND, NZ [36757] : C1807 DFS, SCT [34096] : C1900 PUEBLO, CO, USA [34096] : BENJAMIN 1870-1944 SLOAN, IA, USA [38156] : WILLIAM L. 1843-1923 SLOAN, IA, USA [38156] : THOMAS J. 1807-1881 JAMESTOWN, VA, USA [38156] : C1820 ORANGE CO., IN, USA [38173] : PRE 1775 ELIZABETH, NJ, USA [38173] : PRE 1750 CHARLES, MD, USA [38373] : PRE 1900 PA & NJ, USA & IRL [36542]
GLOYNS 1700-1800 PLYMOUTH, DEV, ENG [37924]
GLUE ALL NTT, ENG [35904] : 1850+ CHELSEA, LND, ENG & NZ [35925]
GLUNZ C1750 OFINGEN, BAD, GER [34239]
GLUVIAS 1625+ WENDRON, CON, ENG [35587] : ALL CON, ENG [37818]
GLUYAS ALL WENDRON, SITHNEY, CON, ENG & AUS [35712]
GLYNN 1400-1700 CON, ENG [37931] : 1713-1785 WINCANTON, DEV, ENG [37931] : C1820 GAL, IRL [35203]
GNOUD 1800S KILRUSH, KID, IRL & AUS [34596]
GOACHER C1877 EASTBOURNE, SSX, ENG [35772] : PRE 1840 CHELSEA, LND, ENG [36035]
GOAD ALL DULWICH, LND, ENG [36744] : PRE 1854 CAMBORNE, CON, ENG [37150] : 1700-1850 LAN, ENG [37858]
GOADBY PRE 1710 LOTHBURY, LND, ENG [34828]
GOAKES PRE 1818 WISBECH, CAM, ENG [36270]
GOATLY PRE 1840 WESTMINSTER, LND, ENG [36474]
GOBBETT PRE 1880 HALESWORTH, SFK, ENG [37287]

GOBBLE PRE 1840 WASHINGTON CO., VA, USA [37604]
GOBEL PRE 1736 GR ZIMMERN, HES, GER [38181] : GEORGE 1700-1780 MORRISTOWN, NJ, USA [38130]
GOBEY 1800+ GLS, ENG [36785]
GOBIN 1500+ WORLDWIDE [38161]
GOBLE 1760+ BROADWATER, SSX, ENG [36827] : PRE 1840 SSX, ENG [37745] : PRE 1700 ROLVENDEN, KEN, ENG [37816] : ELIZABETH 1827-1847 IN, USA [37551] : ELIZABETH PRE 1827 IN, USA [37551]
GODBELL 1700-1800 HARKSTEAD, SFK, ENG [37042]
GODBER C1820 STAPLEFORD, NTT, ENG [34734] : 1800+ ENNISKILLEN, FER, IRL [35194]
GODBILL PRE 1800 WHITTLESEY, CAM, ENG [34884]
GODBY 1750+ WISTOW, HUN, ENG [35499]
GODDARD PRE 1849 ST MARYS & PENRITH, NSW, AUS [34758] : 1880+ SHERBORNE, DOR, ENG [33979] : ALL SOUTHWARK, SRY, ENG [34308] : 1700+ LONDON, ENG [34701] : 1840+ HEMPNALL, NFK, ENG [34710] : 1750-1820 MERE, WIL, ENG [34769] : 1800 BATH, SOM, ENG [35186] : 1808 STOKEWAKE, DOR, ENG [35252] : 1600S CURLAND, SOM, ENG [35558] : 1800+ LONDON, ENG [36049] : 1557+ SFK, ENG [37399] : 1800 LOWDHAM, NTT, ENG [37829] : 1847-1922 BROMLEY BY BOW, LND, ENG [38417] : 1750+ FENNY STRATFORD, BKM, ENG & AUS [36642] : ALL BARBADOS, W.INDIES [35558]
GODDEN C1865 YOUNG, NSW, AUS [36284] : ALL SFK, ENG [34254] : 1700-1800 SSX, ENG [35094] : 1711 HINTON ST GEORGE, SOM, ENG [35252] : PRE 1850 FOLKESTONE, KEN, ENG [36584] : 1800-1850 WOOTEN ST LAWRENCE, HAM, ENG [37222] : 1840-1880 ENG [37877]
GODEN C1720 CHATHAM, KEN, ENG [37735]
GODENCH C1800 KEN, ENG [37715]
GODENZIE 1870S MALDON, VIC, AUS [35044]
GODETH C1520 SHERINGTON, BKM, ENG [34041]
GODFREY 1842+ RICHMOND, TAS, AUS [34910] : 1850S SA, AUS [35743] : 1850+ QLD, AUS [37974] : 1820-1900 ADELAIDE, SA, AUS [38275] : ALL AUS & NZ [33975] : 1800+ BITTON, GLS, ENG [34852] : PRE 1850 PORTLAND, DOR, ENG [35232] : C1800-1819 BRISTOL, GLS, ENG [35358] : 1760-1800 BELTON IN AXHOLM, LIN, ENG [36635] : 1800 BLACK NOTLEY, ESS, ENG [37928] : PRE 1860 MDX, ENG [37974] : 1740-1840 CHATHAM, KEN, ENG [38275] : 1800+ OXF, ENG & AUS [35712] : PATRICK PRE 1821 CARLOW, CAR, IRL [36314] : 1800S EDINBURGH, MLN, SCT [35395] : 1790-1820 ORLEANS, MA, USA [38099] : RUTH 1700S SALEM, MA, USA [38785]
GODFREY FAUSSETT 1600+ HEPPINGTON, KEN, ENG [36756]
GODIER 1820+ LONDON, ENG [38288]
GODIN 1760+ BERTHIER, QUE, CAN [34082] : 1800-1820 AR, USA [38312] : 1650+ USA [38312]
GODINCH C1800 SHEERNESS, KEN, ENG [37715]
GODKIN 1800+ GOREY, WEX, IRL [34008] : 1700+ WEX, IRL [38385]
GODLEY PRE 1900 NTT, ENG [34783] : 1750-1860 BRASTED & SUNDRIDGE, KEN, ENG [36051] : PRE 1850 WORKSOP, NTT, ENG [36403] : PRE 1850 WAR, ENG [37750] : 1700+ YKS, ENG & NZ [36266]
GODMAN ALL LONDON, ENG [34054] : PRE 1920 LONDON, ENG [36765]
GODOFSKY ALL OLKIENIKI, SU [38368]
GODOWSKY 1900+ CT, USA [38368]

GODREY C1841 STREET, SOM, ENG [34157]

GODSAFE 1800+ ESS, ENG [34818]

GODSALL 1800S STOKE EDITH, HEF, ENG [36633]

GODSHALK 1700-1780 MONTGOMERY CO., PA, USA [36738]

GODWARD PRE 1886 MARYLEBONE, LND, ENG [35883]

GODWIN 1820-1850 ESSEX CO., ONT, CAN [36731] : PRE 1850 PORTSEA, HAM, ENG [35710] : ALL ENG [35998] : 1825-1875 GLOUCESTER, GLS, ENG [36109] : 1850 MACCLESFIELD, CHS, ENG [36860] : C1850 WOLVERHAMPTON, STS, ENG [37233] : PRE 1850 ENG [37739] : C1800 BATHEASTON, SOM, ENG [37838] : 1850-1900 LASALLE CO., IL, USA [36731] : ALL WORLDWIDE [36914]

GODWINS C1885 TORONTO, ONT, CAN [34521] : 190+ BETHUNE, SAS, CAN [34521]

GOEBEL ALL MUDTAPILLY, QLD, AUS [37176]

GOEDEGEBUURE ALL WORLDWIDE [38358]

GOEDEKE 1600-1900 SHO, GER [38748]

GOEDEMOND ALL ARGENTINA [38697] : PRE 1700 ANTWERPEN, OVL, BEL [38697] : ALL USA [38697]

GOEDENDORP ALL NL [38351]

GOEGEBUER (SEE GOEDE [38358]

GOENS PRE 1800 MARKE, WVL, BEL [38164]

GOERGE PRE 1790 WINGERODE, PSA, GER [38048]

GOERING PRE 1700 LUE, BRD [38561]

GOERTZEN 1850-1870 ALEXANDERTHAL, TAURIEN, SU [36543]

GOESSLING ALL BOCKHORN BRINKFITGENS, OLD, GER [35767]

GOETJE 1600-1900 SHO, GER [38748]

GOFAUX ALL LODELINSART, CHARLEROI, BEL [35002]

GOFF PRE 1815 DEV, ENG & CAN [33906]

GOFFAERT ALL LODELINSART, CHARLEROI, BEL [35002]

GOFFARD 1761-1802 HAY & NAMUR, LGE & QUE, BEL & CAN [35002]

GOFFART PRE 1802 THIENES, LGE & ONT, BEL & CAN [35002]

GOFFE 1700S NTH, ENG [37566] : 1800S GREAT KINETON, WAR, ENG [37566]

GOFFHEIN PRE 1800 LUETTICH, LUI, BEL [38617]

GOFFIN 1600+ GREAT YARMOUTH, NFK, ENG [33851]

GOFORTH PRE 1900 WORLDWIDE [37749]

GOGGAIN 1800+ COR, IRL & NZ [36850]

GOGGIN ALL WORLDWIDE [37086]

GOGGINS PRE 1864 MEA, IRL [38296]

GOLBY PRE 1800 EYDON & MIDDLETON CHENEY, NTH, ENG [37650]

GOLD PRE 1850 BRIDGWATER, SOM, ENG [35406] : C1790 WEST COWES, IOW, ENG [35860] : JOHN PRE 1841 FROME, SOM, ENG [36314] : PRE 1862 READING, BRK, ENG [36475] : 1790+ HAM, ENG [37168] : RICHARD C1690 BOWERCHALKE, WIL, ENG [38489]

GOLDBLATT PRE 1900 KLIKOL, MAZEIK, LITHUANIA [36455]

GOLDEN 1880S ARMIDALE & URALLA, NSW, AUS [37966] : 1800-1990 NJ, USA [38096] : 1800-1990 PHILADELPHIA CO., PA, USA [38096]

GOLDENSKY 1700-1990 RUSSIA [38096] : 1800-1990 NJ, USA [38096] : 1800-1990 NEW YORK, NY, USA [38096] : 1800-1990 PHILADELPHIA CO., PA, USA [38096]

GOLDER 1750+ MINSTER, KEN, ENG [35398]

GOLDFINCH ALL WORLDWIDE [36107]

GOLDHAWK ABRAHAM 1700S ST PAUL'S WALDEN, HRT, ENG [35634]

GOLDIAN 1800-1900 SHEFFIELD & LEEDS, WRY, ENG [36031]

GOLDIE 1842+ KANGY ANGY, NSW, AUS [34859] : 1832+ HOBART, TAS, AUS [35932] : 1800+ TAS, AUS & SCT [34280] : ALL SLI, IRL [34569] : PRE 1900 WAMPHRAY, DFS, SCT [34254] : PRE 1842 MAUCHLINE, AYR, SCT [34859] : PRE 1760 DAILLY, AYR, SCT [35406] : 1700-1830 EDINBURGH, MLN, SCT [35932]

GOLDING ALL HADLOW, KEN, ENG [34558] : PRE 1900 KEN, ENG [36070] : PRE 1845 MILTON, KEN, ENG [36070] : 1840+ DARTFORD, KEN, ENG [36070] : PRE 1900 YARMOUTH, NFK, ENG [36122] : PRE 1911 BRIXTON, LND, ENG [36290] : PRE 1800 ESS & SFK, ENG [36399] : 1800+ MINGTY, WIL, ENG [36568] : 1850+ BRISTOL, SOM, ENG [37360] : 1792 COR, IRL [35152] : 1650-1783 HEMPSTEAD, WESTCHESTER CO., NY, USA [34366] : 1750-1820 STOKES CO., NC, USA [38119]

GOLDMAN VICTORIA 1914 BALTIMORE, MD, USA [37800]

GOLDRING PRE 1800 ROGATE, SSX, ENG [34112] : 1760+ DOR, ENG [34416] : ALL WORLDWIDE [34825]

GOLDSBOROUGH PRE 1880 IDLE, YKS, ENG [38755]

GOLDSBURY C1848 LEI, ENG [36253]

GOLDSBY PRE 1892 ST ALBANS, HRT, ENG [35036]

GOLDSCHMIDT C1830 WOLFERODE, HAL, DDR [38677] : 1816 GOEDENS, OLD, GER [37509]

GOLDSMITH GEORGE 1880S BALMAIN, NSW, AUS [34427] : GEORGE 1840S PADDINGTON, NSW, AUS [34427] : 1849+ NEWTOWN, NSW, AUS [34979] : PRE 1900 BALLARAT, VIC, AUS [35087] : PRE 1847 IPSWICK, LND, ENG [34979] : PRE 1840 TUNBRIDGE, KEN, ENG [36607] : C1820 EAST HOATHLEY, SSX, ENG [37285] : PRE 1850 BRIGHTON, SSX, ENG [37321] : 1850+ LONDON, ENG [38413] : 1700+ BREMEN, NSA, GER [38578] : 1700+ HAINSTADT, BAW, GER [38578] : 1750+ RAMSAY, IOM [34415] : PRE 1700 ROS, IRL [35216] : ALL IRL [38754]

GOLDSPINKE MARY ALICE PRE 1885 WEST ZORA, ONT, CAN [34216]

GOLDSTON WILLIAM C1780+ WALSHAM LE WILLOWS, SFK, ENG [36945]

GOLDSTONE C1865 SYDNEY, NSW, AUS [35826] : C1840 LEYTONSTONE, ESS, ENG [35826]

GOLDSTRAW ALL LIVERPOOL, LAN, ENG [35514] : 1800+ SALFORD, LAN, ENG [37705]

GOLDSWORTHY PRE 1900 CON, ENG [34536] : PRE 1850 CON, ENG [34783] : 1870+ REDRUTH, CON, ENG [35151] : PRE 1840 REDRUTH, CON, ENG [35496] : PRE 1800 SOM, ENG [36416] : PRE 1850 CON, ENG [36416] : PRE 1930 GWENNAP, CON, ENG [37322]

GOLDTHORPE PRE 1760 SHEPLEY & KIRKBURTON, WRY, ENG [37754] : 1760-1780 THURLSTONE & PENISTONE, WRY, ENG [37754]

GOLLAN PRE 1850 INVERNESS, INV, SCT [33968] : PRE 1798 APPLECROSS, ROC, SCT [34689] : ALL PAISLEY, SCT [35009]

GOLLO 1750+ TINN, NUMEDAL, NOR [36905]

GOLLOP 1400+ NETHERBURY, DOR, ENG [38745]

GOLLUB PRE 1900 STRAUSBURG, NBR, DDR [35323]

GOLOS 1700-1990 EUROPE [38096] : 1700-1990 ESTONIA, RUSSIA [38096] : 1800-1990 CHEMUNG CO., NY, USA [38096]

GOLSBY PRE 1892 ST ALBANS, HRT, ENG [35036] : PRE 1800 BKM, BDF & NTH, ENG [35701]

GOLTZ 1700+ METZELTIEN & HINDENBERG, BRA, GER [35460]

GOLUMBIC 1800-1990 CLINTON CO., PA, USA [38096]

GOMERSALL 1800S YKS, ENG [34715]

GOMMERS 1889-1908 BRUSSELS, BEL [35107]

GONSALVES 1910-1925 REVERE CITY, MA, USA [36337]

GONTHIER JEAN PRE 1666 PARIS, RPA, FRA [38408]

GOOCH PRE 1783 TIMWORTH, SFK, ENG [33992] : C1750-1800 WIX, ESS, ENG [36478] : PRE 1850 MID, NFK, ENG [37718] : C1550 DISS, NFK, ENG [38383] : C1700 BRUNDISH, SFK, ENG [38383] : ELIZABETH PRE 1792 GLS, ENG [38567]

GOOD 1919 BOWRAL, NSW, AUS [34421] : PRE 1860 WALTHAMSTOW, ESS, ENG [34014] : ALL SFK, ENG [34254] : C1800 DROITWICH, WOR, ENG [34655] : C1780-1850S FOVANT, WIL, ENG [36289] : 1820-1888 LYMINGTON, HAM, ENG [37709] : 1740 ALPHAMSTONE, ESS, ENG [37837] : 1740 BURES, SFK, ENG [37837] : PRE 1850 LIM & COR, IRL [37807] : PRE 1830 KKD, SCT [33971] : PRE 1859 SORN, AYR, SCT [35779]

GOODAIR 1900+ SYDNEY, NSW, AUS [35929]

GOODALE 1830-50 JEFFERSON, NY, USA [38054] : 1800 RI, USA [38054]

GOODALL 1828 MEDSTEAD, HAM, ENG [34909] : PRE 1840 CHOLDERTON, WIL, ENG [35346] : PRE 1890 LEEDS & WAKEFIELD, WRY, ENG [36187] : 1800-1855 DOVEDALE, DBY, ENG [36824] : 1800+ SCT & CAN [35778]

GOODARD C1840-1910 COLNEY, HRT, ENG & AUS [38585]

GOODAYRE 1600-1920 HUDDERSFIELD, WRY, ENG [37736]

GOODBODY 1700-1800 EAST RUDHAM, NFK, ENG [37845] : ALL NFK, ENG [38035] : ALL WORLDWIDE [34717]

GOODBRAND 1800+ ABERDEEN, ABD, SCT [34008]

GOODBURN 1797 BOLTON, WES, ENG [38209]

GOODBY PRE 1810 BIRMINGHAM, WAR, ENG [36177]

GOODCHILD 1860+ ESSEX CO., ONT, CAN [35610] : PRE 1805 LONGWICK, BKM, ENG [35578] : 1650-1720 TOSTOCK, SFK, ENG [36213] : 1800-1850 WALWORTH, MDX, ENG [36586] : C1800 IPSWICH, SFK, ENG [37449] : 1800+ KEN, MDX & SRY, ENG & CAN [34467]

GOODDEN ALL WORLDWIDE [36170]

GOODDY PRE 1832 PRESTBURY, CHS, ENG [37138]

GOODDYN 1500-1650 MARTOCK, SOM, ENG [36170]

GOODE PRE 1900 AUS [34196] : 1300-1700 CON, ENG [35283] : C1810 NTH, ENG [35863] : 1850S COVENTRY, WAR, ENG & AUS [35558]

GOODEARE 1600-1920 ENG [37736]

GOODEN C1500-1900 COMPTON DUNDON, SOM, ENG [34158] : 1950+ DOR, ENG [36572]

GOODENOUGH 1800+ CORSTON, DOR, ENG [34777]

GOODENOW C1700 SUDBURY, MA, USA [36319]

GOODENS 1807 NORWICH, NFK, ENG [35259]

GOODERHAM 1757-1820 SCOLE, NFK, ENG [34088]

GOODES PRE 1870 HARROW, MDX, ENG [37622]

GOODEVE PRE 1832 HAM, ENG [34504]

GOODFELLOW 1852-1882 BENDIGO & BALLARAT, VIC, AUS [37968] : 1830S LANARK CO., ONT, CAN [34075] : ALL CAN [34489] : 1821-1841 AMBROISE DE KILDARE, QUE, CAN [35609] : 1730S BEWCASTLE, CUL, ENG [34688] : C1600 BODMIN, CON, ENG [35563] : C1800-1850S WIL, ENG [36289] : PRE 1852 STEPNEY, LND, ENG [37968] : 1780-1810

CREAGIN, ARM, IRL [35609] : 1840-50 NEWTOWNHAMILTON, ARM, IRL [38583] : 1850S COCKBURNSPATH & SELKIRK, BEW, ROX & NBL, SCT & ENG [37853] : 1880+ NE, USA [34368]

GOODGER ALL KEN, ENG [35353] : PRE 1808 PORTSEA, HAM, ENG [36870] : 1808+ WEST ASHLING, SSX, ENG [36870] : 1858+ CHRISTCHURCH, NZ [36870]

GOODHART 1762-1920 EVERCREECH, SOM, ENG [37380]

GOODHEAD PRE 1890 BURTON UPON TRENT, STS, ENG [38390] : C1871 BURTON ON TRENT, HEF & HRT, ENG [38450]

GOODHEART 1812-90 CLERKENWELL & ISLINGTON, MDX, ENG [37380]

GOODHEW 1800S ENG [35161]

GOODHUGH 1700-1834 BIRLING, KEN, ENG [37921]

GOODIER C1860 WHALLEY RANGE, LAN, ENG [35203]

GOODIFF C1800 BOW, LND, ENG [37053]

GOODILL PRE 1900 LECONFIELD, ERY, ENG [34855]

GOODIN C1800+ NSW, AUS [33930] : 1788+ RYDE, NSW, AUS [35857] : 1790+ NFK, ENG & NZ [36850]

GOODING PRE 1816 NORWICH, NFK, ENG [35259] : 1865-80 SAWSTON, CAM, ENG [35259] : PRE 1830 DRAYTON, SOM, ENG [35798] : 1790+ NFK, ENG & NZ [36850] : EMMA ALL FEATHERSTON, NZ [33961] : 1875+ DONIPHAN CO., KS, USA [38343] : 1840+ WASHINGTON CO., OH, USA [38343]

GOODISON 1750-1900 STOCKPORT, CHS & LAN, ENG [34520]

GOODLET 1840+ DUNDEE, ANS, SCT [35938]

GOODLIFFE ALL HANNS, ENG [34561] : 1811 EATON SOCON, BDF, ENG [37723]

GOODMAN 1840+ FARNHAM, QUE, CAN [34379] : C1850 HOLLINWOOD, LAN, ENG [34734] : FRANK ALL NOTTINGHAM, ENG [35164] : THOMAS V. 1918+ ENG [35164] : RICHARD PRE 1820 BDF, ENG [35164] : THOMAS PRE 1811 BDF, ENG [35164] : PRE 1860 EASTON, WIL, ENG [35346] : PRE 1887 LND, ENG [35414] : 1790+ LUCKINGTON, WIL, ENG [35825] : 1700-1900 NTH, ENG [36038] : 1800S LIN, ENG [36038] : ALL STOURPORT, WOR, ENG [36525] : PRE 1847 FINSBURY, MDX, ENG [36866] : PATRICK 1930S LONDON, ENG [36889] : LOUIS 1895-1920 LONDON, ENG [36889] : HARRY 1940+ HOVE, SSX, ENG [36889] : PRE 1885 LEICESTER, LEI, ENG [37346] : PRE 1890 FOWEY, CON, ENG [37622] : 1860+ BRISTOL, SOM, ENG [37622] : C1730-1860 BERKHAMSTED, HRT, ENG [37752] : PRE 1860 LND, ENG [38077] : 1810+ ST ALBANS, VT, USA [34379] : ALBERT &GRACE 1904+ CA & IN, USA [35164] : 1800+ MS, USA [36720] : 1890+ CARLISLE CO., KY, USA [36720] : 1830-1870 AUGUSTA, GA, USA [36737] : 1800-1830 GREENEVILLE, TN, USA [36737] : TILLY 1925-45 NEW YORK, NY, USA [36889] : 1800+ WORLDWIDE [37637]

GOODRAM PRE 1775 SFK, ENG [37280]

GOODRICH C1500 ENG [34395] : 1620 BURY ST EDMUNDS, SFK, ENG [38131] : 1550 HEGESSETT, SFK, ENG [38131] : 1820-1900 PARKER, SD, USA [37464] : 1700-1900 CAYUGA CO., NY, USA [37464] : 1700-1900 TOMPKINS CO., NY, USA [37464] : 1820-1900 SUFFOLK CO., NY, USA [37464]

GOODRICK PRE 1824 FOSDYKE, LIN, ENG [35029]

GOODRIDGE 1784 TREFOREST, GLA, WLS [34726]

GOODRUM 1700-1750 HELMINGHAM, SFK, ENG [36213] : 1700S FUNDENHALL, NFK, ENG [37191]

GOODSALL 1600 STOCK, ESS, ENG [37928]

GOODSELL 1880+ PROSPECT & HILL END, NSW, AUS [37307] : 1800-1900 EWHURST, SSX, ENG [36485]

GOODSIR DAVID PRE 1775 KIRKCALDY, FIF, SCT [37906]

GOODSON PRE 1844 CHELMSFORD, ESS, ENG [33806] : C1800 COGGESHALL, ESS, ENG [37053] : C1780 NTH, ENG [37520] : ALL TRING, HRT, ENG [37692] : 1700+ BALTONSBOROUGH, SOM, ENG [37924]

GOODSTEIN C1850-60 ALITA, RUSLAND [37935]

GOODWIN 1807+ HOBART, TAS, AUS [36312] : THOMAS 1860-1900 MARULAN, NSW, AUS [36316] : C1800 PARRAMATTA & SYDNEY, NSW, AUS [36638] : PRE 1790 BICKNOR, KEN, ENG [34105] : ANDREW 1788 LONDON, ENG [34176] : 1740-1860 BICESTER, OXF, ENG [34440] : PRE 1800 CHAPEL EN-LE FRITH, DBY, ENG [34588] : 1840-1900 OMBERSLEY, WOR, ENG [34677] : 1800-1900 SOUTHMINSTER, ESS, ENG [34697] : 1780-1800 BOCKING, ESS, ENG [34697] : 1800S CON, ENG [34953] : 1743-1856 HOLT, WOR, ENG [36513] : 1800+ SANDBACH AREA, CHS, ENG [36997] : C1810 MANCHESTER, LAN, ENG [37172] : PRE 1600 PONINGTON IN HOLLAND, LIN, ENG [37381] : PRE 1800 KINGSLEY, STS, ENG [37389] : 1894 EAST LONDON, ENG [37898] : PRE 1853 NTT, ENG & AUS [35512] : PRE 1850 IRL [37901] : PRE 1815 CARTER CO., TN, USA [36929] : PRE 1750 MD, USA [37570] : 1719 BUCKS, PA, USA [38022] : ALL USA & SCT [38782] : 1820+ NEWCHURCH, RAD, WLS [36772]

GOODY ALL ESS & SFK, ENG [36399]

GOODYEAR C1850 ESS, ENG [34661]

GOODYER 1600-1920 HUDDERSFIELD, WRY, ENG [37736]

GOOLE C1780 CUMBERNAULD, DNB, SCT [36257]

GOOLEY 1850-1890 GEELONG, VIC, AUS [34682] : PRE 1860 KIK, IRL [34682]

GOOSMAN JOHN EDEN 1840-1900 STRACKHOLT, BRD, GER [38781] : EDWARD EDE J. 1870-1890 STRACKHOLT, BRD, GER [38781] : GERD JANSSEN 1800-1895 OLENDORF, BRD, GER [38781]

GOOSSENS ALL LEBBEKE, OVL, BEL [38170]

GOPPEL MARIA 1778-1842 SPEYER, BAV, GER [33752]

GOPSILL 1800S BIRMINGHAM, WAR, ENG [37083]

GORAM PRE 1836 WITTERSHAM, KEN, ENG [36272]

GORBELL PRE 1852 ST GILES, MDX & LND, ENG [37452]

GORCHUM PRE 1750 WESTHOFEN, RPF, BRD [34245]

GORDEN ALL WORLDWIDE [36221]

GORDLEY 1830-1990 CASS CO., IL, USA [38154] : 1750-1850 CUMBERLAND CO., PA, USA [38154] : 1800-1990 BRACKEN CO., KY, USA [38154] : 1800-1990 FAYETTE CO., KY, USA [38154] : 1800-1990 MASON CO., KY, USA [38154] : 1850-1990 ADAMS CO., OH, USA [38154] : 1827-1990 BROWN CO., IL, USA [38154]

GORDON 1860+ MITTAGONG & GUNDARY, NSW, AUS [34685] : 1890+ NARROMINE & SYDNEY, NSW, AUS [34978] : 1855 SYDNEY, NSW, AUS [35089] : 1890 SYDNEY, NSW, AUS [35508] : PRE 1915 NSW, AUS [36645] : 1850S+ SHERBROOKE, QUE, CAN [38406] : C1850+ MONTREAL, QUE, CAN [38406] : C1840 NORTHUMBERLAND CO., ONT, CAN [38410] : PRE 1842 LIVERPOOL, LAN, ENG [34417] : ALEXANDER 1769+ LONDON, ENG [34910] : 1700S STOKE CLIMSLAND, CON,

ENG [34920] : PRE 1890 LND, ENG [34978] : PRE 1793 HORNCLIFFE, NBL, ENG [35397] : ALL BIRMINGHAM, WAR, ENG [36234] : C1893 YORK, YKS, ENG [36668] : 1790+ NEWCASTLE UPON TYNE, NBL, ENG [36717] : ARTHUR C1897 SALFORD, LAN, ENG [38072] : 1800-1900 GLASLOUGH, MOG, IRL [34615] : C1840S ENNIS, CLA, IRL [35158] : 1800 ENNISKILLEN, FER, IRL [35194] : 1791+ IRL [35266] : 1800-1990 KILHORNE & ANNALONG, DOW, IRL [36398] : 1800+ IRL [37306] : 1840 MOY, DOW, IRL [37445] : C1830 BELFAST, ANT, IRL [38253] : MARGARET C1825 IRL [38298] : ALL BELFAST, IRL [38415] : 1820 NEWRY, DOW, IRL & NZ [36803] : 1700-1800 GLADSMUIR, MLN, SCT [33908] : PRE 1800 SCT [33959] : 1900+ GLASGOW, LKS, SCT [34039] : 1780-1910S INVERESK, MLN, SCT [34359] : C1830 FRASERBURGH, ABD, SCT [34474] : 1750-1820 HADDINGTON, ELN, SCT [34615] : KATHERINE 1844+ TWYNHOLM, KKD, SCT [35615] : 1700-1800 BALMERINO, FIF, SCT [35627] : PRE 1837 SPINNINGDALE, SUT, SCT [35709] : COLIN 1842+ EMBO HOUSE, SUT, SCT [36559] : WILLIAM 1854-1900S EMBO HOUSE, SUT, SCT [36559] : COLIN 1780-C1850 DORNOCH, SUT, SCT [36559] : PRE 1850 GRAITNEY, DFS, SCT [36760] : 1700+ PAISLEY, RFW, SCT [36794] : 1750-1850 BENVIC, KCD, SCT [36824] : 1800+ URQUHART, ROC, SCT [36857] : PRE 1878 FORDLE, FIF, SCT [36888] : 1800+ BERVIE, KCD, SCT [36971] : 1770+ EDINBURGH, MLN, SCT [37333] : 1750-1850 BORGUE & CROSSMICHAEL, KKD, SCT [37644] : 1820S INVERNESS, INV, SCT [38206] : PRE 1820 FARR, SUT, SCT [38457] : 1800 DUNDEE, ANS, SCT [38735] : 1793+ TARBET & GARVE, ROC, SCT & AUS [35150] : 1800-1900 CABRACH, BAN & ONT, SCT & CAN [34479] : JOHN PRE 1780 CURRITUCK, NC, USA [33757] : PRE 1750 VOLUNTOWN, MA, USA [36935] : 1700S GREENE CO., NY, USA [37018] : HUGH C1733-1834 WASHINGTON CO., KY, USA [37527] : PRE 1800 ALBANY, NY, USA [38220] : LEWIS 1800-1860 CINCINNATI, OH, USA [38523] : LEWIS 1750-1800 MONMOUTH CO., NJ, USA [38523] : C1780+ NH, VT & QUE, USA & CAN [38406] : ALL DOMINICA, W.INDIES [34170]

GORE 1800+ CAMPTON, BDF, ENG [34315] : 1700-1900 LIVERPOOL, LAN, ENG [34624] : 1800S RIDLINGTON, NTH, ENG [35024] : ALL AMPTHILL, BDF, ENG [36152] : PRE 1845 ETELLE, BRITTANY, FRA [34858] : C1830 KIK, IRL [33812] : ALL SLI, IRL [34361] : PRE 1800 ROS, IRL [35216] : PRE 1800 SLIGO, SLI, IRL [35770] : 1800-1858 KY, USA [36968] : 1900-1990 SOUTHERN PART, CA, USA [38154] : 1850-1900 MASON CO., IL, USA [38154]

GOREWOOD PRE 1830 POCKLINGTON, NRY, ENG [34127]

GORFORD PRE 1800 EXETER, DEV, ENG [34809]

GORHAM ALL WITTENHAM, KEN, ENG [38487] : PRE 1836 WITTERSHAM, KEN, ENG [36272] : PRE 1800 RUTLAND, POULTNEY, VT, USA [37804]

GORICK ALL WORLDWIDE [36233]

GORICX ALL BEL [36233]

GORING C1845 BATTERSEA, SRY, ENG [37611] : 1813+ HORLEY, SRY, ENG [37611]

GORIQUE ALL FRA [36233]

GORLE ALL NZ [34603]

GORMAN 1826+ HAWKESBURY, NSW, AUS [38208] : PETER 1820+ CHELSEA, LND, ENG [33797] : 1821+ BIRMINGHAM, WAR, ENG [35824] : PRE 1825 BRISTOL, ENG [38208] : 1700+ BALLYMOTE,

SLI, IRL [33797] : C1840 DUBLIN, IRL [34395] : PRE
1862 BALLYMOGORTY, DON, IRL [35197] : 1850+
BELFAST, ANT, DOW & ARM, IRL [35636] : ALL
KIK, IRL [35707] : PRE 1750 GLENAVY, ANT, IRL
[35897] : PATRICK 1830+ BALLIWAY, TIP, IRL
[36367] : ALL ESP. BUFFALO & WESTERN, NY,
USA & IRL [38287]

GORMANLY 1850+ DUBLIN, IRL [34256] : 1870+
LONDONDERRY, LDY, IRL [34256]

GORMIE 1700+ URQUHART, MOR, SCT [34637]

GORMLEY C1840 KILCOMMON, MAY, IRL [36649] :
PRE 1880 GLASGOW, LKS, SCT [34018]

GORMLY 1882 WAGGA WAGGA, NSW, AUS [35970]
: 1800S NEILSTON, SCT [35767]

GORNALL C1830 SOUTHWALK, SRY, ENG [36271] :
1800+ PRESTON, LAN, ENG [36271]

GOROSTIZA 1700-1800 PORTUGALETE, BISCAYA,
ESP [36340]

GORRIDGE C1800 KEN, ENG [37715]

GORRIE 1830+ PERTH, PER, SCT [35039] : PRE 1906
EAST WERNYS, FIF, SCT [38393]

GORRINGE 1840+ CARCOAR, NSW, AUS [35238] :
PRE 1840 SSX, ENG [35238]

GORRY 1870+ KINGS CREEK & O'CONNELL,
NSW, AUS [35132] : ALL WEM, IRL [35063]

GORSALITZ PRE 1860 GORLITZ, WPR, GER [37427]

GORSE 1750-1900 MACKWORTH, DBY, ENG [34714]
: 1750-1900 LEIGH, STS, ENG [34714]

GORST 1825+ THORNTON, CHS, ENG [35114] :
1760S+ LIVERPOOL, LAN, ENG [35331] : 1660-1900
NORTHWICH, LAN, ENG [37919]

GORSUCH 1853+ CARLTON, VIC, AUS [36605] :
PRE 1853 CHICHESTER, SSX, ENG [36605]

GORTLEY 1600+ STAVERTON, DEV, ENG [34747]

GORTNER PRE 1760 PA, USA [37587]

GORTON 1840 CHORLEY, LAN, ENG [37732] : 1700-
1850 NY, USA [33753]

GOSEMEYER 1780+ HAN, GER [37532] : 1840+ USA
[37532]

GOSHAWKE 1850S AUCKLAND, NZ [33934]

GOSLAND C1850 EXETER, DEV, ENG [37378] : ALL
GLASGOW, LKS, SCT [35985]

GOSLETT 1826+ GUNDAROO, NSW, AUS [35331]

GOSLEY PRE 1700 MEVAGISSEY, CON, ENG [37319]

GOSLING 1795-1851 HUNSLET, WRY, ENG [34352] :
PRE 1810 NORWICH, NFK, ENG [34616] : 1880+
KENNINGTON, SRY, ENG [34710] : PRE 1865
BROOMWICH, STS, ENG [35061] : 1800+
SAMPFORD PEVERELL, DEV, ENG [36069] : PRE
1820 SALCOMBE REGIS, DEV, ENG [36069] : 1750-
1850 CHEADLE, CHS, ENG [36416] : C1800
CHISELDON, WIL, ENG [36975] : PRE 1850
WORLINGWORTH, SFK, ENG [37416] : C1812
HAZELGROVE, CHS, ENG [37697]

GOSMER 1400+ CHIDHAM, SSX, ENG [33989]

GOSNELL ALL KENT CO., ONT, CAN [34155] : ALL
COR, IRL [34155]

GOSNEY ALL CREWKERNE, SOM, ENG [36382]

GOSS 1840+ LAUNCESTON, TAS, AUS [34799] :
1790+ TOTTINGTON, NFK, ENG [33942] : PRE
1861 PLYMOUTH, DEV, ENG [35108] : PRE 1850
BODMIN, WITHIEL & ROCHE, CON, ENG [37814]
: 1800+ PLYMOUTH, DEV, ENG [37993] : C1812
GER [37022] : 1670+ LANCASTER, MA, USA
[38520]

GOSSARD 1747 LICHFIELD, STA, ENG [36635]

GOSSHAWKE 1700-1990 UK & AUS [35421]

GOSSIP 1850+ NSW, AUS [35364]

GOSSLAND ALL WORLDWIDE [35985]

GOSSMAN 1850+ BUENA VISTA CO., IA & OH,
USA [36942]

GOSSOW 1810-1840 MILLENBACH, LUX [38691] :
1810-1840 MUHLENBACH, LUX [38711]

GOSSWEIN 1800+ GER [36343]

GOSTLING 1872+ CAMBERWELL &
COLCHESTER, ESS & LND, ENG [37656]

GOSTOMCZYK ALL POM & WOR, GER [38687]

GOSWELL ALL WORLDWIDE [37688]

GOTCHE 1810-30 BUCHENBACH, PRE, GER [38202]

GOTH 1750-1830 BECHELN, PRE, GER [38405]

GOTHAM ALL UK [36062]

GOTHARD C1850 REEFTON, NZ [35998]

GOTHERIDGE 1800+ DBY, ENG [38261]

GOTHORP 1872+ RIPPON, YKS, ENG [35887]

GOTMAN PRE 1900 NIZHNY NOVGAROD, SU
[36889]

GOTSINGER PRE 1840 LONDON &, SRY, ENG
[35946]

GOTT 1800S ULCEBY, LIN, ENG [36847] : 1700+
GER [37993] : PRE 1860 QUINCY & PLUMAS, CA &
MO, USA [38570]

GOTTASON WILLIAM PRE 1644 JSY, CHI [38348]

GOTTHART PRE 1762 HALLE, HAL, DDR [37380]

GOTTLIEB 1800-1950 GRULICH & KRALICKY, CS
[33834]

GOTTLING 1831 GAWLER, SA, AUS [35369]

GOTTS 1790+ GRESHAM, NFK, ENG [35560]

GOTTSCHALK ALL BENNUNGEN, THU, GER
[38637]

GOTZFRID 1824-1890 RASTADT, CHER, SU [38738]

GOUDE PRE 1800 CAMBRIDGE, CAM, ENG [35238]

GOUDGE PRE 1875 BODMIN, ROCHE &
TYWARDRETH, CON, ENG [37814]

GOUDIE C1750-1850 MAYBOLE, AYR, SCT [33845] :
PRE 1842 MAUCHLINE, AYR, SCT [34859] : PRE
1740 MAYBOLE, AYR, SCT [35406] : PRE 1890
GLASGOW, LKS, SCT [36583] : 1800S PARTICK,
GOVAN, LKS, SCT [36642]

GOUDY PRE 1900 SCT [37443]

GOUGE PRE 1795 SPITALFIELDS, MDX, ENG
[35016] : PRE 1850 BOBBING, KEN, ENG [36298] :
PRE 1850 KEN, ENG [36393] : PRE 1900 CARLISLE,
CUL, ENG [37616]

GOUGER PRE 1750 WALKINGTON, ERY, ENG
[36059]

GOUGH PRE 1860+ WINDSOR, NSW, AUS [35237] :
PRE 1895 MARYBOROUGH, VIC, AUS [37960] :
1880+ NSW & QLD, AUS [37974] : 1840-1900
MIDDLESEX CO., ONT, CAN [34153] : ALL SRY,
ENG [33925] : 1750+ EASTHAMPSTEAD, BRK,
ENG [33938] : C1800 HEF, ENG [34153] : 1650+
DORSTONE & WELLINGTON, GLS, ENG [34747] :
PRE 1830 BISHOP NYMPTON, DEV, ENG [34868] :
1836 BRISTOL, GLS, ENG [34868] : 1750-1850
PETERCHURCH, HEF, ENG [36109] : 1600-1800
ODDFALLINGS, STS, ENG [36205] : ALL
HUDDERSFIELD, YKS, ENG [36656] : ALL
ASHLEWORTH & MAISEMORE, GLS, ENG [37681]
: 1550-1650 WIL, ENG [37764] : PRE 1890
LIVERPOOL, ENG [37974] : 1800+ BENGAL
ARMY, IRL &, INDIA [34109] : 1790+ BRANDON,
COR, IRL [35582] : C1832 CUYAHOGA CO., OH,
USA [34153] : BAILEY 1830-1845 GREEN, IL, USA
[38157]

GOUJON PRE 1750 SOHO, LND, ENG & FRA [36396]

GOUKES PRE 1818 WISBECH, CAM, ENG [36270]

GOULD 1860+ CASTLEMAINE, VIC, AUS [34798] :
PRE 1900 CASTLEMAINE, VIC, AUS [35055] : 1853
VIC, AUS [35414] : 1820+ ONT, CAN [36687] : 1820-
1850S SOM, ENG [33835] : 1750 BRK, ENG [34321] :
1760+ SOM, ENG [34532] : PRE 1900 LONDON,
ENG [34671] : PRE 1865 BIRMINGHAM, WAR,
ENG [34736] : EDWARD 1850+ WALWORTH, SRY,

ENG [34810] : C1829 DOR, ENG [34815] : PRE 1815
SOM, ENG [35016] : PRE 1796 CASTLE CARY,
SOM, ENG [35414] : 1700-1845 ASHCOTT, SOM,
ENG [35445] : PRE 1841 ALVESCOTT & BAMPTON,
OXF, ENG [35525] : PRE 1816 KEN, ENG [35532] :
1841-1900 SOUTHWARK, LND, ENG [36117] : 1840
STOKE DAMEREL, DEV, ENG [37204] : C1850
BIRMINGHAM, WAR, ENG [37209] : 1820S KEN,
ENG [37513] : PRE 1850+ HOLWAY TAUNTON,
SOM, ENG [37518] : 1700+ LEEK, STS, ENG [37666]
: PRE 1850 DOW, IRL [34617] : PRE 1850 NEWTON
BUTLER, FER, IRL [34798] : 1800+ TIP, IRL [34880]
: 1835-1856 KER, IRL [36281] : PRE 1900 ANT &
DOW, IRL [37708] : 1680-1800 SUFFOLK CO., NY,
USA [35318] : C1770 SOMERSET CO., MD, USA
[36354] : JOHN E. 1820-1850 TROY, ME, USA [36944]
: 1640-1700 MA, USA [38203] : THOMAS C1740
CHARLESTOWN, RI, USA [38348] : JOSEPH 1911-
1930 NEWPORT, MON, WLS [36707]

GOULD (SEE GOLD) [36314]

GOULDBY PRE 1919 LOWESTOFT, SFK, ENG [36230]

GOULDEN 1800-1900 SHEFFIELD & LEEDS, WRY,
ENG [36031] : 1800S MANCHESTER, LAN, ENG
[37203] : 1830S LAN, ENG [37309] : 1700-1900 PA &
MD, USA [37517]

GOULDER 1750+ MINSTER, KEN, ENG [35398]

GOULDING 1865+ STAFFORD, STS, ENG [35753] :
ALL CUL & ONT, ENG & CAN [37738] : PRE 1833
POWERSCOURT, WIC, IRL [33924]

GOULDSBOROUGH 1770S EAST COWTON, NRY,
ENG [34211]

GOULET JOSEPH 1836+ DE BERTHIER, QUE, CAN
[36678]

GOULSBRA 1700+ LIN, ENG [36133]

GOULSTON 1830 THELNETHAM, SFK, ENG [35067]

GOUPIL 1800+ ST-MICHEL, QUE, CAN [34082] :
1880+ ALPENA, MI, USA [36720] : 1900+
CHEBOYGEN, MI, USA [36720]

GOURDEN ALL WORLDWIDE [36221]

GOURDIN C1840 MONT ST GILBERT, BEL [34521] :
C1905 GRAND CLARIERE, MAN, CAN [34521]

GOURDON ALL WORLDWIDE [36221]

GOURLAY 1853-1920 VIC, AUS [33791] : PRE 1853
INVERNESS, SCT [33791] : INGLERAMUS DE 1175
CERES, FIF, SCT [33791] : PRE 1853 CERES, FIF,
SCT [35217] : 1700+ BALMERINO, FIF, SCT [35627]
: PRE 1860 ST ANDREWS, FIF, SCT [35800] : ALL
RFW, SCT & AUS [35213]

GOURLEY 1870 MARYBOROUGH, VIC, AUS
[37960] : C1820 TYR, IRL [34774] : PRE 1735 ERROL,
PER, SCT [33873] : C1795 ORMIESTON, MLN, SCT
[34239] : 1800-1860S RUTHERLGEN, LKS, SCT
[34882] : 1860+ NEWCASTLE, FIF, SCT [35800] :
1865-1960 GIBSON CO., IN, USA [36553] : 1838-1865
MONROE CO., IN, USA [36553] : 1801-1838
CHESTER DISTRICT, SC, USA [36553] : PRE 1900
WORLDWIDE [35253]

GOUT PRE 1946 JAVA, E. INDIES &, NL [36630] :
PRE 1700 KILDERVEEN, NL [36630]

GOVAN WILLIAM 1775-1885 SCT [34143]

GOVANLOCK 1790S JEDBURGH, ROX, SCT [37145]

GOVE C1880 VIC, AUS [34456] : 1800-1900 TWIGG
CO., GA, USA [34004] : 1650-1900 HAMPTON
FALLS, NH, USA [34004] : 1880-1905 ST
AUGUSTINE, FL, USA [34004]

GOVER 1600-1900 WAREHAM, DOR, ENG [38471]

GOVERNOR 1800S NSW, AUS [34570]

GOW 1800+ ORILLIA, ONT, CAN [36756] : PRE 1883
STENTON COTTAGE, ENG [34797] : PRE 1800
SCONE, PER, SCT [35448] : 1860S LKS, SCT [35799] :
PRE 1800 FETTERCAIRN & BLAIR ATHOL, KCD
& PER, SCT [36371] : 1700+ GLASGOW, LKS, SCT

[36756] : 1700+ EAST KILPATRICK, DNB, SCT
[36756] : 1800+ LITTLE DUNKELD, PER, SCT
[36869] : 1836-1898 JOHNSTON, RFW, SCT & AUS
[35763]

GOWANLOCK C1760 SOUTH DEAN, ROX, SCT
[34358]

GOWANS 1850 HOBART, TAS, AUS & SCT [35079] :
1850S-1870S HALDIMAND, ONT, CAN [34088] :
1860-1870 KILMARNOCK, AYR, SCT [34088] : 1830-
1850 HAMILTON, LKS, SCT [34088]

GOWARD 1850+ BEGA, NSW, AUS [35240]

GOWDY PRE 1780 SUNDERLAND, DUR, ENG
[36202] : C1830 SCT [37513]

GOWER ALL NSW, AUS [33798] : 1800+ KEN, ENG
[35041] : 1800 ABOTS LANGLEY, HRT, ENG [36798]
: PRE 1851+ ROCHFORD, ESS, ENG [37108] : 1800
SHOREHAM, KEN, ENG [37262] : 1800-1850
WAYNE CO., TN, USA [35301]

GOWERS 1820S HAVERHILL, SFK, ENG [35391] :
PRE 1950 ISLEHAM, CAM, ENG [36489] : PRE 1837
STEBBING, ESS, ENG [36589] : ALL UK [36131]

GOWING 1500-1650 STRADBROKE AREA, SFK,
ENG [36335] : 1500-1650 STARSTON AREA, NFK,
ENG [36335]

GOWLAND PRE 1900 ROWLANDS GILL, DUR,
ENG [36113]

GOWLETT PRE 1800 UXBRIDGE, MDX, ENG [35806]

GOWNASS 1750-1800 KILLINGTON, WES, ENG
[37779]

GOY C1630 GENEVA, GE, CH [38348]

GOYER ALL IRL [36118]

GOYMER 1800S ESS & SRY, ENG [37525]

GOZA PRE 1870 AR, USA [38314]

GOZNEY 1795-1857 HUNSLET, WRY, ENG [34352]

GRAAUW (DE) C1800 BETUWE, GEL, NL [38713]

GRABAU 1895+ BALRANALD, NSW, AUS [34906] :
1881-1895 ECHUCA, VIC, AUS [34906]

GRABHAM C1787 BICKENHALL & CURLAND,
SOM, ENG [34195] : ALL YARCOMBE, DEV &
SOM, ENG [37269] : PRE 1650 ENG [38768] : 1600-
1860 DUR & YKS, ENG [38768] : PRE 1700 WLS
[38768]

GRABLE PRE 1729 RPF, BRD [37603] : 1800-1870
FAYETTE, PA, USA [37589] : 1725-1760
PHILADELPHIA CO., PA, USA [37603] : 1764-1800
FREDERICK CO., MD, USA [37603] : 1770S VA,
USA [38202]

GRABOWSKI PRE 1900 KOLACZKOWA, PO, POL
[36941] : 1829S SANOK, POL [38184]

GRACE PIERCE 1840S HOBART, TAS, AUS [34785] :
1830-1870 BALLARAT, VIC, AUS [35850] : PATRICK
1846+ LA & MIDDLESEX CO., ONT, CAN [34154] :
1780+ EVERLEIGH, WIL, ENG [34290] : C1840
LONDON, ENG [34952] : PRE 1845 BRIGHTON &
EASTBOURNE, SSX, ENG [36589] : 1863+
DONCASTER, WRY, ENG [37058] : 1800+ ESS &
KEN, ENG [37058] : 1800+ EWHURST, SSX, ENG
[37816] : PRE 1750 WARBLETON & WARTLING,
SSX, ENG [37816] : 1750+ SEDLESCOMBE, SSX,
ENG [37816] : 1750-1800 HORSLEY, DBY, ENG
[38478] : PRE 1844 IRL [35192] : 1780+ DRINAGH,
COR, IRL [36343] : 1900-1920 NZ & AUS [37816]

GRACIE 1830+ LIVERPOOL, LAN, ENG [35363] :
1730+ CARRON HILL, DFS, SCT [35363]

GRADOLPH 1750-1820 BAV, GER [38740] : 1820-1950
CINCINNATI, OH, USA [38740] : 1820-1950
HAMILTON, OH, USA [38740]

GRADWELL PRE 1725 ULVERSTON, LAN, ENG
[34053]

GRADY 1866+ PT LINCOLN, SA, AUS [34262] :
1851+ FREMANTLE, WA, AUS [35847] : C1832
WEX, IRL [33812] : 1880 CALLAN, KIK, IRL [35350]

: PRE 1835 DUBLIN, IRL [38056] : ALL IRL & USA [36933]

GRAEB 1800S PUSLINCH, ONT, CAN [35635]

GRAENDORF 1800-1875 SELCHOW & BERLIN, GER [36953]

GRAESSER PRE 1745 UNTERSIEMAU, BAY, BRD [35311]

GRAET 1730+ KISKET, NY, USA [34408]

GRAF 1895+ BUCHANAN CO., IA, USA [38323]

GRAFTON 1800-1850 LONDON, ENG [36025]

GRAGERT PRE 1800 BRA, GER [38648]

GRAGG 1790-1810 BALTAMORE, MD, USA [36328] : 1700-1800 OH, USA [36328]

GRAHAM PRE 1830 BRISBANE, QLD, AUS [33932] : 1840+ MACKAY, QLD, AUS [34044] : 1850-1890 BRISBANE, QLD, AUS [34438] : 1850+ MARRICKVILLE, NSW, AUS [35358] : 1850+ OBERON, NSW, AUS [35395] : 1853+ COLAC, VIC, AUS [35437] : JOHN 1881 ADAMSTOWN, NSW, AUS [36367] : 1855+ BALLARAT, VIC, AUS [37109] : 1850S FIGTREE, NSW, AUS [38001] : 1880+ MELBOURNE, VIC, AUS [38018] : 1847+ SCUGOG ISLAND, ONT, CAN [34169] : ELIZABETH PRE 1860 ONT, CAN [34222] : 1830-1900 BROCKVILLE, ONT, CAN [34402] : 1850+ SIMCOE CO., ONT, CAN [34465] : 1790+ GLENGARRY CO., ONT, CAN [36350] : 1827S QUE, CAN [36695] : PRE 1851 RENFREW, ONT, CAN [36695] : 1838-80 TWEED & HASTINGS CO., ONT, CAN [37528] : ROBERT PRE 1851 DERBY, ONT, CAN [38445] : 1840+ VICTORIA CO., ONT, CAN & SCT [38433] : PRE 1760 CHOLLERTON, NBL, ENG [33940] : 1800+ KIRKOSWALD, CUL, ENG [34148] : 1800+ LONDON, ENG [34322] : MARGARET C1810-1893 LIVERPOOL, LAN, ENG [34432] : JANE PRE 1850 CARLISLE, CUL, ENG [34583] : 1740-1810 CUL, ENG [34687] : PRE 1760 LONDON, ENG [34974] : C1820 CARISBROOKE, IOW, ENG [35131] : 1790+ DOLPHINHOLME, LAN, ENG [36040] : 1850-1900 PRESTON, LAN, ENG [36040] : C1840 PRESTWICH & MANCHESTER, LAN, ENG [36147] : PRE 1834 WARDY HILL & ELY, CAM, ENG [36149] : JOHN 1846+ SEATON DELAVEL, NBL, ENG [36367] : 1800+ ENG [36470] : 1700+ HARTLEY, NBL, ENG [36609] : ALL LIVERPOOL, ENG [36811] : C1800 NEW BIDDOCK, DUR, ENG [37112] : 1800+ JARROW, DUR, ENG [37134] : PRE 1837 WESTMINSTER, LND, ENG [37321] : 1650-1800 FARLAM, CUL, ENG [37457] : 1800-1860 BRAFFERTON, DUR, ENG [37872] : 1700S ENG [38336] : PRE 1830 LEX, IRL [33838] : 1800-1900 BELFAST, ANT, IRL [33851] : 1750S TULINNAGRAKIN, SLI, IRL [33898] : 1800S CHARLEVILLE, COR, IRL [33924] : 1800S KILMORE, ARM, IRL [34044] : PRE 1826 BALLYMENA, ANT, IRL [34169] : 1780-1840 ELPHIN, ROS, IRL [34274] : 1825-1845 SLI, IRL [34457] : PRE 1830 DUBLIN, IRL [34494] : PRE 1838 BALLYMENA, ANT, IRL [34881] : HUGH 1800+ BENAGH, DOW, IRL [35219] : 1800S ENNISKILLEN, FER, IRL [35395] : DOROTHY 1850S ARM, IRL [35584] : 1800+ ARM, IRL [35949] : 1800-1900 OMAGH, TYR, IRL [36618] : 1809 IRL [36667] : 1800-1870 IRL [36718] : C1810+ DROMORE, TYR, IRL [36838] : ALL BELFAST, DOW, IRL [37303] : PRE 1905 GLASDRUMMAN, DOW, IRL [37439] : PRE 1840 TYR, IRL [37528] : 1700-1990 TYR, IRL [37549] : PRE 1890 FER, IRL [37601] : 1780 DOW, IRL [37795] : JAMES 1788 DOW, IRL [37801] : 1865+ LIM, IRL [38018] : AMELIA 1877 TIMARU, NZ [36782] : 1788+ GRAHAMSTOWN, CAPE, RSA [34947] : PRE 1860

GLASGOW, SCT [33838] : 1790-1850S GRANGEMOUTH, STI, SCT [33865] : PRE 1880 ARRAN, SCT [33966] : 1400+ KIRKINTILLOCH, DNB, SCT [33989] : 1700-1800S HUTTON & CORRIE, DFS, SCT [34032] : C1700 LIVINGSTONE, WLN, SCT [34118] : 1820+ JEDBURGH, ROX, SCT [34149] : ISOBEL 1700 JOHNSTONE, DFS, SCT [34225] : 1800+ EDINBURGH, MLN, SCT [34232] : 1810+ DUNTOCHER, DNB, SCT [34260] : PRE 1755 HUTTON & CORRIE, DFS, SCT [34501] : PRE 1830 SOUTH KNAPDALE, ARL, SCT [34911] : PRE 1845 BEW, SCT [34959] : 1750+ CRAIGBARNET, STI, SCT [35186] : THOMAS C1848-79 WISHAW, LKS, SCT [35411] : CATHERINE 1830+ EDINBURGH, MLN, SCT [35428] : 1800S KIRKALDY, FIF, SCT [35437] : 1700+ EASDALE IS., ARL, SCT [35825] : 1800+ DUNFERMLINE, FIF, SCT [35969] : 1700-1833 GLASGOW, LKS, SCT [36149] : PRE 1840 KELTON, KKD, SCT [36278] : 1840+ CASTLE DOUGLAS, DFS, SCT [36278] : C1800 IRVINE, AYR, SCT [36431] : 1700S FINTRIE, STI, SCT [36585] : 1820S GLASGOW, SCT [36695] : 1800-1870 SCT [36718] : 1840+ EDINBURGH, MLN, SCT [36884] : 1200 SCT [37008] : 1700+ KIPPEN, STI, SCT [37073] : 1800+ RENFREW, RFW, SCT [37073] : 1786+ DENNY, STI, SCT [37132] : PRE 1835 ISLE OF SKYE, SCT [37142] : PRE 1840 DOUGLAS, LKS, SCT [37332] : C1811 SCT [37474] : 1800S ROC, SCT [37496] : EUPHEMIA 1800 LKS, SCT [37879] : 1840+ NEWHAVEN, AYR, SCT [38247] : 1800+ LOCHMABEN, DFS, SCT [38247] : C1850 VAN BUREN, AR, USA [36934] : C1860 BRUSH CREEK, MO, USA [36934] : 1890-1960 NORMAN, OK, USA [36934] : 1880-1920 ARCADIA LAPEER CO., MI, USA [37528] : 1750-1990 BUTLER CO., PA, USA [37549] : 1760-1790 PHILADELPHIA, PA, USA [37549] : C1861 IN, IA & KS, USA [38112] : 1825 RUSSELLVILLE, KY, USA [38151] : 1900+ NEW YORK CITY, NY, USA [38481]

GRAHAME 1880+ SHEPPARTON, VIC, AUS [33836] : ELIZA 1852+ RICHMOND, SRY, ENG [36180] : 1700-1880 SCT [33836]

GRAINGER PRE 1850 WOR, ENG [34711] : PRE 1840 WALSALL, WAR, ENG [34736] : 1800 TIPTON, STS, ENG [35912] : ALL FROME, SOM, ENG [37617]

GRAISLEY 1840+ LINCOLN CO., ONT, CAN [38448]

GRALERT ALL GUSTROW, MEK, DDR [34812]

GRALEY 1775-1875 LONDON, SRY, ENG [36355]

GRAMANN C1800 WORLDWIDE [33841]

GRAMYK C1930 HAMTON & YORKTON, SAS, CAN [34521] : 1850-1930 STAWCHIN, BUKOVINA, UKRAINE [34521]

GRANAM ALL WORLDWIDE [37676]

GRANAT 1700-1781 VIBY, OSTERGOTLAND, SWE [38346]

GRAND C1500 THONON, HTE SAVOIE, FRA [38348]

GRANDAM C1700S+ WILLAND, DEV, ENG [35163]

GRANDI PRE 1570 VERONA, VENETIA, ITL [38348]

GRANDIN 1750+ GROUVILLE, JSY, CHI [34637]

GRANDINETTI 1890 CALABRIA, ITL [36679]

GRANDPRE RON PRE 1629 SEDAN, CHA, FRA [38563] : RON 1629-1640 NORRKOPING, SWE [38563]

GRANEA ALL WORLDWIDE [37102]

GRANFELD C1830 WOOLWICH, KEN, ENG [37129]

GRANGE 1870-1871 LND, ENG [35414] : 1800+ YKS, ENG [35579] : PRE 1850 WHITTLESEY, CAM, ENG [35821] : PRE 1808 WRY, ENG [38389] : C1835 PARIS, FRA [35414] : 1874+ AUCKLAND, NZ [35414]

GRANGE DIT LA GRANGE C1800 ONEX, GE, CH [38348]

GRANGER C1860 ESPERANCE, TAS, AUS [34586] :
1857+ GUNNING, NSW, AUS [35510] : 1800+
WALSHAM LE WILLOWS, SFK, ENG [34640] :
1800-1860 SHEFFIELD, YKS, ENG [35382] : C1800
NOTLEY, ESS, ENG [37449] : 1550-1650 WITHERN
WITH STAIN, LIN, ENG [38453]

GRANHAGAN 1780+ BSW, GER [35093]

GRANHAM ALL WORLDWIDE [37676]

GRANLAND 1822-1866 BALLARAT, VIC, AUS [36281]

GRANN 1890+ USA [38552]

GRANNIS JOHN 1815-1898 ORANGE CO., NY, USA
[37023]

GRANNUM 1750-1850 BARBADOS [38355] : ALL
WORLDWIDE [37676]

GRANSHAW 1886+ SYDNEY, NSW, AUS [34979] :
PRE 1886 LND, ENG [34979] : ALL EAST
LONDON, MDX, ENG [37700]

GRANT PRE 1900 VIC, AUS [34268] : 1856-1940
DAYLESFORD, VIC, AUS [34462] : 1868+
BALLARAT EAST, VIC, AUS [34685] : 1852+
CHILWELL, VIC, AUS [34685] : 1855-1925
PORTLAND, VIC, AUS [35223] : 1875-1895
COLERAINE, VIC, AUS [35223] : 1873+
WYNDHAM, NSW, AUS [35731] : PRE 1900
MELBOURNE, VIC, AUS [35932] : 1870+ TINGHA,
NSW, AUS [37889] : 1863-1895 FREDERICKTON,
NSW, AUS [38007] : 1890-1910 WOODBURN, NSW,
AUS [38007] : 1873-1883 ALGONQUIN &
KINCARDINE, ONT, CAN [34235] : JOHN 1860+
COLLINGWOOD, ONT, CAN [35648] : ANNE
1900+ MASSIE STN, ONT, CAN [35648] : NELLIE
F. 1802-1850 GLENGARRY, ONT, CAN [38482] :
ALEX. B. 1786-1829 GLENGARRY, ONT, CAN
[38482] : DONALD B. 1802-1842 GLENGARRY,
ONT, CAN [38482] : 1800-1850 LONDON, ENG
[34228] : 1660-1800 KIBWORTH BEAUCHAMP, LEI,
ENG [34258] : C1890 FORMBY, LAN, ENG [34366] :
PRE 1770 BIDEFORD, DEV, ENG [34445] : PRE
1852 MELLS, SOM, ENG [34685] : 1870-1900
EALING, MDX, ENG [34735] : JUDITH PRE 1740
BRADFORD ON AVON, WIL, ENG [34908] : 1640+
POUGHILL & CREDITON, DEV, ENG [35027] :
PRE 1820 RAMSGATE, KEN, ENG [35211] : PRE
1830 ST AUSTELL & VERYAN, CON, ENG [35215] :
1900+ CHERTSEY, SRY, ENG [35335] : PRE 1900
LONDON, ENG [35335] : PRE 1800 KELSHALL,
HRT, ENG [35967] : PRE 1853 LAMBETH, SRY,
ENG [36090] : GEORGE C1779 CHITTERN ST
MARY, WIL, ENG [37002] : CHARLES P. PRE 1850
BICESTER, OXF, WAR & GLS, ENG [37655] : ALL
WINCHESTER, HAM, ENG [37898] : 1850+ EAST
LONDON, ENG [37898] : 1835-1840 GRIMSBY, LIN,
ENG [38007] : C1910 LIVERPOOL, ENG [38168] :
ELIZA 1800+ BRISTOL &, SFK, ENG [38540] : ALL
ULCEBY, LIN & NSW, ENG & AUS [35547] : PRE
1820 TANDRAGEE, ARM, IRL [36692] : 1800-1900
IRL [38041] : 1800-1900 DUNTROON, OTAGO, NZ
[35923] : 1700S ABD, SCT [34053] : PRE 1800
GLENGAULLIE & CROMDALE, MOR, SCT [34235]
: 1800+ GRANTOWN & INVERALLAN, MOR,
SCT [34235] : 1780-1840S KINGUSSIE, INV, SCT
[34268] : JAS & ELSPET C1800 LOWER CRAGGEN,
INV, SCT [34369] : 1750+ SCT [34387] : 1800+
PETERHEAD, ABD, SCT [34560] : 1800+
PETERHEAD, ABD, SCT [34560] : PRE 1840
ABERDEEN, ABD, SCT [34598] : JAMES C1770-1790
STRATHSPEY, MOR, SCT [34646] : 1750+
TARADALE, ROC, SCT [34684] : ALL
BALMERINO, FIF, SCT [34758] : 1750+ ABD, SCT
[35060] : BETSEY 1805-1854 ALVIE, INV, SCT
[35223] : JANE C1832-1925 CROMDALE, MOR, SCT
[35223] : JAMES C1772+ FORRES, MOR, SCT

[35223] : ALEXANDER C1851 CROFTBEG, INV,
SCT [35223] : 1850S GLASGOW, LKS, SCT [35377] :
1800-1900 PITLOCHRY, PER, SCT [35923] : 1800-
1900 DUNNING, PER, SCT [35923] : 1700-1900
CROMDALE, MOR, SCT [35923] : PRE 1828
EDINBURGH, MLN, SCT [35932] : PRE 1820 ABD,
SCT [35983] : JOHN 1600-1800 LATHERON, CAI,
SCT [36001] : DR DAVID 1744-1817 DELACHAPEL
& STRATHSPREY, INV, SCT [36311] : PRE 1890
GLASGOW ELGIN, MOR, SCT [36369] : 1800S
KIRKMICHAEL, BAN, SCT [36607] : PRE 1772
CROMDALE, INV, SCT [36653] : PRE 1840
GLASGOW, LKS, SCT [36777] : PRE 1820 INV, SCT
[37133] : PRE 1840 AUCHINLECK & CUMNOCK,
AYR, SCT [37374] : PRE 1850 ABERDEEN, ABD,
SCT [37832] : 1820+ KEPPOCH, ISLE OF SKYE,
SCT [37889] : C1700-1800 MONQUHITTER, ABD,
SCT [37977] : 1800+ ABERDEEN, ABD, SCT [38213]
: PRE 1855 BEAULY, INV, SCT [38292] : 1750-1950
CROMDALE, MOR, SCT [38355] : 1750+ MOR, SCT
[38425] : DONALD B. 1770-1802 DALCATOIG, INV,
SCT [38482] : ALEXANDER 1740-1829 INV, SCT
[38482] : 1700-1990 UK & AUS [35421] : PRE 1750
STONINGTON, CT, USA [33804] : PRE 1850S ME,
USA [37522] : ALLEXANDER 1770-1790 UPPER
NEW YORK, NY, USA [38482] : 1700+ CARDIFF &
BORNVILLE, WLS & WOR, WLS & ENG [36794]

GRANT DR DAVID 1774-1817 KINGSTON,
JAMAICA, W.INDIES [36311]

GRANTHAM 1596 NORTHENDEN, CHS, ENG
[35097] : PRE 1850 LONDON, ENG [35229] : 1800+
WEST KEAL, LIN, ENG [37487]

GRANTZ PETER C1858 SHO, GER [37024] : 1700-1800
DANZIG, WESTPREUßEN, PRE [38603]

GRANVIK 1888-1930 NEW YORK, NY, USA [38757]

GRANVILLE 1800S RICHMOND, NSW, AUS [35537]

GRASS 1800-1850 GERBACH, BAV, GER [36966] :
1789S SIEN, PRE, GER [36966] : 1850S SONOMA,
CA, USA [36966]

GRASSE 1800S MALLMITZ, SIL, GER [38623]

GRASSICK PRE 1920 LEITH, MLN, SCT [37835]

GRASSIE 1800-1900 MARYCULTER, KCD, SCT
[36951] : 1700-1900 OLD MACHAR, ABD, SCT
[36951]

GRATIOT 1700-1800 LAUSANNE, VD, CH [35283]

GRATON CLAUDE 1650S AUBIGNY, PCH, FRA
[36711]

GRATTAN PRE 1940 DUBLIN, IRL [34547]

GRATTON ALL NORTHLEW, DEV, ENG [37092]

GRATWICK 1750-1800 ERITH, KEN, ENG [34829]

GRATZ 1700+ RPR, GER [38765]

GRAUKE PRE 1855 GER [38191]

GRAUMEN ALL KERZ, TRANSYLVANIA, RO
[38519]

GRAVE 1849+ MELBOURNE, VIC, AUS [36360] :
PRE 1849 LONDON, ENG [36360] : 1550-1650
KESWICK, CUL, ENG [37460]

GRAVEL PRE 1616 DINAN, BRITTANY, FRA [34106]

GRAVELY 1715+ RATCHAM, SSX, ENG [35824]

GRAVENALL ALL WORLDWIDE [33928]

GRAVENER ALL DUDLEY, WOR, ENG [36492] : ALL
ROWLEY REGIS, STS, ENG [36492] : PRE 1830
DOVER, KEN, ENG [37169] : ALL USA [37520]

GRAVER ALL NFK, ENG [38035]

GRAVES PRE 1880 VIC, AUS [34268] : 1845+
GEELONG, VIC, AUS [35218] : 1830+ HOBART,
TAS, AUS [35218] : PRE 1775 GREAT CHISHALL,
ESS, ENG [34840] : 1800+ LND, ENG [35218] :
1750+ KINGS WALDEN, HRT, ENG [35908] :
1880+ HARTLEPOOL, DUR, ENG [35908] : C1800
STANSTEAD, HRT, ENG [36978] : PRE 1840 FER,
IRL [34117] : PRE 1800 IOM, UK [35612] : C1720

SAYBROOK, CT, USA [36319] : PRE 1900 HAMILTON & LOS ANGELES, MT & CA, USA [36899] : 1700S CHARLES CO., MD, USA [37570] : 1600-1700 WETHERSFIELD, CT, USA [37783] : 1605-53 MA, USA [38151]

GRAVESON C1780-1930S CARTMEL, LAN, ENG [37413]

GRAVETT 1793+ WORTHING, SSX, ENG [35716] : ALL BRIGHTON, SSX, ENG [35716]

GRAY 1800+ WILLIAMSTOWN, VIC, AUS [34568] : EBENEZER PRE 1883 HACKNEY, SA, AUS [34587] : THOMAS 1880+ BURRA, SA, AUS [34871] : PRE 1940 VIC, AUS [35055] : EPHRAIM 1850+ HAWTHORN, VIC, AUS [35136] : JAMES ALL WEST WALLSEND, NSW, AUS [35234] : ALLURED 1884+ VIC, AUS [35477] : 1832+ SUTTON FOREST, NSW, AUS [35556] : ALL STAWELL, VIC, AUS [35707] : 1852+ WILLIAMSTOWN, VIC, AUS [35802] : 1869+ ARMIDALE, NSW, AUS [37316] : 1783+ SAINT JOHN, NB, CAN [34470] : 1915+ ONT & ALB, CAN [35802] : 1800S+ GLENELG TWP., ONT, CAN [37458] : 1750+ MONTREAL, QUE, CAN [38377] : 1800+ GILLINGHAM, KEN, ENG [33893] : C1868 NTH SHEFFIELD, YKS, ENG [34193] : 1880+ NEWINGTON, SRY, ENG [34237] : C1860 SOUTH SHIELDS, DUR, ENG [34329] : 1820+ EXMOUTH, DEV, ENG [34568] : 1660-1900 REDRUTH, CON, ENG [34697] : 1700+ THORNFORD, DOR, ENG [34777] : PRE 1838 REDRUTH, CON, ENG [34816] : 1840S TRURO, CON, ENG [34854] : PRE 1831 LOWER PUTNEY, SRY, ENG [35016] : PRE 1730 BASSINGBOURN, CAM, ENG [35070] : PRE 1848 WOODLAND, DEV, ENG [35147] : 1730-1830 SOUTH SHIELDS, DUR, ENG [35153] : 1830S SALISBURY, WIL, ENG [35156] : JAMES C1825 WHITEPARISH, WIL, ENG [35349] : PRE 1700 NBL, ENG [35802] : PRE 1700 YKS, ENG [35802] : ALL SUNDERLAND, DUR, ENG [35802] : 1790S-1900 SSX, ENG [36024] : 1850+ ISLINGTON, LND, ENG [36142] : 1800S STOKE TRISTER, SOM, ENG [36142] : PRE 1850 HEXHAM, NBL, ENG [36224] : 1860-1870S ASTON ABBOTS, BKM, ENG [36289] : C1860S LEIGHTON BUZZARD, BDF, ENG [36289] : 1860 KEA, CON, ENG [36640] : EDMUND 1800-50 EDGBASTON & SHELDON, WAR, ENG [36652] : C1740 WITNEY, OXF, ENG [37053] : ALL LEICESTER, LEI, ENG [37295] : 1800S IOW, HAM, ENG [37349] : CHARLES JOS. 1824-1900 LAMBETH, SRY, ENG [37453] : WILLIAM 1800-1850 LAMBETH, SRY, ENG [37453] : ALL NFK, ENG [37612] : PRE 1850 PITTINGTON, DUR, ENG [37693] : 1820-1860S SUNDERLAND, DUR, ENG [37878] : PRE 1810 LEEDS, YKS, ENG [37913] : SLANEY 1800-1881 SHOREDITCH & BISHOPGATE, LND, ENG [37988] : PRE 1700 WEST KNOYLE, WIL, ENG [38499] : WILLIAM 183+ THORNFORD, DOR, ENG & AUS [33919] : C1770-1830 CARNSAMPSON, ANT, IRL [33845] : 1700-1800S TYR, IRL [35785] : 1800-1850 LOUGHCREW, MEA, IRL [37435] : 1880 KILRUSH, CLA, IRL [37914] : JOHN 1812+ MEA & WIC, IRL [38396] : ALL DUNEDIN & WELLINGTON, NZ [34603] : PRE 1887 INVERCARGILL, SOUTH IS., NZ [35234] : 1852+ NZ [35802] : 1802+ CUYLERVILLE, CAPE, RSA [34947] : 1800S FREUCHIE, FIF, SCT [33811] : 1820-1894 GLASGOW, LKS, SCT [33811] : C1800 ALVAH, BAN, SCT [33842] : ALL EDINBURGH, MLN, SCT [34093] : 1780+ TARVES, ABD, SCT [34326] : PETER PRE 1819 GLASGOW, LKS, SCT [34539] : CATHERINE C1819 GLASGOW, LKS, SCT [34539] : 1700+ LONGHOPE, OKI, SCT [34688] : 1836+ URQUHART & LOGIE WESTER, ROC, SCT

[34764] : PRE 1864 AIRDRIE, LKS, SCT [34961] : 1810 LEITH, MLN, SCT [35027] : PRE 1808 LOWER LARGO & SCOONIE, FIF, SCT [35229] : JAMES ALL SANGUHAR, DFS, SCT [35234] : PRE 1762 CADDER, LKS, SCT [35252] : 1740 DUFFUS, BAN, SCT [35259] : 1750+ EDINBURGH, MLN, SCT [35395] : 1800+ CUPAR & LEUCHARS, FIF, SCT [35395] : 1750-1850 CADDER, LKS, SCT [36261] : PRE 1860 BERWICK, BEW, SCT [36882] : PRE 1830 GLASGOW, SCT [37115] : PRE 1880 SCT [37459] : PRE 1870 BLAIRGOWRIE, PER, SCT [37711] : PRE 1870 EAST MILL, PER, SCT [37711] : 1700-1780 SCT [38373] : PRE 1878 ELLON, ABD, SCT [38412] : JOHN PRE 1800 LKS, SCT [38437] : C1800 BERKSHIRE CO., MA, USA [34395] : WILLIAM C1750-783 WESTCHESTER, NY, USA [34470] : 1790+ GENEVA, NY, USA [36354] : 1700+ GA, USA [36914] : 1830-1930 ST MARYS CO., MD, USA [37583] : 1820-30S NEWTON CO., GA, USA [38314] : 1750-1950 ALLEGHENY CO., PA, USA [38344] : MARY E. 1830+ LEBANON, CT, USA [38766]

GRAYDON WILLIAM 1793-1870 MAGUIRESBRIDGE, FER, IRL [34524] : 1775-1850 FER, IRL [37795]

GRAYGOOSE 1780S MANUDEN, ESS, ENG [37250]

GRAYLESS 1850+ PRESTON, LAN, ENG [37066]

GRAYLIS 1850+ PRESTON, LAN, ENG [37066] : PRE 1850 MAY, IRL [37066]

GRAYSON 1873+ QLD, AUS [37894] : JOHN PRE 1829 PENISTONE & MIDHOPE, WRY, ENG [35250] : C1770-1830 BOLSTERSTONE & MIDHOPE, WRY, ENG [35550] : C1820 LEEDS, YKS, ENG [35723] : PRE 1871 SHEFFIELD, WRY, ENG [36403] : PRE 1800 EGREMONT, CUL, ENG [36431] : 1822 SHEFFIELD, YKS, ENG [37391] : PRE 1820 LURGAN, ARN, IRL [35113] : PRE 1873 LURGAN, ARM, IRL [37894] : 1750+ WASHINGTON, DC & MD, USA [38336]

GRAYSTONE 1800-1900 NORTH LONDON, ENG [38244]

GRAZZILA C1780-1900 NS, CAN & SCT [38248]

GRAZEBROOK 1800+ BRISTOL, ENG [34571]

GREADLE PRE 1806 MANCHESTER & OLDHAM, LAN, ENG [38248]

GREALY 1800+ YACKANDANDAH, VIC, AUS [35028] : PRE 1855 GAL, IRL [35028]

GREARSON C1775 PRESTBURY, CHS, ENG [35095]

GREASLEY 1700+ NTT, ENG [34405]

GREATHEAD 1860+ WOOLLOOMOOLOO, NSW, AUS [37136] : PRE 1850 SHEERNESS, KEN, ENG [37136] : 1750-1890 DUR, ENG [37137]

GREATOREX 1790+ GLASGOW, SCT [34803]

GREAVEN PRE 1900 DOW, IRL [37405]

GREAVES 1845+ GEELONG, VIC, AUS [35218] : 1830+ HOBART, TAS, AUS [35218] : 1860+ BALLARAT, VIC, AUS [35218] : PRE 1910 SHEFFIELD, WRY, ENG [33902] : 1744-1830 BIRSTALL, WRY, ENG [34352] : ALL SOLIHULL & BIRMINGHAM, WAR, ENG [34553] : PRE 1800 SHEFFIELD, YKS & LAN, ENG [34743] : PRE 1800 HILLESDEN, BKM, ENG [35211] : 1800+ LND, ENG [35218] : C1806 BALE, NFK, ENG [35872] : PRE 1706 LAN, ENG [37706] : PRE 1830 SHEFFIELD, YKS, ENG [37913] : 1730-1800 STANHOE, NFK, ENG [38453] : ALL USA [34553]

GREAVES TIDD 1819+ WESTMINSTER, LND, ENG [35414]

GREBBY ALL LIN, ENG [37487]

GREBE PRE 1740 HES, GER [38642] : ALL WORLDWIDE [38677]

GREBER 1855 HUNTER VY, NSW, AUS [33929]

GREDT 1850+ ANTWERPEN, BEL [36533]

GREEDUS ALL WORLDWIDE [37237]

GREEDY ALL LOCHINVAR, NSW, AUS [37950] : ALL WIVERLIPSCOMBE, SOM, ENG [37950]

GREEK 1805+ WEARE GIFFARD, DEV, ENG & USA [36254] : 1805+ LITTLE TORRINGTON, DEV, ENG & USA [36254]

GREEN 1870-1900 ECHUCA, VIC, AUS [34175] : 1850-1880 CASTLEMAINE, VIC, AUS [34175] : C1850 GUNNING & BATHURST, NSW, AUS [35009] : WILLIAM 1828+ BATHURST, NSW, AUS [35066] : GEORGE 1820+ SYDNEY, NSW, AUS [35066] : JOSEPH 1800-1900 NSW, AUS [35103] : 1850+ WINCHELSEA, VIC, AUS [35185] : 1850+ GRASSMERE, VIC, AUS [35185] : 1840+ COWRA & YOUNG, NSW, AUS [35241] : JOHN PRE 1867 CYGNET, TAS, AUS [35258] : JOSEPH 1850-83 GEELONG & WINCHELSEA, VIC, AUS [35411] : 1800-1860 BROUGHTON, SA, AUS [36315] : FREDERICK 1877+ SYDNEY, NSW, AUS [37556] : ELIZA 1850 GLEBE, NSW, AUS [37942] : PRE 1775 LEEDS & RIO DE JANEIRO, WRY, ENG &, BRAZIL [36104] : MARY C1780-1850 YORK CO., NB, CAN [37454] : 1750+ QUEBEC, QUE, CAN [38377] : EDWARD 1860+ ONT, CAN [38419] : PHILIP 1780-1880 ONT, CAN & IRL [34514] : PRE 1870 TOLLARD ROYAL, WIL, ENG [33968] : ANN 1762 AMCOTTS, LIN, ENG [34091] : JOSEPH 1800+ KEN, ENG [34140] : 1800+ HENLEY ON THAMES, OXF, ENG [34236] : 1800+ BKM, ENG [34236] : 1802+ COLWALL, HEF, ENG [34334] : PRE 1896 NFK, ENG [34406] : PRE 1896 SFK, ENG [34406] : FRANCES ELIZA 1843+ MESSING, ESS, ENG [34627] : 1700S CLERKENWELL, LND, ENG [34776] : 1750+ LONDON, ENG [34813] : C1865-1914 BANK TOP, LAN, ENG [35052] : RICHARD 1798 LONDON, ENG [35066] : MARY PRE 1800 TREDINGTON, WAR, ENG [35128] : 1770+ FERSFIELD, NFK, ENG [35157] : ALL GODMANCHESTER, HUN, ENG [35185] : 1750S SHORTHAMPTON, OXF, ENG [35186] : PRE 1900 HUNTINGDON & GODMANCHESTER, HUN, ENG [35255] : ALL TOLLARD ROYAL, WIL, ENG [35297] : WM. FITTON 1843+ BINGLEY, YKS, ENG [35343] : 1800+ FRODINGHAM, LIN, ENG [35377] : ALFRED 1800S HARLESDEN GREEN, LND, ENG [35409] : JOSEPH C1819 NEWPORT, SAL, ENG [35411] : PRE 1843+ CAMBERWELL, SRY, LND & MDX, ENG [35460] : PRE 1885+ HACKNEY, MDX & LND, ENG [35460] : C1805 IPSWICH, SFK, ENG [35552] : PRE 1850 PAUL, CON, ENG [35736] : 1739 LANDSBEACH, CHS, ENG [35769] : 1700S SHEEN, STS, ENG [35830] : 1850+ TATTERSALL BRIDGE, NTT, ENG [35847] : PRE 1900 EVERCREECH, SOM, ENG [35878] : PRE 1900 SSX, ENG [35913] : WILLIAM C1825 WHITECHAPEL, LND, ENG [36000] : 1845-C1900 LAN, ENG [36024] : PRE 1880 BRIERLEY HILL & KINGSWINFORD, STS, ENG [36110] : PRE 1800 LIN, ENG [36143] : 1788-1872 KEMPSEY, WOR, ENG [36190] : PRE 1830 NORWICH, NFK, ENG [36228] : THOMAS A. 1838 HAM, ENG [36316] : PRE 1784 NEEDINGWORTH, HUN, ENG [36425] : MIRIAM PRE 1806 PRISTON, SOM, ENG [36526] : 1700+ BEDLINGTON & COWPEN, NBL, ENG [36609] : 1700+ WOODHORN & HORTON, NBL, ENG [36609] : 1700+ WHELMLY BURN & LONGHORSLEY, NBL, ENG [36609] : MARY 1791 MDX, ENG [36633] : 1750+ TOLLARD ROYAL, WIL, ENG [36825] : 1760+ LACKFORD & KENTFORD, SFK, ENG [36955] : PRE 1760 SFK, ENG [36955] : 1780+ SANDBACH AREA, CHS, ENG [36997] : PRE 1822 RADFORD, NTT, ENG

[37000] : ALICE PRE 1819 KINGSCLIFFE, NTH, ENG [37112] : FREDERICK C1830-1877+ CAMBORNE & CROWAN, CON, ENG [37556] : MARY C1825 BRISTOL, GLS & SOM, ENG [37556] : 1800+ BISHOP AUCKLAND, DUR, ENG [37598] : ALL SFK & ESS, ENG [37612] : ALL NORWICH, NFK, ENG [37629] : PRE 1880 BIRMINGHAM, WAR, ENG [37662] : PRE 1809 KIBWORTH, LEI, ENG [37706] : 1806 ABBOTS RIPTON, HUN, ENG [37723] : C1800S BOSHAM AND SURROUNDS, SSX, ENG [37745] : PRE 1810 PENISTONE & SILKSTONE, WRY, ENG [37754] : 1800S RYE, SSX, ENG [37833] : 1860 BLACKBURN, LAN, ENG [37873] : ELEANOR PRE 1870 LONDON, ENG [37926] : 1700 WIDFORD, ESS, ENG [37928] : ALL CHIPPENHAMDALE, CAM, ENG [37950] : WILLIAM 1830+ STUDHAM, BDF, ENG [38020] : PRE 1850 ROCHESTER, KEN, ENG [38027] : MARY 1820+ WAR & LEI, ENG [38031] : HANNAH 1802 EBBESBOURNE WAKE, WIL, ENG [38489] : 1800+ YKS, ENG [38494] : PRE 1824 SPORLE, NFK, ENG [38512] : HENRY 1857+ ROTHERAM, YKS & COR, ENG & IRL [34836] : PRE 1826 GROSFIEL, MEK, GER [36726] : CATHERINE 1780-1854 LONDONDERRY, LDY, IRL [34514] : C1770 COR, IRL [34521] : 1830+ LOUGHREA, GAL, IRL [35043] : ELLEN 1830S TIP, IRL [36316] : 1720-1850 DUNAMON, ROS & TYR, IRL [37118] : 1878+ BELFAST, ANT, IRL [37930] : ALL IRL [37930] : 1850S ARDFINNAN, TIP, IRL [38223] : 1811+ AUGHALOUGH, DON, IRL & AUS [35056] : 1870+ PORONGAHAU, HB, NZ [33968] : ALFRED 1900+ WELLINGTON, NZ [35409] : JOHN HAMLET 1863 NZ [35714] : 1800+ AUCKLAND, NZ [38273] : C1710 LOGIE, FIF, SCT [34768] : GEORGE 1820-1855 URQUHART & ELGIN, FIF, SCT [36068] : 1750+ LOCHMABEN, DFS, SCT [38388] : PRE 1860 HILLSDALE, NY, USA [34025] : 1677 HAVERHILL, MA, USA [36560] : GEORGE PRE 1860 MONTGOMERY CO., NY, USA [36950] : 1800-1950 ST JAMES PARISH, NEW ORLEANS, LA, USA [37583] : PRE 1815 CLARKE CO., GA, USA [37587] : 1800+ NY, USA [37592] : 1900+ NY, USA [37787] : PRE 1853 LOUISBURG, TN, USA [37817] : 1842+ RED HOOK, NY, USA [37823] : PRE 1843 ALBANY, NY, USA [38052] : 1600-1800 WARREN, PA & NY, USA [38098] : MARY JANE 1858-1882 BARABOO, SAUK CO., WI, USA [38145] : ROBERT 1650+ CANTERBURY, CT, USA [38181] : PRE 1850 WAYNE CO., KY, USA [38231] : JOHN PRE 1800 NJ, USA [38463] : JEANETTE 1956+ SILVER SPRING, MD, USA [38554] : DOUGLAS 1956+ SILVER SPRING, MD, USA [38554] : 1900+ USA & CAN [37930] : 1860+ MOLD, FLN, WLS [36228] : PRE 1907 WREXHAM, CLWYD, WLS [36613]

GREENAIGH 1875+ INVERELL, NSW, AUS [35232]

GREENAWAY 1883+ GRAFTON, NSW, AUS [35088] : 1840+ HUNTER VALLEY, NSW, AUS [37500] : PRE 1900 PLYMOUTH, DEV, ENG [34849] : C1800 BISHOPSGATE, LND, ENG [37449] : PRE 1820 RAMSBURY, WIL, ENG [37687]

GREENBERG PRE 1900 MELBOURNE, VIC, AUS & POL [34439]

GREENBURY 1840 WHITBY, NRY, ENG [37388]

GREENE GODFREY B. 1750-1850 MARCH, ONT, CAN [34514] : GODFREY PRE 1650 ENG [34514] : PRE 1680 NTH, ENG [34514] : 1600-1700 NEWCASTLE, STS, ENG [38474] : PRE 1870 THURLES, IRL [33954] : GODFREY 1600-1850 MOORESTOWN CASTLE, WAT, IRL [34514] : GODFREY 1600-1850 KILMANAHAN CASTLE,

TIP, IRL **[34514]** : PRE 1869 LOCH ERNE, FER, IRL **[36757]** : 1869+ NEWTON & ONEHUNGA, AUCK, NZ **[36757]** : 1900 HELENSBURGH, DNB, SCT **[35881]** : 1700+ BERKSHIRE CO., MA, USA **[34342]** : 1600-1670 SOMERSET CO., MD, USA **[36566]** : JOHN 1640 RI, USA **[37008]** : 1630-1690 KENT CO., RI, USA **[37477]** : 1842+ MELLENVILLE, NY, USA **[37823]**

GREENER PRE 1890 WINLATON, DUR, ENG **[38457]**

GREENFIELD 1910+ BRISBANE, QLD, AUS **[36359]** : C1850 ORANGE, NSW, AUS **[38760]** : PRE C1892 PECKHAM, PLUMSTEAD, LND, ENG **[33978]** : PRE 1780 CRANLEIGH, SRY, ENG **[36752]** : 1600-1800 EDGMOND, SAL, ENG **[38420]**

GREENGRASS 18501-950 BROMLEY, KEN, ENG **[34135]** : 1800S SFK, ENG **[35377]** : 1848 WEST STOW, SFK, ENG **[38209]**

GREENHALGH PRE 1828 MANCHESTER, LAN, ENG **[35247]** : ANN C1820 BLACKBURN, LAN, ENG **[35514]** : PRE 1800 BOLTON & MANCHESTER, LAN, ENG **[36066]** : 1790+ MANCHESTER, LAN, ENG **[36271]** : PRE 1874 RATCLIFFE, LAN, ENG **[38288]**

GREENHAM PRE 1800 NORTON SUB HAMDON, SOM, ENG **[34057]** : 1800+ STRADBALLY, LEX, IRL **[37070]**

GREENHILL ALL WALTON ON THE HILL, SRY, ENG **[34366]** : C1770 WEST HAM, ESS, ENG **[35203]** : PRE 1850 NFK, ENG **[37225]**

GREENHOOD 1700-1750 NORTH FRODINGHAM, YKS, ENG **[37011]**

GREENHORN 1800+ STIRLING, STI, SCT **[35865]** : 1800+ STIRLING, STI, SCT **[38726]**

GREENHOUGH HARRY A. C1860 LAN, ENG **[38383]**

GREENHOW 1760S THRELKELD, CUL, ENG **[33917]** : ALL WORLDWIDE **[36469]**

GREENING 1841+ MELBOURNE, VIC, AUS **[34962]** : 1840+ MUSGRAVETOWN, NFD, CAN **[33852]** : 1800S BONAVISTA BAY, NFD, CAN **[34096]** : 1800-1950 ST PETER PORT, GSY, CHI **[37435]** : PRE 1840 CHEPSTOW, GLS, ENG **[34962]** : ALL GLS, ENG **[36248]** : ALL BIRMINGHAM, WAR, ENG **[37274]**

GREENLAND ALL WORLDWIDE **[37232]**

GREENLAW 1780 ST ANDREWS, NB, CAN **[34129]**

GREENLEAF 1813+ PORTSMOUTH, HAM, ENG **[37855]** : PRE 1800 BOSTON, MA, USA **[37855]**

GREENLEE PRE 1770 WAR, ENG **[37545]** : 1850+ WAYNE CO., IA, USA **[37545]** : 1800-1850 MASON CO., WV, USA **[37545]**

GREENLEES PRE 1900 KILWAUGHTER, ANT, IRL **[35967]** : 1760-1850S KILBARCHAN & LOCHWINNOCK, RFW, SCT **[34359]**

GREENOUGH 1700 WIGAN, LAN, ENG **[35288]** : 1850-1920 PHILLIPSBURG, KS, USA **[34255]**

GREENSHIELDS 1800-1840 LKS, SCT **[36623]** : 1840-1855 EDINBURGH, MLN, SCT **[36623]**

GREENSILL 1800S TIPTON, STS, ENG **[35256]**

GREENSLADE C1830+ EXETER, DEV, ENG **[33812]** : C1824 REWE BY EXETER, DEV, ENG **[34195]** : C1800 WIVERSLIESCOMBE, SOM, ENG **[35038]** : ALL DEV, ENG **[37127]**

GREENSMITH 1400+ MATLOCK, DBY, ENG **[33989]**

GREENSTOCK 1700+ BORDER AREA, SOM & DOR, ENG **[36389]**

GREENTREE THOMAS 1850+ PITT TOWN, NSW, AUS **[36598]** : 1900S TAMWORTH, NSW, AUS **[37910]** : 1708+ HARTING, SSX, ENG **[36875]** : 1750+ HARTING, SSX, ENG **[36997]**

GREENWAY CLARA 1851-1919 OLD SWINFORD, WOR, ENG **[33892]** : PRE 1830 GREAT SOMERFORD, WIL, ENG **[36424]**

GREENWOOD AMY 1900+ WINDSOR & PRAHRAN, VIC, AUS **[38540]** : PRE 1839 SHOREDITCH, MDX, ENG **[34166]** : C1800+ BURNLEY, LAN & YKS, ENG **[34451]** : 1680-1750 ACKWORTH, YKS, ENG **[34762]** : C1850+ HALIFAX, YKS, ENG **[35163]** : 1790 HAWORTH, WRY, ENG **[35282]** : PRE 1900 HALIFAX, WRY, ENG **[36037]** : 1750-1800 S YKS, ENG **[36084]** : PRE 1840 LINGFIELD, SRY, ENG **[36090]** : C1815 SHIPLEY, YKS, ENG **[36302]** : 1775-1875 LONDON, SRY, ENG **[36355]** : C1840 DROYLESDEN, LAN, ENG **[36386]** : C1800 BRISTOL, GLS, ENG **[36585]** : 1800S LEICESTER, LEI, ENG **[37818]** : 1750-1850 BELFAST, ANT, IRL **[33851]** : C1830 MOY, TYR, IRL **[35428]** : GEORGE C1843+ NY, USA **[37764]** : 1841-1900 PHILADELPHIA, PA, USA **[38139]**

GREENYER PRE 1800 SOMPTING, SSX, ENG **[34112]**

GREEP ALL WORLDWIDE **[35931]**

GREER 1900+ PARRY SOUND, ONT, CAN **[35608]** : 1800+ DURHAM, CAN **[35608]** : 1750+ DON, IRL **[34416]** : JOHN ALL ARM, IRL **[34475]** : RICHARD C1833 ARM, IRL **[34475]** : PRE 1860 BELFAST, IRL **[34557]** : PRE 1825 BELFAST, ANT, IRL **[34786]** : 1800+ BAILIEBORO, CAV, IRL **[35608]** : 1840+ ANT, IRL **[36366]** : 1845-1875 SLIGO TOWN, SLI, IRL **[36906]** : PRE 1860 ANT, IRL **[37601]** : JOHN & REBCCA 1775-1830 IRL & SCT **[38216]** : 1800+ SCT **[36906]** : 1920+ CA, USA **[36906]**

GREESHAW EDWARD 1892-1978 GREENWICH, LND, ENG **[36598]**

GREESON PRE 1831 LIMESTONE CO., AL & TN, USA **[37817]**

GREETHAM 1860+ SCARBOROUGH, YKS, ENG **[37376]**

GREGAR 1830 PRAGUE, CS **[37582]**

GREGG 1800+ BRUCE CO., ONT, CAN **[37046]** : ALL ENG **[34758]** : 1750+ NOTTINGHAM, NTT, ENG **[35080]** : 1652-1897 EASTHAM, WOR, ENG **[36513]** : 1806+ SUMERBY, LAN, ENG & AUS **[36238]** : ALL INDIA **[35259]** : PRE 1850 ENNISKILLEN, CAV, IRL **[33874]** : 1630-1712 LONDONDERRY, DRY, IRL **[38019]** : C1790 KILMARNOCK, AYR, SCT **[35259]** : 1833 SOUTH LEITH, MLN, SCT **[35259]** : MARTHA PRE 1869 HAMILTON CO., OH, USA **[37797]** : 1712+ CARLISLE, PA, USA **[38019]** : 1712+ SC, USA **[38019]**

GREGOIRE 1700-1900 FOSSES LA VILLE, NMR, BEL **[38158]**

GREGORY 1850-1900 FLEMINGTON, VIC, AUS **[33834]** : 1800+ SYDNEY, NSW, AUS **[34888]** : 1840+ MORPETH, NSW, AUS **[34888]** : PETER& ELINOR 1860+ MOAMA, NSW, AUS **[35049]** : PETER C1860 CHEWTON, VIC, AUS **[35049]** : 1885-1900 RANDWICK, NSW, AUS **[35187]** : 1870 CRAIGIE, VIC, AUS **[35204]** : WILLIAM C1850 SYDNEY, NSW, AUS **[37106]** : 1800-1853 NTT, ENG **[33834]** : ALL FAVERSHAM, KEN, ENG **[34093]** : 1700+ CHESTERFIELD, DBY, ENG **[34888]** : 1750-1850 ST DOMINICK, CON, ENG **[34920]** : PRE 1870 TROWBRIDGE, WIL, ENG **[34999]** : PRE 1850 LIVERPOOL, LAN, ENG **[34999]** : 1500-1790 OXF, ENG **[35030]** : 1790-1930 BKM, ENG **[35030]** : 1700+ WHITE WALTHAM, BRK, ENG **[35042]** : 1834-1853 MULLION, CON, ENG **[35187]** : 1835 BRISLINGTON, SOM, ENG **[35204]** : C1830 SOUTHAMPTON, HAM, ENG **[35252]** : 1780+ HUNGERFORD, BRK, ENG **[35379]** : PRE 1820 PAULTON, SOM, ENG **[35397]** : 1800S GREAT TEW, OXF, ENG **[35408]** : PRE 1853 MACCLESFIELD, CHS, ENG **[35872]** : PRE 1801 NEWARK, NTT, ENG **[35904]** : PRE 1780 KINGSWINFORD, STS, ENG **[36110]** : 1840S

CHESTERFIELD, DBY, ENG **[36181]** : WILLIAM 1850-1950 LINKINHORNE, CON, ENG **[36286]** : ALL FROME, SOM, ENG **[36393]** : PRE 1900 EXETER, DEV, ENG **[36664]** : 1780+ MARKET DRAYTON AREA, SAL, ENG **[36997]** : WILLIAM C1781 BERMONDSEY, SRY, ENG **[37106]** : ALL GOSPORT & PORTSMOUTH, HAM, ENG **[37214]** : 1820S-1872 CLAPTON, LND, ENG **[37283]** : 1700S BEDFORD, BDF, ENG **[37283]** : 1850-80 ROADE & GREAT DODDINGTON, NTH, ENG **[37283]** : PRE 1886 TAVISTOCK, DEV, ENG **[37575]** : 1900+ BROADBOTTOM, CHS, ENG **[37828]** : 1841 MACCLESFIELD, CHS, ENG **[37828]** : PRE 1754 BASLOW, DBY, ENG **[37875]** : C1850-1900 BANBURY, OXF, ENG **[38034]** : C1850-1900 GRIMSBURY W WARKWORTH, NTH, ENG **[38034]** : 1840 HANSLOPE, BKM, ENG **[38282]** : ELIZABETH PRE 1635 GREAT BENTLEY, ESS, ENG **[38348]** : 1800-1890 BANBURY, OXF, ENG **[38373]** : PRE 1850+ SOUTH SHIELDS, DUR, ENG & AUS **[35064]** : JOHN 1800+ WIC, IRL **[37165]** : 1870S GORE & DUNEDIN, OTAGO, NZ **[35408]** : ALL NZ & AUS **[38068]** : PRE 1920 SCT **[37062]** : PRE 1897+ VA, USA **[35004]** : PRE 1700 CHESTERFIELD CO., VA, USA **[36969]** : ABSALOM 1820+ SIMPSON CO., KY, USA **[37032]** : JOSEPH 1730+ NC, USA **[37032]** : 1832+ WASHINGTON CO., MO, USA **[37032]** : 1800-30 WASHINGTON CO., KY, USA **[37533]** : 1830-45 CLARK CO., MO, USA **[37533]** : 1870+ SHELBY CO., IA, USA **[38323]** : 1780-1795 BEDFORD, NY, USA **[38763]**

GREGSON 1870+ AUS **[34432]** : PRE 1850 CHURCHTOWN, LAN, ENG **[34696]** : 1555-1677 RYLSTONE, YKS, ENG **[34793]** : 1800+ MANCHESTER, LAN, ENG **[35586]** : 1500+ PENWORTHAM & PRESTON, LAN, ENG **[36218]** : 1750-1800 PRESTON, LAN, ENG **[37613]** : PRE 1791 LAN, ENG **[37706]**

GREIG 1870-1888 CARNGHAM & WYCHEPROOF, VIC, AUS **[35594]** : C1834 HOBART & LONGFORD, TAS, AUS **[37144]** : PRE 1800 DALKEITH, MLN, SCT **[33866]** : PRE 1870 INVERESK, ELN & MLN, SCT **[33959]** : 1600+ FINZEAN, ABD, SCT **[34608]** : C1800 LONGSIDE, ABD, SCT **[34608]** : 1600+ BIRSE, ABD, SCT **[34608]** : PRE 1875 ABD, SCT **[34712]** : 1800+ EDINBURGH, MLN, SCT **[35027]** : C1792 ARNGASK, FIF, SCT **[35496]** : 1826 DUNDEE, ANS, SCT **[35594]** : 1870S DUNBAR, ELN, SCT **[35914]** : PRE 1860 FIF, SCT **[35994]** : PRE 1880 ABERDEEN, ABD, SCT **[36792]** : PRE 1800 AYR, AYR, SCT **[37144]**

GREIG (SEE GREGG) **[35259]**

GREINER PRE 1855 BROZFELD, WUE, GER **[34886]** : PRE 1850 BAW, GER **[38669]**

GREIVE 1860+ BATHURST, NSW, AUS **[38760]** : PRE 1860 LARGS, FIF, SCT **[38760]**

GRELCK PRE 1860+ NSW, AUS **[38585]** : PRE 1860 HAMBURG, HBG, BRD **[38585]**

GRENDON C1700-1800 EXBOURNE, DEV, ENG **[37977]**

GRENFELL PRE 1857 PENDEEN, CON, ENG **[34043]** : 1700-1800 ST JUST, CON, ENG **[35968]** : 1800+ BIRMINGHAM, WAR & CON, ENG **[36058]** : ALL WI & CA, USA **[38363]**

GRENIER PRE 1839 QUE, CAN & FRA **[37443]**

GRENYER PRE 1800 WORTHING & STANMER, SSX, ENG **[34112]**

GRESHAM 1850-1900 WORCESTER, WOR & NTT, ENG **[34123]**

GRESLEY JAMES STEPHEN 1850-1890 DERBY, DBY, ENG **[38207]** : 1850-1900 DERBY, DBY, ENG **[38207]**

GRESLEY-JACKSON PRE 1870+ WORLDWIDE **[36265]**

GRESS 1850+ CAN & USA **[38437]** : PRE 1850 ELO, GER **[38437]**

GRESSEL 1745+ USA **[38650]**

GRETER ALL LU, CH **[35954]**

GRETTON 1700-1840 WORSLEY, LAN, ENG & NZ **[36255]**

GREUTZMACHER PRE 1823 MEK, GER **[38572]**

GREVEN 1780S OISTE, HAN, GER **[35865]** : 1778+ RIDDERS, SHO, GER **[37542]**

GREVETT 1840 WORTHING, SSX, ENG **[33810]** : 1786+ LANCING, SSX, ENG **[35716]**

GREVILLE 1700S WIL, ENG **[36873]** : PRE 1788 CRICKLADE, WIL, ENG **[37144]**

GREW 1800-1850 DON, IRL **[38421]**

GREWAR ALL GLENISLA, ANS, SCT **[36704]**

GREWCOCK PRE 1799 BARWELL, LEI, ENG **[36528]**

GREWLOCK 1850-1950 STOKE GOLDING, LEI, ENG **[34135]**

GREY 1856+ MARYBOROUGH & SHEPPARTON, VIC, AUS **[34591]** : WILLIAM C1860 MAIDSTONE, KEN, ENG **[35427]** : 1273+ CHILLINGHAM & HORTON, NBL, ENG **[35723]** : PRE 1680 BITCHFIELD HARTBURN, NBL, ENG **[36502]** : ALL ENG & AUS **[33799]** : 1800+ GLASGOW, LKS, SCT **[36875]** : 1921 CINCINATI, OH, USA **[34498]**

GREY (SEE GRAY) **[37435]**

GREYGOOSE 1753+ STOW-CUM-QUY, CAM, ENG **[36489]** : PRE 1700 BROCKLEY, SFK, ENG **[37655]**

GRIBBEN PRE 1876 SHARKHILL & BELFAST, ANT, IRL **[34695]**

GRIBBLE PRE 1950 BLACKWOOD, VIC, AUS **[35055]** : 1860 FORBES, NSW, AUS **[35529]** : PRE 1850 CON, ENG **[33953]** : 1820S REDRUTH, CON, ENG **[34628]** : C1850 TUNBRIDGE, KEN, ENG **[34836]** : 1760+ GWENNAP, CON, ENG **[35749]** : PRE 1750 DEV, ENG **[36064]** : PRE 1750 CON, ENG **[38004]**

GRICE C1882 HANDWORTH, WAR, ENG **[34009]** : 1700-1900 BOOTLE, CUL, ENG **[37858]** : PRE 1900 LIN, ENG & IRL **[33863]**

GRIDER PRE 1820 PENDLETON DISTRICT, SC, USA **[37029]**

GRIDLEY ALL SOM, ENG **[34817]**

GRIEBEL PRE 1850 OLDENBURG, SHO, GER **[38648]**

GRIEBELS 1700+ GORNITZ, SHO, GER **[37170]**

GRIEF C1790+ NORWICH, NFK, ENG **[35725]** : 1760+ GREAT YARMOUTH, NFK, ENG **[35725]**

GRIEFFEL 1700+ GORNITZ, SHO, GER **[37170]**

GRIEFFENBERG 1700S BERKHOLZ, BRA, GER **[35968]**

GRIEGER 1796 ZULLICHAU, BRA, PRE **[35369]**

GRIEGG 1750+ DUTCHESS CO., NY, USA **[35322]**

GRIEN PRE 1840 HEPPENHEIM, HES, GER **[38029]**

GRIER 1770+ RERRICK, KKD, SCT **[34345]** : ALL WORLDWIDE **[38237]**

GRIERSON PRE 1900 DFS, SCT **[37443]**

GRIESDALE ALL COCKERMOUTH, CUL, ENG **[36822]**

GRIESON PRE 1850 LARBERT, STI, SCT **[34097]**

GRIEVE HELLEN 1875-1962 TARNAGULLA, VIC, AUS **[37111]** : ALL CASTLETON, ROX, SCT **[34254]** : 1700+ HAWICK, ROX, SCT **[35038]** : 1700-1820 SEL, SCT **[38154]** : WALTER 1860+ SCT & AUS **[37111]** : 1820-1900 GREENE CO., OH, USA **[38154]**

GRIEVES 1760S+ TANFIELD, DUR, ENG **[35706]** : PRE 1812 BURNHAM DEEPDALE, NFK, ENG **[37841]** : PRE 1840 FER, IRL **[34117]**

GRIFFEN C1890 DUNNSTOWN, VIC, AUS **[34767]** : 1800-1860 WHISSONSETT, NFK, ENG **[37845]**

GRIFFIN 1855+ BRAIDWOOD, NSW, AUS **[37131]** : C1890 BROMPTON PARK, SA, AUS **[37157]** : PRE

1832 SYDNEY, NSW, AUS **[37982]** : WILLIAM C1850 QUE, CAN **[34395]** : DEBBIE ALL SMITHVILLE, LINCOLN CO., ONT, CAN **[36712]** : 1770+ HINTON AMPNER, HAM, ENG **[33938]** : C1875 SOUTHWARK, SRY, ENG **[34393]** : 1870+ LIVERPOOL, LAN, ENG **[34566]** : C1800-1940 QUEENBOROUGH, KEN, ENG **[34718]** : 1800S SNITTERFIELD & HAMPTON LUCY, WAR, ENG **[34823]** : PRE 1863 WALTON LE DALE, LAN, ENG **[34886]** : 1750+ SHEPTON MALLET, SOM, ENG **[34970]** : PRE 1892 BRISTOL, GLS, ENG **[35002]** : 1826+ LONDON, MDX, ENG **[35112]** : C1820 TIMSBURY, HAM, ENG **[35127]** : PRE 1860 LAN, ENG **[35331]** : PRE 1850 HATHEROP, GLS, ENG **[35515]** : C1800 SHEPTON MALLET, SOM, ENG **[36247]** : PRE 1780 GREAT RISSINGTON, GLS, ENG **[36889]** : 1820+ BRISTOL, SOM, ENG **[36995]** : PRE 1830 MARLBOROUGH, WIL, ENG **[37083]** : PRE 1855 CLENCHWARTON, NFK, ENG **[37131]** : ALL BILLINGTON & LEIGHTON BUZZARD, BDF, ENG **[37937]** : ALL OXF, ENG **[37937]** : 1800-1870 LAN, ENG **[38299]** : PRE 1900 WOR, ENG **[38745]** : PRE 1857 KILRUSH, CLA, ENG **[34886]** : C1850 CORK, COR, IRL **[35038]** : 1850S-1880S CORK CITY, COR, IRL **[35044]** : PRE 1840 CLA, IRL **[35488]** : PRE 1906 DUBLIN, IRL **[35521]** : 1830S ENNISCORTHY, WEX, IRL **[35799]** : 1780+ DINGLE, KER, IRL **[36343]** : 1845-55 CASTLEBAR, MAY, IRL **[38583]** : SGT RICHARD PRE 1950S USA **[37320]** : 1650-1800 OXFORD, CT, USA **[38588]** : JAMES C1864 USA & IRL **[37135]**

GRIFFITH 1850+ NEWCASTLE, NSW, AUS **[34690]** : ROBERT 1870+ ARMIDALE, NSW, AUS **[34690]** : FREDERICK 1870+ ARMIDALE, NSW, AUS **[34690]** : 1819+ CARDIGAN, NB, CAN **[34056]** : 1810-1880 MUSKOKA CO. & SIMCO CO., ONT, CAN **[35602]** : JOHN 1800+ JSY, CHI **[34690]** : PRE 1880 BIRMINGHAM, WAR, ENG **[35523]** : PRE 1850 CHS, ENG **[36380]** : 1600-1800 IRL **[35098]** : 1790-1850 IRL **[36687]** : THOMAS PRE 1780 GOWRAN, KIK, IRL **[38084]** : PRE 1830 IRL **[38457]** : PRE 1750 ISLE OF WIGHT, VA, USA **[33757]** : JOHN B. PRE 1849 FOX LAKE, MN, USA **[37481]** : 1700-1800 FREDERICK CO., MD, USA **[38009]** : 1777 NY, USA **[38192]** : PRE 1850 CHATHAM CO., NC & CA, USA **[38570]** : 1800S CLAY CO. & MACON CO., MO & CA, USA **[38570]**

GRIFFITHS PRE 1862 STEPNEY, SA, AUS **[33890]** : 1850+ SYDNEY, NSW, AUS **[34969]** : THOMAS 1880 GYMPIE, QLD, AUS **[35096]** : C1850+ WARRACKNABEAL, VIC, AUS **[35233]** : 1838+ GLENORCHY & STAWELL, VIC, AUS **[35528]** : PRE 1848+ BATHURST, NSW, AUS **[35759]** : 1800S SYDNEY, NSW, AUS **[36372]** : JOHN C1833+ NORTH RICHMOND, NSW, AUS **[36643]** : WILLIAM 1878-1896 LOWER CLARENCE RIVER, NSW, AUS **[38006]** : 1850-1900 GEELONG, VIC, AUS **[38007]** : 1835+ GLENORCHY & MELBOURNE, VIC, NSW & LAN, AUS & ENG **[35383]** : 1816-1841 CHESTER, CHS, ENG **[33864]** : PRE 1855 LONDON, ENG **[33864]** : PRE 1830 CONDOVER, SAL, ENG **[34370]** : 1800S DITTON, SAL, ENG **[35233]** : PRE 1842 MANCHESTER, LAN, ENG **[35383]** : 1906+ SHEFFIELD, YKS, ENG **[35455]** : 1800+ WEDNESBURY, STS, ENG **[35942]** : 1800+ MANCHESTER, LAN & CHS, ENG **[36087]** : 1760S LAN, ENG **[36858]** : 1700-1800 HEF, ENG **[37762]** : PRE 1800 WHITCHURCH, SAL, ENG **[37893]** : C1846 GLASGOW, LKS, SCT **[35487]** : C1840+ TRETOWER & CRICKHOWELL, BRE, WLS **[33922]** : C1846 BANGOR, AGY, WLS **[35487]** : 1800-1850 NORTHOP, FLN, WLS **[35706]** : 1700+ LLANTWIT,

JUXTA & NEATH, GLA, WLS **[36209]** : 1800+ TREVETHIN, MON, WLS **[36614]** : 1750-1860 LLANDEWY & YSTRADENNY, RAD, WLS **[38006]**

GRIFFY C1855 WOOLSHED CREEK, VIC, AUS **[35028]** : C1820 TEMPLEMALEY, CLA, IRL **[37944]**

GRIGG 1852+ BALLARAT, VIC, AUS **[38205]** : PRE 1850 HALESOWEN, WOR, ENG **[37703]** : PRE 1900 LITTLEHAM BY BIDEFORD, DEV, ENG **[38205]**

GRIGGS 1842+ FRANKLIN, TAS, AUS **[34853]** : PRE 1915+ WA, AUS **[35453]** : PRE 1857+ VIC, AUS **[35453]** : PRE 1840 NEWPORT PAGNELL, BKM, ENG **[34853]** : PRE 1835+ LAN, ENG **[35453]** : 1850+ MDX & SRY, ENG **[36203]** : 1650+ ATTLEBRIDGE, NFK, ENG **[36483]** : 1800 LOUGHTON, ESS, ENG **[37928]**

GRIGNON 1600-1900S ST JEROME, QUE, CAN **[35327]**

GRIGOR 1800+ ELGIN, MOR, SCT **[35428]** : JAMES 1790 KELLAS, MOR, SCT **[35848]** : PRE 1800 NEW SPYNIE, MOR, SCT **[36431]** : 1830+ ELGIN, MOR, SCT **[36885]** : 1750+ ELGIN, MOR, SCT **[37110]**

GRIGSBY C1780 BREDGAR, KEN, ENG **[37007]**

GRIGSON ALL NFK, ENG **[36065]** : 1805-25 IPSWICH, SFK, ENG **[37863]**

GRIJSENHOUD 1762 SCHIEDAM, ZUH, NL **[38706]**

GRILLETT 1800 ST JUST IN PENWITH, CON, ENG **[35023]**

GRIM 1820+ JEFFERSON CO., OH, USA **[37040]** : 1802 VA, USA **[38121]**

GRIMCEY 1700-1800 TENDRING HUNDRED, ESS, ENG **[35178]**

GRIME 1790-1900 DOLPHINHOLME, LAN, ENG **[36040]** : PRE 1850 BENTHAM, WRY, ENG **[36040]** : 1750-1850 WHEELTON, LAN, ENG **[38251]**

GRIMES 1802 HERTFORD, HRT, ENG **[34726]** : C1860-1890 BATH, SOM, ENG **[36161]** : C1840 LYMPSTONE, DEV, ENG **[37757]** : ALBERT J. 1851-1925 BRIGHTON, SSX, ENG **[38549]** : 1800-1825 NC, USA **[37605]** : (THE MISSES) PRE 1920 BROOKLYN, NY, USA **[38305]**

GRIMM 1820-1875 EBERTSHAUSEN, TIERENGA, GER **[36317]** : 1870-1930 IA, USA **[37453]**

GRIMMER 1830 LND, ENG **[35871]** : 1800-1900 EISLINGEN FILS & GOPPINGEN, STUTGART, GER **[38374]**

GRIMMETT ALL WIL, ENG **[34158]**

GRIMSBY ALL WORLDWIDE **[35620]**

GRIMSHAW 1888+ PERTH, WA, AUS **[35857]** : 1800+ HUNTINGDON CO., QUE, CAN **[36664]** : 1750-1900 DROYLSDEN, LAN, ENG **[34520]** : 1840 YKS, ENG **[35120]** : PRE 1890 MANCHESTER, LAN, ENG **[35857]** : PRE 1850 ENG **[37739]** : 1800 MANCHESTER, LAN, ENG **[38047]** : ALL VT, USA **[36664]**

GRIMSON 1750-1900 PUTNEY, SRY & LND, ENG **[35495]** : ALL NFK, ENG **[37612]**

GRIMSTEAD PRE 1825 SOM, ENG **[38399]**

GRIMSTER PRE 1825 SOM, ENG **[38399]**

GRIMWADE PRE 1814 SFK, ENG **[36124]**

GRIMWOOD C1850 NSW, AUS **[33809]** : ALL SPROULTON, SFK, ENG **[33823]** : PRE 1820 SFK, ENG **[35552]**

GRINDER PRE 1800 PA, USA **[36937]**

GRINDLE PRE 1832 DRUM, MOG, IRL **[37473]**

GRINDLEY C1820-1850 SAL, ENG **[35791]** : PRE 1900 CHS, ENG **[37098]** : C1770 RUNCORN, CHS, ENG **[37697]** : 1780-1820 LINLITHGOW, WLN, SCT **[37779]**

GRINDROD PRE 1853 CHORLTON UPON MEDLOCK, LAN, ENG **[34278]** : 1800+ BAMFORD ROCHDALE, LAN, ENG **[37626]**

GRINELL PRE 1850 GREAT MISSENDEN, BKM, ENG [37743]

GRINGLEY ALL YKS & LIN, ENG [36399]

GRINGRAS JOSEPH 1830+ DEBERTHIER, QUE, CAN [36678]

GRINHAM 1750+ FARNHAM, SRY, ENG [36256]

GRINLY 1836+ ALLOA, CLK, SCT [33822]

GRINNEY PRE 1840 LAMBETH, SRY, ENG [33937]

GRINNING C1775 DEV, ENG [34096]

GRINSLADE 1700S WATCHETT, SOM, ENG [34931]

GRINTON ALL WORLDWIDE [36327]

GRINYER 1700-1800 MDX, LND & SRY, ENG [36491]

GRISBY 1800-1900 KEN, ENG [36118]

GRISELL 1752+ DELAWARE CO., PA, USA [37564]

GRISENTHWAITE ALL WORLDWIDE [35470]

GRISS 1700+ LAVENHAM, SFK, ENG [34943]

GRISSELL 1880+ WOODBURN, NSW, AUS [35394]

GRIST ALL SOM & LND, ENG [34729] : PRE 1750 BRADFORD ON AVON, WIL, ENG [34908] : C1742+ BRADFORD ON AVON, WIL, ENG [36276]

GRISWOLD C1600 KENILWORTH, WAR, ENG [36310] : 1748-1773 NORWICH, CT, USA [38741]

GRIVELL ALL OLD SODBURY, GLS, ENG & AUS [33919]

GRIVELLE 1700S WIL, ENG [36873]

GRIZDALE 1841-1900 SYDNEY, NSW, AUS [35559]

GROAT 1880+ MELBOURNE, VIC, AUS [35493] : 1818 LERWICK, SHI, SCT [35855]

GROB 1840+ USA [38728]

GROBLER PRE 1688 TANGERMUNDE, MAG, DDR [36468] : ALL WORLDWIDE [34949]

GROCOCK PRE 1825 NTT, ENG [35745]

GROCOTT ALL WOORE, SAL, ENG [36504]

GROCUTT C1820 BIRMINGHAM, STS & WAR, ENG [35349] : PRE 1825 HALESOWEN, STS, ENG [35967]

GROENENDIJK 1660-1690S KAPELLE, ZEL, NL [38358]

GROENHAGEN ALL WORLDWIDE [38688]

GROESBECK ALL USA [35281]

GROETENHERDT 1744-1944 SCHLEUSINGEN, THURINGIA, GER [38148]

GROFF LORENZA PRE 1800 HOCHETTSTOWN, NJ, USA [35302]

GROGAN PATRICK 1863+ GLEBE, NSW, AUS [33764] : 1850S OFF, IRL & AUS [34845] : HENRY 1798-1903 HAYWOOD CO., NC, USA [38141]

GROMMEN ANNA 1866+ HERMANNSTADT (SIBIU), TRANSYLVANIA, RO [38519] : ALL KERZ, TRANSYLVANIA, RO [38519]

GRONO 1799+ HAWKESBURY, NSW, AUS [34685] : PRE 1799 NEWPORT, PEM, WLS [34685] : PRE 1900 NEWPORT, PEM, WLS [35577]

GRONVALL ALL EURAJOKI & PORI TURUN, UUDENMAANLAAN, FIN [38542]

GROO 1800-1925 SAMARA, SU [34081]

GROOM 1800S NFK, ENG [33972] : 1550-1850 WESTON UNDER REDCASTLE, SAL, ENG [34411] : 1910 CAMBERWELL, LND, ENG [34496] : 1800-1910 ENFIELD, MDX, ENG [34496] : C1810 KINGS WALDEN, HRT, ENG [35840] : PRE 1850 STS & SAL, ENG [37098] : PRE 1850 MID, NFK, ENG [37718] : 1824-1940 LIBERTY, MO, USA [38187] : PRE 1860 WARREN CO., IA, USA [38538]

GROOMBRIDGE 1880-1950 SWANLEY, KEN, ENG [35469]

GROOME PRE 1845 MANCHESTER, LAN, ENG [34959] : 1500-1700 SAL, ENG [36062]

GROOTEWAL 1750-1940 WEST FRIESLAND, NOH, NL [38713]

GROOTHUIZEN 1800+ NIJMEGEN, NBT, NL [34560]

GROSART C1815 TWEEDLE, FIF, SCT [34914] : C1800 EDINBURGH, MLN, SCT [38253]

GROSE PRE 1895 NOOJEE, VIC, AUS [35479] : 1400+ ST BREOCK, CON, ENG [33989] : PRE 1854 ST JUST, CON, ENG [34043] : 1700+ CHIVERTON SANCREED, CON, ENG [35712] : PRE 1875 BODMIN, LANIVET & ROCHE, CON, ENG [37814] : PRE 1900 HOUGHTON CO., MI, USA [37814]

GROSHALOUSH 1810-1870 GER [38199]

GROSIER JOHN 1750-1800 WINDHAM CO., VT, USA [36573]

GROSILL ALL NOR [38470]

GROSKLAGS ALL WORLDWIDE [36719]

GROSMAN 1610+ ST GERMANS, CON, ENG [34804]

GROSS 1830+ LONDON, ENG [34568] : ALL ST ANTHONY & MANACCAN, CON, ENG [35063] : 1760S BETHNAL GREEN, MDX, ENG [37080] : ALL MARKTSCHELKEN, TRANSYLVANIA, RO [38519] : 1860-1880 WESTFIELD, IL, USA [37576] : 1870+ GALENA, IL, USA [38343] : ANNA E. 1859-1875 IL, USA [38732]

GROSSE C1820 WESTMINSTER, LND, ENG [35865] : C1782 STORKOW, BRA, GER [38626]

GROSSER 1750+ KRISCHUTZ, SIL, GER [35468]

GROSSET C1850 EDINBURGH, MLN, SCT [38253]

GROSSKLAGS ALL WORLDWIDE [36719]

GROSSKLEG ALL WORLDWIDE [36719]

GROSSLE 1800-1935 GER [37363]

GROSSMITH 1750-1850 PORTSMOUTH, HAM, ENG [36390]

GROSVENOR ALL DUDLEY, WOR, ENG [36492] : ALL ROWLEY REGIS, STS, ENG [36492] : 1800S KIDDERMINSTER, WOR, ENG [36847]

GROTEN 1796-1820 AACHEN, NRW, GER [38166]

GROTH PRE 1841 KLEIN KRAMS, MSW, GER [38618]

GROTHE ALL BERNDORF, WAL, GER [34861] : ALL WORLDWIDE [38358]

GROTHIER ALL UK [37674]

GROTT 1600+ UCKERMARK, PRE [35460]

GROUND PRE 1841 WHITTLESEY, CAM, ENG [34581]

GROUNDSEL-BROWN 1851+ FREMANTLE, WA, AUS [35847]

GROUNDSELL ALL WORLDWIDE [35847]

GROUT ALBERT 1920+ CAN [36811]

GROVE PRE 1830 BERMONDSEY, SRY, ENG [36073] : ALL LONDON, ENG [36174] : 1700-1900 HOLBORN & CLERKENWELL, MDX, ENG [36398] : MARTHA 1850S ASTON TERRID, BRK & OXF, ENG [37476] : 1800-1856 DUBLIN, IRL [34413] : 1570-1768 GROVEHALL, DON, IRL [38396]

GROVER DAVID 1827+ NSW, AUS [34902] : DAVID 1826+ NSW, AUS [35086] : C1860 BELMORE, QLD, AUS [35807] : 1803+ WINDSOR, NSW, AUS [38490] : PRE 1820 ENG [34245] : 1750-1850 NFK, ENG [34472] : C1805 HAMMERSMITH, MDX, ENG [34518] : DAVID PRE 1828 LEWES, SSX, ENG [34902] : 1813 DUNCTON, SSX, ENG [34909] : 1818+ BKM, ENG [35139] : PRE 1810 NEWINGTON, SRY, ENG [36153] : 1700+ FROYLE, HAM, ENG [37448] : MARTHA C1799 WINCHESTER, HAM, ENG [37992] : 1700-1800S WORPLESDON, SRY, ENG [38490] : 1820-1840 OH, USA [36965]

GROVES ALL UPTON ON SEVERN, WOR, ENG [34160] : 1800+ IOW, ENG [34918] : 1817 LYNMOUTH & LINTON, DEV, ENG [35251] : 1820 FROME, SOM, ENG [35809] : ALL SLOUGH, BKM, ENG [36616] : PRE 1830 EAST HARPTREE, SOM, ENG [38376] : 1800+ BARNSTAPLE, DEV, ENG [38396] : 1840+ ARNOLD, NTT, ENG [38396] : PRE 1830 MINEHEAD, SOM, ENG [38773] : PRE 1873

LIMERICK, LIM, IRL [36508] : 1825-1845 MEXICO [37630] : 1800S POLK CO., IA, USA [36709] : PRE 1860 FAYETTE CO., OH, USA [37565]

GROW JULIE 1860 PONTYPOOL, MON, WLS [37614]

GROWDEN ALL WORLDWIDE [38377]

GROZINGER ALL MAGOLSHEIM, BRD, GER [34938]

GRUB PRE 1832+ KIDDERMINSTER, WOR, ENG [35109]

GRUBB 1855+ TAS, AUS [33786] : 1840+ GOULBURN, NSW, AUS [36296] : 1728+ NTH, ENG [33786] : PRE 1850 LONDON, ENG [34571] : 1817+ UPWAY, DOR, ENG [36296] : 1865+ AUCKLAND, NZ [35960] : 1780+ LARGO, FIF, SCT [35960] : C1860 CERES, FIF, SCT [35960] : 1800-1900 LOUDOUN CO., VA, USA [36937]

GRUBEN 1820+ HAN, GER [35730]

GRUBER 1815 SCHRIESHEIM, BAD, GER [33929] : 1830+ KINGSTON, JAMAICA, W.INDIES [34904]

GRUBERT ALL GER [38648]

GRUBY ALL WESTMINSTER, LND, ENG [34820] : PRE 1850 LND & SRY, ENG [37091]

GRUCHY PRE 1850 WHOLE ISLAND, JSY, CHI, UK [36200]

GRUE 1800-1850 DON, IRL [38421]

GRUENHAG ALL WORLDWIDE [38688]

GRUENHAGE ALL WORLDWIDE [38688]

GRUENHAGEL ALL WORLDWIDE [38688]

GRUENHAGEN ALL WORLDWIDE [38688]

GRUENINGER 1523+ WINNENDEN, BAW, FRG [38660]

GRUETER 1700+ BOTTRUP, WEF, GER [38651]

GRUFFET ALL FRA [34164]

GRUGEL 1800+ LENSAHN, SHO, GER [33996]

GRUHLKE 1800+ GERVIN, PRE, GER [37170]

GRULKE 1800+ GERVIN, PRE, GER [37170]

GRUMMITT PRE 1800 HOUGHTON CONQUEST, BDF, ENG [35967] : 1819-90 CLOPHILL, BDF, ENG & AUS [37946]

GRUN 1800-1900 WUPPERTAL, BAHRMEN, BRD [36958]

GRUNDSTROM 1767+ LOVIISA, UUSIMAA, FIN [38758]

GRUNDY 1900+ NOARLUNGA, SA, AUS [35771] : FRED PRE 1920 NSW, AUS & ENG [37525] : WALTER C1913 VANCOUVER, BC, CAN [37525] : PRE 1860 TOW LAW, DUR, ENG [35255] : 1830-1930 MANCHESTER, LAN, ENG [36098] : 1800+ MANCHESTER, LAN, ENG [36257] : ALL NORBURY, CHS, ENG [36704] : 1780S RIVINGTON, LAN, ENG [37309] : PRE 1920 LAN, ENG [37525] : JOHN C1818 LAN, ENG [37525] : ALFRED C1843 LAN, ENG [37525] : STEPHEN C1813 LAN, ENG [37525] : C1800 CARLETON, WRY, ENG [37859] : GEORGE 1848+ MISTERTON, NTT, ENG [38016]

GRUNSELL PRE 1900 HAM, ENG [36479] : 1720-1800 HUNTON, HAM, ENG [38003]

GRUNSON ALL NBL, ENG [35540]

GRUNTON 1840 KIRKCALDY, FIF, SCT [35609] : ALL WORLDWIDE [36327]

GRUNWALD PRE 1860 OBORSKI, PO, POL [34246]

GRUNWELL 1750+ OTLEY, LEEDS, WRY, ENG [36104] : 1806 ABBOTS RIPTON, HUN, ENG [37723] : PRE 1837 WORLDWIDE [37723]

GRUPP 1800 ST ANDREWS, FIF, SCT [33848]

GRUSH C1873 DRESDEN, IA, USA [36899] : PRE 1960 ASTORIA, OR & IA, USA [36899]

GRUTZMACHER 1800-1880 BERLIN, GER [34469] : ALBERT 1856-1900 GER [38090] : 1860-1880 LEHMKUHLEN, MSW, GER [38331] : FLORIAN 1876-1946 PRZYCIEKA, POL [38090]

GRUTZMAN FLORIAN 1876-1946 PRYZIOK, POL [38090]

GRYNIER PRE 1600 STANMER, SSX, ENG [34112]

GUBB ALL EXETER, DEV, ENG [38753]

GUBBINS C1825 WOOTTON, OXF, ENG [35910]

GUBERNAT 1800+ BEDOWA ZGLOIENSKA, POL [35000] : 1850+ KORZELICE, SU [35000] : 1850+ USA [35000]

GUBIAN ALL LONDON, ENG [36381]

GUDGEON ALL WORLDWIDE [36235]

GUDGER 1600-1920 ENG [37736]

GUDGIN 1700-1750 PULLOXHILL, BDF, ENG [34552]

GUDGSON (SEE GUDGIN) [34552]

GUELLY (SEE GELLY) [36268]

GUENARD PRE 1769 ST GEORGES, BRT, FRA [37819]

GUERARD PRE 1850 JOLIETTE CO., QUE, CAN [34106]

GUERIC PRE 1700 GUINGAMP, BRT, FRA [38420]

GUERIN C1700 GENEVA, GE, CH [38348] : 1800+ KILLALOE, CLA, IRL [38189]

GUERNEY 1820+ LND, ENG [35053]

GUESS C1900+ NORTHCOTE, VIC, AUS [35143] : 1800-1900 FRONTENAC CO., ONT, CAN [36688] : 1850+ DORKING, SRY, ENG [35390] : PRE 1900 TICEHURST, SSX, ENG [35742]

GUEST DAVID PRE 1900 NSW, AUS [34902] : GEORGE 1832+ NSW, AUS [35086] : C1900+ NORTHCOTE, VIC, AUS [35143] : 1868+ SYDNEY, NSW, AUS [35414] : 1868+ BULLI, NSW, AUS [35414] : 1790 NORFOLK ISLAND, NSW, AUS [35877] : 1805 HOBART, TAS, AUS [35877] : PRE 1720 FINSTHWAITE, LAN, ENG [34053] : 1883 EDGBASTON, WAR, ENG [34120] : 1800+ DUDLEY, WOR, ENG [34323] : 1830-1885 GORNAL & PENSNETT, STS & WOR, ENG [35166] : PRE 1864 BARROW IN FURNESS, LAN, ENG [35414] : C1767 PRESTBURY, GLS, ENG [35877] : 1820S-1900 MANCHESTER & SALFORD, LAN, ENG [36024] : 1800S BROADWAS, WOR, ENG [36847] : C1822 KIDDERMINSTER, WOR, ENG [36860] : PRE 1850 LND & SRY, ENG [37091] : ALL WOR, ENG [37950] : C1890 IGATPURI, KURNOOL, INDIA [36092]

GUGGENBERGER ALL WORLDWIDE [38689]

GUIDER 1750+ GRAFFIN & CLONMORE, TIP, IRL [37534]

GUIHOT 1850+ GOULBURN, NSW, AUS [34421] : 1820+ ST MALO, FRA [34421]

GUILAN 1700-1870 ANNAN, DFS, SCT [37734]

GUILBAULT FELIX 1840+ MONTREAL & BERTHIER, QUE, CAN [34161] : ALL WORLDWIDE [34161]

GUILD 1800-1900 KRS, SCT [34054]

GUILDFORD ALL EASTON, WIL, ENG [33975]

GUILFORD ALL EASTON, WIL, ENG [33975]

GUILFOYLE 1836 KNOCKAVILLA, TIP, IRL [35824] : 1800-1900 SCARIFF, CLA, IRL [35845] : 1818+ TULLAMORE, OFF, IRL [35865]

GUILLAUME ALL WORLDWIDE [35832]

GUILLE ALL CHI [36839]

GUILLOT PRE 1800 LOIRE, FRA [36353]

GUILMET NICOLAS PRE 1660 ST ANTOINE NESLE, RPA, FRA [38408]

GUIN 1750+ LANCASTER CO., PA, USA [37507] : PRE 1850 UNION CO., PA, USA [37507] : PRE 1850 NORTHUMBERLAND CO., PA, USA [37507]

GUINAN ALL IRL [36801] : ALL DUNDEE, ANS, SCT [36801]

GUINEE PRE 1880 LIM, IRL [36918]

GUINEFF 1800+ ARMAGH, IRL [34271]

GUINERY 1820+ LND, ENG [35084]

GUINEY MICHAEL 1850 MOYVANE, KER, IRL
[36274]

GUINN 1840+ MO, USA [36919]

GUINNANE 1800+ LISCANNOR, CLA, IRL [38295]

GUINTHER ALL GER [36719]

GUIOU PRE 1900 PEY ROLLES, RHA, FRA [35448]

GUIRY 1820-1840 WAT, IRL [37305]

GUISE 1867+ DROITWICH, WOR, ENG [37230]

GUISELEY ALL WORLDWIDE [37848]

GUIVER ALL WORLDWIDE [35806]

GULDEN 1760+ BERKS CO., PA, USA [37040] : 1700-1900 PA & MD, USA [37517]

GULDENSUPP ALL WORLDWIDE [38648]

GULDIN 1700-1900 PA & MD, USA [37517]

GULDNER PRE 1860 FRANKENHAUSEN, GER [34801]

GULLAND 1780-1800 NORTH BERWICK, ELN, SCT [35609]

GULLEN 1865 ANCASTER, ONT, CAN [35609] : 1865-1875 EAST OXFORD, ONT, CAN [35609] : 1800-1810 LONDON, ENG [35609] : 1818 SHERBORNE, DOR, ENG [35609] : 1840-1920 ROCHDALE, LAN, ENG [37734] : 1800-1870 BURY, LAN, ENG [37734] : 1820-1825 FERMOY, COR, IRL [35609] : 1827 PAISLEY, RFW, SCT [35609] : 1700-1870 HODDAM, DFS, SCT [37734] : 1870-1910 NEW YORK, NY, USA [37734] : 1810 WLS [35609]

GULLETT 1800+ PLYMOUTH, DEV, ENG [34559]

GULLEY 1700+ SOM, ENG & USA [37805]

GULLICK ALL CAMERTON, SOM, ENG [34643] : ALL FOREST OF DEAN, GLS, ENG [34643] : 1800+ SOM, WAR & WIL, ENG [35580]

GULLIFORD ALL ENG [34131]

GULLIKSON 1871 BERGEN, NOR [38470]

GULLIVER SUSANNAH 1800 BANBURY, OXF, ENG [36782] : PRE 1837 DOR & SOM, ENG [37771]

GULLOCK C1760 WITHAM, ESS, ENG [33899] : ALL CAMERTON, SOM, ENG [34643] : 1800+ GLS, WAR & WIL, ENG [35580] : ALL WORLDWIDE [37281]

GULLY 1900+ QLD, AUS [35451] : 1700+ KENWYN, CON, ENG [34808] : 1850-1900 SOUTH PETHERTON, SOM, ENG [35451] : PRE 1806 EXETER, DEV, ENG [38186]

GULS 1809 TRIPASSOE, INDIA [34609]

GULSVIK 1750+ FLAA, HALLINGDAL, NOR [36905]

GUM 1740-1770 ROCKINGHAM CO., VA, USA [36566]

GUMBLETON 1840+ CAMDEN, NSW, AUS [35360] : PRE 1840 DOR & WIL, ENG [35098]

GUMBRECHT PRE 1680 GATTENHOFEN, BAV, GER [35242]

GUMMERY 1790S NEWINGTON & CAMBERWELL, SRY, ENG [34204]

GUMMOW PRE 1842 ST COLUMB MAJOR, CON, ENG [36748]

GUNBY 1820-1890 AMITE CO., MS, USA [35307]

GUNCKEL 1661-1700 GROSSALMERODE, GHE, GER [38748]

GUNDELACH 1807 NASSENSAND, LIP, GER [38749] : 1693-1734 GROSSALMERODE, GHE, GER [38749]

GUNDERSEN 1800+ HAMAR, HEDMARK, NOR [34664] : 1800+ CHRISTIANIA, NOR [34664]

GUNDERSON 1864+ CHRISTCHURCH, CBY, NZ [34049] : 1850+ SWE & NOR [34049]

GUNDRY PRE 1768 WENDRON & SITHNEY, CON, ENG [34881] : 1880-1900 PORTSMOUTH, HAM, ENG [35992] : 1855-1870 KEWEENAW CO., MI, USA [38010]

GUNN 1870-1884 RICHMOND, VIC, AUS [35526] : C1849+ ROKEWOOD, VIC, AUS [37164] : PRE 1848 MATTISHAL, NFK, ENG [33871] : 1800+ MANCHESTER, LAN, ENG [35183] : ALL

HARROW WEALD, MDX, ENG [35417] : ESTHER 1839+ BRIGHTON, SSX, ENG [35716] : PRE 1800 RACKENFORD & OAKFORD, DEV, ENG [35866] : ALL BIRMINGHAM, WAR, ENG [36193] : 1800+ WETHERSFIELD, ESS, ENG [36791] : PRE 1849 LONDON, ENG [37164] : 1780-1850 COR, IRL [35017] : 1850-1900 PORT ELIZABETH, RSA [37914] : 1700+ OKI, SCT [33986] : AGNES ALL GLASGOW, LKS, SCT [34093] : PRE 1850 WICK, CAI, SCT [34287] : 1800+ LATHERON, CAI, SCT [34591] : ROBERT C1760-1830 DUNBEATH, CAI, SCT [34646] : 1600+ ORPHIR & KIRKWALL, OKI, SCT [34722] : PRE 1850 LATHERON, CAI, SCT [35819] : 1650-1750 WICK, CAI, SCT [35961] : 1790+ KILDONAN, SUT, SCT [36865] : PRE 1900 CAMSTER, CAI, SCT [38457] : PRE 1850 MELVICK, SUT, SCT [38457] : PRE 1850 BRAEMORE, CAI, SCT [38457]

GUNNELL 1800+ COLBY, LIN, ENG [34221] : 1850+ LONDON, MDX, ENG [37294] : ALL ENG [37584] : PRE 1810 LITTLE MARLOW, BKM, ENG [37652] : PRE 1838 DUNAS, CLA, IRL & AUS [34845] : ALL PITTSBURGH, PA, USA [37584]

GUNNER PRE 1818 WARWICK, WAR, ENG [35702]

GUNNERTON C1800 NBL, ENG [35203]

GUNNING 1850+ ST KILDA, VIC, AUS [38281] : ALL ENG [38235] : PRE 1881 IRL [37318] : PRE 1900 PORTARLINGTON, LEX, IRL [37521] : 1800S SHANNON, IRL [38281]

GUNNINGHAM 1750-1900 MARYLEBONE, LND & SOM, ENG [37644]

GUNSON PRE 1750 OXF, ENG [34720] : 1750-1880 GUISBOROUGH, NRY & DUR, ENG [37615]

GUNSTON PRE 1750 OXF, ENG [34720]

GUNTER ALL STANFORD IN THE VALE, BRK, ENG [36076]

GUNTHER 1863 ROCKHAMPTON, QLD, AUS [35922] : C1828 FRANKFURT A.M., HEN, GER [35922]

GUNTHORPE C1800 BUCKINGHAM, BKM, ENG [34840] : 1877-1883 WORTLEY, WRY, ENG [34840] : C1774 BUCKINGHAM, BKM, ENG [36945]

GUNTRIP C1774 BUCKINGHAM, BKM, ENG [36945]

GUNWELL PRE 1700 AYLSHAM & FELMINGHAM, NFK, ENG [36593]

GUNYON PRE 1912 HORSHAM & STAWELL, VIC, AUS [34159]

GUPPY 1800+ NORTH WOOTTON, SOM, ENG [35112]

GURA 1880+ ALLEGENY, PA, USA [38185]

GURATZSCH 1720-1800 SACHSENFELD, KSA, GER [38628]

GURDEN C1750-1850 BRACKLEY, NTH, ENG [33876] : ALL WORLDWIDE [36221]

GURDIN ALL WORLDWIDE [36221]

GURDON ALL WORLDWIDE [36221]

GURLEY 1860 NEWCASTLE, NSW, AUS [35800]

GURNEY 1700-1780 STURRY, KEN, ENG [34623] : C1840+ WANDSWORTH, SRY, ENG [35347] : PRE 1820 WARWICK, WAR, ENG [36177] : PRE 1840 LEAMINGTON SPA, WAR, ENG [36177] : 1850S NOTTING HILL, LND, ENG [37369] : PRE 1850 GLS, ENG [37681] : 1780-1815 CORNWALL CO., ENG [38151] : PRE 1808 IRL [34766]

GURR 1852 CHIDDINGLY, SSX, ENG [34120] : ANN 1835+ ULCOMBE, KEN, ENG [34630] : C1837 HYTHE, KEN, ENG [36071] : C1814 SSX, ENG [38177]

GURREY ALL DUNDEE, ANS, SCT [37994]

GURSKI ALL DANZIG, WPR, GER [35315] : 1980S SINDELFINGEN, GER [35315]

GURTNER 1900+ DAYTON, OH, USA [36909]

GURTON C1750 PATTISWICK, ESS, ENG [37053] : PRE 1900 ESS, ENG [37668]

GUSCOTT 1000-1855 EXETER, DEV, ENG [34476] :
ELIZ PRE 1820 EGG BUCKLAND, DEV, ENG
[36634]
GUSEN 1753 HOHENWEPEL, GER [38749]
GUSES 1850+ DDR [34087]
GUSKETT 1740+ BRIXHAM, DEV, ENG [35027]
GUSTAFSON 1840+ ADELAIDE & LARGS BAY, SA,
AUS [35555]
GUSTAFSSON 1864+ PERNAJA, UUSIMAA, FIN
[38758]
GUSTAVSON 1850-1950 NUBRA, SWE [34135]
GUTERMUTH C1816 MARIENWERDER, WPR, GER
[38626]
GUTGESELL PRE 1780 UNTERSIEMAU, BAY, BRD
[35311]
GUTH ALL QLD, AUS [36616]
GUTHMANN PRE 1700 GER [38683]
GUTHRIE 1800-1910 NB, CAN [36718] : PRE 1850
CLA, IRL [35407] : 1850S ARDFINNAN, TIP, IRL
[38223] : 1800S CHRISTCHURCH, NZ [34570] : 1750-
1850 TAIN, ROC, SCT [34523] : 1700-1800
MENMUIR, ANS, SCT [35269] : ALL PLANT CITY,
FL, USA [35302] : 1790-1800 HILLSBORO, NC, USA
[37027] : CALVIN P. 1860-1907 STILLWELL, OK,
USA [38732] : SARAH ANN A. 1860-1885
STILLWELL, OK, USA [38732] : SARAH K. 1880-
1893 STILLWELL, OK, USA [38732]
GUTMAN PRE 1900 NIZHNY NOVGAROD, SU
[36889]
GUTSCHE PRE 1860 CROSSEN ON ODER, BRA,
GER [34801]
GUTSTEIN PRE 1850 SIL, GER [38648]
GUTTEREL 1800+ CHATHAM, KEN, ENG [36559]
GUTTERIDGE PRE 1850 BETHNAL GREEN, MDX,
ENG [36099] : C1750 WHITCHURCH & GORING
HEATH, OXF, ENG [37652]
GUTTORMSGARD 1700+ SKURDAL,
HALLINGDAL, NOR [36905]
GUTZEIT PRE 1801 BRA & BLN, GER [35310]
GUY 1850+ ARARAT & SHEPPARTON, VIC, AUS
[33793] : PRE 1900 RICHMOND, TAS, AUS [34918] :
1840+ SYDNEY, NSW, AUS [35543] : 1838+
NEWTOWN & SYDNEY, NSW, AUS & IRL [37556] :
C1815 LAN, ENG [33793] : PRE 1870 BETHNAL
GREEN, LND, ENG [34277] : PRE 1803 BERKLEY,
GLS, ENG [35157] : 1695+ CHALVINGTON, SSX,
ENG [35436] : PRE 1850 LND, ENG [35556] : C1836
LEEDS, YKS, ENG [35715] : PRE 1800 WHITWELL,
IOW, ENG [36142] : PRE 1855 SRY, ENG [36589] :
1750+ WINDSOR, BRK, ENG [36603] : 1850+
ROEHAMPTON, LND, ENG [36603] : PRE 1800
CHIPPENHAM, WIL, ENG [37695] : PRE 1800 ST
KEW, CON, ENG [37768] : 1700-1750 TAMWORTH,
STS, ENG [37846] : ALL BATH, SOM, ENG [37950] :
1800+ PORTADOWN, ARM, IRL [37625] : 1700+
LLANRHIDIAN, GLA, WLS [35248]
GUY-FRENCH ALL SPALDING, LIN, ENG [36167]
GUYMER ALL SFK, ENG [34436]
GUYVER ALL ESS, ENG [37741]
GWILLAM PRE 1850 LONDON, ENG & WLS [34343]
GWILLIAM ALL WLS [36500]
GWILLIM PRE 1850 LONDON, ENG & WLS [34343] :
PRE 1815 NEW CHURCH, RAD, WLS [37671]
GWYER 1796 BRAMSHAW, WIL, ENG [35252]
GWYNNE 1860+ LISMORE, NSW, AUS [34978] :
C1850 ROSTREVOR, DOW, IRL [35722] : 1700+
CMN, WLS [36009]
GYDE 1600-1860 PAINSWICK, GLS, ENG [38028]
GYLAIN ALL KORTRYK, WVL, BEL [38164]
GYNN C1790 LAUNCESTON, CON, ENG [35865]
GYSLET CATHERINE PRE 1837 NEIDRHOLM,
DDR [35426]

GYTH 1600-1675 SCT [35317]
GYVER PRE 1600 ESS, ENG [35642]
HAAG PRE 1909 HEILBRONN, BAD, GER [34175]
HAAGA PRE 1755 UNTERJESINGEN, WUE, GER
[37587]
HAAJEM PRE 1880 SKODJE, NOR [35932]
HAAKENSON C1847 SODERAKRA, KAL, SWE
[36356]
HAAKER 1860+ HAMBURG, HBG, GER [37889]
HAALCK 1490-1800 BURG DITHM., SHO, GER
[38750]
HAANEL 1840+ BRESLAU, SIL, GER [34367] : 1800S
ST LOUIS, MO, USA [34367]
HAAR PRE 1860 STEPNEY, LND, ENG [35411] : PRE
1850 LILIENTHAL, HAN, GER [35411] : 1860+
KAIAPOI & TEMUKA, CANT, NZ [35411]
HAARBURG 1770+ WPR, GER [34017] : 1770+ OPR,
GER [34017] : 1770+ PRE, GER [34017]
HAASCH PRE 1880 BRD [38238]
HAASDIJK 1935+ USA [34990]
HAASE C1900 WELLINGTON, NZ [35597]
HAAVISTO 1856+ PYHTAA, KYMEN LAANI, FIN
[38758]
HABBIS 1820 LANDBEACH, CAM, ENG [34976]
HABECK C1862 STETTIN, POM, GER [34688]
HABELMAN 1860 TEMPLEBURG, GER [37531]
HABGOOD 1850 BURIN, NFD, CAN [34349]
HABRES 1700+ BADEN, NOE, OES [36303]
HABURNE C1593 COTTINGHAM, YKS, ENG [36544]
HACCHE MARY PRE 1800 GEORGE NYMPTON,
DEV, ENG [34963]
HACHE ALL WORLDWIDE [36934]
HACK 1850-1900 IOW, ENG & CAN [38349] : 1800S
BAD, GER [34102]
HACKBARTH PRE 1740 SCHULITZ, GER [38614] :
1814+ LABISCHIN, PRE, GER [38614] : PRE 1740
SCHULITZ, SWE [38614]
HACKE PRE 1800 BRA & MST, GER [38648]
HACKER PRE 1795 MDX, ENG [34445] : 1700-1850
POUNDSTOCK, CON, ENG [36727] : PRE 1802
FRIEDLAND, MST, GER [38630]
HACKERLEY ALL WORLDWIDE [37350]
HACKESLEY 1800-1900 IRL [37844]
HACKET 1750+ ABERDEEN, ABD, SCT [34606]
HACKETT 1860+ TANTAWANGLO, NSW, AUS
[33870] : 1850+ SOUTH CREEK (ST MARYS),
NSW, AUS [35101] : 1890S REDFERN, NSW, AUS
[35785] : PRE 1850 GREAT STAUGHTON, HUN,
ENG [33870] : 1800-1850 ISLINGTON, MDX, ENG
[34623] : 1800+ FROME, SOM, ENG [35101] : 1830+
GOSPORT, HAM, ENG [35476] : 1800+ FROME,
SOM, ENG [35567] : 1880S BUSHBURY, STS, ENG
[35730] : 1850S LND, ENG [36304] : C1750 LEI, ENG
[37869] : 1800+ CLONMEL, TIP, IRL [34556] : 1800S
OXFORD, CHCH, NZ [35785] : ALL NJ, USA [38733]
HACKLETON 1825 LLANBADARNFAWR, CGN,
WLS [34284] : 1826+ ABERYSTWYTH, CGN, WLS
[34284]
HACKLING 1850+ STEPNEY, LONDON, MDX,
ENG [36989] : 1850+ MILE END, LONDON, MDX,
ENG [36989] : THOMAS 1800+ ENG [36989]
HACKMAN C1833 LANCASTER, PA, USA [37022]
HACKNEY ALL PA, USA [38359]
HACKWOOD PRE 1847 CANNOCKWOOD, STS,
ENG [34797]
HACKWORTH PRE 1850 OH & VA, USA [37604]
HACQUEVILLE 1800+ AIZIER & LA BOUILLE, HN
& BN, FRA [37294]
HADAWAY 1800S ACOL, KEN, ENG [35398]
HADDEN 1853+ AVCTERADA, PER, SCT [33936] :
PRE 1840 PAISLEY, SCT [34667] : PRE 1868
DUNNOTTAR, KCD, SCT [35521] : PRE 1772

NEWBATTLE, MLN, SCT **[37852]** : C1800S
PITGAIR, GAMRIE, BAN, SCT **[37977]** : C1850+
GLASGOW, DNB, VIC & WA, SCT & AUS **[37888]**
HADDERN (SEE HARDERN [37290]
HADDINGTON PRE 1820 CORK, COR, IRL **[34452]**
HADDOCK PRE 1828 WEDNESBURY, STS, ENG
[35514] : 1840S IRL **[34638]** : 1700+ USA **[38336]** :
1700+ ENG &, WLS & SCT **[38336]**
HADDON THOMAS 1800+ YAXLEY, HUN, ENG
[34916] : 1800S STAMFORD, RUT, ENG **[36005]** :
1777 UPHALL, MLN, SCT **[33945]**
HADDOW 1800-1880 TOTTENHAM, MDX, ENG
[37376]
HADDRELL 1800+ STOCKCROSS & NEWBURY,
BRK, ENG **[37705]**
HADE 1800+ CARDIFF, GLA, WLS **[34803]**
HADEGADY 1750-1800 MAY, IRL **[35581]**
HADEN 1700-1800S WOLVERTON, SAL, ENG **[37898]**
: 1800S LANARK, LKS, SCT **[37898]**
HADFIELD PRE 1725 SHIRLAND, DBY, ENG **[35079]**
: 1500-1900 HAYFIELD, GLOSSOP, DBY, ENG
[35944] : C1900 HORNLEY, YKS, ENG **[38168]**
HADINGTON PRE 1685 SEALE, SRY, ENG **[37420]**
HADLAND PRE 1840 NTH, ENG **[37650]**
HADLER ALL WORLDWIDE **[36156]**
HADLEY SAMUEL 1800S DUDLEY, WOR, ENG
[34427] : PRE 1850 BISHOPSGATE, LND, ENG
[36361] : PRE 1880 IDLE, YKS, ENG **[38755]** : C1700
CHESTER CO., PA, USA **[36319]** : 1800-1840 TODD
CO. & LOGAN CO., KY, USA **[37824]**
HADLOW PRE 1860 MAIDSTONE, KEN, ENG
[38033] : 1860+ BERRIEN CO., MI, USA **[38033]**
HADOCK 1800+ BELFAST, ANT, IRL **[36135]**
HAEGE ALL WORLDWIDE **[38693]**
HAEGGI ALL WORLDWIDE **[38693]**
HAEGI ALL WORLDWIDE **[38693]**
HAEGY ALL PA, USA **[38693]**
HAENICHEN 1700-1800 HELMSTEDT, NSA, GER
[38643]
HAENSCH C1827 STORKOW, BRA, GER **[38626]** :
1801-1871 COTTBUS, BRA, GER **[38626]**
HAENSEL 1759-1815 WURZEN, KSA, GER **[38749]**
HAERING PRE 1770 LAUBEN, MEMMINGEN BAV,
GER **[38661]**
HAESZLER 1810+ LIEGNITZ, PRE, GER **[35391]**
HAEUSLER C1880 TERMORA, NSW, AUS **[35585]** :
1846+ LOBETHAL, SA, AUS **[35585]** : C1867
WODONGA, VIC, AUS **[35585]** : PRE 1846
ULBERSDORF & ZULLICHAU, PRE, GER **[35585]**
HAEVES PRE 1870 LITTLE CARLTON, NTT, ENG
[35821]
HAFER JAMES 1898 FILLMORE CO., NE, USA
[38132]
HAFFIELD 1850+ SYDNEY, NSW, AUS **[35360]** : PRE
1850 DUBLIN, IRL **[35360]**
HAFFNER C1880 NSW, AUS **[34963]** : 1830+
KINGSTON, ONT, CAN **[37047]** : C1820
SWARKESTON, DBY, ENG **[34963]** : 1805+ HES,
GER **[37047]** : ALL IRL **[37047]** : ALL SLZ, OES
[37047] : 1750-1850 PA, USA **[36908]** : ALL USA
[37047]
HAFLICH 1780-1831 UNION, PA, USA **[38095]**
HAFNER ALL HES, GER **[37047]**
HAGAN 1851+ GLEBE & WAVERLEY, NSW, AUS
[35092] : 1860+ MELBOURNE, VIC, AUS & IRL
[34864] : 1800+ LEADGATE, DUR, ENG **[36503]** :
PRE 1875 DUNGANNON, TYR, IRL **[34661]** : 1832-
1851 MILTON MALBAY, CLA, IRL **[35092]**
HAGAR SUSANNAH 1790-1834 HAGERSVILLE,
ONT, CAN & GER **[35778]**
HAGARTY 1700S MOHILL, LET, IRL **[38054]**

HAGEDORN PRE 1822 BLUMBERG, HAN, GER
[36726] : 1700+ GREBIN, SHO, GER **[37170]**
HAGEMANN PRE 1850 SCHWEINSBERG, GHE &
HEN, GER **[38606]** : 1700-1800 HUTTENRODE,
NSA, GER **[38643]**
HAGEMEISTER 1691 HABERHAUSEN, GER **[38749]**
HAGEN 1880+ WAVERLEY, NSW, AUS **[34857]** :
1860+ BEECHWORTH, VIC, AUS **[34857]** : C1830
HAMBURG, HBG, GER **[34952]** : PRE 1795
BELFAST, IRL **[36721]**
HAGENAAR 1856+ SCHAGEN, NOH, NL **[35141]**
HAGENBURGER PRE 1800 RPF, GER **[38681]**
HAGENOW 1854+ NSW, AUS **[35874]** : 1700+
DEVEN, MEK, GER **[35874]**
HAGER HARRIET 1806 MARLBORO, MIDDLESEX,
MA, USA **[38183]**
HAGERMAN 1790+ VINELAND, ONT, CAN **[34408]** :
1650+ NORRBARKE & VIKA, KOPPARBERG,
SWE **[37036]** : PRE 1766 ALBANY, NY, USA **[36721]**
HAGERTON 1750-1850 MONROE CO. & JACKSON
CO., AR, USA **[38570]**
HAGERTY GEORGE 1838+ YASS, NSW, AUS **[35787]**
HAGETER 1890+ SPISSKA NOVA VES, CZECH.,
GER **[38185]**
HAGEY ALL PA, USA **[38693]**
HAGGAR 1850+ BOMBALA, NSW, AUS **[36295]** :
ALL GREAT CHESTERFORD, ESS, ENG **[36955]**
HAGGARD 1600 WARE, HRT, ENG **[34204]**
HAGGART ALL ONT, CAN **[37044]** : C1840 PORT
GLASGOW, RFW, SCT **[36806]**
HAGGARTY C1810 COR & TAS, IRL & AUS **[34596]**
HAGGEN MARTA 1840-1930 FILMORE CO., MN,
USA **[38392]**
HAGGER PRE 1860 SHOREDITCH & ST GILES,
LND, ENG **[35576]** : PRE 1780 SFK, ENG **[35642]**
HAGGERTY PRE 1875 DON, MAY & SLI, IRL **[37764]**
HAGGIS 1750+ ENG **[33963]** : PRE 1845 PORTSEA,
HAM, ENG **[37380]**
HAGGLUND 1870+ ARENDAL, AUST AGDER,
NOR **[36795]** : 1800+ ARNAS,
VASTERNORRLAND, SWE **[36795]**
HAGGSTROM ERIC 1884+ SWE **[35641]**
HAGLER 1840-1880 WARREN CO., IL, USA **[36573]** :
JOHN 1750-1800 WILKES CO., NC, USA **[36573]** :
ALL WORLDWIDE **[36573]**
HAGLEY C1800 EXMOUTH, DEV, ENG **[34434]** :
MARIA 1800S ENG **[37800]**
HAGNAUER PRE 1751 AARAU, AG, CH **[37103]**
HAGREEN C1790 HORRINGER, SFK, ENG **[36111]**
HAGUE PRE 1760 ECCLESFIELD, WRY, ENG **[34974]**
: HARRIETT C1811 SHEFFIELD, YKS, ENG **[37383]**
HAGY ALL PA, USA **[38693]**
HAHLBOHM PRE 1900 PSA & HAN, GER **[38648]**
HAHLWEG PRE 1900 DDR **[38616]**
HAHN HENRICH 1800+ JETTENBACK, BAY, BRD
[34171] : 1850+ BECHTOLSHEIM, RPF, BRD **[38530]**
: PRE 1855 ENDERSBACH, WUE, GER **[34886]** :
1850 GER **[36579]** : ALL BAW, GER & BRD **[36656]** :
1700-1800 NY, USA **[35603]**
HAHNEL ALL GER **[38664]**
HAHNEMANN PRE 1740 BERLIN, PRE, GER **[38135]**
HAIDLE 1855+ SYDNEY, NSW, AUS **[34812]** : ALL
STETTEN, WUE, GER **[34812]**
HAIG C1800 ENG **[34654]** : 1860+ JEDBURGH, ROX,
SCT **[34109]**
HAIGH PRE 1895 SYDNEY, NSW, AUS **[34978]** :
JOHN 1760+ WRY, ENG **[34181]** : C1794
ALMONDBURY, WRY, ENG **[35733]** : PRE 1872
MELTHAM, WRY, ENG **[35733]** : 1500-1990
KIRKBURTON & CUMBER WTH, WRY, ENG
[36218] : 1735 PENISTONE, WRY, ENG **[36606]** :
1750-1800 LINGARDS, WRY, ENG **[36635]** : ALL

BRADFORD & HALIFAX, WRY, ENG [37236] :
1600-1920 HUDDERSFIELD, WRY, ENG [37736] :
PRE 1770 THURLSTONE, WRY, ENG [37893]

HAIGHT 1850+ MAN, CAN [34465] : PRE 1800
COLUMBIA CO., NY, USA [37568]

HAIGS PRE 1800 FIF, SCT [36679]

HAIL MOSES C1670-1790 CUL, ENG [37794]

HAILD PRE 1877 MANCHESTER, LAN, ENG [37174]

HAILES C1700 MAMBLE, WOR, ENG [37918]

HAILEY 1880+ UXBRIDGE, MDX, ENG [36535] :
1810-1885 HIGH WYCOMBE, BKM, ENG [36535] :
PRE 1900 OXF, ENG [36535] : 1854+ UT, USA
[36535]

HAILL ALL WORLDWIDE [38725]

HAILS C1797 NEWBOTTLE, DUR, ENG [34972]

HAILY PRE 1900 OXF, ENG [36535]

HAIN C1817 AUCHTERMUCHTY, FIF, SCT [34527] :
ALL FIF, SCT [37704]

HAINAN 1825S COR, IRL [35416]

HAINE 1750+ TINTINHULL & YEOVIL, SOM, ENG
[34913] : ALL DUNDEE, ANS, SCT [36842]

HAINER 1860+ ELGIN CO., ONT, CAN [36710]

HAINES 1841+ SA, AUS [34775] : 1870+
BRAIDWOOD, NSW, AUS [38324] : 1830-1900
VANCOUVER, BC, CAN & ENG [37499] : PRE 1830
LONDON, ENG [33805] : PRE 1840 WIL, ENG
[34775] : 1830S CHELTENHAM, GLS, ENG [35331] :
C1700-1900 ISLINGTON & SHOREDITCH, LND,
ENG [35892] : PRE 1850 STOW IN THE WOLD,
GLS, ENG [36385] : PRE 1875 BRIGHTON, SSX,
ENG [36888] : 1830S ST MARTIN IN FIELDS, LND,
ENG [37080] : PRE 1800 NTH & NJ, ENG & USA
[38746] : 1800+ MALLOW, COR, IRL [35201] : PRE
1900 MALLOW, COR, IRL & AUS [34705] : 1800-
1900S CANTERBURY, NZ [36796] : 1811 BROOME,
NY, USA [38022] : ALL WORLDWIDE [36933]

HAINES (SEE HAYNES) [35866]

HAINEY PRE 1880 HULL, YKS, ENG [33808]

HAINS 1805+ FREMINGTON, DEV, ENG [35822] :
PRE 1800 GER [36933] : PRE 1757 STATEN
ISLAND, NY, USA [37811]

HAINSWORTH PRE 1910 WESTMEAD, NSW, AUS
[34979] : C1860 WORTLEY, WRY, ENG [35470] :
1800-1900 BRADFORD, YKS, ENG [36150]

HAINWORTH PRE 1800 GUISELEY, WRY, ENG
[36159]

HAIR C1910 DULACCA, QLD, AUS [35807] : 1800-1868
ARM, IRL [36440] : PRE 1838 LOUDON, AYR, SCT
[35407] : C1847 CAMPBELTOWN, ARL, SCT [35807]

HAIRD 1760-1850 GREAT BARDFIELD, ESS, ENG
[37859]

HAISELL C1860+ COOLAC, NSW, AUS [34426] :
JOHN PRE 1836 EAST GUILDFORD, SSX, ENG
[33807] : PRE 1800 LYDD, KEN, ENG [34899]

HAISLIP PRE 1900 FAIRFAX CO., VA, USA [35270]

HAK C1900 BETUWE, GEL, NL [38713]

HAKANSDOTTER PRE 1850 TVARRED, ALVSBORG,
SWE [35324]

HAKE 1730+ STAPLE FITZPAINE, SOM, ENG
[35112]

HAKEN 1833+ HAMILTON & NORWICH, ONT,
CAN [36652] : PRE 1833 IPSWICH, SFK, ENG
[36652]

HAKES THOMAS 1800+ LEI & YKS, ENG [37640]

HALAYKO ALL UKRAINE [36719]

HALBERG ALL NZ & DEN [34604] : 1780-1830 PA &
NJ, USA [36908]

HALBROOKS ALL WORLDWIDE [35326]

HALCRO 1700+ CAN [33903] : 1700+ OKI, SCT
[33903]

HALCROW 1780S LERWICK, SHI, SCT [35824]

HALDANE 1840S PLYMOUTH, DEV, ENG & NZ
[36862] : 1853+ AUCTERADA, PER, SCT [33936] :
1850S EDINBURGH, MLN, SCT [35415]

HALDEMAN 1790+ USA & UK [36357]

HALDEN 1840S MELBOURNE, VIC, AUS [35136] :
1750-1850 EDINBURGH, MLN, SCT [34930]

HALDIN ALL HRT, ENG [36978]

HALDSWORTH C1859+ MOORABBIN, VIC, AUS
[35249]

HALE ALL NFD, CAN [35619] : 1800+ ORILLIA,
ONT, CAN [36756] : 1800+ SUDBURY, SFK & ESS,
ENG [33970] : 1800+ BERKLEY, GLS, ENG [34008] :
C1730 LONDON, ENG [34768] : 1922+ ALLERTON,
LAN, ENG [35025] : 1780-1830 CHESTER, CHS,
ENG [35402] : WILLIAM 1830+ LND, ENG [35593] :
ALL STANFORD IN THE VALE, BRK, ENG [36076]
: 1750+ WITHYHAM, SSX, ENG [36088] : 1700+
LITTLE SOMERFORD, WIL, ENG [37328] : ALL
NORWICH, NFK, ENG [37629] : 1636-1781
NEWBURY, MA, USA [35294] : 1750+ USA [38587] :
1750+ PA, USA [38587]

HALES 1852+ COLLINGWOOD, VIC, AUS [34702] :
1750-1850 BENENDEN, KEN, ENG [33785] : 1850+
LEYTONSTONE, ESS, ENG [34272] : 1800-1890
DERBY & UTTOXETER, DBY & STS, ENG [34729] :
1802+ LIN, ENG [35136] : 1800S LOWESTOFT,
SFK, ENG [35377] : 1820+ CORTON, SFK, ENG
[35725] : 1780+ HOPTON, SFK, ENG [35725] : PRE
1840 LUDHAM & NEATTSHEAD, NFK, ENG
[36224] : 1872+ COLCHESTER, ESS, ENG [37656] :
1700-1850 HARTLIP & NEWINGTON, KEN, ENG
[38354] : PRE 1900 KILLESHANDRA, CAV, IRL
[38391] : PRE 1900 EASTON, SOUTH BANK, UK
[37804]

HALEY 1680-1800 ILLINGWORTH 7 BIRSTALL,
WRY, ENG [34352] : 1700S BRADFORD &
BOWLING, WRY, ENG [36263] : PRE 1830 IRL
[35339] : 1800 MAY, OFF, IRL [37170] : 1700-1750
ORANGE CO., VA, USA [36566] : ALL USA & IRL
[38782]

HALFHILL 1780-1830 PA & NJ, USA [36908]

HALFORD PRE 1840S STAFFORD, STS, ENG [34240]
: C1770 NOTTINGHAM, NTT, ENG [34734]

HALFPENNY 1800 STEPNEY, LND, ENG [33778] :
ALL WORLDWIDE [36224]

HALFYARD ALL WORLDWIDE [34250]

HALIAN C1800 KALLINE, OFF, IRL [37911]

HALIDAY C1772 CRAILING, ROX, SCT [34239]

HALKETT ALL HALL HILL OR LA HILL, FIF, SCT
[37673]

HALKEY PRE 1750 MONTROSE, ANS, SCT [35462]

HALKYARD 1880 OLDHAM, LAN, ENG [35201] :
1872-1927 CAMPTONVILLE, CA, USA [33754] :
1872-1927 RENTON, WA & IA, USA [33754]

HALL JOHN 1880 ORANGE, NSW, AUS [34038] :
WILLIAM 1895 MURGA, NSW, AUS [34038] :
C1809+ AUS [34444] : 1840-1890 SA, AUS [34615] :
PRE 1883 ADELAIDE, SA, AUS [34861] : PRE 1850
HOBART, TAS, AUS [34896] : JAMES 1860+
MANGANA, TAS, AUS [34910] : 1900 WARREN &
DUBBO, NSW, AUS [35082] : 1860+ BENDIGO,
VIC, AUS [35390] : 1860-1890 NORWOOD, SA, AUS
[35861] : ALL WA, AUS [35868] : 1850+ SOUTH
BRISBANE, QLD, AUS [36616] : 1884+ WIMMERA
& SHEPPARTON, VIC, AUS [36622] : 1884+
BLEAKHOUSE, VIC, AUS [36622] : ALL
ADELAIDE, SA, AUS & ENG [34561] : 1949 SAINT
JOHN, NB, CAN [34111] : 1850+ WELLINGTON
CO., ONT, CAN [34231] : ALTON 1865
ORANGEVILLE, ONT, CAN [36728] : 1800S
INVERNESS, QUE, CAN [36944] : 1820+ WHITBY
TWP., ONT, CAN [38235] : WILLIAM 1835-1900

MONTREAL, QUE, CAN [38591] : ROBERT 1815-1868 MONTREAL, QUE, CAN & SCT [38591] : 1780+ YAXLEY, HUN, ENG [33836] : 1700-1800+ FOLKINGHAM, LIN, ENG [33889] : C1700-1800+ PRESTWOLD, LEI, ENG [33889] : C1600+ DUNNINGTON UPON THE HEATHER, LEI, ENG [33889] : C1700+ HUGGLESCOTE, LEI, ENG [33889] : C1700+ DUNNINGTON UPON THE HEATHER, LEI, ENG [33889] : 1700-1800+ COTES, LEI, ENG [33889] : 1800+ LEAMINGTON, LEI, ENG [33889] : 1800+ ISLEY, WALTON, LEI, ENG [33889] : PRE 1850 GRETTON, NTH, ENG [33993] : C1760 NEWPORT PAGNELL, BKM, ENG [34041] : PRE 1852 ST EBBS, OXF, ENG [34043] : 1893 JUPON HALL, YORK & KINGSTON, ERY, ENG [34111] : ALL HULL, YKS, ENG [34111] : 1840-1900 CLEASBY, NRY, ENG [34211] : 1700+ CONNINGSBY, LIN, ENG [34221] : PRE 1813 STOCKTON, DUR, ENG [34320] : PRE 1860 NRY, ENG [34320] : 1830+ NEWCASTLE, NBL, ENG [34320] : C1809 BRADFIELD, WRY, ENG [34358] : PRE 1840 BURTON FLEMING & BRIDLINGTON, YKS, ENG [34504] : C1830 NEWCASTLE, NBL, ENG [34556] : 1830-1855 STUDLEY, WAR, ENG [34582] : 1826-1900 BRIDGEWATER, SOM, ENG [34658] : 1820+ MARLESFORD, SFK, ENG [34700] : 1750+ EARTLSOHAM, SFK, ENG [34700] : ALL HARBY, LEI, ENG [34758] : C1822 CONINSBY, LIN, ENG [34765] : DINAH 1800+ ARKENGARTHDALE, YKS, ENG [34810] : PRE 1845 RISELEY, BDF, ENG [34855] : PRE 1688 ST PETERS, NOTTINGHAM, NTT, ENG [34858] : 1850-1900 WES, ENG [34948] : PRE 1874 MALVERN, WOR, ENG [35061] : PRE 1850 BARKING, ESS, ENG [35098] : 1800S PETERBOROUGH, NTH, ENG [35188] : PRE 1840 PAULTON & TAUNTON, SOM, ENG [35231] : C1740 LONG SUTTON, HAM, ENG [35247] : DR. JOHN PRE 1900 SOUTH SHIELDS, DUR, ENG [35337] : C1820 NORTHALLERTON, NRY, ENG [35350] : PRE 1800 NBL, ENG [35377] : 1830S EASTINGTON, DUR, ENG [35390] : C1824 BRANDSBURTON, YKS, ENG [35515] : 1820+ GILLINGHAM, DOR, ENG [35529] : WILLIAM C1802 PAULTON, SOM, ENG [35729] : 1800+ NEWPORT, IOW, ENG [35824] : 1700+ GRINDLEFORD BRIDGE, DBY, ENG [35825] : 1780+ PENISTONE & THURLSTONE, NRY, ENG [35825] : 1800+ DUNFORD BRIDGE, WRY, ENG [35825] : 1800+ ASHBY DE LA ZOUCH, LEI, ENG [35851] : 1820-1860 LIVERPOOL, LAN, ENG [35861] : C1820 BISHOPS LYDEARD, SOM, ENG [35872] : 1750 ILFORD, ESS, ENG [35886] : C1860 DEV, ENG [35910] : 1820 SUNDERLAND, DUR, ENG [35912] : PRE 1890 HULL & SELBY, YKS, ENG [36039] : PRE 1825 HAMPTON, MDX, ENG [36051] : 1700-1800 UXBRIDGE, MDX, ENG [36081] : ALFRED 1925+ ASTON & BIRMINGHAM, WAR, ENG [36108] : C1750 CHESTERFIELD, DBY, ENG [36112] : 1876+ ISLINGTON & HOUNSLOW, MDX, ENG [36171] : BENJAMIN 1825+ WELLINGTON, SAL, ENG [36254] : PRE 1720 OLD SWINFORD, WOR & WAR, ENG [36326] : PRE 1840 SOUTH SHIELDS, DUR, ENG [36364] : 1400-1500 WARNHAM, SSX, ENG [36420] : PRE 1690 RAMPTON, NTT, ENG [36426] : 1801-1823 GRIMLEY, WOR, ENG [36513] : PRE 1837 SHEFFIELD, YKS, ENG [36589] : 1840 ISLINGTON, MDX, ENG [36606] : PRE 1860 HYDE PARK, LND, ENG [36645] : 1650+ FRADSWELL & MILWICH, STS, ENG [36701] : PRE 1700 WILLERSERY, GLS, ENG [36817] : PRE 1630 STRATFORD ON AVON, WAR, ENG [36931] : 1771-1776 NEWBURN, NBL, ENG [36961] : C1798 WASHINGTON, DUR, ENG

[36961] : C1802 FATFIELD, DUR, ENG [36961] : 1700-1800 HOUGHTON LE SPRING, DUR, ENG [36961] : 1800-1890 WEST BROMWICH, STS, ENG [37068] : 1780+ DAWLISH, DEV, ENG [37088] : ROBERT C1750 DENNINGTON, SFK, ENG [37191] : PRE 1850 HARWICK, ESS, ENG [37300] : 1820S POPLAR, LND, ENG [37369] : PRE 1800 CUL, ENG [37450] : 1750+ ORSTON, NTT, ENG [37552] : 1880S AYLESBURY, BKM, ENG [37560] : 1844+ LAMBETH, LND, ENG [37560] : PRE 1825 ST HELENS, LAN, ENG [37573] : THOMAS 1800+ HINCKLEY, LEI, ENG [37640] : 1750-1900 POPLAR, MDX, ENG [37651] : PRE 1800 INSKIP & POULTON, LAN, ENG [37710] : 1820S LIVERPOOL, LAN, ENG [37751] : PRE 1860 NEWCASTLE, NBL, ENG [37899] : 1800S HANLEY & FENTON, STS, ENG [37908] : 1800S CIRENCESTER, GLS, ENG [37910] : PRE 1760 KEN, ENG [38389] : C1880 OSGATHORPE, LEI, ENG [38471] : 1700-1800 HEWORTH, DUR, ENG [38516] : C1840 OLD MALTON, NRY, ENG [38516] : C1800 AMPLEFORTH, NRY, ENG [38516] : 1840-1900 HUSTHWAITE, NRY, ENG [38516] : ALL COOTEHILL, CAV, IRL [33823] : JOHN PRE 1845 KEADY, ARM, IRL [33905] : PRE 1850 ARM, IRL [34502] : PRE 1900 LISNAVEANE, MOG, IRL [34569] : PRE 1900 TYR, IRL [34598] : 1800+ CASTLE CONNELL, LIM, IRL [35358] : 1800+ BELFAST, ANT, DOW & ARM, IRL [35636] : 1839+ KNOCKRAVEN KEADY, ARM, IRL [36863] : PRE 1800 GRANGE, ARM, IRL [38461] : JOHN 1803-1829 ANT, IRL [38522] : JAMES PRE 1800 IRL [38536] : 1863+ ONEHUNGA & MILFORD, NZ [33823] : 1852 DUNDEE, PER, SCT [34224] : 1800-1870 ROX, SCT [34615] : 1800+ CLACKMANNAN, CLK, SCT [35121] : ALL HAWICK, ROX, SCT [35577] : 1750+ CLACKMANNAN, CLK, SCT [35989] : C1830 ROX, SCT [36762] : PRE 1758 GLENISLA, ANS, SCT [37772] : 1820 MCDONOUGH, IL, USA [34248] : GEORGE C1808 NEW YORK, NY, USA [34917] : 1776-1830 YARMOUTH, BARNSTABLE CO., MA, USA [35316] : ELISHA 1780+ MA, USA [35629] : 1600-1670 SOMERSET CO., MD, USA [36566] : 1630+ DORCHESTER BRADFORD, MA & NH, USA [36931] : 1710+ SPRINGFIELD, VT & NH, USA [36931] : PRE 1800 OWEGO, NY & PA, USA [37018] : 1630-1768 NEWPORT CO., RI, USA [37477] : ISAAC 1830-50S ROWAN CO., NC, USA [37585] : DAVID PRE 1860 FRANKLIN CO., OH, USA [37781] : LEMUEL PRE 1840 MUSKINGUM CO., OH, USA [37781] : JESSE 1788 SAGINAW CO., MI, USA [37788] : JAMES 1800S CLIFTON FORGE, VA, USA [37794] : PRE 1835 LOGENSPORT, IN, USA [37820] : 1850-1950 NAVARRO CO., TX, USA [38092] : 1840-1870 SCOTT CO., AR, USA [38092] : 1870-1950 LIMESTONE & MCLENNAN CO., TX, USA [38092] : 1850-1935 TRAVIS CO., TX, USA [38092] : 1860-1886 BASTROP CO., TX, USA [38092] : 1920-1950 PITTSBURG, TX, USA [38092] : 1870 EDGEFIELD CO., SC, USA [38092] : 1860 CHOCTAW & CHICKASAW NATION, OK, USA [38092] : 1830-1840 AL, USA [38092] : 1850 CRAWFORD CO., AR, USA [38092] : PRE 1862 BROOKLYN, NY, USA [38126] : THOMAS 1824-1893 HAYWOOD CO., NC, USA [38141] : MARY ELIZ. 1800 NC, USA [38536] : WILLIAM 1835-1900 MARENGO, IA & CA, USA [38591] : MARY ELIZ. 1868-1899 LA, MOHAVE CO., CA & AZ, USA [38591] : PRE 1850 MON, WLS [37086] : ALL WORLDWIDE ENG

HALLADAY ALL WIL & HAM, ENG [37412]

HALLAM 1853+ AUS [34264] : PRE 1855 LEI, ENG [34264] : 1860 NTT, ENG [34614] : C1747

SHEFFIELD, YKS, ENG [35257] : 1800 +
SHEFFIELD, YKS, ENG [35377] : ALL HOPE, DBY,
ENG [36134] : 1700-1800 DBY, ENG [38321]
HALLARAN PHILIP 1833 COR, IRL [38122] : PHILIP
1909 CHALLIS CUSTER, USA [38122]
HALLAWAY FREDERICK 1920 WINNIPEG, MAN,
CAN [38397] : PRE 1740 PENSHURST, KEN & SSX,
ENG [38397]
HALLBERG ALL DEN & SWE [34604]
HALLDEN ALL HRT, ENG [36978]
HALLDIN ELISABETH 1878 + SWE [38564]
HALLEAD 1850S CAN [35165]
HALLEN 1850S CLONCOMBE, KID, IRL [36862]
HALLENBECK 1750-1800 NY, USA [38113]
HALLENBERGER 1862 MO, USA [37815]
HALLESSEY PRE 1900 DROMAGH, COR, IRL [36168]
HALLET 1865 + BRIDPORT, DOR, ENG [34045]
HALLETT ALEX 1800-1900 LND, ENG [33875] : ALL
ENG [33937] : ALL ALDERSGATE, ST LUKES,
LND, ENG [34820] : ALL ENG [34834] : 1700 +
WEST CHINNOCK, SOM, ENG [35085] : C1780
CHINNOCK, SOM, ENG [36671] : PRE 1819
BLACKBURN, LAN, ENG [37316]
HALLEWELL 1750 + LEEDS, WRY, ENG [35824]
HALLEY 1640-1700 ALFORD, LIN, ENG [38453] : PRE
1900 FIF, SCT [33966] : 1700 + CRIEFF, PER, SCT
[34283] : PRE 1887 TORWOOD, STI, SCT [35113] :
PRE 1850 AUCHTERARDER, PER, SCT [35962]
HALLIDAY PRE 1850 NORTH KEPPEL, ONT, CAN
[36672] : 1820 + PAINSWICK, GLS, ENG [33893] :
ALL LIVERPOOL, LAN, ENG [35514] : 1800 KEN,
ENG [35970] : ALL WIL, DOR & HAM, ENG [37412]
: 1848 + MULL, ARL, SCT [34225] : JAMES 1734-
1179 TINWALD & JOHNSTONE, DFS, SCT [34225] :
1830S MOFFAT, DFS, SCT [34635] : PRE 1832
EDINBURGH, MLN, SCT [35932] : PRE 1800
JOHNSTONE, DFS, SCT [36437] : 1600-1890
HAZELBANK, DFS, SCT [37422] : PRE 1900 DFS,
SCT [37443] : 1830 BRYDEKIRK, DFS, SCT & ENG
[34934] : 1750-1860 STEUBEN CO., NY & MN, USA
[36334]
HALLIFAX C1860 WIGAN, LAN, ENG [37561] : PRE
1900 WOOLWICH, KEN, ENG [37561]
HALLIGAN 1870-1900 BALLARAT, VIC, AUS [34191]
HALLINAN C1859 PYRMONT, NSW, AUS [35827] :
1800S KILCOLMAN, LIM, IRL [35964]
HALLISSEY ALL IRL [34068]
HALLIWELL 1800-1860 CANTERBURY, KEN, ENG
[33758] : 1860-1875 DEAL, KEN, ENG [33758] : PRE
1829 HALIFAX, WRY, ENG [35223] : 1820 +
OLDHAM, LAN, ENG [36568]
HALLMARK 1800 + CHESTER, CHS, ENG [35992]
HALLMURHAGHAN 1970 + USA [34111]
HALLORAN 1840 + TUMUT, NSW, AUS [34978] : PRE
1850 NSW, AUS [38730] : 1700S CLA, IRL [34978] :
PRE 1880 LIM, IRL [36918] : 1840S COOLHALIRA,
CLA, IRL & AUS [34845]
HALLOT C1705 WAPPENHAM, NTH, ENG [36945]
HALLOWELL C1650 NTT, ENG [37698]
HALLOWS 1857 + MELBOURNE, VIC, AUS [33830] :
PRE 1900 CHS, ENG [33830] : PRE 1900
NEWTOWN, MGY, WLS [33830]
HALLPIKE 1700 + GIGGLESWICK & SETTLE, YKS,
ENG [37666]
HALLROW ALL SHI, SCT [36697]
HALLS ALL BIDEFORD, DEV, ENG [34471] : 1854
IPSWICH, SFK, ENG [36281] : 1772 WEST STOW,
SFK, ENG [38209] : 1700-1900 SWALE MEDWAY,
KEN, ENG [38249]
HALLTRIFTS 1970 + CHARLOTTETOWN, PEI, CAN
[34111]
HALM C1665 STUTTGART, BAW, FRG [38660]

HALPIN 1884 ROCKDALE, NSW, AUS [37136] : 1870S
KILBURN, LND, ENG [36175] : PRE 1880 ADARE,
LIM, IRL [33954] : 1864 LIM, IRL [34654] : 1750-1850
DROGHEDA, LOU, IRL [38575]
HALS PRE 1874 DEN [34811] : C1700 BATTLE, SSX,
ENG [35259] : ALL WORLDWIDE [34811]
HALSE 1800S TRURO, CON, ENG [35882]
HALSEY 1800-1900 BUSHEY, HRT, ENG [36977] :
1700-1800 ST ALBANS, HRT, ENG [37898]
HALSTEAD 1891 KITCHENER, ONT, CAN [34129] :
1750-1850 BACUP, LAN, ENG [34520]
HALTER PRE 1855 BIBERACH, WUE, GER [34886]
HALTON C1820 CHS, ENG [34222] : PRE 1810
LANCASTER, LAN, ENG [38755]
HALVERSON PRE 1900 TRONDHJEM, NOR & USA
[38386]
HALVORSEN 1797 ONSOY & SANDE, OST-
VESTFOLD, NOR [34063] : 1880 + SKIEN, NOR
[34430] : C1860 WAALER SOGNE, NOR [38168]
HAM PRE 1900 + VIC, AUS [34877] : PRE 1850 TAS,
AUS [35378] : 1800-1850 ABINGDON, BRK, ENG
[34552] : 1870 + SUNDERLAND, DUR, ENG [35719]
: 1800 + WITNEY, OXF, ENG [35992] : 1730-1880
BRAMLEY, HAM, ENG [37118] : C1800 BRISTOL,
SOM, ENG [38376]
HAMAN ELIZABETH C1652 + LYNN, MA, USA
[35271]
HAMBLETON PRE 1839 ISLINGTON, MDX, ENG
[34166] : 1640-1820 WOKINGHAM, BRK, ENG
[37638]
HAMBLETT ALL WORLDWIDE [38754]
HAMBLEY PRE 1808 CON, ENG [33777] : C1700 ST
CLEER, CON, ENG [36389] : 1840 + WLS &, ENG &
CAN [37525]
HAMBLIN 1830-1900 PETERBOROUGH CO., ONT,
CAN [36688] : 1700-1830 UT, USA [36688]
HAMBLY PRE 1900 GRENFELL, NSW, AUS [35253] :
PRE 1808 CON, ENG [33777] : 1757 PROBUS, CON,
ENG [34808] : 1800S MDX, ENG [37423] : ALL
PADSTOW, CON, ENG [37766] : 1700-1800 +
BODMIN & LANIVET, CON, ENG [37814]
HAMBLYN 1850 + HOBART, TAS, AUS [35062] : ALL
WORLDWIDE [36875]
HAMBRIDGE ALL WORLDWIDE [34712]
HAMBROOK ALL NORTHUMBERLAND CO., NB,
CAN [34404] : C1750 SANDWICH, KEN, ENG
[35203] : PRE 1822 DEAL, KEN, ENG [35781] : ALL
KEN, ENG & AUS [34404] : PRE 1900 IRL [34404] :
1880 + ALBANY CO., NY, USA [34404] : 1865 +
COOK CO., MI, USA [34404] : 1850 + LORAIN CO.,
OH, USA [34404] : 1860 + LENAWEE CO., MI, USA
[34404] : 1850 + KENOSHA CO., WI, USA [34404]
HAMBURDGER ISODORE 1840 + VIEHLEUR, POL
[35803]
HAMBURG 1764-1900 WALTER, SARATOV, SU
[36958]
HAMEL 1840 + ST HELIER, JSY, CHI [36704] : 1660 +
ST AUBIN D'AUREMESNIL, HN, FRA [36678] :
PRE 1850 LE NEUFBOURG, BN, FRA [36704]
HAMENCE 1851 + SUTTON, ISLE OF ELY, CAM,
ENG [33920]
HAMER 1865 + SHERBROOKE & GRANBY, QUE,
CAN [34485] : PRE 1800 BURY, LAN, ENG [34485] :
1880 KENCHESTER, HEF, ENG [36636]
HAMERS 1800 + WEVELGEM, WF, BEL [34163]
HAMES 1792 ST BEES, CUL, ENG [34063] : C1700-
1850 CHARLTON MARSHALL, DOR, ENG [36435] :
1800 BARROW UPON SOAR, LEI, ENG [37082] :
PRE 1650 TRABEN, RPF, GER [38663] : ALL
WORLDWIDE [37091]
HAMILL 1845-1926 KEIGHLEY, YKS, ENG [38067] :
PRE 1846 SEAFORDE, DOW, IRL [33924] : 1840 +

BALLYMENA, ANT, IRL [36827] : PRE 1800 DOW, IRL [38428] : 1940 KNOCKBOY, ANT, IRL [38470]

HAMILTON 1850-1930 NORTH, NSW, AUS [34438] : 1850+ CARISBROOK, VIC, AUS [34459] : 1879+ SOUTH MELBOURNE, VIC, AUS [34595] : ELIZABETH 1830-1861 HOBART, TAS, AUS [34889] : 1840S DUNTROON, ACT, AUS [35226] : 1840+ ILLABO, NSW, AUS [36295] : 1850+ MATILDA, ONT, CAN [34051] : 1795-1820 HOPEWELL, NB, CAN [35314] : 1870+ AMHERSTBURG, ONT, CAN [35610] : PRE 1866 BEAUHARNOIS CO., QUE, CAN [38412] : HUGH C1800-1850 BERWICK, NBL, ENG [34007] : PRE 1860 LAN, ENG [34883] : ADAM 1770S+ LONDON, ENG [35706] : 1800S DURHAM TOWN, DUR, ENG [35987] : FRANCIS PRE 1780 BAKEWELL, DBY, ENG [36192] : PRE 1750 TILLINGTON & PETWORTH, SSX, ENG [38254] : 1840+ NEWCASTLE, ENG [38399] : PRE 1915 DUR, ENG [38594] : PRE 1840 MOG, IRL [34035] : 1700-1900 IRL [34081] : 1700-1800 IRL [34387] : WILLIAM 1730+ RAPHOE, DON, IRL [34515] : 1780+ LIMERICK, IRL [34642] : 1780+ DUBLIN, IRL [34642] : C1850S GREY ABBEY, DOW, IRL [34788] : 1830S BELFAST, ANT, IRL [34793] : 1840S BALLYMENA, ANT, IRL [35508] : 1750-1850 IRL [35600] : 1800+ TULLYISH, DOW, IRL [35995] : 1800+ CUSHENDALL, ANT, IRL [36686] : 1770-1800 ARM, FER & MOG, IRL [36687] : 1800S TULLYISH, DON, IRL [36856] : PRE 1856 LISBURN, DOW, IRL [37138] : PRE 1850 DOW, IRL [37180] : C1700-1800 TOMAREY HILL, ARM, IRL [37977] : PRE 1913 IRVINESTOWN, FER, IRL [37992] : 1770-1840 ANT & DOW, IRL [38004] : PRE 1800 IRL [38399] : C1730 TYR, IRL [38533] : 1867+ MILTON, NZ [33944] : CHARLES 1855+ CHRISTCHURCH, CBY, NZ [34652] : 1861+ GREYMOUTH, NELSON, NZ [35956] : 1880+ GORE, SI, NZ [36628] : C1850 AYR, SCT [33812] : PRE 1860 LANOREEK, LKS, SCT [33868] : PETER PRE 1860 GLASGOW, LKS, SCT [33944] : PRE 1880 KILMORY, ARL, SCT [33966] : 1800S LKS, SCT [34102] : PRE 1775 LANARK & CARLUKE, LKS & DNB, SCT [34127] : C1826 DRYMEN, STI, SCT [34189] : 1700+ LKS & RFW, SCT [34459] : ALL DALZIEL, LKS, SCT [34595] : PRE 1860 EAT KILBRIDE, LKS, SCT [34958] : PRE 1870 KILMARNOCK, AYR, SCT [35118] : PRE 1838 KILWINNING, AYR, SCT [35226] : PRE 1850+ GREENOCK, RFW, SCT [35237] : 1780+ WISHAW, LKS, SCT [35411] : 1860S ARDROSSAN, AYR, SCT [35415] : WALTER 1755+ EDINBURGH, MLN, SCT [35499] : 1780+ KILBRIDE, LKS, SCT [35956] : C1790+ HAMILTON, LKS, SCT [35956] : PRE 1900 MOTHERWELL, LKS, SCT [36067] : JOHN 1700+ CARLUKE, LKS, SCT [36291] : 1800+ GLASGOW, LKS, SCT [36295] : 1850-1900 LEVEN, FIF, SCT [36394] : C1800 LESMAHAGOW, LKS, SCT [36431] : PRE 1820 STONEHOUSE, LKS, SCT [36583] : JAMES 1819+ LANARK, BRIGGS END & KIRKFALS, LKS, SCT [36678] : PRE 1850 HAMILTON & STONEHOUSE, LKS, SCT [36705] : 1700-1850 TORTHORWALD, DFS, SCT [37442] : 1780-1860 GLASSFORD & COATBRIDGE, LKS, SCT [37488] : 1750-1800 CAMBUSLANG, LKS, SCT [37872] : 1750+ LESMAHAGOW, LKS, SCT [38388] : GILBERT PRE 1800 LKS, SCT [38437] : GEORGE WM. 1804-1844 JEDBURGH, ROX, SCT & AUS [34889] : LIZZIE 1850-1900 BOSTON, MA, USA [35706] : 1829+ ROCHESTER, NY, USA [35956] : 1840-1930 GREENVILLE, MERCER CO., PA, USA [36449] : 1780 PRINCE EDWARD CO., VA, USA [36730] : 1820-1830 WESTMORELAND, PA, USA

[36908] : PRE 1800 KY & OH, USA [38043] : 1750-1800 CORNISH, ME, USA [38045] : 1840-1855 SAINT LOUIS, MO, USA [38105] : C1850 SOMERSET CO., NJ, USA [38116] : C1780-1880 PA & NJ, USA [38325] : 1776-1900 NY, USA [38764]

HAMLEN PRE 1840 BATHEASTON & MONKTON COMBE, SOM, ENG [35701]

HAMLET PRE 1864 NEWBURY, BRK, ENG [35031] : PRE 1839 CHATHAM, KEN, ENG [37138] : PRE 1700 MA, USA & ENG [38746]

HAMLEY PRE 1840 TAVISTOCK, DEV, ENG [36095] : PRE 1735 CON, ENG [38389]

HAMLIN 1550+ WIDECOMBE ERMINGTON STAVERTON, DEV, ENG [34747] : 1750-1850 OTHERY, SOM, ENG [36012] : 1847 TAMWORTH, STS, ENG [37594] : 1800-1900 NY, USA [35305]

HAMLING 1700+ DEV, ENG [35062]

HAMLYN 1750+ CLOVELLY, DEV, ENG [34380] : 1820S FALMOUTH, CON, ENG [35815] : PRE 1800 WIDECOMBE IN THE MOOR, DEV, ENG [36790]

HAMM 1800S MISTERTON, SOM, ENG [37442] : EMILY 1905 DUBLIN, IRL [37518]

HAMMAN 1900-1990 SEATTLE, WA, USA [38154]

HAMMAR 1600-1746S LARBRO, GOTLAND, SWE [38346]

HAMMAT 1850+ WILLIAMSTOWN, SA, AUS [35520] : C1800 TRURO, CON, ENG [35520]

HAMMATHER 1748+ LANCASTER, PA, USA [38067]

HAMMER C1883 MARYBOROUGH, QLD, AUS [35515] : 1840-1890 REUTLINGEN, GER [37296] : 1856 FREDEREKSHALD, IDD, NOR [35515] : PRE 1870 NOR [37009]

HAMMERSLEY 1810 BOLLINGTON, CHS, ENG [37697]

HAMMERTON ALL YKS, ENG [34040]

HAMMETT 1850-1900 MELBOURNE, VIC, AUS [33834] : 1848+ VIC, AUS [38539] : 1820-1850 DEV, ENG [33834] : ANN PRE 1800 TAUNTON, SOM, ENG [36192] : ALL KIMPTON, HRT, ENG [36382] : PRE 1830 LYMINGTON & MILFORD, HAM, ENG [37287] : PRE 1850 ENG [37782] : 1820+ DEV, ENG [38539] : 1600-1900 EXETER, DEV, ENG [38579]

HAMMON 1840+ SSX, ENG [37560]

HAMMOND 1840+ COWRA DISTRICT, NSW, AUS [35205] : HARRY ELI 1850-1921 CATHCART & GUNDAGAI, NSW, AUS [35549] : 1838+ MELBOURNE, VIC, AUS [35734] : PRE 1860 BUNGENDORE, NSW, AUS [36369] : 1880+ AUS [37705] : C1835-45 DUDLEY, WOR, ENG [33828] : ALL SOUTHAMPTON, HAM, ENG [33937] : PRE 1900 MDX, ENG [34015] : SARAH C1744 NFK, ENG [34222] : JOHN PRE 1851 SHREWSBURY, SAL, ENG [34437] : PRE 1839 BLAXHALL, SFK, ENG [34689] : 1700+ SOUTH BERSTED, SSX, ENG [34747] : PRE 1880 BRIGHTON, SSX, ENG [34923] : 1750-1850 BLACK COUNTRY AREA, WAR & WOR, ENG [35166] : PRE 1840 GAYTON, NFK, ENG [35212] : 1660S ST GILES IN THE FIELD, LND, ENG [35259] : 1800+ YARMOUTH, NFK & IOW, ENG [35734] : 1750+ UPMINSTER, ESS, ENG [36065] : 1750+ GREAT WARLEY, ESS, ENG [36065] : PRE 1850 MARTLEY & GREAT WITLEY, WOR, ENG [36110] : 1840S CHESTERFIELD, DBY, ENG [36181] : PRE 1900 SFK, ENG [36417] : PRE 1841 ANDOVER, HAM, ENG [36865] : C1833 MILDENHALL, SFK, ENG [37106] : 1800-1875 ISLINGTON, MDX, ENG [37222] : 1700-1900 MARYLEBONE, LND, ENG [37233] : C1860 ISLINGTON, LND, ENG [37233] : 1600-1700 WILBY, SFK, ENG [37250] : 1750-1900 GREAT WALTHAM, ESS, ENG [37477] : PRE 1700 HAM, ENG [37693] : C1900-1920 MILE END &

ISLINGTON, LND, ENG [37865] : C1892+
PECKHAM, PLUMSTEAD, LND, ENG & SCT
[33978] : PRE 1840 ANT, IRL [35205] : MARY PRE
1850 CAPE GIRARDEAU, MO & IL, USA [37529] :
PRE 1850 OH & DE, USA [37565] : PRE 1850
LAWRENCE CO., OH, USA [37604]

HAMMONDS PRE 1870 WIGMORE, HEF, ENG
[37681]

HAMNETT 1830 LIVERPOOL, LAN, ENG [37751]

HAMON PRE 1800 SRK, CHI [38293] : 1860+
COFFEE CO., TN, USA [38323] : 1840+ ROANE
CO., WV, USA [38323]

HAMPSEY ALL IRL [36118]

HAMPSHIRE C1780 HASLEMERE, SRY, ENG [33918]
: EMMA 1840+ ENG [34630]

HAMPSON PRE 1851 LIVERPOOL, LAN, ENG
[34999] : 1830-1930 WIDNES, LAN, ENG [36983] :
1800+ WIGAN, LAN, ENG [37669] : C1840
SALFORD, LAN, ENG [38410]

HAMPTON 1850+ VIC, AUS [35035] : ALL GLS, ENG
[34837] : PRE 1853 ENG [35035] : PRE 1855 ESS,
ENG [35162] : C1825 FUNTINGDON, SSX, ENG
[35746] : WILLIAM 1902+ KETTERING, NTH,
ENG [36959] : LILY 1896-1903 LEICESTER &
KETTERING, LEI & NTH, ENG [36959] : WILLIAM
1890+ LYMINGTON, HAM, ENG [36959] : WM.
JAMES 1904+ UPPER NORWOOD, SRY, ENG
[36959] : HELEN 1900+ LEICESTER, LEI, ENG
[36959] : C1800 STANSTEAD, HRT, ENG [36978] :
ALL HAM, ENG [37658] : 1700-C1740S ROMSEY/N
BADDESLEY, HAM, ENG [38358] : WILLIAM
1871+ MARYLEBONE, LND, ENG & FRA [36959] :
PRE 1850 LOU, IRL [35953] : PRE 1862 CLARE,
DOW, IRL [36856] : ALL ULSTER, IRL [37154] :
ROBERT 1862+ CBY, NZ [36856] : PRE 1851
DUNDEE, MURROES & MONIFIETH, ANS, SCT
[33957] : PRE 1855 PERTH, PER, SCT [33957] :
1700+ LAURENCEKIRK, KCD, SCT [37485] : PRE
1850 ROSS CO., OH, USA [35290] : 1800-1900 OWEN
CO., KY, USA [36939] : 1840-1900 LOGAN, KY, USA
[38095] : 1850-1900 WARREN & BUTLER, KY, USA
[38095] : PRE 1810 KY, USA [38576]

HAMSING PRE 1880 HANNOVER, HAN, GER
[37529]

HANALA 1833 LEI, ENG [34305]

HANAUER PRE 1720 KESSWILL, TG, CH [34115]

HANBURY 1830S BRIERLEY HILL, STS, ENG [35099]

HANCHEN 1800S REPPERSDORF, SIL, GER [34367]

HANCKELL PRE 1801 SOUTHWARK, MDX, ENG
[34142]

HANCOCK 1831-1945 WINDSOR & SYDNEY, NSW,
AUS [34589] : 1800S GOULBURN, NSW, AUS [35009]
: ANN C1820 SYDNEY, NSW, AUS [35089] : C1870
WOODBURN, NSW, AUS [35515] : 1870+
MORUYA, NSW, AUS [35530] : C1818+ SYDNEY,
NSW, AUS [38208] : PRE 1840 BONAVISTA, NFD,
CAN [34096] : 1700+ SCOTLAND VILLAGE, WIL,
ENG [34121] : 1700+ S MOLTON & BISHOPS
NYMPTON, DEV, ENG [34188] : PRE 1890
BOURNEMOUTH, HAM, ENG [34252] : C1830
SKELMERSDALE, LAN, ENG [34329] : PRE 1830
EYAM & STONEY MIDDLETON, DBY, ENG
[34329] : ALL DBY, ENG [34329] : PRE 1910 ENG
[34657] : PRE 1866 CON, ENG [34711] : PRE 1850
STOKE DAMEREL, DEV, ENG [34742] : C1831
EATINGTON, WAR, ENG [34839] : 1870-1882
HURSLEY, HAM, ENG [34839] : 1859 ST AUSTELL,
CON, ENG [34844] : 1780+ PLYMOUTH, DEV,
ENG [34927] : 1841-1861 KIDSGROVE, STS, ENG
[35074] : PRE 1810 CON, ENG [35255] : C1780 NTH,
ENG [35387] : C1848 BRISTOL, ENG [35515] : FDK
CHILDS PRE 1837 LONDON, MDX, ENG [35530] :

PRE 1894 ST AUSTELL & LANIVET, CON, ENG
[36039] : 1800+ CALNE, WIL, ENG [36323] : 1700+
LONDON, ENG [36743] : C1820 ST AUSTELL, CON,
ENG [36806] : 1900-20 ST AUSTELL, CON, ENG
[36909] : C1700 OAKE, SOM, ENG [37053] : PRE 1790
LEONARD STANLEY, GLS, ENG [37146] : C1831
REDRUTH, CON, ENG [37148] : PRE 1900 STOKE
UPON TRENT, STS, ENG [37319] : 1700-1800 ST
MELLION, CON, ENG [37339] : PRE 1810
SHEFFIELD, YKS, ENG [37402] : 1800-1860
BRIGHTON, SSX, ENG [37705] : PRE 1860
PADDINGTON, MDX, ENG [37720] : 1770+
LONDON, ENG [37908] : 1700-1820 WORKSOP,
NTT, ENG [38084] : 1700-1800 SHEFFIELD, WRY,
ENG [38084] : 1803 TETBURY, GLS, ENG [38209] :
PRE 1820 TUNSTALL, STS, ENG [38248] : PRE 1800
MARWOOD & BARNSTAPLE, DEV, ENG [38376] :
1700+ BRADWORTHY, DEV, ENG [38446] : 1600-
1700 WOOLSTANTON, STS, ENG [38474] :
ROBERT 1818+ SRY, ENG & AUS [33840] : ALL
WILKES CO., NC, USA [37789] : ALL PATRICK
CO., VA, USA [37789] : THOMAS 1757-1805
BURLINGTON & SALEM CO., NJ, USA [38127] :
1650+ NEW LONDON, CT, USA [38241] : SUSIE
1866-1870 CRENSHAW CO., AL, USA [38340] :
WILLIAM C1817 GA, USA [38340] : ALL
WORLDWIDE [35875]

HANCOCKE 1600 HAWKESBURY, GLS, ENG [34466]

HANCON 1792+ HEREFORD, HEF, ENG [37886]

HANCORN THOMAS 1822+ CROSS INN
TURNASTONEVOWCHURCH, HEF, ENG [33819]

HANCORNE KATHERINE 1574+ LEDBURY, HEF,
ENG [33819] : PHILIP 1600+ GLASBURY, BRE,
WLS [33819]

HANCOX 1856-1990 DAIRY HILL, VIC, AUS [33885] :
PRE 1857 STS, ENG [33885] : 1760+ COVENTRY,
WAR, ENG [36827] : 1640-1780 FARMINGTON, CT,
USA [37783]

HAND C1900S+ BOURKE, NSW, AUS [38510] : PRE
1864 CALNE, WIL, ENG [34959] : 1806
SLAUGHERFORD & DEVIZES, WIL, ENG [35594] :
ALL NETTLETON, LIN, ENG [35949] : PRE 1700
AYLSHAM, NFK, ENG [36593] : 1800-1900
BRISTOL, GLS, ENG [37403] : 1790-1820
ALVERSTOKE, HAM, ENG [37403] : 1700-1900
WOTTON UNDER EDGE, GLS, ENG [37403] :
1680+ NJ, USA [36347] : 1600-1900 CT, USA [36689]

HANDBY 1800-1870 LONDON, ENG [34687]

HANDCOCK 1740S EXETER, DEV, ENG [35259] :
PRE 1840 TOCKINGTON & OLVESTON, GLS,
ENG [36082] : 1804+ WEXFORD, WEX, IRL [35223]
: ELIAS 1835-1858 STRADBALLY, LEX, IRL [35223]

HANDEBO 1830+ ARMIDALE, NSW, AUS [34599] :
ALL WEM, IRL & AUS [34599]

HANDFORD ALL MUMMULGUM, NSW, AUS
[35561] : 1700S STANTON BY DALE, DBY, ENG
[38478]

HANDLEY 1860 SYDNEY, NSW, AUS [35508] : 1860-
1900 GARSTON, LAN, ENG [35341] : 1800S
UNDERBARROW, WES & WRY, ENG [36868] :
PRE 1800 LEEK, STS, ENG [37722]

HANDS 1700+ STONELEIGH, WAR, ENG [36065]

HANDSTEIN C1800 LUX [38711]

HANDTE ALL KLEINBETTLINGEN, BAW, BRD
[38615]

HANEL 1700-1735 SHORTHAMPTON, OXF, ENG
[35186]

HANELY C1845 GREENDALE, NSW, AUS [37921]

HANEMAN 1830-1850 VERMILLION CO., IN, USA
[36450]

HANEMANN 1735 BLOMBERG, PYR, GER [38749]

HANES 1760-1780 COLUMBIA, PA, USA [36703]

HANEY 1700S CON, ENG [34920] : PRE 1820 DUBLIN & NEWTOWNBARRY, WEX, IRL [34137] : 1800+ BUTLER CO., PA, USA [37040] : 1850S CUMBERLAND CO., OH, USA [38087] : 1800-40 BEAVER, BEAVER CO., PA, USA [38087]

HANFORD 1550-1700 EALING, MDX, ENG [37077]

HANGEN 1800-1850 SPRENDLINGEN, RPF, BRD [38530]

HANGER 1776 DEAL, KEN, ENG [33929] : PRE 1860 NTH, ENG & AUS [36095]

HANGGI PRE 1800 SO, CH [38333]

HANHAM CHARLES G. 1820+ JSY, CHI [37165]

HANIFER PRE 1890 CASTLE BELLINGHAM, LOU, IRL [34441]

HANKEY PRE 1876 GISBURN, YKS, ENG [37242]

HANKIN 1780-1880 CAM & MDX, ENG [38021]

HANKINS C1760 WITNEY, OXF, ENG [37053] : JOHN 1800-1899 SRY, WOR & SSX, ENG [37321] : 1700S NBL, ENG [37857] : WILLIAM 1760-1821 BURGHILL, HEF, ENG [37886] : 1600-1800 DYMOCK, GLS, ENG [37886] : 1700+ NJ, USA [34350] : 1600+ LONG ISLAND, NY, USA [34350]

HANKS C1702 FARMINGTON, GLS, ENG [35259] : PRE 1910 MIDDLESBROUGH, NRY, ENG [36408] : PRE 1762 CT, USA [37037]

HANLAY (SEE HANLY) [38737]

HANLEY 1877+ ADELAIDE, SA, AUS [35731] : 1880+ CASINO, NSW, AUS [35842] : 1850S STANHOPE, NSW, AUS [35842] : 1850+ NEW ENGLAND, NSW, AUS [37944] : 1800S FRONTENAC, ONT, CAN [34353] : 1850 GODERICH, HURON, CAN [35609] : 1860 OSPREY, GREY, CAN [35609] : PRE 1860 LIM, IRL [34886] : 1830 LISBELLAW, FER, IRL [35609] : PRE 1850 SOLOHEAD, TIP, IRL [35842] : PRE 1830 GLIN, LIM, IRL [36325] : C1800 ROSCOMMON, ROS, IRL [37944] : 1855-1880 KEWEENAW CO., MI, USA [38010]

HANLON 1861+ GERALDTON, WA, AUS [37109] : 1840 MALLOW, COR, IRL [34844] : PRE 1860 KIK, IRL [35197] : C1885 ATHLONE, ROS, IRL [36307]

HANLY PRE 1800 SAL, ENG [37681] : 1800-1860 KILRUSH, CLA, IRL [38737] : JOSEPH 1870+ LIMA & OROYA, PERU [37415]

HANN PRE 1900 DOR, ENG [36122] : ALL KERZ, TRANSYLVANIA, RO [38519]

HANNA C1885-1950 MIAMI, MAN, CAN [34101] : 1800+ WELLINGTON CO., ONT, CAN [34215] : PRE 1800 MOG, IRL [34215] : 1700-1900 LDY, IRL [38035] : PRE 1900 FER, IRL [38226] : 1900+ NZ [38226] : PRE 1800 IRVINE, AYR, SCT [34112] : AGNES 1800+ AYR, SCT [34161] : 1910+ AYR, SCT [38226] : PRE 1820 JEFFERSON CO., OH, USA [36709] : 1915+ USA [38226]

HANNABAL 1790+ CLIPSTON, NTT, ENG [38494]

HANNABY PRE 1890 LONGTON, STS, ENG [34261]

HANNAFORD 1650+ HARBERTON & TOTNES, DEV, ENG [34970] : ALL NEWTON ABBOT, DEV, ENG [35438] : C1873-1900 KENTISH TOWN & LAMBETH, LND, ENG [36161]

HANNAH 1860S BALLARAT, VIC, AUS [35390] : 1890S RICHMOND, VIC, AUS [35390] : ALL NORWICH, NFK, ENG [35525] : 1812+ WHITEHAVEN, CUL, ENG [35921] : PRE 1800 DOW, IRL [35572] : 1841-1876 BALLYMENA, ANT, IRL [37891] : 1844-1876 BALLYLOUGH, ANT, IRL [37891] : PRE 1800 DOW, IRL [38057] : WILLIAM 1800+ AYR & KILMARNOCK, AYR, SCT [35033] : THOMAS 1863+ GLASGOW, LKS, SCT [35033] : 1850S DUMFRIES, DFS, SCT [35390] : PRE 1900 MOCHRUM, WIG, SCT [36497]

HANNAM PRE 1800 OTTLEY & FEWSTON, YKS, ENG [36247]

HANNAMAN 1750-1760 NEW YORK, NY, USA [36450] : 1830-1875 SHELBY CO., IL, USA [36450] : 1875-1900 SHELBY CO., IL, USA [36450] : 1820-1830 ROSS CO., OH, USA [36450] : 1800-1850 LIVINGSTON CO., IL, USA [36450] : 1850-1880 KNOX CO., IL, USA [36450] : 1820-1850 HAMILTON CO., IN, USA [36450] : 1770-1796 WOOD CO., WV, USA [36450] : 1830-1840 VERMILLION CO., IN, USA [36450] : 1800-1820 JACKSON CO., WV, USA [36450] : 1800-1820 MARION CO., OH, USA [36450] : 1763-1770 OTSEGO CO., NY, USA [36450] : PRE 1780 CHERRY VALLEY, NY, USA [38135] : PRE 1820 HARRISON CO., VA, USA [38135]

HANNAN 1858+ BENDIGO, VIC, AUS [34174] : 1853-1868 ST KILDA, VIC, AUS [38777] : C1857 MELBOURNE, VIC, AUS [38777] : PRE 1858 CLA, IRL [34174] : 1830-1855 TIP, IRL [37150] : PRE 1850 TIP, IRL [38777] : 1820-1950 AYR, SCT [38377]

HANNEN 1840+ NELSON, NZ [36841]

HANNES PRE 1700 CHIPPING CAMPDEN, GLS, ENG [36065]

HANNESSEN 1700+ NL [35338]

HANNEYSEE PRE 1840 BARKING, ESS, ENG [34576]

HANNIGAN THOMAS 1845-1880 KILMORE, VIC, AUS [33900]

HANNON 1750-1850 BALLYBRICKEN, LIM, IRL [34183] : PRE 1860 BALLYGRADDY, COR, IRL [35197]

HANNS ALL WHITCHURCH, DEV, ENG [33995]

HANNSEN MADTZ 1600-1680 TAARNBORG, SORO, DEN [37547]

HANRAHAN 1800+ BLACK SPRINGS, NSW, AUS [35205] : JOHN 1878+ BUNINYONG, VIC, AUS [37111] : PRE 1835 KILKENNY, KIK, IRL [34368] : PATRICK 1835+ KILMURRY & BALLARAT, CLA & VIC, IRL & AUS [37111]

HANRIEDER ALL WORLDWIDE [37483]

HANS 1860-1890S BRAIDWOOD, NSW, AUS [38324] : 1840-1860S MELBOURNE, VIC & NSW, AUS [38324]

HANSBIE C1833 EDGBASTON, WAR, ENG [35515]

HANSCH PRE 1883 KASSEL, HES, GER [36888]

HANSCHKE PRE 1860 RACKEL, UPPER LUSATIA, GER [34766]

HANSCOMB ALL WORLDWIDE [37857]

HANSDATTER 1800+ VIGERSLEY, DEN [35767] : ANNEK 1800-1860 LILLE NAUSTUED, SORO, DEN [37547]

HANSELL 1700S ISLE OF WIGHT, HAM, ENG [33802] : PRE 1860 PORTSMOUTH, HAM, ENG [38276]

HANSELMANN 1700-1885 MUNSTER CREGLINGEN, WUE, GER [37550] : 1840-1900S MANSON, NC, USA [37550]

HANSEN 1892+ BALMAIN, NSW, AUS [36600] : 1850S WARREN OXLEY, NSW, AUS [37949] : 1840 HUNTER VALLEY & ROCKHAMPTON, NSW & QLD, AUS [38008] : PRE 1900 DEN [34604] : PRE 1860 ALLER, DEN [35339] : LARS 1800-1860 LILLE NAESTUED, SORO, DEN [37547] : 1850S SJAELLAND IS., DEN [37562] : 1900+ OSTERMARIE, BHLM, DEN [37977] : 1848-1865 CARLS, DEN [38738] : PRE 1920 AARHUS, DEN & AUS [33959] : 1800S COPENHAGEN, VIJLE & ODENSE, DEN & GER [36706] : PRE 1854 SHO, GER [34590] : PRE 1900 SHO, GER [37105] : HANS HAUANE 1807+ BRUNLANES, TANUM, NOR [36810] : ANNE KATRINE 1863+ LARVIK, NOR [36810] : 1877 NOR [37493] : PRE 1890 BAY OF ISLANDS, NLD, NZ [36249] : 1904+ NEW YORK,

NY, USA [37977] : 1905+ PHILADELPHIA, PA,
USA [37977] : 1902+ PHILADELPHIA, PA, USA
[37977] : 1891+ PHILADELPHIA, PA, USA [37977]
HANSFORD PRE 1900 BRIDPORT, DOR, ENG
[34089] : PRE 1900 PORTLAND, SOM, ENG [34089] :
PRE 1760 ATHELHAMPTON & PUDDLETOWN,
DOR, ENG [37410]
HANSKE 1775-1830 GER [37150] : 1775-1830 NL [37150]
: 1775-1830 POL [37150] : ALL WORLDWIDE [33975]
HANSLIP ALL SFK, ENG [36179]
HANSLOW C1796+ AUS [34444] : ALL
WORLDWIDE [35068]
HANSON OSCAR C1875-1900 LAKE ALMA, SAS,
CAN [37440] : PRE 1800 YKS, ENG [33959] : 1800S
DORCHESTER, DOR, ENG [34483] : 1800S
WINCHESTER, HAM, ENG [34483] : 1800S
MAIDSTONE, KEN, ENG [34483] : 1880S
NOTTING HILL, MDX, ENG [34738] : 1856
OLDHAM, LAN, ENG [36679] : 1750+
OLDCOATES, NTT, ENG [36772] : C1850
ATTERCLIFFE & SHEFFIELD, WRY & YKS, ENG
[36772] : PRE 1912 LEEDS, WRY, ENG [37202] :
ISAAC 1820+ SALFORD, LAN, ENG [37748] :
1850+ BRADFORD, YKS, ENG [37997] : 1700-1900
SAL, ENG [38073] : PRE 1900 PT CHALMERS,
OTAGO, NZ [33998]
HANSORD 1700+ ENG [37653]
HANSSON 1780S LAPINJARVI & LILJENDAL,
USSIMAA, FIN [36966] : HANS 1883+ NEW YORK,
NY, USA [38550]
HANSTED 1400+ CHIDHAM, SSX, ENG [33989]
HANTON PRE 1851 DUNDEE & MURROES, ANS,
SCT [33957]
HANWAY PRE 1900 KILMACOW, WAT, IRL [36168]
HANWELL PRE 1840 TRING, HRT, ENG [35485] :
ALL ENG [37290] : 1845+ LND, ENG & AUS [35485]
HAPIMANA PRE 1884 ROTORUA, NZ [36748]
HAPKE PRE 1850 HOLTENSEN, HAN, GER [38577]
HAPP 1800+ RPF, GER [37534]
HAPPER PRE 1700 COLDINGHAM, BEW, SCT
[37463]
HAPPERLEY ALL AUS [35933]
HAPPOLD 1650-1950 WUE, GER [37609]
HARBACH ALL UK & GER [37717]
HARBART PRE 1800 CUL, ENG [37089] : PRE 1800
NBL, ENG [37089]
HARBERGER PRE 1852+ LUZERNO CO., USA &
AUS [35064]
HARBIDGE ALL WORLDWIDE [37717]
HARBINSON PRE 1900 GARVAGH, LDY, IRL [38481]
HARBISON 1750-1800 IRL [38115]
HARBONE PRE 1860 EVERSHAM, WOR, ENG
[36015]
HARBOR 1850+ TAS, AUS [34904]
HARBORDT PRE 1860 GER [36927] : PRE 1880 ST
LOUIS, MO, USA [36927]
HARBOTTEL 1300-1700 NBL, ENG [37081]
HARBOTTLE 1300-1700 NBL, ENG [37081]
HARBOUR 1769-1812 QUEBEC CITY, QUE, CAN
[34331] : 1700-1850 CHARD, SOM, ENG [37838] :
1800S+ MDX, ENG [37868] : C1887 WOOLWICH,
KEN, ENG [38485] : C1905 ROCHFORD, ESS, ENG
[38485] : PRE 1840 VA, ENG [37587] : 1840-1860
CHEROKEE CO., AL, USA [37587] : 1860-1905
FLOYD CO., GA, USA [37587]
HARBOURN PRE 1820 SOUTHAMPTON, HAM, ENG
[38700]
HARBOURNE MARY 1685-1750 IRL &, BARBADOS
[36103] : PRE 1870 STRATFORD ON AVON, WAR,
ENG [36015] : PRE 1860 EVERSHAM, WOR, ENG
[36015] : PRE 1829 SOLIHULL, WAR, ENG [37144] :
1880+ CARDIFF, GLA, WLS [36015]

HARBRIDGE 1907+ DAYLESFORD, VIC, AUS
[34787] : PRE 1900 WOR, ENG [36998] : ALL
WORLDWIDE [37717]
HARBURY PRE 1900 ENG [35901]
HARCOMBE 1800+ BATH, SOM, ENG [34550] :
C1600 BICKNOLLER, SOM, ENG [35612]
HARCOURT PRE 1842 SYDNEY, NSW, AUS [35344] :
PRE 1881 LEAMINGTON, WAR, ENG [34031] : PRE
1815 BIRMINGHAM, WAR, ENG [35344]
HARDCASTLE 1600-1850 WRY, ENG [35292] : PRE
1815 BISHOP THORNTON, YKS, ENG [36403] :
ALL LAN, ENG [36500] : 1770-1820 HARTWITH
CUM WINSLEY, YKS, ENG [38690] : ALL YKS,
ENG [38690] : PRE 1770 RIPLEY, YKS, ENG [38690]
: ALL WLS [36500]
HARDEE C1700-1900 SWANSEA, GLA, WLS [33855]
HARDEN 1825-1950 NSW, AUS [34535] : 1875+
SYDNEY, NSW, AUS [34786] : WILLIAM 1875+
NORTH MELBOURNE, VIC, AUS [34916] : 1750+
SHEPPY, KEN, ENG [35947] : 1742 HEADCORN,
KEN, ENG [36679] : 1650-1750 SALISBURY, WIL,
ENG [37232] : 1700-1800 HAM, ENG [37232] : PRE
1800 BECKLEY, SSX, ENG [37833] : MARY 1822-
1884 TATTNALL CO., GA, USA [38340]
HARDER 1650-1860 BARMSTEDT, SHO, GER [37021]
: 1840 WOODSTOCK, IL, USA [36907]
HARDERN 1700-1800 SHEFFIELD, ERY, ENG [37290]
HARDESTER 1850-1880 BATES CO., MO, USA [36968]
HARDIE 1880+ IPSWICH, QLD, AUS [33782] : 1875+
COLLINGWOOD, VIC, AUS [34017] : JOHN 1905
NELSON, BC, CAN [33929] : WILLIAM PRE 1905
AUCHTERARDER, PER, SCT [33929] : PRE 1850
LARBERT, STI, SCT [34097] : 1700-1800 ROX, SCT
[34153] : C1855 STIRLING, STI, SCT [34713] : PRE
1850S FERRY PORT ON CRAIG, FIF, SCT [35544] :
C1750 BO'NESS, WLN, SCT [36431] : PRE 1800 FIF,
SCT [36679] : 1800+ EDINBURGH, MLN, SCT
[37645] : PRE 1860 ABD, SCT [37708]
HARDIMAN 1800+ BATH, SOM, ENG [35370] : 1800S
GALWAY, GAL, IRL & AUS [36642]
HARDIN 1850-1870 TX, USA [38105] : 1815-1835 TN,
USA [38105] : 1685-1735 PRINCE WILLIAM CO.,
VA, USA [38120]
HARDING 1850+ GEELONG, VIC, AUS [35053] :
C1890+ BUNBURY, WA, AUS [35053] : 1850S
HEATHCOTE, VIC, AUS [35136] : 1850+
BELLARINE, VIC, AUS [38205] : 1800+
FRANKLIN, TAS, AUS [38288] : PRE 1879
SYDNEY, NSW, AUS [38585] : 1800+ DEV, ENG
[33948] : 1880+ LONDON, ENG [33979] : C1840
HEMINGTON, SOM, ENG [34016] : 1790+
PICKERING & ELLERBURN, NRY, ENG [34078] :
PRE 1760 LONDON, ENG [34258] : ALL
BRADWORTHY, DEV, ENG [34471] : 1815+ LND,
ENG [35053] : ISABELLA C1818 LONDON, ENG
[35365] : C1840 STEPNEY, LND, ENG [35502] : 1500-
1700 STS, ENG [36062] : PRE 1900 WOKING, SRY,
ENG [36142] : PRE 1800 PIRBRIGHT, SRY, ENG
[36260] : ALL SOUTH PETHERTON, SOM, ENG
[36382] : 1500-1800 DURSLEY, GLS, ENG [36438] :
1890+ WATFORD, HRT, ENG [37070] : 1800+
SHERINGTON, BKM, ENG [37070] : PRE 1800 STS,
ENG [37098] : PRE 1792 GUISBOROUGH, NRY,
ENG [37204] : PRE 1860 TIMSBURY, SOM, ENG
[37300] : GEORGE 1856 LAMBETH, LND, ENG
[37321] : PRE 1775 PILTON, DEV, ENG [37505] :
PRE 1860 KEYNSHAM, SOM, ENG [37729] : PRE
1800 GLS, ENG [37731] : 1700-1800 SEERGREEN,
BKM, ENG [37931] : 1850+ GLS, ENG [38059] : PRE
1900 HURSTBOURNE PRIORS, HAM, ENG [38205]
: PRE 1850 ROMFORD, ESS, ENG [38708] : 1800+
LONDON, ENG & NZ [34632] : 1870+ STODDARD

CO., MO, USA [35262] : 1890 PIKE CO., AR, USA [35262] : JOHN 1700 BRAINTREE, MA, USA [35273] : 1800-1900 OSWEGO, NY, USA [36438] : PRE 1725 MD, USA [37587] : 1800-1900 OH, USA [37599] : 1650+ LAGRANGE CO., IN & PA, USA & ENG [36970]

HARDING (SEE HARDEN) [35947]

HARDINGE 1905+ PAKA TANK, NSW, AUS [34011] : ALL DUBLIN, IRL [36881]

HARDINGHAM 1800S LONDON, ENG [37898]

HARDISTY 1585-1773 FEWTON, YKS, ENG [34793]

HARDLEY 1687+ WHITTLESEY, CAM, ENG [37317] : 1660S+ HARDLEY & MARCHES, NFK, ENG [37317]

HARDMAN 1700S BE, CH [37004] : PRE 1900 LIVERPOOL, LAN, ENG [36380] : PRE 1787 PRESTWICH & MIDDLETON, LAN, ENG [38248] : 1800+ MONTGOMERY CO., OH, USA [37004] : 1830+ ST JOSEPH CO., IN, USA [37004] : 1700S FREDERICK CO., MD, USA [37004] : 1790+ SHELBY CO., KY, USA [37004]

HARDSTAFF PRE 1850 BINGHAM, NTT, ENG [36403]

HARDT 1775 WANGENHAUSEN, GER [34957]

HARDWICH C1890 BRISTOL, ENG [37131]

HARDWICK 1540+ BOURNE, LIN, ENG [34577] : PRE 1850 SHERINGTON, BKM, ENG [34665] : 1839 LINCOLN, LIN, ENG [34940] : PRE 1750 PATTINGHAM, STS, ENG [36110] : PRE 1880 WRY, ENG [36886]

HARDWICKE 1540+ BOURNE, LIN, ENG [34577]

HARDY 1851+ DON, TAS, AUS [35238] : ALL VIC, AUS [35707] : PRE 1800 PORT PHILLIP DIST., VIC, AUS [35752] : 1890+ PORTLAND, VIC, AUS [35752] : JOSEPH 1890-1901 RYLSTONE, NSW, AUS [35787] : THOMAS 1841+ HUNTERS HILL, NSW, AUS [35787] : MARY G. 1870+ NSW, AUS [35787] : 1850S THALABA, NSW, AUS [37500] : 1800S ST HELIER, JSY, CHI [34309] : 1780+ ISLE OF WIGHT, HAM, ENG [33802] : 1700S CHILLINGTON, SOM, ENG [34172] : PRE 1780 ALSOP IN THE DALE, DBY, ENG [34311] : 1800S CAMBERWELL, LND, ENG [34483] : ALL LEI, ENG [34493] : 1560-1780 HOUGHAM, LIN, ENG [34672] : PRE 1855 JARROW, DUR, ENG [34713] : 1850+ MANCHESTER, LAN, ENG [35183] : PRE 1860 NEWARK ON TRENT, NTT, ENG [35238] : HARRIET 1800-1850 ST MARYLEBONE, LND, ENG [35494] : RICHARD 1802+ FINCHINGFIELD, ESS, ENG [35787] : SAMUEL 1808+ FINCHINGFIELD, ESS, ENG [35787] : MARY 1806+ FINCHINGFIELD, ESS, ENG [35787] : ROBERT 1815+ FINCHINGFIELD, ESS, ENG [35787] : SARAH 1802+ FINCHINGFIELD, ESS, ENG [35787] : PRE 1670 TAVISTOCK, DEV & CON, ENG [36594] : WILLIAM PRE 1838 NEWCASTLE ON TYNE, NBL, ENG [36629] : 1750-1800 HELPRINGHAM, LIN, ENG [36682] : C1850 CARLISLE, CUL, ENG [37112] : C1800 STOCKPORT, CHS, ENG [37112] : 1780S WITLEY, SRY, ENG [37309] : 1800-1880 FREISTON, LIN, ENG [37342] : PRE 1800 PUNCKNOWLE & BEAMINSTER, DOR, ENG [37410] : 1650-1850 FARLAM, CUL, ENG [37457] : PRE 1850 MID, NFK, ENG [37718] : ALL RUT, ENG [37738] : 1700S DUR, ENG [37857] : 1783+ BROADWEY, DOR, ENG [38204] : RICHARD 1650-1700 QUADRING, LIN, ENG [38453] : JANE PRE 1880 IDLE, YKS, ENG [38755] : PRE 1860 ARM, IRL [34571] : 1807-1854 BALLINASLOE & LAUGHREA, GAL, IRL [37187] : 1700+ AIRTH, STI, SCT [34977] : PRE 1760 KINTORE, ABD, SCT [37454]

HARE PRE 1851 ESS, ENG [34665] : 1650+ CURLAND, SOM, ENG [35558] : 1600+ SFK & ESS, ENG [36093] : ALL WRY, ENG [36126] : 1650+ CLOPHILL, BDF, ENG [37151] : 1750-1850 DOR, ENG [37609] : 1860+ CLOPHILL, BDF, ENG [37946] : PRE 1832+ CAV, IRL [37912] : PRE 1770 SANQUHAR, DFS, SCT [35406] : DAVID & MARIA 1778+ MANOR TWP., PA, USA [34247] : 1700S BUCKS CO., PA, USA [36926] : ALL WORLDWIDE [38329]

HARE (SEE HAIR) [36440]

HARFIELD C1740 WINCHESTER, HAM, ENG [37898] : C1740 WINCHESTER, HAM, ENG [37898]

HARFORD SUSANNAH 1850S+ EAST MELBOURNE, VIC, AUS [35876] : 1834-1856 LONDON, LND, ESS & SFK, ENG [35940] : 1700-1800 NY, USA [38342]

HARGER 1740+ GIGGLESWICK & SETTLE, YKS, ENG [37666]

HARGEST 1650+ LETTON & NORTON CANON, HEF, ENG [37625]

HARGRAVE PRE 1850 WALLACE TWP., ONT, CAN [34216] : CHARLES 1840+ LND, ENG [33875] : C1500 ENG [34395] : 1800-1870 LEEDS CITY, YKS, ENG [35017] : 1800+ WISBECH, CAM, ENG [36753] : 1650-1700 ALFORD, LIN, ENG [38453] : C1830 ARMAGH, ARM, IRL [35723] : ALL EDINBURGH, MLN, SCT [34619] : 1750-1800 SC, USA [38576] : 1790-1810 KY, USA [38576]

HARGRAVES 1600+ ADELAIDE, SA, AUS & ENG [36303] : PRE 1839 QUE, CAN [33906] : PRE 1820 LAN, ENG [35079]

HARGREAVE 1840+ WAIMEA SOUTH, NELSON, NZ [36806]

HARGREAVES 1856+ VIC, AUS [35136] : PRE 1856 LAN, ENG [35136] : PRE 1870 BLACKBURN, LAN, ENG [35514] : 1850+ GUIDE, LAN, ENG [35942] : 1810-1880 EVERTON, LAN, ENG [37525]

HARGROVE PRE 1770 KIRBY MALZEARD, WRY, ENG [36011] : ALL WHITEHAVEN, CUL, ENG [36822]

HARIE 1600+ ST KEVERNE, CON, ENG [34747]

HARISKY PRE 1829 RICHMOND, NSW, AUS [35419]

HARJU ALL SUDBURY, ONT, CAN [34987]

HARKER JAMES 1680+ MUKER, YKS, ENG [35462] : PRE 1890 SUNDERLAND, DUR, ENG [36121] : PRE 1800 GREENHOWHILL & PATELEY BRIDGE, NRY, ENG [36121] : 1865-1880 KINGSTON UPON HULL, ERY, ENG [36121] : PRE 1850 GRINTON, YKS, ENG [36704] : PRE 1850 MUKER, YKS, ENG [36704] : 1800S LAN, ENG [36710] : PRE 1770 GRINTON, NRY, ENG [36810] : CHARLES PRE 1809 SWINEFORD, MAY, IRL [36453] : PRE 1800 MAY & COR, IRL [36455]

HARKIN 1800+ BALLYGASTEL & LISDOONVARNA, CLA, IRL [33829] : PRE 1910 CRANFORD, DON, IRL [33902] : 1800+ SLIGO, IRL [37907]

HARKINS 1830-1990 CALEDON, ONT, CAN [35833] : PRE 1850 DON, IRL [35833] : 1842 GLASGOW, LKS, SCT [34582]

HARKINSON 1850S MELBOURNE, VIC, AUS [35958] : 1812+ PRIESTHILL, LKS, SCT [35958]

HARKISON 1850S MELBOURNE, VIC, AUS [35958] : 1812+ PRIESTHILL, LKS, SCT [35958]

HARKLESS ALL AYR, SCT [36599]

HARKNESS PRE 1870 HARTON, DUR & NBL, ENG [34869] : GEORGE PRE 1820 LAN & YKS, ENG [36066] : WHITESMITH PRE 1820 LAN & YKS, ENG [36066] : PRE 1800 YKS, ENG [36066] : PRE 1850 DEANSGATE, MANCHESTER, LAN, ENG [36066]

HARLAND 1650+ NRY, ENG [34181] : 1840S BURDON, DUR, ENG [35136] : 1835 NEW SHOREHAM, SSX, ENG [35716] : 1740-1800 WHITBY, NRY, ENG [35813] : 1800S THIXENDALE, ERY, ENG [37357] : PRE 1760 HACKNESS, NRY, ENG [37630] : PRE 1837 MUSSELBURGH, MLN, SCT [36513] : 1840+ COLUMBIANA CO., OH, USA [38018]

HARLE PRE 1790 NEWCASTLE, NBL, ENG [35212] : PRE 1852 NEWINGTON BUTTS, SRY, ENG [37876]

HARLECK 1855-1870 KEWEENAW CO., MI, USA [38010]

HARLEY ALL HALTON, BKM, ENG [35588] : PRE 1825 RUGELEY, STS, ENG [36866] : 1750+ LONGVILLE, NFK, ENG [38204] : ALL FALKIRK, STI, SCT [36846] : ALL UK [37421]

HARLING PRE 1840 DUR, ENG [37137]

HARLOW 1874 RENHOLD, BDF, ENG [34761] : PRE 1800 CHISLET, KEN, ENG [37602]

HARMAN 1775-1852 HAMBLEDEN, BKM, ENG [35815] : PRE 1820 BRIGHTON, SSX, ENG [36035] : PRE 1803 WILMINGTON, KEN, ENG [36866] : C1830 CLONES, MOG, IRL [35336]

HARMANNSEN 1795+ HORSBUELL, DEN [38671]

HARMER 1860+ CASTLEMAINE, VIC, AUS [36620] : 1811 NFK, ENG [35837] : PRE 1800 CARTMEL, LAN, ENG [36726] : ALL BRIGHTON, SSX, ENG [37445] : ALL GLS, ENG [37672] : ALL WORLDWIDE [37183]

HARMON 1806-1825 PA, USA [38101] : 1750-1990 WORCESTER, MD, USA [38136]

HARMOND C1835-45 DUDLEY, WOR, ENG [33828]

HARMS PRE 1900 MENARD, IL, USA [38173]

HARMSEN 1800 DORFNEBST, GER [37170] : 1800S GEL, NL [38358] : ANTONIUS 1872+ USA [38358]

HARNDEL 1650+ RI, USA [38015]

HARNDEN PRE 1712 KEN, ENG [38389]

HARNEP ALL WORLDWIDE [34312]

HARNETT 1800+ RICHIBUCTO & ROGERSVILLE, NB, CAN [36662] : C1800 DOVER, KEN, ENG [34559]

HARNEY 1800-1850 ONT, CAN [35614] : 1800-1850 QUE, CAN [35614] : PRE 1860 NELSON CO., NY, USA [37015] : ALL WORLDWIDE [38015]

HARNIP ALL WORLDWIDE [34312]

HARNISCH C1900 HALLE & SAALE, SAB, GER [36520] : C1860 THU, GER [36520]

HARNOP ALL WORLDWIDE [34312]

HAROD 1880+ NFK & CAM, ENG [37347]

HARP 1860-1890 PARRAMATTA, NSW, AUS [34788] : 1770+ CREWKERNE, SOM, ENG [34788] : 1650 PEASENHALL, SFK, ENG [37928]

HARPER 1854-1928 WAGGA WAGGA & SYDNEY, NSW, AUS [34463] : JOHN C1820 SYDNEY, NSW, AUS [35089] : GEORGE 1822+ PARRAMATTA, NSW, AUS [35484] : 1822 LOCHINVAR, NSW, AUS [35705] : 1815-1836 SYDNEY, NSW, AUS [38208] : 1840+ ONTARIO CO., ONT, CAN [34988] : PRE 1812 LITTLE GRANSDEN, CAM & HUN, ENG [33866] : C1860 EYE, HEF, ENG [34096] : 1910S EGREMONT, CHS, ENG [34096] : 1837 CLEWER, BRK, ENG [34305] : RACHEL& HENRY 1867 BARNSLEY, WRY, ENG [34369] : RACHEL& HENRY 1843 SCULCOATES, YKS, ENG [34369] : C1800+ BURNLEY, LAN & YKS, ENG [34451] : MOLLY 1900+ LIN, ENG [34499] : 1853+ TRURO, CON, ENG [34668] : 1800 MANCHESTER, LAN, ENG [34995] : 1870-1920 MAIDSTONE, KEN, ENG [35172] : C1816 ST AGNES, CON, ENG [35438] : WILLIAM 1810-1842 BOLTON, LAN, ENG [35484] : WILLIAM 1759+ RYLSTONE & HETTONS, YKS, ENG [35484] : JONATHAN 1823+ BOLTON, LAN,

ENG [35484] : 1780+ LONDON, ENG [35929] : PRE 1851 YORK & RIPON, YKS, ENG [36039] : PRE 1800 STS & WOR, ENG [36379] : 1750+ SUTTON MADDOCK, SAL, ENG [36488] : 1800-1900 WOLVERHAMPTON, STS, ENG [36495] : ALL WOLVERHAMPTON, STS, ENG [36537] : C1870 BIRMINGHAM, WAR, ENG [36649] : 1800+ ENG [36662] : SOLOMON 1800-25 CON, ENG [36678] : 1840-62 WOR, ENG [36759] : C1830-40 ISLINGTON, LND, ENG [37552] : PRE 1910 BATTERSEA, LND, ENG [37871] : 1800S WOLVERTON, SAL, ENG [37898] : PRE 1814 WOLVERHAMPTON, ESS, ENG [38208] : 1734 ARKSEY, WRY, ENG [38469] : 1700-1900 KINGSTON UPON HULL, YKS, ENG [38745] : C1840 TAMNEYMORE, DRY, IRL [34395] : C1850+ TYR, IRL [36838] : PRE 1720 LIMAVADY, DRY, IRL [37528] : 1800-1900 SKIRTS OF URNEY, TYR & NSW, IRL & AUS [35422] : 1860+ WAIKOUAITI, OTAGO, NZ [36871] : 1830+ LKS, SCT [34526] : JOHN 1815-1918 TRAQUAIR, PEE, SCT [37499] : WILLIAM C1815 GIRTHON, KKD, SCT [37499] : MATTHEW PRE 1800 NC, USA [33757] : 1860-1870 RICHLAND CO., WI, USA [36444] : 1720-1790 PA, USA [37527] : 1742-54 MIDDLETOWN & WINDSOR, CT, USA [37528] : 1800-65 SALEM CONNEAUT, ASHTABULA CO., OH, USA [37528] : 1771-1800 HARPERSFIELD, NY, USA [37528] : 1865-1940 CLINTON CO., MI, USA [37528] : 1724-1740 BOSTON, MA, USA [37528] : 1754-1771 CHERRY VALLEY, NY, USA [37528] : 1830-1870 GREENE CO., OH, USA [38154] : 1860-1990 WARREN CO., IL, USA [38154] : 1700-1850 ROCKBRIDGE CO., VA, USA [38154] : PRE 1800 ST KITTS, W.INDIES [35929]

HARPHAM PRE 1820 BURGH LE MARSH, LIN, ENG [34311]

HARPUR 1800-1900 WINDSOR & SYDNEY, NSW, AUS & ENG [34632] : C1830 LIVERPOOL, ENG [38488]

HARRAD 1812+ BURTON ON TRENT, STS, ENG [37487]

HARRAN ALL DURHAM, ENG & CAN [38410]

HARRELL PRE 1840 ENG [36755] : PRE 1800 NORWICH, NFK, ENG [37103] : ABEL 1854-1869 CALHOUN CO., IL, USA [35329]

HARRER 1856 EBELSBERG, OES [37582]

HARREWELL 1800S MAIDSTONE, KEN, ENG [34816]

HARRIES 1760+ OISTE, HAN, GER [35865] : 1700-1800 ST DOGWELLS, PEM, WLS [34552] : 1800+ DYFED, CMN, WLS [35296] : PRE 1800 ABERGWILLI, CMN, WLS [36432] : ALL PEM, WLS [36500]

HARRIGADDY 1750-1800 MAY, IRL [35581]

HARRIGAN ALL PEEL CO., ONT, CAN [35833]

HARRIMAN 1860-1880 BLUE EARTH CO., MN, USA [33760] : 1700+ MA, NH & CT, USA [35137]

HARRINGTON C1857 MELBOURNE & BENDIGO, VIC, AUS [34971] : C1880 COLLINGWOOD, VIC, AUS [35014] : 1830-1880 ATW, BEL [37203] : 1825 HARBOUR GRACE, NFD, CAN [38243] : PRE 1800 CARDINGTON, SAL, ENG [34861] : PRE 1600 ESS, ENG [35642] : 1740+ BOOTLE & EGREMONT, CUL, ENG [37073] : 1800+ LONDON, ENG & IRL [38175] : 1840S FEDAMORE, LIM, IRL [33967] : 1840 IRL [36579] : 1850S VAN BUREN CO., MI, USA [36319] : PRE 1850 BENNINGTON, VT, USA [37018] : 1663+ MA, USA [37592] : 1855-1885 KEWEENAW CO., MI, USA [38010] : 1780-1897 CHATHAM, ALEXANDER & ASHE CO., NC, USA [38315] : 1800S OH, USA [38369] : 1850+ MO & MT, USA & IRL [38050]

HARRIOT 1805+ AUCKLAND, DUR, ENG [35706]

HARRIP 1800+ FOWLMERE, CAM, ENG [35554]

HARRIS PRE 1840 SYDNEY, NSW, AUS [34442] :
1861+ BALLARAT, VIC, AUS [34595] : PRE 1843
TAS, AUS [34696] : JOHN 1820S HOBART, TAS,
AUS [34698] : 1870+ LAUNCESTON, TAS, AUS
[34770] : HENRY 1829-1850 HOBART, TAS, AUS
[34844] : DANIEL 1800-1900 NOWRA, NSW, AUS
[34871] : GEORGE 1879-1921 TRURO & KAPUNDA,
SA, AUS [34881] : WILLIAM PRE 1880 ARMIDALE,
NSW, AUS [34902] : DAISY ALL JACKSON, QLD,
AUS [35122] : PRE 1900 ADELAIDE, SA, AUS
[35339] : 1800S TAS, AUS [35531] : 1860+
PINJARRA, WA, AUS [35533] : 1883+
MELBOURNE, VIC, AUS [35746] : GEORGE 1870+
BOURKE, NSW, AUS [35848] : GEORGE C1853
MUDGEE, NSW, AUS [35848] : GEORGE 1860S
DUBBO, NSW, AUS [35848] : 1850S AVOCA, VIC,
AUS [35866] : TED 1920+ BLUE MOUNTAINS,
NSW, AUS [36252] : 1889+ COLLINGWOOD, VIC,
AUS [36279] : 1873+ JUNG, NHILL &
BLEAKHOUSE, VIC, AUS [36622] : 1850+ OUSE,
TAS & NSW, AUS & NZ [36850] : 1875+
MUSKOKA, ONT, CAN [34080] : 1850+
MIDDLESEX, ONT, CAN [34080] : 1770-1850
SOUTHLEIGH & WITNEY, OXF, ENG [33861] :
1841-1865 ST GERMANS, CON, ENG [33865] : PRE
1864 CHATHAM, KEN, ENG [33914] : 1860+
SHREWSBURY, SAL, ENG [33923] : 1700-1800S
BARNSTAPLE, DEV, ENG [33958] : THOMAS
C1803 OWSTON, LIN, ENG [33992] : GEORGE
1787+ GRAVESEND, KEN, ENG [34019] :
WILLIAM 1777+ GRAVESEND, KEN, ENG [34019]
: 1750+ EVESHAM, WOR, ENG [34080] : 1750-1900
SRY, ENG [34135] : PRE 1750 BURRINGTON, DEV,
ENG [34214] : PRE 1836 OLVESTON, GLS, ENG
[34281] : 1800-1850 LAWHITTON, CON, ENG [34337]
: 1800-1850 THROWLEY, KEN, ENG [34337] :
1750+ LITTLE SAXHAM & HOLTON, SFK, ENG
[34416] : ALL DEV, ENG [34471] : PRE 1860 HRT,
ENG [34571] : C1790 CLERKENWELL, LND, ENG
[34579] : PRE 1892 ST ALBANS & LUTON, BDF,
ENG [34757] : 1892+ ST ALBANS & LUTON, BDF,
ENG [34757] : 1700+ BUCKFASTLEIGH, DEV,
ENG [34760] : PRE 1861 CHERITON FITZPAINE,
DEV, ENG [34778] : PRE 1900 SOM, ENG [34848] :
PRE 1900 SOM, ENG [34861] : DANIEL 1750-1850
NEWCASTLE UNDER LYME, STS, ENG [34871] :
PRE 1853 HAGGERSTONE WEST, MDX, ENG
[34909] : C1840 IOW, HAM, ENG [34944] : PRE 1850
BRACKNELL, BRK, ENG [34958] : 1600+ SSX,
ENG [34980] : 1750+ CON, ENG [35060] : ALL
ILLOGAN, CON, ENG [35063] : SARAH 1820
LONDON, MDX, ENG [35067] : C1790 ST ERME,
CON, ENG [35076] : C1865+ OVERBURY, WOR,
ENG [35099] : 1714+ MORETON CORBET, SAL,
ENG [35126] : PRE 1860 BRIGHTON, SSX, ENG
[35128] : 1830S PLYMOUTH, DEV, ENG [35136] :
1815-1845 NEWPORT, IOW, ENG [35196] : 1700S
CAMBRIDGE, CAM, ENG [35238] : C1800
SHERBORNE ST JOHN, HAM, ENG [35247] :
1600+ ST JUST IN ROSELAND, CON, ENG [35306]
: 1600+ GERRANS, CON, ENG [35306] : 1600+
MEVAGISSEY, CON, ENG [35306] : 1600+ ST
ANTHONY IN ROSELAND, CON, ENG [35306] :
PRE 1870 ESS, ENG [35359] : C1846 MARSTON,
BDF, ENG [35478] : PRE 1860 BEDWORTH, WAR,
ENG [35533] : 1810-1850 RINGWOOD, HAM, ENG
[35621] : 1700-1850 EVESHAM, WOR, ENG [35621] :
PRE 1883 ETON & WINDSOR, BRK, ENG [35746] :
PRE 1830 SANDOWN, IOW, ENG [35770] : C1770-
1850 DEV, ENG [35791] : GEORGE 1810+

LIVERPOOL, LAN, ENG [35848] : PRE 1850
TRURO, CON, ENG [35866] : 1750-1900
BIRMINGHAM, WAR, ENG [36057] : PRE 1800
ULLEBY, LIN, ENG [36059] : 1750+ WHITE
LACKINGTON, SOM, ENG [36195] : 1840+
BUSHEY, HRT, ENG [36252] : 1816+
TEDDINGTON, MDX, ENG [36252] : 1840+
WATFORD, HRT, ENG [36252] : 1840+ BUSHEY
HEATH, HRT, ENG [36252] : 1750+
TEDDINGTON, MDX, ENG [36252] : 1870S
SOMERSAL HERBERT, DBY, ENG [36301] : PRE
1840 EARDISLEY, HEF, ENG [36432] : ELIZABETH
S. PRE 1880 ST EWE, CREED, CON, ENG [36575] :
PRE 1860 DEV, ENG [36755] : 1800S LONDON,
ENG [36858] : 1800-1900 HEREFORD, HEF, ENG
[36879] : PRE 1820 HAMPNETT, GLS, ENG [36889] :
C1780 COGGESHALL, ESS, ENG [37053] : 1795
KENWYN, CON, ENG [37186] : C1850
HARTLEBURY, WOR, ENG [37209] : 1680
GOUDHURST, KEN, ENG [37215] : 1840+
HAWKHURST, KEN, ENG [37215] : 1650+
ALDERMASTON & READING, BRK, ENG [37216]
: PRE 1800 MARDEN, KEN, ENG [37228] : 1700-
1800 TROWBRIDGE, WIL, ENG [37232] : 1640-1750
RODE, SOM, ENG [37232] : 1790+
HERSTMONCEUX, SSX, ENG [37301] : PRE 1750
MEVAGISSEY, CON, ENG [37319] : PRE 1900
SHELTON, STS, ENG [37319] : PRE 1850 CHARD &
ILMINSTER, SOM, ENG [37325] : 1775-1825
TEDDINGTON, MDX, ENG [37345] : C1900 EAST
PECKHAM, KEN, ENG [37359] : 1840+
ENGLEFIELD, BRK, ENG [37384] : MARY 1860+
STONEHOUSE, GLS, ENG [37444] : 1800S
MARLOW & LITTLE MARLOW, BKM, ENG
[37652] : 1750-1850 CHICHESTER, SSX, ENG [37765]
: PRE 1733 WESTMINSTER, LND, ENG [37909] :
1803 TETBURY, GLS, ENG [38209] : PRE 1700
PLYMOUTH, DEV, ENG [38745] : ALL ENG & AUS
[35579] : 1850+ BUSHEY, HRT, ENG & AUS [37345]
: 1790+ LONDON, ENG & AUS [38204] : 1800+
LONDON, ENG & NZ [36266] : PRE 1822
NEWBRIDGE, WIC, IRL [35854] : PRE 1800
LENAMORE, LDY, IRL [37450] : PRE 1900
KILMALLOCK, LIM, IRL [37807] : 1780-1822 WEX,
IRL [38404] : PRE 1810 ST VIGEANS, ANS, SCT
[36497] : PRE 1800 PERTH, PER, SCT [36653] : PRE
1820 ARBROATH, ANS, SCT [369E3] : 1600S-1700S
CHARLESTOWN, MA, USA [35291] : 1700-1990
ESSEX CO., CA & NJ, USA [35313] : C1700 PA, USA
[36319] : 1720-1850 WRENTHAM & HARDWICK,
MA, USA [36335] : NICHOLAS 1630-1720
PROVIDENCE, RI, USA [36335] : 1880+ WAPELLO
CO., IA, USA [36582] : WILLIAM 1790-1844
BUNCOMBE, NC, USA [36728] : 1830-1850
CHATOOGA, GA, USA [36735] : 1826 ELBERT, GA,
USA [36735] : 1850-1900 COOSA, AL, USA [36735] :
LYDIA 1887-1955 QUEENSBURRY, NY, USA
[36902] : BENJAMIN ALL NY, USA [36902] : JOHN
J. 1863-1924 NY, USA [36902] : 1850-1920 CO, USA
[37807] : HAMILTON 1800-1830 VA, USA [37815] :
1840-1855 CALLAWAY CO., MO, USA [37815] :
WILLIAM 1825-1875 PATRICK CO., VA, USA
[38044] : 1778-1800 SURRY CO., NC, USA [38107] :
1744-1780 ALBEMARLE CO., VA, USA [38107] :
1855+ ALLAMAKEE, IA, USA [38111] : 1810-1855
NOBLE, OH, USA [38111] : ALL WALWORTH CO.,
WI, USA [38231] : 1800+ DARKE CO., OH, USA
[38587] : 1664+ BLOCK ISLAND, RI & NY, USA &
CAN [34988] : 1500+ NEW LONDON, CT & MA,
USA & ENG [36970] : HENRY 1800+ BARBADOS,
W.INDIES [35558] : ELIJAH ALL CAERLEON,
MON, WLS [34475] : 1853 ABERGAVENNY, MON,

WLS [34595] : 1725+ NEWPORT, WLS [36956] : 1830-1860 MERTHYR TYDFIL, GLA, WLS [37343]

HARRISON 1870 GYMPIE, QLD, AUS [33783] : 1823+ OATLANDS, TAS, AUS [34280] : C1855 MELBOURNE, VIC, AUS [34936] : 1800S COLO, NSW, AUS [35159] : JANE (JONES) 1820+ SYDNEY, NSW, AUS [35816] : 1870+ GRETA, NSW, AUS [36632] : C1800 SYDNEY, NSW, AUS [37500] : 1700-1900S DERBY, DBY, ENG [33958] : PRE 1880 HANDSWORTH, STS, ENG [33993] : WM. JOHN ALL SOUTHAMPTON, HAM, ENG [34065] : PRE 1840 POCKLINGTON, NRY, ENG [34127] : PRE 1900 ESS, ENG [34280] : PRE 1850 WOR & SAL, ENG [34318] : ALL DUR, ENG [34617] : JOHN ALL DUR, ENG [34667] : 1780+ DEWSBURY, WRY, ENG [34915] : WILLIAM 1820+ BATLEY, WRY, ENG [34915] : C1848 PADDINGTON, LND, ENG [34963] : C1810 SUTTON, LIN, ENG [34963] : 1800 RIDLINGTON, RUT, ENG [35024] : 1860-1900 SHEFFIELD, YKS, ENG [35341] : 1830+ RUNCORN, CHS, ENG [35341] : 1800-1880 PRESTON, LAN, ENG [35473] : C1800-90 ROTHERHAM & SHEFFIELD, WRY, ENG [35550] : C1850 MDX, ENG [35761] : C1873 LONDON, ENG [35761] : JANE (JONES) PRE 1820 NOTTINGHAM, NTT, ENG [35816] : 1680+ MARKSE BY SEA, YKS, ENG [35908] : 1850+ DOVER, KEN, ENG [35969] : 1800+ LAN, ENG [36042] : 1750-1800 LIN, ENG [36084] : PRE 1855 NORWICH, NFK, ENG [36086] : 1870+ SNEINTON & NOTTINGHAM, NTT, ENG [36105] : C1700-1900 GREAT YARMOUTH, NFK, ENG [36128] : PRE 1815 BIRMINGHAM, WAR, ENG [36177] : PRE 1841 WIGAN, LAN, ENG [36187] : 1795-1875 CLAYTON & BRADFORD, WRY, ENG [36391] : 1812-1833 SHELF, WRY, ENG [36391] : 1831-91 GREAT DRIFFIELD, ERY, ENG [36412] : 1860-1920 WOLVERHAMPTON, STS, ENG [36495] : 1700-1860 SEDGLEY, STS, ENG [36495] : 1890-1930 LEEDS, YKS, ENG [36495] : ALL SEDGLEY, STS, ENG [36518] : PRE 1900 BYKER, NBL, ENG [36707] : 1790+ GRIMSBY, LIN, ENG [36846] : ALL WOODCHESTER, GLS, ENG [36996] : 1675+ WAKEFIELD, YKS, ENG [37172] : PRE 1850 KIRKHAM, LAN, ENG [37318] : PRE 1850 YKS, ENG [37379] : C1810 BROMPTON, YKS, ENG [37536] : PRE 1865 HINDLEY, LAN, ENG [37573] : 1750-1850 KIRKOSWALD, CUL, ENG [37654] : PRE 1900 ILKESTON, DBY, ENG [37692] : PRE 1850 WAR, ENG [37750] : JOHN 1750-1900 YORK, YKS, ENG [37779] : 1820+ WORCESTER, WOR, ENG [37889] : BENJAMIN 1800-1850 PRESTWICH, LAN, ENG [37934] : BENJAMIN 1800-1850 MANCHESTER, LAN, ENG [37934] : ELIZ. 1800+ WESTON LONGVILLE, NFK, ENG [38204] : 1750-1810 KENTMERE & KENDAL, WES, ENG [38248] : PRE 1950 BURTON IN LONSDALE, YKS, ENG [38464] : DAVID 1818-1872 EAST DEREHAM & BOWRAL, NFK & NSW, ENG & AUS [36341] : PRE 1850 ENG & IRL [38772] : PRE 1848 GREYTOWN, SOM, ENG & NZ [36255] : 1858-1900 HUTTON CRANSWICK, ERY, ENG & USA [38574] : PRE 1900 ROS, IRL [39448] : 1870+ BELFAST, ANT, DOW & ARM, IRL [35636] : PATRICK C1909 SPENSER AVE NW, DUB, IRL [38302] : JOHN C1909 NORTHWALL, DUB, IRL [38302] : 1700+ DUNDEE, FIF, SCT [34789] : PRE 1792 MUTHILL, PER, SCT [37575] : WILLIAM PRE 1821 UK [35473] : 1865 IL & MO, USA [35279] : THOMAS 1700S SMITHTOWN, LONG ISLAND, NY, USA [36321] : JESSE 1800S EL PASO, MCLEAN CO., IL, USA [36321] : EZEKIAL 1751-1834 HARRISONBURG, VA, USA [36321] : ISREAL 1600S OYSTER BAY, LONG ISLAND, NY, USA [36321] : 1700 NJ, USA [36730] : 1820-1872 GALLIA CO., OH, USA [37029] : ANDREW PRE 1752 ESSEX CO., VA, USA [37580] : LAWRENCE PRE 1770 ORANGE CO., VA, USA [37580] : BENJAMIN PRE 1770 FAYETTE CO., PA, USA [37580] : PRE 1800 SOUTHAMPTON CO., VA, USA [37587] : 1850+ JOHNSTOWN, FULTON CO., USA [37889] : 1850+ GLOVERSVILLE, FULTON CO., USA [37889] : JOSEPH 1795 CANAJOHARIE TWP., NY, USA [38142] : C1800-1890S BERKELEY & MORGAN, WV, USA [38348] : ALL WORLDWIDE [35875]

HARROD PRE 1900 WINGATE, DUR, ENG [36056] : ALL CAM & NFK, ENG [36363] : PRE 1800 BUNTINGFORD, HRT, ENG [36588] : 1800+ KEN & SRY, ENG [36871]

HARROLD PRE 1840 WEST BROMWICH, STS, ENG [34904] : CHRISTMAS 1816+ NFK, ENG & AUS [33840] : PRE 1830 NC, USA [38196]

HARRON C1700+ DRUMCHORY, DON, IRL [34246]

HARROP 1840+ BENDIGO, VIC, AUS [35715] : PRE 1820 KNIPTON, LEI, ENG [33771] : PRE 1830 CHS, ENG [34590] : 1800+ OLDHAM, LAN, ENG [35715] : MARTHA 1808 DUKINFIELD OLD CHAPEL, CHS, ENG [36311] : 1880+ AUCKLAND, NZ [36818]

HARROW 1800+ ABERDEEN, SCT [33947] : 1880-90 WAPELLO CO., IA, USA [36582]

HARROWER ALL FIF, PER & STI, SCT [34861]

HARROWFIELD ALL WORLDWIDE [37995]

HARRY 1750-1800 REDRUTH, CON, ENG [34697] : C1782 MULLION, CON, ENG [34752] : ALL REDRUTH, CON, ENG [35082] : PRE 1820 LELANT, CON, ENG [35709] : 1500-1990 MORVAH & ST JUST, CON, ENG [37680] : 1800-1920 FULHAM & MARYLEBONE, MDX, ENG [37877] : ALL LELANT, CON, ENG [38402] : C1700 PA, USA [36319]

HARRYMAN 1800 BIRMINGHAM, WAR, ENG [34309]

HARRYSE C1600 ST GLUVIUS, CON, ENG [34258]

HARSANT ALL NORWICH, NFK, ENG & NZ [34604]

HARSE PRE 1850 GLS, ENG [35413] : PRE 1850 SOM, ENG [35413]

HARSHBARGER 1750-1830 VA, USA [34410] : 1840S CARROLL CO., IN & IL, USA [36546]

HARSLETT C1821 LONDON, ENG [35714]

HARSTON 1897+ GUNNEDAH, NSW, AUS [35254]

HARSTROM 1870+ NY, USA [38552]

HARSUNT 1400+ HARWICH, ESS, ENG [33989]

HART C1862 MT MERCER, VIC, AUS [35478] : 1850+ SIMCOE CO., ONT, CAN [34465] : PRE 1850 PEI, CAN [36700] : PRE 1870+ BRIGHTON, ONT, CAN [37518] : 1800S LEEDS & GRENVILLE CO., ONT, CAN [38414] : PRE 1844 LOUGHBOROUGH, LEI, ENG [34133] : PRE 1860 FARNHAM, SRY, ENG [34428] : PRE 1830 GOOLE, YKS, ENG [34465] : LYDIA 1814 BATH, SOM, ENG [34539] : PRE 1800 WHITTLESEY, CAM, ENG [34884] : WILLIAM 1700+ LND, ENG [34943] : 1800S ST MARYLEBONE, MDX, ENG [34953] : 1790+ HILL CROOME, HEF & WOR, ENG [34953] : 1815+ KEN, ENG [35156] : 1750+ DYMOCK, GLS, ENG [35248] : 1700+ THORNBURY, GLS, ENG [35248] : 1820+ RAVENSTHORPE, NTH, ENG [35387] : PRE 1788 STOWUPLAND & NEWTON, SFK, ENG [35459] : C1806 ST THOMAS, OXF, ENG [35478] : 1780+ FOLKESTONE, KEN, ENG [35560] : 1835-1840 NEWINGTON, SRY, ENG [35865] : JAMES 1830S+ OXFORD, OXF, ENG [35876] : THOMAS 1800S+ OXFORD, OXF, ENG [35876] : PRE 1770 MUNDON & MALDON, ESS, ENG [35902] : ALL THORNHAM, NFK, ENG [35949] : 1741+

BIRMINGHAM, WAR, ENG [35965] : 1700-1800
SFK, ENG [36213] : GEORGE C1798
SHOREDITCH, LND, ENG [36619] : JOHN JOSEPH
1888 OLD TRAFFORD, LAN, ENG [36635] : 1780-
1850 SEIGHFORD, STS, ENG [36746] : ALL
BOWBRICKHILL, BKM, ENG [36789] : GEORGE
C1830 LONDON, MDX, ENG [37239] : 1810
WALMER, KEN, ENG [37520] : 1872-1900
EDMONTON, LND, ENG [36627] : PRE 1870
WARE, HRT, ENG [37627] : 1600S ROMNEY
MARSH AREA, KEN, ENG [37714] : PRE 1846
CHESTER LE STREET, DUR, ENG [37856] : 1700
RETTENDON, ESS, ENG [37928] : PRE 1837 FEN
DITTON, CAM, ENG [37978] : PRE 1860
ANDOVERSFORD, GLS, ENG [38435] : PRE 1850
LEX, IRL [34262] : C1800 GLENFARNE, LET, IRL
[35350] : 1830 SLIGO, SLI, IRL [35372] : 1840+
NELSON, NZ [35058] : 1860+ PALMERSTON
NORTH, MWT, NZ [36746] : 1820+ PATHHEAD,
MLN, SCT [33795] : 1745-1800 KIRKINNER, WIG,
SCT [34695] : LEVI 1818 NY, USA [35629] : SAMUEL
1783-1863 BUCKS CO., PA, USA [36729] : JOSEPH
1745-1797 BUCKS CO., PA, USA [36729] : 1650+
TOMKINS CO., NY, USA [36970] : 1832
OKMULGEE, OK, USA [38012] : 1750 LANCASTER,
PA, USA [38115] : 1650-1800 HARTFORD, CT, USA
[38344] : 1800-1950 TRUMBULL CO., OH, USA
[38344] : 1840+ LLANELLI, CMN, WLS [35248]
HARTE PRE 1820 WIX, ESS, ENG [36478] :
MARGARET PRE 1850+ EMLY, TIP, IRL [38567] :
WILLIAM C1830+ EMLY, TIP, IRL [38567]
HARTEL 1826 ZWICKAU, PSA, GER [35251] : PRE
1950 CHICAGO, IL, USA [37808]
HARTEN ALL WORLDWIDE [34421]
HARTESS 1600+ SFK & NFK, ENG [36203]
HARTFIEL 1880+ FASSIFERN, QLD, AUS [33782]
HARTIGAN 1855+ MELBOURNE, VIC, AUS [37982] :
1800+ CLOONEY, CLA, IRL [35352] : 1832+
ENNISKILLEN, FER, IRL [37982] : PRE 1869 CLA,
IRL [37991] : 1869+ MALTBY, CLA, IRL & AUS
[37111]
HARTIL-LAW PRE 1860 TIPTON, STS, ENG [34904]
HARTIN PRE 1900 DRUMACHOSE, LDY, IRL [35181]
HARTING PRE 1800 OXF, ENG [36183]
HARTINGER 1830-1900 CINCINNATI, OH, USA
[38149]
HARTKOPF 1800-1880 BRD [37822] : 1800-1880 DDR
[37822] : 1800-1880 GER [37822] : 1860-1960
WILLIAMSON CO., IL, USA [37822]
HARTLAND C1840S LANE COVE, NSW, AUS [37309]
HARTLEY BEN 1873 CARLTON, VIC, AUS [34011] :
C1840 TAS, AUS [34678] : 1825-1875
PETERBOROUGH, ONT, CAN [34348] : RICHARD
1700S-1800S MANCHESTER & FAILSWORTH,
LAN, ENG [34181] : PRE 1760 ILLINGWORTH &
OVENDEN, WRY, ENG [34397] : PRE 1896 NFK,
ENG [34406] : PRE 1896 SFK, ENG [34406] : PRE
1759 ESKDALE, CUL, ENG [34452] : ALL
BARROWFORD, LAN, ENG [34564] : PRE 1790
EGREMONT & BECKERMET, CUL, ENG [35085] :
JOHN 1821+ EGREMONT & BECKERMET, CUL,
ENG [35085] : C1809 ROCHDALE, LAN, ENG
[35560] : PRE 1810 WALTON, LEI, ENG [35745] :
PRE 1850 GUISELEY & BAILDON, WRY, ENG
[36159] : 1850+ KEN, ENG [36574] : JAMES PRE
1870 HASLINGDEN, LAN, ENG [37414] : 1710+
WYCOLLAR, COLNE & KEIGHLEY, YKS, ENG
[37581] : 1790+ LONDON, ENG [37699] : 1890+
GARSTANG & BOLTON, LAN, ENG [37710] :
1840+ HELLFIELD & MASONGILL, WRY, ENG
[37710] : PRE 1840 LAN, ENG [37739] : C1770
COLNE, LAN, ENG [37859] : 1706+ ST JOHN

BECKERMET, CUL, ENG [38067] : 1915-1940
ALFREDTON, WAIRARAPA, NZ [35889] : PRE 1915
MASTERTON, WAIRARAPA, NZ [35889]
HARTLY PRE 1900 DYSART, KIK, IRL [38300]
HARTMAN 1853 ERNESTOWN, ONT, CAN [36680] :
1831 ODESSA, ONT, CAN [36680] : JOHANNES
1725-1753 SWR HESSE CASSEL, WUE, DDR [37023]
: 1860+ LONDON, ENG [34230] : 1800-1860
SCHWERIN, GER [38199] : JOHANNES 1753-1783
PHILADELPHIA AREA, PA, USA [37023] : PRE
1900 PIKE CO., IL & MO, USA & CS [38532]
HARTMANN 1840+ CRESWICK, VIC, AUS [34421] :
1860+ LEEDS, WRY, ENG [36034] : C1860
BLACKBURN, LAN, ENG [37873] : PRE 1855 BAD,
GER [34421] : C1757 BUSENWURTH, SHO, GER
[38671] : 1850+ WAIUKU, NZ [33963] : 1770+ LW,
POL [38650] : PRE 1860 SCT [36034] : TOBIAS 1770-
1840 YORKTOWN YORK, PA, USA [38197] : 1843-
1860 SPRINGFIELD CLARK, OH, USA [38197] :
C1900 NEW YORK, NY, USA [38671]
HARTNELL 1770+ PITMINSTER, SOM, ENG [35951]
: 1750-1850 DOR, ENG [36962]
HARTNESS 1878+ SOUTH MELBOURNE, VIC, AUS
[34798]
HARTNETT 1880+ NORTHCOTE, VIC, AUS [35538] :
PRE 1850 MIDLETON, COR, IRL [35522] : 1840S+
CHARLESTON, SC, USA [35522]
HARTNOLL PRE 1700 BRAUNTON, DEV, ENG
[34931]
HARTRICK ALL HOF, BAV, GER [38176]
HARTSHORN C1780 WITNEY, OXF, ENG [37053] :
PRE 1900 LONDON, MDX, ENG [37749]
HARTSHORNE PRE 1861 AYLESBURY, BKM, ENG
[35599] : 1750-1830 DARLASTON, STS, ENG [37632]
HARTT JOB 1750+ VT & ONT, USA & CAN [38241]
HARTWELL ELIZABETH C1777 ST MARYS, WAR,
ENG [36782] : 1800+ CHIPPING CAMPDEN, GLS,
ENG [37838] : PRE 1850 BRADFORD CO., PA &
NY, USA [38309] : 1850+ SMITHFIELD, PA, IA &
NE, USA [38309]
HARTWICK 1820-50 JEFFERSON, NY, USA [38054] :
1840 MONROE, NY, USA [38054] : 1700-90
ALBANY, NY, USA [38054] : 1850+ ROCK, WI,
USA [38054]
HARTWIG C1840 HES, BRD & AUS [35079]
HARTWRIGHT 1840-1900 TIBBERTON, WOR, ENG
[34677]
HARTY 1850+ MALMSBURY & MOOROOPNA, VIC,
AUS [33793] : PRE 1850 DUNDALK, LOU, IRL
[33846]
HARTZ 1820 GER [33910]
HARVEY PRE 1920 TAS & VIC, AUS [33798] : 1925-
1942 TOOWOOMBA, QLD, AUS [33811] : 1860+
INVERLEIGH, VIC, AUS [33915] : 1838+
NEWCASTLE, NSW, AUS [34020] : 1850+ NSW,
AUS [34424] : PRE 1834 BOTHWELL, TAS, AUS
[34576] : 1844+ MACCLESFIELD, SA, AUS [34685] :
ALL VIC, AUS [34907] : 1869+ EAGLEHAWK, VIC,
AUS [35207] : 1870+ TEMPLARS, SA, AUS [35411] :
C1890 MONARO, NSW, AUS [35434] : 1900S
SIDNEY, NSW, AUS [36708] : 1800-1900
CHATEAUGUAY, QUE, CAN [36729] : C1840S
SHROPHAM, NFK, ENG [33915] : ROBERT PRE
1863 BRIGHTON, SSX, ENG [34247] : ANN 1801+
NOTTINGHAM & FARNSFIELD, NTT, ENG
[34247] : PRE 1860 ESS, ENG [34424] : PRE 1740 ST
EWE, CON, ENG [34644] : PRE 1824
WESTERFIELD, SFK, ENG [34696] : CATHERINE
1700+ LONDON, ENG [34701] : C1840 ENG [34907]
: 1700-1800 CON, ENG [35023] : PRE 1870 PAUL,
CON, ENG [35207] : C1842 ESS, ENG [35251] : 1850S
DEV, ENG [35377] : PRE 1840 PEASMARSH, SSX,

ENG [35396] : PRE 1780 ESS, ENG [35642] : 1800+
LND & MDX, ENG [35760] : JAMES 1810+
TAUNTON, SOM, ENG [35822] : PRE 1750 CLENT,
WOR, ENG [35919] : PRE 1900 HORSLEY, GLS,
ENG [35949] : PRE 1800 KINGSBRIDGE, DEV,
ENG [36155] : PRE 1700 ASKHAM, NTT, ENG
[36202] : 1870S BURTON ON TRENT, STS, ENG
[36301] : PRE 1800 WAR, ENG [36429] : ALL
ASHBURNHAM, SSX, ENG [36501] : 1800-1900 LEI,
ENG [36531] : 1800S LONDON, ENG [36708] : ALL
DBY, ENG [36861] : C1780 HASSINGHAM, NFK,
ENG [36978] : PRE 1800 STS, ENG [37098] : PRE
1800 READING, BRK, ENG [37179] : 1750+
GERMANSWEEK, DEV, ENG [37224] : 1750+
BROADHEMPSTON, DEV, ENG [37231] : THOMAS
C1800 LND, ENG [37239] : 1700S GREAT
HALLINGBURY, ESS, ENG [37250] : 1850S ST
EVAL, CON, ENG [37343] : 1800+ EAST LONDON,
LND, ENG [37373] : 1835 WYMONDHAM, NFK,
ENG [37388] : 1835 EAST DEREHAM, NFK, ENG
[37388] : 1800+ ASHWELLTHORPE, NFK, ENG
[37699] : PRE 1750 GRADE & ST KEVERNE, CON,
ENG [37913] : 1810+ GLS, ENG [38257] : PRE 1850
DORCHESTER, GLS, ENG [38257] : MARIA C1840
FRODSHAM, CHS, ENG [38410] : PRE 1920
PLYMOUTH, DEV, ENG [38594] : 1820+ STS, ENG
& AUS [34703] : PRE 1865 GRAHAMSTON, STI,
SCT [34937] : C1750 ABERDEEN, ABD, SCT [35747] :
PRE 1900 RUTHERGLEN & GLASGOW, LKS, SCT
[35991] : C1800+ AYR, AYR, SCT & NZ [36258] :
THOMAS 1730 BUCKS, PA, USA [36447] :
CYNTHIA 1805+ GA, USA [37590] : 1820-1860
CAIRO, NY & MA, USA [37591]

HARVIE 1829S SHAWVILLE, QUE, CAN [36695] :
PRE 1820 MILE END, MDX, ENG [35098] : ALIAS
COLLINS 1834 STIRLING, STI, SCT [35409] : PRE
1900 RUTHERGLEN & GLASGOW, LKS, SCT
[35991] : C1800+ AYR, AYR, SCT [36258] : 1800S
CAMBUSLANG, LKS, SCT [36695]

HARVISON ALL LIN, ENG [37929]

HARWEG ALL WORLDWIDE [38709]

HARWELL LOUDEN 1810 MALBGORD CO., SC,
USA [36330] : JOHN 1871 LAFAYETTE CO., MS,
USA [36330] : LOUDEN 1840-1850 MONTGOMERY
CO., AL, USA [36330] : JOHN 1875 BUTLER CO.,
AL, USA [36330] : JOHN T. 1900-1930 BUTLER CO.,
AL, USA [36330]

HARWICK ALL WORLDWIDE [38709]

HARWIDEL 1800 RHEINSHEIM, BAW, BRD [37028]

HARWIG ALL WORLDWIDE [38709]

HARWIGH ALL WORLDWIDE [38709]

HARWIN 1750-1900 MULBARTON &
SAXLINGHAM, NFK, ENG [37477]

HARWOOD JULIA PRE 1887 BRUNY ISLAND, TAS,
AUS [36634] : ALL HANNS & PERTH, WA, AUS &
ENG [34561] : 1750-1860S STEPNEY, LND, ENG
[33986] : PRE 1855 WOOD GREEN, MDX, ENG
[33997] : PRE 1769 NFK, ENG [34222] : JAMES
C1830 BULBY & HAWTHORPE, LIN, ENG [34302] :
1700-1800 LONDON, ENG [34552] : PRE 1812
BOLTON, LAN, ENG [35020] : PRE 1775 LONDON,
ENG [35238] : 1776+ CAMBRIDGE, CAM, ENG
[35238] : 1818+ ARUNDEL, SSX, ENG [35459] :
CATHERINE 1560+ SHOREDITCH, LND, ENG
[36944] : C1850 BRIDPORT, DOR, ENG [37264] :
1750-1850 SCARBOROUGH, ERY, ENG [37352] :
1700-1812 BANBURY, OXF, ENG [37487] : ALL
YAPTON, SSX, ENG [37637]

HASE ALL NFK, ENG [34493]

HASELDINE 1800S DUR, ENG [35377]

HASELGROVE PRE 1800 RUSTLINGTON, SSX,
ENG [34112] : ALL WORLDWIDE [36100]

HASELWOOD C1790-1830 MDX, ENG [34727]

HASHER 1850 HUDDERSFIELD, YKS, ENG [34305]

HASKELL ALL NY & MA, USA [37502]

HASKETT HENRY PRE 1800 BORIS O KANE, TIP,
IRL [33956] : ANNIE 1852+ BORIS O KANE, TIP,
IRL [33956] : PRE 1900 BELFAST, ANT, IRL [33985] :
PRE 1900 BORIS O KANE, TIP, IRL [33985]

HASKINS 1800+ BITTON & BRISTOL, GLS, ENG
[33764] : ALL OLDLAND & BRISTOL, GLS, ENG
[36163]

HASLAM WILLIAM 1860S STH MELBOURNE, VIC,
AUS [35876] : C1830 PARRAMATTA, NSW, AUS
[36370]

HASLAND C1800-40 ECCLESFIELD, WRY, ENG
[35550]

HASLEGROVE 1744+ TWINEHAM, SSX, ENG
[36212]

HASLETT 1750-1900 MONTREAL, QUE, CAN [34401]
: 1800+ LONDON, ENG [36004] : 1900-1920
BELFAST, ANT, IRL [34401] : 1750-1790 IRL [34408] :
1800S PITTSBURGH, PA, USA [34353]

HASLIP PRE 1846 SOUTHWARK, LND, ENG [35574]

HASSALL 1500-1780 AUDLEM, CHS, ENG [36025] :
1730-1900 TARVIN, CHS, ENG [36025] : 1500-1850
SAL & CHS, ENG [36062] : PRE 1799 STOKE
GOLDING, LEI, ENG [36528] : 1730+ COVENTRY,
WAR & NSW, ENG & AUS [36827]

HASSAN 1840+ MARYHILL, ONT, CAN [34056] :
PRE 1840 IRL [34056]

HASSARD 1720-1800 YKS, ENG [36392]

HASSEL PRE 1860 MAG, DDR [37551] : C1860 MAG,
DDR [37551]

HASSELBACH C1744 RONKEL (NASSAU), FRG
[38698]

HASSELL PRE 1850 KEN, ENG [34593]

HASSELMAN 1800+ STRASBOURG, ALS, FRA
[36304]

HASSETT 1838 CLARE CASTLE, CLA, IRL [36367]

HASSLINGHAUS PRE 1800 SUDERWYCK, NRW,
BRD [38646]

HASSLINGHUIS PRE 1850 ROTTERDAM, ZUH, NL
[38646]

HASSWELL PRE 1799 STOKE GOLDING, LEI, ENG
[36528]

HASTE PRE 1830 STUTTON, SFK, ENG [35406] :
C1730-1750 OVER WYERSDALE, LAN, ENG [36198]

HASTED PRE 1750 SSX, ENG [36172] : PRE 1750
HAM, ENG [36172] : 1650-1800 LONDON, ENG
[36172]

HASTIE PRE 1893 AUGATHELLA, QLD, AUS [34587]
: 1820-1880 LND, ENG [35402] : 1845+ LKS & AYR,
SCT [34373] : ALEX PRE 1850 DUNDEE, ANS, SCT
[35838] : ALL LINLITHGOW, WLN, SCT [37480] :
PRE 1704 PRESTONPANS, ELN, SCT [37852] : PRE
1783 NEWBATTLE, MLN, SCT [37852]

HASTILOW PRE 1830 TAMWORTH, STS, ENG
[34213] : C1800-1900 LONDON, ENG [34213]

HASTINGS 1800+ HOBART, TAS, AUS [34571] :
1800+ WELLINGTON CO., ONT, CAN [34215] :
1800+ LONDON, ENG [34571] : ALL
PORTSMOUTH, HAM, ENG [36409] : PRE 1839
WHITEHAVEN, WLS & CUL, ENG [37840] : 1870+
COR, IRL [35358] : PRE 1856 CLA, IRL [35824] :
C1816-1869 CLOUGHY & PORTAFERRY, DOW,
IRL [38402] : 1883-1935 AUCK, NZ [34680] : 1883-
1935 OTAGO & CHCH, NZ [34680] : ALL LARBERT,
STI, SCT [36846] : ALL GLASGOW, LKS, SCT
[36846]

HASTINGS-PAINE ALL WORLDWIDE [36201]

HASTY PRE 1835 KILMARNOCK, AYR, SCT [34014]

HASWELL ALL LONDON, ENG [34820] : 1700+
STOKE GOLDING, LEI, ENG [35972] : PRE 1835

GUISBOROUGH, NRY, ENG **[37204]** : 1740S
PRESTEIGN, RAD, WLS **[37869]**

HASZ 1860 GER &, WORLDWIDE **[37511]**

HATCH 1857+ SMITHFIELD & YOUNG, NSW, AUS
[34595] : 1880+ CANOBOLAS & MANILLA, NSW,
AUS **[34595]** : 1800+ BRIGHTON, VIC, AUS **[34961]**
: 1760+ CHALFONT ST PETER, BKM, ENG **[37122]**
: 1759-1847 ELTON AND STOCKPORT, CHS, ENG
[37581] : 1790-1850 LONDON, ENG **[38199]** : 1789-
1853 THORNTON LE MEERS & WOODSTOCK,
CHS & ONT, ENG & CAN **[37581]** : C1800 DUBLIN,
IRL **[38072]** : 1700-1860 VT, USA **[33753]** : 1500-1880
IL, USA **[37538]** : 1500-1880 MA, USA **[37538]**

HATCHALL 1870+ JEFFERSON CO., CO, USA
[38310]

HATCHARD 1850+ LND & MDX, ENG **[36430]**

HATCHER 1700+ CROSCOMBE, SOM, ENG **[37328]** :
1700+ STURMINSTER NEWTON, DOR, ENG
[37328] : 1890+ PILTON, SOM, ENG **[37328]** : 1820-
1850 MUSCOGEE CO., GA, USA **[38770]**

HATCLIFFE 1550-1650 GREAT STEEPING, LIN,
ENG **[38453]**

HATER MORRIS 1828 GEORGE ST, SYDNEY, NSW,
AUS **[36311]**

HATFIELD PRE 1783 ELIZABETH, NJ, USA **[34494]**

HATHAWAY 1860+ NSW, AUS **[35498]** : ALL
CHESTERTON, OXF, ENG **[34110]** : 1595-1638
KINGCOTE, GLS, ENG **[38741]** : 1809-1901 ST
CLAIR, MI, USA **[36910]** : 1740-1742 BERKLEY,
MA, USA **[38099]** : 1740-1742 DARTMOUTH, MA,
USA **[38099]** : PRE 1861 PLYMOUTH CO., MA, USA
[38223] : PRE 1830 STARKEY, NY, USA **[38335]** :
1840-1870 OH, USA **[38373]**

HATHERLEY PRE 1850 SHEFFIELD, YKS, ENG
[34485] : ALL ENG **[34485]**

HATHWAY 1600 HORTON, GLS, ENG **[34466]**

HATKILL 1390-1710 SLAIDBURN, WRY, ENG **[38251]**

HATKISS 1780+ SEDGLEY & BILSTON, STS, ENG
[36987]

HATLEY 1840 GREENWICH, KEN, ENG **[37690]** :
1860S LEWISTON, IL & VA, USA **[38223]**

HATRICK 1800+ CARNLOUGH, ANT, IRL **[34008]** :
PRE 1900 PAISLEY, RFW, SCT **[34060]**

HATT PRE 1800 BRK, ENG **[34504]** : ALL STANFORD
IN THE VALE, BRK, ENG **[36076]** : 1700-1800
LAMBOURN & COMPTON, BRK, ENG **[36175]** :
ALL FYVIE, ABD, SCT **[37972]**

HATTAM PRE 1880 REDRUTH, CON, ENG **[33850]**

HATTERSLEY 1785-1850 KEIGHLEY, WRY, ENG
[34827] : C1800 HARTLEY BROOK, YKS, ENG
[35920]

HATTON 1850-1900 KILMORE AREA, VIC, AUS
[33836] : 1750-1850 KEN, ENG **[33836]** : PRE 1850
OLD SWINFORD, WOR, ENG **[34314]** : 1850+
NAZEING, ESS, ENG **[34374]** : 1770+ WHITWICK,
LEI, ENG **[34374]** : 1770+ LONDON, ENG **[35013]** :
1800+ MELBOURNE, DBY, ENG **[35851]** : PRE
1900 DBY, ENG **[37377]** : PRE 1770
WINTERBORNE WHITCHURCH, DOR, ENG
[37410] : PRE 1770 PUDDLETOWN, DOR, ENG
[37410] : 1650+ LONDON, ENG **[37586]** : PRE 1800
DOVER, KEN, ENG **[37652]**

HATTWELL 1865+ WIMMERA, VIC, AUS **[36622]**

HATWELL 1800+ MURCOTT & ASTON, OXF, ENG
[36329]

HATWOOD PRE 1750 BKM, BDF & NTH, ENG
[35701]

HATZELMAN 1800+ STRASBOURG, ALS, FRA
[36304]

HAUCH PRE 1850 OBERMIESAU, BAY, BRD **[35635]**

HAUCK 1800+ HES, GER **[36900]** : 1850-1950 NEW
ORLEANS, LA, USA **[37583]**

HAUESERMAN PRE 1850 EGLISWEIL, AG, CH
[35635]

HAUG 1680-1750 EGLOSHEIM, WUE, GER **[38599]**

HAUGE ALL MADISON & SONDNOR, MN, USA &
NOR **[37440]**

HAUGHTON 1820-1840 BISHOPSGATE &
BLACKFRIARS, LND, ENG **[34738]** : C1750
TUNSTALL, LAN, ENG **[36955]** : MARY 1869
COVENTRY, WAR, ENG **[37444]** : C1837 DUBLIN,
IRL **[33845]** : C1848-1858 DUBLIN, IRL **[35133]** :
C1817 OFF, IRL **[35133]** : C1875-1895 WANGANUI,
NZ **[35133]**

HAUGRUD GULLEK 1879+ BO, TELEMARK, NOR
& CAN **[34481]**

HAUGUE 1700+ WADWORTH, ERY, ENG **[37050]**

HAULBROOK ALL WORLDWIDE **[35326]**

HAULDAY MARY ANN ALL MDX, ENG **[33961]**

HAULTAIN ALL WORLDWIDE **[33886]**

HAUNIT 1800-1900 BERLIN, GER **[38603]**

HAUSBERG 1885+ BRISTOL, GLS, ENG **[35974]**

HAUSBURG 1885+ BRISTOL, GLS, ENG **[35974]**

HAUSCHILD ALL POM, GER **[38630]**

HAUSCHILDT ALL ALTONA, SHO, GER & AUS
[33919]

HAUSER 1870+ MELBOURNE, VIC, AUS **[34178]** :
1600-1800 WUE, GER **[37015]**

HAUSMANN 1800S GER & NZ **[36809]**

HAUSS 1750-1840 ALBERSWEILER, RPF, GER
[38374]

HAUT 1756 MONONGALIA, WV, USA **[37008]**

HAUTON ALL SFK, ENG **[37629]**

HAUTSCHKE C1838 COTTBUS, COT, DDR **[37144]**

HAUVER 1750-1990 NY, USA & CAN **[37486]**

HAVELANGE 1800+ HEURE, NMR, BEL **[35004]**

HAVER 1750+ COLUMBIA CO., NY, USA **[37591]**

HAVERKAMP C1840 CASTROP, WEF, GER **[38023]**

HAVERS ALL WORLDWIDE **[34399]**

HAVILAND 1820+ ST JOHN & FREDERICTON, NB,
CAN **[34056]** : 1890+ ONT, CAN **[38323]** : PRE 1820
DRY, IRL **[34056]** : 1900-1930 LONG BEACH, CA,
USA **[37597]**

HAVOCK C1763 CHEDDINGTON, BKM, ENG
[35095] : ALL WORLDWIDE **[35095]**

HAW 1781 SWABY, LIN, ENG **[34474]** : PRE 1698
BELCHFORD, LIN, ENG **[37318]**

HAWARD PRE 1700 ESS, ENG **[35642]** : 1850+ MON,
WLS **[34459]**

HAWCHET C1625 ENG **[34395]**

HAWCROFT PRE 1850 SHEFFIELD, YKS, ENG
[34031]

HAWES C1880 GLEN INNES, NSW & QLD, AUS
[34971] : 1850+ UPPER CAN, ONT, CAN **[34409]** :
1750-1850 EDDLESBOROUGH, BKM, ENG **[34316]** :
1800+ STOW UPLAND, SFK, ENG **[34640]** : 1800+
KENNINGHALL, NFK, ENG **[34640]** : 1780+
STEBBING, ESS, ENG **[34970]** : 1790+
HAVERHILL, SFK, ENG **[36558]** : 1813 BURNHAM
MARKET, NFK, ENG **[37841]** : PRE 1881 CLA, IRL
[34886] : JOHN 1880-1900 TELLER CO., CO, USA
[37212]

HAWFORD ALL MEOLE, LAN & CHS, ENG **[38043]**

HAWGATE 1700+ WAR, ENG **[34416]**

HAWICH ALL WORLDWIDE **[38709]**

HAWICK PRE 1850 NORTHMAVEN, SHI, SCT **[35022]**

HAWK 1700+ HELSTON, CON, ENG **[35712]** : ALL
WORLDWIDE **[36965]**

HAWKE 1870+ MARYBOROUGH, VIC, AUS **[35135]** :
C1875-1918 BRUCE CO. & RICHMOND HILL, ONT
& SAS, CAN **[36693]** : PRE 1837 TRURO, CON, ENG
[33821] : 1730-1750 WADEBRIDGE, CON, ENG
[36536] : 1800S SOUTH PETHERWIN, CON, ENG
[37122]

HAWKEN 1800S WIL & SOM, ENG [34472] : 1780 ST
BREWARD, CON, ENG [34950] : 1852 HELSTON &
LANTEGLOS, CON, ENG [38761]

HAWKENS 1850+ WALKERTON, ONT, CAN [34051]

HAWKER PRE 1865 HIGHHAM, SOM, ENG [34962] :
ALL DOR, ENG [36500] : C1890+
BOURNEMOUTH, HAM, ENG [36955]

HAWKES 1800S SEYMOUR, VIC, AUS [33849] : 1860S
NSW, AUS [33849] : 1930+ MANLY, NSW, AUS
[35573] : 1854+ ADELAIDE, SA, AUS [37987] : 1800S
ASTON, WAR, ENG [34110] : C1820 WOORE, STS,
ENG [35203] : 1600+ GLS & SAL, ENG [36058] :
1600+ BIRMINGHAM, WAR, WOR & STS, ENG
[36058] : 1800+ THAMES DITTON, SRY, ENG
[36245] : PRE 1837 PERSHORE, WOR, ENG [37282] :
PRE 1837 HARVINGTON, WOR, ENG [37282] : PRE
1837 BUCKLAND, GLS, ENG [37282] : 1700-1900
ELY, CAM, ENG [37738] : ALL ESS, ENG [37741] :
PRE 1880 BETHNAL GREEN & SHOREDITCH,
MDX, ENG [37987] : ALL WORLDWIDE [35797]

HAWKESFORD PRE 1700 WEDNESFIELD &
WOLVERHAMPTON, STS, ENG [36110] : C1820-
1850 BIRMINGHAM, WAR, ENG [36874]

HAWKESMORE 1600+ EAST DRAYTON, NTT,
ENG [34408]

HAWKEY C1800 EAST NEWLYN, CON, ENG [35076]
: 1800S KENWYN, CON, ENG [35076] : 1750+
KENWYN, CON, ENG [35475]

HAWKING PRE 1850 INWARDLEIGH, DEV, ENG
[38418]

HAWKINGS PRE 1780 BUCKFASTLEIGH, DEV,
ENG [35157]

HAWKINS 1840+ CLUNES & MOORPOOPNA, VIC,
AUS [33793] : C1870 BORDERTOWN, SA, AUS
[35091] : 1822+ BATHURST, NSW, AUS [35203] :
1815+ BRISBANE WATERS, NSW, AUS [35240] :
1840+ FORBES, NSW, AUS [35240] : JOHN 1878+
BULLI & LLANDILO, NSW, AUS [35394] : 1800-1880
HAWKESBURY & SPRING HILL, NSW, AUS
[35396] : 1848 WOLLOMBI, NSW, AUS [35407] : 1820-
1850 ORANGE & BATHURST, NSW, AUS [38568] :
ALL FOGO, NFD, CAN [35264] : 1777 WOOL, DOR,
ENG [33967] : 1750+ BRISTOL, SOM, ENG [34100] :
1750-1850 GREAT BEDWYN, WIL, ENG [34687] :
PRE 1850 PADWORTH, BRK, ENG [34719] : C1766-
1777 DERBY, DBY, ENG [35037] : PRE 1857 CON,
ENG [35091] : 1800+ BRK, ENG [35115] : ALL
MOUNTSORREL, LEI, ENG [35177] : 1830+
WINCHESTER, HAM, ENG [35341] : 1781+ SSX,
ENG [35407] : ALL KINGSTON, SOM & DEV, ENG
[35580] : 1660+ GREAT BEDWYN, WIL, ENG
[35587] : 1890 STEPNEY & LONDON, ENG [35716] :
MARY-ANNE 1830S LONDON, ENG [35876] :
C1885 SADDLEWORTH, LAN & YKS, ENG [36028]
: PRE 1840 BARKING & LONDON, ESS, ENG
[36178] : 1800+ WESTMINSTER, LND, ENG [36232]
: 1700+ SEIGHFORD, STS, ENG [36512] : PRE 1850
ASHCOTT, SOM, ENG [36676] : 1750+ NEWBURY
& SPEEN, BRK, ENG [36727] : 1850-1950 BRK, ENG
[37348] : 1850-1990 BKM, ENG [37348] : 1850-1950
SRY, ENG [37348] : 1700-1900 BRISTOL, GLS, ENG
[37829] : PRE 1856 ENG [37885] : 1650-1800
WONSTON, HAM, ENG [38003] : 1800-1890
BANBURY, OXF, ENG [38373] : PRE 1735 WEST
COKER, SOM, ENG [38483] : PRE 1860
HEADCORN, KEN, ENG [38755] : 1860+
ENNISCORTHY, WEX, IRL [33923] : 1788+ CLA,
IRL [34068] : PRE 1867 DUBLIN, IRL [34570] : PRE
1830 WIC, IRL [38457] : 1800S BAGENALSTOWN,
CAR, IRL [38498] : 1850+ ENNIS, CLA, IRL & AUS
[38204] : PRE 1800 RUTHERFORD CO., NC, USA
[36570] : PRE 1810 UNION CO., SC, USA [36570] :

PRE 1750 ORANGE OR AMHERST CO., VA, USA
[36927] : CALVIN 1820-1830S TIOGA CO., NY, USA
[37001] : ALL LAWRENCE, KS, USA [38605]

HAWKS 1600+ BIRMINGHAM, WAR, WOR & STS,
ENG [36058] : ALL SOUTH SHIELDS, DUR, ENG
[37950]

HAWKSHAW ALL IRL [38754]

HAWKSWORTH ALL DONCASTER & BENTLEY,
YKS, ENG [34789] : ALL LEI, ENG [35177]

HAWKSWWORTH 1750-1800 S YKS, ENG [36084]

HAWLEY 1650-1950 ONT, CAN [38128] : 1700+
PAULERSPURY, NTH, ENG [34747] : PRE 1825
STS, ENG [37098] : PRE 1852 BURNSALL, YKS,
ENG [38085] : 1500-1650 ENG [38128] : 1570-1990
FAIRFIELD CO., CT, MA & NY, USA [37523]

HAWORTH 1858+ MERINO & MILDURA, VIC, AUS
[37892] : 1800S EDGWORTH, LAN, ENG [33934] :
C1840 LEEDS, WRY, ENG [37378] : 1800-1920
LIVERPOOL, LAN, ENG [37870] : PRE 1858
HASLINGDEN, LAN, ENG [37892] : 1780-1825
ROCHDALE, LAN, ENG [38259] : RICHARD PRE
1820 CHESTER & LIVERPOOL, LAN, ENG [38540] :
JAMES PRE 1800 CHESTER & LIVERPOOL, LAN,
ENG [38540] : 1867 NEWTON CO., IN, USA [37005]

HAWS PRE 1697 RUISLIP, MDX, ENG [35895] :
ELIZABETH C1697 RUISLIP, MDX, ENG [35895]

HAWSON ALL WORLDWIDE [36126]

HAWSWORTH 1750-1850 LAMBOURNE, BRK, ENG
[37188]

HAWTHORN PRE 1875 DOW, IRL [35949] : JOHN
C1827 MOYNE, ANT, IRL [37155] : 1800-1920
PETERHEAD, MOR, SCT [37290] : 1840-1860
ALLEGHENY, PA, USA [38347]

HAWTHORNE ALEXANDER PRE 1865 SOUTH
GRAFTON, NSW, AUS [34539] : ADAM PRE 1815
TIPPERARY, TIP, IRL [34539] : C1800S TYR, IRL
[35381] : PRE 1875 DOW, IRL [35949] : 1859 ARM,
IRL [36910] : PRE 1850 STRABANE, TYR, IRL
[37906] : 1800S GLASGOW, LKS, SCT [34288] : 1840
KNOX, IL, USA [38317] : 1840 JEFFERSON, PA,
USA [38317]

HAWTIN 1700+ OXF, ENG [35882] : 1872
SHOREDITCH, LND, ENG [36823]

HAWTON 1857-1896 MOREE & PARKES, NSW, AUS
[35092] : 1831-1857 LONDON, MDX, ENG [35092]

HAXBY ALL PATELY BRIDGE, WRY, ENG [35588]

HAY 1839+ LAUNCESTON & CIRCULAR HEAD,
TAS, AUS [34295] : 1849+ BELLINGEN &
KANGAROO VALLEY, NSW, AUS [35735] : PRE
1835 HULL, ERY, ENG [33944] : 1816 LEIGH, LAN,
ENG [34352] : 1700+ BIRKENHEAD, CHS, ENG
[37620] : 1800+ SHEFFIELD, YKS, ENG [37659] :
1800-1930 MULLINGAR, WEM & WEX, IRL [34496]
: C1805 MAGHERACLONE, MOG, IRL [34993] :
1860+ OAMARU, NZ [33944] : 1882+
RICCARTON, CANTY, NZ [36841] : ALL
EDINBURGH, MLN, SCT [34093] : JAMES C1853
ST QUIVOX, AYR, SCT [34300] : C1800
OCHILTREE, AYR, SCT [34713] : 1800+
GLASGOW, LKS, SCT [34956] : ALL DUNDEE,
ANS, SCT [35139] : 1709+ KIRKINTILLOCH, DNB,
SCT [35252] : C1806 ELGIN, MOR, SCT [35260] :
1750-1850 CULLEN, ABD, SCT [35283] : 1783
CULLEN, BAN, SCT [35369] : C1840 MILLERHILL,
FIF, SCT [35502] : C1840 STEVENSTON, AYR, SCT
[35865] : 1840+ DUNDEE, ANS, SCT [35865] : 1700+
FETLAR, SHI, SCT [36266] : PRE 1900 FORFAR,
ANS, SCT [36361] : PRE 1882 EDINBURGH, SCT
[36841] : 1200 SCT [37008] : PRE 1870 BAN & MOR,
SCT [37085] : PRE 1950 BAN, SCT [37835] : 1850+
DUNBAR, ELN, SCT [37881] : 1830+
HADDINGTON, ELN, SCT [37881] : 1860S

ARDENTINNY, ARL, SCT [37881] : 1870+
NEILSTON, RFW, SCT [37881] : 1835-1885
GREENOCK, RFW, SCT & NZ [33944]

HAYBALL 1750+ CHARD, SOM, ENG [37838]

HAYCOCK ALL NB, CAN [35602] : C1810
CAMBRIDGE, CAM, ENG [33940] : C1870 SAL,
ENG [34935] : C1890 WOLVERHAMPTON, STS,
ENG [35014] : 1800-1850 TUENA, IRL [35103]

HAYCOCKS PRE 1760+ LOPPINGTON, SAL, ENG
[35072]

HAYCOX PRE 1890 SAL, ENG [37331]

HAYDEN 1840+ NSW, AUS [34976] : ALL TAS, AUS
[35063] : PRE 1850 CAMPBELLTOWN, NSW, AUS
[35211] : 1880+ TINGHA, NSW, AUS [37889] :
1850+ NSW, AUS [37942] : PRE 1841 CHESTER,
CHS, ENG [34357] : PRE 1840 GOSPORT, HAM,
ENG [34976] : ALL NFK, ENG [37252] : 1850 CAM &
NFK, ENG [37448] : 1700-1800S WOLVERTON, SAL,
ENG [37898] : PRE 1841 WEX, IRL [33775] : PRE
1900 DUB, IRL [35181] : 1874 DUBLIN CITY, IRL
[36296] : PRE 1850 BORRISOLEIGH, TIP, IRL
[37942] : 1800-1860 HARRISON & SHELBY, KY,
USA [37740] : PRE 1700 SUDBURY & BRAINTREE,
MA, USA [37740]

HAYDEN-BROOKS PRE 1900 STH SHIELDS, DUR,
ENG [35048]

HAYDOCK 1600+ USA &, IRL & ENG [38336]

HAYDON 1834 CASHEL, TIP, IRL [36367]

HAYES CATHERINE 1859+ WISEMANS FERRY,
NSW, AUS [33819] : 1862+ GAYNDAH, QLD, AUS
[33819] : 1840 SYDNEY, NSW, AUS [34966] : 1840+
ORANGE, NSW, AUS [35105] : THOMAS 1850+
BOOROWA, NSW, AUS [37555] : 1810
PITMINSTER, SOM, ENG [33783] : PRE 1840S NTT
& LIN, ENG [34240] : 1828-1870 LEEDS, YKS, ENG
[34622] : 1880-1920 TWICKENHAM, MDX, ENG
[34735] : ALL KEN, ENG [34938] : C1824 LEIGH,
LAN, ENG [35090] : PRE 1750 GREAT BEDWYN,
WIL, ENG [35346] : C1766 OTTERBOURNE, HAM,
ENG [35457] : 1810 CANTERBURY, KEN, ENG
[35855] : MARIE A. 1849 ST PANCRAS, LND, ENG
[35972] : PRE 1900 ST HELENS, LAN, ENG [35986] :
1800+ BIRMINGHAM, WAR, ENG [36058] : 1770-
1830 SCORTON, NRY, ENG [36217] : JOHN PRE
1800 MARYLEBONE, MDX, ENG [36309] : PRE
1700 LONDON CITY, ENG [36619] : PRE 1858
SUNDERLAND, DUR, ENG [36777] : 1750-1850
BOURNE, LIN, ENG [37018] : 1600+ OXF & BKM,
ENG [37099] : PRE 1874 WATFORD, HRT, ENG
[37442] : PRE 1845 CHESHAM, BKM, ENG [37442] :
1830-1860 ST ALKMUND, DBY, ENG [37829] :
C1922 LIVERPOOL, LAN, ENG [37865] : JOHN
C1825-1838 BRIDGEHOUSES, SHEFFIELD, YKS,
ENG [37890] : PRE 1855 WROTHAM, KEN, ENG
[38077] : PRE 1795 NTT, ENG [38080] : 1750-1950
SOM, ENG [38377] : PRE 1850 BALLYMENA, ANT,
IRL [34001] : PRE 1830 COR, IRL [34258] :
CATHERINE PRE 1860 CARRIGATOGHER, TIP &
LIM, IRL [34282] : PRE 1854 NICKER, LIM, IRL
[34763] : 1750-1900 ANT, IRL [35645] : 1750-1900
FER, IRL [35645] : 1750-1900 CAV, IRL [35645] :
C1860-61 SKIBBEREEN, COR, IRL [36307] : 1830
CASTLETOWNARRA, TIP, IRL [36620] : 1835
DOON, LIM, IRL [36804] : PRE 1900 BELFAST,
ANT & DOW, IRL [37708] : C1800 LIM, IRL [37890] :
PRE 1856 TIPPERARY, TIP, IRL [37984] : 1860-1900
SOUTH IS., NZ [36777] : 1840-1866 AR, USA [35301] :
1675-1775 CT, USA [36732] : 1775-1825 GRAFTON,
NH, USA [36732] : 1800-1850 NY, USA [36732] : 1775-
1825 ORANGE, VT, USA [36732] : 1800S-1900S
GREENE CO., IN, USA [37028] : 1830
MUSKINGUM CO., OH, USA [37028] : 1790+

WESTCHESTER, NY, USA [37582] : PRE 1800 SC &
GA, USA [38023] : THOMAS 1847+ AL, USA [38187]
: 1801 JAMAICA, W.INDIES [35550] : 1868 IRL &,
WORLDWIDE [37511]

HAYFORD PRE 1800 OXTON, NTT, ENG [34505]

HAYHOE 1837+ EVANDALE, TAS, AUS [34171] :
1880+ SYDNEY, NSW, AUS [34338] : 1900+
DERBY, DBY, ENG [34338] : 1860+ ROUDHAM,
NFK, ENG [34338] : 1800+ HADDISCOE, NFK,
ENG [34338] : PRE 1800 SOHAM, CAM, ENG [34445]
: PRE 1847 ESS, ENG [36124]

HAYHOW ALL ENG & AUS [33799]

HAYHURST 1770-1800S HASLINGDEN, LAN, ENG
[37988]

HAYINCK ALL ATW, BEL [38169]

HAYLEY 1855 GRAMPOUND, CON, ENG [35152] :
PRE 1900 OXF, ENG [36535]

HAYLOCK 1790 ELVEDEN, SFK, ENG [35243] : C1750
RUMBURGH, SFK, ENG [37191]

HAYLOR SARAH C1800-1880 STORRINGTON,
SULLINGTON, SSX, ENG [34432] : PRE 1856
HAILSHAM, SSX, ENG [36281]

HAYMAN 1700-1800S CREECH ST MICHAEL, SOM,
ENG [34483] : 1800S BRIDGEWATER, SOM, ENG
[34483] : 1700-1800S WEST MONKTON, SOM, ENG
[34483] : 1800+ MANCHESTER, LAN, ENG [35166] :
PRE 1860 LAMBETH, LND, ENG [37287] : PRE 1820
ENG [38730]

HAYMES PRE 1660 CANN & SHAFTESBURY, DOR,
ENG [36478]

HAYMET ALL WORLDWIDE [35857]

HAYNE C1860 SCONE, NSW, AUS [33810] : 1910+
WOY WOY, NSW, AUS [35040] : 1800+
LYONVILLE, VIC, AUS [35040] : 1900S SCONE,
NSW, AUS [37910] : 1750+ TINTINHULL &
YEOVIL, SOM, ENG & AUS [34913]

HAYNES 1822+ MULGOA, NSW, AUS [35420] : 1850S
TAMWORTH, NSW, AUS [36285] : 1800S LONDON,
MDX & ESS, ENG [34813] : C1760 GLS, ENG [34993]
: 1850+ OXFORD, OXF, ENG [35027] : PRE 1850
HUN, ENG [35389] : PRE 1822 LND & KEN, ENG
[35420] : PRE 1800 CHIEVELEY, FRILSHAM &
COMPTON, BRK, ENG [35866] : C1800
BADDINGTON, NTH, ENG [35990] : PRE 1810
LONDON (COV GDN), MDX, ENG [36047] : PRE
1920 LEI & WAR, ENG [36216] : 1650-1750
WARMINSTER, WIL, ENG [37038] : 1812
ELLASTONE, STS, ENG [37174] : C1870 IPSWICH,
SFK, ENG [37285] : WILLIAM C1761 LND, ENG
[37453] : 1740-1800 GREAT BOLAS, SAL, ENG
[37762] : 1750+ LND, ENG & AUS [34724] :
ANTHONY PRE 1680 LONDON, ENG & USA
[33757] : BENJAMIN C1820 (TO USA & TO CAN
C1847), IRL [35607] : 1822 RENSSELAER CO., NY,
USA [37531] : PRE 1800 DAUPHIN, PA, USA [38220]
: 1840+ WV, USA [38323] : C1760-1890
HAGERSTOWN, MD & PA, USA [38325]

HAYS 1880+ MELBOURNE, VIC, AUS [33870] : PRE
1880 CHESTERFIELD, DBY, ENG [33870] : 1800-
1830 OH, USA [38180] : 1790+ USA & UK [36357]

HAYSTAFF ALL WORLDWIDE [36042]

HAYTER 1770+ DONHEAD, WIL, ENG [34899] : PRE
1820 PUTNEY, MDX, ENG [34911] : SARAH 1700-
1800 DILTON MARSH, WIL, ENG [35361] : C1830
WINCHESTER, HAM, ENG [38292] : PRE 1900
BOMBAY, MAHARASHTRA, INDIA [37101]

HAYTHORN 1870+ BARROW IN FURNESS, LAN,
ENG [35411]

HAYTON PRE 1850 CUL, ENG [34727] : 1700+
CAMERTON & WORKINGTON, CUL, ENG [35293]
: C1851 LANCASTER, LAN, ENG [37144] : ALL
BRIGSTEER & MILNTHORPE, WES, ENG [38464]

HAYWARD 1820-1875 SYDNEY, NSW, AUS [34778] :
1830S+ PENRITH, NSW, AUS [35108] : 1819+
RICHMOND & COBBORAH, NSW, AUS [35527] :
C1814 RED CLIFF, NFD, CAN [33852] : 1800+
CREWKERNE, SOM, ENG [33893] : C1783
PORTISHAM, DOR, ENG [34389] : 1756-1840
ASCOT UNDER WYCHWOOD, OXF, ENG [34440] :
1700+ MENDLESHAM & STOWMARKET, SFK,
ENG [34508] : C1800 HEATHFIELD, SSX, ENG
[34887] : PRE 1885 WARRINGTON, LAN, ENG
[35022] : C1794+ BEWDLEY, SAL, ENG [35108] :
PRE 1830+ CHADDERTON, LAN, ENG [35527] :
1840+ LIVERPOOL, LAN, ENG [35943] : C1794
GREAT YARMOUTH, NFK, ENG [35990] : 1810+
SOM & HAM, ENG [36207] : C1800 SHERBORNE,
DOR, ENG [36271] : PRE 1734 LAVENHAM, SFK,
ENG [36425] : PRE 1900 SFK, ENG [36754] : JESSIE
1800+ SUTTON BENGER, WIL, ENG [36890] :
1800+ LONDON, ENG [37306] : PRE 1850
THANET, KEN, ENG [37371] : 1850S KEN, ENG
[37751] : 1810+ CLYST ST GEORGE, DEV, ENG
[37986] : 1820S-1900 WANDSWORTH, SRY, ENG
[38443] : SHADRACK PRE 1850 WIL, ENG & AUS
[36852]

HAYWOOD MARY 1830-1860 LAUNCESTON, TAS,
AUS [33900] : 1790 SYDNEY, NSW, AUS [34581] :
1840S-1880S SMYTHSDALE, VIC, AUS [35777] :
1885+ BRUNSWICK, VIC, AUS [37109] : 1700
WHITTINGTON, WOR, ENG [34210] : PRE 1700
WINTERBORNE HOUGHTON, DOR, ENG [34228]
: C1840 CIRENCESTER, GLS, ENG [34239] : C1850
BIRMINGHAM, WAR, ENG [34239] : PRE 1832
BIRMINGHAM, WAR, ENG [34795] : PRE 1830
WHALTON, NBL, ENG [35488] : ALL ALCESTER,
WOR & WAR, ENG [36234] : PRE 1876
GREENWICH, KEN, ENG [36761] : 1800-1900
SHRESWBURY, SAL, ENG [37074] : PRE 1850
NEWHAVEN & BRIGHTON, SSX, ENG [37321] :
1800-1830 SUTTON ON TRENT, NTT, ENG [37929] :
C1890 WORCESTER, MA, USA [34239]

HAZARD PRE 1885 NOTTINGHAM, NTT, ENG
[37725]

HAZARD (SEE HAZZARD) [38358]

HAZEL C1848 BIRMINGHAM, WAR, ENG [36599] :
1840S BRIDGEWATER, SOM, ENG [37167] : 1770
EAST DEVON, DEV, ENG [37733]

HAZELDEN PRE 1850 MANCHESTER, LAN, ENG
[38568]

HAZELDENE ALL NOTTINGHAM, NTT, ENG
[36365]

HAZELETT 1750-1850 BRAMLEY, HAM, ENG [35422]

HAZELHURST 1830-1930 WIDNES, LAN, ENG
[36983]

HAZELL 1800+ CHELSEA, MDX, ENG [34818] : PRE
1850 STROOD, KEN, ENG [36387] : ALL BRISTOL,
ENG [36844]

HAZELMAN 1800+ STRASBOURG, ALS, FRA
[36304]

HAZELTON 1880+ MEDONTE, ONT, CAN [35648] :
1750-1900 NS, CAN [36080] : 1750-1900 CAN [36080] :
1600+ KILLYMAN, DUNGANNON, TYR, IRL
[36080] : 1600+ LURGAN, ARM, IRL [36080] : PRE
1900 GLASGOW, SCT [36080] : ALL WORLDWIDE
[36080]

HAZELWOOD 1800+ ESS, ENG [34818]

HAZLE 1850+ VIC, AUS [37113]

HAZLEDON 1750-1820 KEN, ENG [35238]

HAZLETT PRE 1830 DRUMBALLY RONEY, DOW,
IRL [38538] : PRE 1900 DRY, IRL & AUS [36893] :
C1863 AUCKLAND, NZ [34814]

HAZLEWOOD C1800+ SYDNEY, NSW, AUS [35053]
: 1700S HANWELL & BANBURY, OXF, ENG
[37330]

HAZZARD 1848+ SOUTH GRAFTON, NSW, AUS
[35088] : 1700+ TEMPLECOMBE, SOM, ENG
[36389] : ALL WINSLOW, BKM, ENG [38358] :
1650+ USA [36347]

HEACOCK 1829+ TALLADEGA, AL, USA [38187]

HEAD PRE 1774 YATELEY, HAM, ENG [34689] : PRE
1875 NFK, ENG [34712] : 1800 PENRITH, CUL,
ENG [34940] : 1800+ DOVER, KEN, ENG [35027] :
1836 GREYSTOKE, CUL, ENG [35769] : 1723
SEBERHAM, CUL, ENG [35769] : 1829 PORTSEA,
HAM, ENG [35922] : PRE 1844 NEW FOREST,
HAM, ENG [36079] : 1857 HAMMERSMITH, MDX,
ENG [36287] : 1830+ MILDEN & MONKS ELEIGH,
SFK, ENG [36533] : 1700-1850 NEWBURY, BRK,
ENG [36727] : 1800+ ISLINGTON, LND, ENG
[36768] : ALL PORTSEA, HAM, ENG [36846] : 1800S
WIL, ENG [38468] : PHOEBE 1847-1914
GREYTOWN, WAI, NZ [33961] : 1856-85 MARION
CO., AL, USA [38590]

HEADACH ALL WORLDWIDE [37416]

HEADE C1800 SHOREDITCH, LND, ENG [36431]

HEADEN SAMUEL PRE 1777 VA, USA [36939]

HEADLAND 1700+ SHARNBROOK & SOULDROP,
BDF, ENG [36123] : 1800+ DENFORD, NTH, ENG
[37437] : 1800+ TITCHMARSH, NTH, ENG [37437] :
1800+ WELLINGBOROUGH, NTH, ENG [37437]

HEADLEY 1800S BURY ST EDMUNDS, SFK, ENG
[36874]

HEADS ALL WOLSINGHAM, DUR, ENG [33993]

HEAFIELD 1788-1810 HEATHER, LEI, ENG [37538] :
1840-1888 KANE CO., IL, USA [37538] : 1810-1829
NY CITY, NY, USA [37538]

HEAGEY ALL PA, USA [38693]

HEAGNEY C1870 LIM, IRL [38079]

HEAL 1800+ MIDSOMER NORTON, SOM, ENG
[34263] : 1800 CALBOURNE, IOW, ENG [34890] :
1650+ SOM, ENG [37216] : PRE 1890 CAMERTON
& BATH, SOM, ENG [37322] : 1800S HINTON
BLEWETT, SOM, ENG [37544]

HEALAM JOHN BROOK 1841 ENG [36143]

HEALAN PRE 1840 TIP, IRL [35727]

HEALD 1700-1990 WAKEFIELD, YKS, ENG [34729] :
1700+ NTT, ENG [37839] : PRE 1806
MANCHESTER & OLDHAM, LAN, ENG [38248] :
1650-1750 SPRINGFIELD, MA, USA [37783]

HEALE PRE 1880 LONDON, ENG [33859] : 1650+
SOM, ENG [37216]

HEALEY C1860 MANNING RIVER, NSW, AUS
[35089] : THOMAS C1840+ MULGOA, NSW, AUS
[38510] : PRE 1900 OXF, ENG [36535] : 1700+
BURTON COGGLES, LIN, ENG [36827] : 1850+
CREWE, CHS, ENG [36997] : 1800S ENG [37922] :
1850+ DUBLIN, IRL [34237] : 1800+ CLA, IRL
[37916] : MARY 1855S ARDEE THE GREEN, LOU,
IRL [38233] : PRE 1870 WAT, IRL [38365] : C1866
HORTON, SCT [37106] : PRE 1910 HOPKINTON,
MA, USA [38537]

HEALION (SEE HELION) [38171]

HEALY 1855+ SYDNEY, NSW, AUS [35160] : 1852+
EPSON & MELBOURNE, VIC, AUS [35379] : 1847+
GEELONG, VIC, AUS [35599] : 1800-1860 SYDNEY,
NSW, AUS [38070] : 1840+ KANGAROO FLAT, SA,
AUS & IRL [35555] : JOHN & ELLEN 1838+
MELBOURNE, QUE, CAN [34147] : 1800-1831
O'BRIENS BRIDGE, CLA, IRL [33778] : JOHN
C1830 COR, IRL [34147] : PRE 1841 ADARE, LIM,
IRL [34452] : 1800+ BRIGOWN, COR, IRL [34453] :
PRE 1860 KID, IRL [35206] : PRE 1852 LIM, IRL
[35379] : PRE 1847 CASHEL, TIP, IRL [35599] : 1840S

CORK CITY, COR, IRL [37134] : 1800 MAY, OFF, IRL [37170] : 1800-1900 KIK, IRL [37661] : C1850 ADARE, LIM, IRL [37718] : PRE 1814 CLA, IRL [37866] : 1800+ CLA, IRL [37916] : PRE 1900 KER, IRL [38755] : JOHN & ELLEN C1830 LOWELL, MA, USA [34147] : 1873+ PATERSON & ARLINGTON, NJ & VA, USA [34645] : 1880-1940 BALTIMORE CO., MD, USA [36895]

HEAMAN 1700S BURRINGTON & ASHREIGNEY, DEV, ENG [34214] : PRE 1735 DOLTON, DEV, ENG [34214]

HEAN ROBERT C1800-1834 CON, ENG [35955] : ROBERT C1800-1834 PLYMOUTH, DEV, ENG [35955]

HEANES 1870+ MANORS CREEK, NSW, AUS [38324]

HEANEY 1800-1900 LAN, ENG [34361] : PRE 1819 ENG [34766] : PRE 1820 DUBLIN & NEWTOWNBARRY, WEX, IRL [34137] : ALL ARM, LOU & ANT, IRL [34955] : 1800S CAV, IRL & AUS [37307]

HEANON PRE 1880+ PHILADELPHIA, PA, USA [36578]

HEANY 1880+ DUBBO, NSW, AUS [37307] : PRE 1855 ARRAN IS, GAL, IRL [35765]

HEAP C1800 HALIFAX, WRY, ENG [35744] : C1740-C1850 HASLINGDEN, LAN, ENG [37066] : PRE 1850 BRADFORD, YKS, ENG [37915]

HEAPS 1800S NSW, AUS [37500] : 1750+ LEEDS, YKS, ENG [36793] : 1850+ CREWE AREA, CHS, ENG [36997]

HEAR MARY PRE 1820 LIM, IRL [35371] : PRE 1800 SLI, IRL [37739]

HEARD C1879 ADELAIDE, SA, AUS [37167] : 1882+ HAWTHORN, VIC, AUS [37167] : 1800+ CAN [34490] : 1847+ WHITBY & SIMCOE, ONT, CAN [37467] : PRE 1775 BIDEFORD, DEV, ENG [34445] : PRE 1700 ESS, ENG [35642] : PRE 1879 DEVONPORT, DEV, ENG [37167] : 1750+ SCT [34490]

HEARDER ALL DEV, ENG [36999]

HEARDSHAW 1850+ POLO & OGLA CO., IL, USA [36575]

HEARL DAISY MARIA PRE 1940 SWINDON, WIL, ENG [36646]

HEARN 1840+ SA, AUS [34883] : 1900+ CUNNAMULLA, QLD, AUS [35807] : 1820-1900 CHINGUACOUSY TWP., ONT, CAN [34346] : PRE 1880 BIRMINGHAM, WAR, ENG [34923] : PRE 1852 IPSWICH, SFK, ENG [35242] : PRE 1840 FEERING, ESS, ENG [35406] : 1750+ CANTERBURY, KEN, ENG [36987] : 1800+ SITTINGBOURNE, KEN, ENG [37194] : PRE 1850 WOOBURN & UPTON CUM CHALVEY, BKM, ENG [37410] : 1805-1830 PORTLAW, WAT, IRL [38117]

HEARNE 1840+ SA, AUS [34883] : C1832 PARRAMATTA, NSW, AUS [35557] : 1890+ HAMILTON, VIC, AUS [35752] : ALL DUBBO, NSW, AUS [37115] : 1860+ OXFORD, OXF, ENG [37202]

HEARNSHAW PRE 1880 ROTHERHAM, YKS, ENG [37353] : PRE 1880 DBY, ENG [37353] : PRE 1780 BASLOW, DBY, ENG [37875]

HEARSFIELD ALL FAIRFIELD & BROOKLAND, KEN, ENG [37714]

HEARSON 1750+ NOTTINGHAM, NTT, ENG [33800] : PRE 1800 ARNOLD, NTT, ENG [36387]

HEASELL PRE 1780 NFK, ENG [35212]

HEASMAN 1600+ SSX, ENG [33998] : PRE 1889 WOOLWICH, LND, ENG [34959] : 1600+ SSX & KEN, ENG [37210] : C1800 HENFIELD, SSX, ENG [37513]

HEASON 1750-1900 SOM, DOR & SRY, ENG [35701]

HEATH 1802-1900 AVOCA, TAS, AUS [35195] : 1880+ SYDNEY, NSW, AUS [35735] : 1858-1880 SPRINGSURE & ROCKHAMPTON, QLD, AUS [35735] : 1800 SA, AUS [35873] : 1867+ RICHMOND, VIC, AUS [37120] : 1802-1900 CLEVELAND, TAS, AUS & ENG [35195] : 1800+ LONDON, ENG [33979] : PRE 1840 STOKE ON TRENT, STS, ENG [34633] : 1850+ NEWCASTLE & STOKE, STS, ENG [34714] : WILLIAM PRE 1856 GREAT COMBERTON, WOR, ENG [35258] : 1700S STOKE UPON TRENT, STS, ENG [35322] : WILLIAM PRE 1824 WARMINSTER, WIL, ENG [35583] : PRE 1810 PORTSMOUTH, HAM, ENG [35605] : PRE 1858 DEPTFORD, KEN, ENG [35735] : PRE 1850 ST ALBANS & RIDGE, HRT, ENG [36061] : 1840+ EDMONTON & ENFIELD, MDX, ENG [36061] : 1815+ RIVERHEAD, KEN, ENG [36071] : 1840+ OLD AYLESFORD, HAM, ENG [36981] : 1850-1860 ST GEORGE IN THE EAST, MDX, ENG [37120] : 1871+ BARROW IN FURNESS, LAN, ENG [37120] : PRE 1890 LIMEHOUSE & POPLAR, MDX, ENG [37120] : ALL SEVENOAKS RIVERHEAD, KEN, ENG [37373] : PRE 1800 BURSLEM, STS, ENG [37389] : 1700-1800 ELMLEY CASTLE, WOR, ENG [37643] : PRE 1840 KINGSBRIDGE, DEV, ENG [37948] : 1800S SEVENOAKS, KEN, ENG [38289] : 1940-1956 WESTLAND, NZ [33988] : 1794+ CANTERBURY, MERRIMACK, NH, USA [38571]

HEATHCOAT C1780 KETTLESHULME, CHS, ENG [37697]

HEATHCOTE 1885+ COOTAMUNDRA, NSW, AUS [35872] : PRE 1750 WHITWELL, DBY, ENG [33912] : 1800-1900 LIN, ENG [33952] : 1600+ LITTLEOVER, DBY, ENG [34579] : PRE 1900 ANSTEY, LEI, ENG [35175] : PRE 1900 HACKNEY, LND, ENG [35175] : 1600+ CHELMORTON, DBY, ENG [37172] : PRE 1842 KEN, ENG [37991]

HEATHER 1860-1900 HAMMERSMITH, MDX, ENG [34735] : 1600+ BLENDWORTH, HAM, ENG [36827]

HEATHERBELL ALL WORLDWIDE [34124]

HEATHERINGTON ALL WORLDWIDE [37076]

HEATHERLY PRE 1800 EASTBOURNE, SSX, ENG [37246]

HEATHFIELD ALL BETHERSDEN, KEN, ENG [37015] : 1855-1859 MADISON CO., NY, USA [37015] : 1849-1861 ONEIDA CO., NY, USA [37015]

HEATHWOOD 1856+ QLD, AUS [37992] : PRE 1856 ARM, IRL [37992]

HEATLEY JOHN 1834+ WARWICK, WAR, ENG [35462] : 1800S+ BERWICK ON TWEED, NBL, ENG [38414] : 1800S ROX, SCT [38414]

HEATON 1850+ SYDNEY, NSW, AUS [34977] : 1850S SYDNEY, NSW, AUS [37309] : 1848-1889 TORONTO & MINESING STN, ONT, CAN [34484] : C1822 BRAMHAM, WRY, ENG [33910] : 1700-1900S FARLEY & ALTON, STS, ENG [33958] : 1830S LONDON, ENG [34296] : 1810-1848 WAKEFIELD, YKS, ENG [34484] : PRE 1807 BOLTON, LAN, ENG [36742] : 1650-1750 BINGLEY, WRY, ENG [37411] : PRE 1840 ALMONDBURY, YKS, ENG [38777] : C1850 GREENE CO., IL, USA [36957] : 1750+ ROCKINGHAM CO., VA, USA [36957] : 1850-1870 KEWEENAW CO., MI, USA [38010] : 1825-1850 VA, USA [38010]

HEAUME 1850+ GSY, CHI [34425]

HEAVEN 1848+ SYDNEY & LISMORE, NSW, AUS [33765] : PRE 1850 GEELONG, VIC, AUS [38306] : PRE 1850 GLS, ENG [33765] : 1800S LITTLE DEAN, GLS, ENG [35968] : PRE 1850 GLS, ENG [38306] : C1800 RSA [35032]

HEAVENS PRE 1839 WEYMOUTH, DOR, ENG [34893]

HEAVER C1850 SSX, ENG [37285]

HEAVEY C1811 AUGHALOO, TYR, IRL [35541]

HEAVIELL ALL WORLDWIDE [37843]

HEAVISIDE 1800+ NORWICH, NFK, ENG [36756]

HEAYDON 1900+ LITHGOW, NSW, AUS [34534]

HEBB PRE 1869 WALTHAM, LEI, ENG [35821]

HEBBEND ALL SMETHWICK, STS, ENG [3o/89]

HEBBENKAUSEN ALL WORLDWIDE [38670]

HEBBERD PRE 1842 ALTON, HAM, ENG [34911]

HEBBLETHWAITE 1843-1877 NORTHOWRAM, WRY, ENG [36391]

HEBBLEWHITE 1770+ SCULCOATES & HULL, ERY, ENG [37988]

HEBDEN PRE 1860 LONDON, ENG [33765]

HEBDIGE 1700+ BOTLEY, HAM, ENG [34678]

HEBDITCH 1700+ WIL, ENG [34678] : PRE 1779 STH PETHERTON, SOM, ENG [35252] : PRE 1810 HOLYROOD SOUTHAMPTON, HAM, ENG [35483]

HEBENTON ALL WORLDWIDE [36509]

HEBER 1880S NSW, AUS [34902]

HEBERER 1820+ DARMSTADT, HES, GER [36342] : 1820+ EDWARDSVILLE, IL, USA [36342] : 1820+ ST LOUIS, MO, USA [36342]

HEBERT 1870+ WALLACEBURG, ONT & QUE, CAN [34983] : 1500-1800S SAINT AIGNAN, NOR, FRA [35327] : JOSEPH 1700-1770 FRA [37479]

HEBRON 1850+ MECKLENBURG CO., VA, USA [36903] : 1840-1940 HOWARD & PRINCE GEORGES COS., MD, USA [37583]

HECHT PRE 1820 GINGST, REUGEN, GER [37961] : C1810 GER [38711]

HECK 1770+ BOTETOURT CO., VA & OH, USA [36540] : 1900+ ND, USA [36942]

HECKEL 1800-1900 NEISSE, SIL, GER [36555]

HECKER 1830-1990 GREENVILLE, MERCER CO., PA, USA [36449]

HECKING CATHERINE 1820-1870 MANCHESTER, LAN, ENG [38409]

HECKLER PRE 1775 AUERBACH, HES, BRD [35311] : 1800-1910 BANAT, YU [37539]

HECKMAN 1900+ SYDNEY, NSW, AUS [38729] : MICHAEL 1815-50 STARK CO., OH, USA [38138]

HECKS ALL ENG [34661] : C1812 BRISTOL, GLS, ENG [34661]

HECKY ALL WORLDWIDE [38693]

HEDBERG PRE 1865 GEFLE, SWE [37991]

HEDDEN 1890+ HALDIMAND CO., ONT, CAN [38323]

HEDDERWICK 1700-1850 GLASCOW, LKS, SCT [36556]

HEDDINGTON 1800+ LAUNCESTON, TAS, AUS [38075] : PRE 1850 WAPPING, LND, ENG [38075]

HEDDITCH ALL WORLDWIDE [37416]

HEDDLE 1740+ KIRKWALL, OKI, SCT [34688] : 1790+ LONGHOPE, OKI, SCT [34688]

HEDDON PRE 1720 CON, ENG [35255]

HEDGE C1820 TAS, AUS [35838] : C1847 SA, AUS [35838]

HEDGECOCK 1830+ SITTINGBOURNE, KEN, ENG [37677]

HEDGER 1870+ PORTSEA, HAM, ENG [37291] : 1747 WARWICK, RI, USA [38287]

HEDGES 1910+ SYDNEY, NSW, AUS [34273] : C1870 PURTON, WIL, ENG [34273] : C1802 HARROW, MDX, ENG [35560] : 1820S-1840S HAMPSTEAD, MDX, ENG [35560] : PRE 1800 OZLEWORTH, GLS, ENG [36113] : PRE 1800 SUNNINGWELL & RADLEY, BRK, ENG [36502] : 1780+ HEADINGTON, OXF, ENG [36502] : 1937 DOVER,

KEN, ENG [36781] : PRE 1883 OXFORD, OXF, ENG [36804]

HEDI 1709-1763 BECHHOFEN PFALZ, BAV, GER [37516]

HEDICKE MARGARET PRE 1774 HALFMOON, NY, USA [37809]

HEDLEY 1911+ STAGHORN FLAT, VIC, AUS [35774] : 1880+ NEWCASTLE, NSW, AUS [35874] : PRE 1860 BROOMWICH, STS, ENG [35061] : PRE 1850 DENTON & SUMMERHOUSE, DUR, ENG [35462] : 1842+ WOOLLER, NBL, ENG [35774] : 1700-1850 SCARBOROUGH, YKS, ENG [35862] : 1700+ BIRTLEY, NBL, ENG [35874] : 1867+ OAMARU, NZ [35774]

HEDRECK PRE 1900 KNOXVILLE & AKEA, TN, USA [36899]

HEDRICK 1736-1990 SCHLESWIG HOLSTEIN, SHO, GER [35316] : PRE 1830 RICHLAND CO., OH, USA [37781] : 1829 MD, USA [38121]

HEEB 1700 GER [36579]

HEEDS C1800 CHESTERFIELD, DBY, ENG [36112] : C1820 ORDSALL & E.RETFORD, NTT, ENG [36112]

HEEL 1700S NTH, ENG [35030]

HEELEY 1750-1900 YKS, ENG [34631] : ALL THORPE HESLEY, YKS, ENG [36704] : ALL WENTWORTH, YKS, ENG [36704] : 1820+ KIMBERWORTH, YKS, ENG [36704] : 1820+ ROTHERHAM, YKS, ENG [36704] : PRE 1840 BIRMINGHAM, WAR, ENG [37133]

HEELY 1750-1900 YKS, ENG [34631]

HEENAN ALL TERRYGLASS, TIP, IRL [34441]

HEEP 1623-1709 ALZEY, RPF, BRD [37011]

HEERMANN C1750+ WUE, GER & USA [37520]

HEEROLT 1700+ FRA [35338]

HEESCH 1908+ WILSTER, SHO, GER [36952] : 1880-1908 ASPINWALL, CRAWFORD CO., IA, USA [36952]

HEESOM 1870+ WARRINGTON, LAN, ENG [38539]

HEETER 1760+ BERKS CO., PA, USA [37040]

HEFFENDEN PRE 1847 HARTFIELD, SSX, ENG [36759]

HEFFER EMILY 1860S MALMSBURY, VIC, AUS [35471]

HEFFERNAN 1839-1990 MORUYA, NSW, AUS [33818] : C1857 BEECHWORTH, VIC, AUS [35585] : C1870 NSW, AUS [38077] : JUDITH PRE 1815 TIPPERARY, TIP, IRL [34539] : PRE 1840 GALBALLY, LIM, IRL [35599]

HEFFLER 1750-1850 HALIFAX, NS, CAN [35151]

HEFFNER 1856+ KINGSTON, ONT, CAN [37047]

HEFLIN PRE 1820 NC, USA [37578]

HEFNER 1861+ KINGSTON, ONT, CAN [37047]

HEFT PRE 1770 LANCASTER, PA, USA [38220]

HEGAN 1800+ MOG, IRL [34226]

HEGARTY GEORGE 1853+ BOWNING, NSW, AUS [35787] : ALL COR, IRL [36599] : C1810 COR & TAS, IRL & AUS [34596]

HEGE ALL WORLDWIDE [38693]

HEGEL 1770+ STUTTGART, WUE, GER [38667] : 1500S KAR, OES [38667]

HEGEMAN JOSEPH 1650-1677 POUGHKEEPSIE, NY, USA [38140] : 1700S BROOKLYN & KINGS CO., NY, USA [38182]

HEGGER MARGARET PRE 1774 HALFMOON, NY, USA [37809]

HEGGI ALL WORLDWIDE [38693]

HEGGIE PRE 1800 WORLDWIDE [38693]

HEGGS OLIVER C1880 LONGSIGHT, LAN, ENG [38284] : WALTER C1900 BLACKPOOL, LAN, ENG [38284]

HEGI ALL WORLDWIDE [38693]

HEGIE ALL WORLDWIDE [38693]

HEGIN ALL WORLDWIDE [38693]
HEGIUS ALL WORLDWIDE [38693]
HEGNEY 1800 DERRYLORAN, TYR, IRL [35350]
HEGSTROM 1910+ JACKSON, MI, USA [37206]
HEGUI ALL WORLDWIDE [38693]
HEGUY ALL WORLDWIDE [38693]
HEGWER PRE 1850 KUNITZ, PRE, GER [38768] :
    PRE 1850 SIL, PRE, GER [38768]
HEGY ALL WORLDWIDE [38693]
HEHDEN SARAH PRE 1850 SKELTON, NRY, ENG
    [34567]
HEHIR C1830 KILMALEY, CLA, IRL [34426] : 1800+
    TULLA, CLA, IRL [34871] : PRE 1856 KILDUFF,
    CLA, IRL [35824]
HEICOX 1770S BRISTOL, CT, USA [38537]
HEIDE (SEE VAN DER H [35753]
HEIDEL (SEE HAIDLE) [34812]
HEIDELK 1836+ GER [38531] : PRE 1889 JANSEN,
    NE, USA [38531]
HEIDER ALL SIL, GER, AUS & [36743]
HEIDIMANN 1860+ APLERBECK, WEF, GER
    [34563]
HEIDMAN ALL NY & CT, USA [37787]
HEIDTKE ALL WORLDWIDE [38687]
HEIFNER 1700+ MAINHARDT, BAW, GER [35355]
HEIGHES ALL WORLDWIDE [34201]
HEIGHTON ALL LEEDS, YKS & LEI, ENG [35954]
HEIGHWAY 1890+ SUTTON IN ASHFIELD, NTT,
    ENG [34329]
HEIL PRE 1550 KL UMSTADT, HES, GER [38181]
HEILBORN 1800+ BERLIN, BLN, GER [36583] : PRE
    1820 POZNAN, PO, POL [36583]
HEILIG PRE 1990 GER [38664]
HEIMANN 1800-1900 BERLIN, BLO, GER [38244]
HEIN PRE 1870 BROMBERG, GER [38217] : PRE 1870
    LPZ, GER & DDR [38217]
HEINEMEYER PRE 1900 OES [36765]
HEINEN 1700+ JUNGLINSTER & GRAND USHE,
    LUX [37016] : 1700+ YOUNGLINSTER & GRAND
    USHE, LUX [37016]
HEINEY PRE 1900 WORLDWIDE [38196]
HEININGER 1700+ BAV, GER [34933]
HEINKE 1750-1850 SAB, GER [38035]
HEINOLD PRE 1800 BRETTACH, BAW, BRD [38615]
HEINRICH 1794-1896 SCHLEUSINGEN,
    THURINGIA, GER [38148]
HEINRICHS 1850S TAURIEN, SU [36543]
HEINRICHSEN 1840+ FASSIFERN, QLD, AUS
    [35460] : PRE 1880+ BLUNK, SHO, GER [35460]
HEINS 1800S HANNOVER, HAN, GER [35278]
HEINZ 1700-1900 ENG & PRE, DDR [36169]
HEINZEN C1845+ LOUISVILLE, KY, USA [37447] :
    C1800+ PA & KY, USA [37447]
HEISE 1825 KULM, WPR, GER [34388] : PRE 1710
    BISCHHAGEN, PSA, GER [38048] : 1750+
    LANCASTER CO., PA, USA [34380] : PRE 1790
    SOMERSET, PA, USA [37435]
HEISELBERG ALL DEN [37515]
HEISER PRE 1770 SHO, GER [38669]
HEISLER ALL MAHONE BAY, NS, CAN [34485] :
    1700+ HANOVER, HAN, GER [34485]
HEITMAN JOHN 1855-1857 EAST AURORA, NY,
    USA [34059] : THEODORE 1852-1938 EAST
    AURORA, NY, USA [34059]
HEITMANN CLAN SOCIETY ALL ASENDORF,
    DIEPHOLZ, GER [34059]
HEITON ALL WORLDWIDE [34809]
HELD 1661 HESSLOH HEIDEN, GER [38749] : 1729
    LIEME, GER [38749]
HELDT PRE 1850 HANNOVER, HAN, GER [36260]
HELEM ALL ROX, SCT [35993] : ALL CAI, SCT
    [35993] : ALL WORLDWIDE [35993]

HELENSCHMIDT 1910 ST LOUIS, MO & IL, USA
    [35279]
HELFMANN 1700+ DARMSTADT, HEN, GER
    [37572]
HELFRICH 1800+ GRETHEN (PFALZ BAYERN),
    BAV, GER [38023]
HELGARTNER PRE 1700 FRANKENTHAL, RPF,
    GER [38348]
HELGASON-WALKER ALL WORLDWIDE [35353]
HELIE PRE 1850 CAEN, HN, FRA [37085]
HELION 1820-1900 CLARA, OFF & WEM, IRL [38171]
HELLABY 1750+ LONGFORD, DBY, ENG [36980] :
    ALL WORLDWIDE [37834]
HELLARD 1800S PENRYN, CON, ENG [35127]
HELLAWAY PRE 1855 DEV, ENG [37442]
HELLER SAMUEL 1844-1873 CH [38134] : 1800-1860
    MAURSMUNSTER, DEPT LWR RHINE, FRA
    [36328]
HELLEUR 1840+ SA, AUS [34775] : PRE 1840 GSY,
    CHI [34775]
HELLIER C1875 WALLENDBEEN, NSW, AUS [36284]
    : 1600+ MEMBURY, DEV, ENG [34747] : ALL
    SOM, ENG [35336]
HELLINGA C1760 GROUW, FRI, NL [34390]
HELLINGS 1800-1850 LND, ENG [35178]
HELLIWELL 1700S WRY, ENG [37570] : PRE 1856
    TODMORDEN, LAN, ENG [37866]
HELLMANN 1650+ WILSTER, SHO, GER [38651]
HELLMICH ALL LUESTRINGEN, GER [34861]
HELLUMS PRE 1852 IN, USA [35289]
HELLWEGE 1860-1916 COSTERFIELD, VIC, AUS
    [34171]
HELLYER 1820-1830S TAS, AUS [35785] : 1800-1900S
    SYDNEY, NSW, AUS [35785] : 1800+ NS, CAN
    [34403] : 1700+ JSY, CHI [36761] : 1750-1850 DOR,
    ENG [37188] : PRE 1850 EAST CHINNOCK, SOM,
    ENG [38457] : PRE 1876 WLS [36878]
HELM JOHN F. 1875 KONIGSBERG, BUCHWALD,
    PRE [38142] : ALL HAWICK, ROX, SCT [34466] :
    ALL CAI & ROX, SCT [35993] : JOE 1800S NEW
    HOPE, MO, USA [33752] : CLARENCE 1930S
    VINITA, OK, USA [33752] : CLARENCE 1940S
    ANKENEY, IA, USA [33752] : 1792-1810 NY, USA
    [38529]
HELMAN ALL GER & USA [38043]
HELMEKE 1860 GER &, WORLDWIDE [37511]
HELMORE ALL MDX & DEV, ENG [38376]
HELPS ALL CAN [37427]
HELSHAM PRE 1850 HORNDEAN, HAM, ENG
    [33937]
HELSTROP 1700-1800 NRY, ENG [38269]
HELT PRE 1791 GER [36929] : PRE 1791
    VERMILLION CO., IN, USA [36929]
HELTMANN 1800-1840 CROMBACH, RPR, GER &
    BEL [38528]
HELTZ ALL GLADWIN CO., MI, USA [35302]
HELY 1830+ SYDNEY, NSW, AUS [34977]
HELYAR 1800+ YEOVIL, SOM, ENG [35201] : 1800-
    1857 HARDINGTON MANDEVILLE, SOM, ENG
    [37378]
HELYARD C1874 MOONBI, NSW, AUS [37915] :
    C1847 ENG [37915]
HELYER C1600 WEST COKER, SOM, ENG [37918]
HEMENHAL ALL ENG [37742]
HEMINGWAY 1810+ GRENVILLE, LEEDS &
    SIMCOE, ONT, CAN [37467] : PRE 1810
    GRENVILLE, ONT & VT, CAN & USA [37467] : PRE
    1870 LEEDS & WAKEFIELD, WRY, ENG [36187] :
    1600-1914 DEWSBURY, WRY, ENG [36218] : PRE
    1780 MIRFIELD, WRY, ENG [37754]
HEMMANT PRE 1870S LONG SUTTON, LIN, ENG
    [35702]

HEMMENWAY 1810+ GRENVILLE, LEEDS & SIMCOE, ONT, CAN [37467]

HEMMERICH 1776 WICKENRODE, GHE, GER [38749]

HEMMING PRE 1900 STUDLEY, WAR, ENG [33985] : 1864-1900 QUINTON, GLS, ENG [34658] : C1823 QUINTON, GLS, ENG [34668] : PRE 1895 WANDSWORTH, LND, ENG [34913] : 1800-1850 STROUD, GLS, ENG [35741] : 1700+ BIRMINGHAM & DUDLEY, WOR, ENG [36794] : 1750-1850 WOR, ENG [37038]

HEMMINGER 1800+ USA [38728] : ALL WORLDWIDE [38728]

HEMMINGS PRE 1850 STS, ENG [37403] : 1850+ GLS, ENG [37403] : 1850+ STEPNEY, LND, ENG [37983] : PRE 1880 MON, WLS [37885]

HEMMINGWAY 1810+ GRENVILLE, LEEDS & SIMCOE, ONT, CAN [37467] : PRE 1810 GRENVILLE, ONT & VT, CAN & USA [37467]

HEMMINWAY PRE 1810 GRENVILLE, ONT & VT, CAN & USA [37467]

HEMMY 1830+ MELBOURNE, VIC, AUS [38008]

HEMPEL 1800S ARNSTADT, THURINGEN, DDR [38659]

HEMPHILL 1841+ GUNDAGAI, NSW, AUS & IRL [36313] : 1832-1900 DEBEC, NB, CAN [38454] : PRE 1787 BALLYKELLY, DRY, IRL [36972] : PRE 1700 AGHADOWEY, DRY, IRL [37740] : 1800+ TYR, IRL [38454] : PRE 1800 DRUMKEERAN & BRACKLIN, FER, IRL & AUS [36313] : 1700+ AYR, SCT [38454] : C1806 CHESTER CO., SC, USA [37817]

HEMPSALL ALL WORLDWIDE [37742]

HEMPSON ALL SFK & ESS, ENG [37250]

HEMPSTEAD 1850+ BROOKLYN & SUFF. CO., NY, USA [38182]

HEMS PRE 1890 SHOREDITCH, LND, ENG [37067]

HEMSTOCK 1800+ MONEY CREEK & SPARTA, MN & WI, USA & ENG [38764]

HEMSWORTH 1880S DUBLIN, IRL [33899]

HEMUS 1800-1900 BROMSGROVE, WOR, ENG [37257] : 1800-1900 CATSHILL, WOR, ENG [37257]

HEMY (SEE HEMMY) [38008]

HENAULT 1600-1690 FRA [38779]

HENBEST 1800+ HAM & SSX, ENG [35760]

HENCE 1820+ NSW, AUS [36305]

HENCHEY PRE 1914 SHOREDITCH, MDX, ENG [35031]

HENDEL PRE 1861 KRS. ASCH, SUDETENLAND, OES, CSR &, GER [38649]

HENDER PRE 1865 TYWARDREATH, CON, ENG [33915] : 1620-1670 ST TEATH, CON, ENG [34448]

HENDERSEN PRE 1860 CLYTHMAIN, CAI, SCT [34797]

HENDERSHOT 1790+ NIAGARA DISTRICT, ONT, CAN [38323] : ALL WORLDWIDE [36933]

HENDERSON JOHN 1877+ SYDNEY, NSW, AUS [34901] : 1850+ NATTE YALLOCK, VIC, AUS [37557] : HELEN 1916+ PRAHRAN EAST, VIC, AUS [37906] : GEORGE 1870+ BROUGHTON HALL, NSW, AUS [38006] : JOHN 1875+ BEGA & CANDELO, NSW, AUS [38006] : 1856+ BEECHWORTH, VIC, AUS [38213] : 1890+ HOPETOUN, RYDE, NSW, AUS [38213] : 1884+ WROTHAM PARK, QLD, AUS [38213] : 1800+ BEGA & CANDELO, NSW, AUS [38491] : C1880+ LITHGOW & SYDNEY, NSW, AUS & IRL [37556] : C1880+ NEW YORK, NY, USA &, CAN & IRL [37556] : 1750+ MANCHESTER, LAN, ENG [34639] : C1785+ LAMBETH, SRY, ENG [34800] : 1750+ LONGBENTON, NBL, ENG [36609] : 1860S SUNDERLAND, DUR, ENG [37853] : 1860+ BLYTH & EARSDON, NBL, ENG [37889] : PRE 1800 DURHAM, DUR, ENG [37984] : PRE 1850 WHITEPARISH, WIL, ENG [37989] : 1830 NEWCASTLE ON TYNE, NBL, ENG [38008] : 1800+ HULL & BERWICK, YKS, ENG & SCT [33935] : C1780 RAPHOE, DON, IRL [34515] : PRE 1854 TYR, IRL [35035] : C1800-1913+ KILSKERRY & BALLINAMALARD, TYR & FER, IRL [37556] : PRE 1850S TULLYVANON, TYR, IRL [37557] : PRE 1827 MOG, IRL [37913] : PRE 1850 MOG & CAV, IRL [38391] : PRE 1781 ARDS PENINSULA, DOW, IRL [38428] : 1700S ARM, IRL [38440] : 1750-1800 DERRY, IRL [38529] : JANE C1810-1885 IRL & CAN [36904] : 1862+ OTAGO & KARTIGI, OTAGO, NZ [35885] : PRE 1880 SCT [33799] : PRE 1900 FREUCHIE, FIF, SCT [33966] : PRE 1850 INVERNESS, INV, SCT [33968] : 1800-1900 CAMERON, FIF, SCT [34004] : PRE 1800 GIGHA, ARL, SCT [34156] : PRE 1837 GLASGOW, LKS, SCT [34379] : 1820+ EDINBURGH, MLN, SCT [34420] : 1780+ LADYKIRK, BEW, SCT [34666] : 1700+ ST ANDREWS & ST LEONARDS, FIF, SCT [34768] : PRE 1860 HALKIRK, CAI, SCT [34816] : ALL DUNFERMLINE, FIF, SCT [34861] : 1761+ DUMFRIES, DFS, SCT [34873] : C1700S LONGFORMACUS, BEW, SCT [34873] : ANDREW PRE 1850 NESTING, SHI, SCT [34901] : PRE 1800 KENNOWAY, FIF, SCT [35045] : 1820 EDINBURGH, SCT [35067] : ISABEL C1750 CRAIL, FIF, SCT [35072] : JOHN PRE 1749 CADDER, LKS, SCT [35252] : PRE 1850 GLASGOW, SCT [35255] : PRE 1700 ST MONANCE, FIF, SCT [35627] : MARY 1880+ PAISLEY, RFW, SCT [35786] : 1730+ WHALSAY, SHI, SCT [35824] : PRE 1862 SCOTLANDWELL, KRS, SCT [35885] : C1682-1758 MILNATHORT, KRS, SCT [35885] : 1800+ OLD MONKLAND, LKS, SCT [35977] : PRE 1880 STRICHEN, ABD, SCT [36061] : SARAH 1855 GLASGOW, LKS, SCT [36253] : 1800+ GLASGOW, LKS, SCT [36295] : C1700-1750 FIF, SCT [36327] : PRE 1750 KILMARNOCK, AYR, SCT [36436] : ALL FIF, SCT [36861] : 1800S COATBRIDGE, LKS, SCT [37898] : 1848+ MLN, SCT [38018] : 1840+ OLD DEER, ABD, SCT [38213] : JOHN 1880+ METHLICK, ABD, SCT [38213] : 1850+ PETERHEAD, ABD, SCT [38213] : 1700+ SCT [38336] : 1830+ LATHERON, CAI, SCT [38425] : 1850+ MI, USA [34232] : PRE 1888 HAMILTON CO. & RICHMOND CO., OH & VA, USA [35270] : 1840 BOLIVAR, PA, USA [36444] : 1820-1890 NJ & NY, USA [36675] : 1800-1890 ST CLAIR, MI, USA [36910] : 1880+ CLINTON CO., MI, USA [38018] : PRE 1810 TN, USA [38576]

HENDLER PRE 1847 UNTERBIMBACH, KURHESSEN, GER [38618] : PRE 1900 BIERSS, KOVNA, LITHUANIA [36455]

HENDLEY PRE 1850 LONDON, ENG [35199]

HENDRA PRE 1900 GWINEAR, CON, ENG [33972]

HENDREN 1850+ EMERALD HILL & WILLIAMSTOWN, VIC, AUS [34903] : DAVID 1850-1868 MULGOA & PENRITH, NSW, AUS [34973] : ALL MIDDLETOWN, ARM, ANT & DOW, IRL [34189]

HENDRICK 1860+ MOREE & NARRABRI, NSW, AUS [34978] : 1780-1820 LEUTSMANSDORF, KSA, GER [36555]

HENDRICKS PRE 1900 LAWRENCE CO., MO, USA [36355] : 1680-1750 GERMANTOWN, PA, USA [36738]

HENDRICKSEN 1740+ VALDRIS, OPLAND, NOR [36326]

HENDRICKSON 1847+ OAKLAND, WI, USA [36326] : 1650+ DELAWARE, PA & NJ, USA [37826] : 1890+ ASTORIA, WA, USA [38758]

HENDRIE 1882+ ADELAIDE, SA, AUS [35797] : 1780+ KIRKINTILLOCH, DNB, SCT [34290] : 1800S NETTLEHOLES, LKS, SCT [36032] : PRE 1875 CATRINE SORN, AYR, SCT [36302]

HENDRIKS HEIRONIMUS PRE 1735 BUDINGEN, NL [36453]

HENDRIKSZ JAN 1719 AMSTERDAM, NL [36453]

HENDRIX 1800 TOMPKINS CO., NY, USA [37582] : 1800S MI & OH, USA [38369]

HENDRY 1750+ OUCHTERHOUSE, PER, SCT [34637] : 1790S FOURDOUN, KCD, SCT [35798] : 1800S NEW MONKLAND, LKS, SCT [36032] : 1850+ LKS, SCT [36237] : 1850+ RFW, SCT [36237] : 1750-1990 GLASGOW, LKS, SCT [36394] : PRE 1850 FETTERESSO, KCD, SCT [36696] : 1786-1990 MOR, SCT [37329] : 1870+ GLASGOW, LKS, SCT [37443] : ALL PER, SCT [37704] : PRE 1820 ALYTH, PER, SCT [37727] : PRE 1820 CORTACHY, ANS, SCT [37727]

HENDRY (SEE HENDRIE) [36302]

HENDY PRE 1850 MULLION & MABE, CON, ENG [36899]

HENEAGE C1700-1750 YORK, YKS & LIN, ENG [34727]

HENEKER ALL BELTANA, SA, AUS [34777]

HENERY 1850+ ATHLONE, ROS, IRL [35223] : 1830-1850S DUBLIN, IRL [37308]

HENESS WALTER C1850 AIRDS, NSW, AUS [38207] : SARAH 1863+ TAMBAROORA & BATHURST, NSW, AUS [38567] : 1800-1840 BRISTOL, SOM, ENG [38207] : RICHARD C1770+ BRISTOL CITY, ENG [38567] : ALL WORLDWIDE [38567]

HENEY 1740-1832 ENNISKILLEN, FER, TYR & ARM, IRL [34514]

HENGEVELD 1700-C1740S DOETINCHEM, GEL, NL [38358]

HENGSTELLER 1685 OBERBALDINGEN, BADEN, GER [38574]

HENKEL JOHN 1830 GER [37815]

HENKEL (SEE INKEL) [36678]

HENKEY 1897+ IPSWICH, QLD, AUS [33782]

HENLEY 1750+ NS, CAN [35299] : 1800 MAIDSTONE, KEN, ENG [34844] : C1670 DARTMOUTH, DEV, ENG [36000] : PRE 1870 GRAYS & ORSETT, ESS, ENG [36178] : ALL PETWORTH, SSX, ENG [37285] : PRE 1766 DUNSTABLE & EASTON BRAY, BDF, ENG [37710]

HENLY 1850+ CAN & USA [38261] : 1400+ BRK, WIL & MDX, ENG [38261] : 1850+ S AMERICA [38261]

HENN 1790+ NIAGARA DISTRICT, ONT, CAN [38323] : ALL LND, ENG [35628] : ALL STAFFORD, STS, ENG [36537] : PRE 1850 ERLACH, BAD, GER [38333] : PRE 1850 ERLACH, BAD, GER [38333]

HENNAH 1700S LONDON, LND, ENG [35858]

HENNEMANN PRE 1800 DOSSEL, WARBURG, GER [37569]

HENNES (SEE HENESS) [38567]

HENNESEY PRE 1860 KID, IRL [35206]

HENNESSEY C1881+ HEYWOOD, VIC, AUS [35233] : PATRICK 1800S SYDNEY, NSW, AUS [36291] : MARY ANN 1800S SYDNEY, NSW, AUS [36291] : C1850S TIPPERARY, TIP, IRL [35233] : 1800+ COR, IRL [36135] : C1822 BELFAST, ANT, IRL [36772]

HENNESSY 1870 KAPUNDA, SA, AUS [34844] : 1800+ FULHAM, LND, ENG [36026] : 1800-1850 ARDMAYLE, TIP, IRL [34183] : PRE 1870 SHANAGOLDEN, LIM, IRL [34812] : PRE 1900

COR, IRL [36963] : PRE 1840 FERMOY, COR, IRL [37018]

HENNESY 1830 MIDDLETON, COR, IRL [36907]

HENNEY 1830-1900 VICTORIA, NS, CAN [37489] : 1860+ POCATELLO, ID, USA [37489]

HENNIG PRE 1875 GER [37009]

HENNIGHAUSEN 1200+ NRW, BRD [38601] : 1500+ GREBENSTEIN, HES, BRD [38601] : 1300+ SOEST, NRW, BRD [38601] : 1720+ OPR, SU [38601] : 1780+ LITAUEN, SU [38601] : 1400-1750 REVAL & GOLDENBECK, ESTLAND, SU [38601] : ALL USA [38601]

HENNIKER 1800-1900 ASHFORD & CHALLOCK, KEN, ENG [36118]

HENNING 1880S ALKMAAR, NL [33802]

HENNINGER 1900-1950 NEWARK, NJ, USA [36349]

HENNINGHAM PRE 1860 COLLINGWOOD, VIC, AUS [37133] : ALL LONDON, ENG [37133]

HENNINGS PRE 1820 PSA, GER [38648]

HENNINGSGARD 1800-1990 ALEXANDRIA, MN, USA [34255]

HENNOCK 1858+ YOUNG, NSW, AUS [33763] : PRE 1858 MIHLA, GER [33763]

HENNOW C1700+ GORRAN, CON, ENG [35851]

HENRI 1817-1840 FRA [35092] : C1817-1840 FRA [35843]

HENRIET 1700-1900 ALS & LOR, FRA [36078]

HENRIKSSON 1890+ USA [38758]

HENRY 1920+ WAGGA WAGGA, NSW, AUS [33770] : 1930+ BEGA, NSW, AUS [33770] : JOHN 1870+ MALDON, VIC, AUS [33846] : 1840-1864 SYDNEY, NSW, AUS [35092] : 1800S MANDURAMA, NSW, AUS [35367] : 1843+ SYDNEY, NSW, AUS [35843] : COLIN & ALEX C1860S+ GLEBE, NSW, AUS [36314] : ROBERT C1860S+ GLEBE, NSW, AUS [36314] : WILLIAM 1800S SAS, CAN [36678] : ALEXIS C1812 SAS, CAN [36678] : ALL ST SAMPSONS, GSY, CHI [35433] : 1700+ SUNDERLAND, DUR, ENG [35364] : PRE 1800 FRA [35824] : PRE 1850 ARM, IRL [34999] : 1700+ DONEGORE, ANT, IRL [35874] : MARY 1894+ DON, IRL [36164] : PRE 1900 TYANEE & INISHRUSH, LDY, IRL [36529] : 1800+ ABERDEEN, SCT [33947] : JANE PRE 1851 EDINBURGH, SCT [34587] : 1780+ PAISLEY, RFW, SCT [35027] : 1770S DELTING, SHI, SCT [35824] : PRE 1850 SCT [35913] : 1800S TRANENT, LKS, SCT [36032] : ALEX 1814+ EDINBURGH, MLN, SCT [36314] : JAMES 1650-1776 BOSTON, PA, USA [34303] : PRE 1822 HARRISBURG, PA, USA [35289] : 1829 NY, USA [37531] : 1899 WAUPACA, WI, USA [37531] : 1870+ NEW ORLEANS, LA, USA [37583] : 1900+ NY, USA [37787] : ELIZABETH 1850 KINGSTON, NY, USA [38066] : 1737-1823 PETERSBURG COTTAGE, PA, USA [38094] : 1827-1912 HUNTINGDON CO., PA, USA [38094] : 1781-1856 FAIRFIELD, PA, USA [38094] : ALL FAYETTE CO. & CRAWFORD CO., PA, USA [38522] : 1850+ WORLDWIDE [35352]

HENSCHE 1631-1665 ADORF, WAL, GER [34912]

HENSEL PRE 1860 FRANKFORT MAIN, GER [38222] : 1913-1925 BERLIN, BLN, GER [38749] : 1800-1818 WEISSENFELS, KSA, GER [38749] : 1926 HAMBURG, HBG, GER [38749] : 1848-1925 JESSEN ELSTER, KSA, GER [38749] : 1636-1782 WURZEN, KSA, GER [38749]

HENSEY 1700S LONDON, CLA, IRL & ENG [37018]

HENSHALL PRE 1850 MACCLESFIELD, CHS, ENG [34686] : 1800-1900 POL [37064]

HENSLEY PRE 1760 CAMBORNE, CON, ENG [35517] : 1765+ BROADWAY, WOR, ENG [37265] : 1810+ FRANKFURT, KY, USA [37564]

HENSLIP ALL WORLDWIDE [33984]
HENSLOW PRE 1796 MAIDSTONE, KEN, ENG [34579]
HENSMAN 1600-1700 RUSHDEN, NTH, ENG [33856]
HENSON PRE 1850 CROXTON KEYRIAL, LEI, ENG [34621] : PRE 1820 SILEBY, LEI, ENG [38512] : PRE 1850 JACKSON CO., IL, NC & VA, USA [37529]
HENSTON ALL WORLDWIDE [37271]
HENSTONE ALL WORLDWIDE [37271]
HENTGES PRE 1800 KOBLENZ, RPR, GER [38437]
HENTIG ALL SALZGITTER, NSA, GER [38604]
HENTON EDNA 1917+ ENG & WLS [37356]
HENTSCH 1700+ ENG [37653]
HENTSCHKIE ALL SIL, GER, AUS & [36743]
HENTZE 1744 BLOMBERG, PYR, GER [38749]
HENWOOD 1840-1900 DURHAM CO.& MUSEOKO, ONT, CAN [34250] : PRE 1840S CARDINHAM & ST NEOT, CON, ENG [34250] : 1600-1900S ST NEOT, ENG [35776] : 1700S WADEBRIDGE, CON, ENG [35804] : PRE 1873 PLYMOUTH, DEV, ENG [35895] : PRE 1850 ST ENODER, CON, ENG [37105] : 1873-1930 TARANAKI, NZ [35895]
HENZE PRE 1852 HAN, GER [38190] : 1852+ SAN ANTONIO, TX, USA [38190]
HENZEY 1618+ KINGSWINFORD, STS & WOR, ENG [35013]
HEOWE 1800+ NSW, AUS [34845]
HEPBURN ALL AUS [34874] : 1840 EDINBURGH, SCT [33881] : ALL FORT AUGUSTUS, INV, SCT [34874] : 1872+ TILLICOULTRY, CLK, SCT [35021] : 1800S FORRES, MOR, SCT [36338] : 1300 SCT [37008] : PETER PRE 1850 WASHINGTON, DC, USA [38049]
HEPFER 1802+ BAW, GER [35287] : 1847+ WASHTENAW CO., MI, USA [35287] : 1866+ CLINTON CO., MI, USA [35287]
HEPHBURN C1750-1800 EDINBURGH, MLN, SCT [37572]
HEPP PRE 1750 WEIDENTHAL, RPF, GER [38681]
HEPPER 1850-1900 MOLLAND & ROSE ASH, DEV, ENG [37096]
HEPPLE 1864+ BEDLINGTON, NBL, ENG [36609]
HEPPLER C1750 OFINGEN, BAD, GER [34239]
HEPPLEWHITE 1800+ NEWCASTLE, NBL, ENG [34074]
HEPTER 1700+ PENSHURST, SSX, ENG [37328]
HEPTINSTALL PRE 1900 ENG [37097]
HEPTONSTALL PRE 1850 HUNSLET & GARFORTH, WRY, ENG [34382]
HEPWORTH 1870S FREMANTLE, WA, AUS [33849] : 1810-1850 HALIFAX, WRY, ENG [33767] : ALL TODWICK & WALES, WRY, ENG [34116] : PRE 1822 LEA, LIN, ENG [34501] : 1800+ DEWSBURY, WRY, ENG [34512] : 1800-1900 YKS, ENG [34631] : 1840S-1860 MANCHESTER, LAN, ENG [36319] : PETER 1780+ MORLEY, WRY, ENG [37621]
HERAGHTY C1840 CARROWMORE LAKE, MAY, IRL [34084]
HERAUD C1860+ TARNAGULLA & RHEOLA, VIC, AUS [35525]
HERAULT 1700-1800 JER, CHI [35494]
HERBANK C1800 ENG [34132] : 1815+ BOSTON, MA, USA [34132]
HERBER PRE 1630 HEMMENDORF, BAV, GER [35242]
HERBERT JAMES 1856+ BALLARAT, VIC, AUS [37155] : RALPH 1887+ COLLINGWOOD, VIC, AUS [37155] : 1856 MELBOURNE & IPSWICH, VIC & QLD, AUS [38008] : PRE 1800 MARSKE IN CLEVELAND, NRY, ENG [33956] : 1750-1800 SUDBURY, SFK, ENG [34552] : 1770-1840 MONKS KIRBY & LEAMINGTON, WAR, ENG [34769] :

1782 HANSLOPE, BKM, ENG [35256] : PRE 1850 MINCHINHAMPTON, GLS, ENG [35540] : 1800-1830 BISLEY, GLS, ENG [35741] : PRE 1860 EXETER, DEV, ENG [35882] : PRE 1825 ENSTONE, STS & WAR, ENG [36064] : PRE 1813 AMPREY, YKS, ENG [36064] : PRE 1820 FALMOUTH, CON, ENG [36064] : PRE 1824 ISLEWORTH, MDX, ENG [36064] : PRE 1830 BRK, ENG [36064] : 1834-1900 DEPTFORD, KEN, ENG [36064] : 1780+ WARGRAVE, BRK, ENG [36975] : 1800+ LITTLEWICK GREEN, BRK, ENG [36975] : PRE 1800 CUL, ENG [37089] : PRE 1800 NBL, ENG [37089] : 1830+ OXFORD, OXF, ENG [37202] : 1860+ MARYLEBONE & BATTERSEA, LND, ENG [37445] : 1830+ LIVERPOOL, LAN, ENG [37500] : 1700-1800 MIDTOWN, CUL, ENG [37858] : PRE 1800 GLS, ENG [37941] : 1800+ DUB, IRL [34664] : PRE 1820 IRL [36064] : RICHARD 1880+ AUCKLAND, NZ [33956] : 1848 GLASGOW, LKS, SCT [34224] : 1700-1991 NINDHAM, NH, USA [38200] : 1740-1750 CRICKHOWELL, BRE, WLS [38465]
HERBERTSON C1820 EDGERTON, ROX, SCT [35963]
HERBISON 1700+ KILBRIDE, ANT, IRL [35874]
HERBORT 1750-1850 GER [37599] : 1840-1900 ORLEANS & JEFFERSON PAR., LA, USA [37599]
HERBST 1600+ STUTTGART, BAW, GER [34980] : 1729-1780 HANNOVER, HAN, GER [38626]
HERBSTREIT 1850+ SCARSDALE, VIC, AUS [33772] : 1680+ OHRENSBACH, BAD, GER [33772] : 1750 EISENBACH, BAD, GER [33772] : 1800+ RUDENBERG, BAD, GER [33772] : 1715+ OBER GLOTTERTAL, BAD, GER [33772]
HERCLIFF PRE 1862 YKS, ENG [34578]
HERCOCK 1800+ LND, ENG [36785]
HERD ISAAC 1800-1884 PENRITH, CUL, ENG [36180] : PRE 1790 ABERNETHY, PER, SCT [34285] : PRE 1850 KILCONQUHAR, FIF, SCT [34784]
HERDA C1852+ TEICHENAU, SIL, GER [38598]
HERDER ALL DEV, ENG [36999]
HERDMAN PRE 1900 SIMONBURN & CHOLLERTON, NBL, ENG [36110]
HERDRICH ALL HOF, BAV, GER [38176]
HERDSMAN 1850+ BRISBANE, QLD, AUS [35829]
HERENDEEN PRE 1900 IL, OH & NY, USA [36544]
HEREPATH 1790+ BRISTOL, GLS, ENG [37056]
HERFURTH PRE 1800 FRANKENTHAL, RPF, GER [38681]
HERICHER PRE 1695 LOUVETOT, HN, FRA [34047]
HERINGTON PRE 1850 FAREHAM, HAM & SSX, ENG [36396]
HERIOT PRE 1700 MLN, SCT [34861] : 1750+ PETERHEAD, ABD & MLN, SCT [36090]
HERITAGE 1860+ AUS [33846] : PRE 1810 BIRMINGHAM, WAR, ENG [33846]
HERITY C1850 MOIRA, ONT, CAN [34084]
HERIVEL C1790 ALD, CHI [35998] : 1600+ WORLDWIDE [34690]
HERLEY ALL EXMOUTH, DEV, ENG [36232]
HERMAN SOLOMON 1870+ GEELONG, VIC, AUS [35803] : PRE 1853 COBLENZ, BRD [37998] : 1800+ DEV, ENG [34085] : PRE 1800 LONDON, ENG [36154] : PRE 1853 WALWORTH & NEWINGTON, SRY, ENG [37998] : 1800-1850 NEISSE, SIL, GER [36555] : C1824 BAV, GER [38527]
HERMANIDES ALL NL [36765]
HERMANN C1815+ RUDENBERG, BAD, GER [33772] : PRE 1850 SAIG, BAD, GER [33772]
HERMELING 1700-1840 WESTERKAPPELN, WEF, GER [36957]
HERMES PRE 1900 NEUERBURG, BRD [38615]
HERMITAGE ALL GRIMSBY, LIN, ENG [36168]

HERMON 1800+ THEALE HUNDRED, BRK, ENG [36435]

HERMSEN 1725+ BEEK (BIJ BERGH), GEL, NL [38358]

HERN PRE 1850 WOOBURN & UPTON CUM CHALVEY, BKM, ENG [37410]

HERNANDEZ NINA ALL SANTA CRUZ CO., AZ, USA [35304]

HERNDON 1600-1680 TENTERDEN, KEN, ENG [36566] : C1677 CAROLINE CO., VA, USA [36354] : GEORGE 1862 WOODFORD CO., IL, USA [38132]

HERNE 1870+ SYDNEY, NSW, AUS [34978] : 1750+ OLNEY, BKM, ENG [38001]

HERNI 1750-1870 NEWVEILNOA, HEN, GER [38007]

HERNON 1850 GALWAY, GAL, IRL [33783]

HEROD 1800+ NFK, ENG [35939] : JAMES 1841 ASHTON UNDER LYNE, LAN, ENG [37184] : PRE 1800 NTT, ENG [37893]

HEROLD 1890-1920 LIVERPOOL, LAN, ENG [37630] : PRE 1860 KASSELL, HES, GER [38026] : PRE 1900 HOF, BAV & PRE, GER [38055]

HERON 1841-1855 MAITLAND, NSW, AUS [34693] : 1850+ HAMILTON, VIC, AUS [35752] : 1853+ ADELAIDE, SA, AUS [35811] : 1871 SYDNEY, NSW, AUS [36599] : 1820-65 CAMPBELLS RIVER, NSW, AUS [36648] : 1870-1880 VIC, AUS [37964] : 1853 SOUTHWARK, LND, ENG [35811] : 1800-1850 DOW, IRL [34523] : 1800-1840 ENNISKILLEN, FER, IRL [34693] : 1855-1920 AUCKLAND, NZ [34693] : 1800+ KIRKSOWALD, AYR, SCT [34225] : 1800-1875 INCH, AYR & WIG, SCT [34523] : 1750+ WIG, SCT [35269] : PRE 1850 ABERDEEN, ABD, SCT [35752] : ALEXANDER PRE 1850 SCT [35752] : PRE 1850 KIRKCALDY, FIF, SCT [35752] : C1867 CUPAR, FIF, SCT [35811] : C1820 KIRKCALDY, FIF, SCT [35811] : C1853 CUPAR, FIF, SCT [35811] : PRE 1830 AIRLIE & KIRRIEMUIR, ANS, SCT [37727] : 1800+ KINWIMMING, AYR, SCT [37949] : 1750+ KKD, SCT [38388] : 1825+ BALTIMORE, MD, USA [35269] : 1837+ CONNERSVILLE, IN, USA [35269]

HERR DAVID & MARIA 1778+ MANOR TWP., PA, USA [34247]

HERRENG 1843 SCHRIESHEIM, BAD, GER [33929]

HERREWIJNEN 1650+ ZUH & ZEL, NL [36464]

HERRICK 1600-1700 LEI, ENG [36146] : 1825+ STANMORE, MDX, ENG [37345] : C1830 BIRR, OFF, IRL [34814] : MARIA PRE 1809 COR, IRL [36453] : 1786-1850 WORTHINGTON, MA, USA [36562] : 1629-1660 SALEM, MA, USA [36562] : 1695-1786 PRESTON, CT, USA [36562] : 1662-1708 BEVERLY, MA, USA [36562] : 1850-1940 BOSTON, MA, USA [36562] : 1630+ SALEM, MA, USA [36909]

HERRIDGE ALL BRIGHTON, SSX, ENG [34247] : PRE 1800 LONDON, ENG [34247] : ALL WORLDWIDE [37416]

HERRIES PRE 1855 GLENCAIRN & APPLEGARTH, DFS, KKD & WIG, SCT [37238]

HERRING 1890+ GEURIE, NSW, AUS [36648] : 1870+ DUBBO, NSW, AUS [36648] : 1820-65 CAMPBELLS RIVER, NSW, AUS [36648] : 1820-65 BATHURST, NSW, AUS [36648] : PRE 1800 DEVIZES, WIL, ENG [34974] : 1850-1950 LONDON, ENG [36109] : ALL LONDON &, NFK, ENG [36152] : 1810-50 LONDON, ENG [36648] : ALL BOONEY, NFK, ENG [36846] : ALL ELSING, NFK, ENG [36846] : PRE 1800 CHARSFIELD, SFK, ENG [37191] : 1700 LND, ENG [37733] : 1800-1900 STEPNEY, LND, ENG [38483]

HERRINGSHAW 1600-1800 EAST TORRINGTON, LIN, ENG [35937]

HERRINGTON 1800+ ENG [35793] : PRE 1890 PARISH, MONROE CO., MO & IL, USA [37529] : PRE 1890 GRAND TOWER, JACKSON CO., IL & MO, USA [37529] : 1800S WI, USA [38468] : 1800-1900 LOUISVILLE, KY, USA [38770]

HERRIOT 1850+ GLEN WAVERLEY, VIC, AUS [35749] : 1770-1850 SSX, ENG [37207] : 1700-1780S DUNBLANE & STRATHAVEN, CLK, SCT [35044] : 1800+ ABERDEEN, ABD, SCT [35749]

HERRIOTT PRE 1900 WOOLWICH, KEN, ENG [33965] : PRE 1749 EAST DEAN, SSX, ENG [36668] : 1800+ ANT, IRL [33979] : 1550+ EDINBURGH, MLN, SCT [33979]

HERRLIBERGER PRE 1850 HERRLIBERG, ZH, CH [38665] : PRE 1850 ZURICH, ZH, CH [38665]

HERRMAN ALL NZ & GER [34603]

HERRMANN 1879+ TAWONGA, VIC, AUS [33877] : KATHARINA PRE 1880 KRS. GUMBINNEN, OPR, GER [38649]

HERRMANNSEN C1824 LUNDEN, SHO, GER [38671]

HERROLD 1800-1860 WESTMORELAND CO., PA, USA [36897]

HERRON C1858 SYDNEY, NSW, AUS [35569] : PRE 1825 PORTADOWN, ARM, IRL [35430] : PRE 1855 ARM, IRL [35569] : ALL BANBRIDGE, DOW, IRL [36428] : 1780-1820 BOARDMILLS, DOW, IRL [38347]

HERRON (SEE HERON) [34225]

HERSEY PRE 1823 PETWORTH & WISBOROUGH GREEN, SSX, ENG [34726] : 1635+ MA, ME & CT, USA [38021]

HERSHEY 1650-1750 RPF, CH [38219] : 1600-1700 ALS & LOR, FRA [38219] : 1600-1700 ELO & AAR, FRA [38219] : 1650-1800 LANCASTER CO., PA, USA [38219] : ALL WORLDWIDE [37785]

HERSOVITZ 1890-1930 VONAJ, HU [38236]

HERTEL (SEE HARTEL) [35251]

HERTER ALL WORLDWIDE [38599]

HERTLING PRE 1800 ANDERNACH, RPF, BRD [38617]

HERTOGH PRE 1800 OSTEND, WVL, BEL [38708]

HERTRICH 1880+ FASSIFERN, QLD, AUS [33782] : 1600-1800 MAURSMUNSTER, ALS & LOR, FRA [36328]

HERTZBERG PRE 1877 PRITZIZ KOMMAR, POM, GER [36290]

HERTZBERGER 1800-1850 POS, GER [36522] : 1800-1850 PRE, GER [36522]

HERTZLER 1700S BERKS, PA, USA [38184]

HERTZOG PRE 1800 GER [38600]

HERTZUM 1700-1900S ODENSE, VEJLE & AHINEN, SHO, DEN & GER [36706] : 1700+ WORLDWIDE [36706]

HERVEY PRE 1800 PAPPLEWICK, NTT, ENG [36387]

HERWECH ALL WORLDWIDE [38709]

HERWEG ALL WORLDWIDE [38709]

HERWEGH ALL WORLDWIDE [38709]

HERWICH ALL WORLDWIDE [38709]

HERWIG ALL WORLDWIDE [38709]

HERWIGH ALL WORLDWIDE [38709]

HERWIJNE 1650+ ZUH & ZEL, NL [36464]

HERZBERG 1700+ RIGA, SU [34943] : 1700+ SU [34943]

HERZOG ALL CH [38600]

HESBIN PRE 1750 STOKE FERRY, NFK, ENG [34139]

HESELTON ALL PICKERING, YKS, ENG [34629] : 1700-1900 ENG [37207]

HESKETH PRE 1920 LIVERPOOL, LAN, ENG [38586]

HESLEM C1855 EMERALD HILL, VIC, AUS [35391]

HESLIP 1900+ NEWRY, DOW, IRL [35219] : C1800 MLN, SCT [35057]

HESLOP PRE 1840 TORPENHOW, CUL, ENG [34392] : 1800-1850 GAYLES, NRY, ENG [36217] : 1846 KILKEEL, DOW, IRL [35529]

HESMER 1800+ CROYDON, SRY, ENG [35355]

HESP ALL WORLDWIDE [37281]

HESPE ALL WORLDWIDE [37281]

HESS PRE 1840 BAW, BRD [34180] : 1744-1926 SCHLEUSINGEN, THURINGIA, GER [38148] : PRE 1790 CAAN, RPF, GER [38663] : 1700+ HERBORN, LUX [37016]

HESSE 1900S ORANGE, NSW, AUS [35367] : 1900S ROCKLEY, NSW, AUS [35367] : PRE 1780 DEUNA, PSA, GER [38048]

HESSEL ANNA 1800-1840 SPEYER, BAV, GER [33752]

HESSELL PHOEBE 1713+ WORLDWIDE [34247]

HESSELTINE PRE 1900 NEWCASTLE ON TYNE, NBL & YKS, ENG [35639]

HESSIE PRE 1813-49 JAMAICA & BAHAMAS, W.INDIES [37518]

HESSLEIN 1700-1900 BAV, GER [38128]

HESTER 1800+ SHEFFIELD, YKS, ENG [36493] : 1780+ MDX, ENG [36872] : C1746 DERITEND & BROADESLEY, WAR, ENG [37144] : PRE 1770S VA & NC, USA [37522] : 1690-1810 MECKLENBERG CO., VA, USA [38219]

HETHERINGTON 1880+ RANDWICK, NSW, AUS [36129] : 1880+ SYDNEY, NSW, AUS [36129] : JOSHUA C1700-1768 YKS, ENG [37076] : 1780+ PADSTOW, CON, ENG [37224] : 1700-1800 WIGTON & LONGTOWN, CUL, ENG [37654] : 1800S LET, IRL [35511] : 1830+ MAKENNY, TYR, IRL [36615] : C1825 IRL [37795] : PRE 1875 FALKIRK, STI, SCT [37308] : 1845+ ALBANY, NY, USA [36129] : 1850+ ST LOUIS, MO, USA [36129] : ALL WORLDWIDE [37076]

HETT PRE 1780 LONGSTOWE, CAM, ENG [35070]

HETZEL ALL LETMATHE, WEF, GER [34861] : 1850 WARWICK TWP., NY, USA [38320]

HEUELER 1800 BINSWANGER, GER [36596]

HEUER PRE 1770 STRALSUND, POM, GER [38632]

HEUGH PRE 1844 LINKESFIELD, AYR, SCT [35523] : ALL LINLITHGOW, WLN, SCT [37480]

HEUGHAN 1793+ DUMFRIES, DFS, SCT [36254]

HEUKELBACH ALL WEI, GER [38607]

HEUP 1840+ WI, USA [36542]

HEUSER PRE 1770 SHO, GER [38669]

HEUSTED 1700+ NY & OH, USA [37026]

HEUSTON PRE 1790 TIPPERARY, TIP, IRL [37579]

HEUTELBECK ALL WEI, GER [38607]

HEVENOR PRE 1860 PALLASKENRY, LIM, IRL [34937]

HEWADINE 1900 NOTTINGHAM, NTT, ENG [37829]

HEWAN 1600-1800 YKS, ENG [34513]

HEWARD PRE 1718 AYLESBURY, BRK, ENG [35578]

HEWES C1740 DEWLISH, DOR, ENG [35203]

HEWETSON ALL DFS & KKS, SCT [35222]

HEWETT 1800+ NEWINGTON, SRY, ENG [33814] : C1810 DILTON, WIL, ENG [35076] : PRE 1855 REIGATE, SRY, ENG [36589] : ALL ST FAITHS, NFK, ENG [37689] : 1906+ BOSTON, MA, USA [37626] : 1700+ CARDIFF, WLS [36794]

HEWISON 1900-1990 VANCOUVER, BC & ALB, CAN [37670]

HEWIT PRE 1850 HUTTON, ELN, SCT [33959]

HEWITSON 1900-1990 VANCOUVER, BC & ALB, CAN [37670] : PRE 1853 DFS, SCT [35035]

HEWITT 1850S SYDNEY, NSW, AUS [34607] : PRE 1900 RICHMOND, TAS, AUS [34918] : ISABELLA 1825+ PORT MACQUARIE, NSW, AUS [37906] : HUGH 1860+ PORT PIRIE, SA, AUS & NZ [33840] : 1700-1850 SOM, ENG [33851] : 1700+ YKS, ENG

[34607] : PRE 1920 WADEBRIDGE, CON, ENG [34657] : 1735+ BROUGHTON BY BRIGG, LIN, ENG [35587] : 1800+ WORKSOP, NTT, ENG [35847] : PRE 1780 EDGEFIELD, NFK, ENG [36726] : 1800-1900 APPLETON & STRETTON, CHS, ENG [36740] : 1700+ KINETON & MANCETTER, WAR, ENG [37056] : 1800-1850 NFK, ENG [37233] : VIOLET C1860 CROPREDY, OXF, ENG [37375] : PRE 1880S ERDINGTON, WAR, ENG [37384] : ALL ST FAITHS, NFK, ENG [37689] : PRE 1800 WELFORD, NTH, ENG [37711] : 1800-1900 SHOREDITCH, MDX, ENG [37747] : 1750-1850 ALDWINCLE, NTH, ENG [37747] : 1700-1800 LEEK WOOTTON, WAR, ENG [37858] : 1800S+ GREENWICH, KEN, ENG [37868] : PRE 1783 COVENTRY, WAR, ENG [38512] : 1880+ PALMERSTON, OTAGO, NZ [34607] : 1855+ LESMAHAGOW, LKS, SCT [37661] : 1800S LEWISTON, NY, USA [37442] : 1700+ CARDIFF, WLS [36794]

HEWLETT PRE 1865 LIVERPOOL, LAN, ENG [33863] : PRE 1877 HORNCASTLE, LIN, ENG [33863] : C1811 ILCHESTER, SOM, ENG [35464] : C1750-1800 ENG [36289] : 1840 NORWOOD, SRY, ENG [37080] : PRE 1700 KENCOT, OXF, ENG [37763]

HEWLITT 1800-1900 TUNBRIDGE WELLS, KEN, ENG [34735]

HEWS 1800 SOUTH FAMBRIDGE, ESS, ENG [37928]

HEWSON C1820 LONDON, ENG [35865] : 1600-1700 AUGHTON, ERY, ENG [37411] : PRE 1856 DEEPING ST JAMES, LIN, ENG [38208]

HEXTALL PRE 1840 SUTTON CHENEY, LEI, ENG [35232] : PRE 1651 LEI, ENG [37706]

HEXTER ALL UK & AUS [38288]

HEY 1800+ THORNTON, YKS, ENG [35734] : 1870+ ROCHDALE, LAN, ENG [36523]

HEYBOURN ALL BLEDLOW, BKM & OXF, ENG [34826]

HEYCOCK 1820+ COLWALL, HEF, ENG [34334]

HEYD PRE 1890 DOSSENHEIM S/Z, ALS, FRA [36930]

HEYDEN 1853+ GEELONG & BALLARAT, VIC, AUS [35564] : DAVID PRE 1853 BARLEY, HRT, ENG [35564] : 1600-1800 GLS, ENG [36165] : 1840-1850 LND, ENG [36165]

HEYDON THOMAS G. 1860+ CHARTERS TOWERS, QLD, AUS & ENG [37161] : 1820S UK [35772]

HEYFORD C1790 NORTHAMPTON, NTH, ENG [37536]

HEYL MARIA 1750-1850 LAUTERECKEN, RPF, BRD [33752] : PRE 1888 GER [35280]

HEYLER 1800 BINSWANGER, GER [36596]

HEYMAN PRE 1855 ISLINGTON, LND, ENG [35134]

HEYN PRE 1750 WESTHEIM, BAY, BRD [35311] : 1700+ BREMERVORDE, NSA, GER [38578]

HEYNEMANN PRE 1740 HES, GER [38642]

HEYNEN PRE 1800 SITTARD, LBG, NL [38167]

HEYWOOD 1800S ADELAIDE, SA, AUS [34191] : PRE 1840 WITHERIDGE & OAKFORD, DEV, ENG [35866] : PRE 1840 RACKENFORD, DEV, ENG [35866] : 1700-1800 DISS, NFK, ENG [37246] : 1800S OLDHAM, LAN, ENG [37442] : PRE 1800 MANCHESTER, LAN, ENG [38186] : 1800+ MANCHESTER, LAN, ENG & NZ [36257] : PRE 1800 BRADDAN, IOM, UK [36768]

HEYWORTH C1880 CASTLETON, LAN, ENG [36649]

HIBBARD 1815+ NSW, AUS [33931] : WILLIAM 1831+ SOUTH COAST & PARRAMATTA, NSW, AUS [36638] : C1600 ENG [34395] : 1840S LAN, ENG [34977] : 1600-1991 WINDHAM, CT, USA [38200] : 1781+ VT, USA [38520]

HIBBEN 1750+ WORLDWIDE [35269]

HIBBERD C1800+ BARFORD, WIL, CUL & LAN, ENG **[34040]** : C1840 URCHFONT, WIL, ENG **[34239]** : PRE 1850 GLS, ENG **[35224]** : 1870S DONCASTER, YKS, ENG **[37692]**

HIBBERT 1815+ NSW, AUS **[33931]** : 1896+ STEPNEY, SA, AUS **[34595]** : 1814+ WILBERFORCE, NSW, AUS **[35331]** : 1780S CHS, ENG **[35331]** : 1700-1900 WAR & NTH, ENG **[36007]** : 1800S ANNERSLEY, NTT, ENG **[36511]** : 1840-1929 BRAYWICK, BRK, ENG **[36975]** : 1800S MDX, ENG **[37186]** : 1750-1850 DBY, ENG **[37188]** : C1835 ALDGATE, MDX, ENG **[37239]** : C1815 RUNCORN, CHS, ENG **[37697]** : PRE 1820 DBY, ENG **[37875]** : TITUS 1847 WAYNESBORO, VA, USA **[36698]** : NATHANIEL 1843 WAYNESVILLE, VA, USA **[36698]** : MALCOLM G. 1896 USA **[36698]** : MARGARET D. ALL VA, USA **[36698]** : ELIZABETH 1880 BROOKLYN, NY, USA **[36698]** : ROBERT 1847 CHARLOTTESVILLE, VA, USA **[36698]** : GEORGE WM. ALL TX, USA **[36698]** : WILLIAM 1879 MOUNDSVILLE, VA, USA **[36698]** : ELLEN RUTH ALL GREENSBORO, NC, USA **[36698]**

HIBBIT 1880+ HALTON, YKS, ENG **[34243]** : 1850+ LITTLE ILFORD, ESS, ENG **[34243]** : PRE 1870 HACKNEY, LND, ENG **[34243]**

HIBBS ALL BURNT ISLAND, NFD, CAN **[33823]** : 1800S MANCHESTER, LAN, ENG **[36786]** : PRE 1700 BONSALL, DBY, ENG **[38321]** : C1830 BULLITT & HARDIN, KY, USA **[37527]** : 1667+ WRIGHTSTOWN, PA, USA **[37564]**

HICKEY C1840 QUE, CAN **[38455]** : JOHN 1815+ BRISTOL, GLS, ENG **[35583]** : 1840S CORK CITY, COR, IRL **[34204]** : C1863 KILCOON, MEA, IRL **[34276]** : 1800-1860 THOMASTOWN, KIK, IRL **[34687]** : 1830S CLA, IRL **[34793]** : MARY 1790-1850 KILLALOE, CLA, IRL **[34915]** : 1800+ DERRYGOOLIN, GAL, IRL **[35054]** : 1800 CLA, IRL **[35067]** : 1850 LIMERICK, IRL **[35204]** : C1850 O'BRIENSBRIDGE, CLA, IRL **[35920]** : C1841 KILLALOE, CLA, IRL **[35922]** : MARY 1829-1855 KIK, IRL **[38104]** : 1820S CONCORD TWP., ROSS, OH, USA **[38054]**

HICKFORD ALL WORLDWIDE **[36889]**

HICKLAND PRE 1800 ANT, ARM & DON, IRL **[35897]**

HICKLEY 1700S BISHOPS WALTHAM, HAM, ENG **[36263]**

HICKLING 1815+ SIMCOE CO., ONT, CAN **[34465]** : PRE 1850 LONDON, ENG **[34465]** : THOMAS 1800+ SUTTON BONNINGTON & BEESTON, NTT, ENG **[35712]** : PRE 1800 NTT, ENG **[36140]** : PRE 1735 LEI, ENG **[36184]** : 1790-1860 GREAT YARMOUTH, NFK, ENG **[36663]** : 1750+ SYSTON & ROTHLEY, LEI, ENG **[36794]** : 1840S+ LEAMINGTON, WAR, ENG **[36809]**

HICKMAN 1850+ SYDNEY, NSW, AUS **[37128]** : PRE 1800 BIRMINGHAM, WAR, ENG **[36177]** : 1780-1820 MDX & SRY, ENG **[36491]** : 1850S TIPTON, STS, ENG **[36528]** : 1900 HIGH BARNETT, LND, ENG **[37627]** : 1764 MD, USA **[37795]** : PRE 1750 USA **[38605]**

HICKMANS PRE 1850 WOMBOURNE & SEDGLEY, STS, ENG **[36110]** : PRE 1800 DUDLEY, WOR, ENG **[36518]**

HICKMOT PRE 1840 LAMBERHURST & GOUDHURST, KEN, ENG **[34897]**

HICKMOTT PRE 1840 YALDING & FARLEIGH, KEN, ENG **[34325]**

HICKNER PRE 1855 NECKERSALM, WUE, GER **[34886]**

HICKOX 1830+ NY, USA **[37787]**

HICKS 1830-1840S HOBART, TAS, AUS **[33780]** : 1855+ SYDNEY, NSW, AUS **[34977]** : PRE 1896 ALEXANDRIA, NSW, AUS **[34979]** : PRE 1861+ BULLI & ILLAWARRA, NSW, AUS **[35143]** : C1900 SURREY HILLS, VIC, AUS **[35515]** : 1900+ VIC, AUS **[37149]** : 1815+ MIDLANDS, ENG **[33788]** : PRE 1820 CON, ENG **[33799]** : 1828+ TRURO, CON, ENG **[34045]** : PRE 1859 WITNEY, OXF, ENG **[34585]** : THOMAS C1812 BRISTOL, GLS, ENG **[34661]** : 1750-1850 NORWICH, NFK, ENG **[34822]** : PETER PRE 1760 BRISTOL, GLS, ENG **[34908]** : 1820+ HACKNEY, MDX, ENG **[34977]** : 1800S AYLESBURY & HARTWELL, BKM, ENG **[35123]** : PRE 1866 SONNING, BRK, ENG **[35200]** : C1820 THETFORD, NFK, ENG **[35502]** : PRE 1866 MALDON, ESS, ENG **[35515]** : 1830-40S CAM & LIN, ENG **[35525]** : ALL KEN, ENG **[35566]** : PRE 1800 EWELME, OXF, ENG **[35838]** : PRE 1825 SEA PALLING & WAXHAM, NFK, ENG **[36118]** : ELIZABETH 1700-1799 WISBECH ST MARY, CAM, ENG **[36149]** : ELIZA C1837 WITNEY, OXF, ENG **[37106]** : 1750-1850 LAMBOURNE, BRK, ENG **[37188]** : PRE 1850 TRURO, CON, ENG **[37237]** : 1650-1750 GRIMSHOE, NFK, ENG **[37456]** : 1800+ CON, ENG **[38338]** : PRE 1700 SRY, ENG **[38745]** : ISAAC 1750-1850 HAM & QUE, ENG & CAN **[37496]** : PRE 1797 GLANSHREE, WIC, IRL **[34814]** : PRE 1765 BRISTOL CO., MA & RI, USA **[36544]** : PRE 1840 SULLIVAN CO., TN, USA **[37029]** : 1850+ HURON CO., OH, USA **[38018]** : 1825-1860 IN, USA **[38137]** : 1870S FULTON CO., IL, USA **[38223]** : 1800+ LYNDON, VT, USA **[38520]**

HICKSON 1842 MACLEAY RIVER, NSW, AUS **[37119]** : PRE 1832 STS, ENG **[35090]** : PRE 1800 CHS, ENG **[36066]** : PRE 1841 SHOREDITCH, MDX, ENG **[36072]** : PRE 1810 IRL & CAN **[34068]**

HICKY C1860 NAIRN, SCT & IRL **[35722]**

HIDAY 1800-1855 MARTINSVILLE, IN, USA **[38199]**

HIDE PRE 1800 GODMANCHESTER, HUN, ENG **[35185]**

HIDER ALL SSX & KEN, ENG **[37210]**

HIEMPSALL ALL ENG &, ALGERIA **[37742]**

HIERN 1850+ SA, VIC & TAS, AUS **[37873]** : PRE 1850 DEV, ENG **[37873]**

HIERONYMI 1850-1875 BINGEN AREA, RPR, GER **[38528]**

HIESIER MARIA CATH. 1740 TRAPPE, PA, USA **[38122]**

HIESTAND 1730+ BOTETOURT CO., VA, USA **[35266]**

HIETT C1740 CHESTER CO., PA, USA **[36319]**

HIGBEE 1750-1850 LONDON, ENG **[37038]** : ALL FIF, SCT **[34226]**

HIGG FRED. 1870+ TARNAGULLA, VIC, AUS **[35803]**

HIGGANS 1809S+ BRISBANE, QLD, AUS **[35907]**

HIGGEN 1670-1720 GLS, ENG **[37233]**

HIGGENBOTTOM C1783 LAN, ENG **[38389]**

HIGGENS 1670-1750 SALISBURY, WIL, ENG **[37233]**

HIGGERSON 1767-1900+ SYDNEY, NSW, AUS **[35497]**

HIGGERTY ALL OTTAWA, ONT, CAN **[36662]**

HIGGIN C1780-1858 LANCASTER, LAN, ENG **[36768]**

HIGGINBOTHAM ALL ASHTON, LAN, ENG **[36187]**

HIGGINBOTTOM PRE 1850 YKS, ENG **[36110]**

HIGGINS 1820+ SYDNEY, NSW, AUS **[34424]** : 1900+ WARRAGUL, VIC, AUS **[35140]** : 1900+ SEA LAKE, VIC, AUS **[35140]** : 1870+ CORA LYN & KOOWEERUP, VIC, AUS **[35140]** : 1850+ PORT ARLINGTON, VIC, AUS **[35140]** : RICHARD 1827+ HOBART & NEW NORFOLK, TAS, AUS **[35394]** : ALL STRANGWAYS, VIC, AUS **[35526]** : 1850+

VIC, AUS [35836] : BERNARD C1891 TAREE, NSW, AUS [36284] : 1660+ ST MICHAELS, BARBADOS [38235] : ALL HURON CO., ONT, CAN [38419] : 1820+ DITCHEAT & WRAXHALL, SOM, ENG [33852] : 1860+ PORTSMOUTH, HAM, ENG [35046] : PRE 1855 PRESTWICH, LAN, ENG [35097] : 1830S-1850S CHESTER, CHS, ENG [35483] : ALL LIVERPOOL, ENG [35707] : 1600-1840 BALTONSBOROUGH, SOM, ENG [36865] : 1600S EAST PENNARD, SOM, ENG [36865] : 1700-1850 RHYME INTRINSECA, DOR, ENG [37378] : 1860S CHARLTON, LND, ENG [37853] : 1700-1800 BALTONSBOROUGH, SOM, ENG [37924] : PRE 1850 ENG [38419] : PRE 1856 EGLISH, OFF, IRL [34037] : C1840 BUTTEVANT, COR, IRL [34145] : ANTHONY C1850 WIC, IRL [34935] : ALL 'BENOWN CASTLE', MEA, IRL [34937] : PRE 1825 TULLAMORE, OFF, IRL [34937] : PATRICK 1836-1837 IRL [35046] : PRE 1850 CLA, IRL [35792] : PRE 1875 MAGHEREBOY & BALLAGHADERREEN, MAY & ROS, IRL [35900] : 1830 ROSCREA, TIP, IRL [35903] : C1820-1880 IRL [36580] : ALL DUBLIN, IRL [37503] : 1800-1850 COR, IRL [37765] : ALL IRL [37893] : PRE 1850 IRL [38419] : 1800+ CROAGH, LIM, IRL & AUS [33769] : 1840+ NELSON, NZ [35058] : 1800S DUMBARTON, DNB, SCT [33820] : C1863 PAISLEY, RFW, SCT [33820] : C1885+ GLASGOW, LKS, SCT [33820] : 1800+ AYR, SCT [35140] : 1800+ GLASGOW, SCT [35140] : C1870 LADHOPE, ROX, SCT [35486] : 1800+ PHILADELPHIA CO., PA, USA [36580] : 1780-1810 ESSEX CO., NY, USA [36581] : 1750-1790 BERKSHIRE CO., MA, USA [36581] : ALL GREAT BEND, PA, USA [37503] : MEHITABLE 1758+ GREENLAND, NH, USA [37784] : C1855-1880S HOLYHEAD BANGOR, AGY, WLS [35483]

HIGGINSON PRE 1827 LEICESTER, LEI, ENG [34501] : ALL LEIRE, LEI, ENG [35984] : C1870-1900 WARRINGTON, LAN, ENG [36161] : 1700-1800 SAL, ENG [37924] : 1750+ KNIGHTLEY, STS, ENG [38481] : 1812-1850+ DUBLIN CITY, IRL [36296] : 1878 CORK CITY, IRL [36296] : ALL ANT, IRL [38084]

HIGGS 1850+ RANDWICK, NSW, AUS [35703] : 1828+ CHOLSEY, BRK, ENG [33942] : 1865 DEAL, KEN, ENG [33942] : PRE 1880 ABINGDON, BRK, ENG [34116] : 1830 REDLYNCH, WIL, ENG [34731] : 1700-1850 LONDON, ENG [34975] : C1888 PAINGTON, DEV, ENG [35526] : 1800+ BRK, ENG [35703] : 1800-1860 CHURCHAM, GLS, ENG [36663] : ALL HRT, ENG [37197] : 1750+ KEN, ENG [37266] : PRE 1820 HALESOWEN, WOR, ENG [37331] : PRE 1850 FARINGDON AREA, BRK, ENG [37720] : 1800-1850 BALLYRAGGET, KIK, IRL [33767] : 1792 W.INDIES [34176] : ELIZA ANN 1836+ NASH, MON, WLS [34234]

HIGH PRE 1900 BLOOMFIELD, NFK, ENG [34611] : 1800S KINGS LYNN, NFK, ENG [35187] : PRE 1788 LEWISBURG, SNYDER CO., PA, USA [37574]

HIGHAM PRE 1850 NORWOOD, NSW, AUS [35199] : C1855 NSW, AUS [38485] : PRE 1800 ESS, ENG [35642] : PRE 1780 ESS, ENG [35642] : C1850 MANCHESTER, LAN, ENG [36635] : WILLIAM C1830 CHEADLE HULME, CHS, ENG [37691] : C1845 GREENWICH, KEN, ENG [38485] : C1822 USA [38485]

HIGHLEY ALL WLS [36432]

HIGHMAN PRE 1820 ENG [33999] : ALL BUTLER CO., PA, IN & MO, USA & ENG [38532]

HIGHT WILLIAM W. 1835-1902 HUNTINGDON CO., PA, USA [38371] : 1770-1785 CHARLOTTE CO., VA, USA [38763]

HIGHTON PRE 1832 LIVERPOOL, LAN, ENG [36522]

HIGHTREE-STARK C1840 SCT [35025]

HIGMAN ALL WORLDWIDE [34742]

HIGNETT 1788+ LIVERPOOL, LAN, ENG [37986]

HIGNIGHT PRE 1860 CHARITON CO., MO, USA [36927]

HIGSON PRE 1733 MANCHESTER, LAN, ENG [36386]

HILBERS ALL BOCKHORN, OLD, GER [35767]

HILBERT 1700-1800 WOODFORD, KY, USA [36328]

HILBERT-SCHMIDT 1904 GR KRUSCHIN, STRASBURG, W PRE [35266]

HILBERY PRE 1880 DEPTFORD, SRY, ENG [35727]

HILBOURNE 1800S UXBRIDGE, ONT, CAN [36727]

HILDEBRAND 1840 CASINO, NSW, AUS [37910] : PRE 1750 NIEDER-WIESEL, HES, BRD [34183] : 1700+ DARMSTADT, HES, BRD [35475] : ALL ZURICH, CH [38197] : 1800-1850 LEEDS, YKS, ENG [34183] : C1775 GROSS SARAU, SHO, GER [38671] : PRE 1865 WASHINGTON CO., OH, USA [37505] : 1850-1860 KNOX CO., BUTLER TWP., OH, USA [38105]

HILDER 1800+ AUS [36295]

HILDERBRAND PRE 1835 STRAUSBOURG, ELO, GER [37820] : 1800 CAMBRIA CO., OH, USA [36907]

HILDESHEIMER 1900S CH [37931] : C1830-1917 MANCHESTER, LAN, ENG [37931] : C1830-1917 LONDON, MDX, ENG [37931] : PRE 1870 HALBERSTADT, GER [37931]

HILDINGER PRE 1860 WEISBACH, WOR, GER [38769] : 1840+ IN, USA [38769]

HILDITCH PRE 1840 SAL, ENG [37114]

HILDRED 1840S ABY, LIN, ENG [34677]

HILDRETH 1830+ DARLINGTON, DUR, ENG [36414]

HILES 1860+ GUNDEMAINE, NSW, AUS [35105] : C1860+ MERRIWA, NSW, AUS [35105] : 1840+ HEF, ENG [35105] : PRE 1850 SOM, ENG [38077] : 1830S LIVERPOOL, LAN, ENG [38206]

HILEY ALL BURTON, STS & WAR, ENG [36074] : PRE 1800 STOKE ON TRENT, STS, ENG [37736] : PRE 1800 BURTON ON TRENT, STS, ENG [37736] : ALL WLS [36432]

HILFERS PRE 1858 BREMEN, BRM, GER [37986] : 1790+ HANNOVER, HAN, GER [37986]

HILKE PRE 1834 BONDENFELDE, HAN, GER [36447] : 1834-1960 MONTGOMERY CO., NY, USA [36447]

HILL 1880S WOLUMLA, NSW, AUS [33870] : MARY 1800+ GINGIN, WA, AUS [33878] : MARY C1830 PARRAMATTA, NSW, AUS [33930] : KATHLEEN 1913+ FOOTSCRAY, VIC, AUS [34174] : 1866-1940 BRISBANE, QLD, AUS [34294] : C1868 PLEASANT CREEK, VIC, AUS [34862] : 1860S DENNINGTON & KEW, VIC, AUS [34919] : 1890+ RICHMOND & KEW, VIC, AUS [34919] : EMANUEL 1860+ CASTLEMAINE, VIC, AUS [35065] : 1855+ NEWNHAM, TAS, AUS [35127] : 1860+ ROCKHAMPTON, QLD, AUS [35138] : PRE 1859 MELBOURNE, VIC, AUS [35441] : EDWIN 1850+ AUS [36345] : PRE 1856 HOBART, TAS, AUS [36362] : 1856+ GAYNDAH, QLD, AUS [36362] : 1840+ HOBART, TAS, AUS [37497] : 1850+ VIC, AUS [37497] : GEORGE 1869+ YASS, NSW, AUS [38582] : WILLIAM 1862-1884 SYDNEY, NSW, AUS [38761] : 1900+ FESSERTON, ONT, CAN [34140] : 1830-1860S TORONTO, ONT, CAN [34248] : WILLIAM C1876-1955 SHELBURNE, ONT, CAN [34997] : PETER 1833+ SALFORD, ONT, CAN [35004] : CALVIN G. 1805+ SALFORD, ONT, CAN [35004] : R.D. 1864+ BLUEVALE, HURON CO., ONT, CAN [35004] : REUBEN 1890+ BOISSEVAIN, MAN,

CAN [35004] : CALVIN PRE 1897+ INGERSOLL,
ONT, CAN [35004] : CALVIN G. 1890+
INGERSOLL, ONT, CAN [35004] : PETER PRE 1912
BOISEVAINE, MAN, CAN [35004] : STEPHEN PRE
1897+ FOLDENS CORNERS, ONT, CAN [35004] :
CALVIN PRE 1897+ WINGHAM, ONT, CAN
[35004] : ISABELLE 1827+ MALAKOFF, ONT,
CAN [35615] : THOMAS 1858+ LANCASTER &
GLENGARRY, ONT, CAN [38402] : ALL
AMHERST ISLAND, ONT, CAN [38402] : C1830-40
INKBERROW, WOR, ENG [33828] : 1830+
PIMLICO, LND, ENG [33867] : PRE 1848 ST
HELENS, LAN, ENG [33912] : PRE 1865 BURFORD,
OXF, ENG [33997] : 1750-1820 ILLOGAN, CON,
ENG [34016] : TRISTRAM ALL NORTHLEW, DEV,
ENG [34093] : 1840S CHADDESLEY CORBETT,
WOR, ENG [34198] : ALL DORCHESTER, OXF,
ENG [34236] : 1750-1860 BIRMINGHAM, WAR,
ENG [34431] : C1800+ LUTON, BDF, ENG [34451] :
WILLIAM PRE 1850 LAMBETH, SRY, ENG [34600]
: PRE 1900 HANLEY & WEDNESBURY, STS, ENG
[34611] : MARTHA PRE 1890 LIN, ENG [34613] :
1815-1840 (39TH REGT), ENG [34796] : PRE 1700
BRADFIELD, WRY, ENG [34974] : EMMA PRE
1860 WALWORTH, SRY, ENG [34977] : C1890
WOLVERHAMPTON, STS, ENG [35014] : 1830+
BUSHBURY, STS, ENG [35019] : PRE 1800
TUPTON, DBY, ENG [35029] : JAMES 1840S
BIGGLESWADE, BDF, ENG [35049] : GEORGE &
RUTH 1800+ BIGGLESWADE, BDF, ENG [35049] :
MARY ANN 1840S BIGGLESWADE, BDF, ENG
[35049] : BENJAMIN 1800+ LONDON, MDX, ENG
[35059] : 1720+ BRAMPTON ABBOTTS, HEF, ENG
[35138] : PRE 1840 OAKHILL & FROME, SOM,
ENG [35215] : PRE 1820 SOM, ENG [35255] : 1800S+
CALSTOCK, CON, ENG [35489] : 1800+ CHURCH
LANGTON, LEI, ENG [35505] : 1800+
DRONFIELD, DBY, ENG [35505] : C1813
SHEFFIELD, YKS, ENG [35525] : 1690+
HATHERLEIGH, DEV, ENG [35587] : 1770S LAY
GREEN & ST PAULS WALDEN, HRT, ENG [35840]
: JESSIE 1865 CAMBERWELL, SRY, ENG [35865] :
HANNAH C1834+ SSX, ENG [35885] : 1790-1860
KYRE, WOR, ENG [36109] : 1750-1795
CULMINGTON, SAL, ENG [36109] : PRE 1750
HOLT, WOR, ENG [36110] : PRE 1700
KINGSWINFORD, STS, ENG [36110] : 1700-1800
TIBSHELF, DBY, ENG [36143] : PRE 1740 BILSBY,
LIN, ENG [36159] : HENRY PRE 1845 MANCHESTER,
LAN, ENG [36345] : C1790 PINCHBECK, LIN, ENG
[36370] : 1743-1861 HINDERWELL & STAITHES,
NRY, ENG [36412] : PRE 1770 WITHAM FRIARY,
SOM, ENG [36478] : ALL STAFFORD, STS, ENG
[36537] : 1800S WEST BROMWICH, WAR, ENG
[36666] : 1800S LYE, WOR, ENG [36670] : 1800+
FRENSHAM, SRY, ENG [36811] : 1800+ LONDON,
LND & SRY, ENG [36823] : PRE 1903 SOM, ENG
[36841] : 1600+ NEEDINGWORTH, CAM, ENG
[36922] : PRE 1848 WENDRON, CON, ENG [37189] :
1770+ LOWTON & LEIGH, LAN, ENG [37258] :
C1840 WEST COKER, SOM, ENG [37378] : PRE
1920 TEIGNMOUTH, DEV, ENG [37393] : THOMAS
PRE 1840 COSELEY IN SEDGELEY, STS, ENG
[37529] : 1700-1800 NRY, ENG [37696] : 1890S
BIRMINGHAM, WAR, ENG [37717] : PRE 1820
BATH, SOM, ENG [37726] : PRE 1800 SOUTH
WINGFIELD, DBY, ENG [37739] : MOSES C1860
PANCRAS, LND, ENG [37827] : 1800-1900
LEICESTER, LEI, ENG [37858] : PRE 1850
SHEFFIELD, WRY, ENG [37875] : 1820+
WORCESTER, WOR, ENG [37889] : C1870

WARRINGTON, LAN, ENG [37919] : 1850+
DERBY, DBY, ENG [38418] : FREDERICK K. 1860-
1900 EDMONTON, LND, ENG [38456] : 1800S
WOR, ENG [38468] : TOM 1855-1860 SWINDON,
WIL, ENG [38724] : WILLIAM 1786-1862
AYLESBURY, BKM, ENG [38761] : JEHU 1820+
HEYWOOD, LAN, ENG & AUS [36642] :
BEATRICE 1884 MEERUT, INDIA [37611] : ANN
ALL WEX, IRL [34143] : 1700-1750 LIM, IRL [34408] :
1831+ SAUL, DOW, IRL [34653] : NEIL PRE 1855
BELFAST, IRL [34862] : 1840 KILKEEL, DOW, IRL
[35529] : PRE 1826+ ROCKCORRY, MOG, IRL
[35759] : PRE 1820 ARKLOW, WIC, IRL [36702] :
C1890+ BELFAST, ANT, IRL [36853] :
ALEXANDER PRE 1852 BALLYMENA, ANT, IRL
[38004] : WILLIAM C1780-1840 FINELLY, TYR, IRL
[38402] : ROSAMUND 1830-1916 TIMOLEAGUE,
COR, IRL & SCT [33847] : ANTHONY PRE 1720 NL
[37764] : 1903+ RICCARTON, CANTY, NZ [36841] :
1840-1870S GLASGOW, SCT [33835] : C1780
KIRKCOLM, WIG, SCT [34993] : ALL AYR, SCT
[35139] : 1820-1830 DUNDEE, ANS, SCT [35865] :
1808-1818 KIRKOSWALD & COYLTON, AYR, SCT
[35865] : PRE 1800 PAISLEY, RFW, SCT [36692] :
CHRISTIAN 1770+ KILSPINDIE, PER, SCT [37146]
: PRE 1810 SCOTSDYKE, DFS, SCT [37978] :
DAVID PRE 1897+ IA, USA [35004] : CALVIN G.
PRE 1805 PA, USA [35004] : PRE 1800 BUCKS CO.,
PA, USA [35620] : DANIEL PRE 1876
WESTMORELAND CO., PA, USA [36448] : 1780 VA,
USA [36730] : JAMES PRE 1770 VA, USA [36927] :
PRE 1800 PA, USA [37587] : ANTHONY C1720-26
NEW YORK CITY, NY, USA [37764] : ANTHONY
1726-60 FOX MEADOWS, NY, USA [37764] : POLLY
1779-1851 FARMINGTON, CT, USA [37806] : J.C.
1930S MT LEBANON, PA, USA [38038] : 1650-1800
CAROLINE CO., VA, USA [38119] : CHARLES 1814-
1850 SMYRNA, KENT CO., DE, USA [38127] : ALL
TX, USA [38359]

HILLARD 1879+ MELBOURNE, VIC, AUS [35230] :
1880+ NZ [35230]

HILLAS BARBARA 1801+ SYDNEY, NSW, AUS
[34973] : JOHN 1801+ SYDNEY, NSW, AUS [34973]
: ALL NSW, AUS [38211]

HILLEMANN PRE 1810 HUEPSTEDT, PSA, GER
[38048]

HILLEN 1750+ FRANSHAM, NFK, ENG [34828]

HILLENHINRICHS 1928 WESTERCAPPELN, GER
[38749]

HILLENKAMP 1700-1795 GESEKE, WEF, GER [38749]
: 1821 DETMARSEN, WEF, GER [38749]

HILLER C1840 RAMSGATE, KEN, ENG [35391] :
C1600 HERRENBERG, BAW, FRG [38660]

HILLESS 1860S IPSWICH, QLD, AUS [35158]

HILLHOUSE ALL STIRLING, STI, SCT [38332]

HILLIARD 1855+ STH MELBOURNE, VIC, AUS
[36279] : 1800S ST PANCRAS, LND, ENG [36981]

HILLIDGE FRANCIS 1800-1819 MANCHESTER,
LAN, ENG [35107] : FRANCIS PRE 1800 CHS, ENG
[35107]

HILLIER 1850+ NSW, AUS [33794] : 1840+ YASS,
NSW, AUS [36610] : 1820-1885 CHELTENHAM,
GLS, ENG [34659] : PRE 1900 TIVERTON &
BAMPTON, DEV, ENG [35978] : C1800 BISHOPS
CANNING, WIL, ENG [36610] : 1850S
DORCHESTER, ENG [37493] : 1800+ BISHOPS
CANNINGS, WIL, ENG [38494]

HILLIGEHEKKEN ALL ZEIST, UTR, NL [38694]

HILLINGTON PRE 1850 KEN, ENG [34730]

HILLMAN 1830+ WHITE HILLS, VIC, AUS [34904] :
1860+ BALMAIN, NSW, AUS [34904] :
NATHANIEL 1850+ SOUTH YARRA, VIC, AUS

[35788] : C1804 MIDDLETON, DBY, ENG [34661] :
PRE 1830 WORTHING, SSX, ENG [34904] : ALL
SRY, ENG [35727] : PRE 1854 FROME, SOM, ENG
[36278]

HILLMER ALL WORLDWIDE [37804]

HILLOCK C1805 ARM, IRL [35400] : 1770+ ABOYNE,
ABD, SCT [35521]

HILLOCKS 1770+ FORFAR, ANS, SCT [35560]

HILLS JAMES 1835-1902 NARELLAN, NSW, AUS
[37553] : CHARLES PRE 1938 TINGHA, NSW, AUS
[37553] : CHARLES C1845 NARELLAN, NSW, AUS
[37553] : CHARLES C1883 BINGARA, NSW, AUS
[37553] : ALL ENG [34131] : 1842 ELY, CAM, ENG
[34540] : PRE 1850 CHATHAM, KEN, ENG [34814] :
1810-1820 SUNDERLAND, DUR, ENG [34832] :
PRE 1820 BOUGHTON, SSX, ENG [34911] : JAMES
1818-1835 ESS, ENG [37553] : C1810 LOWER
DINSDALE, NRY, ENG [37627] : 1833+ YARM,
NRY, ENG [37627] : 1700-1750 HEWORTH, NRY,
ENG [38516] : PRE 1850 GODSHILL, IOW, ENG
[38722] : 1640-1775 HARTFORD & TORRINGTON,
CT, USA [33905]

HILLSWORTH PRE 1850 FORREST GATE, HAM,
ENG [34633] : PRE 1850 DUBLIN &, ANT, IRL
[34633]

HILLYARD ALL NTH, ENG [36179] : 1800S
TEMPLEMORE, TIP, IRL [33776]

HILSBERG 1883+ AUS [35550] : 1820-1900 OLD, GER
[35550]

HILSON PRE 1833 NOTTINGHAM, NTT, ENG
[35904]

HILTON 1842+ MULGOA FOREST, NSW, AUS
[35245] : 1842+ MULGOA CAMDEN, NSW, AUS
[35420] : 1800+ BATHURST, NSW, AUS [36288] :
1860+ ARDLETHAN, NSW, AUS [36648] : 1840+
BARGO, NSW, AUS [36648] : 1860+
NARRANDERA, NSW, AUS [36648] : PRE 1850
AVOCA, VIC, AUS [37174] : PRE 1800 ASHTON
UNDER LYNE, LAN, ENG [34581] : PRE 1842
ASHTON UNDER LYNE, LAN, ENG [35420] :
C1800 BURNRIG, CUL, ENG [35592] : 1800+
MANCHESTER, LAN, ENG [35919] : 1750+ LAN,
ENG [36042] : PRE 1850 CLAYTON BRIDGE, LAN,
ENG [36066] : CHRISTOPHER PRE 1680 BURTON,
ORMSIDE, WES, ENG [36180] : C1850 OLDHAM,
LAN, ENG [37233] : PRE 1850 LAN, ENG [37646] :
PRE 1774 EAGLE, LIN, ENG [38248] : PRE 1650
NORTHWICH & GREAT BUDWORTH, CHS, ENG
[38589] : PRE 1600 LAN, ENG [38589] : ALL FYVIE
& KING EDWARD, ABD, SCT [37972] : 1797
MOSCOW, SU [35126] : 1621+ USA [38589] : ALL
WORLDWIDE [38589]

HILYEAR PRE 1820 SHAFTESBURY, DOR, ENG
[36478]

HILYER 1820-1885 CHELTENHAM, GLS, ENG
[34659]

HIMBERT PRE 1850 GUISINGEN, SAA, GER & FRA
[38681]

HIMPFEN 1850+ WORLDWIDE [37387]

HINCH 1870+ QLD, AUS [37554] : PRE 1869 WIC,
IRL [37554]

HINCHCLIFF C1800 GAWBER, YKS, ENG [34031] :
1800+ BRADFORD, YKS, ENG [35947] : PRE 1855
CUL & YKS, ENG [36052]

HINCHCLIFFE 1810+ ST HELIER, JSY, CHI [34963] :
PRE 1800 KEXBOROUGH, YKS, ENG [34963] :
1750-1850 PENISTONE, YKS, ENG [36898]

HINCHEY 1850+ MARYLEBONE, MDX, ENG
[37902]

HINCHLIFFE 1850+ ROCKHAMPTON, QLD, AUS
[37117] : PRE 1799 OSSETT, YKS, ENG [36528] :
1820S LEICESTER, LEI, ENG [36528] : JOS PRE

1850 HUDDERSFIELD, YKS, ENG [37117] : JOSH
PRE 1860 HUDDERSFIELD, YKS, ENG [37117]

HINCHMORE ALL IOM, UK [35136]

HINCKLE 1800+ WV, USA [38235]

HINCKLEY 1800+ SOM, ENG [35632] : PRE 1600
TENTERDEN, KEN, ENG [36972]

HINCKS 1760 WINSON, GLS, ENG [35256] : C1787
BROAD ST GILES, MDX, ENG [35560] : PRE 1844
ST MARGARETS, LEI, ENG [37346]

HIND 1750+ PORTSEA, HAM, ENG [33938] : C1750
ASHWELL, HRT, ENG [35072] : C1828
DARLINGTON, DUR, ENG [35131] : PRE 1828 LIN,
ENG [36002] : PRE 1762 LANCASTER, LAN, ENG
[36204] : 1800+ LONDON, ENG [36386] : 1800+
NOTTINGHAM, NTT, ENG [36386] : ALL
DUDLEY, WOR, ENG [36492] : ALL LEEK, STS,
ENG [36492] : ANNIE 1840+ MARYLEBONE,
LND, ENG [37775] : 1886+ SOUTHWARK, LND,
ENG [37775] : 1840+ NOTTINGHAM, NTT, ENG
[37775] : 1800S EAST RETFORD, NTT, ENG [37857] :
1880+ USA [36002]

HINDE 1864+ GILSTON, QLD, AUS [34807] : ALL
WAR, ENG [34054] : C1854 OLNEY, BKM, ENG
[34807] : PRE 1857 PORTLAND, DOR, ENG [38413]

HINDER 1870+ EMMAVILLE, NSW, AUS [37115] :
1850+ KEMPSEY, NSW, AUS [37115] : ALL
SHERSTON, LIN, ENG [37115] : ALL LIN, ENG
[37115] : ALL LATTON, LIN, ENG [37115] : ALL
GLS, ENG [37115]

HINDERTHUR ALL WORLDWIDE [38602]

HINDES PRE 1800 SFK, ENG [35642] : PRE 1870 LIM,
IRL [33765]

HINDHAUGH 1850+ GEELONG, VIC, AUS [38213]

HINDLE 1800+ BOLTON, LAN, ENG [35847] : 1700-
1900 LEEDS, WRY, ENG [38047]

HINDLEY PRE 1859 SALFORD, LAN, ENG [35061]

HINDMAN ALEXANDER C1785-1867 FER & QUE,
IRL & CAN [36904]

HINDRALL 1850 BIRMINGHAM, WAR, ENG [35061]

HINDS PRE 1849 CHIPPENDALE, NSW, AUS [35419]
: 1850S LEIGHTON BUZZARD, BDF, ENG [35730] :
SARAH 1800-1850S LONDON, ENG [36000] : 1700+
SHIPLAKE, OXF & SRY, ENG [36871] : PRE 1880
KEN, ENG [37668] : 1750+ LEEKE & DUNLUCE,
ANT, IRL [34808] : ALL MADISON CO., AR & CA,
USA [38570]

HINDSON C1860 SOUTH SHIELDS, DUR, ENG
[34329] : PRE 1900 SOUTH SHIELDS, DUR, ENG
[36481]

HINE ALL LONDON, ENG [34669] : PRE 1818
MEERBROOK, STS, ENG [35976] : C1790
WOOLVERTON, HAM, ENG [37168] : ALL
WORLDWIDE [35884]

HINEMAN 1830+ WENTWORTH CO., ONT, CAN
[34051]

HINES PRE 1839 PORTSMOUTH, HAM, ENG [34166]
: C1850+ PORTSMOUTH, HAM, ENG [35565] :
CATHERINE 1790+ WAR, ENG [36600] : PRE 1845
CAMBRIDGE, CAM, ENG [37899] : PRE 1855 GAL,
IRL [35028] : 1800-40 CLA, IRL [38202] : 1900S
BOSTON, MA & PA, USA [36337] : PRE 1800 PIKE,
OH, USA [38220]

HINEY PRE 1830 IRL [35556]

HINGELEY C1800-1820 ROTHERHAM, YKS & WAR,
ENG [36530]

HINGLAND 1800+ DOW, IRL [37170]

HINGST PRE 1900 STOLP & SCHLAWE, POM, GER
[38684]

HINGSTON 1850S+ PATERSON, NSW, AUS [35331] :
1820S GLS, ENG [35331] : PRE 1900 DEV, ENG &
CAN [38391]

HINKLE 1800+ WV, USA [38235]

HINLEY 1830+ COALBROOKDALE, SAL, ENG [37443]

HINNERS PRE 1866 GER &, WORLDWIDE [37511]

HINNRICHSEN PRE 1870 FLENSBURG, SHO, BRD [35023]

HINRICHS PRE 1850 SHO, GER [37009]

HINRICHSEN 1840+ FASSIFERN, QLD, AUS [35460] : PRE 1870 FLENSBURG, SHO, BRD [35023] : PRE 1880+ BLUNK, SHO, GER [35460]

HINSLEY ALL LEICESTER, LEI & DBY, ENG [36074]

HINTERTHUER ALL WORLDWIDE [36930] : ALL WORLDWIDE [38602]

HINTERTHUR ALL WORLDWIDE [38602]

HINTON 1887+ MITCHELL, QLD, AUS [34754] : PRE 1800 SOUTHAMPTON, HAM, ENG [36155] : PRE 1900 BALLOW, SRY, ENG [36288] : PRE 1690 UPTON LOVELL, WIL, ENG [36478] : 1600-1900 WILTON, WIL, ENG [37211] : ALL LONDON, ENG [37743] : 1900-1930 MASON CITY, IA, USA [37211]

HINTZ 1858-1886 BRODHAGEN, ELLICE, ONT, CAN [37550] : ALL VANSBURG WITTUN, PRE, GER [37550] : HENRY 1843-1879 SUDERHASTEDT, SHO, GER [38104] : HENRY 1879-1890 CHICAGO, COOK, IL, USA [38104] : LILLIAN 1915-1970 HOLLYWOOD, CA, USA [38104]

HINXMAN PRE 1820 WINTERSLOW, WIL, ENG [37321]

HINZ 1700-1900 SHO, GER [35630]

HIPKIN 1700-1800 GRISTON, NFK, ENG [35892] : 1830S ROUGHAM, NFK, ENG [36665] : PRE 1800 NFK, ENG [37712] : 1900+ SCT [37278]

HIPPERSON ALL WORLDWIDE [34710]

HIPTHORP ALL ENG [36872]

HIPWOOD 1870+ BRISBANE, QLD, AUS [35814]

HIPWORTH 1870 MELBOURNE, VIC, AUS [36640]

HIRAM ALL WORLDWIDE [36548]

HIRBI ALL BREMGARTEN, BAW, GER [38609] : ALL GRISSHEIM, BAW, GER [38609]

HIRD 1850+ GRINGLEY, NTT, ENG [35847] : PRE 1850 IDLE & BAILDON, WRY, ENG [36159] : ALL AMBLESIDE & GRASMERE, WES & CUL, ENG [38443] : 1820-1900 HUNTLY & ABERDEEN, ABD, SCT [34615] : PRE 1800 BOYNDIE, BAN, SCT [36790]

HIRDES C1780 BEYERLAND, ZEL, NL [38702]

HIRNING ALL MUNSINGEN, BRD, GER [34938]

HIRONS GEORGE C1845 CASTLEMORTON, WOR, ENG [34935] : PRE 1850 IRTHLINGBOROUGH, NTH & HRT, ENG [37708]

HIRSCH PRE 1600 PLEDELSHEIM, BAW, BRD [38509] : 1860-1930 WORMS, RPF, GER [37413] : 1750-1850 GER [37599] : 1700+ WALDGRIMES NAUNHEIM, HES, GER [38578] : PRE 1870 WLOCLAWECK, POL [34675] : 1840-1900 ORLEANS & JEFFERSON PAR., LA, USA [37599]

HIRSCHEL C1800-1900 HAMBURG, GER [35591]

HIRSCHFELD 1815+ NEUTEICH, EL, POL [36254]

HIRSCHFELDER PRE 1840 BAW, GER [34504]

HIRSCHMUELLER ALL OBERGAIL BACH, SAARGEMUND, BRD [37045] : ALL KAISERSLAUTERN, PFALZ, GER [37045]

HIRST C1830 THORNES BY WAKEFIELD, WRY, ENG [33796] : PRE 1827 HUDDERSFIELD, YKS, ENG [35061] : 1700+ MIRFIELD & CLECKHEATON, WRY, ENG [36218] : 1820-1860 HUDDERSFIELD, YKS, ENG [36319] : PRE 1842 ALMONDBURY, WRY, ENG [36807] : PRE 1855 LONDON, MDX, ENG [37647] : 1750-1920 HUDDERSFIELD, WRY, ENG [37736] : PRE 1860 COOLGARN, FER, IRL [37971] : 1900+ LAS ANIMAS, CO, USA [38067]

HIRSTLE C1820-50 PENISTONE, WRY, ENG [35550]

HIRTZMANN PRE 1820 MOSELLE, LOR, FRA [37504]

HIRYATT PRE 1750 SSX, ENG [37875]

HISCOCK PRE 1900 ALL CANNINGS, WIL, ENG [34569] : ALL HAMPSTEAD NORRIS, BRK, ENG [36144] : C1829 UPPER CLATFORD, HAM, ENG [36820] : 1700-1800 SSX, ENG [37207] : ALL YEOVIL, SOM & DOR, ENG [37269] : ALL SSX, ENG [37373]

HISCUTT ALL WORLDWIDE [37361]

HISLOP PRE 1895 EROMANGA, QLD, AUS [34805] : ALL ADELAIDE, SA, AUS & ENG [34561] : 1850S CHICHESTER, SSX, ENG [35720] : ALL GLASGOW, LKS, SCT [34561] : JANET PRE 1834 KIRKNEWTON, MLN, SCT [35072] : ALL HAWICK, ROX, SCT [37176] : ALL SELKIRK, SEL, SCT [37176] : ALL GOVAN, RFW, SCT & AUS [33799]

HISPACH PRE 1800 SINSHEIM & ELSENZ, BAW, GER [38609]

HISSONG C1850 OH & IN, USA [38177]

HITCH 1842 ELY, CAM, ENG [34540]

HITCHCOCK C1690-1755 SANDY & ELSTOW, BDF, ENG [36068] : 1800+ YEOVIL, SOM, ENG [36158] : 1800+ BRISTOL, ENG [36158] : ALL NORWICH, NFK, ENG [36473] : C1829 UPPER CLATFORD, HAM, ENG [36820] : C1805 BAMPTON, OXF, ENG [36975] : 1800-1900 BLOOMSBURY, LND, ENG [37845] : C1700 SPRINGFIELD, MA, USA [36319] : 1720-1800 BALTIMORE CO., MD, USA [37795]

HITCHCOX PRE 1890 LILLINGTON, WAR, ENG [35962] : PRE 1850 COVENTRY, WAR, ENG [35962] : PRE 1890 LEAMINGTON SPA, WAR, ENG [35962]

HITCHIN 1840+ ADELAIDE, SA, AUS [37913] : BRITANNIA 1780+ SAL, ENG [35429] : PRE 1900 WOR & SAL, ENG [37693]

HITCHINGS ALL YARMOUTH, NFK, ENG [36201]

HITCHINS ALL ST AGNES, CON, ENG [35475] : 1800+ ST BLAZEY, CON, ENG [37905] : 1820 CMN, WLS [35516]

HITT 1714-1850 GERMANIA & CULPEPPER CO., VA, USA [37605]

HITZMANN 1800+ HANNOVER, HAN, GER [37116]

HIX PRE 1750 ME, USA [37808]

HIXSON ALL ENG & AUS [37373]

HJAERNE PRE 1596 FROGOL, VERMLAND, SWE [38544]

HJORT THEKLA 1891+ USA [38560]

HJORTH 1853-1863 LONDON, ENG [33960] : 1750-1850 VASTERVIK, SWE [33960]

HNATUICK 1860 WORLDWIDE [36679]

HOAD PRE 1930 WALTHAMSTOW, ESS, ENG [37418] : 1840+ ELTHAM, KEN, ENG [37533] : 1800-40 WOOLWICH, KEN, ENG [37533] : ALL ENG & AUS [38068]

HOADLEY 1800+ EAST CHILTINGTON & LEWES, SSX, ENG [34927]

HOADLY 1751 TICEHURST, SSX, ENG [35260]

HOAR 1850+ BRUCE CO., ONT, CAN [34051] : PRE 1850 DUNSFOLD, SRY, ENG [34850] : PRE 1900 MENHENIOT, CON, ENG [35339] : ALL HAM & DUR, ENG [37195] : 1845-1860 KEWEENAW CO., MI, USA [38009]

HOARE 1801+ SYDNEY & AIRDS, NSW, AUS [33934] : 1853+ MORPETH, NSW, AUS [35842] : 1880+ DUNGARUBBA, NSW, AUS [35842] : 1862S KYNETON, VIC, AUS [35900] : 1872+ QLD, AUS [37894] : PRE 1900 SPARSHOLT, HAM, ENG [33966] : 1700-1900 LONDON, ENG [34054] : C1845 GREAT BEDWYN & WILTON, WIL & HAM, ENG [34836] : PRE 1890 HAM, ENG [34935] : 1830+ ENG [34956] : PRE 1900 MENHENIOT, CON, ENG [35339] : ALL LOSTWITHIEL, CON, ENG [35647] : 1880+ LND, ENG [37051] : 1842+ GILLINGHAM, KEN, ENG

[37051] : C1850-1900 LONDON, MDX & ESS, ENG
[37236] : 1700-1920 SRY, ENG [37348] : 1500+
BEAMINSTER, DOR, ENG [37625] : 1820+
NEWLAND, GLS, ENG [37746] : 1820 NEWLAND,
LEARWELL BREAM, GLS, ENG [37746] : PRE 1872
ALTON, HAM, ENG [37894] : C1830+ OXF, ENG &
NZ [36258] : PRE 1840 BORRIS O'KANE, TIP, IRL
[34452] : PRE 1852 KILMOYLER, TIP, IRL [35842] :
1828+ GALBALLY, LIM, IRL [35900] : PRE 1826
KER, IRL [36270] : C1850-1945 LOWER HUTT, NZ
[35900] : 1680+ WLS [37051] : 1840+ MONMOUTH,
MON, WLS [37746]
HOBART C1800 NEEDHAM MARKET, SFK, ENG
[37679] : 1840+ LIVERPOOL, LAN, ENG [37679] :
ALL ENG [37679] : PRE 1850 HOVE, SSX, ENG
[37913] : 1573-1991 HINGHAM, MA, USA [38200]
HOBBART 1830 LEAMINGTON, WAR, ENG [34793]
HOBBINS 1816 COVENTRY, WAR, ENG [37145]
HOBBIS ALL WANTAGE, BRK, ENG [34218] : 1700-
1900 NORTHFIELD & BIRMINGHAM, WOR, ENG
[37257] : 1700-1900 KINGSNORTON &
BIRMINGHAM, WOR, ENG [37257]
HOBBS 1850S TAMWORTH, NSW, AUS [33934] :
ROBERT 1791+ PITT TOWN, NSW, AUS [33939] :
1823+ CHAMPNEYS, NFD, CAN [33852] : 1700S-
1800S ARGYLE, NS, CAN [35291] : 1754+
DITCHEAT, SOM, ENG [33852] : PRE 1791
BISHOPSGATE, MDX, ENG [33939] : PRE 1848
YALDING & FARLEIGH, KEN, ENG [34325] :
1820-1900 THATCHAM, BRK, ENG [34719] : 1860-
1900 NORTH LONDON, ENG [34719] : 1650+
SOUTH MOLTON, DEV, ENG [34747] : C1813
LONDON, ENG [34806] : REBECCA PRE 1850
NORTH MOLTON, DEV, ENG [34963] : 1770+
LIMINGTON, SOM, ENG [35461] : LUCY 1792+
ASTWOOD, BKM, ENG [35477] : 1800+
TAUNTON, SOM, ENG [35847] : PRE 1870
EDMONTON & ENFIELD, MDX, ENG [36061] :
WILLIAM 1760-1820 DOR & SOM, ENG [36100] :
1830+ THORNBURY, GLS, ENG [36523] : PRE 1834
WHITCHURCH & ST MARY BOURNE, HAM &
BRK, ENG [36668] : 1750+ TODDINGTON, BDF,
ENG [36797] : 1740+ BRISTOL, GLS, ENG [36995] :
PRE 1940 LONDON, ENG [37062] : 1800-1900
ALDERTON, WIL, ENG [37192] : 1884+
POTSGROVE, BDF, ENG [37647] : 1753+ LITTLE
STUKELEY, HUN, ENG [38069] : C1845
TERRYGLASS, TIP, IRL [35541] : 1843 HIGHLAND
CO., OH, USA [35295] : 1780-1820 STURBRIDGE,
MA, USA [38741]
HOBDAY C1840 HASTINGS, SSX, ENG [33918] : 1700-
1750 OMBERSLEY, WOR, ENG [34552] : 1700-1830
WOR, ENG [37849] : ALL ENG & USA [38043]
HOBERT 1800-1991 GROTON, NH, USA [38200]
HOBLYN 1700-1800S LISKEARD, CON, ENG [34483]
HOBSON 1830+ PORT PHILLIP, VIC & TAS, AUS
[36477] : 1800+ STOURBRIDGE, WOR, ENG [34323]
: HENRY PRE 1900 STOKE NEWINGTON, MDX,
ENG [34347] : ALL LEI, ENG [35177] : PRE 1800
BURNLEY, LAN, ENG [35470] : 1750+
SHEFFIELD, WRY, ENG [35824] : PRE 1800 YKS &
LIN, ENG [36399] : 1600+ SPALDING, LIN, ENG
[36477] : PRE 1850 DRIBY, LIN, ENG [36477] :
1790+ EATON SOCON, BDF, ENG [36477] : 1650+
SPRATTON, NTH, ENG [36574] : 1790-1916
GREATER, LND, ENG [38171] : 1700-1800
NEWCASTLE, STS, ENG [38474] : ALL NC, IN &
CA, USA [38363]
HOCBO SANTOS PRE 1850 SAN JOSE, BATANGAS,
PHILIPPINE [34891]
HOCH PRE 1740 DETWANG, BAV, GER [35242] :
ANNA 1853+ BETTWAR, GER [37596] : JOHANN

1780-1843 LICHTEL, GER [37596] : MARIA 1855-
1953 BAYERN, GER [37596] : PRE 1720
HEININGEN, WUE, GER [38661]
HOCK PRE 1723 MESSEL, HES, GER [38181]
HOCKADAY 1880-1920 GOULBURN, NSW, AUS
[35861] : 1800+ DEV, ENG [34703] : 1800-1900 DEV,
ENG [35861] : 1640-1720 ENG [37233]
HOCKEN PRE 1645 NORTH HILL, CON, ENG [34573]
HOCKENSMITH 1839-1880 STARK CO., OH, USA
[35301]
HOCKER 1800+ BREMEN, BRM, GER & AUS [35460]
HOCKEY 1800+ AUS [34426] : PRE 1892 SYDNEY,
NSW, AUS [35236] : 1852+ GUYONG, NSW, AUS
[37313] : PRE 1700 CHARLTON ADAM, SOM, ENG
[33912] : 1700+ MONTACUTE, SOM, ENG [34426] :
PRE 1800 HORSINGTON, SOM, ENG [37833]
HOCKIN 1812+ PHILLACK, CON, ENG [37921] :
1880+ SOUTHALL, MDX, ENG [38402] : ALL
LELANT, CON, ENG [38402]
HOCKING C1876 DAYLESFORD, VIC, AUS [35748] :
1750-1840 EGLOSHAYLE, CON, ENG [34010] : PRE
1850 CAMBORNE, CON, ENG [34644] : 1750-1850
ILLOGAN, CON, ENG [34697] : C1760 EAST
NEWLYN, CON, ENG [35076] : C1800 KENWYN,
CON, ENG [35076] : 1800S ST MELLION, CON,
ENG [36393] : 1800-1850 DEV & CON, ENG [36422] :
PRE 1854 CAMBORNE, CON, ENG [37150] : ALL
ILLOGAN, CON, ENG [37291] : ALL KEN, ENG
[37407]
HOCKLEY ALL STOCK WICKFORD, ESS, ENG
[34669] : PRE 1876 BETHNAL GREEN, LND, ENG
[34669] : PRE 1800 STALISFIELD, KEN, ENG
[35223] : 1770 SOUTHWARK, SRY, ENG [38209]
HOCKNELL ALL LIN, ENG [37929]
HOCKNEY ALL LIN, ENG [37929]
HODBLAKE PRE 1800 CUL, ENG [38708]
HODCROFT PRE 1900 CHS & LAN, ENG [36363]
HODDER ALL AUS [35389] : PRE 1855 SOM, ENG
[35389] : PRE 1730 NETHERBURY, DOR, ENG
[36478] : 1760+ BRIXHAM, DEV, ENG [37132] :
ELIZABETH 1839-1907 FEATHERSTON &
GREYTOWN, ENG & NZ [33961]
HODDING ALL SALISBURY, ENG [38273] : ALL
WAIPUKURAU, HAWKES BAY, NZ [38273]
HODDY ALL SFK, ENG [36046]
HODEY WILLIAM C1800 ENG [34034]
HODGE 1850+ DAYLESFORD, VIC, AUS [35599] :
PRE 1900 CAMASPE, VIC & DEV, AUS & ENG
[37995] : PRE 1589 ST NEOT, CON, ENG [34573] :
PRE 1824 LONG BUCKBY, NTH, ENG [34584] :
PRE 1800 KEN, ENG [34858] : PRE 1830
WENDRON, CON, ENG [35045] : PRE 1635
CONSTANTINE, CON, ENG [35587] : PRE 1849 ST
ERTH, CON, ENG [35599] : 1650+ CONSTANTINE,
CON, ENG [35851] : PRE 1820 DEV, ENG [35866] :
ALL BDF, ENG [35939] : 1750+ SITHNEY, CON,
ENG [36603] : 1800+ LUDGVAN, CON, ENG
[36603] : PRE 1819 PLYMOUTH, CON, ENG [36604] :
C1814-1890 PENRYN, CON, ENG [36632] : 1770
HADLOW, KEN, ENG [38209] : 1750-1910
WATERFORD, WAT, IRL [37244] : PRE 1850 ARM,
IRL [37313] : 1800S TYR, IRL [37313] : 1760+
KILRENNY, FIF, SCT [35525] : PRE 1900
AVONSIDE, STI, SCT [37480] : 1831 ST ANDREWS
& ST LEONARD, FIF, SCT [37952] : PRE 1807 MDL,
SCT [38389] : 1855-1870 KEWEENAW CO., MI, USA
[38010]
HODGEKISS PRE 1850 BIRKENHEAD, LAN, ENG
[36270] : PRE 1850 WOLVERHAMPTON, STS, ENG
[36270] : PRE 1850 STEPNEY, MDX, ENG [36270]
HODGES 1870 GOULBURN, NSW, AUS [34421] :
SAMUEL 1857+ SYDNEY, NSW, AUS [34449] :

1788-1900S MUSWELLBROOK, NSW, AUS [35412] :
1857-1901 BELLTREES, NSW, AUS [35412] : 1880+
FREMANTLE, WA, AUS [36825] : 1850+
MUSWELLBROOK, NSW, AUS [37113] : 1850+
PERTH CO., ONT, CAN [34066] : PRE 1800
LONDON, ENG [34258] : PRE 1850 EVERCREECH,
SOM, ENG [34314] : 1830+ MILTON, NTH, ENG
[34421] : 1799 CHELMSFORD, ESS, ENG [34421] :
PRE 1850 STOKE DAMEREL, DEV, ENG [34742] :
1700-1857 CHARLTON ADAM, SOM, ENG [35412] :
PRE 1770 SEDGLEY, STS, ENG [36110] : 1750+ ST
HELENS & ST PETER, WOR, ENG [36825] :
JOSEPH 1720+ BEACHAMPTON, BKM, ENG
[37165] : 1800-1860 HAMPSTEAD, MDX, ENG
[37253] : C1800 CASTLEMORTON, WOR, ENG
[37320] : C1784 ESSEX CO., VA, USA [36354] : 1800-
1825 IN, USA [38137]

HODGESON ALL WHITBY & SCARBOROUGH,
NRY, ENG [38580]

HODGETT 1500-1700 SOUTH, STS & WOR, ENG
[36062]

HODGETTS PRE 1761 STS, ENG [34270] : PRE 1770
SEDGLEY, STS, ENG [36110] : PRE 1710
BIRMINGHAM, WAR, ENG [37662]

HODGINS ALL STONEY CREEK, NSW, AUS [35541]
: GEORGE C1808-1874 CARISBROOK, VIC, AUS &
IRL [37559] : ALL LONDON, ONT, CAN [35264] :
1910 LONDON, ENG [35194] : 1850 ENNISKILLEN,
FER, IRL [35194] : ALL FER, IRL [35541] :
ANDREW C1845 TERRYGLASS, TIP, IRL [35541] :
JOHN JR. C1845 TIPPERARY, TIP, IRL [35607]

HODGKINSON 1850+ NSW, VIC & SA, AUS [34424] :
C1833 TUNSTALL, STS, ENG [35348] : ELLEN
1813+ WESTHOUGTON, LAN, ENG [35634] :
JOHN 1804-1875 WIGAN, LAN, ENG [35634] :
1750+ TAMWORTH KINGSBURY, STS & WAR,
ENG [36329] : PRE 1850 MAPPLETON, DBY, ENG
[36841] : 1800-1860 ISLINGTON, MDX, ENG [37845]
: 1830+ CARLISLE, CUL, ENG [37997] : PRE 1850
YKS, ENG [38370] : 1850+ RICCARTON, CANTY,
NZ [36841]

HODGKISS PRE 1700 KIDDERMINSTER, WOR,
ENG [38420]

HODGKISS (SEE HODGEK [36270]

HODGSON PRE 1885 GOULBURN, NSW, AUS
[35037] : 1860+ MELBOURNE, VIC, AUS [35877] :
1823+ HOBART, TAS, AUS [35877] : 1850+
ADELAIDE, SA, AUS [38209] : 1700+ CAN [33903] :
PRE 1850 WOLSINGHAM, DUR, ENG [33993] :
PRE 1785 ADDINGHAM, CUL, ENG [34148] : PRE
1785 DUFTON, CUL, ENG [34148] : PRE 1800
SALKELD, CUL, ENG [34148] : JOHN PRE 1815
SEATHWAITE, CUL, ENG [34452] : 1700+
RUGELEY, STS, ENG [34639] : 1750
BUTTERWICK, LIN, ENG [35288] : PRE 1914
CLIFTON, YKS, ENG [35368] : PRE 1820
BROMFIELD, CUL, ENG [35440] : PRE 1844
BLENNERHASSET, CUL, ENG [35440] : 1700+
BRADFORD & BRADFORD MOOR, YKS, ENG
[35460] : PRE 1820 HAWKSHEAD, LAN, ENG
[35877] : 1800+ CROFTS, YKS, ENG [35891] : PRE
1860 YORK, NRY, ENG [36022] : 1787+
KIRKHAM, LAN & LND, ENG [36049] : ALL
TATHAM, LAN, ENG [36144] : 1809-1907 SEATON
& SEAHAM, DUR, ENG [36412] : 1851-83 STANLEY
BURN, DUR, ENG [36412] : PRE 1829 WRY, ENG
[36459] : 1800+ IDLE & THACKLEY, WRY, ENG
[36617] : 1725-1860 LANGFIELD, WRY, ENG [36635]
: 1700+ SUDBURY, SFK, ENG [36949] : C1803
TEALBY, LIN, ENG [37318] : 1790+ KEN, ENG
[37460] : C1790-1850 LONDON, ENG [37460] : 1550-
1850 KESWICK, CUL, ENG [37460] : 1800S

ROTHERHAM, WRY, ENG [37831] : 1700-1800
MORESBY, CUL, ENG [37858] : 1796 LOWTHER,
WES, ENG [38209] : 1800-1900 ST OSWALDS, DUR,
ENG [38269] : ALL WOOD HOUSEHILL,
ROTHWELL, YKS, ENG [38473] : C1830
MANCHESTER & LANCASTER, LAN, ENG &
AUS [35079] : 1900+ NZ [37710] : ALL OKI, SCT
[33903] : 1780-1860 AYR, SCT [37338] : PRE 1850
PHILADELPHIA, PA, USA [34148] : 1900+ SAN
FRANCISCO, CA, USA [34148] : 1750-1800
GUILFORD CO., NC, USA [38108]

HODINOTT 1800S SHERBORNE, DOR, ENG [35187]

HODISON 1800+ MILTON ABBOT, DEV, ENG
[36195]

HODKINSON 1845-1900 NANTWICH, CHS, ENG
[36214]

HODPAL ALL HARTLEPOOL, DUR, ENG [34619]

HODSKINSON 1800S POCKLINGTON, ERY, ENG
[34854]

HODSOLL 1597-1630 COWFOLD, SSX, ENG [36944]

HODSON 1935+ PADDINGTON, QLD, AUS [34030] :
1700+ SUDBURY, SFK, ENG [36949] : C1850
LONDON, ENG [36949] : C1820-1900 OXFORD,
OXF, ENG [36949] : PRE 1861 ENG [38112] : C1850
EMLAGHMORE, ROS, IRL [35216] : PRE 1840
HODSONS BAY, ROS, IRL [35216] : PRE 1840
TWYFORDS, ST JOHNS, ROS, IRL [35216] : ALL
IRL [38754] : 1861+ IN, IA & KS, USA [38112]

HODSON FLIGHT 1800+ KEN, ENG [34313]

HOECKEN 1650+ BOKENDORF VIA BELLERSEN,
WEF, GER [35460]

HOECKY ALL WORLDWIDE [38693]

HOEFER 1800+ GRETHEN (PFALZ BAYERN), BAV,
GER [38023]

HOEFLING 1800-1865 BAY, BRD [36895] : 1850-1900
LOHR, BAV, GER [37914]

HOEGI ALL WORLDWIDE [38693]

HOEHNE 1788 HEMSENDORF, KSA, GER [38750]

HOEKE 1650+ BELLERSEN, WEF, GER [35460]

HOEKEN 1650+ BELLERSEN, WEF, GER [35460]

HOEK VAN DUKE 1750-1800 GOES E.O., ZEL, NL
[38696]

HOELBACH PRE 1815 SILBERHAUSEN, PSA, GER
[38048]

HOENEN PRE 1800 KOBLENZ, RPR, GER [38437]

HOEPPNER 1860 STOLP, POM, GER [34388]

HOERBER 1600+ ROTHENBURG, BAV, GER [37542]

HOES 1750-1800 NY, USA [38113]

HOEY 1850+ NSW, AUS [34902] : 1850S PORT
FAIRY, VIC, AUS [35721] : 1850 BRISBANE, QLD,
AUS [35829] : C1820 WESTMINSTER, LND, ENG
[37112] : 1850+ DUBUQUE CO., IA, USA [37510]

HOF 1600+ GEDERN, HEN, GER [37572]

HOFEDITZ ALL SIELEN, HEN, GER [36552]

HOFER PRE 1810 AG, CH [38029] : PRE 1850 GROSS
AUPA, GER [38674]

HOFF 1850-1898 HBG, BRD [35094] : C1850 ALS &
LOR, FRA [38527] : 1800+ ZIELBECK, LUE, GER
[37170] : 1800 SARKWITZ, GER [37170] : 1700+
BERGZABERN, RPR, GER [38765] : 1700+
KAPSWEYER, RPR, GER [38765] : 1800+
LANDAU, ODESSA, SU [38765] : 1800+
FELSENBERG, ODESSA, SU [38765]

HOFFERT PRE 1800 BUCKS CO., PA, USA [38335]

HOFFHAM 1830-1890 WESTFALEN, TELGTE, BRD,
GER [34002]

HOFFMAN 1852+ KILLARNEY, QLD, AUS [38262] :
1790-1910 MDX & HAM, ENG [37651] : 1750-1900
NEUKIRCHEN, GER [37651] : PRE 1867
OSTERBRUKEN, BAD, GER [37819] : PRE 1852
KAFERTHAL, BAD, GER [38262] : 1700+ GRAND
USHE & YOUNGLINSTER, LUX [37016] : 1700+

GRAND USHE & JUNGLINSTER, LUX **[37016]** :
C1880 WELLINGTON, NZ **[36878]** : 1780-1850
BERKS CO., PA, USA **[35318]** : J.W. 1921+ KANSAS
CITY, MO, USA **[37526]** : ELIZABETH 1740-1826
FRED CO., MD, USA **[38591]**

HOFFMANN PRE 1840 GRADITZ, SIL, GER **[35333]** :
PRE 1840 BRESLAU, SIL, GER **[35333]** : 1821+
KIRN ON NAKE, KOBLUTZ, GER **[35583]** : 1700+
DARMSTADT, HEN, GER **[37572]** : 1700+
REGENSBURG, BAY, GER **[38578]** : PRE 1800
WATTENHEIM, RPF, GER **[38681]** : C1870 RSA
[34756]

HOFFMEISTER 1600-1700 ANGERMUNDE,
UCKERMARK, BRA **[38603]**

HOFFNER PRE 1650 PRASTBOL & FRYKSANDE,
VARMLAND, SWE **[38551]**

HOFFSOMIER 1800-70 ROTHENBURG, HEN, GER
[35866]

HOFGREN LARS 1741-1803 SODERTALJE,
SODERMANLAND, SWE **[38550]**

HOFLUND ALL WORLDWIDE **[38648]**

HOFMAN 1750-1900 HUNFELD, GER **[37651]**

HOFMANN PRE 1850 BLACK FOREST, BAW, BRD
[37225] : PRE 1900 LAMBETH & SOUTHWARK,
SRY, ENG **[37225]** : 1700+ HEMSBACH, BAV, GER
[34933] : 1741-1774 KASHOFEN PFALZ, BAV, GER
[37516] : PRE 1750 HERLINGHAUSEN, NRW, GER
[38642] : PRE 1800 NECKARREMS, WUE, GER
[38661]

HOFSTAEYAN 1500-1600 NMR, MECHELIN, BEL
[36943]

HOG C1750 PENCAITLAND, ELN, SCT **[36276]** :
ELIZ 1810+ BEW, SCT **[37476]**

HOGAN PRE 1900 VIC, AUS **[33798]** : 1820+ NSW,
AUS **[34428]** : ALL IPSWICH, QLD, AUS **[34441]** :
C1895+ LISMORE & CASINO, NSW, AUS **[34449]** :
1870+ MELBOURNE, VIC, AUS **[36605]** : 1800+
STS, ENG **[36829]** : PRE 1860 TOOMEVARA, TIP,
IRL **[33902]** : PRE 1850 LIMERICK, LIM, IRL **[34197]**
: ALL ROSCREA & BORRISOKANE, TIP, IRL
[34441] : 1750+ CLA, IRL **[34684]** : 1852 NENAGH,
TIP, IRL **[35100]** : 1876 TIP, IRL **[35100]** : PRE 1859
LIM, IRL **[35363]** : PRE 1814 FERMOY, COR, IRL
[35561] : PRE 1850 CLA & LIM, IRL **[35866]** : C1835-
1861 CASTLEGAR, GAL, IRL **[35900]** : PRE 1840
LDY, IRL **[35930]** : PRE 1800 DUB, IRL **[36829]** : PRE
1850 WAT, IRL **[37497]** : PRE 1850 IRL **[38196]** :
PATRICK 1840+ HOGANS GARDENS, LACKEN,
WIC, IRL **[38302]** : JOHN 1819-1855 CORK CITY,
COR, IRL **[38322]** : ALL KIK, IRL **[38487]** : PRE 1880
BALLINAMOE, TIP, IRL & USA **[34454]** : C1840-
1900 INVERCARGILL, NZ **[35900]** : 1850-1930
CRIPPLE CREEK, CO, USA **[34441]** : PRE 1880 NY,
USA **[38196]**

HOGAN (SEE HOGGAN) **[37906]**

HOGARTY 1835+ COLUMBIA CO., NY, USA **[36900]**

HOGBEN 1827+ HOBART & LAUNCESTON, TAS,
AUS **[35394]** : PRE 1844 LENHAM, KEN, ENG
[34277] : 1790-1859 DEAL & DOVER, KEN, ENG
[36836] : 1800-1900 NORTH LONDON, MDX, ENG
[38171]

HOGBERG C1858 BYGDEA, VASTERBOTTEN, SWE
[38228]

HOGBIN 1817+ LITTLEBOURNE, KEN, ENG **[35156]**

HOGG 1850+ AUS **[36034]** : 1850+ BINGARA, NSW,
AUS **[36305]** : 1870+ TONBRIDGE, KEN, ENG
[34280] : ALL LAN, ENG **[34938]** : C1870 HOXTON,
MDX, ENG **[35778]** : PRE 1900 LEEDS, WRY, ENG
[36034] : ALL GUISELEY & OTLEY, WRY, ENG
[36159] : C1800 LISBURN, ANT, IRL **[35502]** : C1800
LKS, SCT **[34127]** : PRE 1850 ABERDEEN, ABD,
SCT **[34590]** : 1750-1875 ARY, ELN & PER, SCT

[34615] : 1840+ LADYKIRK, BEW, SCT **[34666]** :
PRE 1845 ROX & MLN, SCT **[35222]** : C1800+
PITLESSIE, FIF, SCT **[35629]** : C1850+ ALLOA,
CLK, SCT **[35629]** : ROBERT 1840-1850 STOW, BEW,
SCT **[35725]** : PRE 1850 COLDINGHAM, BEW, SCT
[36497] : PRE 1830 MONTROSE, ANS, SCT **[36777]** :
1800+ GLASGOW, SCT **[36827]** : 1770+ LARBERT,
STI, SCT **[37767]** : PRE 1715 TRANENT, ELN, SCT
[37852] : 1820+ ABD, SCT **[38253]** : C1795
ATHELSTANEFORD, ELN, SCT **[38761]** : 1750+
SCT & AUS **[35059]** : 1844-1882 NEW BROUGHTON,
JAMAICA, W.INDIES **[34615]**

HOGGAN 1600-1750 KIER & THORNHILL, DFS, SCT
[34513] : MARTHA PRE 1808 DUNFERMLINE, FIF,
SCT **[37906]**

HOGGART 1800+ SHADWELL, MDX, ENG **[36093]** :
MARY PRE 1740 GRAYRIGG, WES, ENG **[36192]** :
PRE 1860 YKS, ENG **[37018]**

HOGGE PRE 1870 SIL, GER **[38648]**

HOGGINS MARY ANN 1800S HOLBORN, MDX,
ENG **[36633]** : C1710 COVENTRY, WAR, ENG
[36635] : PRE 1850 WESTBURY, SAL, ENG **[37681]**

HOGLE 1740+ ONT & QUE, CAN **[36539]**

HOGLUND LARS 1824 LYSVIK, VARMLAND, SWE
[38556]

HOGNO (SEE HAGENOW) **[35874]**

HOHENADEL 1854 CARRICK TWP., ONT, CAN
[34503]

HOHN PRE 1840 HEPPENHEIM, HES, GER **[38029]**

HOHNHORST 1830-1900 CINCINNATI, OH, USA
[38149]

HOILES 1870+ PARKER, ONT, CAN **[34231]**

HOLAHAN ALL LIM, IRL **[34938]**

HOLBEACH PRE 1880 TAMWORTH, STS, ENG
[35232]

HOLBEN 1770 BIGGLESWADE, BDF, ENG **[34204]**

HOLBROCK ALL WORLDWIDE **[35326]**

HOLBROOK 1800+ CAN **[37427]** : PRE 1860S
CHEWTON MENDIP & BATH, SOM, ENG **[35433]** :
1700+ ISLE OF WIGHT, HAM, ENG **[35886]** :
1800+ SHOREDITCH, MDX & ESS, ENG **[37065]** :
1800+ IRL **[37427]** : 1800+ CAR & KIK, IRL **[37427]**
: JOHN 1650 ROXBURY, MA, USA **[35273]** : ALL
WORLDWIDE **[35326]**

HOLBROW 1770-1800 STROUD, GLS, ENG **[35741]** :
1700-1800 BRISTOL, GLS, ENG **[37829]**

HOLBURN PRE 1830 WIG, SCT **[35572]** : PRE 1810
HIGH KILDONAN, IOA, SCT **[38057]**

HOLCOMBE PRE 1600 SANDFORD, DEV, ENG
[36389] : C1650 MIDDLETOWN, CT, USA **[34395]** :
1780-1880 YANCEY CO., NC, USA **[38009]**

HOLCROFT ALL MANCHESTER, LAN, ENG **[36635]**
: 1870+ PADGATE POULTON, LAN, ENG **[36795]**

HOLDBROOK ALL WORLDWIDE **[35326]**

HOLDCROFT 1700S STRETFORD, LAN, ENG **[36635]**

HOLDEN 1800+ PORT SORELL, TAS, AUS **[34541]** :
PRE 1780 ROXTON, BDF, ENG **[33912]** : C1843
BOLTON, LAN, ENG **[33955]** : WILLIAM C1787-
1848 ROCHDALE, LAN, ENG **[34721]** : SAML 1837-
1872 ROCHDALE & BROOKSIDE, LAN, ENG
[34721] : 1617-1646 FEWTON, YKS, ENG **[34793]** :
PRE 1864 ACCRINGTON, LAN, ENG **[34929]** : PRE
1850 HUDDERSFIELD, YKS, ENG **[35061]** : 1800+
BLACKBURN, LAN, ENG **[35362]** : 1865 BURY,
LAN, ENG **[35514]** : PRE 1827 OVER DARWEN,
LAN, ENG **[35514]** : 1700+ WALSALL, STS, ENG
[35749] : C1600-1726 CARDINGTON, BDF, ENG
[36068] : 1880+ BLACKPOOL, LAN, ENG **[36685]** :
PRE 1838 SPILSBY, LIN, ENG **[36748]** : C1800
WISBECH, CAM, ENG **[36753]** : PRE 1857
HALIFAX, WRY, ENG **[36766]** : PRE 1850
CHAIGHLEY, LAN, ENG **[36998]** : PRE 1900 DUR,

ENG [37061] : 1600+ TOCKHOLES, LAN, ENG [37166] : PRE 1700 YORK, ERY, ENG [37650] : PRE 1800 HALIFAX, WRY, ENG [37650] : 1783 LISTON, ESS, ENG [38078] : C1888+ COTGRAVE, NTT, ENG [38401] : PRE 1852 ANT, IRL [35720] : PRE 1900 IRL [37761]

HOLDER 1920+ NSW, AUS [34597] : 1910-1920 MELBOURNE, VIC, AUS [34597] : 1700+ HAM, SRY & SSX, ENG [34597] : 1650+ PAINSWICK, NEWENT & UPLEADEN, GLS, ENG [34747] : C1800 WISBECH, CAM, ENG [36753] : PRE 1850 LND & SRY, ENG [37091] : JOSEPH PRE 1850 GA & SC, USA [38536]

HOLDER-KEEPING 1868+ COONABARABRAN, NSW, AUS [37967] : 1833-67 RHODE, SOM, ENG [37967]

HOLDGATE 1765 MANCHESTER, LAN, ENG [36635] : 1800+ LAMBETH, SRY, ENG [37718]

HOLDING PRE 1890 HUN, ENG [34021] : PRE 1890 HIGH ERCALL, SAL, ENG [35215]

HOLDOM 1800S WALWORTH, SRY, ENG [37494] : 1800S BISHOPSGATE, MDX, ENG [37494] : C1870-80 SCHUYLKILL CO., PA, USA [37494]

HOLDSWORTH C1810+ BALLARAT, VIC, AUS [35053] : 1860S ADELAIDE, SA, AUS [35390] : 1850S DORKING, SRY, ENG [35390] : PRE 1785 BURNHAM, NFK, ENG [36425]

HOLE PRE 1870 WALCOT, SOM, ENG [34201] : PRE 1800 SRY & KEN, ENG [34383] : ALL DBY, ENG [36216]

HOLEBROOK ALL WORLDWIDE [35326]

HOLFORD C1815 NBL & SSX, ENG [35646] : C1812 MARYLEBONE, MDX, ENG [37320]

HOLGATE 1700+ ESS, ENG [33849] : PRE 1801 LAN, ENG [34213] : PRE 1842 YKS, ENG [34216] : C1840-1860 LEEDS, YKS, ENG [35955] : 1750-1850 LAN, ENG [36482] : JOHN PRE 1791 COLNE, LAN, ENG [37002] : 1750-1850 LONDON, MDX, ENG [37077] : 1750-1850 STAINES, MDX, ENG [37077]

HOLGATE (SEE HOLDGAT [37718]

HOLIDAY 1650-1750 PENRITH, CUL, ENG [36098] : 1750-1800 CHORLEY, LAN, ENG [37613]

HOLIERHOEK ALL DELFT, ZUH, NL [33751] : ALL DELFT, ZUH, NL [38692]

HOLIHANE C1830 CLONAKILTY, COR, IRL [36076]

HOLKOM ALL NL [38358]

HOLLADAY 1700S BEVERLY & WOODMANCY, YKS, ENG [38745]

HOLLAH PRE 1800 GULVAL, CON, ENG [35500]

HOLLAND 1850+ NEWTOWN, NSW, AUS [34424] : 1890+ KALGOORLIE, WA, AUS [34866] : PRE 1900 WINDSOR, NSW, AUS [35406] : 1930+ MANLY, NSW, AUS [35573] : 1830+ REDFERN, NSW, AUS [35825] : 1850+ MAITLAND, NSW, AUS [37141] : JOHN 1780+ CHADDERTON, LAN, ENG [34181] : 1830S LONDON &, WIL, ENG [34191] : 1812+ BURGHILL, HEF, ENG [34334] : ALL PYRTON, OXF, ENG [34429] : 1816-1886 SWINESHEAD, LIN, ENG [34651] : C1840S NOTTINGHAM, NTT, ENG [34788] : PRE 1849 STOKE, STS, ENG [34797] : PRE 1821 ALTON, HAM, ENG [35113] : C1850 LOUGHBOROUGH, LEI, ENG [35163] : 1750+ COLCHESTER, ESS, ENG [35370] : PRE 1820 LEYTONSTONE, ESS, ENG [35406] : 1800+ WELLINGTON, SOM, ENG [35825] : PRE 1670 WALSALL, STS, ENG [36110] : 1730-1820 HALIFAX, WRY, ENG [36111] : PRE 1880 GLASSHOUSE GREEN & GLOUCESTER, GLS, ENG [36113] : PRE 1836 LIVERPOOL, LAN, ENG [36522] : PRE 1870 HINTON ST GOERGE, SOM, ENG [36581] : 1600+ OVER, CHS, ENG [36818] : C1800 WORCESTER, WOR, ENG [36835] : C1800-1850 LONDON, ENG

[37141] : PRE 1838 NFK, ENG [37897] : 1790 NORTH MARSTON, BKM, ENG [38209] : 1700-1800 NEWPORT, SAL, ENG [38474] : 1796-1849 RENCOMBE & NORTON, GLS, ENG [38761] : 1810-1900 OXF, ENG & AUS [35718] : 1841-1897 SWINESHEAD, LIN, ENG & NZ [34651] : 1840-1865 COR, IRL [34183] : 1838-1858 BALLYSTEEN & ASKEATON, LIM, IRL [34794] : 1820-1850 ARM, IRL [34866] : C1800 CLONAKILTY, COR, IRL [36076] : PRE 1850 DUBLIN, IRL [37454] : 1780-1830 KIK, IRL [38404] : PRE 1828 GLASGOW, LKS, SCT [37524] : 1890-1930 NEW YORK CITY, NY, USA [37079] : THOMAS J. 1830-1920 STODDARD CO., MO & TN, USA [38532] : ALL NJ, USA [38733]

HOLLANDERS 1882 BREDA, NBT, NL [36307]

HOLLANDS PRE 1821 KEN, ENG [35407] : PRE 1870 SALTWOOD, KEN & ESS, ENG [35517] : ALL ENG [36221] : PRE 1820 BATTLE, SSX, ENG [37875]

HOLLAS 1712+ SOYLAND, WRY, ENG [35815] : PRE 1760 BARKISLAND & SOYLAND, WRY, ENG [37372]

HOLLBROOK ALL WORLDWIDE [35326]

HOLLEY ALL WIL, ENG [37233] : PRE 1842 TIP, IRL [34886]

HOLLICK PRE 1800 BIRMINGHAM, WAR, ENG [34931]

HOLLIDAY PRE 1850 LONDON, MDX, ENG [37097] : HUGH 1845-1937 HAYTON, CUL, ENG [38156] : 1750-1850 COR, IRL [34513] : 1650-1750 SPOTSYLVANIA CO., VA, USA [36566] : ALL WORLDWIDE [37739]

HOLLIDGE PRE 1910 CROYDON, SRY, ENG [36725]

HOLLIGAN 1854+ GEELONG, VIC, AUS [34549]

HOLLIMAN ALL UK [36020]

HOLLINGER ADAM PRE 1780 IRL [35328] : ADAM 1770S IRL [37585] : ADAM 1780+ MT VERNON, AL, USA [35328]

HOLLINGS MARY PRE 1841 ISLINGTON, LND, ENG [34916] : PRE 1850 IDLE & CALVERLEY, WRY, ENG [36159] : ALL BRADFORD, WRY, ENG [37379]

HOLLINGSWORTH C1816 ESS, ENG [35729] : 1600-1800 SOMERSAL HERBERT, DBY, ENG [35775] : 1600-1800 WESTON UNDER LIZARD, STS, ENG [35775] : 1890S EDMONTON, MDX, ENG [37677] : 1856+ RATHFRILAND & BELFAST, DOW, IRL [34528] : PRE 1900 PEORIA, IL, USA [35312] : 1870 APPANOOSE CO., IA, USA [38243] : 1815 CLARK CO., OH, USA [38243] : 1845 OSAGE CO., MO, USA [38243] : 1800-1850 BUNCOMBE CO., NC, USA [38737] : ALL WORLDWIDE [36387]

HOLLINGWORTH 1600-1700S LIN, ENG [34504] : ALL AMPTHILL, BDF, ENG [34789] : 1700+ KIRKBURTON, WRY, ENG [36218] : ALL WORLDWIDE [36387]

HOLLINS 1750-1900 LEIGH, STS, ENG [34714] : PRE 1850 BRISTOL, ENG [38377]

HOLLINSHED 1850+ NEWCASTLE, NSW, AUS [35598]

HOLLIS ALL BKM, ENG [33803] : 1800S SHALFLEET, HAM, ENG [34559] : PRE 1860 LONDON, ENG [35544] : 1850-1900 SOUTHTOWN & GT YARMOUTH, NFK, ENG [35725] : PRE 1860 BRK, ENG [35868] : 1800-1850 LONDON, ENG [36081] : C1800 BIRMINGHAM, WAR, ENG [37944] : PRE 1700 IOW, ENG [38420]

HOLLISTER 1780+ STORMONT CO., ONT, CAN [38411] : C1836 WINTERBOURNE, GLS, ENG [34281] : PRE 1800 CHISELDON, WIL, ENG [36041]

HOLLISTON 1860-80 WOLFORD, ONT, CAN [36722]

HOLLITT 1799+ BDF, ENG [34777]

HOLLMEIER 1680-1990 USA & GER [36442]

HOLLMEYER 1680-1990 USA & GER **[36442]**

HOLLOCKS ALL SFK, ENG **[34744]**

HOLLOLE PRE 1800 LEI & DBY, ENG **[34686]**

HOLLOW 1820+ CON, ENG **[35747]** : 1750+ LONDON, ENG **[36004]**

HOLLOWAY 1864+ BRISBANE, QLD, AUS **[35144]** : 1895+ QLD, AUS **[36305]** : 1800S NFD, CAN **[36558]** : PRE 1900 BETHNAL GREEN, LND, ENG **[34048]** : PRE 1857 GREAT MARLOW, BKM, ENG **[34305]** : 1800-1850 MANSFIELD, NTT, ENG **[34345]** : 1670+ FROME, SOM, ENG **[34408]** : 1700S UPPER CLATFORD, HAM, ENG **[34709]** : PRE 1850 HANDSWORTH, STS, ENG **[34725]** : PRE 1841 SHALDEN, HAM, ENG **[34911]** : 1835+ HARTSHORNE, DBY, ENG **[35144]** : ALL WEST BUCKLAND, DEV, ENG **[35222]** : PRE 1669 ROMSEY, HAM, ENG **[36668]** : ALL OLDBURY, WOR, ENG **[37373]** : ALL DBY, ENG **[37661]** : PRE 1700 SOM & NJ, ENG & USA **[38746]** : PRE 1855 TIP, IRL **[35379]** : 1960+ NY, USA **[34055]** : PRE 1800 USA & SCT **[34410]**

HOLLOWELL ALL PERQUIMANS CO., NC, USA **[36557]**

HOLLSTEN 1600+ MOLNBACKA & SUNNE, VARMLAND, SWE **[38551]**

HOLLY ALL WIL, ENG **[37233]** : ALL CT, USA **[37803]**

HOLLYWELL 1860+ WITHERSLACK, WES, ENG **[37073]**

HOLLYWOOD 1850+ SINGLETON, NSW, AUS **[38582]**

HOLMAN ALL ENG **[34057]** : PRE 1840 CROWAN, CON, ENG **[35045]** : 1850S DEPTFORD, KEN, ENG **[36800]** : ALL WELFORD, NTH, ENG **[37291]** : PRE 1900 STROOD, KEN, ENG **[37405]** : 1880+ SALIDA, CO, USA **[34057]** : 1884+ POCATELLO, ID, USA **[34057]** : 1884+ ST PAUL, MN, USA **[34057]**

HOLMBERG 1863-1885 SWE **[38101]** : 1885-1928 DOUGLAS CO., MN, USA **[38101]** : 1928-1935 CLARK CO., WA, USA **[38101]**

HOLMDEN 1800+ EDENBRIDGE, KEN, ENG **[36088]**

HOLME 1800 LANCASTER, LAN, ENG **[36151]** : 1700S PENDLETON, LAN, ENG **[36585]**

HOLMES MARY PRE 1853 GEELONG, VIC, AUS **[34587]** : 1850S BENDIGO, VIC, AUS **[35390]** : 1920+ PERTH, WA, AUS **[35480]** : 1880+ BURWOOD, NSW, AUS **[35874]** : 1828+ NSW, AUS **[36607]** : 1857+ CENTRAL, VIC, AUS **[37497]** : 1820+ NSW, AUS **[37900]** : 1840+ ADELAIDE, SA, AUS **[37913]** : 1900+ SAS, CAN **[37682]** : 1844+ LONDON, ENG **[33919]** : C1838 SHEFFIELD, YKS, ENG **[34329]** : 1800S TUPTON, DBY, ENG **[34329]** : C1808 TUPTON, DBY, ENG **[34329]** : 1830+ HALIFAX, WRY, ENG **[34397]** : 1815+ OVENDEN, WRY, ENG **[34397]** : 1850+ BERWICK UPON TWEED, NBL, ENG **[34397]** : PRE 1810 LEIGH, LAN, ENG **[34397]** : PRE 1700 SKIPTON, WRY, ENG **[34575]** : 1840 ERY, ENG **[34731]** : PRE 1900 YKS, ENG **[34848]** : PRE 1754 FULBOURN, CAM, ENG **[35070]** : PRE 1780 LEEDS, WRY, ENG **[35079]** : 1830-1855 KEIGHLEY, YKS, ENG **[35196]** : C1820 NORMANBY, LIN, ENG **[35251]** : ANN 1678 KING'S CLIFFE, NTH, ENG **[35369]** : 1830S BIRMINGHAM, WAR, ENG **[35390]** : ALL LEIGHTON BUZZARD, BDF, ENG **[35480]** : C1798 BIRMINGHAM, WAR, ENG **[35552]** : ALL LONDON, ENG **[35608]** : PRE 1813 SHERBORNE, DOR, ENG **[35764]** : 1790 KEIGHLEY, WRY, ENG **[35809]** : WILLIAM 1830-1870 NFK, ENG **[35870]** : 1800+ TANFIELD, DUR, ENG **[35874]** : 1830+ SOUTH SCARLE, NTT, ENG **[35904]** : PRE 1828 TUXFORD, NTT, ENG **[35904]** : PRE 1820 CLARBOROUGH, LIN, ENG **[35904]** : 1812-1870

BOW, LND, ENG **[36049]** : 1780+ ARNOLD, NTT, ENG **[36105]** : 1700 ORTON, WES, ENG **[36151]** : PRE 1867 DERBY, DBY, ENG **[36475]** : PRE 1858 WOODCOTT, HAM, ENG **[36650]** : 1650-1830 WOLSINGHAM & WEARDALE, DUR, ENG **[36961]** : 1699-1800 ROMALDKIRK, YKS, ENG **[36961]** : 1830-1895 WALDRIDGE & EDMONDSLEY, DUR, ENG **[36961]** : 1890+ SACRISTON, DUR, ENG **[36961]** : 1700-1840 LITTLE SUTTON, WAR, ENG **[37068]** : 1800S MANCHESTER, LAN, ENG **[37203]** : PRE 1850 MOUNTSOREL, LEI, ENG **[37497]** : PRE 1850 BARROW UPON SOAR, LEI, ENG **[37497]** : ALL SFK, ENG **[37612]** : 1900+ EALING, LND, ENG **[37682]** : ALL MDX, ENG **[37682]** : 1900+ CHELTENHAM, GLS, ENG **[37682]** : C1814 HUSTWAITE, NRY, ENG **[37710]** : C1780-1860 LEIGH, KEN, ENG **[37752]** : PRE 1850 BISHOPS WALTHAM, HAM, ENG **[37773]** : PRE 1880 PLAISTOW, LND, ENG **[37871]** : PRE 1800 HEPWORTH, WRY, ENG **[37893]** : PRE 1820 LAN, ENG **[37900]** : PRE 1888 LND, ENG **[37940]** : PRE 1888 BATTERSEA, SRY, ENG **[37940]** : PRE 1620 DIDSBURY, LAN, ENG **[38135]** : PRE 1920 BENTHAM & BURNLEY, YKS, ENG **[38464]** : JOHN ALL YKS & WES, ENG **[38464]** : 1842 MOG, IRL **[34965]** : PRE 1840 HOUSTON, RFW, SCT **[38056]** : 1600+ RFW, SCT **[38065]** : 1800S BUCKS CO., PA, USA **[34309]** : 1620-1650 SALEM, MA, USA **[36737]** : 1800-50 SYRACUSE, NY, USA **[37471]** : THOMAS PRE 1850 BALTIMORE, MD, USA **[38049]** : 1730-1740 DUXBURY, MA, USA **[38099]** : 1650-1800 SUSSEX CO., DE, USA **[38342]**

HOLMESTED ALL WORLDWIDE **[37321]**

HOLMFIELD C1825 COPENHAGEN, DEN **[34041]**

HOLMGREN PRE 1840 GOTHENBURG, SWE **[37062]**

HOLMSTEAD 1800-1860 ESS, ENG **[37207]**

HOLMSTEN ALL WORLDWIDE **[38542]**

HOLNESS ALL DEAL, KEN, ENG **[35577]** : ALL WORLDWIDE **[36156]**

HOLOCHER PRE 1850 GER **[38437]** : 1880+ MI & OH, USA **[38437]**

HOLOHAN ALL BAGENALSTOWN, CAR, IRL **[36532]** : PATRICK C1818-1897 IRL & CAN **[36904]**

HOLROYDE PRE 1850S HALIFAX, WRY, ENG **[34873]**

HOLSKAMP ALL MDX & LND, ENG **[35701]**

HOLST PRE 1700 LUE, BRD **[38561]**

HOLSTE C1650 GROSSENHEIDORN, HAN, GER **[38631]** : 1761 BLOMBERG, PYR, GER **[38749]** : 1791-1797 BARNTRUP, LIP, GER **[38749]**

HOLSTINE 1700 VA, USA **[33348]**

HOLSTOCK C1845+ MELBOURNE, VIC, AUS **[35746]** : PRE 1845 BENENDEN, KEN, ENG **[35746]**

HOLSTON 1850+ ADAMINABY, NSW, AUS **[38491]**

HOLSWORTH PRE 1850 LND & DEV, ENG **[37693]**

HOLT 186+ QLD, AUS **[33808]** : ALL VIC, AUS **[33872]** : PRE 1917 YOUNG, NSW, AUS **[35253]** : PRE 1866 BURY, LAN, ENG **[33808]** : 1800+ MIRFIELD, YKS, ENG **[34351]** : CHARLES 1800+ ROCHDALE, LAN, ENG **[35499]** : 1650-1840 THORNBOROUGH & PADBURY, BKM, ENG **[35592]** : ALL N LONDON, MDX, ENG **[36382]** : 1750+ SALFORD, MANCHESTER, LAN, ENG **[36440]** : PRE 1810 HORWICH, LAN, ENG **[36742]** : PRE 1835 MANCHESTER, LAN, ENG **[36761]** : C1730 DARWEN, LAN, ENG **[38283]** : PRE 1800 LONDON, ENG **[38376]** : 1800 PETERBOROUGH, NTH, ENG **[38719]** : 1831 GLOUCESTER, GLS, ENG **[38719]** : PHOEBE PRE 1860 DUB, IRL **[37992]** : 1780+ RUTHERFORD & BEDFORD CO., TN, USA **[38743]** : PRE 1700 ESSEX CO., MA, USA & ENG **[36544]**

HOLT, VON ALL WORLDWIDE [38666]

HOLTAM PRE 1630 WHITCHURCH, WAR, ENG [34995]

HOLTFRETER 1890+ COOLGARDIE, WA, AUS [35857]

HOLTHAM 1700+ ALVECHURCH, WOR & WAR, ENG [36435] : 1800-1870 WOR, ENG [37050] : 1870+ CARDIFF, GLA, WLS [37050]

HOLTHUSEN PRE 1868 HANOVER, GER &, WORLDWIDE [37511]

HOLTKAMP PRE 1820 SCHWELM, NRW, BRD [38636]

HOLTOM 1700+ ALVECHURCH, WOR & WAR, ENG [36435]

HOLTON-JARRET 1880S EVESHAM, WOR, ENG [37230]

HOLTROP PRE 1910 GOOTEGAST, GRO, NL [34218] : PRE 1910 OLDEKERK, GRO, NL [34218]

HOLTZMANN 1849+ MOUNT GAMBIER & PENOLA, SA, AUS [34278] : PRE 1849 HAMBURG, HBG, GER [34278]

HOLWAY ALL SOM, ENG [36231]

HOLWILL PRE 1870 MARWOOD, DEV, ENG [38473]

HOLYER PRE 1820 SOHAM, CAM, ENG [34316]

HOLYHEAD 1861-1879 SRY, ENG [34540]

HOLYOAK PRE 1800 BKM, ENG [34041] : 1800+ BDF, ENG [35939] : 1700+ NEWPORT PAGNELL, BRK, ENG [35939] : 1800+ NORTHAMPTON, NTH, ENG [35939] : C1820 LEICESTER, LEI, ENG [36414] : 1870S SILEBY, LEI, ENG [37692]

HOLYOKE ALL NEW ENGLAND, USA [36713]

HOLZAPPEL PRE 1800 NORDHAUSEN, ERF, DDR [38617]

HOLZER 1700+ DIERSBURG, BAD, GER [38529]

HOLZHAUSER PRE 1850 HOKEFELD, BAD, GER [36298]

HOLZSCHUH 1680-1800 DIETINGEN, WUE, GER [36896]

HOLZWARTH PRE 1770 RIELINGSHAUSEN, WUE, GER [38661]

HOMAN C1830-1870 SOUTHAMPTON, HAM, ENG [35046] : 1700+ CHORLTON, LAN, ENG [36165] : PRE 1837 SOM, ENG [36180] : PRE 1840 CORK, COR, IRL [35046] : 1800+ MALLOW, COR, IRL [35201] : 1800S OH & IN, USA [37028]

HOMANN 1750 HAMBURG, HBG, GER [35773]

HOMAY 1600-1690 LE GUERCHE, PL, FRA [38779]

HOMBACH 1700-1900 KRAFSHOLM, KROFFELBACK, GER [38740]

HOMBURG C1850 UTRECHT, UTR, NL [38702]

HOME 1700-1900 BISHOPS CASTLE, SAL, ENG [36531] : PRE 1800 BEW, SCT [36588]

HOMER PRE 1843 MANSFIELD, NTT, ENG [35029] : 1800+ CRADLEY, WOR, ENG [37266] : 1800-60 WOR & STS, ENG [37271] : 1820+ SHEFFIELD, YKS, ENG [37402] : 1700-1800 YARDLEY, WOR, ENG [38321] : PRE 1700 ENG & WLS [38745] : 1820S WLS [37402]

HOMES PRE 1800 EARSHAM, NFK, ENG [37191] : ALL LONDON, ENG [37252] : 1800S HEF & WOR, ENG [38468]

HOMMEL 1800-1950S QUE, CAN & GER [34202]

HONAN PRE 1850 CROAGH, LIM, IRL [34707]

HONARA ALL DUB, IRL [37407]

HONE PRE 1830 HOBART, TAS, AUS & ENG [35758]

HONEL ALL WORLDWIDE [37330]

HONEY C1820 SOLINA, ONT, CAN [35612] : C1820 DEV, ENG [34456] : 1800S+ GUNNISLAKE, CON, ENG [35489] : 1700S ST CLEER, CON, ENG [37122] : 1790+ BOURBON CO., KY & MO, USA [38050]

HONEYBALL 1885+ WIMBLEDON, SRY, ENG [35725] : 1870-1880 SEVENOAKS, KEN, ENG [35725]

HONEYCOMBE 1800S CALSTOCK, CON, ENG [37178]

HONEYFIELD ALL GILLINGHAM, DOR, ENG [35901]

HONEYMAN 1800+ DUNDEE, ANS, SCT [34326]

HONEYSETT 1811+ AUS [35831] : 1600+ HASTINGS, SSX, ENG [34747] : ALL BURWASH, SSX, ENG [35831]

HONEYWOOD PRE 1759 MARKSHALL, ESS, ENG [37580] : PRE 1759 SFK, ENG [37580] : PRE 1759 HORSHAM, SSX, ENG [37580]

HONISS 1800+ SYDNEY, NSW, AUS [36830] : ALL HASTINGS, SSX, ENG [36830] : 1860+ THAMES, NZ [36830] : ALL WORLDWIDE [36830]

HONNERY 1801+ WINDSOR, NSW, AUS [38490]

HONNIBALL PRE 1840 SOM, ENG [35523]

HONORE C1700 PARIS, FRA [37819]

HONOUR 1600-1800 SHILLINGON & HOLWELL, BDF, ENG [34411] : ALL WORLDWIDE [37330]

HOO ALL ENG [36987]

HOOD 1887-1894 WILCANNIA, NSW, AUS [34844] : C1900 PRINCES HILL, VIC, AUS [35414] : 1910 SYDNEY, NSW, AUS [35414] : 1840+ NSW, AUS [36305] : 1856+ HEXHAM, VIC, AUS [38492] : PRE 1742 OWSTON, LIN, ENG [33992] : C1887 DALSTON, LND, ENG [35414] : PRE 1887 READING, LND, ENG [35414] : 1800 MIDLANDS, ENG [35970] : PRE 1850 BERWICK ON TWEED, NBL, ENG [36224] : AGNES 1821-86 PRESTWICK, AYR, SCT [34300] : 1839-1908 STRAITON, AYR, SCT [34300] : ROBERT 1816 MONKTON, AYR, SCT [34300] : AGNES & SARAH 1848-1933 ST QUIVOX, AYR, SCT [34300] : DANIEL C1790-1870 COYLTON, AYR, SCT [34300] : SARAH & JOHN 1824-88 SYMINGTON, AYR, SCT [34300] : MARGARET 1895-C1933 KILWINNING, AYR, SCT [34300] : ALL OCHILTREE, AYR, SCT [36497] : PRE 1820 MAUCHLINE, AYR, SCT [36583] : 1700+ PAISLEY, RFW, SCT [36794] : PRE 1850 ABERDEEN, ABD, SCT [37693] : PRE 1882 RATTRAY, PER, SCT [37946]

HOODLESS C1842 MIDDLE RASEN, LIN, ENG [36762]

HOOGEN 1750+ NL [36602]

HOOGEVEEN 1850S AMSTERDAM, NL [33802]

HOOGEWERFF 1700-1800 TRIVANDRUM, TRAVANCORE, INDIA [37203]

HOOGLAND C1880 OIJ, NL [36283]

HOOK C1840S NSW, AUS [33794] : 1870+ BARRIE, ONT, CAN [34484] : 1700-1850 DALLINGTON, SSX, ENG [37785] : 1790+ CLAPHAM, SRY, ENG [34484] : THOMAS 1860S HOLBORN, MDX, ENG [34484] : PRE 1790 DORKING, SRY, ENG [34484] : 1720+ BRANSCOMBE, DEV, ENG [35027] : 1800+ BRISTOL, GLS, ENG [35157] : C1853 SOUTHWARK, LND, ENG [35811] : C1830 CHRISTCHURCH, SRY, ENG [35811] : ALL SOM, ENG [36012] : 1700+ PEVENSEY, SSX, ENG [37328]

HOOKE PRE 1850 LEICESTER, LEI, ENG [37246]

HOOKER 1800+ HRT, ENG [36123] : C1803 WESTBOURNE, SSX, ENG [36185] : PRE 1810 DEV, ENG [37180] : C1840 ERITH, KEN, ENG & CAN [36479] : ALL NEW YORK CITY, NY, USA [38361] : ALL SACRAMENTO, CA, USA [38361]

HOOKEY PRE 1800 POOLE & LONDON, DOR & MDX, ENG [36997]

HOOKWAY ALL DEV, ENG [36744] : ALL WORLDWIDE [37393]

HOOLE ALL WEAVERHAM, CHS, ENG [33916] : 1850S BRADFORD, WRY, ENG [35075] : PRE 1900 LAN, ENG [36508]

HOOLEY ANNIE E. 1875-1922 SA & WA, AUS [34034] : JOHN J. 1877-1956 SA & WA, AUS [34034] : JOHN

PRE 1904 SA & WA, AUS & ENG [34034] : C1913 CLAYTON, LAN, ENG [36171] : 1700+ MOBBERLEY, CHS, ENG [37039]

HOOLGRAVES 1700+ ADELAIDE, SA, AUS & ENG [36303]

HOOLIHAN 1800-1860 DOONBEG & KILLARD, CLA, IRL [35244]

HOON GEORGE 1810-20 MERCER CO., PA, USA [38138] : GEORGE 1820-35 BEAVER CO., PA, USA [38138] : GEORGE 1835-50 PORTAGE CO., OH, USA [38138] : JOHN 1850-1900 HARDIN CO., OH, USA [38138]

HOONAKER 1800+ UTR, NL [33769]

HOOPER 1750+ TEMPLECOMBE, OXF, ENG [33963] : 1800+ LND, ENG [33963] : PRE 1834 EXETER, DEV, ENG [34584] : PRE 1862 MERRIOTT, SOM, ENG [34706] : HENRY 1811 ST AUSTELL, CON, ENG [35343] : PRE 1876 CHELSEA, MDX, ENG [35441] : ALL KENWYN, CON, ENG [35588] : PRE 1880 COTLEIGH & STOCKLAND, DEV, ENG [35701] : 1600-1900S CON, ENG [35776] : 1600-1900 ISLE OF SCILLY, CON, ENG [36000] : 1800-1900 ISLINGTON, MDX, ENG [36589] : 1700-1900 SSX, ENG [36589] : PRE 1800 KEN, ENG [36589] : 1800-1900 BERMONDSEY, SRY, ENG [36589] : 1890+ SHEFFIELD, YKS, ENG [36993] : C1760 NORTON FITZWARREN, SOM, ENG [37053] : C1830 BRIXTON, WIL, ENG [37131] : PRE 1860 DEV, ENG [37393] : 1800S SOM, ENG [37442] : PRE 1885 BATH, SOM, ENG [37830] : 1780+ BARNSTAPLE, DEV, ENG [37904] : C1759 JACOBSTOW, CON, ENG [38052] : 1600-1870 DOLTON & DOWLAND, DEV, ENG [38265] : PRE 1845 KENWYN, CON, ENG [38292] : 1750+ PYEWORTHY, DEV, ENG [38446] : 1840+ AUCKLAND, NZ [38671] : 1750-1850 BRIGHSTONE, IOW, UK [34016] : PRE 1810 RUTLAND, VT, USA [37509]

HOOTON PRE 1852 TOTTENHAM, LND, ENG [34305] : 1870+ MACCLESFIELD, CHS, ENG [36826]

HOOVER JAMES BRYANT 1823-1901 DALLAS CO., MO & VA, USA [34481] : C1830 MIAMI, OH, USA [38527]

HOPCOTT ALL ENG [37803]

HOPCRAFT PRE 1859 DEDDINGTON, OXF, ENG [36855]

HOPCROFT 1700+ THAME, OXF, ENG [34640]

HOPE 1856+ APSLEY, VIC, AUS [33833] : 1850+ SIMCOE CO., ONT, CAN [34465] : PRE 1790 WHITEHAVEN, CUL, ENG [33940] : 1700+ IVYBRIDGE, DEV, ENG [34970] : PRE 1859 BIRMINGHAM, WAR, ENG [35083] : C1760 BRIGHTON, SSX, ENG [35260] : PRE 1835 BURBAGE, WIL, ENG [35346] : ALL LEIGH, LAN, ENG [36743] : PRE 1860 HAM, ENG [37127] : 1650-1750 OXF, ENG [37217] : 1650-1780 LND, ENG [37217] : 1870+ WORCESTER, WOR, ENG [37384] : PRE 1856 ANCRUM, ROX, SCT [33833] : PRE 1856 PEE & PER, SCT [33833] : 1800-1890 CARSPHAIRN & KELLS, KKD, SCT [33971] : 1800+ DFS, SCT [35293] : 1700-1850 KELSO, ROX, SCT [36556] : PRE 1870 GRAITNEY & GLASGOW, DFS, SCT [36760] : C1800 EDINBURGH, MLN, SCT [37168] : 1650-1750 AYR, SCT [37217]

HOPEWELL PRE 1775 BEESTON, NTT, ENG [36411] : PRE 1885 LEICESTER, LEI, ENG [37346]

HOPFINGER PRE 1900 OES [37268]

HOPGOOD ALL COMPTON, HAM, ENG [33995] : 1600-1800 CHUTE, WIL, ENG [34343]

HOPKIN 1700+ ELY, CAM, ENG [34747]

HOPKINS 1869+ VIC, AUS [34412] : 1819+ TAS, AUS [35127] : GEORGE 1870+ WALLSEND, NSW, AUS

[35239] : ELLEN 1870+ CATHCART, NSW, AUS [35549] : PRE 1902 NEW TOWN, TAS, AUS [36256] : 1848+ TEWKESBURY, GLS, ENG [33882] : PRE 1830 SOM, ENG [34041] : 1600+ DOWNHAM, CAM, ENG [34221] : C1640 ENG [34395] : 1800+ CHICHESTER, SSX, ENG [34747] : 1700-1900 POYNINGS & HAYSHOTT, SSX, ENG [34749] : C1860 EGHAM, SRY, ENG [34814] : C1786 EAST & WEST WITTERING, SSX, ENG [34936] : 1750+ LND, ENG [35370] : PRE 1850 WILLERSEY, GLS, ENG [36478] : 1730+ BUCKLAND NEWTON, DOR, ENG [37360] : C1850 PRESTON, LAN, ENG [37661] : 1800-1900 SHOREDITCH, LND, ENG [37765] : 1770+ LONDON, ENG [37908] : 1600-1850 SHAFTESBURY, DOR, ENG [38471] : 1800-1930 CHARLTON MARSHALL, DOR, ENG [38471] : PRE 1869 ANT, IRL [34412] : EDWARD ALL WEXFORD, WEX, IRL [38205] : 1902+ NEWCASTLE, NATAL, RSA [36256] : PRE 1820 PAISLEY, RFW, SCT [34613] : PRE 1890 KIRKINNER, WIG, SCT [34675] : GEORGE 1860S USA [35239] : C1654 JAMESTOWNE, VA, USA [36354] : 1800+ NY, USA [36935] : 1810-1830 BENTON CO., TN, IL & RI, USA [37529] : PRE 1820 CHAMPAIGN CO., OH, USA [38135] : C1851 MO, USA [38184] : 1790+ LLANCARFAN, GLA, WLS [35825] : ALL WORLDWIDE [38060]

HOPKINSON PRE 1850 YKS, ENG [35745] : PRE 1845 TIBSHELF & CHESTERFIELD, DBY & NTT, ENG [37267] : 1800 NORTH WINGFIELD, DBY, ENG [37391]

HOPMA PRE 1720 GARMERWOLDE, GRO, NL [34390]

HOPMAN 1650+ SALEM, NJ & PA, USA [37826]

HOPP PRE 1800 OLDENBURG, SHO, GER [38648]

HOPPE ALL VOLMARSTEIN, WEF, GER [34861] : 1650-1850 ELO, GER [35300] : 1770-1800 SIESEBY, SHO, GER [38750] : ALL NY, USA [38037]

HOPPEE ALL LONDON, ENG [36584]

HOPPENBROUWER ALL WORLDWIDE [38358]

HOPPENFELD PRE 1880 WARSAW, POL [34675]

HOPPER ALL NSW, AUS [36288] : SAMUEL 1800+ WIARTON, ONT, CAN [34091] : JOHN 1806-1853 DEER ISLAND, NB, CAN [38785] : PRE 1740 STANHOPE, DUR, ENG [33940] : ALL BRADWORTHY, DEV, ENG [34471] : 1819+ RIPPLE, WOR, ENG [36190] : PRE 1900 KEN, ENG [36288] : PRE 1800 DUR, ENG [37646] : PRE 1860 DUNGANNON, TYR, IRL [34661] : 1780-1850 BALLYGAWLEY, TYR, IRL [36075] : ALL EDINBURGH, MLN, SCT [34619] : 1700-1900 IA & MO, USA [38328]

HOPPES 1730+ PA, USA [38108]

HOPPING PRE 1900 TIVERTON, DEV, ENG [33965]

HOPPIT C1757 GREAT SHELFORD, CAM, ENG [36185]

HOPPS PRE 1850 ARM, IRL [36833] : 1850+ NEW MONKLAND, LKS, SCT [36833]

HOPPY 1700-99 GRANSDEN, CAM, ENG [34315]

HOPS (SEE HOPPS) [36833]

HOPSON ALL WORLDWIDE [36548]

HOPTON 1840S WOOTTON UNDER EDGE, GLS, ENG [34605]

HOPUM 1828-1841 ACTON ROUND, SAL, ENG [37556]

HOPWOOD GEORGE PRE 1815 EGHAM, SRY, ENG [35096] : PRE 1900 LONDON, ENG [35458] : 1750+ BETHNAL GREEN, LND, ENG [36085] : 1840 ASHTON U LYNE, LAN, ENG [36640] : C1800 BLACKBURN, LAN, ENG [37157] : 1800S CASTLEFORD & ALTOFTS, WRY, ENG [37352] : PRE 1859 ROCHDALE, LAN, ENG [37925] : PRE

1787 PRESTWICH & MIDDLETON, LAN, ENG [38248] : ALL LAN, ENG [38514] : 1770+ ENG & AUS [33790] : AVERY 1882+ CLEVELAND, OH, USA [36611]

HORA ALL WORLDWIDE [37653]

HORAN PRE 1850 SYDNEY, NSW, AUS [35400] : PRE 1868 WELLINGTON, NSW, AUS [37911] : PRE 1850 OFF, IRL [34259] : 1800+ NENAGH & CORBALLY, TIP, IRL [35358] : 1780-1850 TRALEE, KER, IRL [36776] : EDWARD 1835+ BORRIS, LEX, IRL [37567] : C1800 KALLINE, OFF, IRL [37911] : 1850-1865 MEDINA, NY, USA [37567] : 1871-1884 LA SALLE CO., IL, USA [37567] : ALL WORLDWIDE [35159]

HORBERRY 1800+ HULL, ERY, ENG [37907]

HORE PRE 1900 BENDIGO, VIC, AUS [34536] : ALL NSW, AUS [35731] : 1850-1900 BRANT CO., ONT, CAN [35605] : PRE 1900 ST AUSTELL, CON, ENG [34536] : ALL LOSTWITHIEL, CON, ENG [35647] : 1680+ WLS [37051]

HOREY ALL GAL, IRL [38084]

HORGAN 1800+ CULCLUCK, COR, IRL [37133]

HORIST 1850-1900 HANNERSDORF, OES [35315]

HORLER 1829 CHARLTON, SOM, ENG [35120] : PRE 1830 KILMERSDON, SOM, ENG [35764]

HORLOCK 1700+ IOW, ENG [35943]

HORN C1859 PIKEDALE & STANTHORPE, QLD, AUS [34305] : 1700+ KEN, ENG [34572] : PRE 1851 MELKINTHORPE, LOWTHER, WES, ENG [34584] : 1850S CHIDHAM, SSX, ENG [34726] : 1800S BIRMINGHAM, WAR, ENG [34953] : PRE 1805 BIRMINGHAM, WAR, ENG [36177] : PRE 1910 LONDON, ENG [37062] : 1750-1850 ISLIP, TRIRAPSTON, NTH, ENG [37747] : PRE 1886 BUBLITZ, POM, GER [36526] : PRE 1800 OLDENBURG, SHO, GER [38648] : JAMES C1816 PARTICK, GLASGOW, SCT [34993] : 1700+ MURROES, ANS, SCT [35644] : ALL WORLDWIDE [37404]

HORNBECK 1922 DETROIT, MI, USA [36679]

HORNBERGER 1800-1830 PA, USA [36908]

HORNBUCKLE 1800+ WALTHAM, LEI, ENG [34863] : 1820-1870 DBY, ENG [37829]

HORNBY PRE 1770 LIN, ENG [34445] : C1886 WEST DERBY, LAN, ENG [35036] : PRE 1881 KENTISH TOWN, LND, ENG [36028] : C1750-1850 MDX, ENG [37323] : C1750-1850 LND, ENG [37323] : JOHN PRE 1818 HULL, YKS, ENG [37383] : 1700+ YKS, ENG [37620]

HORNCASTLE PRE 1860 LIN, ENG [34652] : 1750+ LONDON, ENG [35403]

HORNDEN PRE 1832 LONDON, MDX, ENG [35162]

HORNE JAMES GEORGE 1870+ AUST GOLDFIELDS, AUS [36278] : 1870+ COLLINGWOOD, VIC, AUS [36295] : WALTER 1873+ ENFIELD, NS, CAN [34206] : PRE 1851 MELKINTHORPE, LOWTHER, WES, ENG [34584] : 1700-1900 BERMONDSEY, SRY, ENG [34749] : C1877 EGGINGTON, BDF, ENG [34839] : 1902+ COVENTRY, WAR, ENG [34839] : PRE 1750 KEN, ENG [35548] : 1830-1890 BLACKBURN, LAN, ENG [35638] : 1800S PADIHAM, LAN, ENG [35638] : 1800+ MAIDSTONE, KEN, ENG [36093] : HENRY & MARY C1790 SALISBURY AREA, WIL, ENG [36278] : 1900+ STH NORWOOD, SRY & MDX, ENG [36278] : 1880S MARGATE, KEN, ENG [36741] : 1600+ LONDON, ENG [38278] : 1840+ GUYANA [36509] : ALL IRL [37884] : 1758+ KIRKINTILLOCH, DNB, SCT [35194]

HORNE (SEE HORN) [34572]

HORNECK 1800+ WEX, IRL [34954]

HORNEL ALL WORLDWIDE [37330]

HORNELL ALL WORLDWIDE [35171]

HORNER C1870+ RIPON, NRY, ENG [33772] : MARY 1750+ LEI, ENG [34915] : PRE 1810 CHESTER, CHS, ENG [35770] : ALL LEI, ENG [36429] : PRE 1850 IN, USA [35312] : PRE 1750 LONDONDERRY, NH, USA [36917] : C1750 LLANTWIT MAJOR, GLA, WLS [37330]

HORNERSTONE 1800+ STEPNEY & SHOREDITCH, LND, ENG [37552]

HORNERY PETER 1801+ RICHMOND & KURRAJONG, NSW, AUS [37992] : 1801+ WINDSOR, NSW, AUS [38490] : ALL WORLDWIDE [35541]

HORNICK 1800+ DALKEY, DUB, IRL [34954] : 1800+ WIC, IRL [34954]

HORNIGOLD ALL NFK, ENG [37409]

HORNIMAN ALL ENG [37069]

HORNRY-FORD 1896+ SYDNEY, NSW, AUS [37992]

HORNSBY C1750 WEST HAM, ESS, ENG [35203] : PRE 1850 NEWCASTLE, NBL, ENG [37711]

HORNSEY 1775-1900 STEPNEY, MDX, ENG [34697] : C1775 EARLS BARTON, NTH, ENG [37536]

HORNUNG 1855+ BRISBANE, QLD, AUS [35460] : 1800 FULDA, HES, BRD [37028] : ALL WUE, GER [35460] : ALL FORCHTENBERG, WUE, GER [35460] : 1750-1850 POM, GER [37535] : 1830-1870 CLARION, PA, USA [37535]

HORNY 1805-20 PRE, GER [38202]

HOROBIN 1680+ UTTOXETER, STS, ENG [35824]

HORRABIN PRE 1918 SYDNEY, NSW, AUS [37000] : PRE 1918 RADFORD, NTT, ENG [37000]

HORRELL 1750+ BLACK TORRINGTON, DEV, ENG [37092]

HORRIGAN 1840-1850S CORK CITY, COR, IRL [35727]

HORROCKS 1800S PRESTON, LAN, ENG [37443] : 1850+ SALFORD, LAN & NSW, ENG & AUS [38204]

HORSBROUGH 1800+ HAWSKER, YKS, ENG [35908] : 1750+ NEWHOLM, YKS, ENG [35908]

HORSBURGH 1877+ POOWONG NORTH & NYORA, VIC, AUS [34796] : 1820+ COLINTON, MLN, SCT [34796] : 1711+ WEST LINTON, PEE, SCT [34796] : 1760+ PENICUIK, MLN, SCT [34796] : 1786+ LOANHEAD, MLN, SCT [34796] : 1865+ BONNYRIGG, MLN, SCT [34796] : 1796+ GLENCORSE, MLN, SCT [34796] : C1824 MACKSIDE, MLN, SCT [36302]

HORSCHIG ALL WORLDWIDE [38666]

HORSEFIELD 1800-1990 STANNINGTON, ERY, ENG [34552]

HORSEMAN ELIZABETH 1808 YORK, YKS, ENG [36447] : 1800+ LAMBETH, LND, ENG [36785]

HORSENAIL C1660 INGATESTONE, ESS, ENG [38488]

HORSEY C1631-1703 LONDON, ENG [34296] : 1650+ SOM, ENG [36093]

HORSFALL 1700+ PENISTONE & THURLSTONE, WRY, ENG [35825] : 1843 DERBY, DBY, ENG [36876]

HORSHAM 1850S STOKE, DEV, ENG [35409] : C1900 GREENWICH, KEN, ENG [36171]

HORSLEY 1800S SYDNEY, NSW, AUS [34979] : PRE 1840 POCKLINGTON, NRY, ENG [34127] : PRE 1853 HENNEY, ESS, ENG [35574] : 1580+ MILWICH, STS, ENG [36701] : ALL BETHNAL GREEN, LND, ENG [37231] : 1800-1900 LIVERPOOL, LAN, ENG [37231] : PRE 1723 LAMBOURNE, ESS, ENG [37231] : 1840-52 SCOT CO., IA, USA [37231]

HORSTMANN 1668+ LEER, NDS, BRD [38685]

HORTENSE 1700-1900 HANOVER, GER [37931]

HORTIN ALL WAR, ENG [37164]
HORTLE ALL WORLDWIDE [33869]
HORTON WILLIAM 1885+ DUBBO, NSW, AUS
[35465] : 1870+ ROCKHAMPTON, QLD, AUS
[37117] : 1750-1900 BITTON & HANHAM, GLS,
ENG [34714] : 1850-1950 ROTHERHITHE, SRY,
ENG [34714] : 1600-1750 BRADLEY, STS, ENG
[34783] : PRE 1890 BIRMINGHAM, WAR, ENG
[35031] : 1840 GILLINGHAM, KEN, ENG [36032] :
1700-1800S CORNWOOD, DEV, ENG [36205] : PRE
1850 BIRMINGHAM, WAR, ENG [36275] : PRE 1850
LANGFORD, SOM, ENG [36275] : PRE 1840
MORLISH, KEN, ENG [36361] : 1872
SHOREDITCH, LND, ENG [36823] : EDWARD PRE
1870 STS, ENG [37117] : 1800+ LONDON, MDX,
ENG [38252] : 1800S MACCLESFIELD, CHS, ENG
[38285] : 1880 MADRAS, INDIA [36032] : 1892
CLARKE CO., GA, USA [36903] : BENJAMIN 1794-
1860 PUTNAM CO., NY, USA [36948] : 1800-1830
NEW YORK, NY, USA [37017] : 1843-1900
KEWEENAW CO., MI, USA [38010] : C1911
WORLDWIDE [37235]
HORTSEED 1500+ SFK, ENG [36093]
HORVATH PRE 1900 KAJDACS & TENGELIC,
TOLNA, HU [34335]
HORVELL PRE 1902 CAMBERWELL, LND, ENG
[35948]
HORWOOD C1820 FRAMPTON, GLS, ENG [33918] :
PRE 1900 NORTHWOOD, HAM, ENG [34812] : PRE
1600 SHIRWELL, DEV, ENG [34931] : PRE 1700
MARWOOD & BRAUNTON, DEV, ENG [34931] :
ALL HEADINGTON, OXF, ENG [35009] : 1660-1800
TINGEWICK, BKM, ENG [35030] : 1790+
FINMERE, OXF, ENG [35030] : 1760-1790 HINTON
IN THE HEDGES, NTH, ENG [35030] : PRE 1852
BRISTOL, SOM, ENG [35439]
HORWORD PRE 1800 BERKHAMSTED &
NORTHCHURCH, HRT, ENG [34316]
HOSACK ALL BEW, SCT & CAN [34209] : PRE 1820
OHIO CO., VA, USA [35295]
HOSCROFT PRE 1850 NSW, AUS [37130]
HOSEA C1850 WASHINGTON CO., IN, USA [34395]
HOSEGOOD PRE 1823 WEST WORLINGTON, DEV,
ENG [35189]
HOSEMAN 1800-1840 WESTMINSTER, MDX, ENG
[36803]
HOSEMANN PRE 1850 SIL, GER [38648]
HOSFORD 1781+ VT, USA [38520]
HOSIE 1740-1810 POLLOKSHAWS, RFW, SCT [35813]
: ALL SCT [37857]
HOSKEN PRE 1850 CON, ENG [34686]
HOSKIN JOHN C1890+ DUBBO & FORBES, NSW,
AUS [35230] : PRE 1801 ST MICHAEL CAERWAYS,
CON, ENG [34753] : 1800S GWINEAR, CON, ENG
[35416] : PRE 1770 MADRON, CON, ENG [35736] :
1740-1825 ST IVE, CON, ENG [36734] : ALL
PERRANZABULOE, CON, ENG [37291] : 1800+
CON, ENG [38446]
HOSKING 1750-1800 REDRUTH, CON, ENG [34697] :
1750-1850 PENDEEN, CON, ENG [34871] : PRE 1860
ST HILARY, CON, ENG [34958] : 1770+ ST
HILARY, CON, ENG [35342] : 1800S ST STEPHENS
BY SALTASH, CON, ENG [35438] : PRE 1850
SOHO, LND, ENG [35925] : PRE 1880
BLACKBURN, LAN, ENG [36369] : 1790S CON,
ENG [36877] : C1770-80 ST JUST, CON, ENG [37842]
: JAMES 1850+ IL, USA [34871] : 1870-1900 NEATH,
GLA, WLS [35442]
HOSKINGS 1700+ CREWKERNE, SOM & DOR,
ENG [35580]
HOSKINS 1877-1890 SYDNEY, NSW, AUS [35092] :
PRE 1900 BROKEN HILL, NSW, AUS [35771] : 1784

MINSTER, CON, ENG [34808] : 1843-1877 CON,
ENG [35092] : PRE 1800 YARLINGTON, SOM, ENG
[35771] : PRE 1700 OXTED, SRY, ENG [37087] :
C1650 WINDSOR, CT, USA [34395] : 1700-1850
KNOX CO., KY & VA, USA [38287]
HOSKYNS 1835+ USA [37087]
HOSMER ALL MEREWORTH, KEN, ENG [34558]
HOSMES PRE 1776 SAALSTADT, RPF, GER [38663]
HOSNER PRE 1850 NY, USA [36702]
HOSSACK PRE 1900 VIC, AUS [35055]
HOSTEDE 1594-1652 BUXTEHUDE, NSA, GER
[38750]
HOSTERT 1800+ HOLZHEIM & HOLSTHUM, RPF,
GER [37534] : 1800+ ACHERN, BAD, GER [37534]
HOSTY 1800-1830 CHESHUNT, HRT, ENG [38475]
HOTBLACK PRE 1800 CUL, ENG [38708]
HOTCHKISS 1800+ WESTMINSTER, LND, ENG
[36271] : 1700-1800 SAL, ENG [37924]
HOTHER ALL WORLDWIDE [35776]
HOTMEN ALL LND, ENG [35707]
HOTSON 1881 ELY, CAM, ENG [34540] : C1800
MANCHESTER, LAN, ENG [36635]
HOTTEN C1744 BUCKINGHAM, BKM, ENG [36945] :
ALL WORLDWIDE [36027]
HOTTON PRE 1850 WHOLE ISLAND, JSY, CHI, UK
[36200]
HOTZ PRE 1800 DIRMSTEIN, RPF, GER [38681]
HOTZE PRE 1880 ERFURT, KSA, GER [38690]
HOUCHIN 1750+ GREAT ELLINGHAM, NFK, ENG
[35800] : C1820 WESTMINSTER, LND, ENG [37053]
HOUCIN PRE 1763 NFK, ENG [34660]
HOUDE 1873+ WINNIPEG, MAN, CAN [34159] :
PRE 1615 MANOU, CEN, FRA [38525] : AIME 1925-
1932 DETROIT, MI, USA [38525]
HOUDEN 1820+ SIMCOE CO., ONT, CAN [44465] :
PRE 1850 YKS, ENG [34465]
HOUGH PRE 1900 AUS [35095] : PRE 1860
STORMONT CO., ONT, CAN [38412] : PRE 1850
BERMONDSEY & ROTHERHITHE, LND, ENG
[34316] : PRE 1795 LONDON, MDX, ENG [35095] :
1840 CHORLEY, LAN, ENG [37732] : C1774 PARIS,
RPA, FRA [35095] : C1800-1840 NANTUCKET, MA,
USA [34659] : ALL USA [34659] : 1700-1800 NY, USA
[35603]
HOUGHTALING 1820-1860 ADAMS CO., CT, USA
[37576] : 1840-1925 ULSTER CO., NY, USA [38053]
HOUGHTON 1820-1880 LONGFORD, TAS, AUS
[34542] : 1870+ BOOLARA, VIC, AUS [35043] : 1860
ROSEDALE, VIC, AUS [35043] : 1890+ AUS [36750] :
C1840 CAM, ENG [33812] : 1826 DITTON, LAN,
ENG [35282] : WILLIAM PRE 1790 KENDAL, WES,
ENG [36192] : PRE 1800 STS, ENG [36379] : ALL
SFK, ENG [37629] : PRE 1860 HAGGERSTON,
LND, ENG [37647] : 1750-1820 RUNCORN, CHS,
ENG [37895] : PRE 1800 HAM, ENG [38177] : PRE
1860 LE HAVRE, BN, FRA [34037] : 1790-1850
CULPEPPER CO., VA & IL, USA [36901] : 1830-1870
OK, USA [37895] : 1830-1870 SC, USA [37895] : 1830-
1870 CA, USA [37895]
HOUK C1832 KERB, GER [35335] : THEODORE G.
1880-1900 OCEANA CO., MI, USA [35329]
HOULAHAN 1846-76 TIP, IRL [35100] : 1880-82
LISDUFF, TIP, IRL [35100] : 1877-79
BORRISOKANE, TIP, IRL [35100]
HOULBROOK ALL WORLDWIDE [35326]
HOULDING PRE 1845 UPHOLLAND, LAN, ENG
[34850] : PRE 1750 ESS, ENG [35642]
HOULIHAN 1800+ EINAGH, CLA, IRL [35244]
HOULKER PRE 1850 LAN, ENG [37671] : 1850+
BLACKBURN, LAN, ENG [38481]
HOULSTON 1780-1900 HODNEY SALOP, SAL, ENG
[34069]

HOULT PRE 1790 NFK, ENG **[34139]**

HOULTON PRE 1830 ENG **[36050]**

HOUNDLE 1700-1850 DEV, ENG **[35171]**

HOUNSEL PRE 1840 NSW, AUS **[38773]**

HOUNSELL C1834 PORTISHAM, DOR, ENG **[34389]** : 1900 BRISTOL, ENG **[35881]** : PRE 1820 BRIDPORT, DOR, ENG **[36100]** : PRE 1860 PORTSEA & ROWLANDS CASTLE, HAM, ENG **[37686]** : 1850S + PLYMOUTH, DEV, ENG **[37686]**

HOUNSLOIN C1800-1900 HARDWICK, BKM, ENG **[36632]**

HOURIGAN 1800 + DOON, LIM, IRL **[36642]** : 1835 DOON, LIM, IRL **[36804]**

HOURIHAN PRE 1900 COR, IRL **[36963]**

HOURNE 1838 + SYDNEY, NSW, AUS **[37915]**

HOUSE C1900 + FORBES, NSW, AUS **[38510]** : 1770 + LINCOLN CO., ONT, CAN **[34407]** : C1900 BANWELL & WORLE, SOM, ENG **[34158]** : 1850-1900 BANWELL & WORLE, SOM, ENG **[34158]** : C1500-1900 BURNHAM & MARK, SOM, ENG **[34158]** : PRE 1850 DRAYTON, SOM, ENG **[35853]** : 1820 HOUGHTON LE SPRING, DUR, ENG **[35912]** : 1850 + DOVER, KEN, ENG **[36123]** : 1750-1900 DOR, ENG **[38471]**

HOUSEL 1770-1830 HUNTERDON CO., NJ, USA **[37591]**

HOUSELEY 1200-1990 ENG & USA **[36114]**

HOUSEMAN 1925 + PALMERSTON NORTH, MAN, NZ **[36809]**

HOUSER 1749-1795 WASHINGTON CO., MD, USA **[38118]** : 1825-1895 LOGAN CO., IL, USA **[38118]** : 1795-1825 JESSAMINE CO., KY, USA **[38118]**

HOUSIE 1840-1850S GLASGOW, SCT **[33835]**

HOUSLEY 1200-1990 ENG & USA **[36114]**

HOUSTON C1819 + AUS **[34444]** : PRE 1850 ST MARYLEBONE, LND, ENG **[34669]** : ELIZABETH 1800 MONAGHAN, MOG, IRL **[34091]** : 1880 + BELFAST, ANT, DOW & ARM, IRL **[35636]** : 1800S STIRLING, STI, SCT **[34156]** : C1850 PAISLEY, RFW, SCT **[35841]** : 1850S PAISLEY ABBEY, RFW, SCT **[36788]** : PRE 1800 GLASGOW, LKS, SCT **[37179]** : C1800 DAVIDSON CO., TN, USA **[37536]**

HOUT 1827-1880 STARK CO., OH, USA **[35301]**

HOUTZ 1840 PERRY CO., OH, USA **[36731]**

HOUTZAGER 1800S WORLDWIDE **[36289]**

HOUX PRE 1800 FREDERICK CO., MD, USA **[34138]**

HOVELL ALL CAM, ENG **[36201]**

HOVENDEN 1800-1900 KYNETON, VIC & NSW, AUS **[35103]** : 1825 + SYDNEY, NSW, AUS **[35929]** : PRE 1825 MALLOW, COR, IRL **[35929]**

HOVEY C1750 + ENG **[37292]** : 1700-1900 SHORNE, KEN, ENG **[38354]**

HOVIND ALL CHRISTIANIA, OSLO, NOR **[36743]**

HOVING 1850-1950 EMMEN, NL **[34135]**

HOVORA 1700 + BUDWEIS, CS **[37582]**

HOW ALL MOLE CREEK, TAS, AUS **[34186]** : 1730-1800 SHEFFIELD, NS & NB, CAN **[34123]** : PRE 1870 SOHAM, CAM, ENG **[34186]** : 1810-1850S LONDON, ENG **[34248]** : C1700 ASHWELL, HRT, ENG **[35072]** : 1760-1820 SOHAM, CAM, ENG **[35151]** : JOHN C1780 WROTHAM COMMON, KEN, ENG **[35607]** : PRE 1800 BIRLING, KEN, ENG **[35798]** : 1800 + KEMPSTON, BDF, ENG **[36414]** : 1575 + OUSBY, CUL, ENG **[36701]** : 1802 + LAMBETH, SRY, ENG **[37321]** : PRE 1770 LANARK, LKS, SCT **[37374]**

HOWARD DAVID 1860 + STANLEY, TAS, AUS **[34295]** : C1861 PORT SORELL, TAS, AUS **[34586]** : PRE 1900 NSW, AUS **[34860]** : 1890 + TALLYGAROOPNA, VIC, AUS **[35814]** : 1860 + BENDIGO, VIC, AUS **[35814]** : 1854-1900 BENDIGO, VIC, AUS **[36304]** : JOHN 1848 + GOULBURN &

TARALGA, NSW, AUS **[38072]** : 1968 BELLEVILLE, ONT, CAN **[38472]** : 1850 SANTIAGO, CHILE **[35082]** : C1820 + NFK, ENG **[33812]** : PRE 1820 WENHASTON, SFK, ENG **[34137]** : ANN 1760-1820 KINGSTON UPON HULL, YKS, ENG **[34143]** : 1850 + CHESTERFIELD, DBY, ENG **[34329]** : PRE 1800 ESS, ENG **[34442]** : PRE 1720 BIDEFORD, DEV, ENG **[34445]** : 1850 + LIVERPOOL, LAN, ENG **[34703]** : PRE 1800 EAST DEREHAM, NFK, ENG **[35348]** : JANE PRE 1820S BRISTOL, SOM, ENG **[35408]** : PRE 1860S BODNEY, NFK, ENG **[35433]** : PRE 1700 ESS, ENG **[35642]** : C1844 STEPNEY, LND, ENG **[35746]** : PRE 1880 MDX, ENG **[35932]** : 1800S LND, ENG **[36289]** : 1800-1850 STS, ENG **[36304]** : PRE 1850 ILMINSTER & ILTON, SOM, ENG **[36529]** : ROBERT C1800 KELSALE & NORWICH, NFK, ENG **[36590]** : 1791 BYFLEET, SRY, ENG **[36860]** : 1799 + ARUNDEL & LITTLE HAMPTON, SSX, ENG **[36967]** : 1650-1820 EXETER, DEV, ENG **[36988]** : 1800-1900 BRIGHTON, SSX, ENG **[37192]** : 1860-1900 WEST BROMWICH, STS, ENG **[37283]** : 1780 WYTON, HUN, ENG **[37723]** : PRE 1850 NORWICH, NFK, ENG **[37725]** : JOHN C1801-1851 FARNHAM & PARHAM, SFK, ENG **[38291]** : PRE 1780 DORKING, SRY, ENG **[38730]** : PRE 1750 YKS, ENG **[38768]** : ALL CARLTON, CAM, ENG & AUS **[35518]** : C1863 CLA, IRL **[37994]** : 1880 + NZ **[38271]** : 1800 ROXBURY, MA, USA **[35275]** : 1800-1900 VANBUREN CO., MI, USA **[36924]** : 1780-1860 RUTLAND, VT, USA **[38054]** : 1778 CORNWALL, CT, USA **[38098]** : 1800-1900 NY, USA **[38271]** : 1775-1810 WEST SPRINGFIELD, MA, USA **[38741]** : 1700 + ORANGE CO., NC, USA & ENG **[38175]**

HOWARD-GIBBON 1842 + HASTINGS & ARUNDEL, SSX, ENG & CAN **[36967]**

HOWARTH 1810 NSW, AUS **[36856]** : 1848 + ST PETERS, NSW, AUS **[37917]** : 1780-1830 CHORLEY & ALDERLEY, CHS, ENG **[34464]** : 1853 + HUDDERSFIELD, YKS, ENG **[34790]** : PRE 1806 BOLTON, LAN, ENG **[35020]** : PRE 1828 MANCHESTER, LAN, ENG **[35247]** : 1850 + MACCLESFIELD, CHS, ENG **[35979]** : ALL HULME, MANCHESTER, LAN, ENG **[36063]** : C1700 HATFIELD, WRY, ENG **[36147]** : 1820-1850 GLOSSOP, DBY, ENG **[36345]** : 1810-1835 ASHTON UNDER LYNE, LAN, ENG **[36345]** : 1770-1809 LAN, ENG **[36856]** : C1780 ROCHDALE, LAN, ENG **[37669]** : 1800 + BURY, LAN, ENG **[37669]** : PRE 1850 ENG **[37739]** : PRE 1848 BURY, LAN, ENG **[37917]** : PRE 1820 MANCHESTER CITY, ENG **[37984]** : 1820S WIGAN, LAN, ENG **[38283]** : 1742-1782 HATFIELD, WRY, ENG **[38469]** : ALL UK **[37674]**

HOWATSON ALL LKS, SCT **[34189]**

HOWATT WILLIAM 1800S GAMRIE, BAN, SCT **[34499]** : 1600-1800S BANFF, BAN, SCT **[35327]**

HOWCROFT PRE 1900 ERY, ENG **[37377]**

HOWDEN PRE 1800 YKS, ENG **[34397]**

HOWE C1820 SYDNEY, NSW, AUS **[35089]** : 1806 BRISBANE WATERS, NSW, AUS **[35089]** : C1802 + WINDSOR, NSW, AUS **[35537]** : 1730-1800 SHEFFIELD, NS & NB, CAN **[34123]** : JOS. 1860 GREY CO., ONT, CAN **[38349]** : C1842 ORILLIA, ONT, CAN **[38450]** : PRE 1850 CHESTERFIELD, ESS, ENG **[33917]** : 1700S THRELKELD, CUL, ENG **[33917]** : PRE 1800 EXETER, DEV, ENG **[33968]** : PRE 1840 ESS, ENG **[34428]** : PRE 1765 WINTERBOURN ST MARTIN, DOR, ENG **[34828]** : PRE 1930 ALDERSHOT, HAM, ENG **[36019]** : PRE 1840 TILEHURST, BRK & BKM, ENG **[36099]** : PRE 1900 NEWINGTON, LND, ENG **[36361]** : 1800-1915

YKS, ENG [36577] : ALL KENNETT, CAM, ENG
[36955] : ALL EAST DEREHAM & FOULSHAM,
NFK, ENG [36955] : ALL GREAT CHESTERFORD,
ESS, ENG [36955] : ALL DALHAM & KENTFORD,
SFK, ENG [36955] : 1590 BURY ST EDMUNDS,
SFK, ENG [38131] : WILLIAM 1800 SOM, ENG
[38349] : PRE 1855 TIP, IRL [34578] : 1830 SCARIFF,
CLA, IRL [35223] : PRE 1870 CLA, IRL [37136] :
1720-1800 CUMBERLAND & ADAMS CO., PA, USA
[36953] : 1800-1870 MA, USA [37086] : 1865-1880
KEWEENAW CO., MI, USA [38010] : 1800 + CT, NE
& VA, USA [38764] : ALL WORLDWIDE [33868]

HOWEL PRE 1760 KILMINGTON, SOM & WIL,
ENG [36478]

HOWELL RICHARD 1841 + SYDNEY, NSW, AUS
[35160] : ELIZ 1865 ANCASTER, ONT, CAN [35609] :
1800 + ONT, CAN [38463] : 1830 + BRISTOL &
BATH, GLS, ENG [34568] : PRE 1850 KEN, ENG
[34638] : PRE 1760 HORSLEY, GLS, ENG [34858] :
PRE 1920 BIRMINGHAM, WAR, ENG [35055] :
THOMAS C1833 LONDON, ENG [35121] : 1826-1864
PADDINGTON, LND, ENG [35937] : 1600-1900
SRY, ENG [35944] : LYDIA 1606 +
HURSTPIERPOINT, SSX, ENG [36212] : PRE 1850
LUDHAM & NEATTSHEAD, NFK, ENG [36224] :
PRE 1760 KILMINGTON, SOM & WIL, ENG [36478]
: ALL KIDDERMINSTER, WOR, ENG [36525] :
1840-1892 BILSTON, STS, ENG [36547] : 1750 +
PALGRAVE, SFK, ENG [36989] : 1750 + DISS, NFK,
ENG [36989] : 1680-1780 WIL, ENG [37233] : 1600-
1800 SOM, ENG [37233] : C1800-1820 TOPSHAM,
DEV, ENG [37757] : 1800-1990 BRISTOL, GLS, ENG
[37870] : ALL SEAFORD, SSX, ENG [37875] : 1850 +
DERBY, DBY, ENG [38418] : ALL UPPER
WAIWERA, NZ [34638] : 1800S
WASHINGTONVILLE, NY, USA [36918] : PRE 1800
NJ, USA [38463] : 1800 + FOXHOLE, GLA, WLS
[37116] : PRE 1820 MGY, WLS [37331]

HOWELLS THOMAS PRE 1840 MUNSLOW, SAL,
ENG [35522] : 1780-1830 GLA, WLS [37263]

HOWES 1890 + SYDNEY, NSW, AUS [34533] : C1800
WISSET, SFK, ENG [34933] : 1800S YKS, ENG
[36842] : C1750 + ATTLEBOROUGH, NFK, ENG
[37053] : C1838 STEPNEY, LND, ENG [37053] : 1835
WYMONDHAM, NFK, ENG [37388] : SARAH 1800-
1855 HIGHWORTH, WIL, ENG [38724]

HOWIE 1870 + SYDNEY, NSW, AUS [36370] : 1750-
1900 KRS, SCT [34632] : PRE 1820 GIRVAN, AYR,
SCT [34816] : C1815 MUSSELBURGH, MLN, SCT
[34898] : 1800 OLD MACHAR, ABD, SCT [34950] :
PRE 1852 AYR, SCT [35535] : 1770 NEILSTON,
AYR, SCT [35903] : 1550-1900 AYR, SCT [37434] :
ALL KILMARNOCK, AYR, SCT & NZ [34604]

HOWIS PRE 1839 LEOMINSTER, HEF, ENG [35578] :
PRE 1875 MERTHYR TYDFIL, GLA, WLS [35333]

HOWISON ALL WORLDWIDE [34961]

HOWLAND 1789-1840 BROCKVILLE, ONT, CAN
[36938] : PRE 1900 ENG [34657] : C1861 HARROW
WEALD, MDX, ENG [35417] : PRE 1615
FENSTANTON, HUN, ENG [36944] : C1800-1960
ANDREAS, IOM &, SCT [37413] : 1846-1870 PLANO
& SANDWICH, IL, USA [36938] : ALL OBLONG,
NY, USA [36938] : 1615 + PLYMOUTH, MA, USA
[36944] : PRE 1731 OH, USA [37037] : PRE 1734
PEMBROKE, MA, USA [37820]

HOWLET PRE 1730 SFK, ENG [37897]

HOWLETT PRE 1720 MILDENHALL, SFK, ENG
[34445] : PRE 1820 HOLBROOK &
TATTINGSTONE, SFK, ENG [35215] : PRE 1900
NFK, ENG [36035] : 1800 WATERBEACH, CAM,
ENG [36314] : 1555 + WOOLPIT, SFK, ENG [37399] :

1800 + NORTH WALSHAM, NFK, ENG [37448] :
1700-1900 BOSTON, MA, USA [36550]

HOWLEY 1800 + NSW, AUS [37993] : 1800 + LEX,
IRL [37993]

HOWLING 1920S BRISBANE, QLD, AUS [35907] :
1800-1920 LONDON, ENG [35907] : 1700-1890 ESS,
ENG [35907] : ALL WORLDWIDE [35907]

HOWOOSEE PRE 1858 + CALCUTTA, INDIA [36955]

HOWORTH C1800 CHARLESTOWN, WRY, ENG
[36635] : C1800 HALIFAX, WRY, ENG [36635]

HOWSLEY 1200-1990 ENG & USA [36114]

HOXFORD PRE 1820 UK [37231]

HOY 1841 + BELFAST & PORT FAIRY, VIC, AUS
[35791] : 1810-1955 LIVERPOOL ROAD, NSW, AUS
[38006] : C1780 + FULBOURN, CAM, ENG [33792] :
C1830-1840 LIVERPOOL, LAN, ENG [35791] : PRE
1900 FULBOURN, CAM, ENG [37619] : TIMOTHY
1780-1807 LONDON AREA, MDX, ENG [38006] :
PRE 1750 CHRISHALL, ESS, ENG [38708] : PRE
1750 GER [38769] : C1805 COR, IRL [34521] : C1810-
1820 DUBLIN, IRL [35791] : PRE 1800 ORKNEY
ISLES, OKI, SCT [33792] : 1850S CHICAGO, IL,
USA [35050] : 1750 + GENTRE, PA, USA [38769]

HOYCARD PRE 1845 BOTTOM BOAT, WRY, ENG
[34786]

HOYE 1850 + CAMBRIDGE, CAM, ENG [37619]

HOYER 1783 OBERNKIRCHEN, SLP, GER [38750] :
1828 GROSSENHEIDORN, SLP, GER [38750]

HOYES 1677-1876 NEWARK, NTT, ENG [34672] :
C1860 BRAUT BROUGHTON, LIN, ENG [35807]

HOYLAND C1800 CUMBERWORTH, WRY, ENG
[34974]

HOYLE PRE 1800 ROCHDALE, LAN, ENG [34995] :
1830-1900 HUDDERSFIELD, WRY, ENG [36391] :
1790 + CLOWES & HELMSHORE, LAN, ENG
[38266] : 1800 BENTHAM, YKS, ENG [38478]

HOYSTED 1600 + EAST MALLING, KEN, ENG
[37153] : C1900 RSA [37153] : C1900 CA, USA [37153]

HOYT 1820-1910 NY & MI, USA [37577] : 1638 +
AMESBURY, MA, USA [37802]

HRECK 1840-60 CS [38314]

HROMAS PRE 1890 SAUNDERS CO., NE, USA
[35290]

HUART PRE 1900 MERRICKVILLE, ONT, CAN
[34466]

HUBANKS ALL CA, USA [38359]

HUBBALL 1700 + INGESTRE, STS, ENG [35824]

HUBBARD 1870-1875 BATHURST, NSW, AUS [33768]
: 1875 + SYDNEY, NSW, AUS [33768] : 1860 +
WHITE HILLS, VIC, AUS [34289] : 1800-1900
POPLAR, MDX, ENG [34135] : ALL LND, ENG
[35063] : 1840 + CAISTOR & GT YARMOUTH,
NFK, ENG [35725] : 1750 + AYLESFORD, KEN,
ENG [35915] : 1700 + SUDBURY, SFK, ENG [35915]
: PRE 1870 ENG [36178] : PRE 1870 GRAYS &
ORSETT, ESS, ENG [36178] : 1700 +
ALPHINGTON, DEV, ENG [37735] : PRE 1850 ENG
[37739] : 1770-1820 COWES, IOW, ENG [38003] :
1800-1900 NEW YORK, NY, USA [36733] : 1700 +
NY & OH, USA [37026] : 1830-50 GWINNETT CO.,
GA, USA [37533] : 1800 + COLUMBIA CO., NY,
USA [37572] : JOSEPH 1643-1686 MIDDLETOWN,
CT, USA [38140] : 1820-1991 ROCKWOOD, IL, USA
[38200] : 1590-1991 GUILFORD, CT, USA [38200] :
1600-1991 IPSWICH, MA, USA [38200] : 1600-1991
YORK CO., VA, USA [38200] : 1640-1991 NEW
LONDON, CT, USA [38200] : 1600-1991 POMFRET,
CT, USA [38200] : 1613-1991 LONG ISLAND, NY,
USA [38200] : 1600-1991 WOODSTOCK, CT, USA
[38200] : 1690-1991 BERWICK, ME, USA [38200] :
1600-1991 MIDDLETOWN, CT, USA [38200] : 1690-

1991 SALISBURY, MA, USA **[38200]** : C1630-1700 FAIRFIELD CO., CT, USA **[38767]**

HUBBART THOMAS 1760-1821 HERKIMER CO., NY & CT, USA **[36319]**

HUBBAUER 1786 GROSSINGERSHEIM, BAW, BRD **[38509]**

HUBBEL 1780+ WOR, ENG & CAN **[38341]** : 1640+ WOR, ENG & USA **[38341]**

HUBBELL 1780+ WOR, ENG & CAN **[38341]** : 1640+ WOR, ENG & USA **[38341]**

HUBBLE 1780+ WOR, ENG & CAN **[38341]** : 1640+ WOR, ENG & USA **[38341]**

HUBER ALL MUNSINGEN, BRD, GER **[34938]** : PRE 1820 SIMBACH, BAV, GER **[38191]** : PRE 1720 ALZEY, RPF, GER **[38681]**

HUBERT 1790+ ST MARTIN, JSY, CHI **[34637]** : PRE 1850 TRINITY, JSY, CHI, UK **[36200]**

HUCHES 1730-1830 CARLISLE, CUL, ENG **[37654]**

HUCHINS 1824 VILLARD, MN, USA **[36721]**

HUCKER PRE 1863 BRISTOL, GLS, ENG **[35985]**

HUCKINS JACOB 1825 BRIDGEWATER & GRAFTON CO., NH, USA **[35281]** : DAN 1849-1900 TIFFCITY, MO, USA **[35281]** : FRANK B. 1870-1900 CRESCO, IA, USA **[35281]** : WILLIAM 1859-1900 CEDAR RAPIDS, IA, USA **[35281]** : ERNEST G. 1863-1900 GRISWOLD, IA, USA **[35281]** : CALVIN E. 1800S ME, USA **[35281]** : WILLIAM 1859-1900 GRISWOLD, IA, USA **[35281]** : FRANK 1853-1900 FREMONT, IA, USA **[35281]** : DANIEL 1815 PORTLAND & CUMBERLAND CO., ME, USA **[35281]** : CHARLES F. 1855-1900 CEDAR RAPIDS, IA, USA **[35281]** : WILLIAM 1850-1900 BREMER CO., IA, USA **[35281]** : CHRISTOPHER 1857-1900 EVERETT, KS, USA **[35281]** : ALL WORLDWIDE **[35281]**

HUCKLE C1860 LND, ENG **[34819]** : C1815 BIGGLESWADE, BDF, ENG **[37151]**

HUCKS PRE 1800 LONDON, MDX & HRT, ENG **[34743]**

HUCKSTEP PRE 1827 EASTRY, KEN, ENG **[34281]**

HUDAN C1800 AUGHALOO, TYR, IRL **[35541]**

HUDD PRE 1840 LAYCOCK, WIL, ENG **[37757]**

HUDDLESTON PRE 1840 MIDDLETON ON THE WOLDS, YKS, ENG **[37094]** : JAMES P. 1860-1870 CUMBERLAND CO., IL, USA **[35329]** : SOLOMON 1820-1830 CHAMPAIGN CO., OH, USA **[35329]**

HUDE 1854-1900 VIC, AUS **[36601]** : C1800-1854 AUV, FRA **[36601]** : 1846-1854 PARIS, RPA, FRA **[36601]** : C1800-1854 BEAUMONT, FRA **[36601]**

HUDNUTT PRE 1876 LUDLOW, SAL, ENG **[34935]**

HUDSON PRE 1858 NSW & TAS, AUS **[34696]** : 1840+ TAS, AUS **[34904]** : 1840+ MELBOURNE, VIC, AUS **[34904]** : 1850 COSTERFIELD, VIC, AUS **[35476]** : 1875 MATHOURA, NSW, AUS **[35476]** : 1886+ COLLINGWOOD, VIC, AUS **[35531]** : 1800S HOBART, TAS, AUS **[35531]** : JOHN 1845 SYDNEY, NSW, AUS **[36274]** : JOSEPH 1840 SYDNEY, NSW, AUS **[36274]** : 1870+ EMMAVILLE, NSW, AUS **[37115]** : ALL KEMPSEY, NSW, AUS **[37115]** : 1820 LONDON, ENG **[34614]** : PRE 1640 BRADFIELD, WRY, ENG **[34974]** : PRE 1855 MDX, ENG **[35079]** : 1800S LIVERPOOL, LAN, ENG **[35127]** : PRE 1887 STOCKTON ON TEES, DUR, ENG **[35198]** : C1870+ MIDDLESBROUGH, YKS, ENG **[35198]** : ALL BARTON LE WILLOWS, YKS, ENG **[35198]** : SKINNER C1744-1767 LONDON, MDX, ENG **[35284]** : PRE 1840 BEESTON, WRY, ENG **[35470]** : PRE 1830 WAVENDON, BKM & BDF, ENG **[35701]** : 1500-1850 NARBOROUGH, LEI, ENG **[36130]** : PRE 1850 GUISELEY, WRY, ENG **[36159]** : 1850+ DRAYCOTT, SOM, ENG **[36195]** : PRE 1810 HASLINGDEN, LAN, ENG **[36271]** : ALL BOSTON,

LIN, ENG **[36382]** : MARGARET 1777 SKIPTON IN CRAVEN, YKS, ENG **[36447]** : 1747 CATHILLS, WRY, ENG **[36606]** : 1810-1837 OLD FORD, MDX, ENG **[37056]** : ALL LAN, ENG **[37115]** : ALL TYLDESLEY, LAN, ENG **[37115]** : 1700-1810 EASTRY, KEN, ENG **[37251]** : 1700-1800 WITNEY, OXF, ENG **[37380]** : 1870 BURTON ON TRENT, STS, ENG **[37388]** : 1841 BROOKE, NFK, ENG **[37512]** : PRE 1850 LIN & SSX, ENG **[37695]** : PRE 1850 RAMSGATE AREA, KEN, ENG **[37720]** : PRE 1900 CHATBURN, LAN, ENG **[37774]** : 1900+ HAM, ENG **[38481]** : PRE 1890 AHOGHILL, ANT, IRL **[33985]** : ALL CLONMEL, TIP, IRL **[34002]** : 1830 CLA, IRL **[35201]** : 1800-1840 LOU, IRL **[35813]** : 1900-1960 AUCKLAND, NZ **[33985]** : 1830+ ANNAN, DFS, SCT **[35476]** : C1820 GLASGOW, LKS, SCT **[35502]** : JOSEPH 1900+ UTICA, NY, USA **[37476]** : CHARLES C1859 TAFTON, GRANT CO., WI, USA **[38172]** : PRE 1900 PA, USA **[38218]**

HUDSPITH PRE 1863 TYNEMOUTH, NBL, ENG **[34696]**

HUEBNER 1800S REPPERSDORF, SIL, GER **[34367]**

HUECKER 1971 KASSEL, BRD **[38749]** : 1890 OTTRAU, GHE, GER **[38749]**

HUELIN ALL JSY, CHI **[35222]**

HUESTER PRE 1633 ELSOFF, WEF, BRD **[36954]**

HUESTON PRE 1850 ARM, IRL **[36664]**

HUET 1880+ BRISBANE, QLD, AUS **[35428]** : PRE 1800 CEN, FRA **[36073]**

HUFF JOHN PRE 1830 WINDSOR, NSW, AUS **[33846]** : PRE 1850 GA, USA **[37587]** : 1790+ USA & UK **[36357]**

HUFF (SEE HOUGH) [35095]

HUFFMAN 1770-1800 PA, USA **[36666]** : JACOB 1835-1852 PENDLETON, KY, USA **[38157]**

HUFTON ALL NTT, ENG **[36861]**

HUGGARD 1800 KILLARNEY, KER, IRL **[33848]** : ALL WORLDWIDE **[33969]**

HUGGETT PRE 1813 SSX, ENG **[33998]** : 1550-1650 SRY, ENG **[34697]** : 1650-1750 EAST GRINSTEAD, SSX, ENG **[34697]** : 1770 EASTBOURNE, SSX, ENG **[34708]** : 1710-1810 EAST GRINSTEAD, SSX, ENG **[38003]**

HUGGINS PRE 1880 ABINGDON, BRK, ENG **[34116]** : 1800 STOKE HOLY CROSS, NFK, ENG **[34546]** : 1700-1850 STROUD & GILLINGHAM, KEN, ENG **[34738]** : PRE 1875 BIRMINGHAM, WAR, ENG **[34850]** : PRE 1800 GLS, ENG **[34929]** : PRE 1850 DEV, ENG **[35389]** : 1800-1850 MARTHAM, NFK, ENG **[36663]** : 1600+ BLEWBURY & READING, BRK, ENG **[37216]** : PRE 1850 SFK, ENG **[38577]** : ALL MARION, OH, USA **[38319]** : 1600+ VA, USA **[38326]** : 1700+ ABBEVILLE DISTRICT, SC, USA **[38326]**

HUGGONSON PRE 1850 LAN & WES, ENG **[37246]**

HUGH PRE 1741 PHILADELPHIA, PA, USA **[34096]**

HUGHES 1840-1920 BRANXTON, NSW, AUS **[34438]** : 1900+ SYDNEY, NSW, AUS **[34978]** : JOHN C1900 PERTH, WA, AUS **[35131]** : MARTHA 1841+ HOBART, TAS, AUS **[35137]** : SAMUEL 1831+ HOBART, TAS, AUS **[35137]** : ELIZABETH 1836+ HOBART, TAS, AUS **[35137]** : ROSETTA 1844+ HOBART, TAS & VIC, AUS **[35137]** : MARY ANN 1838+ HOBART, TAS & VIC, AUS **[35137]** : 1855+ NSW, AUS **[35379]** : 1852+ LAUNCESTON, TAS, AUS **[35422]** : 1900+ QLD, AUS **[35465]** : MARY-ANN 1858S MT ARARAT, VIC, AUS **[35593]** : 1881+ PRAHRAN, VIC, AUS **[35746]** : 1844-1847 NORFOLK ISLAND, AUS **[35746]** : C1880+ COLLINGWOOD, VIC, AUS **[35746]** : 1847+ HOBART, TAS, AUS **[35746]** : C1877+ MELBOURNE, VIC, AUS **[35746]** : 1900S SYDNEY,

NSW, AUS [35926] : 1876+ SYDNEY, NSW, AUS [36296] : 1864+ MELBOURNE, VIC, AUS [36296] : ELLEN HELENA 1826-1856 LIVERPOOL, NSW, AUS [37135] : THOMAS 1807+ TAS, AUS [37139] : THOMAS 1800 SYDNEY, NSW, AUS [37139] : 1820+ SYDNEY, NSW, AUS [37500] : 1850S GRAHAM LAKE, ONT, CAN [35626] : 1950S JSY, CHI [37703] : PRE 1775 HOLLINGBOURNE, KEN, ENG [34105] : C1836 LEEDS, YKS, ENG [34157] : 1850+ HIGHCLERE, HAM, ENG [34237] : PRE 1915 BIRMINGHAM, WAR, ENG [34736] : RICHARD 1800+ WINGATE, DUR, ENG [34933] : THOMAS PRE 1900 SOUTH SHIELDS, DUR, ENG [34933] : 1800S BERMONDSEY, SRY, ENG [34978] : EDWIN C1826 WEST DERBY, LAN, ENG [35131] : PRE 1855 BRK, ENG [35379] : 1850-1950 ENFIELD, MDX, ENG [35403] : 1833+ NBL, ENG [35482] : PRE 1882+ IPSWICH, SFK, ENG [35536] : MARY ANN PRE 1893 WAPPING, MDX, ENG [35729] : PRE 1843 TAUNTON, SOM, ENG [35746] : 1940+ PRESTWICH, LAN, ENG [35942] : THOMAS JAMES 1920+ SOUTHAMPTON, HAM, ENG [35942] : PRE 1840 BRIGHTHELMSTONE, SSX, ENG [36079] : PRE 1800 WOMBOURNE & SEDGLEY, STS, ENG [36110] : 1860S-1905 WORCESTER, WOR, ENG [36190] : DAVID 1900-1991 ENG [36430] : PRE 1800 KEN, ENG [36480] : 1800-1880 WESTMINSTER, MDX, ENG [36491] : PRE 1800 SEDGLEY, STS, ENG [36518] : PRE 1852 MELTON MOWBRAY, YKS, ENG [36632] : 1800+ LONG DITTON, SRY, ENG [36756] : PRE 1850 LIVERPOOL, LAN, ENG [36849] : 1860+ ACCRINGTON, LAN, ENG [36955] : 1860-1900 LIVERPOOL, LAN, ENG [36983] : 1800-1860 SSX, ENG [37222] : 1750-1850 LAMBETH, LND, ENG [37246] : JOSEPH 1800-1853 CHILLINGTON, STS, ENG [37283] : JOSEPH 1770S-1830S SAL, ENG [37283] : MARY PRE 1770 MADRON, CON, ENG [37319] : PETER C1850 LIVERPOOL, LAN, ENG [37330] : PRE 1930 ROCHDALE, LAN, ENG [37667] : 1800+ BIRMINGHAM, WAR, ENG [37924] : PRE 1854 LIVERPOOL, LAN, ENG [38085] : 1849-1990 WAKEFIELD, WRY, ENG [38139] : 1790-1851 NOTTINGHAM, NTT, ENG [38248] : C1750-1850 TARVIN & LLANASA, CHS & FLN, ENG & WLS [34370] : 1700-1900S LAN & CHS, ENG & WLS [37221] : C1845 BAMBRIDGE, DOW, IRL [33918] : 1800+ LECK & OLDTOWN, DON, IRL [33996] : C1850 WIC, IRL [34935] : 1800+ COR, IRL [35201] : 1830-1840S IRL [35626] : PRE 1900 BALLYLEAGH, ROS, IRL [35926] : 1830+ DON, IRL [35975] : 1845+ DUBLIN CITY, IRL [36296] : 1860-83 IRVINESTOW, FER, IRL [36816] : 1700-1838 DUNGANNON, TYR, IRL [36913] : PRE 1830 GLASCOUGH, MOG, IRL [37729] : 1875-1889 NAPIER & WELLINGTON, NZ [36836] : PRE 1770 EDINBURGH, MLN, SCT [38135] : PRE 1900 JEFFERSON CO., IL & OH, USA [36544] : 1840S PROVIDENCE, RI, USA [36836] : 1600-1872 VA & OH, USA [37577] : 1780-1820 MADISON, KY, USA [38061] : 1862-1898 ADAMS CO., IL, USA [38101] : 1830-1900 OSWEGO CO., NY, USA [38742] : C1750-1911 LLANBADARN FAWR, CGN, WLS [34589] : 1750+ CAERHUN, CAE, WLS [35377] : 1780S ROWLAND & CAERHUN, CAE, WLS [35377] : DANIEL 1850+ ABERGAVENNY, MON, WLS [35498] : 1830S CAE, WLS [35626] : 1830S CGN, WLS [35626] : ELIZABETH 1821 CMN, WLS [35867] : 1865+ LLANIGON, BRE, WLS [35942] : PRE 1850 PANTOSA, FLN, WLS [36955] : OWEN 1839+ BANGOR, CAE, WLS [37201] : OWEN PRE 1839 AGY, WLS [37201] : OWEN ALL BANGOR, CAE,

WLS [37201] : ROBERT 1777-1850 CLOCAENOG, DEN, WLS [37283] : PETER C1820 GRONANT & HOLYWELL, FLN, WLS [37330] : EDWARD 1700-1860 SWANSEA, GLA, WLS [37330] : ALL CAERWYS, FLN, WLS [37667] : 1813-35 LLANASA, FLN, WLS [37732]

HUGHESMAN 1750+ TONBRIDGE, KEN, ENG [35915]

HUGHLINGS C1820 WORCESTER, WOR, ENG [34760]

HUGHSON 1800+ STUDHOLM, NB, CAN [38225] : PRE 1836 NESTING, SHI, SCT [34901] : 1600S DOBBS FERRY, NY, USA [34353] : ALL WORLDWIDE [38313]

HUGILL C1813 HULL, YKS, ENG [35198]

HUGKULSTONE PRE 1840 ST PANCRAS, MDX, ENG [34187]

HUGO 1600-1800 FEOCK, CON, ENG [34214] : 1800+ ENG [35538]

HUGUELET PRE 1840 VAUFFELIN, BE, CH [36405]

HUGUENIN C1800 CASSEL, HEN, GER [34655]

HUGUET PRE 1800 ESP [36353]

HUIJSDENS PRE 1850 MIDDELBURG, ZEL, NL [38646]

HUISMAN 1700+ VOLLENHOVE, OIJ, NL [35338]

HUKIN 1830+ SHEFFIELD, WRY, ENG [34145]

HULANCE PRE 1850 ALDERTON, WIL, ENG [37403]

HULBERT 1700+ STOCKBRIDGE, HAM, ENG [34405] : 1800+ WINCHESTER, HAM, ENG [34405] : C1878 ATWORTH, WIL, ENG [34584] : 1906 DOVER, KEN, ENG [36781] : 1906 ROYAL GARRISON ART., DOVER, KEN, ENG [36781] : 1880 KENSINGTON, LND, ENG [36781] : PRE 1700 WETHERSFIELD, CT, USA [38225]

HULETT 1850 BALLARAT, VIC, AUS [33848]

HULL C1800+ WINDSOR, NSW, AUS [35570] : PRE 1800 QUE, CAN [34130] : 1800+ ONT, CAN [34130] : PRE 1805 NRY, ENG [36046] : 1770-1860 YETMINSTER, DOR, ENG [37021] : 1880+ CHATHAM, KEN, ENG [37707] : 1600-1700 CREWKERNE, SOM, ENG [37783] : 1690-1750 DOCKING, NFK, ENG [38453] : PRE 1880 DUSTON, NTH, ENG [38464] : C1800 GARVAGH, DRY, IRL [34395] : WILLIAM PRE 1700 LISBURN, ANT, IRL [38731] : 1800-1900 CHAUTAUQUA CO., NY, USA [36924] : JOHN 1788 WASHINGTON CO., PA, USA [38086] : ALL WORLDWIDE [36548]

HULLEN PRE 1840 HANOVER, HBG, BRD [35898]

HULLEY 1890+ OLDHAM, LAN, ENG [34790] : C1700-1860 ECCLESFIELD & ROTHERHAM, WRY, ENG [35550]

HULLIGAN PRE 1844 ONT, CAN [38415]

HULLYER PRE 1820 SOHAM, CAM, ENG [34316]

HULME 1800S EDGLEY, CHS, ENG [33776] : 1600S+ LONGNOR, STS, ENG [37413] : 1820+ LAN, ENG [38286] : PRE 1792 CHS, ENG [38389]

HULOT 1539+ AMPTON, SFK, ENG [37897] : ALL BREST, FRA [37897]

HULSART 1800+ NEW YORK, NY, USA [34140]

HULSE 1835-45 SOUTHAMPTON, HAM, ENG [37217]

HULSEBOS 1768 RECHTEREN DALFSEN, OIJ, NL [34398]

HULSON PRE 1900 CON & DEV, ENG [34718]

HULSTON 1700+ BIRMINGHAM, WAR, ENG [34640] : 1700+ HALESOWEN, WOR, ENG [34640]

HULTMEL 1903+ JAMESTOWN, NY, USA [38559]

HUMAN ALL WORLDWIDE [34949]

HUMANN ALL WORLDWIDE [34949]

HUMBACH 1800-1900 COLOGNE, GER [38740] : 1700-1900 PRE, GER [38740] : 1800-1900 USA [38740] : 1800-1990 LONG ISLAND, USA [38740] : 1800-1900 HAMILTON, OH, USA [38740]

HUMBER 1840+ NOTTINGHAM, NTT, ENG **[36854]** : PRE 1860 LOUGHBOROUGH, LEI, ENG **[36854]**

HUMBLE PRE 1920 VIC, AUS **[35055]** : 1800-1900 ENG **[34135]** : PRE 1900 DUR, ENG **[35413]** : PRE 1900 LND, ENG **[37089]** : PRE 1900 SRY, ENG **[37089]** : 1800+ MONKWEARMOUTH SHOTLEY BRIDGE, DUR, ENG **[37635]**

HUMBLEY C1815 BDF & HUN, ENG **[35330]**

HUMBY 1867+ SOUTH STONEHAM, HAM, ENG **[35418]** : 1890+ HAMPSTEAD, LND, ENG **[35418]** : 1867+ BONCHURCH & VENTNOR, IOW, ENG **[35418]** : 1890+ LONDON, ENG **[35418]** : 1867+ LONG COMMON, HAM, ENG **[35418]** : HARRIET 1843+ SOUTH STONEHAM, HAM, ENG **[36332]** : C1800-1900 LYNDHURST, HAM & CHI, ENG **[36874]** : 1830 SRY, ENG **[37558]**

HUME 1831-1875 FREMANTLE, WA, AUS **[34530]** : 1840+ ARMIDALE, NSW, AUS **[34899]** : ALL NS, NB & NJ, CAN & USA **[38349]** : PRE 1839 ISLINGTON, MDX, ENG **[34166]** : 1831-1875 PLYMOUTH, DEV, ENG **[34530]** : 1830+ CARLISLE, CUL, ENG **[35391]** : 1800+ CLACTON, ESS, ENG **[37046]** : ALL CROMARTY, ROC, SCT **[34674]** : PRE 1800 GLASGOW, LKS, SCT **[36405]** : 1880S SKYE, INV, SCT **[38210]** : ALL UK **[37674]** : 1800 KY & IA, USA **[36540]**

HUMES PRE 1820 HOUGHTON LE SPRING, DUR, ENG **[36202]** : PRE 1820 WASHINGTON, DUR, ENG **[36202]**

HUMFFRES PRE 1600 NAUNTON, GLS, ENG **[35260]**

HUMFREY 1790+ COUNTESTHORPE, LEI, ENG **[37070]**

HUMMEL PRE 1880 BAW, BRD **[38238]** : 1840S ROIGHEIM, WUE, GER **[35050]**

HUMPAGE 1800-1900 GNOSALL, STS, ENG **[37850]**

HUMPERT ALL LETMATHE, WEF, GER **[34861]**

HUMPHREY 1800-1850 TORONTO, ONT, CAN **[36666]** : 1820-1880 MILTON, ONT, CAN **[36666]** : 1700 RODMARTIN, GLS, ENG **[34466]** : 1700 NORTH WRAXHALL, WIL, ENG **[34466]** : PRE 1900 ENG **[34657]** : PRE 1850 EPSOM, SRY, ENG **[35231]** : 1700S STEEPLE BUMPSTEAD, ESS, ENG **[35994]** : PRE 1900 NEWCASTLE UPON TYNE, NBL, ENG **[36110]** : PRE 1820 POLSTEAD, SFK, ENG **[36215]** : 1780+ STOW CUM QUY & CAMBRIDGE, CAM, ENG **[37065]** : 1900+ DURBAN, RSA **[36746]** : PRE 1800 FORDYCE & KEITH, BAN, SCT **[36652]**

HUMPHREYS 1800+ BRISTOL, GLS, ENG **[34591]** : HENRY 1815-1835 ESS, ENG **[34886]** : 1850-1900 ISLINGTON, LND, ENG **[35187]** : 1830S DUNCTON, SSX, ENG **[35187]** : PRE 1850S BROUGHTON, OXF, ENG **[35544]** : 1800S WOOLWICH, KEN, ENG **[35858]** : PRE 1820 BICESTER, OXF, ENG **[36502]** : PRE 1840 AGY, WLS **[35557]** : PRE 1740 MGY, WLS **[36613]** : 1800+ MGY, WLS **[37113]** : ALL WORLDWIDE **[38329]**

HUMPHRIES 1906-1908 ARARAT, VIC, AUS **[34289]** : 1912+ NEWPORT & DONALD, VIC, AUS **[34289]** : 1870-1912 BEAUFORT, VIC, AUS **[34289]** : 1920-1928 HOBART, TAS, AUS **[34289]** : 1890-1928 QUEENSTOWN, TAS, AUS **[34289]** : 1829 SYDNEY, NSW, AUS **[35089]** : C1810 BRISBANE WATERS, NSW, AUS **[35089]** : 1800+ NSW, AUS **[36305]** : C1860-1880+ GUNNEDAH & BOGGABRI, NSW, AUS **[37556]** : ROBERT PRE 1900 ARDLEY, OXF, ENG **[34901]** : 1800+ STOW ON THE WOLD, GLS, ENG **[35395]** : 1750-1800 MANSFIELD, NTT, ENG **[36084]** : 1780 BATH, SOM, ENG **[36798]** : PRE 1828+ ACTON ROUND & WORFIELD, SAL, ENG **[37556]** : 1762 WIC, IRL **[35089]** : 1800+

SAINTFIELD & KILLINCHY, DOW, IRL **[36746]** : 1852-1880 TIP, IRL & AUS **[37946]**

HUMPHRISS PRE 1791 HAZLETON, GLS, ENG **[35260]**

HUMPHRY 1900+ MURRABIT, VIC, AUS **[35140]** : PRE 1840 YALDING & FARLEIGH, KEN, ENG **[34325]** : 1880+ CAMBERWELL, LND, ENG **[35140]** : 1800+ WALWORTH, SRY, ENG **[35140]** : 1800+ ISLE ABBOTS, SOM, ENG **[35140]** : PRE 1900 SOUTHAMPTON, HAM, ENG **[35533]** : 1900+ BLOEMFONTEIN, RSA **[35533]**

HUMPHRYS C1838 LAMBETH, SRY, ENG **[34893]** : C1714 HAWLING, GLS, ENG **[35260]**

HUMPSTONE ALL DBY, ENG **[36532]**

HUMRICKHAUSER C1780 SHENANDOAH, VA, USA **[38348]**

HUN 1723-1770 WETHERSFIELD CO., CT, USA **[38764]**

HUND ALL HES, BRD **[38677]**

HUNDLEY LLEWELLYN 1834-1850 AUGUSTA CO., VA, USA **[38109]**

HUNGERFORD 1828+ MAITLAND, NSW, AUS **[34969]** : 1828+ NSW, VIC & QLD, AUS **[35597]** : PRE 1860 BERMONDSEY, SRY, ENG **[34978]** : PRE 1675 CT, USA **[37570]**

HUNKING 1860S BATHURST, NSW, AUS **[35743]** : 1840S ENG **[35743]** : 1800S ST GERMANS, CON, ENG **[37083]**

HUNN 1843+ OXF, ENG **[34668]**

HUNNEYMAN 1700S HEWORTH, DUR, ENG **[36364]**

HUNNIGHUSEN 1400-1750 REVAL & GOLDENBECK, ESTLAND, SU **[38601]**

HUNNISETT C1850 WARTLING, SSX, ENG **[35990]**

HUNSCOTT ALL WORLDWIDE **[37086]**

HUNT C1845 DAPTO, NSW, AUS **[34273]** : 1822 BELTANA, SA, AUS **[34777]** : 1855+ GEELONG, VIC, AUS **[35379]** : PRE 1895 ARMIDALE, NSW, AUS **[37911]** : 1840+ MELBOURNE, VIC, NSW & ANT, AUS & IRL **[35383]** : 1750+ THORNFORD, DOR, ENG **[33919]** : ALL TRURO, CON, ENG **[33975]** : 1800-1900 TUNBRIDGE WELLS, KEN, ENG **[34135]** : 1794 MARDEN, KEN, ENG **[34540]** : 1750-1800 WALLINGFORD, BRK, ENG **[34552]** : 1830-1857 STROUD, GLS, ENG **[34677]** : 1800+ RODBOURNE & CHENEY, WIL, ENG **[34681]** : PRE 1850 CHURCHTOWN, LAN, ENG **[34696]** : 1760+ SHERBORNE, DOR, ENG **[34777]** : JOHN PRE 1856 STRATFORD ON AVON, WAR, ENG **[34806]** : ALL LEI, ENG **[35177]** : 1817-1864 IOW, ENG **[35196]** : C1800 KEN, ENG **[35331]** : PRE 1855 BRK, ENG **[35379]** : 1820+ MOULTON, NTH, ENG **[35387]** : JAMES 1840-1860 SHERBORNE, DOR, ENG **[35607]** : PRE 1700 SFK, ENG **[35642]** : 1800-1830 BISLEY, GLS, ENG **[35741]** : PRE 1840 LND, ENG **[35902]** : PRE 1800 GRINSHILL, STS, ENG **[35967]** : 1700S SWANWICK, DBY, ENG **[36018]** : PRE 1860 BAGTHORPE, NTT & DBY, ENG **[36148]** : ALL ALCESTER, WOR & WAR, ENG **[36234]** : JAMES 1827+ STOURPAINE, DOR, ENG **[36367]** : 1750-1800 HEMSBY, NFK, ENG **[36663]** : HUMPHREY 1759-60 KEN, ENG **[36678]** : PRE 1800 MUKER, YKS, ENG **[36704]** : PRE 1770 STONE EASTON, SOM, ENG **[36779]** : 1750+ DARWEN, LAN, ENG **[36991]** : PRE 1680 STRATFORD ON AVON, WAR, ENG **[37103]** : 1750-1850 DBY, ENG **[37207]** : 1640-1750 MARLBOROUGH, WIL, ENG **[37233]** : 1600-1750 SOM, ENG **[37233]** : HENRY 1850+ LILLINGTON, WAR, ENG **[37283]** : 1700-1850 STANFORD, LIN, ENG **[37283]** : HENRY 1820-1850 ISLINGTON, LND, ENG **[37283]** : 1850+ BRINKWORTH, WIL, ENG **[37468]** : C1828 COVENTRY & KENILWORTH, WAR, ENG **[37556]**

: 1600-1850 PAMBER, HAM, ENG [37651] : 1750+
HIGH WYCOMBE, BKM, ENG [37735] : 1800S
LAMBETH, SRY, ENG [37834] : PRE 1800
BURWELL & SOHAM, CAM, ENG [37834] : 1780+
SHOREDITCH, MDX, ENG [37834] : 1800-1900
LEICESTER, LEI, ENG [37858] : 1800+ THAXTED,
ESS, ENG [37889] : C1760 FARNHAM, SRY, ENG
[37898] : 1800S SILEBY, LEI, ENG [38285] : ALL
MARYLEBONE, LND, ENG [38357] : JOSEPH
C1800+ EAST QUANTOXHEAD, SOM, ENG
[38510] : 1860+ ISLINGTON, MDX, ENG [38539] :
JAMES 1840-1856 LIN, ENG & AUS [36239] : PRE
1840 STROKESTOWN, ROS, IRL [35189] : PRE 1845
BELFAST, ANT, IRL [35383] : PRE 1875
MAGHEREBOY & BALLAGHADERREEN, MAY
& ROS, IRL [35900] : PRE 1818 BUMBLIN, ROS,
IRL [37911] : 1840+ LET, IRL [38484] : 1750-1950
CORK & LEEDS CO., COR & ONT, IRL & CAN
[36669] : C1900 WAIKAKA & GORE, NZ [35900] :
1850-1920 ST AUGUSTINE, FL, USA [34004] : 1640-
1695 NEW KENT CO., VA, USA [36354] : JOHN
1700S WATERTOWN, MA, USA [36928] : THOMAS
C1800 FT WAYNE, IN, USA [36928] : RUTH F.
1800+ FT WAYNE, IN, USA [36928] : PRE 1730
GUILFORD CO., NC, USA [36929] : LUCINDA 1887
SAN BERADINO, CA, USA [38062] : 1650-1750
BUCKS CO., PA, USA [38119] : JOHN 1850+
LIBERTY, MO, USA [38187] : 1700-1900 MO, UT,
CA, IN, USA [38328] : PRE 1830 ST GENEVIEVE,
MO, USA [38538] : PRE 1800 ELBERT CO., GA, USA
[38538] : ALL WORLDWIDE [38060]

HUNTER ALL AUS [33959] : PRE 1883 HILLSTON,
NSW, AUS [34417] : RUFUS C1890 BROKEN HILL,
NSW, AUS [37159] : PRE 1850 QUEANBEYAN,
NSW, AUS [37901] : 1850S WINNIPEG, MAN, CAN
[34607] : ALEXANDER 1860+ SAS, CAN [36140] :
1820-1910 QUE, CAN [36272] : 1797-1840S LEEDS &
GRENVILLE, ONT, CAN [37490] : C1830 HALIFAX,
WRY, ENG [33830] : PRE 1840 WOOLWICH
(ARSENAL), KEN, ENG [34384] : PRE 1853 NBL,
ENG [34417] : ALL WOOLWICH, KEN, ENG [34564]
: PRE 1830 LOWGATE & HULL, YKS, ENG [34941]
: 1600-1800 YORK, ERY, ENG [35283] : 1840+ LND,
ENG [36254] : PRE 1857 SALFORD, LAN, ENG
[36513] : PRE 1870 SOUTH SHIELDS, DUR, ENG
[36514] : PRE 1875 DEV, ENG [37020] : THOMAS
PRE 1801 LND, ENG [37103] : WILLIAM C1860
PRESTON, LAN, ENG [37159] : 1862 LND, ENG
[37493] : 1800-1870 DURHAM, DUR, ENG [37615] :
1800-1890 REDESDALE, NBL, ENG [37835] : PRE
1800 NEWBROUGH, NBL, ENG [37835] : 1710-1800
BURY ST EDMUNDS, SFK, ENG [38003] : MARY
ANN C1820 HASWELL, DUR, ENG [38269] :
1830S+ SEAHAM HARBOUR, DUR, ENG [38269] :
1840S-50S BISHOPWEARMOUTH, DUR, ENG
[38269] : 1700S BEVERLY & WOODMANCY, YKS,
ENG [38745] : ALL CON, ENG & AUS [34024] :
C1870 CALCUTTA, INDIA [38659] : PRE 1831
KILTINNEY & COLERAINE, LDY, IRL [33906] :
CATHERINE PRE 1832 TYR, IRL [34247] : C1880
BELFAST, ANT, IRL [34385] : C1850 DOAGH, ANT,
IRL [34385] : PRE 1850 LDY, IRL [34575] : 1920+
TIMARU, CANT, NZ [34607] : 1700-1800
KIRKMAHOE, KKD, SCT [34107] : 1840+
JEDBURGH, ROX, SCT [34109] : PRE 1800 IRVINE,
AYR, SCT [34112] : C1800 ABD, SCT [34400] : 1700+
PAISLEY & GLASGOW, SCT [34607] : PRE 1900
EDINBURGH, MLN, SCT [34784] : PRE 1800
ABINGTON & WISTON, LKS, SCT [34835] : 1750-
1850 KILMARNOCK, AYR, SCT [35151] : 1830-1855
ALLOA, CLK, SCT [35196] : 1811 AYR, SCT [35336] :
1750+ HOOVE, WEISDALE, SHI, SCT [35719] : PRE

1750 HOOVE, WEISDALE, SHI, SCT [35719] : 1830S
GLASGOW, LKS, SCT [35730] : PRE 1800 NEW
CUMNOCK, AYR, SCT [36041] : PRE 1830
GLASGOW, LKS, SCT [36140] : PRE 1830 AYR,
MLN & RFW, SCT [36140] : 1750-1800 SCT [36239] :
1700-1820 CLK, SCT [36272] : ALEX 1800+ EAST
KILBRIDE, LKS, SCT [36471] : PRE 1800 HUTTON,
BEW, SCT [36497] : PRE 1750 SCT [36537] : 1845+
AYR, SCT [36632] : 1800+ PAISLEY, RFW, SCT
[36692] : ALL FRASERBURG, ABD, SCT [36743] :
1800+ CUMBERNAULD, DNB, SCT [36875] :
THOMAS PRE 1800 KELSO, ROX, SCT [37103] :
C1855 BLAIRINGONE, KRS, SCT [37148] : 1840+
EDINBURGH, MLN, SCT [37483] : PRE 1880 RFW
& LKS, SCT [37554] : 1880-1930 KEITH, BAN, SCT
[37835] : PRE 1852 EASTHOUSES & NEWBATTLE,
MLN, SCT [37852] : PRE 1791 NEWBATTLE, MLN,
SCT [37852] : PRE 1800 DFS, SCT [38463] : JESSIE
C1830 CLACKMANNAN, CLK, SCT [38477] : 1850-
1930 DUMBARTON, DNB, SCT [38659] : 1850-1870
DUNFERMLINE, FIF, SCT [38763] : 1880+
CREIFF, PER, SCT & AUS [35056] : ALL UK [37674]
: ALL SRY & ALL, UK [37674] : 1750+ PA, USA
[36537] : PRE 1850+ PA, USA [36578] : 1730+
CARLISLE, PA & MO, USA [36917] : 1770S VT, USA
[37490] : C1900 NEW ORLEANS, LA, USA [37593] :
DANIEL PRE 1870 GA & AR, USA [38314] : 1890+
CHICAGO, IL, USA [38463] : HOPE ALL
WORLDWIDE [34835]

HUNTINGDON PRE 1870 PRESTON, LAN, ENG
[37169]

HUNTINGTON 1800S NORTH SYDNEY, NSW, AUS
[34427] : 1800+ BETHNAL GREEN, LND, ENG
[36245]

HUNTLEY 1680-1850 PILTON & LAYCOCK, SOM &
WIL, ENG [34012] : 1750+ MANNINGFORD, WIL,
ENG [34291] : ALL AUCKLAND, NZ [34561] : 1820-
1860 OTSEGO CO., NY, USA [36334]

HUNTOON 1700-1900 VT, USA [38154] : 1880-1930
SONOMA CO., CA, USA [38154]

HUNTRESS ALL DUR, ENG [37704] : ALL NBL, ENG
[37704]

HUNTZ PRE 1830 NORTHUMBERLAND CO., PA,
USA [38135]

HUOLOHAN PATRICK C1818-1897 IRL & CAN
[36904]

HURAMAN 1800+ ONT, CAN [34500]

HURBURGH 1805+ GREENWICH, KEN, ENG
[34017] : 1820+ WORLDWIDE [34017]

HURCOMB 1700+ STROUD, GLS, ENG [34664]

HURD 1847+ WHITBY & SIMCOE, ONT, CAN
[37467] : 1800-1830 DIERHEIM, BAD, GER [36953]

HURDER ALL DEV, ENG [36999]

HURDITCH C1870 BRISTOL, ENG [37131]

HURDLE 1800+ LONDON, ENG [37194]

HURFORD 1780+ BROADHEMPSTON, DEV, ENG
[34700] : MORRIS 1820S YEOVIL, SOM, ENG [35361]
: RICHARD PRE 1830 YEOVIL & TAUNTON,
SOM, ENG [35361] : PRE 1753 WASHFIELD &
TIVERTON, DEV, ENG [37103]

HURLBERT 1865 HAYDEN, ONT, CAN [36680]

HURLE 1864+ MAUDE, NSW, AUS [35185] : PRE
1903 MARYBOROUGH, VIC, AUS [35185] : 1800+
AUS & ENG [33769] : PRE 1848 WIL, ENG [35185]

HURLEY 1883+ CLIFTON, QLD, AUS [35335] :
1842+ BRAIDWOOD, NSW, AUS [35335] : PRE 1850
SYDNEY, NSW, AUS [36632] : 1880+
MARYBOROUGH, QLD, AUS [36632] : 1844+ HILL
END & SYDNEY, NSW, AUS [36632] : 1861+ LND,
ENG [35814] : 1840+ DEV, ENG & NZ [36850] : PRE
1866 COR, IRL [35088] : PRE 1855 COR, IRL [35378] :
1800+ COR, IRL [36000] : PRE 1830

DESERTSERGES, COR, IRL [36652] : PRE 1850
CORK, COR, IRL [38420] : PRE 1820 SCT [33812] :
C1834 OH, USA [38184]

HURLSTONE 1857+ EAST TRENTHAM &
KYABRAM, VIC, AUS [36622] : 1857+ TYLDEN,
KYABRAM & COLLINGWOOD, VIC, AUS [36622] :
PRE 1841 DOR, ENG [35895] : 1841-1876
TARANAKI, NZ [35895]

HURN PRE 1880 BIRMINGHAM, WAR, ENG [34923]

HURR ALL WORLDWIDE [34813]

HURRELL C1810 LND, ENG [37239]

HURREN 1850+ ADELAIDE, SA, AUS [36286]

HURRY PRE 1800 CAM, ENG [34660]

HURS PRE 1795 SILVERSTONE, NTH, ENG [35926]

HURST SARAH 1840+ SYDNEY, NSW, AUS [35394] :
1865+ ARMIDALE, NSW, AUS [37316] : 1870+
ADELAIDE, SA, AUS [37987] : CHARLES WM.
C1880S TORONTO, ONT, CAN [38452] : C1790-1800
CHIDINGFOLD, SRY, ENG [33845] : ALL
COCKERMOUTH, CUL, ENG [34100] : PRE 1900
HUDDERSFIELD, YKS, ENG [34638] : PRE 1790S
LEIGH, LAN, ENG [34873] : 1800 CLAYBROOK,
LEI, ENG [35023] : 1800+ KEN & SSX, ENG [35555]
: 1450-1550 OXFORD, OXF, ENG [36017] : 1500-1750
LECKHAMSTEAD, BKM, ENG [36017] : WILLIAM
JAMES 1900+ NEWCASTLE UPON TYNE, NBL,
ENG [36075] : 1800-1850 CHEADLE, CHS, ENG
[36084] : 1873 GREAT WALSINGHAM, NFK, ENG
[36287] : PRE 1891 BLACKBURN, LAN, ENG [36613]
: 1750+ EASTBOURNE, SSX, ENG [36793] : 1800+
CULCHETT, LAN, ENG [36857] : 1700+
MANCHESTER, LAN, ENG [36857] : C1860
PORTSEA, HAM, ENG [37865] : C1880
MARYLEBONE, LND, ENG [37865] : CHARLES
WM. C1860 ENG [38452] : ALL IRL [36075] :
ROBERT 1915-1950 NEW YORK, NY, USA [36075] :
1850 LANCASTER CO., PA, USA [38235]

HURT 1750-1820 NTT, ENG [37829]

HURTT 1850+ SAUNDERS CO., NE, USA [38310]

HURTUBISE ALL WORLDWIDE [36660]

HURTZBUAG PRE 1877 PRITZIZ KOMMAR, POM,
GER [36290]

HUSBAND 1800+ WHITECHAPEL, MDX, ENG
[37729]

HUSH PRE 1812 NBL, ENG [37901]

HUSK PRE 1820 BOXTED, SFK, ENG [37345]

HUSKISSON PRE 1879 NTH, ENG [34979]

HUSS 1700-1860S HODERSLEBEN, SCHLESWIG,
DEN [38524] : 1730+ ESSLINGEN, BAW, FRG
[38660]

HUSSELL ALL WIL, ENG [36975] : ALL GLS, ENG
[36975]

HUSSEY ALL ENG [34671] : 1700+ SHIPLEY, SSX,
ENG [34747] : 1750-1850 MANCHESTER, LAN,
ENG [36416] : C1650-1800 BROADWINSOR, DOR,
ENG [36478] : 1700-1850 LONDON, MDX, ENG
[38115] : 1800+ HAM, ENG & AUS [35592] :
CHRISTOPHER PRE 1736 NEWCASTLE CO. &
NANTUCKET, DE & MA, USA [37003] : 1635-1700
ROCKINGHAM CO., NH, USA [38119] : 1750S
WRIGHTSBORO, GA, USA [38531]

HUSSONG 1600-1870 STRASBURG, ELO, GER [38026]

HUST ALL WORLDWIDE [36651]

HUSTED 1690-1759 STAMFORD, CT, USA [36310]

HUSTER ALL WEF, GER [35310]

HUSTON C1835+ MONTREAL, QUE, CAN [38406] :
1800+ DRY, IRL [37175] : 1810 FRANKLIN CO.,
VA, USA [38066]

HUSTWAIT 1700S BYTHORN, HUN, ENG [35830]

HUTCHENS 1850S BEECHWORTH, VIC, AUS [34875]
: 1800 FROME, SOM, ENG [35370] : 1600+
HARWELL, BRK, ENG [37166]

HUTCHEON PRE 1770 ABD, SCT [33914] : PRE 1884
INVERKEITHNY, BAN, SCT [34840]

HUTCHERSON 1800-1804 HARRISON CO., KY, USA
[33761]

HUTCHESON 1840S NB, CAN [35721] : PRE 1839
POYNTYPASSE, ARM, IRL [37915] : PRE 1900
DNB, SCT [35386] : 1800S AYR, SCT [37915]

HUTCHESSON 1870+ WIMMERA, VIC, AUS [36622]

HUTCHIN 1860+ HOMERTON, MDX, ENG [34272] :
PRE 1800 FINSBURY, LND, ENG [34272] : 1860+
LEYTONSTONE, ESS, ENG [34272] : C1800
ALBURY, HRT, ENG [36978]

HUTCHINGS 1875+ ROCKHAMPTON, QLD, AUS
[33893] : 1800 ST HELIER, JSY, CHI [36758] : 1850S
HATHERLEIGH, DEV, ENG [33893] : PRE 1816
SHEPTON BEAUCHAMP, SOM, ENG [34270] : PRE
1825 LONDON, ENG [34428] : PRE 1900 HARROW,
LND, ENG [35055] : PRE 1800 SOM, ENG [36100] :
PRE 1890 KINGSTON, SRY, ENG [36286] : 1800+
TAVISTOCK, DEV, ENG [36758] : PRE 1856
FROME, SOM, ENG [36788] : PRE 1800
PLYMOUTH, DEV, ENG [36891] : ALL
PORTSMOUTH, HAM, ENG [37214] : 1650-1760
TAUNTON, SOM, ENG [37233] : 1841
HARDINGTON MANDEVILLE, SOM, ENG [37378]
: PRE 1820 SSX & HAM, ENG [37882] : 1840
HANSLOPE, BKM, ENG [38282]

HUTCHINS 1830-1920 HOBART, TAS, AUS [34551] :
1842+ LITTLE HAMPTON, TAS, AUS [35258] :
1750-1850 SHALBOURNE, WIL, ENG [34687] :
1790+ HATHERLEIGH, DEV, ENG [35587] : 1890+
KINGSTON, SRY, ENG [36286] : PRE 1850
AYLSHAM, NFK, ENG [36385] : LYDIA 1831+
ALBURY, HRT, ENG [36679] : ALL ALRESFORD,
HAM, ENG [37044] : PRE 1900 ENG [37805] : PRE
1842 COR, IRL [35258]

HUTCHINSON 1872-1963 CHARTERS TOWERS,
QLD, AUS [33811] : 1830+ DUNKELD, VIC, AUS
[33882] : 1825 HARTLEY, NSW, AUS [35082] : 1850+
STAWELL, VIC, AUS [35533] : C1840 YASS, NSW,
AUS [36271] : 1870+ TOTTENHAM, NSW, AUS
[36271] : C1850 ROCHESTER, VIC, AUS [36271] :
1840-1900 STONEHENGE, NSW, AUS [36315] :
1880+ PORT MELBOURNE, VIC, AUS [37157] :
1886+ SYDNEY, NSW, AUS [38288] : 1870S PARRY
SOUND, ONT, CAN [37157] : C1842 PICKERING &
SCARBORO, ONT, CAN [37467] : C1800-1855
BRUCEFIELD, ONT, CAN & ENG [37790] : 1848-
1865 HELWITH, NRY, ENG [33811] : C1780
HUNSTANWORTH, DUR, ENG [33940] : HENRY
C1852 YKS, ENG [34070] : HANNAH C1835 YKS,
ENG [34070] : DAVID C1835 YKS, ENG [34070] :
1860S LAMBETH, LND, ENG [34175] : 1800+
HITCHIN, HRT, ENG [34345] : PRE 1830
MANCHESTER, LAN, ENG [34855] : PRE 1900
DUR, ENG [35386] : PRE 1860 RIPON & WATH,
YKS, ENG [35533] : C1806 NEWCASTLE, NBL,
ENG [35764] : PRE 1860 HAWNBY, YKS, ENG
[35932] : 1870+ BRISTOL, GLS, ENG [35974] :
1809+ EARBY HALL, NRY, ENG [35974] : JANE
PRE 1858 TANFIELD, DUR, ENG [36164] : 1850+
CHARNOCK RICHARD, LAN, ENG [36241] : PRE
1850 DENTON, LIN, ENG [36387] : PRE 1720 EAST
RETFORD, NTT, ENG [36426] : GRACE PRE 1686
NOTTINGHAM, NTT, ENG [36532] : C1800
ALLENDALE, NBL, ENG [37112] : 1850+ BARTON
ON IRWELL, LAN, ENG [37157] : 1830S ECCLES,
LAN, ENG [37157] : 1830+ MANCHESTER, LAN,
ENG [37157] : C1790 DARWEN, LAN, ENG [37157] :
C1830 BRIGHTON, SSX, ENG [37285] : C1750
HATHERN, LEI, ENG [37536] : PRE 1850 BELPER
& BRASSINGTON, DBY, ENG [37736] : 1800S+

NEWCASTLE UPON TYNE, NBL, ENG [38436] :
PRE 1839 BALLYMENA, ANT, IRL [35381] : 1800 +
MONASTEREVIN, KID, IRL [35499] : PRE 1840
BALLYMENA, ANT, IRL [36271] : 1800-1900 DON,
IRL [36344] : PRE 1900 WEX, IRL [37750] : 1800-1840
INV, SCT [36315] : 1800 + PHILADELPHIA CO., PA,
USA [36344] : 1750-1780 NORTH ANDOVER, MA &
NH, USA [36913] : ALL USA & CAN [38782]

HUTCHISON ALL NSW, AUS [35377] : 1850 +
PRAHRAN, VIC, AUS [35476] : 1890 + FITZROY,
VIC, AUS [35476] : PRE 1900 SYDNEY, NSW, AUS
[37136] : C1890 BRUNSWICK, VIC, AUS [37159] :
1863 + FORDWICH, ONT, CAN [34080] : C1800-1855
BRUCEFIELD, ONT, CAN & ENG [37790] : 1800-
1900 ST PANCRAS, LONDON, ENG [35600] : PRE
1720 SSX, ENG [37875] : SIR WILLIAM ALL ENG &
RSA [38487] : 1860 + INDIA [35377] : 1850S
MONEYMORE, LDY, IRL [37879] : PRE 1863 SCT
[34080] : 1850 LONGSIDE, ABD, SCT [34474] : PRE
1821 SCT [35572] : ANNA PRE 1870 EDINBURGH
& LEITH, SCT [36575] : C1860 LASSWADE
DALKEITH, MLN, SCT [37159] : PRE 1870 DYSART
& KIRKCALDY, FIF, SCT [37727] : 1800
NEMPHLAR, LKS, SCT [37879] : PRE 1820
PAISLEY, RFW, SCT [38056] : PRE 1860
GLASGOW, SCT [38057] : PRE 1850 FOCHABERS,
BAN & NEI, SCT & NZ [35961]

HUTH C1826 CELLE, HAN, GER & AUS [35391]

HUTLEY PRE 1830 STANSTEAD, ESS, ENG [35835] :
WILLIAM 1870 + SUTTON, ESS, ENG [37664]

HUTMACHER 1700 + RPR, GER [38765]

HUTSON 1800 + COALVILLE, LEI & NTT, ENG
[34066] : SKINNER C1744-1767 LONDON, MDX,
ENG [35284] : 1770 + SRY, MDX & SSX, ENG
[36574] : C1800 EAST HOATHLEY, SSX, ENG
[37285]

HUTT PRE 1840 MAIDSTONE, KEN, ENG [34325] :
THOMAS 1780-1850 MAIDSTONE, KEN, ENG
[34325] : 1800-1860 STANDLAKE & COTE, OXF,
ENG [37194] : 1650-1800 RYDE, IOW, HAM, ENG
[37333] : 1700 + ANSTRUTHER EASTER, FIF, SCT
[35395] : 1700 + PITTENWEEM & CARNBEE, FIF,
SCT [35395] : 1650-1800 FIF, SCT [37333]

HUTTER EVA 1820-1840 GERMESCHEIN, BAV, GER
[38482]

HUTTNER 1840-1890 COLN, RPR, GER [38528]

HUTTO 1850 + GA & FL, USA [38739]

HUTTON 1840-1870 ADELAIDE, SA, AUS [38082] :
PRE 1880 SMITHS FALLS, ONT, CAN [34376] : PRE
1826 BKM, ENG [34041] : 1800S WETHERAL, CUL,
ENG [34110] : 1680 + MARSKE BY SEA, YKS, ENG
[35908] : PRE 1800 BAILDON, WRY, ENG [36165] :
ALL SWYNCOMBE, OXF, ENG [36231] : 1750-1880
BRAMLEY, HAM, ENG [37118] : 1780-1850 ROXBY,
NRY, ENG [37615] : PRE 1850 SNAITH, WRY, ENG
[37856] : C1700-1850 FIF, SCT [34040] : C1750-1800
FIF, SCT [36327] : PRE 1800 BEW, SCT [36588] :
1800 + PORTMOAK, KRS, SCT [36705] : PRE 1750
CHESTER CO., PA, USA [36319] : JOHN 1828-1898
WILL CO., IL, USA [37014]

HUWER 1700-1800 ILLINGEN, SAA, BRD [38617]

HUXFORD 1800-1850 GREENE CO., NY, USA [38113]
: J775-1800 HARTFORD, CT, USA [38113]

HUXHAM C1750-1850 MALBOROUGH &
DEVONPORT, DEV, ENG [34952]

HUXLEY EDWARD P. 1848 + NARRABRI, NSW,
AUS [37312] : THOMAS 1804 + WINDSOR, NSW,
AUS [37312] : 1800 + LONDON, ENG [34556] :
C1768-1791 LND & MDX, ENG [34886] : PRE 1839
LEOMINSTER, HEF, ENG [35578] : 1690 +
BENGAL &, BDF, ENG &, INDIA [34109]

HUXOLL PRE 1630 BUCHHOLZ, WEF, GER [38631]

HUXTABLE PRE 1884 MALLALA, SA, AUS & ENG
[35763] : PRE 1800 FILLEIGH, DEV, ENG [34908]

HUYCK C1600 + NEW YORK, NY, USA [34339]

HUZZARD 1800-1830 HULL & SCULCOATES, YKS,
ENG [36392]

HUZZELL ALL GLS, ENG [36975] : ALL WIL, ENG
[36975]

HYAM PRE 1800 ESS, ENG [35642]

HYAMS HENRY SNR. PRE 1840 LONDON
(WATCHMAKER), ENG [33816] : HENRY PRE 1846
LONDON, ENG [33816]

HYANAM C1800-1860 DUBLIN, IRL [33876]

HYATT 1830-1880 ST MARYLEBONE, LND, ENG
[36127] : 1880-1930 KENSAL TOWN, LND, ENG
[36127] : 1900-1950 PADDINGTON, LND, ENG
[36127] : 1870-1900 KILBURN, LND, ENG [36127] :
1600-1800 ASCOT UNDER WYCHWOOD, OXF,
ENG [36653] : 1800 + LONDON, ENG [38725] :
MARY 1780 MD, USA [38109] : 1920-1950 +
CARMARTHEN, WLS [36127] : ALL WORLDWIDE
[36127]

HYDE 1915 + WAWOTA, SAS, CAN [34521] : C1865
HAMTON & YORKTON, ONT, CAN [34521] :
1910 + WINNIPEG & WOODLANDS, MAN, CAN
[34521] : 1810 + MARQUETTE, MAN, CAN [34521] :
C1940 DUMAS, SAS, CAN [34521] : 1820-1850
BOLDRE & GORLEY, HAM, ENG [34291] : 1479-
1830 ROCKFORD, HAM, ENG [34291] : C1830-1854
BRIDGE, KEN, ENG [34437] : 1800-1840 WALSALL,
STS, ENG [34448] : PRE 1838 HORSLEY, GLS, ENG
[34463] : 1600 + HASTINGS, SSX, ENG [34747] : PRE
1850 BRIGHTON, SSX, ENG [34763] : PRE 1900
CLAPHAM, LND, ENG [34825] : 1920 +
WALLASEY, LAN, ENG [35025] : 1793 CAUNDLE
PURSE, DOR, ENG [35252] : 1700 + TICKNALL,
DBY, ENG [35851] : PRE 1865 WALTON ON
THAMES, SRY, ENG [35976] : 1800 + SALISBURY,
WIL, ENG [36474] : ALL DOR & SOM, ENG [36479] :
C1840 BIRMINGHAM, WAR, ENG [36649] :
LUCRETIA 1600 ENG [36890] : 1891 +
BIRMINGHAM, WAR, ENG [37265] : 1700 +
LEIGH & ECCLES, LAN, ENG [38047] : C1790 +
HAMTON & YORKTON, COR, IRL [34521] : C1874
DRUMCREE, ARM, IRL [34805] : 1750-1850
BUXTON, ME, USA [38045] : 1800 + CARDIFF,
GLA, WLS [34803] : 1800 + LLANDOGO, MON,
WLS [37885] : 1700 + WORLDWIDE [38774]

HYDEN 1700-1800S CANNOCK, STS, ENG [37898]

HYDER ALL SSX & KEN, ENG [37210]

HYDRON PRE 1800 WLS, ENG [35287]

HYDZIK 1842S SANOK, POL [38184]

HYEMPSALL ALL WORLDWIDE [37742]

HYETT C1860 + VIC, AUS [33930] : 1800-1850
GLOUCESTER, GLS, ENG [36663]

HYHAM C1820 BOXFORD, SFK, ENG [36215]

HYLAND 1851 + GLEBE & WAVERLEY, NSW, AUS
[35092] : 1828 + SYDNEY, NSW, AUS [35857] : PRE
1800 TICEHURST, SSX, ENG [35857] : PRE 1860
BARMING, KEN, ENG [37359] : 1870 +
SKELMERSDALE & BICKERSTAFFE, LAN, ENG
[37968] : 1827-1851 RATHDRUM, WIC, IRL [35092] :
C1814 CASTLEBAR, MAY, IRL [36366] : 1750 + TIP,
IRL [36602] : ALL TOORTAUN, LEX, IRL [37968]

HYMAN C1870 + TAMWORTH, NSW, AUS [35163] :
PRE 1820 ENG [33999] : PRE 1900 LND, ENG [36399]
: PRE 1850 FALMOUTH, CON, ENG [37300]

HYMERS PRE 1880 ENG [38585]

HYMETTE 1865 + KENSINGTON BROMPTON,
LND, ENG [35418] : 1880 + MARGATE &
RAMSGATE, KEN, ENG [35418] : ALL FRA [35418]

HYND 1800 + DUNFERMLINE, FIF, SCT [35969]

HYNDMAN C1760+ BALLYMENA, ANT, IRL [34672] : 1760-1834 GREENOCK, RFW, SCT [35782]

HYNDS PRE 1860 LANARK, LKS, SCT [36191]

HYNE C1800-1850 STOKE DAMEREL & MARLBOROUGH, DEV, ENG [34952]

HYNES 1880+ SYDNEY, NSW, AUS [34979] : JAMES PRE 1878 CLA, IRL [34979] : C1840-1850S GAL, IRL [36337]

HYNESS 1860 GAL, IRL [35325]

HYSLOP 1800-1850 TOMAGO, NSW, AUS [35094] : ALL GOSPORT, IOW, HAM, ENG [35936] : 1764+ KKD, SCT [33790] : 1790S LESMAHAGOW, LKS, SCT [35406] : 1800+ DFS, SCT [36869] : PRE 1900 MOUSWALD & LOCHMABEN, DFS, SCT [37821] : 1800+ DFS, SCT [38247] : 1800+ DFS, SCT & AUS [34705]

HYSON C1880 TINTINHULL, SOM, ENG [37378]

HÄRWICH ALL WORLDWIDE [38709]

HÄRWICK ALL WORLDWIDE [38709]

HÄRWIG ALL WORLDWIDE [38709]

HÄRWIGH ALL WORLDWIDE [38709]

IBBERSON 1880S EAST RETFORD, NTT, ENG [34854]

IBBESON 1860+ WORSBOROUGH, YKS, ENG [35364]

IBBS PRE 1830 HIGHAM FERRERS, NTH, ENG [33860]

IBONAS ALL PHILIPPINE [38730]

IDDENDEN PRE 1650 HAWKHURST, KEN, ENG [36972]

IDE 1860-1880 UELITZ, MSW, GER [38331] : ALL WORLDWIDE [34936]

IDEN PRE 1780 ROLVENDEN, KEN, ENG [36272]

IDIENS PRE 1810 TRYSULL, STS, ENG [37710]

IDSTEIN 1800+ MITTELHEIM, HEN, GER [34693]

IESLER ALL GER [35618]

IFE C1860 HOBART & FRANKLIN, TAS, AUS [35388] : PRE 1750 SFK, ENG [37280]

IGOE 1800-1840 LONGFORD, LOG, IRL [33994]

IHDE 1860-1880 UELITZ, MSW, GER [38331]

IHLE 1800-1900 NOR [34631]

IJNZONIDES 1791+ OLDEBOORN, FRI, NL [34990]

IJZENDOORN VAN 1738+ ROTTERDAM, ZH, NL [38712]

IKIN PRE 1800 WELLINGTON, SAL, ENG [34711] : 1755+ WHIXALL, SAL, ENG [34926]

ILDAU 1790+ OLD, GER [37509]

ILES 1830+ TAS, AUS [35062] : 1800-1850 TOMAGO, NSW, AUS [35094] : 1860+ HUNTER REGION & NEWCASTLE, NSW, AUS [35239] : C1801 CHIPPING SODBURY, AVN, ENG [34685] : PRE 1830 WIL, ENG [36755] : HENRY PRE 1840 BRISTOL, ENG [37406] : C1860 YKS, ENG [37760]

ILET 1780-1820 THORLEY, HRT, ENG [36017] : 1770-1820 MATCHING, ESS, ENG [36017] : 1775-1825 THORLEY, HRT, ENG [36017]

ILETT 1700+ HAUXTON, CAM, ENG [37166]

ILIFFE PRE 1850 GUILSBOROUGH, NTH, ENG [35863] : 1700-1850 KIBWORTH, LEI, ENG [36314] : PRE 1592 ASHBY MAGNA, LEI, ENG [37706]

ILLFELD 1850S BATTENBURG, GER [35156]

ILLIDGE 1850-1900 GYMPIE, QLD & NSW, AUS [34589] : PRE 1855 LEAMINGTON, WAR, ENG [34589]

ILLINGWORTH 1800 AUS [35481] : C1708-1848 WAKEFIELD, WRY, ENG [33862] : ALL BRADFORD, YKS, ENG [34604] : 1670+ LAN, ENG [35481]

ILLMAN ALL ENG [35362]

ILLMANN 1800-1880 ST CATHERINESBURG, BOHEMIA [38033] : PRE 1800 OES [38033] : 1880+ MI, USA [38033]

ILLSLEY PRE 1850 BLACKFORDBY, LEI, ENG [36387]

IMBER 1860S BOWENFELS, NSW, AUS [35105] : 1870+ MUDGEE, NSW, AUS [35105] : 1863+ HASSANS WALLS, NSW, AUS [35105] : 1801+ NSW, AUS [38389] : C1750-1880 SHAFTESBURY, DOR, ENG [36478] : C1799 ENG [38389]

IMBRY 1600-1900 BORDER TOWNS, BEW, ROX & SEL, SCT [36461]

IMELE ALL SCHELINGEN, BAD, GER [38534]

IMLAY 1780-1830 SCT [38201]

IMMS 1751+ RUGELEY, STS, ENG [34939]

IMPEY ALFRED 1880+ VIC, AUS [35803] : 1750-1820 EDDLESBOROUGH, BKM, ENG [34316] : PRE 1850 SHEFFORD & AMPTHILL, BDF, ENG [35229] : PRE 1900 AMERSHAM, BKM, ENG [37753]

IMRAY 1800+ ABERDEEN, ABD, SCT [34882]

IMRIE 1800S MOSGEIL, OTO, NZ [36799] : 1800S DUNEDIN, OTO, NZ [36799] : 1800-1900 SCT [34135] : 1600-1900 BORDER TOWNS, BEW, ROX & SEL, SCT [36461]

INALL 1800S LAUNCESTON, TAS, AUS [35491] : PRE 1830 LONDON, ENG [35491]

INCE C1900 SOUTHAMPTON, HAM, ENG [37378]

INCH 1850-1865 ST IVES, CON, ENG [33865] : PRE 1850 PENHALLOW, CON, ENG [36909] : ALL CON, ENG [37020] : ALL DEV, ENG [37020]

INCHES PRE 1710 CLUNIE, PER, SCT [37852]

IND AMBROSE C1785 LONDON, ENG [35714] : ALL TETBURY, WIL, ENG [35750] : JOHN PRE 1848 LACOCK, WIL, ENG [37184] : 1827+ KEEVIL, WIL, ENG [37184]

INDGE C1861 WESTMINSTER, LND, ENG [35348] : PRE 1872 ALTON, HAM, ENG [37894]

INESON 1863 BATLEY, YKS, ENG [38449]

INETT PRE 1800 WORCESTER, WOR, ENG [38420]

INFIELD 1800-1900 STARK CO., OH, USA [38770]

INFUSINI PRE 1920 MARTONE, CALABRIA, ITL [36271]

ING C1804 DOWNTON, WIL, ENG [34898] : 1830S+ BKM, ENG [35139]

INGALL 1790+ LONDON, ENG [35171]

INGALLS 1895-1627 SKIRBECK, LIN, ENG [38571] : 1792-1942 BRIDGTON, ME, USA [35294]

INGE 1700S VA, USA [36926]

INGERSOLL 1795+ DUCHESS CO.& FREDRICKSBURGH, NY & ONT, USA & CAN [34109]

INGERSON PRE 1800 NORTH TAWTON, DEV, ENG [36662]

INGHAM MYERS 1829+ NSW & QLD, AUS [37131] : PRE 1780 ILLINGWORTH & OVENDEN, WRY, ENG [34397] : 1650+ PENDLE FOREST, LAN, ENG [35169] : 1800+ NOTTINGHAM, NTT, ENG [35543] : JAMES 1814-1883 ENG [35615] : PRE 1815 ST WERBY BRIDGE, WRY, ENG [36202] : 1880+ LEICESTER, LEI, ENG [37112] : 1820 LEEDS, YKS, ENG [37112] : PRE 1815 LAN, ENG [37131] : PRE 1800 WRY, ENG [37402] : PRE 1885 SHEFFIELD, YKS, ENG [37686] : 1800-1870 CAYUGA CO., NY, USA [36738]

INGLE ALL MANCHESTER, LAN, ENG [36989] : 1860+ CANNING TOWN, LONDON, ESS, ENG [36989]

INGLEBY C1850 YKS, ENG [33809]

INGLEDEW GEORGE PRE 1852 SKELTON, NRY, ENG [34567] : PRE 1863 ENG [37897] : PRE 1863 SCT [37897]

INGLEFINGER PRE 1850 WUERTTENBURG, GER [34914]

INGLESBY PRE 1811 MEA, IRL [36338] : 1800+ PHILADELPHIA, PA, USA [36338]

INGLESON C1834 BRADFORD, YKS, ENG **[34305]**
INGLIN PRE 1850 SATTEL, SZ, CH **[38686]**
INGLIS 1800+ LESMAHAGOW, LKS, SCT **[33948]** :
C1760 DOUGLAS, LKS, SCT **[34118]** : 1791-1851 ST
ANDREWS, FIF, SCT **[34622]** : PRE 1850S PAISLEY
& GLASGOW, RFW, SCT **[35433]** : 1900 PAISLEY,
SCT **[37829]** : C1800-1850 GLASGOW, MLN, SCT
[38541] : 1820+ ST ANDREWS & MOTUEKA, FIF &
NLN, SCT & NZ **[34622]** : ALL WORLDWIDE
[33959]
INGLISH C1800 KENTON, SFK, ENG **[33910]** : 1850+
SOUTHSEA, HAM, ENG **[35377]** : 1779 WYTON,
HUN, ENG **[37723]**
INGOLDSBY 1770-1850 CARRICKMACROSS, MOG,
IRL **[34346]** : 1700+ MEA, IRL **[36338]** : PRE 1750
LIMERICK & DUBLIN, IRL **[38084]**
INGRAHAM 1782 RI, USA **[36900]**
INGRAM 1860+ WAGGA WAGGA, NSW, AUS
[35203] : 1851+ MELBOURNE, VIC, AUS **[35203]** :
ELIZABETH 1830+ MELBOURNE, VIC, AUS
[35593] : PRE 1905 WAGGA WAGGA, NSW, AUS
[35781] : 1830+ VIC, AUS **[35831]** : 1750-1820
STAPLEHURST, KEN, ENG **[34623]** : PRE 1800
SOUTH CAVE, ERY, ENG **[34866]** : PRE 1850
GRAYS THURROCK, ESS, ENG **[35203]** : PRE 1810
FYFIELD, WIL, ENG **[35211]** : 1700-1850 WIL, ENG
[35862] : PRE 1685 LODDISWELL, DEV, ENG
[35895] : 1750-1850 BANWELL, SOM, ENG **[36012]** :
PRE 1815 BROMSGROVE, WOR, ENG **[36518]** :
1770+ OLD WARDEN, BDF, ENG **[37151]** : ALL
CASTLE CARY, SOM, ENG **[37378]** : ALL
WINSLOW/N MARSTON, BKM, SCT **[38358]** :
1807+ CLAPTON, NTH, ENG & AUS **[33919]** :
1800+ FERNISKY, ANT, IRL **[36304]** : 1860+
GALGORM, ANT, IRL **[36304]** : PRE 1820
FRASERBURGH, ABD, SCT **[36673]** : PRE 1850 AYR,
SCT **[38039]** : PRE 1800 CUMBERLAND CO., PA,
USA **[34138]** : 1870+ USA **[36304]** : PRE 1840
NEWTOWN, MGY, WLS **[33830]** : ALL
WORLDWIDE **[37036]**
INGS 1851-1861 MELBOURNE, VIC, AUS **[34673]** :
PRE 1851 WINCANTON, SOM, ENG **[34673]** : 1920S
WIL, ENG **[35243]** : 1700S SEMLEY & DONHEADS,
WIL, ENG **[36211]** : 1861+ DUNEDIN, NZ **[34673]**
INKEL 1840+ QUE, CAN **[36678]**
INKIN ALL WLS **[36133]** : ALL WORLDWIDE **[36133]**
INKPEN ALL LAUGHTON, SSX, ENG **[35588]**
INKSTER ALL OKI, SCT **[34362]**
INMAN ALL ST LUKES & SHOREDITCH, LND,
ENG **[34820]** : 1800+ LONDON, ENG **[35608]** : PRE
1900 DONCASTER, WRY, ENG **[36048]** : 1800
WICKLOW, WIC, IRL **[37422]**
INNES 1750+ BROCKHAMPTON & SOLERSHOPE,
HEF, ENG **[34747]** : 1750+ MUCH MARCLE, HEF,
ENG **[34747]** : 1600-1850 CUMNOR, BRK, ENG
[35937] : ALL HEF & GLS, ENG **[37269]** : 1800+
ABERDEEN, SCT **[33947]** : 1835+ NETHERMILL,
ABD, SCT **[35584]** : PRE 1840 ANS, SCT **[35950]** :
1808 TRANSSENT, SCT **[37898]** : ALL
SPEYMOUTH, MOR, SCT **[38357]**
INNIS (SEE ENNIS) **[34044]**
INNOCENT PRE 1800 ALFRETON, DBY, ENG **[35079]**
INNS 1820+ LIDLINGTON, BDF & YRK, ENG
[35701] : PRE 1840 WAVENDON, BKM, ENG **[35701]**
: PRE 1840 WAR, NTT & OXF, ENG **[35735]**
INSAN PEDRO PRE 1770 MOBILE, AL, USA **[35328]**
INSCO PRE 1800 NEWBERRY CO., SC, USA & IRL
[36969]
INSLEY ALL LEICESTER, LEI & DBY, ENG **[36074]** :
1800+ HURLEY & DRAYTON BASSETT, STS,
ENG **[37608]**
INSTONE 1866 MDX, ENG **[35872]**

INTERMANN PRE 1867 HAN, GER **[35042]**
INVERARITY 1600 WORLDWIDE **[33783]**
INWOOD C1760 THURSLEY, SRY, ENG **[37420]**
ION C1600 WES, ENG **[33827]** : 1600-1800 ORTON,
WES, ENG **[36151]**
IONN C1600 WES, ENG **[33827]**
IONSON PRE 1900 MELBOURNE, VIC, AUS **[35435]**
IOTTE 1800 QUEBEC, QUE, CAN **[37484]**
IPSEN 1710-1780 BRINGSTRUP, SORO, DEN **[37547]**
IRELAND 1880+ NARRABRI, NSW, AUS **[35159]** :
1900+ WINNIPEG, MAN, CAN **[35614]** : 1900+
VANCOUVER, BC, CAN **[35614]** : 1790-1850 PEI,
CAN **[38007]** : PRE 1850 CANTERBURY, KEN,
ENG **[33935]** : PRE 1875 LAMBETH, SRY, ENG
[44450] : 1833+ GLASTONBURY, SOM, ENG **[34777]**
: 1800S SFK, ENG **[34813]** : PRE 1860 SOUTH
PETHERTON, SOM, ENG **[34865]** : PRE 1860 HRT,
ENG **[34929]** : 1820+ ALCONBURY WESTON,
HUN, ENG **[35141]** : EDMUND PRE 1812 DEV,
ENG **[35234]** : 1800+ IOW, ENG **[35824]** : ALL
ALCESTER & REDDITCH, WAR & WOR, ENG
[36234] : PRE 1900 WEST BRADFORD, LAN, ENG
[37774] : C1814 CASTLEBAR, MAY, IRL **[36366]** :
PRE 1900 ANS, SCT **[34053]** : 1600+ ST MONANCE,
FIF, SCT **[34637]** : 1809+ DUNDEE, ANS, SCT
[34637] : PRE 1840 KINGSKETTLE, FIF, SCT **[35045]**
: C1827 NY, USA **[36923]** : 1880+ SANTA
BARBARA, CA, USA **[36923]** : 1900+ DE KALB,
USA **[37206]**
IREMONGER C1500 RUDGE, STS, ENG **[38348]**
IRESON C1750-1860 BENEFIELD & BULWICK,
NTH, ENG **[37770]**
IRETON ALL AUS **[35746]** : 1800S ONT, CAN **[38393]** :
ALL CLA, IRL **[35746]** : PRE 1829 IRL **[38393]**
IRISH 1790+ ONT, CAN **[34380]** : 1855+ DEKALB
CO., IL, USA **[34380]** : 1780-1859 LITTLE
COMPTON, VT, USA **[37810]**
IRONMONGER 1790+ LND, ENG **[37983]**
IRONS RUTH 1825+ WHEATHAMPSTEAD, HRT,
ENG **[35634]** : 1850+ SHEFFIELD, WRY, ENG
[36772]
IRONSIDE 1760+ WAKEFIELD, WRY, ENG **[35905]** :
JAMES 1800+ ASHOGLE, TURRIFF, ABD, SCT
[36712] : ALL WORLDWIDE **[36019]**
IRTON 1700S IRTON, CUL, ENG **[35877]** : ALL
IRTON, CUL & LND, ENG **[36477]**
IRVIN 1800+ ORILLIA, ONT, CAN **[35608]** : 1790
LISNAWESNAGH, FER, IRL **[35085]** : PRE 1860
DON, IRL **[36854]** : 1820S BELFAST, IRL **[38288]** :
ELIZABETH C1760-1830 HUNTINGDON CO., PA,
USA **[38371]** : PRE 1900 WORLDWIDE **[36932]**
IRVINE ALEXANDER 1863 SYDNEY &
MELBOURNE, NSW & VIC, AUS **[36712]** : 1920+
BECHARD, SAS, CAN **[36509]** : 1870+
WESTBOURNE, MAN, CAN **[36704]** : C1790
KILSKERRY, TYR, IRL **[33910]** : PRE 1870 KESH &
IRVINESTOWN, FER, IRL **[34018]** : ALL MEA, IRL
[34386] : 1830-1850 OMAGH & DRUMRAGH, TYR,
IRL **[34386]** : ELEANOR C1809-1888 LARNE, ANT,
IRL **[36244]** : 1800+ DOW, IRL **[37170]** : PRE 1850
BALLYCLARE, ANT, IRL **[38411]** : MARGARET
1864+ MISSION SCHOOL, MADAGASCAR **[36712]**
: C1800 PERTH, PER, SCT **[34084]** : PRE 1800
IRVINE, AYR, SCT **[34112]** : 1840+ STROMNESS,
OKI, SCT **[34614]** : PRE 1800 ANNAN, DFS, SCT
[36209] : 1820-1920 GLASGOW, LKS, SCT **[36663]** :
1842+ KENMORE, PER, SCT **[36704]** : ALL
FORTINGALL, PER, SCT **[36704]** : WILLIAM 1770-
1849 KING EDWARD, ABD, SCT **[36712]** :
WILLIAM 1770+ NEW DEER, ABD, SCT **[36712]** :
WILLIAM 1835-1849 NEW PITSLIGO & TYRIE,
ABD, SCT **[36712]** : CHRISTINA 1835-1849 NEW

PITSLIGO & TYRIE, ABD, SCT [36712] : ANN 1770-1859 ASHOGLE, TURRIFF, ABD, SCT [36712] : ALL SHI, SCT [37340] : SAMUEL PRE 1850 GLASGOW, SCT [37443] : PRE 1810 COLINTON, MLN, SCT [37463] : 1740+ SHI, SCT [37527] : ALL ANS, SCT [37727] : 1850-1870 DUNFERMLINE, FIF, SCT [38763] : PRE 1900 WORLDWIDE [36932]

IRVING C1850 WA, AUS [34186] : 1850+ VIC, AUS [34186] : DANIEL 1800S TAS, VIC & SA, AUS [35127] : 1919 BROKEN HILL, NSW, AUS [35452] : 1949+ ROCKHAMPTON, QLD, AUS [35452] : 1912 GYMPIE, QLD, AUS [35452] : PRE 1850 CUL, ENG [34186] : 1840S DALSTON, CUL, ENG [34688] : 1853 CARLISLE, CUL, ENG [35452] : PRE 1850 GRASSINGTON, YKS, ENG [35490] : PRE 1850 ASKRIGG, YKS, ENG [35490] : DAVID 1800+ NEWCASTLE UPON TYNE, NBL, ENG [36823] : 1700-1900 CON, ENG [36977] : PRE 1768 BURGH BY SANDS, CUL & DFS, ENG & SCT [37623] : PRE 1840 NEWRY, DOW, IRL [36295] : 1825 KINCARON O'REAL, ABD, SCT [35041] : PRE 1840 LKS, SCT [37332] : W.W. 1800-1820 DFS, SCT [37465] : 1800-1855 SEL, SCT [38199] : PRE 1800 GRETNA, DFS, SCT [38390] : ALL GRETNA GREEN, DFS, SCT [38411] : 1750-1800 DORNOCK, DFS & CUL, SCT & ENG [35624] : 1750+ TARRYTOWN & MANHATTAN, NY, USA [35924] : 1860-1890 OLYMPIA, WA, USA [37465] : 1800-1860 DAUPHIN CO., PA, USA [38219] : PRE 1900 WORLDWIDE [36932]

IRWIN JOHNSTONE 1880S BINNAWAY, NSW, AUS [34788] : 1902+ WEST WYALONG, NSW, AUS [34900] : 1878+ SHEPPARTON, VIC, AUS [35379] : 1870+ BRISBANE, QLD, AUS [38278] : C1830 RAWDON, QUE, CAN [34367] : 1820-1990 BEAUHARNOIS DIST, QUE, CAN [34377] : 1800S LAMBTON CO., ONT, CAN [38414] : 1800+ DEV, ENG [35057] : JOSEPH PRE 1859 CATCHGATE, DUR, ENG [36164] : JOHN S. 1879 MANCHESTER, LAN, ENG [36635] : JOHNSTONE 1820S EASKEY, SLI, IRL [34788] : C1802 LOU, IRL [35247] : C1820S IRL [35340] : PRE 1850 BRACKEY, ARM, IRL [35871] : PRE 1880 ARM & WAT, IRL [37136] : 1600-1900 BELFAST, IRL [38278] : 1800S TYR, IRL [38414] : 1750+ FER, IRL [38476] : WM & SARAH 1821+ MIDDLETOWN, ARM, IRL [38567] : ELIZA C1821 MIDDLETOWN, ARM, IRL [38567] : 1400-1650 ABERDEEN, SCT [38115] : ARTHUR C1812+ OH, USA [35272] : JAMES C1848+ PA & IL, USA [35272] : 1840+ PA, USA [37030] : 1800+ OH, USA [37030] : PRE 1900 WORLDWIDE [36932]

IRWIN (SEE IRVINE) [34386]

IRWINE PRE 1900 WORLDWIDE [36932]

IRWING PRE 1900 WORLDWIDE [36932]

IRWING (SEE IRVINE) [34386]

ISAAC PRE 1785 YATE & HORTON, GLS, ENG [33771] : 1773 MELCOMBE REGIS, DOR, ENG [33967] : 1700+ HIGH BICKINGTON & BIDEFORD, DEV, ENG [34970] : C1770-1841 BISHOPSTONE, WIL, ENG [37271] : C1841 SCHMALL KALDEN, HEN, GER [35864] : PRE 1760 ALSING (ALTESE), GER [38690] : 1815+ NEUTEICH, EL, POL [36254] : C1870 CAMBUSNETHAN, LKS, SCT [34556] : C1810+ TRETOWER & CRICKHOWELL, BRE, WLS [33922] : 1858+ CRICKHOWELL, BRE, WLS [34288] : 1800S LLANGAMARCH, BRE, WLS [34288]

ISAACS PRE 1889 LANDPORT & SOUTHAMPTON, HAM, ENG [33890] : PRE 1850 KEN, ENG [36480] : 1830+ LND, ENG [37309] : PRE 1900 DOR, ENG [37941] : PRE 1900 DEV, ENG [37941]

ISAACSON PRE 1820 HRT & BDF, ENG [35701] : C1880+ MEKINOCK, ND, USA [34203]

ISAAKSOHN 1777 VAREL, OLD, GER [37509]

ISABROOK ALL WORLDWIDE [37231]

ISAMBERT 1850+ WARWICK, QLD, AUS [35147] : PRE 1850 LORCH, HEN, GER [35147]

ISARD 1700+ CROYDON, SSX, ENG [38235] : PRE 1800 ENG [38235]

ISBELL PRE 1850 NFK, ENG [37718]

ISBILL ALL NFK, ENG [37612]

ISBISTER PRE 1860 SUNDERLAND, DUR, ENG [36765]

ISCHER 1700-1900S LATTERBACH, BE, CH [37550] : 1800-1889 RIDGEWAY, NC, USA [37550]

ISHAM ALL ENG [35914]

ISHERWOOD C1820 BOROUGHBRIDGE, YKS, ENG [35708] : PRE 1900 CLITHEROE & BASHALL EAVES, LAN, ENG [37774] : PRE 1800 BOLTON, LAN, ENG [38708]

ISING PRE 1824 EMMERICH, REES, GER [37569]

ISLES C1820 DEPTFORD, LND & KEN, ENG [34556] : 1750+ WIL, ENG [35062] : 1750+ TIDWORTH & KIMPTON, HAM, ENG [35062] : 1800+ KEN, ENG [35821] : PRE 1860 DUNDEE, ANS, SCT [35959]

ISLIP PRE 1900 MELCHBOURNE, BDF, ENG [37780] : PRE 1900 PERTENHALL, BDF, ENG [37780]

ISMOND C1650-1750 FLUSHING, NY, USA [38767]

ISOM 1786 HAVERSHAM, BKM, ENG [35256]

ISON ALL CAM, ENG [34182] : 1850+ IBSTOCK & MARKFIELD, LEI, ENG [34329] : C1775+ ENG [35537] : ALL MAURITIUS [34170]

ISRAEL PRE 1790 MDX, ENG [34262] : PRE 1850 LONDON, ENG [36583] : ALL USA [37562]

ISSACS 1822+ BURIN, NFD, CAN [34349]

ISSBEHN C1749 HAMBURG, HBG, GER [37819]

ISSITT 1850+ EAST LONDON, ENG [37898]

ISSLER ALL ONT, CAN [34488]

ISSOTT 1883 LIVERPOOL, LAN, ENG [36770]

ISTED 1800+ DALLINGTON, SSX, ENG [33785] : ALL WORLDWIDE [35898]

IVANY 1740+ ENGLISH HARBOUR, NFD, CAN [33852]

IVATT C1873 CAM, ENG [37830]

IVE 1854-1900 MARYLEBONE, LND, ENG [37756]

IVENS 1600+ WAR, ENG [34950]

IVERIS (SEE IVERY) [34290]

IVERSON 1818 OSLO, NOR [38533]

IVERY 1800+ LEX, IRL [34290]

IVES 1860-1900 BALMAIN, NSW, AUS [35857] : C1860 TOOWOOMBA, QLD & NSW, AUS [38485] : 1800-1860 LONDON, MDX, ENG [35857] : PRE 1855 CHARLTON, KEN, ENG [36064] : 1800-1900 CHERTSEY, SRY, ENG [37858] : 1800S SRY, ENG [37868] : 1700 YOXFORD, SFK, ENG [37928] : 1800S SOUTHALL, MDX, ENG [38402] : C1830 BRAMPTON, SFK, ENG [38485] : PRE 1900 NFK, ENG & AUS [34301] : 1700S SALEM, MA, USA [35291]

IVEY 1834+ NORTHUMBERLAND CO., ONT, CAN [37446] : C1693 ST MERRYN, CON, ENG [33992] : THOMAS 1802 GOLDSITHNEY, CON, ENG [34844] : PRE 1834 BLISLAND, CON, ENG [37446] : PRE 1820 SITHNEY, CON, ENG [38263] : 1850-1930 AL, USA [36449]

IVIL 1780+ FARNHAM, SRY, ENG [36232]

IVORY PRE 1750 GREAT GADDESDEN, HRT, ENG [34041] : PRE 1790 NFK, ENG [34139]

IVY PRE 1650 BREDE, SSX, ENG [34974] : 1700+ SITHNEY, CON, ENG [35712]

IZARD 1900+ AUS [37682] : ALL LND, ENG [37682] : ALL MDX, ENG [37682] : ALL KEN, ENG [37682] : PRE 1700 ENG [38235]

IZZARD 1877-1971 ONT, CAN & ENG [34055] : 1887-1973 BROMLEY, KEN, ENG [34055] : PRE 1755 SPITALFIELDS, LND, ENG [37261] : ALL KEN, ENG [37682]

IZZITT 1850 EAST LONDON, ENG [37898]

JAAG 1650-1950 WUE, GER [37609]

JABLONSKI 1800-1900 THORN, WESTPREUβEN, POL [38603]

JACHENS 1767 LEUCHTENBURG, BRM, GER [35828] : 1730+ VORWOHLDE LESUM, BRM, GER [35828]

JACK 1800S MELBOURNE, VIC, AUS [35797] : 1881+ PICTOU, NS, CAN [38335] : PRE 1850 NOTTINGHAM, NTT, ENG [34725] : CHARLES PRE 1888 ISLINGTON, MDX, ENG [35553] : 1800-1870 LONDON, MDX, ENG [37716] : PRE 1775 INCHTURE, PER, SCT [33873] : 1800S MONTROSE, ANS, SCT [34028] : PRE 1800 IRVINE, AYR, SCT [34112] : PRE 1823 ROX, SCT [34489] : C1750 AUCTERLESS, ABD, SCT [34713] : 1800+ EDINBURGH, MLN, SCT [34713] : C1770 MONQUHITTER, ABD, SCT [34713] : C1725 MARNOCH, BAN, SCT [34713] : 1877 WISHAW, LKS, SCT [34761] : JANE 1866+ HAMILTON, LKS, SCT [35033] : WILLIAM C1850 HAMILTON, LKS, SCT [35033] : 1833 SOUTH LEITH, MLN, SCT [35260] : 1700+ CARNBEE, FIF, SCT [35627] : 1750+ GOVAN, LKS, SCT [36642] : PRE 1850 URQHUART, ROC, SCT [36879] : PRE 1850 PERTH, PER, SCT [37395] : PRE 1840 NEW DEER, ABD, SCT [37716] : PRE 1830 ROBERTON & WISTON, LKS, SCT & CAN [34835]

JACKA 1750-1850 CON, ENG [37156]

JACKAMAN 1750+ STOKE BY NAYLAND, SFK, ENG [33938] : ALL LND, KEN & SFK, ENG [35222]

JACKEL ALL WORLDWIDE [35868]

JACKLIN 1790-1890 HAWKESBURY AREA, NSW, AUS [35092] : 1760-1790 SCOTTON & LINCOLN, LIN, ENG [35092]

JACKMAN 1800+ DEV, ENG [33948] : 1840+ PORTSMOUTH & SOUTHSEA, HAM, ENG [36163] : ALL DEV, ENG [36163] : ALL DEVON, DEV, ENG [36253] : JOHN 1800+ WEEDON, BKM, ENG [36471] : JOHN 1860+ HARDWICK, BKM, ENG [36471] : ALL IOW, HAM, ENG [37730] : 1740-1840 LONG PRESTON & SETTLE, WRY, ENG [38251]

JACKSON 1801-1850 AIRDS, NSW, AUS [33817] : 1843+ HUNTERS HILL, NSW, AUS [33896] : 1840-1900 ALBURY, NSW, AUS [34175] : 1860+ REDFERN, NSW, AUS [34542] : 1900+ LEICHHARDT, NSW, AUS [34542] : 1814-1825 COWPASTURES, NSW, AUS [34542] : 1870+ BALLARAT, VIC, AUS [34574] : 1885+ ORANGE, NSW, AUS [35073] : 1833-1877 SYDNEY, NSW, AUS [35092] : PRE 1900 NEWCASTLE, NSW, AUS [35225] : 1826+ PARRAMATTA, NSW, AUS [35410] : 1852+ MELBOURNE, VIC, AUS [35710] : 1900+ MELBOURNE, VIC, AUS [35752] : JOHN 1879+ STRATHFIELD, NSW, AUS [36367] : ADELAIDE C1849 SYDNEY, NSW, AUS [37106] : 1870S BALMAIN, NSW, AUS [37309] : 1830S TAS & SA, AUS [37873] : HENRY 1832+ HOBART, TAS, AUS [37954] : STEPHEN PRE 1900 CORNWALLIS DISTRICT, NS, CAN [34206] : C1885 GANANOQUE, ONT, CAN [34521] : 1890-1920 MARQUETTE, MAN, CAN [34521] : 1880+ ST ANNE & MEADOW LEA, MAN, CAN [34521] : 1920+ WAWOTA, SAS, CAN [34521] : 1800+ PORTLAND, ONT, CAN [35633] : 1880+ HOLLAND, MAN, CAN [36704] : JONATHAN 1840-1880S THOROLD & MERRITON, ONT, CAN [36729] : PRE 1840 NEWFOUNDLAND, CAN [38248]

: 1800+ BRANCEPETH, DUR, ENG [33774] : PRE 1750 DARTMOUTH, DEV, ENG [33998] : JOHN 1800-1830 YKS, ENG [34078] : WILLIAM 1820-1900 CASTLETOWN, STS, ENG [34143] : C1530-1610 MORLAND, WES, ENG [34296] : 1800S ARMBOTH, CUL, ENG [34542] : 1838+ HALESWORTH, SFK, ENG [34668] : C1825 MARTON IN CRAVEN, WRY, ENG [34675] : PRE 1850 CHURCHTOWN, LAN, ENG [34696] : PRE 1817 CHICHESTER, SSX, ENG [34753] : 1700S BURTON LEONARD & STH STAINLEY, NRY, ENG [34776] : 1734 DEANE, HAM, ENG [34909] : 1750 MEDSTEAD, HAM, ENG [34909] : PRE 1820 PUTNEY, MDX, ENG [34911] : PRE 1880 HIGH YEWDALE, LAN, ENG [34958] : 1800+ LIN, ENG [34980] : C1890 ISLINGTON, LND, ENG [35014] : 1810-1833 STAFFORD, STS, ENG [35092] : 1750-1850 HINSTOCK, SAL, ENG [35203] : WILLIAM 1834+ CUL, ENG [35343] : JOHN 1756 KING'S CLIFFE, NTH, ENG [35369] : VALENTINE 1900+ WANDSWORTH, SRY, ENG [35418] : THOMAS 1800+ ENG [35554] : ROBERT 1833+ ST JOHNS WOOD, ENG [35554] : PRE 1850 PORTSEA, HAM, ENG [35710] : C1820 LONDON, ENG [35747] : 1700S DONCASTER, YKS, ENG [35830] : PRE 1855 WALWORTH, SRY, ENG [35863] : LUCY 1820S+ PENZANCE, CON, ENG [35876] : 1800 DUDLEY, WOR, ENG [35912] : PRE 1850 MORTLAKE, LND, ENG [35945] : 1800-1880 HULL, ERY, ENG [36059] : 1800-1850S ST PANCRAS & MARYLEBONE, MDX, ENG [36095] : ALL LOZELLS & BIRMINGHAM, WAR, ENG [36234] : 1800+ BOSTON, LIN, ENG [36251] : PRE 1880 FARNSFIELD, NTT, ENG [36265] : 1780-1900 TATTERSHALL, LIN, ENG [36346] : JOHN 1827 BISHOP AUCKLAND, NBL, ENG [36367] : 1800-1900 GOODMANHAM, YKS, ENG [36724] : 1700-1860 NORFOLK, NFK, ENG [36773] : ALL BIRMINGHAM, WAR, ENG [36774] : PRE 1880 MIDDLESBROUGH, YKS, ENG [36800] : WILLIAM 1827-92 OLDBURY, WAR, ENG [36816] : EMMA 1800S KENSINGTON, MDX, ENG [36817] : CAPT. GEORGE C1805-1880 LIVERPOOL, LAN, ENG [36838] : 1700+ LUTON, BDF, ENG [36922] : PRE 1800 DBY, ENG [36923] : 1880+ CREWE AREA, CHS, ENG [36997] : C1826 MITCHAM, SRY, ENG [37106] : PRE 1900 TOTTENHAM, ESS, ENG [37133] : PRE 1850 ST MICHAELS, LAN, ENG [37179] : 1850+ SITTINGBOURNE, KEN, ENG [37213] : 1850-1900 BETHNAL GREEN, LND, ENG [37252] : ROBERT PRE 1850 BOLTON BY BOWLAND, LAN, ENG [37414] : MARIA PRE 1879 CAMBERWELL, SRY & LND, ENG [37452] : C1786-1813 HUMBLETON & HULL, ERY, ENG [37556] : HARRY 1800-1904 LEAMINGTON SPA, WAR, ENG [37614] : C1700-1850 GLS & WIL, ENG [37642] : 1700-1800 DBY, ENG [37661] : PRE 1900 AUDLEY, STS, ENG [37722] : PRE 1840 LONDON, ENG [37743] : 1830S DBY & STS, ENG [37751] : PRE 1600 CHURCH BROUGHTON, DBY, ENG [37873] : 1760-1870 ISLINGTON & HAMMERSMTIH, LND, ENG [37943] : HENRY PRE 1831 LAN, ENG [37945] : PRE 1850 HIGH HALSTOW & ST MARYS HOO, KEN, ENG [38027] : PRE 1786 NTT, ENG [38080] : 1795 MORLAND, WES, ENG [38209] : JOHN BESTALL 1814-1864 LEADENHAM, LIN, ENG & AUS [33892] : RICH. BESTALL 1846-1909 PT LINCOLN & ADELAIDE, SA, ENG & AUS [33892] : ALL CAMGART, FER, IRL [34644] : PRE 1841 CASHEL, IRL [35399] : 1856 CAVAN, CAV, IRL [35769] : C1883 DUB, IRL [36276] : 1840+ AVOCA, WIC, IRL [36772] : PRE 1780 BALLYSIMON, LIM, IRL [36840] : PRE 1865 DAVIDSTOWN, KID, IRL [36888] : ALL ANT,

IRL [38226] : 1700+ SHILLELAGH, WIC, IRL
[38385] : 1750+ RATHVILLY, CAR, IRL [38385] :
JAMES PRE 1840 CAV, IRL [38391] : CATHERINE
C1833-1885 ENNISKILLEN, FER, IRL & AUS
[34942] : PRE 1800 JAMAICA [37873] : 1841+
NELSON, NZ [33945] : PRE 1920 NZ [36773] : 1843+
RAGOUSSA, OES [38212] : 1810-1840 LKS, SCT
[34175] : 1830-1850 EDINBURGH, MLN, SCT [34175]
: C1775+ OLD RATTRAY, PER, SCT [34203] :
1800+ RFW & LKS, SCT [35395] : JAMES 1800-1930
GLASSFORD, LKS, SCT [36282] : 1760+
METHVEN, PER, SCT [36704] : 1830+ KINNAIRD,
PER, SCT [36704] : 1810+ ABERDALGIE, PER, SCT
[36704] : 1838+ LONGFORGAN, PER, SCT [36704] :
PRE 1840 PORT GLASGOW, RFW, SCT [36806] :
JOHN PRE 1843 ST HELENS, WIG, SCT [37819] :
ALL UK [37674] : 1840+ MERCER CO., IL, USA
[35278] : DAVID 1800-1900 ALBANY &
RENSSELAER, NY, USA [35292] : ALL DYLAN
PARK, FL, USA [35302] : 1856 IL, USA [35325] : PRE
1800 COXSAKIE, NY, USA [35633] : 1800+ SANTA
FE, NM, USA [36251] : PRE 1850 NJ, USA [36347] :
1800-1900 WEVER, IA, USA [36548] : 1890+
EMERSON, NE, USA [36704] : 1720-1800
CUMBERLAND & YORK CO., PA, USA [36953] :
1813 MONTGOMERY CO., TN, USA [37536] : 1740-
1800 NJ & OH, USA [37577] : PRE 1800 NOTTAWAY
CO., VA, USA [37587] : 1815-1865 HENRY &
NEWTON CO., GA, USA [37587] : 1800-1815
CLARKE CO., GA, USA [37587] : 1865+ WALTON
& DEKALB CO., GA, USA [37587] : 1840+ NY, USA
[37621] : PRE 1892 BELL, TX, USA [37819] : 1720S
PHILADELPHIA, PA, USA [37873] : C1796 VA, USA
[38026] : 1850+ BUCHANAN CO., VA, USA [38044] :
LEONA ONIE 1805 GA, USA [38155] : C.A. 1830-
1900 RED WOOD FALLS, MN & OH, USA [38392] :
ALL CRAWFORD CO., PA, USA [38522]

JACOB PRE 1850S COLKIRK, NFK, ENG [35819] :
PRE 1630 WALDINGFIELD, SFK, ENG [36341] :
1800+ BAUGHURST, HAM, ENG [36376] : PRE
1800 BRADING, IOW, ENG [38700] : 1788+
WATERFORD, WAT, IRL [35720] : 1829
LIBERTIES, DUB, IRL [35720]

JACOBI PRE 1851 ZELLERFELD, HARZ, GER
[34766] : 1820-1850 BLN & HES, GER [36896] : PRE
1850 CARLSBERG & MAINZ, RPF, GER [38681]

JACOBS 1840+ RICHMOND, TAS, AUS [34650] :
1856+ GAWLER, SA, AUS [34775] : ALL
DENDERMONDE, WVL, BEL [38170] : ALL CAN
[36919] : GEO. WASH. 1825+ ONT, CAN [37438] :
1700S WINCHESTER, HAM, ENG [33802] : C1810
WOOTTON BASSETT, WIL, ENG [33918] : ALL
DEV & CON, ENG [34318] : 1770+
WESTMINSTER, MDX, ENG [34650] : PRE 1850
BRK, ENG [34775] : PRE 1850 ST PANCRAS, LND,
ENG [35199] : PRE 1840 CON, ENG [35346] : JOHN
1790-1841 HACKNEY, MDX, ENG [35955] :
CATHERINE C1818 LEYTON, SRY, ENG [35955] :
PRE 1900 MILE END, MDX, ENG [36107] : 1870
LONDON, ENG [36995] : 1860S LND, ENG [37309] :
1700+ QUEBEC, CAN &, GER & USA [36341] :
C1860 OES [33809] : PRE 1895 VIENNA, OES [37574]
: 1850+ NE, USA [36919] : 1800-1850 BRANCH CO.,
MI, USA [36924] : DAVID C1759 GREENE CO., PA,
USA [37036] : 1750+ MA, USA [37438] : ELLA
FRANCES 1876+ BOLTON, WORCESTER, MA,
USA [38183]

JACOBSDATTER 1856 IDD, NOR [35515]

JACOBSEN 1800-1900 HELIGOLAND IS., DEN
[35228] : PRE 1836 ODENSE, DEN [36604] : PRE
1900 SHO, GER [37105]

JACOBSON 1800-1900 HELIGOLAND IS., DEN
[35228]

JACOBUSSE 1760-1790S BAARLAND, ZEL, NL
[38358]

JACOBY 1750-1850 POM & BRA, GER [36662] : 1868+
SU [38058]

JACOMB 1738+ ENFIELD & MELBOURNE, LND &
VIC, ENG & AUS [34109]

JACOMBS PRE 1860 BAMFORD, WAR, ENG [34638] :
PRE 1910 CHRISTCHURCH, NZ [34638]

JACQUEMIN PRE 1761 MAASTRICHT, LMB, NL
[38647]

JACQUES PRE 1850 TICKNALL, DBY, ENG [34655] :
ALL BROUGHTON ASTLEY, LEI, ENG [36532] :
C1780 LUTTERWORTH, LEI, ENG [37053]

JACQUIN PRE 1850 FRA [38029]

JAECKEL 1850-1950 USA [35308]

JAEGER 1900S MUSWELLBROOK, NSW, AUS [37910]
: PRE 1850 BAY, GER [38029]

JAENSCH PRE 1945 MUENSTERBERG, SIL, GER
[38606] : 1830 HERZOGSWALDAU, LG, POL [38495]

JAFFA PRE 1900 JERUSALEM, ISRAEL [35635]

JAFFE ALL WORLDWIDE [38368]

JAFFERIS PRE 1828 WROUGHTON, WIL, ENG
[35016]

JAFFRAY PRE 1830 ST FERGUS, ABD, SCT [34197]

JAGER PRE 1845 OBERERTAL, BAV, GER [38321] :
ALL OLDAMBT, GRO, NL [38705]

JAGGARD 1700-1800 HOLTON ST MARY, SFK, ENG
[36717]

JAGGER PRE 1800 BRADFORD & HUDDERSFIELD,
WRY, ENG [36104] : C1800 ALMONDBURY &
HUDDERSFIELD, WRY, ENG [36147] : 1680-1860
CROFTON, WRY, ENG [38028]

JAGO AMELIA 1867+ RICHMOND, VIC, AUS
[36611] : C1859+ BENDIGO, VIC, AUS [36838] : PRE
1840 PELYNT, CON, ENG [34445] : C1830+
LONDON, ENG [36838] : 1776-1800 BANDON,
COR, IRL [37859] : C1854+ NZ [36838] : 1857+
DUNEDIN, NZ [38082]

JAGOE 1780+ SKIBBEREEN, COR, IRL [35971]

JAGTMAN 1760+ AMSTERDAM, NOH, NL [38691] :
1760+ AMSTERDAM, NOH, NL [38711]

JAHAN ALL FRA [38178] : 1189-1458 FRA [38178] :
ALL WORLDWIDE [38178]

JAHAN DIT LA VIOLETT 1630+ WORLDWIDE
[38178]

JAHN PRE 1793 NIESIG & FULDA, HES, GER [38663]

JAHNS 1780+ BSW, GER & AUS [35093]

JAIKENS ALL HUN, ENG [37409]

JAKEMAN C1884 LEEDS, YKS, ENG [37865] : C1902
MARYLEBONE, LND, ENG [37865]

JAKINS 1800S AUS [35161] : PRE 1850 TAS, AUS
[35238] : PRE 1835 BKM, ENG [35238] : 1800+ HUN,
ENG [37409]

JAKOBSEN 1850+ VORDINGBORG, SJAELLAND,
DEN [37160]

JALINK 1582+ GOOR, OIJ, NL [34398]

JAMES 1850+ VIC, AUS [34368] : 1850+
WOLLONGONG, NSW, AUS [34969] : C1789
SYDNEY, NSW, AUS [35089] : PRE 1895 HUNTER
RIVER, NSW, AUS [35097] : PERCY 1915+
MELBOURNE, VIC, AUS [35220] : 1800S
COLLINGWOOD, VIC, AUS [35500] : ANN 1834-
1897 DAYLESFORD, VIC, AUS [36598] : ANNIE
C1876 BRISBANE, QLD, AUS [36616] : WILLIAM
PRE 1878 MOLONGLO, NSW, AUS [37901] :
WILLIAM C1886-1923 MELBOURNE, VIC, AUS &
ENG [37559] : PRE 1750 FRESSINGFIELD, SFK,
ENG [34258] : PRE 1900 HOLCOMBE &
CROSCOMBE, SOM, ENG [34314] : BENJAMIN
1737-1827 WLS & SOM, ENG [34314] : PRE 1800

HUN, ENG [34324] : PRE 1834 BRISTOL, ENG
[34368] : 1700-1750 OXFORD, OXF, ENG [34552] :
1800-1850 NORTH CRAWLEY, BKM, ENG [34552] :
PRE 1800 FOREST OF DEAN, GLS, ENG [34643] :
PRE 1820 NEWLYN EAST & CUBERT, CON, ENG
[34795] : SAMUEL C1784-1802 CHELMSFORD, ESS,
ENG [34886] : 1780-1850 HELSTON, CON, ENG
[35017] : 1877-1910 MANCHESTER, LAN, ENG
[35107] : 1870-1885 CARLISLE, CUL, ENG [35107] :
1800S GULVAL, CON, ENG [35138] : PRE 1890
BATH, SOM, ENG [35253] : PRE 1750 CON, ENG
[35255] : 1800+ WEDNESBURY, STS, ENG [35358] :
PRE 1860 CUBERT, CON, ENG [35384] : 1600-1900S
WEEK ST MARY, CON, ENG [35424] : PRE 1850
NEWLANDS EAST, CON, ENG [35435] : PRE 1849
DENTON & SUMMERHOUSE, DUR, ENG [35462] :
1800S EXETER, DEV, ENG [35500] : 1857 LONDON,
ENG [35500] : PRE 1814 HARTLEBURY, WOR,
ENG [35574] : 1710+ KENWYN, CON, ENG [35587]
: PRE 1844 GREENWICH, KEN, ENG [35863] : PRE
1875 ROTHERSTHORPE, NTH, ENG [35888] :
1740+ BRISTOL, SOM, ENG [35924] : PRE 1840
ROCHFORD, ESS, ENG [35959] : 1500-1600 STS,
ENG [36062] : 1800-1930 BETHNAL GREEN &
LEWISHAM, MDX & KEN, ENG [36101] : 1807+
NORTH PETHERTON, SOM, ENG [36278] : ALL
CAVERSHAM, OXF, ENG [36326] : 1860+
BRAINTREE, ESS, ENG [36439] : 1880-1917
LONDON, MDX, ENG [36439] : 1750+ OLNEY,
BKM, ENG [36439] : PRE 1820 GAYDON &
CHADSHUNT, WAR, ENG [36516] : GREGORY
C1700 DEV & CON, ENG [36594] : ANNIE 1854+
SLOUGH, BKM, ENG [36616] : 1600S PETWORTH,
SSX, ENG [36679] : 1831-74 LYNEHAM, OXF, ENG
[36759] : 1800S CHATTON, NBL, ENG [36776] :
C1730 HINTON BLEWETT, SOM, ENG [36779] :
C1891 MILE END OLD TOWN, MDX, ENG [36876]
: C1868-1891 STEPNEY, MDX, ENG [36876] : C1868-
1891 SHADWELL, MDX, ENG [36876] : PRE 1681
RADFORD, NTT, ENG [37000] : PRE 1850
CHELTENHAM, GLS, ENG [37253] : PRE 1850
CARISBROOK, IOW, ENG [37321] : ALL SFK, ESS
& KEN, ENG [37674] : PRE 1800 CANTERBURY,
KEN, ENG [37692] : 1750-1850 BROMYARD, HEF,
ENG [37765] : 1800+ NEWINGTON, SRY, ENG
[38288] : HENRY 1800-1870 KEN, ENG [38337] :
THOMAS 1800S CONSTANTINE & ADELAIDE,
CON & SA, ENG & AUS [33981] : 1800-1900
PLYMOUTH, DEV & QLD, ENG & AUS [35422] :
PRE 1920 LONDON, ENG & IRL [33883] :
RICHARD 1917+ ENG & WLS [37356] : JOSEPH
1870+ BELFAST, ANT, IRL [34340] : ARTHUR
1900+ BELFAST, ANT, IRL [34340] : 1700+ WEX,
IRL [38385] : WILLIAM 1790+ IRL & CAN [35611] :
1875+ INVERCARGILL, SLD, NZ [35888] : PRE
1824 MORAY, MOR, SCT [37971] : ALL UK [37674] :
JOSEPH 1910+ CLEVELAND, OH, USA [34340] :
ARTHUR 1920+ CLEVELAND, OH, USA [34340] :
1800-1900 ALLAMAKEE CO., IA, USA [34477] :
JOSHUA 1750 HOLMES CO., MS, USA [35328] :
1830-1850 ATHENS CO., OH, USA [36731] : PRE
1830 CLINTON, IN, USA [37010] : A.J. 1824-1909
MONTGOMERY CO., VA, USA [37014] : PRE 1758
NORTHUMBERLAND CO., VA, USA [37029] :
1840+ BATESVILLE, AR, USA [37549] : JOSHUA
1860S TENSUS PARISH, LA, USA [37585] : COPP
1860S BILOXI, MS, USA [37585] : PRE 1800 VA, USA
[37795] : 1860-1880 KEWEENAW CO., MI, USA
[38009] : JAMES 1770 FRANKLIN CO., VA, USA
[38066] : 1800-1900 BERGEN CO., NJ, USA [38337] :
JOHN 1800+ SWANSEA, GLA, WLS [35248] :
1860+ LLANELLI, CMN, WLS [35248] : PRE 1850

BEDWELLTY, MON, WLS [35540] : JOSEPH 1800-
1850 WLS [35602] : BENJAMIN C1800 PEM, WLS
[36279] : PRE 1850 SPITTAL, PEM, WLS [36500] :
PRE 1850 PENTRAYTHLYN, CGN, WLS [37804] :
THOMAS 1820+ LLANGOVAN, MON, WLS [37827]
JAMESON THOMAS 1800+ HULME &
MANCHESTER, LAN, ENG [37165] : C1874
CAMBERWELL & LAMBETH, SRY & LND, ENG
[37452] : 1870-1920 EDINBURGH, MLN, SCT [33978]
: 1770+ SANDSTING & AITHSTING, SHI, SCT
[35719] : 1796 PA, OH & MI, USA [36910] : 1770-1852
NEWBURGH, NY, USA [37470]
JAMIESON 1900+ VIC & WA, AUS [34459] : JOHN
C1850 CAMPBELLS CREEK, VIC, AUS [37159] :
WILLIAM 1810+ INVERNESS, QUE, CAN [34200] :
1890 ORILLIA, ONT, CAN [35637] : 1771-1851
OSWEGO & DURHAM, ONT, CAN [37470] : 1850+
NEW RICHMOND, QUE, CAN & USA [37486] :
PRE 1850 CHI, ENG [36840] : PRE 1830 DOW, IRL
[35983] : 1771-1851 IRL & USA [37470] : JOHN 1700-
1850 LEITH, MLN, SCT [34514] : PRE 1850 AYR,
SCT [35354] : 1860S AIRDRIE, LKS, SCT [35516] :
PRE 1800 HIGH KILDOUNAN, WIG, SCT [35572] :
C1830+ ABERCORN, WLN, SCT [35629] : 1770+
SANDSTING & AITHSTING, SHI, SCT [35719] :
ALL SANDSTING, SHI, SCT [36789] : 1750+
KIRKOSWALD, AYR, SCT [36869] : PRE 1810
HIGH KILDONAN, IOA, SCT [38057] : 1850+
MON, WLS [34459]
JANCA 1840-72 CS [38314]
JANCKE ALL KLEIN TROMNAU &
KLOSTERCHEN, WPR, GER [37529]
JANES PRE 1860 CARBONEAR, NFD, CAN [33852] :
1850+ TORONTO, ONT, CAN [37761] : 1700-1900
HUGHENDEN & WENDOVER, BKM, ENG [36175]
: 1700+ EDLESBOROUGH, BKM, ENG [37092] :
1600-1700 HAMBLEDEN, BKM, ENG [37761] : PRE
1650 BKM, ENG [37761] : PRE 1600 CAM, ENG
[37761] : ALL KIRTLING, SOM, ENG [37761] : ALL
WORLDWIDE [37761]
JANION PRE 1900 RSA [37517]
JANIS 1800+ SOMERTON, SOM, ENG [35573]
JANKE C1820S BANKOW, PRE, GER [34238]
JANNER ALL WORLDWIDE [35391]
JANSEN JAN REEMS 1757 BALTRUM (INSELN),
OST & FRI, FRG [38706] : PRE 1650 HAARLEM,
SALEE, NL [34366] : 1700S BEEK (BIJ BERGH),
GEL, NL [38358] : 1850+ TONSBERG, VESTFOLD,
NOR & SWE [34568] : 1650-1783 LONG ISLAND,
NY, USA [34366] : 1650-1750 NEW YORK, NY, USA
[38113]
JANSEN VAN RENSBURG PRE 1820 MIDDELBURG,
CAPE, RSA [36468]
JANSE VAN VUUREN ALL WORLDWIDE [34949]
JANSSEN C1780 HEEREWAARDEN, GEL, NL
[38705]
JANTAYS ALL QUE & ONT, CAN [36539]
JANTON PRE 1850 QUE, CAN [38512]
JANVRIN 1800+ ST PETER PORT, GSY, CHI [35847]
JAQUEMAIN 1870S PARIS, FRA [34579]
JAQUES 1820+ NB, CAN [36710] : 1835-1900
CRAMAHE TWP., ONT, CAN [37011] : 1800+ NBL,
ENG [35862] : 1770-1835 STAITHES, YKS, ENG
[37011]
JAQUET ALL JAMAICA [37623]
JARAM 1800S COWICK SNAITH, WRY, ENG [37568]
JARDEN 1920S AUS [34636] : 1830+ ARM, IRL [34636]
: 1800+ LOCKERBIE, DFS, SCT [34636]
JARDINE 1841+ MONARO SHIRE, NSW, AUS
[35414] : PRE 1900 DOW, IRL [37807] : 1800+
STONEHOUSE, LKS, SCT [34670] : PRE 1840
CASTLETON, ROX, SCT [35215] : PRE 1840-56

TROQUEER, DFS, SCT [35414] : C1820 KKD, SCT
[35414] : PRE 1823 GLENCAIRN, DFS, SCT [37238]
JARDYNE 1880+ SYDNEY, NSW, AUS [36295]
JAREK 1800-1920S FRYSZTAK, RZ, POL [36940] :
1800-1910S ODRZYKON, KS, POL [36940]
JARL CHARLOTTE 1850+ STOCKHOLM, SWE
[36138]
JARLETT 1600-1750 GUILDFORD & DORKING,
SRY, ENG [36727]
JARMAN 1865-1900 BRAZIL [36336] : 1790S
EWHURST, SSX, ENG [35260] : PRE 1700 ENG
[36336] : 1800 HONEYBOURNE, GLS & WOR, ENG
[37299] : PRE 1910 KEN, ENG [38419] : 1790+
CUMBERLAND CO., NC, USA [36336] : 1675-1730
CALVERT CO., MD, USA [36336] : C1767-1818
LENOIR CO., NC, USA [38340]
JARMANY 1760 STOCKTON, NFK, ENG [37841]
JARMOLOWSKI 1800-1900 KAMIONKA, POL [38232]
: 1900-1990 PA, USA [38232]
JARMOND PRE 1800 BRIXHAM, DEV, ENG [34333]
JARMY PRE 1790 NFK, ENG [34445]
JARRAD ALL ETON, BKM, ENG & AUS [33919]
JARRARD C1800 ESS, ENG [35349] : PRE 1840 GA,
USA [37587]
JARRATT ALL WORLDWIDE [36014]
JARRET 1800-1900 PORT HOPE, ONT, CAN [36688] :
ALL WORLDWIDE [36014]
JARRETT 1839+ DUNGOG, NSW, AUS [35573] :
1847+ ECCLESTON, NSW, AUS [35573] : 1750-
1800+ PICKLESCOTT, SAL, ENG [35573] : ALL
CHERINGTON, WAR, ENG [36014] : ALL
MICKLETON, GLS, ENG [36014] : ALL WOR, ENG
[36014] : 1850+ BIRMINGHAM, WAR, ENG [36014]
: ALL CHERINGTON, WAR, ENG [36807] : 1808+
MICKLETON, GLS, ENG [36807] : 1830S-1890S
LONDON, MDX, ENG [37634] : 1910S-1927
BROADSTAIRS, KEN, ENG [37634] : 1923-24
SPRING POINT, MDX, ENG [37634] : 1810S
BRISTOL, AVON, ENG [37634] : C1832 ENG [37947]
: 1800+ RSA [36014] : ALL WORLDWIDE [36014]
JARRITT ALL WORLDWIDE [36014]
JARROLD PRE 1909 CAMBRIDGE, CAM, ENG
[38403]
JARROT ALL WORLDWIDE [36014]
JARROTT ALL WORLDWIDE [36014]
JARVIE PRE 1872 KILSYTH, STI, SCT [37925]
JARVIS ROBERT 1780+ SOULDERN, OXF, ENG
[33956] : 1800 SHEPPY, KEN, ENG [34565] : PRE
1858 SAL, ENG [34858] : 1800S NEL, ENG [35024] :
PRE 1840 SSX, ENG [36361] : 1700 WHALEY, DBY,
ENG [36514] : 1830 PETERBOROUGH, NTH, ENG
[37112] : 1750+ SWAFFHAM, NFK, ENG [37160] :
1840+ STRATFORD, MDX, ENG [37274] : ALL
THURNBY & LEICESTER, LEI, ENG [37692] : 1890-
1920 LOUGHTON, ESS, ENG [37717] : PRE 1890
NORWOOD, SRY, ENG [37769] : PRE 1870 SAL,
ENG [37807] : 1820S ST TOTHAM, ESS, ENG & AUS
[35558] : PRE 1872 CHRISTIAN CO., IL, USA [37797]
: 1830+ GUERNSEY CO., OH, USA [37797] :
WILLIAM PRE 1855 WASHINGTON CO., OH, USA
[37797] : 1690+ NORTHAMPTON CO., VA, USA
[38032]
JARZINSKY PRE 1840 POL [38681]
JASPER 1878+ SOUTH WEST, NSW, AUS [34534] :
PRE 1900 SALTFORD, SOM, ENG [34536] : 1780-
1800 NORTH HILL, CON, ENG [34793] : 1800S
CALLINGTON, CON, ENG [36896] : PRE 1900
SHREWSBURY, SAL, ENG [37616] : PRE 1900
CAMBRIDGE, CAM, ENG [37616] : PRE 1650
REDGRAVE, SFK, ENG [38745]
JAUCH PRE 1800 WALDMOESSINGEN, WUE, GER
[38679]

JAY 1780S ALDERTON, SFK, ENG [34205] :
STEPHAN 1750-1800 LITTLE FALLS, NY, USA
[38038]
JAYNE ANNA 1700-1800 ORANGE CO., NY, USA
[38130]
JEALOUS 1820+ NSW, AUS [35391] : 1820+
MELBOURNE, VIC, AUS [35391] : 1700+
WISBECH, CAM, ENG [35391] : 1820 KELVEDON,
ESS, ENG [36729]
JEAN (SEE JEHAN) [36660]
JEANES C1836 WINCANTON, SOM, ENG [35826] :
1770-1860 YETMINSTER, DOR, ENG [37021]
JEANNIN 1800S CAPE GIRARDEAU CO., MO, USA
[37562]
JEANNOT 1850+ FRA [34323]
JEANS ANN 1825+ STOURPAINE, DOR, ENG
[36367]
JEANTON PRE 1850 QUE, CAN [38512]
JEANTY PRE 1780 MONS, HNT, BEL [36630]
JEARY ALL NFK, ENG [37612]
JEATT 1821-1824 SMITH'S GAP, NFK, ENG [34389] :
1831-1834 WARDEN POINT, KEN, ENG [34389]
JEBB 1500-1700 SAL & STS, ENG [36062]
JECKS 1860+ CAN [37726]
JEECK C1812 KIEL, SHO, GER [37819]
JEEMS 1880+ STROUD, GLS, ENG [38324]
JEENS THOMAS PRE 1860 GLOUCESTER &
BRISTOL, GLS, ENG [36590]
JEFCOATE 1880+ BIRMINGHAM, WAR, ENG
[36592]
JEFFARES PRE 1840 WEX, IRL [33954]
JEFFERIES 1859+ CARLSRUHE, VIC, AUS [35709] :
1859+ KYNETON, VIC, AUS [35709] : 1770S
MINCHINHAMPTON, GLS, ENG [35560] : PRE
1830 OLDLAND COMMON, SOM, ENG [36121] :
1800+ WESTON SUPER MARE, SOM, ENG [36158]
: 1600+ SHRIVENHAM, BRK & WIL, ENG [37625]
JEFFERIS 1880-1910 BRISTOL, GLS, ENG [35586]
JEFFERS PRE 1859 SWE [35709] : PRE 1830 NY, USA
[37510]
JEFFERSON 1860+ MELBOURNE, VIC, AUS [38568]
: 1820-1880 BRANDESBURTON & SKERNE, YKS,
ENG [33861] : 1780+ NEWPORT PAGNELL, BKM,
ENG [37070] : PRE 1850 MANCHESTER, LAN,
ENG [38568]
JEFFERY 1900+ KOOWEERUP & DANDENONG,
VIC, AUS [35140] : 1800S HASELBURY
PLUCKNETT, SOM, ENG [34688] : 1794+
PLYMOUTH, DEV, ENG [34808] : 1770
MEDSTEAD, HAM, ENG [34909] : C1780 ELMDON,
ESS, ENG [34936] : PRE 1800 WENDRON, CON,
ENG [35151] : C1843 BRENCHLEY, KEN, ENG
[36803] : 1500-1990 ST KEVERNE & WEST
PENWITH, CON, ENG [37680] : PRE 1755 CON,
ENG [38389] : PRE 1700 BRADING, IOW, ENG
[38420]
JEFFERYES 1902 MIRBOO NTH, VIC, AUS [35529]
JEFFERYS 1800+ LIVERPOOL, LAN, ENG [34688]
JEFFES THOMAS 1800S LONG COMPTON, OXF,
ENG [35876]
JEFFORD 1700S SHEERNESS, KEN, ENG [34715] :
1750-1800 COR, IRL [35494]
JEFFRESON PRE 1854 HAM, ENG [38306]
JEFFREY ALL NAPOLEON'S LEAD, VIC, AUS
[35474] : PRE 1850 CAMBORNE, CON, ENG [34916]
: 1800S DEV, ENG [35377] : PRE 1850
FOLKESTONE, KEN, ENG [36584] : 1700+
ILLOGAN, CON, ENG [38745] : 1800-1860
'TWIZEL', BERWICK ON TWEED, NBL, ENG &
AUS [35778] : PRE 1850 DOW, IRL [35277] : 1800+
CANISBAY, CAI, SCT [35428] : C1873 ROX, SCT

[36856] : 1700-1900 ALFORD, ABD, SCT [36951] : PRE 1835 GORDON, BEW, SCT [37610]

JEFFREYS 1700S HORNCASTLE, LIN, ENG [34808] : ALL ENG & AUS [35579]

JEFFRIES 1800-1900 TAS, AUS [38070] : PRE 1822 BASFORD, NTT, ENG [34661] : PRE 1850 SHRIVENHAM, BRK, ENG [35866] : PRE 1860 HEMINGFORD ABBOTS, HUN, ENG [36486] : 1750+ WEYBREAD, SFK, ENG [36989] : 1750+ DISS, NFK, ENG [36989] : 1750+ SANDY, BDF & CAM, ENG [37065] : PRE 1850 BRK, ENG [37416] : 1811+ POSEY CO., IN, USA [35286] : JOHN 1880 WAYNE & RICHLAND CO., IL, USA [35286] : 1870+ HAMILTON CO., IL, USA [35286] : 1840+ HENRY CO., IN, USA [37527] : C1819 LOUDOUN CO., VA, USA [37527] : 1840S BULLITT CO., KY, USA [37527] : 1820+ GREENBRIER CO., WV, USA [37527] : C1799-1832 WASHINGTON CO., KY, USA [37527] : 1800+ MERTHYR TYDFIL, GLA, WLS [37988] : ANDERSON ALL WORLDWIDE [37527]

JEFFRYES 1750-1850 SHOREDITCH, MDX, ENG [37747]

JEFFS PRE 1830 DOR, ENG [35866] : PRE 1800 WAR, ENG [36429] : ALL COVENTRY, WAR, ENG [37404] : 1650-1725 LEI, NTH & RUT, ENG [38229] : PRE 1877 WORLDWIDE [36249]

JEGGINS PRE 1715 BRADWELL, ESS, ENG [35157]

JEHAN ALL WORLDWIDE [36660]

JEKYLE C1850-1900 NEWCASTLE, NBL, ENG [34372] : C1875 LONDON, ENG [34372]

JELINSKI PRE 1926+ MALA, WARSAW, POL [35109]

JELLEFF 1650+ CATHERINGTON, HAM & SSX, ENG [36827]

JELLEY 1800-1860 HAMMERSMITH, MDX, ENG [36150] : 1800-1900 NTT, ENG [36531] : ALL ENG [37857] : PRE 1800 LONDON, SRY, ENG [38512] : 1790+ IRL [38460]

JELLICOE 1800+ NESTON, CHS, ENG [35611]

JELLINEK 1700+ ZNOJMO, MORAVIA, CS [37088] : 1890+ LND, ENG [37088]

JELLY 1800-1900 WORPLESDON, SRY, ENG [37403]

JELLYMAN 1800S GLS, ENG [36865] : 1840+ NELSON, NZ [35058]

JEMSON 1750+ KEN, ENG [36093]

JENKIN 1750+ PLYMOUTH, DEV, ENG [34747] : C1800 CAMBORNE, CON, ENG [35034] : PRE 1864 ILLOGAN, CON, ENG [35911] : 1700S ILLOGAN, CON, ENG [37343]

JENKING PRE 1855 CON, ENG [35074]

JENKINS PRE 1829 SYDNEY, NSW, AUS [34304] : PRE 1906 SCARSDALE, VIC, AUS [35221] : 1880+ BOULDER, WA, AUS [35866] : 1850+ IPSWICH, QLD, AUS [36300] : WM & ELIZA PRE 1843+ SYDNEY & MAITLAND, NSW, AUS [38567] : WM & ELIZA 1847+ GEELONG & PENTLAND HILLS, VIC, AUS [38567] : WM & ELIZA 1857 BACCHUS MARSH, VIC, AUS [38567] : EDWARD 1835+ VANCOUVER, BC, CAN [34134] : PRE 1900 HAMILTON, ONT, CAN [38390] : PRE 1850 BITTON, GLS, ENG [33850] : PRE 1870 FONTMELL MAGNA, DOR, ENG [33968] : 1860 WANDSWORTH, LND, ENG [34084] : 1798+ COLWALL, HEF, ENG [34334] : 1750-1860 WENDRON, CON, ENG [34687] : PRE 1882 GLS, ENG [34993] : C1820 GWENNAP, CON, ENG [35153] : 1800S DEVONPORT, DEV, ENG [35768] : PRE 1853 KILTON, SOM, ENG [35779] : 1780+ SHOREDITCH, LONDON, MDX, ENG [36263] : C1760-1811 AYLESBURY, BKM, ENG [36425] : 1850+ ENG [36470] : 1700+ HARTLEY & EARSDON, NBL, ENG [36609] : 1750+ FONTMELL MAGNA, DOR, ENG [36825] : C1805 CLIFFE, KEN,

ENG [37007] : 1800+ STEPNEY & SILVERTOWN, MDX, ENG [37251] : WILLIAM 1832 HORSLEYDOWN, SRY, ENG [37345] : THOMAS J. 1867-1889 SHOREDITCH, LND, ENG [37345] : WILLIAM 1836-1843 BIRMINGHAM, WAR, ENG [37345] : THOMAS J. 1837-1866 BIRMINGHAM, WAR, ENG [37345] : 1850+ WESTMINSTER, SRY, ENG [37746] : PRE 1850 FOREST OF DEAN, GLS, ENG [37746] : 1525+ LYMING, KEN, ENG [37802] : ELIZA C1850 DAWLEY, SAL, ENG [37883] : ALL ROCHESTER, KEN, ENG [38027] : 1805 STINCHCOMBE, GLS, ENG [38209] : WILLIAM C1820 LONDON, ENG [38567] : 1700+ WIL, ENG & AUS [34189] : C1808 WAR, ENG & AUS [34807] : 1850+ ROTHESAY, BUT, SCT [34614] : ALEXANDER C1740+ ELGIN, MOR, SCT [35848] : 1820S ELDRIE, LKS, SCT [35866] : 1750+ ST NINIANS, STI, SCT [36827] : 1766-1886 MOR, SCT [37329] : PRE 1858 SCRANTON, PA, USA [35711] : 1650+ MERCER, IL & MA, USA [36931] : 1840+ HANCOCK, GA, USA [36946] : 1863 CIVIL WAR, USA [36965] : 1808+ SHENANDOAH CO., VA, USA [36965] : 1836+ OH, USA [36965] : 1850+ CHAMPAIGN CO., IL, USA [36965] : MATTHEW 1818-1860 POPE CO., IL, USA [37590] : SADIE 1790S PENDELTON CO., SC, USA [37590] : JOHN 1810-1818 RUTHERFORD CO., TN, USA [37590] : 1850-1855 FRANKFORT, KY, USA [38227] : C1840+ MAESTEG, GLA, WLS [33922] : EDWARD 1800+ ABERYSTWYTH, CGN, WLS [34134] : EDWARD 1830+ BRECON, BRE, WLS [34134] : ANNE 1832+ BRECON, BRE, WLS [34134] : PRE 1800 RUDBAXTON, PEM, WLS [34319] : CAROLINE C1862 CAERLEON, MON, WLS [34475] : WILLIAM ALL CAERLEON, MON, WLS [34475] : C1890 BARGOED, GLA, WLS [35391] : 1890+ MOUNTAIN ASH, GLA, WLS [35391] : PRE 1858 ABERCARN & RISCA, MON, WLS [35711] : C1600 PAMTEG, MON, WLS [36185] : 1700+ NEATH, GLA, WLS [36209] : PRE 1850 NEWGALE & ROCH, PEM, WLS [36260] : PRE 1917 GLA, WLS [37201] : PRE 1830 PONTYPOOL, MON, WLS [37716]

JENKINSON PRE 1900 BOX HILL, VIC, AUS [34858] : RICHARD 1840-1851 RICHMOND & SPRINGS, TAS, AUS [35725] : 1854+ BENDIGO, VIC, AUS [35725] : 1880+ BUNDABERG, QLD, AUS [35725] : 1900+ KALGOORLIE, WA, AUS [35725] : JOHN PRE 1850 BARROWBY, LIN, ENG [34916] : 1815-1860 TOTTENHAM, MDX, ENG [35725] : 1600-1700 CITY, LND, ENG [36588] : C1800 HOLBORN, LND, ENG [36874] : 1780-1900 TANNAGH & AUGHNACLOY, TYR, IRL [36075] : 1870+ LEITH, MLN, SCT [35486] : PRE 1850 UK & IRL [35496] : WILLIAM C1809 UK & IRL [35496]

JENKS 1780-1900 BIRMINGHAM, WAR, ENG [36130] : PRE 1900 PADDINGTON, LND, ENG [36361] : 1700S HEF, ENG [37331]

JENKYN 1542+ ST ENODER, CON, ENG [36961]

JENKYNS C1820 CHILDERDITCH, ESS, ENG [35998]

JENNAWAY ALL ENG [36538]

JENNER ALL ADELAIDE & PERTH, SA & WA, AUS & ENG [34561] : PRE 1813 SSX, ENG [33998] : ALL SSX & KEN, ENG [34254] : 1700S BREDE, SSX, ENG [35881] : 1750+ FINCHLEY & CAMDEN TOWN, MDX, ENG [36219] : 1800-1870 TUNBRIDGE WELLS, KEN, ENG [36795] : 1700+ KEYMER, SSX, ENG [37166] : 1800+ ISLINGTON, LND, ENG [37620] : 1750-1850 KEN, ENG [37644] : PRE 1780 SSX, ENG [37875] : 1840+ USA [38728] : ALL WORLDWIDE [38728]

JENNESS 1790+ SHEFFIELD, VT, USA [38411]

JENNETT C1779 PORTADOWN, ARM, IRL [34474]

JENNINGS 1840+ BRAIDWOOD, NSW, AUS [35537] :
1855+ REDFERN & SYDNEY, NSW, AUS [38541] :
HENRY 1800+ PENZANCE & GWENNAP, CON,
ENG [34511] : 1800-1850 GWENNAP, CON, ENG
[34697] : C1730 ST JUST IN ROSELAND, CON,
ENG [34768] : PRE 1900 SOM, ENG [34861] : PRE
1855 GWENNAP, CON, ENG [34876] : PRE 1870
BOW, LONDON, MDX, ENG [35029] : 1790-1840
BIRMINGHAM, WAR, ENG [35517] : PRE 1840
SALISBURY, WIL, ENG [35517] : 1880+
BIRMINGHAM, WAR, ENG [36592] : 1800+
NEWENT, GLS, ENG [36825] : ALL AINTREE,
LIVERPOOL, ENG [36830] : GEORGE 1800-1850
ISLINGTON & PENTONVILLE, MDX, ENG [36864]
: C1785 HILL FARRANCE, SOM, ENG [37053] :
PRE 1762 EVERCREECH, SOM, ENG [37380] :
WILLIAM 1811-1881+ ATHERSTONE, WAR &
LAN, ENG [37546] : JANE 1834-1881+
ATHERSTONE, WAR & LAN, ENG [37546] : ALL
SFK, ENG [37612] : PRE 1900 CASTLEFORD, YKS,
ENG [37746] : PRE 1850 LEE MOOR, YKS, ENG
[37746] : PRE 1825 LND, ENG [37941] : PRE 1825
HRT, ENG [37941] : PRE 1855 KENTISH TOWN,
LND, ENG [38541] : PRE 1880 IDLE, YKS, ENG
[38755] : PRE 1840 COR, IRL [33821] : WILLIAM
C1840 AUGHRIM, GAL, IRL [38301] : 1870+
DARLINGTON, WI, USA [34876] : 1760
FAIRFIELD, CT, USA [37582]

JENNISON PRE 1800 IBLE & DUFFIELD, DBY, ENG
[37736]

JENSDATTER C1790 SIROP, JUTLAND, DEN [34654]

JENSEN 1886+ BUNDABERG, QLD, AUS [35452] :
1900+ MELBOURNE, VIC, AUS [36423] : PRE 1820
DEN [33959] : 1840+ KEMMELTAFT, DEN [34308] :
PRE 1920 VIBY, ODENSE, DEN [34657] : C1858
RINKJOBING, DEN [36762] : CHRISTIAN C1850-
1870 COPENHAGEN, DEN [37553] : PRE 1838
KIRK FLINTERUP, DEN [38738] : CHRISTIAN
C1850 FRANKFURT & FRANKCOP, GER [37553] :
1890-1900+ CAPE, RSA [36423] : 1940+
ROCHESTER, NY, USA [36512] : CHRISTINA
1860S CHICAGO, IL, USA [38315]

JENSON 1600-99 STOCKTON, WAR, ENG [34315]

JENSSON HEMMING PRE 1684 TAARNBORG,
SORO, DEN [37547]

JENTSCH 1798 GOERLITZ, PRE, GER [35575]

JENVEY PRE 1750 HAM, ENG [36380] : WILLIAM
1770S BROCKENHURST, HAM, ENG [37025] :
ETHEL 1893-1900 CHICAGO, COOK CO., IL, USA
[37025] : SUSAN 1880S MI, USA [37025]

JENYNS JOSHUA 1835-1913 BRISBANE, QLD, AUS
[37146] : PRE 1830 WATERBEACH, CAM, ENG
[37146]

JEOFFRY 1630+ RI, USA [38015]

JEPHS PRE 1800 WAR, ENG [36429]

JEPHSON PRE 1870 LISTOWEL, KER, IRL [34262]

JEPSON PRE 1930 SALE & TIMPERLEY, CHS, ENG
[36363] : 1750+ DARWEN, LAN, ENG [36991] : 1600-
1750 ECCLESFIELD, WRY, ENG [37339] : 1810
SOUTH NORMANTON, DBY, ENG [37391] : 1500+
LIN, RUT & LEI, ENG [38261] : 1770S BOLTON,
LAN, ENG [38283] : PRE 1840 SWE [34816]

JEPSOP ALL ENG [34938]

JERG PRE 1845 GER [35028] : PRE 1850 WUE, GER
[38675]

JERICHO 1670+ EISENACH, THU, GER [38606]

JERICO 1890+ BELMONT, OH, USA [38185]

JERMAN 1700-1800 SFK, ENG [35094] : PRE 1880
BIRMINGHAM, WAR, ENG [38002] : PRE 1920
TARANAKI, NZ [33985]

JERMIN 1865-1900 BRAZIL [36336]

JERMY ALL GREAT YARMOUTH, NFK, ENG
[37689]

JERNBERG C1700 FALUN, KOPPARBERG, SWE
[37036]

JERNEGAN 1100+ WORLDWIDE [35403]

JERNIGAN ALL USA [36545]

JERNINGHAM 1500+ WORLDWIDE [35403]

JEROME PRE 1820 LND, SRY & WIL, ENG [34848] :
1750S BINSTEAD, IOW, ENG [35973]

JERONIMUS 1750+ NL [38691] : 1750+ NL [38711]

JERRAM C1813 SPONDON, DBY, ENG [34661]

JERRETT ALL WORLDWIDE [36014]

JERRUM ALL WORLDWIDE [34848]

JERRY 1700+ BOWER, CAI, SCT [34981]

JERVIS ALL LONDON &, STS, ENG [34671] : C1830
STAPLEFORD, NTT, ENG [34734] : PRE 1870 SAL,
ENG [37807] : 1900+ RI, USA [34734] : 1780-1880
YANCEY CO., NC, USA [38009]

JESKIE 1800-1900 GER [37464] : 1800-1900 RUSSIA
[37464]

JESS JOHN C1815 DROMORE, DOW, IRL [35607] :
1880+ NZ [36871]

JESSE 1900+ LONDON & WINDSOR, ENG [36456] :
C1910 NEW YORK, NY, USA [36456]

JESSETT 1774+ ISLIP, OXF, ENG [34110]

JESSIMAN ALL WORLDWIDE [37442]

JESSON ANN 1784 ENG [34126] : PRE 1800 WEST
BROMWICH, STS, ENG [36379] : 1900+ GRIMSBY,
LIN, ENG [36511] : PRE 1830 LEICESTER ST
MARGARETS, LEI, ENG [36511] : 1860+
GLASGOW, LKS, SCT [34559]

JESSOP 1812+ TAS, AUS [35531] : ANN 1828-1928
SPALDING & CROWLAND, LIN, ENG [33952] :
PRE 1850 GREAT HOCKHAM, NFK, ENG [35491] :
PRE 1850 ERISWELL, SFK, ENG [35491] : 1800S
NORWICH, NFK, ENG [35899] : 1600-1700
BOURNE, LIN, ENG [38287]

JESSOP (SEE JESSUP) [35819]

JESSUP 1855+ BEECHWORTH, VIC, AUS [35819] :
1855+ CASTERTON, VIC, AUS [35819] : PRE 1855
GREAT HOCKHAM, NFK, ENG [35819]

JESTICE CLARISSA 1855+ WASHINGTON CO.,
OH, USA [37797]

JESTICO C1815 BERMONDSEY, LND, ENG [34972]

JESTON 1617+ OLD SWINFORD, WOR, WAR &
LND, ENG [35013]

JEUKEN ALL WORLDWIDE [34778]

JEUNE 1800S ST BRELADE, JSY, CHI [35041]

JEW 1860+ GYMPIE, QLD, AUS [34763] : PRE 1850
ARNOLD, NTT, ENG [34763]

JEWEL 1810-1880 COLUMBIANA CO., OH, MD &
PA, USA [37529]

JEWELL 1850+ SA & VIC, AUS [34962] : 1848+ VIC,
AUS [35035] : 1850+ GEELONG, VIC, AUS [37557] :
1800+ CAMBORNE, CON, ENG [34916] : PRE 1848
DBY, ENG [35035] : PRE 1764 CHATHAM &
COBHAM, KEN, ENG [35723] : 1827+ FOWEY &
POLRUAN, CON, ENG [35723] : 1700+
LINGFIELD, SRY, ENG [36088] : 1520+ DEV, ENG
[36549] : 1806-1915 WINNERSH & WOKINGHAM,
BRK, ENG [37638] : PRE 1780 TORRINGTON & ST
GILES AREA, DEV, ENG [37941]

JEWES PRE 1770 ACTON, MDX, ENG [36619]

JEWILL PRE 1900 LIVERPOOL & LONDON, ENG
[36399]

JEWITT ALL KIRK DEIGHTON, WRY, ENG [35588]

JEWKES ALL DUDLEY, WOR, ENG [35967] : ALL
STS, ENG [35967]

JEX 1700-1850 NFK, ENG [37207] : PRE 1895 NFK &
ESS, ENG [37726]

JEYNES 1700+ LUDLOW SALOP, HEF, ENG [36256]
: EDMUND 1800+ MARYLEBONE, MDX, ENG
[36256] : 1850+ WORCESTER, WOR, ENG [37384]
JEZEK ALL PRAHA, BOHEMIA, GER & USA [36916]
JHNSON 1841 ASHTON UNDER LYNE, LAN, ENG
[37184]
JIFFERAYES PRE 1670 WESTERLEIGH, GLS, ENG
[34908]
JIGGINS 1857+ WANDSWORTH, SRY, ENG [35827]
: PRE 1800 ESS, ENG [37749]
JILLARD PRE 1825 ENG [34383]
JILLETT 1820 HOBART, TAS, AUS [34456] : ALL
NFD, CAN [34207]
JINKINS 1830+ HOBART, TAS, AUS [35831]
JINKS 1840S HOBART, TAS, AUS [34750] : PRE 1874
MALVERN, WOR, ENG [35061] : ALL ENG [36613]
JOADIN ALL WORLDWIDE [33858]
JOAN PRE 1888 SHOREDITCH, LND, ENG [36475]
JOARLETTE 1751-1831 FOSSES LA VILLE, NMR,
BEL [38158]
JOB 1800S AUS [35161] : 1800+ HULL, YKS & LIN,
ENG [34727] : 1650-1840 GWENNAP, CON, ENG
[34793] : PRE 1810 BIRMINGHAM, WAR, ENG
[36177] : 1650 GER [38598]
JOBBER ALL UK [35791]
JOBE 1750-1890 IRL [38366] : 1830S BUTLER, OH,
USA [38366] : 1800-1875 FAYETTE CO., IN, USA
[38366] : 1800-1840 WILLIAMSON, TN, USA [38576]
JOBEY 1800+ GLS, ENG [36785]
JOBLING 1840-1888 MORPETH, NSW, AUS [35348] :
1820-1840 HEPWORTH, DUR, ENG [35348] : 1800+
MORPETH, NBL, ENG [36093] : JOHN & MARY
1817-1848 STOCKTON ON TEES, DUR, ENG &
SCT [34889]
JOBSON 1860+ WALCHA, NSW, AUS [35740] : 1800S
HORNCASTLE & HALTHAM, LIN, ENG [36511] :
1860S GATESHEAD, DUR, ENG [36867] : PRE 1850
WAR, ENG [37273] : PRE 1900 SAL, ENG [37273] :
1890+ BEDWELLTY, MON, WLS [37273]
JOBST 1826+ NSA, GER [38186]
JOCE 1850+ NORTH MOLTON, DEV, ENG [35825]
JOCKISCH 1800+ HESSE DARMSKEDT, KSA, GER
[37001]
JOE 1740+ STRACATRHO, ANS, SCT [34713]
JOEL ALL CGN, WLS [37250]
JOERG 1300S NOERDLINGEN, BAY, GER [38608]
JOERGENSEN C1500 FLENSBURG, SHO, GER
[38608]
JOHADE 1600-1750 ZANZHAUSEN, POS, GER
[37535]
JOHANNES PRE 1980 SCHMALKALDEN, THU,
GER [36458]
JOHANNESEN ALL AUS [35115] : PRE 1890
TOLSTREY, ROSKILDE, DEN [35115] : PRE 1874
NOR [36807] : PRE 1874 SWE [36807]
JOHANNS PRE 1800 PSA, GER [38648]
JOHANNSEN PRE 1890 SHO, GER [37009] : 1789+
DRELSDORF, SHO, GER [37148]
JOHANNSON SWAN MANFRED ALL SWE [34164]
JOHANSDOTTER 1600-1740S DALHAM, GOTLAND,
SWE [38346] : ELIN 1888+ MINNIAPOLIS, MN,
USA [38557]
JOHANSDTR CATH B. PRE 1723 GAVLE, FIN &
SWE [38564]
JOHANSEN 1840S BRETH, VJELE, DEN [35953] :
1730-1760 TILLITSE, DEN [37515] : CHRISTIAN
C1850-1870 COPENHAGEN, DEN [37553] :
CHRISTIAN C1850 FRANKFURT & FRANKCOP,
GER [37553] : PRE 1850 NESNA, NORDLAND,
NOR [36326] : 1891-1968 DOUGLAS CO., NE, USA
[37538]

JOHANSSON PRE 1840 COPENHAGEN, DEN [37137]
: MARIA BRITA PRE 1900 JUNSELE,
VASTERNORRLAND, SWE [34481] : PRE 1900
SANDSJO, JONKOPLING, SWE [35324] : ALL
HALMSTAD, SWE [36331] : LILLY 1909+
ROCHESTER, NY, USA [38546] : 1900+ NEOLA,
IA, USA [38552]
JOHN 1750-1900 MDX, ENG [37651] : 1831+ ST
MARYLEBONE, MDX, ENG [37651] : PRE 1945
TETSCHEN, GER [38674] : PRE 1860 PEM, WLS
[35868] : PRE 1850 NEWGALE & ROCH, PEM, WLS
[36260] : ALL WORLDWIDE [38666]
JOHNMAN ELIZABETH C1742 DUNNING, PER,
SCT [37106] : 1750-1850 DUNNING, PER, SCT
[38511]
JOHNS 1850+ GAWLER, SA, AUS [34279] : JOHN
1870S CORNISHTOWN, VIC, AUS [35070] : C1900
SYDNEY, NSW, AUS [35585] : 1892 HUGHENDEN,
QLD, AUS [37952] : MARY-ANN PRE 1840 BEER
FERRES, DEV, ENG [34652] : PRE 1900 HELSTON
& ST KEVERNE, CON, ENG [34865] : JOHN C1836-
60 CON, ENG [35070] : C1724 ALTARNUN, CON,
ENG [35335] : C1854 HELSTON, CON, ENG [35585] :
PRE 1850 DEV, ENG [35913] : C1810 REDRUTH,
CON, ENG [37148] : 1800-1900 PLYMOUTH, DEV,
ENG [37211] : 1800-1860 LAUNCESTON, CON,
ENG [37211] : 1800S HULL, ERY, ENG [37299] :
1800-1900 PLYMOUTH, DEV, ENG [37365] : 1850S
ST WINNOW, CON, ENG [37641] : RICHARD PRE
1730 ST AGNES, CON, ENG [37995] : ALL
PLYMOUTH, DEV, ENG & AUS [34561] :
ELIZABETH C1806 UK & IRL [35496] : PRE 1900
WESTERN COUNTIES, PA, USA [38218] : 1780-1830
GLA, WLS [37263] : 1790+ HAVERFORD WEST,
PEM, WLS [37443] : 1850+ PEMBROKE DOCK,
PEM, WLS [38481]
JOHNSMAN 1860-1940 MERCER CO., OH, USA
[36901]

JOHNSON JAMES 1847+ BRAIDWOOD, NSW, AUS
[33813] : PRE 1883 IPSWICH, QLD, AUS [33832] :
PRE 1869 MACKAY, QLD, AUS [34044] : 1902+
PORT MELBOURNE, VIC, AUS [34568] : PRE 1870
HOBART, TAS, AUS [34603] : MARYANN 1835+
BOWENFELS, NSW, AUS [34843] : 1830+
BOWENFELS, NSW, AUS [34843] : 1870+
NEWCASTLE, NSW, AUS [35075] : PETER 1850+
HORSHAM, VIC, AUS [35240] : 1840+ COWRA &
YOUNG, NSW, AUS [35241] : 1846 COLDSTREAM
RIVER, NSW, AUS [35251] : 1890+
QUEANBEYAN, NSW, AUS [35410] : 1850+
RICHMOND, NSW, AUS [35419] : C1840
HAWKESBURY RV, NSW, AUS [35434] : C1840
PENRITH, NSW, AUS [35434] : 1800S NORTH, TAS,
AUS [35715] : 1839 PARRAMATTA, NSW, AUS
[35920] : 1800S ARNCLIFFE, NSW, AUS [36372] :
1850+ KILMORE, VIC, AUS [36610] : 1850+
HOBART, TAS, AUS [36766] : 1860+ EMMAVILLE,
NSW, AUS [37115] : 1900+ MOREE, NSW, AUS
[37115] : 1900+ BINGARA, NSW, AUS [37115] :
JULIA MARY 1860S BALLARAT, VIC, AUS [37151]
: RICH'D & MARY 1860S BALLARAT, VIC, AUS
[37151] : JAMES 1828+ MONARO, NSW, AUS
[37155] : WILLIAM 1845-1919 MONARO, NSW, AUS
[37155] : GEORGE 1885+ LAURIETON, NSW, AUS
[37175] : CHRISTIAN C1882-1894 UPPER
BINGARA & TINGHA, NSW, AUS [37553] :
CHRISTIAN 1878-1882 GULGONG, NSW, AUS
[37553] : C1802 NSW, AUS [38485] : ANNIE ALL
BRISBANE, QLD, AUS & ENG [35122] : ALL BRD
[38607] : PRE 1879 ONT, CAN [34252] : 1850+
YORK CO., ONT, CAN [34407] : 1820+ SIMCOE
CO., ONT, CAN [34465] : WILLIAM 1850+

HAMIOTA, MAN & ONT, CAN [34519] : 1850-1950
KINGSTON, ONT, CAN [36990] : PETER C1875-
1900 OVERLAND, SAS, CAN [37440] : MARGARET
1828+ PARIS, ONT, CAN [37443] : PRE 1860
ROSTOCK, RST, DDR [37115] : CHRISTIAN C1850-
1870 COPENHAGEN, DEN [37553] : C1828
LARDEN, LIN, ENG [33793] : JAMES PRE 1827
KEN, ENG [33813] : PRE 1820 SOUTH SHEILDS,
DUR, ENG [33937] : PRE 1740 HOUGHTON LE
SPRING, DUR, ENG [33940] : PRE 1910 LONDON,
ENG [33960] : RICHARD 1750+ LONDON, ENG
[34013] : 1800+ BEDFORD, ENG [34049] : 1850
LONDON, ENG [34098] : PRE 1800 WIL, ENG
[34139] : 1695+ GUISBOROUGH, NRY, ENG
[34181] : PRE 1880 SOUTH SHIELDS, DUR, ENG
[34293] : 1800-99 CAMPTON, BDF, ENG [34315] :
KATHERINE PRE 1605 STOCKPORT, CHS, ENG
[34573] : PRE 1840 LONDON, ENG [34576] : PRE
1879 GREAT AMWELL, HRT, ENG [34584] : PRE
1850 YORK CITY, YKS, ENG [34588] : 1841+
NOTTINGHAM, NTT, ENG [34609] : PRE 1820
SUTTON IN ASHFIELD, NTT, ENG [34612] : PRE
1850 WETWANG, YKS, ENG [34686] : PRE 1900
WEST BROMWICH, STS, ENG [34711] : C1800
ROYSTON, HRT, ENG [34840] : C1810 DEPTFORD,
WIL, ENG [34843] : 1880S EAST RETFORD, NTT,
ENG [34854] : WILLIAM PRE 1837 ASPENDEN,
HRT, ENG [34873] : WILLIAM PRE 1850
LAMBETH, LND, ENG [34916] : PRE 1803
PENDLETON, LAN, ENG [34959] : C1720 BREDE,
SSX, ENG [34974] : 1800+ YKS, ENG [35060] : PRE
1870 SEATON DELAVAL, NBL, ENG [35075] :
C1850 LND, ENG [35089] : 1830+ KNOWSLEY,
LAN, ENG [35114] : 1850+ REPTON, DBY, ENG
[35183] : C1845 BURTON UPON TRENT, STS, ENG
[35183] : C1850 DERBY, DBY, ENG [35183] : PRE
1810 ALTHORPE, LIN, ENG [35255] : SARAH C1820
SOM, ENG [35336] : THOMAS 1690 GEDNEY, LIN,
ENG [35369] : PRE 1818 ISLE OF ELY, CAM, ENG
[35419] : WILLIAM C1837 DOVER, KEN, ENG
[35560] : C1850 MANCHESTER, LAN, ENG [35586] :
PRE 1780 SFK, ENG [35642] : 1800+ COCKING,
SSX & HAM, ENG [35760] : JOSEPH 1795+
MEDMENHAM, BKM, ENG [35815] : 1700+
RUNTON, NFK, ENG [35824] : 1870S EXETER,
DEV, ENG [35865] : 1820-1842 NEWINGTON, SRY,
ENG [35865] : C1829-1885 REDHILL, SRY, ENG
[35885] : 1798+ KETTERING, NTH, ENG [35921] :
C1850 HAWKHURST, KEN, ENG [35931] : 1710-
1800S DARTMOUTH, DEV, ENG [35938] : PRE 1850
CHS, ENG [35945] : 1700+ BOXGROVE, SSX, ENG
[35987] : 1800+ FULHAM, LND, ENG [36026] : PRE
1800 BKM & HRT, ENG [36042] : 1700-1800
GREYSTOKE, CUL, ENG [36098] : 1700-1765
ROTHERHITHE & LAMBETH, SRY, ENG [36184] :
ANN 1820+ CHS, ENG [36214] : 1800+ BLETSOE,
BDF, ENG [36257] : WILLIAM 1790+ BRADFORD,
WRY, ENG [36263] : PRE 1752 PARWICH, DBY,
ENG [36281] : PRE 1800 CHATTERIS, CAM, ENG
[36388] : ANN 1759-1784 BISHOP BURTON, ERY,
ENG [36391] : 1750-1850 MANCHESTER, LAN,
ENG [36416] : 1650S HURST, BRK, ENG [36425] :
1700+ FISHLEY, NFK, ENG [36434] : WILLIAM
PRE 1900 SUNDERLAND, NBL, ENG [36529] :
1790-1815 BRETTON, WRY, ENG [36606] : C1810-
1900 FRAMLINGHAM, SFK, ENG [36632] : PRE
1825 KIRKBY IRELETH, LAN, ENG [36701] : PRE
1860 STAFFORD, STS, ENG [36701] : 1800S ST
GEORGE EAST, LND, ENG [36764] : 1800S
BIRMINGHAM, WAR, ENG [36764] : 1800S
WAKEFIELD, WRY, ENG [36837] : 1880-1920
CROYDON, SRY, ENG [36990] : 1750-1860 GREAT

YARMOUTH, NFK, ENG [36990] : PRE 1870
HORSEY, NFK, ENG [37078] : PRE 1850 STEPNEY,
LND, ENG [37102] : JACOB C1849
GUILSBOROUGH, NTH, ENG [37106] : TIMOTHY
C1789 COLD ASHBY, NTH, ENG [37106] :
SOLOMON C1770 COLD ASHBY, NTH, ENG
[37106] : 1720-1820 TAMWORTH, STS, ENG [37283] :
1820-1890 WILLENHALL, STS, ENG [37283] : PRE
1845 HANLEY, STS, ENG [37298] : PRE 1889 SRY,
ENG [37358] : 1850 CHESTER LE STREET, DUR,
ENG [37388] : PRE 1800 HEREFORD, HEF, ENG
[37393] : 1860 OLD ST PANCRAS, MDX, ENG
[37418] : 1800-1900 BOZEAT, NTH, ENG [37495] :
1830S HOUGHTON, NFK, ENG [37568] : PRE 1900
CRICKLEWOOD, LND, ENG [37622] : 1780+
KIRKANDREWS ON ESK, CUL, ENG [37628] :
ALL EVERTON, CHS, ENG [37667] : ALL SFK, ESS
& KEN, ENG [37674] : PRE 1806 FARNWORTH,
LAN, ENG [37697] : PRE 1716 ORMSKIRK, LAN,
ENG [37706] : PRE 1800 ENG [37721] : 1790+
SOUTHWARK & NEWINGTON, SRY, ENG [37721]
: PRE 1800 SANDON, STS, ENG [37722] : 1800-1860
EAST PECKHAM & TONBRIDGE, KEN, ENG
[37752] : PRE 1852 GOSBERTON, LIN, ENG [37866]
: 1700+ WAR, ENG [37868] : JAMES PRE 1850
HAMPSTEAD HEATH, LND, ENG [37961] : PRE
1798 GRINGLEY ON THE HILL, NTT, ENG [37978]
: HENRY C1833 NORWICH, NFK, ENG [37981] :
PRE 1867 NTH, ENG [37991] : EDWARD PRE 1830
SALFORD, LAN, ENG [38004] : PRE 1840
LEICESTER, LEI, ENG [38056] : PRE 1800
READING, BRK, ENG [38084] : C1860 RIPON,
YKS, ENG [38168] : 1750+ HOLBORN, LND, ENG
[38375] : 1840S NEWLAND, YKS, ENG [38422] :
MICHAEL 1700-1800 WEST KEAL, LIN, ENG
[38453] : 1830+ CHESTERFIELD, DBY, ENG [38488]
: 1830-72 LONDON, ENG & AUS [35535] :
CHRISTIAN C1850-1870 FRANKFURT &
FRANKCOP, GER [37553] : 1800-1945 LIEGNITZ,
SIL, GER [38607] : 1800-1945 GOLDBERG, SIL, GER
[38607] : MARY 1845+ DUB, IRL [33801] : PRE 1856
COLERAINE, DRY, IRL [34407] : C1800 DUBLIN,
IRL [34843] : 1850+ LEA, LEX & KID, IRL [36087] :
PRE 1881 IRL [37318] : PRE 1832 DRUM, MOG, IRL
[37473] : C1812 IRL [37474] : 1750-1875
BALLYMENA, ANT, IRL [38024] : 1790+ BELFAST
& TINKEY PARK, ANT & IL, IRL & USA [37581] :
PRE 1890 STAVANGER, NOR [36035] : 1850-1880
KRISTIANNA, NOR [36331] : OLE PRE 1870
LILLEHAMMER, NOR [37782] : 1870
HELENSVILLE, NORTHLAND, NZ [33968] : 1870+
CHRISTCHURCH, NZ [34603] : C1859 RANGIORA,
NZ [35885] : GEORGE 1875+ INVERCARGILL, NZ
[37175] : JOSEPH 1801+ TINGWALL, SHI, SCT
[34627] : ALL TINGWALL, SHI, SCT [34627] : 1800+
WISHAW, LKS, SCT [34934] : C1830 UNST, SHI,
SCT [35708] : BRAGANZA 1847 SCT [36452] : 1800+
SHI, SCT [36857] : 1786+ MID SOUTH YELL, SHI,
SCT [36875] : NELS PRE 1890 MALMOHUS, SWE
[36723] : CHAS ALBERT 1800S SMOLAND,
OSTERGOTLAND, SWE [36918] : ALL UK [37674] :
JAMES 1850+ CHARLOTTE, MI, USA [34232] :
PRE 1880 DETROIT, MI, USA [34252] : ELIZABETH
C1815+ TN, USA [35272] : 1800-1900S MO & KS,
USA [35304] : 1800-1855 PHILADELPHIA, PA, USA
[35320] : ENOCH G. 1865-1878 VAN BUREN CO.,
MI, USA [35329] : JACOB S. 1880-1894 VAN BUREN
CO., MI, USA [35329] : WILLIAM 1776-1800
WESTERN COUNTIES, MD, USA [35329] : ENOCH
G. 1835-1855 HOCKING CO., OH, USA [35329] :
GEORGE W. 1860-1870 MERCER CO., OH, USA
[35329] : WILLIAM 1804-1835 FAIRFIELD CO., OH,

USA [35329] : ENOCH G. 1806-1835 FAIRFIELD CO., OH, USA [35329] : DAVID B. 1865-1878 MERCER CO., OH, USA [35329] : BENJAMIN 1817-1838 HOCKING CO., OH, USA [35329] : ENOCH G. 1855-1865 MERCER CO., OH, USA [35329] : JOSEPH C. 1840-1845 HOCKING CO., OH, USA [35329] : SAMUEL 1790-1860 PUTNEY, VT, USA [36319] : ABRAM 1850+ WHITESIDE CO., IL, USA [36334] : C1815-50 KY & MO, USA [36337] : GUSTAV 1878 SANTA CLARA CO., CA, USA [36356] : NELS PRE 1900 ELBOW LAKE, MN, USA [36723] : NEWBERRY 1790-1880 ONEIDA CO., NY & IL, USA [36901] : 1880-1910 HAYWOOD CO., TN, USA [36912] : GIDEON 1700+ SURRY CO., VA, USA [36934] : 1750-1900 ALBANY CO., NY, USA [36962] : CHARLOTTE 1822 STAFFORD, TOLLAND, MA, USA [37025] : ELIZABETH C1820 TN, USA [37030] : GEORGE J. 1850+ BELLVILLE, IL, USA [37426] : 1800 NC, USA [38362] : CARRIE BELLE 1800+ USA [38451] : 1880+ OTTUMUA, IA, USA [38552] : BAILEY PRE 1848 LAUDERDALE, NEWTON CO., MS, USA [38569] : PRE 1700 MA, USA [38745] : 1750-1770 HUNTERDON CO., NJ, USA [38763]

JOHNSON-GIBB ALL WORLDWIDE [35383]

JOHNSSON ISAAC 1765-1850 GOTHENBORG, SWE [36320]

JOHNSTON CAPT. 1864 SYDNEY, NSW, AUS [33826] : 1870 CHARTERS TOWERS, QLD, AUS [33826] : 1840S+ ORANGE & NYNGAN, NSW, AUS [35331] : 1848-1870 MELBOURNE, VIC, AUS [35436] : 1850+ GISBORNE, VIC, AUS [36277] : 1860+ GERRINGONG, NSW, AUS [36615] : 1850+ WALLAN, VIC, AUS [36620] : 1925+ SYDNEY, NSW, AUS [36792] : 1800+ TAS, AUS [36850] : 1865+ KANGALOON, NSW, AUS [37971] : 1817+ BATHURST & DINGO CREEK, NSW, AUS & SCT [37130] : 1823+ TABUSINTAC, NB, CAN [34056] : 1800-1930 NORTHUMBERLAND CO., NB, CAN [34404] : 1820+ SIMCOE CO., ONT, CAN [34465] : 1850+ TORONTO, ONT, CAN [34465] : 1833+ KIRKWALL, ONT, CAN [34507] : SAMUEL 1850+ KILSYTH, ONT, CAN [36697] : ALL ELGIN CO., ONT, CAN [36702] : 1875-1930 NB, CAN [36718] : 1817+ NEWCASTLE, NB, CAN [37443] : 1840+ RENFREW CO., ONT, CAN [37474] : WILLIAM 1848-1927 LAUREL, ONT, CAN [38451] : ALL CUL, ENG [35293] : 1880-1911 BRACKNELL, BRK, ENG [35604] : GEORGE 1750+ (BRITISH ARMY), ENG [35975] : JAMES PRE 1897 EDMONTON, MDX, ENG [36167] : C1851-52 MANCHESTER, LAN, ENG [36307] : PRE 1838 LONDON, MDX, ENG [37840] : 1870+ ALLAHABAD, INDIA & AU [36405] : 1750-1850 ROCKFIELD & BALLYBAY, MOG, IRL [33826] : ALL CORKEERAN, MOG, IRL [33826] : ALL AUGHNAMULLEN & CASTLEBLAYNEY, MOG, IRL [33826] : 1750-1835 DUBLIN, IRL [33826] : 1750-1850 THORNHILL & DRUMINICAN, MOG, IRL [33826] : 1840 BELFAST, DOW, IRL [34546] : PRE 1870 GLENARM, ANT, IRL [34585] : 1800+ BELFAST, ANT, IRL [35121] : 1800S BELFAST, ANT, IRL [35233] : PRE 1850 ARM, IRL [35297] : 1800+ BELFAST, ANT, IRL [35436] : 1800-40 BELFAST, IRL [35612] : ALL BELFAST, ANT, IRL [35628] : PRE 1830S MAGHERA, LDY, IRL [35702] : C1838 BARRAGH, CAV, IRL [35708] : JOHN KENT 1830+ DUBLIN, IRL [35975] : 1750+ LEA & PORTARLINGTON, LEX & KID, IRL [36087] : PRE 1935 GRANGE, TYR, IRL [36437] : ALL HAMILTON, ANT, IRL [36697] : ALL TULLYVALLON & NEWTOWN, ANT, IRL [36697] : WILLIAM PRE 1880 BAWNBOY, CAV, IRL [36723] : PRE 1900 KILREA, LDY, IRL [36750] : 1780 IRL

[37008] : 1820-1850S KILDRESS & COOKSTOWN, TYR, IRL [37308] : PRE 1830 ENNISKILLEN, FER, IRL [37729] : PRE 1864 KISH, FER, IRL [37971] : PRE 1830 TAMYBRAKE, ANT, IRL [38292] : THOMAS C1796+ FER & QUE, IRL & CAN [36904] : THOMAS C1796+ ARM & QUE, IRL & CAN [36904] : ELIZA C1822+ FER & QUE, IRL & CAN [36904] : ELIZA C1822+ ARM & QUE, IRL & CAN [36904] : 1850-1865 LYTTLETON, NZ [35582] : 1859+ RANGIORA, CANTY, NZ [36792] : JOHN C1720+ PERTH, PER, SCT [33950] : PRE 1800 GLADSMUIR, ELN, SCT [33959] : PRE 1850 ANS, SCT [34053] : PRE 1823 ANNAN, DFS, SCT [34056] : 1785 BARONY GLASGOW, LKS, SCT [34118] : DAVID PRE 1825 KIRKINTILLOCK, DNB, SCT [34127] : JAMES C1799 CLACKMANNAN, DNB, SCT [34127] : PRE 1830 STONEHOUSE, LKS, SCT [34197] : 1800S PETERHEAD, ABD, SCT [34336] : 1812-1890 GLASGOW, LKS, SCT [34635] : 1700+ OLD DEER, ABD, SCT [34637] : C1800 ISLAY, ARL, SCT [34644] : 1750-1850 MARNOCH, BAN, SCT [34771] : PRE 1820S DUMFRIES, DFS, SCT [34873] : 1820S ISLAY, ARL, SCT [34911] : PETER 1830+ LERWICK, SHI, SCT [35240] : JOHN C1730 CADDER, LKS, SCT [35252] : 1750+ CRANSHAWS, BEW, SCT [35475] : C1830 SHI, SCT [35476] : 1700+ AUCHTERHOUSE, ANS, SCT [35644] : 1790+ FALKIRK, STI, SCT [35921] : ALL LKS, SCT [35961] : 1842+ DELTIN, SHI, SCT [36237] : PRE 1850 CAI, SCT [36277] : C1770 COLDINGHAM, BEW, SCT [36302] : 1820S AUCHINLECK, DFS, SCT [36620] : 1830S AUCHINLECK, AYR, SCT [36620] : 1800S SHOTTS, LKS, SCT [36764] : PRE 1800 ECHT, ABD, SCT [36792] : PRE 1860 ABERDEEN, ABD, SCT [36792] : 1831+ BANNOCKBURN, STI, SCT [37205] : WILLIAM 1740+ HODDOM, DFS, SCT [37443] : JOHN 1780-1785 EDINBURGH, SCT [37815] : FRANCIS PRE 1840 SCT [37913] : 1822 AUCHERTOOL, FIF, SCT [37946] : PRE 1900 PAISLEY, RFW, SCT [38076] : 1700-1990 ANNANDALE, DFS, SCT & AUS [35421] : CAPT. 1864 SAN FRANCISCO, CA, USA [33826] : 1863 EAST WASHINGTON, USA [33826] : 1768+ FAIRFAX CO., VA, USA [36895] : ALL NY, USA [38451] : 1807+ AMESBURY, ESSEX, MA, USA [38571] : ALL WORLDWIDE [36333]

JOHNSTONE 1900 RICHMOND, MELBOURNE, VIC, AUS [35769] : 1839+ WALLAN, VIC, AUS [37154] : 1840-1845 BROCKVILLE, ONT, CAN [34402] : 1820+ SIMCOE CO., ONT, CAN [34465] : 1850+ MOOSEJAW, SAS, CAN [35627] : C1870-1900 BECKENHAM, KEN, ENG [34372] : JAMES 1860 PENRITH, CUL, ENG [36818] : JOSEPH PRE 1838 WAR, ENG & IRL [38437] : 1745-1900 LISBELLAW, FER, IRL [34402] : 1866-1890 BALLYMENA, ANT, IRL [34545] : PRE 1935 GRANGE, TYR, IRL [36437] : JAMES 1700S JOHNSTONE, DFS, SCT [34225] : PRE 1714 WESTERKIRK, DFS, SCT [34501] : 1833 GALASHIELS, SEL, SCT [34507] : BARBARA PRE 1819 GLASGOW, LKS, SCT [34539] : PRE 1820 PETTY, INV, SCT [34613] : C1800 BARONY, LKS, SCT [35525] : 1800+ DUNFERMLINE, FIF, SCT [35627] : 1780+ FIF, SCT [35880] : PRE 1820 BEW, SCT [36201] : PRE 1855 LOCHMABEN, DFS, SCT [36437] : 1800S SHOTTS, LKS, SCT [36764] : 1770-1870 MUIRAVONSIDE, STI, SCT [37205] : 1780-1870 LOCKERBIE, DFS, SCT [37422] : C1850 MLN, SCT [37527] : 1780S CRAWFORD, DFS, SCT [37751] : THOMAS 1863-1883 GLASGOW, SCT [37940] : 1800+ LOCHMABEN, DFS, SCT [38247] : 1700+ DFS, SCT [38385] : PRE 1870 ECCLEFECHAN, DFS,

SCT [38411] : 1820 ST CYRUS, KCD, SCT [38470] : ANNE 1800+ DFS, SCT & AUS [34161]

JOHNSTONE OF WESTRAW PRE 1700 LKS, SCT [38561]

JOICE (SEE JOYCE) [37812]

JOICEY ALL UK [37240]

JOINER 1850+ SYDNEY, NSW, AUS [35373] : 1860+ WHITSTABLE, KEN, ENG [37213]

JOLICOEUR 1700-1990 QUE, CAN [36699]

JOLIN 1700 LOR, FRA [36418] : 1700 ST GERMAIN EN LAYE, RPA, FRA [36418]

JOLIVET 1620-1740 BOUTE D'ILE, QUE, CAN & FRA [34514]

JOLLAND 1790+ LEI, ENG [37869]

JOLLEY PRE 1780 ISLEHAM, CAM, ENG [34445] : ALL GREAT BILLING, NTH, ENG [34838] : 1800+ LAN, ENG [36363] : 1850+ ST JOSEPH, MO, NE & WY, USA [36942]

JOLLIFFE PRE 1800 OLD PERLICAN, NFD, CAN [37513] : 1700+ PORTISHAM, DOR & SOM, ENG [34933] : PRE 1700 MOTCOMBE, DOR, ENG [36478] : 1800-1900 CREWKERNE, SOM, ENG [37709]

JOLLIN 1700 ST GERMAIN EN LAYE, RPA, FRA [36418] : 1700 LOR, FRA [36418]

JOLLY 1855+ BENDIGO, VIC, AUS [35468] : 1800S LADOCK, CON, ENG [35023] : 1700+ DEOPHAM, NFK, ENG [35411] : 1800S LAN, ENG [35468] : PRE 1880 CROGHAN, ROS, IRL [34084] : SAMUEL 1833-1859 DRUMMORE, KKD, SCT [35615] : PRE 1875 CHANGUE & CUMNOCK, AYR, SCT [36302] : 1830+ DUNDEE, ANS, SCT [36320] : 1600-1900 PHILADELPHIA, PA, USA [36689]

JOLSBERG 1850 DEN [35246]

JONAH 1760+ ALBERT CO., NB, CAN & USA [37486]

JONAS 1800S+ LONDON, ENG [35342] : PRE 1880 HAMBURG, HBG, GER [36583]

JONASEN 1880+ TOWNSVILLE, QLD, AUS [35548] : ALL LARVIK, NOR [35548] : PRE 1872 UPPER PASTERAL DALSLAND, SWE [35443]

JONASON 1750-1900 NOR [34631]

JONASSON 1880+ NY, USA [38552]

JONES 1845 MUDGEE, NSW, AUS [33783] : JOHN C1850S NSW, AUS [33794] : JAMES GOULD 1848-1860 STANLEY, TAS, AUS [33900] : JAMES GOULD 1860-1895 MORNINGTON, VIC, AUS [33900] : PRE 1900 MARYBOROUGH, VIC, AUS [33997] : ISAAC 1900-1956 MAFFRA, VIC, AUS [34006] : C1860-1900 BRIGHT, VIC, AUS [34006] : EDWARD 1843+ HEIDELBURG, VIC, AUS [34036] : BARNABAS 1840+ SYDNEY, NSW, AUS [34036] : RICHARD 1860S VIC, AUS [34186] : CATHERINE 1852+ SYDNEY, NSW, AUS [34449] : JOHN 1852+ SYDNEY, NSW, AUS [34449] : JOHN 1853+ EDEN, NSW, AUS [34461] : ELIZA 1853+ EDEN, NSW, AUS [34461] : BENJAMIN PRE 1905 DEVONPORT, TAS, AUS [34539] : ROBERT PRE 1874 RICHMOND, VIC, AUS [34553] : WILLIAM DAVYS 1835-1912 VIC, AUS [34578] : 1850+ VIC, AUS [34874] : SARAH PRE 1880 SYDNEY, NSW, AUS [34978] : WILLIAM 1820S-1866 WINDSOR & ROUSE HILL, NSW, AUS [35108] : W.F. ALL WA, AUS [35139] : 1850S DUNGOG, NSW, AUS [35156] : JOHN ALLAN 1850S WILLOUGHBY, NSW, AUS [35373] : 1880S MALDON, VIC, AUS [35390] : 1810 SYDNEY, NSW, AUS [35407] : ELIZA ANN PRE 1860-70 EDINGLASSIE, NSW, AUS [35412] : JOHN PRE 1853 CAMPBELLTOWN, TAS, AUS [35459] : 1900S BULLI, NSW, AUS [35727] : 1880S COLLINGWOOD, VIC, AUS [35728] : THOMAS 1850S MUDGEE, NSW, AUS [35743] : C1879+ MELBOURNE, VIC, AUS [35746] : C1876+ PARRAMATTA, NSW, AUS [35746] : WILLIAM 1819-1893 GRANVILLE, NSW, AUS [35784] : LORANDO 1819-1893 GRANVILLE, NSW, AUS [35784] : LOREANDER 1865+ GRANVILLE, NSW, AUS [35784] : 1850+ RUTHERGLEN, VIC, AUS [35829] : 1880+ BRISBANE, QLD, AUS [35854] : PRE 1878 WARRNAMBOOL, VIC, AUS [36249] : HUGH O. 1850+ VIC & TAS, AUS [36885] : EDWARD 1855+ BURRA BURRA, SA, AUS [37310] : WILLIAM 1815-1827 RICHMOND & WINDSOR, NSW, AUS [37553] : WILLIAM 1827+ SINGLETON, NSW, AUS [37553] : MARY ANN PRE 1860 BENALLA, VIC, AUS [37901] : RICHARD 1850+ PADDINGTON, NSW, AUS [37944] : SARAH 1860+ BALLARAT, VIC, AUS [38213] : 1840+ WARWICK, QLD, AUS [38262] : JOSEPH 1914 TAS, AUS & CAN [34539] : C1768 ENGLISH HARBOUR, NFD, CAN [33852] : 1840+ RIDGETOWN, ONT, CAN [37484] : ROBERT V. 1736-1990 POWNAL, PEI, NB & BC, CAN [37499] : 1867+ ST PETER PORT, GSY, CHI [34688] : HERBERT PRE 1750 ST DUNSTAN, STEPNEY, MDX, ENG [33757] : C1820S LONDON, ENG [33794] : ROBERT PRE 1860 LIVERPOOL, LAN, ENG [33814] : ANN 1823+ CLEHONGER, HEF, ENG [33819] : ELIZA C1815-1864+ EDGBASTON & BIRMINGHAM, WAR, ENG [33847] : 1800+ LEIGHTON, SAL, ENG [33855] : JAMES GOULD PRE 1848 LONDON, ENG [33900] : 1850+ SHAPWICK, SOM, ENG [33982] : 1725-1900 LUCKINGTON, WIL, ENG [34012] : 1750-1850 PYWORTHY, DEV, ENG [34108] : WILLIAM 1850+ KIDDERMINSTER, WOR, ENG [34113] : C1830 DUDLEY, WOR, ENG [34145] : C1829 LONDON, ENG [34305] : 1800-1820 LONDON, ENG [34307] : THOMAS PRE 1830 CONDOVER, SAL, ENG [34370] : EDWARD PRE 1890 KEN, ENG [34481] : MARY 1920S LIVERPOOL, LAN, ENG [34510] : 1750-1800 CLAINES, WOR, ENG [34552] : 1835+ WIGSTON, LEI, ENG [34578] : 1789 COLEFORD, GLS, ENG [34609] : PRE 1900 DRIFFIELD, ERY, ENG [34617] : JOSEPH 1814+ LIVERPOOL, LAN, ENG [34698] : JAMES WALTER 1820-1840 CON, ENG [34751] : 1834 MEARE, SOM, ENG [34777] : ALL BETHNAL GREEN, LND, ENG [34820] : C1800 MADELEY, SAL, ENG [34822] : 1880+ GREAT GRIMSBY, LIN, ENG [34836] : WILLIAM 1718 BRISTOL, GLS, ENG [34908] : ALL SSX, ENG [34980] : 1800-1900 KEN, ENG [34980] : MARIA ANNE 1800S HUNGERFORD, WIL, ENG [35023] : C1850 HUN, ENG [35121] : HENRY 1868+ MARYLEBONE, LND, ENG [35144] : ROWLAND PRE 1846 MANCHESTER, LAN, ENG [35232] : PRE 1860 WYCOMBE, BKM, ENG [35255] : THOMAS 1822 NEWINGTON BUTTS, LND, ENG [35369] : PRE 1835 KEN, ENG [35397] : 1816+ MARSHBALDON, OXF, ENG [35463] : JOHN PRE 1860 BOULDON, SAL, ENG [35522] : PRE 1876 FOLKESTONE, KEN, ENG [35746] : 1830 WARLINGHAM, SRY, ENG [35746] : 1890+ WANDSWORTH, LND, ENG [35814] : 1918+ CON, ENG [35893] : MARIA 1845+ DARLASTON, STS, ENG [35942] : 1810+ DARLASTON, STS, ENG [35942] : 1900+ MANCHESTER, LAN, ENG [35943] : 1800S ISLINGTON, MDX, ENG [35987] : ISAAC 1840S+ MANCHESTER, LAN, ENG [36024] : PRE 1898 HULL & HOWDEN, ERY, ENG [36039] : 1800-1850 BISHOPSGATE, LND, ENG [36047] : RACHEL 1825+ BESSES O' THE BARN, LAN, ENG [36149] : PRE 1835 BROADWAY & SEDGEBERROW, WOR, ENG [36171] : PRE 1850 HARVINGTON, WOR, ENG [36171] : 1850+ ECKINGTON & CHURCH LENCH, WOR, ENG [36171] : PRE 1870 PANDY, HEF, ENG [36178] : WILLIAM PRE 1800

PERSHORE, WOR, ENG [36190] : PRE 1900
DAWLEY & MALINS LEE, SAL, ENG [36196] :
1850-1900 BOLTON, LAN, ENG [36198] : WILLIAM
HENRY 1903+ NEWINGTON, SRY, ENG [36212] :
JAMES WALTER 1810+ CON, ENG [36239] :
MARY 1854 BILSTON, STS, ENG [36253] :
CAROLINE 1810+ MARYLEBONE, MDX, ENG
[36367] : PRE 1850 SEDGLEY, STS, ENG [36379] :
WILLIAM PRE 1840 MDX, ENG [36388] : PRE 1800
SHEFFIELD, WRY, ENG [36480] : MARY 1890+
CHESTER, CHS, ENG [36523] : JOHN 1750-1825
BRISTOL CO., SOM, ENG [36555] : 1600-1850
BRIDGNORTH, SAL, ENG [36556] : EDWARD 1800
TREFONEN & OSWESTRY, SAL, ENG [36568] :
1830+ OLDHAM, LAN, ENG [36568] : 1690-1740
HEADLEY & KINGSLEY, HAM, ENG [36595] :
EDWARD C1840 WOR, ENG [36759] : JOSEPH
C1819-1840 TIPTON, STS, ENG [36838] : JOSEPH
1839 DUDLEY, WOR, ENG [36838] : PRE 1855
COLCHESTER, ESS, ENG [36876] : WILLIAM 1800
IGHTHAM, KEN, ENG [36887] : PRE 1900 NTH,
ENG [36893] : ELIZABETH PRE 1836 DERBY, DBY,
ENG [36980] : JOSEPH PRE 1914 OXF, ENG [36996]
: 1760+ CHALFONT ST PETER, BKM, ENG [37122]
: ISAAC ALL MEDWAY, KEN, ENG [37228] :
1800+ CHS, ENG [37306] : PRE 1810 HEF & SAL,
ENG [37331] : 1840 STAFFORD, STS, ENG [37388] :
1770+ LAN, ENG [37482] : WILLIAM 1789-1814
MDX, ENG [37553] : PRE 1900 MAIDSTONE, KEN,
ENG [37561] : 1863+ DERBY, DBY, ENG [37662] :
SARAH C1800-1900 PONTESBURY, SAL, ENG
[37681] : PRE 1875 GUILDFORD, SRY, ENG [37753]
: 1700-1800 ALVESCOT, OXF, ENG [37763] : MARY
JANE 1886 LIVERPOOL, LAN, ENG [37769] : PRE
1750 BETTWS Y CRWYN, SAL, ENG [37816] :
DAVID MORGAN 1810+ WALTERSTONE, HEF,
ENG [37827] : 1600-1800 POULSHOT, WIL, ENG
[37843] : GEORGE C1850 DAWLEY, SAL, ENG
[37883] : ANNIE 1887+ BOURNEMOUTH, HAM,
ENG [37886] : WM. & MARY C. 1855+
HEREFORD, HEF, ENG [37886] : THOMAS PRE
1900 BRAMPTON BIERLOW, WRY, ENG [37979] :
1820-50 LONDON, ENG [38073] : 1700-1900
BIRMINGHAM, WAR, ENG [38321] : 1700-C1740S
LOUGHTON & WHADDON, BKM, ENG [38358] :
EVAN 1750-1850 FITZ, SAL, ENG [38453] : DAVID
& D.L. 1870+ WARRINGTON, LAN, ENG [38539] :
EDITH ROSE PRE 1900 GILLINGHAM, KEN,
ENG & CAN [34481] : JAMES C1810+ WIL, ENG &
FRA [36086] : GEORGE VICARS ALL READING,
BRK, ENG & NZ [33981] : JAMES C1836
CHELMSFORD & TEMPLETON, ESS & CANT,
ENG & NZ [34622] : CATHERINE C1878-1913
LIVERPOOL, LAN, ENG & WLS [34622] : 1700-
1900S LAN & CHS, ENG & WLS [37221] : PRE 1830
OAKENGATES, SAL & STS, ENG & WLS [38254] :
GEORGE C1850 NEWRY, ARM, IRL [34006] :
MARY JANE 1860-1880S BELFAST, ANT, IRL
[34018] : C1840 MAY, IRL [34189] : PRE 1840
BALLYMORE, ARM, IRL [34835] : PRE 1850 WIC,
IRL [34874] : FRANCIS 1600-1700 LEX, IRL [36898] :
PRE 1860 PORTADOWN, ARM, IRL [38262] :
SUSAN C1830 COR, IRL & AUS [35592] :
ELIZABETH 1800+ IRL & WLS [35784] : ALL
INVERCARGILL, NZ [34603] : SAMUEL 1840S-1868
MOTUEKA, NLN, NZ [34622] : 1840-1900
WELLINGTON, WN, NZ [36773] : 1840-1900
DUNEDIN, OTAGO, NZ [36773] : JOSEPH 1843
WANGANUI, NZ [36838] : JOSEPH 1840
WELLINGTON, NZ [36838] : CATHERINE 1875+
GLASGOW, SCT & AUS [38564] : ALL ESS & SFK,

UK [37674] : 1750+ VA, USA [33761] : 1840+
FOUNTAIN CO., IN, USA [35262] : MATILDA
LYDIA C1794-1848 LINCOLN CO., ME, USA [35263]
: 1840-1920 ALBANY, NY, USA [35300] :
ELIZABETH ALL LA RUE CO., KY, USA [35304] :
1800+ HANFORD, OH & CA, USA [35313] : MARY
ANNA 1853+ SUSSEX CO., DE, USA [36319] :
1750+ PHILADELPHIA, PA, USA [36347] :
MARTHA 1800 ELBERT, GA, USA [36946] : 1864+
CIVIL WAR, USA [36965] : 1864-1880
SWITZERLAND CO., IN, USA [36965] : WILLIAM
1850S ST LOUIS, MO, USA [36974] : ROBERT
1785+ COLUMBIA CO. & RICHMOND CO., GA,
USA [37003] : PRESTON KING C1850 UTICA, NY,
USA [37017] : C.V. 1921+ CHICAGO, IL, USA
[37526] : PRE 1780 MD, USA [37587] : 1833-1900S VA
& TX, USA [37812] : 1744-1780 ALBEMARLE CO.,
VA, USA [38107] : ALFRED SNR. 1805+ GA, USA
[38125] : ABSOLOM 1860 MARSHALL CO., IL, USA
[38132] : BURR RICH. 1882-1904 BARABOO, SAUK
CO., WI, USA [38145] : THOMAS C1795-C1840 OH &
IN, USA [38324] : C1750-1850 WASHINGTON CO.,
PA & MD, USA [38325] : 1890S LUZERNE CO., PA,
USA [38339] : PRE 1860 OH, USA [38363] : SILAS
1850+ DELAWARE CO., IN, USA [38374] : SILAS
1815+ DE, USA [38374] : SILAS 1894 DEXTER,
STODDARD CO., MO, USA [38374] : SILAS 1841+
ROSS CO., OH, USA [38374] : SILAS 1851+
HUNTINGTON CO., IN, USA [38374] : CHARLES
A. C1800 PHILADELPHIA, PA, USA [38533] : C1820
FESTINIOG, MER, WLS [33918] : BENJAMIN
C1870+ MAESTEG, GLA, WLS [33922] : WILLIAM
C1840+ CMN, WLS [33922] : ANN C1810+
TRETOWER & CRICKHOWELL, BRE, WLS [33922]
: 1840-1862 NEWPORT, MGY, WLS [34050] : MARY
1810+ LLANDDEW, BRE, WLS [34134] : GWEN
1700+ CRICARDAN, BRE, WLS [34134] : PRE 1850
LLANFYRNACH, PEM, WLS [34311] : EDWARD
PRE 1815 PANDY BODR, FLN, WLS [34370] : 1850-
1900 RHYD-Y-FOEL, DEN, WLS [34411] : ROBERT
C1851 WLS [34553] : EMILY 1840-1880 CHEPSTOW,
MON, WLS [34637] : LLEWELLYN 1815+
ABERDARE, GLA, WLS [34954] : 1815 BRECON,
BRE, WLS [35066] : MOSES C1800 WLS [35178] :
1750+ DEN, WLS [35377] : 1750+ CAE, WLS [35377]
: 1850S MAESTAG, GLA, WLS [35390] : DAVID
C1816 TALGARTH, BRE, WLS [35391] : PRE 1858
CLANGERNEW, DEN, WLS [35727] : 1820S
ABERDARE, GLA, WLS [35728] : WILLIAM 1819-
1893 MERTHYR TYDFIL, GLA, WLS [35784] :
LORANDO 1819-1893 MERTHYR TYDFIL, GLA,
WLS [35784] : WATKIN 1820+ MERTHYR
TYDFIL, GLA, WLS [35784] : ERNEST 1883+
LLANDUDNO, CAE, WLS [35848] : 1857
WAENLLYS, MGY, WLS [35854] : PRE 1880
LLANFYLLIN, MGY, WLS [35854] : GOMER PRE
1900 WLS [35954] : PRE 1840 LLANGUNLLO, RAD,
WLS [36110] : PRE 1850 BRYNSIENCYN, AGY,
WLS [36168] : PRE 1870 ABERGAVENY, MON,
WLS [36178] : C1844 BASSALLEG, MON, WLS
[36185] : 1750+ NEATH, GLA, WLS [36209] :
HIRAM 1850 PEN-Y-CRAIG, GLA, WLS [36443] :
PRE 1900 CONWAY, CAE, WLS [36518] : WILLIAM
C1820-1896 LLANAELHAEURN & TALSARNAU,
CAE & MER, WLS [36590] : JANE C1740 NEFYN,
CAE, WLS [36590] : GRIFFITH 1860+
RHOSHIRWAN, CAE, WLS [36590] : HANNAH
1800+ VALE OF CLWYD, DEN, WLS [36614] : PRE
1840 HAWARDEN & EWLOE, FLN, WLS [36849] :
REV WILLIAM 1840+ NEFYN, CAE, WLS [36885] :
1884-1937 SWANSEA, WLS [36910] : DAVID 1849
YSPYTTY, DEN & CAE, WLS [37147] : 1826+

CRICEITH, CAE, WLS **[37147]** : 1850+ YSPYTTY, DEN & CAE, WLS **[37147]** : MARY 1761 BRONANT, CGN, WLS **[37250]** : JOHN 1700S CWM RHEIDOL, CGN, WLS **[37250]** : JOSEPH PRE 1840 BANGOR, CAE, WLS **[37261]** : PRE 1840 ANGLESEY, AGY, WLS **[37484]** : ANNE 1794 ABERGELE, DEN, WLS **[37649]** : MATILDA C1840-1920 SWANSEA, GLA, WLS **[37813]** : EVAN PRE 1831 LLANFYLLIN, MGY, WLS **[37897]** : 1820+ MOLD, FLN, WLS **[37908]** : 1850+ WREXHAM, DEN, WLS **[37908]** : 1800-1870 LLANWNOG, MGY, WLS **[37934]** : 1780-1810 TREFEGLWYS, MGY, WLS **[37934]** : RICHARD C1800 RHAYADER, RAD, WLS **[37944]** : JOHN 1636-1660 MAES-Y GARNEDD, MER, WLS **[38145]** : PRE 1875 FLN, WLS **[34337]** : 1750-1850 LLANBRYNMAIR, MGY, WLS **[38524]** : ALL FLN, WLS & AUS **[35213]** : CAPT GRIFFITH 1819-1867 NEFYN & HULL, CAE & ERY, WLS & ENG **[36590]** : 1820+ LLANELLI, CMN, WLS & NZ **[36257]**

JONES-PRITCHARD 1871+ MELBOURNE, VIC, AUS **[36611]**

JONES-ROSWELL 1800 RUTLAND CO., VT, USA **[36925]**

JONETT 1750-1837 HARDEN, WRY, ENG **[37278]**

JONKVORST 1730-1830 ZWARTSLUIS, OIJ, NL **[34398]**

JONS 1706 BATTLE, SSX, ENG **[35260]**

JONSDOTTER PRE 1850 TVARRED, ALVSBORG, SWE **[35324]**

JONSON PRE 1900 MELBOURNE, VIC, AUS **[35435]**

JONSSON ALL BYN, BRUNSKOG, SWE **[36881]** : EMIL PRE 1884 BEXHEDA JONKOPING, SWE **[38543]** : IDA PRE 1884 BEXHEDA JONKOPING, SWE **[38543]** : SMEDMAN OLOF 1752+ SMEDSERUD, SWE **[38549]** : IDA 1884 NEW YORK, NY, USA **[38543]** : EMIL 1884 NEW YORK, NY, USA **[38543]**

JONZEN 1850+ NEWCASTLE, NSW, AUS **[37310]**

JOOST C1755 WANFRIED WERRA, HES, BRD **[38659]**

JOPLEN ALL WORLDWIDE **[36474]**

JOPLING PRE 1865 SCHUYLKILL CO., PA, USA **[37574]**

JORANSDOTTER ANNA PRE 1720 MALMO, SWE **[38553]**

JORDAN 1860+ MELBOURNE & SHEPPARTON, VIC, AUS **[33793]** : C1834 EVAN, NSW, AUS **[35090]** : PRE 1900 KINDRED & FORTH, TAS, AUS **[35433]** : C1900 TUNGAMAH, VIC, AUS **[35434]** : PRE 1852 MUSWELLBROOK, NSW, AUS **[35781]** : 1800+ VALENTIA, ONT, CAN **[34169]** : ED. 1845+ ONT, CAN **[37438]** : PRE 1800 HACKNEY, MDX & LND, ENG **[34177]** : 1872 BEDFORD, BDF, ENG **[34761]** : 1800+ WOR, ENG **[35812]** : C1750 COVENTRY, WAR, ENG **[36635]** : ABRAHAM PRE 1793 LIVERPOOL, LAN, ENG **[37769]** : PRE 1800 SSX, ENG **[37771]** : 1750-1850 HRT, ENG **[37829]** : 1800 SHOREDITCH, LND, ENG **[37928]** : 1700-1860 STROUD, GLS, ENG **[38003]** : PRE 1806 BALLYNAHINCH, DOW, IRL **[34169]** : PRE 1836 LIM, IRL **[34959]** : PRE 1874 DUBLIN, IRL **[35761]** : LYDIA 1875-1900 IRL **[38383]** : 1820-1890 BROWN CO., OH, USA **[33760]** : 1790+ BROWN CO., OH, USA **[35278]** : 1782 NEW ASHFORD, MA, USA **[37594]** : 1750-1850 ULSTER CO., NY, USA **[37783]** : 1822 RUSSELL CO., VA, USA **[38151]** : 1855-70 AL, USA **[38151]** : 1800-50 BOSTON, SUFFOLK CO., MA, USA **[38153]** : 1820-1848 OXFORD CO., ME, USA **[38201]**

JORDEN PRE 1700 OXF, ENG **[36183]** : C1850 KIDDERMINSTER, WOR, ENG **[37556]**

JORDON PRE 1850 MD & OH, USA **[34116]**

JORGENSEN PRE 1870 COPENHAGEN, DEN **[33968]** : PRE 1873 VJELBY, DEN **[35767]** : 1800+ RORAS, S TRNDLG, NOR **[36326]** : PRE 1800 NESNA, NORDLAND, NOR **[36326]**

JORINI 1800S MILAN, ITL **[35491]**

JORY 1800+ WENDRON, CON, ENG **[36785]**

JOSE 1858+ GEELONG, VIC, AUS **[37109]** : 1735 KENWYN, CON, ENG **[34214]** : 1831+ CON, ENG **[37109]**

JOSENHANS ALL WORLDWIDE **[36922]**

JOSEPH ALL ENG **[34318]** : 1750 VECHTA, OLD, GER **[37509]** : PRE 1695 STOCKHOLM, SWE **[37036]** : 1813+ BRIDGEND, GLA, WLS **[34684]**

JOSEY ALL ENG **[37416]**

JOSLIN PRE 1850 TORONTO, ONT, CAN **[34222]** : MARY 1666 LANCASTER, MA, USA **[36944]**

JOSLING C1840 ONT, CAN **[35398]** : 1800-1860 ENG **[35398]** : 1880S PLYMOUTH, DEV, ENG **[37773]** : PRE 1750 BARNSTAPLE & ASHREIGNEY, DEV, ENG **[37773]**

JOSLYN 1760-1800 BERKSHIRE CO., MA, USA **[37013]** : C1810-40 KNOX CO., OH, USA **[38173]**

JOULE PRE 1820 CHS, ENG **[37650]** : ALL WORLDWIDE **[34588]**

JOURNEAUX PRE 1840 GROUVILLE, JSY, CHI **[36696]**

JOWETT 1900+ SURBITON, SRY, ENG **[36300]** : PRE 1823 WAKEFIELD, YKS, ENG **[37383]** : C1870 BIRKENSHAW, YKS, ENG **[38168]**

JOWITT PRE 1800 BURTON SALMON, YKS, ENG **[37463]**

JOWSEY JOSEPHINE C1837 OLD STREET, LND, ENG **[36225]**

JOY PRE 1850 ALVERDISCOTT, DEV, ENG **[36516]** : PRE 1850 CHRISTCHURCH, HAM, ENG **[37173]** : 1860-1918 CREWKERNE, SOM, ENG **[37709]** : 1820-1920 ISLINGTON, MDX, ENG **[37757]** : 1810S IA, USA **[36729]**

JOYCE 1880+ PORTLAND, VIC, AUS **[38213]** : 1864 WINDSOR, NSW, AUS **[38288]** : 1850+ WHITCHURCH TWP., ONT, CAN **[34259]** : C1840+ TYENDINAGA & BELLEVILLE, ONT, CAN **[35466]** : PRE 1965 TORONTO, ONT, CAN **[37611]** : 1800S LONDON, ENG **[34871]** : PRE 1874 HAM, ENG **[36282]** : 1850-1940 BIRMINGHAM, WAR, ENG **[36349]** : ALL LND, ENG **[36805]** : 1905+ SOUTHWARK, SRY, ENG **[37611]** : C1800 FULHAM, LND, ENG **[37770]** : 1836 LND, ENG **[38288]** : 1800+ INDIA **[35963]** : PRE 1845 MUCKALEE, KIK, IRL **[34259]** : PRE 1796+ WESTPORT, MAY, IRL **[34423]** : PRE 1800 ARMAGH, IRL **[37474]** : 1850-1870 GALWAY, GAL, IRL **[38763]** : PRE 1820 WESTPORT, MAY, IRL & AUS **[35056]** : 1874+ WAIMATE, NZ **[36282]** : PRE 1870 PER, SCT & IRL **[37496]** : 1750-1900S VA, NC, GA, LA, USA **[37812]**

JOYNER 1850+ SYDNEY, NSW, AUS **[35373]** : 1880+ SYDNEY, NSW, AUS **[37942]** : PRE 1800 WORMINGHALL, BKM & OXF, ENG **[36502]** : PRE 1880 TUAM, GAL, IRL **[37942]**

JOYNES ALL NORTHAMPTON CO., VA, USA **[36557]**

JOYNT ALL MAY, IRL **[36196]**

JUBB PRE 1770 KELFIELD, LIN, ENG **[33992]**

JUBBER ALL WORLDWIDE **[36871]**

JUCHEREAU 1500S LA FERTE & VIDAME, FRA **[35617]**

JUDD 1800-1850 ENG **[34422]** : C1800 NORTHWOOD, HAM, ENG **[34812]** : PRE 1860 BRIGHTON, SSX, ENG **[35128]** : PRE 1700 ESS, ENG **[35642]** : 1880+ SWINDON, WIL, ENG **[36118]** : 1700-1850 LEIRE, LEI, ENG **[36410]** : PRE 1885 NOTTINGHAM, NTT, ENG **[37725]** : 1600-1700 LANGLEY, ESS, ENG

[37783] : PRE 1812 COVENTRY, WAR, ENG [38512] : C1650 MA, USA [34395] : PRE 1720S CT, MA & NY, USA [37522] : 1800-1850 NY, USA [38529] : ALL WORLDWIDE [36548]

JUDE 1811 HEIGHAM & LAKENHAM, NFK, ENG [36263] : ALL LONGBENTON, NBL & DUR, ENG [37129]

JUDEFEIND PRE 1916 HBG, GER [38669]

JUDEIKIS PRE 1900 LITHUANIA [36136]

JUDGE 1846+ WEST MAITLAND, NSW, AUS [35088] : 1750+ TYSOE, WAR, ENG [34435] : ALL SSX, ENG [34980] : ALL NTH, ENG [36179] : 1800 ARMAGH, ARM, IRL [35186]

JUDKINS 1700+ ME, USA [38116]

JUDSON 1860+ WEST HARTLEPOOL, DUR, ENG [34333] : PRE 1820 STANGROUND, CAM, ENG [34884] : C1800 PETERBOROUGH, CAM, ENG [34884] : 1764 NORTH FERRIBY, YKS, ENG [35737] : PRE 1850 LND, ENG [37731] : ALL HOVINGHAM, YKS, ENG [37744]

JUERGENS PRE 1817 BRAUNSCHWEIG, BSW, GER [38608] : 1700+ HEIDE, SHO, GER [38608] : 1706 MASPE, GER [38749] : 1794 BLOMBERG, PYR, GER [38749]

JUFFES CAROLINE 1800S LONG COMPTON, OXF, ENG [35876]

JUGERE 1800 QUE, CAN [35272] : C1814 QUE, CAN [37030]

JUGGINS 1740-1760 LONDON, ENG [34230]

JUKE 1833 WICKLOW, WIC, IRL [35903]

JUKES 1800+ DUDLEY, WOR, ENG [35342] : 1800+ TIPTON, STS, ENG [35972] : 1850S TIPTON, STS, ENG [36528]

JUKES (SEE JEWKES) [35967]

JULEFF ALL WORLDWIDE [35082]

JULIAN JOHN 1853 MACLEAY RV DIST., NSW, AUS [35816] : JOHN PRE 1853 WITHIEL, CON, ENG [35816] : 1800+ LIZARD AREA, CON, ENG [37913]

JULIER 1800+ BETHNAL GREEN, LND, ENG [35006]

JULL C1870 KEN, ENG [33809] : ALL ENG [35868]

JULYAN PRE 1740 ST EWE, CON, ENG [34139]

JUMAN 1869+ NEWPORT, IOW, ENG [35459] : 1875+ BRIGHTON, SSX, ENG [35459] : C1811 CALCUTTA, INDIA [35459] : PRE 1869 NEWPORT & TIPPERARY, TIP, IRL [35459]

JUNG PRE 1830 STRASBOURG, ELO, GER [37820] : PHILIPP PRE 1725 OFFENTHAL, HES, GER [38181] : PRE 1650 OSTHEIM & HANAU, HES, GER [38348] : JOHANN PRE 1680 BUCHHOLZ, WEF, GER [38631] : 1608+ BROKREIHE BEI HODORF, SHO, GER [38667] : PRE 1850 HOERINGEN, RPF, GER [38681] : 1641+ MONNICKENDAM, NL [38667] : 1840+ GERMANTOWN, WI, USA [38530] : ALL WORLDWIDE [34318]

JUNGBECK PRE 1860 ZEHOLFING, BAV, GER [38191]

JUNGE PRE 1700 KETTENBACH, GER [37587] : 1608+ BROKRETHE BEI HODORF, SHO, GER [38667] : 1641+ MONNICKENDAM, NL [38667]

JUNGEN ALL KOBLENZ, RPR, GER [38637]

JUNGERT PRE 1660 HUFFENHARDT, WUE, GER [36972]

JUNGIUS 1608+ BROKREIHE BEI HODORF, SHO, GER [38667] : 1641+ MONNICKENDAM, NL [38667]

JUNGJOHANN PRE 1800 RUSSEE, SHO, BRD [35809]

JUNKEN JANET C1740+ ELGIN, MOR, SCT [35848]

JUNKIN ALL IRL [34280] : ALL WORLDWIDE [38533]

JUNKINS SUSANNAH 1750+ YORK, ME, USA [36563]

JUPE ALL NUTHURST, SSX, ENG [37054] : 1750+ CUCKLINGTON, SOM, ENG [37756]

JUPP 1920-1940 BRIGHTON, SSX, ENG [34384] : 1850+ MEDWAY RIVER "BARGEMEN", KEN, ENG [34810] : PRE 1840 HORSHAM, SSX, ENG [34873] : PRE 1810 SSX, ENG [35238] : 1600-1800 HORSHAM, SSX, ENG [35445] : 1830+ ICHINGFIELD, SSX, ENG [35543] : ALL NUTHURST, SSX, ENG [37054] : ALL ENG [37214] : 1850-1940 WELLINGTON, NZ [34641]

JUPPE ALL NUTHURST, SSX, ENG [37054]

JURAN ALL SLOVAKIA, CS [34634]

JURKOVIC VLAIC ALL GABELA, BOSNIA & HERC, YU [36775]

JURY ALL SOM, ENG [34730] : PRE 1826 KEN, ENG [38389]

JUST C1852 LEIPZIG, LPZ, DDR [38631]

JUSTICE PRE 1827 MACCLESFIELD, CHS, ENG [33862] : 1827+ ALL SAINTS, HUN, ENG [33862] : ALL DROMARA, DOW, IRL [34627] : 1859+ DUNEDIN, OTAGO, NZ [33957] : PRE 1856 PERTH, PER, SCT [33957] : PRE 1850 PERTH, PER, SCT [37832] : 1850-1900 COOSA, AL, USA [36735] : 1850 DALE, AL, USA [36735] : 1795-1830 JONES, GA, USA [36735]

JUSTIN 1830+ DROMARA, DOW, IRL [35219]

JUSTINS ALL WORLDWIDE [33913]

JUSTIS 1650+ DELAWARE, PA, USA [37826]

JUTTEN ALL WORLDWIDE [37371]

JUTTON ALL WORLDWIDE [37371]

JUX ALL NUTHURST, SSX, ENG [37054]

JUZAN GABRIEL 1730S JUSAN, PYRENEES, FRA [37585] : PETER PRE 1770 MOBILE, AL, USA [35328] : PIERRE 1780S MOBLINE, AL, USA [37585]

KAARSTAD PRE 1880 UTVIK, NORDFJORD, NOR [37821]

KABAT PRE 1880 GDANSK, GD, POL [36941]

KABLE JOHN PRE 1800 JEFFERSON, WV, USA [37023]

KACENAK PRE 1900 CZ, POL [36575] : 1900+ NY, USA [36575]

KACHEL 1950-1965 FRANKFURT, HES, GER [38679]

KADEL PRE 1750 NEULUSSHEIM, BAD, GER [38681]

KADING 1750-1850 PRE, GER [38342]

KADWELL 1400-1850 KEN, ENG [36383] : ALL WORLDWIDE [36517]

KAEGELER PRE 1880 GENTIN, MAG, GER [34588]

KAGIN PRE 1850 SAINTFIELD, DOW, IRL [36760]

KAGINBURGIN PRE 1800 BERLIN, PA, USA [37010]

KAHANEK 1850-70 CS [38314]

KAHL 1909+ ROCKHAMPTON, QLD, AUS [33920] : PAULINE PRE 1890S PRESTON, ONT, CAN [34216]

KAHLER 1800+ ZIELBECK, LUE, GER [37170]

KAHLER (SEE KOEHLER) [37511]

KAHN 1700+ ARHEILGEN, HEN, GER [37042] : PRE 1870 ESCHWEGER, SAX, GER [37931] : PRE 1870 HALBERSTADT, GER [37931] : 1800-1900 ERIE CO., PA, USA [38588]

KAHNT ALL WORLDWIDE [38431]

KAIFFER 1750-1900 ALS, FRA & USA [38574]

KAIN 1825S COR, IRL [35416] : PRE 1840 CLARE, IRL [35532]

KAINES C1814 GSY, CHI [35478] : C1800 MANSTON, DOR, ENG [33937] : PRE 1870 LND, ENG [35709] : C1850 LAMBETH, LND, ENG [38276]

KAINZ 1850+ AUGSBERG, BAV, GER [38534] : 1889+ MARATHON & SHAWANO COS., WI, USA [38534]

KAISER 1800 BRUSSEL, BEL [33751] : 1800 BRUSSELS, BEL [38692] : ALL NORFOLK CO., VA, USA [36557] : 1830-1900 CINCINNATI, OH, USA [38149]

KAITAJARVI 1888-1930 NEW YORK, NY, USA [38757]

KALBER 1600+ OEDHEIM, GER [35566]

KALFF JACOB J. 1920 DEN HELDER, NL [36782] :
CHRISTOPHER 1870 DEN HELDER, NL [36782]

KALLEN 1600-1700 FRUTIGEN, BE, CH [35283]

KALLENBACH 1800+ HESSE DARMSKEDT, KSA,
GER [37001] : 1850-1860S CASS CO., IL, USA [37001]

KALLWEIT PRE 1800 DEDEN, OPR, GER [33901]

KALMS PRE 1855 PRAUSCHWITZ, POS, GER [34766]

KALTENBACH ALL SCHELINGEN, BAD, GER
[38534]

KALTENBERGER 1868+ SU [38058]

KALTENECKER ALL GER & USA [37036]

KALWAR ALL WORLDWIDE [38682]

KALWIET (SEE KALLWEI [33901]

KALWIG ALL WORLDWIDE [37718]

KAMPERMAN 1795+ HOOGEVEEN, DRN, NL
[34398] : 1640+ GORSSEL, GEL, NL [34398] : 1760+
HOLTEN, OIJ, NL [34398]

KAMPS 1800 SITTARD, LBG, NL [38167] : ALL
WORLDWIDE [36922]

KANALY 1840+ SUSQUEHANNA CO., PA & NY,
USA [35299]

KANANOVICH 1890-1920 VILNA, LITHUANIA
[38123] : 1910-1950 SOUHT RIVER, NJ, USA [38123]

KANE C1840 HAWKESBURY RV, NSW, AUS [35434] :
1854-1910 WOODEND, VIC, AUS [37156] : 1800+
SHO, BRD [34703] : 1870+ OLDHAM, LAN, ENG
[34790] : 1812 LND, ENG [35434] : PATRICK 1860-
1900 WALSALL, STS, ENG [37632] : PRE 1900
BANBRIDGE, DOW, IRL [35962] : PRE 1850 LIM,
IRL [36325] : PATRICK 1800+ DUNMORE, WEX,
IRL [37632] : JOHN 1800S IRL [37800] : TERESA
1885+ NEWRY, ARM, IRL [38233] : JAMES 1860S
WEM, IRL [38233] : DAVID 1870S KILBEGGAN,
WEM, IRL [38233] : AUGUSTIN 1895+ ARM, IRL
[38233] : 1900+ CHICAGO, IL, USA [36325] : JOHN
LEO 1891-1951 PORT RICHMOND, NY, USA
[37800]

KANEY 1820 BAD, GER [37799]

KANGLEY 1850-1900 WILL CO., IL, USA [38154] :
1900-1950 HAWK EYE, IA, USA [38154] : 1930-1970
WATERLOO, IA, USA [38154] : 1900-1950 WEST
UNION, IA, USA [38154]

KANMACHER PRE 1850 ELO, GER [38437]

KANNENBERG PRE 1870 PRE [38217]

KAPHEIM 1848 MEK, GER [34468]

KAPITZ PRE 1700 BOEMISCHDORF, SIL, GER
[33901]

KAPLAN PRE 1900 BIERSS, KOVNA, LITHUANIA
[36455]

KAPMEIER PRE 1800 RINTELN, NSA, BRD [37513]

KAPPENBERG 1700+ BOTTROP, WEF, GER [38651]

KAPPIE ALL NEW YORK, NY, USA [35468]

KAPPMEYER ALL WORLDWIDE [38189]

KAPPS ALL SINDOLSHEIM, BAW, BRD [35264]

KARCHER PRE 1690 HEN, GER [38669]

KARGER 1830S WILDENOW, PRE, GER [34957]

KARI 1700-1800 FRUTIGEN, BE, CH [35283]

KARKKAINEN ALL MYLLYKOSKI, KYMI, FIN
[35334]

KARL 1764-1900 WALTER, SARATOV, SU [36958]

KARLSSON 1900+ STOCKHOLM, SWE [36138]

KARMODY PRE 1880 INDIA [36955]

KARN 1864 SOUTH KENSINGTON, LND, ENG
[37694]

KARNEY FRANCIS 1794-1868 STREETSVILLE, ONT,
CAN [34524]

KARP ALL POL [38481]

KARPF 1840 BRD, GER [38221] : 1840+ CO & TX,
USA [38221]

KARR 1800-1860 WILLIAMSBURG, NY, USA [38523]

KARRAN ANN C1850 IOM [34215]

KARRICK 1800-1900 BATH CO., KY, USA [38089]

KARST 1880+ CHRISTCHURCH, CANT, NZ [34643]

KARSTENS 1700+ WEDDINGSTEDT, SHO, GER
[37542]

KARTHEISER 1750-1810 COOK CO., IL, USA [38024]

KASA 1400-1850 NISSEDAL, TELEMARK, NOR
[35292]

KASLER 1800-1900 GROβ BUCHWALDE,
OSTPREUβEN, GER [38603]

KASPRZYK 1930 GOLDAP, OPR, GER [35082]

KASSEL PRE 1725 OVL, BEL [38697]

KASSELL ALL OPPELN, POL [38379]

KATELY PRE 1850 SSX, ENG [35438]

KATES (SEE CATES) [35106]

KATESBY C1802 NSW, AUS [38485]

KATHSTEDE ALL NRW, FRG [38717]

KATONA ALL UNGVAR & UZOROD, HU [36532]

KATTLER ALL SATULMARE, BUKOVINA, RO
[34488]

KATZ 1600-1900 PHILADELPHIA, PA, USA [36689]

KATZE (SEE KATZ) [36689]

KAUFFMAN 1750-1760 BERKS, PA, USA [36908] : ALL
GERMAN YORK CO., PA, USA & CH [38197]

KAUFMANN 1870-1990 MILWAUKEE, WI, USA
[38588]

KAUFNER 1878S MELBOURNE, VIC, AUS [35593]

KAUL 1750+ SINSHEIM & ELSENZ, BAW, GER
[38609] : PRE 1800 WORMS, RPF, GER [38609]

KAUPP 1700-1800 HILDRIZHAUSEN, WUE, GER
[38652]

KAVANAGH 1900-1990 MELBOURNE & MALDON,
VIC, AUS [33778] : 1847-1890 ADELAIDE, SA, AUS
[34025] : 1800+ GLENGARRY, ONT, CAN [35614] :
PRE 1841 ENNISCORTHY, WEX, IRL [35088]

KAVANAUGH 1750+ CAR & WEX, IRL [36343]

KAVELMAN PRE 1860 MAG, GER [36726]

KAVENY C1847 CLA, IRL [34652]

KAY 1818-C1900 NEWCASTLE & MOREE, NSW, AUS
[37556] : 1820+ TOTTINGTON, LAN, ENG [35937] :
1770 BURY, LAN, ENG [36032] : 1810
DUKINFIELD, CHS, ENG [36032] : C1830
WARMINGTON, WAR, ENG [36370] : 1800+
RAINTON, YKS, ENG [36791] : C1830 WINCHAM,
CHS, ENG [36806] : C1795-C1818 LANCASTER,
LAN & YKS, ENG [37556] : 1780+ CHAIGLEY,
LAN, ENG [38020] : 1800 MIDDLETON TYAS,
NRY, ENG [38379] : PRE 1850 MAROWN, IOM
[36260] : PRE 1850 HAMILTON, LKS, SCT [34097] :
1810+ DYSART, FIF, SCT [34542] : C1800
OCHILTREE, AYR, SCT [34713]

KAY (SEE HAY) [34956]

KAYE 1869+ BEECHWORTH, VIC, AUS [34577] :
1870+ ELTHAM & N FITZROY, VIC, AUS [35059] :
JOSEPH 1770+ EMLEY, WRY, ENG [34181] : 1800-
1900 SKELMANTHORPE, YKS, ENG [37495]

KAYS C1870 SOUTH ISLAND, NZ [34767]

KAYSER PRE 1700 NIEDER DORFELDEN, HES,
GER [38348]

KAZSAS ALL LAGY, VALPALFARA, HU [36695]

KAZY ALL NEW YORK, NY, USA [35468]

KEABLE 1780+ SIBTON, SFK, ENG [38291]

KEACH 1833+ CAMPBELL TOWN, TAS, AUS [34280]
: 1832+ HOBART, TAS, AUS [36855] : PRE 1900
LONDON, ENG [34280] : PRE 1832 LONDON, ENG
[36855]

KEADY C1845 WASHINGTON CO., IL, USA [37817]

KEAL (SEE KELL) [34532]

KEALEY 1800+ GATINEAU CO., QUE, CAN [34199] :
1850+ CARLETON CO., ONT, CAN [34199]

KEALO 1905+ VIC, AUS [35193]

KEAM C1847 PENZANCE, CON, ENG [34893]

KEAN HENRY 1821 LONDON, ENG [34176] :
CHRISTOPHER PRE 1837 EXETER, DEV, ENG
[37954] : 1870+ BELFAST, ANT, DOW & ARM, IRL
[35636] : C1767 LINCOLN CO., ME, USA [35263]

KEANE 1850-1910 BACCHUS MARSH, VIC, AUS
[37156] : 1840 MELBOURNE, VIC, AUS [37163] :
HENRY 1821 LONDON, ENG [34176] : 1800+
WALSALL, STS, ENG [37632] : 1800+
BALLYLANDERS, LIM, IRL [34453] : 1840 CLA,
IRL [35067] : PRE 1850 ENNISTYMON, CLA, IRL
[35095] : PRE 1900 KILFYAN, MAY, IRL [35181] :
PRE 1880 CLA, IRL [35814] : ALL TIP, IRL [36854] :
PRE 1886 CAPPOQUIN, WAT, IRL [37113] : 1800+
GLASGOW, LKS, SCT [36875]

KEARFOOT 1800+ VA & MD, USA [37478]

KEARLEY 1800+ HERMITAGE BAY, NFD, CAN
[36684] : 1730+ BLANDFORD FORUM, DOR, ENG
[37056] : 1730+ TARRANT GUNVILLE, DOR, ENG
[37056] : PRE 1800 CRANBORNE, DOR, ENG
[38700]

KEARNES ALL ENG [37833]

KEARNEY 1870+ CUMNOCK, NSW, AUS [34759] :
1850+ HOBART, TAS, AUS [35459] : 1883
ROCKHAMPTON, QLD, AUS [35769] : C1856 TAS,
AUS [38485] : PRE 1876 LOU, IRL [33871] : PRE 1820
DONOUGHMORE, DON, IRL [35157] : 1860 CORK,
COR, IRL [35769] : C1821 IRL [38485] : PRE 1840
COR, IRL [38777] : 1800-40 ROCHESTER, NY, USA
[37007]

KEARNEY (SEE KARNEY) [34524]

KEARNS C1816 SYDNEY, NSW, AUS [34839] : C1840
MAITLAND, NSW, AUS [35431] : 1850+
BALLARAT, VIC, AUS [35986] : 1890+
LIVERPOOL, LAN, ENG [38274] : BRIDGET 1800-
1821 KILLARNEY, KER & CLA, IRL [33941] :
1800+ KINVARA, GAL, IRL [35201] : C1860
GALWAY, GAL, IRL [35963] : 1850S GAL, IRL
[35986] : PRE 1886 KILMOODS & NEWTONARDS,
DOW, IRL [36509] : 1860+ ROSCOMMON, IRL
[38274]

KEARSE ALL WORLDWIDE [34667]

KEARTON 1850+ AUS [35927] : 1760+ ISLAND OF
ST VINCENT, CARIBBEAN [35927] : 1800+
LONDON, ENG [35927] : 1700+ WIL, ENG [35927] :
1800+ CUL, ENG [35927] : 1800+ ALSTON, CUL,
ENG [35927] : 1800+ BATH, SOM, ENG [35927] :
1500+ NRY, ENG [35927] : 1800+ CHS, ENG
[35927] : 1900+ FRA [35927] : 1800+ USA [35927]

KEARVELL ALL WORLDWIDE [35954]

KEARY PRE 1847 BALLINA, MAY, IRL [37454]

KEAST 1842+ MACLEAY RIVER, NSW, AUS [37119]
: C1800 CALLINGTON, CON, ENG [35494] : PRE
1700 ST NEOT & CLEER, CON, ENG [37434] : PRE
1900 CON, ENG [37749] : 1600+ ST NEOT & ST
CLEER, CON, ENG & AUS [35776]

KEATES 1840+ ONT, CAN [34213] : PRE 1850
CHEADLE, STS, ENG [33954] : EDWARD C1815-
1840 ENGLAND [34213] : 1860+ USA [34213]

KEATING C1881 YOUNG, NSW, AUS [35391] :
C1880+ GIPPSLAND, VIC, AUS [35399] : PRE 1875
PARRAMATTA, NSW, AUS [35399] : C1875
BOMBALA, NSW, AUS [35399] : PRE 1892
BRISTOL, GLS, ENG [35002] : PRE 1830
COOLBAWN & SMITHSTOWN, KIK, IRL [33775] :
PRE 1816 KILKENNY, KIK, IRL [35419] : PRE 1825
WEX, IRL [35424] : 1700+ TIP, IRL [36602] : 1750-
1850 ME, USA [37808]

KEATS 1860-1888 HILLEND & ROCKDALE, NSW,
AUS [35092] : 1843-1860 SWANAGE, DOR, ENG
[35092] : 1830-1880 SRY, ENG [36118]

KEATY C1890 LISGIBBON & CURRANA, TIP, IRL
[37135] : 1864+ BANSHA, TIP, IRL [37135]

KEAY 1900+ MDX & SRY, ENG [36955]

KEAYS 1820-1860 RATHDOWNEY, LEX, IRL [35717]

KEDDIE C1750 HAWICK, ROX, SCT [35038] : 1780+
DYSART, FIF, SCT [35977] : PRE 1780 FIF, SCT
[36679] : 1800+ EDINBURGH, MLN, SCT [37572]

KEDDY 1850+ NS, CAN [36404]

KEDGE 1820+ AUS [36026] : 1700+ CAN [36026] :
1560+ BKM, ENG [36026] : 1800+ BDF, ENG
[36026] : 1780+ FULHAM, LND, ENG [36026] :
1600+ NFK, ENG [36026] : 1600+ LND, ENG
[36026] : 1800+ ST PANCRAS, LND, ENG [36026] :
1800+ LIN, ENG [36026] : 1750+ ESS, ENG [36026] :
1600+ SFK, ENG [36026] : 1700+ SRY, ENG [36026]
: 1800+ KEN, ENG [36026] : 1840+ NZ [36026] :
1945+ RSA [36026] : 1620+ USA [36026]

KEDING 1800+ DANZIG, PRE, GER [34932]

KEDWELL ALL WORLDWIDE [36517]

KEDZIE C1750 HAWICK, ROX, SCT [35038]

KEDZLIE PRE 1856 MUSSELBURGH, MLN, SCT
[35856]

KEEBLE PRE 1830 ALDHAM, SFK, ENG [35406] :
PRE 1800 SFK, ENG [36050] : 1750+ BROCKFORD,
SFK, ENG [37262] : 1800S MARKSTEY &
KELVEDON, ESS, ENG [37677] : 1870+ WITHAM
& ROMFORD, ESS, ENG [37677] : 1850+ SOHO,
LND, ENG [37677]

KEECH 1800S TOLLER PORCORUM, DOR, ENG
[35964]

KEEFE DANIEL & LUKE 1854+ ALBURY, NSW,
AUS [35357] : DANIEL 1876+ WAGGA WAGGA,
NSW, AUS [35357] : JOHN 1854+ ALBURY, NSW,
AUS [35357] : JOHANNA 1874 NEWMARKET,
COR, IRL [33929] : LUKE PRE 1836 COR, IRL
[35357] : C1833 TULLA, CLA, IRL [35746] : PRE 1860
TIPPERARY, TIP, IRL [36765] : 1750-1850
CASTLEISLAND, KER, IRL [36776] : 1830 CORK,
COR, IRL [38756]

KEEFER 1800-1900 ONT, CAN [37466] : 1800-1830
SOMERSET CO., PA, USA [36901]

KEEGAN ALL AUS [34759] : PRE 1930
ENNISKILLEN, NB, CAN & IRL [38447] : 1815-1895
WEX, IRL [36293]

KEEHN 1853 HUNTER VY, NSW, AUS [33929]

KEEL C1800 KEN, ENG [35045]

KEELE 1850+ MELBOURNE, VIC, AUS [34178] :
1700+ SRY, ENG [36434]

KEELER PRE 1900 LONDON, MDX, ENG [37561] :
PRE 1900 SELLING, KEN, ENG [37561] : 1800+
MONEY CREEK, MN & PA, USA [38764]

KEELEY JOHN C1820 ST GILES, LND, MDX, ENG
[36519] : JOHN PRE 1802 COR, IRL [36519] : JOHN
1802+ COR, IRL [36519] : 1831-1870+ GAL, IRL &
AUS [35497]

KEELING ALL MANCHESTER, LAN, ENG [34837] :
ALL STOCKPORT, CHS, ENG [34837] : 1700S
HANLEY, STS, ENG [35830]

KEELY 1800+ ONT, CAN [34252] : PRE 1860 LND,
ENG [35902] : PRE 1799 CORK CITY, COR, IRL
[34252]

KEEMER 1870 ENG [34757] : 1843 GER [34757]

KEEMISH 1710+ CHERITON, HAM, ENG [36388]

KEEN 1880+ MOLONG, NSW, AUS [34759] : 1750+
WETHERINGSETT, SFK, ENG [34710] : 1800S
TWIDALE, STS, ENG [35409] : C1840+ OXF, ENG
[36258] : 1750+ TAMWORTH, STS & WAR, ENG
[36329] : PRE 1825 RADFORD, NTT, ENG [37000] :
PRE 1890 LIVERPOOL, LAN, ENG [37553] : C1750-
1850 WEYBRIDGE, SRY, ENG [37618] : 1800+
LONDON, ENG [37718] : 1920+ MA, USA [37468] :
ALL WORLDWIDE [37721]

KEENAN FRANCIS 1860+ EMERALD HILL, VIC,
AUS [33956] : 1820-1870 SYDNEY, NSW, AUS

[34306] : 1827 BOWENFELS, NSW, AUS [34788] : 1833 + MELBOURNE & IPSWICH, VIC, QLD & TIP, AUS & IRL [38008] : JAMES 1870 + BARRIE, ONT, CAN [34484] : 1800 + LIVERPOOL, ENG [33825] : PRE 1850 CAVAN, CAV, IRL [33805] : FRANCIS 1826 + DOW, IRL [33956] : PRE 1825 AGHALOO, TYR, IRL [34259] : 1800-1890 BALLYMORE, WEM, IRL [34306] : 1840 + WHITEHOUSE, ANT, IRL [34484] : PRE 1882 BELFAST, ANT & DOW, IRL [35046] : PATRICK 1832-1890 KILDARE, KID, IRL [35136] : PHILLIP 1832-1890 KILDARE, KID, IRL [35136] : THOMAS 1838-1880 KILDARE, KID, IRL [35136] : JAMES 1790-1880 KILDARE, KID, IRL [35136] : ALL FER, IRL [35139] : 1840S BALLYSILLAN, ANT, IRL [35508] : PRE 1850 AGALOO, TYR, IRL [35833] : 1800-1900 ENNISKILLEN, FER, IRL [35845] : 1700 + DOW, IRL [36261] : 1798 ANT, IRL [36691] : 1800 + DERRYBOY & KILLINCHY, DOW, IRL [37405] : FRANCIS 1866 + CATLINS, OTAGO, NZ [33956] : 1850 + OTG, NZ [36261] : 1860 + AUCKLAND, NZ [36620] : 1800-1860 LKS, SCT [35845] : 1800 WORLDWIDE [36944]

KEENE CHARLES 1880 + SYDNEY, NSW, AUS [34544] : 1700 + EFFINGHAM, SRY, ENG [34544] : C1865 LND, ENG [35552] : 1800-1850 CHERTSEY, SRY, ENG [36474] : PRE 1860 BATH, SOM, ENG [36754] : C1750-1850 WEYBRIDGE, SRY, ENG [37618] : ALL WORLDWIDE [37721]

KEENEY PRE 1700 CT & MA, USA [38746]

KEENS PRE 1900 GODALMING, SRY, ENG [34377] : 1700 + AMPTHILL, BDF, ENG [37632]

KEEP PRE 1900 KINDRED & FORTH, TAS, AUS [35433] : C1840 ENG [35786] : 1800 + WOOTEN, BDF, ENG [35825] : C1787 KINGSCLERE, HAM, ENG [37168]

KEEPENCE 1849 + PARRAMATTA, NSW, AUS [34979] : C1786 WIL, ENG [34858] : PRE 1849 NORTH NEWTOWN, WIL, ENG [34979]

KEEPER PRE 1835 PA, USA [38314]

KEER 1560-1590S AALST, OVL, BEL [38358] : 1600S DREISCHOR, ZEL, NL [38358]

KEERSHAN PRE 1900 CARNARVON, WA, AUS [33795]

KEET 1800-1850 LIVERPOOL, LAN, ENG [36390]

KEETLEY 1780-1850 DBY, ENG [35916] : 1800-1900 NTT, ENG [36531]

KEEVES PRE 1900 WORLDWIDE [37874]

KEFFER PRE 1700 ZESELBERG, RPF, GER [38681]

KEGLER PRE 1865 MEK, GER [38235]

KEHOE MARY PRE 1858 QUE, CAN [34993] : 1770-1850 WEX, IRL [34346] : C1830 WEX, IRL [38435]

KEHRBERGER PRE 1850 BRONNHOLZHEIM, WUE, GER [38333]

KEHRMEYER PRE 1830 BAV, GER [38191]

KEIDLING PRE 1740 DETWANG, BAV, GER [35242]

KEIG 1850 + COR & IOM, IRL & ENG [38050]

KEIGHLEY 1815-1860S SHOREDITCH & FINSBURY, LND, ENG [36836] : 1860 + PIRONGIA & TE AWAMUTU, NZ [36836]

KEIGHRAN 1900-1930 CANOWINDRA, NSW, AUS [36315] : 1800-1900 ROSEDALE, NSW, AUS [36315]

KEIGHTLEY 1850 + WATFORD, HRT, ENG [37437]

KEIGHTLY PRE 1780 IRL [38084]

KEIJSER (SEE DE KEIJ [38358]

KEIL KILE 1855 + FRANKLIN, TAS, AUS [37954] : PRE 1906 CALGARY, ALB, CAN [35380] : PRE 1906 EDMONDTON, ALB, CAN [35380]

KEILBACH 1850-1900 NEW YORK, NY, USA [37021]

KEILER PRE 1852 OH, USA [37037]

KEILEY 1750-1850 KIK, IRL [37137]

KEILT ROSE ELLEN C1890 BUNGENDORE, NSW, AUS [37106] : PATRICK C1877 LDY, IRL [37106]

KEILY JOHN PRE 1802 COR, IRL [36519]

KEIMER C1750 HAUSEN, HOH, GER [38604]

KEIR PRE 1780 BAN, SCT [34646] : 1778 + FALKIRK, STI, SCT [35921] : PRE 1865 RFW, SCT [36363] : 1750-1860 GARTMORE, PER, SCT [36788]

KEIRCE PRE 1863 BALLYVAUGHAN, CLA, IRL [35206]

KEIRLE 1800 + CURRY RIVEL, SOM, ENG [35734]

KEIRNAN C1796 WEM, IRL [35922]

KEISER 1860S OH, USA [37600] : 1780-1830S PA, USA [37600]

KEITH PRE 1866 POPLAR, MDX, ENG [35242] : PRE 1800 ENG & SCT [38399] : PRE 1805 MONIFIETH, PER, SCT [34014] : 1838 GLASGOW, LKS, SCT [34529] : 1780-1850 KEITH, BAN, SCT [34771] : PRE 1851 ISLAY, ARL, SCT [34911] : 1750 + OLD DEER, ABD, SCT [38446] : GEORGE 1777 + VA & IL, USA [35272] : 1800 + TN, USA [37030] : 1770 + VA, USA [37030] : PRE 1810 RUTLAND, VT, USA [37509] : 1853 BANNER, VA, USA [38151]

KEITHLEY ALL USA [36896]

KEIZER 1840 LEER, PRUISEN, FRG [33751] : 1840 LEER, PRUISEN, FRG [38692]

KELBIE 1800 + DUNDEE, ANS, SCT [34326]

KELBRICK 1760 + LANCASTER, LAN, ENG [37666] : 1700-1800 FYLDE, LAN, ENG [38251]

KELK C1744 WRY, ENG [36126] : 1800 FRISKNEY, LIN, ENG [38756]

KELL 1740 + GSY, CHI [34532] : PRE 1850 RALOO, ANT, IRL [37636] : 1860-1930 BALLYCARRY, ANT, IRL [37636]

KELLAND ALL WORLDWIDE [37709]

KELLARD 1840 + WAKEFIELD, YKS, ENG [37134]

KELLAS 1800S STRATHDON, ABD, SCT [35411] : C1800 STRATHDON, ABD, SCT [36607] : 1800 + SCT & RSA [38425]

KELLAWAY 1860 + QLD, AUS [35253] : PRE 1800 ABBOTTSBURY, DOR, ENG [33984] : 1790 + ASHMORE, WIL, ENG [34899] : PRE 1860 DOR, ENG [35253] : PRE 1840 TAVISTOCK, DEV, ENG [36095] : PRE 1830 HALSTOCK, DOR, ENG [38135] : ALL WORLDWIDE [36095]

KELLEHER 1807-1834 CLA, IRL [36281] : ALL COR, IRL [36545] : 1800-1846 MILSTREET, COR, IRL [36915] : ALL USA [36545] : 1846-1988 BOSTON, MA, USA [36915]

KELLER PRE 1850 BADEN BADEN, BAW, BRD [37565] : 1820-1900 SIMCOE CO., ONT, CAN [36703] : ALL AG, CH [38037] : 1800 + BODMIN, CON, ENG [35155] : FREDERIC 1830 MELSHEIM, ALS, FRA [36930] : 1840-60 GER [38151] : 1700 + DIERSBURG, BAD, GER [38529] : PETER 1820 + MONTGOMERY CO., NY, USA [36950] : 1845 + ROSS CO., OH, USA [37565] : 1860-70 COVINGTON, KY, USA [38151] : PRE 1820 WILKINSON CO., MS, USA [38190]

KELLESEY 1830S GEAUGA CO., OH, USA [36729] : 1840-1850S ATCHISON CO., MO, USA [36729]

KELLETT ANN 1855-1895 NSW, AUS [35086] : PRE 1780 KIRKBY IRELETH, LAN, ENG [34053] : C1800-1900 AUDENSHAW & ASHTON UNDER LYNE, LAN, ENG [35591] : C1800-1900 HYDE & GERARDS WERNETH, CHS, ENG [35591] : 1823-1850 IOM & ENG [36910] : ALL CAV, IRL & AUS [34301] : 1823-1850 MI, USA [36910]

KELLEY PETER PRE 1856 CAVAN, CAV, IRL [38174] : 1825 + CALAIS & MACHIASPORT, ME, USA [37048] : 1812 OKMULGEE, OK, USA [38012] : 1800-1950 FAYETTE CO., PA, USA [38344] : 1800-1950

GREENE CO., PA, USA [38344] : ALL WORLDWIDE [35707]

KELLIE 1750+ URQUHART, MOR, SCT [34637]

KELLINGTON ALL WORLDWIDE [34485]

KELLMAN 1800-1850S MADRAS & BANGALORE, INDIA [35815]

KELLNER 1852+ MAITLAND & SINGLETON, NSW, AUS [37966] : ALL OES [37268]

KELLOCH ANN ALL FIF, SCT [38595]

KELLOCK 1750-1878 DFS, SCT [38463]

KELLOGG C1500 DEBDEN, ESS, ENG [34395] : 1845-1860 KEWEENAW CO., MI, USA [38010]

KELLOND ALL WORLDWIDE [37709]

KELLOW WILLIAM JOHN 1860+ OATLANDS, TAS, AUS [35803] : 1750+ BISHOPSTONE, WIL, ENG [34899] : 1800+ BODMIN, CON, ENG [35155] : PRE 1800 ST KEW, CON, ENG [37768]

KELLOWAY 1838+ CAMDEN, NSW, AUS [34899]

KELLY JOHN 1866+ ADELAIDE, SA, AUS [33797] : 1870s ADELAIDE, SA, AUS [34191] : 1848+ WELLINGTON, NSW, AUS [35007] : 1847+ HARTLEY, NSW, AUS [35007] : PRE 1873 THE OAKS, NSW, AUS [35245] : 1873+ THE OAKS, NSW, AUS [35245] : C1835+ WOLLONGONG, NSW, AUS [35249] : C1864+ JAMBEROO, NSW, AUS [35249] : 1800+ QLD, AUS [35352] : 1865+ OLLERA, NSW, AUS [35753] : NED ALL NSW, AUS [35831] : C1830 SYDNEY, NSW, AUS [35859] : 1812-1844 DUNGOG, NSW, AUS [36281] : ELIZABETH B. 1890+ COLLINGWOOD, VIC, AUS [36295] : 1870-1920 STANTHORPE, QLD, AUS [36315] : MARGARET C1890 SOUTH BRISBANE, QLD, AUS [36616] : JOHN 1850+ GANMAIN, VIC & NSW, AUS [37135] : ROSANNA 1850-1880 MONARO, NSW, AUS [37155] : C1870-90S TAMBO, QLD, AUS [37178] : DOMINEC 1850+ GRESFORD, NSW, AUS [37907] : PATRICK 1845 THE OAKS, NSW, AUS [37911] : 1870-1900 BALLARAT, VIC, AUS [37996] : JOHN C1859 DELORAINE, TAS, AUS & IRL [34596] : 1780+ YORK CO., NB, CAN [34138] : 1800S CAVAN & DURHAM, ONT, CAN [36727] : 1850-1925 BETHNAL GREEN, MDX, ENG [34242] : 1800S DEV, ENG [34715] : 1800-1900 MANCHESTER, LAN, ENG [34895] : C1815 SOUTHWARK, LND, ENG [36076] : 1800+ LAN, ENG [37482] : NICHOLAS PRE 1830 PLYMOUTH, DEV, ENG [37579] : PRE 1855 PORT ST MARY, IOM [35446] : 1700+ IOM [37482] : THOMAS 1780 IOM [37514] : 1790+ DOUGLAS, IOM & ENG [36967] : 1800+ KILKENNY, KIK, IRL [33800] : DAVID 1870-1900S COMBER, DOW, IRL [33895] : SAMUEL ALL DOW, IRL [33895] : JAMES 1868-1900S DOW, IRL [33895] : CATHERINE 1760-1800 CLA, IRL [33941] : 1820+ TIP, IRL [33982] : PRE 1860 ENNIS, CLA, IRL [34039] : ALL TERRYGLASS, TIP, IRL [34441] : PRE 1877 MARYBOROUGH, LEX, IRL [34879] : THOMAS PRE 1857 CASTLEREA & BALLINAKILL, GAL, IRL [34942] : 1700-1800 SLIGO, SLI, IRL [34975] : PRE 1800 SHANAGOLDEN, LIM, IRL [35007] : PRE 1844 GRAIGUENAMANAGH, KIK, IRL [35083] : 1800-1950 COORACLARE, CLA, IRL [35244] : C1800 GLENFARNE, LET, IRL [35350] : JAMES PRE 1825 KILDARE, KID, IRL [35578] : 1700-1800 GORMANSTON, MEA, IRL [35614] : 1780+ BELFAST, ANT, DOW & ARM, IRL [35636] : CATHERIN 1800S TIP, IRL [35768] : PRE 1870 CAPPAPOE, TIP, IRL [35913] : 1700+ PAISLEY, GAL, IRL [35918] : JAMES 1800S LOUGHLAN, CAR, IRL [36290] : 1850S BORRISAFERNEY, TIP, IRL [36315] : 1750+ CAR & WEX, IRL [36343] : 1848 SHANAGOLDEN, LIM, IRL [36640] : WILLIAM

1832-1843 CARNEW & BENRAW, DOW, IRL [37514] : GUY & JOHN 1832+ LEPPOCKS, DOW, IRL [37514] : THOMAS & WM. 1807+ DOW, IRL [37514] : 1800+ SLIGO, IRL [37907] : PATRICK C1814 CANAGH CASTLE, ROS, IRL [37911] : PRE 1862 LOG, IRL [37991] : C1827 BALLINASLOE, ROS, IRL [38052] : PETER PRE 1856 CAVAN, CAV, IRL [38174] : 1860+ CLOONSHANVILLE, ROS, IRL [38274] : ALL BONNETSTOWN, KIK, IRL [38300] : HENRY 1883-1900S COMBER, DOW, IRL & AUS [33895] : 1800S BALLYGALVERT, WEX, IRL & ENG [36874] : 1870+ NZ [35414] : 1855+ NEW PLYMOUTH, NZ [35446] : PRE 1830 FIF, SCT [34576] : 1890-1920 GLASGOW, SCT [34813] : PRE 1760 WIGTOWN, WIG, SCT [35242] : C1851 GLASGOW, SCT [35414] : 1845-50 GLASGOW, LKS, SCT [36262] : 1800-1900 NEWTON STEWART, WIG, SCT [36262] : 1850+ STRANRAER, WIG, SCT [36971] : 1850+ PETERHEAD, ABD, SCT [36971] : HELEN C1806 PATHHEAD, ELN, SCT [37168] : HELEN C1806 GARVALD, ELN, SCT [37168] : HELEN C1806 SPOTT, ELN, SCT [37168] : 1750-1850 CALLEGARY, INV, SCT [37188] : CATHERINE C1840-1865 GLASGOW, SCT [37572] : PRE 1808 PRESTONPANS, ELN, SCT [37852] : 1815-1850 KILMARNOCK, AYR, SCT [37996] : EDWARD 1823+ IOM, UK [36164] : 1847+ TRENTON, NJ, USA [36326] : WILLIAM 1843-1874 PITTSBURGH, PA, USA [37514] : WILLIAM 1870-1884 LODA, IL, USA [37514] : 1790+ USA & IRL [36357]

KELM 1700S SOMERSET, PA, USA [38184]

KELMAN C1790 ABD, SCT [38253]

KELSCH PRE 1864 PALTINOSSA, BUKOVINA, OES [37481]

KELSEY C1625 ENG [34395] : 1840+ POCKLINGTON, ERY, ENG [35977] : 1800S WEAVERTHORPE, YKS, ENG [36636] : 1840+ CRIGGLESTONE, WRY, ENG [36636] : PRE 1800 MARKET WEIGHTON, ERY, ENG [36636] : 1800S HUTTON CRANSWICK, ERY, ENG [36636] : PRE 1850 HAGGERSTON, LND, ENG [37871] : ROBERT C1740-1800 BUCKS CO., PA, USA [35284] : 1840-1900 SHIAWASSEE CO., MI, USA [38010] : 1845-1855 KEWEENAW CO., MI, USA [38010] : 1708S KILLINGWORTH, CT, USA [38184]

KELSO 1914+ EAST HILLS, NSW, AUS [37904] : PRE 1880 TEMPLEPATRICK, ANT, IRL [34115] : 1880+ LONDONDERRY, LDY, IRL [35315] : PRE 1800 DRY & ANT, IRL [38055] : PRE 1800 COCKBURNSPATH, BEW, SCT [36497] : 1881 GLASGOW, LKS, SCT [38210] : 1855 SCT [38210] : ROBERT C1740-1800 BOURBON CO., KY, USA [35284] : HENRY C1700-1790 BUCKS CO., PA, USA [35284] : ARCHIBALD C1700-1750 BUCKS CO., PA, USA [35284] : ANDREW C1690-1760 BUCKS CO., PA, USA [35284] : 1866-1870 SAN FRACISCO, CA, USA [37136]

KELSON 1770-1870 KENT CO., ONT, CAN [36703]

KELTIE PRE 1740 FOSSOWAY, KRS, SCT [36272]

KELTY JAMES 1828 ARMAGH, IRL [35484]

KEMBER 1857+ NEWTOWN, NSW, AUS [34979] : PRE 1857 KEN, ENG [34979]

KEMBLE 1600-1700 VA, USA [36934]

KEMISTER ALL LIVERPOOL, NSW, AUS [35234]

KEMMA 1831-1899 HAN, GER [36948] : SOPHIA 1831-1899 PHILADELPHIA, PA, USA [36948]

KEMP ALL COOMA & TUMUT, NSW, AUS [34024] : C1898 COOLGARDIE, WA, AUS [34577] : 1839 PORTLAND, NSW, AUS [35082] : 1852+ ARALUEN, NSW, AUS [35537] : BERT 1900+ ONT, CAN [35184] : C1890 KINGSTON, ONT, CAN [38455] : C1880 KEN, ENG [33809] : 1750-1840 STYTHIANS,

CON, ENG [34016] : PRE 1870 LONGTON, STS, ENG [34261] : PRE 1692 ST DOMINICK, CON, ENG [34573] : 1830 MERTHER, CON, ENG [34668] : 1800+ TOPCROFT, NFK, ENG [34710] : 1840+ GREAT YARMOUTH, NFK, ENG [34710] : PRE 1763 BOWDON, ENG [35097] : 1550-1650 CHILHAM, KEN, ENG [35283] : ELIZABETH 1600-1700 TICEHURST, SSX, ENG [35361] : 1821+ ICKLETON, CAM, ENG [35537] : PRE 1743 ILLOGAN, CON, ENG [36277] : PRE 1858 BRIGHTLING, SSX, ENG [36281] : 1700 CARLETON RODE, NFK, ENG [36483] : ALL ESS, ENG [36500] : ALL HOUSEHOLE, CON, ENG [36506] : 1700+ MILTON & GRAVESEND, LND, ENG [36818] : 1680+ BOCKING, ESS, ENG [36871] : 1800+ BOW & MILE END, MDX & LND, ENG [37065] : PRE 1857 NTT & CUL, ENG [37267] : PRE 1833 BAGSHOT, SRY, ENG [37442] : 1500-1900 SANCREED & MADRON, CON, ENG [37680] : THOMAS C1866 ELTHAM, KEN, ENG [37691] : PRE 1750 LONDON, ENG [37703] : 1800+ HERNE BAY & WHITSTABLE, KEN, ENG [37707] : PRE 1837 NFK, ENG [38080] : 1700+ DEV, ENG [38235] : 1700-1800 RAMSGATE, KEN, ENG [38524] : C1750-1850 DINGWALL, ROC, SCT [33874] : 1770+ CROMRIE, PER, SCT [34956] : 1800S EDINBURGH, MLN, SCT [35715] : 1650+ KENT CO., MD & IN, USA [37010] : PRE 1763 GOOCHLAND CO., VA, USA [38190] : ELIZABETH 1740-1826 FRED CO., MD, USA [38591] : ALL WORLDWIDE [35884]

KEMPENFELT 1718-1782 OF 'ROYAL GEORGE', UK [36638]

KEMPER 1800S CUYAHOGA CO., OH, USA [38369]

KEMPF PRE 1830 WHITECHAPEL, LND, ENG [37841] : PRE 1830 FRANKFURT, GER [37841]

KEMPLE 1750-1840 STYTHIANS, CON, ENG [34016]

KEMPSON 1800-1900 WONERSH, SRY, ENG [36095] : MARY C1840-5 GOREY, WEX, IRL [35184]

KEMPSTER 1824 TIPPERARY, TIP, IRL [37694] : 1850 WELSHPOOL, MGY, WLS [37694]

KEMPTHORNE 1650-1700 MULLION, CON, ENG [34697]

KEMPTON 1864+ MAIDENHEAD, BRK, ENG [36975] : 1782+ ELY, CAM, ENG [36975] : PRE 1630 LONDON, MDX, ENG [37049] : HENRY 1838+ MARYLEBONE & GREYTOWN, MDX, ENG & NZ [33961] : THOMAS 1836-1910 MARYLEBONE & GREYTOWN, MDX, ENG & NZ [33961] : EMILY JANE 1840-1865 GREYTOWN, WAI, NZ [33961] : SARAH 1844-1937 GREYTOWN, WAI, NZ [33961] : 1623+ PLYMOUTH, MA, USA [37049] : ALL WORLDWIDE [37049]

KEMSEY PRE 1685 LONDON WALL, LND, ENG [37610]

KENAN MARY PRE 1816 TIPPERARY, TIP, IRL [34539]

KENDAL PRE 1870 DUR, ENG [38585]

KENDALL 1750-1850 STALLEN, CON, ENG [34028] : 1600S ULVERSTON, LAN, ENG [34053] : 1750+ WIL, ENG [34664] : PRE 1800 NORTH THORESBY, LIN, ENG [34849] : PRE 1850 LANLIVERY, CON, ENG [34953] : PRE 1880 TORVER, LAN, ENG [34958] : 1750+ LITTLE BOWDEN, NTH, ENG [35921] : PRE 1810 LEEDS, WRY, ENG [36011] : 1700 ARKSEY, WRY, ENG [36112] : PRE 1800 NORWICH, NFK, ENG [36381] : 1860 IDLE & THACKLEY, WRY, ENG [36617] : ALL ILKLEY & APPLETREEWICK, YKS, ENG [37078] : 1800+ ST BREOCK, CON, ENG [37343] : 1830+ ROCKHAMPTON, GLS, ENG [37343] : 1800S HENBURY, GLS, ENG [37343] : C1852 ST KEW & CROWAN, CON, ENG [37556] : ALL ISEL &

MORLAND, CUL, ENG [37735] : 1750-1850 CON & DOR, ENG [37943] : 1850+ ENG [38059] : 1850S GLASGOW, LKS, SCT [34605] : PRE 1810 BROWN CO., OH & KY, USA [34410]

KENDELL 1800+ HERMITAGE BAY, NFD, CAN [36684]

KENDERDINE 1780+ STAFFORD, STS, ENG [34334]

KENDREW 1842-1901 HARROGATE, YKS, ENG [37352]

KENDRICK 1850-1940 ENG & RSA [37525]

KENEDY CHARLES 1860 MCCLEAN CO., IL, USA [38132]

KENEFICK ALL COBH, COR, IRL [37526] : WILLIAM 1865+ KANSAS CITY, MO, USA [37526] : KATE 1865+ KY, USA [37526]

KENELL 1864-1939 HARKAWAY, VIC, AUS [35047]

KENGEN ALL BISDOM LUIK, LMB, NL [38702]

KENISK 1805 MORESBY, CUL, ENG [37960]

KENN ALL SCT & AUS [34955]

KENNA PRE 1865 TIP, IRL [34886] : PRE 1861 TIP, IRL [35088]

KENNAR PRE 1746 DEV, ENG [35895]

KENNARD 1820+ LONDON & BERMONDSEY, SRY, ENG [35579] : PRE 1842 DEV, ENG [35895] : PRE 1800 SITTINGBOURNE AREA, KEN, ENG [37720] : ALL ORE & GUESTLING, SSX & KEN, ENG [38230] : JOHN 1850-1860 HOCKING CO., OH, USA [35329]

KENNAUGH 1850+ PATRICK, IOM & MT, UK & USA [38050]

KENNEAR 1800+ FOURNIER, ONT, CAN [38462]

KENNEDY PRE 1900 TAS, AUS [34536] : ALL DELORAINE, TAS, AUS [34555] : 1830+ WINDSOR, NSW, AUS [35150] : CHARLES PRE 1847 PORT FAIRY, VIC, AUS [35431] : JOHN 1838+ RICHMOND, VIC, AUS [35467] : C1900 GRANTVILLE, VIC, AUS [35748] : DONALD 1804+ NEPEAN, NSW, AUS [35831] : 1879 GATINEAU HILLS, QUE, CAN [34224] : 1840 CARBONEAR, NFD, CAN [34349] : 1851+ ONT, CAN [34368] : 1800+ CURRAN, ONT, CAN [36686] : DOUGLAS 1937+ KENSINGTON, LND, ENG [35154] : KATHLEEN C1937 KENSINGTON, LND, ENG [35154] : PRE 1898 LND, ENG [35528] : 1800+ SUNDERLAND, DUR, ENG [35719] : C1700 OCKENDEN, ESS, ENG [36490] : 1800+ ESS, ENG [37088] : 1700 ROCHFORD, ESS, ENG [37145] : DOUGLAS 1904+ SIMLA, INDIA [35154] : ALL CAV, IRL [33854] : 1850 BOHERBUE, COR, IRL [33929] : PRE 1848 IRL [34357] : PRE 1850 LIM, IRL [34593] : PRE 1870 INCH, DOW, IRL [34895] : PRE 1864 CARRICK ON SUIR, KIK, IRL [35197] : JEREMIAH PRE 1850 KILLANANE, TIP, IRL [35750] : MICHAEL 1800S BALLINGARRY, TIP, IRL [35768] : 1830-1860 NEWRY, DOW, IRL [35992] : 1820+ TULLYLISH, DOW, IRL [35992] : 1820+ BANBRIDGE, DOW, IRL [35992] : 1800-1950 BALLYMACARBERRY, WAT, IRL [36565] : JAMES 1800+ WATERFORD CITY, WAT, IRL [36620] : PRE 1850 BALLITORE, KID, IRL [36821] : PRE 1850 KILKENNY, KIK, IRL [37544] : ANNE 1800+ IRL [37942] : C1850 ARM, IRL [37946] : 1827+ ROSCREA, TIP, IRL [37982] : PRE 1800 DRY & ANT, IRL [38055] : 1800-35 TIP, IRL [38202] : PRE 1900 CRAAN & BUNCLODY, WEX, IRL [38300] : 1800+ CAPPAMORE, LIM, IRL & AUS [36642] : JOHN C1828 BELFAST & GLASGOW, ANT & LKS, IRL & SCT [35467] : 1890+ HUNTLEY, NZ [35567] : 1900-1990 NZ [36565] : THOS 1940 DUNEDIN, NZ [36620] : C1880 SADDLE HILL, OTAGO, NZ [36806] : PRE 1850 DFS, SCT [34013] : ALL ST MARGARET'S HOPE, OKI, SCT [34362] : 1844

COLDSTREAM, ROX, SCT [34529] : ALL LAGGAN, INV, SCT [34558] : 1750+ URQUHART, INV, SCT [35511] : PRE 1839 DULL, PER, SCT [35525] : DONALD 1759+ SCT [35831] : 1750S FIF, SCT [36327] : 1750+ ELGIN, MOR, SCT [37110] : 1675+ FOSS & DRUMNAKYLE, PER, SCT [37447] : PRE 1900 GREENOCK, RFW, SCT [37500] : 1857+ DALSERF PARISH, LKS, SCT [37879] : 1750+ LANARK, LKS, SCT [38492] : PRE 1840 GLEN GARRY, INV, SCT [38773] : ANGUS PRE 1800 INV, SCT [38773] : ROBERT C1860 SCT & INDI [35154] : WILLIAM C1901 SCT & INDI [35154] : PRE 1850 AYR, SCT & IRL [38039] : 1860+ WYANDOTTE, MI, USA [34983] : 1800-1850 GREENE CO., PA, USA [36958] : 1834-1864 GREENWICH, CT, USA [37803] : SAMUEL 1797+ EMANUEL CO., GA, USA [38340]

KENNEFECK 1800S CARRIGALINE, COR, IRL & AUS [34596]

KENNELLY 1850-1930 WINNESHEIK CO., IA, USA [37538] : 1830-1850 BULLOCH CO., GA, USA [37538]

KENNERLEY PRE 1900 NORTHWICH, CHS, ENG [36487]

KENNETT-SMITH ALL ENG [36805]

KENNEWEELS ALL WORLDWIDE [38161]

KENNEWELL ALL AUS [33798] : ALL NTT & LIN, ENG [33798]

KENNEY DAVID 1837+ SOUTHWARK, LND, ENG [37270] : JAMES 1930S CROYDON, SRY & LND, ENG [37270] : SARAH 1842+ SOUTHWARK, LND, ENG [37270] : JAMES 1841+ SOUTHWARK, LND, ENG [37270] : JOSEPH 1877+ STEPNEY, LND, ENG [37270] : ELIZABETH 1839+ SOUTHWARK, LND, ENG [37270] : 1870-1930 STEPNEY, LND, ENG [37270] : MARY ANNE 1831+ SOUTHWARK, LND, ENG [37270] : PATRICK 1836+ SOUTHWARK, LND, ENG [37270] : CATHERINE 1846+ SOUTHWARK, LND, ENG [37270] : 1840+ NEW YORK, NY, USA [37823] : 1780+ WORCESTER CO., MA, USA [38050] : 1850-1900 ONEIDA, NY, USA [38111]

KENNIE 1600-1750 ST MONANCE, FIF, SCT [35627]

KENNIFECK ALL TIP, IRL [35809]

KENNIFORD ALL ENG & WLS [36019]

KENNINGTON PRE 1900 AUS [34196]

KENNISH 1799 WHITEHAVEN, CUL, ENG [37960] : 1805 MORESBY, CUL, ENG [37960] : 1790+ DOUGLAS, IOM & USA [36967] : PRE 1700 MAUGHOLD & BRADDAN, IOM, UK [35866]

KENNISON HANNAH 1831-1871+ FRYEBURG, ME, USA [36948]

KENNIWELL 1818+ AUS [35241] : 1750+ NTT, ENG [35241]

KENNON 1830-1850 WAR, ENG [34153] : 1700-1900 ENG,, IRL & SCT [34153]

KENNY 1839-1990 MORUYA, NSW, AUS [33818] : 1855+ VIC, AUS [34578] : 1860+ SOUTH COAST, NSW, AUS [37133] : 1840+ GOORAMBAT EAST, VIC, AUS [37171] : 1840+ BENALLA, VIC, AUS [37171] : PRE 1817 CHATHAM, NB, CAN [36721] : 1800+ LIVERPOOL, LAN, ENG [34563] : ROBEY ALL HAM, ENG & IRL [35975] : ROBEY 1840+ HAM, ENG & IRL [35975] : PRE 1855 TIP, IRL [34578] : 1850+ BOHERBRADDA ADARE, LIM, IRL [34960] : C1800-1851 TIP, IRL [35389] : PRE 1835 BLACKWATER, WEX, IRL [36372] : 1795 IRL [36721] : PRE 1840 CLA, IRL [37133] : 1800 BALLINASLOE, GAL, IRL [37791] : 1840+ OLD MONKLAND, LKS, SCT [35138] : C1800 AYR, SCT [36694]

KENOYER FRED 1800+ WA, USA [34511]

KENSINGTON ALL WORLDWIDE [33946]

KENT 1863+ BRISBANE, QLD, AUS [34020] : 1850+ CARRISBROOK, VIC, AUS [35489] : THOMAS 1840+ ULLADULLA & SHOALHAVEN, NSW, AUS [36600] : ANN C1825 PARRAMATTA, NSW, AUS [37106] : PRE 1840 WATHEROP, GLS, ENG [33860] : JAMES 1780-1840 STOKE ON TRENT, STS, ENG [34143] : PRE 1900 STOKE ON TRENT, STS, ENG [34548] : PRE 1860 MERTHER, CON, ENG [34682] : 1700-1750 BENNINGTON, HRT, ENG [34697] : PRE 1900 WEST HACKNEY, LND, ENG [34825] : 1800S+ MERTHER, CON, ENG [35489] : 1800-1840 TRURO, CON, ENG [36536] : ANN C1802 LONDON, LND, ENG [37106] : 1500-1800 BALSHAM, CAM, ENG [37342] : 1850+ ALDERSHOT, HAM, ENG [37437] : 1720-1900 CORFE CASTLE, DOR, ENG [37676] : PRE 1820 WESTMINSTER, LND, ENG [38292] : 1650-1850 TIP, IRL [36097] : 1900+ PHILLIPINE [37251] : ALL SCT [36002] : 1700-1840 PRESTONPANS, WLN, SCT [37251] : 1800-1860 DALKEITH, MLN, SCT [37251] : 1790+ WESTRAY, OKI, SCT [37881]

KENTESBER ALL WORLDWIDE [36430]

KENTISH ALL LITTLE BARDFIELD HALL, ESS, ENG [34778]

KENWARD C1800 BUXTED, SSX, ENG [36090] : PRE 1860 CATSFIELD, SSX, ENG [37260]

KENWORTHY PRE 1840 HALIFAX, YKS, ENG [35404] : 1820-1850 HUDDERSFIELD, YKS, ENG [36319] : 1770-1870 SCAMMONDEN & RIPPONDEN, WRY, ENG [38003]

KENYON 1875+ MANCHESTER, LAN, ENG [37902] : 1750-1850 WIG, SCT [34229]

KENZIL 1850 PARIS & LONDON, FRA & ENG [38540]

KENZLER PRE 1910 MULHEIM, GER [34269]

KEOGH PRE 1840 DUBLIN, IRL [34555]

KEOGHAN 1800+ ENG [35880] : 1750-1850 IRL [34687] : 1700+ MOG, IRL [35880]

KEOGHOE PRE 1840 LONDON, ENG [37743]

KEON PRE 1830 ENNISKILLEN, FER, IRL [38447]

KEOUGH 1809 CLARE, CLA, IRL [34176]

KEPPIER 1831+ PATERSON, NSW, AUS [35394]

KERCHER PRE 1814 OVERTON, HAM, ENG [36650]

KEREECH 1800+ PHILADELPHIA, PA, USA [36965]

KEREER 1800+ PHILADELPHIA, PA, USA [36965]

KERFOOT 1792 FREDERICK CO., VA, USA [35295] : PRE 1800 WORLDWIDE [34746] : 1800 WORLDWIDE [35873]

KERFORD PRE 1800 WORLDWIDE [34746]

KERKHAM ALL LONG SUTTON, LIN, ENG [35258]

KERKMANN 1700+ LEMBECK, WEF, GER [38651]

KERLEY PRE 1870 SPETTISBURY, DOR, ENG [36417] : JEMIMA PRE 1850 ENG [36634] : 1750+ IWERNE MINSTER, DOR, ENG [36825] : 1750-1850 DOR, ENG [36962] : PRE 1900 CRANBORNE, DOR & WIL, ENG [37335] : C1780 ALVEDISTON, WIL, ENG [38489] : C1850 LIMERICK, LIM, IRL [34688]

KERLEY (SEE CARLEY) [34532]

KERMEEN PRE 1790 MAUGHOLD, IOM, UK [35866]

KERMENEUR PRE 1650 BRT, FRA [37428]

KERMODE PRE 1850 KIRK GERMAN, IOM [36260]

KERMON PRE 1765 LOUTH, LIN, ENG [37069]

KERMOND 1820S STEPNEY, LND, ENG [36292]

KERN PRE 1750 SODEN & BAD SODEN, GHE, GER [38610] : ALL HONNINGEN, RPR, GER [38637] : C1856 COLOMBO, SRI LANKA [35887] : 1884 SCOTT CO., VA, USA [38151]

KERNAGHAN 1800+ BELFAST, IRL [38456]

KERNAHAN 1790-1828 ATHLONE, WEM, IRL [38779]

KERNAN 1850 MELBOURNE, VIC, AUS [35194]

KERNES C1805 CLOGHER, TYR, IRL [37556]

KERNEY 1780-1830 TRUMBULL, OH & PA, USA [37529]

KERNEY (SEE KARNEY) [34524]

KERNOHAN 1820+ GRENVILLE CO., ONT, CAN [37586]

KERR 1880+ QLD, AUS [34368] : 1880+ WOLLONGONG, NSW, AUS [35075] : 1842 MELBOURNE, VIC, AUS [35089] : 1829+ HOBART & FIREFLY CRK, TAS & NSW, AUS [35189] : WILLIAM PRE 1927 CHELSEA, VIC, AUS [35788] : 1879+ MARYBOROUGH & ROCKHAMPTON, QLD, AUS [35814] : THOMAS 1860S FIREFLY CRK, NSW, AUS [35848] : THOMAS 1840+ DUNGOG, NSW, AUS [35848] : 1860+ MACLEAY RIVER, NSW, AUS [37349] : 1920+ QLD, AUS [37974] : 1840+ HUNTINGDON CO., QUE, CAN [34138] : 1880S NORTH GOWER, ONT, CAN [35078] : C1850 CROOKDAKE, CUL, ENG [34515] : 1850S ALNWICK, NBL, ENG [35075] : PRE 1845 MAYFAIR, LND, ENG [36153] : PRE 1827 HOLBORN, LND, ENG [36153] : PRE 1824 CAV, IRL [34368] : ANN PRE 1840 IRL [34977] : PRE 1850 NEWTOWNARDS, DOW, IRL [35722] : ALL WARRENPOINT, DOW, IRL [35814] : 1750-1890 SHEETRIM & EMYVALE, MOG, IRL [36075] : PRE 1910 BELFAST AREA, IRL [37745] : 1800+ STRABANE, TYR, IRL [38379] : 1847-1902 GROOMSPORT & CRAIGBOY, DOW, IRL & AUS [33847] : JAMES C1808-1873 IRL & CAN [36904] : ALL NELSON, NZ [35058] : 1860 BOTHKENNAR, STI, SCT [33810] : 1832-1871 MONTROSE, ANS, SCT [33811] : PRE 1845 KILBIRNIE, AYR, SCT [33845] : 1800+ PAISLEY, RFW & WIG, SCT [33970] : 1700S PANBRIDE, ANS, SCT [34053] : 1700-1900 KIRKCONNELL, KKD, SCT [34107] : 1800 STRANRAER, WIG, SCT [34214] : 1800+ ANS, SCT [34226] : PRE 1823 ROX, SCT [34489] : JOHN BLACK PRE 1850 DUMFRIES, DFS, SCT [34621] : 1830S REIFF, ROC, SCT [35151] : GEO & JAMES PRE 1760 KELSO, ROX, SCT [35371] : 1780-1820 DALRY, AYR, SCT [35391] : 1750+ AYR, AYR, SCT [35558] : 1800 DRUMMOND, MLN, SCT [35755] : THOMAS C1809 COLDSTREAM, BEW, SCT [35848] : PRE 1900 MOCHRUM, WIG, SCT [35915] : C1828 EDGERTON, ROX, SCT [35963] : 1830-1860 EDINBURGH, SCT [35981] : 1750-1870 NEW CUMNOCK, AYR, SCT [35981] : PRE 1848 ELGIN, MOR, SCT [36848] : 1780-1910 STRAITON, AYR, SCT [37338] : 1728-1840 BEITH, AYR, SCT [37338] : 1830-1990 DALMELLINGTON, AYR, SCT [37338] : ROBERT PRE 1830S FIF, SCT [37349] : PRE 1741 TOMTAIWAN & DULL, PER, SCT [37852] : PRE 1930 LKS, SCT [37974] : 1750-1800 DOUGRIE, BUT, SCT [38465] : 1880+ CA, USA [34368] : C1900 COOS, NH, USA [34368] : 1865+ VT, USA [34368] : 1770S PA, USA [37533] : 1799-1837 MO, USA [37533] : 1900-1920 CUSTER, CO, USA [38465]

KERRE 1750+ SUTTON MADDOCK, SAL, ENG [36488] : 1750+ STOTTESDON, SAL, ENG [36488]

KERRIDGE ALL WORLDWIDE [36048]

KERRUISH PRE 1760 MAUGHOLD, IOM, UK [35866]

KERRY ALL GREAT MASSINGHAM, NFK, ENG [37181] : C1812 CORK, COR, IRL [35854]

KERS 1700S ZONNEMAIRE, ZEL, NL [38358]

KERSEY 1840+ FAKENHAM MAGNA, SFK, ENG [34710] : 1820S NORTHAMPTON, ENG [36146] : PRE 1616 BODICIT, OXF, ENG [36929] : 1700+ SHILLELAGH, WIC, IRL [38385] : 1650+ PA NC IN & IA, USA [36319]

KERSHAW C1840 OLDHAM, LAN, ENG [34734] : 1820+ ROCHDALE, LAN, ENG [35169] : JOHN PRE 1825 SHUTTLEWORTH, LAN, ENG [35514] :

1800 ENG [37391] : PRE 1900 ENG [37739] : 1750-1850 OLDHAM, LAN, ENG [37807]

KERSHLER 1852+ CAMPBELLTOWN, NSW, AUS [33817]

KERSLAKE ALL LAUNCESTON, TAS, AUS [34674] : ALL EUROA, VIC, AUS [34674] : 1840+ LAUNCESTON, TAS, AUS [34770] : C1860 NSW, AUS [37830] : C1820 NTH TAMERTON, CON, ENG [37144] : 1750+ ST GILES IN THE HEATH, CON, ENG [37224] : 1750+ VIRGINSTOW, DEV, ENG [37224] : C1815 WIVELISCOMBE, SOM, ENG [37830]

KERSLEY 1750-1850 ODIHAM, HAM, ENG [34464] : PRE 1820 MEDSTED, HAM, ENG [35016]

KERSTEN 1870-1900 SHAWANO CO., WI, USA [36546]

KERSWELL 1874-1916 BURRAGORANG, NSW, AUS [34966] : PRE 1812 MODBURY, DEV, ENG [35128]

KERVILE ALL WORLDWIDE [38068]

KERVILL ALL WORLDWIDE [38068]

KERVILLE ALL WORLDWIDE [38068]

KERWIN PRE 1850 KEN, ENG [37371] : 1839-1861 SILVERMINES & NENAGH, TIP, IRL [37988]

KESBY ALL KEMPSEY, NSW, AUS [37115] : PRE 1800 KEN, ENG [34252]

KESLER JOHN 1860 SHIAWASSEE CO., MI, USA [38142]

KESSEL 1723+ EGLOSHAYLE, CON, ENG [34374]

KESSLER 1800 LUSTEN, CH [33751] : 1800 LUSTEN, CH [38692] : C1860 DANVILLE, PA, USA [36803] : C1854 MI, USA [36923] : 1876+ ELLIS CO., KS, USA [38057]

KESTELL C1852 ST KEW & CROWAN, CON, ENG [37556]

KESTER PRE 1853 HARDWICK, CAM, ENG [36629]

KESTING ALL GER [34861]

KESTLER PRE 1800 GRUENSTADT, RPF, GER [38681]

KETCH C1837 ALVERSTOKE, HAM, ENG [35515] : 1791 STARKSBORO, CHITTENDEN, VT, USA [38188] : 1810 BRISTOL, ADDISON, VT, USA [38188]

KETCHIN 1782-1806 STOW, MLN, SCT [37329] : 1840-1960 PEE, SCT [37329]

KETCHUM 1800S YORK CO., ONT, CAN [37458] : 1751 LONG ISLAND, NY, USA [36680]

KETLAND 1800 CUL, ENG [34088]

KETNER PRE 1850 PA, USA [38218]

KETTERINGHAM PRE 1900 NFK, ENG [37737]

KETTLE 1821+ SYDNEY, NSW, AUS [35336] : ELLWOOD C1780 STS, ENG [35336] : C1808 PER, SCT [35729]

KETTLETY 1800+ SOM & BRK, ENG [35433]

KETTLEWELL ALL LIN, ENG [34436] : PRE 1880 KETTERING, NTH, ENG [36617]

KETTNER 1796-1871 PA, USA [38101]

KETURAH 1780 BRITWELL SALOME, OXF, ENG [35067]

KEUROVOST 1800+ THE HAGUE, NL [36662]

KEVEN PRE 1840 LONDON, ENG [36765]

KEVERN PRE 1750 ST KEVERNE, CON, ENG [37913]

KEVERS ALL WORLDWIDE [37274]

KEVEY C1848 MANCHESTER, LAN, ENG [35990]

KEVIS 1900+ ALB, CAN [37274] : ALL WORLDWIDE [37274]

KEW PRE 1800 STEVENTON, BRK, ENG [34347] : PRE 1800 SHERBORNE ST JOHN, HAM, ENG [34347] : PRE 1840 LOUTH & LACEBY, LIN, ENG [37402] : PRE 1725 HEYSHAM & LANCASTER, LAN, ENG [38248] : 1800S BRK, ENG & NZ [36607] : ALL WORLDWIDE [34347]

KEWEN 1750+ IOM [37306]

KEY PRE 1832 KISLINGBURY, NTH, ENG [34941] : PRE 1900 ENG [35055] : 1600-1840 ADSTOCK & BEACHAMPTON, BKM, ENG [35592] : PRE 1860

CALSTOCK, CON, ENG [36000] : 1700+
DIPTFORD, DEV, ENG [36209] : ALL
MOLLINGTON, OXF, ENG [36922] : 1700+
WORKINGTON, CUL, ENG [37735]
KEYATTA ALL WORLDWIDE [38445]
KEYES 1800+ NSW, AUS [38484] : 1860+ QLD, AUS
[38484] : 1880+ NORTH-WEST, QLD, AUS [38484] :
1750-1850 BUSHMILLS, ANT, IRL [34513]
KEYMAR PRE 1800 AYLSHAM & NORWICH, NFK,
ENG [36593]
KEYMER PRE 1800 AYLSHAM & NORWICH, NFK,
ENG [36593]
KEYS 1880+ NORTH-WEST, QLD, AUS [38484] :
1860+ QLD, AUS [38484] : 1800+ NSW, AUS [38484]
: 1700-1800 BRADWELL NEAR-THE SEA, ESS,
ENG [34872] : C1710 KEN, ENG [38389] : 1820
LONDONDERRY, LDY, IRL [35194] : 1820-1860
RATHDOWNEY, LEX, IRL [35717] : PRE 1840
PAISLEY, RFW, SCT [36793]
KEYSER PRE 1675 GOCHSHEIM, BAY, BRD [35311]
KEYWORTH PRE 1900 WELLINGLEY, WRY, ENG
[36126]
KIBBLE PRE 1864 HALSTEAD, ESS, ENG [37346]
KIBBLER C1808 HAMPTON IN ARDEN, WAR, ENG
[34239]
KIBILIN PRE 1850 BALLINA, SLI, IRL [37568]
KIBLER 1840 OH, USA [33910]
KIBLINGER 1700S BERKS CO., PA, USA [37028] :
1760+ BERKS CO., PA, USA [38330]
KICKBUSCH PRE 1900 QLD, AUS [37973]
KIDALL 1800S SWAFFHAM, NFK, ENG [34151]
KIDD C1852 HOBART, TAS, AUS [37556] : 1855
MELBOURNE, VIC, AUS [37556] : 1873+ SYDNEY,
NSW, AUS [37556] : 1800+ CAN [37427] : PRE 1780
GARBOLDISHAM, NFK, ENG [35571] : 1840-1900
MANCHESTER, LAN, ENG [38259] : 1800+ ANS,
SCT [34226] : C1820 GAMRIE, ABD, SCT [34400] :
ALL FORGUE & TURRIFF, ABD, SCT [34861] :
1809+ FIF, SCT [35720] : 1800+ KILWINNING,
AYR, SCT [38247] : 1800+ LOCHMABEN, DFS, SCT
[38247] : 1848+ NEW YORK CITY, NY, USA [37086]
: JAMES 1780-1795 MECKLENBURG CO., VA, USA
[38155] : ZACARIAH 1795-1804 OGLETHORPE CO.,
GA, USA [38155] : JAMES 1860-1888 RANDOLPH
CO., AL, USA [38155] : JAMES 1802-1825
OGLETHORPE CO., GA, USA [38155] : JAMES 1816
WILKERSON CO., GA, USA [38155]
KIDDER PRE 1750 COLUMBIA CO., NY, USA [37568]
KIDGELL ALL SHEFFIELD & VICTORIA, YKS,
ENG [34558]
KIDMAN PRE 1800 CAM, ENG [34660] : C1800
CAMBRIDGE, CAM, ENG [37718] : PRE 1830
STEPNEY & BOW, LND & MDX, ENG [38254]
KIDNEY PRE 1870 HARROW, MDX, ENG [37622]
KIDSLEY PRE 1838 WEEDON, NTH, ENG [33821]
KIDWELL 1800+ HANLEY, STS, ENG [34693] : PRE
1820 LONDON, ENG [38383] : PRE 1880 PRINCE
GEORGE CO., CHAS CO., MD, USA [36914] : ALL
WORLDWIDE [36517]
KIEFT 1800 COEVORDEN, DRN, NL [35338]
KIEL 1672 BOEMIGHAUSEN, WAL, GER [34912]
KIELEY ELIZA ALL GAWLER, SA, AUS [35223] :
1902+ BRISBANE, QLD, AUS [37171]
KIELOW PRE 1840 TURNOW, BRA, LOWER
LUSATIA, GER [34766]
KIELY 1900+ MAITLAND & SINGLETON, NSW,
AUS [37966] : PRE 1840 KER, IRL [34368] : C1837
LIMERICK, LIM, IRL [35131] : ALL GLENSTAL &
LIMERICK, LIM, IRL [36326] : PRE 1800 CARRICK
ON SUIR, WAT, IRL [37579]
KIEMELE ALL ALT FREUDENTAL, UKRAINE,
GROSSLIEBENTAL, SU [38372]

KIERCE PRE 1863 BALLYVAUGHAN, CLA, IRL
[35206]
KIERNAN 1875+ MACKAY, QLD, AUS [34044] : PRE
1865 HUNTINGDON, QUE, CAN [34368] : PRE 1860
MAIDSTONE, KEN, ENG [36888] : PRE 1875
VIRGINIA, CAV, IRL [34044] : PRE 1860 CARAN,
CAV, IRL [37521]
KIERNON C1850 HAY VALLEY, SA, AUS [34025]
KIERZEK THERESE C1820 POS, GER [36452] :
CONSTANZIA 1845 BOMST, POS, GER [36452]
KIFFE (SEE KIFT) [35223]
KIFT C1760 MIDDLEZOY, SOM, ENG [35223]
KIGHTLEY PRE 1856 PITSFORD, NTH, ENG [35070]
KIKER ALL AUS [35382]
KILBOURN PRE 1870 BETHNAL GREEN, LND,
ENG [37832]
KILBURN PRE 1870 WINGATE, DUR, ENG [36056]
KILBY 1850+ LAUNCESTON, TAS, AUS [35068] :
1860 BIGGLESWADE, BDF, ENG [35024] : 1800S
LONDON, ENG [35068] : PRE 1840 OFFLEY &
KINGS WALDEN, HRT, ENG [35701] : PRE 1850
BIRMINGHAM, ENG [37245] : 1750-1800 RAMSEY,
IOM, UK [35068]
KILDAY PRE 1806 TYR, IRL [33924] : 1830-1930 OFF,
IRL [34165]
KILDERRY 1800S CLA, IRL [37186]
KILDOFF ALL WORLDWIDE [37530]
KILDUFF JOHN C1840+ MOORE, ROS, IRL [37530] :
ALL WORLDWIDE [37530]
KILE 1812 PICKAWAY, OH, USA [37008]
KILEY 1806+ TIP, IRL [38291]
KILFORD ALL ENG [35069]
KILFOYLE PRE 1850 CAR, KIK & WEX, IRL [37427] :
ALL WORLDWIDE [37427]
KILGORE PRE 1830 OMAGH, TYR, IRL [34113] :
MARTHA FRANCI 1814-1860 MO & TN, USA
[34481] : 1820-1860 MADISON CO., OH, USA [37576]
: 1773-1990 WISE & SCOTT, VA, USA [38136]
KILGOUR ALEX 1840+ HOBART, TAS, AUS [34461] :
ALEX 1850+ WILLIAMSTOWN, VIC, AUS [34461] :
ALEX PRE 1790 DUNDEE, ANS, SCT [34461] : 1801
KIRKCALDY, FIF, SCT [34529] : PRE 1700 FIF, SCT
[35627] : 1750-1850S DUNDEE, ANS, SCT [35938] :
1700-1750S GLAMIS, ANS, SCT [35938]
KILHAM 1880+ SYDNEY, NSW, AUS [34693] : 1800-
1870 BURY, SSX, ENG [34693] : 1820-1880 BIGNOR,
SSX, ENG [34693]
KILHOLAND JOHN 1895-1940+ MACON CO., MO,
USA [37567] : ROSA 1889-1950+ MACON CO., MO,
USA [37567] : RUTH 1893-1990 BEVIER, MACON,
MO, USA [37567]
KILKIE 1819+ INVER, DON, IRL [38291]
KILLAR PRE 1870 TERNOPOL GALICIA, OES &
POL [36679]
KILKIE 1819+ INVER, DON, IRL [38291]
KILLDOFF ALL WORLDWIDE [37530]
KILLDUFF ALL WORLDWIDE [37530]
KILLEN MARY 1838-1868 MAY & DUB, IRL [36776] :
PRE 1829 IRL & CAN [34068]
KILLEY 1803+ RUSHEN, IOM [34288] : 1700S NJ,
USA [37018]
KILLICK 1731-1804 BLACKFRIARS, LND, ENG
[35597] : PRE 1900 MANNINGTREE, ESS, ENG
[36477]
KILLICOAT ALL WORLDWIDE [37879]
KILLIN C1810-1820 MAUCHLINE, AYR, SCT [33845]
KILLINGBACK 1837 ELMDON, ESS, ENG [35903]
KILLINGBECK C1812 WITHERSFIELD, SFK, ENG
[37167]
KILLINGER ALL ENG [37630]
KILLINGSWORTH PRE 1900 BUCKINGHAM, BKM,
ENG [33776]

KILLINGWORTH PRE 1900 BUCKINGHAM, BKM, ENG [33776]
KILLIP ALL BIRKENHEAD, CHS, ENG [35115] : ALL IOM, UK [35115]
KILLMAN 1800-1850S MADRAS & BANGALORE, INDIA [35815]
KILLMASTER C1750 MINCHINHAMPTON, GLS, ENG [37838]
KILLMORE 1800S NY, USA [36851] : 1800 HERKIMER, NY, USA [38098]
KILLOOLEY 1844+ BOMBALA, NSW, AUS [34966]
KILLOR 1820 BELFAST, ANT, IRL [34774]
KILLOUCH 1820 BELFAST, ANT, IRL [34774]
KILLOWAY 1820+ INDIA [35136] : PRE 1820 SLI, IRL [35136]
KILLWICK ALL CAM, ENG [36829] : ALL ESS, ENG [36829] : ALL SFK, ENG [36829] : ALL NFK, ENG [36829]
KILMARTIN PRE 1860 ROS, IRL [35546]
KILMASTER ALL WORLDWIDE [37198]
KILMER 1800+ ONT, CAN [38235]
KILMINSTER PRE 1828 BATH, SOM, ENG [35234] : ALL WORLDWIDE [37198]
KILMISTER ALL WORLDWIDE [37198]
KILPATRICK PRE 1842 SINGLETON, NSW, AUS [35472] : 1870+ HORSHAM, VIC, AUS [35493] : 1863+ VIC, AUS [37586] : 1830-1950 HURON CO., ONT, CAN [36901] : 1820+ GRENVILLE CO., ONT, CAN [37586] : PRE 1870 SRY, ENG [35493] : 1800-1840 SURINAM, INDIA [35472] : PRE 1900 ANT, IRL [37601] : 1600-1720 DOW, IRL [38045] : 1600-1720 LDY, IRL [38045] : 1600-1720 TYR, IRL [38045] : 1600-1720 ANT, IRL [38045] : 1880+ CA, USA [37601]
KILPIN PRE 1850 LEEDS, WRY, ENG [37246] : 1900+ BKM, ENG [37347]
KILSBY ALL KETTERING, NTH, ENG [36830]
KILTY C1812 KEN, ENG [35133] : C1836 WESTMINSTER ST JAMES, MDX, ENG [35133] : ALL CLA, IRL [35248]
KILVINGTON PRE 1810 STOCKTON ON FOREST, YKS, ENG [35983] : 1800S RAINTON, YKS, ENG [36791]
KILWORTH ALL CRICK & WEST HADDON, NTH, ENG [37730]
KIMBALL 1500S IPSWICH, SFK, ENG [35617]
KIMBER 1855+ PATERSON, NSW, AUS [34421] : 1820S TAS, AUS [35877] : 1800S ASHURST, KEN, ENG [34205] : 1490 FAIRFORD, GLS, ENG [34421] : ALL CLERKENWELL, LND, ENG [34723] : PRE 1750 BURBAGE, WIL, ENG [35346] : 1800-1814 BRK, ENG [35850] : PRE 1800 BURBAGE, WIL, ENG [37687] : 1840+ NEWBURY, BRK, ENG [38541] : PRE 1850 USA [36298]
KIMBERLEY ALL COVENTRY & BIRMINGHAM, WAR, ENG [36234]
KIMBLE ALL CRAZIES HILL & SHINFIELD, BRK, ENG [36407] : ALL WANDSWORTH & EPSOM, SRY, ENG [36407] : 1840+ JACKSON & LAWRENCE CO., OH, USA [37565]
KIMMERLY PRE 1800 LENNOX & ADDINGTON, RICHMOND, ONT, CAN [38428]
KIMMEY PRE 1800 WORLDWIDE [38345]
KIMMINS C1800 TIVERTON, DEV, ENG [35038]
KIMPEL WILLIAM PRE 1890S PRESTON, ONT, CAN [34216]
KIMPTON THOMAS 1807-1889 LAMBETH, LND, ENG [33961] : 1760+ BOURN, CAM, ENG [36772]
KINANE 1800S TIPPERARY, TIP, IRL [34574]
KINCADE ALL AUS [34196]
KINCAID ALL AUS [34196] : 1850+ DAYLESFORD, VIC, AUS [35823] : PRE 1850 CAPETOWN, RSA [35823] : PRE 1700 CAMPSIE, STI, SCT [35252]

KINCH 1700S PRIORS MARSTON, WAR, ENG [36431]
KINCHIN 1700 STEPNEY, MDX, ENG [34210] : 1842+ FLADBURY, WOR, ENG [37265]
KIND PRE 1837 LEI, ENG [34773]
KINDBLOM PRE 1870 LINKOPINGSLAN, OSTERGOTLAND, SWE [37821]
KINDER ALL DBY, ENG [36506] : 1600-1750 GER [38224] : 1830S ROSCOE, OFF, IRL [34075] : JACOB PRE 1760 ROTTERDAM, HOLLAND, NL [34992] : C1790 WYTHE CO., VA, USA [38044]
KINDERMANN 1681 WARBURG, GER [38749]
KINDESS HENRY 1879-1908 INVERURIE, ABD, SCT [37023]
KINDLY PRE 1715 GLADSMUIR, ELN, SCT [37852]
KINDNESS HENRY 1908-1958 CHICAGO, IL, USA [37023]
KINDRED 1840S-60S LONDON, ENG [35243] : C1906 WEST HARTLEPOOL, DUR, ENG [36270]
KINDT C1730S RICHMOND TWP, BERKS CO., PA, USA [34126]
KINEFECH 1800S CARRIGALINE, COR, IRL & AUS [34596]
KING 1847+ CANOWINDRA, NSW, AUS [34773] : 1891+ ECHUCA, VIC, AUS [34906] : ALL RICHMOND, TAS, AUS [35063] : EMMA 1841-1903 NSW, AUS [35086] : 1800S PENGUIN, TAS, AUS [35377] : QUINTON 1856+ BEECHWORTH, VIC, AUS [35484] : 1870+ LISMORE, NSW, AUS [35521] : THOMAS J. 1855+ PORT ADELAIDE, SA, AUS [35585] : THOMAS J. 1883+ SYDNEY, NSW, AUS [35585] : 1856+ PORT ALBERT, VIC, AUS [35599] : WILLIAM 1846+ NSW, AUS [35831] : RHODA 1864+ MOUNT COLE, VIC, AUS [35831] : 1846+ FAIRY MEADOW, NSW, AUS [35863] : 1841+ SMITHFIELD, NSW, AUS [35874] : WILLIAM 1854+ SYDNEY, NSW, AUS [36600] : PRE 1900S MUSWELLBROOK, NSW, AUS [37910] : WILLIAM 1850+ BATHURST AREA, NSW, AUS [38290] : C1840+ VIC, AUS & PT [34907] : C1811 BROAD COVE, NFD, CAN [33852] : 1850+ WELLINGTON CO., ONT, CAN [34231] : PRE 1850 SEYMOUR TWP., ONT, CAN [34365] : PRE 1700 ROXTON, BDF & HUN, ENG [33866] : 1830S MANUDEN, ESS ENG [33870] : ISAAC 1700S BRISTOL, GLS, ENG [33918] : C1820 FRAMPTON, GLS, ENG [33918] : C1830 DEV, ENG [33937] : WILLIAM ALL MDX, ENG [33961] : MARY ANN 1804-1882 MDX, ENG [33961] : 1835 WANDSWORTH, SRY, ENG [34336] : PRE 1800 SRY, ENG [34383] : C1850 KEN, ENG [34395] : 1800-1840 LONDON, ENG [34448] : C1834 WALWORTH, SRY, ENG [34452] : 1700-1750 HAINES (HAYNES), BDF, ENG [34552] : 1835 STROUD, GLS, ENG [34594] : PRE 1850 EYNESBURY & ST NEOTS, CAM, ENG [34611] : PRE 1858 STOKE BY NAYLAND, SFK, ENG [34648] : 1820-1900 FLAXBOURTON, SOM, ENG [34658] : MARIA PRE 1832 NORWICH, NFK, ENG [34902] : SAMUEL PRE 1834 AYLESBURY, BKM, ENG [34992] : RICHARD 1800S SYDENHAM, OXF ENG [35024] : GEORGE PRE 1860 BARTON UPON HUMBER, LIN, ENG [35024] : C1850 FENNY STRATFORD, BKM, ENG [35038] : ALL LEI, ENG [35246] : GEORGE PRE 1810 WIL, ENG [35252] : DANIEL 1760S STROUD, GLS, ENG [35560] : 1860-1880 WHITE HILL, SSX, ENG [35565] : 1854-1887 SOUTHAMPTON, HAM, ENG [35565] : THOMAS J C1874 SOUTHAMPTON, HAM, ENG [35585] : THOMAS J. 1817+ HYTHE, KEN, ENG [35585] : THOMAS J. C1840 GLOUCESTER, GLS, ENG [35585] : PRE 1856 NEWBURY, BRK, ENG [35599] : 1800+ LONG WHATTON, LEI, ENG [35712] :

1700+ NORTH NEWNTON, WIL, ENG [35874] :
C1833 TACKLEY, OXF, ENG [35910] : 1700-1800
NTH, ENG [36038] : 1800-1850 WESTMINSTER,
LND, ENG [36047] : PRE 1870 OLD & ROLLESTON,
NTH, ENG [36082] : GEORGE PRE 1850 CARLTON
& BREWELL, NFK & HRT, ENG [36082] : 1800-1900
CHADHUNT, WAR, ENG [36097] : PRE 1840
GATESHEAD, DUR, ENG [36102] : ELIZABETH
1760+ ALBOURNE & SHERMANBURY, SSX,
ENG [36212] : PRE 1847 BOXFORD, SFK, ENG
[36215] : ALL LITTLEWORTH & LONGWORTH,
BRK & OXF, ENG [36231] : 1840 DBY, ENG [36250] :
1821 WIX, ESS, ENG [36287] : ELIZABETH PRE
1841 BRISTOL, GLS, ENG [36309] : 1800+
HILLINGTON, MDX & OXF, ENG [36326] : PRE
1850 SHOREDITCH, LND, ENG [36380] : 1840-1930
UPPER HOLLOWAY, MDX, ENG [36485] : 1850-
1870 TORQUAY, DEV, ENG [36530] : 1811+
WALWORTH, SRY, ENG [36621] : JOHN 1800S
BRADFORD, YKS, ENG [36633] : PRE 1850
STREET, SOM, ENG [36676] : PRE 1900 BECCLES,
SFK, ENG [36765] : WILLIAM 1898 QUEEN
VICTORIA ST, LND, ENG [36782] : GEORGE 1905
WEEDON, NTH, ENG [36782] : WILLIAM 1900
BECKENHAM, KEN, ENG [36782] : GEORGE 1890
EAST HADDON, NTH, ENG [36782] : WILLIAM
1840 HOLDENBY, NTH, ENG [36782] : WILLIAM
1800+ FARNBOROUGH, WAR, ENG [36782] :
C1847 BRENCHLEY, KEN, ENG [36803] : PRE 1800
BILLESDON TUGBY, LEI, ENG [36817] : ALL
COMBWICH TAUNTON, SOM, ENG [36834] : ALL
BRIDGWATER, SOM, ENG [36834] : 1850S
CROYDON, LND, ENG [36848] : PRE 1804 LONG
CRENDON, BKM, ENG [36866] : 1700S HRT, ENG
[36872] : 1797+ BAMPTON, OXF, ENG [36975] :
PRE 1812 RADFORD, NTT, ENG [37000] : 1500+
OXF & BKM, ENG [37099] : ALL GLS, ENG [37115] :
ALL WIL, ENG [37115] : JOHN C1883-1917
LONDON, ENG [37173] : 1848 STOKE DAMEREL,
DEV, ENG [37204] : PRE 1850 HEADCORN, KEN,
ENG [37214] : 1830+ WIVELSFORD, SSX, ENG
[37214] : 1780-1840 FRECKENHAM, SFK, ENG
[37223] : 1700+ HAYNES, BDF, ENG [37304] :
BEATRICE 1870-1904 IPSWICH, SFK, ENG [37311] :
OLIVER 1867-1900 CHELMONDISTON, SFK, ENG
[37311] : ALBERT C1820+ CHELMONDISTON,
SFK, ENG [37311] : DAVID H. 1767+
WINTERSLOW, WIL, ENG [37321] : GEORGE 1790-
1860 HARLOW, ESS, ENG [37488] : 1750-1850 DOR,
ENG [37609] : PRE 1830 ASPLEY, WAR, ENG
[37621] : ALL LIVERPOOL, LAN, ENG [37751] :
1800-1900 GREAT YARMOUTH, NFK, ENG [37757]
: 1700-1900 DEV & DUR, ENG [37829] : PRE 1800
BLETCHINGTON, OXF, ENG [37832] : PRE 1890
BRAMLEY & ASHTEAD, SRY, ENG [37834] : ALL
HINCKLEY, LEI, ENG [37868] : 1800S DRAYTON,
MDX, ENG [37910] : C1800 WARMINSTER, WIL,
ENG [37918] : 1700 PEASENHALL, SFK, ENG
[37928] : PRE 1870 PADDINGTON, LND, ENG
[37987] : 1550+ ENG [38241] : DANIEL PRE 1840
CHAPEL ALLERTON, SOM, ENG [38290] :
DANIEL 1780+ BATH, SOM, ENG [38290] : 1800S
BRK, GLS & WIL, ENG [38468] : 1730-1850
MARLESFORD, SFK, ENG [38483] : C1770
EBBESBOURNE WAKE, WIL, ENG [38489] : PRE
1775 BROOKLAND, KEN, ENG [38708] : PRE 1600
SFK, ENG [38746] : 1876+ POONA, INDIA [34667] :
C1858 CASTLE ISLAND, KER, IRL [34935] : ALL
DUBLIN, IRL [34938] : ALL POMEROY, TYR, IRL
[35460] : 1830+ DUBLIN CITY, IRL [35529] :
HANORA C1863 MILLTOWN, CLA, IRL [35786] :
1800+ LEENANE, GAL, IRL [35963] : RICHARD

1843 NEW ROSS, WEX, IRL [36782] : 1830
ATHLONE, WEM, IRL [37558] : 1800S TUAM, GAL,
IRL & AUS [34198] : 1920-1929 BALLYGALVERT,
WEX, IRL & NZ [36874] : JOHN 1890+ TIMARU &
DUNEDIN, NZ [33918] : 1880 GREYTOWN,
WAIRAPARA, NZ [36250] : 1815 BAY OF ISLANDS,
NZ [36300] : PRE 1888 NAPIER, NZ [36848] : 1871+
DUNEDIN, NZ [37155] : 1830+ WEST ISLAND, PT
& AUS [34703] : 1810+ CAMBUSLANG, LKS, SCT
[33956] : ALEXANDER 1780+ BARONY, LKS, SCT
[33956] : C1840 EDINBURGH, MLN, SCT [34713] :
C1800 KIRKWALL, OKI, SCT [34713] : 1880+
AVOCH, ROC, SCT [34810] : 1800 PETERHEAD &
ABERDEEN, ABD, SCT [35027] : 1880+
GLASGOW, RFW, SCT [35825] : 1800-1900 BEITH,
AYR, SCT [35923] : ALL STRICHEN, ABD, SCT
[36061] : 1700-1800 FIF, SCT [36394] : PRE 1878
CRAFTHEAD & LINLITHGOW, WLN, SCT [36888]
: PRE 1795 KILBIRNIE, AYR, SCT [37144] : PRE
1764 TRANENT, ELN, SCT [37852] : 1750+ LKS,
SCT [38260] : 1750+ COATBRIDGE & AIRDRIE,
LKS, SCT [38260] : BENJAMIN 1800S WICK &
REAY, CAI, SCT [38290] : 1900S PITTSBURGH, PA,
USA [35460] : C1890 SAN FRANCISCO, CA, USA
[35963] : PHILLIP 1850-1895 PEORIA CO., IL, USA
[36573] : JESTON C1800+ KY & IN, USA [37003] :
HENRY C1838 CHESTER, PA, USA [37155] : PRE
1930 NEW BEDFORD, MA, USA [37223] : WESLEY
PRE 1824 LANCASTER CO., PA, USA [38023] :
CHARLES ALL WYTHE & SMYTHE CO., VA, USA
[38060] : 1857-1900 KNOX, IL, USA [38097] : 1820 TN,
USA [38143] : ALL MA, OH, KS, CA, USA [38363] :
PRE 1918 CARMARTHEN, CMN, WLS [36181]

KINGDOM ALL NEW ENGLAND, NSW, AUS [36632]
: 1852+ BALLARAT, VIC, AUS [38205] : 1866 MDX,
ENG [35872]

KINGDON PRE 1900 SWIMBRIDGE, DEV, ENG
[38205] : C1760-1815 DULVERTON & NORTH
PETHERTON, SOM, ENG [38309]

KINGE 1650+ COSBY, LEI, ENG [36827]

KINGERY 1800 OH, USA [35275]

KINGHAN C1700 BALLYMACRAN, LDY, IRL [36818]
: ALL NZ [36818]

KINGMAN PRE 1900 SOM, ENG [35433] : ANN 1700S
CASTLETON, DOR, ENG [36633] : 1900+
BUFFALO, NY, USA [34011]

KINGS ALL ROCK, WOR, ENG [35417]

KINGSBOROUGH 1800S DRUMCREE, ARM, IRL
[36607]

KINGSBURY 1687 WORMINGFORD, ESS, ENG
[34142] : C1800-1900 STEPNEY & LAMBETH, LND,
ENG [37102] : 1860S HOXTON & SHOREDITCH,
LND, ENG [37102] : PRE 1940 CHELSEA &
FULHAM, LND, ENG [37102] : 1587 GREAT
WALDINGFIELD, SFK, ENG [37837] : ALL
WORLDWIDE [34324]

KINGSELL 1840-1990 GOULBURN & ILLAWARRA,
NSW, AUS [34294]

KINGSFORD 1600-1900 WORLDWIDE [35944] : ALL
WORLDWIDE [36310]

KINGSLEY ALL LONDON &, DEV, ENG [34671] :
ALL LONDON, ENG [37392] : 1800-1870S MENAI,
AGY, WLS [36522] : ALL WORLDWIDE [37145]

KINGSNORTH 1700-1896 BETHERSDEN, KEN, ENG
& NZ [36874]

KINGSTON PRE 1868 YOUNG, NSW, AUS [35472] :
PRE 1700 THORNEY ABBEY, CAM, ENG [34204] :
C1840 SHEPTON MALLET, SOM, ENG [34556] :
1700S STRENSALL, YKS, ENG [34569] : PRE 1850
BURTON AGNES, YKS, ENG [34569] : 1650-1850
PETERBOROUGH, NTH, ENG [37223] : 1700-1800S

SOUTH STOKE, SOM, ENG [37544] : PRE 1900 BAWNAHOW, COR, IRL [35814]

KINGSTONE PRE 1840 UPWELL, CAM, ENG [35354] : 1700-1850 UPWELL & GUYHIRNE, CAM, ENG [37642]

KINGSWEL PRE 1830 IOW, HAM, ENG [37271]

KINGWELL 1800-1990 PLYMOUTH AREA, DEV, ENG [36398]

KINGWILL ALL SALE, VIC, AUS [35345] : ALL BOVEY TRACEY, DEV, ENG [35345]

KINIRY 1775-1850 COR, IRL [36318] : ALL USA [36318]

KINKADE ALL AUS [34196] : 1850-1900 ONT, CAN [36355] : PRE 1850 LDY, IRL [36355]

KINKAID ALL AUS [34196]

KINKEAD ALL IRL [34571] : ALL WORLDWIDE [34196]

KINKEADE ALL WORLDWIDE [34196]

KINKED ALL AUS [34196]

KINLEY PRE 1880 BANBRIDGE, DOW & ANT, IRL [37708]

KINLOCH PRE 1860 KILMALCOLM, RFW, SCT [33906] : C1760 OLD KILPATRICK, DNB, SCT [35252]

KINLYSIDE 1830S BEW, SCT [36843]

KINNAIRD 1849 KIRKLISTON, WLN, SCT [37165]

KINNANE (SEE GUINNAN [38295])

KINNASTON PRE 1890 HIGH ERCALL, SAL, ENG [35215]

KINNEAR 1840+ SYDNEY, NSW, AUS [35207] : 1817-1840 LONDON, MDX, ENG [35207] : 1870+ OAMARU, NZ [33944] : PRE 1870 MONTROSE, ANS, SCT [33944] : 1770-1790 MONTROSE, ANS, SCT [35207] : 1600-1800 DYSART, FIF, SCT [36556] : MARY 1800-1860 OLD MONKLAND, LKS, SCT [37488] : 1750-1800 EDINBURGH, MLN, SCT [38465]

KINNEN PRE 1821 ANACARTY, TIP, IRL [34285]

KINNERSLEY 1800S BRISTOL AREA, GLS, ENG [34483] : 1700-1800S HANDSWORTH, STS, ENG [34483] : PRE 1805 STEPNEY, MDX, ENG [34570]

KINNEY C1846+ KILWINNING, AYR, SCT [38067] : 1600+ MA, USA [38241] : ALL CT & IN, USA [38287]

KINNIN PRE 1870 DEPTFORD, KEN, ENG [36072]

KINNINMONT 1750+ AUCHTERMUCHTY, FIF, SCT [34768]

KINNISON 1850 DUNDEE, ANS, SCT &, INDIA [34708] : PRE 1850 ANS, SCT [36072]

KINNMONT C1860+ DUNDEE, PER, SCT [35053]

KINREAD PRE 1800 CASTLETOWN, MALEW, IOM [34137]

KINROSS PRE 1800 DUNBLANE, PER, SCT [34621]

KINSELA PRE 1840 ROSE BAY, NSW, AUS [34857]

KINSELLA C1830 WEX, IRL [34145] : PRE 1900 DUB, IRL [35742] : 1850+ CLARA, KIK, IRL [36763] : 1700+ DUBLIN, IRL [37284] : ALL DUB, IRL [37407] : SUSAN 1819-1891 DUBLIN, IRL [38724]

KINSEY PRE 1850 ASHBY DE LA ZOUCHE, LEI, ENG [36188] : 1750-1830 LAN, ENG [36297] : PRE 1850 ENG [37554] : 1700-1800 STS, ENG [37762] : PRE 1867 RUNCORN, LAN, ENG [38415] : 1850+ MIAMI CO., OH & MO, USA [38050]

KINSLAER 1770-1845 HARRISON CO., KY, USA [33761] : PRE 1765 MD, USA [33761]

KINSMAN PRE 1850 ST AGNES & REDRUTH, CON, ENG [34753] : PRE 1800 KILKHAMPTON, CON, ENG [35255]

KINVIG 1860+ LEITH, MLN, SCT [34125] : ALL WORLDWIDE [34125]

KINZER 1820+ STEARNS CO., MN & WA, USA [34988]

KINZETT PRE 1842 WAR, ENG [36841] : PRE 1842 OXHILL, WAR, ENG [36888] : 1842+ NELSON, NZ [36841]

KIOVICH ALL UNGVAR & UZOROD, HU [36532]

KIPLING 1800+ COOKRIDGE, YKS, ENG [38395]

KIPP 1810+ POTS DAM, POT, DDR [35073]

KIPPAX ALL KIRKBURTON, WRY, ENG [37372]

KIPPEN ALL KENMORE, PER, SCT [36704] : ALL FALKIRK, STI, SCT [38298] : ALL GLASGOW, LKS, SCT [38298]

KIPPS ALL WORLDWIDE [37083]

KIRBY 1800+ AUS [35538] : PRE 1720 PACKINGTON, LEI, ENG [34311] : 1800S SEDGEFORD, NFK, ENG [35256] : ALL DBY, ENG [35467] : 1800+ ENG [35538] : PRE 1800 HAMPSTEAD, LND, ENG [35592] : CHARLES 1826+ BALLINGDON, ESS, ENG [35634] : 1740-1820 SKIPTON & WHITBY, YKS, ENG [35813] : 1800-1890 LND, ENG [36095] : C1880 MAIDSTONE, KEN, ENG [37359] : PRE 1765 LEI, ENG [37706] : JOHN 1790-1830 HIGHWORTH, WIL, ENG [38724] : MARGARET 1836-1850 IRL [37567] : 1700-1750 HANOVER CO., VA, USA [36554] : 1865+ ST LOUIS, MO, USA [36645] : 1765+ SC, USA [38340] : 1776-1830 TALBOT CO., MD, USA [38764]

KIRBYE 1850-1890 COLLINGWOOD & HEATHCOTE, VIC, AUS [37488]

KIRCHER ALL BAW, FRG [38657]

KIRCHNER 1850+ BRISBANE, QLD, AUS [34020] : 1850+ HAMILTON, VIC, AUS [35798]

KIRFOOT PRE 1800 WORLDWIDE [34746]

KIRGAN 1800-1900 DUNLOY, ANT, IRL [36115]

KIRK 1800-1900 HALIFAX CO., NS, CAN [34225] : 1825-1900 KIRKS FERY, QUE, CAN [34514] : C1790 NOTTINGHAM, NTT, ENG [33928] : 1830-1875 ABY, LIN, ENG [34677] : 1800+ BETHNAL GREEN, MDX, ENG [34818] : PRE 1881 BOCKENFIELD, NBL, ENG [35026] : 1680-1800 DRAYTON PARSLOW &GRANDBOROUGH, BKM, ENG [35701] : PRE 1850 LEICESTER, LEI, ENG [36082] : 1800S ENG [36289] : 1778 SIMONBURN, NBL, ENG [36386] : JOHN PRE 1736 NOTTINGHAM, NTT, ENG [36532] : 1700-1750 NORTH FRODINGHAM, YKS, ENG [37011] : CHARLOTTE PRE 1837 LEEDS, YKS, ENG [37610] : PRE 1810 NOTTINGHAM, NTT, ENG [37866] : JAMES 1850 STRAITON, AYR, IRL [34091] : THOMAS 1780-1830 LONDONDERRY, LDY, IRL [34514] : 1813-1886 BELFAST, IRL & USA [36960] : 1700-1800 ARBROATH, ANS, SCT [34225] : ALL ROX, SCT [36999] : C1717 LANCASTER CO., VA, USA [36354] : 1750-1850 SPRINGFIELD, VT, USA [38131] : 1700-1900 WORLDWIDE [36977]

KIRKALDY 1800+ ANSTRUTHER, FIF, SCT [33955]

KIRKBRIDE ALL CUL, ENG [35579]

KIRKBY 1828+ EVANDALE, TAS, VIC & NSW, AUS [33970] : 1600+ BARTON IN FABIS, NTT, DBY & BDF, ENG [33970] : 1820+ STANSTEAD ABBOTS, HRT, ESS & LND, ENG [33970] : 1800+ ENG [34132] : C1820 STAPLEFORD, NTT, ENG [34734] : 1750-1850 WHITBECK, CUL & LAN, ENG [35624] : 1800+ COVENTRY, WAR, ENG [36257] : 1800+ LANCASTER, LAN, ENG [37666]

KIRKE PRE 1900 AUS [36477] : PRE 1900 EAST MARKHAM, NTT, ENG [36477]

KIRKER ALL AUS [35382]

KIRKHAM 1850+ VIC, AUS [37579] : 1700+ KNUTSFORD, CHS, ENG [34163] : 1800+ POPLAR, LND, ENG [37579] : PRE 1880 ENG [37739]

KIRKHART PRE 1850 VA & PA, USA [38181]

KIRKHOPE ALL DFS, SCT [36429]

KIRKLAND 1825-50 RENFREW CO., ONT, CAN [36722] : 1825-75 WOLFORD, ONT, CAN [36722] : PRE 1830 ARM, IRL [36722] : ALL STRATHAVEN, LKS, SCT [37480] : 1700-1850 AVONDALE, LKS,

SCT **[38076]** : 1750-1850 ORANGE CO., NC, USA
[38342] : 1850-1900 DENTON CO., TX, USA **[38367]**

KIRKMAN 1842 + SYDNEY, NSW, AUS **[35365]** :
JOHN 1839 HEATON NORRIS, CHS, ENG **[37184]**

KIRKNESS 1800 + OKI, SCT **[37426]**

KIRKPATRICK 1800 + BROMLEY, KEN, ENG **[37116]**
: C1700-1830 CARNSAMPSON, ANT, IRL **[33845]** :
1200-1300 CLOSEBURNE, DFS, SCT **[37027]** : 1700S
WATTIESNEACH, DFS, SCT **[37027]** : 1800S SCT &
ENG **[35161]**

KIRKWOOD 1845 + BRISBANE, QLD, AUS **[36632]** :
1820 + ONT, CAN **[37492]** : 1850 + ASHFORD,
KEN, ENG **[35501]** : 1835 MAYFIELD, STS, ENG
[37174] : 1760 + KIRKINTILLOCH, DNB, SCT
[34290] : ALL KILBARCHAN, RFW, SCT **[34644]** :
1800 + RUTHERGLEN, LKS, SCT **[35027]** : 1700 +
POLMONT, STI, SCT **[35085]** : 1880 + LEITH, MLN,
SCT **[35486]** : PRE 1870 BLANTYRE, LKS, SCT
[37242] : 1700 + LOCKWINNOCH, RFW, SCT
[37492] : PRE 1815 MOREBATTLE, ROX, SCT
[38056]

KIRSCH 1700S KAULWITZ, SIL, GER **[33901]** : PRE
1700 FUSS, RPF, GER **[38681]**

KIRSCHLER PRE 1852 ILVESHEIM, BAD, BRD
[33817] : 1840 + USA **[33817]**

KIRSCK C1838 COTTBUS, COT, DDR **[37144]**

KIRSH 1900 + WEXBURN, SAS, CAN **[38434]** : PRE
1900 BUDAPEST, HU **[38434]**

KIRSHAW 1810-1840 AIRDS, NSW, AUS **[33817]**

KIRSOP PRE 1800 SIMONBURN, NBL, ENG **[36110]**

KIRSTATTER PRE 1600 OBERGIMOERN, WUE,
GER **[36972]**

KIRSTING C1870 BOW, MDX, ENG **[34086]**

KIRTLETON 1840S HELENSBURGH, DNB, SCT
[38283]

KIRTON 1600 + ALSTON, CUL, ENG **[35927]** : 1840 +
HOVE, SSX, ENG **[35927]** : 1700 + LONDON, ENG
[35927] : 1750 NEW DEER & SAVOCH, ABD, SCT
[37628] : C1800 SCT **[38729]**

KIRWAN 1823 + BATHURST THE LESS, NSW, AUS
[36291] : OF DALGIN C1600 DALGAN, IRL **[34005]** :
1800 + DUB, GAL & ANT, IRL **[34005]** : PRE 1788
MYSHALL, CAR, IRL **[35578]** : C1800 GELSTON,
KKD, SCT **[34005]** : 1800 USA **[34005]**

KIRWIN 1875 IRL **[34540]**

KISHERE ALL WORLDWIDE **[35879]**

KISHPAUGH 1750S SUSSEX, NJ, USA **[36966]** : 1750
SUSSEX CO., NJ, USA **[38192]**

KISILEWICZ PRE 1860 GALICIAL, UKRAINE, OES
[36679]

KISS PRE 1853 WARWICK, WAR, ENG **[35702]**

KISSANE 1843 LAHESROUGH, KER, IRL **[33967]**

KISSEL PRE 1750 GROSS KARLBACH, RPR, GER
[35983] : 1700 + GROSSKARLBACH, BAV, GER
[36869] : 1850S CLINTON CO., PA, USA **[38339]**

KISSINGER 1800-1900 LINCOLN CO., KY, USA
[37586]

KISSLING C1750 HOLZHAUSEN, BAW, FRG **[38660]**

KITCATT ALL ENG **[36166]**

KITCH (SEE KETCH) [38188]

KITCHEN 1800 + GLENGARRY, ONT, CAN **[35614]** :
PRE 1750 COLTON, LAN, ENG **[34053]** : C1799 STH
PETHERTON, SOM, ENG **[35252]** : ELEANOR
C1806 CUL, ENG **[35607]** : 1750-1890 LONDON,
ENG **[35775]** : PRE 1850 LEI, ENG **[36054]** : 1820-
1870 NORTHALLERTON, NRY, ENG **[36867]** :
1805 + FORRES, MOR, SCT **[35208]** : C1752
SOLEBURY, PA, USA **[38220]**

KITCHENER 1800 + MARYLEBONE, MDX, ENG
[35905] : 1820 NORWOOD, SRY, ENG **[37080]**

KITCHENHAM PRE 1850 WADHURST, SSX, ENG
[34611] : PRE 1850 LINTON, KEN, ENG **[34611]**

KITCHIN PRE 1837 IRTON, CUL, ENG **[37103]**

KITCHING 1700 + BRISBANE, QLD, AUS & NZ
[36266] : PRE 1850 ALDBOROUGH, NRY, ENG
[33860]

KITE C1827 DOWNTON, WIL, ENG **[37830]**

KITELEY PRE 1750 LONDON, ENG **[34364]** :
HANNAH J. 1745-69 BALTIMORE, MD, USA
[38086]

KITERINGHAM PRE 1720 NFK, ENG **[37737]**

KITSON JAMES 1880 + WA, AUS **[35465]** : 1851 +
GREENWICH, KEN, ENG **[35465]** : 1820 + LEEDS,
WRY, ENG **[35465]** : ALL LONDON, ENG **[36748]** :
1825 ECCLESHILL, YKS, ENG **[37174]** : 1820-84
IDLE, YKS, ENG **[37174]** : 1820 BRADFORD, YKS,
ENG **[37174]** : 1790 BOMBAY, INDIA **[35067]** : PRE
1836 MALLOW, COR, IRL **[33924]**

KITTEL ALL NEISSE, SIL, GER **[38685]**

KITTERINGHAM 1839 ROTHERHITHE, SRY, ENG
[33810]

KITTLE PRE 1910 IL, USA **[37525]**

KITTO 1870 + MOONTA, SA, AUS **[34035]** : 1850 +
VIC, AUS **[36993]** : 1837-1870 TUCKINGMILL, RED
RIVER, CON, ENG **[34035]** : 1750 + MEVAGISSEY,
CON, ENG **[35306]** : ALL REDRUTH, CON, ENG
[36801] : PRE 1766 CON, ENG **[36993]** : 1775-1850
BREAGE, CON, ENG **[37160]**

KITTOE PRE 1800 KENWYN, CON, ENG **[34214]**

KIVER PRE 1800 WIMBORNE, DOR, ENG **[34655]** :
1850 + CHRISTCHURCH, CBY, NZ **[34655]**

KJERBYE CHRISTOFFER 1845-1850 ADELAIDE, SA,
AUS **[37488]** : 1750-1890 DEN **[37488]** :
CHRISTOFFER 1820-1845 COPENHAGEN, KBN,
DEN **[37488]**

KJERRULF 1448 + WORLDWIDE **[38546]**

KJOLSTAD 1750 + SOR ODAL, HEDMARK, NOR
[34664]

KLAARWATER 1624 + ROTTERDAM, NL **[35963]**

KLAN CHRISTIAN PRE 1877 ALBRETCHTS, WPR,
GER **[34567]**

KLAPP HENRY PRE 1820 LANCASTER CO., PA,
USA **[36925]**

KLASCHKE PRE 1910 SU & POL **[37510]**

KLASSEN ALL GER **[38610]** : ALL USA **[38610]**

KLATT ALL MSW, GER **[34488]**

KLATTEN AUF DEM KUTZENHUFKEN C1790
COLLBERG, THU, GER **[34688]**

KLAUSER ALL CH **[38611]** : ALL FLUMS, SG, CH
[38611] : ALL TOGGENBURG, SG, CH **[38611]** : ALL
ZURICH, ZH, CH **[38611]** : ALL SCHMIEDRUED,
AG, CH **[38611]** : ALL TG, CH **[38611]** : ALL
WORLDWIDE **[38611]**

KLAWIKOWSKI 1707-1890 SIANOWO, GDANSK,
POL **[38148]**

KLAY 1815-1881 JESSEN ELSTER, KSA, GER **[38749]**

KLEESS PRE 1800 WILLMEROTH, HES, BRD **[38617]**

KLEEVBLATT PRE 1640 JURBY, UPPLAND, SWE
[38544]

KLEFFERSTEIN PRE 1800 NYSA, OP, POL **[38617]**

KLEIMENHAGEN 1790-1800S WILLIAMSPORT, PA,
USA **[34059]**

KLEIMEYER 1840-1930 BATESVILLE, IN, USA
[38149]

KLEIN 1853 + TOOWOOMBA & ALPHA, QLD, AUS
[37178] : PRE 1680 HILSCHBACH, BRD **[38615]** :
PRE 1914 REUTLINGEN, WUE, GER **[34175]** : PRE
1853 STRUTH, GER **[37178]** : CHARLES 1860
HOUSTON CO., MN, USA **[34378]**

KLEINE CHRISTION PRE 1880 NORDHEMMERN,
NRW, BRD **[36575]** : CHRISTION 1880 + LOGAN
CO. MT PULASKI, IL, USA **[36575]**

KLEINEG-LINK ALL AMSTERDAM, NL **[36894]**

KLEINGARN PRE 1850 FEHMARN ISLAND, SHO, GER [35725]

KLEINGARTNER C1700 MEK, GER [37036]

KLEINHERENBRINK ALL WORLDWIDE [34095]

KLEINIG PRE 1850 CORTNITZ, UPPER LUSATIA, GER [34766]

KLEINKNECHT 1820+ WATERLOO CO., ONT, CAN [34502] : PRE 1818 WUE, GER [34502] : 1818+ LANCASTER CO., PA, USA [34502]

KLEINMEYER 1840-1930 BATESVILLE, IN, USA [38149]

KLEINSCHMIDT PRE 1862 HES, BRD [35083] : 1610-1658 GIEBRINGHAUSEN, WAL, GER [34912]

KLEINSCHROD ALL WORLDWIDE [38612]

KLEINSCHRODT ALL WORLDWIDE [38612]

KLEINSCHROT ALL WORLDWIDE [38612]

KLEINSCHROTH ALL WORLDWIDE [38612]

KLEMM ALL WAIBSTADT & OBERGIMPERN, BAD, GER [38534] : ALL HEDDESHEIM, BAD, GER & AUS [33895]

KLEMME 1819 MASSBRUCH, GER [38749] : 1732 BRAKE, WEF, GER [38749]

KLEMMER PRE 1795 NRW, GER [38630] : ALL WORLDWIDE [38630] : 1795+ WORLDWIDE [38630]

KLEMT ALL SIL, GER [38607]

KLENK ALL ENZWEIHINGEN, WUE, GER [38333] : 1867+ BUFFALO, NY, USA [38333] : 1840+ USA [38728]

KLEPEC ALL WORLDWIDE [37808]

KLEPMAN PRE 1860 OBORSKI, PO, POL [34246]

KLEPS PRE 1900 RYPIN, BY, POL [34246]

KLERING ALL WORLDWIDE [38613]

KLERINGS ALL WORLDWIDE [38613]

KLEWENO PRE 1767 TRUPPEN, POM, GER [38590] : 1767+ JAGODNAJA, SU [38590]

KLIGGE ALL PADERBORN, WEF, GER [36822]

KLINE ALL LONDON, SRY, ENG [36498] : PRE 1830 CHILLISQUAQUE, PA, USA [38335] : ALL PA, USA [38369]

KLINETOB ALL WORLDWIDE [36548]

KLINGBIEL 1700-1900 GER [34624]

KLINGE 1862+ TOOWOOMBA, QLD, AUS [35147] : PRE 1862 LUTTERBERG, HAN, GER [35147]

KLINGENBERGER 1780 GOERLITZ, PRE, GER [35575]

KLINGENSMITH 1770-1810 WESTMORELAND CO., PA, USA [33760]

KLINGHJERDT 1734+ SKOVDE & ULRICEHAMN, SKARABORG, SWE [37036]

KLINK PRE 1876 KOCHERSTETTEN, WUE, GER [36809]

KLINSTROM C1740-1760S GEL, NL [38358]

KLIPSTEIN 1800-1900 GER [36589]

KLISKEY ALL WORLDWIDE [34724]

KLITTICH PRE 1850 BAW, BRD [34180]

KLIX ALL WORLDWIDE [38664]

KLOEPPER MARIA PRE 1880 NORDHEMMERN, NRW, BRD [36575]

KLOHN ALL WORLDWIDE [37464]

KLOOTS 1800-1850 WERKENDAM & WOUDRICHEM, NBT, NL [37187]

KLOPP 1800S GROSS JANNEWITZ, POM, GER [35340]

KLOSE 1900+ CRANTZ, OSTPREUβEN, GER [38603]

KLOTH PRE 1750 LANDSBERG, OPR, GER [38648]

KLOTZ C1751 KIEL, SHO, GER [37819]

KLUBERDANZ 1835-1865 BAV, GER [38528]

KLUESS PRE 1835 GOEHLEN, MSW, GER [38618] : 1880+ HORNKATEN, MSW, GER [38618] : ALL WORLDWIDE [38618]

KLUNK ALL ST MALO, BRT, FRA [33902]

KMETZ ALL WORLDWIDE [38733]

KNAB 1750-1850 REIMERSWILLER, ALS, FRA [36898]

KNABB 1725-1900 BERKS CO., PA, USA [35318]

KNABENBAUER PRE 1922 HAGEN, NRW, BRD [35021]

KNAGGS PRE 1810 MIDDLETON ON THE WOLDS, YKS, ENG [37094] : 1800S DUBLIN, IRL [35738] : 1700+ MOUNTMELLICK, LEX, IRL [38498] : 1500+ IRL [38498]

KNAPP C1827-1840S CRANBROOK, KEN, ENG [33950] : 1600-1900 GLS, ENG [36130] : ALL MAINHARDT, BAW, FRG [38657] : 1845-1917 GREYTOWN, WAIRARAPA, NZ [33950] : 1840S USA [35165] : 1807+ NY, USA [37592] : 1750-1870 SUFFOLK CO., NY, USA [37783] : 1760+ WINDHAM, CUMBERLAND, ME, USA [38571] : 15902-1880 ATHENS CO., OH, NY & CT, USA & ENG [38532]

KNAPPING PRE 1823 ESS, ENG [34280]

KNAPTON 1860 LANARK CO., ONT, CAN [38243] : 1650S FORDINGTON, DOR, ENG [33967] : 1850-1915 YEOVIL, SOM, ENG [34996] : 1810 WEYMOUTH, DOR, ENG [38243] : 1877 DOUGLAS CO., MN, USA [38243]

KNAUF PRE 1858 KASSEL, HES, BRD [38069]

KNAUTH PRE 1880 TRECHTINGSHAUSEN, RPF, GER [35147] : ALL WORLDWIDE [35147]

KNAUTHE 1779 GOERLITZ, PRE, GER [35575]

KNEALE C1860 MELBOURNE, VIC, AUS [34178] : 1853 BUNINYONG, VIC, AUS [34878] : 1850 RUTHERGLEN & WATERLOO, VIC, AUS [35538] : C1857 ADELAIDE, SA, AUS [35746] : 1853+ MELBOURNE, VIC, AUS [35746] : C1867+ DURHAM LEAD, VIC, AUS [35746] : C1855+ CRESWICK, VIC, AUS [35746] : PRE 1786 BRIDE, IOM [35185] : ALL IOM, UK [35746]

KNEBEL ALL WORLDWIDE [38739]

KNEEBONE 1780 LIFTON, DEV, ENG [37080] : 1640 MENHENIOT, CON, ENG [37080]

KNEELANDS (SEE NEELA) [37599]

KNEEN PRE 1881 JURBY, IOM [35185]

KNEIB ALL WORLDWIDE [38613]

KNEIP ALL WORLDWIDE [38613]

KNEIPP ALL WORLDWIDE [38613]

KNELAND 1200-1350 KILSPINDIE IN THE GOWRIE, PER & TAY, SCT [37599] : 1310-1650 CLELAND & MOTHERWELL, LKS, SCT [37599]

KNELL 1803-1820 RICHMOND, NSW, AUS [37553] : C1781-1801 HAM, ENG [37553]

KNELLER PRE 1800 BROWN CANDOVER, HAM, ENG [35247]

KNEMEYER 1727 FRONHAUSEN, GER [38749]

KNESTER ALL WORLDWIDE [38636]

KNETZER PRE 1828 MASON, KY, USA [36929]

KNEVELS 1750+ MEIERSBERG, LUE, GER [35370]

KNEVITT 1900+ RSA [34760]

KNEWSTED ALL WORLDWIDE [38060]

KNEWSTEP 1947+ BREMERTON & KITSAP CO., WA & BC, USA & CAN [38060] : ALL USA & ENG [38060]

KNIBLO C1800 KIRKMAIDEN, WIG, SCT [35820]

KNIE C1866-1895 LOCKEN, OPR, GER [34083]

KNIEHOF 1600-1700 ANGERMUNDE, UCKERMARK, BRA [38603]

KNIERIEMEN PRE 1780 WINGERODE, PSA, GER [38048]

KNIES ALL GUSTROW, MEK, DDR [34812]

KNIFE ALL ENG [37561]

KNIFTON 1700-1860 EAST LEAKE, NTT, ENG [36018]

KNIGGE PRE 1900 WORLDWIDE [33987] : ALL WORLDWIDE [38577]

KNIGHT WILLIAM 1838+ BALMAIN, NSW, AUS [33764] : 1850+ SYDNEY, NSW, AUS [34979] : PRE 1844+ MELBOURNE, VIC, AUS [35088] : ETHEL & EDITH 1904+ CATHCART, NSW, AUS [35549] : ELEANOR 1875+ CATHCART, NSW, AUS [35549] : DOROTHY 1901+ CATHCART, NSW, AUS [35549] : EMMA 1903+ CATHCART, NSW, AUS [35549] : RICHARD 1871-1910 CATHCART, NSW, AUS [35549] : 1850+ REDFERN, NSW, AUS [36364] : 1850+ NSW, AUS [37900] : 1850+ VIC, AUS [37900] : 1816-1850 PERTH & RENFREW, ONT, CAN [34371] : MARY 1870-1911 BARRIE, ONT, CAN [34484] : 1800+ HASTINGS, KEN, ENG [34167] : PRE 1830 CHEVENING & PENSHURST, KEN, ENG [34325] : PRE 1850 BUCKLAND NEWTON, DOR, ENG [34347] : 1750-1850 WEST BRIDGFORD, NTT, ENG [34371] : 1775+ ALMER & DORCHESTER, DOR, ENG [34416] : PRE 1859+ EWHURST, SSX, ENG [34423] : 1800S WIL & SOM, ENG [34472] : 1866-1870 BATTERSEA & CLAPHAM, SRY, ENG [34484] : 1800+ HARDWICKE, GLS, ENG [34681] : ROBT 1800+ LEI, ENG [34915] : PRE 1841 HUNTLY, ENG [35088] : 1600+ YARCOMBE, DEV, ENG [35112] : 1800+ BUCKLAND ST MARY, SOM, ENG [35112] : PRE 1800 WESTMINSTER, LND, ENG [35181] : ALL LEIGH, KEN, ENG [35260] : C1790 LANDRAKE, CON, ENG [35349] : C1875 BINSTED, HAM, ENG [35457] : RICHARD 1800+ UPHAMPTON & OMBERSLEY, WOR, ENG [35549] : LEAH 1844+ UPHAMPTON & OMBERSLEY, WOR, ENG [35549] : THOMAS 1829+ UPHAMPTON & OMBERSLEY, WOR, ENG [35549] : PRE 1800 KENSINGTON, MDX, ENG [35758] : PRE 1840 ILFORD, ESS, ENG [35866] : C1819 PORTSEA, HAM, ENG [35990] : 1811+ ITCHINGFIELD, SSX, ENG [36071] : ALL EAST RETFORD, NTT, ENG [36174] : 1800-1835 WHITSTABLE, KEN, ENG [36264] : PRE 1760 SOUTH LEVERTON, NTT, ENG [36434] : C1809 COSTOCK, NTT, ENG [36532] : HANNAH 1790 GLS, ENG [36596] : 1750+ MILWICH, STS, ENG [36701] : 1700+ GLEN PARVA, LEI, ENG [36756] : 1800-1870 TUNBRIDGE WELLS, KEN, ENG [36795] : 1800+ SRY, ENG [36811] : 1842 PORTSEA, HAM, ENG [36859] : 1840S NORWOOD, SRY, ENG [37080] : PRE 1825 KINGS NYMPTON, DEV, ENG [37104] : ALFRED JAMES 1900S NORTON MANDEVILLE, ESS, ENG [37151] : SAMUEL C1880S DODDINGHURST, ESS, ENG [37151] : ALL DEVIZES, WIL, ENG [37285] : PRE 1880 NETHERWALLOP, HAM, ENG [37287] : PRE 1780 CHAWTON & FARRINGDON, HAM, ENG [37321] : 1800S SHOREDITCH, LND, ENG [37765] : PRE 1850 BIRMINGHAM, WAR, ENG [37900] : PRE 1859+ LONDON, LND, ENG [37912] : HENRY 1770-1780 MANCHESTER, LAN, ENG [37929] : PRE 1840 WESTMINSTER & HOLBORN, MDX, ENG [38258] : GEORGE 1841-1906 UPHAMPTON & COTHERIDGE, WOR, ENG & AUS [35549] : JULIA 1840-1932 UPHAMPTON & OMBERSLEY, WOR, ENG & AUS [35549] : LEONARD C1800 DEV, ENG & AUS [37995] : 1700+ IRL [34408] : PRE 1860 BANDON, COR, IRL [34588] : 1800+ ANS, SCT [34226] : 1750-1900 BOHARM & KEITH, BAN, SCT [36783] : PRE 1800 DUDDINGSTON & NEWTON, MLN, SCT [37852] : ALL ELGIN, MOR, SCT [38357] : ALL UK [37674] : 1908 GRADY CO., OK, USA [35262] : PRE 1830 KY, USA [35290] : 1720-1840 LANCASTER, MA, USA [38131] : THOMAS 1855-1946 GREENVILLE CO., SC, USA [38141] : 1850S MONMOUTH, MON, WLS [35804]

KNIGHTBRIDGE PRE 1700 GREAT WALTHAM, ESS, ENG [37718]

KNIGHTS WILLIAM 1817-1850 CHELSEA, MDX, ENG [34484] : SARAH A. 1845+ MILE END, NEWTOWN, MDX, ENG [34484] : WALTER 1849+ CHELSEA, MDX, ENG [34484] : ROBERT W. 1844+ MILE END, NEWTOWN, MDX, ENG [34484] : WILLIAM 1850+ CHELSEA, MDX, ENG [34484] : MARY P. 1847+ CHELSEA, MDX, ENG [34484] : 1820 THELNETHAM, SFK, ENG [35067] : 1750+ ASHWELL, HRT, ENG [35592] : 1800-1900 CAISTER ON SEA, NFK, ENG [36663] : 1800-1900 SOUTH, NFK, ENG [37052] : ADAM 1740-1816 KENNINGHALL, NFK, ENG [37052] : 1850+ CASTON, NFK, ENG [37376] : 1650-1740 CARLETON RODE, NFK, ENG [37376] : 1850+ GRISTON, NFK, ENG [37376] : 1840-1900 CARBROOKE, NFK, ENG [37376] : PRE 1870 GISSING, NFK, ENG [37512] : 1860-1930 EALING, LND, ENG [37614] : ALL SFK, ENG [37629] : 1886+ SOUTHWARK, LND, ENG [37775] : JOHN 1830+ TOPCROFT, NFK, ENG [37775]

KNILL 1750+ CUXTON & ROCHESTER, KEN, ENG [37677]

KNIPFER 1770+ BURGLEMNITZ, SAX, GER [38529]

KNIPPEL 1800+ GER & USA [38065]

KNIPPER PRE 1830 SOLINGEN, RPR, GER [38647]

KNISCIA 1900-1850 ZOELSELEN, OPR [38427]

KNISEL PRE 1846 BAW, BRD [34180]

KNISTON 1700+ POUGHILL, DEV, ENG [35027]

KNOBLAUCH PRE 1880 BAW, BRD [38238]

KNOEDLER ALL BAW, FRG [38657]

KNOELLER 1931 AUS [38749] : 1958-1959 ESSEN, RPR, BRD [38749]

KNOEPFEL PRE 1774 GRAUDENZ, GER [38614]

KNOEPFELIUS PRE 1774 GRAUDENZ, GER [38614]

KNOEPPEL 1860-1930 MILWAWKEE, WI, USA [36349]

KNOLL 1871+ GREY & BRUCE, ONT, CAN [36714] : 1856-C1871 WATERLOO, ONT, CAN [36714] : 1818-1856 MACHENHEIM, BAD, GER [36714] : PRE 1720 HOLZBRONN, WUE, GER [38681]

KNOP PRE 1900 POM, GER [38636]

KNOPF 1850+ GUTTSTADT, SUED, AMERIKA [38614] : 1850+ GUTTSTADT, DDR [38614] : PRE 1774 GRAUDENZ, GER [38614] : 1850+ GUTTSTADT, GER [38614] : 1600-1750 DRAMMEN & TOTEN, NOR [36335] : 1850+ GUTTSTADT, RSA [38614] : 1850+ GUTTSTADT, USA [38614]

KNOPP PRE 1945 POM, GER [38636] : PRE 1830 VA, USA [38196]

KNOPPERT 1700S WERKHOVEN, UTR, NL [38358]

KNORRE PRE 1860S HANNOVER, HAN, GER [37529]

KNOT ELIZABETH 1750+ ST PAUL'S WALDEN, HRT, ENG [35634]

KNOTT 1850 GLENELG, SA, AUS [34594] : 1820+ STOURBRIDGE, WOR, ENG [33933] : PRE 1755 THAME, OXF, ENG [35046] : PRE 1838 BURY, LAN, ENG [35514] : PRE 1830 STROOD, KEN, ENG [36272] : 1820 MANCHESTER, LAN, ENG [36818] : 1858 ASHFORD, KEN, ENG [37690]

KNOWD 1800S KILRUSH, KID, IRL & AUS [34596]

KNOWLDEN 1850+ TENTERDEN, KEN, ENG [38509]

KNOWLER ALL KEN, ENG [37595]

KNOWLES 1845-C1900 GUNNEDAH, NSW, AUS [33847] : 1850+ VIC, AUS [35888] : 1842+ GOULBURN, NSW, AUS [38008] : ALL BARROW IN FURNESS, LAN, ENG [34074] : PRE 1860 WAKEFIELD & HUNSLET, WRY, ENG [34382] : 1792 WIGAN & MILLGATE, LAN, ENG [34609] :

1750-1890 LONDON, ENG [34615] : PRE 1770
WENLOCK, SAL & WOR, ENG [36110] : RUTH
PRE 1780 STAUNTON, DBY, ENG [36192] : ALL
WIGAN & TUNSTALL, LAN, ENG [36587] : 1750-
1830 LANGFIELD, WRY, ENG [36635] : 1750-1890
LYMM & APPLETON, CHS, ENG [36740] : 1700-
1900 CON & DEV, ENG [36899] : PRE 1700
SLAPTON & VICINITY, DEV, ENG [36899] :
SARAH 1840 DUKINFIELD, CHS, ENG [37184] :
PRE 1800 KIDDERMINSTER, WOR, ENG [37377] :
1750+ BLACKBURN, LAN, ENG [38034] : PRE
1620 HULL, YKS, ENG [38135] : 1851+ ARKSEY,
WRY, ENG [38469] : 1850+ WAVERTREE,
LIVERPOOL, LAN, ENG [38539] : 1824+ ENG &
AUS [33793] : 1870+ KAITANGATA & OWAKA,
OTG, NZ [35888] : PRE 1870 EDINBURGH, MLN,
SCT [35888] : PRE 1870 KCD, SCT [35888] :
GEORGE 1780-1840 INVERKEILLOR & DUNDEE,
ANS, SCT [38483] : 1640-1745 PLYMOUTH, MA,
USA [36944] : 1600-1800 EASTHAM, MA, USA
[36944] : 1830-1850 HAMPDEN, ME, USA [36944]
KNOWLING 1750-1830 BRISTOL, ENG [38299]
KNOWLTON 1790 PODINGTON, BDF, ENG [34708] :
PRE 1750 BRAMSHAW, WIL, ENG [35252]
KNOX ELIZA 1838+ STAWELL, VIC, AUS [36598] :
MARY 1875+ STAWELL, VIC, AUS [36598] : 1830+
CARISBROOK, IOW, HAM, ENG [34063] : C1800
LIVERPOOL, LAN, ENG [35573] : ALL DROMARA,
DOW, IRL [34627] : JOSEPH 1846+ DRUMQUIN,
TYR, IRL [34973] : C1806 FER, IRL [35824] : 1800+
FER, IRL [35918] : 1800+ BELTURBET, CAV, IRL
[35963] : ELLEN 1800+ GLENWHERRY, ANT, IRL
[35995] : 1800-1850 KILLALA, MAY, IRL [36390] :
JAMES 1834+ WATERFORD, IRL [36598] : 1700
STRABANE, TYR, IRL [38379] : JOHN C1815+
DRY & QUE, IRL & CAN [36904] : JOHN C1792-
1871 DRY & QUE, IRL & CAN [36904] : 1700-1800
ABERDEEN, ABD, SCT [34107] : PRE 1918
GLASGOW, LKS, SCT [35985] : ANNIE 1850+ LKS,
SCT [35995] : PRE 1850 SCT [36726] : 1825-1900 ABD,
SCT [38253] : PRE 1890 SPOKANE, WA, USA [35137]
KNUBBE 1700+ MEK, GER [35874]
KNUBER 1615+ NEUENSTADT, DDR [38667] :
1615+ NEUSTADT, DDR [38667]
KNUCKEY PRE 1800 WENDRON, CON, ENG [33992]
: 1650-1850 STITHIANS, CON, ENG [34411] : PRE
1842 ST MAWGAN INRYDEN, CON, ENG [34616] :
1700+ REDRUTH, CON, ENG [35385] : 1600-1800
STITHIANS, CON, ENG [37457]
KNUDSDATTER BERGDAL AASNE 1858-1943
VINJE, TELEMARK & ALB, NOR & CAN [34481]
KNUDSEN PRE 1820 DEN [33959] : C1830+
BANDHOLM, MARIBO CO. DEN, USA & CAN
[34203]
KNUEPFER 1600+ NEUSTADT AN DER ORLA,
GRA, DDR [38667]
KNUEPPEL ALL GOLLNOW, GER & USA [36916]
KNUPFER 1600+ NEUSTADT AN DER ORLA, GRA,
DDR [38667]
KNUTH C1800+ RHEDA, GD, POL [35834]
KNYVETT 1850+ MDX & SRY, ENG [36203]
KOBARG 1800S SHO, GER [36552]
KOCH 1840+ WOODSIDE, SA, AUS [34883] : 1870+
CAMPASPE, VIC, AUS [35725] : PRE 1930 QLD,
AUS [37986] : C1600 GUSTEN, HAL, DDR [37918] :
ALL DELLE, ELO, GER [34861] : FREIDRICH 1820-
1840 NARAMAWITZ, POS, GER [35725] : C1879
WITTENBURG, MSW, GER [35820] : 1858
PAMPRIN, MSW, GER [35820] : WILLIAM 1800+
SAX-WEIMAR, GER [38064] : C1850 STETTIN &
MASSOW, POM, GER [38065] : PRE 1800
BEAUMARAIS, SAA, GER [38681] : 1850+ ROSS

CO., OH, USA [38064] : 1750-1850 BANAT, YU
[37539]
KOCHENDOERFER ALL WUE, GER [38333]
KOCHENDORFFER 1845+ GER [35190]
KOCHER ALL WIE, OES [37268]
KOCUR 1900+ RZESZOW, POL [35000] : 1800+
BEDOWA ZGLOBIENSKA, POL [35000] : 1900+
KORZELICE & BOBRYCA, SU [35000]
KOEHLER 1838 ST ANDEASBURG, HAN, GER
[34195] : 1800+ GRABEN, BAD, GER [34791] :
1780+ OLD, GER [37532] : PRE 1840 NORKA,
VOLGA, SU [36543] : PRE 1882 NORKA, SU &
WORLD [37511]
KOEHNE 1697-1755 BARNTRUP, LIP, GER [38749]
KOEHORN 1600-1990 NL [33983] : 1550-1950 GRO,
FRI & BRA, NL [38704]
KOEIJERS (SEE DE KOE [38358]
KOELEMAN ALL HOLLAND, NL [38703]
KOELEN VAN PRE 1757 SOEST, UTR, NL [38706]
KOELSCH 1623-1649 ADORF, WAL, GER [34912]
KOEN PRE 1730 FRANEKER, FRI, NL [35008]
KOENIG PRE 1840 BRETTHEIM, WUE, GER [37510] :
1750-1890 POM, GER [37535] : PRE 1837
FISCHHAUSEN, PRE, GER [38614] : PRE 1800
CHROSTNIKI, LU, POL [38617]
KOENIGSTEIN PRE 1900 WORLDWIDE [36930]
KOENS ALL ZUID BEVELAND, ZEL, NL [38714]
KOEPKE PRE 1870 POM, GER [37009]
KOERBER PRE 1856 ALTEN-BUSECK, HES, GER
[33824]
KOESTER GEORGE C. 1822+ MONTREAL, QUE,
CAN [38384] : M.A. 1815+ BRADING, IOW, ENG
[38384] : GEORGE C. 1810+ BRADING, IOW, ENG
[38384] : GEORGE C. 1783+ MAINZ, GER [38384] :
C1752 ST MICHAELISDONN, SHO, GER [38671] :
A.T. 1841+ DETROIT, MI, USA [38384]
KOESTER (SEE KOSTER) [34812]
KOFFORD PRE 1830 SONDERBORG, DEN [34886]
KOFOED C1700-1800 OSTERMARIE, BHLM, DEN
[37977]
KOHL PRE 1853 COBLENZ, BRD [37998] : PRE 1853
WALWORTH & NEWINGTON, SRY, ENG [37998]
KOHLBERGER ALL BITTELBOURN &
MOCKMUHL, WUE, GER [38176]
KOHLER PRE 1799 MUNCHHAUSEN, HES, BRD
[34840] : PRE 1850 BUREN, SO, CH [38333] : KARL
GUSTAV 1875-1890 FRA [38550] : 1800+
ZIELBECK, LUE, GER [37170] : JOHAN 1707+
GER [38550] : JOHAN 1707-69 VADSTENA,
OSTERGOTLAND, SWE [38550]
KOHLHAUSEN PRE 1800 GROSSENRITTE, GHE &
HEN, GER [38606]
KOHN 1900+ MAITLAND & SINGLETON, NSW,
AUS [37966]
KOHORN 1800-1925 CS [33983] : 1800-1990 USA [33983]
KOHOUT ALL KOVANICE, PRAGUE, CS [35264]
KOHRS 1846-1880 BUXTEHUDE, HAN, GER [36952] :
1882-1892 LYONS, CLINTON CO., IA, USA [36952]
KOIMER PRE 1800 AYLSHAM & NORWICH, NFK,
ENG [36593]
KOITILA 1870-1930 KEWEENAW CO., MI, USA
[38010]
KOLB PRE 1730 RPF, BRD [38448] : PRE 1810
LANCASTER CO., PA, USA [38448] : PRE 1810
BUCKS CO., PA, USA [38448]
KOLBATSCH 1905-1940 NEWARK, NJ, USA [36349]
KOLI 1830-1890 HU [36331]
KOLL PRE 1870 ROS, IRL [37510]
KOLLEWE PRE 1815 LUEBEN, SIL, GER [36954]
KOLOTYLO 1800+ POL [36602] : 1800+ USA [36602]
KOLP PRE 1810 BUCKS CO., PA, USA [38448]
KOLSCH PRE 1800 EDENKOBEN, BAV, GER [37630]

KOLTER ALL WORLDWIDE [36930]
KOMINITZ PRE 1850 KOVNO, LITHUANIA, USSR [35635]
KOMP ALL GER [38319] : 1860 AL, USA [38319] : 1800S USA [38319]
KONEMANN 1875 NEUKIRCHEN, POM, GER [35575]
KONICTZKA 1900-1850 GLOUCH, KRIES, OPR [38427]
KONIG PRE 1875 GER [37009] : 1800+ MALENTA, SHO, GER [37170] : PRE 1750 WORLDWIDE [38542]
KONIGH ALL WORLDWIDE [38542]
KONING PRE 1750 WORLDWIDE [38542]
KONINGI ALL WORLDWIDE [38542]
KONINKI ALL WORLDWIDE [38542]
KONKEL 1930S POL [35906]
KONNOLE PRE 1900 CLA, IRL &, WORLDWIDE [38305]
KONOS PRE 1900 DOMAZLICE, TAUS, CS [35290]
KONRAD 1800S SILBER, SIL, GER [38623]
KONTNER 1850-1920 BALTIMORE, MD, USA [38770]
KONVICKA 1840-80 OES [38314]
KOOIJMAN ALL NL [38701] : ALL UTR, NL [38716]
KOOISTRA RUURD 1750-1830 FRI, NL [34990] : KIEMPE 1821 GARIJP, FRI, NL [35607]
KOOLE 1700S ZIERIKZEE, ZEL, NL [38358]
KOONS C1860 DANVILLE, PA, USA [36803]
KOONTZ C1720-1730 GER [35275]
KOOPER 1800-25 ANKUM, HAN, GER [38202]
KOOT PRE 1877 UTRECHT, UTR, NL [36307]
KOP PRE 1860 HUZARD, SAA, GER & FRA [38681]
KOPHAL PRE 1870 PERVER, PSA, GER [38648]
KOPP PRE 1860 NUSSDORF & MAGSTADT, BAW, BRD [34581] : PRE 1700 BLAUFELDEN, WUE, GER [37510] : 1827-1930 BAV, GER [38308] : PRE 1870 BISSENDORF, HAN, GER [38632] : ALL WORLDWIDE [38624]
KORBY 1750-1850 BRAMLEY, HAM, ENG [35422]
KORCK PIETER PRE 1816 GER [36453]
KORDICK PRE 1890 CHICAGO, IL, USA [38042]
KORDOWSKI 1700-1800 CULM, WPR, GER [38652]
KORIE ALL WORLDWIDE [36709]
KORLIN 1848 + HOLLOLA, HAME, FIN [38758]
KOROCH PRE 1912 GUENTHAL, VOLHYNIA, SU [37545] : PRE 1912 ROMANOFKA, VOLHYNIA, SU [37545]
KORODCHUCK 1800 + KRICHILSK, WN, SU [34087]
KORODCZUK 1900 + KRICHILSK, WN, POL [34087]
KOROTCHUCK 1900 + CHOROSTOW, WN, POL [34087]
KORSTEN ALL SCHERPENISSE, ZEL, NL [38694]
KORT 1740-1846 BORBY, SHO, GER [38750]
KORTRIGHT C1868 WARRNAMBOOL, VIC, AUS [34563]
KOSBAB PRE 1880 SHO, BRD [36338]
KOSCHEL 1780-1860 NEU FREUDENTAL, UKRAINE, GROSSLIEBENTAL, SU [38372]
KOSTE 1700-1800 DRAKENSTEDT, PSA, GER [38643]
KOSTER ALL GUSTROW, MEK, DDR [34812] : 1839-1921 GLAMBECK, BRA, GER & AUS [35763] : ALL WORLDWIDE [38615]
KOSTYMICK 1860 SNIATYN, OES & POL [36679]
KOTZ 1600-1800 MOHRUNGEN, OPR, GER [38654]
KOUTH PRE 1800 NRW & RPF, BRD [38616]
KOVER C1800 READING, PA, USA [36969]
KOWLESKEY ALL WORLDWIDE [34724]
KOZAK 1850 + REWYATICHYL, POL & SU [34087]
KOZIELSKI ALL LIDZIANKA, VOL, SU [37041]
KRABB PRE 1800 LARSMO, VAASA, FIN [34858]
KRABBE PRE 1830 MSW, GER [38191]
KRACH PRE 1760 OBERSTEINBACH, GER [38681]
KRACHENBUEHL ALL SA, AUS [35070]

KRACHT 1835-1990 MILWAUKEE, WI, USA [38588]
KRAEHENBUELL ALL CH [35070]
KRAEHLER ALL WORLDWIDE [37012]
KRAFFT PRE 1640 ROTHENBURG, BAV, GER [35242]
KRAFT C1875 ROCKHAMPTON & TOWNSVILLE, QLD, AUS [35786] : C1848 GREAT LAKES, USA [35786]
KRAGE PRE 1848 MELDORF & GLUCKSTADT, SHO, GER [37774]
KRAGENBRINK PRE 1840 CASGLOW, GER [35333]
KRAGER 1800-1900 MDX, ENG [37651]
KRAHE PRE 1850 SAXONY, KSA, GER [33874]
KRAKOWIENSKA PRE 1900 DANZIG, GER & POL [33966]
KRAL ALL VELENKA, PRAGUE, CS [35264]
KRAMBRICH PRE 1856 OESTRICH, PPF, GER [33824]
KRAMER 1750+ BRISTOL, SOM, ENG [37717] : PRE 1680 REICHELSHOFEN, BAV, GER [35242] : PRE 1800 MENNIGHUFFEN, WEF, GER [36957] : ALL ARIENDORF, RPR, GER [38637] : PRE 1850 SCHUYLKILL CO., PA, USA [37508] : C1835+ NEW YORK, NY, USA [38182]
KRANTZ 1750-1850 COOK CO., IL, USA [38024] : 1830-1900 CINCINNATI, OH, USA [38149]
KRANZ 1830-1900 CINCINNATI, OH, USA [38149]
KRATZER PRE 1851 BROWN CO., OH, USA [37037]
KRAUSE FRIEDRICH PRE 1885 LICHTFILD, WPR, GER [34567] : CHRISTIAN 1870-1900 RAHMEL, GER [35315] : PRE 1840 WOHLAU, SIL, GER [35333] : PRE 1840 SCHILKOWITZ, SIL, GER [35333] : 1880-1910 JACKSON CO., IL, USA [36912]
KRAUSENECK ALL STALLUPONEN, EAST PRUSSIA, GER [34131]
KRAUSHAAR ALL WORLDWIDE [36441]
KRAUSS 1859 + WARIALDA, NSW, AUS [38069] : PRE 1750 WALDBACH, WUE, GER [35242]
KRAUT 1700 + JAGSTFELD, GER [35566]
KRAUTH (SEE KRAUT) [35566]
KREBS PRE 1754 NEW HANOVER, PA, USA [37574]
KREES 1750-1900 SYRACUSE, NY, USA [35318]
KREFFORD PRE 1650 UK [34746]
KREFT 1707-1890 SIANOWO, GDANSK, POL [38148]
KREICK 1890S + SARATOW CO., HUCK, SU [38318]
KREIDER 1780-1840 WESTMORELAND, PA, USA [36908]
KREIJ HENRIK JOHAN 1700S REVAL & SVARTAA, ESTLAND &, FIN [38564] : FREDR HINDR PRE 1718 FIN & SWE [38564] : OTTO ROBERT 1900 GLASGOW, SCT [38564] : AGNES LOVISA 1904+ GLASGOW, SCT & AUS [38564] : NILS THEODOR 1901+ GLASGOW, SCT & AUS [38564] : NILS TEODOR PRE 1907 GLASGOW, SCT, SWE & [38564] : ERIC 1750+ FALUN, SWE [38564] : JOHAN ALBERT 1857+ ULRICA, SWE [38564] : ANDERS PETER 1854+ ULRICA, SWE [38564] : OTTO GUSTAF 1707+ GAVLE, SWE [38564] : KARL OSKAR 1862+ ULRICA, SWE [38564] : JOENS 1700S KALVSVIK, SWE [38564] : HENRIK W. PRE 1823 MALMOE, SWE & GER [38564] : PHILIP 1863+ NY, USA [38564] : CHARLES 1873+ NY, USA [38564] : MARIA 1878+ NY, USA [38564] : ALBERT FABIAN 1861+ NY, USA & SWE [38564] : CARL FABIAN C1861+ NY, USA & SWE [38564] : ALL WORLDWIDE [38564]
KREISE PRE 1900 AUGSBURG, BAY, BRD [36963]
KREISSELER 1700+ KISKET, NY, USA [34408]
KREITZER PRE 1850 NJ, USA [38708]
KREJ ALL WORLDWIDE [38564]
KREJCIK PRE 1770 LAUCIN, NYMBURK, CS [38618] : 1878+ STRUHY, MLADA BOLESLAV, CS [38618] : ALL WORLDWIDE [38618]

KREKE PRE 1845 NEVENKIRCHEN, OLD, GER [37034]

KREMER 1855-1900 KEWEENAW CO., MI, USA [38010]

KREPEL PRE 1858 PRE, GER [38577]

KREPP 1800+ TAS, AUS [35538] : 1800+ WORLDWIDE [35538]

KREPS PRE 1877 GER [34567]

KRESS PRE 1860 PRE, GER [36935] : ALL CLARKSTON, MI, USA [36935] : 1870-1900 DUBUQUE CO., IA, USA [38092] : 1875-1930 MARSHALL CO., KS, USA [38092] : 1875-1940 SMITH CO., KS, USA [38092]

KRESSIG ALL GER [38664]

KREUTER PRE 1830 GER [34090]

KREUTZ PRE 1900 STETTIN, SZ, POL [34089]

KREUTZMANN ALL GUSTROW, MEK, DDR [34812]

KREUTZMUELLER 1800+ EISBERGEN, WEF, GER [38023]

KREY LUDVIG HENRIK PRE 1705 RPF, BRD & SWE [38564] : HANS 1700S DEN [38564] : ALL REVAL, ESTLAND [38564] : FREDR HINDR PRE 1718 FIN & SWE [38564] : ALL ROSTOCK, MEK, GER [38564] : ALL STETTIN, POM, GER [38564] : AUGUST F.W. PRE 1886 PRE, GER [38564] : ALL STRALSUND, MEK, GER [38564] : JOHAN BERNARD C1825 ROSTOCK, GBRG, MEK, GER & SWE [38564] : JOHAN PRE 1656 KILBERG, POM, GER & SWE [38564] : ALL RIGA, LETTLAND [38564] : JOCHUM N. PRE 1770 NOR [38564] : HANS H. 1600S NOR [38564] : JOCHUM C. PRE 1767 NOR & SCT [38564] : NILS TEODOR PRE 1907 GLASGOW, SCT, SWE & [38564] : HENRIK PRE 1658 SWE [38564] : GEORG NICLAS 1700S STOCKHOLM, SWE [38564] : EVA CAROLINA 1874+ SWE & USA [38564] : OSKAR FREDRIK 1876+ SWE & USA [38564] : PRE 1715 PHILADELPHIA CO., PA, USA [38017] : ALL WORLDWIDE [38564]

KREYER CARL 1823-1909 BAV, GER [37596]

KREYMBORG ALL AUS [35933]

KRIEGER 1857+ QLD, AUS [36362] : 1852+ GRAFTON, NSW, AUS [38597] : PRE 1857 NOTEFELDEN, HESSEN KASSEL, GER [36362] : PRE 1852 BERKHEIM, WUE, GER [38597]

KRIEHN 1800-1875 DANZIG & KONIGSBERG, ALT-DOLLSTADT, PRE [36953]

KRIEL ALL TULBACH, CAPE, RSA [34945]

KRIJGSMAN PRE 1800 ZUH, NL [34180]

KRILL PRE 1860 COLOGNE, GER [37875]

KRIM PRE 1852 BAV, GER [37786] : PRE 1850 BUFFALO, NY, USA [37786]

KRINGER PRE 1705 BE, CH [37811]

KRINITZ 1800S NEW YORK, NY, USA [38369]

KRISTOFFERSDOTTER ANNA KRISTINA PRE 1940 GAFSELE, VASTERBOTTENS, SWE [34481]

KROEGER 1850+ FASSIFERN, QLD, AUS [35460] : 1600+ SHO, GER [35460] : PRE 1860 ANEMOLTER, HAN, GER [38577]

KROEHLER ALL BRD [37012]

KROENER PRE 1825 LENGERICH, NRW, GER [38663]

KROENING PRE 1920 SU [34478]

KROENK (SEE KRONK) [34172]

KROFT GEORGE M. 1845-1923 LEUTZENBORN, GER [37596]

KROG PRE 1877 AALBORG, DEN [35197]

KROHN PRE 1850 DASSAW, SWR, GER [35945] : PRE 1872 WPR, GER [37819]

KROME ALL WORLDWIDE [38612]

KROMER 1715-1740 BORSTEL, HEN, GER [38528] : 1790+ EDWARDSVILLE, IL, USA [36342]

KROMMINGA ALL WORLDWIDE [38634]

KRONA 1830-1880 HAN, GER [36948] : FREDERICK 1830-1897 PHILADELPHIA, PA, USA [36948] : CAROLYN 1859-1929 PHILADELPHIA, PA, USA [36948]

KRONE PRE 1868 LEVERN, WEF, BRD [38685]

KRONEN 1800 POS, GER [37170]

KRONENBERGER ALL WORLDWIDE [38613]

KRONING PRE 1850 POL [34478]

KRONK 1880+ BENDIGO, VIC, AUS [35725] : 1840S BATAVIA, E.INDIES [34591] : 1800S HEIDE, SHO, GER [34172]

KROON 1775 S'GRAVENLAND, NOH, NL [38706] : ALBERT 1865+ KS & MO, USA [38064]

KROON GIJSBERT 1740 S'GRAVENLAND, NOH, NL [38706]

KROPF PRE 1883 KRS. ASCH, SUDETENLAND, OES, CSR &, GER [38649]

KROTOWICH 1927+ WINNIPEG, MAN, CAN [34087] : 1850+ REWYATICHYL, POL & SU [34087]

KROTOWICZ 1850+ REWYATICHYL, POL & SU [34087]

KROTTENTHALER 1787 SCHORNDORF, BAV, GER [38322]

KRPAN ALL LICKO CERJA, GRACAC, YU [38063]

KRUCHER ALL WORLDWIDE [36377]

KRUCK 1700-1800 DANZIG, WESTPREUβEN, PRE [38603]

KRUEGER PRE 1828 GROSFIEL, MEK, GER [36726] : EMILE 1842 POM, GER [38322] : 1870+ QUINCY, ADAMS CO., IL, USA [36952]

KRUEKEBERG ALL BRD [36545]

KRUESE 1700-C1740S GEL, NL [38358]

KRUG PRE 1725 GOCHSHEIM, BAY, BRD [35311] : 1700S UDENHAUSEN, HES, BRD [35635]

KRUGER 1865+ FASSIFERN, QLD, AUS [33782] : 1850+ SA, AUS [37186] : PRE 1845 STEBBE & STIBBE, POM, GER [34584] : 1850S LIPPINGHAUSEN, WEF, GER [36952] : PRE 1860 ANEMOLTER, HAN, GER [38577] : 1858-1870 QUINCY, ADAMS CO., IL, USA [36952] : ALL WORLDWIDE [34949]

KRUIJSEN 1881 BOXTEL, NBT, NL [36307]

KRUITHOFF 1800 OSTFRIESLAND, PRE, GER [38039]

KRUK 1880 KASSEL HESS, GER [36730]

KRUPICEK ALL WORLDWIDE [36377]

KRUSE C1800 AHRENSHOFT, SHO, GER [37148] : 1700+ GETTORF, SHO, GER [37542] : 1800-1830 WELPLAGE, HAN, GER [38528]

KRUSS 1700+ BAD, GER [38529]

KUCHEL 1816 ZULLICHAU, BRA, PRE [35369]

KUCHENMEISTER 1840-1860 WARNKENHAGEN AG BUTZOE, MSW, GER [35810] : PRE 1840 HOHEN LUKOW AG BUTZOW, MSW, GER [35810]

KUCHINKA PRE 1850 ZICI & ZITEC, JINDRICHUV, HRADEC, CS [38461]

KUCKENS 1600+ STEDINGEN WESERMARSCH, BRM, GER [35828] : 1700+ DELMENHORST, BRM, GER [35828] : 1794+ VEGESACK, BRM, GER [35828]

KUEBLER 1840+ VORN. BARBARA, USA [38661] : 1832 VORN. CHRISTOPH, USA [38661]

KUEHL PRE 1900 OLDENBURG, SHO, GER [38648]

KUEMMICH PRE 1800 ALTENRIET, GER [37587]

KUFLER ALL WORLDWIDE [34222]

KUGENER 1800S LXM, LXM [36851]

KUHHAUPT PRE 1700 KUELTE, HES, GER [38642]

KUHL PRE 1862 SCHWERIN, SWR, DDR [38738]

KUHLOW ALL ANH, GER [35310]

KUHN 1873+ TOWNSVILLE, QLD, AUS [35138] : 1850 OESTRICH, HEN, GER [33929] : 1840S DEUTCHKRONE, WPR, GER [35138] : PRE 1796

LEIPZIG, LPZ & PSA, GER [38499] : ALL
HEILSBERG, OPR, GER [38664] : PRE 1800
URPHAR, GER [38676]
KUHNEL C1870 PETERSWALD, BOHEMIA, OES
[37148]
KUHNER PRE 1832 MOSBACH, BAD, GER [37819]
KUHNLE PRE 1748 KALTENWESTEN, WUE, GER
[38181]
KUHORN 1500-1800 WUE, GER [33983]
KUIPER 1775+ EMLICHHEIM, NSA, BRD [34398] :
1880+ HOLLAND, MI, USA [34398]
KUIPERS 1840+ HOOGEVEEN, DRN, NL [34398]
KUJATH 1830 LUBASZ, PI, POL [38495]
KUKLA WIKTORIA 1849-1937 POL [38090]
KUKURA 1940+ ROCHESTER, NY, USA [36512]
KULCHYSKI 1875-1910 SOKAL & GIMLI, MAN,
CAN & OES [34063]
KULHAVY 1900+ DURANGO, CO, USA [36909]
KULLANDER C1700+ VARMLANDS, SWE [36651]
KULLEN 1667+ HUELBEN, WUE, GER [38667]
KULMUS ALL WORLDWIDE [38613]
KULP PRE 1810 BUCKS CO., PA, USA [38448]
KULSER PRE 1850 DIRMSTEIN, RPF, GER [38681]
KULT JORAN 1663-1698 HEDEMORA, SWE [38563]
KUMLIE 1800-1851 BE, CH [38374]
KUMMER 1750-1900 ZITTAU, KSA, GER [38628]
KUNDE 1900+ DELORAINE, TAS, AUS [34770] :
1800+ ZARPEN, SHO, GER [34688] : C1790
COLLBERG, THU, GER [34688]
KUNKEL 1661-1700 GROSSALMERODE, GHE, GER
[38749] : 1800-1950 WESTMORELAND CO., PA,
USA [38154] : 1800-1950 ALLEGHENY CO., PA, USA
[38154] : 1700-1850 PA, USA [38154]
KUNKLE 1850-1950 WESTMORELAND CO., PA, USA
[38154] : 1900-1990 LA CO., CA, USA [38154] : 1850-
1950 ALLEGHENY CO., PA, USA [38154]
KUNNEN 1750+ EMLICHHEIM, NSA, BRD [34398]
KUNST 1840+ FRI & NOH, NL [35753]
KUNTZ JOSEPH ALL CHICAGO, IL, USA [37440]
KUNZ JOSEPH ALL CHICAGO, IL, USA [37440] :
1865-1875 KEWEENAW CO., MI, USA [38010] : 1800
WORLDWIDE [35873]
KUNZE THERESIA 1700-1900S DRESDEN, PSA,
GER & USA [35304]
KUPFER PRE 1760 HEN, GER & USA [38016] : 1890+
ST LOUIS, MO, USA [36912]
KURAASEN ALL RORAS, S TRNDLG, NOR [36326]
KURITTU 1600-1867 VEHKALAHTI & SIPPOLA,
KYMI, FIN [38562]
KURLANSIK PRE 1900 KOVNO, LITHUANIA, USSR
[35635]
KURRE 1800+ ANGERSTEIN, PRE, GER [37116]
KURRER C1485 HERRENBERG, BAW, FRG [38660]
KURTEKNAB 1716 DETMARSEN, WEF, GER [38749]
KURTH PRE 1812 SIEGBURG, NRW, GER [35280]
KURTZ 1856+ DARLING DOWNS, QLD, AUS [37894]
: 1600-1750 ALS & LOR, FRA [38219] : 1600-1750
ELO & LU, FRA [38219] : 1800S BAW, GER [37048] :
1650-1750 BAW, GER [38219] : 1860-1920
BOLECHOWICE, KR, POL [35717] : 1836+
SACRAMENTO CO., CA, USA [37048] : 1700-1760
LANCASTER CO., PA, USA & CH [38219]
KURTZMAN ALL WORLDWIDE [37496]
KURZ 1840 ALTFRAUTAUTZ, BUCKOVYNA, [36655]
: 1450-1650 OBERURBACH, BAW, BRD [38654] :
PRE 1855 SCHOANBACH, WUE, GER [34886] : PRE
1856 NECKERSUHR, WUE, GER [37894] : PRE 1720
HOLZBRONN, WUE, GER [38681] : 1860-1920
BOLECHOWICE, KR, POL [35717]
KURZA 1860-1920 BOLECHOWICE, KR, POL [35717]
KUSIA ALL WORLDWIDE [34060]
KUSSLER ALL GER [38678]

KUSWORM ALL WORLDWIDE [36962]
KUTACH 1850-70 CS [38314]
KUTCH 1800 LINCOLN, KY, USA [37027] : 1790
LINCOLN, NC, USA [37027] : ALL USA [37027]
KUTZNER PRE 1870 POS, GER [38627]
KUYKENDAL 1700-1800 MINISINK, NY, USA [37435]
KWIATKOWSKI PRE 1880 SEB, POL [37139]
KYDD ALL ANS, SCT [34226] : PRE 1850
ARBROATH, ANS, SCT [34274]
KYLANDER PRE 1640 LINKOPING, SWE [38544]
KYLE PRE 1830 NEWTON STEWART, TYR, IRL
[34494] : 1800-1900 BALLYMENA, ANT, IRL [34631]
: PRE 1860 ROS, IRL [37104] : 1800+
LISMACLOON, TYR, IRL [37949] : C1840
CLONMEL, TIP, IRL [38292] : 1800+ MOR, SCT &
IRL [34326]
KYME ALL ENG [35868]
KYMER PRE 1800 AYLSHAM & NORWICH, NFK,
ENG [36593]
KYMPTON EDWARD 1780-1840 BOVINGDON,
MDX, ENG [33961]
KYNE 1800+ IRL [33963]
KYNOCH 1750+ ABD, SCT [35499]
KYNOCK PRE 1784 SKENE, ABD, SCT [37315]
KYSH PRE 1850 ANTIGUA, W.INDIES [35413]
KYTE 1867+ AKRON, OH, USA & ENG [36254]
LAAGER 1835 GL, CH [38518]
LA BELLE C1886 ST ANNE & MEADOW LEA, ONT,
CAN [34521]
LA BOMASCUS ALL TRAKEHNIN, PRE, GER
[38191]
LABORIE PRE 1750 CARDIALLAC, MP, FRA [37821]
LA BRANCHE ADAM 1600-1800S SYRACUSE,
ONONDAGA, NY, USA [35327]
LABRASH ALL ONT, CAN [37044]
LABRENZ 1700-1850 RAWA-MAZ, WA, POL [38652]
LABROSSE 1800+ ST EUGENE, CAN [36686]
LABTON C1750 BIDEFORD, DEV, ENG [34456]
LABUTT ALL WORLDWIDE [36574]
LACANDELA ALL WORLDWIDE [36030]
LACE PHILIP 1826-1832 LIVERPOOL, LAN, ENG
[37794] : WILLIAM 1830 LIVERPOOL, LAN, ENG
[37794] : 1840+ PATRICK, IOM [35185] : PRE 1900
ANDREAS, IOM [35185] : WILLIAM 1864+ EGAN,
TX, USA [37794]
LACERTE GUILLAUME PRE 1670 ANGERS, PL,
FRA [38408]
LACEY PRE 1891 KAPUNDA, SA, AUS [33866] :
1870+ COLLINGWOOD, VIC, AUS [35524] : ALL
SHARDLOW, DBY, ENG [34261] : 1800+ LISS,
HAM, ENG [34514] : PRE 1900 EASINGTON, DUR,
ENG [34562] : C1849 KEN, ENG [34685] : PRE 1809
KELSTON, SOM, ENG [35223] : 1700-1900 GREAT
HAMPDEN & HUGHONDEN, BKM, ENG [36175] :
1800-1900 LONDON, MDX, ENG [36438] : 1800
SYSTON, LEI, ENG [37829] : PRE 1850 LEICESTER,
LEI, ENG [38056] : 1400+ DUBLIN, WIC, IRL
[33989] : 1800+ BRAINTRIM, PA, USA [36356] :
C1655 SUFFOLK CO., MA, USA [36356]
LACHANCE 1800S LEEDS & GRENVILLE CO., ONT,
CAN [38414]
LACK 1800+ CAMPBELLTOWN, NSW, AUS [35511] :
1800-1900 SHOREDITCH, LND, ENG [34872] : 1800-
1850 WALSINGHAM, NFK, ENG [35524] : PRE 1900
HOLKHAM, NFK, ENG [37724] : PRE 1900 WELLS
NEXT THE SEA, NFK, ENG [37724]
LACKEN ALL BALLINA & ARDNAREE, MAY &
SLI, IRL [38084]
LACKENBY 1800+ ALNWICK, NBL & DUR, ENG
[34905]

LACKEY 1840+ GOULBURN, NSW, AUS [34774] :
PRE 1900 NSW, AUS [35028] : 1830+ CAR, IRL
[34774] : PRE 1836 ST LEVE, LOG, IRL [35028]
LACKIE PRE 1860 INISTIOGE, KIK, IRL [33820]
LACKLAND ALL PA, MD & DE, USA [36319]
LACKLEN ALL PA, MD & DE, USA [36319]
LACOMBE 1600-1900 NIAX, ARIEGE, FRA [33758]
LACON PRE 1700 MD, USA [37587]
LACOUME 1600-1900 VICDESSOS ARCONAC,
ARIEGE, FRA [33758]
LACOUR PRE 1718 PELHAM, MA, USA [35616]
LACROIX PRE 1880 QUE, CAN [36720]
LACY 1800S WOOTTON, LIN, ENG [36393] : 1800
NOTTINGHAM, NTT, ENG [37391] : C1760-1770
LIN, NBL & LAN, ENG [37938] : 1700-1800 YKS,
ENG [37938] : PRE 1850 TIP, IRL [34021] : JOHN
PRE 1870 TINAHELY, WIC, IRL [38305] : 1882+
COLLIN CO., TX, USA [37824] : 1870
INDEPENDENCE CO., AR, USA [37824] : 1880
IZARD CO., AR, USA [37824] : JOHN PRE 1870+
BALTIMORE, MD, USA [38305] : PRE 1900
TINAHELY, WIC, IRL &, WORLDWIDE [38305]
LADBROOK PRE 1830 LONDON, ENG [33805] : 1700-
1950 ESS, ENG [37344] : PRE 1860 BETHNAL
GREEN, MDX, ENG [37681] : C1800+ WAR, ENG
& NZ [36258]
LADBURY 1850 FRECKENHAM, SSX, ENG [37829]
LADD 1750-1800 CANTERBURY, KEN, ENG [35017] :
1790+ LONDON, ENG [36749] : PRE 1800
ROCKINGHAM CO., NH, USA [36544]
LADIEU ALL CAN & USA [36539]
LADIMIR 1850S HOMBURG, GER [35156]
LADLOW 1845+ MOUNT GAMBIER, SA, AUS
[34010]
LADOO ALL CAN & USA [36539]
LADUE ALL CAN & USA [36539]
LAFAVE ALL USA & CAN [37502]
LAFFIN PRE 1858 GOOLWA, SA, AUS [35709]
LAFFOLEY PRE 1840 ST SAVIOUR, JSY, CHI [36696]
LAFLIN 1840-1860 BOONE CO., KY, USA [36566]
LA FORCE 1600+ HENRICO & GOOCHLAND, VA,
USA [38326]
LAFRENZ 1700 WORLDWIDE [35873]
LAGARCE 1700-1800 NS, CAN [36579] : ALL FRA
[36579]
LAGARDE 1600-1900S ST JEROME, QUE, CAN
[35327]
LAGERLOF 1876+ COPENHAGEN, DEN [38559]
LAGERSTAM 1822+ PERNAJA, UUSIMAA, FIN
[38758]
LAGERWAY ALL AMSTERDAM, NL [36894]
LAGERWIJ 1700S WOUDENBERG, UTR, NL [38358]
LAGOASSE PRE 1800 GERS, FRA [35620]
LAGRUE PRE 1800 CEN, FRA [36073]
LAHD 1800-1900 PARK RIVER, ND, USA [34255] :
1850-1950 RINGLING, ND, USA [34255]
LAHEE 1837-C1870 MOETAKI, OTAGO, NZ [34659]
LAHENY PRE 1860 SLI, IRL [38365]
LAHEY 1810-1837 KER, IRL [34659]
LAHIFF PRE 1823 CLA, IRL [37916]
LAHRHEIM ALL WORLDWIDE [38613]
LAIDLAW 1750-1900 ENG [35136] : 1700-1800
JOHNSTONE, DFS, SCT [34225] : C1768 HOBKIRK,
ROX, SCT [34358] : C1800 ROX, SCT [35032] : 1870+
DALKEITH, MLN, SCT [35486] : ELIZABETH S.
PRE 1910 MANN'S LAND BLANTYRE, LKS, SCT
[36646] : JAMES PRE 1910 SMELLIES LAND
BLANTYRE, LKS, SCT [36646]
LAIDLER 1700S WHICKHAM, DUR, ENG [35408] :
1800-1850 HARTLEPOOL, DUR, ENG [36205]
LAINCHBURY PRE 1770 LADBROKE, WAR, ENG
[34629] : C1880 INVERCARGILL, NZ [36878]

LAINE 1739-1830 FOSSES LA VILLE, NMR, BEL
[38158]
LAINE-PREECE PRE 1839 ORCOP, OXF, ENG [38540]
LAING 1885+ HOBART, TAS, AUS [34670] : 1840+
MORUYA & BOMBALA, NSW, AUS [34977] : ALL
LAUNCESTON, TAS, AUS [35353] : 1700+ ONT,
CAN [34126] : 1820+ CRAIGHURST, ONT, CAN
[34465] : ALL ONT, CAN [34465] : 1800+ GSY, CHI
[34149] : PRE 1850 SWALBACH, HEN, GER [35523] :
JAMES PRE 1820 KINGSTON, JAMAICA [36692] :
1848+ DUNEDIN, OTAGO, NZ [36766] : PRE 1874
GLASGOW, ARL & LKS, SCT [33919] : 1700+
LEGERWOOD, BEW, SCT [34126] : 1800+ OLD
MELDRUM, ABD, SCT [34326] : PRE 1825
KILSYTH, STI, SCT [34465] : PRE 1840 ABD, SCT
[34977] : 1800S DUNDEE, ANS, SCT [35134] : ALL
REDDING, POLMONT, STI, SCT [35353] : C1840
PER, SCT [35786] : 1820+ DURRISDEER, DFS, SCT
[35886] : PRE 1850 CRIEFF, PER, SCT [36766] : PRE
1900 SCT [37061] : WILLIAM C1740 LOGIE PERT,
ANS, SCT [38383] : ALL WORLDWIDE [37785]
LAINSBURY 1908 CAVERSHAM, OXF, ENG [36301]
LAIRD ROBERT 1855+ TENTERFIELD, NSW, AUS
[35788] : ALL PONOKA, ALB, CAN [34220] : 1800+
PARIS, ONT, CAN [37443] : PRE 1850 ANT, IRL
[35277] : 1700-1900 LETTERKENNY, DON, IRL
[36727] : 1800+ MOTHERWELL, LKS, SCT [35152] :
1780-1800 MONTROSE, ANS, SCT [37485] : PRE
1900 WEST GREENOCK, RFW, SCT [37745] : 1830-
1880 CARRON, STI, SCT [38331] : 1800-1850
RANKIN CO., MS, USA [36573]
LAIRSON C1837 ASHTABULA CO., OH, USA [37782] :
PRE 1837 NY, USA [37782]
LAITHWAITE 1826+ WIGAN, LAN, ENG [34873]
LAITY PRE 1900 CON, ENG & AUS [35433]
LAKE 1850 ARMIDALE, NSW, AUS [34892] : DANIEL
P. 1810+ ERNESTOWN TWP. ADDINGTON CO.,
ONT, CAN [34486] : C1784+ LEN & ADD CO.,
ONT, CAN [36651] : 1700-1900 IPPOLLITTS,
PIRTON, HRT, ENG [34411] : PRE 1770
BIDEFORD, DEV, ENG [34445] : PRE 1930 ENG
[34657] : 1830+ HETHERSETT, NFK, ENG [34710] :
ALL NORTH SHIELDS, NBL, ENG [35009] : 1862+
TRURO, CON, ENG [35335] : C1841 STOKE
DAMEREL, DEV, ENG [35335] : C1814
ALTARNUN, CON, ENG [35335] : C1845-1861 ST
COLUMB, CON, ENG [35335] : 1800+ ENG [36470] :
PRE 1868 WANDSWORTH, LND, ENG [36475] :
PRE 1800 DEV, ENG [37231] : C1800 WITHAM, ESS,
ENG [37449] : ALL NORWICH, SFK & NFK, ENG
[37612] : 1735 DUNSFORD, DEV, ENG [37869] : ALL
WHITCHURCH, HAM, ENG & NZ [33959] : 1909+
NZ [37115] : C1640-C1759 LONG IS. & ALBANY
CO., NY, USA [36651] : 1820-1850 GREENE CO.,
NY, USA [38113]
LAKEMAN PRE 1800 DEV, ENG [33998] : PRE 1777
MODBURY, DEV, ENG [35895]
LAKEY PRE 1839 WEST BRADENHAM, NFK, ENG
[37726] : 1789+ CHIVELSTONE, DEV, ENG [38469]
LAKIN 1650S GROTON, MA, USA [36944]
LALANDE 1650-1700 LIMOGES, LMS, FRA [34514]
LALLANCE 1780+ MEIGS CO., OH, USA [36897]
LALLMANN 1800-1850 RELLINGHAUSEN, RPR,
GER [38750]
LALLY 1800+ IRL [33788]
LALONDE PRE 1885 MONTREAL, QUE, CAN [38525]
LA LONDE ALL USA &, CAN & FRA [38287] : ALL
USA & CAN [38287]
LALOR 1865+ ENFIELD, NSW, AUS [35101] : 1850+
SOUTH CREEK (ST MARYS), NSW, AUS [35101] :
C1876 MAXWELLTON, QLD, AUS [35158] : 1830-
1850S LEX, IRL [34027] : PATRICK PRE 1810

TINNAKILL & ABBEYLEIX, LEX, IRL **[34061]** :
C1858 CASTLEKELLY, KIK, IRL **[35158]** : ALL
BALLYROAN, LEX, IRL **[37367]** : 1700+ LEX, IRL
[37826] : ALL WORLDWIDE **[34061]**

LA MAMRE PRE 1864 ST SAMPSONS, GSY, CHI
[35575]

LAMANT PRE 1800 ELSTOW, BDF, ENG **[34588]**

LAMAR 1880+ WHITLEY CO., IN, USA **[36897]**

LAMARTINE ALL WORLDWIDE **[34316]**

LAMB 1837-1875 JERUSALEM (COLEBROOK), TAS,
AUS **[35725]** : PRE 1900 LITHGOW, NSW, AUS
[36372] : 1858+ BRAIDWOOD, NSW, AUS **[37911]** :
1895+ ARMIDALE, NSW, AUS **[37911]** : 1850-1875
NORFOLK CO., ONT, CAN **[34364]** : 1850+
BOWLING GREEN, ONT, CAN **[38451]** : 1770+
DORCHESTER & SHERBORNE, DOR, ENG **[33979]**
: 1800+ PLYMOUTH, DEV, ENG **[33979]** :
ELIZABETH 1670 ALTHORPE, LIN, ENG **[34091]** :
PRE 1840S LONDON, ENG **[34240]** : 1790-1820
CORTON DENHAM, SOM, ENG **[34448]** : ALL
SHERBORNE, DOR, ENG **[34817]** : PRE 1900 STS,
ENG **[34848]** : 1800S YKS, ENG **[34854]** : ALL CHS,
ENG **[34938]** : PRE 1888 YORK, YKS, ENG **[35368]** :
PRE 1860 MALDON, ESS, ENG **[35374]** : PRE 1837
FARNDON, NTT, ENG **[35725]** : 1790+ NEWARK
ON TRENT, NTT, ENG **[35725]** : 1730-1740
BOURNE, LIN, ENG **[35725]** : 1850+ SWERFORD,
OXF, ENG **[35846]** : 1800S NBL & DUR, ENG **[35862]**
: PRE 1855 ASHBURTON, DEV, ENG **[36155]** :
FRANCIS PRE 1894 DUR, ENG **[36164]** : PRE 1850
BISHOPS CAUNDLE, DOR, ENG **[36271]** : ALL
TETBURY, GLS, ENG **[37249]** : PRE 1800
STOCKBURY, KEN, ENG **[37602]** : PRE 1791 ESS,
ENG **[37656]** : PRE 1832 HULL, YKS, ENG **[37911]** :
PRE 1885 HOVE, SSX, ENG **[37913]** : ALL
MILVERTON, WAR, ENG **[37950]** : PRE 1860
DUBLIN, IRL **[35206]** : PRE 1880 MOG, IRL & AUS
[33881] : 1869+ NZ **[33988]** : 1869+ DUNEDIN,
OTAGO, NZ **[33988]** : 1760S ELN, SCT **[33959]** :
C1870 NAIRN, NAI, SCT **[34362]** : 1820 STRICHEN
& METHLICK, ABD, SCT **[35027]** : 1800+
CROOKBOAT, LKS & RFW, SCT **[35999]** : 1800+
LIVINGSTON, ELN, SCT **[36815]** : C1864 ABD, SCT
[36856] : ALL STIRLING, STI, SCT & NZ **[34604]** :
1886+ VACAVILLE, CA, USA **[36569]** : 1886+ SAN
FRANCISCO, CA, USA **[36569]** : 1800-1850 TN, USA
[36926] : PRE 1850 ROBESON CO., NC, USA **[36946]**
: 1793+ NY, USA **[37802]** : JAMES 1851-1919
LINCOLN, NE & IL, USA **[38124]** : C1800-1830
CAMDEN CO., MD, USA **[38325]** : JOSIAH 1810+
WAYNE CO., IN, USA **[38374]** : JOSIAH 1750+ NC,
USA **[38374]** : JOSIAH 1790+ RANDOLPH CO., NC,
USA **[38374]**

LAMBARD 1830+ MELBOURNE, VIC, AUS **[34547]** :
1700+ LONDON, ENG **[34547]**

LAMBDEN 1890+ MELBOURNE, VIC, AUS **[34798]** :
ALL VIC, AUS **[35055]** : PRE 1890 BASINGSTOKE,
HAM, ENG **[34798]** : PRE 1800 BASINGSTOKE,
HAM, ENG **[35055]** : PRE 1830 EAST GARSTON,
BRK, ENG **[35503]**

LAMBE 1800S LONDON & STAINES, LND & KEN,
ENG & CAN **[36967]**

LAMBERT C1860 MT GAMBIER & CASTERTON, SA
& VIC, AUS **[33812]** : 1865+ LAUNCESTON, TAS,
AUS **[34271]** : 1800+ SIDMOUTH, TAS, AUS **[34271]**
: CLAUDE 1917+ YOUNG, NSW, AUS **[34885]** :
1828+ BATHURST, NSW, AUS **[35147]** : 1800S+
SHOALHAVEN, NSW, AUS **[35331]** : 1862+
BRISBANE, QLD, AUS **[35455]** : PRE 1896
WENTWORTH, NSW, AUS **[35708]** : 1800S PRINCE
EDWARD CO., ONT, CAN **[34052]** : 1784-1800S
NIAGARA CO., ONT, CAN **[34052]** : 1786+

FREDERICKSBURGH, ONT, CAN **[34052]** : 1840S
NORTHUMBERLAND CO., ONT, CAN **[34052]** :
PRE 1900 DUR, ENG **[34617]** : 1865-1900 STROUD,
GLS, ENG **[34658]** : PRE 1850 BETHNAL GREEN,
LND, ENG **[34669]** : PRE 1800 ASTON ON TRENT,
DBY, ENG **[34822]** : 1817 KILMERSDON, SOM,
ENG **[35120]** : 1782 HORNSEY, MDX, ENG **[35282]** :
WILLIAM 1790+ LONDON, ENG **[35865]** : PRE
1760 WITHAM FRIARY, SOM, ENG **[36478]** : PRE
1736 NOTTINGHAM, NTT, ENG **[36532]** : PRE 1832
BENTLEY, SFK, ENG **[36804]** : 1750+ WARE, HRT,
ENG **[36978]** : ALL SFK, ENG **[37612]** : C1750-1850
CHERTSEY, SRY, ENG **[37618]** : 1700+ STEPNEY,
LND, ENG **[37843]** : 1797 BOLTON, WES, ENG
[38209] : WILLIAM PRE 1789 CHICHESTER, SSX,
ENG **[38335]** : 1800 BLACKFRIARS, LND, ENG
[38756] : 1832-1857 BANAGHER, TIP, IRL **[35455]** :
ALL COR, IRL & AUS **[35213]** : 1770+ LW, POL
[38650] : 1830 CUMNOCK, AYR, SCT **[35372]** : C1835
SWE **[35708]** : 1700S TEWKESBURY TWP., NJ, USA
[34052] : PRE 1802 HUNTERDON CO., NJ, USA
[34052] : 1640-1800 ESSEX CO., NJ, USA **[36924]** :
1770-1870 WYTHE CO., VA, USA **[38044]** : ALL OH,
USA **[38369]** : PRE 1920 PHILADELPHIA, PA, USA
& GER **[37587]**

LAMBERTI 1800+ ITL **[35762]**

LAMBERTON 1500S ST MARY'S WHITE HALL,
LND, ENG **[35617]** : PRE 1874 KILMARNOCK,
AYR, SCT **[33953]**

LAMBETH JOHN PRE 1690 NORFOLK, VA, USA
[36448] : JOHN 1745 NORFOLK, VA, USA **[36448]** :
NDM 1905 LYNCHBURG (CAMPBELL), VA, USA
[36448] : MEREDITH 1745 NORFOLK, VA, USA
[36448]

LAMBIE 1793-1877 MAUCHLINE & STEVENSON,
AYR, SCT **[35780]**

LAMBKIN 1876 PYRMONT, NSW, AUS **[35099]** :
SYDNEY 1900S NZ **[35099]**

LAMBLE ALL BOVEY TRACEY, DEV, ENG **[35345]**

LAMBORN 1800 BASINGSTOKE, HAM, ENG **[34909]**

LAMBOURN PRE 1840 DENCHWORTH, BRK, ENG
[35523] : 1850+ HEREFORD, HEF, ENG **[37070]**

LAMBOURNE 1800+ ROPLEY, HAM, ENG **[35393]** :
1800+ BUCKLAND, BRK, ENG **[35598]** : PRE 1850
OXF, ENG **[37097]** : PRE 1850 BRK, ENG **[37097]**

LAMBRECHT C1860 NSA, FRG **[38660]**

LAMERTON 1700+ PALYNT & TALLAND, CON,
ENG **[35172]**

LAMEY 1890+ ADELAIDE, SA, AUS **[36309]** : 1800-
1900 TURNHOUT, ATW, BEL **[38170]**

LAMIN ALL HARBY, LEI, ENG **[34758]** : PRE 1900
LINBY & ARNOLD, NTT, ENG **[36387]**

LAMING PRE 1850 DEAL, KEN, ENG **[33804]** : 1750
ST MARGARET AT CLIFF, KEN, ENG **[34964]** :
1790+ RINGWOULD, KEN, ENG **[34964]** : 1785+
RIPPLE, KEN, ENG **[34964]**

LAMKIN 1700 STATFORD, NH, USA **[38131]**

LAMMAS 1835 SOUTH HACKNEY, MDX, ENG
[38288]

LAMMEREE 1900+ STEENBERGEN, NBT, NL
[35141]

LAMMERS PRE 1870 BISSENDORF, HAN, GER
[38632]

LAMMIE 1870-1980 DALRY, AYR, SCT **[37205]**

LAMMING 1860+ ROCHESTER, NY, USA **[34964]**

LAMMLE PRE 1850 WUE, GER **[38675]**

LAMOND ALL ANS & PER, SCT **[37727]** : JAMES
1780-1840 ISLE OF MULL, ARL, SCT **[38409]**

LAMONT 1852+ HORSHAM, VIC, AUS **[37115]** :
1852+ VIC, AUS **[37115]** : ELIZA 1792-1879
GOULBOURN, ONT, CAN **[37441]** : EUPHEMIA
1880-1905 CHATHAM, ONT, CAN **[38409]** : 1850S

MAGHERA, ANT, IRL [34636] : DAVID C1884 GLASGOW, SCT [34222] : PRE 1812 GREENOCK, DNB, SCT [34501] : PRE 1846 GREENOCK, RFW, SCT [35232] : 1750+ DNB, SCT [35924] : 1807 PERTH, PER, SCT [36536] : ALL INV, SCT [37115] : PRE 1852 ISLE OF SKYE, INV, SCT [37115] : ELIZA 1792-1879 PER, SCT [37441] : PRE 1850 ISLAY, ARL, SCT [38403]

LAMONTAGNE 1750-1850 MASKINONGE, QUE, CAN [36703]

LAMOTHE 1800+ DE DE CALUMET, QUE, CAN [38727]

LAMP 1960+ ELGIN, USA [37206]

LAMPARD C1857 WELLINGTON, SA, AUS [35384] : PRE 1835 ENG [37760]

LAMPE 1750-1900 DANZIG, PRE, GER [35205] : PRE 1700 BREMEN, BRM, GER [35205] : C1750+ DELMENHORST, BRM, GER [35828]

LAMPEL PRE 1830 DETMOLD, NRW, GER [38029]

LAMPELA 1927+ CHICAGO, IL, USA [38542]

LAMPLUGH 1700S LAMPLUGH, CUL, ENG [35877]

LAMPMANN 1800+ CASTROP, WEF, GER [38023]

LAMPORT PRE 1911 ASH, SRY, ENG [34959]

LAMPRECHT 1830-1882 BASSDORF, BRA, GER [37973]

LAMPRELL ALL LND, ENG [34723] : ALL BOCKING, ESS, ENG [37994]

LAMPREY 1750+ KENTISBEARE, DEV, ENG [35587]

LAMY ALL QUE, CAN [34245]

LA NAGE 1840+ AUS [35975] : 1840+ PORTSMOUTH, HAM, ENG & BEL [35975]

LANARD 1850+ USA [38481]

LANAU 1790-1860 BALTIMORE CITY, MD, USA [36911]

LANCASTER ALL MANILLA, NSW, AUS [34595] : PRE 1900 NSW, AUS [34705] : 1830S ST CHARLES, QUE, CAN [38422] : PRE 1740 THORNEY ABBEY, CAM, ENG [34204] : 1860+ BRADFORD, WRY, ENG [34355] : ALL BUTTERMERE & LORTON, CUL, ENG [34595] : RICHARD 1750-1800 LIVERPOOL, LAN, ENG [35844] : RICHARD 1800+ MANCHESTER & COLNE, LAN, ENG [35844] : PRE 1880 RAINHILL, LAN, ENG [36779] : 1753 ALLENDALE, NBL, ENG [37019] : PRE 1805 HULL, YKS, ENG [37383] : ALL PREESALL & RAMPSIDE, LAN, ENG [37673] : 1800S CARLISLE, CUL, ENG [38422]

LANCE 1861+ SYDNEY, NSW, AUS [35373] : PRE 1820 BLACKWATER, CON, ENG [34031]

LANCELEY PRE 1850 SRY, ENG [34848]

LAND C1750 ASKWITH & WESTON, WRY, ENG [35079] : PRE 1750 ESS, ENG [35642] : ALL NFK, ENG [36234] : 1825 HONLEY, YKS, ENG [38209] : ROBERT PRE 1857 PORTLAND, DOR, ENG [38413] : 1850+ ERIE CO., NY, USA [36962]

LANDAU 1853 KLEIN WESSNBERG, DEN [37690]

LANDEGENT PRE 1800 DREISCHOR, ZEL, NL [36630]

LANDELLS PRE 1850 ALNWICK, NBL, ENG [37300]

LANDER 1822+ SYDNEY, NSW, AUS [33771] : 1750-1850 ST NEOT, CON, ENG [34250] : 1740-1800 MERE, WIL, ENG [34769] : PRE 1850 NFK, ENG [36073] : PRE 1800 BELPER, DBY & NTT, ENG [38254] : PRE 1860 GREAT TORRINGTON, DEV, ENG & NZ [35997] : PRE 1800 SCHAUERHOF, RPF, GER [38681]

LANDERKIN 1819 WELLESLEY TWP., ONT, CAN [34503]

LANDERS PRE 1902 NORTHAMPTON, NTH, ENG [35956] : 1842 SALFORD, LAN, ENG [37184] : ALL IRL [36784] : 1800-1825 KY, USA [38137] : 1825-1850 FOUNTAIN CO., IN, USA [38137] : PRE 1790 VA & KY, USA [38242]

LANDES PRE 1800 ALTLEININGEN, RPF, GER [38681]

LANDGADE 1500 LANDGALL, CUL, ENG [34466]

LANDIS 1735-1810 CHESTER CO., PA, USA [36738] : 1780 PA, USA [38143]

LANDISS 1700-1850 GRANVILLE CO., NC, USA [36565] : 1800-1900 BARDLEY, MO, USA [36565]

LANDLES PRE 1850 LINLITHGOW, STI, SCT [34097]

LANDMANN 1600+ GEDERN, HEN, GER [37572]

LANDON 1790-1850 LEEDS, ONT, CAN [38097] : ALL ABERFORD, YKS, ENG [36822]

LANDORF ALL AUS [35746] : ALL PRE, GER [35746] : ALL NZ [35746]

LANDRAGIN 1795-1842+ WASIGNY, CHA, FRA & ENG [33847]

LANDROCK PRE 1860 SAXONY, PSA, GER [37875]

LANDRY 1840-1940 NEW ORLEANS, LA, USA [37583]

LANDSAAT 1700S UTRECHT, UTR, NL [38358]

LANDSBERG C1810 POM, GER [38630]

LANDSDALE 1780-1820 NELSON CO., KY, USA [38108]

LANDT 1800-1900 GER [36962]

LANDZION 1950+ GLENDALE, CA & MI, USA [34244]

LANE ALL TAS, AUS [33791] : 1848-1920 SYDNEY, NSW, AUS [34438] : 1840+ NEWCASTLE, NSW, AUS [34544] : 1801+ SYDNEY, NSW, AUS [34905] : WILLIAM C1837 PITTWATER, TAS, AUS [35431] : C1870 MELBOURNE, VIC, AUS [35515] : 1878 DALBY, QLD, AUS [35807] : 1838+ PITTWATER & SORELL, TAS, AUS [36600] : WILLIAM 1864+ HAY & WODONGA, NSW & VIC, AUS [36600] : 1864 HAY & DARLINGTON PT, NSW, AUS [36600] : C1830 RICHMOND, NSW, AUS [38568] : 1800+ LINCOLN CO., ONT, CAN [34114] : GORDON 1905+ BC, CAN [34234] : 1800S DEAL & DOVER, `KEN, ENG [33779] : PRE 1851 PLYMOUTH, DEV, ENG [33866] : 1842-1864 CHARLTON, LND, ENG [34002] : PRE 1900 BIRMINGHAM, SRY, ENG [34207] : 1850-1925 BETHNAL GREEN, MDX, ENG [34242] : C1830 WEST HARNHAM, WIL, ENG [34281] : 1890+ BARNSLEY, WRY, ENG [34306] : 1800-1850 FOWEY, CON, ENG [34438] : PRE 1810 HERMITAGE, DOR, ENG [34544] : C1788-1808 BRISTOL, GLS, ENG [35037] : ALL BKM, ENG [35139] : JOSEPH ALL NEWARK UPON TRENT, NTT, ENG [35353] : CHARLES ALL NEWARK UPON TRENT, NOTTINGHAM, NTT, ENG [35353] : 1810 DEVONPORT, DEV, ENG [35706] : 1837+ BERE FERRERS, DEV, ENG [35706] : 1700+ REDRUTH, CON, ENG [35749] : 1880-1930 GATESHEAD, DUR, ENG [36090] : 1841-1909 WESTMINSTER, MDX, ENG [36117] : PRE 1830 OXF, ENG [36117] : 1900+ CHISWICK, LND, ENG [36117] : 1861-1920 STAINES, MDX, ENG [36117] : ALL LONDON, ENG [36174] : 1770+ WEST PUTFORD, DEV, ENG [36254] : PRE 1820 BRINGSTY, HEF, ENG [36518] : 1600+ KING BROMLEY, STS, ENG [36756] : SAMUEL 1800-1850 PENTONVILLE & ISLINGTON, MDX, ENG [36864] : PRE 1806 EYNSFORD, KEN, ENG [36866] : PRE 1848 SUTTON AT HONE, KEN, ENG [36866] : C1812 KINGSDON, SOM, ENG [37144] : C1800 DEV, ENG [37180] : PRE 1870 MINWORTH, WAR, ENG [37331] : 1800S TORQUAY, DEV, ENG [37643] : 1650+ WOKINGHAM, BRK, ENG [37842] : C1810 STOURBRIDGE, STS, ENG [37883] : 1400-1600 HEREFORD, HEF, ENG [38026] : PRE 1800 NEWARK, NTT, ENG [38248] : JAMES C1800 ENG [38268] : ALFRED C1860 DALSTON, MDX, ENG

[38268] : 1832-1858 CHRISTON, DEV, ENG & AUS [37643] : LETITIA 1830+ DOUGLAS, IOM [36638] : PRE 1820 COR, IRL [34984] : C1850+ BURNHORT, COR, IRL [35249] : JOSEPH 1861-1881 (1ST ROYAL SCOTS), UK [35353] : 1870+ AL, USA [35262] : C1820 NY, USA [36923] : WILLIAM 1840+ CALHOUN CO., MS, USA [37004] : WILLIAM 1820S SC, USA [37004] : PRE 1760 WESTCHESTER CO., NY, USA [37018] : MARY ANN PRE 1850 BALTIMORE, MD, USA [38049] : PRE 1800 MONMOUTH CO., NJ, USA [38448] : PRE 1775 MON, WLS [37040]

LANEY 1800+ HAM, ENG [37160] : JOHN 1790-1850 MONTGOMERY, NYS, USA [36447]

LANFEAR 1825 KINTBURY, BRK, ENG [34731]

LANG ALL GEELONG, VIC, AUS [36605] : 1860+ SALE, VIC, AUS [36622] : 1830-1870 SIMCOE CO., ONT, CAN [38033] : 1855+ ONT, CAN [38650] : PRE 1756 STH PETHERTON, SOM, ENG [35252] : PRE 1870 CHEDDAR, SOM, ENG [36605] : 1850+ TAUNTON, SOM, ENG [37396] : ALL CON & DEV, ENG [38735] : PRE 1880 DERDINGER & BADEN, GER [36918] : PRE 1730 LIPPOLDSWEILER, WUE, GER [38661] : 1770-1830 BELTURBET, CAV, IRL [33767] : PRE 1840 IRL [38033] : C1770 BRIDGE OF WEIR, RFW, SCT [34926] : 1870S GLASGOW, SCT [35799] : 1850+ MI, USA [38033]

LANG (SEE LAING) [35353]

LANGAN 1850 BALLYCASTLE, MAY, IRL [34708]

LANGBEIN 1860-1880 WELLINGTON, NSW, AUS [34844]

LANGBRIDGE C1850 HUON, TAS, AUS [35747] : 1853+ MUDGEE, NSW, AUS [38541] : 1800S TOTNES, DEV, ENG [38541]

LANGBURN ALL WORLDWIDE [34341]

LANGDALE 1700-1900 BARNET, HRT, ENG [36589] : PRE 1850 MALTON, ERY, ENG [38457]

LANGDON PRE 1857 CARISBROOK, VIC, AUS [33896] : 1926+ CARLTON, VIC, AUS [34011] : 1868+ GOULBURN DISTRICT, NSW, AUS [35854] : 1700-1800 GOULBURN, ONT, CAN [34107] : PRE 1800 ST MEWAN & ST AUSTELL, CON, ENG [34753] : PRE 1851 CHISELBOROUGH, SOM, ENG [35258] : ALL WEST CHINNOCK, SOM, ENG [35854] : 1700S LANTEGLOS BY CAMELFORD, CON, ENG [36961] : PRE 1850 ST ENODER, CON, ENG [37105] : 1776-84 LONG ISLAND, NY, USA [38151] : MERCY 1790 MA & CT, USA [38734]

LANGDOWN 1750+ LYTCHETT MATRAVERS, DOR, ENG [36276]

LANGE 1850+ BALLARAT, VIC, AUS [34421] : ALL DDR [35913] : ALL FLENSBURG, DEN & AUS [33959] : 1830 ZEDLITZ, SIL, GER [34195] : C1877 PAPENBURG, OLD, GER [38691] : C1877 PAPENBURG, OLD, GER [38711] : ALL NOR [38710] : PRE 1891 HOPE, NLN, NZ [36249] : ELISABETH 1878+ SWE [38564]

LANGEDAM 1880S ALKMAAR, NL [33802]

LANGELAAN 1850+ ENG & USA [36491]

LANGELIER 1617 FRA [34516] : 1500 NORMANDIE, FRA [34516]

LANGENBACH 1860+ GOONDIWINDI, QLD, AUS [35335] : C1829 BEUTELSBACH, WUE, GER [35335]

LANGENECKER PRE 1847 BAW, BRD [36542]

LANGEVELT C1700 NOORDWIJK, ZUH, NL [34990]

LANGEVIN PRE 1825 QUE, CAN & FRA [38386]

LANGFIELD GEORGE C1786 HENSALL, YKS, ENG [37143]

LANGFORD 1840-1880 GOULBURN, NSW, AUS [33838] : 1820-1860 GOULBURN, NSW, AUS [37140] : PRE 1929 MAGNETEWAN, ONT, CAN [38450] : PRE 1900 PERSHORE & BIRLINGHAM, WOR, ENG [37097] : 1700-1750 IGHTFIELD, SAL, ENG

[38474] : 1800S ROSENALLIS, LEX, IRL [38498] : 1824-1900 BRADFORD CO., PA, USA [37013] : 1780-1825 BERKSHIRE CO., MA, USA [37013]

LANGHAM C1840 STOW CUM QUY, CAM, ENG [35367]

LANGHORN 1726-1780 AIRMYN, WRY, ENG [37326] : 1780-1900 HOLME ON SPALDING MOOR, ERY, ENG [37326]

LANGHORNE C1800 BRISTOL, GLS, ENG [34952] : 1726-1780 AIRMYN, WRY, ENG [37326] : 1780-1900 HOLME ON SPALDING MOOR, ERY, ENG [37326] : PRE 1850 KENDAL, WES, ENG [38722]

LANGHORST 1775-1825 YORK, ONT, CAN [37435]

LANGHOUT 1817+ OLDEBOORN, FRI, NL [34990]

LANGILLE PRE 1850 NORTH SHORE, NS, CAN [35635]

LANGKOWSKI 1800+ OSTERWICK, WPR, GER [34932]

LANGLEY 1803+ SYDNEY, NSW, AUS [37909] : 1830-1870S WESTMINSTER, MDX, ENG [33962] : PRE 1800 WYCOMBE, BMK, ENG [34131] : PRE 1850 LONDON, ENG [34799] : PRE 1821 HENFIELD, SSX, ENG [34906] : PRE 1854 LONDON, ENG [35363] : PRE 1752 WOKINGHAM, BRK, ENG [36425] : 1800+ KEN & LAN, ENG [36574] : ANN C1820 BRADFORD, YKS, ENG [36638] : PRE 1803 SOUTHWARK, LND, ENG [37909] : 1860+ NEW ALBANY, IN, USA [37781] : ALL WORLDWIDE [36500]

LANGMAID PRE 1805 PLYMOUTH, DEV, ENG [36154] : ALL LANSALLOS, CON, ENG [38446]

LANGMAN PRE 1720 DOWNHAM, CAM, ENG [34445] : 1700-1900 ALTARNUN, CON, ENG [35381] : PRE 1780 EXETER, DEV, ENG [37701]

LANGMEAD ALL MOONTA, SA, AUS [35012]

LANGOULANT 1820+ PARIS, RPA, FRA [33788]

LANG QUAY 1800 QLD, AUS [35465]

LANGRIDGE PRE 1820 HORSTED KEYNES, SSX, ENG [34245] : C1870 LND, ENG [35034] : PRE 1850 E GRINSTEAD, SSX, ENG [36061] : 1850+ NZ [36778] : 1850+ TEMUKA, NZ [36778]

LANGRISH PRE 1800 ROPLEY, HAM, ENG [35247] : PRE 1785 COLMORE, HAM, ENG [37420]

LANGSFORD PRE 1780 ST NEOT, CON, ENG [37579]

LANGSTAFF 1750+ NBL & DUR, ENG [36176]

LANGSTON C1600 ENG [34395] : 1850+ LONDON, MDX, ENG [37847]

LANGSTRATH PRE 1897+ SEAFORTH, ONT, CAN [35004]

LANGTON PRE 1853 MELBOURNE, VIC, AUS [35384] : 1850-1980 LEICESTER AREA, LEI, ENG [34512] : PRE 1850 LOUTH, LIN, ENG [36168] : PRE 1870 CHORLEY, LAN, ENG [36198] : PRE 1900 SRY, ENG [36216]

LANGTRY 1830S MEA, IRL [35136]

LANHAM 1850+ BRISBANE, QLD, AUS [35199] : PRE 1860 ST GEORGE, MDX, ENG [35199] : 1750-1850 TOPCROFT, NFK, ENG [37477] : PRE 1875 BURY ST EDMUNDS, SFK, ENG [37753] : 1826 OHIO CO., KY, USA [35295] : 1830S MO, USA [37533]

LA NICCA ALL GR, CH [36982]

LANIGAN ELIZABETH 1841+ TIP, IRL & AUS [37161]

LANIGAN-SPROULE 1870-1890S COLLINGWOOD, VIC, AUS [37161]

LANKEY PRE 1910 MI, USA [35371]

LANKFORD 1800-1880 YANCEY CO., NC, USA [38009]

LANKOW 1700-1900 ELMENHORST, MEK, GER [34624]

LANKOWSKI CARL PRE 1877 KIRCHDORF, WPR, GER [34567]

LANKSBURY PRE 1800 CON, ENG [38735]

LANKTREE PRE 1800 MEA, IRL [34876]

LANNGUTH 1840 ODENBACK, REINPFALZ, BRD [38327]

LANNING PRE 1800 LONDON, ENG [38428] : PRE 1850 GUERNSEY CO., OH, USA [38584] : C1860 PARIS, IA, USA [38584]

LANNO (SEE LANAU) [36911]

LANNON C1791 ROSEMEILAN, TYR, IRL [37288] : PRE 1860 KILKENNY, KIK, IRL [37521]

LANOUETTE 1859-1944 ST ANNE DE LA PERADE, QUE, CAN [35639]

LANREY 1815+ BARKING, ESS, ENG [37656]

LANSDALE 1600-1800 NFK, ENG [35377]

LANSDELL FREDERICK 1825+ HOBART, TAS, AUS [37301] : 1800+ LND, MDX & KEN, ENG [34597] : 1600-1800 NFK, ENG [35377] : 1815-1825 BEXHILL, SSX, ENG [37301] : 1790+ WORTH, SSX, ENG [37301]

LANSDOWN PRE 1834+ GOULBURN, NSW, AUS [35759] : PRE 1825 GLS, ENG [37040]

LANSKEY PRE 1870 LUBNA GONEZ, GER [35339]

LANSLEY PRE 1830 BROUGHTON, HAM, ENG [37287]

LANSON PRE 1794 NTT, ENG [38080]

LANT 1875+ RUGELEY, STS, ENG [36866]

LANTEIGNE JEAN N. 1650+ NO, FRA [37429]

LANTHIER PRE 1910 CAN [35371] : PRE 1910 MI, USA [35371]

LANTINGA JANTJE 1852 YLST, NL [35607]

LANYON PRE 1600 CON, ENG [34139]

LANZERATH PRE 1800 NRW & RPF, BRD [38616]

LANZO PRE 1870 CALABRIA, ITL [36679]

LAPIERRE 1800+ ALUMETTE ISLAND, QUE, CAN [35613] : 1800+ PEMBROKE, ONT, CAN [35613] : PRE 1900 SOHO, LND, ENG [35435]

LAPIN PRE 1850 PORTADOWN, ARM, IRL [35918]

LAPOINT ALL USA & CAN [37502]

LAPPAN C1813 DERRYLORAN, TYR, IRL [33924]

LAPWORTH PRE 1800 ALVESCOT, OXF, ENG [34384]

LARABIE ALL CAN [34212] : ALL USA [34212]

LARABY ALL CAN [34212]

LARAD ALL ENG [37827]

LARAGY 1800+ CHURCHTOWN, WEM, IRL & AUS [35093] : 1800-1900 IRL & AUS [35778] : 1900+ USA [35778]

LARAN 1800S CAARON, ROS, IRL [38281]

LARARD ALL ENG [37827]

LARBALESTIER 1600-1750 ST HELIER, JSY, CHI [34552]

LARBY 1750-1825 FARNHURST, SSX, ENG [37253]

LARCELLES ALL WORLDWIDE [35901]

LARCHER 1800+ SHOREDITCH & POPLAR, LND, ENG [37660]

LARCOMBE JAMES 1750-1850 SOM, ENG [36813]

LARCUM ALL YKS, ENG [36636]

LARDNER PRE 1850 OXF, ENG [36702]

LARGE 1650+ YKS, ENG [34408] : PRE 1810 WINDRUSH, GLS, ENG [36541] : JOSIAH C1815+ LANGHAM, NFK, ENG [36767] : PRE 1818 LEX, IRL [33838] : JAMES 1880S BROOKLYN, NY & OH, USA [38369] : 1900+ CUYAHOGA CO., OH & NY, USA [38369]

LARGEY AMBROSE C1915+ NEW YORK, NY, USA [38593]

LARIMBE 1700-1800 PORTUGALETE, BISCAYA, ESP [36340]

LARIVIERE 1650-1700 LIMOGES, LMS, FRA [34514]

LARK 1900 COLLINGWOOD, VIC, AUS [34682] : 1837-1900S GREAT YARMOUTH, NFK, ENG [36876] : PRE 1850 BECCLES, SFK, ENG [36876] : 1750+ ILK ST MARGARETS, SFK, ENG [37191]

LARKE 1700+ NFK, ENG [36086] : PRE 1830 DEV & CON, ENG [36673]

LARKIN 1800+ VIC, AUS [35352] : 1840-1900 HUNTERS HILL, NSW, AUS [35559] : MARTIN 1860+ MELBOURNE, VIC, AUS & IRL [34864] : 1790+ CRANBROOK, KEN, ENG [33946] : 1700+ STS, ENG [33973] : 1780+ EWHURST, SSX, ENG [36749] : THOMAS PRE 1855 BANAGHER, OFF, IRL [34449] : ALL RAHAN, OFF, IRL [36784] : PRE 1830S DOW, IRL [37529] : C1817 BALLYNEACOMBS, LDY, IRL [38052] : 1840+ GAL, IRL [38484]

LARKING 1800-99 GREENWICH, LND, ENG [37272]

LARKUM ALL WORLDWIDE [37220]

LARKWORTHY PRE 1900 DEV, ENG [36639]

LARNACH 1850+ OBERON & BATHURST, NSW, AUS [35395]

LARNEY PRE 1900 AUCKLAND, NZ [33964] : PRE 1910 MORRINSVILLE, WKT, NZ [33964]

LAROCHE PRE 1812 MONTREAL, QUE, CAN [37473]

LA ROCHE 1600+ LONDON, ENG [36123] : 1600+ ANGERS, FRA [36123]

LA ROSE PRE 1860 LEVEN, BEL [35818]

LAROSE PRE 1812 MONTREAL, QUE, CAN [34115]

LARRABEE 1650+ NEW LONDON, CT, MA & NY, USA & ENG [36970]

LARRACY 1874+ TENTERFIELD, NSW, AUS [35253]

LARRAD ALL ENG [37827]

LARRARD ALL ENG [37827]

LARRED ALL ENG [37827]

LARRINGTON PRE 1900 CAM, ENG & USA [38386]

LARRISON 1700+ NJ, USA [34121]

LARROD ALL ENG [37827]

LARSDATTER 1832 SANDE, VESTFOLD, NOR [34063]

LARSDOTTER MATHILDA 1897-1900 NELSON, MO, USA [38559]

LARSEN PRE 1870 JUTLAND, DEN [34003] : PRE 1873 VIGERSLEY & VJELBY, DEN [35767] : C1700-1800 OSTERMARIE, BHLM, DEN [37977] : 1830-1870 CHRISTIANIA, NOR [35442] : PRE 1900 LARVIK, NOR [35548] : 1790+ ARENDAL, AUST AGDER, NOR [36326] : 1775+ RORAS, S TRNDLG, NOR [36326]

LARSON OLE 1816-1900 NESS, NOR [36672] : PRE 1850 HALLINGDAL, NOR [38054] : PRE 1865 TROMSO, TOMS, NOR [38600] : HENRY 1825-1890 SWE [36331] : ALL LIMBECK, VAMHUS, SWE [36919]

LARSSEN SVEN C1845-1869 CLAY CO., KS, NE & IA, USA & SWE [38535]

LARSSON ALFRED 1870S NYBO, SIMTUNA, SWE [37025] : GUDMUND PRE 1731 HJO, VASTERGOTLAND, SWE [38550]

LARTER 1840+ SYDNEY, NSW, AUS [35360] : 1800-1900 CHARLOTTETOWN, PEI, CAN [34996]

LA RUE 1660+ QUE, CAN [34152] : 1600-1660 BN, FRA [34152]

LARUE PRE 1910 TX, USA [36947]

LARUSH (SEE LAROCHE) [37473]

LASCELLES C1850 HAREWOOD, WRY, ENG [37650]

LASHAM 1850-1860 SALE, VIC, AUS [35725] : PRE 1794 SELBORNE, HAM, ENG [35247]

LASHBROK ALL WORLDWIDE [37624]

LASHBROOK PRE 1900 MENHENIOT, CON, ENG [35339] : PRE 1850 DEV, ENG [37807] : 1890+ LOS ANGELES, CA, USA [37807] : ALL WORLDWIDE [37624]

LASHBROOKE ALL WORLDWIDE **[37624]**
LASHBROOKS ALL WORLDWIDE **[37624]**
LASHMAR PRE 1700 SSX, ENG **[37875]**
LASHMORE PRE 1775 SSX, ENG **[37736]**
LASHPROK ALL WORLDWIDE **[37624]**
LASKA ALL OES **[37268]**
LASKEY 1700+ WOLBOROUGH & NEWTON ABBOT, DEV, ENG **[35587]** : 1600-1800 CON, ENG **[36806]**
LASKOWSKI PRE 1882 BISCHOSSTEIN, OPR, GER **[38647]**
LASLEY 1770-1800 WASHINGTON CO., PA, KY & OH, USA **[37529]**
LASSAM ALL DEV, ENG **[36469]** : PRE 1775 CRANLEY, SRY, ENG **[37112]**
LASSCOCK PRE 1900 SWAFFHAM, NFK, ENG **[35862]**
LASSELL 1750-1800 PERQUEMANS CO., NC, USA **[36349]** : 1800-1860 IN, USA **[36349]**
LASSEN 1800+ NORRE & OGUM, JUT, DEN **[35448]**
LASSEY 1810S FEWSTON, YKS, ENG **[37643]**
LAST 1760+ BRADFIELD ST GEORGE, SFK, ENG **[34020]** : 1830+ WETHERINGSETT, SFK, ENG **[34710]** : 1835-1906 WOODBRIDGE, SFK, ENG **[37071]**
LASTINGS PRE 1906 BELGAUM, INDIA **[34667]**
LATCHAM PRE 1840 WEDMORE, SOM, ENG **[33874]** : 1860+ LONDON, ENG **[34213]**
LATCHFORD C1800 WHEATHAMPSTEAD, HRT, ENG **[38489]**
LATCHMORE C1848 LEI, ENG **[36253]**
LATEWOOD 1700+ SAL, ENG **[36135]**
LATHAM 1830-1860 HAZELGROVE, CHS, ENG **[33982]** : PRE 1820 ASHTON IN MAKERFIELD, LAN, ENG **[33982]** : ELIZA PRE 1850 ESS, ENG **[34583]** : 1700+ LIVERPOOL, LAN, ENG **[35971]** : 1600S ENG **[36560]** : PRE 1850 SOUTHWARK, SRY, ENG **[38205]** : PRE 1884 IRL **[35618]** : 1600-1850 IRL **[36130]** : ALL GLASGOW, SCT **[35177]** : PRE 1700 MA, USA **[38746]**
LATHBURY 1675+ FRADSWELL, STS, ENG **[35824]**
LATHROPE 1800S OTTERY ST MARY, DEV, ENG **[34857]**
LATHWELL C1690-1718 ST ALBANS, HRT, ENG **[36068]**
LATIMER 1750-1800 BRAMPTON, CUL & LAN, ENG **[35624]** : 1800+ NEWCASTLE, NBL, ENG **[36135]** : 1810+ CUL, WES & LAN, ENG & CAN **[34467]** : C1700-1832 KILMORE, MOG, IRL **[34246]** : 1864 BOYLE, ROS, IRL **[35855]** : C1820 BELFAST, ANT, IRL **[37106]** : ALL PORTADOWN, ANT, IRL **[37295]** : 1730-1800 DOONEREAGH, LET, IRL **[37613]** : PRE 1800 CANONBIE, DFS, SCT **[34025]** : THOMAS C1770 DUMFRIES, DFS, SCT **[37106]** : JOHN C1795 CANONBIE, DFS, SCT **[37106]**
LATIMORE CATHERINE PRE 1814 WARWICK BIRMINGHAM, WAR, ENG **[36646]**
LATOURETTE 1500-1700 OSSE BEARN, FRA **[36556]**
LATOUR-FORGET PRE 1850 QUE, CAN **[34106]**
LA TROBE-BATEMAN 1750+ CON, WRY & SRY, ENG **[36058]**
LATTA 1844+ NSW, AUS **[35356]** : 1840+ ADELAIDE & BULL CREEK, SA, AUS **[35888]** : 1800+ RIVER HIBERT, NS, CAN **[34107]** : 1860+ BALCLUTHA & OWAKA, OTG, NZ **[35888]** : JEAN C1795-C1835 COYLTON, AYR, SCT **[34300]** : PRE 1844 GLASGOW, SCT **[35356]** : PRE 1840 ALLOA, CLK, SCT **[35888]** : 1750-1783 CUMBERLAND, PA, USA **[36908]**
LATTENKAMP 1700+ STERKRADE, RPR, GER **[38651]**

LATTER PRE 1858 SHEFFIELD, YKS, ENG **[37002]** : GEORGE C1882 LEIGH, KEN, ENG **[37345]**
LATTERMANN 1800-1900 BERLIN, GER **[38603]**
LATTIMER PRE 1900 IRL **[38226]**
LATTIMORE 1800+ WAR, ENG **[36600]**
LATURELL PRE 1800 ALTHEIM, RPF, BRD **[36964]**
LATZ PRE 1850 SAARLAND, SAA, GER **[36935]**
LAUBENSTEIN ALL ALT FREUDENTAL, UKRAINE, GROSSLIEBENTAL, SU **[38372]**
LAUBER PRE 1880 NORTHAMPTON CO., PA, USA **[36359]**
LAUBSCH 1829 WOLLSTIEN, POS, GER **[34195]**
LAUBSCHER ALL MIECOURT, BE & JU, CH **[38600]** : PRE 1860 TAEUFFELEN, BE, CH **[38600]**
LAUCHLAN C1803 BEITH, AYR, SCT **[37144]**
LAUCK 1900+ CA, USA **[38333]** : 1850+ CINCINNATI, OH, USA **[38333]**
LAUDENBERGER 1743-1850S PHILADELPHIA CO., PA, USA **[38308]**
LAUDER 1885+ CHARTERS TOWERS, QLD, AUS **[33932]** : 1750+ CLOVERHILL, DON, IRL **[34299]** : PRE 1920 TAURANGA, NZ **[36290]** : 1800S NEW SNEDDON, PAISLEY, RFW, SCT **[33856]** : PRE 1885 CAMBUSNETHAN, LKS, SCT **[33932]** : PRE 1883 WISHAW, DFS, SCT **[36855]** : 1870 BLACKFORD, PER, SCT **[37690]**
LAUDERDALE 1056-1990 BEW & TN, SCT & USA **[37523]**
LAUDRUM PRE 1885 LONDON, ENG **[34519]**
LAUER PRE 1780 OBERNDORF, WUE, GER **[38679]**
LAUFF 1850+ AUS **[37308]**
LAUGHEAD 1821 SLI, IRL **[38227]**
LAUGHLAN PRE 1832 GALSTON, AYR, SCT **[37575]**
LAUGHLEN 1790+ STI, SCT **[35632]**
LAUGHLIN 1850+ SYDNEY, NSW, AUS & IRL **[34913]** : 1800-60 SALEM & CONNEAUT, OH, USA **[37528]** : 1849-1935 ALLAMAKEE, IA, USA **[38111]**
LAUGHMAN ALL WORLDWIDE **[37570]**
LAUGHTON 1700S HAXEY, LIN, ENG **[36635]** : 1650-1850 LIN & NTT, ENG **[37695]**
LAUK ALL ERLACH, BAD, GER **[38333]**
LAUNDESS 1853+ GRENFELL, NSW, AUS **[35022]** : PRE 1853 ATHENS, GR **[35022]**
LAURANCE PRE 1760 CREWKERNE, SOM, ENG **[36581]**
LAURENCE PRE 1839 MULGOA, NSW, AUS **[34275]** : 1800S ST AUBINS, JSY, CHI **[36018]** : C1800-1840 UFTON NERVET, BRK, ENG **[34628]** : PRE 1800 RYE, SSX, ENG **[34858]** : 1850 FROME, SOM, ENG **[34584]**
LAURENSON ALL ONT & QUE, CAN **[35602]** : 1776+ WHALSAY, SHI, SCT **[36875]**
LAURIE 1860S WENTWORTH, NSW, AUS **[37178]** : PRE 1895 PHYBELT, SA, AUS **[37955]** : 1840+ DFS, SCT **[33790]** : 1761+ SOUTH WEST DISTRICTS, SCT **[34918]** : PRE 1829+ STOBE & PEEBLES, PEE, SCT **[35237]**
LAURISON PRE 1883 MULLABRACK, ARM, IRL **[35852]**
LAUT 1860+ CARCOAR AREA, NSW, AUS **[36316]**
LAUTARD PRE 1900 RODEZ, AUV, FRA **[34104]**
LAUTENBERGER 1700-1850 NORTHAMPTON CO., PA, USA **[38308]**
LAUTHERS PRE 1800 PA, USA **[37603]**
LAUTRE PRE 1850 GIBEL, MP & AUV, FRA **[34945]**
LAUWERS PRE 1800 BERGHEM, OVL, BEL **[38697]**
LAUZON MARIE C1790+ ST BENOIT, DEUX MONTAGNES, QUE, CAN **[34506]**
LAVAL 1600-1690 GENEVA, GE, CH **[38779]**
LAVALLEY 1800+ NEPEAN, ONT, CAN **[35613]** : 1800+ SOREL, QUE, CAN **[35613]** : PRE 1800 FRA **[35613]**

LAVDIJ 1876 ROOSENDAAL EN NISPEN, NBT, NL [36307]

LAVELLE PRE 1930 MANCHESTER, LAN, ENG [36201] : PRE 1950 IRL [36201]

LAVENDER 1860S+ BELLINGEN, NSW, AUS [35735] : 1800-1900+ CAN [37648] : 1300-1400+ SSX, ENG [37648] : 1800S HASTINGS, SSX, ENG [37714] : PRE 1800 ESS, ENG [37718]

LAVER PRE 1851 TAUNTON, SOM, ENG [37396] : C1811 NORTH PETHERTON, SOM, ENG [37396] : PRE 1840 STANFORD LE HOPE, ESS, ENG [37885] : 1880S WHITHORN, SCT [36659]

LAVERICK 1856+ BALLARAT, VIC, AUS [35564] : 1860S SYDNEY, NSW, AUS [35926] : C1807 MONKWEARMOUTH, DUR, ENG [35564] : JOHN C1850 DEPTFORD & SUNDERLAND, DUR, ENG [35564] : PRE 1860 MANCHESTER, LAN, ENG [35926]

LAVEROCK PRE 1823 YKS, ENG [34494]

LAVERS ALL DEV, ENG [35063] : PRE 1740 DEV, ENG [37882]

LAVERTY 1860S WORTH, IRL [36264] : 1880S GLASGOW, SCT [36264]

LAVERY ALL MANLY, NSW, AUS [33765] : PRE 1870 RATHMULLAN, DOW, IRL [37405]

LAVICTOIRE BENECHE ALL ST JEROME, QUE, CAN [35327] : 1600-1900S ST JEROME, QUE, CAN [35327]

LAVIN 1845+ ROS, IRL [35201] : PRE 1850 COR, IRL [38196]

LAVIS PRE 1854 PITNEY, SOM, ENG [35117] : 1820S-1850S LOWER BRISEHAM, DEV, ENG [36337]

LAVOIE ALL QUE, CAN [34517]

LAVOR PRE 1730 STH PETHERTON, SOM, ENG [35252]

LAW 1872+ SYDNEY, NSW, AUS [34978] : C1861 MIDDLE PLAINS, TAS, AUS [35391] : C1861 DELORAINE, TAS, AUS [35391] : JANE SELINA 1842-1891 WOR & STS, ENG [34314] : PRE 1800 BETHERSDEN, KEN, ENG [34563] : 1780-1850 LIVERPOOL, LAN, ENG [34762] : PRE 1860 TIPTON, STS, ENG [34904] : 1840+ BROOKLANDS, CHS, ENG [34978] : PLEASANT PRE 1840 BETHERSDEN, KEN, ENG [35077] : 1899+ HEADCORN, KEN, ENG [35759] : 1800+ WOODBRIDGE, SFK, ENG [36093] : 1830-1950 KIDDERMINSTER, WOR, ENG [36556] : 1600-1850 BRIDGNORTH, SAL, ENG [36556] : 1800+ IDLE & THACKLEY, WRY, ENG [36617] : ROBERT C1800-1856 BALLYWILLAN & PORTRUSH, ANT & LDY, IRL [36244] : 1800+ CARNMONEY & TEMPLEPATRICK, ANT, IRL [37425] : 1875+ BELFAST, ANT & DOW, IRL [37425] : 1700+ CASTLEBAR, MAY, IRL & ENG [35403] : THOMAS C1850 SCT [34222] : PRE 1700 ST ANDREWS, FIF, SCT [35227] : PRE 1860 EDINBURGH, MLN, SCT [36793]

LAWER ALL NEWLYN EAST, CON, ENG [35235] : 1870+ OTAGO, NZ [35235]

LAWERENCE SARAH 1609-1684 NEWARK, NJ, USA [35271]

LAWERENZ ALL WORLDWIDE [38687]

LAWES PRE 1860 COOMBE BISSET, WIL, ENG [33850] : PRE 1854 WINCHESTER, HAM, ENG [34696] : 1750-1800 WHITBURY, WIL, ENG [36213]

LAWFORD 1750-1850 EDGEWARE, MDX, ENG [36165]

LAWLER 1831+ NSW, AUS [33768] : PRE 1840 KIK, IRL [35758] : 1830-1850S LEX, IRL [34027] : PRE 1856 PAULSTOWN, KIK, IRL [35113] : C1858 CASTLEKELLY, KIK, IRL [35158] : PRE 1848 DUBLIN, IRL [36204]

LAWLESS PIERCE C1890S AUS [35852] : PRE 1852 LANCASTER, LAN, ENG [35097] : 1858-1930 DUBLIN CITY &, KID, IRL [34165] : ALL CASTLECOMER, KIK, IRL [34593] : PRE 1830 TIPPERARY, TIP, IRL [34901]

LAWLEY 1800-1850 BRIDGNORTH, SAL, ENG [33767] : 1800S BIRMINGHAM, WAR, ENG [35744] : 1820 AL, USA [38198]

LAWLISS 1809+ SYDNEY & GUNNING, NSW, AUS [34839]

LAWLOR 1865+ NSW, AUS [34812] : 1790+ KILLARNEY, KER, IRL [33946] : C1815 KER, IRL [34145] : 1870-1910 DUB, IRL [34191] : PRE 1865 ASKEATON, LIM, IRL [34812] : C1858 CASTLEKELLY, KIK, IRL [35158]

LAWLOR (SEE LAWLER) [36204]

LAWNS PRE 1908 BARRHEAD, RFW, SCT [34706]

LAWRANCE C1820 SHOREDITCH, LND, ENG [35260] : 1880+ DUMBARTON, DNB, SCT [34260]

LAWRASON (SEE LARRIS [34121]

LAWRENCE STEPHEN 1848+ SYDNEY, NSW, AUS [34449] : 1900+ ALBANY & PERTH, WA, AUS [35136] : 1890S BRUNSWICK, VIC, AUS [35136] : ALL ST LEONARDS, TAS, AUS [35136] : 1860+ SYDNEY, NSW, AUS [35400] : 1860S MELBOURNE, VIC, AUS [35855] : 1850S PORT LINCOLN, SA, AUS [35855] : 1855+ CASTLEMAINE, VIC, AUS [37911] : 1857-1873 INGLEWOOD, VIC, AUS [37911] : 1660+ ST MICHAELS, BARBADOS [38235] : 1800S SHOREDITCH, MDX, ENG [33898] : PRE 1860S STS, ENG [34240] : PRE 1900 TOVIL & MAIDSTONE, KEN, ENG [34325] : 1700 WARMINSTER, WIL, ENG [34466] : C1800-1840 UFTON NERVET, BRK, ENG [34628] : 1700+ YORK, ENG [34703] : 1800 BRADFORD ON AVON, WIL, ENG [34890] : 1800+ YORK, ENG [34907] : 1850+ GRIMSBY, LIN, ENG [35125] : 1850+ HULL, YKS, ENG [35125] : ALL NORTH SHIELDS, NBL, ENG [35136] : C1820 SHOREDITCH, LND, ENG [35260] : ALL FONTMELL MAGNA, DOR, ENG [35297] : PRE 1800 SSX, ENG [35407] : ISABELLA C1810+ LONDON, ENG [35427] : PRE 1800 ESS, ENG [35642] : 1800+ WOR, ENG [35812] : 1850+ LIVERPOOL, LAN, ENG [35979] : 1750+ SFK & NFK, ENG [36058] : ALL NTT, ENG [36174] : ALL WISSET, SFK, ENG [36938] : C1750 BRAUGHING, HRT, ENG [36978] : 1660-1760 WOODHAY, HAM, ENG [37233] : C1850 SHEFFIELD, YKS, ENG [37233] : PRE 1940 MAIDSTONE, KEN, ENG [37359] : GEORGE 1750-1850 STEPNEY & LAMBETH, LND, ENG [37644] : 1800+ SHOREDITCH & POPLAR, LND, ENG [37660] : 1600-1900 ST KEVERNE & ST HILARY, CON, ENG [37680] : 1800+ LONDON, ENG & NZ [36850] : 1848 PETERHEAD, ABD, SCT [35855] : PRE 1900 LONGSIDE, ABD, SCT [36061] : 1750+ OLD DEER, ABD, SCT [38446] : 1750-1800 MONMOUTH, NJ, USA [37435] : 1817-1848 DEARBORN CO., IN, USA [37563] : 1875-1910 ATLANTA, GA, USA [38126] : PRE 1875 RI, USA [38126] : 1790+ PA, USA [38735]

LAWRENSON PRE 1831 GOOSNARGH & INGLEWHITE, LAN, ENG [37710]

LAWREY ALL CON, ENG [35500]

LAWRIE 1850+ GREENOCK, RFW, SCT [35461] : PRE 1800 WLN, SCT [37374] : PRE 1800 LKS, SCT [37374]

LAWRIE-LYLE 1900-1930 GLASGOW, LKS, SCT [35025]

LAWRY PRE 1800 ROCHESTER, KEN, ENG [33869] : 1400+ LUXULYAN, CON, ENG [33989] : 1750-1850 GULVAL, CON, ENG [34535] : ALL GULVAL, CON, ENG [35500] : ALL ST AGNES, CON, ENG [35500] :

1800+ SANCREED, CON, ENG [36795] : 1650+
TYWADREATH & GORRAN, CON, ENG [36827] :
PRE 1746 ST AGNES, CON, ENG [37939] : ALL
WORLDWIDE [35500]

LAWS THOMAS 1855 LND, ENG [35575] : 1700S TEST
VALLEY, HAM, ENG [38350] : PRE 1850
WINLATON, DUR, ENG [38457] : C1690
BOWERCHALKE, WIL, ENG [38489]

LAWSON ARCHIBALD 1854+ VIC, AUS [33915] :
1864+ KILKIVAN, QLD, AUS [34678] : 1886
GYMPIE, QLD, AUS [36368] : 1830S NEWCASTLE,
NSW, AUS [36365] : 1860+ SYDNEY, NSW, AUS
[36365] : 1850+ VIC, AUS [37113] : 1835+ ONT,
CAN [34465] : JAMES 1869+ ONT, CAN [35641] :
GEORGE PRE 1876 ONT, CAN [35641] : C1809
LITTLE GOMERSAL, YKS, ENG [34434] : C1870
SOUTHWARK, SRY, ENG [36099] : PRE 1881
NEWCASTLE ON TYNE, NBL, ENG [36475] :
1840+ NEWBIGGIN, NBL, ENG [36609] : 1710+ ST
BEES, CUL, ENG [38067] : C1588 LND, ENG [38348]
: 1866-1931 LIVERPOOL & NEW PLYMOUTH,
LAN, ENG & NZ [34622] : PRE 1800 IOM [36380] :
ARCHIBALD PRE 1854 BALLYCASTLE, ANT, IRL
[33915] : PRE 1840 DRUMFIN, SLI, IRL [34465] :
MATTHEW PRE 1862 DON, IRL [36678] : GEORGE
PRE 1862 DON, IRL [36678] : 1800+ BLACKFORD,
PER, SCT [34098] : 1800-1900 SCT [34135] : 1780+
LIBERTON, MLN, SCT [34420] : 1750-1820 AYR,
SCT [34615] : PRE 1808 SCOONIE, FIF, SCT [35229] :
1600-1800 FIF, SCT [35627] : 1840S HADDINGTON,
SCT [36358] : PRE 1883 LOCHMABEN, DFS, SCT
[36855] : 1800-1900 HAMILTON, LKS, SCT & AUS
[33991] : 1600+ SWE [37805] : 1864-1870
CUMBERLAND, PA, USA [36558] : 1840-1864
FRANKLIN CO., OH, USA [36558] : C1780
ORANGE CO., NY, USA [37810] : RICHARD 1890+
ND, USA [38431] : C1920 HOLYHEAD, AGY, WLS
[34622]

LAWTON 1838+ WEYMOUTH, DOR, ENG [33920] :
1780+ ASHTON UNDER LYNE, LAN, ENG [34290]
: 1730-1900 WINWICK & CULCHETH, LAN, ENG
[34352] : PRE 1880S HANLEY, STS, ENG [35439] :
C1885 SADDLEWORTH, LAN & YKS, ENG [36028]
: PRE 1840 TUNSTALL, STS, ENG [36504] : 1816+
WIGAN, LAN, ENG [37560]

LAWTY PRE 1873 HUNMANBY, ERY, ENG [34241]

LAX C1860 COVENTRY, WAR, ENG [33932] : 1700+
BRANCEPETH, DUR, ENG [35511] : ALL
WORLDWIDE [33932]

LAXEN ALL NFK, ENG [36122]

LAXTON ALL NTT, ENG [35904]

LAY PRE 1800 HILLSCHEID, RPF, GER [38663]

LAYBOURNE PRE 1850 ENG [38403]

LAYBUTT ALL WORLDWIDE [36574]

LAYCOCK C1800 TADCASTER, WRY, ENG [33796] :
PRE 1930 BURNLEY, LAN, ENG [34050] : ALL
ENG [35618] : ALL TADCASTER, YKS, ENG [37252]
: 1710+ WYCOLLAR, COLNE & KEIGHLEY, YKS,
ENG [37581] : 1860+ BRIGHTON, SSX, ENG [38539]
: 1750+ NOTTINGHAM, NTT, ENG & NZ [36765]

LAYDEN C1690-1756 SULHAM & BURGHFIELD,
BRK, ENG [36068]

LAYLAND 1850+ PANCRAS, MDX, ENG [34738] :
PRE 1850 LAN, ENG [37885]

LAYT 1857+ SYDNEY, NSW, AUS [35160] : PRE 1857
BKM, WAR & WOR, ENG [35160]

LAYTON PRE 1850 MILTON ERNEST, BDF, ENG
[34311] : ALL WINDSOR, BRK, ENG [34571] : ALL
WEST HAM, LND, ENG [35353] : ALL LONDON,
ENG [35842] : JOHN PRE 1800 ST JAMES
WINCHESTER, LND, ENG [36899] : JOHN PRE
1800 HIGHGATE, LND, ENG [36899]

LAZAROW 1840+ BREMEN, BRM, GER & BRD
[35062]

LAZARUS ALL LINCOLN, LIN, ENG [34318]

LAZENBY 1700-1900 SHINCLIFF, DUR, ENG [35857]
: 1810+ MIDDLETON TYAS, NRY, ENG [37635] :
PRE 1800 MD, USA [37587] : 1800-1850 NEWTON &
COLUMBIA CO., GA, USA [37587]

LEA PRE 1900 HORTON, WRY, ENG [33830] : PRE
1750 OLD SWINFORD, WOR, ENG [34711] : PRE
1770 KINGSWINFORD, STS, ENG [36110] : PRE
1850 SOMERFORD MAGNA, WIL, ENG [37403] :
1760S PHILADELPHIA, PA, USA [38531]

LEACH ELIZA JANE 1886+ MICHELAGO, NSW,
AUS [34885] : 1880+ SYDNEY, NSW, AUS [34978] :
1800S PORTAGE LA PRAIRIE, MAN, CAN [34218] :
ALL LANARK CO., ONT, CAN [34376] : 1851+
DARLINGTON, ONT, CAN [35601] : GRACE
1750+ STRATTON, CON, ENG [34078] : ESTHER
1836+ STOKE NEWINGTON, LND, ENG [34630] :
1840+ GRAVESEND, KEN, ENG [34978] : 1700S
CAMBRIDGE, CAM, ENG [35018] : PRE 1760
HEDENHAM, NFK, ENG [35173] : 1800+
WALSOKEN, NFK & CAM, ENG [35342] : 1850+
BURY, LAN, ENG [35442] : PRE 1851 DEV, ENG
[35601] : 1700-1900 MDX & LND, ENG [36007] :
1800S CLERKENWELL, LND, ENG [36055] :
GEORGE 1820+ ISLINGTON, MDX, ENG [36068] :
1800+ WIL & HAM, ENG [36697] : 1800-1870
BRISTOL, GLS, ENG [36795] : 1750+ DARWEN,
LAN, ENG [36991] : ALL EAST CHINNOCK, SOM,
ENG [37378] : ALL GRUNDISBURGH, SFK, ENG
[37487] : C1850 LIVERPOOL, LAN, ENG [37508] :
1750-1820 HOGHTON & BRINDLE, LAN, ENG
[37613] : PRE 1850 MORCHARD BISHOP, DEV,
ENG [37722] : 1500-1600 MARTOCK & ASH, SOM,
ENG [37783] : WILLIAM 1800-1870 BLACK DOG,
DEV, ENG [38456] : ALL CON & DEV, ENG [38735] :
PRE 1820 WEX, IRL [34376] : C1800 RUPERT
MANOR, LET, IRL & CAN [35078] : 1812 KY, USA
[36908] : C1796 NY, USA [38590] : 1835-60
RANDOLPH CO., IN, USA [38590] : WILLIAM 1800
WLS [34363]

LEACH (SEE LEAH) [35133]

LEADBEATTER PRE 1845 SEYMOUTH, VIC, AUS
[35763]

LEADBETTER ALL NIPPISSING, ONT, CAN [36679] :
ALL ROCKWOOD & WEDDIFIELD, ONT, CAN
[36679] : PRE 1900 LND, SSX & SRY, ENG [37195] :
ALL ASHLAND, MA & MI, USA [38369]

LEADER PRE 1890 TUMUT, NSW, AUS [34978]

LEADLE 1871+ MIDDLESBROUGH, NRY, ENG
[36412]

LEADLEY 1700+ REDMIRE, YKS, ENG [38034]

LEAH C1806 STROUD, GLS, ENG [35133] : 1787+
MACCLESFIELD, CHS, ENG [36875]

LEAHY 1860-1880 ECHUCA, VIC, AUS [34175] : 1840-
1900 RICHMOND, VIC, AUS [34175] : 1810+
COOTAMUNDRA, NSW, AUS [34198] : PRE 1950
ALBURY, NSW, AUS [35386] : PRE 1854
JERUSALEM, TAS, AUS [35459] : C1847
MELBOURNE, VIC, AUS [35515] : ALL ONT, CAN
[36539] : 1790-1840 YOUGHAL, COR, IRL [34175] :
1840-1860 TIP, IRL [34183] : PRE 1850 NEWCASTLE
WEST, LIM, IRL [34198] : 1800S TIP, IRL [35017] :
1818+ CASL, COR, IRL [36296]

LEAK PRE 1870 SCARBOROUGH & YORK, NRY,
ENG [34241] : 1700-1800 PRESTON, LAN, ENG
[36618]

LEAKE 1800+ KIRTON & ALGARKIRK, LIN, ENG
[34916] : CHARLES 1900+ WINDSOR, LND, ENG
[34916] : 1880 NORTH WINGFIELD, DBY, ENG
[37829]

LEAKER PRE 1810 SHELDON, DEV, ENG **[37406]** :
1840+ BRISTOL, ENG **[37406]**

LEAKEY 1700-1900 SOM, ENG **[36531]** : ALL
SHOREDITCH, LND, ENG **[37647]**

LEALL C1750-1820 GOSPORT & IOW, HAM, ENG
[36051]

LEAMING 1890S AUCKLAND, NZ **[36283]**

LEAMON ALL EPSOM & HORTON, SRY, ENG
[38332]

LEAN PRE 1855 ADELAIDE, SA, AUS **[36768]** : 1840+
ADELAIDE, SA, AUS **[36892]** : 1650-1800
GWENNAP, CON, ENG **[34793]** : 1852 GWENNAP,
CON, ENG **[34878]** : PRE 1840 GWENNAP, CON,
ENG **[35496]** : ALL BRISTOL, GLS, ENG **[36789]** :
1790 GWENNAP, CON, ENG **[36892]**

LEANING 1640-1840 WAWBY, LIN, ENG **[34658]** :
ALL UK **[37421]**

LEANY 1700S TONBRIDGE, KEN, ENG **[35260]**

LEAR 1843+ CAMPBELLTOWN, NSW, AUS **[34966]** :
PRE 1840 GILLINGHAM, DOR & SOM, ENG
[37410] : JOHN 1500-1620 ENG **[37784]** : PRE 1876
DEV, ENG **[37892]** : PRE 1830 GLS, ENG & AUS
[36095] : 1800-1860 HARRISON CO., KY, USA
[37740]

LEAR-GARFIELD C1850+ BINGHAM, NTT, ENG
[38401]

LEARIE 1848-1868 ONT, CAN **[36654]**

LEARY PRE 1780 LAMBERHURST, KEN, ENG
[36883] : PRE 1845 COR, IRL **[33781]** : PRE 1876
COLLUM, LOU, IRL **[34695]** : 1800+
CHURCHTOWN, COR, IRL **[35847]** : 1805+ COR,
IRL **[37560]** : 1700+ WORLDWIDE **[38774]**

LEASK MARIA PRE 1857 BIRSEY, OKI, SCT **[37948]**

LEASON C1775-1990S BELFAST HARBOR, ME, USA
[38308]

LEATHAM 1890+ GRETA & GRANVILLE, NSW,
AUS **[35075]** : 1850S LITTLE OUSEBURN, WRY,
ENG **[35075]** : PRE 1830 LEEDS, YKS, ENG **[38690]**

LEATHEARD ALL DUR, ENG **[36090]**

LEATHERLAND 1800S BROUGHTON & ASTLEY,
LEI, ENG **[35187]**

L'EAU 1700+ NS, CAN & FRA **[34500]**

LEAVELY PRE 1874 PITSMOOR, YKS, ENG **[34814]**

LEAVENS PRE 1820 CALVERLEY, WRY, ENG
[36583] : 1634+ ROXBURY, MA, USA **[37802]**

LEAVER PRE 1783 RICHMOND, SRY, ENG **[38248]**

LEAVEY 1830-1900 SHOREDITCH, LND, ENG **[36047]**
: 1800-1900 BASINGSTOKE, HAM, ENG **[36047]**

LEAVITT C1600 ENG **[37820]** : C1730 PEMBROKE,
MA, USA **[37820]**

LEAVITT (SEE LEVITT) **[33898]**

LEBACK 1650+ NTH, BKM & BDF, ENG **[36574]**

LEBARRE PRE 1845 CARLETON PLACE, ONT, CAN
[37568]

LE BAS PRE 1860 ST CLEMENT, JSY, CHI **[35440]**

LEBAS 1600-1660 ROUEN, HN, FRA **[34514]**

LEBATT ALL WORLDWIDE **[36574]**

LEBER ALL SCHELINGEN, BAD, GER **[38534]** : PRE
1900 OES **[37574]**

LE BLANC 1900+ AUS **[36750]**

LEBLANC ALL CAN **[34212]**

LE BLANC 1880+ HAMILTON, ONT, CAN **[34512]**

LEBLANC 1883-1936 COMPTON CO., QUE, CAN
[35639]

LE BLANC C1800 CAPE BRETON, NS, CAN **[36694]** :
1800-1860 NEW RICHMOND, QUE, CAN **[38131]**

LEBORNE ALL QUE, CAN **[35005]**

LEBOUVIER ALL WORLDWIDE **[34218]**

LE BRETON PRE 1840 TRINITY, JSY, CHI **[36696]**

LEBRETON 1776-1820 DIJON & NLLE-ORLEANS,
BRG & LA, FRA & USA **[34136]**

LE BROCQ 1807+ ST BRELADE, JSY, CHI **[35041]**

LE BRUN 1800S ST HELIER, JSY, CHI **[36874]**

LEBUTT ALL WORLDWIDE **[36574]**

LECAIN 1812-1900 HALIFAX, NS, CAN **[36550]**

LECK PRE 1820 GLASGOW, LKS, SCT **[36431]** : PRE
1815 MOREBATTLE, ROX, SCT **[38056]**

LECKIE 1750+ PENCAITLAND, ELN, SCT **[36276]** :
PRE 1761 AUCHTERTOOL & AREA, FIF, SCT
[37842]

L'ECLUSE 1780-1830 MOLENBEEK ST JEAN, BEL
[37203]

LE COCQ PRE 1880 ALOERNEY, CHI, ENG **[37855]**

LECOP ALL NOR, FRA **[37385]**

LECOUTRE 1870-1900 ROUBAIX, NOR, FRA **[38166]**

LEDDRA 1700-1758 ST IVES, CON, ENG **[37842]**

LEDEL PRE 1756 GER **[37289]** : 1750+ NOR & SWE
[37289]

LEDERMANN 1786-1956 VORSTETTEN, BAV, GER
[35287] : 1606+ GUNDELFINGEN, BAV, GER
[35287] : 1850+ SANDUSKY CO., OH, USA **[35287]**

LEDGER PRE 1730 DBY & LAN, ENG **[36176]** : 1700-
1920 CLAYWORTH & CLAREBOROUGH, NTT,
ENG **[36176]** : 1900+ CHESTERFIELD, DBY, ENG
[36176] : 1700-1920 EAST RETFORD, NTT, ENG
[36176] : PRE 1730 YKS & LIN, ENG **[36176]** : 1700-
1900 LIN, ENG **[36176]** : 1700+ RETFORD, NTT,
ENG **[37735]**

LEDICA ALL GER **[37529]**

LEDINGHAM PRE 1814 RAYNE, ABD, SCT **[35083]** :
1800+ BANCHORY, ABD, SCT **[35466]**

LEDOUX ALL CAN & USA **[36539]**

LEDREW ALL NFD, CAN **[35619]**

LEDSAM PRE 1820 DUBLIN, IRL **[34581]**

LEDSTER PRE 1860 SHOTTS & LANARK, LKS, SCT
[36191]

LEDUC JOSEPH 1840-1920 SOUTH PLANTAGENET,
ONT & QUE, CAN **[38779]**

LEDWARD 1600-1950 CHS, ENG **[36983]** : ALL
WORLDWIDE **[36983]**

LEE 1849+ GLEBE, NSW, AUS **[34695]** : PRE 1843
TAS, AUS **[34696]** : 1860+ VIC, AUS **[34703]** : 1880
GAWLER, SA, AUS **[34844]** : C1860 GORDON, VIC,
AUS **[34907]** : 1828+ HOBART, TAS, AUS **[35721]** :
1850+ PORT FAIRY, VIC, AUS **[35721]** : HENRY
1840-1860 SYDNEY, NSW, AUS **[35803]** : 1870+
BRUNSWICK & CARLTON, VIC, AUS **[37908]** :
MARY ANN 1900S GRAFTON, NSW, AUS **[37910]** :
1888+ SA, AUS **[37994]** : GEORGE PRE 1860
LINDSAY, ONT, CAN **[34068]** : 1800-1900+
FORTUNE BAY, NFD, CAN **[36684]** : 1780-1800+
HERMITAGE BAY, NFD, CAN **[36684]** : 1802
LONDON, ENG **[33783]** : 1860S CHESTERFIELD,
DBY, ENG **[33870]** : PRE 1830 WAVENDON, BKM,
ENG **[33876]** : SOPHIA BUDDIE 1812+
HAMBLEDON, SRY, ENG **[34011]** : 1865+
BRIDPORT, DOR, ENG **[34045]** : 1874
SMETHWICK, STS, ENG **[34224]** : C1870 SSX, ENG
[34808] : PRE 1870S ATHERTON, LAN, ENG **[34873]**
: C1840 ENG **[34907]** : PRE 1843 NTH PETHERTON,
SOM, ENG **[34909]** : PRE 1811 COGHILL'S HILL,
ESS, ENG **[34917]** : PRE 1823 MANSFIELD, NTT,
ENG **[35029]** : JAMES 1815 STOCKPORT, CHS,
ENG **[35041]** : ROSE C1887 ENG **[35346]** : C1879
BETHNAL GREEN, MDX, ENG **[35464]** : 1800-1880
PRESTON, LAN, ENG **[35473]** : PRE 1830
HOLBORN & LAMBETH, LND, ENG **[35517]** : PRE
1850 PENZANCE, CON, ENG **[35589]** : PRE 1820
SUTTON, NTT, ENG **[35745]** : 1800+ TROWELL,
NTT, ENG **[35847]** : 1780+ WOOTTON, OXF, ENG
[35974] : PRE 1880 MANCHESTER, LAN, ENG
[36019] : PRE 1900 LEEDS, WRY, ENG **[36034]** :
C1825-1860 RAMSGATE & MINSTER, KEN, ENG
[36051] : 1700-1800 KETTERING, NTH, ENG **[36057]**

: 1700+ CANTERBURY, KEN, ENG [36135] : ALL ADDINGHAM, WRY, ENG [36159] : 1859 ARDWICK, LAN, ENG [36253] : PRE 1844 MANCHESTER, LAN, ENG [36513] : 1700-1800 BRADFORD, WRY, ENG [36682] : C1780 WESTHOUGHTON, LAN, ENG [36742] : 1861 POPLAR, LND, ENG [36781] : 1840 SFK, ENG [36781] : 1800S DREWSTEIGNTON, DEV, ENG [36817] : RUTH PRE 1781 NORTHHOLME, LIN, ENG [36880] : ALL SRY & KEN, ENG [36978] : 1840 DUKINFIELD, LAN, ENG [37184] : ALL COLEBROOKE & CREDITON, DEV, ENG [37195] : PRE 1864 STEPNEY, MDX, ENG [37259] : PRE 1864 SHOREDITCH, MDX, ENG [37259] : 1700-1900 ALSTON, CUL, ENG [37290] : ALL RYE, SSX, ENG [37355] : 1850-1900 ASHTON UNDER LYNE, LAN, ENG [37373] : 1750+ PINXTON, DBY, ENG [37391] : PRE 1870 GRANTHAM, LIN, ENG [37392] : JOSEPH 1801-1851+ GORTON & DENTON, LAN, ENG [37546] : JAMES 1824-1871 GORTON & DENTON, LAN, ENG [37546] : 1850+ YKS, ENG [37620] : PRE 1820 BRILLEY, HEF, ENG [37671] : 1870+ ESS, ENG [37677] : PRE 1800 WROCKWARDINE, SAL, ENG [37693] : ALL IPSWICH, SFK, ENG [37700] : PRE 1780 NTH, ENG [37706] : PRE 1800 KEN, ENG [37715] : PRE 1850 LONDON, ENG [37743] : 1845+ LONDON, ENG [37908] : 1800S MELDRITH, CAM, ENG [37910] : AGNES P. C1898 PANCRAS, MDX, ENG [37992] : PRE 1850 YKS, ENG [38293] : C1871 BIRMINGHAM, ENG [38450] : 1500-1675 MOTTINGHAM, KEN, ENG [38523] : PRE 1800 CAV, IRL [33905] : 1750-1830 GOREY, WEX, IRL [34071] : 1750-1850 ATHLONE, ROS, IRL [35228] : PRE 1800 DUBLIN, IRL [35253] : PRE 1872 MOG, IRL [35932] : 1700+ MONASTEREVAN, KID, IRL [36087] : C1865 LISDOONVARNA, CLA, IRL [37994] : PRE 1850 DUBLIN, IRL [38457] : JOHN 1800-1900 TYR & MO, IRL & USA [38050] : 1940+ AUCKLAND, NZ [33811] : PRE 1751 RATHEN, ABD, SCT [36673] : 1800-1900 CUMNOCK, AYR, SCT [37338] : ALL HAYWOOD, UK [34961] : WILLIAM 1739-1795 STRATFORD, VA, USA [36684] : RICHARD 1732-1794 STRATFORD, VA, USA [36684] : PRE 1910 KNOXVILLE, TN & WA, USA [36899] : 1850-1900 ASPEN, CO, USA [36951] : MARY 1900S AMHERST, WI, USA [37024] : WILLIAM 1840 ALBANY & BROOKLYN, NY, USA [37501] : 1600-1825 VA, USA [38154] : 1850-1990 WARREN CO., IL, USA [38154] : 1790-1850 WASHINGTON CO., KY, USA [38154] : 1700-1825 CLAIBORNE CO., TN, USA [38154] : 1790-1850 FAYETTE CO., KY, USA [38154] : 1860-1990 SAN DIEGO, CA, USA [38154] : 1850-1990 MASON CO., IL, USA [38154] : 1700-1825 DAVIDSON CO., TN, USA [38154] : 1860-1990 LA CO., CA, USA [38154] : 1860-1990 SAN BERNARDINO, CA, USA [38154] : 1825-1880 CASS CO., IL, USA [38154] : 1700+ VA, USA [38195] : 1675-1800 HEMPSTEAD, NY, USA [38523] : ALL WHITFORD, FLN, WLS [37667]

LEECE 1801-1860 IOM &, ENG & USA [36910]

LEECH 1900+ MARYBOROUGH, VIC, AUS [34871] : 1850+ BENDIGO, VIC, AUS [35360] : 1800+ DAYLESFORD, VIC, AUS [35829] : PRE 1850 NANTWICH, CHS, ENG [33796] : PRE 1850 BLACKBURN & EGREMONT, LAN & CUL, ENG [33883] : 1808 KIMBLE, BKM, ENG [34120] : 1860-1900 LAN, ENG [34510] : 1800-1900 WOODBRIDGE, SFK & DEV, ENG [34632] : PRE 1850 WELLINGTON, HRT, ENG [35360] : C1800 MANCHESTER, LAN, ENG [35525] : 1790+ HOLT, NFK, ENG [35989] : 1750+ KEN, ENG [36093] : ALL

WOGGLESWORTH, WRY, ENG [36144] : 1700+ NEWENT, GLS, ENG [37328] : C1823 DUNDALK, LOU, IRL [37919] : C1800 RUPERT MANOR, LET, IRL & CAN [35078]

LEECH (SEE LEITCH) [36727]

LEEDER 1848+ ILLFORD, NFK, ENG [38212] : 1730-1759 BARKING AREA, SFK, ENG [38465]

LEEDHAM 1830+ LONDON, ENG [34338]

LEEDS GEORGINA 1800+ GREAT FINBOROUGH, SFK, ENG [34889] : EDWARD 1800+ GREAT FINBOROUGH, SFK, ENG [34889]

LEEGAARD ALL DEN [36856]

LEEGARRDT ALL DEN [36856]

LEEIJWENSTEIN 1792 UTR, NL [38716]

LEEK 1800+ TORONTO, ONT, CAN [34062] : 1800+ CODSALL, STS, ENG [36370]

LEEMING 1700+ MANCHESTER & SALFORD, LAN, ENG [35971] : PRE 1792 BILTON IN HINSTY, ERY, ENG [37852]

LEEN ALL TRALEE, KER, IRL [34643] : ALL NL [38303]

LEENACKER 1800-1908 KOEHLAR, SARATOV, USSR [38133]

LEENSTRA PRE 1850 OOSTHEM, FRI, NL [38646]

LEEPER 1800-1990 WV, USA [35313]

LEER 1880 NSW, AUS & NZ [34976] : PRE 1804 SRY & KEN, ENG [34976] : 1700+ NL [34180]

LEES PRE 1828 SYDNEY, NSW, AUS [34859] : 1850+ TUGGERAH, NSW, AUS [34859] : 1797+ CASTLEREAGH, NSW, AUS [35090] : MARY 1811+ SYDNEY, NSW, AUS [37951] : 1817-1900 FALLBROOKE, ONT, CAN [35638] : 1880-1900 ARGYLE, MAN, CAN [35638] : PRE 1800 CLARKSFIELD, LAN, ENG [34522] : PRE 1822 MANCHESTER, LAN, ENG [34859] : PRE 1801 BRIGGAT & LEEDS, ENG [35090] : 1850+ WEDNESBURY, STS, ENG [35121] : 1836+ TIPTON, STS, ENG [35597] : PRE 1750 BRIGGATE LEEDS, WRY, ENG [35825] : JOSE 1920+ OXFORD UNI., OXF, ENG [36471] : PRE 1580 BIDDULPH, STS, ENG [36701] : WILLIAM 1812-1842 NEWCASTLE, STS, ENG [36757] : 1843-1880 BREWOOD, STS, ENG [36757] : 1760+ ASHTON UNDER LYNE, LAN, ENG [37255] : PRE 1900 SHAW, LAN, ENG [37704] : 1880+ PONSONBY, AUCK, NZ [36757] : 1800 ROX, SCT [35638] : C1850 ABERLADY, ELN, SCT [36370] : PRE 1900 WORLDWIDE [34522]

LEESON 1886+ GOULBURN, NSW, AUS [35741] : PRE 1850 DOW, IRL [34001] : C1840+ RATHDRUM, WIC, IRL [35741] : CATH 1787+ LIM, IRL & AUS [35093]

LEET ALL WORLDWIDE [35391] : ALL WORLDWIDE [35577]

LEETCH 1770S TRINITY GASK, PER, SCT [35260]

LEETE ALL WORLDWIDE [35391] : ALL WORLDWIDE [35577]

LEEVES 1500+ DORKING, SRY, ENG [37206] : 1670+ TORTINGTON, SSX, ENG [37206] : 1500+ UCKFIELD, SSX, ENG [37206] : 1600+ HEATHFIELD, SSX, ENG [37206] : 1500+ WRINGTON, SOM, ENG [37206] : 1500+ STOKE ABBOT, DOR, ENG [37206] : 1500+ CRANBROOK, KEN, ENG [37206]

LE FEBRE PRE 1683 MER, FRA [36458]

LEFEBVRE PRE 1700 MARCHIENNE AUFONT, HNT, BEL [38167] : HENRI 1873-1948 ST CHARLES SUR RICHELIEU, QUE, CAN [35639] : PRE 1760 TROIS RIVIERES, QUE, CAN [37537] : 1800+ AIZIER & LA BOUILLE, HN & BN, FRA [37294] : ALL USA & CAN [37502]

LEFEE 1600-1800 LONDON, MDX, ENG [36233]

LEFEVERE 1500+ WORLDWIDE **[38161]**
LEFFLER PRE 1850 MEK, GER **[36726]**
LEFLEY ALL WORLDWIDE **[37656]**
LEFORT 1790S LONDON, ENG **[34296]**
LE FRANCOIS CHS C1575 DIEPPE, HN, FRA **[36681]**
LEGAARDT ALL DEN **[36856]**
LEGACY C1850 BRANTFORD, ONT, CAN **[36671]**
LEGARDEUR 1500S BN & HN, FRA **[35617]**
LEGARE NICOLAS 1670+ QUEBEC, QUE, CAN **[34168]** : NICOLAS 1650-1690 PARIS, FRA **[34168]** : GILLES 1650-1690 PARIS, FRA **[34168]** : ALL WORLDWIDE **[34168]**
LEGARTH ALL WORLDWIDE **[36856]**
LEGATE ALL WORLDWIDE **[36063]**
LEGEAR PRE 1709 RPF, BRD **[33862]** : 1709+ LIM, IRL **[33862]**
LE GENDRE 1600 ROUEN, HN, FRA **[37703]**
LEGER DIT LAROSETTE JACQUES 1660+ FRA **[37429]**
LE GEYT C1800 KEN, ENG **[36993]**
LEGG PRE 1880 BRISTOL, GLS, ENG **[35215]** : 1800S ISLINGTON, MDX, ENG **[35987]** : PRE 1900 WOOLWICH, LND, ENG **[36067]** : PRE 1860 SOUTH SHIELDS, DUR, ENG **[37442]** : JOHN 1804 MACDUFF, BAN, SCT **[34499]**
LEGGAT 1800+ WISHAW, LKS, SCT & ENG **[34934]**
LEGGATT 1845+ ADELAIDE, SA, AUS **[35218]** : 1850+ VIC, AUS **[35218]** : C1740 FARLINGTON, HAM, ENG **[37321]** : 1770-1800S BRIGHTON, SSX, ENG **[37445]** : 1850 WOKINGHAM, BRK, ENG **[37690]** : C1815 WEM, IRL **[34041]** : 1828 DUBLIN, IRL **[35218]** : C1770 WEXFORD, WEX & WIC, IRL **[38391]** : PRE 1750 SKYE, SCT **[38391]** : ALL WORLDWIDE **[36063]**
LEGGE C1850 FULHAM, LND, ENG **[34277]** : PRE 1870 BRK, ENG **[35949]** : PRE 1830 HEF, ENG **[37671]**
LEGGETT 1880+ SALE, VIC, AUS **[34421]** : 1590-1880 SFK, ENG **[35916]** : C1790-1930 SRY, ENG **[38242]** : C1815 WEM, IRL **[34041]** : 1830 TANDERAGEE, ARM, IRL **[35809]** : PRE 1837 LARGS, RFW, SCT **[35407]** : ALL WORLDWIDE **[36063]**
LEGGO 1500-1990 MADRON, ST JUST & SITHNEY, CON, ENG **[37680]**
LEGGOTT 1940S BC, CAN **[38422]** : 1790S OWSTON, LIN, ENG **[38422]** : 1800S CAMBLESFORTH, YKS, ENG **[38422]** : ALL WORLDWIDE **[36063]**
LE GRANDE 1815-1875 WARREN CO., KY, USA **[36553]**
LE GROS 1840S JSY, CHI **[36848]** : 1860+ FULHAM, MDX, ENG **[34650]** : C1600 SUR LE MEIN, FRANCFORT, FRA **[34568]** : ALL WORLDWIDE **[36890]**
LEGROVE C1750-1850 BASING, HAM, ENG **[37770]**
LEGROW PRE 1880 NEW LISKEARD, ONT, CAN **[38445]** : 1881+ PETERBOROUGH, ONT, CAN **[38445]** : PRE 1850 QUE, CAN **[38445]**
LEHANY PRE 1860 SLI, IRL **[38365]**
LE HARTEL 1873 FALDOUET, JSY, CHI **[35761]**
LE HERON PRE 1820 GSY **[35111]**
LEHMAN 1868+ STOCKTON, NSW, AUS **[38568]** : 1800-1850 CH **[38238]** : PRE 1840 AMSTERDAM, NL **[38568]**
LEHMANN 1800S BRUTZEN, GER **[34172]** : 1775-1820 RAHMEL, GER **[35315]** : PRE 1850 KROSSEN, PRE, GER **[35379]** : PRE 1834+ FRANKFORT ON ODER, PRE, GER **[36307]** : 1850-1900 LEIPZIG & PEGAU, SAX, GER **[36953]** : PRE 1850 POS, GER **[38490]** : PRE 1843 HERMSDORF, PSA, GER **[38618]** : 1900 CULM, WPR, POL **[35315]** : REV. JAN 1920+ CULM, POL **[35315]**
LEHMITZ PRE 1858 PAMPRIN, MSW, GER **[35820]**

LEHOAR PRE 1850 DALSERT, LKS, SCT **[34245]**
LEHRER 1700+ DIERSBURG, BAD, GER **[38529]**
LEHRLE C1790 MINSTER, KEN, ENG **[35411]** : 1825+ STEPNEY, LND, ENG **[35411]** : 1860+ BARROW IN FURNESS, LAN, ENG **[35411]**
LE HUQUET 1790S JSY, CHI **[38396]**
LEICHT 1830-1860 HAN, GER **[37996]**
LEID PRE 1852 ABERDOUR, ABD, SCT **[37982]**
LEIDENHAM C1800S MONQUHITTER, ABD, SCT **[37977]**
LEIGH 1740 BROMPTON RALPH, SOM, ENG **[34204]** : 1780+ LEIGH, LAN, ENG **[34290]** : PRE 1800 MAIDEN BRADLEY, WIL, ENG **[34304]** : 1800+ ROCHDALE, LAN, ENG **[34363]** : C1815 BRISTOL, GLS, ENG **[34661]** : 1600-1800S CON, ENG **[35424]** : PRE 1800 COMBWICH, SOM, ENG **[35779]** : PRE 1682 ENG **[36972]** : 1840+ SNEYD, STS, ENG **[36997]** : PRE 1750 DAVENHAM, CHS, ENG **[37103]** : ALL PENZANCE, CON, ENG **[37160]** : 1400-1675 STONELEIGH, WAR, ENG **[38216]** : 1810-1910 LIVERPOOL, LAN, ENG & AUS **[34769]** : ALL WHITFORD, FLN, WLS **[37667]** : 1600-1820 CARMARTHEN, CMN, WLS **[38216]**
LEIGHTON PRE 1850 GILBERDYKE, YKS, ENG **[38091]** : PRE 1900 BIRMINGHAM, WAR, ENG & USA **[37096]** : PRE 1860 SLIGO, SLI, IRL **[35001]** : PRE 1866 WIC, IRL **[35001]** : PRE 1860 LOG, IRL **[35001]** : 1800+ DUBLIN, IRL **[38423]** : 1780-1830 ABERDEEN, ABD, SCT **[34400]** : 1800+ DUMFRIES, DFS, SCT **[34650]** : ALL TARBOLTON, AYR, SCT **[37176]**
LEIJS 1700S OUDELANDE, ZEL, NL **[38350]**
LEIJTEN PRE 1780 BAARLE NASSAU, NBT, NL **[35008]**
LEIMBACH PRE 1850 ILVESHEIM, BRD **[34544]**
LEINACKER 1900-1930 IL, USA **[38133]**
LEINGANG 1700+ RPR, GER **[38765]**
LEININGER 1830+ ALBANY, NY, USA **[38530]**
LEINSEIDER PRE 1873 GALACIA, OES **[37574]**
LEIPER 1884+ SYDNEY, NSW, AUS **[36647]** : PRE 1840 AVONDALE, LKS, SCT **[34187]** : 1750-1930 RHYNIE, ABD, SCT **[34615]** : 1825+ GLASGOW, SCT **[36647]**
LEIPOLDT ALL GER **[35753]** : C1780 STEINAU, HEN, GER **[35753]** : ALL NL **[35753]** : ALL RSA **[35753]**
LEIPPI ALL WORLDWIDE **[33903]**
LEIR PRE 1840 BRUTON, SOM & DOR, ENG **[37410]**
LEISHMAN 1800-1840S LARBERT & AIRTH, STI, SCT **[34359]** : 1740+ DFS, SCT **[38385]**
LEISS PRE 1850 NECKARSULM, BAW, GER **[33874]**
LEITCH 1900S AUS **[33843]** : 1900S LONDON, ENG **[33843]** : 1800S GLASGOW, LKS, SCT **[34598]** : PRE 1742 MUIRMOUTH, PER, SCT **[35260]** : 1700-1850 DUNFERMLINE, FIF, SCT **[36727]** : 1800+ ROX, SCT **[37170]** : 1800-1860 EDINBURGH, MLN, SCT **[37437]** : 1800S GLASGOW, SCT **[38281]**
LEITH PRE 1850 ABBOTSHALL, FIF, SCT **[35125]** : ALL GLAMIS & KIRRIEMUIR, ANS, SCT **[37727]**
LEITHMAN 1750-1850 SACON, OPR, GER **[37599]** : 1860-1920 MONTGOMERY CO., KS, USA **[37599]** : 1840-1900 ORLEANS & JEFFERSON PAR., LA, USA **[37599]**
LEITHWOOD ALL WORLDWIDE **[34401]**
LEIVERS PRE 1850 GREASLEY & SELSTON, NTT, ENG **[36516]**
LEJEUNE ALL BEAULIEU & BOLDRE, HAM, ENG **[36211]**
LELAND PRE 1900 HOWTH, DUB, IRL **[38305]** : PRE 1900 USA &, WORLDWIDE **[38305]**
LE'LARCH 1800+ SHOREDITCH & POPLAR, LND, ENG **[37660]**

LE LEIVRE 1700+ JSY, CHI **[35499]**

LE LORRAIN PRE 1900 TILDONCK, BEL **[36474]**

LEMAIRE 1690+ LACHINE & DE DU CALUMET, QUE, CAN & IRL **[38727]** : 1500-1620 ROMORANTIN, CEN, FRA **[34514]**

LE MAIRE (SEE MAIRE) **[35967]**

LE MAISTRE 1800-1890 ST HELIER, JSY, CHI **[35048]**

LEMAN 1860+ WATERLOO, NSW, AUS **[35360]** : PRE 1850 BEL **[35360]** : 1750+ BRIDGEWATER, SOM, ENG **[34100]** : PRE 1850 FRA **[35360]**

LEMAR ELIZABETH 1800 BULLS CREEK, SA, AUS **[35361]**

LE MARCHANT 1850+ ST PETER PORT, GSY, CHI **[35847]**

LE MASSON NICOLAS C1600 FRA **[37429]**

LE MASURIER 1720-1774 TRINITY, JSY, CHI **[38396]** : 1841-1851 ST HELIER, JSY, CHI **[38396]** : 1774-1841 ST BRELADE, JSY, CHI **[38396]** : 1851-1901 CLAPHAM, SRY, ENG **[38396]**

LEMBERG 1800+ WODKE, POM, GER **[37949]**

LEMEN 1860-1920 PETERHEAD, MOR, SCT **[37290]**

LEMERES C1750 SPITALFIELDS, MDX, ENG **[38516]**

LE MESSURIER C1840 GLENELG, SA, AUS **[34425]** : 1840+ ADOLPHUS, SA, AUS **[34425]** : 1880+ OSWALD, QLD, AUS **[34425]**

LEMIERE PRE 1873 PORT LOUIS, MAURITIUS **[33762]**

LEMIEUX 1630-1990 CAN & USA **[34124]**

LEMKE 1830+ SCHNITTRIGE, POM, DDR **[38530]**

LEMLEY ALL WORLDWIDE **[37036]**

LEMMENES C1827 NL **[38052]**

LEMMER 1834 CASTROP, WEF, GER **[38749]** : 1899 KOELN, RPR, GER **[38749]**

LEMMERS 1700+ BOSTON, MA, USA **[35857]**

LEMMON 1850+ LAUDERDALE, SC, USA **[35135]** : ALL WORLDWIDE **[37347]**

LEMON 1870+ COONABARABRAN, NSW, AUS **[34788]** : PRE 1820 GLENORCHY, TAS, AUS **[35217]** : 1860+ WATERLOO, NSW, AUS **[35360]** : 1800+ LONDON, ENG **[34341]** : 1820 HONINGHAM, NFK, ENG **[34788]** : 1840+ TILNEY ST LAWRENCE, NFK, ENG **[34788]** : 1800+ DEV, ENG **[34818]** : ALL NFK, ENG **[36234]** : 1750-1825 KENTISBEARE, DEV, ENG **[37222]** : PRE 1800 LND, ENG **[37420]** : PRE 1837 DOR & SOM, ENG **[37771]** : PRE 1780 DEV, ENG **[37807]** : ALL EPSOM & HORTON, SRY, ENG **[38332]** : 1883+ BELFAST, IRL **[34528]** : PRE 1926 BALLYWALTER, DOW, IRL **[35047]**

LE MONTAIS ALL JSY, CHI **[35222]**

LE MOTTEE 1878+ AUS **[38286]** : PRE 1879 CHI **[38286]**

LEMPP PRE 1650 PLEDELSHEIM, BAW, BRD **[38509]**

LEMUNYAN ALL WORLDWIDE **[37764]**

LENANDER 1850+ NE, USA **[36919]**

LENANE 1800-1900 WAT, IRL **[37661]**

LENAU 1850-1865 CUYAHOGA CO., OH, USA **[38144]**

LENAW 1850-1865 CUHAHOGA CO., OH, USA **[38144]**

LENCHFORD PRE 1900 ENG **[37595]**

LENDRUM PRE 1850 FIVE MILE TOWN, FER, IRL **[37927]**

LENEHAN C1850S SYDNEY, NSW, AUS **[33794]** : PRE 1850 CORK, IRL **[33794]** : 1800+ BALLYLANDERS, LIM, IRL **[34453]** : 1819 ROS, IRL **[37911]**

LENEY 1865+ ALLORA, QLD, AUS **[34812]** : PRE 1865 ENG **[34812]**

LENFESTY ALL NIPPISSING, ONT, CAN **[36679]** : 1920 ROCKWOOD & WEDDIFIELD, ONT, CAN **[36679]** : 1920 NIPPISSING, ONT, CAN **[36679]** : ALL ROCKWOOD & WEDDIFIELD, ONT, CAN **[36679]**

LENG 1884-1894 MELBOURNE, VIC, AUS **[36757]** : 1770+ SCALBY, NRY, ENG **[36757]** : ALL YKS, ENG **[37407]** : 1894+ NORTH IS, NZ **[36757]**

LENIHAN 1860+ QLD, AUS **[34588]** : PRE 1860 FULLALACE, LIM, IRL **[34588]** : PRE 1864 TULLYLEASE, LIM, IRL **[35197]**

LENNAN 1720+ CORK, COR, IRL **[35749]**

LENNARD PRE 1800 DITTISHAM, DEV, ENG **[33998]** : PRE 1840 IRL **[37428]**

LENNIE ALL CAN **[36672]**

LENNON PRE 1905 ARMIDALE, NSW, AUS **[33832]** : PRE 1950 MID NORTH, SA, AUS **[35352]** : C1872 ENG & AUS **[35417]** : C1800 BELFAST, ANT, IRL **[34788]** : PRE 1850 IRL **[38075]**

LENNOX ALL NSW, AUS **[38730]** : 1850S BERMUDA **[38226]** : 1890S DEVONPORT, DEV, ENG **[38226]** : 1880S KILWARLIN, DRY, IRL **[38226]** : 1810S IRL **[38226]** : 1890S NICARAGUA **[38226]** : 1860-1890 RSA **[36392]** : 1770-1810 MAUCHLINE, AYR, SCT **[36392]** : 1780-1810 QUEENSFERRY S., WLN, SCT **[36392]** : 1750-1840 AUCHINLECK, AYR, SCT **[37338]** : 1829 CAMBUSLANG, LKS, SCT **[37575]** : 1800+ DEANSTON, PER, SCT **[38726]** : 1890S TRINIDAD **[38226]** : 1900+ USA **[38226]** : 1890S ST CROIX, VIRGIN IS. **[38226]**

LENOT C1818 FRA **[35414]**

LENOURY 1800-1950 ST PETER PORT, GSY, CHI **[37435]**

LENS PRE 1700 ANTWERPEN, OVL, BEL **[38697]** : 1850S AMSTERDAM, NL **[33802]**

LENT 1750+ WESTCHESTER CO., NY, USA & CAN **[35611]**

LENTAL PRE 1800 DBY & WRY, ENG **[37589]**

LENTHALL 1750-1800 DBY & WRY, ENG **[37589]**

LENTON JOSEPH 1828+ CAMPBELLTOWN, NSW, AUS **[35703]** : ALL DEV, ENG **[34838]** : CHARLES C1770 CHILVERS COTON, WAR, ENG **[35252]** : PRE 1778 GRETTON, NTH, ENG **[35597]** : JOSEPH 1800+ COVENTRY, WAR, ENG **[35703]** : C1760 GIRTON, CAM, ENG **[37420]** : 1790-1850 SOUTHWARK & ST PANCRAS, LND, ENG **[37420]**

LENTS 1780 NELSON CO., KY, USA **[38143]**

LENTY JOHN C1810 YKS, ENG **[34447]**

LENTZ 1815+ NSW, AUS **[38485]** : ALL ENG **[37561]** : PRE 1815 LONDON, ENG **[38485]** : 1750+ PHILADELPHIA, PA, USA **[36347]**

LENTZ (SEE LENZ) **[33901]**

LENZ 1600S OEHRINGEN, WUE, GER **[33901]** : 1744-1890 SCHLEUSINGEN, THURINGIA, GER **[38148]** : 1798-1890 SCHLEUSINGEN, THURINGIA, GER **[38148]**

LENZEN 1880+ ST LOUIS & JEFFERSON CO., MO & IL, USA **[37796]**

LEO ALL BUFFALO, NY, USA **[37438]**

LEONARD ALL KENTON NORTH, NBL, ENG **[34074]** : 1700-1800 GAZELEY, SFK, ENG **[35094]** : PRE 1774 SOHAM, CAM, ENG **[37144]** : 1550-1600 BILSTON, STS, ENG **[37783]** : PRE 1800 LIMEHOUSE & CHELSEA, MDX, ENG **[37833]** : PRE 1860 HURST, CHS, ENG **[37939]** : C1750-1850 OXF, ENG **[38242]** : 1827+ LONDON, ENG & AUS **[34773]** : PRE 1820 DUBLIN, IRL **[37133]** : 1800S LOU & MEA, IRL **[37969]** : PRE 1838 MEA, IRL **[38075]** : 1700+ NFD, CAN &, UK & IRL **[38774]** : 1760 WESTFIELD, MA, USA **[37006]** : RITCHIE PRE 1839 WASHINGTON CO., OH, USA **[37580]** : RITCHIE PRE 1810 ALEXANDRIA, DC, USA **[37580]** : RITCHIE PRE 1790 NJ, USA **[37580]** : 1630-1750 SPRINGFIELD, MA, USA **[37783]** : 1651-1700 REHOBOTH, MA, USA **[38151]**

LEONARDS C1792 ENG **[36594]**

LEONHARDT FREDERICK 1830-1850 PRE, GER [38150] : 1900S KY, USA [35313] : 1850-1890 FLORIDA, OH, USA [38150]

LEONHART 1841+ BAD, GER [38572]

LEOPARD 1900-1990 WATERLOO, IA, USA [38154] : 1850-1950 ST CLOUD, MN, USA [38154] : 1900-1940 MINNEAPOLIS, MN, USA [38154]

LEOPOLD 1850-1860 KEWEENAW CO., MI, USA [38009] : ALL WORLDWIDE [37453]

LE PAGE ALL ATW, BEL [38169] : 1800S GSY, CHI & ENG [35137]

L'EPEE ALL NEU, CH [36405]

LEPELTACK ALL STAVENISSE, ZEL, NL [38694]

LEPERE C1830 DUNFERMLINE, FIF, SCT [35078]

LEPOIDEVIN 1850-1975 ST PETER PORT, GSY, CHI [37435]

LE POTIER 1580-1640 LA FLECHE, FRA [34514]

LEPPARD LENARD 1870+ HOLLAND LANDING, ONT, CAN [35648]

LEPPER ALL STAPLEHURST, KEN, ENG [34284] : ALL MAIDSTONE, KEN, ENG [36774]

LEPPINGTON 1856+ MINTO & ALBION, ONT, CAN [36716] : 1876+ STOCKTON & SALTCOATS, SAS, CAN [36716]

LEPPLA 1750-1800 ROTH & ODENBACH, RPF, BRD [35311]

LEPSCHELY C1725 GENEVA, GE & VD, CH [38348]

LE QUESNE PRE 1880 WHOLE ISLAND, JSY, CHI, UK [36200]

LERICK 1700S SURAT, INDIA [36786]

LERIGER-LAPLANTE LOUIS 1840+ ST EDOUARD, QUE, CAN [36678]

LERMAN 1800S ENG [38369]

LE ROI PRE 1933 NORBURY, LND, ENG [36313]

LEROI 1827 YEBLERON, HN, FRA [38163]

LEROUX ALL ONT & QUE, CAN [36539] : 1600-1680 VITRY LE FRANCOIS, CHA, FRA [34514] : 1600-1700 ROUEN, HN, FRA [34514]

LE ROUX PRE 1688 BLOIS, FRA [36458]

LE ROY 1800+ HAWKESBURY, ONT, CAN [36686] : DAVID H. PRE 1767 CH [37321] : PRE 1880 ST SAMPSONS, GSY, CHI [35575] : ALL GSY, CHI [36839] : 1849+ GREAT BARRIER IS, AKL, NZ [36839]

LE RUEZ C1869 ST CLEMENT, JSY, CHI [33893]

LESAGE PRE 1800 HAMBURG, GER [37873]

LESAN C1775-1900S SEBEC, BOOTHBAY, ME, USA [38308]

LESAR 1700-1850 LONDON, MDX, ENG [36233]

LE SAUVAGE ALL JSY & GSY, CHI [36696] : C1820 GSY, CHI [37112]

LESCHKE 1800+ GROSSDORF, POS, GER [37170]

LESCHMANN 1750-1850 BANAT, YU [37539]

LESCURE PRE 1800 GERS, FRA [35620]

LE SEELLEUR 1600+ JSY, CHI [34152]

LESHEIR 1725-1850 BERKS CO., PA, USA [35318]

LESHINSKY PRE 1900 SKULSK, BYDGOSZCZ, POL [36455]

LESIEUR JULIEN PRE 1660 DEAUVILLE, BN, FRA [38408]

LESINSKE PRE 1938 SKULSK, BYDGOSZCZ, POL [36455]

LESLEY 1775+ SFK, ENG [34416] : PRE 1848 MDX, ENG [38437] : 1700+ COLDSTREAM, ROX, SCT [34163] : PRE 1780 DORNOCH, SUT, SCT [37913]

LESLEY (SEE LESLIE) [37577]

LESLIE 1890S FREMANTLE, WA, AUS [34006] : 1900-1925 BAYSWATER, WA, AUS [34006] : 1880S-1910 SYDNEY, NSW, AUS [34693] : 1850-1887 DUNGIVEN, LDY, IRL [34693] : 1800S-1900S KER, IRL [36856] : C1800 IRL [37180] : 1820-1830 DUBLIN, IRL [38475] : PRE 1770 ABD, SCT [33914] : 1800-1860

KIRKINTILLOCH, DNB, SCT [34359] : 1050+ SCT [34513] : 1800 CERES, FIF, SCT [34637] : ALL ABERDEEN, ABD, SCT [34674] : 1600-1800 ABERDEEN, ABD, SCT [34695] : THEODORE 1851 BUCKSBURN, ABD, SCT [35369] : 1760+ ARDCLACH, NAI, SCT [35905] : 1700-1800 LEDUCKIE, PER, SCT [36246] : ALL ROTHES, MOR, SCT [37767] : 1800+ BANCHORY, ABD, SCT [38425] : 1750-1853 NC & OH, USA [37577] : 1750-1830 PA, USA [38344]

LESPERANCE 1800+ TICONDEROGA, NY, USA [34408]

LESSELS PRE 1800 FIF, SCT [35745]

LESSEPS 1800-1950 PLAQUENINES PAR. NEW ORLEANS, LA, USA [37583]

LESSER ALL SHO, BRD [38620] : ALL HBG, BRD [38620] : ALL DDR [38620]

LESSLIE 1767-1836 ABERDEEN, ABD, SCT [33811] : 1700-1900 CAMERON, FIF, SCT [34004]

LESSLIE (SEE LESLIE) [36246]

LESTER C1780 HAM, ENG [33772] : PRE 1800 WELLINGTON, SAL, ENG [34711] : 1848 SSX, ENG [34808] : 1872 SOUTHAMPTON, HAM, ENG [34808] : PRE 1880 SUDBURY, SFK & ESS, ENG [36050] : PRE 1900 NEWINGTON, LND, ENG [36361] : PRE 1800 SAL, ENG [37389] : 1800+ POPLAR, MDX, ENG [37729] : PRE 1842 COR, IRL [36338] : 1800-1900 JONES CO., GA, USA [34004] : BRYANT PRE 1800 VA & NC, USA [38536]

L'ESTRANGE 1850-1880 SYDNEY, NSW, AUS [33838]

L'ESTREIGN 1600-1700 GIEN, PL, FRA [34123]

LE SUEUR PRE 1800 TRINITY, ST JOHN, JSY, CHI [36696]

LETCHER PRE 1866 CON, ENG [34711] : 1800S LADOCK & ILLOGAN, CON, ENG [38745]

LETCHFORD C1850 BALLARAT, VIC, AUS [36362]

LETENDRE DIT BATOCHE C1800 SAS, CAN [36678]

LE TERRIEN 1400-1980 PL, FRA [38493]

LETHAM PRE 1890 BARONY, LKS, SCT [34632]

LETHERIDGE PRE 1837 PORT ISAAC, CON, ENG [36856]

LE TISSIER ALL GSY, CHI [37229] : ALL WORLDWIDE [37229]

LETT 1805+ SOUTH COAST, NSW, AUS [36638] : STAFFORD PRE 1780 LONDON, ENG [34461] : 1847+ MISSISSIPPI CO., MO, USA [38187]

LETTANIE ALL MECHELEN, ATW, BEL [36230]

LETTAU ALL ENG [34406] : PRE 1900 GER [34406] : ALL WORLDWIDE [34406]

LETTS PRE 1870 SRY, ENG [37034]

LEUCHARS PRE 1800 STRATHMIGLO, FIF, SCT [35496]

LEUCHS 1828 NUREMBERG, GER [34793]

LEUTHOLD 1780-1850 POLENZ, KSA, GER [38628]

LEUTKIRCHNER C1600 NUERNBERG, BAY, FRG [38660]

LEUVEN VAN PRE 1725 S'GRAVENLAND, NOH, NL [38706]

LEVACH 1823+ HOBART, TAS, AUS [37954] : PRE 1823 WICK, CAI, SCT [37954] : PRE 1823 LYTH, CAI, SCT [37954]

LE VALLEE PRE 1800 ALD, CHI [34984]

LEVENTHALL 1800+ HAMBURG, HBG, BRD [36961]

LEVEQUE 1800+ ABBEVILLE & AMIENS, NOR, FRA [37294]

LEVER C1875 WALLSEND & NEWCASTLE, NSW, AUS [37992] : PRE 1841 STANDISH CHORLEY, LAN, ENG [34667] : 1800 RICHMOND, SRY, ENG [34890] : 1700+ SFK, ENG [34943] : C1800-1825 ASHTON UNDER LYNE, LAN, ENG [36037] : 1800+ CROPREDY, OXF, ENG [37375] : WILLIAM C1840 CROPREDY, OXF, ENG [37375] : 1800+

HARBURY, WAR, ENG **[37375]** : 1800+
CHESTERTON, OXF, ENG **[37375]** : 1880S SCT &
ENG **[36659]** : ALL THAILAND **[36659]**
LEVERINGTON C1762 ATTLEBOROUGH, NFK,
ENG **[35714]**
LEVERSAGE 1855+ PERTH CO., ONT, CAN **[34066]** :
1800+ MACCLESFIELD, CHS, ENG **[34066]**
LEVERSIDGE 1800+ HARWORTH, CAM, ENG
[36772]
LEVERTON 1730+ GOSBERTON & SURFLEET,
LIN, ENG **[38443]**
LEVESON 1815+ NEUTEICH, EL, POL & ENG
[36254]
LE VESQUE C1770-1884 HOLBORN, LND & CHI,
ENG **[36874]**
LEVET 1800+ SOHAM, CAM, ENG & NZ **[36257]**
LEVETT 1850+ GRENFELL, NSW, AUS **[36269]** :
1840+ MERTON, NSW, AUS **[36269]** : 1800+
TENTERDEN, KEN, ENG **[36269]** : PRE 1800
CHICHESTER, SSX, ENG **[36588]** : PRE 1800
TARING NEVILLE, SSX, ENG **[37321]**
LEVI C1850 ST AUSTELL, CON, ENG **[35722]** :
ISRAEL 1868-1870 PHILADELPHIA, PA, USA
[38134] : ALL WORLDWIDE **[34318]**
LEVICK 1820-1900 YORK TWP., ONT, CAN **[34346]** :
1830+ STAPLETON, YKS, ENG **[35491]** : PRE 1850
DRUNFIELD, DBY, ENG **[35491]** : ALL
SHEFFIELD, YKS & MDX, ENG & AUS **[35723]**
LEVIDO 1850-1900 WALLAROO, SA, AUS **[35861]** :
1820-1850 COLOGNE, RPR, GER **[35861]** : PRE 1820
WORLDWIDE **[35861]**
LEVINE 1880-1940 LONDON, ENG **[38380]** : 1800-1880
UKRAINE, SU **[38380]** : 1850+ CHICAGO, IL, USA
[36962]
LEVINGSTONE 1800+ MEETING OF THE
WATERS, AVOCA, WIC, IRL **[36642]**
LEVISCHANE PRE 1900 GER **[35533]**
LEVISON ALL AUS **[34685]** : PRE 1850
WHITEHAVEN, CUL, ENG **[34685]**
LEVISTON PRE 1800 ST JOHNS, DUB, IRL **[35217]**
LEVITT 1820 ESSEX, ONT, CAN **[35809]** : 1800S
MELBOURN, CAM, ENG **[33898]** : 1820S GREAT
BARDFIELD, ESS, ENG **[35026]** : PRE 1854
CASTLEBLAYNEY, MOG, IRL **[38289]**
LEVY C1819 SYDNEY, NSW, AUS **[35335]** : 1850+
AUS **[35356]** : 1830+ SYDNEY, NSW, AUS **[35509]** :
C1850 ST AUSTELL, CON, ENG **[35722]** : 1812
LONDON, ENG **[36618]** : PRE 1847
GAINSBOROUGH, LIN, ENG **[37908]** : C1800-1900
HAMBURG, GER **[35591]** : 1850-1875 SU **[38236]** :
ABRAHAM 1804 FREDERICK, MD, USA **[38348]** :
ALL WORLDWIDE **[34318]**
LEWANDOWSKA FRANCISZKA 1857-1900 POL
[38090]
LEWARNE 1700+ ST COLUMB MINOR & ST
MAWGAN, CON, ENG **[36961]**
LE WARNE 1805+ MAKER, CON, ENG **[37921]**
LEWCUN ALL WORLDWIDE **[37233]**
LEWELLIN 1951 CHELMSFORD, ESS, ENG **[34577]**
LEWES 1700+ RYE, SSX, ENG **[35943]** : PRE 1840
ROLVENDEN, KEN, ENG **[38730]**
LEWIS RICE 1870-1917 PETERSHAM, NSW, AUS
[33933] : 1824+ HAWKESBURY RIVER, NSW, AUS
[34273] : MARY ANNE 1834-1862 PARRAMATTA &
PENRITH, NSW, AUS **[34662]** : 1860S FORBES,
NSW, AUS **[34937]** : 1865+ TARNAGULLA, VIC,
AUS **[35039]** : PRE 1900 VIC, AUS **[35055]** : 1852+
ORANGE & BATHURST, NSW, AUS **[35075]** : 1850-
1896 TOMAGO, NSW, AUS **[35094]** : PRE 1875
COORANBONG, NSW, AUS **[35097]** : PRE 1848+
HOBART, TAS, AUS **[35109]** : 1833+ BATHURST,
NSW, AUS **[35132]** : 1820-1850 HOBART, TAS, AUS

[35151] : MARY PRE 1850 ROCKHAMPTON, QLD,
AUS **[35232]** : C1880 SYDNEY, NSW, AUS **[35859]** :
PRE 1880 MELBOURNE, VIC, AUS **[36305]** :
WILLIAM 1820 PITT TOWN, NSW, AUS **[36596]** :
1880+ CLUNES, VIC, AUS **[36622]** : 1807+
ARMIDALE, NSW, AUS **[37316]** : 1800+ LOCHEIL,
NSW, AUS **[38491]** : 1880-1920 SAS, CAN **[34141]** :
1850-1890 ONT, CAN **[34141]** : 1800S DUNDAS CO.,
ONT, CAN **[34150]** : LOUISA 1912-1917 LEVIS,
QUE, CAN **[34200]** : 1778+ KEN, ENG **[33867]** :
C1780-1870 PIPE ASTON, HEF & NBL, ENG **[34040]**
: WILLIAM 1800 BETHNAL GREEN, MDX, ENG
[34204] : WILLIAM 1820+ KEN, ENG **[34289]** :
COCKY 1800+ LONDON, ENG **[34455]** : ALL ESS,
ENG **[34493]** : C1800 ENG **[34654]** : C1847 LONDON,
ENG **[34752]** : 1800S LONDON, ENG **[34800]** : PRE
1868 BROMLEY, KEN, ENG **[34816]** : CHARLES
HENRY 1844+ LONDON, ENG **[35039]** : PRE 1840
BREMHILL, WIL, ENG **[35045]** : C1812 HENLEY
IN ARDEN, WAR, ENG **[35046]** : PRE 1852 LOPEN,
SOM, ENG **[35075]** : 1800+ BRK, ENG **[35115]** : PRE
1841 LOSTWITHIEL, CON, ENG **[35335]** : 1800+
BADMINTON, GLS, ENG **[35448]** : C1830
BETHNAL GREEN, MDX, ENG **[35502]** : 1820
BROBURY, HEF, ENG **[35912]** : ALL WAR, ENG
[35924] : 1800S ARDLEIGH, ESS, ENG **[35987]** : PRE
1810 ESS, ENG **[36124]** : ALL ECKINGTON, WOR,
ENG **[36171]** : SARAH 1830+ SHOREDITCH, LND,
ENG **[36378]** : 1730-1820 TUNBRIDGE WELLS,
KEN, ENG **[36595]** : C1800 COVENTRY, WAR,
ENG **[36649]** : PRE 1840 EALING, MDX & GLS,
ENG **[36967]** : PRE 1870 TOXTETH, LIVERPOOL,
LAN, ENG **[36986]** : PRE 1850 LND, ENG **[37057]** :
PRE 1700 HAWKINGE, KEN, ENG **[37069]** : PRE
1800 TIDENHAM, GLS, ENG **[37085]** : 1800+
STILTON, CAM, ENG **[37181]** : 1800+ EAST
LONDON, ENG **[37416]** : PRE 1842 TAVISTOCK,
DEV, ENG **[37575]** : PRE 1891 ESS, ENG **[37656]** :
1780-1840 MARYLEBONE, MDX, ENG **[37696]** :
PRE 1870 WORTHEN, SAL, ENG **[37722]** : 1800-1830
ISLINGTON, MDX, ENG **[37845]** : 1700-1800
BIRMINGHAM, WAR, ENG **[37924]** : 1810
BERKELEY, GLS, ENG **[38209]** : PRE 1870
PIMLICO, LND, ENG & AUS **[34454]** : WILLIAM
1780+ LONDON, ENG & WLS **[34662]** : MARY
ANNE 1814-1834 LONDON, ENG & WLS **[34662]** :
1830-1850 IRL **[34141]** : PRE 1884 KILLALA, MAY,
IRL **[34720]** : MARGARET PRE 1856 PETERS
WELL, GAL, IRL **[35564]** : 1800S DUBLIN, IRL
[35738] : PRE 1860 WAIROA, NZ **[33944]** : 1740-
1850S, ST SYLVESTER, QUE & VT **[34200]** : 1850-
1870 LORRAIN CO., OH, USA **[34141]** : 1850-1870
DETROIT AREA, MI, USA **[34141]** : 1772+ NC,
USA **[34507]** : 1750-1820 SPARTENBURG, SC, USA
[36737] : PRE 1799 CARTER CO., TN, USA **[36929]** :
1935+ FARGO, ND, USA **[37171]** : 1800-1900 NY &
MI, USA **[37577]** : 1840-1930 MINERSVILLE, PA,
USA **[37722]** : 1625-1700 FARMINGTON, CT, USA
[37783] : LUCY 1890+ PEEKSKILL, NY, USA
[37796] : OLIVER 1760 FARMINGTON, CT, USA
[38142] : HENRIETTA 1839-1931 ANTELOPE CO.,
NE, USA **[38156]** : RICHARD 1864 WLS **[33855]** :
JOSEPH 1827 WLS **[33855]** : RICE 1840-1870
MERTHYR TYDFIL, GLA, WLS **[33933]** : C1780-
1909 CGN & GLA, WLS **[34589]** : PRE 1850
LLANYCHAER, PEM, WLS **[34729]** : JOHN 1815+
ABERDARE, GLA, WLS **[34954]** : RICHARD 1830+
ABERDARE, GLA, WLS **[34954]** : WILLIAM
C1818+ PEM, WLS **[35447]** : 1700+ NEATH, GLA,
WLS **[36209]** : PRE 1850 AGY, WLS **[36380]** : JOHN
PRE 1800 LLANGATTOCK, BRE, WLS **[36432]** :
HENRY 1700S CARDIFF, GLA, WLS **[36585]** : PRE

1820 HAWARDEN & EWLOE, FLN, WLS [36849] : PRE 1870 ABERDARE, GLA, WLS [37393] : 1849+ BRIDGEND, GLA, WLS [37401] : PRE 1800 PEM, WLS [38461]

LEWKNOR PRE 1500 SSX, ENG [35866]

LEWRY C1805 MARESFIELD, SSX, ENG [35397] : 1800+ SLAUGHAM, SSX, ENG [37206]

LEWTHWAITE 1700-1800 BOOTLE, CUL, ENG [37858]

LEWTON PRE 1820 BITTON, GLS, ENG [36095]

LEY 1850+ AUS [36395] : 1800+ DEV, ENG [35362] : 1800-1900 ISLINGTON, DEV, ENG [36395] : 1748+ ST CLEER, CON, ENG [36961] : PRE 1800 HILLSCHEID, RPF, GER [38663]

LEYBOURN PRE 1820 NEWCASTLE, NBL, ENG [36019]

LEYBUT ALL WORLDWIDE [36574]

LEYDEN PRE 1839 SKIPTON, WRY, ENG [34675] : 1837 TYR, IRL [37605]

LEYDON PRE 1839 SKIPTON, WRY, ENG [34675] : 1865 GLASGOW, LKS, SCT [34529]

LEYENDECKER PRE 1808 WEILERSWIST, NRW, GER [38630]

LEYH ALL WORLDWIDE [35383]

LEYLAND C1728 ILKLEY, YKS, ENG [34926]

LEYMAN 1844+ PA, USA [36560]

LEYNE C1670 LESMAHAGOW, LKS, SCT [34118]

LEYRER 1830+ PHILADELPHIA, PA, USA [36356]

LEYSHAN 1860S OMEO & BAIRNSDALE, VIC, AUS [35391]

LEYSHON CLARA 1890S REDFEARN, SA, AUS [35467]

LEYTON 1815 KILMUCKACRANY, SLI, IRL [37911]

L'HER 1700S JSY, CHI [35048]

L'HEUREUX ALL ST CHARLES SUR RICHELIEU, QUE, CAN [35639]

L'HOMMEDIEU 1762 SOUTHHOLD, NY, USA [36358]

LHONNEUX C1820 JANDRAIN JANDRE, BBT, BEL [38160] : 1981+ MAUNGATUROTO, WAN, NZ [38160]

LIA 1800S TAVERNA, CATANZARO, ITL [34371]

LIBEAU DIADONNE 1831 SAIVE, LGE, BEL [34924]

LIBERDA 1840-72 CS [38314]

LIBERSAN 1640-1690 RAZAC SUR-L'ISLE, FRA [38779]

LICHFIELD PRE 1812 RADFORD, NTT, ENG [37000]

LICHTE PRE 1800 FRA & GER [35604]

LICHTE (SEE LIGHT) [38030]

LICHTENSTEGER 1816 NIEDERHELFENSCHWIL, SG, CH [33754]

LICHTENSTEIN 1857 JEVER, OLD, GER [37509]

LICHTI PRE 1800 FRA & GER [35604]

LICHTIG PRE 1900 BERDITCHEV, UKRAINE, USSR [35635]

LICHTY 1700+ PA, USA [38241]

LICKELY C1830 FINTRAY, ABD, SCT [36875]

LICKIS 1600-1900 ENG [36169]

LICKISS ALL YORK, YKS, ENG [36557] : ANN 1800S HULL, YKS, ENG [37383]

LIDBETTER 1800S ULVERSTON, LAN, ENG [34178]

LIDDEL 1700+ LKS, SCT [36515]

LIDDELL C1794 SUNDERLAND, DUR, ENG [34157] : PRE 1850 SEDGFIELD, DUR, ENG [34335] : 1850-1900 WITTON GILBERT, DUR, ENG [36217] : 1750S GREAT COXWELL, BRK, ENG [38206] : C1880 COLERAINE, LDY, IRL [34223] : PRE 1852 ST NINIANS, STI, SCT [33822] : ALL PAISLEY, RFW, SCT [34046] : HELEN C1858 GLASGOW, LKS, SCT [34369] : PRE 1770 ST ANDREWS, FIF, SCT [35223] : 1700-1900 FALKIRK, STI, SCT [35923] : 1700-1900 DENNY, STI, SCT [35923] : ALL WORLDWIDE [34593]

LIDDIARD 1800-1930S LONDON, MDX & ESS, ENG [34813]

LIDDLE 1650-1838 ALSTON, CUL, ENG [38026] : PRE 1850 LINLITHGOW, STI, SCT [34097] : 1700-1900 DENNY, STI, SCT [35923] : 1850+ AIRTH, STI, SCT [37213]

LIDDY MATTHEW 1790-1850 KILLALOE, CLA, IRL [34915] : 1800+ CLA, IRL [35407] : PRE 1850 TULLA, CLA, IRL [36760]

LIDDYCOAT 1793+ ST ERVAN, CON, ENG [33781] : PRE 1780 ST ERVAN, CON, ENG [33992]

LIDGETT ALL WORLDWIDE [36063]

LIDIARD 1830+ GEORGETOWN, DEMERARA, GUIANA [35130]

LIDSTON PRE 1800 LONDON, ENG [34655]

LIDWELL C1800-1855 CLONMORE & CORMACKSTOWN, TIP, IRL [37415]

LIEB PRE 1900 AUGSBURG AREA, BAY, BRD [36963]

LIEBER C1735 FREIENSEEN, BRD [38658]

LIEBEZEIT ALL WORLDWIDE [38621]

LIEBHART C1815 YORK CO., PA, USA [38172]

LIEBREICH PRE 1850 GADEBUSCH, MEK, GER [36583]

LIECHTI PRE 1760 RUDERSWIL, BE, CH [38686] : 1750-1850 SOLOTHURN, SO, CH [38686]

LIECHTY ALL FC & ALS, FRA [38686] : ALL USA [38686]

LIEPE 1700-1830 DOBERITZ, BLN, GER [36340]

LIERE 1700-C1740S SCHOUWEN DUIVELAND, ZEL, NL [38350]

LIERSCH ALL BRD [34212] : ALL CAN [34212] : ALL DDR [34212]

LIFLY ELIZABETH PRE 1747 BURTON ON THE HILL, GLS, ENG [36817]

LIFORD ALL WORLDWIDE [37691]

LIGGETT ALL WORLDWIDE [36063]

LIGGINS ALL WAR, ENG [37404]

LIGGIT PRUDENCE PRE 1830 VA & OH, USA [38181]

LIGHT PRE 1837 PRESTON, GLS, ENG [35798] : ALL WIL, ENG [37086] : C1820 COLERNE & RODMARTEN, WIL & GLS, ENG [37838] : C1750-1800 BERKELEY CO., VA, USA [38030]

LIGHTBODY 1700-1825 DOW, IRL [34523]

LIGHTBOURNE PRE 1860S BERMUDA [34458]

LIGHTBOWN 1750+ DARWEN, LAN, ENG [36991]

LIGHTBURN 1600S KIRKLAND, CUL, ENG [38440]

LIGHTCAP C1700 KREFELD, GER [37040]

LIGHTERNESS PRE 1850 HACKNEY, MDX, ENG [37144]

LIGHTFOOT PRE 1920 AUS [36272] : 1797 ORRELL, LAN, ENG [35282] : PRE 1800 LANSALLOS, CON, ENG [35823] : PRE 1850 CON, ENG [36272] : RALPH C1690 WARRINGTON, LAN, ENG [37002] : 1640+ CAM, ENG [37564]

LIGHTON C1680-1715 N & S LEITH, MLN, SCT [36327]

LIGNON 1807-1890 ALS & LOR, FRA [38308]

LIHOU C1824 SYDNEY, NSW, AUS [37978]

LIKELY MARTHA BELLE 1850-1924 MERCER CO., IL, USA [38371]

LILBURN 1700+ TYNEMOUTH, NBL, ENG [34933] : 1800+ LKS, SCT [34933]

LILBURNGON PRE 1800 ENG [37833]

LILENTHAL 1700+ HUTTENBACH SCHNAITTACH, BAY, GER [38578]

LILJEGREN ALL BJORNA, SWE [38175]

LILL PRE 1800 LONDON, ENG [36154] : PRE 1850 WITHERN & BARROW, LIN, ENG [37402]

LILLEY 1852-1990 BEAUFORT & RAGLAN, VIC, AUS [33885] : 1837+ BULL DOG FLAT, VIC, AUS [35425] : PRE 1853 WEKLEY, NTH, ENG [33885] :

PRE 1837 NEWCASTLE UPON TYNE, YKS, ENG
[35425] : PRE 1810 CAMBRIDGE, CAM, ENG
[36201] : 1800S LIN, ENG [36851] : 1800+ YORK,
YKS, ENG [36975] : 1750+ CAM, ENG [37113] :
C1760 DOVER, KEN, ENG [38389] : PRE 1850
HAWICK, ROX, SCT [35934]

LILLICO ALL ROX, SCT [35032]

LILLIE PRE 1830 WAT, IRL [37497] : 1700-1850
KELSO, ROX, SCT [36556]

LILLIS C1800-1860 LIM, IRL [35389]

LILLY 1800+ HERMITAGE BAY, NFD, CAN [36684]
: C1750 DEAL, KEN, ENG [35203] : PRE 1882
DEAL, KEN, ENG [35781] : 1700-1850 CON, ENG
[37453] : C1850 SRY, ENG [37453] : 1802+
COLCHESTER & WEELEY, ESS, ENG [37656]

LILLYWHITE C1830 ENG [35998]

LIMA 1813 CIRCLEVILLE, OH, USA [35295]

LIMB 1700-1800 DBY, ENG [35862] : 1700 AULT
HUCKNALL, DBY, ENG [36018] : ALL
WORLDWIDE [36394]

LIMBART PRE 1800 GARFORTH, WRY, ENG [34382]

LIMBERG 1850 BUETOW, POM, GER [34388]

LIMBERY C1730S BDF, ENG [36289]

LIMBRICK 1650-1750 CHARFIELD, GLS, ENG [37222]

LIMBURG PRE 1824 EMMERICH, REES, GER
[37569]

LIMEBEER ALL AUS [35001] : ALL LONDON, ENG
[35001] : PRE 1840 DEV, ENG [35001] : ALL USA
[35001]

LIMER ALL WORLDWIDE [35875]

LIMINGTON 1800 CALNE, WIL, ENG [34890]

LIMMER 1814+ COWLINGE, SFK, ENG [35487]

LIMON 1600-1700 ESP [37822]

LINACRE 1840-1898 VIC & NSW, AUS [35841] : PRE
1840 LIVERPOOL, LAN, ENG [35841]

LINCEN PRE 1832+ BALAVIA, JVA, E.INDIES
[37912]

LINCHEVSKI ALL WORLDWIDE [38481]

LINCOLN C1730-1942 GREAT WITCHINGHAM &
MORTON, NFK, ENG [36128] : ALL NFK, ENG
[36234] : NANCY PRE 1840 BOSTON, MA, USA
[37797] : CORNELIUS 1809 COHASSET, MA, USA
[38193]

LIND 1872+ MACKAY, QLD, AUS [34768] : 1859+
BENDIGO, VIC, AUS [35468] : 1850-1900 DEN
[34135] : 1700S-1800S BJERT, DEN [35468] : 1830S
SHOREHAM, SSX, ENG [36486] : C1800 WEST
CALDER, MLN, SCT [34367] : PRE 1880
VARMLAND, SWE [34169] : C1800 SWE [34367] :
1880+ DENVER, CO, USA [34169]

LINDALL 1800+ HASSLEHOLM, KRISTIANSTADS,
SWE [34432]

LINDAMEN 1835+ OH, USA [36542]

LINDBERG 1800-1865 GOTEBORG & BOHUS, SWE
[37591]

LINDBORG 1860+ PERNAJA, UUSIMAA, FIN
[38758]

LINDE 1600+ AUE, WEF, GER [38622] : 1650+
WINGESHAUSEN, WEF, GER [38622] : 1550+
BERLEBURG, WEF, GER [38622] : 1550+
WITTGENSTEIN (STATE), WEF, GER [38622] :
1550+ SAYN WITTGENSTEIN BERLEBURG,
WEF, GER [38622] : 1760+ BERGHAUSEN, WEF,
GER [38622]

LINDEKAM PRE 1860 SANGERHAUSEN, PSA, GER
[37346]

LINDEMANN 1700-1900 GHE & HEN, GER [35630] :
1738 LESUM, BRM, GER [35828]

LINDEN 1600+ AXMINSTER, DEV, ENG [34408]

LINDEN VAN DER 1700-1900 CULEMBORG, GEL,
NL [38712]

LINDER C1715 OHRENSBACH, BAD, GER [33772]

LINDERMAN 1740-60 UNKENBACH, GER [38151] :
1680-1750 GERMANTOWN, PA, USA [36738] : 1736-
92 ORANGE CO., NY, USA [38151]

LINDFIELD 1800-1900 SHIPLEY, SSX, ENG [34749] :
PRE 1825 SHIPLEY, HORSHAM & BRIGHTON,
SSX, ENG [36384]

LINDGREN OLGA 1890+ KAGERODS
FORSAMLING, M-LAN, SKANE, SWE [38759] :
AUGUST 1898+ KAGERODS FORSAMLING, M-
LAN, SKANE, SWE [38759] : 1900+ USA [38759]

LINDHORST 1750-1816 CELLE, HAN, GER [38626]

LINDLAGE 1650+ DSNABRUECK, HAN, GER
[38651]

LINDLEY 1840-1850 HOWARD CO., IN, USA [37005] :
JOHN 1862+ MARION, IL, USA [37596]

LINDNER ALL GERMANY, QLD, AUS [36881] : ALL
SAGAN, SIL, GER [38623]

LINDORES PRE 1812 HADDINGTON, ELN, SCT
[33846]

LINDQUIST 1882+ NE, USA [36919]

LINDRAGE C1765 HIGH HALDEN, KEN, ENG
[38389]

LINDSAY 1906+ MELBOURNE, VIC, AUS [34042] :
C1833 EMU BAY, TAS, AUS [35391] : THOMAS 1874
HEATHCOTE, VIC, AUS [35529] : 1840S
CARDINGTON & WELLINGTON, NSW, AUS
[35546] : 1850+ BALLARAT, VIC, AUS [36368] : PRE
1820 SRY, ENG [33925] : 1900+ SHEFFIELD, YKS,
ENG [34049] : 1800+ WHITEHAVEN, CUL, ENG
[36368] : ISABELLA 1800 DURHAM, DUR, ENG
[36928] : 1840+ WELLINGTON, SAL, ENG & SCT
[36254] : C1811 SESKINORE, TYR, IRL [34926] :
PRE 1825 WIC & DUB, IRL [35488] : DAVID 1800+
DUNLAVY, DOW, IRL [36813] : 1800S MENMUIR,
ANS, SCT [33899] : 1800+ PAISLEY, RFW, SCT
[34049] : C1700 LANARK, LKS, SCT [34118] : 1750-
1850 PITTENWEEM& ANSTRUTHER EASTER,
FIF, SCT [34359] : C1840 LIBERTON, LKS, SCT
[34556] : C1870 CARNWARTH, LKS, SCT [34556] :
PRE 1857 KINROSS, PER, SCT [34683] : PRE 1856
ARBROATH, ANS, SCT [35129] : 1800+ DFS, SCT
[35407] : PRE 1860 DUNDEE, ANS, SCT [35423] :
THOMAS 1820+ FIF, SCT [35529] : PRE 1837 ISLE
OF SKYE, SCT [35546] : 1700-1800
KILCONQUHAR, FIF, SCT [35627] : 1800+
TWEEDSMUIR, DFS, SCT [35909] : 1848-1900
GLASGOW, SCT [35999] : MARION 1800+
EAGLESHAM, AYR, SCT [36471] : AGNES PRE
1910 HAMILTON, LKS, SCT [36646] : 1700+
KINNEFF & CATTERLINE, KCD, SCT [36971] :
1720+ STRATHAVEN, LKS, SCT [37399] : 1800S
RAVENSHALL, KKD, SCT [37499] : 1600+
KERRICK, KKD, SCT [37734] : 1850-1900
BALMAGIE, KKD, SCT [37734] : PRE 1810
KILCONQUHAR & CARNBEE, FIF, SCT [37913] :
PRE 1860 LKS, SCT [37923] : 1770+ ROX, SCT
[38274] : 1900+ KEARNY, NJ, USA [34049] : PRE
1850 NEW PROVIDENCE, BAHAMAS IS.,
W.INDIES [35546]

LINDSELL 1740-1871+ PRITTLEWELL, ESS, ENG
[37108]

LINDSEY 1800S COATES, CAM, ENG [35188] : PRE
1880 OXF, ENG [37739] : 1700-1780 CAROLINE CO.,
VA, USA [36566] : 1850-1900 CHEROKEE CO., TX,
USA [37533] : 1830-50 CHOCTAW CO., MS, USA
[37533]

LINE 1750 PORCHESTER, HAM, ENG [34204] : C1720
WESTBURY, WIL, ENG [37063] : JEDIDAH 1790-
1838 LITTLE EGG HARBOR, NJ, USA [38127]

LINEBAUGH JAMES 1786-1859 COSHOCTON, OH,
USA [36322]

\

LINEBERGER PRE 1788 GUILFORD CO., NC, USA [37029]

LINEHAM PRE 1820 ST ALBANS, HRT, ENG [37687]

LINEHAN PRE 1860 IRL [37015]

LINEHANN PRE 1830 THOMAS TOWN, KIK, IRL [35533]

LINES PRE 1750 RIDLEY, KEN, ENG [34911] : PRE 1854 WATER STRATFORD, BKM, ENG [35111] : PRE 1800 LONDON, ENG [36154] : 1760+ BRISTOL, GLS, ENG [36995] : 1700 CHEDISTON, SFK, ENG [37928] : ALL WOLVERTON & RUGBY, WAR, ENG [38258] : PRE 1850 HRT, ENG [38258]

LINFIELD PRE 1800 BILLINGSHURST, SSX, ENG [34112]

LING 1849+ BRISBANE, QLD, AUS [34808] : 1888+ MELBOURNE, VIC, AUS [35059] : 1855+ NW COAST, TAS, AUS [38492] : PRE 1769 STERNFIELD, SFK, ENG [34205] : 1800+ NAPTON, WAR, ENG [34315] : 1820S ECCLES, NFK, ENG [35151] : 1700-1850 BROCKFORD, SFK, ENG [37042] : 1700+ PEVENSEY, SSX, ENG [37328] : 1813+ EAST HARLING, NFK, ENG [38492]

LINGARD 1785-1856 THORNTON, YKS, ENG [34793] : PRE 1900 WRY, ENG [35978] : ALL GRIMSBY, LIN, ENG [37355]

LINGE PRE 1846 WHITECHAPEL, MDX, ENG [37546]

LINGENBERG 1850S FOXHOW, VIC, AUS [35127] : C1830 DANTZIC, PRE, GER [35127]

LINGENFELTER ALL ARMSTRONG & JEFFERSON CO., PA, USA [38036]

LINGLEY PRE 1900 LONDON, MDX, ENG [36709] : ALL NORWICH, NFK, ENG [37689]

LINGO PRE 1820 SUSSEX CO., DE, USA [36957]

LINGS ALL LEICESTER, LEI, ENG [37334] : ALL WORLDWIDE [37334]

LINGWOOD C1600 ENG [34395]

LINHARDT PRE 1800 AG, CH [38029]

LINK PRE 1765 KEN, ENG [38389] : 1800-1850 PA, USA [37597] : 1890+ CANTON, OK, USA [37597]

LINKE ALL MAGDEBURG DRESDEN, GER [35767]

LINKHORN PRE 1860 LIVERPOOL, LAN, ENG [36768]

LINKLATER JOHN 1880+ AUROR, ONT, CAN [34247] : ALEX 1856+ YORK CO., ONT, CAN [34247] : 1800S TANKERNESS, OKI, SCT [34353]

LINKLETER (SEE LINKL [34247]

LINN 1840+ SA, AUS [35888] : PRE 1700 TRIPPSTADT, RPF, GER [38681] : PRE 1700 IRL [37032] : ALL ABERCORN & KIRKLISTON, WLN, SCT [35888] : C1700 MA, USA [37032] : JOHN 1740+ SOMERSET CO., NJ, USA [37032]

LINN (SEE LYNN) [34126]

LINNETT PRE 1812 LONDON, ENG [36010] : PRE 1874 CLAYCOTTON & CATTHORPE, NTH, ENG [36290]

LINNEY 1800 HAM, ENG [35043] : 1850-1860 WAR, ENG [36845]

LINNINGTON ALL ENG [34715] : 1630+ LONG ISLAND, NY, USA [34392]

LINSDELL ALL LONDON, UK & AUS [34599]

LINSELL 1700S+ BISHOPS STORTFORD, ESS, ENG [34339]

LINSEY 1700-1800 LANGFORD, BRK, ENG [37380]

LINSKILL 1700+ TYNEMOUTH, NBL & YKS, ENG [35723]

LINSTEAD PRE 1800 LODDON, NFK, ENG [36073]

LINSTROT 1500+ BURGSTEINFURT, WEF, GER [38065]

LINTER PRE 1700 EHRINGSHAUSEN, WUE, GER [37510]

LINTERN 1760+ DITCHEAT, SOM, ENG [33852] : C1795 DITCHEAT, SOM, ENG [34393]

LINTHERN C1830 MARSTOW, SOM, ENG [34393]

LINTHWAITE ALL LEI, ENG [35177] : 1800+ MARYLEBONE, LND, ENG [35800]

LINTON PRE 1855 CYGNEY, TAS, AUS [33786] : 1820+ HOBART, TAS, AUS [34547] : 1843+ EVANDALE, TAS, AUS [35578] : PRE 1890 SHEFFIELD, TAS, AUS [36775] : MARY 1740-1832 MARKET WEIGHTON, YKS, ENG [34143] : PRE 1800 GOATHLAND, NRY, ENG [34333] : 1800S SCARBOROUGH AREA, ERY, ENG [34333] : 1795-1819 BRIXHAM, DEV, ENG [34333] : 1750-1835 YORK, YKS, ENG [37011] : 1790-1850 SOUTHWARK & ST PANCRAS, LND, ENG [37420] : 1840 ARM, IRL [35024] : ALL DOW, IRL [36853] : 1905+ OREPUKI, SLD, NZ [36853] : 1800-1850 FRANKLIN & GUERNSEY CO., OH, USA [37599]

LINTS ALL NY, USA [37502]

LINTZ C1758 AMHERST, VA, USA [37819]

LIONNAIS 1705+ BAIC DU FEBURE, QUE, CAN [36678]

LIONNAISE MARIE C1818 SAS, CAN [36678]

LIPCAMON FREDRICK 1820-1830S GER [37001]

LIPE 1870-1990 JACKSON, IL, USA [38588]

LIPKA 1920 ROCKWOOD & WEDDIFIELD, ONT, CAN [36679] : 1920 NIPPISSING, ONT, CAN [36679]

LIPMAN 1820S LONDON, ENG [35509]

LIPPELT 1700+ BREMEN, BRM, GER [36303]

LIPPERT PRE 1710 ROTHENBURG ODT, BAY, BRD [35311] : 1700S LINGELRACH, HES, BRD [35635] : C1866-1895 LOCKEN, OPR, GER [34083]

LIPSCOMB 1840+ MAITLAND, NSW, AUS [35826] : 1800-1900 KENT CO., ONT, CAN [34094] : PRE 1900 ENG [34812] : C1840 READING, BRK, ENG [35826]

LIPSCOMBE PRE 1886 PETERSHAM, NSW, AUS [35232] : PRE 1760 BKM, ENG [37498]

LIPSETT 1843-C1902 BALLYSHANNON, DON, IRL & AUS [33847]

LIPSEY C1732 TYR, IRL [37527] : PRE 1830 IN, USA [37527] : 1830+ HARDIN CO., KY, USA [37527]

LIPSON 1700S CREDITON, DEV, ENG [34766]

LISCOM PHILIP 1750 CANTON, MA, USA [35273]

LISENBY PRE 1850 CLARK, AR, USA [37819]

LISHMAN PRE 1713 NEWBY WISKE, NRY, ENG [37852]

LISIIECKI ALL LOMZA, POL [37041]

LISK PRE 1830 DERRYCORN, ARM, IRL [35430]

LISKA PRE 1847 VISKY, ROKYCANY, CS [38618]

LISSAMAN ALL WORLDWIDE [37868]

LIST ALL PFULLINGEN, BAW, BRD [38624] : 1500-1700 GOETLISHOFEN, BAW, BRD [38624] : ALL SCHLITZ, HES, BRD [38624] : ALL BISCHOFSZELL, TG, CH [38624] : ALL CH [38624] : ALL FRA [38624] : C1870 GER [33809] : ALL GER [38624] : PRE 1834 DUBLIN, IRL [36451] : ALL OES [38624] : ALL UK & USA [38624] : ALL WORLDWIDE [38624]

LISTER 1700+ DOR, ENG [34416] : PRE 1795 TORKSEY, LIN, ENG [34501] : ALL SFK, ENG [34744] : PRE 1720 CARLTON IN LINDRICK, NTT, ENG [36426] : 1720+ STURTON LE STEEPLE, NTT, ENG [36426] : PRE 1820 SCARBOROUGH, YKS, ENG [36838] : C1820+ LONDON, ENG [36838] : 1750-1870 LEEDS, YKS, ENG [36983] : 1800-1900 LEEDS, WRY, ENG [37643] : C1800 EDINBURGH, MLN, SCT [37552]

LISTON 1600+ HASTINGS, SSX, ENG [34747] : 1600+ WLN, FIF & PER, SCT [35999] : 1870-1915 CARDONALD, RFW, SCT & INDI [35999]

LITCHFIELD C1800 GREAT BADDOW, ESS, ENG [35203] : PRE 1840 LONDON, MDX, ENG [35857] :

PRE 1756 BOURN, CAM, ENG [36604] : ALL ESS, ENG [37741] : PRE 1630 KEN, ENG [38135] : PRE 1840 BECKAMPORE, ORISSA, INDIA [35857]

LITEL (SEE LITTLE) [34433]

LITHERLAND C1813 APPLEBY, LEI, ENG [36253] : C1848 BURTON ON TRENT, DBY, ENG [36253] : PRE 1836 ASHBY DE LA ZOUCH, LEI, DBY & RUT, ENG [37840]

LITSTER 1750-1850 ST ANDREWS, FIF, SCT [33800] : ALL SCT [34254] : 1800+ DUNFERMLINE, FIF, SCT [35969]

LITT 1920-1930S NYC, NY, USA [36936]

LITTLE STEPHEN 1826+ SYDNEY, NSW, AUS [36600] : 1852+ RICHMOND, VIC, AUS [37120] : NELLIE C1854-1906 COBOURG & HAMILTON, ONT, CAN [33759] : JOHN PRE 1885 THOROLD, ONT, CAN [33762] : 1850+ SIMCOE CO., ONT, CAN [34465] : C1790+ ESSEX & KENT CO., ONT, CAN [34493] : 1700-1800 ALB, MAN & ONT, CAN [38764] : 1700S WOOTTON BASSETT, WIL, ENG [33918] : C1800-1830 MARYPORT, CUL, ENG [34727] : PRE 1830 WORKINGTON, CUL, ENG [34795] : PRE 1860 LITTLE CANFIELD, ESS, ENG [35200] : PRE 1800 CUL, ENG [35423] : 1769-1849+ BRAMPTON, CUL, ENG [35497] : 1715+ BROUGHTON BY BRIGG, LIN, ENG [35587] : PRE 1800 WOLVERHAMPTON & PENN, STS, ENG [36110] : 1650+ STEVINGTON & SHARNBROOK, BDF, ENG [36123] : ALL GOOD EASTER, ESS, ENG [36500] : STEPHEN C1810+ LND & SRY, ENG [36600] : 1750-1850 LAMBOURNE, BRK, ENG [37188] : 1750-1900 HALTWHISTLE & SIMONBURN, NBL, ENG [37395] : 1840+ TYNEMOUTH & WALLSEND, NBL, ENG [37395] : 1700+ STANHOPE, DUR, ENG [37460] : 1750-1850 CARLISLE, CUL, ENG [37654] : PRE 1800 SLI, IRL [33905] : 1300-1800 IRL [34493] : PRE 1818 DUBLIN, IRL [35117] : PRE 1870 DRUMMULLY & CLONES, MOG & FER, IRL [35997] : C1825 IRL [37795] : PRE 1700 DFS, SCT [34493] : PRE 1714 WESTERKIRK, DFS, SCT [34501] : PRE 1900 LANGHOLM, DFS, SCT [37821] : C1780 DETROIT, MI, USA [34493] : C1700 LANCASTER CO., PA, USA [34493] : C1700 MD, USA [34493] : C1700 ALLEGHENY CO., PA, USA [34493] : 1700-1777 VA, USA [36939] : PRE 1720 BRISTOL, RI, USA [37804] : RACHEL 1774 ROWAN CO., NC, USA [38086] : C1750-1890 TN & MO, USA [38242] : 1890S RENO CO., KS, USA [38243] : JOHN 1750+ LEBANON, CT, USA [38766] : ALL NEWTOWN, MGY, WLS [35566]

LITTLEBOYS PRE 1840 SPARKHAM, NFK, ENG [36828]

LITTLEFIELD 1820 STREATHAM, SRY, ENG [37080] : 1868-1663 WELLS, YORK, ME, USA [38571]

LITTLEHALE C1790 PONTESBURY, SAL, ENG [38052]

LITTLEJOHN 1854+ SYDNEY, NSW, AUS [38541] : 1800S DOWNSVIEW, ONT, CAN [37458] : PRE 1854 LKS, SCT [38541]

LITTLEJOHNS ALL ENG [38735]

LITTLEJON 1700+ INVERKEITHNY, BAN, SCT [34420]

LITTLER 1830+ NORTHWICH, CHS, ENG [35341] : 1800 ELTON, CHS, ENG [35341] : 1690+ CHS, ENG [38487] : C1735 FREDERICK CO., VA, USA [37788] : 1690+ USA [38487]

LITTLETON 1852+ ADELAIDE & CASTLEMAINE, SA & VIC, AUS [35064] : PRE 1850+ PLYMOUTH, DEV, ENG [35064] : PRE 1850 LUMLIVERY, CON, ENG & AUS [35064]

LITTLEWOOD PRE 1880 SA, AUS [38755] : 1800+ LANGLEY, NFK, ENG [35358] : C1787

ALMONDBURY, WRY, ENG [35733] : 1600+ HUDDERSFIELD, WRY, ENG [36104] : 1800-1850 ORMESBY ST MICHAEL, NFK, ENG [36663]

LITTRELL ALL NC, SC & TN, USA [38739]

LITZENBERGER 1775-1815 ODENBACH, RPF, BRD [35311]

LIUM 1820+ NOR [38533]

LIVARD 1700-1850 IBSTON, BKN, ENG [36653]

LIVENGOOD 1740-1820 NORTHAMPTON, PA, USA [38095]

LIVERD ALL WORLDWIDE [37691]

LIVERMORE C1910-1918 MELBOURNE, VIC, AUS [37355] : PRE 1950 WILBRAHAM, CAM, ENG [36489] : 1680+ CAMBRIDGE, CAM & ESS, ENG [37065] : C1910-1940 EASTBOURNE, SSX, ENG [37355] : ALL RYE & WESTFIELD, SSX, ENG [37355] : ALL BATTLE & HASTINGS, SSX, ENG [37355] : 1910S HAMMERSMITH & ST PANCRAS, LND, ENG [37355] : 1800S ESS, ENG [37885] : C1900-1940 NEW YORK, NY, USA [37355] : FREELOVE 1807-1890 VERMONT, VT, NY & MI, USA [37806] : 1840-1860 KEWEENAW CO., MI, USA [38009] : 1860-1880 OAKLAND CO., MI, USA [38009] : C1910-1950 SWANSEA & BARRY, GLA, WLS [37355]

LIVERSAGE PRE 1802 WYBUNBURY, CHS, ENG [35368] : PRE 1766 GNOSALL, STS, ENG [37762] : 1797+ CHS, ENG [38212]

LIVERTON ALL NZ &, WORLDWIDE [33798]

LIVESEY 1816+ WALTON LE DALE, LAN, ENG [34522] : PRE 1670 PLEASINGTON, LAN, ENG [34522] : 1850+ PRESTON, LAN, ENG [34522] : C1680 WALTON LE DALE, LAN, ENG [34522] : 1700+ WORLDWIDE [34522]

LIVINGSTON 1750-1850 ENNISKILLEN, FER, IRL [34513] : PRE 1840 LKS, SCT [33971] : 1800-1850 MULL, ARL, SCT [34345] : 1150 SCT [37008] : PRE 1800 DUDDINGSTON & NEWTON, MLN, SCT [37852] : PRE 1799 PRESTONPANS, ELN, SCT [37852] : 1800S GLASGOW, SCT [37898] : 1600-1700 SCT [38319] : PRE 1850 ISLAY, ARL, SCT [38403] : 1770-1850 WASHINGTON, NY, USA [38373] : ALL WORLDWIDE [37785]

LIVINGSTONE C1851 GREY CO., ONT, CAN [37474] : DONALD C1730 FT WILLIAM, ARL, SCT [33849] : C1806 ST ANDREWS, FIF, SCT [35096] : PRE 1850 AYR, SCT [35354] : C1816 SCT [37474] : 1800-1840 LOUDOUN, AYR, SCT [37996] : 1850+ SCT [38059]

LIVSEY 1820+ ACCRINGTON, LAN, ENG [38266]

LIVY ALL WORLDWIDE [34453]

LIZARS PRE 1875 CLERKENWELL, MDX, ENG [37753] : ALL WORLDWIDE [36257]

LIZENBY PRE 1850 CLARK, AR, USA [37819]

LIZT PRE 1834 DUBLIN, IRL [36451]

LLEWELLEN 1838+ SYDNEY, NSW, AUS [35033] : PRE 1860 CARDIFF, GLA, WLS [36451]

LLEWELLIN 1790+ LONDON, MDX, ENG [38171]

LLEWELLYN 1866+ BRISBANE, QLD, AUS [35557] : 1890S BOURKE, NSW, AUS [35557] : 1882+ ARMIDALE, NSW, AUS [37310] : MARYANN C1839 WOR, ENG [34222] : 1830S BRISTOL, GLS, ENG [35557] : 1700+ GENESEE, NY, USA [37826] : 1850S RHOSCROWTHER, PEM, WLS [34603] : PRE 1845 TREVETHIN, MON, WLS [37948]

LLEWHELLIN 1800-1840 PEM & GLA, WLS [37263]

LLOYD JOHN 1832+ HOBART & FRANKLIN, TAS, AUS [35388] : SARAH PRE 1860 FRANKLIN, TAS, AUS [35388] : WILLIAM 1850+ FRANKLIN & LONGFORD, TAS, AUS [35388] : THOMAS 1865+ FRANKLIN, TAS, AUS [35388] : LUTHER 1880+ PERTH, WA, AUS [35388] : GEORGE 1832+ HOBART & FRANKLIN, TAS, AUS [35388] : LUTHER 1855+ FRANKLIN, TAS, AUS [35388] :

BURGESS 1880+ PERTH, WA, AUS [35388] :
DANIEL C1921 MOREE, NSW, AUS [35852] : ADA
REBECCA C1921 MOREE, NSW, AUS [35852] :
JOHN 1809-1815 AUS [37113] : 1840-1930 CLARE &
EMU FLAT, SA, AUS [37905] : 1870 STUART HILL,
VIC, AUS [37984] : JOHN 1860+ DUNGOG, NSW,
AUS [38729] : PRE 1850 SOM, ENG [33851] : 1750-
1900 HOPESAY, SAL, ENG [34632] : 1800-1842
ALBERBURY, SAL, ENG [34844] : C1900 MOSELEY
& BIRMINGHAM, STS, ENG [35306] : JOHN 1783+
OSWESTRY, SAL, ENG [35388] : 1860S DBY, ENG
[36531] : 1800 TREFONEN & OSWESTRY, SAL,
ENG [36568] : PRE 1828 MANCHESTER, LAN,
ENG [36642] : HENRY 1812-1872 BRISTOL, GLS,
ENG [37056] : 1810+ BIRMINGHAM, WAR, ENG
[37074] : C1840 NOTTING HILL, MDX, ENG [37859]
: C1875 LIVERPOOL, LAN, ENG [37865] : C1860
DUDLEY, WOR & STS, ENG [37865] : 1750+
ANDOVER, HAM, ENG [37868] : 1800-1910
MUCHELNEY, SOM, ENG [37905] : PRE 1860
LIVERPOOL, ENG [37984] : 1780 WESTON
ZOYLAND, SOM, ENG [38209] : 1800+ WALTHAM
ABBEY, LND, ENG & NZ [35896] : 1700+ DON,
IRL [35080] : 1860+ CHRISTCHURCH, NZ [35896] :
1840S ROCKTON, WI & IL, USA [37017] : SOPHIA
1823 HARTFORD CO., CT, USA [38734] : 1809+
BRIDGEND, GLA, WLS [34684] : STEPHEN PRE
1866 LLERTAI LLANFIHANGEL, WLS [34992] :
STEPHEN PRE 1866 ABERGWESYN, WLS [34992] :
PRE 1845 RAD, WLS [35386] : 1800S
ABERYSTWYTH, CGN, WLS [36205] : PRE 1850
LLANELIAN, DEN, WLS [36416] : 1861-79
CARDIFF, GLA, WLS [37144] : PRE 1860
CRIGGION, MGY, WLS [37242] : PRE 1851 DEN,
WLS [37946] : ALL WLS & AUS [34301]
LLOYDD 1800+ HARTFORD, CT, USA [33989]
LNENIKA ALL LITMYSOL, BOHEMIA, CS [36881]
LOACH PRE 1900 OLDBURY, WOR, ENG [37681]
LOADER PRE 1850 ARSON, OXF, ENG [33884] : PRE
1835 SRY, ENG [35083] : 1700+ SPETTISBURY,
DOR, ENG [35965] : 1800S LONDON, ENG [35965] :
C1815 CHICHESTER, SSX, ENG [36215] : 1720+
LAMBETH & ST PANCRAS, LND, ENG [37420] :
ALL BRK, ENG [37420]
LOAGUE C1800 STRABANE, TYR, IRL [34426]
LOANE 1700S CORK, COR, IRL [35597]
LOBARSUS 1873 FALDOUET, JSY, CHI [35761]
LOBB ALL TRURO, CON, ENG [33975]
LOBBAN ALL KNOCKANDOO & ELGIN, MOR,
SCT [35460]
LOBER 1821+ GURWITZ & WARDRISCH, SIL, GER
[35391]
LOBLEY C1800 CRAKKE, NRY, ENG [37710] :
C1750+ BATLEY & AREA, WRY, ENG [37842]
LOCEY 1750-1800 PA, USA [38529]
LOCHEARN 1830+ SCT [34373]
LOCHEL KATE 1760-1800 KILLARNEY, KER &
CLA, IRL [33941]
LOCHER PRE 1850 HASLE, BE, CH [38747]
LOCHHEAD PRE 1900 DUNFERMLINE, FIF, SCT
[35823] : PRE 1900 LASSWADE, MLN, SCT [35823]
LOCHNER PRE 1800 HELSHOFEN, WUE, GER
[37510] : 1850+ MILWAUKEE CO., WI, USA [36962]
LOCK CHARLES PRE 1888 NORTH ADELAIDE, SA,
AUS [33890] : FANNY ALL LIVERPOOL, NSW,
AUS [35234] : PRE 1875 LAURA, SA, AUS [37955] :
PRE 1900 CAMPBELLFORD, ONT, CAN [38438] :
CHARLES PRE 1888+ NFK, ENG [33890] : PRE
1700 SFK, ENG [34258] : ALL CURRY RIVEL, SOM,
ENG [34298] : PRE 1830 NORTH LEIGH, OXF,
ENG [34466] : 1800S ST PANCRAS, MDX, ENG
[34953] : JOHN PRE 1855 COLSBURN, GLS, ENG

[35234] : PRE 1850 DEANPRIOR, DEV, ENG [35330]
: PRE 1810 STANION ST GABRIEL, DOR, ENG
[35597] : 1890S MINEHEAD, SOM, ENG [36528] :
PRE 1745 ALTON, HAM, ENG [37420] : 1800
SHALFLEET, IOW, ENG [37733]
LOCKE 1865+ FREMANTLE, WA, AUS [34781] :
1866+ QUEANBEYAN, NSW, AUS [34806] : 1840+
MERRITT'S HARBOR, NFD, CAN [34074] : PRE
1900 CAMPBELLFORD, ONT, CAN [38438] :
CHARLES 1853 MORTON IN MARSH, GLS, ENG
[34806] : JONAS 1856 LONDON, ENG [34806] : PRE
1650 CANN, DOR, ENG [36478] : 1650-1750
BROOKE, NFK, ENG [36483] : 1700+ WYLYE,
WIL, ENG [36818] : 1600-1800 CHESTERTON, NFK
& SFK, ENG [38194] : 1800S DEAN PRIOR &
BUCKFASTLEIGH, DEV, ENG [38468] : C1788
PARTON, KKD, SCT [37981] : AYRES PRE 1820
ENFIELD, CT, USA [36345] : AYRES 1820-1835
ALLEGANY CO., NY, USA [36345] : SARAH 1850S
ROWAN CO., NC, USA [37585]
LOCKER PRE 1800 STS, ENG [37389]
LOCKETT C1869 BIRMINGHAM, ENG [35515] : ALL
TRURO, CON, ENG [37558]
LOCKEY PRE 1900 BRISBANE, QLD, AUS [34978] :
1820+ ROTHWELL, YKS, ENG [38473]
LOCKHART PRE 1800 ABBOTSHALL, FIF, SCT
[34861] : 1750-1850 KILMARNOCK, AYR, SCT
[35151] : KATHERINE PRE 1800 MONTROSE,
ANS, SCT [35462] : PRE 1841 BEITH, AYR, SCT
[37575] : 1828 NORTH LEITH, MLN, SCT [38364]
LOCKHOFF PRE 1885 GER [34383]
LOCKIE C1800 MANCHESTER, LAN, ENG [36635] :
1720-1800 BEW, SCT [34615]
LOCKING ALL WORLDWIDE [34361]
LOCKINGS 1850S BENWICK, CAM, ENG [34884] :
C1800-1880 RAMSEY, HUN, ENG [34884]
LOCKLEY PRE 1830S CANNOCK & PENKRIDGE,
STS, ENG [34240]
LOCKMAN 1790+ BIRMINGHAM, WAR, ENG
[35152] : C1869 HEREFORD, HEF, ENG [37886] :
1750-1850 ORANGE CO., NC, USA [38342]
LOCKSLEY 1880+ FOOTSCRAY, VIC, AUS [35065] :
1867+ GEELONG, VIC, AUS [35065] : PRE 1867
CONGROVE, STS, ENG [35065]
LOCKWOOD 1809 ERNESTOWN, ONT, CAN [36680]
: PRE 1890 HUDDERSFIELD, WRY, ENG [33943] :
1850 SCOTBY, CUL, ENG [35194] : PRE 1900
HECKMONDWIKE, WRY, ENG [36069] : PRE 1900
LND, ENG [36288] : PRE 1860 KELLINTON, WRY,
ENG [36516] : 1800 NEEDHAM MARKET, SFK,
ENG [37122] : PRE 1800 SOMERSTOWN, MDX,
ENG [37137] : 1826 LIVERPOOL, LAN, ENG [37445]
: 1604-1884 GREENWICH, CT, USA [37803]
LOCKYER 1700-1900 BERE REGIS, DOR, ENG
[34714] : 1800+ RUGBY, WAR, ENG [35461] : 1800+
LONDON, MDX, ENG [35461] : PRE 1830
SEAVINGTON ST MICHAEL, SOM, ENG [36581] :
MARY 1760S KEN, ENG [36679] : 1700+ SSX, ENG
[37210] : PRE 1850 PLYMOUTH, DEV, ENG [38376]
LODDER ALL NL [38701] : ALL UTR, NL [38716]
LODDING PRE 1800 NEUSTADT, HAN, GER [38186]
LODER ALL BRK, ENG [37420]
LODEWICK PRE 1800 ALBANY, NY, USA [36935]
LODGE ALL TAS, AUS [33786] : PRE 1854
CATALINA, NFD, CAN [34096] : THORNTON
1872+ MAPLETON, NS, CAN [34340] : PRE 1900
WIL & DOR, ENG [34317] : 1800S CHISWICK,
MDX, ENG [36708] : PRE 1800 ENG [37133] : C1700
SHERBURN IN ELMET, YKS, ENG [37144] : 1800-
1900 YKS, ENG [37495] : C1777 HUDSWELL, NRY,
ENG [37627] : ALL YARM, NRY, ENG [37627] :
C1828 WORSALL, NRY, ENG [37627] : INGLETON

PRE 1858 SHOREDITCH, LND, ENG [37647] : PRE 1875 HUDDERSFIELD, YKS, ENG [38730] : THORNTON C1905-1960 HOLLYWOOD, CA, USA [34340]

LOERKE 1800+ WALDORF, WPR, GER [37542]

LOESSER 1800-1840S GER [35298] : 1850-1860S NEW YORK, NY, USA [35298] : 1870-1890 KALAMAZOO, MI, USA [35298]

LOETSCH PRE 1788 RHEINBROHL, RPF, GER [38663]

LOEW 1450-1650 MUEHLHAUSEN NECKAR, BAW, BRD [38654]

LOEWENHEIM 1800S BERLIN, BRA, GER [36921] : 1870S VICKSBURG, MS, USA [36921]

LOFFEL PRE 1825 OTTENHEIM, BAD, GER [37817]

LOFFLER PRE 1925 BREITENWORBIS, THU, GER [38636]

LOFTHOUSE 1800S SHERBURN IN ELMET, YKS, ENG [36847]

LOFTS 1700-1850 DOWNHAM, CAM, ENG [37188]

LOFTUS 1873+ ROCKHAMPTON, QLD, AUS [35138] : C1870 CHESTERFIELD, DBY, ENG [37131] : 1878+ WIGAN, LAN, ENG [37131] : ALL ROSCOMMON, IRL [34879] : C1844 IRL [37131]

LOFTY 1600+ SSX, ENG [34980]

LOGAN 1850+ MAITLAND, NSW, AUS [34969] : GEORGE 1747-1834 ROGERS HILL, NS & ROC, CAN & SCT [37499] : 1700+ DRUMIGNY, DON, IRL [33986] : PRE 1850 CLONDAVADDOCK, DON, IRL [34611] : JAMES C1800-1867 BANBRIDGE, DOW, IRL [36001] : GEORGE 1700-1784 DOWNPATRICK, DOW, IRL [36001] : PRE 1851 BELFAST, ANT, IRL [37939] : PRE 1856 MAYBOLE, AYR, SCT [33845] : 1700+ CATHCART, RFW, SCT [35395] : C1840 DUMBARTON, DNB, SCT [35594] : PRE 1850 TRANENT, ELN, SCT [35823] : WILLIAM 1750-1820 AYR, AYR, SCT [36001] : JOHN RONALD C1774-1858 AYR, AYR, SCT [36001] : QUINTIN 1750+ AYR, AYR, SCT [36001] : 1800+ GLASGOW, LKS, SCT [37628] : 1700-1990 KILBIRNIE, AYR, SCT [37628] : PRE 1800 GLASGOW, SCT [37939] : 1850S ROW, DNB, SCT [38283] : FRANCIS 1784-1862 DUNLOP, AYR, SCT & NZ [36001] : GEORGE 1650+ ABERDEEN, ABD, SCT & USA [36001] : PRE 1910 LAKE, MS, USA [36543] : 1840-1990 LEAVENWORTH CO., KS, USA [37798] : 1840-1870 ATCHISON CO., KS, USA [37798] : 1850 GADSDEN, AL, USA [38198] : ALL WORLDWIDE [36001]

LOGANE ALL WORLDWIDE [36001]

LOGEN ALL WORLDWIDE [36001]

LOGGAN ALL WORLDWIDE [36001]

LOGGANE ALL WORLDWIDE [36001]

LOGIE PRE 1790 REDHALL & BAUDS, MOR, SCT [34056]

LOGIER PRE 1850 DUBLIN, IRL [34877]

LOGIN ALL WORLDWIDE [36001]

LOGON ALL WORLDWIDE [36001]

LOGSDON PRE 1886 WAITSBURG, WA, USA [34064] : 1720-1750 BALTIMORE CO., MD, USA [38137] : PRE 1775 FREDERICK CO., VA & MD, USA [38314]

LOGUE PRE 1860 ALTNAGELVIN, LDY, IRL [35545] : 1798+ DRUMAHOE, LDY, IRL [35545] : C1863 DRY, IRL & AUS [34971]

LOHAN 1700S SILBER, SIL, GER [38623]

LOHMANN PRE 1900 BAV, GER [36339] : 1750-1900 WULFTEN, HAN, GER [37798] : C1786 WERTHEIM, BAW, GER [38626] : ALL USA [36339] : 1860-1920 PEORIA CO., IL, USA [37798]

LOHR PRE 1750 BRD [34180]

LOHRHEIM ALL WORLDWIDE [38613]

LOHRUM PRE 1900 BENDORF, RPF, GER [38663] : ALL WORLDWIDE [38613]

LOHSE 1830-1865 GROSENDORF, SHO, GER [37973]

LOISEL 1750-1890 LITTLE CORNARD, SFK, ENG [35775]

LOISIDIS 1870-1990 PHAPHOS, CYPRUS [34771]

LOIZIDIS 1870-1990 PHAPHOS, CYPRUS [34771]

LOKER 1700-1750 CHITTLEHAMPTON, DEV, ENG [37602] : C1800 INGRAVE, ESS, ENG [37918] : ALL NATICK, MA & MI, USA [38369]

LOLLBACH 1730+ KAFERTAL, BAD, GER & AUS [37132]

LOMAS 1840+ BOMBALA, NSW, AUS [36295] : 1860-1900 GREY CO., ONT, CAN [35277] : 1800+ LONDON, ENG [34256] : PRE 1750 STAMFORD, LIN, ENG [36295] : C1850-1890 STOCKPORT, CHS, ENG [36523] : C1800 LAN, ENG & AUS [35079]

LOMAX 1850+ PRESTON, LAN, ENG [33894] : 1880+ BATH, SOM, ENG [36521] : PRE 1794 BOLTON LE MOORS, LAN, ENG [36742] : 1700-1800 NEWCASTLE ON TYNE, NBL, ENG [37747] : C1800 WELLINGTON, NZ [35089]

LOMBARGE 1700-1750 LA ROCHELLE, POITOU, FRA [38523]

LONCIN 1795-1871 VELM, LBG, BEL [38158]

LONDON 1810+ RICHMOND & APPIN, NSW, AUS [36600] : 1650-1750 OXFORD, OXF, ENG [34552] : 1850+ ISLINGTON, LND, ENG [37620]

LONE PRE 1805 EAST HANNINGFIELD, ESS, ENG [34837]

LONERGAN 1800+ QUEANBEYAN, NSW, AUS [35562] : PRE 1882 WARWICK, QLD, AUS [36632]

LONEY PRE 1890 RICHHILL, ARM, IRL [36877]

LONG 1849+ LAUNCESTON, TAS, AUS [33880] : 1850S BAIRNSDALE, VIC, AUS [33934] : WILLIAM 1870 ADELAIDE, SA, AUS [35066] : PRE 1840 SYDNEY, NSW, AUS [35400] : 1830+ NSW & QLD, AUS [35854] : SAMUEL 1800-1880 DALBY & ROMA, QLD, AUS [36634] : RICHARD 1800S LENNOX & ADDINGTON, ONT, CAN [34392] : 1900+ MAN, CAN [37836] : 1900+ WIN, CAN [37836] : 1811+ WYMONDHAM, NFK, ENG [33880] : ALL WITNEY, OXF, ENG [34046] : 1850S CLERKENWELL, MDX, ENG [34187] : 1820-1845 PHILLEIGH, CON, ENG [34191] : PRE 1829 GWENNAP, CON, ENG [34279] : 1910 SPALDING, LIN, ENG [34565] : 1899 WISBECK, CAM, ENG [34565] : JOHN PRE 1855 HAGGERSTON, LND, ENG [34652] : C1781 DURSLEY & ULEY, GLS, ENG [35223] : 1820S DURNFORD, WIL, ENG [35243] : HANNAH C1810 BURBAGE, WIL, ENG [35346] : PRE 1795 KINGSTON DEVERILL, WIL, ENG [35517] : 1850+ BATH, SOM, ENG [35586] : 1720-1750 CRANWELL, LIN, ENG [35725] : 1790-1810 CRAINOCK, LIN, ENG [35725] : PRE 1791 ALLINGTON, DOR, ENG [35895] : MARY C1791 ALLINGTON, DOR, ENG [35895] : THOMAS PRE 1841 MAIDSTONE, KEN, ENG [36309] : PRE 1780 PRISTON, SOM, ENG [36526] : 1800+ ISLE SHEPPY, KEN, ENG [36662] : PRE 1715 LYDDEN, KEN, ENG [37069] : 1750-1850 BAKEWELL BUXTON, DBY, ENG [37255] : C1740 SUTTON BONNINGTON, NTT, ENG [37536] : 1600-1836 ACTON, SFK, ENG [37638] : 1750-1900 PAMBER, HAM, ENG [37651] : 1750-1800 CARLISLE, CUL, ENG [37654] : 1830+ SITTINGBOURNE, KEN, ENG [37677] : 1700+ ROPLEY & BEDHAMPTON, HAM, ENG [37836] : 1600-1900 EARLS COLNE, ESS, ENG [38579] : 1840S WOOLWICH, KEN, ENG & NZ [36803] : PRE 1830 FEENAGH, LIM, IRL [33766] : C1811 DUBLIN, IRL [35854] : ALL TIP, IRL [36030] : 1800-1850 BORRISAFERNEY, TIP, IRL

[36315] : PRE 1843 INVER, DON, IRL [38291] : 1750-1850 CARRICKFERGUS, ANT, IRL [38588] : 1818-1854 WHITEOAK TWP, HIGHLAND CO., OH, USA [33761] : 1780-1815 FAYETTE TWP, ALLEGHENEY CO., PA, USA [33761] : 1818-1871 CONCORD TWP, HIGHLAND CO., OH, USA [33761] : GEORGE 1788-1910 SOMERSET CO., PA, OH & IN, USA [36901] : WILLIAM PRE 1850 FAYETTE CO., OH, USA [37565] : 1850-1884 KEWEENAW CO., MI, USA [38009] : 1650+ RI, USA [38015] : PHILLIP 1820-1880 PORTAGE CO., OH, USA [38138] : ALL WOOD CO., OK, USA [38230] : JOHN M. 1828-1868 NC, USA [38732]

LONGBOTHAM PRE 1800 OTTLEY & FEWSTON, YKS, ENG [36247]

LONGBOTTOM PRE 1900 BRADFORD, WRY, ENG [33830] : 1650+ NRY, ENG [34181]

LONGBOURNE ALL WORLDWIDE [34341]

LONGBURN ALL WORLDWIDE [34341]

LONGDEN 1871+ PORTAGE, MAN, CAN [36704] : ALL CRANAGE, CHS, ENG [36704] : 1840+ NORBURY, CHS, ENG [36704] : 1850+ ST CROIX FALLS, WI, USA [36704] : ALL WORLDWIDE [36704]

LONGDON PRE 1830 LONDON, ENG [37107] : ALL WORLDWIDE [36704]

LONGEWAY ALL WORLDWIDE [38386]

LONGFORD 1800 CIRENCESTER, GLS, ENG [36155] : PRE 1870 DUBLIN, IRL [34733]

LONGHORN 1780-1900 HOLME ON SPALDING MOOR, ERY, ENG [37326] : 1726-1780 AIRMYN, WRY, ENG [37326]

LONGHORNE 1726-1780 AIRMYN, WRY, ENG [37326] : 1780-1900 HOLME ON SPALDING MOOR, ERY, ENG [37326]

LONGHOUSE (SEE LANGH [37435]

LONGHURST PRE 1800 RUDGWICK, SSX, ENG [33845] : PRE 1815 LEATHERHEAD, SRY, ENG [34314] : C1803 WEST GRINSTEAD, SSX, ENG [36071] : 1830+ SRY, ENG [36071] : C1800 WOTTON & OCKLEY, SRY, ENG [36215]

LONGLAND PRE 1850 CAM, ENG [36216]

LONGLEY C1820+ SHEFFIELD, WRY, ENG [34145] : PRE 1850 WAKEFIELD, WRY, ENG [36159] : PRE 1800 DETROIT, MI, USA [34252]

LONGMAN 1800+ ISLINGTON, LND, ENG [35951]

LONGMORE PRE 1895 NANDARRA, NSW, AUS [37174] : PRE 1700 UPPER ARLEY, STS, ENG [38420]

LONGMUIR C1840 GLASGOW, SCT [35034] : ALL FERN, ANS, SCT [35438] : 1700+ OLD MACHAR, KCD, SCT [36824]

LONGNECKER JULIA 1868 CORNELLA, IL, USA [38156] : JULIA 1889 WAYNE, NE, USA [38156] : C1800 CUMBERLAND CO., PA, USA [38367]

LONGRIG TYSON 1852+ NY, USA [34234]

LONGSTAFF 1819+ ONT, CAN [34982] : PRE 1819 BROUGH UNDER STAINMORE, WES, ENG [34982] : PRE 1819 KIRBY ST STEPHEN, WES, ENG [34982] : 1750+ NBL & DUR, ENG [36176] : 1800-1900 NEWCASTLE UPON TYNE, NBL, ENG [36176] : 1750+ SOULBY & KIRKBY STEPHEN, WES, ENG [36869]

LONGSTAFFE 1700 KIRKBY STEPHEN, WES, ENG [36151]

LONGSTREET 1750-1850 CAYUGA CO., IL, USA [36957]

LONGSTRETH 1790-1810 BEDFORD CO., PA, USA [38137]

LONGTHORNE 1750-1850 HARROGATE, YKS, ENG [36724]

LONGTON PRE 1840 LIVERPOOL, LAN, ENG [36849]

LONIE ATHOL 1967 LONDON, ENG [34499] : 1700-1850 FIF, SCT [34229] : PRE 1858 EDINBURGH, SCT [34626]

LONNERSTADTER 1700-1900 BAV, GER [38128]

LONNSTROM 1839+ KOTKA, KYMEN LAANI, FIN [38758]

LONSDALE JOSEPH C1850 LONDON, ENG [35049] : PRE 1800+ CHURCH & OSWALDTWISTLE, LAN, ENG [36955] : PRE 1732+ PADIHAM, LAN, ENG [36955] : C1850 ACCRINGTON, LAN, ENG [36955] : JOSEPH PRE 1836+ ENG & AUS [35064]

LOO 1881 HARA, JAMTLAND, SWE [38101] : 1837-1885 HADE, DALERNA, SWE [38101] : 1885-1928 DOUGLAS CO., MN, USA [38101]

LOOIJENSTIJN C1770 WASSENAAR, ZUH, NL [38698]

LOOKER 1700-1840 HAM, ENG [33998] : PRE 1870 WARRINGTON, LAN, ENG [35967] : PRE 1770 FARRINGDON, BRK, ENG [36072] : 1840 MAIDENHEAD, BKM, ENG [37388]

LOOMAN 1800 HELLENDOORN, OIJ, NL [35338]

LOOMES ALL NEW BILTON & RUGBY, WAR, ENG [34629]

LOOMIS 1620-1680 HADLEY, MA, USA [34395]

LOONE PRE 1850 BIRMINGHAM, WAR, ENG [35151]

LOONEY C1850+ BURNFORT, COR, IRL [35249] : PRE 1834 CORK, COR, IRL [35842] : PRE 1854 IOM, UK [35091] : ALL VA, TN, AR, CA, USA [38363]

LOOSE C1840 DOVERIDGE, DBY, ENG [35998] : 1700+ NFK, ENG [36863]

LOOSELY 1800S LONDON, ENG [36708]

LOOSEMORE C1796 CHITTLEHAMPTON, DEV, ENG [34563] : 1846+ NORTH MOLTON, DEV, ENG [35825] : 1750-1875 ATHRINGTON, DEV, ENG [38216]

LOOSER ALL BORBEC, BRD & DDR [38013]

LOPDELL PRE 1800 GORT, GAL, IRL [35521]

LOPER C1750-1850 PA & VA, USA [38242]

LOPPACHER 1700-1900 HERISAU, AAR, CH [35292]

LORAM PRE 1810 DEV, ENG [33999]

LORD 1830+ SHEFFIELD, TAS, AUS [36635] : PRE 1800 BACUP, LAN, ENG [33886] : 1819 BURNLEY, LAN, ENG [33942] : 1830-1910 BATH, SOM, ENG [34735] : 1870-1900 STAINES, MDX, ENG [34735] : 1830-1880 HOLBORN & HAMMERSMITH, MDX, ENG [34735] : 1675-1830 ULEY, GLS, ENG [34735] : JAMES C1800 WARDLE, LAN, ENG [35560] : 1600-1900S ST NEOT, CON, ENG [35776] : ALL ESS, ENG [36006] : PRE 1860 ACCRINGTON, LAN, ENG [36022] : PRE 1900 WAR, ENG [36508] : 1800S MANCHESTER, LAN, ENG [36635] : C1780 LANGFIELD, WRY, ENG [36635] : 1600-1800 BACUP, LAN, ENG [36635] : C1800+ ST NEOT & CLEER, CON, ENG [37434] : JOHN 1722-1850 CRAWSHAWBOOTH, LAN, ENG [37988] : PRE 1850 LITTLEHAM BY BIDEFORD, DEV, ENG [38205] : 1624+ ROCHDALE, LAN, ENG & AUS [37243] : PRE 1678 ANDOVER, MA, USA [38348] : WARD 1814-1860 SARATOGA CO., NY, USA [38734]

LORDING 1650-1900 LYDD, KEN, ENG [37326]

LORENSEN PRE 1870 RAPSTEEK, SHO, BRD [35330]

LORENZ CARL 1842 NEUSTADT, WUE, GER [38193] : LOHRENTZ ALL POM & WPR, GER [38687] : 1786 BARNTRUP, LIP, GER [38749]

LORENZINI 1900+ VIC, AUS [35136]

LOREY 1750-1850 GULVAL, CON, ENG [34535]

LORIMER ELIZ. A. 1851+ TORONTO, ONT, CAN [37825] : THOMAS C1830+ ULSTER, IRL [37825] : 1710-1740S KILRENNY & ANSTRUTHER EASTER, FIF, SCT [34359] : ELIZ. A. 1851+ ROCHESTER, NY, USA [37825]

LORING PRE 1800 BERMONDSEY, LND, ENG [34316] : 1800-1850 LONDON, ENG [34436]

LORNEY PRE 1800 PER, SCT [36327]

LORNIE PRE 1800 PER, SCT [36327]

LOROCQUE 1800-1950S QUE & NY, CAN & USA [34202]

LORRAWAY 1880+ ROCKHAMPTON, QLD, AUS [33893]

LORUM ALL WORLDWIDE [38613]

LORY PRE 1800 ST KEVERNE, CON, ENG [37913]

LOSCHKE 1800+ GROSSDORF, POS, GER [37170]

LOSCOMBE PRE 1860 BATH, SOM, ENG [35798]

LOSEBY 1802+ HARBY, LEI, ENG & AUS [36238]

LOSER 1855-1898 ADAMS CO., IL, USA [38101] : 1835-1855 FRANKLIN CO., OH, USA [38101]

LOSH CATHERINE C1770+ YORK CO., PA, USA [37604]

LOSSI PRE 1626 GENEVA, GE, CH [38348]

LOTCHO PRE 1840 LND, ENG [37655]

LOTH PRE 1849 BAD, GER [34977]

LOTT PRE 1890 BROOKLYN, NY, USA [38126]

LOTTIN ALL ZWEVEGEM, WVL, BEL [38164]

LOTZ CHRISTIAN 1840-1850 LIVERPOOL, LAN, ENG [38246]

LOUCH PRE 1750 SONNING, OXF & BRK, ENG [36099]

LOUCKS PRE 1800 LENNOX & ADDINGTON, RICHMOND, ONT, CAN [38428] : PRE 1850 ULSTER CO., NY, USA [36702] : 1800+ WESTMORELAND, PA, USA [36908]

LOUDEN 1930+ MT LAWLEY, WA, AUS [33782] : 1855+ ONT, CAN [37446] : 1800+ ARM, IRL [34408] : 1850S SHOTTS, LKS, SCT [34618]

LOUDENBERGER 1800-1890S CAMERON CO., PA, USA [38308] : 1800-1890S LUZERNE & NORTHAMPTON COS., PA, USA [38308] : ALL WORLDWIDE [38308]

LOUDENBURG 1800-1870S LUZERNE CO., PA, USA [38308]

LOUDENBURGHER ALL GER [38308]

LOUDERMILK 1750-1840 WASHINGTON CO., TN, USA [38009]

LOUDIN 1600-1790 DUNFERMLINE, FIF, SCT [36894]

LOUDON PRE 1850 FORRES, MOR, SCT [36761] : PRE 1855 PAISLEY, RFW, SCT [37446] : 1700+ CUMBERLAND CO., PA, USA [37004]

LOUGEE ALL WORLDWIDE [37236]

LOUGEVILLE C1830 WEX, IRL [34145]

LOUGH 1800+ WINCHESTER, ONT, CAN [36662] : PRE 1769 LESBURY, NBL, ENG [35026] : 1750 ABINGTON, PA, USA [36446]

LOUGHBOROUGH ALL DURHAM, DUR, ENG [36928]

LOUGHERY 1775+ PITTSBURGH, PA, USA [37462]

LOUGHLIN 1850+ SYDNEY, NSW, AUS & IRL [34913] : JOHN 1780+ MOUNTAIN, ONT, CAN & IRL [34514] : C1830 TRINCOMOLEE, CEYLON [34913] : PRE 1840 CASTLECONNELL, LIM, IRL [33775] : C1830 IRL [34913] : ALL IRL & ENG [35934]

LOUGHMAN 1750-1860 JOHNSTOWN, KIK, IRL [38045]

LOUGHREY 1750-1850 NY, USA [36552]

LOUGHRIDGE 1900+ PERTH, WA, AUS [35857] : ALL BALLYMENA, ANT, IRL [33923]

LOUIS CHARLES F. 1855+ GUNNEDAH, NSW, AUS [34973] : CHARLES F. 1840+ FRA [34973] : PRE 1856 PETERS WELL, GAL, IRL [35564]

LOUKS 1825 SUTTON TWP., QUE, CAN [36323] : 1830+ NORFOLK CO., ONT, CAN [36323] : 1790-1830 HIGHGATE, VT, USA [36323]

LOUSBEY 1851+ GOSBERTON & SPALDING, LIN, ENG [34528]

LOUTHAN ALL LONDON, ENG [36174]

LOUTTIT 1800+ LATHERON, CAI, SCT [34606] : PRE 1811 HARRAY, OKI, SCT [35021] : 1850+ DEERNESS, OKI, SCT [35106]

LOUTTITT 1820+ MUSSELBURGH, MLN, SCT & AUS [33926]

LOUVEISER PRE 1820 ENG [35946]

LOUX 1800+ WESTMORELAND, PA, USA [36908]

LOVABOND C1600-1900 SOM & DOR, ENG [37953]

LOVATT 1800S WESTBURY, TAS, AUS [34871] : 1763 STONE, STS, ENG [34011] : 1700-1800 NEWCASTLE UNDER LYME, STS, ENG [34871] : 1600-1800 DRAYCOTT IN THE MOORS, STS, ENG [36226] : C1800 SANDON, STS, ENG [36623] : ALL STS, SAL & WAR, ENG [38754]

LOVE 1791-1827 SYDNEY & APPIN, NSW, AUS [33934] : 1791+ NSW, AUS [35878] : JOSEPH 1793+ SYDNEY & PARRAMATTA, NSW, AUS [33934] : SAMUEL 1850+ HURON CO., ONT, CAN [34075] : 1500 AYNHO, SOM, ENG [34466] : PRE 1800 LONDON, ENG [34568] : 1800+ NFK, ENG [34710] : 1700+ CUL, ENG [35080] : PRE 1791 ENG [35878] : 1700-1750 ASH & STAPLE, KEN, ENG [37602] : PRE 1850 MERE, WIL, ENG [37914] : PRE 1870 COTSGROVE, NTT, ENG [38004] : 1850+ ENG [38481] : PRE 1841 ENNISCORTHY, WEX, IRL [35088] : C1860 DUNNALONG, TYR, IRL [35247] : PRE 1840 FER, IRL [35719] : PRE 1900 GLASGOW, LKS, SCT [34391] : 1861+ JOHNSTON, RFW, SCT [34926] : 1808 POLMONT, STI, SCT [35260] : PRE 1800 SCT [35910] : 1800S AIRDRIE, LKS, SCT [36032] : ALL USA [36567] : 1802-1820 HAYWOOD CO., NC, USA [38144] : ALL WORLDWIDE [35731]

LOVEBOND PRE 1700 SOM, DOR & IOW, ENG [37953]

LOVEBONDE PRE 1700 SOM, DOR & IOW, ENG [37953]

LOVEDAY 1860S NTH EDMUNDS, ENG [34793] : PRE 1836 ESS, ENG [35739] : C1835 LAMBETH, SRY, ENG [38268]

LOVEGROVE 1850-1950 CASSILIS & COOLAH, NSW, AUS [35422] : PRE 1946 ROSEVILLE, NSW, AUS [35521] : 1800S BRK, ENG [34102] : 1700-1800 MATTINGLEY & BRAMLEY, HAM, ENG [35422] : 1850+ BRK, ENG [36239] : PRE 1850 LONDON, ENG [37743] : ALL WORLDWIDE [36060]

LOVEGROWE ALL WORLDWIDE [36060]

LOVEJOY 1850-1900 EGHAM, SRY, ENG [34735] : ALL MAPLE DURHAM, OXF & BRK, ENG [36326] : 1500+ ENG [38498] : JAMES C1730-1755 BRK, BKM & OXF, ENG [38498]

LOVELACE BENJAMIN ALL FREDERICK CO., MD & KY, USA [35304]

LOVELAND PRE 1845 GUILDFORD, SRY, ENG [34719]

LOVELESS 1790+ USA & UK [36357]

LOVELL JOSEPH 1887+ SYDNEY, NSW, AUS [37155] : C1750-1800 MILLBROOK, BDF, ENG [33845] : PRE 1800 COMPTON MARTIN, SOM, ENG [33912] : 1760-1800 MELCOMBE REGIS, DOR, ENG [34337] : ELLEN 1918+ WEST KENSINGTON, LND, ENG [34484] : ELLEN C1930 HAMMERSMITH, SRY, ENG [34484] : PRE 1800 BRISTOL, GLS, ENG [34711] : 1802 ALDERBURY, WIL, ENG [35369] : PRE 1895 BRISTOL, GLS, ENG [36149] : C1830 KINGSCLERE, HAM, ENG [36215] : 1890-1899 BARNES & SHEPHERDSBUSH, MDX, ENG [36423] : 1700-1800 LONDON, MDX, ENG [36438] : PRE 1600 DOR, ENG [36679] : 1848-1875 AYLESBURY, BKM, ENG [36836] : 1750+ OLNEY,

BKM, ENG [36872] : 1640-1750 STEVENTON, HAM, ENG [38003] : 1840+ BLANDFORD FORUM, DOR, ENG [38204] : 1900+ CAPE, RSA [36423] : 1832 OKMULGEE, OK, USA [38012]

LOVELOCK 1800-1900 DRY PLAINS, NSW, AUS [36315] : 1700+ SHIPTON MOYNE, GLS, ENG [37328]

LOVERIDGE C1792+ WINDSOR, NSW, AUS [35537] : PRE 1860S SEATON & BEER, DEV, ENG [35544] : 1790S NORTON, GLS, ENG [36190]

LOVERING PRE 1690 BIDEFORD, DEV, ENG [34445]

LOVERSIDGE 1800+ HARWORTH, CAM, ENG [36772]

LOVETT 1700+ SUTTON COLDFIELD, WAR, ENG [34416] : 1793+ ILKETSHALL ST ANDREW, SFK, ENG [35824] : 1766+ TOPCROFT, NFK, ENG [35824] : 1750-1950 LONDON &, MDX, ENG [37344] : 1800S BARROW UPON SOAR, LEI, ENG [37497] : 1650+ USA [36347] : 1800-1900 FRANKLIN CO., NY, USA [37783]

LOVEY 1800+ WOOLWICH, KEN, ENG [33927]

LOVIBOND 1600+ IOW, ENG [37953] : C1600-1900 SOM, ENG [37953] : ALL WORLDWIDE [37953]

LOVICK ALL NORWICH, NFK, ENG [37629]

LOVYBOND C1600-1900 SOM & DOR, ENG [37953]

LOW C1810-1880 SOUTH HANNINGFIELD, ESS, ENG [37664] : 1800+ MITTELHEIM, HEN, GER [34693] : PRE 1850 GLASGOW, SCT [33992] : PRE 1800 MONTROSE, ANS, SCT [34041] : PRE 1760 BRECHIN, ANS, SCT [34053] : 1700-1830 MONTROSE, ANS, SCT [34753] : ALL BALMERINO, FIF, SCT [34758] : PRE 1780 AUCHTERDERRAN, FIF, SCT [34861] : PRE 1840 ABD, SCT [35055] : DAVID 1822 DUNDEE, ANS, SCT [35369] : ISABELLA 1817 CRUDEN, ABD, SCT [35369] : 1700+ BAN, SCT [35627] : 1750+ EDINBURGH, MLN, SCT [37572]

LOWBER 1670S-1880 KENT CO., DE, PA & NY, USA & NL [37529]

LOWBRIDGE 1700-1900 WALSALL, STS, ENG [36256]

LOWDEN 1820-1880S LIFF, LOCHEE & DUNDEE, ANS, SCT [34359]

LOWDON PRE 1728 CARLUKE, LKS, SCT [34501]

LOWE PRE 1850 ARMIDALE, NSW, AUS [34892] : 1930+ SYDNEY, NSW, AUS [34921] : 1816+ NSW, AUS [35241] : 1884+ CRESWICK & MELBOURNE, VIC, AUS [38277] : 1857+ BALLARAT & BARRYS REEF, VIC, AUS [38277] : RICHARD PRE 1856 BRK, ENG [34153] : PRE 1850 LEIGH, LAN, ENG [34370] : PRE 1841 STANDISH CHORLEY, LAN, ENG [34667] : PRE 1760 ST MARYS, NOTTINGHAM, NTT, ENG [34858] : THOMAS 1810 ASHLEY, CHS, ENG [35184] : PRE 1800 ASHLEY, CHS, ENG [35184] : 1750+ DBY, ENG [35241] : 1700 WIGAN, LAN, ENG [35288] : PRE 1860 LIVERPOOL, LAN, ENG [35423] : ALL WAR & WOR, ENG [36234] : PRE 1880 LAN, ENG [36363] : PRE 1849 SANDBACH, CHS, ENG [36403] : PRE 1830 SEDGLEY, STS, ENG [36518] : 1800 PRESTON, LAN, ENG [36745] : PRE 1850 WOODFORD, ESS, ENG [37097] : C1845 NOTTINGHAM, NTT, ENG [37148] : ALL NTT & DBY, ENG [37412] : C1780 KETTLESHULME, CHS, ENG [37697] : 1828-1856 WEARDALE, DUR, ENG [38277] : C1530 BISHOPS STORTFORD, HRT, ENG [38348] : 1903+ WESTPORT, BULLER, NZ [38277] : ALL GSY, CHI, UK [37730] : LOUISA 1885-1908 STOUTSVILLE, MO, USA [36322] : PRE 1840 MD, USA [38126] : PRE 1930 LLANDUDNO, CAE, WLS [34921]

LOWEN ALL ESS, ENG [37409]

LOWENKI ALL WORLDWIDE [35298]

LOWENSTEIN 1700+ BREIDENBACH, HES, GER [38578]

LOWER 1800S BENDIGO, VIC, AUS [35377] : ALL NEWHAVEN, SSX, ENG [35260] : 1840+ NEWHAVEN, SSX, ENG & NZ [36850]

LOWERRE GEORGE 1921+ KANSAS CITY, MO, USA [37526]

LOWERY PRE 1800 BYWELL ST PETER, NBL, ENG [37663] : 1850+ COVINGTON CO., MS, USA [37796] : PATSY 1830 KY, USA [38109] : C1740-1840 VA & TN, USA [38242]

LOWES PRE 1800 SUNDERLAND, DUR, ENG [36202] : C1800-1860 LONDON, MDX, ENG [38264] : ALL BALLYCLARE, ANT, IRL [38319]

LOWGROVE ALL WORLDWIDE [36060]

LOWGROW ALL WORLDWIDE [36060]

LOWING 1853+ PARKES, NSW, AUS [35207] : ALL ENG [34396] : PRE 1853 LONDON, MDX, ENG [35207]

LOWN 1800-1900 KINGS LYNN, NFK, ENG [34337]

LOWNDES CHARLOTTE 1896-1948 SYDNEY, NSW, AUS [37310] : 1840+ CANNOCK & PENKRIDGE, STS, ENG [35019] : 1830S MEA, IRL [35136]

LOWNDS 1847 TAMWORTH, STS, ENG [37594]

LOWNES 1840+ CANNOCK & PENKRIDGE, STS, ENG [35019]

LOWREY MARY 1880+ BURNIE, TAS, AUS [38729]

LOWRIE C1939 LANE COVE, NSW, AUS [35025] : 1860S MELBOURNE, VIC, AUS [35855] : 1850S PORT LINCOLN, SA, AUS [35855] : PRE 1800 ST MONANCE, FIF, SCT [35627] : 1840S PETERHEAD, ABD, SCT [35855] : 1848 KIRKLISTON, WLN, SCT [37165] : PRE 1860 GLASGOW, LKS, SCT [37179]

LOWRY PERCY ALL SYDNEY, NSW, AUS [35122] : LAURA ALL SYDNEY & MOUNT LARCOM, NSW & QLD, AUS [35122] : ALL LND, ENG [35096] : 1600-1900 CLERKENWELL, LND, ENG [35944] : PRE 1746 KEA, CON, ENG [37939] : 1850+ TULSK, ROS IRL [37560] : 1790+ ARL, SCT [35622] : 1850+ PITTSBURG, PA, USA [38413]

LOWSBY PRE 1880 MANCHESTER & SALFORD, LAN, ENG [34683]

LOWSLEY ALL WORLDWIDE [35130]

LOWSONE 1600-1800 FIF, SCT [35627]

LOWTHER PRE 1800 KILBURN, NRY, ENG [34588] : C1700-1920 GRESSINGHAM & BOLTON LE SANDS, LAN, ENG [36227] : 1830+ LIVERPOOL, LAN, ENG [36227] : 1700+ KIRBY LONSDALE, WES, ENG [36227] : PRE 1889 CARNFORTH, LAN, ENG [36227] : PRE 1730 BUCKS CO., PA, USA [35620]

LOWTON 1816+ WIGAN, LAN, ENG [37560] : PRE 1850 WORTHINGTON, LAN, ENG [38708]

LOXLEY ALL ENG [34730]

LOXSTON PRE 1843 NTH PETHERTON, SOM, ENG [34909]

LOXTON GIDEON 1753+ SOM, ENG [34065] : 1816-1825 EAST HARPTREE, SOM, ENG [34065] : 1880+ PRIDDY, SOM, ENG [35112] : PRE 1820 WELLS, SOM, ENG [35112]

LOYAL 1750-1900 ST HUBERT, BANAT, YU [37539]

LOYDE WILLIAM 1750-1822 MUCHELNEY & NEARBY, SOM, ENG [37905] : 1800+ MUCHELNEY, SOM, ENG [37905] : WILLIAM 1770-1820 MUCHELNEY, SOM, ENG [37905]

LOYEN PRE 1850 ATW, BEL [37385] : 1850-1920 DOUAI, NOR, FRA [37385]

LOYNS 1700-99 DUNCHURCH, WAR, ENG [34315]

LOYTERTON 1700+ ELY, CAM, ENG [34747]

LOZIER PRE 1850 DUBLIN, IRL [34877]

LOZO BUCKE PRE 1900 LUBANA GONEZ, GER [35339]

LUBCKE ALL MSW, GER [34488]

LUBECK 1870+ VIC, AUS [35841] : 1800S GOTEBORG, SWE [35841]

LUBERDA ALL POL [38769]

LUBEY 1835 COR, IRL [37605]

LUBIN ALL WORLDWIDE [36378]

LUBOMIRSKI 1800+ GESTFMAINS, PRE, GER [34932]

LUBRICH PRE 1789 NEUDAMM, BRA, GER [36954]

LUBY C1860 MITCHELSTOWN, COR, IRL [36599]

LUC 1740-1800 LES CEDRES & SOULANGES, QUE, CAN [34514]

LUCAS 1870+ BOMBALA, NSW, AUS [34977] : 1800+ SA, AUS [36756] : 1856-1900 GOONDIWINDI, QLD, AUS [37919] : 1840-1865 MINGAN, QUE, CAN [33994] : 1800+ ALLIANCE, ALB, CAN [36756] : ALL CAN [37427] : 1785+ LENNOX & ADDINGTON, ONT, CAN [38517] : 1680-1750 HASLEMERE, SRY, ENG [34004] : 1700-1900 BEWDLEY, WOR, ENG [34004] : 1550-1700 BURY ST EDMUNDS, SFK, ENG [34486] : 1780-1850 EAST GRINSTEAD, SSX, ENG [34697] : FRANK PRE 1890 BISHOPSTONE & WILTON, WIL, ENG [34779] : C1825 TROWBRIDGE, WIL, ENG [34999] : ALL STOKE CLIMSLAND, CON, ENG [35048] : 1844 BIRMINGHAM, WAR, ENG [35152] : PRE 1700 ESS, ENG [35642] : PRE 1780 LOSTWITHIEL, CON, ENG [35973] : 1700-1800 KETTERING, NTH, ENG [36057] : 1810 LONDON, ENG [36146] : ALL NTT, ENG [36174] : BART 1700-1800 DUNCHIDEOCK, DEV, ENG [36813] : PRE 1860 NTH, ENG [37291] : 1841 HARDINGTON MANDEVILLE, SOM, ENG [37378] : 1700-1900 PAGHAM, SSX, ENG [37964] : 1810S ORRELL, LAN, ENG [38283] : PRE 1700 KEN, ENG [38389] : PRE 1730 JUELICHERLAND, RPR, GER [38644] : PRE 1820 KIK & CAR, IRL [34376] : 1840+ MT LUCAS, PHILIPSTOWN, OFF, IRL [34486] : PRE 1800 CAR & KIK, IRL [37427] : PRE 1860 MOG, IRL [37443] : 1776-1830S LECROPT, STI & AYR, SCT [34635] : JANE C1795 SAYBROOK, CT & NY, USA [36319] : 1870S LICKING CO., OH, USA [38323] : 1709+ NJ, USA [38517] : 1750+ ALBANY, NY, USA [38517] : 1866+ CHICAGO, IL, USA [38644] : PRE 1810 RAD, WLS [35211] : 1700+ LLANGATTOCK NIGH USK, MON, WLS [36756]

LUCE 1640+ BRISTOL, GLS, ENG [33754] : PRE 1670 HORTON, GLS, ENG & WLS [38135] : 1640-1990 MA,VT,IA & CA, USA [33754]

LUCERNE 1920-1958 NEWCASTLE, NSW, AUS [34694]

LUCHFORD 1860+ STROOD, KEN, ENG [37405]

LUCIER PRE 1665 PARIS, FRA [37503]

LUCINI C1880 ALICE CASTELLO, VERCELLI, ITL [37691]

LUCK 1871 BEALIBA, VIC, AUS [35529] : 1750-1800 MANFIELD, NRY, ENG [34552] : 1800-1850 BORDEN, KEN, ENG [35857] : PRE 1770 LEI, ENG [36179] : 1826-1846 LIVERPOOL, LAN, ENG [37490] : PRE 1728 LUBENHAM, LEI, ENG [37706]

LUCKETT 1800+ BLOXHAM, OXF, ENG [35905] : 1780-1830 HAMMERSMITH, MDX, ENG [36150]

LUCKHURST HENRIETTA 1850 FAVERSHAM, KEN, ENG [36749] : PRE 1700 KEN, ENG [38389]

LUCKIE 1830S JEDBURGH, SEL, SCT [36843]

LUCKING PRE 1807 WRITTLE, ESS, ENG [35112] : 1750+ ESS, ENG [37885]

LUCKINGS C1830S MAITLAND, NSW, AUS [33794]

LUCOCK 1850+ DUDLEY, WOR, ENG [34782]

LUCOS 1590-1670 LIMOGES & D'AUREIL, LMS, FRA [34514]

LUCY 1794 STRATFORD ON AVON, WAR, ENG [35194] : PRE 1900 IRL [36933] : PRE 1890S KNOCKBUE, DRIMOLEAGUE, COR, IRL [37909]

LUDBROOK 1650 PEASENHALL, SFK, ENG [37928]

LUDBY 1807 SUTTON, SSX, ENG [37952]

LUDDINGTON 1750-1920 WOLLASTON & NORTHAMPTON, NTH & NSW, ENG & AUS [35422]

LUDECKE PRE 1875 HAGEN, NRW, BRD [35021]

LUDEKE 1700+ BREMEN, BRM, GER & BRD [35062]

LUDGATE ALL ENG [36430]

LUDINGTON 1820-1920 POPLAR, MDX & NSW, ENG & AUS [35422]

LUDLAM 1790+ NOTTINGHAM, NTT, ENG [36219]

LUDLOW 1869+ BALLARAT, VIC, AUS [37109] : PRE 1800 LONDON, ENG [34275] : 1700-1800 WIL, ENG [37645] : 1800-1850 HAM, ENG [37645] : 1700-1900 IFFLEY & ABINGDON, BRK, ENG [37877] : 1840+ KILLESHANDRA, CAV, IRL [37109] : 1800-1850 TOMPKINS CO., NY, USA [38153] : ALL WORLDWIDE [37645] : ALL WORLDWIDE [38533]

LUDTKE PRE 1875 HAGEN, NRW, BRD [35021] : C1815-1918 ZARNGLAFF, POM, GER & USA [38309]

LUDWAR ALL CHUMA, BOHEMIA, CS [37045]

LUDWICK 1650+ DORCHESTER, MD & DE, USA [37826]

LUDWIG PRE 1740 PA, USA [36937] : ALL WORLDWIDE [35945]

LUEDECKE PRE 1875 HAGEN, NRW, BRD [35021]

LUEDTKE 1841-1918 VALLEY CO., NE, TX & WI, USA & GER [38309]

LUEKE PRE 1856 MUENSTER, WEF, GER [37563]

LUERY PRE 1860 CRANBROOK, KEN, ENG [36017] : 1850-1925 TUNBRIDGE WELLS, SSX, ENG [36017]

LUETCHFORD PRE 1850 SEVENOAKS, KEN & LND, ENG [36396]

LUETTIC ALL WORLDWIDE [35136]

LUFF PRE 1900 TUMBALONG, NSW, AUS [33807] : PRE 1800 STEDHAM, SSX, ENG [34112] : PRE 1750 HIGH LITTLETON, SOM, ENG [34466] : 1760-1830 EASTBOURNE, SSX, ENG [34834] : ALL HRT & BDF, ENG [37738]

LUFFMAN 1870-1940 LONDON, ENG [34722] : 1820+ BRISTOL, ENG [34722] : 1830+ INDIA [34722]

LUGAR 1850+ STAWELL & MELBOURNE, VIC, AUS [35533] : PRE 1850 COLCHESTER, ESS, ENG [35533]

LUGG 1700-1900 BERE REGIS, DOR, ENG [34714] : ALL PENZANCE & MADRON, CON, ENG [34724] : 1780-1830 STROUD, GLS, ENG [37442]

LUGROVE ALL WORLDWIDE [36060]

LUHAN 1700S SILBER, SIL, GER [38623]

LUHNING ALL GER & AUS [35045]

LUITJES HUIBERTHA 1915 OOSTERGEST, NL [36782]

LUJA PRE 1856 KALLUNBORG, DEN [34633]

LUKE 1860-1900 ORANGE, NSW, AUS [34422] : 1795-1847 HANNOVER, BRD [37803] : JOHN & MARY 1837+ GWENNAP, CON, ENG [33819] : 1700-1750 ILLOGAN, CON, ENG [34697] : 1695 PORTSEA, HAM, ENG [34836] : 1800+ DUR, ENG [34846] : ALL EASINGTON, DUR, ENG [36407] : 1830-1870 ST BREOCK, CON, ENG [36422] : 1770+ KINCARDINE BY DOUNE, PER, SCT [34650]

LUKEN 1625 ESS, ENG [36358]

LUKENS 1800S MONROE CO., OH, USA [38531]

LUKER PRE 1850 FARINGDON, BRK, ENG [35554] : PRE 1770 FARRINGTON, BRK, ENG [36072] : 1750-1810 SUNNINGWELL, BRK, ENG [37602]

LUKEY ALL WORLDWIDE [34258]

LULAND 1820+ REDFERN, NSW & MDX, AUS & ENG [38204]

LULHAM 1828+ BROOKFIELD, NSW, AUS [35157] : 1757 KINGSTON UPON THAMES, SRY, ENG [35157]

LULMANS C1650 BREMEN, BRM, GER [37819]

LUMB 1712+ BARKISLAND, WRY, ENG [35815]

LUMBARD 1650-1750 SOM, ENG [37233] : 1800+ MA, USA [35629]

LUMBIES PRE 1900 BEDFORD, BDF, ENG [36473]

LUMBIS ALL BEDFORD & GOLDINGTON, BDF, ENG [36473] : ALL SANDY & RENHOLD, BDF, ENG [36473] : ALL HERTFORD, HRT, ENG [36473] : ALL NOTTINGHAM, NTT, ENG [36473] : ALL WORLDWIDE [36473]

LUMBY EVA 1860-1910 TRANMERE, CHS, ENG [38259]

LUMLEY PRE 1860 HULL, ERY, ENG [34380] : GEORGE 1840S REDRUTH, CON, ENG [35593]

LUMM 1630-1700 FARMINGTON, CT, USA [37783]

LUMMIS ALL LONDON, ENG [37285]

LUMSDEN 1830+ KANGAROO VALLEY & BELLINGEN, NSW, AUS [35735] : C1866 BURNSIDE SCOONIE, FIF, SCT [35457] : 1750-1990 DYSART, FIF, SCT [36394] : PRE 1800 PITTENWEEM, FIF, SCT [37693]

LUN 1700+ HAWICK, ROX, SCT [35038]

LUNA PRE 1850 SAN JOSE, BATANGAS, PHILIPPINE [34891]

LUNAN 1850+ HUNTINGDON, QUE, CAN [36272] : ALL FORFAR, ANS, SCT [37684]

LUND PRE 1835 BEVERLEY, ERY, ENG [34358] : C1836 LONDON, ENG [35350] : 1800S KEIGHLEY, YKS, ENG [35734] : 1720-1860 NORDLAND, NOR [35317]

LUNDBERG ERIK 1829 HAMRANGE, GASTRIKLAND, SWE [38556]

LUNDIE PRE 1850 MOG, IRL & RSA [38772] : 1850S LEITH, MLN, SCT [35260] : PRE 1860 ARBROATH, ANS, SCT [36963] : PRE 1773 ARBIRLOT, ANS, SCT [37442]

LUNDWALL 1650-1750 DALBY & LUND, MAL, SWE [36320]

LUNDY 1600+ AXMINSTER, DEV, ENG [34408]

LUNHAM 1860+ PALMERSTON, OTAGO, NZ [34666] : 1840+ CHIRNSIDE, BEW, SCT [34666]

LUNN 1780-1880 YKS, ENG [35600] : PRE 1850 CHELMSFORD, ESS, ENG [36154] : 1800-1991 ENG [36430] : 1700+ CLEEVE & DEFFORD, WOR, ENG [36462] : 1800+ IDLESTOP, LIN, ENG [37050] : 1800 FINCHAMPSTEAD, BRK, ENG [37170] : PRE 1810 HOBKIRK, ROX, SCT [35430]

LURAAS 1600+ TINN, TELEMARK, NOR [36905]

LURRINGS 1700 HADLEIGH, ESS, ENG [37928]

LUSCHER ALL AG, CH [36941]

LUSCOMBE WILLIAM 1850S+ MELBOURNE, VIC, AUS [35876]

LUSH 1763+ ENG [36312] : PRE 1700 DONHEAD, WIL, ENG [36478] : ESAU 1740 BOWERCHALKE,

WIL, ENG [38489] : 1700 BROADCHALKE, WIL, ENG [38489]

LUSHER 1887 PUTNEY, SRY, ENG [35720]

LUSK ALL SCT [37621] : 1790+ SALEM, NY, USA [38572] : PRE 1830 MS, USA [38783]

LUSKEY 1650-1700 NORTH HILL, CON, ENG [34793] : PRE 1700 NORTH HILL, CON, ENG [35973]

LUSSENHOP ALBERT 1898-1961 MORTON, MN & KS, USA [38124]

LUSTED PRE 1800 SSX, ENG [36501] : 1700+ NINFIELD, SSX, ENG [37328]

LUSTY 1780+ KINGSTANLEY, GLS, ENG [36865] : C1820-1870 CHELTENHAM, GLS, ENG [37249] : 1840+ NELSON, NZ [35058]

LUT C1650 AKEN, FRG [38698]

LUTERBACHER PRE 1850 STEINHOF, SO, CH [38747]

LUTH 1910 CHARLEVOIX CO., MI, USA [38062]

LUTHER JOHN 1763-1784 HOUSE OF COMMONS LONDON, ENG [37683] : JOHN 1739 ONGAR, ESS, ENG [37683] : CHARLOTTE 1735 ONGAR, ESS, ENG [37683] : JAMES 1594 CORFE CASTLE, DOR, ENG [37683] : JOHN 1786 PETWORTH, SSX, ENG [37683] : RICHARD 1700 ONGAR, ESS, ENG [37683] : 1820-60 WATERFORD, WAT, IRL [33846] : JOHN 1635 ON BOARD SHIP HOPEWELL, UK & USA [37683] : 1790-1860 WESTERN NY, NY & PA, USA [33760] : ALL LIVINGSTON CO., NY, USA [38222] : ALL WORLDWIDE [37683]

LUTKENS C1706 HAMBURG, HBG, GER [35990]

LUTLEY C1787 BICKENHALL, SOM, ENG [34195]

LUTMAN 1750-1880 FULHAM, WESTMINSTER, MDX, ENG [37756]

LUTON HENRY 1902+ SOUTH GUNDAGAI, NSW, AUS [34885]

LUTTERLOH 1930+ WA, USA [38323]

LUTTIC ALL WORLDWIDE [35136]

LUTTICK ALL WORLDWIDE [35136]

LUTTON PRE 1700 KNAPTON, YKS, ENG [35897] : PRE 1850 ANT, ARM & DON, IRL [35897]

LUTTRELL 1830+ TUAM, GAL, IRL & CAN [37070] : ALL NC, SC & TN, USA [38739]

LUTYENS 1740+ LONDON, ENG [35990]

LUTZ 1800S WOOLWICH, LND, ENG [35377] : 1750+ MAINE, FRA [34408] : 1600 SCHWAIGERN, WUE, GER [38574] : PRE 1800 ODENHEIM, BAW, GER [38609] : ALL HU & YU [35606] : PRE 1895 ZYRARDO, POL [34519] : 1725-1800 BERKS CO., PA, USA [35318] : PRE 1900 DALLES, IN & OR, USA [36899] : 1815-1990 LANCASTER, PA, USA [37022] : ALL WORLDWIDE [38308]

LUURMAN 1777 SOEST, UTR, NL [38716]

LUXFORD C1900+ BATHURST, NSW, AUS [38510] : 1780S WISBOROUGH GREEN, SSX, ENG [33899] : 1814+ HORSHAM, SSX, ENG [33899]

LUXON 1800+ ST AUSTELL, CON, ENG [37443] : PRE 1810 TALLAND, CON, ENG [38049]

LUXON (SEE LUXSON) [35866]

LUXSON PRE 1750 DEV, ENG [35866]

LUXTON 1800+ BLACK TORRINGTON, DEV, ENG [37092]

LUYA ALL LIVERPOOL, LAN & LND, ENG [34686]

LYAL 1700+ GAMRIE, BAN, SCT [35627]

LYALL PRE 1800 MONTROSE, ANS, SCT [34028] : C1750-1800 PER, SCT [36327] : 1800S EDZELL, SCT [37474]

LYDALL 1800S SWANNINGTON, LEI, ENG [36511]

LYDFORD 1750-1850 WINCANTON, SOM, ENG [37765]

LYDON PETER PRE 1860 CONNEMARA, GAL, IRL [35077]

LYE PRE 1900 DUNKERTON, SOM, ENG [37322]

LYELL PRE 1802 MAUCHLINE, AYR, SCT [34339]

LYERS PRE 1744 LANLIVERY, CON, ENG [35973]

LYFORD C1800 BRK, ENG [37715] : ALL WORLDWIDE [37691]

LYLE 1850+ GREY CO., ONT, CAN [34485] : 1929+ ALB, CAN [34485] : ALL TWEEDMOUTH, NBL, ENG [36878] : 1800S BANBRIDGE, DOW, IRL [35968] : JOHN 1800 RFW, SCT [37025] : 1870+ HANNAH, ND, USA [34485]

LYMAN PRE 1850 PHILADELPHIA, PA, USA [33804]

LYMBERY 1700+ WATERFORD, IRL [38001]

LYMBURNER 1765+ QUE, CAN [34129] : ALL AYR, SCT [34129] : 1600-1900S KILMARNOCK, AYR, SCT [35327]

LYMN (SEE LIMB) [36018]

LYN 1850+ KRICHILSK, WN, POL & SU [34087]

LYNAM 1830+ SYDNEY & CONDOBOLIN, NSW, AUS [35533] : 1830+ TARLO & NARROMINE, NSW, AUS [35533] : PRE 1830 THOMAS TOWN, KIK, IRL [35533] : PRE 1930 NEW BEDFORD, MA, USA [37223]

LYNARD PRE 1800 DITTISHAM, DEV, ENG [33998]

LYNAS PRE 1850 YKS, ENG [36481]

LYNCH ALL MUDGEE & TARLO GAP, NSW, AUS [33765] : 1870+ SOUTH COAST, NSW, AUS [34425] : 1800+ BALLARAT, VIC, AUS [36830] : WILLIAM 1833+ HOBART, TAS, AUS [37954] : BRIDGET 1850 COCKFIGHTERS CREEK, NSW, AUS [38500] : BRIDGET 1850-88 COONAMBLE, NSW, AUS [38500] : 1838+ WOLLOMBI, NSW, AUS [38592] : 1837+ RIMOUSKI, QUE, CAN [34368] : 1850+ LINCOLN CO., ONT, CAN [36710] : PRE 1854 HORSLEY DOWN, LND, ENG [34277] : PRE 1831 STALISFIELD, KEN, ENG [35223] : 1800+ BICKERSTAFFE, LAN, ENG [37968] : PRE 1865 LIMERICK, LIM, IRL [33805] : 1800S CARNAMOYLE, LDY, IRL [33880] : 1820S TIP, IRL [33934] : 1840S ASKEATON, LIM, IRL [33967] : JAMES 1840-1895 MOUNT NUGENT, CAV, IRL [34165] : PRE 1830 CAV, IRL [34368] : 1800-1860S TULLA, CLA, IRL [34431] : 1700-1775 DUBLIN, IRL [34707] : PRE 1850 MIDDLETON, COR, IRL [35519] : PRE 1836+ LOCHAIT, CLA, IRL [35759] : 1800-1900 KILLARNEY, KER, IRL [36565] : 1850-1870 O'BRIENS BRIDGE, CLA, IRL [38007] : 1850-1870 KILLALOE, CLA, IRL [38007] : 1800-1850 KILKEE, CLA, IRL [38045] : MARGARET 1880S ARDEE, LOU, IRL [38233] : PRE 1790 KIK, IRL [38460] : PRE 1875 FALKIRK, STI, SCT [37308] : PRE 1800 MONMOUTH CO., NJ, USA [36702]

LYNDALL ALL WORLDWIDE [38383]

LYNDE PRE 1750 MALDEN & LEICESTER, CT, USA [33905]

LYNDON 1870+ BENALLA & BEECHWORTH, VIC, AUS [33896] : LUCY 1700-1800 WAR, ENG [33952]

LYNDS 1750-1850 MEOPHAM, KEN, ENG [34911]

LYNEHAM ALL AUS [33887] : 1870+ SYDNEY & CONDOBOLIN, NSW, AUS [35533] : 1800+ LIDLINGTON, BDF, ENG [33887]

LYNESS C1850 DRUMGOR & SEAGOE, ARM, IRL [36259]

LYNN 1860S BALLARAT, VIC, AUS [34793] : 1912 MOREE, NSW, AUS [36312] : 1850+ BALLARAT, VIC, AUS [34366] : 1820S MONTREAL, QUE, CAN [34793] : 1800S ROUGHAM, NFK, ENG [36665] : 1790S FETHARD, WEX, IRL [36366] : C1825 PHILADELPHIA, PA & KS, USA [34126]

LYNST ALL CORNWALL, ONT, CAN & IRL [37503]

LYON 1800S FRONTENAC, ONT, CAN [34353] : 1600+ YKS, ENG [34408] : 1800+ MANCHESTER, LAN, ENG [35586] : PRE 1800 ESS, ENG [36019] : ALL STS, ENG [37400] : ALL WALSALL, STS, ENG [37400] : 1870-1912 RUGBY, WAR, ENG [37400] : PRE 1815 RAINFORD, LAN, ENG [37573] : 1903-1906 AHMEDABAD, GUJURAT, INDIA [37400] : 1870+ NZ [37400] : 1895-1903 QUETTA, PAKISTAN [37400] : PRE 1775 BANCHORY DEVENICK, KCD, SCT [34613] : ALEXANDER 1800+ GLASGOW, LKS, SCT [35377]

LYONS 1838+ SUTTON FOREST, NSW, AUS [34534] : 1935+ FAIRFIELD & PRESTON, VIC, AUS [34702] : EDMOND 1850+ PYRMONT, NSW, AUS [35104] : 1860+ MELBOURNE, VIC, AUS [35190] : 1870+ BERRIMA, NSW, AUS [35567] : 1834+ GUILDFORD & SWAN, WA, AUS [35772] : MARY ARNOT 1890+ RENMARK, SA, AUS [36295] : 1800+ FREDERICTON, NB, CAN [34138] : ALL NFK, ENG [34758] : C1860 SPALDING, KEN, ENG [34935] : 1850+ LND, ENG [35390] : 1880 MANCHESTER, LAN, ENG [36032] : 1800 LONDON, ENG [36146] : ALL NFK, SFK & SSX, ENG [37078] : 1800+ GALWAY, GAL, IRL [34684] : DENIS PRE 1840 OFF, IRL [34800] : PRE 1868 CLA, IRL [35746] : 1700-1850 RHODE, OFF, IRL [37228] : C1830 KINSALE & NOHOVAL, COR, IRL [37908] : 1863+ CAV, IRL [38212] : JAMES 1800-1815 TUAM, GAL, IRL [38780]

LYS PRE 1947 YORKTON, SAS, CAN [38438]

LYSAGHT 1800+ TIPPERARY, TIP, IRL [33996] : PRE 1841 TIP, IRL [35185]

LYSTER C1880+ ORANGE, NSW, AUS [38510] : PRE 1800 BROSELEY, SAL, ENG [37389] : 1730 MOUNTMELLICK, MOG, IRL [36667]

LYTHGOE 1816-1875 LEIGH & CULCHETH, LAN, ENG [34352] : PRE 1880 BRADFORD, YKS, ENG [36508] : C1876+ PONTIFRACT, YKS, ENG [37888]

LYTHGOW 1870S WIRRAL, CHS, ENG [35848]

LYTLE 1760-1774 ORANGE CO., NC, USA [38118] : 1749-1760 LANCASTER CO., PA, USA [38118]

LYTLE (SEE LITTLE) [34493]

LYTTLE 1837+ SYDNEY, NSW, AUS [34979] : 1800S TYR, IRL [34979]

LYTTLETON C1870 ADELADIE, SA, AUS [35066]

MAAS C1700-1770 LEMBERG, RPR, GER [38316]

MAASS C1700-1770 LEMBERG, RPR, GER [38316] : PRE 1850 MANZELEN, RHEINLAND, GER & NL [35890]

MAASZ C1700-1770 LEMBERG, RPR, GER [38316]

MAATZ ALL GER [38664]

MABBERLY 1830+ BRISBANE WATER, NSW, AUS [36648]

MABBOTT C1850 MAITLAND, NSW, AUS [35090] : PRE 1810 MALDEN & RIDGEMOUNT, BDF, ENG [33846]

MABBUTT 1700-1850 CHESTERTON, CAM, ENG [37756] : 1840-1950 FULHAM, LND, ENG [37756]

MABEN (SEE MABON) [34126]

MABERLY 1830+ BATHURST, NSW, AUS [36648] : 1830+ BRISBANE WATER, NSW, AUS [36648] : 1800S LAMBOURNE, BRK, ENG [36648] : 1800+ BRENTFORD, MDX, ENG [36885] : PRE 1830 EAST GARSTON, BRK, ENG [38596]

MABEY 1845+ WEYMOUTH, DOR, ENG [33920] : PRE 1802 MYTHE, DOR, ENG [35976] : PRE 1810 SIDBURY, DEV, ENG [35976]

MABIE 1500-1600 BRA, FRA [36943]

MABLEY 1600+ WAVENDON, BKM, ENG [38241]

MABON HELEN 1777 BEW, SCT [34126] : JANE 1800S ABD & KCD, SCT [37476]

MADAN ALL WORLDWIDE [38754]

MADDAFORD WILLIAM 1880-1925 WOOLLOONGABBA & BRISBANE, QLD, AUS [34662] : WILLIAM 1861-1925 PLYMOUTH, DEV, ENG [34662]

MC and MAC (see page 366)

MADDEN 1820+ CAMPBELLTOWN & YOUNG, NSW, AUS [33763] : 1850 RICHMOND, VIC, AUS [34025] : 1858 SYDNEY, NSW, AUS [35753] : 1850+ HEATHCOTE AREA, VIC, AUS [35793] : 1850+ SYDNEY, NSW, AUS [35843] : ALL YOUNG, NSW, AUS [35843] : MARGARET 1841+ SINGLETON, NSW, AUS [35852] : JOSEPH 1843 FLINT & EXETER FM, LUDDENHAM, NSW, AUS & WLS [36311] : 1875+ YORK CO., ONT, CAN [34129] : ALL RICHMOND & KINGSTON, SRY, ENG [36043] : PRE 1820 GAL, IRL [33763] : 1800S CASTLECONNELL, LIM, IRL [35843] : ALL WAT, IRL [36043] : 1800-1840 CORK CITY, COR, IRL [37843] : ALL WORLDWIDE [38754]

MADDER 1700-1850 NFK, ENG [36873]

MADDERN 1600-1900 SENNEN & ST BURYAN, CON, ENG [37680]

MADDICK C1840 BROADHEMPSTON, DEV, ENG [35807] : PRE 1833 DEV, ENG [37180]

MADDING ALL WORLDWIDE [38754]

MADDISON 1918+ NEWCASTLE, NSW, AUS [33800] : 1850+ LONDON, ENG [36070] : 1600-1900 LIN, ENG [36070] : WILLIAM PRE 1858 TANFIELD, DUR, ENG [36164]

MADDOCK RACHEL 1840-1890 ALB & SAS, CAN [37878] : 1770-1870 PLYMOUTH & SHAUGHPRIOR, DEV, ENG [36214] : 1800+ ELTON AREA, CHS, ENG [36997] : BETSY 1830+ OVER & NORTHWICH, CHS, ENG [37546]

MADDOCKS 1600-1850 WEM & OSWESTRY, SAL, ENG [34411] : ALL STS & SAL, ENG [36062]

MADDOX 1863+ HARTLEY, NSW, AUS [35105] : PRE 1840+ SYDNEY, NSW, AUS [35105] : ALL STS & SAL, ENG [36062] : 1700-1920 NESTON, CHS, ENG [36983] : 1750+ STOKE DAMEREL, DEV, ENG [37735] : PRE 1840 IL, USA [36947] : 1850+ MO, USA [36947] : PRE 1830 TN, USA [36947] : 1890+ LAMAR CO., TX, USA [36947]

MADEJA ALL CRACOW, POL [38769]

MADELEY PRE 1920 PONTESBURY, SAL, ENG [35055]

MADEN PRE 1800 BACUP, LAN, ENG [33886] : ALL WORLDWIDE [38754]

MADGWICK 1849+ VIC & NSW, AUS [35222] : ALL SRY & HAM, ENG [35222] : 1700+ SRY & SSX, ENG [38323]

MADIGAN 1848 SHANAGOLDEN, LIM, IRL [36640]

MADILL 1800S MONAGHAN, MOG, IRL [38272] : PRE 1830 IRL [38736]

MADIN 1850-1890 NOTTINGHAM, NTT, ENG [34735] : ALL WORLDWIDE [38754]

MADISON C1700 KING & QUEEN CO., VA, USA [36354] : 1830-1850 MS, USA [38576] : PRE 1830 NC, USA [38576]

MADLANGBAYAN PRE 1850 BATANGAS, BATANGAS, PHILIPPINE [34891]

MADOX 1863+ HASSANS WALLS, NSW, AUS [35105]

MADSEN ALL SOMMERSTED, DEN [34308] : 1850-1870S JEGINDA & LEMVIG, SJELLAND, DEN [36285] : PRE 1836 ODENSE, DEN [36604] : PRE 1876 DEN [36878]

MAEER 1913 TOTTENHAM, LND, ENG [36781]

MAEERS PRE 1852 LONDON & BUDLEIGH, SRY & DEV, ENG [37452]

MAEGLI ALL FRA [38625] : ALL GER [38625] : 1750+ USA [38625]

MAEHRLE PRE 1900 NOERDLINGEN, BAY, BRD [36963]

MAENNEL 1900+ STRASBOURG, ALS, FRA [38644] : PRE 1730 LOBENSTEIN, THU, GER [38644]

MAENNER PRE 1700 KIRCHBERG, WUE, GER [38683]

MAERIER PRE 1613 HOTTINGEN, ZH, CH [36954]

MAERKSCH 1800-1850 ZIEBINGEN, BRA, GER [38599]

MAETZE 1860+ SA, AUS [36611]

MAEYENS 1595-1990 KNESSELANE, OVL, BEL [38165]

MAFFENGEL ALL GER [38610]

MAFFIN 1650-1900 NORTHEAST, ESS, ENG [37042]

MAGAA C1840 LARRAS LAKE, NSW, AUS [33930]

MAGAN C1840 LARRAS LAKE, NSW, AUS [33930]

MAGANTE PRE 1874 MARAGONDON, CAVITE, PHILIPPINE [34891]

MAGAREY PRE 1880 ANT, IRL [37987]

MAGEE C1840 LARRAS LAKE, NSW, AUS [33930] : ROSEANNE C1870 CARCOAR, NSW, AUS [35104] : PRE 1835 ENNISKILLEN, FER, IRL [34043] : ROSEANNE 1840+ CLOGHANEELY, DON, IRL [35104] : 1830+ DON, IRL [35975] : PRE 1935 EAST BELFAST, ANT, IRL [37745] : MARGARET C1909 NORTH WILLIAM ST PARISH, DUB, IRL [38302] : MARGARET C1909 NORTHWALL, DUB, IRL [38302] : ROBERT H. C1898 TEMPLEMICHAEL PARISH, LOG, IRL [38302] : PRE 1850 DOW, IRL [38391] : 1840 EDINBURGH, SCT [36579] : 1851+ WHIPPANY, NJ, USA [36572]

MAGENNIS 1842 KINGS PLAINS, NSW, AUS [34038] : C1800 BALLYOONAN, LOU, IRL [34296]

MAGER C1800 NETHERBURY, DOR, ENG [38272] : PRE 1800 SEEBACH, RPF, GER [38681]

MAGGS PRE 1950 SOUTHALL, MDX, ENG [33997] : PRE 1850 HOLCOMBE, SOM, ENG [34314] : 1852 CLUTTON, SOM, ENG [34878] : 1850+ MILE END OLD TOWN, MDX, ENG [37088] : 1700+ MERE & ZEALS, WIL, ENG [37088]

MAGICK 1855+ COBBORAH, NSW, AUS [35527]

MAGILL 1790 DRY, IRL [38522] : 1800-1847 BELFAST, ANT & DOW, IRL & CAN [34244]

MAGIN PRE 1840 GATESHEAD, TYNE & WEAR, ENG [36028]

MAGINNES PRE 1900 LEEDS, WRY, ENG [36228]

MAGINNIS 1650+ DELAWARE, PA, USA [37826]

MAGLADDERY 1800+ BELFAST, ARM, IRL [36369]

MAGLI ALL FRA [38625] : ALL GER [38625] : 1750+ USA [38625]

MAGLON 1813 ST MARTINS IN THE FIELD, MDX, ENG [38078]

MAGNAN 1650-1730 QUE, CAN [36703]

MAGNANI 1800+ ITL [35762]

MAGNER 1700+ COR, IRL [38299]

MAGNOSAPA PRE 1830 CASALBORDINO, CHIETI, ITL [34127]

MAGNUSKI 1800-1870 KALISZ, KL, POL [37615]

MAGNUSON ALBREKT 1900-1930 MIAMI, FL, USA & SWE [38564]

MAGOR ALL MELBOURNE, VIC, AUS [35087] : 1400+ ST KEA, CON, ENG [33989]

MAGRATH 1840+ BAGENALSTOWN, CAR, IRL [34237] : UNITY 1750+ KERRY, CLA, IRL [34970] : PRE 1852 BALLYCASTLE & DUBLIN, IRL [35077]

MAGREGOR 1700-1900 PER, SCT [35179]

MAGRUDER PRE 1650 SCT [37587] : PRE 1715 MD, USA [37587]

MAGSON 1865 YKS, ENG [37493] : 1800-1890 MANCHESTER & PRESTON, LAN, ENG [38251]

MAGUE C1805 BISLEY, GLS, ENG [36649]

MAGUIRE PRE 1855 WINDSOR, NSW, AUS [35236] : 1870 ORBOST, VIC, AUS [35755] : 1860 GISBORNE, VIC, AUS [35755] : WILLIAM 1880+ BRUNSWICK, VIC, AUS [35792] : 1844+ HOBART, TAS, AUS [37954] : PETER 1840+ NORTHUMBERLAND CO.,

ONT, CAN [38410] : 1800 + LIVERPOOL, ENG [33825] : PRE 1844 WALTHAM ABBEY, ESS, ENG [37954] : THOMAS 1800S NEWRY, ARM, IRL [34499] : C1760 PETTIGO, FER, IRL [34672] : PRE 1800 MONAGHAN, MOG, IRL [35095] : JAMES 1822-1900 ENNISKILLEN, FER, IRL [35172] : 1800-1850 DUB, IRL [35402] : PRE 1863 FLORENCE COURT, FER, IRL [35792] : MARY PRE 1863 FER, IRL [36855] : ALL SHILLELAGH, WIC, IRL [38300]

MAHADY 1800-1860 MULLINGAR, WEM, IRL [35732] : 1800-1860 GRANARD & LONGFORD, LOG, IRL [35732] : 1800-1860 ROSCOMMON, ROS, IRL [35732] : 1800-1860 BALLINA, MAY, IRL [35732]

MAHAFFEY ALL IPSWICH, QLD, AUS [36616] : PRE 1850 LOUGHBRICKLAND, DOW, IRL [33939]

MAHAN PRE 1775 VA, USA [37570]

MAHAR PRE 1900 NFD & NS, CAN [38391]

MAHEDY 1800-1860 ROSCOMMON, ROS, IRL [35732] : 1800-1860 BALLINA, MAY, IRL [35732] : 1800-1860 MULLINGAR, WEM, IRL [35732] : 1800-1860 GRANARD & LONGFORD, LOG, IRL [35732]

MAHER 1850 + WOLLOMBI, NSW, AUS [33963] : PRE 1850 YARRAWONGA, VIC, AUS [34170] : C1870 BALLARAT, VIC, AUS [35895] : ROSE MARIE 1893 LARGS, NSW, AUS [36633] : 1870S BARMEDMAN, NSW, AUS [37309] : PRE 1866 CAR, IRL [33822] : PRE 1850 THURLES, TIP, IRL [34013] : PRE 1865 TEMPLEMORE, TIP, IRL [34022] : 1840 + BAGENALSTOWN, CAR, IRL [34237] : PRE 1850 BORRISOLEIGH, TIP, IRL [35050] : PRE 1870 TIP, IRL [35895] : 1817-1837 TIP, IRL [36281] : PRE 1886 VALENTIA ISL., KER, IRL [37537] : PRE 1860 THURLES, TIP, IRL [37537]

MAHLER PRE 1865 BEHIM, SHO, BRD [37012]

MAHLSTEDT PRE 1870 WILSTER, SHO, GER [34431]

MAHNCKE 1860 + USA [36974]

MAHNKE C1885-1900 MELBOURNE, VIC, AUS [33971] : C1860-1880S ROTHENBURG, BAV, GER [33971]

MAHODY 1800-1860 ROSCOMMON, ROS, IRL [35732] : 1800-1860 MULLINGAR, WEM, IRL [35732] : 1800-1860 BALLINA, MAY, IRL [35732]

MAHON 1945 + SA, AUS [35771] : CATHERINE 1837-1914 RICHMOND & PENRITH, NSW, AUS [36643] : 1890S BRADFORD, WRY, ENG [34827] : 1800 + MOHILL, CAV, IRL [34574] : PRE 1870 BALLYMACWARD, ANT, IRL [34797] : EDWARD PRE 1840 DUBLIN, IRL [35713] : EUGENE 1855 + FINISKLIN, LET, IRL [38233]

MAHONEY MICHAEL 1819 + BATHURST, NSW, AUS [34030] : 1860S HAMILTON, VIC, AUS [34175] : 1823 + HOBART, TAS, AUS [35378] : 1847 + HOBART, TAS, AUS [35746] : C1850 BRISBANE, QLD, AUS [36616] : WILLIAM 1895-1925 MOREE, NSW, AUS [38083] : 1860S NB, CAN [36710] : PRE 1830 ENG [35378] : JOHN 1800 + LIM, IRL [34161] : 1840S CLONAKILTY, COR, IRL [34175] : PRE 1874 DRIMOLEAGUE, COR, IRL [35197] : PRE 1846 BAWDON, COR, IRL [35746] : 1890 BROOKLYN, NY, USA [37521] : C1872 + WLS & ENG [35453]

MAHONY JERIMAH 1810 + INCHIGEELAGH, COR, IRL [34171] : 1830-1845 CORK CITY, COR, IRL [34457] : 1816-1830 CORK CITY, COR, IRL [35132] : 1820-1870 DOON & KILCROHANE, KER, IRL [36763]

MAHY 1830 + ST ANDREWS, GSY, CHI [34916]

MAIA 1790-1820 WUE, GER [37593]

MAIDEN PRE 1760 LLANMYNECH, SAL, ENG [34370] : 1750 + OLD SWINFORD, WOR, ENG [35812] : PRE 1800 ENG & IRL [38754] : PRE 1797 AUGUSTA, VA, USA [38220]

MAIDMENT ALL DOR & WIL, ENG [35069] : JAMES PRE 1816 WEST KNOYLE, WIL, ENG [36621] : ALL SOM, ENG [37084] : C1848 MELBURY ABBAS, DOR, ENG [38489] : 1800-1900 WIL, ENG & AUS [37914]

MAIER PRE 1850 KIEFERLING, BAY, BRD [38658] : C1837 MELLE, HAN, GER [35507] : JOHANNES 1784 GRUPPENBACH, WUE, GER [38193] : ALL NEUFRA, WUE, GER [38333] : PRE 1750 MUEHLHEIM, WUE & HOH, GER [38679]

MAIERHOFFER PRE 1879 RADATZ, BUKOVINA, OES & CAN [37481]

MAIGRET PRE 1550 DINANT, BEL [38658]

MAIL 1897 + ROOKWOOD, NSW, AUS [35445] : ALL SFK, CAM & LIN, ENG [37742]

MAILING PRE 1805 CAMBRIDGE, CAM, ENG [34691]

MAILLARD ELIZABETH 1867 + RICHMOND, VIC, AUS [36611] : 1700 + NS, CAN & FRA [34500]

MAILLE 1800 + QUE, CAN [36568]

MAILLET PRE 1870 KENT CO., NB, CAN [38447]

MAILLIARD 1750 + ST PETER PORT, GSY, CHI [35847]

MAIN 1800 + BEVERLY TWP., ONT, CAN [34231] : ALL JSY, ALD & GSY, CHI [35891] : PRE 1810 LONGHORSLEY, NBL, ENG [33905] : 1900 + CHARLTON, LND, ENG [35335] : ALL PORTSEA, HAM, ENG [36163] : 1750-1850 SOUTH SHIELDS, DUR, ENG [37395] : C1820 + TYNEMOUTH & WALLSEND, NBL, ENG [37395] : 1820 CARRIDEN, WLN, SCT [33810] : PRE 1880 BURGHEAD, MOR, SCT [33993] : PRE 1811 FINDHORN, MOR, SCT [36673] : PRE 1830 PA, USA [37034]

MAINES 1860 + YOUNGSVILLE, PA, USA [34231]

MAINEY PRE 1889 KEMPSEY, NSW, AUS [35425]

MAINS JOSEPH 1790 + BALLYSHIEL, ARM, IRL [35274] : ROBERT ALL IRL [35274] : ROBERT 1800 + BALLYMORE, ARM, IRL [35274] : 1790 + TANDRAGEE, ARM, IRL [35274] : ALL SCT & IRL [35274] : ROBERT 1810-1837 SCT & IRL [35274] : 1790 + SCT & IRL [35274] : ROBERT 1810-1838 WORLDWIDE [35274]

MAINWARING C1840 + MAESTEG, GLA, WLS [33922]

MAINZ 1867 WARSAW, POM, GER [38322]

MAIR 1850 + NSW, AUS [37128] : C1780 IRL [37609] : 1898 + RIVERTON, SI, NZ [36611] : C1760-1810 LOUDON, AYR, SCT [34635] : PRE 1776 KILMARNOCK, AYR, SCT [35561] : C1800 ABD, SCT [36856] : 1835-36 GRENADA, W.INDIES [37609]

MAIRE PRE 1800 FRA [35967]

MAIRS ALL DOW, IRL [38298] : ALL ANT, IRL [38298]

MAISH PRE 1800 MAIDEN BRADLEY, WIL, ENG [34304] : PRE 1813 WELLOW, SOM, ENG [34304] : PRE 1800 HORNINGSHAM, WIL, ENG [34304]

MAITLAND 1800 + ONT, CAN [34827] : 1780 + SOHO, LND, ENG [34550] : ALL MAIDSTONE, KEN, ENG [36743] : 1800 + MANCHESTER, LAN, ENG [37134] : 1660-1800 GLASGOW, LKS, SCT [34827] : 1700-1900 WEST, SCT [35179] : 1790 + ROC & INV, SCT [35486] : 1800-1990 GLASGOW, LKS, SCT [37628] : 1830S GLASGOW, LKS, SCT [38206] : PRE 1804 CAMPBELTOWN, ARL, SCT [38438]

MAITRAT PRE 1805 STRASBOURG, ALS, GER [34582]

MAJOR 1800-1900 TODDINGTON, GLS, ENG [33758] : 1800-1900 BATH, SOM, ENG [33758] : PRE 1830 BIDEFORD, DEV, ENG [36516] : 1800-1900 LND, ENG [36780] : PRE 1836 MANCHESTER, LAN, ENG [37866] : PRE 1830 ELSTREE, HRT, ENG [38075] : PRE 1830 ALDENHAM, HRT, ENG [38075]

: PRE 1850 NETHERBURY, DOR, ENG [38272] :
1700+ PHILADELPHIA, PA & MD, USA [37826]

MAJOR WEST PRE 1850 N.IRL &, ENG [34013]

MAJOUE PRE 1870 BEL [36353] : PRE 1870 FRA
[36353]

MAJOURITIS JOHN PRE 1850 MEMEL, OPR [37314]

MAKAY ROBERT 1783+ YORK CO., NB, CAN
[37443]

MAKCUBYN ALL SCT [36348]

MAKEMAN ALL WORLDWIDE [37100]

MAKEPEACE 1815+ BKM, ENG [37165] : 1820-1860
HALTWHISTLE, NBL, ENG [38259]

MAKEPIECE 1854+ ENG [34528]

MAKER ALL ENG [33959]

MAKIM ALL WORLDWIDE [35331]

MAKIN 1800+ HAMILTON, TAS, AUS [33933] : PRE
1841 NSW, AUS [34412] : EMMA 1800+
COVENTRY, WAR, ENG [34078] : 1882-1948
EDINBURGH, MLN, SCT [33891]

MAKIN (SEE MEAKIN) [36369]

MAKLEIN 1742-70 NY, USA [38151]

MALADY PRE 1870 IRL [37510] : 1840+ DUBUQUE
CO., IA, USA [37510]

MALAN PRE 1820 ENG [35945] : 800+ WORLDWIDE
[36464]

MALARD 1840+ WALSALL, STS, ENG [34768] : PRE
1655 MAGNY & METZ, LOR, FRA [36954]

MALCOLM 1800+ KENT & BRANT, ONT, CAN
[37484] : 1842+ NELSON, NZ [35929] : ALL
MUIRAVONSIDE, STI, SCT [34765] : PRE 1842
GLASGOW, LKS, SCT [35929] : 1750-1850 SCT
[37461] : 1794-1900 KINROSS, KRS, SCT & AUS
[36874] : JAMES 1816 ROCKINGHAM CO., NC,
USA [35328] : PRE 1850 ALBANY, NY, USA [37541] :
1900S MARION CO., KS, USA [37541] : LANDRETH
1810-90S ROCKINGHAM, NC, USA [37585]

MALCOM 1850+ SIMCOE CO., ONT, CAN [34465]

MALCOMSON 1850+ HAMILTON, ONT, CAN
[34688] : PRE 1860 BELFAST, IRL [34557] : PRE 1860
DUBLIN, IRL [34557] : 1700+ LONGHOPE, OKI,
SCT [34688]

MALE PRE 1810 CAM, ENG [33998] : C1700
NOTGROVE, GLS, ENG [35260] : 1800-1850
KINSBURY EPISCOPI, SOM, ENG [35806] : 1750-
1850 MARTOCK, SOM, ENG [36688] : 1800S
TAUNTON, SOM, ENG [37299] : 1700-1850
HEMINGFORD, HUN, ENG [37642]

MALES THOMAS 1815-1850 AYOTT ST PETERS,
HRT, ENG [36634]

MALIN ALL ENG [36093]

MALING 1868+ PARRAMATTA, NSW, AUS [34691] :
C1840 CAM, ENG [33812] : PRE 1805 CAMBRIDGE,
CAM, ENG [34691]

MALISON 1946 CINCINNATI, OH, USA [34498]

MALISZEWSKI 1400-1900 VARIOUS, LITHUANIA
[38232] : 1600-1990 LOMZA, BIALYSTOK, POL
[38232] : 1400-1600 LOMZA, BIALYSTOK, POL
[38232] : 1400-1900 PRE [38232]

MALKIN 1650+ LEEK, STS, ENG [36701] : PRE 1850
LEATHERHEAD, SRY, ENG [38721]

MALLABAR C1800 HANBURY, STS, ENG [35998]

MALLAN 800+ WORLDWIDE [36464]

MALLANTS 1700-C1740S YERSEKE, ZEL, NL [38350]

MALLARD 1700-1750 ST HILARY, CON, ENG [34697]
: PRE 1850 MINETY, WIL, ENG [34727] : PRE 1900
WOOTTON & BUGBROOKE, NTH, ENG [38280]

MALLEN 1748 BURWASH, SSX, ENG [35260]

MALLERET 1620-1690 LIBOURNE & BORDEAUX,
FRA [34514]

MALLERY PRE 1832 ENG [34720]

MALLET PRE 1780 KNAPTON, NFK, ENG [35046] :
C1825 DJAKARTA, JAVA, INDONESIA [38711] :
PRE 1850 SWANSEA, WLS [37030]

MALLETT PRE 1875 CON, ENG [34679] : 1800+
LOWESTOFT & KESSINGLAND, SFK, ENG [34903]
: 1799 SANGTREE, DEV, ENG [35272] : PRE 1800
TYSOE, WAR, ENG [37371] : C1700-1900 ST NEOT
& CLEER, CON, ENG [37434] : 1500-1850 ST
GLUVIAS, CON, ENG [37680]

MALLEY ALL PEI & NB, CAN [34202] : PRE 1810
ENG & IRL [36052]

MALLIN 1790S-1860 WEST BROMWICH, STS, ENG
[35044]

MALLINCKRODT PRE 1700 DORTMUND, WEF,
GER [38644]

MALLINSON 1861+ AUS [35490] : 1800+
KNUTSFORD, CHS & YKS, ENG [35490] : C1800
YORK, YKS, ENG [36975]

MALLISON PRE 1830 ASHTON UNDER LYNE,
LAN, ENG [35420] : 1850+ LONDON, ENG [37847]

MALLOCH C1850 FIF, SCT [34527]

MALLON 1860+ TAREENA, SA, AUS [33824] : 1800+
ARBOE, TYR, IRL [33829] : CHARLES PRE 1850
ARBOE & AGHOCOLUMB, TYR, IRL [34061] :
1700-1800 FER, IRL [37126]

MALLORIE 1820-1860 LEEDS, YKS, ENG [33861]

MALLORY 1800+ DURHAM TWP., ONT, CAN
[38410] : EDWARD, EDWIN ALL NY, USA [35304] :
WELLINGTON ALL SANTA CRUZ CO., AZ & NY,
USA [35304] : 1750+ CT & VT, USA [38410]

MALLOWS 1800-1900 BOZEAT, NTH, ENG [37495]

MALLOY 1854+ VIC, AUS [34590] : PRE 1850 IRL
[36935] : PRE 1854 DUNDEE, ANS, SCT [34590]

MALLPRESS ALL ENG [37409]

MALMOTH HENRY 1770-1810S BLANDFORD
FORUM, DOR, ENG [37559]

MALO PRE 1750 ZWIESIGKO, KSA, GER [38750] :
1811 LEBIEN, KSA, GER [38750]

MALON 1830-1900 COPENHAGEN, DEN [34952] :
C1830 HAMBURG, HBG, GER [34952]

MALONE 1880+ ROCKHAMPTON, QLD, AUS
[34021] : C1850-1900 SYDNEY, NSW, AUS [37987] :
1800S WESTMEATH, IRL [34028] : PRE 1900
TULLOW, CAR, IRL [34784] : 1815-1836 ARM, IRL
[36281] : PRE 1883 LIM, IRL & AUS [34773] : WOOD
1770S WARREN CO., NC, USA [35328] : PRE 1790
SULLIVAN CO., TN, USA [37029] : 1840+ PA, USA
[37438] : EDWARD 1850S MOBILE, AL, USA [37585]
: EDWARD 1860S GALVESTON, TX, USA [37585] :
WOOD 1770S WARREN CO., NC, USA [37585] :
PRE 1840 BANGOR, CAE, WLS [38286]

MALONEY 1868 LEARMONTH, VIC, AUS [35204] :
1860+ EAST MAITLAND, NSW, AUS [35239] :
1880+ TOWNSVILLE, QLD, AUS [36305] : 1800+
MELBOURNE, VIC, AUS [36746] : 1880+
MACLEAY RIVER, NSW, AUS [37997] : 1847+ VIC,
AUS [38281] : PRE 1845 NEWMARKET, CLA, IRL
[35077] : PRE 1848+ WATERFORD, WAT, IRL
[35453] : 1820 GORTUSSA, TIP, IRL [35809] : 1800-
1900 WHITEGATE, CLA, IRL [35845] : THOMAS
PRE 1840 IRL [36532] : 1800S DONASS, CLA, IRL
[38281] : 1813+ WATERFORD, WAT, IRL [38291] :
C1800+ CHRISTCHURCH, CBY, NZ [36746] :
1847+ WESTLAND, NZ [38281]

MALPAS PRE 1812 TEWKESBURY, GLS, ENG
[36177]

MALPASS PRE 1840 SHOREDITCH, MDX, ENG
[34691] : 1785 BIRMINGHAM, WAR, ENG [35808]

MALPRESS 1880+ WIMBLEDON, SRY, ENG [35725]
: 1866+ SYDENHAM, KEN, ENG [35725] : C1780-
1870 MEPAL, CAM, ENG [35725]

MALROY ALL AYR, SCT [34040]

MALTBY ALICE 1878 HUNTERS HILL, NSW, AUS [34898] : ALL AUS [34898] : 1720-1790S THORNER, WRY, ENG [34898] : 1725-1780S FARNLEY, WRY, ENG [34898] : PRE 1800 HULL, ERY, ENG [36298] : ALL BDF, ENG [37738] : 1800 GOTHAM, NTT, ENG [37829]

MALTPRESS 1850-1870 MEPAL, CAM, ENG [35725]

MAMMATT 1700+ MEASHAM, DBY, ENG [35874]

MAMMO PRE 1875 MALTA [38659]

MAMOND 1790S BATLEY, WRY, ENG [35815]

MANALLOCK PRE 1845 CON, ENG [35425]

MANBY 1915-1960 WOODHALL SPA, LIN, ENG [37400] : 1800+ LAN, ENG [37400]

MANCHESTER PRE 1857 HARBY, LEI, ENG [34758] : 1800S PORTSEA, HAM, ENG [35186] : 1800+ MANCHESTER, LAN, ENG [37598] : 1830+ DAYTON, OH, USA [37598]

MANDEN PRE 1720 NYEVEEN, OIJ & DRN, NL [36283] : 1830-1860S JOHNSTON, NC & OH, USA [36283]

MANDER PRE 1800 ARDLEY, OXF, ENG [34112] : C1780 WOLVERHAMPTON, STS & WAR, ENG [35349]

MANDERS ALL SCHAYK, NBT, NL [38703]

MANDERSON PRE 1850 EDINBURGH, MLN, SCT [35713]

MANDEVILLE PRE 1809 LONDON, MDX, ENG [35090]

MANDLEBAUM 1845-1859 KEWEENAW CO., MI, USA [38009]

MANFIELD C1840 CLONMEL, TIP, IRL [38292]

MANGAN 1800+ HOBART, TAS, AUS [34904] : 1835+ AGHADOE, KER, IRL [35380] : MARY 1846+ ASKEATON, LIM, IRL [36367]

MANGELSDORF 1700+ COOLAMON, NSW, AUS & GER [36303]

MANGER C1762 OFINGEN, BAD, GER [34239]

MANGHAM 1809-1850 WENTWORTH & ROTHERHAM, YKS, ENG [35365]

MANGUAL PRE 1805 MAYAGUEZ, PR, USA [37819]

MANIFIELD PRE 1900 TICKHILL, WRY, ENG [37979]

MANION 1815-1903 LANARK CO., ONT, CAN [34071] : 1780-1830 GAL, IRL [34071]

MANIS 1790-1900 ANSON & GREENE CO., NC & TN, YU [37539]

MANKELOW 1800+ WROTHAM, KEN, ENG [36092]

MANKLON 1800+ LONDON, ENG [36092]

MANLEY 1853+ PRAHRAN, VIC, AUS [34446] : PRE 1900 COLLINGWOOD, VIC, AUS [34536] : PRE 1900 CON, ENG [34536] : 1800+ HILLINGDON, MDX, ENG [35214] : C1800+ LONDON, ENG [35834]

MANLOVE PRE 1800 KENT CO., DE, USA [38538]

MANN 1855+ CRESWICK, VIC, AUS [34039] : 1854+ CASTLEMAINE, VIC, AUS [35533] : PRE 1930 BRACKNELL, TAS, AUS [35962] : 1844+ OAKS, TAS, AUS [35962] : PRE 1900 OATLANDS, TAS, AUS [37777] : 1890+ VIC, AUS [37149] : 1850 OSHAWA, ONT, CAN [38395] : ANN 1800 SHEFFIELD, YKS, ENG [33956] : PRE 1872 BEXLEYHEATH, KEN & SSX, ENG [33957] : PRE 1872 LONDON, ENG [33957] : 1830-1850 ULLINGSWICK, HEF, ENG [34039] : C1710-1820 ILLINGWORTH & OVENDEN, WRY, ENG [34397] : 1800+ NORWICH, NFK, ENG [34597] : 1790-1870 HARBURY, WAR, ENG [34677] : 1700-1800 SILKSTONE, YKS, ENG [34762] : ALL GLS, ENG [34837] : 1700S ST ERTH, CON, ENG [34920] : C1860 OLNEY & NEWPORT PAGNAL, BKM, ENG [35387] : C1847 MARYLEBONE, LND & MDX, ENG [35460] : 1800-1900 PAUL & ST BURYAN, CON, ENG [35736] : 1796 ALDERBURGH, SFK, ENG [35903] : PRE 1880 STIVICHALL, WAR, ENG [35962] : PRE 1890 LEAMINGTON SPA, WAR, ENG [35962] : PRE 1900 STRETTON ON DUNSMORE, WAR, ENG [35962] : PRE 1900 BOURTON ON DUNSMORE, WAR, ENG [35962] : PRE 1900 HALIFAX, WRY, ENG [36037] : C1730-1904 SWANTON MORLEY, NFK, ENG [36128] : 1834-1856 NFK, ENG [36281] : 1800-1850 PAUL, CON, ENG [36833] : 1820+ BURWELL, CAM, ENG [36846] : PRE 1890 LONDON, ENG [37237] : 1830S HADLEIGH, SFK, ENG [37418] : 1859-1860S MOUNTNESSING & MARGARETTING, ESS, ENG [37418] : PRE 1860 SOUTH SHIELDS, DUR, ENG [37442] : ALL SFK, ENG [37612] : PRE 1900 ENG [37787] : ALL ESS, ENG [37832] : 1819 MAULDEN, BDF, ENG [37946] : 1800+ BENENDEN, SSX, ENG & CAN [34467] : ALL PODE HOLE, LIN, ENG & USA [36916] : 1800 TANDERAGEE, ARM, IRL [35809] : 1400+ CARSTAIRS, LKS, SCT [33989] : 1880+ GRANTOWN, MOR, SCT [34810] : 1860-1880 AVOCH, ROC, SCT [34810] : 1780+ INVERNESS, INV, SCT [34810] : PRE 1850 DUNDEE, TAY, SCT [35533] : 1750-1820 SCT [38139] : CHRISTOPHER PRE 1800 NJ & KY, USA [34410] : PRE 1863 USA [37787] : 1815-1860 NEW YORK CITY, NY, USA [38139] : C1880 SYRACUSE, NY, USA [38263]

MANNERS PRE 1769 NEWBATTLE, MLN, SCT [37852]

MANNESS ALL WORLDWIDE [34508]

MANNEWELL C1820-30 KEN, ENG [35860]

MANNIN ALL LAMBETH, LND, ENG [35260]

MANNING 1870+ BRISBANE, QLD, AUS [33932] : PRE 1872 MELBOURNE, VIC, AUS [35792] : 1850+ BENDIGO & EAGLEHAWK, VIC, AUS [36297] : C1815+ QUE, CAN [38406] : PRE 1870 BARDWELL, SFK, ENG [33932] : C1830-1890 MOULTON, YKS, ENG [33935] : PRE 1840 HIGHBURY, ESS, ENG [34205] : C1852 FOLESHILL, WAR, ENG [34358] : PRE 1900 LONDON, ENG [34825] : PRE 1850 NEWBURY, BRK, ENG [34869] : 1700-1890 WAR, ENG [35180] : C1720 HOLBORN, LND, ENG [35260] : C1811 ESS, ENG [35560] : PRE 1880 BEER, DEV, ENG [35792] : PRE 1820 SPALDWICK & GAMLINGAY, HUN & CAM, ENG [35866] : 1800 MANCHESTER, LAN, ENG [35871] : CHARLES 1780-1830 SHEFFIELD, YKS, ENG [36297] : 1750-1800S ROUGHAM, NFK, ENG [36665] : 1807 BURWELL, CAM, ENG [37131] : ALL TOTTENHAM, ESS, ENG [37133] : PRE 1850 KIRBY LE SOKEN, ESS, ENG [37300] : C1850+ DENFORD, NTH, ENG [37437] : PRE 1800 GREAT YARMOUTH, NFK, ENG [37716] : 1614+ CAMBRIDGE, CAM, ENG [37802] : 1800 WESTLETON, SFK, ENG [37928] : PRE 1842 CRUSHENLINGH, CAV, IRL [35225] : PRE 1840 ANNA, CAV, IRL [35225] : PRE 1860 TUAM, GAL, IRL [35792] : CATH 1817+ KIK, IRL & AUS [35093] : 1780-1850 ESSEX CO., NY, USA [36581] : PRE 1850 INDIAN VALLEY, VA, USA [37595]

MANNINGE 1600+ UFFCULM, DEV, ENG [34747]

MANNINGS C1770 KEN, ENG [38389]

MANNION 1800+ GALWAY, GAL, IRL & AUS [36875]

MANNIS 1800-1860 CRAWFORD CO., PA, NY & OH, USA [37529]

MANNIX C1882+ BRIGHTON, VIC, AUS [35746] : 1810-1842 NARELLAN & UPPER MINTO, NSW, AUS [38006] : 1840S LIMERICK, LIM, IRL [33967] : 1800+ MOYNE CO., CLA, IRL [35566] : 1850 COR, IRL [36579] : PATRICK C1766 CORK, COR, IRL [38724]

MANNOCK 1700-1900 LAN, ENG [35292]

MANNS PRE 1800 AUS &, WORLDWIDE [33941]

MANROW PRE 1850 NRY, ENG [36046]

MANSBRIDGE 1835 PORTSMOUTH, HAM, ENG [34628] : C1750-1850 BASING, HAM, ENG [37770]

MANSEL PRE 1820 STOW ON WOLD, OXF, ENG [34727] : PRE 1820 ENG [36873]

MANSELL ALL SAL, ENG [37681] : PRE 1850 BURSLEM, STS, ENG [37945]

MANSER 1820+ SYDNEY, NSW, AUS [34860] : 1841-1900 WOLLOMBI, NSW, AUS [37904] : PRE 1800 MDX, ENG [34739] : ALL SHOREDITCH, LND, ENG [34820] : ALL SSX, ENG [34858] : 1850+ KEN, SRY & SSX, ENG [35762]

MANSFIELD 1852+ BRIDGEWATER, TAS, AUS [33786] : CHARLES 1858+ SINGLETON, NSW, AUS [33939] : 1858+ BRANXHOLME, VIC, AUS [34685] : 1837+ MOOREBANK, NSW, AUS [35088] : 1870+ MELBOURNE, VIC, AUS [35515] : 1858-1990 KEW, VIC, AUS [35592] : 1840-1900 GEELONG, VIC, AUS [37156] : PRE 1900 SYDNEY, NSW & DEV, AUS & ENG [34439] : PRE 1858 BALSHAM, CAM, ENG [33939] : PRE 1800 BARKWAY, HRT, ENG [34547] : PRE 1860 HARTSHORNE, DBY & LEI, ENG [34686] : 1804+ HARTSHORNE, DBY, ENG [35144] : C1800-1850 HEYDON & GREAT CHISHALL, ESS, ENG [35592] : PRE 1800 ESS, ENG [36379] : PRE 1840 LONDON, ENG [36882] : PRE 1800 EPPING, ESS, ENG [37832] : 1800+ BETHNAL GREEN, LND, ENG [37832] : 1815-30 IRL [33828] : 1870+ NE & IL, USA [38739] : 1800-1870 NY & IL, USA [38739]

MANSION PRE 1820 ZEURANGE, FRA [38681]

MANSNERUS 1722+ DANDERYD, STOCKHOLM, SWE [38544]

MANSON 1886+ BRISBANE, QLD, AUS [36290] : 1838+ HOBART, TAS, AUS [37954] : 1500-1630 ENG [37784] : PRE 1850 LARNE, ANT, IRL [36191] : 1840+ DUNROSSNESS, SHI, SCT [33982] : 1786+ BOWER, CAI, SCT [35013] : PRE 1800 ULBSTER, OKI, SCT [36436] : PRE 1860 WATTEN, CAI, SCT [36793] : 1750 STROMNESS, OKI, SCT [37170] : PRE 1838 WICK, CAI, SCT [37954]

MANSUS ALL KOVIK, FIN & CAN [34164]

MANTEI 1800+ UNTERBRUCK, BRA, GER [37170]

MANTEUFEL C1841 REDLIN, WPR, GER [35733]

MANTHEY 1800+ UNTERBRUCK, BRA, GER [37170]

MANTHORNE ALL WORLDWIDE [35299]

MANTLE 1810-40 KEN, ENG [35516] : ALL CINDERFORD, GLS, ENG [36359] : ALL WORLDWIDE [35884]

MANTON PRE 1850 HOBART, TAS, AUS [33786] : C1890+ SOUTH YARRA & HAWTHORN, VIC, AUS [37158] : 1828+ SYDNEY & YASS PLAINS, NSW, AUS [37158] : 1863 DARLINGHURST, NSW, AUS [37158] : PRE 1850 ONT, CAN [37217] : 1700-99 COTTESBROOKE, NTH, ENG [34315] : 1550-1700 WOR, ENG [37217] : PRE 1842+ TIP, IRL [37912]

MANUEL 1700 EXETER, DEV, ENG [34409] : 1800+ GWENNAP, CON, ENG [36254] : ALL WORLDWIDE [38244]

MANUS 1850S AMSTERDAM, NL [33802]

MANUSSET ALL PCH, FRA [36078]

MANWARING PRE 1857 CRANBROOK, KEN, ENG [35117]

MANZER HENRY 1847 LEROY, NY, USA [38140]

MAP THOMAS PRE 1750 BROMFIELD, WOR, ENG [36619]

MAPES PRE 1840 NFK, ENG [35745]

MAPLES 1600-1700 NAVENBY, LIN, ENG [37039]

MAPLEY 1600+ WAVENDON, BKM, ENG [38241]

MAPPIN ALL ENG & RSA [38772]

MAPPLEY 1850+ LONDON, ENG [37847]

MAPSTONE 1840S CHEW MAGNA, SOM, ENG [35557] : ALL WESTBURY, SOM, ENG [35804]

MAQUE 1400+ DUBLIN, WIC, IRL [33989]

MARA 1840-1890 BATESFORD, GEELONG, VIC, AUS [37156]

MARABLE MARTHA 1818-1873 DOLOGANA & GOSHEN, GA, USA [35265]

MARACHEE PRE 1870 INDIA [36955]

MARAIS 1683-1980 DRAKENSTEIN, CAPE, RSA [34947]

MARBIN 1700-1800 UPMINSTER, ESS, ENG [36438]

MARBLE 1780-1830 MA & VT, USA [36968]

MARBURY 1750-1775 NEWBERRY CO., SC, USA [38088]

MARBY C1770 LAN, ENG [38177]

MARCEAU 1600S LUCON, PCH, FRA [34371]

MARCH 1850+ BURRA, SA & NSW, AUS [34955] : C1871 TRUNKEY, NSW, AUS [35028] : 1904+ NTH CARLTON, VIC, AUS [36279] : EDGAR 1940+ OLD PERLICAN, NFD, CAN [36678] : 1800+ BEXLEY, KEN, ENG [34927] : PRE 1857 SOM, ENG [35028] : 1800+ ENG [35171] : 1690-1780 DODSBROOKE, DEV, ENG [36155] : PRE 1800 DEV, DOR & SOM, ENG [36166] : 1800S DAGENHAM, ESS, ENG [36263] : PRE 1820 SOUTHWARK, LND & SRY, ENG [36612] : PRE 1780 WOODLEIGH, DEV, ENG [37169] : PRE 1820 BROUGHTON, NTH, ENG [37346] : 1700+ ATHERSTONE & CHEAPSIDE, WAR & LND, ENG [37735] : ALL WORLDWIDE [37785]

MARCHAND C1830 CAPE BRETON, NS, CAN [34675] : PRE 1870 QUE, CAN [38033]

MARCHANT 1910+ MELBOURNE, VIC, AUS [35747] : PRE 1910 GAWLER, SA, AUS [35747] : 1850-1871 MACLEAY, NSW, AUS [37915] : ALL CH [36545] : 1700-1900 POYNINGS & NEWTIMBER, SSX, ENG [34749] : PRE 1840 PAULTON & TAUNTON, SOM, ENG [35231] : 1763+ ELM & CHATTERIS, CAM, ENG [35999] : PRE 1850 BRIGHTLING, SSX, ENG [36393] : ALL SRY, ENG [36811] : 1750+ AYNHO, OXF, ENG [37194] : PRE 1790+ SEVENOAKS, KEN, ENG [38053] : ALL USA [36545] : 1857-1900 BROOKLYN, NY, USA [38053]

MARCHESSAULT 1630-1710 LUCON, PCH, FRA [34514]

MARCHMAN PRE 1870 WIL, ENG [35913]

MARCHMENT ALL WORLDWIDE [34285]

MARCKERT PRE 1670 HEMMENDORF, BAV, GER [35242]

MARDEL PRE 1800 CS [35971] : PRE 1800 MONTPELLIER, LGD, FRA [35971] : PRE 1800 HU [35971] : ALL PT [35971]

MARDELL PRE 1850S ESS, ENG [34240] : PRE 1890 BRENTWOOD, ESS, ENG [36516]

MARDEN 1850+ NSW, AUS [38389] : 1592-1787 EASTBOURNE, SSX, ENG [34706] : PRE 1856 MEREWORTH, KEN, ENG [34886] : PRE 1850 ENG [38389]

MARE C1800 CHERITON FITZPAINE, DEV, ENG [35050]

MAREK IGNATZ J. 1900-1983 PARACHANIE, POSEN, POL [38090] : KATARZYNA 1879-1942 PARACHANIE, POSEN, POL [38090] : JOSEPH 1857-1900 POL [38090]

MARES 1700-1800 MAIDSTONE, KEN, ENG [36438]

MARETT 1650+ JSY, CHI [34532] : PRE 1850 WHOLE ISLAND, JSY, CHI, UK [36200]

MARGATE ALL HAM, ENG [35493]

MARGERISON ALL TONG, ILKLEY & COLLINGHAM, WRY, ENG [36159]

MARGETTS 1700-1820 MDX, LND & SRY, ENG [36491]

MARGGRAFF PRE 1707 MINDEN, WESTFALEN, GER [38563] : 1707-1742 GOTEBORG, VASTERGOTL, SWE [38563]

MARGIN ALL SSX, ENG [34858]

MARGRIE C1852 LONDON, ENG [35827]

MARGUERETTAZ 1690 BOSSES, AOSTA, ITL [37691]

MARIANI PRE 1861 CAMPO, ITL [37519]

MARICHAL PRE 1821 JEREZ DE LA FRONTERA, ESP [37819]

MARINA PRE 1900 CAMPO, ITL [37519]

MARINER PRE 1800 ARNOLD, NTT, ENG [37901]

MARION 1620-1750 GUINGAMP, BRT, FRA [38420]

MARION WEEKS WILLIAM 1867-1890 IA & OH, USA [36321]

MARIOT PRE 1600 WITNEY, OXF, ENG [37277] : PRE 1600 BN, FRA [37277] : PRE 1600 HN, FRA [37277]

MARIOTT PRE 1600 WITNEY, OXF, ENG [37277]

MARJORAM PRE 1800 SFK, ENG [35642] : 1700S FRESSINGFIELD, SFK, ENG [37250]

MARK 1700+ ROCHE, CON, ENG [35235] : 1800+ LONDON, ENG [36815] : 1780-1880 MUSSELBURGH, MLN, SCT [36776]

MARKEY ALL GLS, ENG [34837] : C1828 KELLS, MEA, IRL [34814] : PRE 1850 CARRICKMACROSS, MOG, IRL [35750]

MARKHAM ALL WOODBRIDGE, SFK, ENG [36076] : C1820 CHELSEA, LND, ENG [36076] : 1835+ OXFORD, OXF, ENG [37181] : PRE 1720 REDGRAVE & BOTESDALE, SFK, ENG [37420] : C1860 ST PANCRAS, LND, ENG [38417]

MARKLAND WILLIAM 1800+ BOLTON, LAN, ENG [35484]

MARKLE 1800-1850 ONT, CAN [37466]

MARKS 1860-1920 MOLONG & GRENFELL, NSW, AUS [35546] : 1880+ SYDNEY, NSW, AUS [36129] : 1880+ RANDWICK, NSW, AUS [36129] : 1880+ MCPHAIL, NSW, AUS [36129] : 1850+ MELBOURNE, VIC, AUS [38290] : C1800 BRISTOL, GLS, ENG [33841] : PRE 1860 SANCREED, CON, ENG [33870] : 1830+ STEEPLE ASHTON, WIL, ENG [34299] : PRE 1840 WEST COKER, SOM, ENG [35045] : PRE 1859+ CAMBORNE, CON, ENG [35453] : JOSEPH PRE 1870S LONDON, ENG [35546] : PRE 1854 CAMBORNE, CON, ENG [37150] : 1750-1850 TAUNTON, SOM, ENG [38290] : PRE 1900 OLDENBURG, SHO, GER [38648] : PRE 1850 BALLINDERRY, LDY, IRL [36722] : 1800-1870 GA, USA [37587] : PRE 1800 SOUTHAMPTON CO., VA, USA [37587]

MARKUS 1803+ CAPE TOWN, CAPE, RSA [34947]

MARKWELL PRE 1800 LIN, ENG [34808] : 1800-1840+ LIN, ENG [36440]

MARLAN 1890 BINALONG, NSW, AUS [37997]

MARLAND ALL MARLAND, LAN, ENG [35145] : PRE 1800 ASHTON UNDER LYNE, LAN, ENG [35145] : PRE 1800 ROCHDALE, LAN, ENG [35145] : PRE 1874 TIP, IRL [35895] : 1879+ NZ [35145] : 1873+ IL, USA [35145]

MARLAR C1500 ENG [34395]

MARLBOROUGH 1800+ STEPNEY, MDX, ENG [37827]

MARLER PRE 1870 WALCOT, SOM, ENG [34201]

MARLEY PRE 1863 DONEGAL, DON, IRL [33820] : 1860+ PAISLEY, RFW, SCT [33820]

MARLING PRE 1820 OHIO CO., VA, USA [35295]

MARLOW C1850+ BLACKPOOL, LAN, ENG [35163] : 1750-1850 BEXWELL, NFK, ENG [36410] : HORATIO 1784-1794 FREDERICK CO., MD, USA [38145]

MARMAUTE 1600-1690 GENEVA, GE, CH [34514]

MARMO 1850+ GEELONG, VIC, AUS [35806]

MAROFKE PRE 1854 WARSZAWA, POL [38629]

MAROHE 1792 RICHLIEU, QUE, CAN [38364]

MARONEY 1830+ NSW, AUS [34424]

MAROTTE 1792 RICHLIEU, QUE, CAN [38364]

MARPACH PRE 1700 GER [38683]

MARPLES ALL BASLOW, DBY, ENG [37875]

MARQUAND ALL ST ANDREWS, GSY, CHI [34916]

MARQUARD PRE 1670 HEMMENDORF, BAV, GER [35242]

MARQUARDT ALL FALKENBURG & DARMBURG, POM, GER [37607]

MARQUART MARIA ALL CAPETOWN, CAPE, RSA & AUS [35122]

MARQUET CHRISTOPH PRE 1863 HOFELDH, GER [34779]

MARR C1850 SYDNEY, NSW, AUS [34682] : 1850-1900 MELBOURNE, VIC, AUS [34682] : 1870 CRAIGIE, VIC, AUS [35204] : 1920 MILDURA, VIC, AUS [35204] : 1800+ SYDNEY, NSW, AUS [35721] : PRE 1620 BLYTH, NTT, ENG [36426] : PRE 1880 PENNINGTON & FURNESS, LAN, ENG [37353] : 1800 KILLARNEY, WIC, IRL [34610] : 1750+ ABERDEEN, ABD, SCT [34606] : 1700+ FIF, SCT [35627]

MARRATT ALL LIN, ENG [37487]

MARRETT 1873+ COOKTOWN, QLD, AUS [35857] : 1800-1870 OSTACAMUND, MADRAS, INDIA [35857]

MARRIETTE ALL ST SAMPSONS, GSY, CHI [35433] : ALL CHI, ENG [36671]

MARRINER C1774 THORNTON IN LONSDALE, WRY, ENG [36955] : PRE 1751+ BARNINGHAM, NRY, ENG [36955] : PRE 1800 ARNOLD, NTT, ENG [37901] : ALL WORLDWIDE [37595]

MARRIOT C1800 OLD DALBY, LEI, ENG [36403] : PRE 1600 WITNEY, OXF, ENG [37277] : PRE 1600 BN, FRA [37277] : PRE 1600 HN, FRA [37277]

MARRIOTT 1873 KEMPSEY, NSW, AUS [35827] : 1850+ SYDNEY, NSW, AUS [37337] : PRE 1830 SWAVESEY, CAM, ENG [34197] : 1800+ HARPURHEY, LAN, ENG [34870] : PRE 1838 WESTMINSTER, MDX, ENG [35211] : 1800S ENG [36289] : ELIZABETH C1819 GUILSBOROUGH, NTH, ENG [37106] : PRE 1600 WITNEY, OXF, ENG [37277] : 1700+ ASHOVER & CHESTERFIELD, DBY, ENG [37337] : 1750+ NETHER HEYFORD, NTH, ENG [37357] : 1800S NORTH WINGFIELD, DBY, ENG [37391] : 1760+ WHATTON, NTT, ENG [37552] : PRE 1890 ENG & NZ [36840] : 1800-1920 RSA [37277] : PRE 1600 DEDHAM, NORFOLK CO., MA, USA [38745] : ALL HALKYN, FLN, WLS [37667]

MARRIS 1700-1840 KEELBY, LIN, ENG [36059]

MARRYWELL 1800S MAIDSTONE, KEN, ENG [34816]

MARSCHAL 1750-1850 BANAT, YU [37539]

MARSDEN 1884+ NEUTRAL BAY, NSW, AUS [34906] : 1800+ SHEFFIELD, WRY, ENG [34020] : ALL STANDISH, LAN, ENG [34730] : C1780-1825 DARWEN & BANK TOP, LAN, ENG [35052] : 1860+ MANCHESTER, LAN, ENG [35183] : 1775-1830 OLDHAM, LAN, ENG [35320] : 1900+ OSWALDTWISTLE, LAN, ENG [35942] : 1900+ LOWER DARWEN, LAN, ENG [35942] : 1840+ LEEDS, WRY, ENG [36228] : 1750-1800 MIDDLESMOOR, NRY, ENG [36228] : PRE 1760 NRY, ENG [36228] : 1800-1840 MASHAM, NRY, ENG [36228] : PRE 1950 SUNDERLAND, DUR, ENG [36502] : PRE 1829 WAKEFIELD, YKS, ENG [36954] : 1800-1880 SHEFFIELD, WRY, ENG [36966] : 1750+ DARWEN, LAN, ENG [36991] :

MARGARET 1840+ NELSON, LAN, ENG [37085] : 1750-1850 BRAMPTON, DBY, ENG [37188] : 1790 WINSTER, DBY, ENG [37215] : JOHN HENRY C1874 SHEFFIELD, WRY, ENG [37960] : GEORGE PRE 1874 SHEFFIELD, WRY, ENG [37960] : 1910 VT, USA [34496] : ALL WORLDWIDE [36228]

MARSDON C1780-1825 DARWEN & BANK TOP, LAN, ENG [35052]

MARSEILLE PRE 1880 MARBURG, GER [36927]

MARSEILLES 1700-1900S MARSEILLES, FRA & CAN [34133]

MARSH 1800+ SYDNEY, NSW, AUS [34459] : 1870+ SHEPPARTON, VIC, AUS [35379] : JAMES 1870S+ ECHUCA, VIC, AUS [35876] : 1875+ MARNHULL, DOR, ENG [34045] : PRE 1813 WELLOW, SOM, ENG [34304] : PRE 1830 SIDMOUTH, DEV, ENG [34304] : PRE 1830 COLATON RALEIGH, DEV, ENG [34304] : PRE 1800 MAIDEN BRADLEY, WIL, ENG [34304] : PRE 1800 SALISBURY, WIL, ENG [34304] : PRE 1800 HORNINGSHAM, WIL, ENG [34304] : 1832+ HAVERHILL, SFK, ENG [34334] : C1805 HANNAH, STS, ENG [34588] : C1880 WESTMINSTER, LND, ENG [34819] : PRE 1840 HASELBURY PLUCKNETT, SOM, ENG [35128] : PRE 1860 HASELBURY, SOM, ENG [35378] : 1800S DOR, ENG [35379] : ALL DOVER, KEN, ENG [35566] : 1850+ CREWKERNE, SOM & DEV, ENG [35580] : C1860 BOLTON, LAN, ENG [35622] : PRE 1788 WEST WRATTING, CAM, ENG [35770] : 1832 SOM, ENG [35808] : 1750-1850 PENISTONE & THURLSTONE, WRY, ENG [35825] : 1800S BALTONSBOROUGH, SOM, ENG [35899] : PRE 1792 GOSPORT & PORTSEA, HAM, ENG [36051] : ELIZABETH 1780+ LONDON, ENG [36378] : PRE 1850 SEDGLEY, STS, ENG [36379] : 1700-1900 SHEFFIELD & LIVERPOOL, YKS & LAN, ENG [36531] : PRE 1812 WESTHOUGHTON, LAN, ENG [36742] : PRE 1820 BROUGHTON, NTH, ENG [37346] : BENJAMIN 1836 SHIAWASSEE CO., MI, USA [38142] : THOMAS PRE 1650 MD, USA & ENG [37529] : JOHN 1819-1891 KINGSTON DEMONDRILLE & SYDNEY, JAMAICA & AUS, W.INDIES [36311]

MARSHAL 1700+ DRAYTON, NTT, ENG [35847]

MARSHALL PRE 1900+ BALLARAT, VIC, AUS [34877] : 1879 ROCKHAMPTON, QLD, AUS [35452] : 1850S+ BALLARAT & WANTHAGGI, VIC, AUS [35489] : 1834 MAITLAND, NSW, AUS [35705] : 1850S SANDHURST, VIC, AUS [35855] : FREDERICK 1850-1890 MELBOURNE, VIC, AUS [36884] : 1870+ GEELONG, VIC & WA, AUS [37552] : 1800S NS, CAN [38418] : 1824-1902 RICHIBUCTO, NB, CAN [38421] : 1750+ NOTTINGHAM, NTT, ENG [33800] : RICHARD 1760+ LASTINGHAM, NRY, ENG [34078] : PRE 1830 SFK, ENG [34090] : SAMUEL PRE 1840S STS, ENG [34240] : C1870 SHEERNESS, KEN, ENG [34395] : 1920 CAMBERWELL, LND, ENG [34496] : 1800-1915 ENFIELD, MDX, ENG [34496] : 1800-1990 STANNINGTON, ERY, ENG [34552] : PRE 1850 CHATHAM & GILLINGHAM, KEN, ENG [34660] : PRE 1824 NOTTINGHAM, NTT, ENG [34806] : PRE 1850 NEWBURY, BRK, ENG [34869] : 1813 DUNCTON, SSX, ENG [34909] : 1870 LUND, YKS, ENG [35452] : PRE 1850 HALIFAX, YKS, ENG [35491] : 1750+ LONDON, ENG [35825] : 1600+ CALKE & TICKNALL, DBY, ENG [35851] : PRE 1874 YKS, ENG [35985] : ALL LEI, ENG [36005] : 1742+ DORKING, SRY, ENG [36071] : PRE 1925 GRAVESEND, KEN, ENG [36090] : ALL WEST DRAYTON, NTT, ENG [36174] : C1730-1780 ENG [36289] : PRE 1850 NORTH MEOLS, LAN, ENG

[36385] : C1630 RAMPTON, NTT, ENG [36426] : 1790-1840 MARNHAM, NTT, ENG [36426] : 1800-1900 DERBY & SNEINTON, DBY & NTT, ENG [36531] : 1800-1900 BURTON, NTH, ENG [36688] : 1830S ST ALBANS, HRT, ENG [36827] : C1820-1875 HACKNEY & STEPNEY, MDX, ENG [36836] : WILLIAM H. 1820+ WAPPING, MDX, ENG [37083] : MARY C1823 ERISWELL, SFK, ENG [37106] : PRE 1840 BEDNAL, STS, ENG [37331] : ALL ASHTON UNDER LYNE, LAN, ENG [37373] : 1840 WHITBY, NRY, ENG [37388] : 1800+ MARKET WEIGHTON, ERY, ENG [37422] : C1830 CLERKENWELL, MDX, ENG [37552] : CHARLES 1820+ BIRMINGHAM, WAR, ENG [37632] : 1790+ KINGS NORTON, WAR, ENG [37632] : 1550-1650 ST PETROCK, EXETER, DEV, ENG [37783] : 1730-1855 BRINGTON, HUN, ENG [38003] : 1700-1900 SWALE MEDWAY, KEN, ENG [38249] : IVY F. 1941 PLAISTOW, LND, ENG [38259] : 1800-1850 MANCHESTER, LAN, ENG [38737] : PRE 1860 FER, IRL [38392] : C1830 KINGSLIST, DOW, IRL [37129] : 1800-1850 IRL [38737] : 1860+ TAITA, WEL, NZ [35943] : 1875+ INVERCARGILL & WELLINGTON, NZ [36836] : PRE 1824 CLK, SCT [33906] : 1780-1800 STRATHAVEN, LKS, SCT [34088] : ALL EDINBURGH, MLN, SCT [34861] : 1793-1825 LERWICK, SHI, SCT [35855] : 1700+ SUT, SCT [35880] : 1800+ THURSO, SUT, SCT [35947] : PRE 1900 GLASGOW, LKS, SCT [36067] : PRE 1875 FALKIRK, STI, SCT [37308] : C1765-95 GRETNA, DFS, SCT [37447] : 1880S WA & NY, USA [36729] : 1800+ LLANDOGO, MON, WLS [37885]

MARSHAM PRE 1810 BRADFIELD, BRK, ENG [36811]

MARSHFEEDLE 1500 HORTON, GLS, ENG [34466]

MARSHMAN C1800 HILPERTON, WIL, ENG [34999] : 1760-1850 DILTON, WIL, ENG [35076] : 1640-1780 WARMINSTER, WIL, ENG [35076] : PRE 1870 WIL, ENG [35913] : 1600-1700 WIL, ENG [37233] : 1600-1700 BRISTOL, GLS, ENG [37233] : 1800+ MOUNTAIN ASH, GLA, WLS [36158]

MARSKELL ALL LONDON, MDX & BRK, ENG [34054]

MARSLAND 1750-1900 AUDENSHAW, LAN, CHS & WAR, ENG [34520] : C1800 HEPTONSTALL, WRY, ENG [36391] : 1890-1940 ASHTON UPON MERSEY, CHS, ENG [38380]

MARSMAN 1770-1865 RECHTEREN DALFSEN, OIJ, NL [34398]

MARSON 1850+ STAFFORD, STS, ENG [35019]

MARSTERS 1800+ PALMERSTON ATOLL, COOK IS. [35969]

MARSTON 1830+ BERMUNDAH & MULGOA, NSW, AUS [35028] : 1870+ WALTHAMSTOW, ESS, ENG [34693] : 1840+ LANDPORT, CON, ENG [34693] : 1800+ KEIGHLEY, WRY, ENG [35970] : 1850+ DERBY, DBY, ENG [36257] : 1650-1950 NORTON & DEERHURST, GLS, ENG [36556] : 1820+ SPITALFIELDS, LND, ENG [37132] : 1800+ ENDERBY, LEI, ENG [37640] : PRE 1800 LEIGH, STS, ENG [37722] : CHARLOTTE C1839 MA, NH & VT, USA [38406]

MARTEL PRE 1870 QUE, CAN [34102] : 1800+ ST PETER PORT, GSY, CHI [35847] : PRE 1700 LYON, RHA, FRA [34253]

MARTELL PRE 1800 CAMBERLEY, SRY, ENG [36155] : 1750-1850 PORTSEA, HAM, ENG [36697] : PRE 1820 ALVERSTOKE & PORTSMOUTH, HAM, ENG [37214]

MARTEN CHARLES C1820-1875 CANTERBURY, KEN, ENG [34437] : PRE 1900 WALWORTH, SRY, ENG [35020] : 1900+ EASTBOURNE, SSX, ENG

[35020] : C1850-1900 LONDON, SRY & MDX, ENG [37236] : ALL SSX, ENG [37236] : ALL BRADFORD, WRY, ENG [37236] : CYRIL 1868-1950 CLIFTONVILLE, KEN, ENG [38255] : C1850-1890 JAVA, INDONESIA [37236]

MARTENS 1700-1990 SHO, GER & USA [35630]

MARTENSZN 1580 HARDERWYK, GEL, NL [33751] : 1580 HARDERWYK, GEL, NL [38692]

MARTI VICTO 1519-1715 BIRR, AG, CH [34992]

MARTIN WILLIAM HENRY 1850+ VIC, AUS [33798] : PRE 1862 SANDHURST, VIC, AUS [33862] : 1850+ INGLEWOOD, VIC, AUS [34173] : DENIS 1835+ SYDNEY, NSW, AUS [34449] : MICHAEL 1855+ IPSWICH, QLD, AUS [34449] : 1855+ STANLEY, TAS, AUS [34845] : 1870+ MELBOURNE, VIC, AUS [34904] : PRE 1898 NSW, AUS [34968] : 1854+ HOBART, TAS, AUS [35059] : 1820+ TAS, AUS [35062] : 1865+ NSW & QLD, AUS [35073] : 1850S BOOROWA, NSW, AUS [35075] : 1877+ CHARTERS TOWERS, QLD, AUS [35347] : SARAH 1846+ HOBART, TAS, AUS [35388] : 1800+ HOBART, TAS, AUS [35422] : 1870S TINGHA, NSW, AUS [35530] : TOM PRE 1837 HOBART, TAS, AUS [35792] : 1870+ COOKTOWN, QLD, AUS [36288] : 1840S+ PATERSON, NSW, AUS [36637] : JAMES 1805+ SYDNEY & SOUTH COAST, NSW, AUS [36638] : MARY ANN 1833+ SOUTH COAST, NSW, AUS [36638] : STEPHEN 1862 MELBOURNE, VIC, AUS [36772] : 1885+ WANDONG, VIC, AUS [37303] : 1894+ RICHMOND, VIC, AUS [37303] : 1854-1919 SYDNEY & ARMIDALE, NSW, AUS [37310] : 1855+ ORANGE, NSW, AUS [37313] : 1870S MYALL LAKES, NSW, AUS [37500] : 1850+ NAVARRE, VIC, AUS [37557] : PRE 1900 BALLARAT, VIC, AUS [38289] : JOSEPH PRE 1900 BOOROWA & YASS, NSW, AUS & ENG [33890] : 1838+ CAYUGA, ONT, CAN [34132] : 1700+ HALIFAX CO., NS, CAN [34225] : 1850+ SIMCOE CO., ONT, CAN [34465] : DIT ST JEAN 1680-1750 MONTREAL & SOULANGES, QUE, CAN [34514] : 1800-1900 MIDDLESEX CO., ONT, CAN [36605] : 1860+ ONT, CAN [37482] : CHARLES H. 1781-1782 HALIFAX, NS, CAN [37580] : CHARLES H. 1776-1777 QUEBEC, QUE, CAN [37580] : 1900-1915 INVERMAY, SHEHO, SAS, CAN [38473] : 1880S+ ROUNTHWAITE, MAN, CAN [38473] : GEORGE PRE 1844 SSX, ENG [33812] : PRE 1761 STITHIANS, CON, ENG [33995] : 1700+ STOWELL, SOM, ENG [34306] : JOHN 1852 SPRATTON, NTH, ENG [34309] : 1800+ LONDON, ENG [34367] : CHARLES C1820-1875 CANTERBURY, KEN, ENG [34437] : JOHN & JAMES PRE 1807 ORMSKIRK, LAN, ENG [34461] : 1780+ DORKING & CLAPHAM, SRY, ENG [34484] : ALL ENG [34561] : PRE 1880 CLIFTON UPON DUNSMORE, WAR, ENG [34562] : 1840+ PHILLACK, CON, ENG [34628] : 1700-1750 EAST GRINSTEAD, SSX, ENG [34697] : 1820-1900 PERRANARWORTHAL, CON, ENG [34697] : 1870+ LONDON, ENG [34710] : 1700-1750 STITHIANS, CON, ENG [34793] : PRE 1900 LND, ENG [34848] : PRE 1688 ST PETERS, NOTTINGHAM, NTT, ENG [34858] : PRE 1871 BRISTOL, GLS, ENG [35061] : 1780-1820 TWYWELL, NTH, ENG [35192] : 1850+ MDX, ENG [35241] : C1830 ST BLAZEY, CON, ENG [35349] : C1780 ST AGNES, CON, ENG [35349] : GEORGE 1700 TICEHURST, SSX, ENG [35361] : THOMAS 1600 TICEHURST, SSX, ENG [35361] : 1750+ RICKINGHALL, SFK, ENG [35475] : PRE 1800 KENWYN, CON, ENG [35500] : PRE 1800 BURTON JOYCE & SHELFORD, NTT, ENG [35512] : ALL FARNWORTH, LAN, ENG [35514] : JOHN ALXDR

PRE 1860 LONDON, MDX, ENG [35530] : C1800 OLD SODBURY, GLS, ENG [35563] : 1850+ KEN, ENG [35566] : 1800+ HRT & LND, ENG [35579] : PRE 1851 DEV, ENG [35601] : PRE 1800 BROADHEMBURY & PLYMTREE, DEV, ENG [35701] : 1818 FAVERSHAM, KEN, ENG [35824] : PRE 1820 WIL, ENG [35853] : 1880S LONDON, SRY, ENG [35865] : 1750+ BELBROUGHTON, WOR, ENG [35919] : PRE 1840 LONDON &, SRY, ENG [35946] : 1700-1800 HEF & SAL, ENG [36003] : 1750-1900 BKM, ENG [36007] : PRE 1900 ISLINGTON, MDX, ENG [36019] : PRE 1860 DARLINGTON, DUR, ENG [36121] : PRE 1800 DOR, ENG [36166] : 1400-1600 SSX, ENG [36420] : C1792 ENG [36594] : 1800S BOLTON, LAN, ENG [36708] : C1770-1780 WEMBURY, DEV, ENG [36788] : 1780+ FEOCK, CON, ENG [36793] : PRE 1838 KENSINGTON, MDX, ENG [36848] : 1700-1900 LONDON, ENG [36894] : JAMES C1773+ ROCHESTER, KEN, ENG [37019] : PRE 1870 LND, ENG [37057] : FAITHFUL PRE 1850 N BOVEY, DEV, ENG [37083] : PRE 1850 KEN, ENG [37091] : 1800+ EASTBOURNE, SSX, ENG [37206] : 1800+ HEATHFIELD, SSX, ENG [37206] : 1800+ HAILSHAM, SSX, ENG [37206] : 1400+ FRAMFIELD, SSX, ENG [37206] : 1400+ WALDRON, SSX, ENG [37206] : 1700+ SSX & KEN, ENG [37210] : PRE 1820 ST STITHIANS, CON, ENG [37343] : 1800S GWENNAP, CON, ENG [37343] : ALL FURNESS, CUL, ENG [37379] : CHARLES H. 1759-1776 COGGESHALL, ESS, ENG [37580] : CHARLES H. 1759-1776 LONG MELFORD, SFK, ENG [37580] : CHARLES H. 1759-1776 SSX & KEN, ENG [37580] : PRE 1700 MIDDLETON TYAS, NRY, ENG [37635] : 1850-70 NEWCROSS & DEPTFORD, LND, ENG [37670] : PRE 1850 HORSINGTON, WINCANTON, SOM, ENG [37670] : 1800+ EAST LONDON, ENG [37699] : 1910+ ACTON, LND, ENG [37719] : 1910+ GREENWICH, LND, ENG [37719] : 1871-1912 ST PANCRAS, LND, ENG [37719] : 1847 EYNESFORD, HUN, ENG [37723] : 1800+ BASFORD, NTT, ENG [37829] : PRE 1800 CUL, ENG [37923] : 1800 SHOREDITCH, LND, ENG [37928] : PRE 1840 SOURTON, DEV, ENG [37948] : PRE 1920 BETHNAL GREEN, LND, ENG [38205] : 1750-1900 QUEEN CAMEL, SOM, ENG [38471] : WILLIAM C1790 TRURO, CON, ENG [38489] : ANN C1821 KEA, CON, ENG [38489] : 1817 PLYMOUTH DOCK, DEV, ENG [38499] : 1700+ SOUTH PETHERWIN, CON & DEV, ENG [38735] : MARY PRE 1795 ENG & IRL [36100] : 1900+ ENG & IRL [37930] : 1850+ BOW, DEV, ENG & NZ [37096] : 1620-1699 MONTALAMBERT, PCH, FRA [38779] : 1800+ GIBRALTAR [37699] : PRE 1850 GALWAY, GAL, IRL [34173] : PRE 1840 LISBURN, ANT & DOW, IRL [34201] : PRE 1855 LUSMAGH & BANAGHER, OFF, IRL [34449] : DENIS C1900 GALWAY CITY, GAL, IRL [34449] : RICHARD C1900 GALWAY CITY, GAL, IRL [34449] : PRE 1870 ATHLONE, WEM, IRL [34585] : C1820 CRUMLIN, ANT, IRL [34586] : PRE 1890 MAGHERA, DRY, IRL [34632] : PRE 1845 MILFORD, DON, IRL [34804] : C1889 CONLIG, BANGOR, DOW, IRL [34972] : ALL CLA & CAR, IRL [35002] : PRE 1850 ANT, IRL [35224] : 1830-1845 IRL [35317] : PRE 1877 LIM, IRL [35347] : 1750+ DUB, IRL [35370] : PRE 1790 FER, IRL [35385] : 1800-1850 DOW, IRL [35600] : 1700-1780 LOU, IRL [35813] : JANE C1780 KILCRONAGHAN, DRY, IRL [35848] : HUGH PRE 1900 MILLISLE, DOW, IRL [35917] : PRE 1858 SLI, IRL [36288] : JOSEPH PRE 1850 CORK, COR, IRL [36432] : PRE 1900 ANNAGHLONE, DOW, IRL [36437] : 1750+ GAL, IRL [36772] : DAVID C1837 COR, IRL [37239] :

ALL BELFAST, DOW, IRL [37303] : 1700+ KIK, IRL [37826] : PRE 1800 GAL, IRL [37984] :
BERNARD PRE 1850 CAVAN, CAV, IRL [38049] : JAMES PRE 1842 FER, IRL [38291] : JAMES PRE 1842 PETTIGO, FER & DON, IRL [38291] : PRE 1815 ARDARRAGH, LOUGHORNE, DOW, IRL [38473] : PRE 1832 DUB, IRL & AUS [34773] : 1870+ CHARLESTON, NZ [37206] : 1870+ INVERCARGILL, NZ [37206] : 1800+ CHRISTCHURCH, NZ [37206] : 1870+ TEKOPURU, NZ [37206] : 1900+ NZ & AUS [33948] : C1800 MADEIRA IS., PT [35582] : JAMES 1800+ GOVAN, LKS, SCT [33784] : PRE 1823 ELN, SCT [33959] : PRE 1900 SUNNYSIDE, BEW, SCT [33959] : 1800-1900 DUNDEE, ANS, SCT [34098] : PRE 1800S DUMFRIES, DFS, SCT [34265] : MARGARET PRE 1825 PERTH, PER, SCT [34583] : WILLIAM PRE 1825 PAISLEY, RFW, SCT [34613] : ALL SCT [34758] : PRE 1824 ABERDEEN, ABD, SCT [34769] : 1830 EDINBURGH, SCT [34793] : PRE 1836 CAMPBELTOWN, ARL, SCT [34887] : 1820-1850 DUNFERMLINE, FIF, SCT [35102] : 1726 THORNHILL MADDERTY, PER, SCT [35260] : 1700+ DFS, SCT [35293] : PRE 1830 EDINBURGH, MLN, SCT [35724] : PRE 1800 SCONE, PER, SCT [36436] : PRE 1860 DONNYBRIDGE, DNB, SCT [37912] : PRE 1750 CRAIL, FIF, SCT [37913] : 1750+ KILRENNY, FIF, SCT [37913] : ANEAS C1750 KILMUIR, SKYE, SCT [38391] : 1850+ MI, USA [34465] : 1840-1860 NEW YORK, NY, USA [35317] : 1738 LOUDON CO., VA, USA [36446] : 1840-1920 EDGAR CO., IL, USA [36901] : 1630+ ACCOMACK CO, NORTHAMPTON CO., VA, USA [36914] : PRE 1800 BELMONT CO., OH, USA [36957] : JOHN 1770S VA, USA [37001] : 1900+ ELGIN, USA [37206] : ABRAM 1716 CAROLINE CO., VA, USA [37509] : CHARLES H. 1777-1789 RI & CT, USA [37580] : CHARLES H. 1789-1815 WASHINGTON CO., OH, USA [37580] : CHARLES H. 1815-1838 LICKING CO., OH, USA [37580] : CHARLES H. 1789-1796 PA, USA [37580] : PRE 1900 NY, USA [37787] : 1800 VA, USA [37792] : 1850S WAYNE CO., MS, USA [37792] : 1880-1905 ADAMS CO., CO, USA [37822] : 1880-1905 ARAPAHOE CO., CO, USA [37822] : BERNARD C1820 PHILADELPHIA, PA, USA [38049] : 1800 DUBLIN, NH, USA [38131] : 1830+ POTTSVILLE, PA, USA [38324] : PRE 1679 IPSWICH, MA, USA [38348] : LIZZIE 1800S BROOKLYN, NY, USA [38369] : SARAH 1800S OH, USA [38369] : 1900+ USA & CAN [37930] : 1850+ SWANSEA, GLA, WLS [36105] : 1770+ GLA, WLS [37923] : ALL WORLDWIDE [36333]

MARTINDALE PRE 1775 CUL, ENG [35423] : PRE 1850 UPHOLLAND, LAN, ENG [38708]

MARTINE PRE 1697 CAMERON, FIF, SCT [34285]

MARTINEAU 1800-1850 QUE, CAN [34476]

MARTING 1750-1875 ST HUBERT, BANAT, YU [37539]

MARTINS 1729 GROSSALMERODE, GHE, GER [38749]

MARTYN 1830+ GSY, CHI [33984] : 1677+ NORTH TAMERTON, CON, ENG [36875] : 1781 HALWILL, DEV, ENG [37080] : 1780S-1860S WERRINGTON, DEV, ENG [37080]

MARTZKE ALL GROB DUBSOW, POM, GER [36571]

MARUFKA PRE 1854 WARSZAWA, POL [38629]

MARUNDE C1830 TRAVEN, POM, GER [34768]

MARWEDEL PRE 1860 HOBART, TAS, AUS & BRD [35758]

MARWOOD ALL LIN, ENG [37487]

MARX 1780-1860 SIL, GER [36555]

MARYON PRE 1795 SHELLEY, ESS, ENG [37568] : ALL WORLDWIDE [36036]

MASAGORE 1800+ PARRAMATTA, NSW, AUS [35387]

MASCARIEN 1820+ SCT [38289]

MASCAUX PRE 1900 BEL [38218]

MASCHKE ALL KOSE, KOSEMUHL & STOLP, POM, GER [38621]

MASCRAFT 1700+ CT, USA [37026]

MASEFIELD ALL WORLDWIDE [38754]

MASFEN ALL WORLDWIDE [38754]

MASH PRE 1800 HUN, ENG [34324]

MASHITER 1800S ELLEL, LAN, ENG [36847]

MASIC PRE 1880 LICKO CERJA, GRACAC, YU [38063]

MASICH DEWEY 1880-1967 EVELETH, DETROIT & ST LOUIS, MN, USA [38063]

MASILUNGAN ENRICO PRE 1850 SAN JOSE, BATANGAS, PHILIPPINE [34891]

MASKELL 1844 NORTHVIEW, PURTON, WIL, ENG [35120]

MASKER 1892-1895 NEWARK, NJ, USA [37810]

MASLEN 1700-1800S STANTON ST BERNARD, WIL, ENG [34032] : PRE 1900 ALL CANNINGS, WIL, ENG [34569] : C1700 ALL CANNINGS, WIL, ENG [35260] : 1730S HAWLING, GLS, ENG [35260] : 1820-1900 WORLDWIDE [34399]

MASLIN PRE 1850 PEWSEY, WIL, ENG [35404] : PRE 1870 WOODLEIGH, WIL, ENG [35711] : C1824 KEMPSFORD, GLS, ENG [36975]

MASMEJAN 1728-1849 LES VANS, LGD, FRA [34136]

MASON 1850+ NSW, AUS [34526] : EVELYN ANNIE 1920+ STAWELL, VIC, AUS [35779] : HELEN PRE 1885 TAS, AUS [36619] : PRE 1870 NSW, AUS [37500] : PRE 1860 LIVERPOOL, LAN, ENG [33814] : 1700-1800 HEIGHINGTON, DUR, ENG [34211] : 1750+ CONNINGSBY, LIN, ENG [34221] : PRE 1780 SMEETONG WESTERBY, LEI, ENG [34501] : 1700+ SYDENHAM & MARYLEBONE, KEN, ENG [34749] : 1800+ DROYLESDEN, LAN, ENG [34870] : 1700-1800 PAINSWICK, GLS, ENG [34872] : 1800+ KEN, ENG [35041] : PRE 1850 LND, ENG [35063] : PRE 1860 LIVERPOOL, LAN, ENG [35129] : 1800+ BIRMINGHAM, WAR, ENG [35152] : 1880 BURTON ON TRENT, STS, ENG [35376] : PRE 1833 YORK, YKS, ENG [35407] : 1800-1840 WALTHAM ABBEY, ESS, ENG [35582] : C1850 LONDON, ENG [35998] : 1850-1900 WORCESTER, WOR, ENG [36109] : ALL ADDINGHAM & KILDWICK, WRY, ENG [36159] : 1810-1880S HILL CROOME & RUPPLE, WOR, ENG [36190] : ALL HANDWORTH & BIRMINGHAM, WAR, ENG [36234] : PRE 1710 BURNHAM, NFK, ENG [36425] : THOMAS PRE 1820 SPITALFIELDS, LND, MDX, ENG [36432] : JOHN 1800+ TUNBRIDGE WELLS, KEN, ENG [36471] : ALL MANCHESTER, LAN, ENG [36498] : 1810-1820 LITTLE THURROCK, ESS, ENG [36595] : SARAH 1790S LONDON, ENG [36636] : 1800+ OXFORD, OXF, ENG [36685] : 1770+ LANCASTER, LAN, ENG [36768] : PRE 1856 ROMFORD, ESS, ENG [36800] : ALL DBY, LEI & NTT, ENG [37078] : 1700-1800 SALISBURY, WIL, ENG [37233] : 1800+ ALBRIGHTON, SAL & STS, ENG [37266] : PRE 1830 LAUNCESTON, CON, ENG [37320] : 1700+ N WALSHAM, NFK & SRY, ENG [37321] : 1780+ WHATTON, NTT, ENG [37552] : C1700-1800 SHOREDITCH, MDX, ENG [37742] : PRE 1725 GUILSBOROUGH, NTH, ENG [37772] : 1800+ BOW, LND, ENG [37839] : 1800-1925 CHESTER, CHS, ENG [38074] : PRE 1900 NBL, ENG & AUS [38585] : CAROLINE M. ALL BRIGHTON, ENG & CAN [34481] : 1750-1900 LND,

ENG & NZ [35961] : C1724 MOON, KID, IRL [34579] : ELLEN 1800+ CORK CITY, IRL & AUS [34864] : 1870 CHRISTCHURCH, NZ [35582] : JOHN 1906+ PIETERMARITZBURG, NATAL, RSA [36471] : JOHN 1899+ LADYSMITH, NATAL, RSA [36471] : PRE 1850 ABERDEEN, ABD, SCT [35713] : 1770+ PITTENWEEN, FIF, SCT [35822] : PRE 1800 LKS, SCT [36955] : 1700-1990 UK & AUS [35421] : PRUDA ANN ALI MI, USA [35302] : 1790-1880 GARRARD CO., KY, IN & IL, USA [36334] : 1750-1850 GREENWICH, MA, USA [36335] : 1800-1820 SPARTENBURG, SC, USA [36737] : ALL OK, USA [36919] : ALL NC, USA [36919] : 1620+ MA, CT & ME, USA [38021]

MASS C1700-1770 LEMBERG, RPR, GER [38316]

MASSA PRE 1920 SORRENTO, ITL [36408]

MASSART 1800S VOLENCIENAS, LILLE, FRA [35409]

MASSE PRE 1620 FRA [34106]

MASSENA 1750+ BRD [35080] : ALL WORLDWIDE [34391]

MASSENGAIL ALL GER [38610]

MASSENGEIL PRE 1783 OBERNHOF & NASSAU, HEN, GER [38610] : ALL GER [38610] : PRE 1719 OSTHEIM & BUTZBACH, GHE, GER [38610]

MASSENKEIL ALL GER [38610]

MASSEY PRE 1877 WADDINGWORTH, LIN, ENG [33863] : 1750-1850 SHALBOURNE, WIL, ENG [34687] : 1700+ LISKEARD, CON, ENG [34742] : 1800+ MDX, ENG [35062] : C1870 HINSTOCK, SAL, ENG [35203] : C1850 STOKE UPON TERN, SAL, ENG [35203] : C1890 AUDLEM, CHS, ENG [35203] : PRE 1840 LINCOLN, LIN, ENG [35934] : PRE 1815 WAVENDON, BKM, ENG [35955] : SAMUAL PRE 1850 OXF, ENG [36453] : 1700+ POCKLINGTON, YKS, ENG [36568] : PRE 1840 AYLESBURY, MDX, ENG [38004] : 1750-1850 SPITALFIELDS, LND, ENG [38483] : 1800+ LIM, IRL [35370] : 1850-1900 JEFFERSON CO., IL, USA [38154] : 1850-1900 BROWN CO., IL, USA [38154] : C1700-1820 VA & KY, USA [38242] : 1840-1880 BENTON CO., IN, USA [38367]

MASSINGHAM ALL DOWNHAM MARKET, NFK, ENG [37213] : ALL PETERBOROUGH, HUN, ENG [37213]

MASSLING 1760-90 HAWLING, GLS, ENG [35260]

MASSOM PRE 1820 IRTHLINGBOROUGH, NTH & BDF, ENG [37708]

MASSON PRE 1850 ABERDEEN, ABD, SCT [35713] : PRE 1850 PAISLEY, RFW, SCT [35962] : 1884 ABD, SCT [38470]

MASTA MATHURIN 1693+ TERREBONNE, QUE, CAN [38417]

MASTAW 1800+ MI, USA [38417]

MASTERS 1837+ NSW & VIC, AUS [34780] : 1845+ SA, AUS [34883] : 1852-1878 CAMPBELLTOWN, NSW, AUS & NZ [33981] : PRE 1937 KEARNEY, ONT, CAN [37439] : PRE 1900 LIVERPOOL, LAN, ENG [34406] : PRE 1837 PEASMARSH, BREDE & RYE, KEN & SSX, ENG [34780] : 1780 WOLFHAMPCOTE, WAR, ENG [34950] : 1834+ FROME, SOM, ENG [35101] : 1796+ COMBE HAY, SOM, ENG [35567] : CHARLES 1850S CON, ENG [36316] : 1800-1860 BIRMINGHAM, WAR, ENG [37068] : 1800-1830 WARWICK, WAR, ENG [37068] : 1770-1799 MARTON & RADFORD SEMELE, WAR, ENG [37556] : 1750-1820 LONDON, ENG [38774] : ALL UK & IRL [38774] : 1843-1865 KEWEENAW CO., MI, USA [38009] : PRE 1900 WORLDWIDE [34406]

MASTERSON ANN 1830S LIVERPOOL, NSW, AUS [34698]

MASTERTON 1888+ BRIGHTON, VIC, AUS [34579] : 1800+ DUMBARTON, DNB, SCT [34260] : 1840S KIRKLISTON, WLN, SCT [34618] : PRE 1855 AUCHTERARDER, PER, SCT [35386] : PRE 1900 DUNFERMLINE & CARNOCK, FIF, SCT [37096]

MASTERTOUN PRE 1855 AUCHTERARDER, PER, SCT [35386]

MASTIN PRE 1830 MONTGOMERY & FLOYD COS., VA, USA [36334] : 1720-1800S NORTH WILKESBORO, NC, USA [38195]

MASZ C1700-1770 LEMBERG, RPR, GER [38316]

MASZLER 1700-1900 POL [38128]

MATCHETT PRE 1827 CLONCORE, ARM, IRL [36259]

MATEER 1840-90 ARM, IRL & AUS [37946]

MATEREAUX 1790-1830 BALTIMORE CITY, MD, USA [36911]

MATHEIS 1850+ TRENTON, NJ, USA [36326]

MATHER 1890+ NERRIGUNDAH, NSW, AUS [35408] : PRE 1700 WOR, ENG [34477] : 1600-1800 WIRKSWORTH, DBY, ENG [34739] : 1700-1800 SSX, ENG [35069] : 1800S SUNDERLAND, DUR, ENG [35408] : 1700S WALSALL, STS, ENG [35408] : 1780+ GATESHEAD, DUR, ENG [35408] : 1700S BILLINGE, LAN, ENG [36742] : 1840+ WEST DERBY, LAN, ENG [36815] : 1850+ PENKETH, LAN, ENG [36815] : 1800+ LIVERPOOL, LAN, ENG [36815] : 1700+ TOXTETH PARK, LAN, ENG [36815] : 1650-1900 COCKERHAM, LAN, ENG [36983] : 1800+ NTT, ENG [37699] : 1800+ LONDON, ENG [37699] : 1860+ LYTTLETON, CANT, NZ [35408] : PRE 1800 STOW, WLN & ELN, SCT [37353] : MARGARET 1831 BATH, NY, USA [38142]

MATHERS 1800+ ONT, CAN [34477] : 1729+ KIRBY BELLARS, LEI, ENG [37860] : 1800+ COOKRIDGE, YKS, ENG [38395] : JOHN C1827 SHANKILL & SEAGOE, ARM, IRL [36259] : ALL DUNDEE, ANS, SCT [34594]

MATHES 1820-1900 DARMSTADT, HEN, GER [37535] : PRE 1910 CHOLIN, CHOLNO, SU [37510] : 1810-1879 NIAGARA, NY, USA [37535]

MATHESON 1840-1880 WOLLONGONG, NSW, AUS [37349] : DUNCAN 1910+ WINNIPEG, MAN, CAN [35888] : 1923+ SKIEN, NOR [34430] : 1800+ DRUMBUIE, ROC, SCT [33993] : 1850-1950S ELGIN, MOR, SCT [34000] : PRE 1750 SKYE, INV, SCT [34364] : FLORA PRE 1837 PLOCKTON, ROC, SCT [34539] : PRE 1820 ISLE OF SKYE, INV, SCT [34959] : PRE 1900 BOWLING, DNB, SCT [35077] : PRE 1837 PLOCKTON, ROC, SCT [35086] : C1825 EDINBANE SKYE, INV, SCT [35260] : CHRISTY 1800 INV, SCT [35429] : ALL DRUMBUIE, ROC, SCT [35888] : PRE 1848 ROC, SCT [36299] : PRE 1837 ARL, SCT [37349] : 1700+ ROC, SCT [37349]

MATHEWS 1860+ PORT PIRIE, SA, AUS [34179] : 1860+ CRYSTAL BROOK, SA, AUS [34179] : 1880+ BOGGABRI, NSW, AUS [34902] : GEORGE PRE 1870 NEW ENGLAND, NSW, AUS [34902] : 1857+ NSW, AUS [36305] : PRE 1884 BYROCK & BOURKE, NSW, AUS [36631] : PRE 1857+ UXBRIDGE, MDX, ENG [35454] : ALL COLEFORD, GLS, ENG [36359] : C1850 OXFORD, OXF, ENG [37053] : 1750-1850 DOR, ENG [37188] : 1880 HOLBORN, MDX, ENG [37690] : ALL KEA, CON, ENG [37939] : 1805+ MILLFIELD, LDY, IRL [33880] : 1600-1840S DUNMURRY, ANT, IRL [33880] : 1600-1840S BRIARFIELDS & BLACK MOUNTAIN, ANT, IRL [33880] : PRE 1825 COLERAINE, LDY, IRL [34116] : PRE 1850 KILLYCOLPY, TYR, IRL [34395] : 1865 ARM, IRL [34636] : NANCY C1820 FRANKLIN, PA, USA

[34573] : ANNA 1834+ PROSPECT, CT, USA [35391] : FLETCHER 1700-1800 ORANGE CO., NY, USA [38130] : NATHANIEL 1820-1835 BRACKEN, KY, USA [38157] : 1425-1599 CASTELL Y MYNACH, GLA, WLS [33880]

MATHEWSON C1900 MAFFRA, VIC, AUS [37167] : PRE 1850 LDY & TYR, IRL [35238] : CHARLOTTE 1850-1860 KENT CO., MI, USA [35329] : JOHN E. 1880-1900 KENT CO., MI, USA [35329]

MATHIAS 1830 WHITECHAPEL, LND, ENG [37841] : C1850 SAO MIGUEL, AZORES, PT [37551]

MATHIE 1850+ SOUTH COAST, NSW, AUS [36637] : PRE 1855 STRATHMIGLO & LOGIE, FIF, SCT [35496]

MATHIESEN PRE 1870 RAPSTEEK, SHO, BRD [35330]

MATHIESON ALL GLASGOW, LKS, SCT [34119]

MATHIEU 1850+ NEW ORLEANS, LA & MS, USA & FRA [37796]

MATHISON 1700S ASHKIRK & MELROSE, ROX & SEL, SCT [33806] : 1700+ PEEBLES, PEE, SCT [33887]

MATHISONE 1600-1800 FIF, SCT [35627]

MATIMO 1815 KILMUCKACRANY, SLI, IRL [37911]

MATKIN 1800+ LONDON, ENG [36135]

MATKINS ALL USA & ENG [36901]

MATLEY JOHN PRE 1794 ASTON UNDER LYNE, LAN, ENG [37546] : JOSEPH 1830-1866 STOCKPORT, CHS & LAN, ENG [37546] : DAVID 1853-1930+ DENTON, LAN & RI, ENG & USA [37546]

MATLOCK PRE 1830 AL, USA [38314]

MATRAVES 1806-1862 ST MICHAEL, SOM, ENG & AUS [35763]

MATSSON MATS 1683+ GRODINGE, SODERMANLAND, SWE [38550]

MATTEI 1790+ CEVID, CH [34453]

MATTERN C1810 HES, GER [37536] : 1860-1910 CO, USA [36909]

MATTERSON NEALS 1790S-1800S MDX, ENG [35366] : 1840+ WAPPING, MDX, ENG [37312]

MATTES 1700+ WALDLAUBERSHEIM, RPR, GER [37042]

MATTESEN 1922+ TILBURY DOCKS, ESS, ENG [37935]

MATTET CALLETTE PRE 1900 BRUSSELS, BEL [38776]

MATTHAUS C1835 GER [34041]

MATTHES PRE 1716 GR ZIMMERN, HES, GER [38181]

MATTHEW THOMAS 1870+ MUDGEE, NSW, AUS [36600] : ALL BARTON LE WILLOWS, YKS, ENG [35198] : C1800 MABE, CON, ENG [36899] : 1843 ST VIGEANS, ANS, SCT [34950] : ALL MONTROSE, ANS, SCT [37082] : ALL ANS, SCT [37480] : PRE 1800 KIRRIEMUIR, ANS, SCT [37727]

MATTHEWS 1849+ VIC, AUS [34412] : C1918 DACEYVILLE, NSW, AUS [34694] : 1870+ LAUNCESTON, TAS, AUS [34770] : 1870+ COONAMBLE, NSW, AUS [34774] : GEORGE 1840+ NEW ENGLAND, NSW, AUS [34902] : C1872 DAYLESFORD, VIC, AUS [34971] : JANE 1800S BATHURST, NSW, AUS [35361] : 1820+ PROSPECT, NSW, AUS [35511] : MARGARET 1902+ TALLANGATTA, VIC, AUS [35522] : PRE 1884 BYROCK & BOURKE, NSW, AUS [36631] : 1870+ BROWNS CREEK, NSW, AUS [36641] : 1850-1990 MONTREAL, QUE, CAN [34249] : 1834+ NORFOLK CO., ONT, CAN [37490] : 1800S ALFORD, SRY, ENG [34172] : 1800-1990 SHOREDITCH, LND, ENG [34249] : 1740+ PAUL, CON, ENG [34258] : PRE 1815 WORCESTER, WOR,

ENG [34285] : 1800+ HARSTON, CAM, ENG [34299] : PRE 1800 CLAPHAM, BDF, ENG [34311] : PRE 1849 SANCREED, CON, ENG [34412] : 1800-1840 MORCHARD BISHOP, DEV, ENG [34448] : 1811 PENZANCE, CON, ENG [34595] : 1800-1900 WANDSWORTH, LND, ENG [35020] : 1800S MADRON, CON, ENG [35023] : 1900+ STRATFORD, ESS, ENG [35029] : PRE 1870 BOW, LONDON, MDX, ENG [35029] : C1760 ENFIELD, MDX, ENG [35095] : WILLIAM PRE 1840 SALISBURY, WIL, ENG [35232] : JOHN MARTIN C1861 PLYMOUTH, DEV, ENG [35391] : 1750+ CHESHAM, BKM, ENG [36100] : 1700-1850 SILVERTON & BRADNINCH, DEV, ENG [36205] : 1549-1909 HURSTPIERPOINT & SHERMANBURY, SSX, ENG [36212] : 1800-50 WAKEFIELD, YKS, ENG [36262] : C1899 BANHAM, NFK, ENG [36307] : PRE 1875 PORTSEA, HAM, ENG [36475] : 1952 DUNSTABLE, BDF, ENG [36781] : 1950 BUFFALOS, DUNSTABLE, BDF, ENG [36781] : 1800+ DEDDINGTON, OXF, ENG [36846] : ALL SEAVIEW, IOW, ENG [36846] : 1900+ CHS, ENG [36997] : GEORGE 1810 GUILSBOROUGH, NTH, ENG [37106] : CHARLES 1800S LND, ENG [37151] : ALL EMSWORTH, HAM & SSX, ENG [37195] : ALL MEMBURY, DEV, ENG [37378] : 1800+ LIVERPOOL, LAN, ENG [37625] : PRE 1850 LAN, ENG [37739] : PRE 1800 DOR, ENG [37760] : PRE 1900 EALING, LND, ENG [37864] : 1800+ STEPNEY, MDX, ENG [37885] : WILLIAM 1841 PLYMPTON ST MARY, DEV, ENG [38193] : C1826 KIMPTON, HRT, ENG [38489] : 1800+ CHACEWATER, CON, ENG [38726] : 1800+ GWENNAP & ST CLEER, CON, ENG & AUS [36254] : ALL NEWQUAY, CON, ENG & NZ [33981] : ANNIE 1801 IRL [35607] : 1800+ BELFAST, ANT, DOW & ARM, IRL [35636] : 1770 MOUNTMELLICK, MOG, IRL [36667] : 1848+ AUCKLAND, NTH IS., NZ [35027] : PRE 1930 GRAHAMSTOWN, CAPE, RSA [35932] : 1850S VA & OH, USA [35577] : ALL SOUTH, WLS [36613]

MATTHIEU ALL KENT CO., ONT, CAN [34154]

MATTICE 1650-1970 SCHOHARIE & LEEDS CO., NY & ONT, USA & CAN [36669]

MATTINGLY 1700S YARMOUTH, NS, CAN [35291] : JOHN 1850+ KY & IN, USA [36925]

MATTINSON 1850+ LANCASTER, LAN, ENG [37073]

MATTISON 1830+ HILLSBOROUGH, DOW, IRL [33946]

MATTJETSCHECK 1800+ HAN, GER [37019] : 1849+ HACKENSACK, NJ & NY, USA [37019]

MATTOCK 1780 TAUNTON, SOM, ENG [34204]

MATTOCKS ALL CRAWFORD CO., PA & NJ, USA [38522]

MATTSON PRE 1900 COPENHAGEN, DEN [38769]

MATU PRE 1835 KAPALONNA, BORSOD, HU [37547]

MATURIN ALL WORLDWIDE [33946]

MATUSIK 1870-1890S KROSNO, KS, POL [36940] : JOSEPH 1920-1930S NASHUA, NH, USA [36940]

MATZ PRE 1900 ERIE, PA, USA [37529]

MATZINGER 1600-1730 GER [37784] : 1730-1830 PHILADELPHIA, PA, USA [37784]

MATZKE PRE 1910 SU [37510]

MAUCH PRE 1855 FEUERBACH, WUE, GER [35393]

MAUCHAN PRE 1900 ABD, SCT [38412]

MAUCHER 1700-1850 WUE, GER [37015]

MAUDE ALL LEEDS, WRY, ENG [37366]

MAUDER GRACE PRE 1800 DEV, ENG [34963]

MAUDLIN PRE 1850 WAYNE CO., IN, USA [35312]

MAUDY PRE 1600 HYTHE & SANDWICH, KEN, ENG [36423]

MAUE C1840 SELEN, RPF, BRD **[36961]**

MAUGER DANIEL 1800+ ST ANDREWS, GSY, CHI **[34916]** : 1800S ST MARTIN, GSY, CHI **[35926]** : C1850 GUERNSEY, CHI, ENG **[36671]**

MAUGHAM ALL GAL, IRL **[35417]**

MAUGHAN 1800+ SOUTHAMPTON, HAM, ENG **[36673]** : 1850+ BELFAST, ANT, DOW & ARM, IRL **[35636]**

MAUGLE ALL BEDFORD, PA, USA **[36571]**

MAULE 1600-1750 SCT **[36081]**

MAULEY ALL NEU, CH & USA **[36405]**

MAUND PRE 1801 LND, ENG **[34979]** : 1700-1741 NORFOLK CO., VA, USA **[38009]**

MAUNDER 1750-1837 HORTON, OXF, ENG **[34687]** : PRE 1820 TIVERTON, DEV, ENG **[36015]** : PRE 1879 DEV, ENG **[36839]** : 1879+ NZ **[36839]**

MAUNDERS 1800+ CAMDEN TOWN, MDX, ENG **[34650]**

MAUNDRELL 1600+ UPTON SCUDAMORE, WIL, ENG **[35355]**

MAUNDS (SEE MOUNDS) **[35872]**

MAUNET 1650-1750 FRUTIGEN, BE, CH **[35283]**

MAUNSELL 1800+ FORT EYRE, IRL **[35429]** : ALL MONKSTOWN, DUB, IRL **[36881]**

MAUNT ALL HEADLEY, HAM, ENG **[33842]**

MAUNTON 1550-1760 WOR, ENG **[37217]**

MAUPAS 1950+ HN, FRA **[38430]** : ALL ST MARTIN DE VAUDRY, VIRE, BN, FRA **[38430]** : 1950+ BH, FRA **[38430]** : ALL FRA **[38430]**

MAUREPAS ALL MAUREPAS, FRA **[38430]**

MAURER C1830 SULZBACH, HEN, GER **[35144]** : PRE 1860 SULZBACK, NASSAU, GER **[37104]** : JACOB 1779-1815 ESCHRINGEN, SAA, GER **[38127]** : 1800-1850 LEHIGH, PA, USA **[36449]**

MAURICE 1711 HINTON ST GEORGE, SOM, ENG **[35252]** : PRE 1755 SUTTON BONNINGTON, NTT, ENG **[37754]**

MAURIER 1841-1907 LAC A LA TORTUE, QUE, CAN **[35639]**

MAURY 1600-1900 AUZAT, ARIEGE, FRA **[33758]**

MAVIN ALL WORLDWIDE **[34152]**

MAVING ALL WORLDWIDE **[34152]**

MAVINS ALL WORLDWIDE **[34152]**

MAW C1820 NORTH RUNCTON, NFK, ENG **[35974]**

MAWBY C1860 BOERN, LIN, ENG **[35807]**

MAWER 1800+ NOTTINGHAM, NTT, ENG **[36434]** : PRE 1935 NOTTINGHAM, NTT, ENG **[37726]**

MAWHINNEY 1700-1800S CASTLE DAWSON, LDY, IRL **[36837]** : 1800+ DUNDEE, ANS, SCT **[34049]**

MAWN 1900+ LONDON, ENG **[34496]**

MAWSON 1856+ LEOPOLD & STAWELL, VIC, AUS **[37300]** : 1750+ SPOFFORTH, YKS, ENG **[35370]** : PRE 1860 KESWICK, CUL, ENG **[37300]** : PRE 1800S LEEDS, YKS, ENG & CAN **[34133]** : ALL BRADFORD, YKS, ENG & NZ **[34604]**

MAXEY 1880+ POLK CO., AR, USA **[37003]**

MAXFIELD PRE 1780 WELLINGTON, SAL, ENG **[34711]** : C1761 PATELEY BRIDGE & LINTON, WRY, ENG **[37002]** : JOHN C1802 SHEFFIELD, YKS, ENG **[37383]** : ALL WORLDWIDE **[38754]**

MAXHAM C1785 MA, USA **[38184]** : ALL WORLDWIDE **[36133]**

MAXIEMME 1500+ AUNIS, FRA **[36133]** : ALL WORLDWIDE **[36133]**

MAXIM ALL ENG **[37249]** : 1500+ AUNIS, FRA **[36133]** : MABEL MAY 1896-1975 NY, USA **[36902]** : ALL WORLDWIDE **[36133]**

MAXIN ALL WORLDWIDE **[36133]**

MAXSOM ALL WORLDWIDE **[36133]**

MAXSON RICHARD PRE 1660 PORTSMOUTH, RI, USA **[38348]** : 1500+ PORTSMOUTH, RI & MA, USA & ENG **[36970]** : ALL WORLDWIDE **[36133]**

MAXSTED 1822 MARKET RASEN, LIN, ENG **[33848]**

MAXTEAD PRE 1856 KEN, ENG **[38541]**

MAXTED 1850-1900 GEELONG, VIC, AUS **[38007]** : PRE 1832 ICKHAM, KEN, ENG **[35462]** : 1790-1920 ELTHAM, KEN, ENG **[37533]**

MAXUM ALL WORLDWIDE **[36133]**

MAXWELL JOHN&THERESA 1856+ MULGOA & BURRAGORANG, NSW, AUS **[34418]** : 1860+ YASS & BURROWA, NSW, AUS **[35159]** : 1850+ TUMUT, NSW, AUS **[35872]** : 1850+ NS, CAN **[34403]** : PRE 1800 MONTREAL & JOILIETT, QUE, CAN & SCT **[34161]** : 1840-1880S BIRKENHEAD, CHS, ENG **[34510]** : 1700+ LIN, ENG **[36093]** : 1784+ IRL **[33761]** : 1800+ BELFAST, ANT, DOW & ARM, IRL **[35636]** : PRE 1850 MAGHERALIN, DOW, IRL **[35866]** : WILLIAM PRE 1900 STONEYFORD & LISBURN, ANT, IRL **[37755]** : 1800-1900 PORTAFERRY, ANT, IRL **[38004]** : 1817-25 PORT GLENONE, ANT, IRL **[38202]** : 1700+ CRAIL, FIF, SCT **[34768]** : 1800+ DFS, SCT **[35293]** : 1800S GRANGEMOUTH, STI, SCT **[35442]** : PRE 1830 KILMADOCK & DUNBLANE, PER & STI, SCT **[36125]** : PRE 1869 MINNIGAFF & PENNINGHAME, KKD & WIG, SCT **[37238]** : 1750+ CURRIE, MLN, SCT **[37666]** : 1600+ KIRKINNER, WIG, SCT **[37734]** : 1798-1800 FAYETTE TWP, ALLEGHENY CO., PA, USA **[33761]** : 1850+ CAMILLUS, NY, USA **[33762]** : 1830-1910 PERRY CO., IL, USA **[36912]** : 1800-1850 BEDFORD CO., TN, USA **[36912]** : 1845+ YELL CO., AR, USA **[36912]** : PRE 1915 CO, USA **[38217]**

MAY WILFRED 1880+ WA, AUS **[34855]** : 1840+ ADELAIDE, SA, AUS **[34855]** : 1850+ NEWCASTLE, NSW, AUS **[35800]** : FRANK 1875+ BELIZE **[37593]** : C1842 CON, ENG **[33863]** : 1770+ LAN, ENG **[34181]** : 1700S FEOCK, CON, ENG **[34214]** : 1700-1770 MYLOR, CON, ENG **[34274]** : 1750-1800 FEOCK, CON, ENG **[34697]** : 1700-1800 MYLOR, CON, ENG **[34742]** : PRE 1850 ST GERMAIN, CON, ENG **[34855]** : PRE 1800 GLOUCESTER, GLS, ENG **[34931]** : PRE 1765 WOODCHURCH, KEN, ENG **[35157]** : 1700S STAYTHORPE, NTT, ENG **[35186]** : 1800S LINCOLN, LIN, ENG **[35186]** : PRE 1856 BODMIN, CON, ENG **[35225]** : 1780S TONBRIDGE, KEN, ENG **[35260]** : 1700-1800 BRAMLEY SHERBOURNE ST JOHN, HAM, ENG **[35422]** : 1800+ MALDON, ESS, ENG **[35706]** : PEGGY PRE 1856 NEWLYN EAST, CON, ENG **[35788]** : 1700+ DEAL, KEN, ENG **[35896]** : 1700-50 WOKINGHAM, BRK, ENG **[36425]** : ANNE PRE 1644 DEV & CON, ENG **[36594]** : 1750+ SYSTON & BERMONDSEY, LEI & SRY, ENG **[36794]** : 1800-1900 WEST HANNINGFIELD, ESS, ENG **[37342]** : C1700 DEV, ENG **[37356]** : C1800 MALDON, ESS, ENG **[37449]** : 1780-1890 ILLOGAN, CON, ENG **[37488]** : ALL TREGONY, CON, ENG **[37730]** : C1800 LAMBETH, SRY, ENG **[37770]** : 1905 FARNHAM, HAM, ENG **[37865]** : C1900 WANDSWORTH, LND, ENG **[37865]** : 1700-1850 WOKINGHAM, BRK, ENG **[38084]** : PRE 1850 STOKE RIVERS, DEV, ENG **[38205]** : 1788-1810 SECKERWITZ, SIL, POL **[35850]** : 1800S MONTROSE, ANS, SCT **[34028]** : ELIZA 1820+ UK **[36621]** : PRE 1790 ALBANY, NY, USA **[34480]** : 1856 MAGOFFIN, KY, USA **[38022]** : WILLIAM 1818 PORTSMOUTH CO., OH, USA **[38152]** : 1760-1775 CHARLOTTE CO., VA, USA **[38763]**

MAYALL PRE 1850 YKS & LAN, ENG **[36380]**

MAYBERRY 1898-1673 BALLYMONEY, ANT, IRL **[38571]** : HARRIET PRE 1900 RAYMOND, ME, USA **[36563]**

MAYBERY PRE 1900 IRL & WLS **[38772]**

MAYBURY ALL WORLDWIDE [37834]

MAYCOCK PRE 1800 LONDON, ENG [37383]

MAYCROFT 1833 STURSTON, NFK, ENG [33942]

MAYELL 1750-1850 LND, ENG [35300] : 1790+ BORAD BLUNSDON, WIL, ENG [36975] : ALL WLS [37742]

MAYER PRE 1800 BARNARDISTON, SFK, ENG [33998] : 1840+ LEEK, STS, ENG [36819] : PRE 1775 UNTERJESINGEN, WUE, GER [37587] : PRE 1700 BACKNANG, WUE, GER [38683]

MAYERS ALL BUCKLEBURY, BRK, ENG [34223] : PRE 1845 WEYMOUTH, DOR, ENG [36079] : 1650-1750 GODALMING, SRY, ENG [37838]

MAYES 1780+ COPLE, BDF, ENG [35112]

MAYGER PRE 1837 SOMERSET, KEN, ENG [35532]

MAYHEW 1830 SOUTHWARK, LND, ENG [34788] : 1788 CASTLE THORPE, BKM, ENG [35256] : PRE 1800 ESS, ENG [36379] : ALL DARSHAM, SFK, ENG [36774] : 1700S NORTHERN, BKM, ENG [38350]

MAYHNE 1840+ BLYTH, NBL, ENG [38324]

MAYKIN PRE 1841 NSW, AUS [34412]

MAYMAN C1850-1900 MUCKLEFORD, VIC, AUS [35221]

MAYNARD 1860+ NOARLUNGA, SA, AUS [35771] : ANN PRE 1890 CON, ENG [34481] : 1840+ WALSALL, STS, ENG [34768] : ALL SSX, ENG [34825] : PRE 1752 GREAT HASELEY, OXF, ENG [35046] : PRE 1790 ROTHERFIELD, SSX, ENG [35406] : FRANCES PRE 1765 ENFIELD, MDX, ENG [36180] : 1750+ MDX, SRY & BKM, ENG [36574] : PRE 1850 COVENTRY, WAR, ENG [37225] : 1600-1700 WINCHESTER, HAM, ENG [37233] : 1600-1700 WIL, ENG [37233] : 1860+ SOUTHWARK, SRY, ENG [37560] : (STATIONERS) 1880 LONDON, ENG [38287] : PRE 1900 UK [37804] : 1740-1800 SUDBURY, MA, USA [38131]

MAYNE 1840+ LONDON, ENG [37294]

MAYNOR 1790-1810 BURKE, GA, USA [36911]

MAYO 1833+ SYDNEY, NSW, AUS [37119] : C1850 QUEDGLEY, GLS, ENG [34734] : 1800+ MANCHESTER, LAN, ENG [35183] : ALL LONDON, ENG [35939] : PRE 1800 HARTPURY, GLS, ENG [37681] : ALL MDX, ENG [37682] : PRE 1832 CHESHAM, BKM, ENG [37899] : 1700+ CHESTERFIELD CO., VA, USA [38032] : 1700+ HENRICO, VA, USA [38032] : PRE 1700 MA, USA & ENG [38745]

MAYOH 1840+ YOUNG, NSW, AUS [35533] : PRE 1840 TURTON, LAN, ENG [35533]

MAYOR 1860+ MILNTHORPE, WES, ENG [34092]

MAYOTT 1590-1700 LONDON, ENG [36010]

MAYS SUSANNA 1780+ NORWICH, NFK, ENG [37640]

MAYSE 1750+ KILMORE, ARM, IRL [37492]

MAYSON PRE 1830 ASPATRIA, CUL, ENG [34835]

MAYTUM THOMAS 1815+ OTHAM, KEN, ENG [35634] : PRE 1900 SITTINGBOURNE, KEN, ENG [36298]

MAZAK 1825 KALUSZ, LW, POL [38495]

MAZE ALL ENG [37283]

MAZENGARB ALL WORLDWIDE [37718]

MAZEY ALL WAR, ENG [38514]

MAZOYER 1709-1767 CLUNY, BRG, FRA [34136]

MAZUR 1800+ PASZNOWA, GALICIA, POL [36686]

MCCACKIN C1840 CAMPSIE, STI, SCT [35206]

MCADAM 1800+ LOCHMABEN, DFS, SCT [37422]

MCADAM PRE 1850 TYENDINAGA TWP., ONT, CAN [34117] : PRE 1860 CASTLE DOUGLAS, DFS, SCT [35200] : PRE 1847 GLASGOW, LKS, SCT [37138] : 1863-1935 KILMARNOCK, AYR, SCT & AUS [35784]

MCADIE 1831+ WICK, CAI, SCT [33882] : PRE 1850 WICK, CAI, SCT [36793]

MCAFEE PRE 1850 DRUMBEG, DOW, IRL [37927]

MCAINSH ALL PER, SCT [38215]

MCALANEY PRE 1914 GLASGOW, LKS, SCT [34373]

MCALEESE PRE 1890 BELFAST, ANT & DOW, IRL [35046] : ALL BALLYMENA, ANT, IRL & UK [36333]

MCALISTER JOHN 1841-1863 MORUYA, NSW, AUS [35848] : PRE 1865 CLONAVADDY & DUNGANNON, TYR, IRL [34897] : 1750-1900 BALLYCASTLE, ANT, IRL [36115] : 1875+ NYAPARA & OAMARU, OTA, NZ [34897] : PRE 1800 ARRAN, BUT, SCT [34419] : C1730 CAMPSIE, STI, SCT [35252] : DONALD 1790-1840 ISLAY, ARL, SCT [35848] : 1830-1890 FRANKLIN CO., MS, USA [36543]

MCALLAN ALL STI, SCT [35924]

MCALLISTER C1863 ORANGE, NSW, AUS [35843] : C1860S GOULBURN, NSW, AUS [35843] : 1840+ NORTHUMBERLAND CO., ONT, CAN [38410] : 1800-1900 PENDLETON, ONT, CAN & IRL [34514] : 1800S BALLYMENA, ANT, IRL [34336] : PRE 1840 LARNE, ANT, IRL [34575] : PRE 1848 BALLINTOY, ANT, IRL [34695] : C1809 KILRUSH, CLA, IRL [34942] : 1800+ CUSHENDALL, ANT, IRL [36686] : 1800 DON, IRL [36691] : 1835 NEW ROSS, WEX, IRL [36907] : PRE 1860 STI, SCT [37704] : 1750-1890 ALBANY, NY, USA [35300] : 1880+ KS, USA [36942]

MCALONEY ALL COLERAINE, LDY, IRL & CAN [34093]

MCALPHINE 1800-1850 NEWRY, DOW, IRL [35228]

MCALPIN 1812+ RICHMOND & BULGA, NSW, AUS [38756] : 1745+ KILLIN, PER, SCT [38756]

MCALPINE 1900+ ACCRINGTON, LAN, ENG [34263] : 1800-1850 LONDON, ENG [34464] : 1800+ PAISLEY, RFW, SCT [34263] : 1780-1830 EDINBURGH, SCT [34464] : ALL SCT & AUS [36348] : ALL USA [36348]

MCALPINE 1830S ISLAY, ARL, SCT [37999]

MACALUSO PRE 1850 RRIZZI, ITL [36964]

MCANALLY ALL ANT, IRL [34287] : 1700+ FER, IRL [34903] : ALL ARM, IRL [36300] : 1820S LAWRENCE CO., TN, USA [37027] : 1820S WAYNE CO., TN, USA [37027] : ALL WORLDWIDE [36300]

MCANDREW 1820-1851 BANFF, SCT [38101] : 1851-1903 CLARK CO., WA, USA [38101]

MCANERIN HERBERT ALL BARNET, HRT, ENG [38413] : WILLIAM ALL FER, IRL [38413]

MACANINY 1840S BRIDGEMAN, NSW, AUS [35156]

MCANTEE 1850-1870 WESTMINSTER, MDX, ENG [33962]

MACANULTY 1860S ADELAIDE, SA, AUS [34191]

MCANULTY 1850+ ENG [34373] : 1850+ BELFAST, ANT, IRL [34373]

MCAPPION 1850S+ HILL END, NSW, AUS [35331]

MCARA PRE 1910 CRIEFF, PER, SCT [34377] : JOHN 1830+ PER, SCT [34620] : MARY 1867+ LOGIEALMOND, PER, SCT [34620] : PRE 1900 CLYDEBANK, DNB, SCT [35378]

MCARDLE C1860 SYDNEY, NSW, AUS [35859] : 1838 MANCHESTER, LAN, ENG [37174]

MACAREE PRE 1890 SHOREDITCH, MDX, ENG [35031]

MCARTHOUR 1720-1800 ABBEY PAISLEY, RFW, SCT [36682]

MACARTHUR PRE 1882 MT GAMBIER, SA, AUS [37315] : C1761 UIG, ROC, SCT [34491] : ALL ABERNETHY & BIRNIE, MOR, SCT [34560] : 1700+ ELGIN, MOR & INV, SCT [35460]

MCARTHUR 1852+ CLUNES, VIC, AUS [35057] : 1857+ EVANDALE, TAS, AUS [35353] : HUGH

1900+ PERTH, WA, AUS [35487] : PRE 1861
LOCHGILPHEAD, ARL, SCT [34252] : DUNCAN
PRE 1825 GREENOCK, RFW, SCT [34310] : 1700+
INV & ARL, SCT [34572] : C1825 GLASGOW, LKS,
SCT [35057] : 1827+ KINTRA, MULL, ARL, SCT
[35057] : C1800 ARL, SCT [35057] : ALL
CAMBUSLANG, LKS, SCT [35353] : 1700+ ELGIN,
MOR & INV, SCT [35460] : ALL ABERNETHY &
BIRNIE, MOR, SCT [35460] : HUGH 1800+ ARL,
SCT [35487] : PRE 1800 GLASGOW, LKS, SCT
[36436] : ALL ISLAY, ARL, SCT [36451] : 1840+
GLASGOW, LKS, SCT [37575] : 1871
INNERCRAIGIE, PER, SCT [37769] : 1750+ ABD,
SCT [38349] : 1700+ PER & GLS, SCT, ENG &
[36266] : PERCY 1880-1920 ST LOUIS, MO, USA
[38349] : JOHN 1852 ST LAWRENCE CO., NY, USA
& CAN [38140]

MACARTNEY 1640+ ANT & ARM, IRL [38720]

MCASKILL 1853+ NSW, AUS [36608] : 1810+
DUNVEGAN, INV, SCT [36608]

MCASLAN 1700+ BLANTYRE & GLASGOW, LKS,
SCT [36705] : PRE 1865 BARONY, LKS, SCT [37852]

MCATAMNEY C1876 ANT, IRL [34792]

MCATANNEY PRE 1900 IRL [37496]

MCCAUGHEY 1850+ MN, USA [38222]

MACAULAY 1750-1850 STORNOWAY, ROC, SCT
[36240] : 1800+ N UIST, INV, SCT & CAN [34403]

MCAULAY 1850S CLARENCE RIVER, NSW, AUS
[35260] : C1800 COSHLETTER SKYE, INV, SCT
[35260] : C1834 SCT [37474]

MCAULEY 1850+ SYDNEY, NSW, AUS [38582] :
1800-1835 BELFAST, ANT, IRL [33994] : 1830S
KILLINCHY, DOW, IRL [34359] : PRE 1850 LDY,
IRL [35863] : 1800-1900 BALLYCASTLE, ANT, IRL
[36115] : GEORGE C1790+ LARNE, ANT, IRL
[36244] : 1800+ CUSHENDUN, ANT, IRL [36686] :
PRE 1835 STRABANE, TYR, IRL [37138] : PRE 1905
BALLYNAHINCH, DOW, IRL [37439] : 1800-1850
FER, IRL [37678] : 1750-1900 BALLYMENA, ANT,
IRL [38024] : 1700-1850 DUNFERMLINE, FIF, SCT
[36727] : 1812+ SCT & CAN [34200]

MCAULIFFE 1845 BLAYNEY, NSW, AUS [34038] :
FLOURANCE 1866+ GINNINDERRA, NSW, AUS
[34885] : PRE 1860 KANTURK, COR, IRL [33835] :
1800-1900 COR, IRL [34071] : 1800+ ROCKLAND,
ME & COR, USA & IRL [38225]

MCAULLIFFE 1800S COR, IRL [35379]

MACAULY (SEE MCAULEY [36727]

MCAUSLAND 1800+ UK [33948]

MCAUSLANE 1830 BONHILL, DNB, SCT [34474]

MACAW PRE 1900 KILREA & INISHRUSH, LDY,
IRL [36529]

MCBAIN WILLIAM PRE 1851 ABD, SCT [33951] :
1780+ KINGUSSIE, INV, SCT [34268] : 1826+
DIOMISH, INV, SCT [34954] : 1800 SCT [38531]

MCBARN C1855 SYDNEY, NSW, AUS [37971]

MCBARRON PRE 1870 FER, IRL [34779] : PRE 1855
COOLGARN, FER, IRL [37971]

MCBEAN ANNE PRE 1851 ABD, SCT [33951] : PRE
1815 URQUHART, ROC, SCT [34689] : PRE 1880
KILTARLITY, INV, SCT [34923]

MCBEATH PRE 1740 BOWER, CAI, SCT [33873]

MCBEE G.C. 1799-1820 KNOX CO., TN, USA [38144] :
1500+ HALIFAX CO., VA, NC & AL, USA & SCT
[36970]

MACBETH 1790S LESMAHAGOW, LKS, SCT [35406]

MCBETH C1850 WOODSTOCK, ONT, CAN [34491] :
C1800 ARM, IRL [36671]

MCBRIAR 1875+ VIC, AUS [35550] : C1800-75 ARM &
DOW, IRL [35550]

MACBRIDE PRE 1884 COCKERMOUTH, CUL, ENG
[37610]

MCBRIDE 1860+ TAREE, NSW, AUS [34690] :
ELLEN 1890+ SYDNEY, NSW, AUS [37035] :
1845+ NORFOLK CO., ONT, CAN [34114] : 1850+
QUE, CAN [38171] : 1874-1941 ST JOHNS, NFD,
CAN & USA [36960] : 1870+ COULSDON &
CROYDON, SRY, ENG [33865] : PRE 1880
LIVERPOOL, LAN, ENG [35430] : 1800+
NEWCASTLE, NBL, ENG [35644] : PRE 1830
HARRINGTON, CUL, ENG [36204] : 1750-1900
BELFAST, ANT, IRL [33851] : PRE 1900 MILFORD,
DON, IRL [33902] : 1800-1850 LONDONDERRY,
LDY, IRL [34114] : 1820+ IRL [34290] : 1800-1870
TYR, IRL [34346] : PRE 1840 BAILY, WEX, IRL
[35088] : 1750-1930 CULFEIGHTRIN, ANT, IRL
[36115] : 1750-1930 GLENSHESK, ANT, IRL [36115] :
PRE 1845 DROMORE, TYR, IRL [37035] : 1800-1900
ROSNOWLAGH, DON, IRL [38171] : 1850-1890S
DALMELLINGTON, AYR, SCT [33865] : 1828-1850S
CROSSHILL, AYR, SCT [33865] : 1800+ DUNDEE,
ANS, SCT [34049] : 1750+ KKD, SCT [34345] : 1789-
1846 LAMLASH, ARRAN IS., SCT [36960] : 1750-
1850 RERRICK, KKD, SCT [37644] : 1820-1882
LAMLASH, ARRAN IS., SCT & NFD [36960] : ALL
KS, USA [34155] : 1800-1876 YELL CO., AR, USA
[36939] : FRED 1920-1950 NEW YORK, NY, USA
[38240] : PRE 1830 NJ, USA [38240] : WILLIAM 1800-
1850 CINCINNATI, OH, USA [38240]

MCBRYDE 1750-1900 WIG & LKS, SCT [34229]

MCBRYDE (SEE MCBRIDE [36204]

MCBURNEY ALL IRL [35011] : 1700-1990
ENNISKILLEN, FER, IRL & AUS [35421]

MCBURNIE 1850S RUSHCUTTERS BAY, NSW, AUS
[36857] : 1800+ BALLYMORE, ARM, IRL [36857]

MCCABE ALL ADJALA, SIMCOE, ONT, CAN [35833]
: 1820-1850 PIMLICO, LND, ENG [36763] : PRE 1840
LIVERPOOL, LAN, ENG & IRL [36849] : 1790+
BENGAL, INDIA [35032] : ALL ARM, IRL [34475] :
C1846-1873 DERRYGONNELLY, FER, IRL [34635] :
PRE 1829 CLONES, MOG, IRL [34806] : PRE 1850
PORTADOWN, ARM, IRL [35430] : 1700S
BALLMONY, ANT, IRL [36709] : 1800 LOU, IRL
[37027] : 1750-1840 CASTLEBLAYNEY, MOG, IRL
[38045]

MCCAFFERTY PRE 1864 KILBIRNIE, AYR, SCT
[33845]

MCCAFFERY PRE 1860 ADELAIDE, SA, AUS [35128]
: PRE 1885 BELFAST, IRL [34519]

MCCAFFREY 1850+ QLD, AUS [38539] : 1850+ VIC,
AUS [38539] : 1700-1800 LONDON, MDX, ENG
[36438] : 1800+ MILL TOWN, DUB, IRL [38539] :
1800+ MILLTOWN, CAV, IRL [38539] : 1820+
ENNISKILLEN, FER, IRL [38539] : 1800+ RED
HILLS, CAV, IRL [38539]

MCCAGHAN PRE 1860 BUSHMILLS, ANT, IRL
[37179]

MCCAGUE PRE 1785 DOW, IRL [38348]

MCCAHON 1750+ KILREA, DRY, IRL [37160]

MCCAIG 1800+ KILLINCHY, DOW, IRL [34190]

MCCAIN PRE 1840 TIPTON CO., TN, USA [38783]

MCCALL ALL IRL [37927] : 1800S ARM, IRL [38422] :
DAVID 1848 IRL & SCT [36902] : JOHN & BARB.
1849-C1965 STEVENSTON, AYR, SCT [34300] :
MARY & ELIZ. C1876-C1950 STEVENSTON, AYR,
SCT [34300] : C1884-C1960 PAISLEY, RFW, SCT
[34300] : PRE 1820 GREENOCK, RFW, SCT [34615] :
PRE 1850 SANQUHAR, DFS, SCT [35406] : ALL
FALKIRK, STI, SCT [37308] : 1840 MONROE CO.,
AL, USA [37792] : 1830-1900 CINCINNATI, OH,
USA [38149]

MCCALLAN PRE 1853 LDY, IRL [34779]

MCCALLEN ALL USA [38287]

MCCALLISTER 1734-1780 BLADEN CO., NC, USA [38107]

MCCALLUM 1750+ ARDCHATTAN, ARL, SCT [34419]

MCCALLUM 1890S CLIFTON HILL, VIC, AUS [34936] : C1850 MIDDLESEX CO., ONT, CAN [35605] : PRE 1840 KEMPTVILLE, ONT & RFW, CAN & SCT [33905] : 1860-1880 LIVERPOOL, LAN, ENG [38515] : PRE 1850 DRY & LDY, IRL [34013] : 1850 MOG, IRL [35535] : 1770-1840 GLASGOW, LKS, SCT [34010] : PRE 1854 DURNESS, SUT, SCT [34039] : 1800+ FEARNAN, PER, SCT [34075] : 1700-1800 MUCKAIRN, ARL, SCT [34225] : 1800+ STIRLING, STI, SCT [35865] : 1840+ BARONY & GLASGOW, LKS, SCT [36749] : PRE 1900 SOUTHEND, ARL, SCT [36761] : 1700+ PAISLEY, RFW, SCT [36794] : PRE 1880 LISMORE, ARL, SCT [36877] : 1700+ MULL, ARL, SCT [37480] : PRE 1900 ARL, SCT [38434] : 1730-1830S GLASGOW, LKS, SCT [38515] : PRE 1850 PA, USA [35605]

MCCALMAN 1700S IONA & MULL, ARL, SCT [33849]

MCCAMBRIDGE 1750-1940 BALLYCASTLE, ANT, IRL [36115]

MCCAMEY ALL AUS & IRL [35345] : PRE 1850 AUGHNACLOY, TYR, IRL [34850]

MCCAMLEY 1800+ BELFAST, YKS, ENG [37640]

MCCAMMON 1800+ BROOKLYN, NY, USA [36935] : 1840+ SYRACUSE, NY, USA [36935]

MCCAMPBELL 1750-1850 ROCKBRIDGE CO., VA, USA [38154]

MCCANDLISH PRE 1874 GLASGOW, LKS, SCT [34706]

MCCANN 1860+ OBERON, NSW, AUS [35586] : 1855+ SYDNEY, NSW, AUS [37987] : 1841-1895 SYDNEY & BEECHWOOD, NSW, AUS [38761] : 1800-1900 PERTH CO., ONT, CAN [34106] : HUGH CHASE 1820-1900 KEMPTVILLE, ONT, CAN [34514] : C1835 SEAGOE, ARM, IRL [34474] : HUGH CHASE 1820-1850 IRL [34514] : 1840S CARRICKMACROSS, MOG, IRL [35138] : 1800+ ANT, IRL [36251] : 1800+ SLI, IRL [37175] : PRE 1900 CASTLECONNELL, LIM, IRL [37987] : 1750-1900 BALLYMENA, ANT, IRL [38024] : 1802-1841 DRUMSNAT, MOG, IRL [38761] : PRE 1875 DUB, IRL [38772] : C1800S IRL & CAN [34133] : 1810-1846 SAINTFIELD, DOW, IRL & CAN [34244] : 1800-1900 CA, USA [38024] : 1860 IRL &, WORLDWIDE [37511]

MCCANNA 1800S WOLLOMBI, NSW, AUS [35159]

MCCAREY 1820-1860 BALLYCARRY, ANT, IRL [34751]

MCCARLIN 1750-1850 DROGHEDA, LOU, IRL [38575]

MCCARMIE 1820-35 ROBISON TWP., BERKS, PA, USA [38054]

MCCARNEY C1850 BATHURST & FORBES, NSW, AUS [34009] : 1840+ NSW, AUS [38771] : PRE 1860 LOWTHERSTOWN, FER, IRL [38771]

MCCAROLL ALL BALLYMENA, ANT, IRL [36822]

MCCARRAGHER 1800+ E BOSTON, MA, USA [37079]

MCCARRISON PRE 1900 BANBRIDGE, DOW, IRL [35962] : PRE 1900 KILBARCHAN, RFW, SCT [35962] : PRE 1900 PHILADELPHIA, PA, USA [35962] : PRE 1990 WORLDWIDE [35962]

MCCARROLL C1760 PA, USA [37536]

MCCARRY 1750-1900 MURLOUGH, ANT, IRL [36115]

MCCARSLARE C1800 SCT [34487]

MCCARTENAY 1920 ROCKWOOD & WEDDIFIELD, ONT, CAN [36679] : 1920 NIPPISSING, ONT, CAN [36679]

MCCARTHY 1887+ REDBANK, VIC, AUS [34174] : 1935+ FAIRFIELD & PRESTON, VIC, AUS [34702] :

T.M. 1864+ PINDARI, NSW, AUS [35088] : MARY C1858 ROSEBROOK & MAITLAND, NSW, AUS [35104] : C1835 SYDNEY, NSW, AUS [35400] : 1830-1850S SYDNEY, NSW, AUS [35589] : 1790+ SYDNEY, NSW, AUS [36236] : C1860 BALLINA, NSW, AUS [36284] : 1835+ SYDNEY, NSW, AUS [36372] : C1840 WOOLWICH, KEN, ENG [36041] : PRE 1860 LAN, ENG [36599] : 1800+ COR, IRL [33788] : 1830S COR, IRL [33934] : C1847 SKIBBEREEN, COR, IRL [34586] : 1830S CLASHMORE, WAT, IRL [34618] : 1820+ COR, IRL [34764] : ALL YOUGHAL, COR, IRL [34886] : 1800+ COR, IRL [34933] : PRE 1838 COR, IRL [35088] : PRE 1823 YOUGHAL, COR, IRL [35088] : MARY 1834+ TRALEE, KER, IRL [35104] : PRE 1858 ENNISTIMON, CLA, IRL [35113] : PRE 1840 LIM, IRL [35589] : 1800+ COR, IRL [36000] : PRE 1900 GLOUNBRACK, COR, IRL [36168] : 1750+ COR, COR, IRL [36236] : 1775-1850 COR, IRL [36318] : JUSTIN 1830 IRL [36443] : 1830S CORK, COR, IRL [36691] : PRE 1835 MITCHELSTOWN, COR, IRL [37035] : 1800+ KILLALOE, CLA, IRL [38189] : 1840+ KIELMABEA, COR, IRL [38484] : ALL GAL, IRL & AUS [35213] : 1847-1900 HOWICK, AUCK, NZ [36832] : ALL PHILA & CHESTER CO., PA, USA [36318]

MCCARTIN 1880+ GEELONG, VIC, AUS [35869]

MCCARTNEY ALL WALKERTON GODRICH, ONT, CAN [34133] : 1851 TORPENHOW, CUL, ENG [35769] : 1847 BRIDEKIRK, CUL, ENG [35769] : 1700+ LIVERPOOL, LAN, ENG [35970] : 1850+ HULME, MANCHESTER, LAN, ENG [36066] : WILLIAM PRE 1870 (PORK BUTCHER) MANCHESTER, LAN, ENG [36066] : 1800+ CARNAHAGH, ARM & ANT, IRL [33857] : PRE 1863 COMBER, DOW, IRL [34588] : 1800+ MAUCHLINE, AYR, SCT [33948] : 1700-1850 SCT [35136] : 1700+ GIRVAN, AYR, SCT [37620] : C1859+ PARTICK, LKS, SCT [38067] : 1900+ PHILADELPHIA, PA, USA [36066] : ALL WORLDWIDE [38346]

MCCARTY C1860+ ABBEYSVILLE, LIM, IRL [36838] : PRE 1793 MIDDLESEX CO., NJ, USA [37811] : 1787-1817 HARDWICK, NJ, USA [37811] : PRE 1830 VA, USA [38576]

MCCAUGHAN 1750-1930 BALLYCASTLE, ANT, IRL [36115]

MCCAUGHIE ALL PORTSMOUTH, HAM, ENG [36232] : ALL WHITECHAPEL, LND, ENG [36232]

MCCAUGHTY 1800-1850S BELFAST, ANT, IRL [34028]

MCCAUL E. ELIJAH 1818-1900 BRIDGESTONE, HUMBERSTONE, ONT, CAN [38426] : REV ALEXANDER 1750-1830 DRUMMONDVILLE, NEWARK, CAN [38426] : ALL IRL [37927] : REV ALEXANDER PRE 1830 SKYE, SCT [38426]

MCCAULEY PRE 1900 ANT, IRL [35915] : 1800-1850 DERRYGONNELLY, FER, IRL [37678] : JOHN J. PRE 1850 FLINT, MI, USA [38049]

MCCAULL 1850 TULLA, CLA, IRL [36274]

MCCAUSLAND 1700-1800 FRUIT HILL, DRY, IRL [35600] : 1850+ FALCARRAGH, DON, IRL [38011] : 1800+ UK [33948]

MCCAUSLIN 1800+ DEV, ENG & SCT [33948]

MCCHESNEY 1800 LANARK CO., ONT, CAN & SCT [38349]

MCCLAFFERTY 1800 WISHAW, DON, IRL [37125]

MCCLAIN 1850-70 AR, USA [37533] : 1810-1930 BATH CO., KY, USA [38089]

MCCLANAHAN 1770-1800S SC & AL, USA [37812]

MCCLAREY PRE 1830 COMBER, DOW, IRL [34588]

MCCLATCHEY 1768-1893 HILLSBOROUGH, DOW, IRL [37524]

MCCLEAN ALL STOCKTON ON TEES, DUR & MDX, ENG [34561] : 1800+ LYLEHILL & CARNMONEY, ANT, IRL [37425] : 1800+ BALLYLINNEY & TEMPLEPATRICK, ANT, IRL [37425] : 1800+ BALLYAUTOGUE & UMGALL, ANT, IRL [37425] : DANIEL PRE 1907 ANT, IRL [37601]

MCCLEARY ALL RASHEE & TEMPLEPATRICK, ANT, IRL [34287] : 1820+ FAYETTE, ROSS & CLARK CO., OH, USA [37565]

MCCLEERY 1800-1890S GLASGOW, LKS, SCT [34018]

MCCLELAN PRE 1812 TIBBERMORE, PER, SCT [33957]

MACCLELLAND PRE 1870 MONEYMORE, LDY, IRL [36260]

MCCLELLAND ALL BALLYMONEY, ANT, IRL [33842] : 1806 LOUDON, AYR, SCT [35560] : MARY PRE 1800 WASHINGTON CO., PA, USA [38536]

MCCLEMENT EVANGELINE 1870-1900S HOBART, TAS, QLD & NSW, AUS, ENG & [36311]

MCCLENAGHAN 1600-1850 BELLAGHY, LDY, IRL [33851] : PRE 1860 ANT, IRL [34763]

MCCLENAHEN PRE 1760 DON, IRL [38769]

MCCLINTOCK 1860+ MELBOURNE, VIC, AUS [35734] : 1800-1900 ENNISKILLEN, FER, IRL [35600] : 1700-1800 TREANTAGH (TRINTAGH), DON, IRL [35600] : 1800-1880 WESTPORT, MAY, IRL [35600] : 1800+ RFW, SCT [33948]

MCCLOSKEY 1860+ LYNDHURST, NSW, AUS [36316] : ALL IRL [37930] : ALL IRL & USA [36933]

MCCLOUD PRE 1850 BISHOPSGATE, LND, ENG [36361]

MCCLOY 1850+ PERTH CO., ONT, CAN [34056] : PRE 1850 ANT, IRL [34056] : ALL AGHADOWEY, LDY, IRL [34287] : PRE 1850 LARNE, ANT, IRL [38726]

MCCLUGHAN MARY NEED ALL BALLYCASTLE, ANT, IRL [33921]

MCCLURE 1850+ CAMPERDOWN, NSW, AUS [36648] : 1900S QUEANBEYAN, NSW, AUS [36648] : 1850+ NARRANDERA, NSW, AUS [36648] : 1800S GLENARM, ANT, IRL [34080] : PRE 1850 CLONDAVADDOCK, DON, IRL [34611] : 1800+ RAPHOE, DON, IRL [36648] : EDWARD 1840 DALKIETH, MLN, SCT [33956] : WILLIAM C1895 DALRY, AYR, SCT & USA [34300]

MCCLURG PRE 1910 KILLYLEAGH, DOW, IRL [36761]

MCCLUSKEY 1840S TARA, MEA, IRL [35560]

MACCLUSKIE ALL SCT [36339] : ALL USA [36339]

MCCLUSKIE ALL SCT [36339] : ALL USA [36339]

MCCLYMONT 1800+ SCT [33948] : 1865 GLASGOW, LKS, SCT [34529] : 1838 EDINBURGH, MLN, SCT [34529] : PRE 1800 GIRVAN, AYR, SCT [35406]

MCCOLE ALL INV, SCT [34593]

MCCOLEDONICH 1700+ KILTARLITY, INV, SCT [34639]

MCCOLL 1870+ ELGIN CO., ONT, CAN [38431] : PRE 1886 DON, IRL [33862] : ALL IRL [37927] : PRE 1854 STRABANE, TYR, IRL [37994] : PRE 1840 MULL, ARL, SCT [33814] : 1890+ DUMBARTON, DNB, SCT [34260] : 1860+ GLASGOW, LKS, SCT [34260] : PRE 1860 GLASGOW, LKS, SCT [36592] : PRE 1880 LISMORE, ARL, SCT [36877] : ALL LISMORE ISLAND, ARL, SCT [38431] : 1877+ KILMARNOCK, AYR, SCT & USA [35150] : 1900+ SCHENECTADY, NY, USA [35150]

MCCOLLUM 1750-1775 BEDFORD CO., PA, USA [38137] : ALL NC, IN, IL, IA, USA [38363]

MCCOLM JOHN PRE 1793 TYR, IRL [37014] : DAVID 1809-1901 ADAMS CO., OH, USA [37014] : 1775-1820 VA & OH, USA [37577]

MCCOM BENJAMIN PRE 1776 MA, USA [36925]

MCCOMAS PRE 1825 GILES, VA, USA [37819]

MCCOMB 1650-1850 ENG [36988] : 1850+ POYNTZPASS, DOW, IRL [36368] : 1650-1900 RSA [36988] : 1800+ AYR, SCT [35140] : 1750-1850 BOSTON, SUFFOLK CO., MA, USA [38153]

MCCOMBES 1836-1891 NELSON, NZ & IRL [36255]

MCCOMBIE 1800+ RSA [35032]

MCCOMISKEY ALL LISBURN, ANT, IRL [36697]

MACCON C1770 LIM, IRL [36000]

MCCONACHY 1850-1900 GEELONG, VIC, AUS [38007]

MCCONAGHY 1750-1900 BALLYCASTLE, ANT, IRL [36115]

MCCONAUGHEY PRE 1900 USA [38303]

MCCONKEY PRE 1800 RADEERPARK, MOG, IRL [35151]

MACCONNELL ALL PICTOU CO., NS, CAN [36713]

MCCONNELL PRE 1878 MYRTLEFORD, VIC, AUS [37901] : 1880-1910 ASSINIBOIA, MAN, CAN [34101] : PRE 1900 ANDERGARNAY, DON, IRL [33966] : C1800 NEWRY, ARM, IRL [34006] : C1850 ROSTREVOR, DOW, IRL [35722] : C1790+ BELFAST, ANT, IRL [35741] : PRE 1820+ CRUSHYBRACKEN, ANT, IRL [35759] : PRE 1870 ANT, IRL [36077] : PRE 1800 LIM & COR, IRL [37807] : 1800+ ARDROSSAN, AYR, SCT [33948] : JOHN C1821 MONKTON, AYR, SCT [34300] : C1900+ MISSOULA, MT, USA [34101] : C1900+ SEATTLE, WA, USA [34101]

MCCONNICO ELIZ. 1700S NC & VA, USA [38536]

MCCONOMY C1800 STRABANE, TYR, IRL [34426]

MCCOOK 1815 COLERAINE, ANT, IRL [34814] : 1790+ ARMOY, ANT, IRL [35815] : 1600-1900 ARRAN, ARL, SCT [34537] : PRE 1800 JAMAICA, W.INDIES [35521]

MCCOOL 1820-1870 BALLYMONEY, ANT, IRL [33947] : 1800-1860 GWEEDORE, DON, IRL [34880]

MCCORD 1840S WEM, IRL [34172] : JAS 1890+ BELFAST, N IRL [36291] : JAS 1800S PORTADOWN, ARM, N IRL [36291]

MCCORKILL PRE 1820 LETTERKENNY, DON, IRL [38056]

MACCORMACK 1920+ SYDNEY & PEAKHURST, NSW, AUS [36600]

MCCORMACK C1900 ALLANDALE AREA, VIC, AUS [36278] : 1780-1860 LOG, IRL [34514] : PRE 1837 KILMURRY MCMAHON, CLA, IRL [34900] : 1800S TIP, IRL [35379] : C1850 O'BRIENSBRIDGE, CLA, IRL [35920] : C1840 BALLYMENA, ANT, IRL [36278] : 1800S DON, IRL [37497]

MCCORMICK PRE 1923 COWANGIE, VIC, AUS [33997] : 1850+ HOBART, TAS, AUS [34871] : PRE 1840 IRL [34368] : LUKE 1840+ MULLINGAR, WEM, IRL [34871] : 1800+ KILKEEL, DOW, IRL [35529] : C1820 PORTAFERRY, DOW, IRL & SCT [37143] : PRE 1870 OAMARU, OTG, NZ [33997] : 1850+ NZ [35952] : 1820S CAMPBELTOWN, ARL, SCT [34156] : 1840+ GREENOCK, RFW, SCT [34156] : ALL ISLE OF MULL, ARL, SCT [35952] : ALL ISLE OF MULL, ARL, SCT [37154] : 1830S ROBISON TWP., BERKS, PA, USA [38054] : PRE 1870 MONTOUR CO., PA, USA & IRL [36917]

MCCORQUODALE 1740-1760 ARL, SCT [34408]

MCCORT 1798-1887 HAGERSVILLE, ONT, CAN & IRL [34164]

MCCOSH PRE 1780 STAIR, AYR, SCT [35406]

MCCOUAIG 1800-1900 RATHLIN ISLAND, ANT, IRL [36115]

MCCOUL 1780-1900 GLASGOW, LKS, SCT [34557]

MCCOURT PRE 1900 BELFAST, DOW, IRL [36707] :
JAMES 1869-1927 TYR & ARM, IRL [37800] :
CHARLIE 1800S IRL & USA [37800]

MCCOWAN 1838+ BRUCEFIELD, ONT, CAN [37451]
: 1840S TYR, IRL [37577] : ALL DURA, ARL, SCT
[37451] : ALL BALLACHULISH, INV, SCT [37451] :
ALL FORT WILLIAM, INV, SCT [37451] : 1600+
WORLDWIDE [38388]

MCCOY C1800+ AUS [34444] : 1850+ BRISBANE,
QLD, AUS [36632] : 1880+ MOOSEJAW, SAS, CAN
[35627] : 1772 ERNESTOWN, ONT, CAN [36680] :
1830-1860 YORK CO., ONT, CAN [38033] : 1830+
PLYMOUTH, DEV, ENG [35943] : 1700+ MOG, IRL
[34572] : 1800+ BELFAST, ANT, IRL [35627] : 1750+
DUBLIN &, SLI, IRL [36087] : 1830+ BELFAST,
MOG, IRL [36641] : PRE 1820 HILLSBOROUGH,
DOW, IRL [37811] : 1800-1900 OWEN CO., KY, USA
[36939] : 1860+ MI, USA [38033] : 1815-1835 TN, USA
[38105]

MCCRACKEN 1880+ STAWELL, VIC, AUS [35207] :
1868+ BEAUFORT, VIC, AUS [35487] : 1800-1880
ARM, IRL [34774] : 1850+ NEWRY, DOW, IRL
[35219] : JN & MARYANN 1832 BENRAW, DOW,
IRL [37514] : PRE 1850 DOW, IRL [37807] :
WILLIAM 1864+ PORTPATRICK, WIG, SCT
[34627] : PRE 1860 STRANRAER, WIG & LKS, SCT
[34958] : PRE 1880 PORT PATRICK, WIG, SCT
[35207] : 1800+ PAISLEY, AYR, SCT [35487]

MCCRAE 1850+ VIC, AUS [35379] : C1895
MELBOURNE, VIC, AUS [36762] : 1830+ NEW
RICHMOND, QUE, CAN & USA [37486] : C1800+
GLENWHERRY, ANT, IRL [35995] : PRE 1900
GLASGOW, SCT [35055] : C1851+ DALRY, AYR,
SCT [35995]

MCCRAIG PRE 1850 DOWN PATRICK, DOW, IRL
[38772]

MCCRATH 1840+ BOWENFELS, NSW, AUS [34843]

MCCREA ALL TEMPLEPATRICK, ANT, IRL [34287] :
ALL STRABANE, TYR, IRL [35888] : 1800+
DUNGANNON, TYR, IRL [36135] : 1800S BIG
PARK, DON, IRL [37818]

MCCREADIE PRE 1850 ANT, IRL [37923] : C1846
IRVINE, AYR, SCT [35486] : C1855 GLASGOW,
LKS, SCT [35486] : 1820+ LKS, SCT [37923]

MCCREADY 1865 PENRITH, NSW, AUS [36273] :
1828+ SYDNEY, NSW, AUS & NZ [35814] : 1800-
1960 LINCOLN CO., ONT, CAN [34114]

MCCREARY 1850-IL & NE, USA [35279] : 1769-1900
TUSCARAWAS CO., OH & IN, USA [36901]

MCCREATH 1850+ IPSWICH, QLD, AUS [35814]

MCCREDIE PRE 1830 STONEYKIRK, WIG, SCT
[38773]

MCCREESH C1850-1870 MIDDLESEX CO., MA, USA
[36337]

MCCRILLIS 1500-1650 IRL [37784]

MCCRONE 1800+ FIF, SCT [35865] : C1800 OLD
CUMNOCK, AYR, SCT [37772]

MCCRORY C1770 TYNAN, ARM, IRL [34672] : 1750+
TYNAN & COOKSTOWN, ARM, IRL & NZ [36850]

MCCROSIN PRE 1800 NEWBATTLE, MLN, SCT
[37852]

MCCROSSAN NEIL C1850 DON, IRL [38397] : NEIL
1874 GLASGOW, SCT [38397]

MCCROSSEN C1860 YOUNG, NSW, AUS [36284] :
PRE 1860 TYR, IRL [34763]

MCCRUM ROBERT 1839+ ANT & SLI, IRL [35426] :
JOHN 1819+ DROMORE, DOW, IRL [35426]

MCCRUTCHIE ALL WORLDWIDE [34471]

MCCUAIG PRE 1866 BEAUHARNOIS CO., QUE,
CAN [38412]

MCCUBBIN PRE 1860 DFS, SCT [34617] : ALL SCT &
AUS [36348] : ALL USA & CAN [36348]

MCCUDDEN ALL AUS [34759]

MCCUE 1800S MUNDERRY, DON, IRL [34342] : PRE
1788 TIP, IRL [35157] : ALL IRL & USA [36933] :
C1851 GLASGOW PORT, RFW, SCT [34277] : 1800+
BATHGATE, WLN, SCT [38279]

MCCUEN (SEE MCCOWAN) [37577]

MACCUISH 1800S CAPE BRETON CO., NS, CAN
[34253]

MCCUISH 1785+ INV, SCT [34148]

MCCULLAGH 1800+ ANNAGHMORE &
TRICKVALLEN, TYR, IRL [33829] : PATRICK PRE
1900 TYR & COR, IRL [36453]

MCCULLEY PRE 1786 UPPER SEAGOE, ARM, IRL
[36259] : PRE 1820 OHIO CO., VA, USA [37781] :
1820-1880 GUERNSEY CO., OH, USA [37781]

MCCULLOCH 1800+ SYDNEY, NSW, AUS [35505] :
1902-1920 BALMAIN, NSW, AUS [37911] : 1925+
NEWCASTLE, NSW, AUS [37911] : DANIEL 1822-
1875 PICTOU CO., NS, CAN [38421] : HELEN
1833+ GLASGOW, LKS, SCT [36367] : MARY
1841+ GLASGOW, LKS, SCT [36367] : PRE 1890
RFW, SCT [36433] : 1780-1880 EAGLESHAM, RFW,
SCT [37783] : C1725-1800 ROC, SCT [37790] : ALL
EAST KILBRIDE, LKS, SCT [38057] : 1779+
DAILLY, AYR, SCT [38067] : C1900 CARDIFF,
GLA, WLS [37356]

MCCULLOCK C1839 MAUCHLINE, AYR, SCT
[37144]

MCCULLOUGH C1850 VIC, AUS [33793] : ALL ARM,
IRL [34054] : 1833+ DONEGAL, DON, IRL [34509] :
PRE 1860 GLENALLEN, DOW, IRL [36297] : 1650-
1890 ULSTER CO., NY, USA [37783] : ISAAC 1860
WOODFORD CO., IL, USA [38132]

MCCULLUM 1800+ CARNLOUGH, ANT, IRL
[34008] : C1864 UK [36707]

MCCULLY 1800-1860 YORK CO., SC, USA [38129]

MCCUMBER PRE 1900 CT, USA [38622]

MCCUMSTIE ALL WORLDWIDE [35331]

MCCUNE 1800-1900 IRL [38041] : 1850-1900 LA
SALLE CO., IL, USA [38041]

MCCURDIE 1810-1910 GLASGOW & LANARK, LKS
& MLN, SCT [34635]

MCCURDY C1840 CUSHENDALL, ANT, IRL [36860] :
1660-1810 BALLINTOY, ANT, IRL [37821]

MCCURE PRE 1878 SYDNEY, NSW, AUS [34898]

MCCURLEY ALL WORLDWIDE [37621]

MCCUSKAY 1800-1850 ARM, IRL [34846]

MCCUSKER 1800-1900 IRL & AUS [35778]

MCCUTCHAN PRE 1820 STAUNTON, VA, USA
[37545]

MCCUTCHEON 1791+ STAIR & SYMINGTON,
AYR, SCT [34039] : ALL AUCHAMULLAN, TYR,
IRL &, WORLDWIDE [34645]

MCDAID PRE 1870 KILMACRENAN, DON, IRL
[35833]

MCDANIEL PRE 1790 ORANGE CO., NY, USA
[34094] : ELEANOR 1840 POSEY CO., IN, USA
[35286]

MCDAVID C1820 HELENSBURGH, DNB, SCT
[35203]

MCDEARMOTT C1800S GAL & CLA, IRL [36337]

MCDERMID 1830-1860 COLLINGWOOD, ONT, CAN
[36658] : PRE 1850 IRL [33959]

MCDERMOT C1854 NEW YORK, NY, USA [35221]

MACDERMOTT 1790+ SLIGO, SLI, IRL [35461]

MCDERMOTT 1918+ NEWTOWN, NSW, AUS
[34030] : 1871+ KEMPSEY, NSW, AUS [37115] :
1850+ BYLANDS & KILMORE, VIC, AUS [37994] :
JAMES 1840-1920 EGANVILLE, ONT, CAN [34514] :
1860+ NBL, ENG [37889] : BRIDGET 1830-1850 TIP,

IRL [33900] : PRE 1825 DUB, IRL [34265] : MARY IRWIN 1800-1900 IRL [34514] : PRE 1883 STRAW, LDY, IRL [34598] : PRE 1860S CAV, IRL [36757] : 1700-1850 DUNAMON, ROS & TYR, IRL [37118] : 1800-1850 KILLENE, WEM, IRL [37188] : 1800-1850 BROLLAGH, FER, IRL [38526] : JOHN W. 1780-1880 IRL [38779] : 1864+ NEWTON & ONEHUNGA, AUCK, NZ [36757] : ANN C1820 FIF, SCT [37904]

MCDIARMID DUNCAN C1770-1836 LANARK, ONT, CAN [37441] : 1800S ONT, CAN [38393] : PRE 1839 COMRIE, PER, SCT [34911] : DUNCAN C1770-1836 PER, SCT [37441] : PRE 1840 SCT [38393] : 1825+ TULLYMET, PER, SCT [38413]

MCDONAGH C1870 IRL [35820]

MACDONALD 1838+ NORTHERN RIVERS, NSW, AUS [36272] : 1840+ LAUNCESTON, TAS, AUS [38289] : 1850+ GREY CO., ONT, CAN [34051] : 1780-1990 OSNABRUCK, ONT, CAN [34077] : 1800-1850 PICTON CO., NS, CAN [34253] : MURDOCH 1900 CUYAHOGA, OH, CAN [36678] : WILLIAM PRE 1887 KINCARDINE, ONT, CAN [36678] : WILLIAM 1887 CHILLIWACK, BC, CAN [36678] : 1800+ HERMITAGE BAY, NFD, CAN [36684] : 1830+ ONT, CAN [38589] : 1830+ NB, CAN [38589] : PRE 1890 PEI & NS, CAN [38746] : 1800-1850 LONDON, ENG [34850] : 1820+ TINSLEY & SHEFFIELD, WRY, ENG [36772] : 1800-1900 BIRMINGHAM, WAR, ENG [37068] : MICHAEL A. 1916 RICHMOND, SRY, ENG [37677] : 1884 DUNDALK, LOU & CLA, IRL [35405] : PHILIP 1850+ CLEGGAN & CLIFDEN, GAL, IRL [36884] : COLIN PRE 1900 WALLACETOWN, SLD, NZ [34613] : C1820 SKYE, INV, SCT [33918] : 1800+ TYREE, ARL, SCT [33982] : 1800+ FIF, SCT [34226] : PRE 1800 URQUHART, INV, SCT [34253] : REV. PATRICK 1800 KILMORE & KILBRIDE, ARL, SCT [34890] : PRE 1818 ABD, SCT [35113] : C1851 GLASGOW, SCT [35414] : 1750+ GLEN URQUHART, INV, SCT [35524] : ALL PLOCKTON, ROC, SCT [35888] : 1800-1850 ISLE OF SKYE, INV, SCT [36240] : JAMES C1690 DALVILLE, SKYE, INV, SCT [36272] : PRE 1800 PERTH, PER, SCT [36653] : 1780+ MOIDART, ARL, SCT [36865] : 1800S ROGART, SUT, SCT [37332] : 1800-1850 GLASGOW, SCT [37593] : PRE 1840 DORES & BOLESKINE, INV, SCT [37936] : 1700+ ROGART, SUT, SCT [38385] : PRE 1906 EAST WERNYS, FIF, SCT [38393] : 1800-1840 BALLAMORE, ROC, SCT [38475] : 1800+ TARBERT, INV, SCT [38481] : 1790-1840 INV, SCT [38589] : C1810 INVERNESS, INV, SCT [38700] : 1810-1900 INVERNESS, SCT & CAN [34395] : 1800-1900 AL & NC, USA [36272] : JOHN C1800+ FAYETTEVILLE, MOORE CO., NC, USA [36272] : MURDOCH 1929 NEW YORK, NY, USA [36678]

MCDONALD ANNIE C1850S NSW, AUS [33794] : CHRISTINE A. 1894 ADELAIDE, SA, AUS [34193] : C1800+ AUS [34444] : ALLAN 1862+ DALBY, QLD, AUS [34449] : PETER 1850+ MELBOURNE, VIC, AUS [34864] : ALLAN PRE 1900 STRATHDOWNIE EAST, VIC, AUS [34879] : PRE 1862 ST ALBANS, VIC, AUS [34959] : 1841+ QLD, AUS [34976] : 1860 REEDY CREEK, VIC, AUS [35204] : JOHN 1839+ CLARENCETOWN, NSW, AUS [35260] : DONALD 1852 BALLARAT, VIC, AUS [35260] : ARCHY 1850S CLARENCE RIVER, NSW, AUS [35260] : 1880S MOUNT MORGAN, QLD, AUS [35260] : BARBARA PRE 1860 BATHURST & SYDNEY, NSW, AUS [35336] : JOHN 1850+ BEECHWORTH, VIC, AUS [35391] : 1850+ RYLSTONE, NSW, AUS [35450] : DAVID 1860+ WOLLONGONG, NSW, AUS [35499] : C1894 BALMAIN, NSW, AUS [35515] : C1856 SEAHAM,

NSW, AUS [35515] : 1862 ORANGE, NSW, AUS [35807] : C1880 SURAT, QLD, AUS [35807] : 1870 ONDIT, VIC, AUS [35807] : 1862-1870 OXLEY, QLD, AUS [36241] : 1865+ KILKIVAN, QLD, AUS [36241] : 1835+ MONARO, NSW, AUS [36295] : SANDY 1846+ PORT ARTHUR, TAS, AUS [37113] : HUGH 1837+ COOMA & MOURUYA, NSW, AUS [37117] : 1837+ QUEANBEYAN, CANBERRA, NSW, AUS [37117] : JOHN 1871+ MELBOURNE, VIC, AUS [37329] : ALL BENDIGO, VIC, AUS [37950] : GEORGE PRE 1868 BULLENBALONG, MONARO, NSW, AUS [37965] : CATHERINE PRE 1854 SALTWATER RIVER, VIC, AUS [37965] : 1790-1850S WEST LINCOLN, ONT, CAN [34094] : RONALD PRE 1852 NS, CAN [34449] : JOHN 1859+ BRUCE CO., ONT, CAN [34519] : 184+ PIGEON HILL, QUE, CAN [34528] : JOHN WILSON 1830+ ONT, CAN [35426] : DONAL 1960+ ROLAND, MAN, CAN [35988] : 1800+ HERMITAGE BAY, NFD, CAN [36684] : 1835+ BRUCEFIELD, ONT, CAN [37451] : GEORGE C1838 PEI, CAN [37965] : 1875+ BARRIE, ONT, CAN [38059] : 1800+ YORK TWP., ONT, CAN [38410] : 1786 ERNSTTOWN, ONT, CAN [38593] : ELIZABETH 1839+ ONT, CAN & AUS [35426] : 1841 NOTTINGHAM, NTT, ENG [34540] : C1842 KESWICK, CUL, ENG [35990] : 1800+ MANCHESTER, LAN, ENG [36614] : C1800-1850 ENG [37790] : 1600-1900 ANT, IRL [35121] : 1800+ DUBLIN, IRL [35206] : PRE 1840 MOG, IRL [35406] : RONALD C1787-1857 BALLYCASTLE, ANT, IRL [36244] : CATHERINE 1750-1800 ENNISKILLEN, FER, IRL [37740] : ALEXANDER 1850+ NZ [37113] : 1850+ MASTERTON, NZ [37113] : 1867-1913 GLASGOW, LKS, SCT [33811] : 1867-1908 BALLACHULISH, ARL, SCT [33811] : ALEX PRE 1860 GLASGOW, SCT [33992] : PRE 1853 ARISAIG, INV, SCT [34010] : C1790 DALNOE, PER, SCT [34203] : 1800+ PORTREE, INV, SCT [34252] : DONALD PRE 1825 CAWDOR, NAI, SCT [34278] : ANN PRE 1831 KILININ, ARL, SCT [34310] : 1800+ LARBERT, STI, SCT [34326] : PRE 1850 DURRIS, KCD & ABD, SCT [34360] : MARGARET 1830+ PER, SCT [34620] : PRE 1850 BALLACHULISH, ARL, SCT [34719] : C1847 BARRHEAD, LKS, SCT [34858] : ALL FORT WILLIAM, INV, SCT [34879] : PRE 1830 ISLAY, ARL, SCT [34911] : C1730 ISLE OF ULVA, ARL, SCT [34926] : 1841 POOLEWE, ROC, SCT [34976] : KATE C1850 HAMILTON, LKS, SCT [35033] : MARY 1870S ALISSARY, INV, SCT [35081] : JOHN 1760S BOURG MULL, ARL, SCT [35260] : PRE 1820 BRACADALE SKYE, INV, SCT [35260] : DONALD 1801 ARDHOUL SKYE, INV, SCT [35260] : JOHN 1821 GOMETRA ULVA, ARL, SCT [35260] : 1820-40 SNIZORT SKYE, INV, SCT [35260] : PRE 1855 PER, SCT [35386] : EMILY 1800+ INV, SCT [35391] : JOHN WILSON 1800+ ARL, SCT [35426] : PRE 1844 SNIZORT, INV, SCT [35450] : C1840 INVERGORDON, ROC, SCT [35502] : PRE 1800 ISLE OF MULL, SCT [35573] : PRE 1855 SPINNINGDALE, SUT, SCT [35709] : DONALD 1900+ DRAINE, INV, SCT [35988] : C1839 LEITH, MLN, SCT [35990] : 1800+ INVERNESS, INV, SCT [36241] : 1800+ ABERDEEN, ABD, SCT [36241] : 1800-70 TOBERMORY, ARL, SCT [36262] : 1800+ NEW MONKLAND, LKS, SCT [36288] : 1800+ INVERMORISTON, INV, SCT [36641] : ALL FORTINGALL, PER, SCT [36704] : CAPT. 1800-1865 TOBERMORY, MULL, ARL, SCT [36712] : SARA 1740-1780 MORTLACH, BAN, SCT [36783] : FLORA 1800+ ULLAPOOL, ROC & INV, SCT [36877] : ARCH PRE 1837 LOCHHOURN GLENELG, INV, SCT [37117] : PRE 1835 ISLE OF SKYE, SCT [37142] :

1815 ROC, SCT [37163] : PRE 1820 IONA, ARL, SCT [37179] : 1750-1850 SKYE, INV, SCT [37188] : CATHERINE 1800+ HARRIS, INV, SCT [37304] : 1800S FERINTOSH, ROC, SCT [37329] : NEIL 1818-1819 PAISLEY, RFW, SCT [37442] : ALL DORES, INV, SCT [37451] : ALL LEDAIG, ARL, SCT [37451] : PRE 1840 BARONY, LKS, SCT [37852] : CATHERINE C1834 FORT WILLIAM, INV, SCT [37965] : PETER PRE 1834 FORT WILLIAM, INV, SCT [37965] : PRE 1860 ISLE OF SKYE, SCT [37989] : PRE 1830 WICK, CAI, SCT [38457] : WILLIAM W. 1840+ KIPPEN, STI, SCT [38568] : ROBERT 1841+ KIPPEN, STI, SCT [38568] : JAMES C1800+ ABERLOUR, BAN & ONT, SCT & CAN [34479] : 1700-1900 PERTH & CARLETON CO., PER & ONT, SCT & CAN [36669] : PRE 1860 GLASGOW, LKS & MAY, SCT & IRL [36191] : 1840+ THURSO & ACHNAVAST, CAI, SCT & NZ [36819] : PRE 1790 ORANGE CO., NY, USA [34094] : 1750+ ST LOUIS CO., MO, KY & NC, USA [36917] : PRE 1900 NY, USA [37787] : 1800-1830 WASHINGTON CO., KY, USA [38154] : 1830-1880 CASS CO., IL, USA [38154] : 1685-1750 NEW CASTLE, DE, USA [38154] : 1750-1800 MONTGOMERY CO., VA, USA [38154] : NEHEMIAH 1809-1857 NICHOLAS CO., KY, USA [38732] : GEORGE W. 1875-1900 SCOTT CO., IL, USA [38732]

MCDONAUGH PETER 170+ TUBERCURRY, SLI, IRL [33797]

MCDONELL PRE 1835 INV, SCT [35745] : 1780+ INV, SCT [36343] : PRE 1832 BALLICHULISH, ARL, SCT [37982]

MCDONNEL 1800+ KID, IRL [36165]

MACDONNELL 1800 KEPPOCH LINE, INV, SCT [34890]

MCDONNELL 1870+ CUMNOCK, NSW, AUS [34759] : C1850 ALD, CHI [38760] : PRE 1850 HOSPITAL, LIM, IRL [34018] : 1800+ CAR, IRL [34237] : PRE 1850 BROADFORD, CLA, IRL [35128] : PRE 1890 TRALEE, KER, IRL [38303] : C1800 INV, SCT [35859] : 1860+ EASTHAMPTON, MA, USA [38015]

MACDONOGH 1870+ TWICKENHAM, SRY, ENG [35461]

MCDONOUGH 1827 OUGHTERARD, GAL, IRL [34176] : 1860-1910 BLAIR CO., PA, USA [38106]

MCDORMAND 1760+ DIGBY CO., NS, CAN [34138] : 1820+ NORFOLK & ELGIN CO., ONT, CAN [36323]

MCDOUCH 1840-1900 IRL [34165]

MACDOUGAL 1800 KERRERA, ARL, SCT [36635] : PRE 1800 PER, SCT [36754]

MCDOUGAL 1800S ABERDEEN, ABD, SCT [33811] : 1780S BORLAND PARK, PER, SCT [35260] : PRE 1861 GREENOCK, RFW, SCT [37242]

MCDOUGALD PRE 1820 ARRAN, BUT, SCT [34419]

MACDOUGALL 1850-1860 RECHERCHE BAY, TAS, AUS [34697] : 1770+ PEI, CAN [38460] : 1700+ EASDALE IS., ARL, SCT [35825]

MCDOUGALL ALL LANARK, ONT, CAN [35637] : C1830 CLERKENWELL, MDX, ENG [37552] : HENRY PRE 1800 HAM, ENG [37926] : HENRY 1800-1870S PORTSMOUTH & PORTSEA, HAM, ENG [37926] : JAMES 1857-90 HAM, ENG [37926] : 1840S BALLACHULISH, ARL, SCT [33811] : 1840-1868 EDINBURGH, MLN, SCT [33945] : PRE 1820 ARRAN, BUT, SCT [34419] : 1700+ INV & ARL, SCT [34572] : PRE 1854 LUSS, DNB, SCT [34695] : C1816 GIRVAN, AYR, SCT [34972] : JANET C1840 GLASGOW, SCT [35120] : PRE 1800 ISLE OF MULL, SCT [35573] : 1800+ PAISLEY, RFW, SCT [35786] : C1809 KILFINAN, ARL, SCT [35854] : 1829 GLASGOW, SCT [35906] : PRE 1880 PER, SCT

[36754] : 1700+ ALLOA, CLK, DEV & LND, SCT [37735] : 1840S MILTON, DNB, SCT [38423]

MCDOWALL PRE 1870 DOW, IRL [38286] : 1869+ CANTERBURY, NZ [38286] : C1870 GLASGOW, LKS, SCT [34122] : 1860+ MAYBOLE, AYR, SCT [34345] : 18450-1860 GIRVAN, AYR, SCT [34345] : ALL NEWTON STEWART, WIG, SCT [36497]

MCDOWELL PRE 1835 ANT, IRL [34758] : 1832 AGHADOWEY, ANT & LDY, IRL [35202] : 1868 ARMAGH, ARM, IRL [35202] : C1800-1805 BALLYMONEY, ANT, IRL [35202] : C1835 ROYAL OAK, CAR, IRL [35560] : C1861 DRUMMINICK, CAV, IRL [35826] : 1800S ANT, IRL [35968] : 1600-1800 BANBRIDGE, DOW, IRL [36556] : 1850-1950 VERMILION CO., IL & MO, USA [38025]

MCDUEL JOHN 1770S CAR, IRL [36880]

MCDUFF 1700-1850 IRL [34242] : PRE 1850 CRIEFF, PER, SCT [36361] : PRE 1800 GLASGOW, SCT [37133]

MCDUGGAL 1780S AUCHTERARDER, PER, SCT [35260]

MACE 1890+ LAUNCESTON, TAS, AUS [34770] : PRE 1840 LONDON, ENG [34421] : PRE 1800 DOR, ENG [34647] : 1830+ KINGS LYNN, NFK, ENG [36301] : 1790-1850 GREEN CO., TN & IN, USA [36901] : 1800-1850 JOHNSTON CO., NC, USA [38009] : 1760-1800 EDGECOMBE CO., NC, USA [38009] : 1792-1870 LUZERNE CO., PA, USA [38101]

MCEACHERN PRE 1800 IONA, ARL, SCT [37179]

MCEACHREN JOHN PRE 1840 FRONTENAC, ONT, CAN [34353]

MCEARHERN 1840-50S GOULBURN, NSW, AUS [35111]

MACEFIELD ALL WORLDWIDE [38754]

MCELDERRY 1700S LONDONDERRY, ANT, IRL [36709]

MCELDOWNEY ALL USA [38287]

MCELFRESH PRE 1695 MLN, SCT [37014] : JOHN P. 1828-1855 MONTGOMERY CO., MD, USA [37014]

MCELHANY 1795 VA, USA [36730]

MCELHATTON ELLIE PRE 1931 NY, USA [36902]

MCELHINNEY 1850-1900 BURNER & MT BARKER, SA, AUS [34897] : PRE 1850 PAISLEY & GLASGOW, RFW & LKS, SCT [34897]

MCELLIGOTT 1843 DUAGH, KER, IRL [36274] : ALL KER, IRL [36854]

MCELREA ALL CAN [34489] : PRE 1840 TYR, IRL [34489]

MCELREAVY 1850+ LEEDS, QUE, CAN [36704] : ALL COLERAINE, LDY, IRL [36704]

MCELREVY 1877+ MACGREGOR, MAN, CAN [36704]

MCELROY PRE 1830 LIMAVADY, LDY, IRL [34494] : 1880 EAST KILBRIDE, LKS, SCT [37690] : 1600-1800 WORLDWIDE [35289]

MCELWAIN 1800S BUTLER, PA, USA [34353]

MCELWEE 1860 LAVEY, CAV, IRL [36264] : PRE 1859 NEWTOWN & LIMAVADY, DRY, IRL [37981]

MCENALLY PRE 1832 NEWRY, ARM & DOW, IRL [33813]

MCENERY 1850+ WELLINGTON CO., ONT, CAN [37492] : 1770+ IRL [37492]

MCENTEE 1850-1870 BATTERSEA, SRY, ENG [33962] : 1850-1870 WESTMINSTER, MDX, ENG [33962] : 1870+ AUCKLAND, NZ [33962]

MCENTYRE 1860-1880 TX, USA [38331]

MCEVERS PRE 1870 PIKE CO., IL, OH & NY, USA & SCT [38532]

MCEVOY PRE 1859 CAMPBELLTOWN, TAS, AUS [33806] : 1800+ MONARO, NSW, AUS [35159] : 1800+ CLA, IRL [37916]

MACEWAN 1800S NEWBURGH, ABD, SCT [38402]

MCEWAN OWEN 1859+ CAMPBELLS CREEK, VIC, AUS [34877] : C1854+ CAMPBELLTOWN, TAS, NSW & QLD, AUS [35547] : PRE 1840 LARNE, ANT, IRL [34575] : BERNARD 1850+ KIK, IRL [34877] : 1852+ CARNMONEY, ANT, IRL [35801] : ALL SCT [33959] : C1780 CRIEFF, PER, SCT [35260] : 1770S WESTHILL MADDERTY, PER, SCT [35260] : 1600+ SCT [38388] : 1860-70 NY, USA [35260]

MCEWEN 1820+ DRUMBANAGHER, ARM, IRL & AUS [38204] : PRE 1800 GIRVAN, AYR, SCT [35406] : 1861 ABERFELDY, PER, SCT [38364] : 1790-1850 LKS, SCT & USA [36913] : ALL WORLDWIDE [38329]

MCEWIN PRE 1850 AUS & SCT [34705] : 1800+ KKD, SCT [35951]

MCFADDEN C1899 DARLINGHURST, NSW, AUS [36284] : 1854+ GLENLYON, VIC, AUS [37109] : 1820-1870 LOUGHCLOO, DOW, IRL [36867] : PRE 1850S KILLYBEGS AND SURROUNDS, DON, IRL [37745] : ALL DOW, IRL [38228] : ALL ANT, IRL [38228] : PRE 1860 DON, IRL [38771] : 1800-1870 KILFINICHEN, ARL, SCT [35228] : 1850-1940 BAY CITY, MI, USA [35625] : 1880+ BROOKLYN, NY, USA [38011]

MCFADGEN 1850-70 SA, AUS [36831]

MCFADYEN 1820+ STRATHLACHLAN, ARL, SCT [37881] : C1815 MURRAYS ISLES, KIR, SCT [38592] : C1841 CAMPBELTOWN, ARL, SCT [38592]

MCFADZEAN C1750-1825 STRANRAER, WIG, SCT [34214]

MCFADZEN JANET 1806-1880 COYLTON, AYR, SCT [34300]

MCFAHAN 1840-1870 NITSHILL, RFW, SCT [33931]

MCFALL C1840-1900 BALT, MD, USA [38182]

MCFALLS 1740-1800 BEDFORD CO., VA, USA [38009]

MACFARLAN CATHERINE C1840+ SYDNEY, NSW, AUS [36643]

MCFARLAN 1783-1990 CHARLOTTE CO., NB, CAN [34124]

MACFARLAND 1800+ PINTOU, NS, CAN [37821]

MCFARLAND 1880+ MURRUMBURRAH & HARDEN, NSW, AUS [34899] : 1850+ LDY, IRL [33973] : C1853 BOCKETS & KILLEESHILL, TYR, IRL [34189] : PRE 1850 OMAGH, TYR, IRL [34611] : PRE 1718 TYR, IRL [36972] : 1700-1820 TYR, IRL [37599] : ALL OK, MO & KS, USA [36916] : 1780-1850 RUSSELL, VA, USA [38061]

MACFARLANE 1876+ EMMAVILLE & BINGARA, NSW, AUS [36600] : ALL CAN [34124] : PRE 1855 OMAGH, TYR, IRL [35022] : PRE 1835 MULL, ARL, SCT [34274] : PRE 1880 PAISLEY, RFW, SCT [34562] : C1791 ISLE OF MULL, ARL, SCT [34926] : 1800S LEWIS, ROC, SCT [36041] : PRE 1800 RICCARTON, AYR, SCT [36802] : C1780 ARROCHAR, DNB, SCT [37131] : ROBERT PRE 1912 GLASGOW & GARTMOOR, SCT [37491] : PRE 1800 PER, SCT [38004] : 1800-1930 TARBERT, ARL, SCT [38355]

MCFARLANE 1863+ MARYBOROUGH, QLD, AUS [34588] : PRE 1868 TUMUT, NSW, AUS [34978] : 1868+ SYDNEY, NSW, AUS [34978] : 1870-1935 NEWCASTLE, NSW, AUS [37911] : PRE 1850 VIC, AUS [38277] : ALL NB, CAN [34124] : 1890+ OAK LAKE, MAN, CAN [37451] : PRE 1871 PUGWASH, NS, CAN [38335] : ALL BALLYMONEY, ANT, IRL [33842] : 1840+ BALLYMONEY, ANT, IRL [33842] : PRE 1863 BELFAST, ANT, IRL [34588] : PRE 1850 GORTIN & ROUSKY, TYR, IRL [34772] : PRE 1855 OMAGH, TYR, IRL [35022] : NIEL 1830 AIRDRIE, LKS, SCT [33956] : 1800-1900 GLASGOW, LKS, SCT [34557] : PRE 1853 CLACKMANNAN, CLK, SCT [34585] : PRE 1853 STIRLING, STI, SCT [34585] : C1801 DUMBARTON, DNB, SCT [34911] : 1800S

CAMPSIE, STI, SCT [35186] : PRE 1834 AUCHTERARDER, PER, SCT [35209] : PRE 1845 PER, SCT [35463] : 1700S KILMADOCK, PER, SCT [35858] : C1820 SCT [35906] : ANDREW 1850+ GLASGOW, LKS, SCT [35952] : KIRSTY 1850+ GLASGOW, LKS, SCT [35952] : PRE 1749 CROFTPARDON & DULL, PER, SCT [37852] : PRE 1855 PAISLEY, RFW, SCT [37925] : C1830 ARL, SCT [38277]

MCFAUL C1800+ PRINCE EDWARD CO., ONT, CAN [36651] : C1750-1800 CUTCHESS CO., NY, USA [36651]

MCFAWN PRE 1860 DON, IRL [33931]

MACFIE ARCHIBALD 1800+ CAN [35429] : PETER 1800 KILMUIR, INV, SCT [35429]

MCFIE PRE 1840 ARL, SCT [33814] : PRE 1870 GLASGOW, LKS, SCT [34598]

MCFIGGANS 1800S AUCHTERDERRAN, FIF & KRS, SCT [36874]

MCGAAN 1820+ RICCARTON, AYR, SCT [36749]

MCGACHEN PRE 1840 EDINBURGH, SCT [35055]

MCGAFFIN 1800+ BRUCE CO., ONT, CAN [34492] : 1700S ARM, IRL [34492] : 1700S DOW, IRL [34492]

MCGAHAN THOMAS PRE 1830 LOU, IRL [34310]

MCGALL JOHN C1860-1880 IRL [35324]

MCGANN PRE 1860 IRL [35750] : 1800S CLA, IRL & AUS [35422] : 1820-1990 TIP, IRL & AUS [35718]

MCGANNON ALL BELFAST, ANT, IRL [36916]

MCGAREY 1831 EMIG LIVERPOOL ENG 1898, IRL [38038]

MCGARRAH 1790-1816 CHESTER, SC, USA [38347]

MCGARRITY ALL BIRMINGHAM & CORNWALL, MI & ONT, USA & CAN [37503]

MCGARRY 1834-1836 MAUCHLINE, AYR, SCT [35583]

MCGARVEY 1850+ SYDNEY, NSW, AUS [38582]

MCGARVIE PRE 1844 CRAWDAWS, DRY, IRL [34014] : PRE 1844 ENNISKILLEN, FER, IRL [34014]

MCGATHAN 1800S KILMARNOCK, LKS, SCT [36642]

MCGAUGHEY 1850+ MN, USA [38222]

MCGAVERN PRE 1840 CAV, IRL [35129]

MCGAVIN ALLAN 1770-1950 VANCOUVER, BC, CAN [38482]

MCGAW PRE 1820 IRL [37103]

MCGAY 1833+ NEW YORK, NY, USA [37462]

MCGEAGH 1750+ COOKSTOWN, TYR, IRL [37462] : 1833+ USA [37462]

MCGEARY C1870 BOND HEAD, ONT, CAN [34251]

MCGECHIE 1800+ NEWBATTLE, MLN, SCT [34188]

MACGEE PRE 1930 GRIMES CO. & MADISON CO., TX, USA [37320]

MCGEE 1849+ WESTBURY, TAS, AUS [34596] : 1860-189S GEELONG, VIC, AUS [35044] : 1886 MANCHESTER, LAN, ENG [37691] : 1820 DONEGAL, DON, IRL [33996] : 1700-1800 MUNDERRY, DON, IRL [34342] : 1819 NTH, IRL [37141] : MARGARET C1909 NORTH WILLIAM ST PARISH, DUB, IRL [38302] : MARGARET C1909 NORTH WALL, DUB, IRL [38302] : PRE 1884 BELFAST, ANT, IRL [38541] : ALL DON, IRL [38760] : C1830+ MAY & TAS, IRL & AUS [34596] : 1674-1720 SOMERSET CO., MD, USA [36354] : 1850-1950 BOSTON, MA, USA [36733]

MCGEEAN PRE 1800 BELFAST, ANT, IRL [34028]

MCGEENEY 1800-1900 UK [38244]

MCGEOCH ALL WORLDWIDE [38754]

MCGEORGE 1870+ MAITLAND & SYDNEY, NSW, AUS [34978]

MCGETTIGAN 1840+ SHELLHARBOUR, NSW, AUS [37133] : 1700-1900 DON, IRL [36165] : 1800+ IRL [37133]

MCGHEE 1838 PENRITH, NSW, AUS [38756] : PRE 1840 TAMLAGHT, DRY, IRL [34758] : 1700+ DON, IRL [37826] : PRE 1923 DNB & LKS, SCT [34391] : 1780+ BEDFORD CO., VA, USA [37443]

MCGIBBON PRE 1850 BELFAST, ANT & DOW, IRL [38084] : PRE 1850 BEITH, AYR, SCT [35719] : 1846 CALLANDER, PER, SCT [35821] : 1851 NEWLANDS, PEE, SCT [35821] : 1849+ OLD MONKLAND, LKS, SCT [35821] : ELEANOR PRE 1804 ISLAY, ARL, SCT [35848]

MCGIFFERT PRE 1760 SCT [34895]

MCGIFFORD (SEE MCGIF [34895]

MCGILL HARRIET 1909-1928 LONDON, ENG [33888] : 1808-1860 WOOLWICH, LND, ENG [34002] : THOMAS 1874 ATHLONE, ROS & WEM, IRL [33888] : ALICE ROSE 1909-1928 MEENAKILLEW, GLENTIES, DON, IRL [33888] : PRE 1870 IRL [33959] : C1855 ARM, IRL [34273] : 1790-1820S DUBLIN, IRL [35777] : PRE 1829 ANT, IRL [36613] : 1800-1847 BELFAST, ANT & ARM, IRL & CAN [34244] : JANE 1820 AYR, SCT [34091] : 1800S PITTENWEEM, FIF, SCT [34144] : PRE 1853 EDINBURGH, MLN, SCT [35863] : 1800S ST QUIVOX, AYR, SCT [36275]

MCGILLICUDDY PRE 1839 TRALEE, KER, IRL [35406]

MCGILLIPICK ALL ROC, SCT [38215]

MCGILLIVRAY DONALD 1886+ OTTAWA, ONT, CAN & SCT [34164] : 1790S BOURG MULL, ARL, SCT [35260] : 1810 CULLEN, BAN, SCT [35369] : 1700S ARDNAMURCHAN & MULL, SCT [36314] : PRE 1850 JURA & ISLAY, ARL, SCT [38403]

MCGILLVRAY 1820+ KEPPOCH, ISLE OF SKYE, SCT [37889]

MCGILP 1700S-1800S CRARAE, ARL, SCT [35126]

MCGILVRA 1805+ KINTRA, MULL, ARL, SCT [35057] : C1800 GLASGOW, LKS, SCT [35057]

MCGILVRAY 1900+ ONT, CAN [35184] : BIRTIE 1910+ SCT [35184] : 1750-1825 NY, USA [36688]

MCGIMPSEY 1850+ ENG [38481]

MCGINLEY PRE 1900 CRANFORD, DON, IRL [33902]

MCGINNESS PRE 1883 IRL [37991]

MCGINNIS 1850+ SIMCOE CO., ONT, CAN [34465] : 1830S WELLAND, ONT, CAN [35625] : 1830S WOLFORD TWP., ONT, CAN [35625] : 1770-1840 ADDISON CO., VT, NY & MI, USA [36913]

MCGINTY PRE 1870 KILMACRENAN, DON, IRL [35833] : 1850-1900 SONOMA, CA, USA [35833]

MCGIRL 1850+ CASTLERAHAN, CAV, IRL & AUS [33926]

MCGIRR 1850 STREETE, LOG, IRL [35410] : PRE 1870 PORTADOWN, ARM, IRL [35911]

MCGIVEN (SEE MCGIBBO [38084]

MCGLADDERY 1880+ NEWRY, DOW, IRL [35219]

MACGLAMERY C1745 SOMERSET CO., MD, USA [36354]

MCGLASHEN 1817 NEWBURGH, FIF, SCT [33848]

MCGLEN C1833 RELAGH & CORNULLA, LET, IRL [35900]

MCGLYNCHEY 1800+ LONDONDERRY, DRY, IRL [35809]

MCGOEY ALL ADJALA & TECUMSETH, ONT, CAN [35833]

MCGOLDRICK PRE 1890 BELCOO, FER, IRL [33871] : C1860 IRL [35820]

MCGONIGAL 1750-1900 BELFAST, ANT, IRL [38024]

MCGOREY PRE 1826 IRL [35824]

MCGOUGAN 1600S PER, SCT [34937]

MCGOUGH 1850-1900 LIVERPOOL, ENG [35602] : 1880+ MOG, IRL [34190] : C1800 LOU, IRL [35247]

MCGOULRICK ALL SLI, IRL [34569] : ALL DUNDEE, PER, SCT [34569]

MCGOVERAN (SEE MCGOV [36796]

MCGOVERN 1750-1950 LONDON &, MDX, ENG [37344] : ALL CAV, IRL [36796] : 1800S BELFAST, IRL [36851] : MARY PRE 1850 CAVAN, CAV, IRL [38049] : 1800S HOKITIKA, WESTLAND, NZ [36796] : C1800+ DUNDEE, ANS, SCT [33792] : MARY PRE 1870 PHILADELPHIA, PA, USA [38049]

MCGOWAN 1890+ AUS [35617] : 1875 LIVERPOOL, ENG [35617] : 1810-1860 LIVERPOOL, ENG [37145] : 1780+ DOWNPATRICK, DOW, IRL [34408] : C1830S DUNDALK, DOW, IRL [35340] : 1800S COR, IRL [35617] : MARY 1820+ DUBLIN, IRL [37825] : PRE 1800 DOW, IRL [38428] : 1740+ GLENLING, WIG, SCT [34993] : 1800S ABERDEEN, SCT [35617] : 1870S GLASGOW, SCT [35799] : PRE 1841 GLASGOW, LKS, SCT [37138] : 1830-1900 INYO, CA, USA [37038] : C1840+ JAMAICA, W.INDIES [35834]

MCGRADY 1850+ OH, USA [36942]

MCGRANE 1800+ AUS [33769]

MCGRAPH PRE 1900 IRL & USA [36933]

MCGRATH 1870 BENDIGO, VIC, AUS [33881] : 1877-1880 QLD, AUS [34693] : 1880+ WATERLOO, NSW, AUS [34693] : MICHAEL 1809 WINDSOR, NSW, AUS [35082] : MATHEW 1850 SYDNEY, NSW, AUS [35082] : 1850+ NORTH EASTERN, VIC, AUS [35106] : PRE 1850 SYDNEY, NSW, AUS [35339] : 1864+ NSW, AUS [35407] : 1850+ IPSWICH, QLD, AUS [35814] : 1843 MELBOURNE, VIC, AUS [35903] : C1872 CORAKI, NSW, AUS [36284] : JAMES 1846+ LA CO., ONT, CAN [34154] : 1850 CLA, IRL [33881] : 1800+ COR, IRL [33963] : ELLEN C1830 COR, IRL [34147] : PRE 1850 TUAM, GAL, IRL [34433] : PRE 1860 INAGH, CLA, IRL [34588] : 1860-1880 CLA, IRL [34693] : MICHAEL 1809 KILKENNY, IRL [35082] : C1835 TIPPERARY, IRL [35090] : PRE 1850 CLA, IRL [35106] : PRE 1860 INAGH, CLA, IRL [35197] : C1830 BALLYVAUGHAN, CLA, IRL [35206] : 1810+ KILKENNY, KIK, IRL [35223] : 1800S BROUGHSHANE, ANT, IRL [35468] : PRE 1849 CLA, IRL [35776] : 1836 KNOCKAVILLA, TIP, IRL [35824] : MARY PRE 1853 IRL [36621] : JOHN PRE 1834 CASHEL, TIP, IRL [37945] : PRE 1852 SAN FRANCISCO, CA, USA [34433] : 1850-1860 BROOKLYN, NY, USA [34693] : ALL WORLDWIDE [36135]

MCGRAW 1820+ LIVERPOOL, LAN, ENG [36871] : PRE 1850 NEWBURY, BRK, ENG [37150] : PRE 1830 DOW, IRL [36871]

MCGREAL 1830S GOULBURN, NSW, AUS [35099] : ALL WORLDWIDE [35579]

MCGREEHAN C1840 DROMORE, DOW, IRL [35502]

MACGREGOR 1853+ CAMPBELLTOWN, NSW, AUS [35239] : C1880 BARNSLEY, WRY, ENG [36635] : C1850 MANCHESTER, LAN, ENG [36635] : PRE 1840 ARDTORNISH, ARL, SCT [34192] : PRE 1850 BONHILL, DNB, SCT [34533] : PRE 1850 OBAN, ARL, SCT [34533] : 1890S FORRES, INV, SCT [35988] : ALL KILMADOCK, PER, SCT [36635] : ALL ABERFELDY, PER, SCT & NZ [33981]

MCGREGOR 1860+ HAMILTON, SA, AUS [33824] : 1860+ WENTWORTH, NSW, AUS [33824] : 1850-1920 CASTLEMAINE, VIC, AUS [34191] : 1800-1850 JINDABYNE, NSW, AUS [34307] : 1852+ MELBOURNE, VIC, AUS [34780] : 1880+ BREWARRINA, NSW, AUS [34780] : PRE 1830 STOKE DAMEREL, DEV, ENG [34660] : 1820-1850 SUNDERLAND, DUR, ENG [36392] : C1800S FIVE MILE TOWN, TYR, IRL [35381] : C1800-1880S

KILSKERRY & ENNISKILLEN, TYR & FER, IRL [37556] : MARY 1820S STRABANE, TYR, IRL [37906] : ALL AUCKLAND, NZ [36744] : ALL COROMANDEL, NZ [36744] : PRE 1828 BURNT ISLAND, FIF, SCT [33812] : 1800+ DRYMEN & BUGHLYVIE, STI, SCT [34189] : 1700+ FORTINGALL & DULL, PER, SCT [34419] : ROB ROY 1700-1800 SCT [34487] : PRE 1855 GLENGARRY, SCT [34593] : 1750+ ROC, SCT [34684] : 1890S FORRES, MOR, SCT [34764] : PRE 1852 ROW & LUSS, DNB, SCT [34780] : 1760S INV, SCT [34991] : ALL LAUDER & EARLSTON, BEW, SCT [35293] : ANGUS 1800+ LOCHBROOM, ROC, SCT [35917] : 1820-1850 FORRES, MOR, SCT [36392] : JOHN PRE 1820 MILLER OF GLASGOW, LKS, SCT [36405] : PRE 1800 DULL, PER, SCT [36436] : ALL GLENQUAICH, PER, SCT [37451] : 1820+ CAMBUSLANG, LKS, SCT [37575] : ELIZABETH PRE 1824 CRIEFF, PER, SCT & AUS [33840] : MOSES C1780 WORLDWIDE [36635]

MCGREGOR-SKINNER 1845 LISCARD, CHS, ENG [35356]

MCGREW 1675+ TYR, IRL [37564] : 1800+ IL, USA [37462]

MCGRIGOR C1750 BALQUHIDDER, PER, SCT [36635]

MCGRODER 1819+ MOLONG, NSW, AUS [34030]

MCGRUER PRE 1900 GLENMORRISTON, INV, SCT [36260]

MCGUCKIN PRE 1850 LDY, IRL [37313]

MCGUFFICKE 1870+ INVERELL, NSW, AUS [35159]

MCGUFFOG 1780-1870 NEWTON STEWART, WIG, SCT [34687] : 1800 KIRKMAIDEN, WIG, SCT [35820]

MCGUGAN ALL MIDDLESEX, ONT, CAN [33854] : C1803 BALLYCASTLE, ANT, IRL [34474]

MCGUIGAN C1880 DESERT MARTIN, LDY, IRL [36762]

MCGUINESS C1828+ COWRA, NSW, VIC & CLA, AUS & IRL [35547] : ALL IRL [33959] : PRE 1915 MASTERTON, WAIRARAPA, NZ [35889]

MCGUINNES 1805+ HOBART, TAS, AUS [35190]

MCGUINNESS MARY PRE 1843+ NSW, AUS [34592] : 1800+ MELBOURNE, VIC, AUS [36746] : PRE 1855 TULLA, CLA, IRL [34431] : 1800-1870 ARM, IRL [35228] : 1800+ IRL [35566] : HUGH C1825-80 DON, MAY & SLI, IRL [37764] : C1850+ NEW YORK CITY, NY, USA [37764]

MCGUIRE PETER PRE 1803 NORFOLK ISLAND & SYDNEY, NSW, AUS [35217] : PRE 1855 WINDSOR, NSW, AUS [35236] : 1842 PATERSON, NSW, AUS [35535] : PRE 1839 KILGLASS, ROS, IRL [34585] : PRE 1839 KILGLASS, LOG, IRL [34585] : PRE 1800 MONAGHAN, MOG, IRL [35095] : ALL LET & LOG, IRL [38346] : 1830+ KILKENNY, KIK, IRL & AUS [34864] : C1800 AYR, SCT [36694] : 1850+ MO, USA [36942] : 1810-1850 BLAIR CO., PA, USA [38106] : 1780-1850 CAMBRIA CO., PA, USA [38106] : 1830+ ROCKFORD, IL, OH & IA, USA & IRL [37796]

MCGUIRK PATRICK 1890S WICKLOW, WIC, IRL [33928] : BERNARD 1770-80 KILSHERDONY & KILMORE, IRL [36440] : ISABELLA PRE 1870 COOKSTOWN, TYR, IRL [37436]

MCGURK PRE 1860 CASTLEBLAYNEY, MOG, IRL [34039] : 1820+ USA [34039]

MCGUSSY 1861 AUS [33932]

MACH ALL BOHEMIA, CS [37440]

MACHADO 1870S-1880S PICO, AZORES IS., PT [36337] : 1915+ CONTRA COSTA CO., CA, USA [38323]

MCHAFFIE 1840-1900 OLDHAM, LAN, ENG [38521] : C1820 CARRICKFERGUS, ANT, IRL & SCT [37143]

: 1800-1850 DNB, SCT [38521] : 1800-1900 GLASGOW, LKS, SCT [38521] : 1800+ GLASGOW, LKS, SCT & IRL [34326]

MCHALE PRE 1880 GLASGOW, LKS & MAY, SCT & IRL [36191]

MCHARDY 1820S ROTHIEMAY, ABD, SCT [37442] : 1700+ STRATHDON, ABD, SCT & NZ [36607]

MCHARG PRE 1831 BALLYMENA, ANT, IRL & SCT [33906] : PRE 1743 BARRLOCKHART, WIG, SCT [34993]

MCHARRY 1800+ ARDKEEN, DOW, IRL [36867]

MACHATTIE PRE 1780 DUMFRIES, DFS, SCT [34253]

MACHEN 1855+ LAUNCESTON, TAS, AUS [35116] : PRE 1855 NFK, ENG [35116]

MCHENRY PRE 1880 SINGLETON, NSW, AUS [34978] : ALL AUS [35840] : 1780-1800 JEFFERSON CO., OH, USA [36328] : 1790-1800 HARDIN CO., KY, USA [36328]

MACHIN 1800S MDX, ENG [34181] : PRE 1847 ROTHERHAM & SCHOLES, WRY, ENG [35212] : PRE 1885 SHEFFIELD, WRY, ENG [37318]

MACHON 1700S TRINITY, JSY, CHI [38396]

MCHUGH 1820+ LAUNCESTON & EVANDALE, TAS, AUS [34910] : PRE 1850 MAY, IRL [34046] : C1800+ RINN, LET, IRL [37447] : C1850+ MOHILL, LET, IRL [37447] : SARAH 1829-1860 IRL [37567] : PRE 1900 BALLYADAMS, LEX, IRL [38300]

MCILHINNEY 1720-1860 LETTERKENNY, DON, IRL [37118]

MCILHINNY 1720-1860 LETTERKENNY, DON, IRL [37118]

MCILLVANY 1900S STIRLING, STI, SCT [35535]

MCILMENE THOMAS PRE 1600 KIRKCUDBRIGHT TOWN, KKD, SCT [37644]

MCILMOYLE 1797+ LEEDS & GRENVILLE, ONT, CAN [37490]

MCILROY 1800+ ONT, CAN [34490] : 1850+ COR, IRL [33857] : 1782+ ANT, IRL [34490] : C1825 ANT, IRL [34668] : PRE 1850 ANT, IRL [35207] : 1740+ STI, SCT [33986]

MCILVANIE 1850+ SAND CO., MI, USA [34218]

MCILWAIN 1934+ ISLANDMAGEE, ANT, IRL [34934] : 1650+ LONDONDERRY, LDY, IRL & ENG [34934] : 1720+ NJ, USA [34934]

MCILWAINE 1669+ LOUGHNEAGH, LDY, IRL [34934] : 1770+ CARRIGANS, DON, IRL [34934] : 1650+ LONDONDERRY, LDY, IRL [34934]

MCILWEE C1810 KILLIBEGS, DON, IRL [34494] : 1750-1875 DON, IRL [38024] : 1750-1875 BELFAST & BALLYMENA, ANT, IRL [38024]

MCILWRAITH PRE 1820 RFW & AYR, SCT [37816]

MCILWRATH PRE 1820 KILLINCHY, DOW, IRL [34895]

MCINDEOR DONALD PRE 1808 BOWMORE, ARL, SCT [35848]

MCINDOE 1765+ CADDER, LKS, SCT [34122] : JANE C1847 EDINBURGH, SCT [34993]

MCINEARN 1780+ IRL [38279]

MCINERNEY 1850-1915 CLA, IRL [33891] : 1877+ KILDYSERT, CLA, IRL [34900] : 1805 CLA, IRL [36860] : PRE 1900 ENNIS, CLA, IRL [38484]

MCINERNY 1800-1880 MADRAS & SIBI, BELOOCHISTAN, INDIA [37203]

MCINIFF PRE 1865 EDINBURGH, SCT & IRL [37852]

MACINNES C1820 CHALEUR, NB, CAN [35612]

MCINNES PRE 1850 NSW, AUS [34809] : 1840-1870 KANMANTOO, SA, AUS [35191] : 1852+ GEELONG, VIC, AUS [35774] : 1862+ DURHAM LEAD, VIC, AUS [35774] : 1820-1900 SPRINGFORD, ONT, CAN [36556] : 1880+ BIRMINGHAM, WAR, ENG [36592] : 1822+ GLASGOW, STI, SCT [33936] : 1800 PORTREE, INV, SCT [33936] : C1820

MORVERN, ARL, SCT [35260] : PRE 1852
SNIZORT, ISLE OF SKYE, INV, SCT [35774] : PRE
1860 BROADFORD, INV, SCT [36592] : 1829+
PORTREE, INV, SCT [37178] : ALL
CAMPBELTOWN, ARL, SCT [37303] : 1850+
GLASGOW, LKS, SCT & AUS [36592]

McINNIS COLIN 1815-1850 GLENGARRY, ONT,
CAN [38482] : COLIN 1790-1820 TYREE, ARL, SCT
[38482] : ISABELLE 1860-1890 FARIBAULT, MN,
USA [38482]

McINTIRE ROBERT 1800 CHESTER CO., PA, USA
[37501]

MACINTOSH PRE 1830 PETTY, INV, SCT [34613] :
PRE 1772 CROMDALE, INV, SCT [36653]

McINTOSH 1844+ MORUYA, NSW, AUS [34979] :
1840+ BALLARAT, VIC, AUS [35053] : 1880+ QLD,
AUS [37114] : 1800+ FRANKLIN, TAS, AUS [38288]
: ALEX 1792-1855 GOULBOURN, ONT, CAN
[37441] : 1830S BRISTOL, ENG [34452] : 1830-1850
LND, ENG [35916] : DOUGLAS C1882 SIMLA,
INDIA [35154] : CATHERINE 1883+ SINLA,
INDIA [35154] : 1860+ SHAG POINT, OTAGO, NZ
[35885] : PRE 1828 BURNT ISLAND, FIF, SCT
[33812] : WILLIAM 1800 DAVIOT & DUNLICHTY,
INV, SCT [33970] : 1700+ OKI, SCT [33986] : PRE
1850 KILCHRENAN, ARL, SCT [34419] : PRE 1820
DRAINIE, MOR, SCT [34452] : AGNES PRE 1850
PERTH, PER, SCT [34583] : JOHN C1825 NEW
SCONE, PER, SCT [34583] : 1800+ GLENMUICK &
LESLIE, ABD, SCT [34591] : 1800+ INVERNESS,
INV, SCT [34810] : 1800S CLK, SCT [34979] : 1750+
GLASGOW, SCT [35152] : ALL CAMSERNEY,
DULL, PER, SCT [35334] : PRE 1792 SALINE, FIF,
SCT [35525] : C1818 CULLEN, BAN, SCT [35585] :
PRE 1840S INV, SCT [35727] : PRE 1863 GLASGOW,
SCT [35885] : C1800 STRATHDON, ABD, SCT
[36607] : 1750+ GLEN URQUHART, INV, SCT
[36815] : PRE 1821 INVERNESS, INV, SCT [36955] :
1800-1860 HELENSBURGH, DNB, SCT [36990] :
1870-1910 CRAIL, FIF, SCT [36990] : 1850-1880
KIRKCALDY, FIF, SCT [36990] : PRE 1830 DFS,
SCT [37133] : C1832 CADDER, LKS, SCT [37148] :
ALEX 1792-1855 PER, SCT [37441] : 1810+ PETTY,
INV, SCT [37575] : PRE 1870 INV, SCT [38286] :
1740+ SUT, SCT [38385] : PRE 1850 TONGUE, SUT,
SCT [38457] : AGNES PRE 1850 PER, SCT & AUS
[33840] : ALL PER, SCT & AUS [35547] : 1800-1890
DUNBEATH, CAI, SCT & NZ [33991] : 1860+
LLANSAMLET, GLA, WLS [35486]

MACINTYRE 1956 BANGALORE, INDIA [34609] :
1700-1800 KILCHRENAN, ARL, SCT [34225] :
1860+ SCT [34609] : 1882+ COLOMBO, SRI
LANKA [34609] : SUSAN 1850S NEW ORLEANS,
LA, USA [34266]

McINTYRE 1860S WINCHELSEA, VIC, AUS [35390] :
1840+ MERINO & CASTLEMAINE, VIC, AUS
[37176] : 1850+ DALBY, QLD, AUS [37176] : 1848+
GERRINGONG, NSW, AUS [37942] : 1800+
BATHURST & YOUNG, NSW, AUS [37993] :
HECTOR 1800+ VIC, AUS & SCT [34572] : C1800-
1950 ADMASTON & RENFREW, ONT, CAN [38464]
: 1825+ DEVONPORT, DEV, ENG [35482] : PRE
1885 GRANARD, LOG, IRL [35872] : PRE 1920
DONEMANA, TYR, IRL [36437] : PRE 1850 CORK
CITY, COR, IRL [36514] : PRE 1848
CLONMACNOISE, OFF, IRL [37942] : 1750S PER,
SCT [34188] : 1850 AYR, SCT [34190] : PRE 1867
NEW MONKSLAND, LKS, SCT [34412] : 1750+
GLENORCHY & KILCHRENAN, ARL, SCT [34419]
: 1850S ARL, SCT [35390] : C1830 SLEAT, ISLE OF
SKYE, SCT [35391] : PRE 1884 ABERFOYLE, PER,
SCT [35601] : 1750+ KILLIN, PER, SCT [35886] :

1806+ COMRIE, PER, SCT [35886] : 1800+
KILMALLIE, ARL, SCT [35909] : PRE 1841 PER,
SCT [36650] : 1800+ CUMBERNAULD, DNB, SCT
[36875] : PRE 1857 ISLE BARRA & SKYE, INV, SCT
[36882] : 1780+ ARROCHAR, DNB, SCT [37131] :
PRE 1900 NTH KNAPDALE, ARL, SCT [37176] :
1700-1800 SORN, AYR, SCT [37188] : DONALD
1809+ HOUSTON, RFW, SCT [37424] : PRE 1850
KILLIN, PER, SCT [38364] : PRE 1850 PER, SCT
[38464] : PRE 1800 SCT [38736] : THOMAS C1860
NIAGARA FALLS, NY, USA [37424] : PRE 1850 ST
LAWRENCE, NY, USA [38736] : 1850-1910
TREMPEALEW & WAUPAEA, WI, USA [38736]

McISAAC 1880+ DARJEELING, INDIA [35886] :
1750+ COMRIE, PER, SCT [35886]

McISSAAC PRE 1860 GLASGOW, SCT [33838]

MACIVER PRE 1900 STORNAWAY, ROC, SCT
[37496]

McIVER 1839+ NSW, AUS [38485] : ALL ONT, CAN
[34471] : C1800 DUBLIN, IRL [38485] : PRE 1850
KNOCK CARLOWAY, LEWIS, ROC, SCT [34491] :
PRE 1850 LOWER SHADER, LEWIS, ROC, SCT
[34491] : C1833 ARL, SCT [38485]

MCIVOR C1795+ PETTIGO, FER, IRL [34672] : ALL
WORLDWIDE [33858]

MACK GOTTLIEBEN C1860-1880 MORNINGTON
WATERLOO, PERTH CO, ONT, CAN [34103] : 1810-
1850 POTTON, BDF, ENG [34832] : GOTTLIEBEN
1838-1860S MUNDELSHEIM, WUE, GER [34103] :
1845 IRL [37558] : PRE 1700 CT & MA, USA [38746]

McKAIN ALL WICK, ELGIN, SCT [33954]

McKANE ALL GSY, CHI [33954] : PRE 1880 ANT,
IRL [34633] : CATHERINE C1798-1850 ANT, IRL
[36782] : 1900+ BELFAST, ANT & DOW, IRL [37425]

MCKASH 1750-1850 ERROL, PER, SCT [34523]

McKAUGHAN PRE 1860 BUSHMILLS, ANT, IRL
[37179]

MACKAY C1860 ROOTY HILL & SYDNEY, NSW,
AUS [33765] : 1850+ CALVERT, QLD, AUS [34812] :
1800S GLADSTONE, QLD, AUS [35501] : 1840-1880
BUNGAY & WINGHAM, NSW, AUS [35546] :
1800+ LOOWEE & MUDGEE, NSW, AUS [35567] :
1865+ SOUTH EAST AREA, QLD, AUS [37896] :
CAPT. JOHN 1880S QLD, AUS [37898] : WILLIAM
1870+ ESSENDON, VIC, AUS [38071] : DONALD
R. C1846-1901 ONT, CAN [33759] : JAMES 1810-1890
MACKAY ISLAND, DOW, IRL [36180] : PRE 1860
DORNOCH ASSYNT, SUT, SCT [34812] : PRE 1900
WATTEN, CAI, SCT [34816] : JANET C1797-1838
SUT, SCT [35108] : PRE 1840 THURSO, SUT, SCT
[35546] : C1864 ABD, SCT [36856] : ISABELLA PRE
1858 SUT, SCT [36886] : PRE 1858 SUT, SCT [36886] :
ROBERT PRE 1858 SUT, SCT [36886] : PRE 1865
THURSO AREA, CAI, SCT [37896]

McKAY C1850 VIC, AUS [33793] : 1845-1904
ROEBOURNE, WA, AUS [34530] : 1870+ TINGHA,
NSW, AUS [37889] : 1750-1800 MALPEQUE, PEI,
CAN [34123] : 1790+ MAN, CAN [37426] : HUGH
1789+ NORTHUMBERLAND CO., NB, CAN
[37443] : JAMES PRE 1870 HAM, ENG [35976] :
1860+ BICESTER & OXFORD, OXF, ENG [36502] :
PRE 1870 WOBURN & VERSHOLT, BDF, ENG
[36502] : JAMES PRE 1900 PORTSTEWART, ANT,
IRL [35976] : 1800+ ANT, IRL [36746] : PRE 1876 N.
IRL [36878] : 1870+ LITTLE RAKAIA &
SOUTHBRIDGE, CBY, NZ [36746] : PRE 1879
CALITZDORP, CAPE, RSA [36459] : DONALD
C1846-1901 CAI, SCT [33759] : ALEXINA PRE 1830
LAIRG, SUT, SCT [33874] : ALEXANDER PRE 1830
LAIRG, SUT, SCT [33874] : CHRISTIAN PRE 1788
DUNDEE, ANS, SCT [34461] : 1845-1904 ISLE OF
SKYE, SCT [34530] : 1820-1830 NEW MILNS, AYR,

SCT **[34582]** : C1817 PAISLEY, RFW, SCT **[35251]** : C1820 MORVERN, ARL, SCT **[35260]** : 1820S BARONY, LKS, SCT **[35728]** : WILLIAM PRE 1830 LOSSIEMOUTH, MOR, SCT **[35848]** : PRE 1840 PAISLEY, RFW, SCT **[35913]** : 1800+ THURSO, SUT, SCT **[35947]** : 1800-1860 DUNDEE, ANS, SCT **[36150]** : PRE 1870 BRYDEKIRK, DFS, SCT **[36502]** : 1850-1890 GLASGOW, LKS, SCT **[36663]** : C1800 AYR, SCT **[36694]** : 1800+ ABERDEEN, ABD, SCT **[36769]** : MARGARET C1830+ GLASGOW, SCT **[36853]** : 1830-1860 CARRINGTON, MLN, SCT **[36884]** : 1800-1880 KIRKINTILLOCH, DNB, SCT **[37456]** : PRE 1845 ABERFOYLE & BRIG O'TURK, PER, SCT **[37842]** : PRE 1850 CAI, SCT **[38457]** : PRE 1850 RACY, SUT, SCT **[38457]** : 1825-1875 NEW YORK CITY, NY, USA **[36724]**

MCKAY (SEE MACKAY) [33759]

MCKEAG 1800-1900 SCT **[35742]**

MCKEAGE 1870-1925 ST CECILE, QUE, CAN **[38407]** : 1830+ COLERAINE, DRY, IRL & NZ **[36869]**

MCKEAN 1840+ DALKEITH & NEWBATTLE, MLN, SCT **[35513]**

MCKEAND 1861 AUS **[35910]**

MACKECKNIE PRE 1860 GLASGOW, SCT **[33906]**

MCKEE 1830+ PORT HOPE, ONT, CAN **[34484]** : 1870+ MIDHURST & BARRIE, ONT, CAN **[34484]** : PRE 1850 CUL, ENG **[34186]** : C1875 MANCHESTER, LAN, ENG **[34360]** : PRE 1832 BALLYMENA, ANT, IRL **[34262]** : 1700-1900 ARDARA, DON, IRL **[34537]** : SARAH 1800 TANDRAGEE & PORTADOWN, ARM, IRL **[34919]** : PRE 1880 BALLYNASKEAGH, DOW, IRL **[36437]** : PRE 1780 KIK, IRL **[37133]** : PRE 1908 BALLYNAHINCH, DOW, IRL **[37439]** : 1700-1990 IRL & AUS **[35421]** : ALL NEWTONARDS, DOW, IRL & USA **[34645]** : 1800+ SOMERSET CO., PA, USA **[36897]** : 1750-1800 CUMBERLAND CO., PA, USA **[37808]** : 1800-1820 CENTRE CO., PA, USA **[37808]** : THOMAS 1800+ CA, OH & PA, USA **[38023]** : 1810-1880 COLUMBIANA CO., OH, USA & IRL **[37529]**

MCKEEN 1860+ KAPUNDA, SA, AUS **[37186]** : 1800S CLA, IRL **[37186]** : PRE 1890 PA, USA & IRL **[38746]**

MCKEEVER ALL ST JOHNSTON, DRY, IRL **[34569]** : 1750+ IRL **[36558]** : PRE 1850 LOU, IRL **[37537]** : 1800-1990 ALLEGHENY CO., PA, USA **[37549]** : C1763+ PHILADELPHIA, PA, USA **[38067]**

MCKEGG (SEE MCCAIG) [34190]

MCKEGGIE C1840 DUMBARTON, DNB, SCT **[35594]**

MCKELL 1845+ BATHURST, NSW, AUS **[34009]** : 1840-1850S EAST MORTON, WRY, ENG **[33780]** : PRE 1850 SCT **[33780]**

MACKELLAR C1750-C1850 LOCHGOILHEAD & ARDACHIE, ARL, SCT **[34589]**

MCKELLAR 1850+ MAN & ONT, CAN **[34496]** : ALL HALIFAX, YKS, ENG **[38332]** : C1800 INVERARY, ARL, SCT **[35502]** : 1800-1810 STRACHUR, ARL, SCT **[36606]** : ALL LOCH LOMOND, SCT **[38332]**

MCKELVAY 1750-1760 BALLYMENA, ANT, IRL **[38347]**

MCKELVEY PRE 1800 BALLYSIMON, LIM, IRL **[36840]** : 1800-1825 CHAMPAIGN CO., IL, USA **[38137]**

MCKELVIE C1838 DOW, IRL **[35820]** : 1800-1850 STONEYKIRK, AYR & WIG, SCT **[34523]** : ALL DNB & RFW, SCT **[35647]** : 1851-1856 STONEYKIRK, WIG, SCT **[35820]**

MACKEN 1852+ AUS **[33764]** : 1853 CHELSEA, MDX, ENG **[35720]** : PRE 1890 PUTNEY, SRY, ENG **[35720]**

MCKENDRICK PRE 1830 LETTERKENNY, DON, IRL **[34613]** : 1700+ PER, SCT **[35450]** : C1800

FALKIRK, STI, SCT **[36846]** : PRE 1857 ELDERSLIE, RFW, SCT **[37925]**

MCKENDRY C1827 ABERDEEN, ABD, SCT **[35391]**

MCKENNA PRE 1900 TAS, AUS **[38305]** : JAMES 1800-1850 NEWCASTLE ON TYNE, NBL, ENG **[36623]** : C1820 ENG & AUS **[35417]** : JOHN 1829-1914 NEWCASTLE UPON TYNE, NBL, ENG & AUS **[37153]** : 1800 DERRY, DRY, IRL **[33848]** : 1800+ DUBLIN, IRL **[34918]** : PRE 1870 TYR, IRL **[35005]** : PRE 1900 GLENGARRIFF, COR, IRL **[36893]** : PRE 1900 HOWTH, DUB, IRL **[38305]** : 1700+ LEE, VA, USA **[34163]** : 1880+ SCRANTON, PA, USA **[38011]** : C1850+ BALT, MD, USA **[38182]**

MCKENNEY ROBERT 1810+ EAST LUTHER TWP., ONT, CAN **[34524]** : C1850+ BALT, MD, USA **[38182]**

MCKENNITT ALL DON, IRL **[34223]**

MCKENNY PRE 1900 TAS, AUS **[38305]** : 1800+ DUBLIN, IRL **[36087]** : 1850S DUB, IRL **[36741]** : PRE 1900 HOWTH, DUB, IRL **[38305]**

MACKENZIE 1822+ BATHURST, NSW, AUS **[35203]** : JOHN D. 1910+ SYDNEY, NSW, AUS **[35888]** : 1883+ SYDNEY, NSW, AUS **[35919]** : 1888+ SYDNEY, NSW & QLD, AUS **[38485]** : C1868 OTTAWA, ONT, CAN **[37148]** : 1800S PAPCASTLE, COCKERMOUTH, CUL, ENG **[35017]** : PRE 1850 HAM, ENG **[35523]** : 1700S STOKE DAMEREL, DEV, ENG **[35830]** : 1850+ MANCHESTER, LAN, ENG **[35919]** : 1830-1850 DONAGHADEE, DOW, IRL **[36536]** : 1830+ NZ **[38433]** : 1800+ FIF, SCT **[34226]** : 1750+ LOCHBROOM & DINGWALL, ROC, SCT **[34403]** : 1800+ KILTEARN, ROC, SCT **[34403]** : C1800 MID BORVE, LEWIS, ROC, SCT **[34491]** : 1750+ LATHERON, CAI, SCT **[34606]** : 1440-1800 GAIRLOCH, ROC, SCT **[35203]** : PRE 1915 PLOCKTON, ROC, SCT **[35888]** : MARY 1800+ ULLAPOOL, ROC, SCT **[35917]** : 1800S STORNOWAY, ROC, SCT **[36041]** : PRE 1800 INVERNESS, INV, SCT **[36201]** : PRE 1900 KILTARLITY, INV, SCT **[37619]** : 1792-1882 DUMFRIES, DFS, SCT **[38433]** : C1856 CUPAR & DUNFERMLINE, FIF, SCT **[38485]** : WILLIAM 1770 SAVANNAH, GA, USA **[35328]** : 1930+ WINNETKA, IL, USA **[35974]**

MCKENZIE C1869+ SOUTH PARA, SA, AUS **[34035]** : 1870+ KYABRAM, VIC, AUS **[34550]** : SAMUEL 1860+ SYDNEY, NSW, AUS **[34901]** : 1840 SODWALL, NSW, AUS **[35089]** : 1850+ BULLI, NSW, AUS **[35143]** : PRE 1857+ STANLEY, VIC, AUS **[35143]** : C1863+ CANOWINDRA, NSW, AUS **[35143]** : C1863+ GRENFELL, NSW, AUS **[35143]** : C1863+ GLENLOGAN, NSW, AUS **[35143]** : 1837+ WOLLONGONG, NSW, AUS **[35143]** : C1840+ GOULBURN, NSW, AUS **[35143]** : C1863+ COWRA, NSW, AUS **[35143]** : 1800S DROUIN, VIC, AUS **[35926]** : 1850+ CASTLEMAINE, VIC, AUS **[37997]** : C1929 WINDSOR, ONT, CAN **[34153]** : 1930S PRINCE ALBERT, SAS, CAN **[34937]** : 1900S MONTREAL, QUE, CAN **[34937]** : MARGARET PRE 1851 WEST ZORRA, ONT, CAN **[36678]** : PRE 1850 INVERNESS CO., NS, CAN **[38447]** : C1849 SUNDERLAND, DUR, ENG **[34972]** : 1800S LONDON, ENG **[35804]** : 1850+ MANCHESTER, LAN, ENG **[35919]** : ALEXANDER 1840+ ROTHERHITHE, LND, ENG **[36254]** : SYDNEY PRE 1877 NBL, ENG **[36453]** : 1850 KIMBERWORTH, YKS, ENG **[37829]** : C1842 CLONMAIN, ARM, IRL **[33821]** : JOHN PRE 1800 SLI, IRL **[33846]** : 1840+ DUBLIN, IRL **[33921]** : 1860+ BALLYCASTLE, ANT, IRL **[33921]** : 1890+ NZ **[33921]** : PRE 1863+ OTAGO, NZ **[35143]** : KENNETH 1859+ PALMERSTON NORTH,

MANAWATU, NZ [36877] : 1817+ ALVAH, BAN, SCT [33842] : PRE 1880 BURGHEAD, MOR, SCT [33993] : PRE 1840 HARRIS, INV, SCT [34197] : PRE 1830 KINNOUL, PER, SCT [34389] : 1750+ LOCHBROOM & DINGWALL, ROC, SCT [34403] : PRE 1800 CONTIN, ROC, SCT [34403] : 1800+ KILMARNOCK, AYR, SCT [34415] : PRE 1850 DFS, SCT [34617] : C1805 LETTOCH, ROC, SCT [34713] : SAMUEL PRE 1854 INVERNESS, SCT [34901] : 1870-1920 ELGIN, MOR, SCT [34937] : C1780 KIRKHOLM, WIG, SCT [34993] : C1800-1837 ISLE OF SKYE, INV, SCT [35143] : CHARLES 1790 CULLEN, BAN, SCT [35369] : 1800-1850 KINGUSSIE, INV, SCT [35494] : C1850 DINGWAL, ROC, SCT [35502] : C1800 FORT WILLIAM, INV, SCT [35773] : JAMES PRE 1770 BIRNIE, MOR, SCT [35848] : 1820S EDINBURGH, MLN, SCT [35865] : PRE 1830 MORANKIE, ROC, SCT [35932] : ALEXANDER PRE 1837 ISLE OF SKYE, INV, SCT [36629] : 1870+ DUMBARTON, DNB, SCT [36705] : DUNCAN 1860+ GOVAN & GLASGOW, LKS, SCT [36749] : 1700+ FERRINTOSH, ROC, SCT [36857] : JOHN PRE 1860 FODDERTY, ROC, SCT [36877] : C1790 INV & NAI, SCT [37263] : 1820+ SCOURIE, SUT, SCT [37881] : 1860+ OKI, SCT [37881] : 1760-1860 RRASAY, INV, SCT [37964] : ALEX 1800+ ROC, SCT [37997]

MCKEON PRE 1860 SYDNEY, NSW, AUS [34812] : 1850+ IPSWICH, QLD, AUS [34812] : 1800+ KILLARGA, LET, IRL [35248]

MCKEOWN 1880+ IPSWICH, QLD, AUS [35511] : 1852+ CAMPBELLS CREEK, VIC, AUS [35801] : 1899+ ALLANDALE, VIC, AUS [36278] : 1865+ LIVERPOOL, LAN, ENG [34566] : 1800+ DOW, IRL [33829] : PRE 1870 LURGAN, ARM, IRL [33932] : 1850S GILFORD, DOW, IRL [33967] : 1800+ ARM, IRL [34408] : PRE 1845 DUBLIN, IRL [34566] : 1800-1900 ANT, IRL [34631] : PRE 1886 GLENARNE, ANT, IRL [34779] : 1800+ ACHILL ISLAND, MAY, IRL [35511] : PRE 1856 NEWRY, ARM, IRL [36278] : 1940+ NJ, USA [34566] : 1930+ NEW YORK, NY, USA [34566]

MCKERCHAR PRE 1838 TULLYMET, PER, SCT [38413]

MACKEREL 1840-1860 HOBART, TAS, AUS [34551]

MACKERELL 1800S GORLESTON, SFK, ENG [34086]

MACKERILL 1830-1852 HALIFAX, YKS, ENG [38207]

MACKERLEY PRE 1813 MORRIS, NJ, USA [34573]

MCKERNAN HARRY 1898+ REDFEARN, SA, AUS [35467] : PRE 1820 CANTERBURY, KEN, ENG [34021] : 1820+ LURGAN, ARM, IRL [34021] : 1800-1850 TYR, IRL [34346] : 1862+ ANT, IRL [34609]

MCKERRACHER PRE 1820 PERTH, PER, SCT [36660]

MCKERRAL PRE 1878 TAMLAGHT, TYR, IRL [34437] : PRE 1878 BELFAST, ANT & DOW, IRL [34437] : PRE 1848 CAMPBELTOWN, ARL, SCT [35807]

MCKERRAS ALL MOR, SCT [35932]

MCKERRIN 1860+ BALLARAT, VIC, AUS [35792]

MCKERROW 1862+ SCOTTSDALE, TAS, AUS [36644] : 1852+ FOREST CREEK, VIC, AUS [36644] : C1735 CRAIGMALLOCH, AYR, SCT [36644]

MCKERRULE PRE 1878 TAMLAGHT, TYR, IRL [34437]

MCKERSEY C1868 MARYLEBONE, MDX, ENG [33955]

MCKERSIE 1859-C1910 BRIGHTON, VIC, AUS [34794]

MACKESON ALL SCT &, WORLDWIDE [36125]

MACKESSAN ALL SCT &, WORLDWIDE [36125]

MCKEW C1880S+ SYDNEY, NSW, AUS [35537] : C1800S+ NEWCASTLE ON TYNE, NBL, ENG [35537]

MACKEWN 1800S NEWBURGH, ABD, SCT [38402]

MACKEY 1850+ PORT PHILLIP, VIC, AUS [34900] : 1818-1913 CARLETON CO., ONT, CAN [36666] : PRE 1800 LONDON, MDX & HAM, ENG [36379] : 1700S IRL [36666]

MCKIBBEN 1700+ MARTINSVILLE, KY & VA, USA [38336]

MCKIBBEN (SEE MCGIBB [38084]

MCKIBBON 1850+ ANT, IRL [35627]

MACKIE PRE 1900 BLACKWOOD, VIC, AUS [35055] : 1890+ BARINGHUP, VIC, AUS [36304] : 1750-1770 IRL [37740] : 1880-1990 FIF, SCT [34393] : 1700+ MARNOCH, BAN, SCT [34420] : PRE 1840 SLAINS & CRUDEN, ABD, SCT [35055] : 1650+ ST MONANCE, FIF, SCT [35627] : 1740+ AYR, SCT [35909] : 1800+ COLMONELL & GIRVAN, AYR, SCT [35989] : 1800+ GARLIESTOWN, WIG, SCT [35989] : 1800-1850 DALRY, AYR, SCT [36304] : PRE 1700 DUNDEE, ANS, SCT [36432] : PRE 1750 WLN, SCT [37463] : ALL BOTHWELL & UDDINGSTON, LKS, SCT [37684]

MCKIE 1800+ THORPEDALE, VIC, AUS [34271] : 1900+ TRARALGON, VIC, AUS [34271] : THOMAS 1868+ KIRKCOWAN, WIG, SCT [34627]

MCKIERNAN PRE 1830 CAV, IRL [34368] : 1850+ LET, IRL [38484]

MACKIESON ALL SCT &, WORLDWIDE [36125]

MCKILDUFFE ALL WORLDWIDE [37530]

MCKILLOP 1940 MONTREAL, QUE, CAN [35194] : 1850+ ELGIN CO., ONT, CAN [38431] : PRE 1820+ CRUSHYBRACKEN, ANT, IRL [35759]

MCKIM 1790+ SWITZERVILLE, ONT, CAN [36688] : 1650-1800 LDY, IRL [36688] : 1750-1790 COPENHAGEN, NY, USA [36688] : 1740-1800 BRADYWINE, DE, USA [36688]

MACKIN PRE 1900 MULLINGAR, WEM, IRL [36941]

MACKINDER 1800-1875 WISBECH, CAM, ENG & AUS [35422]

MCKINDLAY ALL WORLDWIDE [34961]

MCKINERY ALL WORLDWIDE [33814]

MCKINLAY 1780+ GLASGOW AREA, LKS, SCT [35851] : C1750 KILMADOCK, PER, SCT [36635] : C1750 CALLANDER, PER, SCT [36635] : PRE 1852 EASTHOUSES & NEWBATTLE, MLN, SCT [37852] : 1800S+ GLASGOW, SCT [38436]

MCKINLEY 1850-1887 SYDNEY, NSW, AUS [35092] : 1800+ CUSHENDUN, ANT, IRL [35054] : C1814 CLONAMULLOG, FER, IRL [35260] : 1750-1900 BALLYCASTLE, ANT, IRL [36115] : 1820 NEWRY, DOW, IRL [36599] : 1799+ CUSHENDUN, ANT, IRL [36686] : 1800S DON, IRL [37497] : 1750+ DNB, SCT [34459] : PRE 1839 WASHINGTON CO., IL & OH, USA [37817]

MCKINNA PETER PRE 1900 NEWTON STEWART, DFS, SCT [35471]

MCKINNAN 1700+ INV, SCT [37949]

MCKINNEL PRE 1870 GREENOCK, RFW, SCT [36072]

MCKINNEY 1800+ DUBLIN, IRL [36087] : 1840-50 SEAGOE, ARM, IRL [38583] : 1800-1900 MD, USA [34749] : ALL USA [35313] : 1800+ GUILFORD, NC, USA [38517]

MCKINNEY (SEE MCKENN [34524]

MACKINNON 1848+ GEELONG, VIC, AUS [33876] : 1853+ VIC, AUS [35379] : PRE 1900 NB, CAN [33904] : PRE 1800 DERRYGUAIG, ARL, SCT [33876] : PRE 1853 PORTREE, INV, SCT [35379]

MCKINNON 1800+ BULLA BULLA, VIC, AUS [35077] : 1860+ MOUNT GAMBIER, SA, AUS [35493] : C1800S+ YASS, NSW, AUS [35537] : 1835+ CAVAN & YASS, NSW, AUS [35561] : 1850S CARNGHAN, VIC, AUS [35721] : DONALD 1848+

SYDNEY, NSW, AUS [35863] : 1897 NORTHAM, WA, AUS [36863] : 1907 FREMANTLE, WA, AUS [36863] : 1890+ TRURO, NS, CAN [34251] : C1860-1890 HANTS CO., NS, CAN [34251] : 1796+ SNIZORT, SKYE, INV, SCT [34122] : 1830+ LKS, SCT [34189] : LACHLAN PRE 1826 KILININ, ARL, SCT [34310] : 1700+ KILCHRENAN, ARL, SCT [34419] : C1846 COLL, ARL, SCT [34815] : 1853 MOTHERWELL, LKS, SCT [35152] : C1833 SLEAT, ISLE OF SKYE, SCT [35391] : PRE 1830 KNOYDART, INV, SCT [35430] : C1849 ISLE OF SKYE, INV, SCT [35502] : PRE 1835 SLEAT, INV, SCT [35561] : JOHN C1780 PORTREE, SKYE, SCT [38397] : 1700-1770 ANNE ARUNDEL CO., MD, USA [37605]

MCKINSTRY 1860-1898 BELFAST, IRL [33976] : PRE 1884 ANT, IRL [34720] : PRE 1900 ANT, IRL [35915]

MACKINTOSH ADAM 1855-1865 INV, SCT [35486] : C1820 GARIOCH, ABD, SCT [35486] : 1750+ GLEN URQUHART, INV, SCT [36815] : PRE 1880 KINGUSSIE, INV, SCT [37114] : ADAM 1860-1890 STIRLING, STI, SCT & WLS [35486]

MACKISON PRE 1850 BANNOCKBURN & STIRLING, STI, SCT [36125] : PRE 1830 MENTEITH & DOUNE, PER & STI, SCT [36125] : ALL SCT &, WORLDWIDE [36125]

MCKISON ALL SCT &, WORLDWIDE [36125]

MCKISSOCK PRE 1860 GLASGOW, LKS, SCT [33944] : JANE PRE 1811 FOCHABERS, MOR, SCT [35848]

MCKISSON PRE 1776 PA, USA [37786] : SAMUEL PRE 1783 HARFORD CO., MD, USA [37786]

MCKITERICK 1850+ ONT, CAN [36705]

MCKITTRICK ALL ARMAGH, ARM, IRL [35633]

MACKLAN 1850+ LITTLE ELTHAM, VIC, AUS [35853] : PRE 1850 DBY, ENG [35853]

MACKLIN 1840 ASHTON U LYNE, LAN, ENG [36640] : C1850 BANBRIDGE, DOW, IRL [34223] : ALL WORLDWIDE [35875]

MACKLIN-SHAW 1870 EMMAVILLE, NSW, AUS [36640]

MACKMAN ALL WORLDWIDE [37100]

MACKMIN ALL WORLDWIDE [37100]

MACKMURDIE ALL WORLDWIDE [36420]

MACKNESS 1800+ BRAMPTON, HUN, ENG [35121]

MCKNIGHT 1870S CASTLEMAINE, VIC, AUS [35044] : C1899 BRISBANE, QLD, AUS [37919] : PRE 1850 LND & STS, ENG & IRL [38746] : C1780 DONAGHMORE, DOW, IRL [37524] : ALL AYR, SCT [37805] : 1850-1920 MACOMB CO., MI, USA [34505]

MCKONE 1814-1900 SYDNEY, NSW, AUS [35735] : PRE 1812 LONDON, ENG [35735]

MCKOWAN 1600+ WORLDWIDE [38388]

MCKOWEN PRE 1860 LARNE, ANT, IRL [36793]

MCKOWN JULIA ISABEL 1800+ USA [38451]

MACKRELL 1790-1855 WOODTON & THWAIT, NFK, ENG [37477] : 1700+ CASTLE BLAYNEY, MOG, IRL [34226] : ALL WORLDWIDE [35538]

MACKRETH PRE 1700 ENG [36184]

MACKRILL 1800S ENG [36289]

MACKRISS ALL LIN, ENG [37487]

MACKWIRTH 1880+ NEW YORK, NY, USA [37796]

MCKYE PRE 1882 SCT [38437]

MACLACHLAN PRE 1840 MORVEN, ARL, SCT [34192] : PRE 1825 GLASGOW, LKS, SCT [35344] : 1760-1850S MULL, ARL, SCT [35938]

MCLACHLAN 1850+ SYDNEY, NSW, AUS [35111] : C1865 BET BET, VIC, AUS [35127] : 1868+ RYLSTONE, NSW, AUS [35450] : C1830-1840 SORN, AYR, SCT [33845] : ANGUS C1845 ARL, SCT [35111] : MARY 1800-1850 ABERDEEN, ABD, SCT [35377] :

C1836 STIRLING, STI, SCT [35478] : ALL INV, SCT [35993]

MCLAGAN 1844 MOULIN, PER, SCT [34224]

MCLAGGAN 1890+ CAN [35150] : 1835+ ABERFELDY & PERTH, PER, SCT & AUS [35150]

MACLAIN 1800+ ISLE OF MULL, SCT [37478]

MACLAINE PRE 1851 TARBERT, ARL, SCT [34501]

MCLARAN 1750+ COMRIE, PER, SCT [35886]

MACLAREN 1800S LONDON, ENG [35068] : 1850S MARYLEBONE, MDX, ENG [36741] : C1812 IRL [35344] : C1847 GLASGOW, LKS, SCT [35344]

MCLAREN C1830+ ARMIDALE, NSW, AUS [34755] : 1840+ REGENTVILLE, NSW, AUS [36273] : 1900+ VIC, AUS [37152] : PRE 1877 MARYLEBONE, LND, ENG [38288] : 1860S MUSSELBURGH, ELN, SCT [33955] : 1800-1900 AYR, SCT [34182] : ALEX 1830+ MOULIN, PER, SCT [34620] : MARGARET 1901+ LOGIEALMOND, PER, SCT [34620] : JAMES 1867+ BALQUHIDDER, PER, SCT [34620] : C1845 PER, SCT [34761] : 1801+ CALLANDER, PER, SCT [35090] : C1760 OLD KILPATRICK, DNB, SCT [35252] : JAMES 1780-1850 BALQUHIDDER, PER, SCT [35377] : C1820 DUNFERMLINE, FIF, SCT [35457] : 1800S FALKIRK, STI, SCT [35627] : 1900+ DUNDEE, ANS, SCT [35888] : C1832 KINCARDINE BY DOUNE, PER, SCT [37148] : ELIZA C1775+ CALLENDER, PER, SCT [37441] : PRE 1880 ALLOA, SCT & NZ [33959] : 1900+ FLINT, MI, USA [35888]

MCLATCHIE PRE 1857 IRL [36509] : C1750 EDINBURGH, MLN, SCT [34713] : PRE 1780 STAIR, AYR, SCT [35406] : 1700+ AYR, SCT [37620] : C1800 OLD CUMNOCK, AYR, SCT [37772]

MCLAUCHLAN 1856+ KYNETON, VIC, AUS [38760] : PRE 1850 CROOK, DUR, ENG [38013] : 1780-1870 NEWTON STEWART, WIG, SCT [34687] : 1800S GALSTON & LESMAHAGOW, LKS, SCT [35391] : PRE 1840 SCT [38013]

MCLAUGHLAN 1800+ VIC, AUS [33793] : PRE 1850 LONDONDERRY, IRL [34941]

MACLAUGHLIN PRE 1900 NB, CAN [33904]

MCLAUGHLIN 1830-1870 GREENSBOROUGH, VIC, AUS [33801] : 1900+ DUNGOG, NSW, AUS [38729] : PRE 1905 WORKINGTON, CUL, ENG [35639] : 1780-1870 LDY, IRL [34687] : PRE 1830 LONDONDERRY, LDY, IRL [34707] : PRE 1852 NEWTOWNARDS, DOW, IRL [35245] : 1840 DON, IRL [36264] : PRE 1900 DOWNPATRICK, DOW, IRL [37405] : 1785+ SCT [33761] : 1840-1920 JERSEY CITY, NJ, USA [37003] : 1850-60 BEAVER, BEAVER CO., PA, USA [38087]

MCLAUGLIN 1750-1850 BURTON, STS, ENG [37188]

MCLAUREN 1839+ NSW, AUS [38018] : 1800-1838 DUNOON, AYR, SCT [38018]

MCLAURIN 1838+ YARRA YARRA, NSW, AUS [34979] : 1838+ NSW, AUS [35719] : 1700S DUNOON, ARL, SCT [34979] : PRE 1850 BEITH, AYR, SCT [35719]

MCLAVERTY 1800+ ANT, IRL [35121]

MCLAY 1820-1880 POLMONT, STI, SCT [33879] : ALL WORLDWIDE [33868]

MACLEAN 1880+ SYDNEY, NSW, AUS [33768] : C1880-1905 HORSHAM, VIC, AUS [35525] : COTTNAM C1850+ QLD, AUS [35525] : PRE 1862 GYRANDA, QLD, AUS [37982] : 1840+ SYDNEY, NSW, AUS [37982] : 1850-1880 MORUYA, NSW, AUS [38007] : HECTOR 1852+ MELBOURNE, VIC, AUS & NZ [35525] : 1800-1850 RICHMOND CO., NS, CAN [34253] : ALL PICTOU CO., NS, CAN [36713] : ALL N SYDNEY, NS, CAN [37478] : PRE 1800 DOW, IRL [33768] : 1800+ BELFAST, IRL [34200] : PRE 1800 NORTH UIST, INV, SCT [34253] : PRE

1830 ELGIN, MOR, SCT [35460] : 1860 KILBRIDE, BUT, SCT [37307] : 1750+ ISLE OF MULL, SCT [37478] : 1797+ KILTARLITY, INV, SCT & AUS [35150]

MCLEAN 1900S INVERELL, NSW, AUS [33781] : 1860+ GEELONG, VIC, AUS [34550] : DAVID 1850+ BALLARAT, VIC, AUS [34683] : 1862 GEELONG, VIC, AUS [34761] : 1837+ MORUYA, NSW, AUS [34979] : C1873+ MELBOURNE, VIC, AUS [35221] : JOHN 1839+ CLARENCETOWN, NSW, AUS [35260] : 1850S MANNING RIVER, NSW, AUS [35260] : 1867+ WOODS POINT, VIC, AUS [35407] : 1852 RYLSTONE, NSW, AUS [35450] : 1870S BINDANGO, QLD, AUS [35450] : 1838-1900 STUART TOWN, NSW, AUS [35559] : 1861+ QLD, AUS [35854] : 1885+ QLD, AUS [36305] : 1830-1950S BOURGET, ONT, CAN [34202] : C1855 ZORRA, ONT, CAN [34491] : 1800+ OTTAWA CO., QUE, CAN [34504] : PETER 1880-1900 CARLYLE, SAS, CAN [34515] : 1840+ QUE, CAN [36539] : 1800-1880 ALMONTE, ONT, CAN [36658] : LACHLIN C1885 KINLOSS, ONT, CAN [37424] : 1852 SUNDERLAND, ONT, CAN [37439] : PRE 1900 CARLISLE, CUL, ENG [37616] : PRE 1860 BOYLE, ROS, IRL [33876] : PRE 1840 LISBURN, ANT & DOW, IRL [34201] : PRE 1827 CAV, IRL [34368] : PRE 1830 ANT, IRL [34380] : PRE 1847+ LET, IRL [37108] : PRE 1890 ANT, IRL [37601] : PRE 1800+ JAMAICA [33921] : 1850+ DIPTON, SOUTHLAND, NZ [34607] : 1780+ APPLECROSS, ROC, SCT [33993] : PRE 1890 GLASGOW, LKS, SCT [34018] : PRE 1824 ROSEMARKIE, ROC, SCT [34058] : 1815-1853 ROC, SCT [34175] : 1700+ ISLE OF COLL, ARL, SCT [34309] : 1725+ CAMPBELTOWN, ARL, SCT [34416] : 1700+ INV & ARL, SCT [34572] : 1700+ GLASGOW & APPIN, ARL & PER, SCT [34607] : 1750+ ROC, SCT [34684] : PRE 1851 ISLE OF SKYE, INV, SCT [34911] : PRE 1837 ISLE OF MULL, ARL, SCT [34979] : 1800+ CREICH, ARL, SCT [35057] : 1850+ LOCHBROOM, ROC, SCT [35150] : HECTOR 1800S DRIMMIN, ARL, SCT [35260] : PRE 1867 FORT WILLIAM, ARL, SCT [35407] : MURDOCH 1800 INV, SCT [35429] : ALL DUNVEGAN, INV, SCT [35460] : PRE 1830 ELGIN, MOR, SCT [35460] : MARGARET 1890S EDINBURGH, MLN, SCT [35498] : C1810 ARL, SCT [35509] : PRE 1838 TYREE, ARL, SCT [35559] : PRE 1820 PAISLEY, RFW, SCT [35587] : 1800+ DALIBURGH, INV, SCT [35611] : DONALD PRE 1900 INV, SCT [35742] : 1800S NEWTON MEARNS, RFW, SCT [35797] : C1801 KILMODAN, ARL, SCT [35854] : 1750-1850 MULL, ARL, SCT [35961] : 1800-1860 BOWMORE, ARL, SCT [36658] : ALEXANDER 1750-1850 LORN, KILNINIAN, ARL, SCT [36712] : 1800S ARL, SCT [37566] : PRE 1860 SCOBUL, ISLE OF MULL, ARL, SCT [37925] : MARION 1813+ ISLE OF SKYE, SCT & AUS [37146] : 1900S STIRLING, STI, SCT & INDI [35535] : WILLIAM PRE 1905 EDINBURGH, MLN, SCT & NZ [35542] : 1840S EDINBURGH, SCT & NZ [36809]

MCLEANS 1750-1810 UISKEN & MULL, ARL, SCT [36712]

MCLEARY 1750-1870 NEW CUMNOCK, AYR, SCT [35981]

MCLEAY 1810 BOGALLEN, ROC, SCT [35135]

MCLEELY ALL WORLDWIDE [36807]

MCLEISH 1830+ MELBOURNE, VIC, NSW & TAS, AUS [34177]

MCLELAND 1700+ NY, USA & SCT [36341]

MCLELLAN 1790 CABRAGH, DOW, IRL [35085] : 1780+ ROSENEATH, DNB, SCT [34550] : PRE 1800 PAISLEY, RFW, SCT [38383]

MCLELLAND C1760-1800 MAUCHLINE, AYR, SCT [33845] : C1854 GLASGOW, LKS, SCT [34972] : 1848 EDINBURGH, MLN, SCT [37263]

MCLEMAN 1760-1870 FRASERBURGH, ABD, SCT [37333] : 1700-1770 AVOCH, ROC, SCT [37333]

MCLENAGHAN PRE 1848 ANT, IRL [36299]

MCLENEGHAN PRE 1872 BALLYMENA, ANT, IRL [34277]

MACLENNAN PRE 1837 KINTAIL, ROC, SCT [34696] : PRE 1850 KILLEARNAN, ROC, SCT [34713] : PRE 1837 BALMACARA, ROC, SCT [35086] : 1800+ KILCOY, ROC, SCT [35214] : PRE 1850 LOCHBROOM, ROC, SCT [37423] : 1800+ ULLAPOOL, ROC, SCT [37478] : GEORGE C1816 CONTIN, ROC, SCT [38724] : 1890+ MORRISON, IL, USA [35150]

MCLENNAN 1857+ LAUNCESTON, TAS, AUS [33806] : 1850-1900 VIC, AUS [34175] : CATHERINE 1842 GREENWICH, EBOR, NSW, AUS [34539] : 1850S BRANXHOLME, VIC, AUS [35766] : 1853+ GOLDEN POINT, VIC, AUS [36644] : 1863+ SCOTTSDALE, TAS, AUS [36644] : 1800-1920 BOWEN, QLD, AUS [38070] : AGNES C1806-1891 QUE, CAN [36904] : 1800S WHITCHURCH YORK, ONT, CAN [38440] : 1860+ SLD, NZ [34283] : PRE 1860 FORTEVIOT & TIBBERMORE, PER, SCT [33957] : PRE 1860 ABERDALGIE & PERTH, PER, SCT [33957] : 1850-1880 INV, SCT [34050] : 1750-1850 ROC, SCT [34175] : 1800+ ROC, SCT [34283] : DONALD PRE 1837 PLOCKTON, ROC, SCT [34539] : FARQUAR PRE 1820 PLOCKTON, ROC, SCT [34539] : CATHERINE 1811 PLOCKTON, ROC, SCT [34539] : 1805-1840 GAIRLOCH, ROC, SCT [34582] : PRE 1850 KILLEARNAN, ROC, SCT [34713] : 1860-1894 ROSS, SCT [34844] : PRE 1837 PLOCKTON, ROC, SCT [35086] : PRE 1860 LOCHALSH LOCH CARRON, ROC, SCT [36260] : PRE 1860 PLOCKTON SALLACHY, ROC, SCT [36260] : PRE 1853 FODDERTY, ROC, SCT [36644] : 1750+ REDCASTLE & KILLEARNAN, ROC, SCT [36869] : 1790S INV & ROC, SCT [37263] : 1700+ ROC, SCT [37949] : 1800S INV, SCT [38440] : GEORGE C1816 CONTIN, ROC, SCT [38724] : 1837+ KILTARLITY, INV, SCT & USA [35150]

MCLENNON 1870+ CANTERBURY, NZ [36750] : 1810 BOGALLEN, ROC, SCT [35135] : 1750+ ROC, SCT [38001]

MACLEOD PRE 1850 RICHMOND CO., NS, CAN [34253] : 1800+ NS, CAN & SCT [34500] : 1790-1839 WOOLWICH & OLD CHARLTON, KEN, ENG [37187] : PRE 1850 CAVAN, CAV, IRL [37459] : PRE 1850 GARADICE, LET, IRL [37459] : 1850+ BELTURBET, CAV, IRL [37459] : 1800S STORNOWAY, ROC, SCT [34044] : 1780+ BRORA TO NS, SUT, SCT [34403] : ALL LATHERON, CAI, SCT [36846] : ALL WICK, CAI, SCT [36846] : ALL NEWPORT, FIF, SCT [36846] : ALL ULLAPOOL, ROC, SCT [36846] : 1775+ SNIZORT, INV, SCT [37459]

MCLEOD 1840-1852 THOMASTOWN, VIC, AUS [34198] : C1914 PINJARRA, WA, AUS [34456] : 1890+ STAWELL, VIC, AUS [36622] : 1700+ GLEN CTY, ONT, CAN [34167] : DONALD 1818-1878 ST CASIMIR, QUE, CAN [34489] : 1800-1900 COLLINGWOOD, ONT, CAN [37464] : ALLAN J. 1904+ PUGWASH, NS, CAN [38335] : MURDOCH PRE 1866 CAPE JOHN, NS, CAN [38335] : JOHN 1891+ CAPE JOHN, NS, CAN [38335] : MURDOCH 1800S NS & NB, CAN [38349] : JOHN ALL NB, CAN [38445] : C1850 GATESHEAD, NBL, ENG [35764] : 1850+ MANCHESTER, LAN, ENG [35919] : 1872+ AUCKLAND, NZ [35960] : WILLIAM 1886+

LYTTELTON, NZ [36877] : C1820 SKYE, INV, SCT [33918] : 1700+ ISLE OF SKYE, INV, SCT [34167] : 1900+ GLASGOW, LKS, SCT [34260] : 1850+ GREENOCK, RFW, SCT [34473] : C1784 UIG, ROC, SCT [34491] : 1830 LAIRG, SUT, SCT [34890] : WILLIAM 1810S-1830S EDDRACHILLIS, SUT, SCT [35108] : ANN C1800 BRACADALE SKYE, INV, SCT [35260] : NORMAN PRE 1900 INV, SCT [35742] : 1800S LOCHBROOM, ROC, SCT [35960] : 1830+ FORT WILLIAM, INV, SCT [36761] : 1850-1860 HOLBORNE, ARL, SCT [36845] : JOHN 1800+ ULLAPOOL, ROC & INV, SCT [36877] : ALL STORNAWAY, ROC, SCT [37496] : 1760-1860 RAASAY, INV, SCT [37964] : DONALD PRE 1803 BARVAS, ROC, SCT [38335] : 1800+ STORNOWAY, INV, SCT [38481] : 1800-1890 LATHERON, CAI, SCT & NZ [33991] : C1839-1883 WIGGS & NIGG, ROC, SCT & USA [36960] : 1750-1806 PHILADELPHIA CO., PA, USA [34476] : 1872-1951 BOSTON, MA, USA [36960]

MCLEOWNAN C1720 MAYBOLE, AYR, SCT [36431]

MCLERNON 1880 ORVILLE, VIC, AUS [35350] : C1800 DERRYLORAN, TYR, IRL [35350]

MCLEROY 1810-1850 SOCIAL CIRCLE, GA, USA [35307] : 1860-1910 MARSHALL CO., MS, USA [35307]

MCLEVEN PRE 1820 GLASSARY, ARL, SCT [37423]

MCLIESH PRE 1800 LITTLE DUNKELD, PER, SCT [34610]

MCLINN PRE 1850 IRL [33814]

MCLINTOCK 1800-1880 GLASGOW, LKS, SCT [34625]

MCLISTER 1750-1900 BALLYCASTLE, ANT, IRL [36115]

MACLOCHLAN CATHERINE C1800 LIVERPOOL, LAN, ENG [37429]

MCLOON 1862 GEELONG, VIC, AUS [34761]

MCLOUD (SEE MCLEOD) [34476]

MCLOUGHLEN 1800+ BIRR, OFF, IRL [36000]

MACLOUGHLIN PRE 1900 NB, CAN [33904]

MCLOUGHLIN 1850+ VIC, AUS [34578] : 1920+ SABDEN, LAN, ENG [35935] : 1900+ BLACKBURN, LAN, ENG [35935] : 1800+ THURLES, TIP, IRL [33825] : ALL SLIGO, SLI, IRL [36822] : 1865+ GLASGOW, LKS, SCT [35416]

MCLUCAS C1797 MOVILLE, DON, IRL [37007] : 1790-1800 GRAND ISLE, VT, USA [38133]

MCLUCKIE 1800S LENNOXTOWN, STI, SCT [35186] : 1808 POLMONT, STI, SCT [35260]

MCLURE C1862 YEA, VIC, AUS [35249] : 1900S COVENTRY, WAR, ENG [37610] : C1794+ GLENELG, INV, SCT [35249]

MACLUSKIE ALL SCT [36339] : ALL USA [36339]

MCLUSKIE ALL SCT [36339] : ALL USA [36339]

MCMACHON C1800+ CAV, IRL [35851] : 1800+ DUNDEE & BLAIRGOWRIE, PER, SCT [35851]

MCMAHON 1800-1850 JINDABYNE, NSW, AUS [34307] : 1890+ SYDNEY, NSW, AUS [35373] : C1862+ BALLARAT, VIC, AUS [35746] : 1885-1888 NORTH SYDNEY, NSW, AUS [36845] : THOMAS GORE 1865+ CASINO, NSW, AUS [38597] : OWEN 1834+ TURRAMURRA & PYMBLE, NSW, AUS [38597] : ALL CAN [35293] : PRE 1880 CAMBERWELL, LND, ENG [35011] : 1840-1863 LIMERICK, LIM, IRL [33778] : 1800+ MOG, IRL [33829] : 1830S ENNIS, CLA, IRL [34175] : 1850S LIM, IRL [34854] : ALL ARM & DON, IRL [35293] : 1700+ KILSHANNIG BY MALLOW, COR, IRL [35364] : 1747 NEWBERRY, COR, IRL [35560] : PRE 1862 CLA, IRL [35746] : 1800-1900 IRL [35778] : C1800+ CAV, IRL [35851] : C1840 KILCORCORAN, CLA, IRL [36307] : PRE 1860 IRL [37563] : 1800+ NORTH, CLA, IRL [38295] : MARTIN ALL KILKEE & PORT FAIRY (BELFAST), CLA & VIC, IRL & AUS [35467] : PRE 1800 PA & MA, USA [34062] : 1870+ CASS CO., IA, USA [37563] : 1800+ SEAGERTON, PA, USA [38295]

MACMAIN 1800+ ONT, CAN [34062]

MCMAIN 1800+ PLYMOUTH, DEV, ENG [37924] : 1700+ CA, PA & OR, USA [34062]

MACMAINS ALL SCT & IRL [35274]

MCMAKIN 1800 VA, USA [38320]

MCMANN 1800+ ONT, CAN [34062] : ELLEN C1800-1850 BERWICK, NBL, ENG [34007]

MCMANUS C1850 GUNNING, NSW, AUS [35336] : 1788 SYDNEY COVE, NSW, AUS [35920] : C1850-1921 MAITLAND, ONT, CAN [35078] : PRE 1850 LANARK CO., ONT, CAN [38445] : 1815 PLYMOUTH, DEV, ENG [35041] : 1800+ THURLES, TIP, IRL [33963] : JOHN ALL ARM, IRL [34475] : CATH ALL FER, IRL [35093] : PRE 1875 DROOGAN & KESH, FER, IRL [35430] : 1808-1831 GALLOON, FER, IRL [36281] : 1800+ LOG, IRL [36602] : 1800S ROS, IRL [37566] : 1800S IRL [38445] : PRE 1860 IRL [38722] : 1800+ PA, USA [36908]

MCMASTER 1850+ WELLINGROVE & GLEN INNES, NSW, AUS [34185] : 1870 DAYLESFORD, VIC, AUS [35204] : 1837+ SYDNEY & WINGHAM, NSW, AUS [38541] : 1800+ KILKEEL, DOW, IRL [35529] : 1870S BELFAST, IRL [37879] : PRE 1820 KIRKOSWALD, AYR, SCT [34713] : PRE 1840 STRONTIAN, ARL, SCT [36877] : PRE 1836 AYR, SCT [38541]

MCMASTERS 1840 LONGFORD, TAS, AUS [35089]

MCMEEKIN C1860 ROMFORD, ESS, ENG [38253] : PRE 1850 ANT, IRL [38253] : 1500-1900 NEWLUCE, WIG, SCT [34975] : 1890+ GLASGOW, LKS, SCT [38253] : 1870+ EDINBURGH, MLN, SCT [38253] : ALL WORLDWIDE [38253]

MCMEENS PRE 1836 ST CLAIR CO., IL, USA [37015]

MCMEIKAN PRE 1900 KKD, SCT & NZ [33959]

MCMENEMY 1855+ BELFAST, ANT, IRL [34373]

MCMICHAEL 1780-1930 BALLYCASTLE, ANT, IRL [36115] : PRE 1850 NEW GALLOWAY, KKD, SCT [36497]

MACMILLAN 1800+ ARGYLLE SHORE, PEI, CAN [34256] : ALLAN 1752-1823 GLENGARRY, ONT, CAN [38466] : JOHN ROG. 1758-1841 GLENGARRY, ONT, CAN [38466] : EWEN C1813 SAS RIVER, SAS, CAN [38466] : COL. ALEX C1814 GLENGARRY, ONT, CAN [38466] : RONALD C1807 KINGSTON & ST ANDREWS, JAMAICA [38466] : PRE 1840 SKYE, INV, SCT [34192] : 1770+ COLONSAY, ARL, SCT [34256] : 1740+ KILMALLIE & MORVERN, ARL, SCT [35909] : MARY C1790-1830 KENMORE, PER, SCT [37441] : HELEN C1813 COLUMBIA RIVER, WA, USA [38466] : ARCHIE C1804 PORT AU PRINCE, TRINIDAD, W.INDIES [38466]

MCMILLAN 1860+ ARMIDALE, NSW, AUS [34421] : 1850+ LAUNCESTON, TAS, AUS [34421] : C1860 ELSTERNWICK, VIC, AUS [34579] : 1923+ SA, AUS [35513] : 1860S POMEROY & GOULBURN, NSW, AUS [35546] : 1837+ NSW, AUS [37349] : 1880+ BUCKINGHAM, QUE, CAN [36350] : C1900 WEBBWOOD, ONT, CAN [36350] : 1793+ LOCHIEL, ONT, CAN [36350] : 1840+ CUMBERLAND, ONT, CAN [36350] : 1800+ LIVERPOOL, LAN, ENG [35033] : 1836 LIVERPOOL, LAN, ENG [38515] : PRE 1860 DUNGANNON, TYR, IRL [35546] : PRE 1800 DOW, IRL [35572] : PRE 1847 ARMEE, ANT, IRL [36509] : 1700-1800 DALKEITH, MLN, SCT [33908] : 1800S GREENOCK, RFW, SCT [33934] : PRE 1880 NITSHILL, RFW, SCT [34001] : PRE 1765

DALGAIN, AYR, SCT [34214] : PRE 1800 ARRAN, BUT, SCT [34419] : 1800+ EDINBURGH, MLN, SCT [34922] : PRE 1837 GLASGOW, AYR, SCT [35117] : C1820 KILLMARNOCK, AYR, SCT [35225] : EUPHEMIA 1800 GLASGOW, SCT [35361] : PRE 1867 KIRKMAIDEN, WIG, SCT [35572] : 1830+ KILDALTON, ARL, SCT [35625] : 1740+ KILMALLIE & MORVERN, ARL, SCT [35909] : PRE 1800 INVERNESS CITY, INV, SCT [35911] : 1800S ISLE OF SKYE, INV, SCT [37349] : ALL EASDALE ISLAND, ARL, SCT [37442] : 1800S GLASGOW, LKS, SCT [37442] : 1840-1870S THORNHILL, DFS, SCT [37540] : 1790+ ROTHESAY, BUT, SCT [37540] : PRE 1836 GOVEN & GLASGOW, LKS, SCT [37852] : PRE 1855 KIRKPATRICK DURHAM, KKD, SCT [37981] : PRE 1805 STONYKIRK, WIG, SCT [38057] : ALL EAST KILBRIDE, LKS, SCT [38057] : 1830+ IRVINE, AYR, SCT [38067] : PRE 1830 ISLE OF ISLAY, SCT [38393] : 1800+ GLASGOW, LKS, SCT [38515] : 1890 MICHIGAMME, MI, USA [36350] : C1820 IL, USA [36923] : 1875+ BOSTON, SUFFOLK, MA, USA [37540] : 1770-1870S ALLEGHANY & ASHE CO., NC, USA [38315]

MCMILLEN PRE 1840 MD, USA [34410]

MCMILLIN PRE 1850 BALLYMOTE, SLI, IRL [36760]

MCMILLON C1850 FORT WILLIAM, INV, SCT [34815]

MCMINN 1800-1900 BATHURST, NB, CAN [36934] : 1800-1845 DONAGHADEE, DOW, IRL [34625] : 1805 MAGHERACLONE, MOG, IRL [34993] : ALL SCT [33959] : 1829 MUIRKIRK, AYR, SCT [35594]

MCMONAGLE C1820-1880 PHILADELPHIA CO., PA, USA [36580]

MCMONIGLE C1820-1880 PHILADELPHIA CO., PA, USA [36580]

MCMORROW 1800+ KILLARGA, LET, IRL [35248] : 1850 DUNDEE, ANS, SCT [34149]

MCMULLAN PRE 1863 LURGAN, ARM, IRL [34021] : 1750+ LISBELLNAGROAH, ANT, IRL [34415] : 1800S ANT, IRL [36858]

MCMULLEN 1840S SINGLETON, NSW, AUS [35134] : C1850 SARNIA, ONT, CAN [34521] : 1820-1880 BALLYMONEY, ANT, IRL [33947] : PRE 1895 DUBLIN, IRL [35363] : 1840-1850 ANT, IRL [38583] : ZACH 1750-1950 OSEDODE, ULSTER & ONT, IRL & CAN [36669] : C1798 PA, USA [38769]

MCMULLIN 1800+ HENDERSON CO., KY, USA [38091]

MCMULLN 1800+ ARM, IRL [34956]

MCMURDO 1800S VAL CARTIER, QUE, CAN [34937] : 1850S PROTON TWP., ONT, CAN [34937] : 1871+ BANNOCKBURN, STI, SCT [35886]

MCMURRAY 1875+ STRATHBOGIE, VIC, AUS [33837] : 1800+ MULLAGHBRACK, ARM, IRL [33837] : 1855+ BELFAST, IRL [35220] : C1800 ARM, IRL [35434] : PRE 1800 ARMAGH, IRL [37474] : PRE 1865 EDINBURGH, SCT & IRL [37852]

MCMURRER C1800 MOG, IRL [34356]

MCMURRY ALL GLASLOUGH, MOG, IRL [35706]

MCMURTRIE C1810 MOTHERWELL, LKS, SCT [35089] : 1872 PRESTWICK, AYR, SCT [35089] : PRE 1740 MAYBOLE, AYR, SCT [35406]

MCMURTRY THOMAS 1824-1894 NORTHUMBERLAND CO., ONT, CAN [36677] : 1860S CARRICKFERGUS, ANT, IRL [35728]

MCNAB 1910 WILLIAMSTOWN, VIC, AUS [34702]

MCNAB 1630+ CAN [33903] : PRE 1870 LIVERPOOL, LAN, ENG & SCT [36849] : PRE 1820 DUNOON & KILMUN, ARL, SCT [35430] : 1745+ COMRIE, PER, SCT [35886] : ALL KENMORE, PER, SCT [36704] : C1846 ISLAY, ARL, SCT [36820] : 1850-1910 AIRTH, STI, SCT [37213] : 1700+ BRIDGE OF MICHAEL, PER, SCT [38726] : 1700-1990 PERTH & OSGOODE, PER, SCT & CAN [36669]

MCNABB PRE 1801+ ERROL, PER, SCT [38567] : 1600+ UK [33903]

MCNAB-LOWRIE C1936 QLD, AUS [35025]

MCNABOLA MARY 1852+ MOHILL, LET, IRL [38233]

MCNAE ALL DFS, SCT [36766]

MCNAIR 1885+ VIC, AUS [34412] : 1818+ NEW RICHMOND, QUE, CAN [37486] : 1874+ NZ [34412] : 1900+ RSA [34280] : PRE 1850 BUT, SCT [34280] : PRE 1874 LKS, SCT [34412] : 1700+ INVERARAY, ARL, SCT [34414] : JANE C1800 GOVAN, LKS, SCT [35848] : 1750+ TORPHICHEN, WLN, SCT [35979] : 1750+ FALKIRK, STI, SCT [35979] : ARCH. 1830+ BOSTON, MA, NY & ME, USA [37486] : JAMES 1849+ ALVIN, TX, USA [37486]

MCNALLY MARY C1845 TAMWORTH, NSW, AUS [34935] : 1850-1905 WESTBURY, TAS, AUS [35195] : PATRICK 1866+ HAPPY VALLEY, VIC, AUS [36278] : MARY-ANN 1880+ CHARLTON, VIC, AUS [36278] : 1816+ NEW BRUNSWICK, NS, CAN [36960] : 1855-1935 HALIFAX, NS, CAN & USA [36960] : 1880+ LIVERPOOL, LAN, ENG [37732] : C1853 COOKSTOWN, TYR, IRL [34807] : 1827-1865 TIP, IRL [35195] : 1800-90 DUB, IRL & USA [37732]

MCNAMARA 1826-1860 WAGGA WAGGA & WYALONG, NSW, AUS [33897] : 1800S JAMBEROO, NSW, AUS [36372] : 1820-1910 CLA, IRL [33947]

MCNAMARA GUSTAVUS 1876+ MELBOURNE, VIC, AUS [33797] : THOMAS 1854+ CARLTON, VIC, AUS [33797] : 1826-1860 WAGGA WAGGA & WYALONG, NSW, AUS [33897] : PRE 1900 AUS [34196] : 1870-1880 BACCHUS MARSH, VIC, AUS [34767] : 1879+ SALE, VIC, AUS [34767] : 1870+ MERRIWA, NSW, AUS [35105] : 1870+ RICHMOND, VIC, AUS [35359] : C1856 TAS, AUS [38485] : 1820+ QUEBEC CITY & LONGUEUIL, QUE, CAN [34138] : 1833+ LND, ENG [35359] : JOHN ALL CLA, IRL [33872] : 1800S LIMERICK, LIM, IRL [33972] : PRE 1850 HOSPITAL, LIM, IRL [34018] : MICHAEL C1815 CLOONEY, CLA, IRL [34176] : MICHAEL 1800-1860 ENNIS, CLA, IRL [34769] : 1820S ENNIS, CLA, IRL [35260] : 1800S CLA, IRL [35379] : PRE 1855 ENNIS, CLA, IRL [36241] : PRE 1845 ENNIS, CLA, IRL [36325] : 1800-1855 ATHLEAGUE, GAL & CLA, IRL [36337] : 1800-1850 CLA, IRL [36780] : C1826 CLA, IRL [38485] : MICHAEL C1840-1906 CLA, IRL & AUS [34942]

MCNAMEE PRE 1900 AUS [34196]

MCNANLEY 1860+ MANCHESTER, LAN, ENG [35529]

MCNARY PRE 1818 WASHINGTON CO., PA, USA [37817]

MCNATTY PRE 1850 SAINTFIELD, DOW, IRL [36760]

MCNAUGHT PRE 1828 CORNWALLIS, NS, CAN [37450] : PRE 1820 DFS & KKD, SCT [34197]

MCNAUGHTAN 1700+ FORTINGALL & WEEM, PER, SCT [34419]

MCNAUGHTON ALL ONT, CAN [37044] : C1800+ LONDON, ONT, CAN & SCT [34339] : 1830 GLENARTNEY, PER, SCT [35135] : 1750+ COMRIE, PER, SCT [35886] : ALL ARL, SCT [37044] : 1700S DUNNING, PER, SCT [37106] : PRE 1744 BALLEDMUND & DOWALLY, PER, SCT [37852]

MCNAUGTON ALL EDINBURGH, MLN, SCT [34093]

MCNAULL C1800-1875 TYR, IRL [36836] : 1875+ PATERANGI & TE AWAMUTU, NZ [36836]

MCNEALUS ALL WORLDWIDE [36579]

MACNEE PRE 1748 BIRTLEY, NBL, ENG [37635] : C1905 RENTON, DNB, SCT [36835]

MCNEE 1869+ COLLINGWOOD, VIC, AUS [35708] : 1820S DRUMMOND, ONT, CAN [35638] : 1835+ HUNTINGDON, QUE, CAN [36272] : 1865-1900 SAN FRANCISCO, CA, USA [36272]

MCNEICE 1600-1950 GLENAVY, ANT, IRL [35897]

MCNEIL 1790-1850 KENT CO., ONT, CAN [36703] : PRE 1845 CHATHAM, KEN, ENG & AUS [37911] : PRE 1850+ GREENMEADOWS, HB, NZ [35928] : PRE 1935 GLASGOW, LKS, SCT [34122] : JOHN 1800+ FORT WILLIAM, INV, SCT [34332] : 1830+ PAISLEY, RFW, SCT [34455] : 1760S BOURG MULL, ARL, SCT [35260] : 1800S EDINBURGH, MLN, SCT [35422] : 1800 AYR, SCT [36239] : 1700+ PAISLEY & ISLE OF BARRA, RFW & INV, SCT [36794]

MACNEILL 1780+ ARL, SCT [34387]

MCNEILL 1800-1940 CULFEIGHTRIN, ANT, IRL [36115] : PRE 1900 CARNLOUGH, ANT, IRL [36529] : PRE 1900 IRVINE, AYR, SCT [33966] : 1800-1850 OLD KILPATRICK, DNB, SCT [38521]

MCNEILLY PRE 1852 KILLALEE, DOW, IRL [36629]

MCNEISH 1780-1860 LKS, SCT [38199] : ALL INVERESK & GLADSMUIR, ELN & MLN, SCT & NZ [33959]

MCNELIS 1800+ ARDARA, DON, IRL [36769]

MCNETH PRE 1770 SCT [37591]

MCNICHOL PRE 1845 IRL [38734] : C1806 DRYMAN, STI, SCT [34911] : PRE 1850 PHILADELPHIA, PA, USA [38734]

MCNICKLE 1857+ PICTON & WAGGA, NSW, AUS [34772] : PRE 1857 GORTIN & ROUSKY, TYR, IRL [34772]

MCNICOL 1870-1920 AUS [37779] : 1845-1865 MANCHESTER, LAN, ENG [37779] : 1800+ BON HILL, DNB, SCT [35631] : 1750-1800 KYLES OF BUTE, ARL, SCT [37779] : 1800-1840 EDINBRUGH, MLN, SCT [37779] : 1859 KILLIN, PER, SCT [38364] : 1850-1900 NEW YORK, NY, USA [37779]

MCNIECE PRE 1839 BALLYMENA & BELFAST, ANT, IRL [35381] : PRE 1820 BALLYMENA, ANT, IRL [36271] : PRE 1830 BALLYMENA, ANT, IRL [36271] : MENACES PRE 1820S BALLYMENA, ANT, IRL [37906]

MCNITT 1850 BROWN, IL, USA [38143]

MCNIVEN 1839+ PATERSON, NSW, AUS [34188] : 1839+ MORVEN, ARL, SCT [34188] : 1700+ ARL & LKS, SCT [34419] : 1750+ COMRIE, PER, SCT [35886]

MCNIVIEN 1790-1830 BARONY & GLASGOW, SCT [36985]

MCNULTY 1900+ BUCHANAN RIVER, WA, AUS [35857] : 1850+ ENG [34373] : PRE 1900 SCARBOROUGH, YKS, ENG [34908] : 1850+ BELFAST, ANT, IRL [34373] : PRE 1900 GLASGOW, LKS, SCT [34908]

MCNUTT ALL TYR, IRL [35888] : PRE 1875 CASTLEFINN & TAUGHBOY, DON, IRL [36787] : PRE 1875 LONDONDERRY, LDY, IRL [36787] : PRE 1875 CARRIGANS, DON, IRL [36787] : 1874+ DUNEDIN & OWAKA, OTG, NZ [35888]

MACOMBER 1900S VT, USA [34496] : PRE 1900 CT, USA [38622]

MCOMIE 1700-1800 EDINBURGH, USA & SCT [35289]

MCOWAN 1600+ WORLDWIDE [38388]

MCPARLAND 1800S ARM, IRL [35126]

MCPARTLAN 1845-1899 ARM, IRL [34331]

MCPEAK WILLIAM 1787-1800 NORTHERN, IRL [38145] : ALL MOG, IRL [38174] : WILLIAM 1800-1813 VA, USA [38145] : JAMES & WM. 1813-1826

SPARTA, WHITE CO., TN, USA [38145] : JAMES 1826-1845 MAGOUPIN CO., IL, USA [38145] : WILLIAM 1826-1845 MAGOUPIN CO., IL, USA [38145]

MCPEARSON 1830S INV, SCT [35516]

MACPHAIL DUNCAN 1815+ KILCHRENAN & DALAVICH, ARL, SCT [34128]

MCPHAIL 1856+ DAPTON, NSW, AUS [33781] : 1850+ BRUCE CO., ONT, CAN [34051] : MARY 1800+ ARGYLLE SHORE, PEI, CAN [34256] : 1829 MILNGAVIE, ARL, SCT [33936] : 1780+ MULL, ARL, SCT [34256] : PRE 1870S TYREE, ARL, SCT [37439]

MCPHAN 1870+ VIC & NSW, AUS [33931]

MCPHEE C1850 BALLARAT, VIC, AUS [36362] : ALL BENDIGO, VIC, AUS [37950] : 1859+ EXETER, ONT, CAN [34528] : C1870 WAKEFIELD, QUE, CAN [36350] : C1900 WEBBWOOD, ONT, CAN [36350] : C1890 BUCKINGHAM, QUE, CAN [36350] : 1870S WENTWORTH, ONT, CAN [38475] : C1800 DRIMMIN, ARL, SCT [35260] : 1800+ INVERNESS, INV, SCT [35355] : PRE 1830 KNOYDART, INV, SCT [35430] : 1800-1860 BOWMORE, ARL, SCT [36658] : PRE 1862 AYR, AYR, SCT [36788] : PRE 1852 ISLE OF ISLAY, SCT [38393] : 1840S GREENOCK, RFW, SCT [38475]

MACPHERSON 1870+ TOWNSVILLE, QLD, AUS [35111] : 1854+ KANGAROO FLAT, VIC, AUS [35801] : 1853+ MELBOURNE, VIC, AUS [35801] : PRE 1880 LIVERPOOL, LAN, ENG [38753] : PRE 1875 TAUGHBOYNE, DON, IRL [36787] : PRE 1875 CASTLEFINN, DON, IRL [36787] : PRE 1875 CARRIGANS, DON, IRL [36787] : PRE 1875 LONDONDERRY, LDY, IRL [36787] : 1878+ DURRY, NZ [36787] : 1880+ TARANAKI & ASHBURTON, NZ [36787] : PRE 1840 BADENOCH, INV, SCT [34268] : PRE 1850 DUFFTOWN, BAN, SCT [34809] : 1840 LAGGAN, INV, SCT [34890] : 1848+ KINGSBURGH, INV, SCT [35801] : 1850 PORTREE, INV, SCT [35801] : COLIN 1809+ KENMORE, PER, SCT [37441] : 1700-1800 STRACHAN, ABD, SCT [37485] : PRE 1840 BARONY, LKS, SCT [38753]

MCPHERSON 1840+ NUNDLE, NSW, AUS [35098] : 1840-50S GOULBURN, NSW, AUS [35111] : PRE 1870 FOOTSCRAY, VIC, AUS [35479] : 1840S-1880S BALLARAT, VIC, AUS [35777] : 1830-1900 BATHURST, NB, CAN [36934] : 1830+ BELMONT, ONT, CAN [38584] : C1797 HILLSBOROUGH, DOW, IRL [38485] : C1879 WELLINGTON, NZ [35515] : 1860+ NZ [36761] : PRE 1840 PITMAIN, INV, SCT [33876] : 1786+ CADDER, LKS, SCT [34122] : 1750-1850 ACHARACLE, ARL & INV, SCT [34572] : 1816-1846 ALVIE, INV, SCT [34582] : PRE 1870 INV & KRS, SCT [34876] : 1880S FORRES, PER, SCT [34937] : JOHN 1750+ DUNOON, ARL, SCT [35013] : ANN 1860S ARISAIG, INV, SCT [35081] : PRE 1840 ISLE OF SKYE, SCT [35098] : 1750+ LEITH, MLN, SCT [35370] : PRE 1850 PAISLEY, RFW, SCT [35389] : PRE 1820 DUNOON & KILMUN, ARL, SCT [35430] : 1840+ EDINBURGH, SCT [35515] : PRE 1800 ISLE OF MULL, SCT [35573] : 1700+ STI, SCT [35627] : PRE 1860 JOHNSTON, RFW, SCT [35820] : 1800S EDINBURGH, SCT [35906] : 1803-1900 EDDERTON, ROC, SCT [35922] : PRE 1850 COLL, ARL, SCT [37169] : PRE 1840 DUIRINISH, SKYE, INV, SCT [37925]

MCPHILIMEY 1815+ MUIRKIRK, AYR, SCT [37909]

MACPHILLAMY 1830+ BATHURST, NSW, AUS [34969] : PRE 1786 NEWTOWN STEWART, TYR, IRL [37909]

MCPIKE CATHERINE 1870+ AUS [35337]

MCQUADE C1850 ADELAIDE, SA, AUS [34907] :
1800+ NSW & VIC, AUS & SCT [34703] : PRE 1820
IRL [37133] : 1800+ IRL & SCT [37306]

MCQUAID ALL PEI, CAN [34356] : ALL
BALLYSHANNON, DON, IRL [36774]

MCQUAKER 1750-1850 COLMONELL, AYR, SCT
[34523]

MACQUARRIE PRE 1830 INVERNESS CO., NS, CAN
[38447] : PRE 1801 DERVARG, ARL, SCT [34501] :
ALL MULL, ARL, SCT [35961] : 1780-1840 ISLE OF
MULL, ARL, SCT [38409] : PRE 1900 WORLDWIDE
[36191]

MCQUARRIE ALL MULL, ARL, SCT [35961]

MCQUARY CHARLES B. 1851+ MO, USA [36723]

MCQUEAR ALL WORLDWIDE [34262]

MCQUEEBIN JANE 1900+ FORRES, MOR, SCT
[34764]

MACQUEEN 1800-1900 ST BEES, CUL, ENG [37858]

MCQUEEN 1909-1950 KENNINGTON, SLD, NZ
[36853] : 1769-1890 WIGTON, WIG, SCT [34649] :
PRE 1800 CRAWFORD, LKS, SCT [34835] : 1880S
FORRES, PER, SCT [34937] : 1772 KILMADOCK,
PER, SCT [35090] : 1830+ DALKEITH &
LIVERTON, MLN, SCT [35513] : 1757 LANRICK,
PER, SCT [36635] : ALL BORGUE, KKD, SCT
[36853]

MCQUEENIE 1845+ LAIDLEY, QLD, AUS [34276] :
C1840 DRUMSHAWBO, LET, IRL [34276]

MCQUESTON ALL ANT, IRL [34298]

MCQUIBAN ALL ELGIN & FORRES, INV, SCT
[35988] : ALL WORLDWIDE [35988]

MACQUIBBAN ALL WORLDWIDE [35988]

MCQUILTY 1850-1990 NIMBIN, NSW, AUS [33818]

MCQUIRE PRE 1900 STRABAND, TYR, IRL [33975]

MCQUIRTER (SEE MCWHI [36727]

MACQUISTEN 1850+ BROCKVILLE, ONT, CAN
[36985] : 1850+ MONTREAL, QUE, CAN [36985] :
1870-1900 INVERKIP, RFW, SCT [36985]

MCQUISTEN PRE 1826 GLASGOW, SCT [36985]

MCQUISTON 1850+ MONTREAL, QUE, CAN [36985]
: ALL BELFAST, ANT, IRL [34298] : 1780-1830
GLASGOW, SCT [36985]

MACRAE 1838+ ISLE OF SKYE, SCT [34528] : PRE
1837 KINTAIL, ROC, SCT [34696] : PRE 1840 ROC,
SCT [34883]

MCRAE 1912+ DRYSDALE, VIC, AUS [34577] :
1850+ MERRIWA, NSW, AUS [35105] : 1894+
WIMMERA, VIC, AUS [36622] : 1800+
LIVERPOOL, NSW, AUS [38001] : 1800+
GLENGARRY, ONT, CAN [36343] : C1800+
GFENWHERRY, ANT, IRL [35995] : PRE 1840 ROC,
SCT [34883] : 1826+ BRACADALE, INV, SCT [34954]
: C1804 BRACADALE SKYE, INV, SCT [35260] :
1850+ BREAKISH, ISLE OF SKYE, INV, SCT
[35825] : C1851+ DALRY, AYR, SCT [35995] : PRE
1850 LOCHALSH LOCH CARRON, ROC, SCT
[36260] : PRE 1860 PLONKTON, SALLACHY, ROC,
SCT [36260] : PRE 1865 LOGIE EASTER, ROC, SCT
[36888] : 1750-1860 AYR, SCT [37338] : JOHN C1832
URRAY & MUIR OF TARRADALE, ROC, SCT
[37684] : 1760+ KINTAIL, ROC, SCT [38001] :
ALEXANDER C1794-1885 KINTAIL, ROC & QUE,
SCT & CAN [36904]

MACRAE (SEE MCRAE) [38001]

MCREA PRE 1865 LOGIE EASTER, ROC, SCT [36888]

MCREATH 1850+ IPSWICH, QLD, AUS [35814]

MACROBERTS 1830+ OTTAWA VALLEY, ONT,
CAN [37443]

MCROBERTS PRE 1900 VA, USA [34115] : PRE 1850
WORLDWIDE [36191]

MCROBIE 1750-1850 PERTH, SCT [38224]

MCRORIE 1840-1890 VESTA CHESLEY, ONT, CAN
[36724] : 1790-1850 COMRIE, PER, SCT [36724]

MCRORY C1855 MARIPOSA, ONT, CAN [34058] :
1750+ TYNAN & COOKSTOWN, ARM, IRL & NZ
[36850]

MACROW 1790+ TOTTINGTON, NFK, ENG [33942]

MCSEVENY 1831+ AYR, SCT [34039]

MCSHANE PRE 1820 DRAPERSTOWN, DRY, IRL
[33869] : 1800+ MA, MO & NY, USA [36574]

MCSWAIN 1854+ WARRNAMBOOL, VIC, AUS
[35557] : PRE 1854 BALACHUIRN, RAASAY, SCT
[35557]

MCSWANE 1830-1925 VANDERBURGH CO., IN,
USA [38234] : 1830-1925 WARRICK CO., IN, USA
[38234]

MCSWEEN 1830+ VICTORIA, ONT, CAN [38387] :
ALL RAASAY IS, INV, SCT [35433] : 1815+ SKYE,
SCT [38387]

MCSWEENEY PRE 1803 GSY, CHI [37841] : C1890
ISLINGTON, LND, ENG [34237] : 1830 IRL [34237] :
PRE 1854 TIPPERARY, TIP, IRL [37106] : 1865+
CAMBRIDGE, WAIKATO, NZ [34700]

MCSWINEY 1830+ COLUMBIA CO., PA, USA [38011]

MCTAGGART 1783-1900 MT VIEW, ONT, CAN
[37011] : 1860+ NZ [33988] : PRE 1830 SOUTH
KNAPDALE, ARL, SCT [34911] : MARGARET 1813
ISLAY, ARL, SCT [35848] : 1800+ APPIN, ARL, SCT
[36254] : PRE 1850 TONGLAND, KKD, SCT [36705] :
1760+ KNAPDALE, ARL, SCT [36827] : 1700-1774
GALLOWAY, DFS, SCT [37011] : 1774-1784
TYRONE CO., NY, USA [37011]

MCTAGGET 1860+ DUNEDIN, OTAGO, NZ [33988]

MCTAGUE PRE 1850 LIVERPOOL, LAN, ENG [35199]

MCTAINSH C1850 CARRINGTON, MLN, SCT [36884]

MACTAVISH PRE 1600 ARL, SCT [38561]

MCTAVISH 1750S APPIN, ARL, SCT [34188] : 1820-
1860 KILMONIVAIG, INV, SCT [35717]

MCTERNAN 1770+ DERINVOHER, LET, IRL [35152]

MCTIERNAN 1850-1887 SOOEY & RIVERSTOWN,
SLI, IRL & AUS [33847]

MCTIMNEY PRE 1850 CORK CITY, COR, IRL [36514]

MCTURK 1750-1860 CUMNOCK, AYR, SCT [37338]

MCVAE 1805 DOW, IRL [34993]

MCVAY 1845 IRL [37558]

MCVEAN C1800 STRACHUR, ARL, SCT [37881]

MCVERRY 1850+ FORKHILL &
CARRICKNAKELLY, DOW, IRL [35970]

MCVEY PRE 1850 BALLYMENA, ANT, IRL [34001] :
C1800 AYR, SCT [36694] : PRE 1867
CARRONSHORE, STI, SCT [37978]

MACVICAR 1830+ CAPE BRETON CO., NS, CAN
[34253] : PRE 1830 NORTH UIST, INV, SCT [34253]

MCVICAR PRE 1871 NSW, AUS & SCT [35028] : PRE
1845 CAMPSIE, STI, SCT [35206] : PRE 1800 PER,
SCT [36361]

MCVITTIE PRE 1850 CASTLETON, ROX, SCT [34665]
: ALL WORLDWIDE [38760]

MCVORAN JANE C1808 JURA, ARL, SCT [35848]

MCVOY PRE 1862 WAT, IRL [34578]

MCWATERS PRE 1781 ARDS PENINSULA, DOW,
IRL [38428]

MCWATTERS 1800+ ONT, CAN [35297] : ALL DOW,
IRL [35297] : ALL KILLEVY BARONY, ARM, IRL
[35297]

MCWHA C1846 BELFAST, IRL [35332]

MCWHAE PRE 1792+ SEL, SCT [35237]

MCWHINNEY 1850+ ROMA, QLD, AUS [34276] :
C1815 DRUMSHAWBO, LET, IRL [34276] : 1846
AUGHATARRAGH, ARM, IRL [38526] : 1800+
DUNDEE, ANS, SCT [34049]

MCWHIRTER 1800S ANT & ARM, IRL [36727] :
1800+ BALLANTRAE, AYR, SCT [33781] : 1800-50
NEWTON STEWART, WIG, SCT [36262]
MCWHORTER PRE 1775 STATESVILLE, NC, USA
[38536]
MCWILLIAM PRE 1773 MORTLACH, BAN, SCT
[34205] : C1824 WIGTOWN, WIG, SCT [36356] : PRE
1850 KILCHRENZIE, ARL, SCT [36583] : PRE 1836
LKS, SCT [37354]
MCWILLIAMS 1780+ STORMONT CO., ONT, CAN
[38411]
MACWOOD ALL WORLDWIDE [36569]
MCWOOD ALL IOM & ENG [36569] : ALL IRL [36569]
: ALL SCT [36569] : 1849-1910 SAN FRANCISCO,
CA, USA [36569] : ALL USA [36569] : ALL
WORLDWIDE [36569]
M'DONALD C1790 DALNOE, PER, SCT [34203]
MEAD 1850+ PATERSON, NSW, AUS [35395] : 1890S
YKS, ENG [33925] : 1700S WENDOVER, BKM,
ENG [34032] : PRE 1839 AYLESBURY, BKM, ENG
[34166] : 1810-1840 LIMEHOUSE, LND, ENG [34469]
: 1800+ LEYTONSTONE, ESS, ENG [34541] : PRE
1849 BKM, ENG [35037] : PRE 1725 CHESTERTON,
CAM, ENG [35238] : PRE 1850 TILSHEAD, WIL,
ENG [35346] : PRE 1850 CAMBERWELL, LND,
ENG [35431] : 1840+ LIVERPOOL, LAN, ENG
[35768] : C1800 LAVERTON, SOM, ENG [36247] :
PRE 1860 PORTSMOUTH, HAM & OXF, ENG
[36396] : 1700S HAWKHURST, KEN, ENG [36874] :
1850-1890 EAST LULWORTH, DOR, ENG [37943] :
1800+ LONDON, MDX & KEN, ENG & AUS
[34705] : PRE 1850 MEA, IRL [37066] : 1630-1727
GREENWICH, CT, USA [36310] : HENRY 1650-1710
PREAKNESS, BERGEN CO., NJ, USA [36317] :
NATHANIEL 1768-1841 DUCHESS CO., NY, USA
[38140]
MEADE C1850 PRESTON, LAN, ENG [37066] : PRE
1850S DUBLIN CITY, IRL [35433] : CATHERINE
PRE 1869 QUEENSTOWN, COR, IRL & AUS [34447]
: 1855-1867 KEWEENAW CO., MI, USA [38009] :
1805-1990 RUSSELL, VA, USA [38136] : ALL WLS
[37201]
MEADON 1641 FORDINGTON, DOR, ENG [33967]
MEADOR PRE 1876 MILAN, MO, USA [34064] :
1876+ ASOTIN, WA, USA [34064]
MEADOW PRE 1735 LAN, ENG [37706]
MEADOWS 1850+ LEICESTER AREA, LEI, ENG
[34512] : 1800+ MDX, ENG [35364] : 1800-1850
WYMONDHAM, NFK, ENG [35595] : PRE 1800
WALSHAM LE WILLOWS, SFK, ENG [37287] :
C1900 HARMONSWORTH, LND, ENG [38464] :
PRE 1875 DUSTON, NTH, ENG [38464]
MEADOWS-JONES 1800S THURMASTON, LEI,
ENG [36511]
MEADS 1700+ IOW, ENG [35943] : PRE 1800
MARLOW, BKM & BRK, ENG [37089]
MEAGAN PRE 1860 COR, IRL [37416]
MEAGER PRE 1798 BDF, ENG [37946]
MEAGHER 1800+ THURLES, TIP, IRL [33963] : 1800
CASHEL, TIP, IRL [36493]
MEAKER 1896+ NEWCASTLE, NSW, AUS [37920]
MEAKIN HARRIET 1840+ HANOVER SQUARE,
MDX, ENG [34475] : JOHN FORSTER C1820
HANOVER SQUARE, MDX, ENG [34475] : C1830
HINSTOCK, SAL, ENG [35203] : 1800+ ENG [35581]
: PRE 1850 SALFORD, LAN, ENG [36369] : 1780
ELLASTONE, STS, ENG [37174]
MEAKINS 1773-1837 POTTERSPURY, NTH, ENG
[37860] : C1819 UK [35772]
MEALE 1790+ LEEDS, WRY, ENG [36868]
MEALING PRE 1805 CAMBRIDGE, CAM, ENG
[34691] : 1835+ MAIDENHEAD, BRK, ENG [37134]

: C1835 OXF, ENG [38487] : 1856+
CHRISTCHURCH, NZ [38487]
MEALMAKER PRE 1767 TEALING, ANS, SCT [34979]
MEANS PRE 1800 BUCKS CO., PA, USA [36729]
MEAR C1800 CHERITON FITZPAINE, DEV, ENG
[35050]
MEARING 1800S EAST END, LND, ENG [33893] :
1800 ASHAMPSTEAD, BRK, ENG [37170]
MEARNS 1800-1900 ANT, N.IRL [38053] : 1860-1980
NE, USA [38053] : 1848-1925 SULLIVAN CO., NY,
USA [38053]
MEARS 1850S BATHURST, NSW, AUS [35598] : PRE
1853 KNIPTON & CROXTON KEYRAIL, LEI,
ENG [33771] : 1700+ STS, ENG [33973] : 1650S
WHITTLESEA, CAM, ENG [34204] : 1850S
BRISTOL, SOM, ENG [35050] : PRE 1842 STS, ENG
[36841] : 1842+ NELSON, NZ [36841]
MEASE ELIZABETH PRE 1750 LUND, ERY, ENG
[36192]
MEASURES PRE 1850 GILMORTON, LEI, ENG
[37346]
MEATH C1850 PRESTON, LAN, ENG [37066]
MEBAN PRE 1865 KILMOYLE, IRL [36888]
MECARTEA 1800S WOODFORD CO., IL, USA [35278]
MECHENICH 1845+ WI & MN, USA [36542]
MECKLENBURGH PRE 1800 NEW BUCKENHAM,
NFK, ENG [35026] : C1918 LEISTON, SFK, ENG
[35026] : 1812+ CHELMSFORD, ESS, ENG [35026]
MECKLER V. PRE 1713 MAINZ, HESSEN, GER
[38563] : V. 1713-1754 UPPLAND, SWE [38563]
MEDARIA PRE 1870 HAMILTON CO., OH & PA,
USA [37504]
MEDARY PRE 1870 HAMILTON CO., OH & PA, USA
[37504]
MEDCALF 1811+ WIC, IRL [35780]
MEDCALFE 1900+ HEMEL HEMPSTEAD, HRT,
ENG [37387]
MEDD PRE 1800 SEAMER, NRY, ENG [35633]
MEDDER PRE 1900 ST HELIER, JSY & DEV, ENG
[34632]
MEDDIN C1650-1800 GUILDFORD, SRY, ENG
[37618]
MEDE PRE 1700 CON, ENG [34258]
MEDERNACK 1840 RPF, GER [36907]
MEDHURST ALL LEIGH, KEN, ENG [35260] : ALL
EDENBRIDGE, KEN, ENG [35260] : PRE 1790
ROTHERFIELD, SSX, ENG [35406] : 1800S
ISLINGTON, LND, ENG [36055] : 1900S
TOTTENHAM, LND, ENG [36055] : PRE 1840
GRAVESEND, KEN, ENG [37142]
MEDINA 1895-1930 LIVERPOOL, LAN, ENG [37255] :
1895-1930 COLOMBO, SRI LANKA [37255]
MEDLAND ALL POUNDSTOCK & ST GENNYS,
CON, ENG [34263] : 1930+ SIDMOUTH, DEV, ENG
[35553] : PRE 1864 WIDEMOUTH, CON, ENG
[37144] : 1860+ NZ [34263]
MEDLEY 1700+ SUNDERLAND, DUR, ENG [35364]
: 1750+ WORKSOP, NTT, ENG [37056] : 1800+
LONDON, ENG [37158] : 1700-C1740S
THORNBOROUGH, BKM, ENG [38350] : 1830+
JEFFERSON CO., MO, KY & TN, USA [37796] :
1830+ CAPE GIRARDEAU CO., MO, KY & TN,
USA [37796]
MEDLIN 1700S KENWYN, CON, ENG [34214]
MEDLYN 1700S WENDRON, CON, ENG [35045] :
PRE 1798 WENDRON, CON, ENG [37975]
MEDRO PRE 1735 SHO, GER [38604]
MEDWAY 1840-1900 DOULTON, NSW, AUS [37895]
MEDWIN 1841+ CIRCULAR HEAD, TAS, AUS
[35399] : PRE 1841 WOBURN, BKM, ENG [35399] :
1840 WYCOMBE, BKM, ENG & AUS [34845]

MEE PRE 1856 DERBY, DBY, ENG [36980] : 1850 CHILWELL, NTT, ENG [37829]

MEECH 1700+ DEV, ENG [35377] : 1700+ DOR, ENG [35377] : SARAH 1820-1840 SCIOTA CO., OH, USA [38573]

MEEHAN 1900+ TOOWOOMBA, QLD, AUS [33842] : PRE 1900 NSW & QLD, AUS [35512] : PRE 1860 JSY, CHI [34958] : PRE 1866 MIDDLESBROUGH, NRY, ENG [37204] : 1819+ TIP, IRL [33880] : 1840 CLA, IRL [35067] : PRE 1850 CLA, IRL [37018] : 1850 CORK, COR, IRL [38699] : PRE 1860 MAURITIUS [34958] : PRE 1845 GREENOCK, RFW, SCT [36844]

MEEK MARGARET 1781-1876 ST FOY, QUE, CAN [34489] : ALL QUE, CAN [34489] : PRE 1840 MAIDSTONE, KEN, ENG [34816] : C1850 BILSTON, STS, ENG [36090] : PRE 1850 MEASHAM, DBY, ENG [36105] : 1800+ NOTTINGHAM, NTT, ENG [36105]

MEEKER ISABELLA 1831-1851 SPRINGFIELD, OH, USA [36322] : LOUISA 1831-1850 MONROE CITY, MO, USA [36322]

MEEKIN 1840S SSX, ENG [34788]

MEEKING 1750-1900 LAVENHAM, SFK, ENG [34632]

MEEKS PRE 1800 CAM, ENG [36183]

MEEN ALL SFK, ENG [37250]

MEENAN ALL TYR, IRL [38228] : ALL DOW, IRL [38228] : ALL ANT, IRL [38228] : ALL USA [38228]

MEER 1840+ TAS, AUS [35847] : 1800+ BISHOPS LYDEARD, SOM, ENG [35847]

MEERLEVE ALL WORLDWIDE [38161]

MEERS 1820S+ MUDGEE, NSW, AUS [35831] : 1800-1850 LND, ENG [37084]

MEESE 1830S KINGSWINFORD, STS, ENG [36848]

MEESON 1700-1800 STS, ENG [36062] : PRE 1815 STAFFORD, STS, ENG [36701]

MEEUWENOORD ALL NOORDWYK, ZUH, NL [38703]

MEGAFFIN 1800+ BRUCE CO., ONT, CAN [34492] : 1700S DOW, IRL [34492] : 1700S ARM, IRL [34492]

MEGARRY PRE 1900 ANT, IRL [35915]

MEGAW PRE 1863 DRUMSALLAGH, DOW, IRL [35779]

MEGER 1870-1900 SHAWANO CO., WI, USA [36546]

MEGERLE 1700+ EICHACH, BAW, GER [35355]

MEGGISON 1700-1800 HELMSLEY, NRY, ENG [37858]

MEGILL PRE 1890 QUE, CAN [34159] : C1890 MIAMI, MAN, CAN [34159]

MEGLEY 1840S ARDMORE, WAT, IRL [34618]

MEGLI ALL FRA [38625] : ALL GER [38625] : 1750+ USA [38625]

MEGOW PRE 1900 STETTIN, SZ, POL [34089] : ALL WORLDWIDE [34089]

MEGSON ALL WORLDWIDE [36391]

MEGUIRE 1800+ LIVERPOOL, ENG [33825]

MEHAN 1800-1850 TIP, IRL [37027]

MEHARG 1780+ LONDONDERRY, DRY, IRL [34190] : ALL BELFAST & NEWTOWNARDS, DOW & ANT, IRL [34733]

MEHARRY C1859 SLAMANNAN, STI, SCT [34542]

MEHEGAN ALL CASTLE TOWN ROCHE, COR, IRL [34460]

MEHLENBACHER PRE 1850 OTTWEILER, BAY, BRD [35635]

MEHRER ALL GER & USA [37805]

MEHRTENS JOHN HENRY 1829-1893 ROCKY RIVER, NSW, AUS & GER [36371]

MEIER PRE 1900 NSW, AUS [34860] : 1860+ QLD, AUS [37554] : PRE 1860 SG, CH [37554] : 1700+ TREUFELD, SHO, GER [37170] : 1876+ ELLIS CO., KS, USA [38057]

MEIERHOFF PRE 1890 GNOIEN, MSW, GER [38125]

MEIERN 1700+ SCHONWEIDE, SHO, GER [37170]

MEIERS PRE 1870 NORDEN, HBG, BRD [34626] : CHRISTOPH 1750 PERLEBERG, BRA, GER [37509]

MEIGH PRE 1850 DERBY, DBY, ENG [36980]

MEIKLE 1850-1900 BRUCE, ONT, CAN [36724] : 1726 SORN, AYR, SCT [34214] : 1800S LINLITHGOW AREA, WLN, SCT [34483] : 1800S KIRKLISTON, WLN, SCT [34483] : PRE 1762 CARLUKE, LKS, SCT [34501] : 1750+ TORPHICHEN, WLN, SCT [35979] : PRE 1850 STRATHAVEN, LKS, SCT [36583] : 1800-1850 SCT [36724]

MEIKLEJOHN 1700+ SALINE, FIF, SCT [34420] : 1800S DUNBLANE, PER, SCT [34621]

MEINCKE 1826-1852 OTTENSEN & ALTONA, SHO, GER [34582] : JOHN PRE 1858 PRE, GER [37192]

MEINHARDT PRE 1805 SILBERHAUSEN, PSA, GER [38048]

MEIR 1850S TUNSTALL, STS, ENG [35730] : 1850S KANKAKEE, IL, USA [36928] : PRE 1840 HAMBURG, NY, USA [36928]

MEIRLEVE ALL WORLDWIDE [38161]

MEIRLEVEDE ALL WORLDWIDE [38161]

MEIRS FREDRICA 1852+ LIVERPOOL, LAN, ENG [33956]

MEISE 1650+ BELLERSEN, WEF, GER [35460]

MEJTER ALL WORLDWIDE [38547]

MEKEOWN 1850 WILLUNGA, SA, AUS [35801]

MELANOPHY 1800-1850 CUMBERLAND CO., NSW, AUS [34307]

MELBOURNE MAUDE MAY PRE 1900 HARLESDEN, MDX, ENG [35124]

MELCHER 1860-1900 ADELAIDE, SA, AUS [35861]

MELCHERT PRE 1880 STOLP, POM, GER [34929]

MELDRUM 1800+ WINCHESTER, ONT, CAN [36662] : 1860+ OREWA & AUCKLAND, NZ [36245] : PRE 1890 PIETERMARITZBURG, NATAL, RSA [36426] : 1750+ ABD, SCT [35060] : 1763-1800 KINROSS, KRS, SCT [36874] : PRE 1880 STI, SCT [37114] : 1800S EDINBURGH, SCT [37134]

MELHUISH PRE 1700 CON, ENG [34139] : C1717 MOREBATH, DEV, ENG [35131] : 1700+ EXETER, DEV, ENG [35972] : C1878 BROMLEY, KEN, ENG [36838] : 1800S CAMBERWELL, LND, ENG [36868] : PRE 1850 DULVERTON & EXFORD, SOM & DEV, ENG [37322]

MELIA PRE 1839 ATHLONE, WEM, IRL [34585]

MELIN ALL HAARNOSAND, VASTERNORLAND, SWE & USA [38175]

MELIUS ALL SCHWABSBURG, BAY, BRD [37012]

MELLEN 1915-1940 TILLEY, ALB, CAN [34255] : 1800-1900 TYR, IRL [34255] : 1850-1916 CHICKASAW, IA, USA [34255] : 1850-1916 PHILLIPSBURG, KS, USA [34255] : ALL WORLDWIDE [34255]

MELLER PRE 1829 MARYLEBONE, MDX, ENG [36309] : PRE 1900 PADDINGTON, LND, ENG [36361] : PRE 1823 KIDDIMORE GREEN, STS, ENG [36866] : 1828+ BRIGHTON, SSX, ENG [37677] : 1830-1860 DROITWICH, WOR, ENG [38207] : ALL WORLDWIDE [37366]

MELLERT 1825-1900 BERKS CO., PA, USA [35318]

MELLIN PRE 1850 NANTES, PL, FRA [36270]

MELLING PRE 1865 LIVERPOOL, LAN, ENG [36522] : 1860S BALHAM & LYTHAM, LAN, ENG [37710]

MELLINGTON MARY ANN 1851+ GOLD FIELDS, NSW & VIC, AUS [34449] : JOHN 1851+ GOLD FIELDS, NSW & VIC, AUS [34449]

MELLIS PRE 1841 ELGIN, MOR, SCT [35260] : ALL ELGIN, MOR, SCT [38357]

MELLISH C1826 BRISTOL, GLS, ENG [37148]

MELLODY 1780+ WIGAN, LAN, ENG [38046]

MELLON 1840+ SINGLETON, NSW, AUS [38582] : 1800-1900 TYR, IRL [34255] : 1750-1800 TYR, IRL

[34255] : ALL LONGFORD, LOG, IRL [35769] : C1840 DUB, IRL [36772] : 1850+ NEWPORT, TIP, IRL [36772]

MELLOR C1798-1848 WAKEFIELD, WRY, ENG [33862] : PRE 1850 MANCHESTER, LAN & WRY, ENG [35354] : C1807 HOLMFIRTH, WRY, ENG [35478] : PRE 1864 UPPERTHONG, WRY, ENG [35733] : PRE 1850 ILAM, STS, ENG [36841] : 1800+ SHEEN, STS, ENG [37666] : 1831 WIRKSWORTH, DBY, ENG [38022] : PRE 1850 NETHERSEALE, DBY, ENG [38457] : GEORGE PRE 1765 LINTHWAITE, WRY, ENG [38480] : PRE 1840 ROTIDALE, YKS, ENG [38568]

MELLORS PRE 1800 ARNOLD, NTT, ENG [36105] : PRE 1900 ARNOLD, NTT, ENG [36387]

MELLOW 1700-1800 ST STEPHEN IN BRANNEL, CON, ENG [37457]

MELLOWS 1700-1800 LONDON, ENG [36081] : 1800+ REEPHAM, LIN, ENG [37448]

MELLROSS PRE 1861 NEW GALLOWAY, KKD & DFS, SCT [35330]

MELOCHE 1800+ HUBBELL, MI, USA [36662]

MELTON PRE 1880 EAGLE, LIN, ENG [35363] : ALL LONG SUTTON, LIN, ENG [35702] : 1800S MDX, ENG [35959] : OLLIE C1825 LA, USA [37801]

MELVILL 1600-1750 GLASGOW, LKS, SCT [36335] : 1690-1850 NEWPORT, RI, USA [36335]

MELVILLE 1750-1830 WORKINGTON, CUL, ENG [34762] : PRE 1800 SSX, ENG [35500] : PRE 1800 MARKINCH, FIF, SCT [34285] : ALL EAST KILBRIDE, LKS, SCT [38057] : ALL WORLDWIDE [37803]

MELVIN 1890+ INGHAM & CAIRNS, QLD, AUS [34852] : 1800-1900 CHESTER CO., NS, CAN [34225] : 1831+ GLASGOW, LKS, SCT [33951] : 1800+ LEITH, MLN, SCT [34852] : PRE 1686 CHARLESTOWN, MA, USA [34225]

MELZER PRE 1860 KARLSBAD AREA, BOHEMIA, CS [36963]

MEMBREY 1870-1882 MACARTHUR MT ECCLES, VIC, AUS [34279] : 1870+ PRAHRAN, VIC, AUS [34279] : ALL LONDON, ENG [35474] : 1820S KEN, ENG [35799]

MEMORY 1600+ STAVERTON, DEV, ENG [34747]

MENACES (SEE MCNEIEC [37906]

MENANTEAU 1830S ROCHEFORT, FRA [34164]

MENARD 1830-1950S QUE & ONT, CAN [34202]

MENCKE 1629-1710 LUEWEBURG, HAN, GER [38626]

MENDENHALL PRE 1840 ATHENS, AL, USA [37804] : PRE 1880 VA & NC, USA [38217]

MENDES C1680-1800 LONDON, ENG [36630]

MENDES DA COSTA 1882-1991 LA PLATA & BAHIA BLANCH, ARGENTINA [36630] : 1880-1991 BRUSSELS & ANTWERP, BEL [36630] : 1680-1991 LONDON, ENG [36630] : 1850-1991 FRA [36630] : 1680-1991 AMSTERDAM, NL [36630] : 1450-1680 TANCOSO, BEIRA ALTA, PT [36630] : 1800-1991 USA [36630] : ALL WORLDWIDE [36630]

MENDOSA 1840+ CO & TX, USA [38221]

MENEFEE 1600+ USA [38326]

MENEGUZZI 1800-1900 BELLUNO, ITL [38337]

MENGEL PRE 1920 DARKEHMEN, OPR, GER [38647]

MENHEERE ÁLL WESTKERKE, ZEL, NL [38694]

MENHENIOTT C1841 STOKE DAMEREL, DEV, ENG [35335]

MENIAN 1659+ GER [38598]

MENKE 1772-1957 HANNOVER, HAN, GER [38626]

MENKOFIELD C1840 SHOREDITCH, MDX, ENG [35553]

MENMUIR 1850 KINCARDINE, ABD, SCT & AUS [37307]

MENNEH MENA JURGENS 1800-1895 GER [38781]

MENNEKE 1900+ JACKSON CO., IA, USA [38323]

MENNIE 1850-1920 NSW, AUS [36282] : 1868+ PORT MELBOURNE, VIC, AUS [37962] : ALL MARYLEBONE, LND, ENG [37937] : ALEX PRE 1930 ABERDEEN, ABD, SCT [36282] : PRE 1868 ABERDEEN, ABD, SCT [37962]

MENNILL 1800-1860 NRY, ENG [37858]

MENNONS C1876 SEVRES, FRA [35216]

MENOGUE ALL KIK, IRL [33872]

MENSFORTH C1840+ LAUNCESTON, TAS, AUS [35834] : C1848+ ADELAIDE, SA, AUS [35834] : 1700+ KIRKHEATON, YKS, ENG [35834] : C1820-1834 IONIAN ISLANDS, GR [35834]

MENTON 1550-1760 WOR, ENG [37217]

MENZEL C1873 RADNITZ CROSSEN ON ODER, BRA, GER [34195] : 1860S NAKEL, POS, GER [34223]

MENZIES 1900+ TOWNSVILLE & BRISBANE, QLD, AUS [35111] : 1750+ BALLINTRA, DON, IRL [34408] : 1800+ WEEM & ABERFELDY, PER, SCT [34008] : 1700+ FORTINGALL & DULL, PER, SCT [34419] : PRE 1829 WESTER CAPUTH, PER, SCT [34797] : PRE 1900 KILSYTH, STI, SCT [35111] : 1700-1800S LEITH, SCT [35424] : 1821 ABERFELDY, PER, SCT [35769] : 1750-1870 DUNDONALD, AYR, SCT [35790] : 1782 SCT [35906] : 1800 GLASGOW, LKS, SCT [35937] : 1800S ABERFELDIE, PER, SCT [35987] : PRE 1760 WEEM, PER, SCT [36704]

MEOPHAM (SEE MEPHAM) [35546]

MEPHAM 1840+ SYDNEY, NSW, AUS [37889] : 1770+ MAYFIELD & BURWASH, SSX, ENG [34473] : ALL BEXHILL, SSX, ENG [35546] : 1800+ WITHYHAM, SSX, ENG [37889]

MEPHRINGHAM ANTHONY PRE C1800 NOTTINGHAM, NTT, ENG [36645]

MERAND C1700 PARIS, FRA [37819]

MERCER 1860+ BARRINGTON, TAS, AUS [34541] : 1860+ PENGUIN, TAS, AUS [34541] : C1810 HARBOUR GRACE, NFD, CAN [33852] : 1794+ YORK CO., ONT, CAN [37458] : 1700-1850 BRADFORD, YKS, ENG [35285] : 1800-1860 BRIGHTON, SSX, ENG [36167] : PRE 1865 WARNHAM, SSX, ENG [36215] : PRE 1850 LND, ENG [37731] : SAMUEL 1780S CROSBY SQUARE, LONDON, MDX, ENG [38396] : 1650-1700 PINCHBECK, SAL, ENG [38453] : 1700+ PRESCOTT & FARNSWORTH, LAN, ENG [38745] : 1800-1822 TIP, IRL [35776] : PRE 1850 KILLUCAN, WEM, IRL [36277] : 1800+ IRL [38226] : JEAN PRE 1760 KELSO, ROX, SCT [35371] : PRE 1855 PER & STI, SCT [37981] : PRE 1855 KIRKPATRICK DURHAM, KKD, SCT [37981] : C1783 KINCLAVEN, PER, SCT [37981] : JOHN C1819 EDINBURGH, MLN, SCT & AUS [37143] : PETER 1821-1902 SCT & AUS [37981] : 1890-1920 LAFAYETTE CO., FL, USA [35315] : REDMOND ALL BRUNSWICK CO., NC, USA [37789] : ALL BLADEN CO., NC, USA [37789] : SOLOMON ALL ROBESON CO., NC, USA [37789] : ALL NORFOLK CO., VA, USA [37789] : ALL WORLDWIDE [38237]

MERCEREAU 1500-1700 MOISE SAINTONGE, FRA [36556]

MERCH 1858-1864 KEWEENAW CO., MI, USA [38009]

MERCHANT 1750-1850 NY, MA & NJ, USA [36319] : 1830 MERCER, PA, USA [38317] : 1820 WESTMORELAND, PA, USA [38317]

MERCOVICH PRE 1870 TRAPANJ, YU [33839]

MERCURIO 1920-1950 PROVIDENCE, RI, USA
[36272]

MEREDITH C1770+ AUS [34444] : 1788+
LIVERPOOL & BANKSTOWN, NSW, AUS [35513] :
1820S TULLOW, CAR, IRL [34602] : PRE 1845 RAD,
WLS [35386] : FREDERICK PRE 1788
PRESTEIGNE & KINGTON, POWYS, WLS [35513]

MEREWEATHER PRE 1850 BRISTOL, ENG [37289]

MERIE ALL WORLDWIDE [34986]

MERIET ALL WORLDWIDE [38775]

MERIMAN PRE 1700 SHEPSHED, LEI, ENG [37295]

MERIOT PRE 1600 WITNEY, OXF, ENG [37277] :
PRE 1600 HN, FRA [37277] : PRE 1600 BN, FRA
[37277]

MERITON ALL WORLDWIDE [33875]

MERKEL 1922 BAD PYRMONT, PYR, GER [38749] :
1849 BEVERUNGEN, WEF, GER [38749] : 1814
BRUCHHAUSEN, WEF, GER [38750]

MERLEVE ALL WORLDWIDE [38161]

MERLEVEDE 1500+ WORLDWIDE [38161]

MERMILLOD PRE 1650 ONEX, GE, CH [38348]

MERRALL PRE 1800 MAIDSTONE, KEN, ENG
[34819] : PRE 1800 NTH & LEI, ENG [37706]

MERRATT ALL WORLDWIDE [38775]

MERRELL ATHEW 1853+ TENTERFIELD, NSW,
AUS [35788]

MERRETT 1840+ SA, AUS [34263] : 1890+ SYDNEY,
NSW, AUS [37136] : PRE 1885 BIRDLIP, GLS, ENG
[37136] : 1700-1850 ALL CANNINGS, WIL, ENG
[37843] : ALL WORLDWIDE [38775]

MERREY ALL WORLDWIDE [33922] : ALL
WORLDWIDE [34986]

MERRICK 1868+ YARRAWONGA, VIC, AUS [35731]
: 1830+ TORONTO, ONT, CAN [36652] : 1850+
ENG [38481] : PRE 1830S BALLINDINE, MAY, IRL
[36652] : 1800S NC, USA [38536]

MERRIE ALL WORLDWIDE [34986]

MERRIFIELD C1764 LINCOLNS INN, LND, ENG
[35013] : 1740S EXETER, DEV, ENG [35260] : PRE
1819 EXETER, DEV, ENG [37703]

MERRIHEW 1807+ LONG ISLAND, NY, USA [38151]

MERRILEES 1700-1800 PAISLEY, RFW & AYR, SCT
[36802]

MERRILL 1810+ NEW NORFOLK & WINDSOR,
TAS, AUS [35394] : DOROTHY I. 1892-1950 NJ &
NY, USA [37800] : JAMES E. 1800S NJ, USA [37800] :
1846-1638 NEWBURY, ORANGE, VT, USA [38571]

MERRIMAN ALL SHEPSHED, LEI, ENG [37295]

MERRINGTON 1800S LONDON, ENG [34953] : PRE
1800 ONGAR, ESS, ENG [34953]

MERRIOTT ALL WORLDWIDE [38775]

MERRITT 1800-1900 MELBOURNE, VIC, AUS [34872]
: 1850+ DERBY, TAS, AUS [35116] : GERTRUDE
1799-1890 ONT, CAN [38146] : 1800-1900 SHIPLEY &
WEST GRINSTEAD, SSX, ENG [34749] : C1850
SOUTHAMPTON, HAM, ENG [35807] : 1800
ASHAMPSTEAD, BRK, ENG [37170] : 1780-1820
MONROE CO., NY, USA [36555] : 1744+ SURREY
CO., VA, USA [37564] : ALL WORLDWIDE [38766] :
ALL WORLDWIDE [38775]

MERROTT ALL WORLDWIDE [38775]

MERRY 1700-1800 LUDGERSHALL, BKM, ENG
[34986] : 1790+ HASELEY & ROWINGTON, WAR,
ENG [37834] : 1600-1900 LONDON, ENG [38278] :
ALL WORLDWIDE [33922] : ALL WORLDWIDE
[34986]

MERRYE ALL WORLDWIDE [34986]

MERRYFIELD C1850 USA [36671]

MERRYMAN PRE 1700 SHEPSHED, LEI, ENG [37295]

MERRYWEATHER 1900+ LONDON, ENG [35783] :
1826+ MIDDLETON TYAS, NRY, ENG [37635]

MERSON 1854+ MELBOURNE, VIC, AUS [35710] :
1780-1820 ERFIELD, HRT, ENG [35710] : 1800+
SHOREDITCH, MDX, ENG [35710] : 1700S BANFF,
BAN, SCT [35710]

MERTON KITTY 1900+ NSW, AUS [36471]

MERVILL ALL WORLDWIDE [36739]

MERWYNS 1500-1600 NMR, BEL [36943]

MERY ALL WORLDWIDE [34986]

MERYE ALL WORLDWIDE [34986]

MERYT ALL WORLDWIDE [38775]

MESCHKE 1850-1889 JESSEN ELSTER, KSA, GER
[38749]

MESICK 1780-1880 ALBANY & ADAMS, NY, USA
[38537]

MESPLAIT PRE 1790 NEW ORLEANS, LA & MO,
USA [36917]

MESS C1909 FLORA, IL, USA [38650]

MESSENGER 1840+ MELBOURNE, VIC, AUS
[34962] : PRE 1840 LOUGHTON, ESS, ENG [34962] :
1580+ BURBAGE & SAPCOTE, LEI, ENG [36827] :
1800S BIRMINGHAM, WAR, ENG [37299] : 1650+
HARTFORD CO., CT, USA [37802] : 1900+ MI, USA
[38739]

MESSER PRE 1800 FINSTERROT, BAW, BRD [38615]
: 1800+ EDINBURGH, MLN, SCT [34718]

MESSERLY 1800-1860 NEU, CH [34751] : C1820-30
BERNE, CH [36722] : 1850-1900 MONROE CO., OH,
USA [36722] : 1845-50 HERKIMER CO., NY, USA
[36722]

MESSINGER 1815+ BIRMINGHAM, WAR, ENG
[37258]

MESSNER 1864-1879 KEWEENAW CO., MI, USA
[38009]

MESTEL ALL WORLDWIDE [37366] : ALL
WORLDWIDE [37750]

MESTON ALL WORLDWIDE [33971]

MESTREZAT DENYS C1500 THONON, HTE
SAVOIE, FRA [38348]

METAXAS 1900-1929 ACTON, LND, ENG [37219] :
1900-1954 KENSINGTON, LND, ENG [37219] : 1860-
1906 PARIS, RPA, FRA [37219]

METCALF 1880S BYKER NEWCASTLE ON TYNE,
NBL, ENG [34198] : PRE 1840 MASHAM, NRY,
ENG [34588] : PRE 1800 RIPLEY, WRY, ENG [36048]
: PRE 1800 BURY ST EDMUNDS, SFK, ENG
[37253] : 1880 WESTFIELD, IL, USA [37576] : 1760-
1880 ONEIDA, NY & MA, USA [38194]

METCALFE 1850-1920 JUNEE, NSW, AUS [34537] :
1900S MOSS VALE, NSW, AUS [35567] : FRASER
1940-1960 LONDON, ONT, CAN [38409] : 1805+
LANGTON, YKS, ENG [35112] : 1703 ARNCLIFFE,
NRY, ENG [35282] : 1860-1890S LAN, ENG [35347] :
1787-1850 ROXTON, BDF, ENG [35706] : 1700-1787
FORDHAM, CAM, ENG [35706] : 1850S
CAMBERWELL, LND, ENG [36799] : PRE 1850
AYSGARTH, NRY, ENG [37414] : PRE 1798
RICHMOND MARSKE & SWALEDALE, NRY,
ENG [37635] : PRE 1873 SEDGBURGH, CUL, ENG
[37769] : 1700-1900 WHORLTON & HELMSLEY,
NRY, ENG [37858] : PRE 1850 YKS, ENG [38039] :
1678-1698 FORT ST GEORGE, MADRAS, INDIA
[35706] : C1860-1920 IRL [36835] : PRE 1859
WHITFORD, FLN, WLS [37667]

METEREAU 1790-1830 BALTIMORE CITY, MD, USA
[36911]

METHER ALL WORLDWIDE [38547]

METHERELL ALL DEV, ENG [36790]

METHERINGHAM ANTHONY PRE C1800
NOTTINGHAM, NTT, ENG [36645]

METHVEN 1780+ KIRKCALDY & SCOONIE, FIF,
SCT [34473]

METTAM 1870+ CAMBERWELL, NSW, AUS [36615]

METTEN 1624 RHENEGGE, WAL, GER [34912]

METTEPENNINGEN 1775-1875 HAMME, OVL, BEL [38405]

METTERNICH PRE 1820 NRW & RPF, BRD [38616] : 1840-1870 PRE [38149] : 1870-1900 BATESVILLE, IN, USA [38149]

METTLER PRE 1756 HUNTERDON CO., NJ, USA [37574]

METTYEAR 1850+ HAM, ENG [38350]

METYARD PRE 1800 DOR, ENG [38211]

METYCH 1900+ SU & POL [35000]

METZ 1700+ BARDEN, GER [37993]

METZGER C1791 KINGDOM OF, BAW, GER [36855] : 1800-1870 ALBISHEIM, KIRKHEIM BOLANDEN, RHEIN-BEIREN, GER [38374] : ALL SCHLIENGEN, BAW, GER [38609]

METZNER 1744-1890 SCHLEUSINGEN, THURINGIA, GER [38148]

METZROTH PRE 1820 ESPENSCHIED, RPF, GER [38681]

MEUDELL 1900+ VIC, AUS [35106] : 1850+ CAN [35106] : ALL POOLE, DOR, ENG [35106] : 1800+ USA [35106]

MEULEMAN 1850+ ZWOLLE, OIJ, NL [35338]

MEULMAN C1850 HOLLAND, UTR, NL [38702]

MEURER C1865 GRAFTON, NSW, AUS [36312]

MEW PRE 1900 IOW, ENG [34825] : PRE 1850 HAM & DOR, ENG [36054] : PRE 1850 SOUTHWARK, SRY, ENG [36153] : 1800 NTT, ENG [37570] : PRE 1850 ARRETON, IOW, ENG [38722] : 1770-1850S DUNDEE, ANS, SCT [35938]

MEWETT ALL WORLDWIDE [37340]

MEWHA PRE 1848 CRIVILLY VALLEY, ANT, IRL [34598] : PRE 1840 CONNOR, ANT, IRL [38292]

MEWKILL 1800+ LONDON, ENG [34455] : 1890+ CHRISTCHURCH, NZ [34455] : ALL WORLDWIDE [34455]

MEYBOHM PRE 1700 BREMEN, BRM, GER [38049]

MEYER 1750 LANDESBERGEN, HAN, BRD [38327] : C1850 WALKERTON, ONT, CAN [33902] : 1852+ WATERLOO, WELLINGTON CO., ONT, CAN [34056] : PRE 1865 MILE END OLD TOWN, MDX, ENG [37138] : 1750-1870 NEHWEILER, ALS, FRA [36898] : C1840 HAN, GER [34875] : 1860S HAN, GER [36952] : 1700+ GREBIN, SHO, GER [37170] : REBECCA 1766 BERNE, OLD, GER [37509] : PRE 1882 VISSELHOUEDE, HAN, GER [37563] : PRE 1860 KRUKENBERG, HEN, GER [38577] : 1825 BLOMBERG, PYR, GER [38749] : 1786 ELBRINXEN, LIP, GER [38749] : SUS. 1600-1800 AUSTRO HUNGARY EMPIRE, HU [37931] : PRE 1890 KIMBERLEY, CAPE, RSA [36468] : JOHN 1800-29 LEHIGH CO., PA, USA [38086] : 1850-1900 GASCONADE CO., MO, USA [38532]

MEYERS CHARLES PRE 1873 MELBOURNE, VIC, AUS [35471] : FREDRICA 1852+ LIVERPOOL, LAN, ENG [33956] : 1860S LUX [38339] : CHRISTOPHER 1820+ EDINBURGH, SCT [35049] : MARGARET 1820+ EDINBURGH, SCT [35049] : 1835 SCHUYLKILL, PA, USA [34388]

MEYERS (SEE MYERS) [38197]

MEYRELEVEDE ALL WORLDWIDE [38161]

MEYRICK PRE 1850 YKS, ENG [37245]

MEZALUCK ALL WORLDWIDE [36709]

M'GREGOR PRE 1860 NEW PLYMOUTH, NZ [35898]

MIATT 1800S CLERKENWELL, LND, ENG [36055] : 1800S HOLBORN, LND, ENG [36055] : ALL WORLDWIDE [36235]

MICHAEL PRE 1677 CHICHESTER, SSX, ENG [34573]

MICHAELIS C1820 HAN, PRE [38487]

MICHAELS PRE 1875 BRM & HAN, GER [37548] : 1833 WYANDOTTE CO., OH, USA [38192]

MICHAELSEN 1728+ BUSUM, SHO, GER [37542]

MICHALIUK 1860 GALICIA, POL [36679]

MICHALYK ALL GALICIA, SU & POL [34146]

MICHAUD ALL QUE, CAN [34517]

MICHEEL PRE 1850 MSW, GER [38191]

MICHEL ALL GWINEAR, CON, ENG [34877] : 1800+ GWENNAP, CON, ENG [35708] : 1620-1710 MAILLEZAIS, PCH, FRA [34514] : REV. C1770 ROUEN, FRA [34678] : C1900 FONTENAY TRESIGNY, RPA, FRA [38166] : C1750 CHARLEVILLE MEZIERES, FRA [38698] : C1900 BERLIN, BLN, GER [38166] : 1840-1850 NEWCASTLE, NATAL, RSA [34678]

MICHELIN PR-FRS 1700-1770 FRA [37479]

MICHELL ALL GWINEAR, CON, ENG [33972] : 1800-1900 BRUTON, SOM, ENG [34135] : 1700S KENWYN, CON, ENG [35076] : PRE 1850 REDRUTH, CON, ENG [35540] : JANE ALL EALING, LND, ENG [36212] : 1800S ST IVES, CON, ENG [36506] : 1800-1840 BENTLEY HAY, STS, ENG [36536] : PRE 1700 ILLOGAN, CON, ENG [38745]

MICHELS 1820-1840 GER [36913] : 1800-50 WEF, GER [38189] : 1840-1910 MCLEAN CO., IL & WI, USA [36913]

MICHELSDOTTER 1600-1780S LARBRO, GOTLAND, SWE [38346]

MICHENER 1650+ PA, USA [36319]

MICHIE ALL GREENVALE, VIC, AUS [35526] : PRE 1800 STRATHDON, ABD, SCT [35955] : C1838 CAIRNEY HILL & CARNOCK, SCT [36855] : 1800S STRATHDON, ABD, SCT & NZ [36607]

MICHL PRE 1900 AUGSBURG, BAY, BRD [36963]

MICK PRE 1720 WIRGES, RPF, GER [38681]

MICKAEL PRE 1835 SCHOHARIE CO., NY, USA [37034]

MICKE ANNA 1700-1900S BRESLAU, GER & USA [35304]

MICKELSON ELIAS 1849+ FIN [36776]

MICKLEBORO 1830+ WORLDWIDE [38462]

MICKLEBOROUGH 1830+ CAMBRIDGE & ST THOMAS, ONT, CAN [38462] : ALL SFK, ENG [38462] : ALL WORLDWIDE [38462]

MICKLEBOURG 1830+ ONT, CAN [38462]

MICKLETHWAITE 1800S YKS, ENG [38468]

MICKLEWRIGHT 1760-1850 WARWICK & BERKSWELL, WAR, ENG [36541] : 1860+ MDX, ENG [36541] : 1865+ BROMLEY & DEPTFORD, KEN, ENG [36541] : 1800+ USA [36541]

MICKMAN ALL WORLDWIDE [37883]

MICKS 1800-1875 ESSA SIMCOE CO., ONT, CAN [36703]

MICOCK 1836 WINDSOR & KURRAJONG, NSW, AUS [36600]

MICUE PRE 1950 ME, USA [37804]

MICUS 1759 GRUNDSTEINEN, GER [38749]

MIDDEKE 1700-1850 HAN, GER [35300]

MIDDING 1897+ ROGATE, SSX, ENG [36215]

MIDDLEBROOK 1880+ GRANTVILLE, VIC, AUS [35059] : 1834 LANESBORO, MA, USA [37594]

MIDDLEDITCH PRE 1750 MILDENHALL, SFK, ENG [34445] : C1700-1750 CHEVINGTON, SFK, ENG [37287]

MIDDLEMAS CATHERIN 1810+ ROXBURGH AREA, ROX, SCT [36636]

MIDDLEMAST 1820S WYLAM, NBL, ENG [33940]

MIDDLEMISS ALL BERWICK UPON TWEED, NBL, ENG [37704] : 1800+ BERWICK ON TWEED, BEW, SCT [36763]

MIDDLETON 1890-1950 WARBURTON, VIC, AUS [34568] : DOROTHY 1942+ BOTANY, NSW, AUS

[34568] : C1850 MELBOURNE, VIC, AUS [34903] :
1870+ BALMAIN, NSW, AUS [35240] : 1830-1900
CHAPEL, DUR, ENG [33991] : PRE 1800
ROSEDALE, NRY, ENG [34127] : 1700 STEPNEY,
MDX, ENG [34210] : 1800S HOLLINGSWORTH,
CHS, ENG [34404] : 1800S MARYLEBONE, MDX,
ENG [34483] : 1796+ DOVER, KEN, ENG [35027] :
PRE 1840 NFK, ENG [35128] : PRE 1842 LONDON,
ENG [35335] : 1852+ WES, ENG [35359] : ALL
LEEDS, WRY, ENG [35470] : 1830+ HUISH
EPISCOPI, SOM, ENG [35734] : 1800 ENG [35873] :
C1790 CHESTERFIELD, DBY, ENG [35920] : JOHN
1870S STOCKPORT, LAN, ENG [36867] : PRE 1840
BRISTOL, SOM, ENG [36955] : 1900+
MAIDSTONE, KEN, ENG [36955] : 1825+
MARYLEBONE & ST PANCRAS, MDX, ENG
[36955] : 1870+ TOTTENHAM & UPPER
HOLLOWAY, MDX, ENG [36955] : 1900+ FAWLEY
& PORTSMOUTH, HAM, ENG [36955] : 1840+
CARSHALTON & CROYDON, SRY, ENG [36955] :
1900+ HILLINGDON, MDX, ENG [36955] : C1842
NEWINGTON & WALLINGTON, SRY, ENG
[36955] : PRE 1900 HALIFAX, ERY, ENG [37000] :
1700-1900 BARTON UNDER NEEDWOOD, STS,
ENG [37487] : 1700-1900 SWADLINCOTE, DBY,
ENG [37487] : 1746-1784 HEYSHAM, LAN, ENG
[37524] : 1800-1900 GREENWICH, LND, ENG
[37850] : 1800 ANT, IRL [34466] : 1810-1860 WEX,
IRL [38301] : 1800S SCT [34000] : C1800 ABERDEEN
& DUNDEE, ANS, SCT [34568] : 1840+ GLASGOW,
LKS, SCT [35240] : 1700+ LEUCHARS, FIF, SCT
[35395] : 1800-1900 LINCOLN CO., KY, USA [37586] :
PRE 1800 GA, USA [37587]

MIDGLEY PRE 1800 LEEDS, WRY, ENG [35079] :
PRE 1820 STANSFIELD & HEPTONSTALL, WRY,
ENG [37372] : PRE 1830 TOTTENHAM, LND, ENG
[37647] : PRE 1880 CALDER VALLEY, WRY, ENG
[37754]
MIDLAM PRE 1900 CONWAY, CAE, WLS [36518]
MIDLANE C1800 SSX, HAM & LND, ENG [35891]
MIDONA ALL WORLDWIDE [36497]
MIEHR PRE 1850 BRA, GER [38627]
MIELCZAREK ALL ZDONSKA WOLA, POL [34266]
MIELENTZ PRE 1783 SCHWEDT & CRIEWEN, BRA,
GER [34083]
MIELL 1860+ SYDNEY, NSW, AUS [35400] : PRE
1860 WIL, ENG [35400]
MIER C1850 WALKERTON, ONT, CAN [33902] :
1700+ YORKSHIRE, DUR, ENG [36609] : PRE 1850
BRA, GER [38627]
MIERENDORFF PRE 1850 HBG, GER [36270]
MIERHS PRE 1850 GER [38627]
MIERISCH PRE 1800 GER [38627]
MIERS 1872+ FISHERMANS BEND, VIC, AUS
[34568] : 1860S+ RICHMOND, VIC, AUS [35188] :
PRE 1870 AUS [38627] : PRE 1870 BRAZIL [38627] :
PRE 1800 ENG [38627] : 1600S BERKHOLZ, BRA,
GER [35968] : PRE 1800 SHO, GER [38627] : PRE
1870 NZ [38627] : PRE 1860S LIBA, RUSSIA [35188] :
PRE 1830 USA [38627] : ALL WORLDWIDE [38627]
MIERSCH PRE 1850 GER [38627]
MIERSCHE 1600S BERKHOLZ, BRA, GER [35968]
MIERSEN ALL SHO, GER [38627]
MIEVIS 1827-1898 VELM, LBG, BEL [38158]
MIFFON C1750-1800 CERNEX, GE, CH [38348]
MIFFORD (SEE MYFORD) [34956]
MIGHELL 1850+ LINDFIELD, SSX, ENG [34785] :
PRE 1820 BRIGHTON, SSX, ENG [36752]
MIGHELLS PRE 1751 BRIMFIELD, MA, USA [37086]
MIGNAN ALL WORLDWIDE [37339]
MIGNEREY 1600 FRA [34500]

MIHEGAN ALL CASTLETOWNROCHE, COR, IRL
[34460]
MIHELL PRE 1600 STANMER, SSX, ENG [34112]
MIHILL C1840 LONDON, ENG [33893]
MIHR PRE 1850 BRA, GER [38627]
MIKESELL ALL USA [38020]
MIKKELSEN 1850-1870S THISTED, JUTLAND, DEN
[36285] : 1890-1990S KENOSHA, WI, USA [36285]
MIKUSKA 1880 SD, USA [35279]
MILARD PRE 1757 NOVIOUS, CHA, FRA [38178]
MILBANK 1790-1870 LONDON, MDX, ENG [36769]
MILBERT 1850S DARMSTADT, HES, BRD [36952] :
1880+ QUINCY, ADAMS CO., IL, USA [36952]
MILBOURNE PRE 1850 PORT ADELAIDE, SA, AUS
[34191]
MILBURN 1780-1790 ST JOHN'S, DUR, ENG [34832] :
1800+ NORTH SHIELDS, NBL, ENG [34852] : 1800-
1850 DEV & CON, ENG [36422] : PRE 1775
CARLISLE, CUL, ENG [36431] : PRE 1850
WHICKHAM, YKS, ENG [37392]
MILCHSACK PRE 1788 HOTTENBACH, RPF, GER
[38663]
MILDENHALL 1700+ NEWBURY, BRK, ENG [35475]
: ALL PECKHAM, LND, ENG [36744]
MILDNER 1800-1850 POLENZ, KSA, GER [38628] :
1590-1650 NIEDEROTTENDORF, KSA, GER [38628]
MILDRED ALL WORLDWIDE [37279]
MILDREN ALL AUS [37913] : ALL CON, ENG [37913]
MILDWATER ALL SYDNEY, NSW, AUS [33765] :
PRE 1850 SHERBORNE, DOR, ENG [33765] : ALL
WORLDWIDE [36599]
MILES PRE 1900 AUS [34196] : 1890+ SYDNEY,
NSW, AUS [35493] : 1850+ SYDNEY, NSW, AUS
[37128] : PRE 1850 ONT, CAN [35620] : 1600-1800
ONT, CAN [38128] : 1892 NEWPORT, NS, CAN
[38470] : PRE 1900 CARNBOURN, DOR, ENG
[33966] : PRE 1800 ICKLEFORD & PIRTON, HRT,
ENG [34551] : ALL DOWNHAM, ESS, ENG [34837] :
ALL WICKFORD, ESS, ENG [34837] : ALL
HOCKLEY, ESS, ENG [34837] : PRE 1851
SEVENOAKS, KEN, ENG [35016] : 1700S
TOWCESTER, NTH, ENG [35030] : 1750S
LONDON, MDX, ENG [35186] : PRE 1850
CROYDON, SRY, ENG [35604] : 1830+
LIVERPOOL, LAN, ENG [35749] : 1600-1800
MAIDEN BRADLEY, WIL, ENG [36106] : PRE 1849
URCHFONT, WIL, ENG [36629] : 1792 CLIFTON
CAMPVILLE, STA, ENG [36635] : ALFRED
ROBERT 1886+ PETERBOROUGH, CAM, ENG
[36638] : C1827+ BRADFORD ON AVON, WIL,
ENG [36753] : 1750-1860 HEREFORD, HEF, ENG
[36879] : 1813-1873 KINGSCLERE, HAM, ENG
[37168] : 1760-1820 CROYDON, SRY, ENG [37252] :
PRE 1856 PLYMOUTH, DEV, ENG [37313] : 1700+
SHERSTON, WIL, ENG [37328] : 1850+
BRINKWORTH, WIL, ENG [37468] : 1700+
KINGSCLERE, HAM, ENG [37638] : PRE 1850
ENFIELD, MDX, ENG [37753] : DAVID 1820+
FULTON CO., NY, USA [36950] : 1760S VA, USA
[38017] : C1834 RIPLEY, IN, USA [38769] : 1800-1855
ABERDARE, GLA, WLS [34844] : ALL
PENRHIWCEIBER, GLA, WLS [35391]
MILEY PRE 1835 WIC, IRL [38733]
MILFORD 1600-1800 EXETER, DEV, ENG [34303] :
PRE 1900 DODDISCOMBSLEIGH, DEV, ENG
[36998] : ELIZA PRE 1800 CECIL CO., MD, USA
[38536]
MILGATE 1838+ RAYMOND TERRACE, NSW, AUS
[35157] : 1650-1750 KEN, ENG [35157]
MILGROVE PRE 1875 FROME, SOM, ENG [35764]

MILHOUS 1649+ CARRICKFERGUS, ANT, IRL
[37564]

MILIANI 1868-1906 OMAHA, NE, USA [36338]

MILIUS 1700-1800 NOCKENHEIM, PRE, GER [36898]

MILL C1699 CHIBBURN, NBL, ENG [35026] : 1780+
INVERESK, MLN, SCT [34922] : 1700-1800 ST
MONANCE, FIF, SCT [35627] : 1600+ PERTH, PER,
SCT [37141]

MILLANE 1870+ BALLARAT, VIC, AUS [34804] :
1791-1850 MALLOW, COR, IRL [34071]

MILLAR 1850+ MELBOURNE & MIRBOO NORTH,
VIC, AUS [35379] : C1840+ WINDSOR, NSW, AUS
[35537] : PRE 1850 NS, CAN [34160] : PRE 1798
ASPULL, LAN, ENG [34873] : PRE 1870 BRIXTON,
SRY, ENG [36437] : ALL BALLY BLACK, DOW,
IRL & NZ [34645] : C1771 INCHTURE, PER, SCT
[34389] : C1860+ PARTICK, LKS, SCT [35108] : PRE
1850 LEITH & EDINBURGH, MLN, SCT [35379] :
1790S DUNDONALD, AYR, SCT [35612] : JOHN
1800+ INVERQUHARITY, ANS, SCT [35917] :
ELIZABETH 1800+ INVERQUHARITY, ANS, SCT
[35917] : JOHN 1800+ KIRRIEMUIR, ANS, SCT
[35917] : MARGARET PRE 1865 RFW, SCT [36363] :
PRE 1850 GRAITNEY, DFS, SCT [36760] : 1800-1900
DUNDEE ST VIGEANS, ANS, SCT [36777] : PRE
1830 MONTROSE, ANS, SCT [36777] : 1840+
NORTH BERWICK, ELN, SCT [36871] : PRE 1750
WALLS, OKI, SCT [36883] : 1750+ KILMAURS,
AYR, SCT [37205] : 1850-1870 DUNFERMLINE, FIF,
SCT [38763]

MILLARD EMANUEL 1846 SINGLETON, NSW, AUS
[34785] : 1842+ BRIGHTON, VIC, AUS [34794] :
1800-1990 GLADSTONE, QLD, AUS [38070] : C1828
HAM, ENG [33880] : 1800S BRISTOL, GLS, ENG
[33958] : ALL LONDON, ENG [34151] : 1800+
MIDSOMER NORTON, SOM, ENG [34263] : PRE
1809 SOUTHWARK, SRY, ENG [34452] : PRE 1834
WALWORTH, SRY, ENG [34452] : ALL WAR, ENG
[34730] : PRE 1850 BRISTOL, GLS, ENG [34776] :
1800S SHOREDITCH, LND, ENG [34776] : 1850+
DUDLEY, WOR, ENG [34782] : 1813-1842 SRY,
ENG [34794] : 1760+ CARDINGTON, BDF, ENG
[35812] : 1800+ WOKING, SRY, ENG [36746] :
SUSAN 1800 CHELSEA, MDX, ENG [36890] : PRE
1845 TODDINGTON, BDF, ENG [37647] : PRE 1800
ULEY, GLS, ENG [38383]

MILLBURN 1840 ST BEES, CUL, ENG [38317] : 1850
DURHAM, DUR, ENG [38317]

MILLEN PRE 1840 KEN, ENG [38389]

MILLER PETER 1864+ CRYSTAL BROOK, SA, AUS
[34279] : PETER C1886 NHILL, VIC, AUS [34279] :
1870+ SYDNEY, NSW, AUS [34977] : 1880+
LYONVILLE, VIC, AUS [35040] : 1870+
WALHALLA, VIC, AUS [35040] : 1868+ FARADAY,
VIC, AUS [35040] : 1854+ FOREST CK, VIC, AUS
[35040] : C1850 GEELONG, VIC, AUS [35225] :
1850+ CASTLEMAINE, VIC, AUS [35242] : 1850+
BENDIGO, VIC, AUS [35416] : 1860+ YASS &
GUNDAGAI, NSW, AUS [36600] : 1839+
ADELAIDE, SA, AUS [37913] : 1850+ MAITLAND
& SINGLETON, NSW, AUS [37966] : 1825+
ADELAIDE, ONT, CAN [34375] : 1820+ SIMCOE
CO., ONT, CAN [34465] : PRE 1840 WILMOT, ONT,
CAN [35290] : PERMELIA C1800+
FREDERICKSBURG, ONT, CAN [37441] : JACOB
1796+ WENTWORTH CO., ONT, CAN [38751] :
SAMUEL 1840+ NORFOLK CO., ONT, CAN
[38751] : ELIJAH C1815 WENTWORTH CO., ONT,
CAN [38751] : 1800-1850 HOLSTIEN, DEN [35397] :
1800-1853 LND, ENG [33834] : PRE 1850 BUNGAY,
SFK, ENG [33935] : 1718 POWERSTOCK, DOR,
ENG [33967] : RICHARD 1777-1848 CHICHESTER,

SSX, ENG [34314] : 1835 WANDSWORTH, SRY,
ENG [34336] : 1775+ FINEDON, NTH, ENG [34416]
: 1860 MDX, ENG [34540] : PRE 1850 YKS, ENG
[34544] : PRE 1802 WOOTTON FITZPAINE, DOR,
ENG [34689] : 1680+ BUNWELL, NFK, ENG [34710]
: PRE 1810 BARLEY, HRT, ENG [34840] : DANIEL
PRE 1844 LONDON, MDX, ENG [34929] : 1800
WEST DERBY & LIVERPOOL, LAN, ENG [35006] :
PRE 1740 MAIDS MORETON, BKM, ENG [35030] :
PRE 1820 CANNOCK, STS, ENG [35061] : PRE 1860
SOM, ENG [35255] : MATILDA ANN C1840 ST
PETERS, KEN, ENG [35391] : ELIZABETH PRE
1904 STREATHAM, LND, ENG [35449] : EDWARD
C1785 CROWHURST, SSX, ENG [35560] : PRE 1800
CARLISLE, CUL, ENG [35592] : PRE 1900 MDX,
ENG [35604] : PRE 1893 HIGH WYCOMBE, BKM,
ENG [35772] : PRE 1860 KEN, ENG [36067] : PRE
1760 NEWCASTLE UPON TYNE, NBL, ENG
[36110] : 1890S-1900 SOUTHAMPTON, BRIXHAM,
DEV, ENG [36337] : 1910+ PLYMOUTH, DEV,
ENG [36376] : PRE 1800 ORMSKIRK, LAN, ENG
[36382] : PRE 1910 SOUTHWOLD, SFK, ENG [36486]
: SAMUEL 1870+ PIMLICO & BELGRAVIA, LND,
ENG [36510] : 1840+ CALNE, WIL, ENG [36697] :
1820+ RANMORE, SRY, ENG [36811] : THOMAS
1875-1952 WEDNESFIEL, STS, ENG [37085] : ALL
EAST BOLDRE, HAM, ENG [37637] : 1750-1850
WOODBURN, BKM, ENG [37735] : HENRY 1860S
LONDON, ENG [37743] : 1750-1850 WISBECH,
CAM & NFK, ENG [37765] : C1812 STEPNEY, LND,
ENG [37968] : PRE 1700 TINTAGEL, CON, ENG
[38214] : PRE 1810 LEI & WAR, ENG [38229] :
WILLIAM C1902 MANCHESTER, LAN, ENG
[38283] : C1530 ST ALBANS, HRT, ENG [38348] :
PRE 1850 WANBOROUGH, WIL, ENG [38383] :
C1850 ALS & LOR, FRA [38527] : PRE 1885
STRAKHOLT, OLD, GER [38173] : 1715-1749 GER
[38318] : PRE 1850 OPR & WPR, GER [38435] : ALL
BALLYMAGUIGAN, LDY, IRL [33823] : PRE 1800
TIP & LEX, IRL [33905] : PRE 1800 LIM, IRL [34060]
: PRE 1845 BELFAST, IRL [34270] : 1800S
ENNISKILLEN, FER, IRL [35134] : PRE 1800 ANT,
IRL [36271] : PRE 1820 ANT, IRL [36271] : JAMES
1800+ WIC, IRL [37165] : 1800+ TIPPERARY, TIP,
IRL [37422] : REBECCA PRE 1858 DUBLIN, IRL
[37481] : PRE 1820 DOWNPATRICK, DOW, IRL
[38190] : 1840+ CAMBRIDGE & PAEROA, NZ
[33823] : 1860+ PICTON, MBH, NZ [36746] : PRE
1764 LATHERON, CAI, SCT [33873] : PRE 1900
IRVINE, AYR, SCT [33966] : 1750+ ARDROSSAN &
SALTCOATS, AYR, SCT [34008] : 1700-1875 ARL,
SCT [34067] : 1731+ KILMAURS, AYR, SCT [34110]
: PRE 1806 DUNDEE, ANS, SCT [34336] : 1750-1850
KINNELL, ANS, SCT [34523] : PRE 1800 THURSO,
CAI, SCT [34576] : JESSIE PRE 1855+ WIG, SCT
[34592] : C1840 GLASGOW, LKS, SCT [34752] : PRE
1853 CASTLETOWN, CAI, SCT [34797] :
ELIZABETH 1760+ WEBSTER, CAI, SCT [34884] :
1750+ GLASGOW, SCT [35152] : 1819+ OLD &
NEW KILPATRICK, DNB, SCT [35579] : 1800-1850
OKI, SCT [35806] : 1778 EDINBURGH, SCT [35906] :
1750-1850 HALKIRK, CAI, SCT [35961] : 1800-65
CRIEFF, PER, SCT [36583] : PRE 1850 PER, SCT
[36754] : C1790+ EDAY, OKI, SCT [37413] : PRE
1850 LKS, SCT [37562] : C1842 FIF, SCT [37631] :
PRE 1925 BONNYBRIDGE, STI, SCT [37631] : 1700-
1800 DUNDONALD, AYR, SCT [37654] : PRE 1900
PAISLEY, RFW, SCT [38076] : 1750+ WICK, CAI,
SCT [38425] : 1600-1650 ROWLEY, MA, USA [34395] :
JOHN C1764-1826 PICKAWAY CO., OH, USA
[35284] : JOHN C1814-1900 FAYETTE CO., OH, USA
[35284] : PHILLIP ALL LA RUE CO., KY, USA

[35304] : JOHN 1822+ TN, USA [35312] : 1750-1850 BERKS CO., PA, USA [35318] : 1500-1900 USA [36114] : JOSEPH C1807-1870S CHESTER CO., PA, USA [36319] : BENJAMIN I. 1845+ CHESTER CO., PA, USA [36319] : ANNA L. 1858+ CHESTER CO., PA, USA [36319] : C1860-1883 EAU CLAIRE CO., WI, USA [36337] : 1815+ WAYNE CO., NY, USA [36342] : 1815+ PENFIELD, NY, USA [36342] : 1680-1720 MIDDLESEX CO., VA, USA [36737] : PRE 1800 PA, USA [36937] : MARIA 1700-1800 NY, USA [36962] : JOSEPH 1820S HUNTINGDON CO., PA, USA [37001] : 1820-1830S HICKMAN CO., TN, USA [37027] : JOHN 1840-1900 ONONDAGA CO., NY, USA [37541] : EZRA 1875-1925 POMONA, CA, USA [37544] : CYRUS 1830S ROWAN CO., NC, USA [37585] : C1850 SCOTLAND CO., MO, USA [37782] : 1834 OKMULGEE, OK, USA [38012] : WILLIAM 1808-1831 MA, USA [38124] : ELLE 1863-1926 LINCOLN, NE & CO., USA [38124] : 1790-1820 BUTLER CO., OH, USA [38137] : 1760 WESTMORELAND CO., PA, USA [38143] : 1800-1820 ERIE CO., PA, USA [38201] : 1749-1830S PA, USA [38318] : 1852+ GUTHRIE CO., IA, USA [38318] : PETER P. 1783-1852 MEYERSDALE, PA, OH & IA, USA [38532] : 1700+ WINDHAM, CUMBERLAND, ME, USA [38571] : 1750-1900 CROCUS, ADAIR CO., KY, USA [38574] : 1780-1900 BEDFORD CO., PA, USA [38735] : ANDREW 1865+ CERRO GORDO CO., IA, USA [38751] : JOHN 1921 SAC CO., IA, USA [38751] : ABRAHAM 1900 WOODWARD CO., OK, USA [38751] : ALL WORLDWIDE [37111]

MILLET DIT BEAUCHEMI ISABEL C1825 SAS, CAN [36678]

MILLETT 1700+ VA & CO, USA [34062] : 1775-1825 COLUMBIA CO., NY, USA [36555]

MILLETTE JEAN PRE 1650 ST SURIN, PCH, FRA [38408]

MILLEVILLE 1650S THORNEY ABBEY, CAM, ENG [34204]

MILLGATE 1900 ORANGE & PEAK HILL, NSW, AUS [37307] : 1820 BIRCHINGTON, KEN, ENG [34395]

MILLHOUS 1800+ BERLIN, PA, USA [37010]

MILLHOUSE ALL WOOLSTHORPE & SPALDING, LIN, ENG [37673]

MILLIARD CHARLES 1830+ MONTREAL, QUE, CAN [36138]

MILLICHAP 1800+ LEIGHTON, SAL, ENG [33855]

MILLIE 1839-1900 ADELAIDE & KUNGARILLA, SA, AUS [35524] : 1900-1930 CHILWELL, VIC, AUS [35524] : 1800-1850 COLOMBO, SRI LANKA, INDIA [35524] : 1700-1750 WEMYSS, FIF, SCT [33767] : 1800+ LARGO 'BALHOUSIE', FIF, SCT [35524]

MILLIGAN JOHN ALL AMARANTH, ONT, CAN [37440] : 1700-1900 ST ALBANS, HRT, ENG [38073] : PRE 1750 DONAGHCLONEY, DOW, IRL [35897] : JEAN 1835 AYR, SCT [34091] : 1800+ PETERHEAD, ABD, SCT [34560]

MILLIKIN PRE 1787 LND, ENG [36972]

MILLINER PRE 1898 LONG PRESTON, YKS, ENG [37242]

MILLINGTON C1890 HOBART, TAS, AUS [35865] : PRE 1820 WIL, ENG [35853] : C1750-1830 DERBY, DBY, ENG [36980] : PRE 1866 MIDDLESBROUGH, NRY, ENG [37204] : PRE 1800 BROSELEY & BENTHALL, SAL, ENG [37389] : EDWARD 1830-1889 MELVERLEY & GRINSHILL, SAL, ENG [37546] : 1854+ GRINSHILL & WEM, SAL, ENG [37546] : ALL ENG & WLS [36152] : PRE 1810 HAWARDEN & EWLOE, FLN, WLS [36849]

MILLIS 1850+ KINGSTON ON THAMES, SRY & MDX, ENG [37088]

MILLIST ALL WORLDWIDE [35136]

MILLMAN 1850+ VIC, AUS [38539] : 1800-1850 DEV, ENG [33834] : 1750-1850 SAL & WOR, ENG [35768] : 1800+ HEF, ENG [37328] : 1800+ DEV, ENG [38539]

MILLMORE PRE 1800 IOW, ENG [35342]

MILLNER PRE 1898 LONG PRESTON, YKS, ENG [37242]

MILLS JOSEPH ALL AUS [34320] : 1849+ SYDNEY, NSW, AUS [35443] : 1830+ CASTLEREAGH, NSW, AUS [35511] : ALL AUS [35831] : ELEANOR 1850S MELBOURNE, VIC, AUS [35958] : 1870+ MELBOURNE, VIC, AUS [36605] : 1880+ WIMMERA, VIC, AUS [36622] : 1880+ MAITLAND & SINGLETON, NSW, AUS [37966] : C1890+ COONAMBLE, NSW, AUS [38510] : 1830+ YORK CO., ONT, CAN [34482] : 1800-1900 BRANT CO., ONT, CAN [35605] : PRE 1850 NS, CAN [38386] : PRE 1800 ROGATE, SSX, ENG [34112] : PRE 1800 ROGATE, SSX, ENG [34112] : PRE 1850 SFK & NFK, ENG [34320] : 1850+ GREAT YARMOUTH, NFK, ENG [34482] : PRE 1794 STOCKTON ON TEES, DUR, ENG [34487] : 1830S CROYDON, SRY, ENG [34518] : MARY 1775 GREAT GADDESDEN, HRT, ENG [34539] : PRE 1835 MAIDSTONE, KEN, ENG [34689] : 1650+ UPLOWMAN, DEV, ENG [34747] : 1782+ SHILBOTTLE, NBL, ENG [35026] : PRE 1772 BILTON BARNS, NBL, ENG [35026] : C1703 CHIBBURN, NBL, ENG [35026] : 1780 KNAPTON, NFK, ENG [35046] : 1800-1850 DILTON, WIL, ENG [35076] : 1800-1850 MDX, ENG [35098] : 1850S WOR & CHS, ENG [35123] : C1640 HASCOMBE, GLS, ENG [35216] : 1700S READING & WANTAGE, BRK, ENG [35375] : PRE 1849 CROYDON, SRY, ENG [35443] : PRE 1820 BERMONDSEY, LND, ENG [35548] : 1760-1860 EXETER, DEV, ENG [35916] : ELEANOR 1822+ SHOREDITCH, LND, ENG [35958] : PRE 1800 NEWPORT, IOW, ENG [36021] : 1728-1800 TUDELEY & CAPEL, KEN, ENG [36049] : 1750-1850 CORTON, SFK, ENG [36057] : C1690-1765 CARDINGTON, BDF, ENG [36068] : PRE 1890 STS, ENG [36095] : JAMES PRE 1894 LIVERPOOL, LAN, ENG [36164] : 1750+ CORSHAM, SWINDON, WIL & BRK, ENG [36329] : 1800-1820 ST BRIDES, LND, ENG [36586] : ROBERT PRE 1820 HOLLINWOOD, MANCHESTER, LAN, ENG [36617] : 1600+ HILDERSTONE, STS, ENG [36701] : JAMES PRE 1770 BURFORD, OXF, ENG [36889] : RICHARD PRE 1735 BURFORD, OXF, ENG [36889] : PRE 1850 BOLDRE, HAM, ENG [37173] : C1800 BRAMPTON, SFK, ENG [37191] : 1800+ LONDON, ENG [37194] : 1858+ OXFORD, OXF, ENG [37202] : 1650-1720 MARLBOROUGH, WIL, ENG [37233] : PRE 1810 LONGPARISH, HAM, ENG [37273] : PRE 1800 BRADSHAW, HAM, ENG [37273] : ALL NYMPSFIELD, GLS, ENG [37279] : PRE 1800 SOUTH EAST, SFK, ENG [37420] : 1800+ ACTON & LONG MELFORD, SFK, ENG [37638] : 1720-1792 HULL, ERY, ENG [37638] : 1700 GERMANSWEEK, DEV, ENG [37733] : 1800 MOUNT BURES, ESS, ENG [37928] : 1800+ MOG, IRL [33829] : PRE 1850 FAIRYMOUNT, ROS, IRL [35216] : 1830+ TRAMORE, WAT, IRL [35719] : C1800 ULSTER, IRL [37795] : 1880+ PALMERSTON NORTH, MWT, NZ [36746] : GEORGE 1890+ FEILDING, NZ [36889] : 1750+ EDINBURGH, MLN, SCT [34420] : PRE 1863 ARBROATH, PER, SCT [35441] : 1800+ DUNOON, ARL, SCT [36746] : PETER 1660+ WINDSOR, CT, USA [36335] : STEPHEN 1776 FAIRFIELD, CT, USA [36447] : STEPHEN 1756-1845 TIOGA, NYS, USA [36447] : MEHITIBEL 1721-1825 TIOGA, NYS, USA [36447] : STEPHEN 1756

WESTCHESTER, NYS, USA [36447] : PRE 1760
DUTCHESS CO., NY, USA [37018] : PRE 1800S NY,
USA [37522] : ALL OH & IL, USA [38043]

MILLSTEAD 1838+ SYDNEY, NSW, AUS [37915] :
PRE 1838 ROLVENDON, KEN, ENG [37915]

MILLWARD PRE 1831 KIDDERMINSTER, WOR,
ENG [36230] : ALL KENDAL, WES, ENG [36230] :
1874+ LEVENSHULME, LAN, ENG [36230] : 1830-
80 WEST BROMWICH, STS, ENG [37283] : 1760-
1820 LONGBRIDGE, WAR, ENG [37632]

MILN 1855+ CANTERBURY, NZ [35584] : C1740
STRACATHRO, ANS, SCT [34713] : 1780-1867
DRON, PER, SCT [35584]

MILNE 1890+ HOBART, TAS, AUS [34904] : JOHN
1866+ RIVERTON, SA, AUS [34922] : ALL
STRANGWAYS, VIC, AUS [35526] : 1890+
MELBOURNE, VIC, AUS [36825] : 1857+ SYDNEY,
NSW, AUS [38211] : 1880+ LONDON, ENG [34922] :
1840+ WEDNESBURY, STS, ENG & NZ [36819] :
1800 ABERDEEN, ABD, SCT [34210] : 1843
LOCHGELLY, FIF, SCT [34529] : 1830S LESLIE,
ABD, SCT [34591] : 1811+ EDINBURGH, MLN,
SCT [34922] : 1780+ INVERESK, MLN, SCT [34922]
: 1700+ AIRTH, STI, SCT [34977] : 1782
FOCHABERS, MOR, SCT [35848] : 1800S
INVERURIE, ABD, SCT [36843] : 1728+ ST
NICHOLAS, ABD, SCT [37260] : 1805 MORTLACH,
BAN, SCT [37260] : C1650-1800 OLD MACHAR,
ABD, SCT [37260] : 1834 BRECHIN, ANS, SCT
[37260] : PRE 1857 ABERDEEN, ABD, SCT [38211] :
1800+ PETERHEAD, ABD, SCT [38253] : 1862
FETTERESSO, KCD, SCT [38470] : JAMES C1820-
1851 KIRKWALL, OKI, SCT & AUS [37559]

MILNER 1974+ BRISBANE, QLD, AUS [35455] : PRE
1810 HYLTON, DUR, ENG [34594] : ALL
PRESTON, LAN, ENG [35058] : 1798
HUDDERSFIELD, YKS, ENG [35061] : 1907+
BIRMINGHAM, WAR, ENG [35455] : 1800 WELL,
NRY, ENG [36147] : 1834-1860 THORALBY, NRY,
ENG [36217] : 1800+ JARROW, DUR, ENG [37134] :
PRE 1898 LONG PRESTON, YKS, ENG [37242] :
PRE 1900 MANCHESTER, LAN, ENG [37353] :
1700-1900 BRIDGNORTH, SAL, ENG [38073] : 1800-
1900 BIRMINGHAM, WAR, ENG [38073]

MILNES PRE 1880 NETHER BROUGHTON, LEI,
ENG [38568]

MILORD PRE 1757 NOVIOUS, CHA, FRA [38178] :
1757-1990 WORLDWIDE [38178]

MILROY 1840+ GIPPSLAND, VIC, AUS [35776] :
1890S LEEDS, WRY, ENG [34854] : ALL AYR, SCT
[34040] : PRE 1800 KKD, SCT [34197]

MILSAPPS C1850 MARSHALL, AK, USA [36899]

MILSOM 1750-1900 BITTON & HANHAM, GLS,
ENG [34714]

MILSON ALL BEVERLEY & SHEFFIELD, YKS,
ENG [36405]

MILSOP 1800-1900 BERGEN CO., NJ, USA [38337]

MILSTED ALL FAVERSHAM, KEN, ENG [34093]

MILSTEIN PRE 1900 BERDITCHEV, UKRAINE,
USSR [35635]

MILTHORP C1857 BEECHWORTH, VIC, AUS [35585]

MILTON 1900+ SOUTH, AFRICA [37920] : THOMAS
1814 NSW, AUS [35831] : 1836+ ADELAIDE, SA,
AUS [37913] : 1840+ NEWCASTLE & WALLSEND,
NSW, AUS [37920] : PRE 1851 MDX, ENG [34661] :
1800S MDX, ENG [35959] : 1750-1850
WATERBEACH, CAM, ENG [37747] : 1780-1801
HACKNEY, LND, ENG [37920] : JAMES 1800-1828
ISLINGTON, LND, ENG [37920] : PRE 1900
PLYMOUTH, DEV, ENG [37949]

MILVERTON 1857+ SYDNEY, NSW, AUS [34905]

MILWAIN 1800+ ALBANY CO., NY, USA [36962]

MILWARD JAMES PRE 1820 LEI, ENG [34311] : PRE
1800 CHURCH LENCH, WOR, ENG [37703]

MIMMS 1600-1800S NTH, BDF & LEI, ENG [36173] :
1600-1800S MDX, SRY & HRT, ENG [36173] : 160Q-
1800S BKM, OXF & WAR, ENG [36173]

MIMS 1600-1800S NTH, BDF & LEI, ENG [36173] :
1600-1800S MDX, SRY & HRT, ENG [36173] : 1600-
1800S BKM, OXF & WAR, ENG [36173]

MINARD PRE 1850 KING & VAUGHAN TWP., ONT,
CAN [36696]

MINARIKA PRE 1900 BLATNA, BOHEMIA, CS
[37569]

MINAUD JEAN 1600+ FRA [37429]

MINCH PRE 1845 GER [35028]

MINCHIN 1870+ NSW, AUS [33765] : C1846 BRK,
ENG [34668] : 1700+ LONDON, ENG [36291] : 1800-
1840 IRL [35192] : 1800-1840 ELPHIN, ROS, IRL
[35192]

MINCHINTON 1800S NORTON SUB HAMDON,
SOM, ENG [37544]

MINCK ALL MEK, GER [34603] : 1820 HESSE
DARMSTADT, GER [36900]

MINDELSOHN ALL WORLDWIDE [34318]

MINDENHALL 1750-1850 LONDON, MDX, ENG
[36769]

MINDRUP ALL OSTFRIESLAND, NDS, BRD [38685]

MINEHAN 1800S IRL [37309]

MINER 1800-1850 VT, USA [33753] : PRE 1860
BOWLING GREEN, KY, USA [37394] : ALL
WORLDWIDE [37394] : ALL WORLDWIDE [38766]

MINERS JAMES 1848+ MONARO, NSW, AUS
[33815] : JOHN 1848+ MONARO, NSW, AUS [33815]
: WILLIAM 1848+ MONARO, NSW, AUS [33815] :
1850+ BLACKSTOCK, ONT, CAN [38395] : 1750+
CREED, CON, ENG [37224] : PRE 1850 TRURO,
CON, ENG [37394] : 1912 FALMOUTH, CON, ENG
[37975] : ALL PA, USA [37394] : ALL WORLDWIDE
[37394]

MINETT 1820+ BISHOPS CLEEVE, GLS, ENG
[35138]

MING ALL BKM, ENG [37345]

MINHINNICK 1830+ BODMIN, CON, ENG [34128]

MINIFIE PRE 1800 WESTMINSTER, LND, ENG
[36474] : ALL BROADHEMBURY, DEV, ENG
[37617]

MINNABARRIET PRE 1860 BASQUE, FRA [34164]

MINNE 1500+ WORLDWIDE [38161]

MINNEY PRE 1840 LND, ENG [33830]

MINNICK 1783+ LANCASTER CO., PA & OH, USA
[36540]

MINNIS 1870+ WINDSOR, ONT, CAN [34983] : PRE
1857 ARM, IRL [36509] : PRE 1755 DON & DOW,
IRL [38311] : 1800-1860 CRAWFORD CO., PA, NY &
OH, USA [37529] : JOHN PRE 1780 ORANGE CO.,
NC, USA [37786] : PRE 1760 VA, USA [38311] : PRE
1755 PA, USA [38311]

MINNISS JANE 1800+ DOW, IRL [36813]

MINNOCK PRE 1900 CLARA, OFF, IRL [36596]

MINNOGUE PRE 1863 BALLYVAUGHAN, CLA, IRL
[35206]

MINNS 1700-40 HOLT, NFK, ENG [35524] : 1830+
EDGEFIELD, NFK, ENG [35524]

MINOGUE ALL KIK, IRL [33872] : PRE 1870 LIM,
IRL [34555] : C1800-1848 COR, IRL [35389] : 1800+
TOMGRANEY, CLA, IRL [35566]

MINOR ALL WORLDWIDE [37394]

MINORGAN PRE 1806 FIF, SCT [35223]

MINORS ALL WORLDWIDE [37394]

MINSELL PRE 1765 BREEDON ON THE HILL, LEI,
ENG [37754]

MINSHELL PRE 1765 BREEDON ON THE HILL,
LEI, ENG [37754]

MINSHEW 1600+ WOR, ENG [38185]

MINSHULL 1790+ BIRMINGHAM, WAR, ENG [36045] : PRE 1875 STS, ENG [37098]

MINTER C1800 LAMBETH, SRY & LND, ENG [35495] : ALL THANET, KEN, ENG & AUS [34040]

MINTO 1738 ALWINTON, NBL, ENG [38269] : 1800-1990 SPENNYMOOR, DUR, ENG [38269]

MINTOFT PRE 1800 PICKERING, NRY, ENG [38356]

MINTON 1550-1760 WOR, ENG [37217] : SIMON PRE 1780 CAMPBELL, VA, USA [33757] : WILLIAM PRE 1780 VA, USA [33757]

MINTY 1774+ STONEHOUSE, GLS, ENG [35815] : ALL BROMHAM, WIL, ENG [37972] : 1857-1890S MADRAS, INDIA [35815] : ALL ABD, SCT [34861]

MINTZ ALL PRINCE EDWARD CO., ONT, CAN [35608]

MINVILLE 1775+ STE ELIZABETH, QUE, CAN [34082]

MIONEYHAN C1801+ KER, IRL & AUS [36642]

MIOTK 1707-1890 SIANOWO, GDANSK, POL [38148]

MIRAMS ALL AUS & UK [34961]

MIRANDA 1700+ LANCASTER, PA & OH, USA & ENG [38336]

MIRAU ELEANORE 1820+ DANZIG, GER [35712]

MIREHOUSE 1650-1850 ASPATRIA, CUL, ENG [37654]

MIRKOVIC PRE 1870 TRAPANJ, YU [33839]

MIRKOVICH PRE 1870 TRAPANJ, YU [33839]

MIRS ALL GER [38627]

MISCAMPBELL ALL BELFAST, DOW, IRL [37303]

MISCHKE ALL POM & WPR, GER [38687]

MISKIMMINS 1867-1874 BELFAST, ANT, IRL [35820] : 1853 CARRICKFERGUS, ANT, IRL [35820]

MISKIMMINS (SEE SKIM [35820]

MISON 1711+ HORSEHEATH, CAM, ENG [34334]

MISSEN 1850-1900 CHRISTCHURCH, NZ [37969]

MISSIAEN CAROLUS PRE 1800 TORHOUT, WVL, BEL [34061]

MISSIN PRE 1950 DOWNHAM, CAM, ENG [36489]

MISSON ROBERT 1840-1860 STETCHWORTH, CAM, ENG [36018]

MIST PRE 1800 CARISBROOK, IOW, ENG [37321]

MITCHEL PRE 1804 CORTACHY, ANS, SCT [34447]

MITCHELE PRE 1860 LND, ENG [34819]

MITCHELL 1850 CRESWICK, VIC, AUS [34421] : EDWARD PRE 1893 AUGATHELLA, QLD, AUS [34587] : 1900+ NORTHAM, WA, AUS [34764] : CORNELIUS 1840+ ADELAIDE, SA, AUS [35429] : JOHN BUTLER 1900+ AUS [35429] : 1856+ STH YARRA, VIC, AUS [35825] : JAMES D. 1860S+ MELBOURNE, VIC, AUS [35876] : C1860 HOBART, TAS, AUS [36793] : WILLIAM 1880-1900 NARRABRI, NSW, AUS [37904] : 1885+ MELBOURNE, VIC, AUS [38059] : 1840 WINDSOR, NSW, AUS [38214] : 1800S WALLSEND, NSW, AUS [38490] : 1880+ KAMERUKA, NSW, AUS [38491] : JOHN 1842-1894 CRAIGIE, VIC, AUS & ENG [37559] : HENRY 1837-1920S ARCHDALE, VIC, AUS & ENG [37559] : JOSEPH 1841-1919 MAJORCA, VIC, AUS & ENG [37559] : GEORGE 1848-1923 COROWA, NSW, AUS & ENG [37559] : 1890+ LONDON, ONT, CAN [34982] : ELIZABETH PRE 1876 ONT, CAN [35641] : 1800S MIDDLESEX CO., ONT, CAN [38414] : 1823+ PEI, CAN [38460] : 1800S REDRUTH, CON, ENG [33834] : 1750-1850 CRANTOCK, CON, ENG [34028] : PRE 1800 SOMERTON, OXF, ENG [34112] : WILLIAM 1750-1850 PER, ENG [34143] : 1850+ RUSHTON, DOR, ENG [34266] : PRE 1828 ST KEVERNE, CON, ENG [34275] : 1819+ DOR, ENG [34308] : 1700 SHEFFORD, BRK, ENG [34321] : 1750-1850 LAWHITTON, CON, ENG [34337] : 1800+

WHITTLESEY, CAM, ENG [34421] : 1820+ YAXLEY, HUN, ENG [34421] : 1840 PORT ISAAC, CON, ENG [34565] : PRE 1860 SOM, ENG [34638] : ALL GWINEAR, CON, ENG [34877] : 1800S KENWYN, CON, ENG [35076] : C1771 STUDLEY, WIL, ENG [35090] : 1853 ST AUSTELL, CON, ENG [35152] : ALL STAMFORD, LIN, ENG [35177] : PRE 1900 HUNTINGDON & GODMANCHESTER, HUN, ENG [35255] : C1800 CHATHAM, KEN, ENG [35350] : JOHN BUTLER 1850+ YKS, ENG [35429] : THOMAS 1800+ WOOLWICH, KEN, ENG [35429] : 1800+ ROXETH & HARROW, MDX, ENG [35436] : PRE 1827 ZENNOR, CON, ENG [35441] : ALL BATH, SOM, ENG [35474] : 1851-59 DURHAM, DUR, ENG [35482] : 1790+ BLYTHE, NBL, ENG [35482] : 1800S+ GOLANT, CON, ENG [35489] : 1800-1900 CALSTOCK, CON, ENG [35489] : C1700 MEVAGISSEY, CON, ENG [35563] : 1900+ BRADFORD, YKS, ENG [35734] : C1800 HALIFAX, WRY, ENG [35744] : 1800+ NORTHAM, DEV, ENG [35768] : 1830+ BETHNAL GREEN, MDX, ENG [35825] : 1750+ RAMSEY, HUN, ENG [35825] : 1810+ BURY, LAN, ENG [35825] : ALL SSX, ENG [35998] : 1600-1800 WESTMINSTER, MDX, ENG [36106] : 1800-1850 SHOREDITCH, LND, ENG [36111] : JANE 1856+ BRENTFORD & EALING, MDX, ENG [36212] : C1850 GLOSSOP, DBY, ENG [36242] : JONATHAN C1800 SHEFFIELD, WRY & SFK, ENG [36479] : 1800+ BAYSWATER, MDX, ENG [36685] : PRE 1860 CLAPHAM, SRY, ENG [36793] : PRE 1885 SPARKBRIDGE, LAN, ENG [36888] : 1680-1900 KENWYN, CON, ENG [36961] : PRE 1879 SOUTHAMPTON, HAM, ENG [36993] : PRE 1844+ MARIZION, CON, ENG [37108] : ALL HAMMERSMITH, LND, ENG [37355] : 1841 HARDINGTON MANDEVILLE, SOM, ENG [37378] : 1780+ SNEINTON, NTT, ENG [37391] : MARY 1852-1877 ST BLAZEY, CON, ENG [37443] : PRE 1865 MANCHESTER, LAN, ENG [37573] : 1780-1840 TYLDESLEY, LAN, ENG [37573] : 1840+ GOLBORNE, LAN, ENG [37573] : PRE 1660 BIDEFORD, DEV, ENG [37587] : 1750+ LEI, ENG [37598] : PRE 1740 HOLBETON, DEV, ENG [37610] : C1800 WELFORD, NTH, ENG [37711] : C1870 SETTLE, YKS, ENG [37711] : C1800 LONG BUCKBY, NTH, ENG [37711] : PRE 1836 CON, ENG [38069] : 1766-1840 ALTARNUM, CON, ENG [38151] : 1700-1800 HOLBETON, DEV, ENG [38516] : ROBERT C1804-1886 BRYANSTON, DOR, ENG & AUS [37559] : ALL INDIA [36300] : HENRY E. 1860+ BAREILLY, INDIA [36300] : ALL COLERAINE, LDY, IRL [34160] : PRE 1840 KILLERA, ARM, IRL [35075] : PRE 1834 GAL, IRL [35090] : JOHN C1820 BALLINTOY, ANT, IRL [35501] : 1840 KILKEEL, DOW, IRL [35529] : 1800+ BELFAST, ANT, DOW & ARM, IRL [35636] : 1800+ TIP, IRL [35951] : 1800+ DONNYBROOK, DUB, IRL [37598] : ALL LEX, IRL [38293] : 1800+ GLENDERMOTT, LDY, IRL [38379] : PRE 1823 LEX, IRL [38460] : 1910 NZ [34421] : 1860+ CHRISTCHURCH, NZ [34638] : 1885+ INVERCARGILL, SI, NZ [36628] : 1800+ BALLANTRAE, AYR, SCT [33781] : PRE 1900 EDINBURGH, MLN, SCT [33799] : EBENEZER 1800+ TILLICOULTRY, CLK, SCT [33846] : JAMES 1890 MAYBOLE, AYR, SCT [34091] : JAMES 1869 WIGTOWN, SCT [34091] : 1800+ LOCHGAIR, ARL, SCT [34232] : 1860+ GALASHIELS, ROX, SCT [34379] : PRE 1850 STI, SCT [34466] : PRE 1912 BARRHEAD, RFW, SCT [34706] : 1800+ PENICUIK, MLN, SCT [34852] : JAMES 1844 BALBEGGIE, PER, SCT [35463] : C1810 DALGETY,

FIF, SCT [35714] : 1770+ CRAIL, FIF, SCT [35822] :
ROBERT 1800S ST ANDREWS, FIF, SCT [35876] :
1800+ CUMBERNAULD, DNB, SCT [36257] : 1740-
1780 MORTLACH, BAN, SCT [36783] : MARGARET
1780S MUTHILL, PER, SCT [37106] : PRE 1800
ABERDEEN, ABD, SCT [37245] : JAMES C1843
TEALING, FORFAR, ANS, SCT [37684] : ALL
ALYTH, PER, SCT [37744] : 1700-1800 GLASGOW,
SCT [37898] : 1800S FIF, SCT [38490] : 1700+
SAUCHENS, PER, SCT [38726] : 1900+ DETROIT,
MI, USA [34232] : 1800-1900 DARLINGTON,
BEAVER CO., PA, USA [36449] : 1700+ KNOX CO.,
TN, USA [37004] : SOLOMON 1840S
WASHINGTON, VA, USA [37604] : 1834
OKMULGEE, OK, USA [38012] : 1885+ LOS
ANGELES, CA, USA [38059] : PRE 1866 AUGUSTA,
GA, USA [38126] : 1845-70 MARSHALL CO., IL,
USA [38151] : 1894+ WORLDWIDE [35482]

MITCHELMORE 1750-1880 STOKE CLIMSLAND,
CON & DEV, ENG [37339]

MITCHEM C1800 TAZEWELL CO., VA, USA [38044]

MITCHEN ALL ENG [37269]

MITCHENER ALL ENG [34970] : 1770S NEWHAVEN,
SSX, ENG [35260] : 1700S-1800S LND, ENG [35531]

MITCHESON 1850+ NEWBIGGIN, NBL, ENG
[36609]

MITCHLEY 1700-1820 WISBECH, CAM, ENG [38381] :
1700-1890 NFK, ENG [38381]

MITLENER PRE 1945 GROSS AUPA, GER [38674]

MITTELSTAEDT ALL POS, GER [37529]

MITTEN PRE 1810 ROCHDALE, LAN, ENG [36102] :
PRE 1840 CHURCH STOKE, MGY, WLS [37137]

MITTENS PRE 1850 BETHNAL GREEN, LND, ENG
[34825]

MITTON C1880 LONDON, ENG [35014]

MIVILLE PRE 1700 CARTIGNY, GE, CH [38348]

MIXON LOUISA C1844 WASHINGTON, LA, USA
[37801]

MIZE 1750 LUNENBURG, VA, USA [38198]

MIZEN PRE 1900 SOUTH WRAXALL, WIL, ENG
[37248] : PRE 1900 BRADFORD ON AVON, WIL,
ENG [37248]

MIZSER PRE 1832 RADABANYA & SZUHOGY,
BORSOD, HU [37547]

MOAD SARAH PRE 1876 ONT, CAN [35641]

MOAT PRE 1810 WHITBY, NRY, ENG [38580]

MOATE PRE 1900 SYDNEY, NSW, AUS [34978]

MOBBERLEY ALL WORLDWIDE [34286]

MOBBS 1798+ PENNANT HILLS, NSW, AUS [34685]
: 1800+ PENNANT HILLS, NSW, AUS [35360] :
C1898 NSW, AUS [35807] : 1800S PENNANT HILLS
& CARLINGFORD, NSW, AUS [37988] : PRE 1798
MDX, ENG [34685] : PRE 1790 LONDON, ENG
[35360] : 1800-1900 LEICESTER, LEI, ENG [37858] :
ALL MDX, ENG [37868] : 1700S BKM, ENG [38350] :
1700S OXF, ENG [38350]

MOBERLEY ALL CHS, ENG [34286] : ALL
WORLDWIDE [34286]

MOBERLY ALL CAN [34286] : ALL HAM & CHS,
ENG [34286] : ALL WORLDWIDE [34286]

MOCABEE 1790+ USA & UK [36357]

MOCATTA ALL WORLDWIDE [38211]

MOCHRIE 1750-1800 BO'NESS, WLN, SCT [36431]

MOCKER 1832-1910 STEGLITZ, BRA, GER & AUS
[35763]

MOCKLAR 1808+ PARRAMATTA, NSW, AUS
[34967]

MODE 1788-1800 ABD, SCT [38407]

MODENA PRE 1897 BRIGHTON, SSX, ENG [36215]

MOE 1710-1880 NH, USA [38054]

MOEBUS C1800+ SCHIEBUS, BRA, GER [35834]

MOELLER PRE 1837 STEINHAUS, KURHESSEN,
GER [38618] : 1980 BAD PYRMONT, PYR, GER
[38749] : 1912 ELBRINXEN, LIP, GER [38749] : 1782
BARNTRUP, LIP, GER [38749] : ALL
WORLDWIDE [37366]

MOELLINGER ALL FRA [36342] : ALL ST LOUIS,
MO, USA [36342]

MOENCH PRE 1760 WINGERODE, PSA, GER [38048]

MOERKE 1870-1900 SHAWANO CO., WI, USA [36546]

MOES (SEE MOSE) [36883]

MOESELER ALL HUESTEN, WEF, GER [34861]

MOESSINGER 1650-1750 AUERBACH, HES, BRD
[35311]

MOFFAT PRE 1860 ENG [35352] : ALL OMAGH,
TYR, IRL [34863] : 1860+ OREWA & AUCKLAND,
NZ [36245] : AGNES PRE 1760 NEW BATTLE,
MLN, SCT [33807] : C1800-1840 ROX, SCT [34479] :
ALL DFS, SCT [35293] : 1670 LINN MILL, DFS, SCT
[35350] : C1700+ NEWLANDS, PEE, SCT [35834] :
ALL DFS, SCT [36429] : 1700S TWEEDSMUIR, PEE,
SCT [37329] : 1740-1790 BARONY, LKS, SCT [37872]

MOFFATT 1840-1950 HURON CO., ONT, CAN [36901]
: ALL ST WINNOW & LANLIVERY, CON, ENG
[33823] : 1800S CONVOY, DON, IRL [35134] : 1700-
1850 BALLENY, ANT, IRL & USA [36918]

MOFFETT PRE 1850 AUGUSTA CO., VA, KY & OH,
USA [38570]

MOFFITT 1800-1850 NSW, AUS [36440] : PRE 1750
BELLINGHAM, NBL, ENG [37635] : 1800+
IRVINESTOWN, FER, IRL [38001] : 1842+ WEM,
IRL [38018] : JOHN 1830S GLASGOW, SCT [36316]

MOGG C1807 BRISTOL, ENG [35748] : PRE 1800
HEYTESBURY, WIL & SOM, ENG [37410] : 1835+
BRISTOL, GLS, ENG [37986] : PRE 1856 CARDIFF,
WLS [37986]

MOGGE PRE 1700 SCHACHTEN, HES, GER [38642]

MOGGRIDGE PRE 1775 DARTMOUTH, DEV, ENG
[34389]

MOGINI ALL WORLDWIDE [34050]

MOGINIE 1890+ CA, USA [34050] : ALL
WORLDWIDE [34050] : ALL WORLDWIDE [34050]

MOGINIER ALL CHESALLES, FR, CH [34050]

MOGRIDGE 1810-1900 MOLLAND & KNOWSTONE,
DEV, ENG [37096]

MOHLACK C1909 BLUFF SPRINGS, FL, USA [37022]

MOHODY 1800-1860 GRANARD & LONGFORD,
LOG, IRL [35732]

MOHR 1916 NEWTOWN, NSW, AUS [34694] :
EUSTACE PRE 1837 NEIDRHOLM, DDR [35426] :
GEORGE FRED. 1837+ NEIDRHOLM, DDR &
AUS [35426] : 1800S STOCKPORT, CHS, ENG
[35595] : PRE 1870 KUSEL, RPR, GER [35930] : PRE
1870 BISCHBERG, BAV, GER [35930]

MOILES PRE 1860 COOLBANAGHER, LEX, IRL
[36581] : 1800-1860 ROSCREA, TIP, IRL [36581]

MOIR JOHN 1660 WAULKMILL OF BALVENIE,
BAN, SCT [34479] : C1760 LOGIE PERT, ANS, SCT
[34814] : PRE 1855 DUNDEE, ANS, SCT [34922] :
1750-1790 DYSART, FIF, SCT [36268] : ALL PER,
SCT [36429] : PRE 1780 KINNEFF AND
CATTERLINE, KCD, SCT [37253] : 1800+ ABD,
SCT [37443] : 1700+ YORWOOD, STI, SCT [38726]

MOLD C1870 ONDIT, VIC, AUS [35807] : 1830+ AUS
[37557] : C1850 MARYLEBONE, LND, ENG [37053] :
PRE 1850 MIDDLETON CHENEY, NTH, ENG
[37557]

MOLDEN 1700+ LYDIARD TREGOZE, WIL, ENG
[36512]

MOLE ALL WEST CHEVINGTON, NTH, ENG
[36869] : 1750-1920 PLYMOUTH, DEV, ENG [37211]

MOLE (SEE MOULE) [34552]

MOLENAAR 1802-1869 NOH, NL [38711]

MOLES C1780 ST JOHN'S, NFD, CAN [34096]

MOLESWORTH 1800+ BASIL (BALSALL) HEATH, ENG [35584] : 1800+ KINGS NORTON, ENG [35584] : DAVID 1800-1870 BIRMINGHAM, WAR, ENG [36814] : FREDERICK 1800+ BIRMINGHAM, WAR, ENG [36814] : C1780-1810 PORTSMOUTH, HAM, ENG [37943] : 1810-1850 CHICHESTER, SSX, ENG [37943]

MOLHOEK 1700S ZUID BEVELAND, ZEL, NL [38350]

MOLLAND 1840 LIVERPOOL, LAN, ENG [38020]

MOLLARD PRE 1880 TAVISTOCK, DEV, ENG [35709] : 1875-1892 RUSSELL, NZ [35709]

MOLLER 1850-1870S TAARS, JUTLAND, DEN [36285]

MOLLETT 1600-1850 NORWICH, NFK, ENG [37670]

MOLLINS 1850+ OXFORD CO., ONT, CAN [36710]

MOLLISON 1750-1850 INVERKEILLOR, ANS, SCT [34523] : 1840-1860 DUNMORE, ARL, SCT [35102]

MOLLOY MARGARET 1872+ GUNDY, NSW, AUS [35412] : 1890+ OLDHAM, LAN, ENG [34790] : 1860S IRL [34937] : PRE 1841 OFF, IRL [35399] : 1821-1891 HEMLOCK, MI, USA [38102]

MOLONEY 1840+ BRAIDWOOD, NSW, AUS [35510] : PATRICK PRE 1839 MEELICK, CLA, IRL [35083] : 1800 KILFEACLE, TIP, IRL [35809]

MOLONY 1860+ SA, AUS [33789] : 1800+ CLA, IRL [33789] : PRE 1870 THURLES, TIP, IRL [37415]

MOLROY 1821-1891 HEMLOCK, MI, USA [38102]

MOLSHER PRE 1850 ENG [35771]

MOLSOME 1800-1875 HOLBEACH, LIN, ENG [35422]

MOLT 1830-1850 ALFDORF, WURTTEMBERG, GER [38689] : 1850-1870 LORCH, WUE, GER [38689]

MOLTENBREY 1878+ BOSTON, MA, USA [37823]

MOLTON JOSEPH 1780-1800 MILFORD, CT, USA [38138]

MOLYNEAUX 1750+ WIGAN, LAN, ENG [38260] : 1750+ ADLINGTON, LAN, ENG [38260] : 1750+ MANCHESTER, LAN, ENG [38260] : 1750+ GLOSSOP & TINTWISTLE, DBY, ENG [38260] : 1750+ ROCHDALE, LAN, ENG [38260]

MOLYNEUX PRE 1848 ST HELENS, LAN, ENG [33912] : 1820 LIVERPOOL, LAN, ENG [35282] : 1750+ TOOTING, LND, ENG [36232] : C1780 WESTHOUGHTON, LAN, ENG [36742] : 1790+ BIRMINGHAM, WAR, ENG [37258] : 1850-1886 WIGAN, LAN, ENG [37262] : 1886+ WARNFORD, HAM, ENG [37262] : 1700+ ORMSKIRK, LAN, ENG [37262] : PRE 1830 WESTMINSTER, MDX, ENG [37729] : PRE 1900 WIGAN, LAN, ENG [37892] : 1900-1911 SOUTHAMPTON & UPHAM, HAM, ENG [37892] : 1300+ ENG [38021] : 1840S WIGAN, LAN, ENG [38283]

MOMNEY 1860+ TILBURY, ONT, CAN [34983]

MONAGHAN ALL FREMANTLE, VIC & WA, AUS [34561] : 1830S MAITLAND, NSW, AUS [35226] : 1814-1830 GRANARD, LOG, IRL [35044] : PRE 1830 GAL, IRL [35226] : C1860 IRL [35820] : 1700-1900 DUB, IRL [38073] : 1915-1936 GLASGOW, LKS, SCT [35820] : C1890 OLD KILPATRICK & DUNTOCHER, DNB, SCT [35820]

MONAHAN 1840-1870 GRENVILLE CO., ONT, CAN [34407] : 1870+ SIMCOE CO., ONT, CAN [34407]

MONAR 1844+ BENDIGO, VIC, AUS [35384] : PRE 1844 GLASGOW, SCT [35384]

MONCKTON 1885+ ARMIDALE, NSW, AUS [37316]

MONCRIEF PRE 1830 EDINBURGH, MLN, SCT [35748]

MONCRIEFF MARGARET C1847-1915 AYR, AYR, SCT [34300]

MONCRIEFFE 1850S LOXTON, SOM, ENG [36741]

MONCUR 1600-1700 DUNDEE, ANS, SCT [34513] : 1756-1774 ABBOTSHALL, FIF, SCT [36770]

MONDAY PRE 1919 ROSENEATH, ONT, CAN [38450]

MONDS PRE 1800 SLI, IRL [33905]

MONETTE 1800S GATINEAU CO., QUE, CAN [34199]

MONEY 1800-1930 PETERSFIELD & LISS, HAM, ENG [34514] : PRE 1865 GRAFFHAM, SSX, ENG [36215] : PRE 1750 NFK, ENG [37712] : 1870S NASEBY, SI, NZ [35509] : 1720-1800 CECIL, MD, USA [38768]

MONEYPENNY PRE 1850 ARM, IRL [37927]

MONGAN PRE 1859 DROMORE, TYR, IRL [34582] : 1858 WI, USA [34582]

MONGOMERY PRE 1700 AYR, SCT [38321]

MONILAWS PRE 1675 LONGNIDDRY, ELN, SCT [37852]

MONK 1800-1870 LONDON, ENG [34464] : ALL HARTLEPOOL, DUR, ENG [34619] : PRE 1800 LONDON, MDX, ENG [36379] : ALL OCKHAM, SRY, ENG [36430] : ALL SRY, ENG [36430] : 1700+ CHESHUNT, HRT, ENG [36434] : 1800+ TETSWORTH, OXF, ENG [36434] : PRE 1797 CHEDDINGTON, BKM, ENG [37909] : PRE 1800 IRL [33869]

MONKHOUSE PRE 1800 CUL, ENG [35423] : C1750 LONGSLEDDALE, WES, ENG [36779] : C1850 NEWPORT, MON, WLS [36779]

MONKLAND 1820+ WORCESTER, WOR, ENG [37889]

MONKLEY 1850+ LONDON, ENG [34415]

MONKS PRE 1800 IRL [33869] : PRE 1850 BAGENALSTOWN, CAR, IRL [35444] : 1800+ DUBLIN, IRL [36236] : 1872+ NAPIER, NZ [35444] : 1800S ALVA, CLK, SCT [36041]

MONLEZUN ALL FRA [35620]

MONNELL 1800-1860 NRY, ENG [37858]

MONNICH 1770-1860 WULFTEN, HAN, GER [37798]

MONRO JEAN C1846 ALYTH, PER, SCT [38207]

MONROE 1855-1858 SYRACUSE, NY, USA [33762] : 1830-1978 ROSS CO., OH, USA [35316] : 1797-1853 LOUDOUN CO., VA & OH, USA [35777] : JAMES J. 1812+ CUMBERLAND CO., NC, USA [37794] : ARCHIBALD P. 1800+ CUMBERLAND CO., NC, USA [37794]

MONSARRAT PRE 1770 FRA [37381]

MONSEES 1750-1800 OSTERHOLZ SCHARMBECK, HAN, GER [38516]

MONSER 1840+ USA & UK [36524]

MONSHOUWER 1700-1900 GORINCHEM, ZH, NL [38712]

MONSON PRE 1850 YKS, ENG [35994] : 1750-1850 BOYLE, ROS, IRL [38523]

MONTAG 1700-1800 NOCKENHEIM, HEN, GER [36898]

MONTAGUE 1850+ GEELONG, VIC, AUS [35793] : PRE 1830 DARTFORD, KEN, ENG [34779] : C1860 LEWISHAM, KEN, ENG [35401] : 1797+ LONDON, ENG [35793] : 1780+ WOOLWICH, KEN, ENG [35965] : 1700-1900 BDF & BKM, ENG [36007]

MONTAMBAULT 1660+ QUE, CAN & USA [37475]

MONTAMBAUT 1660+ QUE, CAN & USA [37475]

MONTAMBEAU 1660+ QUE, CAN & USA [37475]

MONTAMBEAULT 1660+ QUE, CAN & USA [37475]

MONTAMBO 1660+ QUE, CAN & USA [37475]

MONTAMBOS 1660+ QUE, CAN & USA [37475]

MONTANARO 1850+ ENG [36986] : PRE 1850 MALTA [36986] : 1850+ SCT [36986]

MONTANBAU 1660+ QUE, CAN & USA [37475]

MONTANBAULT 1660+ QUE, CAN & USA [37475]

MONTANBEAULT 1660+ QUE, CAN & USA [37475]

MONTANBO 1660+ QUE, CAN & USA [37475]

MONTCALM 1800+ ST ISADORE, ONT, CAN [36686]

MONTEATH 1700+ SALINE, FIF, SCT **[34420]** :
C1810 DUNBLANE, PER, SCT **[37512]**

MONTEITH 1797+ BELFORD, NBL, ENG **[38436]** :
C1807-1862 KINGSWINFORD & BRIERLEY HILL,
STS, ENG & NZ **[34651]** : 1820+ MOVILLE, DON,
IRL **[37007]** : PRE 1860 ARM, IRL **[38081]** : PRE 1860
FALKIRK, STI, SCT **[34682]** : PRE 1780 CRIEFF,
PER, SCT **[38290]**

MONTELEONE PRE 1850 SANTA MAGUERITA, ITL
[36964]

MONTEMBAULT 1660+ QUE, CAN & USA **[37475]**

MONTEMBEAU 1660+ QUE, CAN & USA **[37475]**

MONTEMBEAULT 1660+ QUE, CAN & USA **[37475]**

MONTENARO ALL MALTA **[37247]**

MONTEY ALL WORLDWIDE **[35037]**

MONTGOMERIE PRE 1750 KILMARNOCK, AYR,
SCT **[36436]** : PRE 1795 KILBIRNIE, AYR, SCT
[37144]

MONTGOMERY 1880+ MOUNT BRITTON, QLD,
AUS **[35141]** : 1841+ MONO TWP, PEEL CO., ONT,
CAN **[34502]** : PRE 1888 BIRMINGHAM & AREA,
ENG **[34391]** : 1820+ DERBY, DBY, ENG **[36138]** :
1800S GLENARM, ANT, IRL **[34080]** : PRE 1841
FER, IRL **[34502]** : 1700-1850 BUSHMILLS, ANT,
IRL **[34513]** : 1750-1900 MOVILLE, LDY, IRL **[35600]**
: PRE 1883 ANT, IRL **[36855]** : PRE 1719
KILLALLO, MAY, IRL **[37528]** : JAMES 1777-1800
TYR, IRL **[38150]** : GEORGE PRE 1840 IRL **[38585]** :
1781-1805 FER, IRL & SCT **[38038]** : 1820S STI, SCT
[33934] : PRE 1830 OLD DEER, ABD, SCT **[34197]** :
1811 ORMISTON, ELN, SCT **[35906]** : C1817
DUNLOP, AYR, SCT **[36302]** : C1907 ROX, SCT
[36856] : DUNCAN C1831 SCT **[38177]** : PRE 1700
AYR, SCT **[38321]** : 1760+ SCT & ENG **[34387]** :
1809+ WIGTOWN & KNIGHTSWOOD, WIG &
DNB, SCT & IRL **[35579]** : PRE 1810 SCT & IRL
[35713] : ALL IL & VA, USA **[35313]** : 1800-1830 NEW
YORK, NY, USA **[37017]** : 1800-50 SALEM
CONNEAUT, ASHTABULA CO., OH, USA **[37528]** :
1720-40 HOPKINTON, MA, USA **[37528]** : 1770-1830
TRUMBULL CO., OH & PA, USA **[37529]** : 1790
LANCASTER, PA, IN & KS, USA **[38054]** : 1800-1857
BUTLER CO., OH, USA **[38150]** : 1830-1840
FRANKLIN CO., IN, USA **[38150]** : ALL PUTNAM
CO., MO & OR, USA **[38230]** : 1700-1900 KY, VA &
IN, USA **[38328]** : 1825-1890 BUTLER CO., PA, USA
[38344] : 1825-1890 ALLEGHENY CO., PA, USA
[38344]

MONTGUMRIE 1760+ GOVAN, LAN, ENG **[34290]**

MONTIETH PRE 1850 ROX & SEL, SCT **[35934]**

MONTIMNEY 1840+ TILBURY, ONT & QUE, CAN
[34983]

MONTMAGNY 1630+ MONTMAGNY, QUE, CAN
[34983]

MONTPAS ALL MAN, CAN **[38430]** : ALL QUE, CAN
[38430] : ALL CAN **[38430]** : 1830+ CT, USA **[38430]** :
1850+ POWERS, MI, USA **[38430]** : ALL USA **[38430]**

MONUMENT ALL NFK, ENG **[38035]**

MOOAR PRE 1870 BISCHBERG, BAV, GER **[35930]** :
PRE 1870 KUSEL, RPR, GER **[35930]**

MOOCER ALL ENG **[36524]**

MOODIE 1800S MARKINCH, FIF, SCT **[34473]** : ALL
KIRKCALDY & DYSART, FIF, SCT **[34473]** : PRE
1870 DUNDEE, ANS, SCT **[34473]** : ALL
TINGWALL, SHI, SCT **[34627]** : 1740+
LONGFORGAN, PER, SCT **[35152]** : PRE 1830 PER,
SCT **[35983]** : 1800S AUCHTERDERRAN, FIF, SCT
[36874] : PRE 1850 EDINBURGH, MLN, SCT **[38376]**
: 1910+ OH, USA **[38552]**

MOODY 1700+ ST MICHAELS, BARBADOS **[38235]** :
1800+ YORK, ONT, CAN **[34054]** : 1800-1880 LIN,
ENG **[34329]** : ALL IOW, HAM, ENG **[34724]** : 1820+
BRIGHOUSE & BRADFORD, WRY, ENG **[36111]** :
1500-1870 NEWMARKET, SFK, ENG **[36397]** : 1800-
1865 BERMONDSEY, SRY, ENG **[36627]** : PRE 1750
BURY ST EDMUNDS, SFK, ENG **[37473]** : 1700-
1850 HARTLEY WINTNEY, HAM, ENG **[37838]** :
1750S WINCHESTER, HAM, ENG **[37898]** : ALL
NBL & DUR, ENG & USA **[38754]** : PRE 1860
NEWRY, DOW, ARM & DUB, IRL **[35940]** : DAVID
C1816-20 POYNTZPASS, ARM, IRL **[36715]** :
ROBERT C1815-20 LISRAU, ARM, IRL **[36715]** :
PRE 1840 LENAMORE, LDY, IRL **[37450]** : PRE
1840 COLERAINE, ANT, IRL **[37450]** : 1840+ NH &
CT, USA **[37450]** : 1880+ PAYETTE, ID, USA **[37450]**
: PRE 1750 BURLINGTON CO., NJ, USA **[37473]** :
1910+ OH, USA **[38552]** : 1910+ KY, USA **[38552]** :
1780-1900 CROCUS, ADAIR CO., KY, USA **[38574]**

MOOERS 1730+ MAUGERVILLE & SHEFFIELD,
NB & NS, CAN **[34123]** : 1700+ NEWBURG, ME,
USA **[34123]**

MOOK PRE 1850 RILLINGTON, ERY, ENG **[36048]**

MOON 1850+ DAPTO & KIAMA, NSW, AUS **[34785]** :
1820-1990 SYDNEY, NSW, AUS **[34829]** : 1850+
ADELAIDE & CASTLEMAINE, SA & VIC, AUS
[35064] : PRE 1847 WINDSOR, NSW, AUS **[35236]** :
1820+ APPIN, NSW, AUS **[35497]** : ALICE
SHELTON 1900S DOUBLE BAY, NSW, AUS **[36633]**
: 1600S MORTENHOE, DEV, ENG **[34931]** : PRE
1850 PASCOE, CON, ENG **[35064]** : ALL
LEICESTER, LEI & DBY, ENG **[36074]** : PRE 1780
SKELTON, YKS, ENG **[36673]** : 1700+ ST
WINNOW, CON, ENG **[36961]** : PRE 1817 YKS,
ENG **[37671]** : PRE 1838 ROLVENDON, KEN, ENG
[37915] : JOHN C1850 LND, ENG **[38391]** : ALL
VERYAN & TREGONY, CON, ENG & AUS **[35712]**
: PRE 1860 IL, USA **[36544]**

MOONEY 1852+ SYDNEY, NSW, AUS **[34786]** :
C1857 BRIGHTON, TAS, AUS **[35391]** : 1865+
SALE, VIC, AUS **[35391]** : 1820+ NSW, AUS **[36305]** :
1840-1900 VIC, AUS **[36780]** : 1850 MELBOURNE &
GEELONG, VIC, AUS **[37307]** : PRE 1870
ENNISKILLEN, NB, CAN & IRL **[38447]** : ALL
SHANGHAI, CHINA **[35568]** : PRE 1840 BELFAST
& DONEGORE, ANT, IRL **[34391]** : 1772 WIC, IRL
[35089] : 1800+ ROS, IRL **[35201]** : BRIDGET
C1840+ OFF, IRL **[35499]** : PRE 1880 ATHBOY,
MEA, IRL **[35574]** : C1852 TEMPLEMORE, IRL
[35827] : 1700-1800 LEX, IRL **[36780]** : 1790-1820
DRUMSNAT, MOG, IRL **[38465]** : C1847 IRL & AUS
[37556]

MOONLIGHT PRE 1850 STRICHEN, ABD, SCT
[36061]

MOOR 1650-1780 BADSWORTH, YKS, ENG **[34762]** :
PRE 1700 LEICESTER, LEI, ENG **[35046]** : PRE 1743
LANCHESTER, DUR, ENG **[37635]** : 1850-1950
DARLINGTON, NRY, ENG **[38513]** : 1720+
PEMBROKE, NH, USA **[37492]**

MOORBY 1800 PRESTON, LAN, ENG **[36151]** : 1700-
1880 DARWEN & PRESTON, LAN, ENG **[38251]**

MOORCOCK 1930S AUS **[36856]** : ALL WORLDWIDE
[36856]

MOORCROFT ALL COVENTRY, WAR, ENG **[36005]**
: C1880-1895 SOUTHPORT, LAN, ENG **[37553]**

MOORE 1877-1935 SYDNEY, NSW, AUS **[34289]** :
1810+ SYDNEY, NSW, AUS **[34428]** : HANNAH
1840+ GEORGETOWN, TAS, AUS **[34541]** : 1880S
ST LEONARDS, TAS, AUS **[34845]** : 1800+ TAS,
AUS **[34845]** : 1850S WESTBURY, TAS, AUS **[34845]** :
PRE 1850 BATHURST, NSW, AUS **[34883]** : 1800+
TAS & VIC, AUS **[35062]** : 1855 GLEBE & SYDNEY,
NSW, AUS **[35089]** : JAMES PRE 1939 CREMORNE,
NSW, AUS **[35104]** : JAMES 1876+
WINBURNDALE & BATHURST, NSW, AUS **[35104]**

: PRE 1850+ SYDNEY, NSW, AUS [35237] : 1890S
ROCKHAMPTON, QLD, AUS [35260] : 1840+
BUCKLAND, VIC, AUS [35391] : 1830+
PARRAMATTA, NSW, AUS [35396] : EDMUND
1815+ FREEMANS REACH, NSW, AUS [35431] :
1914 BALMAIN, NSW, AUS [35705] : 1830 HOBART,
TAS, AUS [35705] : CLAUDIUS WM 1845+
BATHURST, NSW, AUS [35737] : JOHNSON 1840+
BATHURST, NSW, AUS [35737] : ROBERT 1840-
1888+ BATHURST, NSW, AUS [35737] : 1840+
MONARO, NSW, AUS [36295] : ROBERT 1840+
SYDNEY, NSW, AUS [36295] : C1860 REDFERN,
NSW, AUS [36641] : 1820+ SYDNEY, NSW, AUS
[37670] : ESTELLA PRE 1875 NS, CAN [35371] :
C1845-50 WOLFORD, ONT, CAN [36722] : 1864
BOLTON, ONT, CAN [38187] : PRE 1900
INVERNESS CO., NS, CAN [38447] : PRE 1774
THORNFORD, DOR, ENG [33919] : WILLIAM
1846+ HESSAY, YKS, ENG [33956] : HENRY 1798
PATRINGTON, YKS, ENG [33956] : 1700-1900
WISBECH, CAM, ENG [34537] : GEORGE PRE 1850
WYLAM, NBL, ENG [34583] : SARAH PRE 1850
WYLAM, NBL, ENG [34583] : JOHN PRE 1860
BEDFORD, BDF, ENG [34585] : 1800+ NORWICH,
NFK, ENG [34591] : ISAAC 1883+ WALSHAM LE
WILLOWS, SFK, ENG [34627] : C1823 DBY, ENG
[34661] : PRE 1850 LYME REGIS, DOR & DEV,
ENG [34716] : PRE 1900 CROYDON, SRY, SSX &
KEN, ENG [34743] : 1736+ SHERBORNE, DOR,
ENG [34777] : PRE 1850 HORSEY, NFK, ENG
[34909] : JOSEPH 1700+ WELLCOME, DEV, ENG
[34970] : C1840 NFK, ENG [35089] : ALL KEN, ENG
[35139] : PRE 1840 WORTHING, SSX, ENG [35200] :
C1800 REDRUTH, CON, ENG [35223] : 1870+
CRAWLEY, SSX, ENG [35240] : C1859 BOMBSON,
DEV, ENG [35251] : C1856 WOOLWICH, KEN,
ENG [35260] : THOMAS 1600 SELSIDE, YKS, ENG
[35429] : ANN 1840S BELPER, DBY, ENG [35471] :
ALL BATH, SOM, ENG [35474] : 1800+ RAMSEY,
HUN, ENG [35499] : 1750S SEDGLEY &
WOLVERHAMPTON, STS, ENG [35512] : PRE 1750
DOR, ENG [35701] : 1700S CLITHEROE, LAN, ENG
[35830] : PRE 1700 DEV, ENG [35866] : PRE 1850
CUL, ENG [35884] : C1800 SRY, ENG [35916] : PRE
1870 CHALLOCK, KEN, ENG [35932] : PRE 1900
ROCHESTER, KEN, ENG [36035] : 1700-1800 LIN,
ENG [36057] : PRE 1880 HEXHAM, NBL, ENG
[36224] : 1900S YOXFORD, SFK, ENG [36230] : PRE
1775 BEESTON, NTT, ENG [36411] : 1796-1828
DEPTFORD, KEN & MDX, ENG [36582] : 1850
WHITEHAVEN, CUL, ENG [36606] : CARTER 1800-
1870 BARKING, IPSWICH, SKF, ENG [36717] :
1700S BILLINGSHURST, SSX, ENG [36760] : ALL
BKM, ENG [36789] : 1700-1800S WOR, GLS & HEF,
ENG [37221] : PRE 1891 MDX, ENG [37358] : PRE
1896 BIRMINGHAM, WAR, ENG [37367] : 1788-
1820S WADDINGTON, LIN, ENG [37490] : 1800S
BAMPTON, DEV, ENG [37497] : 1860 LAMBETH,
LND, ENG [37558] : PRE 1830 WAKEFIELD &
ROTHWELL, YKS, ENG [37662] : PRE 1872
DERBY, DBY, ENG [37662] : PRE 1770 LEI, ENG
[37706] : C1800 HEANOR, DBY, ENG [37739] : 1800-
1900 EGREMONT, CUL, ENG [37858] : ALL
EASTHAM, ESS, ENG [37884] : 1800-1900 SRY,
ENG [37884] : ROBERT PRE 1800S
WANDSWORTH, SRY, ENG [37909] : PRE 1855
THAXTED, ESS, ENG [37917] : 1750 WEST
HANNINGFIELD, ESS, ENG [37928] : PRE 1809
CRANAGE, CHS, ENG [37948] : 1850-1900
WOOLWICH, KEN, ENG [37980] : PRE 1842 KEN,
ENG [37991] : MARGARET 1764+ GOSFORTH,
CUL, ENG [38067] : PRE 1812 NEWCASTLE, NBL &

DUR, ENG [38306] : RICHARD 1600-1700
PINCHBECK, LIN, ENG [38453] : 1880-1920
KIRKSTALL LEEDS, YKS, ENG [38513] : 1850-1950
DARLINGTON, NRY, ENG [38513] : 1800-1900
NORTHALLERTON, NRY, ENG [38513] : PRE 1870
HUDDERSFIELD, YKS, ENG [38730] : 1600+
NETHERBURY, DOR, ENG [38745] : KATHLEEN
1911+ NOWAGHER, INDIA [35154] : EDWARD
1901+ CALCUTTA, INDIA & IR [35154] : PRE 1840
PATRICK, IOM [35185] : 1815-30 IRL [33828] : 1800+
LISBRANNAN, MOG, IRL [33977] : PRE 1840
MAGHERALOUGH, TYR, IRL [34137] : PRE 1850
GIANT'S CAUSEWAY, ANT, IRL [34160] : 1750-
1875 ANT, IRL [34340] : JAMES 1847-1931
BELFAST, ANT, IRL [34340] : C1742 CROOKED
STONE, ANT, IRL [34385] : C1870 LARNE, ANT,
IRL [34385] : C1803 INVER, ANT, IRL [34385] :
C1870 LARGEY KILLEAD, ANT, IRL [34385] : 1750-
1850 BROUGHSHANE, ANT, IRL [34572] : ALL
TEMPO, FER, IRL [34644] : GUSTANES C1750
MEA, IRL [34682] : C1873 BANGOR, DOW, IRL
[34972] : 1840 ARM, IRL [35024] : DANIEL C1843
DROGHEDA, LOU, IRL [35154] : PRE 1880 WEM,
IRL [35339] : JOHN PRE 1830 LDY, IRL [35371] :
PATRICK PRE 1810 KID, IRL [35497] : PRE 1830
LIM, IRL [35705] : PRE 1870 LOUGHNEASE, TYR,
IRL [36437] : ROSE 1820S ARM, IRL [36634] :
C1890+ BELFAST, ANT, IRL [36853] : C1800
BELFAST, ANT, IRL [37952] : 1750-90 DON, IRL
[38221] : PRE 1900 FIER & BALLYOUSKIL, KIK,
IRL [38300] : DANIEL PRE 1837 BURNFOOT
FARM, LDY, IRL [38595] : ANNE C1782-1852
DUNFEENEY, MAY & QUE, IRL & CAN [36904] :
STEBBINGS 1880+ AUCKLAND & WHANGAREI,
NZ [36818] : WILLIAM 1800+ GLASGOW, LKS,
SCT [34933] : 1700+ CAMPBELTOWN, ARL, SCT
[35391] : WILLIAM 1841+ GLASGOW, LKS, SCT
[36367] : PRE 1815 AYR, SCT [37142] : PRE 1800
OLRIG & DUNNET, CAI, SCT [37727] : C1800
SLAMANNAN, STI, SCT [37898] : C1900 SCT &
AUS [33881] : C1945 PHILADELPHIA, PA, USA
[34385] : 1750-1850 NC, USA [34749] : PRE 1790 SC &
NC, USA [35098] : 1820-1850 EDMONSON CO., KY,
USA [36573] : HENRY 1745+ ESSEX CO., VA, USA
[36895] : PRE 1825 JEFFERSON CO., IN, USA
[36923] : JACOB 1785 MONONGALIA, WV, USA
[37008] : 1821-1860 TUSCALOOSA CO., AL, USA
[37029] : 1741-1821 EDGECOMBE CO., NC, USA
[37029] : 1780+ BARNET, VT, USA [37492] : ISAAC
1820-1940 LAWRENCE CO., OH, USA [37525] :
JOHN PRE 1810 FREDERICK CO., VA, USA [37580]
: PRE 1800 ROCKINGHAM CO., NC, USA [37587] :
C1880 LUCASVILLE, OH, USA [38065] : 1840-1870
WINSTON CO., MS, USA [38088] : MOSE 1866
RICHMOND, KY, USA [38109] : EDWARD 1805
RANDOLPH, NC, USA [38122] : DANIEL W. 1804
SUDBURY, MIDDLESEX, MA, USA [38183] : ALL
OK, USA [38230] : JOHN TAYLOR 1880+ PIERCE
CO., NE, USA [38323] : 1700S MORRIS CO., NJ,
USA [38531] : JAMES 1847-1918 MILLICAN,
BRAZOS CO., TX, USA [38724] : MARGARET C.
C1884 MILLICAN, TX, USA [38724] : 1800S TENBY,
PEM, WLS [36856]

MOOREHEAD ALL QUEBEC CITY, QUE, CAN
[34074] : 1780-1870 LDY, IRL [34687]

MOOREN ALL LAN & YKS, ENG & IRL [37353]

MOORES PRE 1825 CHS, ENG [37098] : 1850-1920
ROCHDALE, LAN, ENG [38251]

MOOREY PRE 1750 KIRBY HILL, YKS, ENG [37643]

MOORFOOT 1650-1750 LIN, ENG [36057]

MOORHEAD JAMES C1856 BALLYBUNDEN, DOW,
IRL [36715] : GEORGE 1847 BALLYBUNDEN,

DOW, IRL [36715] : DAVID C1765-70
BALLYBUNDEN, DOW, IRL [36715] : THOMAS
C1767 BALLYBUNDEN, DOW, IRL [36715] :
FREDERICK C1856 BALLYBUNDEN, DOW, IRL
[36715] : DAVID C1708 BALLYMACASHEN, DOW,
IRL [36715] : SUSANNA C1767 BALLYBUNDEN,
DOW, IRL [36715] : 1820+ PA, USA [35275]

MOORHOUSE PRE 1800 KEIGHLEY & BINGLEY,
YKS & LAN, ENG [34383] : PRE 1830
BRAITHWELL, YKS, ENG [35898] : 1700-1800
HELMSLEY, NRY, ENG [37858] : 1870+ BELFAST,
ANT, DOW & ARM, IRL [35636]

MOORMAN 1852 WILLITON, SOM, ENG [36860] :
1900+ NE, USA [33903]

MOORTGAT ALL ATW, BEL [38169]

MOORTON 1700-1850 NEWPORT, SAL, ENG [38474]

MOOS ANTON 1825-1845 BAV, GER [38482] :
ANTON 1845-1850 PORT CLINTON, OH, USA
[38482]

MOOSER ALL ENG [36524]

MOOTE 1790+ LINCOLN CO., ONT, CAN [34114] :
1767-1800 CANAJOHARIE, NY, USA [34114]

MOOTH LYDIA 1825 SHIAWASSEE CO., MI, USA
[38142]

MORALEE 1750-1920 SUNDERLAND, DUR, ENG
[37419] : 1800-1860 TYNEMOUTH, NBL, ENG
[37419] : 1700-1860 HORNBY, DUR, ENG [37419] :
1800-1900 SOUTH SHIELDS, DUR, ENG [37419] :
1700-1870 STOCKTON, DUR, ENG [37419] : 1700-
1870 NEWCASTLE ON TYNE, NBL, ENG [37419]

MORAN PRE 1860 RICHMOND & BENALLA, VIC,
AUS [35792] : 1800-1930 QLD, AUS [38070] : 1700+
TARADALE, VIC & TIP, AUS & IRL [36303] : 1840+
CHESTERVILLE, ONT, CAN [34152] : 1820S+
ADJALA TWP., ONT, CAN [34259] : C1878
HAMPTONWICK, MDX, ENG [35121] : PRE 1842
CAR, IRL [34056] : 1800-1900 BALLYMORE, WEM,
IRL [34411] : PRE 1800 IRL [34428] : 1821+
DUBLIN, IRL [34781] : 1822-1950 RATHOWEN,
WEM, IRL [35044] : ALL KINGSTOWN, DUB, IRL
[35063] : PRE 1845 COR, IRL [35134] : PRE 1854
BALLINAKILL, GAL, IRL [35792] : C1830
ROSCOMMON, ROS, IRL [35990] : 1850-1900 ND,
USA [34515]

MORASCHINELLI LORANZO 1887+ APRICA &
KALGOORLIE, ITL & AUS [37111] : ALL
WORLDWIDE [37111]

MORCHEL 1650-1755 AUERBACH, HES, BRD [35311]

MORCOM 1852+ BALAKLAVA, SA, AUS [37189] :
ALL ST MARTIN N MENEAGE, CON, ENG [37189]

MORCOMB 1650-1720 GWENNAP, CON, ENG
[34793]

MORDEN PRE 1743 YKS, ENG [37811] : ALL
WORLDWIDE [34377]

MORE PRE 1880 BURGHEAD, MOR, SCT [33993] :
1770+ AVOCH, ROC, SCT [34810]

MOREAU ALL WORLDWIDE [35832]

MOREAUX ALL WORLDWIDE [35832]

MOREHEAD 1800+ BALTIMORE, MD, USA [38321]

MOREHOUSE 1700-1850 HOLMFIRTH, WRY, ENG
[37736]

MOREL 1839+ ADELAIDE, SA, AUS [33773] : 1800+
BOULOGNE SUR MER, FRA [36239]

MORELAND 1865+ VIC, AUS [38539] : 1840+
LONDON, ENG [38539] : 1800+ DEV, ENG & AUS
[35137] : MARY C1815 DROMORE, DOW, IRL
[35607]

MORELY 1700+ ALLINGTON, DOR, ENG [38745]

MOREN CHARLES C1834 YATELEY, HAM, ENG
[34935]

MORETON 1800+ NFD, CAN [34637] : 1800+
EPPING, ESS, ENG [34637] : ALL PORTSEA, HAM,

ENG [36255] : C1818 PORTSMOUTH, HAM, ENG
[36859]

MOREY 1400+ HAVANT, HAM, ENG [33989] : 1880-
1900 MIDDLE CLAYDON, BKM, ENG [34850] :
C1856 WOOLWICH, KEN, ENG [35260] : ALL
ELSTED, SSX, HAM & LND, ENG [35891] : 1730S-
1750S DARTMOUTH, DEV, ENG [36337]

MOREY (SEE MURREY) [35260]

MORFORD 1670+ MONMOUTH CO., NJ, USA
[36917]

MORGAN 1840+ BOOROWA, NSW, AUS [33763] :
1830+ TAS, AUS [34283] : C1860 ESPERANCE, TAS,
AUS [34586] : ELIZABETH PRE 1877+ VICTOR
HARBOUR, SA, AUS [34592] : 1880+ BRISBANE &
IPSWICH, QLD, AUS [34853] : PRE 1871
NEWTOWN, NSW, AUS [35781] : 1868 MUDGEE,
NSW, AUS [35786] : 1852+ CAMPBELLS CREEK,
VIC, AUS [35801] : 1856+ TOOWOOMBA
DISTRICT, QLD, AUS [35854] : GEORGE PRE 1855
NEWCASTLE, NSW, AUS [36634] : C1872-1895
HOBART, TAS, AUS [36836] : 1892 BALMAIN,
NSW, AUS [37911] : 1866 NEWPORT, VIC, AUS
[37963] : 1780-1990 OSNABRUCK, ONT, CAN [34077]
: PRE 1840+ GUELPH, ONT, CAN [34504] :
HENRY PRE 1860 ONT, CAN [35371] : HANNAH
1830+ GSY, CHI [38394] : 1700+ PORTSMOUTH,
HAM, ENG [33814] : ELIZA 1800+ ST PANCRAS,
LND, ENG [33938] : PRE 1850 WOLSINGHAM,
DUR, ENG [33993] : PRE 1860S ST MICHAELS,
BRISTOL, GLS, ENG [34115] : 1700+
WOODSTOCK & DEDDINGTON, OXF, ENG
[34121] : JOHN PRE 1887 NBL, ENG [34278] : 1700+
FROME, SOM, ENG [34283] : 1700+ ELLESMERE,
SAL, ENG [34405] : 1800+ LIVERPOOL, CHS, ENG
[34405] : PRE 1840 HALESWORTH, SFK, ENG
[34504] : ALL HACKNEY, MDX, ENG [34545] : PRE
1912 LONDON, ENG [34545] : C1858 MONMOUTH,
DEV, ENG [34653] : PRE 1850 SOUTHWARK &
BERMONDSEY, SRY, ENG [34719] : 1854 WIL,
ENG [34761] : C1820 BRISTOL, GLS, ENG [34853] :
C1860 MIDDLESBROUGH, YKS, ENG [34853] :
1780 ROPLEY, HAM, ENG [34909] : PRE 1750
BENENDEN, KEN, ENG [35227] : 1750+ LND,
ENG [35370] : 1830S BRISTOL, GLS, ENG [35516] :
PRE 1880 SSX, ENG [35742] : C1834 LONDON,
ENG [35786] : JEMIMA 1859-1942 WHITECHAPEL,
LND, ENG [35815] : 1880S LUDLOW & CRAVEN
ARMS, SAL, ENG [36512] : ALL CHEDDAR, SOM,
ENG [36605] : ALL LASHAM, HAM, ENG [37044] :
1700-1800 SFK, ENG [37084] : C1827
KINGSTANLEY, GLS, ENG [37144] : C1900
WOLVERHAMPTON, STS, ENG [37233] : 1690-1850
SALISBURY, WIL, ENG [37233] : 1680-1770
NORTON ST PHILIP, SOM, ENG [37233] : PRE 1850
BETHNAL GREEN, LND, ENG [37261] : PRE 1800
GREAT WALTHAM, ESS, ENG [37718] : 1720-1739
HANLEY, WOR, ENG [38465] : 1800+ OLNEY,
NTH, ENG [38488] : DOLLY 1933+ MANCHESTER
& BURY, LAN, ENG [38593] : 1820-1922
DRUMINTEE, ARM, IRL [34058] : 1820S
YOUGHAL, COR, IRL [34175] : PRE 1830 OFF, IRL
[34702] : 1847 MONTPELIER, LIM, IRL [35364] :
PRE 1840 BALBRIGGAN, DUB, IRL [36532] :
C1890+ BELFAST, ANT, IRL [36853] : EDWARD
1800+ FEES TCE, LOG, IRL [38302] : THOMAS
C1810+ BELFAST, ANT, ARM & DOW, IRL [38593]
: PRE 1942 DUNEDIN, OTO, NZ [36853] : 1900-1980
AUCKLAND, NZ [38465] : MALACHY C1924+
WELLINGTON, NZ [38593] : PRE 1913
FINDHORN, MOR, SCT [34816] : 1700-1800
TORRYBURN, FIF, SCT [35094] : C1824 COCKPEN,
MLN, SCT [35854] : C1849 PRESTONHOLME, MLN,

SCT [35854] : PRE 1920 INVERNESS, INV, SCT [37619] : 1790-1830 CT, USA [34153] : ROBERT HUGH PRE 1914 DALLAS CO., MO, USA [34481] : MARY JANE PRE 1900 MI, USA [35371] : 1780 MONROE, PA, USA [38022] : 1725-1775 NEWBERRY CO., SC, USA [38088] : 1805 SANG CO., IL, KY & NC, USA [38287] : PRE 1770 RICHMOND & NORTHUMBERLAND, VA, USA [38311] : RIDLEY 1760-1835 BEDFORD CO., TN & KY, USA [38569] : RIDLEY 1760-1835 GRANVILLE CO., NC, USA [38569] : RIDLEY 1760-1835 PENDLETON DIST., SC, USA [38569] : JOHN 1700-1786 GRANVILLE CO., NC & VA, USA [38569] : 1800-1840 WARRICK, IN, USA [38576] : EILEEN 1937+ KEARNY & NEWARK, NJ, USA [38593] : PRE 1840 GLA, WLS [33763] : 1827+ ABERGAVENNY, BRE, WLS [33955] : 1750-1890 CHRISTCHURCH, MON, WLS [34234] : WILLIAM 1800S TREDEGAR, MON, WLS [34842] : C1850 PONTYPOOL, MON, WLS [35045] : C1800 GLA, WLS [35153] : ELIZABETH 1880+ KIDWELLY, CMN, WLS [35338] : 1840+ ABERDARE, GLA, WLS [35390] : PRE 1860 MERTHYR TYDFIL, GLA, WLS [35540] : 1852+ CARDIFF, WLS [35801] : PRE 1850 LLANHAMLACH, BRE, WLS [36041] : JOHN PRE 1860 BLAINA & EBBW VALE, MON, WLS [36082] : 1795+ ST ISHMAELS, PEM, WLS [36254] : 1800+ BRECONTOWN, BRE, WLS [36614] : 1800+ MYNYDDISLWYN, MON, WLS [36614] : 1850+ TREVETHIN, MON, WLS [36614] : 1800S PRESVEIGN, RAD, WLS [36764] : PRE 1900 BLAENAVON, MON, WLS [36801] : 1800+ MON, WLS [36956] : RICHARD 1747 LLANBADARN FAWR, CGN, WLS [37250] : PRE 1850 MERTHYR TYDFIL, GLA, WLS [37343] : 1607+ LLANDAFF, GLA, WLS [37564] : HANNAH 1830+ USH, MON, WLS [38394] : MARY PRE 1873 NEWPORT, MON, WLS [38580] : ALL WORLDWIDE [37688]

MORGANS ALL AL, KY & TN, USA [38197] : PRE 1800 PWLLCROCHAN, PEM, WLS [34319] : PRE 1900 MARDY, GLA, WLS [34611] : JOHN PRE 1842 TREGARON, CGN, WLS [34992] : 1700S BRONANT, CGN, WLS [37250]

MORIARITY 1780 IRL [37008]

MORIARTY 1852-1900 CAMDEN, NSW, AUS [33766] : 1925-1930 SYDNEY, NSW, AUS [34867] : 1925-1935 NEW ENGLAND AREA, NSW, AUS [34867] : 1930-1936 DORRIGO AREA, NSW, AUS [34867] : TIMOTHY PRE 1900 HALIFAX, NS, CAN [34206] : MICHAEL PRE 1923 HALIFAX, NS, CAN [34206] : 1785-1815 OKEHAMPTON, DEV, ENG [36594] : PRE 1840 CAHIRCIVEEN, KER, IRL [33766] : MICHAEL PRE 1850 KER, IRL [34206] : PRE 1875 TRALEE, KER, IRL [35443] : 1875+ TINWALD, SI, NZ [35443] : 1880-1925 GLASGOW, SCT [34867] : PRE 1850 TIPTON, IN, USA [33854]

MORIER PRE 1800 CHATEAU D'OEX, CH [36295] : PRE 1800 SRY, ENG [36295] : 1800+ GLASGOW, LKS, SCT [36295]

MORIN 1614+ QUE, CAN [34068] : 1837-1887 BEAUJEU, RHA, FRA [34136] : 1580-1660 PIRGNAC, PCH, FRA [34514]

MORISON DAVID 1852+ SYDNEY & NEWCASTLE, NSW, AUS [35394] : GEORGE 1870+ HOTHAM, VIC, AUS [35803] : C1824 BUCHANAN, STI, SCT [34156] : PRE 1730 INVERARY, ARL, SCT [35227] : C1780 CRIEFF, PER, SCT [35260] : C1805 AUCHTERARDER, PER, SCT [35260] : GEORGE 1810+ ERROLL, PER, SCT [35803] : C1750 ANS, SCT [36327] : C1770 DRYMEN, STI, SCT [36788] : PRE 1792 MUTHILL, PER, SCT [37575] : PRE 1820 CAIRNIE, ABD, SCT [37835]

MORISSON PRE 1860 CARLINGFORD, NSW, AUS [35232]

MORLEDGE PRE 1800 IBLE & BELPER, DBY, ENG [37736]

MORLEY PRE 1875 HOBART, TAS, AUS [35388] : 1850+ LAUNCESTON, TAS, AUS [35422] : 1880S HEATHCOTE, VIC, AUS [35777] : 1830 BURGATE, SFK, ENG [34546] : 1550-1851 HOUGHAM & MARSTON, LIN, ENG [34672] : 1700S PORTSMOUTH, HAM, ENG [34715] : 1700S CON, ENG [34920] : 1800+ LND, ENG [35156] : 1800-1838 BIRMINGHAM, WAR, ENG [35436] : PRE 1750 LAKENHEATH, SFK, ENG [35742] : PRE 1830 KIRTON, LIN, ENG [35746] : PRE 1865 ORSTON, NTT, ENG [35819] : PRE 1745 ELTON, NTT, ENG [35904] : PRE 1870 GORLESTON, NFK, ENG [36067] : ALL NEWARK, NTT, ENG [36174] : ALL GRIMSTON, LEI, ENG [36174] : PRE 1830 SFK, ENG [36179] : PRE 1860 MILDEN & MELFORD, SFK, ENG [36479] : PRE 1830 CHELMSFORD, ESS, ENG [37137] : 1700+ ORSTON & WHATTON, NTT, ENG [37552] : PRE 1900 ASHTON UNDER LYNE, LAN, ENG [37821] : 1800+ BRANSTON & LEICESTER, LEI, ENG [38425] : 1800+ HIGH HARROGATE, YKS, ENG [38425] : 1830+ CHESTERFIELD, DBY, ENG [38488]

MORLEY-MEE C1835+ NTT, ENG [38401]

MORLING PRE 1810 LEISTON, SFK, ENG [35406]

MORMAN 1800-1990 CAN [33903]

MOROFKE PRE 1819 BIELINY, WARSZAWA, POL [38629] : 1854+ SLADOW, WARSZAWA, POL [38629] : ALL WARSZAWA, POL [38629] : ALL WORLDWIDE [38629]

MORONEY 1850S SOUTH BRISBANE, QLD, AUS [33870] : MARY C1800 TAS, AUS [33984] : 1840-1890 VIC, AUS [33984] : 1870+ MELBOURNE, VIC, AUS [35147] : 1865+ MYRTLEFORD & MELBOURNE, VIC, AUS [35190] : PRE 1870 IRL [35147] : 1820 DERRAFA, CLA, IRL [36274] : PRE 1900 DUNEDIN, NZ [35147]

MORPHET ALL WORLDWIDE [35797]

MORPHETT ALL WORLDWIDE [35797]

MORPHY 1800S TORONTO, ONT, CAN [36670] : PRE 1800 LITTLETON, TIP & OFF, IRL [33905]

MORR PRE 1800 EIBINGEN, RPF, GER [38681]

MORRALL C1850 WELLINGTON, SAL, ENG [35791] : 1550-1700 WOR, ENG [37217] : PRE 1700 BN, FRA [37217]

MORRATT 1700-1850 DEV, ENG [36395]

MORRELL 1839+ KENSINGTON, SA, AUS [33773] : 1825+ PANNAL, WRY, ENG [34915] : 1854-1872 CHIPPENHAM, WIL, ENG [35594] : 1800+ YKS, ENG [35891] : 1820+ ENG [36242] : 1800+ HELPERBY & THOLTHORPE, NRY, ENG [36791] : 1700-1900 TIVERTON, DEV, ENG [38579] : 1800+ BANBRIDGE, DOW, IRL [35644] : 1800S NEW YORK, NY, USA [38182]

MORRET 1600+ SAXTON IN ELMET, YKS, ENG [34408]

MORRETT 1850-1900 JSY, CHI [36395]

MORREY C1790+ SAL, ENG [37762]

MORRICE ALL ABERDEEN, ABD, SCT [34877] : 1837+ CRUDEN BAY, ABD, SCT [35584] : PRE 1830 ABD, SCT [38277]

MORRILL 1790+ BRIER ISLAND, NS, CAN [34138] : PRE 1632 ENG [35165] : 1890S MCPHERSON CO., KS, USA [38243]

MORRIS 1920S+ HARDEN, NSW, AUS [33930] : PRE 1900 COBRA, NSW, AUS [35118] : ALL COBRA, NSW, AUS [35118] : 1866+ MALMSBURY, VIC, AUS [35525] : SILAS 1880+ RICHMOND, VIC, AUS [35725] : SILAS 1865-1880 CALIFORNIA GULLY,

VIC, AUS [35725] : 1890+ ADELAIDE, SA, AUS [36309] : PRE 1862 WEST MAITLAND, NSW, AUS [37899] : 1850+ KILMORE & GEELONG, VIC, AUS [38277] : 1800-1865 MINGAN, QUE, CAN [33994] : 1800 WESTMORELAND CO., NB, CAN [34991] : 1800-1900 PENDLETON, ONT, CAN & IRL [38779] : 1700+ ONT, CAN & USA [34062] : PRE 1788 ISLE OF WIGHT, HAM, ENG [33995] : PRE 1818 TRURO, CON, ENG [34036] : C1845 WOODSTOCK, OXF, ENG [34358] : 1600+ NEWTON ST CYRES, DEV, ENG [34747] : 1829+ PORTSMOUTH, HAM, ENG [34900] : C1763 COVENTRY, WAR, ENG [35090] : 1727 SALEHURST, SSX, ENG [35260] : 1800+ BLACKBURN, LAN, ENG [35362] : PRE 1800 LONDON, ENG [35548] : 1700S MARSHFIELD, GLS, ENG [35548] : 1870+ TOTTENHAM & ISLINGTON, MDX & LND, ENG [35701] : RICHARD 1840-1860 GREAT RISSINGTON, GLS, ENG [35725] : 1600-1900 BKM, ENG [35944] : PRE 1860 SOUTHAMPTON, HAM, ENG [36019] : PRE 1930 ALDERSHOT, HAM, ENG [36019] : 1848-1900 MANCHESTER, LAN, ENG [36024] : CATHERINE M. 1860-1870 LONDON, ENG [36101] : 1800-1900 MUCH COWARNE, HEF, ENG [36109] : C1700-1980 REEPHAM & NEWCASTLE, NFK & NBL, ENG [36128] : 1800+ LONDON, ENG [36135] : PRE 1825 BIRMINGHAM, WAR, ENG [36177] : 1790-1810S TENBURY & CLAINES, WOR, ENG [36190] : 1600-1800 DUNTON BASSETT, LEI, ENG [36410] : 1750-1900 LUTTERWORTH, LEI, ENG [36410] : 1800+ SSX, ENG [36470] : 1628 STOTTESDON, SAL, ENG [36488] : 1594-1805 EASTHAM, WOR, ENG [36513] : PRE 1795 LEWES, SSX, ENG [36589] : 1800-1840 BARFORD, BIRMINGHAM, WAR, ENG [36649] : 1700-1800 WESTMINSTER, LND, ENG [36828] : C1801-1885 STEPNEY & BOW COMMON, MDX, ENG [36836] : JAMES C1720+ SRY, ENG [36880] : C1770 ALBURY, HRT, ENG [36978] : PRE 1825 HARDINGTON, SOM, ENG [37067] : 1800+ ENG [37306] : 1800+ LAN, ENG [37482] : JANE 1790-1860 EPPING & HARLOW, ESS, ENG [37488] : 1800+ STOKESLEY, YKS, ENG [37525] : ALL WRY, ENG [37704] : 1820+ DEWSBURY, WRY, ENG [37704] : PRE 1755 SUTTON BONNINGTON, NTT, ENG [37754] : 1750+ KEMERTON, WOR, ENG [37763] : PRE 1750 BLAISDON, GLS, ENG [37763] : C1700 EAST COKER, SOM, ENG [37918] : 1800-1850 DARCY LEVER, LAN, ENG [37934] : PRE 1800 MAIDSTONE, KEN & SSX, ENG [38254] : 1890 SALE, CHS, ENG [38267] : PRE 1884 LAN, ENG [38289] : PRE 1830 BANDON, COR, IRL [34177] : C1798-1833 SLIGO, SLI, IRL [34214] : PRE 1830 MAY, IRL [34696] : PRE 1863 NEWTOWNSTEWART, TYR, IRL [34763] : 1850-60S CARROWNBAUN, GAL, IRL [35525] : 1820S GAL, IRL [36292] : 1863+ TYR, IRL & AUS [34763] : 1865+ AUCKLAND, NZ [34609] : 1906-1967 WEST COAST & NELSON, NZ [35895] : ALL FIF, SCT [34593] : 1700+ PITTENWEEN, FIF, SCT [35395] : 1725+ ST ANDREWS, FIF, SCT [35558] : C1841 PRIFICK, AYR, SCT [36253] : 1851-1930 ABERDEEN, ABD, SCT & AUS [35469] : 1830+ OH, USA [35629] : 1871-1910 ST LOUIS, MO, USA [36974] : PRE 1800S IN, TN & NC, USA [37522] : JOHN PRE 1840 WESTERN, NY, USA [37804] : JOHN D. 1810-1820 BUCKS CO., PA, USA [37815] : 1820+ NEW YORK, NY, USA [37956] : 1850 WALPOLE, NH, USA [38131] : RICHARD IVEY 1839 GA, USA [38155] : 1830-1860 DENTON CO., TX, USA [38367] : 1700+ GREENE CO. & ALBERMARLE CO., VA, USA [38765] : 1890S+ FERNDALE, WLS [33930] : PRE 1840 LLANFYLLIN, MGY, WLS [34395] :

GEORGE 1860+ WARREN, PEM, WLS [35338] : 1906-1930 MON, WLS [35895] : ROBERT PRE 1870 NANTYGLO & BLAINA, MON, WLS [36082] : 1700+ LLANMYNECH & CARREGHOVA, MGY, WLS [37625] : TOM 1885 BALA, MER, WLS [37694] : 1840 LLANARTHNEY, CMN, WLS [38282] : THOMAS C1846 WLS & ENG [37525] : ALL WORLDWIDE [36551] : ALONZO 1820+ WORLDWIDE [37956]

MORRISBY PRE 1788 CAWOOD, YKS, ENG [34547]

MORRISH 1700+ STOKE IN TEIGNHEAD, DEV, ENG [34602] : 1800S CON, ENG [34684] : PRE 1820 ILLOGAN, CON, ENG [34795] : 1800S ENG [35161] : 1750-1850 SHEBBEAR, DEV, ENG [37339]

MORRISON ROBERT 1858+ MELBOURNE, VIC, AUS [35149] : 1862-65 WALGETT, NSW, AUS [35226] : 1840S DUNTROON, ACT, AUS [35226] : C1848-62 ILFORD, NSW, AUS [35226] : 1800+ BADDECK, NS, CAN [34500] : 1800+ BASTARD TWP, LEEDS CO., ONT, CAN [36664] : 1850+ VARNEY GREY CO., ONT, CAN [37443] : 1800S GREY CO., ONT, CAN [38393] : PRE 1840 BRISTOL, GLS, ENG [34711] : 1840S THONG, KEN, ENG [34738] : 1800-1850 BERMONDSEY, SRY, ENG [34753] : PRE 1879 EWELL, KEN, ENG [36613] : PRE 1675 STS, ENG [37098] : 1870+ NRY, ENG [37733] : ALL LONDON, ENG [37743] : PRE 1900 BRAMPTON BIERLOW, WRY, ENG [37979] : 1780+ TARVES KEILYFORD, ABD, SCT &, FIJI [34008] : PRE 1870 CAWNPORE, INDIA [36262] : MARGARET 1853 DON, IRL [35149] : ABRAHAM 1840 DON, IRL [35149] : ROBERT 1837 RATHMULLEN, DON, IRL [35149] : JOHN 1804 LONDONDERRY, DON, IRL [35149] : PRE 1860 FER, IRL [37443] : 1800-1833 LET, IRL & CAN [34244] : 1700-1900 TRANENT, MLN, SCT [33908] : PRE 1850 SCT [33999] : PRE 1855 ULLAPOOL, ROC, SCT [34014] : 1850+ METHLICK & UDNEY, ABD, SCT [34374] : JAMES C1800-1840 KEITH, BAN, SCT [34479] : PRE 1850 CRUDEN, ABD, SCT [34784] : 1800 ULLAPOOL & LEWIS, ROC, SCT [35194] : 1790+ KILLEARNAN, ROC, SCT [35214] : PRE 1839 CASTLE MOYLE, SKYE, INV, SCT [35226] : PRE 1750 OLD KILPATRICK, DNB, SCT [35227] : 1868-93 HAWICK, ROX, SCT [35260] : 1820-50 CRAIG & MADDERTY, PER, SCT [35260] : 1800S KINCARDINE O'NEIL, ABD, SCT [35409] : JOHN C1827 PAISLEY, RFW, SCT [35411] : 1815+ ISLE OF ISLAY, ARL, SCT [36316] : C1750 ANS, SCT [36327] : 1802-1841 INVERCHAOLAIN, ARL, SCT [36606] : MARGARET C1853 TOBERMORY & MULL, ARL, SCT [36712] : 1800+ LANARK, LKS, SCT [36791] : 1700S FORGUE, BAN, SCT [36843] : C1832 CADDER, LKS, SCT [37148] : 1806+ PORTREE, INV, SCT [37178] : 1790+ KINLOCHBERVIE, SUT, SCT & CAN [35611] : 1890S CHICO KITSAP, WA, USA [35260] : C1813 NC, USA [36358] : NATHANIEL 1800-28 FAYETTE CO., KY, USA [38086] : PETER PRE 1825 MADISON CO., AL, USA [38314] : PRE 1900 LAKE CO., CA & AR, USA [38570] : JEMIMA ALL WORLDWIDE [35291]

MORRISROE ALL IRL [36551]

MORRISS 1850-1920 COLLINGWOOD, VIC, AUS [34191] : PRE 1818 CROYDON, SRY, ENG [34036] : PRE 1830 PYTCHLEY, NTH, ENG [35215] : JAMES 1750 BARNACK, NTH, ENG [35369] : 1700+ CLAINES, WOR, ENG [37694] : 1800+ LONGFORD, LOG, IRL [38213]

MORRISSEY PRE 1860 IRL [33798] : PRE 1830 LEX, IRL [34273] : PRE 1856 THURLES, TIP, IRL [35028]

MORRITT 1840-1850S PRESTON & CANDOVER, HAM, ENG [36285] : 1700-1850 DEV, ENG [36395] : 1700+ WHITKIRK, WRY, ENG [37426]

MORROTT 1700-1850 DEV, ENG [36395]

MORROW 1846+ BALACLAVA, SA, AUS [34685] : 1853-1905 CAMPERDOWN, NSW, AUS [35530] : 1800-1900 SIMCOE CO., ONT, CAN [36688] : 1834+ RENFREW CO., ONT, CAN [37474] : 1800-1815 CAV, IRL [34088] : 1700-1900 KESH, FER, IRL [34537] : 1870S LIMERICK, LIM, IRL [34688] : PRE 1852 NEWTOWNARDS, DOW, IRL [35245] : PRE 1834 IRL [37474] : 1806+ CARROLL CO., OH, USA [35266] : WILLIAM 1862-1880 WARREN CO., KY, USA [36734] : PRE 1850 LAKE CHARLES, LA, USA [37740] : 1775-1928 SC, TN & TX, USA [37812]

MORSCHEL 1750-1870 DARMSTADT, HEN, GER [38007]

MORSE 1788 ROCHDALE, LAN, ENG [34474] : 1750+ VERYAN, CON, ENG [35208] : PRE 1800 SFK, ENG [35701] : ALL OXF, ENG [36189] : 1860+ HEANOR, DBY, ENG [36189] : PRE 1860 GREAT FARINGDON, BRK, ENG [36189] : PRE 1793 WICKENBY, LIN, ENG [37318] : PRE 1650 ESS & SFK, ENG [38746] : 1750-1850 CANTON, MA, USA [36915] : 1750 COVENTRY, RI, USA [37008] : 1840+ CT, USA [37803] : 1790+ WASHINGTON CO., OH, USA [38343]

MORSON 1870S LITHGOW, NSW, AUS [38541]

MORTENSEN 1810-1850S TAARS, JUTLAND, DEN [36285]

MORTER ALL THURSFORD & SCULTHORPE, NFK, ENG [36171] : 1840-1900 BURTON ON TRENT, STS, ENG [37850] : 1890+ DERBY, DBY, ENG [37850] : ALL WORLDWIDE [36171]

MORTIER 1800 VEERE, ZEL, NL [38696]

MORTIMER 1860-1900 VIC, AUS [34191] : PRE 1833 TAS, AUS [34959] : 1860S POMEROY & GOULBURN, NSW, AUS [35546] : 1860-1930 YORK CO., ONT, CAN [34482] : 1790+ RUFFORTH, YKS, ENG [33956] : PRE 1815 BRENTFORD, MDX, ENG [34959] : C1750-1850S AYLESBURY, BKM, ENG [36289] : PRE 1800 ISLEWORTH, MDX, ENG [36423] : 1800+ CHADDERTON OLDHAM, LAN, ENG [36568] : 1750-1800 MELTON, NFK, ENG [37456] : PRE 1860 CLONDAVADDOG, DON, IRL [35546] : 1880+ CHRISTCHURCH, CBY, NZ [34049]

MORTIMORE 1880+ PLYMOUTH, DEV, ENG [34703]

MORTIN PRE 1840 CHAPEL EN-LE FRITH, DBY, ENG [34588]

MORTLEY PRE 1841 HAWKHURST, KEN, ENG [35578]

MORTLOCK 1800+ CLARE, SFK, ENG [33857] : 1800+ CHATHAM ROCHESTER, KEN, ENG [33857] : PRE 1770 SFK, ENG [34445] : 1700+ SFK, ENG [34943] : 1800 GLEMSFORD, SFK, ENG [34976]

MORTOMER 1750-1800 EAST LONDON, MDX, ENG [38516]

MORTON 1850+ VIC, AUS [34866] : 1824+ BATHURST, NSW, AUS [35090] : 1800+ BATHURST, NSW, AUS [35911] : 1854-1867 NSW, AUS [38389] : 1860+ QUEBEC, QUE, CAN [34228] : 1840+ OMEMEE, ONT, CAN [35625] : ALL MORPETH & MITFORD, NBL, ENG [35579] : REBECCA PRE 1805 STAUNTON, DBY, ENG [36192] : 1790-1850 LONDON, MDX, ENG [36239] : 1830+ MANCHESTER, LAN, ENG [37322] : ANTHONY C1815 WARMSWORTH, YKS, ENG [38247] : PRE 1846 CARLISLE, CUL, ENG [38399] : HENRY PRE 1840 FER, IRL [34392] : C1840S ARM, IRL [34866] : 1790 MONAGHAN, MOG, IRL [35067] : 1820S CAR, IRL [35557] : 1600-1660 CAV, IRL [37613]

: 1750-1850 KILMARNOCK, AYR, SCT [35151] : PRE 1900 PAISLEY, RFW, SCT [35433] : 1650-1800 ST MONANCE, FIF, SCT [35627] : C1800 LOUDON, AYR, SCT [35773] : PRE 1800 LKS, SCT [36277] : PRE 1860 PER, SCT [36754] : PRE 1820 PAISLEY, RFW, SCT [37333] : 1700-1850 ATHOL & NEW SALEM, MA, USA [36335] : 1800-1860 STANLY CO., NC, USA [36897] : 1880-1990 LA CO., CA, USA [38154] : PRE 1850 USA [38389] : 1800+ USA & NZ [36850] : 1800+ AMLWCH, AGY, WLS [36277]

MORTSON C1795 ERY, ENG [33910]

MORVEL PRE 1900 NEGUAC, NB, CAN & FRA [38447]

MORYS PRE 1940 TP, POL [36497]

MOSCHINI ALL FLORENCE, ITL [33954]

MOSCROP PRE 1850 CUL, ENG [35423] : PRE 1820 BOLTON, LAN, ENG [38261] : 1820+ BKM & MDX, ENG [38261] : ALL WORLDWIDE [33858]

MOSDELL 1880+ NEWBURY, BRK, ENG [36975]

MOSE PRE 1800 LAMBERHURST, KEN, ENG [36883] : 1750+ DEAL & CANTERBURY, KEN, ENG [37251]

MOSEL 1840-1990S BLAIR CO., PA, USA [37021]

MOSELEY PRE 1850 ENG [34222] : 1800+ ENG [34956] : PRE 1860 BEWDLEY & DUDLEY, WOR, ENG [35940] : 1700-1800S TENTERDEN AREA, KEN, ENG [37714] : PRE 1680 LONDON, ENG [38044] : PRE 1775 HENRICO CO., VA, USA [38126]

MOSER PRE 1900 GODERICH, ONT, CAN [36716] : 1856+ WELLESLEY & MORNINGTON, ONT, CAN [36716] : C1560 HERRENBERG, BAW, FRG [38660] : 1700+ DIERSBURG, BAD, GER [38529] : 1700-1820 GOLS, BUR, OES [36957]

MOSES PRE 1780 CARLISLE, CUL, ENG [34162] : ALL CUL, ENG [34558] : 1800S LONDON, ENG [35743] : PRE 1800 KEN, ENG [36399] : ELLEN C1880 LONDON, ENG [37334] : ALL LONDON, ENG [37334] : 1610-1650 SCT [34162] : 1500-1900 USA [36114]

MOSGROVE 1830+ WELLINGTON CO., ONT, CAN [34231]

MOSHER ALL WASHINGTON CO., NY, USA [35312] : 1850-1900 MI, USA [35603] : 1630+ RI, USA [38015] : THOMAS 1780-1850 WASHINGTON CO., NY, USA [38130] : 1500+ DARTMOUTH, MA, RI & ME, USA & ENG [36970]

MOSIUK PRE 1900 NIWRA & BORSZCZOW, GALICIA, SU & POL [34146]

MOSLEY 1840-1860 KINGSTANLEY, GLS, ENG [35725] : 1645-1820 NORTH WINGFIELD, DBY, ENG [36907] : 1770+ LND, ENG [37074] : 1799-1901 IRL [35316]

MOSMAN C1850+ NSW & QLD, AUS [34589]

MOSQUERA ALL LA CORUNA, GALICIA, ESP [34732]

MOSS WILLIAM 1867+ CHARTERS TOWERS, NSW, AUS [36367] : 1840S LAUNCESTON AREA, TAS, AUS [37307] : GEORGE H. 1864-1903 LONDON &, VIC, AUS & ENG [34680] : PRE 1845 PYRTON, OXF, ENG [33866] : PRE 1840 CONGLETON, CHS, ENG [33937] : 1750-1870 BIRMINGHAM, WAR, ENG [34431] : 1800-1840 LONDON, ENG [34448] : 1850+ NEWCASTLE & STOKE, STS, ENG [34714] : C1840 GLOUCESTER, GLS, ENG [34734] : 1750+ VERYAN, CON, ENG [35208] : PRE 1850 ESS, ENG [35238] : THOMAS PRE 1851 WOLVERHAMPTON, STS, ENG [35330] : C1777 SHOREDITCH & HACKNEY, LND, ENG [35560] : PRE 1800 SFK, ENG [35701] : PRE 1865 FRAXFIELD, WIL, ENG [35932] : PRE 1860 SAPPERTON, GLS, ENG [35971] : 1850+ CHELFORD, CHS, ENG [35979] : WILLIAM 1842+

LEEK, STS, ENG [36367] : PRE 1900 LIVERPOOL & LONDON, ENG [36399] : PRE 1900 PENWORTHAM & PRESTON, LAN, ENG [36508] : EMMA PRE 1884 COLNBROOK, BKM, ENG [36510] : EMMA 1890+ CLERKENWELL, LND, ENG [36510] : 1700S SHADWELL, LND, ENG [36585] : 1830-40 EAST BERGHOLT, SFK, ENG [36816] : 1600-1700 MANCHESTER, LAN, ENG [36898] : C1770 WETHERDON, SFK, ENG [36945] : 1800-1850 SHEFFIELD, WRY, ENG [36966] : ALL BRISTOL, ENG [36995] : PRE 1860 LND, ENG [37057] : 1750+ EAST LONDON, ENG [37252] : PRE 1840 SUDBURY AREA, SFK, ENG [37307] : 1700S+ RUSHTON, STS, ENG [37413] : 1750+ LAN, ENG [37482] : C1900 WOOD GREEN, LND, ENG [38168] : PRE 1900 INWORTH, ESS, ENG [38205] : PRE 1930 ISLINGTON, LND, ENG [38205] : PRE 1898 OLDHAM, LAN, ENG [38580] : C1806 TERMONAMONGAN, TYR, IRL [33924] : PRE 1863 TYR, IRL [34582] : PRE 1840 TYR, IRL [34984] : GEORGE H. 1864-1903 ROSS & HOKITIKA, NZ [34680] : GEORGE H. 1880-1990S HOKITIKA, LYTTLETON & CHCH, NZ [34680] : 1612-1642 NEW HAVEN, CT, USA [37803] : 1640-1913 VA, IN, IA, KS, USA [37812] : 1875+ CARDIFF, GLA, WLS [36995]

MOSSES 1850+ LIVERPOOL & BLACKPOOL, LAN, ENG [36683]

MOSSMAN C1850+ NSW & QLD, AUS [34589] : 1700-1800 NEWBANK, PEE, SCT [35094] : 1800+ BEW, SCT [35909]

MOSSOP ALL CAN & ENG [34140] : ALL ST BEES & PRIOR SCALES, CUL, ENG [37735] : 1600-1900 ROTTINGTON, CUL, ENG [37858]

MOSSY PRE 1800 RHA, FRA [36353]

MOSTERT 1672 CAPE, RSA [38382]

MOSTYN PRE 1850 LONDON, ENG [34536] : 1700S SURAT, INDIA [36786]

MOTE 1826 WALWORTH, SRY, ENG [34808]

MOTH ALL IOW, HAM, ENG [34724]

MOTHERLOVE ALL ENG & IRL [37061]

MOTHERSHALL 1650-1740 CRAYTHORNE, ERY, ENG [34552]

MOTHERSHAW C1820 DARLASTON, STS, ENG [34239]

MOTHERSILL PRE 1830 KILDARE, KID, IRL [37473]

MOTHERWELL PRE 1840 YKS, ENG [36360]

MOTLEY 1700-1800S BOSTON, MA, USA [36837]

MOTSCH PRE 1800 BRD & GER [36964]

MOTT PRE 1900 HAMILTON, VIC, AUS [34536] : 1840+ MACCLESFIELD, SA, AUS [34685] : PRE 1840 EAST HANNINGFIELD, ESS, ENG [33833] : 1700+ STANFORD RIVERS, ESS, ENG [33849] : 1750+ COCKFIELD, SFK, ENG [34020] : ALL NFK & SFK, ENG [34286] : C1550 ESS, ENG [34286] : 1650+ LONDON, ENG [34286] : PRE 1900 BKM, ENG [34536] : PRE 1840 EAST HANNINGFIELD, ESS, ENG [34685] : 1790+ SFK & ESS, ENG [35632] : PRE 1700 ESS, ENG [35642] : ALL SRY, ENG [37115] : ALL CROYDON, SRY, ENG [37115] : 1840+ NFK, ENG [37347] : 1700 INWORTH, ESS, ENG [37928] : 1700S DUTCHESS CO., NY, USA [36710]

MOTTLEY PRE 1800 LONDON, ENG [38658]

MOTTRAM PRE 1850 YKS, ENG [37245]

MOTZ PRE 1800 BRD & GER [36964]

MOUAT ALL KCD, SCT [34381] : 1850+ MONTROSE, ANS, SCT [36971]

MOUBRAY 1700+ AYR, SCT [34408]

MOUCER ALL ENG [36524]

MOUDY PRE 1802 WEAKLEY CO., TN, USA [36939]

MOUEL ALL ENG [38258]

MOULD 1800+ PARRAMATTA, NSW, AUS [35073] : PRE 1880 COPPENHALL, CHS, ENG [33765] : PRE 1799 ESS, ENG [34886] : 1800S LONDON, ENG [37969] : 1600-1700 NEWCASTLE, STS, ENG [38474] : 1850-1900 CHRISTCHURCH & WELLINGTON, NZ [37969] : 1700S ROCKBRIDGE CO., VA, USA [38044]

MOULDEN PRE 1888 SOUTH STOKE, OXF, ENG [36475]

MOULDEY PRE 1750 SPEEN, BRK, ENG [35889]

MOULDING PRE 1845 BRAMPTON, CUL, ENG [34911] : PRE 1900 KEIGHLEY, WRY, ENG [36126] : 1840 LEICESTER, LEI, ENG [36528]

MOULDS PRE 1900 LEICESTER, LEI, ENG [36113]

MOULE 1880+ MACKAY, QLD, AUS [35825] : 1700-1770 WORCESTER, WOR, ENG [34552] : 1680-1880 NORTH MOLTON, DEV, ENG [35825] : ALL ENG [35933]

MOULTON ALL SAWSTON, CAM, ENG [37189] : MARTHA 1750+ YORK, ME, USA [36563] : PRE 1840 MON, WLS [35895]

MOUNCE 1700-1900 PA, IN & IA, USA [38328]

MOUNCEY 1800-1850 SKIBBEREEN, COR, IRL [38290]

MOUNDS C1777 LONDON, ENG [35872]

MOUNGER JOHN 1615-1670 ENG [36317] : ROBERT 1666-1730 ISLE OF WIGHT CO., VA, USA [36317]

MOUNSEY 1750-1900 MORLAND & BAMPTON, WES, ENG [34632] : 1850+ CUMBERLAND, CUL & YKS, ENG [35579] : 1800+ MARYPORT, CUL, ENG [37073] : 1840-87 LAN, WAR & WOR, ENG [37762]

MOUNSTER 1700+ BRIDPORT, DOR, ENG [38745]

MOUNT 1800+ DOVER, KEN, ENG [35980] : 1776+ PRESTON, KEN, ENG [35980] : 1800+ BARHAM, KEN, ENG [35980] : ALL HERNE BAY, KEN, ENG [37707]

MOUNTAIN PRE 1921 NSW, AUS [36856] : PRE 1870 THREE RIVERS, QUE, CAN [34683] : 1793+ QUE, CAN [34778] : ALL THWAITE HALL, NFK, ENG [34778] : 1700-1800S BRISTOL, GLS, ENG [36856] : 1750+ HEVENINGHAM, SFK, ENG [37321] : 1823 PETERBOROUGH, NTH, ENG [37462] : 1795+ STIBBINGTON, HUN, ENG [37462]

MOUNTFIELD 1750S MINSHULL VERNON, CHS, ENG [37751]

MOUNTFORD 1830S ENG [37024] : PRE 1800 STOKE, STS, ENG [37893]

MOUNTJOY ALL BRADWORTHY, DEV & CON, ENG [38446]

MOUNTS 1700-1900 PA, IN & IA, USA [38328]

MOUNTSTEPHEN 1660+ PITMINSTER, SOM, ENG [35112]

MOURIE ALL WORLDWIDE [33903]

MOURIER JEAN 1600+ FRA [37429]

MOURILYAN ALL WORLDWIDE [34742]

MOURNE 1800+ ATHENS CO., OH, USA [37032]

MOURNIER ALL ESS, ENG [37741]

MOUSELL ALL FOREST OF DEAN, GLS, ENG [37746]

MOUSHALL PRE 1860 MANCHESTER, LAN, ENG [33835]

MOUSIER ALL UK [36524]

MOUSIN ALL UK [36524]

MOUSIR ALL WORLDWIDE [36524]

MOUSLEY PRE 1750 FOSTON, DBY, ENG [34311]

MOUSSA ALL ENG [36524]

MOUSSIER ALL UK [36524]

MOVAT 1750-1790 LEAVENWICK, SHI, SCT [38407]

MOW 1640-1710 PLYMOUTH, MA, USA [38054] : 1730-1780 BARRINGTON, NH, USA [38054] : 1640-1710 NY, USA [38054]

MOWAT JOHN 1852-1853 TORONTO, ONT, CAN [34247] : 1830-1900 BROCKVILLE, ONT, CAN

[34402] : PRE 1810 WHITBY, NRY, ENG [38580] :
PRE 1900 EDINBURGH, SCT [34148] : PRE 1900
ABERDEEN, SCT [34148] : JOHN PRE 1852 OKI,
SCT [34247] : ALL MONTROSE, ANS, SCT [34381] :
ALL KINNEFF, KCD, SCT [34381] : ALL KCD, SCT
[34381] : 1830-1860 ORKNEY IS, CAI, SCT [34402] :
DON C1770-1850 CAI, SCT [34646] : 1700-1850
TURRIFF, ABD, SCT [34771] : PRE 1800 CAI, SCT
[35800] : JOHN 1750+ FRESWICK, CAI, SCT [36813]
: 1750+ GOURDON, KCD, SCT [36971] : 1700+
KINNEFF & CATTERLINE, KCD, SCT [36971] :
1750+ BERVIE, KCD, SCT [36971]

MOWATT PRE 1800 WICK, CAI, SCT [36436]

MOWBERY ALL WORLDWIDE [35739]

MOWBRAY 1700+ DUNFERMLINE, FIF, SCT
[35969] : PRE 1890 TREDEGAR, MON, WLS [37716] :
ALL WORLDWIDE [35739]

MOWBRY PRE 1850 SPETCHLEY & BRENDON,
WOR, ENG [37716]

MOWE ALL ENG & USA [38054] : 1710-1880
GRAFTON, NH, USA [38054]

MOWERS PRE 1883 PORT BRUCE &
COPENHAGEN, ONT, CAN [37518] : PRE 1870+
BRIGHTON & WAUBASHENE, ONT, CAN [37518]
: 1700-1860 NY, USA [33753]

MOWRY 1800-1850 MERCER, PA, USA [36449]

MOXHAM 1830-1900 HAMILTON, TAS, AUS [34551] :
PRE 1830 EBBESBOURNE WAKE, WIL, ENG
[34551] : ALL EBBESBOURNE WAKE, WIL, ENG
[38489] : ALL ALVEDISTON, WIL, ENG [38489]

MOXLEY 1800+ LONDON, ENG [37160]

MOXON 1750-1820 CARLETON, YKS, ENG [34762]

MOYER PRE 1900 FIF, SCT [33966] : SOLOMON
1790+ HERKIMER CO., NY, USA [36950] : HENRY
1750+ HERKIMER CO., NY, USA [36950] :
JEREMIAH 1790-1820+ HERKIMER CO., NY,
USA [36950] : FREDERICK 1780+ HERKIMER
CO., NY, USA [36950]

MOYES PRE 1850 BERGH APTON, NFK, ENG
[37512] : 1860S KILMARNOCK, AYR, SCT [34088]

MOYLAN ALL COR & KID, IRL [36580]

MOYLE 1850+ BOTANY, NSW, AUS [35149] : C1860
MOONTA, SA, AUS [37159] : 1848+ ADELADIE,
SA, AUS [37189] : PRE 1850 HELSTON, CON, ENG
[33814] : 1700-1800 WENDRON, CON, ENG [35151] :
1655+ WENDRON, CON, ENG [35587] : JAMES
PRE 1890 REDRUTH, CON, ENG [35962] : JAMES
PRE 1890 PENRYN, CON, ENG [35962] : ALL
WENDRON, CON, ENG [37189]

MOYLES ALL WORLDWIDE [36581]

MOYNIHAN PRE 1870 KILLARNEY, KER, IRL
[34901] : ALL KER, IRL & NZ [36854]

MOYSES 1735 OELDE, WEF, GER [37509]

MOYSEY 1840+ VIC & NSW, AUS [35233] : 1800+
LIN, ENG [35233]

MOYTHAN 1700+ HEF, ENG [36552]

MOZELY (SEE MOSELEY) [34956]

MOZISEK 1833-80 CS [38314]

MOZLEY C1800 GAINSBOROUGH, LIN, ENG
[36515]

MUCH PRE 1890 POM, GER [34837]

MUCHALL C1840 SMESTOW, STS, ENG [37143]

MUCHEN PRE 1830 CLUNAS, FER, IRL [38412]

MUCKEL MARY ANN C1863 BATHURST, NSW,
AUS [35104]

MUCKEY 1818-1848 PA, USA [35301]

MUCKLEY PRE 1837 CREW, CHS, ENG [34942] : PRE
1838 WEDNESBURY & MOXLEY, STS, ENG
[34942]

MUDD PRE 1870 ENG [36747]

MUDDEN ALL OXF, NTH & LND, ENG [38754]

MUDDLE 1800S DEAL & BRASTED, KEN, ENG
[38289]

MUDFORD 1800+ BROMBOROUGH, CHS, ENG
[35611]

MUDGE 1800-1900 NEWTON ABBOT, DEV, ENG
[35614] : 1800+ TAVISTOCK, DEV, ENG [36266]

MUDIE C1860 JAMBEROO, NSW, AUS [35249] :
1840+ LND, ENG & AUS [36254] : PRE 1812
DUNDEE, ANS, SCT [34979] : 1880+ LEITH, MLN,
SCT [35486] : 1800S LOCHEE, DUNDEE, ANS, SCT
[36246]

MUEHLENBRUCH 1850+ USA [36974]

MUEHLHEIM PRE 1850 SCHEUREN, BE, CH [38747]

MUELLER 1945 WOLFSBURG, NSA, BRD [38749] :
1600-1900 HERISAU, AAR, CH [35292] : PRE 1880
CANTON AARRGON, CH [36918] : 1655+ BE, CH
[37004] : PRE 1850 UROJANKE, DDR [38616] : 1750-
1870 NEHWEILER, ALS, FRA [36898] : 1700S
TSCHECHEN, SIL, GER [33901] : WILHELM 1854
BRA, GER [34195] : ALL DAISBACH, BAD, GER
[34238] : 1800+ MEK, GER [35874] : 1839
ANDISLEBEN, PRE, GER [36900] : 1830-1866
RUGEN ISLAND, GER [37165] : JOHAN 1830-1864
MECKLENBERG, STETIN, GER [38104] : PRE 1823
ALTENTREPTOW, POM, GER [38630] : PRE 1800
HOHENSOLMS, HEN, GER [38681] : PRE 1700
GERHARDSBRUNN, RPF, GER [38681] : 1977-1979
BAD PYRMONT, PYR, GER [38749] : 1835 LEBIEN,
KSA, GER [38750] : 1811 HEMSENDORF, KSA,
GER [38750] : 1738-1845 JESSEN ELSTER, KSA,
GER [38750] : WILHELM ALL ELMA, NY, USA
[34059] : JOHN 1839-1914 HAMILTON CO., OH,
USA [36973] : JOHN 1870-1908 CHICAGO, COOK,
IL, USA [38104] : JOHN 1864-1870 DENISON,
CRAWFORD, IA, USA [38104] : HENRIETTA W.
PRE 1899 NEW YORK, NY, USA [38477] : 1840+
GERMANTOWN, WI, USA [38530]

MUELMANS 1550-1650 NMR, BEL [36943]

MUERMANN ALL WEI, GER [38607]

MUES 1868+ COLENFELD, NSA, BRD [38631] : 1580
OSNABRUCK, WEF, GER [38631] : ALL
MILOSLAWITZ, POS, GER [38631] : ALL
CINCINNATI, OH, USA [38631]

MUESKE ALL POS, GER [37529]

MUFF C1820 DUR, ENG [37112]

MUGGERIDGE 1700-1800 SLAUGHAM, SSX, ENG
[35288]

MUGGIN 1700-1740 LANERSBACH, TIROL, OES
[35850]

MUGGLESTONE C1770 BARWELL, LEI, ENG [37053]

MUGGLETON PRE 1850 ROCKINGHAM, NTH &
KEN, ENG [37339] : ALL UK [36020]

MUGLISTON 1770+ DISEWORTH, LEI, ENG [34374]

MUHSS C1648 ALTENHAGEN, HAN, GER [38631]

MUIR PRE 1852 HAMILTON & RIVER OUSE, TAS,
AUS [35459] : WILLIAM ALL PRAHRAN,
MELBOURNE, VIC, AUS [35593] : MARION 1860+
CHARTERS TOWERS, QLD, AUS & SCT [37161] :
C1850-1900 BRUCE CO., ONT, CAN [37453] : C1860
SOUTH SHIELDS, DUR, ENG [34329] : C1800+
GLASGOW, LKS, SCT [33971] : 1750+ PAISLEY,
RFW, SCT [33986] : C1744 LANARK, LKS, SCT
[34118] : 1840+ KIRKCALDY, FIF, SCT [34260] :
1820+ AUCHTERDERRAN, FIF, SCT [34260] : PRE
1890 HAMILTON, LKS, SCT [34598] : C1808-1910
MUSSELBURGH, MLN, SCT [34635] : PRE 1851
GLASGOW, LKS, SCT [34873] : PRE 1800 ST
ANDREWS, FIF, SCT [35126] : JOHN 1800
GLASGOW, SCT [35361] : ALEXANDER PRE 1841
RENFREW, RFW, SCT [35380] : ALEXANDER 1845
PAISLEY, RFW, SCT [35380] : ALEXANDER PRE
1851 BARONY, GLASGOW, LKS, SCT [35380] :

1800S STRAITON, AYR, SCT [35558] : 1800-1850
OKI, SCT [35806] : 1800+ DALGETY, FIF, SCT
[35969] : ALL ISLAY, ARL, SCT [36451] :
EUPHEMIA PRE 1830 PER, SCT [36619] : 1800
FORT AUGUSTUS, INV, SCT [36641] : 1780-1850
CREETOWN, KKD, AYR & RFW, SCT [36802] :
C1820 CUMBERNAULD, DNB, SCT [36875] : 1820-
50 MUSSELBURGH, MLN, SCT [36884] : PRE 1850
MAYBOLE, AYR, SCT [37169] : 1710+
MUIRAVONSIDE, STI, SCT [37205] : 1750+
STRATHAVEN, LKS, SCT [37333] : C1800 GOVAN,
RFW, SCT [37333] : C1830 MULL, ARL, SCT [37453] :
C1800 SLAMANNAN, STI, SCT [37898] : PRE 1770
EDINBURGH, MLN, SCT [38135] : 1750+
LESMAHAGOW, LKS, SCT [38388]
MUIR (SEE MOIR) [36268]
MUIRE 1740S-1790S KILRENNY & ANSTRUTHER
EASTER, FIF, SCT [34359]
MUIRHEAD 1875+ CANTERBURY, NZ [38286] : PRE
1870 EDINBURGH & GLASGOW, MLN, SCT
[34845] : PRE 1880 RFW, SCT [36363] : 1770-1800
CUMBERNAULD, DNB, SCT [37779]
MUIS D'ENTREMONT 1500S BN & HN, FRA [35617]
MUKIN PRE 1874 PITSMOOR, YKS, ENG [34814]
MULBURGER ALL USA & GER [38369]
MULCAHEY PRE 1850 LIM, IRL [36325]
MULCAHY JOHN 1830+ YOUGHAL, COR, IRL
[34954] : 1850+ NEWCASTLE WEST, LIM, IRL
[34960] : 1820+ BALLYPOREEN, TIP, IRL [34960] :
1800+ MILLTOWN, KER, IRL [35054] : 1820
MILLTOWN, KER, IRL [35054] : 1820-1880 TIP, IRL
& AUS [35718]
MULCASTER PRE 1840 CARLISLE, CUL, ENG
[38722]
MULCHALL C1800+ MOTHILL, KIK, IRL [33792]
MULCOCK 1830S ESS, ENG [34603] : ALL NZ [34603]
MULCORNY 1800S CLA, IRL [35379]
MULDON PRE 1868 CANDABA, PAMPANGA,
PHILIPPINE [34891]
MULDOON PRE 1840 QUEANBEYAN, NSW, AUS
[34265] : 1825+ MICHELAGO, NSW, AUS [35410] :
JOHN 1841-1851+ RATCLIFF & LIMEHOUSE,
MDX, ENG [37546] : 1775-1870 GAL, IRL [34071] :
1800+ CLARA, OFF, IRL [35080] : 1800 OFF, IRL
[35410]
MULFORD 1820+ EXETER, DEV, ENG [34568]
MULHAIR PRE 1865 EDINBURGH, SCT & IRL
[37852]
MULHALL C1800+ MOTHILL, KIK, IRL [33792]
MULHARE PRE 1900 COURTWOOD, LEX, IRL
[38300]
MULHOLLAND 1860+ BINALONG, NSW, AUS
[35105] : C1870+ COONAMBLE, NSW, AUS [35105]
: 1860+ DUBBO, NSW, AUS [35105] : C1841+
SYDNEY, NSW, AUS [35105] : ALL DERRY, LDY,
IRL [33993] : SARAH 1800-1850 ANT, IRL [35006] :
PRE 1832 ANT, IRL [37496]
MULLALY C1860 STITTOVILLE, ONT, CAN [34988] :
PRE 1850 IRL [36532]
MULLAM PRE 1750 DUR, ENG [37693]
MULLAN 1800-1930 COLERAINE, LDY, IRL [36115] :
1700+ GATEHOUSE OF FLEET, KKD, SCT [34414]
MULLANE 1860 CORK, IRL [34844] : PAT 1840S KER,
IRL [37169]
MULLANEY 1750+ IRL [33963] : PRE 1900
THURLES, TIP, IRL [34013]
MULLARD 1780 CRESSAGE, SAL, ENG [34708]
MULLARKEY 1870S PADDINGTON, NSW, AUS
[37309] : 1840S CLA, IRL [37309]
MULLEN 1864+ OXLEY CREEK, QLD, AUS [35392] :
1880-1900 LAMBTON CO., ONT, CAN [34153] : 1880
HASTINGS CO., ONT, CAN [36655] : ALL SOUTH

SHIELDS, DUR, ENG [37950] : 1850-1900 BELFAST,
IRL [35094] : PRE 1864 CAV, IRL [35392] : 1870
PORTGLENONE, ANT, IRL [36655] : 1800+ FIF,
SCT [34226] : 1900-1915 DETROIT, MI, USA [34153]
MULLEN-TURNER PRE 1857 NEW YORK CITY,
NY, USA [35704]
MULLER 1848+ PORT LINCOLN, SA, AUS [35040] :
1600-1900 HERISAU, AAR, CH [35292] : C1700
GIERSLEBEN, HAL, DDR [37918] : NARCISSE
C1811 BOULOGNE, NOR, FRA [35848] : C1785
NUSSLOCH, BAD, GER [34239] : PRE 1848
WILDEMANN, HAN, GER [35040] : PRE 1850
HAYNDYEBERG, HEN, GER [35523] : C1725
KRAHENBERG PFALZ, BAV, GER [37516] : 1710-
1730 LOSHEIM AREA, SAA & RPR, GER [38528] :
1650-1730 SCHWIGERN, WUE, GER [38574] :
1860+ PICTON, MBH, NZ [36746]
MULLIGAN 1915+ KENSINGTON, NSW, AUS
[35843] : 1800+ PONTIAC CO., QUE, CAN [34199] :
1800+ CARLETON CO., ONT, CAN [34199] : 1780-
1860 LOG, IRL [34514] : PRE 1865 GAL, IRL [34911] :
1800+ SLI, IRL [35998] : ALL IRL [37893] : 1845-55
CASTLEBAR, MAY, IRL [38583] : 1800+ NZ & UK
[35963]
MULLIN C1800+ GASPE, QUE, CAN [38406] : ALL
BELFAST, ANT, IRL & AUS [35213] : 1800+ OH &
IA, USA [38735]
MULLINER 1800+ SAL & STS, ENG [35019]
MULLINEUX ALL WORLDWIDE [35331]
MULLINGER PRE 1780 BLO NORTON, NFK, ENG
[35973]
MULLINIX 1769-1880 MD, MC & IN, USA [36901]
MULLINS 1855+ REDBANK PLAINS, QLD, AUS
[34449] : 1832+ TAS, AUS [35127] : 1840+
NORTHUMBERLAND CO., ONT, CAN [38410] :
1830 ST GILES CRIPPLEGATE, LND, ENG [36863] :
1839 ST LUKES FINSBURY, LND, ENG [36863] :
1829+ CHRISTCHURCH & NEWGATE, LND,
ENG [36863] : 1840 ST LEONARDS SHOREDITCH,
LND, ENG [36863] : 1750-1900 EAST COKER, SOM,
ENG [37378] : PRE 1900 ESS, ENG [37693] : 1600-
1850 HARTHILL, WRY, ENG [38265] : ALL FYANS
IS., LIM, IRL [34299] : PRE 1850 TULLA, CLA, IRL
[34431] : PRE 1855 BALLYHALE, KIK, IRL [34449] :
PRE 1830 GLIN, LIM, IRL [34449] : PRE 1859
NEWTOWN & LIMAVADY, DRY, IRL [37981] :
1854 LIMERICK, LIM, IRL [37984] : PRE 1850
CORK, COR, IRL [38420] : 1800-1850 DUBLIN, IRL
[38455] : 1800-1838 WIC, IRL [38455] : PRE 1850
EASTERN, KY, USA [36972] : JONATHAN 1800-
1835 CALLOWAY CO., KY, USA [38569]
MULLIS JOHN 1814-1895 DENISON, IA, USA [37014]
MULLISS 1700-1900 WAR & LEI, ENG [37858]
MULLONEY 1830 GAL, IRL [34793]
MULQUEENY 1800S IRL & AUS [33881]
MULQUINNEY 1870+ VIC, AUS [34574]
MULRANEY 1840S OFF, IRL & AUS [34845]
MULREADY 1820+ RHODE, OFF, IRL [36647] :
1850+ BOSTON, MA, USA [36647]
MULROONEY PRE 1866 CAR, IRL [33822] :
JOHANNA C1855 TIP, IRL [35541] : 1850+ CLARA,
KIK, IRL [36763]
MULROY 1840S KINGS MEADOWS, TAS, AUS
[34845]
MULRY 1850+ NSW, AUS [35148] : PRE 1855 GAL,
IRL [35148]
MULSO PRE 1495 CREATINGHAM, SFK, ENG
[34573]
MULVAY ALL WA, AUS [36889] : ALL IRL [36889] :
ALL NZ [36889]
MULVEY 1800-1850 LOUGHCREW, MEA, IRL [37435]
: ALL WORLDWIDE [36889]

MULVIHILL 1840S SHANAGOLDEN, LIM, IRL [35136]

MUMBY ALL LIN, ENG [35628] : 1870+ LONDON, LND, ENG [37048]

MUMFORD 1800+ DOR, ENG [34228] : 1700+ UGLEY, ESS, ENG [36402] : 1875+ ISLINGTON & UPPER HOLLOWAY, MDX, ENG [36955]

MUMMA 1650+ PA, USA [38241]

MUMMERY PRE 1884 NSW, AUS [35351] : 1700+ BERMONDSEY, LND, ENG [34664]

MUNACOTT C1700 ST BUDEAUX, DEV, ENG [37770]

MUNBY 1600-1800 ERY, ENG [36393]

MUNCASTER 1864+ NEWCASTLE, NSW, AUS [35394]

MUNCKTON 1878 QLD, AUS [37894] : PRE 1878 EAST LAMBROOK, SOM, ENG [37894]

MUNDAY ALL GOULBURN, NSW, AUS [34869] : PRE 1883 PONTVILLE, TAS, AUS [35553] : CHARLOTTE 1850-1890 COLLINGWOOD & HEATHCOTE, VIC, AUS [37488] : 1840+ LONDON, MDX, ENG [34049] : PRE 1850 NETHERHAMPTON, WIL, ENG [35229] : C1800 LONDON, ENG [35755] : ALL HAM & OXF, ENG [37373] : CHARLOTTE 1820-1845 ARUNDEL, SSX, ENG [37488] : PRE 1800 BUCKLAND, BKM, ENG [37726] : 1832+ ROCHESTER, KEN, ENG [37921] : 1846-1865 GRANGEMOUTH, STI, SCT [33951] : 1865-1875 KEWEENAW CO., MI, USA [38009]

MUNDEE C1880 PAISLEY & GLASGOW, RFW & LKS, SCT [35786]

MUNDELL 1847+ SCUGOG ISLAND, ONT, CAN [34169] : PRE 1826 BALLYMENA, ANT, IRL [34169] : 1700-1820 BALLYNASCREEN, LDY, IRL [35603] : 1850-1900 MI, USA [35603]

MUNDEN PRE 1900 HAM & DOR, ENG [34317] : PRE 1900 LONDON, ENG [34406] : PRE 1760 KILMINGTON, SOM & WIL, ENG [36478] : ALL LONDON, ENG [37334] : PRE 1824 NC, USA [38366] : PRE 1900 WORLDWIDE [34406] : ALL WORLDWIDE [37334]

MUNDY 1780-1850 HELSTON, CON, ENG [35017] : C1798 KINGSCLERE, HAM, ENG [37168] : 1846-1865 GRANGEMOUTH, STI, SCT [33951] : PRE 1910 WORLDWIDE [37235]

MUNE 1800+ WEEM & ABERFELDY, PER, SCT [34008]

MUNFORD PRE 1892 DRAYTON, NFK, ENG [36828] : 1770 CREWKERNE, SOM, ENG [37733]

MUNGEAM PRE 1838 SITTINGBOURNE, KEN, ENG [35553]

MUNGER 1870-1900S USA [37600]

MUNGOVAN 1830-1990 ENNIS, CLA, IRL [36620]

MUNKER PRE 1900 FERNDORF, NRW, BRD [38636]

MUNN 1750-1850 EDDLESBOROUGH, BKM, ENG [34316] : 1817-1866 HEADCORN, KEN, ENG [36071] : PRE 1840 GREENOCK, RFW, SCT [34615] : ALL AYR, SCT [36497] : 1837-1884 JOHNSTON, RFW, SCT & AUS [35763] : 1790 SOUTH BURY, CT, USA [38518]

MUNNEERUDDIN 1835-58 CALCUTTA, INDIA [36955]

MUNNINGS 1725+ NORTH ELMHAM, NFK, ENG [35824]

MUNNIS ALL ANT, IRL [35706]

MUNNOCK 1800+ ST NINIANS, STI, SCT [38726]

MUNNS 1860+ COONABARABRAN, NSW, AUS [37967] : 1864 KEN, ENG [34654] : 1850+ BROUGHTON, HUN, ENG [35567] : 1831-1860S WAPPING, MDX, ENG [37071] : 1793-1840S WAPPING, MDX, ENG [37071] : 1917 PECKHAM, LND, ENG [37418] : 1830-1860 NEW ORLEANS, LA, USA [37071]

MUNRO C1860 THAMESFORD, ONT, CAN [34491] : 1800-1900 QUEBEC, QUE, CAN [36246] : LYDIA 1788 KINGSTON UPON THAMES, SRY, ENG [34176] : 1850 BIRMINGHAM, WAR, ENG [37209] : 1811 LINCOLN, LIN, ENG [37209] : 1811 CHELMSFORD, ESS, ENG [37209] : C1750-1850 ABD, SCT [34400] : 1800+ KILTEARN, ROC, SCT [34403] : 1700-1900 GOLSPIE, SUT, SCT [34537] : 1700-1900 DORNOCK, SUT, SCT [34537] : 1800+ AUDERN, NAI, SCT [34606] : PRE 1800 PETTY, INV, SCT [34613] : 1862+ LONGHOPE, OKI, SCT [34688] : MORE 1800+ ASSYNT, SUT, SCT [34764] : PRE 1800 ALNESS, ROC, SCT [35857] : ALL ISLE OF RASSAL, SKYE, SCT [36743] : 1800+ ALNESS, ROC, SCT [36857] : PRE 1780 LANARK, LKS, SCT [37374] : 1780+ ARDROSS, ROC, SCT [37628] : C1819 SALTBURN, ROC, SCT [38592] : DAVID C1820+ PAISLEY, RFW & LKS, SCT [38593] : C1810 KILTEARN, ROC, SCT [38700] : FINLAY 1750-1803 SCT & ENG [38003]

MUNROE PRE 1820 LIVERPOOL, LAN, ENG [34588] : PRE 1850 NRY, ENG [36046]

MUNS 1750-1850 NEWTON FLOTMAN, NFK, ENG [37477]

MUNSTER 1900+ NUNDAH, QLD, AUS [34957]

MUNT 1850+ HUNTER RIVER, NSW, AUS [38006] : 1400-1990 WHEATLEY, OXF, ENG [34124] : 1400-1990 MINCHINHAMPTON, GLS, ENG [34124] : PRE 1800 ILFORD, ESS, ENG [35125]

MUNTER PRE 1850 SIL, GER [38648]

MUNTIN (SEE MUNTON) [34812]

MUNTON ALL AUS [34812] : PRE 1850 BOSTON, LIN, ENG [34812] : PRE 1900 ROCKHAMPTON, DEV, ENG [35976] : 1860+ DALSTON & HACKNEY, MDX, ENG [37677]

MUNYARD 1800+ GEELONG & BELLERINE, VIC, AUS [35987] : C1800 GREENWICH, KEN, ENG [35863] : C1874 WESTMINSTER, MDX, ENG [37148] : ALL WORLDWIDE [35863]

MUNZELL C1780+ BRUFELS, HAN, GER [33792]

MUNZER 1850S BADEN BADEN, BAD, GER [36966]

MURALT PRE 1900 CH [34478]

MURAS 1800+ STANNINGTON, NBL & DUR, ENG [34905]

MURAT PRE 1900 CH [34478]

MURBERG 1850+ STORA KOPINGE, MAL, SWE [36320]

MURCH C1874 ENG [35906]

MURCHISON C1856+ BOX FOREST, VIC, AUS [35249] : C1814 GLENELG, INV, SCT [35249] : PRE 1850 LOCHBROOM, ROC, SCT [37423]

MURDEN 1700-1900 PENSELWOOD, SOM, ENG [37747]

MURDOCH 1850+ NSW, AUS [34526] : 1840+ NSW, AUS [36295] : 1890+ WA, AUS [37149] : 1900+ PORT ELGIN, ONT, CAN [34521] : 1910-1950 MOOSE JAW, SAS, CAN [34521] : C1889 KINCARDINE, ONT, CAN [34521] : 1900+ BETHUNE, SAS, CAN [34521] : ALL RSA [36515] : C1860 FORRES, MOR, SCT [33776] : PRE 1805 GLASGOW, LKS, SCT [33971] : 1800+ MAUCHLINE, AYR, SCT [34521] : PRE 1810 WANLOCKHEAD, DFS, SCT [34835] : PRE 1850 NEWMILNS, AYR & LKS, SCT [35354] : 1750+ GALSTON, AYR, SCT [35503] : ALL DFS, SCT [36515] : ALL KKD, SCT [36515] : C1815 HUNTLY, ABD, SCT [36949] : 1860-1900 OCHILTREE, AYR, SCT [37969] : 1800+ GLASGOW & LIVERPOOL, LKS & LAN, SCT & ENG [34326]

MURDOCK C1810 MOTHERWELL, LKS, SCT [35089] : C1784 WILLOCHGTON, AYR, SCT [37144]

MURE PRE 1731 CARLUKE, LKS, SCT [34501]

MURFEE JOHN 1786 GUILFORD CO., NC, USA **[37590]**

MURFET PRE 1830 CAM, ENG **[34445]**

MURFIN 1640+ HANES GREEN, MANSFIELD, NTT, ENG **[34408]** : PRE 1850 DBY, ENG **[37739]** : PRE 1805 DBY, ENG **[37875]** : PRE 1700 NTT, ENG **[38745]**

MURFITT C1700-1850 STRETHAM, CAM, ENG **[35238]** : PRE 1774 LITTLE THETFORD, HUN, ENG **[36278]**

MURGAN PRE 1780 KRS, SCT **[37463]**

MURGATROYD 1750+ IDLE & SHIPLEY, WRY, ENG **[36263]** : 1800S HEATON, WRY, ENG **[38206]**

MURGEY PRE 1865 PORT HOPE, ONT, CAN **[36680]**

MURIE JOHN 1851+ IRL **[34389]** : PRE 1861 GLASGOW, LKS, SCT **[37238]**

MURISON 1820+ STRICHEN, ABD, SCT **[35027]**

MURK ALL SCHOONHOVEN, ZUH, NL **[38703]**

MURLEY ALL GWINEAR, CON, ENG **[34877]** : 1700S CON, ENG **[34920]** : 1800S ST BURYAN, CON, ENG **[35723]** : 1707-1990 VA & KY, USA **[35313]**

MURNAGHANHALL 1970+ CHARLOTTETOWN, PEI, CAN **[34111]** : 1970+ USA **[34111]**

MURNAN ALL IN, USA **[33854]**

MURNANE 1828 CLA, IRL **[35535]**

MURPHY 1850-1900 BUENOS AIRES, ARGENTINA **[36468]** : PRE 1893 URANA, NSW, AUS **[33770]** : WILLIAM 1842-1880 MULGOA, NSW, AUS **[34693]** : 1850-1870 WALLAN, VIC, AUS **[35043]** : C1850S SMYTHDALE, VIC, AUS **[35136]** : 1900+ BROKEN HILL, NSW, AUS **[35185]** : 1850+ WOODFORD, VIC, AUS **[35185]** : 1850+ GRASSMERE, VIC, AUS **[35185]** : 1850-1880 HEATHCOTE, VIC, AUS **[35191]** : ANDREW 1872+ HOBART, TAS, AUS **[35209]** : C1830 PENRITH, NSW, AUS **[35211]** : 1880+ SPRINGSURE, QLD, AUS **[35398]** : 1900+ ROCKHAMPTON, QLD, AUS **[35405]** : FRANCES 1896+ GUNDY, NSW, AUS **[35412]** : THOMAS 1850-1890 SUTTON FOREST, NSW, AUS **[36316]** : 1888 INGLEWOOD, VIC, AUS **[37174]** : JOHN 1847 NOWRA, NSW, AUS **[37942]** : PRE 1902 RUTHERGLEN, VIC, AUS **[37960]** : ALL MOUNT MORGAN, QLD, AUS **[38361]** : PATRICK PRE 1900 SYDNEY, NSW, AUS **[38585]** : PRE 1830 PENRITH, NSW, AUS **[38773]** : ALICE 1860+ QUEBEC, QUE, CAN **[34147]** : 1840+ QUEBEC, QUE, CAN **[34228]** : ALL MANCHESTER, LAN, ENG **[33823]** : 1860-1920 SALFORD, LAN, ENG **[36523]** : PRE 1860 MANCHESTER, LAN, ENG **[36604]** : ALL AINTREE, LIVERPOOL, ENG **[36830]** : JOHN PRE 1830 HULL, YKS, ENG **[37942]** : PRE 1839 SUMMERHILL, MEA, IRL **[33770]** : PRE 1845 IRL **[33777]** : JOHN PRE 1830 COOLMINE, DUB, IRL **[33944]** : PRE 1860 CAHERAGH, SKIBBEREEN, COR, IRL **[33957]** : 1841 KILLEA, WAT, IRL **[33967]** : 1810-1835 DUBLIN, IRL **[34022]** : 1860-1926 DRUMINTEE, ARM, IRL **[34058]** : ALICE 1830-1860 BLACKWATER, WEX, IRL **[34147]** : THOMAS 1793-1850 BLACKWATER, WEX, IRL **[34147]** : PRE 1840 LDY, IRL **[34228]** : PRE 1841 KNOCK & BEKAN, MAY, IRL **[34305]** : MICHAEL ALL HILLTOWN, DOW, IRL **[34308]** : 1780-1820 LISBURN, DOW, IRL **[34440]** : WILLIAM PRE 1842 WEX, IRL **[34693]** : PRE 1900 WEX, IRL **[34772]** : JOHN 1840+ WIC, IRL **[34781]** : JEREMIAH PRE 1860 KINSALE, COR, IRL **[34836]** : C1840 CORK, COR, IRL **[35038]** : ANNIE 1800+ THOMASTOWN, LDY, IRL **[35315]** : JOHN PRE 1835 KILBONANE, KER, IRL **[35380]** : MARGARET 1835+ KIK & LIM, IRL **[35426]** : JOHN C1840 NENAGH, TIP, IRL **[35522]** : PRE 1867 CASTLEDERMOT, KID, IRL **[35535]** : PRE 1862 GALBALLY, LIM, IRL **[35900]** : C1800-1847 YOUGHAL, COR, IRL **[35931]** : PRE 1830 ARDEE, LOU, IRL **[35953]** : 1800S NEWCASTLE WEST, LIM, IRL **[35964]** : ARTHUR 1834+ BALLYSCULLION, ANT, IRL **[35989]** : 1790+ BALLYSCULLION, ANT, IRL **[35989]** : C1836 IRL **[36204]** : 1800+ ANT, IRL **[36251]** : THOMAS 1840 WEX, IRL **[36316]** : 1775-1850 COR, IRL **[36318]** : PRE 1850 CAPPAWHITE, TIP, IRL **[36468]** : ALL BALLYQUIN, KER, IRL **[36784]** : 1806+ LISTOWEL, KER, IRL **[36821]** : 1750+ WEX, IRL **[37026]** : 1850+ BALLYDULANY & KILKEEL, DOW, IRL **[37405]** : PRE 1860 EMLY, TIP, IRL **[37537]** : 1835-45 ARM, IRL **[38583]** : THOMAS 1790+ BAGOT, LIM, IRL & CAN **[35611]** : 1860+ AUCKLAND & THAMES, NZ **[33823]** : ALL CLUNE, BRAEFOOT & PT GLASGOW, SCT **[34002]** : ROSANNA C1800 BARONY, LKS, SCT **[35525]** : 1835+ SUSQUEHANNA CO., PA, USA **[35299]** : 1880+ SAN FRANCISCO, CA, USA **[35405]** : ALL PHILA & CHESTER CO., PA, USA **[36318]** : 1700-1850 NEWPORT, RI, USA **[36335]** : SPENCER 1770S PITT CO., NC, USA **[37585]** : ALEXANDER 1790S SPARTANBURG CO., SC, USA **[37590]** : 1794-1889 CLEVELAND, OH, USA **[38102]** : NANCY 1841 COWETA CO., GA, USA **[38155]** : 1800+ BEVERLY, MA, USA **[38175]** : 1880+ CLEVELAND, OH, USA **[38369]** : 1720-1800 MD, USA **[38529]**

MURR ALL ENG **[34980]**

MURRAY 1845 KINGS PLAINS, NSW, AUS **[34038]** : 1821+ SYDNEY, NSW, AUS **[34544]** : ALL FREMANTLE, WA, AUS **[34561]** : 1855+ PENTRIDGE, VIC, AUS **[34579]** : C1930 SANDFORD, VIC, AUS **[34767]** : 1865-1876 PENSHURST, VIC, AUS **[34767]** : 1820+ BOMBALA, NSW, AUS **[34960]** : HENRY C1898 CARLTON, VIC, AUS **[35391]** : MARIA 1824+ MELBOURNE, VIC, AUS **[35467]** : C1870 ANGORICHINA, SA, AUS **[35744]** : GEORGE C1876-1955 BRISBANE, QLD, AUS **[36616]** : 1850S GRAFTON, NSW, AUS **[37911]** : 1856+ ARMIDALE, NSW, AUS **[37911]** : FRANK 1924+ BOTANY, NSW, AUS **[37912]** : PRE 1884 VIC, AUS **[38289]** : ALL PICTOU CO., NS, CAN **[36713]** : 1800-1930 BATHURST, NB, CAN **[36934]** : 1800+ PEI, CAN **[38460]** : 1800+ CARLISLE, CUL, ENG **[34243]** : PETER 1880+ NEWCASTLE UPON TYNE, NBL, ENG **[34243]** : PRE 1841 ASHTON UNDER LYNE, CHS, ENG **[35368]** : PRE 1825 DEV, ENG **[36594]** : 1700-1825 STANHOPE CO., DUR, ENG **[37460]** : 1880+ BARROW, LAN, ENG **[37930]** : 1700+ AUGHNAMULLEN, MOG, IRL **[33826]** : 1807 ANNAGH, CAV, IRL **[33893]** : DARBY 1803 DUBLIN, IRL **[34176]** : 1820+ RATHKEALE, LIM, IRL **[34960]** : 1800+ CAV, IRL **[35201]** : JAMES C1818 BELFAST, ANT, IRL **[35391]** : MARIA PRE 1824+ CAV, IRL **[35467]** : ALL KILMACOW, WAT, IRL **[36168]** : 1835+ LOUGHGILLY, ARM, IRL **[37560]** : PRE 1850 GAL, IRL **[37893]** : PRE 1850 IRL **[37901]** : 1890+ BELFAST, ANT, IRL **[37930]** : 1800-1820 TULLAMORE, OFF, IRL **[38421]** : PRE 1800 OFF, IRL **[38460]** : 1860+ GLASGOW, LKS, SCT **[33820]** : PRE 1860 DUNDEE, ANS, SCT **[33820]** : 1796+ MORREL, SUT, SCT **[33882]** : 1800-1870 MACDUFF, BAN, SCT **[33955]** : PRE 1772 ESKDALE, DFS, SCT **[34056]** : PRE 1800 STEVENSON, AYR, SCT **[34112]** : C1800 BARONY GLASGOW, LKS, SCT **[34118]** : PRE 1780 CUMNOCK, AYR, SCT **[34274]** : ALL DUMFRIES, DFS, SCT **[34485]** : CHARLES PRE 1800 CANONBIE, DFS, SCT **[34494]** : ALL GLASGOW, LKS, SCT **[34561]** : C1820 DUNDONALD, AYR, SCT **[34972]** : C1640 LANGHOLM, DFS, SCT **[35038]** : PRE 1840 EDINBURGH, SCT **[35055]** : 1790+

GLASGOW, LKS, SCT [35194] : CHRISTINA C1837 HAWICK, ROX, SCT [35486] : PRE 1800 LITTLE DUNKELD, PER, SCT [35525] : 1750+ LONGFORGAN, PER, SCT [35644] : 1650-1730 BALQUHIDDER, PER, SCT [36635] : 1750-1900 AYR & GALSTON, AYR, SCT [36802] : 1830+ CROSSHILL, AYR, SCT [36803] : 1600-1800 KINTORE, ABD, SCT [36951] : 1600+ ALFORD, ABD, SCT [36951] : 1600-1800 TOUGH, ABD, SCT [36951] : PRE 1861 ABERDEEN, ABD, SCT [37315] : PRE 1860 ABD, SCT [37708] : PRE 1800 NEWBATTLE, MLN, SCT [37852] : C1700 MONZIE, PER, SCT [37918] : PRE 1860 HALKIRK & THURSO, CAI, SCT [37987] : PRE 1870 GLASGOW, LKS, SCT [38276] : 1740+ DORNOCH, SUT, SCT [38385] : 1750+ LONGSIDE, ABD, SCT [38446] : 1800+ CADDER, LKS, SCT [38476] : 1890+ FAIRFIELD & WATERVILLE, ME, USA [36934] : 1890S BROOKLYN, NY, USA [36936] : 1870-1900S NYC, NY, USA [36936] : 1850+ SPRINGFIELD, MO & KS, USA [36942] : 1900+ USA & CAN [37930] : 1780+ LAUGHARNE, CMN, WLS [36209]

MURREY 1820S KINGSTON ON THAMES, LND, ENG [35260]

MURRISH 1800S ST JUST, CON, ENG [35723]

MURRY 1850+ IRL [38481] : PRE 1845 MORRISVILLE, OH, USA [37574]

MURTAGH WILLIAM 1835 KILSHANROE, KID, IRL [36274] : 1750-1850 WEM, IRL [37850] : PRE 1925 HOWTH, DUB, IRL [38305] : PRE 1925 TAS, AUS &, NZ & USA [38305]

MURTHA PRE 1925 HOWTH, DUB, IRL [38305] : PRE 1925 TAS, AUS &, NZ & USA [38305]

MURTON PRE 1850 NFK, ENG [37739]

MURTY PRE 1860 ARM, IRL [37510]

MUSCHIN 1600+ LITTLEHAMPTON, SSX, ENG [34747]

MUSCHLER 1780-1860 JONESTOWN, PA, USA [38093] : 1800-1865 JONESTOWN, PA, USA [38093]

MUSCULUS 1514-1581 FRANKFURT A.D. ODER, FFO, DDR [38659]

MUSCUTT PRE 1850+ BERMONDSEY, LND, ENG [37108]

MUSGRAVE ROBERT 1862+ NEWCASTLE AREA, NSW, AUS [37992] : PRE 1851 SHORE, LND, ENG [35893] : PRE 1867 PENRITH, CUL, ENG [36227] : 1850+ KEN, ENG [36574] : ROBERT PRE 1862 DUR, ENG [37992] : 1800 KILSKERRY, TYR, IRL [33910] : PRE 1850 PA, USA [38605]

MUSGROVE 1862+ CAMPBELLFIELD, VIC, AUS [34036] : MATTHEW 1862+ NEWCASTLE AREA, NSW, AUS [37992] : 1850-1990 AUS [38224] : PRE 1900 WOOLWICH, KEN, ENG [33965] : PRE 1900 HACKNEY, LND, ENG [33965] : 1800+ TRURO, CON, ENG [34036] : C1794 DEVONPORT, DEV, ENG [35457] : 1828 OVING, SSX, ENG [36117] : PRE 1908 SIDBURY, DEV, ENG [37256] : 1700-1800 CUL, ENG [38224] : PRE 1800 DBY, ENG [38745] : 1800-1850 NORTH, IRL [38224]

MUSHENS PRE 1780 COXGREEN & PENSHAW, DUR, ENG [36202]

MUSHET 1800-1900 GLASGOW, LKS, SCT [34557]

MUSKET BRIDGETT 1611+ N SALEM, MA, USA [35271]

MUSKETT ALL NFK, ENG [34139] : 1750+ LND & MDX, ENG [37323]

MUSPRATT 1800+ BATLEY, WRY, ENG [34328]

MUSS 1750 PERLEBERG, BRA, GER [37509] : C1610 BUCHHOLZ, WEF, GER [38631]

MUSSELL ALL SALISBURY, WIL, ENG [34558]

MUSSELY ALL WORLDWIDE [36982]

MUSSEN ALL ANT & DOW, IRL [38084] : ALL WORLDWIDE [38084]

MUSSER MICHAEL 1770 LANCASTER CO., PA, USA [38127]

MUSSETT C1850 MAITLAND, NSW, AUS [35090]

MUSSINNEN 1600 ALTENHAGEN, HAN, GER [38631]

MUSSON ALL HARBY, LEI, ENG [34758]

MUSTARD 1780+ AVOCH, ROC, SCT [34810]

MUSTE 1700S SCHOUWEN DUIVELAND, ZEL, NL [38350]

MUSTER PRE 1850 POS, GER [38490]

MUSTEY 1770-1850 BLACKBOURTON, OXF, ENG [33861]

MUSTIEN 1600+ LITTLEHAMPTON, SSX, ENG [34747]

MUSTOLER 1790+ BEDFORD CO., PA, USA [38093]

MUTCH 1800+ BIRKENHEAD, CHS, ENG [38034] : 1700+ ENG [38034]

MUTCHLER 1760-1800 HARMONY TWP., NJ, USA [38093] : 1751-1800 WARREN CO., NJ, USA [38093] : 1780-1830 LEBANON CO., PA, USA [38093] : 1760-1800 LANCASTER CO., PA, USA [38093] : 1800-1830 SUSSEX CO., NJ, USA [38093] : 1790 BEDFORD CO., PA, USA [38093] : 1751-1800 BERKS CO., PA, USA [38093]

MUTH PRE 1767 MANNHEIM, BAW, BRD [34114] : ALL GER [36551] : PRE 1820 FRANKFORT MAIN, GER [38222] : 1767-1800 CANAJOHARIE, NY, USA [34114]

MUTLOW 1650+ SOLERSHOPE & HOW CAPEL, HEF, ENG [34747]

MUTON PRE 1870 BARBADOS [36486]

MUTRIE 1800+ PAISLEY, RFW, SCT [34435]

MUTSCHLER 1751 PHILADELPHIA, PA, USA [38093] : 1751-1800 BERKS CO., PA, USA [38093] : 1780-1800 LEBANON CO., PA, USA [38093] : 1800-1830 NORTHUMBERLAND, PA, USA [38093] : 1800-1840 LANCASTER CO., PA, USA [38093]

MUTSE (SEE MUSTE) [38350]

MUTTON 1795-1850 LANE EAST, CON, ENG [38151] : 1845-75 MARSHALL CO., IL, USA [38151]

MUXLOW 1840+ NSW & VIC, AUS [33798] : PRE 1850 LIN, ENG [37893]

MUXWORTHY PRE 1850 SWIMBRIDGE, DEV, ENG [38473]

MUZELL 1650-1700 SHORNE, KEN, ENG [38354]

MUZZELL ALL WORLDWIDE [37260]

MVEIGH 1800S ANT, IRL [37496]

MYATT 1700-1900 STS, ENG [37703]

MYCHELL PRE 1650 COLYTON, DEV, ENG [38746]

MYER 1700+ NEWCASTLE ON TYNE, NBL, ENG [36609] : PRE 1860 GLEN AHERLOWE, TIP, IRL [37135] : 1898 TIPPERARY HOSPITAL, TIP, IRL [37135] : HYNDERT PRE 1840 AMELAND, NL [35371] : C1784 FREDERICK, MD, USA [38348]

MYERS PRE 1900 SYDNEY, NSW, AUS [33859] : 1829+ SUTTON FOREST, NSW, AUS [37131] : PRE 1850 ONT, CAN [35620] : FREDRICA 1852 LIVERPOOL, LAN, ENG [33956] : 1770-1840 LIVERPOOL, LAN, ENG [34274] : PRE 1810 LND, ENG [34819] : PRE 1850 BAILDON & GUISELEY, WRY, ENG [36159] : PRE 1829 LAN, ENG [37131] : PRE 1870 DUB & VIC, IRL & AUS [37705] : 1840-60 CRAWFORD CO., OH, USA [36909] : 1800-1990

HUNTINGDON & BLAIR COS., PA, USA [37021] :
1800+ IL, USA [37592] : ARTHUR PRE 1909
STAUNTON, VA, USA [37794] : PRE 1900
STAUNTON, VA, USA [37794] : ARTHUR 1909+
CLIFTON FORGE, VA, USA [37794] : PRE 1800 NC,
USA [38017] : C1750-1800 BERKELEY CO., VA, USA
[38030] : 1790+ VA, USA [38050] : 1770-1830
SHREWBURY, YORK CO., PA, USA [38197] :
NANCY 1824 KNOX CO., OH, USA [38784]

MYERSCOUGH PRE 1900 PRESTON, LAN, ENG
[35163]

MYFORD 1830+ ENG [34956]

MYHILL ALL WORLDWIDE [33974]

MYHLE ALL WORLDWIDE [38666]

MYLAM ALL WORLDWIDE [36406]

MYLECHARANE 1700S JURBY, IOM, UK [35007] :
PRE 1830 BALLAUGH, IOM, UK [35007] : 1700-1830
JURBY, IOM, UK [36618]

MYLES 1850-1950 HURON CO., ONT, CAN [36901] :
ALL FER, IRL [34494] : PRE 1900 KIRRIEMUIR,
ANS, SCT [36361]

MYLORD PRE 1757 NOVIOUS, CHA, FRA [38178]

MYLREA 1700+ ANDREAS, IOM [37175]

MYNER ALL WORLDWIDE [37394]

MYNERS ALL WORLDWIDE [37394]

MYNOR ALL WORLDWIDE [37394]

MYNORS PRE 1790 STAFFORD, STS, ENG [36701] :
ALL WORLDWIDE [37394]

MYNTY 1750-1850 LAMBOURNE, BRK, ENG [37188]

MYORS 1850+ BEVERIDGE, VIC, AUS [35427] : PRE
1846 SOUTH LOPHAM, NFK, ENG [35427]

MYOTT 1700+ BARLASTON, STS, ENG [36701]

MYRACH PRE 1770 ANKLAM, POM, GER [38630]

MYRAM C1850 SSX, ENG [35998]

MYRICK PRE 1800 EASTHAM, MA, USA [36944]

MYRRIE ALL WORLDWIDE [34986]

MYRRY ALL WORLDWIDE [34986]

MYTTON 1880-1940 CAN [37096] : PRE 1920
CAMBERWELL & CROYDON, LND, ENG [37096] :
PRE 1930 PADDINGTON, LND, ENG [37096] :
1840-1940 BRIGHTON, SSX, ENG [37096] : 1850+
NELSON, NZ [37096] : PRE 1840 CHURCH STOKE,
MGY, WLS [37137]

NAC ALL WORLDWIDE [35257]

NACE 1700-1900 MONTGOMERY CO., PA, USA
[38147]

NADEAU FRANCIS 1846-1851 WORCESTER, MA,
USA [37025]

NADENBOUSCH PRE 1785 PRE, GER [36972]

NADER ALL BRAZIL [37162] : ALL BNICHAAI,
LEBANON [37162] : ALL BENACHI, LEBANON
[37162]

NADIN 1790+ BAKEWELL, DBY, ENG [34790]

NAEF PRE 1800 CH [38238]

NAEFS PRE 1820 OLDENBURG, SHO, GER [38648]

NAEREBOUT ALL WALCHEREN, ZEL, NL [38705]

NAEVE PRE 1820 OLDENBURG, SHO, GER [38648]

NAGEL C1760 MINDEN, NRW, FRG [38660] : 1800
KLEINNUCHEL, GER [37170] : C1820-C1900
CAHER, TIP, IRL [36648]

NAGELI JOHN L. 1700+ BIRSTEN, HES, BRD [34161]

NAGHTEN 1810+ GAL, IRL [35969]

NAGLE 1870+ VIC, AUS [35190] : 1750+
ATTERCLIFFE & SHEFFIELD, WRY, ENG [36772]
: 1750-1820 MALLOW, COR, IRL [34071] : 1800-1850
MALLOW, COR, IRL [36915]

NAGY PRE 1800 SZENDROLAD, BORSOD, HU
[37547]

NAHOS ALL WORLDWIDE [38445]

NAIRN 1762+ SHOREDITCH, HOXTON, LND, ENG
[36600] : SUZANNAH PRE 1800 SHOREDITCH,

LND, ENG [36646] : ALL THAMES, NZ [35998] :
1800+ FIF, SCT [34226]

NAIRNE C1750-1800 SANDWICH, KEN, ENG [34395]

NAISH 1750-1850 CLUTTON, SOM, ENG [36109] :
C1850 GLOUCESTER, GLS, ENG [36109] : 1700-
1800S HAM, ENG [36289]

NAISMITH 1820+ LANARK CO., ONT, CAN [36955] :
1830+ LKS, SCT [34983] : 1800+ DUNOON, ARL,
SCT [36746] : 1830+ HUTCHESONTOWN, LKS,
SCT [36955] : PRE 1835 GLASGOW & BARONY,
LKS, SCT [36955]

NAJVAR 1850-80 OES [38314]

NALDER PRE 1875 BRK, ENG [37897]

NALLY PRE 1840 TUAM, GAL, IRL [33846]

NANCARROW 1800+ REDRUTH, CON, ENG [35223]
: 1800-1875 DEVONPORT, DEV, ENG [35422] : ALL
GRAMPOUND & CREED, CON, ENG [35736] :
1700-1800S ILLOGAN, CON, ENG [35804] : PRE
1850 STOKE DAMEREL, DEV, ENG [35818] : PRE
1820 ILLOGAN, CON, ENG [35818] : PRE 1840
CON, ENG [37901] : ALL CON, ENG & AUS [34301]

NANCE LOUISA 1850S CON, ENG [36316]

NANCHOLAS ALL WORLDWIDE [36404]

NANCOLAS ALL WORLDWIDE [36404]

NANCOLLAS ALL WORLDWIDE [36404]

NANCOLLIAS ALL WORLDWIDE [36404]

NANCOLLIS ALL WORLDWIDE [36404]

NANGLE 1400-1675 COSTELLO, MAY, IRL [38054] :
1675-1725 MULLINGAR, WEM, IRL [38054]

NANJULIAN 1400+ LUXULYAN, CON, ENG [33989]
: 1600+ LUXULYAN, CON, ENG [36827]

NANKERUIS 1848-1865 KEWEENAW CO., MI, USA
[38009]

NANKERVIS 1850-1950 AUS [34535] : 1900 DIAMOND
CRK, VIC, AUS [34892] : 1860+ BEECHWORTH,
VIC, AUS [36622] : PRE 1857 ST JUST IN
PENWITH, CON, ENG [35804]

NANKERVIS (SEE NANKE [38009]

NANKEWELL PRE 1760 LONDON, ENG [36619] :
C1750 MDX, ENG [37239]

NANKIVELL 1400+ CON, ENG [35951]

NANSCAWEN 1853+ BALLARAT, VIC, AUS [36644] :
PRE 1853 LANDULPH, CON, ENG [36644]

NAPIER C1830 BINGLEY, WRY, ENG [33796] : PRE
1900 LEWISHAM, LND, ENG [36069] : 1820+
NEWCASTLE ON TYNE, NBL, ENG [37889] : PRE
1900 LITTLE, DUB, IRL & RSA [38772] : 1800-1850
THE GORBALS, RFW, SCT [34187] : 1700+ DNB,
ARL & RFW, SCT [35999] : PRE 1603 DNB, SCT
[36973]

NAPIONTES 1700+ BREMEN, BRM, GER [36303]

NAPPER 1863 LAUNCESTON, TAS, AUS [37177] :
1850+ TAS, AUS [37177] : C1800 SOM, ENG [34393] :
PRE 1900 SEAVINGTON & SOUTH PETHERTON,
SOM, ENG [34865] : PRE 1900 SSX, ENG [35742] :
PRE 1900 COMPTON DUNDUN, SOM, ENG
[36676]

NAPTHALI PRE 1817 SPITALFIELDS, LND, ENG
[38596]

NARCISSE 1800-1900 WESTMINSTER, MDX, ENG
[36106]

NARES 1859 HAVERFORDWEST, PEM, WLS [34577]

NARROWAY 1700-1900 ACTON, LND, ENG [35229]

NARUM PRE 1870 KOLBU, GUDBRANDSDAL,
NOR [37821]

NASE 1700-1900 SALFORD, PA, USA [38147] : 1700-
1900 PERKASIE, PA, USA [38147] : 1800-1900
BUCKS CO., PA, USA [38147] : 1700-1900
TYLERSPORT, PA, USA [38147]

NASH PRE 1860S SYDNEY, NSW, AUS [35433] :
1870+ SYDNEY, NSW, AUS [36203] : 1800S
SYDNEY, NSW, AUS [38490] : 1800S SYDNEY,

NSW, AUS [38490] : ALL ALDERMASTON, BRK, ENG [34002] : PRE 1835 LONDON, ENG [34177] : 1800+ SSX, ENG [34237] : EDWARD 1850 TARDEBIGGE, WOR, ENG [34363] : CHARLES 1816+ TROWBRIDGE, WIL, ENG [34785] : ALL SOM, GLS & LND, ENG [34951] : C1800 HILPERTON, WIL, ENG [34999] : PRE 1817+ LONDON, MDX, ENG [35109] : 1830-1860 ENG [35317] : PRE 1800 HAM, ENG [35902] : THOMAS 1590-1702 HARPENDEN & WHEATHAMSTED, HRT, ENG [36068] : PRE 1890 BRENTWOOD, ESS, ENG [36516] : 1800+ NEWMILTON, HAM, ENG [36989] : 1800+ BOLDRE, HAM, ENG [36989] : PRE 1885 BIRDLIP, GLS, ENG [37136] : 1800-1860 ST GEORGE BRISTOL, GLS, ENG [37222] : 1780-1860 KEN, ENG [37338] : RACHEL PRE 1814 WEST LAVINGTON, WIL, ENG [37995] : 1820+ WIL, ENG [37999] : 1879 RUSPIDGE, GLS, ENG [38470] : PRE 1837 HENLEY UPON THAMES, ENG [38490] : PRE 1890 MDX, ENG [38722] : C1850 IRL [35906] : 1780-1860 BUTTEVANT, COR, IRL [36769] : 1860-1900 BAY CITY, MI, USA [35317] : 1850-1880 DAYTON, OH, USA [35317] : PRE 1860 TREDEGAR, MON, WLS [37716] : ALL WORLDWIDE [35875] : ALL WORLDWIDE [36235]

NASMYTH 1800S EDINBURGH, MLN, SCT [35422]

NASON PRE 1850 CRAWFORD CO., PA, USA [33804] : 1800-1870 ME, USA [38737]

NASS 1750-1800 KLEIN RADOWISK, WPR, GER [38599]

NASTIUK 1900S TORONTO, ONT, CAN [36670]

NATE 1700+ HELDEN, GER & USA [34988]

NATHAN PRE 1920 STOKE NEWINGTON, MDX, ENG [37890] : PRE 1815 ENG & AUS [33799] : C1800S LONDON, ENG & AUS [34133]

NATION 1820-1900 HUONVILLE, TAS, AUS [38761] : 1790-1830 MOREBATH & BAMPTON, DEV, ENG [38761]

NATIONS 1820-40 AL, USA [37533] : 1840-50 YALOBUSHA CO., MS, USA [37533]

NATTE PRE 1760 MARSEILLE, PCA, FRA [38033] : 1700S SCHOUWEN DUIVELAND, ZEL, NL [38350]

NATTRASS 1898+ WIMMERA, VIC, AUS [36622] : 1700+ STANHOPE, DUR, ENG [35972]

NAUGHTEN 1845-1854 GRAFTON, NSW, AUS [37911] : 1800-1893 CHARTERS TOWERS, QLD, AUS [37911] : 1854-1887 ARMIDALE, NSW, AUS [37911] : PRE 1840 STROKESTOWN, ROS, IRL [35189] : 1814 STROKESTOWN, ROS, IRL [37911]

NAUGHTON 1845+ TUMUT, NSW, AUS [34978] : PRE 1845 WEM, IRL [34978] : PATRICK 1800-1810 ROSCOMMON, ROS & GAL, IRL [38780]

NAUMANN PRE 1650 OBERNEISSEN & LIMBURG, HES, BRD [36954]

NAUSCHULTZ 1887 GATTON, QLD, AUS [37174]

NAVIN 1800 SYDNEY, NSW, AUS [37125]

NAYLOR 1850+ MELBOURNE, VIC, AUS [34640] : 1850+ WATERLOO & HURON CO., ONT, CAN [34075] : C1800 NOTTINGHAM, ENG [33915] : 1700+ WARSOP & SOUTHWELL, NTT, ENG [33955] : 1700-1860 WARRINGTON, LAN, ENG [34928] : 1852+ WESTMINSTER, MDX, ENG [35054] : 1840-50S CHESTER LE STREET, DUR, ENG [35525] : 1840-50S PELTON FELL, DUR, ENG [35525] : PRE 1750 ESS, ENG [35642] : PRE 1840 YKS, ENG [35745] : C1700+ SOUTHWARK, SRY, ENG [36810] : C1800+ MDX, ENG [36810] : C1800+ MDX, ENG [36810] : 1820+ BOLTON & LEIGH, LAN, ENG [37258] : 1700+ HALIFAX, YKS, ENG & USA [33955]

NEADES ALL FROME & BEDMINSTER, SOM, ENG [38357]

NEAGLE PRE 1850 COR, IRL [35750]

NEAL PRE 1900 TAMWORTH, NSW, AUS [34590] : JAMES 1803-1820 RICHMOND, NSW, AUS [37553] : PRE 1880 GUELPH, ONT, CAN [38390] : PRE 1820 MDX, ENG [34442] : PRE 1830 ALSTON, HAM, ENG [34903] : ALL SRY, ENG [34951] : PRE 1800+ SHIRSTON, WIL, ENG [35109] : WILIAM 1846+ LIN, ENG [35583] : ALL NFK, ENG [35628] : 1800+ WOODFORD, ESS, ENG [35942] : MARY C1845 WOODFORD, ESS, ENG [35942] : 1750-1850 FAKENHAM, NFK, ENG [36081] : 1800+ LAMBERHURST, KEN, ENG [36219] : GEORGE 1790S-1840 CHICHESTER, SSX, ENG [36880] : ALL WAR, ENG [36886] : PRE 1796 IRL [37142] : JOHN 1750+ PITTSYLVANIA CO., VA, USA [38044]

NEALE PRE 1800 SOHO, LND, ENG [34117] : 1600 HAWKESBURY, GLS, ENG [34466] : 1812-1884 STROUD, GLS, ENG [34658] : C1850 CHELTENHAM, GLS, ENG [34734] : 1800+ LND, ENG [35370] : C1810 ST FAITHS, NFK, ENG [35458] : C1880 WAR, ENG [35931] : 1870 BIRMINGHAM, WAR, ENG [36649] : ALL WAR, ENG [36886] : PRE 1870 LIVERPOOL, LAN, ENG [36993] : ALL YATE, GLS, ENG [37154] : 1600-1700 SOUTHAMPTON, HAM, ENG [37233] : PRE 1820 CULWORTH, NTH, ENG [37249] : HENRY 1670 BRAINTREE, MA, USA [35273] : RUTH 1670 BRAINTREE, MA, USA [35273]

NEALEN 1820+ LIVERPOOL, LAN, ENG [34566]

NEALIS 1700+ BIRR, OFF, IRL [34642] : 1800-1855 BIRR, OFF, IRL [36824] : 1750-1850 STRABANE, TYR, IRL [36824] : 1800+ ONEHUNGA, AUCK, NZ [34642]

NEALON ALL MCHENRY, IL, USA [37537]

NEALSON PRE 1720 ULVERSTON, LAN, ENG [36701]

NEARY MARY 1910 SANMARTIN, CA, USA [37024]

NEASE 1880+ WHITLEY CO., IN, USA [36897]

NEASHAM 1894 KIRKLEATHAM, NRY, ENG [38719]

NEATE PRE 1860 ENG [34661] : PRE 1750 BISHOPS CANNINGS, WIL, ENG [35346] : 1780S-1850S CHELTENHAM, GLS, ENG [36541] : 1860S-1940S BECKENHAM, KEN, ENG [36541] : 1850S-1900 ST PANCRAS, MDX, ENG [36541] : ALL WIL, ENG [36607] : PRE 1750 MALMSBURY, WIL, ENG [37034] : 1700-1900 LND, ENG [37858]

NEAVE PRE 1800 GREAT YARMOUTH, NFK, ENG [33762] : PRE 1800 LIVERPOOL, LAN, ENG [36416] : 1750-1850 MANCHESTER, LAN, ENG [36416] : 1750+ SOUTHREPPS, NFK, ENG [37276] : C1640-1700 ETON, BKM, ENG [37618] : PRE 1850 HERNE, KEN, ENG [37773] : 1600-1700 DUNDEE & DISTRICT, ANS, SCT [37702]

NEAVES PRE 1850 LIVERPOOL, LAN, ENG [35344]

NEAVOY 1700-1750 DUNDEE, ANS, SCT [36081]

NEBELIN 1750 PERLEBERG, BRA, GER [37509]

NECK PRE 1800 MORETON HAMPSTEAD, DEV, ENG [36662]

NEDDEN 1800S WI, USA [33903]

NEDWILL PRE 1850 LONDONDERRY, LDY, IRL [34611]

NEECE 1840 HENDRICKS CO., IN, USA [38324]

NEED 1750-1810 WASHINGTON CO., PA, OH & IN, USA [36901]

NEEDHAM 1848 ADELAIDE, SA, AUS [35136] : 1788 SYDNEY, NSW, AUS [35721] : 1833+ MIDDLESEX CO., ONT, CAN [34380] : PRE 1850 LIVERPOOL, LAN, ENG [35994] : PRE 1800 MISTERTON, NTT, ENG [36514] : PRE 1880 MANCHESTER, LAN, ENG [37217] : PRE 1870 PONTEFRAUT, YKS, ENG [37442] : 1960+ ORANGE, CA & MI, USA [34244]

NEEDS 1830+ DULVERTON & WINSFORD, SOM, ENG [37322] : PRE 1842 LANGPORT, SOM, ENG [37957]

NEEFF 1571-1630 ZOELEN, NL [36317]

NEEGKEN C1700 NEUHANAU, HES, GER [38348]

NEEL 1740+ NC, USA [38340]

NEELANDS 1600-1820 TYR & DOW, IRL [37599]

NEELEY 1700-1800 ORANGE CO., NC, USA [38764]

NEELS ALL WORLDWIDE [38170]

NEELY 1862 EUPHRASIA, ONT, CAN [34224]

NEEMES 1800+ MORESBY CO., CUL, ENG [35269]

NEENAN ALL GOULBURN, NSW, AUS [34869]

NEER 1800-1900 VA, USA [36937]

NEES 1700-1900 FRANCONIA, PA, USA [38147] : 1700-1850 OLD GOSHENHOPPEN, PA, USA [38147]

NEEVE PRE 1830 HETHERSETT, NFK, ENG [34931]

NEEVEY 1860 DUDLEY, WOR, ENG [34224]

NEGELE JOHN L. 1700+ BIRSTEN, HES, BRD [34161]

NEGLEY JOHN L. 1700+ BIRSTEN, HES, BRD [34161] : 1745-1800 WELSH-RUN CUMBERLAND CO., PA, USA [38197]

NEGRI 1800+ ITL [35762]

NEGUS 1800-1880 HACKNEY, LND, ENG [36130] : PRE 1852 GODMANCHESTER & FENSTANTON, HUN & CAM, ENG & AUS [34705]

NEHER C1790 ROCKINGHAM CO., VA & OH, USA [36540]

NEHMITZ ALL POM & WPR, GER [38687]

NEHRENHEIM 1884+ TAS, AUS [35865] : C1850 DARKEHMEN, OPR, GER [35865]

NEHRING 1700-1850 RADZYMIN, WA, POL [38652]

NEIDEFFER 1700-1850 PA & TN, USA [38768]

NEIDEL 1900 ST LOUIS, MO & IL, USA [35279]

NEIDERHOFFER ALL WORLDWIDE [38768]

NEIDHOEFFERIN PRE 1780 GUTENACKER & KOERDORF, LAHNKREIS, GER [38690]

NEIDHOFFER ALL WORLDWIDE [38768]

NEIGER 1900+ BRONX, NY, USA [35717]

NEIGHANGER 1867-1879 KEWEENAW CO., MI, USA [38009]

NEIGHBOUR 1700-1850 PYRTON, OXF, ENG [36653] : ALL WORLDWIDE [36422]

NEIL PRE 1850 LANARK CO., ONT, CAN [38445] : 1830S ALBION, ONT, CAN & ENG [34164] : BENTLEY 1850+ KNAPWELL, CAM, ENG [35164] : MARTHA 1840+ KNAPWELL, CAM, ENG [35164] : PRE 1900 NEWCASTLE UPON TYNE, NBL, ENG [36110] : C1780 DONAGHMORE, DOW, IRL [37524] : 1800S IRL [38445] : PRE 1850 ABD, SCT [33914] : PRE 1823 ELN, SCT [33959] : 1890+ DUMBARTON, LKS, SCT [34260] : PRE 1854 EDINBURGH, SCT [35074] : PRE 1849 GLASGOW, LKS, SCT [35407] : 1800+ DYSART, LKS, SCT [35977] : C1820 LESMAHAGOW, LKS, SCT [36431] : PRE 1751 TRANENT, ELN, SCT [37852] : 1806 GLASGOW, LKS, SCT & IRL [37524]

NEILAN C1840 KILCORCORAN, CLA, IRL [36307]

NEILAND PRE 1900 HOWTH, DUB, IRL [38305]

NEILAND (SEE NYLAND) [38305]

NEILANDS PRE 1820 MAGHERALOUGH, TYR, IRL [34137]

NEILL 1900+ WA & VIC, AUS [34846] : PRE 1865 MAITLAND, NSW, AUS [37142] : 1852+ BROADFORD, VIC, AUS [37303] : 1700-1850 TIP, IRL [34846] : ALL HILLSBOROUGH, DOW, IRL [37303] : ANDREW 1852+ KIRKOSWALD, AYR, SCT [34039] : WILLIAM 1826-1838 STRAITON, AYR, SCT [34039] : PRE 1822 MUSSELBURGH, MLN, SCT [35709] : 1847 KILMARNOCK & IRVINE, AYR, SCT [35903] : 1800S GREENOCK, RFW, SCT [37566]

NEILLEY ALL AUS [34937] : 1700S FRA [34937] : ALL CARRICKFERGUS, ANT, IRL [34937]

NEILLIS PRE 1890 GLASGOW, LKS & MAY, SCT & IRL [36191]

NEILSEN 1840S HOBART, TAS, AUS [33918] : 1880 STANTHORPE, QLD, AUS [37914]

NEILSON 1880+ IPSWICH, QLD, AUS [33782] : 1870+ GLADSTONE, NSW, AUS [34873] : 1850S MELBOURNE, VIC, AUS [35855] : C1790 SIROP, JUTLAND, DEN [34654] : PRE 1840 COPENHAGEN, DEN [37137] : C1700-1870 COPENHAGEN, DEN [37642] : 1820 EAST KILBRIDE, LKS, SCT [34546] : PRE 1780 GLASGOW, LKS, SCT [35227] : 1844 INVERESK, MLN, SCT [35855] : 1790-1855 AIRDRIE & GLASGOW, LKS, SCT [38053] : 1730-1850S GRETNA, DFS, SCT [38390]

NEINDORF PRE 1850 TUCHEIM, PRE, GER [38490]

NEIS 1700-1800 FREDERICK, PA, USA [38147]

NEISH 1790-1870S CAMPSIE, STI, SCT [34359] : 1900+ LAS ANIMAS, CO, USA [38067]

NEISS 1700-1850 FALKNER SWAMP, PA, USA [38147]

NEIST PRE 1906 GEISENHEIM, RPR, GER [36273]

NELDER ALL WORLDWIDE [37738]

NELL ALL ENG [37827]

NELLIGAN 1830S MALLOW, COR, IRL [35780]

NELLIS PRE 1710 RPF, BRD [37473]

NELLIST ALL WORLDWIDE [36481]

NELLY C1830 GALWAY, GAL, IRL [33992]

NELMS PRE 1859 LONG CRENDON, BKM, ENG [33862]

NELSEY PRE 1860 WAINFLEET, LIN, ENG [36168] : 1700-1750 LIN, ENG [38453]

NELSON 1840+ ADELAIDE, SA, AUS [34263] : 1862+ WALHALLA, VIC, AUS [34578] : 1860'+ LONGFORD, TAS, AUS [34770] : 1855-1890 CLUNES, VIC, AUS [35151] : 1800+ ONT, CAN [37468] : C1800 COLKIRK, NFK, ENG [33796] : C1800 BARKING, ESS, ENG [33918] : 1869 HATTENLAW, NBL, ENG [35089] : DAVID PRE 1874 MANCHESTER, LAN, ENG [35449] : C1815 MAIDSTONE, KEN, ENG [35464] : PRE 1860 BRIDEKIRK, CUL, ENG [35914] : 1850-1895 BOLTON, LAN, ENG [35914] : 1850S MOOR PIT, DUR, ENG [36503] : 1850+ LANCASTER, LAN, ENG [37073] : PRE 1850 LONDON & KEN & SRY, ENG [37087] : ALL YKS, ENG [37468] : ALL NFK, ENG [37612] : C1763 WINEWALL, LAN, ENG [37988] : 1875-1962 OLDHAM, LAN, ENG [38370] : ALL FORDON, PRE, GER & AUS [33799] : 1700-1830S MOG, IRL [34246] : PRE 1882 BELFAST, ANT & DOW, IRL [35046] : 1800-1860 KILLEVAN, MOG, IRL [35151] : 1800-1850 GREENVALE, TYR, IRL [35422] : 1830+ MAKENNY, TYR, IRL [36615] : PRE 1860 DON, IRL [36854] : 1800S DOW & ANT, IRL [37260] : PRE 1780 IRL [37795] : 1800+ MAKENNY, TYR, IRL [38001] : C1840-1890 BELFAST, ANT, IRL [38323] : MARGARET PRE 1850 IRL [38734] : PRE 1870 DROMARA, DOW & WIG, IRL & SCT [37238] : PRE 1862 KRISTIANSAND, NOR [34578] : PRE 1900 NOR & USA [38386] : 1820-1875 MINIGAFF, KKD, SCT [38370] : 1840S ST PETERSBURG, SU [34542] : PRE 1872 VASTERVIK, KALMAR, SWE [36800] : PETER 1600+ SWE [37805] : ANNA C1850 LINKOPING, SWE [38064] : 1750-1850 BERKLEY CO., SC, USA [34749] : 1800S BATH CO., KY, USA [37028] : 1900+ DE KALB, USA [37206] : 1700S LONG ISLAND, NY, USA [38038] : 1780-1830 HENRY CO., VA, USA [38119] : ALL DEWITT, IL & OK, USA [38230] : SAMUEL ROBERT 1900+ TX, USA [38323] : TENA 1953+ ELM CREEK, NE, USA [38554]

NEMEC PRE 1845 KORNATICE, ROKYCANY, CS [38618]

NEMECEK 1830-1850 CHRAST, MLADA BOLESLAV, CS [38618]

NERGAARD 1820S TRONDHEIM, NOR [35906]

NES 1700-1900 FRANCONIA, PA, USA [38147]

NESBIT 1850+ PENRITH, CUL, ENG [34349] : ANN 1821 IRL [37518] : 1400+ BOTHWELL, LKS, SCT [33989] : 1714 GLASGOW, LKS, SCT [34224] : PRE 1889 CRIEFF, STI, SCT [35473] : 1830S AYR, SCT [38206]

NESBIT-ROBINSON C1843-6 FARNHAM, EAST, CAN [37518]

NESBITT PRE 1830 DOW, IRL [34060] : PRE 1900 BALLYMACWARD & LISBURN, ANT, IRL [37755] : PRE 1851 STIRLING, SCT [35258]

NESFIELD PRE 1885 BURTON FLEMING & BRIDLINGTON, ERY, ENG [36039]

NESOM 1600-1900 NRY & DUR, ENG [36472]

NESS PRE 1866 PORTAFERRY, DOW, IRL [35335] : PRE 1900 ALESUND, NOR [37440] : ANN PRE 1825 MLN, SCT [36297] : 1700-1850 LARGO, FIF, SCT [36776] : 1860+ MUSSELBURGH, MLN, SCT [36892] : 1700-1900 FRANCONIA, PA, USA [38147]

NETCOTT ALL WORLDWIDE [37672]

NETHAWAY 1770-1850 DUCHESS CO., NY, USA [37591]

NETHERCLIFT 1740-1860 SILCHESTER, HAM, ENG [37118]

NETHERCOOK PRE 1630 SOHAM, CAM, ENG [34445]

NETHERCOTE 1800 MOULTON, NTH, ENG [34546] : ALL WORLDWIDE [38293]

NETHERCOTT C1780 SIDMOUTH, DEV, ENG [37356] : PRE 1760 CUTCOMBE, SOM, ENG [37622]

NETHERSOLE 1750+ WORTH, KEN, ENG [35891] : ALL E KEN, ENG [36137] : ALL WORLDWIDE [36137]

NETHERTON ALL DEV, ENG [35063]

NETHERY 1800+ EDERAY, FER, IRL [34075] : 1800+ CLOGHERNY, TYR, IRL [34863]

NETLEY 1700-1882 PULBOROUGH, SSX, ENG [36828] : 1810 PULBOROUGH, SSX, ENG [37691]

NETTELL PRE 1850 ILLOGAN, CON, ENG [36416]

NETTLE PRE 1850 ILLOGAN, CON, ENG [36416] : 1650+ ILLOGAN & CAMBOURNE, CON, ENG [38745] : 1700S CHARLES, MD, USA [38373]

NETTLESHIP 1770-1830 EAST RETFORD, NTT, ENG [36426] : PRE 1670 BLYTH, NTT, ENG [36426]

NETTLETON 1849 TAS, AUS [34039] : 1855 WARRNAMBOOL, VIC, AUS [34039] : C1850 TAS, AUS [35399] : 1750+ CAMBERWELL, SRY, ENG [34109] : C1830 LONDON, ENG [35399] : 1798 BRANDESBURTON, YKS, ENG [35452]

NEUENDORF 1830-1870 QLD, AUS & GER [37973] : PRE 1850 TUCHEIM, PRE, GER [38490] : 1850-1920 DODGE CO., WI, USA [38199]

NEUFELD (SEE NEUFELD [34356]

NEUFELDT 1870+ MENNONITE WEST RESERVE, MAN, CAN [34356]

NEUFFER 1862-1865 CORUNNA, MI, USA [38009]

NEUMAN PRE 1840 OPR, PRE & WPR, GER [38176]

NEUMANN C1821 BERLIN, GER [33864] : C1820-1850S GER [36289] : 1800 TREBENOW, POM, GER [37170] : PRE 1830 LIBAU, LATVIA, SU [38690] : PRE 1880 BORSTIG, VASTERGOTLAND, SWE [37821]

NEUNZLING PRE 1855 DEIDESHEIM, BAV, GER [34886]

NEUTZLING 1790+ PRE, GER [37532] : 1840+ POMEROY, OH, USA [37532]

NEVAY 1700-1750S MILTON IN THE GLEN, ANS, SCT [35938]

NEVE 1851+ NSW, AUS [34534] : PRE 1851 WITHYHAM, SSX, ENG [34534] : PRE 1850 LONDON, MDX, ENG [37647] : 1580-1900 KEN, SSX & LND, UK, AUS & [37644]

NEVELL 1849+ MUDGEE, NSW, AUS [35807]

NEVELU PRE 1880 BRNO & BRUSBURG, MORAVIA, OES [36918]

NEVEN 1650-1700 NEW YORK, NY, USA [38113]

NEVENS 1800S SOUTH SHIELDS, DUR, ENG [36364]

NEVES C1790 LENHAM, KEN, ENG [35920]

NEVIL PRE 1900 SYDNEY, NSW, AUS [33799]

NEVILL 1600+ LICHFIELD & SHENSTONE, STS, WAR & WOR, ENG [36058] : C1840 PECKHAM, SRY, ENG [36704] : 1880-1940 BREEDON, DBY, ENG [38471] : JAMES 1830-1860 SOM, ENG & NZ [35999]

NEVILLE 1850+ HOVELLS CK, NSW, AUS [33931] : 1820+ COWRA, NSW, AUS [35205] : PRE 1800 NS, CAN [34403] : PRE 1832 BLOXHAM, OXF, ENG [34806] : PRE 1825 RETTENDON, ESS, ENG [35488] : C1100+ NBL, ENG [35723] : 1600+ LICHFIELD & SHENSTONE, STS, WAR & WOR, ENG [36058] : 1840 POPLAR & EDMONTON, MDX, ENG [36263] : ALL COKER, SOM, ENG [37233] : 1815-1860 INDIA [34722] : PRE 1860 LIM, IRL [33931] : 1700-1860 MARYBOROUGH, LEX, IRL [34722] : PRE 1850 ASKEATON & RATHKEALE, LIM, IRL [35205] : 1800+ LEA, LEX, IRL [35499]

NEVIN PRE 1870 SHEFFIELD, YKS, ENG [36181] : C1800-1860 DONAGHADEE, DOW, IRL [37141]

NEVINS 1790S NEWCASTLE, NBL, ENG [36364] : 1850S IRL [36579]

NEVINSON ALL CUL, ENG [37274] : ALL WES, ENG [37274]

NEVIUS 1594-1634 ZOELEN, NL [36317] : 1627-1672 ZOELEN, NL [36317]

NEW PRE 1850 BARYULGIL, NSW, AUS [38730] : PRE 1800 ROGATE, SSX, ENG [34112] : 1820 LONDON, ENG [36146] : 1812 KINGSTON ON THAMES, SRY, ENG [36860] : 1800 MITCHAM, SRY, ENG [37080] : ALL BATTLE & HASTINGS, SSX, ENG [37355] : ALL RYE & WESTFIELD, SSX, ENG [37355] : 1800+ GLS, ENG [38257]

NEWALL ALL ARDROSSAN, AYR, SCT [34835] : 1820-1900 DALBEATTIE, DFS, SCT [38433]

NEWARK 1857 SYDNEY, NSW, AUS [34425]

NEWBERRY 1700+ ST BARTS BY THE EXCHANGE, LND, ENG [36088] : 1800-1850 HAM, ENG [37645]

NEWBERY 1840+ CLIFFORD CHAMBERS, WAR, ENG [34113]

NEWBOLD DAVID C1820-1850 LONDON, ENG [34007] : C1870-1908 DERBY, DBY, ENG [34659] : C1713 SHEFFIELD, YKS, ENG [35257] : ALL LINTON, DBY, ENG [36074] : 1840+ LONDON, ENG [36146] : PRE 1800 MOUNTSORREL, LEI, ENG [36146]

NEWBON PRE 1695 STRETHAM, CAM, ENG [34445]

NEWBORN 1867+ DONCASTER, WRY, ENG [38469]

NEWBOURNE 1650+ ELY, CAM, ENG [34747]

NEWBY PRE 1800 GREAT YARMOUTH, NFK, ENG [33762] : C1883 JOHNSON CO., TX, USA [37032]

NEWCOM 1750-1861 OH & PA, USA & IRL [37577]

NEWCOMB 1880+ RICHMOND, VIC, AUS [36360]

NEWCOMBE PRE 1800 NTT, ENG [36171]

NEWCOMM PRE 1880 MO, USA [38217]

NEWDICK PRE 1700 LND & CAM, ENG [37103]

NEWELL 1800+ TAS & NSW, AUS [34976] : 1820-1930 DUNGOG, NSW, AUS [36647] : 1838-1970+ NEWTOWN & SYDNEY, NSW, AUS [37556] : 1833-

1838+ HOBART, TAS, AUS [37556] : 1824+ DUFFERIN CO., ONT, CAN [34407] : PRE 1700 MARWOOD & BARNSTAPLE, DEV, ENG [34741] : C1878 COLCHESTER, ESS, ENG [35348] : PRE 1867 TIBSHELF, DBY & BDF, ENG [37267] : PRE 1852 TODMORDEN, WRY, ENG [37866] : PRE 1857 LEEDS, YKS, ENG [38288] : C1620 HRT, ENG [38348] : 1700-1900 LEEDS, YKS, ENG [38579] : 1770-1820S DOWNPATRICK, DOW, IRL [34407] : 1780-1870 MOG, IRL [34615] : PRE 1800 FINABROGUE, DOW, IRL [34895] : 1800 DUBLIN, IRL [34976] : C1860 BAILIEBOROUGH, CAV, IRL [35826] : PRE 1833 DUBLIN, IRL [37556] : PRE 1800 PA & VA, USA [37580] : 1780-1810 WASHINGTON CO., PA, USA [38331] : PRE 1880 NEWTOWN, MGY, WLS [35333]

NEWENS PRE 1730 CHEDDINGTON, BKM, ENG [37909]

NEWETT C1815+ AUS [34444]

NEWEY PRE 1820 WOLVERHAMPTON, STS, ENG [34851]

NEWHAM PRE 1870+ FITZROY, VIC, AUS [33890] : PRE 1870 HULL, YKS, ENG [33890] : 1700-1875 REEPHAM, NFK, ENG [36879] : 1870+ STREATHAM, SRY, ENG [36879]

NEWHOUSE 1760-1880 ONEIDA, NY & MA, USA [38194]

NEWIN PRE 1800 CARISBROOKE, HAM, ENG [34812]

NEWING PRE 1850 GRAVESEND, KEN, ENG [34733] : 1800-1900 BATTERSEA & WANDSWORTH, LND, ENG [34749]

NEWINGTON PRE 1820 DOVER, KEN, ENG [37652]

NEWIS PRE 1765 SHEPTON BEAUCHAMP, SOM, ENG [34270]

NEWITT PRE 1900 SINGLETON, NSW, AUS [34269]

NEWITT (SEE NEWETT) [34444]

NEWKIRK JAMES 1828 SULLIVAN CO., NY, USA [38142]

NEWLAND 1840+ WOLLONGONG, NSW, AUS [35535] : ALL MANCHESTER, LAN, ENG [34837] : 1800S HORSLYDOWN, SRY, ENG [34887] : 1770+ EAST MEON, HAM, ENG [35905] : 1700+ ESS, ENG [36922] : PRE 1836 EDINBURGH, MLN, SCT [33893] : 1635-1690 DUXBURY & SANDWICH, MA, USA [36944]

NEWLANDS 1800+ ASTON, ENG [35396]

NEWLING ALL CAM, ENG [35577] : 1805-1855 ICKLETON & DUXFORD, CAM, ENG [37988]

NEWLOVE 1700+ HARPHAM & GREAT DRIFFIELD, ERY, ENG [36516]

NEWMAN 1840+ MAITLAND, NSW, AUS [34424] : 1842+ MAITLAND, NSW, AUS [34596] : 1851+ GUNNING, NSW, AUS [34839] : 1837+ EVANDALE, TAS, AUS [34910] : 1850+ ARMIDALE, NSW, AUS [35147] : 1811+ PARRAMATTA, NSW, AUS [35147] : 1851+ MELBOURNE, VIC, AUS [35238] : 1854+ KILMORE, VIC, AUS [35797] : 1902 MT MORGANS, WA, AUS [35919] : 1860+ KAPUNDA, SA, AUS [37186] : 1800S HEREFORD, HEF, ENG [33780] : C1700-1850 SOUTHROP, GLS, ENG [33855] : C1700-1838 WOOTTON WAWEN, WOR, ENG [33855] : ALL DOR, ENG [34079] : EDWARD 1700+ ENG [34079] : ALL ISLE OF PORTLAND, DOR, ENG [34079] : PRE 1840S BETHNAL GREEN & ENFIELD, MDX, ENG [34240] : C1856 FINGRINGHOE, ESS, ENG [34358] : ALL ENG [34493] : 1700-1800 DARTMOUTH, DEV, ENG [34742] : 1700+ BINSTED, PETWORTH &EASTBOURNE, SSX, ENG [34747] : ALL LONDON & SALISBURY, WIL, ENG [34820] :

1767+ BATH & TAUNTON, SOM, ENG [34926] : GREGORY 1700-1760 BOURN, CAM, ENG [35070] : 1830S SALISBURY, WIL, ENG [35156] : PRE 1845 HUNSDON, HRT, ENG [35238] : C1845-1850S CAM, ENG [35238] : PRE 1828 FOXTON, CAM, ENG [35748] : 1800S IPING, SSX, ENG [35797] : C1828 STEEPLE MORDEN, CAM, ENG [35860] : C1860 LIVERPOOL, LAN, ENG [35919] : 1800S NTT, ENG [36038] : 1817+ SHERMANBURY, SSX, ENG [36212] : 1754+ STOW-CUM-QUY, CAM, ENG [36489] : C1800 LEI, ENG [36694] : C1850-1900 BARROW IN FURNESS, CLOUGHFOLD, LAN, ENG [36835] : PRE 1761 RADFORD, NTT, ENG [37000] : 1800+ CAMBRIDGE, CAM, ENG [37065] : 1770+ LEYTON, ESS, ENG [37186] : 1800+ HACKNEY, MDX, ENG [37186] : 1750-1850 FEERING, ESS, ENG [37223] : C1760 FARNHAM, SRY, ENG [37420] : PRE 1850 STEPNEY, LND, ENG [37832] : 1650 STOCK, ESS, ENG [37928] : PRE 1890 MAIDSTONE, KEN, ENG [38270] : 1900-1930 FOLKESTONE, KEN, ENG [38513] : ALL KINSALE, COR, IRL [34312] : PRE 1840 IRL [34835] : THOMAS PRE 1811 DUBLIN, IRL [35147] : ALL WAT, IRL [35901] : ALL KINSALE, COR, IRL [35901] : 1800S THURLES, TIP, IRL & AUS [34596] : ANDREW 1877+ CAV, IRL & CAN [34164] : 1850+ NAPIER, NZ [37186] : PAT ALL NEW YORK, NY, USA [34164] : 1850+ USA [37186] : PRE 1800 PATRICK CO., VA, USA [38044] : 1800+ DARTFORD, KEN & MDX, ENG, WORLDWIDE [37065]

NEWNHAM 1890+ VIC, AUS [33979] : 1830+ KINGSTON UPON HULL, ERY, ENG [33979] : 1780+ NEWPORT, IOW, ENG [35977] : ALL WORLDWIDE [35868]

NEWPORT 1760+ HRT, ENG [34290] : 1800+ BABCARY & SPARKSFORD, SOM, ENG [35028] : 1700S GREAT HAMPDEN, BKM, ENG [35899] : PRE 1800 KEN, ENG [36480] : PRE 1842 MISSENDEN, BKM, ENG [36841] : 1842+ NELSON, NZ [36841]

NEWSHAM PRE 1780 WIGAN, LAN, ENG [34576] : PRE 1800 MURROW, CAM, ENG [35521] : 1700-1900 PRESTON & GARSTANG, LAN, ENG [38251]

NEWSOME 1860+ BALLARAT & GEELONG, VIC, AUS [34185] : 1875+ GLEN INNES, NSW, AUS [34185] : 1800+ NTT, ENG [37839] : 1800+ BIRMINGHAM, ENG [37839] : 1680+ MA, USA [37576]

NEWSON 1822+ MAITLAND & GLEN INNES, NSW, AUS [34185] : PRE 1822 CARBROOKE, NFK, ENG [34185] : C1800-1850 MDX & SRY, ENG [34484] : PRE 1700 KNODDISHALL, SFK, ENG [37420]

NEWSTEAD C1829 HILLINGTON, NFK, ENG [35729] : C1770 KINGS LYNN, NFK, ENG [37053]

NEWTON C1935 ROSEVILLE, NSW, AUS [34694] : C1900-1921 QLD, AUS [34694] : C1935 NORTHBRIDGE, NSW, AUS [34694] : 1900+ WA, AUS [35352] : 1871+ NEWCASTLE, NSW, AUS [35356] : PRE 1860 MT GAMBIER, SA, AUS [35789] : JOHN ALL BRISBANE, QLD, AUS & ENG [35122] : LESLIE ALL KINGAROY & BRISBANE, QLD, AUS & ENG [35122] : 1952-1979 WINNIPEG BEACH, MAN, CAN [34101] : PRE 1900 ONT, CAN [38434] : PRE 1880 HETTON LE HOLE, DUR, ENG [33859] : PRE 1828 SUTTON BONNINGTON & REPTON, NTT & DBY, ENG [33890] : 1880-1911 BRISTOL, ENG [34101] : 1830 CHESTER, DBY, ENG [34120] : 1869 EVERSHOLT, BDF, ENG [34309] : 1840S GRENDON, BKM, ENG [34518] : 1800-1950 ZENNOR, CON, ENG [34535] : 1800-1950 ST ERTH, CON, ENG [34535] : 1693+ CROWCOMBE, SOM,

ENG [34840] : PRE 1800 WORKSOP, NTT, ENG [34897] : 1800+ MANCHESTER, LAN, ENG [35129] : 1750-1900 GEE CROSS & HYDE, CHS, ENG [35591] : 1700+ HINDERWELL, YKS, ENG [35908] : ALL NOTTINGHAM, NTT, ENG [35993] : JOHN PRE 1795 TAUNTON, SOM, ENG [36192] : C1800+ SELBORNE, HAM, ENG [36265] : 1800+ LONG SUTTON, LIN, ENG [36370] : ELLEN C. PRE 1843 DOVER & BUCKLAND, KEN, ENG [36532] : 1700+ DUDLEY & CLAINES, WOR, ENG [36794] : 1600+ WESTBURY ON SEVERN, GLS, ENG [37051] : 1865+ LAMBETH, LND, ENG [37051] : C1807 COLCHESTER, ESS, ENG [37298] : 1600-1800 COLSTERWORTH, LIN, ENG [37342] : ALL YORK, YKS, ENG [37433] : C1700 TURNDITCH, DBY, ENG [37834] : 1800-1900 MILLOM, CUL, ENG [37858] : WILLIAM C1790-1815 ASTBURY, CHS, ENG [38055] : THOMAS ALL BRADFORD & BRISBANE, WRY & QLD, ENG & AUS [35122] : PRE 1856 MILLTOWN, KER, IRL [35765] : PRE 1856 KILLARNEY, KER, IRL [35765] : 1600-1700 CORBALLY, LEX, IRL [36898] : 1800S KILLALOE, CLA, IRL [38510] : 1805+ MANNING RIVER, OFF, IRL & AUS [37130] : 1800S+ BRUNNER & TAYLORVILLE, CHCH, NZ [34680] : PRE 1770 INCHTURE, PER, SCT [33873] : 1890+ DUNDEE, ANS, SCT [33873] : 1874-1950S RENFREW, SCT [33976] : PRE 1930 IOW, UK [34207] : 1797+ ROSELLE, IL, USA [34101] : 1800+ NE, USA [34511] : 1816 BRECKENRIDGE CO., KY, USA [35295] : BENJAMIN 1803 WAYNE CO., PA, USA [36736] : 1628+ RI, USA [38015] : PRE 1900 WORLDWIDE [35352] : SIR ISAAC 1600+ WORLDWIDE [35993]

NEWTON-LEWIS ALL WORLDWIDE [37091]

NEX 1600+ BRADNINCH, DEV, ENG [35821]

NEYER PRE 1840 DAUPHIN, PA, USA [37804]

NIBLETT 1800+ CINDERFORD, GLS, ENG [36058]

NIBLOCK 1800 KIRKMAIDEN, WIG, SCT [35820]

NICE PRE 1900 KITAMAT VILLAGE, BC, CAN [33858] : ALL ENG [35933] : 1700S WICKHAM ST PAUL, ESS, ENG [37568] : 1680-1760 BOXTED, SFK, ENG [37638] : 1800 SFK, ENG [37869]

NICHELSON PRE 1850 SPILSBURY, LND, ENG [36677]

NICHOL 1860+ HOBART, TAS, AUS [34670] : C1844 TORONTO, ONT, CAN [34133] : PRE 1830 NORFOLK CO., ONT, CAN [36702] : ALL KENDAL, WES, ENG [36159] : 1700-1800 CARLISLE, CUL, ENG [37654] : PRE 1900 KILCROW, MOG, IRL [34466] : 1800+ SCT [34408] : 1800-1875 MINTO, ROX, SCT [34649] : 1780+ SCT [34803] : 1750+ MCDUFF, BAN, SCT [35627]

NICHOLAS 1887 SYDNEY, NSW, AUS [36608] : 1650+ SANCREED, CON, ENG [34747] : 1800S TRURO, CON, ENG [35076] : 1800S ST AGNES, CON, ENG [35965] : 1750-1850 EDDINGTON, SOM, ENG [36012] : 1800+ LIVERPOOL, LAN, ENG [36241] : 1800S PENZANCE, CON, ENG [36608] : PRE 1800 SENNEN, CON, ENG [37379] : PRE 1750 WENTNOR, SAL, ENG [37722] : 1840 GENOA, ITL [35705] : 1700+ GROSSMONT, MON, WLS [36209]

NICHOLLE 1800S GSY, CHI [36809]

NICHOLLS 1870+ BURRA, NSW, AUS [33807] : PRE 1890 GOULBURN, NSW, AUS [34417] : 1880+ SYDNEY, NSW, AUS [35374] : 1900+ LUCKNOW, NSW, AUS [35567] : ALL ONT, CAN [38419] : JOSEPH PRE 1836 DURSLEY, GLS, ENG [33807] : PRE 1850 SOUTHWARK, LND, ENG [34316] : 1700+ KIDDERMINSTER, WOR, ENG [34711] : 1685-1740 GWENNAP, CON, ENG [34793] : PRE 1816 HARLESTON, NFK, ENG [34828] : C1854 ASHELWORTH, GLS, ENG [34939] : 1824

TEWKESBURY, GLS, ENG [34950] : 1700-1850 LONDON, ENG [34975] : 1800-1850 CHESHUNT, HRT, ENG [35151] : PRE 1880 CHESTER, CHS, ENG [35374] : 1750S-1850S ST AGNES & KENWYN, CON, ENG [35489] : JOHN 1784 LEOMINSTER, HEF, ENG [35560] : 1800S ST AUSTELL, CON, ENG [35567] : 1800S REDRUTH, CON, ENG [35567] : PRE 1840 CHESTERFIELD, DBY, ENG [35946] : 1830+ BERMONDSEY, LND, ENG [35974] : C1800 HATFIELD, HRT, ENG [35974] : 1800+ TAMWORTH, STS, ENG [36058] : 1850S GREAT LINFORD, BKM, ENG [36292] : PRE 1812 HAMPSTEAD NORRIS, BRK, ENG [36668] : 1840 BLOXWICH & WALSALL, STS, ENG [36887] : 1800+ PRESTON & GARSTANG, LAN, ENG [37066] : 1880+ TRELEIGH, CON, ENG [37343] : PRE 1836 SSX, ENG [37978] : PRE 1850 WISBECH, CAM, ENG [38386] : C1876 CURRAGH, KID, IRL [35374] : PRE 1821 CORK, COR, IRL [37454] : 1890+ RSA [35224]

NICHOLS 1750-1900 ONT, CAN [38128] : 1775-1880 MONTREAL, VALLEYFIELD, QUE, CAN [38147] : 1800-1860 CHATEAUGAY, QUE, CAN [38147] : PRE 1794 CARLTON COLVILLE, SFK, ENG [33762] : 1785 OTTRINGHAM, ERY, ENG [33910] : 1700+ DEV, ENG [34271] : PRE 1796 WHITTLESEY, CAM, ENG [34660] : PRE 1827 HOLBORN, LND, ENG [34800] : 1835 WESTMINSTER, LND, ENG [34808] : 1800+ PACKWOOD, WAR, ENG [35436] : ISAAC C1790-1830 ST AGNES, CON, ENG [35725] : PRE 1840 CHESTERFIELD, DBY, ENG [35946] : 1700+ BRIGHTLINGSEA, ESS, ENG [36794] : 1700+ BARROW IN FURNESS, LAN, ENG [36794] : 1780 ROYDEN, NFK, ENG [37181] : 1860S BATTERSEA, SRY, ENG [37271] : PRE 1884 STRATFORD, ESS, ENG [38412] : PRE 1839 HORSLEY, GLS, ENG & AUS [34845] : 1819-1900 BRADFORD CO., PA, USA [37013] : C1750-1850 BERKELEY CO., VA, USA [38030] : 1700-1820 FAUQUIER, VA, USA [38054] : 1850-1900 CHURUBUSCO, NY, USA [38147]

NICHOLSEN C1820-1850S IRL [36289]

NICHOLSON 1850+ GEELONG, VIC, AUS [35439] : 1870S FORBES, NSW, AUS [35557] : 1820+ SYDNEY, NSW, AUS [35557] : 1858+ GOULBURN, NSW, AUS [35557] : ALL ST KILDA, VIC, AUS [36852] : 1850-1990 WENTWORTH CO., ONT, CAN [34377] : 1821+ LANARK CO., ONT, CAN [36955] : C1831+ NEWCASTLE, NB, CAN & SCT [34339] : PRE 1781 BRANCEPETH, DUR, ENG [33774] : ALICE C1880+ BRISTOL, GLS, ENG [34862] : 1700+ EGREMONT, CUL, ENG [34888] : 1840S CROYDON, SRY, ENG [35177] : PRE 1820 MANCHESTER, LAN, ENG [35557] : PRE 1860 HULL, ERY, ENG [36039] : PRE 1850 BURNESTON, NRY, ENG [36159] : ALL LEEDS & WAKEFIELD, WRY, ENG [36187] : PRE 1832 KENDAL, WES, ENG [36230] : ALL LOFTUS, NRY, ENG [36402] : ALL EGTON, NRY, ENG [36402] : ALL EASINGTON, NRY, ENG [36402] : ALL BOULBY, NRY, ENG [36402] : ALL SKINNINGROVE, NRY, ENG [36402] : PRE 1800 GRINTON, NRY, ENG [36588] : ALL WESTMINSTER, MDX, ENG [37994] : 1700-1800 BARTON, WES, ENG [38516] : PRE 1808 COR, IRL [34377] : 1800+ BELFAST, ANT, DOW & ARM, IRL [35636] : 1825 PORTREE, INV, SCT [33936] : 1700+ LONGHOPE, OKI, SCT [34688] : PRE 1860 DORNOCH ASSYNT, SUT, SCT [34812] : 1750+ DUNBLANE, PER, SCT [35558] : PRE 1800 ST MONANCE, FIF, SCT [35627] : PRE 1821 INVERNESS, INV & PER, SCT [36955] : ELIZABETH PRE 1780 EDINBURGH, SCT [37514] : 1800S GREENOCK, RFW, SCT [37566] : DUNCAN

PRE 1800 SCT [38536] : ELIZABETH 1782 NEWBURGH, NY, USA [37514] : PRE 1815 ANTIGUA, W.INDIES [35359] : ROBERT 1787+ HOLYHEAD, AGY, WLS [35515]

NICKEL 1810-1860 BERNSDORF, KSA, GER [35402] : 1870-1920 VOLT & MT LAKE, MT & MN, USA [36675]

NICKELL 1728 TYR, IRL [38054] : 1728-1990 AUGUSTA, VA, KY & WA, USA [38054]

NICKERSON 1600-1750 NFK, ENG [38224]

NICKLAS PRE 1800 CHS, ENG [35238]

NICKLER PRE 1648 TIR, OES [38667]

NICKLESS 1800S OLDBURY, WOR, ENG [35256]

NICKLINSON PRE 1895 LIVERPOOL, LAN & DBY, ENG [37840]

NICKOLDS 1850+ NFK, ENG [37347]

NICKOLLES PRE 1816 LOWESTOFT, SFK, ENG [34828]

NICKOLLS 1700+ KIDDERMINSTER, WOR, ENG [34711]

NICLAS PRE 1750 MUENSTER, RPF, GER [38681]

NICOL 1870+ HAMILTON, ONT, CAN [35004] : 1870+ BRANDON, MAN, CAN [35004] : 1800+ DONBRIDGE, ABD, SCT [34107] : C1830 LONGSIDE, ABD, SCT [34400] : 1700+ PERTH, PER, SCT [34637] : 1700+ PAISLEY, SCT [34664] : C1850 DALRYMPLE, AYR, SCT [35158] : C1810 ISLE OF ARRAN, BUT, SCT [35158] : 1750-1875 KEMNAY, CHAPEL OF GAIROCH, ABD, SCT [35981] : PRE 1900 CLK, SCT [36433] : PRE 1900 STI, SCT [36433] : PRE 1840 FORFAR, ANS, SCT [36617] : 1750-1890 ABERDEEN, ABD, SCT [37432] : 1800S WICK & REAY, CAI, SCT [38290]

NICOLAI ALL ATHANASIENHOF, POS, GER [38372]

NICOLAS PRE 1825 CMN, WLS [35867] : ELIZA PRE 1825 CMN, WLS [35867]

NICOLAY 1800+ SOUTH EAST, ASIA [33795] : 1800+ CAN [33795] : 1720+ COURT OF ST JAMES, ENG [33795] : 1700+ ENG [33795] : PRE 1800 SCG, GER [33795] : ALL DURBAN, RSA [33795]

NICOLL 1820 CAPE BRETON CO., NS, CAN [34253] : 1875+ WINNEPEG, MAN, CAN [38059] : C1750 HRT, ENG [36978] : 1800+ ABERDEEN, ABD, SCT [34008] : PRE 1820 SCT [34253] : THOMAS 1839 DUNDEE, ANS, SCT [35369] : 1850+ FORTEVIOT, PER, SCT [35450] : 1850+ KCD, SCT [38059]

NICOLLE PRE 1800 JSY, CHI [36696]

NICOLS C1794 OLD SODBURY, GLS, ENG [37144]

NICOLSON C1800 INTERSALL, NTT, SCT [37381] : ALL TRANENT, ELN, SCT [33959] : PRE 1800 KENNOWAY, FIF, SCT [35045] : 1780+ PORTREE, INV, SCT [37178] : PRE 1870 GREENOCK, RFW, SCT [37242] : ALL CAI, SCT [37727]

NIDDREY C1750-1800 ANS, SCT [36327]

NIDDRIE C1750-1800 ANS, SCT [36327]

NIDEVER 1700-1850 PA & TN, USA [38768]

NIDREY C1750-1800 ANS, SCT [36327]

NIECE PRE 1830 IRL [33907]

NIEDERSTEIN 1760-1810 BONN, RPR, GER [38528]

NIEHOFF PRE 1830 NRW, GER [38029]

NIELD PRE 1848 YKS, ENG [37760]

NIELSDATTER INGEBURRIG 1640-1700 TAARNBORG, SORO, DEN [37547]

NIELSEN 1880+ BUNDABERG, QLD, AUS [35158] : PRE 1820 DEN [33959] : C1840 BANDHOLM, MARIBO CO., DEN [34203] : 1800+ FREDERICKSHAVN, HJORRING, DEN [34664] : 1850-1870 HOLBERG, DEN [35158] : PRE 1872 ULLBULL, DEN [35443] : 1800S TUENDAL & COPENHAGEN, DEN [35816] : ELIAS 1690-1770 TAARNBORG, SORO, DEN [37547] : C1863-1876

LECK, SHO, GER [33950] : C1876-1915 MATARAWA, WAIRARAPA, NZ [33950]

NIELSEN (SEE NEILSEN [33918]

NIELSON PRE 1861 MAARUP, DEN [38738] : ALL NOR [38273] : PRE 1830 LKS, SCT [37332]

NIEMANN 1890-1895 MELBOURNE, VIC, AUS [33971] : 1860-1870 BENDIGO, VIC, AUS [35725] : 1880+ COLLINGWOOD, VIC, AUS [35725] : PRE 1860 TUCHEIM, PSA, GER [34801] : PRE 1837 BARTH, MEK, GER [35048] : C1830 BREMEN, GER [35725] : C1860-1880 CHRISTCHURCH, NZ [35725]

NIEMEYER 1840-55 BISCHOFSPOHL, HAN, GER [38202]

NIENSDORFF (SEE VON [37728]

NIESLER ALL AUS [36289] : ALL SCHNEIDNITZ, GER [36289]

NIEUWENHUIS C1900 LISSE, ZUH, NL [38713]

NIEVA PRE 1711 MALAGA, ESP [37819]

NIGGELER PRE 1850 DOTZIGEN, BE, CH [38747]

NIGH 1847 HERKIMER CO., NY, USA [35295]

NIGHTINGALE PRE 1830 BKM, ENG [35030] : 1800+ BURNLEY, LAN, ENG [35949] : 1837+ CHARLWOOD, SSX & SRY, ENG [36212] : PRE 1889 SRY, ENG [37358] : PRE 1800 BIRMINGHAM, WAR, ENG [37371] : ANN 1830-1900 MANCHESTER, LAN, ENG [37543] : WILLIAM 1830-1900 MANCHESTER, LAN, ENG [37543] : 1795+ KENNINGTON & SYDNEY, BRK & NSW, ENG & AUS [35155] : ALL WORLDWIDE [36651]

NIKULSEN DALEN TOLLEF 1829+ VINJE, TELEMARK, NOR [34481]

NILE 1760-1900 MERTHER & ST MICHAEL PENKEVIL, CON, ENG [35576]

NILES 1700+ OSTEGO CO.& ADOLPHUSTOWN, NY & ONT, USA & CAN [34109]

NILLES 1700+ YOUNGLINSTER, LUX [37016] : 1700+ JUNGLINSTER, LUX [37016]

NILSDOTTER KARNA 1839 ANDRARUM, KRISTIANSTADT, SWE [38193] : MARIT 1820 LYSVIK, VARMLAND, SWE [38556]

NILSEN ALL KONGSVINGER, NOR [38273]

NILSSON PRE 1862 GOTEBORG, SWE [34177] : KRISTOFFER D. PRE 1900 ADALSLIDEN PARISH, VASTERBOTTENS, SWE [34481] : ALL BRUNSKOG, VARMLAND, SWE [36881] : PRE 1860 ALINGSAS, VASTERGOTLAND, SWE [37821] : 1820-1880 DINGTUNA & NORA, VASTMANLAND, SWE [37821] : ERIK 1800-1900 VANNAS, VASTERBOTTEN, SWE [38104] : 1600-1780S OTHEM, GOTLAND, SWE [38346] : OLOF 1825 LYSVIK, VARMLAND, SWE [38556] : C1870 HELSINGBORG, MALHOMUS, SWE [38769]

NIMMO 1800+ SCT [34299] : ALL ABERDEEN, ABD, SCT [35334] : 1700+ FAULDHOUSE, WLN, SCT [36261]

NIMMONS 1800+ IRL [38726]

NIMNEY PRE 1900 IRL [36499]

NIND PRE 1873 LONDON, ENG [36124] : PRE 1840 LND, ENG [37370]

NINER ALL EXETER & TIVERTON, DEV, ENG [36664]

NINIAN PRE 1850 DYSART, FIF & MLN, SCT [37727]

NIPPRESS 1850+ RICHMOND, NSW, AUS [35088] : 1829+ SYDNEY, NSW, AUS [35759] : PRE 1850 WIL, ENG [35088]

NISBET PRE 1850 LONDON, ENG [34463] : PRE 1767 COLDINGHAM PARISH, BEW, SCT [34491] : PRE 1870 EDINBURGH, SCT [35330] : PRE 1700 ELN, SCT [36679] : 1859+ STANE, LKS, SCT [37205] : MARY 1820-30 EYEMOUTH, BEW, SCT [37476]

NISSEN PRE 1876+ ADELAIDE, SA, AUS [33890] : PRE 1870 GRAM, HADERSLEV, DEN [38111] : PRE

1876 APENRADE, SHO, GER **[33890]** : GERTRUD PRE 1722 HADERSLEBEN, NOR **[36453]**

NISSON PRE 1900 NZ & DEN **[34603]**

NITSCHKE ALL CAN **[36661]** : PRE 1800 LASGEN, SIL, PRE **[35795]** : ALL USA **[36661]** : ALL WORLDWIDE **[36661]**

NITSHCHKE 1794 ZULLICHAU, BRA, PRE **[35369]**

NITZEL 1837+ GER **[38531]**

NIVEN 1875+ INVERELL, NSW, AUS **[35232]** : 1780-1850 DONAGHADEE, DOW, IRL **[36776]** : PRE 1790 FORTEVIOT, PER, SCT **[33957]** : PRE 1840 ORWELL, KRS, SCT **[37621]**

NIX PRE 1850 ABD, SCT **[37693]** : ALL WORLDWIDE **[35190]**

NIXON 1818+ RICHMOND & WINDSOR, NSW, AUS **[35586]** : 1840+ MONTREAL, QUE, CAN **[34144]** : PRE 1800 MACCLESFIELD, CHS, ENG **[34686]** : PRE 1850 WOR, ENG **[34977]** : C1800 RIPLEY, WAR, ENG **[35586]** : 1750+ RAMSEY, HUN, ENG **[37409]** : 1831 LOWFELL, DUR, ENG **[37975]** : PRE 1896 LEEK, STS, ENG **[38490]** : 1820+ ENNISKILLEN, FER, IRL **[34075]** : PRE 1840 IRL **[34144]** : JOHN 1780 MACGUIRES BRIDGE, FER, IRL **[35328]** : C1830-1850 NEWRY, ARM, IRL **[36768]** : 1800S DUB, IRL **[36837]** : JAMES 1733-1826 GRAVAGHY, TYR, IRL **[37317]** : PRE 1826 FER, IRL **[37601]** : PRE 1881 CLOGHER, MAY, IRL **[37955]** : JOHN 1806+ NEW ORLEANS, LA, USA **[35328]** : ADELINE 1820-60S NEW ORLEANS, LA, USA **[37585]**

NOAD PRE 1860 BATH, SOM, ENG **[34865]** : PRE 1853 WIDCOMB, SOM, ENG **[35379]** : JOHANNA 1813+ PAULTON, SOM, ENG **[35729]**

NOAH PRE 1825+ WHITECHAPEL & STEPNEY, LND, ENG **[34423]** : 1800+ KEN, ENG **[37907]**

NOAKE CHARLES W. 1843 WORCESTER, WOR, ENG **[36633]**

NOAKES 1854-1874 ROSSMORE, NSW, AUS **[34966]** : C1819-1841 BREDE, SSX, ENG **[33950]** : PRE 1760 SSX, ENG **[34858]** : 1760S BREDE, SSX, ENG **[35260]** : PRE 1850 SSX, ENG **[36584]** : 1800-1900 SSX, ENG **[37207]** : PRE 1800 SSX, ENG **[37741]** : 1854-1869 GREYTOWN, WAIRARAPA, NZ **[33950]**

NOALL PRE 1800 ST IVES, CON, ENG **[35385]**

NOBEL 1800S ALTENBURG, SAB, GER **[34914]**

NOBELS C1740 WALCHEREN, ZEL, NL **[38705]**

NOBES JOHN C1770+ ENG **[33892]**

NOBIS 1650-1720 RANSWEILER, RHINELAND, GER **[36561]**

NOBLE 1880+ IPSWICH, QLD, AUS **[33782]** : 1836+ SA, AUS **[34179]** : 1841+ (PER 'RUNNYMEDE'), NSW, AUS **[35410]** : 1850+ MURRUMBURRAH, NSW, AUS **[38001]** : ALBERT 1912 NSW, AUS **[38269]** : 1800+ NORTHUMBERLAND CO., CAN **[34126]** : 1870S MULMER, ONT, CAN **[34937]** : 1900S NEVILLE, SAS, CAN **[34937]** : PRE 1800 LONDON, ENG **[34112]** : 1700+ WEST WRATTING, CAM, ENG **[34179]** : PRE 1830 BEDWORTH, WAR, ENG **[34769]** : PRE 1880 HIGH YEWDALE, LAN, ENG **[34958]** : 1800+ NORTH FRODINGHAM, YKS, ENG **[35112]** : PRE 1891 PLYMOUTH, DEV, ENG **[35339]** : 1750-1820 ISLINGTON, LND, ENG **[35382]** : ALL WALTON, WRY, ENG **[35588]** : 1700+ SHARNBROOK, BDF, ENG **[36123]** : PRE 1826 HALIFAX, WRY, ENG **[36411]** : C1650-1850 WHITEPARISH, WIL, ENG **[36478]** : 1800+ ROYSTON, YKS, ENG **[36512]** : 1800-1900 DBY & NTT, ENG **[36531]** : 1780-1830 BOLTON, LAN, ENG **[37779]** : 1830-1900 LIVERPOOL, LAN, ENG **[37779]** : HENRY 1860-1917 DUR, ENG **[38269]** : 1800-1900 BELFAST, ANT, IRL **[33851]** : ALEXANDER C1783 ENNISKILLEN, FER, IRL **[34126]** : 1800+

CLONES, FER, IRL **[35410]** : PRE 1839+ ENNISKILLEN, FER, IRL **[35453]** : PRE 1830 NEWTOWNBARRY, WEX, IRL **[36652]** : PRE 1840 DRUMKERRAN, FER, IRL **[38214]** : C1700-1800 MAUCHLINE, AYR, SCT **[34339]** : 1800+ STRICHEN, ABD, SCT **[34870]** : PRE 1850+ PAISLEY, RFW, SCT **[35453]** : 1800-1820 KNOCKBAIN, ROC, SCT **[36783]** : 1846-1902 NEWBATTLE, MLN, SCT **[37165]** : 1850-1870 AURORA, IN, USA **[34914]** : 1600-1865 RAYMOND, ME, USA **[35294]** : PRE 1800 WASHINGTON CO., NY, USA **[38017]** : 1750-1800 SUFFOLK CO., MA, USA **[38119]** : 1870+ JEFFERSON CO., CO, USA **[38310]** : ALL WORLDWIDE **[36333]** : ALL WORLDWIDE **[36333]**

NOBLES 1700+ SHARNBROOK, BDF, ENG **[36123]** : PRE 1850 IRA, CAYUGA, NY, USA **[38027]**

NOBLET PRE 1850 NANTES, PL, FRA **[36270]** : PRE 1820 TIGLIN, WIC, IRL **[37179]**

NOCK 1844+ SA, AUS **[34179]** : 1850+ WALHALLA, VIC, AUS **[34421]** : PRE 1844 TIPTON, STS, ENG **[34179]** : PRE 1790 ROWLEY REGIS, STS, ENG **[37369]** : 1766-1860 SHADWELL, LND, ENG **[37369]** : PRE 1900 SMETHWICK, STS, ENG **[37681]** : 1900+ JOHANNESBURG, TVL, RSA **[37369]** : ALL WORLDWIDE **[37369]**

NOCKE 1845+ PADDINGTON, MDX, ENG **[37165]**

NOCKELS ALL WORLDWIDE **[37083]**

NODDINS 1700-1800 ROXBY, YKS, ENG **[37011]**

NOE PRE 1824 SCHWEDT & ANGERMUENDE, BRA, GER **[34083]**

NOEL 1727-1793 FOSSES LA VILLE, NMR, BEL **[38158]** : PRE 1900 HARBOUR GRACE, NFD, CAN **[33852]** : PRE 1874 FALDOUET, JSY, CHI **[35761]**

NOESSELT C1850 SCHWEIDNITZ, SIL, GER **[34083]**

NOEST PRE 1750 KOLDERVEEN, NL **[36630]**

NOFFKE ALL WORLDWIDE **[33974]**

NOGUERA 1700-1990 ALICANTE, ESP **[38346]**

NOICE 1800S LND & BKS, ENG **[38541]**

NOISE C1750 ALDBOURNE, WIL, ENG **[37335]**

NOKES C1800 SHEERNESS, KEN, ENG **[34296]**

NOLAN 1840+ VIC, AUS **[33798]** : 1850+ COLERAINE, VIC, AUS **[35587]** : PRE 1900 TAMWORTH, NSW, AUS **[36288]** : 1865-1930 GYMPIE, QLD, AUS **[36297]** : 1864+ MELBOURNE, VIC, AUS **[37994]** : PRE 1860 ENG **[33798]** : ANDREW 1800+ CON, ENG **[35911]** : PRE 1842 KIK, IRL **[34214]** : 1750-1850 GAL, IRL **[34572]** : ALL IRL **[34938]** : 1820+ ARDAGH, LIM, IRL **[34960]** : 1830-1860 ATHLONE, WEM, IRL **[35151]** : 1840S TIP, IRL **[35855]** : 1800+ IRL **[35911]** : PETER 1800-1850 TIP, IRL **[36297]** : PRE 1850 LIM, IRL **[36840]** : ANN C1840 KILLARNEY, KER, IRL **[37664]** : MICHAEL 1870 DUBLIN, IRL **[37791]** : 1700+ KIK, IRL **[37826]** : PRE 1864 KILKENNY, KIK, IRL **[37994]** : 1800-1870S CLA, LND & MA, IRL, ENG & **[36337]** : 1850S AUCKLAND, NZ **[35855]** : ALL RSA & IRL **[34945]** : 1890+ SUPERIOR, WI, USA **[34368]** : ALL SPRINGFIELD, IL, USA **[37558]**

NOLAN (SEE NOWLAN) **[37555]**

NOLL 1670-1704 WICKENRODE, GHE, GER **[38749]** : 1712-1772 GROSSALMERODE, GHE, GER **[38749]** : 1872-1920 SHENANDOAH, PA, USA **[38619]**

NOLLEY 1810-1850 VA & AL, USA **[38340]**

NOLTE PRE 1850 BRIENTENBERG & OBERNFELD, NSA, GER **[38029]**

NOLTEN PRE 1850 SALATIGA, JAVA, E. INDIES &, NL **[36630]**

NOMMAIRE CHARLOTTE C1600 VALREUILLE, NO, FRA **[37429]**

NONNAST PRE 1827 RIEMERSTHEIDE &
BORKENDORF, SIL, GER [34083]
NOON ALL BURTON DASSETT, WAR, ENG [35746] :
PRE 1873 ASHBY ST LEDGERS, NTH, ENG [36290]
: 1800+ CLOONSHEE, ROS, IRL [36493] : 1700-1850
DUNAMON, ROS & TYR, IRL [37118]
NOONAN 1800-1880 BENDIGO, VIC, AUS [33879] :
1850+ SYDNEY, NSW, AUS [38484] : 1780-1850
CLA, IRL [33879] : 1800+ SCARIFF, CLA, IRL
[36758] : 1830+ BALLYSIMON, LIM, IRL [37181] :
MAURICE JAMES PRE 1840 UK & IRL [35496]
NOONE 1700+ LND, ENG [34062]
NOONEY 1880S BIRKENHEAD, LAN, ENG [36207]
NOORDBEEK 1820+ BERGUM & OLDEBOORN,
FRI, NL [34990]
NOORE 1790-1800 BLAIR CO., PA, USA [38087]
NOOTH PRE 1700 DEV, SOM & WIL, ENG [37623] :
PRE 1700 LND, ENG [37623] : PRE 1700 ENG [37623]
: PRE 1830 NFK, ENG [37623] : PRE 1700
WORLDWIDE [37623]
NOPPER C1792 OFINGEN, BAD, GER [34239]
NORBISRATH ALL GER [34861]
NORBURY C1836 MACCLESFIELD, CHS, ENG
[37263]
NORCLIFFE PRE 1800 STAINLAND & LINDLEY,
WRY, ENG [37372]
NORCOTT 1700-1860 LAUNCESTON & STH
PETHERWIN, CON, ENG [35581]
NORCROSS C1750 RIBCHESTER, LAN, ENG [37066]
NORDABY 1750-1820 ERY, ENG [34320]
NORDIN C1800 LAMBOURN, BRK, ENG [35512] :
CARL 1800S NORSJO, VASTERBOTTENS, SWE
[38445] : CARL 1890S KULM, ND, USA [38445]
NORFOLK 1920+ BOURNEMOUTH &
PORTSMOUTH, HAM, ENG [38403] : 1600+
STOKE BY NAYLAND, SFK, ENG [38745]
NORFORD PRE 1852 ST MARYS BLANDFORD,
DOR, ENG [37192]
NORGROVE 1800+ GLYMPTON, OXF, ENG [36892]
NORMAN 1869+ REDBANK, VIC, AUS [34174] :
1850+ PADDINGTON, NSW, AUS [35105] : 1850+
PRAHRAN, VIC, AUS [35476] : C1890 HOBART,
TAS, AUS [35797] : 1825+ HOBART, TAS, AUS
[37312] : 1840-1870 LOUGHBOROUGH, LEI, ENG
[34337] : 1852 BRISTOL, SOM, ENG [34540] : PRE
1850 RYE, SSX, ENG [35232] : 1700S WINSON, GLS,
ENG [35256] : 1800S CHEDWORTH, GLS, ENG
[35256] : 1700+ GRANDBOROUGH, BKM, ENG
[35476] : 1800+ ISLINGTON, MDX & LND, ENG
[35701] : CHARLES PRE 1893 WAPPING, MDX,
ENG [35729] : 1800S UFCULME, DEV, ENG [35797] :
C1780-1970 NORWICH & FELTHORPE, NFK, ENG
[36128] : PRE 1850 NEWBOLD ON AVON, WAR,
ENG [36380] : 1800S GUILDFORD, SRY, ENG
[36409] : PRE 1820 SSX, ENG [36577] : 1800+ YKS,
ENG [36577] : 1870+ LAN, ENG [36577] : ALL SOM,
ENG [36834] : 1810+ CAMERTON, CUL, ENG
[37073] : 1865+ CLIFTON, CUL, ENG [37073] :
1825+ MARYPORT, CUL, ENG [37073] : 1775+
DEAN & BRIGHAM, CUL, ENG [37073] : 1760+
WORKINGTON, CUL, ENG [37073] : 1660+
LORTON, CUL, ENG [37073] : 1860+ BRIDEKIRK
& BRIDGEFOOT, CUL, ENG [37073] : 1840+
SEATON & GREAT BROUGHTON, CUL, ENG
[37073] : ALL HEF, ENG [37103] : 1830-70
WATNALL CHAWORTH, NTT, ENG [37215] :
1806+ CARBURTON, NTT, ENG [37215] : PRE 1860
CUTCOMBE & WHEDDON CROSS, SOM & WIL,
ENG [37556] : ALL LIVERPOOL, CHS, ENG [37667]
: 1770S LAGORE, MEA, IRL [37869] : C1870
GREENOCK, RFW, SCT [34222] : JOSEPH C1850
SCT [34222] : 1790-1850 CULPEPPER CO., VA & OH,

USA [36901] : 1792+ SPENCER CO., KY, USA
[38091] : PRE 1800 RUTHERFORD CO., NC, USA
[38091] : PRE 1820 VA, USA [38196]
NORMANDEAU 1600-1850 QUE, CAN [38033]
NORMANN PRE 1800 VIEREGGE, RUEGEN, DDR
[38604]
NORMAVILLE 1777+ BROMPTON BY
NORTHALLERTON, YKS, ENG [36704]
NORMENT PRE 1775 MECKLENBURG &
CAROLINE, VA, USA [38348]
NORMILE 1800+ LIMERICK, LIM, IRL & AUS
[38204]
NORMINGTON PRE 1810 DENHOLME, WRY, ENG
[36011]
NORMINTON PRE 1864 WEST DERBY, LAN, ENG
[37651]
NORMORE 1840+ CUTWELL ARM, NFD, CAN
[34074]
NORMOYLE PRE 1870 LIMERICK, LIM, IRL [35136]
NORQUAY 1836+ ST MARGARET'S HOPE, OKI,
SCT [34688]
NORRIE PRE 1844 ABD, SCT [35083] : 1800S
PETERHEAD, ABD, SCT [35906] : PRE 1890
FORRES, MOR, SCT [36338]
NORRIS 1837+ CAMDEN, NSW, AUS [34874] :
1830+ SOUTH CREEK, NSW, AUS [37500] : 1872-
1890 WOMBAT & YOUNG, NSW, AUS [37968] :
1820-1850 BEEFORD, YKS, ENG [33861] : ALL
SOM, ENG [34131] : 1600+ HAM, ENG [34303] :
1846 LANDPORT, HAM, ENG [34757] : PRE 1849
CHILD OKEFORD, DOR, ENG [34874] : 1700+
PORTSEA, HAM, ENG [35080] : 1700+ IOW, ENG
[35080] : C1843 ST MARYLEBONE, LND, ENG
[35244] : C1848 HUNGERFORD, BRK, ENG [35244] :
1830S ST GEO IN EAST, LND, ENG [35408] : ALL
CORSHAM, WIL, ENG [35433] : PRE 1810
NEWINGTON, SRY, ENG [36153] : PRE 1880 WAR,
ENG [36508] : 1850-1930 NEW MALDEN, SRY,
ENG [36708] : 1800S LONDON, ENG [36708] : 1830+
MANCHESTER, LAN, ENG [37134] : PRE 1840
DONYATT, SOM, ENG [37692] : C1800 KEN, ENG
[37715] : PRE 1875 BATTERSEA, SRY, ENG [37753] :
C1860-1900 FULHAM, MDX, ENG [37778] : C1900-
1930 MITCHAM, SRY, ENG [37778] : C1800-1860
CHELSEA, MDX, ENG [37778] : 1860-1960S STOKE
DRY, RUT, ENG [37780] : ALFRED C1898
PANCRAS, MDX, ENG [37992] : EMMA PRE 1850
TROWBRIDGE, WIL, ENG [38049] : JAMES C1833
KELMINGTON, DEV, ENG [38406] : 1850+
OMAGH & DRUMRAGH, TYR, IRL [37317] : 1800+
GOVAN, LKS, SCT [34290] : 1790-1800 SUSSEX CO.,
NJ, USA [35287] : 1800-1865 SENECA CO., NY, USA
[35287] : 1865+ CLINTON CO., MI, USA [35287] :
1650 ST MARYS CO., MD, USA [36731] : C1989
ROME, GA, USA [37780] : 1831 BALTIMORE, MD,
USA [37817]
NORRISH WILLIAM 1832 RAWDON, QUE, CAN
[34091] : WILLIAM 1779 EXETER, DEV, ENG
[34091] : 1680+ CREDITON, DEV, ENG [35027] :
1780+ LYDFORD, DEV, ENG [36865] : C1800 SRY,
DEV & MDX, ENG [36978] : PRE 1900 CON & DEV,
ENG [37749]
NORTH PRE 1900 NSW, AUS [34968] : 1830-1900 ONT,
CAN [34364] : 1550S MELBOURN & ARRINGTON,
CAM, ENG [34204] : ALL NEWBURY, BRK, ENG
[34292] : ALL HITCHIN & STEVENAGE, HRT,
ENG [34292] : 1700+ LOUGHBOROUGH, LEI,
ENG [34414] : 1700+ HUN, ENG [34414] : ALL LEI,
ENG [34493] : 1800-1900 BRIGHTON, SSX, ENG
[35069] : 1719+ STAPLE FITZPAINE, SOM, ENG
[35112] : 1775+ NEWARK ON TRENT, NTT, ENG
[35194] : 1850 LAMBETH, MDX, ENG [35256] :

1760+ WAKEFIELD, WRY, ENG [35905] :
WILLIAM PRE 1830 WHITECHAPEL, LND, ENG
[38731] : PRE 1840 DUBLIN, DUB, IRL [37909] :
1800S RSA [34292] : 1830+ IL, USA [36912]

NORTHACE 1700+ NOTTINGHAM, NTT, ENG
[37248]

NORTHCOTE 1842+ DEV & NSW, ENG & AUS
[35579]

NORTHCOTT PRE 1842 PLYMOUTH, DEV, ENG
[34616] : PRE 1860 LAPFORD, DEV, ENG [35496] :
1870+ LONG ASTON, GLS, ENG [35969] : 1833
HOLLACOMBE, DEV, ENG [36804]

NORTHERN PRE 1873 DRYPOOL, YKS, ENG [37369]

NORTHEY PRE 1851 CHACEWATER & TRURO,
CON, ENG [34881] : PRE 1850 TRURO, CON, ENG
[34923] : ALL KEA, CON, ENG [37939]

NORTHMORE 1600-1700 SHEEPSTOR &
SAMPFORD SPINEY, DEV, ENG [37411] : ALL
WORLDWIDE [37411]

NORTHOVER 1850+ WA, USA [36942]

NORTHROP OLIVER ALL BRADFORD CO., PA,
USA [37584] : ALL TOMPKIN CO., NY, USA [37584]
: ALL CT, USA [37584]

NORTHROPE 1800S HARSTON, CAM, ENG [33898]

NORTHWAY PRE 1820 CHITTLEHAMPTON, DEV,
ENG [36514]

NORTON PRE 1894 WILUNGA, SA, AUS [33935] :
REV. JAMES 1880+ VIC & SA, AUS [35844] : 1850+
MANNING RV., NSW, AUS [35844] : 1700 RUT,
ENG [34321] : 1827+ ENG [34609] : ALL
MERRIOTT, SOM, ENG [34665] : PRE 1880
WILLITON, SOM, ENG [34730] : 1600+
KETTERING, NTH, ENG [35776] : PRE 1900 DUR
& NRY, ENG [37061] : PRE 1915 MAIDSTONE,
KEN, ENG [37359] : PRE 1850 MID, NFK, ENG
[37718] : 1500+ YKS, ENG & BEL [37010] : 1800
EGLISH, OFF, IRL [35844] : PRE 1850 WIC, IRL
[38457] : PETER 1800-1810 ROSCOMMON, ROS &
GAL, IRL [38780] : 1865+ AUCKLAND &
WHANGAREI, NZ [34609] : 1868+ LISBON, PT
[34609] : DOROTHY MAY 1810+ ONTARIO CO.,
NY, USA [36575]

NORVAL PRE 1838 GLASGOW, LKS, SCT [37238]

NORWOOD 1887-1912 FITZROY, VIC, AUS [34549] :
1789+ BERKHAMSTED, HRT, ENG [36071] : 1820-
1830 GWINNETT CO., GA, USA [37533]

NOSEWORTHY PRE 1860 HARBOUR GRACE, NFD,
CAN [33852]

NOSKE 1790-1850 SCHERLANTRY, PRE, GER [35798]

NOSSETER MARY 1700S SHERBORNE, DOR, ENG
[36633]

NOSWORTHY 1800+ DEV, ENG [36470]

NOTCUTT PRE 1764 IPSWICH, SFK, ENG [33919] :
1764+ IPSWICH, SFK, ENG [34777]

NOTDRUFT 1700+ EICHACH, BAW, GER [35355]

NOTEN PRE 1800 GREAT AYTON, NRY, ENG
[35212]

NOTLEY C1750+ LONDON & ALL, ENG [34589] :
PRE 1711 CUDWORTH, SOM, ENG [34900] : PRE
1900 HENDON, LND, ENG [35175] : PRE 1800
LITTLE BENTLEY, ESS, ENG [36409] : C1790
LAMBETH, SRY, ENG [38209]

NOTMAN PRE 1850 ROX, SCT [35934]

NOTT 1838-1918 INVERELL, NSW, AUS [36313] :
1800S LONDON, ENG [34930] : PRE 1808 SOM,
ENG [37104] : C1850-1880 CALSTOCK, CON, ENG
[37214] : PRE 1700 STAUNTON ON WYE, HEF,
ENG [37816]

NOTTAGE THOMAS 1757 HENHAM, ESS, ENG
[38307]

NOTTER 1750-1850 WEST CARBURY BARONY,
COR, IRL [34513]

NOTTINGHAM 1800 YKS, ENG [35871] : 1680+
NORTHAMPTON CO., VA, USA [38032]

NOTWELL PRE 1790 GWENNAP, CON, ENG [35496]

NOUD 1850+ NSW, AUS [34425] : 1850+ QLD, AUS
[34425]

NOVACK 1860+ MILWAUKEE, WI, USA [36542]

NOWACK 1870+ PERTH CO., ONT, CAN [37455] :
PRE 1870 PRE, GER [37455]

NOWAK TERESA 1810-1899 POL [38090]

NOWELL 1800S LND, ENG [35377]

NOWLAN 1843-1854+ EAST MAITLAND, NSW, AUS
[35088] : 1837+ BOOROWA, NSW, AUS [37555] :
1860+ FISH RIVER & REIDS FLAT, NSW, AUS
[37555] : 1850+ BEECHWORTH, AUS [38289] : 1780-
1850 KID, IRL [34514]

NOWLAND C1761 ENG & AUS [33863] : 1750-1820
COR, IRL [34307]

NOWLIN PRE 1840 PATRICK CO., VA, USA [38044]

NOWODWORSKI 1900-1810 ZABIELLEN, KRIES,
OPR [38427] : 1900-1810 GROSWALDE, KRIES, OPR
[38427]

NOY 1900+ TONGALA, VIC, AUS [36622]

NUBER 1800S BANAT, YU [37539]

NUDD 1850+ HICKLING, NFK, ENG [34322]

NUESSMEYER PRE 1800 LENGERICH, NRW, GER
[38663]

NUGENT 1870+ CUMNOCK, NSW, AUS [34759] :
1853+ SOUTH YARRA, VIC, AUS [37158] : C1780-
1810 FALMOUTH, CON, ENG [37158] : PRE 1850
ARDAGH, LIM, IRL [34198] : PRE 1900 BODAL,
KIK, IRL [34274] : PRE 1890 KIK, IRL [35750] :
1750+ WAT, IRL [36602] : 1850+ ALBANY, NY,
USA [38530]

NUIJENS ALL WORLDWIDE [37461]

NULISCH ALL WORLDWIDE [36926]

NUNAN PRE 1840 UK & IRL [35496]

NUNEMAKER 1826-1900 WASHINGTON CO., MD,
USA [38139]

NUNGESSER 1680-1780 AUERBACH, HES, BRD
[35311]

NUNLEY 1900+ FINEDON, NTH, ENG [37437]

NUNN 1840S SYDNEY, NSW, AUS [33934] : C1842
LAUNCESTON, TAS, AUS [37177] : 1800+
WICKHAMBROOK, SFK, ENG [35341] : 1700-1990
LND, ENG [35421] : C1850 LAWSHALL, SFK, ENG
[35838] : PRE 1900 BARKWAY, HRT, ENG [36061] :
PRE 1873 READING, BRK, ENG [36475] : C1800
GATELY, NFK, ENG [37498] : PRE 1817
GLEMSFORD, SFK, ENG [37568] : C1770 GREAT
CHISHALL, CAM, ENG [38209]

NUNNEY 1630-1890 BURFORD, OXF, ENG [37380]

NUNNS 1700-1850 SRY & SSX, ENG [37880] : 1500-
1990 RUSHTON, NTH, ENG [38502] : 1700S
KINGSTHORPE, NTH, ENG [38502] : 1800S
BROCKHALL, NTH, ENG [38502] : 1700S
MOULTON, NTH, ENG [38502] : 1800S LEEK, STS,
ENG [38502] : 1840-1880 SWANSEA AREA, GLA,
WLS [38502]

NURCOMBE C1800 SOM, ENG [38488]

NURSE 1750-1850 BARBADOS [38355] : 1830+
SOUTH MONAGHAN, ONT, CAN [34507] : PRE
1830 EASTRINGTON, YKS, ENG [34507] : 1830+
PULHAM ST MARY, NFK, ENG [34710] : 1845-1903
WESTMINSTER, MDX, ENG [36117] : 1500-1630
ENG [37784] : FRANCIS 1618 NFK, ENG [37809] : JOHN
1600+ BOUGHTON, NFK, ENG [37809] : FRANCIS
1638-1695 SALEM, MA, USA [37809]

NURSEY 1813 LOWESTOFT, SFK, ENG [36860]

NURTON 1800+ HOXTON, MDX, ENG [34272]

NUSS PRE 1874 COOMA, NSW, AUS [34421] : PRE
1800 GOCKLINGEN, RPF, BRD [36964] : PRE 1848
BAD, GER [34421]

NUTCOMBE PRE 1740 NUTCOMBE, DEV & SOM, ENG [34741]

NUTHACK 1650+ STOLP, POM, GER [34388]

NUTHAL C1800+ MDX, ENG [36810]

NUTHALL 1790+ BLUNDESTON, SFK, ENG [34205]

NUTLEY 1850+ AUS [36286] : 1700-1860 COLLINGBOURNE KINGSTON, WIL, ENG [36286] : 1870+ FAREHAM, HAM, ENG [37360]

NUTT PRE 1850 TETSWORTH, OXF, ENG [34104] : 1720+ SOMERTON, SOM, ENG [35462]

NUTTALL 1884+ MELBOURNE, VIC, AUS [37807] : 1850+ EDDINGTON, VIC, AUS [34588] : PRE 1830 DBY, ENG [35745] : C1863+ ACCRINGTON, LAN, ENG [36955] : PRE 1900 LAN, ENG [37807] : PRE 1856 BURY, LAN, ENG [37956] : ALL NTT, ENG & AUS [35056] : 1890+ CHESTER, PA, USA [37807]

NUTTER ALL CAM, ENG [36201]

NUTTING 1600S GROTON, MA, USA [36944]

NUTZ PRE 1900 ULREICHSBERG, NOE, OES [34691]

NUYENS ALL WORLDWIDE [37461]

NYBERG PRE 1900 SWE [38364]

NYCE ALL WORLDWIDE [33858]

NYE PRE 1882 ISLINGTON, MDX, ENG [34726] : PRE 1800 HORSHAM, SSX, ENG [37602] : 1500+ BIDDENDEN, KEN, ENG [38745]

NYLAND PRE 1900 HOWTH, DUB, IRL [38305] : PRE 1900+ USA &, WORLDWIDE [38305]

NYLEN ALL VARMLAND, SWE [34353]

NYT 1822-1900˙NL & AUS [35056]

OAG ALL WICK, CAI, SCT & AUS [35518] : 1780-1880 UK [38271]

OAKDON PRE 1852 ATHERSTONE, WAR, ENG [35344]

OAKES 1903 SOFALA, NSW, AUS [35066] : 1850+ WOLSTANTON, STS, ENG [35730] : 1800S STS, ENG [35994] : PRE 1900 KANKAKEE, IL, USA [36355]

OAKHILL PRE 1860 BATH, SOM, ENG [35253]

OAKLEY 1878+ SOUTH YARRA, VIC, AUS [34577] : 1900+ PORTLAND, VIC, AUS [35149] : 1872-75 GRIMSBY, ONT, CAN [36582] : 1831-51 HALTON CO., ONT, CAN [36582] : 1851 EVERSHOLT, BDF, ENG [34309] : 1793 NORTH MORETON, BRK, ENG [34474] : PRE 1833 CHERTSEY, SRY, ENG [34873] : 1800+ DUDLEY, WOR, ENG [35077] : PRE 1750 SEDGLEY, STS, ENG [34110] : PRE 1800 WOLVERHAMPTON, STS, ENG [37389]

OAKMAN PRE 1880 STEPNEY, MDX, ENG [34693]

OAKY 1840S PHILLACK, CON, ENG [34628]

OATES 1870+ TRARALGON, VIC, AUS [33868] : PRE 1870 DENHAM, ENG [33868] : 1800S REDRUTH, CON, ENG [34684] : 1860S MARAZION, CON, ENG [35099] : 1800S ST JUST, CON, ENG [35723] : 1750-1900 HULL OR ALSTON, ERY & CUL, ENG [37290] : FLORA 1929-90 DOR, ENG [37926] : 1820 KENWYN, CON, ENG [38317]

OATES (SEE OATS) [34558]

OATS 1875+ CHILTERN, VIC, AUS [35039] : ALL ST JUST IN PENWITH, CON, ENG [34558] : 1850S ST JUST, CON, ENG [35039] : C1820 REDRUTH, CON, ENG [36276]

OBEE C1800+ NSW, AUS [33930] : 1800S MAIDSTONE, KEN, ENG [34223]

OBEIRNE 1800S CAARON, ROS, IRL [38281]

O'BEIRNE 1880+ GEELONG, VIC, AUS [33935] : 1800+ DUBLIN, IRL [33935]

O'BEIRNE (SEE BEIRNE [33927]

OBERBERGER 1870 CREUTZBERG, GER [36907]

OBERHOLZER PRE 1845 SG, CH [38048]

OBERLAENDER PRE 1720 HARDENBURG, RPF, GER [38681]

OBERLIN 1840-1890 ONT, CAN [34141] : 1830-1850 BAS RHIN, ALS, FRA [34141] : 1840-1870 LORRAIN CO., OH, USA [34141]

OBERT C1675 MIDDLESEX CO., VA, USA [37032]

O'BIERNE (BERN) 1840-1885 SYDNEY, NSW, AUS [35782]

OBRAY ALL AUS [36689] : 1500-1900 PEMBROKE, PEM, WLS [36689]

O'BRIAN 1860S DON, IRL [35415]

OBRIEN 1840S NEW LONDON, CAN [37169]

O'BRIEN 1863-1990 MALMSBURY, VIC, AUS [33778] : 1853+ QLD, AUS [34588] : 1850+ ROSEWOOD, QLD, AUS [34812] : 1855+ KILMORE & SHEPPARTON, VIC, AUS [35379] : DENIS 1841+ NEVILLE, NSW, AUS [35513] : ALL MORUYA, NSW, AUS [35520] : 1855+ TAMWORTH, NSW, AUS [35765] : BRIDGET C1843 SYDNEY, NSW, AUS [35843] : C1850 MELBOURNE, VIC, AUS [35859] : MARGARET 1850S+ DERRIMUT, VIC, AUS [35876] : C1874 BALLARAT, VIC, AUS [35895] : EDWARD 1855+ PORT CYGNET, TAS, AUS [37159] : PRE 1850 LAMBING FLAT, NSW, AUS [38214] : 1837+ ELDERSLIE & BRANXTON, NSW, AUS [38592] : EDWARD 1840+ CHAFFEY'S LOCK, ONT, CAN [36652] : JAMES 1750-1867 ONT, CAN & USA [34514] : JOHN 1850-1880 LONDON, ENG [35003] : 1939-40 MDX, ENG [36181] : EDWARD 1840+ WOOLWICH & DEPTFORD, LND, ENG [37159] : 1870-90 ENG [37701] : 1802+ ADARE, LIM, IRL [33880] : C1850 TOOMEVARA, TIP, IRL [33902] : PRE 1853 CAPPAWHITE, TIP, IRL [34588] : DANIEL 1870S ARDMORE, WAT, IRL [34618] : JOHN 1840S CLASHMORE, WAT, IRL [34618] : PRE 1870 DONASKEIGH, TIP, IRL [34812] : JOHN 1790-1860 SKIBBEREEN, COR, IRL [35003] : BRIDGET 1823-1844 GAL, IRL [35092] : ALL DUBLIN, IRL [35246] : 1800 CORK, COR, IRL [35352] : PRE 1855 TIP, IRL [35379] : 1700+ CONG, GAL & MAY, IRL [35580] : 1845+ LIMERICK, LIM, IRL [35765] : MATTHEW 1800+ GAL, IRL [35843] : BRIDGET C1823-1843 GAL, IRL [35843] : PRE 1874 TIP, IRL [35895] : 1850+ LIMERICK, LIM, IRL [35943] : C1875 RATHKEALE, LIM, IRL [36906] : 1850-1890 HOLY CROSS, LIM, IRL [36906] : MARGARET C1897 CLONMEL, TIP, IRL [37519] : C1897 OLD BRIDGE, WAT, IRL [37519] : JOHN C1867 OLD BRIDGE, WAT, IRL [37519] : JOHN C1867 CLONMEL, TIP, IRL [37519] : ELLEN PRE 1900 CLONMEL, TIP, IRL [37519] : MARY C1897 CLONMEL, TIP, IRL [37519] : PRE 1860 PILTOWN, KIK, IRL [37521] : C1812 ATHLONE, ROS, IRL [38052] : PRE 1840 OATFIELD, O'CALLAGHANS MILLS, CLA, IRL [38079] : JOHN PRE 1900 IRL [38140] : THOMAS C1800 GALWAY, GAL, IRL [38290] : HONORA 1840-50 MALLOW, COR, IRL & AUS [36884] : 1907+ SOUTH IS., NZ [35895] : MARY PRE 1843 ST HELENS, WIG, SCT [37819] : JEREMIAH 1880+ FORT WORTH, TX, USA [35003] : 1850+ EASTHAMPTON, MA, USA [38015] : LEROY 1892-1949 RUSSELL, ST LAWRENCE CO., NY, USA [38140]

O'BRIENS 1890+ BALMAIN, NSW, AUS [36600]

O'BRYAN 1800-1832 CORK CITY, COR, IRL [35903] : PRE 1790 NC, USA [37587]

O'CALLAGHAN 1883+ NORTH CARLTON, VIC, AUS [34430] : 1860+ VIC, AUS [35352] : MARGARET C1833 CAV, IRL [37960]

O'CARROLL 1870S+ IRL [37145]

OCHS 1800S PUSLINCH, ONT, CAN [35635] : ALL GER [37584]

OCHTERBECK 1860-1900 ST LOUIS, MO, USA [36349]

OCKBURN 1830+ LONDON, ENG [35982]

O'CONNELL ALL MORUYA, NSW, AUS [35520] :
ALL NANA GLEN, NSW, AUS [35520] : 1861+
GEELONG, VIC, AUS [35599] : 1860+
CAMPERDOWN, NSW, AUS [37944] : 1820+ PEEL,
YORK, ONT, CAN [34982] : C1920 GUNNISLAKE,
CON, ENG [35489] : PRE 1863 CAHIRCIVEEN,
KER, IRL [34252] : 1800-1950 NEWBRIDGE &
GLIN, LIM, IRL [34411] : PRE 1865
BALLYBRICKEN, LIM, IRL [35189] : PRE 1860
WEM, IRL [35382] : PRE 1861 IRL [35599] : PHILIP
PRE 1860 TIP, IRL [35816] : 1800 KER, IRL [35970] :
ALL COR, IRL [36318] : KATHLEEN 1875-1881
LIM, IRL [36374] : NORA 1878-1885 KILLARNEY,
KER, IRL [36374] : BARBARA 1878-1882 LIM, IRL
[36374] : KATHLEEN 1875-1881 KILLARNEY, KER,
IRL [36374] : MICHAEL PRE 1855 KILLARNEY,
KER, IRL [36374] : NORA 1878-1885 LIM, IRL
[36374] : MICHAEL PRE 1855 LIM, IRL [36374] :
BARBARA 1878-1882 KILLARNEY, KER, IRL
[36374] : C1820 TEMPLEMALEY, CLA, IRL [37944] :
ALL PHILA & CHESTER CO., PA, USA [36318] :
1800+ AMENIA, NY & KER, USA & IRL [38225]
OCONNOR PRE 1866 BARAVORE FORD, WIC, IRL
[34959]
O'CONNOR 1866+ MOLONG, NSW, AUS [33867] :
1850+ IPSWICH, NSW, AUS [33929] : JOHN PRE
1841 QUEANBEYAN, NSW, AUS [34942] : JANE
1844-1875 SINGLETON, NSW, AUS [34942] : 1800+
VIC, AUS [35352] : JOHN 1800S+ RICHMOND,
NSW, AUS [35831] : 1870+ QLD, AUS [36305] :
1800+ GUYSBOROUGH, NS, CAN [35627] : 1800+
WOOLWICH, KEN, ENG [33927] : 1780-1990
ELFIN, ROS, IRL [33818] : 1848 KILCOLMAN, LIM,
IRL [33967] : PRE 1841 ADARE, LIM, IRL [34452] :
PRE 1870 CUSHENDUN, ANT, IRL [34955] : C1800-
1850 KER, IRL [35389] : PRE 1850 WEM, IRL [35404]
: 1851 BARRAVORE, WIC, IRL [35837] : C1800+
ROSCOMMON, ROS, IRL [35851] : C1850 IRL
[35906] : 1840 CLONMEL, TIP, IRL [36032] : PRE
1870 CASTLE IS, KER, IRL [36757] : PRE 1900
PORTARLINGTON, LEX, IRL [37521] : 1800S
TRALEE, KER, IRL [38243] : WILLIAM 1838+ ST
MARY'S CLONMEL, TIP, IRL & AUS [37161] : 1870-
1936 AUCKLAND, NZ [36757] : 1890-1910 TE
AWAMUTU, BOP, NZ [36757]
O'CONNORS PRE 1780 IRL [37428]
ODDY 1600-1850 TICKHILL & ROTHERHAM, WRY
& LND, ENG [37339] : 1842+ HUDDERSFIELD,
WRY, ENG [37754] : PRE 1790 BATLEY &
BIRSTALL, WRY, ENG [37754] : 1790-1860 SPEN
VALLEY, WRY, ENG [37754] : C1780 FOLLIFOOT
& SPOFFORTH, WRY, ENG [37988]
ODEA C1830 KILMALEY, CLA, IRL [34426]
O'DEA 1800+ KILRUSH, CLA, IRL [35244]
ODELL 1790-1800 NB & NS, CAN [35314] : 1800+
CAMPTON, BDF, ENG [34315] : ALL PULLOXHILL
& FLITTON, BDF, ENG [34789] : ALL
CRANFIELD, BDF, ENG [34789] : 1874+ ODELL,
BDF, ENG [35144] : PRE 1900 BDF, ENG [35954] :
ALL AMPTHILL, BDF, ENG [36152] : ALL TEMPLE
GRAFTON, WAR, ENG [38502] : 1785-1810
ALBANY CO., NY, USA [38227] : RUTH 1890+
HAVASTRAW, NY, USA [38233] : C1770-1850S
ALBANY & SCHENECTADY, NY, USA [38479]
ODENBROT PRE 1880 KRS. GUMBINNEN, OPR,
GER [38649]
ODENDAAL ALL WORLDWIDE [36460]
ODGER 1650+ PHILLEIGH & ST ANTONY
R.LAND, CON, ENG [34747]
ODGERS PRE 1777 WENDRON, CON, ENG [33992] :
PRE 1828 ILLOGAN, CON, ENG [34616] : ALL
WORLDWIDE [36467]

O'DOHERTY PRE 1850 OMAGH, TYR, IRL [33822] :
1850+ DRUMAGARNER, LDY, IRL [35824] : PRE
1840 SCT [35824]
O'DOHERTY (SEE DOHER [33927]
O'DONAHUE 1820-1880 DUNMANWAY, COR, IRL
[35402]
O'DONNELL 1900+ QLD, AUS [35465] : 1860S
BENDIGO, VIC, AUS [35793] : PRE 1900
WARWICK, QLD, AUS [36290] : 1860-1940 SCONE
& FLEMINGTON, NSW, AUS [38541] : JOHN
1846+ LA & MIDDLESEX CO., ONT, CAN [34154] :
JOHN PRE 1808 LND, ENG [35541] : PRE 1860
CLOGHEEN, TIP, IRL [35793] : PRE 1880
KILCLOGHER, CLA, IRL [35814] : PRE 1860 TIP,
IRL [36854] : 1700+ DON, IRL [37826] : PRE 1860
ARDFINNAN, TIP, IRL [38541] : 1850-1870
GALWAY, GAL, IRL [38763] : 1850-1950 LUZERNE,
PA, USA [36733]
O'DONOGHUE 1890S CRAYFORD, KEN, ENG
[37083] : 1880S TARBERT, KER, IRL [37083]
O'DONOHUE PRE 1870 KER, IRL [36840]
O'DONOVAN JAMES 1870S+ SOUTH BRIGHTON,
VIC, AUS [35522]
O'DOWD 1800-1900 AUS [33941] : JOHN 1840-1889
WALCHA, NSW, AUS [33941] : MARY 1840-1904
WALCHA, NSW, AUS [33941] : PATRICK 1760-1800
KILLARNEY, KER & CLA, IRL [33941]
O'DRISCOLL C1860-61 SKIBBEREEN, COR, IRL
[36307] : PRE 1870 WAT, IRL [38365]
O'DWYER 1800S MASHAM & RIPON, NRY, ENG
[33916] : 1750-1820 PARIS & CALAIS, FRA [33916] :
1700-1750 SOLOHEAD, TIP, IRL [33916] : PRE 1850
CAPPAWHITE, TIP, IRL [34588] : PRE 1880
DUNDALK, LOU, DUB & DOW, IRL [35354] :
PATRICK PRE 1841 RATHCLOGH, CASHEL, TIP,
IRL [36314] : FRANCIS C1840-C1870 DUALLA,
CASHEL, TIP, IRL [36314] : CAREW ALL
WORLDWIDE [33916]
OEDEL 1816+ RATHKEALE, LIM, IRL [35824]
OEHLER PRE 1820 GROSSINGERSHEIM, BAW,
BRD [38509]
OEHLMANN PRE 1872 POM, GER [35310]
OEHMIG 1750-1850 DRESDEN, KSA, GER [38628]
OELE 1700S ZUID BEVELAND, ZEL, NL [38350]
OELSCHIG ALL WORLDWIDE [36930]
OELZE AUGUST 1884-1922 MAG, DDR [37551] :
FREDERICK PRE 1884 MAG, DDR [37551]
OERTEL 1650+ RONNEBURG, THU, GER [38651]
OESCHGER ALL WORLDWIDE [38657]
OESTREICHER CHRIST C1840 SCHOPFLOHE, GER
[37596] : H. 1861-1925 BAYERN, GER [37596] :
MARIA 1880-1938 BAYERN, GER [37596]
OETZEL PRE 1800 VOCKENROTH, GER [38676]
OEVERDIEK ALL WORLDWIDE [38648]
O'FARRELL 1850+ MELBOURNE, VIC, AUS [34174] :
1850 CASTLEMAINE, VIC, AUS [37163] : ANDREW
PRE 1881 BURFORD, ONT, CAN [38445] :
ANDREW PRE 1881 IRL [38445]
OFFEN PRE 1750 KEN, ENG [36588] : ALL SFK, ENG
[37629]
OFFICER PRE 1820 LONDON, ENG [34613] : PRE
1840 CRAMMACHMORE, KCD, SCT [34613]
OFFIELD ALL WORLDWIDE [37252]
OFFORD 1800+ LONDON, ENG [34455] : 1830+ SRY
& MDX, ENG [38008]
OFIELD 1300-1400+ LEI, ENG [37648] : 1300-1400+
DBY, ENG [37648] : ALL WORLDWIDE [37252]
O'FLAHERTY PRE 1860 KIK, IRL [34682]
OG PRE 1910 SEAHAM HARBOUR, DUR, ENG
[37179] : ALL GER [37179]
O'GALLAGHER 1840S TIP, IRL [35855]
O'GARA C1841+ BOYLE, ROS, IRL [36276]

OGATT C1798 DURHAM & MONKSWEARMOUTH, DUR, ENG [37710]

OGBURNE PRE 1829 BRISTOL, SOM, ENG [35414]

OGDEN 1800-1900 TORONTO, ONT, CAN [37466] : PRE 1850 POCKTHORPE & NORWICH, NFK, ENG [34287] : JOHN PRE 1850 (SEA CAPTAIN), ENG [36066] : PRE 1800 WAKEFIELD, YKS, ENG [36066] : 1800+ SALFORD & MANCHESTER, LAN, ENG [36066] : 1884-1905 WIGAN, LAN, ENG [36253] : 1865 KEARSLEY, LAN, ENG [36253] : 1800S BRADFORD & DENHOLME, WRY, ENG [36263] : 1700+ ROCHDALE, LAN, ENG [36961] : C1860 LND, ENG [37449] : 1800-1850 YKS, ENG [37495] : 1850-1990 IL, USA [37466]

OGG C1820 GLENMUICK, ABD, SCT [34591]

OGILVEY-MIDDLETON C1800 ABERDEEN, SCT [34568]

OGILVIE C1850 MUSWELLBROOK, NSW, AUS [35585] : 1850+ IPSWICH & ROCKHAMPTON, QLD, AUS [38290] : C1855 AUCKLAND, NZ [35585] : C1792 KEITH, BAN, SCT [35585] : PRE 1900 ANS, SCT [35950] : ALL ANS, SCT [37480] : 1700-1800 ROX, SCT [37747] : PRE 1780 CRIEFF, PER, SCT [38290] : ALL WORLDWIDE [34949]

OGILVY 1853+ VIC, AUS [36366] : PRE 1900 ANS, SCT [35950] : 1690-1840S LERWICK, SHI, SCT [36366] : 1840S+ EDINBURGH, MLN, SCT [36366] : ALL ANS, SCT [37480] : PRE 1758 LINTRATHEN, ANS, SCT [37772]

OGLE C1704 BURTON JOYCE & GEDLING, NTT, ENG [34836] : PRE 1800 GEDLING, NTT & DBY, ENG [34836] : 1700+ FENROTHER, NBL, ENG [36609] : 1700+ LONGFRAMLINGTON, NBL, ENG [36609]

OGLESBY PRE 1840 BARNETBY, LIN, ENG [35024] : 1856+ KID, IRL [36287]

O'GORMAN 1850+ OTTAWA, ONT, CAN [36662] : 1750+ WAT, IRL [36602]

OGRADY 1850+ BALMAIN, NSW, AUS [34857]

O'GRADY 1920+ CUNNAMULLA, QLD, AUS [35158] : C1880S BATHURST, NSW, AUS [35158] : PRE 1907 SOUTHAMPTON, HAM, ENG [33802] : PRE 1862 CLA, IRL [34673] : 1800+ TROUGH, CLA, IRL [35190] : PRE 1880 IRL [36840] : 1888+ OAMARU, NZ [34673]

OGRAM PRE 1803 MILLINGTON, ERY, ENG [37710]

O'GREADY 1850+ MERRULEBALE, NSW, AUS [35028] : 1850+ YACKANDANDAH, VIC, AUS [35028] : 1800-1880 ST MARTINS, LA, USA [38219]

O'GUIN ALL NORTHUMBERLAND CO., PA, USA [37507] : 1800+ TN, USA [37507] : 1700+ NC, USA [37507]

OGWIN 1800+ TN, USA [37507] : 1700+ NC, USA [37507]

O'HAGAN 1860+ CAMPERDOWN, VIC, AUS [35721] : PRE 1876 LOU, IRL [33871] : ALL GREENORE, DOW, IRL [34732] : ALL COOKSTOWN, TYR, IRL [35721]

O'HALLERAN PRE 1850 ENNIS, CLA, IRL [37018]

O'HALLORAN PRE 1850 ENNISTYMON, CLA, IRL [35095] : 1800-1850 DUNASS, CLA, IRL [37996]

O'HANLON 1690-1900 DUBURREN, ARM, IRL [37326]

OHARA FRANCIS 1860 CARROLS GAP, NSW, AUS [37123] : FRANCIS 1816 LONDON, ENG [37123]

O'HARA C1870S MARYBOROUGH, QLD, AUS [35158] : 1838+ MOUNT KEIRA, NSW, AUS [36597] : ALL SPITALFIELDS, LND, ENG & IRL [34820] : PRE 1855 BELFAST, ANT, IRL [34373] : PRE 1870 DUBLIN, IRL [34652] : C1846 COR, IRL [35158] : C1820-1880 IRL [36580] : PRE 1838 NEWTOWN LIMAVADY, DRY, IRL [36597] : 1790-1830 LOUGHREA, GAL, IRL [37187] : 1810+ IRL [38416] : 1800+ PHILADELPHIA CO., PA, USA [36580]

O'HARE C1894+ WARRAGUL, VIC, AUS [35399] : C1875 BOMBALA, NSW, AUS [35399] : 1861+ MACEDON, VIC, AUS [35419] : 1859+ ADELAIDE, SA, AUS [35419] : C1880 HASLINGDEN, LAN, ENG [35514] : PRE 1855 BELFAST, ANT, IRL [34373] : C1800 ARMAGH, ARM, IRL [35859] : 1800+ DUNSFORT, DOW, IRL [37405]

OHDE 1816-1896 SHO, GER [36952] : 1878+ MANNING, CARROLL CO., IA, USA [36952] : 1880-1892 ASPINWALL, CRAWFORD CO., IA, USA [36952] : 1864-1878 CLINTON CO., IA, USA [36952]

O'HEA PRE 1892 SKIBBEREEN, COR, IRL [34241]

O'HEARN PATRICK 1806+ TIP, IRL [38291]

O'HERLIHY 1840-1950 COR, IRL [35308]

OHLIGER PRE 1820 REICHWEILER, RPR, GER [34137]

OHLROGGE 1900 NEUSCHOO FRIESLAND, NSA, GER [38750] : 1869 BRAKE, NSA, GER [38750]

OHMART 1770+ SHENANDOAH CO., VA & OH, USA [36540]

OHNEWEHR C1761 NEUKIRCHEN, HAN, GER [38711]

OJA ALL FIN [38445]

O'KANE 1750-1900 BELFAST, ANT, IRL [38024] : 1750-1900 LOUGHGUILE, ANT, IRL [38024]

OKE ALL DEV, ENG [34471] : C1810 EXETER, DEV, ENG [35211] : C1817 ST COLUMB MAJOR, CON, ENG [35251] : PRE 1890 DEV & CON, ENG [38004]

O'KEEFE PRE 1910 INNISFAIL, QLD, AUS [34269] : DANIEL & LUKE 1854+ ALBURY, NSW, AUS [35357] : DANIEL 1876+ WAGGA WAGGA, NSW, AUS [35357] : JOHN 1854+ ALBURY, NSW, AUS [35357] : 1884+ MARYBOROUGH, QLD, AUS [38008] : 1840+ SYDNEY, NSW, AUS [38484] : 1875+ CLONCURRY, QLD, AUS [38484] : 1800+ LEEDS, ONT, CAN [36343] : PRE 1874 NEWMARKET, COR, IRL [33929] : PRE 1850 ENNISTYMON, CLA, IRL [35095] : PRE 1856 LIMERICK, LIM, IRL [35231] : LUKE PRE 1836 COR, IRL [35357] : THOMAS C1820 TYREDAGH, CLA, IRL [36274] : MARY 1825 TYREDAGH, CLA, IRL [36274] : JEREMIAH 1828 TYREDAGH, CLA, IRL [36274] : PRE 1900 LIM, IRL [36288] : 1884 KANTURK, COR, IRL [38008] : 1800+ VT, USA [38116]

O'KEEFFE RICHARD 1867+ ALBURY, NSW, AUS [35357] : DANIEL 1876+ WAGGA WAGGA, NSW, AUS [35357] : JOHN 1854+ ALBURY, NSW, AUS [35357] : DANIEL & LUKE 1854+ ALBURY, NSW, AUS [35357] : LUKE PRE 1836 COR, IRL [35357] : PRE 1830 CORK, COR, IRL [38288] : C1831 KIK, IRL [38487] : 1800+ VT, USA [38116]

O'KELLY PRE 1890 FETHARD, TIP, IRL [35111] : 1835+ CAPPAMORE, LIM, IRL [36326]

OLA HAUGRUD PRE 1900 BO, TELEMARK, NOR [34481]

OLAN ALL NOVAR & KENDAL, ONT, CAN [33854]

OLBRICH PRE 1885 RATIBOR, SIL, GER [38618]

OLD PRE 1843 ST MERRYN, CON, ENG [33781] : C1749 ST ERVAN, CON, ENG [33992] : 1700+ KINGSTON, SOM, ENG [34538] : 1630-1720 CONSTANTINE, CON, ENG [34793] : 1650+ WHITSTONE, CON, ENG [34804] : C1820 BRISTOL, GLS, ENG [34952] : 1830+ PIDDLETRENTHIDE, DOR, ENG [37360] : 1780+ ST MAUGHAN ON PYDER, CON, ENG & NZ [36850]

OLDACRE PRE 1850 MILLBANK, ENG [33878]

OLDAGE 1595-1625 ENG [37803] : ANN 1645 DORCHESTER, MA, USA [35273] : PRE 1665 WINDSOR, CT, USA [37510]

OLDAKER PRE 1850 MILLBANK, ENG **[33878]** : 1850+ COR, IRL **[33878]**

OLDAKOWSKI 1600-1990 KONOPKI, POL **[38232]**

OLDBURY 1700-1900 NOTTINGHAM, NTT, ENG **[34658]** : 1500-1900 ENG &, NZ & AUS **[36169]**

OLDCOTT PRE 1800 BURSLEM, STS, ENG **[38248]**

OLDE 1800+ SYDNEY, NSW, AUS **[34538]** : 1800+ BATHURST, NSW, AUS **[34538]** : 1800+ LAUNCELLS, CON, ENG **[34108]**

OLDENBURG 1830S ALTHARMHURST, SHO, BRD **[35638]**

OLDER PRE 1800 ENG **[34597]**

OLDFATHER 1836+ WUE, GER **[38572]** : 1770+ OH & IN, USA **[37823]** : C1890 JERSEY CITY, NJ, USA **[38572]**

OLDFIELD JAS 1800+ SKIPTON, WRY, ENG **[34915]** : PRE 1900 BOLLINGTON, CHS, ENG **[35865]** : C1790 CHESTERFIELD, DBY, ENG **[35920]** : SARAH 1800-1850 THORNTON IN LONSDALE, WRY, ENG **[35955]** : HANNAH 1813 HOPE, DBY, ENG **[36576]** : ELIAS 1784-1861 HOPE, DBY, ENG **[36576]** : WILLIAM 1761-1841 GREAT HUCKLOW & HOPE PARISH, DBY, ENG **[36576]** : WILLIAM 1816 HOPE, DBY, ENG **[36576]** : ELIZABETH 1811 HOPE, DBY, ENG **[36576]** : THOMAS 1818 HOPE, DBY, ENG **[36576]** : 1860-1900 OLDHAM, LAN, ENG **[38370]** : 1810-1860 BOSTON & GAINSBOROUGH, LIN, ENG **[38370]** : 1700-1800S LAN, ENG & WLS **[37221]** : 1675-1725 JAMAICA, L.I., NY, USA **[38194]**

OLDFSDDR MARIA SOPHIA 1829-1900 VANNAS, VASTERBOTTEN, SWE **[38104]**

OLDHAM PRE 1818 SOM, ENG **[34421]** : PRE 1860 MACCLESFIELD, CHS, ENG **[34870]** : 1600S LANCASTER, ENG **[35291]** : 1700-1800 SUTTON ON TRENT, NTT, ENG **[36527]** : 1856 BURY & BREDBURY, LAN, ENG **[36980]** : 1700-1850 OXF, ENG **[37064]** : 1860+ HYDE, CHS, ENG **[37384]** : ALL NORWICH, NFK, ENG **[37689]** : JOHN 1917+ STREATHAM, LND, ENG **[37756]** : 1750-1800 HUDDERSFIELD, WRY, ENG **[37779]** : 1600+ DARBY, ENG **[38241]** : PRE 1812 COVENTRY, WAR, ENG **[38512]** : PRE 1700 DBY, ENG **[38746]** : 1800+ PA & MD, USA **[38023]** : ALL WORLDWIDE **[36548]**

OLDHAMSTEAD PRE 1930 SOUTH OCKENDON, ESS, ENG **[37685]**

OLDRIDGE PRE 1840 CHARLETON & CHIVELSTONE, DEV, ENG **[34025]** : 1750+ EAST DEVON, DEV, ENG **[37733]**

OLDROYD 1889+ GEELONG, VIC, AUS **[35379]** : PRE 1825 YKS, ENG **[34712]** : PRE 1889 DEWSBURY, YKS, ENG **[35379]**

OLDS 1876+ ADELAIDE, SA, AUS **[37998]**

O'LEARY 1880+ TARAGO, NSW, AUS **[34773]** : ALL VIC, AUS **[34877]** : 1850+ BERRY, NSW, AUS **[37133]** : ALL MOG, IRL **[34877]** : WILLIAM PRE 1860 BALLYHOOK, COR, IRL **[36270]** : 1800-1900 KILLARNEY, KER, IRL **[36565]** : 1800+ CULCLUCK, COR, IRL **[37133]** : PRE 1880 COR, IRL & AUS **[34773]** : 1858-1930 MONAGHAN, MOG, IRL & AUS **[35469]**

OLEDATTER 1815+ SEIDRE, OPLAND, NOR **[36326]**

OLESDATTER PRE 1800 DEN **[33959]**

OLESEN 1840S LYNGSA, HJORRING, DEN **[35953]**

OLHABER PRE 1825 ZARNEKOW, POM, GER **[38125]**

OLIFFE 1850+ AUS **[35878]** : PRE 1850 COR, IRL **[35878]**

OLIN PRE 1737 RI, USA **[37037]** : ALL CT, USA & WLS **[33854]**

OLIPHANT PRE 1740 ANSTRUTHER, FIF, SCT **[35525]**

OLIVE ALL MDX & SRY, ENG **[36179]** : 1840S CANTERBURY, KEN, ENG **[36799]** : 1750-1950 LONDON &, MDX, ENG **[37344]** : 1880S MIDDLEMARCH, OTO, NZ **[36799]**

OLIVEIRA ALL HONOLULU, HI, USA **[33756]**

OLIVER 1850-1900 MELBOURNE, VIC, AUS **[33834]** : 1860 GLEN INNES, NSW, AUS **[34878]** : 1860+ BOMBALA, NSW, AUS **[34977]** : C1800 BARRINGTON, TAS, AUS **[35089]** : ALL GOORNONG, VIC, AUS **[35211]** : C1884 HOBART, TAS, AUS **[35772]** : CALEB C1859+ MOONTA, SA, AUS **[35834]** : CALEB 1880S WARRACKNABEAL, VIC, AUS **[35834]** : ALL AUS **[36295]** : 1880+ WOLLONGONG, NSW, AUS **[37136]** : GEORGE 1836+ FINGAL, TAS, AUS **[38492]** : ALL PEI, CAN **[35933]** : 1860S ORANGEVILLE, ONT, CAN **[38423]** : 1800-1850 GSY, CHI **[33834]** : PRE 1840 ISLE OF WIGHT, HAM, ENG **[33802]** : PRE 1860 LONDON, ENG **[34177]** : C1800 BRADMORE, NTT, ENG **[34319]** : 1750+ NRY, ENG **[34456]** : ALL SCARBOROUGH, YKS, ENG **[34619]** : 1800-1990 OMBERSLEY, WOR, ENG **[34677]** : 1836 CON, ENG **[34793]** : C1855 LND, ENG **[34861]** : JOHN 1796+ CON, ENG **[35272]** : C1826 TYSOE & WELSBOURNE, WAR, ENG **[35363]** : PRE 1800 BREAGE, CON, ENG **[35500]** : 1700S TICEHURST, SSX, ENG **[35501]** : PRE 1800 PAUL & MADRON, CON, ENG **[35736]** : CALEB C1800-1859 CON, ENG **[35834]** : 1500+ ST NEOT & GORRAN, CON, ENG **[35851]** : 1765 GOUDHURST, KEN, ENG **[35872]** : 1700+ NBL & DUR, ENG **[35891]** : 1820+ NEWARK, NTT, ENG **[35904]** : PRE 1789 HAWKSWORTH, NTT, ENG **[35904]** : 1700S CLERKENWELL, LND, ENG **[36055]** : 1800S ISLINGTON, LND, ENG **[36055]** : PRE 1780 SKIRPENBECK, ERY, ENG **[36059]** : 1600+ KEN, ENG **[36093]** : PRE 1770 ROCK, WOR, ENG **[36110]** : C1750+ NORTHIAM, SSX, ENG **[36258]** : 1700-1900 LONDON, ENG **[36261]** : 1700S DAGENHAM, ESS, ENG **[36263]** : C1700 ST CLEER, CON, ENG **[36389]** : 1700-1900 TRURO AREA, CON, ENG **[36398]** : 1900+ BIRMINGHAM, WAR, ENG **[36592]** : 1900+ HEREFORD & BROMYARD, HER, ENG **[36592]** : 1780+ ELLINGTON, NBL, ENG **[36609]** : 1870 BRISTOL, SOM, ENG **[36995]** : 1800-1900 HAM, ENG **[37064]** : PRE 1700 HEXTON, HRT, ENG **[37089]** : 1780-1810 BRISTOL, GLS, ENG **[37122]** : 1600+ BARKWAY, HRT, ENG **[37166]** : 1771-1840S TAMERTON & TETCOTT, CON, ENG **[37317]** : 1830+ DEPTFORD, KEN, ENG **[37560]** : 1850S WATERLOO, LND, ENG **[37692]** : PRE 1800 POWICK, WOR, ENG **[37736]** : PRE 1830 READING, BRK, ENG **[37842]** : PRE 1848 BEDFORD, BDF, ENG **[37961]** : 1729-1900S MERRINGTON, DUR, ENG **[38269]** : PRE 1800 ERY, ENG **[38383]** : C1760 HIGH HALDEN, KEN, ENG **[38389]** : 1829+ ENFIELD, MDX, ENG **[38441]** : 1870+ REEFTON, NZ **[34678]** : PRE 1831 KELSO, ROX, SCT **[33906]** : 1800+ JOHNSTONE, RFW, SCT **[34049]** : 1800 ABERDEEN, ABD, SCT **[34210]** : C1760 JEDBURGH, ROX, SCT **[34358]** : VIOLET 1790-1860 ROX, SCT **[34525]** : PRE 1850 IRVINE, AYR, SCT **[35758]** : 1820 GALASHIELS, SEL, SCT **[35912]** : 1700+ JEDBURGH, ROX, SCT **[36295]** : PRE 1780 ROX, SCT **[37145]** : ALL DUNDEE, ANS, SCT **[37303]** : 1811-1884 ROXBURGH, ROX, SCT **[37581]** : 1800+ ALBANY, NY, USA **[36295]** : 1700-1760 JONES CO., NC, USA **[36354]** : 1800+ ALBANY CO., NY, USA **[36962]** : ALL WORLDWIDE **[36235]**

OLIVERO PRE 1856 SOMMARIVA BOSCO, PIEDMONT, ITL [38085]

OLIVEY PRE 1700 ST KEVERNE, CON, ENG [37913]

OLIVIER PRE 1776 CAPE, RSA [36459]

OLLER PRE 1790 MADISON CO., KY, USA [38314]

OLLERENSHAW ALL CHAPEL EN-LE FRITH, DBY, ENG [34588]

OLLEY PRE 1853 NEWNHAM, HRT, ENG [35425] : 1800+ NEWNHAM, HRT, ENG [35524]

OLLIER 1700+ CHS, ENG [34309] : 1600+ OVER & NORTHWICH, CHS, ENG [36818] : 1855+ CREWE & ACCRINGTON, CHS & LAN, ENG [36997]

OLLINGTON ALL SFK, ENG [34744]

OLLIS PRE 1860 OLDLAND COMMON, GLS, ENG [33850]

OLLIVER PRE 1850 LONDON, ENG [35953] : 1550+ LYMINSTER & FERRING, SSX, ENG [36827]

OLM 1800-1860 BRA, GER [37535]

OLMANT 1400+ CHIDHAM, SSX, ENG [33989]

OLMSTEAD 1900+ BC, CAN [34510] : 1900+ VANCOUVER, BC, CAN [34510] : 1800S ONT, CAN [38468] : 1900+ MT, USA [34510] : 1700S MA, NY & VT, USA [38468]

OLNEY 1700+ CODICOTE, HRT, ENG [34416] : 1800+ SOUTHILL, BDF, ENG [37304]

OLOFOR PRE 1700 HEXTON, HRT, ENG [37089]

OLOFSDOTTER STINA PRE 1875 LUNSJON, VASTERBOTTENS, SWE [34481]

OLOFSDR HANNA K. 1882-1970 VANNAS, VASTERBOTTEN, SWE [38104]

OLOFSSON OSKAR PRE 1900 JUNSELE, VASTERNORRLAND, SWE [34481] : OLOF 1853-1940 VANNAS, VASTERBOTTEN, SWE [38104] : JOHAN 1880-1970 VANNAS, VASTERBOTTEN, SWE [38104] : ZACRIS 1817-1900 VANNAS, VASTERBOTTEN, SWE [38104] : 1880+ WAHOO, NE, USA [38552]

O'LOUGHLIN 1870S SANDHURST, VIC, AUS [35136] : 1800-1900 LIM, IRL [36780]

OLPALKA PRE 1900 STRAUSBURG, BRA, GER [35323]

OLSDATTER INGEBORG PRE 1865 VINJE, TELEMARK, NOR [34481]

OLSDTR ANLAU 1800-1900 ARENDAL, TELEMARK, NOR [35292]

OLSEN 1890+ GIPPSLAND, VIC, AUS [35399] : C1900 SYDNEY, NSW, AUS [35859] : 1884 SYDNEY, NSW, AUS [36312] : PRE 1800 KIKHAVN, ZEALAND, DEN [33957] : 1850+ VORDINGBORG, SJAELLAND, DEN [37160] : PRE 1888 CHELTENHAM, GLS, ENG [37940] : 1754+ SANDE, VESTFOLD, NOR [34063] : 1730+ RORAS, S TRNDLAG, NOR [36326] : ANNA PRE 1888 GRIMSTAD, AUS AGDER, NOR [37940] : C1860 FREDERIKSTAD, NOR [38168] : PRE 1900 NOR & USA [38043]

OLSEN BAKHUS KNUDT PRE 1865 VINJE, TELEMARK, NOR [34481]

OLSON 1890+ CLAREMONT, WA, AUS [36611] : 1905-1930 WINNIPEG, MAN, CAN [34521] : 1925+ KAMSACK, SAS, CAN [34521] : 1860+ CAN [36919] : CARL 1856+ LND, ENG [37861] : 1800+ LND, ENG [37861] : C1865 NEFSTAD, VANG, NOR [37007] : ALL NORLAND, NOR [38470] : 1863+ NE, USA [36919] : HULDA E. 1869-1944 KNOX CO., IL, USA [38371] : JOHN 1903+ ENGLEWOOD & CHICAGO, IL, USA [38551] : JOHN 1800+ WORLDWIDE [37861] : 1800+ WORLDWIDE [37861]

OLSSON 1830 COPENHAGEN, DEN [35376] : PRE 1832 SWE [35893]

OLSZEWSKI 1400-1990 MEZENIN BIALYSTOK, POL [38232]

OLTRA ALL WORLDWIDE [38346]

OLTRAMARE PRE 1600 GENEVA, GE, CH & ITL [38348]

OLTSMAN 1700+ NL [35338]

OLVER C1888 PAINGTON, DEV, ENG [35526] : C1700 ST CLEER, CON, ENG [36389] : C1831 LISKEARD, CON, ENG [38069] : 1800+ LIFTON, DEV, ENG [38213]

O'MADDEN 1720-1880 IRL [34386]

O'MAHONEY ALL VIC, AUS [34578] : PRE 1840+ DUNMORE, WAT, IRL [35453]

O'MALLEY 1918+ SYDNEY, NSW, AUS [33923] : 1850+ VIOLET TOWN, VIC, AUS [34174] : 1835 CULROSS TWP., ONT, CAN [34503] : 1860-1900 SHREWSBURY, SAL, ENG [33923] : 1900-1918 BIRMINGHAM, WAR, ENG [33923] : 1820+ SLI, IRL [34174] : 1820-50 MOUNTBELLEW, GAL, IRL & AUS [36884] : ALL IRL & USA [36933]

OMAND 1836+ LONGHOPE, OKI, SCT [34688]

OMANSON 1852-1970+ NORKOPING, SUTHERMALAND, SWE [38308]

O'MARA PHILIP 1845+ TOONGABBIE, VIC, AUS [36279] : LAWRENCE 1848+ HEIDELBERG, VIC, AUS [36279] : MICHAEL 1862+ BALLARAT EAST, VIC, AUS [36279] : 1795-1825 MIDDLEMOUNT, LEX, IRL [35340] : PRE 1830 NENAGH, TIP, IRL [37124] : PRE 1900 NIRE VALLEY, WAT, IRL [37519]

O'MEAGHER 1780-1820 TIP, IRL [35017]

O'MEARA 1800S MELBOURNE, VIC, AUS [35965] : PRE 1830 NENAGH, TIP, IRL [37124]

OMERY PRE 1801 ENG [38490]

ONA SANTOS PRE 1850 SAN JOSE, BATANGAS, PHILIPPINE [34891]

O'NEAL 1700-1750 LONDONDERRY, IRL [38373] : MARGARET PRE 1888 DOUGLAS CO., IL, USA [36322] : 1730-1760 OTSEGO CO., NY, USA [36450] : 1750-1780 CULPEPPER, VA, USA [38373]

O'NEIL PRE 1900 BLACKHEATH, NSW, AUS [35245] : 1857+ MELBOURNE, VIC, AUS [37982] : PATRICK 1800-1860 DRUMCREE, WEM, IRL [34514] : ALL GAL, IRL [35139] : C1840 BARNA, GAL, IRL [35865] : PRE 1800+ TYR, IRL [35928] : PRE 1870 WAT, IRL [38365] : ALL ENNIS, CLA, IRL & NZ [36854] : PRE 1850+ GREENMEADOWS, HB, NZ [35928]

ONEILL JOHN 1860+ BURRA, SA, AUS [37162] : 1820+ RATHKEALE, LIM, IRL [34960]

O'NEILL 1870-1928 SERPENTINE, VIC, AUS [34794] : 1869+ VIC, AUS [38539] : OWEN EUGENE C1900 TORONTO, ONT, CAN [38452] : 1800S DOW, IRL [33895] : 1830S POWERSCOURT, WIC, IRL [33924] : ALL SCOLBOA, ANT, IRL [34287] : 1800-1930 BALLYNEASE, LDY, IRL [36115] : ALL CLONAKILTY, COR, IRL [36168] : 1880+ BALLYMENA, ANT, IRL [36690] : C1800-1900 RATHFRILAND, DOW, IRL [36821] : 1800S WIC, IRL [36851] : 1800+ BALLYSHEEN, CLA, IRL [37244] : 1750+ WATERFORD, WAT, IRL [37244] : PRE 1790 TYR, IRL [38321] : PRE 1790 ANT, IRL [38321] : 1780-1822 WEX, IRL [38404] : 1840+ MEA, IRL [38539] : PRE 1850 GIRVAN, AYR, SCT [34262] : 1920+ FL, USA [36690] : 1860+ DURANGO, CO, USA [37534] : 1840S NH, USA [37534] : JOHN 1862-1888 BOSTON & HOLYOKE, MA, USA [38301]

ONELY 1700-99 CARLTON, BDF, ENG [34315]

ONESS (SEE ONUS) [38756]

ONGLEY C1600 GOUDHURST, KEN, ENG [37513]

ONGLY C1788 BRENCHLEY, KEN, ENG [35786]

ONIELL PRE 1865 PT ADELAIDE, SA, AUS [34858]

ONION 1500-1850 SFS, WOR & WAR, ENG [36169]

ONIONS 1800+ WELLINGTON, SAL, ENG [36104]
ONLEY PRE 1835 CHELSEA, MDX, ENG [35795] :
ALL WORLDWIDE [35795]
ONUS 1780 KEN, ENG [38756]
OOST ALL BROMLEY, KEN, ENG [37674] : ALL
WLS [37674]
OOSTDIJK 1700-C1740S YERSEKE, ZEL, NL [38350]
OOSTER 1750-1815 KEERBERGEN, BBT, BEL [38405]
OOSTHOEK ALL ZUID BEVELAND, ZEL, NL
[38714]
OP DEN GRAEFF PRE 1715 PHILADELPHIA CO.,
PA, USA [38017]
OPENSHAW C1852 HOBART, TAS, AUS [37556] :
1800+ FARNWORTH, LAN, ENG [37669]
OPFERMAN ALL GOTTINGEN, BRD [34765]
OPIE 1854+ BALLARAT, VIC, AUS [36622] : 1854+
CLUNES, SANDHURST & BENDIGO, VIC, AUS
[36622] : 1900+ SYDNEY & LISMORE, NSW, AUS
[36622] : PRE 1850 PERRANARWORTHAL, CON,
ENG [34750] : 1750+ KENWYN, CON, ENG [36000]
: 1845-1865 KEWEENAW CO., MI, USA [38009]
OPPEDISANO PRE 1920 MARTONE, CALABRIA,
ITL [36271]
OPPERMAN 1940+ PHILADELPHIA, PA, USA
[36578] : PRE 1940 BROOKLYN & QUEENS, NY,
USA [36578]
OPPY 1800-1840 STITHIANS, CON, ENG [35576] :
C1824 TRURO, CON, ENG [36000]
OPTENDYCK 1624+ NEW AMSTERDAM, NY, USA
[38015]
O'QUIN 1800+ TN, USA [37507] : ALL
NORTHUMBERLAND CO., PA, USA [37507] :
1700+ NC, USA [37507]
ORAM 1777+ COLWICH, STS, ENG [34334] : PRE
1770 DOR, ENG [36100] : 1864+ SHERMANBURY,
SSX, ENG [36212] : ALL HAVANT &
BEDHAMPTON, HAM, ENG [36994] : PRE 1833
DUNDEE, ANS, SCT [33957]
ORANGE C1860 BUNDABERG, QLD, AUS [35431] :
1800+ LEICESTER & LITTLE GLEN, LEI, ENG
[36414] : 1740+ ROSCREA, TIP, IRL [33862] : ALL
NZ [36414]
ORAS ALL OES [38369]
ORBY 1600S LONDON, ENG [33918]
ORCHARD 1816+ NSW, AUS [38212] : 1900+
LONDON, ONT, CAN [36654] : 1700-1850
GOSPORT, HAM, ENG [33814] : 1750+ WOTTON
UNDER EDGE, GLS, ENG [34283] : ALL
POLESWORTH, WAR, ENG [34665] : 1792 BATH,
GLS, ENG [34939] : 1820+ SOULBURY, BKM, ENG
[35730] : PRE 1821 MAWGAN IN MENEAGE, CON,
ENG [36277] : 1850+ LONDON, ENG [36654] : PRE
1776 SOM, ENG [37144] : C1720 CREWKERNE,
SOM, ENG [37381] : 1900 LONG EATON, DBY,
ENG [37829] : 1850+ DUBLIN, IRL [36654] : 1880S
CARBONDALE, PA, USA [35074]
ORDIGE ALL NSW, AUS [33799] : ALL WAR, ENG
[33799]
OREDDAN PRE 1800 CLA, IRL [37916]
O'REDDAN PRE 1800 CLA, IRL [37916] : 1300+ CLA,
IRL [37916]
O'REDDING PRE 1849 CLA, IRL [34797]
O'REGAN 1800S COR, IRL [35017] : PRE 1842
DRUMAGARNER, LDY, IRL [35824]
O'REILEY WILLIAM 1780-1790S CAV, IRL [35298]
O'REILLY 1860+ SANDHURST & MELBOURNE,
VIC, AUS [35190] : C1830 COLUMBKILLE, CAV,
IRL [33812] : 1780-1800 RATHOWEN, WEM, IRL
[34149] : 1800-1845 DUBLIN, IRL [34625] :
CATHERINE PRE 1852 DUBLIN, IRL [34701] : PRE
1879 CAV, IRL [34779] : ALL DUBLIN, IRL [34938] :

1850+ WELLINGTON, NZ [35785] : PHOEBE 1812-
1891 NJ, USA [36319]
OREILLY (SEE RILEY) [34421]
ORFORD 1830+ HASTINGS CO., CAN [34090] : PRE
1830 SFK, ENG [34090]
ORGAN 1880+ BENALLA, VIC, AUS [34595] : 1895+
ADELAIDE, SA, AUS [34595] : ALL NFD, CAN
[34207] : ALL MEVAGISSEY & PENZANCE, CON,
ENG [34595] : 1840+ PENZANCE, CON, ENG
[35034] : PRE 1900 EL DORADO CO., CA, USA
[35312]
ORLEDGE 1600-1900 PILTON, SOM, ENG [36130]
ORLING ANDERS 1756-1812 STOKHOLM, SWE
[38550]
ORMAN PRE 1830 WORLDWIDE [36202]
ORMANDY ALL LAN, ENG [37761]
ORMANROYD 1830-1900 BRADFORD, WRY, ENG
[35402]
ORME 1800+ WINDSOR, BRK & BKM, ENG [34236]
: C1760 LONGFORD, DBY, ENG [37834] : 1800-1860
ATHBOY, MEA, IRL [34440]
ORMEROD 1830+ CLIVIGER, LAN, ENG [33942] :
1700-1850 YKS & LAN, ENG [34067] : 1780 BACUP,
LAN, ENG [36635] : PRE 1900 STANSFIELD, WRY,
ENG [36998] : 1720-1770 KIRKBY MALHAM, WRY,
ENG [37934] : 1750-1850 DARCY LEVER, LAN,
ENG [37934] : 1818-1870 SKIPTON, WRY, ENG
[37934]
ORMESHER ALL LAN, ENG [37761]
ORMESTON C1830 MANCHESTER, LAN, ENG
[36635] : ISABELLA 1835 SCT [36635]
ORMISTON 1810+ LONDON, LND, ENG [37533]
ORMOND-MIDDLETON C1820+ FORFAR &
DUNDEE, ANS, SCT [34568]
ORMROD 1700-1900 WRY, ENG [37934]
ORMSBY PRE 1850 WORLDWIDE [36180]
ORNERY PETER C1800 CHELMSFORD, ESS, ENG
[37992]
ORNORT 1750+ ALBANY CO., NY, USA [36962]
O'ROURKE DANIEL 1862+ KILLARNE, VIC, AUS
[35209] : 1882+ MELBOURNE, VIC, AUS [35379] :
1820+ NSW, AUS [37900] : 1830-1840S ST HELIER,
JSY, CHI [36285] : PRE 1886 DON, IRL [33862] :
MAURICE 1800-1875 TRALEE, KER, IRL [34699] :
FLORENCE 1850-1875 TRALEE, KER, IRL [34699] :
1860+ KILBEGGAN, WEM, IRL [35138] : DANIEL
PRE 1862 CAR, IRL [35209] : PRE 1882 TIP, IRL
[35379] : JOHN PRE 1870 ENNISCORTHY, WEX,
IRL [36619] : PRE 1800 IRL [37984]
ORPETH C1748 ROTHBURY, NBL, ENG [35026]
ORPWOOD C1500 SHREWSBURY, SAL, ENG [38348]
ORR 1840-1850 PERTH CO., ONT, CAN [34106] :
1818+ HALTON & PEEL COS., ONT, CAN [34407] :
1800+ WINNIPEG, MAN, CAN [35765] : 1820+
MONTREAL, QUE & TX, CAN & USA [34116] : PRE
1825 IRL [34116] : PRE 1800 TYR, IRL [34407] : PRE
1880 STRABANE, TYR, IRL [34809] : PRE 1860
INNISHANNON, COR, IRL [35765] : C1800
DONAGHMORE, DOW, IRL [37524] : 1770-1870
INNISHANNON, COR, IRL [37859] : JAMES C1824
MAUCHLINE, AYR, SCT [34300] : 1800 AYR &
PEE, SCT [35336] : C1770+ KIRKLISTON, MLN,
SCT [35629] : 1775-1871 DAHLONEGO, WAPELLO
CO., IA, USA [35316] : 1870+ AMESBURY, MA,
USA [37450] : 1700-1900 MO & TX, USA [38328]
ORR (SEE HOARE) [34956]
ORRELL 1820S WIGAN, LAN, ENG [38266]
ORRIS 1700-1850 HINDRINGHAM &
HILHOUGHTON, NFK, ENG [37246]
ORROCK C1891-1913+ DONALD, VIC, AUS [34289] :
C1804 ABERDOUR, FIF, SCT [35714]

ORROK 1867 WOODSIDE, VIC, AUS [35708] : C1844 JAMAICA [35708]

ORSBORN 1700-1850 SSX, ENG [36007]

ORSMAN ALL NZ [36818]

ORTH 1800S YORK CO., ONT, CAN [37458] : 1800-1900 ALS, GER [37064]

ORTLIEB 1800S PRE, GER [36683]

ORTLIP 1750+ PHILADELPHIA, PA, USA [36347]

ORTON 1720+ KEN, ENG [37087] : 1840+ CARLISLE, CUL, ENG [37635]

ORTWEIN PRE 1855 BIBERACH, WUE, GER [34886]

ORVINE PRE 1900 WORLDWIDE [36932]

OSBAN PRE 1867 CLARK CO., MO, USA [36672]

OSBORN C1800 STEPNEY, LND, ENG [34117] : 1900+ SOUTH LAMBETH, LND, ENG [34313] : 1700+ DEV, ENG [34313] : 1786 BASSINGBOURN, CAM, ENG [34761] : 1800+ BROMLEY, MDX, ENG [34857] : PRE 1850 FOXHALL, SFK, ENG [35898] : PRE 1851+ CHELSEA, LND, ENG [37108] : 1771+ PRITTLEWELL, ESS, ENG [37108] : HENRY PRE 1900 LND, ENG [37273] : 1810+ WIGGENHALL ST MARY MAGDALEN, NFK, ENG [37902] : C1800 LITTLE CLACTON, ESS, ENG [37952] : PRE 1800 SALEHURST, SSX, ENG [38744] : PRE 1800 BORDER AREA, KEN & SSX, ENG [38744] : PRE 1867 CLARK CO., MO, USA [36672] : PRE 1860 PA, USA [36672] : 1719+ SALEM, MA, USA [37802] : 1800-1850 SUSSEX CO., NJ, USA [38201] : ALEXANDER PRE 1800 NJ, USA [38536]

OSBORNE PRE 1857 MELBOURNE, VIC, AUS [34895] : 1863+ ORANGE, NSW, AUS [34977] : 1850-1900 HOBBYS YARDS, NSW, AUS [36316] : 1853+ ST GEORGE, ONT, CAN [34528] : 1800S PEI, CAN [36727] : 1800S RODE, SOM, ENG [33958] : 1800S BENACRE, SFK, ENG [34151] : 1750-1825 GLS, ENG [34307] : PRE 1830 ST BURYAN, CON, ENG [34575] : 1800+ RADFOR, NTT, ENG [34790] : PRE 1863 LND, ENG [34977] : PRE 1814 BURGHFIELD, WIL, ENG [35016] : 1800+ GRAYS, ESS, ENG [35712] : PETER C1864 LIVERPOOL, LAN, ENG [35777] : C1840 BROADHEMPSTON, DEV, ENG [35807] : PRE 1850 BLACKBURN, LAN, ENG [36369] : PRE 1863 ST AGNES, CON, ENG [36432] : 1700 KESWICK, NFK, ENG [36483] : PRE 1850 SOM, ENG [36986] : 1750-1850 DBY, ENG [37064] : PRE 1900 ST ENODER, CON, ENG [37105] : HENRY PRE 1900 LND, ENG [37273] : 1870-90 CASTON, NFK, ENG [37376] : C1812 TAUNTON & BRISTOL, SOM, ENG [37396] : 1800S MARDEN, KEN, ENG [37816] : PRE 1700 ALDBURY, HRT, ENG [37980] : 1800S TILBURY, ESS, ENG [38373] : 1840S ANNACOLTY, LIM, IRL [33967] : PRE 1880 TYR, IRL [35913] : ISABELLA C1810+ EDENFOGARY (OMAGH), TYR, IRL [37906] : PRE 1829 DERNSEER, TYR, IRL [38211] : JANE C1822-1893 STRAITON, AYR, SCT [34300] : PRE 1820 GRAYSON, VA, USA [36567] : 1820+ LEWIS, MO, USA [36567] : 1800-1850 SUSSEX CO., NJ, USA [36731] : 1860-1870 KEWEENAW CO., MI, USA [38009]

OSBOURN HENRY PRE 1900 LND, ENG [37273]

OSBOURNE HENRY PRE 1900 LND, ENG [37273] : ASENATH PRE 1845 BATH, SOM, ENG [38776]

OSBURN C1830 VA, USA [38177]

OSCAR C1848 MANCHESTER, LAN, ENG [35216]

OSEEN C1840 ALMEBODA, SMALAND, SWE [34395]

OSGOOD 1778 FROXFIELD, HAM, ENG [34909] : 1500-1640 WHERWELL, HAM, ENG [36733] : 1630-1900 NH, USA [36733] : 1630-1900 ESSEX, MA, USA [36733] : 1630-1900 VT, USA [36733] : 1630-1900 OXFORD, ME, USA [36733]

O'SHAUGHNESSY 1840-1889 KEW, VIC, AUS [37305] : JOHANNA ALL AUS [38075] : PRE 1860 HAMILTON & KINGSTON, ONT, CAN [37534] : 1810-1840 ATHENRY, GAL, IRL [37305] : 1830S OATFIELD, O'CALLAGHANS MILLS, CLA, IRL [38079] : 1870+ SOUTH BEND, WA, USA [37534]

O'SHAY PRE 1830 CULCLUCK, COR, IRL [37133]

O'SHEA 1863-1880 BUCKLAND, VIC, AUS [33778] : 1830+ LONDON, ENG [36600] : 1800+ WATERFORD, WAT, IRL [33861] : PRE 1880 MACROOM, COR, IRL [34809] : PRE 1857 LIM, IRL [35378] : JAMES C1836 DROGHEDA, LOU, IRL [36274] : 1848 LOUGHILL, LIM, IRL [36640]

O'SHEA (SEE SHEA) [36946]

OSKAMP 1826 UTR, NL [38716]

OSLAND 1800S MANNINGFORD, WIL, ENG [33934]

OSLER ALL VIC, AUS [34574] : ALL HORNINGSEA, CAM, ENG [34574] : 1770-1800 CURRY RIVEL, SOM, ENG [35798]

OSMAN PRE 1814 BURGHFIELD, WIL, ENG [35016] : C1800 SOM, ENG [38488]

OSMOND 1800-1840 CORTON DENHAM, SOM, ENG [34448] : 1840+ LONDON, ENG [35043] : PRE 1825 SHENLEY, HRT, ENG [35098] : PRE 1820 CHULMLEIGH & SWIMBRIDGE, DEV, ENG [35128] : 1850+ TOTTENHAM, LND, ENG [36818]

OSMUNDSEN 1820-1870 SKUDESNES, ROGALAND, NOR [35102]

OSSEFORT PRE 1904 GREEN BAY & DEPERE, IL & WI, USA [35002]

OSSENKOP ALL LISTRINGEN, NSA, GER [38637]

OSSI 1800-1900 SAN VITO CADORE, BELLUNO, ITL [38337] : 1860-1910 PASSAIC CO., NJ, USA [38337]

OST PRE 1910 ENGHIEN, HAINAUT, BEL [35173]

OSTAFIJOW PRE 1895 BILCZEZLOT, TP & PD, POL [37410]

OSTDIEK PRE 1846 OESTERWIEHE, WEF, GER [37563] : 1846+ LEE & POTTAWATTAMIE, IA, USA [37563]

OSTER 1790-1850 YORK, ONT, CAN [37435]

OSTERLOH C1830 BS-WENDEN, NSA, FRG [38660] : 1870+ OHRUM, NSA, FRG [38660]

OSTERLOO 1860 BUFFALO, WI, USA [38320]

OSTERVALD ALL WORLDWIDE [38633]

OSTERVALD DE ALL WORLDWIDE [38633]

OSTERWALD ALL WORLDWIDE [38633]

OSTERWALDE ALL WORLDWIDE [38633]

OSTERWALDER ALL WORLDWIDE [38633]

OSTIN 1800-1900 SAL, ENG [37884]

OSTLER 1850-1930 EAST BRIGHTON, VIC, AUS [38207] : MARY ANN 1850-1930 EAST BRIGHTON, VIC, AUS [38207] : PRE 1850 SOMERTON, SOM, ENG [35462] : 1820-1860 WISBECH, CAM, ENG [38207] : 1600S CURRY RIVEL, SOM, ENG [38745]

OSTRANDER 1780-1830 LINCOLN CO., ONT, CAN [34407] : 1790+ NORFOLK & ELGIN CO., ONT, CAN [36323]

OSTROWSI 1886-1938 WARSAW, POL [34063]

OSTRYK PRE 1900 GALICIA, SU & POL [34146]

O'SULLIVAN 1840-1990 BRISBANE, QLD, AUS [35308] : C1890 INDIA [36010] : CATHERINE 1844 ADARE & KILEEDY, LIM, IRL [34070] : MICHAEL 1841 ADARE & KILEEDY, LIM, IRL [34070] : PATRICK 1840 ADARE & KILEEDY, LIM, IRL [34070] : 1700-1900 KER, IRL [35308] : 1700-1900 COR, IRL [35308] : ALL GLOUNBRACK, COR, IRL [36168] : 1840S CLA, IRL [36264] : 1750-1816 KER, IRL [36618] : ALL KER, IRL [36784] : 1800+ KILLORGLIN, KER, IRL [36821]

OSWALD 1840-1855 GODSTONE, SRY & LND, ENG [36175] : 1820 ALS, FRA [37006] : 1800S BADEN, BRD, GER [34791] : PRE 1800 FIF, SCT [34571]

OSWIN PRE 1750 LEI, ENG [37706]
OTHBERG ALL WORLDWIDE [38346]
OTLEY PRE 1760 WHEPSTEAD, SFK, ENG [35391]
O'TOOLE PRE 1820 WIC, IRL [37087] : HANNAH
PRE 1849 FOX LAKE, MN, USA & IRL [37481]
OTT 1850+ ALEXANDRIA, EGYPT [36982]
OTTEN 1670+ MARNE, SHO, GER [37542] : 1750-1900
VENLO & DEN BOSCH, LI & ND, NL [38712]
OTTENHEIMER 1700+ NORDSTETTEN, BAW, GER
[38578]
OTTENSTEYN ALL LEIDEN, ZUH, NL [38703]
OTTER 1841+ NORTHAMPTON, NTH, ENG [34609] :
1700+ LIN, ENG [36133] : PRE 1850 LIN & NTT,
ENG [37695] : 1855+ CANNAMORE, INDIA [34609]
OTTERBEIN 1800 MUS, HES, BRD [37028]
OTTEY 1870+ CASTLEMAINE, VIC, AUS [36279] :
1750-1850 EDGBASTON, WAR, ENG [35857]
OTTLEY 1880+ ENG [37653]
OTTLIK PRE 1836 WOJNOWICE, SIL, GER [38618]
OTTO C1770 LONDON, ENG [36010] : PRE 1850
LONDON, ENG [36765] : PRE 1860 ZWICKAU,
WPR, GER [35853] : 1813 CRICHTON, MLN, SCT
[37165] : PRE 1718 SWE & FIN [38564]
OTTOSON 1864-1941 KNOX CO., IL, USA [38371]
OTWAY 1850+ VIC & WA, AUS [35137] : 1920+
DUNLOP, AYR, SCT [34341] : 1819+ UK [35137] :
1819+ PA, LA & NY, USA [35137]
OUDERKIRK 1760-99 CAYUGA CO., NY, USA [38153]
OUDNEY ALL EDINBURGH, SCT [35899]
OUDSHOORN 1880+ ENG [37453]
OUELLET ALL QUE, CAN [34517]
OUGH RICHARD 1800+ CON, ENG [34481] :
SIDNEY EGBERT PRE 1900 SALTASH, CON, ENG
& CAN [34481]
OUGHTON 1860+ NEWCASTLE, NSW, AUS [34905] :
1500-1850 BIRMINGHAM, WAR, STS & SAL, ENG
[36169]
OULCOTT 1800+ BURSLEN, STS, ENG [38410]
OULD 1800+ ST ENODER, CON, ENG [34666]
OULDES C1820 SRY, ENG [36838]
OULTON 1850+ BELVEDERE, KEN, ENG [36807] :
1850+ BEXLEYHEATH, KEN, ENG [36807]
OUSELEY 1200-1990 WORLDWIDE [36114]
OUSLEY PRE 1850 ILMINSTER, SOM, ENG [37084] :
1200-1990 WORLDWIDE [36114]
OUTHIT 1600+ MIDDLETON TYAS, NRY, ENG
[37635] : 1600+ MARSKE & SWALEDALE, NRY,
ENG [37635]
OUTHWAITE 1600+ MIDDLETON TYAS, NRY,
ENG [37635] : 1600+ MARSKE & SWALEDALE,
NRY, ENG [37635]
OUTRAM 1759-1785 PENISTONE, WRY, ENG [36606]
: 1819 SILKSTONE, WRY, ENG [36606] : ALL ENG
[37858]
OUTTRIM 1850+ MARYBOROUGH, VIC, AUS
[35986] : ALL WORLDWIDE [35986]
OVEL PRE 1760 KEN, ENG [36584]
OVEN C1802 WESTMINSTER, MDX, ENG [37834]
OVENDEN C1780 CANTERBURY, KEN, ENG [35350]
: C1880 CHATHAM, KEN, ENG [35350]
OVENS PRE 1840 FER, IRL [35001] : PRE 1866 WIC,
IRL [35001] : 1850-1940 CORRY, FER, IRL [38526] :
1800-1850 BROLLAGH, FER, IRL [38526] : 1800+
PEE, SCT [34515] : 1860-1930 BARRHEAD, RFW,
SCT [38526] : 1870-1930 ADDIWELL, MLN, SCT
[38526]
OVENSTONE ALL ELIE, FIF, SCT [37704]
OVER PRE 1800 ISLINGTON & EDMONTON, MDX,
ENG [37402]
OVERALL PRE 1919 PREES & WEM, SAL, ENG
[34213] : PRE 1838 MARYLEBONE, LND, ENG
[34213]

OVERBEEK 1600 AMSTERDAM, NL [38379]
OVERBOCK 1840-1860 WALDO CO., ME, USA [37576]
OVERBY 1820-1850 HALIFAX, VA, USA [38342]
OVERHOLT 1790-1881 ONT, CAN [34106] : 1790+
NIAGARA DISTRICT, ONT, CAN [38323] : PRE
1780 BUCKS CO., PA, USA [34741] : PRE 1796
BUCKS CO., PA, USA [37811] : 1850+ IA, USA
[38323]
OVERLACK HEINRICH C1896 TOWNSVILLE, QLD,
AUS [34266] : ALL RHINELAND, NRW, GER
[34266] : 1850+ KOLN, NRW, GER [34266] : PRE
1850S KOLN, NRW, GER [34266]
OVERMIRE 1840 PERRY CO., OH, USA [36731]
OVERS PRE 1850 WINDSOR, NSW, AUS [35199] :
1815-1900 ORO TWP., ONT, CAN [34346]
OVERSETH PRE 1870 BOVERBRU,
GUDBRANDSDAL, NOR [37821]
OVERSON ALL CONGHAM, NFK, ENG [38762] :
ALL KINGS LYNN, NFK, ENG [38762] : ALL
GRIMSTONE, NFK, ENG [38762]
OVERSTREET 1794-1850 EMANUEL CO., GA, USA
[38340] : ALL WORLDWIDE [38060]
OVERTON 1840+ SYDNEY, NSW, AUS [35703] :
1800+ MANSEL LACY, HEF, ENG [34363] : 1800-
1840 BRAMPTON, CUL, ENG [35703] : 1750+
ASTLEY, WOR, ENG [37209] : 1800+
BIRMINGHAM, WAR, ENG [37209]
OVETT PRE 1800 BRIGHTON, SSX, ENG [34247]
OVEY 1742 MORTON MORRELL & AVON
DASSETT, WAR, ENG [35013]
OWCZAREK ALL SIERADZ, SI, POL [38164]
OWEN 1828+ PATTERSON RD, NSW, AUS [34020] :
1850+ ARARAT, VIC, AUS [34690] : 1880S MANLY,
NSW, AUS [37309] : 1700+ KINNERLEY, SAL,
ENG [34370] : C1800 DUR, ENG [34456] : 1700+
BRADLEY & PENKRIDGE, STS, ENG [35019] :
PRE 1820 ARNOLD, NTT, ENG [35462] : C1837
CHIPPING NORTON, OXF, ENG [35478] : C1816
CARLISLE, CUL, ENG [35478] : PRE 1800
BRINKLOW, WAR & BKM, ENG [35588] : PRE 1805
WEST BUCKLAND, SOM, ENG [35727] : THOMAS
1830 LONDON, ENG [35827] : HENSHALL MOSS
1860S+ MANCHESTER, LAN, ENG [35876] : ALL
WIDNES, LAN, ENG [36063] : C1710 OVER
WHITLEY, CHS, ENG [36520] : 1800S LIVERPOOL
OR BLACKPOOL, LAN, ENG [36683] : ROBERT
1800S KINGS NORTON, WOR, ENG [37299] : 1800S
SAL, ENG [37309] : PRE 1815 MEOPHAM, KEN,
ENG [37325] : ALL COVENTRY, WAR, ENG [37404]
: PRE 1800 MILVERTON, SOM, ENG [37410] :
1850+ LAMBETH & WANDSWORTH, SRY &
LND, ENG [37707] : 1792-1883 SAL, ENG & AUS
[36642] : 1820+ MADISON CO., KY, USA [35275] :
ALL OHIO, OH, USA [37619] : PRE 1880
WREXHAM, DEN, WLS [34622] : 1880+
LLANELLI, CMN, WLS [35248] : PRE 1890
LLANGWYLLOG, AGY, WLS [35430] : 1700-1800
LLANFIHANGEL, MGY, WLS [36025] : JANE PRE
1715 NEFYN, CAE, WLS [36590] : 1750+
GLAMORGAN, GLA, WLS [37619] :
MARGARETTA 1698 DOLGELLEY, MER, WLS
[37649]
OWENS 1800+ NSW, AUS [35352] : 1900+
SCARBOURGH, ONT, CAN [34993] : 1835+
LIVERPOOL, LAN, ENG [36168] : PRE 1870 FER,
IRL [34555] : PRE 1890 ENNISKILLEN, FER, IRL
[34585] : C1838 JULIANSTOWN, MEA, IRL [35247] :
1800S CREAVE, ROS, IRL [36290] : 1800+
BALLITORE, KID, IRL [36821] : C1749 IRL [37527] :
C1800 FAUQUIER CO., VA, USA [37527] : JAMES
1850+ IL, USA [38324] : ALL CA, USA [38359] :
1839+ LLANSADWYN, AGY, WLS [37201] :

ELLEN PRE 1872 LLANSADWYN, CAE, WLS [37201] : C1780 BETTISFIELD, FLN, WLS [37508] : MARY ANN PRE 1875 GRESFORD, DEN, WLS [37886] : 1800S OSWESTRY, MGY, WLS [37899] : 1800S RHONDA & SOUTH, WLS [38753]

OWERS 1600-1750 LITTLE SALING, ESS, ENG [37250]

OWLD PRE 1843 ST MERRYN, CON, ENG [33781]

OWLER C1775 BLAIRGOWRIE, PER, SCT [34203]

OWNBY 1870 NASHVILLE, TN, USA [35325] : 1890 DALLAS, TX, USA [35325]

OWSLEY 1200-1990 WORLDWIDE [36114]

OWST 1672-1730 BAINTON, ERY, ENG [35996] : 1742-1858 WILBERFOSS, ERY, ENG [35996]

OWTRAM ALL ENG [37858]

OXBY 1700S HARMSTON, LIN, ENG [37039]

OXENBOULD ALL WORLDWIDE [38279]

OXFORD GEORGE 1835+ SYDNEY, NSW, AUS [35541] : 1750-1810 OXF, ENG [34074] : 1730+ WINTERBORNE STICKLAND, DOR, ENG [34228] : PRE 1835 DOR, ENG [35541] : 1800+ BRIXHAM, DEV, ENG [37231]

OXLADE HARRY 1880+ BALLARAT, VIC, AUS [35803] : BENJ. 1820+ LONDON, ENG [35803]

OXLEY 1750+ NRY, ENG [34456] : PRE 1800 DONCASTER, YKS, ENG [37553] : 1840-1900 DEPTFORD, LND, ENG [38247]

OXNARD 1800 WAR, ENG [34363]

OXYER ALL FRA [38287]

OYSTER 1700+ DELLANBURG, GER & OES [38735]

OYSTRYK 1920+ RHEIN, SAS, CAN [34521] : 1900-1920 HAMTON, SAS, CAN [34521] : 1890S STAWCHIN, BUKOVINA, UKRAINE [34521]

OZANNE ALL ST SAMPSONS, GSY, CHI [35433]

OZDYCH ALL KOLACZKOWA, PO, POL [36941]

OZIAS 1790-1850 PREBLE CO., OH, USA [38108]

PACE 1790+ ABINGER, SRY, ENG [36263] : PRE 1800 BURSLEM, STS, ENG [37389] : PRE 1871 TUNSTALL, STS, ENG [37726]

PACEY 1830+ SYDNEY, NSW, AUS [34905] : 1815+ LONDON, ENG [34905] : ALL WORLDWIDE [34361]

PACK PRE 1971 BROMLEY, KEN, ENG [35029] : PRE 1892 FORESTGATE, ESS, ENG [35029] : 1800+ TONBRIDGE WELLS, KEN & LND, ENG [37065] : PRE 1700 HAWKHURST, KEN, ENG [37185] : THOMAS PRE 1800 FREDERICK CO., MD & VA, USA [35304] : C1880 SEARCY, AR, USA [36899] : PRE 1840 NC, USA [38040] : 1800-1900 TN, USA [38040]

PACKARD JOHN 1839 ENG & CAN [36677] : 1890+ BROCKTON, MA, USA [33867]

PACKE 1600+ STAVERTON, DEV, ENG [34747]

PACKER DANIEL 1875 KURRAJONG, NSW, AUS [35831] : 1750+ BARBADOS [38355] : PRE 1780 WARMLEY, GLS, ENG [35079] : PRE C1830 GLOUCESTER, GLS, ENG [35904] : 1650-1800 GROOMBRIDGE, KEN, ENG [38355] : PRE 1796 POTTERSBURY, NTH, ENG [38490] : C1810-40 COLUMBIANA CO., OH, USA [38173]

PACKHAM PRE 1925 CHATHAM, KEN, ENG [37067]

PACKMAN 1835+ FAVERSHAM, KEN, ENG [34374] : PRE 1880 KEN, ENG [37358]

PACKWOOD ALL WILBURTON, CAM, ENG [34772]

PADDEN PRE 1838 NORTHAM & LITTLEHAM, DEV, ENG [38580]

PADDICK 1800 MAIDSTONE, KEN, ENG & AUS [36239]

PADDISON PRE 1820 HIGH BRAY, DEV, ENG [35523] : 1800+ CLEETHORPES, LIN, ENG [36059] : PRE 1800 BRIGSLEY, LIN, ENG [36059] : PRE 1850

GREAT CARLTON, LIN, ENG [36168] : 1700-1800 TEALBY, LIN, ENG [37487]

PADDOCK 1605-1787 MA, USA [37803] : 1790+ SALEM, NY, USA [38572] : 1820+ CAYUGA CO., NY, USA [38572]

PADDON PRE 1800 BRIXHAM, DEV, ENG [34333] : PRE 1900 EXETER, DEV, ENG [36145] : PRE 1838 NORTHAM & LITTLEHAM, DEV, ENG [38580]

PADFIELD 1850+ OAKHILL, SOM, ENG [37322]

PADGEN 1800+ ENG [35106]

PADGET ALL NAILSEA, SOM, ENG [36407]

PADGETT C1860 HARROGATE, NRY, ENG [33772] : ALL NEWPORT, MON, WLS [36407]

PADGHAM PRE 1839 BREDE, SSX, ENG [35189]

PADLEY 1900+ KAMSACK, SAS, CAN [34521] : 1890-1950 LEEDS, WRY, ENG [34521] : THOMAS 1800S CHIPPING NORTON, OXF, ENG [35876] : 1800+ LONDON, ENG [37699] : 1800+ NTT, ENG [37699]

PADRAZOLLA ALL WORLDWIDE [37366]

PADWICK 1800-1900 HORSHAM, SSX, ENG [34117] : NICK 1816-1822 LONDON, ENG [38397] : MARY C1800 LONDON, ENG [38397]

PAE C1793 COLDINGHAM, BEW, SCT [36302]

PAESLER ALL BRA, GER [34801]

PAFF C1860 SLIEDRECHT, ZUH, NL [38705] : C1820 ZIERIKZEE, ZEL, NL [38705]

PAFFORD 1800+ NF, CAN [34998] : PRE 1850 DEV, ENG [34998] : ALL SCT [37028] : 1800+ GA & KY, USA [34998] : 1700S NC, USA [37028]

PAGE 1840+ MELBOURNE, VIC, AUS [34547] : 1875+ TOWNSVILLE, QLD, AUS [35335] : 1851+ ADELAIDE, SA, AUS [37189] : 1856-1876 MIDDLESEX CO., ONT, CAN [34153] : 1910-1950 EDMONTON, ONT, CAN [36990] : 1800-1850 BRIDGNORTH, SAL, ENG [33767] : 1830+ LAMBETH, SRY, ENG [34092] : PRE 1800 WIL, ENG [34139] : PRE 1856 BRK, ENG [34153] : 1750-1850 NTH, ENG [34258] : 1700+ HEMPNALL, NFK, ENG [34420] : 1700-1800S ASHFORD, KEN, ENG [34483] : 1700+ KEN, ENG [34547] : 1850+ HEADINGTON, OXF, ENG [34655] : 1600+ HASTINGS, SSX, ENG [34747] : 1800+ ESS, ENG [34818] : 1800S SRY, ENG [34845] : ALL MARGATE, KEN, ENG [34879] : 1830 EMBERTON, BKM, ENG [34950] : PRE 1815 FORDHAM, ESS, ENG [34976] : PRE 1700 SHIPBOURNE, KEN, ENG [35321] : PRE 1700 LONDON, ENG [35321] : PRE 1700 SHORNE, KEN, ENG [35321] : PRE 1700 ALDINGTON, KEN, ENG [35321] : PRE 1866 HERTFORD, HRT, ENG [35335] : ISAAC 1800+ LONDON, ENG [35905] : PRE 1850 GRAVESEND & DARTFORD, KEN, ENG [36178] : 1700-1800 BRISTOL, GLS, ENG [36205] : ELEANOR PRE 1828 LONDON, ENG [36314] : 1594 EAST BEDFONT, MDX, ENG [36358] : 1700S LONDON, MDX, ENG [36438] : 1750+ ENG [36470] : 1800 KEN, ENG [36480] : NICHOLAS PRE 1660 NTT, ENG [36619] : 1750-1850 LONDON, ENG [36708] : PRE 1825 STROOD, KEN, ENG [37067] : 1500-1700 BEDFONT, MDX, ENG [37077] : 1500-1700 WEMBLEY, MDX, ENG [37077] : JOHN PRE 1839 ARMY, LND, ENG [37143] : PRE 1851 BETHNAL GREEN, MDX, ENG [37189] : GEORGE 1750+ STH ELMHAM ALL SAINTS, SFK, ENG [37191] : 1600S STRADBROKE & SOUTH ELMHAM, SFK, ENG [37250] : PRE 1850 HADLEIGH, SFK, ENG [37279] : C1780 KEN, ENG [37536] : PRE 1840 BETHNAL GREEN, MDX, ENG [37617] : PRE 1900 LND & ESS, ENG [37693] : PRE 1780 GREAT YARMOUTH, NFK, ENG [37716] : PRE 1900 DEV, ENG [38594] : ALL ENG & NZ [34679] : 1830S WIC, IRL [38082] : 1750+ KIRKCALDY & BURNT ISLAND, FIF, SCT [34473]

: SANFORD 1835 HAMILTON CO., IL, USA [35286] : 1650+ BRANFORD, CT, USA [35321] : ALL LIVINGSTON, NY, USA [35321] : ELIZABETH 1850 ROCKINGHAM CO., NC, USA [35328] : 1650-1800 WILLIAMSBURG, VA, USA [37077] : 1650+ BURLINGTON, NJ, USA [37826] : PRE 1690 YORK CO., VA, USA [38066]

PAGEL PRE 1900 STOLP & SCHLAWE, POM, GER [38684]

PAGERIE 1750+ BN & HN, FRA [35614]

PAGE-ROBERTS 1850+ ENG [34099]

PAGET 1600-1900 IBSTOCK, LEI, ENG [34004] : C1800 WAKEFIELD, YKS, ENG [34952] : ALL NAILSEA, SOM, ENG [36407] : 1800+ WAR & WOR, ENG [36462] : 1804-C1820S WINLATON HILL, DUR, ENG [37634] : 1830S-1880S LONDON, MDX, ENG [37634] : 1700-1800 THRAPSTON, NTH, ENG [37747] : ALL NEWPORT, MON, WLS [36407]

PAGETT ALL NAILSEA, SOM, ENG [36407] : ALL NEWPORT, MON, WLS [36407]

PAGGINTON C1800 HULLAVINGTON, WIL, ENG [36975]

PAHL PRE 1824 SCHWEDT & VIERRADEN, BRA, GER [34083] : PRE 1843 BARDOWICK, HAN, GER [34911] : PRE 1860 GRUNENPLAN, HAN, GER [36454] : 1861-1880 GRUNENPLAN, HAN, GER & RSA [36454] : 1880S-1915 KALKBANK, TRANSVAAL, RSA [36454]

PAICE C1850 SYDNEY, NSW, AUS [36265] : C1839 DATCHETT, BKM, ENG [36265] : C1840-1850 ETON, BKM, ENG [36265] : 1800+ SWALLOWFIELD, BRK, ENG [36892] : 1800+ BASINGSTOKE, HAM, ENG [37400] : 1850+ AUCKLAND, NZ [36265] : ALL WORLDWIDE [34944]

PAIGE PRE 1860 THOROLD, ONT, CAN [34741] : 1800-1840 KINGSBRIDGE, DEV, ENG [35102] : ALL BLACK TORRINGTON, DEV, ENG [37092] : ALL ENG & NZ [34679] : ALL USA [33842]

PAIGE (SEE PAGE) [34153]

PAIKI 1800S CANTERBURY, NZ [35906]

PAILET ALL LONDON, ENG [38368] : ALL PARIS, FRA [38368] : ALL VILNA, SU [38368] : ALL OLKIENIKI, SU [38368] : ALL PINASHASHUK, SU [38368] : 1800+ RICHMOND, VA, USA [38368]

PAILLIART 1841 RELLINGHAUSEN, RPR, GER [38750]

PAILTHORPE 1800-1900 ENG [34422]

PAIN 1845+ ADELAIDE, SA, AUS [35524] : EDITH PRE 1915 ST KILDA, VIC, AUS [36621] : PRE 1730 NUNNEY, SOM, ENG [36478] : 1600S CIRENCESTER, GLS, ENG [36585] : 1700+ HEATHFIELD, SSX, ENG [37206] : PRE 1790 ESHER, SRY, ENG [38512] : 1755+ NOR [37289] : 1800+ SWE [37289]

PAIN (SEE PAYNE) [35065]

PAINE 1837+ NSW, AUS [34780] : MARY PRE 1873 MELBOURNE, VIC, AUS [35471] : 1900S GRAFTON, NSW, AUS [37910] : MARTHA 1838 LONDON, ENG [34091] : ALL ENG [34131] : C1770 TARRANT HINTON, DOR, ENG [34426] : PRE 1900 ENG [34978] : C1800 SOUTHAMPTON, HAM, ENG [35252] : PRE 1800 ROTHERFIELD, SSX, ENG [35406] : ALL MILDENHALL, SFK, ENG [35858] : 1750-1800 WINGRAVE, BKM, ENG [36987] : PRE 1900 WADHURST, SSX, ENG [37335] : C1748 KENARDINGTON & WOODCHURCH, KEN, ENG [37714] : C1861 EBONY, KEN, ENG [37714] : 1900S WORTHING, SSX, ENG [37714] : 1800S BECKLEY, SSX, ENG [37910] : PRE 1700 REHOBOTH BRISTOL, RI, USA [37804] : ROYAL

1848 VT, USA [38124] : PRE 1730 NJ, USA & ENG [38745]

PAINE (SEE PAYNE) [35866]

PAINTER 1887+ SYDNEY, NSW, AUS [37175] : 1750+ SHROTON OR IWERNE COURTNAY, DOR, ENG [34650] : PRE 1810 GRAMPOUND & CREED, CON, ENG [35736] : PRE 1850 BETHNAL GREEN, MDX, ENG [36095] : 1770-1900 BROADWAY & ASHILL, SOM, ENG [36373] : 1854+ LONDON, ENG [37175] : 1790-1839 WALBERTON & ARUNDEL, SSX, ENG [37187] : 1726+ ROCKINGHAM, VA, USA [38054]

PAISLEY C1675-1795 GRETNA, DFS, SCT [37447]

PAITSON PRE 1900 CUL, ENG [34335]

PAKES 1857+ SYDNEY, NSW, AUS [37987] : ALL OLNEY, BKM, LND & MDX, ENG [37987]

PAKULSKA WIKTORIA 1849-1937 POL [38090] : THERESA 1810-1899 POL [38090]

PAKULSKI MICHAL 1820-1890 POL [38090]

PAKUSA C1835 POS, GER [38618]

PALAMOUNTAIN C1800-60 CON, ENG [36877] : 1861+ MILTON, OTAGO, NZ [36877]

PALETTE ALL LONDON, ENG [38368]

PALFERMAN PRE 1750 CHAPEL EN-LE FRITH, DBY, ENG [34588]

PALFREE 1700+ DBY, ENG [37839] : 1700+ WAR, ENG [37839] : 1700+ NTT, ENG [37839] : 1700+ WOR, ENG [37839]

PALFREY PRE 1730 WHIMPLE, DEV, ENG [37643]

PALFREYMAN 1700S MANCETTER, WAR, ENG [34385]

PALIN 1750-1850S BILSBY & ALFORD, LIN, ENG [34745] : ALL LEI, ENG [36005] : PRE 1800 NTT, ENG [37739]

PALKE 1500+ DEV, ENG [36208] : 1660+ MELTON MOWBRAY & ALL, LEI, ENG [36208]

PALLATT 1850+ LEICESTER, LEI, ENG [35169]

PALLENDER 1800+ LONDON, ENG [36404]

PALLETT 1720+ ESS, ENG [34322] : C1875 ESSENDON, HRT, ENG [36490] : C1800 HERTFORD, HRT, ENG [37449] : PRE 1825 STOKE GOLDINGTON, BKM, ENG [37655]

PALLISER C1826 RIPON, YKS, ENG [34157] : PRE 1880 NORTHALLERTON, NRY, ENG [36870] : 1880+ TIMARU, NZ [36870]

PALLISTER 1835+ ONT, CAN [34380]

PALLOT PRE 1820 GROUVILLE, JSY, CHI [34923] : ALL ST HELIER, JSY, CHI, ENG [35474] : ALL CAPETOWN, RSA [37256]

PALM BERTHA 1886-1922 MAG, DDR [37551] : ANDREW PRE 1886 MAG, DDR [37551]

PALMER 1820-1850 HOBART, TAS, AUS [33778] : 1847+ TAS, AUS [33786] : 1890+ INVERELL, NSW, AUS [33836] : 1870-1890 RUTHERGLEN & BEECHWRTH, VIC, AUS [33836] : 1920-1990 GILGANDRA, NSW, AUS [34294] : 1801-1837 SYDNEY, NSW, AUS [34649] : 1930+ BONDI, NSW, AUS [36632] : 1850+ MELBOURNE, VIC, AUS [36761] : 1859+ WARIALDA, NSW, AUS [37894] : C1852-1858 MT PLEASANT, VIC, AUS [37894] : JOHN JAMES PRE 1943 CANLEY VALE, SYDNEY, NSW, AUS [37992] : C1830 PARRAMATTA, NSW, AUS [38209] : 1832-1842 LAUNCESTON, TAS, AUS [38209] : 1846+ GEELONG & MELBOURNE, VIC, AUS [38209] : 1850+ SYDNEY, NSW, AUS [38484] : JOHN 1780-1848 NFK, ENG [33871] : 1800S ST ERME, CON, ENG [33981] : PRE 1810 TEIGNMOUTH, DEV, ENG [33999] : 1814 GOODMANSFIELD, MDX, ENG [34204] : 1760+ BATH, SOM, ENG [34261] : 1750-1850 HUNGERFORD, BRK, ENG [34343] : PRE 1834 BIRMINGHAM, ENG [34443] : 1822 HEF,

ENG [34446] : 1800+ WOODSTOCK, OXF, ENG [34455] : 1750+ STILTON, HUN, ENG [34455] : ISABELLA 1826 LUDHAM, NFK, ENG [34539] : ALL KINGSTON UPON THAMES, SRY, ENG [34595] : 1760-1801 FLAMPSTEAD, HRT, ENG [34649] : 1800+ DEV, ENG [34818] : 1850+ SOMERTON, SOM, ENG [35066] : THOMAS 1839 WROUGHTON, WIL, ENG [35120] : PRE 1757 STH PETHERTON, SOM, ENG [35252] : C1861 WESTMINSTER, LND, ENG [35348] : PRE 1857 SOM, ENG [35393] : PRE 1850 ERISWELL, SFK, ENG [35491] : 1690+ EAST TEIGNMOUTH, DEV, ENG [35587] : ROBERT 1812-1881 ST PANCRAS, MDX, ENG [35725] : FRED 1848-1925 ST PANCRAS & ISLINGTON, MDX, ENG [35725] : SYDNEY C1920-1945 GREAT YARMOUTH, NFK, ENG [35725] : 1830+ WARLINGHAM, SRY, ENG [35746] : 1753+ WADDINGTON, LIN, ENG [35746] : PRE 1750 NOCTON, LIN, ENG [35746] : 1830S MILTON BY GRAVESEND, KEN, ENG [35780] : PRISCILLA 1800 MDX, ENG [35975] : 1600+ KEN, ENG [36093] : ALL SCALEBY, CUL, ENG [36144] : ALL RUGBY, WAR, ENG [36162] : 1800+ CLARBOROUGH, NTT, ENG [36176] : PRE 1820 YARMOUTH, NFK, ENG [36201] : ALL CAMBRIDGE, CAM, ENG [36201] : C1750 PARKHAM, DEV, ENG [36254] : WILLIAM 1770+ STONDON MASSEY & DAGENHAM, ESS, ENG [36263] : C1881 BRANDON, SFK, ENG [36307] : PRE 1880 OKEHAMPTON, DEV, ENG [36424] : PRE 1820 NFK, ENG [36629] : PRE 1873 HARROLD, BDF, ENG [36866] : 1873+ PETERBOROUGH, NTH, ENG [36866] : PRE 1850 KIMBOLTON, HUN, ENG [36866] : PRE 1850 HAIL WESTON, ENG [36866] : ALL LAKENHEATH & MILDENHALL, SFK, ENG [36955] : 1700+ WADWORTH, ERY, ENG [37050] : PRE 1900 NEEN SOLLARS, SAL & WAR, ENG [37096] : C1743 CAM, ENG [37144] : JANE 1847+ ODIHAM, HAM, ENG [37168] : 1740-1860 KIMPTON, HRT & BDF, ENG [37194] : 1650-1750 WELLOW, HAM, ENG [37233] : 1650-1750 WELLOW, WIL, ENG [37233] : SARAH 1800S SOUTH PETHERTON, SOM, ENG [37544] : PRE 1880 LONDON, ENG [37646] : 1860+ EVERSHOLT, BDF, ENG [37647] : PRE 1845 TODDINGTON, BDF, ENG [37647] : 1900+ ASPLEY GUISE, BDF, ENG [37647] : PRE 1851 NORWOOD, SRY, ENG [37700] : PRE 1852 HAM, ENG [37894] : JOHN 1828 BOW, MDX, ENG [37992] : C1824 LAMBETH, SRY, ENG [38209] : 1700-1800 SUNDERLAND BRIDGE, DUR, ENG [38269] : JAMES 1836-1921 NORTHAMPTON & IPSWICH, NTH & SFK, ENG [38280] : 1790+ BRISTOL, GLS & DOR, ENG & USA [37990] : ALL WEM, IRL [34027] : BARNABUS PRE 1750 IRL [35328] : BARNABUS 1750 COR, IRL [37585] : 1820-1886 OTAGO & STHLND, NZ [34649] : 1840 STIRLING, PER, SCT [34098] : PRE 1900 DUMFERMLINE, FIF, SCT [36451] : PRE 1650 REHOBOTH, MA, USA [33804] : PRE 1783 DUTCHESS CO., NY, USA [34494] : BARNABUS 1750+ ROCHESTER, NH, USA [35328] : 1860 JACKSON CO., MN, USA [36444] : ALL BANGOR, ME, USA [36713] : 1650-1800 MONROE CO., NY, USA [36924] : GEORGE PRE 1828 TUSCARAWAS CO., OH, USA [36925] : 1700-1800 PA, USA [37466] : 1829 OH, USA [38121] : C1820S BERKELEY & MORGAN, WV, USA [38348]

PALMER-COX 1750-1850 VENTNOR, IOW, HAM, ENG [36324]

PALMETIER C1760 NY, USA [38052]

PALMHOUT ALL BEL [36982]

PALSER 1837-1917 SYDNEY & HUNTERS HILL, NSW, AUS [38761] : 1778-1837 FRAMPTON COTTERELL, GLS, ENG [38761]
PALUMBO PRE 1861 CAMPO, ITL [37519]
PALUSKA 1800+ OSIVATZ, OES [35278]
PAMANT 1700+ WORLDWIDE [37606]
PAMMANT 1700+ WORLDWIDE [37606]
PAMMENT 1830+ INDENTED HEAD, VIC & CAM, AUS & ENG [37606] : 1700+ WORLDWIDE [37606]
PAMONT 1700+ WORLDWIDE [37606]
PAMPHILION 1820-1904 LONDON, ENG [37165]
PAMPLIN PRE 1858 CAM, ENG [34886]
PANDEL 1650-1780 WESTERWALD REGION, GER [36340]
PANGBURN 1880-1910 BROWN, OH, USA [38054]
PANKHURST PRE 1730 BREDE, SSX, ENG [34974]
PANKO PRE 1890 PROCHIM, BRA, GER [38173]
PANNALL 1857+ CHEWTON, VIC, AUS [36644] : PRE 1857 POPLAR, LONDON, MDX, ENG [36644]
PANNELL PRE 1800 LONDON, ENG [35285] : 1800-1860 CLERKENWELL, MDX, ENG [35285] : 1860-1910 NEWINGTON, SRY, ENG [35285] : PRE 1870 STEEPLE BUMPSTEAD, ESS, ENG [35994] : 1760 E KEN, ENG [36679]
PANNELL (SEE PANNALL [36644]
PANNER 1830 RHEINBAYERN, GER [36900]
PANNIFER PRE 1873 IKEN, SFK, ENG [36230]
PANSA 1870S DRESDEN, KSA, DDR [35018] : 1860S KARL MARX STADT, KSA, DDR [35018]
PANTEL (SEE PANDEL) [36340]
PANTER PRE 1720 TINTAGEL, CON, ENG [38214]
PANTHER PRE 1840 PYTCHLEY, NTH, ENG [35215]
PAPALLO PRE 1920 MARTONE, CALABRIA, ITL [36271]
PAPE PRE 1830 DETMOLD, NRW, GER [38029] : ANNA 1862-1899 COVINGTON, KY & NSA, USA & BRD [34481]
PAPILLAU ALL CAN & USA [35640]
PAPILLON ALL CAN & USA [35640]
PAPIN 1550-1700 SABLE, BRT, FRA [35283]
PAPPIN 1840+ SA, AUS [36267]
PAPWORTH 1700S-1800S TOFT, CAM, ENG [36211]
PAR ALL WORLDWIDE [37742]
PARADINE PRE 1860 BDF, ENG [36086]
PARADIS 1800 LACADIE, QUE, CAN [36907]
PARAMON 1716 BROMPTON RALPH, SOM, ENG [34204]
PARBY ALL WORLDWIDE [37036]
PARCELL 1860+ HARRISVILLE, QLD, AUS [36286] : PRE 1800 PEM, WLS [38461]
PARDE 1800+ STOURBRIDGE, WOR, ENG [34323]
PARDEY C1795 RINGWOOD, HAM & DOR, ENG [37760] : ALL WORLDWIDE [37173]
PARDOE PRE 1870 OLD SWINFORD, WOR, ENG [36870] : 1870+ CHRISTCHURCH, NZ [36870]
PARDY 1800S GSY, CHI [35137] : 1820+ GSY, CHI [37112] : 1700+ CLONFERT, GAL, IRL [34970] : ALL WORLDWIDE [37173]
PAREDES ALL WORLDWIDE [37742]
PARENTEAU MARIE C1800 SAS, CAN [36678]
PARFETT PRE 1849 KINGSLEY, HAM, ENG [34587] : 1800-1900 BRK, ENG [37348]
PARFITT 1500-1900 BRISTOL, GLS, ENG [36130] : 1800+ OAKHILL & ASHWICK, SOM, ENG [37322] : PRE 1851 BANSTEAD, SRY, ENG [38075] : PRE 1851 SRY, ENG [38075] : PRE 1830 WOODMANSTERNE, SRY, ENG [38075] : 1700+ EGHAM, SRY, ENG [38498] : PRE 1800 CLUTTON, SOM, ENG [38745]
PARFORD C1811 RAME & MAKER, CON & DEV, ENG [34836]

PARFREY 1840+ VIC & NSW, AUS [35233] : 1800+ BRISTOL, GLS, ENG [35233]

PARHAM 1700-1900 PORTSMOUTH, HAM, ENG [38249]

PARIS 1600+ FRAMFIELD, SSX, ENG [37365] : 1500+ SSX & SRY, ENG & FRA [36006]

PARISH 1790-1850 LEEDS, ONT, CAN [38097] : 1790-1858 ARKESDEN, ESS, ENG [34035] : C1826 LND, ENG [35552] : JAMES PRE 1800 CARDINGTON, BDF, ENG [35805] : PRE 1850 WOODFORD, ESS, ENG [37097] : PRE 1850 LND & DEV, ENG [37693] : 1910+ YALDHURST, NZ [36359] : 1866-1990 POTTAWATTAMIE, IA, USA [38097] : 1857-1900 KNOX, IL, USA [38097] : 1849-1855 LEE, IA, USA [38097]

PARK 1857 ROBINSON CRUSOE GULLY, VIC, AUS [35391] : 1910+ SYDNEY, NSW, AUS [37119] : 1797+ LONG POINT, ONT, CAN [34235] : PRE 1880 LAN, ENG [34958] : PRE 1850 NRY, ENG [35620] : 1800 LAN, ENG [35873] : 1820 BROUGHTON IN FURNACE, LAN, ENG [36798] : C1780 WAKEFIELD, YKS, ENG [37508] : 1830-1860 BATH, SOM, ENG [38377] : PRE 1835 BALLYWALTER, DOW, IRL [36264] : 1800-1837 DOW, IRL [36958] : C1750 IRL & SCT [36969] : PRE 1800 FIF, SCT [34571] : 1820+ STRICHEN, ABD, SCT [35027] : 1853 GRETNA GREEN, DFS, SCT [35391] : 1740-1800 AYR, SCT [35813] : ROBERT 1780+ OLD KILPATRICK, DNB, SCT [35848] : 1750+ STONEYKIRK & LUCE, WIG, SCT [37110] : PRE 1800 SCT [37216] : ALL METHLIC & STRICHEN, ABD, SCT [37972] : PRE 1870 GLASGOW, LKS, SCT [38276] : 1760-1837 OXFORD FURNES, NJ, USA [34235] : PRE 1790 CHESTER CO., SC, USA [37817]

PARKE PRE 1880 HEYBRIDGE, ESS, ENG [34261] : ALL DONEGAL, DON, IRL [37127] : PRE 1840 SCHLESIEN [38669] : PRE 1730 OLD KILPATRICK, DNB, SCT [35227]

PARKER 1840+ MONARO, NSW, AUS [33765] : 1898+ WARWICK, QLD, AUS [34805] : 1855-1865 HOBART, TAS, AUS [34910] : THOMAS 1882+ MANGANA, TAS, AUS [34910] : MARY 1930 SYDNEY, NSW, AUS [34967] : 1830+ BRISBANE WATER, NSW, AUS [35226] : MARY ANNE 1881-1897 QUAMBATOOK, VIC, AUS [35522] : 1886+ WEST WALLSEND, NSW, AUS [35800] : JOHN ALL AUS [35828] : MARY C1860 WIMMERA, VIC, AUS [35848] : MARY 1855+ PORTLAND, VIC, AUS [35848] : 1857-1888 BOWRAL, NSW, AUS [35864] : JOHN 1838+ PARRAMATTA, NSW, AUS [36641] : 1851+ KEILOR & NUMURKAH, VIC, AUS [37962] : W.T. 1830+ PETERSHAM, NSW, AUS [38204] : 1800S+ JERRYS PLAINS, NSW, AUS [38490] : 1818-1905 WESTBURY, TAS, AUS & ENG [35195] : 1839-1990 AUS & RSA [35009] : 1870+ WINDSOR, ONT, CAN [34983] : 1820+ ELGIN CO., ONT, CAN [38235] : ALL STAFFORD, STS, ENG [33823] : 1850-1950 BROMLEY, KEN, ENG [34135] : PRE 1850 HATHERLEIGH, DEV, ENG [34218] : 1800 HECKMONDWIKE, WRY, ENG [34328] : PRE 1800 CARLTON IN CRAVEN, WRY, ENG [34675] : 1750-1900 OWERMOIGNE, DOR, ENG [34714] : PRE 1898 LEEDS, YKS, ENG [34805] : C1813 LANGFORD, BRK, ENG [34936] : MARY 1906 LONDON, ENG [34967] : 1700-1900 BRADFORD ON AVON, WIL, ENG [34975] : 1700-1900 TROWBRIDGE, WIL, ENG [34975] : 1780+ HULL, YKS, ENG [35009] : ALL ASPLEY, STS, ENG [35009] : JAMES 1800S GRANTHAM, LIN, ENG [35127] : JAMES C1853 LONDON, MDX, ENG [35127] : JAMES 1800S BURTON ON TRENT, STS, ENG [35127] : ALL BKM, ENG [35139] : PRE 1850 BRISTOL, GLS, ENG [35215] : GEORGE PRE 1886 HAMMERSMITH, LND, ENG [35449] : PRE 1600 ESS, ENG [35642] : PRE 1886 AYLSHAM, NFK, ENG [35800] : 1807 FLETCHING, SSX, ENG [35824] : PRE 1846 KINGSTHORPE, NTH, ENG [35864] : 1810-1842 NEWINGTON, SRY, ENG [35865] : THOMAS 1808-1832 MDX, ENG [35895] : PRE 1865 MDX & HAM, ENG [35895] : SARAH C1865 MDX, ENG [35895] : 1800+ ISLINGTON, LND, ENG [35924] : PRE 1890 BRISTOL, SOM, ENG [36121] : 1700-1800 IDLE & CALVERLEY, WRY, ENG [36263] : WILLIAM C1823 WOLVERHAMPTON, STS, ENG [36274] : 1800-1850 LIVERPOOL, LAN, ENG [36390] : 1800+ ESS & HRT, ENG [36574] : WILLIAM S. 1840+ GLOUCESTER & HASTINGS, GLS & SSX, ENG [36590] : PEACH PRE 1800 BERKELEY & GLOUCESTER, GLS, ENG [36590] : 1720-1820 WAINFLEET, LIN, ENG [36595] : PRE 1830 FRANT, SSX, ENG [36612] : 1650+ BOOTLE, CUL, ENG [36701] : 1845+ IVYBRIDGE, DEV, ENG [36761] : C1850-1900 BARROW IN FURNESS, LAN, ENG [36835] : C1750 HOBY, LEI, ENG [37053] : 1750S CHELSEA, LND, ENG [37145] : ALL BANWELL, SOM, ENG [37164] : JOHN PRE 1852 SSX, ENG [37210] : 1700+ ALLER & CURRY RIVEL, SOM, ENG [37322] : 1700-1800 SEVENOAKS, KEN, ENG [37365] : PRE 1745 ALTON, HAM, ENG [37420] : EDWIN 1811+ COLCHESTER, ESS, ENG [37443] : 1800+ NEWHALL, DBY, ENG [37552] : PRE 1900 ENG [37595] : EMILY 1860-1954 CHELTENHAM, GLS, ENG [37614] : PRE 1820 LAN & DBY, ENG [37739] : 1700-1837 UTTOXETER & INGESTRE, STS, ENG [37762] : C1870-1930 BATTERSEA, LND, ENG [37778] : PRE 1880 ABBOTSLEY, BDF, ENG [37780] : C1885 WANSTEAD, ESS, ENG [37780] : PRE 1875 PEMBRIDGE, HEF, ENG [37816] : 1700-1850 BOOTLE, CUL, ENG [37858] : 1600-1900 WASHINGTON & FINDON AREA, SSX, ENG [37859] : C1700 NEEN SOLLARS, SAL, ENG [37918] : C1800 LONDON, MDX, ENG [37918] : 1840-1880 BAGBOROUGH, SOM, ENG [37983] : HERBERT D. 1915+ HULL, ERY, ENG [38280] : PRE 1900 FEN DISTRICT, LIN, ENG [38280] : JOHN ROBERT 1860+ WISBECH, CAM, ENG [38280] : PRE 1900 WISBECH, CAM, ENG [38280] : JAMES JOHN 1854+ WISBECH, CAM, ENG [38280] : 1700-1900 EXETER, DEV, ENG [38579] : ALL CHS, ENG & AUS [35518] : PRE 1840 LIM & CLA, IRL [33765] : PRE 1840 ENNISCORTHY, WEX, IRL [35132] : PRE 1830 IRL [35226] : WILLIAM C1830 PORT STEWART, DRY, IRL [35848] : 1800+ ANT, IRL [36304] : PRE 1828 SPRINGFIELD, FER, IRL [37035] : 1800-1850 KILLENE, WEM, IRL [37188] : 1800 BALLINASLOE, GAL, IRL [37791] : 1800 DUBLIN, IRL [37791] : 1844 DUMBARTON, DNB, SCT [35808] : 1640+ NJ, USA [34408] : C1855 MD, USA [36116] : BEN 1759-1836 NELSON & HARDIN, KY, USA [37527] : 1960S USA [37778] : 1850-1860 BUXTON, ME, USA [38099] : SARAH ELIZ. 1851-1924 SACRAMENTO, CA, USA [38183] : ANDREW (JACK) PRE 1903 PHILLIPS, ME, USA [38477] : C1850 CAE, WLS [36803] : ALL WORLDWIDE [34471]

PARKERSON 1700-1800S ENG [36837] : 1830-1850 OH, USA [38137]

PARKES 1860+ SYDNEY, NSW, AUS [35360] : 1850S-1860S MILA & BOMBALA, NSW, AUS [35777] : 1850-72 IPSWICH, QLD, AUS [37171] : 1870+ TOWNSVILLE, QLD, AUS [37171] : ALL DENDERMONDE, OVL, BEL [37171] : PRE 1870 CHARLOTTE TOWN, PEI, CAN [38116] : C1767

HALESOWEN, WOR, ENG [33924] : PRE 1800 DBY, ENG [36172] : PRE 1800 SHEFFIELD, WRY, ENG [36172] : ALL EAST LONDON, MDX, ENG [36379] : 1830+ BERMONDSEY, SRY, ENG [36803] : C1825 NORTHFIELD, WOR, ENG [36876] : 1800+ WEST BROMWICH, STS, ENG [36987] : PRE 1900 MANSFIELD, NTT, ENG [37171] : 1500+ HEATHFIELD, SSX, ENG [37206] : PRE 1860 WESTMINSTER, MDX, ENG [37729] : C1840-1930 POPLAR, LND, ENG [37752] : 1800-1870 ST PANCRAS, MDX, ENG [37752] : RICHARD 1818 BIRMINGHAM, WAR, ENG [38122] : PRE 1840 DROMORE, DOW, IRL [33884] : 1900S YELLOWSTONE, WY, USA [37171] : 1900+ DULUTH, MN, USA [37171] : 1950+ LOS ANGELES, CA, USA [37171] : RICHARD 1863 PHILADELPHIA, PA, USA [38122]

PARKHOUSE 1830-1856 HALBERTON & TIVERTON, DEV, ENG [38761]

PARKHURST PRE 1880 CAMBERWELL, LND, ENG [35011]

PARKHURSTE PRE 1630 SHERE, SRY, ENG [36179]

PARKIN PRE 1874 BRADFORD, WRY, ENG [33943] : 1850 SHEFFIELD, WRY, ENG [36480] : 1700-1850 EXETER, DEV, ENG [36988] : 1700-1850 ATHERINGTON, DEV, ENG [36988] : PRE 1800 BOSTON, LIN, ENG [37371] : 1800+ BARWICK IN ELMET, WRY, ENG [37426] : 1819+ MIDDLETON TYAS, NRY, ENG [37635] : PRE 1880 WAKEFIELD, WRY, ENG [37708] : 1800+ NBL, ENG [37993] : 1820-1884 HOYLAND & ECCLESFIELD, YKS, ENG & AUS [35365]

PARKINSON PRE 1900 VIC, AUS [34268] : 1860-1890 BRUNSWICK, VIC, AUS [34793] : 1841+ MUSWELLBROOK, NSW, AUS [37136] : 1850+ SA, AUS [37913] : PRE 1850 MANCHESTER, LAN, ENG [34268] : ALL LANCASTER & HALTON, LAN, ENG [34732] : 1760 DANBY WISKE, NRY, ENG [34793] : 1795 TRIMDON, DUR, ENG [34793] : ALL BOTTON, LAN, ENG [34837] : ALL STOCKPORT, CHS, ENG [34837] : C1833 LONDON, ENG [35121] : PRE 1800 FYLDE, LAN, ENG [36073] : PRE 1920 LEI, NTT & WAR, ENG [36216] : PRE 1855 LONDON, ENG [36766] : PRE 1800 GREENWICH, KEN, ENG [36810] : PRE 1841 CATON, LAN, ENG [37136] : 1839-1953 MANCHESTER, LAN, ENG [37263] : PRE 1682 GOOSNARGH, LAN, ENG [37706] : PRE 1870 INCH, DOW, IRL [34895] : ALL BELFAST, IRL [36094] : C1824 IRL [37263] : PRE 1835 INCH & DOWNPATRICK, DOW, IRL [37913] : C1770 ULSTER, IRL [38769] : ALL GLASGOW, SCT [36094] : 1854 OKMULGEE, OK, USA [38012] : 1770+ PA, USA [38769]

PARKISON 1814+ MADISON CO., OH, USA [38318] : 1880S+ GUTHRIE CO., IA, USA [38318] : 1850S+ ROSEDALE, IN, USA [38318]

PARKS ALL SHOREDITCH, LND, ENG [34820] : 1900-1960 TOLWORTH, SRY, ENG [36786] : 1860+ HAILSHAM, SSX, ENG [36786] : PRE 1750 STS & DBY, ENG [37098] : 1740+ BATTLE, SSX, ENG [37260] : 1800+ HANLEY, STS, ENG [38013] : C1750-1820 DUMFRIES, DFS, SCT [36355] : 1820-1900 JEFFERSON CO., IN, USA [36355] : 1820 ALLEGHANY, NY, USA [38143] : PRE 1900 USA & CAN [36933]

PARLE C1840 WEX, IRL [37697]

PARLEE ALL CAN & USA [34494]

PARLETT PRE 1800 FAREHAM, HAM, ENG [36396] : GERTRUDE 1898-90 LONDON, ENG [37926]

PARLIAMENT 1788-1900 MT VIEW, ONT, CAN [37011] : LYDIA 1800-1900 PRINCE EDWARD CO., ONT, CAN [37567] : LYDIA 1778+ MA, USA [37567]

PARLOW PRE 1880 BRD [38238]

PARMENTER 1900S MOSS VALE, NSW, AUS [35567] : 1830+ BERRIMA, NSW, AUS [37136] : C1780 STAMBOURNE, ESS, ENG [33796] : PRE 1800 ESS, ENG [33998] : PRE 1800 SFK, ENG [33998] : C1835 LONDON, ENG [35350]

PARMENTIER 1770-1850 DUCHESS CO., NY, USA [37591]

PARMER ALL MILDENHALL, SFK, ENG [36955]

PARNABY ALL ROTHWELL, MIDDLETON, YKS, ENG [38473] : ALL STONEGRAVE, HOVINGHAM, YKS, ENG [38473]

PARNELL PRE 1800 COMBE PALFORD, DEV, ENG [34576] : 1800+ KINGSTON, SRY, ENG [34852] : 1750+ OLVESTON, GLS, ENG [35499] : ALL HOLM HELE, NFK, ENG [36743] : PRE 1900 COVENTRY, WAR, ENG [37225] : 1800-1900 SPALDING, LIN, ENG [37378]

PARNHAM PRE 1820 MANSFIELD WOODHOUSE, NTT, ENG [34612]

PARNWELL 1920+ ISLINGTON, MDX, ENG [35725]

PARR 1833+ LAUNCESTON, TAS, AUS [36296] : 1845+ NIAGARA, ONT, CAN [33908] : 1850+ CAMDEN TOWN & TUFNEL PARK, LND, ENG [34669] : 1859+ SOUTHWARK, SRY, ENG [35418] : 1847+ DEPTFORD, KEN, ENG [35418] : 1895+ TILEHURST, BRK, ENG [35418] : 1853+ WALWORTH, SRY, ENG [35418] : 1871+ BATTERSEA, SRY, ENG [35418] : C1800 PRESCOT, LAN, ENG [36112] : 1812+ CARLTON COLVILLE, SFK, ENG [36296] : C1800 LEI, ENG [37770] : PRE 1800 WIGAN, LAN, ENG [38708] : 1700 ESSEX, VA, USA [38027] : 1870-1920 EL PASO & CORPUS CHRISTI, TX, USA [38312] : C1869 SACRAMENTO & GRASS VALLEY, CA, USA [38746]

PARRATT 1780+ NOTTINGHAM, NTT, ENG [37391]

PARR-BURMAN 1880-1916 EAST LONDON & DURBAN, RSA [36559] : ALL WORLDWIDE [36559]

PARRCELLS PRE 1837 ALVERSTOKE, HAM, ENG [36475]

PARRELL 1800-1900 PLACENTIA BAY, NFD, CAN [35103] : 1780-1850 IRL [35103]

PARRETT PRE 1800 ROCHESTER, KEN, ENG [36588] : 1853+ NEWBERG, OR, USA [35468]

PARRIS PRE 1870 MEMBURY & YARCOMBE, DEV, ENG [35701]

PARRISH PRE 1856 LONDON, ENG [35047] : 1750+ LIN, ENG [35812] : PRE 1850 WOODFORD, ESS, ENG [37097] : 1778-1850 GA & FL, USA [38340]

PARROT RICHARD 1616 VA, USA [38122]

PARROTT 1822+ SYDNEY & MAITLAND, NSW, AUS [34786] : 1824 NEWINGTON, SRY, ENG [34677] : 1790-1920 NJ, VA & MO, USA [38050]

PARRY 1860+ LISMORE, VIC, AUS [34695] : 1852+ GOSFORD, NSW, AUS [35419] : 1800+ HEREFORD, HEF, ENG [33814] : 1850+ IBSTOCK & MARKFIELD, LEI, ENG [34329] : 1550-1750 LONDON, WAR & WOR, ENG [35305] : PRE 1900 PLYMOUTH, DEV, ENG [35339] : PRE 1838 LIVERPOOL, LAN, ENG [35419] : 1700-1860 ENG [35581] : 1750+ LIVERPOOL, ENG [36811] : PRE 1800 DEVONPORT & PLYMOUTH, DEV, ENG [37740] : 1800S AYMESTREY, HEF, ENG [37833] : 1750-1800 ROCHDALE, LAN, ENG [38259] : C1820 FESTINIOG, MER, WLS [33918] : PRE 1875 TREHAFOD, GLA, WLS [35333] : PRE 1906 MON, WLS [35895] : DAVID 1724-1807 NEFYN, CAE, WLS [36590] : PRE 1840 BANGOR, CAE, WLS [36986] : 1750-1900 ABERDARON, CAE, WLS [37858]

PARSELL ALL KYNETON & TUNGAMAH, VIC, AUS [35379] : ALL HITCHIN, HRT, ENG [35379]

PARSLEY 1800S CONGRESBURY, SOM, ENG [37729]

PARSLOW PRE 1720 CAM, COALEY, GLS, ENG [37101]

PARSONAGE ALL CANNOCK, STS, ENG [36031]

PARSONS WILLIAM 1836-1876 GLEBE & SYDNEY, NSW, AUS [33933] : 1800S PENGUIN, TAS, AUS [35377] : 1870+ DALBY, QLD, AUS [35807] : ANNIE 1858+ MOREE, NSW, AUS [38083] : WILLIAM 1895-1925 MOREE, NSW, AUS [38083] : MALCOLM 1860+ COOGEE BAY, NSW, AUS [38083] : C1855+ SINGLETON, NSW, AUS [38541] : 1840+ HARBOUR GRACE, NFD, CAN [34349] : PRE 1850 CARPONEAR, NFD, CAN [38412] : PRE 1850 WIL, ENG [33953] : 1826+ LND, ENG [34036] : PRE 1800 LONDON, ENG [34112] : 1700-1850 SANDRIDGE, HRT, ENG [34411] : PRE 1818 SOM, ENG [34421] : ALL MALMESBURY, WIL, ENG [34466] : ALL HIGH LITTLETON, SOM, ENG [34466] : ALL HULLAVINGTON, WIL, ENG [34466] : ALL BATH, SOM, ENG [34466] : ALL HULLAVINGTON & MALMESBURY, WIL, ENG [34484] : C1770 HORSINGTON, SOM, ENG [34581] : 1750+ WEYMOUTH, DOR, ENG [34714] : 1800S READING, BRK, ENG [34715] : 1650+ KINGSSTANLEY,BLAISDON,NEWENT, GLS, ENG [34747] : 1700-1900 POYNINGS, SSX, ENG [34749] : 1840+ BOSWORTHFIELD, WAR, ENG [34777] : 1797 ST JUILOT, CON, ENG [34808] : PRE 1850 SOUTHAMPTON, HAM, ENG [34836] : PRE 1820 WINCANTON, SOM, ENG [34836] : PRE 1820+ CHARLTON ADAM, SOM, ENG [35412] : C1800 AYLMERTON, NFK, ENG [35560] : 1852 WATERLOO, SRY, ENG [35720] : 1887 CLAPHAM, SRY, ENG [35720] : 1760-1860 CON, ENG [35916] : PRE 1840 WINKFIELD, BRK, ENG [35949] : 1900S ISLINGTON, LND, ENG [36055] : 1900S TOTTENHAM, LND, ENG [36055] : 1800+ CINDERFORD, GLS, ENG [36058] : 1780 BOLNEY, SSX, ENG [36384] : 1754+ NORTH EAST AREA, DOR, ENG [36400] : JOHN PRE 1841 ENG [36532] : 1600-1700 TAKELEY, ESS, ENG [37250] : ALL LYTCHETT MATRAVERS, DOR, ENG [37287] : PRE 1800 DOR & SOM, ENG [37771] : PRE 1890 ROCHE & ST AUSTELL, CON, ENG [37814] : PRE 1860 BROMLEY, LND, ENG [37871] : PRE 1850 LND, ENG [38746] : PRE 1850 CAV, IRL [35330] : JOHN 1815-1870 DUBLIN, IRL [38724] : PRE 1896 BARKLY EAST, CAPE, RSA [36459] : 1650+ YORK, ME, USA [36931]

PARTIN 1770-1794 IRL [38340]

PARTINGTON PRE 1850 GLS, ENG [33869] : C1706 PRESTWICH, LAN, ENG [33917] : C1785 LITTLE HULTON, LAN, ENG [36742] : 1800+ MANCHESTER, LAN, ENG [36818] : C1848 MIDDLETON, LAN, ENG [38284]

PARTNER ALL ESS, ENG [34493]

PARTON PRE 1850 WELLINGTON, SAL, ENG [34711] : PRE 1800 WELLINGTON, SAL, ENG [37736]

PARTRIDGE 1900+ EIDSVOLD & MANY PEAKS, QLD, AUS [35395] : 1850+ MORPETH, NSW, AUS [35395] : 1820-1890 ST THOMAS, ONT, CAN [34073] : 1860-1940 TORONTO, ONT, CAN [34525] : PRE 1800 DEV, ENG [33948] : 1750-1820 DEV, ENG [34073] : 1750-1820 CREDITON, DEV, ENG [34073] : PRE 1800 WEST BROMWICH, STS, ENG [34139] : ALL TRESHAM, GLS, ENG [34466] : 1800+ LONDON, ENG [34608] : PRE 1860 CREDITON, DEV, ENG [34958] : THOMAS PRE 1797 HOUGHTON REGIS, BDF, ENG [34992] : 1700+ HARDINGTON & MANDEVILLE, SOM, ENG [35395] : PRE 1750 DEV, ENG [35866] : 1840+ ROTHERHITHE, LND, ENG [36615] : PRE 1900 CLERKENWELL, LND, ENG

[37261] : 1800 BURES, SFK, ENG [37928] : 1600-1900 MIDLANDS, ENG [38278] : 1860+ MARTON, NZ [34608]

PASCALL 1792 DOVER, KEN, ENG [36781] : 1800S HRT & STS, ENG & WLS [37525] : ALL WORLDWIDE [36781]

PASCO PRE 1830 FALMOUTH, CON, ENG [34804]

PASCOE 1900+ ROCKHAMPTON, QLD, AUS [35405] : 1868+ ROCKHAMPTON, QLD, AUS [37982] : PRE 1863 SYDNEY, NSW, AUS [37982] : PRE 1800 WENDRON, CON, ENG [34753] : PRE 1800 WENDRON, CON, ENG [35045] : 1800S TRURO, CON, ENG [35076] : 1864+ LONDON, ENG [35193] : ALL SITHNEY, CON, ENG [35500] : C1770 WENDRON & SITHNEY, CON, ENG [35576] : 1600+ WENDRON, CON, ENG [35587] : PRE 1850 LONDON, MDX, ENG [35862] : ELIZA JANE 1800-1848 SITHNEY & WENDRON, CON, ENG [36814] : 1874 BUDOCK, CON, ENG [37975] : PAUL 1845-1870 ENG [38324] : SIR EDWIN 1850-1930 ENG [38324] : 1850-1870 KEWEENAW CO., MI, USA [38009]

PASFIELD C1575 ENG [34395]

PASH ALL DEV, ENG [37411]

PASHLER 1878+ LONGWARRY EAST, VIC, AUS [34430]

PASHLEY PRE 1800 LONDON, MDX, ENG [36379]

PASKA ALL FALKENBURG & DARMBURG, POM, GER [37607]

PASKE 1700S ESS, ENG [35994] : ALL FALKENBURG & DARMBURG, POM, GER [37607]

PASKINS 1785-1900S SOUTHAMPTON & IOW, HAM, ENG [34458]

PASLOW 1800+ BATH, SOM, ENG [35566]

PASMORE 1845 ENG [37493]

PASS 1800+ NS, CAN & ENG [34500] : PRE 1900 LIN & NTT, ENG [34335]

PASSFIELD C1870 TAMWORTH, NSW, AUS [37944]

PASSINGHAM ALL BRIGHTON & HOVE, SSX, ENG [34057] : 1800+ BUCOCK, CON, ENG [34057]

PASSINIER ALL WORLDWIDE [37803]

PASSMORE 1850+ BARNSTAPLE, DEV, ENG [35586] : 1830S WITHYCOMBE, SOM, ENG [36138] : C1819 HAM, ENG [36859] : PRE 1790 BODMIN, CON, ENG [38389]

PASTORET 1865-1875 KEWEENAW CO., MI, USA [38009]

PASTORIN 1800+ GENOA, ITL [36934]

PATCH ALL ENG [33937] : PRE 1865 ENG [34543] : 1597+ PETHERTON, SOM, ENG [37802]

PATCHETT 1800+ WAR & WOR, ENG [36462]

PATCHING 1890S SHOREHAM, SSX, ENG [36486]

PATE 1820+ SYDNEY, NSW, AUS [34978] : PRE 1830+ BALDOCK, HRT, ENG [35105] : PRE 1800 LONG SUTTON, LIN, ENG [37371] : 1740+ INVERESK, MLN, SCT [33986] : PRE 1790 SHOTTS, LKS, SCT [34384] : JOHN 1800-1811 MARY GREEN, LKS, SCT [36678] : GEORGE C1750-1840 LKS, SCT [38437]

PATELLE NORMAN C1904+ VIC, AUS [38567]

PATEMAN PRE 1798 LONG BENNINGTON, LIN, ENG [34765] : PRE 1800 EAST PECKHAM, KEN, ENG [38383]

PATEN 1750-1860 AYLESBURY, BKM, ENG [35196]

PATENAUDE ALL CAN & USA [36539]

PATERSON 1846+ GEELONG, VIC, AUS [34922] : ARCHIBALD 1847-1893 CLARE & KADINA, SA, AUS [35132] : 1860+ SCOTCHMANS LEAD, VIC, AUS [35525] : 1854+ BALLARAT, VIC, AUS [36193] : 1850+ LEARMONTH, VIC, AUS [36627] : 1819+ TORONTO, ONT, CAN [36652] : 1837 ALNWICK, NBL, ENG [34540] : 1780-1805 MADRAS, INDIA

[34695] : 1790+ KIRKINRIOLA, ANT, IRL [35989] : PRE 1900 DUMFRIES, DFS, SCT [33776] : C1690 LAMINGTON, LKS, SCT [34118] : PRE 1855 BONHILL, DNB, SCT [34533] : PRE 1800 FINDON, KCD, SCT [34608] : PRE 1840 KNOCKBAIN, ROC, SCT [34613] : PRE 1840 ABBY ST BATHANS, BEW, SCT [34648] : 1700+ LESLIE, FIF, SCT [34768] : JOHN 1791+ NEW KILPATRICK, DNB & CAI, SCT [34881] : 1800+ WISHAW & MOTHERWELL, LKS, SCT [34934] : PRE 1860 SCT [34958] : 1825 BALLATER, ABD, SCT [35041] : 1700-1800 ABERDOUR, FIF, SCT [35094] : PRE 1860 GLASGOW, SCT [35113] : PRE 1870 BEW, SCT [35400] : 1850S TURRIFF, ABD, SCT [35415] : 1843 SCT [35906] : 1870+ EDINBURGH, MLN, SCT [35914] : JANET PRE 1900 PETERHEAD, ABD, SCT [35917] : 1900+ BAILLIESTON, LKS, SCT [35969] : 1800+ DUNFERMLINE, FIF, SCT [35969] : ALL KILMARNOCK, AYR, SCT [36193] : C1700-1750 N & S LEITH, MLN, SCT [36327] : PRE 1775 COCKBURNSPATH, BEW, SCT [36405] : PRE 1750 KILMARNOCK, AYR, SCT [36436] : PRE 1870 SCT [36627] : PRE 1853 ALLOA, CLK, SCT [36627] : PRE 1819 BLANTYRE, LKS, SCT [36652] : HUGH 1780-1830 KNOCKBAIN & ROSEMARKIE, ROC, SCT [36783] : 1800S SELKIRK, SEL, SCT [36874] : PRE 1780 ABBOTSHALL, FIF, SCT [37333] : JANE C1810 FALKIRK, STI, SCT [37424] : C1890 KILMARNOCK, AYR, SCT [37556] : THOMAS 1820S SCT [38281] : THOMAS 1820S SCT [38281] : PRE 1800 DUNBAR, ELN, SCT [38383] : JAMES 1780+ MIDMAR, ABD, SCT [38400] : 1800S AYR, SCT [38490] : ALEX 1800+ LEITH, SCT [38540]

PATEY ALL LND, ENG [36501]

PATIENT C1800 CORTON, WIL, ENG [35563]

PATMAN PRE 1798 LONG BENNINGTON, LIN, ENG [34765]

PATMORE ALL HOBART & SCOTTSDALE, TAS, AUS & NZ [35432] : 1800-1850 ORILLIA, ONT, CAN [36676] : C1840 NEWCASTLE UNDER LYME, STS, ENG [34880] : PRE 1800 BISHOPS STORTFORD, HEF, ENG [36676] : C1840-C1900 DOVER, KEN, ENG [37634]

PATNODE ALL CAN & USA [36539]

PATON C1827-1876 PARRAMATTA, NSW, AUS [34942] : 1816+ PARRAMATTA & MAITLAND, NSW, AUS [35420] : 1850+ MITTA MITTA, VIC, AUS [35719] : 1750-1860 AYLESBURY, BKM, ENG [35196] : ALL DOW, IRL [34938] : C1740 LANARK, LKS, SCT [34118] : 1750S AYR, SCT [34367] : PRE 1890 STEVENSTON, AYR, SCT [34913] : PRE 1800 CRAIG, ANS, SCT [35127] : 1800+ MONTROSE, ANS, SCT [35127] : PRE 1850 BEITH, AYR, SCT [35719] : PRE 1840 AYR, SCT [37434] : 1800+ AVONSIDE, STI, SCT [37480] : 1753+ LANARK, LKS, SCT [38492]

PATRICK ALL TALBRAGAR & GULGONG, NSW, AUS [33765] : PRE 1900 ISLINGTON, MDX, ENG [36019] : PRE 1830 LONDON, ENG [37663] : PRE 1850 FRENSHAM, SRY, ENG [37743] : PRE 1850 BINSTED, HAM, ENG [37743] : PRE 1830 IRL & USA [38043] : 1890S BALLINGRY, FIF, SCT [34605] : 1760-1820 BANTON, STI, SCT [36763] : 1780 SCT [37006]

PATRICKSON PRE 1822 FERBANE, OFF, IRL [34781]

PATRIE PRE 1870 NEGUAC, NB, CAN & USA [38447]

PATRONE PRE 1892 SAN FRANCISCO, CA, USA & ITL [38570]

PATRONI 1850S SERINO, ITL [34574]

PATRU PRE 1600 GENEVA, GE, CH [38348]

PATRY 1830-1950S QUE & ONT, CAN [34202]

PATSCHULL 1800+ POGORCH, GER [35315]

PATTEN PRE 1800 SITHNEY, CON, ENG [33814] : C1800 ESS, ENG [35349] : 1841 HARDINGTON MANDEVILLE, SOM, ENG [37378] : PRE 1700 ESS & SFK, ENG [37712] : PRE 1700 HELSTON, CON, ENG [38180] : PRE 1830 EAST CHINNOCK, SOM, ENG [38457] : 1840-1850S MILLS CO., IA, USA [36729] : 1830S HANCOCK CO., IL, USA [36729]

PATTENDEN PRE 1809 HAILSHAM, SSX, ENG [35020] : 1785+ HAILSHAM, SSX, ENG [35436] : C1800 LND, ENG [38397]

PATTERSON 1900-1990 MELBOURNE, VIC, AUS [33778] : ISABELLA PRE 1856 MCLAREN VALE, SA, AUS [33941] : 1850+ HASTINGS, VIC, AUS [34424] : 1850-1920 BALLARAT, VIC, AUS [34551] : 1800S NUMURKAH, VIC, AUS [34570] : 1859+ PORTLAND, VIC, AUS [35599] : PRE 1859 WYNDHAM, WA, AUS [35599] : PRE 1910 BALLARAT, VIC, AUS [35796] : ALL BATHURST, NSW, AUS [36613] : 1840-60 GIPPSLAND, VIC, AUS [36648] : PRE 1868 GYMPIE, QLD, AUS [37315] : PRE 1880 LAMBTON CO., ONT, CAN [38042] : C1765+ GASPE, QUE, CAN [38406] : ALL YKS, ENG [34131] : 1885-1900S WHITEHAVEN, CUL, ENG [34680] : 1763 BREDE, SSX, ENG [35260] : 1830-1900 TERRINGTON ST CLEMENT, NFK, ENG [36394] : PRE 1900 NBL, ENG [36934] : THOMAS 1820S LAN, ENG [38281] : 1850+ DON, IRL [33973] : 1840S-60S ULSTER, IRL [35243] : 1600-1820+ RAPHOE, DON, IRL [35759] : 1790+ BALLYSCULLION, ANT, IRL [35989] : PRE 1863 BELFAST, ANT, DOW, IRL [36242] : ALL BANBRIDGE, DOW, IRL [36428] : ALL BELFAST, DOW, IRL [37303] : PRE 1850 DON & FER, IRL [37446] : 1750-1800 DRUMLANE, CAV, IRL [37613] : 1600-1870 RAPHOE, DON, IRL [37784] : PRE 1840 ARM, IRL [37913] : 1840+ LISNARABLE, TYR, IRL [38508] : 1885-1900 RUNUNGA, CHCH, NZ [34680] : 1860-1870 HASTINGS, NZ [36845] : WILLIAM PRE 1860 DFS & AYR, SCT [34197] : PRE 1820 RICCARTON, SCT [34816] : 1700+ BAN, SCT [35627] : PRE 1600+ PER, SCT [35759] : PRE 1850 ALLOA, CLK, SCT [35853] : 1750-1900 DFS, SCT [36130] : PRE 1841 EDINBURGH, SCT [36613] : C1813 CAMBUSLANG, LKS, SCT [36644] : 1800S MUIRKIRK, AYR, SCT [36648] : 1800S KILWINNING, AYR, SCT [36648] : 1750-1900 AYR & GALSTON, AYR, SCT [36802] : PRE 1780 KIRKCALDY, FIF, SCT [37333] : THOMAS 1820S SCT [38281] : PRE 1859 SWE [35599] : C1750 OXFORD, NY, USA [34395] : LYDIA 1780+ BOSTON, MA, USA [35276] : 1806-1905 SO. CHARLESTON, CLARK CO., OH, USA [35316] : PRE 1800 BUCKS CO., PA, USA [36729] : 1800-1850 BUTLER CO., CH & IN, USA [36913] : ELIZABETH 1820-1850 PORTAGE CO., OH, USA [37784] : ALL IL & KS, USA [38043] : 1730-1800 BRIMFIELD & WARE, MA, USA [38047] : 1800-1840 PARIS & POMPEY, NY, USA [38047] : 1830-1900 ROCHESTER, NY, USA [38047] : 1820-1860 MORGAN, OH, USA [38111] : 1855-1900 ALLAMAKEE, IA, USA [38111] : 1800-1880 CHAUTAUQUA, NY, USA [38529] : 1780+ USA & CAN [35778] : PRE 1900 OH & PA, USA & SCT [35270]

PATTERSON (SEE PATER [34608]

PATTIE PRE 1822 ST ANDREWS, FIF, SCT [34622]

PATTIN PRE 1700 HELSTON, CON, ENG [38180]

PATTINSON 1750-1850 CALDBECK, CUL, ENG [36098]

PATTISON 1883 EDGBASTON, WAR, ENG [34120] : PRE 1850 DUR, ENG [35153] : PRE 1850 EASBY & EASINGTON, NRY & DUR, ENG [36159] : 1600+ PLAWORTH, DUR, ENG [36685] : PRE 1907

NEWCASTLE, NBL, ENG [37704] : 1800S +
WHICKHAM, DUR, ENG [38436] : PRE 1890
GLASGOW, LKS, SCT [34018] : PRE 1840 DFS &
AYR, SCT [34197] : 1832 + DUNOON, ARL, AYR &
DUB, SCT & IRL [35013] : ALL WORLDWIDE
[37738]

PATTISSON C1800 MALDON, ESS, ENG [37449]

PATTON C1850 GEELONG & BALLARAT, VIC, AUS
[37143] : 1850 + WANDONG & KILMORE, VIC,
AUS [37157] : 1850 + HURON CO., ONT, CAN
[34075] : 1830 + PEEL, SIMCOE, ONT, CAN [34982] :
PRE 1845 MANCHESTER, LAN, ENG [36345] :
C1830 CONWAL, DON, IRL [37143] : 1840 +
EDINBURGH, MLN, SCT [37157] : 1750-1850
KIRKWALL, OKI, SCT [37157] : PRE 1860
WASHINGTON CO., IL & OH, USA [37817] : 1800-
1900 DES MOINES, IA & MO, USA [38025] :
REBECCA 1880 BREATHITT CO., KY, USA [38062]
: 1800 + LICKING CO., OH, USA [38240] : C1825
KY, USA [38527]

PATTY JAMES 1840 + NSW, AUS [34973] : 1800 +
BAILIEBOROUGH, CAV, IRL [34973]

PATULLO 1841 + VIC, QLD & NSW, AUS [37962] :
1788 + AUS [37962] : GEORGE PRE 1899 VIC, AUS
[38567] : JAMES C1820 + VIC, AUS [38567] : PRE
1841 DUNDEE AREA, ANS & PER, SCT [37962]

PATUREAU ALL AMBOISE, PL, FRA [36492]

PAUCHONG C1925 LAVENDER BAY, NSW, AUS
[37963]

PAUFREYMAN PRE 1740 LEI, ENG [34258]

PAUL 1860 BLAYNEY, NSW, AUS [34038] : 1800 QLD,
AUS [35465] : 1860 + BALLARAT, VIC, AUS [35489] :
C1872 DALBY, QLD, AUS [35807] : PRE 1855
WINDSOR & SYDNEY, NSW, AUS [37988] : 1800S
SPRINGHILL, NS, CAN [38418] : 1800-1900
POPLAR, MDX, ENG [34135] : 1700-1800 ST
AGNES, CON, ENG [35489] : PRE 1850 STEPNEY,
MDX, ENG [37371] : ALL SEAVINGTON, SOM,
ENG [37378] : 1600-1800 PAUL, CON, ENG [37680] :
1700S REDRUTH, CON, ENG [37921] : PRE 1850
UPTON ON SEVERN, WOR, ENG [38383] : 1860 +
PUHOI & AUCKLAND, NZ [36245] : 1843-1885
KEWEENAW CO., MI, USA [38009] : 1600 + PA, VA
& NC, USA [38326] : THOMAS 1700 +
CURRITOCK, ORANGE & CASWELL, NC, USA
[38326] : 1650-1750 ORANGE & CASWELL, NC,
USA [38326] : 1600 + BARBADOS, W.INDIES [38326]
: ALL WORLDWIDE [38418]

PAULDING 1830S ST CATHERINES, ONT, CAN
[36729] : 1750-1880 NY, USA [36935]

PAULET PRE 1800 HADDENHAM, CAM, ENG
[35391]

PAULEY ALL CON, ENG [36610] : 1800 + BERAGH,
TYR, N IRL [36291]

PAULGER 1900 + YORKTON, SAS, CAN [36716]

PAULHEMUS ALL LYCOMING CO., PA, USA [38035]

PAUL-HUS BRUNO 1844 + ST DAVID, YAMASKA,
QUE, CAN [36723] : PIERRE 1848 + ST
BONAVENTURE, QUE, CAN [36723] : PASCHAL
1796-1818 ST PIERRE DE SOREL, QUE, CAN
[36723]

PAULI 1620 RHENEGGE, WAL, GER [34912]

PAULING PRE 1800 ENG [37739]

PAULL PRE 1820 ST AGNES, CON, ENG [35441] :
PRE 1850 CON, ENG [35540] : ALL ILLOGAN,
CON, ENG [37291] : 1843-1885 KEWEENAW CO.,
MI, USA [38009]

PAULSEN MARIE 1845-1879 SUDERHASTEDT,
SHO, GER [38104] : MARIE 1879-1927 CHICAGO,
COOK, IL, USA [38104]

PAULSON 1810-1860 MANSFIELD, NTT, ENG [34397]
: C1800 KEGWORTH, LEI, ENG [34397] : PRE 1850

LEEDS, WRY, ENG [34397] : 1910 + CLEVELAND,
OH, USA [36325]

PAUMIERE 1580-1660 CHEMIRE EN CHARNIE,
FRA [34514]

PAUW 1700S SCHOUWEN DUIVELAND, ZEL, NL
[38350]

PAVARIN PRE 1930 FONTE ALTO, TREVISO, ITL
[36363]

PAVATT 1810-1860 TN, USA [36349]

PAVEY 1750-1800 HAMPTON, MDX, ENG [34552] :
1830 + BRISTOL, GLS, ENG [35948] : 1882
BRISTOL, GLS, ENG [38210] : 1880-1900 SAN
FRANCISCO, CA, USA [35638] : 1860-1880
BOULDER, CO, USA [35638]

PAVITT 1750-1850 DOR, ENG [37188]

PAVORD 1750-1850 DOR, ENG [37188]

PAWLAK PRE 1900 PO, POL [36941]

PAWLEY C1805 SYDNEY, NSW, AUS [35089] : PRE
1800 GALLOW, NFK, ENG [37737]

PAWSEY 1750 + LONDON &, SFK, ENG [34415]

PAWSON PRE 1840 OTLEY, WRY, ENG [36883] : PRE
1750 PANNAL, YKS, ENG [37610]

PAWTHORNE ALL WORLDWIDE [36420]

PAWTON PRE 1720 SEDGLEY, STS, ENG [36110]

PAXFORD (SEE PAXTON) [34812]

PAXMAN PRE 1930 LONDON, ENG [33883] : JAMES
1800 + SFK, ENG [38423]

PAXTON 1670-1845 FINMERE, OXF, ENG [35030] :
1600-1720 BALLYMONEY, ANT, IRL [38342] :
C1786 PATHHEAD, ELN, SCT [37168] : C1786
GARVALD, ELN, SCT [37168] : C1786 SPOTT, ELN,
SCT [37168] : 1800 LKS, SCT [38478] : ALL WLS
[34812]

PAY PRE 1850 DOVER, KEN, ENG [37652] : ALL
CHARTHAM, KEN, ENG [38497]

PAYAN 1580-1660 PARIS, RPA, FRA [34514]

PAYARD 1840 UCKERMARK POLSSEN, POS, GER
[34940] : 1688-1800 WODDOW, BRA, GER [38377]

PAYLOR 1880-1950 KAMSACK, SAS, CAN [34521]

PAYMENT PRE 1685 SOHAM, CAM, ENG [34445]

PAYN 1800 + ST HELIER, JSY, CHI [36758] : PRE
1900 KEN, ENG [36387]

PAYNE 1850 + BEECHWORTH & BENALLA, VIC,
AUS [34789] : C1890 + BUNBURY, WA, AUS [35053]
: 1861 + BRISBANE, QLD, AUS [35455] : 1840 +
MAITLAND & BURRAWANG, NSW, AUS [35511] :
1881 + WILLOWIE, SA, AUS [35811] : 1889 +
MELBOURNE, VIC, AUS [35811] : ALL BEGA,
NSW, AUS [37176] : ALL MT MORT & IPSWICH,
QLD, AUS [37176] : 1820 + SIMCOE CO., ONT,
CAN [34465] : 1700-1800 ST HELIER, JSY, CHI
[34552] : JAMES THOMAS PRE 1870 LONDON,
ENG [33765] : ALL SOUTHAMPTON, HAM, ENG
[33802] : 1808 + LIN, ENG [33867] : C1820
WOOTTON BASSETT, WIL, ENG [33918] : ALL
DOVER, ENG [34131] : PRE 1810 SOUTHAMPTON
& LONDON, ENG [34240] : PRE 1900 ENG [34317] :
PRE 1850 NEWMARKET, SFK, ENG [34465] : 1700-
1800S CHELMSFORD, ESS, ENG [34483] : ANN
1764 TRING, HRT, ENG [34539] : 1816 +
FELTHAM, LND, ENG [34577] : MARY ANN PRE
1874 + LONDON, ENG [34592] : 1800 +
WORTHING, SSX, ENG [34749] : ALL
HOUGHTON CONQUEST & STOTFOLD, BDF,
ENG [34789] : ALL HARLINGTON & SUNDON,
BDF, ENG [34789] : C1854 EAST HORNDEN, ESS,
ENG [34893] : C1850 NTT, ENG [35034] : 1770S
EAST GRINSTEAD, SSX, ENG [35065] : PRE 1870
PECKHAM, SRY, ENG [35077] : PRE 1850 LEE
LEWISHAM, LND, ENG [35173] : 1832 + BURY ST
EDMUNDS, SFK, ENG [35455] : 1800-1870
BIRMINGHAM, WAR, ENG [35456] : C1856 SOM,

ENG [35811] : PRE 1820 CORFE CASTLE, DOR,
ENG [35866] : C1803 STAPLEHURST, KEN, ENG
[35872] : ALL BANWELL, SOM, ENG [36012] : 1700-
1800+ LEI, ENG [36038] : 1800+ STEYNING, SSX,
ENG [36219] : 1796+ FROME, SOM, ENG [36276] :
PRE 1779 WEST LYDFORD, SOM, ENG [36386] :
PRE 1840 SAL, ENG [36480] : PRE 1760 EASTRY,
KEN, ENG [36532] : 1750+ HEF, ENG [36552] : PRE
1800 DUNSFORD, DEV, ENG [36662] : 1700-1830
FROME, WARMINSTER, WIL, ENG [36688] : 1731
BOURTON ON THE WATER, GLS, ENG [36797] :
1850+ LYMINGTON, HAM, ENG [36989] : 1750-
1850 BENTLEY, SFK, ENG [37042] : WILLIAM
C1792 BANNINGHAM, NFK, ENG [37052] : 1900
NORWICH, NFK, ENG [37052] : PRE 1884
STAVELEY, DBY & WAR, ENG [37267] : 1800+
WALLSEND, NBL, ENG [37395] : PRE 1825
LIVERPOOL, LAN, ENG [37463] : 1800-1900
WESTMINSTER, MDX, ENG [37747] : PRE 1850
WIL, ENG [37804] : PRE 1820 INGRAVE, ESS, ENG
[37885] : ALL WESTCAMPBELL, SOM, ENG [37950]
: 1833 LIM, IRL [34785] : 1800+ KILLARGA, LET,
IRL [35511] : 1915 KILKEEL, DOW, IRL [35529] :
1877 KILKEEL, DOW, IRL [35529] : 1840S
CLONCUMBER, KID, IRL [36862] : C1850
CHRISTIAN CO., KY, USA [37527] : PRE 1785
CULPEPER, VA, USA [37819] : C1856 WLS & ENG
[35811] : ALL WORLDWIDE [36651]

PAYNTER 1850+ BRAIDWOOD & QUEANBEYAN,
NSW, AUS [35736] : PRE 1850 REDRUTH, CON,
ENG [34187] : 1800-1850 LAMBETH, SRY, ENG
[35595] : PRE 1850 IWERNE COURTNAY, DOR,
ENG [37105] : C1720-1750 ST IVES, CON, ENG
[37842]

PAYTEN 1800+ SYDNEY, NSW, AUS [37500]

PAYZE ALL ENG [38375]

PEACH 1700S ELLINGTON, HUN, ENG [33886] :
1800+ HUN, ENG [35121] : 1700 ALFRETON, DBY,
ENG [36018] : PRE 1810 STAFFORD, STS, ENG
[36701] : 1700-1850 DBY, ENG [36824] : ALL DOR,
ENG [37063] : ALL LEI & RUT, ENG [37738] : 1780S
BRIGSTOCK, NTH, ENG [37780] : PRE 1800 IOW,
ENG [38700]

PEACHEY 1868+ COLLINGWOOD, VIC, AUS [34017]
: C1855 DBY & YKS, ENG [34365] : PRE 1830 BRK,
MDX & SRY, ENG [35846] : 1750+ CAMBRIDGE,
CAM, ENG [36257] : C1780+ GRAVESEND, KEN,
ENG [38279] : PRE 1900 BURWELL & SWAFFHAM
BULBECK, CAM, ENG [38403]

PEACOCK 1840+ CASTLEREAGH RIVER, NSW,
AUS [33923] : 1800-1850 LAUNCESTON, TAS, AUS
[34307] : C1967 MELBOURNE, VIC, AUS [34694] :
1855+ MELBOURNE, VIC, AUS [35238] : 1841+
GEELONG, VIC, AUS [37175] : PRE 1795
SOUTHGATE, MDX, ENG [34115] : 1760+
HISTON, CAM, ENG [34190] : PRE 1775
TERRINGTON, NRY, ENG [34333] : PRE 1800
EASINGWOLD, YKS, ENG [34588] : 1750-1900
BITTON & HANHAM, GLS, ENG [34714] : ALL
FARNDALE, YKS, ENG [35198] : 1830+
CAMBRIDGE, CAM, ENG [35238] : PRE 1830
CHESTERTON, CAM, ENG [35238] : PRE 1865
WHALTON & NEWCASTLE UPON TYNE, NBL,
ENG [35488] : PRE 1700 GRAVENHURST, BDF,
ENG [35967] : 1827+ MANCHESTER, LAN, ENG
[37175] : 1802+ ERY, ENG [37175] : 1827+ REETH,
YKS, ENG [37175] : C1810 LONDON, ENG [37180] :
1750-1850 SWALEDALE, NRY, ENG [37615] :
MARY PRE 1779 HAUGHTON GREEN, LAN,
ENG [38384] : MARY 1779+ MANCHESTER, LAN,
ENG [38384] : PRE 1850 BALLYSHANNON, DON,
IRL [35211] : 1890+ HAWKES BAY, NAPIER, NZ

[33889] : PRE 1837 AYR, SCT [36650] : 1700+
PAISLEY, RFW, SCT [36794] : 1841+ AGY, WLS
[36650] : PRE 1887 LLANGEFNI, AGY, WLS [36650]

PEAGAM ALL WORLDWIDE [36995]

PEAK PRE 1600 MULCHELNEY, SOM, ENG [38135]

PEAKE PRE 1880 CAM & NFK, ENG [36363] : 1849+
ISLEWORTH, LND, ENG [36959] : 1800 MOUNT
BURES, SFK, ENG [37928] : 1800+ WLS [33955]

PEAKIC PRE 1880 SREMSKA MITROVICA,
VOJVODINA, YU [38063]

PEAR 1800S ASTON, WAR, ENG [37299]

PEARCE 1934 BALMAIN, NSW, AUS [34878] : 1915
LEEDERVILLE, WA, AUS [34878] : 1915 BLAIR
ATHOL, QLD, AUS [34878] : 1847 BUNINYONG,
VIC, AUS [34878] : 1850+ SYDNEY, NSW, AUS
[34978] : PRE 1885 VIC, AUS [34978] : 1850S
ADELAIDE, SA, AUS [35136] : C1854+ BALLARAT,
VIC, AUS [35746] : 1847-C1854 ADELAIDE, SA, AUS
[35746] : C1862+ DURHAM LEAD, VIC, AUS
[35746] : 1861+ BEECHWORTH & CHILTERN,
VIC, AUS [36597] : 1855+ BURRA, SA, AUS [36597] :
1794+ SEVEN HILLS, NSW, AUS [38211] : C1850
PLYMOUTH, DEV, ENG [33870] : 1800+ CON,
ENG [33948] : PRE 1900 LEIGH ON SEA, ESS, ENG
[34131] : PRE 1839 SHOREDITCH, MDX, ENG
[34166] : PRE 1776 GOUDHURST & CRANBROOK,
KEN, ENG [34351] : 1750-1870 WOR, ENG [34615] :
1770-1837 WENDOVER, BKM, ENG [34687] : PRE
1866 ST JUST, CON, ENG [34711] : 1880+
PLYMOUTH, DEV, ENG [34754] : ROSE 1943
LONDON, ENG [34790] : 1750-1850 SOM & WIL,
ENG [34801] : PRE 1880 ST KEVERNE &
HELSTON, CON, ENG [34865] : PRE 1840
BRIDGEWATER, SOM, ENG [34897] : PRE 1840
STOGUMBER, SOM, ENG [34897] : 1800S TEMPLE
CLOUD, SOM, ENG [34978] : PRE 1850 GREAT
MISSENDEN, BKM, ENG [35173] : ST
COLUMB MINOR, CON, ENG [35235] : PRE 1830
CAMELEY, SOM, ENG [35368] : C1800
LOCKERLEY, HAM, ENG [35456] : PRE 1835
PENZANCE, CON, ENG [35517] : PRE 1854
REDRUTH, CON, ENG [35536] : STEPHEN PRE
1865 SYDENHAM, KEN, ENG [35725] : C1819+
SAINT BLAZEY, CON, ENG [35746] : PRE 1830
REDRUTH, CON, ENG [35955] : PRE 1820
CLAPHAM, SRY, ENG [36107] : 1775+
PYWORTHY, DEV, ENG [36254] : 1700-1830
KERWIN, CON, ENG [36440] : 1700-1800
MEVAGISSEY, CON, ENG [36538] : PRE 1855
TUCKINGMILL & ROSKEAR, CON, ENG [36597] :
JOHN 1870+ NORTHAM, DEV, ENG [36813] :
1840+ CAMBORNE, KEHELLAND, CON, ENG
[36819] : 1780+ DEV, ENG [36858] : MARY 1650+
OF BRISTOL, GLS, ENG [36890] : 1875+
CHADDLEWORTH, BRK, ENG [36975] : 1820
BRIDGWATER, SOM, ENG [37080] : C1750
RAMSBURY, WIL & HAM, ENG [37335] : PRE 1907
SRY, ENG [37358] : 1850S NOTTING HILL, LND,
ENG [37369] : 1800 WHITECHAPEL, LND, ENG
[37841] : C1760 ST ALBANS, HRT, ENG [37898] :
C1760 ST ALBANS, HRT, ENG [37898] : PRE 1801
COW HONEYBOURNE, WOR, ENG [37909] : C1830
BUDEHAVEN, CON, ENG [38078] : 1780S
CAMBRIDGE, CAM, ENG [38206] : PRE 1794
KINGS LANGLEY, HRT, ENG [38211] : 1700-1900
SWALE MEDWAY, KEN, ENG [38249] : PRE 1884
STRATFORD, ESS, ENG [38412] : 1780+
SELMESTON, SSX, ENG [38549] : 1866+
DUNEDIN, NZ [34711] : C1820 CARDIFF, GLA,
WLS [37144]

PEARCEY 1750-1820 DAMERHAM, WIL, ENG [36155]

PEARCY 1700S LITCHBOROUGH, NTH, ENG [35030]

PEARDON 1800 CON, ENG [36860] : PRE 1790 KILKHAMPTON, CON, ENG [37320]

PEARL PRE 1835 IRL [35649]

PEARMAN 1850+ HOBART, TAS, AUS [37989] : PRE 1800 CAMBERWELL, LND, ENG [34819] : 1800S MAIDSTONE, KEN, ENG [35964] : 1798-1840 WYTHE CO., VA, USA [37029]

PEARNE WILLIAM 1760 ISLE OF SHEPPEY, KEN, ENG [35096] : 1790S WEST LOOE, CON, ENG [35914]

PEARS 1836+ CAMPBELL TOWN, TAS, AUS [33786] : PRE 1872 BUCKINBAR & MOLONG, NSW, AUS [35028]

PEARSALL 1800-1850 MT VIEW, ONT, CAN [37011] : PRE 1825 BIRMINGHAM, WAR, ENG [37736]

PEARSE 1650+ BROADHEMPSTON & CHULMLEIGH, DEV, ENG [34747] : 1650+ SOUTH MOLTON, DEV, ENG [34747] : 1700S WASHFIELD, DEV, ENG [35131] : PRE 1883 WIL, ENG [35536] : C1790-C1850 SSX, ENG [36024] : PRE 1850 DEV, ENG [36052] : 1700 PETHERWIN, CON, ENG [37997]

PEARSEY ALL WORLDWIDE [33975]

PEARSON 1860S HAMILTON, VIC, AUS [34175] : 1870-1890 VIC, AUS [34175] : 1860+ SYDNEY, NSW, AUS [34533] : 1850+ BALLARAT, VIC, AUS [34533] : 1865-1890 NARACOORTE, SA, AUS [35191] : 1900-1915 LOCKHART, NSW, AUS [35191] : 1850-1930 ADELAIDE, SA, AUS [35191] : 1848-1870 KANMANTOO, SA, AUS [35191] : 1910+ THALLON, QLD, AUS [35335] : 1875+ BOURKE, NSW, AUS [35335] : 1800 NIAGARA FALLS, ONT, CAN [34188] : 1800S + LANARK CO., ONT, CAN [37458] : 1830-1900 WOODSTOCK, ONT, CAN [38026] : 1680-1800 TUDELEY & CAPEL, KEN, ENG [33785] : DAMARIS C1830-1850 WATERSIDE, CAM, ENG [34007] : 1600+ NTH, ENG [34062] : ALL ASHENDON, BKM, ENG [34261] : KEZIAH PRE 1823+ GOUDHURST, KEN, ENG [34592] : PRE 1880 TONBRIDGE, KEN, ENG [34671] : 1760S LANERCOST, CUL, ENG [34688] : 1800+ CARLISLE, CUL, ENG [34688] : PRE 1857 STOCKPORT, CHS, ENG [34711] : 1700-1900 BEESTON, NTT, ENG [34729] : 1800+ TWICKENHAM, MDX, ENG [34882] : PRE 1879 BONGATE, WES, ENG [34911] : PRE 1908 FAKENHAM MITFORD, NFK, ENG [34982] : 1853+ STOCKPORT, CHS, ENG [35452] : PRE 1820 ALMONDBURY, WRY, ENG [35733] : C1860 LIVERPOOL, LAN, ENG [35919] : 1765+ WHITEHAVEN, CUL, ENG [35921] : JANE PRE 1819 WISBECH ST MARY, CAM, ENG [36149] : 1800+ CUL, ENG [36368] : PRE 1800 DERBY, DBY, ENG [36493] : LUKE 1800+ NUNNINGTON, YKS, ENG [36609] : 1803+ ORTON, WES, ENG [36620] : 1800-1908 LONDON, ENG [36847] : ALL BRIERLEY HILL, STS, ENG [36998] : 1740+ TICKHILL, WRY, NTT & LIN, ENG [37056] : PRE 1840 BIRMINGHAM, WAR, ENG [37133] : PRE 1850 NEWCASTLE ON TYNE, ENG [37497] : 1700-1852 LONG MELFORD, SFK, ENG [37638] : JOSEPH 1800+ HINCKLEY & WARWICK, ENG [37640] : 1650-1838 ALSTON, CUL, ENG [38026] : PRE 1842 APPLEDORE, KEN, ENG [38389] : 1800+ FRAMPTON, LIN, ENG [38413] : PRE 1825 WHITBY & SCARBOROUGH, NRY, ENG [38580] : ALL NBL & DUR, ENG & USA [38754] : AGNES C1825 ARMAGH, ARM, IRL [34176] : 1700-1860 LETTERKENNY, DON, IRL [37118] : 1750+ KRS, SCT [34054] : 1830S GLASGOW, LKS, SCT [34175] : ALL EDINBURGH, MLN, SCT [34593] : 1780-1840 GLASGOW, LKS, SCT [35191] : 1840+ OKI, SCT

[36892] : 1834+ GLASGOW, SCT & AUS [36238] : 1700 EASTERN SHORE, MD, USA [37582] : PRE 1840 AUGUSTA, GA, USA [38126] : 1835+ MS, USA [38360] : 1795+ SC, USA [38360] : C1870 GRAND RAPIDS, MI, USA [38466] : 1890+ LINCOLN, NE, USA [38552] : PRE 1850 ANTIGUA, W.INDIES [35413]

PEASE ELIZABETH 1856 ESCOMB, DUR, ENG [36367] : ELIZABETH 1833 COUNDON, DUR, ENG [36367] : 1750-1850 NRY, ENG [36472] : C1860 TERREHAUTE, IN, USA [36803]

PEASGOOD PRE 1840 LIMEHOUSE, MDX & LIN, ENG [36099]

PEASLAND ALL WORLDWIDE [33930]

PEASLEY 1804+ PARRAMATTA, NSW, AUS [33930] : SARAH 1816-1841 CHARLESTOWN & CARBONDALE, RI & PA, USA [36948]

PEAT 1700S HOLME CULTRAM, CUL, ENG [36431] : PRE 1850 DURRIS, KCD & ANS, SCT [34360] : PRE 1790 SHOTTS, LKS, SCT [34384] : 1730-1850 LARGO, FIF, SCT [36776] : PRE 1830 LKS, SCT [38437]

PEATE C1788 SHREWSBURY, SAL, ENG [35560]

PEATTIE 1700-1900 LARGO, FIF, SCT [36776]

PEATZMAN ALL GER & USA [38043]

PEBODY PRE 1800 WELFORD, NTH, ENG [37711]

PECHE PRE 1895 MOCKER, LEOBSCHUTZ, GER [36458]

PECHMANN C1600 GUSTEN, HAL, DDR [37918]

PECK 1820-1832 CAMDEN, NSW, AUS [34966] : WILLIAM 1877+ CESSNOCK, NSW, AUS [38083] : PRE 1830 GREAT BADDOW, ESS, ENG [33935] : 1770 EYEWORTH, BDF, ENG [34204] : 1793-1820 STUTTON, SFK, ENG [34966] : JOHN W. 1848+ HOLBEACH & LONG SUTTON, LIN, ENG [35583] : 1800+ ENG [36287] : 1800-1900 SUTTON IN ASHFIELD, NTT, ENG [36531] : 1650-1800 HARKSTEAD, SFK, ENG [37042] : 1700+ BROCKFORD, SFK, ENG [37262] : SAMUEL 1858+ NEWARK, NTT, ENG [38083] : PRE 1870 COLCHESTER, ESS & NSW, ENG & AUS [37130] : 1800+ MANSFIELD, NTT, ENG & CAN [36791] : ALL NZ [35058] : CHARLES 1800-1832 SARATOGA, NYS, USA [36447] : 1810 CHITTENDEN, VT, USA [36907] : 1840 BRECKSVILLE, OH, USA [36907] : 1850-1870 PEORIA CO., IL, USA [37798] : 1500+ REHOBOTH, MA, CT & RI, USA & ENG [36970]

PECKER AMY 1800S SITTINGBOURNE, KEN, ENG [35634]

PECKHAM C1810 NORTHIAM, SSX, ENG [33940] : PRE 1800 STANMER, SSX, ENG [34112] : PRE 1830 BURY ST EDMUNDS, SFK, ENG [38270] : PRE 1900 MA, USA [37804]

PECKSTON 1800-1900 HUTTON CRANSWICK, ERY, ENG & USA [38574]

PECKTEL PRE 1800 RHINEBECK, NY, USA & GER [38386]

PECKWELL PRE 1800 ROGATE, SSX, ENG [34112]

PECORE 1800+ MAXWELL, ONT, CAN [36662]

PEDDER C1860 POPLAR, LND, ENG [33796] : ALL BROMPTON, LND, ENG [34002] : PRE 1850 NOTTINGHAM, NTT, ENG [35205] : PRE 1724 GARSTANG, LAN, ENG [37706]

PEDDIE 1850+ MELBOURNE, VIC, AUS [38568] : 1700-1800 PERTH, PER, SCT [36440] : PRE 1840 LEITH, MLN, SCT [38568]

PEDDLE PRE 1843 WELLS & SOMERTON, SOM, ENG [34955]

PEDEN 1838+ CAMDEN & GOULBURN, NSW, AUS [34418] : ALL BROCKVILLE, ONT, CAN [37431] : 1834 ARL, SCT [34195] : 1600+ ARL, SCT [34418] : 1750+ GALSTON, AYR, SCT [35503] : ALL SCT [37431]

PEDERSDATTER 1800-1839 ELSINORE, DEN **[37172]** : ELLSE 1625-1700 TAARNBORG, SORO, DEN **[37547]**

PEDERSEN PRE 1828 LYNES, THORUP, ZEALAND, DEN **[33957]** : PRE 1835 VIGERSLEY, DEN **[35767]** : 1870S HJORRING, DEN **[35953]** : 1830-1850S TAARS, JUTLAND, DEN **[36285]** : SOREN 1700-1860 VEMELEV, SORO, DEN **[37547]** : JENNY 1867 AALBORG, DEN **[38193]** : PRE 1905 DEN **[38393]** : 1800-1890 EIDSBERG, OSTFOLD, NOR **[34523]** : 1800-1900 NOR **[34631]** : 1800-1900 ARENDAL, AUSTAGDER, NOR **[35292]** : PRE 1800 NESNA, NORDLAND, NOR **[36326]** : 1700 RORAS, S TRNDLG, NOR **[36326]**

PEDERSSON JORAN PRE 1700 MALMO, SWE **[38553]**

PEDLER 1800+ WORLDWIDE **[37147]** : 1800+ WORLDWIDE **[37147]**

PEDLEY 1829 FENSTANTON, HUN, ENG **[34976]** : PRE 1720 ELTISLEY, CAM, ENG **[36604]**

PEDOTT ALL WORLDWIDE **[34318]**

PEDRETTI PRE 1865 BRUSIO, GR, CH **[35750]**

PEDWELL PRE 1860 SRY, ENG **[33925]**

PEEBLES PRE 1850 AYR, SCT **[34345]** : 1750+ LONGFORGAN, PER, SCT **[35644]** : 1800 OUTERTOWN, SCT **[37170]**

PEED 1790+ GREAT MELTON, NFK, ENG **[34710]** : PRE 1830 CAM, NFK & SFK, ENG **[37646]**

PEEK 1800+ HOO, KEN, ENG **[37328]** : 1800S KINGS LYNN, NFK, ENG **[38753]** : 1862 ST JOSEPH CO., MI, USA **[37788]**

PEEL PRE 1800 NS, CAN & ENG **[34403]** : 1800+ NS, CAN & USA **[34403]** : C1867 PECKHAM & CAMBERWELL, SRY, ENG **[34235]** : PRE 1860 NEWCASTLE, NBL, ENG **[35862]** : 1800 NOTTINGHAM, NTT, ENG **[37391]**

PEELE C1700 RALEIGH, NC, USA **[38367]**

PEELER 1800 UK **[38719]**

PEEP PRE 1800 BRISTOL, GLS, ENG **[35079]**

PEER PRE 1900 LND, ENG **[37724]** : 1810-1840 SOUTHAMPTON, HAM, ENG **[37724]** : PRE 1800 MARYLEBONE, LND, ENG **[37724]**

PEERBAKAS PRE 1870 INDIA **[36955]**

PEERDEN PRE 1606 MEER, ATW, BEL **[35008]**

PEERLESS PRE 1760 ASH NEXT RIDLEY, KEN, ENG **[37325]**

PEERS 1590+ HOLLINS GREEN, LAN, ENG **[37581]** : C1860 DUDLEY & BIRMINGHAM, WOR & STS, ENG **[37865]** : 1841+ LIVERPOOL, LAN, ENG & AUS **[35763]**

PEET 1850+ DALBY, QLD, AUS **[34044]** : 1894+ PERTH, WA, AUS **[36645]** : 1849+ SOUTH MELBOURNE & BALLARAT, VIC, AUS **[37962]** : 1600+ RUT, ENG **[35180]** : ANN 1830+ HESKET NEWMARKET, CUL, ENG **[35343]** : ALL ARMSKIRK, LAN, ENG **[36382]** : PRE 1750 NTT, ENG **[36619]** : PRE 1865 NOTTINGHAM, NTT, ENG **[36645]** : 1815-1871 RAINFORD, LAN, ENG **[37573]** : PRE 1815 BILLINGE, LAN, ENG **[37573]** : 1871+ GOLBORNE, LAN, ENG **[37573]** : PRE 1849 DERBY, DBY, ENG **[37962]** : PRE 1900 RAINFORD & KIRKBY, LAN, ENG **[38586]** : 1865+ ST LOUIS, MO, USA **[36645]**

PEETERS ALL MECHELEN, ATW, BEL **[36230]**

PEEVER 1850+ LONDON, MDX, ENG **[37847]**

PEGG 1870+ JUNEE, NSW, AUS **[36370]** : ALL ONT, CAN **[34493]** : ALL NFK, ENG **[34493]** : ALL KEXBY, ERY, ENG **[36144]** : 1842 POPLAR & EDMONTON, MDX, ENG **[36263]** : 1800+ HISTON, CAM, ENG **[36370]** : 1765-1833 GAMLINGAY, CAM, ENG **[36820]** : ALL POTTON, BDF, ENG **[36820]** : PRE 1800 STS & DBY, ENG **[37098]** : PRE

1900 LONDON, ENG **[37190]** : 1730+ LITTLEOVER, DBY, ENG **[37258]** : 1830+ BIRMINGHAM, WAR, ENG **[37258]**

PEGGIE PRE 1840 AUCHTERMUCHTY, FIF, SCT **[33868]**

PEGLAR 1850+ MACKAY, QLD, AUS **[35825]** : 1750-1890 THORNBURY, GLS, ENG **[35825]**

PEGMAN C1820 ZWOLLE, OIJ, NL **[35338]**

PEGRAM REBECCA 1876 BREDBO, NSW, AUS **[34885]** : AGNES 1900+ BREDBO, NSW, AUS **[34885]**

PEGUS 1800-1989 BURNIE, TAS, AUS **[35089]**

PEHRSSON 1830 VARBERG, HAL, SWE **[34890]** : PRE 1900 KARLSHAM, BLE, SWE **[35433]** : 1600-1780S LARBRO, GOTLAND, SWE **[38346]**

PEIER 1800S GER **[37814]**

PEIKER PRE 1861 KALDAUN, LEOBSCHUTZ, GER **[36458]** : PRE 1928 MUHLHAUSEN, THU, GER **[36458]** : PRE 1893 LOWITZ, GER **[36458]** : ALL WORLDWIDE **[36458]**

PEIL 1700-1800 WORKINGTON, CUL, ENG **[34762]** : PRE 1800 ULLOCK, CUL, ENG **[38708]**

PEIN PRE 1876 RITZEBUTTEL, NSA, GER **[38632]** : 1800+ SWE **[37289]**

PEIRCE PRE 1850 BIRMINGHAM, WAR, ENG **[35491]** : PRE 1849 RYDE, IOW, HAM, ENG **[36526]** : C1790 NORTHAMPTON, NTH, ENG **[37536]** : 1750-1830 HARWICH, ESS & SFK, ENG **[37779]**

PEIRSON 1600-1850 NRY, ENG **[36472]** : PRE 1850 PA & DE, USA **[36319]**

PEISLEY ALL AUS **[33930]** : 1850-1910 COWRA, NSW, AUS **[34422]** : C1800 SSX, ENG **[33930]**

PEKAR PRE 1864 PALTINOSSA, BUKOVINA, OES & CAN **[37481]**

PEKSA PRE 1900 STETTIN, SZ, POL **[34089]**

PELCHEY 1800+ ENG **[36662]**

PELESKY ALL WORLDWIDE **[34150]**

PELHAM C1824+ AUS **[34444]** : 1900S CAN **[36800]** : PRE 1858 CHELSEA, LND, ENG **[36800]** : 1810-1860 GREENE, NY, USA **[38111]** : 1855+ CLINTON, IA, USA **[38111]**

PELL 1851+ VIC, AUS **[33793]** : 1700S RUSKINGTON, LIN, ENG **[33793]** : 1840 MOULTON, NTH, ENG **[34546]** : JOSEPH PRE 1840 ASLACKBY, LIN, ENG **[35798]** : PRE 1878 GREAT YARMOUTH, NFK, ENG **[35956]**

PELLET ALL MONTREAL, QUE, CAN **[38368]** : ALL LONDON, ENG **[38368]**

PELLETIER 1630-1700 MONTREAL, QUE, CAN **[35283]**

PELLETT 1730-1810 BILLINGSHURST, SSX, ENG **[35643]** : 1890+ BIDDENDEN, KEN, ENG **[35980]**

PELLING PRE 1854 SCT **[37504]** : 1857+ KENTON CO., KY, USA **[37504]** : PRE 1857 PROVIDENCE, RI, NY & LKS, USA & SCT **[37504]**

PELLOW ALL CON, ENG **[36506]**

PELLY PRE 1900 GAL, IRL **[38301]** : PRE 1900 OFF, IRL **[38301]** : MARTIN 1890-1930 CHICAGO, IL, USA **[38301]**

PELMAN 1700-1800 MERE, WIL, ENG **[34769]**

PELSENAIRE ALL WORLDWIDE **[35596]**

PELSENER ALL WORLDWIDE **[35596]**

PELTON NATHAN 1789 MIDDLESEX CO., CT, USA **[38142]** : NATHAN 1789 HARTFORD CO., CT, USA **[38142]**

PELVIN 1700+ KENSINGTON, KEN, ENG **[35882]**

PEMBERTHY 1845-1880 KEWEENAW CO., MI, USA **[38009]**

PEMBERTON 1800S WHITWICK, LEI, ENG **[36511]** : PRE 1900 WEM & PREES, SAL, ENG **[36757]** : 1900+ MANCHESTER, LAN, ENG **[36757]** : 1800+ ATHERTON & LEIGH, LAN, ENG **[37258]**

PEMBLE PRE 1880 TAS & NSW, AUS [38271] : 1700-1880 BOSTON, MA, USA [38271]

PEMBROKE 1818+ HARTLEY, NSW, AUS [34030]

PEMERTON C1640-1700 ETON, BKM, ENG [37618]

PEMPLETON PRE 1850 ENG [36387]

PENAAT 1800-1900 WEENER, LINGEN-EMS, NIEDERSACHSEN, FRG [38710] : 1840-1940 BUREN, LIPPE, FRG [38710]

PENALIGON PRE 1800 ST BREOCK AREA, CON, ENG [36272]

PENALUNA 1580+ WENDRON, CON, ENG [35587]

PENBERTHY 1920+ BALMAIN, NSW, AUS [34421] : 1800+ ROBOROUGH, DEV, ENG [34700] : PRE 1900 HELSTON & ST HILARY, CON, ENG & NZ [35997]

PENDER 1790+ WRY, ENG [34692]

PENDERGAST 1800+ WINDSOR & CORNWALLIS, NSW, AUS [38592] : JOHN C1760 DUBLIN, IRL [38724]

PENDERGRASS JOHN C1760 DUBLIN, IRL [38724]

PENDERGRAST ALL WORLDWIDE [36131]

PENDLEBURY ALL AUS [35135] : 1893+ ROSEDALE, VIC, AUS [35748] : 1860+ MT GAMBIER, SA, AUS [36622] : 1800 MANCHESTER, LAN, ENG [35135] : 1750+ MANCHESTER, LAN, ENG [35748] : 1800+ WEST HOUGHTON, LAN, ENG [37626] : 1830+ MIDDLETON, LAN, ENG [37828] : J.T. 1823-1885 MANCHESTER, LAN, ENG [38259] : 1916 CAPETOWN, RSA [34193]

PENDLETON PRE 1890 DUR, ENG [36499] : 1820+ STONINGTON, CT, USA [38187]

PENDREIGN 1820S GIFFORD, ELN, SCT [36308]

PENDRILL 1650-1870 BOSCOBEL, SAL, ENG [34431]

PENELUNA 1700+ WENDRON & GWENNAP, CON, ENG [34970]

PENFOLD 1830+ CUCKFIELD, SSX, ENG [34785] : PRE 1864 ASHFORD & TONBRIDGE, KEN, ENG [36051]

PENFOLDS 1900S MOSS VALE, NSW, AUS [35567]

PENFORD ALL KINGSCLERE, HAM, ENG [37373] : PRE 1900 BRK, ENG & NZ [35950]

PENFOUND ALL WORLDWIDE [36474]

PENGALLY 1870+ CLUNES, VIC, AUS [36622]

PENGELLY 1600-1800 ILSINGTON, DEV, ENG [36106] : 1750+ BEAWORTHY, DEV, ENG [37733] : 1700+ WLS [35580]

PENGILLY 1800S YARNSCOMBE, DEV, ENG [34380] : 1700+ ENG [35580] : C1800 DEV, ENG [37180]

PENGLASE 1840+ ADELAIDE, SA, AUS [35811] : 1840+ AUS [35811] : PRE 1840 REDRUTH, CON, ENG [35811]

PENGLAZE PRE 1855 CON, ENG [35162]

PENGLAZE (SEE PENGLA [35811]

PENHALIGON PRE 1800 ST BREOCK AREA, CON, ENG [36272]

PENHALLIGON 1800+ NEWLYN EAST, CON, ENG [35235]

PENICK PRE 1750 HENRICO & PRINCE EDWARD, VA, USA [36927]

PENKETH 1840 WEAVERHAM, CHS, ENG [37690]

PENMAN 1900+ AUS [34993] : 1758+ ENG [34387] : C1789 BERWICK UPON TWEED, NBL, ENG [35702] : ALL DUR, ENG [37704] : DAVID 1825+ ARBUCKLE & NEW MONKLAND, LKS, SCT [34369] : 1700-1860 GLASCOW, LKS, SCT [36556]

PENN PRE 1856 COVENTRY, WAR, ENG [35008] : JOSHUA WM. C1812 COVENTRY, WAR, ENG [35607] : 1600+ OXF & BKM, ENG [37099] : 1800S-1900S CHS & LAN, ENG [37221] : 1879-1907 HULL, YKS, ENG [37493] : PRE 1731 CHURCHILL, WOR, ENG [37662] : 1880S HACKNEY (WEST), MDX, ENG [37677] : 1700-1800 BIRMINGHAM, WAR, ENG [37924] : 1709+ CAROLINE CO., VA, USA [38044] : 1800+ LLANDILO, CMN & MON, WLS [35580]

PENNA C1830 CON, ENG [33796]

PENNELL 1850+ COSTERFIELD, VIC, AUS [35379] : PRE 1870 FOOTSCRAY, VIC, AUS [35796] : PRE 1900 HORNSEY, MDX, ENG [33966] : 1800S WOOLWICH, KEN, ENG [35379] : ALL TOPSHAM & MALBOROUGH, DEV, ENG [36211] : ALL WORLDWIDE [36832]

PENNEY 1840+ QUEANBEYAN, NSW, AUS [35410] : PRE 1850 WOR & SAL, ENG [34318] : 1800-1850 BERMONDSEY, SRY, ENG [34753] : 1752+ NEW GLOUCESTER & GUILFORD, ME, USA [36915]

PENNICOTT THOMAS 1880S WINDSOR, BRK, ENG [36880]

PENNIMAN 1600-1700 CHIPPING ONGAR, ESS, ENG [37633] : 1650-1800 HOWDEN, ERY, ENG [37633] : 1600-1700 GREAT BROMLEY, ESS, ENG [37633]

PENNING 1793-1849 BARNTRUP, LIP, GER [38749]

PENNINGTON 1700S COLTON & ULVERSTON, LAN, ENG [34053] : ALL HUDDERSFIELD, WRY, ENG [34701] : ALL ASPULL MOOR, LAN, ENG [36743] : 1750+ RETFORD, NTT, ENG [37735] : 1800+ CHESTER & WREXHAM, CHS, ENG [37735] : 1750-1840 KENDAL, WES, ENG [38511] : MARTHA 1785-1856 PHILADELPHIA & LAKE WINOLA, PA, USA [36948] : PRE 1800 BUCKS CO., PA & NJ, USA [37018]

PENNO 1800+ CON, ENG [37153]

PENNOCH ALL YKS, ENG [37407]

PENNOCK PRE 1700 SFK, ENG [35642]

PENNY ALL ENGLISH HARBOUR TRINITY, NFD, CAN [34093] : 1700-1800 NS, CAN [36579] : PRE 1860 TEFFONT, WIL, ENG [33850] : PRE 1850 EVERCREECH, SOM, ENG [34314] : 1700+ TOTNES, DEV, ENG [34970] : PRE 1864 BIRMINGHAM, WAR, ENG [35095] : PRE 1842 EDMONSHAM, DOR, ENG [35407] : C1820-1880 BROAD CHALKE, WIL, ENG [36289] : PRE 1860 DEVONPORT, DEV, ENG [36923] : PRE 1750 LULWORTH & BRADFORD PEVERIL, DOR, ENG [37410] : 1838+ HANLEY, STS, ENG [37945]

PENNY (SEE PENNEY) [34318]

PENNYMAN 1700-1800 EMBLETON, NBL, ENG [37633] : 1700-1850 MONKWEARMOUTH, DUR, ENG [37633] : 1650-1700 LONGHOUGHTON, NBL, ENG [37633] : 1600-1850 THORPE NEXT NORWICH, NFK, ENG [37633] : 1700-1800 WHITEHAVEN, CUL, ENG [37633] : 1700-1850 BISHOP MIDDLEHAM, DUR, ENG [37633] : 1700-1850 BISHOPWEARMOUTH, DUR, ENG [37633] : 1650-1750 LESSINGHAM, NFK, ENG [37633]

PENRITH 1835 WIGTON, CUL, ENG [35815] : ALL WORLDWIDE [34944]

PENROD C1800 ENG [34395]

PENROSE JOHN 1720-1800 MARKET WEIGHTON, YKS, ENG [34143] : C1800 DEV, ENG [35137] : PRE 1800 SOUTH CAVE BRANTINGHAM, ERY, ENG [35940] : 1800S DUKINFIELD, CHS, ENG [37299] : 1604+ WHELDRAKE, YKS, ENG [37564] : ALL WORLDWIDE [37379]

PENSON 1700-1750 EPPING, ESS, ENG [36081] : 1600-1700 CLEOBURY MORTIMER & HIGHLEY, SAL, ENG [37257] : 1700-1800 ENFIELD & ENVILLE, STS, ENG [37257] : PRE 1850 LAMBETH, LND, ENG [37287]

PENSTONE 1500-1660 BRK, ENG [35180] : ALL STANFORD IN THE VALE, BRK, ENG [36076]

PENTEN 1750-1900 POPLAR, MDX, ENG [37651]

PENTENEY 1820+ SRY, ENG [34484]

PENTLAND 1840+ AUS [33932] : C1824+ AUS [34444] : PRE 1820 PORTADOWN, ARM, IRL [35866] : PRE 1781 ARDS PENINSULA, DOW, IRL [38428] : PRE 1850 EDINBURGH, MLN, SCT [38364]

PENTON 1750-1900 POPLAR, MDX, ENG [37651]

PENWARDEN 1760-1860 CON & DEV, ENG [35916]

PENWELL PRE 1759 ESS & SSX, ENG [37580] : PRE 1759 SCT [37580]

PENYMAN 1558 WESTBURY ON SEVERN, GLS, ENG [37633] : 1550-1750 NEWCASTLE UPON TYNE, NBL, ENG [37633] : 1700-1750 LESBURY, NBL, ENG [37633] : 1550-1650 BACTON, NFK, ENG [37633]

PENYMON 1750-1850 BRISTOL, GLS, ENG [37633]

PENZER 1800+ ALVECHURCH & BROMSGROVE, WOR, ENG [37257] : 1700-1900 ENFIELD & ENVILLE, STS, ENG [37257]

PEPLOE PRE 1890 ENG [36747]

PEPLOW 1804+ WELLINGTON, SAL & STS, ENG [37762]

PEPPER 1850+ NOWRA, NSW, AUS [34871] : PRE 1890 FOSTON, LIN, ENG [34612] : ALL DAY DODDINGTON, LIN, ENG [34765] : ALL WESTBOROUGH, LIN, ENG [34765] : 1830S WOR, ENG [34765] : 1800+ KNAVESTOCK, ESS, ENG [35505] : PRE 1850 ROYSTON, HRT, ENG [35865] : 1700+ BDF, ENG [35880] : 1800+ LIDLINGTON, BDF, ENG [35947] : ALL WRY, ENG [36126] : C1810-1840 LIDLINGTON, BDF, ENG [36803] : PRE 1840 MELDRETH, CAM, ENG [37137] : PRE 1800 STOCKBURY, KEN, ENG [37602] : 1845+ GREENE CO., OH, USA [37781]

PEPPERALL THOMAS C1787 BRIDGWATER, SOM, ENG [36367]

PEPPERELL 1840+ WINDSOR, VIC, AUS [35877]

PEPPERILL PRE 1835 SOUTHEND, ESS, ENG [37142]

PEPPIN PRE 1800 WILLITON & BICKNOLLER, SOM, ENG [35612] : PRE 1870 EXFORD, SOM, ENG [37622]

PERCHARD 1750-1820 LONDON, ENG [34550]

PERCIVAL PRE 1900 AUS [33849] : 1859+ SYDNEY, NSW, AUS [37909] : 1700+ THORNTON, LEI, ENG [34370] : ALL DBY, ENG [35009] : PRE 1870 KEN, ENG [35331] : PRE 1780 BRISTOL, GLS, ENG [36388] : PRE 1850 APPLETON & STRETTON, CHS, ENG [36740] : 1650+ EMPINGHAM, RUT & LEI, ENG [37266] : PRE 1860 EYE, HEF & WOR, ENG & NZ [35940]

PERCY PRE 1820 CANTERBURY & DOVER, KEN, ENG [34316] : 1800+ BLANDFORD, DOR, ENG [35410] : PRE 1668 LONG CRENDON, BKM, ENG [36866] : PRE 1880 COWPEN VILLAGE, NBL, ENG [38218] : 1830-1883 WISHAW, LKS, SCT [33955] : ALL SCT [35804]

PERDUE PRE 1860 BOYLE, ROS, IRL [33876]

PEREIRA ALL TOTTENHAM, LND, ENG [37647] : ALL SOUTHWARK, LND, ENG [37647] : 1700S TRINQUEBAR, INDIA [38659] : PRE 1920 PERRINA, LIPARI ISL., ITL [36271]

PEREN (SEE PERRIN) [36608]

PERENA 1700-1830 HUESCA, ESP [36937]

PEREZ 1830+ VALPARAISO, CHILE &, AUS [33926]

PERFECT 1758+ WEST MALLING, KEN, ENG [36558]

PERHAM C1850-1930 TORONTO, ONT, CAN [37351] : PRE 1750 DEV, DOR & SOM, ENG [36166] : PRE 1860 BRK, SRY & BKM, ENG [37351]

PERIAM PRE 1850 ENG [34099]

PERIE 1843 BLAYNEY, NSW, AUS [34038]

PERIGNY ALL CAN [35640]

PERIGO 1830 ADAMS CO., IL, USA [36444]

PERIGO (SEE PERRIGO) [36883]

PERKIN C1797 EAST STONEHOUSE, DEV, ENG [36376] : 1800+ CASHEL, TIP, IRL [33825]

PERKINS PRE 1857 MELBOURNE, VIC, AUS [37982] : 1783+ SAINT JOHN, NB, CAN [34470] : JAMES PRE 1818 NS, CAN [38421] : 1800+ LONDON, ENG [34455] : ALL HORNCHURCH, ESS, ENG [34758] : PRE 1820 WARWICK, HUN, ENG [35141] : 1800S PLYMPTON & ST MARY, COLEBROOK, DEV, ENG [35437] : PRE 1850 SWAFFHAM, NFK, ENG [35462] : PRE 1820 KILMERSDON, SOM, ENG [35764] : 1700-1800 ROTHWELL, NTH, ENG [36057] : PRE 1850 SPITALFIELDS, MDX, ENG [36065] : ALL BARKING, ESS, ENG [36065] : PRE 1800 BROMPTON & CHATHAM, KEN, ENG [36423] : PRE 1800 WINKTON & CHRISTCHURCH, HAM, ENG [36423] : C1837 CARLTON CURLIEU, LEI, ENG [37053] : C1900 ISLINGTON, LND, ENG [37053] : C1770 HINCKLEY, LEI, ENG [37053] : C1840 RAMSGATE, KEN, ENG [37053] : C1799 BARWELL, LEI, ENG [37053] : SARAH 1789-1866 LND, ENG [37055] : SALLY 1789-1866 LND, ENG [37055] : 1820-1860S WAPPING, MDX, ENG [37071] : 1800 BURTON ON TRENT, STS, ENG [37487] : 1800S PRITTLEWELL & SOUTHEND, ESS, ENG [37677] : 1750 MARKET DEEPING, LIN, ENG [37952] : 1836+ RICHMOND, SRY, ENG [37982] : PRE 1820 STS, ENG [38056] : 1800+ CASHEL, TIP, IRL [33825] : PRE 1783 NORTHCASTLE, NY, USA [34470] : 1600-1850 VT & MA, USA [35292] : 1860+ GREENE CO., GA, USA [36903] : 1620-1680 NH, USA [38119] : 1800 TN, USA [38320] : 1800+ LLANGYNIDR, BRE, WLS [34082]

PERKS 1850+ LIVERPOOL, LAN, ENG [36845]

PERLICK 1850-1900 PRE, GER [38041] : 1850-1900 CHICAGO, IL, USA [38041]

PERLITZ PRE 1880 BRD [38238]

PERMEWEN PRE 1830 ST BURYAN, CON, ENG [34575]

PERRAS LOUIS 1880+ ST EDOUARD, QUE, CAN [36678]

PERRATON PRE 1822 LOWER BASTON, DEV, ENG [38214]

PERREAUX ALL WORLDWIDE [35832]

PERREN (SEE PERRIN) [36608]

PERRET C1800 LAVERTON, SOM, ENG [36247]

PERRETT PRE 1840 SOUTH PERROTT, DOR, ENG [33874] : 1643-1860 HILL FARRANCE, SOM, ENG [37053] : C1750-1850 CUTCOMBE & WHEDDON CROSS, SOM, ENG [37556] : 1750+ WARMINSTER, WIL, ENG [37847]

PERREY C1862 CHINGFORD, ESS, ENG [37302]

PERRIAM 1800+ HAMMERSMITH, MDX, ENG [35975] : PRE 1750 DEV, DOR & SOM, ENG [36166]

PERRIER 1800+ MOOSE CREEK, ONT, CAN [36686] : C1700 ROLLE, VD & GE, CH [38348]

PERRIGO PRE 1613 CATSFIELD & HASTINGS, SSX, ENG [36883] : 1760-99 CAYUGA CO., NY, USA [38153]

PERRIN 1850+ NSW & VIC, AUS [36608] : 1843+ TAS, AUS [38485] : C1893-1960 PERTH, WA, AUS [38541] : C1887-1945 STRATHFIELD & TEAGARDENS, NSW, AUS [38541] : GEORGE C1883-1944 BOLIVIA, NSW, AUS [38541] : C1730 OVER PEOVER, CHS, ENG [34474] : 1814 WHITCHURCH, BKM, ENG [35123] : PRE 1850 ILFORD, ESS, ENG [35866] : 1700-1800 KEN, ENG [36491] : WILLIAM H. 1862-1892 MANCHESTER, LAN, ENG [36564] : C1808 EASTWICKHAM & ELTHAM, KEN, ENG [38485] : 1826 RAGUSA, OES [36608] : PRE 1853 TRIESTE & RAGUSA, OES [38541] : PRE 1660 HENRICO CO., VA, USA [36973] :

1637-1695 HENRICO CO., VA, USA **[38120]** : 1826 DUBROVNIK, YU **[36608]**

PERRING 1700+ HARBERTON & TOTNES, DEV, ENG **[34970]** : 1800-1900 COMBE FLOREY, SOM, ENG **[37378]**

PERRINS 1750-1830 DARLASTON, STS, ENG **[37632]**

PERRIOTT PRE 1824 ALLINGTON, DOR, ENG **[35895]**

PERRIS C1900 SHEFFORD, BRK, ENG **[36975]**

PERRIT 1850S MARSTON, WIL, ENG **[36253]**

PERRON 1840 FISH HOEK, CAPE, RSA **[34332]**

PERROT 1710 HOUGHTON CONQUEST, BDF, ENG **[36798]**

PERROTT ALL NORTH LEIGH, OXF, ENG **[34466]** : PRE 1841 ALLINGTON, DOR, ENG **[35895]** : 1841-1870 TARANAKI, NZ **[35895]**

PERRY ALL MONARO & GOULBURN, NSW, AUS **[33765]** : 1845 MUDGEE, NSW, AUS **[33783]** : EMILY 1882+ WALHALLOW, NSW, AUS **[34942]** : 1850+ SYDNEY, NSW, AUS **[34978]** : 1840S MANGROVE, NSW, AUS **[35134]** : JAMES ALL SURRY HILLS, NSW, AUS **[35234]** : JOHN 1830-1840S SYDNEY, NSW, AUS **[35735]** : HENRY 1850-1867 YOUNG, NSW, AUS **[36316]** : PRE 1900 AILSIA CRAIG, ONT, CAN **[34477]** : C1784+ LEN & ADD CO., ONT, CAN **[36651]** : 1700-1850 ONT, CAN **[38128]** : 1785+ LENNOX & ADDINGTON, ONT, CAN **[38517]** : PRE 1870 STOWFORD, DEV, ENG **[33995]** : CHARLES PRE 1850 CLERKENWELL, LND, ENG **[34131]** : PRE 1900 ESS, ENG **[34317]** : ALL ESS, ENG **[34493]** : 1780 TRYSULL, STS, ENG **[34950]** : PRE 1803 CAMELEY, SOM, ENG **[34978]** : 1630+ SIDMOUTH & BRANSCOMBE, DEV, ENG **[35027]** : 1810 ALTON PRIORS, WIL, ENG **[35067]** : 1880S GOLDEN HILL, STS, ENG **[35074]** : C1800 WRIVENBURY, SAL, ENG **[35203]** : FREDERICK PRE 1890 ROMFORD, ESS, ENG **[35232]** : GEORGE PRE 1820 SRY, ENG **[35234]** : 1870+ MANCHESTER, LAN, ENG **[35240]** : JOHN 1781-1838 TONBRIDGE WELLS, KEN, ENG **[35391]** : 1700-1860 ENG **[35581]** : 1600+ WENDRON, CON, ENG **[35587]** : PRE 1740 KINGSWINFORD, STS, ENG **[36110]** : 1700S-1800S SAFFRON WALDEN, ESS, ENG **[36211]** : 1800+ WENNINGTON & DEGENHAM, ESS, ENG **[36263]** : PRE 1700 BETHNAL GREEN, LND, ENG **[36295]** : EDWARD PRE 1830 PLYMOUTH, DEV, ENG **[36309]** : PRE 1830 WHITWICK & OSGATHORPE, LEI, ENG **[36511]** : ALL WOLVERHAMPTON, STS, ENG **[36537]** : C1588-C1640 DEV, ENG **[36651]** : PRE 1910 LONDON, ENG **[37062]** : PRE 1840 READING, BRK, ENG **[37179]** : 1800+ BIRMINGHAM, WAR, ENG **[37557]** : C1831 CHILCOMPTON, SOM, ENG **[37830]** : C1825 WALCOT, SOM, ENG **[37830]** : C1600 ALL CANNINGS, WIL, ENG **[37918]** : ALL LONDON, ENG **[38287]** : PRE 1800 WOTTON UNDER EDGE, GLS, ENG **[38299]** : JAMES C1829 DUB, IRL **[33765]** : 1700-1900 LEX, IRL **[34717]** : 1800-70 SLI, IRL **[37807]** : PRE 1900 PT CHALMERS, OTAGO, NZ **[33998]** : 1700-1860 NEWLUCE, WIG, SCT **[34975]** : RACHEL MINERV 1894-1990 DEWITT CO., IL, USA **[35329]** : 1850-60 SACRAMENTO, CA, USA **[36349]** : FRANKLIN 1780-1820 WOODFORD CO., KY, USA **[36573]** : C1640-C1780 REHOBOTH, MA, USA **[36651]** : 1760S ALBEMARLE CO., VA, USA **[37027]** : PRE 1870 WASHINGTON CO., OH, USA **[37505]** : 1813-1840 ORLEANS CO., NY, USA **[37576]** : 1868-1900 KEWEENAW CO., MI, USA **[38010]** : WESLEY 1824-1870 COLUMBIA CO., PA, USA **[38732]**

PERRYMAN PRE 1800 MARLEBONE, LND, ENG **[33912]** : 1550-1700 ALDENHAM, HRT, ENG **[37633]**

PERSDOTTER MARIT 1821 LYSVIK, VARMLAND, SWE **[38556]** : HILDA 1887+ USA **[38560]** : ELIANA 1887+ USA **[38560]**

PERSEHOUSE PRE 1770 SEDGLEY, STS, ENG **[36110]**

PERSHOUSE 1857+ GLADSTONE, QLD, AUS **[35452]**

PERSIAN 1900+ WEBBWOOD, ONT, CAN **[36350]**

PERSIANI PRE 1900 LEGHORN, TUSCANY, ITL & AUS **[33799]**

PERSIS-SIMMONDS 1835 DOVER, KEN, ENG **[36781]**

PERSONS 1700-1800 BRISTOL, CT, USA **[37783]**

PERSSON ERIK 1820-1843 BRANDVAL, HEDMARK, NOR **[38556]** : PRE 1850 TVARRED, ALVSBORG, SWE **[38556]** : FILIP R. 1901+ ANGELHOLM, L-LAN, SWE **[38560]** : ARVID RUDOLF 1898+ HELSINGBORG, M-LAN, SWE **[38560]** : JOHAN B.R. 1901-1919 VEDBY, L-LAN, SWE **[38560]** : ANNA 1901+ ANGELHOLM, L-LAN, SWE **[38560]** : ROSA A. 1899+ ANGELHOLM, L-LAN, SWE **[38560]** : ASTRID A. 1901+ ANGELHOLM, L-LAN, SWE **[38560]** : JENNY A. 1901-1919 VEDBY, L-LAN, SWE **[38560]** : JANNE 1872+ STOCKHOLM, SWE **[38560]** : ESTER A. 1901+ ANGELHOLM, L-LAN, SWE **[38560]** : NILS PETER 1882+ USA **[38560]** : AMANDA 1874+ BROOKLYN, USA **[38560]**

PERT C1896 HETHERSETT, NFK, ENG **[35249]** : 1800+ FERRYDEN, ANS, SCT **[36971]**

PESCHKE JOHANN C1850 BOMST, POS, GER **[36452]**

PESSINER 1876-1889 DRE, DDR **[38520]**

PESSNER 1889-1910 MANHATTAN, NY, USA **[38520]**

PESTELL PRE 1841 ISLINGTON, MDX, ENG **[36072]** : 1750+ HUNTINGDON, ENG **[38001]**

PESTER ALL NORTH PERROTT & WEST COKER, SOM, ENG **[36161]**

PETCH ROBERT 1805-1850 YKS, ENG **[34078]** : 1700+ KIRKBY MOORSIDE, NRY, ENG **[34380]** : PRE 1830 HULL, YKS, ENG **[34941]** : PRE 1718 MONKWEARMOUTH, DUR, ENG **[37635]**

PETER C1839 SYDNEY, NSW, AUS **[37968]** : PRE 1800 AMHERST CO., VA, USA **[36965]** : 1815+ SANGAMON CO., IL, USA **[36965]** : 1800+ WASHINGTON CO., KY, USA **[36965]**

PETERHBRIDGE 1853+ MAITLAND, NSW, AUS **[34977]**

PETERS 1854 ORANGE, NSW, AUS **[34038]** : C1894 SYDNEY, NSW, AUS **[35515]** : C1905 FITZROY, VIC, AUS **[35708]** : 1865 PORTLAND, VIC, AUS **[35777]** : 1900+ BRISBANE, QLD, AUS **[37116]** : 1841+ NIMMITYBELLE, NSW, AUS **[37313]** : PETER PRE 1840 NSW, AUS **[38773]** : PRE 1840 CORRYONG, VIC, AUS **[38773]** : 1783+ NB, CAN **[34504]** : 1720-1780 STYTHIANS, CON, ENG **[34016]** : 1873 BRISTOL, SOM, ENG **[34540]** : 1700-1840 ST AGNES, CON, ENG **[34697]** : 1722 GWENNAP, CON, ENG **[34793]** : ALL TIVERTON, DEV, ENG **[34847]** : C1850 WORLE, SOM, ENG **[34914]** : PRE 1860 CAM, ENG **[34929]** : PRE 1850 SOMERSHAM, HUN, ENG **[35323]** : PRE 1852+ BRISTOL, GLS, ENG **[35454]** : PRE 1825 ST ANTHONY IN MENEAGE, CON, ENG **[35496]** : 1800+ GWENNAP, CON, ENG **[35708]** : 1900 BRISTOL, ENG **[35881]** : PRE 1840 HARLTON, CAM, ENG **[36224]** : ALL BATTLE, SSX, ENG **[36664]** : 1830+ EXETER, DEV, ENG **[36664]** : 1800+ TAUNTON, SOM, ENG **[36756]** : ALL ST GERMANS, CON, ENG **[37451]** : 1819-1850 BAV, GER **[35287]** : PRE 1850 SHO, GER **[37009]** : PRE 1790 DUNAGHY, ANT, IRL **[34995]** : PRE 1841 TIP, IRL **[37313]** : 1864-1888 DUNEDIN, NZ **[35708]** : ALL GROSS KRAUKOW, POL **[38634]** : FRANK 1890+ RSA

[34847] : C1850 KCD, SCT [35515] : C1800 MUSSELBURGH, ELN, SCT [35646] : 1800S EDINBURGH, MLN, SCT [36246] : PETER 1800 DUNDEE, ANS, SCT [36842] : JOHN 1880+ OH, USA [34847] : 1850+ OH, USA [35287] : 1845-1850 PA, USA [35287] : 1650S-1720 ANDOVER, MA, USA [36310] : 1855-1880 KEWEENAW CO., MI, USA [38009] : C1780 PEMBROKE DOCK, PEM, WLS [35457] : ALL WORLDWIDE [35832]

PETERSEN 1890+ CHARTERS TOWERS, QLD, AUS [35108] : C1850-1895 GIPPSLAND, VIC, AUS [35755] : PRE 1820 COPENHAGEN, DEN [33959] : PRE 1880 FALKERSLOV, DEN [35451] : 1901-1990 FLENSBERG, DEN [36248] : 1801-1900 FLENSBERG, DEN [36248] : PRE 1836 ODENSE, DEN [36604] : MADS C1860 HORSENS, VEJLE, DEN [37982] : CARL 1861 COPENHAGEN, DEN [38193] : PETER 1861 COPENHAGEN, DEN [38193] : 1856-1870S CARLUM, FLENSBUG, SHO, GER [33950] : 1860+ LUBECK, LUE, GER [34688] : PETER 1870S MATARAWA, WAIRARAPA, NZ [33950]

PETERSOHN 1840-1890 KINGS, QUEENS, NY CITY, NY, USA [34067]

PETERSON C1975 SYDNEY, NSW, AUS [34694] : 1900+ TRARALGON, VIC, AUS [35476] : 1880+ WIMMERA, VIC, AUS [36622] : ALL WETASKIWIN, ALB, CAN [36919] : 1700+ SOUTH HACKNEY, MDX, ENG [34547] : 1850-1950S CHRISTCHURCH, NZ [34000] : ALL SHI, SCT [38215] : C1820 JONSTORP & STROVELSTORP, MALMO, SWE [34654] : PRE 1882 UDDEVALLA, SWE [35598] : 1850+ CROSBY, MN, USA [35598] : 1850+ MI, USA [35598] : ISABELLA 1840-1850 SPRINGFIELD, MO, USA [36322] : PRE 1750 CT & MA, USA [38746]

PETERSSON EVA 1852+ SAINT PAUL, MN, USA [38557]

PETHEBRIDGE 1800+ TOCAL, NSW, AUS [38001] : PRE 1830 ALVERDISTOCK, DEV, ENG [38001]

PETHER 1800+ AUS [33769]

PETHERAM PRE 1840 CON, ENG [36877]

PETHERBRIDGE PRE 1853 ASHBURTON, DEV, ENG [34977]

PETHERHAM C1800 SOM, ENG [36307]

PETHERICK 1832-1853 HALLOCOMBE, DEV, ENG [36771] : 1802+ ASHWATER, DEV, ENG [36771] : 1780+ ASHWATER, DEV, ENG [37224]

PETHICK 1810-1880 CON, ENG [35074] : 1882 CARBONDALE, PA, USA [35074]

PETIT 1700-1850 VARENNES, QUE, CAN [34242] : PRE 1870 ENG [35722]

PETITT 1871+ EMMAVILLE, NSW, AUS [37115]

PETRE C1750 CHARLEVILLE MEZIERES, FRA [38698]

PETRI ALL WEF, GER [35310]

PETRIE PRE 1850 SHOREDITCH, MDX, ENG [37362] : PRE 1850 SRY, ENG [37362] : ALL EDINBURGH, MLN, SCT [34093] : PRE 1845 STRICHEN & LUMPHANAN, ABD, SCT [34870] : PRE 1810 RAFFORD, MOR, SCT [36338] : 1800+ EDINBURGH, SCT [37134]

PETROFF ALL WORLDWIDE [37549]

PETRUSCH C1880 KONIGSBERG, OPR, GER [36520]

PETRY PRE 1855 BLENHEIM, ONT, CAN [36345]

PETTAK PRE 1850 BRA & MST, GER [38648]

PETTEE 1700-1750 WEYMOUTH, MA, USA [35314]

PETTER PRE 1800 ROGATE, SSX, ENG [34112]

PETTERSON 1858-1876 GOTHENBURG, BOHUS, SWE & AUS [33896]

PETTET 1800+ FIRLE, SSX, ENG [37293]

PETTEY PRE 1865 WELLS, SOM, ENG [37406]

PETTICAN PRE 1860 COLCHESTER, ESS, ENG [36116]

PETTIFER PRE 1800 OXF & NTH, ENG [38754]

PETTIGREW 1865+ NSW, AUS [34534] : 1900+ BALLYMONEY, ANT, IRL [35395] : PRE 1740 CARLUKE, LKS, SCT [34501] : PRE 1800 LKS, SCT [37374]

PETTINGILL 1850+ VIC, AUS [35836] : 1700+ NFK & SFK, ENG [35836]

PETTIT 1900-1990 MALDON, VIC, AUS [33778] : 1878+ MELBOURNE & FAIRFIELD, VIC, AUS [34685] : 1850S GEELONG, VIC, AUS [34793] : 1900+ HEYFIELD & SALE, VIC, AUS [36622] : C1860S+ HARTLEY, NSW, AUS [38510] : 1790+ BRADFIELD ST GEORGE, SFK, ENG [34020] : FRANCIS PRE 1900 BETHNAL GREEN, MDX, ENG [34347] : PRE 1852+ WORLINGWORTH, SFK, ENG [34423] : C1860 IPSWICH, SFK, ENG [34685] : 1830S HUN, ENG [34793] : C1800 BARLEY, HRT, ENG [34840] : C1775 GREAT CHISHALL, ESS, ENG [34840] : PRE 1800 STANFORD RIVER, ESS, ENG [36500] : PRE 1900 KEN, ENG [37377] : 1895+ WELWYN, HRT, ENG [37398] : 1895+ SACOMBE, HRT, ENG [37398] : C1800-1900 CASTLE CAMPS, CAM, ENG [37398] : 1600-1965 HORSEHEATH, CAM, ENG [37398] : 1895+ TONWELL, HRT, ENG [37398] : 1895+ WIDFORD, HRT, ENG [37398] : C1700-1900 SHUDY CAMPS, CAM, ENG [37398] : 1920+ RSA [38288] : PRE 1878 AYR, AYR, SCT [34685] : ELSINE 1847-1924 MEDFORD, NJ, USA [38134]

PETTITT PRE 1800 HETHERSETT, NFK, ENG [34931] : 1782-1844 ST IVES, HUN, ENG [35922] : C1846 LONDON, MDX, ENG [36253] : 1300-1400+ SSX, ENG [37648] : ALL SSX, ENG [37875] : 1800-1880 LONDON, ENG & AUS [35365]

PETTRIE C1750 COLLESSIE, FIF, SCT [34768]

PETTS 1800S MINSTER, KEN, ENG [35398] : 1812-77 MAYFIELD, STS, ENG [37174] : PRE 1900 THE HADHAMS, HRT, ENG [37387] : PRE 1900 THE HADHAMS, ESS, ENG [37387]

PETTY 1820+ YASS, NSW, AUS [36610] : THOMAS C1780 CHILVERS COTON, WAR, ENG [35252] : 1789 RILSDON, WRY, ENG [35282] : 1800S NUNEATON, WAR, ENG [35535] : GEORGE 1840S (SOLDIER), SOM, ENG [35607] : ALL BOLTON ABBEY, WRY, ENG [36144] : 1698-1850S ILKLEY & BOLTON ABBEY, WRY, ENG [37988] : 1800S GUILFORD CO., NC, USA [37028] : C1700 ESSEX, VA, USA [38348]

PETYT ALL BOLTON ABBEY, WRY, ENG [36144] : ALL LONDON, ENG [36144]

PEUNNER PRE 1854 ALTONA HAMBURG, HBG, BRD [38525]

PEUTRILL ALL LEI, ENG [34400]

PEVEHOUSE PRE 1790 SURRY CO., NC, USA [38538]

PEVER 1700S ILLOGAN, CON, ENG [38745]

PEVERELL 1770S NOTTINGHAM, NTT, ENG [34594] : PRE 1850 WAREHAM & CORFE, DOR, ENG [38483]

PEVERETT ALL DBY, ENG [35009] : ALL GRAHAMSTOWN, CAPE, RSA [35009]

PEVERILL 1770S NOTTINGHAM, NTT, ENG [34594]

PEW 1700 HENRICO, VA, USA [38198]

PEWSEY PRE 1845 NEW FOREST, HAM, ENG [36079] : ALL WORLDWIDE [37291]

PEXER PRE 1900 STETTIN, SZ, POL [34089]

PEXSA PRE 1900 STETTIN, SZ, POL [34089]

PEXSTERS 1772-1990 HASPENGOUW, LBG, BEL [38158]

PEXTON 1865 HULL, YKS, ENG [37493]

PEYLA C1700 ONEX, GE, CH [38348]

PEZENAS PRE 1900 BESSUEZOULS, AUV, FRA [34104]

PFADLER PRE 1720 LAUBEN, MEMMINGEN BAV, GER [38661]

PFAFFENBACH 1880+ MECKELSDORF, HES, GER [35315]

PFAFFLE PRE 1852 WEINSBERG, BAW, GER [35387]

PFAU 1630-1700 ALTONA, HBG, GER [38626]

PFEFFER 1800S OBERJOSSA, GHE, GER [38354]

PFEIFER C1900+ FORT SASKATCHENAN, ALB, CAN [34356] : ALL WORLDWIDE [34356]

PFEIFFER PRE 1800 ODENHEIM, BAW, GER [38609]

PFEIFFER (SEE PFEIFE [34356]

PFENNING 1770-1872 DETMOLD, GER [38749]

PFENNINGWERTH 1860+ LAUNCESTON, TAS, AUS [34770]

PFERSICH 1600-1700 PFEFFINGEN, WUE, GER [38599]

PFISTERER PRE 1700 WINNENDEN, WUE, GER [38683]

PFITZER C1720 VORN. LUDWIG, WUE, GER [38661]

PFITZNER C1835 BORKENDORF, SIL, GER [34083]

PHAFFLEN PRE 1770 WEINSBERG, BAW, GER [35387]

PHAIR 1750+ TERAROE KINAWLEY, FER, IRL [35851] : ALL DOW, IRL [36856] : C1810 EDINBURGH, MLN, SCT [34713]

PHARAR ALL CAVERSHAM, OXF, ENG [36326]

PHARO PRE 1700 NTT & NJ, ENG & USA [38746]

PHAROLE (SEE FERRELL [34758]

PHARRELL 1800S TAS & VIC, AUS [35137]

PHAYER 1850+ PLUMSTEAD, KEN, ENG [36107]

PHAYRE ALL DOW, IRL [36856]

PHEE 1850S NEW MONKLAND, LKS, SCT & AUS [35075]

PHEFLEY 1855+ WODONGA, VIC, AUS [35387]

PHELAN 1853+ AXEDALE, VIC, AUS [34174] : 1880+ STRATHFIELDSAYE, VIC, AUS [34174] : 1800+ GUYSBOROUGH, NS, CAN [35627] : PRE 1875 LIVERPOOL, ENG [35761] : 1850+ CLONMEL, TIP, IRL [33797] : PRE 1852 LEX, IRL [34174] : PRE 1860 ROSSMORE, LEX, IRL [34275] : 1825+ WATERFORD, WAT, IRL [38291] : 1800S TIP, IRL & CAN [36710]

PHELPS 1500-1700 HEF & GLS, ENG [34739] : 1730+ SHEPTON BEAUCHAMP, SOM, ENG [34900] : PRE 1823 LAMBETH, SRY, ENG [35016] : PRE 1857 PENTONVILLE, MDX, ENG [35335] : PRE 1850 ST MARYLEBONE, MDX, ENG [36425] : ALL UK [36505] : ZURIAH 1729 HEBRON, CT, USA [35273] : THERSA ALL DEVEREAUX, MI, USA [35302] : 1820-1870 SPENCER, IN, USA [38095] : 1790-1820 WARREN, KY, USA [38095] : 1820-1860 WARRICK, IN, USA [38095] : 1790-1890 EDMONSON & MCCRACKEN, KY, USA [38095] : 1790-1890 BUTLER & OHIO, KY, USA [38095] : ABIRHAM 1811-50 TRUMBULL CO., OH, USA [38138] : PRE 1890 HAMPDEN CO., MA, USA [38365]

PHEMISTER PRE 1780 DFS, SCT [37133]

PHENEY PRE 1900 ST PANCRAS, MDX, ENG [34638] : 1850+ NEW PLYMOUTH, NZ [34638]

PHIBBS C1827 LADYWOOD, BIRMINGHAM, WAR, ENG [34972]

PHILBEY 1880+ KERANG, VIC, AUS [35230] : C1890+ KOETONG, VIC, AUS [35230]

PHILIP 1855-1875 ARTHUR, ONT, CAN [34205] : PRE 1809 FYVIE, ABD, SCT [34205]

PHILIPO ALL WORLDWIDE [36083]

PHILIPOT 1600S KEN, ENG [38373]

PHILIPPO ALL WORLDWIDE [36083]

PHILIPPS 1750-1850 MOYLGROVE, PEM, WLS [34345]

PHILIPPSOHN 1835 JEVER, OLD, GER [37509]

PHILIPS PRE 1834 BOTHWELL, TAS, AUS [34576] : 1785 NORTH WALTHAM, HAM, ENG [34309] : 1750-1825 CHITTLEHAMPTON, DEV, ENG [37602] : 1700+ KILMUCKRIDGE, WEX, IRL [34749] : C1850 ALVAH, ABD, SCT [34515]

PHILIPSON 1700-1750 STANHOPE, DUR, ENG [38516]

PHILLEMORE 1894-1910+ BURWOOD, NSW, AUS [34294]

PHILLIPO ALL WORLDWIDE [36083]

PHILLIPPI 1790+ TRIER & ORMOND, RPF, GER [37534] : 1790+ ELO, GER & FRA [37534]

PHILLIPPO ALL WORLDWIDE [36083]

PHILLIPPS C1780-1850 BAD, GER [38325]

PHILLIPS 1875+ PRAHRAN, VIC, AUS [33877] : 1890+ PERTH, WA, AUS [33927] : 1838+ MAITLAND, NSW, AUS [34288] : PRE 1864 BANNOCKBURN, VIC, AUS [34412] : 1850S+ SYDNEY, NSW, AUS [34791] : PRE 1930 STANLEY, TAS, AUS [34918] : 1861+ ROCKHAMPTON, QLD, AUS [35260] : 1875+ SOUTH YARRA, VIC, AUS [35436] : 1857-1875 DAYLESFORD, VIC, AUS [35436] : 1896+ VIC, AUS [35453] : PRE 1888+ SA, AUS [35453] : 1868+ NUNAWADING, VIC, AUS [35531] : 1873+ COLLINGWOOD, VIC, AUS [35531] : 1880+ BEAUFORT, VIC, AUS [35538] : WILLIAM C1860 BEAUFORT, VIC, AUS [35838] : 1722-1856 CAMPBELLS CK, VIC, AUS [36371] : C1860 GEELONG, VIC, AUS [36612] : 1850+ BEECHWORTH, VIC, AUS [37134] : 1850 DANDENONG, VIC, AUS [37163] : PRE 1910 NSW, AUS [38730] : 1780-1990 OSNABRUCK, ONT, CAN [34077] : 1850S BURRITS RAPIDS, ONT, CAN [35078] : 1870+ CAN [37720] : 1700+ JSY, CHI [34789] : 1790S JSY, CHI [37134] : PRE 1850 DINDER, SOM, ENG [34314] : 1832 PORT ISAAC, CON, ENG [34565] : 1760+ GRAFTON, WOR, ENG [34580] : EDMUND & JOHN 1819+ GRAFTON, WOR, ENG [34580] : SAMUEL 1831+ GRAFTON, WOR, ENG [34580] : PHILIP 1831+ GRAFTON, WOR, ENG [34580] : BENJAMIN 1870-1915 SHIPTON MOYNE, GLS, ENG [34580] : 1790+ MANCHESTER & WIGAN, LAN, ENG [34609] : PRE 1840 COLDWALTHAM, SSX, ENG [34621] : PRE 1884 STEPNEY, MDX, ENG [34689] : PRE 1786 TAUNTON, SOM, ENG [34696] : 1600+ HASTINGS, SSX, ENG [34747] : 1700-1800S LND & MDX, ENG [34791] : 1700S STITHIANS, CON, ENG [34793] : JOEL C1835 WEST BROMWICH, STS, ENG [34898] : PRE 1880 GLS, ENG [34993] : PRE 1880 CHS, ENG [35055] : 1800+ CON, ENG [35060] : PRE 1840 MODBURY, DEV, ENG [35128] : C1840 DARTFORD, KEN, ENG [35260] : 1830S ST MARTIN IN THE FIELDS, LND, ENG [35260] : 1700+ ST CLEARS, CON, ENG [35355] : 1800S BAINTON, LIN, ENG [35531] : 1800S DUDDINGTON, NTH, ENG [35531] : PRE 1700 ESS, ENG [35642] : WILLIAM C1850 ST PANCRAS, MDX, ENG [35725] : PRE 1860S CHORLTON CUM HARDY, LAN, ENG [35728] : 1850+ CON, ENG [35771] : 1850-1870 WALWORTH & CLERKENWELL, LND, ENG [36044] : WILLIAM 1777 ST MARYLEBONE, LND, ENG [36279] : 1722-1856 STITHIANS, CON, ENG [36371] : ALL CHELSEA, LND, ENG [36407] : PRE 1800 KINGSWOOD, GLS, ENG [36441] : PRE 1875 BURSLEM, STS, ENG [36514] : 1725-1850 CHEPSTOW CO., GLS, ENG [36555] : C1780+ LIVERPOOL, LAN, ENG [36838] : 1800+ PLYMOUTH, DEV, ENG [36885] : SUSAN 1820S MILDENHALL, SFK, ENG [37106] : 1820+

KENSINGTON, LND, ENG [37134] : 1750-1900
BARNET, MDX, ENG [37207] : PRE 1850
AMESBURY & DEVIZES, WIL, ENG [37320] :
C1700-1900 TWEEDMOUTH & NORHAM, NBL,
ENG [37395] : THOMAS 1838-40 ALBERBURY,
SAL, ENG [37694] : PRE 1820 CHATHAM AREA,
KEN, ENG [37720] : 1750-1900 CLERKENWELL,
MDX, ENG [37747] : 1800+ SUCKLEY, WOR, ENG
[38020] : 1800-1900 BIRMINGHAM, WAR, ENG
[38321] : 1800S BEAUCHAMP, WOR, ENG [38745] :
1820 HIGHGATE HILL, LND, ENG [38756] :
THOMAS 1760-1803 ENG & IRL [36100] : 1780+
DERRY, LDY, IRL [33927] : 1850+ DON, IRL
[34342] : PRE 1860 BRAY, WIK, IRL [36612] : 1830
MONTENEGRO, OES [36798] : 1800+ LARBERT &
GLASGOW, STI & LKS, SCT [34326] : ALL DFS,
SCT [35293] : C1781 CRAIL, FIF, SCT [35854] : ALL
GLASGOW, SCT [36094] : C1800 GLASGOW, LKS,
SCT [37143] : ALL UK [36131] : SILAS 1839-1905
HUMASVILLE, POLK CO., MO, USA [36321] :
SILAS 1839-1905 KANSAS CITY, JACKSON, MO,
USA [36321] : SILAS 1839-1905 FUNKS GROVE,
MCLEAN CO., IL, USA [36321] : PRE 1710 VA, USA
[36927] : PRE 1800 MOORE CO., NC & VA, USA
[37010] : DR NATHAN 1828+ GRIGGSVILLE,
PIKE CO., IL, USA [37797] : PRE 1808 KNOX CO.,
IN, USA [38017] : HENDRICK C1690-1750
DUTCHESS CO., NY, USA [38055] : WM. AUSTIN
1875 SHIAWASSEE CO., MI, USA [38142] :
MICHAEL C1659 NEWPORT, RI, USA [38172] :
JOHN 1850+ USA & CAN [34580] : EDMUND
1850+ USA & CAN [34580] : C1802+ NEW YORK,
NY, USA & ENG [35108] : 1810-1880 GELLIGAER,
GLA, WLS [34234] : PRE 1850 LLANFYRNACH,
PEM, WLS [34311] : 1820S MON, WLS [34853] :
THOMAS PRE 1842 TREGARON, CGN, WLS
[34992] : 1800+ FISHGUARD, PEM, WLS [35436] :
ALL LLANDAFF, GLA, WLS [35474] : 1860+
NEATH, GLA, WLS [36209] : 1700-1860 BEGELLY,
PEM, WLS [36209] : 1850+ SWANSEA, GLA, WLS
[36257] : PRE 1850 CONWIL ELFET, CMN, WLS
[36432] : 1871 LLANFYLLIN, MGY, WLS [37694] :
THOMAS 1838-40 MGY, WLS [37694] : NOAH
C1800-1900 BYNEA, WLS [37813] : 1840-1927 GLA,
WLS & AUS [33926] : 1825-1900 BRE, WLS & ENG
[36703] : PRE 1900 WORLDWIDE [36933] : ALL
WORLDWIDE [38060]

PHILLIPSON ALL LAN, ENG [37692]

PHILLIS 1840+ SYDNEY, NSW, AUS [35569] : 1700+
ANT, IRL [34572]

PHILLPOTTS 1818-1851 ST WEONARDS, HEF, ENG
[35720]

PHILLY 1700-1890 SCHENANGO, NY, USA [38529]

PHILO ALL WORLDWIDE [37651]

PHILOE ALL WORLDWIDE [37651]

PHILP ALL SCT [34758] : C1720-1920S CRAMOND,
MLN, SCT [37413]

PHILPOT 1790+ HATFIELD HEATH, ESS, ENG
[34577] : 1700-1800 KENNINGTON, MDX, ENG
[34623] : 1800-1900 WISHFORD, WIL, ENG [36438]

PHILPOTT ALL HERRING NECK, NFD, CAN
[35264] : PRE 1770 SHELWICH, KEN, ENG [34445] :
1800+ FAVERSHAM, KEN, ENG [35951] : PRE
1850 NEWMARKET, COR, IRL [34725]

PHILPS 1850+ LEE CO., IA, USA [37704]

PHIMISTER 1790S ELGIN, MOR, SCT [35260]

PHIN 1800+ LIFF & BENVIE, ANS, SCT [34637]

PHIPP PRE 1900 LONDON, ENG [36755]

PHIPPEN 1800-1950 HEMINGTON, SOM, ENG
[35288] : 1580-1633 CON, DEV & DOR, ENG [37764] :
1633-50 MA, USA [37764]

PHIPPS PRE 1940 TORONTO, ONT, CAN [37337] :
1850+ ONT, CAN [38323] : ALL FOREST OF
DEAN, GLS, ENG [34241] : HARRIET R. PRE 1853
OXF, ENG [34310] : C1800 SHOREDITCH, LND,
ENG [35527] : PRE 1830 NORTHWICH, CHS, ENG
[35945] : PRE 1780 REARSBY, LEI, ENG [36976] :
C1840 HAREFIELD, MDX, ENG [37552] : PRE 1840
WESTBURY LEIGH, WIL, ENG [38214] : PRE 1750
RIVER, KEN, ENG [38708] : 1750-1800
GLOUCESTER CO., VA, USA [36737] : C1940S
DAYTONA BEACH, FL, USA [37337]

PHISTER 1870+ GLENDALE, CA, USA [34922]

PHLLIPS ELIZABETH 1768+ BRILLEY, HEF, ENG
[33819]

PHYSIC ALL HORNCHURCH, ESS, ENG [34758]

PHYSICK PRE 1780 TAVISTOCK, SOM, ENG [36011]

PIAGET ALL WORLDWIDE [38303]

PIANOWSKA 1877-1910 SOKAL & GIMLI, MAN,
CAN & OES [34063]

PIANTA PRE 1870 BRUSIO, GR, CH [35750]

PICARD 1800+ KENMORE, ONT, CAN [36662]

PICHET LOUIS 1820+ MASKINONGE, QUE, CAN
[36678]

PICHIN 1856-1930 KYNETON, VIC, AUS [35469]

PICK PRE 1800 MELTON MOWBRAY, LEI, ENG
[34314] : 1794 WARTHILL, YKS, ENG [34581] : ALL
LEI, ENG [35177] : RALPH PRE 1670 LEI, ENG
[36619]

PICK (SEE VAN DER PI [38350]

PICKALL C1790 BOLTON LE SANDS, LAN, ENG
[36227]

PICKARD 1870+ ELGIN CO., ONT, CAN [34480] :
1783+ NIAGARA, ONT, CAN [34480] : ALL
WARWICK, WAR, ENG [37247] : PRE 1780 LEI,
ENG [37706] : PRE 1790 WESTMORELAND, PA,
USA [34480]

PICKART 1800S MUS, HES, BRD [37028]

PICKER 1600-1800 WELBOURN, LIN, ENG [37039]

PICKERDEN ALL WORLDWIDE [38252]

PICKERING 1852+ STAWELL & ILLAWARRA, VIC,
AUS [33793] : 1881+ MELBOURNE, VIC, AUS
[33880] : 1850+ WERONA & WATCHEM, VIC, AUS
[34962] : 1800+ AUS [35241] : 1890+ ZEEHAN, TAS,
AUS [35241] : 1820+ TAS, AUS [35241] : 1800+
SYDNEY, NSW, AUS [35513] : PRE 1890
NEWTOWN, NSW, AUS [35781] : PRE 1850
SYDNEY, NSW, AUS [37309] : 1850+
BUNINYONG, VIC, AUS & IRL [34864] : C1660-
1852 BLOCKLEY, WOR, ENG [33793] : 1858+
HENDON, MDX, ENG [33880] : JONATHAN C1850
CARLTON GARDENS, LND, ENG [33880] : PRE
1800 BILLINGHAM, DUR, ENG [34908] : 1810+
LITTLE SUTTON & THORNTON, LAN, ENG
[35114] : 1750+ YKS, ENG [35241] : 1800S
BRETTON, YKS, ENG [35379] : C1794
BRANDSBURTON, YKS, ENG [35515] : PRE 1800
RILLINGTON & SCAMPSTON, ERY, ENG [36048] :
PRE 1750 NRY, ENG [37498] : 1800-1890 WEST
DERBY, LAN, ENG [37651] : 1860-1940 ST
MARYLEBONE, MDX, ENG [37651] : 1860-1940 ST
PANCRAS, MDX, ENG [37651] : 1790-1860
WEETON & HALSHAM AREA, ERY, ENG [37859] :
PRE 1810 WRY, ENG [38577] : 1830+ KILKENNY,
KIK, IRL & AUS [34864] : 1800-1925 NY, IA & CA,
USA [35305]

PICKERSGILL 1750-1850 BETHNAL GREEN, LND,
ENG [37644]

PICKESS ALL WORLDWIDE [35884]

PICKET 1650-1750 CHITTLEHAMPTON, DEV, ENG
[37602]

PICKETT 1800+ WITNEY, OXF, ENG [35992] : ALL
LIN, ENG [36498] : PRE 1850 LND, ENG [36605] :

C1750 HRT, ENG [36978] : 1800-1890 DUNGIVEN, LDY, IRL & NZ [33991]

PICKFAT PRE 1840 LONDON, ENG [36967]

PICKFORD ALL NFD, CAN [35619] : PRE 1855 CAMELEY, SOM, ENG [34978] : JAMES & ELIZ PRE 1800 LANGPORT, SOM, ENG [35573] : HUBERT FOOT 1810-1840 YEOVIL, SOM, ENG [35714] : ALL MACCLESFIELD, CHS, ENG [36826] : C1860 BATH, SOM, ENG [37757] : ALL UK [36020]

PICKINSON PRE 1899 SHORE, LND, ENG [35893]

PICKLE 1800+ MONTREAL, QUE, CAN [34051] : MARY ANN 1852+ HALIFAX, NS, CAN [34206] : THOMAS 1800+ HALIFAX, NS, CAN [34206]

PICKLES C1910 LIVERPOOL, ENG [38168] : C1900 NOTTON, YKS, ENG [38168] : C1920 S. AFRICA [38168]

PICKMAN PRE 1780 MUNDON & MALDON, ESS, ENG [35902]

PICKSTOCK PRE 1800 STOCKPORT, CHS, ENG [34904] : 1820+ NORTHWICH, CHS, ENG [36214] : PRE 1821 STOCKPORT, LAN, ENG [36754]

PICKTON PRE 1840 LND, ENG [37370]

PICKUP 1750+ DARWEN, LAN, ENG [36991]

PICKWELL 1600-1700 FREISTON, LIN, ENG [35288]

PICKWORTH PRE 1874 WISBECH, CAM, ENG [36855]

PICQUIGNY PRE 1088 PIC, FRA [37764]

PICTON PRE 1840 LND, ENG [37370] : THOMAS ALL GLA, WLS [36443]

PIDD C1980 ESSENDON, VIC, AUS [34694]

PIDDING 1836+ SYDNEY, NSW, AUS [35261] : 1793 PADDINGTON, LND, ENG [35260] : C1825 BLACKHEATH, KEN, ENG [35260]

PIDDUCK 1800 KEN, ENG [36480]

PIDGEON 1850+ BENDIGO, VIC, AUS [35725] : 1775+ YARMOUTH, ENG [34387] : ALL KEN, ENG [35063] : C1830-1850 BIRMINGHAM, WAR & WOR, ENG [35725] : ALL WINCHCOMBE, GLS, ENG [36998] : 1800S CHINGFORD ESSEX, LND, ENG & AUS [36642]

PIDSLEY 1700S COLEBROOK, DEV, ENG [35830]

PIDWELL PRE 1860 SRY, ENG [33925]

PIECE 1859+ BRANTFORD, ONT, CAN [34528]

PIECZONKA PRE 1900 OPR, GER [38632] : PRE 1900 POL [38632]

PIELOU 1689-1990 ENG & IRL &, CAN & USA [34124]

PIEPER 1855+ BENDIGO, VIC, AUS [35725] : 1800-1847 MAGDEBURG, PRE, GER [35725]

PIERCE PAUL 1827+ HOBART, TAS, AUS [35394] : PRE 1776 GOUDHURST & CRANBROOK, KEN, ENG [34351] : PRE 1865 ESS, ENG [36116] : 1900-1920 LONDON, ENG [36116] : 1750-1830 HARWICH, ESS & SFK, ENG [37779] : 1740-1850 MAIDSTONE, KEN, ENG [37880] : ALL CHESTER, CHS, ENG [38074] : ALL ARDFERT, KER, IRL [36854] : 1600-1700 REHOBOTH, MA, USA [34749] : PRE 1870 WI, USA [35290] : C1850 MCMINN & ROANE CO., TN, USA [36934] : 1750-1820 CORNWALL, CT, USA [38098] : PRE 1800 WASHINGTON CO., OH, USA [38231] : 1767-1850S MONHEGAN, MA, USA [38308]

PIERCY 1710+ KERDISTON, NFK, ENG [35046]

PIERPOINT 1800S WOR, ENG [35984] : 1790-1850 EARL STONHAM, SFK, ENG [36717]

PIERRE 1800-1950 ST BERNARD PARISH NEW ORLEANS, LA, USA [37583]

PIERREHUMBERT 1790-1860 CORTAILLOD, NEU, CH [34751]

PIERS PRE 1920 DUBLIN, IRL [35738]

PIERSMA PRE 1850 NIJLAND, FRI, NL [38646]

PIERSON 1750-1850 KEN, ENG [34572]

PIERT ALL KIK, IRL [35525]

PIESCHE PRE 1945 TETSCHEN, GER [38674]

PIESS ALL WORLDWIDE [36378]

PIESSE ALL WORLDWIDE [36378]

PIETERS PRE 1850 BOSCHKAPELLE, ZEL, NL [38697]

PIETRZAK PRE 1900 PO, POL [36355]

PIETY PRE 1780 NC, USA & ENG [36917]

PIETZ 1860-1890 WAUSHARA CO., WI, USA [36546]

PIEZZI 1840 GUIMAGLIO, TICINO, CH [35903]

PIFER PRE 1900 IL, OH & PA, USA [36544]

PIGEON 1800 SYDNEY, NSW, AUS [36312] : 1750-1900 STOW BARDOLPH, NFK, ENG [36394]

PIGG 1806 CHRISHALL, ESS, ENG [35808] : MOSES 1797-1813 HARDIN, KY, USA [38157]

PIGGFORD ALL AUS [33887] : ALL DUR, ENG [33887]

PIGGIN PRE 1900 RACKHEATH, NFK, ENG [36122]

PIGGINS 1850-1900 ORANGE, NSW, AUS [34422] : ALL FOLKINGHAM, LIN, ENG [35258]

PIGGOT 1750-1850 ABINGDON, BRK, ENG [34552]

PIGGOTT 1860 HAMILTON, VIC, AUS [34594] : 1860S BENDIGO, VIC, AUS [35390] : ALL ONT, CAN [35139] : 1830 LONDON, ENG [34594] : 1850+ OLDBURY, WOR, ENG [34782] : ALL HADDENHAM, BKM, ENG [35139] : ALL WADDESDON, BKM, ENG [35139] : 1830+ WISBECH, CAM, ENG [35390] : 1700+ WADDESDON, BKM, ENG [35555] : PRE 1825 LONDON, ESS & MDX, ENG [36709] : PRE 1855 GRAVESEND, KEN, ENG [37142] : PRE 1890 GUILDEN MORDEN, CAM, ENG [37989]

PIGOT C1810 ST JOHN'S, NFD, CAN [34096] : 1420-1500 BEACHAMPTON, BKM, ENG [34716] : PRE 1780 FORFAR, ANS, SCT [34096]

PIGOTT 1700-1850 WEM, IRL [35494] : 1700-1850 MEA, IRL [35494] : ALL NEW YORK, NY, USA [36076]

PIGRUM ALL WORLDWIDE [34451]

PIJTTERS 1778+ OLDEBOORN, FRI, NL [34990]

PIKE ALL NFD, CAN [33852] : 1840+ BURIN, NFD, CAN [34349] : C1913 SHERBROOKE, QUE, CAN [35973] : 1816+ DOVER, KEN, ENG [35027] : 1750+ BRIXHAM, DEV, ENG [35027] : ALL NFK, ENG [36580] : 1800+ BULFORD, WIL, ENG [36785] : 1730-1772 WICKMERE AREA, NFK, ENG [38465] : 1817+ SURRY CO., NC, USA [38044] : SAMUEL 1737 PASQUOTANK, NC, USA [38152] : ROBERT C1610 PROVIDENCE, RI, USA [38172] : JAMES 1800S MEADE CO., KY, USA [38312] : PRE 1780 ST MARYS CO., MD, USA [38312]

PIKESLEY ALL LONDON & EDINBURGH, ENG & SCT [36006]

PILCH PRE 1800 NFK, ENG [37712] : ALL NFK, ENG [38035]

PILCHER 1830+ MAITLAND, NSW, AUS [34969] : 1870+ BATHURST, NSW, AUS [34969] : 1880+ STRATHFIELD, NSW, AUS [34969] : ALL DODINGTON, KEN, ENG [34564] : 1870+ BARNSTAPLE, DEV, ENG [34969] : PRE 1830 ROCHESTER, KEN, ENG [34969] : PRE 1700 CANTERBURY, KEN, ENG [36532] : 1750-1900 THANET, KEN, ENG [37644]

PILCOCKE ALL ENG [36086]

PILE PRE 1800 CHEDDON FITZPAINE, SOM, ENG [37381]

PILET 1700-1990 QUE, CAN [36699] : 1100-1700 CH [36699] : 1600-1800 RPA, FRA [36699] : ALL WORLDWIDE [36699]

PILFOLD 1775-1800 BRIGHTON, SSX, ENG [36035]

PILGER 1700+ BAD, GER [38529]

PILGRIM PRE 1700 ESS, ENG [35642] : 1800 GREENWICH, KEN, ENG [37083] : 1800-1900 ENG

[37207] : 1800-1850 ABBEVILLE, SC, USA [38088] : 1865+ USA [38533]

PILKINGTON 1820-1940 DAYLESFORD, VIC, AUS [34462] : PRE 1900 WA, AUS [36645] : 1650 LONDON, ENG [33918] : PRE 1820 BRANCEPETH, DUR, ENG [34462] : 1850+ LAN, ENG [35362]

PILL ALL GORRAN, CON, ENG [35723] : ALL WORLDWIDE [37379]

PILLANS PRE 1815 EDINBURGH, MLN, SCT [35430]

PILLE ALL WORLDWIDE [38664]

PILLEY 1700 TOLLESHUNT KNIGHTS, ESS, ENG [37928] : C1800 CHELTENHAM, GLS, ENG [37943]

PILLILLAH 1780 JEDBURGH, ROX, SCT [34149]

PILLIN PRE 1841 COLNE, LAN, ENG [36022]

PILLING C1862 MT COLE, VIC, AUS [37177] : C1886+ TAS, AUS [37177] : 1820+ BURY, LAN, ENG [35442] : PRE 1841 COLNE, LAN, ENG [36022] : 1800+ HASLINGDEN, LAN, ENG [36271] : C1750 BACUP, LAN, ENG [36635] : ALL TOP O THE HUTTOCK, LAN, ENG [37177]

PILLINGER PRE 1850 HASFIELD & GLOUCESTER, GLS, ENG [36113]

PILLINGS 1800+ MDX & LAN, ENG [37525] : H.W. C1911 RSA [37525]

PILLMAN 1820-1850 TAMWORTH, ONT, CAN [34394]

PILLOKAT PRE 1880 KRS. GUMBINNEN, OPR, GER [38649]

PILLOW C1715 ESSEX CO., VA, USA [36354] : 1776-1782 ROCKINGHAM CO., NC, USA [36354]

PILON 1610-1690 BAYEUX, BN, FRA [34514]

PILSBURY 1850S SOUTH, STS, ENG [35099]

PILSON 1819-1853 WIC, IRL [38455] : ALL IRL [38455]

PIM PRE 1807 LND, SRY & HRT, ENG [37760]

PIMBLOT 1700 BUTLEY, CHS, ENG [37697]

PIMM 1500+ CHILHAM, KEN & LND, ENG [36049] : ALL BATTLE, SSX, ENG [36664]

PINARD 1800+ CAN [38493] : 1649+ FRA [38493] : 1800+ USA [38493]

PINCH ELIZABETH 1816+ ROCHE, CON, ENG [35343] : ALL ENG [37561] : PRE 1850 ST KEW & TREQUITE, CON, ENG [37768]

PINCHEM JOHN ALL SMITH CO., TN, USA [35304]

PINCHEN 1850+ WOLLOMBI, NSW, AUS [35420] : PRE 1850 HILCOTT, WIL, ENG [35420] : 1700 HILCOTT, WIL, ENG [35874]

PINCHIN PRE 1900 BOX, WIL, ENG [37248] : PRE 1900 SOUTH WRAXALL, WIL, ENG [37248] : 1850-1920 MONKTON COMBE, SOM, ENG [37248]

PINCKNEY 1066-1650 ENG [37764] : C1630-49 NEW ENGLAND, USA [37764] : C1649-64 FAIRFIELD, CT, USA [37764] : 1664+ EASTCHESTER, NY, USA [37764]

PINDER 1830-1870 WAWNE & STH DALTON, YKS, ENG [33861] : 1790+ WRY, ENG [34692] : PRE 1900 WITHERNSEA, YKS, ENG [36035] : 1500-1860 HINDERWELL AREA, NRY, ENG [37859]

PINE PRE 1756 BRISTOL, GLS, SOM & DEV, ENG [37289] : 1650+ LONG ISLAND, NY, USA [34392]

PINEL ALL WORLDWIDE [36832]

PINEO 1667+ LYONS, FRA [37499]

PINER 1800+ HEDGERLEY, BKM, ENG [35909]

PINFOLD 1800-1870 PRIORS MARSTON, WAR, ENG [36795] : PRE 1850 TAYNTON, OXF, ENG [36889] : ALL OXF, ENG [36889]

PINGNEY PRE 1791 DRUMBROUGH, CUL, ENG [35440]

PINION 1600+ BATTLE, SSX, ENG [34939]

PINK PRE 1755 THURSLEY & GODALMING, SRY, ENG [34382] : 1778 PRIVETT, HAM, ENG [34909] : ALL BUCKLEBURY & BASILDON, BRK, ENG [36163]

PINKARD 1700+ BKM, NTH & BDF, ENG [36574]

PINKERTON 1830S YORK MILLS, ONT, CAN [38422] : 1800S ANT, IRL [38422] : ALL KAMO, NZ [34561] : ALL LKS, SCT [34561] : 1800-1838 PAISLEY, RFW, SCT [34842] : PRE 1835 PAISLEY, RFW, SCT [38596]

PINKESS C1847 LIVERPOOL, LAN, ENG [37155] : 1874+ DUNEDIN, NZ [37155]

PINKHAM 1751-1849 PQ, CAN [37577] : 1758-1644 DOVER & DOVER NECK, NH, USA [38520]

PINKNEY PRE 1860 BRIDLINGTON & LANGTON, YKS, ENG [34865] : ALL DUR, ENG [36046] : C1810 FELIXKIRK, NRY, ENG [37710] : C1810 THORNTON LE STREET, NRY, ENG [37710] : 1700S MD, USA [37764]

PINKSTON MESHOOK PRE 1760S ENG [37585]

PINN 1700-1800S BRISTOL, GLS, ENG [36856]

PINNELL C1850+ BRINKWORTH, WIL, ENG [36258] : PRE 1900 BRINKWORTH, WIL, ENG [36282] : 1800+ WLS & ENG [36885]

PINNER ALL BIRMINGHAM, WAR, ENG [37133]

PINNEY ALL CREWKERNE, SOM, ENG [36382] : 1550-1600 BROADWAY, SOM, ENG [37783]

PINNICK PRE 1900 DOR, ENG [34364]

PINN-MOUNTAIN ALL WORLDWIDE [36856]

PINNOCK 1700-1800 KETTERING, NTH, ENG [36057] : ALL HADLOW, KEN, ENG [36469]

PINSELER C1700 OSMARSLEBEN, HAL, DDR [37918]

PINTO 1855+ GEELONG & BALLARAT, VIC, AUS [37994]

PION ALL CAN & USA [35640]

PIOTT 1850-1900 RICHMOND, NRY, ENG [34211]

PIPER CONNIE 1800+ BATHURST, NSW, AUS [33878] : JOHN 1820+ HOBART, TAS, AUS [33898] : 1870S NEWCASTLE & SYDNEY, NSW, AUS [34458] : 1850-1880 MARYBOROUGH, VIC, AUS [34682] : C1835 LAUNCESTON, TAS, AUS [35865] : PRE 190 KEN, ENG [33953] : HUGH PRE 1803 LAUNCESTON, CON, ENG [34019] : C1840 BROADSTAIRS, KEN, ENG [34395] : PRE 1835 CAMBERWELL, SRY, ENG [34458] : 1790-1850S WESTMINSTER, MDX, ENG [34458] : C1850 BOSCALLA, CON, ENG [34682] : 1839-1900 PIMLICO & DULWICH, LND, ENG [34829] : GEORGE PRE 1840 REIGATE, SRY, ENG [34847] : WILLIAM PRE 1826 NEW ALRESFORD, HAM, ENG [34847] : 1900S BIRMINGHAM, WAR, ENG [34909] : PRE 1813 EAST MALLING, KEN, ENG [35016] : 1788 COLYTON, DEV, ENG [35203] : ALICE PRE 1750 NFK, ENG [35212] : ALL HAM, ENG [35365] : C1841 TAUNTON, SOM, ENG [35720] : C1814 BRIGHTON, SSX, ENG [35865] : C1780 ENG [35998] : C1800 WEST HOATHLY, SSX, ENG [36107] : C1850 HEATHFIELD, SSX, ENG [36271] : C1810 BURWASH, SSX, ENG [36271] : 1800+ PLAYDEN, KEN, ENG [36785] : 1800S KENWYN, CON, ENG [36961] : C1790 BUCKLAND, DEV, ENG [36961] : 1700-1900 LONDON & CAMBERWELL, SRY, ENG [37257] : 1800-1900 LONDON & BETHNAL GREEN, MDX, ENG [37257] : 1800-1900 LONDON & BERMONDSEY, SRY, ENG [37257] : 1300-1400+ SSX, ENG [37648] : PRE 1850 ENG [37901] : 1780+ RATHKEALE, LIM, IRL [37172] : JOHN PRE 1792 MAYBOLE, AYR, SCT [34019] : HUGH PRE 1803 MAYBOLE, AYR, SCT [34019] : JOHN PRE 1773 MAYBOLE, AYR, SCT [35578] : ALL THURSO, CAI, SCT [37303] : ALL WORLDWIDE [35831]

PIPPARD PRE 1850 SOUTH PETHERTON, SOM, ENG [33876]

PIPPIN C1750+ BILLESDON, LEI, ENG [36258]

PIPR PRE 1870 ST LAWRENCE SEAL, KEN, ENG [35016]

PIPSON PRE 1840 BOGNOR, SSX, ENG [35913]
PIRIE 1870-1878 BALMAIN, NSW, AUS [36293] : 1850-1900 BALLARAT, VIC, AUS [36293] : 1710-1970 CAIRNEY BY HUNTLEY, ABD, SCT [34771] : 1840+ EDINBURGH, MLN, SCT [37483] : 1906-1990 CHICAGO, IL, USA [34771]
PIRRET 1800S EDINBURGH, MLN, SCT [36742]
PISFORD PRE 1850 NEWPORT, ESS, ENG [36676]
PISKOSKI ALL FALKENBURG & DARMBURG, POM, GER [37607]
PISOR PRE 1842 BRD [36020]
PISTORIUS PRE 1700 WINNENDEN, WUE, GER [38683]
PITCHER ALL ENGLISH HARBOUR TRINITY, NFD, CAN [34093] : PRE 1875 GUELPH, ONT, CAN [34849] : ALL DOR, ENG [33803] : 1700-1850 NFK, ENG [34081] : PRE 1784 NETHERBURY, DOR, ENG [34275] : PRE 1800 HELLINGLY, SSX, ENG [35020] : C1800 BEAMINSTER, DOR, ENG [35612] : C1803 ATTLEBOROUGH, NFK, ENG [35714] : C1700-1900 COLCHESTER, ESS, ENG [36425] : 1650-1750 SOM, ENG [37233]
PITCHES C1880 SYDENHAM, KEN, ENG [34362] : PRE 1875 FORDHAM, CAM, ENG [35561]
PITCHFORD PRE 1720 DOWNHAM, CAM, ENG [34445] : 1815 STANTON, SAL, ENG [34926]
PITE ALL WORLDWIDE [38445]
PITELIN 1600-1700 BROME, SFK, ENG [37457]
PITFIELD 1586 ALLINGTON, DOR, ENG [33967]
PITHER PRE 1830 HURST, BRK, ENG [37069]
PITHOUSE PRE 1840 BKM, ENG [34445]
PITKIN ALL POPLAR, LND, ENG [37871]
PITMAN 1850+ QLD, AUS [37974] : PRE 1857 PODIMORE, SOM, ENG [35464] : PRE 1850 LONDON, ENG [37743] : PRE 1860 SOM, ENG [37974] : PRE 1770 RICHMOND, SRY, ENG [38248]
PITSENBARGER 1800-1860 DARKE CO., OH, USA [33760]
PITSON ALL BAGSHOT, SRY, ENG [35231]
PITSONBARGER 1850-1855 PENDLETON CO., VA & IA, USA [37815]
PITSTOCK 1820+ TAS, AUS [34904]
PITT 1870-1890S GOODNA, QLD, AUS [35044] : PRE 1810 BRISTOL, GLS, ENG [34445] : PRE 1800 HAWKESBURY, GLS, ENG [34466] : C1880 SAWSTON, CAM, ENG [35121] : PRE 1850 BIRMINGHAM, WAR, ENG [35151] : C1844 CHS, ENG [35202] : RACHAEL 1800+ KIDDERMINSTER, ENG [35429] : PRE 1850 MORTLAKE, LND, ENG [35945] : 1700-1900 LND & SFK, ENG [36007] : ALL BIRMINGHAM, WAR, ENG [36216] : THOMAS 1829-1900 COLCHESTER, ESS, ENG [36876] : 1800S COLCHESTER, ESS, ENG [36876] : PRE 1900 LONDON, ENG [37062] : 1800S LEIGH, LAN, ENG [37083] : 1850S SRY, ENG [38017] : PRE 1830S POOLE, DOR, ENG [38396] : WILLIAM ALL BRIGHTON, ENG & CAN [34481] : 1700+ GIRVAN, AYR, SCT [37620] : 1840S EDINBURGH, MLN, SCT [38206]
PITTARD PRE 1852 GENEVA, CH [35189] : PRE 1806 LONG SUTTON, SOM, ENG [35464] : PRE 1840 BRISTOL, AVON, ENG [35795]
PITTAWAY 1866 BIRMINGHAM, WAR, ENG [34120] : PRE 1869 BARROW ON FURNESS, LAN, ENG [34786] : 1840+ WEST BROMWICH & TIPTON, STS, ENG [36254]
PITTILLA PRE 1850 LKS & MLN, SCT [37496]
PITTILLO PRE 1828 PENICUIK, MLN, SCT [33821]
PITTMAN PRE 1750 YATE, GLS, ENG [33771]
PITTOCK PRE 1850 DEAL, KEN, ENG [33804]
PITTS 1800S CATTLE, YKS, ENG [35379] : 1840+ FULHAM, MDX, ENG [36791] : PRE 1810 ESS, ENG

[37668] : PRE 1800 WOR, ENG [38745] : PRE 1910 KS, USA [37668] : 1770+ YORK CO., ME, USA [37784]
PITTSEN ALL BAGSHOT, SRY, ENG [35231] : PRE 1749 NUNAN COURTNEY, OXF, ENG [35231]
PITTY PRE 1830+ GREAT CHISHALL, ESS, ENG [35453]
PIVEY 1820-1860 BATHAMPTON, SOM, ENG [36262]
PIZANNE 1795+ QUE, CAN [34068]
PLACE 1842-1893 FREMANTLE & PERTH, WA, AUS [34582] : PRE 1869 TAMAR HEADS, TAS, AUS [35109] : 1790-1850 EAST WITTON, YKS, ENG [33861] : 1814-1876 WELL & SNAPE, NRY, ENG [34352] : ALEXANDER 1817+ HALIFAX, WRY, ENG [35353] : GEORGE 1834+ ST ANDREWS, HOLBORN, LND, ENG [35353] : 1600-1700 ENG [36898] : PRE 1825 ENG [38288]
PLADON 1800-1900 LONDON, ENG [36766]
PLAICE PRE 1800 YORK, NRY, ENG [34648]
PLAISTED ALL WORLDWIDE [36651]
PLANE ALL WORLDWIDE [37656]
PLANK 1790+ USA & GER [36357]
PLANT PRE 1859 LONG CRENDON, BKM, ENG [33862] : PRE 1850 NOTTINGHAM, NTT, ENG [34570] : JOHN PRE 1855 BURSLEM, STS, ENG [34935] : PRE 1850 STS, ENG [35394] : 1750+ SYSTON & LOUGHBOROUGH, LEI, ENG [36794] : PRE 1820 FRADSWELL, STS, ENG [37085] : ALL WORLDWIDE [36482]
PLANTE 1890+ MELBOURNE, VIC, AUS [34570] : 1621 LA ROCHELLE, AUNIS, FRA [38364]
PLASTOW C1836 WINDSOR, BRK, ENG [37148]
PLATE PRE 1800 SCHOLEN & STOPHEL, PRE, GER [36363]
PLATER 1840+ WALSALL, STS, ENG [34768] : ALL BKM, ENG [35139]
PLATFOOT 1700S WATTON, NFK, ENG [38745]
PLATT 1807 WIDNES, LAN, ENG [35282] : PRE 1850 YKS & LAN, ENG [36380] : PRE 1851 MIDDLEWICH, CHS, ENG [36403] : ALL ENG [36613] : PRE 1620 WARE, HRT, ENG [38135] : 1600+ TARBOCK, LAN, ENG [38745] : PRE 1850 DRUMCREE, ARM, IRL [36607] : 1835-1918 BATH, NY & ME, USA [33891] : C1650 MIDDLETOWN, CT, USA [34395] : PRE 1855 MI & IN, USA [36968] : JOHN 1719 BURLINGTON, NJ, USA [38152]
PLATTEN PRE 1750 KOBLENZ, RPR, GER [38437]
PLATTNER GEOFFREY 1880S IPSWICH, QLD, AUS [34044]
PLATTS 1800+ NOTTINGHAM, NTT, ENG [35342] : PRE 1850 DBY, ENG [36298] : 1853 ALBIAN PRAIRIE, WI, USA [38362]
PLATZ PRE 1855 HEDDESHEIM, BAD, GER [37894]
PLATZOEDER 1600+ SCHAUERHEIM, BAV, GER [37542]
PLAXTON 1750-1850 ENG [36688]
PLAYER 1750-1850 SALISBURY, WIL, ENG [34343] : PRE 1820 MALMESBURY, WIL, ENG [36113]
PLAYFAIR ALL FIF, SCT [36394]
PLAYFOOT 1860 LAMBERHURST, KEN, ENG [35041]
PLAYFORD PRE 1838 PEASMARSH, SSX, ENG & AUS [34463]
PLAYLE ALL NSW, AUS [35702] : ALL DUNTON, ESS, ENG [34837]
PLAYSTED 1735+ WADHURST, SSX, ENG [35013]
PLAYTER ALL ONT, CAN & ENG [36707]
PLEASANCE PRE 1850 NFK, ENG [34317] : ALL CAMBRIDGE, CAM, ENG [37884] : PRE 1870 CAMBRIDGE & BURWELL, CAM, ENG [38403]
PLEASANTS 1528 NORWICH, NFK, ENG [36337]
PLEDGE PRE 1800 HORSHAM, SSX, ENG [37602]

PLEES ALL WORLDWIDE [35997]
PLEHMAN JACOB 1690S-1770S LANCASTER CO., PA, USA [38141]
PLEMMONS THOMAS 1733+ GER [38141] : PETER 1715-1763 ROWAN CO., NC, USA [38141] : PETER 1804-1872 BUNCOMBE CO., NC, USA [38141]
PLESSEUS ALL BADHOEVEDORP, NL [36894]
PLETSCH 1800S NIEDERJOSSA, GHE, GER [38354]
PLIM 1800-1980 SYDNEY, NSW, AUS [36186] : EDWIN CURTIS 1820-1880 LONDON, MDX, ENG [36186] : HUGH 1650-1700 EGHAM, SRY, ENG [36186] : BENJAMIN 1850 ADAMS CO., PA, USA [36186] : DANIEL 1810-1850 POTTSGROVE MONTGOMERY CO., PA, USA [36186] : CHRISTIAN 1810-1850 DOUGLAS MONTGOMERY CO., PA, USA [36186] : ALL WORLDWIDE [36186]
PLIME ALL WORLDWIDE [36186]
PLIMM ALL WORLDWIDE [36186]
PLIMME ALL WORLDWIDE [36186]
PLIMMER 1807 LEIGHTON, SAL, ENG [35390]
PLISCH PRE 1820 LANDSBERG, OPR, GER [38648]
PLOCK 1800 SPIER, WUE, GER [35871]
PLOEGER 1756 BRAKE, WEF, GER [38749] : 1675-1695 IN DER LUETTE, WEF, GER [38749]
PLOESCH ALL WORLDWIDE [38747]
PLONKEY ALL KENT CO. & MARINE CITY, ONT & MI, CAN & USA [37503]
PLOTTS BENJAMIN 1834-1901 PROCTORSVILLE, HUGHESVILLE, PA, USA [37813]
PLOUGHMAN C1830-57 OAKLAND CO., MI, USA [37528] : C1758-C1830 ORANGE CO., NY, USA [37528]
PLOWMAN 1780+ CROYDON, SRY, ENG [37250] : C1850 IN, USA [34395] : C1830-57 OAKLAND CO., MI, USA [37528]
PLOWRIGHT 1840+ LONDON, ENG [35989] : PRE 1860 NTT, ENG [36645] : 1780-1810 NTT, ENG [37829] : 1700-1830 FOLKINGHAM & BOOTHBY PAGNELL, LIN, ENG [38287] : PRE 1850+ NTT, ENG [38401]
PLOWS 1800S SFK, ENG [35509]
PLOZZA 1869+ VIC, AUS [33773] : PRE 1869 CH [33773] : PRE 1869 TIRANO, LOMBARDIA, ITL [33773] : PRE 1880 LOMBARDY, ITL [37105]
PLOβ PRE 1870 KRS. ASCH, SUDETENLAND, OES, CSR &, GER [38649]
PLUCKNETT 1800+ QUEEN CAMEL, SOM, ENG [34933]
PLUM (SEE PLUMB) [36133]
PLUMB 1870 ROCKHAMPTON, QLD, AUS [34021] : C1850 LIVERPOOL, LAN, ENG [34556] : PRE 1833 GARBOLDISHAM, NFK, ENG [35571] : 1700+ SFK, ENG [36133] : 1600+ GAZELEY, SFK, ENG [36402] : C1750 BRAUGHING, HRT, ENG [36978]
PLUMBLEY C1820 FARNWORTH, LAN, ENG [35261]
PLUMBLY 1750-1950 LONDON &, MDX, ENG [37344]
PLUMBRIDGE PRE 1840 FULHAM, MDX, ENG [37644]
PLUMER 1750-1900 KENILWORTH, WAR, ENG [34004]
PLUMLEY ALL ENG [33869]
PLUMM ALL LOMPOC, CA, USA [38361]
PLUMMER 1790-1860 ONT, CAN [37461] : DANIEL 1792+ WALSHAM LE WILLOWS, SFK, ENG [34627] : EMILY ELLEN 1853+ SPROWSTON, NFK, ENG [34627] : C1880 LONDON, ENG [35014] : 1760S PROBUS, CON, ENG [35076] : 1782+ ASHBURNHAM & HASTINGS, SSX, ENG [35560] : 1800+ WESTMINSTER, LND, ENG [35566] : PRE 1820 KILMERSDON, SOM, ENG [35764] : PRE 1800 HIGHWORTH, WIL, ENG [35898] : 1858 BURY ST

EDMUNDS, SFK, ENG [36287] : 1660-1850 WHITTLESEY, CAM, ENG [37461] : C1757 AUGHNAMULLEN, MOG, IRL [33826] : 1620-1690 MA, USA [35317] : ALL COYCHURCH, GLA, WLS [38027]
PLUMPTON PRE 1750 MILDENHALL, SFK, ENG [34445] : C1700 HALBERTON, DEV, ENG [37264]
PLUMTON 1750+ CARLETON RODE, NFK, ENG [36483]
PLUNKETT 1858+ NEWCASTLE, NSW, AUS [34755] : 1859 GEELONG, VIC, AUS [34761] : 1815+ PARRAMATTA, NSW, AUS [36638] : PRE 1880 HOBART, TAS, AUS [38506] : PRE 1900 IRL [36481] : MARY C1826-1876 DUBLIN, IRL [36782] : PRE 1828 ENNISKILLEN, FER, IRL [37035] : PRE 1800 ORANGE CO., VA, USA [36927]
PLYM RALPH 1400 EXETER, DEV, ENG [36186] : ALL WORLDWIDE [36186]
PLYME 1400-1600 BARNSTAPLE, DEV, ENG [36186]
PLYMM 1400-1600 BISHOPS TAUNTON, DEV, ENG [36186]
PLYMME 1400-1600 PLYMOUTH, DEV, ENG [36186]
PLYMMER C1550 ELLASTONE, STS, ENG [37661]
POACHER 1600-1850 SFK, ENG [37457]
POBJAY 1640-1750 NORTON ST PHILIP, SOM, ENG [37233]
POBJOY 1884+ SYDNEY, NSW, AUS [34544] : ALL NORTON ST PHILIP, SOM, ENG [34284]
POCKERIDGE PRE 1820 MALMSBURY, WIL, ENG [37034]
POCKLINGTON PRE 1870 SELBY, YKS, ENG [37094] : 1800+ PORTSEA, HAM, ENG [37861] : EMILY 1800+ ENG [37861] : 1800+ LND, ENG [37861] : WILLIAM 1800+ ENG [37861]
POCKNALL 1850+ NSW, AUS [35472] : 1800+ VIC, AUS [36800] : 1800-1865 EYNSFORD, KEN, ENG [35472] : PRE 1900 CHATHAM, KEN, ENG [36800]
POCKNELL 1830+ NEWINGTON, SRY, ENG [36300]
POCKRAND ALL WORLDWIDE [37464]
POCOCK C1839 TILEHURST, BRK, ENG [34157] : PRE 1850 LONDON, ENG [34314] : 1700S BREDE, SSX, ENG [35881] : C1679 CATSFIELD, SSX, ENG [36679] : PRE 1880 EALING, MDX, ENG [37914]
PODE PRE 1800 DEV, ENG [34445]
PODGER 1750+ BROMLEY, KEN & LND, ENG [37065]
PODLICH CLARA 1890-1925 SAN FRANCISCO, CA, USA [36911]
PODMORE ALL MANCHESTER, LAN, ENG [36878] : PRE 1800 SANDON, STS, ENG [37722]
POE PRE 1850 DONNYBROOK, TIP, IRL [34682]
POEL 1870+ HARDERWIJK, OIJ, NL [35338]
POFF ALL WORLDWIDE [38576]
POGANY PRE 1772 SZUHOGY, BORSOD, HU [37547]
POGGE PRE 1855 GER [37563] : 1855+ LEE & POTTAWATTAMIE, IA, USA [37563]
POGSON 1740-1800 BARKISLAND, WRY, ENG [38003]
POGUE PRE 1830 WHITEWATER, IN, USA [38135] : PRE 1800 NC, USA [38135] : PRE 1880 MARION CO., IN, USA [38135]
POHL 1860+ BENDIGO, VIC, AUS [35725] : PRE 1860 KARLSBAD AREA, BOHEMIA, CS [36963]
POHLHAMMER PRE 1880 SMOLANT, OSTERGOTLAND, SWE [36918]
POHLING PRE 1837 GUTEBORN, PSA, GER [38618]
POHLMANN 1633 RHENEGGE, WAL, GER [34912]
POILE PRE 1877 SOUTHWARK, SRY & SSX, ENG [37452]
POINDEXTER 1680-1780 JAMES CITY CO., VA, USA [38119]

POINTER C1750 SHERFIELD ENGLISH, HAM, ENG [33841] : C1775 BKM, ENG [34041] : 1800+ LANREATH, CON, ENG [36254] : ALL GLS, ENG [37681] : ALL ST FAITHS, NFK, ENG [37689]

POINTON PRE 1890 SHIFNAL, SAL, ENG [36877] : 1820 STS, ENG [38317] : 1880+ NZ [36877] : 1850 MERCER, PA, USA [38317] : 1840 WLS [38317]

POINTS 1000-1990 WORLDWIDE [36114]

POIRIER ALL CAN [34212] : 1825-1890 ONT, CAN [36331] : 1630-1730 LATUS & POITIERS, PCH, FRA [34514]

POIRRIER 1888+ SYDNEY, NSW, AUS [34755] : 1856-1907 LONDON, ENG [34755] : PRE 1856 SAINS EN GOHELLE, NOR, FRA [34755]

POISSON 1560-1650 MORTAGNE, BN, FRA [34514]

POIZER 1680+ STATHERN, LEI, ENG [37829]

POLAN C1930 GARY, IN, USA [38455]

POLAND C1890S PERTH, WA, AUS [36762] : 1600-1900 LONDON, MDX, ENG [36438]

POLDERMAN ALL KLOETINGE, ZEL, NL [38350]

POLDRACK C1860 AUS [35865] : C1840 HOCHKIRCH, KSA, GER [35865]

POLE 1860+ DONALD, VIC, AUS [35834] : 1800+ WEST PANARD, SOM, ENG [35834] : 1700-1850 BAWDRIP, SOM, ENG [35865]

POLEN 1828-1860 MONROE CO., OH, USA [36734]

POLFLIET ALL WORLDWIDE [38159]

POLHEMUS ALL WORLDWIDE [38035]

POLITIEK 1791+ OLDEBOORN, FRI, NL [34990]

POLK 1800-1860 UNION CO., NC, USA [36897]

POLKEY ALL LOUGHBOROUGH, LEI, ENG [34032] : 1740+ LOUGHBOROUGH & ALL, LEI, ENG [36208]

POLKINGHORN 1780+ BURAGE, CON, ENG [35847]

POLKINGHORNE 1820+ REDRUTH, CON, ENG [34628] : 1800S REDRUTH, CON, ENG [35965] : PRE 1860 ST AGNES, CON, ENG [36909] : 1800+ REDRUTH, CON, ENG [37343]

POLL 1840+ CATTON, NFK, ENG [34710] : 1790+ ELSING, NFK, ENG [34710] : PRE 1880 LND, ENG [36514]

POLLARD PRE 1859 GLENELG & ADELAIDE, SA, AUS [33812] : HENRY 1814+ SYDNEY, NSW, AUS [34427] : 1800+ QLD, AUS [35352] : 1800+ CHARLTON WOOLWICH, KEN, ENG [34313] : HENRY PRE 1814 BATH, SOM, ENG [34427] : PRE 1858 LEEDS, YKS, ENG [34779] : 1790-1880S EPPING, ESS, ENG [35011] : 1588+ SOUTH MOLTON, DEV, ENG [35130] : 1850+ SOLIHULL, WAR & BDF, ENG [36123] : 1900+ LONDON, MDX, ENG [36423] : 1860 CROUGHTON, NTH, ENG [36423] : C1742 ARLINGTON & HAILSHAM, SSX, ENG [36679] : PRE 1749 BISHOPS NYMPTON, DEV, ENG [36995] : C1750 RUMBURGH, SFK, ENG [37191] : PRE 1860 CRAWSHAWBOOTH, LAN, ENG [37414] : PRE 1900 BDF & BKM, ENG [37749] : PRE 1760 SPEN VALLEY, WRY, ENG [37754] : 1760-1790S COSGROVE, NTH, ENG [38350] : 1800 GEORGETOWN, DEMERARA, GUIANA [35130] : ALL IRL [37061] : 1630+ ST MICHAELS, BARBADOS, W.INDIES [35130] : 1620 PEMBROKE TRIBE, BERMUDA, W.INDIES [35130] : 1850 PORT OF SPAIN, TRINIDAD, W.INDIES [35130]

POLLETT PRE 1850 HRT & ESS, ENG [37321]

POLLEY 1704 WEST BERGHOLT, ESS, ENG [34142] : LETITIA 1780-1850S SFK & ESS, ENG [36776]

POLLIFRONE ALL ITL [37520]

POLLINGTON ALL KEN, ENG [35706] : ALL TUNBRIDGE, KEN, ENG [36743] : ALL DEV, ENG [36999]

POLLITT 1910+ IPSWICH, QLD, AUS [34853] : C1850 LEIGH, LAN, ENG [34853] : C1820 NEWCASTLE,

STS, ENG [34853] : PRE 1800 BARTON ON IRWELL, LAN, ENG [36066]

POLLOCK PRE 1850 CASTLE FENNELL, DON, IRL [35719] : PRE 1900 KILLYNAUGHT, TYR, IRL [36437] : 1780+ EDINBURGH, MLN, SCT [35112] : PRE 1883 CLK, SCT [36392] : ALL EAST KILBRIDE, LKS, SCT [38057] : 1860-1890S AYR, SCT [38434]

POLLOWYN 1660-1700 LANDEWEDNACK, CON, ENG [34697]

POLMANN 1600-1700 ANGERMUNDE, UCKERMARK, BRA [38603]

POLNER 1850-1890 PERTH CO., ONT, CAN [34101]

POLON C1930 GARY, IN, USA [38455]

POLS ELEANOR C1860-1950 LONDON, ENG [37926] : WILLIAM PRE 1870 LONDON, ENG [37926]

POLSON 1840+ OXLEY ISLAND, NSW, AUS [35785] : 1905+ SYDNEY, NSW, AUS [37527] : PRE 1769 KINGS STANLEY, GLS, ENG [37610] : PRE 1800 ABERDEEN, ABD, SCT [34618] : 1800+ CATTHSPEY, CAI, SCT [35785] : C1889-C1919 DUNDEE, ANS, SCT [37527] : 1740+ SHI, SCT [37527] : 1890-1935 RIVERSIDE, CA, USA [36582]

POMERLEAU PRE 1900 ST JOSEPH DE BEAUCE, QUE, CAN [36941]

POMEROY PRE 1900 ST JOSEPH DE BEAUCE, QUE, CAN [36941] : ALL CON & DEV, ENG [36844] : ALL BEAMINSTER, DOR, ENG [37233] : ALL COKER, SOM, ENG [37233] : 1700-1800 MA, USA [35502] : 1650+ DOVER & PORTSMOUTH, NH & ME, USA [36931] : 1790-1833 FRANKLIN, VT, USA [38741] : ALL WORLDWIDE [36054] : ALL WORLDWIDE [38037]

POMERY PRE 1900 HELSTON, CON, ENG [35232]

POMFRET ALL LAN, ENG [36189]

POMFRETT 1857-1900 MAITLAND, NSW, AUS [37969] : 1850-1900 BERDEN, ESS, ENG [37969]

POMPEY C1720 EXNING, SFK, ENG [34157]

POMPHERY 1830-1900 EAST KILBRIDE, LKS, SCT [37783]

POND C1817 TROWBRIDGE, WIL, ENG [35760] : 1700S SHEPTON BEAUCHAMP, SOM, ENG [37307] : ALL MASTERTON, NZ & ENG [34604]

PONEY ALL UK [36086]

PONS 1804+ MONTPELLIER, LGD, FRA [38691] : 1804+ MONTPELLIER, LGD, FRA [38711]

PONSFORD PRE 1831 BRISTOL, ENG [36290] : ELIAS 1700-1800 DREWSTEIGNTON, DEV, ENG [36817]

PONT PRE 1800 HEATHFIELD, SSX, ENG [36761] : 1800+ ICKLESHAM, SSX, ENG [37560]

PONTIN 1850+ MELBOURNE, VIC, AUS [35877] : PRE 1840 LONDON, ENG [35877]

PONTING 1750+ STANWELLMOOR, MDX, ENG [33963] : PRE 1800 WROUGHTON, WIL, ENG [35016] : 1860-1900 SWINDON, WIL, ENG [37243]

PONTON C1800S+ ANDOVER, HAM, ENG [37868]

PONZO ALL ITL [37520]

POOK ALL SSX, ENG [36501] : 1850+ WANDSWORTH, LND, ENG [36517]

POOL 1880+ VIC, AUS [37128] : 1600+ BUCKLAND, SOM, ENG [35558] : PRE 1780 ESS, ENG [35642] : 1800 ST EARTH, CON, ENG [35755] : 1700-1800 LIN, ENG [36057] : ALL SEDGLEY, STS, ENG [36518] : 1780+ CRUDWELL & POOLE, WIL & DOR, ENG [36997] : ALL BARKING, ESS, ENG [37125] : 1790-1850 MARTON IN CRAVEN, WRY, ENG [37934] : 1800-1830 WESTMORELAND, PA, USA [36908] : 1720-1725 GLOUCESTER, MA, USA [38099]

POOLE 1788 SYDNEY, NSW, AUS [35920] : 1800+ BEGA, NSW, AUS & ENG [33769] : 1800+ SIMCOE

CO., ONT, CAN [34062] : 1800S SIMCOE CO., ONT, CAN [38440] : PRE 1900 ENG [34046] : 1700+ BIRMINGHAM, WAR, ENG [35050] : 1833 BIRMINGHAM, WAR, ENG [35152] : 1846-1920+ ISLINGTON, LND, ENG [35497] : PRE 1780 ESS, ENG [35642] : 1820S MADRON, CON, ENG [35730] : 1840-1870 BETHNAL GREEN, LND, ENG [35916] : 1600-1700 WOR, ENG [36003] : PRE 1900 DOR, ENG [36054] : ALL SEDGLEY, STS, ENG [36518] : 1881+ GLOUCESTER, GLS, ENG [36538] : PRE 1817 WIL, ENG [36538] : PRE 1870 ROMILEY, CHS, ENG [37359] : 1800-1920 ACTON, SFK, ENG [37638] : 1790+ BROSELEY, SAL, ENG [37908] : 1850+ FENTON, STS, ENG [37908] : ALL ESS, ENG [37973] : 1750+ FRYERNING, ESS, ENG [38488] : 1836-1898 KERSLEY & HARSLEY, WAR, ENG & AUS [35763] : 1700+ SOM, GLA & GLS, ENG & WLS [37827] : JAMES C1820-35 BRANNOCK, ARM, IRL [36715] : PRE 1890 RUSSELL, NLD, NZ [36249] : 1700S BUCKS CO., PA, USA [36926] : 1800 TOMPKINS CO., NY, USA [37582] : PRE 1903 LIVERPOOL & WAVERTREE, LAN, ENG &, W.INDIES [35997]

POOLEY 1856+ BARNAWARTHA, VIC, AUS [38213] : PRE 1855 NECTON, NFK, ENG [37067] : PRE 1830 CAM, NFK & SFK, ENG [37646] : 1800+ LIFTON, DEV, ENG [38213] : 1800+ LAUNCESTON, CON, ENG [38213]

POOLMAN PRE 1860 ENG [34589] : 1750+ CHITTERNE, WIL, ENG [37847] : 1825+ WARMINSTER, WIL, ENG [37847]

POOR 1750-1800 DOWNTON, WIL, ENG [36213] : 1790-1850 GALLIA CO., OH, USA [38108] : 1750S-1840S IL, IN & NC, USA & ENG [37522]

POORE PRE 1580 GLS, ENG [36944]

POORTVLIET 1700S COLIJNSPLAAT, ZEL, NL [38350]

POPE C1865 DAYLESFORD, VIC, AUS [34748] : 1850+ SA, AUS [34883] : 1840+ BOTANY, NSW, AUS [35149] : ISABELLA 1884+ GYMPIE, QLD, AUS [35477] : 1850+ QLD, AUS [35517] : 1880-1912 HACKNEY, MDX, ENG [34172] : PRE 1748 DEV, ENG [34213] : 1800+ WINGLINGTON, CAM, ENG [34972] : EPHRAIM 1854 KEN, ENG [35409] : C1902 CHELSEA, LND, ENG [35418] : PRE 1840 GLS & WOR, ENG [35517] : C1860-1880 SYDENHAM, KEN, ENG [35725] : C1783+ REDRUTH, CON, ENG [35746] : SUSAN C1849 SOM, ENG [36332] : PRE 1800 SHEPTON MALLET, SOM, ENG [36396] : ALL MANCHESTER, LAN, ENG [36881] : PRE 1900 FORDINGBRIDGE, HAM, ENG [37335] : 1790 OXTED, SRY, ENG [37841] : PRE 1800 FROME, SOM, ENG [38270] : 1700S-1800S DEV, ENG [38436] : 1800-1900 FOLKESTONE, KEN, ENG [38513] : 1800+ DON, IRL [38274] : PRE 1850 LOTH, SUT, SCT [33883] : 1855-1875 KEWEENAW CO., MI, USA [38009]

POPENHAGEN C1819 GER [35887]

POPHAM 1850+ LAMAR CO., TX, USA [36947]

POPLE 1800+ SOM, ENG [35060] : 1760+ BUCKLAND NEWTON, DOR, ENG [37360]

POPLIN ALL WILKES CO., NC, USA [37789]

POPP 1863+ HERVEY BAY, QLD, AUS [33887] : 1958 OLDENBUETTEL, SHO, BRD [38749] : PRE 1860 FORCHTEMBERG, WUE, GER [33887] : PRE 1845 LEIBOLTSGRUN, BAV, GER [38321] : 1850+ PELHAM, NY, USA [35489] : 1845+ BALTIMORE, MD, USA [38321]

POPPER 1830 WIE, OES [37582]

POPPLESTONE PRE 1730 BOTUS FLEMING, CON, ENG [34214] : 1600-1814 ALTARNUM, CON, ENG [35335] : ALL WORLDWIDE [36155]

POPPLEWELL ALL BIRMINGHAM, WAR, ENG [37058] : ALL WRY, ENG [37058]

POPPY 1400+ HARWICH, ESS, ENG [33989] : PRE 1750 SFK, ENG [35642] : 1700S EAST ANGLIA, ENG [36484]

PORCH 1700-1890 TROWBRIDGE, WIL, ENG [34975]

PORCHER 1700-1800 YAXLEY, SFK, ENG [37457]

PORCHMOUTH C1830 PORTSMOUTH, HAM, ENG [35401]

PORRETT ALL NFK, ENG [37712]

PORSNER ALL OPENDORF, YU [38369]

PORT 1800S BASINGSTOKE, HAM, ENG [35127] : 1821 SHERFORD, DEV, ENG [37418]

PORTAS PRE 1780 LANGTON BY PARTNEY, LIN, ENG [36148]

PORTE 1850S TUSCARAWAS CO., OH, USA [38339]

PORTEOUS C1880 BALLARAT, VIC, AUS [37891] : 1800-1900S NSW, AUS [38490] : C1880 MALTON, NRY, ENG [35350] : PRE 1900 INVERESK & GLADSMUIR, ELN & MLN, SCT [33959] : PRE 1854 CARLUKE, LKS, SCT [34501] : C1650 LINN MILL, DFS, SCT [35350] : PRE 1850 INVERESK, MLN, SCT [35823] : 1830+ MUSSELBURGH, MLN, SCT [35905] : PRE 1800 BIGGAR, LKS, SCT [37463] : 1750+ LESMAHAGOW, LKS, SCT [38388] : 1800S MLN, SCT [38490]

PORTEOUSS 1856+ NEWCASTLE, NSW, AUS [35160] : PRE 1856 ESS, ENG [35160]

PORTER 1880+ MAITLAND, NSW, AUS [34424] : 1800+ ADELAIDE, SA, AUS [34915] : 1850+ VIC, AUS [35836] : 1862+ PYMBLE & SYDNEY, NSW, AUS [38597] : 1900+ ELM CREEK, MAN, CAN [34996] : 1800-1900 RENFREW CO., ONT, CAN [34996] : PRE 1831 CORNWALLIS, NS, CAN [36800] : 1845-1900 WELLINGTON & YORK, ONT, CAN [37456] : THOMAS 1800S DEER ISLAND, NB, CAN [38785] : 1880+ SASKATOON, SAS & BC, CAN & USA [37322] : 1700-1800 ADDINGTON, KEN, ENG [33785] : 1850S LIVERPOOL, LAN, ENG [33810] : 1600-1750 PREES, SAL, ENG [34411] : 1853 HANDSWORTH, YKS, ENG [34581] : CHARLOTTE PRE 1816 SPAXTON, SOM, ENG [34630] : PRE 1850 CON, ENG [34742] : PRE 1900 SOM, ENG [34848] : WILLIAM 1800+ ESS, ENG [34915] : 1840 RICKINGHALL SUPERIOR, SFK, ENG [34950] : C1838 LONDON, ENG [35121] : 1790+ LEATHERHEAD, SRY, ENG [35214] : PRE 1910 SAMBROOK, HOLBROOK & IPSWICH, ENG [35255] : 1800S WORLINGHAM & ELLOUGH, SFK, ENG [35398] : THOMAS PRE 1820 HOLBORN, LND, ENG [35574] : PRE 1750 ESS, ENG [35642] : 1700+ ASHBY FOLVILLE, LEI, ENG [35836] : PRE 1700+ ENG [35956] : 1700+ KEN, ENG [36093] : WILLIAM C1799-1850 CRICH, DBY, ENG [36218] : 1800S LIN, ENG [36289] : 1701-1812 EASTHAM, WOR, ENG [36513] : RICHARD PRE 1860 LEI, ENG [36619] : 1853+ MDX, ENG [36810] : 1825+ SANDBACH AREA, CHS, ENG [36997] : PRE 1850 CHURCHTOWN, LAN, ENG [37179] : C1800 WITHAM, ESS, ENG [37449] : PRE 1860 NFK, ENG [37456] : PRE 1850 DRIFFIELD, ERY, ENG [37630] : 1780+ LONG SUTTON, LIN, ENG [38494] : PRE 1860 BIRMINGHAM, WAR & LEI, ENG [38512] : 1800+ JABALPUR, BENGAL, INDIA [35956] : 1750-1900 DOW, IRL [34229] : PRE 1828 VIRGINIA, CAV, IRL [34270] : PRE 1850 DOW, IRL [38393] : 1860+ GISBORNE, BOP, NZ [35956] : 1800S LKS, SCT [36660] : 1700-1850 NEW HANOVER CO., NC, USA [34749] : 1750-1850 BEAVER CO., PA, USA [36353] : 1800 HAMPDEN, ME, USA [36944] : ROBERT 1785-1860 OGLETHORPE CO. & GREENE CO., GA, USA [37003] : JAMES 1815+ OGLETHORPE CO. &

GREENE CO., GA, USA [37003] : 1650-1750
FARMINGTON, CT, USA [37783] : 1772-1859
UNION CHURCH, PA, USA [38094] : WILLIAM
1890-1910 KEEWENAW CO., MI, USA [38573] :
PAULINE 1900-1910 KING CO., WA, USA [38573] :
THOMAS 1800S CUMBERLAND CO., ME, USA
[38785]
PORTES 1800+ NBL & DUR, ENG [38754]
PORTEUS 1750-1800 APPLEBY, WES, ENG [38440] :
ALL HOLYWOOD, DOW, IRL [34758] : PRE 1850
TIP, IRL [35722]
PORTIER PRE 1750 PARIS, RPA, FRA [36353] : PRE
1800 SURAKARTA, JAVA, E. INDIES &, NL [36630]
PORTINGTON PRE 1700 HOWDEN, ERY, ENG
[36011]
PORTMANN ALL DEGERFELDEN, BAW, BRD
[38686]
PORTON 1750-1790 BRITFORD, WIL, ENG [37271]
PORTOR 1700-1800 LOUTH, LIN, ENG [37487]
PORTUFIELD 1800+ ENG [37352]
POSEY 1600S KEN, ENG [38373] : 1760S NEWBERRY
CO., SC, USA [38243]
POSICH 1790-1820S PALERMO, SICILY, ITL [38744]
POSKITT ALL BARNBY DUN & CANTLEY, WRY,
ENG [33916]
POST 1732-1846 ZWARTSLUIS & SCHUTSLOOT,
OIJ, NL [34398] : PRE 1829 MONMOUTH CO., NJ,
USA [37029] : PHEBE 1750+ LEBRON, CT, USA
[38766]
POSTAN 1840 WITHINGTON, HEF, ENG [35024]
POSTANS PRE 1914 BRISBANE, QLD, AUS [37316]
POSTEL 1900+ ZITTAU, SACHSEN, GER [38603]
POSTHILL PRE 1850 YKS, ENG [36841]
POSTICH ALL VOLUSCO & OPATIJA, OES & YU
[37164] : ALL WORLDWIDE [37164]
POSTIJ (SEE POSTICH) [37164]
POSTLE PRE 1920 NORWICH, NFK, ENG [37685]
POSTLETHWAITE 1700-1800 ALDINGHAM, LAN,
ENG [37858] : ALL WORLDWIDE [38371]
POSTON PRE 1850 GLS & HEF, ENG [38258]
POSTONS C1800 CLEOBURY, SAL, ENG [35456]
POTBURY ALL WINDSOR, BRK, ENG [34897] : ALL
SIDMOUTH, DEV, ENG [34897]
POTE PRE 1841 CON & DEV, ENG [36820]
POTHIER 1909-1912 MORINVILLE, ALB, CAN
[34251]
POTHOFF 1879 ST LOUIS, MO, USA [35279]
POTHS 1820S PANROD, BAW, BRD [34581]
POTT 1700S PRESTBURY, CHS, ENG [37697]
POTTAGE ALL YKS, ENG [36020]
POTTEN PRE 1820 CRANBROOK, KEN, ENG [34816]
POTTER 1854+ COLLINGWOOD, VIC, AUS [35708] :
1850+ MT FRANKLIN, VIC, AUS [36275] : ALL
NORTH BAY, ONT, CAN [38432] : ALL SRY, ENG
[33925] : JOHN 1780 MANCHESTER, LAN, ENG
[34091] : 1700S FEOCK, CON, ENG [34214] : 1800+
WINDSOR, BRK & BKM, ENG [34236] : 1825+
HINDLEY, LAN, ENG [34238] : 1700-1850 FEOCK &
MYLOR, CON, ENG [34274] : 1884+ BURGHILL,
HEF, ENG [34334] : 1800+ NEWCASTLE, NBL,
ENG [34556] : 1858+ TORQUAY, DEV, ENG [34700]
: 1810+ STAVERTON, DEV, ENG [34700] : 1700+
ROTHERFIELD & PENSHURST, SSX, ENG [34970]
: C1775 BATTLE, SSX, ENG [35261] : PRE 1852
ATHERSTONE, WAR, ENG [35344] : 1600+
YALDING, KEN, ENG [35355] : 1800 ORTON, WES,
ENG [36151] : 1800+ BOSTON, LIN, ENG [36251] :
1800 BRAINTREE, ESS, ENG [36275] : 1839+
MEDWAY, KEN, ENG [37051] : 1700S
SEDGEFORD, NFK, ENG [37083] : 1700+
SAMPFORD COURTENEY & S TAWTON, DEV,
ENG [37411] : 1800S KELVEDON & FEERING, ESS,

ENG [37677] : 1820-1850 WIL, ENG [37996] : C1850
YKS, ENG [38168] : ALL LANGHAM, SFK, ENG &
AUS [33919] : PRE 1827 KURNING, BERNSTEIN,
GER [35463] : 1300-1652 GER [36457] : 1652-1990
GER [36457] : C1840 GAL, IRL [37883] : 1780-1840
GAL, IRL [38054] : 1700S BIEZELINGE, ZEL, NL
[38350] : 1700-1850 TORTHORWALD, DFS, SCT
[37442]
POTTERS 1693 WEST BRABANT, NBT, NL [38715]
POTTERTON JAMES PRE 1800 BRIGHTON, SSX,
ENG [34539] : MARY PRE 1819 BRIGHTON, SSX,
ENG [34539]
POTTHOFF 1879 ST LOUIS, MO, USA [35279]
POTTICARY 1744+ LONGPARISH, HAM, ENG
[37321]
POTTINGER C1800 BIRMINGHAM, WAR, ENG
[34274] : 1700-1800 ALL CANNINGS, WIL, ENG
[37843]
POTTLE PRE 1830 TOLLARD ROYAL, WIL, ENG
[37320]
POTTS ROBERT 1820+ NSW, AUS [35831] : C1833-
1885 CLARKE TWP., ONT, CAN [36693] : 1800+
NEWCASTLE, NBL, ENG [33837] : PRE 1800
LONDON, ENG [34314] : 1800S STONE, WOR, ENG
[34715] : 1850+ LEEDS, WRY, ENG [35170] : 1800-
1850 DARLINGTON, DUR, ENG [35170] : PRE 1800
BERWICK, NBL, ENG [35170] : 1720S+
HARROGATE, YKS, ENG [35831] : 1700+
LONGHORSLEY, NBL, ENG [36609] : 1700-1900S
NEWARK, NTT, ENG [36796] : PRE 1910 NEW
MILLS, DBY, ENG [37359] : 1830 YORK, YKS, ENG
[37391] : PRE 1800 SUNDERLAND, DUR, ENG
[37693] : PRE 1850 NTH, ENG [37741] : JOHN 1862-
1890 BELFAST, ANT, IRL [34340] : C1807-1833
TATTINDERRY & LISNASKAE, FER, IRL [36693] :
1800-1900S WESTLAND, NZ [36796] : MELVILLE
C1900+ CINCINNATI, OH, USA [34340] : JOHN
C1890-1936 CINCINNATI, OH, USA [34340]
POULDRON PRE 1880 LEWISTON, ME, USA [35649]
POULSON ALL SFK, ENG [34744] : PRE 1800
LOUGHBOROUGH, LEI, ENG [38494]
POULTER PRE 1840 CRONDALL, HAM, ENG [35934]
: PRE 1860 WEATHERSFIELD, MDX, ENG [35976]
POULTNEY PRE 1834 LEEK, STS, ENG [35525]
POULTON 1840S TAS, AUS [34979] : 1877+
DELEGATE, NSW, AUS [34979] : ALL BREAMORE,
HAM, ENG [33823] : 1850-1910 LONDON, ENG
[33843] : 1800S WOR, ENG [33843] : ALL
AYLESBURY, BKM, ENG [34863] : 1600S
COOKHAM, BRK, ENG [36585] : PRE 1860
WENDOVER, BKM, ENG [36754] : 1720S GREAT
BADDOW, ESS, ENG [36981] : 1800S CAM, GLS,
ENG [37343]
POUND 1865-1925 QUE, CAN & USA [36068] : JAMES
1800+ BIRMINGHAM, WAR, ENG [36068] :
JAMES 1800+ STEPNEY, LND, ENG [36068] : PRE
1830 WIL, ENG [36755] : PRE 1730 COMPTON
PAUNCEFOOT, SOM, ENG [37442]
POUNDER 1650+ ENNISCORTHY, WEX, IRL
[38476] : ALL WORLDWIDE [38476]
POUNDS PRE 1850 HUNGERFORD, BRK, ENG
[37687]
POUNTAIN PRE 1770 BOYLESTONE, DBY, ENG
[34311] : 1680+ BIRLING, KEN, ENG [37921]
POUNTNEY C1836 LONDON, ENG [37919]
POVEY 1800S TAS, AUS [35531] : C1800 LND, ENG
[34274] : PRE 1792 BURGHFIELD, WIL, ENG
[35016] : 1800-1900 LONDON &, KEN, ENG [38171]
POWDRILL ALL LEI, ENG [34400]
POWE 1865+ TOOWOOMBA & IPSWICH, QLD, AUS
[36134] : ALL TORQUAY, DEV, ENG [36134] : ALL
NEWCASTLE UPON TYNE, ENG [36881]

POWEL ALL SALISBURY, WIL, ENG **[36881]**

POWELL MAUD C1900 SYDNEY, NSW, AUS **[33765]** : 1880-1890 BALLARAT, VIC, AUS **[34748]** : ROBERT 1826-1873+ THE BLAND, NSW, AUS **[35497]** : RUTH 1886+ ORBOST, VIC, AUS **[37906]** : 1900-1980 ALB, CAN **[34135]** : 1830+ PERTH CO., ONT, CAN **[34502]** : 1850+ HURON CO., ONT, CAN **[34502]** : 1775+ NFD, CAN **[34749]** : 1800+ JSY, CHI **[34556]** : 1670+ KEN, ENG **[34181]** : 1820+ BURGHILL, HEF, ENG **[34334]** : 1700-1850 ALDBOURNE, WIL, ENG **[34343]** : PRE 1800 FOREST OF DEAN, GLS, ENG **[34643]** : 1774 BOURTON ON THE HILL, GLS, ENG **[34995]** : PRE 1800 EXETER, DEV, ENG **[35032]** : 1800S LONDON, ENG **[35068]** : PRE 1750 WEM, SAL, ENG **[35181]** : JANE C1871-3 SHREWSBURY, SAL, ENG **[35184]** : PRE 1857 WOR, ENG **[35247]** : THOMAS SYKES 1829+ ST GEORGE, LAN, ENG **[35426]** : 1800+ KEN, ENG **[35429]** : PRE 1890 GLOUCESTER, GLS, ENG **[36113]** : PRE 1816 BIRMINGHAM, WAR, ENG **[36177]** : 1800-1860 MASHAM, NRY, ENG **[36228]** : JOHN PRE 1850 BRISTOL, SOM, ENG **[36432]** : 1840S SHELTON & TUNSTALL, STS, ENG **[36504]** : PRE 1739 HANLEY WILLIAM, WOR, ENG **[36513]** : 1840-1892 BILSTON, STS, ENG **[36547]** : PRE 1837 SRY, ENG **[36589]** : JANE 1760S CAMBERWELL, SRY, ENG **[36633]** : 1860S GATESHEAD, DUR, ENG **[36867]** : 1600-1700 ENG **[36898]** : 1830+ BIRMINGHAM, WAR, ENG **[37074]** : 1830S-1870S ORSETT & WEST THURROCK, ESS, ENG **[37320]** : PRE 1880 WHITNEY & CLIFFORD, HEF, ENG **[37320]** : C1800 ULLEY, GLS, ENG **[37403]** : 1300-1400+ SSX, ENG **[37648]** : 1890 LAMBETH, MDX, ENG **[37690]** : PRE 1900 ENG **[37787]** : PRE 1890 LONDON & KENTISH TOWN, MDX, ENG & AUS **[34705]** : 1850+ LIMERICK, LIM, IRL **[35943]** : PRE 1830 JAMAICA **[37630]** : C1874 SPRING GROVE, NELSON, NZ **[35885]** : ALL UK **[37674]** : ISAAC C1860 SCOTT CO. & LOGAN CO., AR, USA **[37003]** : ISAAC 1790+ COLUMBIA CO. & TALAPOSSA CO., GA & AL, USA **[37003]** : JOSEPH PRE 1800 FAIRFAX CO., VA, USA **[37590]** : 1800-1900+ USA **[37648]** : PRE 1900 NY, USA **[37787]** : SARAH JANE 1847-1866 MONTGOMERY CO., OH, USA **[38732]** : PRE 1833 WLS **[34502]** : 1750+ NEATH, GLA, WLS **[35829]** : 1750-1850 BRYNGWYN, RAD, WLS **[36109]** : PRE 1850 OVERTON, FLN, WLS **[36385]** : C1760 LLANGATTOCK VIBON AVEL, MON, WLS **[36779]** : C1800 LLANSOY, MON, WLS **[36779]** : C1730 LLYWEL, BRE, WLS **[36779]** : 1750+ PEMBROKE DOCK, PEM, WLS **[37356]**

POWELL-TUCK 1800-1900 LLANBEDR PAINSCASTLE, RAD, WLS **[36109]**

POWER 1880-1920 PEAK HILL, NSW, AUS **[34759]** : PRE 1860 SYDNEY, NSW, AUS **[34812]** : 1878 ROCKHAMPTON, QLD, AUS **[34452]** : 1850S BATHURST & ORANGE, NSW, AUS **[35557]** : PRE 1892 GEELONG, VIC, AUS **[36276]** : 1863+ MELBOURNE, VIC, AUS **[37165]** : LAWRENCE 1820+ HULME & MANCHESTER, LAN, ENG **[37165]** : PRE 1860 CORK, COR, IRL **[34018]** : PRE 1892 SKIBBEREEN, COR, IRL **[34241]** : PRE 1814 WATERFORD, WAT, IRL **[34696]** : PRE 1825 WAT, IRL **[34804]** : 1800+ CLA, IRL **[35358]** : 1869 CASTLE CONNELL, LIM, IRL **[35452]** : 1850+ TRAMORE, WAT, IRL **[35719]** : 1850+ CARRIGAVANTRY, WAT, IRL **[35719]** : PRE 1900 MULLINVAT, WAT, IRL **[36168]** : 1831-1856 PORTLAW, WAT, IRL **[38117]** : PRE 1840 WATERFORD, WAT, IRL **[38291]** : 1850-1880 WAT, IRL & AUS **[35064]** : PRE 1900 TRINITY WITHOUT,

WAT, IRL & NZ **[36840]** : PRE 1900 CLA, IRL & USA **[38305]** : 1820S WESTMORELAND CO., PA, USA **[38590]** : ALL WORLDWIDE **[35159]**

POWERS PRE 1828 KEN, ENG **[35472]** : 1629+ CUMBRIA, ENG **[37592]** : JAMES ALL KY & MO, USA **[35304]** : 1855-1875 KEWEENAW CO., MI, USA **[38009]** : 1900-1920 BURLINGTON, IA, USA **[38154]** : 1850-1920 WASHINGTON DC, MD, USA **[38154]** : 1900-1990 LA CO., CA, USA **[38154]**

POWIS C1846 BISHOPS CASTLE, SAL, ENG **[35336]** : ALL STAFFORD, STS, ENG **[36537]** : C1850 LND, ENG & AUS **[35512]**

POWLAS PRE 1800 VA, USA **[38196]**

POWNCEBY 1750+ LONDON, ENG **[37160]**

POWNEY PRE 1830 WYCOMBE, BKM, ENG **[35255]** : 1800-1900 LONDON, ENG **[35845]** : PRE 1670 WIL, ENG **[37941]**

POWNING PRE 1816 PLYMOUTH, DEV, ENG **[37998]**

POWRIE PRE 1839 ARBROATH, ANS, SCT **[34691]**

POYER C1785 LAWRENNY, PEM, WLS **[35457]** : 1600-1700 PEM, WLS **[38194]**

POYNER PRE 1886 LIVERPOOL, LAN, ENG **[36522]** : PRE 1870 BN, FRA **[36522]** : PRE 1870 HN, FRA **[36522]**

POYNTELL 1700+ CHIPPING NORTON, OXF, ENG **[36572]**

POYNTER C1775 BKM, ENG **[34041]** : ALL MAIDSTONE, KEN, ENG **[34131]** : PRE 1800 HAM, ENG **[35902]** : 1500+ ENG **[37099]**

POYNTON 1850+ LND, ENG **[37983]**

POYNTZ 1000-1990 WORLDWIDE **[36114]**

POYSER PRE 1800 BENDIGO, VIC & MDX, AUS & ENG **[37995]**

POYZER 1880-1900 NOTTINGHAM, NTT, ENG **[37829]** : 1800 MELTON MOWBRAY, LEI, ENG **[37829]**

PRAIN 1700+ SCT **[36291]**

PRALL 1650-1840 ST JOHN, NB, CAN & FRA **[38225]** : PRE 1830 BRENCHLEY & FARLEIGH, KEN, ENG **[34325]**

PRANCE 1800 STOCK, ESS, ENG **[34204]** : ALL WORLDWIDE **[36206]**

PRANGE 1780+ OISTE, HAN, GER **[35865]** : PRE 1856 HAN, GER **[37811]**

PRANGNELL ALL PADDINGTON, LND, ENG **[33823]** : PRE 1820 CARISBROOKE, IOW, ENG **[36142]** : 1879+ CHRISTCHURCH, NZ **[33823]**

PRANNCE ALL WORLDWIDE **[36206]**

PRANSE ALL WORLDWIDE **[36206]**

PRASSE ANNA 1879+ SEIFHENNERSDORF, SAX, GER **[35641]** : ALWIN 1857+ SEIFHENNERSDORF, OBERDORF, GER **[35641]**

PRAT PRE 1760 WEYMOUTH, MA, USA **[36319]**

PRATER 1855+ NSW & VIC, AUS **[35379]** : PRE 1855 GREAT SHEFFORD, BRK, ENG **[35379]** : 1600S CHEDWORTH, GLS, ENG **[36585]**

PRATLEY PRE 1881 LND, ENG **[37991]**

PRATS PRE 1800 MENORCA, ESP **[36353]**

PRATT 1861+ GOODOOGA, NSW, AUS **[34806]** : 1857+ SALE, VIC, AUS **[34977]** : MARGARET 1850+ ADELAIDE, SA, AUS **[35529]** : 1800S ONT, CAN **[36679]** : 1830+ ONT, CAN **[38235]** : PRE 1855 WOOD GREEN, MDX, ENG **[33997]** : PRE 1800 YKS, ENG **[34177]** : 1700+ CHICHESTER & WOOLAVINGTON, SSX, ENG **[34747]** : ALFRED HIRAM 1824+ NOTTINGHAM, NTT, ENG **[34806]** : 1750+ TAUNTON, SOM, ENG **[34817]** : PRE 1857 HRT, ENG **[34977]** : 1830+ STRATFORD, ESS, ENG **[35125]** : 1800+ NTH, ENG **[35492]** : 1700+ OAKTHORPE, DBY, ENG **[35874]** : 1800+ CHELSEA & NOTTING HILL, MDX, ENG **[35915]** : 1600-1850 WARWICK & SALFORD, WAR, ENG

[35937] : PRE 1790 PORTSEA, HAM, ENG [35973] : 1750-1770 WOODHAM WALTER, ESS, ENG [36010] : 1800-1900 HAM, ENG [36207] : PRE 1830 MANCHESTER, LAN, ENG [36583] : MARIA PRE 1804 ASH & WROTHAM, KEN, ENG [36767] : 1790+ HARLTON, CAM, ENG [36772] : ALL HAWES, YKS, ENG [36774] : 1780-1880 BRISTOL, GLS, ENG [37233] : 1640-1880 SOM, ENG [37233] : 1850-1880 LEICESTER, LEI, ENG [37266] : PRE 1825 BIRMINGHAM, WAR, ENG [37367] : PRE 1800 MARSKE BY RICHMOND, NRY, ENG [37505] : 1881+ DARLINGTON, DUR, ENG [37505] : C1840 LND, ENG [37552] : PRE 1885 CREWE, CHS, ENG [37831] : 1850S THRINTOFT, NRY, ENG [38269] : 1860S ANDERBY STEEPLE, NRY, ENG [38269] : 1770S-1803 PATRICK BROMPTON, NRY, ENG [38269] : 1870S-1940S SPENNYMOOR, DUR, ENG [38269] : 1830+ DUBLIN CITY, IRL [35529] : PRE 1870 RATHDOWNEY, LEX, IRL [38293] : 1850+ NZ [37552] : PRE 1854 KINGSKETTLE, FIF, SCT [34001] : C1770-1850 FIF, SCT [34040] : C1750-1800 FIF, SCT [36327] : 1750-1850 ABERDEEN, ABD, SCT [37367] : MEHITABLE 1700 PLYMOUTH, MA, USA [35273] : 1630-1700 PLYMOUTH & BRIDGEWATER, MA, USA [37432] : 1800+ VT, USA [38235] : PRE 1860 GLA, WLS [37901]

PRATTEN 1800-1900 BEDWELLTY, MON, WLS [35094]

PRAY PRE 1700 MA, USA & ENG [38745]

PRAYLL (SEE PLAYLE) [34837]

PREBBLE ROBERT 1550-1650 DENTON, KEN, ENG [36563] : ROBERT 1500-1600 WOOTTON, KEN, ENG [36563] : WALTER 1440-1540 EAST FARLEIGH, KEN, ENG [36563]

PREBLE JOHN PRE 1875 BRADFORD, ME, USA [36563] : NATHANIEL 1650+ SCITUATE, MA, USA [36563] : SAMUEL R. PRE 1850 RAYMOND, ME, USA [36563] : EDWARD 1750+ YORK, ME, USA [36563] : HERBERT E. PRE 1900 EAST BOSTON, MA, USA [36563]

PRECIOUS PRE 1830 YORK, YKS, ENG [36051] : 1750-1800 HARWICH, ESS, ENG [37779]

PREDDY 1860-1900 SWINDON, WIL, ENG [37243]

PREECE 1900+ MAITLAND & SINGLETON, NSW, AUS [37966] : 1840+ NASH, SAL, ENG [33956] : THOMAS 1807+ TENBURY, WOR, ENG [33956] : 1800-1900 WIGMORE, HEF, MDX & HRT, ENG [34382] : 1820+ HEREFORD, HEF, ENG [35998] : PRE 1800 PRESTON ON WYE, HEF, ENG [36188] : PRE 1850 CALLOW, HEF, ENG [36188] : 1750+ CLEDBURY MORTIMER, SAL, ENG [36488] : 1800S BURFORD, WOR, ENG [36764] : ALL ENG [37468]

PREEDY 1700S CHARLBURY, OXF, ENG [37083]

PREEN PRE 1850 LEIGH, GLS, ENG [34725]

PREHN 1850+ ST LOUIS, MO, USA [36912]

PREISS 1850 BRUCE CO., ONT, CAN [34503] : PRE 1851 HAN, GER [35351]

PRELL 1848 SELB, BAV, GER [37531] : 1849 MILWAUKEE, WI, USA [37531]

PRENCE 1631 EASTHAM, MA, USA [36944] : PRE 1700 MA & GLS, USA & ENG [38745]

PRENDERGAST 1820+ SYDNEY, NSW, AUS [34428] : 1860-1870S NS, CAN [36936] : PRE 1858 TUAM & LEITRIM, GAL, IRL [33812] : PRE 1857 WEX, IRL [34412] : MICHAEL PRE 1843+ BUNRATTY, CLA, IRL [34592] : ALL KIK, IRL [35707] : PRE 1860 TULLA, CLA, IRL [35824] : 1860-1870S NYC, NY, USA [36936] : 1860-1870S PHILADELPHIA, PA, USA [36936] : 1860-1870S BOSTON, MA, USA [36936]

PRENDERGAST (SEE PRE [36131]

PRENDERVILLE ALL DROMCOLLIHER, LIM, IRL [37988]

PRENDEVILLE JOHANNA 1874 NEWMARKET, COR, IRL [33929] : WILLIAM 1869 BOHERBUE, COR, IRL [33929] : MICHAEL 1869 RATHDUANE, COR, IRL [33929]

PRENDIVILLE PRE 1860 EAST MINARD, KER, IRL [34187]

PRENTICE WILLIAM 1800-1870 SEYMOURT NORTHUMBERLAND, ONT, CAN [34072] : PRE 1840 SHUDY CAMPS, CAM, ENG [35798] : PRE 1850 WOBURN, BDF, ENG [36369] : ALL OAKLEY, BDF, ENG [36866] : 1850+ ENNISKILLEN, FER, IRL [36615] : 1799+ CORK, IRL & AUS [36238] : PRE 1838 SCT [33777] : 1800S CARNSWORTH, LKS, SCT [34336] : PRE 1862 HAMILTON, LKS, SCT [35885]

PRENTIS PRE 1750 NEWTON, MA, USA [33804]

PRENTISS 1870S LONDON, ENG [35018]

PRESBURY 166S-1990 DBY & STS, ENG [34729]

PRESCHIO 1700S+ LAURENCEKIRK, KCD, SCT [37485]

PRESCOT TOM 1810+ PRESCOT & LIVERPOOL, LAN, ENG [35114] : JOHN 1832+ PRESCOT & HUYTON, LAN, ENG [35114]

PRESCOTT 1700S KEN, ENG [34181] : 1850+ HUYTON, LAN, ENG [35114] : 1800S VAUXHALL, SRY, ENG [36868] : PRE 1700 DOVER, KEN, ENG [36891]

PRESDEE 1750+ WOR, ENG [38020]

PRESGRAVE PRE 1850 WORLDWIDE [34099]

PRESICK 1800S KILMORE, ARM, IRL [34044]

PRESLEY 1800+ ONT, CAN [36539] : 1800-1950 NC & TN, USA [37539]

PRESMALL ALL WORLDWIDE [37651]

PRESNELL 1700-1800S ENG [35340]

PRESS ALL NFK, ENG [36393] : ALL HUN, ENG [37409] : 1800S CLEWER, BRK, ENG [38285]

PRESSER ALL BUKOVINA, RO [34488]

PRESSEY PRE 1700 PORTSMOUTH, HAM, ENG [38420]

PREST 1840+ CARLTON, WRY, ENG [34957] : 1800 COVERHAM, NRY, ENG [34957] : THOMAS C1800 RIPON & LEEDS, WRY, ENG [35164]

PRESTIDGE ALL NTH, ENG [36790]

PRESTON GEORGE 1860S KYNETON, VIC, AUS [35471] : 1850 BRANTFORD TWP., ONT, CAN [34357] : 1820 GLEMSFORD, SFK, ENG [34976] : 1650-1750 PINCHBECK, LIN, ENG [35288] : C1850 KESWICK, CUL, ENG [35349] : 1880+ YORK, YKS, ENG [35460] : ANNE 1676 WORFIELD, SAL, ENG [35794] : 1860+ OSWALDTWISTLE, LAN, ENG [35942] : ALL CHEADLE, STS, ENG [36196] : PRE 1898 KENDAL, WES, ENG [36230] : 1800+ TAMWORTH, MARCHINGTON, STS & WAR, ENG [36329] : PRE 1700 OTTERY ST MARY, DEV, ENG [36389] : 1800S BRISTOL, ENG [36799] : 1780+ KIRKBY LONSDALE, WES, ENG [36821] : 1790+ MARKET DRAYTON AREA, SAL, ENG [36997] : ROGER PRE 1635 ST ALPHAGE, LND, ENG [38348] : PRE 1800 LONDON, ENG [38658] : 1750+ PORTADOWN, ARM, IRL [35918] : ANNIE 1850+ BELFAST, ANT, IRL [35942] : 1800S ARM, IRL [36858] : PRE 1900 BAILLIESTON, LKS, SCT [36067] : RACHEL PRE 1806 DUNFERMLINE, FIF, SCT [36308] : EDWARD 1800-1895 PAISLEY & LEICESTER, SCT & ENG [37640] : PRE 1850 NEW YORK, NY, USA [34357] : GENERAL C1780 DUXBURY, MA, USA [37810] : 1807-1852 DALLAS CO., MO, USA [38120] : ROSINA 1830-1850 OH, USA [38240] : 1790-1820 LUZERNE CO., PA, USA [38342] : 1700-1800 BEDFORD CO., VA & KY, USA [38524]

PRESTWOOD PRE 1900 WELLINGTON, SAL, ENG [34711]

PRESWICK 1600S-1700S MARKSE IN CLEVELAND, NRY, ENG [34181]

PRETORIUS PRE 1896 DEALESVILLE, RSA [36458]

PRETTIE 1860-1900 YORK CO., ONT, CAN [34482]

PRETTY 1929+ DANDENONG, VIC, AUS [34430] : 1896+ PRAHRAN, VIC, AUS [34430] : 1890 MELBOURNE, VIC, AUS [35774] : 1940 MOOROOPNA, VIC, AUS [35774] : 1900 JINDIVICK, VIC, AUS [35774] : 1870S EPSOM, VIC, AUS [35774] : 1836+ ADELAIDE, SA, AUS [37913] : 1800-1960 DILDO, NFD, CAN [34208] : PRE 1835 SFK, ENG [37913] : 1600-1800 DENTON & HOMERSFIELD, NFK & SFK, ENG [38194]

PREVETT DAVID 1872+ BRIGHTON, SSX, ENG [34247]

PREVOST PRE 1600 GENEVA, GE, CH [38348]

PREWETT 1870 ST CLAIR, AL, USA [38198]

PREWIT 1830+ BRISTOL, GLS, ENG [35948]

PRIAL ALL WORLDWIDE [37883]

PRIAULX PRE 1880 GUERNSEY, CHI, ENG [37855]

PRICE 1840S LAUNCESTON, TAS, AUS [34542] : 1854+ HEYWOOD DISTRICT, VIC, AUS [34681] : 1890+ MELBOURNE, VIC, AUS [34767] : VIOLET 1925+ WOLLONGONG, NSW, AUS [34885] : 1850+ VIC, AUS [35379] : 1834-1850 LIVERPOOL, NSW, AUS [35582] : PRE 1850S SYDNEY, NSW, AUS [37309] : 1840-1900 BROCKVILLE, ONT, CAN [34402] : 1750-1850 NEWARK, CAN [38426] : 1800S WELLAND CO., ONT, CAN [38440] : 1800+ WOODSTOCK, NB, CAN [38454] : 1700-1870 GAGETOWN, NB & NY, CAN & USA [38225] : PRE 1865 LIVERPOOL, LAN, ENG [33863] : ALL ROCHFORD AREA, ESS, ENG [33899] : 1800-1871 ESSENDON, HRT, ENG [33960] : 1857-1862 SOUTH MOLTON, DEV, ENG [33960] : 1868-1900 BRADFORD, LAN, ENG [33960] : 1800-1870 ENG [34099] : 1780-1800 BIDEFORD & NORTHAM, DEV, ENG [34448] : C1750-1770 LIVERPOOL, LAN, ENG [34448] : JOHN PRE 1845 STS, ENG [34541] : PRE 1854 HAMPTON POYLE, OXF, ENG [34681] : PRE 1833 ROSS ON WYE &BRAMPTON ABBOTTS, HEF, ENG [34823] : 1800S GLOUCESTER, GLS, ENG [34931] : C1750 ISLINGTON, LND, ENG [35203] : PRE 1850 ST AUSTELL & VERYAN, CON, ENG [35215] : 1800+ STAPLETON, GLS, ENG [35248] : 1800S OLDBURY, WOR, ENG [35256] : ANN C1871 LEIGHTON BUZZARD, BDF, ENG [35778] : PRE 1870 BURSLEM, STS, ENG [35854] : 1830-1880 LIMEHOUSE, MDX, ENG [35955] : WILLIAM HENRY C1809 DEPTFORD, KEN, ENG [35955] : PRE 1830 BRAMPTON BRYAN & WIGMORE, HEF, ENG [36110] : 1840+ BRIERLEY HILL, STS, ENG [36110] : 1660+ STOTTESDON, SAL, ENG [36488] : 1700+ LYDIARD TREGOZE & PURTON, WIL, ENG [36512] : JANE PRE 1804 WOLVERHAMPTON, STS, ENG [36532] : WILLIAM HENRY 1800S POPLAR, MDX, ENG [36633] : 1750-1900 WOLVERHAMPTON & WEST BROMWICH, STS, ENG [36786] : JOHN 1800S STAUNTON, HEF, ENG [36803] : PRE 1797+ CHATHAM GREEN, ESS, ENG [37108] : 1700+ BRK, ENG [37166] : 1830-1860 WOR, ENG [37233] : PRE 1861 BRISTOL, GLS, ENG [37318] : PRE 1890 CLIFFORD, HEF, ENG [37320] : PRE 1900 SMETHWICK, STS, ENG [37681] : PRE 1860 CLIFTON (BRISTOL), GLS, ENG [38004] : PRE 1857 WIL & LND, ENG & AUS [34845] : ALL LAN, ENG & NZ [34604] : ELIZABETH 1827-1889+ GRINSHILL, SAL & MGY, ENG & WLS [37546] : PRE 1850 DEVENISH, FER, IRL [34201] : PRE 1860 LIMERICK, LIM, IRL [34454] : PRE 1850 WICKLOW, WIC, IRL [35229] : JAMES C1834 FER, IRL & AUS [34942] : JOHN C1816 ABERDEEN, ABD, SCT [34541] : 1750+ GLASGOW, LKS, SCT [34684] : WILLIAM 1750+ KILMARNOCK, AYR, SCT [34684] : 1780-1810 BOSTON, MA, USA [36561] : 1815-1865 COLUMBUS, OH, USA [36561] : 1780-1810 PA, USA [36561] : PRE 1780 HUNTERDON CO., NI & PA, USA [36917] : 1600-1800 ESSEX CO., NJ, USA [36924] : EDWARD PRE 1843 RI, USA [37504] : PRE 1830 ROSS CO., OH, USA [37580] : JOHN WESLEY PRE 1880 BALTIMORE, MO, USA [38049] : JOHN WESLEY PRE 1860 BROOKLYN, NY, USA [38049] : 1790-1830 FRANKLIN, KY, USA [38061] : 1755-1877 CAROLINE & ADAIR CO., VA & KY, USA [38315] : 1750-1850 YELLOW BREECHES, PA, USA [38426] : DAVID 1700-1850 MOHAWK VALLEY, NY, USA [38426] : 1600S ELIZABETHTOWN, NJ, USA [38440] : PRE 1850 ABERDEW, CGN, WLS [35379] : 1800-1850 BOUGHROOD, RAD, WLS [36047] : PRE 1840 LLANGUNLLO, RAD, WLS [36110] : PRE 1792 CAERNARVON, CAE, WLS [36204] : PRE 1803 BRECON, WLS [36632] : 1859+ BRECON, WLS [36632] : LLEWELLYN 1800S SWANSEA, WLS [36633] : PRE 1830 BRYNGWYN, RAD & MON, WLS [37320] : PRE 1875 LLANPIHANGER CRUCORNEY, MON, WLS [37771] : FLOYD C1825-C1876 WLS & ENG [37320]

PRICHARD ARTHUR SELWYN 1910+ BC, CAN [36993]

PRICKETT 1800-1850 LONDON, ENG [35192] : PRE 1705 OXF, ENG [37069]

PRIDDLE 1700-1860 STH PETHERTON, SOM, ENG [33884] : 1873 DEVONPORT, DEV, ENG [35870]

PRIDE 1864+ MELBOURNE, VIC, AUS [35059] : 1860+ SYDNEY, NSW, AUS [37136] : 1700-1900 KINGSKETTLE, FIF, SCT [36394]

PRIDEAUX PRE 1847 CRESWICK, VIC, AUS [34878] : 1847+ ADELAIDE, SA, AUS [35746] : PRE 1847 CAMBORNE, CON, ENG [35746]

PRIDHAM PRE 1880 HOLDSWORTHY, DEV, ENG [35118] : ALL HOLDSWORTHY, DEV, ENG [35118]

PRIDITH 1700+ NEWENT, GLS, ENG [34747]

PRIDMORE 1830 WILBARSTON, NTH, ENG [35024] : 1747+ LITTLE BOWDEN, NTH, ENG [35921]

PRIESS PRE 1850 OLDENBURG, SHO, GER [38648]

PRIEST 1780+ LAMBETH, MDX, ENG [36872] : PRE 1800 HEF & WAR, ENG [37404] : PRE 1810 DENBY & SILKSTONE, WRY, ENG [37754] : PRE 1700 KEN, ENG [38389]

PRIESTLEY C1690+ ALTOFTS & NORMANTON, WRY, ENG [34397]

PRIESTLEY CASEY C1860-87 ST MARYLEBONE, MDX, ENG [36153] : 1918+ CAMBRIDGE, MA, USA [36153]

PRIESTLY 1760-1825 THORNTON, YKS, ENG [34793]

PRIESTMAN 1850+ MIDDLETON TYAS, NRY, ENG [37635]

PRIESTNER PRE 1861 LYMM & KINGSLEY, CHS, ENG [36740]

PRIESTWOOD 1700+ CON, ENG [38725] : 1700+ WATERFORD, WAT, IRL [38725]

PRIME PRE 1850 GREAT BARRINGTON, CAM, ENG [36073] : 1800+ ESS & VIC, ENG & AUS [37152]

PRIMETT PRE 1885 ICKLEFORD, HRT, ENG [34802]

PRIMROSE PRE 1870 HAM, ENG [36372] : 1849-1866 CAV, IRL [36801] : PRE 1836 TULLIALLAN, PER, SCT [33822] : 1800+ ABERDEEN, SCT [33947] : PRE 1804 TULLIALLAN, PER, SCT [34037] : PRE 1860 KINCARDINE, PER, SCT [34037] : ALL LESLIE, FIF, SCT [36801]

PRINCE 1850S HARROW ON THE HILL, MDX, ENG [34450] : PRE 1810 HUNGERFORD, BRK, ENG [35503] : C1750 STOKE GABRIEL, DEV, ENG [35938] : 1750-1780 SHERBURN IN ELMET, WRY, ENG [36136] : 1800-1850 CHESTER, CHS, ENG [36229] : ALL DBY, ENG [36326] : 1600-1870 NORTH HEATH, WINTERBOURNE, BRK, ENG [36485] : ALL HUBY, YKS, ENG [36557] : 1600S ALLHALLOWS, LND, ENG [36944] : 1800+ MDX, ENG [37868] : C1840 DOVER, KEN, ENG [37888] : 1740-1783 NJ, USA [34366] : 1850+ TRENTON, NJ, USA [36326] : 1780-1810 HAWARDEN, FLN, WLS [36229] : 1835-1935 GRESFORD, DEN, WLS [36229]

PRIND ALL AUS [35565] : C1830 DEV, ENG [35565] : 1800+ ENG [35565]

PRINEVILLE C1834 LIM, IRL [34752]

PRING C1850 BALLARAT, VIC, AUS [36362] : 1800+ CROYDON, SRY, ENG [35355] : 1740-1860 BRASTED & SPELDHURST, KEN, ENG [36051] : PRE 1850 LND & SRY, ENG [37091] : PRE 1900 SOM, ENG [37322]

PRINGLE 1864+ FREMANTLE, WA, AUS [34530] : 1790-1900 LA CO., ONT, CAN [34520] : 1800S GREY CO., ONT, CAN [37423] : 1810+ LND, ENG [38288] : C1900 RATHGAR, DUB, IRL [35521] : 1840-1900 INNERLEITHEN, SEL, SCT [33991] : GEORGE 1834+ DUNS, BEW, SCT [34954] : 1800S SCT [35906] : 1780-1855 ETTRICK, SCT [38199] : 1600-1800 USA & ENG [35289]

PRINZ PRE 1839 ODENTHAL, RPR, GER [38647]

PRIOR PRE 1900 DAPTON, NSW, AUS [33781] : 1885+ SYDNEY, NSW, AUS [34302] : HENRY 1860+ ELSTERNWICK ,MELBOURNE, VIC, AUS [35593] : SARAH 1861+ BOWNING, NSW, AUS [35787] : PATRICK 1861 BOWNING, NSW, AUS [35787] : 1924+ WINDSOR, ONT, CAN [37380] : 1873+ ST HELIER, JSY, CHI & UK [34302] : PRE 1852 MALMESBURY, WIL, ENG [33806] : C1736 WENDRON, CON, ENG [33992] : PRE 1839 LONDON, ENG [34166] : PRE 1860 HOMERTON, MDX, ENG [34272] : LYDIA KATE PRE 1890 KEN, ENG [34481] : 1700-1770 ABINGDON, BRK, ENG [34552] : 1800S MAIDSTONE, KEN, ENG [34793] : C1840 MDX, ENG [34898] : 1880+ HAM, ENG [35565] : 1600-1900 ESS, MDX & LND, ENG [35944] : 1800S CORSCOMBE, DOR, ENG [35964] : PRE 1800 FAREHAM, HAM, ENG [36396] : 1700+ HRT, ESS & MDX, ENG [36574] : PRE 1850 HATFIELD BROADOAK, HEF, ENG [36676] : 1700S GREAT HALLINGBURY, ESS, ENG [37250] : C1744 LEI, ENG [37706] : PRE 1775 KEN, ENG [38389] : 1804-1826 OLD SODBURY & BRISTOL, GLS, ENG [38761] : PRE 1870 BALLYDUFF, WAT, IRL [34302]

PRIOR-WOOD 1780 CHEAM, SRY, ENG [34204]

PRISK PRE 1775 WENDRON, CON, ENG [33992] : 1700+ WENDRON & GWENNAP, CON, ENG [34970] : PRE 1856 CON, ENG [37901]

PRISMALL ALL WORLDWIDE [37651]

PRISNALL ALL WORLDWIDE [37651]

PRISTMELL ALL WORLDWIDE [37651]

PRISTON PRE 1860 EXETER, DEV, ENG [35882]

PRITCHARD 1810-C1880 IVINGTON & LEOMINSTER, HEF, ENG [33847] : PRE 1860 LND, ENG [34819] : C1870 HOXTON, MDX, ENG [35778] : PRE 1840 ISLINGTON, MDX, ENG [36072] : PRE 1803 WOLVERHAMPTON, STS, ENG [36532] : 1700-1850 MARYLEBONE, LND, ENG [37361] : PRE 1850 BIRMINGHAM, WOR, WAR & STS, ENG [37703] : 1700 AYMESTREY, HEF, ENG [37928] : 1750-1850 FER, IRL [35494] : 1750-1870 ARM, IRL [36440] : PRE 1845 KINFAUNS, PER, SCT [35463] : 1818+ ONEIDA CO., NY, USA [37510] : 1700-1800 WLS

[34387] : PRE 1840 ABERYSTWYTH, CGN, WLS [35079] : 1686+ BRE, WLS [37399]

PRITCHET PRE 1797 BARWELL, LEI, ENG [36528]

PRITCHETT C1780-1866 WOR & WAR, ENG [37762] : EDWARD 1855 WOODFORD CO., IL, USA [38132] : 1800-1900 IN, USA [38328]

PRITZ C1900 MELBOURNE, VIC, AUS [35859]

PRITZKOW PRE 1900 BRA, GER [38648]

PRIVETT 1860+ MDX, ENG [37525] : PRE 1823 ENG [37897]

PRIZMELL ALL WORLDWIDE [37651]

PROBASCO ALL WORLDWIDE [38073]

PROBER ALL WORLDWIDE [37750]

PROBERT PRE 1836 CRANHAM, GLS, ENG [33860] : PRE 1839 TOTTENHAM, MDX, ENG [34166] : ALL LYONSHALL, HEF, ENG [34553] : C1820 WORCESTER, WOR, ENG [36649] : 1800-1900 BIRMINGHAM, WAR, ENG [37068]

PROBST ALL WUE, GER [38333]

PROBY 1700+ LE GRAND LEMP, GRENOBLE, FRA [34323] : 1700+ DUBLIN, IRL [34323]

PROBYN 1700-1800 TENBURY WELLS, WOR, ENG [36003]

PROCH 1780-1850 REHDEN, WPR, GER [38599]

PROCTER 1850+ ECCLESHALL & FENTON, STS, ENG [34714] : PRE 1820 CHULMLEIGH, DEV, ENG [35128] : C1744+ TRAWDEN & COLNE, LAN, ENG [37988] : 1635-1985 ESSEX CO., MA, USA [36562]

PROCTOR 1850+ NORWOOD, SA, AUS [36638] : 1850+ LONDON, ONT, CAN [34473] : PRE 1800 BRIXHAM, DEV, ENG [34333] : 1709-1860S SHOULDHAM, NFK, ENG [34649] : 1834+ BRETTENHAM, SFK, ENG [35567] : 1812+ PALGRAVE, SFK, ENG [35567] : 1800+ LND, ENG [35762] : PRE 1870 YKS, ENG [35949] : PRE 1850 GUISELEY, WRY, ENG [36159] : 1650-1750 NEWCASTLE UPON TYNE, NBL, ENG [36220] : 1820+ BRADFORD, YKS, ENG [36638] : 1800S ELLEL, LAN, ENG [36847] : PRE 1847 LIVERPOOL, LAN, ENG [37840] : PRE 1840 CAV, IRL [36255] : C1800-1890 IRL & NZ [36835] : 1700-1800 DUNDEE, PER, SCT [36220] : 1800+ LOCKSBURG, TN, USA [36351] : 1800+ MCNAIRY CO., TN, USA [36351] : 1800+ GA, USA [36351] : 1635-1985 ESSEX CO., MA, USA [36562]

PROCTOR-THOMPSON 1850S CAMBERWELL, SRY, ENG [34204]

PROFET PRE 1300 ABERDEEN & FARFAR, SCT [38586]

PROFFITT 1740-1880 MIDDLE BARTON, OXF, ENG [34440] : 1800+ LAN, ENG [37462] : 1800+ LIVERPOOL, LAN, ENG [38586] : 1700-1800 WAVERTREE & LIVERPOOL, LAN, ENG [38586] : PRE 1900 WALTON & LIVERPOOL, LAN, ENG [38586]

PROFKE 1880+ FASSIFERN, QLD, AUS [35460] : ALL HINDENBERG VIA TEMPLIN, BRA, GER [35460] : PRE 1880+ KRENZKRUG, BRA, GER [35460]

PROFSER THOMAS 1735+ CRICARDAN, BRE, WLS [34134] : ROGER 1700+ CRICARDAN, BRE, WLS [34134]

PROLE 1700-1880 ENG [36169]

PRONCE ALL WORLDWIDE [36206]

PRONSE ALL WORLDWIDE [36206]

PROOM 1750-1850 STUTTON, SFK, ENG [37042]

PROPER 1930+ CHICAGO, IL, USA [34132]

PROPHET 1700+ GREAT SANKEY, LAN, ENG [38586]

PROPHETE PRE 1300 YKS, ENG [38586]

PROSSER 1840-1860S SODBURY, GLS, ENG [33835] : PRE 1900 LONDON, ENG [35901] : PRE 1860

BRISTOL, ENG [37974] : 1870+ JEFFERSON CO., CO, USA [38310] : ANN 1773+ LLANDEVALLEY, BRE, WLS [34134] : C1816 TALGARTH, BRE, WLS [35391] : ALL WLS [35901] : 1800-1835 TREVETHIN, MON, WLS [37671]

PROST C1710 DEV & CON, ENG [36594]

PROTT 1600S LEMGO, WEF, GER [38750]

PROTZEL 1700-1800 HERZBERG, NSA, GER [38643]

PROU 1620-1700 GOURNAY & POITIERS, PCH, FRA [34514]

PROUD 1845-1990 MELBOURNE, VIC, AUS [36832] : PRE 1850 LANCHESTER, DUR, ENG [33993] : 1843-1868 BRIGHTLINGSEA, ESS, ENG [34582] : PRE 1750 THIRSK, NRY, ENG [34588] : C1797 SHARP, WES, ENG [35764] : PRE 1716 LANCHESTER, DUR, ENG [37635] : 1841-1990 AUCKLAND, NZ [36832]

PROUDFOOT 1850-1950 CAN [34135] : 1750-1800 BARTON, WES, ENG [38516] : 1800+ ANS, SCT [33862] : PRE 1882 DFS, SCT [37318] : 1700-1750 JOHNSTONE, DFS, SCT [38516]

PROUDLOVE 1800-1850 ODDROOE, CHS, ENG [38250]

PROUDMAN PRE 1900 KIDDERMINSTER & ASTLEY, WOR, ENG [33883]

PROULX PRE 1800 MONTREAL, QUE, CAN [38033]

PROUSE 1600-1800 ILSINGTON, DEV, ENG [36106] : 1700+ CLOVELLY & BUCKLAND BREWER, DEV, ENG [36516]

PROUT 1880+ MACKAY, QLD, AUS [35825] : 1860+ TAS, AUS [38005] : PRE 1730 NORTH TAMERTON, CON, ENG [34304] : 1788 TINEO, DEV, ENG [34804] : 1600-1800 ARLINGTON, DEV, ENG [35825] : 1700-1900 NORTH MOLTON, DEV, ENG [35825] : ALL BUDE & STRATTON, CON & DEV, ENG [35940] : PRE 1760 INKPEN, BRK, ENG [37638] : 1700-1860 CON, ENG [38005] : 1780-1850 STROUD, GLS, ENG [38407]

PROUTEN 1874 TOOWOOMBA, QLD, AUS [37174] : PRE 1877 JSY, CHI [37174] : PRE 1828 PAGHAM, SSX, ENG [37174]

PROVAN C1700 ROBRESTOWN, LKS, SCT [35051] : 1730+ CADDER, LKS, SCT [35051] : 1840+ ANDERSTON, GLASGOW, LKS, SCT [35051] : 1852+ ARDROSSAN, AYR, SCT [35051] : 1879+ AUCHTERDERRAN, FIF, SCT [35051]

PROVEST 1848+ NEW WINDSOR, BRK, ENG [35598] : 1815+ WYRADISBURY, BKM, ENG [35598]

PROVIS ALL COLEFORD, GLS, ENG [36359] : 1800+ ESS & GLS, ENG [37597] : 1850+ PONTYPOOL, MON, WLS [37597]

PROVOST 1820-1870 QUE, CAN [37547] : 1840-1885 RUTLAND, VT, USA [37547] : 1840-1885 CHAMPLAIN, NY, USA [37547]

PROWD 1848+ MELBOURNE, VIC, AUS [34925] : 1840+ ARMAGH, ARM, IRL [34925] : ALL SCT & ENG [34925] : ALL WORLDWIDE [34925]

PROWSE 1800+ PENZANCE, CON, ENG [34934] : 1600-1800 ILSINGTON, DEV, ENG [36106] : RICHARD PRE 1836 BUCKFASTLEIGH, DEV, ENG [37014] : ALL LAN, ENG [38514] : RICHARD 1830-1862 MCHENRY CO., IL, USA [37014] : JOHN 1839-1886 MCHENRY CO., IL, USA [37014]

PROZEL 1700-1800 HERZBERG, NSA, GER [38643]

PRPIC 1884-1975 WHITING, IN & MI, USA [38063] : PRE 1880 LICKO CERJA, GRACAC, YU [38063]

PRUDENCE PRE 1870 EDMONTON & ENFIELD, MDX, ENG [36061] : PRE 1900 EAST LONDON, ENG [37416]

PRUDHOME PRE 1800 DANBY, YKS, ENG [36481]

PRUE C1860 BANBURY, OXF, ENG [34935]

PRUITT ALL USA [36540]

PRUSSIANI C1500-C1780 CASTELLEONE DI SUASA, ITL [36139]

PRYCE PRE 1830 LND, ENG [36538]

PRYOR 1839+ WEST MAITLAND, NSW, AUS [33794] : 1800S WENDRON, CON, ENG [35127] : PRE 1830 WENDRON, CON, ENG [35151] : 1565+ WENDRON, CON, ENG [35587] : PRE 1900 MELBOURN, CAM, ENG [37137] : 1700+ WOOTEN FITZPAINE, DOR, ENG [38745] : ALLEN CYRUS 1835 VT, USA [34511] : C1813 BULLITT CO., KY, USA [37527] : 1875-1950 TN, USA [37593] : 1900+ WORLDWIDE [37593]

PRYSE PRE 1900 LETHBRIDGE, ALB, CAN [35135]

PUCK PRE 1909 BALLARAT, VIC, AUS [34907] : PRE 1909 BRD [34907] : 1820+ KIEL, SHO, BRD & AUS [34703] : PRE 1909 DDR [34907]

PUCKERIDGE 1801+ SYDNEY, NSW, AUS [34979] : PRE 1801 MDX, ENG [34979]

PUCKEY ALL HELSTON, CON, ENG [35749]

PUCKNELL 1750-1800 BERMONDSEY, LND, ENG [36378]

PUDDEN C1865 COKER, SOM, ENG [37233]

PUDDICOMBE C1795 EXETER, DEV, ENG [35131] : ALL WORLDWIDE [37264]

PUDDIFOOT 1800-99 WATFORD, HRT, ENG [37272]

PUDDY C1500-1900 BURNHAM & MARK, SOM, ENG [34158] : 1800+ MARK, SOM, ENG [35565]

PUDNEY PRE 1840 BUCKLAND, KEN, ENG [36752]

PUDSEY ALL WORLDWIDE [35987]

PUE 1800S NORWICH, NFK, ENG [35899]

PUFFER PRE 1850 NORTHUMBERLAND CO., ONT, CAN [37446] : 1640+ SAPCOTE & DESFORD, LEI, ENG [36827]

PUGH C1800+ LIVERPOOL, LAN, ENG [34451] : PRE 1800 HEF, ENG [34929] : PRE 1850 LIVERPOOL, LAN, ENG [35423] : C1774 LYONSHALL, HEF, ENG [35560] : 1800S NORWICH, NFK, ENG [35899] : ALL HEF, ENG [36197] : 1750-1850 SEDGLEY, STS, ENG [36495] : 1674-1867 EASTHAM, WOR, ENG [36513] : PRE 1850 LONDON, ENG [37078] : 1761-1889 GRAYSON CO., VA, USA [38315] : 1790-1850 GLA, WLS [35153] : ALL WLS [36197] : PRE 1861 MGY, WLS [36968] : LEWIS 1698 DOLGELLEY, MER, WLS [37649] : 1850S RUABON, DEN, WLS [37946] : 1600-1825 CARMARTHEN, CMN, WLS [38216]

PUGSLEY C1814 BLACK TORRINGTON, DEV, ENG [35057] : 1760-1800 YORK CO., ME, USA [38108]

PUIGCERVER 1700-1990 ALICANTE, ESP [38346]

PULFORD JOHN PRE 1836 SFK, ENG [34701]

PULIN 1800-1950 SHAVINGTON, CHS, ENG [36983]

PULKER PRE 1860 OXFORD, OXF, ENG [36015]

PULLAR C1800-1880 NEWCASTLE ON TYNE, NBL, ENG [33862] : ALL SCT & AUS [33990]

PULLEN 1860S LOUISA CREEK & MEROO, NSW, AUS [38006] : 1870S CARLETON PLACE, ONT, CAN [37568] : HENRY 1821 LONDON, ENG [34176] : 1600+ CHICHESTER, SSX, ENG [34747] : 1800+ BRISTOL, GLS, ENG [35812] : PRE 1862 SRY, ENG [37358] : 1790S OLD WINDSOR, BRK, ENG [37568] : 1800+ COR, IRL [35812]

PULLER MARRION 1860 HOBART, TAS, AUS [37123] : CATH 1860 LIVERPOOL, LAN, ENG [37123] : DAVID 1834 FIFE, SCT [37123] : ALL WORLDWIDE [37123]

PULLEY PRE 1788 THETFORD, NFK, ENG [35090] : 1760+ ENG [35101]

PULLIAM 1680-1750 SPOTSYLVANIA CO., VA, USA [36566]

PULLIN 1800+ LONDON, ENG [36494] : C1840 TY & VA, USA [35401]

PULLING C1843 BRISTOL, ENG [35827] : PRE 1850 BISHOPS FROME, HEF, ENG [36051]

PULLINGER PRE 1808 PORTSEA, HAM, ENG [36870]

PULMAN 1800-90 SOLUM, NOR [37031]

PUMFREY C1920+ ISLINGTON, MDX, ENG [35726]

PUMMEROY ALL WORLDWIDE [35707]

PUMPHREY 1830+ PINJELLY, WA, AUS [35857]

PUNCH 1800+ AUS [34424]

PUNLER PRE 1841 DUNFERMLINE, FIF, SCT [36308]

PUNNETT PRE 1836 SSX, ENG [37978]

PUNT 1820S LANGFORD, ESS, ENG [36393]

PUNTER 1800+ SRY, ENG [36430]

PUNTON 1870+ NEWCASTLE, NSW, AUS [35703] : 1864+ BALLARAT, VIC, AUS [35703] : 1800+ NEWCASTLE ON TYNE, NBL, ENG [35703] : PRE 1850 GATESHEAD, DUR, ENG [35821]

PUPIC PRE 1880 RAGUSA, OES [35895]

PUPICH 1880-1913 WEST COAST & CHRISTCHURCH, NZ [35895] : PRE 1880 RAGUSA, OES [35895]

PUPLETT 1800+ GREENWICH, LND, ENG [36069] : PRE 1820 SRY, ENG [37034] : 1900-1990 CROYDON, SRY, ENG [37914]

PURCAS 1680+ BOCKING, ESS, ENG [36871]

PURCELL 1850+ VIC, AUS [34550] : 1860S NSW & WA, AUS [35331] : 1841+ VIC, AUS [35399] : C1890 NSW, AUS [35807] : 1895+ MONTREAL, QUE, CAN [34368] : 1850+ KIDDERMINSTER, WOR, ENG [34113] : 1800+ CLERKENSWELL, LND, ENG [34550] : 1800S HACKNEY, LND, ENG [34953] : 1800-1900 LONDON, MDX, ENG [33642] : 1850+ RAWTENSTALL, LAN, ENG [37066] : PRE 1890 ROSSENDALE, LAN, ENG [37414] : 1800-1830 TIP, IRL [34183] : 1830S STRADBALLY, IRL [35331] : PRE 1841 CASHEL, TIP, IRL [35399] : PRE 1841 GALBALLY, LIM, IRL [35599] : 1800+ THOMASTOWN, KIK, IRL [35992] : PRE 1850 BALLINGARRY, TIP, IRL [37066] : WILLIAM C1803+ DUNFEENEY, MAY & QUE, IRL & CAN [36904] : JOHN C1773-1868 DUNFEENEY, MAY & QUE, IRL & CAN [36904]

PURCHALL PRE 1800 NEWBURY, BRK, ENG [37259] : ALL MDX, ENG [37259] : 1860+ LAMBETH, LND, ENG [37259] : 1840+ CAMBERWELL & PECKHAM, LND, ENG [37259] : 1780-1850 ISLINGTON & SHOREDITCH, MDX, ENG [37259] : ALL SRY, ENG [37259] : ALL HAM, ENG [37259]

PURCHAS 1750+ CHRISTCHURCH, HAM, ENG & FRA [34508]

PURCHASE C1855+ GEELONG, VIC, AUS [35053] : 1880S ARMIDALE & URALLA, NSW, AUS [37966] : 1750-1900 BERE REGIS, DOR, ENG [34714] : ALL WORLDWIDE [37803]

PURCHASS 1750+ CHRISTCHURCH, HAM, ENG & FRA [34508]

PURCHES 1700+ BRIDPORT, DOR, ENG [34532] : ALL WORLDWIDE [36690]

PURCHIS 1750+ CHRISTCHURCH, HAM, ENG & FRA [34508]

PURCIL (SEE PURCELL) [35599]

PURDEY 1878+ RIVERTON, SA, AUS [34437] : PRE 1837 FRAMINGHAM, NFK, ENG [34437] : 1837-1900S SHOTESHAM ALLSAINTS, NFK, ENG [34437]

PURDIE 1890 RICHMOND, VIC, AUS [35204] : 1800 CON, ENG [36860] : 1825+ SCT [34373] : 1800+ EDINBURGH, SCT [38001] : 1750+ LESMAHAGOW, LKS, SCT [38388]

PURDOM 1800+ CARLISLE, CUL, ENG [36823] : 1830+ PIKE CO., MO, USA [38050]

PURDON ALL SPRING BAY, TAS, AUS [34663] : ALL HULL, ERY, ENG [37738] : PRE 1850 NEWMARKET, COR, IRL [34725] : 1750-1850 KILLALOE, CLA, IRL [37844]

PURDUE PRE 1840 ISLINGTON, LND, ENG [36377]

PURDY 1878+ RIVERTON, SA, AUS [34437] : 1800+ NS, CAN [38460] : 1800S DEVONPORT, DEV, ENG [33842] : CHRISTOPHER 1890-1978 BROMLEY, KEN, ENG [34055] : PRE 1837 FRAMINGHAM, NFK, ENG [34437] : 1837-1900S SHOTESHAM ALLSAINTS, NFK, ENG [34437] : 1750-1850 TITTLESHALL, NFK, ENG [35624] : 1750-1850 LITTLE WALSINGHAM, NFK, ENG [35624] : 1700-1960 STIFFKEY & WIVERTON, NFK, ENG [36128] : 1851 ROCHDALE, LAN, ENG [36640] : PRE 1850 IRL [38403] : PRE 1820 CLONES, MOG, IRL [38428] : JOEL 1860 SONOMA, CA, USA [38320]

PURFUERST 1830-1870 ST CHARLES & ST LOUIS, MO, USA [36912]

PURGETT C1778-1837 HAMPSHIRE CO., VA, USA [35284]

PURKESS PRE 1841 NEW FOREST, HAM, ENG [36079]

PURKIS 1871+ LONDON, ENG [35193] : PRE 1800 ESS, ENG [36379]

PURKISS 1880+ ST MARYS, NB, CAN [34256] : 1800-1840 COLNE ENGAINE & ARDLEIGH, ESS, ENG [36987]

PURKS 1800S BETHNAL GREEN, LND, ENG [36764]

PURNELL 1793 STROUD, GLS, ENG [35560] : 1650-1750 LONDON, ENG [37231] : 1750+ TROWBRIDGE, WIL, ENG [37705]

PURRIER PRE 1800 WORLDWIDE [37089]

PURSELEY ALL NFK, ENG [37181]

PURSELY 1700-1800S KILSKEERY AREA, TYR, IRL [34483]

PURSER 1700+ LYTTLETON, MDX, ENG [35972] : 1810-1850S CLAINES & KEMPSEY, WOR, ENG [36190] : PRE 1833 BIRLINGHAM, WOR, ENG [36190] : C1850 STOURPORT ON SEVERN, WOR, ENG [37209] : 1700+ HANLEY CASTLE, WOR, ENG [37209] : 1750+ HUN, ENG [37409]

PURSEY PRE 1820 CANTERBURY & DOVER, KEN, ENG [34316]

PURSHOUSE 1750+ LONDON, MDX, ENG [36462]

PURSSER C1790 CANTERBURY, KEN, ENG [35350]

PURTELL 1870+ OMAHA, DOUGLAS, NE, USA [36338]

PURTILL 1849+ WAVERLEY, NSW, AUS [34857] : 1790+ KILCORNAN, LIM, IRL [34857]

PURTON C1884 DENVER, CO, USA [34522]

PURVES ALL KCD, SCT [34381] : ALL ANS, SCT [34381] : ALL LAUDER & EARLSTON, BEW, SCT [35293] : PRE 1840 NENTHORN, BEW, SCT [35962] : PRE 1900 AUCHTERMUCHTY, FIF, SCT [38116]

PURVIS 1850+ NEWCASTLE ON TYNE, DUR, ENG [35806] : C1809 HEWORTH, DUR, ENG [36364] : 1800S SOUTH SHIELDS, DUR, ENG [36364] : 1700S NEWBURN, NBL, ENG [36364] : 1816-1850 ANTRIM, ANT, IRL [34114] : C1850 TYR, IRL [35974] : C1870 AUCKLAND, NZ [35974]

PURYER PRE 1805 OCKLEY, SRY, ENG [37568] : PRE 1800 WORLDWIDE [37089]

PUSCH 1800S SAGAN, SIL, GER [38623]

PUSEY PRE 1845 NEW FOREST, HAM, ENG [36079]

PUSTKUCHEN 1754-1815 BLOMBERG, PYR, GER [38749]

PUTLAND 1852+ GUNDAGAI, NSW, AUS [34806] : PRE 1800 WESTHAM, SSX, ENG [34806] : PRE 1850 WILLINGDON, SSX, ENG [35898] : 1800+ CATSFIELD, SSX, ENG [37260]

PUTMAN 1700-1950 HRT, ENG [38471] : 1780 ST JOHNSVILLE, MONT. CO., NY, USA [37006] : 1780-1830S PA, USA [37600] : 1600-1800 CULPEPPER CO., VA, USA [38154] : 1800-1850 CHAMPAIGN CO., OH, USA [38154] : 1830-1990 BROWN CO., IL, USA [38154] : 1695-1800 CULPEPER CO., VA, KY & OH, USA & ENG [38309]

PUTNAM 1750+ CT, MA & NH, USA [35137] : 1825-1830 WABASH & KNOX CO., IL & IN, USA [38092] : 1850-1860 FANNIN CO., TX, USA [38092] : 1825-1860 DUBUQUE CO., IA, USA [38092]

PUTT 1810-1840 TUSCAWASA CO., OH, USA [36328]

PUTTER 1652-1990 RSA [36457]

PYATT 1800-1850 BIRMINGHAM, WAR, ENG [37074]

PYCROFT PRE 1800 NTT, ENG [36140]

PYE 1850+ BALLARAT, VIC, AUS [36368] : 1791+ AUS [36632] : 1800+ ESS, ENG [33857] : 1780+ CARLETON, LAN, ENG [34092] : PRE 1760 FALMOUTH, CON, ENG [34139] : 1700+ COLD NORTON & MOUNTNESSING, ESS, ENG [34789] : 1904 EDMONTON, MDX, ENG [35575] : 1700-1800 WESTBURY ON SEVERN, GLS, ENG [35968] : 1800+ BRISTOL, ENG [36368] : 1800S BREDGAR & SITTINGBOURNE, KEN & MDX, ENG [37677]

PYGOT PRE 1500 CLOTHERHAM, YKS, ENG [34716]

PYKE 1880-1920 BALLARAT, VIC, AUS [34191] : ALL PA & KS, USA [35304]

PYKE (SEE PIKE) [38465]

PYLE 1750+ WEST MEON, HAM, ENG [33938] : PRE 1840 DEV, ENG [34463] : 1700+ USA [38065]

PYM 1500+ CHILHAM, KEN, ENG [36049]

PYMAN 1600-1850 SANDSEND, NRY, ENG [37665] : 1850+ WEST HARTLEPOOL, DUR, ENG [37665]

PYMBLE 1821+ PYMBLE, NSW, AUS [35547]

PYNE 1880S CRESWICK, VIC, AUS [34191] : 1850+ GUNNEDAH, NSW, AUS [34913] : 1850+ PETERSHAM, NSW, AUS [38204] : PRE 1756 BRISTOL, GLS, SOM & DEV, ENG [37289] : C1805 KILMURRY, CLA, IRL [34942] : 1755+ NOR [37289]

PYOTT 1850-1900 RICHMOND, NRY, ENG [34211] : PRE 1770S KIRRIEMUIR, ANS, SCT [36405]

PYPER COLIN C1839 TARBOLTON, AYR, SCT [34300]

PYWELL 1800 NTH, ENG [34057] : PRE 1765 LEI, ENG [37706]

PYZER 1680+ STATHERN, LEI, ENG [37829]

QUACKENBUSH 1800-1850 ONT & FRI, CAN & NL [37446]

QUADE PRE 1850 POS, GER [35323]

QUADT PRE 1867 NRW, GER [38630]

QUAGLIANI C1500-C1780 CORINALDO, ITL [36139]

QUAIFE C1875 ROCKHAMPTON & TOWNSVILLE, QLD, AUS [35786] : C1817 BRENCHLEY, KEN, ENG [35786]

QUAIL 1860+ WALLSEND, NSW, AUS [35105] : C1880 PT & AUS [35079]

QUAILE 1800+ LIVERPOOL, LAN, ENG [34591]

QUAILEY 1840+ NSW, AUS [34426]

QUAILL 1878+ SYDNEY, NSW, AUS [37914]

QUAIN C1890 QLD, AUS [34807] : 1859+ BALLYHOOLY, COR, IRL [34807]

QUAIT ALL WORLDWIDE [37069]

QUAK ALL NL [36240]

QUALMANN PRE 1770 HOHENKIRCHEN, MSW, GER [38632]

QUALY ALL WORLDWIDE [34500]

QUANDT 1700-1800+ KROPITZ, BLN, GER [37814] : PRE 1800 BRA, GER [38627] : 1900+ WAYNE CO., MI, USA [37814]

QUANT 1800+ BAMPTON, DEV, ENG [35006]

QUANTOCK PRE 1810 SOM, ENG [37957]

QUANTRILL PRE 1792 NORWICH, NFK, ENG [34222] : 1800 NFK, ENG [34261]

QUANY 1800S BRIDE, IOM [34288]

QUARINTON PRE 1830 STROOD, KEN, ENG [34819]

QUARLES PRE 1800 SFK, ENG [36829] : PRE 1800 NFK, ENG [36829] : 1760 KING WILLIAM, VA, USA [38198]

QUARMBY PRE 1840 HUDDERSFIELD, WRY, ENG [37385] : 1700-1920 HUDDERSFIELD, WRY, ENG [37736]

QUARRIE ALL WORLDWIDE [36044]

QUARRY 1700-1750 BDF, ENG [36044] : 1740-1770 BKM, ENG [36044] : 1830-61 LONDON, ENG [37341] : 1860S CHELSEA, LND, ENG [37341] : ALL WORLDWIDE [36044]

QUARTERMAIN ALL WORLDWIDE [33836] : ALL WORLDWIDE [37837]

QUARTERMAINE ALL THAME, OXF, ENG [35139] : ALL WORLDWIDE [33836]

QUARTERMAN ALL OXF, ENG [35139] : 1750L+ OXFORD, OXF, ENG [37837] : 1750+ LONDON, ENG [37837] : 1600-1890S CONLEY, OXF, ENG [37837] : 1629+ SUNNINGWELL, BRK, ENG [37837] : 1700S ASCOT UNDER WYCHWOOD, OXF, ENG & NZ [35186] : ALL WORLDWIDE [33836] : ALL WORLDWIDE [37837]

QUARTERMANE ALL WORLDWIDE [33836]

QUARTLY ALL DULVERTON, SOM & DEV, ENG [37322]

QUARY ALL WORLDWIDE [36044]

QUATREMAINS ALL FRA [37837] : ALL CAEN, FRA [37837]

QUAYLE 1860S-1880S PAISLEY, ONT, CAN [34103] : MARY ANN 1848-1860S RAMSAY, IOM, UK [34103]

QUEALLY C1830 KILMALEY, CLA, IRL [34426]

QUEE ALL BELFAST & DUBLIN, IRL [36486]

QUEEN JOSEPH 1800+ GLASGOW, LKS, SCT [37496] : PRE 1930 LKS, SCT [37974]

QUELCH 1878+ CHARTERS TOWERS, QLD, AUS [34852] : 1854 LONDON, ENG [34808] : 1800+ THAME, OXF, ENG [34852]

QUENNELL 1400+ CHIDDINGFOLD, SRY, ENG [37218]

QUEREE 1800+ TRINITY, JSY, CHI [36795]

QUERIPEL 1900+ SYDNEY, NSW, AUS [35926] : PRE 1990 FOREST, GSY, CHI [35926]

QUESTED 1827+ HOBART, TAS, AUS [35394] : 1700S KEN, ENG [34404] : 1800+ KEN, ENG [35465]

QUIBBLE 1750+ RETFORD, NTT, ENG [37735]

QUIBELL ALL EAST MARKHAM, NTT, ENG [35904]

QUICK 1850+ BALLARAT, VIC, AUS [36622] : 1850+ CLUNES, BLACKWOOD & CRESWICK, VIC, AUS [36622] : PRE 1800 CON, ENG [33972] : PRE 1815 DUNSTER, SOM, ENG [37144] : ALL ST IVES, CON, ENG [37873] : ALL ULSTER CO., NY, USA [37584] : 1800-1850 SUSSEX CO., NJ, USA [38201]

QUIGG C1860 CHINCHILLA, QLD, AUS [35807] : PRE 1880 DON, MAY & SLI, IRL [37764] : 1900+ AUCKLAND, NZ [36871]

QUIGGIN C1853-1907 WYNYARD, TAS, AUS [38072] : PRE 1840 KIRK MICHAEL, IOM, UK [38072]

QUIGLEY 1830+ ROS, SLI & MEA, IRL [38079] : ALL UK & IRL [37240] : 1880+ MI, USA [34368] : PRE 1899 RENSSELAER, NY, USA [38321]

QUILAN 1920 ROCKWOOD & WEDDIFIELD, ONT, CAN [36679] : 1920 NIPPISSING, ONT, CAN [36679]

QUILLERET ALL WORLDWIDE [36308]

QUILTER 1700+ ESS, ENG [36093] : 1830S DAWDON, DUR, ENG [38269]

QUILTON PRE 1800 LONDON, MDX, ENG [37006]

QUIN 1850+ EPSOM & HUNTLY, VIC, AUS [35379] : C1853 KILLEESHIL, TYR, IRL [34189] : PRE 1850

SIX MILE BRIDGE, CLA, IRL [35379] : 1700-1850 MONAGHAN, MOG, IRL [35937] : 1700+ IRL [36261] : PRE 1900 KILLINANE, CAR, IRL [36361] : C1850-1900 GLASGOW, LKS, SCT [35730] : 1750+ LANCASTER CO., PA, USA [37507] : PRE 1850 NORTHUMBERLAND CO., PA, USA [37507] : PRE 1850 UNION CO., PA, USA [37507]

QUINANE 1800S TIPPERARY, TIP, IRL [34574]

QUINBY ISAAC 1790-1866 PARSIPPANY, MORRIS CO., NJ, USA [37023]

QUINCY 1750-1810 BRINGTON, HUN, ENG [38003]

QUINLAN 1860+ DARLING DOWNS, QLD, AUS [33871] : 1840+ VIC & NSW, AUS [36299] : D. 1873+ MELBOURNE, VIC, AUS [38289] : 1865+ SYDNEY, NSW, AUS [38597] : PRE 1860 BALLYLONGFORD, KER, IRL [33871] : CONNOR 1760-1800 KILLARNEY, KER & CLA, IRL [33941] : PRE 1855 MITCHELSTOWN, COR, IRL [34582] : 1800S INAGH, CLA, IRL [35398] : PRE 1840 LEX, OFF & TIP, IRL [36299] : PRE 1863 MULLINAHONE, TIP, IRL [36361]

QUINLIVAN ALL IRL [35190]

QUINN 1860+ QLD, AUS [34588] : 1880+ DUNGOG & MAITLAND, NSW, AUS [37966] : 1850S IRISH CREEK, ONT, CAN [35078] : 1800S HASTINGS CO., ONT, CAN [38445] : 1770+ PEI, CAN [38460] : 1800-1860 SOM, ENG [34738] : 1850+ BIRTLEY & SUNDERLAND, DUR, ENG [36503] : 1879 ILKESTON, DBY, ENG [37694] : 1800+ MOORTOWN & ARBOE, TYR, IRL [33829] : PRE 1870 LEITRIM, IRL [34443] : PRE 1860 INAGH, CLA, IRL [34588] : 1750+ COR, IRL [34933] : 1700+ IRL [34970] : 1800 MONAGHAN, MOG, IRL [35067] : 1830+ TULLAMORE, OFF, IRL [35240] : C1850 OFF, IRL [35398] : C1810 DUNDALK, LOU, IRL [35434] : PRE 1860 TIP, IRL [35750] : 1850+ FORKHILL, DOW, IRL [35970] : MARY 1800-1880 GAL, IRL [36297] : PRE 1860 FER & TYR, IRL [36503] : 1830+ DUBLIN, IRL [36691] : 1810+ TANDRAGEE, ARM, IRL [36728] : ALL LET, IRL [36844] : 1830-1860 LOUGHREA, GAL, IRL [38117] : 1800-50 FER, IRL [38189] : PRE 1900 KILLIMACARDLE, TYR, IRL [38300] : PRE 1825 ARM, IRL [38445] : 1750-1850 LET, IRL [38575] : ALL TIP, IRL & NZ [36854] : 1850-1876 DALRY, AYR, SCT [35937]

QUINNELL 1860+ BRISBANE, QLD, AUS [35232] : 1850+ INVERELL, NSW, AUS [35232] : 1775+ BRISTOL, GLS, ENG [35232] : 1600+ TRALEE, KER, IRL [37218] : 1830+ SWANSEA, GLA, WLS [35232]

QUINNEY PRE 1856 PRESTON CAPES, NTH, ENG [36841] : PRE 1870 PEEL, IOM [35986] : 1856+ NELSON, NZ [36841]

QUINT PRE 1842 ST HELIER, JSY, CHI [35258]

QUINTAL 1850-1915 SCOTT CO., IL, USA [36546]

QUINTON 1825+ NFD, CAN [33852] : C1830 RED CLIFFE, NFD, CAN [34096] : 1811 WELLS, SOM, ENG [36011] : 1800+ SOM, ENG [37827]

QUIREY 1860+ CARNMONEY, ANT, IRL & AUS [35372]

QUIRK PRE 1882 MT GAMBIER, SA, AUS [37315] : 1840-1843 NB, NS & PEI, CAN [37816] : 1800-1900 BALLYMCELLIGOTT, KER, IRL [33785] : PRE 1840 WAT, IRL [34800] : MAY 1800S IRL [34902] : JOHN PRE 1850 IRL [34902] : 1834-1840 JAMAICA [37816] : PRE 1862 LAMBFELL, IOM, UK [35108]

QUIRT 1830 OGDENSBURG, NY, USA & IRL [38349]

QUITMEYER 1870 RODEVALD, HAN, GER [36730]

QUITTENTON C1810 LONDON, ENG [33914]

QUOIT 1824-1854 NANTES, FRA [36601]

QUY PRE 1900 EAST HAM, LND, ENG [36260]

QVERNBERG 1750+ SOR ODAL, HEDMARK, NOR [34664]

RAASCH PRE 1945 SCHLENZIG, POM, GER [38636]

RABBATTS C1843 GREENWICH, LND, ENG [37627]

RABBICH ALL DEV, ENG [34415]

RABBITS PRE 1875 PORTSEA, HAM, ENG [33944]

RABBITT PATRICK 1829-1860 IRL [37567] : MARY ETHEL 1894-1990 MO, USA [37567] : MARTIN 1890-1940 NOVINGER, ADAIR, MO, USA [37567] : BERNARD 1901-1990 MO, USA [37567] : JAMES LEO 1897-1990 MO, USA [37567] : MICHAEL 1854-1900+ HUDSON (HOBOKEN TWP), NJ, USA [37567]

RABBITTS PRE 1900 BISHOPWEARMOUTH, DUR, ENG [33944] : PRE 1874 WIL, ENG [36204]

RABE 1788-1810 HERMSDORF, SIL, POL [35850] : 1790+ MD & KY, USA [38050]

RABETT 1700-1850 FRANT, SSX, ENG [36612]

RABIN 1884+ LONDON, ENG [36995] : PRE 1884 SALANT, COVENAY GOURBERNEY, SU [36995]

RABINEL 1750-1850 CEYLON [37306]

RABJOHNS 1700-1900 DEV, ENG [36118]

RABNOTT PRE 1920 MT MORGAN, QLD, AUS [34868] : PRE 1880 LONDON, ENG [34868]

RABON PRE 1800 BRD & GER [36964]

RABRANT 1800-1840 MEA, IRL [34200]

RABY ALL CAN [34212] : 1850 BURY, LAN, ENG [34015] : 1830-50S GAYWOOD, NFK, ENG [36301] : 1700-1800 DOWNHAM, CAM, ENG [37188] : 1700-1850 SRY, ENG [37618]

RACE JAMES 1883+ NORTH SYDNEY, NSW, AUS [34427] : JAMES PRE 1883 DUR, ENG [34427]

RACEY 1750+ BATH, SOM, ENG & CAN [34467]

RACHAOU PRE 1680 PRASTBOL & FRYKSANDE, VARMLAND, SWE [38551]

RACHELSON PRE 1900 LND, ENG [36399]

RACHER 1770+ BASSINGBOURN, CAM, ENG [35368] : 1885-1910 FINSBURY PARK, LND, ENG [37657] : 1800-1900 BASSINGBOURN, CAM, ENG [37657]

RACHOW PRE 1680 PRASTBOL & FRYKSANDE, VARMLAND, SWE [38551]

RACINE VETAL 1837 CAN [38062]

RACKEMANN PRE 1864 HANNOVER, LOWER SAXONY, GER [34766]

RACKLIFF ALL WORLDWIDE [36235]

RACKSTRAW C1818 READING, BRK, ENG [35990] : 1800-1850 LITTLE MARLOW, BKM, ENG [37652] : ALTISEDORA 1849+ WATLINGTON, OXF, ENG [37958]

RACKUFF ALL ENG [36055]

RADABAUGH 1700S RPF, BRD [37028] : 1800S OH, USA [37028] : 1700S PA, USA [37028]

RADBURN 1750S-1950S OXF & SSX, ENG [36541]

RADCLIFF 1800S WREXHAM, DEN, WLS [37134]

RADCLIFFE 1850S FRYERS CREEK, VIC, AUS [33934] : PRE 1865 BIRMINGHAM, WAR, ENG [34736] : 1700-1870 MELLOR & AREA, DBY, CHS & WRY, ENG [37934] : 1870+ GOVERNORS BAY, NZ [35986] : 1750+ FAYETTE CO., PA, USA [36956]

RADCLIFFE (SEE RATCL [34444]

RADCLYFFE PRE 1745 LONDON, MDX, YKS & LAN, ENG [34743]

RADDATZ 1872+ BRISBANE, QLD, AUS [36290] : PRE 1877 GERMAN STATION, QLD, AUS [36290] : PRE 1877 PRITZIZ KOMMAR, POM, GER [36290]

RADDE 1800S BLN, GER [37814]

RADDEKER 1834 GOTTINGEN, HAN, GER [35808]

RADDEN C1820 GSY, CHI [37112]

RADDEY 1800-1840 HELSTON & PENZANCE, CON, ENG [34751]

RADDON PRE 1720 STOCKLAND & OFFWELL, DEV, ENG [35701]

RADER 1700 SHENODOAH, VA, USA [38054]

RADFORD C1860-1952 ADELAIDE, SA, AUS [33950] : 1850+ ALEXANDRIA, NSW, AUS [35360] : 1850+ COLLINGWOOD, VIC, AUS [35524] : 1800+ KENTISBEARE, DEV, ENG [33950] : 1760 NORMANTON, DBY, ENG [34120] : PRE 1847 ALBURY, OXF, ENG [34815] : PRE 1850 BUCKLAND, GLS, ENG [36171] : 1750S-1780S DARTMOUTH, DEV, ENG [36337] : PRE 1735 POTTERHANWORTH, LIN, ENG [37318] : 1850+ LIVERPOOL & BOOTLE, LAN, ENG [37679] : 1830-1860 SHOREDITCH AREA, MDX, ENG [37859] : ALL WORLDWIDE [37979]

RADI ALL UNGVAR & UZOROD, HU [36532]

RADIEL 1700 GER [38531]

RADJIER 1820-1840 DORFSTADT, SHO, GER [35726]

RADLEY 1858+ NUNDLE, NSW, AUS [34859] : 1800+ LIVERPOOL, LAN, ENG [34415] : ALL SHEFFIELD, YKS, ENG [36994] : PRE 1800 EPPING, ESS, ENG [37718] : PRE 1858 USA [34859]

RADLOFF ALL DINGO, QLD, AUS [35118] : PRE 1875 GER [35118] : ALL WORLDWIDE [36467]

RADNOR PRE 1780 SEAFORD, SSX, ENG [36701]

RADSHAW 1750-1900 BIRMINGHAM, WAR, ENG [37068]

RADSTOK 1800-1900 BAARN, UTR, NL [34069]

RAE 1895+ OMEO & BAIRNSDALE, VIC, AUS [35840] : 1800+ ANT, IRL [35121] : PRE 1850 LETTERKENNY, DON, IRL [35823] : 1831+ GLASGOW, LKS, SCT [33951] : PRE 1850 MIDMAR, ABD, SCT [33999] : 1750+ GLASGOW, LKS, SCT [34008] : 1700+ UDNY, ABD, SCT [34560] : 1800+ BELHELVIE, ABD, SCT [34560] : PRE 1850 PAISLEY, RFW, SCT [34809] : 1800+ DFS, SCT [35293] : 1750+ ABOYNE, ABD, SCT [35466] : GEORGE 1820-1900 ABD, SCT [36316] : PRE 1800 COLDINGHAM, BEW, SCT [36497] : 1750-1800 GLASGOW, LKS, SCT [36682] : PRE 1784 SKENE, ABD, SCT [37315] : 1750+ LESMAHAGOW, LKS, SCT [38388] : PRE 1840 ANNAN, DFS, SCT [38722]

RAE (SEE ROWE, JAMES [37556]

RAEBURN 1900+ NZ [36645]

RAESIDE 1768+ KILMAURS, AYR, SCT [34110]

RAFFE PRE 1910 LONDON, ENG [37062]

RAFFEL 1770+ DFS & KKD, SCT [34345]

RAFFELL C1840 SWINDLEY PARK, BRK, ENG [34675]

RAFFERTY PRE 1825 ROS, IRL [37104] : 1800+ LKS, SCT [38279] : 1844 CLEVELAND, OH, USA [38102] : ABNER 1800 BOURBON CO., KY, USA [38152]

RAFFN 1500-1600 MALMO, MAL, SWE [36320]

RAFTER 1750+ KILMANAGH, KIK, IRL [33963] : SARAH 1880-1900 MOYDERWELL, KER, IRL [38233]

RAFUSE ALL LUNENBURG, NS, CAN [36713]

RAGEOT ALL WORLDWIDE [34068]

RAGG 1700+ LEATHERHEAD, SRY, ENG [36760] : 1800+ NURBASFORD, NTT, ENG & AUS [35056] : 1790S LARBERT, STI, SCT [36431]

RAGGETT C1840 LIVERPOOL, LAN, ENG [35778] : PRE 1881 MDX, ENG [37358] : ALL IRL [37358]

RAGIN 1825+ BUTTERVANT, COR, IRL [35507]

RAGOLE 1880-1900 GHENT, BEL [38537]

RAGOTTE ALL WORLDWIDE [34068]

RAGSDALE PRE 1820 WOR, ENG [37643]

RAHAL PRE 1853 CAV, IRL [34412]

RAHARDT 1853+ PENRITH, NSW, AUS [34693] : 1770+ GEISENHEIM, HEN, GER [34693] : 1800+ MITTELHEIM, HEN, GER [34693]

RAHIL PRE 1853 CAV, IRL [34412]

RAHILLY 1850S BALLARAT, VIC, AUS [35855] : 1854 AUCKLAND, NZ [35855]

RAHN ALL GER & USA [38043]

RAICHE 1700 CAN [38493]

RAIFORD 1190-1679 CREDITON, DEV, ENG [35319] : 1796-1989 JEFFERSON, GA, USA [35319] : 1679-1989 ISLE OF WIGHT, VA, USA [35319] : 1700-1989 BLADEN, NC, USA [35319]

RAIFSTANGER PRE 1850S ROMMELSHAUSEN, WUE, GER [36628]

RAILL 1800S WEM, IRL & AUS [36642]

RAILTON PRE 1775 CUL, ENG [35423]

RAIMENT 1690+ DARRIEN, CT, USA [34140] : ALL WORLDWIDE [35174]

RAINBIRD PRE 1780 EPPING, ESS, ENG [35587] : PRE 1800 WALSHAM LE WILLOWS, SFK, ENG [36121] : 1700+ NAVESTOCK, ESS, ENG [36263]

RAINBOW PRE 1822 HANSLOPE, BKM, ENG [37655]

RAINE PRE 1830 WEARDALE, DUR, ENG [38277]

RAINES PRE 1855 MDX, ENG [36299] : PRE 1800 SOM, ENG [36299] : ALL WORLDWIDE [36299]

RAINEY PRE 1865 CLONAVADDY & DUNGANNON, TYR, IRL [34897] : 1810S DRY, IRL [38226] : 1883-1971 WYCONDA, CLARK CO., MO, USA [35316]

RAINGS PRE 1850 MORLISH, KEN, ENG [36361]

RAINNIE 1700S EDINBURGH, MLN, SCT [35395]

RAINS PRE 1855 MDX, ENG [36299] : EMILY F. 1844-1917 SLOAN, IA, USA [38156] : ALL WORLDWIDE [36299]

RAINSFORD PRE 1835 DAWLEY, SAL, ENG [34851] : PRE 1850 DUBLIN, IRL [34918] : PRE 1700 BLESSINGTON, WIC, IRL [36030]

RAISBECK PRE 1800 ENG [36993]

RAISKIO ALL RIITIALA, FIN [38445]

RAISTRICK PRE 1850 IDLE & THACKLEY, WRY, ENG [36617] : PRE 1830 YKS, ENG [37923]

RAIT PRE 1890 FALMOUTH, CON, ENG [35962] : 1800 CRUDEN, ABD, SCT [35369] : PRE 1890 DUNFERMLINE, FIF, SCT [35962] : PRE 1890 EDINBURGH, MLN, SCT [35962] : 1700-1750 ANS, SCT [36081] : 1800-1900 CAMBUSNETHAN, LKS, SCT [38515] : 1730-1800 BOTHWELL, LKS, SCT [38515] : 1850-1900 GLASGOW, LKS, SCT [38515]

RAITHBY PRE 1780 BILSBY, LIN, ENG [36148]

RAITT 1850+ WAIHOLA, OTAGO, NZ [35962] : PRE 1860 PANBRIDE, ANS, SCT [35962]

RAIWET 1800+ EVRHAILLE, NMR, BEL [35004]

RAJECKI ALL ZAGORZE, KRAKOW, POL [38678]

RAJEZKI ALL ZAGORBZE, KRAKOW, POL [38678]

RAJOTTE ALL WORLDWIDE [34068]

RAKAU PRE 1680 PRASTBOL & FRYKSANDE, VARMLAND, SWE [38551]

RAKE C1868 ROTHERHITHE, LND, ENG [34972]

RAKESTRAW PRE 1800 PRINCES RISBOROUGH, BKM, ENG [37652] : PRE 1800 SAUNDERTON, BKM, ENG [37652]

RAKOU PRE 1680 PRASTBOL & FRYKSANDE, VARMLAND, SWE [38551]

RAKOWER ALL WARSAW, POL [38481]

RALF 1800+ ZARPEN, SHO, GER [34688]

RALFEN (SEE RALF) [34688]

RALFS ALL PORTSEA & POOLE, HAM & DOR, ENG [36697]

RALLINGS 1900+ AUS [33859] : PRE 1900 LONDON, ENG [33859]

RALPH PRE 1850 SYDNEY, NSW & DEV, AUS & ENG [34439] : PRE 1836 LIVERPOOL, ENG [35258] : PRE 1853 YATTON KEYNELL, WIL, ENG [35594] : PRE 1800 COLLINGBOURNE KINGSTON, WIL, ENG [36286] : PRE 1800 CROWAN, CON, ENG [36416] : 1745 LONDON, ENG [36558] : 1750

LANDEWEDNACK, CON, ENG [36640] : 1800 +
CROWAN, CON, ENG [37149] : 1750-1850
PENZANCE, CON, ENG [37943] : 1830-1860S
ROTHES, MOR, SCT [34764] : 1820-1849 RODMAN,
NY, USA [37005] : 1775 DARTMOUTH, MA, USA
[37005]

RALPHS C1785 BILLERICAY, ESS, ENG [37533]

RALSTON 1800-1850 BELFAST, ANT, IRL [34440] :
PRE 1850 LONDONDERRY, IRL [34941]

RAMAGE ALL VIOLET TOWN, VIC, AUS [37139] :
1815 + ALLOA, CLK, SCT [34122] : 1840 DOUGLAS,
LKS, SCT [34618] : 1800S GLASGOW, SCT [37139] :
C1855 FOSSOWAY, KRS, SCT [37148] : 1700-1800S
LKS, PEE & DFS, SCT [38437]

RAMAIGNAN 1500-1600 NMR, BEL [36943]

RAMBRIDGE ALL WORLDWIDE [34712]

RAMIREZ PRE 1874 MARAGONDON, CAVITE,
PHILIPPINE [34891]

RAMIREZ DE ARELLANO 1500-1630 SANTO
DOMINGO, STO DOMING [36340]

RAMM PRE 1720 RIGA, KURLAND, LATVIA [37808]

RAMMAGE 1852-56 NSW, AUS [37182] : 1750 +
LONDON &, DUR & NBL, ENG [37182]

RAMP 1700-1800 KOUDEKERK, ZUH, NL [34479]

RAMPTON 1777 FROYLE, HAM, ENG [34909] : PRE
1820 TADLEY, HAM, ENG [37579] : 1770-1900
WHITCHURCH, HAM, ENG [38003]

RAMSAUER 1890-1930 LONDON, ENG & OES [37243]

RAMSAY 1849 + FREMANTLE, WA, AUS [34530] :
1870-1934 ADELAIDE, SA, AUS [35191] : 1865 +
BRISBANE, QLD, AUS [35442] : 1880 +
THESSALON & ALGOMA, ONT, CAN [37491] :
1840-1860 PORT STANLEY, ONT, CAN [37491] :
1800 + MARTLESHAM, SFK, ENG [34205] : 1850
HOUGHTON LE SPRING, DUR, ENG [35912] :
ELEANOR 1764 GARRIGILL & ALSTON, CUL,
ENG [37019] : PRE 1862 NEWCASTLE ON TYNE,
NBL, ENG [37897] : 1700-1900 IRL [34081] : 1800 +
JAMAICA [37491] : 1800 + ANS, SCT [33862] : 1800 +
UDNY, ABD, SCT [34560] : PRE 1820 GLASGOW &
BARONY, LKS, SCT [34706] : 1600 + NEWHAVEN,
MLN, SCT [34718] : C1830 PAISLEY, RFW, SCT
[35251] : PRE 1800 STIRLING, STI, SCT [35442] :
1800-1865 PAISLEY, RFW, SCT [35442] : C1800 + ST
NINIANS, STI, SCT [35629] : 1780-1840 LASSWADE,
MLN, SCT [36724] : 1825 + FORFAR, ANS, SCT
[37172] : C1845-1854 DUNDEE, ANS, SCT [37172] :
1850 + BANCHORY TERNAN, KCD, SCT [37491] :
1700 + BIRSE, ABD, SCT [37491] : ALL DUNDEE,
ANS, SCT [37619] : PRE 1770 ARL, SCT [38460] :
ALL OAKLANDS, CA, USA [37308] : HANNAH
1684-1760 NY, USA [37453]

RAMSBARGER 1800S TOPEKA SHAWNEE CO., KS,
USA [36918]

RAMSDALE C1824 LEIGH, LAN, ENG [35090] : PRE
1920 SOUTH SHIELDS, DUR, ENG [37405]

RAMSDELL 1600-1700 MA, USA [34749]

RAMSDEN 1800 + LONDON, ENG [34597] :
CHARLOTTE PRE 1825 HUDDERSFIELD, WRY,
ENG [35955] : ALL ASTON & MIDDLETON, LAN,
ENG [36187] : C1760 MDX, ENG [37239] : 1800 +
BURY, LAN, ENG [38266]

RAMSEIER PRE 1800 DIRMSTEIN, RPF, GER & CH
[38681]

RAMSEY 1800-1860 ST CATHERINES, ONT, CAN
[38045] : 1850 + SOM, ENG [36050] : PRE 1800
GREAT BURSTEAD, ESS, ENG [36050] : PRE 1800
LONDON, ENG [36050] : 1800 + WHITECHAPEL,
MDX, ENG [36219] : PRE 1860 YORK, YKS, ENG
[38783] : PRE 1850 DUBLIN, IRL [34305] : MARY
1830 + ROCHESTER, NY, USA [37825] : PRE 1850
MACON CO., MO, USA [38231]

RAMSHAW PRE 1850 KEN, ENG [35620] : 1850-1880
SOUTH SHIELDS, DUR, ENG [36867]

RAMSLAND 1903 + KOTKA, KYMI, FIN [38562] :
PRE 1903 GRIMSTAD, AUST-AGDER, NOR [38562]

RAMTHUN 1700-1820 DORINGSHAGEN, POM, GER
[38372]

RANCE 1892-1935 BICESTER & OXFORD, OXF,
ENG [34829] : 1800-1935 BRIGHTON, SSX, ENG
[34829] : 1880-1892 WESTMINSTER, LND, ENG
[34829] : ALL ENG [34831] : ALL INDIA [34831]

RANCIER 1700S FRONTENAC, ONT, CAN [34353]

RANCK PRE 1750 UNGSTEIN, RPF, GER [38681]

RAND 1600-1900 SFK, ENG [35178]

RANDAL PRE 1830 MORTON IN MARSH, GLS,
ENG [34806] : C1787-1862 ST WALSHAM, NFK,
ENG [36876]

RANDALL PRE 1888 ESK, QLD, AUS [33832] : JOHN
1797 + SYDNEY & WINDSOR, NSW, AUS [35394] :
PRE 1800 NS, CAN [34403] : PRE 1888 BRIGHTON,
SSX, ENG [33832] : PRE 1850 NEWBURY, BRK,
ENG [34869] : ALL DOR, SOM & DEV, ENG [35264]
: C1810 WIL, ENG [35863] : PRE 1730
NEEDINGWORTH, HUN, ENG [36425] : PRE 1850
BOOKHAM, SRY, ENG [37062] : PRE 1900
PORTSMOUTH, HAM, ENG [37062] : PRE 1760
BKM, ENG [37498] : PRE 1814 WESTMINSTER,
LND, ENG [37701] : 1840 + KEN, ENG [37701] :
1820S LEWISHAM, LND & KEN, ENG [37701] :
PRE 1780 EXETER, DEV, ENG [37701] : PRE 1870
LONDON, ENG [38306] : PRE 1800
CHIDDINGSTONE, KEN, ENG [38700] : 1921
OWATONNA, MN, USA [38751]

RANDELL PRE 1780 BURNHAM, BKM, ENG [34588]
: 1800S LONDON, ENG [37898]

RANDERSON ALL WORLDWIDE [37979]

RANDLE PRE 1815 DARTMOUTH, DEV, ENG [34389]
: ALL DOR, SOM & DEV, ENG [35264] : 1750-1870
EXHALL, WAR, ENG [37211]

RANDON ALL WORLDWIDE [37291]

RANDS 1890 + LAVENHAM, MAN, CAN [36704] :
ALL NORTH KELSEY, LIN, ENG [36704] : 1820 +
ROTHERHAM, YKS, ENG [36704] : ALL
WADDINGHAM, LIN, ENG [36704]

RANFT 1800 BAY, BRD [37028]

RANGELEY 1550-1850 TICEHURST, SSX & KEN,
ENG [35394]

RANGER ALL LND, KEN & SRY, ENG [34325] : PRE
1850 SSX, ENG [35913] : ALL SSX, ENG [37285] :
1600-1690 LA ROCHELLE, PCH, FRA [34514]

RANKEN C1800 STIRLING, STI, SCT [35261]

RANKILOR C1700 ELIE, FIF, SCT [35072]

RANKIN MARGARET C1860-1908 BROCKVILLE &
MAITLAND, GRENVILLE, ONT, CAN [34103] :
1750 + YKS, ENG [35241] : PRE 1847
WHITECHAPEL STEPNEY, LND, ENG [35418] :
MARGARET 1823-1850S IRL [34103] : 1800 +
GLASGOW, ARL, SCT [34416] : PRE 1750 BAN, SCT
[34646] : 1830S GLASGOW, SCT [35099] : 1750-1850
MLN, SCT [35136] : 1800-1900 TOBERMORY &
MULL, ARL, SCT [35961] : PRE 1800 LKS, SCT
[37374] : 1800 + GLASGOW, LKS, SCT & AUS
[35579]

RANKINE C1834 NEW MONKLAND, LKS, SCT
[34752]

RANN 1850 + NORTH COAST, NSW, AUS [37140] :
PRE 1850 ROWLEY REGIS, STS, ENG [34725] :
1750 + GLS, ENG [37140]

RANNIE 1780S SHIELDS, NBL, ENG [34336]

RANSBY 1700-1800 SFK, ENG [34697]

RANSLEY 1839 + LLANDILO & PENRITH, NSW,
AUS [35394] : 1827 + NEW NORFOLK & HOBART,
TAS, AUS [35394] : 1700 + KEN, ENG [34572] : 1550-

460

1850 ALDINGTON & BILSINGTON, KEN, ENG
[35394] : 1550-1850 TICEHURST & RYE, SSX, ENG
[35394] : 1855+ DEPTFORD, KEN, ENG [36093] :
1890+ BOUGHTON MALHERBE, KEN, ENG
[37945] : PRE 1765 KEN, ENG [38389] : 1866+
CHRISTCHURCH, NZ [35394]

RANSLY 1550-1850 KENNARDINGTON, KEN &
SSX, ENG [35394]

RANSOM PRE 1900 ENG [34657] : ALL MDX, ENG
[35115] : ROBERT 1800 MANCHESTER, LAN, ENG
[35429] : PRE 1775 VA, USA [36927]

RANSOME PRE 1900 ENG [34657] : 1800+
NORWICH, NFK, ENG [35513]

RAPER 1850-1900 LONDON, ENG [35723] : PRE 1850
ROTHWELL, YKS, ENG [35723] : PRE 1866 YKS,
ENG [36761]

RAPP JOANNA PRE 1839 STUTTGART, BAW, BRD
[35471] : 1800S IMSBACH, RPR, GER [37814] : C1835
BAV, GER & AUS [35079] : 1900+ WAYNE CO., MI,
USA [37814] : C1775-1820 BUCKS CO., PA, USA
[38055] : 1830+ GENESEO & NIAGARA CO., NY,
USA [38055]

RAPPE PRE 1804 LGE, BEL [35002]

RAPPOLD PRE 1900 FRANKENBACH, BAW, BRD
[38615]

RAPSON 1800S KEN, ENG [33758]

RASBURY 1789-1826 KERSHAW DISTRICT, SC, USA
[37029]

RASCHEN 1767+ BLUMENTHAL, BRM, GER [35828]
: C1660 ST MAGNUS LESUM, BRM, GER [35828] :
1704 VEGESACK, BRM, GER [35828] : 1738 LESUM,
BRM, GER [35828]

RASE PRE 1822 FRANKFURT AM MAIN, GER
[35236]

RASHLEY 1700 CONSTANTINE, CON, ENG [34793] :
C1700 IOW, ENG [36257]

RASHOTTE ALL WORLDWIDE [34068]

RASKY 1840S ZARPEN, SHO, GER [34688]

RASMUS PRE 1735 LANGELAND, DEN [38632]

RASMUSEN LARS 1700-1860 VEMELEV, SORO, DEN
[37547]

RASMUSSEN PRE 1870 JUTLAND, DEN [34003] :
1860-80 LOLLAND, DEN [35638] : JEP 1600-1650
TAARNBORG, SORO, DEN [37547] : 1800 HULL,
YKS, ENG [33935]

RASTALL 1793+ BROADWAY, WOR, ENG [37265]

RASTRICK 1800-1860 ADDLESTONE, SRY, ENG
[37618]

RATASCHAK PRE 1933 BREMEN, BRM, BRD [38525]

RATCHFORD PRE 1900 IRL & CAN [38391]

RATCLIFF 1815+ ENG [38416]

RATCLIFFE C1816+ AUS [34444] : 1790+ VIC, AUS
[34915] : 1850+ LYONVILLE, VIC, AUS [35040] :
JOSEPH 1890 SYDNEY, NSW, AUS [35484] : PRE
1745 LONDON, MDX, YKS & LAN, ENG [34743] :
PRE 1840 ENG [35246] : PRE C1860 DAISY HILL,
YKS, ENG [35904] : 1850-1920 MANCHESTER,
LAN, ENG [36495] : 1570-1700 ASHBOURNE, DBY,
ENG [36495] : PRE 1880 MANCHESTER, ENG
[37203] : C1800 ROCHDALE, LAN, ENG [37807] :
PRE 1836 MANCHESTER, LAN, ENG [37866] :
1700-1870 MELLOR & AREA, DBY, CHS & WRY,
ENG [37934] : 1850-1900 FARNWORTH, LAN, ENG
[37934] : 1850S WHITFIELD, DBY, ENG [37934] :
1840S MARPLE, CHS, ENG [37934] : 1840S
LUDWORTH, DBY, ENG [37934] : PRE 1750
DURHAM PARISH, MD, USA [38783]

RATE PRE 1800 LANGTOFT, LIN, ENG [37463]

RATEL 1580-1650 ROUEN, HN, FRA [34514]

RATH 1600+ STUTTGART, BAW, GER [34980] : PRE
1837 ENNISCORTHY, WEX, IRL [35136]

RATHBONE THOMAS 1837 HOBART, TAS, AUS
[37106] : THOMAS 1870 CASSILIS, NSW, AUS
[37106] : PRE 1855 MACCLESFIELD, CHS, ENG
[34870] : THOMAS 1790S COLESHILL, WAR, ENG
[37106] : 1700-1900 SUTTON COLDFIELD, WAR,
ENG [38321] : ALL WORLDWIDE [38015]

RATHBORN PRE 1800 CHS, ENG & IRL [38754]

RATHBOURNE 1750-1850 MANCHESTER, LAN,
ENG [36416]

RATHBUN 1500+ NEW LONDON, CT, RI & ID, USA
& ENG [36970] : ALL WORLDWIDE [38015]

RATHERAM ALL BIRMINGHAM, WAR, ENG
[35984]

RATHGEB 1850 FINCHLEY, MDX, ENG [34029]

RATHGEBER ALL AURICH, WUE, BRD [37045] :
ALL NEUDORF, GALICIA, OES [37045]

RATHJEN 1700 GER [35873]

RATHSACK PRE 1836 MEK, GER [35310]

RATJEN 1700 GER [35873]

RATLEY ALL BIRMINGHAM, TYSOE &
ARMSCOTE, WAR, ENG [34823]

RATLIFF 1750-1850 DE, USA [36566] : 1750-1825
CECIL, MD, USA [37795]

RATSTOK 1800-1900 BAARN, UTR, NL [34069]

RATT 1860+ BALLARAT, VIC, AUS [34299]

RATTARY 1850-99 SCT [37605]

RATTAY PRE 1870 NECKLA HAULAND, POSEN,
POL [34801]

RATTEAUX ALL HAM, ENG [38350]

RATTEI PRE 1870 NECKLA HAULAND, POSEN,
POL [34801]

RATTER 1800S SHETLANDS, SHI, SCT [36585]

RATTLE ALL ENG [37833]

RATTRAY 1820+ RSA [34946] : 1700+ MONIFIETH,
ANS, SCT [34637] : 1740-1800 AIRLIE, ANS, SCT
[36320] : 1900+ LONG BEACH, CA, USA [34510]

RATZ 1850+ SABOLIN OR JOSEPHIN, POL [36683]

RATZBORG PRE 1850 OLDENBURG, SHO, GER
[38648]

RAU PRE 1836 CRIESBRAC, WUE, GER [34031] :
1700+ RPR, GER [38765]

RAUCH 1750+ GL, CH [36343] : 1700+ DIERSBURG,
BAD, GER [38529]

RAUDIES PRE 1800 TILSIT, OPR, GER [34753]

RAUFER 1800+ MELBOURNE, VIC, AUS [35391] :
1700+ LONDON, ENG [35391]

RAULIN 1750+ ST PETER PORT, GSY, CHI [35847]

RAUNER 1860+ PUHOI & AUCKLAND, NZ [36245]

RAUSCH PRE 1800 NRW & RPF, BRD [38616]

RAUTMANN ALL WORLDWIDE [36460]

RAVALD 1888-1930 NEW YORK, NY, USA [38757]

RAVALL 1888-1930 NEW YORK, NY, USA [38757]

RAVELTON 1730+ CAMBUSNETHAN, LKS, SCT
[38492]

RAVEN 1880S STRZELECKI, VIC, AUS [34793] : PRE
1800 HEDENHAM, NFK, ENG [35173] : PRE 1800
COVENTRY, WAR, ENG [37367] : 1750 BLACK
NOTLEY, ESS, ENG [37928] : 1840S SCHELWIG,
GER [34793] : 1700+ QUICKBORN, SHO, GER
[37542]

RAVENE ALL WORLDWIDE [38675]

RAVENHILL 1700+ LONGNEY & WHADDON, GLS,
ENG [35172] : 1800 BROBURY, HEF, ENG [35912]

RAVENS C1690-1750 COPLE & CARDINGTON, BDF,
ENG [36068]

RAVENSCROFT 1804+ WINDSOR, NSW, AUS
[35394]

RAVENSHAW 1700-1900 LONDON, MDX, ENG
[36438]

RAW PRE 1900 NRY, ENG [34617] : PRE 1773
MUKER, NRY, ENG [36955]

RAWCLIFF 1815+ ENG [38416]

RAWE JOHANN WILHEL PRE 1850 HASELUNNE, NSA, BRD [34481] : WILLIAM PRE 1850 HASELUNNE, NSA, BRD & ENG [34481] : HERMAN CASPER 1839-1937 COVINGTON, KY & NSA, USA & BRD [34481]

RAWES 1700S CROSBY RAVENSWORTH, WES, ENG [35804]

RAWET 1700-1800 PERTH, PER, SCT [36440]

RAWKINS PRE 1700 HAM, ENG [38420]

RAWLE C1840 LIVERPOOL, LAN, ENG [35778]

RAWLENCE 1790+ NORTH BRADLEY, WIL, ENG [36195]

RAWLES C1800 SPALDING, LIN, ENG [37378]

RAWLEY C1808 OXF, ENG [35478] : GEORGE 1800S+ BRIZE NORTON, OXF, ENG [35876] : 1700S WLS [37027]

RAWLING 1850+ ONT, CAN [34477] : 1900+ ALB, CAN [34477] : PRE 1800 YKS, ENG [34477] : 1700S BUDOCK & CAMBORNE, CON, ENG [36277]

RAWLINGS 1700-1770 MUCH COWARNE, HEF, ENG [34552] : 1799 HEF, ENG [35243] : PRE 1810 CUBBINGTON, WAR, ENG [36177] : PRE 1837 TACHBROOK, WAR, ENG [36177] : 1820+ BECKINGTON, SOM, ENG [36195] : ALL SEAVINGTON, SOM, ENG [36382] : PRE 1900 LND, ENG [36399] : 1820-42 BERMONDSEY & NEWINGTON, SRY, ENG [36955] : 1800S+ BEXLEY & HOLBORN, KEN & MDX, ENG [37868] : C1800 MORBORNE, ALWALTON, HUN, ENG [38078] : 1800+ CAM, ENG [38324]

RAWLINS 1870S CLAY CROSS, DBY, ENG [33870] : C1840S NETHERAVON, WIL, ENG [35158] : PRE 1850 MEDWAY & SHEPPEY, KEN, ENG [36479] : PRE 1775 GRAVESEND, KEN, ENG [37142] : ALL ENG [38369]

RAWLINSON 1700-1900 LAN, ENG [34624] : PRE 1802 ST NICHOLAS LIVERPOOL, LAN, ENG [35483] : ALL LIN, ENG [35878] : PRE 1789 WOLSTANTON, STS, ENG [38055]

RAWLL C1790 BARKING, ESS, ENG [36010]

RAWLS 1650-1800 NANSEMOND CO., VA, USA [38129]

RAWS C1773 INGLETON, WRY, ENG [36955]

RAWSON ALL AUS [34578] : 1800+ ONT, CAN [35778] : PRE 1900 ARNOLD BASFORD, NTT, ENG [34342] : 1800-1840 NETHER WASDALE, CUL, ENG [34345] : PRE 1862 YKS, ENG [34578] : PRE 1750 BURNLEY, LAN, ENG [36159] : 1730+ IDLE & THACKLEY, WRY, ENG [36617] : 1867+ ASTON BIRMINGHAM, WAR, ENG [37319] : 1633-1673 MELLING, LAN, ENG [37524] : ALL UK [36062]

RAWSTRON C1850 HABERGAM, LAN, ENG [36649]

RAY 1846+ BAIRNSDALE, VIC, AUS [33837] : PRE 1850 HOBART, TAS, AUS [34541] : PRE 1850 GRAFTON, NSW, AUS [35548] : 1830-1850S WOLLONGONG, NSW, AUS [35589] : C1800S ENG [34133] : 1750-1800 WALLINGFORD & OXFORD, BRK & OXF, ENG [34552] : 1850S LONDON, ENG [34953] : 1793 SOUTHAMPTON, HAM, ENG [35905] : 1779+ LODDON & PULHAM, NFK, ENG [37841] : 1770-1860 ST MARY BOURNE, HAM, ENG [38003] : ALL POMEROY, TYR, IRL [35460] : 1816 AYR, SCT [34541] : 1770-1850 WASHINGTON, NY, USA [38373]

RAYBURN PRE 1900 OH & KY, USA [37565] : 1850+ COVINGTON CO., MS, USA [37796]

RAYCROFT ALL WORLDWIDE [36639]

RAYMANT ALL WORLDWIDE [35174]

RAYMENT PRE 1800 ESS, ENG [37712] : 1800-1850 LONDON AREA, MDX, ENG [38006] : ALL WORLDWIDE [35174]

RAYMER 1754+ IPSWICH, SFK, ENG & AUS [35056]

RAYMINT ALL WORLDWIDE [35174]

RAYMOND 1867+ BRUCE CO., ONT, CAN [36690] : 1880+ ONT, CAN [38739] : PRE 1800 QUE, CAN & FRA [38386] : C1830 BARROW, SOM, ENG [34393] : PRE 1800 SIDBURY, DEV, ENG [38540] : 1690+ DARRIEN, CT, USA [34140] : 1775+ MANCHESTER, VT, USA [38027] : ALL WORLDWIDE [34373]

RAYMONT 1800+ WHITCHURCH, DEV, ENG [35511] : PRE 1850 BROADWOODKELLY & WINKLEIGH, DEV, ENG [37195] : ALL WORLDWIDE [35174]

RAYNE C1550 SUTTON CUM LOUND, NTT, ENG [36426] : PRE 1850 WINLATON, DUR, ENG [38457]

RAYNER 1830+ TAS, AUS [34601] : 1847+ VIC, AUS [34601] : 1830+ NSW, AUS [34601] : 1891 CARCOAR, NSW, AUS [34965] : 1800+ NSW, AUS [34976] : 1800S-1900S YASS, NSW, AUS [35117] : 1866+ TIARO, QLD, AUS [35244] : ROBERT 1847+ MUDGEE & CASSILIS, NSW, AUS [37307] : 1857+ ROMA DISTRICT, QLD, AUS [37896] : 1775+ LIN, ENG [34416] : 1750-1850 LONDON, SRY, ENG [34601] : 1750-1850 LONDON, MDX, ENG [34601] : 1750-1850 CHELMSFORD, ESS, ENG [34601] : 1800 HASLINGTON, CAM, ENG [34976] : 1800+ HACKNEY, LND, ENG [35235] : 1790-1900 ATTLEBOROUGH, NFK, ENG [35244] : 1824-1907+ WIVENHOE, ESS, ENG [35497] : 1750-1800 MIDDLESMOOR, NRY, ENG [36228] : ALL THURROCK, ESS, ENG [36500] : ALL HYTHE, KEN, ENG [36822] : ALL HYTHE, KEN, ENG [36826] : 1660+ BOCKING, ESS, ENG [36871] : PRE 1800 STURRY, KEN, ENG [37371] : PRE 1856 ELLESBOROUGH, BKM, ENG [37896] : 1860+ WAIKATO, AUCK, NZ [36826] : 1870+ THAMES, AUCK, NZ [36826]

RAYNES PRE 1800 SOM, ENG [36299] : ALL WORLDWIDE [36299]

RAYNOLD 1800-1850 MELCOMBE REGIS, DOR, ENG [34337]

RAYNOR C1805 MARKET BOSWORTH, LEI, ENG [34548] : 1800+ LEI, ENG [34548] : 1750-1825 MORRISTOWN, NJ, USA [38523]

RAYSON PRE 1587 BRK & LND, ENG [37706]

RAZEY 1860 LINN CO., KS, USA [37586]

REA 1850+ NSW, AUS [35933] : PRE 1770 KIDDERMINSTER, WOR, ENG [34711] : ALL LONDON, ENG [35933] : PRE 1860 ROCK & ASTLEY, WOR, ENG [36110] : DANIEL PRE 1630 ENG [37784] : 1841 PLUMSTEAD, KEN, ENG [38499] : 1843+ RASHARKIN, ANT, IRL [33882] : 1750+ BALLYMENA, ANT, IRL [34416] : ALL POMEROY, TYR, IRL [35460] : 1800+ BALLYAUTOGUE & UMGALL, ANT, IRL [37425] : 1800+ BALLYLINNEY & TEMPLEPATRICK, ANT, IRL [37425] : PRE 1800 LIM, IRL & NZ [36840] : 1850 FORFAR, ANS, SCT [37952]

REACHER ALL WORLDWIDE [37094]

READ 1886+ CARLTON, VIC, AUS [35526] : SEPTER 1911+ MELBOURNE, VIC, AUS [37958] : 1750-1800 NORTH CRAWLEY, BKM, ENG [34552] : 1820+ HEMPNALL, NFK, ENG [34710] : 1890+ NELSON & BURNLEY, LAN, ENG [34790] : 1850-1900 WES, ENG [34948] : 1800-1850S ENG [35011] : PRE 1800 ALCESTER, WAR, ENG [35181] : SARAH C1800 ENG [35350] : PRE 1850 OWERMOIGNE, DOR, ENG [35407] : 1800+ LANGPORT, SOM, ENG [35734] : C1820 NORTH PETHERWIN, CON, ENG [35744] : 1770+ HORNING, NFK, ENG [35824] : C1700-1900 HOXTON & SHOREDITCH, LND, ENG [35892] : PRE 1815 BKM, ENG [36086] : PRE 1860 CHS & LAN, ENG [36363] : ALL PECKHAM, LND, ENG [36744] : PRE 1813 HARTFIELD, SSX, ENG

[36759] : C1850 RIPE, SSX, ENG [37285] : 1800+
UPWEY, DOR, ENG [37378] : 1820S HINTON ST
GEORGE, SOM, ENG [37533] : 1850-70
BEAMINSTER & BROADWINDSOR, DOR, ENG
[37533] : 1828+ POLSTEAD & COLCHESTER, ESS
& SFK, ENG [37656] : PRE 1900 ISLINGTON, MDX,
ENG [37753] : JAMES 1835+ PADDINGTON,
MDX, ENG [37958] : SEPTER 1871-1911
PADDINGTON, MDX, ENG [37958] : 1800S
BOZRAH TWP., CT, USA [36896] : 1800S VA, USA
[37795]

READE 1565-1857 ENG [37803] : PRE 1807
WHITCHURCH, SAL, ENG [37893] : 1800+
WINDGAP & KILKENNY, KIK, IRL [34934]

READER ALL STAPLEHURST, KEN, ENG [34284] :
1840+ BIRMINGHAM, WAR, ENG [35356] : PRE
1819 SWANNINGTON, NFK, ENG [35863] : PRE
1800 BRENCHLEY, KEN & SSX, ENG [38254]

READETT 1850+ NEW ENGLAND, NSW, AUS
[37889]

READFORD 1815+ EMU PLAINS, NSW, AUS [34019]

READING 1870+ WA, AUS [35139] : PRE 1850
GRETTON, NTH, ENG [33993] : 1830 DEPTFORD,
KEN, ENG [34731] : ALL BIRMINGHAM, WAR,
ENG [35139] : ALL LONDON, ENG [35139] : 1700+
BIRMINGHAM, WAR, ENG [36892] : PRE 1910
HIGH WYCOMBE & CHESHAM, BKM, ENG
[38580]

READMAN PRE 1871 WHITBY, NRY, ENG [38580] :
1800S GLASGOW, LKS, SCT [35987]

READY PRE 1881 SOUTH BURGESS, ONT, CAN
[38434] : PRE 1825 TIP, IRL [34428]

REAH C1700 FERRYHILL, DUR, ENG [37388]

REAKES 1660-1862 EVERCREECH, SOM, ENG
[37380]

REAM 1700+ PA, USA [38023]

REAMAN 1700-1800 BROTHERSVALLEY, PA, USA
[37435]

REANEY 1750-1820 DRONFIELD, DBY, ENG [34762] :
1860+ BENAGH, DOW, IRL [35219]

REAPER 1700+ GRANGE, BAN, SCT [34160]

REARDAN 1830-1900 COR, IRL & AUS [37134]

REARDEN 1820-1850 FRANKLIN, KY, USA [38373]

REARDON 1850+ SYDNEY, NSW, AUS [34544] :
1840+ SYDNEY, NSW, AUS [34544] : 1895 SA, AUS
[34777] : MARY PRE 1831 TAS, AUS [35788] : C1890
IGATPURI, KURNOOL, INDIA [36092] : PRE 1857
CLA, IRL [34911] : JOHN PRE 1790 KILLARNEY,
KER, IRL [35713] : 1780+ TIP, IRL [35768] : C1800-
1830S RAYMORE, KER, IRL [36314] : ALL CORK,
COR, IRL [36826] : ALL NZ [36826] : 1874-1990
WANGANUI, NZ [36832] : C1840 ISLE OF ST
VINCENT, W.INDIES [34544]

REASON PRE 1823 WESTMINSTER, LND, ENG
[35702]

REASY PRE 1860 COLLINGBOURNE KINGSTON,
WIL, ENG [36286]

REAUME PIERRE 1700+ KENT & ESSEX CO., ONT,
CAN [34154]

REAY 1820+ SYDNEY, NSW, AUS [35589] : 1800S+
BENTINCK TWP., ONT, CAN [37458] : 1820-1890
CUL, ENG [35589] : PRE 1860 WIGTON, CUL, ENG
[35589] : 1750+ ASPATRIA & MARYPORT, CUL,
ENG [37073] : 1815+ ALLONBY, CUL, ENG [37073]

REBBECK 1910+ APPELA YARROWIE, VIC, AUS
[37212] : 1910 HAMILTON, VIC, AUS [37212] :
1856+ GAWLER, SA, AUS [37212] : 1900-1916
KALGOORLIE, WA, AUS [37212] : 1915+ HYDE
PARK, SA, AUS [37212]

REBHORN 1450-1550 GAISBURG, BAW, BRD [38654]

REBOLLEDO C1821 JEREZ DE LA FRONTERA, ESP
[37819]

REBSTOCK PRE 1850 NEUFRA, WUE, GER [38333]

RECETT 1830S GENOA, ITL [37390]

RECK PRE 1810 SAFENWIL, AG, CH [38029]

RECKERS 1814 BLOMBERG, PYR, GER [38749]

RECORD PRE 1775 KEN, ENG [38389] : 1810-1820
HIGHLAND CO., OH, USA [38334]

RECTOR 1740-1800 FAUQUIER CO., VA & KY, USA
[36901]

REDBURG 1880+ PEARSON, WA, USA [38069]

REDDALL 1880+ NSW, AUS [37128] : 1820+
LEICESTER, LEI, ENG [34260] : PRE 1870
WOBURN & EVERSHOLT, BDF, ENG [36502]

REDDAN 1800+ CLA, IRL [37916]

REDDAWAY 1800+ AUS [35505]

REDDICK 1840-1890 BROWN CO., OH, USA [33760] :
JOHN 1860-1855 HOCKING CO., OH, USA [35329]

REDDIE PRE 1819 PENZANCE, CON, ENG [34452] :
1800-1840 HELSTON & PENZANCE, CON, ENG
[34751] : 1820+ EDINBURGH, MLN, SCT [34452] :
PRE 1790+ INVERKEITHY & KINGHORN, FIF,
SCT [35525] : 1850+ ABERDOUR, FIF, SCT [35977]

REDDIN 1800S STOCKWELL, SRY, ENG [34800]

REDDING PRE 1850 SOHO, LND, ENG [35925] : PRE
1910 HIGH WYCOMBE & CHESHAM, BKM, ENG
[38580] : MATHIAS 1820 DEARBORN CO., IN, USA
[36925] : 1680-1700 DORCHESTER, MA, USA [36943]

REDDISH 1800S DBY & NTT, ENG [35858]

REDETZKE PRE 1850 POS, GER [37009]

REDFERN 1800-1862 HANLEY, STS, ENG [34693] :
1800S LONDON, ENG [34813] : PRE 1750
ALFRETON, DBY, ENG [35079] : 1820-1850
GLOSSOP, DBY, ENG [36345] : 1810-1835 ASHTON
UNDER LYNE, LAN, ENG [36345] : PRE 1860
HANLEY, STS, ENG [36881] : 1800-1940
LIVERPOOL, LAN, ENG [37870] : 1775-1850
BETLEY, STS, ENG [38474] : 1690-1800 AUDLEM,
CHS, ENG [38474] : 1862+ PAPAROA, NZ [34693] :
ALL HALKYN, FLN, WLS [37667]

REDFORD PRE 1850 GUISELEY, WRY, ENG [36159]

REDGATE 1700+ CALVERTON, NTT, ENG [35970]

REDGROVE C1838 OLNEY, BKM, ENG [37963]

REDHEAD 1850-1890 LEEDS, YKS, ENG [33861] :
PRE 1815 TORVER, LAN, ENG [34053] : PRE 1800
FURNESS, LAN, ENG [35165] : PRE 1870 KINGS
LYNN, NFK, ENG [37140]

REDHOUSE ALL WORLDWIDE [37741]

REDINGER 1862+ TOOWOOMBA, QLD, AUS [37894]
: PRE 1862 HEDDESHEIM, BAD, GER [37894] :
PRE 1848 ECHTERNACH, LUX [37817]

REDINGTON ELLEN 1875+ QUEANBEYAN, NSW,
AUS [34885] : ALL WORLDWIDE [36500]

REDMAN C1895+ KEN, ENG [35099] : C1865+
WALTHAMSTOW, ESS, ENG [35099] : GILES C1750
KIRBY LONSDALE, WMD, ENG [36635] : 1750-1800
HEVERSHAM, WES, ENG [37779] : PRE 1871
WHITBY, NRY, ENG [38580] : MARTHA 1840
POSEY CO., IN, USA [35286] : 1780-1810 VA, KY &
IL, USA [36913]

REDMAYNE PRE 1850 PENRITH, CUL, ENG [37252]

REDMOND PRE 1840 MALLOW, COR, IRL [33808] :
JANE PRE 1811 LEX, IRL [34539] : 1800+
KILMASKIN, WEX, IRL [34956] : C1800 TINTERN,
WEX, IRL [35744] : C1840 BALLYGARRETT, WEX,
IRL [35920] : 1840+ BALLYMENA, ANT, IRL
[36827] : PRE 1900 CLONEGAL, CAR, IRL [38300] :
1700+ IA, IN & PA, USA [38764]

REDPATH 1750+ MLN, SCT [34718] : 1770+
PITTENWEEM, FIF, SCT [35822] : PRE 1800
PITTENWEEM, FIF, SCT [37693] : 1800S
MACKERSTON, ROX, SCT [38414]

REDROP 1700-1850 NEAR WRENBURY, CHS, ENG
[36440]

REDSHAW ALBERT PRE 1862+ TAS, AUS **[34592]** : C1580 SUTTON CUM LOUND, NTT, ENG **[36426]** : PRE 1800 LONGFORD, DBY, ENG & USA **[36980]**

REDSTON ALL KEN, ENG **[34961]**

REDWOOD 1790 HARWICH, ESS, ENG **[34204]** : C1790 HAUGHLEY, SFK, ENG **[36945]** : PRE 1918 CARMARTHEN, CMN, WLS **[36181]**

REE PRE 1834 BIRMINGHAM, ENG **[34443]**

REEB PRE 1700 HERMERSBERG, RPF, GER **[38681]**

REECE ISAAC 1839-1870S MUDGEE & VARIOUS, NSW, AUS **[35396]** : PRE 1840 PEASMARSH, SSX, ENG **[35396]** : ALL BURY, LAN, ENG **[35514]** : 1850-1888 OES & HU **[38236]** : 1850-1888 ROM **[38236]** : 1750-1850 NC, TN & MO, USA **[36552]** : PRE 1847 GLA, WLS **[36828]**

REED WM. & MARTHA C1900 PETERSHAM, NSW, AUS **[33765]** : PRE 1916 SANDHURST, VIC, AUS **[35384]** : PRE 1863 BRAIDWOOD, NSW, AUS **[35705]** : PRE 1948 TERANG & GEELONG, VIC, AUS **[36276]** : PRE 1886 EAGLEHAWK, VIC, AUS **[36276]** : PRE 1949 STH YARRA, VIC, AUS **[36276]** : C1860+ STEIGLITZ & NORTH MELBOURNE, VIC, AUS **[36276]** : 1859+ AVOCA, CLUNES & BALLARAT, VIC, AUS **[36622]** : 1660+ ST MICHAELS, BARBADOS **[38235]** : JOSEPH C1839 CRUMPSALL, LAN, ENG **[33917]** : 1740-1840 STYTHIANS, CON, ENG **[34016]** : 1825+ ROTHERHITHE, SRY, ENG **[34063]** : ALL LIN, ENG **[34361]** : 1800-1840 PADDINGTON & BLACKFRIARS, LND, ENG **[34448]** : PRE 1850 KENWYN & S GENNYS, CON, ENG **[34742]** : 1750 LEZANT, CON, ENG **[34793]** : 1800+ BRENCHLEY, KEN, ENG **[34980]** : ALL KEN, ENG **[35353]** : 1800+ LOFTUS, YKS, ENG **[35364]** : C1840 KINGSTON UPON HULL, YKS, ENG **[35582]** : 1780-1860 CHICHESTER, SSX, ENG **[35720]** : 1832 BARKING, ESS, ENG **[35906]** : PRE 1760 NEWCASTLE UPON TYNE, NBL, ENG **[36110]** : 1700S LITTLEBURY & SAFFRON WALDEN, ESS, ENG **[36211]** : THOMAS 1800S CHITTLEHAMPTON & MESHAW, DEV, ENG **[36211]** : 1780-1864 WOOTTON ST LAWRENCE, HAM, ENG **[36229]** : C1822+ REDRUTH, CON, ENG **[36276]** : 1800-1890 YORK, NRY, ENG **[36397]** : 1840S NEWCASTLE, NBL, ENG **[36843]** : 1860S CORTON, SFK, ENG **[36843]** : 1810S TANFIELD, DUR, ENG **[36843]** : C1753 CAM, ENG **[37144]** : ALL NFK, ENG **[37379]** : 1810+ LONDON, ENG **[37586]** : PRE 1840 TOTTENHAM, LND, ENG **[37743]** : 1875+ WEYBRIDGE, SRY, ENG **[37777]** : 1880 MDX, ENG **[37836]** : ALL LONDON, MDX, ENG **[37950]** : C1793 HOXTON, LONDON, MDX, ENG **[38079]** : THOMAS C1530+ BARTON COURTS, BRK, ENG **[38183]** : 1700-1900 SWALE MEDWAY, KEN, ENG **[38249]** : 1800S ERY, ENG **[38468]** : ALL SLI, IRL **[34361]** : PRE 1910 MORRINSVILLE, WKT, NZ **[33964]** : PETER PRE 1830 WESTMORELAND CO., PA, USA **[34410]** : 1840+ LINCOLN CO., TN, USA **[35262]** : 1815-1860 PA, USA **[35317]** : 1825-1870 TRUMBULL CO., OH, USA **[35317]** : 1750-1800 FLEMING CO., KY, USA **[36566]** : 1850+ LAMAR CO., TX, USA **[36947]** : PRE 1830 SUMNER, TN, USA **[36947]** : 1900+ CHOCTAW CO., OK, USA **[36947]** : 1830-1850 GREENE CO., IL, USA **[36947]** : PRE 1812 WAYNE CO., NY, USA **[36968]** : ROBERT C1811 MONROE CO., VA, USA **[38044]** : 1886-1990 HASKELL CO., TX, USA **[38092]**

REEDE (SEE READ) **[37285]**

REEDER 1700-1800 LONDON, ENG **[34742]** : EDMUND PRE 1800 KELSALE, NFK, ENG **[36590]** : ALL SURINAME **[38692]** : ALL WORLDWIDE **[33751]**

REEDS C1770 ALFRISTON, SSX, ENG **[35261]**

REEDY 1800S OH, USA **[38369]**

REEK 1780-1820 TILNEY, NFK, ENG **[37586]**

REEKIE 1600+ ST MONANCE, FIF, SCT **[35627]**

REEKS 1680+ CHRISTCHURCH, HAM, ENG **[34972]** : C1863 WEYMOUTH, DOR, ENG **[35251]** : 1851 GREAT MARYLEBONE, MDX, ENG **[36606]**

REEL 1600S LIMERICK, IRL **[35617]**

REES MAGGIE 1915+ QUEANBEYAN, NSW, AUS **[34885]** : DAVID 1818+ PARRAMATTA (CONVICT), NSW, AUS **[34973]** : 1880S MALDON, VIC, AUS **[35390]** : 1850+ VIC, AUS **[38771]** : PRE 1870 CHATHAM & ROCHESTER, KEN, ENG **[34660]** : 1700-1900 STRETFORD, LAN, ENG **[36261]** : PRE 1900 LND, ENG **[36829]** : 1800 GREAT CLACTON, ESS, ENG **[38379]** : ESTHER PRE 1800 LLANFYRNACH, PEM, WLS **[34311]** : 1840+ HAVELOCK, GLA, WLS **[35390]** : 1800-1870 GLA, WLS **[36346]** : 1800+ BLAENAVON, MON, WLS **[36614]** : JONATHAN C1830 CARDIGAN, CGN, WLS **[37330]** : PRE 1880 RHYMNEY, MON, WLS **[37716]** : 1800S SOUTH, WLS **[38753]**

REESE 1871+ STONES CORNER, QLD, AUS **[34957]** : 1821 WANGENHAUSEN, GER **[34957]**

REEVE 1830 BARRINGTON, TAS, AUS **[35089]** : PRE 1830 ASHFORD, KEN, ENG **[34623]** : ALL LONDON, ENG **[34648]** : PRE 1840 HINDERCLAY, SFK, ENG **[34911]** : 1830+ CAM, ENG **[35116]** : PRE 1800 HEDENHAM, NFK, ENG **[35173]** : 1675-1837 SUTTON COLDFIELD, WAR, ENG **[35552]** : PRE 1780 SFK, ENG **[35642]** : 1700+ EPSOM & CLAPHAM, SRY, ENG **[35737]** : ALL NORTHAMPTON, NTH, ENG **[35956]** : C1700-1960 PULHAM MARKET & WINFARTHING, NFK, ENG **[36128]** : 1728+ TWINEHAM, SSX, ENG **[36212]** : MARY ANN C1880S MILE END, LND, ENG **[36880]** : PRE 1826 ESS, ENG **[37668]** : JOHN 1700+ HEPWORTH THETFORD, SFK, ENG **[38540]**

REEVES 1870+ BALMORAL, VIC, AUS **[35116]** : JACOB C1900 STOTTS CREEK, NSW, AUS **[36284]** : ALICE 1880S TORONTO, ONT, CAN **[34103]** : 1700-1950 ONT, CAN **[38128]** : ALICE 1863-1880S SUTTON, SRY, ENG **[34103]** : 1700+ TANGMERE, BOSHAM & GRAFFHAM, SSX, ENG **[34747]** : 1810 BKM, ENG **[35243]** : 1890+ BIDDENDEN, KEN, ENG **[35980]** : PRE 1900 OXFORD, OXF, ENG **[36015]** : 1700-1850 DODSBROOKE, DEV, ENG **[36155]** : PRE 1809 WESTERN ON THE GREEN, OXF, ENG **[36281]** : C1820 ELCOMBE, WIL, ENG **[36284]** : 1700 LAUNTON, OXF, ENG **[36649]** : 1800+ KEN, ENG **[36749]** : 1800 BIRMINGHAM, WAR, ENG **[36860]** : 1660+ HENLEY, OXF, ENG **[36981]** : PRE 1813 HINSTOCK, SAL & CHS, ENG **[37762]** : 1833-1837 HASTINGS, SSX, ENG **[37921]** : 1840 STAVERTON, NTH, ENG **[38047]** : 1780-1837 HIMLEY & SEDGLEY, STS, ENG **[38248]** : 1800S MAINE, ME, USA **[35116]** : PRE 1700 PLYMOUTH, MA, USA **[37049]** : 1650+ SALEM, NJ & DE, USA **[37826]** : 1800-1960 JACKSON, IL, USA **[38588]** : ALL WORLDWIDE **[38237]**

REFFIN 1780S LEI, ENG **[35066]** : PRE 1805 NOTTINGHAM, NTT, ENG **[38208]**

REFORD PRE 1900 BALLINDERRY, ANT, IRL **[36077]**

REGAN PRE 1840 DOUBLE BAY, NSW, AUS **[34857]** : 1880 HOBBYS YARDS, NSW, AUS **[36641]** : 1880+ WOLLOMBI, NSW, AUS **[38582]** : PRE 1900 MONTREAL, QUE, CAN **[38442]** : 1830+ GOLDEN, TIP, IRL **[33946]** : 1825+ BUTTERVANT, COR, IRL **[35507]** : PRE 1850 LOUGHGLINN, ROS, IRL **[36504]** : 1830+ LET & MO, IRL & USA **[38050]**

REGGETT C1815-30 ARM, IRL **[36722]**

REGLER 1750-1850 FRIEDRICHSDORF, POM, GER [38628]

REGULI 1800+ NIZNEH, ORAV, CZECH [37484] : PRE 1900 NIZNEH, ORAV, CZECH [37484]

REHARDT 1853+ PENRITH, NSW, AUS [34693] : 1770+ GEISENHEIM, HEN, GER [34693] : 1800+ MITTELHEIM, HEN, GER [34693]

REHBERG ALL MEK, GER [38037]

REHBOCK 1800-1900 CINCINNATI, OH, USA [38149]

REICH 1700-1800 POS, GER [37535]

REICHARD 1800-1900 GER [36589]

REICHARDT PRE 1750 GER [38640]

REICHERT 1862+ ELMIRA, ONT, CAN [36716]

REICHSTEIN PRE 1870 IRESLAU, PRE, GER [34268]

REICHWINE 1760 LANCASTER, PA & IN, USA [38054]

REID 1858+ HAZEL GLEN, VIC, AUS [33934] : HENRY 1900+ YUNDAGA, WA, AUS [34171] : JOSEPH 1850+ MARKDALE, NSW, AUS [34171] : JOSEPH 1835-1850 PERTH, WA, AUS [34171] : 1850+ MELBOURNE, VIC, AUS [34414] : JAMES 1842+ SYDNEY, NSW, AUS [34449] : ANN JANE 1842+ SYDNEY, NSW, AUS [34449] : 1855+ NSW, AUS [34875] : 1855+ QLD, AUS [34875] : 1900S PATRICK, NSW, AUS [35367] : 1830+ CAMDEN, NSW, AUS [35562] : C1850 HOBART, TAS, AUS [35747] : MICHAEL 1861+ YASS, NSW, AUS [35787] : 1840+ GOULBURN, NSW, AUS [36295] : 1840+ COOPERS CK, QLD, AUS [36295] : 1850+ TUMBARUMBA, NSW, AUS [36295] : 1850S CASTLEMAINE, VIC, AUS [36797] : 1900S SCONE, NSW, AUS [37910] : 1860+ HOBART, TAS, AUS & ENG [35079] : WILLIAM 1850+ EGREMONT, ONT, CAN [37424] : 1800S LAMBTON CO., ONT, CAN [38414] : ROBERT C1856 HURON CO., ONT, CAN [38584] : 1750+ NEWCASTLE ON TYNE, NBL, ENG [34414] : HANNAH PRE 1860 ENG [35255] : 1750+ SHAFTESBURY, DOR, ENG [35370] : PRE 1860 LIVERPOOL, LAN, ENG [35423] : C1870 POPLAR, LND, ENG [36525] : JAMES 1870 LIVERPOOL, ENG [36811] : MARINER 1870+ LIVERPOOL, ENG [36811] : 1800+ LAMBETH, SRY & BRK, ENG [37065] : JOHN HANCOCK PRE 1841 WAPPING, MDX, ENG [37083] : ELEANOR 1851+ BETHNAL GREEN, MDX, ENG [37083] : 1830-1845 HOLBORN, MDX, ENG [37336] : 1810-1815 BOROUGH, SRY, ENG [37336] : 1845-1855 WESTMINSTER, MDX, ENG [37336] : 1885-1925 ISLINGTON, MDX, ENG [37336] : 1813+ ECCLES & SALFORD, LAN, ENG [38410] : 1780+ GATESHEAD & EDINBURGH, DUR & MLN, ENG & SCT [35579] : PRE 1856 TIEVEMORE & PETTIGO, DON, IRL [35779] : 1860-1883 IRL [36594] : 1800S BALLINA & ARDNAREE, MAY, IRL [36794] : 1800+ PORTADOWN, ARM, IRL [36833] : ISAAC C1811 KILLEVY, ARM, IRL [37106] : THOMAS C1790 KILLEVY, ARM, IRL [37106] : PRE 1850 GLENARM & BUCKNA, ANT, IRL [37246] : PRE 1860 INISHARGY, DOW, IRL [37636] : 1800S IRL [38414] : 1877 BALLYMENA, ANT, IRL [38470] : 1850+ TYR, IRL [38531] : 1750-1950 BALLEMENA & OSGOODE, ANT & ONT, IRL & CAN [36669] : MARTHA C1800-1879 FER & QUE, IRL & CAN [36904] : MARTHA C1800-1879 ARM & QUE, IRL & CAN [36904] : 1890+ NZ [33889] : JOHN 1850S KAWAU ISLAND, NZ [35408] : CHARLES 1848-1990 DUNEDIN, OTAGO, NZ [36832] : PRE 1877 AKAROA, NZ [37948] : 1870+ CHRISTCHURCH, NZ & AUS [36362] : PRE 1860 SORN, AYR, SCT [33845] : ROSIE PRE 1950 BUCKIE, BAN, SCT [33907] : 1804+ GLASGOW, STI, SCT [33936] : PRE 1861 LESMAHAGOW, LKS, SCT [33971] : PRE 1850 MIDMAR, ABD, SCT [33999] : 1800S ABD, SCT [34053] : 1780S GOREBRIDGE, GLASGOW, SCT [34188] : 1800+ DALKEITH, ELN, SCT [34188] : 1773 SORN, AYR, SCT [34214] : ISABELLA WARK C1850 GLASGOW, SCT [34222] : MARGARET 1750-1850 GLASGOW, LKS, SCT [34229] : PRE 1850 ARBROATH & MONTROSE, ANS, SCT [34274] : 1830S DUNFERMLINE, FIF, SCT [34793] : 1700+ AYR, SCT [34875] : 1800+ LKS, SCT [34983] : SADIE 1900+ SHOTTS, LKS, SCT [35184] : PRE 1855 INVERNESS, SCT [35384] : PRE 1820 PAISLEY, RFW, SCT [35503] : C1800 ARBROATH, ANS, SCT [35773] : PRE 1780 EDINBURGH, MLN, SCT [35983] : 1850+ AYR, AYR, SCT [36275] : 1800-1900 OLD RAYNE, ABD, SCT [36653] : 1700+ PAISLEY, RFW, SCT [36794] : C1868 SLAMANNAN, STI, SCT [36875] : WILLIAM 1813+ DENNY, STI, SCT [37424] : JAMES PRE 1772 DUNIPACE, STI, SCT [37424] : 1800-1910 BOTHWELL, LKS, SCT [37432] : 1600-1820 STI & LKS, SCT [37456] : PRE 1820 EDINBURGH, MLN, SCT [37496] : ALL WICK, CAI, SCT [37627] : PRE 1739 RAIT, MOR, SCT [37772] : PRE 1805 FARNELL, ANS, SCT [38483] : PRE 1890 PEACH ORCHARD, KY, USA [34245] : 1809-1914 IN, USA [35316] : ALL WORLDWIDE [34245]

REIDENBACH ALL USA [36339]

REIDINGER 1838 HEDDESHEIM, BAD, GER [37174]

REIDY 1830-1900 RATHKEALE, LIM, IRL [36906] : PRE 1869 CLA, IRL [37554] : KATE C1880 NEW YORK, NY, USA [38452]

REIERS 1650 TONSEL, GEL, NL [33751] : 1650 TONSEL, GEL, NL [38692]

REIGLE 1800S JASPER CO., IN, OH & PA, USA [36552] : JACOB 1750+ PA, USA [37032]

REIJMERS ALL MILLINGEN A/D RIJN, GEL, NL [38350]

REILEY WILLIAM 1800-1840S DRAKESVILLE, NJ, USA [35298]

REILLY 1850S HOBART, TAS, AUS [33838] : 1885+ SINGLETON, NSW, AUS [34568] : 1853+ HOBART, TAS, AUS [35531] : 1851+ ONT, CAN [34368] : 1810-1830 EPPING FOREST, LND, ENG [35556] : 1852-1929 LISNASKEA, FER, IRL [34233] : 1800+ ANNAGH BELTURBET, CAV, IRL [34568] : HANNAH PRE 1841 CAVAN, CAV, IRL [34805] : PRE 1855 MEA, IRL [34876] : 1818+ DUBLIN, IRL [35416] : 1775-1830 IRL [36724] : PRE 1850 CAVAN, CAV, IRL [37521] : 1831-1933 CASTLEBAR, MAY, IRL [38102] : 1850S CLA, IRL & AUS [36268] : 1831-1933 CLEVELAND, OH, USA [38102]

REIM ALL WORLDWIDE [38383]

REIMANN PRE 1861 MICHELSDORF, LEOBSCHUTZ, GER [36458]

REIMER 1966 LIMBURGERHOF, PFALZ, BRD [38749] : PRE 1900 STOLP & SCHLAWE, POM, GER [38684] : 1930 RUCHHEIM, PFALZ, GER [38749] : ALL WORLDWIDE [33913]

REIMERS 1696-1700 WORDEN, SHO, GER [38528] : PRE 1852 CUXHAVEN, NSA, GER [38632]

REIMS PRE 1848 BRK, ENG [35379]

REINDL ALL ZVIRETIC, BOHEMIA, GER & USA [36916]

REINECKE 1831 GEHRZEN, HAN, GER [34195]

REINER (SEE RINER) [38030]

REINERS JOHN 1935 HAMILTON CO., OH, USA [38062]

REINHARD 1829-1852 RHODEN, WAL, GER [38749]

REINHART 1750-1841 NEUBRUNN, BAV, BRD [36553] : 1841-1990 GIBSON CO., IN, USA [36553]

REINICK ALL GUSTROW, MEK, DDR [34812]

REINING (SEE REINICK) [34812]

REINOLDS 1700-1750 SSX, ENG [35238]

REINSCH ALL USA [36310]

REIS 1820+ TAS, AUS [33790]

REISBERGER PRE 1900 AUGSBURG, BAY, BRD [36963]

REISS PRE 1825 GROSS SCHREIONITZ, KSA, PRE [35795]

REISTAD 1850+ OSLO AREA, AKERSHUS, NOR [36335]

REISWICH 1764-1900 WALTER, SARATOV, SU [36958]

REISZ FERDINAND C1842 MECKLENBERG, GER [34792]

REITER PRE 1800 ST MICHAEL & LUNGAU, SLZ, OES [38609]

REITH PRE 1800 BANCHORY & DEVENICK, KCD, SCT [34608]

RELF 1790S LONDON, ENG [34709] : ALL BRIGHTLING, SSX, ENG [36393] : 1850+ FRIERN BARNET, MDX & LND, ENG [37707] : C1765 HIGH HALDEN, KEN, ENG [38389]

RELPH 1800+ ENG [36662] : ALL STREATHAM, SRY, ENG [36879]

RELYEA 1845+ ROCHESTER, NY, USA [36935] : PRE 1800 GUILDERLAND, NY, USA [36935] : 1800+ SYRACUSE, NY, USA [36935]

REMACLE 1842-1890 FOSSES LA VILLE, NMR, BEL [38158]

REMBERT PRE 1850 SC, USA [38237]

REMBOT PRE 1700 LAUFFEN, WUE, GER [38683]

REMIG 1848 EDENKOBEN, PFALZ, GER [38184]

REMILLARD 1852-1928 ST ETIENNE DE BOLTON, QUE, CAN [35639]

REMINGTON PRE 1800 CAM, ENG [34660] : 1800+ SHEFFIELD, WRY, ENG [36772] : C1860-1919 MALDON & CHELMSFORD, ESS, ENG [37664] : ALL YKS & LIN, ENG [37842] : EBEN 1911 FENTON, MI, USA [38062]

REMLINGER PRE 1855 BIBERACH, WUE, GER [34886] : 1816+ BIBERACH, WUE, GER [35465]

REMMI 1868+ ELIMAKI, KYMEN LAANI, FIN [38758]

REMMINGTON 1700-1800 KETTERING, NTH, ENG [36057] : ALL TIP, IRL [34060]

REMNANT C1800 SRY, ENG [34258]

REMUSAT PRE 1778 LE VERNET, RHA & PCA, FRA [38085]

RENCHER PRE 1710 LEI, ENG [37706]

RENDA ALL GER [38635]

RENDALL ALL DOR, SOM & DEV, ENG [35264] : PRE 1814 WESTMINSTER, LND, ENG [37701] : PRE 1864 WESTRAY, OKI, SCT [35002]

RENDE ALL GER [38635]

RENDEL 1850+ WEYMOUTH, DOR, ENG [37378]

RENDELL 1865+ ROCHESTER, VIC, AUS [34434] : ALL DOR, SOM & DEV, ENG [35264] : 1700-1920 SOM, ENG [37348] : PRE 1780 EXETER, DEV, ENG [37701] : PRE 1898 GLA & DEV, WLS & ENG [35757]

RENDLE ALL DEVONPORT, DEV, ENG [36664] : 1800+ EXETER, DEV, ENG [36664] : 1700+ CHITTLEHAMPTON, DEV, ENG [36995] : PRE 1860 DEV, ENG [37807] : 1850+ ILFRACOMBE, DEV, ENG [38376]

RENES H. 1850-1950 ARNHEM, GEL, NL [38405]

RENFREY 1860S BALDHU & GWENNAP, CON, ENG [34854]

RENKIN PRE 1765 WORKINGTON, CUL, ENG [34795]

RENNEBERG PRE 1900 BALMAIN, NSW, AUS [37969] : C1900 USA [37969]

RENNEHVAMMEN 1650+ UVDAL, NUMEDAL, NOR [36905]

RENNER 1780-1860 NEU FREUDENTAL, UKRAINE, GROSSLIEBENTAL, SU [38372] : ALL CHI, UK [36844]

RENNICK PRE 1842 BRD [36020] : PRE 1820 CLONES, MOG, IRL [38428] : PRE 1820 HAWICK, ROX, SCT [34465]

RENNICKE C1830 WOLFERODE, HAL, DDR [38677]

RENNIE PRE 1799 LONDON, ENG [35702] : 1700S EDINBURGH, MLN, SCT [35395] : 1780+ BARONY, LKS, SCT [35977] : 1750+ NEW DEER & TYRIE, ABD, SCT [37628]

RENNISON 1900+ WESTMINSTER TWP., ONT, CAN [34480] : PRE 1880 BALLYMENA, ANT, IRL [34480]

RENOLD ALL WORLDWIDE [37103]

RENOOY 1700-1990 NOH, NL [38713]

RENOUF 1600+ JSY, CHI [34152]

RENOW 1900+ PERTH, WA, AUS [37966]

RENSHAW 1750-1900 YKS, ENG [34631] : 1800S STEPNEY, LND, ENG [35409] : 1800+ SALFORD, LAN, ENG & NZ [36257]

RENTON 1800+ NBL, ENG [34846] : 1800-1900 DUR, ENG [34846] : PRE 1820 CALVERLEY, WRY, ENG [36583] : 1700+ TRANENT, ELN, SCT [34008] : PRE 1880 SCT [34543] : 1860-1885 EDINBURGH, MLN, SCT [35442] : PRE 1830 HUTTON, BEW, SCT [36497]

RENTOUL 1795+ LONDON, ENG [38204] : PRE 1900 BURNT ISLAND, FIF, SCT [33966] : PRE 1900 GLASGOW, DNB, SCT [33966] : ALL WORLDWIDE [35899]

RENTOWELL 1700+ BALMERINO, FIF, SCT [35627]

RENTSCH C1840 HOCHKIRCH, KSA, GER [35865]

RENWICK 1850+ LND & MDX, ENG [36430] : PRE 1700 MONIAIVE, DFS, SCT [34013] : PRE 1900 DFS, SCT [34013] : PRE 1820 HAWICK, ROX, SCT [34465] : 1800+ TWEEDSMUIR, DFS, SCT [35909] : PRE 1850 HAWICK, ROX & SEL, SCT [35934]

RENZOW PRE 1742 MUMMENDORF, MSW, GER [35157]

REPONTE ALL PHILIPPINE [38730]

REPPER C1760 CON, ENG [36877]

REPPERT C1888 CHICAGO, IL, USA [38650]

RESAN (SEE RESIN) [38080]

RESCORLA C1700 CON, ENG [34686]

RESIN PRE 1745 NTT, ENG [38080]

RESKILLY PRE 1750 MULLION, CON, ENG [38263]

RESPAILLE ALL WORLDWIDE [38162]

RESSER 1700+ EICHACH, BAW, GER [35355]

REST PRE 1729 RADFORD, NTT, ENG [37000]

RETALLACK 1670+ LADOCK, CON, ENG [36961] : 1860-1904 KEWEENAW CO., MI, USA [38009]

RETHAGE ALL WORLDWIDE [38636]

RETHAGEN 1880+ WORLDWIDE [38636]

RETSCHKUS PRE 1880 KRS. GUMBINNEN, OPR, GER [38649]

RETTIE 1800S TYRIE, ABD, SCT [38422]

RETTIG 1852 SAAFELD, MOHRUNGEN, GER [35463]

REUHL PRE 1800 BAW, FRG [38708]

REUTTER 1713 WICKENRODE, GHE, GER [38749]

REVANS ALL WORLDWIDE [36246]

REVEL C1789 REVELSTOKE, DEV, ENG [36803]

REVELL PRE 1850 LONGHOUGHTON, NBL, ENG [34835] : PRE 1860 BASSINGBOURN, CAM, ENG & AUS [34463] : 1830 LIMERICK, IRL [35376] : C1800 KILLEVY, ARM, IRL [37106] : 1600-1680 SOMERSET CO., MD, USA [36566] : 1814-1850 DARLINGTON DISTRICT, SC, USA [38340]

REVERS 1730-1812 SCHIEDAM, ZH, NL [38712]

REVILL 1700-1800 YKS, ENG [37217] : PRE 1850 NTT, ENG [37739]

REVITT 1836+ SA, AUS [34179] : 1800-1990 STANNINGTON, ERY, ENG [34552]

REW C1806 TAUNTON, SOM, ENG [37168] : 1600+
DEV, ENG [38235] : ALL WORLDWIDE [37922]

REWER PRE 1900 CH [38159] : PRE 1900 GER [38159] :
ALL UK [38159]

REX 1800+ GREENE CO., PA, USA [36958]

REY JEAN-PIERRE PRE 1700 CARTIGNY, GE, CH
[38348] : ANTOINE PRE 1846 RUMILY, FRA [34164]
: 1700-1990 CASTELNAU DE MEDOC, GIRONDE,
ILE MAURICE, FRA [36465]

REYMENT ALL WORLDWIDE [35174]

REYNOLDS ALL AUS [34264] : 1830+ SYDNEY,
NSW, AUS [34428] : PRE 1841 QUEANBEYAN,
NSW, AUS [34942] : 1875+ BOMBALA, NSW, AUS
[34966] : 1840 SODWALL, NSW, AUS [35089] : 1830+
PARRAMATTA, NSW, AUS [35396] : 1850+
MELBOURNE, VIC, AUS [35793] : 1860+
ROKEWOOD & INVERLEIGH, VIC, AUS [36622] :
1864+ PORT ADELAIDE, SA, AUS [36632] : 1911+
PADDINGTON, NSW, AUS [38277] : 1800-1950
ONT, CAN [38128] : C1850 KEN, ENG [33809] : 1650-
1800 BADMINTON & BATH, GLS & SOM, ENG
[34012] : 1700+ PADSTOW, CON, ENG [34028] :
1871 KINGS NORTON, WOR, ENG [34224] : 1745+
ECCLES, NOR, ENG [34374] : PRE 1840 MDX, ENG
[34428] : PRE 1850 HANDSWORTH, STS, ENG
[34725] : 1675-1745 GWENNAP, CON, ENG [34793] :
PRE 1876 LUDLOW, SAL, ENG [34935] : PRE 1860
CREDITON, DEV, ENG [34958] : 1700-1750 SSX,
ENG [35238] : 1800+ BETHNAL GREEN, MDX,
ENG [35436] : PRE 1700 BURSTON, NFK, ENG
[35571] : PRE 1700 BANHAM, NFK, ENG [35571] :
PRE 1873 ROCHE & LANIVET, CON, ENG [36039] :
1700-50 KIRKBRIDE, CUL, ENG [36431] : 1750+
BIRMINGHAM, WAR & STS, ENG [36435] : PRE
1850 WOLVERHAMPTON, STS, ENG [36664] : 1800-
1900 TENTERDEN, KEN, ENG [37326] : 1700-1800
WONSTON, HAM, ENG [38003] : 1600-1850 ENG
[38128] : 1600-1700 BOURNE, LIN, ENG [38287] :
PRE 1855 LUDLOW, SAL, ENG [38306] : 1853
ROYSTON, CAM, ENG [38364] : 1800-1900
ALTARNUN, CON, ENG & AUS [35381] : C1870
CLASHMORE, WAT, IRL [34618] : PRE 1871 GAL,
IRL [35332] : PRE 1820+ CAV, IRL [35793] : PRE
1850 IRL [37565] : PRE 1900 ANT, IRL [37601] : 1850S
SAN FRANCISCO, CA, USA [36569] : PRE 1850
COLD SPRINGS, NY, USA [36569] : 1630-1740
WASHINGTON CO., RI, USA [37477] : 1850+
SCIOTO CO., OH, USA [37565] : 1800-1870
MONROE CO., NY, USA [37798] : 1825-1925
STEUBEN CO., NY, USA [37798] : 1749-1829
PATRICK CO., VA, USA [38044] : 1820-1860
RICHLAND, OH, USA [38095] : ALL TX, USA
[38359] : PRE 1870 LLANLLWCHAIARN, MGY,
WLS [37681]

REYS C1780 LISBON, PT [38079]

REZEAU 1750-1800 MONMOUTH, NJ, USA [37435]

REZIN 1800-1950 HUNTLY, ABD, SCT [38355]

RHALL 1840 NEWCASTLE, NSW, AUS [35970]

RHEA ALL POMEROY, TYR, IRL [35460]

RHEIN ALL BONN, NRW, FRG [38717]

RHEINLANDER PRE 1860 PLAISTOW, ESS, ENG
[37138]

RHEINLAUDER 1820 KIRN ON NAKE, KOBLUTZ,
GER [35583]

RHEMREV ALL WORLDWIDE [33751] : ALL
WORLDWIDE [38692]

RHIND 1800+ ELGIN, MOR, SCT [34785] : PRE 1850
HUNTLEY, SCT [35435]

RHOADERMER 1890+ SHANNONVILLE, ONT,
CAN [34466] : 1840 LANCASTER, PA, USA [34466] :
1838+ URBANA, OH, USA [34466]

RHOADES 1700-1900 WELLS, NFK, ENG [37929] :
1650-1750 MIDDLESEX CO., VA, USA [36737] :
1700-1800 USA & ENG [35289]

RHOADS 1800-1855 WARRICK, IN, USA [38576]

RHODE PRE 1700 DEN [38553]

RHODEN ALL ENG [37846]

RHODES THOMAS 1855+ SYDNEY, NSW, AUS
[34979] : C1874 HALLS GAP, VIC, AUS [35848] : PRE
1851 BOURNE, LIN, ENG [34421] : C1825-1830
BRADFORD, WRY, ENG [34628] : THOMAS C1813
ENG [34979] : PRE 1895 HORSFORTH, YKS, ENG
[35985] : ALL GUISELEY & KIRKBYOVERBLOW,
WRY, ENG [36159] : 1870+ SHIPLEY, SSX, ENG
[36212] : JOSEPH PRE 1820 HULL, ERY, ENG
[36432] : PRE 1820 CALVERLEY, WRY, ENG [36583]
: C1720 HAWORTH, YKS, ENG [37288] : 1750-1850
NEWCASTLE ON TYNE, NBL, ENG [37419] : PRE
1840 PHILADELPHIA, PA & OH, USA [37018] :
1675-1725 JAMAICA, L.I., NY, USA [38194] : 1825
ASHEVILLE, NC, USA [38198] : C1650-1800
QUEENS CO., NY, USA [38767]

RHODES CORDINGLEY 1800+ BRADFORD, YKS,
ENG [35163]

RHORER 1725-1750 LANCASTER CO., PA, USA
[38118]

RHYND (SEE RHIND) [34785]

RIACH 1790+ ROTHES, MOR, SCT [34764]

RIBLET 1780-1820 UNION, PA, USA [38095] : 1790-
1990 RICHLAND, OH, USA [38095] : 1735-1775
NORTHAMPTON, PA, USA [38095]

RICARDS ALL KER & COR, IRL [37664]

RICCARDI 1700S-1800S MADRID, ESP [35126]

RICCIUS PRE 1800 BERNSTADT, PSA, GER [38675]

RICE 1880S MELBOURNE, VIC, AUS [35136] : 1890+
GOLDEN, BC, CAN [34368] : PRE 1880 SMITHS
FALLS, ONT, CAN [34376] : C1850 HORSLEY, GLS,
ENG [35038] : 1700+ TRURO, CON, ENG [35385] :
PRE 1790 SHERSTON MAGNA, WIL, ENG [36113] :
ALL NFK, ENG [36234] : PRE 1830S LEICESTER,
LEI, ENG [36652] : ALL SIDBURY, DEV, ENG
[36789] : 1850-1900 SHOREDITCH, LND, ENG
[37765] : 1750-1850S BLOOMSBURY, MDX, ENG
[37765] : 1700+ WADDESDON, BKM, ENG & AUS
[35555] : PRE 1800 LIM, IRL [34265] : PRE 1884
MALLOW, COR, IRL [34705] : 1835+ KANTURK,
COR, IRL [35136] : PRE 1841 DUBLIN, IRL [35162] :
1806 KANTURK, COR, IRL [35201] : 1800+
MALLOW, COR, IRL [35201] : PRE 1800+ TYR,
IRL [35928] : 1800S LOUGHLAN, CAR, IRL [36290] :
EDWARD 1849-1913 CORK CITY, COR, VIC &
NSW, IRL & AUS [35239] : PRE 1850 PAISLEY,
RFW, SCT [34365] : PRE 1800+ ROC & INV, SCT
[35928] : 1810-1870 AMITE CO., MS, USA [35307] :
JOHN 1650 RI, USA [37008] : 1865-1875
KEWEENAW CO., MI, USA [38009] : ELIZABETH
1775+ BOSTON & KINGSVILLE, MA & OH, USA
[38241] : 1800-1840 CLAIBORNE CO., TN, USA
[38367]

RICH 1867+ GRENFELL, NSW, AUS [33763] : C1750
LIMEHOUSE, MDX, ENG [33918] : 1750+ LND,
ENG [33963] : CHARLES C1830 CON, ENG [34792] :
PATRICK C1810 CON, ENG [34792] : ERNEST
C1860 QUAINTON, BKM, ENG [34792] : 1860-1900
QUAINTON, BKM, ENG [34792] : 1800+ TIPTON,
STS, ENG [35972] : 1750+ KINGSWEAR, DEV,
ENG [36000] : PRE 1830 TIPTON, STS, ENG [36528] :
C1800 DEV, ENG [37180] : 1850S NETHER
STOWEY, SOM, ENG & USA [38309] : 1872-88
NORTHMOOR GREEN, SOM, ENG & USA [38309]

RICHARD PRE 1850 KENT CO., NB, CAN [38447] :
PRE 1791 STITHIANS, CON, ENG [33995] : PRE
1655 MAGNY & METZ, LOR, FRA [36954] : 1820-

1860 HAMILTON CO., OH, USA [36940] : 1883
SENECA CO., OH, USA [37788]

RICHARDS JOHN PRE 1846 MAITLAND, NSW, AUS
[34935] : 1880 HAMILTON, VIC, AUS [35048] : ALL
BENDIGO, VIC, AUS [35063] : C1850 TAS, AUS
[35091] : 1900+ PARKDALE, VIC, AUS [35140] :
1858+ MOORABBIN, VIC, AUS [35408] : 1810+
RICHMOND, NSW, AUS [35537] : CHARLES 1890S
VIC & WA, AUS [35780] : 1840+ WINGHAM, NSW,
AUS [36295] : SEYMOUR 1879+ BALMAIN,
SYDNEY, NSW, AUS [37906] : THOMAS W.M. 1855-
1932 BALMAIN, SYDNEY, NSW, AUS [37906] :
FREDERICK 1879+ BALMAIN, SYDNEY, NSW,
AUS [37906] : 1800S MAITLAND, NSW, AUS [37910]
: 1850+ ADELAIDE, SA, AUS [38209] : 1819+
CARDIGAN, NB, CAN [34056] : JOHN 1827 QUE,
CAN [36319] : EVELINE 1827+ QUE, CAN [36319] :
PRE 1880 HANDSWORTH, STS, ENG [33993] :
MARY 1800-1880 LIVERPOOL, LAN, ENG [34143] :
1740 WIVELISCOMBE, SOM, ENG [34204] : 1800+
PLYMOUTH, DEV, ENG [34532] : 1800+
HOLBORN, LND, ENG [34550] : 1700+ DUDLEY,
WAR, ENG [34640] : 1700-1750 ILLOGAN, CON,
ENG [34697] : PRE 1850 WELLINGTON, SAL, ENG
[34711] : HENRY ALL ENG [34737] : C1831 RUAN
MINOR & GRADE, CON, ENG [34752] : 1800-1900
STS, ENG [34783] : PRE 1816 HILTON, DOR, ENG
[34828] : ALL MEMBURY, DEV, ENG [34838] : PRE
1821 COMBE FLOREY, SOM, ENG [34840] :
SOPHIA 1800S LONDON, ENG [34889] : CHARITY
PRE 1750 TRINTISHOE, DEV, ENG [34963] : PRE
1850 HALBERTON, DEV, ENG [35063] : 1820S GLS,
ENG [35084] : PRE 1813+ STONEHENGE, WIL,
ENG [35109] : 1816-1850 REDRUTH, CON, ENG
[35146] : 1840S ST LUKE & CLERKENWELL, LND,
ENG [35408] : 1800S LEA, HEF, ENG [35408] : PRE
1827 ZENNOR, CON, ENG [35441] : 1756+ LONG
SUTTON, SOM, ENG [35464] : 1800+ BREAGE,
CON, ENG [35476] : PRE 1780 LAPFORD, DEV,
ENG [35496] : C1782+ WOLVERHAMPTON, STS,
ENG [35537] : 1590+ WENDRON, CON, ENG
[35587] : ANN 1820-1840 REDRUTH, CON, ENG
[35726] : CAROLINE 1840+ ENG [35762] : C1750
WETTEN BRIDGE, IOW, ENG [35860] : 1842
SHREWSBURY, SAL, ENG [35903] : EDWARD
1890S+ SW LONDON, SRY & KEN, ENG [35907] :
1800S DOVER, KEN, ENG [35907] : STEPHEN
1850S CHARLTON, KEN, ENG [35907] : 1800+
LONDON, ENG [35939] : 1700-1800 KETTERING,
NTH, ENG [36057] : ALL DOVER, KEN, ENG
[36094] : PRE 1790 WITHAM FRIARY, SOM, ENG
[36478] : ALL ST IVES, CON, ENG [36506] : 1725+
TAVISTOCK, DEV, ENG [36594] : EDWARD CHAS.
PRE 1907 SHEERNESS, KEN, ENG [36646] : PRE
1800 ST KEVERNE, CON, ENG [36788] : 1860+
BRISTOL, ENG [36995] : PRE 1850 NEWQUAY,
CON, ENG [37105] : PRE 1850 CHESTER, CHS,
ENG [37289] : 1800+ ILLOGAN, CON, ENG [37291]
: 1800S REDRUTH, CON, ENG [37343] : ANN
1774+ CON, ENG [37453] : WILLIAM 1829-1870
STS & HRT, ENG [37525] : MOSES 1750-1850 STS,
ENG [37525] : 1800+ HRT & STS, ENG [37525] :
1600-1850 PAUL, CON, ENG [37680] : C1834
MANCHESTER & HULME, LAN, ENG [37691] :
PRE 1830 STAUNTON HAROLD, LEI, ENG [37754]
: 1800-1900 CADBY, LEI, ENG [37931] : 1750
HIGHHAM & WESTON ZOYLAND, SOM, ENG
[38209] : C1863 CLOTH FAIR, LND, ENG [38721] :
ALL BERE FERRERS, DEV, ENG & AUS [35712] :
ALL ENG & WLS [35579] : C1647+ WEXFORD,
WEX, DUB & CLA, IRL [35738] : ALL KER & COR,
IRL [37664] : PRE 1885 NORSEWOOD, HKY, NZ

[33964] : 1870+ CHRISTCHURCH, CANT, NZ
[35408] : GEORGE 1800S NEW YORK, NY, USA
[36321] : PRE 1930 BEDIAS & MADISON CO., TX,
USA [37320] : 1845-1890 PITTSBURGH, PA, USA
[37605] : ALL JEFFERSON CO., PA, USA [38036] :
SARA PRE 1850 BALTIMORE, MD, USA [38049] :
1637-66 FARMINGTON, CT, USA [38518] : 1700+
WREXHAM, DEN, WLS [34303] : 1850S PEM, WLS
[34603] : THOMAS C1824 LLANSTADWELL, PEM,
WLS [34836] : C1784 PEMBROKE DOCK, PEM,
WLS [34457] : PRE 1817 GARDIFFAITH, MON,
WLS [36995] : ALL RAD, WLS [37332]

RICHARDSON 1890+ ALBION, BRISBANE, QLD,
AUS [33782] : 1855+ WOOLSTHORPE, VIC, AUS
[35203] : ALL HOBART, TAS, AUS [35432] : C1900
TOWNSVILLE, QLD, AUS [35507] : ALL
STRANGWAYS, VIC, AUS [35526] : JOHN PRE 1831
TAS, AUS [35788] : 1836-1866 BALLARAT, VIC, AUS
[36281] : 1820+ CRAIGHURST, ONT, CAN [34465] :
1835+ ALB, CAN [34465] : 1820+ YORK CO., ONT,
CAN [34465] : PRE 1900 LONDON, ENG [33914] :
1650+ KESWICK, CUL, ENG [33973] : PRE 1800
OWSTON, LIN, ENG [33992] : 1650-1900 SOUTH
SHIELDS, DUR, ENG [34004] : 1700-1900
COVENTRY, WAR, ENG [34004] : PRE 1850 ENG
[34046] : 1850+ SHEFFIELD, YKS, ENG [34190] :
PRE 1850 YKS, ENG [34465] : PRE 1770
ROCHDALE, LAN, ENG [34474] : PRE 1900
HUDDERSFIELD, YKS, ENG [34638] : PRE 1850
ATHERTON, LAN, ENG [34730] : GEOFFREY
1833+ SUTTON COLDFIELD, WAR, OXF & STS,
ENG [35013] : GEOFFREY 1833+ AVON DASSETT,
WAR, OXF & STS, ENG [35013] : C1830
NEWCASTLE ON TYNE, NBL, ENG [35203] :
C1760 LIVERPOOL, LAN, ENG [35331] : PRE 1800
NTH, ENG [35377] : PRE 1850+ CROYDON, SRY,
ENG [35453] : 1800-1850 LEGSBY, LIN, ENG [35602]
: 1870+ DURHAM, DUR, ENG [35704] : 1800S
JARROW, NBL, ENG [35706] : 1800
MANCHESTER, LAN, ENG [35881] : 1800+
SAFFRON WALDEN, ESS, ENG [35914] :
ANTHONY PRE 1720 NETHER POPPLETON,
YKS, ENG [35983] : PRE 1770 MARESFIELD, SSX,
ENG [36107] : 1800-1930 BRIGHOUSE, WRY, ENG
[36111] : 1750-1800 SHEFFIELD, WRY, ENG [36126]
: PRE 1780 STEBBING, ESS, ENG [36589] : 1852+
COWPEN & BEDLINGTON, NBL, ENG [36609] :
PRE 1840 BREDE, SSX, ENG [36752] : 1814
FADMOOR, YKS, ENG [36907] : PRE 1900 NBL,
ENG [36934] : ALL PYECOMBE, SSX, ENG [36938] :
1700S WILSTHORP, LIN, ENG [37018] : 1800 ST
GEORGE IN THE EAST, LND, MDX, ENG [37082] :
PRE 1820 SRY, ENG [37107] : PRE 1827 LEI, ENG
[37207] : 1800+ IFORD, SSX, ENG [37293] : 1840+
LONDON, ENG [37294] : C1852 BRIGHTON, SSX,
ENG [37302] : 1300-1400+ SSX, ENG [37648] : 1800-
1850 BRAMPTON, CUL, ENG [37711] : 1800+
HULL, ENG [37907] : ALL WESTMINSTER, LND,
ENG [37994] : ELIZA 1849+ STOPHAM, SSX, ENG
[38549] : 1800S BELGAUM & BOMBAY, INDIA
[37203] : 1600-1900 LISBURN, DOW, IRL [34717] :
PRE 1839 DUBLIN, IRL [35189] : 1800S WIC, IRL
[37203] : 1873+ AUCKLAND, NZ [34609] : PRE 1871
EDINBURGH, SCT [33906] : PRE 1820 HAWICK,
ROX, SCT [34465] : 1800 JEDBURGH, ROX, SCT
[34468] : 1700-1800 FORDYCE, BAN, SCT [36652] :
1600+ PERTH, PER, SCT [37141] : PRE 1870+
KILMARNOCK, AYR, SCT [37556] : 1850+
PICKFORD, MI, USA [34465] : 1835+ MT, USA
[34465] : 1835+ MI, USA [34465] : 1860-1890 AR, USA
[36934] : 1800-1950 LANCASTER, WI, USA [36938] :
1861-1891 GIBSON CO., IN, USA [37826] : 1650-1861

GENESEE CO., NY, USA [37826] : PRUDENCE 1800-1834 BURLINGTON CO., NJ, USA [38127] : PRE 1805 BEDFORD & SHELBY CO., TN, USA [38743] : PRE 1900 WORLDWIDE [36840]

RICHART C1775-1810 NORTHUMBERLAND CO., PA, USA [38055]

RICHE PRE 1853 MAG, DDR [37551] : 1853-1926 MAG, DDR [37551]

RICHER C1820-1840 STE SCHOLASTIQUE, QUE, CAN [34047] : C1698-1800 MONTREAL, QUE, CAN [34047] : 1850+ OTTAWA, ONT & QUE, CAN [34047]

RICHES 1700+ HEMPNALL, NFK, ENG [34420] : PRE 1886 OLDHAM, LAN & NFK, ENG [34443] : ALL NFK, ENG [34493] : BATHSHEBA 1785+ HOXNE, SFK, ENG [34572] : 1750+ NFK, ENG [35241] : JOHN RICHARD 1800S NFK, ENG [35361] : ALL SFK, ENG [37612] : 1700-1800 NORWICH & DISTRICT, NFK, ENG [37702]

RICHESON 1700+ FRANKLIN, VA, USA [38343] : 1850+ APPLE RIVER & GALENA, IL, USA [38343] : 1800+ WASHINGTON CO., OH, USA [38343]

RICHINSON C1600-1700S BDF, ENG [36289]

RICHMAN PRE 1825 ESS, ENG [36050] : PRE 1850 HAM & BRK, ENG [36380] : 1738-1739 DARNBY UPON DON, WRY, ENG [38469]

RICHMIRE 1780+ DUNDAS, ONT, CAN [38411]

RICHMOND 1802+ YORK, YKS, ENG [38071] : 1730+ FOTHERBY, LIN, ENG [35587] : 1750-1850 FAILSWORTH, LAN, ENG [35775] : PRE 1825 ESS, ENG [36050] : PRE 1800 WESTON, NFK, ENG [36122] : 1650-1750 COCKERHAM, LAN, ENG [36983] : ALL SADBERGE, NRY, ENG [37627] : 1870+ GLADSTONE, STH, NZ [34446] : 1850+ AIRDRIE, LKS, SCT [33978] : 1760+ EDINBURGH, MLN, SCT [35813] : PRE 1870 DARNHAY, AYR, SCT [37446] : ALL SCT [37572] : C1789 ANNAPOLIS MD, WA, USA [37627] : C1769 UPPER MARLBOROUGH, WA, USA [37627] : ALL WORLDWIDE [36933]

RICHTER ALL GER [38664] : ALL OES [37268]

RICHWINE 1760+ LANCASTER, PA & IN, USA [38054]

RICK 1850S NOTTINGHAM, NTT, ENG [36506]

RICKARD 1860+ WOODSPOINT, VIC, AUS [34936] : 1796 DINTON, BKM, ENG [34120] : 1750-1850 MYLOR, CON, ENG [34274] : C1780 REDRUTH, CON, ENG [34644] : C1800S CON, ENG [35381] : EDWARD 1873 DEVONPORT, DEV, ENG [35870] : C1835 TREGONY, CON, ENG [35922] : PRE 1850 PROBUS, CON, ENG [35930] : ALL TRURO, CON, ENG [37237] : 1840+ CAMBORNE, KEHELLAND, CON, ENG & NZ [36819] : ALL KER & COR, IRL [37664] : 1850-1880 KEWEENAW CO., MI, USA [38009] : PRE 1860 IL, USA [38017]

RICKARDS 1891 ANNANDALE, NSW, AUS [35479] : PRE 1865 MELBOURNE, VIC, AUS [35479] : 1850+ CLACTON & WESTBURY, ESS, ENG [34714] : C1860 GLOUCESTER, GLS, ENG [35920] : ALL KER & COR, IRL [37664] : PRE 1700 WORLDWIDE [38345]

RICKENBACHER PRE 1740 RICKENBACH, BL, CH [36972]

RICKERT 1850+ CRESWICK, VIC, AUS [34421]

RICKETTS 1868+ SA, AUS [34777] : 1880+ CAMPERDOWN, NSW, AUS [34978] : 1848-1873 WOOL, DOR, ENG [34389] : PRE 1855 GLS, ENG [34853] : 1800S LND, ENG [34978] : 1785+ WILMINGTON, KEN & STS, ENG [37266] : 1700+ BROKENBOROUGH, WIL, ENG [37328] : 1800-1830 ISLINGTON, MDX, ENG [37845]

RICKEY HANNA 1800-1900 OH, NJ & MD, USA [38392]

RICKMANN 1900+ NEUBRANDENBURG, MECKLENBURG, GER [38603]

RICKS X. ALL CORSHAM, WIL & BRK, ENG [36329] : JOHN C1815 GA, USA [37801] : NAPOLEON C1848 WASHINGTON, LA, USA [37801] : NANCY C1805 GA, USA [37801]

RICKSON ALL GILLINGHAM, KEN, ENG & NZ [36840]

RICKWOOD 1800-1900 ROYAL TUNBRIDGE WELLS, KEN, ENG [37695]

RIDDALL ALL ENG [37833]

RIDDEL 1851+ PAISLEY, RFW, SCT [33882]

RIDDELL C1885 RICHMOND, VIC, AUS [35526] : ROBERT 1839 SYDNEY, NSW, AUS [36367] : 1830-1870 DURHAM CO., ONT, CAN [34484] : PRE 1858 RADSTOCK, SOM, ENG [34858] : 1857+ MILTON, OTAGO, NZ [35956] : 1780+ TEVIOTDALE, ROX, SCT [34092] : FRANCIS 1800S PETERHEAD, ABD, SCT [34499] : PRE 1830 OLD DEER, ABD, SCT [34576] : PRE 1857 FARR, INV, SCT [35956] : PRE 1858 BONAR BRIDGE, INV, SCT [36855] : PRE 1850 CASTLETON, ROX, SCT [36877] : ADAM 1822 ESTILL CO., KY, USA [38109] : ROBERT 1799 STOKES CO., NC, USA [38109]

RIDDERBUSCH 1802 BARNTRUP, LIP, GER [38749]

RIDDETT PRE 1800 PORTSMOUTH, HAM, ENG [34559]

RIDDICK C1837+ LIVERPOOL, LAN, ENG [34432] : ALL DUMFRIES, DFS, SCT [34432]

RIDDIOUGH 1800+ ORMSKIRK, LAN, ENG [36818]

RIDDLE C1930 TOWNSVILLE, QLD, AUS [35038] : 1870S KANIMBLA, NSW, AUS [37309] : 1840S MANNING RIVER, NSW, ENG [37309] : C1900 NEW YORK, YKS, ENG [35038] : C1833 BELFAST, ANT, IRL [36259] : 1800+ GLASGOW, SCT [33948] : 1750+ HAWICK, ROX, SCT [35038] : C1730 SHREWSBURY, NJ, USA [34366] : PRE 1820 CUMBERLAND CO., KY, USA [37820] : C1769 RIDDLES FERRY, NC, USA [37820] : PRE 1840 ROWAN CO., NC, USA [37820] : JOHN 1860-1865 MADISON CO., KY, USA [38109]

RIDDLER ALL ENG & AUS [35213]

RIDDLESTON PRE 1725 ESS, ENG [35642]

RIDDOCH 1837-1860 AUCHTERARDER, PER, SCT [36635]

RIDDY PRE 1780 BDF, ENG [35701]

RIDEN ELIZABETH 1800+ DEV, ENG [34078]

RIDEOUT C1800 ASHMORE, DOR, ENG [34426] : ALL FONTMELL MAGNA & ASHMORE, DOR, ENG [35297] : ALL TOLLARD ROYAL, WIL, ENG [35297] : ADA 1874+ PORTSMOUTH & SOUTHSEA, HAM, ENG [38255]

RIDER ALL VIC, AUS [34554] : C1800 BARNWOOD, GLS, ENG [34258] : 1550+ UGBOROUGH, DEV, ENG [34747] : PRE 1808 COVERDALE & LEEDS, NRY, ENG [37710] : 1840S NELSON, NZ [34554]

RIDGARDS 1800S DERBY, DBY, ENG [34995] : 1830 DERBY, DBY, ENG [34995]

RIDGE PRE 1910 SHEFFIELD, WRY, ENG [33902] : 1700+ WADDESDON, BKM, ENG [35555] : PRE 1830 DUFFIELD, DBY, ENG [36403] : C1747 BARNBY IN THE WILLOWS, NTT, ENG [37007] : 1800 CROYDON, SRY, ENG [37082]

RIDGES ALL WORLDWIDE [36469]

RIDGEWAY PRE 1860 STROUD, NSW, AUS [35236] : PRE 1799 GREAT HORWOOD, BKM, ENG [35737] : 1820+ PIKE & ROSS COS., OH, USA [38323]

RIDGEWELL EMILY 1860-70 HARLESDEN, MDX, ENG [35124]

RIDGLEY 1750-1880 PRINCES RISBOROUGH, BKM, ENG [36175]

RIDGWAY C1889 ROSEDALE, VIC, AUS [35748] : C1840 CLYDE, VIC, AUS [35748] : PRE 1811 THORNBOROUGH, BKM, ENG [35748]

RIDGWELL 1800+ SAFFRON WALDEN, ESS, ENG [35914]

RIDING 1849+ BRISBANE, QLD, AUS [35462] : PRE 1849 BURNLEY & PADIHAM, LAN, ENG [35462]

RIDINGS PRE 1850 MANCHESTER, LAN & WRY, ENG [35354] : 1833 NEWTON, LAN, ENG [35369] : 1830+ OLDHAM, LAN, ENG [35586] : 1820+ MARIETTA & CHEROKIE, GA, USA [38197] : 1790+ RUTHERFORD CO., TN, USA [38197]

RIDLAND 1790+ DUNROSSNESS, SHI, SCT [33982]

RIDLEY 1860-1920 ROOKWOOD & LIDCOMBE, NSW, AUS [34294] : 1800-1860 KEN, ENG [34294] : 1840S NBL, ENG [34875] : PRE 1750 COLLERTON & NEWCASTLE, NBL, ENG [36110] : ALL TUNBRIDGE, KEN, ENG [36743] : PRE 1890 CAMBERWELL, SRY, ENG [37321] : 1730-1850 WHITTLESEY, CAM, ENG [37461] : ALL NBL & DUR, ENG & USA [38754]

RIDOUT PRE 1860 TAM O'SHANTER BELT & ADELAIDE, SA, AUS [35339] : 1700-1900 GILLINGHAM, DOR, ENG [35069]

RIDOUTT 1852 SOUTH YARRA, VIC, AUS [35468] : 1800S PORTSMOUTH, HAM, ENG [35468]

RIDPATH ALL WORLDWIDE [37361]

RIDSDILL PRE 1858 BOLTEN PERCY, YKS, ENG [34779]

RIEBERGER PRE 1860 KLASTERDORF ODESSA, KSA, GER & CAN [37481]

RIEBESEL 1800-1860 HAN, GER & USA [36552]

RIECK 1870+ FASSIFERN, QLD, AUS [35460] : PRE 1880+ KILPEIN, UCKERMARK, PRE [35460]

RIED CATHERINE PRE 1850 LUNENBERG, VA, USA [38536]

RIEDE 1600-1800 RATSHAUSEN, WUE, GER [37015]

RIEDEL 1820+ DOEBELN, SAX, DDR [34803] : 1750-1840 ALBERSWEILER, RPF, GER [38374]

RIEDMEYER PRE 1800 WINGERODE, PSA, GER [38048]

RIEDY 1830-1900 RATHKEALE, LIM, IRL [36906]

RIEGLER 1600-1700 GOCHSHEIM, BAY, BRD [35311]

RIEHL 1830+ WATERLOO & PERTH CO., ONT, CAN [37455] : PRE 1850 ALS, FRA [37455] : PRE 1850 GHE, GER [37455] : CHRISTIAN 1790-1799 ALSACE LORRAINE, ELO, GER [38780]

RIEKIE 1600+ ST MONANCE, FIF, SCT [35627]

RIEL (SEE REEL) [35617]

RIELLY PRE 1900 NEW HAVEN, CT, USA [38537]

RIEMAN (SEE REAMAN) [37435]

RIEMER PRE 1855 KREMMIN, POM, GER [38018]

RIENEK ALL SU & CHINA [35568]

RIENHARDT 1450-1650 MUEHLHAUSEN, BAW, BRD [38654]

RIENKS PRE 1800 GIETHOORN, NL [36630]

RIEPENHAUSEN C1750 BREMKE, NSA, BRD [37513]

RIETH 1800+ HERISAU, AAR, CH [35239]

RIETKERK 1850-1900 LEIDEN, ZUH, NL [34479]

RIEWE 1700-1850 MICHELSDORF, LUBLIN, POL [38652]

RIFKIND PRE 1900 SAD, KOVNA, LITHUANIA [36455]

RIGBY 1840+ GOORAMBAT EAST, VIC, AUS [37171] : 1840+ BENALLA, VIC, AUS [37171] : 1800-1900 SNEDSHILL SALOP, SAL, ENG [34069] : PRE 1770 FYLDE, LAN, ENG [36073] : C1850 WARRINGTON, LAN, ENG [36092] : 1800S BOLTON, LAN, ENG [36708] : 1800+ IA, USA [35305]

RIGBYE 1780-1820 ECCLESTON, LAN, ENG [35017]

RIGDEN 1600+ FAVERSHAM, KEN, ENG [36096] : 1600-1800 EAST, KEN, ENG [36096]

RIGG PRE 1800 YORK, YKS, ENG [34588] : PRE 1850 DALTON IN FURNESS, LAN, ENG [36259]

RIGGALL 1700+ FULSTOW, LIN, ENG [34221]

RIGGS 1850+ KINDRED & FORTH, TAS, AUS [35433] : C1782 WINFRITH NEWBURGH, DOR, ENG [34586] : PRE 1833 WINFRITH, DOR, ENG [35976] : ZOPHAR 1800 MORRIS CO., NJ, USA [35276]

RIGHTON 1750-1800 CHESTERTON, WAR, ENG [34677] : C1826 BRIGHTON, SSX, ENG [35261] : C1836 SPILLABY, LIN, ENG [35515]

RIGLAR C1750-1850 DOR, ENG [36435]

RIGNEY 1700+ OFF & GAL, IRL [34572] : PRE 1840 BIRR, OFF, IRL [34576] : JOHN 1760 BEAUFORT CO., NC, USA [35328] : MURPHY 1760S BEAUFORT CO., NC, USA [37585]

RIGOLEAU 1700+ LUNENBURG, NS, CAN & FRA [34500]

RIGSBY 1780-1860 SHEBBEAR, DEV, ENG [34469]

RIJCKMANS C1821 PARIS, RPA, FRA [38711] : C1836 MORLAIX, BRI, FRA [38711]

RIJKEWAART C1730 LEIDEN, ZUH, NL [38698]

RILENER ALL IRL [35399]

RILES ALL BEDWORTH & ATHERSTONE, WAR, ENG [34955]

RILEY 1840+ SYDNEY, NSW, AUS [34421] : PRE 1850+ CAMPERDOWN, NSW, AUS [34423] : C1885 TAS, AUS [34775] : BERNARD 1832+ PARRAMATTA, NSW, AUS [34885] : 1850+ PATERSON & WINGHAM, NSW, AUS [35189] : JOHN 1802+ AIRDS, NSW, AUS [35358] : ANN 1883+ GUNDY, NSW, AUS [35412] : MARTHA 1852+ WINDSOR & KURRAJONG, NSW, AUS [36600] : JOHN 1792+ PROSPECT & KURRAJONG, NSW, AUS [36600] : C1800 LEEDS, WRY, ENG [33796] : 1875-1910 LONDON, ENG [34331] : C1800+ KIRKBY IRELETH, LAN, ENG [34374] : 1750-1900 BACUP, LAN & WRY, ENG [34520] : PRE 1831 THURLASTON, LEI, ENG [34548] : EDIE 1880-1944 SWANSEA & BATH, SOM, LND & KEN, ENG [36443] : EDWARD 1788+ SHOREDITCH, LND, ENG [36600] : EDWARD PRE 1800 SHOREDITCH, LND, ENG [36646] : PRE 1920 MOUNTNESSING & WRITTLE, ESS, ENG [36765] : C1846 ACCRINGTON, LAN, ENG [36955] : PRE 1830 ALREWAS, STS, ENG [36980] : 1811+ SOUTHWARK, SRY, ENG [37270] : 1750-1850 HULL, ERY & SFK, ENG [37290] : PRE 1800 TREDINGTON, WOR, ENG [37371] : JOHN PRE 1900 (HMS DUNCAN), ENG [37436] : PRE 1836 STOCKTON ON TEES, DUR, ENG [37662] : PRE 1900 AUDLEY, STS, ENG [37722] : JAMES 1847 ST PANCRAS, LND & STS, ENG & IRL [36443] : CISSIE 1909-1955 BATH & SWANSEA, ENG & WLS [36443] : 1800-1850 MACOSQUIN, LDY, IRL [34244] : PRE 1817 CAV, IRL [35400] : PRE 1850 CASTLEBAR, MAY, IRL [36310] : 1800+ NEW ROSS, KIK, IRL [38494] : C1905 NEW FRANKLIN, MO, USA [34157] : 1840+ FOUNTAIN CO., IN, USA [35262] : 1812-1891 NJ, USA [36319] : FRANCIS 1820-1828 GIBSON, IN, USA [36908] : JACOB C1850 HAMILTON CO., OH, USA [37001] : 1830-1850 OH, USA [38105] : EDIE 1880-1944 GLA, WLS [36443] : SARAH 1860 GLA, STS & LND, WLS & ENG [36443]

RILEY (SEE REILLY) [34805]

RIMBY 1800S BALTIMORE, MD, USA [36921] : 1800S NJ, USA [36921]

RIMEL PRE 1752 WESTON SUB EDGE, GLS, ENG [37909]

RIMES PRE 1865 BRATTON & WOOKEY HOLE, SOM, ENG [35132]

RIMINGTON PRE 1824 WORKSOP & RETFORD, NTT & DBY, ENG [37267]

RIMMER 1910+ SYDNEY, NSW, AUS [37119] : PRE 1860 LIVERPOOL & MANCHESTER, LAN, ENG [34865]

RINCKES ALL WORLDWIDE [36755]

RINDFLEICH PRE 1860 CLEVELAND, OH, USA [37034]

RINDFLEISCH 1650-1750 AUERBACH, HES, BRD [35311]

RINEHART 1750-1780 FREDERICK CO., MD, USA [38310]

RINER 1800-1820 FREDERICK CO., MD, USA [38030] : C1750-1782 LANCASTER CO., PA, USA [38030] : 1782-1803 WASHINGTON CO., MD, USA [38030]

RING ALL ULLADULLA, NSW, AUS [35727] : PRE 1842 OXF, ENG [35727] : EDMUND 1750+ KILSHANNIG BY MALLOW, COR, IRL [35364] : 1787 KILSHANNIG, COR, IRL [35560] : 1630-1750 PLYMOUTH, MA, USA [37432]

RINGER PRE 1853 LAKENHAM & NORWICH, NFK, ENG [37655]

RINGHAM 1700+ LIN & RUT, ENG [35891]

RINGLEB ALL DITTICHENRODE, THU, GER [38637] : ALL BERLIN, BLN, GER [38637]

RINGNALDA PRE 1800 SNEEK, FRI, NL [38646]

RINGROSE 1900+ NSW, AUS [35771] : 1920 ROCKWOOD & WEDDIFIELD, ONT, CAN [36679] : 1920 NIPPISSING, ONT, CAN [36679] : ALL ENG [35998] : ALL NOTTINGHAM, ENG [36679] : PRE 1842 LET & GAL, IRL, NZ [36628]

RINGSTEAD C1800 NFK, ENG [35998]

RINGWOOD PRE 1820 CHALDON, SRY, ENG [34205]

RINN 1800S MCKILLOP & HURON, ONT, CAN [36727]

RINNAN 1700-1900 LEVANGER, N-TLG, NOR [38745]

RINNELL C1815 STOKE DAMEREL & PLYMOUTH, DEV, ENG [37330]

RINSCHE 1913-1953 LUEGDE, LIP, GER [38749]

RINTOUL PRE 1900 GLASGOW, DNB, SCT [33966] : PRE 1900 BURNT ISLAND, FIF, SCT [33966] : PRE 1790 KRS, SCT [37463] : ALL WORLDWIDE [35884] : ALL WORLDWIDE [35899]

RINTOULE 1860+ NHILL, VIC, AUS [35493]

RIORDAN 1800-1950 NEWBRIDGE & ASKEATON, LIM, IRL [34411] : PRE 1860 MILLTOWN, KER, IRL [35765] : PRE 1860 KILLARNEY, KER, IRL [35765] : 1800-1850 BROADFORD, CLA, IRL [37996] : 1834-1903 KER, IRL & AUS [33926] : 1830-1900 COR, IRL & AUS [37134] : ALL WORLDWIDE [35875]

RIOUX ALL QUE, CAN [34344]

RIPBOUTH 1750+ RAINHAM, KEN, ENG [37677]

RIPLEY C1800+ SSX, ENG [33812] : 1700-1800 HECKMONDWIKE, WRY, ENG [34328] : PRE 1800 COVERHAM & HORSEHOUSE, NRY, ENG [37498] : PRE 1780 MASHAM, NRY, ENG [37498] : DAVID 1857 HINGHAM, MA, USA [38193]

RIPP 1740-1780 BERSTHEIM, ALS, FRA & GER [38528]

RIPPATH (SEE REDPATH [35822])

RIPPER 1800+ ELTHAM, LND, ENG [34927]

RIPPEY PRE 1780 NC, USA [37786]

RIPPMANN C1700 GER [38598]

RIPPON 1850+ VIC, AUS [37152]

RIRIE ALL LND & KEN, ENG [35182]

RISAR PRE 1684 ENG [37886]

RISBRIDGER ALL SRY, ENG [36179]

RISBY 1830+ MAITLAND & GLEN INNES, NSW, AUS [34971] : 1807+ HOBART, TAS, VIC & SA, AUS

[34971] : 1750+ COCKFIELD, SFK, ENG [34020] : PRE 1762 KETTLEBASTON, SFK, ENG [37655]

RISEBOROUGH ALL NORWICH, NFK, ENG [36473]

RISEBROW 1980-1990 JSY, CHI [34249] : 1850-1990 CROMER & NORWICH, NFK, ENG [34249] : 1900-1990 LONG ISLAND, NY, USA [34249]

RISHTON PRE 1840 LAN, ENG [38293]

RISK 1750 LONDONDERRY, IRL [34844]

RISLEY PRE 1906 LAN, ENG [38286] : 1848-1924 WASHINGTON CO., AR, USA [35301]

RISON (SEE RESIN) [38080]

RISSMAN 1900S PARRAMATTA, NSW, AUS [36316]

RISTE ALL WORLDWIDE [35868]

RISTOW 1700-1800 POS, GER [37535]

RITCHETT 1794+ ASLACKBY, LIN, ENG [34421]

RITCHIE PRE 1914 TYNONG, VIC, AUS [34036] : WILLIAM JOHN 1862 WALLAMBA RIVER, NSW, AUS [36371] : 1865 LANE COVE, NSW, AUS [37963] : 1855 MEROO, NSW, AUS [37963] : 1860+ INDIA [35136] : 1820+ RANDLTOWN, ANT, IRL [34407] : PRE 1862 FER, IRL [35083] : PRE 1900 KILREA, LDY, IRL [36529] : C1850 BELFAST, ANT, IRL & CAN [36677] : PRE 1820 SCONE, PER, SCT [33869] : 1700-1800 AUCHENTIBBER, ELN & WLN, SCT [34107] : C1750 CARMICHAEL, LKS, SCT [34118] : C1900 GRANGEMOUTH, STI, SCT [34381] : C1806 DALRY, AYR, SCT [34972] : PRE 1860 WATTEN, CAI, SCT [35136] : PRE 1811 ELGIN, MOR, SCT [35261] : 1800+ INVERNESS, INV, SCT [35355] : 1830+ DALMELLINGTON, AYR, SCT [35798] : 1700S KIRKCONNEL, DFS, SCT [35858] : 1830S SANQUHAR, DFS, SCT [35966] : PRE 1900 PITSLIGO, ABD, SCT [36061] : ALL ABD, SCT [36429] : 1800+ ST CYRUS, KCD, SCT [36971] : C1800 FORFAR, ANS, SCT [37172] : ALL PER, SCT & NZ [33981] : 1825+ ONEIDA, NY, USA [36974]

RITER 1810+ WATERLOO CO., ONT, CAN [37492]

RITMEESTER 1860+ AUS [35367] : PRE 1860 NL [35367] : ALL WORLDWIDE [35367]

RITTAOJA ALL FIN [38445] : ALL MN, USA [38445]

RITTER 1898-1937 MELBOURNE, VIC, AUS [34794] : PRE 1695 BAD, GER [36972] : 1700+ BINGEN, PRUSSER, GER [37993] : FRANKLIN 1700-1900S DRESDEN, PSA, GER & USA [35304] : 1760+ FRANKLIN CO., VA, USA [37004] : 1800+ UNION CO., IN, USA [37004] : ALL NY & PA, USA [37502] : PRE 1820 ASHEVILLE, NC, USA [38196] : SAMUEL 1846-1908 MCDONOUGH CO., IL, USA [38371] : SAMUEL 1822+ UNION CO., PA, USA [38371]

RITTMEISTER ALL WORLDWIDE [35367]

RIVE 1620-1700 GOURNAY & POITIERS, PCH, FRA [34514]

RIVEROLL 1895+ CA, USA [38059]

RIVERS ALL ALDERMASTON, BRK, ENG [34002] : 1700+ BATTERSEA, LND, ENG [34664] : 1720+ SFK, ENG [36093] : 1600-1850 IPSWICH, SFK, ENG [36588] : ALL EAST HAGBOURNE, BRK, ENG [37743] : 1700-1800 ALL CANNINGS, WIL, ENG [37843]

RIVET C1818 PARIS, FRA [35414]

RIVETT 1836+ SA, AUS [34179] : 1800-1860 NFK, ENG [34179]

RIVIERE 1925-1950 CORNWALL, ONT, CAN [34242]

RIVINGTON ALL TIP, IRL [34060]

RIVITT 1798+ WILBY, NTH, ENG [35921]

RIX 1849+ MARULAN, NSW, AUS [34009] : PRE 1849 NFK, ENG [34009] : 1680S LND, ENG [35261] : PRE 1750 ENG [38460]

RIXON ALL NSW, AUS [35731] : 1770+ CARISBROOK, IOW, ENG [35342] : ALL WORLDWIDE [35159]

ROACH CAPT. JOHN 1820+ MELBOURNE & SEYMOUR, VIC, AUS **[35077]** : 1863 + VIC, AUS **[37114]** : ALL CORNWALL & BIRMINGHAM, ONT & MI, CAN & USA **[37503]** : 1834 LETCOMBE, BRK, ENG **[34120]** : C1800 KEN, ENG **[34239]** : 1913 BRIGHTON, SSX, ENG **[34384]** : 1930-1940 ST PANCRAS, LND, ENG **[34384]** : JOHN (R.N.) 1780+ ENG **[35077]** : PRE 1854 TOWEDNACK, COM, ENG **[35192]** : C1800 ST IVES, CON, ENG **[35747]** : C1800 HORSLEYDOWN, LND, ENG **[35772]** : 1800+ REDRUTH, CON, ENG **[36266]** : ALL ST IVES, CON, ENG **[36506]** : ALL BELFAST, ANT, IRL **[33842]** : 1841 LIMERICK, CLA, IRL **[35123]** : ALL KILALLA, MAY, IRL **[35181]** : HENRIETTA 1630+ IRL **[36890]** : 1800-1826 MALLOW, COR, IRL **[36915]** : WILLIAM PRE 1800 VA, USA **[33757]** : DAVID 1770 PITT CO., NC, USA **[35328]** : C1840 OK, USA **[36934]** : PRE 1750 LOUDOUN CO., VA, USA **[36972]** : 1700-1850 SCOTT & HAWKINS CO., VA & TN, USA **[37539]** : 1750+ ALBANY CO., NY, USA **[38176]** : PRE 1900 MON, WLS & AUS **[34603]**

ROACH (SEE ROCHE) **[33957]** : **[38597]**

ROACHE JAMES C1842 TIPPERARY, TIP, IRL **[34266]**

ROACHE (SEE ROCHE) **[35100]**

ROADHOUSE 1600-1835 MONKFRYSTON, YKS, ENG **[37011]**

ROADLEY 1850+ LIN, ENG **[35515]** : 1800+ BINGHAM, NTT, ENG **[36892]** : C1765 BARNBY IN THE WILLOWS, NTT, ENG **[37007]**

ROADS 1600+ AYLESBURY & QUAINTON, BKM, ENG **[36494]** : PRE 1900 LONDON, SRY, BRK & SFK, ENG **[38512]**

ROALS C1830 STOGURSEY, SOM, ENG **[37112]**

ROAN 1820+ TROQUEER, KKD, SCT **[36254]**

ROB 1743 LONGFORGAN, PER, SCT **[35152]**

ROBARDS (SEE ROBERTS **[38060]**

ROBATI 1750+ COOK IS. **[35969]**

ROBB 1860S+ NSW, AUS **[33930]** : SAMUEL 1850+ WELLINGTON CO., ONT, CAN **[36697]** : C1846 LISLAID, TYR, IRL **[35057]** : SAMUEL 1800+ BELFAST &, TYR, IRL **[36697]** : 1840S+ ANS, SCT **[33930]** : 1880+ AYR, SCT **[34526]** : 1770-80 ERROL, PER, SCT **[35152]** : C1851 LOW BLANTYRE, LKS, SCT **[35565]** : JANET C1840+ KINCARDINE, PER, SCT **[35629]** : JANET PRE 1830 GLASGOW, LKS, SCT **[36294]** : 1730-1850 LARGO, FIF, SCT **[36776]** : 1830-1900 DUNDEE, ANS, SCT **[37988]** : ALL WHITBURN, WLN, SCT **[38489]** : C1800 ABD & ONT, SCT & CAN **[34203]** : 1835 OKMULGEE, OK, USA **[38012]**

ROBBERDS ALL WORLDWIDE **[37103]**

ROBBIE C1867 BOMBALA, NSW, AUS **[35414]** : PRE 1867 SCT **[35414]**

ROBBINS C1600 THEDDINGWORTH, LEI, ENG **[33791]** : PRE 1800 WINTERBOURNE & HOUGHTON, DOR, ENG **[34347]** : PRE 1750 OKEFORD FITZPAINE, DOR, ENG **[34347]** : PRE 1810 WATER EATON, BKM, ENG **[34633]** : PRE 1880 LND, ENG **[34819]** : 1880-1920 CERNE ABBAS, DOR, ENG **[36136]** : PRE 1800 STRETTON ON FOSSE, WAR, ENG **[36516]** : 1700S CHEDWORTH, GLS, ENG **[36585]** : C1793 GUNNISLAKE, CON, ENG **[36949]** : ALL WAR, ENG **[37404]** : CAROLA 1980 SHI, SCT **[34847]** : 1630-1760 PLYMOUTH, MA, USA **[37432]**

ROBENOLT ALL NY, PA, OR, OH, USA & GER **[37502]**

ROBENS PRE 1850 CT & NY, USA **[36319]**

ROBERG C1866 NORDFJORD, NOR **[38052]**

ROBERGE ALL FRA **[35617]**

ROBERSON ALL WAPENGO & BEGA, NSW, AUS **[34024]** : 1850S BIBBENLUKE, NSW, AUS **[34976]** : 1750+ BETHNAL GREEN, LND, ENG **[33963]** : 1852-1990 WATERBEACH, CAM, ENG **[34024]** : 1820 WATERBEACH, CAM, ENG **[34976]** : 1810-1930 BATH CO., KY, USA **[38089]**

ROBERT PRE 1700 ONEX, GE, CH **[38348]**

ROBERTS 1850S CASTLEMAINE, VIC, AUS **[34175]** : GEORGE C1836 AUS **[34444]** : PRE 1858 MOONTA, SA, AUS **[34683]** : 1857-1890 GIPPSLAND, VIC, AUS **[34697]** : 1850+ TAS, AUS **[35063]** : 1850+ NORTHERN RIVERS, NSW, AUS **[35117]** : 1880+ HORSHAM, VIC, AUS **[35476]** : 1865+ GREAT WESTERN, VIC, AUS **[35476]** : 1851+ JERRALONG & GOULBURN, NSW, AUS **[35506]** : 1850+ SUTTON FOREST, NSW, AUS **[35741]** : 1815-1819 PARRAMATTA, NSW, AUS **[35741]** : GEORGE W. 1850+ PADDINGTON, NSW, AUS **[36367]** : 1824+ HOBART, TAS, AUS **[37954]** : GEORGE C1837-1924 TAS, AUS & ENG **[35799]** : 1860+ PEI, CAN **[37540]** : PRE 1845 GSY, CHI **[35330]** : ALL JSY, ALD & GSY, CHI **[35891]** : JAMES PRE 1830 SMETHWICK, STS, ENG **[33776]** : CAROLINE 1814+ SOUTHAMPTON, HAM, ENG **[34065]** : 18101-1850 LIVERPOOL, LAN, ENG **[34099]** : ALL SOM, ENG **[34131]** : PRE 1850 GEDNEY, LIN, ENG **[34144]** : PRE 1830 MADRON, CON, ENG **[34197]** : AUBREY 1885 SAL, ENG **[34231]** : PRE 1800 STANTON ST BERNARD, WIL, ENG **[34291]** : 1750+ MANNINGFORD BRUCE, WIL, ENG **[34291]** : 1700+ CAMBORNE, CON, ENG **[34414]** : 1650-1750 COTHERIDGE, WOR, ENG **[34552]** : WILLIAM PRE 1719 ST COLUMB MAJOR, CON, ENG **[34573]** : 1800-1900 LIVERPOOL, LAN, ENG **[34762]** : ALL LANDRAKE, CON, ENG **[34897]** : 1860 BIGGLESWADE, BDF, ENG **[35024]** : C1770 ST COLUMB MAJOR, CON, ENG **[35034]** : PRE 1860 WIL, ENG **[35063]** : PRE 1837 PRESTON, LAN, ENG **[35117]** : PRE 1810 EXETER, DEV, ENG **[35211]** : C1800 PRESTON, LAN, ENG **[35225]** : C1877 LONDON, ENG **[35363]** : ALL NBL & YKS, ENG **[35540]** : PRE 1840 SFK, ENG **[35556]** : CHARLES 1813+ GREENWICH & LANGTON GREEN, KEN, ENG **[35560]** : CHARLES C1785 SRY, ENG **[35560]** : 1870+ WIMBORNE, DOR, ENG **[35587]** : 1786-1815 MONMOUTH, HEF, ENG **[35741]** : 1835+ LIVERPOOL, LAN, ENG **[36168]** : MARY 1630+ COWFOLD, SSX, ENG **[36212]** : 1700+ CLERKENWELL, MDX, ENG **[36256]** : GEORGE W. 1800+ TUNBRIDGE WELLS, KEN, ENG **[36367]** : 1900-1950 BECKENHAM, KEN, ENG **[36439]** : PRE 1850 BROSELEY, SAL, ENG **[36478]** : 1800+ YKS, ENG **[36568]** : C1752 SUDBURY, SFK, ENG **[36949]** : 1850-99 ISLINGTON, MDX, ENG **[37070]** : JOHN PRE 1800 ST GEORGE HAN SQ, MDX, ENG **[37083]** : JOHN FRANCIS 1850+ LAMBETH, SRY, ENG **[37083]** : GEORGE C. 1820S POPLAR, MDX, ENG **[37083]** : G.H.J. 1850+ LAMBETH, SRY, ENG **[37083]** : CHARLES EDWIN 1850+ LAMBETH, SRY, ENG **[37083]** : PRE 1820 BIRLINGHAM & PERSHORE, WOR, ENG **[37097]** : EMMA 1800+ SOTHERTON, SFK, ENG **[37191]** : 1850+ BIRMINGHAM, WAR, ENG **[37258]** : ALL YEOVIL, SOM & DOR, ENG **[37269]** : THOMAS C1850 LIVERPOOL, LAN, ENG **[37330]** : 1879 YKS, ENG **[37493]** : PRE 1820 GOUDHURST, KEN, ENG **[37652]** : PRE 1850 WITHIEL, COLAN & KENWYN, CON, ENG **[37814]** : PRE 1850 LANIVET, ROCHE & ST AUSTELL, CON, ENG **[37814]** : 1700-1800 GLS, ENG **[37829]** : 1840+ LANGTOFT, LIN, ENG **[37837]** : 1850S NEWCASTLE, NBL, ENG **[37853]** : 1800S ALPHINGTON, DEV, ENG **[37954]** : 1800S

LONDON, MDX, ENG **[37954]** : PRE 1840
TOOTING, SRY, ENG **[37986]** : PRE 1830
AMPTHILL, BDF, ENG **[38075]** : 1810-1876
LYDBROOK, GLS, ENG **[38275]** : PRE 1850 DEAL,
KEN, ENG **[38288]** : 1700-1800 DOVER, KEN, ENG
[38381] : JANE C1829 LONDON, MDX, ENG **[38389]**
: C1841-1895 CHS, ENG & NZ **[34651]** : 1860+
TRURO, CON & NV, ENG & USA **[38050]** : 1820S
GIBRALTAR **[34175]** : PRE 1825 HILLSBOROUGH,
DOW, IRL **[34895]** : JOSEPH PRE 1841 NEWTOWN
BARRY, WEX, IRL **[35084]** : 1750-1850 COR, IRL
[35494] : 1750-1900 CAV, IRL **[35494]** : 1700S-1900S
WATERFORD, WAT, IRL & ENG **[35738]** : 1875+
WESTPORT, NZ **[38275]** : 1800S EDINBURGH, SCT
[35797] : C1750 PHILADELPHIA, PA, USA **[34096]** :
1870 TX, USA **[35325]** : C1850 MARSHALL, AK,
USA **[36899]** : C1800 KY & NC, USA **[36923]** : PRE
1870 WI & MI, USA **[37446]** : 1885+ BOSTON,
SUFFOLK, MA, USA **[37540]** : 1800-1900
BALTIMORE CITY, MD, USA **[37583]** : DECIE PRE
1900 WILLIAMSBURG & FLORENCE, CO, USA
[37671] : 1900+ HOUGHTON & WAYNE CO., MI,
USA **[37814]** : 1625 YORK, ME, USA **[38022]** : ALL
NC, USA **[38060]** : PRUDENCE 1870 MONROE CO.,
KY, USA **[38109]** : DANIEL 1850 ESTILL CO., KY,
USA **[38109]** : 1750+ BALBOUR CO., WV, USA
[38235] : C1880 SHELBY, IL, USA **[38263]** : C1830
AMLWCH, AGY, WLS **[35476]** : 1600S
HAWARDEN, FLN, WLS **[35899]** : PRE 1900
LLANYCIL, MER, WLS **[36761]** : 1700S MOSTYN,
FLN, WLS **[37221]** : PRE 1862 CRIGGION, MGY,
WLS **[37242]** : PRE 1862 ALBERBURY, MGY, WLS
[37242] : PRE 1890 GROSMONT, MON, WLS **[37320]**
: 1840+ BRIDGEND, GLA, WLS **[37401]** : ALL
TREMEIRCHION, FLN, WLS **[37667]** : JOHN PRE
1870 FFESTINIOG & TRAWSFYNYDD, MER, WLS
[37671] : 1750-1890 ABERDARON, CAE, WLS **[37858]**
: PRE 1850 WREXHAM, DEN, WLS **[37961]** : 1810-
1876 NANTYGLO, BRE, WLS **[38275]** : PRE 1875
FLN, WLS **[38437]**

ROBERTSHAW 1700-1768 THORNTON, YKS, ENG
[34793]

ROBERTSON 1852+ BALLARAT, VIC, AUS **[35223]** :
RICHARD 1901+ ENFIELD, NSW, AUS **[37146]** :
1852+ SWANSWATER, VIC, AUS **[38077]** :
ALEXANDER 1850+ BUNINYONG, VIC, AUS
[38082] : NATHANIEL 1900+ OTTAWA, ONT, CAN
[34234] : JAMES 1840+ COLOMBO, CEYLON
[33886] : PRE 1770 ESS, ENG **[35642]** : ALL
MONKWEARMOUTH, DUR, ENG **[36046]** : 1840S
ROCKLAND ST MARY, NFK, ENG **[36843]** :
SARAH C1839 IRL **[33951]** : JAMES C1800 CUPAR,
FIF, SCT **[33886]** : 1740+ INVERESK, MLN, SCT
[33986] : 1800+ MUTHILL TILLICOULTRY, CLK,
SCT **[33996]** : PRE 1850 SCT **[33999]** : PRE 1835
METHVEN, PER, SCT **[34140]** : PRE 1830
GLENRINNES, BAN, SCT **[34192]** : 1820+
AUCHTERDERRAN, FIF, SCT **[34260]** : 1770+
DOLPHINGTON, LKS, SCT **[34290]** : 1836 SKYE,
INV, SCT **[34421]** : ALL BLAIR ATHOL, PER, SCT
[34558] : PRE 1850 EDINBURGH, ELN, SCT **[34611]** :
1700-1900 GLASGOW, LKS, SCT **[34624]** : JEROME
1775+ WALLS, SHI, SCT **[34627]** : UMPHREY
1770+ WALLS, SHI, SCT **[34627]** : 1830+
LONGHOPE, OKI, SCT **[34688]** : PRE 1850
BO'NESS, WLN, SCT **[34733]** : PRE 1900 DUNDEE,
ANS, SCT **[34758]** : PRE 1860 LKS, SCT **[34958]** :
1770S ABERFELDY, PER, SCT **[34991]** : C1830
CUMBRAE, BUT, SCT **[35158]** : PRE 1830
MILLPORT, BUT, SCT **[35158]** : C1835-8 DUNDEE,
ANS, SCT **[35184]** : 1750S AUCHENBOWE, STI, SCT
[35186] : JEAN C1786 BENDOCHY, PER, SCT

[35196] : 1800+ ELIE & AUCHTERDERRAN, FIF,
SCT **[35223]** : 1826 DUNDEE, ANS, SCT **[35251]** :
ALL MILTON OF STRATHBRAAN, PER, SCT
[35334] : 1848+ ST MONANCE, FIF, SCT **[35347]** :
ALL LKS, SCT **[35415]** : ALL MLN, SCT **[35415]** :
ALL KNOCKANDOO & ELGIN, MOR, SCT **[35460]**
: PRE 1852 GLASGOW, LKS, SCT **[35473]** : 1750+
HADDINGTON, ELN, SCT **[35475]** : 1700+
KILMANY, FIF, SCT **[35627]** : PRE 1850
CUMBRAE, SCT **[35853]** : C1740-1840 KINROSS,
KRS, SCT **[35885]** : 1830 LESLIE, FIF, SCT **[35912]** :
PRE 1800 CARLUKE, LKS, SCT **[35929]** : PRE 1840
ANS, SCT **[35950]** : ROBERT PRE 1880
EDINBURGH, MLN, SCT **[35962]** : ROBERT PRE
1880 EARLSTON, BEW, SCT **[35962]** : 1856+
NORTHMAVINE, SHI, SCT **[36237]** : PRE 1880
ABERDEEN, ABD, SCT **[36241]** : 1700-1850
PITNACREE, PER, SCT **[36246]** : 1700-1850
LOANING, FORNETH, PER, SCT **[36246]** : 1820S ST
ANDREWS, FIF, SCT **[36292]** : JANE 1820-1860
ABD, SCT **[36316]** : ALL STRAUN, PER, SCT **[36362]**
: PRE 1810 WHITSOME, BEW, SCT **[36497]** : PRE
1830 FORRES, MOR, SCT **[36673]** : JAMES A. 1800
PAISLEY, RFW & WIG, SCT **[36814]** : PRE 1800
KINROSS, KRS, SCT **[36874]** : C1820 KING
EDWARD, BAN, SCT **[36877]** : 1600-1800
DRUMBLADE, ABD, SCT **[36951]** : ALL
RUTHERGLEN, LKS, SCT **[36955]** : 1800+
RENFREW, RFW, SCT **[37073]** : PRE 1790
KILCONQUHAR, FIF, SCT **[37146]** : 1800
STROMNESS, OKI, SCT **[37170]** : 1800 ROX, SCT
[37170] : PRE 1800 GARVALD, ELN, SCT **[37353]** :
ELIZ 1872-1940 NIGG, KCD, SCT **[37476]** : BILL
1950 ABERDEEN, SCT **[37621]** : C1858 CLK, SCT
[37631] : PRE 1850 IRVINE & AYR, AYR, SCT
[37736] : JOHANNA M. 1855 SCT **[37769]** : PRE 1890
AULDEARN, NAI, SCT **[37772]** : 1800-1870
EDINBURGH, SCT **[37806]** : C1813 ST NINIANS,
STI, SCT **[37834]** : C1820 JEDBURGH, ROX, SCT
[37834] : 1820+ MUSSELBURGH, MLN, SCT **[37834]**
: 1732+ GLASGOW, LKS, SCT **[37834]** : PRE 1784
DULL, PER, SCT **[37852]** : PRE 1805 MOULIN, PER,
SCT **[37852]** : PRE 1860 LKS, SCT **[37923]** : ALL
RERRICK & KIRKCUDBRIGHT, KKD, SCT
[37972] : MARGARET C1759 BARR, AYR, SCT
[38067] : PRE 1852 HARRIS, INV, SCT **[38077]** : PRE
1790 GLASGOW, SCT **[38460]** : 1848 BENHOLM,
KCD, SCT **[38470]** : PRE 1811 LUNAN, ANS, SCT
[38483] : PETER 1799+ FIF, SCT **[38595]** : JOHN
1839-1900 ST LOUIS, MO, WA & CA, USA **[33754]** :
1800+ APPLING, GA, USA **[38185]** : 1770+ USA &
CAN **[38261]**

ROBESON PRE 1856 REIGATE, SRY, ENG **[37138]**
ROBEY ALL FARLEY, WIL, ENG **[38357]**
ROBIATO ALL PHILIPPINE **[38730]**
ROBICHAUD PRE 1850 KENT CO., NB, CAN **[38447]**
ROBIN 1870S CHILTERN, VIC, AUS **[35039]** : 1800+
ADELAIDE, SA, AUS & ENG **[35555]** : 1802+ GSY,
CHI **[35039]**
ROBINETT 1700S ENG **[37829]**
ROBINI 1700-1920 WORLDWIDE **[37348]**
ROBINS 1830+ HOBART, TAS, AUS **[34550]** : 1830-
1850 BRISBANE, QLD, AUS **[35454]** : PRE 1800
DEV, ENG **[34319]** : PRE 1820 TEBWORTH &
TODDINGTON, BDF, ENG **[34633]** : PRE 1900
PORTSEA, HAM, ENG **[35247]** : FREDERICK
C1874 ENG **[35247]** : 1890-1920 SUTTON
COLDFIELD, WAR, ENG **[37068]** : PRE 1885
EASTERHOUSES, DUR, ENG **[37068]** : 1770-1800
UPPER SWELL, GLS, ENG **[37320]** : 1770-1800
STOW ON THE WOLD, GLS, ENG **[37320]** : 1841
HARDINGTON MANDEVILLE, SOM, ENG **[37378]**

: C1790-1820 BIRMINGHAM, WAR, ENG [37943] :
1810-1860 LONDON, ENG [37943] : PRE 1815
DAUPHIN CO., PA, USA [37574]

ROBINSON HENRY 1850+ CASTLEMAINE, VIC,
AUS [33846] : 1798-1860 SYDNEY & APPLIN, NSW,
AUS [33934] : 1850-1900 VIC, AUS [34641] : PRE 1930
TOOWOOMBA, QLD, AUS [34868] : PRE 1900
IPSWICH, QLD, AUS [34868] : PRE 1870S VIC, AUS
[34937] : 1863+ BINGARA, NSW, AUS [35393] :
ANDREW 1880+ ADAMSTOWN, NSW, AUS
[35396] : THOMAS 1850+ PROSPECT, NSW, AUS
[35409] : 1863+ MAUDE, VIC, AUS [35439] : 1860+
MARYBOROUGH, VIC, AUS [35589] : 1900
RICHMOND, NSW, AUS [35769] : 1907
RICHMOND, MELBOURNE, VIC, AUS [35769] :
1836+ AUS [36362] : 1870-1900 RAYMOND
TERRACE, NSW, AUS [36682] : JOHN 1854+
OBERON, NSW, AUS [37556] : WILLIAM 1854+
SALTWATER RIVER, VIC, AUS [37965] : WILLIAM
PRE 1854 SALTWATER RIVER, VIC, AUS [37965] :
MARY JANE 1866 GEELONG, VIC, AUS [37982] :
1800+ BRANTFORD, DEREHAM & NIAGARA,
ONT, CAN [34357] : 1800+ JARVIS, ONT, CAN
[34497] : C1850 LANARK CO., ONT, CAN [34988] :
CHRISTOPHER 1750+ CAPE BRETON, NS, CAN
[35328] : 1840+ DUNDAS CO., ONT, CAN [36662] :
JOHN 1861-71 EUPHEMIA & LAMBTON, ONT,
CAN [37518] : JOHN 1861-71 ENNISKILLEN &
PLYMPTON, ONT, CAN [37518] : PHILIP 1874
LAMBTON CO., ONT, CAN [37518] : 1840+ JSY,
CHI [34969] : 1752+ EAST BRANDON, DUR, ENG
[33774] : PRE 1856 RICHMOND, YKS, ENG [33813] :
PRE 1800 BILLINGSHURST, SSX, ENG [34112] :
PRE 1900 DUR, ENG [34301] : PRE 1800 SCALBY
AREA, NRY, ENG [34333] : C1829 EGTON &
BACKBARROW, LAN, ENG [34374] : C1854+
SWARTHMOOR & ULVERSTON, LAN, ENG
[34374] : 1700+ NFK, ENG [34572] : 1700+ SFK,
ENG [34572] : PRE 1890 WHITTLESEY &
CHATTERIS, CAM, ENG [34581] : PRE 1870 LAN,
ENG [34696] : ELLEN 1812-1850 ROCHDALE &
SHAWCLOUGH, LAN, ENG [34721] : PRE 1850
FINSBURY & STEPNEY, LND, ENG [34776] : PRE
1850 LND, ENG [34819] : ACHILLES C1830
CHELTENHAM, GLS, ENG [34851] : EDWARD
C1880+ CAMBERWELL, LND, ENG [34862] : PRE
1851 HORNINGSEA, CAM, ENG [34976] : PRE 1840
KNARESBOROUGH, YKS, ENG [35098] :
ANDREW 1840+ BYKER & NEWCASTLE, NBL,
ENG [35396] : 1900+ CAMBERWELL, SRY & LND,
ENG [35495] : 1792 MARYLEBONE, LND, ENG
[35560] : PRE 1770 ESS, ENG [35642] : 1800-1850
OAKHAM, KEN, ENG [35861] : HENRY PRE 1812
ISLINGTON, MDX, ENG [35867] : JOHN PRE 1830
RANDWICK, CUL, ENG [35867] : PRE 1790
TETNEY, LIN, ENG [35983] : PRE 1790 WILSDEN,
WRY, ENG [36011] : WILLIAM 1815-1880
AMBLESIDE, CUL & LAN, ENG [36082] : 1750+
NEW CROSS, KEN, ENG [36093] : 1750+
STRATFORD, ESS, ENG [36093] : PRE 1760
DUDLEY, WOR, ENG [36110] : PRE 1850
BAILDON & GUISELEY, WRY, ENG [36159] :
SAMUEL 1780+ LEWES & BRIGHTON, SSX, ENG
[36167] : JOSEPH 1870-1900 STOCKPORT, CHS,
ENG [36214] : CAROLINE 1865-1900 ISLINGTON,
MDX, ENG [36214] : JAMES 1865-1900
ISLINGTON, MDX, ENG [36214] : C1760
PRESTON, LAN, ENG [36271] : PRE 1933
NORBURY, LND, ENG [36313] : 1645 CLEASBY,
YKS, ENG [36358] : 1800-1920 YORK, NRY, ENG
[36397] : PRE 1790 DARFIELD, YKS, ENG [36426] :
PRE 1899 MANSFIELD, NTT, ENG [36475] : 1750-

1840 HELPRINGHAM, LIN, ENG [36682] : W.J.
1853-1900 SOUTHWARK, LND, ENG [36717] : R.E.
1830+ ST PANCRAS, MDX & YKS, ENG [36717] :
JAMES 1820 MANCHESTER, LAN, ENG [36818] :
1700+ NATLAND, WES, ENG [36821] : MARK
ANTHONY PRE 1810 YORK, NRY, ENG [37083] :
HENRY PRE 1840 YORK, NRY, ENG [37083] : PRE
1850 LYTHE, YKS, ENG [37094] : PRE 1900 STS,
ENG [37098] : 1810+ BIRMINGHAM, WAR, ENG
[37145] : C1864 GUISBOROUGH, NRY, ENG [37204]
: 1670-1720 CUL, ENG [37233] : PRE 1850
ROTHERHAM, YKS, ENG [37245] : C1775
TEDDINGTON, MDX, ENG [37345] : 1790-1840
SHADWELL, LND, ENG [37369] : THOMAS PRE
1837 AUDLEY & AREA, STS, ENG [37406] : 1700-
1800 NETHER COULDERTON, CUL, ENG [37858] :
1700-1800 SESSAY, NRY, ENG [37872] : PRE 1880
SRY, ENG [37901] : PRE 1812 NBL, ENG [37901] :
1775+ LONDON, MDX, ENG [37923] : C1800-80
DUR, ENG [37987] : PRE 1850 YKS, ENG [38039] :
1785-1900 IRESHOPEBURN, DUR, ENG [38053] :
1800+ MORESBY, CUL, ENG [38067] : PETER
1840-1925 DISTINGTON, CUL, ENG [38067] : 1830-
1860 MANCHESTER, LAN, ENG [38248] : 1760S
WRAY, LAN, ENG [38283] : PRE 1850 MALTON,
ERY, ENG [38457] : PRE 1900 GREYSTOKE, CUL,
ENG [38457] : PRE 1820 ENG [38730] : PRE 1900
YKS & VIC, ENG & AUS [34301] : ROBERT 1800+
MANCHESTER, LAN, ENG & AUS [38204] :
HENRY 1800-50 HAMBURG, HBG, GER [33846] :
JANE PRE 1840 DUNGANNON & MOY, TYR, IRL
[33816] : C1850 IRL [34395] : PRE 1840 ARM, IRL
[34429] : PRE 1821 MUCKAMORE, ANT, IRL [34895]
: GODFREY 1750+ DUB, IRL [35093] : 1830S FER,
IRL [35136] : JOHN PRE 1830 LDY, IRL [35371] :
PRE 1850 GLENBOY, LET, IRL [35406] : PRE 1860
ALTNAGELVIN, LDY, IRL [35545] : PRE 1930
WAT, IRL [35639] : ALL BALLYMENA, ANT, IRL
[36750] : 1800S PORTADOWN, ARM, IRL [36833] :
1840 ROKEL, ANT, IRL [36887] : PRE 1850 LARNE
& GLENARM, ANT, TYR & FER, IRL [37246] :
JOHN PRE 1854 LOUGH NEAGH & LURGAN,
ARM, IRL [37556] : PRE 1850 ANT, IRL [37923] :
1770-1825 LDY, IRL [38216] : FRANCES PRE 1820
ANT, IRL [38222] : JAMES 1840S LEGG,
INNISHMACSAINT, FER, IRL [38396] : ELIZ. ANN
PRE 1800 TYR, IRL [38536] : C1833 IRL & SCT
[37180] : 1900+ MEXICO [35935] : 1850-1900
NELSON, NZ [34641] : JAMES 1840 MOTUEKA &
NELSON, NZ [36818] : 1850+ LINLITHGOW, STI,
SCT [35953] : WILLIAM C1835 GLASGOW, SCT
[37965] : PRE 1800 ORKNEY ISLANDS, SCT & SWE
[34357] : PRE 1850 UK [37804] : MARTHA 1925 SAN
FRANCISCO, CA, USA [33754] : HEZEKIAH PRE
1790 CUMBERLAND, VA, USA [33757] : GEORGE
PRE 1823 PROVIDENCE, RI, USA [35258] : JAMES
H. 1748-1784 CHARLESTON, SC, USA [35265] :
JAMES H. 1725-1786 CATAMBA CO., NC, USA
[35265] : 1800 FRANKLIN CO., PA, USA [35276] :
CHRISTOPHER PRE 1750 EXETER, NH, USA
[35328] : C1866 DE KALB CO., GA, USA [36903] :
1760-1775 CAMDEN DISTRICT, SC, USA [37460] :
PRE 1760 VA, USA [37460] : C1890 CALEDONIA,
MI, USA [37521] : CHRISTOPHER 1750S ESSEX,
MA, USA [37585] : PRE 1790 LINCOLN CO., NC,
USA [37587] : 1825-1875 PHILADELPHIA, PA, USA
[37740] : ISSACHER 1753-1833 SARATOGA CO.,
NY, USA [38140] : PRE 1800 CROSS CREEK, PA,
USA [38708] : 1750 ST MICHAEL, BARBADOS,
W.INDIES [35769]

ROBINSON-NESBIT C1843-6 FARNHAM, EAST,
CAN [37518]

ROBISON JOHN 1739+ BALDERNOCK, STI, SCT [36880] : 1842-1850 LOUISVILLE, KY, USA [36965]

ROBJANT 1800S SHOREDITCH ST LEONARDS, LND, ENG [36642]

ROBLEY 1770S COBHAM, SRY, ENG [35557]

ROBSON 1839-1870 PEEL'S RIVER, NSW, AUS [34251] : 1818+ SYDNEY & SHOALHAVEN, NSW, AUS [35117] : 1850+ LAL LAL, VIC, AUS [35475] : 1890+ NEWCASTLE, NSW, AUS [35874] : C1842 BUCTON, NRY, ENG [33863] : PRE 1813 HALTWHISTLE, NBL, ENG [34452] : PRE 1900 DUR, ENG [34951] : 1880S BARRINGTON, NBL, ENG [35026] : PRE 1818 BRISTOL, ENG [35117] : 1830 HEXHAM, NBL, ENG [35404] : 1800S COWPEN, NBL, ENG [35874] : ALL LONDON, ENG [36152] : ANTHONY C1816-1888 PRUDHOE, NBL, ENG [36244] : JOHN C1798+ OVINGHAM, NBL, ENG [36244] : PRE 1862 NEWCASTLE UPON TYNE, NBL, ENG [36270] : 1900+ TANTOBIE, DUR, ENG [36503] : PRE 1852 MARKET DRAYTON, STS, ENG [36604] : 1800S SHOTLEY BRIDGE, DUR, ENG [36847] : 1800+ ST PANCRAS, LND, ENG [36863] : JOHN 1777+ BLACKFRIARS, LND, ENG [36880] : 1700-1900 SLINGSBY, NRY, ENG [37281] : 1700-1900 WRELTON, NRY, ENG [37281] : PRE 1850 HEXHAM, NBL, ENG [37395] : 1750-1800 MONKWEARMOUTH, DUR, ENG [37859] : ALL WESTRAY, OES [35002] : 1760-1785 MORTON, DFS, SCT [38117]

ROBY ALL LIVERPOOL, LAN, ENG [38074] : 1838-1911 LOGAN, OH & MI, USA [36910]

ROBYNS 1765+ ST JUST IN PENWITH, CON, ENG [35138]

ROCH 1800-1832 ALSACE LORRAINE, FRA [38092] : 1800-1832 BADEN BADEN, GER [38092]

ROCHE C1880+ MELBOURNE, VIC, AUS [33957] : PRE 1875 MOOROOPNA, VIC, AUS [34170] : 1840-1890 SCONE & ST GEORGE, NSW & QLD, AUS [38592] : 1840-1890 QUIRINDI & MURRURUNDI, NSW, AUS [38592] : 1850-1890 LIVERPOOL, LAN & CHS, ENG [34526] : PRE 1867 BALLYHOOLY, COR, IRL [33957] : 1800-1840 KILKENNY, KIK, IRL [34018] : 1854 CLONMEL, TIP, IRL [35100] : 1830+ CORK, COR, IRL [35100] : 1800+ COR & WAT, IRL [35190] : PRE 1863 TIP, IRL [37114] : PRE 1890 IRL [38303] : PRE 1815 AGHADA, COR, IRL [38597] : 1875+ PT CHALMERS, OTAGO, NZ [33957] : ALL BIRMINGHAM & CORNWALL, MI & ONT, USA & CAN [37503] : 1850+ ROCKFORD, IL & WI, USA & IRL [37796]

ROCHESTER PRE 1875 NORTH SHIELDS, NBL, ENG [35009] : 1770S LESBURY, NBL, ENG [36364]

ROCHFORD C1800 CLA, IRL [35032]

ROCHON 1800S TERREBONNE & MONTREAL, QUE, CAN [33934]

ROCHTE 1800-1832 ALSACE LORRAINE, FRA [38092] : 1800-1832 BADEN BADEN, GER [38092] : 1845-1900 HENRY CO., OH, USA [38092] : 1846-1864 WOOD CO., OH, USA [38092] : 1886-1944 MI, USA [38092] : 1830-1845 NY, USA [38092]

ROCK JOSEPH C1830-1880 QUE, CAN [35284] : PRE 1800 HEF, ENG [34929] : C1820 DARMSTADT, HES, GER [37022] : JOSEPH C1830-1880 FRANKLIN CO., VT, USA [35284]

ROCKALL 1800-1900 OXF & MDX, ENG [34337]

ROCKER ALL WORLDWIDE [34731]

ROCKETT PRE 1870 STOCKLAND, DEV, ENG [35701] : PRE 1880 TAUNTON, SOM, ENG [37325] : PRE 1850 STOKE DAMEREL, DEV, ENG [37410] : PRE 1900 WAT, IRL [37519] : PRE 1900 CARRICK ON SUIR, TIP, IRL [37519]

ROCKLIFF PRE 1850 KIRK SMEATON, YKS, ENG [35491] : PRE 1800 ALFORD, LIN, ENG [35491]

ROCKWELL PRE 1895 PA, USA [37787]

RODABAUGH 1870-1900 ST CLAIR CO., MO, USA [33760] : 1770-1810 WESTMORELAND CO., PA, USA [33760] : 1810-1880 DARKE CO., OH, USA [33760]

RODBERD C1790-1851 HASELBURY & WEST COKER, SOM, ENG [36161]

RODD 1800+ NSW, AUS [34902]

RODDA 1750-1900 GULVAL, CON, ENG [34535] : PRE 1857 CROWAN, CON, ENG [34750] : 1600-1700 SANCREED, CON, ENG [34760] : 1700-1900 CROWAN, CON, ENG [36130] : PRE 1800 PENZANCE, CON, ENG [36469] : C1760-1860 HAYLE, CON, ENG [36877] : 1845-1855 KEWEENAW CO., MI, USA [38009]

RODDAM PRE 1850 LANCHESTER, DUR, ENG [36270] : PRE 1774 CHESTER LE STREET, DUR, ENG [36270]

RODDAN PRE 1875 DFS, SCT [34617] : PRE 1830 GLASGOW, SCT [37133]

RODDICK 1798 DFS, SCT [36721]

RODDY PRE 1850 LOUGHGLINN, ROS, IRL [36504] : C1825 SCT [37513]

RODDY (SEE RODY) [34172]

RODE PRE 1700 DEN [38553] : PRE 1790 ANT, IRL [36271]

RODEK PRE 1860 PRAGUE AREA, BOHEMIA, CS [36963]

RODEN PRE 1774 WELLINGTON, SAL, ENG [34711] : 1689 WORFIELD, SAL, ENG [35794] : 1750+ WOR, ENG [35812] : ALL ENG [37846] : 1750-1875 MEERFELD & STEININGEN, RHEINLAND, GER [38534] : 1853+ HENNIGEN & WRIGHT COS., MN, USA [38534] : 1865+ COOK CO., IL, USA [38534] : 1848+ OZAUKEE & WASHINGTON CO., WI, USA [38534]

RODENBACH ALL USA [33760]

RODER 1750-1850 ZELLERFELD, NSA, GER [38643]

RODERICK 1860+ MORPETH, NSW, AUS [36362] : 1792 MD, USA [38121]

RODERIGO EMMA 1800 QLD, AUS [35361]

RODERIGUES 1700-1900 LIVERPOOL, LAN, ENG [35923]

RODERIQUE 1800-1900 NZ [35923]

RODERMOND PRE 1750 NYEVEEN, OIJ, NL [36283]

RODEY PRE 1870 NEW ENGLAND, NSW, AUS [36632]

RODGER PRE 1850 HAMILTON, LKS, SCT [34097] : C1750 LANARK, LKS, SCT [34118] : 1800S PER, SCT [34937]

RODGERS 1930+ BENDIGO, VIC, AUS [34568] : PRE 1900 DERBY, DBY, ENG [34909] : ALL LOU, IRL [35139] : 1700-1899 KILLYMAN, DUNGANNON, TYR, IRL [36080] : PRE 1850S KILLYBEGS AND SURROUNDS, DON, IRL [37745] : C1750+ ST JOHNSTON, DON, IRL & NZ [36258] : 1800+ EDINBURGH, MLN, SCT [34670] : 1700-1890 KILSPINDIE, PER, SCT [36653] : 1840-1880 NJ, USA [38733]

RODGERS (SEE ROGERS) [35599]

RODHAM (SEE RODDAM) [36270]

RODIER 1830-1900 BULLAROOK, VIC, AUS [34748] : 1830-1840 ADELAIDE, SA, AUS [34748]

RODMAN JOHAH 1802+ SOUTHERN DISTS., TAS, AUS [35816] : JONAH PRE 1802 CROMHALL, GLS, ENG [35816] : 1800-1820 JEFFERSON CO., OH, USA [36328]

RODNEY C1825 LONDON, ENG [34176]

RODONI 1800+ BIASCO, TI, CH [37116]

RODRIGUES 1880+ CONTRA COSTA CO., CA, USA [38323]

RODWAY PRE 1784 ALDERLEY, GLS, ENG [36113] : 1800-1900 WINTERBOURNE, GLS, ENG [37222]

RODWELL 1750-1850 SOUTH KIRKBY, WRY, ENG [33916] : PRE 1880 HOLBROOK, NFK, ENG [36468]

RODY 1800S CLOONE, LET, IRL [34172]

ROE 1850+ SIMCOE CO., ONT, CAN [34465] : ALL CAN [37427] : ALL LINTON, CAM, ENG [34772] : THOMAS 1780+ EDGMOND, SAL, ENG [35429] : 1700+ LIDLINGTON, BDF, ENG [35947] : ALL SHEPSHED, LEI, ENG [37295] : 1800+ PLYMOUTH, DEV, ENG [37985] : 1750+ BALLYCANEW, WEX, IRL [37244] : C1828+ DAILLY, AYR, SCT [38067] : ABRAHAM 1750-1825 COLUMBIA CO., NY, USA [36555] : MILLICENT 1800-1876 HORTON TOWN, NY, USA [36948]

ROE (SEE ROWE, JAMES [37556]

ROEBUCK 1820 WAKEFIELD, WRY, ENG [36606] : PRE 1870 HEPWORTH, WRY, ENG [37893]

ROELANDSE C1710 LEIDEN, ZUH, NL [38698]

ROELOFFZE ALL WORLDWIDE [34949]

ROELOFS ALL AMSTERDAM, NL [36894]

ROELOFSE ALL WORLDWIDE [34949]

ROEN 1750+ NES, HALLINGDAL, NOR [36905]

ROEPKE PRE 1881 STETTIN, POM, GER [38112]

ROES PRE 1850 LND, ENG & GER [34776]

ROESE PRE 1820 FRANKFURT AM MAIN, GER [35236]

ROESENER PRE 1850 OLDENBURG, SHO, GER [38648]

ROETGEN PRE 1788 DOSSEL, WARBURG, GER [37569]

ROETS PRE 1900 BARKLY EAST, CAPE, RSA [36459]

ROETTGER 1880 JACKSON, MO, USA [38320]

ROFE 1800+ ROBERTSBRIDGE, SSX, ENG [38488]

ROFFEY PRE 1829 ISLEWORTH, LND, ENG [33860] : 1800-1900 WOLVERHAMPTON, STS, ENG [36495]

ROFFMAN PRE 1899 ODESSA, SU [35757]

ROGAN PRE 1880 DEV, ENG [34847] : 1800-1990 LEEDS CITY, WRY, ENG [37031] : 1800-1840 EASKEY, SLI, IRL [38178]

ROGER 1870+ NSW & WA, AUS [35550] : ALL LANARK, LKS, SCT [34595]

ROGERS 1840-1880S BOMBALA, NSW, AUS [33934] : 1876+ HAWKESBURY RIVER, NSW, AUS [34273] : REVERAND 1850+ LAUNCESTON, TAS, AUS [34770] : 1836 ADELAIDE, SA, AUS [35027] : 1866+ NORTH FITZROY, VIC & SA, AUS [35108] : 1840+ DIGBY, VIC, AUS [35385] : 1848+ SYDNEY & GOSFORD, NSW, AUS [36365] : 1860S NEWCASTLE, NSW, AUS [37172] : 1810S-1850S WEST LINCOLN, ONT, CAN [34094] : 1777-1860 NB, CAN [36718] : 1900-1990 ALB, CAN [37348] : 1810 NORTHILL, BDF, ENG [33848] : PRE 1769 BLOXHAM, OXF, ENG [33866] : 1750+ BRISTOL, ENG [33963] : 1800-1845 KEN, ENG [34022] : PRE 1800 UPPER HEYFORD, OXF, ENG [34112] : ALL ENG [34131] : PRE 1700 ROLLESTON, NTT, ENG [34144] : 1700S NEWARK, NTT, ENG [34144] : 1800S GRANTHAM, LIN, ENG [34144] : 1700S BLANDFORD FORUM, DOR, ENG [34228] : 1730+ WINTERBORNE STICKLAND, DOR, ENG [34228] : 1700-1740 SOUTH HAYLING, HAM, ENG [34228] : 1842 IOW, ENG [34273] : 1750-1900 EDDLESBOROUGH, BKM, ENG [34316] : PRE 1850 WOR & SAL, ENG [34318] : PRE 1740 EYNSHAM, OXF, ENG [34466] : 1800+ BRISTOL, SOM, ENG [34550] : 1865 CAMBERWELL, KEN, ENG [34636] : 1750+ EASTON, SFK, ENG [34700] : ALL SALEHURST, SSX, ENG [34805] : C1830 DEV, ENG [34866] : 1810+ WESTMINSTER, LND, ENG [35027] : PRE 1864 NEWBURY, BRK, ENG [35031] : 1865 PLYMOUTH, DEV, ENG [35108] : C1814 ST BLAZEY, CON, ENG [35438] : C1825 BELGRAVE, LND, ENG [35478] : 1700-40 HOLT, NFK, ENG [35524] : PRE 1849 ST ERTH, CON, ENG [35599] : PRE 1880 ST PANCRAS, MDX, LND & HAM, ENG [35701] : 1800-1850 TREGONY, CON, ENG [35736] : 1800 ST EARTH, CON, ENG [35755] : PRE 1820 LINKINHORNE, CON, ENG [35818] : PRE 1850 STOKE DAMEREL, DEV, ENG [35818] : PRE 1900 MAIDENHEAD, BRK, ENG [35954] : 1860-1880 HOLBORN & CLERKENWELL, LND, ENG [36044] : 1850+ MDX, ENG [36123] : 1815+ DUDLEY, WOR, ENG [36254] : PRE 1750 ADMINGTON, GLS, ENG [36260] : PRE 1848 NOTTINGHAM, NTT, ENG [36365] : 1700S SHERBORNE, DOR, ENG [36484] : C1800 BATH, SOM, ENG [36835] : PRE 1750 BODMIN, CON, ENG [36891] : 1800-1920 LONDON, ENG [36894] : PRE 1842 LONDON & EALING, MDX & SFK, ENG [36967] : 1700+ GLS & BKM, ENG [37099] : PRE 1780 LONDON, ENG [37133] : WILLIAM PRE 1852 SSX, ENG [37210] : 1780-1900 LADOCK & GERRANS, CON, ENG [37224] : RICHARD C1870 LIVERPOOL, LAN, ENG [37330] : 1650-1850 LEEK & MEERBROOK, STS, ENG [37650] : 1887+ COLCHESTER, ESS, ENG [37656] : PRE 1840 HANLEY, STS, ENG [37893] : 1800+ WESTMINSTER, LND, ENG [37985] : 1750-1850 MANCHESTER, LAN, ENG [38005] : WILLIAM 1711-1787 HELSTON, CON, ENG [38180] : PRE 1800 NEWARK, NTT, ENG [38257] : PRE 1800 GRANTHAM, LIN, ENG [38257] : WILLIAM PRE 1800 'TUSMORE' ORCOP, OXF, ENG [38540] : PRE 1850 CLUTTON, SOM, ENG [38745] : ALL STS, SAL & WAR, ENG [38754] : 1830-1848 CALAIS, FRA [36365] : 1840 MALAHIDE, DUB, IRL [34636] : ALL LOU, IRL [35139] : C1800 KILLINKERE, CAV, IRL [35203] : C1780 ANT, IRL [35926] : 1800S MOUNTMELLICK, LEX, IRL [38498] : C1870 AUCKLAND, NZ [35974] : 1800S AUCKLAND, NZ & AUS [35023] : 1700-1800 MA, USA [35023] : C1730-1810 CUMBERLAND CO., ME, USA [35263] : MATTHEW PRE 1800 HAMPSHIRE CO., VA, USA [35304] : ALL NELSON & OHIO CO., KY & MO, USA [35304] : ALL NY, USA [36571] : 1750-1850 TN, USA [36939] : CHAUNCEY 1800 MA, USA [37509] : PRE 1700 VA, USA [37587] : 1615+ CT, USA [37592] : ANN 1813-1892 PA, USA [37813] : 1855-1875 KEWEENAW CO., MI, USA [38009] : 1750-1875 PATRICK CO., VA, USA [38044] : 1790+ NJ, OH & MO, USA [38050] : 1630-50 MA, USA [38151] : 1800+ ORANGE & PERSON CO., NC, USA [38175] : 1700-1750 HUNTINGTON, NY, USA [38767] : 1500+ NEW LONDON, CT & MA, USA & ENG [36970] : C1850+ MAESTEG, GLA, WLS [33922] : PRE 1850 PEMBROKE, PEM, WLS [36019] : PRE 1800 LOVESTON, PEM, WLS [36019] : 1820S RUABON, DEN, WLS [37172] : 1850 MERTHYR TYDFIL, GLA, WLS [37172] : 1863+ WREXHAM, WLS & AUS [35547]

ROGERS (SEE RODGERS) [37745]

ROGERSON PRE 1848 ROCHDALE, LAN, ENG [35514] : 1800-1850 LIVERPOOL, LAN, ENG [36390] : PRE 1531 TINWALD, DFS, SCT [38390] : WILLIAM 1800+ DFS, SCT & AUS [34161] : ALL PERQUIMANS CO., NC, USA [36557]

ROGGASCH 1750+ DANZIG, WPR, GER [36338]

ROGGE PRE 1800 BIRKUNGEN, PSA, GER [38048]

ROGGENDORF 1918+ MANNING, CARROLL CO., IA, USA [36952] : 1894-1918 ASPINWALL, CRAWFORD CO., IA, USA [36952]

ROGOWSKI 1827S SANOK, POL **[38184]**

ROHDE 1850S HAMBURG, GER **[38153]** : PRE 1900 PHILADELPHIA, PA, USA **[36926]** : 1900-1912 MANNING, CARROLL CO., IA, USA **[36952]**

ROHLFS 1700 GER **[35873]**

ROHLOFF 1830-1870S HAMBURG, HBG, BRD **[37513]**

ROHRBACH 1700-1850 FRANKFURT AM MAIN, BRD **[36958]**

ROHRBECK ALL POM, GER **[38037]**

ROHRER 1750-1850 ASCH, OES **[38194]**

ROHWEDDER PRE 1852 GAUSHORN, SHO, GER **[35616]** : 1852+ JONES CO., IA, USA **[35616]**

ROIL PRE 1842 ALTON, HAM, ENG **[34911]** : ALL WORLDWIDE **[38634]**

ROILE 1650+ CHICHESTER, SSX, ENG **[36827]**

ROING 1705 RUETHEN, GER **[38749]** : 1789 GESEKE, WEF, GER **[38749]**

ROIZ A.T. 1790+ MADRID, ESP **[38384]**

ROKE 1800S GUILDFORD, SRY, ENG **[36409]**

ROL ALL BADHOEVEDORP, NL **[36894]**

ROLES CHARLES 1800+ KEN, ENG **[35429]**

ROLF PRE 1720 MILDENHALL, CAM, ENG **[34445]**

ROLFE C1762 WHEPSTEAD, SFK, ENG **[34358]** : 1700+ ANDOVER, HAM, ENG **[34405]** : PRE 1840 MDX, ENG **[34463]** : 1700+ KEN, ENG **[34572]** : PRE 1845 CAMBERWELL, LND, ENG **[34584]** : PRE 1746 TRING, HRT, ENG **[35095]** : 1800+ MAIDSTONE, KEN, ENG **[36093]** : 1780-1830 LAWSHALL, SFK, ENG **[36111]** : 1700-1800S KINGSCLERE, HAM, ENG **[36289]** : PRE 1600 NFK, ENG **[37570]**

ROLIN 1800-1950 SHAVINGTON, CHS, ENG **[36983]**

ROLINDI 1700+ STI, SCT **[34970]**

ROLINSON PRE 1880 ENG **[35757]**

ROLL C1800 NBL & NFK, ENG **[35646]** : 1849+ BETSCHE, POS, GER **[36974]** : 1775-1860 MELZOW, BRA, GER **[36974]**

ROLLAN C1876 BARRENGARRY, NSW, AUS **[34807]**

ROLLAND PRE 1800 PIERREFONTEIN DOUB, FC, FRA **[38383]** : ALL FORFAR & ARBROATH, ANS, SCT **[37684]**

ROLLASON 1807-1854 BIRMINGHAM & COVENTRY, WAR, ENG **[34024]** : 1790-1903 ERDINGTON & WEST BROMWICH, WAR, ENG **[35044]** : PRE 1817+ FOLESHILL, WAR, ENG **[35453]** : PRE 1830 DUDLEY, WOR, ENG **[36110]** : PRE 1850 SEDGLEY, STS, ENG **[36518]**

ROLLER 1700-1800 WUE, GER **[38652]**

ROLLESTON PRE 1850 NTH & LEI, ENG **[36082]**

ROLLING 1800+ DARTON, YKS, ENG **[33855]**

ROLLINGS SARAH PRE 1898 ONT, CAN **[35641]** : 1800S PEPPARD & BIX, OXF, ENG **[34335]** : PRE 1800 CAM, ENG **[34445]** : PRE 1814 LITTLEHAMPTON, SSX, ENG **[37144]** : PRE 1850 DEENE, NTH, ENG **[37321]** : 1780+ UPTON, AILSWORTH, NTH, ENG **[38078]** : C1900 TOTTENHAM, MDX, ENG **[38078]**

ROLLINGSON C1865 DBY, ENG **[34521]**

ROLLINS PRE 1900 SYDNEY, NSW, AUS **[33799]** : PRE 1870 MEDWAY & DARTFORD, KEN, ENG & CAN **[36479]** : PRE 1848 ANT, IRL **[38435]** : 1790 RANDOLPH CO., NC, USA **[38143]** : PRE 1830 AL, USA **[38783]**

ROLLINSON 1830+ POINT PIPER, NSW, AUS **[34857]** : PRE 1800 LAN, ENG **[34857]** : PRE 1880 ENG **[35757]** : ALL WAINFLEET, LIN, ENG **[36168]**

ROLLO PRE 1840 INDIA **[36102]**

ROLLS 1900+ EAST HAM, ESS, ENG **[34818]** : PRE 1860 BKM, ENG **[37249]** : C1820 UK **[35827]**

ROLPE 1800+ WORTH, WOODNESBOROUGH, KEN, ENG **[35891]**

ROLPH ALL FULBOURN, CAM, ENG **[35577]** : 1830-1920 WALTHAMSTOW, ESS, ENG **[36136]**

ROLSON PRE 1772 KIBWORTH, LEI, ENG **[37706]**

ROLSTON MARY PRE 1830 LDY, IRL **[35371]** : PRE 1840 EGLISH, ARM, IRL **[35997]** : ALL ARM, IRL & CAN **[38349]** : JAMES 1800S GLASGOW & INDIAN RLY, SCT & INDI **[36311]**

ROMANEL PRE 1850 LND & MDX, ENG **[34791]**

ROMANYSHYN ALL UKRAINE **[36719]**

ROMARY 1833 TUNBRIDGE WELLS, KEN, ENG **[35906]**

ROMBERGER ALL DAUPHIN CO., PA, USA **[35304]**

ROMBOUGH 1780-1990 OSANBRUCK, ONT, CAN **[34077]**

ROMER C1550 MARBACH, BAW, BRD **[38509]**

ROMERIL ALL ST HELIER, JSY, CHI, ENG **[35474]**

ROMILLY 1900+ FINCHLEY, MDX, ENG **[34029]**

RONALD PRE 1800 MONTROSE, ANS, SCT **[37832]**

RONALDSON 1857+ BALLARAT, VIC, AUS **[34683]** : PRE 1857 EDINBURGH, SCT **[34683]** : PRE 1857 ISLE SKYE & HADDINGTON, INV & ELN, SCT **[36882]**

RONAN 1800+ DAMARAND, WAT & COR, IRL **[36435]**

RONCZKA PRE 1880 PLANIA, SIL, GER **[38618]**

RONDA 1700-1800 CALLOSA, VALENCIA, ESP **[36340]**

RONDEAU ALL RI, USA **[34985]**

RONEY 1867+ ADELAIDE, SA, AUS **[38209]** : 1805-1855 FLETCHING, SSX, ENG **[38209]** : C1800 SELLING, KEN, ENG **[38209]** : 1800+ CARLOW, CAR, IRL **[37160]**

RONK 1790+ BOTETOURT CO., VA & IL, USA **[36540]**

RONKSLEY 1750-1870 STANNINGTON & SHEFFIELD, ERY, ENG **[34552]**

RONNEBERG 1862-1900 REFVIG, SELJE, NOR **[37969]**

RONSON PRE 1730 LAN, ENG **[37706]**

ROOCROFT 1900 CHORLEY, LAN, ENG **[34332]**

ROOK MARY 1780-1840 KIRBY KNOWLE, YKS, ENG **[34143]** : PRE 1784 SOUTHILL, BDF, ENG **[35728]** : PRE 1740 DOWNTON & WHITEPARISH, WIL, ENG **[36478]** : PRE 1880 BOUGHTON, KEN, ENG **[36584]** : PRE 1853 CHILDERLEY, CAM, ENG **[36629]** : 1850S BATES CO., MO, USA **[36968]** : 1825-1828 GRAINGER, TN, USA **[36968]**

ROOKE 1840+ SYDNEY, NSW, AUS **[34544]** : 1600+ BDF, ENG **[34980]** : PRE 1933 DNB, SCT **[36313]**

ROOKS 1770-1880 POSEY CO., IN & SC, USA **[38532]**

ROOM 1750-1890 STORWOOD, ENG **[37290]** : ALL EATON BRAY, BDF, ENG **[37746]** : ALL NORTHALL, BKM, ENG **[37746]** : ALL EDENBRIDGE, KEN, ENG **[37746]**

ROOME 1750-1880 LND, ENG **[35178]** : 1780-1830 KINGS LYNN, NFK, ENG **[37252]**

ROOMES 1870+ NOTTINGHAM, NTT, ENG **[36105]**

ROOMS ALL MECHELEN, ATW, BEL **[36230]**

ROONAN C1800 GORT, GAL, IRL **[36860]**

ROONEY 1850+ GEELONG, VIC, AUS **[36612]** : 1880+ TINGHA, NSW, AUS **[37889]** : 1840+ WARWICK, QLD, AUS **[38262]** : PRE 1854 IRL **[34696]** : PRE 1850 ATHLONE, WEM, IRL **[36612]** : PRE 1865 BELFAST, IRL **[38262]** : 1800S SHANNON, IRL **[38281]** : MARGARET 1916 CARROWKEEL & HACKETT, MAY & ACT, IRL & AUS **[36311]** : 1850-1870 PHILADELPHIA, PA, USA **[38106]** : 1870-1900 BLAIR CO., PA, USA **[38106]**

ROOP C1858 LAFAYETTE, IN, USA **[37467]**

ROOS 1814+ KARJAA, UUSIMAA, FIN **[38758]** : 1750-1875 DIERHEIM, BAD, GER **[36953]** : PRE

1840 BAD, GER **[38333]** : PRE 1800 ZUH, NL **[34180]** : 1840+ CINCINNATI, OH, USA **[38333]**

ROOSE 1700-1860 LAWHITTON & STH PETHERWIN, CON, ENG **[35581]** : 1700+ CAMELFORD, CON, ENG **[36833]**

ROOT 1800-1850 LEEDS, ONT, CAN **[38097]** : 1750-1850 LND, ENG **[37064]** : PRE 1700 BADBY, NTH & HAM, ENG **[38746]** : 1650-1850 MONROE CO., NY, USA **[36924]** : 1814 LIVINGSTON, NY, USA **[38022]** : 1630+ MA & CT, USA **[38745]**

ROOTE 1800-1950 PRINCE EDWARD CO., ONT, CAN **[36688]** : 1700-1800 MA, USA **[35502]**

ROOTES 1850+ CAMDEN, NSW, AUS **[35360]** : PRE 1850 NORTHIAM, SSX, ENG **[35360]** : 1700+ SSX, ENG **[35407]** : 1550-1950 SSX, ENG **[36485]**

ROOTHAM 1916-1925 MIMICO, ONT, CAN **[34123]** : 1890-1914 NE, USA **[34123]**

ROOTS 1860+ GEELONG, VIC, AUS **[34969]** : ALL SSX, ENG **[34858]** : C1870 LND, ENG **[35053]** : PRE 1873 KEN, ENG **[35351]** : WILLIAM 1800S HORNCHURCH, ESS, ENG **[36817]** : 1700-1800 LAMBOURNE, ESS, ENG **[36817]** : 1880-1910 LONGFIELD, KEN, ENG **[37219]** : PRE 1880 KEN, ENG **[37358]** : PRE 1750 KEN, ENG **[38389]**

ROPE C1761 ROCHFORD, ESS, ENG **[35090]** : 1760+ ENG **[35101]**

ROPER PRE 1840 WEYMOUTH, DOR, ENG **[34269]** : PRE 1851 NOTTINGHAM, NTT, ENG **[35519]** : HANNAH 1740+ LONDON, ENG **[36378]** : 1700-1800 WHERSTEAD, SFK, ENG **[37042]** : PRE 1825 WRY, ENG **[37402]** : PRE 1680 SAXMUNDHAM, SFK, ENG **[37420]** : 1680 NEW KENT, VA, USA **[38198]** : 1750 CHESTERFIELD, VA, USA **[38198]**

ROPNER 1850-1900 LANRICK, PER, SCT **[36635]**

RORHIG 1787 OBERSINN, BAV, GER **[36358]**

RORKE SARAH 1850+ WATERLOO, NSW, AUS **[35703]** : 1800+ SIMCOE CO., ONT, CAN **[34465]** : SARAH 1830+ ARM, IRL **[35703]**

ROSAR ALL GER **[38678]**

ROSBOROUGH 1700-1900 CLAUDY, LDY, IRL **[34624]** : 1700-1900 OH, MO, IA, VA, USA **[38328]**

ROSCOW 1860+ FARNWORTH, LAN, ENG **[37934]** : 1780-1880 DARCY LEVER & GREAT LEVER, LAN, ENG **[37934]** : 1780+ BOLTON, LAN, ENG **[37934]**

ROSE 1800+ NSW, AUS **[34261]** : 1800+ BAUHINIA DOWNS, QLD, AUS **[34261]** : 1900 SYDNEY, NSW, AUS **[34271]** : 1885+ MORUYA, NSW, AUS **[34979]** : 1865 WOODSPOINT, VIC, AUS **[35065]** : 1867 RICHMOND, VIC, AUS **[35065]** : 1861 BAIRNSDALE, VIC, AUS **[35065]** : PRE 1850 PENRITH, NSW, AUS **[35199]** : WILLIAM 1819-1881 HAWKESBURY & HUNTER REGIONS, NSW, AUS **[35239]** : 1860S+ SYDNEY, NSW, AUS **[35537]** : 1835-1860 NSW, AUS **[35589]** : JAMES C1900 PORT MELBOURNE, VIC, AUS **[37159]** : 1900+ MAITLAND & SINGLETON, NSW, AUS **[37966]** : PRE 1860 LEVEN, BEL **[35818]** : 1850+ SIMCOE CO., ONT, CAN **[34465]** : ROBERT R.R. 1800+ ST HELIER, JSY, CHI **[34690]** : GEORGE 1850+ JSY, CHI **[34690]** : ALL MAIDENHEAD, BRK, ENG **[34002]** : 1650+ LEI, ENG **[34054]** : 1700+ WARWICK, WAR, ENG **[34054]** : CHARLES C1825 LONDON, ENG **[34176]** : 1800+ DOR, ENG **[34228]** : 1700-1850 GREASEBOROUGH, WRY, ENG **[34827]** : WM. JOSEPH 1860-1903 BICESTER & OXFORD, OXF, ENG **[34829]** : WM. JOSEPH 1860-1892 WESTMINSTER, LND, ENG **[34829]** : C1800 LND, ENG **[35180]** : PRE 1834 ALL CANNINGS AREA, WIL, ENG **[35251]** : 1712 KEMSING, KEN, ENG **[35261]** : 1830S SWERFORD, OXF, ENG **[35408]** : PRE 1900 ESS, ENG **[36006]** : 1800-1875 MDX & LND, ENG **[36007]** : PRE 1850 DEBENHAM, SFK,

ENG **[36048]** : PRE 1837 READING, BRK, ENG **[36190]** : 1850S MARSTON, WIL, ENG **[36253]** : PRE 1725 BIRMINGHAM, WAR, ENG **[36326]** : 1800+ WIGAN, LAN, ENG **[36587]** : 1800+ SHADWELL, LND, ENG **[36623]** : 1700+ LEXDEN, ESS, ENG **[36794]** : ALL WIL, DOR & HAM, ENG **[37412]** : 1881+ RAYLEIGH, ESS, ENG **[37664]** : 1800-1860 SOUTHAMPTON, HAM, ENG **[37709]** : PRE 1775 STOURBRIDGE, WOR, ENG **[37736]** : PRE 1722 YORK & NEWBY WISKE, NRY, ENG **[37852]** : 1700-1850 ECKINGTON, DBY, ENG **[38265]** : PRE 1820 GILLINGHAM, DOR & NFD, ENG & CAN **[37410]** : PRE 1650 SFK & MA, ENG & USA **[38745]** : PRE 1861 BIELEFELD, PRE, GER **[35065]** : 1816+ RATHKEALE, LIM, IRL **[35824]** : PRE 1885 INV, SCT **[34979]** : PRE 1855 INV, NAI & MOR, SCT **[35496]** : 1793 AULDEARN, NAI, SCT **[35905]** : PRE 1840 NIGG, ROC, SCT **[35925]** : 1700+ KILRAVOCK, INV, SCT **[35956]** : PRE 1860 LKS, SCT **[36754]** : 1800-1880 DUTHIL, INV, SCT **[37329]** : C1870 INVERNESS, INV, SCT **[37772]** : EMMANUEL 1840+ USA **[37532]** : PRE 1850 LYCOMING CO., PA, USA **[37914]** : 1792-1885 ULSTER CO., NY, USA **[38113]** : 1875-1900 ROCHESTER, NY, USA **[38118]** : PRE 1805 HANCOCK CO., GA, USA **[38190]** : 1746+ GRANVILLE CO., NC, USA **[38190]** : C1835 PENROSE, MON, WLS **[35597]**

ROSECRANTZ 1800 ULSTER, NY, USA **[38015]**

ROSEMAN 1800-1850 MANCHESTER, LAN, ENG **[38737]**

ROSEN 1681 HERBRAM, GER **[38749]**

ROSENBAUM 1887-1905 NEW YORK, NY, USA **[38236]**

ROSENBERG ALL DUBLIN, POL **[38481]** : ALL ESTONIA, SU **[37742]**

ROSENFELOT 1882+ FITZROY, VIC, AUS **[35391]**

ROSENOW 1775-1860 MELZOW, BRA, GER **[36974]**

ROSENSTENGEL PRE 1697 ALERTSHAUSEN & ELSOFF, WEF, BRD **[36954]**

ROSENTHAL 1850+ STRATHALBYN, SA, AUS **[38582]** : KATHERINE 1870-1890 TEIGNMOUTH, DEV, ENG **[38409]** : 1700+ VEHLFELD, BAY, GER **[38578]** : 1810-1900 NIAGARA, NY, USA **[37535]**

ROSER ALL DARLING DOWNS, QLD, AUS **[36288]** : C1837+ SINGLETON, NSW, AUS **[38541]** : 1800+ WALDRON, SSX, ENG **[34970]**

ROSEVEAR 1700+ MADRON, CON, ENG **[36000]** : ALL DBY, ENG **[36005]**

ROSEWARNE ALL CON, ENG **[35063]** : 1750-1900 PAUL & MADRON, CON, ENG **[35736]** : 1700+ BREAGE & KENWYN, CON, ENG **[36961]**

ROSEWELL 1700-1900 ALMONDSBURY, GLS, ENG **[36589]** : PRE 1660 DUNKERTON, SOM, ENG **[36628]** : 1660-1750 ROTHERHITHE, SRY, ENG **[36628]** : 1700S HACKNEY, MDX, ENG **[36628]**

ROSGEN PRE 1857 GER **[35280]**

ROSHONG 1800-1850 STARK CO., OH, USA **[38770]**

ROSIE ALL WORLDWIDE **[34981]**

ROSIER PRE 1834 LANGHAM, SFK, ENG **[35441]**

ROSS JAMES C1840 MELBOURNE, VIC, AUS **[33917]** : JAMES C1860 GEELONG, VIC, AUS **[33917]** : 1800-1900 SINGLETON & TEXAS, NSW, AUS **[33926]** : 1880 ST LAWRENCE, QLD, AUS **[33932]** : ALEXANDER 1848+ HAMILTON, VIC, AUS. **[34171]** : 1890 NEWTOWN, NSW, AUS **[34306]** : 1840-1930 HOBART, TAS, AUS **[34551]** : 1860+ MACLEAN, NSW, AUS **[35143]** : 1857+ WOLLONGONG, NSW, AUS **[35143]** : 1860+ PALMERS ISLAND, NSW, AUS **[35143]** : D. H. MCK. 1866+ STANTHORPE, QLD, AUS **[35428]** : 1860 DALBY, QLD, AUS **[35450]** : PRE 1852

HAMILTON & RIVER OUSE, TAS, AUS **[35459]** :
CATHERINE 1881+ TEXAS, QLD, AUS **[35852]** :
1850+ SYDNEY, NSW, AUS **[37128]** : 1803-20
LONGFORD, TAS, AUS **[37144]** : ALEXANDER
C1852+ BRANXHOLME, VIC, AUS **[37164]** : 1800-
1900 QUEBEC, QUE, CAN **[36246]** : PIERRE 1820+
MASKINONGE, QUE, CAN **[36678]** : 1800S+
DOWNSVIEW, ONT, CAN **[37458]** : 1860+
ECCLESFIELD, WRY, ENG **[34306]** : 1840+
LONDON, ENG **[34628]** : 1870+ OLDHAM, LAN,
ENG **[34790]** : PRE 1830 PUTSEY, YKS, ENG **[35225]**
: 1800+ TERRINGTON, ST CLEMENT, NFK, ENG
[35342] : 1800+ REDRUTH, CON, ENG **[35385]** :
1850 PLYMOUTH, DEV, ENG **[35943]** : 1830+
CAMBERWELL, LND, ENG **[36393]** : PRE 1850
ERY, ENG **[36393]** : C1800 LEI, ENG **[36694]** : 1800+
POPLAR, MDX, ENG **[36810]** : C1850+
GRAVESEND, KEN, ENG **[36810]** : ALL
GREENWICH, KEN, ENG **[36810]** : GEO. OR
JOHN C1829 LE HAVRE & NEWCASTLE, NOR &
NSW, FRA & AUS **[36311]** : PRE 1760
ISENBURGISCHEN, HESSE, GER **[36543]** : 1800-
1850 WIEWIORKEN, WPR, GER **[38599]** : PRE 1870
OLDENBURG, SHO, GER **[38648]** : PRE 1840
ROSSCAIRN, FER, IRL **[35793]** : PRE 1850 TULLY
CORBET, MOG, IRL **[36705]** : 1865+ KINSALE,
COR, IRL **[37079]** : JOHN C1851 BELFAST, ANT,
IRL **[37135]** : ALL MAGHERALIN, DOW, IRL
[38298] : HENRY PRE 1850 MAGHERALIN, DOW,
IRL **[38298]** : 1760-1840 TATTRACONAUGHT, TYR,
IRL **[38537]** : JOHN 1770-1834 TYR, IRL & AUS
[33926] : ANN 1800+ WEM, IRL & AUS **[34864]** :
C1870+ NZ **[35143]** : PRE 1880 LOTH & OLRIG,
SUT, CAI & ROC, SCT **[33883]** : 1788 MUIR OF
ORD, ROC, SCT **[33924]** : 1827 HILLOCHEAD, SCT
[34058] : 1800S DUNDEE, ANS, SCT **[34172]** :
DAVID 1793-1858 TAIN, ROC, SCT **[34524]** : 1700+
INVERNESS, INV, SCT **[34560]** : PRE 1821
LOCHCARRON, ROC, SCT **[34689]** : 1780+
DAILLY, AYR, SCT **[34713]** : 1760+ GIRVAN, AYR,
SCT **[34713]** : 1810+ COLMONELL, AYR, SCT
[34713] : 1829-1857 ALNESS, ROC, SCT **[35143]** : D.
H. MCK. 1800+ WICK, CAI, SCT **[35428]** : 1857
SNIZORT, INV, SCT **[35450]** : 1700-1800 FIF, SCT
[35627] : PRE 1840 NIGG, ROC, SCT **[35710]** : 1807-
1900 EDDERTON, ROC, SCT **[35922]** : PRE 1820
ALNESS, ROC, SCT **[35932]** : PRE 1850
CROMARTY, ROC, SCT **[36260]** : 1826+
EDINBURGH, MLN, SCT **[36276]** : 1800S
BONARBRIDGE, ROC, SCT **[36800]** : GEORGE
PRE 1851 LOGIE EASTER, ROC, SCT **[37164]** :
GEORGE 1837-47 KINCARDINE, ROC, SCT **[37164]**
: GEORGE PRE 1828 FEARN, ROC, SCT **[37164]** :
1800 KRS, SCT **[37170]** : 1880S ABD, SCT **[37500]** :
1700-1800 AMAT, ROC, SCT **[37654]** : JOHN 1802
FORRES, MOR, SCT **[37684]** : SINCLAIR ALL SCT
[37684] : PRE 1750 EWES, DFS, SCT **[38461]** : JANET
C1815 CATERLOCH, ROC, SCT **[38724]** : JANET
C1815 ROSSKEEN, ROC, SCT **[38724]** : PRE 1840
NORKA, VOLGA, SU **[36543]** : 1750-1850
NATCHITOCHES, LA, USA **[35267]** : JON 1750-1838
NJ, USA **[35271]** : ALL ONIEDA & HERKIMER
CO., NY, USA **[37502]** : 1880+ MILWAUKEE, WI,
USA **[38125]** : PRE 1900 WESTERN, PA, USA **[38218]**
: 1820-1830 HIGHLAND CO., OH, USA **[38334]** :
1775-1825 MIFLIN CO., PA, USA **[38342]** : PRE 1820
KY, USA **[38576]** : C1750-1850 FRANKLIN,
SOMERSET, PA, USA & IRL **[35305]**

ROSSALL PRE 1867 GREAT ECCLESTON &
LANCASTER, LAN, ENG **[37710]**

ROSSELL C1800 OCKBROOK, DBY, ENG **[35502]**

ROSSER 1900+ BALLARAT, VIC, AUS **[34541]** : 1800S
LONDON, ENG **[34930]** : 1900+ RSA **[34541]**
ROSSETTI C1890 LONDON, ENG **[38002]**
ROSSI ALL APRIGLIANO (VICO), COSENZA, ITL
[34047]
ROSSIGNOL 1867-1990 VILLEFRANCHE &
MONTREAL, LGD & QUE, FRA & CAN **[34136]**
ROSSITER 1863+ SYDNEY, NSW, AUS **[34979]** :
1870+ MORNINGSIDE, QLD, AUS **[35392]** : 1852+
IPSWICH AREA, QLD, AUS **[37896]** : 1820-1850S
MELBOURNE PORT, ENG **[33835]** : 1828+
DOULTING, SOM, ENG **[34446]** : PRE 1863
SHOREDITCH, LND, ENG **[34979]** : 1840+
ALDERSHOT, HAM, ENG **[35377]** : 1840+ DEV,
ENG **[35377]** : PRE 1853 DOULTING, SOM, ENG
[35392] : 1730+ CHILD OKEFORD, DOR, ENG
[37360] : PRE 1852 CAMERTON, SOM, ENG **[37896]**
: PRE 1900 CHEDDAR, SOM, ENG **[38226]** : PRE
1840 WEX, IRL **[35592]**
ROSSKOPF 1832-50 FRITZ-LAS, HESSIA CAPEL,
GER **[38151]** : 1855-1883 COVINGTON, KY, USA
[38151]
ROSSON ALL LONDON, ENG **[35984]** : ALL
BIRMINGHAM, WAR, ENG **[35984]**
ROSSWINKEL 1700+ OLK KREIS FRIER &
METZOORF, GER **[37016]**
ROSTNEL 1850-1870 OARE, JAMTLAND, SWE
[35102]
ROSTRON C1880 CHADDERTON, LAN, ENG **[34734]**
ROSYPAL ALL OES **[37268]**
ROTE ALL WORLDWIDE **[37453]**
ROTH PRE 1870 BADEN BADEN, GER **[34443]** : PRE
1900 ITTENDORF, BAW, GER **[38609]** : ALL
MARKTSCHELKEN, TRANSYLVANIA, RO **[38519]**
: STEPHEN L. 1796-1849 MEDIASH,
TRANSYLVANIA, RO **[38519]** : 1870-1900S NYC,
NY, USA **[36936]** : PRE 1733 LANCASTER CO., PA,
USA **[36972]** : 1717-1800 NORTHAMPTON CO., PA,
USA **[38153]** : JOHN C1753 NORTHAMPTON, PA,
USA **[38348]**
ROTHACKER PRE 1850 BERLIN, BLO, GER **[33868]** :
ALL WORLDWIDE **[33868]**
ROTHELIE ALL CH **[38029]**
ROTHERHAM PRE 1750 WHITWELL, DBY, ENG
[33912] : PRE 1860 LAN, ENG **[38286]**
ROTHERMEL 1820-1900 FAYETTE CO., PA, USA
[38344]
ROTHEROE ALL GLA, WLS **[37373]**
ROTHERY PRE 1810 UNDLEY & HUDDERSFIELD,
WRY, ENG **[37372]** : 1790S COCKERMOUTH, CUL,
ENG **[38221]**
ROTHFOSS 1771 VEGESACK, BRM, GER **[35828]** :
1767+ BLUMENTHAL, BRM, GER **[35828]**
ROTHLEY ALL WORLDWIDE **[37572]**
ROTHMAHLER ALL WORLDWIDE **[38237]**
ROTHON 1800-1840 STEPNEY, MDX, ENG **[35098]**
ROTHSCHILD 1700+ HELDENBERGEN, HEN,
GER **[37042]**
ROTHWELL C1960 ST MARGARETS, NSW, AUS
[35367] : PRE 1850 BURY, LAN, ENG **[33808]** : PRE
1850 LAN, ENG **[34730]** : PRE 1876 MANCHESTER,
LAN, ENG **[37235]** : 1800+ SKELMERSDALE,
LAN, ENG **[37262]** : PRE 1720 BATLEY, WRY, ENG
[37754] : 1780-1860 CLIFTON, LAN, ENG **[38028]** :
PRE 1812 MIDDLETON, LAN, ENG **[38248]** : ALL
HASLINGDEN, LAN, ENG **[38266]** : 1930
MANCHESTER, LAN, ENG **[38267]**
ROTT 1800-1865 BAY, BRD **[36895]** : 1700-1800
BADENHAUSEN, NSA, GER **[38643]** : 1870-1960
BALTIMORE CITY, MD, USA **[36895]**
ROTTENSTEINER PRE 1750 ST MICHAEL &
LUNGAU, SLZ, OES **[38609]**

ROTTLINGSCHOEFFER 1600+ ALTHEIM, BAV, GER **[37542]**

ROTTMAN ALL WORLDWIDE **[34126]**

ROTTON ALL ENG **[34415]** : 1800S BATTERSEA, LND, ENG **[37167]**

ROUFOSSE PRE 1800 HERVE, LUI, BEL **[38617]**

ROUGEAU EDOUARD 1880+ ST EDOUARD, QUE, CAN **[36678]**

ROUGEAU DIT BERGER JEAN 1684 NOTRE DAME DE LA RICHE, TOURS, FRA **[36678]**

ROUGH ALL NC, USA **[38325]**

ROUGHEAD 1854+ VIC, AUS **[35056]** : 1800-1865 LARBERT, STI, SCT **[37205]**

ROUGHLEY SARAH C1830+ ENG **[35447]**

ROUGHTON ALL WORLDWIDE **[37370]**

ROULSTON PRE 1779 NTT, ENG **[37829]** : PATRIC & JANE 1800+ CLA & TYR, IRL **[35049]**

ROULSTONE 1760S LANE END, STS, ENG **[35261]**

ROUND ELIJAH 1850+ HOBART, TAS, AUS **[34770]** : OSWOLD C1850 PORTLAND, VIC, AUS **[37984]** : PRE 1880 NEWBOLD ON AVON, WAR, ENG **[34562]** : PRE 1880 HADLEIGH & DAWLEYMAGNA, SAL, ENG **[36502]** : 1820-1850 WOLVERHAMPTON, STS, ENG **[37233]**

ROUNDHILL 1800-50 HEYWOOD, LAN, ENG **[36419]**

ROUNDTREE 1780-1810 ORANGEBURG CO., SC, USA **[35307]** : C1752 GOACHLAND CO., VA, USA **[37820]** : C1759 HART CO., KY, USA **[37820]** : C1820 KNOX CO., KY, USA **[37820]**

ROUNDY 1678-1850 BEVERLY, MA, USA **[36550]**

ROUNTREE 1875+ HAMILTON, VIC, AUS **[35208]** : ALL USA **[38340]**

ROURKE BRYAN 1823+ BATHURST THE LESS, NSW, AUS **[36291]** : THOMAS 1849+ PER "SUCCESS", NSW, AUS **[36314]** : LAWRENCE 1849+ PER "SUCCESS", NSW, AUS **[36314]** : MARY 1840+ PARRAMATTA, NSW, AUS **[36314]** : MAURICE 1800-1875 TRALEE, KER, IRL **[34699]** : FLORENCE 1850-1875 TRALEE, KER, IRL **[34699]** : BRYAN 1800+ KER, IRL **[36291]** : JERH 1700S KER, IRL **[36291]** : MARY PRE 1840 TULLAMORE, OFF, IRL **[36314]**

ROUSE PRE 1855 HOSE, LEI, ENG **[33806]** : 1830+ ST COLOMB, CON, ENG **[34666]** : 1840+ ILLOGAN, CON, ENG **[34666]** : ALL NBL, ENG **[35540]** : 1700-1860 LAWHITTON & STH PETERHWIN, CON, ENG **[35581]** : 1800+ BERMONDSEY, LND, ENG **[36512]** : 1870+ METHVEN, CANTY, NZ **[34666]** : KATE 1900S BURNHAMWOOD, WI, USA **[37024]**

ROUSEAU 1837 TORQUAY, DEV, ENG **[37418]**

ROUSEE 1600-1900 VICDESSOS ARCONAC, ARIEGE, FRA **[33758]**

ROUSEL ANN 1784+ EAST HARPTREE, SOM, ENG **[34065]**

ROUSH 1736-1827 POCAHONTAS CO., VA & OH, USA & GER **[37577]**

ROUSSEAU PRE 1855 ENG **[35386]** : PIERRE C1725-1780 LOIX, PCH, FRA **[38408]**

ROUTLEDGE 1880+ IPSWICH, QLD, AUS **[33782]** : 1800-1900 SSX, ENG **[37207]** : 1853 MONTROSE, ANS, SCT **[34637]**

ROUTLEFF ALL DEV, ENG **[34320]**

ROUTLEY 1833 HOLLACOMBE, DEV, ENG **[36804]**

ROW 1850+ MIDDLESEX CO., ONT, CAN **[35605]** : 1690-1720 ST TEATH, CON, ENG **[34448]** : C1700 ST ALLEN, CON, ENG **[35076]**

ROWAN ELIZA 1840+ PARRAMATTA, NSW, AUS **[34461]** : C1850 BATHURST, NSW, AUS **[35028]** : 1850+ ONT, CAN **[34496]** : 1850+ LIVERPOOL, ENG **[35566]** : EDWARD PRE 1800 GLENDERMONT, LDY, IRL **[34461]** : ELIZA PRE

1830 GLENDERMONT, LDY, IRL **[34461]** : 1800+ MOYNE CO., CLA, IRL **[35566]** : PRE 1840 NEWTOWNHAMILTON, ARM, IRL **[35744]** : 1780+ MULLAGHBRACK, ARM, IRL **[36254]** : PRE 1781 ARDS PENINSULA, DOW, IRL **[38428]** : 1750-1800 BO'NESS, WLN, SCT **[36431]**

ROWAND PRE 1790 PAISLEY, RFW, SCT **[34358]**

ROWAT PRE 1830 CARMUNNOCK, DNB, SCT **[34127]** : C1860+ DUNDEE, PER, SCT **[35053]**

ROWATT 1800+ CUMBERNAULD, DNB, SCT **[34459]**

ROWBERRY 1800+ TAS, AUS **[34647]** : PRE 1900 HEF, ENG **[34647]**

ROWBOTHAM 1860+ READING, BRK, ENG **[35095]** : C1810 MACCLESFIELD, CHS, ENG **[35095]** : C1775 PRESTBURY, CHS, ENG **[35095]**

ROWBOTTOM C1840 TAS, AUS **[33881]** : 1855+ BALLARAT, VIC, AUS **[37968]** : PRE 1840 ENG **[33881]** : 1820S MDX, ENG **[34175]** : 1750-1850 BIRMINGHAM & WARWICK, WAR, ENG **[34520]** : HANNAH 1876-1922+ DENTON, LAN, ENG **[37546]** : ALL MANCHESTER, LAN & DBY, ENG **[38174]**

ROWCLIFF 1850S SANDHURST, VIC, AUS **[35127]** : ALL DEV, ENG **[34320]** : C1822 PRESTON, LAN, ENG **[35127]**

ROWDEN 1800-1900 CLERKENWELL, MDX, ENG **[33830]** : ALL ENG **[34812]** : ALL ENG **[37846]**

ROWE JOHN 1840+ THEBARTON & GOLDEN GROVE, SA, AUS **[34279]** : JOHN 1860S CARAMUT, VIC, AUS **[34279]** : 1850-1950 AUS **[34535]** : RICHARD 1850+ BALLARAT & GEELONG, VIC, AUS **[34916]** : 1880+ RAVENSWOOD, QLD, AUS **[35138]** : 1820+ LAUNCESTON, TAS, AUS **[35865]** : 1850S ARARAT, VIC, AUS **[36277]** : JAMES 1822-1850 SYDNEY & GOULBURN, NSW, AUS **[37556]** : 1877+ NSW, AUS **[37556]** : 1830S NSW, AUS **[37947]** : PRE 1850 CAN & USA **[38386]** : C1800 FALMOUTH, CON, ENG **[33841]** : PRE 1860 DRIFT, CON, ENG **[33870]** : 1800+ PYWORTHY, DEV, ENG **[34108]** : CATHERINE 1790-1860 NORTHERN ETCHELLS, CHS, ENG **[34143]** : PRE 1839 CANTERBURY, KEN, ENG **[34269]** : JOHN 1830-1838 ST DAY & REDRUTH, CON, ENG **[34279]** : JOHN PRE 1829 RUAN LENNIHORNE & GWENNAP, CON, ENG **[34279]** : ALL NEWTON ST PETROCK, DEV, ENG **[34471]** : 1750-1850 GULVAL, CON, ENG **[34535]** : 1800+ CAMBORNE, CON, ENG **[34785]** : 1812 PLYMOUTH, DEV, ENG **[34808]** : 1857 DEPTFORD, KEN, ENG **[34808]** : C1780 LOSTWITHIEL, CON, ENG **[34808]** : C1865 FARNCOMBE, SRY, ENG **[34893]** : 1800 TYWANDREATH, CON, ENG **[35023]** : ALL CURY & SITHNEY, CON, ENG **[35063]** : 1820 PLYMOUTH, DEV, ENG **[35067]** : 1880 ALTARNUM, CON, ENG **[35089]** : JOHN C1849 CROWAN, CON, ENG **[35131]** : 1800+ MADRON, CON, ENG **[35138]** : WILLIAM 1810-1850 GULVAL & MADRON, CON, ENG **[35208]** : 1700-1850 ST KEVERNE & BREAGE, CON, ENG **[35496]** : 1800-1850 TAVISTOCK, DEV, ENG **[35602]** : 1800+ BURAGE, CON, ENG **[35847]** : C1790 LANEAST & LAUNCESTON, CON, ENG **[35865]** : 1750-1860 SFK, SRY & ESS, ENG **[36242]** : 1840-42 EXETER, DEV, ENG **[36242]** : PRE 1750 DUR, ENG **[36242]** : 1750-1860 LONDON, MDX, ENG **[36242]** : PRE 1850 CAMBORNE, CON, ENG **[36277]** : JOSEPH 1880-1950 BERMONDSEY, SRY, ENG **[36286]** : 1500+ PLAWORTH, DUR, ENG **[36685]** : PRE 1806 CON, ENG **[36775]** : RICHARD 1700+ DODDISCOMBSLEIGH, DEV, ENG **[36813]** : 1700-1900 SITHNEY & HELSTON, CON, ENG **[36899]** :

1870+ BRISTOL, SOM, ENG [36995] : C1862
BETHNAL GREEN, MDX, ENG [37279] : PRE 1900
ISLINGTON, MDX, ENG [37279] : PRE 1877 ST
KEW & CROWAN, CON, ENG [37556] : JAMES
1800-1822 SUNDERLAND & NOTTINGHAM,
DUR, ENG [37556] : 1790-1934 BRENTFORD, MDX,
ENG [37657] : 1788-1800 ACTON, MDX, ENG [37657]
: 1755-1790 CREDITON, DEV, ENG [37657] : 1750-70
CON, ENG [38151] : ALL CON, ENG [38522] : PRE
1900 DEV, ENG [38594] : 1875+ TEMUKA, STH IS.,
NZ [34893] : 1750-1825 COLUMBIA CO., NY, USA
[36555] : 1850-80 HOBART, NY, USA [36685] : JOHN
1838-1840 W.INDIES [34279] : PRE 1835 TENBY,
PEM, WLS [34893]

ROWELL 1750S BULWICK, NTH, ENG [33967] :
1800+ YAXLEY, HUN, ENG [34421] : PRE 1841
BELMONT, DUR, ENG [36604] : PRE 1832
MANCHESTER, LAN, CHS & WRY, ENG [37840]

ROWEN 1700+ CUMBERLAND CO., PA, USA [37004]

ROWGHAN 1790-1870 BKM & BRK, ENG [36100]

ROWIES PRE 1600 RATCLIFF, STEPNEY, LND,
ENG [36944]

ROWING PRE 1855 WENDLING, NFK, ENG [37067]

ROWLAND C1900 THE ROCK, NSW, AUS [37553] :
1872+ WANGARATTA, VIC, AUS [37553] : C1846
PERTH, WA, AUS [37553] : PRE 1868 ENG [35148] :
1870+ COWFOLD & SHERMANBURY, SSX, ENG
[36212] : GEORGE 1810+ BRISTOL, GLS, ENG
[36314] : GEORGE PRE 1834 LONDON, ENG [36314]
: 1600+ HARGRAVE, SFK, ENG [36402] : 1850+
WESTHAM, LND, ENG [36402] : 1850+
LEATHERHEAD, SRY, ENG [36533] : 1900+
SUTTON IN ASHFIELD, NTT, ENG [36533] : PRE
1860 DUKINFIELD, CHS, ENG [36617] : 1811
MAIDSTONE, KEN, ENG [37006] : PRE 1860
LANGFORD, OXF, ENG [37763] : PRE 1868
BERGEN OPS ZOOM, NL [35148] : PRE 1900 ME,
USA [36933]

ROWLANDS ALL LIVERPOOL, LAN, ENG [34160] :
1880-1910 SALFORD, LAN, ENG [35565] : 1800+
CHESTER, CHS, ENG [37732] : 1860+ LIVERPOOL,
LAN, ENG [37732] : ALL NORTH, CGN, WLS
[37250] : PRE 1860 HOLYHEAD, AGY, WLS [37962]

ROWLANDSON 1860-1900 WINSFORD, CHS, ENG
[36831]

ROWLEDGE C1800 RIPLEY, WAR, ENG [35586]

ROWLEN ALL GER [35618]

ROWLER 1750 BATH, SOM, ENG [36798]

ROWLES PRE 1800 SHERSTON MAGNA, WIL, ENG
[36113] : 1800+ CANTERBURY, KEN, ENG [36756]
: 1734-1804 BALTIMORE, MD, USA [38529]

ROWLEY 1750+ RUGELEY, STS, ENG [34639] :
THOMAS 1757+ BENTLEY, SAL, ENG [35794] :
RICHARD 1740S WORFIELD, SAL, ENG [35794] :
JOHN 1685 WINSCOTE, SAL, ENG [35794] : JOHN
1660S NEWTON, SAL, ENG [35794] : PRE 1720
KINGSWINFORD, SAL, ENG [36110] : PRE 1760
COUND, SAL, ENG [37383] : PRE 1865 AUDLEY,
STS, ENG [37406] : C1815 WALTHAM ABBEY, ESS,
ENG [37973] : PRE 1776 BIDDULPH, STS, ENG
[38055] : PRE 1900 WEDNESBURY, STS, ENG
[38581] : 1780-1835 IRL [35320] : C1863 ROWLEY, NZ
[34814] : JAMES 1780-1835 PAISLEY, RFW, SCT
[35320]

ROWLING 1600+ HARGRAVE, SFK, ENG [36402]

ROWLINGS 1830-1850S CAMBRIDGE, CAM, ENG
[36285]

ROWLINGSON 1800S LONDON, ENG [34028]

ROWLINSON 1800S LONDON, ENG [34028] : PRE
1850 BIRMINGHAM, WOR, WAR & STS, ENG
[37703]

ROWLSTON PRE 1690 NOTTINGHAM, NTT, ENG
[36532]

ROWNEY PRE 1780 CARDINGTON, BDF, ENG
[33912]

ROWORTH PRE 1892 LEI, NTT & LIN, ENG [37754]

ROWS 1750-1850 BROMLEY, ESS, ENG [36256] :
1860+ MIDDLESBROUGH, ERY, ENG [36636] :
PRE 1830 INGLETON, NRY, ENG [36636]

ROWSE C1790+ ERNESTTOWN TWP., ONT, CAN &
USA [34339] : ALL ST AUSTELL, CON, ENG [36759]

ROWSELL C1800 CHARD, SOM, ENG [38079]

ROWSON ALL SAL, ENG [36866]

ROWSWELL PRE 1854 SHEPTON BEAUCHAMP,
SOM, ENG [34886]

ROWTCLIFF ALL DEV, ENG [34320]

ROWTER C1750 ST EWE, CON, ENG [34644]

ROXBOROUGH 1800S+ MONTREAL, QUE, CAN
[38406]

ROXBURGH 1878+ NORTH SYDNEY, NSW, AUS
[34427] : 1820-1850 HAMILTON, LKS, SCT [34191] :
1780+ IRVINE, AYR, SCT [36254]

ROY 1875+ PIMPINIO & HORSHAM, VIC, AUS
[37555] : 1850+ LOBETHAL, SA, AUS [37555] :
1900+ CHINA [35771] : 1600-1660 MARANS, PCH,
FRA [34514] : PRE 1800 JAMAICA [33869] : PRE
1850 POZAN, PO, POL [37555] : 1780+
BLACKFORD, PER, SCT [35450] : 1730 NJ, USA
[37006]

ROYAL 1800-1900 BATH & WALCOT, SOM, ENG
[37877] : 1800-1900 GOOCHLAND, VA, USA [38588] :
ALL WORLDWIDE [36498]

ROYALL PRE 1850 YARMOUTH, NFK, ENG [37906] :
ALL WORLDWIDE [36498]

ROYCE PRE 1700 MARTOCK, SOM & CT, ENG &
USA [38746] : PRE 1800 RI, USA [37804]

ROYDEN PRE 1875 LIVERPOOL, LAN, ENG [34999]

ROYE PRE 1700 LONDON, ENG [35181]

ROYER 1780-1850 LANCASTER CO., PA, USA [37782]
: JACOB 1820-80 STARK CO., OH, USA [38138]

ROYLANCE 1880+ SYDNEY, NSW, AUS [34978] :
PRE 1880 LEEDS, YKS, ENG [34978]

ROYLE PRE 1842 MANCHESTER, LAN, ENG [37072]
: 1700 PRESTBURY, CHS, ENG [37697] : WILLIAM
HENRY 1911-C1985 CA, USA [36498] : ALL
WORLDWIDE [36498]

ROYLES ALL WORLDWIDE [36498]

ROYSTON MARY 1820 BLACKBURN, LAN, ENG
[35805] : 1850S CAMBERWELL, LND, ENG [36799] :
1800+ LOVERINGTON, CAM, ENG [37598] : 1820-
1900 MANCHESTER, LAN, ENG [37598] : 1790-1850
MACCLESFIELD, CHS, ENG [37598] : 1800+ HRT,
ENG [37598] : 1800+ BOOTHY GRAFFOE, LIN,
ENG [37598]

ROYTHORNE 1700-1800 NFK, ENG [36873]

ROY-WRAY C1800 LOUISEVILLE, QUE, CAN [34985]

ROZELL 1870-1910 TX, USA [36445] : 1900-1960 NM,
USA [36445]

ROZIER 1800S MDX, ENG [37186] : 1849 INDIA
[34609]

RUAULT 1620-1690 BAYEUX, BN, FRA [34514]

RUBEN PRE 1900 SKULSK, BYDGOSZCZ, POL
[36455]

RUBENSTEIN PRE 1818 LND, ENG [34036]

RUBERG ALL LETMATHE, WEF, GER [34861]

RUBERY 1800+ LONDON, ENG [37699]

RUBIN PRE 1850S GALS, BE, CH [35525] : PRE 1900
SKULSK, BYDGOSZCZ, POL [36455]

RUCH ALL WORLDWIDE [36965]

RUCKER JOHN PRE 1908 ELBERT, GA, USA [36946]

RUCKLE ALL USA [33760]

RUCKSER PRE 1690 GATTENHOFEN, BAV, GER
[35242]

RUDD 1915+ ECHUCA, VIC, AUS [35220] : 1800+ LONGFORD, TAS, AUS [35806] : 1820-1870 ST HENRI, QUE, CAN [36944]

RUDDELL 1757 BOURBON CO., KY, USA [38187]

RUDDERFORTH 1760-1800S WESTMINSTER, LND, ENG [37445]

RUDDICK 1875 ST ARNAUD, VIC, AUS [35204] : 1830 RAMSGATE, KEN, ENG [35204] : 1800-1830 PORTADOWN, ARM, IRL [36671]

RUDDLE 1600-1850 KINGSCLERE, HAM, ENG [37651] : PRE 1600 BISHOPS CANNINGS, WIL, ENG [37687]

RUDDLE DE COATE PRE 1650 ALL CANNINGS, WIL, ENG [35346]

RUDDOCK 1840+ MELBOURNE, VIC, AUS [34904] : 1840+ HOBART, TAS, AUS [34904] : PRE 1750 GARBOLDISHAM, NFK, ENG [35571] : PRE 1900 RICHHILL, ARM, IRL [35915]

RUDDY PRE 1863 PORTADOWN, ARM, IRL [34044]

RUDE 1750+ LEBANON, CT, USA [38766]

RUDELT 1820+ DOEBELN, SAX, DDR [34803]

RUDGARD PRE 1850 DBY, ENG [36105]

RUDGWAY 1700-1800 BRISTOL, SOM, ENG [37843]

RUDIGER PRE 1800 PLAU 7 CROSSEN, BRA, PER [35795]

RUDKIN ALL EMPINGHAM, RUT, ENG [33916]

RUDLAND PRE 1800 TIMWORTH, SFK, ENG [33992] : C1850 KINGS LYNN, NFK, ENG [37326]

RUDOLPH 1850+ SYDNEY, NSW, AUS [38568] : PRE 1850 PRE, DDR [38568]

RUDOWSKA ALL NIWA, KALISCH, POL [38678]

RUDOWSKI ALL KRASNIK, KALISCH, GER [38678]

RUDSDALE PRE 1900 WHITBY & DANBY, NRY, ENG [37616]

RUE 1822+ BATHURST, NSW, AUS [37110] : 1600+ TINN, TELEMARK, NOR [36905] : 1780+ GLASGOW, LKS, SCT [37110] : 1800-1900 ND, USA [34255] : 1850-1950 MT, USA [34255]

RUECKERT 1819+ KIRCHHAUSEN, GER [35465]

RUEDE ALL BARTHOLOMEW CO., IN, USA [36924]

RUEHLING PRE 1750 CAMBERG, RPF, GER [38681]

RUELBERG 1696 GROSSALMERODE, GHE, GER [38749]

RUETE PRE 1615 BREMEN, BRM, GER [37819]

RUETLINGER 1800-1890 KINGS, QUEENS, NY CITY, NY, USA [34067]

RUETTER 1860 GER & USA [36349]

RUFF C1855 AMBERLEY, SSX, ENG [34936] : 1700+ LONDON, MDX, ENG [35886]

RUFFETT PRE 1785 CHEDDINGTON, IVINGHOE, BKM & BDF, ENG [36668]

RUFFLE 1700S LITTLE SALING, ESS, ENG [37250]

RUFFLIN 1600 SCHWAIGERN, WUE, GER [38574]

RUGG 1750 SOM, ENG [34532] : PRE 1920 KNOCKILLY, COR, IRL [34013]

RUGGE 1600-1700 HRT & HUN, ENG [37670]

RUGLESS PRE 1900 LONDON, ENG [34850]

RUGMAN ALL GRAFFHAM, SSX, ENG [35146]

RUHL 1670-1710 NIEDER RAMSTADT, HEN, BRD [38342] : PRE 1850 GHE, GER [37455] : 1800-1900 KOEHLAR, SARATOV, USSR [38133] : ALL WORLDWIDE [36930]

RUHLAND ALL BERLIN, GER [38672]

RUHLE CATHARINE 1852 GER [38193]

RUHRADE PRE 1850 GER [36773]

RULE 1900+ KOGARAH, NSW, AUS [34275] : HENRY 1853+ VIC, AUS [34278] : PRE 1855 ADELAIDE, SA, AUS [35148] : HENRY PRE 1849 LONDON, ENG [34278] : PRE 1830 CUL, ENG [38718] : C1720 LINLITHGOW, WLN, SCT [36431] : 1820+ HUNTLY, ABD, SCT [36792] : PRE 1820 BOLTON, MLN, SCT [36792] : ALL WORLDWIDE [36295]

RULER 1842+ CAN [34216] : PRE 1842 YKS, ENG [34216] : ALL WORLDWIDE [34216]

RULF ALL TUCHEIM, PSA, GER [34801]

RULLER 1842+ CAN [34216] : WILLIAM PRE 1842 RAWCLIFFE BY GOOLE, WRY, ENG [34216] : PRE 1842 YKS, ENG [34216] : ALL WORLDWIDE [34216]

RULON 1686-1865 NJ, USA [37810]

RUMBALL SOPHRONIA 1864+ MELBOURNE, VIC, AUS [36611] : ALL NEVENDON, ESS, ENG [34837] : 1800-1865 THORLEY, HRT, ENG [36017] : 1800-1865 BISHOPS STORTFORD, HRT, ENG [36017] : 1865-1890 M.E.O.T. & STEPNEY, MDX, ENG [36017]

RUMBELLOW 1720-1800 THORNHAM, NFK, ENG [38453]

RUMBELOW PRE 1900 THORNHAM, NFK, ENG [37686]

RUMBLE C1851 BRISTOL, AVON, ENG [35391] : ALL PETERBOROUGH, CAM, ENG [37127]

RUMBOLD PRE 1757 SHIPDHAM, NFK, ENG [34275] : PRE 1815 LITTLE MAY DEACON, KEN, ENG [35728] : PRE 1640 HATFIELD, ENG [35866] : 1790+ HAM, ENG [37168] : ALL WORLDWIDE [35987]

RUMBOLD (SEE RUMBALL [34837]

RUMENS ALL PETERSHAM, SRY, ENG [37827]

RUMERY 1856+ RIVERSTONE, NSW, AUS [35569]

RUMLER 1788-1810 HERMSDORF, SIL, POL [35850]

RUMLEY PRE 1800 MEOPHAM, KEN, ENG [37325] : 1800 MO, USA [37605]

RUMMERY PRE 1839 SSX, ENG [35569] : 1800-1900 ETCHINGHAM, SSX, ENG [36071] : ALFRED C1900-1912 MOUNTFIELD, SSX, ENG [37436]

RUMMY 1400+ HAVANT, HAM, ENG [33989]

RUMP C1860 DILHAM, NOR, ENG [35121] : 1884 WITTENBURG, MSW, GER [35820] : 1754-1778 GESEKE, WEF, GER [38749]

RUMPFF ALL FRANKFURT, GER [37167]

RUMSBY PRE 1888 NORWICH, NFK, ENG [37442] : 1907 WREXHAM, DEN, WLS [37975]

RUMSEY ALL STUTTON, SFK, ENG [34789] : PRE 1825 GREAT BARDFIELD, ESS, ENG [35026] : ALL WORLDWIDE [36130]

RUNCHMANN 1800+ WORLDWIDE [35555]

RUNDEL 1700-1800 CON, ENG [34258] : 1791-1825 GREENVILLE, NY & PA, USA [37086]

RUNDLE JOHN R. 1840+ ADELAIDE, SA, AUS [35865] : 1830 PLYMOUTH, DEV, ENG [34214] : PRE 1800 MALBOROUGH, DEV, ENG [34214] : ALL ST EWE, CON, ENG [34644] : ALL TREGONY, CON, ENG [35712] : C1816 LOSTWITHIEL, CON, ENG [35865] : 1800-1850 TREGONY, CON, ENG [36623] : C1750 TRURO, CON, ENG [36945]

RUNION (SEE RUNYON) [38060]

RUNIONS 1850-1900 ST LAWRENCE CO., NY & IL, USA [38532]

RUNNALLS PRE 1840 ST BREWARD, CON, ENG [36752] : PRE 1850 CON, ENG [37749]

RUNNELLS PRE 1800 GARBOLDISHAM, NFK, ENG [35571]

RUNYON 1700 BLAND CO. & WARREN CO., VA, USA [38060]

RUPP PRE 1684 BEESSHEIM, BAW, BRD [38615] : 1770-1870 MEISSEN, KSA, GER [38628]

RUPRECHT PRE 1860 GER [37145]

RUS 1850-1900 WEISBADEN, GER [37969]

RUSBRIDER 1400-1500 SRY, ENG [36420]

RUSBRIDGE 1775+ DENTON & SEAFORD, SSX, ENG [35560] : C1806 SEAFORD, SSX, ENG [36668]

RUSE 1700-1850 LAWHITTON & STH PETHERWIN, CON, ENG [35581] : 1810+ CON, ENG [38539]

RUSH PRE 1790 NTH, ENG [35030] : JOHN PRE 1600 OXF, ENG [38023] : PRE 1841 MEA & WEM, IRL [35824] : 1800+ OH, PA & CA, USA [38023] : ALL WORLDWIDE [38023]

RUSHBROOK ALL SFK, ENG [34744]

RUSHBROOKE ALL SFK, ENG [34744]

RUSHBY 1840+ MUDGEE, NSW, AUS [37553] : PRE 1890 YKS, ENG [37309] : 1750-1850 DONCASTER, YKS, ENG [37553]

RUSHFORTH 1600+ HORBURY & MIRFIELD, WRY, ENG [36218]

RUSHMAN PRE 1800 ROGATE, SSX, ENG [34112]

RUSHTON 1840S MAITLAND, NSW, AUS [35516] : 1770 BOROUGHBRIDGE, NRY, ENG [34731] : PRE 1805 HALLIWELL, LAN, ENG [36742] : PRE 1800+ CHURCH & OSWALDTWISTLE, LAN, ENG [36955] : 1800+ ACCRINGTON & BLACKBURN, LAN, ENG [36955] : PRE 1800 BIRMINGHAM, WAR, ENG [37736]

RUSHWORTH 1860-1900 ALEXANDRIA, NSW, AUS [36682] : 1740-1810 BRADFORD, WRY, ENG [36682]

RUSK 1860-1890 CHELSEA, MDX, ENG [37940] : JAMES ALL NORTHERN, IRL [38450]

RUSS PRE 1880 WIL & LND, ENG [37057] : 1940-1973 SANTA MONICA, CA, USA [33853]

RUSSEL 1750+ BLACKHILL & INSCH, ABD, SCT [34387]

RUSSELL 1863+ BURRAGA & BOOROWA, NSW, AUS [33763] : PRE 1862 SANDHURST, VIC, AUS [33862] : 1898+ BRISBANE, QLD, AUS [33932] : PRE 1860 HAWTHORN, VIC, AUS [35200] : ELIZABETH 1830+ MUDGEE, NSW, AUS [35831] : 1875+ BALLARAT, VIC, AUS [35865] : 1800+ NEWCASTLE, NSW, AUS [35911] : 1875-1930 BOOROWA, NSW, AUS [36624] : C1865 SANDRIDGE, VIC, AUS [37500] : 1857+ URALLA, NSW, AUS [38208] : 1848 DORCHESTER, ONT, CAN [34357] : 1844-1890 STELLARTON, NS, CAN [34525] : JANE C1666 HORTON, GLS, ENG [33771] : 1750-1820 PORCHESTER, HAM, ENG [33787] : PRE 1776 ASH, KEN, ENG [33821] : PRE 1820 DEV, ENG [33999] : C1830-1900 EGERTON, KEN, ENG [34101] : PRE 1800 STANMER, SSX, ENG [34112] : 1570 ARRINGTON, CAM, ENG [34204] : 1800+ LONDON, ENG [34271] : PRE 1836 DEPTFORD, KEN, ENG [34462] : 1700 RODMARTIN, GLS, ENG [34466] : 1770+ MAYFIELD & BURWASH, SSX, ENG [34473] : PRE 1849 MARKET HARBOROUGH, LEI, ENG [34584] : PRE 1850 CRANBROOK, KEN, ENG [34611] : EDITH 1870 LENHAM, KEN, ENG [34630] : WILLIAM 1840+ EAST SUTTON, KEN, ENG [34630] : PRE 1920 LONDON, ENG [34657] : PRE 1920 EGERTON, KEN, ENG [34657] : PRE 1791 DEV, ENG [34758] : PRE 1810 MAIDSTONE, KEN, ENG [34816] : 1830+ BYKER, NBL, ENG [35027] : PRE 1850 MAIDSTONE, KEN, ENG [35200] : PRE 1834 BKM, ENG [35419] : PRE 1853 ISLINGTON, MDX, ENG [35532] : 1690+ GREAT BEDWYN, WIL, ENG [35587] : CAROLINE 1809 CUXTON, KEN, ENG [35607] : 1800+ LND & MDX, ENG [35760] : 1740-1790 WANTAGE, BRK, ENG [35813] : 1770-1840 FARNHAM, SRY, ENG [35813] : 1800+ MAIDSTONE, KEN, ENG [35915] : PRE 1800 BRIXTON, IOW, ENG [36142] : PRE 1854 BRIGHTLING, SSX, ENG [36281] : 1800-1900 SOM, ENG [36531] : 1805+ IDLE & THACKLEY, WRY, ENG [36617] : LUCY PRE 1827 AYLESFORD, KEN, ENG [36767] : 1800-60 EAST LONDON, ENG [37252] : PRE 1840 HOVE, SSX, ENG [37325] : ALL CHARD, SOM & NTT, ENG [37692] : 1800-1840 LND, ENG [37696] : 1800-1840 BRIGHTON, SSX, ENG [37696] : PRE 1837 INGOE, NBL, ENG [37744] : PRE 1856

DEEPING ST JAMES, LIN, ENG [38208] : 1700-1800 WINWICK, HUN, ENG [38523] : PRE 1898 FENAGH, ANT, IRL [33932] : PRE 1840 ANT, IRL [34280] : PRE 1848 IRL [34357] : 1750+ PORTADOWN, ARM, IRL [35918] : 1700-1899 STEWARTSTOWN, TYR, IRL [36080] : ALL BANBRIDGE, DOW, IRL [36428] : PRE 1900 MOUNT RUSSELL & CHARLEVILLE, COR, IRL [37415] : JOHN 1822 CHURCHHILL, DON, IRL [37509] : PRE 1772 HILLSBOROUGH, DOW, IRL [37524] : 1800-1900 KILKEE, CLA, IRL [38045] : MARY 1839 DUBLIN CITY, DUB, IRL [38322] : C1857-1917 FOXTON & LEVIN, WGTN, NZ [34651] : C1820-1860+ WELLINGTON, WGTN, NZ [34651] : ALEXANDER C1865+ AUCKLAND, NZ & SCT [36559] : WILLIAM C1865 DUNEDIN, NZ & SCT [36559] : PRE 1850 LARBERT, STI, SCT [34097] : 1800S CARNWARTH, LKS, SCT [34336] : 1800-1870 GLASGOW, LKS, SCT [34373] : PRE 1810 AYR, AYR, SCT [34501] : 1800S SCT [34526] : 1867 FRASERBURGH, ABD, SCT [34529] : 1800+ RUTHERGLEN, LKS, SCT [35027] : ANGUS ALL LKS, SCT [35122] : PRE 1890 SOUTH QUEENSFERRY, WLN, SCT [35457] : PRE 1855 BANNOCKBURN, STI, SCT [35782] : 1800+ MULL, ARL, SCT [35938] : PRE 1750 STRAWFRANK, LKS, SCT [36436] : PRE 1820 AIRDRIE, LKS, SCT [36509] : 1600-1850 DYSART NEWBURGH, FIF, SCT [36556] : 1800-1890 NEW ELGIN & BISHOPMILL, MOR, SCT [36559] : C1800+ CUMBERNAULD, DNB, SCT [36875] : PRE 1780 WHITBURN, WLN, SCT [37374] : 1770S CRAWFORD, LKS, SCT [37751] : 1840 LAUDERDALE, BEW, SCT [38270] : 1790-1850 ERROLL, PER, SCT [38511] : 1750-1850 CADDER, LKS, SCT [38515] : ELIZABETH ALL ARDEN & BRISBANE, LKS & QLD, SCT & AUS [35122] : THOMAS C1797-1900 LKS, SCT & NZ [38437] : 1820-1850 LKS, SCT & USA [36913] : ANDREW PRE 1770 AUGUSTA CO., VA, USA [35328] : 1850-1990 SANTA ROSA, FL, USA [36449] : ALL GREAT BEND, PA, USA & IRL [37503]

RUSSELL-JONES 1854 SURRY HILLS, NSW, AUS [35855]

RUSSEN ALL TWICKENHAM, MDX, ENG [35500]

RUSSENBERGER ALL BRAZIL [35334] : ALL SCHLEITHEIM, SH, CH [35334] : VERONIKA 1850+ USA [35334]

RUSSILL 1780+ KINGSTON ON THAMES, SRY, ENG [37250]

RUSSON 1800+ STOURBRIDGE, WOR, ENG [34323] : PRE 1720 KINGSWINFORD, STS, ENG [36110] : ALL BIRMINGHAM, WAR, ENG [37367]

RUST 1700+ BDF, ENG [37304] : 1866+ MST, GER [34577] : 1650+ BREMEN, BRM, GER [35460] : 1890+ ELK POINT, SD, USA [38751]

RUSTAD PRE 1900 TRONDHJEM, NOR & USA [38386]

RUSTON 1837 KENNINGTON, SRY, ENG [35827]

RUTH 1800 NC, USA [38143]

RUTHERFORD 1860+ MELBOURNE & DAYLESFORD, VIC, AUS [34919] : 1865+ ROCKHAMPTON & TOWNSVILLE, QLD, AUS [35222] : 1800S DUNCAS CO., ONT, CAN [34150] : 1800+ CAMBRIDGE, CAM, ENG [35027] : PRE 1900 LND, ENG [35541] : PRE 1800 HALTWHISTLE & CHOLLERTON, NBL, ENG [36110] : PRE 1650 ROCHESTER, NBL, ENG [36502] : 1800S CHATTON, NBL, ENG [36776] : 1884 HOUGHTON LE SPRING, DUR, ENG [37611] : C1760 NBL, ENG [37788] : 1800S BAILIEBOROUGH, CAV, IRL [34919] : 1770-1830 ROXBURGH, ROX, SCT [34479] : 1815-1936 SELKIRK, SEL, SCT [34525] : PRE 1865 ROX &

SEL, SCT **[35222]** : PRE 1800 JEDBURGH, ROX, SCT **[35351]** : 1790-1840 JEDBURGH, ROX, SCT **[35602]** : 1780 AIRDRIE, LKS, SCT **[36032]** : ROBERT 1830-1870 JEDBURGH, ROX, SCT & NZ **[35999]** : 1850+ NOBLE CO., OH, USA **[36956]** : C1800 WYTHE CO., VA, USA **[37824]** : 1620S ELIZABETH CITY CO., VA, USA **[37824]** : 1790-1800 MONTGOMERY CO., VA, USA **[37824]** : C1800 WASHINGTON CO., VA, USA **[37824]**

RUTHERFURD C1870 ADELAIDE, SA, AUS **[38072]** : C1830 BRT & BN, FRA **[38072]**

RUTHVEN PRE 1855 TORRYBURN, FIF, SCT **[36437]**

RUTHY 1880 ALS, FRA **[37576]** : 1885-1990 CHICAGO, IL, USA **[37576]**

RUTKOWSKI ALL KRAKOW, POL **[37041]**

RUTLAND 1700-1850 GREAT KIMBLE, BKM, ENG **[34687]** : ALL ALFORD & ULCEBY, LIN, ENG **[34745]**

RUTLEDGE C1882 LONDON, ENG **[35786]** : C1826 LET, IRL **[36860]** : 1740-1800 DERRYLIN, FER, IRL **[37613]** : 1700-1840 DUPLIN CO., NC, USA **[37549]** : 1800-1850 CHEROKEE CO., AL, USA **[37549]**

RUTT 1780+ FYFIELD, HAM, ENG **[35214]** : C1780 LND, ENG **[37449]** : MARY C1770 PEWSEY, WIL, ENG **[38489]**

RUTTER 1850+ PARRAMATTA, NSW, AUS **[35410]** : C1856 SYDNEY, NSW, AUS **[35575]** : 1800+ WOR, ENG **[33855]** : PRE 1800 LAMBERHURST & GOUDHURST, KEN, ENG **[34897]** : ALL BURITON, HAM, ENG **[35493]** : PRE 1800 CAM, ENG **[35500]** : ALL FAIRFIELD, WOR, ENG **[35984]** : 1730 HELSTON, CON, ENG **[36640]** : 1800-1870 FAYETTE, PA, USA **[37589]**

RYALL 1880+ BOWRAVILLE, NSW, AUS **[34185]** : 1830+ AUS **[38771]** : ALL MILTON ABBOT, DEV, ENG **[33995]** : PRE 1800 SOM, ENG **[35181]** : PRE 1860 MITCHELLSTOWN, COR, IRL **[35077]** : ALL TIP, IRL **[38771]** : 1850 BOYLE CO., KY, USA **[38103]**

RYAN 1838-1880 GLENORCHY, TAS, AUS **[33934]** : JOHN 1856+ URALLA, NSW, AUS **[33939]** : MICHAEL 1819-1838 AIRDS, NSW, AUS **[33939]** : 1840+ MAITLAND & GLEN INNES, NSW, AUS **[34185]** : 1800+ LAUNCESTON, TAS, AUS **[34271]** : ELIZ PRE 1867 BALLARAT, VIC, AUS **[34652]** : MARRIANNE 1830S+ NSW, AUS **[34902]** : PATRICK 1850-1905 WESTBURY, TAS, AUS **[35195]** : ALL SYDNEY, NSW, AUS **[35258]** : 1883+ BRISBANE, QLD, AUS **[35335]** : C1861+ MELBOURNE, VIC, AUS **[35746]** : C1854-C1861 ADELAIDE, SA, AUS **[35746]** : 1868+ WOLLONGONG, NSW, AUS **[35825]** : MARGARET 1860S CONCORD, NSW, AUS **[36316]** : 1850-1860 NORTH SYDNEY, NSW, AUS **[36845]** : 1849+ SWAN REACH, NSW, AUS **[37136]** : 1835+ NSW, AUS **[37900]** : TIMOTHY 1864-1890S BUNGAREE, VIC, AUS & IRL **[37559]** : 1820+ KINGS CO., NB, CAN **[35610]** : 1800+ GLENGARRY, ONT, CAN **[35614]** : 1800+ CURRAN, ONT, CAN **[36686]** : C1800 CAPE BRETON, NS, CAN **[36694]** : 1800-1990 ONT, CAN **[37466]** : 1800+ LONDON, ENG **[33982]** : PRE 1879 PRESTWICH, LAN, ENG **[35097]** : PRE 1880 LIVERPOOL, LAN, ENG **[35430]** : C1850-C1870 LONDON, MDX, ENG **[37066]** : 1900 SALE, CHS, ENG **[38267]** : ANN 1824-1864 CANNANORE & MADRAS, INDIA **[35132]** : ALL LIM, IRL **[33773]** : PRE 1850 KILLALOE, CLA, IRL **[33805]** : 1800+ TIP, IRL **[33927]** : 1780+ LIM, IRL **[33982]** : 1820S CULLENSTOWN, WEX, IRL **[34044]** : PATRICK PRE 1840 BORRIS O'KANE, TIP, IRL **[34452]** : 1800 TIPPERARY, TIP, IRL **[34574]** : PRE 1830 TIP, IRL **[34588]** : PRE 1840 ENNIS, CLA, IRL **[34769]** : WILLIAM PRE 1854 KILSHAN, TIP, IRL **[34901]** :

1850 TEMPLEMORE, TIP, IRL **[34940]** : PRE 1878 KILADE, TIP, IRL **[34979]** : PRE 1861 HOLYWOOD, DOW, IRL **[35046]** : PATRICK 1820-1865 TIP, IRL **[35195]** : ELLEN PRE 1868 KIK, IRL **[35209]** : PRE 1857 KIK, IRL **[35332]** : C1825 LIMERICK CITY, LIM, IRL **[35389]** : ALL NENAGH, TIP, IRL **[35474]** : PRE 1854 TIP, IRL **[35746]** : ROGER PRE 1840 THURLES & BALLYCAHILL, TIP, IRL **[35750]** : C1832 CLA, IRL **[35772]** : NANCY 1821+ THURLES, TIP, IRL **[35787]** : 1830+ BALLINGRANNE, LIM, IRL **[35905]** : WILLIAM 1787-1828 SOLAHID (SOLLOGHODBEG ?), TIP, IRL **[36711]** : 1750-1850 TIP, IRL **[36780]** : C1800 CAR, IRL **[37066]** : CATH 1816 KILKENNY, IRL **[37123]** : 1840S LIM, IRL **[37309]** : ANDREW C1830-1890 UPPERCHURCH & THURLES, TIP, IRL **[37415]** : 1800-1840 MAY, IRL **[37489]** : PRE 1835 CORK, COR, IRL **[37900]** : DANIEL PRE 1848+ LIM, IRL **[37912]** : C1864 LIM, IRL **[37994]** : 1750-1860 JOHNSTOWN, KIK, IRL **[38045]** : REV. THOMAS 1735-1807 CAHIRCORNEY, LIM, IRL **[38084]** : THOMAS 1800-1875 TIPPERARY, TIP, IRL **[38194]** : PATRICK 1800-1830 WAT, IRL **[38404]** : 1800+ IRL & AUS **[33769]** : TIMOTHY C1853 TIP & QLD, IRL & AUS **[35512]** : JAMES M. 1852-1919 CLA, IRL & AUS **[37153]** : 1880+ BROOKLYN, NY, USA **[34044]** : C1860+ NH, USA **[34494]** : 1868 IRL &, WORLDWIDE **[37511]**

RYCKAERT ALL OOSTWINKEL, OVL, BEL **[38694]** : ALL THOLEN, ZEL, NL **[38694]**

RYCKMANS C1821 PARIS, RPA, FRA **[38691]** : C1836 MORLAIX, BRI, FRA **[38691]**

RYCRAFT C1793 LITTLE BENTLEY, ESS, ENG **[34518]** : PRE 1800 GREAT BROMLEY, ESS, ENG **[36409]**

RYCROFT PRE 1848 BIRMINGHAM, WAR, ENG **[34391]**

RYDE 1880S LONDON, SRY, ENG **[35865]**

RYDER MATILDA C1900 BUNDARRA, NSW, AUS **[35852]** : GEORGE C1870S BUNDARRA, NSW, AUS **[35852]** : C1800 GLS, ENG **[34258]** : 1700-1900 MORETON SAY, SAL, ENG **[34411]** : 1850 FULHAM, MDX, ENG **[35194]** : SARAH C1849 FROXFIELD, WIL, ENG **[35852]** : 1850-1900 SOLIHULL, WAR, ENG **[36530]** : 1870S SALTASH, CON, ENG **[36865]** : PRE 1800 DEV, ENG **[37180]** : C1808 MASHAM, NRY, ENG **[37710]** : 1800+ GAL, IRL **[35201]** : C1800+ MOHILL, LET, IRL **[37447]** : 1870S SC, USA **[36530]** : ALL WORLDWIDE **[38754]**

RYDING PRE 1800 PADIHAM, LAN, ENG **[35462]**

RYDINGS 1751 MANCHESTER, LAN, ENG **[35369]** : 1830+ OLDHAM, LAN, ENG **[35586]**

RYE 1848+ COLAC, VIC, AUS **[35157]** : PRE 1810 SOUTH LOPHAM, NFK, ENG **[35157]** : PRE 1766 KEN, ENG **[38389]**

RYLAND 1800S LONDON, ENG **[35068]** : 1800+ STEPNEY, LND, ENG **[36111]** : 1800-1900 GREATER, LND, ENG **[38171]**

RYMELL ALL UK **[36505]**

RYMER 1790 CROSTON, LAN, ENG **[36798]**

RYMUS 1803+ VT, USA **[37592]**

RYSELL 1870+ USA **[38558]**

RYTER 1750+ USA **[37492]**

RYTON 1750-1830 WOLVERHAMPTON, STS, ENG **[37609]** : 1650-1800 OXF, ENG **[37609]**

SAAL PRE 1861 KAFERTAL, BAD, GER **[35744]**

SAATHOFF ALL OSTFRIESLAND, NDS, BRD **[38685]**

SABEAN CAPT. 1903+ SAINT JOHN, NB, CAN **[34206]** : CAPT. PRE 1954 CAMBRIDGE, MA, USA **[34206]** : LEMUEL PRE 1954 BOSTON, MA, USA **[34206]**

SABERY ALL CARDINGTON, SAL, ENG **[34861]**

SABIEN PRE 1886 YULGILBAR, NSW, AUS [37315]
SABIN PRE 1864 WESTMINSTER, MDX, ENG [35335]
: PRE 1820S USA [38226]
SABINE 1880+ IPSWICH, QLD, AUS [34853] : C1860
ILMINGTON, WAR, ENG [34853]
SABOE PRE 1900 HU & YU [36709]
SABRA PRE 1818 CARTER CO., TN, USA [36929]
SACHAN ALL WORLDWIDE [35121]
SACHS 1864+ GREY, ONT, CAN [36714] : 1857-C1864
WATERLOO, ONT, CAN [36714] : PRE 1806 PRE,
GER [36714] : 1806-1857 KIRCHAIN, HES, GER &
BRD [36714]
SACHTEL 1700S FREDERICK CO., MD, USA [38325]
SACK 1850 PRE [34468]
SACKER 1750+ NFK, ENG [35458]
SACKERS JOHANNES C1640 WESEL CITY, NRW &
WEF, GER [34656] : HENDRICK 1670+ WESEL
CITY, NRW & WEF, GER [34656] : JOHANNES
1697-1789 UTRECHT CITY, UTR, NL [34656]
SACKERT JOHANN 1697-1789 WESEL CITY, NRW &
WEF, GER [34656] : JAN C1640 WESEL CITY, NRW
& WEF, GER [34656] : HENDRICK 1670+ WESEL
CITY, NRW & WEF, GER [34656]
SACKETT ALL USA & ENG [34252]
SACRE 1800-1850 CLERKENWELL, MDX, ENG
[37845]
SADDLER 1780+ WISTON & CARMICHAEL, LKS,
SCT [36749]
SADDLETON 1790+ GAYTON, NFK, ENG [36301]
SADLER 1860+ NEWCASTLE, NSW, AUS [34905] :
1740+ PICKERING, NRY, ENG [34078] : 1700-1860
EDGBASTON, WAR, ENG [35228] : PRE 1900 SFK,
ENG [35352] : ALL NFK, ENG [35628] : PRE 1770
SFK, ENG [35642] : PRE 1850 GORLESTON, NFK,
ENG [36067] : ALL WIL, ENG [36197] : 1750+
NEWBIGGIN, NBL, ENG [36609] : 1800+
LONGBENTON, NBL, ENG [36609] : PRE 1800
CHS, ENG [37098] : 1870S POPLAR, MDX, ENG
[37677] : 1600-1720 TATTERFORD, NFK, ENG
[38453] : 1850 CROGHAN, ROS, IRL [34084] : 1840
YORK TOWNSHIP, ADDISON, IL, USA [38327] :
ALL WORLDWIDE [35875]
SADOWIE ALL WORLDWIDE [38445]
SAEGEBRECHT 1875 DEMMIN, POM, GER [34388]
SAFEGUARD C1650 ST IVES, CON, ENG [33841]
SAFFELL PRE 1875 GREAT WALTHAM, ESS, ENG
[37753]
SAFFREY PRE 1900 STROOD, KEN, ENG [37405]
SAFFRON 1830S HOBART, TAS, AUS [35702]
SAFRAHN 1860+ HAMBURG, HBG, GER [37889]
SAFRENSKI C1700-1850 COPENHAGEN, DEN
[37642]
SAGAR 1860S NELSON, LAN, ENG [36264]
SAGE C1860+ TAMWORTH, NSW, AUS [34277] :
PRE 1844 LENHAM, KEN, ENG [34277] : PRE 1826
SOM, ENG [34633] : 1780-1850 LIVERPOOL, LAN,
ENG [34762] : C1780 HOLINGBOURNE, KEN,
ENG [35920] : 1820S OTTERY ST MARY, DEV,
ENG [36086] : C1797 CHEWTON MENDIP, SOM,
ENG [36816] : 1750-1900 FRESTON, SFK, ENG
[37042] : 1650+ BRISTOL, ENG [38299] : ROBERT
1770 ONSLOW CO., NC, USA [35328] : 1830-1876
CASS CO., MI, USA [36342] : 1639-1876
MIDDLETOWN, CT, USA [36342] : ROBERT 1770S
ONSLOW CO., NC, USA [37585] : ALL CT, OH & IA,
USA & WLS [34116]
SAGGERS 1740-1860 BASSINGBOURNE, CAM, ENG
[37118]
SAGGUS 1740-1860 BASSINGBOURNE, CAM, ENG
[37118]
SAGO ALL ENG [33842]
SAGSBY 1750 THEBERTON, SFK, ENG [37928]

SAIGEON 1730+ MAINE, FRA [34408]
SAIM 1700-1800 UNTERSIEMAU, BAY, BRD [35311]
SAIN 1800+ ENG [37889]
SAINDON 1800+ QUE, CAN [36568]
SAINS ALL WORLDWIDE [37193]
SAINSBURY ALL KENT CO., ONT, CAN [36325] :
C1800 TROWBRIDGE, WIL, ENG [34999] : PRE
1820 EASTERTON, WIL, ENG [35853] : 1800+
BECKINGTON, SOM, ENG [36195]
SAINT 1700+ WOODHORN, NBL, ENG [36609]
SAINT-PIERRE ALL QUE, CAN [34517]
SAINTY ALL AUS [38744] : ALL NFK, ENG [38744]
SAKER PRE 1850 ST LAWRENCE SEAL, KEN, ENG
[35016]
SAKKERS HENDRICK 1737-1814 UTRECHT CITY,
UTR, NL [34656]
SALAMON PRE 1850 LONDON, ENG [36583]
SALAMONSEN 1700-1900 MOLDE, NOR [36261]
SALANT PRE 1900 JERUSALEM, ISRAEL [35635]
SALATHIN PRE 1850 SO, CH [38333]
SALE PRE 1800 WOLSTANTON, STS, ENG [38055]
SALE (SEE SAYLE) [34112]
SALER 1743-1840 FLEMING CO., KY, USA [35316]
SALES 1798-1838 TONBRIDGE WELLS, KEN, ENG
[35391] : 1846 OH, USA [37008]
SALGREN 1901+ ASPEN, CO, USA [38554] : 1902
KANSAS CITY, KS, USA [38554] : 1875+ PHELPS
CO., NE, USA [38554]
SALINGER 1860+ ARARAT & MELBOURNE, VIC,
AUS [35595]
SALISBURY 1850+ NSW & VIC, AUS [34780] : C1818
EVERSHOLT, BDF, ENG [34972] : PRE 1840 WEST
CHINNOCK, SOM, ENG [35211] : PRE 1818
WISBECH, CAM, ENG [36270] : ALL NTH, ENG
[36830] : ALL SOM, ENG [37249] : C1860
BIRKENHEAD, CHS, ENG [37302] : 1841
HARDINGTON MANDEVILLE, SOM, ENG [37378]
: PRE 1833 GREYTOWN, SOM, ENG & NZ [36255] :
TOBIAS 1817-1893 ALBANY & WOODHULL, NY,
USA [35271] : 1750-1850 USA [36962]
SALKEILD PRE 1700 NBL, ENG [37081]
SALKELD C1820 RAUGHTON HEAD, CUL, ENG
[35877] : C1550 CUL, ENG [36490] : 1500-1900 YKS,
ENG [37081] : 1450-1900 NBL, ENG [37081] : 1500-
1900 DUR, ENG [37081] : ALL CUL, ENG [37081] :
ALL WES, ENG [37081] : 1700-1900 DOR, ENG
[37081] : 1750-1850 KENDAL, WES, ENG [38440]
SALKER ALL BRD [34212]
SALKIND 1890+ NORWICH, NFK, ENG [34109]
SALLAWAY 1881 NSW, AUS [35356]
SALLIS PRE 1838 DUMBLETON, GLS, ENG [38399]
SALLOWS 1800S GUELPH & WELLINGTON, ONT,
CAN [36727] : 1700 PEASENHALL, SFK, ENG
[37928]
SALMON 1818+ CASTLEREAGH, NSW, AUS [34967]
: 1860+ ARMIDALE, NSW, AUS [35842] : 1894+
BRISBANE, QLD, AUS [35842] : ALL
MARSHFIELD, GLS, ENG [36152] : 1800+
BLOOMSBURY, LND, ENG [36510] : PRE 1815
HOLLINGBOURNE, KEN, ENG [36510] : 1800+
CLERKENWELL & HOLBORN, LND, ENG [36510]
: ALL KETTERING, NTH, ENG [36830] : C1650-
1750 CHS, ENG [38055] : 1850-1920 GLASGOW,
LKS, SCT [37783] : 1650-1800 WORCESTER CO.,
MD, USA [38342]
SALOMON ALL NSW, AUS & IRL [35498] : 1830S
DUBLIN, IRL & AUS [35498]
SALONEN ALL MYLLYKOSKI, KYMI, FIN [35334]
SALOW 1870-1900 FARMINGTON, MI, USA [36551]
SALSBURY 1850-1880 CAMBERWELL, SRY, ENG
[36586] : ALL KETTERING, NTH, ENG [36830]

SALT C1800+ SUTTON, BDF, ENG [35070] : SARAH C1780 BERMONDSEY, SRY, ENG [37106] : GEORGE PRE 1850 CHEADLE, STS, ENG [37319] : 1790+ SHELTON, STS, ENG [37908]

SALTAU 1957 TOORAK, VIC, AUS [36606]

SALTER 1829-1884 ADELAIDE, SA, AUS [34530] : 1829-32 WINDORAH, QLD, AUS [37178] : 1800+ BRUCE CO., ONT, CAN [37046] : 1829-1884 SOUTHWARK, MDX, ENG [34530] : C1650-1760 LONDON, ENG [35305] : ALL LONDON, ENG [35702] : C1840-70 CHELSEA, MDX, ENG [36153] : PRE 1820 FERSFIELD, NFK, ENG [37512] : ALL ENG [37833] : 1830-1870 ENG [38742] : ALL FLENSBURG, SHO, GER [34869] : C1820 FYVIE, ABD, SCT [36753]

SALTMARSH PRE 1784 MDX, ENG [34853] : PRE 1839 YKS, ENG [35351]

SALTSMAN PRE 1751 RPR, GER [37040]

SALVAGE ALL PRIDDY, SOM, ENG [35391]

SALVETER 1870 PA, USA [35325]

SALVIN 1750-1850 BARLBOROUGH, DBY, ENG [34623]

SAMBLOWSKY ALL BRD [34212]

SAMMERS ELIZABETH C1780 HUN, ENG [35164]

SAMMON 1850+ KILCUMIN, OFF, IRL [34956]

SAMMONS ALL IRL [36545]

SAMPHIRE ALL ALVERSTOKE & PORTSEA, HAM, ENG [36051]

SAMPLE C1850-1930 WEST BROMWICH, STS, ENG [34898]

SAMPSEL PRE 1880 NORTHAMPTON CO., PA, USA [36359]

SAMPSON C1890 WATERLOO, VIC, AUS [35223] : 1856+ KOORINGA, SA, AUS [37901] : SARAH PRE 1865 ENG [34902] : PRE 1821 WRY, ENG [35162] : C1822 BELTON, LIN, ENG [35223] : C1822 GOOLE, ERY, ENG [35223] : 1700+ MDX, ENG [35241] : 1700+ LND, ENG [35241] : C1870 BROMLEY, KEN, ENG [35331] : 1680+ BREAGE, CON, ENG [35587] : ELIZ 1750-1825 BEDMINSTER, SOM, ENG [36555] : 1750-1825 PENZANCE, CON, ENG [37160] : PRE 1760 CUXTON, KEN, ENG [37325] : C1770 WINCHESTER, HAM, ENG [37898] : C1770 WINCHESTER, HAM, ENG [37898] : PRE 1856 CON, ENG [37901] : PRE 1650 HAWKCHURCH, DOR, ENG [38746] : C1830 PRE, GER [34296] : 1750-1850 FORFAR, ANS, SCT [34523] : 1855-1875 KEWEENAW CO., MI, USA [38009]

SAMS 1900+ MUDGEE, NSW, AUS [35373] : 1800S+ SOMERTON, SOM, ENG [35543]

SAMSON ANNIE 1873+ MONTREAL, QUE, CAN [36904] : GEORGE 1869+ MONTREAL, QUE, CAN & USA [36904] : 1750-1850 DROR, ENG [37609] : GEORGE C1830-1879 FORFAR, ANS & QUE, SCT & CAN [36904]

SAMUEL 1800+ SUNDERLAND, DUR, ENG [33982] : PRE 1800 AMSTERDAM, NL [33982]

SAMUELS PRE 1925 POLAR, LND, ENG [34968] : ALL NFK, ENG [35628] : 1700S SHENFIELD, ESS, ENG [36872] : 1800S NOTTINGHAM, NTT, ENG [37977]

SAMUELSSON 1890S CHEHALIS CO., WA, USA [38243]

SAMWAYS PRE 1800 PIDDLETRENTHIDE, DOR, ENG [34347] : PRE 1800 ALTON PANCRAS, DOR, ENG [34347] : 1500+ NETHERBURY, DOR, ENG [38745]

SAMWELL PRE 1879 CAMBERWELL, SRY & LND, ENG [37452] : PRE 1859 IRL [35744]

SANBORN PRE 1817 DOON, ONT, CAN [36726] : 1600-1974 HAMPTON, NH, USA [35294]

SANCHEZ PRE 1873 CALUMPIT, BULACAN, PHILIPPINE [34891]

SANDALL 1800+ PINCHBECK, LIN, ENG [37223] : ALL LIN, ENG [37407]

SANDAY 1650 COTGRAVE, NTT, ENG [36440]

SANDBERG MARIA CH. 1721-1761 STOCKHOLM, SWE [38550]

SANDELANDS E.JELF 1750+ ENG [33963]

SANDENBERGH HERCULES PRE 1714 DRONTHEIM, NOR [36453]

SANDER 1800 KENSINGTON, LND, ENG [36493] : PRE 1899 UMTATA, RSA [33860]

SANDERCOCK PRE 1860 PLYMOUTH, DEV, ENG [36788] : PRE 1730 LOOE & ST GERMANS, CON, ENG [37320]

SANDERLIN ALL CAMDEN CO., NC, USA [38060]

SANDERS PRE 1870 LAUNCESTON, TAS, AUS [35238] : 1895-1908 KYABRAM, VIC, AUS [35238] : PRE 1882 HACKNEY, MDX, ENG [34689] : ALL LND, ENG [35063] : 1800-1850 TAVISTOCK, DEV, ENG [35076] : PRE 1870 ABBOTSHAM, DEV, ENG [35199] : PRE 1800 SSX, ENG [35238] : 1750 LONDON, ENG [35770] : 1700+ MYLOR & GORRAN, CON, ENG [35851] : ALL WOR, ENG [35984] : C1875 PLYMPTON, DEV, ENG [36376] : 1850S TIPTON, STS, ENG [36528] : C1800 BETHNAL GREEN, LND, ENG [37053] : 1700-1800 OXF, ENG [37064] : 1800+ BIRMINGHAM, WAR, ENG [37074] : 1740+ OLD WARDEN, BDF, ENG [37151] : 1800+ PLYMOUTH, DEV, ENG [37924] : PRE 1819 CLOPHILL, BDF, ENG [37946] : 1650-1850 BUTTERWORTH, LEI, ENG [38115] : PRE 1900 OXFORD, OXF, ENG [38116] : PETER PRE 1870 IRTHLINGBORO, NTH, ENG [38776] : 1800+ CAVE SPRINGS, GA, USA [34749] : 1750-1900 ALBANY & RENSSELAER, NY, USA [35292] : SILAS 1880-1890 ST FRANCOIS CO., MO, USA [35329] : DEMPSEY PRE 1810 PEEDEE RIVER, SC, USA & ENG [37529]

SANDERSON 1850+ NSW, AUS [34977] : 1849+ ADELAIDE, SA, AUS [37987] : JOHN 1860S THOROLD, ONT, CAN [36729] : 1770-1800 ALMONDBURY, YKS, ENG [34834] : GEORGE 1800 LAN, ENG [34844] : C1875 DORE, DBY, ENG [35515] : PRE 1861 SPILLABY, LIN, ENG [35515] : C1873 BRADWAY, DBY, ENG [35515] : C1869 STICKFORD, LIN, ENG [35515] : ALL DUR, ENG [35868] : PRE 1850 NEWCASTLE, NBL, ENG [36019] : 1830+ MANCHESTER, LAN, ENG [36019] : C1850 CARLISLE, CUL, ENG [36803] : 1750-1820 BRINKBURN, NBL, ENG [37300] : 1650+ GREAT AYTON, YKS & DUR, ENG [37987] : 1870+ BURY, LAN, ENG [38481] : 1780-1820 STANHOPE, DUR, ENG [38516] : PRE 1820 LEEDS, YKS, ENG [38690] : 1850-1870 ST HELENS, LAN, ENG [38763] : C1800-1827 NEWCASTLE UPON TYNE, NBL, ENG & GER [34740] : MARY ANN ALL COR, IRL [34889] : 1800+ CANNINGSTOWN, CAV, IRL [37478] : ALL KIRKWALL, ORKNEY, SCT [34820] : 1800+ (MCDONNELL CLAN), SCT [34889] : C1850 ROTHIEMAY, BAN, SCT [35860] : C1805 OLRIG & LATHERON, CAI, SCT [37684]

SANDFORD PRE 1839 AYLESBURY, BKM, ENG [34166] : PRE 1900 NFK, ENG [34317] : 1800-1850 YEOVIL, SOM, ENG [37435] : PRE 1800 WOUTTUN RIVERS, WIL, ENG [37687] : ALFRED J. PRE 1877+ NZ [34592]

SANDHAGEN ALVENA 1863 BENSONVILLE, IL, USA [37596]

SANDHAM 1890+ AUS & NZ [34158] : 1780+ CARLETON, LAN, ENG [34092] : C1700-1900

BOLTON LE SANDS, LAN, ENG [34158] : 1800S
PILLING, LAN, ENG [38285]
SANDILANDS PRE 1851 EDINBURGH, MLN, SCT
[34590] : 1800 + LKS, SCT [36749] : 1820S
CARMICHAEL, LKS, SCT [37879]
SANDIMAN PRE 1800 SETTRINGTON, ERY, ENG
[37913] : 1790 + ROC & INV, SCT [35486]
SANDLES 1800+ LEWES, SSX, ENG [36434]
SANDON 1850+ SYDNEY, NSW, AUS [33765]
SANDOVAL PRE 1720 SANLUCAR DE
BARRAMEDA, CADIZ, ESP [36937] : PRE 1940
JIQUILIPAN, MICHOACAN, MEXICO [37565]
SANDRY 1860-1990 MUDGEE & GILGANDRA, NSW,
AUS [34294] : 1800 + MUDGEE, NSW, AUS [34538] :
1800+ VITTORIA, NSW, AUS [34538]
SANDS 1853 + GOULBURN, NSW, AUS [36296] :
1853+ GUNNING, NSW, AUS [36296] : 1890
FAIRHOLME, ONT, CAN [34055] : 1800S
FRONTENAC, ONT, CAN [34353] : 1800S
LONDON, ENG [34178] : 1800S CAMBRIDGE,
CAM, ENG [34178] : PRE 1800 FRISKNEY &
TRUSTHORPE, LIN, ENG [35255] : ALL GRIMSBY,
LIN, ENG [35337] : PRE 1850 LEICESTER, LEI,
ENG [36188] : JOHN PRE 1730 NOTTINGHAM,
NTT, ENG [36619] : PRE 1682 LANCASTER, LAN,
ENG [36972] : 1790 + BRISTOL, GLS & DOR, ENG
[37990] : 1870 PORTGLENONE, ANT, IRL [36655] :
1800+ LIMERICK, LIM, IRL [37560] : 1700S LAKE
MEUTEITH, PER, SCT [34621] : 1850-1870S EAU
CLAIRE CO., WI, USA [36337] : PRE 1785
CHESTER CO., PA, USA [36972] : 1751-1853
LLANDOUGH, GLA, WLS [36296] : PRE 1890
WORLDWIDE [34055]
SANDTNER PRE 1875 OES [37009]
SANDWICH ALL HAM, ENG [36131]
SANDY PRE 1833 BRISTOL, GLS, ENG [34695] : PRE
1842 EDMONSHAM, DOR, ENG [35407] : PRE 1900
HAM, ENG [36828] : MATILDA C1909
CAPETOWN, RSA [34193] : 1890+ RSA [34946]
SANDYS 1758 + SFK, GLS & DUB, ENG & IRL
[34109] : 1758 + LDY, KIK & WAT, IRL [34109] :
1758+ ARM, IRL [34109]
SANFORD PRE 1832 WEST COKER & NORTON,
SOM, ENG [34057] : PRE 1900 ABBOTSLEY, BDF,
ENG [37780]
SANG ALL SCT [37767]
SANGER 1820+ GILLINGHAM, DOR, ENG [35529] :
1690-1780 WIL, ENG [37233] : PRE 1860
DURNFORD, WIL, ENG [37989] : ALL ELO, GER
[38742] : ALL PRE [38085] : ALL RUSSIA [38085] :
ALL SAN FRANCISCO, CA, USA [38085]
SANGSTER 1850-1890 MANCHESTER & SALFORD,
LAN, ENG [36024] : PRE 1840 INDIA [37882] : PRE
1830 GLASGOW, RFW, SCT [34769] : 1800+ ABD,
SCT [36971] : C1800 ABD, SCT [37245] : C1800
PETERHEAD, ABD, SCT & AUS [35079]
SANGWELL 1850+ TAS, AUS [34590] : PRE 1850
LONDON, ENG [34590]
SANKEY 1705 MUCH WENLOCK, SAL, ENG [34708] :
1800-1837 CRADELEY, STS, ENG [36008] : 1837+
CHURCH GRESLEY, DBY, ENG [36008] : PRE 1600
LAN, ENG [38744] : ALL NFK, ENG [38744]
SANLY 1870+ LONGSWAMP, PA, USA [38335]
SANNDERSON 1823 + CAV, IRL [36608]
SANSBERRY 1744 CHISWICK, MDX, ENG [36051]
SANSBURY 1800S POOLE, DOR, ENG [36637] : 1800S
UPTON, WOR, ENG [36637]
SANSOM 1700S TIDEFORD, CON, ENG [34817] :
1800+ DOR, ENG [35144] : PRE 1850
NOTTINGHAM, NTT, ENG [37739] : GEORGE PRE
1830 SUNDERLAND, DUR, ENG [38509] : 1700+
USA [38235]

SANSOME 1750-1860 OXF, ENG [34667]
SANSON 1750-1860 OXF, ENG [34667]
SANTILLA PRE 1825 MANCHESTER, LAN, ENG
[35592]
SANTINI PRE 1830 CASALBORDINO, CHIETI, ITL
[34127]
SANTOS PRE 1950 SUNDERLAND, DUR, ENG
[36502]
SANTOUX C1675 ONEX & VANDOEUVRES, GE, CH
[38348]
SANTS 1800-1950 ENG [37233]
SANXAY ALL WORLDWIDE [36993]
SAPARA ALL BERGSTADT, PISEK, CS [37045]
SAPE PRE 1765 NORTHAM, DEV, ENG [38580]
SAPSFORD PRE 1700 GREAT HALLINGBURY, ESS,
ENG [37250]
SARA PRE 1849 TRURO, CON, ENG [34750]
SARAH PRE 1880 PROBUS, CON, ENG [33850] :
JOHN PRE 1850 MARY TAVY, DEV, ENG [33850]
SARATO PRE 1880 AXBRIDGE, SOM, ENG [34713]
SARAU PRE 1800 OLDENBURG, SHO, GER [38648]
SARDEN PRE 1865 KNOXVILLE, TN, USA [37817]
SARFAS ALL WORLDWIDE [35939]
SARGEANT 1880+ AVOCA, VIC, AUS [35801] : 1854
BINFIELD, BRK, ENG [34120] : 1690 BINFIELD,
BRK, ENG [34731] : PRE 1850 SALTFLEET BY ST
PETER, LIN, ENG [36168] : PRE 1866
SHOREDITCH, MDX, ENG [34750]
SARGEAUNT C1750-1850 EARLS BARTON, NTH,
ENG [33876]
SARGENT 1880 MARYBOROUGH, VIC, AUS [35801] :
1825+ PETERBOROUGH, ONT, MAN & BC, CAN
[34348] : C1791 LANGHAM, ESS, ENG [34518] : PRE
1800 CLAPHAM, LND, ENG [34655] : 1600+
HASTINGS, SSX, ENG [34747] : 1800S LAN, ENG
[35017] : 1800S WINTERBOURNE, GLS, ENG
[35187] : PRE 1850 HULL, ERY, ENG [35724] : PRE
1850 GRANTHAM & STAMFORD, LIN, ENG
[35724] : 1800+ BINFIELD, BRK, ENG [35806] : PRE
1740 KEELBY, LIN, ENG [36059] : 1562+
COURTEENHALL, NTH, ENG [37802] : C1760
LISKEARD, CON, ENG [38209] : 1820 SSX, ENG
[38719] : PRE 1825 MITCHELSTOWN, COR, IRL
[34348]
SARGESON 1850 HULL & KINGSTON, ERY, ENG
[34111]
SARGOOD ALL WORLDWIDE [37843]
SARJANT PRE 1700 ESS, ENG [35642]
SARLUIS 1800-1870 EAST END, LONDON, ENG &
GER [37194]
SARNIAK 1850-1900 WARSAW, WA, POL [37615]
SARRE ALL GSY, CHI [37229] : ALL WORLDWIDE
[37229]
SARROW 1790 + SCIOTO, OH, USA [38054]
SARTAIN C1740 VA, USA [37032]
SARTORI 1870+ STAWELL, VIC, AUS [35493]
SARTORIS ALL WORLDWIDE [34472]
SARTORIUS 1700+ LONDON, ENG [36756]
SARVER PRE 1800 LANCASTER CO., PA, USA
[36345] : 1800-1820 WASHINGTON CO., MD, USA
[36345]
SASANKA 1900+ DETROIT, MI, USA [34148]
SASBACH 1800-1900 AMSTERDAM, NOH, NL [34069]
SASS ALL WORLDWIDE [38633]
SASSE 1900+ FREMANTLE & PERTH, WA, AUS
[34841] : 1800S MITCHAM, SRY, ENG [36817] : 1893-
1975 WESTOENNEN, GER [38749]
SASSEN 1700+ QUICKBORN, SHO, GER [37542]
SASSEVILLE 1600+ FRA [37479]
SATCHELL 1763 COVENTRY, WAR, ENG [36649]
SATCHWELL ALL AUS [33975] : C1700-1850 BURY
NR TOTNES, DEV, ENG [34508] : 1820S

HARBURY, WAR, ENG [35123] : C1816
GUILDFORD, SRY, ENG [35828] : 1850-1860 WAR,
ENG [36845] : ANN 1800S COVENTRY & CROFT
CHETHAM, WAR, ENG [37317]
SATES PRE 1800 KENCOT, OXF, ENG [37763]
SATRES C1860 DEV, ENG [35910]
SATTERLY MARY 1848 + SA & VIC, AUS [33840]
SATTERWHITE ALL USA [36545]
SATTLER PRE 1855 NIEDERWALLUF, HEN, BRD
[36629]
SAUBERLI ALL TEUFENTHAL, AG, CH [34719]
SAUBERT C1560 NUERNBERG, BAY, FRG [38660]
SAUER 1850 TRIEVELESHT, BUCKOVYNA, [36655] :
1855 + TOOWOOMBA, QLD, AUS [37894] : PRE
1857 HESSE NASSAU, BRD [36338] : PRE 1855
HEDDESHEIM, BAD, GER [37894] : ALL WEI,
GER [38607] : 1857-1866 BROOKLYN, KINGS, NY,
USA [36338]
SAUL 1853 + NORTHERN RIVERS, NSW, AUS
[35117] : PRE 1853 ST BEES & WHITEHAVEN,
CUL, ENG [35117] : 1800-70 ROTHENBERG, HEN,
GER [35866]
SAULDE 1570-1640 LA FLECHE, FRA [34514]
SAULL 1865 + SYDNEY, NSW, AUS [34545] : 1815-
1865 LONDON, ENG [34545]
SAULS SAM 1770 + GA, USA [38185] : SAM 1770 +
VA, USA [38185]
SAULT 1900 ASHOPTON, HOPE WOODLANDS,
DBY, ENG [34995] : 1862 LEICESTER, LEI, ENG
[34995]
SAUNDERS 1840 + CASTLEREAGH RIVER, NSW,
AUS [33923] : 1894 ADELAIDE, SA, AUS [34193] :
PRE 1900 AUS [34196] : 1880 + ESK, QLD, AUS
[34585] : PRE 1900 VIC, AUS [34657] : PRE 1900 VIC,
AUS [34657] : 1879 + POLICE FORCE, NSW, AUS
[36632] : PRE 1900 MELBOURNE, VIC, AUS [38082]
: 1820 + CAN [37427] : 1800 + ST HELIER, JSY, CHI
[35393] : 1830-1860S ST HELIER, JSY, CHI [36285] :
1810-1850 ARKESDEN & WICKEN BONANT, ESS,
ENG [34035] : PRE 1850 PORTLAND, DOR, ENG
[34089] : PRE 1791 ESS, ENG [34189] : 1800-1820
CUDHAM, KEN, ENG [34205] : 1871 KINGS
NORTON, WOR, ENG [34224] : 1700-1800 MYLOR,
CON, ENG [34274] : 1795-1816 SSX, ENG [34371] :
ALL BIDEFORD, DEV, ENG [34471] : ALL
SAUNDERSTEAD & LONDON, MDX, ENG [34645]
: C1840 CHELMSFORD, HRT, ENG [34654] : 1810 +
LYDEARD ST LAWRENCE, SOM, ENG [34726] :
PRE 1800 LONDON, MDX, ENG [34743] : PRE 1852
BETHNAL GREEN, LND, ENG [34814] : PRE 1780
CANNOCK, STS, ENG [34974] : PRE 1760
WESTFIELD, SSX, ENG [35128] : THOMAS PRE
1815 NEWBOLD ON AVON, WAR, ENG [35431] :
MARY 1750S SSX, ENG [35501] : 1825 HORSLEY,
GLS, ENG [35770] : 1800 + CON, ENG [35836] : 1833
ELMDON, ESS, ENG [35903] : 1700-1800 LONDON,
ENG [36081] : 1750 + TAKELEY, ESS, ENG [36123] :
PRE 1850 HITCHIN, HRT, ENG [36154] : 1800-1900
PRINCES RISBOROUGH, BKM, ENG [36175] :
1800-1900 PRESTWOOD, BKM, ENG [36175] : PRE
1831 + BROADBLUNSDON, WIL, ENG [36307] :
1700-1900 MISTLEY & MANNINGTREE, ESS,
ENG [36409] : PRE 1879 UFFINGTON, BRK, ENG
[36632] : C1856 SWINDON, WIL, ENG [36975] :
C1730 DEV, ENG [37180] : GEORGE PRE 1820
ISLINGTON & LAMBETH, LND, ENG [37321] :
1700-1950 ESS, ENG [37344] : C1862 MARDEN,
KEN, ENG [37359] : PRE 1838 STRATFORD, ESS,
ENG [37442] : PRE 1850 TIBENHAM, NFK, ENG
[37512] : 1300-1400 + SSX, ENG [37648] : PRE 1850
BRAINTREE, ESS, ENG [37726] : C1851 DUNMOW,
ESS, ENG [37726] : PRE 1850 NOTTINGHAM, NTT,

ENG [37729] : PRE 1890 MDX, SOM & LAN, ENG
[37882] : PRE 1800 OTTEREY SIDBURY, DEV, ENG
[38540] : PRE 1800 IOW, ENG [38700] : PRE 1850
KINGSTON ON THAMES, SRY, ENG & AUS
[34845] : ALL WROUGHTON, WIL, ENG & AUS
[35213] : HARRIET 1832 + HIGH WYCOMBE,
BKM, ENG & AUS [37161] : 1700 + WICKLOW,
WIC, IRL [37422] : PRE 1880 CORK, COR, IRL
[38299] : 1900 + JOHANNESBURG, RSA [34215] :
ALL DUNDEE, ANS, SCT [36999] : C1800
FOSSOWAY, KRS, SCT [37463] : 1840 + MERCER
CO., IL, USA [35278] : 1790S FREDERICK CO., VA,
USA [35278] : ALL PA, USA [38359] : ALL
MERTHYR TYDFIL, GLA, WLS [35588] :
(DRAPERS) ALL WORLDWIDE [38540]
SAUNDERS (NEE SANDER [35076]
SAUNDERS-LODER 1850S GEORGETOWN,
CANTERBURY, NZ [35906]
SAUNDERSON 1780-1850 BALLYGAWLEY, TYR,
IRL [36075]
SAUNDERSON (SEE SANN [36608]
SAUNDRY 1700 + BREAGE, CON, ENG [34538]
SAUSBURY C1834 BANGALORE, MYSOR, INDIA
[38069]
SAUVE 1620-1690 LIBOURNE & BORDEAUX, FRA
[34514]
SAUZIERE 1700 CAN [38493]
SAVAGE 1860 HOBART, TAS, AUS [33810] : C1840
MELBOURNE, VIC, AUS [35089] : 1900 +
MELBOURNE, VIC, AUS [37152] : 1750 +
COLNBROOK, MDX, ENG [33963] : 1750 + KEN,
ENG [33973] : 1850 + NOTTINGHAM, NTT, ENG
[34329] : PRE 1860 NORTHAMPTON, NTH, ENG
[34329] : EDWARD 1780 + COLNBROOK, BKM &
MDX, ENG [34486] : PRE 1800 HUCKNALL &
TORKARD, NTT, ENG [34739] : PRE 1821
BUCKINGHAM, BKM, ENG [34840] : WILLIAM
1810 + LAMBETH, SRY, ENG [35046] : 1860-1900
NORTON, WOR, ENG [35341] : 1890-1937
RUNCORN, CHS, ENG [35341] : C1770 CODFORD,
WIL, ENG [35349] : PRE 1790 NTT, ENG [35745] :
1750-1767 TITCHFIELD, HAM, ENG [35903] : 1700-
1800 LEICESTER, LEI, ENG [36081] : PRE 1834
LANCASTER, LAN, ENG [36227] : DANIEL PRE
1730 LONDON, ENG [36619] : PRE 1840
HORSFORD, NFK, ENG [36828] : 1850 + HAM,
ENG [37128] : GEORGE 1799 + BEACHAMPTON,
BKM, ENG [37165] : C1730 SHOREDITCH, MDX,
ENG [37239] : 1780 + NFK, ENG [37409] : JOB 1785-
1840 MANCHESTER, LAN, ENG [37543] : MARY
1785-1840 MANCHESTER, LAN, ENG [37543] :
1800-1880 BLACKBURN, LAN, ENG [37547] :
1900 + LIVERPOOL, LAN, ENG [37831] : 1700-1900
SWALE MEDWAY, KEN, ENG [38249] : ALL
ROMSEY & MICHELMERSH, HAM, ENG [38350] :
C1790 BELFAST, ANT & LDY, IRL [35773] : PRE
1890 KER, IRL [36840] : PRE 1900 DUBLIN, IRL
[37831] : 1850 + DUNEDIN, NZ [33963] : EDWARD
1861 + DUNEDIN, NZ [34486] : 1750-1850 HUDSON
RIVER AREA, NY, USA [38153] : GORDON
EDWARD 1945 GLEN COVE, LONG ISLAND, NY,
USA [38183] : C1861 LLANDINAM, MGY, WLS
[34893]
SAVEALL 1720 + WEST HANNINGFIELD, ESS,
ENG [36981]
SAVERY 1820 + BOVEY TRACEY, DEV, ENG [35114]
SAVILE PRE 1250 OLLERTON & NORMANDY,
NTT, ENG & FRA [36104]
SAVILL PRE 1818 BARLEY, HRT, ENG [34840] :
1800 + ESS, ENG [35999] : ALL ESS, ENG [37741]
SAVILLE 1870 + NORTH-EAST, TAS, AUS [34017] :
1800S WEST HAM, ESS, ENG [34086] : ALL ESS,

ENG [34877] : C1803 LND & LAN, ENG [35137] :
1870+ DOWNHAM, CAM & NFK, ENG [35999] :
1750S STEBBING, ESS, ENG [37250] : 1788+
DEWSBURY, YKS, ENG [38499] : ALL NEWPORT,
ESS, ENG [38502] : 1730-1740 CHESTER CO., PA,
USA [38334]
SAVIN PRE 1819 BLETCHINGDON, OXF, ENG
[34281]
SAVORY 1800+ NFK, ENG [37699] : 1800+
LONDON &, NFK, ENG [37699] : 1650-1707 LITTLE
COMPTON, RI, USA [37810]
SAWALLISCH 1800-1900 DANZIG, WESTPREUβEN,
PRE [38603]
SAWARD C1730 COGGESHALL, ESS, ENG [37063]
SAWDEN 1700S GRINDALE, YKS, ENG [34569]
SAWELL 1750 NORTH CHURCH, HRT, ENG [36798]
SAWERS C1895 SLD, NZ [36853] : 1750-1850 LKS, SCT
[34229] : PRE 1900 WIG, SCT [36853]
SAWKILL ALL DUR, ENG [37293]
SAWLE 1500-1800 GERRANS & FOWEY, CON, ENG
[35576]
SAWTELL PRE 1832 LANGPORT, SOM, ENG [34616]
: 1852+ CHRISTCHURCH, CANT, NZ [34616]
SAWYER C1860+ WA, AUS [35053] : 1857-1857
HAWTHORN, VIC, AUS [37911] : ROBERT C1881-
1971 WEST GWILLIMBURY, ONT, CAN [34997] :
PRE 1800 HEMINGFORD, HUN, ENG [34003] :
PRE 1940 BATH, SOM, ENG [35433] : PRE 1850
MAIDSTONE, KEN, ENG [36298] : PRE 1800 CITY,
LND, ENG [36432] : 1670-1820 WELLOW, HAM,
ENG [37233] : 1670-1750 WOODHAY, HAM, ENG
[37233] : 1670-1820 WELLOW, WIL, ENG [37233] :
JOHN C1800 PANCRAS, LND, ENG [37239] : 1834
NORTH MEOLS, LAN, ENG [37911] : 1600-1900
LONDON, ENG [38278]
SAWYERS WILLIAM 1850+ AVISFORD &
WINDEYER, NSW, AUS [37310] : 1848-1855 ESS,
ENG [37310] : JOSEPH 1760+ EWELL, SRY, ENG
[37310] : 1745-1765 AUGUSTA CO., VA, USA [38144]
SAXBY PRE 1874 BUNGAY & WINGHAM, NSW,
AUS [35546] : 1855+ VIC, AUS [35731] : PRE 1841
BATTLE, SSX, ENG [35546] : 1750 METFIELD, SFK,
ENG [37928] : 1800+ UK [36683]
SAXER PRE 1776 SAALSTADT, RPF, GER [38663]
SAXLER 1848+ COOK CO., IL, USA [38534]
SAXON 1820+ PRESTWICH, LAN, ENG [37669] :
1750-1850 MANCHESTER, LAN, ENG [38005]
SAXPEACH 1800S LONDON, ENG [34634]
SAXPEY PRE 1800 MOUNTFIELD &
WHATLINGTON, SSX, ENG [37875]
SAXTON 1740 DBY, ENG [36440] : PRE 1850
LONDON, MDX & ESS, ENG [37749]
SAY ALL AUS [34759] : PRE 1838 NORTH BRADLEY,
WIL, ENG [34759] : C1836 LITTLE DURHAM, NFK,
ENG [35225]
SAYCE PRE 1900 HEF, ENG [34647]
SAYER ALL THWAITES FARM, YKS, ENG [34155] :
ALL YKS, ENG [34155] : 1700-1800 KEWSTOKE,
SOM, ENG [34158] : SAMUEL J. PRE 1860
BUNGAY, SFK, ENG [36590] : WILLIAM 1870-1900
NORWICH, NFK, ENG [36876] : 1670-1820
WELLOW, HAM, ENG [37233] : 1670-1820
WELLOW, HAM, ENG [37233] : 1670-1750
WOODHAY, HAM, ENG [37233] : PRE 1900
WHITBY & BROTTON, NRY, ENG [37616] : 1650
GREAT WALTHAM, ESS, ENG [37928] : WILLIAM
PRE 1870 INDIA [36876]
SAYERS 1860+ VIC, AUS [38719] : 1900+
BRANTFORD, ONT, CAN [34145] : PRE 1750 WEST
CHILTINGTON, SSX, ENG [33899] : C1840
BRIGHTON, SSX, ENG [34145] : 1816+ YAPTON,
SSX, ENG [34237] : PRE 1900 LONDON, ENG

[34590] : 1500-1900 SSX, ENG [35643] : 1840-1860
DOVER, KEN, ENG [36071] : C1896 RIVERHEAD,
KEN, ENG [36071] : 1800+ TWINEHAM, SSX, ENG
[36212] : C1800 MDX, ENG [36810] : 1800+
MITCHAM, SRY, ENG [36871] : ALL SSX, ENG
[37922] : C1800 INDIA [37770]
SAYLE 1850 VIC, AUS [35776] : PRE 1800
BILLINGSHURST, SSX, ENG [34112] : ALL
BALLAUGH, IOM [35776]
SAYLOR PHILLIP 1818-1845 MORGON CO., OH,
USA [35329]
SAYWELL PRE 1800 BEXLEY, KEN, ENG [34707] :
PRE 1848 RADFORD, NTT, ENG [34773] : 1810-1841
RADFORD, NTT, ENG [35864] : 1700-1900 SWALE
MEDWAY, KEN, ENG [38249]
SCADDEN 1840S CAMBORNE, CON, ENG [35728]
SCADTZ C1587 RUMMEN, BBT, BEL [38160]
SCALES PRE 1860 WOLVERHAMPTON, STS & CUL,
ENG [34958] : PRE 1800 DONCASTER, WRY, ENG
[37589] : 1850S MAGHERA, ANT, IRL [34636] :
1890+ CHRISTCHURCH, SI, NZ [36628] : 1730-1752
RICHMOND, VA, USA [36354]
SCALING THOMAS 1760-1820 KINGSTON UPON
HULL, YKS, ENG [34143]
SCALLEY C1834 CUSHENDALL, ANT, IRL [36860]
SCAMELL 1700+ FROME, SOM, ENG [36591] :
1650+ SALISBURY, WIL, ENG [36591] : 1800+
LAMBETH & SOUTHWARK, LND, ENG [36591] :
1650+ WYLYE VALLEY, WIL, ENG [36591] : ALL
WORLDWIDE [36591]
SCAMMEL PRE 1916 VIC, AUS [36622] : PRE 1854
SOM, ENG [36622]
SCAMMELL PRE 1830 TEWINWATER, HRT, ENG
[34003] : PRE 1830 ISLE OF WIGHT, HAM, ENG
[34014] : C1799 PORTSEA, HAM, ENG [34836] :
1770+ THORLEY, IOW, ENG [35342] : 1700-1800
RINGWOOD, HAM, ENG [36226] : 1700+ FROME,
SOM, ENG [36591] : 1800+ LND, ENG [36591] :
1800+ BERMONDSEY, LND, ENG [36591] : 1650+
TISBURY & SEMLEY, WIL, ENG [36591] : ALL
WORLDWIDE [36591]
SCANDLEAN 1860+ TIP, IRL [34774] : 1860+ LIM,
IRL [34774]
SCANLAN 1883+ BRISBANE, QLD, AUS [35335] :
PRE 1882 OATLANDS, TAS, AUS [35459] : 1900+
ADELAIDE, SA, AUS [35565] : 1865+
ROCKHAMPTON, QLD, AUS [35753] : PRE 1883
BALLYBOFEY, DON, IRL [35335] : PRE 1845
KILLALOE, CLA, IRL [35753]
SCANLON 1920+ WAVERLEY & SYDNEY, NSW,
AUS [37966] : 1800+ CASHEL, TIP, IRL [34556] :
1800+ KERRY, CLA, IRL [34970] : 1829+ IRL
[36312] : 1750+ TIP, IRL [36602]
SCANTLEBURY 1800-1850 DEV & CON, ENG [36422]
SCARBORO 1840 IRTHLINGBOROUGH, NTH, ENG
[35376]
SCARBOROUGH PRE 1870 COLLINGWOOD, VIC,
AUS [34600] : 1866+ BUNDAMBA, QLD, AUS
[35392] : 1835+ MELBOURNE, VIC, AUS & ENG
[35498] : C1750-1820 MILLBROOK, BDF, ENG
[33845] : 1824+ CAISTOR, LIN, ENG [35392] : PRE
1846 BARTON ST MARY, LIN, ENG [35392] :
1800+ HOLME UPON SPALDING MOORE, ERY,
ENG [37989] : 1830+ BARTON, LIN, ENG [37989]
SCARBROW 1850+ CAMDEN TOWN, LND, ENG
[36981]
SCARCE PRE 1850 SAXMUNDHAM, SFK, ENG
[35215]
SCARDEFIELD 1800S PORTSEA, HAM, ENG [36409]
SCARFF 1858+ MARYBOROUGH, VIC, AUS [33882] :
ALL SFK, ENG [37279]
SCARFFE PRE 1750 IOM [37646]

SCARLETT ALL AUS [34578] : 1840-1930
MELBOURNE, VIC & WA, AUS [34815] : 1856
TORONTO, ONT, CAN [37493] : PRE 1841 WAR,
ENG [34578] : PRE 1800 SFK, ENG [36124] : PRE
1837 CAV, IRL [33845] : PRE 1826 FER, IRL [37601] :
JAMES 1911+ GAL, IRL [37601] : 1700+ ORANGE
CO., NC, USA & ENG [38175]

SCARONI CESARE 1900 DARRARA, BROADFORD
NEWCASTLE, LIM, IRL [34070]

SCARPALANI PRE 1900 ITL [38125]

SCARR PRE 1870 LND, ENG [36843] : PRE 1659
AYSGARTH, WRY, ENG [37685]

SCARRETT PRE 1756 PORTSEA, HAM, ENG [35973]

SCARROTT PRE 1800 WELLINGTON, SAL, ENG
[35181]

SCARSI 1850S SERINO, ITL [34574]

SCARTH 1760-1850S YKS, ENG [34178]

SCAT C1348 BRUSSEL, BBT, BEL [38160]

SCATS C1363 BRUSSEL, BBT, BEL [38160] : C1591
HERCK DE STAD, LBG, BEL [38160]

SCATTE C1374 BRUSSEL, BBT, BEL [38160]

SCATTERGOOD PRE 1842 THURCASTON, LEI,
ENG [34661] : 1700-1800 NOTTINGHAM, NTT,
ENG [37829]

SCAWLAN 1880+ LONGREACH &
ROCKHAMPTON, QLD, AUS [35222]

SCAYSBROOK C1800 TODENHAM, GLS, ENG
[35033] : 1853+ BIRMINGHAM, WAR, ENG [35033]

SCEDGELL C1810 DEV, ENG [37180]

SCHAAF PRE 1750 ARNSTADT, PSA, GER [38681]

SCHAAK 1800-1945 GER [37363]

SCHACKE 1825-1880 LINGEN-EMS,
NIEDERSACHSEN, FRG [38710] : ALL LIPPE, FRG
[38710]

SCHADTS C1622 RUMMEN, BBT, BEL [38160]

SCHAEFER ALL BERNDORF, WAL, GER [34861] :
JOHANN 1815+ BAD, GER [37532] : 1877-1957
ELBRINXEN, LIP, GER [38749] : 1845+
POMEROY, OH, USA [37532]

SCHAEFFER 1690 EILENBURG, GER [38749] : 1759
WURZEN, KSA, GER [38749]

SCHAFER ELIZA 1880+ MECKELSDORF, HES,
GER [35315] : 1800-1830 SUSQUEHANNA CO., PA,
USA [36736]

SCHAFFARINSKY C1700-1850 COPENHAGEN, DEN
[37642]

SCHAFFER 1870+ BRISBANE, QLD, AUS [35460]

SCHAFNER PRE 1800 ANNAPOLIS, NS, CAN [37049]

SCHAGEN 1864-1894 NOH, NL [38711]

SCHAKE 1840-1940 BUREN, LIPPE, FRG [38710]

SCHALCK PRE 1720 DETWANG, BAV, GER [35242]

SCHALKWIJK PRE 1800 ZUH & UTR, NL [34180]

SCHALOW 1870-1900 SHAWANO CO., WI, USA
[36546]

SCHAN PRE 1800 CLK, SCT [36272]

SCHAND ALL ENAHOFEN, BRD, GER [34938]

SCHANZ 1758+ MENGEN & MULLHEIM, BAD,
GER [37504]

SCHAPER C1830 BRAUNSCHWEIG, NSA, FRG
[38660] : PRE 1850 WESTERKAPPELN, WEF, GER
[36957]

SCHARFENBERG PRE 1849 PRE, GER [35340]

SCHARHAG PRE 1851 OBERWALLUF, BAD, BRD
[33817] : 1840+ USA [33817]

SCHARNINGHAUSEN PRE 1850 HAN, GER [38577]

SCHAT C1337 BRUSSEL, BBT, BEL [38160]

SCHATS C1386 ANTWERPEN, ATW, BEL [38160] :
C1687 WEELDE, ATW, BEL [38160] : C1652
RUMMEN, BBT, BEL [38160]

SCHATTE C1406 BRUSSEL, BBT, BEL [38160]

SCHATVET 1800+ FET & OSLO AREA, AKERSHUS,
NOR [36335]

SCHAU SHAW A. 1884-1950 NEW YORK, NY, USA
[36564]

SCHAUBER ALL BIETINGEN, BAW, FRG [38657]

SCHAUBLIN 1600S OBERDORF, BL, CH [38374]

SCHEAFFER ALL WORLDWIDE [38533]

SCHEER ALL BAD, GER [38742] : 1850-1990
WARREN CO., OH, USA [38742]

SCHEERDER 1767-1836 NOH, NL [38711]

SCHEERER 1860S GLEN INNES, NSW, AUS [37104]

SCHEFFE PRE 1850 GER [35604]

SCHEFFLER 1885 MARYBOROUGH, QLD, AUS
[34754]

SCHEFFNER 1948 WESSUM AHAUS, NRW, BRD
[38749] : 1975-1984 STADTLOHN, NRW, BRD [38749]

SCHEIBEL PRE 1884 SHOALHAVEN, NSW, AUS
[34978]

SCHEIBLEIN PRE 1840 GER [38437]

SCHEIDE PRE 1730 POLLEBEN, BRD [38658]

SCHEIDEGGER PRE 1880 CANTON BERN, CH &
USA [36918]

SCHEIDT 1750-1850 STRASBOURG, ALS, FRA [38024]

SCHEIER PRE 1850 WI, USA [38052]

SCHEILE 1698 ALTENHAGEN, HAN, GER [38631]

SCHELBACH CHARLES PRE 1877
LANGENBIELAU, SIL, GER [34567]

SCHELLE PRE 1845 HES, GER [38669]

SCHELLEKENS PRE 1824 OOSTERHOUT, NBT, NL
[35008]

SCHELLENBERGER 1744-1890 SCHLEUSINGEN,
THURINGIA, GER [38148]

SCHELLINGER 1839-1920 WASHINGTON CO.
FOND DU LAL, WI, USA [36542]

SCHELLINX PRE 1650 NL [38768]

SCHELLY PRE 1835 BAV, GER [36972]

SCHEMPP 1840 WURTEMBURG, WUE, BRD [38327]
: 1840 PHILADELPHIA, PA, USA [38327]

SCHENCK 1800+ GER & USA [38065]

SCHENK 1880+ BUNGAREE & ROMSEY, VIC, AUS
[35186] : 1862+ LONDON, MDX, ENG [35186] :
1800+ BUSUM, SHO, GER [37542] : 1859-1862
URRAY, ROC, SCT [35186]

SCHERER PRE 1850 ZUSCH, GER [38033] : 1850+
BERRIEN CO., MI, USA [38033]

SCHERF ALL EMMAVILLE, NSW, AUS [37115]

SCHERLE 1850 BUCKOVYNA, [36655]

SCHERMER 1780-1820 LEUTSMANSDORF, KSA,
GER [36555] : ALL GER [36694] : 1750-1990 WEST
FRIESLAND, NOH, NL [38713]

SCHERMHOUR PRE 1900 ODESSA, ONT, CAN
[36680]

SCHERMUKSZNAT PRE 1896 KRS. GUMBINNEN,
OPR, GER [38649]

SCHERNER PRE 1900 SIL, GER [38648]

SCHERZER PRE 1900 FILIPPDORF, BOEHMEN, CS
[36377]

SCHEU PRE 1860 WALDBACH, WUE, GER [35242] :
PRE 1740 DETWANG, BAV, GER [35242]

SCHEUER PRE 1900 RPR, GER [36339] : 1700+
HELDENBERGEN, HEN, GER [37042] : ALL USA
[36339]

SCHEUERER ALL BAD, GER [38333]

SCHEUERMANN ALL NIDDY OBERLAIS, HESSE,
GER [37550] : ALL JAGODNAJA, SARATOV, SU
[37550] : PRE 1875 CLEVELAND, OH, USA [37034]

SCHEUNERT 1750-1850 BRA & POM, GER [36662]

SCHEURER 1750+ USA [38728]

SCHEWITZER KATHRYN PRE 1900 PONTIAC, MI,
USA [35371]

SCHEX 1450-1650 MUEHLHAUSEN NECKAR, BAW,
BRD [38654]

SCHIACH PRE 1850 INVERNESS, INV, SCT [35925]

SCHIELKE 1800+ NEUENBURG, WPR, GER [37542]

SCHIEREN ALL DUESSELDORF, WEF, GER [34861]
SCHIERHOLTZ ALL ELMIRA, ONT, CAN & GER [34137]
SCHIERONI CESAR C1873 LONDON, ENG [34070] : CESARE 1900 DARRARA, BROADFORD NEWCASTLE, LIM, IRL [34070]
SCHIESEL C1860+ SIL, GER [37728]
SCHIEVELBEIN PRE 1872 POM, GER [37009]
SCHIFFFLIN 1773+ MONTREAL, QUE, CAN [34130]
SCHILAK 1700-1850 DIERSBUETTEL, HAN, GER [38652]
SCHILD C1755 DETMOLD, LIP, GER [37819]
SCHILDMEYER 1816-1907 DAMME & ROTTERDAM, OLD & ZH, FRG & NL [38712]
SCHILKA PRE 1840 WERBEN, BRA, LOWER LUSATIA, GER [34766]
SCHILLER 1700-1800 BAV, GER [38128]
SCHILLING ALL METZELTIEN VIA TEMPLIN, BRA, GER [35460] : PRE 1780 BEBERSTEDT, PSA, GER [38048]
SCHILPZAND C1800 ZANDVOORT, NOH, NL [38713]
SCHIMMELPFENG ALL WORLDWIDE [38677]
SCHINDEHUETTE PRE 1700 HES, GER [38642]
SCHINDLER JOHANN PRE 1898 KRS. ASCH, SUDETENLAND, OES, CSR &, GER [38649]
SCHINLE PRE 1780 PIRONTEN, BAV, GER [38679]
SCHINTLER 1850-1900 ADELONG, NSW, AUS [34436]
SCHIPANSKI 1790-1890 DARKEHMEN, OPR, GER [38647]
SCHIRMER PRE 1836 NICKERN, BRA, GER [33866] : PRE 1860 WUE, GER [38333] : 1824-1870 SACHS, ALTENBURG, SAB [36317] : 1800-1900S USA [38369]
SCHITTNER ALL SAFFIG, RPR, GER [38637]
SCHLAEGER ALL MSW, GER [34488]
SCHLAGEL 1600-1650 EDIGHEIM, BAV, GER [36898]
SCHLARBAUM 1830-1880 KITCHENER, ONT, CAN [38026] : 1700-1830 KASSELL, HES, GER [38026]
SCHLEGEL PRE 1700 WAIBLINGEN, WUE, GER [38683]
SCHLEINING 1840 NORKA, SU & WORLD [37511]
SCHLENKER PRE 1800 KRZECZYN MALY, LU, POL [38617]
SCHLESIER 1745-1810 FRANKENHEIM, SAB, GER [38528]
SCHLEUNING 1830 NORKA, SU & WORLD [37511]
SCHLEUTERS 1700+ QUICKBORN, SHO, GER [37542]
SCHLIETER 1841 GRABO, KSA, GER [38750]
SCHLINTZ 1700-1860S TARNOW, MEK, GER [38524]
SCHLITT PRE 1890 CHICAGO, IL, USA [38042]
SCHLOBACH EDWARD 1857 MELBOURNE, VIC, AUS [37683] : FRITZ 1921 CHICAGO, IL, USA [37683]
SCHLOEMP PRE 1850 OPR, GER [38648]
SCHLOTTMANN 1711+ PERLIN, MEK, GER [38671]
SCHMALHAUS PRE 1830 VOELKERSHAUSEN, THU, GER [38606]
SCHMALZ PRE 1830 BADEN, BAD, GER [34238] : 1700-1800 RPR, GER [38765] : 1800+ LANDAU, ODESSA, SU [38765]
SCHMEL 1740-1800 HAYCOCK TWP., PA, USA [37011]
SCHMELLER 1780-1820 NEUENBURG, WPR, GER [37542]
SCHMELZEL ALL WORLDWIDE [36930]
SCHMICK ALL BUDINGEN, HESSE, GER [37550] : ALL JACODNAJA, SARATOV, SU [37550] : 1886-1894 WHITEWATER, KS, USA [37550]
SCHMID 1450-1600 FRUTIGEN, BE, CH [35283] : C1847 BERN, BE, CH [37022]

SCHMIDT 1725-1800 GRAEFENNEUSAS, BAY, BRD [35311] : 1750-1800 SOTEPPACH, BAY, BRD [35311] : 1956 LINDEN, SHO, BRD [38749] : 1850S CHRISTIANSFELD, JUTLAND, DEN [34266] : C1870 GER [33809] : JOHANNA PRE 1854 EICHELBERG, WUE, GER [34806] : 1770-1820 RANSWEILER, RHINELAND, GER [36561] : 1800-1900 STEBNITZ, PRE, GER [36898] : CHRISTINA 1770+ KARLSRUHE, BAD, GER [37504] : CARL PRE 1820 GINGST, REUGEN, GER [37961] : FRIEDA 1875-1895 KARLSRUHE, GER [38134] : JOHANNES PRE 1718 GR ZIMMERN, HES, GER [38181] : LOUISA PRE 1860 MEK, GER [38222] : SOPHIA 1835-1865 BAV, GER [38528] : PRE 1860 ANEMOLTER, HAN, GER [38577] : 1900S ESSEN, RPR, GER [38749] : ELIZ 1800+ WEM, IRL [34161] : CARL C1844 POCLITZ STETTIN, SZ, POL [36873] : PRE 1866 OBORNIKI, PA, POL [36882] : JOHANN 1840-1896 PO, POL [36941] : 1800-1925 EKATRINESLAV, UKRANE, SU [34081] : 1830-1935 TAGNAROG, KUBAN, SU [34081] : CARL 1816-1884 LUTHERAN CHURCH, MN, USA [38785] : 1854+ LEMBERG, STRASBURG, W PRE [35266]
SCHMIDTKE 1800+ STRENOW, POM, GER [37949]
SCHMIED PRE 1855 DOMBACH, WUE, GER [34886] : MARTIN 1820+ DANZIG, GER [35712]
SCHMITT 1800+ ALS, FRA [36343] : 1830-1870 ALBANY, NY, USA [38530] : 1850-1900 GASCONADE CO., MO, USA & CAN [38532]
SCHMITZ PRE 1856 ORENHOFEN, BRD [38615] : 1856 WILESBURG, BRD [38738] : 1800-25 ANKUM, HAN, GER [38202] : PRE 1800 KOBLENZ, RPR, GER [38437]
SCHMITZER PRE 1880 NSW, AUS & GER [37130]
SCHMOL ALL OES [37268]
SCHMOLL PRE 1830 GUNTERBERG, UCKERMARK, GER [34766] : 1880+ WIE, OES [37268]
SCHMONSEES 1750-1800 OSTERHOLZ SCHARMBECK, HAN, GER [38516]
SCHNABEL PRE 1829+ WUE, GER [37314] : 1850-1900 HENDERSDORF, SIL, GER [38599]
SCHNABLY 1800-1880 CAMBRIA CO., PA, USA [36897]
SCHNAIDT PRE 1875 UNTERJESINGEN, WUE, GER [37587]
SCHNARR PRE 1800 GHE, GER [36726]
SCHNEBELY PRE 1730 CH [38769]
SCHNEIDER 1860+ QLD, AUS [36362] : PRE 1862 ZAHMEN, HES, BRD [35083] : 1750-1825 ODENBACH, RPF, BRD [35311] : 1700-1800 WESTERBURG, HES, BRD [38617] : PRE 1850 FISCHENGEN, TG, CH [37554] : 1800+ VELBERT, RPR, GER [34560] : 1785-1860 GEISENHEIM, HEN, GER [34693] : PRE 1860+ RANSEL, GER [36362] : PETER 1780-1810 OFFENBACH HUNDHEIM, RPR, GER [38127] : 1820+ WOLFHAGEN, HES, GER [38186] : ALL KRS. ZEITZ, KSA, GER [38649] : ALL KRS. ASCH, SUDETENLAND, OES, CSR &, GER [38649] : C1700-1850 GERHARDTSBRUN, RPF & PA, GER & USA [35305] : 1850 ST CHARLES CO., MO, USA [37582] : 1830+ GERMANTOWN, WI, USA [38530]
SCHNEITER ALL LU, CH [35954]
SCHNETTLER ALL BRD [38636]
SCHNIEDER 1758 LIEME, GER [38749] : 1686 BREITENHEIDE LAGE, GER [38749]
SCHNIEPP 1720-1760 OBERWALDEN, WUE, GER [38689]
SCHNITZLEIN ALL WORLDWIDE [38645]
SCHNIZLEIN ALL WORLDWIDE [38645]

SCHNOEPPEL PRE 1860 NOERDLINGEN, BAY, BRD [36963]

SCHNORR C1830 BAY, BRD [37536]

SCHNUR 1791-1864 STRUECKEN, SLP, GER [38750]

SCHNUZLEIN ALL WORLDWIDE [38645]

SCHNYTZLEIN ALL WORLDWIDE [38645]

SCHOBEL PRE 1932 ROTTWEIL, BAD, GER [34175]

SCHOBELL 1850S SYDNEY, NSW, AUS [37947]

SCHOCH ALL WORLDWIDE [38657]

SCHOEN PRE 1850 TETBURY, GLS, ENG [34958] : PRE 1821 POZNAN, POS, GER [38190] : 1862+ BROOKLYN, NY, USA [38190]

SCHOENBERGER PRE 1800 SANKT BARBARA, SAA, GER [38681]

SCHOENFELDT 1800-1900 KAMENKA, SARATOV, USSR [38133]

SCHOENKNECHT 1680-1920 SIL, GER [38634]

SCHOENMANN 1675-1750 GOCHSHEIM, BAY, BRD [35311]

SCHOEPHER 1900+ DETROIT, MI, USA [37572]

SCHOFIELD ALL MONARO, NSW, AUS [33765] : 1850S TAMWORTH, NSW, AUS [36285] : 1850+ VIC, AUS [38539] : 1700+ HECKMONDWIKE, WRY, ENG [34328] : BETTY 1817+ ROCHDALE & SPOTLAND, LAN, ENG [34721] : ALICE 1836-1913 ROCHDALE & BROOKSIDE, LAN, ENG [34721] : 1780-1900 WANDSWORTH, SRY & LND, ENG [35495] : 1750+ CLARBOROUGH, NTT, ENG [36434] : 1790-1820 DARTFORD, KEN, ENG [37056] : 1800-1900 EMLEY, YKS, ENG [37495] : PRE 1850 BIRSTALL, WRY, ENG [37704] : 1870+ SHEFFIELD, YKS, ENG [38539] : 1850+ BROMLEY, LND, ENG [38539]

SCHOLEFIELD 1700S HOLLINGREAVE, LAN, ENG [35126] : 1835-1900 SOUTHWARK, LND, ENG [36117]

SCHOLES 1880-1925 NEW CARLISLE, QUE, CAN [37665] : ALL CHELMSFORD, ESS, ENG [34684] : 1500+ EDENHAM, LIN, ENG [37665] : 1860+ FOUNTAIN CO., IN, USA [35262] : 1880+ FAIRMONT, MN, USA [37665]

SCHOLEY PRE 1734 POTTERHANWORTH, LIN, ENG [37318] : PRE 1854 LEEDS, YKS, ENG [37913]

SCHOLL ALL WORLDWIDE [38657]

SCHOLLER JOHANN 1753-1789 TAUBERZEU, GER [37596]

SCHOLLITT PRE 1840 YKS, ENG [37671]

SCHOLLMEYER ALL WORLDWIDE [38189]

SCHOLTING C1830 LYON, RHA, FRA [34591]

SCHOLTS 1800+ AMSTERDAM, NL [33802]

SCHOLZ PRE 1850 SCHWEIDNITZ, SIL, GER [34083] : ALL WORLDWIDE [38633] : ALL WORLDWIDE [38666]

SCHONE 1650-1780 MILTITZ, KSA, GER [38628]

SCHONHER C1820 CAN [37017]

SCHONKNECHT ALL POM & WPR, GER [38687] : PRE 1860 PRE [38081]

SCHOOLCRAFT ALL QUE, CAN [36539]

SCHOOLEY 1560+ ST MARYS, BDF, ENG [34408] : 1834 SPICELAND, HENRY CO., IN, USA [36319]

SCHOON 1940+ AUSTINMER, NSW, AUS [33770]

SCHOONDERBECK ALL WORLDWIDE [34095]

SCHOONDERBEEK ALL NL [38351]

SCHOONEMAN 1850-1929 NOH, NL [38711]

SCHOONHOVEN 1740 S'GRAVENLAND, NOH, NL [38706]

SCHOPP 1750-1809 BUISDORF, RPR, GER [38528]

SCHOPPACH PRE 1750 BREITENBACH, GHE & HEN, GER [38606]

SCHORIZIN ALL NIZHNY NOVGAROD, SU [36889]

SCHORN 1850-1950 DURBAN, NATAL, RSA [34947]

SCHOTT 1750-1820 BAY, BRD [35311]

SCHOUNHEIR C1820 CAN [37017]

SCHOUT PRE 1700 IRL [34312]

SCHOUTEN 1780+ ERNESTOWN & ADDINGTON CO., ONT, CAN [34486]

SCHOWE PRE 1900 LENGERICH, NRW, GER [38663]

SCHRA 1830-1850 SNEEK, FRI, NL [34398] : ALL UTRECHT, UTR, NL [34398]

SCHRAA 1784+ DEN HELDER TEXEL, NOH, NL [34398] : 1711+ ZWARTSLUIS, OIJ, NL [34398]

SCHRADER PRE 1848 HOBART, TAS, AUS [35109] : 1850+ NSW, AUS [38356] : PRE 1795+ LONDON, ENG [35109] : 1750-1800 LONDON, ENG [35151]

SCHRAM ALL ATW, BEL [38169] : PETER 1750-1850 OFFENBACH, RFP, BRD [33752] : PHILIP 1780-1845 LAUTERECKEN, RPF, BRD [33752] : JOHN 1832-1860 SPEYER, BAV, GER [33752] : GEORG 1803-1861 SPEYER, BAV, GER [33752] : PRE 1865 ISLE OF TEXEL, NL [34936]

SCHRAMKA ALL WORLDWIDE [36785]

SCHRAMM C1723 HANNOVER, HAN, GER [38626]

SCHRASSERT 1750-1850 HOLLAND, ZUH, NL [38702]

SCHRASSERT BERT ALL HOLLAND, ZUH, NL [38702]

SCHREFER PRE 1820 UNTER STEINBACH BURGER, WUE, GER [34031]

SCHREIBER 1571 EISLEBEN, GER [38750] : 1634-1685 HARTUM, WEF, GER [38750] : 1731-1753 LEBIEN, KSA, GER [38750]

SCHREINER PRE 1856 ALTEN-BUSECK, HES, GER [33824] : PRE 1800 WATTENHEIM, RPF, GER [38681]

SCHRIJVER ALL SCHERPENISSE, ZEL, NL [38694]

SCHRIMPE 1640 BUCHHOLZ, WEF, GER [38631]

SCHROCK 1750S BERKS, PA, USA [38184]

SCHRODER 1854 GAWLER & ADELAIDE, SA, AUS [35369] : ALL GUSTROW, MEK, DDR [34812]

SCHRODERN 1800 BARKAU, GER [37170]

SCHROEBLE 1800-1826 RUTHERFORD CO., NC, USA [35301]

SCHROEDER PRE 1842 MADGEBURGERFORTH, MAG, DDR [34462] : 1750-1800 LONDON, ENG [35151] : PRE 1823 WRANGLESBURG, POM, GER [38125] : 1780-1843 DAMP, SHO, GER [38750] : 1870-1900 SHAWANO CO., WI, USA [36546]

SCHROEER IN VOERDE ALL VOERDE, WEF, GER [34861]

SCHRYVER C1800 LEIDERDORP, ZUH, NL [38713] : 1750-1900 LEROY & PLEASANT GROVE, MN, PA & NY, USA [38392]

SCHUBERT 1900S MERRIWA, NSW, AUS [37910] : PRE 1860 LIEGNITZ, GER [34801] : 1860+ BUCHHOLZ, PSA, GER [35073] : 1735 WURZEN, KSA, GER [38749]

SCHUCHART PETER 1700-1900S WIESENFELD, PSA, GER & USA [35304]

SCHUELER 1744-1903 SCHLEUSINGEN, THURINGIA, GER [38148]

SCHUETT 1600+ WILSTER, SHO, GER [38651]

SCHUETZE PRE 1800 WINGERODE, PSA, GER [38048]

SCHUH PRE 1700 AICHELBACH, WUE, GER [38661] : PRE 1800 SHENANDOAH, VA, USA [37457]

SCHUHARDT PRE 1849 GOEHLEN, MSW, GER [38618]

SCHUHMANN 1840S FRANKENBERG, PRE, GER [35050]

SCHULDHAM WILLIAM 1770+ BECCLES, SFK, ENG [34884]

SCHULER 1826 SZ, CH [33754] : 1820 KUPPENHEIM, BAD & WUR, GER [36730] : C1800 SCHLATT, HOH, GER [38604] : 1820-1828 CUMBERLAND CO., PA, USA [35301]

SCHULLANDER 1835-1850 CARLSTADT, SWE [38144] : 1850-1865 CUHAHOGA CO., OH, USA [38144]

SCHULTE PRE 1816 GIELGEN, NRW, GER [38630] : 1750+ HELDEN, GER & USA [34988]

SCHULTZ 1850+ WODONGA, VIC, AUS [35387] : PRE 1855 PRUSKOWO, POS, GER [34766] : PRE 1843 HAN, GER [34911] : PRE 1840 PRE, GER [35387] : CARL PRE 1877 GER [36621] : PRE 1900 RYPIN, BY, POL [34246] : PRE 1906 STEPHAN, WN, POL [37545] : PRE 1906 EICHENHAGEN, PO, POL [37545] : 1700-1850 MICHELSDORF, LUBLIN, POL [38652]

SCHULZ HEINRICH 1880+ MECKELSDORF, HES, GER [35315] : PRE 1880 MEK, GER [38037]

SCHULZE 1750-1860 PRE, GER [35300]

SCHUMACHER PRE 1800 STOMMELN, BRD [38615] : 1820-1870 MEK, GER [35317] : PRE 1862 GOLLMITZ, PRE, GER [35393] : 1855-1900 SAGINAW, MI, USA [35317] : C1885+ TRAILL CO., ND & ALB, USA & CAN [34203] : C1820-1885 WI, USA & LUX [34203]

SCHUMAN C1822 BAV, GER [38527]

SCHUMANN PRE 1916 GULLEWA & DAY DAWN, WA, AUS [36622]

SCHUNEMANN 1800+ GERVIN, PRE, GER [37170]

SCHUPELIUS PRE 1851 GHEGATTIN, PRE, GER [34766]

SCHUPP PRE 1852 BOENICH, GER [34285]

SCHUPPEL PRE 1854 LEIMEN, BAD, GER [34273]

SCHURICHT 1838+ ST LOUIS, MO, USA [36912]

SCHUTTE 1700+ STREUKEL, OIJ, NL [35338]

SCHUTTEMAN 1700-C1740S DOETINCHEM, GEL, NL [38350]

SCHUTZBACH ALL MAHLSTETTEN, BAW, FRG [38657]

SCHUWER ALL BURBACH, SAA, GER [36935]

SCHUYBROEK 1769 ESSEN ANTWERPEN, BEL [38715]

SCHWAB 1800+ AUS & HU [38065] : 1840 ONT, CAN [34231] : 1850S GALS, BE, CH [35525] : 1813 EDENKOBEN, PFALZ, GER [38184]

SCHWABE 1825 SCHWETZ, WPR, GER [34388]

SCHWACH PRE 1900 POL [33966]

SCHWAEGERMANN ALL WORLDWIDE [38612]

SCHWALB PRE 1900 NECKARGARTACH, BAW, BRD [38615]

SCHWAN PRE 1845 STETTIN, PRE, GER [38191] : 1800S ASHLAND CO., OH, USA [36552]

SCHWANCK C1885 SOUTH SHIELDS, DUR, ENG [34329]

SCHWARTE 1819 HOLZHAUSEN, PYR, GER [38750]

SCHWARTZ 1800+ RPF, BRD [35190] : 1800+ MONTREAU, QUE, CAN [35627] : 1700-1800 CH [35627] : 1850S HAMBURG, GER [36800] : MARGARETHA 1830-1850 ROSENKOPF, SAA, GER [38127] : PRE 1700 ZIERENBERG, HES, GER [38642] : 1850-1865 MADISON CO., OH, USA [37781] : WILHELMINA 1800S PRESTON, MN, USA [38785]

SCHWARZ C1750-1940S LANDAU, RPF, GER [37413] : PRE 1840 MESEKENHAGEN, POM, GER [37416] : 1810 POMMERBY, SHO, GER [38750] : ALL MARKTSCHELKEN, TRANSYLVANIA, RO [38519] : 1824-1950 STEARNS CO., MN, USA [37538] : PRE 1796 FRANCONIA, PA, USA [37811] : 1880+ ALLEGENY, PA, USA [38185]

SCHWARZE 1800+ LOBETHEL, SA, AUS [35364]

SCHWARZLOSE 1800S GER [38490]

SCHWEEN 1800S SHO, GER [36552]

SCHWEICH ALL WORLDWIDE [38189]

SCHWEICHART (SEE SWE [38220]

SCHWEIKERT 1800S+ DEN [35831]

SCHWEINLIN PRE 1600 TUERCKHEIM, ALS, FRA [38615]

SCHWEITZER 1850 ALTRAUTAUTZ, BUCKOVYNA, [36655] : ALL SAARBRUCKEN, SAA, BRD [35924] : PRE 1750 ULM, WUE, GER [37361] : 1800+ MIDDELBURG & VLISSINGEN, ZEL, NL [35924]

SCHWERDTMANN 1712-1752 OBERNKIRCHEN, SLP, GER [38750]

SCHWERIN 1800+ KONITZ, WPR, GER [34932]

SCHWERTFEGER C1696 VOELKSEN, HAN, GER [38626]

SCHWERTLE 1700-1800 SCHWIEBERDINGEN, WUE, GER [38652]

SCHWIETERS 1800+ LEGDEN, GER & USA [34988]

SCHWIND 1700-1860 VIENNA, WIE, OES [35300] : 1800-1880 BUFFALO, NY, USA [35300]

SCHWINGHAMMER PRE 1800 SIMBACH, BAV, GER [38191]

SCLATER C1700 LEI, ENG [37706]

SCOBIE 1854+ ARARAT, VIC, AUS [36193] : 1847+ FALKIRK, STI, SCT [34039] : ALL KRS, SCT [36193]

SCOBLE PRE 1890 KADINA, SA, AUS [35012]

SCOFIELD C1700-C1750 GREAT FINBOROUGH, SFK, ENG [36425] : 1830+ WATERFORD, WAT, IRL [36620]

SCOGGINS ALL LONDON, ENG [34948] : ALL SFK & NFK, ENG [34948]

SCOGIN ALL SFK & NFK, ENG [34948]

SCOGINGS ALL SFK & NFK, ENG [34948]

SCOLES 1800+ AUS [37665] : 1880-1925 NEW CARLISLE, QUE, CAN [37665] : 1600-1830 EDENHAM, LIN, ENG [36147] : 1500+ EDENHAM, LIN, ENG [37665] : 1812 KILMARNOCK, AYR, SCT [36860] : 1880+ FAIRMONT, MN, USA [37665] : 1863+ RHINEBECK, DUTCHESS CO., NY, USA [38223]

SCOLLARD 1750-1880 KNOCKNAGASHEL, KER, IRL [36776]

SCOLLAY 1700+ FETLAR, SHI, SCT & NZ [36266]

SCOLTOCK C1853 NSW, AUS [34009] : PRE 1850 LND & MDX, ENG [34633] : C1860 NZ [34009]

SCONDRETT 1689-1814 EASTHAM, WOR, ENG [36513]

SCORAH C1840 FELKIRK, YKS, ENG [36302]

SCORER ALL NBL & DUR, ENG [38754]

SCOREY ALL ALRESFORD, HAM, ENG [37044] : ALL LASHAM, HAM, ENG [37044] : ALL BISHOP WALTHAM, HAM, ENG [37044] : ALL WORLDWIDE [36469]

SCORTHALS 1050+ GER & BEL [37415] : PRE 1170 WLS & BEL [37415]

SCOT ALL ENG [36221] : PRE 1770 ST ANDREWS, FIF, SCT [35223] : PRE 1900 ANON, DFS, SCT [38434]

SCOTT SOPHIA 1824+ HARTLEY, NSW, AUS [34030] : PRE 1890 EAST BRUNSWICK, VIC, AUS [34184] : 1850-1890 CRESWICK, VIC, AUS [34865] : PRE 1836 PARRAMATTA, NSW, AUS [35245] : PRE 1838 GOULBURN, NSW, AUS [35245] : CATHERINE 1870+ AUS [35337] : ROBERT 1865+ BRISBANE, QLD, AUS [35521] : 1930-1950 PERTH, WA, AUS [35595] : ROBERT 1870S LAUNCESTON, TAS, AUS [35772] : ALL BEACONSFIELD, TAS, AUS [37177] : C1840 TAS, AUS [37177] : 1800-1900 LAUNCESTON, TAS, AUS [38070] : HARRY C1912+ AUS & NZ [34340] : 1890+ CAN [35595] : 1800+ FOURNIER, ONT, CAN [38462] : 1800+ NAFFERTON & BRANDESBURTON, YKS, ENG [38861] : WILLIAM 1752+ BURTON STATHER, LIN, ENG [34091] : PRE 1858 READING, BRK, ENG [34184] : GEORGE PRE 1850 LONDON, ENG [34298] : 1650-1700 SUDBURY, SFK, ENG [34552] : 1800-1850

493

OXFORD, OXF, ENG **[34552]** : C1820
SHOREDITCH, LND, ENG **[34556]** : 1863 +
HARTLEPOOL, DUR, ENG **[34619]** : PRE 1875
BENFIELDSIDE, DUR, ENG **[34778]** : 1800 +
MOSTON, LAN, ENG **[34870]** : 1820 +
BEDLINGTON, NBL, ENG **[35027]** : 1800 +
ALSTON, CUL, ENG **[35112]** : 1800 + LIN, ENG
[35377] : PRE 1878 LEYTON, ESS, ENG **[35515]** :
ELIZABETH PRE 1850 STOKE, DEV, ENG **[35548]** :
1872S NEWCASTLE ON TYNE, NBL, ENG **[35639]** :
PRE 1800 ESS, ENG **[35642]** : PRE 1700 CAM, ENG
[35642] : PRE 1824 SHOREDITCH, ST LEONARDS,
LND, ENG **[35821]** : 1810S ISLINGTON, MDX,
ENG **[35914]** : PRE 1820 FINSBURY, MDX, ENG
[36099] : PRE 1820 HARTBURN & SIMONBURN,
NBL, ENG **[36110]** : PRE 1900 PENZANCE, CON,
ENG **[36145]** : PRE 1790 BISHOP'S STORTFORD,
HRT, ENG **[36201]** : ALL ENG **[36221]** : 1800 + DUR,
ENG **[36246]** : 1910 + MITCHAM, SRY, ENG **[36378]**
: PRE 1750 BRISTOL, GLS, ENG **[36380]** : 1829-1873
NORTHOWRAM, WRY, ENG **[36391]** : 1830-1901
HAMPSTEAD & ST MARYLEBONE, LND, ENG
[36425] : PRE 1830 BURY ST EDMUNDS, SFK,
ENG **[36425]** : PRE 1850 IDLE & THACKLEY, WRY,
ENG **[36617]** : 1800 NEWCASTLE ON TYNE, NBL,
ENG **[36892]** : WILLIAM PRE 1806 KINGS LYNN,
NFK, ENG **[37228]** : 1700-1780 NORTHWOOD, IOW,
ENG **[37335]** : ALL GREENWICH, KEN, ENG
[37338] : 1770 + CHIPPENHAM, CAM, ENG **[37705]** :
1830-75 MALTON, YKS, ENG **[37705]** : 1850-1900
LEI, ENG **[38229]** : W.G. & RHODA 1700-C1740S
EASTLEIGH, HAM, ENG **[38350]** : THOS.
COLLIAR 1760-1790S BKM, ENG **[38350]** : JOHN
1800 + OLD SWENFORD, WOR, ENG **[38540]** :
WILLIAM 1800 + STOURBRIDGE, WOR, ENG
[38540] : PRE 1800 LONDON, ENG **[38658]** : PRE
1800 IOW, ENG **[38700]** : WILLIAM PRE 1806
GIBRALTAR **[37228]** : C1800-1860 DUBLIN, IRL
[33876] : DORCAS & ANNE PRE 1840 DUBLIN &
GALWAY, IRL **[34254]** : HARRY C1880 +
BELFAST, ANT, IRL **[34340]** : JANE PRE 1830
MONAGHAN, MOG, IRL **[35713]** : PRE 1840
LONDONDERRY, DRY, IRL **[35782]** : PRE 1826
IRL **[35824]** : 1800-1900 KILLARNEY, KER, IRL
[36565] : PRE 1856 BELFAST, IRL **[37113]** : PRE 1850
DUBLIN, IRL **[37454]** : 1840S TYR, IRL **[38221]** :
1800 WATERFORD, IRL & AUS **[37911]** : PRE 1757
ASHKIRK, ROX & SEL, SCT **[33806]** : 1800 +
ABERDEEN, SCT **[33947]** : HENERY PRE 1860
EILDRIG, SCT **[34000]** : PRE 1880 ST ANDREWS,
FIF, SCT **[34018]** : 1800 + DUNDEE, ANS, SCT
[34049] : C1714 LIBERTON, LKS, SCT **[34118]** : 1700-
1900 BOG HOLLOW, SCT **[34135]** : PRE 1850
PERTH, SCT **[34170]** : PRE 1830 ST ANDREWS,
LLANBRYDE, MOR, SCT **[34192]** : JANET PRE
1800 GLENHILL, DFS, SCT **[34282]** : 1800 +
FORGUE, ABD, SCT **[34326]** : ANDREW PRE 1894
DUNDEE, ANS, SCT **[34447]** : 1770-1860
SINGDEAN, CASTLETON, ROX, SCT **[34479]** : PRE
1850 DUMFRIES, DFS, SCT **[34574]** : WILLIAM
PRE 1851 EDINBURGH, SCT **[34587]** : PRE 1870
DUNDEE, ANS, SCT **[34617]** : ALL FORRIS, MOR,
SCT **[34619]** : PRE 1810 SOUTH LEITH &
EDINBURGH, MLN, SCT **[34619]** : ALL
EDINBURGH, MLN, SCT **[34619]** : 1700-1900 LKS,
SCT **[34624]** : PRE 1850 KIRKCONNEL, DFS, SCT
[34626] : 1600 + DUNDEE, ANS, SCT **[34637]** : ALL
DUNDEE, ANS, SCT **[34758]** : ALL RUTHERGLEN,
ROX, SCT **[34846]** : PRE 1850 DUNKELD, PER, SCT
[34865] : 1700S SOUTH LEITH, MLN, SCT **[34930]** :
1800 + ABERDEEN, ABD, SCT **[35015]** : DR.
WILLIAM ALL MOFFAT, DFS, SCT **[35337]** : REV.

THOMAS ALL DFS, SCT **[35337]** : DONALD PRE
1852 SOUTH LEITH, MLN, SCT **[35380]** : THOMAS
1827 + JEDBURGH, SCT **[35584]** : 1800-1860
BONNET HILL, DUNDEE, ANS, SCT **[35595]** : PRE
1885 ABERFOYLE, PER, SCT **[35601]** : JANE PRE
1830 GLASGOW, LKS, SCT **[35713]** : 1800S EAST
KILBRIDE, LKS, SCT **[35797]** : 1800 + FIF, SCT
[35865] : PRE 1850 PITSLIGO, ABD, SCT **[36061]** :
1700 + UDDINGTON, LKS, SCT **[36261]** : C1800
WAUCHOPE, ROX, SCT **[36803]** : ALL INV, SCT
[36807] : WILLIAM C1892-1960 ABD, SCT **[36807]** :
1780S MACDUFF, BAN, SCT **[36877]** : PRE 1844
SALCOATS, AYR, SCT **[37575]** : ALL EAST
KILBRIDE, LKS, SCT **[37767]** : PRE 1850 PEE, SCT
[38306] : PRE 1740 DFS, SCT **[38587]** : C1750-1950
SCONE & RIBBERMUIR, PER, SCT & AUS **[34040]** :
DAVID ALL OH & IA, USA **[34116]** : C1640 CT, USA
[34395] : THEODOSIA PRE 1800 PA & VA, USA
[34410] : 1800-1845 PA, USA **[35317]** : 1900 + USA
[36145] : ANDREW PRE 1840 ONEIDA CO., NY,
USA **[36345]** : 1830-1900 CARROLL CO. &
HOWARD CO., IN, USA **[36940]** : JOSEPH 1720-1840
TN, USA **[36940]** : C1800 PHELPS, NY, USA **[37017]** :
1850 + LAFAYETTE & LINCOLN, IN & NE, USA
[37467] : JOHN C1741-C1841 HARDIN CO., KY,
USA **[37527]** : 1800S TN, USA **[37539]** : 1845-1870
KEWEENAW CO., MI, USA **[38009]** : ANN PRE
1850 WASHINGTON, DC, USA **[38049]** : 1800-1836
UINION, PA, USA **[38095]** : 1835-1920 RICHLAND
& CRAWFORD, OH, USA **[38095]** : 1848-1876
CLAYTON CO., IA, USA **[38133]** : 1790-1848 ISLE
LA MOTTE, VT, USA **[38133]** : 1760-1800 ALBANY,
NY, USA **[38133]** : AUSTIN ANDREW 1839-1860
MERCER CO., PA, USA **[38145]** : JAMES 1828-1850
MERCER CO., PA, USA **[38145]** : HARRIET S. 1828-
1838 MERCER CO., PA, USA **[38145]** : PRE 1820
WILKINSON CO., MS, USA **[38190]** : WILLIAM
1790 + VA, USA **[38374]** : WILLIAM 1820 GREEN
CO., OH, USA **[38374]** : WILLIAM 1851 +
HUNTINGTON CO., IN, USA **[38374]** : WILLIAM
1850 + DELAWARE CO., IN, USA **[38374]**

SCOTTION 1830S LEEK, STS, ENG **[33780]**

SCOUGAL 1870-1958 DUNS, PEE, SCT **[33978]**

SCOULAR PRE 1850 HUTTON, BEW, SCT **[36497]** :
PRE 1840 LKS, SCT **[37354]** : 1700 + STRATHAVEN
& GLASGOW, LKS, SCT **[37399]**

SCOURIE PRE 1820 ANT, IRL **[36271]**

SCOUT PRE 1700 IRL **[34312]**

SCOVELL ALL IOW, HAM, ENG **[37730]**

SCOWEN PRE 1840 SYDNEY, NSW, AUS **[36372]** :
1840 + ESS, ENG **[37376]**

SCOWN WILLIAM PRE 1810 LAUNCESTON, CON,
ENG **[35124]**

SCRACE PRE 1850 FRANT & HORSTED KEYNES,
SSX, ENG **[37871]**

SCRANNAGE 1500-1900 WOR, WAR & SFS, ENG
[36169]

SCREATON 1800-1850 WAR & LEI, ENG **[37858]** :
PRE 1900 LAN & LEI, ENG & USA **[36481]**

SCREEN 1820 + HOBART, TAS, AUS **[35151]** : C1850
EXETER, DEV, ENG **[35841]** : 1880 +
ROCKHAMPTON, GLS, ENG **[37343]**

SCREETON 1830-1990 TORONTO, ONT, CAN **[38308]**

SCRIBNER ALL SPROUGHTON, SFK, ENG **[33823]**

SCRIMGEOUR 1803 + CLUNIE, PER, SCT **[36509]** :
PRE 1762 DONNIEVORICH & DULL, PER, SCT
[37852]

SCRIVEN 1870 + CRYSTAL BROOK, SA, AUS **[34600]**
: PRE 1880 CREWKERNE, SOM, ENG **[34730]** : PRE
1860 ALMONDSBURY & PILNING, GLS, ENG
[36589] : 1750-1870 WELLS, SOM, ENG **[37508]** :

C1780 CHARLETON MACKERELL, SOM, ENG [37508]

SCRIVENER 1500+ SFK, ENG [36093] : 1750+ STREATLEY, BDF, ENG [37304] : PRE 1790 NH, USA [37509]

SCRIVENOR 1920S BRENTFORD, ESS, ENG [37677]

SCRIVENS 1860+ CHATHAM, KEN, ENG [37836] : PRE 1800 KEN, ENG [38235]

SCROGGIN 1700+ SCT [36958]

SCROOM 1800S HUN, ENG [37868]

SCROONEY CAESAR 1900 DARRARA, BORADFORD NEWCASTLE, LIM, IRL [34070]

SCROOP PRE 1700 MUGGINTON, DBY, ENG [34311]

SCROPE 1600-1700 BRISTOL, GLS, ENG [37783]

SCRUSE 1893+ SHOALHAVEN & SYDNEY, NSW, AUS [34786]

SCRUTCH 1820 PLYMOUTH, DEV, ENG [35067]

SCUDAMORE 1700+ HOLM LACY, HEF, ENG [35824]

SCUDDER 1800+ LEWISHAM & SYDENHAM, KEN, ENG [35525] : ALL ENG [37803]

SCULLY 1850 PORTLAND, VIC, AUS [35755] : 1859+ SYDNEY, NSW, AUS [35843] : ALL MANLY, NSW, AUS [35843] : C1850-1880 MELBOURNE, VIC, AUS [35982] : C1865 BALLARAT, VIC, AUS [36362] : 1750+ LONDON, ENG [34813] : C1830-1880 LONDON, ENG [35982] : 1862-1902 SOUTHWARK, SRY, ENG [37611] : PRE 1920 KNOCKILLY, COR, IRL [34013] : PRE 1800 IRL [34780] : 1800 GOULDEN, TIP, IRL [35755]

SCULTHORPE PRE 1819 KINGSCLIFFE, NTH, ENG [37112]

SCURFIELD 1816+ TANFIELD, DUR, ENG [36270]

SCUSZ 1850-1900 HU [36331]

SCUTCHINGS PRE 1840 GUERNSEY, CHI, UK [38306]

SCUTT ELLEN 1800+ WOOL, DOR, ENG [33875] : C1800-1875 STORRINGTON, SSX, ENG [34432] : LOIS 1830-1850S ENG [35366]

SCYPHERS PRE 1840 PA & VA, USA [37604]

SEABORN JOHN 1812-1876 BRE, WLS & USA [38016]

SEABRIDGE C1811 SWINNERTON, STS, ENG [36356] : ALL UK [36062]

SEABRIGHT 1796 ADDLETHORPE, LIN, ENG [34808] : C1840 WINCHESTER, HAM, ENG [35826]

SEABROOK C1850 HOBART, TAS, AUS [35747] : 1700-1900 HRT, ENG [36422] : ALL WORLDWIDE [34945] : ALL WORLDWIDE [36206]

SEABROOKE 1500+ SEABROOK, BKM & ESS, ENG [36093] : ALL WORLDWIDE [36206]

SEABURY 1851+ SA, AUS [34861] : ALL ATCHAM & BERRINGTON, SAL, ENG [34861]

SEACOLL PRE 1600 BANBURY, OXF, ENG [38420]

SEAGE PRE 1775 CHITTLEHAMPTON, DEV, ENG [37602]

SEAGER PRE 1700 KINGSWINFORD, STS, ENG [36110] : 1765-1793 BRENTFORD, MDX, ENG [37657]

SEAGRAVE PRE 1850 SALFORD, LAN, ENG [36369]

SEAGROTT PRE 1915 AUS [36645]

SEAGULL PRE 1870 CHATHAM & STROOD, KEN, ENG [37067]

SEAL C1850-1900 BIRMINGHAM, WAR, ENG [35791] : C1810-1820 HANDSWORTH, STS, ENG [35791] : 1700S GREAT BOWDEN, LEI, ENG [35858]

SEALE PRE 1845 MAYFAIR, LND, ENG [36153] : PRE 1824 WESTMINSTER, LND, ENG [36153] : 1750-1825 MARYBOROUGH, LEX, IRL [38407]

SEALEY ALL HERRING NECK, NFD, CAN [35264] : ALL ST JOHNS, NFD, CAN [35264] : ALL DEV & KEN, ENG [35264] : 1750S EWHURST, SSX, ENG [35501]

SEALS 1860-1890 BROOKLYN, NY, USA [38126]

SEAMAN PRE 1830 NORTH TUDDENHAM, NFK, ENG [36269] : 1900+ NTH, ENG [37437] : 1630-1722 NASSAU CO., NY, USA [37477]

SEAMARK 1640-1747 BIRLING, KEN, ENG [37921]

SEAMONE JOHN 1918-20 AKRON, OH, USA [38109]

SEANIGER PRE 1860 BRISTOL, ENG [37974]

SEANOR PRE 1810 ROTHWELL & ABERFORD, WRY, ENG [34382]

SEAR C1800-1900 LONDON, ENG [34372] : C1850-1900 BERLIN, BLN, GER [34372]

SEARCY 1800-1900 OWEN CO., KY, USA [36939]

SEARE 1797-1861 BERKHAMSTED, HRT, ENG [36071]

SEARGANT 1842 GLASGOW, LKS & AYR, SCT [35801]

SEARING 1850-1900 SOUTH LONDON, ENG [34719]

SEARL C1832 CON, ENG [37912] : PRE 1835 IRL [35649]

SEARLE GEORGE 1912+ SYDNEY, NSW, AUS [36192] : DANIEL 1901 ALMA PLAINS, SA, AUS [37155] : PRE 1875 GUELPH, ONT, CAN [34849] : 1750-1840 SIDBURY, DEV, ENG [34834] : C1843 CAMBERWELL, SRY, ENG [35460] : PRE 1744 LANLIVERY, CON, ENG [35973] : PRE 1801 ST JUST IN R & ST AUSTELL, CON, ENG [36039] : 1700+ EDENBRIDGE, KEN, ENG [36088] : WILLIAM PRE 1791 TAUNTON, SOM, ENG [36192] : 1500S CHAGFORD, DEV, ENG [36527] : 1860-1900 PLYMOUTH, DEV, ENG [36536] : PRE 1880 STREET, SOM, ENG [36676] : PRE 1840 HRT, ENG [36755] : PRE 1910 EAST END, LND, ENG [38581] : PRE 1850 WERRINGTON & ALL, DEV & NSW, ENG & AUS [38772] : ALL CAPETOWN, CAPE, RSA [38772] : 1066-1750 UK [38107] : 1700S BYFIELD, MA, USA [36560]

SEARLES DANIEL 1894 RHYNIE, SA, AUS [37155] : SAMUEL 1805 ONONDAGA CO., NY, USA [38062]

SEARLS PRE 1730 DEV, ENG [35866]

SEARS 1820+ TAS, AUS [35865] : 1850+ VIC, AUS [35865] : 1860+ MARYBOROUGH & MELBOURNE, VIC, AUS [38209] : C1860 SEVENOAKS, KEN, ENG [35348] : C1800 LONDON, ENG [35865] : 1700+ BKM, ENG [35880] : 1750+ DARTFORD & HADLOW, KEN, ENG [38209] : SIMEON C1760-1800 PAWLET, VT, CT & MA, USA [38055] : PRE 1700 MA & SOM, USA & ENG [38745]

SEASTON 1700+ SUTTON IN ASHFIELD, NTT, ENG [37058] : ALL BIRMINGHAM, WAR, ENG [37058]

SEATER 1800+ WESTRAY, OKI, SCT [37881]

SEATES 1890S CHEDWORTH, GLS, ENG [35256]

SEATH 1870+ MELBOURNE, VIC, AUS [35059]

SEATON GEORGE PRE 1860 ENG [35164] : 1800+ RAMSAY, HUN, ENG [35396] : 1800+ WHITTLESEA, CAM, ENG [35396] : JOHN 1765-1775 COTTINGHAM, YKS, ENG [35737] : PRE 1800 YKS & LIN, ENG [36399] : 1778-1823 LIVERTON, NRY, ENG [36412] : 1800+ BUTTERWICK, LIN, ENG [37448] : C1865 GREENOCK, RFW, SCT [35211] : 1855 AUCHINLECK, AYR, SCT [36599] : ALL ARBROATH WING, RUT, SCT & ENG [34645] : ALL WORLDWIDE [38344]

SEATRE 1620-1720 SKELTON, CUL, ENG [36098]

SEATREE ALL BRITON FERRY, GLA, WLS [37133]

SEAVEY 1770-1800 RYE, NH, USA [37576]

SEAWELL 1875-1883 TOMBSTONE, AZ, USA [35148]

SEAY 1800S LDY, IRL [36837]

SEBASTIAN 1700-1800 REMMESWEILER, SAA, BRD [38617]

SEBELIN 1800+ ALTENKREMPE, SHO, GER [33996]

SEBIRE PRE 1870 GSY, CHI [38004]

SECCOMBE 1820-1880 LANDEWEDNACK, CON, ENG [34115] : ALL POOLE, DOR, ENG [34663] : 1740S GERMANSWEEK, DEV, ENG [37080]

SECKER PRE 1900 NFK, ENG [34317] : 1750+ ST FAITHS, NFK, ENG [35458] : 1750+ NFK, ENG [35458] : 1700+ HOLM HELE, NFK, ENG [36743]

SECKOLD 1835+ AUS [34418] : 1838+ CAMDEN, NSW, AUS [34418] : ALL WORLDWIDE [34418]

SECOMBE 1800+ ILLOGAN, CON, ENG [38539]

SECORD PRE 1860 CAN & NZ [36255]

SEDDEN C1840 ECCLES, LAN, ENG [38410]

SEDDING PRE 1790 THAMES DITTON, SRY, ENG [38512]

SEDDON 1862+ BALLARAT EAST, VIC, AUS [36279] : PRE 1850 WESTHOUGHTON, LAN, ENG [34397] : PRE 1800 DEANE, LAN, ENG [34397] : 1870+ BELFAST, ANT, DOW & ARM, IRL [35636]

SEDELSTEN 1865+ BENALLA, VIC, AUS [36279]

SEDERHOLM 1885+ USA [36320]

SEDGER 1830+ DEPTFORD, KEN, ENG [37560]

SEDGEWICK ALL KENDAL, WES, ENG [37939] : 1870+ SHEFFIELD, YKS, ENG [38539]

SEDGLEY 1820+ CHARLESTON, SC, USA [35595]

SEDGWICK 1785+ LEEDS, YKS, ENG [37443] : 1750+ ST PANCRAS, LND, ENG [37735] : 1780+ STEPNEY & BETHNAL GREEN, MDX & LND, WORLDWIDE [37065]

SEDORE ALL WORLDWIDE [34485]

SEE PRE 1888 ESK, QLD, AUS [33832] : PRE 1888 NSW, AUS [33832] : PRE 1888 CANTON, CHINA [33832]

SEEBECK ALL USA [37961]

SEED 1832+ BRADFORD, WRY, ENG [34628] : PRE 1800 LIVERPOOL, LAN, ENG [37692] : PRE 1847 LIVERPOOL, LAN, ENG [37840] : PRE 1870 KILKEEL, DOW, IRL [33944] : 1850+ MILTON, NZ [33944]

SEEGER PRE 1850 PRE, GER [38490]

SEELAENDER PRE 1595 WEFERLINGEN, NSA, BRD [38639]

SEELBACH ALL WEI, GER [38607]

SEELENDER PRE 1595 BUELSTRINGEN, NSA, BRD [38639]

SEELEY ALL NEW ENGLAND, USA [36713] : 1740S-1770 OVENCAANON, CT, USA [38038]

SEELIG C1920 KASTANIENBAUM, LU, CH [34655] : 1800+ CASSEL, HEN, GER [34655] : 1900 CHICAGO, IL, USA [34655]

SEENER 1770+ CALVERLEY, WRY, ENG [36263]

SEERS 1850+ VIC, AUS [35865] : 1800+ LONDON, ENG [34455] : 1800+ LAMBETH, SRY, ENG [34455] : C1800 LONDON, ENG [35865] : 1700+ BKM, ENG [35880]

SEETS HANNAH 1750+ TUDELEY & CAPEL, KEN, ENG [33785]

SEEX PRE 1600 ESS, ENG [35642]

SEFTLY (SEE SEPLEY) [37310]

SEFTON 1850+ VIC, AUS [37497] : 1780-1850 LIVERPOOL, LAN, ENG [34762] : PRE 1841 DOW, IRL [34570]

SEGAL 1700-1990 BUCHAREST, ROUMANIA [38096] : 1880-1990 PHILADELPHIA CO., PA, USA [38096]

SEGERS 1800+ ZWOLLE, OIJ, NL [35338]

SEGROTT PRE 1835 EXNING, SFK, ENG [37978]

SEGUIN 1800-1950S QUE & NY, CAN & USA [34202] : 1600S D'ONS-EN-BRAY, RPA, FRA [34371]

SEHL 1850+ CAN & USA [38437] : PRE 1800 KOBLENZ, RPR, GER [38437]

SEHLIGER 1700-1800 HUTTENRODE, NSA, GER [38643]

SEIBEL 1620+ QUICKBORN, SHO, GER [37542]

SEIBERT PRE 1750 PA, USA [37587]

SEIBOTH 1800S KS, POL [33972]

SEIDEL 1830 HERZOGSWALDAU, LG, POL [38495]

SEIDELMANN GEORG A. 1796 MARKT BERGER, GER [37596] : GEORGE 1764-1816 MARKT BERGER, GER [37596] : JOHANN 1732-C1800 MARKT BERGER, GER [37596] : GEORG M. 1793 MARKT BERGER, GER [37596] : ANNA K. 1800-1844 MARKT BERGER, GER [37596] : JOHANN G. 1850+ MARKT BERGER, GER [37596] : ANNA 1795-1858 MARKT BERGER, GER [37596] : MARIA B. 1798-1862 MARKT BERGER, GER [37596]

SEIDL PRE 1880 HOEHENBERG, BAY, BRD [36338]

SEIGNETTE 1800 JARNAC, FRA [36596]

SEILS C1850 STOLP, POM, GER [34388]

SEIMONS ALL AUS [33836] : 1880+ SHEPPARTON, VIC, AUS [33836] : 1800-1900 HANNOVER, GER [33836]

SEINIGER PRE 1860 KARLSBAD AREA, BOHEMIA, CS [36963]

SEIP ALL KURHESSEN, WOLLMAR, MARBURG, BRD [35115]

SEISTRUP PRE 1870 REDDING, SHO, BRD [35330]

SEITHUEMER ALL DUESSELDORF, WEF, GER [34861]

SEITZER MARIA CATH. 1770 TRAPPE, PA, USA [38122]

SEL 1600-1700 PARIS, RPA, FRA [34514]

SELBACH PRE 1750 KOBLENZ, RPR, GER [38437]

SELBY 1776+ ASHBY DE LA ZOUCH, LEI, ENG [34260] : 1800+ LEICESTER, LEI, ENG [34260] : 1847-1900 STROUD, GLS, ENG [34658] : 1200S+ NBL, ENG [35096] : 1600S+ IGHTHAM MOTE, KEN, ENG [35096] : 1800+ LONGTON, STS, ENG [35121] : 1820+ NEWTON, CAM, ENG [37902] : 1800+ IFFLEY, OXF, ENG [38279] : 1820-1860S OH, USA [37600] : PRE 1820 MIDDLETOWN, OH, USA & ENG [36969]

SELDEN 1850-1990 HALIFAX, NS, CAN & USA [36182] : 1785-1990 OLD TOWN HASTINGS, SSX, ENG [36182] : 1812-1867 HURST & ASHTON UNDER LYNE, LAN, ENG [36182] : 1198 AMSTERDAM, NL [36182] : 1763-1990 HADLYME, CT, USA [36182] : 1643-1990 HADLEY, MA, USA [36182]

SELEMONAVICH C1900 IL, USA [38023]

SELENDER PRE 1595 BUELSTRINGEN, NSA, BRD [38639]

SELES PRE 1800 ZUH, NL [34180]

SELF PRE 1845 SAXMUNDHAM, SFK, ENG [35215] : 1700-1850 LOPHAM, NFK, ENG [36491] : PRE 1850 BRADFORD UPON AVON, WIL, ENG [37739]

SELFE 1700-1800 TROWBRIDGE, WIL, ENG [36205]

SELG 1800-1850 WUE, GER [38528]

SELIGER 1800-1900 BERLIN, GER [38603]

SELIGMANN 1750-1850 REIMERSWILLER, ALS, FRA [36898]

SELKIRK REV JAMES PRE 1800 WHITEHAVEN, CUL, ENG [36180] : 1650-1730 WEMYSS, FIF, SCT [33767]

SELLARS PRE 1900 CLK & LKS, SCT [38081]

SELLCKE 1874+ MARYBOROUGH, QLD, AUS [35144] : PRE 1874 GER [35144]

SELLECK 1858+ BUNINYONG, VIC, AUS [38277] : PRE 1824 CT, USA [38226]

SELLER PRE 1800 BEMPTON, ERY, ENG [34285] : 1700S SIDBURY, DEV, ENG [34715]

SELLERS 1800+ HARROGATE, WRY, ENG [36194]

SELLERY 1800-1840 ISLE OF WIGHT, HAM, ENG [38091] : 1820-1850 GLASGOW, SCT [38091]

SELLICK 1620 LYDEARD ST LAWRENCE, SOM,
ENG [34204] : ELIZA PRE 1840 SOM, ENG [34310] :
ALL ISLINGTON, DEV, ENG [36790]
SELLINGS PRE 1800 BURWASH, SSX, ENG [35406]
SELLMAN PRE 1800 OXF, ENG [37739]
SELLON 1861 HALIFAX CO., NS, CAN [38470] :
1700S MARLOW, BKM, ENG [36585]
SELMAN ALL ONT, CAN [34133] : PRE 1900
FRONTENAC CO., ONT, CAN [35604] : 1750-1850
MALMESBURY, WIL, ENG [34623]
SELMES 1887+ SYDNEY, NSW, AUS [37175] : PRE
1840 BECKLEY & RYE, SSX, ENG [35117] : 1863+
LONDON, ENG [37175]
SELSBY 1700+ ESS, ENG [37735]
SELTZER 1750-1850 BERKS CO., PA, USA [35318]
SELVES 1800-1900+ MAIDSTONE, KEN, ENG
[36803]
SELWAY 1855 BALLARAT, VIC, AUS [35728] : 1820S
ABERTILLERY, GLA, WLS [35728]
SELWOOD ALL ORANGE, NSW, AUS [38487] : PRE
1870 BOWERCHALKE, WIL, ENG [36255]
SEMER PRE 1800 SOM, ENG [36180]
SEMMELINK ALL WORLDWIDE [36458]
SEMMENS 1800S REDRUTH, CON, ENG [34684]
SEMMES 1790-1820 KY, USA [37029]
SEMOTIUK PRE 1860 SNIATYN, UKRAINE, OES
[36679]
SEMPLE 1900+ NSW, AUS [33859] : 1860S LONDON,
ENG [34709] : PRE 1900 GLASGOW, LKS, SCT
[33859] : PRE 1834 GLASGOW, LKS, SCT [34897] :
1780+ OLD KILPATRICK, DNB, SCT [35848]
SEMPLE-OUTRAM 1856+ ROTHESAY, BUT, SCT
[35025]
SENDALL ALL WORLDWIDE [37629]
SENDERS 1870S STRATUM, NBT, NL [35557]
SENECAL 1700-1850 VARENNES, QUE, CAN [34242]
SENER 1800+ LAN, ENG [37482]
SENGSTOCK PRE 1940 MARYBOROUGH, QLD,
AUS & GER [37948]
SENIOR PRE 1840 LEEDS, YKS, ENG [38288]
SENN C1821 RSA [34756]
SENNICKSEN 1850-1870 SKIPPING & SKIVINGE,
DEN [35158]
SENTER 1845-1865 KEWEENAW CO., MI, USA
[38009]
SENTINELLA 1830+ NORWICH, NFK, CAM &
MDX, ENG [34882]
SEPHTON PRE 1900 SCARISBRICK AND ST
HELENS, LAN, ENG [36487]
SEPLEY 1857+ WINDEYER, NSW, AUS [37310]
SERAO PRE 1793 FUNCHAL, IS. OF MADEIRA, PT
[35223]
SERAPHINA 1800+ MONTROSE, ANS, SCT [36971]
SERAPHINI 1800+ LEGHORN, TOSCANA, ITL
[36971] : 1880+ REDLANDS, CA, USA [36971]
SERCOMBE PRE 1900 TANJA, NSW, AUS [33781] :
1820S EXETER, DEV, ENG [35261]
SERENIUS ALL FINLAND [37444] : ALL SWE [37444]
SERGANT THOMAS 1700S NINFIELD, SSX, ENG
[35501]
SERGEANT MARTHA C1830 SYDNEY, NSW, AUS &
IRL [37556]
SERGEJEFF 1850+ HELSINKI, UUSIMAA, FIN
[38758]
SERGUIER PRE 1600 FRA & BEL [36140]
SERJEANT 1850-1910 STOKE NEWINGTON, MDX,
ENG [34735] : 1700-1800 NEWTIMBER, SSX, ENG
[34749] : C1830-1850 COLDWALTHAM, SSX, ENG
[36828]
SERL ALL NTT, ENG [36196]
SERLE C1700 ST ERME, CON, ENG [35076]
SERLE (SEARLS) [35866]

SERMON ALL GLS & OXF, ENG [37090]
SEROCOLD PRE 1830 LONDON, ENG [37873]
SEROI (SEE SEROY) [38451]
SERONG ALL AUS [35223] : 1824+ SYDNEY, NSW,
AUS [35835] : 1850+ WARRNAMBOOL, VIC, AUS
[35835]
SERONG (SEE SERAO) [35223]
SEROY 1860S QUE, CAN [38451]
SERPELL PRE 1830 MENHENIOT, CON, ENG
[34197]
SERRIL 1750+ GRITTLETON, WIL, ENG [34970]
SERROT 1790+ SCIOTO, OH, USA [38054]
SERVER 1800-1820 LOGAN, KY, USA [38576] : ALL
WORLDWIDE [38576]
SERVIFS 1800S DUNDAS CO., ONT, CAN [34150]
SERVOS 1786+ WEST LINCOLN, ONT, CAN [34094]
: 1700-1750 HUDSON VALLEY, NY, USA [34130]
SESSIONS PRE 1820 BIBURY, GLS, ENG [34725] :
WILLIAM PRE 1830 BRK, ENG [36619]
SESTERFLETH PRE 1700 GER [37808]
SESTON ALL BIRMINGHAM, WAR, ENG [37058]
SETCHELL 1698+ MILDENHALL, SFK, ENG [36489]
: 1820+ STETCHWORTH, CAM, ENG [36489]
SETFORD C1855 RICHMOND, VIC, AUS [37302] :
C1825 HADLOW, KEN, ENG [37302]
SETON 1840 CHELSEA, MDX, ENG [37080] : 1814
LAMBETH, SRY, ENG [37080] : 1370 SCT [37008] :
ALL WORLDWIDE [38344]
SETTER GEORGE PRE 1827 DUNSFORD, DEV,
ENG [35788] : RICHARD 1796+ EXETER, DEV,
ENG [35788]
SETTERFIELD 1800-1900 THANET, KEN, ENG
[37757]
SETTLE 1830S DEBENHAM, SFK, ENG [33934] :
1798-1820 BATLEY, WRY, ENG [35815]
SETZER 1700+ MAINHARDT, BAW, GER [35355] :
1860 GER [38017] : PRE 1890 HBG & MO, GER &
USA [38746]
SEUFERT PRE 1900 LEBENHAN, BAVARIA, GER
[34061]
SEUNTJENS PETRUS 1863 RETHY, BRA, BEL [38695]
: ANTONIUS 1814 RETHY, BRA, BEL [38695] :
JOH. BAP. 1835 RETHY, BRA, BEL [38695] : SICHT.
JOH. PRE 1800 BEL [38695] : JOH. BAP. 1774
RETHY, BRA, BEL [38695] : HENR. LUD. 1762
RETHY, BRA, BEL [38695] : HENRY PRE 1800 BEL
[38695]
SEVERE NANCY C1800 WV, USA [34126]
SEVERIN PRE 1635 RIBE, JUTLAND, DEN [38632]
SEVERN 1800-1900 KENSINGTON &
PADDINGTON, LND, ENG [34749]
SEVERNS 1800+ YKS, ENG [35403] : JOHN 1790-1833
HUNTERDON & BURLINGTON CO., NJ, USA
[38127]
SEVIER (SEE SEVERE) [34126]
SEWARD PRE 1760 MEMBURY & AXMINSTER,
DEV & DOR, ENG [35701] : 1600-1700
DREWSTEIGNTON, DEV, ENG [36817]
SEWELL 1851+ CRESWICK, VIC, AUS [35709] :
1880+ COCKERMOUTH, CUL, ENG [34100] : 1800S
GREAT YARMOUTH, NFK, ENG [34914] : PRE
1850 GOSFORTH, CUL, ENG [35709] : PRE 1854
GREAT YARMOUTH, NFK, ENG [35956] : PRE
1780 SIMONBURN, NBL, ENG [36110] : C1880
CAMBERWELL, LND, ENG [36175] : 1700-1860
WARCOP, WES, ENG [36256] : ALL YARMOUTH,
NFK, ENG [36393] : 1840+ CARLISLE
WETHERAL, CUL, ENG [37635] : PRE 1800 LIN,
ENG [37893] : C1812 BRIGHTON, SSX, ENG [37973]
: 1790-1900 LINCOLN, LIN, ENG [38511] : PRE 1907
RSA [35709] : 1905+ USA [35709] : 1700+ CLINTON
CO., OH & VA, USA [38336]

SEWILL PRE 1900 LIVERPOOL & LONDON, ENG
[36399]

SEWING ALL WEF, GER [35310]

SEWRY PRE 1842 ALTON, HAM, ENG [34911]

SEXBY (SEE SAXBY) [35546]

SEXEY C1822 FAREHAM, HAM, ENG [36259] :
1849+ SAN FRANCISCO, CA, USA [36259]

SEXTON 1850+ HEATHCOTE & COSTERFIELD,
VIC, AUS [35379] : 1860+ SHOREDITCH, LND,
ENG [33893] : PRE 1850 NORWICH, NFK, ENG
[35379] : 1750+ NFK, ENG [35403] : 1750+
LONDON, ENG [35403] : 1847+ MILLTOWN, DUB,
IRL [34653] : 1850S KILCORCORAN, CLA, IRL
[36307] : 1800+ KID, IRL [36863] : ALL IRL [37061] :
ALL CLOONLAHAN, CLA & GAL, IRL [37133] :
1840-1860 UNION CO., SC, USA [38188] : 1810-1840
SPARTANBURG CO., SC, USA [38188]

SEYBERT 1750+ EIBINGEN, HEN, GER [34693]

SEYBOLDT 1450-1750 ROMMELSHAUSEN, BAW,
BRD [38654]

SEYDEL 1750-1850 KNAUTTKLEEBURG &
LEIPZIG, SAX, GER [36953]

SEYFFARTH BERNHARD PRE 1872
BRANDENBERG, PRE, GER [38776]

SEYFRIED 1600-1800 WUE, GER [37015]

SEYLER PRE 1830 SELCHENBACH, RPR, GER
[34137]

SEYMOUR ALL NSW, AUS [35731] : 1750-1837
BLEDLOW, BKM, ENG [34687] : 1798
HILMARTON, WIL, ENG [34708] : 1800+
LONDON, ENG [35032] : CHARLES 1800S
TUNBRIDGE WELLS, KEN, ENG [35361] : 1830S
BRISTOL, ENG [35508] : C1793 LONDON, ENG
[36010] : PRE 1800 SHAFTESBURY, DOR, ENG
[36478] : 1700+ WALFORD, HEF, ENG [36756] :
PRE 1870 YEOVIL, SOM, ENG [37067] : 1750-1920
BRISTOL, ENG [37757] : PRE 1864
CASTLETOWNARRA, TIP, IRL [35407] : 1844
BALTIMORE, MD, USA [35808] : 1800-1900
JAMAICA, W.INDIES [36324]

SHACKELFORD 1800+ FAYETTE CO., OH, USA
[37565] : 1796-1850 SC & AL, USA [38340]

SHACKELL 1800+ MAYFAIR, LONDON, ENG
[35342] : 1800-1820 STANMORE, MDX, ENG [36044]
: 1780S TIVERTON & HOLCOMBE ROGUS, DEV,
ENG [36373] : 1880-1920 CARDIFF, GLA, WLS
[36373]

SHACKELTON 1850 KIMBERWORTH, YKS, ENG
[37829]

SHACKLES 1800 DRYPOOL, YKS, ENG [35370]

SHACKLETON 1800 BURNLEY, LAN, ENG [36560] :
ELIZABETH 1800S BINGLEY, YKS, ENG [36633] :
JANE PRE 1782 BRADFORD, WRY, ENG [38016]

SHACKLEY 1850+ ROWESHAM, BKM, ENG [36611]

SHACKLOCK 1800S ECKINGTON, DBY, ENG
[33776]

SHAD 1800-50 CH [37541]

SHADBURN 1750-80 VA, USA [38202]

SHADLEY 1850+ IA, USA [35287] : 1760+
FREDERICK CO., VA, USA [35287] : 1800+ OH,
USA [35287]

SHADLOW 1819+ ST MARYS & LLANDILO, NSW,
AUS [35394]

SHADWICK C1820 MANCHESTER, LAN, ENG
[35592]

SHAFER 1801 WAYNE CO., PA, USA [36736] :
NELSON 1868 BARTON CO., MO, USA [36736] :
NELSON 1865 HENRY, IL, USA [36736] : NELSON
1858 TISKELIVA, IL, USA [36736] : 1888 MCCOMB,
MO, USA [36736] : NELSON 1830 SUSQUEHANNA
CO., PA, USA [36736] : PETER 1800
SUSQUEHANNA CO., PA, USA [36736] : 1888

WRIGHT CO., MO, USA [36736] : GEORGE 1764
BERKS CO., PA, USA [38086]

SHAFFER 1800 FULDA, HES, BRD [37028] : 1800-1830
SUSQUEHANNA CO., PA, USA [36736] : 1850
MERCER, PA, USA [38317] : 1840
WESTMORELAND, PA, USA [38317]

SHAFTESBURY PRE 1660 ENG [36030]

SHAFTO 1800+ LIVERPOOL, LAN, ENG [35979]

SHAILER 1866+ SLACKS CREEK, QLD, AUS [34802]
: PRE 1840 PUTNEY, MDX, ENG [34802]

SHAKELEY PRE 1800 WESTMORELAND CO., PA,
USA [37040]

SHAKESPEARE PRE 1770 COLEORTON &
BREEDON, LEI, ENG [34311]

SHALDERS 1800-1850 ERPINGHAM & NORWICH,
NFK, ENG [34834] : 1880-1890 LEEDS, YKS, ENG
[34834] : PRE 1880 LND, ENG [37057] : ALL
WORLDWIDE [34834]

SHALDRICK 1750+ LYNN, NFK, ENG [34642] :
1800+ ONEHUNGA, AUCK, NZ [34642]

SHALES 1800+ TERRINGTON, NFK, ENG [37181]

SHALTZ 1780+ BRISTOL, GLS, ENG [36263]

SHAMBROOK ALL WORLDWIDE [37862]

SHAMBROOKE ALL WORLDWIDE [37862]

SHANAHAN 1800+ COLAC, VIC, AUS [36622] :
1800+ CASHEL, TIP, IRL [33825]

SHAND C1832 RICHMOND, NSW, AUS [35583] :
WILLIAM 1900+ BC, CAN [33784] : 1900+
CHELSEA, LND, ENG [36118] : 1780-1850 CITY,
LND, ENG [36432] : JAMES 1820+ ABD, SCT
[33784] : PRE 1830 GLENRINNES, BAN, SCT [34192]
: C1800 PITSLIGO, ABD, SCT [34400] : 1700+
INVERKEITHNY, BAN, SCT [34420] : 1750-1835
MORTLACH, BAN, SCT [34479] : PRE 1766
FORGUE, ABD, SCT [34861] : PRE 1790
ARBROATH, ANS, SCT [36432] : 1870+ KEITH,
BAN, SCT [36673] : 1800S SCT [37474]

SHANDY 1700-1800 NC, USA [38324]

SHANE 1800S CALLAWAY, MO, USA [38605]

SHANK PRE 1860 MARKHAM, CAN [34090] : 1660-70
BERN, BE, CH [38518]

SHANKLE PRE 1900 PA & NJ, USA [38218]

SHANKLEY 1780-1860 LKS, SCT [34751]

SHANKLY 1750+ SCT & AUS [36239]

SHANKS 1860+ WARRACKNABEAL, VIC, AUS
[34685] : PRE 1860 BALLYLINNY, ANT, IRL [34685]
: PRE 1840 PORTAFERRY, DOW, IRL [37636] :
1812+ SLAMANNAN, STI, SCT [35194] : PRE 1800
FALKIRK, STI, SCT [35377]

SHANLEY 1826+ AUS [36295]

SHANN 1750+ LEEDS, WRY, ENG [35824]

SHANNAHAN 1800+ LIM, IRL [36758]

SHANNAN 1700-1900 DFS, SCT [37480]

SHANNON PRE 1858 NSW, AUS [35407] : PRE 1900
BALLARAT, VIC, AUS [36372] : PRE 1900
TEMPLEPATRICK, ANT, IRL [34115] : PRE 1850
STROKESTOWN, ROS, IRL [34613] : 1815-1872
WEXFORD, IRL & USA [36960] : 1700-1900 DFS,
SCT [37480] : 1841-1923 BOSTON, MA, USA [36960]

SHAPLAND CHRISTOPHER C1740 NORTH
MOLTON, DEV, ENG [34963] : JOAN C1740
NORTH MOLTON, DEV, ENG [34963] : MARY PRE
1800 GEORGE NYMPTON, DEV, ENG [34963] :
CHRISTOPHER PRE 1800 GEORGE NYMPTON,
DEV, ENG [34963] : 1800+ WIVERLIESCOMBE,
SOM, ENG [35038]

SHAPLEY 1845-1875 KEWEENAW CO., MI, USA
[38009]

SHAPTER 1850+ PLYMOUTH, DEV, ENG [34482]

SHAPTON PRE 1850 AWLISCOMBE, DEV, ENG
[34314]

SHARADIN C1800 WEST TIEGNMOUTH, DEV, ENG [36271]

SHARD PRE 1800 LONDON, ENG [33968]

SHARDALOW 1800+ THORPE N HADDISCOE, NFK, ENG [34916]

SHARDLOW 1690-1840 ASTON ON TRENT, DBY, ENG [34822] : 1700-1850 NTT, ENG [35394]

SHARE 1800+ SYDNEY, NSW, AUS [38001]

SHARER PETER 1801 WAYNE CO., PA, USA [36736] : ROBERT 1799 WAYNE CO., PA, USA [36736]

SHARKEY C1850 GEELONG, VIC, AUS [34903] : ALICE 1853+ MELBOURNE & GREYTOWN, VIC, AUS & NZ [33961] : 1800-1860 GWEEDORE, DON, IRL [34880] : PRE 1850 OMAGH, TYR, IRL [34903] : ALL GLASGOW, SCT [36094] : 1850-1920 POUGHKESPIE, NY, USA [38102] : 1900-1960 CLEVELAND, OH, USA [38102]

SHARKIE ALL BELFAST, IRL [36094] : PRE 1864 KILKENNY, KIK, IRL [37994]

SHARLAND 1800+ SIDMOUTH & UPTON PYNE, DEV, ENG [35027]

SHARMAN 1850+ NEW ENGLAND, NSW, AUS [37889] : C1800+ LONDON, ENG [33812] : 1700-99 STOCKTON, WAR, ENG [34315] : 1700-1800 HUN, ENG [36038] : ALL RUGBY, WAR, ENG [36162] : PRE 1880 LONDON, ENG [37392] : 1800+ WISBECH, CAM, ENG [38280]

SHARNBERG 1800 MALENTA, SHO, GER [37170]

SHARP PRE 1909 CORINDHAP, VIC, AUS [35478] : 1854+ SOUTH MELBOURNE, VIC, AUS [37908] : 1880S MACKAY, QLD, AUS [37946] : 1837+ BATHURST & YOUNG, NSW, AUS [37993] : 1750+ ADOLPHUSTOWN, ONT, CAN [34109] : C1830 MONTREAL, QUE, CAN [37908] : 1800+ CRACOE, WRY, ENG [33814] : 1850+ GUILDFORD, SRY, ENG [34066] : C1860 LONDON, ENG [34117] : JAMES PRE 1850 CLERKENWELL, LND, ENG [34131] : PRE 1772 INGHAM, LIN, ENG [34501] : 1830S MAULDEN, BDF, ENG [35156] : 1800+ SCAWBY, LIN, ENG [35223] : 1720S TICEHURST, SSX, ENG [35261] : PRE 1880 SADDLEWORTH, LAN & YKS, ENG [36028] : 1800-1900 LIVERPOOL, LAN, ENG [36151] : 1600-1800 ORTON, WES, ENG [36151] : 1758-1841 LYDDEN, KEN, ENG [36865] : 1700+ WADWORTH, ERY, ENG [37050] : PRE 1840 KEN, ENG [37370] : PRE 1840 LAN, ENG [37701] : SAMUEL 1810+ DRONFIELD, DBY, ENG [37748] : 1840+ NELSON, NZ [35058] : PRE 1841 GRANGEMOUTH, STI, SCT [33951] : C1843 CLACKMANNAN, CLK, SCT [34122] : 1760S DUBHEAD & MADDERTY, PER, SCT [35261] : THOMAS 1840S+ CAMPBELTOWN, ARL, SCT [35876] : ALL SCT [35913] : 1700-1800 PER, SCT [36327] : 1870+ DUNDEE, ANS, SCT [36777] : 1830-1900 ABERDEEN, ABD, SCT [36777] : 1800+ FIF, SCT [37993] : 1800 SCT [38320] : 1850-1870 DUNFERMLINE, FIF, SCT [38763] : 1810-1820 SHARPSBERG, BATH CO., KY, USA [36328]

SHARPAROWE 1400-1650 BKM & BDF, ENG [35292]

SHARPE 1850S MAITLAND, NSW, AUS [35340] : 1855+ SINGLETON, NSW, AUS [35425] : 1850+ EDITHBURY, SA, AUS [37500] : 1880S YORKETOWN, SA, AUS [37500] : CHARLES 1840-1890 ALB & SAS, CAN [37878] : 1850+ MUSKOKA, ONT, CAN [38463] : 1784 RENNINGTON, NBL, ENG [33942] : PRE 1800 WIGTOFT, LIN, ENG [34311] : PRE 1820 RUDDINGTON, NTT, ENG [34319] : PRE 1855 BDF, ENG [35425] : 1840-1860S HAMPSTEAD, MDX, ENG [35560] : 1700+ PORTSMOUTH, HAM, ENG [36004] : PRE 1840 KEN, ENG [37370] : ALL SFK & ESS, ENG [37612] : PRE 1799 GRANTHAM, LIN, ENG [37726] : 1881+

KINGSCLIFFE, NTH, ENG [37878] : LOVE C1800 MEA, IRL [35494] : C1800 RATHDRUM, WIC, IRL [35563] : PRE 1840 BALLYCASTLE, ANT, IRL [37315] : 1750+ CAV, IRL [37478] : PRE 1885 GLASGOW, LKS, SCT [35985]

SHARPHOUSE 1600-1850 WRY, ENG [35292]

SHARPLES PRE 1858 LIVERPOOL, LAN, ENG [34587] : 1850+ LONDON, ENG [35812] : 1800+ HUDDERSFIELD, WRY, ENG [36777] : 1782-1900 BROUGHTON & PRESTON, LAN, ENG [37066] : 1800+ LAN, ENG [37462] : NATHANIEL 1800S OSWALDTWISTLE, LAN, ENG [38284] : JOHN THOMAS 1860 HABERGHAM EAVES, LAN, ENG [38284]

SHARPLESS 1869+ ORANGE, NSW, AUS [34595]

SHARRATT PRE 1853 DBY, ENG [34816]

SHARROCK 1848+ VIC, AUS [35836] : 1700+ NTH, ENG [35836] : 1800 LAN, ENG [36042]

SHARROD PRE 1844 SEVENOAKS, KEN, ENG [35238]

SHARRY 1840S ENNISTYMON, CLA, IRL [35136]

SHATSWELL 1600+ BITTESWELL, LEI, ENG [37784]

SHATTLES 1854+ HAWKESBURY RIVER, NSW, AUS [34273]

SHATTUCK 1800-1900 NORWICH, ONT, CAN [36556] : 1800-1950 SPRINGFORD, ONT, CAN [36556] : ALL ENG [37803]

SHATWELL 1800+ LIVERPOOL, LAN, ENG [34323]

SHAU 1800 GER [35873]

SHAUL 1750+ NFK & SFK, ENG [37347]

SHAVER 1800+ DUNDAS CO., ONT, CAN [34051] : 1795-1825 LINCOLN CO., ONT, CAN [37578] : 1825-1916 MIDDLESEX CO., ONT, CAN [37578] : 1700-1800 NY, USA [35603] : PRE 1795 SUSSEX CO., NJ, USA [37578] : PRE 1830 CRAWFORD, OH, USA [38112] : 1770-1820 ALBANY CO., NY, USA [38342]

SHAW SIMON 1800+ GINGIN, WA, AUS [33878] : ALL MOUNT VINCENT & WOLLOMBI, NSW, AUS [34595] : 1878+ LUSCOMBE, QLD, AUS [34893] : JAMES 1820+ NSW, AUS [34902] : JOSEPH 1831-1840 NEW NORFOLK, TAS, AUS [34910] : 1850-1910 SYDNEY, NSW, AUS [34989] : C1891 LANCEFIELD, VIC, AUS [35249] : C1842 HUNTER VALLEY, NSW, AUS [35251] : 1820+ CASTLEREAGH, NSW, AUS [35511] : JAMES 1852 ADELAIDE, SA, AUS [35529] : JOHN HENRY 1860S+ KEW, VIC, AUS [35876] : 1870 EMMAVILLE, NSW, AUS [36640] : ANNIE EMMA 1882-1922 SA & WA, AUS [34034] : 1800+ BADDECK, NS, CAN [34500] : PRE 1800 HUDDERSFIELD, YKS, ENG [33937] : EMMA 1700-1800 ENG [34034] : PRE 1800 NEWPORT, SAL, ENG [34275] : PRE 1820 CHRISTCHURCH, SRY, ENG [34316] : C1819 ILFORD, ESS, ENG [34518] : C1796 NOTTINGHAM, NTT, ENG [34595] : 1750-1850 OTLEY, YKS, ENG [34762] : 1890+ NELSON & BURNLEY, LAN, ENG [34790] : C1860 WENTWORTH, YKS, ENG [34893] : PRE 1795 THORPE HESLEY, YKS, ENG [34893] : PRE 1720 BRADFIELD, WRY, ENG [34974] : PRE 1900 LIVERPOOL, LAN, ENG [34999] : 1800-1870 LEEDS, YKS, ENG [35017] : JOHN PRE 1852 LIVERPOOL, LAN, ENG [35042] : PRE 1950 ENG [35352] : JOSEPH C1815 HARLESTONE, NTH, ENG [35391] : 1750+ BURY & TOTTINGTON, LAN, ENG [35511] : 1790+ LND, ENG [35511] : JAMES 1820+ LONDON, ENG [35529] : 1800S CHRISTCHURCH, MDX, ENG [35965] : C1613 NUTHURST, SSX, ENG [35990] : 1600 CHEBSEY, STS, ENG [36062] : 1800-1840 BRIGHOUSE & HALIFAX, WRY, ENG [36111] : 1800-1900 EAST RETFORD, NTT, ENG [36176] : JOHN 1784-1847 MERTON, SRY, ENG [36180] :

PRE 1850 MANCHESTER, LAN, ENG [36275] : PRE 1850 WAKEFIELD, YKS, ENG [36426] : PRE 1790 DARFIELD, YKS, ENG [36426] : JOHN C1800S SHEFFIELD, YKS, ENG [36585] : C1750 ALMONDBURY, WRY, ENG [36635] : 1800+ APPLEBY, WES, ENG [36869] : PRE 1890 DURHAM, DUR, ENG [37068] : ALL SOUTHAM & DAVENTRY, WAR & NTH, ENG [37090] : PRE 1790 ENG [37142] : PRE 1870 HUDDERSFIELD, WRY, ENG [37385] : 1800+ LONDON AREAS, LND, ENG [37496] : C1750-1830 SEDGLEY, STS, ENG [37642] : C1700-1800 LONDON, ENG [37718] : 1700-1920 HUDDERSFIELD, WRY, ENG [37736] : RALPH C1810-C1860 MELLOR, DBY, ENG [37934] : 1868 HAUGHTON, YKS, ENG [37986] : 1862+ WALES, YKS, ENG [37986] : 1827+ HONLEY, WAR, ENG [38209] : PRE 1760 PRESTON PATRICK, WES, ENG [38248] : 1840+ LIVERPOOL, LAN, ENG [38515] : 1700S THORP ARCH, WRY, ENG [38577] : ROBERT C1800 ENG & AUS [34034] : KENZIAS C1800 ENG & AUS [34034] : 1890-1925 KARACHI, INDIA [34989] : PRE 1842 KIK, IRL [33812] : 1850+ BELFAST, ANT, DOW & ARM, IRL [35636] : ALL BANBRIDGE & DUBLIN, DOW & DUB, IRL [36428] : 1750-1913 BANDON & CORK CITY, COR, IRL [36652] : PRE 1770 BELFAST, ANT, IRL [36917] : 1770-1790 DUBLIN, DUB, IRL [37869] : PRE 1849 SLI, IRL & AUS [34773] : 1700 KINGSTON, JAMAICA [36438] : 1850+ PIETERMARITZBURG, NATAL, RSA [36426] : 1800+ RICCARTON, AYR, SCT [34190] : C1818 KINGUSSIE, INV, SCT [34840] : C1847 GAMRIE, BAN, SCT [34840] : MATILDA C1846 IRVINE, AYR, SCT [35486] : JANET 1800S AYR, SCT [35501] : PRE 1810 SCT [36052] : 1600-1700 CRATHIENARD, FIF, SCT [36438] : 1700-1800 EDINBURGH, FIF, SCT [36438] : 1800-1900 DAVIOT, INV, SCT [36724] : JAMES C1759+ BARR, AYR, SCT [38067] : 1750-1850 CUMBERNAULD, SCT [38199] : 1800+ TARBERT, INV, SCT [38481] : PRE 1800 DUTCHESS CO., NY, USA [34495] : 1700-1850 LANESBORO & PITTSFORD, MA & VT, USA [36669] : 1650+ NEW LONDON CO., CT & NY, USA [36917] : 1822 PA, USA [37008] : PRE 1840 BRISTOL, RI, USA [37804] : CHRISTOPHER 1695-1720 FAIRFIELD, CT, USA [38130] : WILLIAM 1850 IL, USA [38152] : WILLIAM 1820 NC, USA [38152] : PRE 1810 DAUPHIN CO., PA, USA & IRL [36917]

SHAW (SEE SHEW) [35100]

SHAWCROSS ALL REDDISH, LAN, ENG [34674] : ALL MANCHESTER, LAN & DBY, ENG [38174] : C1820 ECCLES, LAN, ENG [38410]

SHAWL 1750+ NFK & SFK, ENG [37347]

SHAWVER SEBASTIAN 1730-1750 GER [37025] : SARAH 1880-1890 MADISON CO., IA, USA [37025]

SHAYLER 1600-1700 SHIPTON U WYCHWOOD, OXF, ENG [37380] : 1700-1800 CHADLINGTON, OXF, ENG [37380]

SHEA 1850+ PERTH, WA, AUS [34530] : 1831+ MAITLAND, NSW, AUS [35226] : 1870+ COLLINGWOOD, VIC, AUS [35524] : 1850 LONDON, ENG [37841] : ALL CLONMEL, TIP, IRL [34643] : PRE 1819 CARRICK ON SUIR, TIP, IRL [35162] : PRE 1831 OHMEA, KER, IRL [35226] : 1800+ MACROOM, COR, IRL [35358] : PRE 1807 OFF, IRL [35399] : 1790+ MIDLETON, COR, IRL [36946] : 1840-1865 CORK, COR, IRL [38117] : CATHERINE 1800-1850 KID, IRL [38779]

SHEAD 1880+ WEST HACKNEY, MDX, ENG [34452]

SHEADY 1806-1830 LIM, IRL [36281]

SHEAHAN 1840+ MUTTUMA & BURROWA, NSW, AUS [35159] : C1840 LIMERICK, LIM, IRL [33918] : PRE 1845 CLA, IRL [35077]

SHEARD PRE 1900 MIRFIELD, YKS, ENG [34351] : 1780+ OVENDEN, WRY, ENG [34397] : 1800+ WITNEY, OXF & BRK, ENG [36802] : ALL BATLEY, WRY, ENG [37621] : PRE 1842 ENG [38222] : ALL YKS, ENG & NZ [36840] : 1840+ NY, USA [37621]

SHEARER 1857+ SCOTTSDALE, TAS, AUS [36644] : C1850+ SINGLETON, NSW, AUS [38541] : 1837 MANCHESTER, LAN, ENG [34581] : C1700 ARM, NC & KY, IRL & USA [34203] : 1700+ CANISBAY, CAI, SCT [34414] : PRE 1850 CRUDEN, ABD, SCT [34784] : PRE 1835 PAISLEY, RFW, SCT [34814] : JANET C1740+ ELGIN, MOR, SCT [35848] : C1738 BOTRIPHNIE, BAN, SCT [36644] : C1850 MLN, SCT [37527]

SHEARGOLD 1840+ SYDNEY, NSW, AUS [35330] : 1900+ BRISBANE, QLD, AUS [35807] : 1790-1900 KENSINGTON, MDX, ENG [36876]

SHEARING 1850+ SA, AUS [35048] : 1840+ AUS [35241] : PRE 1830 SALISBURY, WIL, ENG [35048] : 1750+ NFK, ENG [35241]

SHEARMAN PRE 1780 READING, BRK, ENG [35946] : 1700+ NEWGATE & ILFORD, LND & ESS, ENG [36794] : 1800-1865 KIK, IRL [37156] : ALL NZ [34603]

SHEARS C1890 ULUPNA, VIC, AUS [35136] : 1870S BULLARTO, VIC, AUS [35136] : 1830S PLYMOUTH, DEV, ENG [35136] : C1825 BRISTOL, SOM, ENG [35807] : PRE 1860 WINTERSLOW, WIL, ENG [37287] : ALL WORLDWIDE [33959]

SHEARS (SEE SHIERS) [35578]

SHEASBY 1500-1990 WAR, ENG [36130]

SHEATH PRE 1780 BRADING, IOW, ENG [35770]

SHEATHER C1860+ MACLEAN, NSW, AUS [35143] : C1860+ PALMERS ISLAND, NSW, AUS [35143] : 1839+ MAITLAND AREA, NSW, AUS [35143] : PRE 1839+ NINFIELD, SSX, ENG [35143] : 1800S HASTINGS, SSX, ENG [35881] : 1760+ CATSFIELD, SSX, ENG [37260] : C1870+ WHAKATANE, NZ [35143]

SHECKELL 1780-1900 WELLINGTON, SOM, ENG [36373]

SHECKLER PRE 1900 INDIANA CO., PA, USA [38218]

SHEDDEN C1895 CATRINE, AYR, SCT [35826]

SHEDLOCK C1880 MANCHESTER, LAN, ENG [37263]

SHEEAN ALL IRL & AUS [35171]

SHEEDY PATRICK PRE 1841 IRL [33807] : JOHANNA PRE 1841 IRL [33807] : 1820 BRUFF, LIM, IRL [37122]

SHEEHAN 1880S WARRNAMBOOL, VIC, AUS [35136] : C1834 BALLYLANDELS, LIM, IRL [33936] : PRE 1840 WEX, IRL [35088] : MICHAEL PRE 1853 KILBONANE, KER, IRL [35380] : MICHAEL PRE 1835 AGHADOE, KER, IRL [35380] : ALL WATERFORD, WAT, IRL [36043] : C1860+ ABBEYSVILLE, LIM, IRL [36838] : PRE 1880 COR, IRL [38589] : PRE 1880 DUB, IRL [38589] : DANIEL PRE 1861 PITTSBURGH, PA, USA [35380] : 1850+ MA, USA [38589]

SHEEHY PRE 1850 DOON, LIM, IRL [35842] : MARTIN 1815 DUAGH, KER, IRL [36274] : MORGAN 1820 DUAGH, KER, IRL [36274] : PATRICK 1825 KILCARRAMDORE, KER, IRL [36274] : BRIDGET 1823+ ASKEATON, LIM, IRL [36367]

SHEEN PRE 1910 HACKNEY & ISLINGTON, MDX, ENG [34335] : LOUISA 1850 WOR, ENG [38183]

SHEEPY PRE 1702 LEICESTER, LEI, ENG [35046]

SHEER PRE 1710 ALTARNUM, CON, ENG [35335]

SHEERAN PRE 1866 BALLYVAUGHAN, CLA, IRL [34262]

SHEERING PRE 1700 GARBOLDISHAM, NFK, ENG [35571]

SHEFFER ALL WORLDWIDE [35337]

SHEFFIELD ALL SYSTON, LEI, ENG [34254] : PRE 1850 EARLS BARTON, NTH, ENG [37357] : 1750-1800 NC, USA [36911] : 1700+ NEW LONDON, CT, USA [38241]

SHEFFORD PRE 1800 WIL, ENG [36282] : 1880+ NZ [36282]

SHEGOG ALL DERRY, IRL [36360]

SHEHAN 1800-1814 MALLOW, COR, IRL [37172]

SHEIDOW 1800+ PEI, CAN [34297] : 1800S RATHMOLYON, MEA, IRL [34297] : ALL IRL [34297]

SHEIRCLIFFE 1800+ BANDON, COR, IRL [35201]

SHEIRSON 1875+ DUBLIN, DUB & SRY, IRL & ENG [35013]

SHELBOURNE C1806-1829 DUBLIN, IRL [34704]

SHELDON C1800 SHOREDITCH ST LEONARDS, MDX, ENG [33841] : PRE 1900 HANLEY & WEDNESBURY, STS, ENG [34611] : 1800S WOOTTEN BASSETT, WIL, ENG [35899] : 1750+ APPLEBY MAGNA, LEI, ENG [36603] : PRE 1870 STS, ENG [37500] : 1740S NY, USA [34342] : C1740 MA & NY, USA [34395] : 1770-1800 DUTCHESS CO., NY, USA [38763]

SHELDRAKE PRE 1824 WESTERFIELD, SFK, ENG [34696] : 1800+ EAST LONDON, ENG [37416] : PRE 1750 KETTLEBURGH, SFK, ENG [37420]

SHELDRICK 1800+ VERNON, ONT, CAN [35613] : 1800+ ENG [35613]

SHELDRICKS PRE 1800 ENG [35613]

SHELENSKI PRE 1900 STETTIN, GER & POL [33966]

SHELFORD PRE 1850 CHESTERFIELD, ESS, ENG [33868]

SHELHAM ALL ADELAIDE, SA, AUS [34561] : ALL MAURITIUS [34561]

SHELIOR PETER PRE 1860 BROWN CO., OH, USA [37037] : SARAH PRE 1926 CLERMONT CO., OH, USA [37037]

SHELL 1856 BATH, SOM, ENG [36860]

SHELLADY PRE 1900 NEW CASTLE CO., DE, USA [36359]

SHELLEW ALL CLA, IRL & AUS [35213]

SHELLEY C1780 SYDNEY, NSW, AUS [35089] : ELIZ. 1820+ BRIGHTON, SSX, ENG [35803] : PRE 1917 AUCKLAND, AKD, NZ [36262]

SHELSWELL JOHN 1880+ ORO, ONT, CAN [35648] : ALFRED 1880+ ORO, ONT, CAN [35648]

SHELTON JOSEPH ALL RICHMOND & CASTLEREAGH, NSW, AUS [36643] : 1780 AYLESBURY, BKM, ENG [34120] : 1700S NORTH SHIELDS, NBL, ENG [35322] : 1840-1860 KINGSTANLEY, GLS, ENG [35726] : PRE 1830 LOUGHBOROUGH, LEI, ENG [35798] : C1850 ETON, LEI, ENG [35807] : PRE 1900 YKS, ENG [36110] : PRE 1800 LONDON, MDX, ENG [36379] : C1810 LONDON, ENG [37180] : EMMA C1820 ENG [37735] : 1827+ STANWAY, ESS, ENG [37963] : ALL STS, SAL & WAR, ENG [38754] : ALL ELIZABETH CITY CO., VA, USA [36557]

SHEMPP 1870 PITTSBURGH, PA, USA [38327]

SHENAULT 1824-1855 HARDEMAN CO., TN, USA [38092] : 1800-1824 SURRY CO., NC, USA [38092] : 1800-1824 MS, USA [38092]

SHENSTONE PRE 1763 HALESOWEN, WOR, ENG [37662] : PRE 1816 BIRMINGHAM, WAR, ENG [37662]

SHENTON PRE 1855 BRIGHTON, SSX, ENG [36167] : 1800-1900 WILLASTON, CHS, ENG [37931]

SHENTSON 1700S SOUTHFLEET, KEN, ENG [37019]

SHEPARD 1800-1900 ST PETER PORT, GSY, CHI [37435] : 1890+ NORTHAMPTON, NTH, ENG [35971] : 1878 LONDON, ENG [36281]

SHEPHARD (SEE SHEPHE [33898]

SHEPHEARD 1700-1850 WAR & NTH, ENG [36007]

SHEPHERD C1860+ GOULBURN, NSW, AUS [33898] : C1833+ CAMDEN, NSW, AUS [33898] : 1868+ GYMPIE & CHARTERS TOWERS, QLD, AUS [34044] : PRE 1936 TINGHA, NSW, AUS [38075] : ANDREW 1883+ MOONGULLA, NSW, AUS [38083] : JOHN 1870S MOREE, NSW, AUS [38083] : PRE 1849 SOUTHAM, WAR, ENG [34009] : PRE 1868 NORTH PETHERTON, SOM, ENG [34044] : 1850 DRIFFIELD, ERY, ENG [34111] : 1850+ RIPPLE, WOR, ENG [34160] : 1800-1850 HEIGHINGTON, DUR, ENG [34211] : ALL LIN, ENG [34663] : PRE 1750 WEM, SAL, ENG [34711] : 1820 KIRKBY STEPHEN, WES, ENG [34731] : 1850+ TEDINGTON, BDF, ENG [34747] : 1700S BARWICK & GARFORTH, WRY, ENG [34776] : C1832 HURSLEY, HAM, ENG [34898] : ALL BRAILES, WAR, ENG [35009] : C1728 BILTON, NBL, ENG [35026] : C1850 BANWEIL, SOM, ENG [35885] : PRE 1860 DONCASTER, YKS, ENG [35898] : PRE 1820 NEEN SOLLARS, SAL & HEF, ENG [35940] : PRE 1770 FARRINGDON, BRK, ENG [36072] : 1750-1890 SRY, ENG [36090] : ALL ISLE OF SHEPPEY, KEN, ENG [36094] : 1700-1800 BERKSWELL, WAR, ENG [36541] : PRE 1860 EAST LONDON, ENG [37416] : ALL LONDON, ENG [37743] : C1780 RICKMANSWORTH, HRT, ENG [37838] : 1800S SFK, ENG [37910] : PRE 1830 ELSTREE, HRT, ENG [38075] : PRE 1851 HORNSEY, MDX, ENG [38075] : PRE 1830 ALDENHAM, HRT, ENG [38075] : PRE 1880 LIN, ENG [38435] : 1700-1800 PREES, SAL, ENG [38474] : 1700-1800 HOLBETON, DEV, ENG [38516] : PRE 1835 DROMARA, DOW, IRL [35411] : 1800+ SEAGAHAN & PORTADOWN, ARM, IRL [36753] : 1824+ ROSEMARKIE, ROC, SCT [34058] : 1800+ ABD, SCT [34420] : 1750-1850 FORFAR, ANS, SCT [34523] : C1835 DUNNING, PER, SCT [35963] : ALEXANDER 1851 LKS, SCT [36367] : 1800+ PHILADELPHIA, PA, USA [36578] : MARY ELIZ. 1854+ OH, USA [36723] : 1680-1800 QUEEN ANNS CO., MD, USA [36731] : JAMES PRE 1795 PA & VA, USA [37580] : 1800S BARBADOS, W.INDIES [38406]

SHEPPARD 1912+ WARRNAMBOOL & MELBOURNE, VIC, AUS [34008] : 1850+ MACLEAY RV, NSW, AUS [34306] : PRE 1850 HOBART, TAS, AUS [34433] : PRE 1900 EUROA, VIC, AUS [34433] : ALL WARRNAMBOOL, VIC, AUS [35082] : PRE 1950 WODONGA, VIC, AUS [35386] : 1855+ ADELAIDE, SA, AUS [35587] : PRE 1870 FOOTSCRAY, VIC, AUS [35796] : 1810+ NFD, CAN [33852] : 1850+ RAMSGATE, KEN & BRK, ENG [34008] : 1850 DRIFFIELD, ERY, ENG [34111] : PRE 1750 WINTERBORNE STICKLAND, DOR, ENG [34228] : PRE 1720 HAM, ENG [34504] : ALL FROME, SOM, ENG [34550] : ALL SOM, ENG [34550] : PRE 1600 WIL, ENG [34550] : 1550 BRAUNTON & BARNSTAPLE, DEV, ENG [34747] : 1550 HALBERTON, DEV, ENG [34747] : PRE 1840 KEWSTOKE, SOM, ENG [35360] : 1780-1830 CHESTER, CHS, ENG [35402] : PRE 1853 CHOLDERTON & ALLINGTON, WIL, ENG [35588] : JESSE 1800+ MERE, WIL, ENG [35803] : PRE 1870 ST PANCRAS, MDX & GLS, ENG [36090] : C1805 CHELTENHAM, GLS, ENG [37063] : PRE 1810 DOVER, KEN, ENG [37371] : 1825-1893 MANCHESTER, LAN, ENG & AUS [36642] : 1870+ PHILADELPHIA, PA, USA [36578]

SHEPPERD PRE 1810 OXF, ENG [37739]
SHEPSTON 1885 CARDIFF, GLA, WLS [34839]
SHEPSTONE PRE 1854 BRISTOL, GLS, ENG [34805]
SHEPTON 1730-74 PRESTBURY, CHS, ENG [37697]
SHEPTON (SEE SHIPTON [36278]
SHERBINE PRE 1870 OH & PA, USA [38217]
SHERBORN ALL LONDON, MDX, ENG [37077] :
1650-1850 ISLEWORTH, MDX, ENG [37077] : 1650-
1850 HESTON, MDX, ENG [37077] : ALL
BEDFONT, MDX, ENG [37077] : ALL ASHFORD,
MDX, ENG [37077] : 1650-1800 HOUNSLOW, MDX,
ENG [37077] : ALL FULHAM, MDX, ENG [37077]
SHERBORNE 1660-1820 GLS, ENG [37870]
SHERBUD 1760+ ENG & AUS [33790]
SHERER C1820 PRE, GER [37022]
SHERET 1800-1890 MONTROSE, ANS, SCT [37495]
SHERGOLD 1830 REDLYNCH, WIL, ENG [34731] :
PRE 1860 WIL, ENG [36289]
SHERIDAN 1800+ NSW, AUS [34424] : 1870+
MAITLAND, NSW, AUS [34969] : PRE 1900 MT
GAMBIER, SA, AUS [35789] : 1856+ TAMWORTH,
NSW, AUS [37314] : 1850+ QLD, AUS [37314] :
1860+ DUNGOG, NSW, AUS [38729] : 1850-1910
ONT, CAN [38774] : 1750+ STOKE ON TRENT,
STS, ENG [34314] : C1800 WEST TIEGNMOUTH,
DEV, ENG [36271] : C1820 EXETER, DEV, ENG
[36271] : 1840 RALAGHE, MEA, IRL [33848] : PRE
1870 DRUMEASAN, DON, IRL [35833] : 1600-1700S
DUBLIN, IRL [36837] : 1817-1856 CAV, IRL [37314] :
DENNIS 1837+ BLACK HILL, MEA & WEM, IRL
[37314] : 1800+ CLA, IRL [37916] : 1850+ NEW
BRITAIN, CT, USA [37314]
SHERIFF PRE 1850 ABERDEEN, ABD, SCT [35713]
[37699]
SHERINGHAM 1800+ SHERINGHAM, NFK, ENG
[37699]
SHERLAN PRE 1870 HUTTON, ELN, SCT [33959]
SHERLIFOU 1840+ WA, USA [36942]
SHERLOCK 1825+ GEORGETOWN, TAS, AUS
[34921] : 1836+ SYDNEY, NSW, AUS [37104] : ALL
ENG [34757] : 1880 HAM, ENG [34757] : 1780+
WIRRAL, CHS, ENG [34921] : PRE 1850 SRY, ENG
[36589] : 1800+ CHILHAM & SELLING, KEN, ENG
[37707] : ALL ORMSKIRK, LAN, ENG & USA
[35289] : PRE 1871 KILMACSHALGEN, SLI, IRL
[35597] : ALL WORLDWIDE [37286]
SHERMAN PRE 1750 ESS, ENG [35642] : PRE 1830
WIL, BRK & HAM, ENG [35902] : PRE 1780
READING, BRK, ENG [35946] : PRE 1730
IPSWICH, SFK, ENG [37420] : PRE 1833 LND, ENG
[38077] : PRE 1625 DEDHAM, ESS, ENG [38135] :
PRE 1800 MONMOUTH CO., NJ, USA [36702] :
1700-1850 SUFFOLK CO., NY, USA [37783] :
ELMIRA 1815-1915 RED WOOD FALLS, MN & OH,
USA [38392]
SHERRACK 1851+ MINTO, NSW, AUS [33817]
SHERRARD 1688+ LONDONDERRY, LDY, IRL
[35194]
SHERRATT PRE 1875 BURSLEM, STS, ENG [36514] :
1600+ LEEK, STS, ENG [36701] : C1720+
BADDESLEY ENSOR, WAR, ENG [36753]
SHERRELL WILLIAM 1820 EGG BUCKLAND, DEV,
ENG [36634]
SHERRIFF PRE 1843 FORFAR, ANS, SCT [34691] :
PRE 1850 ABERDEEN, ABD, SCT [35713]
SHERRILL C1650-1800 MD, USA [38242]
SHERRING WILLIAM C1862 GUM FLAT, NSW, AUS
[37106] : WILLIAM C1834 LONDON, ENG [37106]
SHERRINGHAM 1801+ SOUTH CREEK &
WINDSOR, NSW, AUS [35394] : PRE 1801
KETTLESTONE, NFK, ENG [34758]
SHERRIT 1800+ FORDOUN, KCD, SCT [34560] :
1700+ ARBUTHNOTT, KCD, SCT [34560]

SHERRITT 184+ HILLSGREEN, ONT, CAN [34085] :
PRE 1868 SHARDLOW, DBY, ENG [36475]
SHERRY 1894 ORANGE, NSW, AUS [34965] : JOHN
1836 HAMILTON CO., IL, USA [35286] : 1900+
SCOTT CO., MO, USA [35286]
SHERVEY 1850+ QLD & NSW, AUS [37176] : 1800+
RODNEY STOKE, SOM, ENG [36195] : ALL SOM,
ENG [37176]
SHERWELL 1806 CHICHESTER, SSX, ENG [34446]
SHERWIN C1858 MONMOUTH, DEV, ENG [34653] :
PRE 1854 WINCHESTER, HAM, ENG [34696] :
C1874 ULVERSTON, LAN, ENG [35887] : 1797
BARWELL, LEI, ENG [36528]
SHERWOOD 1856+ CHILTERN, VIC, AUS [33932] :
C1831 NEW NORFOLK, TAS, AUS [35729] : PRE
1830 LEEDS, WRY, ENG [33932] : C1800 BETHNAL
GREEN, MDX, ENG [36099] : ALL
ALDERMASTON, BRK, ENG [37044] : PRE 1800
YKS, ENG [37669] : PRE 1860 HULL, ERY, ENG &
NZ [35940] : 1700+ WIC, IRL [35627] : 1700-1880
GLENOSHEEN, LIM, IRL [37422] : 1700-1800 MA,
USA [37538]
SHEVELAN 1790+ DON & LOU, IRL [36503] : 1790-
1850 FER, MOG & TYR, IRL [36503] : ALL
WORLDWIDE [36503]
SHEVLIN PRE 1900 LKS, SCT [34373]
SHEW 1830+ CORK, COR, IRL [35100] : ALL
WORLDWIDE [37292]
SHEWARD 1865+ KINGSWINFORD, STS, ENG
[36110] : PRE 1895 OLDBURY & ASTLEY, WOR,
ENG [36110]
SHIEFENMUELER ALL ENG [34588]
SHIEL 1885+ IPSWICH, QLD, AUS [36305]
SHIELD 1782 GOSPORT, HAM, ENG [36051]
SHIELDS 1914+ ENFIELD, SA, AUS [33920] : PRE
1880 SKIPTON & BALLARAT, VIC, AUS [35087] :
1848+ HOBART, TAS, AUS [35831] : THOMAS
1800-1876 CUMBERLAND CO., NS, CAN [38421] :
1860S LONDON, ENG [34605] : 1800S
DILLONSTOWN, LOU, IRL [37027] : 1800+
BELFAST, ANT, IRL [38726] : 1750+
TORPHICHEN, WLN, SCT [35979] : 1700+ AYR,
SCT [37620] : 1809-1884 ROXBURGH &
STRATHROY, ROX & ONT, SCT & CAN [37581] :
SAMUEL 1830-1840S WHITE CO., IL, USA [37001] :
WILLIAM 1800-1810S MADISON, IN, USA [37001] :
ROBERT 1870-1790S TN, USA [37001] : ROBERT
1760-1770S ROCKINGHAM CO., VA, USA [37001] :
SAMUEL 1820S EDGAR CO., IL, USA [37001] : 1835
OKMULGEE, OK, USA [38012] : 1720-1780 KENT
CO., DE, USA [38119] : 1720-1750 ACCOMAC CO.,
VA, USA [38119] : FRANK 1800-40 MIFFLIN CO.,
PA, USA [38138]
SHIELS PRE 1820+ DOW, IRL [35453] : 1780-1880
LOU, IRL [37844]
SHIERLAW C1916 ROBERTSON, NSW, AUS [34648] :
PRE 1860 OLD CAMBUS, BEW, SCT [34648]
SHIERS PRE 1784 LONDON, ENG [35578]
SHIFLETT 1850-1930 COUNCIL GROVE, KS & CA,
USA [38043]
SHILCOCK 1800-1850 NFK, LND & SRY, ENG [36422]
SHILDRICK 1870+ ONT, CAN [38323]
SHILLING 1800+ NEWTON, HAM, ENG [35644]
SHILLINGFORD PRE 1850 LONDON, ENG [38002]
SHILLINGLAW 1840S MELBOURNE, VIC, AUS
[34563] : 1800+ ESS, ENG [34563] : 1790+ ELN, SCT
[36871]
SHILLITO PRE 1880 WESTMORELAND CO., PA,
USA [35270]
SHILLOM 1832 AVENING, GLS, ENG [38209]
SHILLUM 1800 GRAVESEND, LND, ENG [38756]

SHILSON PRE 1855 DEV, ENG [34116] : PRE 1787 TIVERTON, DEV, ENG [35496]

SHILSTON PRE 1800 CREDITON, DEV, ENG [37264]

SHILTON PRE 1860 BURBAGE, LEI, ENG [35246] : C1720 BADDESLEY ENSOR, WAR, ENG [36753]

SHILVOCK ALL UK [37058]

SHIMELD PRE 1926 SHEFFIELD, WRY, ENG [36403]

SHIMELL PRE 1850 ST LUKES OLD STREET, MDX, ENG [37753]

SHIMMEN 1839+ KIRK GERMAN, IOM [34288]

SHIMMIN 1800 GERMAN, IOM [34890] : C1800 PEEL, IOM, UK [35034]

SHIMMING PRE 1775 HASKETON, SFK, ENG [37420]

SHINABARGER 1900+ OR, USA [37597]

SHINAULT 1824-1855 SHELBY CO., TN, USA [38092] : 1824-1855 FAYETTE CO., TN, USA [38092] : 1860-1950 NAVARRO CO., TX, USA [38092] : 1870-1940 LIMESTONE & MCLENNAN CO., TX, USA [38092] : 1853-1950 FREESTONE CO., TX, USA [38092] : 1800-1824 SURRY CO., NC, USA [38092] : 1824-1855 HARDEMAN CO., TN, USA [38092] : 1850 DE SOTO CO., MS, USA [38092]

SHINE PRE 1919 GLIN, LIM, IRL [36631] : CATHERINE C1840+ GAL, IRL [37530] : C1860+ MOORE, ROS, IRL [37530]

SHINGLES ALBERT PRE 1900 SWAN HILL, VIC, AUS [35124] : PRE 1900 RACKHEATH, NFK, ENG [36122]

SHINKLE 1820+ ROSS & HIGHLAND CO., OH, USA [37565]

SHINKWIN ALL WORLDWIDE [35793]

SHINN PRE 1876 BRANDON, NFK, ENG [37955]

SHINNERS 1858 ROSEWOOD & SURAT, NSW, AUS [38592] : 1890+ BRISBANE & NORTH QLD, QLD, AUS [38592]

SHINNICK 1841 SYDNEY, NSW, AUS [36367]

SHIP C1840 PIDLEY, HUN, ENG [35877] : ALL ENG [37664]

SHIPHERDLY 1776 AMERSHAM, BKM, ENG [34708]

SHIPMAN 1600+ ALL CANNINGS, WIL, ENG [37843]

SHIPP 1850+ VIC, AUS [37152] : 1800S DOR, ENG [34817] : ALL BURNWALL, CAM, ENG [35467] : C1817 STANFORD, NFK, ENG [37144] : 1775 ROTHERHITHE, SRY, ENG [38499]

SHIPPAM ALL NTT & YKS, ENG [36399]

SHIPPEE 1640+ RI, USA [38015] : 1640+ RI, USA [38015]

SHIPPEN PRE 1830 OXF, ENG [35592]

SHIPPERBOTTOM 1700+ BOLTON, LAN, ENG [36198]

SHIPPOBOTHAM 1700+ BOLTON, LAN, ENG [36198]

SHIPPOBOTTOM 1700+ BOLTON, LAN, ENG [36198]

SHIPPY 1639 HENRICO, VA, USA [38198]

SHIPTON 1600-1700 ANDOVER, HAM, ENG [36226] : PRE 1793 NORTH PETHERTON, SOM, ENG [36278] : 1842-70 MON & GLA, WLS [36873]

SHIRE ALL SOM, ENG [38431]

SHIRLEY PRE 1880 BALLARAT, VIC, AUS [35885] : CORPORAL C1940 AUS [37375] : ARTHUR 1914+ ONT & SAS, CAN [37375] : PRE 1880 BANBURY, OXF, ENG [35885] : PRE 1852 HORSINGTON, SOM, ENG [36800] : C1900 CHILWELL, NTT, ENG [37375] : J.W. 1912+ MANCHESTER, LAN, ENG [37375] : GEORGE 1864 NOTTINGHAM, NTT, ENG [37375] : JOHN WILLIAM C1912 LAN & STS, ENG [37375] : 1600 EYAM, DBY, ENG [37375] : 1600 FAWFIELD HEAD, STS, ENG [37375] : 1600+ LONGNOR, STS, ENG [37375] : J.W. 1912+

LIVERPOOL, LAN, ENG [37375] : 1770S DBY & STS, ENG [37751] : 1843 AYLESBURY, BKM, ENG [38209] : WALTER 1937 LONG ISLAND, NY, USA [37375] : WALTER 1923 NEW YORK, NY, USA [37375]

SHIRREFF 1790S LONDON, ENG [34296]

SHISLER 1819+ MO, USA [37592]

SHISTEL ALL WORLDWIDE [37440]

SHIVAS 1840+ ABERDEEN, ABD, SCT [35584]

SHIVELY 1785 MONONGALIA CO., VA, USA [36446] : 1770 PA, USA [36446] : C1751+ PA, USA [38067] : 1700S FREDERICK CO., MD, USA [38374] : 1700S LANCASTER CO., PA, USA [38374]

SHIVERS 1776-1782 EDGECOMB CO., NC, USA [36354]

SHLAR PRE 1870 BADEN BADEN, GER [34443]

SHOALE ALL WORLDWIDE [36416]

SHOBER 1700S PA, USA [38374]

SHOBERT 1841-1851 IL, USA [38101] : 1851-1914 CLARK CO., WA, USA [38101] : 1806-1840 LUZERNE CO., PA, USA [38101]

SHOCKLEY C1766 WORCESTER CO., MD, USA [36354]

SHOEBOTTOM ALL LONDON, ONT, CAN [35264] : ALL STONEY ACRES, TIP, IRL [35264]

SHOEBRIDGE 1720S TONBRIDGE, KEN, ENG [35261] : PRE 1826 KEN, ENG [35746] : ALL WORLDWIDE [36107]

SHOEBROOK 1700-1800 TAUNTON, SOM, ENG [37843]

SHOESMITH 1850S WOODVILLE & JONES ISLAND, NSW, AUS [35546] : 1700S BEXHILL, SSX, ENG [35156] : PRE 1840 BEXHILL, SSX, ENG [35546] : 1500-1900 LAUGHTON, SSX, ENG [36461]

SHOLE ALL WORLDWIDE [36416]

SHOLL PRE 1815 KENWYN, CON, ENG [35865] : 1810-1890 LONDON, ENG [35865] : ALL WORLDWIDE [36416]

SHONE HENRY 1820+ TAS, AUS [34105] : 1826+ MAITLAND, NSW, AUS [34277] : PRE 1837 LONDON, ENG [34105] : PRE 1825 ELLESMERE, SAL, ENG [34277] : ALL WORLDWIDE [34105]

SHONFIELD 1846 DARMSTADT, GER [37799]

SHONROCK PRE 1879 POSEN, POS, GER [34648]

SHOOBRIDGE 1856-1931 BURRAGORANG, NSW, AUS [34966] : 1832-1856 ROLVENDEN, KEN, ENG [34966]

SHOOK HARVEY 1860-1890 RICHLAND CO., IL, USA [36734] : PRE 1830 MONTEZUMA, IN, USA [37010]

SHOOSMITH 1500-1900 LAUGHTON, SSX, ENG [36461] : PRE 1800 LAUGHTON, SSX, ENG [36589]

SHOOTER 1900+ WA, AUS [34045] : 1800+ NTT, ENG [34045] : ALL LEEDS, WRY, ENG [37208] : 1815 MANSFIELD, NTT, ENG [37208] : 1845 MANSFIELD, NTT, ENG [37208] : PRE 1838 KIRKBY, NTT & DBY, ENG [37267] : 1645-1656 BRAINTREE, MA, USA [37208]

SHOPLAND PRE 1850 DEV & SOM, ENG [37771]

SHORDAR PRE 1850 HBG, GER [36270]

SHORE PRE 1860 ALBURY, NSW, AUS [38773] : WILLIAM PRE 1860 NSW, AUS [38773] : PRE 1844 NTT, ENG [34886] : 1750+ LIN, ENG [35812] : 1810+ STOCKPORT, CHS, ENG [37384] : 1800+ WELLS, NFK, ENG [37411] : ALL MANCHESTER, LAN & WA, ENG & AUS [34705]

SHORING PRE 1870 POPLAR, MDX, ENG [35440] : PRE 1823 RATCLIFFE, MDX, ENG [35440]

SHORLAND 1800S PORTSEA, HAM, ENG [35186]

SHORROCK 1820-39 DARWEN, LAN, ENG [35638] : 1750+ DARWEN, LAN, ENG [36991]

SHORT C1788 SYDNEY, NSW, AUS [35089] : 1870S COLAC, VIC, AUS [36276] : CYNTHIA 1860-1960 BRIGHTON, ONT, CAN [37567] : PROSPER 1860-1990 BRIGHTON, ONT, CAN [37567] : 1850-1990 BRIGHTON, ONT, CAN [37567] : JOEL 1856-1950 BRIGHTON, ONT, CAN [37567] : PRE 1850 DEPTFORD, KEN, ENG [33765] : 1800+ LONDON, ENG [34571] : PRE 1800 SOLIHULL, WAR, ENG [34743] : PRE 1850 WOOTTON BASSETT & BRINKWORTH, WIL, ENG [34753] : 1700S LANGTON MATRAVERS, DOR, ENG [34931] : WILLIAM PRE 1840 HELSTON, CON, ENG [35232] : PRE 1820 DOR, ENG [35525] : C1850-1890 LEIGHTON BUZZARD, BDF, ENG [35730] : PRE 1850 NFK, ENG [35730] : C1820 ST PANCRAS, LND, ENG [36276] : WILLIAM C1828 SOUTHGATE, HEF, ENG [36276] : C1800 MORPETH, NBL, ENG [36276] : PRE 1840 SALISBURY, WIL, ENG [36474] : 1820 ALLENDALE, NBL, ENG [36851] : C1800 PORTSMOUTH, HAM, ENG [36859] : 1800+ STRATTON, CON, ENG [36971] : PRE 1800 MANSFIELD, NTT, ENG [37739] : 1700+ BETHNAL GREEN, LND, ENG [37832] : 1750+ ADBASTON, STS, ENG [38481] : 1700+ THROWLEIGH, DEV, ENG [38745] : 1790-1990 SCT [37870] : 1800S EDINBURGH, MLN, SCT & NZ [36791] : PRE 1850 WILKES CO., GA, USA [37797]
SHORTALL PRE 1850 STRADBALLY, LEX, IRL [37415] : ALL KILRORY & STRADBALLY, LEX, IRL [38300]
SHORTELL 1839 NB, CAN [37509]
SHORTEN PRE 1838 CORK CITY, COR, IRL [37124]
SHORTER PRE 1834 GREENWICH, ENG [34589] : PRE 1810 LEE, KEN, ENG [35440] : 1800+ HARTLEY WINTNEY, HAM, ENG [36989] : 1850 WOKINGHAM, BRK, ENG [37690]
SHORTHOUSE C1827+ IBSTOCK, LEI, ENG [35583]
SHORTLAND 1820S PLYMOUTH, DEV, ENG [36011] : 1650-1750 ROTHWELL, NTH, ENG [36057] : PRE 1860 BETHNAL GREEN, MDX, WES & STS, ENG [37681]
SHORTLE PRE 1830 IRL [37509]
SHORTRIDGE 1880+ CHARLTON, VIC, AUS [36278]
SHOTBOULT 1760+ PINCHBECK, LIN, ENG [36370]
SHOTT 1800+ ASTON INGHAM, HEF, ENG [34236] : 1500-1991 WLS &, ENG & BRD [34236]
SHOTTER PRE 1850 LND, MDX & SSX, ENG [37731]
SHOTTON 1830-1875 NEWCASTLE ON TYNE, NBL, ENG [34373] : PRE 1950 RICHMOND, NRY, ENG [36489]
SHOTWELL 1700S NC & VA, USA [36552]
SHOULDERS 1850+ ARMIDALE, NSW, AUS [34902] : JOHN PRE 1850 BKM, ENG [34902]
SHOULTS 1850+ CAPE GIRARDEAU CO., MO, KY & TN, USA [37796] : 1850+ JEFFERSON CO., MO, KY & TN, USA [37796]
SHOWALTER 1760 ROANOKE CO., VA, USA [36540] : 1770 CHESTER CO., PA, USA [36540]
SHOWELL PRE 1825 NEWBURY & THATCHAM, BRK, ENG [34669] : 1800-1900 SCT [34373]
SHOYER 1840S LONDON, ENG [36862]
SHREEVES C1840 KEN, ENG [35920]
SHREWSBURY ALL USA & ENG [38287]
SHRIGLEY 1744-1790 BUCKS CO., PA, USA [37578] : 1790-1860 AL, USA [37578]
SHRIMPTON ALL COVENTRY, WAR, ENG [34663] : ALL LONDON, MDX, ENG [36978] : PRE 1850 STEPNEY, LND, ENG [37067] : C1780 SHOREDITCH, MDX, ENG [37834] : ALL WORLDWIDE [35984]
SHRIVER 1800-1900 VA, USA [36937]

SHROUDER 1862-1925 STEPNEY, LND, ENG & AUS [35784]
SHUCKFORTH C1816 ATTLEBOROUGH, NFK, ENG [37053]
SHUFELT PRE 1800 RHINEBECK, NY, USA [38386]
SHUFFLEBOTHAM 1700-1900 SFS, CHE & DBY, ENG [36169] : PRE 1760 ASTBURY & CONGLETON, CHS, ENG [38055]
SHUGG PRE 1812+ CON, ENG [35759] : ALL WORLDWIDE [37291]
SHUIRR ALL WORLDWIDE [38533]
SHUKER C1770 MARKET DRAYTON, SAL, ENG [35203]
SHULDT 1700 GER [35873]
SHULER JACOB 1763-1830 LEHIGH CO., PA, USA [38086]
SHULL 1750-1800 DAUPHIN, PA, USA [38095] : 1780-1800 NORTHAMPTON, PA, USA [38095] : 1740-1860 NORTHAMPTON, PA, USA [38095] : PRE 1800 PA, USA [38769]
SHUNN ALL WORLDWIDE [34399]
SHURTLEFF 1700+ NY & OH, USA [37026]
SHUTER PRE 1850 LND, MDX & SRY, ENG [34383]
SHUTLER C1846 ST LAWRENCE CO., NY, USA [38435]
SHUTT ALL YKS, ENG [33975] : C1830 DUDLEY, WOR, ENG [34145] : PRE 1820 KIRKBY OVERBLOW, YKS, ENG [35470]
SHUTTER 1800+ SHERBORNE, DOR, ENG [34817]
SHUTTLES 1854+ HAWKESBURY RIVER, NSW, AUS [34273]
SHUTTLESWORTH C1805 WIL, ENG [34273]
SHUTTLEWORTH 1845-1990 AMHERST, VIC, AUS [33885] : 1845-1990 HEIDELBERG, VIC, AUS [33885] : 1848+ ADELAIDE, SA, AUS [36275] : 1850+ EAGLEHAWK, VIC, AUS [36275] : 1900+ SYDNEY, NSW, AUS [38541] : PRE 1845 ENG [33885] : ALL WES, ENG [33953] : 1800 STROUD, GLS, ENG [36275] : 1700 RIBBLETON, LAN, ENG [36275] : 1800S MARKET HARBOROUGH, LEI, ENG [36275] : 1800 LONDON, ENG [36275] : PRE 1850 LOTHERSDALE, YKS, ENG [37085] : PRE 1887 MANCHESTER, LAN & CUL, ENG [37267] : 1781-1855 TOTTENHAM, MDX, ENG [37921] : 1700 EAST HANNINGFIELD, ESS, ENG [37928]
SHUTTS 1800-1850 ST ARMAND, QUE, CAN [37486]
SHYING ALL WORLDWIDE [35541]
SIBBALD PRE 1900 VIC, AUS [38288] : PRE 1900 NBL, ENG [36934] : ALL SCT [33842] : ALL HADDINGTON, ELN, SCT [34462]
SIBBELIUS 1670+ WORLDWIDE [38546]
SIBBETT 1840+ CHIPPIWA, ONT, CAN [37442] : PRE 1840 ARM, IRL [37442]
SIBBIT PRE 1900 DOW, IRL [35011]
SIBBONS PRE 1844 MON, WLS [35895]
SIBLEY PRE 1801 LONDON, ENG [35704] : C1820-1880 NEWINGTON & CAMBERWELL, SRY, ENG [35997] : ANNE 1800-1900 NEWTOWN BEDFORD, MDX, ENG [36890] : PRE 1900 THE HADHAMS, ESS, ENG [37387] : 1900+ OCKENDON, HRT & ESS, ENG [37387] : PRE 1900 THE HADHAMS, HRT, ENG [37387] : PRE 1900 OCKENDON, HRT & ESS, ENG [37387]
SIBSEY PRE 1785 NTT, ENG [35745]
SICHTER 1800+ GUNTERBERG, UKERMARK, GER [35121]
SICKAFUS C1800 WASHINGTON CO., MD, USA [36544]
SICKING PRE 1900 VENLO, LMB, NL [38717]
SICKLEMORE 1780 IPSWICH, SFK, ENG [34950]
SICKOLD 1755 BEL [34418] : 1750+ MITTLEHEIM, HEN, GER [34418] : 1840+ USA [34418]

SICKOLD (SEE SECKOLD [34418]

SICOLT (SEE SECKOLD) [34418]

SIDAWAY 1800-1900 DUDLEY, WOR, ENG [34399] : 1850-1920 KINGSWINFORD, STS, ENG [34399] : 1750+ ROWLEY REGIS, STS & WOR, ENG [37266]

SIDDALL ALL SHEFFIELD, WRY, ENG [34145]

SIDDEN PRE 1850 CARISBROOKE, IOW, ENG [38722]

SIDDENS 1700-1800 HUN, ENG [36038]

SIDDLE 1840 ERY, ENG [34731]

SIDDONS PRE 1890 LONDON, ENG [36486] : ALL WORLDWIDE [34944]

SIDDY ELEAZOR C1880 LEVENSHULME, LAN, ENG [38284] : 1800S LYMME, CHS, ENG [38284]

SIDEBOTTOM 1880+ AVENEL, VIC, AUS [35230] : PRE 1842 TINTWISTLE, CHS, ENG [34285] : 1700+ MIDDLETON, LAN, ENG [35824] : PRE 1750 WAKEFIELD, WRY, ENG [36159]

SIDELINGER 1700-1800S NEWBURG, ME, USA [36944]

SIDGWICK 1700+ REDMIRE, YKS, ENG [38034]

SIDLINGER 1844-1896 LIBERTY CENTER, OH, USA [38150]

SIDNELL 1750-1877 EAST LONDON, MDX, ENG [38441]

SIDNEY 1800-1900 LND & SRY, ENG [36422] : PRE 1840 GRANTHAM, LIN, ENG [37726]

SIDOTI ALL WORLDWIDE [38445]

SIDRONSKI ALL WORLDWIDE [38368]

SIDWELL 1840+ GOULBURN, NSW, AUS [36269] : 1760+ TROWBRIDGE, WIL, ENG [36269] : C1845 IRL [37556]

SIEBERT 1800 TORNHEIM HAFSSEN, DARMSTADT, BRD [38327] : 1823 MAGDEBURG, DDR [34195] : ALL POTSDAM, DDR [34801] : PRE 1880 KAROW & JERICHOW, PSA, GER [34801] : ALL MAGDEBURG, PSA, GER [34801]

SIEBRECHT PRE 1843 BARDOWICK, HAM, GER [34911]

SIEDBRUECKBURG ALL WORLDWIDE [38682]

SIEDE 1800S DRESDEN, DRE, DDR [34914] : 1850-1856 NEW YORK, NY, USA [34914]

SIEGISMUND 1800S TSCHIEBSDORF, SIL, GER [38623]

SIEMON 1871 ROCKHAMPTON, QLD, AUS [35808]

SIETHOFF PRE 1863 ISERLOHN, WEF, GER [38647]

SIEVERS 1884+ BELLARINE, VIC, AUS [38307]

SIEVZAC 1650-1850 UK &, BARBADOS [38355]

SIEWERT 1800+ GER [35465]

SIGGENDOLLAR 1840-1870S BE, CH [37600]

SIGGROEN PRE 1814 POM, GER [38630]

SIGGS 1860+ TAS, AUS [37117] : PRE 1680 WALDRON, SSX, ENG [37069] : PRE 1860S SSX, ENG [37117]

SIGNORACCI ALL WORLDWIDE [36139]

SIGSTON 1840S KINGSTEIGNTON, DEV, ENG [33870]

SIGSWORTH 1800S FRONTENAC, ONT, CAN [34353]

SIKES PRE 1788 SKEFFINGTON, LEI, ENG [34501] : 1780-1820 VA, USA [38115]

SILBER 1750-1800 FREDERICK CO., MD, USA [38009]

SILBERSTEIN 1900+ BROMMA, SWE [37935]

SILCOCK C1917 MAITLAND, NSW, AUS [37963] : 1880 BATHURST, NSW, AUS [37963] : PRE 1890 STS, ENG [34868] : ALL SOM, ENG [37712] : PRE 1811 SOM, ENG [37957]

SILCOCKS C1861 ROAD, SOM, ENG [37913]

SILFISTER THOMAS PRE 1660 CHARD, SOM, ENG [38452]

SILK WILLIAM C1800+ DUFFERIN CO., ONT, CAN [37441] : PRE 1800 WOOLWICH, KEN, ENG [35385]

: C1840 PIDLEY, HUN, ENG [35877] : PRE 1870 MARCH, CAM, ENG [37989]

SILKEY ALL HBG, GER [35618]

SILKSTONE PRE 1800 DBY, ENG [34661] : ALL ENG [34661]

SILL 1728-1850 ULVERSTON & CARTMEL, LAN, ENG [35044] : 1600+ CLIBURN, WES, ENG [36256]

SILLARS 1750+ ISLE OF ARRAN, BUT, SCT [35499] : 1802 KILMARNOCK, AYR, SCT [35903]

SILLENCE PRE 1877 MOTISFONT & MICHELMERSH, HAM, ENG [37226]

SILLEY ALL EXETER, DEV, ENG [37321] : C1770 FORDINGBRIDGE, HAM, ENG [37335]

SILLICK PRE 1840 SOM & DEV, ENG [33869]

SILLIKER PRE 1750 WESTCHESTER CO., CT, USA [38460]

SILLJER ALL WORLDWIDE [36709]

SILLS 1800S FRONTENAC, ONT, CAN [34353] : SARAH PRE 1806 BRK, ENG [36810] : 1765-1785 TIOGA, NY, USA [34408]

SILLWOOD PRE 1826 DEVIZES, WIL, ENG [34584]

SILVA C1830-1860S FAYAL, AZORES IS., PT [36337]

SILVEN 1890+ JERSEY CITY, NJ, USA [36320]

SILVER 1820 KINGS SUTTON, NTH, ENG [36649] : 1700-1850 HARTLEY WINTNEY, HAM, ENG [37838] : 1750-1800 FREDERICK CO., MD, USA [38009] : 1750-1790 FREDERICK CO., MD, USA [38137] : 1790-1800 BEDFORD CO., PA, USA [38137]

SILVERMAN PRE 1900 ODESSA, RUSSIA [37574]

SILVERSTEIN C1850 ROTZ, POL [37935]

SILVERTHORNE PRE 1850 SHOREDITCH, MDX, ENG [36099] : C1820 SUSSEX CO., NJ, USA [37032] : 1500 WORLDWIDE [34321]

SILVESTER PRE 1850 YATELEY & HAWLEY, HAM, ENG [34311] : 1700+ SUTTON COLDFIELD & BIRMINGHAM, WAR, ENG [34416] : ALL ELLENHALL, STS, ENG [37265] : ALL WORLDWIDE [38452]

SILVUS SUSANNAH PRE 1842 WESTMORELAND CO., PA, USA [36448]

SIM 1800+ DOWALLY, PER, SCT [33800] : C1790 DUN, ANS, SCT [34713] : C1700 ELIE, FIF, SCT [35072] : C1890-1930 DUNFERMLINE, FIF, SCT [35078] : 1700S KINGSBARNS, FIF, SCT [35126] : PRE 1770 KILMENY, FIF, SCT [35227] : PRE 1800+ FORFAR, ANS, SCT [35928] : PRE 1900 PER, SCT [36612]

SIM (SEE SIME) [35704]

SIMCO PRE 1860 WORLDWIDE [37280]

SIMCOX 1700 DUDLEY, WOR, ENG [34210]

SIME 1842+ JOHNSONVILLE, NI, NZ [35704] : 1768 FORDYCE, BAN, SCT [35369] : PRE 1836 FORFAR, ANS, SCT [35704] : PRE 1800+ ERROL, PER, SCT [35928] : PRE 1800+ FORFAR, ANS, SCT [35928] : ALL DUNDEE, ANS, SCT [37619]

SIMECKA PRE 1880 BRNO & BRUSBURG, MORAVIA, OES [36918]

SIMES 1660-1710 SOM, ENG [37233]

SIMINSTER PRE 1817 WESTBURY LEIGH, WIL, ENG [38214]

SIMIONE ALL LEGHORN, ITL [33954]

SIMISTER ALL WORLDWIDE [37739]

SIMKIN 1853 AUS [35135] : PRE 1800 ESS, ENG [37718]

SIMKINS 1780+ WESTMINSTER, MDX, ENG [34710] : 1690+ NORTHAMPTON CO., VA, USA [38032]

SIMMELL 1730+ PATSHULL, STS, ENG [35749] : 1750+ GNOSALL, STS, ENG [35749] : 1760+ BROMSTEAD, STS, ENG [35749] : 1730+ PENKRIDGE, STS, ENG [35749]

SIMMERS C1746 CRAIL, FIF, SCT [35072]

SIMMIE 1750S THORNHILL MADDERTY, PER, SCT **[35261]**

SIMMONDS 1870+ CAULFIELD, VIC, AUS **[35768]** : PRE 1880 LAUNCESTON, TAS, AUS **[35772]** : 1850-1900 DUNDAS, ONT, CAN **[34402]** : PRE 1750 SOUTH MORETON, BRK, ENG **[35181]** : 1800S DEPTFORD, KEN, ENG **[35377]** : 1700-1950 NORTON, GLS, ENG **[36556]** : 1861 POPLAR, LND, ENG **[36781]** : 1800+ SLAUGHAM, SSX, ENG **[37206]** : PRE 1822 SHOREDITCH, LND, ENG **[37610]** : PRE 1850 KINGSWORTHY, HAM, ENG **[37855]** : GEORGE 1780+ ENG & IRL **[36100]** : 1750-1885 ALSACE, ALS, FRA **[35172]** : SAMUEL ALL TYR, IRL **[36697]**

SIMMONS 1833+ BATHURST, NSW, AUS **[34295]** : EMILY 1860+ TAS, AUS **[35063]** : 1840+ MERRIWA, NSW, AUS **[35406]** : 1810-1850 OXF, ENG **[34191]** : PRE 1833 FALMOUTH, CON, ENG **[34295]** : 1800S RINGWOOD, HAM, ENG **[34309]** : PRE 1850 KEN, ENG **[34593]** : C1800 CAMBORNE, CON, ENG **[34644]** : 1800 AMERSHAM, BKM, ENG **[34708]** : PRE 1700 ST MARYS, NOTTINGHAM, NTT, ENG **[34858]** : SAM 1700S DOWNEND, GLS, ENG **[34908]** : PRE 1860 BRIGHTON, SSX, ENG **[35128]** : PRE 1780 SOHAM, CAM, ENG **[35151]** : PRE 1826 TAUNTON, SOM, ENG **[35406]** : PRE 1850 RICKMANSWORTH, HRT, ENG **[35589]** : 1700-1850 DEV & CON, ENG **[36422]** : 1814 DOVER, KEN, ENG **[36781]** : PRE 1910 LONDON, ENG **[37062]** : 1750+ NFK, ENG **[37304]** : PRE 1820 STRENSHAM, WOR, ENG **[37384]** : 1760+ WARBLETON, SSX, ENG **[37560]** : JOHN 1888-1944 SOUTHWARK, SRY, ENG **[37611]** : WILLIAM 1857-1904 SOUTHWARK, SRY, ENG **[37611]** : PRE 1800 ENG **[37721]** : 1800S NEWINGTON & CAMBERWELL, SRY, ENG **[37721]** : JOHN 1938-95 LONDON, ENG **[37926]** : 1797 EAST GRINSTEAD, SSX, ENG **[38209]** : ALL WEX, IRL **[34054]** : 1700S PER, SCT **[34937]** : 1760+ KINDERHOOK, NY, USA **[34408]** : PRE 1860 IN, USA **[36968]** : FRANCES 1832 BRUNSWICK, NY, USA **[38734]**

SIMMS 1830+ SYDNEY, NSW, AUS **[35360]** : 1780 IRL **[38362]** : 1790-1820 KY, USA **[37029]**

SIMNETT C1882 LOWESTOFT, SFK, ENG **[35131]** : C1856 KIRKLEY, SFK, ENG **[35131]** : C1850 DERBY, DBY, ENG **[35183]** : C1845 BURTON UPON TRENT, STS, ENG **[35183]** : 1600-1900 ENG **[36169]**

SIMON ALL ST SAMPSONS, GSY, CHI **[35433]** : ALL GSY, CHI **[37229]** : PRE 1600 BN & HN, FRA **[37229]** : 1700+ ARHEILGEN, HEN, GER **[37042]** : 1850 BERLIN, GER **[38379]** : PRE 1788 KIRN, RPF, GER **[38663]** : PRE 1800 GWERNAFIELD, FLN, WLS **[35706]** : 1800-1820 NERGUIS, FLN, WLS **[35706]** : ALL WORLDWIDE **[37229]**

SIMONI GIOVANNIA 1905 NEW YORK, NY, USA **[38109]**

SIMONS 1798-1870 HANSLOPE, BKM, ENG **[34677]** : ALL CON, ENG **[35139]** : 1800-1900 BIRMINGHAM, WAR, ENG **[37068]** : VAZIE 1850+ ENG **[37653]** : 1880+ BAY CITY, MI, USA **[35614]** : 1790+ TN, KY & MO, USA **[38050]** : 1900-1950 CA, USA **[38100]**

SIMONSEN 1860+ DEN **[34667]** : 1803-1886 ASSENS, DEN **[36317]**

SIMPKIN 1830+ NTT, ENG & NZ **[35584]**

SIMPKINS 1690+ NORTHAMPTON CO., VA, USA **[38032]**

SIMPSON 1874+ BALD HILLS, QLD, AUS **[34277]** : ALEX 1840+ ADELAIDE, SA, AUS **[34602]** : 1880+ BRISBANE & WARWICK, QLD, AUS **[35460]** : 1850+ VIC, AUS & NZ **[34617]** : C1910-1915 LONDON, ONT, CAN **[34153]** : 1900+ CAN **[38261]** : 1875-1880 HALIFAX, NS, CAN **[38537]** : PRE 1800 MORPETH, NBL, ENG **[33905]** : 1780 OTTRINGHAM, ERY, ENG **[33910]** : 1750+ HADLEIGH, SFK, ENG **[33938]** : PRE 1800 WHICKHAM, DUR, ENG **[33940]** : 1800+ HAZELWOOD, WRY, ENG **[34020]** : ED. COLEMAN 1822+ SOUTH EAST, KEN, ENG **[34181]** : EDWARD 1790+ SOUTH EAST, KEN, ENG **[34181]** : SAMUEL PRE 1825 NTH, ENG **[34310]** : C1800+ MILLOM, CUL, ENG **[34374]** : 1830S BRISTOL, ENG **[34452]** : ALL BEDALE, NRY, ENG **[34617]** : C1802 BARLOW, DBY, ENG **[34661]** : 1800-1900 MORLAND, WES, ENG **[34872]** : 1734 SILCHESTER, HAM, ENG **[34909]** : PRE 1860 WOLVERHAMPTON, STS, ENG **[34958]** : 1821-41 HEMSWORTH, WRY, ENG **[35211]** : 1750S NEWHAVEN, SSX, ENG **[35261]** : 1829 LIVERPOOL, LAN, ENG **[35282]** : 1800 PYTCHLEY, NTH, ENG **[35376]** : 1830 BURTON LATIMER, NTH, ENG **[35376]** : 1845+ YORK & BRADFORD, YKS, ENG **[35460]** : ALL KIRKBY MOORSIDE & KIRKDALE, NRY, ENG **[35460]** : C1850 LIN, ENG **[35515]** : GEORGE 1800+ KEN, ENG **[35737]** : STEPHEN 1800+ KEN, ENG **[35737]** : 1700S WADWORTH, YKS, ENG **[35830]** : ALL COLCHESTER, ESS, ENG **[35936]** : 1750 WIRKSWORTH, DBY, ENG **[35970]** : PRE 1775 MILBURN, WES, ENG **[36180]** : C1856 GRANTHAM, LIN, ENG **[36253]** : C1800 WESTMINSTER, LND, ENG **[36271]** : PRE 1850 YORKSHIRE DALES, NRY, ENG **[36416]** : PRE 1850 AUCKLAND, DUR, ENG **[36481]** : PRE 1900 NEWCASTLE, NBL, ENG **[36583]** : 1720-1990 HOWDEN, YKS, ENG **[36832]** : 1655+ SEIGHFORD AREA, STS, ENG **[36997]** : C1750 CLAYPOLE, LIN, ENG **[37007]** : PRE 1800 HULL, ERY, ENG **[37082]** : PRE 1800 PURLEY, BRK, ENG **[37416]** : 1600-1712 POULTON LE SANDS, LAN, ENG **[37524]** : PRE 1800 LEEK, STS, ENG **[37650]** : 1700-1800 SUNBRICK, LAN, ENG **[37858]** : PRE 1810 NOTTINGHAM, NTT, ENG **[37866]** : PRE 1850 SHEFFIELD, WRY, ENG **[37893]** : PRE 1800 LIN, ENG **[38261]** : PRE 1800 GREAT YARMOUTH, NFK, ENG **[38389]** : 1888 DENTON, CUL, ENG **[38699]** : 1799+ WHITBY, NRY, ENG & AUS **[36238]** : PRE 1843 ENG & SCT **[33812]** : PRE 1874 BALLYMENA, ANT, IRL **[34277]** : 1865+ LET & LOG, IRL **[34680]** : PRE 1860 TAMLAGHT & BALLYMENA, ANT, IRL **[34763]** : 1800+ CASHEL, TIP, IRL **[34918]** : PRE 1880 CLOONY AUGHNALOO, LDY, IRL **[35013]** : 1700-1838 DOW, IRL **[35266]** : 1757 ARM, IRL **[35266]** : 1835+ BELFAST, ANT, IRL **[35391]** : C1856 TYR, IRL **[36312]** : C1830 NEWTON LIMAVADY, LDY, IRL **[36806]** : PRE 1850 IRL **[37923]** : 1860+ ANT, IRL & AUS **[34763]** : 1800-1864 DRUMREAGH & GOVAN, DOW & LKS, IRL & SCT **[36642]** : 1860+ ANT, IRL & USA **[34763]** : 1909+ NZ **[37115]** : 1865+ HOKITIKA, WGTN & TAS, NZ & AUS **[34680]** : 1865+ INVERCARGILL, NZ & AUS **[34680]** : C1795 ORMIESTON, MLN, SCT **[34239]** : 1835+ LKS & AYR, SCT **[34373]** : 1780-1790 CAMPBELTOWN & KINTYRE, ARL, SCT **[34387]** : PRE 1820 DRAINIE, MOR, SCT **[34452]** : JOHN 1750+ TARADALE, ROC, SCT **[34684]** : ALL FIF, SCT **[34758]** : PRE 1854 KIRKCALDY, FIF, SCT **[34914]** : C1780 CERES, FIF, SCT **[34914]** : 1800-1830S FALKIRK, STI, SCT **[35136]** : 1854 HADDINGTON, ELN, SCT **[35535]** : 1600-1800 FIF, SCT **[35627]** : C1839-1855 STRAITON & DALMELLINGTON, AYR, SCT **[35739]** : PRE 1850 WICK, CAI, SCT **[35913]** : 1750+ OLD MONKLAND, LKS, SCT **[35979]** : PRE 1900

LONMAY, ABD, SCT **[36061]** : PRE 1860 FORT WILLIAM, ARL, SCT **[36201]** : C1845 WEMYSS & DALGETY, FIF, SCT **[36268]** : PRE 1799 RATHEN, ABD, SCT **[36673]** : PRE 1850 FIF, SCT **[36679]** : PRE 1800 LARBERT, STI, SCT **[37341]** : PRE 1700 LONGSIDE, ABD, SCT **[37513]** : PRE 1800 KINNOUL, PER, SCT **[37659]** : 1750 + BO'NESS, WLN, SCT **[37666]** : PRE 1771 EDINBURGH, MLN, SCT **[37852]** : 1840 + LKS, SCT **[37923]** : 1760-1785 MORTON, DFS, SCT **[38117]** : PRE 1900 OCHILTREE, AYR, SCT **[38298]** : PRE 1900 CUMNOCK, AYR, SCT **[38298]** : PRE 1860 ABERDEEN, ABD, SCT **[38537]** : PRE 1800 STRICHEN, ABD, SCT & AUS **[38537]** : 1835 + JENNINGS CO., IN, USA **[35266]** : PRE 1800 NEW HANOVER CO., NC, USA **[36702]** : 1840-1900 FRANKLIN CO., NY, USA **[38742]**

SIMS ALL CALLINGTON, SA, AUS **[34561]** : 1890 GOONDIWINDI, QLD, AUS **[35807]** : PRE 1871 SA, AUS & ENG **[33840]** : PRE 1825 BENDIGO, VIC & CON, AUS & ENG **[37995]** : C1824 + CAMBORNE, CON, ENG **[35746]** : PRE 1847 DEV, ENG **[36052]** : PRE 1930 POTTERIES, STS & CON, ENG **[36502]** : PRE 1807 FACCOMBE & ST MARY BOURNE, HAM, ENG **[36668]** : PRE 1806 CON, ENG **[36775]** : C1818 LONDON, ENG **[36949]** : PRE 1730 HURSLEY, HAM, ENG **[37259]** : PRE 1848 BABWORTH & LANEHAM, NTT, ENG **[37267]** : PRE 1850 BRADFORD UPON AVON, WIL, ENG **[37739]** : 1600 + ALL CANNINGS, WIL, ENG **[37843]** : PRE 1830 ENG **[38217]** : PRE 1802 SOM, ENG **[38291]** : 1700S ROMSEY, HAM, ENG **[38350]** : 1750-1800 PER, SCT **[34937]** : C1700 RICHMOND, VA, USA **[38348]** : 1885 CARDIFF, GLA, WLS **[34839]**

SIMSON 1700S LEWISHAM, KEN, ENG **[35858]**

SIMURDA ALL SALZBURG, SLZ, OES **[34086]**

SINCLAIR C1870 BARRABA, NSW, AUS **[34251]** : 1839 + BATHURST, NSW, AUS **[35504]** : 1870 + NSW, AUS **[36682]** : HUGH 1840 + QUEANBEYAN, NSW, AUS **[37117]** : 1840 + TOODYAY, WA, AUS **[37892]** : WILLIAM 1780 + MAN, CAN **[37426]** : 1800-1900 TYNEMOUTH, NBL, ENG **[37137]** : 1800 + CUL, ENG **[37274]** : PRE 1900 BALLINTOY, ANT, IRL **[37636]** : PRE 1850 DERRIAGHY, ANT, IRL **[37927]** : 1855 + PIRINOA, WAIRARAPA, NZ **[36877]** : PRE 1775 HALKIRK, CAI, SCT **[33873]** : PRE 1874 AYR, SCT **[33953]** : C1812 ALTON, INV, SCT **[34142]** : ALL BAN, SCT **[34160]** : PETER PRE 1830 OBAN, SCT **[34310]** : MARY 1776-1840S PORTMOAK, KRS & FIF, SCT **[34447]** : C1800 KINLOCH, PER, SCT **[34527]** : MARGARET C1790-1820 CAI, SCT **[34646]** : 1700S-1800S CRARAE, ARL, SCT **[35126]** : PRE 1856 CAMPBELTOWN, ARL, SCT **[35222]** : PRE 1800 KILMODAN, ARL, SCT **[35430]** : 1760 + KENMORE, PER, SCT **[35503]** : PRE 1839 DUNFERMLINE, FIF, SCT **[35504]** : PRE 1845 THURSO, CAI, SCT **[35704]** : C1824 + ROX, SCT **[35885]** : PRE 1850 WICK, CAI, SCT **[35913]** : 1830 + AUCHTERDERRAN, FIF, SCT **[35977]** : PRE 1800 MUIRHOUSE, RFW, SCT **[36436]** : 1800-1850 SCT **[36718]** : 1800 + PAISLEY, RFW, SCT **[36768]** : JOHN PRE 1870 STRONTIAN & BENDERLOCH, ARL, SCT **[36877]** : PRE 1860 RATHVEN, CAI & SUT, SCT **[36963]** : C1730 + ORPHIR, OKI, SCT **[37413]** : WILLIAM PRE 1780 EASTAQUAY, OKI, SCT **[37426]** : PRE 1840 AULDEARN, NAI, SCT **[37892]** : 1805 + EDINBURGH, SCT **[38289]** : 1750 INVERNESS, SCT **[38379]** : 1750 + INVERNESS, INV, SCT **[38476]** : NEIL 1850-1990 RFW, SCT & AUS **[34783]**

SINCOCK PRE 1800 ST IVES, CON, ENG **[35385]**

SINDALL 1800 + BETHNAL GREEN & SHOREDITCH, LND, ENG **[34747]** : 1650 + ELY, CAM, ENG **[34747]**

SINDERSON PRE 1768 GLENTHAM, LIN, ENG **[37318]** : CHARLES 1855-1876 LOGAN, IL, USA **[38157]**

SINDIN 1790S EWHURST, SSX, ENG **[35261]**

SINE 1830-1900 HASTINGS CO., ONT, CAN **[34996]** : 1800-1840 COLBORNE, ONT, CAN **[34996]**

SINETT 1790 BRISTOL, GLS, ENG **[36798]**

SINEY PRE 1860 TULLAMORE, OFF, IRL **[34039]**

SINGELE C1800 SCHLATT, HOH, GER **[38604]**

SINGER PRE 1839 PORTSEA, HAM, ENG **[34166]** : C1870 FROME, SOM, ENG **[35826]** : C1750 WIL, ENG **[38389]** : 1850-1900 EDINBURGH, MLN, SCT **[36246]** : 1700-1900 FYVIE, ABD, SCT **[36246]** : 1800-1900 GLASGOW, LKS, SCT **[36246]**

SING HEE 1900 + SURRY HILLS, NSW, AUS **[35373]**

SINGLE 1700-1850 COMBE ST NICHOLAS, SOM, ENG **[36065]** : 1700-1850 CHARD, SOM, ENG **[36065]**

SINGLETON 1792 + NSW, AUS **[35331]** : PRE 1846 LIN, ENG **[34859]** : PRE 1752 CHS, ENG **[35331]** : PRE 1840 YKS, ENG **[36754]** : 1770 ENG **[37006]** : PRE 1850 TANWORTH, WAR, ENG **[37725]** : 1700-1820 ARNOLD, NTT, ENG **[38381]** : HANNAH C1822 + MUNCASTER, CUL, ENG **[38567]** : PRE 1810 LINTHWAITE, YKS, ENG **[38690]** : PRE 1870 DUBLIN, IRL **[34733]** : PRE 1860 KILMORE, ARM, IRL **[35128]** : C1850 DROMTARRIFF, COR, IRL **[35931]** : WILLIAM 1830 HENDRICKS CO., IN, USA **[36925]** : THOMAS 1782 + BRUNS CO. & AUGUSTA CO., VA & IN, USA **[36925]**

SINGRAVEN 1665-1705 VELDHAUSEN, NSA, BRD **[34398]**

SINGRUEN ALL BAD & WUE, GER **[36078]**

SINGS 1700 + DULOE, CON, ENG **[35965]**

SINKE 1700-C1740S ZUID BEVELAND, ZEL, NL **[38350]**

SINKINS PRE 1855 LONDON, ENG **[34811]**

SINN PRE 1900 BUSCH, BAW, BRD **[38615]**

SINNETT 1790 + IRL & CAN **[35611]**

SINNOTT 1800 + MELBOURNE, VIC & WA, AUS **[34638]** : ALL INDIA **[34638]** : ALL DUB & WEX, IRL **[34496]** : ALL WEX, IRL **[34638]**

SINTON 1800-1850 JEDBURGH, ROX, SCT **[37628]**

SIPES 1800S DUNDAS CO., ONT, CAN **[34150]** : 1700 + IA & IN, USA **[38764]**

SIPLE JN & MICHAEL 1840S ONT, CAN **[37472]** : JUSTIN 1820-50 ONT, CAN **[37472]**

SIPONIUS 1858 + SIPPOLA, KYMI, FIN **[38562]** : 1879 + VIIPURI, FIN **[38562]**

SIPPEL 1800 + BUDINDEN, HES, BRD **[37581]**

SIPPO 1906 + MN & WI, USA **[38562]**

SIPPRELL 1783 + SAINT JOHN, NB, CAN **[34470]** : 1500S FRA **[34470]** : C1700-1783 PA, USA **[34470]**

SIPPU 1544 + VEHKALAHTI & SIPPOLA, KYMI, FIN **[38562]** : 1820 + ST PETERSBURG, RUSSIA **[38562]** : 1906 + MN & WI, USA **[38562]**

SIPUNIUS 1879 + VIIPURI, FIN **[38562]** : 1858 + SIPPOLA, KYMI, FIN **[38562]**

SIRE 1846-86 CHILWELL, VIC, AUS **[37919]** : 1840-1847 HOBART TOWN, TAS, AUS **[37919]** : C1813 BANHAM, NFK, ENG & AUS **[37919]**

SIRED ALL ENG & AUS **[35555]**

SIRETT 1800 + ADSTOCK, BKM, ENG **[38213]**

SIRGER 1700-1850 WUE, GER **[37015]**

SIRIANNI 1890 CALABRIA, ITL **[36679]**

SIRKETT ALL LONDON, ENG **[35939]**

SIRRS MARY J. 1837-1914 MOG, IRL **[34215]**

SIRSE ALL KAPEL, GEMEINDE, YU & OES **[38369]**

SISCO 1770-1850 CAN **[38742]**

SISK 1900 + MARTINSBURG, WV, USA **[36909]**

SISLEY 1843-1863 KEN, ENG [36071]
SISSEY ALL ENG [37833]
SISSINGH 1814+ GRO & FRI, NL [34990]
SISSON PRE 1831 KENDAL, WES, ENG [36230] : PRE 1650 IRL [37706] : 1740-1820 MANDILLO, NY, USA [38133]
SISSONS PRE 1900 LAMBETH, LND, ENG [34825] : ALL SHEFFIELD, YKS, ENG [37383] : PRE 1750 DONCASTER, WRY, ENG [37589] : C1800S YKS, ENG & CAN [34133]
SISTERMANS ALL MONNICKENDAM, NOH, NL [38703]
SITCH 1840 LONDON, MDX, ENG [35067]
SITTERDING ALL GER & USA [36581]
SIVER 1650-1900 GUELDERLAND, ALBANY CO., NY, USA [34004]
SIVERLY ALL WORLDWIDE [35278]
SIVERTSEN ALL KOPENHAGEN, DEN & NZ [34603]
SIVIER 1680-1910 NORTHWOOD, IOW, ENG [38420]
SIXSMITH TOBIAS 1800+ WEX & WAT, IRL [34954]
SIZELAND 1840-1850S WELLS, SOM, ENG [33835]
SIZEMORE 1818-1825 SYDNEY, NSW, AUS [34649] : 1805-1818 ENG [34649] : 1830S-1860 WAIKOUAITI, OTAGO, NZ [34649]
SIZER 1880+ WILLOWIE, SA, AUS [34777] : PRE 1774 SOHAM, CAM, ENG [37144] : THOMAS 1810-1858 NEW LONDON, CT, USA [38134]
SJOHOLM 1771+ PERNAJA, UUSIMAA, FIN [38758]
SJOTVET 1883 NOR [37493]
SKAE 1700-1800 BANCHORY DEVENICK, KCD, SCT [36824]
SKAHILL PRE 1855 GORT, GAL, IRL [34868]
SKAINES 1820-1890 SALISBURY, WIL, ENG [37233] : 1800-1890 SOUTHAMPTON, HAM, ENG [37233] : ALL WORLDWIDE [35253]
SKARADICK ALL WORLDWIDE [37768]
SKARAH PRE 1881 LINCOLN, MN, USA [36678]
SKATES PRE 1861+ SYDNEY & WAGGA WAGGA, NSW, AUS [34423]
SKEAD WILLIAM 1790-1870 WHITEHAVEN, CUL, ENG [36180]
SKEAINES 1820-1890 SALISBURY, WIL, ENG [37233] : 1800-1890 SOUTHAMPTON, HAM, ENG [37233]
SKEAT 1856-1925 HOLT, WOR, ENG [36513]
SKECK ALL NY, USA [36935]
SKEDGELL C1810 DEV, ENG [37180]
SKEEN 1850+ BATTERSEA & WANDSWORTH, SRY, ENG [37401]
SKEER ALL WORLDWIDE [36540]
SKEETE PRE 1750 SNODLAND, KEN, ENG [34725]
SKEETS PRE 1730 BRK, ENG [35866]
SKEFFINGTON 1700-1900 SLI, IRL [37031] : 1700-1900 ROS, IRL [37031]
SKEGGS 1820S STANSTEAD ABBOTS, HRT, ENG [34152]
SKELLERN 1893+ SYDNEY, NSW, AUS [34979]
SKELLY PRE 1884 BRADFORD, YKS, ENG [34566] : C1840 DROGHEDA, LOU, IRL [34138] : THOMAS 1840S-1870S DUBLIN, IRL [34924] : PETER FRANCIS 1860S DUBLIN, IRL [34924]
SKELTON 1830-1900 MILLERS FOREST, NSW, AUS [35559] : 1850-1900 STUART TOWN, NSW, AUS [35559] : ALL JSY, CHI [35222] : PRE 1840 YKS, ENG [33873] : PRE 1840 FINNINGLEY, NTT, ENG [33959] : 1802 DEVONPORT & STOKE DAMEREL, DEV, ENG [34195] : 1700-1800 WORKINGTON & BOLTON, CUL, ENG [34762] : 1750+ LIN, ENG [35812] : 1750+ HARRINGTON, CUL, ENG [37073] : 1830+ CROSSCANONBY & BRIDEKIRK, CUL, ENG [37073] : C1810 LONDON, ENG [37180] : 1760+ FISHKNEY & BOSTON, LIN, ENG [37317] : PRE 1840 KEN, ENG [37370] : 1770-1850 OVENDEN

& ILLINGWORTH, WRY, ENG [37754] : 1700+ YKS & QUE, ENG & CAN [36341] : 1820+ TYR, IRL [33812]
SKENE 1850+ BEECHWORTH, VIC, AUS [38213] : 1880+ BRISBANE, QLD, AUS [38213] : 1800+ TARLAND, ABD, SCT [38213]
SKEPPER PRE 1700 ENG [37758]
SKERRIT 1920-1980 TAS, AUS [38465] : PRE 1617 TAVISTOCK & WHITCHURCH, DEV, ENG [36594]
SKERRITT C1800 MANCHESTER, LAN, ENG [37988]
SKEVINGTON 1820+ NOTTINGHAM, NTT, ENG [35342] : ALL BDF, ENG [37738]
SKEWER PRE 1900 ESS, ENG [37750]
SKEWES 1700-1820 MULLIN, CON, ENG [34697]
SKEWIS 1850-70 SHULLSBURG, WI, USA [36909]
SKEWS PRE 1845 KENWYN, CON, ENG [38292]
SKIDMORE PRE 1700 KINGSWINFORD, STS, ENG [36110] : 1800+ GLS, ENG [36118] : 1700+ RICKMANSWORTH, HRT, ENG [36981] : PRE 1830 BRIERLEY HILL, STS, ENG [37671] : ALL BARNSLEY, WRY, ENG [37979] : ALFRED THOMAS C1880 BIRMINGHAM, ENG [38452] : 1728-1825 MONMOUTH CO., NJ, USA [36558] : 1700+ CLINTON CO., IN & PA, USA [37010] : 1780-1840 GASTON, NC, USA [38576]
SKIERRA (SEE SKARAH) [36678]
SKIFFINS ALL WORLDWIDE [34910]
SKILES WILLIAM 1783 PGH, ALLEGHENY CITY, PA, USA [36576] : MARY 1834 PGH, ALLEGHENY CITY, PA, USA [36576]
SKILL C1750 MINCHINHAMPTON, GLS, ENG [37838]
SKILLINGTON PRE 1800 GREAT PONTON, LIN, ENG [37712]
SKILTON PRE 1770 EASTLING, KEN, ENG [34445]
SKIMMINS 1874-1921 GLASGOW, LKS, SCT [35820]
SKIMMINS (SEE MISKIM) [35820]
SKINGLEY 1750+ NAVESTOCK, ESS, ENG [36263]
SKINNER 1830+ ASHBY, VIC, AUS [33991] : 1880+ SA, AUS [35771] : 1863+ TWEED RIVER, NSW, AUS [37140] : 1840-1900 NSW, AUS [37140] : 1835+ WINGHAM, NSW, AUS [38541] : C1845-1891 MUSWELLBROOK & INVERELL, NSW, AUS & ENG [36313] : 1800-1888 NORFOLK CO., ONT, CAN [34364] : 1800+ HERMITAGE BAY, NFD, CAN [36684] : C1787 OTTERY, ST MARY, NFK, ENG [33880] : JOHN C1777 INGHAM, SFK, ENG [33992] : 1800+ BRISTOL, GLS, ENG [34082] : 1776 BOXLEY, KEN, ENG [34176] : ALL HATFIELD PAVERELL, ESS, ENG [34460] : PRE 1848 BRIGHTLING, SSX, ENG [34886] : 1835 HORNSEY, MDX, ENG [35041] : C1820 CARISBROOKE, IOW, ENG [35131] : PRE 1849 TORQUAY, DEV, ENG [35578] : PRE 1650 ESS, ENG [35642] : 1700-1800 MARYLEBONE, MDX, ENG [36106] : 1700-1750 LAXTON, NTT, ENG [36112] : C1840 IFIELD, SSX, ENG [36175] : PRE 1870 SOUTH BOROUGH, KEN, ENG [36486] : PRE 1851+ WALCOT, SOM, ENG [37108] : 1750-1850 SSX, ENG [37140] : 1800-1850 ELY & WISBECH, CAM, ENG [37187] : 1780-1810 RAUNDS, NTH, ENG [37187] : PRE 1830 CALLINGTON, CON, ENG [37320] : PRE 1870 SRY, ENG [37358] : PRE 1800 GLS, ENG [37941] : 1802 BUCKFASTLEIGH, DEV, ENG [37952] : C1700-1800 WOLSTANTON, STS, ENG [38055] : 1650-1850 WOODHOUSE HALL, CUCKNEY, NTT, ENG [38084] : C1880-1900 LEWES, SSX, ENG [38264] : PRE 1800 TAUNTON, SOM, ENG [38399] : 1809+ BENGAL ARMY &, SRY, ENG &, INDIA [34109] : PRE 1850 PEORIA, IL, USA [35312] : C1770 SOMERSET, PA, USA [38023] : 1802-1824 LYME, NH, USA [38741]

SKINSLEY PRE 1800 ESS, ENG [37832]
SKIPPER 1850-1870 COLLINGWOOD, VIC, AUS [35384] : C1749 INGHAM, SFK, ENG [33992] : 1800+ KINGS LYNN & NORWICH, NFK, ENG [35513] : PRE 1860 HINGHAM, NFK, ENG [36747] : ALL ENG [37561] : PRE 1700 ENG [37758]
SKIPPIN 1570+ WOOLPIT, SFK, ENG [37399]
SKIPWORTH PRE 1850 HOLGATE, LIN, ENG [35255] : 1800S HALTON HOLGATE, LIN, ENG [35340]
SKIRROW 1618-1680 MELLING, LAN, ENG [37524]
SKIRTH ALL LEI, ENG [37291]
SKIRVING ALL WORLDWIDE [37517]
SKITCH ALL WORLDWIDE [37320]
SKIVER ALL WORLDWIDE [38310]
SKOFF PRE 1880 FARRELL, SLOVAKIA & MERCER, PA, USA &, SLOVAKIA [38063]
SKOG JOHANN 1860+ WASA, FIN [38183]
SKONE PRE 1800 JEFFREYSTON, PEM, WLS [36019]
SKOTS PRE 1725 DOWNTON, WIL, ENG [36478]
SKOTTOW ALL WORLDWIDE [35948]
SKOV ALL SOMMERSTED, DEN [34308]
SKOWRONEK 1850+ BERLIN, GER [34367]
SKRPAN ALL POL &, UKRAINIA [38021]
SKUCE 1836 ADELAIDE, SA, AUS [35027] : 1770+ CRAWLEY, SSX, ENG [35027] : 1700-1850 CRAWLEY WORTH, SSX, ENG [37985]
SKULLEY ALL LONDON, MDX, ENG [37950]
SKUSE PRE 1836 HOBART, TAS, AUS [35344]
SKYNNER ALL WORLDWIDE [34642]
SKYRME PRE 1813 HEF, ENG [36432]
SLABBERT PRE 1896 DEALESVILLE, RSA [36458]
SLACK PRE 1871 INVERELL, NSW, AUS [33807] : 1800+ LEEDS, ONT, CAN [36343] : 1750-1800 NIAGARA, ONT, CAN [36703] : RICHARD 1801+ DUFFERIN CO., ONT, CAN [37441] : 1820-1850 LEEDS, ONT, CAN [38097] : PRE 1868 BERWICK ON TWEED, NBL, ENG [33932] : THOMAS PRE 1790 CUL, ENG [34164] : C1803 SOHAM, CAM, ENG [35391] : 1700+ CRICH & ASHOVER, DBY, ENG [36218] : 1800+ SANDBACH AREA, CHS, ENG [36997] : 1830-1880 MANCHESTER, LAN, ENG [38259] : HENRY PRE 1819 CUL, ENG & CAN [34164] : ALL WORLDWIDE [36651]
SLACKFORD 1700-1900 KEN, ENG [38115]
SLADDEN ALICE C1870 TUNBRIDGE WELLS, SSX, ENG [38397]
SLADE ELIAS 1880S NSW, AUS [35831] : PRE 1800 WESTMINSTER, LND, ENG [34117] : PRE 1800 PELYNT, CON, ENG [34285] : PRE 1850 MARYLEBONE, LND, ENG [34466] : 1700-1850 HANSLOPE, BKM, ENG [34760] : 1880+ OXFORD, OXF, ENG [36015] : PRE 1850 GREAT BARRINGTON, GLS, ENG [36015] : C1870-1890 FAIRFORD, GLS, ENG [36015] : C1842 LIDLINGTON, BDF, ENG [36803] : 1800+ AVENING & STROUD, GLS, ENG [36868] : ALL COKER & YEOVIL, SOM, ENG [37269] : 1750-1800 BISHOPS WALTON, HAM, ENG [38276] : 1650-1750 WEST COKER, SOM, ENG [38483]
SLAGHT 1865+ ONT, CAN [38323]
SLAMA PRE 1879 TRI STUDNE, NOVA MESTA, CS [36338] : 1879+ SALINE, NE, USA [36338]
SLANY PRE 1638 LND, ENG [38348]
SLATER 1850+ GIPPSLAND, VIC, AUS [34936] : 1820-1840 PATTERSON, NSW, AUS [35857] : PRE 1820 BLACKBURN, LAN, ENG [34442] : 1800S LONDON, ENG [34709] : PRE 1830 LAN, ENG [35246] : PRE 1900 LEICESTER, LEI, ENG [35470] : ANN 1844+ YKS, ENG [35615] : PRE 1851 SRY, ENG [35720] : ALL ENG [35913] : C1718-1840S CALDBERGH & COVERHAM, NRY, ENG [35996] : PRE 1794 LIVERPOOL, LAN, ENG [36204] : 1750-

1850 OXF, ENG [36482] : PRE 1800 KIRKBY IRELETH, LAN, ENG [36701] : PRE 1850 PINXTON, DBY, ENG [36854] : 1700+ NOTTINGHAM, NTT, ENG [37248] : JAMES PRE 1700 DALTON IN FURNESS, LAN, ENG [37353] : 1800 PINXTON, DBY, ENG [37391] : 1801-1821 WHALLEY, LAN, ENG [37490] : ALL STAINBURN, WRY, ENG [37621] : 1813+ WANSTEAD & COLCHESTER, ESS & LND, ENG [37656] : PRE 1800 BELPER, DBY, ENG [37692] : 1841 UP WALTHAM, SSX, ENG [37952] : ALL NZ [35913] : PRE 1870 DALKEITH, MLN, SCT [37711] : PRE 1900 BLAIRGOWRIE, PER, SCT [37711] : 1800-1860 CRAWFORD CO., OH, USA [37529]
SLATTERY PATRICK C1840+ MONARO, NSW, AUS [33765] : 1842+ MELBOURNE, VIC, AUS [34285] : C1860 KURRAJONG, NSW, AUS [35095] : 1850+ MENANGLE, NSW, AUS [35095] : C1840-1900 KYNETON, VIC, AUS [35136] : 1848+ OBERON, NSW, AUS [35410] : 1854+ BELFORD, NSW, AUS [35842] : 1860+ MELBOURNE, VIC, AUS [35842] : JOHANNA PRE 1850 KER, IRL [34206] : PRE 1833 TIP, IRL [34959] : PRE 1850 ENNISTYMON, CLA, IRL [35095] : 1850S TIP, IRL [35332] : 1800+ BALLYCLERIHAN, TIP, IRL [35410] : PRE 1850 TOOMEVARA, TIP, IRL [35842] : PRE 1863 MULLINAHONE, TIP, IRL [36361] : ALL IRL [36551] : 1700+ TIP, IRL [36602] : CLARENCE 1880 SAN FRANCISCO & OAKLAND, CA, USA [37501] : ALL SWANSEA, GLA, WLS [36501]
SLATYER 1865+ GOULBURN, NSW, AUS [34275]
SLAUENWHITE 1700+ HALIFAX CO., NS, CAN [34225]
SLAUGHTER 1700+ EDBURTON, SSX, ENG [33785] : C1870-1900 LONDON, ENG [34372] : PRE 1876 NFK, ENG [35618]
SLAUSON PRE 1608 SRY, ENG [38226] : 1608+ USA [38226]
SLAVIN 1700S VA, GA & IN, USA [38325]
SLAYMAN PRE 1820 PETWORTH, SSX, ENG [37724]
SLAYSER CATHERINE PRE 1850 IRL [34902]
SLEATOR ALL ARMAGH & BELFAST, ARM & ANT, IRL [36428]
SLEE 1848+ MOONTA, SA, AUS [37189] : 1500+ DEV, ENG [34777] : 1700+ KIRKBY STEPHEN, WES, ENG [35908] : 1900 PENRITH, CUL, ENG [36818] : 1750-1850 MARWOOD, DEV, ENG [36988] : 1500-1900 SHIRWELL, DEV, ENG [36988] : PRE 1848 MERTON, DEV, ENG [37189] : 1800-1900 BRADFORD, YKS, ENG [38471]
SLEEMAN 1800+ TAVISTOCK, DEV, ENG [36610] : 1800+ REDRUTH, CON, ENG [36887] : 1700S TETCOTT, DEV, ENG [37317]
SLEEP 1850+ EGHAM, SRY, ENG [35598]
SLEET PRE 1810 WOODBRIDGE, SFK, ENG [33992]
SLEIGH 1818+ AUS [35241] : 1750+ MDX, ENG [35241] : 1750+ LND, ENG [35241]
SLEIGHT ALL LIN, ENG [37195]
SLEIGHTHOLM PRE 1776 ROSEDALE, NRY, ENG [34127] : PRE 1900 WHITBY, NRY, ENG [37616]
SLEIGHTHOLME ALL KIRKBY MOORSIDE, NRY, ENG [34380]
SLEMANS ALL WORLDWIDE [37724]
SLEMINGS ALL WORLDWIDE [37724]
SLEMMING ALL WORLDWIDE [37724]
SLEMMINGS JOHN 1861-1865 PA, USA [37724] : ALL WORLDWIDE [37724]
SLEMMONDS ALL WORLDWIDE [37724]
SLEMONDS ALL WORLDWIDE [37724]
SLENTER PRE 1850 BERLIN, BLO, GER [33868]
SLEPER 1800 OSTFRIESLAND, PRE, GER [38039]
SLEYMANS ALL WORLDWIDE [37724]

SLIGHTAM 1800S STONEY MIDDLETON, DBY, ENG [36670]

SLIMAN PRE 1800 LKS & AYR, SCT [38437]

SLINGER 1800S NORTH OWRAN, WRY, ENG [38468]

SLINGO CAROLINE 1835+ OXF, ENG [36611] : 1766+ COMBE, OXF, ENG [36611]

SLINGSBY ALL PUDSEY, WRY, ENG [35470] : PRE 1900 YKS, ENG [36676]

SLINN ALL NORTHAMPTON & CRICK, NTH, ENG [35005]

SLOAN C1860 EUGOWRA & BATHURST, NSW, AUS [34009] : 1800 + WHITEHAVEN, CUL, ENG [34374] : 1824-1898 LIVERPOOL BLACKS, IRL &, ENG & NZ [34680] : 1700-1800 BELFAST, ANT, IRL [34107] : 1824-1898 DOW, IRL [34680] : PRE 1850 TANNYBROOK, ANT, IRL [36345] : PRE 1847 ARMEE, ANT, IRL [36509] : 1800+ LOCHWINNOCH, RFW, SCT [37205] : PRE 1861 APPLEGARTH & GLENCAIRN, DFS, SCT [37238] : FERGUS PRE 1775 STATESVILLE, NC, USA [38536]

SLOANE GEORGE 1858 + BATHURST & ORANGE, NSW, AUS [34545] : 1800S KILBURNIE, AYR, SCT [34288] : 1834-1885 GLASGOW, LKS, SCT [37205] : PRE 1824 FRANKLIN, PA, USA [34573] : 1850+ LAUDERDALE, SC, USA [35135]

SLOBODA PRE 1914 HU [37519] : PRE 1914 VIENNA, OES [37519] : PRE 1914 YU [37519]

SLOCUM PRE 1780 MA, USA [37018]

SLOEY PETER 1838+ ORANGE, NSW, AUS [34545] : C1860 ORANGE, NSW, AUS [34806] : PRE 1800 CLONE, MOG, IRL [34806]

SLOSS 1820+ ARM, IRL [33788] : 1820+ DALMELLINGTON, AYR, SCT [33788]

SLOTHER 1780+ NEWCASTLE UPON TYNE, NBL, ENG [35322]

SLOTWINSKI 1800-1850 UKRAINE, POL [36331]

SLOW 1833 WILTON, SALISBURY, HAM, ENG [34654] : ALL HEMEL HEMPSTEAD, HRT, ENG [36981]

SLOWEY CORNELIUS 1750+ CLUNES, MOG, IRL [34545]

SLUIJTER 1600S DREISCHOR, ZEL, NL [38350]

SLUMAN PRE 1700 ENG [38746]

SLUTTE 1855-1885 KEWEENAW CO., MI, USA [38009]

SLUTTS 1757-1830 SOMERSET CO., PA, USA [36901]

SLY 1853-1900 ARMIDALE, NSW, AUS [37911] : 1790-1850 LEEDS, ONT, CAN [38097] : 1860S LONDON, ENG [36146] : 1790 + BLOOMSBURY, LND, ENG [36868] : PRE 1818 LONDON, ENG [37911] : ELIZABETH 1850 POSEY CO., IN, USA [35286]

SLYN ALL NTH, ENG [35005]

SLYNE ALL NTH, ENG [35005]

SMAHA PRE 1915 JAZIENICA, OES [34519]

SMAIL 1840+ SYDNEY, NSW, AUS [37349] : PRE 1850S SYDNEY, NSW, AUS [37349]

SMAILES 1800+ GOOLE, SNAITH, WRY, ENG [36772] : 1600+ KILBURN, NRY, ENG [36772] : 1550+ HAWNBY, NRY, ENG [36772] : 1800+ GOWDALL, SNAITH, WRY, ENG [36772]

SMALE ALL EAST LONDON, MDX, ENG [37700] : C1784 SUTTON AT HOME, KEN, ENG [38485]

SMALES 1859 + FINCHLEY, LND, ENG [36772] : 1800+ GOOLE, SNAITH, WRY, ENG [36772] : 1550+ HAWNBY, NRY, ENG [36772] : 1600+ KILBURN, NRY, ENG [36772] : 1800+ GOWDALL, SNAITH, WRY, ENG [36772]

SMALFIT PRE 1830 HINDERWELL, NRY, ENG [37776]

SMALL 1870+ CUMNOCK, NSW, AUS [34759] : PRE 1860 PENRITH, NSW, AUS [34759] : 1788 SYDNEY, NSW, AUS [35251] : 1895+ NARRABRI, NSW, AUS

[35254] : CHARLES PRE 1940 SYDNEY, NSW, AUS [35541] : 1900S MERRIWA, NSW, AUS [37910] : 1900+ NS, CAN [34513] : ALL ARRETON, ISLE OF WIGHT, HAM, ENG [33802] : PRE 1850 DEV, ENG [35913] : 1730-1800 BIRMINGHAM, WAR, ENG [37145] : C1880 LND, ENG [37627] : 1800+ WAR, ENG [37924] : PRE 1845 NETHERSEALE, DBY, ENG [38457] : PRE 1850 DOW, IRL [36073] : 1870+ MIDHURST, TARANAKI, NZ [36806] : 1600-1750 DUNDEE, ANS, SCT [34513] : PRE 1670 ST ANDREWS, FIF, SCT [35227] : PRE 1750 ST MONANCE, FIF, SCT [35627] : 1700-1750 DUNDEE, ANS, SCT [36081] : PRE 1683 UK [38590] : 1850+ TREVETHIN, MON, WLS [36614]

SMALLBONE 1784-1810 WOOTTON ST LAWRENCE, HAM, ENG [36229]

SMALLBONES ALL BKM, ENG [38350]

SMALLDON 1850+ DEV, ENG [38417] : 1878-1958 PLAISTOW, LND, ENG [38417]

SMALLEY 1851-1853 EMU BOTTOM, VIC, AUS [35192] : 1800S NEWTON, CAM, ENG [34930] : 1750+ DARWEN, LAN, ENG [36991]

SMALLFIELD FREDERICK 1829-1915 LONDON, ENG [34314]

SMALLHORN 1800S DUBLIN, IRL [36873] : C1849 DUBLIN, IRL [37144]

SMALLMAN ALL WORLDWIDE [38460]

SMALLPAGE 1800+ LEEDS, YKS, ENG [37705]

SMALLPIECE PRE 1830 HINDERWELL, NRY, ENG [37776]

SMALLRIDGE PRE 1820 DEV, ENG [38377]

SMALLSHIRE C1800 ECCLESHALL, STS, ENG [37209]

SMALLWOOD C1768 ETON, NRY, ENG [34127] : 1650+ CALKE & HARTSHORNE, DBY, ENG [35851] : PRE 1775 RANTON, STS, ENG [36701]

SMART C1860S SARNIA, ONT, CAN [36310] : 1780 WIL, ENG [34731] : PRE 1860 LITTLEBURY, ESS, ENG [34869] : 1690 PETWORTH, SSX, ENG [34909] : PRE 1858 CROUGHTON, NTH, ENG [34935] : 1800-1850 BRISTOL, SOM, ENG [35192] : C1650-1750 GLS, ENG [35305] : 1800+ STEPNEY, MDX, ENG [35972] : ALL GREENS NORTON, NTH, ENG [36144] : 1800-1900 ANDOVER, HAM, ENG [36175] : C1869 BROAD BLUNSDON, WIL, ENG [36307] : PRE 1800 SEDGLEY, STS, ENG [36518] : C1857 ENG [36878] : PRE 1820 WOUTTUN RIVERS, WIL, ENG [37687] : 1700-1800 BURFORD, OXF, ENG [37763] : 1700-1800 GLS, ENG [37829] : 1770+ ALWALTON, ORTON WATERVILLE, HUN, ENG [38078] : PRE 1800 WANBOROUGH, WIL, ENG [38383] : PRE 1850 DOW, IRL [38393] : 1770-1840S KILSYTH & FALKIRK, STI, SCT [34359] : 1750+ COLLESSIE, FIF, SCT [34768] : C1874 GLASGOW, LKS, SCT [34768] : 1800-1900 AUCHTERMUCHTY, FIF, SCT [35094] : 1800+ LITERTIE, ABD, SCT [35911] : PRE 1820 BRECHIN, ANS, SCT [36310] : 1900 HALBEATH, FIF, SCT [38470]

SMARTT 1870 GEMBROOK, VIC, AUS [35774] : PRE 1870 ENFIELD, MDX, ENG [35774]

SMEAL 1820+ EDINBURGH, SCT [38204]

SMEATH C1780 EXETER, DEV, ENG [35920]

SMEATON 1815+ PER, SCT [35427]

SMEDLEY PRE 1920 WELLINGTON, NSW, AUS [37911] : 1830+ ASHBY DE LA ZOUCH, LEI, ENG [37911] : ELIZABETH PRE 1870S LEICESTER & MATLOCK, DBY, ENG [38031] : ALL GLS & GLA, ENG & WLS [37269]

SMEE 1870+ BATHURST, NSW, AUS [38568] : 1793+ LND, ENG [35414] : ALEXANDER 1750-1850 KEN, ENG [35494] : 1700 BLACK NOTLEY, ESS, ENG [37928] : PRE 1868 ESS, ENG [38568]

SMEED 1827+ HOBART, TAS, AUS **[35394]** : PRE 1870 MONKS HORTON, KEN, ENG **[35932]** : PRE 1903 MIDDLESEX, ENG **[36249]** : ALL KEN & E SSX, ENG **[37714]** : ALL WORLDWIDE **[38230]**

SMEETON ALL WORLDWIDE **[37070]**

SMELLIE 1800+ BRISBANE, QLD, AUS **[34538]** : 1800+ SYDNEY, NSW, AUS **[34538]** : 1833 CONVENT GARDEN, MDX, ENG **[34808]** : 1700+ DALERE, LKS, SCT **[34538]** : 1700+ CAMBUSNETHAN, LKS, SCT **[38492]** : ALL WORLDWIDE **[36467]**

SMET ALL HAMME, OVL, BEL **[38162]** : ALL WORLDWIDE **[38162]**

SMETHAM PHOEBE PRE 1800 TAUNTON, SOM, ENG **[36192]**

SMETHURST ALL HALIFAX, YKS, ENG **[38332]**

SMID 1620-1700 TAARNBORG, SORO, DEN **[37547]**

SMIDT 1750-1800 SCHENECTADY, NY, USA **[38178]**

SMILEY C1850 BRANTFORD, ONT, CAN **[36671]** : 1820+ DON, IRL **[36958]**

SMILLIE 1780+ ABERDEEN, ABD, SCT **[37122]** : PRE 1870 AYR, AYR, LKS & DNB, SCT **[37238]**

SMILOVITZ 1840-1886 ROM **[38236]**

SMIT 1768-1933 LUTJEBROEK, NOH, NL **[38711]**

SMIT (SEE DE SMIT) **[38350]**

SMITH 1835+ DAPTO, NSW, AUS **[33781]** : PRE 1928 BERMAGUI, NSW, AUS **[33781]** : ALL NSW, AUS **[33799]** : SARAHANNE PRE 1859 GLENELG & ADELAIDE, SA, AUS **[33812]** : FREDERICK 1918+ NSW, AUS **[33813]** : ARTHUR 1926+ NSW, AUS **[33813]** : JOHN R. 1889+ WUTTAGOONA STN, NSW, AUS **[33813]** : HERBERT PRE 1905 IPSWICH, QLD, AUS **[33832]** : 1845+ HYNAM, SA, AUS **[33833]** : WILLIAM C1865 MANSFIELD, VIC, AUS **[33883]** : HENRY 1830+ SYDNEY, NSW, AUS **[33931]** : MARY ROBBINS 1860 CHILTERN, VIC, AUS **[34038]** : JOSEPH 1883 CHILTERN, VIC, AUS **[34038]** : ELIZA 1867 CHILTERN, VIC, AUS **[34038]** : GEORGE 1856 ADELAIDE, SA, AUS **[34193]** : CHARLES 1842+ HOBART, TAS, AUS **[34262]** : DAVID 1903+ KARRIDALE, WA, AUS **[34282]** : DANIEL 1852+ ESSENDON & EVERSLEY, VIC, AUS **[34295]** : 1860 DUNGOG, NSW, AUS **[34421]** : 1920+ NOWRA, NSW, AUS **[34421]** : 1840 NIMMITABEL, NSW, AUS **[34421]** : 1888+ BOMBALA, NSW, AUS **[34421]** : EWART 1949+ SURREY HILLS, VIC, AUS **[34430]** : 1822+ TAS, AUS **[34463]** : JOHN 1875+ SYDNEY, NSW, AUS **[34533]** : JOHN 1800+ DANDENONG, VIC, AUS **[34541]** : ELLEN AGNES PRE 1863+ TAS, AUS **[34592]** : ALL SPRING BAY, TAS, AUS **[34663]** : 1851+ BALLARAT, VIC, AUS **[34685]** : JOHN 1840S HOBART, TAS, AUS **[34698]** : CLARA 1852+ BEECHWORTH, VIC, AUS **[34698]** : HENRY PRE 1922 TAMWORTH, NSW, AUS **[34698]** : EMMA 1852+ BEECHWORTH, VIC, AUS **[34698]** : CALEB 1860+ LAUNCESTON, TAS, AUS **[34770]** : MARTHA 1879+ KENSINGTON, NSW, AUS **[34786]** : CATHERINE 1883+ SHOALHAVEN, NSW, AUS **[34786]** : CHAS ALFRED 1860S BALLARAT, VIC, AUS **[34793]** : JAMES 1842-1866 GAYNDAH, QLD, AUS **[34852]** : JAMES 1870+ SHOALHAVEN, NSW, AUS **[34977]** : ALYDIA PRE 1877 TOWAMBA, NSW, AUS **[34979]** : CHARLES C1857 ROSEBROOK & MAITLAND, NSW, AUS **[35104]** : PETER 1868 BALLARAT, VIC, AUS **[35123]** : 1819+ TAS, AUS **[35127]** : ALICIA 1839 SYDNEY, NSW, AUS **[35152]** : EDWARD 1835 SYDNEY, NSW, AUS **[35152]** : GRACE 1867 SYDNEY & GULGONG, NSW, AUS **[35159]** : WILLIAM 1835+ WARKWORTH, NSW, AUS **[35197]** : DR JAMES 1890-1922 LAUNCESTON, TAS, AUS **[35222]** : JOHN 1853-C1890 MAITLAND, NSW, AUS **[35222]** : PHOEBE 1865+ COOKTOWN, QLD, AUS **[35232]** : CHARLES PRE 1860 SA, AUS **[35255]** : THOMAS C1860 SYDNEY, NSW, AUS **[35336]** : C1909 PERTH, WA, AUS **[35348]** : 1900+ FARINA & HAWKER, SA, AUS **[35352]** : JOHN 1879 COBURG, VIC, AUS **[35356]** : GEORGE THOMAS PRE 1882 OATLANDS, TAS, AUS **[35459]** : EMANUEL PRE 1854 JERUSALEM, TAS, AUS **[35459]** : RICHARD PRE 1918 AUS **[35628]** : JOHN THOMAS C1915 STRATHALBYN, SA, AUS **[35744]** : GEORGE 1855+ PEACHEY BELT, SA, AUS **[35744]** : THOMAS 1867+ BRIGHTON & SOUTH PRESTON, VIC, AUS **[35780]** : HENRY 1892 MELBOURNE, VIC, AUS **[35805]** : C1883 DALBY, QLD, AUS **[35807]** : TY 1860+ STAWELL, VIC, AUS **[35823]** : 1890S MORAYFIELD & STAFFORD, QLD, AUS **[35854]** : JOHN T. 1840 NSW, AUS **[35970]** : 1865+ GYMPIE, QLD, AUS **[36241]** : GEORGE 1859-1907 LAUNCESTON, TAS & VIC, AUS **[36268]** : HENRY PRE 1900 BRISBANE, QLD, AUS **[36290]** : JOHN 1847-1870 WOLLONGONG, NSW, AUS **[36293]** : JOHN 1860-1884 TAMWORTH, NSW, AUS **[36293]** : JOHN 1860+ GOSFORD, NSW, AUS **[36365]** : THOMAS 1847+ SMITHFIELD, NSW, AUS **[36611]** : DAVID 1878 ORANGE, NSW, AUS **[36634]** : SAMUEL 1840+ DUNGOG, NSW, AUS **[36647]** : 1900+ BINGARA, NSW, AUS **[37115]** : ALL JERILDERIE, NSW, AUS **[37115]** : 1900+ MOREE, NSW, AUS **[37115]** : 1890+ DUBBO, NSW, AUS **[37115]** : ALL HORSHAM, VIC, AUS **[37115]** : CHARLOTTE 1890+ MURWILLUMBAH, NSW, AUS **[37140]** : WILLIAM HENRY C1880S SALE & LUCKNOW, VIC, AUS **[37151]** : C1858 WALKERVILLE, ADELAIDE, SA, AUS **[37167]** : THOMAS 1850+ DUNOLLY, VIC, AUS **[37557]** : THOMAS 1838+ BATHURST, NSW, AUS **[37557]** : 1820+ NSW, AUS **[37900]** : ALL MULGUNNIA, NSW, AUS **[37909]** : CUMMINGS C. PRE 1933 NEWCASTLE, NSW, AUS **[37911]** : JOSIAH 1849+ ADELAIDE, SA, AUS **[37913]** : 1865+ HANGING GARDENS, VIC, AUS **[37920]** : 1855+ YARRAWONGA, VIC, AUS **[37994]** : JAMES 1890-1910 NEWTOWN, NSW, AUS **[38083]** : PRE 1850 LAMBING FLAT, NSW, AUS **[38214]** : CHARLES 1850+ HILL END, NSW, AUS **[38500]** : CHARLES 1850+ TAMBAROORA, NSW, AUS **[38500]** : JOHN C1820+ PROSPECT, NSW, AUS **[38510]** : WILLIAM C. 1870S GOLDFIELDS & CASTLEMAINE, VIC, AUS **[38541]** : WILLIAM 1836-1849 SYDNEY & GOULBURN, NSW, AUS **[38761]** : ELIZABETH 1821+ BRUSSELS, BEL **[36180]** : CLAUD 1900-1950 EAGLE VALLEY & MOUND, ALB, CAN **[34072]** : WILLIAM 1880+ NORFOLK CO., ONT, CAN **[34128]** : JOHN C1835 CAMPBELLFORD, ONT, CAN **[34133]** : 1780+ LINCOLN CO., ONT, CAN **[34407]** : 1850+ BARRIE, ONT, CAN **[34466]** : EDWARD 1829-1855 HUDSON'S BAY CO.(YORK), ONT, CAN **[34688]** : PRE 1929 EMSDALE, ONT, CAN **[37439]** : 1856-1943 WENTWORTH, ONT, CAN **[37469]** : MARTIN 1850-1900 NS, CAN **[38421]** : EVERETT C1897 TORONTO, ONT, CAN **[38455]** : HENRY 1800S DEER ISLAND, NB, CAN **[38785]** : JAMES C1820+ SAINT JOHN, NB, CAN & SCT **[34339]** : ELIZABETH 1860+ PAISLEY & BOTHWELL, ONT, CAN & SCT **[34983]** : GILBERT 1766-1846 VICTORIA CO., ONT, CAN & SCT **[38433]** : PRE 1850 JSY, CHI **[35823]** : JOHN PRE 1820 CAMBERWELL, SRY, ENG **[33774]** : FOSTER 1800S SUNDERLAND, DUR, ENG **[33776]** : C1825 CHELTENHAM, GLS, ENG **[33793]** : ALL HULL, YKS, ENG **[33799]** : JOHN PRE 1810 ESS, ENG

[33813] : PRE 1824 WOLLESTON, NTH, ENG [33860] : JOHN & WM. 1800+ ST PANCRAS, LND, ENG [33938] : 1800S ERPINGHAM, NFK, ENG [33972] : HENRY 1820+ BREDE, SSX, ENG [34011] : JAMES PRE 1818 WOLVERHAMPTON, STS, ENG [34036] : FRANCES C1770S KEN, ENG [34040] : C1520 SHERINGTON, BKM, ENG [34041] : C1780 NEWPORT PAGNELL, BKM, ENG [34041] : WILLIAM 1850+ GUILDFORD, SRY, ENG [34066] : JOHN 1838 LONDON, ENG [34091] : ALL GLS & SOM, ENG [34093] : 1690S-1830S THORNTON BY POCKLINGTON, YKS, ENG [34094] : 1690S-1830S YAPHAM, YKS, ENG [34094] : LAVOICA C1865 MDX, ENG [34102] : PRE 1800 ROGATE, SSX, ENG [34112] : JOHN 1814 ST GEORGE MARTYR, MDX, ENG [34142] : 1850+ SHEFFIELD, YKS, ENG [34190] : CHRISTOPHER G 1825 BATHEALTON, SOM, ENG [34195] : JOHN 1762+ HEMYOCK & DUNKESWELL, DEV, ENG [34195] : PRE 1830 NTH CRAWLEY, NTH, ENG [34197] : THOMAS 1750 PORCHESTER, HAM, ENG [34204] : 1800 BRAMPTON BRYAN, HEF, ENG [34210] : 1800 LAMBETH, SRY, ENG [34210] : 1750+ E KIRKBY, LIN, ENG [34221] : 1800+ MILTON ABBAS, DOR, ENG [34228] : JOHN 1804-1873 NOTTINGHAM, NTT, ENG [34238] : PRE 1830 FLETCHING, SSX, ENG [34245] : 1650-1750 KIBWORTH BEAUCHAMP, LEI, ENG [34258] : 1650-1750 APPLEBY MAGNA, LEI, ENG [34258] : 1820+ GREAT CHISHALL, ESS, ENG [34299] : WILLIAM 1800+ LEATHERHEAD, SRY, ENG [34314] : PRE 1830 SCULCOATES & HULL, ERY, ENG [34320] : HERBERT C1885 SOUTH SHIELDS, DUR, ENG [34329] : 1800S DEAL, KEN, ENG [34336] : 1750-1850 SALISBURY, WIL & MDX, ENG [34343] : ALL LIN, ENG [34361] : GEORGE C1830+ MOLASH (MOLDASH), KEN, ENG [34374] : 1860+ TEYNHAM, KEN, ENG [34374] : PRE 1825 KEIGHLEY, YKS, ENG [34383] : PRE 1850 KIDDERMINSTER, WOR, ENG [34383] : 1760+ MIDDLETON BY OLDHAM, CHS, ENG [34408] : 1800+ DUDLEY, WOR, ENG [34420] : PRE 1834 FLORE, NTH, ENG [34421] : PRE 1720 LISSINGTON, LIN, ENG [34445] : THOMAS GEORGE C1840 BATH, SOM, ENG [34475] : PRE 1900 SWANAGE, DOR, ENG [34477] : 1800+ LANDPORT & SOUTHAMPTON, HAM, ENG [34477] : RICHARD PRE 1820 WHITEHAVEN, CUL, ENG [34494] : STEPHEN 1883 MARKET DEEPING, LIN, ENG [34511] : JOSEPH PRE 1875 BIRMINGHAM, WAR, ENG [34533] : JOHN 1800+ BRISTOL, GLS, ENG [34541] : PRE 1830 ENG [34571] : 1750-1850 MAIDSTONE, KEN, ENG [34572] : THOMAS PRE 1859 WOODSTOCK, OXF, ENG [34585] : THOMAS PRE 1859 WITNEY, OXF, ENG [34585] : WILLIAM C1836 CLEWERS, BRK, ENG [34586] : PRE 1800 EYNESBURY & ST NEOTS, CAM, ENG [34611] : PRE 1800 RATCLIFFE, LND, ENG [34612] : JOSEPH PRE 1880 MANCHESTER & LEEDS, LAN & YKS, ENG [34622] : MARY ANN 1815+ SHOREDITCH, LND, ENG [34684] : 1860+ BILLESDON, LEI, ENG [34710] : 1830+ WETHERINGSETT, SFK, ENG [34710] : PRE 1857 STOCKPORT, CHS, ENG [34711] : PRE 1850 NOTTINGHAM, NTT, ENG [34734] : 1700+ PAULERSPURY & NORTHAMPTON, NTH, ENG [34747] : C1755 CLAYPOLE, LIN, ENG [34765] : 1750-1890 ECCLESHILL, YKS, ENG [34793] : PRE 1900 SALFORD, LAN, ENG [34848] : PRE 1860 BATH, SOM, ENG [34848] : PRE 1690 ST MARYS, NOTTINGHAM, NTT, ENG [34858] : 1700-1800 DEPTFORD, KEN, ENG [34872] : PRE 1850

UXBRIDGE, MDX, ENG [34909] : ARTHUR 1916+ NEWBOLD, DBY, ENG [34921] : REV. THOMAS 1800+ SOM, ENG [34933] : PRE 1830 KISLINGBURY, NTH, ENG [34941] : PRE 1786 CALNE, WIL, ENG [34959] : GEORGE 1800+ ENGLEFIELD, BRK, ENG [34970] : MARY C1680 ECCLESFIELD, WRY, ENG [34974] : PRE 1800 HULL, ERY, ENG [34984] : PRE 1830 WIGTON, CUL, ENG [35020] : MARIA PRE 1835 BRADFORD, WRY, ENG [35023] : C1699 CHIBBURN, NBL, ENG [35026] : GEORGE 1885+ BIRMINGHAM, WAR, ENG [35033] : HENRY C1850 BIRMINGHAM, WAR, ENG [35033] : JULIA 1890+ BIRMINGHAM, WAR, ENG [35033] : JOHN 1800+ FULFORD, STS, ENG [35042] : 1850 BIRMINGHAM, WAR, ENG [35061] : 1800+ STRATFORD ON AVON, WAR, ENG [35062] : PRE 1832 ST AUSTELLS, CON, ENG [35091] : SABRINA 1822 BIRMINGHAM, WAR, ENG [35152] : 1830S MAULDEN, BDF, ENG [35156] : PRE 1780 HEDENHAM, NFK, ENG [35173] : C1830 MILLBANK, WRY, ENG [35221] : WILLIAM PRE 1806 WARWICK, WAR, ENG [35232] : 1840S-60S DURRINGTON, WIL, ENG [35243] : ABIGAIL 1750+ FROME, SOM, ENG [35248] : JOSEPH 1800+ BRISTOL, GLS, ENG [35248] : WILLIAM 1730S CHIDDINGSTONE, KEN, ENG [35261] : C1800 BOUGHTON & FAVERSHAM, KEN, ENG [35350] : C1800 ROCHESTER & CHATHAM, KEN, ENG [35350] : SARAH 1850+ BLACKBURN, LAN, ENG [35362] : WILLIAM PRE 1810 WAR, ENG [35407] : JOHN C1840+ GLAISDALE, YKS, ENG [35447] : ISABELLA C1840+ GLAISDALE, YKS, ENG [35447] : MARY ANN C1817 NUNEATON, WAR, ENG [35496] : PRE 1839 NUNEATON, WAR, ENG [35496] : RICHARD PRE 1880 BRISTOL, GLS, ENG [35525] : MARY PRE 1786 LONDON, ENG [35578] : 1800+ LONDON, ENG [35608] : GEORGE PRE 1870 LND, ENG [35628] : PRE 1800 SFK, ENG [35642] : PRE 1840 OFFLEY & KINGS WALDEN, HRT, ENG [35701] : WM. SYDNEY C1840-1880 GREAT YARMOUTH, NFK, ENG [35726] : JEREMIAH C1800 HALIFAX, WRY, ENG [35744] : CHARLES 1862 ENFIELD, MDX, ENG [35805] : C1850 HANLEY, STS, ENG [35854] : 1700S GREAT BOWDEN, LEI, ENG [35858] : CHARLES 1830+ ISLINGTON, MDX, ENG [35867] : HERBERT PRE 1888 PECKHAM, LND, ENG [35867] : CONSTANCE 1891+ PECKHAM & CAMBERWELL, LND, ENG [35867] : AUBREY PRE 1889 MINSTER IN SHEPPEY, KEN, ENG [35867] : PERCIVAL PRE 1879 EAST ISLINGTON, MDX, ENG [35867] : HENRY 1850+ ISLINGTON, MDX, ENG [35867] : GEORGE PRE 1910 LAMBETH & STOCKWELL, LND, ENG [35867] : PRE 1872 BURFORD, OXF, ENG [35898] : WILLIAM PRE 1900 WOOLWICH, LND, ENG [35901] : ABRAHAM PRE 1841 LND, ENG [35910] : C1685 NEWNHAM, GLS, ENG [35920] : 1746+ BRAFIELD ON-THE-GREEN, NTH, ENG [35921] : PRE 1874 LICHFIELD, WAR, ENG [35932] : 1800+ CHERTSEY, SRY & BRK, ENG [35947] : JOSEPH C1785 DINGLEY, NTH, ENG [35955] : FREDERICK 1700 LAUNCESTON, CON, ENG [35970] : SAMUEL C1790 MIDDLETON CHENEY, NTH, ENG [35974] : GEORGE 1820+ DEDDINGTON, OXF, ENG [35974] : 1770+ POCKLINGTON, ERY, ENG [35977] : 1800S ARDLEIGH, ESS, ENG [35987] : 1700-1800 TENBURY WELLS, WOR, ENG [36003] : 1700-1800 ORLETON, HEF, ENG [36003] : HENRY & ANNE 1840-1860 COALEY & DURSLEY, GLS, ENG [36018] : PRE 1860 CLERKENWELL, MDX, ENG [36019] :

1816+ WAKES GREEN, ESS, ENG [36026] : PRE
1930 STRADISHALL, SFK, ENG [36046] : 1827-1900
BLOOMSBURY, LND, ENG [36047] : 1811-1845
IDEN, SSX, ENG [36071] : 1849+ STAPLEHURST,
KEN, ENG [36071] : PRE 1890 WITHAM, ESS, ENG
[36077] : 1900+ SOUTHFLEET, KEN, ENG [36107] :
PRE 1730 SEDGLEY, STS, ENG [36110] : C1700-1900
THURGARTON & WHITWELL, NFK, ENG [36128]
: WILLIAM JOHN 1820-1877 MANCHESTER, LAN,
ENG [36130] : EBENEZER R. 1820-1851
MANCHESTER, LAN, ENG [36130] : HUGH
LATHAM 1825-1884 MANCHESTER, LAN, ENG
[36130] : WILLIAM PRE 1890 NOTTINGHAM, NTT,
ENG [36148] : PRE 1800 ASHBY PUERORUM, LIN,
ENG [36168] : C1761 ROGATE, SSX, ENG [36185] :
EMANUEL C1788-1822 DYMOCK &
MINSTERWORTH, GLS, ENG [36190] : PRE 1842
NEWTON, SFK, ENG [36215] : PRE 1850
MEONSTOKE, HAM, ENG [36224] : 1790-1850
BIRCHANGER, ESS, ENG [36229] : 1800-1850
STANSTED MOUNTFITCHET, ESS, ENG [36229] :
PRE 1863 BOOTLE, LAN, ENG [36241] : 1800+
ISLINGTON, LND, ENG [36245] : 1800S BKM, ENG
[36289] : DANIEL PRE 1802 BRISTOL, GLS, ENG
[36309] : CHARLES PRE 1855 SANGFORD, SOM,
ENG [36310] : PRE 1775 SITTINGBOURNE, KEN,
ENG [36326] : PRE 1765 PANGBOURNE, BRK,
ENG [36326] : PRUDENCE PRE 1780 SEDGLEY,
STS, ENG [36374] : PRE 1899 MANSFIELD, NTT,
ENG [36475] : ALL YORK, YKS, ENG [36500] :
GEORGE C1865 LEICESTER, LEI, ENG [36532] :
HENRY B. C1851 BROMLEY, MDX, ENG [36582] :
WILLIAM 1720+ CARLTON & THACKLEY, WRY,
ENG [36617] : GLADYS MAY 1890S WEST DERBY,
LAN, ENG [36633] : PRE 1800 ST MARY
STAINING, LND, ENG [36636] : 1850
BIRMINGHAM, WAR, ENG [36649] : 1800+
OVERTON, HAM, ENG [36650] : PRE 1840
BRIDGNORTH, SAL, ENG [36660] : PRE 1807
AYLESBURY, BKM, ENG [36668] : SAMUEL 1870S
MANCHESTER, YKS, ENG [36741] : PRE 1850
NORTHAMPTON, NTH, ENG [36748] :
ELIZABETH 1787-1860 SCALBY, NRY, ENG [36757]
: WILLIAM 1800S CUDDINGTON, SRY, ENG
[36817] : PRE 1765 BILLESDON TUGBY, LEI, ENG
[36817] : JOHN 1800-65 LIN, ENG [36820] : JOHN
1700 WORKINGTON, CUL, ENG [36822] :
WILLIAM 1872 SHOREDITCH, LND, ENG [36823] :
PRE 1800 SOUTHWOLD, SFK, ENG [36829] : ALL
ISLINGTON, LND, ENG [36830] : PRE 1950
KETTERING, NTH, ENG [36830] : PRE 1930
HARTHILL & TODWICK, WRY, ENG [36854] :
HANNAH 1800S BROCKENHURST, HAM, ENG
[36874] : ROSE PRE 1885 WRY, ENG [36886] :
MATTHEW PRE 1860 BURFORD, OXF, ENG
[36889] : MATTHEW PRE 1810
MINCHINHAMPTON, GLS, ENG [36889] : 1870+
EDMONDSLEY, DUR, ENG [36961] : 1700-1824
TANFIELD & WASHINGTON, DUR, ENG [36961] :
REV. JOHN PRE 1635 DOR, ENG [36972] :
THOMAS 1680S FLAMSTEAD, HRT, ENG [36981] :
1750-1850 SCORTON, LAN, ENG [36983] :
CHARLES C1830 NAPLES, ENG [37007] :
WILLIAM C1800 BOW, LND, ENG [37053] : C1800
ATTLEBOROUGH, NFK, ENG [37053] : WILLIAM
1780+ HORNINGSEA & CAMBRIDGE, CAM &
LND, ENG [37065] : JOSEPH PRE 1680
STRATFORD ON AVON, WAR, ENG [37103] :
JOSEPH C1830 HAILEY, OXF, ENG [37106] :
SUSANNA C1830 HAILEY, OXF, ENG [37106] :
WILLIAM C1849 STANDISH, LAN, ENG [37131] :
1800 ASHAMPSTEAD, BRK, ENG [37170] : ALL

SSX, ENG [37210] : 1880S REDDITCH, WOR, ENG
[37230] : 1700-1820 BATH, SOM, ENG [37233] :
C1775-1894 BROADWAY, WOR, ENG [37265] :
EMILY C1920-1950 MDX, ENG [37268] : EMILY
1880S-1909 KENSINGTON, LND, ENG [37268] :
PRE 1755 ALDBOURNE, WIL, ENG [37288] :
ISAAC 1800S COVENTRY & CROFT CHETHAM,
WAR, ENG [37317] : ROBERT PRE 1900 COW
HONEYBOURNE, WOR & GLS, ENG [37319] :
ESTHER 1780-1830 CAM, GLS, ENG [37320] :
BENJAMIN PRE 1800 BLETCHINGLEY, SRY,
ENG [37321] : 1800+ QUENNINGTON, GLS, ENG
[37328] : PRE 1800 DOVER, KEN, ENG [37371] : 1800
LOFTUS, NRY, ENG [37388] : 1750+ RAMSEY,
CAM, ENG [37409] : AMELIA 1744-1884
WESTMINSTER, LND, ENG [37453] : ALL
BRINKWORTH, WIL, ENG [37468] : ALL
BRIGHTON, SSX, ENG [37468] : PRE 1640
HALIFAX, WRY, ENG [37484] : ALL
GRUNDISBURGH, SFK, ENG [37487] : 1700-1800
EAST KIRKBY, LIN, ENG [37487] : WILLIAM 1750-
1800 MOUNTFIELD, SSX, ENG [37541] : PRE 1787
PRESTWICH, LAN, ENG [37573] : EDWARD 1790+
SOUTHWARK, LND, ENG [37579] : 1859
TAMWORTH, STS, ENG [37594] : 1750-1800 DEAN,
CUL, ENG [37613] : JANE PRE 1900 CAMBRIDGE,
CAM, ENG [37619] : ALL HORNE, SRY, ENG
[37627] : 1300-1400+ SSX, ENG [37648] : PRE 1800
DAVENTRY, NTH, ENG [37650] : 1800-50 ST
PETERS & SITTINGBOURNE, KEN, ENG [37677] :
WILLIAM PRE 1872 LND, ENG [37687] : PRE 1900
SHRAWLEY, WOR, ENG [37703] : GEORGE C1780
LAN & WES, ENG [37706] : C1800 LONDON, ENG
[37715] : PRE 1850 NORWICH, NFK, ENG [37725] :
ALL EDENBRIDGE, KEN, ENG [37746] : PRE 1800
CHIDDINGSTONE, KEN, ENG [37746] : WILLIAM
1860+ LONDON & SWINDON, WIL, ENG [37748] :
PRE 1810 PAR KIRKBURTON, WRY, ENG [37754] :
MARTHA 1770+ LECHLADE, GLS, ENG [37763] :
BRIDGET 1700-1800 DUNTON, NFK, ENG [37845] :
1600-1800 COWLING, NRY, ENG [37854] : 1750-1880
CODDINGTON, NTT, ENG [37858] : 1700-1800
FORDHOUSE, CUL, ENG [37858] : 1800S ASTLEY,
WAR, ENG [37868] : 1810S LIVERPOOL, LAN, ENG
[37869] : OLIVER PRE 1859 BRIDGWATER, SOM,
ENG [37876] : OLIVER 1870 STROUD, GLS, ENG
[37876] : PATRICK 1860+ NBL, ENG [37889] : 1832-
1850 LONDON, ENG [37891] : RICHARD PRE 1829
BEXLEY, KEN, ENG [37892] : PRE 1820 ESS, ENG
[37900] : PRE 1788 WESTON SUB EDGE, GLS, ENG
[37909] : CUMMINGS C. 1897+ GATESHEAD,
DUR, ENG [37911] : 1650 THORINGTON, SFK,
ENG [37928] : EMMA 1870+ KENNINGHALL,
NFK, ENG [37937] : WILLIAM PRE 1870 GREAT
NESTON, CHS, ENG [37989] : JENNINGS C1780-
1843 CON, ENG [37998] : WILLIAM 1760-1850 ENG
[38003] : ELIZA C1790 SALFORD, LAN, ENG
[38034] : JOHN C1790 SALFORD, LAN, ENG [38034]
: PRE 1830 AMPTHILL, BDF, ENG [38075] : 1800+
STEPNEY, LND, ENG [38247] : GEORGE 1803 COX
GREEN, DUR, ENG [38269] : GEORGE 1890-1943
SPENNYMOOR, DUR, ENG [38269] : GEORGE
1840S NEWFIELD, DUR, ENG [38269] : ANNIE
C1870-1938 SPENNYMOOR, DUR, ENG [38269] :
GEORGE 1870-1939 SPENNYMOOR, DUR, ENG
[38269] : ABRAHAM EVANS 1860-1920S
SPENNYMOOR, DUR, ENG [38269] :
(STATIONERS) 1880 LONDON, ENG [38287] : PRE
1870 KNUTSFORD, CHS, ENG [38292] : THOMAS
1880S NORTON, ERY, ENG [38356] : THOMAS
GROOM PRE 1880 LONDON, ENG [38356] : 1820-
1850 CHADDERTON, LAN, ENG [38370] : PRE 1870

CAM, ENG [38386] : THOMAS 1815 GLOUCESTER, GLS, ENG [38394] : BENJAMIN 1830+ COLCHESTER, ESS, ENG [38402] : FRANCES W. 1912+ PORTSMOUTH, HAM & CAM, ENG [38403] : STEPHEN PRE 1910 KEN, ENG [38419] : WILLIAM PRE 1876 ASTON & BIRMINGHAM, WAR, ENG [38437] : PRE 1750 OSWESTRY, SAL, ENG [38461] : JOHN 1733+ SCARBOROUGH, YKS, ENG [38499] : THOMAS 1800S WALTHAM ABBEY, ESS, ENG [38500] : PRE 1800 NEWTOWN LINFORD, LEI, ENG [38512] : MARY 1800-1851 KNOTTINGLEY, WRY, ENG [38580] : PRE 1930 DUR, ENG [38594] : WILLIAM 1820-1836 FRAMPTON COTTERELL, GLS, ENG [38761] : WILLIAM C1849+ HASTINGS, SSX & NSW, ENG & AUS [35547] : THOMAS ALL LONDON, ENG & NZ [33981] : OWEN 1881-1954 MANCHESTER & INVERCARGILL, LAN & STHLND, ENG & NZ [34622] : 1800S LAN, ENG & NZ [35134] : 1850+ LONDON, ENG & NZ [37132] : CHARLES C1830+ ROSTOCK, MEK, GER [35104] : ANNA 1790-1799 ALSACE LORRAINE, ELO, GER [38780] : JOHN 1854+ PRUSSIA, GER & AUS [35712] : DR JAMES 1867-1890 MADRAS, INDIA [35222] : 1800-1900 IOM [36130] : PRE 1870 FER, IRL [34555] : PRE 1851 LOUGHALL, ARM, IRL [34685] : JAMES 1840S CAV, IRL [35123] : BENJAMIN C1840-3 GOREY, WEX, IRL [35184] : 1800+ BANDON, COR, IRL [35201] : 1800+ ATHENRY, GAL, IRL [35521] : OWEN 1800+ NAVAN, MEA, IRL [35525] : JOHN 1821+ WEX, IRL [35713] : PRE 1850 CAVANDARRAGH, TYR, IRL [35897] : 1832 CORK CITY, COR, IRL [35903] : C1840 PARKANNESLEY, WEX, IRL [35920] : 1780-1860 CASTLE BLAYNEY, MOG, IRL [36130] : 1780-1860 CLONES, MOG, IRL [36130] : 1730-1850 CORK, COR, IRL [36130] : JOSEPH 1790+ IRL [36667] : WILLIAM 1800S TYR, IRL [36801] : WILLIAM C1830 CARRIGHNE, DON, IRL [37007] : 1800 SLIEVENISKI, DOW, IRL [37028] : ALL DUBLIN, IRL [37503] : PRE 1880 BALLYCONNEL, CAV, IRL [37808] : C1800-1840 BANDON, COR, IRL [37859] : 1833+ REFEARA, MOG, IRL [37994] : GEORGE 1870S ANT, IRL [38266] : LAWRENCE 1839 DUBLIN CITY, DUB, IRL [38322] : PRE 1900 KOVNA, KOVNA, LITHUANIA [36455] : ALFRED 1850-1950S SKIPPERS, QUEENSTOWN, OTAGO, NZ [34000] : THOMAS 1880+ PONSONBY, AUCK, NZ [34282] : 1857+ DUNEDIN, NZ [34711] : JANE C1850-1915 MARYBANK, WANGANUI, NZ [35885] : 1860+ WAIUKU & AUCKLAND, NZ [36245] : SOPHRONIA 1862+ RIVERTON, SI, NZ [36611] : GEORGE C1860 LITTLE RIVER, CHCH, NZ [36878] : GEORGE PRE 1912 HASTINGS, NZ [36889] : FRED PRE 1900 NAPIER & HASINGS, NZ [36889] : SUSSANNA PRE 1898 BOKSBURG, RSA [34862] : THOMAS PRE 1860 PORT ELIZABETH, NATAL, RSA [36426] : JOHN PRE 1806 BAN, SCT [33822] : PRE 1839 OXNAM, ROX, SCT [33833] : JAMES 1840+ DUNDEE, ANS, SCT [33862] : JAMES 1750-1850 RESCOBIE, ANS, SCT [34004] : PRE 1848 BRECHIN, PER, SCT [34031] : WILLIAM 1770S+ KETTLE & STRATHMIGLO, FIF, SCT [34040] : JAMES C1785 THORNMUIR & CARLUKE, LKS & DNB, SCT [34127] : ELIZA C1803 GIGHA, ARL, SCT [34156] : NEIL C1770 GIGHA, ARL, SCT [34156] : PRE 1850 RATHVEN, BAN, SCT [34192] : PRE 1830 LONGSIDE, ABD, SCT [34197] : MARGARET C1850 SCT [34222] : WILLIAM PRE 1800 GLENHILL, DFS, SCT [34282] : DANIEL PRE 1852 PERTH, PER, SCT [34295] : ALL EDINBURGH, MLN, SCT [34466] : PRE 1735 AYR, AYR, SCT

[34501] : DAVID 1800+ FOURDOUN, KCD, SCT [34560] : 1820+ GOREBRIDGE, MLN, SCT [34621] : 1790+ AULDEARN, NAI, SCT [34666] : 1700+ LONGHOPE, OKI, SCT [34688] : THOMAS 1800+ KINNELL, ANS, SCT [34852] : ALL FORGUE, ABD, SCT [34861] : MARY PRE 1894 GAULDRY, FIF, SCT [35026] : JOHN PRE 1854 DALKEITH, MLN, SCT [35035] : ANDREW 1800+ SCONE, PER, SCT [35042] : C1850 TILLICOULTRY, CLK, SCT [35121] : C1865 GREENOCK, RFW, SCT [35211] : JAMES 1837 CULLEN, BAN, SCT [35369] : JESSIE 1800 WOODSIDE, ABD, SCT [35369] : CHRISTINA 1800+ LKS, SCT [35429] : 1835+ PORT ERROLL, ABD, SCT [35584] : JANET 1810-1850 ST NINIANS, STI, SCT [35602] : JOHN PRE 1821 KILMARNOCK, AYR, SCT [35713] : ANDREW PRE 1836 PERTH & SCONE, PER, SCT [35729] : PRE 1800 OXNAM, ROX, SCT [35823] : 1800+ HAWICK, ROX, SCT [35823] : ANDREW 1844 INVERESK, MLN, SCT [35855] : JANE C1836-1860 CAMPSIE, STI, SCT [35885] : ELIZABETH C1700 KINROSS, KRS, SCT [35885] : 1880 ROTHESAY, BUT, SCT [35943] : EUPHEMIA PRE 1860 ROTHIEMAY, BAN, SCT [35952] : JOHN PRE 1860 ROTHIEMAY, BAN, SCT [35952] : ALEXANDER C1790 HAMILTON, LKS, SCT [35956] : ALEXANDER PRE 1800+ HAMILTON, LKS, SCT [35956] : ALEX AUGUSTUS 1750+ MONTROSE, ANS, SCT [35969] : PRE 1800 PAISLEY, RFW, SCT [36041] : 1750-1850 GLENCAIRN, DFS, SCT [36130] : ELIZABETH PRE 1862 STI, SCT [36262] : DUNCAN 1815 ISLE OF ISLAY, ARL, SCT [36316] : JOSEPH PRE 1850 DUMFRIES, DFS, SCT [36388] : JEAN 1800+ WIGTOWN, WIG, SCT [34471] : 1720-1800 ABBEY PAISLEY, RFW, SCT [36682] : CHRISTOPHER ALL SHI, SCT [36697] : WILLIAM 1800S ABD, SCT [36801] : JOHN 1700+ ABD, SCT [36801] : JAMES 1800+ CUMBERNAULD, DNB, SCT [36875] : MARGARET C1750 DUNCRUB, PER, SCT [37106] : ALEXANDER C1749 DUNCRUB, PER, SCT [37106] : ALL GLASGOW, SCT [37115] : PRE 1806 BEITH, AYR, SCT [37144] : 1800 ROX, SCT [37170] : THOMAS PRE 1838 PER, SCT [37557] : ANDREW PRE 1850 DUNDEE, ANS, SCT [37619] : C1860 GLASGOW, LKS, SCT [37661] : JOHN C1827 OLD MONKLAND, LKS, SCT [37684] : THOMAS C1827 OLD MONKLAND, LKS, SCT [37684] : PRE 1772 NEWBATTLE, MLN, SCT [37852] : 1750+ KIRKMAHOE, DFS, SCT [38247] : GEORGE C1780 OXNAM, ROX, SCT [38269] : C1825 DUNDEE, ANS, SCT [38292] : JAMES PRE 1900 ABERDEEN & OLRIG, ABD & CAI, SCT & NZ [33883] : CLAUD 1879-1900 LINCOLN & LENNOX, SD, USA [34072] : 1800-1900 NY, USA [34135] : JOHN ROCK 1600S LONG ISLAND, NY, USA [34392] : MARGARET ANNE PRE 1919 DALLAS CO., MO, USA [34481] : CHAS ALFRED 1830S NEW YORK, NY, USA [34793] : 1810-1820 GREEN CO., TN, USA [36337] : 1800-1900 GRANT PARISH, LA, USA [36449] : 1800-1900 BOWLESVILLE & GALLATIN CO., IL, USA [36565] : 1900+ GREENE, MO, USA [36567] : PRE 1900 RUSSELL, KY, USA [36567] : JAMES M. 1857-1893 DALLAS CO., TX, USA [36573] : ALEXANDER 1800-1830 BLOUNT & WILSON, TN, USA [36573] : MILBEY 1830-1870S PICKAWAY CO., OH, USA [36729] : 1750-1810 MIDDLEFIELD, MA, USA [36738] : JOHN PRE 1850 NORTHUMBERLAND CO., PA, USA [36917] : PRE 1797 TOPSHAM, VT, USA [36923] : AARON 1820+ MONTGOMERY CO., NY, USA [36950] : 1775-1850 MASON CO., KY, USA [36953] : 1720-1800 CUMBERLAND & ADAMS CO., PA, USA [36953] : 1838-1870 SWITZERLAND CO.,

IN, USA [36965] : 1740-1800 COLEBROOK &
GLASTONBURY, CT, USA [37086] : 1800+ LEWIS,
NY, USA [37484] : 1640+ DEDHAM, MA, USA
[37484] : ALL GREAT BEND, PA, USA [37503] :
HATTIE C1851+ NY, USA [37530] : JEREMIAH
PRE 1850 CLARK CO., OH, USA [37565] :
ANTHONY PRE 1840 VA, USA [37565] : PRE 1810
FRANKLIN & HABERSHAM CO., GA, USA [37587]
: PRE 1870 LYCOMING CO., PA, USA [37587] :
PHILEMON C1783-1834 PUTNAM VALLEY, NY,
USA [37764] : LEMUEL C1783-1835 PUTNAM
VALLEY, NY, USA [37764] : PHILEMON 1760-83
STAMFORD, CT, USA [37764] : ABRAHAM PRE
1700 LONG ISLAND, NY, USA [37764] : ABRAHAM
C1741+ PUTNAM VALLEY, NY, USA [37764] :
SAMUEL 1700S STAMFORD, CT, USA [37764] :
ASAHEL C1783+ NY, USA [37764] : ABRAHAM
PRE 1741 WESTCHESTER CO., NY, USA [37764] :
1843 VEVAY, IN, USA [37810] : 1881-1885 HEBRON,
NE, USA [37810] : RICHARD 1630+ RI, USA [38015]
: JOSEPH C1750-1890 FREDERICK CO., MD, USA
[38030] : DAVID 1760-1830S OVENCAANON, CT,
USA [38038] : NEHEMIAH PRE 1800+ SOUTH
EAST, NY, USA [38053] : NEHEMIAH JR 1804+
THOMSON, NY, USA [38053] : JONATHAN 1790
ULSTER CO., NY, USA [38062] : CHILIAS 1630+
SALEM, MA, USA [38066] : SAMUEL 1745-90
BALTIMORE, MD, USA [38086] : 1720-1725
MUDDLEBORO, MA, USA [38099] : GEORGE
1700+ BURLINGTON CO., NJ, USA [38127] :
ADELINE 1818-1852 JEFFERSON CO., NY, USA
[38145] : 1800-1900 MONTPELIER, VT, USA [38147] :
ALL USA [38151] : 1750-1800 SCHENECTADY, NY,
USA [38178] : ALL ST CLAIR CO., MI & NY, USA
[38287] : IVY-FORMAN 1820-38 MADISON CO., AL,
USA [38314] : JOSEPH BROCK 1860+ JACKSON
CO., IA, USA [38323] : C1800-1840 PA & IL, USA
[38325] : PENELOPE PRE 1799 NC, USA [38340] :
1800 KY, USA [38362] : HENRY C1800 JONES CO.,
NC, USA [38367] : HENRY C1776 PA, USA [38367] :
DURANT C1825 SURRY CO., NC, USA [38367] : DR
JOSEPH D. 1831-1900 IL, USA [38371] : ELIZABETH
1700S EASTERN SHORE, MD, USA [38374] :
OLIVER 1780-1853 BERKSHIRE CO., MA, USA
[38569] : 1780+ WATERBORO, YORK, ME, USA
[38571] : JOSEPH 1739 BURLINGTON CO., NJ, USA
[38734] : HELLCAT C1835 TN, MO & OR, USA
[38746] : HENRY P. PRE 1908 IL, VA & PA, USA
[38746] : IRA 1892+ ELK POINT, SD, USA [38751] :
CHAUNCEY 1785-1795 DORSET, VT, USA [38763] :
1717-1760 CAPE MAY CO., NJ, USA [38764] :
THOMAS 1862-1932 HICKORY, WI, USA [38785] :
PRE 1900 EBBW VALE, MON, WLS [34848] :
ARTHUR 1890S GLA, WLS [35084] : ALL
BRIDGEND, GLA, WLS [35474] : 1805-1860 MON,
WLS [38269] : PHILIS 1805-1840S MON, WLS [38269]
: GEORGE 1805-1840S MON, WLS [38269] :
THEOPHILUS W. 1770-1843 WORLDWIDE [36635]

SMITHARD 1924 HASLAND, DBY, ENG [37723]

SMITHEN PRE 1880 FOLKESTONE, KEN, ENG
[36841]

SMITHERINGALE 1800S LONDON, MDX, ENG
[37954]

SMITHERS 1862+ GRAFTON, NSW, AUS [34534] :
1800+ YOUNG, NSW, AUS [38491] : 1800+
TONBRIDGE, KEN, ENG [33785] : PRE 1850
GODALMING, SRY, ENG [33935] : 1880 LONDON,
ENG [34084] : PRE 1830 STONEHOUSE, DEV, ENG
[35739] : PRE 1903 PORTSEA, HAM, ENG [36475] :
PRE 1800 WORPLESDON, SRY, ENG [37832] :
1800+ TOWER HAMLETS, LND, ENG [37832]

SMITHIES PRE 1850 GISBURN, WRY & LAN, ENG
[37246]

SMITHSON 1817+ SOUTH MONAGHAN, ONT,
CAN [34507] : ALL WISBECH, CAM, ENG [34054] :
ALL SUTTON ST JAMES, LIN, ENG [34054] : PRE
1817 SLAIDBURN, YKS, ENG [34507] : PRE 1840
SALISBURY, WIL, ENG [35913] : PRE 1780
SHERIFF HUTTON, YKS, ENG [35983] : 1760-1800
YORK, ERY, ENG [36228] : 1572-1593 ELTHAM,
LONDON, MDX, ENG [36770] : PRE 1900 NRY,
ENG [37061] : ALL LONDON, ENG [37743] : 1680-
1790 NORTON LE CLAY & CUNDALL, NRY, ENG
[37754] : 1750-1830 MIRFIELD & SPEN VALLEY,
WRY, ENG [37754]

SMITH-THOMAS C1800 ORSETT, ESS, ENG [36978]

SMITHURST 1890+ SAN FRANCISCO, CA, USA
[34770]

SMITH WILSON WILLIAM 1850+ DARLINGTON,
NSW, AUS [37904]

SMITTEN C1760-1800 SEVENOAKS, KEN, ENG
[37453]

SMOAKHAM 1700S RAMSBURY, WIL, ENG [34205]

SMOCK PRE 1654 NL [38367] : C1654 NEW
UTRECHT, NY, USA [38367] : 1800S CRAWFORD
CO., PA, USA [38522]

SMOKER 1760S HUNGERFORD, BRK, ENG [34205]

SMOKHAM 1796 LONDON, MDX, ENG [35471]

SMOLENAARS ALL LMB, NL [36627]

SMOLENAERS ALL LMB, NL [36627]

SMOOT 1820-1840 COLUMBIA CO., OH, USA [36328]

SMOOTHEY 1750+ ESS, ENG [35975]

SMOTH ALL WORLDWIDE [35036]

SMUIN 1800S RADLEY, BRK, ENG [38745]

SMURFOOT PRE 1830 HINDERWELL, NRY, ENG
[37776]

SMURTHWAITE PRE 1830 HINDERWELL, NRY,
ENG [37776]

SMY JOHN C1800 DEBENHAM, SFK, ENG [37191] :
1750-1800 IPSWICH, SFK, ENG [37779]

SMYE PTE. C1914-1919 (WW1), LND, ENG [37756]

SMYLLIE ALL DERRY, LDY, IRL [33993]

SMYTH PRE 1831+ NEWCASTLE, NSW, AUS [35237]
: CHARLES 1860+ MELBOURNE, VIC, AUS
[36276] : 1880+ GLEBE, NSW, AUS [36316] : 1850+
NSW, AUS [37128] : 1880+ NSW, AUS [38771] :
HARRY C1940 BRUSSELS, BEL [37984] : ROSE
ANN 1800-1890 AYLMER, QUE, CAN [34514] :
C1850 ST AUSTELL, CON, ENG [35722] : C1730
SHERBORNE, DOR, ENG [36271] : THOMAS PRE
1865 RAMSEY, IOM & IRL [36967] : ALL NEWRY,
ARM, IRL [34054] : 1750-1850 CLA, IRL [34346] :
1800S DUBLIN, IRL [34647] : LETITIA 1800
BAILIEBOROUGH, CAV, IRL [34919] : PRE 1850
DRUMLOCHAN, LIM, IRL [34937] : 1700-1899
MULLYASH, MOG, IRL [36080] : CHARLES C1855
DUB, IRL [36276] : ALL ULSTER, IRL [36333] : 1780-
1880 LOU, IRL [37844] : THOMAS PRE 1850
BELFAST & DROMORE, DOW & ANT, IRL [38391]
: PRE 1880 TRIM, MEA, IRL [38771] : 1880+
EDINBURGH, MLN, SCT [37984] : 1880
ABERDEEN, ABD, SCT [37984] : 1900+ LOS
ANGELES, CA, USA [34647] : 1800-1900
BOWLESVILLE, IL, USA [36565] : ALL
WORLDWIDE [36333]

SMYTHE 1875+ MELBOURNE, VIC, AUS [35439] :
ALL SPROUGHTON, SFK, ENG [33823] : ALL
ALDEBURGH & FRANLINGHAM, SFK, ENG &
CAN [36967] : PRE 1860 DUBLIN, IRL [35439] :
MARY 1819-1902 ARM, IRL [38595] : CATHERINE
1820-1920 ANT, IRL & CAN [38779]

SMYTHIES 1851+ NZ [34570]

SNADDEN 1960+ AUS [37631] : C1907 ALLOA, CLK, SCT [37631] : C1876 WESTFIELD, CLK, SCT [37631] : C1858 CLK, SCT [37631]

SNADDON 1880-1884 TULLICOULTRY, CLK, SCT [33822] : 1810S OLD MONKLAND, LKS, SCT [35261] : ALL BO'NESS, WLN, SCT [36509]

SNADEN PRE 1880 ALLOA, CLK, SCT [35857]

SNAITH 1800 ALLENDALE, NBL, ENG [34890]

SNAPE 1790+ PATRICROFT, LAN, ENG [34370] : 1912-1933 BROMSGROVE, WOR, ENG [35047] : 1857-1897 BAKEWELL, DBY, ENG [35047] : PRE 1904 NORTHAMPTON, NTH, ENG [35047] : 1885 CHESTER, CHS, ENG [36606] : 1790+ WITHNELL, LAN, ENG [36991] : PRE 1845 DERBY, DBY, ENG [37298] : PRE 1750 SALFORD, LAN, ENG [38410] : 1875 FALL RIVER, MA, USA [35935]

SNAVELY 1850+ CAMBRIA CO., PA, USA [36897]

SNEAD 1744-1780 ALBEMARLE CO., VA, USA [38107]

SNEAL PRE 1925 WOODLAND, PA, USA [38222]

SNEDDAN PRE 1820 GLASGOW, LKS, SCT [34259]

SNEDDEN 1821+ RAMSAY TWP., ONT, CAN [34259] : 1830-75 FALKIRK, STI, SCT [35261]

SNEDDON JAMES 1900+ SURREY HILLS, VIC, AUS [35059] : ANDREW PRE 1830 CLACKMANNAN & ALLOA, CLK, SCT [33846] : PRE 1820 STI, SCT [35863] : PRE 1899 DUNOON, ARL, SCT & AUS [33919]

SNEED 1800+ LOUISA CO., VA, USA [36895]

SNELGROVE ALL LONGBRIDGE DEVERILL, WIL, ENG [34466]

SNELL 1840S MT BARKER, SA, AUS [33838] : 1867+ CLUNES, VIC, AUS [34530] : ALL SFK, ENG [34744] : 1780+ CON, ENG [35060] : 1860+ ST PANCRAS & MARYLEBONE, LND, ENG [35418] : ALBION C1825 SOUTH MOLTON, DEV, ENG [35418] : 1890+ HENDON, MDX, ENG [35418] : 1790S MEDMENHAM, BKM, ENG [35815] : PRE 1859 WELLS NEXT SEA, NFK, ENG [35872] : 1710+ TALLAND & PELYNT, CON, ENG [36254] : 1800-1900 STAMFORD COURTNEY, DEV, ENG [37227] : 1750+ NEEDHAM MARKET, SFK, ENG [37262] : 1600S-1700S DEV, ENG [37818] : JOHN 1770+ BRISTOL, ENG [38595]

SNELLING PRE 1940 TORONTO, ONT, CAN [37337] : C1780 HASLEMERE, SRY, ENG [33918] : ALL ST MARY'S CRAY, KEN, ENG [34558] : 1700+ NEWTON ABBOT, DEV, ENG [34602] : 1785+ FITTLEWORTH, SSX, ENG [34693] : 1780-1800 PORTSEA, HAM, ENG [35720] : 1750-1820 IOW, HAM, ENG [36873] : 1800+ GREATER LONDON, MDX, ENG [37337] : 1870-1890 BIRMINGHAM, WAR, ENG [37337] : 1865-1875 BURTON ON TRENT, STS, ENG [37337] : 1890+ NOTTINGHAM, NTT, ENG [37337] : ALL CHARTHAM & CANTERBURY, KEN, ENG [37337] : ALL BRENCHLEY & HORSMONDEN, KEN, ENG [37627] : C1940S DAYTONA BEACH, FL, USA [37337]

SNELLINGS 1837 SOM, ENG [33848]

SNELSON ALL AUS [38074] : ALL CHS, ENG [38074] : ALL GRESFORD, DEN, WLS [38074]

SNEVE ALL WORLDWIDE [37464]

SNEY PETER 1827+ SPAXTON, SOM, ENG [34630]

SNIDER 1730-1783 PHILADELPHIA, PA, USA [34366] : LEWIS PRE 1926 CLERMONT CO., OH, USA [37037] : JOHN PRE 1853 PITTSBURG, PA, USA [37037]

SNIPE 1750+ KILREA, DRY, IRL [37160]

SNOAD 1700-1900 KEN, ENG [37964]

SNOOK 1700S FRONTENAC, ONT, CAN [34353] : PRE 1848 EAST KNOYLE, WIL, ENG [35517] : 1800+ HINDON, WIL, ENG [36474] : PRE 1800 POOLE, DOR, ENG [36997] : PRE 1839 SHERBORNE, DOR, ENG [37201] : PRE 1839 SHERBORNE, DOR, ENG [37201] : 1846 SHERBORNE, DOR, ENG [37201] : C1800 BISHOPSTOKE, HAM, ENG [37201] : C1890 MENAI, CAE, WLS [37201] : 1890+ MENAI, CAE, WLS [37201] : ALL WORLDWIDE [37201]

SNOSWELL C1750+ ENG [37292]

SNOW 1850+ VIC & NSW, AUS [34274] : 1850+ VIC & NSW, AUS [35073] : 1850S+ LAKE BATHURST, NSW, AUS [35537] : 1860+ INDIGO, VIC, AUS [38069] : PRE 1900 CONCEPTION BAY, NFD, CAN [33904] : 1700-1855 ST GLUVIAS & GWENNAP, CON, ENG [34274] : 1780+ NORTHAM, DEV & CON, ENG [34559] : 1600-1850S NORTH & SOUTH MOLTON, DEV, ENG [35096] : ALL LEI, ENG [35177] : HANNAH C1890 LND & MDX, ENG [35418] : C1820+ ESSEX, ESS, ENG [35537] : PRE 1600 BOW, LND, ENG [36944] : PRE 1837 WAR, ENG [37103] : PRE 1870 DEV & SOM, ENG [37393] : 1700+ LAN, ENG [37620] : 1700+ ESS, ENG [37620] : 1750 WHITE NOTLEY, ESS, ENG [37928] : C1822 GWENNAP, CON, ENG [38069] : 1826 ST MARYLEBONE, LND, ENG [38282] : 1855+ USA [34274] : SARAH 1828 HAMPDEN, ME, USA [36944] : 1880+ BUCHANAN CO., IA, USA [38323]

SNOWBALL 1835+ WITTON GILBERT, DUR, ENG [37878]

SNOWDEN 1857-1870 INVERLEIGH, VIC, AUS [34452] : 1870S MULMER, ONT, CAN [34937] : PRE 1813 HALTWHISTLE, NBL, ENG [34452] : 1800S WAKEFIELD, YKS, ENG [34715] : ALL NBL & DUR, ENG [38754] : 1840+ DOVER, KEN & WA, ENG & AUS [37888]

SNOWDON 1650-1800 ALSTON, CUL, ENG [37290] : ALL NBL & DUR, ENG [38754] : 1840+ DOVER, KEN & WA, ENG & AUS [37888]

SNOWMAN PRE 1870 PEMBROKE DOCK, PEM, WLS [38718]

SNOXTON ALL UK [36062]

SNUGGS PRE 1900 BRK & BKM, ENG [34472]

SNUSHELS DANIEL PRE 1756 THORNEY & WISBECH, CAM, ENG [36149] : DANIEL PRE 1756 SANDTOFT, YKS, ENG [36149]

SNUTCH C1800 LEI, ENG [36694]

SNYDER PRE 1839 FRONTENAC, ONT, CAN [38434] : C1830 STEENWYKERWOLD, OIJ, NL [36283] : 1735+ KNOWLTON TWP., NJ, USA [34130] : 1832-1881 COOPERSTOWN, BROWN CO., IL, USA [35316] : JOHN 1850-1855 PHILADELPHIA, PA, USA [35320] : 1800-1850 LEHIGH, PA, USA [36449] : TYRUS 1840-1890 DAUPHIN, PA, USA [36908] : 1750+ FAYETTE CO., PA, USA [36956]

SOADY C1821 ST MARTIN, CON, ENG [35251]

SOANE 1750 CHEDISTON, SFK, ENG [37928]

SOANES 1780+ CORTON, SFK, ENG [35726] : 1860 ENG [36655] : PRE 1820 FOREST HILL, OXF, ENG [37832]

SOAR PRE 1802 NOTTINGHAM, NTT, ENG [37298] : ALL ST JUST IN ROSELAND, CON, ENG [37298] : PRE 1800 NTT, ENG [37739] : PRE 1830 GREASLEY & EASTWOOD, NTT & DBY, ENG [38254]

SOARES 1875-1890S AZORES, PT [36337]

SOBIESKI 1648 KRAKOW, KR, POL [35369]

SOBOTKA 1850-1899 SEDLICE, CS [34251]

SOCKETT 1860+ YKS, ENG & CAN [37525]

SOCKLIN C1650-1700S CLIFTON, BDF, ENG [36289]

SODEN 1840S LET, IRL [34223]

SODER 1898+ TOOTING GRAVENEY, LND, ENG [36519]

SODERBERG 1750+ LERSJOFORS & SUNNE, VARMLAND, SWE [38551]

SODERLUND KAROLINE K. PRE 1900 ADALSLIDEN PARISH, VASTERNORRLAND, SWE [34481]

SODERSTROM 1825-1880 SWE [36331]

SOEDER PRE 1845 GER [38437]

SOFTLEY PRE 1840 BRITON FERRY, GLA, WLS [37133]

SOHIER 1750-1800 JER, CHI [35494] : 1750-1800 QUETTREVILLE, BN, FRA [34552]

SOHLBERG 1720-800 OSTRA VEMMENHOG, MAL, SWE [36320]

SOHLGREN 1620-1800 STOCKHOLM, SWE [36320]

SOIRDET 1798-1885 BROMPTON, LND, ENG [34002]

SOLDER 1790-1860 BAV, GER [38199]

SOLE 1810S CHISLEHURST, KEN, ENG [35261] : PRE 1837 SRY & SSX, ENG [37771]

SOLE (SEE SOUL) [33844]

SOLESBURY PRE 1800 MILTON ERNEST, BDF, ENG [34311]

SOLHEIM 1600+ UVDAL, NUMEDAL, NOR [36905]

SOLITT C1859 BRIDLINGTON, NRY, ENG [36759]

SOLIVAN 1700-1830 CAYEY, CAGUAS & SAN JUAN, PUERTO RICO, USA [36937]

SOLLERMANN C1800 LEER, NDS, BRD [38685]

SOLLEY 1820 PRESTON, KEN, ENG [35912] : ALL WORLDWIDE [37083]

SOLLY STEPHEN PRE 1800 CANTERBURY, KEN, ENG [37083] : ALL WORLDWIDE [37083]

SOLOMAN PRE 1727 CON, ENG [33777]

SOLOMON LION 1800+ HOBART, TAS, AUS [33875] : WILLIAM 1850+ NEWTOWN, NSW, AUS [34979] : 1700+ TAS & KEN, AUS, ENG & [36266] : 1750-1825 PHILIPSBURG, QUE, CAN & USA [37486] : 1800S TRURO, CON, ENG [34292] : PRE 1794+ EWHURST & BODIAM, SSX, ENG [34423] : 1800+ ST ENODER, CON, ENG [34666] : PRE 1800 ST COLUMB MINOR, CON, ENG [35500] : 1700-1850 PLYMOUTH, DEV, ENG [36025] : 1700+ LAMBETH, SRY, ENG [36256] : 1700-1830 LND & SRY, ENG [36491] : LOUIS 1872+ ST CLEMENT DANES, MDX, ENG [36519] : RACHEL 1878+ ST CLEMENT DANES, MDX, ENG [36519] : MICHAEL 1839+ ST ANNES WESTMINSTER, MDX, ENG [36519] : 1800-1850 LIVERPOOL, LAN, ENG [36618] : ELIZ. 1780+ NORWICH, NFK, ENG [37640] : PRE 1858 CANNINGTON, SOM, ENG [37876] : 1870+ WESPORT, NZ [34292] : 1850+ PORT CHALMERS, OTG, NZ [36261] : PRE 1900 GALICIA, SU & POL [34146]

SOLOMONS 1880S+ REDFERN, NSW, AUS [37309] : PRE 1900 MILE END, MDX, ENG [36107] : 1790+ LONDON, ENG [36995] : 1830S LND, ENG [37309]

SOLSBY PRE 1750 SNODLAND, KEN, ENG [34725]

SOLTERBECK PRE 1794 SHO, GER [38669]

SOLWAY PRE 1850 DRAYTON, SOM, ENG [35853] : ALL WORLDWIDE [36796]

SOMERFELDT PRE 1860 POS, GER [38052]

SOMERS PRE 1850 WALTON, SOM, ENG [36676] : 1820-1910 CURROW, CASTLE ISLAND, KER, IRL [33947] : 1820-1880 GLASGOW, LKS, SCT [34928] : PRE 1872 MI & NY, USA [37574]

SOMERSET (SEE SUMMER [35261]

SOMERVILLE C1832-1870 HOBART, TAS, AUS [35726] : PRE 1830+ ENNISKILLEN, FER, IRL [35453] : PRE 1859 SCALLON & KILSKEERY, FER, IRL [35779] : PRE 1870 CAV, IRL [36255] : 1800+ ENNISKILLEN, FER, IRL [37172] : 1800+ CHURCH HILL, FER, IRL [37172] : ALL LKS, SCT

[33975] : C1785 CARLUKE, LKS, SCT [34127] : ALL EDINBURGH, MLN, SCT [34619] : PRE 1849 CAMBUSLANG, LKS, SCT [34706] : 1800S GLASGOW, LKS, SCT [35767] : 1066 SCT [37008]

SOMERVILLE-WOODIWISS ALL WORLDWIDE [37059]

SOMES JOHN PRE 1788 TRING GROVE, HRT, ENG [34992]

SOMMERVILL 1710-1790 AUCHTERARDER, PER, SCT [36635]

SOMMERVILLE 1794 SYDNEY & PARRAMATTA, NSW, AUS [35082]

SOMNER PRE 1844 SCHULZDOLF, POM, GER [34584]

SONDERGAARD 1860-1880S THISTED, JUTLAND, DEN [36285]

SONE PRE 1930 LONDON, ENG [33883]

SONES C1800 CHEDISTON, SFK, ENG [37191]

SONKEY PRE 1600 LAN, ENG [38744]

SONNEN PRE 1870 DUSSELDORF, NRW, GER [38663]

SONNENBURG 1700-1780 GRABAU, POS, GER [38372]

SONNERSEN 1850-1870 SKIPPING & SKIVINGE, DEN [35158]

SONNIUS ALL WALCHEREN, ZEL, NL [38702]

SONNTAG ALL MARKTSCHELKEN, TRANSYLVANIA, RO [38519]

SONTER 1840+ PENNANT HILLS, NSW, AUS [35360] : PRE 1840 NORTHIAM, SSX, ENG [35360]

SOOVER 1849 MEDINA, OH, USA [36338]

SOPER PRE 1850 WOOLWICH, LND, ENG [37630] : ALL MORETONHAMPSTEAD, DEV, ENG [37722] : 1840-1900 DEV, ENG [38259] : 1700-1750 TAUNTON, MA, USA [38151]

SOPKE 1860 STOLP, POM, GER [34388]

SORBIE 1800+ CAMBUSNETHAN, LKS, SCT [36749]

SORE PRE 1839 SFK, ENG [36124] : PRE 1800 NTT, ENG [37739]

SORENSDATTER 1800+ VJELBY, DEN [35767] : 1830-1850S TAARS, JUTLAND, DEN [36285]

SORENSEN 1829-1888 CASINO, NSW, AUS [36281] : ALL COPENHAGEN, QLD, AUS [36881]

SORENSON 1850 YDING, DEN [34666] : 1870+ CANTY, NZ [34666]

SORLEY PRE 1861 LONG DALMAHOY, RATHO, MLN, SCT [34584]

SOROSEN 1887 WILCANNIA, NSW, AUS [34844]

SORRELL 1800 HEMPSTEAD, ESS, ENG [35067] : 1880+ HYTHE, KEN, ENG [35560] : 1850S HASTINGS, SSX, ENG [35560] : 1860+ ESS, ENG [37656] : PRE 1820 HUNDON, SFK, ENG [37913] : 1066-1750 UK [38107]

SORRELS 1744-1780 ALBEMARLE CO., VA, USA [38107]

SORROW HENRY 1800-1811 OGLETHORPE CO., GA, USA [38155]

SORRY PRE 1770 ABD, SCT [33914]

SORTER PRE 1750 BENDORF, RPR, GER [37811]

SOTRES C1860 DEV, ENG [35910]

SOUDER 1650-1750 LANCASTER CO., PA, USA [38118] : ALL WORLDWIDE [37785]

SOUERBERY ELIZA 1857+ COLLINGWOOD, VIC, AUS [35590]

SOUERBREY ELIZA 1857+ COLLINGWOOD, VIC, AUS [35590] : ELIZA PRE 1857 LONDON, ENG [35590]

SOUGHWEED 1800S USA [36569] : 1800S SAN FRANCISCO, CA, USA [36569] : ALL WORLDWIDE [36569]

SOUL ALL THE OLD PARK, RICHMOND, LND, ENG [33844]

SOULE PRE 1600 HAWKHURST, KEN, ENG [36972]
SOULEY 1800-1850 EGLISH, ARM, IRL [35006]
SOULIE ALL SCT [34373]
SOULIGNY DIT RAZEAU ALL QUE, CAN [38287]
SOULS PRE 1836 STONEHOUSE, GLS, ENG [37978]
SOULSBY ALL DUR, ENG [34293] : 1800 +
WALLSEND, NBL, ENG [37395] : PRE 1800
TANFIELD, DUR, ENG [37395]
SOUNSELVELLE PRE 1900 WORLDWIDE [36933]
SOUR 1800 + NY, USA [34129]
SOURBERY ELIZA PRE 1857 LONDON, ENG [35590]
SOUTAR C1832 STS, ENG [35854] : PRE 1860
DUNDEE, ANS, SCT [33845] : 1700 + PERTH, PER,
SCT [34419] : PRE 1860 SUT, SCT [36201]
SOUTER C1765-1863 CHEDBURGH & BURY ST
EDMUNDS, SFK, ENG [36874] : ALL SCT [33959] :
1880 + URQUHART, MOR, SCT [35460]
SOUTH PRE 1800 FAWLEY & SOUTHAMPTON,
HAM, ENG [36155] : C1856 ENG [36616] : THOMAS
PRE 1856 VIRGINIA WALTER, SRY, ENG [37481] :
PRE 1830 GREAT WIGBOROUGH, ESS, ENG
[37712] : PRE 1830 FINGRINGHOE, ESS, ENG
[37712] : PRE 1880 LONDON, ENG [38004] : 1760S
HAM, ENG [38206]
SOUTHALL 1800-1850 WOR, ENG [37038] : C1815
DUDLEY, WOR & WAR, ENG [37883] : PRE 1800
BIRMINGHAM, WAR, ENG [38084] : PRE 1750
KIDDERMINSTER, WOR, ENG [38420] : PRE 1800
WOR, ENG [38746]
SOUTHAM 1900-1990 SYDNEY, NSW, AUS [33778] :
1900 + STS, ENG [36183] : PRE 1900 OXF, ENG
[36183] : ALL UXBRIDGE, MDX, ENG [36743]
SOUTHAN OLIVER 1822-1897 GLOUCESTER, GLS,
ENG [38394]
SOUTHCOMBE 1850S + WINCHESTER, HAM, ENG
[38270]
SOUTHEE 1650-1900 CANTERBURY, KEN, ENG
[37251]
SOUTHEN PRE 1875 WALTHAM &
HASTINGLEIGH, KEN, ENG [36883]
SOUTHER 1700-1800 NEWCASTLE, NBL, ENG
[35094]
SOUTHERDEN ALL WORLDWIDE [37890]
SOUTHERN MARY PRE 1849 NEWTOWN, LEX, IRL
[36314]
SOUTHEY C1810 DURHAM, DUR, ENG [37834] :
1850S GRANGE, CUL, ENG [37834]
SOUTHGATE 1850 + LEARMONTH, VIC, AUS
[35856] : C1880 CAMBERWELL, LND, ENG [34862] :
1850 SWANDERTON, NFK, ENG [34890] : 1800 +
ENG [36287] : C1750-1900 WIX, ESS, ENG [36478] :
1750-1900 TATTINGSTONE, SFK, ENG [37042]
SOUTHON 1700-1900 BENENDEN, KEN, ENG
[37338] : 1700-1900 ROTHERFIELD, SSX, ENG
[37338] : ALL WORLDWIDE [37338]
SOUTHORN ALL MIDLANDS, ENG [37375]
SOUTHWARD PRE 1830 PRESTON & KIRKHAM,
LAN, ENG [38254]
SOUTHWELL PRE 1830 MARCH, CAM, ENG [34197]
: 1847 BRIGHTON, SSX, ENG [36280] : 1804 +
LONDON, MDX, ENG [36280] : C1801
WEDNESFIELD, STS, ENG [36280] : 1880
LONDON, MDX, ENG [36280] : 1769 +
WHITTLESEY, CAM, ENG [38069] : C1800
LOCKERLEY, HAM, ENG [38700] : 1760 +
DUBLIN, IRL [36280] : 1811-1836 MAY, IRL [38492] :
ALL WORLDWIDE [33916]
SOUTHWICK 1870 LENAWEE CO., MI, USA [38192]
SOUTHWOOD C1870 DEV, ENG [34195] : PRE 1874
HONINGTON, LIN, ENG [35895] : PRE 1850 SOM,
ENG [37695]
SOUTHWORTH PRE 1850 LAN, ENG [35473]

SOUTTER 1750 + STEPNEY, LND, ENG [33986] :
1750-1830 ABERDEEN, ABD, SCT [33767] : PRE
1800 ANS, SCT [34041] : C1800 KCD, SCT [34041] :
PRE 1914 PER, SCT [34053] : 1850 + FERRYDEN,
ANS, SCT [36971] : 1800 + FETTERESSO, KCD, SCT
[36971]
SOVEY 1800 + CAYUGA, ONT, CAN [34132]
SOWARD 1829-1900 MDX, ENG [34683]
SOWDEN 1800 CAMBORNE, CON, ENG [34890] :
1700S STOKE CLIMSLAND, CON, ENG [34920] :
1700-1860 CAMBORNE, CON, ENG [38005]
SOWDER 1700 + MYLOR & GORRAN, CON, ENG
[35851]
SOWERBY ELIZA PRE 1857 LONDON, ENG [35590]
SOWERMIRE 1680-1700 MIDDLETON, WMD, ENG
[36635]
SOWERS 1880-1910 BROWN, OH & PA, USA [38054]
SOWTER 1840 + AUS [34871] : C1800 SHIRLAND,
DBY, ENG [35079] : 1812-81 DERBY, DBY, ENG
[37860]
SOWTON 1800 BERE ALSTON, DEV, ENG [35023]
SPACEY C1828 ISLIP, OXF, ENG [34281]
SPACKMAN ALL BRENTWOOD, ESS, ENG [36743]
SPAETH 1800-1900 LIMBACH, KMS, DDR [37798] :
ALL SASSENBACH WEIDEN, BAD, GER [36573]
SPAIN PRE 1900 MT GAMBIER, SA, AUS [35789] :
1700-1800S DEAL AREA, KEN, ENG [37714] : 1740-
1800 FORDWICH, KEN, ENG [37880]
SPALDING 1849 + SYDNEY, NSW, AUS [35443] :
PRE 1849 CROYDON, SRY, ENG [35443] : C1810
EDINBURGH, MLN, SCT [34713] : C1830 PORT
AUGUSTUS, INV, SCT [35859] : 1800 + KY, USA
[36965] : 1750-1860 BRIDGEWATER, NH, USA
[38045]
SPANN 1813 CALVELEY, CHS, ENG [35120]
SPANSWICK PRE 1860 EASTON, WIL, ENG [35346]
SPANTON PRE 1880 DUR, ENG [34293] : 1850 +
GREAT YARMOUTH, NFK, ENG [35726] : PRE
1810 NFK, ENG [36541] : 1820-1900 EAST OF
LONDON, MDX, ENG [36541] : 1900 +
BOKSBURG, TVL & CAPE, RSA [36541]
SPAREHAM 1763 + STAPENHILL, DBY, ENG [34011]
SPARHAWKE ALL WHITCHURCH, OXF, ENG
[36326]
SPARK PRE 1850 TOTNES, DEV, ENG [34268] : PRE
1775 CANTLAYHILLS, KCD, SCT [34613]
SPARKE 1880 + GRETA, NSW, AUS [36632]
SPARKES 1852 + SYDNEY, NSW, AUS [35801] :
1860 + DUBBO, NSW, AUS [36648] : 1780
TAUNTON, SOM, ENG [34204] : 1842
WOODBRIDGE, SFK, ENG [35639] : 1852 +
WANDSWORTH, SRY, ENG [35801] : PRE 1900
MAIDENHEAD, BRK, ENG [35954] : 1840 +
WESTMINSTER, MDX, ENG [36795] : MARIANNE
C1873-1963 LEICESTER & HALIFAX, WRY, ENG
[37311] : ARTHUR LEE C1840 + BURSLEM &
FARNDON, NTT, ENG [37311]
SPARKMAN 1800 + GOSPORT, HAM, ENG [36263] :
1750S ENG [37006]
SPARKS 1820S ST LUKES, MDX, ENG [34738] : 1795
ALVERSTOKE, HAM, ENG [36051] : PRE 1755
MITCHAM, SRY, ENG [37913] : 1790 + SCT [38423]
SPARLING 1860 + AUS [33859] : 1700 + CLACTON,
ESS, ENG [37376] : 1700 + THORPE LE SOKEN,
ESS, ENG [37376] : 1700 + KIRBY LE SOKEN, ESS,
ENG [37376] : 1700 + HOLLAND, ESS, ENG [37376]
: PRE 1860 DUBLIN, IRL [33859] : 1709 +
KILSCANNELL, LIM, IRL [33862]
SPARNON 1700-1900 ILLOGAN, CON, ENG [34697]
SPARROW 1920 + MOONEE PONDS, VIC, AUS
[35771] : C1813 BRISTOL, SOM, ENG [34195] : PRE
1900 NORTH LEIGH, OXF, ENG [34466] : 1830 +

LONDON, ENG [35982] : PRE 1900 LONDON, MDX, ENG [37749] : 1800S HANKERTON, WIL, ENG [37831] : C1780 LONG MELFORD, SFK, ENG [38078] : 1809 CAMBERWELL, SRY, ENG [38078] : 1850 ST PANCRAS, MDX, ENG [38078] : 1700-1900 HAVERHILL, SFK, ENG [38579] : PRE 1700 KEN & MA, ENG & USA [38746] : 1790-1820 ORLEANS, MA, USA [38099]

SPARTAN 1850+ GREAT YARMOUTH, NFK, ENG [35726]

SPASER 1780+ HISTON, CAM, ENG [34190]

SPASHETT ALL ENG [37228]

SPATH GEORGE 1830-1860 BAD, GER [36573] : PRE 1700 PETERZELL, WUE, GER [38679]

SPATHELI PRE 1650 HORNBERG, BAD, GER [38679]

SPATZ 1770-1820S PA, USA [37600]

SPAULDING 1800+ KY, USA [36965]

SPAVOLD 1780S EVERTON & RETFORD, NTT, ENG [36018]

SPEAGLE 1850-1880 SHELBY CO., IN, USA [36336]

SPEAK 1830-1880 SHEFFIELD, YKS, ENG [36262] : 1700-1850 SHEFFIELD & HANDSWORTH, WRY, ENG [36727] : PRE 1890 CAWNPORE, INDIA [36262] : PRE 1900 AUCKLAND, AKD, NZ [36262] : PRE 1900 THAMES, AKD, NZ [36262]

SPEAKMAN PRE 1800 LIVERPOOL, LAN, ENG [37389] : 1850-1870 ST HELENS, LAN, ENG [38763] : C1800 COR, IRL [33793]

SPEAR PRE 1900 BRATTON CLOVELLY, DEV, CON & GLA, ENG & WLS [37339]

SPEARBALL 1900 BOOROWA, NSW, AUS [37997]

SPEARING 1780 ALVERTSTOKE, HAM, ENG [34204] : ALL WORLDWIDE [33946]

SPEARNS 1700+ WORLDWIDE [38774]

SPEARS 1806 BRISBANE WATERS, NSW, AUS [35089] : JAMES 1804+ SYDNEY, NSW, AUS [36638] : 1773 LYE, SOM, ENG [35089] : PRE 1835 GREENLAW, BEW, ROX & ELN, SCT [33905] : C1850 AR, USA [36934] : 1817-1900 LAWRENCE CO., TN, USA [37029]

SPEASER PRE 1824 COR, IRL [33793]

SPECHT 1780-1800 RPF, GER [36908] : 1780-1850 DAUPHIN, PA, USA [36908]

SPECK ALL SHERBURN, ERY, ENG [35633] : 1800+ NORTON BY MALTON, YKS, ENG [35891]

SPECKENBACH ALL GER [34861]

SPEDDING ALL SUMMERGROVE, CUL, ENG [35009] : ALL WHITEHAVEN, CUL, ENG [35009] : 175001850 CUL & WES, ENG [36063] : ALL DUNEDIN, NZ [35467] : ALL AYR & GEELONG, AYR & VIC, SCT & AUS [35467]

SPEECHLEY 1750+ PETERBOROUGH, NTH, ENG [37223]

SPEED 1850+ WARRNAMBOOL, VIC, AUS [38082] : 1900+ MOOSEJAW, SAS, CAN [35627] : C1800 HEYDON, ESS, ENG [35592] : 1800S SALFORD, LAN, ENG [38290]

SPEEDY ALL BERWICK UPON TWEED, NBL, ENG [37704]

SPEELER C1816+ GOETHE, ANH, GER [35272] : C1850 OH, USA [37030]

SPEER ALL NELSON, NZ & IRL [36861]

SPEERS PRE 1900 MELBOURNE, VIC, AUS [35435] : PRE 1825 DON & ARM, IRL [35435]

SPEIDEL ALL LUNENBURG, NS, CAN [36713]

SPEIER 1700+ HELDENBERGEN, HEN, GER [37042]

SPEIGHT 1800S BROUGHTON IN FURNESS, CUL, ENG [36803] : PRE 1860 LEEDS, YKS, ENG [37094] : PRE 1675 LAN & WES, ENG [37706]

SPEIR 1840+ GLASGOW, SCT [38274] : 1791-1830 SARATOGA, NY, USA [38347]

SPEIRS 1812+ STRATHAVEN & FLEMING, LKS, SCT [37399]

SPEISER PRE 1840 BRETTHEIM, EHRINGSHAUSEN, WUE, GER [37510]

SPELLESY 1860+ COLLINGWOOD, VIC, AUS [35379]

SPELLMAN 1890-1923 BIRKENHEAD, LAN, ENG [36207] : 1800+ GALWAY, GAL, IRL & NZ [36257]

SPELTER PRE 1870 GREVENBROICH, NRW, GER [38663]

SPENCE 1850-1900 FARNHAM, NSW, AUS [35559] : 1850-1900 GOULBURN, NSW, AUS [35559] : 1800+ NFD, CAN [34637] : C1820 BIRMINGHAM, WAR, ENG [34456] : 1800+ WOODBRIDGE, SFK, ENG [34637] : 1700-1880 MASHAM, NRY, ENG [36472] : JOHN PRE 1810 YKS, ENG & CAN [35778] : PRE 1870 AHOGHILL, ANT, IRL [33964] : 1700+ DRUMCHORY, DON, IRL [34246] : C1820S BALLYMURPHY, DOW, IRL [34788] : C1873 BANGOR, DOW, IRL [34972] : 1700-1800S PORTGLENONE, ANT, IRL [36289] : 1700-1800S AHOGHILL, ANT, IRL [36289] : PRE 1860 MOR, ABD & BAN, SCT [34615] : 1770+ STROMNESS, OKI, SCT [35461] : 1750+ AYR, SCT [35499] : PRE 1841 DUNFERMLINE, STI, SCT [35559] : 1770-1860 HUNTLY, ABD, SCT [36762] : 1848-1990 SALCUTTS, AYR, SCT & AUS [34024] : 1800S BALT, MD, USA [38182]

SPENCELEY PRE 1949 OXSPRING, NTH SHEFFIELD, WRY, ENG [35751] : PRE 1730 GRINTON, YKS, ENG [37671]

SPENCER 1880+ QLD, AUS [33932] : 1867+ SCOTCHMAN'S LEAD, VIC, AUS [35487] : 1853+ CHEWTON, VIC, AUS [36644] : 1870+ WYNYARD, TAS, AUS [36644] : 1850+ SA, AUS [37186] : 1847+ HOBART, TAS, AUS [38262] : SAM 1725+ SHEPTON MALLET, SOM, ENG [34200] : MAGDALEN PRE 1800 LONDON, ENG [34247] : 1850-1914 BURNLEY, LAN, ENG [34408] : PRE 1850 PAULTON, SOM, ENG [34739] : FRANK C1850-1900 BRADFORD, YKS, ENG [34745] : FRANCIS PRE 1898 LEICESTER, LEI, ENG [34745] : C1870 HALIFAX, WRY, ENG [34752] : 1800S WALWORTH, LND, ENG [35126] : PRE 1830 MANCHESTER, LAN, ENG [35238] : PRE 1850 TARLETON, LAN, ENG [35473] : 1825+ DAWLISH, DEV, ENG [35487] : PRE 1700 ESS, ENG [35642] : 1800S HALIFAX, WRY, ENG [35744] : PRE 1831 GLS, ENG [35757] : 1800+ RADWAY, WAR, ENG [35970] : PRE 1900 BARKWAY & ROYSTON, HRT, ENG [36061] : C1800 WOODBRIDGE, SFK, ENG [36076] : 1800-1900 SOHO, MDX, ENG [36106] : 1800+ ROSSENDALE, LAN, ENG [36194] : PRE 1900 LEEDS, WRY, ENG [36228] : 1865+ SOUTHWALK, SRY, ENG [36271] : 1790+ MANCHESTER, ENG [36271] : 1820+ ROCHDALE, LAN, ENG [36271] : PRE 1800 KIDDERMINSTER, WOR & GLS, ENG [36379] : PRE 1780 CLARBOROUGH, NTT, ENG [36426] : 1840+ EAST RETFORD, NTT, ENG [36426] : STEPHEN PRE 1850 EAST, LND, ENG [36479] : STVN 1796-1860 THURSFORD, NFK, ENG [36564] : THOS 1700 GUNTHORPE, NFK, ENG [36564] : PRE 1850 DUR, ENG [36639] : PRE 1853 SWINFORD, LEI, ENG [36644] : PRE 1800 DOR, ENG [36679] : 1800+ LONDON, LND, ENG [36791] : ANN MARY 1844+ PETERSFIELD, HAM, ENG [36959] : ELIZABETH 1813+ BOSHAM, SSX, ENG [36959] : SAMUEL 1849+ PETERSFIELD, HAM, ENG [36959] : 1800S MDX, ENG [37186] : 1800+ RETFORD, NTT, ENG [37241] : 1860S NORWICH, NFK, ENG [37341] : C1700 SIDMOUTH, DEV, ENG [37356] : ALL

PENDLE, LAN, ENG [37379] : 1800-1900 WOTTON UNDER EDGE, GLS, ENG [37403] : C1770
BELTON, LEI, ENG [37536] : PRE 1850 NORWICH, NFK, ENG [37718] : C1700 WIRKSWORTH, DBY, ENG [37834] : 1500-1800 NEWCHURCH IN PENDLE, LAN, ENG [38251] : 1700-1840 SLAIDBURN, WRY, ENG [38251] : PRE 1880 CLAVERING, ESS, ENG [38262] : PRE 1880 RICKLING, ESS, ENG [38262] : BISHOP C1830-1860 MADRAS, INDIA [33952] : 1700-1780 BALLYMENA & LISBURN, ANT, IRL [37187] : 1900S NZ [36809] : 1700+ LEE, VA, USA [34163] : DAVID 1773-1780 WESTFIELD UNION CO., NJ, USA [36734] : MOSES 1800-1824 ALLEGANY CO., MD, USA [36734] : 1700+ WEST SUFFIELD, CT, USA [37026] : PRE 1830S ME, USA [37522] : 1805+ SC, USA [37592] : 1771-1832 SPENCERTOWN, NY, USA [38038] : 1760+ SPRINGFIELD, VT, USA [38235]
SPENDLEY PRE 1900 MANNINGTREE, ESS, ENG [36477]
SPENDLOVE PRE 1893 DERBY, DBY, ENG [34909]
SPERANZA PRE 1830 CASALBORDINO, CHIETI, ITL [34127]
SPERBECK ALL ALBANY CO., NY, USA [38176]
SPERNON ALL CON, ENG [34742]
SPERRIN 1850-1890 ISLINGTON, LND, ENG [36990] : AGNES 1870+ WLS & USA [37320]
SPERRYN 1600-1860 SOM, ENG [34722] : 1830-1860 BRISTOL, ENG [34722] : 1830-1860 INDIA [34722]
SPETHMANN 1800S ZARPEN, SHO, GER [34688]
SPETS ALL VARMLAND, SWE [34353]
SPETZ ALL VARMLAND, SWE [34353]
SPHAR THEODORUS 1780-1808 BERKELEY, WV, USA [38157] : PRE 1760 WILLIAMSBURG, VA, USA & CH [36969]
SPIBEY PRE 1900 BOLTON, LAN, ENG [37443]
SPICE 1840 KNOWSLEY & LANCASTER, LAN, ENG [35114] : C1830 HARTLIP, KEN, ENG [37007] : 1790 GOUDHURST, KEN, ENG [37215]
SPICER 1880+ QLD, AUS [33782] : C1900 ARTHURS CRK, VIC, AUS [35434] : 1840+ BOMBALA, NSW, AUS [35510] : 1840-1900 MELBOURNE, VIC, AUS [38082] : 1760 ENG [33910] : 1850+ LONDON, ENG [33960] : PRE 1850 ST PAULS WALDEN & HITCHIN, HRT, ENG [34450] : 1750-1825 LEICESTER, LEI, ENG [35320] : 1700-1800 WHITCHURCH & HANNINGTON, HAM, ENG [35422] : 1764 FOLKESTONE, KEN, ENG [35560] : PRE 1850 ENG [35945] : 1500-1700 BASCHURCH, SAL, ENG [36062] : GEORGE 1845-1924 BROMLEY, KEN, ENG [36180] : C1800-1850S HALESBURY, BKM, ENG [36289] : PRE 1870 ENG [37137] : 1888 KINGSBURY, SRY, ENG [37445] : 1800 USA [33910] : PRE 1875 GRENADIER IS, NY, USA [34365]
SPICKETT ALL LONDON, ENG [37743]
SPICKNELL ALL ENG [37273]
SPIEGL ALL GER & DDR [36656]
SPIERS C1800-1850 HIGHBROOK & EAST GRINSTEAD, SSX, ENG [36053] : 1750+ LONG CRENDON, BKM, ENG [36088] : 1811-1838 CHARLTON, NTH, ENG [38761] : C1847 BARRHEAD, LKS, SCT [34858] : 1840+ GLASGOW, SCT [38274] : 1800-1860S RUTHERGLEN, LKS, SCT & NZ [34882]
SPIES 1880 SHO, GER [37576]
SPIKE 1880+ QLD, AUS [35848]
SPIKER PRE 1800 PA, USA [36702]
SPILER C1816+ GOETHE, ANH, GER [35272] : C1850 OH, USA [37030]
SPILLARD PRE 1860 SYDNEY, NSW, AUS [37901]
SPILLER ALL DEV, ENG [34838] : 1690+ YARCOMBE, DEV, ENG [35112] : C1850 LONDON,

ENG [35807] : 1700-1890 LONDON, ENG [36894] : ALL SOM, ENG [37268] : 1850-1900 HENDERSDORF, SIL, GER [38599] : 1890-1912 TREHERBERT, GLA, WLS [37268]
SPILSBURY ALL STOCKPORT, CHS, ENG [34837] : PRE 1850+ BIRMINGHAM, ENG [35237]
SPILSTED 1780+ BATTLE, SSX, ENG [34288] : 1820+ SEDLESCOMBE, SSX, ENG [34288]
SPINDLEY C1796 HOLTON LE MOOR, LIN, ENG [35990]
SPINK PRE 1800 CAM, ENG [36388] : PRE 1830 SETTRINGTON, ERY, ENG [37913]
SPINKS 1850S THOROLD, ONT, CAN [36729] : HANNAH 1794 MELBURY SAMPFORD, DOR, ENG [34091] : HANNAH 1822 LONDON, ENG [34091] : 1839 BODHEY, NFK, ENG & AUS [34845]
SPINNER 1750+ WORTH, SANDWICH, KEN, ENG [35891] : PRE 1800 NORTHBOURNE, KEN, ENG [36532] : ALL CENTRALIA, IL, USA [35548]
SPINNEWEBER C1800 PRE, GER [34988]
SPINNEY PRE 1650 MANCHESTER, LAN, ENG [34162]
SPINNING ALL USA & ENG [38287]
SPITE MICHIEL PRE 1628 LIEGE, BEL [38563] : MICHIEL 1628+ NORRKOPING, SWE [38563]
SPITTAL ALL WORLDWIDE [35217]
SPITTALL 1530+ STIRLING, STI, SCT [35217] : ALL WORLDWIDE [37167]
SPITTLE PRE 1745 WESTERN ON THE GREEN, OXF, ENG [36281] : ALL ENG [37595]
SPITTLER 1774+ WIMSHEIM, WUE, GER [38667]
SPITTLES PRE 1900 KEN, ENG [37377]
SPITZ C1905 WINNIPEG, MAN, CAN [34521]
SPITZHIRN 1831 CHAM, BAV, GER [38322]
SPITZIG C1844-C1863 PERTH, ONT, CAN [36714] : 1863+ BRUCE, ONT, CAN [36714] : 1669-C1834 TAUBERBISCHOFSHEIM, BAD, GER [36714] : C1834-1844 USA [36714]
SPIVAK 1870+ OLKHOVETS, UKR, SU [34256]
SPIVEY 1700+ HECKMONDWIKE, WRY, ENG [34328] : 1790-1820 MIRFIELD, WRY, ENG [36111]
SPLAN 1820+ ONT, CAN [36687]
SPLIEHALOVA ALL BOHEMIA, CS [36881]
SPOARD ALL ENG [37846]
SPODE 1821+ AUS [37846] : ALL ENG [37846]
SPOHN ALL WORLDWIDE [38616]
SPOHR ALL WORLDWIDE [35541]
SPONG PRE 1890 STOURMOUTH, KEN, ENG [35045] : PRE 1890 BLOOMSBURY, LND, ENG [35045] : 1500+ ENG [38498] : 1700-1800 CHERTSEY, SRY, ENG [38498]
SPONHEIMER ALL HIGHWORTH, LND & MDX, ENG [34614] : ALL DARMSTADT, HEN, GER [34614]
SPOONER 1820+ BDF, ENG [34764] : PRE 1750 LND, ENG [34804] : SAMUEL 1700S LONDON, ENG [36527] : 1750-1800 HACKNEY, MDX, ENG [36527] : 1840-1920 MDX, ENG [36527] : 1800+ VT, USA [38235]
SPOOR 1840+ HOBART, TAS, AUS [36622] : 1850+ COLLINGWOOD, KYNETON & TYLDEN, VIC, AUS [36622] : PRE 1830 NEWCASTLE, NBL, ENG [36583] : PRE 1840 LONDON, ENG [36622]
SPORAN 1500+ NORE, NUMEDAL, NOR [36905]
SPORLE 1860-1870 COLN, RPR, GER [38528]
SPORNE 1700-1800 STANHOE, NFK, ENG [38453]
SPOTSWOOD 1600-1850 BELLAGHY, LDY, IRL [33851]
SPRACKLIN ALL NFD, CAN & USA [38352]
SPRACKLING PRE 1900 DORCHESTER, DOR, ENG [36529]

SPRAGG 1783-1900 KINGS CO., NB, CAN & USA [34366] : 1650-1783 HEMPSTEAD, FISHKILL, NY, USA [34366]

SPRAGUE 1800S ARTHURETTE, NB, CAN [37423] : 1870S EXETER, DEV, ENG [35865] : C1820 WHITESTONE, DEV, ENG [36265] : 1820S DUXBURY, MA, USA [38223] : 1820 NY, USA [38362]

SPRAKE PRE 1780 DOR & SOM, ENG [35098] : PRE 1880 IOW, ENG [35745]

SPRANKLE PRE 1850 USA [37604]

SPRATLEY PRE 1770 ABINGER, SRY, ENG [33905]

SPRATT 1850+ SMITHFIELD, NSW, AUS [35874] : 1870+ CHICHESTER, SSX, ENG [34338] : 1800 KEN, ENG [34940] : ALL WOOTTON RIVERS, WIL, ENG [35874] : 1800-1900 EXETER, DEV, ENG [37378] : 1895+ NZ [34338] : 1830+ AYTON, BEW, SCT [35341] : PRE 1850+ PHILADELPHIA, PA, USA [36578]

SPRAY 1700+ NTT, ENG [34405] : 1870+ SNEINTON & NOTTINGHAM, NTT, ENG [36105] : PRE 1800 SSX, ENG [36501] : 1700+ MILTON & GRAVESEND, LND, ENG [36818] : PRE 1830 OH, USA [38217]

SPREADBURY PRE 1940 FREMANTLE, WA, AUS [36976]

SPREIGHTON ALL WORLDWIDE [34951]

SPRENCKEL PRE 1800 WORLDWIDE [37604]

SPRENGER 1887 INGOLSBY, QLD, AUS [37174] : PRE 1884 GRUMS, POM, GER [37174] : ALL WORLDWIDE [37968]

SPRENKEL PRE 1850 USA [37604]

SPRIET ALL ZWEVEZELE, WVL, BEL [38656] : ALL TIELT, WVL, BEL [38656] : PRE 1845 SERAING, LGE, BEL [38656] : ALL PITTEM, WVL, BEL [38656] : ALL EGEM, WVL, BEL [38656] : ALL WINGENE, WVL, BEL [38656] : PRE 1928 ONT, CAN [38656] : PRE 1850 TOURCOING, NOR, FRA [38656] : PRE 1850 ARMENTIERES, NOR, FRA [38656] : PRE 1907 LOWELL, MA, USA [38656] : PRE 1893 MOULINE, IL, USA [38656] : PRE 1905 FRASER, MI, USA [38656] : PRE 1893 DETROIT, MI, USA [38656] : PRE 1920 KANSAS CITY, KS, USA [38656] : PRE 1909 BAKER, OR, USA [38656]

SPRIGGS 1875+ SA, AUS [34777] : ALL CAM, ENG [34660] : PRE 1823 GRETHAM, RUT, ENG [35091] : 1775+ BKM, ENG [35476]

SPRIGHTON ALL WORLDWIDE [34951]

SPRILING PRE 1877 KIRCHDORF, WPR, GER [34567]

SPRIMICH 1800S RAGUSU, DALMATIA, YU [33972]

SPRINAGE C1820 FINSBURY, MDX, ENG [36099]

SPRING 1880S COOMA, NSW, AUS [34198] : C1800 WATFORD, HRT, ENG [34223]

SPRINGALL C1800-1900 LND & NFK, ENG [34007] : 1825+ CASTLEACRE, NFK, ENG [37483]

SPRINGER 1880+ KY, USA [38058]

SPRINGETT 1836 LOOSE, KEN, ENG [34142] : PRE 1860 COLCHESTER, ESS, ENG [36116] : 1820-1850 WISSINGTON, ESS, ENG [36116]

SPRINGFORD HUDSON 1840+ MELBOURNE, VIC, AUS [34904] : 1840+ TAS, AUS [34904]

SPRINGHALL C1800-1900 SALLE, NFK, ENG [34007] : 1770-1825 LONDON &, WIL, ENG [34191]

SPRINGHAM PRE 1791 ENG [33777]

SPRINGLE C1700-1800 SALLE, NFK, ENG [34007]

SPRINGOLD C1600-1700 NFK, ENG [34007]

SPRINGSTEEL ALL SPRINGFIELD, IL, USA [34409]

SPRINGSTEEN 1786+ WEST LINCOLN, ONT, CAN [34094]

SPRINKLE PRE 1850 USA [37604]

SPRINKS 1800-1850 LONDON, MDX, ENG [38115]

SPRINT 1800S PORTADOWN, ARM, IRL [36858]

SPROTT 1500+ BUTLER CO., PA, USA & SCT [36970]

SPROTTE 1811+ SOMMERFELD, BRA, GER [35391]

SPROULE JOHN C1815-1861 WESTBROOK, NS, CAN [34340] : 1800S CANNINGTON, ONT, CAN [38418] : JOHN 1771-C1815 LONDONDERRY, LDY, IRL [34340] : JAMES 1831+ TYR, IRL & AUS [37161]

SPRUCE PRE 1879 WOLVERHAMPTON, STS, ENG [35864]

SPRUHAN 1800-1860 THOMASTOWN, KIK, IRL [34687]

SPRURER 1914+ RICHMOND, VIC, AUS [34568]

SPRY 1849+ PORT ELLIOTT, SA, AUS [35443] : 1821 EAST STONEHOUSE, DEV, ENG [34195] : PRE 1825 LEWTRENCHARD, DEV, ENG [34504] : ALL CON, ENG [35628] : 1800+ LITTLE BRICKHILL, BKM, ENG [36756] : 1600+ ASHWATER & TETCOTT, DEV, ENG [37356] : C1880 PLYMOUTH & SIDMOUTH, DEV, ENG [37356] : 1865+ WANGANUI, NZ [35443] : C1900 CARDIFF, GLA, WLS [37356] : ALL WORLDWIDE [37356]

SPUFFORD 1910S STAINES, MDX, ENG [37332]

SPUITH PRE 1855 TRAKEHNIN, PRE, GER [38191]

SPUR ALL WORLDWIDE [36463]

SPURGEON 1750-1850 LOWESTOFT, SFK, ENG [34822] : 1720-1750 FREDERICK CO., MD, USA [37011]

SPURGIN 1850-1860 KNOX CO., OH, USA [38105]

SPURR 1840+ TAS, AUS [36754] : 1650-1800 NEWBOULD & CHESTERFIELD, DBY & WRY, ENG [36147] : PRE 1840 SHEFFIELD, WRY, ENG [36754] : ALL WORLDWIDE [36463]

SPURRE ALL WORLDWIDE [36463]

SPURRIER 1914+ RICHMOND, VIC, AUS [34568]

SPURRILL 1850+ CASTLEFORD, YKS, ENG [36846]

SPURWAY ALL WORLDWIDE [37264]

SQUARE 1680+ BRIXHAM, DEV, ENG [36000]

SQUIBB PRE 1840 LISSAN GROVES & HOUGHTON, SA, AUS & ENG [33890] : 1756 FORDINGTON, DOR, ENG [33967] : ALL BRISTOL, GLS, ENG [36744] : 1600+ STOKE ABBOT, DOR, ENG [37206] : 1800+ LONDON, MDX, ENG [37483]

SQUIER 1730S WOOTTON BASSETT, WIL, ENG [33918] : 1790 PA, USA [38143]

SQUIRE 1830+ WARKWORTH, NSW, AUS [33893] : JOHN 1850+ ARMIDALE, NSW, AUS [35462] : WILLIAM 1857+ IPSWICH, QLD, AUS [35462] : 1770S STANFORD, BDF, ENG [33893] : 1800+ HERTFORD, HRT, ENG [33893] : 1840+ ROBOROUGH, DEV, ENG [34075] : PRE 1850 PITNEY & SOMERTON, SOM, ENG [35462] : PRE 1700 DOR, ENG [36679] : 1800-1850 LONDON & ST LEONARDS, LND, ENG [37187] : ALL ST PANCRAS, LND, ENG [37321] : 1650-1730 SKIPTON & SLAIDBURN, WRY, ENG [38251] : 1860S ST NINIANS, STI, SCT [35075] : 1850-1920 LENINGRAD, SU [37670]

SQUIRES C1807 THURCASTON, LEI, ENG [34661] : CHARLOTTE PRE 1835 LONDON, ENG [35234] : ALL WADDINGTON, LIN, ENG [35746] : ALL STICKFORD, LIN, ENG [35746] : ALL WELLINGORE, LIN, ENG [35746] : ALL HOUGH ON THE HILL, LIN, ENG [35746] : 1750-1900 YEOVIL, SOM, ENG [37378] : PRE 1910 BIGGLESWADE, BDF, ENG [37671] : ALL PERQUIMANS CO., NC, USA [36557] : 1790-1850 NORTH HERO, VT, USA [38133]

SRYGLEY 1744-1790 BUCKS CO., PA, USA [37578] : 1790+ GREEN CO., KY, USA [37578] : 1790-1860 AL, USA [37578]

STAAB 1860-1880 MERCER CO., OH, USA [38573] : 1855-1865 KNOX CO., OH, USA [38573]

STABEL PRE 1800 BRETZENHEIM, RPF, GER [38681]

STABEN 1860-1880 BENDIGO, VIC, AUS [35726] : 1880-1910 POOWONG, VIC, AUS [35726] : 1810-1855 DORFSTADT, SHO, GER [35726]

STABLE 1750+ LND, ENG [36858]

STABLEFORTH PRE 1900 HULL, YKS, ENG [37433]

STABLER PRE 1870 DEERHAM, CUL, ENG [33870] : C1800-1850 DARLINGTON, DUR, ENG [36053] : 1700-1760 SKIPSEA, YKS, ENG [37011]

STABLES PRE 1788 YKS, ENG [38080] : 1800-1810 ABD, SCT [37263]

STACE PRE 1867 PIDDINGHOE, SSX, ENG [37610] : PRE 1800 SSX, ENG [37875]

STACEY 1800S SORELL, TAS, AUS [34971] : 1870 DAYLESFORD, VIC, AUS [35204] : PRE 1900 OATLANDS, TAS, AUS [36777] : 1860+ NSW, AUS [37176] : 1836+ ELGIN CO., ONT, CAN [37490] : ALL DONCASTER & CONISBOROUGH, YKS, ENG [34789] : ALL PONTEFRACT & AUSTERFIELD, YKS, ENG [34789] : C1831 WOLVERHAMPTON, STS, ENG [34893] : 1700S WADWORTH, YKS, ENG [35830] : WILLIAM 1814 HAM & MDX, ENG [35870] : 1800-1860 BATHAMPTON, SOM, ENG [36262] : C1800S FOVANT, WIL, ENG [36289] : PRE 1850 WOORE, STS, ENG [36488] : 1850+ LICHFIELD, STS, ENG [36488] : PRE 1850 MUCKLESTONE & MUCKLETON, STS & SAL, ENG [36488] : C1825 KEN, ENG [36490] : 1750-1850 LANGPORT, SOM, ENG [36776] : PRE 1880 AUCKLAND, AKD, NZ [36262]

STACK HENRY THOMAS PRE 1844 ST GILES, ENG [34557] : PRE 1850 CORK, COR, IRL [35323] : MARY 1879+ KER, IRL [38233]

STACKELROTH PRE 1837 GER [34840]

STACKER 1850+ OTTAWA CO. & CUYAHOGA CO., OH, USA [38369] : ALL USA & GER [38369]

STACKHOUSE ALL WORLDWIDE [36347]

STACY ALL CON & DEV, ENG [38735] : PRE 1690 BURLINGTON, NJ, USA [34573] : 1800-1830 FRANKLIN CO., NC, USA [38770]

STADHAM PRE 1794 HAMPDEN, BKM, ENG [37726]

STADLER 1800-1925 KAMENKA, SARATOV, USSR [38133]

STAEDTNER ALL WORLDWIDE [35606]

STAER 1890-1930 DETROIT, MI, USA [35084]

STAERKEL PRE 1850 NORKA, SU & WORLD [37511]

STAFF PRE 1750 NFK, ENG [34707] : 1780-1850+ NORWICH, NFK, ENG [35594] : PRE 1900 NFK, ENG [37256]

STAFFORD MICHEAL C1891 ADELAIDE, SA, AUS [35729] : MICHEAL C1910 DUNGOG, NSW, AUS [35729] : MICHEAL 1910-1930 BANKSTOWN, NSW, AUS [35729] : 1880+ ST MARY'S, NB, CAN [34256] : 1900S VANCOUVER, BC, CAN [37331] : 1722 MELLOR, DBY, ENG [34474] : ALL LEI, NTH & DBY, ENG [34821] : ALL LND, NTT & DEV, ENG [34821] : ALL STS, WAR & WOR, ENG [34821] : PRE 1865 LAN, CHS & STS, ENG [35137] : PRE 1880 STAMFORD, LIN, ENG [37171] : RHODA 1852+ LEI, ENG [37312] : PRE 1819 CLAYBROOK, LEI, ENG [37346] : PRE 1860 CAV, IRL [35113] : 1818+ MONAGHAN, MOG, IRL [35416] : PRE 1850 FLORENCE COURT, FER, IRL [35818] : MICHEAL 1863-1867 WAIKATO & AUCKLAND, NZ [35729] : ALL USA [34821]

STAGG 1850-1948 BENDOC, VIC, AUS [33934] : C1850 NFD, CAN [33852] : C1850 COKER, SOM, ENG [37233] : ALL COKER & YEOVIL, SOM, ENG [37269] : C1750-1850 NTH & NTT, ENG [37520] : ALL

MILTON LILBOURNE, WIL, ENG [38489] : WILLIAM 1820+ NELSON, NZ [34667]

STAHL JOHN H. 1870-1890 VIENNA, OES [38134] : 1770+ LW, POL [38650]

STAHLEN 1730+ KELLINGHUSEN, SHO, GER [37542]

STAHLHUT ALL AUS [37316] : PRE 1832 HANNOVER, HBG, GER [37316]

STAIG 1800S KIRKCALDY, FIF, SCT [34914]

STAINES 1842+ SYDNEY, NSW, AUS [35439] : C1800 MOUNTNESSING, ESS, ENG [33841] : PRE 1850 ESS, ENG [33847] : 1850+ LEICESTER, LEI, ENG [35169] : PRE 1842 NORTH KILWORTH, LEI, ENG [35439] : C1790 COGGESHALL, ESS, ENG [37053]

STAINES (SEE STAYNES [34376]

STAINFORTH 1770 MARYLEBONE, LND, ENG [35261]

STAINTON 1840+ MIDDLESEX, ONT, CAN [34527] : PRE 1840 SCARBOROUGH, ONT, CAN [34527] : C1840 NORTHUMBERLAND & DURHAM CO., ONT, CAN [34527] : PRE 1840 KENDAL, WES, ENG [34527] : 1860+ MT, USA [34527]

STAIR 1700S UPPER CLATFORD, HAM, ENG [34709]

STAIRMAND 1875+ DARLINGTON, DUR, ENG [34873]

STAIT 1870+ MAN, CAN [34160]

STAITE ALL WORLDWIDE [36922]

STAKE KAJSA 1820-1845 OSTMARK, VARMLAND, SWE [38556]

STAKER 1873+ ALLENS CK, KAPUNDA, SA, AUS [35771] : 1940+ BROKEN HILL, NSW, AUS [35771]

STALDER C1926 HABERFIELD, NSW, AUS [35515] : C1870 STS, ENG [35515] : C1880 BIRMINGHAM, ENG [35515]

STALENHOEF ALL AMERSFOORT, LITR, NL [33751] : ALL AMERSFOORT, UTR, NL [38692]

STALEY ALL NY, USA [36664] : 1700S-1820 HAGERSTOWN, MD, VA & OH, USA [38050]

STALF 1840-1880 DARMSTADT, HES, BRD [36952] : 1880+ QUINCY, ADAMS CO., IL, USA [36952]

STALKER DUNCAN 1844+ HOBART, TAS, AUS [35209] : 1810S-1900 SATTERTHWAITE & HAWSHEAD, LAN, ENG [38443] : DUNCAN PRE 1844 PER, SCT [35209] : PRE 1850 CLEISH, KRS, SCT [35457] : 1600-1781 DUNFERMLINE, FIF, SCT [36894]

STALLABRASS 1853 ROYSTON, CAM, ENG [38364]

STALLARD C1880 SYDENHAM, KEN, ENG [34362] : 1800+ NEWTON, HAM, ENG [35644]

STALLIBRASS ALL WORLDWIDE [37741]

STALLINGA PRE 1850 SNEEK, FRI, NL [38646]

STALLION 1650+ NORWICH, NEW LONDON CO., CT, USA [38745]

STALLWORTHY 1870+ HAY, NSW & VIC, AUS [38213] : 1780+ FAKENHAM, NFK, ENG [34092] : 1800+ PADBURY, BKM, ENG [38213]

STAM 1748-1808 ZWARTSLUIS & SCHUTSLOOT, OIJ, NL [34398]

ST AMAND PRE 1843 ST POLYCARPE, QUE, CAN & FRA [37443]

STAMATOPOULOS 1880-1920 MEGALOPOLIS, PELOPONESUS, GR [38123] : 1910-1960 CAMBRIDGE, MA, USA [38123]

STAMBAZZE PRE 1900 ITL [38125]

STAMFORD 1850+ LONDON, MDX, ENG [38263]

STAMM 1800S WURZBERG, HES, BRD [35340]

STAMMERS PRE 1839 ANGMERING, SSX, ENG [37972]

STAMP PRE 1800 HOTHAM, ERY, ENG [36059] : 1700-1990 BRIXHAM, DEV, ENG [36398] : ALL KEN, ENG [37407] : 1800+ EXETER, DEV, ENG [37617]

STAMPER 1860+ MOOSEJAW, SAS, CAN [35627] :
1856 MORGAN, KY, USA [38022]

STAMPS PRE 1800 NOR, ENG [34383] : 1750-1795
FAUQUIER CO., VA, USA [38763]

STANAWAY 1800-1850 DEV & CON, ENG [37411]

STANBROOK C1800S+ ANDOVER, HAM, ENG
[37868]

STANCLIFFE ALL ADDINGHAM, WRY, ENG
[38577]

STANDAGE C1795 ROTHWELL, YKS, ENG [37002]

STANDEN 1850+ NSW, AUS [35472] : PRE 1850 SA,
AUS [35472] : 1800S MAITLAND, NSW, AUS [35881]
: 1800S MELBOURNE, VIC, AUS [35926] : JOHN
PRE 1770 BREDE & WESTFIELD, SSX, ENG
[34847] : PRE 1721 WHATLINGTON, SSX, ENG
[35211] : PRE 1860 EGERTON, KEN, ENG [35799] :
1800S HOLLINGTON, SSX, ENG [35881] : C1722
HARTFIELD & BOLNEY, SSX, ENG [36384]

STANDERFER PRE 1860 IL, USA [36544] : C1860
MOULTRIE CO., IL, USA [36544] : ALL
WORLDWIDE [36965]

STANDEVEN PRE 1820 HALIFAX, YKS, ENG [38512]

STANDGROOM C1840 YEOVIL, SOM, ENG [35714]

STANDIDGE PRE 1795 LEEDS AREA, YKS, ENG
[37002]

STANDING ALL NSW, AUS [35520] : PRE 1860
FOLKESTONE, KEN, ENG [36067] : PRE 1850
STEPNEY, MDX, ENG [37259] : 1700+ SSX, ENG
[38261]

STANDISH 1700S PETERBOROUGH, NTH & HUN,
ENG [34032] : C1640 ENG [34395] : PRE 1760 LAN,
ENG [34397] : 1630-1850 MA, USA [37538]

STANDLEY 1830 SOHO, LND, ENG [34731] : PRE
1850 WARBOROUGH, LEI, ENG [36387]

STANDON 1780+ BRIGHTON, ENG [35520]

ST ANDREW ALL WORLDWIDE [37379]

STANDRING 1700S MANCHESTER &
HOLLINWOOD, LAN, ENG [34181] : 1791-1811
ROCHDALE, LAN, ENG [36606]

STANFIELD JOSEPH 1824-1835 EXETER FM, NSW,
AUS & CAN [36311] : C1750 GOSPORT, HAM, ENG
[34456] : PRE 1789 ENG [34547] : ALL NFK & YKS,
ENG [35460] : PRE 1900 SHEFFIELD, WRY & LIN,
ENG [36477] : 1860S IRL [38226] : D'ARCY A. 1861-
1901 (ACTOR) LEEDS, WRY, ENG &, RSA & AUS
[36311] : JOSEPH 1808-1875 CLWYD &
LUDDENHAM, EXETER FM, NSW, WLS & AUS
[36311]

STANFORD 1800-1850S ENG [35011] : 1817+
AIBOURNE, SSX, ENG [36212] : ALL DUR, ENG
[37929] : 1850+ LONDON, MDX, ENG [38263] : PRE
1780 BOARDMAN, POLAND, OH, USA [38231] :
PRE 1850 WALWORTH CO., WI, USA [38231]

STANFORTH ALL NRY, ENG [37929]

STANHOPE PRE 1850 KIRKHAM, LAN, ENG [37318]
: 1800-1850 LEI, ENG [38478] : 1800-1850 RUT, ENG
[38478]

STANIFORD ALL HAM, ENG [34218]

STANIFORTH 1770 MARYLEBONE, LND, ENG
[35261]

STANILAND PRE 1794 NEWARK & EAST
DRAYTON, NTT, ENG [38248]

STANLAKE 1840+ FOOTSCRAY, VIC, AUS [34796] :
1814+ DARTINGTON, DEV, ENG [34796] : 1759+
NORTH PETHERWIN, CON, ENG [34796] : 1781+
ST KEW, CON, ENG [34796]

STANLEY 1841+ QLD, AUS [35144] : PRE 1890
NEWTOWN, NSW, AUS [35781] : 1850-1900
LAMBETH, LND, ENG [34469] : PRE 1870
CHESTERFIELD, DBY, ENG [34736] : C1817
CARLISLE, CUL, ENG [34851] : C1840
STOCKPORT, CHS, ENG [34851] : C1860

HANDSWORTH, STS, ENG [34914] : JOHN PRE
1830 HAM, ENG [35713] : 1700-1900 WAR & NTH,
ENG [36007] : GEORGE 1840-1850 CLAPTON,
WOR, ENG [36018] : 1750+ TAKELEY, ESS, ENG
[36123] : 1800+ ST JOHN BAPTIST HOXTON,
LND, ENG [36863] : ALL FOLESHILL, WAR, ENG
[37265] : PRE 1850 YKS, ENG [37646] : 1800-1900S
CAMBERWELL, LND, ENG [37780] : 1800-1900
LONDON, ENG [38070] : 1770+ BIGGLESWADE,
BDF, ENG [38078] : ALL SOUTHAMPTON, HAM,
ENG [38332] : C1800 ENG & AUS [33793] : 1819-1841
DERRYGRATH, TIP, IRL [35144] : PRE 1860
KILRAORAN, TIP, IRL [35818] : PRE 1840
DRUMBANE, TIP, IRL [35818] : C1840 LEX, IRL
[37697] : ALL NC, IL & IN, USA [38363] : 1700S
COVENTRY, TOLLAND CO., CT, USA [38745] :
PRE 1800 VA, USA [38746]

STANLEY-CLARKE 1850+ TONBRIDGE & BENGAL
ARMY, KEN, ENG &, INDIA [34109]

STANNARD C1850 WA, AUS & ENG [35014] : 1800-
1850 WYMONDHAM, NFK, ENG [34073] : C1820
KILLEVY, ARM, IRL [37106] : 1850+ GARVALD,
PEE, SCT [34515]

STANNOWSKI PRE 1900 LANDSBERG, OPR, GER
[38648]

STANROYD PRE 1800 WISBECH, CAM, ENG [36477]

STANSBURY 1899 ST LOUIS, MO, USA [35279]

STANSFIELD 1740-1800 HALIFAX, WRY, ENG
[33767] : 1800-1854 HEPTONSTALL & KEIGHLEY,
WRY, ENG [34352] : ALL BARROWFORD, LAN,
ENG [34564] : C1800-1900 AUDENSHAW, LAN,
ENG [35591] : C1800-1900 HYDE & STOCKPORT,
CHS, ENG [35591] : 1820S MANCHESTER, LAN,
ENG [36024] : PRE 1855 CUL & YKS, ENG [36052] :
1700-1800 IDLE & CALVERLEY, YKS, ENG [36642]
: 1700-1800S MANCHESTER, LAN, ENG [36837] :
1850+ MURRAYVILLE, IL, USA [34564]

STANSWOOD ALL WORLDWIDE [36222]

STANSWORTH PRE 1820 ENG [35589]

STANTON 1890S ADELONG, NSW, AUS [37947] :
1820-1860S WALSALL, STS, ENG [33962] : 1800S
HOXTON, MDX, ENG [34518] : PRE 1855 ST
JAMES, LND, ENG [34862] : JOSEPH 1819
THORNTON, LEI, ENG [35343] : PRE 1800
KEMPSEY, WOR, ENG [35542] : 1800S LEIGH &
NORTON, GLS, ENG [35542] : ALL
LITCHBOROUGH & WOOTTON, NTH, ENG
[36179] : ALL CHELTENHAM, GLS, ENG [36996] :
1810S BIRMINGHAM, ENG [37024] : C1800 IRL
[34518] : PRE 1820 IRL [36064] : 1830-1850S
GALWAY, GAL, IRL [36936] : 1830-1850S COR, IRL
[36936] : C1800 MAY, IRL [38744] : 1860S+
AUCKLAND, NZ [33962] : PRE 1908 GERMISTON,
TVL, RSA [34862] : 1835 RUSH, IN, USA [38022] :
ALL WORLDWIDE [36996]

STANWAY 1860S PORT ALBERT, VIC, AUS [35599] :
1880S RICHMOND, VIC, AUS [35599] : 1860-1862
PORT ALBERT, VIC, AUS [35599] : PRE 1850 LEEK,
STS, ENG [36385] : 1650+ LOSTOCK GRALAM,
CHS, ENG [37039]

STANWELL 1890+ PARKES, NSW, AUS [35367]

STANWOOD PRE 1700 ESS, ENG [35642]

STAPELBERG 1768-1989 GRAAF REINETT, CAPE,
RSA [34947]

STAPLE 1750+ GWENNAP, CON, ENG [35847]

STAPLEFORD 1840S BERWICK BASSETT, WIL,
ENG [35156] : ALL MELTON MOWBRAY, LEI,
ENG [36174]

STAPLES 1890+ PORT MACQUARIE, NSW, AUS
[38582] : 1800+ COBOURG, ONT, CAN [37434] :
1800+ LEADENHAM, LIN, ENG [34002] : PRE 1660
SOHAM, CAM, ENG [34445] : 1800+ MOULTON,

SFK, ENG [34650] : C1772 SWANLEY, KEN, ENG [35090] : 1816 CHATHAM, KEN, ENG [35369] : 1927+ PLYMOUTH, DEV, ENG [36771] : PRE 1771 LONGBRIDGE DEVERILL, DEV, ENG [36771] : 1809+ WARMINSTER, WIL, ENG [36771] : C1820 KENNINGTON, KEN, ENG [37007] : PRE 1880 KEN, ENG [37686] : PRE 1818 GOREY, WEX, IRL [37454] : 1820 MONROE, CT, USA [38066] : 1680-1730 TAUNTON, MA, USA [38151]

STAPLETON 1800-1900 PLACENTIA BAY, NFD, CAN [35103] : 1800-1900 LONDON, ENG [34151] : C1810 BARNSTAPLE, DEV, ENG [35848] : MARY C1765 LANGPORT, SOM, ENG [36367] : 1750+ SYSTON & LOUGHBOROUGH, LEI, ENG [36794] : 1798 LISKEARD, CON, ENG [38209] : 1780-1850 IRL [35103] : ALL WORLDWIDE [38304]

STAPLETON ADKINS 1850-1950 SEVENOAKS, KEN, ENG [34946]

STAPLEY 1838+ PENRITH, NSW, AUS [34534] : 1776+ KEN, ENG [34140] : PRE 1838 ROTHERFIELD, SSX, ENG [34534] : PRE 1838 PENSHURST, KEN, ENG [34534] : SAMUEL 1700 WADHURST, SSX, ENG [35361] : 1800+ USA [34140]

STAPP 1600-1700 ENG [36898]

STAPYLTON-ADKINS 1870+ RSA [34946]

STAR 1689 WIDDINGTON, ESS, ENG [34939]

STARBUCIC PRE 1850 LEI, ENG [37078]

STARBUCK PRE 1750 NTT, ENG [37739] : ALL WORLDWIDE [37803]

STARGARDT 1882+ RICHMOND, VIC, AUS [34452]

STARINGER PRE 1725 WONSHEIM, PFALZ, GER [38135]

STARK 1800-1900 ONT, CAN [38774] : 1750+ CHRISTCHURCH, HAM, ENG [34508] : 1800+ GAINSBOROUGH, LIN, ENG [36515] : PRE 1800 SOM, ENG [37695] : 1830+ LONDON, ENG & AUS [37134] : 1709+ RATHKEALE, LIM, IRL [35874] : 1800+ FIF, SCT [34226] : PRE 1900 CALDER, WLN, SCT [34784] : PRE 1720 KILMENY, FIF, SCT [35227] : C1709 KIRKINTILLOCH, DNB, SCT [35252] : ALL PEE, SCT [36515] : PRE 1800 LKS, SCT [36515] : 1750+ STI, SCT [38476] : 1835 OKMULGEE, OK, USA [38012]

STARKEL (SEE STAERKE [37511]

STARKEY 1750-1800 HUDDERSFIELD, WRY, ENG [33767] : ALL ST LUKES, MDX, ENG [34801] : 1800-1880 GREENWICH, KEN, ENG [36874] : 1740+ RASTRICK, WRY, ENG [36900] : ALL WORLDWIDE [36187]

STARKS 1859-1975 COUNCIL BLUFFS, POTTAWATTAMIA, IA, USA [35316]

STARLING 1830S WISE, ESS, ENG [33981] : 1700-1850 NFK, ENG [34081] : 1840+ GREAT YARMOUTH, NFK, ENG [35939] : 1845+ SOMERS TOWN, LND, ENG [35939] : PRE 1850 CAM & HUN, ENG [36216] : 1880S WEST HACKNEY, MDX, ENG [37677] : PRE 1830 SSX & HAM, ENG [37882]

STARMAR 1800+ BRIGSTOCK, NTH, ENG [38204]

STARMORE PRE 1708 BELCHFORD, LIN, ENG [37318]

STARN 1815-1890 JEFFERSON CO., OH, USA [37040]

STARNES PRE 1924 CASTLETON, LAN, ENG [35417]

STARR ALL VIC, AUS [35702] : PRE 1850 HILLINGTON, MDX, ENG [33804] : C1790 MOUNTFIELD, SSX, ENG [33917] : 1940+ CARMARTHEN, WLS [36127] : ALL WORLDWIDE [35501]

STARRATT 1800-1821 MALIN & PRIESTFIELD, DON, IRL [38421]

STARRETT 1750-1820 TULLYAUGHNISH, DON, IRL [34074] : 1750-1820 FAHAN & TULLY, DON, IRL [34074] : 1750-1820 STRABANE, TYR, IRL [34074] : 1820-1860 WALDO CO., ME, USA [37576] : 1825-1860 WILLIAMSBURG, NY, USA [38523]

STARRITT 1800-1821 MALIN & PRIESTFIELD, DON, IRL [38421]

START PRE 1800 LONDON, MDX, ENG [36379] : PRE 1875 WEYBRIDGE AND AREA, SRY, ENG [37745]

STAS NICOLAS PRE 1836 LBG, BEL [37430]

STATHAM 1750-1820 HAM, ENG [34930]

STATHAMS PRE 1794 HAMPDEN, BKM, ENG [37726]

STATHER PRE 1690 WORLDWIDE [36180]

STATHERS 1800S POCKLINGTON, ERY, ENG [34854]

STATON 1915-1990 YANDINA, QLD, AUS [36306] : PRE 1930 SHEFFIELD, YKS, ENG [36306]

STATTNER ALL WORLDWIDE [35606]

STATTON 1820+ VA, USA [34510]

STAUBACH 1800 HERBSTEIN, HES, BRD [37028]

STAUDLE PRE 1750 GER [38683]

STAUDTER 1800-1850 SIERSHAN WIRGES, GER [37597]

STAUFFER 1880+ NEW YORK & PEEKSKILL, NY, USA & CH [37796]

STAUNTON PRE 1700 ESS, ENG [35642] : C1800 MAY, IRL [38744]

STAVELEY 1757+ NORTH DALTON, ERY, ENG [37443]

STAWELL ALL WORLDWIDE [37646]

STAYNES ALL ENG [34376] : PRE 1900 LEICESTER, LEI, ENG [34376]

ST BERNARD ALL HAM, IOW & WIL, ENG [35418]

ST CLAIR ALL CUL, ENG [37497] : ALL WORLDWIDE [37497]

ST CLARENCE 1800S LANGLOAN, STI, SCT [37898]

STEAD ALL ERY, ENG [35002] : ALL WALTON, WRY, ENG [35588] : C1790 RAMSGATE, KEN, ENG [37053] : PRE 1842 NY, USA [34463] : 1820+ ABERGAVENNY, MON, WLS & AUS [34591]

STEADMAN 1800S TORONTO, ONT, CAN [36670] : 1827 CAM, ENG [35535] : C1790 LENHAM, KEN, ENG [35920] : PRE 1820 BARNINGHAM, NRY, ENG [35974]

STEADWELL 1840 MONTGOMERY CO., NY, USA [37582]

STEALEY PRE 1900 SMETHCOTE, SAL, ENG [34569]

STEAN 1865+ HOBART, TAS, AUS [34770]

STEANE 1800S OXF, ENG [38206]

STEAR (SEE STEER) [37421]

STEARNS PRE 1830 LINCOLN CO., ME, USA [35263]

STEBBIN PRE 1710 SOHAM, CAM, ENG [34445]

STEBBING PRE 1870 SANDHURST & BENDIGO, VIC, AUS [35796] : 1740-1900 POPLAR, MDX, ENG [37651] : PRE 1880 MDX, ENG [37987]

STEBBINGS 1800-1830S KINGS LYNN, NFK, ENG [36264]

STEBBINS 1750+ WETHERDEN, SFK, ENG [37262] : PRE 1720 NEW LONDON CO., CT, USA [36917]

STECK PRE 1880 BRA, BRM & HAN, GER [37548] : 1640-1700 MUSBERG, WUE, GER [38599] : PRE 1915 PA, USA [37587]

STEDFORD 1870-1910 GOULBURN, NSW, AUS [34842] : ALL WORLDWIDE [34842]

STEDING PRE 1565 BREMEN, BRM, GER [37819]

STEDMAN 1750-1850 ROCHESTER & GILLINGHAM, KEN, ENG [34738] : 1400-1500 OCKLEY, SRY, ENG [36420] : PRE 1650 BEDDENHAM, KEN, ENG [36571] : PRE 1900 HORSHAM, SSX, ENG [36828] : 1700+ SFK, ENG [37659] : 1700+ NFK, ENG [37659] : ALL KINROSS, KRS, SCT [37659]

STEDMOND ALL WEX, IRL [35949] : ALL WORLDWIDE [35949]

STEED ALL GREAT WALDINGFIELD, SFK, ENG [34663] : 1850-1920 FINGLESHAM & NONINGTON, KEN, ENG [36137] : ALL KEN, ENG [36137] : 1800-1860 CRAIGS, ANT, IRL [35243] : 1725-1775 BRUNSWICK CO., VA, USA [38088] : 1820+ ABERGAVENNY, MON, WLS & AUS [34591]

STEEDEN 1850+ CHINGAUCOUSY, ONT, CAN [38413] : 1800+ TINGEWICK, BKM, ENG [38413]

STEEDMAN 1885+ ROTHERHAM, YKS, ENG [35455] : C1800+ KINROSS, KRS, SCT [37659] : C1700+ DUNNING, PER, SCT [37659] : C1700+ DRON & ABERNETHY, PER, SCT [37659] : C1700 FORTEVIOT & FORGADENNY, PER, SCT [37659]

STEEDS PRE 1817 WESTBURY LEIGH, WIL, ENG [38214]

STEEL C1750 LITTLE DEAN, GLS, ENG [33841] : 1800+ ASHMANSWORTH, HAM, ENG [34788] : 1800-1850 SUNDERLAND, DUR, ENG [35153] : 1800+ HACKNEY, LND, ENG [35235] : PRE 1810 ALDINGBOURNE, SSX, ENG [36843] : 1800-1900 HAM, ENG [37064] : C1850-C1870 LONDON, MDX, ENG [37066] : 1600-1800 FELTWELL, NFK, ENG [37456] : C1830 HETTON, DUR, ENG [37615] : 1858-1940 PORTSEA, HAM, ENG & AUS [35784] : C1830 MOVILLE, DON, IRL [34426] : PRE 1880 NZ [34603] : PRE 1710 CARLUKE, LKS, SCT [34501] : PRE 1770 COLDINGHAM, BEW, SCT [36302] : PRE 1900 DUNDEE, ANS, SCT [36777] : C1740 AUCHTERARDER, PER, SCT [37066] : 1700-1900 NEW CUMNOCK & AYR, AYR, SCT [37251] : ALL LANARK, LKS, SCT [37480] : ALL LESMAHAGOW, LKS, SCT [37480]

STEELE 1855+ MAITLAND, NSW, AUS [35073] : 1890S CRAMLINGTON, NBL, ENG [34688] : ALL BATH, SOM, ENG [35566] : 1800+ WHITEHAVEN, CUL, ENG [35821] : 1830-1860 HAMMERSMITH, MDX, ENG [36229] : 1790+ MARKET DRAYTON AREA, SAL, ENG [36997] : 1863+ ISLIP, OXF, ENG [37202] : PRE 1690 NOKE, OXF, ENG [37202] : 1580-1850 ST BEES, CUL, ESS & NFK, ENG [37246] : 1855-1865 SOUTHAMPTON, HAM, ENG [37251] : 1865-1880 CHELTENHAM, GLS, ENG [37251] : 1850-1860 READING, BRK, ENG [37251] : 1880+ HAMMERSMITH, MDX, ENG [37251] : 1802+ WIL, ENG & AUS [33790] : 1878 LIMERICK, LIM, IRL [34688] : 1600-1820+ RAPHOE, DON, IRL [35759] : ALL BALLYMONEY, ANT, IRL & NZ [34441] : 1780+ FYVIE, ABD, SCT [34008] : 1655+ LESMAHAGOW, LKS, SCT [34118] : JOHN 1800+ AYR, SCT [34161] : 1830 LEITH, MLN, SCT [35282] : PRE 1600+ EDINBURGH, SCT [35759] : PRE 1890 ABINGTON, LKS, SCT [36149] : ALL LESMAHAGOW, LKS, SCT [37480] : ALL LANARK, LKS, SCT [37480] : HELEN 1850-1930 RFW, SCT & AUS [34783] : 1845+ IN, USA [38151]

STEELEY 1840 MUSCOGEE, GA, USA [37792] : 1850S COVINGTON CO., AL, USA [37792]

STEEN PRE 1860 STORMONT CO., ONT, CAN [38412] : 1898-1910 MANNING, CARROLL CO., IA, USA [36952]

STEENSON ALL MOG, IRL [34226]

STEEP ALL RHEINLAND, RPF, BRD [35874] : 1830+ THOROLD, ONT, CAN [35874] : 1709+ KILCOOLY, TIP, IRL [35874] : ALL KILFINNANE, LIM, IRL [36232] : 1709-1870 KILFINNANE, LIM, IRL [37422]

STEER PRE 1900 ENG [35571] : C1749 DEV, ENG [36337] : ALL EXMOOR, SOM, ENG [36790] : ALL UK [37421]

STEERE PRE 1650 OCKLEY, SRY, ENG [36179]

STEERS C1830 BRIGHTON, SSX, ENG [35525] : 1800+ BRANSTON, LEI, ENG [38425]

STEFANSKA KATARZYNA 1879-1942 PARACHANIE, POSEN, POL [38090]

STEFANSKI MICHAL 1883-1934 ORLOWO, POL [38090]

STEFES PRE 1702 SUCHTELN, PRE, GER [38181]

STEFFEN 1800-99 CAMPTON, BDF, ENG [34315] : 1800-1860S WEGORZEWO, POM, GER [38524]

STEFFENS PRE 1745 MSW, GER [37819]

STEFFENSEN ALL JERSLEY, LOT, DEN [34308] : C1853 SKOVSBOG, SJELLAND, DEN [34752]

STEGEMANN PRE 1880 RUGEN, POM, GER [37774]

STEGGAL C1699-1817 HAUGHLEY & GREAT FINBOROUGH, SFK, ENG [36425]

STEGGALL PRE 1900 ENG [38286] : 1855+ NZ [38286]

STEGGALLS 1800+ LONDON, ENG [35296] : EMMA PRE 1880 ST PANCRAS, LND & MDX, ENG [36443] : FRANCIS 1837 KENTISH TOWN, LND, ENG [36443]

STEGGALS C1800-1872 NORTHWOLD & DOWNHAM MARKET, NFK, ENG [36425]

STEGGLES 1700-1850 BARNINGHAM, SFK, ENG [38003] : 1700-1850 RICKINGHALL SUPERIOR, SFK, ENG [38003]

STEHR ALL BRD [34212] : ALL CAN [34212] : ALL DDR [34212]

STEIN 1800+ BUDAPEST, HU [38481]

STEINACKER ALL SCHLITZ, HES, BRD [35264]

STEINBERG 1860 LUEBBECKE, OLD, GER [37509]

STEINBRUCH 1730-1800 BERKS CO., PA, USA [37011]

STEINER MARIA ANNA 1880 EISENBACH, WUE, BRD [33754] : JOHANN 1826-1888 SCHWYZ, SZ, CH [33754]

STEINERT 1912 DRESDEN, DDR [35110] : PRE 1854+ STEINAVA DODER, SILESIA, GER [35110]

STEINFELD PRE 1777 POM, GER [38553] : ALL SHO, GER [38553] : PRE 1700 KIEL, SHO, GER [38553] : LORENTZ 1640-1680 KIEL, SHO, GER [38553] : LORENTZ 1640-1680 POM, GER [38553] : PRE 1700 LUBECK, SHO, GER [38553] : ALL POM, GER [38553] : PRE 1777 WISMAR, POM, GER [38553] : LORENTZ 1640-1680 LUBECK, SHO, GER [38553] : LORENTZ ALL POM, GER [38553] : LORENTZ 1670-1726 MALMO, SWE [38553]

STEINGRIEB 1750-1850 MONTGOMERY CO., NY, USA [35318]

STEINHAGEN PRE 1870 GER [35005]

STEINHARDT 1885 MARYBOROUGH, QLD, AUS [34754] : 1870 SCHABROW, POM, GER [34754]

STEINHAUSER 1884+ BALLARAT, VIC, AUS [36278]

STEINHAVER PRE 1870 KOBLENZ, BRD [35574]

STEINHOFF PRE 1884 ONT, CAN [35302] : 1700-1800S CROWLAND, ONT, CAN [37442]

STEINKE PRE 1870 GER [37009]

STEINLEITNER PRE 1850 PASSAU, BAV, GER [36957]

STEINMANN 1850+ LIVERPOOL, LAN, ENG [37020] : ALL GER [37020] : 1900+ NY, USA [37020]

STEITZ WILHEMINA B. 1863-1939 STUTTGART, WUE, GER & USA [33827]

STELMACH ALL GALICIA, SU & POL [34146]

STEMP 1856+ IPSWICH, QLD, AUS [38075] : 1750S HOLLINGTON, SSX, ENG [35501] : PRE 1820 SRY, ENG [38075]

STEMPER PRE 1855 LXM, BEL [36722] : 1912-35 LIVINGSTON, MT, USA [36722] : 1855-80 IA, USA [36722]

STEMPLE 1840-1860 MARIN CO., CA, USA [36968]

STENDER 1700+ GORNITZ, SHO, GER [37170]

STENERSEN 1800+ HISOY & ARENDAL, NOR [33789]

STENFORD 1850+ LONDON, MDX, ENG [38263]

STENGEL 1830-1850 PHILADELPHIA, PA, USA [37740]

STENGER PRE 1840 MOEBRIS, BAD, GER [37563] : 1840+ IN & IA, USA [37563]

STENHOUSE 1740-1800 ROX, SCT [34615] : 1750-1840 INVERKEITHING & DYSART, FIF, SCT [36268] : C1750-1800 SCT [36327]

STENNER 1800+ BRISTOL, SOM, ENG [35489]

STENNET C1820 SYDNEY, NSW, AUS [35089] : C1771 DIGBY, LIN, ENG [35746]

STENNETT 1800+ MANCHESTER, LAN, ENG [34866] : ALL LIN, ENG [37830]

STENNING 1920+ KARRINYUP, WA, AUS [34906] : 1871+ MOONEE PONDS, VIC, AUS [34906] : 1883+ NEUTRAL BAY, NSW, AUS [34906] : 1865-1883 ECHUCA, VIC, AUS [34906] : PRE 1824 HENFIELD, SSX, ENG [34906] : C1857 CHELMSFORD, ESS, ENG [35337]

STENSON ALL ALVASTON, DBY, ENG [36162]

STENT C1880+ MELBOURNE, VIC, AUS [38510] : PRE 1800 WORTHING, SSX, ENG [34112]

STENZEL 1865+ FASSIFERN, QLD, AUS [36616]

STEPHAN PRE 1860 LIEGNITZ, GER [34801] : ALL NEISSE, SIL, GER [38685]

STEPHANI ALL WORLDWIDE [38666]

STEPHEN 1887+ YASS, NSW, AUS [33898] : C1845 MOORE TWP., ONT, CAN [34259] : 1834 LAUNCESTON, CON, ENG [36860] : 1700-1820 DOVENBORF, ALS, FRA [38024] : 1750+ MONTROSE, ANS, SCT [36397] : C1800 PETERHEAD, ABD, SCT [37245] : 1800-1920 PETERHEAD, MOR, SCT [37290] : PRE 1860 IOM, UK [37882]

STEPHENS 1895+ SYDNEY, NSW, AUS [33820] : 1885+ MELBOURNE, VIC, AUS [33820] : 1826+ LAUNCESTON, TAS, AUS [33820] : 1873+ KADINA, SA, AUS [33882] : C1840 VIC, AUS [33930] : 1800+ LAUNCESTON, TAS, AUS [34271] : DANIEL 1861+ WILLUNGA & MAITLAND, SA, AUS [34295] : 1850-1900 GIPPSLAND, VIC, AUS [34641] : 1862+ BALLARAT, VIC, AUS [35379] : 1870+ MELBOURNE, VIC, AUS [35379] : 1865+ GOLDEN SQUARE, VIC, AUS [35416] : 1898S QUORN, SA, AUS [35416] : 1800S KAPUNDA, SA, AUS [35984] : 1856+ BUNINYONG, YARRAVILLE & COLAC, VIC, AUS [36622] : 1856+ DURHAM LEAD & BEECHWORTH, VIC, AUS [36622] : 1856+ FOOTSCRAY & SCOTCHMANS LEAD, VIC, AUS [36622] : 1856+ BALLARAT, CLUNES & PORTLAND, VIC, AUS [36622] : 1858-1863 BENDIGO, VIC, AUS [37968] : 1862-1891 COWRA, NSW, AUS [37968] : 1880-1940 CONDOBOLIN, NSW, AUS [37968] : RICHARD 1860-80 BENDIGO & SANDHURST, VIC, AUS [38500] : PRE 1900 MERRICKVILLE, ONT, CAN [34466] : ROBERT 1850+ CHERRY VALLEY & ATHOL TWP., PE CO.& ONT, CAN [34486] : 1860+ HAMILTON, OWEN SOUND, ONT, CAN [36326] : PRE 1750 SITHNEY, CON, ENG [33814] : C1790 NASH, HEF, ENG [33820] : PRE 1850 ST TEATH & CAMBORNE, CON, ENG [34360] : 1730-1830 ST BARTHOLOMEW BY EXCHANGE, LND, ENG [34650] : 1800-1850 SOM, ENG [34666] : PRE 1860 ST COLUMB, CON, ENG [34684] : C1739 GRADE, CON, ENG [34752] : 1630-1700 GWENNAP, CON, ENG [34793] : PRE 1900 PEMBRIDGE, HEF, ENG [34807] : C1820 CROWAN, CON, ENG [35131] : EDMUND 1780-1820 PROBUS, CON, ENG [35208] : PRE 1900 BRISTOL, SOM, ENG [35612] : C1834 CON, ENG [35717] : PRE 1880 IOW, ENG [35745] : PRE 1850S ST AUSTELL, CON, ENG [35804] : PRE 1850

CHELTENHAM, GLS, ENG [35846] : PRE 1850 ALSTONE, GLS, ENG [35846] : PRE 1870 REDRUTH, CON, ENG [35959] : PRE 1760 OLD SWINFORD, WOR, ENG [36110] : 1858 PORTSMOUTH, HAM, ENG [36264] : PRE 1850 RUAN MINOR, CON, ENG [36788] : CHARLES 1930 IPSWICH, SFK, ENG [36877] : 1830S DBY, ENG [37024] : 1788-1809+ LYDFORD, DEV, ENG [37108] : 1750-1900 SHERBORNE, GLS, ENG [37207] : JOSEPH PRE 1793 MEDWAY, KEN, ENG [37228] : ALL DENTON & LEWES, SSX, ENG [37285] : 1500-1990 ST HILARY, ST GLUVIAS, MORVAH, CON, ENG [37680] : PRE 1800 RAMSBURY, WIL, ENG [37687] : PRE 1852 STEPNEY, LND, ENG [37968] : ROBERT 1720-1783 HELSTON, CON, ENG [38180] : 1850S SMALL HEATH, ENG [38321] : 1800-1857 SALFORD, LAN, ENG [38321] : 1700-1800 GLS, ENG [38321] : 1800-1900 BIRMINGHAM, WAR, ENG [38321] : JOHN C1810 BETHNAL GREEN, MDX, ENG [38441] : PRE 1800 BRADLEY, WIL, ENG [38745] : ROBERT PRE 1795 BLENNERVILLE & ANNAGH, GAL, IRL [34254] : SAMUEL PRE 1795 GALWAY, GAL, IRL [34254] : 1600-1900 CAV, IRL [34717] : PRE 1830+ CAV, IRL [35759] : 1869+ OTEPOPO, OTAGO, NZ [34570] : 1870+ MID CANTERBURY, NZ [34666] : 1903+ WANGANUI, NZ [36877] : ALL BOSTON, MA, USA [34466] : 1800 PULASKI CO., KY, USA [37570] : 1855-1875 KEWEENAW CO., MI, USA [38009] : 1800-1900 CARDIFF, WLS [34641] : 1850-1870 BRIDGEND, GLA, WLS [34666] : PRE 1862 SWANSEA, GLA, WLS [35379] : PRE 1900 LLANDEFEILOG, CMN, WLS [36432]

STEPHENSON 1850-1915 GOULBURN, NSW, AUS [35861] : PRE 1884 ONT, CAN [34391] : PRE 1907 COLTON & SEATHWAITE, LAN, ENG [34053] : 1600-1900 KESWICK, CUL, ENG [34717] : 1700+ ALMONDBURY, YKS, ENG [34927] : C1714 ROTHBURY, NBL, ENG [35026] : C1860 SHEFFIELD, YKS, ENG [35251] : C1832 BRANDSBURTON, YKS, ENG [35515] : 1800-1850 LEEDS, KEN, ENG [35861] : PRE 1850 STEPNEY, LND, ENG [35967] : MARY PRE 1775 BURTON LEONARD, ERY, ENG [36192] : ISABELLA PRE 1788 FIRBANK ST JOHN, WES, ENG [36192] : PRE 1850 BARNSLEY, YKS, ENG [36704] : 1800S DOVER, KEN, ENG [36876] : PRE 1850 HIGH HYLAND, WRY, ENG [37402] : PRE 1825 LONDON, ENG [37416] : PRE 1860 MOULTON, NTH, ENG [37708] : PRE 1750 WESTON UPON TRENT, STS, ENG [37722] : 1700-1800 WHITEHAVEN, CUL, ENG [37735] : PRE 1750 HEYSHAM & LANCASTER, LAN, ENG [38248] : PRE 1870 INDIA [36876] : PRE 1830 LDY, IRL [33845] : 1750-1815 MELROSE, SCT [38154] : 1890-1920 LAFAYETTE CO., FL, USA [35315] : C1830 VICKSBURG, MS, USA [36969] : 1870S MATTOON, IL, USA [37010] : 1900S LAWRENCE CO., IN, USA [37028] : 1800S GUILFORD CO., NC, USA [37028] : 1700-1850 GREENVILLE & SIMPSON, SC & KY, USA [38027] : 1815-1860 UNION CO., IN, USA [38154] : 1815-1860 BUTLER CO., OH, USA [38154]

STEPNEY PRE 1800 TROTTON, SSX, ENG [34112] : 1800+ MONKTON DEVERILL, WIL, ENG [36521]

STEPP 1837 CLARK CO., MO, USA [38287]

STEPTOE C1900 NEWBURY, BRK, ENG [36975] : PRE 1895 LND, ENG [37955] : ALL WANTAGE, BRK, ENG [38279]

STERCZER ALL WORLDWIDE [34335]

STERKEN 1686+ HOOGEVEEN, DRN, NL [34398]

STERLING PRE 1840 NBL, ENG [35918] : PRE 1884 BELFAST, ANT, IRL [38541] : 1760-1785 HUNTERDON, NJ, USA [36908]

STERN ALL POM, GER [38037]

STERNBERG 1840+ DANZIG, PRE, GER [34932]

STERRAT 1857-1921 GLASGOW, LKS, SCT [33891]

STERRIT 1857-1921 GLASGOW, LKS, SCT [33891]

STERRY ALL GLS, ENG [34837] : 1400-1990 UK [36218]

STERZER ALL WORLDWIDE [34335]

STETNER ALL WORLDWIDE [35606]

STETTER C1806-20 BAD, GER [37022]

STETTIFORD 1827 EXETER, DEV, ENG [37952] : ALL EXETER, DEV, ENG &, INDIA [34561]

STETTLER ALL WORLDWIDE [35606]

STETTNER ALL WORLDWIDE [35606]

STETZEL ALL WORLDWIDE [37362]

STEUDEL 1700S SCHWEIDNITZ, SIL, GER [33901]

STEVEN GEORGE 1780+ TONNACK, CAI, SCT [34884] : 1750+ GUTHRIE, ANS, SCT [35644]

STEVENS 1840+ THERESA PARK, THE OAKS, NSW, AUS [35420] : 1840+ NSW, AUS [35520] : JOHN 1890+ ADELAIDE, SA, AUS [36212] : 1855+ BENDIGO, VIC, AUS [36304] : PRE 1840 SYDNEY, NSW, AUS [36372] : 1900+ BENDIGO, VIC, AUS [36622] : C1830 BOW, LND, ENG [33893] : C1790 CHATHAM, KEN, ENG [33914] : 1800+ HASTINGS, SSX, ENG [33918] : SUSAN C1825-1850 GREAT MISSENDEN, BKM, ENG [34007] : PRE 1800 STEDHAM, SSX, ENG [34112] : 1780+ WIL, ENG [34290] : PRE 1850 ST TEATH & CAMBORNE, CON, ENG [34360] : PRE 1750 WARMINSTER, WIL, ENG [34466] : C1815 DEVIZES, WIL, ENG [34581] : PRE 1760 PAPPLEWICK, NTT, ENG [34612] : 1790+ MANSFIELD WOODHOUSE, NTT, ENG [34612] : PRE 1900 ENG [34657] : C1823 SPONDON, DBY, ENG [34661] : PRE 1835 MEOPHAM, KEN, ENG [34720] : 1800+ KEN, ENG [34815] : 1800+ CHELSEA, MDX, ENG [34818] : NATHANIEL PRE 1800 CAMBRIDGE, CAM & SRY, ENG [35032] : WILLIAM 1800+ CON, ENG [35060] : PRE 1840 YORK, YKS, ENG [35215] : 1800-40 ZENNOR, CON, ENG [35416] : PRE 1840 NEAR DEVIZES, WIL, ENG [35420] : 1800+ AYLESBURY, BKM, ENG [35520] : SARAH JANE 1840+ KEN, SRY & SSX, ENG [35762] : 17650 PAPPLEWICK, NTT, ENG [36032] : 1860+ BRENTFORD & HANWELL, MDX, ENG [36212] : ALL LND & MDX, ENG [36212] : 1800+ IPSWICH, SFK, ENG [36251] : 1800+ BRISTOL, GLS, ENG [36251] : 1800+ HARWICH, ESS, ENG [36251] : C1670-1750 WIL, ENG [36289] : PRE 1910 HAMMERSMITH, LND, ENG [36361] : C1800 LAMBETH, SRY, ENG [36978] : PRE 1930 LONDON, ENG [37062] : PRE 1850 SWINDON, WIL, ENG [37101] : 1750+ CITY OF LONDON, ENG [37223] : 1850-1920 WEYMOUTH, DOR, ENG [37233] : ALL ABBOTSBURY, DOR, ENG [37233] : 1785-1820 YETMINSTER, DOR, ENG [37233] : PRE 1862 BETHNAL GREEN, MDX, ENG [37279] : ALL SEAFORD, SSX, ENG [37285] : 1700+ EXMOOR, SOM & DEV, ENG [37322] : 1902 PRIBRIGHT, SRY, ENG [37345] : C1800 SSX, ENG [37698] : PRE 1750 GREAT WALTHAM, ESS, ENG [37718] : PRE 1800 SOUTH MOLTON, DEV, ENG [37725] : PRE 1700 OXF, ENG [37739] : PRE 1800 SHIPTON GORGE, DOR, ENG [37760] : 1800-1860 SHIPTON GORGE & WHITCHURCH, DOR, ENG [37859] : C1870 FINCHLEY, MDX, ENG [37859] : 1800S SSX & SRY, ENG [37868] : 1814-1870 CAMBERWELL, SRY, ENG [38171] : 1790-1830 BRK & BKM, ENG [38171] : 1880S BEXHILL ON SEA, SSX, ENG [38223] : C1852 BETHNAL GREEN, MDX, ENG [38441] : 1770S+ LIVERPOOL, LAN, ENG [38443] : C1740

NYEVEEN, OIJ, NL [36283] : DIANA 1790+ WICK, CAI, SCT [34884] : OZIAS 1816 WV, USA [36320] : 1630-1850 CHESHIRE & NAUGATUCK, CT, USA [36335] : 1800-1880 GREENE, NY, USA [36346] : 1750-1850 CT, USA [36346] : 1820-1880 TIOGA, NY, USA [36346] : 1840+ CINCINATTI, OH & IA, USA [36542] : 1750-1790 ORANGE CO., VA, USA [36566] : PRE 1807 SCHENECTADY, NY, USA [36923] : PRE 1770 BALTIMORE CO., MD, USA [36923] : 1740-1780 BALTIMORE CO., MD, USA [37021] : ALVERDA 1840-1870 WILLIAMS CO., OH, USA [37529] : HARMON 1848-1938 STOCKBRIDGE, WI, USA [37596] : ALL CINCINNATI, OH, USA [37799] : PRE 1830 CAROLINE, NY, USA [38335] : PRE 1790 MA, USA [38746] : 1700-1990 BASTARD, VT & ONT, USA & CAN [36669] : EVA T. 1850+ CLEVELAND, OH, USA & ENG [37322] : ALL WORLDWIDE [35875]

STEVENS (SEE STEPHEN [37680]

STEVENSON 1854+ SCONE, NSW, AUS [34774] : JOHN 1850S+ ARARAT, VIC & NSW, AUS [35239] : 1850-1960 OBERON, NSW, AUS [35395] : 1856+ VIC, AUS [35404] : PRE 1931 ISIS FORD, QLD, AUS [35507] : C1831 NEW NORFOLK, TAS, AUS [35729] : 1890-1920 MAN, CAN [34510] : 1810-1900 ONT, CAN [37461] : PRE 1850 PLYMOUTH, DEV, ENG [34742] : 1750-1850 LONDON, ENG [34846] : 1650-1750 HOUGHTON, STS, ENG [35288] : 1851-1919 BOOTLE, LAN & CHS, ENG [35490] : PRE 1830 CON, ENG [36078] : PRE 1750 HORNBY & HUNTON, NRY, ENG [36159] : C1840 ROCHDALE, LAN, ENG [36271] : C1890 BRIGG, LIN, ENG [36271] : PRE 1834 WINLATON, DUR, ENG [36459] : 1750+ PLYMOUTH, DEV, ENG [36858] : 1855+ LIANAFIFFY & BANBRIDGE, DOW, IRL [34528] : 1854+ STRABANE, TYR, IRL [34774] : 1830+ ARM, IRL [34956] : ELINA 1830-1860 ARM, IRL [35017] : C1873 DEERMATTERY, ARM, IRL [35507] : C1859 PORTADOWN, ARM, IRL [35507] : C1800 CORK, COR, IRL [35563] : 1800S LONDONDERRY, LDY, IRL [36833] : 1700-1850 DUBLIN, IRL [37461] : WILLIAM PRE 1750 IRL [38536] : DANIEL C1850-1880 AIRDRIE, LKS, SCT [33978] : 1800+ KILBARCHAN, RFW, SCT [34049] : 1780 JEDBURGH, ROX, SCT [34149] : C1800 KIRKOSWALD, AYR, SCT [34345] : 1830 ELLON, ABD, SCT [34474] : PRE 1850 MUTHILL & LOGIE, PER, SCT [34753] : 1800+ CAMPSIE, STI, SCT [35194] : PRE 1750 OLD KILPATRICK, DNB, SCT [35227] : 1700S CATHCART, RFW, SCT [35395] : 1700-1780 KILMARNOCK, AYR, SCT [35813] : C1826 FALKIRK, STI, SCT [35863] : 1817+ SCT [35963] : 1600-1878 DUNFERMLINE, FIF, SCT [36894] : PRE 1850 ABERDEEN, ABD, SCT [37832] : PRE 1900 LEITH, MLN, SCT [37835] : JAMES 1900+ NEWTON MEARNS, RFW, SCT [37879] : 1800+ MENSTRIE & ALVA, CLK, SCT & AUS [35150] : 1837+ MENSTRIE & ALVA, CLK, SCT & USA [35150] : 1770-1900 FAYETTE CO., KY, USA [38154]

STEVES PRE 1850 NRW & RPF, BRD [38616]

STEVINS JOHN PRE 1684 ENG [37886]

STEVSON ALL CHRISTIANIA, OSLO, NOR [36743]

STEWARD PRE 1770 SFK, ENG [35701] : PRE 1630 BIRSTALL & DRIELINGTON, WRY, ENG [36202] : 1750 TYR, IRL [38336] : 1770-1810 PA, USA [37029] : ALL IL, USA [38013]

STEWART 1840+ PARRAMATTA, NSW, AUS [33874] : JAMES 1842+ SYDNEY, NSW, AUS [34449] : C1860 SYDNEY, NSW, AUS [35049] : WM. & ANNE 1863+ SYDNEY, NSW, AUS [35049] : C1900 HAMILTON, VIC, AUS [35049] : 1852+ WERRIBEE, VIC, AUS [35137] : CHARLES 1863+

STANTHORPE, QLD, AUS [35428] : 1860-90
BREWARRINA, NSW, AUS [35511] : 1860-1890
LAGGAN, NSW, AUS [35559] : PRE 1840 SYDNEY,
NSW, AUS [35559] : 1840-1900 GOULBURN, NSW,
AUS [35559] : 1820-1900 QUE, CAN [33753] : 1780+
NORTHUMBERLAND CO., CAN [34126] : 1800+
DURHAM CO., ONT, CAN [34232] : C1845 SIGHT
POINT, MABOU, NS, CAN [34395] : THOMAS PRE
1878+ BRUCE CO., ONT, CAN [35004] : MARTHA
A. 1878+ BRUCE CO., ONT, CAN [35004] : 1860+
STAYNER, ONT, CAN [35269] : JAMES 1813-1893
DRUMMOND TWP., ONT, CAN [37458] : 1850-70
ST SYLVESTER, QUE, CAN [37528] : 1848
GRINTON, NRY, ENG [33811] : PRE 1870
LONDON, ENG [34261] : 1864 WINDSOR, LND,
ENG [34540] : MARY PRE 1853 THRIPLOW, CAM,
ENG [35564] : PRE 1770 SFK, ENG [35701] : PRE
1820 CRONDALL, HAM, ENG [35934] : EMMA
1890S WINGATE, DUR, ENG [36559] : 1840S
LOWICK, NBL, ENG [36636] : 1820S BANGALORE,
INDIA [33811] : 1800-1830 ULSTER, IRL [33753] :
PRE 1870 MAGHERAFELT, LDY, IRL [33977] :
1780+ COR, IRL [34126] : THOMAS PRE 1878
ENNISKILLEN, IRL [35004] : C1800 THE WARD,
DUB, IRL [35152] : C1858 TYR, IRL [35247] : PRE
1880 ARM, IRL [35918] : 1850+ BELFAST, ANT,
IRL [36135] : PRE 1850 ULSTER, IRL [37528] : PRE
1840 MAGHERAGALL, ANT, IRL [37927] :
ROBERT 1877 TIMARU, NZ [36782] : PRE 1850
DUNDEE, ANS, SCT [33868] : PRE 1830
DINGWALL, ROC, SCT [33874] : ALL LAUDER,
BEW, SCT [33959] : C1800-190 PER, SCT [34040] :
1850 DUNDEE, ANS, SCT [34149] : 1840+
ARDSHEAL, ARL, SCT [34188] : PRE 1840
STIRLING, STI, SCT [34428] : PRE 1840
INVERNESS, INV, SCT [34428] : 1850 BOLESKINE,
INV, SCT [34468] : PRE 1870 STONEHOUSE, LKS,
SCT [34598] : 1767+ ROTHESAY, BUT, SCT [34614] :
1820-1920 HUNTLY, ABD, SCT [34615] : 1800-1859
LITTLE DUNKELD, PER, SCT [34649] : 1800+
LONGHOPE, OKI, SCT [34688] : 1750+ ST
MARGARET'S HOPE, OKI, SCT [34688] : PRE 1827
DALGUISE, PER, SCT [34695] : PRE 1839
BALQUHIDDER, PER, SCT [34911] : C1854
GLASGOW, LKS, SCT [34972] : ROBERT & MARY
1800+ GLASGOW, SCT [35049] : C1800+
AUCHINLECK, AYR, SCT [35108] : 1800S APPIN,
ARL, SCT [35137] : DANIEL 1786-1795
BENDOCHY, PER, SCT [35196] : JAMES 1759-C1798
FINCASTLE, PER, SCT [35196] : DANIEL C1830-
1835 RATTRAY, PER, SCT [35196] : JAMES C1800-
1829 MONEYDIE, PER, SCT [35196] : 1860+
BRECHIN, ANS, SCT [35269] : PRE 1851
GLENBERVIE, KCD, SCT [35269] : 1700-1850
LEUCHARS & CARNBEE, FIF, SCT [35395] : 1700-
1850 ANSTRUTHER WESTER, FIF, SCT [35395] :
JAMES PRE 1820 KEAL APPIN, ARL, SCT [35426] :
ISABELL 1815+ KEAL APPIN, ARL, SCT [35426] :
CHARLES 1830+ EDINBURGH, MLN, SCT [35428]
: ALL BLAIR ATHOLL, PER, SCT [35456] : JEAN
C1760 PER, SCT [35729] : THOMAS C1740 PER, SCT
[35729] : 1766-1830 GREENOCK, RFW, SCT [35782] :
1802-1856 INCH, WIG, SCT [35820] : ALISTER ALL
SCT [35821] : PRE 1877 RENFREW, RFW, SCT
[35863] : C1834 BANKFORD, PER, SCT [35922] :
1838 ABERDEEN, ABD, SCT [35922] : JANET PRE
1856 EDINBURGH, MLN, SCT [36623] : 1830
SPROUSTON, ROX, SCT [36636] : 1800+ CURRIE
& LASSWADE, MLN, SCT [36705] : CHARLES
1800+ TORBREX, STI, SCT [36728] : 1820+
STONEHAVEN, KCD, SCT [36772] : DAVID ALL
EDINBURGH, MLN, SCT [36846] : DAVID ALL

DUNDEE, ANS, SCT [36846] : 1200 SCT [37008] :
DONALD 1800+ ARL, SCT [37304] : JAMES C1800
GLASGOW, LKS, SCT [37429] : 1780-1800 BIRSE,
ABD, SCT [37485] : DONALD PRE 1800-50
AVERNISH KYLE OF LOCHALSH, ROC, SCT
[37518] : PRE 1749 CROFTPARDON & DULL, PER,
SCT [37852] : PRE 1865 BARONY, LKS, SCT [37852] :
PRE 1741 DULL, PER, SCT [37852] : PRE 1858
EDINBURGH, MLN, SCT [37892] : 1800-80 CUPAR,
FIF, SCT [37946] : 1823 MEIGLE, ANS, SCT [37952] :
C1840S SOUTHWICK, KKD, SCT [37981] :
MALCOLM 1720-1857 STRATHGROY & BLAIR
ATHOLL, PER, SCT [37988] : 1700+ CRACHAVIE,
PER, SCT [38726] : NEIL 1860+ STORNOWAY,
ROC, SCT & CAN [34467] : PRE 1866 NY, USA
[33822] : 1800S PITTSBURGH, PA, USA [34353] : 1795
VA, USA [36730] : 1815 OH, USA [36730] : 1857+
MUS, OH, USA [36910] : 1740S NEW CASTLE, DE,
USA [37027] : WILLIAM 1830+ COVINGTON CO.,
MS, NC & SC, USA [37796] : PRE 1835
LOGENSPORT, IN, USA [37820] : 1775-1900 POLK
CO., GA, USA [38107] : 1788-1835 DAVIDSON &
WILSON COS., TN, USA [38330] : 1800 VA, USA
[38362] : 1700+ ONONDAGA CO., NY, USA [38745]
: ALL WORLDWIDE [35253]

STEWART (SEE STUART) [34247]

STEYAERT PRE 1800 GENT, OVL, BEL [38700]

STEYN 1800-1900 SOLINGEN & ROTTERDAM, ZH,
FRG & NL [38712]

ST GERMAIN 1700+ DE DU CALUMET, QUE, CAN
[38727]

ST HELIER PRE 1850 CAEN, HN, FRA [37085]

STIANSEN 1800+ HISOY & ARENDAL, NOR [33789]

STIBBARD ALL ONT, CAN & ENG [38410]

STIBBS PRE 1707 DEV, ENG [38330] : 1790
SOMERSET CO., NJ, USA [38330]

STIBER PRE 1785 BAW, BRD [37428]

STICHBURY 1700+ WHITECHAPEL, MDX, ENG
[34650]

STICKA PRE 1854 RASTADT, CHER, SU [38738]

STICKLAND C1850 COLLINGWOOD, VIC, AUS
[35764] : ALL DOR, ENG [36427] : C1800
LONGFORD, WIL, ENG [37378]

STICKLER C1750 WITHAM FRIARY, SOM, ENG
[34376] : C1700-1850 WITHAM FRIARY, SOM, ENG
[36478]

STICKLES ALL LUTON, BDF, ENG [36891]

STICKLEY 1900+ CAN & USA [33904] : PRE 1750
DOR, ENG [33904]

STIDOLPH 1675-1775 DEPTFORD & CHATHAM,
KEN, ENG [36486]

STIFF PRE 1848+ SFK, ENG [35759] : 1760-1870
NORTON & CHEDBURGH, SFK, ENG [36111] :
C1804+ IRON ACTON, GLS, ENG [38443]

STIGLINGH 1755+ RSA [36466]

STILES PRE 1882 MONCK TWP., ONT, CAN [36680] :
PRE 1800 GOUDHURST, SSX, ENG [35113] : PRE
1842 BKM, ENG [36839] : 1700-1900 RENSSELAER,
NY, USA [35292] : 1600-1900 ALBANY, NY, USA
[35292] : 1840S HURON CO., OH, USA [38331] :
1840S FRANKLIN CO., OH, USA [38331]

STILL 1846+ WELLINGTON, NSW, AUS [37313] :
1600-1900 BRISTOL, ENG [34722] : 1820-1940
LONDON, ENG [34722] : PRE 1880 KENTISH
TOWN, LND, ENG [36028] : 1500+ KEN, ENG
[36093] : 1800-1851 PYECOMBE, SSX, ENG [36938] :
1830-1920 INDIA [34722] : ALL USA [36334]

STILLER PRE 1877 LANGENBIELAU, SIL, GER
[34567]

STILLWELL C1750 BYFLEET, SRY, ENG [36860] :
1650-1680 KINGS CO., NY, USA [37477]

STILWELL 1783+ QUEENS CO., NB, CAN [36323] :
1820+ SUTTON, SRY, ENG [34514]

STIMPSON 1800-1875 KEN, ENG [37771] : PRE 1791
SOUTHWARK, LND, ENG [37909]

STINCHCOMB 1740-1800 WICKWAR, GLS, ENG
[37870]

STINCHCOMBE 1890+ CALGARY, ALB, CAN
[36523] : 1820+ THORNBURY, GLS, ENG [36523] :
C1920 LOS ANGELES, CA, USA [36523]

STINE 1810S LINCOLN CO., NC, USA [38066]

STINGERS 1834+ ALSTON, CUL, ENG [33775]

STINSON 1841+ BUNGENDORE, NSW, AUS [33923]
: 1840+ MERIVALE, ONT, CAN [33851] : 1600-1850
BELFAST, ANT, IRL [33851] : ALL BALLYMENA,
ANT, IRL [33923] : ALL ARM, IRL [34475]

STINTON RICHARD PRE 1760 STOKE BLISS, HEF,
ENG [36619]

STIPP ALL KEN & SRY, ENG [34325]

STIRLING 1840 MELBOURNE, VIC, AUS [37163] :
1800+ PER, SCT [34283] : 1880+ BRIDGE OF
ALLEN, STI, SCT [34283] : 1830+ SCT [34777] : 1790-
1850 KIRKINTILLOCH, DNB, SCT [35960] : MARY
C1770 MUTHILL, PER, SCT [37106]

STIRNAMAN PRE 1835 RANDOLPH CO., IL, USA
[37820]

STIRNIMANN PRE 1800 CANTON, AG, CH [37820]

STIRRAT 1857-1921 GLASGOW, LKS, SCT [33891] :
1700-1810 BATTURICK, DARBY, AYR, SCT [34074]
: 1800+ PAISLEY, RFW, SCT [37879]

STIRRUP PRE 1820 ST ALBANS, HRT, ENG [35232]

STIRTON AGNES C1804 DUNNICHEN &
RESCOBIE, ANS, SCT [34447] : 1700-1890 ST
NICHOLAS, ABD, SCT [36653]

STIRZAKER 1790S WEETON, LAN, ENG [37751]

STITES 1600+ HEMPSTEAD, NY & OH, USA & ENG
[38336]

STITT 1800 NEW CUMNOCK, AYR, SCT [36667]

STITTLE 1800S GRANTCHESTER, CAM, ENG
[33898]

STITTS C1890 GLASGOW, LKS, SCT [38463]

STIVENSEN 1880+ ADELAIDE, SA, AUS [33789]

ST JOHN ALL HAM, IOW & WIL, ENG [35418] :
1810S SC & NC, USA [38314]

ST LAURENT C1825 ST THOMAS, DWI [37819]

ST LAWRENCE 1750+ CLA, IRL [34684]

ST LEGER PRE 1823 BORRISOKANE, TIP, IRL
[34781]

ST LEON ALL WORLDWIDE [38073]

ST-MARTIN PIERRE PRE 1880 RIMOND-ARRIEGE,
MONTPELLIER, MP, FRA [34061]

STOAKES PRE 1865 MANSFIELD, NTT, ENG [34265]
: PRE 1864 SELLINGE, KEN, ENG [35799]

STOATES CAROLINE PRE 1820 LONDON, ENG
[36000]

STOBART 1800-1900 HARROGATE, YKS, ENG
[38380]

STOBBART PRE 1800 BARNARD CASTLE, DUR,
ENG [35448]

STOBBIE C1800 MONZIE, PER, SCT [35563]

STOBBO PRE 1850 FIF, SCT [37693]

STOBBS 1797+ PATELEY BRIDGE, WRY, ENG
[34827]

STOBER ALL LINKENHEIM, BAD, BRD [38342]

STOBIE ALL WORLDWIDE [37517]

STOBO 1840S PAISLEY, RFW, SCT [33934]

STOBS PRE 1800 WOLSINGHAM, DUR, ENG [33993]

STOCK PRE 1700 ESS, ENG [35642] : PRE 1914 LAN,
ENG [35895] : PRE 1850 ESS, ENG [36639] : C1892
BALTIMORE, MD, USA [38650] : C1884
PATERSON, NJ, USA [38650]

STOCKBRIDGE 1800S MELBOURN, CAM, ENG
[33898]

STOCKDALE ALL UK [35896]

STOCKER C1797+ RICHMOND, NSW, AUS [35537] :
1800+ WAR, ENG [37924]

STOCKERS PRE 1900 CAPE, RSA [38600] : PRE 1880
STOCKHOLM, SWE [38600]

STOCKFORD 1700+ WOOTTON, OXF, ENG [34121] :
ALL ENG [34671] : 1800-1850 SOM, ENG [35595]

STOCKHAM 1850S BRISTOL, SOM, ENG [36829]

STOCKLEY 1800S HRT, ENG [34684] : 1800+ LAN,
ENG [36042] : 1880S WESTMINSTER, MDX, ENG
[36230] : 1881+ DERBY, DBY, ENG [36230]

STOCKMAN PRE 1850 BRIXHAM, DEV, ENG [37393]
: C1800 MARYLEBONE, MDX, ENG [37718] :
1900+ NZ [34412]

STOCKMANN PRE 1850 POL [34478]

STOCKS C1810+ AUS [34444] : PRE 1914 LAN, ENG
[35895] : 1790 ILKESTON, DBY, ENG [36032] :
1810+ PINXTON, DBY, ENG [36854] : 1870+
SHIREOAKS, NTT, ENG [36854] : C1904 ELLBAY,
MAY, IRL [35895] : 1929+ NZ [35895]

STOCKTON ALL GIPPSLAND, VIC, AUS [35345] :
1800 ENG [35023] : ALL CHELSEA, MDX, ENG
[35345] : C1840 WHITECHAPEL, LND, ENG [37053]
: PRE 1934 ENG & AUS [33799]

STOCKWELL C1832 REDMILE, LEI, ENG [34358] :
1806 LONDON, ENG [34761] : PRE 1825 HYTHE,
KEN, ENG [34900] : PRE 1819 ULEY & DURSLEY,
GLS, ENG [35223] : PRE 1900 MANCHESTER,
LAN, ENG [35443] : 1700+ LONDON, ENG [36266] :
PRE 1850 OXF, ENG [37064]

STODALSKI ALL USA &, EUROPE [38369]

STODART 1839-1905 NAIRNE MAGILL, SA, AUS
[36757] : 1905-1910 MATATA, HB, NZ [36757] :
1910+ AUCKLAND, NZ [36757]

STODDART C1870 MUDGEE, NSW, AUS [35859] :
1853+ MELBOURNE, VIC, AUS [38008] : C1800
ROX, SCT [35032] : C1830 PORT AUGUSTUS, INV,
SCT [35859] : PRE 1800 YARROW, SEL, SCT [38376]
: EDWARD C1949 ARLINGTON & NEWARK, NJ,
USA [35786]

STODHART RALPH 1725+ NORTON, DUR, ENG
[35219]

STOELKE PRE 1825 LENGERICH, NRW, GER
[38663]

STOEL VAN DER 1750-1900 ROTTERDAM, ZH, NL
[38712]

STOFFER PRE 1840 ELBURG, GEL, NL [33751] : PRE
1840 ELBURG, GEL, NL [38692]

STOFFREGEN PRE 1850 BADINGEN, PSA, GER
[38648]

STOKELD MARY 1844 DURHAM, DUR, ENG [37334]

STOKER (SEE STOOKER) [38694]

STOKES 1849+ MAITLAND, NSW, AUS [34421] :
1840S SYDNEY, NSW, AUS [37104] : 1850-1900
HORNSBY, NSW, AUS [37969] : PRE 1897
DESERONTO, ONT, CAN [38480] : PRE 1850
HILLINGDON, MDX, ENG [33804] : ALL
BREAMORE, HAM, ENG [33823] : 1800S LONDON,
ENG [34178] : PRE 1860 LEI, ENG [34652] : 1715-
1845 BIRMINGHAM, WAR, ENG [34799] : WM. &
JOSEPH PRE 1860 BRADFORD, WRY, ENG [35164]
: PRE 1860 LITTLE CANFIELD, ESS, ENG [35200] :
PRE 1827 WIL, ENG [35236] : PRE 1700 ESS, ENG
[35642] : PRE 1900 HECKMONDWIKE, WRY, ENG
[36069] : PRE 1660 KINGSWINFORD, STS, ENG
[36110] : C1787 GRAVESDEN, KEN, ENG [36259] :
BRIDGET 1800-1850 LND, ENG [36297] : 1850S
DUNDRY, SOM, ENG [37969] : 1790 KILCORNAN,
LIM, IRL [34857] : 1830-1840 TIPPERARY, TIP, IRL
[37027] : 1860+ HOKITIKA, NZ [35967] : ALL CAPE,
RSA [38600] : PRE 1820 BRECHIN, PER, SCT [34031]

: 1850-1893 EDINBURGH, SCT [37469] : 1840S NEW HAVEN CO., CT, USA [37027]

STOKES BUTLER C1860 GLA, WLS [36803]

STOKES-BUTLER C1860 DANVILLE, PA, USA [36803]

STOLBERG PRE 1750 VACHA, THU, GER [38606]

STOLDOR C1869 BIRMINGHAM, ENG [35515]

STOLE ALL WORLDWIDE [37646]

STOLIKER 1775-1850 GANANQUA, ONT, CAN [38194]

STOLLZNOW PRE 1880 GUNTERBERG, UCKERMARK, GER [34766]

STOLTENBERG 1724 WELDA, GER [38750]

STOLTENBOER 1700-1855 BORK & ROTTERDAM, ZH, FRG & NL [38712]

STOMMEL PRE 1817 MUCH, RPR, GER [38647]

STONAL 1780S SEVERN STOKE, WOR, ENG [36190]

STONE 1850+ NSW, AUS [34424] : 1869+ SYDNEY, NSW, AUS [34979] : 1848+ SURRY HILLS, NSW, AUS [34979] : C1853+ VIC, AUS [35746] : 1817 WELLESLEY TWP., ONT, CAN [34503] : 1800+ WYKE REGIS, DOR, ENG [33774] : 1850+ SOUTHAMPTON, HAM, ENG [33774] : PRE 1857 SOUTH PETHERTON, SOM, ENG [33822] : PRE 1830 LYDEARD ST LAWRENCE, SOM, ENG [34201] : C1829 BIRMINGHAM, WAR, ENG [34972] : PRE 1848 BRK, ENG [34979] : PRE 1869 BIRMINGHAM, WAR, ENG [34979] : 1700-1870 BKM, ENG [35030] : PRE 1757 KINGSTON UPON THAMES, SRY, ENG [35157] : PRE 1835 PORTLAND, DOR, ENG [35211] : PRE 1800 TWICKENHAM, MDX, ENG [35500] : C1833 MILTON, KEN, ENG [35746] : C1800+ MELBOURNE, DBY, ENG [35851] : 1800-1840 BUSHEY & WATFORD, HRT, ENG [36044] : C1765 DORKING, SRY, ENG [36071] : PRE 1700 RUSPER, SSX, ENG [36179] : 1800+ DEPTFORD, KEN, ENG [36263] : C1780 EXETER, DEV, ENG [36271] : PRE 1830 BRADFORD ABBAS, DOR, ENG [36424] : PRE 1800 SHAFTESBURY, DOR, ENG [36478] : HERBERT 1870 HASTINGS, SSX, ENG [36633] : 1800S STOKENCHURCH, BKM, ENG [36708] : 1800S BIRMINGHAM, WAR, ENG [36764] : ROBERT PRE 1820 WESTMINSTER, LND, ENG [37321] : ALL HAM, ENG [37682] : 1854 DOVER, KEN, ENG [37690] : PRE 1865 RAMSGATE AREA, KEN, ENG [37720] : PRE 1871 LEATHERHEAD, SRY, ENG [37834] : 1915+ EXETER, DEV, ENG [37890] : PRE 1830 SEAL, KEN, ENG [38700] : C1740-1900 NORTH PETHERTON, SOM, ENG & USA [38309] : 1810-1870 WARREN CO., KY, USA [36734] : 1830 MI & NY, USA [38098] : JAMES 1826 PUTNAM CO., GA, USA [38155] : 1800S WI & NY, USA [38468] : PRE 1860 SC, USA [38576] : 1888+ VALLEY CO., NE, USA & ENG [38309] : PRE 1900 WLS & AUS [38746]

STONEHAM 1700S SOUTHFLEET, KEN, ENG [37019]

STONEHEWER PRE 1815 BIDDULPH, STS, ENG [36701]

STONEHOUSE 1600 ST ALBANS, HRT, ENG [34466] : ALL DUR & ERY, ENG [35002] : PRE 1771 NEWBATTLE, MLN, SCT [37852]

STONELL 1830-1840 BRIXTON, SRY, ENG [34832]

STONEMAN PRE 1820 ILLOGAN, CON, ENG [34795] : PRE 1850 DEV, ENG [36639]

STONER 1783+ ONT, CAN [38396] : 1805-1810 IRL [38201] : PRE 1855 PA, OH & IA, USA [34116] : 1777-1783 ONESKETHAU, ALBANY CO., NY, USA [38396]

STONES 1700-1870 BKM, ENG [35030] : 1800+ PATELEY BRIDGE, YKS, ENG [35891] : SARA 1820+ MANCHESTER & SALFORD, LAN, ENG [37748] : 1863+ SILKSTONE, WRY, ENG [38469]

STONESTREET C1800 BRIGHTLING, SSX, ENG [38397]

ST ONGE 1800-1850 DRUMMOND IS, ONT, CAN [36703] : 1840 NEW RICHMOND, QUE, CAN [38131]

STONIER PRE 1840 ASTBURY, CHS, ENG [36504] : PRE 1815 DILHORNE, STS, ENG [36701]

STOODLEY 1700-1800 CHARD & THORNCOMBE, SOM & DOR, ENG [37838] : 1880S PONTYPRIDD, GLA, WLS [37230]

STOOKE 1750S DAWLISH, DEV, ENG [34266] : 1500-1800 TEIGN & CHUDLEIGH VALLEY, DEV, ENG [34266]

STOOKER PRE 1820 HARLINGEN, FRI, NL [38694]

STOOKEY 1650-1737 CH [37784] : JACOB 1737-1900 USA [37784]

STOOPS C1825 ARMAGH, ARM, IRL [34223]

STOPCZYNSKI C1813 SANOK, POL [38184]

STOPP 1700+ OXFORD, OXF, ENG [35080]

STOPPS C1879 KYNETON, VIC, AUS [35133] : ALL LONDON, ENG [36152]

STORAASLI 1600-1900 TELEMARK, NOR [38588]

STORCK 1770-1865 LORCH, HEN, BRD [34010] : PRE 1750 SEEBACH, RPF, GER [38681]

STOREN 1880+ SOUTH MELBOURNE, VIC, AUS [35039] : 1865+ CAMPBELL'S CK, VIC, AUS [35039] : 1820+ O'BRIENSBRIDGE, CLA, IRL [35039]

STORER 1847+ SA, AUS [33789] : 1750-1880 WIRKSWORTH & DERBY, DBY, ENG [33789] : PRE 1753 ROTHBURY, NBL, ENG [35026] : PRE 1800 LONDON, ENG [35500] : C1791 BILLESDON, LEI, ENG [36803] : 1800+ NEWHALL, DBY, LEI & NTT, ENG [37552] : PRE 1900 INDIA [34562]

STORES 1830-45 MAITLAND, NSW, AUS [37921]

STOREY 1860+ CRESWICK, VIC, AUS [35525] : C1800 GRANTHAM, LIN, ENG [33793] : 1500-1900 TROUTBECK & WINDERMERE, WES, ENG [34158] : PRE 1850 NBL, ENG [36481] : 1700+ EARSDON & HARTLEY, NBL, ENG [36609] : 1820+ LONDON, ENG [37165] : 1800-1840 CUL, ENG [37613] : 1900S WINDERMERE, CUL, ENG [37853] : ALL NRY, ENG [37929] : PRE 1880 LONDON, SRY, ENG [38512] : 1700+ MONASTEREVAN & DUBLIN, KID, IRL [36087] : 1700-1900 LETTERKENNY, DON, IRL [36727] : 1775-1850 FER, IRL [37795] : 1790+ DOUGLAS, IOM, UK [34158] : WILLIAM 1760-1790 MONTVILLE, CT, USA [38134] : WILLIAM 1760-1790 PRESTON, CT, USA [38134] : JAMES WILLIAM 1815-1866 NORWICH, CT, USA [38134] : WILLIAM JAMES 1815-1866 NORWICH, CT, USA [38134]

STORIE 1830S LANARK & RENFREW, ONT, CAN [36695] : 1850S SHAWVILLE, QUE, CAN [36695] : 1800 FALKIRK, STI, SCT [34602] : PRE 1830 MOTHERWELL, SCT [36695]

STORK PRE 1800 CHESTER CO., PA, USA [38017]

STORKS 1700 LONGBRIDGE DEVERILL, WIL, ENG [34466]

STORM PRE 1900 ROBIN HOODS BAY, YKS, ENG [36481]

STORMER 1860+ WOLFHAGEN, HES, GER [38186]

STORMONT 1800+ BELFAST, ANT & DOW, IRL [37425]

STORMS C1813 BULLITT CO., KY, USA [37527]

STORR 1875-1940 ELLOUGHTON, ERY, ENG [36703] : 1840 WHITBY, NRY, ENG [37388]

STORRAR C1750-1800 FIF, SCT [36327]

STORRIER ALL WORLDWIDE [35884]

STORRS 1730-1820 STURTON LE STEEPLE, NTT, ENG [36426] : PRE 1520 SUTTON CUM LOUND, NTT, ENG [36426]

STORTZ PRE 1822 FRANKFURT AM MAIN, GER [35236]

STORY 1830+ TAS, AUS [37134] : 1850-1870 YORK CO., ONT, CAN [34482] : ALL ENG [34131] : 1770+ DUR, ENG [34408] : 1770+ CARLISLE, CUL, ENG [34688] : JAMES WILLIAM 1815-1866 NORWICH, CT, USA [38134] : WILLIAM JAMES 1815-1866 NORWICH, CT, USA [38134] : WILLIAM 1760-1790 PRESTON, CT, USA [38134] : WILLIAM 1760-1790 MONTVILLE, CT, USA [38134]

STOTE PRE 1750 HAM, ENG [36380]

STOTT 1860S+ BENDIGO, VIC, AUS [35706] : PRE 1857 BOLTON, LAN, ENG [33763] : C1830 RIPON, WRY, ENG [34025] : 1820S-1830S HOUGHTON LE SPRING, DUR, ENG [35706] : ALL DUR, ENG [35706] : 1798-1880 LEEDS & HUDDERSFIELD, WRY, ENG [36391] : 1800+ BAMFORD ROCHDALE, LAN, ENG [37626] : ALL HOLYWELL GREEN, YKS, ENG [38332] : PRE 1850 FOVERAN, ABD, SCT [34784] : 1790+ DUNROSSNESS, SHI, SCT [35855]

STOTTS 1880+ ONT, CAN [38463] : 1800S LAWRENCE CO., IN, USA [37028]

STOUPP PRE 1844 IRL [34645]

STOURTON PRE 1801 BLOOMSBURY, LND, ENG [36047] : PRE 1800 TEALBY, LIN, ENG [36047] : PRE 1800 WALESBY, LIN, ENG [36047]

STOUT C1870+ MELBOURNE, VIC, AUS [35053] : 1700+ GUILDFORD, SRY, ENG [35560] : PRE 1650 BURTON JOYCE PARISH, NTT, ENG [36972] : C1780 HOLLAND, ZUH, NL [38702] : 1700+ LONGHOPE, OKI, SCT [34688] : 1756+ KIRKW, SHI, CAI & OKI, SCT [35002] : 1790+ DUNROSSNESS, SHI, SCT [35855] : 1790-1860 DELTING, SHI, SCT [36762] : PRE 1810 LONGHOPE, OKI, SCT [36883] : ALL MO, USA [38320] : C1750 FAYETTE CO., OH, USA [38367] : 1790S-1900 BROWNING, GREEN CO., IL & PA, USA [38532]

STOVER 1700-1850 MARKHAM, ONT, CAN [36727] : 1785+ LENNOX & ADDINGTON, ONT, CAN [38517] : PRE 1814 CARTER CO., TN, USA [37551]

STOVIN PRE 1840 ENG [36677]

STOVOLD PRE 1800 SRY, ENG [34660]

STOW 1910+ VIC, AUS [35136] : PRE 1900 LONDON, ENG [35229]

STOWARD PRE 1811 COGHILL'S HILL, ESS, ENG [34917]

STOWE 1866+ CAMBERWELL, NSW, AUS [34942] : 1866-1930 SINGLETON, NSW, AUS [34942] : 1830+ TYWADREATH, CON, ENG [34881] : C1828 NTH, ENG & AUS [34942]

STOWELL C1835 NSW, AUS [35410] : ALL AXBRIDGE, SOM, ENG [34362] : 1800 LAN, ENG [35410] : 1800-1900 LIVERPOOL, LAN, ENG [37508] : 1700-1800S LAN & CHS, ENG & IOM [37221] : ALL WORLDWIDE [37646]

STOWELLS ALL WORLDWIDE [37366]

STOWEY 1800+ BRISTOL, GLS, ENG [34082]

STOYLE ALL WORLDWIDE [34833]

STOYLES ALL WORLDWIDE [34833]

ST PIERRE 1870+ WALLACEBURG, ONT, CAN [34983]

STRACHAN PRE 1830 ANS, SCT [34053] : 1800 DUNDEE, ANS, SCT [34098] : 1700-1900 LKS, SCT [34624] : PRE 1860 ALVAH, BAN, SCT [34840] : 1800+ BEW, SCT [35909] : PRE 1836 FETTERESSO, KCD, SCT [36308] : PRE 1900 EDINBURGH, MLN, SCT [37561] : PRE 1860 NEW MACHAR, ABD, SCT [37708] : PRE 1800 ELLON, ABD, SCT & AUS [35079]

STRADER 1770-1850 MUHLENBERG CO., KY, USA [38120]

STRADLING ALL DEV, ENG [37020] : ALL SOM, ENG [37020]

STRAHAN PRE 1900 LONDON, ENG [34611] : PRE 1850 SHOREDITCH & BETHNAL GREEN, MDX, ENG [37768] : 1800-1920 WESTCHESTER, NY, USA [36445]

STRAIGHT C1700 ST ALLEN, CON, ENG [35076] : ALL WORLDWIDE [36548]

STRAIN PRE 1884 BELFAST, ANT, IRL [35601] : PRE 1800 DOW, IRL [38057] : 1700-1850 STONEYKIRK, WIG, SCT [35572] : PRE 1850 VERMILLION CO., IN, USA [36929]

STRAITH 1830+ UDNEY & NEW MACHAR, ABD, SCT [34374]

STRALEY C1758 AMHERST, VA, USA [37819] : PRE 1785 GILES, VA, USA [37819] : PRE 1830 TAZEWELL, IL, USA [37819]

STRANAHAN ALL DOW, IRL [37506] : ALL USA [37506]

STRAND C1690 AMSTERDAM, NL [36459] : SVEN GUSTAF 1950+ GRANNA LANDSFORSAMLING, JONKOPINGS LAN, SWE [38548] : 1880+ POLK CO., WI, USA [34473]

STRANEY 1820-1840 LIVERPOOL, LAN, ENG [35431] : PRE 1820 DOWNPATRICK, DOW, IRL [35431]

STRANG 1690S ARLINGTON, GLS, ENG [35261] : 1760+ FORFAR, ANS, SCT [35560]

STRANGE PRE 1850 SA, AUS [35743] : 1800+ GREENWICH, KEN, ENG [34415] : 1800 OXF, ENG [35793] : 1800S MILTON BY GRAVESEND, KEN, ENG [36211] : PRE 1800 THORNDON, SFK, ENG [37442] : JOSEPH 1850S ASTON TERRID, BRK & OXF, ENG [37476] : PRE 1685 BIDEFORD, DEV, ENG [37587] : 1700-1775 NEW KENT & HALIFAX CO., VA, USA [37587]

STRANGEWAYS 1800+ BERWICK UPON TWEED, NBL, ENG [34702] : 1700+ CON & DEV, ENG [34742]

STRANIELLO PRE 1800 ITL [34984]

STRAPP 1860+ LONDON, ENG [36070] : PRE 1900 BDF, ENG [36070] : 1700-1900 CLOPHILL, BDF, ENG [36070] : 1800S LEIGHTON BUZZARD, BDF, ENG [36070] : 1860+ TUNBRIDGE WELLS, KEN, ENG [36070] : 1800S TODDINGTON, BDF, ENG [36070]

STRAT C1826 BLENBURY, BRK, ENG [36975]

STRATFIELD ALL MARSWORTH, HRT, ENG [35480]

STRATFORD 1850S LONDON, ONT, CAN [37566] : 1833+ BRANTFORD, ONT, CAN [37566] : 1833+ WOODSTOCK, ONT, CAN [37566] : PRE 1800 LONDON, MDX & SSX, ENG [34733] : PRE 1890 DRAYTON, BKM, ENG [34978] : PRE 1890 DRAYTON, BKM, ENG [35368] : PRE 1820 LONDON, MDX & KEN, ENG [36379] : 1760 COATES, GLS, ENG [37209] : 1782 TEWKESBURY, GLS, ENG [37209] : 1772+ BEACONSFIELD, BKM, ENG [37566] : 1764+ HIGH WYCOMBE, BKM, ENG [37566] : 1696-1911 KLIPHEUWEZ, CAPE, RSA [34947]

STRATFUL ALL MARSWORTH, HRT, ENG [35480] : ALL CHEDDINGTON, BKM, ENG [35480]

STRATH C1750 RATHEN, ABD, SCT [34400]

STRATHAM PRE 1820 RFW, SCT [33999]

STRATIELD ALL CHEDDINGTON, BKM, ENG [35480]

STRATTEN 1820+ SCT [38293]

STRATTON 1850+ ADELAIDE, SA, AUS [34755] : PRE 1850 ST PAULS WALDEN & KIMPTON, HRT, ENG [34450] : C1819-1848 LILSFORD, WIL, ENG [34755] : C1670-1750 WILCOT, WIL, ENG [34755] : C1730-1809 WOODBOROUGH, WIL, ENG [34755] : ALL KEN, ENG [34961] : PRE 1750 SHRIVENHAM,

STROH 1870-1890 KEWEENAW CO., MI, USA [38009]
STROHM PRE 1840 BOUS, PRE, GER [38333]
STROHM (SEE STROME) [34503]
STROME 1810+ WATERLOO TWP., ONT, CAN [34503]
STRONACH 1910+ TORONTO, ONT, CAN [35346] : 1880+ LEEDS, YKS, ENG [35346] : PRE 1900 LONDON, ENG [35346]
STRONG 1820+ LINCOLN CO., ONT, CAN [34130] : ALL WHITBY, YKS, ENG [34724] : 1800S HOCKWORTHY & CULLOMPTON, DEV, ENG [35188] : ROBERT 1750-1860 STH PETHERWIN, CON, ENG [35581] : 1800S SRY, ENG [35965] : 1800-1850 ASTON, WAR, ENG [36057] : 1790-1880 SHALDON, DEV, ENG [36069] : 1850+ SAMPFORD PEVERELL, DEV, ENG [36069] : ALL STANFORD IN THE VALE, BRK, ENG [36076] : 1700-1830 WIL, ENG [36130] : 1800+ LND & MDX, ENG [36430] : PRE 1650 SOM & CAE, ENG & WLS [38746] : 1630-1900 IL, USA [37538] : 1630-1900 MA, USA [37538] : 1835-1847 POMFRET, VT, USA [38099] : CHARLES E. 1860+ NEW HAVEN, CT, USA [38766]
STRONGWELL PRE 1800 KEN, ENG [37006]
STROUD 1875+ DUBBO, NSW, AUS [35238] : PRE 1835 SPEEN, OXF, ENG [34043] : PRE 1855 LONDON, ENG [35238] : 1840+ NOTTINGHAM & BEESTON, NTT, ENG [36105] : 1800+ DERBY, DBY, ENG [36257] : PRE 1840 CITY OF WESTMINSTER, LND, ENG [36377] : 1600-1800 UK [36324] : 1800+ FORESTVILLE, MI, USA [37422]
STROVER PRE 1850 BRISTOL, GLS, ENG [35215]
STROWBRIDGE ALL DEV, ENG [37717]
STROYAN 1800S LANRICK, PER, SCT [36635]
STRUBI ALL CH [36661]
STRUBY ALL CAN [36661] : ALL USA [36661]
STRUCKMANN 1850+ DARKEHMEN, OPR, GER [35865]
STRUDLING PRE 1820 WAPPING & WHITECHAPEL, LND, ENG [38731]
STRUDWICK 1875+ WAIL & HORSHAM, VIC, AUS [37555] : 1851+ MYPONGA & YANKALILLA, SA, AUS [37555] : 1750+ WISBOROUGH GREEN & PETWORTH, SSX, ENG [34726] : 1822-1840 BRASTED, KEN, ENG [36136] : PRE 1851 HERNE, KEN, ENG [37555]
STRUDWICKE ALL AUS [35550] : 1720+ ENG [35550]
STRUEBY ALL CAN [36661] : ALL USA [36661]
STRUGNELL ALL DEV, ENG [35423] : 1695 BISHOPS WALTHAM, HAM, ENG [36263] : PRE 1730 DROXFORD, HAM, ENG [36396]
STRUGNELLE PRE 1826 DOR, ENG [36679]
STRUMMEY 1700-1850 SSX, ENG [34975]
STRUNK LUDWIG 1819-1883 WEITEFELD, WEF, GER [38127] : 1700+ DAADEN, RPF, GER & USA [38016]
STRUTHERS 1860-1900 AUS [34928] : 1840-1860 MADRAS, INDIA [34928] : PRE 1916 HAMILTON & MOTHERWELL, LKS, SCT [35007]
STRUTT PRE 1820 DEPTFORD & LAMBETH, SRY, ENG [37321]
STRUTZBECKEN C1711 RUDESBURG, SHO, GER [37819]
STUART C1840 VIC, AUS [33881] : CHARLES 1880+ JUNEE & WINCHENDONVALE, NSW, AUS [35230] : JESS 1880+ JUNEE & WINCHENDONVALE, NSW, AUS [35230] : 1900 MOLONG, NSW, AUS [37133] : PRE 1830 OXFORD, OXF, ENG [34197] : PRE 1820 BOLTON LE MOORS, LAN, ENG [34487] : PRE 1800 KENWYN, CON, ENG [35500] : 1815+ LIVERPOOL, LAN, ENG [36502] : GEORGE PRE 1910 LONDON, ENG [36526] : PRE 1840 MOG, IRL [33881] : ROBERT PRE 1832 TYR, IRL [34247] : 1821 NTH, IRL [37141] : PRE 1840 DRUMBESS, CAV, IRL [38292] : 1750-1800 DERRY, IRL [38529] : JAMES C1800-1870S BELFAST & BALLYMENA, ANT, IRL [38593] : 1700-1815 GENOA, ITL [36502] : PRE 1860 GLASGOW, SCT [33906] : PRE 1900 EDINBURGH, SCT [34001] : 1770 DUNKELD, PER, SCT [34084] : PRE 1800 ABERLOUR, BAN, SCT [34192] : 1770-1850 KEITH, BAN, SCT [34479] : C1800 KILBARCHAN, RFW, SCT [34644] : 1700-1850 ANSTRUTHER WESTER, FIF, SCT [35395] : 1700S SCT [37330] : 1600-1900 PERTH & CARLETON, PER, SCT & CAN [36669] : 1850+ LAPEER CO., MI, USA [36720] : 1500+ MUHLENBERG CO., KY, IL & NC, USA & SCT [36970]
STUBBERFIELD 1800+ NINFIELD, SSX, ENG [35629]
STUBBING 1700+ CHESTERFIELD, DBY, ENG [36493]
STUBBINGS PRE 1880 ACCRINGTON, LAN, ENG [34675] : PRE 1871 HEMPSTEAD, ESS, ENG [35517] : PRE 1900 LAKENHEATH, SFK, ENG [35742] : 1700 HEMPSTEAD, ESS, ENG [37125] : 1854-1931 ICKLETON, CAM, ENG & NZ [34651]
STUBBINS ALL AUS [37487]
STUBBLE 1800 EVERSLEY, BRK, ENG [37170]
STUBBLETY 1850+ MELBOURNE, VIC, AUS [33789] : PRE 1850 CON, ENG [33789]
STUBBLETZ PRE 1850 GER [33789]
STUBBS 1830-1900 CAMDEN, NSW, AUS [34438] : 1791+ WINDSOR, NSW, AUS [35427] : 1840-1900 HUNTERS HILL, NSW, AUS [35559] : ALL ORANGEVILLE & CALEDON, ONT, CAN [37518] : ALL LAMBTON CO., ONT, CAN [37518] : 1800-1875 SPENNYMOOR, DUR, ENG [33955] : C1820 BRIXTON, DEV, ENG [35778] : C1770 CHEADLE, STS, ENG [35920] : 1880+ WALWORTH, LND, ENG [36430] : 1850+ LEEDS, YKS, ENG [36797] : C1850 NORTHWICH, CHS, ENG [36806] : PRE 1783 SHERBURN IN ELMET, YKS, ENG [37144] : ALL YKS, ENG & NZ [36840]
STUBELER C1835+ WUE, GER [35272]
STUBINGER 1750-1830 QUE, CAN [36737]
STUCHBURY ALL ENG [36221]
STUCKAR PRE 1854 RASTADT, CHER, SU [38738]
STUCKEY 1800+ AUS [33769] : 1800+ GOULBURN, NSW, AUS [38356] : PRE 1750 SOM, ENG [36166] : 1820-1890 HUNTINGDON, HUN, ENG [36675] : PRE 1642 CHEDDON FITZPAINE, SOM, ENG [37876]
STUCKI 1700-1900S LATTERBACH, BE, CH [37550]
STUDDERT 1800+ CLA & LIM, IRL [34692] : PRE 1850 KILKEE, CLA, IRL [35829]
STUDDS 1800+ MDX, ENG [36987]
STUDLEY ALL WORLDWIDE [33858]
STUETZEL PRE 1800 FREINSHEIM, RPF, GER [38681]
STUFFEN 1500-1600 WARSOP, NTT, ENG [36802]
STUFFLEBEAM C1810-1840 PICKAWAY CO., OH, USA [35284]
STUHM 1800+ WESSELBUREN, SHO, GER [35616]
STUKENBROK 1676-1765 HOLZHAUSEN, PYR, GER [38750] : 1765 HOLZHAUSEN, PYR, GER [38750] : 1828 ELBRINXEN, LIP, GER [38750]
STUMBAUGH PRE 1850 HIGHLAND CO., OH, USA [37565]
STUMBLES PRE 1750 DEV, ENG [34707] : PRE 1900 DEV, ENG & AUS [34679]
STUMP C1850 RANDOLPH CO., IN, USA [38367]
STUPAKOFF ALL WORLDWIDE [36172]

STURDEVANT JOSEPH 1783-1862 YORK, PA & MI, USA [37813]

STURDOCK 1600+ STROOD, KEN, ENG [35355]

STURE PRE 1746 LODDISWELL, DEV, ENG [35895]

STURGE ALL OLVESTON, GLS, ENG [36881]

STURGEON 1822+ OATLANDS, TAS, AUS [35443] : 1700-1800 RISBY, SFK, ENG [35094] : PRE 1800 STANTON, SFK, ENG [35443] : 1750-1900 ENG & AUS [34632] : 1800-1900 DUMFRIES, DFS, SCT [37779]

STURGES 1750+ MONKTON DEVERILL, WIL, ENG [36521]

STURGIS 1819+ NSW, AUS [35510] : 1750+ MONKTON DEVERILL, WIL, ENG [36521]

STURM C1740 HAMBURG, GER [36638] : 1700S ZEL, NL [38350] : 1850+ WESTMORELAND CO., PA, USA [37549]

STURMAN 1830-1860 BUNWELL, NFK, ENG [37376]

STURROCK 1750-1850 FORFAR, ANS, SCT [34523]

STURTEVANT MARY PRE 1800 GA, USA [38536]

STURZAKER ALL WORLDWIDE [35817]

STUT (SEE STOUT) [36883]

STUTCHBURY ALL ENG [36221] : ALL WORLDWIDE [37991]

STUTE PRE 1850 BRD [38238]

STUTLEY ALL LONDON, ENG [34742]

STUTSMAN C1774+ LANCASTER, PA, USA [38067]

STUTT C1872-1918 TEESWATER & RICHMOND HILL, ONT & SAS, CAN [36693] : C1840-1916 CULROSS & TEESWATER, ONT & SAS, CAN [36693] : C1910-1930 TEESWATER & YORK CO., ONT & SAS, CAN [36693] : C1833-1891 CLARKE TWP., ONT, CAN [36693] : 1750-1850 LISNASKEA, FER, IRL [35151] : C1812-1832 BOYHILL & TATTINDERRY, FER, IRL [36693]

STUTTARD 1700-1830 COLNE, LAN, ENG [37859] : 1830-1860 WIGHILL, WRY, ENG [37859]

STUTZIENS 1700+ MAINHARDT, BAW, GER [35355]

STYCHNOW ALL CHRUSZOBROD, KRAKOW, POL [38678]

STYLES 1794 MARDEN, KEN, ENG [34540] : ALL SALEHURST, KEN, ENG [35706] : 1762 KEN, ENG [35872] : C1800 LAMBETH & EAST HORSLEY, SRY, ENG [37420] : JAMES C1860 CLAPHAM, SRY, ENG [38268] : ROBERT 1800 LOU, IRL [37791] : 1860 DUBLIN, IRL [37791]

STYRING PRE 1800 DONCASTER, WRY, ENG [36011]

SUAREZ PRE 1805 HORMIGUEROS, PR, USA [37819]

SUBRA (SEE SABRA) [36929]

SUCH 1780 ERY, ENG [34731] : 1800-1860 BIRMINGHAM, WAR, ENG [35166]

SUCKER PRE 1790 NFK, ENG [35458]

SUCKLING 1800+ NEATHERSFIELD, ESS, ENG [35847] : ALL ENG [35868]

SUDBURY 1940+ DUNGOG, NSW, AUS [38494] : PRE 1800 CLIPSTON, NTT, ENG [38494]

SUDDABY 1880 ERY, ENG [34731]

SUDDES PRE 1800 DURHAM, DUR, ENG [36056]

SUDDICK ALL MIDDLESBROUGH, YKS, ENG [35767]

SUDDOUS PRE 1800 DURHAM, DUR, ENG [36056]

SUDE 1611-1782 RHENEGGE, WAL, GER [34912] : 1611-1714 GIEBRINGHAUSEN, WAL, GER [34912]

SUDICK PRE 1806 DUR, ENG [34982]

SUDLOW 1879 WEST DERBY, LAN, ENG [38470]

SUEL 1700+ GREAT MUSGRAVE, WES, ENG [35908]

SUERIZIN ALL NIZHNY NOVGAROD, SU [36889]

SUFF 1820S MON, WLS [35156]

SUGAR PRE 1700 BETHNAL GREEN, LND, ENG [36295] : PRE 1720 WOR, ENG [36619]

SUGARMAN ALL MANCHESTER, ENG & POL [35757]

SUGDEN 1890 MAITLAND, NSW, AUS [37963] : 1882+ SYDNEY, NSW, AUS [37987] : 1800+ KEIGHLEY, YKS, ENG [35734] : 1820+ BRADFORD, YKS, ENG [36638] : C1842 YKS, ENG [37963]

SUGEL ALL WORLDWIDE [37808]

SUGG PRE 1840 SHAPWICK, SOM, ENG [35346] : ALL WORLDWIDE [36324]

SUGGATE 1843+ NSW & VIC, AUS [35222] : ALL SFK, KEN & LND, ENG [35222]

SUGGETT 1600-1700 RINGSTEAD, NFK, ENG [38453]

SUGGIT 1600+ NRY, ENG [34181]

SUIDWEG (SEE ZUIDWEG [38350]

SUITTIE (SEE SUTIE) [36268]

SULLINGS PRE 1900 ROCKY RIVER, NSW, AUS [33949]

SULLIVAN 1850-1900 GIPPSLAND, VIC, AUS [33879] : 1841+ GRAFTON & TENTERFIELD, NSW, AUS [34198] : MARY PRE 1890 BATHURST & ORANGE, NSW, AUS [34545] : 1841+ GRAFTON, NSW, AUS [34596] : ELLEN 1840-1846 BROULEE, NSW, AUS [34699] : ELLEN 1830-1846 HAWKESBURY RV DIST, NSW, AUS [34699] : WILLIAM 1800-1850 HAWKESBURY RV DIST, NSW, AUS [34699] : 1840-1990 BRISBANE, QLD, AUS [35308] : JOHN 1860S SYDNEY, NSW, AUS [35988] : 1840 MELBOURNE, VIC, AUS [37163] : MARY ANN 1827+ SINGLETON, NSW, AUS [37553] : MARY ANN 1821-1827 RICHMOND & WINDSOR, NSW, AUS [37553] : JAMES 1885 BINGARA, NSW, AUS [37553] : 1750 YARMOUTH CO., NS, CAN [34162] : CATHERINE PRE 1860 HALIFAX, NS, CAN [34206] : PRE 1924 ST HELIER, CHI [36372] : PRE 1850 LIVERPOOL, LAN, ENG [33814] : PRE 1860 WINGATE, DUR, ENG [34933] : MARY-ANNE 1785-1810S TAUNTON, SOM, ENG [36880] : JAMES C1775 MDX, ENG [37553] : MARY ANN 1805-1820 MDX, ENG [37553] : C1840 CLA, IRL [33881] : 1800S OUGHTERARD, GAL, IRL [34930] : 1840+ NENAGH, TIP, IRL [35100] : 1830+ GOLDING, TIP, IRL [35218] : 1700-1950 COR, IRL [35308] : 1700-1900 KER, IRL [35308] : 1800+ COR, IRL [35448] : 1830-60 BANTRY, COR, IRL [35516] : C1848 KILLARNEY, KER, IRL [35920] : 1802+ CARRIGALINE, COR, IRL [35921] : 1800S NEWCASTLE WEST, LIM, IRL [35964] : C1800-1830S RAYMORE, KER, IRL [36314] : PRE 1860 COR, IRL [36963] : 1800+ KIL, IRL [37306] : PRE 1840 KILMARE, TIP, IRL [37945] : JEREMIAH 1800S CARRIGALINE, COR, IRL & AUS [34596] : MARY 1846 COR, IRL & USA [37481] : JOHN PRE 1846 COR, IRL & USA [37481] : JOHN 1840 COR, IRL & USA [37481] : TOM 1841-1990 DUNEDIN, OTAGO, NZ [36832] : 1855-1865 KEWEENAW CO., MI, USA [38009] : PRE 1860 WHITE PIGEON, IL, USA [38365] : 1900+ PEN-Y-CRAIG, GLA, WLS [34921]

SULLIVANT C1750 LUNENBURG CO., VA, USA [37536]

SULLY 1830-1880 BELFAST, ANT, IRL [35006]

SULTON C1850 WILLITON, SOM, ENG [36860]

SUMBLER PRE 1745 WIL, ENG [34959]

SUMERVILLE 1880S WALLS, SHI, SCT [35881]

SUMICHRAST 1800-1880 VIENNA, OES [37747]

SUMMERBELL 1850S SUNDERLAND, DUR, ENG [37853]

SUMMERELL C1860 SSX, ENG [36878] : 1600+ KINGSTON UPON HULL, YKS, ENG [38745]

SUMMERER ALL BAV, GER [34086]

SUMMERFIELD 1750+ WOLLASTON, NTH, ENG [36123] : 1750+ ODELL & SHARNBROOK, BDF, ENG [36123]

SUMMEROUR 1914-1928 MONT, USA [36445] : 1920-1928 ID, USA [36445] : 1800-1890 WALTON, GA, USA [36445]

SUMMERS PRE 1894 KADINA & MOUNT BARKER, SA, AUS [33890] : 1820+ LONGFORD, TAS, AUS [34770] : 1870+ MELBOURNE, VIC, AUS [36361] : JOHN PRE 1869 MELROSE & KADINA, SA, AUS & ENG [33890] : 1800-1900 SUMMERSTOWN, ONT, CAN [37807] : PRE 1850 YKS, ENG [34037] : PRE 1850 HEREFORD, HEF, ENG [34037] : PRE 1831 EGLINGHAM, NBL, ENG [34198] : 1820S-1850 BIRLINGHAM & PERSHORE, WOR, ENG [36190] : 1700-1850 GLS, ENG [36541] : PRE 1850 SEDGLEY, STS, ENG [37085] : 1750+ HRT & SRY, ENG [37304] : PRE 1866 SRY, ENG [37358] : ALL NBL, ENG [37704] : 1750-1860 HARESFIELD, GLS, ENG [38003] : PRE 1850S LIMERICK, LIM, IRL [34037] : 1860+ DUBLIN, IRL [35712] : PRE 1900 KILLINANE, CAR, IRL [36361] : PRE 1900 HAMILTON, LKS, SCT [36893] : PRE 1850 MACONCO, MO, USA [38231]

SUMMERSELL 1740S LAMBETH, LND, ENG [35261] : C1700 ST KITTS, W.INDIES [35261] : ALL WORLDWIDE [35261]

SUMMERSGILL 1800S OLDHAM, LAN, ENG [37442]

SUMMERTON PRE 1800 OXHILL, WAR, ENG [37371]

SUMMERVILLE PRE 1860 ARM, IRL [35953]

SUMMITT 1790 LINCOLN CO., NC, USA [38017]

SUMMY ALL USA [36896]

SUMNER 1860+ BOMBALA, NSW, AUS [34977] : 1850+ VIC, AUS [35489] : 1804 1800-1899 DUFFERIN CO., ONT, CAN [37441] : 1780+ WAR, ENG [33790] : 1788-1880 KINETON, WAR, ENG [35123] : ALL GRANTHAM, ROWSTON & DIGBY, LIN, ENG [35746] : 1800+ LONDON, ENG [36257] : 1725+ ASTON, CHS, ENG [37039]

SUMPTER 1750+ HISTON HALL, CAM, ENG [35824]

SUMPTION 1700+ CASTLE COMBE, WIL, ENG [34970]

SUNCKELL 1750+ WES, ENG [33986]

SUNDERHAUS 1835-1870 HAMILTON CO., OH, USA [38573] : 1835-1870 MERCER CO., OH, USA [38573]

SUNDERLAND 1830+ KURRAJONG, NSW, AUS [34755] : C1870 DUBBO, NSW, AUS [34755] : 1808+ SYDNEY, NSW, AUS [34755] : 1700-1890 YKS, ENG [36844] : 1850-1800 PA, USA [34410]

SUNDERMEYER 1940-1950 FARGO, ND, USA [38092]

SUNDSTRUP ALL WORLDWIDE [35809]

SUNLEY C1860 BRIDLINGTON, YKS, ENG [34653] : 1827 SHOREDITCH, MDX, ENG [37380] : 1851-57 SOUTHAMPTON, HAM, ENG [37380] : 1794-1854 CLERKENWELL, MDX, ENG [37380]

SUNSBURG ALL WORLDWIDE [34740]

SUPPLE PRE 1847 PORT FAIRY, VIC, AUS [35431] : 1846 BELFAST & HAY, VIC & NSW, AUS [36600] : 1900 MANCHESTER, LAN, ENG [35881] : C1847 NOTTINGHAM, NTT, ENG [37148] : C1795 ST MARYS, DUB, IRL [37148]

SUPPWELL 1846 BELFAST & HAY, VIC & NSW, AUS [36600]

SURGAY ALL WORLDWIDE [36140]

SURGEY ALL WORLDWIDE [36140]

SURGUY ALL WORLDWIDE [36140]

SURMAN ALL WAR & WOR, ENG [37090] : PRE 1862 MDX, ENG [37358]

SURRIDGE 1840-1880 HAMMERSMITH, MDX, ENG [36150] : C1903+ WALTHAMSTOW, ESS & ONT, ENG & CAN [36693]

SURTEES PRE 1861 WELSINGTON, DUR, ENG [35507] : PRE 1800 TANFIELD & SUNDERLAND, DUR, ENG [35605] : ALL WORLDWIDE [38329]

SURTES 1800+ BURSLEM, STS, ENG [38410]

SUSHAM PRE 1830 CASTON, NFK, ENG [35151]

SUSSAMS PRE 1830 CASTON, NFK, ENG [35151]

SUSSEX PRE 1800 LITTLEHAM, DEV, ENG [33780] : 1700+ ST GILES, DEV, ENG [35511]

SUSTINS 1800+ LOWESTOFT & KESSINGLAND, SFK, ENG [34903]

SUTCLIFFE 1842 HOBART, TAS, AUS [35705] : PRE 1904 YKS, ENG [34775] : PRE 1842 ROOF TOP, YKS, ENG [35705] : 1750-1830 LANGFIELD, WRY, ENG [36635] : 1750-1850 OLDHAM, LAN, ENG [36898] : 1790+ ACCRINGTON, LAN, ENG [36955] : 1790+ NEWCHURCH IN ROSSENDALE, LAN, ENG [36955] : 1800S WHALLEY, LAN, ENG [37490] : LYDIA 1860S COLNE, LAN, ENG [38284] : THOMAS 1822 MYTHOLMROYD, LAN, ENG [38284] : PRE 1811 CALVERLEY, WRY, ENG [38469]

SUTER 1800+ WANDSWORTH, SRY, ENG [37171] : 1800+ PUTNEY, SRY, ENG [37171] : 1850+ GLASGOW, INV, SCT [36369] : 1780-1840 PA, USA [36908]

SUTERS HENRY &MARTHA 1856-1903 (ARMY), UK & INDIA [34889]

SUTHERLAND 1850+ VIC, AUS [33793] : 1850-1870 TAMWORTH, NSW, AUS [34251] : ALL EUROA, VIC, AUS [34674] : 1874+ BRISBANE, QLD, AUS [35015] : C1900 MELBOURNE, VIC, AUS [35068] : PRE 1844 MELBOURNE, VIC, AUS [35088] : 1848+ WALCHA, NSW, AUS [35740] : 1855-1865 HEXHAM, VIC, AUS [36623] : 1850+ PORTLAND, VIC, AUS [38082] : 1824 ONT, CAN [34474] : 1859-1927 FISHERS GRANT, NS & BC, CAN [37499] : C1784 GLENGARRY, ONT, CAN [38466] : PRE 1820 SUNDERLAND, DUR, ENG [34588] : 1800+ HOLBORN & HACKNEY, MDX, ENG [34882] : PRE 1775 LATHERON, CAI, SCT [33873] : 1800-1870 FORSE, CAI, SCT [33991] : 1800+ DORNOCH, SUT, SCT [34260] : ROBERT PRE 1837 WICK, CAI, SCT [34310] : C1780 WICK, CAI, SCT [34362] : C1825 ST MARGARET'S HOPE, OKI, SCT [34362] : 1750+ SCT [34387] : 1740+ BURNT ISLAND, FIF, SCT [34473] : 1700-1900 DORNOCK, SUT, SCT [34537] : ISAAC 1831 WATTEN & WICK, CAI, SCT [34580] : ISAAC C1808 LATHERON, CAI, SCT [34580] : ISAAC C1845 KIRKWALL, OKI, SCT [34580] : 1800+ DRAINIE, MOR, SCT [34606] : 1780+ LATHERON, CAI, SCT [34606] : 1840+ ABERDEEN, ABD, SCT [34606] : 1700+ ELGIN, MOR, SCT [34637] : ALL LOTHBEG, SUT, SCT [34674] : 1780+ LONGHOPE, OKI, SCT [34688] : 1800+ ABERDEEN, ABD, SCT [35015] : 1700S KILRENNY, FIF, SCT [35395] : PRE 1851 BRORA, SUT, SCT [35530] : PRE 1848 TORRYBURN, FIF, SCT [35740] : 1825 THURSO, CAI, SCT [35906] : PRE 1793 CAI, SCT [36412] : 1800-1855 SOUTH RONALDSAY, OKI, SCT [36623] : 1800+ CAI, SCT [36869] : 1780+ LOANHEAD, MLN, SCT [36871] : PRE 1800 SCT [37133] : PRE 1840 TARBAT BY FEARN, ROC, SCT [37137] : 1800 STROMNESS, OKI, SCT [37170] : PRE 1840 LATHERON, CAI, SCT [37627] : 1830+ LATHERON, CAI, SCT [38425] : C1828 EDINBURGH, MLN, SCT [38499] : ALL ABD, SCT & AUS [35417]

SUTHOFF HENRY 1800-1870 PASSAIC CO., NJ, USA [38337]

SUTIE 1720-1760 DYSART, FIF, SCT [36268]

SUTTIE 1711 MONTROSE, ANS, SCT [35808]

SUTTIE (SEE SUTIE) [36268]

SUTTLES JULIA C1830+ JACKSON CO., IA, USA [37014]

SUTTON WILLIAM F. 1886 LAUNCESTON, TAS, AUS [34295] : 1880+ NEWCASTLE, NSW, AUS [34424] : PRE 1850 ARMIDALE, NSW, AUS [34892] : MARTHA 1860+ SYDNEY, NSW, AUS [35033] : 1850+ VIC, AUS [35391] : 1855+ WILLIAMTOWN, NSW, AUS [35462] : C1866 IPSWICH, QLD, AUS [35843] : 1790-1820 SYDNEY, NSW, AUS [36595] : PRE 1850 VAUGHAN TWP., ONT, CAN [36696] : SAMUEL C1850 BROCKVILLE, ONT, CAN [37436] : MARY C1850 BROCKVILLE, ONT, CAN [37436] : WILLIAM C1851-1865 LANARK, ONT, CAN [37436] : PHILIPPA 1867+ BROCKVILLE, ONT, CAN [37436] : SALLY 1861+ BROCKVILLE, ONT, CAN [37436] : 1880+ MUSKOKA DISTRICT, ONT, CAN [38419] : 1800S DOVER, KEN, ENG [33779] : 1850+ PRESTON, LAN, ENG [33894] : PRE 1855 PINCHBECK, LIN, ENG [34043] : 1650-1990 CHALFORD, GLS, ENG [34124] : 1750-1850 BENACRE, SFK, ENG [34151] : PRE 1854 WEYMOUTH, DOR, ENG [34269] : PRE 1819 EASTRY, KEN, ENG [34281] : 1780-1860S BROOKLAND, KEN, ENG [34458] : ALL MALMESBURY, WIL, ENG [34466] : 1750+ SALISBURY, WIL, ENG [34664] : 1780S CARLISLE, CUL, ENG [34688] : 1600+ HASTINGS, SSX, ENG [34747] : MARTHA 1843+ LONDON, ENG [35033] : 1600+ TENTERDEN, KEN, ENG [35275] : C1800-1850 CALLINGTON, CON, ENG [35391] : PRE 1855 WICKHAMBREAUX & ASH, KEN, ENG [35462] : PRE 1846 BORTON, WAR, ENG [35827] : C1800 STOURMOUTH, KEN, ENG [35912] : 1790S HOCKLEY, ESS, ENG [35959] : 1820-1840 SOUTHWARK, LND, ENG [36044] : 1860-1890 CLERKENWELL, LND, ENG [36044] : 1800+ KEN, ENG [36093] : PRE 1800 WILBURTON, CAM, ENG [36183] : ALL ASTON & BIRMINGHAM, WAR, ENG [36234] : CHARLES 1830-40S CAMBERWELL, KEN, ENG [36253] : PRE 1845 MANCHESTER, LAN, ENG [36345] : 1800+ WOLVERHAMPTON, STS, ENG [36370] : PRE 1850 NANTWICH, CHS, ENG [36385] : PRE 1850 ASHBY DE LA ZOUCH, LEI, ENG [36387] : PRE 1800 SWAVESEY, CAM, ENG [36388] : 1750-1850 LAN, ENG [36482] : 1720-1800 LONDON, ENG [36595] : 1800+ STOCKPORT & MANCHESTER, ENG [37640] : C1850 SHEFFIELD, WRY, ENG [37873] : PRE 1850 NEWTON, WAR, ENG [37873] : WILLIAM 1835-1842 DODCOTT, CHS, ENG [37934] : 1800+ MARBURY CUM QUOISLEY, CHS, ENG [37934] : 1845-1885 WHITCHURCH, SAL, ENG [37934] : 1782 LITTLEPORT, CAM, ENG [38209] : PRE 1880 GLS & NRY, ENG [38419] : C1819 RADCLIFFE, LAN, ENG [38499] : PRE 1850 RICHFORDSTOWN, COR, IRL [35818] : SAMUEL PRE 1850 WEX, IRL [37436] : MARY PRE 1850 WEX, IRL [37436] : PRE 1820 WEX, IRL [37454] : 1700-1770 CAROLINE CO., VA, USA [36566] : 1825+ EMANUEL CO., GA, USA [38340] : 1800-1850 CAYAUGA, NY, USA [38531]

SUTTON-MURRAY 1800S ENG [34483] : 1800S LONDON AREA, ENG [34483]

SUTTOR 1840S+ YASS, NSW, AUS [35159]

SUURD 1700+ DRN & FRI, NL [36464]

SUYDENHAM C1500 LYNFORD, DEV, ENG [34395]

SUZUKI 1900+ JAPAN [36417]

SVENSDOTTER LANDIN C. 1851 OLMSTADS FORSAMLING, JONKOPINGS, SWE [38548]

SVENSSON PRE 1900 TVARRED, ALVSBORG, SWE [35324] : ALMA 1884-1897 HOSSNA, ALVSBORG, SWE [35324] : PRE 1900 KARLSHAM, BLE, SWE

[35433] : EMANUEL 1893+ USA & CAN [35324] : ALMA 1897+ USA & CAN [35324]

SVOBODA 1880+ HOWARD CO., NE, USA [36942]

SWAANE 1700S+ ZIERIKZEE, ZEL, NL [38350]

SWABY 1830+ ABBOTS LANGLEY, HRT, ENG [35054] : 1800+ GREAT GADDESDEN, HRT, ENG [35054] : ALL HRT, ENG [35868] : 1830-1900 SKIDBY, ERY, ENG [36059] : ALL MARSHCHAPEL, LIN, ENG [36059] : 1880-1920 ROTHERHAM, WRY, ENG [36059]

SWACKHAMMER C1870 BENTON CO., IA, USA [38173]

SWADDELL C1810 YKS, ENG & CAN [34988]

SWADLIN C1720 NORTH HINKSEY, BRK, ENG [36076]

SWAENE 1600S ZIERIKZEE, ZEL, NL [38350]

SWAFFER JAMES 1841+ GUNNEDAH, NSW, AUS [38567] : ALL WOODCHURCH, KEN & SSX, ENG [38230] : JAMES C1820+ WOODCHURCH, KEN, ENG [38567] : RICHARD PRE 1820+ WOODCHURCH, KEN, ENG [38567]

SWAFFIELD 1870+ NSW, AUS [34532]

SWAFFING C1700 BRIXHAM, DEV, ENG [34333]

SWAIL 1800-1900 USA & CAN [37502]

SWAILES PRE 1917 HORSFORTH, YKS, ENG [35985] : 1920+ NAPIER, HBY, NZ [35985]

SWAIM ALL NY, IN, MS, IA, USA [37812]

SWAIN 1896+ MUDGEE & RYLSTONE, NSW, AUS [34534] : C1865 PECKHAM & CAMBERWELL, SRY, ENG [34235] : 1800+ DERBY, DBY, ENG [34291] : 1825-1850S BIGGLESWADE, BDF, ENG [34372] : C1890 BEDFORD, BDF, ENG [34372] : ALL PICKERING, YKS, ENG [34629] : PRE 1875 HILPERTON, WIL, ENG [34999] : PRE 1800 GRAVELEY, HRT, ENG [35229] : 1800-1900 CHIPPENHAM, WIL, ENG [36158] : 1700+ BKM, NTH & BDF, ENG [36574] : PRE 1818 GOREY, WEX, IRL [37454] : ALL WORLDWIDE [37364]

SWAINE PRE 1845 GOULBURN, NSW, AUS [37314] : 1845+ GOULBURN, NSW, AUS [37314] : PRE 1750 BIRMINGHAM, WAR, ENG [36326] : ALL WORLDWIDE [37364]

SWAINSON 1875+ OAKHAM, RUT, ENG [35716]

SWAISLAND ALL ENG [36122] : PRE 1870 GRAVESEND & DARTFORD, KEN, ENG [36178]

SWALES 1820S POCKLINGTON & MARKET WEIGHTON, ERY, ENG [34854] : PRE 1880 LIN, ENG [34868] : PRE 1874 NEWINGTON, SRY, ENG [35948] : MARIA BRIGGS PRE 1907 SHEERNESS, KEN, ENG [36646]

SWALEY PRE 1800 LEEDS, WRY, ENG [37643]

SWALLOW PRE 1720 FISHLAKE, WRY, ENG [37589] : PRE 1740 NTT, ENG [37589] : 1700-1850 HOLMFIRTH, WRY, ENG [37736] : PRE 1790 YKS, ENG [38080] : JOSEPH 1800+ LEEDS ROTHWELL, WRY, ENG [38540]

SWALWELL PRE 1900 WHITBY & STOKESLEY, NRY, ENG [37616]

SWAN 1835+ ALEXANDRIA & SYDNEY, NSW, AUS [34979] : 1850+ WELLINGTON, NSW, AUS [35556] : 1869+ CADOW & WARROO, NSW, AUS [35557] : 1850+ SIMCOE CO., ONT, CAN [34465] : PRE 1800 BELFORD, NBL, ENG [33776] : PRE 1775 HOLLINGBOURNE, KEN, ENG [34105] : 1840-1880 UGLEY, ESS, ENG [34399] : C1800-1870 MARDEN, KEN, ENG [34432] : 1830 EAST PECKHAM, KEN, ENG [34432] : 1700-1800 DALHAM, SFK, ENG [35094] : PRE 1840 IPSWICH, SFK, ENG [35556] : PRE 1874 LICHFIELD, WAR, ENG [35932] : 1700+ LONGHORSLEY, NBL, ENG [36609] : 1750-1850 MONKWEARMOUTH, DUR, ENG [37859] : 1750 THEBERTON, SFK, ENG [37928] : PRE 1800

STAPLEHURST, KEN, ENG [38383] : HENRY
C1780-1850 NBL & BEW, ENG & SCT [34366] :
WILLIAM 1850S BALLINA, WEX & DUB, IRL
[36244] : 1758+ STELLENBOSCH, CAPE, RSA
[34947] : C1811 CAPE OF GOOD HOPE, RSA [36433]
: ALL LAUDER, BEW, SCT [33959] : ALL
ABERFOYLE, PER, SCT [33975] : PRE 1835
DUNDEE, ANS, SCT [34979] : PRE 1800 FIF, SCT
[35496] : PRE 1850 HAWICK, ROX, SCT [35635] :
1780-1800 DUNDEE, ANS, SCT [36433] : 1700-1850
FIF & MLN, SCT [36556] : 1800+ DUNDEE, ANS,
SCT [37395] : PRE 1825 PERTH, PER, SCT [37395] :
C1700 PERTH, PER, SCT [37918] : JOHN 1850S
TROY, NY, USA [36244] : 1800-1850 JEFFERSON,
NY, USA [38061] : 1840-60 IL, USA [38151] : 1700-
1800 FRANKLIN CO., PA, USA [38524]

SWANCOTT 1860-1947 LLANBISTER, RAD, WLS
[37400]

SWANE ALL WORLDWIDE [37364]

SWANEY 1870+ NZ [36870] : PRE 1870 OKI, SCT
[36870]

SWANK 1700-1990 KY, USA [35313]

SWANKIE JOSEPH 1830+ DUNDEE, ANS, SCT
[34637]

SWANN 1850-1920 HOBART, TAS, AUS [34551] : 1800-
1900S SLINGSBY, YKS, ENG [36796] : 1800
CAMBERWELL, SRY, ENG [36928] : 1600-1650
DENTON & SOUTHSLEETE, KEN, ENG [38041] :
1609-1650 JAMESTOWN, VA, USA [38041]

SWANNE ALL WORLDWIDE [37364]

SWANSON 1800-1850 WICK, CAI, SCT [36390] : 1830S
ORKNEY ISLES, OKI, SCT [38206] : 1860S
HAGRYD, GOTLAND, SWE [35050] : 1875
BURLINGTON, NJ, USA [35279] : 1863+ NE, USA
[36919]

SWANTON ALL WORLDWIDE [37084]

SWANWICK 1830-1850 NOTTINGHAM, NTT, ENG
[35798] : 1800+ BINGHAM, NTT, ENG [36892] :
ALL SEIGHFORD, STS, ENG [37265]

SWARBRICK 1880S MANCHESTER, LAN, ENG
[38283] : 1800S LEYLAND, LAN, ENG [38444]

SWARBROOK PRE 1800 CHS, ENG [37650]

SWARESBRICK C1745 YKS & LAN, ENG [33827]

SWARTZ C1840-92 GER [38309] : 1800+ BUCKS CO.,
PA, USA [36540] : 1875-1920 DENVER, CO, USA
[36951]

SWARZ 1700+ BUSENBURG, BAY, GER [38578]

SWASBRICK (SEE SWARE [33827]

SWAYN 1850S+ MOUNT MORIAC, VIC, AUS [35477]
: ALL WORLDWIDE [37364]

SWAYNE 1700+ WESTBURY, WIL, ENG [34121] :
1880-1925 CAMBERLEY, SRY, ENG [36662] : 1800
LIVERPOOL, LAN, ENG [36805] : ALL
WORLDWIDE [37364]

SWAYZE ALL WORLDWIDE [37461]

SWEARENGIN PRE 1900 DOUGLAS & JACKSON,
MO & TN, USA [36899]

SWEATMAN 1850+ HAMMERSMITH, LND, ENG
[35442]

SWEDHELM 1800 ST GEORGE IN THE EAST, LND,
MDX, ENG [37082]

SWEEM (SEE SWAIM) [37812]

SWEENEY 1830-1900 CALEDON, ONT, CAN [35833] :
PRE 1870 ENNISKILLEN, NB, CAN & IRL [38447] :
PRE 1855 MANCHESTER, LAN, ENG [34187] : PRE
1858 ALTAN, DON, IRL [33939] : PRE 1850
BROADFORD, CLA, IRL [35128] : ALL KERRY,
KER, IRL [35514] : HUGH PRE 1850
KILMACRENAN, DON, IRL [35833] : CATHERINE
PRE 1856 TIP, IRL [35852] : 1830+ TIP, IRL & AUS
[33926] : 1825-1880 KUNGSBUCKA, SWE [36331]

SWEENY JOHN 1834-1896 ST JOHN, NB, CAN [38591]
: JOHN 1834-1896+ NEEDLES, SB CO., CA, USA
[38591] : JOHN 1888-1896+ NEEDLES &
GLENWOOD, SB CO. &, MOHAVE CO., USA
[38591]

SWEET 1830+ CAYUGA, ONT, CAN [34132] : 1820+
ST MEWAN, CON, ENG [34435] : 1818 DEV, ENG
[35204] : C1750 CHISWICK, MDX, ENG [36051] :
PRE 1800 SOM, ENG [36166] : 1700-1900 DEV, ENG
[36491] : PRE 1905 CHS, ENG [36839] : ALL CURRY
RIVAL, SOM, ENG [37269] : 1650-1750 SWAINBY,
NRY, ENG [37858] : 1770-1800 PITTSFORD, VT,
USA [34495] : PRE 1900 USA [36933] : 1650+ RI,
USA [38015] : 1790-1900 MENDON, MA, CT & OH,
USA [38025] : SYLVANUS 1772+ HAMILTON CO.,
RI, USA [38140] : 1700S DUTCHESS CO., NY, USA
[38153] : JOHN 1800-1900 RED WOOD FALLS, MN
& PA, USA [38392] : PRE 1851 BLAINA, MON, WLS
[36230]

SWEETAPPLE ALL WORLDWIDE [37855]

SWEETE PRE 1619 ST NEOT, CON, ENG [34573]

SWEETENHAM PRE 1850 ALVERSTOKE &
GOSPORT, HAM, ENG [36037]

SWEETINGHAM ALL SOUTHAMPTON, HAM, ENG
[35802]

SWEETMAN PRE 1849 RYDE, IOW, HAM, ENG
[36526] : PRE 1950 CLONMEL, TIP, IRL [37519]

SWEIGERT PRE 1761 LANCASTER, PA, USA [38220]

SWEMER 1700S ZUID BEVELAND, ZEL, NL [38350]

SWENARTON ALL WORLDWIDE [36194]

SWENERTON ALL WORLDWIDE [36194]

SWENSSON PRE 1870+ GOTTEBORG, SWE [35536]

SWEPSTON C1500 ASTWOOD, BKM, ENG [34041]

SWETMAN ALL WINCANTON & SHEPTON
MALLET, SOM, ENG [34861] : PRE 1750 SOM &
DOR, ENG [36166]

SWICK ALL CAN [34129]

SWIFT 1860 HOBART, TAS, AUS [34262] : 1848-1865
VIC, AUS [37150] : ELIZA C1800 SHEFFIELD,
WRY, ENG [34369] : PRE 1828 CONDOVER, SAL,
ENG [34370] : PRE 1840 SAXMUNDHAM, SFK,
ENG [35215] : 1800S LEE, KEN, ENG [35408] : PRE
1900 BARNSLEY, WRY, ENG [36126] : 1836-1848
DUKINFIELD, CHS, ENG [37150] : PRE 1860
SHEERNESS, KEN, ENG [37405] : PRE 1820
TINGEWICK, BKM, ENG [37716]

SWIGGS 1738-1809 TALLAND, CON, ENG [37641] :
1625-1721 MENHENIOT, CON, ENG [37641] :
JOHN 1800 PLYMOUTH, DEV, ENG [38193]

SWINARTON ALL WORLDWIDE [36194]

SWINBOURNE C1875-1900 BIRMINGHAM, WAR,
ENG [35791]

SWINBURN 1840+ SHOALHAVEN, NSW, AUS
[35147] : ALL AUS [35331] : 1700-1780
WORKINGTON, CUL, ENG [34762] : PRE 1840
PRESTBURY, CHS, ENG [35147] : 1790+ CHS,
ENG [35331] : ALL CAPHEATON, NBL, ENG
[36098] : 1850+ MANCHESTER, LAN, ENG [36098] :
1600-1850 CUL & WES, ENG [36098] : C1830S IRL
[35331] : ALL WORLDWIDE [36098]

SWINBURNE ALL YARM, NRY, ENG [37627]

SWINDAIL C1880+ AUCKLAND & THAMES, NZ
[36258]

SWINDELL ALL AUS [37487] : ALL LEI, ENG [37487]

SWINDELLS PRE 1793 MELLOR, DBY, ENG [34474] :
C1750+ STOCKPORT, CHS, ENG [36258]

SWINDLEHURST PRE 1800 LAN, ENG [36022] :
1860+ LAN, ENG & USA [36022]

SWINDLER PRE 1810 VA, USA [37603]

SWINGLEHURST PRE 1800 LAN, ENG [36022] :
1860+ LAN, ENG & USA [36022]

SWINLASS PRE 1800 LAN, ENG [36022]

SWINLEHURST PRE 1800 LAN, ENG [36022]
SWINNE ALL BEL [38640] : 1900-1990 GER [38640] :
ALL NL [38640] : 1700-1990 RIGA, LIVLAND, USSR
[38640] : 1650-1990 TUKKUMS, KURLAND, USSR
[38640]
SWINNERTON PRE 1600 WHITMORE, STS, ENG
[36701] : ALL WORLDWIDE [36194]
SWINNEY PRE 1775 PENSHAW & COXGREEN,
DUR, ENG [36202] : PRE 1820 SCT [33999]
SWINNINGTON ALL WORLDWIDE [36194]
SWINSON MARY MARIA F. 1814+ EALING, MDX,
ENG [34484]
SWINYARD ALL WORLDWIDE [37857]
SWIRE 1790-1850 LAN, ENG [34175] : PRE 1637 UK
[36324]
SWISHER 1800+ CUMBERLAND, PA, USA [36558]
SWISICK 1700S VA, USA [37028]
SWITALLA ALL HAMBURG, GER & POL [33966] :
ALL WORLDWIDE [33966]
SWITZER ALL ONT, CAN [34060] : ALL IRL [34060] :
PRE 1900 TIP, IRL [34097] : ALL NY, USA [34060]
SWOPE 1800-1878 CLERMONT CO., OH, USA [37037]
SWORDS PRE 1864 DUB, IRL [38296]
SWYNNERTON ALL WORLDWIDE [36194]
SYASSEN PRE 1816 OLD, GER [37986]
SYDAL 1780+ ST IVES, CON, ENG [37873] : PRE 1800
NFK, ENG [37873]
SYDENHAM 1700-1850 LONDON, ENG [34975] :
1600+ TAUNTON, SOM, ENG [37843]
SYDER 1700-1850 WYMNDON, NFK, ENG [34081] :
1700-1850 NORWICH, NFK, ENG [34081]
SYDNEY 1800-1900 LND & SRY, ENG [36422]
SYE 1650S THORNEY ABBEY, CAM, ENG [34204]
SYKES 1750-1850 FOLKSWORTH, HUN, ENG [33908]
: 1700-1740 SWILLINGTON, WRY, ENG [34228] :
1740+ ACKWORTH, WRY, ENG [34228] : C1850
YKS, ENG [34239] : PRE 1840 MANCHESTER,
LAN, ENG [34299] : PRE 1800 HERTFORD, HRT,
ENG [34655] : 1800+ KIRBY, LAN, ENG [34852] :
C1804 ALMONDBURY, WRY, ENG [35733] : C1812
HUDDERSFIELD, WRY, ENG [35733] : SAMUEL
1820-1840 LINTHWAITE, WRY, ENG [35955] : PRE
1850 BARNSLEY, WRY, ENG [36479] : 1740-60
ALMONDBURY, YKS, ENG [37011] : 1839
HEATON NORRIS, CHS, ENG [37184] : PRE 1800
YKS, ENG [38080] : 1800S PILLING, LAN, ENG
[38285] : 1840S CAMBLESFORTH, YKS, ENG
[38422] : PRE 1900 OSWEGO & BENNINGTON, NY
& VT, USA [38027] : 1840+ WORLDWIDE [36850]
SYLVESTER 1851 L'ORIGNAL, ONT, CAN [35272] :
PRE 1900 NORTH LEIGH, OXF, ENG [34466] : PRE
1800 SEIGHFORD, STS, ENG [37103] : C1825-1865
FAYAL, AZORES IS., PT [36337] : BENJAMIN 1700
BRAINTREE, MA, USA [35273] : PRE 1891 BUTTE,
MT, USA [37030] : ALL WORLDWIDE [38452]
SYM 1750-1850 WALSTON, LKS, SCT [37329] : 1800+
FRANKLIN CO., NY, USA [35611]
SYME 1818-1823 PERTH, PER, SCT [35196] : PRE 1791
TRANENT, ELN, SCT [37852]
SYMES PRE 1790 BURSTOCK, DOR, ENG [35252] :
1800S BALTONSBOROUGH, SOM, ENG [35899] :
C1800 STOKE SUB HAMDON, SOM, ENG [36247] :
1660-1710 SOM, ENG [37233] : 1700-1800
HAZELBURY PLUNKNETT, SOM, ENG [37654] :
1730-1780 CREWKERNE, SOM, ENG [38028] : ALL
WORLDWIDE [33773]
SYMM 1650-1800 TREGONY & LAMORRAN, CON,
ENG [35576]
SYMMONS 1700-1900 LONDON, ENG [36025]
SYMON C1830 ELGIN, MOR, SCT [35428] : ALL CAI,
PER & SUT, SCT [37727]

SYMONDS EDWARD 1800-1900 HOBART, TAS, AUS
[33875] : 1868 VIC, AUS [35414] : C1850+
BRUNSWICK, VIC, NSW & TAS, AUS [35547] : ALL
ISLE OF WIGHT, HAM, ENG [33802] : 1600-1900
WINFRITH NEWBURGH, DOR, ENG [33875] :
JOHN 1800-1900 BEXLEY, LND, ENG [33875] :
1700+ WANTAGE, BRK, ENG [34110] : 1700+
CASTLEMORTON, WOR, ENG [34160] : 1730+
DOR, ENG [34228] : 1750-1800 SAUNDERTON,
BKM, ENG [34687] : ALL SFK, ENG [34744] : C1840
BINSEY, OXF, ENG [35414] : PRE 1832 BALSHAM,
CAM, ENG [35770] : PRE 1883 OXFORD, OXF,
ENG [36804] : PRE 1883 LYMINGTON, HAM, ENG
[36804] : ALL NORWICH, NFK, ENG [37629] : 1800-
1900 MADEIRA [33875] : 1750-1800 LITTLE
NEWCASTLE, PEM, WLS [34552] : HANNAH ALL
WORLDWIDE [35291]
SYMONS WILLIAM C1868 BALLARAT, VIC, AUS
[33915] : 1830+ LONGFORD, TAS, AUS [34770] :
RICHARD C1900 WA, AUS [35131] : JAMES C1900
WA, AUS [35131] : PRE 1860 BURRA BURRA, SA,
AUS [35200] : PRE 1890 CLUNES, VIC, AUS [36360] :
1800 SYDNEY, NSW, AUS [37125] : CHARLES PRE
1860 ROCHE & ST AUSTELL, CON, ENG [33915] :
1700+ LND, ENG [34062] : C1850 HELSTON, CON,
ENG [34608] : C1750 CROWAN, CON, ENG [35131] :
PRE 1740 CON, ENG [35255] : PRE 1814 NBL, ENG
[35440] : 1770+ BURY ST EDMUNDS, SFK, ENG
[35706] : 1876+ DULOE, CON, ENG [35887] : PRE
1863 HELSTON & BREAGE, CON, ENG [35997] :
1775+ LIFTON, DEV, ENG [36254] : 1800+
PERRANUTHNOE, CON, ENG [36885] : PRE 1850
ST COLUMB MAJOR, CON, ENG [37105] : 1760+
ST COLUMB MAJOR, CON, ENG [37905] : 1760+
INDIAN QUEENS, CON, ENG [37905] : 1690-1728
LADOCK & ST ENODER, CON, ENG [37905] : 1800
LIFTON, DEV, ENG [38213] : 1850+ NEATH, GLA,
WLS [35442]
SYMONS (SEE SYMONDS) [34552]
SYMS 1800S TOTNES, DEV, ENG [37442] : C1840-1847
DUBLIN, IRL [35931]
SYMSOME 1600-1800 FIF, SCT [35627]
SYNDEN 1790S EWHURST, SSX, ENG [35261]
SYNDER PRE 1860 IL, USA [38017]
SYNNETT PRE 1790 WEX, IRL [37428]
SYNOKIS ALL GALICIA, SU & POL [34146]
SYPHER 1857+ QLD, AUS [37894] : PRE 1857
CHRISTIAN MALFORD, WIL, ENG [37894]
SYRETT 1800+ ADSTOCK, BKM, ENG [38213]
SYTEK PRE 1900 KOLACZKOWA, PO, POL [36941]
SYZMIKOWSKICH 1707-1890 SIERAKOWICE,
GDANSK, POL [38148]
SZELDER 1880+ ALLEGENY, PA, USA [38185]
SZENTES PRE 1900 ISTENSEGITS, BUHOVINA, HU
[35616]
SZIDAT PRE 1897 KRS. GUMBINNEN, OPR, GER
[38649]
SZOK ALL POL [36941]
SZOR PRE 1835 KAPALONNA, BORSOD, HU [37547]
SZRAMA 1809 OBORNIKI, PO, POL [38495]
SZUBERT 1840 OES [36679]
TAAFFE 1947+ DEVONPORT, NZ [34811] : ALL
WORLDWIDE [37026]
TABAULT 1580-1660 PRIGNAC, PCH, FRA [38779]
TABB PRE 1780 BODMIN, CON, ENG [38389]
TABEL ALL CHI [36839]
TABELL C1800 WORLDWIDE [33841]
TABERKAUSEN ALL WORLDWIDE [38670]
TABERNER 1750-1900 LAN, ENG [36042]
TABINER 1840S WIGAN, LAN, ENG [38266]

TABOR 1890S BIRMINGHAM, WAR, ENG [36592] :
ALL WARMINSTER, WIL, ENG [37617] : C1800
WARMINSTER, WIL, ENG [37918]

TABRETT PRE 1860 ASHFORD, KEN, ENG [36113]

TABUTEAU 1860+ HAWKES BAY, NAPIER, NZ
[33889]

TACEY 1890+ MT MORGAN, QLD, AUS [35254] :
1870+ BRISBANE, QLD, AUS [35254] : 1850+
GUNNEDAH, NSW, AUS [35254] : 1875+
BOURKE, NSW, AUS [35254] : 1860+
NORTHFLEET, KEN, ENG [35254] : 1760+
NEWCASTLE UPON TYNE, YKS, ENG [35254] :
1830+ ROTHERHITHE, SRY, ENG [35254] : 1820+
LIVERPOOL, LAN, ENG [35254] : C1850-70 IRL
[36877] : ALL WORLDWIDE [35254]

TACHELL 1855+ HALDIMAND CO., ONT, CAN
[38323]

TACKABERRY 1700+ KILMUCKRIDGE, WEX, IRL
[34749] : 1740-1950 WEXFORD & LEEDS CO., WEX
& ONT, IRL & CAN [36669] : 1700+ IL, USA [34749]

TACKEN PRE 1750 SCHACHTEN, HES, GER [38642]

TACKMANN ALL GUSTROW, MEK, DDR [34812]

TADD 1820+ DEPTFORD, MDX, ENG [33950]

TAFE ALL WORLDWIDE [37026]

TAFF ALL WORLDWIDE [37026]

TAFFORA ALL ACQUAVIRA PICENA, MARCHE,
ITL [37510] : ALL USA [37510]

TAFT 1860-1900 CHS, ENG [36831] : 1750+ WAR,
ENG [37868] : 1890 WESTON, VT, USA [38131]

TAGGART PRE 1852 DRY, IRL [34039] : ALL ANT,
IRL [34488] : JAMES PRE 1866 ANT, IRL [37601]

TAGGERT MICHAEL PRE 1840 SWORDS, DUB, IRL
[34039]

TAGGETT 1812-1826 LITCHFIELD CO., CT, USA
[37810] : 1836-1901 OAKLAND CO., MI, USA [37810]

TAGNEY ALL IRL & ENG [37515]

TAIF ALL WORLDWIDE [37026]

TAILBY 1800S+ NSW, AUS [34902]

TAILFORD PRE 1850 ALTONSIDE, NBL, ENG
[36270]

TAILLEFER C1665 ST GERMAIN MESNIL, BN, FRA
[36681]

TAILOR PRE 1800 BEDLINGTON, NBL, ENG [33905]
: PRE 1725 ESS, ENG [35642]

TAINSH PRE 1800 PER, SCT [37127]

TAINTON PRE 1900 RSA [37517]

TAINTOR PRE 1650 CT, USA & WLS [38745]

TAIT ROBERT 1854+ CASTLEREAGH & PENRITH,
NSW, AUS [35164] : 1660+ ST MICHAELS,
BARBADOS [38235] : 1810-50 BATHURST, ONT,
CAN [35638] : 1800+ ETAL, NBL, ENG [35611] :
C1800 CARLISLE, CUL, ENG [36431] : PRE 1831
AGHALEE, ANT, IRL [35344] : 1750 LOCHMABEN,
DFS, SCT [34088] : 1700+ GIRVAN & CHAPEL
DONAN, AYR, SCT [34927] : ROB & JANET C1840
CAIRNCROSS NEAR COLDINGHAM, BEW, SCT
[35164] : ROBERT 1846-1926 CAIRNCROSS NEAR
COLDINGHAM, BEW, SCT [35164] : 1700+
MOFFAT, DFS, SCT [35909] : 1700+
TWEEDSMUIR, DFS, SCT [35909] : C1800 PEE, SCT
[36271] : C1820 ROX, SCT [36978] : PRE 1830 STOW,
WLN, SCT [37353] : 1815+ MYNIGAFF, KKD, SCT
[37499] : PRE 1865 SHETTLESTON, GLASGOW,
SCT [37925]

TAIT-BLACK 1790+ EDINBURGH, MLN, SCT [35025]

TAITE 1800S GLASGOW, LKS, SCT [34288]

TALANT PRE 1750 SFK, ENG [34258]

TALASKA PRE 1940 HANNOVER, HAN, GER [38674]

TALBART 1841-1952 BAYE, BRT, FRA [34136]

TALBOT 1829+ NEWTOWN, SYDNEY, NSW, AUS
[37556] : PRE 1880 SA, AUS [38270] : PRE 1900
SPARSHOLT, HAM, ENG [33966] : C1800

ROMFORD, ESS, ENG [35582] : 1750-1870
MARYLEBONE, LND, ENG [36130] : 1840-1860
DEWSBURY, YKS, ENG [36319] : C1700-1850
CHALDON HERRING, DOR, ENG [36435] : 1626+
NORTON & WOOLPIT, SFK, ENG [37556] : PRE
1829 SOM, ENG [37556] : 1800S WAR, ENG [37910] :
PRE 1800 NORTH SCARLE, LIN, ENG [38248] :
1860 NEWPORT, ENG [38470] : 1797 LAWSHALL,
SFK, ENG [38518] : 1864 CORK, IRL [37163] : 1850+
IRL [38481] : PRE 1740 AMELIA CO., VA, USA
[38126]

TALBOTT 1800+ NSW, AUS [34976] : 1800 SOM, ENG
[34976] : 1870+ IL, USA [38058] : PRE 1880 CASS
CO., IN, USA [38783]

TALBOYS 1800-1850 OXFORD, OXF, ENG [36530]

TALLAMY PRE 1788 DEV, ENG [38580]

TALLENTIRE 1750+ ISEL, CUL, ENG [37735]

TALLEY 1750-1800 HENRICO CO., VA, USA [36554] :
GEORGE 1771-1837 LOUISA CO., VA, USA [36573] :
ALL WORLDWIDE [36573]

TALLKE ALL NZ [35058]

TALLY 1700+ BARBADOS, W.INDIES [35558] : ALL
WORLDWIDE [35558]

TALMAGE 1700-1800 SFK, ENG [34740]

TALMASH ALL SFK, ENG [37250]

TAMBLING ALL WORLDWIDE [35172]

TAMBLYN 1850+ VIC, AUS [35060] : 1750+ CON,
ENG [35060] : ALL WORLDWIDE [35172]

TAME 1850+ OXFORD, OXF, ENG [35027] : C1806
WOOTTON COURTNEY, SOM, ENG [37144] : PRE
1850 WOOTTON COURTNEY & SELWORTHY,
SOM, ENG [37622]

TAMLYN 1690-1730 LANTEGLOS BY CAMELFORD,
CON, ENG [34448]

TAMMAGE ALL HAMBLEDON, HAM, ENG [36405]

TAMMS PRE 1797 SHO, GER [38669]

TAMPLIN ALL CLA, IRL [35746]

TAMS ALL STS, ENG [37617]

TAMSETT 1837+ PORT STEPHENS, NSW, AUS
[34773] : 1837-1900 BAULKHAM HILLS, NSW, AUS
[35864] : 1800+ RYE, SSX, ENG [35105] : PRE 1837
BREDE & ICKLESHAM, SSX, ENG [35864]

TAMSITT ALL WORLDWIDE [35501]

TANCEE PRE 1863 AMOY, CHINA [37167]

TANCRED ALL WORLDWIDE [36595]

TANDY PRE 1900 STUDLEY, WAR, ENG [33985] :
1850+ BIRMINGHAM, STS, ENG [35306] : PRE
1784 HAWKESBURY, GLS, ENG [36113] : PRE 1800
ASHFORD, KEN, ENG [36190] : 1800-1870
KEMPSEY, WOR, ENG [36190] : 1800S ASTON,
WAR, ENG [37299]

TANE 1860-1900 BRADFORD, WRY, ENG [34827] :
1830S MOUNTMELLICK, LEX, IRL [34827]

TANGEE C1863 SALE, VIC, AUS [37167]

TANGHE 1600-1700 WEVELGEM, WF, BEL [34163]

TANGNEY ALL IRL & ENG [37515]

TANGYE ALL WORLDWIDE [36789]

TANKARD 1850+ MELBOURNE, VIC, AUS [34542] :
1750-1881 CLAYTON & BRADFORD, WRY, ENG
[36391]

TANN PRE 1785 BEESTON, NFK, ENG [35212] : ALL
LONDON, ENG [36174]

TANNAHILL PRE 1840 KILMARNOCK, AYR, SCT
[34003]

TANNATT 1700-1800 LLANSANTFFRAID YM
MECHAIN, MGY, WLS [34411]

TANNER 1880+ HOBART, TAS, AUS [34670] : 1852+
HASTINGS CO., ONT, CAN [34153] : ALL
WOODHAM FERRERS, ESS, ENG [34460] : 1700-
1800 PLYMOUTH, DEV, ENG [34742] : PRE 1750
CON, ENG [34742] : 1930S CASTLE CARY, SOM,
ENG [35553] : PRE 1872+ BATH, SOM, ENG [35553]

: PRE 1705 NORTHLEIGH, DEV, ENG [35587] :
1800S LEWISHAM, KEN, ENG [35858] : 1800 +
SNODLAND, KEN, ENG [35972] : 1700 + EAST
MALLING, KEN, ENG [35972] : HENRY 1820
HENLEY ON THAMES, OXF, ENG [36526] : PRE
1780 DRAYCOT CERNE, WIL, ENG [36526] : PRE
1820 HENLEY ON THAMES, OXF, ENG [36526] :
1500-1900 LONDON, MDX, ENG [36689] : 1700-1850
NEWBURY, BRK, ENG [36727] : PRE 1914
BIRMINGHAM, WAR, ENG [37265] : PRE 1852
COR, IRL [34153] : 1855 + TEMPLEMARTIN &
MOSKEAH, COR, IRL [34926] : 1840-1900
LEXINGTON & LOUISVILLE, PN & KY, USA
[37539] : L.D. 1866 + HAMILTON CO., OH, USA
[37797] : C1850 CINCINNATI, OH, USA [38166] :
1660 HENRICO, VA, USA [38198]

TANNOTA PRE 1850 ITL [34984]

TANSER 1800-1900 REARSBY, LEI, ENG [37858]

TANSLEY 1900 + NEWMARKET, ONT, CAN [34062]

TANSWELL PRE 1833 SHAFTESBURY, DOR & SOM,
ENG [34955]

TAPE ALL KENT CO., ONT, CAN [34155] : ALL DEV,
ENG [34155] : ALL COR, IRL [34155]

TAPERELL 1890 + SYDNEY, NSW, AUS [35357] : PRE
1860 TAVISTOCK, DEV, ENG [34582] : PRE 1850
CON & DEV, ENG [35357] : C1860 WELLINGTON,
NZ [35357]

TAPLEY C1870 ECHUCA, VIC, AUS [34434] : 1820-
1840 WENTWORTH CO., ONT, CAN [33911] : C1813
LOUGHBOROUGH, LEI, ENG [37053] : C1787
OTTERTON, DEV, ENG [37053] : 1600-1800 CITY
OF LONDON, ENG [38516]

TAPLIN 1786 + THAME, OXF, ENG [36975]

TAPLING PRE 1840S WRAWBY, LIN, ENG [35706]

TAPLINGER 1700-1990 GER [38096] : 1700-1990
RUSSIA [38096] : 1800-1990 PHILADELPHIA CO.,
PA, USA [38096]

TAPOLA 1634-1867 VEHKALAHTI & SIPPOLA,
KYMI, FIN [38562]

TAPP ALL HASTINGS, SSX, ENG [34263] : PRE 1805
ENG [37428] : PRE 1773 WENDLEBURY, OXF,
ENG [37655]

TAPPING PRE 1830 STOKE MANDEVILLE, BKM,
ENG [35578]

TAPPS 1800 + SUTTON, SRY, ENG [35112]

TAPRELL 1827 WESTMINSTER, LND, ENG [34582] :
PRE 1827 EXETER, DEV, ENG [34582]

TARANTO PRE 1920 CANNETO, LIPARI ISL., ITL
[36271]

TARBELL 1610-1647 ENG [37809] : 1647-1678
WATERTOWN, MA, USA [37809]

TARBOX 1700-1775 BIDDEFORD, ME, USA [38045] :
PRE 1630 CT, LAN & HRT, USA & ENG [38746]

TARGETT 1700 + WOODGREEN, WIL, ENG [34121] :
1700-1800 BOWER CHALK, WIL, ENG [36205]

TARJESON PRE 1850 TROMOY, AUST AGDER,
NOR [36326]

TARLETON 1740 + LIVERPOOL, LAN, ENG [34174]

TARPEY 1800S STS, ENG [36038]

TARPHY C1800-1840 BALLINASLOE, GAL, IRL
[35389]

TARPY 1750S + MAY, IRL [36038]

TARR 1840 + WINSFORD, SOM, ENG [35825] : PRE
1850 KINGSDON, SOM, ENG [36716] : C1812
KINGSDON, SOM, ENG [37144] : PRE 1850 ASH
PRIORS, SOM, ENG [37322]

TARRANT 1850 + BALLARAT, VIC, AUS [36610] :
1810 ALTON PRIORS, WIL, ENG [35067] : ALL
NEWINGTON & POOLE, SRY & DOR, ENG [36997]
: C1700 ALTON PRIORS, WIL, ENG [37918] : 1819 +
LONDON, ENG [38018] : 1800 + CASL, COR, IRL

[36296] : 1870 + ROCHESTER, MT, USA [38018] :
ALL WORLDWIDE [36610]

TARRATT 1700-1750 KEGWORTH, LEI, ENG [36081]

TARRON 1800 WHITECHAPEL, LND, ENG [37841]

TARRUN 1700-1850 MICHELSDORF, LUBLIN, POL
[38652]

TARTE PRE 1890 LND & STS, ENG & IRL [38746]

TARVEL PRE 1875 + PRE, GER [34645]

TASH 1800 MAYS LANDING, NJ, USA [35275]

TASKER 1856 + KILMORE & MYRTLEFORD, VIC,
AUS [35564] : JAMES 1820 + BROADMARSH, TAS,
AUS [35564] : PRE 1900 ENG [33965] : 1800 BATH,
SOM, ENG [35186] : JAMES C1785 BKM, ENG
[35564] : JAMES PRE 1820 SOUTH HINKSEY, BRK,
ENG [35564] : 1550 + CHIPPENHAM, WIL, ENG
[36158] : 1690 + STANTON ST BERNARD, WIL,
ENG [36158] : 1740 + ALL CANNINGS, WIL, ENG
[36158] : ALL MDX & SRY, ENG [36179] : 1750-1910
DEEPING ST NICHOLAS, LIN, ENG [37194] : 1840
DUNDEE, FIF, SCT [35912]

TASSELL 1874 + DAYLESFORD, VIC, AUS [34787]

TASSIKER ALL WORLDWIDE [35817]

TATAM ALEXANDER 1857 + BENDIGO, VIC, AUS
[34171]

TATE 1820S-1830S JSY, CHI [34088] : PRE 1860 ENG
[33953] : 1800-1820 CHALFORD, GLS, ENG [34088] :
PRE 1815 PONTELAND, NBL, ENG [34102] : PRE
1750 CHOLLERTON & HEXHAM, NBL, ENG
[36502] : PRE 1800 FINDON, SSX, ENG [37179] :
PRE 1850 NORWICH, NFK, ENG [37725] : 1750 +
HARRINGTON, CUL, ENG [37735] : 1800S
WESTMINSTER, MDX, ENG [37834] : PRE 1860
HARBROUGH, LIN, ENG [38111] : ALL
WORLDWIDE [37785]

TATERSAL ALL BRIGHTON, SSX, ENG [35261]

TATESON ALL WORLDWIDE [37103]

TATFORD ALL WORLDWIDE [36172]

TATHAM PRE 1758 HEPTONSTALL & HAWORTH,
YKS, ENG [35459]

TATLOCK PRE 1800 SCOLES & ECCLESTON, LAN,
ENG [36779]

TATLOCK (SEE TETLOCK [36660]

TATLOW 1856 + STANLEY, TAS, AUS [38292] :
1802 + ROCHDALE, LAN, ENG [35815]

TATNALL PRE 1900 MARYLEBONE, LND, ENG
[34450]

TATOR 1835-1900 COLUMBIA CO., NY, USA [37591]

TATTAM 1834 + NSW & QLD, AUS [33939] : PRE 1834
BKM, ENG [33939]

TATTERSALL C1880 CHESTERFIELD, DBY, ENG
[34329] : 1880 + OLDHAM, LAN, ENG [35241]

TATTERSELL 1880-1900 ALDEBURGH, SFK, ENG
[35261]

TATTON 1880 + BRISBANE, QLD, AUS [35111] : ALL
WAR, ENG [37404] : PRE 1890 KILFINNANE, LIM,
IRL [35111]

TATUM 1815 + LONDON, ENG [34627] : SAMUEL
PRE 1735 MADISON CO., KY, USA [37784]

TAUBMAN 1982-1989 NUERNBERG, BAY, BRD
[38750] : 1950 LIVERPOOL, ENG [38750]

TAUDEVAN RACHEL PRE 1810 BRT, FRA [38049]

TAUGHER 1840 CULROSS TWP., ONT, CAN [34503] :
ALL IRL [36545]

TAUNTON 1845 + PARKESBOURNE, NSW, AUS
[38077] : PRE 1840 MONTACUTE, SOM, ENG
[33766]

TAVENER 1860 + GOULBURN, NSW, AUS [35509] :
1820S SOM, ENG [35509]

TAVENIER 1600S KAPELLE, ZEL, NL [38350]

TAVENNER PRE 1730 LONDON, MDX, ENG [36972]

TAVERNER PRE 1840 CHELMSFORD, ESS, ENG
[35406] : PRE 1800 MORETON HAMPSTEAD, DEV,
ENG [36662]

TAWLER PRE 1725 ESS, ENG [35642]

TAWNEY PRE 1796 HANDSWORTH, STS, ENG
[35013]

TAYLER C1767 BRINGTON, NTH, ENG [34584] : PRE
1800 SOMERTON, OXF, ENG [37763]

TAYLOR 1870-1875 BATHURST, NSW, AUS [33768] :
1860+ BEGA, NSW, AUS [33870] : FRANCIS 1842+
TASMAN PENINSULAR, TAS, AUS [33886] : 1850+
NSW, AUS [34534] : C1868 WALLAROO, SA, AUS
[34798] : 1891+ SOUTH MELBOURNE, VIC, AUS
[34798] : 1840 FISH RIVER, NSW, AUS [35089] :
EDWARD 1813+ PARRAMATTA, NSW, AUS
[35155] : JOHN 1850+ GEELONG, VIC, AUS [35224]
: PRE 1880 WARKWORTH, NSW, AUS [35225] :
C1890+ BRANXHOLME, VIC, AUS [35233] : 1919+
RAINBOW, VIC, AUS [35233] : C1860+ SUNBURY,
VIC, AUS [35233] : 1880S DENILIQUIN, NSW, AUS
[35508] : 1850+ RUTHERGLEN, VIC, AUS [35829] :
1850+ ARMIDALE, NSW, AUS [35842] : 1800S
OATLANDS, TAS, AUS [36289] : MARGARET K.
1811+ SYDNEY & SOUTH COAST, NSW, AUS
[36638] : JOHN 1802+ COROMANDEL I &
PARRAMATTA, NSW, AUS [36638] : JOHN 1806+
YORK STREET, SYDNEY, NSW, AUS [36638] :
JOHN 1820+ SOUTH COAST & SYDNEY, NSW,
AUS [36638] : 1860+ MACLEAY RIVER, NSW, AUS
[37104] : ELIZABETH C1840 MAITLAND, NSW,
AUS [37141] : 1850 MOUNT BARKER, SA, AUS
[37186] : THOMAS 1865+ SOUTH EAST AREA,
QLD, AUS [37896] : PRE 1820 BONG BONG, NSW,
AUS [37901] : 1850+ MAITLAND & SINGLETON,
NSW, AUS [37966] : ALEXANDER 1840+ FINGAL,
TAS, AUS [38492] : 1800S NFD, CAN [36558] : 1899+
STOCKTON, SAS, CAN [36716] : 1830-1882 STE
CATHERINE, QUE, CAN [37809] : PRE 1835
CARBONEAR, NFD, CAN [38412] : 1900+
HAMILTON & DUNDAS, ONT, CAN [38481] : PRE
1870 LND, ENG [33768] : 1700+ ADDINGTON,
KEN, ENG [33785] : PRE 1850 MANUDEN, ESS,
ENG [33870] : FRANCIS 1810-1842 DARLASTON,
STS, ENG [33886] : 1800-1900 PETERBOROUGH,
HUN, ENG [33908] : PRE 1840 LAN, ENG [33943] :
PRE 1830 GAWBER, YKS, ENG [34031] : PRE 1777
LND, ENG [34056] : HARRIET 1815-1831
WOOLTON, LAN, ENG [34174] : 1800+
SOMERTON, OXF, ENG [34236] : PRE 1840
WEYBRIDGE, MDX, ENG [34269] : GEORGE PRE
1859 THORNBURY, GLS, ENG [34287] : 1750-1850
HUNGERFORD, BRK & SRY, ENG [34343] : 1900+
LIN, ENG [34361] : 1845 TEDDINGTON, MDX,
ENG [34388] : PRE 1760 WIGAN, LAN, ENG [34397]
: CLARA 1840-1890 LEI, ENG [34400] : 1700+
SUTTON COLDFIELD, WAR, ENG [34416] :
EDWARD PRE 1785 ESS, ENG [34461] : 1800-1870
NEWCHURCH, LAN, ENG [34520] : 1700-1770
BROMYARD, HEF, ENG [34552] : 1750-1800
KEMPSEY, WOR, ENG [34552] : 1750-1800 THORP,
SRY, ENG [34552] : PRE 1872 HILMARTON, WIL,
ENG [34588] : PRE 1874 LIDLINGTON, BDF, ENG
[34588] : 1850 WALKER, NBL, ENG [34614] : PRE
1845 BLAXHALL, SFK, ENG [34669] : PRE 1814
WINDLESHAM, SRY, ENG [34689] : 1815
MORLAND, WES, ENG [34731] : 1880
PORTSMOUTH, HAM, ENG [34757] : ALL ROSS
ON WYE &BRAMPTON ABBOTTS, HEF, ENG
[34823] : PRE 1880 MDX, ENG [34848] : THOMAS
1800+ ST PANCRAS & ISLINGTON, MDX, ENG
[34882] : 1780+ ALMONDBURY, WRY, ENG [34934]
: PHILIP C1858 CROUGHTON, NTH, ENG [34935] :

1700+ CASTLE COMBE, WIL, ENG [34970] : PRE
1878 LIVERPOOL, LAN, ENG [34999] : MARY 1830
WILBARSTON, NTH, ENG [35024] : 1800
ALTARNUM, CON, ENG [35089] : JOHN C1823-
1851+ HILPERTON & TROWBRIDGE, WIL, ENG
[35133] : JOHN C1801+ CHEW MAGNA, SOM,
ENG [35133] : 1750-1850 ENG [35136] : PRE 1875
ACTON, DEV, ENG [35211] : PRE 1840 PYTCHLEY,
NTH, ENG [35215] : PRE 1850 BDF, ENG [35224] :
1800-1850 BIRMINGHAM & LONDON, ENG
[35228] : 1700-1800 SSX & SRY, ENG [35238] : 1800S
BILSTON, STS, ENG [35256] : 1900S STAVELEY,
DBY, ENG [35256] : JANE C1830 PRESTON, LAN,
ENG [35261] : SAMUEL C1770 BATTLE, SSX, ENG
[35261] : 1850+ BLACKBURN & GT HARWOOD,
LAN, ENG [35362] : 1700+ HACKFORD, NFK,
ENG [35411] : PRE 1890 BISHOPS FROME, HEF &
WOR, ENG [35417] : 1840+ CHELSEA, MDX, ENG
[35458] : 1830S BURNHAM THORPE, NFK, ENG
[35525] : C1819 SOUTHWARK, LND, ENG [35527] :
PRE 1883 LONDON, ENG [35536] : 1800S
TEWKESBURY, GLS, ENG [35542] : 1800-1830
ANWICK, LIN, ENG [35643] : C1804
ALMONDBURY, WRY, ENG [35733] : PRE 1820
YKS, ENG [35745] : PRE 1880 BOLTONGATE, CUL,
ENG [35764] : JAMES C1785 BARKBY, LEI, ENG
[35773] : C1845 LIVERPOOL, LAN, ENG [35791] :
C1850 SOUTHAMPTON, HAM, ENG [35807] :
1800+ BATTERSALL, NTT, ENG [35847] : 1830+
ADDLESTONE, SRY, ENG [35880] : 1700+ BDF,
ENG [35880] : 1750+ TWYNING, GLS, ENG [35886]
: 1750+ BELBROUGHTON & CLENT, WOR, ENG
[35919] : PRE 1860+ LAN, ENG [35928] : PRE 1880
MDX, ENG [35932] : 1800+ ADDLESTON &
LIDLINGTON, SRY & BDF, ENG [35947] : ALL
LYMINGTON, HAM, ENG [35998] : PRE 1830
BERMONDSEY, LND, ENG [36035] : PRE 1890
FORDHAM, ESS, ENG [36077] : PRE 1795 SFK,
ENG [36124] : PRE 1840 CHARD, SOM, ENG [36142]
: ALL WHITWELL, DBY, ENG [36174] : JOHN
1784+ BOTTON, LAN, ENG [36180] : ALL LAN,
ENG [36189] : 1800+ PRESTON & BARROW, LAN,
ENG [36218] : PRE 1830 BURY, LAN, ENG [36271] :
C1700-1800S HAM, ENG [36289] : C1798 SOM, ENG
[36307] : ALL THANET, KEN, ENG [36393] : PRE
1850 CADDENHAM, SFK, ENG [36409] : 1790+
DOR, ENG [36435] : JOSEPH 1790+ ST MARYS,
SCILLIES, CON, ENG [36435] : PRE 1850 NORTON
AT THE MOORS, STS, ENG [36502] : PRE 1850
BUCKNALLCUM BAGNALL, STS, ENG [36502] :
1840S TUNSTALL, STS, ENG [36504] : PRE 1868
LIVERPOOL, LAN, ENG [36522] : PRE 1884 SFK,
ENG [36526] : DANIEL PRE 1850 LONDON, ENG
[36527] : DANIEL 1850-1900 SOUTHWARK, SRY,
ENG [36527] : 1825-1912 HALESWORTH &
HAVERHILL, SFK, ENG [36558] : 1800+ YKS, ENG
[36568] : 1900+ BRADFORD, YKS, ENG [36568] :
ASPIN 1700S BRAY, BRK, ENG [36585] : 1650+
MILWICH, STS, ENG [36701] : 1850+
ORPINGTON, KEN, ENG [36708] : ALL
MAIDSTONE, KEN, ENG [36743] : 1800+ LAN,
ENG [36745] : C1790+ WISBECH, CAM, ENG
[36753] : 1808-1840 SEAL, KEN, ENG [36770] : 1761-
1807 BOURTON ON THE WATER, GLS, ENG
[36770] : 1882 ETCHINGHAM, SSX, ENG [36770] :
1800+ HUDDERSFIELD, WRY, ENG [36777] :
THOMAS 1700+ LUCCOMBE, SOM, ENG [36813] :
PRE 1840 SHIREOAKS, NTT, ENG [36854] : 1790+
WEYMOUTH, DOR, ENG [36868] : 1840-1860
COLCHESTER, ESS, ENG [36913] : C1764
ACCRINGTON, LAN, ENG [36955] : C1760
LACKFORD, SFK, ENG [36955] : 1700-1900 NFK,

ENG [36977] : C1747 BARNBY IN THE WILLOWS, NTT, ENG [37007] : THOMAS C1814 LEICESTER, LEI, ENG [37053] : 1810+ BIRMINGHAM, WAR, ENG [37074] : STEPHEN 1700+ EAST MALLING, KEN, ENG [37088] : 1700+ STAPLEHURST & CRANBROOK, KEN, ENG [37088] : PRE 1836 LONDON, ENG [37104] : PRE 1775 CAM, ENG [37144] : HESTER C1750-1820 DEVONPORT, DEV, ENG [37158] : C1800 BRAILSFORD, DBY, ENG [37215] : 1880S YARDLEY, WOR, ENG [37230] : RICHARD 1740-1800 DEV, ENG [37231] : ALL MADLEY, HEF, ENG [37281] : ALL DEWSALL, HEF, ENG [37281] : ALL CLEHONGER, HEF, ENG [37281] : ALL EATON BISHOP, HEF, ENG [37281] : ALL GALLOW, HEF, ENG [37281] : PRE 1900 ASHMORE, DOR, ENG [37291] : PRE 1850 KIRKHAM, LAN, ENG [37318] : JANE PRE 1771 PENZANCE, CON, ENG [37319] : PRE 1844 ST MARGARETS, LEI, ENG [37346] : PRE 1820 SLAMMONDEN & BARKISLAND, WRY, ENG [37372] : 1800-1900 MANGOTSFIELD, GLS, ENG [37403] : PRE 1750 NRY, ENG [37498] : JOHN C1780 WAKEFIELD, YKS, ENG [37508] : 1800+ WEDNESBURY, STS, ENG [37608] : ALL DEPTFORD, LND, ENG [37627] : JOHN 1790-1820 ROWLEY REGIS, WOR, ENG [37632] : JOHN 1850+ DARLASTON, STS, ENG [37632] : HANNAH 1770+ BRENCHLEY, KEN, ENG [37664] : PRE 1908 ROCHDALE, LAN, ENG [37667] : PRE 1850 OLDBURY & BIRMINGHAM, WOR, WAR & STS, ENG [37703] : JOSEPH 1830-1860 LIVERPOOL, LAN, ENG [37779] : MARY PRE 1640 HALIFAX, WRY, ENG [37806] : MARY PRE 1635 HALIFAX, WRY, ENG [37806] : 1800-1850 CITY OF LONDON, ENG [37877] : 1800-1850 CLERKENWELL, MDX, ENG [37877] : JAMES 1855 WHALLEY, LAN, ENG [37888] : 1800S WILLINGTON, DUR, ENG [37899] : 1760+ MUCHELNEY, SOM, ENG [37905] : 1800+ BIRMINGHAM, WAR, ENG [37924] : 1820 WHITCHURCH, SAL, ENG [37946] : 1800+ BRIGHTON, SSX, ENG [37985] : PRE 1900 EVENSWOOD, DUR, ENG [38013] : PRE 1800 ROCHESTER, KEN, ENG [38027] : CHARLES C1875 NEWCASTLE ON TYNE, NBL, ENG [38207] : 1815-1950 ROCHDALE & OLDHAM, LAN, ENG [38370] : 1875-1900 CREWE, CHS, ENG [38370] : 1840+ WORSLEY & SALFORD, LAN, ENG [38410] : 1863 NEW MILLS, DBY, ENG [38449] : PRE 1820 GREYSTOKE, CUL, ENG [38457] : 1800+ GNOSALL, STS, ENG [38481] : HENRY C1809 DEVIZES, WIL, ENG [38489] : 1850 NETHERAVON, WIL, ENG [38489] : SARAH 1863 PEWSEY, WIL, ENG [38489] : PRE 1830 LEEDS, YKS, ENG [38512] : ALL ENG & AUS [35213] : 1700+ ST LAWRENCE, NY, USA &, ENG & CAN [36341] : JOHN 1809-1920 BELFAST, IRL [34200] : MARGARET ELIZ 1819 (M. JOHN HODGINS JR), TIP, IRL [35607] : MARGARET ELIZ C1840 TIPPERARY, TIP, IRL [35607] : PRE 1840 FAHAN, DON, IRL [35842] : 1820+ BALLYNAKILL, GAL, IRL [35970] : JOHN 1600-1700 DRUMLECH, ARM, IRL [36321] : PRE 1860 DONAGHADEE, DOW, IRL [37141] : 1700-1900 SCARIFF & MOUNTSHANNON, CLA, IRL [37244] : PRE 1800 LEX, IRL [37498] : 1810-1830 KIK, IRL [37809] : PRE 1865 COR, IRL [37896] : 1872+ PARANUI, NZ [34588] : 1874+ WESPORT, NZ [34588] : PRE 1790 LATHERON, CAI, SCT [33873] : PRE 1770 ERROL, PER, SCT [33873] : PRE 1850 CURRIE, EDINBURGH, ELN & MLN, SCT [33959] : 1800+ DUNFERMLINE, FIF, SCT [33970] : JOHN 1775+ BURNBANK, PER, SCT [34075] : 1800-1900 AUCHTERARDER, PER, SCT [34098] :

MARGARET PRE 1822 DUNDEE, ANS, SCT [34461] : JAMES 1800S CUMINESTOWN, ABD, SCT [34499] : EUPHAN PRE 1825 PERTH, PER, SCT [34583] : 1840 STROMNESS, OKI, SCT [34614] : 1780+ ABDIE, FIF, SCT [34637] : 1845 PER, SCT [34761] : 1841 FIF, SCT [34793] : 1750-1850 STI, WLN & MLN, SCT [34920] : 1836 BATHGATE, WLN, SCT [35251] : ELSPET 1775 KEITH, BAN, SCT [35369] : ISABEL 1768 FORDYCE, BAN, SCT [35369] : C1777 LEUCHARS, FIF, SCT [35854] : 1808+ PORT GLASGOW, RFW, SCT [35854] : ROBERT 1828-1868 ANSTRUTHER, FIF, SCT [35865] : 1800S SCT [35906] : 1750+ TORPHICHEN, WLN, SCT [35979] : PRE 1880 PERTH, PER, SCT [36077] : PRE 1900 ABERDEEN, ABD, SCT [36201] : JOHN 1800-1860 AYR, SCT [36239] : PRE 1880 GLASGOW, LKS, SCT [36754] : PRE 1900 ARBROATH, SCT [36773] : 1700-1850 CABRACH, ABD, SCT [36783] : HENDRIE 1698-1800+ DUNDURCAS & KEITH, BAN, SCT [36783] : C1811 ABD, SCT [36856] : C1800 GLASGOW, LKS, SCT [37141] : 1800-1810 ABD, SCT [37263] : ISABELLA 1810-1830 SCT [37443] : 1790+ BO'NESS, WLN, SCT [37666] : PRE 1900 BAN, SCT [37835] : 1800-1850 ARL, SCT [37891] : C1786 CAPUTH, PER & FIF, SCT [37972] : RICHARD HUGH PRE 1860 BRUNSWICK CO., VA, USA [35264] : OLIVE 1750+ GROTON CO., NH, USA [35276] : 1790+ BERKELEY CO., WV, USA [35278] : 1725-1800 EDGEFIELD CO., SC, USA [36354] : ALL CASEY, KY, USA [36567] : PRE 1760 DERRY, PA & NJ, USA [36917] : 1800 MARIETTA, OH, USA [37028] : 1700S VA, USA [37028] : 1813-1860 BLOUNT CO., TN, USA [37029] : JAMES 1859-1866 ST LOUIS, MO, USA [37035] : 1600S CT, USA [37570] : 1855-1870 KEWEENAW CO., MI, USA [38009] : 1850-1860 KNOX CO., OH, USA [38105] : 1800-1990 WORCESTER, MD, USA [38136] : GEORGE Z. 1870S LICKING CO., OH, USA [38323] : EDWIN 1783+ NC, USA [38340] : PRE 1890 GRAINGER CO., TN & CA, USA [38570] : 1800S JAMAICA, W.INDIES [37186]

TAYLORSEN 1870S NRY & ERY, ENG [38356]

TAYMAN ALL WORLDWIDE [36015]

TAYTON ALL CONINGSBY & TATTERSHALL, LIN, ENG [34765]

TCENNES CARL 1893+ SWE [38564]

TEAGE 1700+ KINGSWEAR, DEV, ENG [36000]

TEAGUE 1860+ SA, AUS [34279] : 1855 VIC, AUS [35776] : 1840-1877 CON, ENG [35092] : C1849 DEVONPORT, DEV, ENG [35251] : PRE 1800 WHITEPARISH, WIL, ENG [36496] : PRE 1700 ST HILARY, CON, ENG [37319] : ALL IA & KS, USA [37812] : ALL MD, NC & IN, USA [37812]

TEARLE PRE 1876 LUTON, BDF, ENG [37955]

TEASDALE 1852+ KANGAROO FLAT, VIC, AUS [35801] : PRE 1789 ENG [36594] : PRE 1775 OUSBY, CUL, ENG [36701] : PRE 1839 MANCHESTER, LAN, ENG [37267] : 1650-1838 ALSTON, CUL, ENG [38026] : 1852+ MANCHESTER, INV, SCT [35801]

TEATHER ALL WORLDWIDE [37672]

TEBB ALL LIN, ENG [34324]

TEBBET PRE 1900 SOHAM, CAM, ENG [35168]

TEBBIT PRE 1760 SOHAM, CAM, ENG [34445] : PRE 1900 SOHAM, CAM, ENG [35168] : 1800S HANSLOPE, BKM, ENG [35256]

TEBBITT PRE 1900 SOHAM, CAM, ENG [35168]

TEBBS 1774+ DONNINGTON, ENG [35465] : 1831+ DBY, ENG [35465]

TEBBUTT 1800+ KEN, ENG [36574] : PRE 1845 EARLS BARTON, NTH, ENG [36748]

TEBO 1800S BROWN CO., IL, USA [36896]

TEBOT PRE 1900 SOHAM, CAM, ENG [35168]

TEBOW PRE 1867 HAMILTON CO., OH, USA [37015]

TECHIM PRE 1857 BRESEGARD, MSW, GER [35820]

TECK 1790-1840 MLN & ELN, SCT [36724]

TECKENTRUP PRE 1880 HOERDE, WEF, GER [38690] : ALL GER [38690]

TEDDER PRE 1783 WINDLESHAM, SRY, ENG [34689]

TEDFORD PRE 1860 ARM, IRL [37974] : PRE 1780 SUSSEX CO., NJ, USA [38116]

TEDMON PRE 1850 HIGH HALSTOW, KEN, ENG [38027]

TEE ALL MAIDWELL, NTH, ENG [35888] : 1874+ WAIMATE, CBY, NZ [35888]

TEEBOON 1800 GRETTON, NTH, ENG [38288]

TEED PRE 1815 CANTERBURY, NB, CAN [37454]

TEELE 1800+ ENNISKILLEN, FER, IRL [35194]

TEEPLE 1820+ NELSON TWP., ONT, CAN [34231] : 1820+ BEVERLY TWP., ONT, CAN [34231]

TEETER 1800-1900 ONT, CAN [37466] : ALL PA, USA [38067]

TEETGEN PRE 1765 HAN, GER [37069]

TEEUWEN PRE 1800 STRAELEN, FRG [38705] : ALL LEIDEN, ZUH, NL [38705]

TEEVENS 1797-1866+ DUBLIN, IRL & USA [36960] : 1840-1894 DUBLIN, IRL & USA [36960]

TEFFT 1800-1820 RI, USA [36901] : ALL USA [37015]

TEGNER 1775-1875 YSTAD, MAL, SWE [36320]

TEGTMEIER ALL HEERSUM, NSA, GER [38637]

TEICHROEW ALL WORLDWIDE [37505]

TEIRNEY 1700-1949 COOTE HILL, CAV, IRL [36894]

TEIXEIRA DE MATTOS C1650-1991 AMSTERDAM, NL [36630]

TELFER 1856+ ARARAT, VIC, AUS [35715] : ALL AUS [35715] : C1800 ROX, SCT [35032] : 1700+ LANGHOLM, DFS, SCT [35038] : 1800S LAMMINGTON, LKS, SCT [35408] : 1800+ JEDBURGH, ROX, SCT [35715] : 1750-1805 ROX, SCT [38416]

TELFORD 1933+ WIMMERA, VIC, AUS [36622] : PRE 1800 BEWCASTLE, CUL, ENG [35165] : 1800S SUNDERLAND, DUR, ENG [35408] : PRE 1830 BEWCASTLE, CUL, ENG [35525] : C1840 GREENHEAD, NBL, ENG [36270] : 1830+ CARLISLE, CUL, ENG & CAN [34467] : PRE 1880 ANT, IRL [34633] : C1867 ARM, IRL [36312] : 1740+ MONTEITH, DOW, IRL [37478] : 1750-1805 ROX, SCT [38416]

TELFORD (SEE TAILFOR [36270]

TELLEP ALL WORLDWIDE [38369]

TELLER PRE 1880 MEK, GER [38037]

TELLING 1800-1850 TOMAGO, NSW, AUS [35094] : PRE 1870 BETHNAL GREEN, LND, ENG [34277]

TEMBY ALL CON, ENG [35063]

TEMPEL PRE 1750 LEISELHEIM & WORMS, RPF, GER [38681]

TEMPERTON PRE 1800 HULL, ERY, ENG [36298]

TEMPEST ALL WORLDWIDE [37235]

TEMPLE 1888+ CARRUM DOWNS, VIC, AUS [35207] : PRE 1888 HOLBECK, WRY, ENG [35207] : 1750+ CON, ENG [35306] : PRE 1850 NTT & ERY, ENG [36387] : C1800 POPLAR, MDX, ENG [36790] : C1820 NEWSHAM, NRY, ENG [37627] : 1900+ SUNDERLAND, DUR, ENG [37878] : 1400+ BROADWINSOR, DOR, ENG [38745] : PRE 1811 HAWICK, ROX, SCT [37878] : 1750+ DFS, SCT [38385]

TEMPLEMAN 1700+ WRY & ERY, ENG [38468] : PRE 1800 USA [37804]

TEMPLETON 1846 SYDNEY, NSW, AUS [35855] : 1848+ SYDNEY, NSW, AUS [38277] : PRE 1900 CARLISLE, CUL, ENG [36725] : PRE 1900 BALLYRAINE, DON, IRL [33966] : SARAH ALL

IRL [34571] : 1880+ MILTON, OTG, NZ [33966] : 1913 GLASGOW, LKS, SCT [33811] : 1800S KILMAURS, AYR, STI & LKS, SCT [35767]

TENBARGE 1704-1846 EIBERGEN, GEL, NL [36553] : 1846-1990 GIBSON CO., IN, USA [36553] : 1846-1990 VANDERBURGH CO., IN, USA [36553]

TEN BRINK PRE 1850 ALKEMADE, ZUH, NL [34613]

TENDESON ALL AUS [33959]

TENES AGNES 1890+ WREXHAM CLWYD CO., WLS & ENG [36572]

TENISON 1700+ DILLONSTOWN, LOU, IRL [34299]

TENNANT 1832 ENG [34609] : 1865+ PANCRAS, LND, ENG [34669] : C1908 STOURBRIDGE, WOR, ENG [36171] : C1650-1700S BDF, ENG [36289] : PRE 1870 LND & MDX, ENG & AUS [35213] : 1885 MASULIPATAM, INDIA [34609] : PRE 1780 ABD, SCT [33914] : ALL FIF, LKS & MLN, SCT [34861] : 1744 GLASGOW, SCT [37008]

TENNENT PRE 1850 ABERNETHY, PER, SCT [34587] : 1800-1850 PAISLEY, RFW, SCT [38521]

TENNEY 1773-1794 BENNINGTON, VT, USA [38741] : ALL WORLDWIDE [37084]

TENNISON 1780-1900 WARRINGTON & SPENCER, IN, USA [38095]

TENNYSON 1883+ GYMPIE, QLD, AUS [34807] : 1854-1883 ARM & TYR, IRL [34807]

TER BRUGGEN 1592+ HANAU, HEN, GER [38667]

TERENTIUK PRE 1875 SNIATYN, UKRAINE, OES & POL [36679]

TERHUNE PRE 1764 GRAVESEND, NY, USA [38126]

TERLINGEN 1800+ NL [33769]

TERNAN WILLIAM 1790+ SYDNEY, NSW, AUS [37139] : WILLIAM 1770-1790 PLYMOUTH, DEV, ENG [37139]

TERNENT 1840+ BELFORD, NBL, ENG [34198] : PRE 1900 NBL, ENG [36934] : 1790S MARSHALL MEADOWS, BEW, SCT [34198]

TERNES 1857-1910 LORAIN CO., OH, USA [38106]

TERNUS PRE 1852 BOPPARD, GER [38738]

TERPENNING 1760+ SCHOHARIE CO., NY, USA [38176]

TERRACE PRE 1850 ALBERT CO., NB, CAN [38447]

TERREL ALL USA [37812]

TERRELL WILLIAM 1840-1905 ADELAIDE, SA, AUS [33892] : 1850-1860 KEWEENAW CO., MI, USA [38009]

TERRETT PRE 1860 CLA, LIM & LEX, IRL [35866]

TERREY 1800S ENG [37857]

TERRIEN 1400-1980 AUS & NZ [38493] : 1400-1980 BEL [38493] : 1840-1875 HERIVILLE, QUE, CAN [37547] : 1400-1989 PL, FRA [38493] : 1666+ DIEPPE, NOR, FRA [38493] : 1656+ LA ROCHELLE, PCH, FRA [38493] : 1400-1980 IRL & ENG [38493] : 1400-1980 PAYS BAYS [38493] : 1400-1980 SCANDINAVI [38493] : 1400-1980 UK [38493]

TERRIENNE 1400-1989 PL, FRA [38493]

TERRILL 1620+ BARBADOS, W.INDIES [34230]

TERRION PRE 1800 QUE, CAN [38445] : 1800S HASTINGS CO., ONT, CAN [38445] : ALL WORLDWIDE [35832]

TERRY 1880+ WEST MAITLAND, NSW, AUS [35384] : 1915+ ALLANDALE, ONT, CAN [34498] : PRE 1840 LONDON, ENG [33821] : PRE 1840 HAILSHAM, SSX, ENG [34755] : ALL EXETER, DEV, ENG [36145] : ALL OXFORD, OXF, ENG [36145] : PRE 1750 BOLTON CASTLE CUM REDMIRE, NRY, ENG [36159] : 1830+ RAMSGATE, KEN, ENG [36254] : PRE 1850 CROYDON, LND & SRY, ENG [36385] : PRE 1806 ROWLING, KEN, ENG [36804] : 1840S BRIGHTON, SSX, ENG [37080] : C1700 PORTSMOUTH, HAM,

ENG **[37513]** : 1700S ROMSEY, HAM, ENG **[38350]** : C1640S WINDSOR, CT, USA **[34395]** : 1740-1806 BUCKS CO., PA, USA **[34476]** : LOU IZA ALL NC, USA **[35304]** : 1800-1900 NEWPORT, NY, USA **[37464]** : 1800 MARSHALL CO., TN, USA **[38743]**

TERSON C1700 PORTARLINGTON, LEX, OFF & DUB, IRL **[37381]**

TERVIN 1753 PRESTWICH, LAN, ENG **[35369]**

TESINA PRE 1880 KRALOVIC, PLZEN, CS **[35290]**

TESKE PRE 1883 NEU STETTIN, POS, GER & POL **[37529]**

TESKEY C1850 LINDSAY, ONT, CAN **[34058]**

TESSEYMAN 1650-1850 ENG **[36988]**

TESSIER PRE 1760 SPITALFIELDS, LND, ENG & FRA **[37261]**

TESSMANN PRE 1875 BISMARK, WPR, GER **[36839]**

TESTER 1700-1800 WESTMINSTER, MDX, ENG **[36106]** : SAMUEL 1840-50 ALLEN CO., OH, USA **[38086]**

TESTERMAN ALL BIG SANDY, WV, USA **[38036]**

TETFORD ALL WORLDWIDE **[36172]**

TETHER PRE 1850 LIN, NTT & YKS, ENG **[37517]** : ALL WORLDWIDE **[37672]**

TETINGER PRE 1790 HAUTE VIGNEULLES, LOR, FRA **[38658]** : PRE 1770 NARBE FONTAINE, LOR, FRA **[38658]**

TETLEY C1800-1850 BRADFORD, WRY, ENG **[34628]** : PRE 1850 NTT & DBY, ENG **[37412]**

TETLOCK PRE 1800 NEW & OLD ROSS, WEX, IRL **[36660]**

TETLOW SAMUEL 1843 HURST, LAN, ENG **[37184]**

TETREAU MARIE 1850-1875 MALONE, NY, USA **[38408]** : EDOUARD 1890+ MALONE, NY, USA **[38408]**

TETREAULT 1634-1950 QUE, CAN **[34217]**

TETT 1700-1900 IRL **[37849]** : 1700-1900 WICK, IRL **[37849]**

TETTERSELL ALL BRIGHTON, SSX, ENG **[35261]**

TETTHER ALL WORLDWIDE **[37672]**

TEUNISSE (SEE THEUNI) **[38694]**

TEUNISSEN 1880-1959 RANDWYCK, ZETTEN, NL **[34242]**

TEVELEIN PRE 1850 CANTERBURY, KEN, ENG **[34291]**

TEW ALL WOODFORD HALSE, NTH, ENG **[35924]**

TEWART ALL ENG & SCT **[36119]**

THACKER 1730+ BUCKNALL, LIN, ENG **[35587]** : 1500-1650 WISBECH, CAM, ENG **[37342]** : 1500-1600 HOLBEACH, LIN, ENG **[37342]** : 1800-1880 LONDON, ENG **[37783]** : 1800-1880 CANTERBURY, KEN, ENG **[37783]** : 1690-1790 HOLME NEXT THE SEA, NFK, ENG **[38453]**

THACKERAY 1700-1800 THIRSK, NRY, ENG **[36472]**

THACKHAM ALL HAM, ENG **[34218]**

THACKRAY 1750-1900 MASHAM, NRY, ENG **[36141]** : PRE 1800 YKS, ENG **[37760]**

THAKE ALL WORLDWIDE **[37741]**

THALLER ALL OES **[38369]**

THARP 1860+ LABETTE CO., KS, USA **[38310]** : 1800-1830 MOSKINGOM CO., OH, USA **[38310]** : 1805-1840 OH, USA **[38324]** : 1800-1820 SC, USA **[38324]** : 1760-1840 NEW ENGLAND, USA **[38531]**

THATCHER 1780S+ LONDON, ENG **[33849]** : 1600+ HASTINGS, SSX, ENG **[34747]** : PRE 1866 SONNING, BRK, ENG **[35200]** : PRE 1750 SHRIVENHAM, BRK, ENG **[35866]** : ALL CHEDDAR, SOM, ENG **[36605]** : 1850+ GREENWICH, MDX, ENG **[36872]** : PRE 1700 SOM, ENG **[38745]** : 1752-1788 KY, USA **[38741]**

THAUBERGER PRE 1861 WORLDWIDE **[37481]**

THEAKER 1800-1880 SHEFFIELD, YKS, ENG **[35600]**

THEAKSTON PRE 1850 RIPON, NRY, ENG **[36121]**

THEEDE 1900 ND, USA **[38434]**

THEEUF 1850+ AUS **[33808]** : PRE 1850 THANAT & CANTERBURY, KEN, ENG **[33808]**

THEILEN 1800+ OVELGONNE, OLD, GER **[37116]**

THEISINGER 1860 PORTLAND, VIC, AUS **[34594]**

THEISS 1750+ LINDENSTRUTH, HES, BRD **[35475]**

THEMUS PIERRE 1700+ KENT & ESSEX CO., ONT, CAN **[34154]**

THEOBALD 1836-1847 ALPHETON, SFK, ENG **[37418]** : 1800-1850S ESS & NSW, ENG & AUS **[37988]**

THEOBALDS 1827 FOULMERE, CAM, ENG **[34761]** : 1800+ PRESTON PATRICK, WES, ENG **[37196]** : 1600+ SETTLE, YKS, ENG **[37196]** : 1800+ FARLETON, WES, ENG **[37196]** : 1700+ KENDAL, WES, ENG **[37196]**

THERIEN PRE 1800 QUE, CAN **[38445]**

THERRIEN 1840-1875 MONTREAL, QUE, CAN **[37547]** : 1800+ CAN **[38493]** : 1800+ USA **[38493]**

THERRY PRE 1830 LIMERICK CITY, LIM & COR, IRL **[37018]**

THESSMAN 1875+ NZ **[36839]**

THEUER 1820+ DETROIT, MI, USA **[35084]**

THEUNISSE ALL ODIJK, UTR, NL **[38694]**

THEUNISSEN ALL NL **[38303]**

THEURICH 1800S SILBER, SIL, GER **[38623]**

THEURIG 1800S SILBER, SIL, GER **[38623]**

THEVENET 1723-1942 CHANDON & MACON, PL & BRG, FRA **[34136]**

THEW 1820+ RICHMOND & BURWOOD, NSW, AUS **[33996]** : 1800+ BON, LONDON, MDX, ENG **[36263]**

THEWLIS 1700-1900 NORTH SHIELDS, NBL, ENG **[35165]**

THEXTON PRE 1837 CARNFORTH, LAN, ENG **[36180]** : 1800S PATTERDALE, WES, ENG **[38440]**

THIBAULT PRE 1840 TERILIS, PCA, FRA **[35098]**

THIBODEAU 1830-1950S NB, CAN **[34202]** : 1760+ LABADIE, QUE & NB, CAN **[37503]**

THICKETT 1650+ ROYSTON, WRY & LAN, ENG **[34520]** : 1780-1860 ECCLESFIELD & PENISTONE, WRY, ENG **[35550]**

THICKNESSE 1850+ BETLEY, STS, ENG **[34243]**

THICTHENER PRE 1805 STRASBOURG, ALS, FRA **[35229]**

THIEDT 1780 WASDOW, MSW, GER **[38125]**

THIEL HANS PRE 1710 STOCKHOLM, SWE **[37036]**

THIELAN 1870 LENAWEE CO., MI, USA **[38192]**

THIELE 1800+ ANK, GER **[35951]** : WILLIAM 1820-1840S HAN, GER **[37001]** : 1800+ CHRISTCHURCH, CANT, NZ **[35951]**

THIERY 1700-1800 ATW, BEL **[38170]**

THIFFAULT 1600-1900S TROIS RIVIERE, QUE, CAN **[35327]**

THIJSSEN C1730 REKEM, BEL **[38698]**

THILL 1870S LUX **[38339]**

THIMME ALL GOTTINGEN, BRD **[34765]**

THINGER 1700+ OXF & NTH, ENG **[34236]**

THIRKLE PRE 1760 ANT, ARM & DOW, IRL **[35897]**

THIRLBY PRE 1800 IBSTOCK, LEI, ENG **[34686]**

THIRLWELL PRE 1800 TANFIELD, DUR, ENG **[36883]**

THIRWALL PRE 1850 SHITTLEBOTTLE, NBL, ENG **[34816]**

THISE PRE 1875 EMB HJORRING, DEN **[35197]**

THISTLETHWAITE PRE 1870 WHITBY, CHS, ENG **[33997]** : 1800+ NBL & DUR, ENG **[38754]**

THISTLETON ALL NFK, ENG **[37236]**

THLE 1900+ FREIBERG, SACHSEN, GER **[38603]**

THODE 1800+ SHO, GER [36662] : PRE 1830
CUXHAVEN, NSA, GER [38632] : 1850-1900
HOLSTEIN, IA & WI, USA [36662]

THODEY 1750-1790 WETHERSFIELD, ESS, ENG
[37859]

THOERNER 1700+ OSNABRUECK, HAN, GER
[38651]

THOLE 1840+ IA & WI, USA [36542]

THOM 1780+ GLEIME, SAX, GER [38529] : PRE 1770
ABD, SCT [34053] : PRE 1800 ABERDEEN, SCT
[36466]

THOMAS 1849+ ADELAIDE, SA, AUS [33763] :
1860+ TAREENA, SA, AUS [33824] : 1870+
MACLEAY RV, NSW, AUS [34306] : 1850-1940
SYDNEY, NSW, AUS [34438] : PRE 1890 TAS, AUS
[34904] : 1920 BEDGEREBONG, NSW, AUS [34967] :
1878+ GOULBURN, NSW, AUS [34967] : 1876
MARYBOROUGH, VIC, AUS [34967] : 1880+
BENDIGO, VIC, AUS [35040] : 1880-1920
FOOTSCRAY, VIC, AUS [35479] : 1873
CASTLEMAINE, VIC, AUS [35479] : 1875-1880
WOODEND, VIC, AUS [35479] : 1855+ SYDNEY,
NSW, AUS [35505] : 1870S+ WILLENABRINA, VIC,
AUS [35522] : ISABELLA C1856 SYDNEY, NSW,
AUS [35575] : 1850S SYDNEY, NSW, AUS [35582] :
HENRY 1865-1866 BALLARD RAILWAY CAMP,
QLD, AUS [35726] : HENRY 1866-1867 TARADALE
& BENDIGO, VIC, AUS [35726] : ALL MORANG,
VIC, AUS [36852] : 1850S KEMPSEY, NSW, AUS
[37500] : C1872 WANGARATTA, VIC, AUS [37553] :
PRE 1869 SHOALHAVEN, NSW, AUS [37948] :
1841+ COLLINGWOOD & THOMASTOWN, VIC,
AUS [37962] : ALL ORANGE, NSW, AUS [38487] :
1750+ BARBADOS [38355] : 1800+ NIAGARA,
ONT, CAN [33908] : PRE 1900 MONT LAURIER,
QUE, CAN [34245] : PRE 1858 GUELPH, ONT, CAN
[35618] : 1900+ PETERBOROUGH, ONT, CAN
[36716] : 1840+ HALIFAX, NS, CAN [37432] : 1878
FENELON FALLS, ONT, CAN [37493] : PRE 1923
HUNTSVILLE, ONT, CAN [38450] : 1770+ ST
HELIER, JSY, CHI [34532] : 1800+ GSY, CHI [37112]
: 1910 TONGSHAN, CHINA [34967] : 1800+ YKS,
ENG [33973] : GRACE 1846-1870 BREAGE, CON,
ENG [34035] : PRE 1800 STOKE DAMEREL, DEV,
ENG [34139] : 1750-1850 WENDRON, CON, ENG
[34194] : 1700-1800 LONDON, ENG [34258] : PRE
1800 WOTTON UNDER EDGE, GLS, ENG [34466] :
PRE 1800 HOWARTH, YKS, ENG [34655] : 1700+
ST JUST IN ROSELAND, CON, ENG [34768] :
1749+ PAINSWICK, GLS, ENG [34939] : DAVID
1906 LONDON, ENG [34967] : W.F. 1804 LONDON,
MDX, ENG [35252] : 1800+ CHESTER, CHS, ENG
[35358] : PRE 1872 TUCKINGMILL, CON, ENG
[35479] : PRE 1850 ROSKEAR, CON, ENG [35479] :
PRE 1800+ FALMOUTH, CON, ENG [35505] : PRE
1850 CAMBORNE & ILLOGAN, CON, ENG [35540]
: 1820+ LONDON & BERMONDSEY, SRY, ENG
[35579] : 1600+ BREAGE, CON, ENG [35587] :
WILLIAM 1824-1860 ST AGNES, MINGOOSE &
MT HAWKE, CON, ENG [35726] : JAMES 1800-1820
ST AGNES, CON, ENG [35726] : WILLIAM 1824-
1860 BANNS, CON, ENG [35726] : C1682
WESTBURY, GLS, ENG [35920] : GEORGE PRE
1826 HALIFAX, WRY, ENG [36411] : 1800+ HEF,
ENG [36552] : JANE PRE 1750 ORMESBY, YKS,
ENG [36673] : PRE 1860 LIN, ENG [36793] : 1840+
CAMBORNE, KEHELLAND, CON, ENG [36819] :
1795-1830 ATHERSTONE & ANSLEY, WAR, ENG
[36820] : 1800+ MAIDSTONE, KEN, ENG [36885] :
PRE 1880 LIVERPOOL, ENG [36935] : PRE 1825
CON, ENG [37020] : 1825+ DEV, ENG [37020] :
1869+ GILLINGHAM, KEN, ENG [37051] : PRE

1800 STORRINGTON, SSX, ENG [37069] : 1782-
1869+ MARAZION, CON, ENG [37108] : PRE 1788
CRICKLADE, WIL, ENG [37144] : JOHN C1820-
1860 HAMPRESTON, DOR & SOM, ENG [37287] :
1770+ GREAT MARLOW, BKM, ENG [37566] :
1850S LANLIVERY, CON, ENG [37641] : PRE 1850
ST KEW & TREQUITE, CON, ENG [37768] : PRE
1890 BATTERSEA, LND, ENG [38276] : PRE 1854
CON, ENG [38487] : 1876 GLOUCESTER, GLS,
ENG [38719] : EMMA 1815-1903 MARIZION, CON,
ENG & AUS [33892] : PRE 1870 LIVERPOOL, LAN,
ENG & IOM [36849] : PRE 1850 OSWESTRY, SAL,
ENG & WLS [36188] : 1758-1990 CLUNY &
BEAUJEU, BRG & RHA, FRA [34136] : ALL
HAMELIN, HAN, GER [36571] : 1550-1800
GOHRISCH, KSA, GER [38628] : 1850S
GIBRALTAR [37178] : PRE 1890 CASTLE
BELLINGHAM, LOU, IRL [34441] : 1850+
THAMES & WAIHI, WKT, NZ [36746] : 1850+
AUCKLAND, NZ [36746] : JOHN 1700S DUTCHESS
CO., NY, USA [34392] : HENRY W. C1815+ TN,
USA [35272] : 1833 HAMMONDVILLE, USA [35906] :
C1800 BEDFORD CO., VA, USA [36354] : 1860-1940
CLARKSTON, MI, USA [36935] : 1700S
PHILADELPHIA, PA, USA [37018] : 1920 MORGAN
HILL, CA, USA [37024] : HENRY W. C1820 TN,
USA [37030] : DAVID 1830 BEDFORD CO., TN,
USA [37509] : PRE 1850 REMSEN, STEUBEN, NY,
USA [37510] : ELIZABETH 1650+ ANN ARUNDEL
CO., MD, USA [37551] : 1830-1860 JACKSON CO.,
MO, USA [37782] : C1800 SCOTT CO., KY, USA
[37782] : HANNAH PRE 1786+ HIGHGATE, VT,
USA [37809] : HANNAH 1750-1786 HALFMOON,
NY, USA [37809] : 1855-1875 KEWEENAW CO., MI,
USA [38009] : MASSEY 1800-1818 OHIO, KY, USA
[38157] : 1683 WESTOWN, PHILADELPHIA &
BUCKS, PA, USA [38287] : ALL CULPEPPER CO.,
VA, USA [38287] : 1780-1850 JEFFERSON CO., WV,
USA [38310] : 1700-1850 FREDERICK CO., MD,
USA [38310] : 1740-1800 PRINCE GEORGE CO., VA,
USA [38366] : 1790+ USA & UK [36357] : JOHN
1850+ GARTHBRENGY, BRE, WLS [34134] :
WILLIAM 1800+ TALACHDDU, BRE, WLS [34134]
: JOHN PRE 1800 PENRYDD, PEM, WLS [34311] :
1800-1850 HAVERFORDWEST, PEM, WLS [34552] :
SARAH PRE 1853 LAUGHARNE, CMN, WLS
[34567] : PRE 1890 NEWCHURCH, CMN, WLS
[34569] : 1730-1900 LLANYCHLLWYDOG, PEM,
WLS [34729] : THOMAS 1860+ SOUTH WALES,
WLS [34757] : THOMAS PRE 1860 SOUTH WALES,
WLS [34757] : 1891 PORT TALBOT, GLA, WLS
[34757] : PRE 1875 PONTYPRIDD, GLA, WLS
[34967] : 1800S COYCHURCH HIGHER &
PENCOED, GLA, WLS [35780] : PRE 1830
PEMBROKE, PEM, WLS [36019] : PRE 1870
NEWPORT, PEM, WLS [36178] : PRE 1887
PONTYPRIDD, GLA, WLS [36230] : ANNE 1740+
ST MARY CHURCH, GLA, WLS [36296] : PRE 1850
OLD COLWYN, DEN, WLS [36416] : PRE 1782
MGY, WLS [36613] : 1750+ TREOS & LLANGAN,
GLA, WLS [36746] : 1856 MORRISTOWN, GLA,
WLS [36910] : PRE 1845 MGY, WLS [36968] : C1770+
ST CLEARS, CMN, WLS [37447] : C1879 SWANSEA
HIGHER, GLA, WLS [37631] : C1925
PONTARDAWE, GLA, WLS [37631] : 1800-1900
ABERSYTWITH & TREGARON, CGN, WLS [37702]
: WILLIAM 1850-1870 CWYM AVON, GLA, WLS
[37740] : DAVID C1840-1920 SWANSEA, GLA, WLS
[37813] : 1780-1850 MOSTYN, FLN, WLS [37870] :
1800-1900 ROACH, PEM, WLS [37884] : 1830+
LLANDOGO, MON, WLS [37885] : JANE 1800+
WLS [38394] : PRE 1855 CAE, WLS [38437]

THOMASEN 1870S BJERRE, VJELE, DEN [35953] : 1760+ ARENDAL, AUST AGDER, NOR [36326]

THOMASIN 1650+ STAFFOR CO., VA, USA [36572]

THOMASON 1800-1870 MANCHESTER & LYMM, CHS, ENG [36740] : 1730S SAFFRON WALDEN, ESS, ENG [37080]

THOMASSON 1700+ CLAINES CARDIFF, WOR, ENG & WLS [36794]

THOMERSON 1800 SHOREDITCH, LND, ENG [37080] : ALL WORLDWIDE [37097]

THOMLINSON 1848-1869 TORONTO & MINESING STN, ONT, CAN [34484] : 1810-1848 WAKEFIELD, YKS, ENG [34484]

THOMPKINSON PRE 1830 MISTERTON, NTT, ENG [38016]

THOMPSON 1800S PENNANT HILLS, NSW, AUS [34427] : 1870+ NERANG, QLD, AUS [34585] : 1867+ MOOROOPNA & YALCA, VIC, AUS [34874] : CHARLOTTE 1810+ SYDNEY, NSW, AUS [34901] : 1850+ SOUTH CREEK (ST MARYS), NSW, AUS [35101] : JAMES 1806+ SYDNEY & PENRITH, NSW, AUS [35394] : C1863+ CAMPBELLTOWN, NSW & QLD, AUS [35547] : 1840+ MITTA MITTA, VIC, AUS [35719] : 1860+ FREMANTLE, WA, AUS [35847] : C1900 MOREE, NSW, AUS [35852] : THOMAS PRE 1883 WARWICK, QLD, AUS [35852] : JOHN 1850+ PARRAMATTA, NSW, AUS [35874] : 1830+ TAS, AUS [35887] : 1940-1965 GOSNELLS, WA, AUS [36084] : 1860 MACLEAY RIVER, NSW, AUS [37119] : DUNCAN 1906 CARRINGTON, NSW, AUS [37123] : CATH 1856 BALLARAT, VIC, AUS [37123] : ALFRED 1900+ GUNNEDAH, NSW, AUS [37312] : WILLIAM 1807+ HOBART, TAS, AUS [37954] : 1890 BOOROWA, NSW, AUS [37997] : 1800S AVOCA, VIC, AUS [38272] : 1836+ NSW, AUS [38485] : 1825+ SCUGOG ISLAND, ONT, CAN [34232] : 1700+ UPPER CAN, ONT, CAN [34409] : JAMES C1844 PORTNEUF, JACQUES CARTIER, QUE, CAN [35607] : ALBERT 1900+ HILLSDALE, ONT, CAN [35648] : JOHN 1900+ KIRKLAND LAKE, ONT, CAN [35648] : GEORGE 1805-1850 NORTH GWILLIMBURY, ONT, CAN [35648] : CHARLES 1880+ MEDONTE, ONT, CAN [35648] : 1800+ BEDFORD TWP, FRONTENAC CO., ONT, CAN [36664] : WILLIAM 1810+ BROCKVILLE, ONT, CAN [37001] : 1840+ RENFREW CO., ONT, CAN [37474] : C1839 SUNDERLAND, DUR, ENG [34157] : 1810 HERTFORD CITY, HRT, ENG [34204] : 1775+ WINTERTON, LIN, ENG [34232] : 1700-99 CARDINGTON, BDF, ENG [34315] : 1700-1820 NORTHALLERTON, NRY, ENG [34320] : PRE 1900 BLACK HILL AREA, DUR, ENG [34333] : 1800S DOVER, KEN, ENG [34336] : 1800+ BKM, ENG [34416] : PRE 1865 BUXTON, NFK, ENG [34443] : 1840S BETHNAL GREEN, MDX, ENG [34518] : 1840S CAM, ENG [34603] : 1700-1800 BOYLESTONE, DBY, ENG [34623] : 1815 MORLAND, WES, ENG [34731] : 1800S SRY, ENG [34738] : PERCY 1870+ NEWINGTON & WANDSWORTH, SRY, ENG [34738] : 1800S GRAVESEND, KEN, ENG [34738] : 1800S MDX, ENG [34738] : 1830S HAMMERSMITH, MDX, ENG [34738] : PRE 1740 BARWICK & GARFORTH, WRY, ENG [34776] : PRE 1900 DRINGHOUSES, NRY, ENG [34776] : 1840S ST PANCRAS, MDX, ENG [34952] : PRE 1845 LAMBETH, SRY, ENG [35016] : PRE 1778 ROTHBURY, NBL, ENG [35026] : 1840+ SOTTERLEY, SFK, ENG [35219] : 1800-1850 HUDDERSFIELD, YKS, ENG [35243] : 1860S-1900 RAMSGATE, KEN, ENG [35243] : 1866 SOUTHPORT, LAN, ENG [35282] : BENJAMIN 1830 HULL, YKS, ENG [35593] : 1817 DACRE, CUL,

ENG [35769] : HENRY C1850 ENG [35786] : 1800+ TROWELL, NTT, ENG [35847] : PRE 1860+ OLDHAM, LAN, ENG [35928] : 1800S HIGHGATE, LND, ENG [36055] : 1800+ SOUTHAMPTON, HAM, ENG [36086] : PRE 1820 ECCLESALL BIERLOW, WRY, ENG [36102] : 1573+ KIRKBY STEPHEN, WES, ENG [36132] : PRE 1820 GREAT HALE, LIN, ENG [36148] : JOHN PRE 1810 PADIHAM, LAN, ENG [36192] : SUSANNAH PRE 1840 MACCLESFIELD, CHS, ENG [36192] : PETER PRE 1825 MACCLESFIELD, CHS, ENG [36192] : 1800-1900 PUTNEY, LND, ENG [36213] : JULIAN 1780S SHOREDITCH, LONDON, MDX, ENG [36263] : SARAH C1842 EIGHTON BANKS, DUR, ENG [36270] : 1870+ PLYMPTON, DEV, ENG [36376] : 1775+ EAST STONEHOUSE & DEVONPORT, DEV, ENG [36376] : 1798+ STOKE DAMEREL, DEV, ENG [36376] : 1750-1800 CARLISLE, CUL, ENG [36431] : 1600-1800 HUDSWELL & RICHMOND, NRY, ENG [36472] : ALL DARTFORD AREA, KEN, ENG [36501] : WILLIAM 1875-1890 BILLY ROW, CROOK, DUR, ENG [36503] : JOHN 1850S LEADGATE, DUR, ENG [36503] : PRE 1900 MANCHESTER, LAN, ENG [36578] : 1800S FAIRFIELD, STS, ENG [36670] : MARY 1794-1860S SCALBY, NRY, ENG [36757] : PRE 1860 LIN, ENG [36793] : 1850S SMETHWICK, STS, ENG [36848] : 1790+ CONISTON, LAN, ENG [36868] : 1750+ DARWEN, LAN, ENG [36991] : C1800 BOW, LND, ENG [37053] : C1797 SOLIHULL, WAR, ENG [37144] : 1750+ PETERBOROUGH, NTH, ENG [37223] : MARY PRE 1791 PORTSEA, HAM, ENG [37228] : PRE 1725 HEATH, DBY, ENG [37242] : WILLIAM 1851+ RUGBY, WAR, ENG [37312] : PRE 1853 LIVERPOOL, LAN, ENG [37318] : PRE 1832 ENG [37474] : JAMES 1790S OTLEY & DENTON, WRY, ENG [37650] : PRE 1900 PETERBOROUGH, NTH, ENG [37753] : PRE 1746 KILBURN, NRY, ENG [37852] : C1830 STEPNEY, MDX, ENG [37859] : 1882-4 NORTHAMPTON, NTH, ENG [37863] : PRE 1890 DEAL, KEN, ENG [37871] : JOHN C1850 WEST BROMWICH, WAR, ENG [37944] : 1700+ REETH, YKS, ENG [38034] : ERNEST 1874+ PORTSMOUTH & SOUTHSEA, HAM, ENG [38255] : JOHN C1813+ FILBY & RUNHAM, NFK, ENG [38255] : 1800S WEST BROMWICH, STS, ENG [38272] : 1700 RICHMOND, NRY, ENG [38379] : 1800+ DUR, ENG [38454] : C1779 BERWICK ON TWEED, NBL, ENG [38485] : 1700+ BURGHAM & WEST NEWTON, NFK, ENG [38745] : RACHEL 1820+ LIVERPOOL & SYDNEY, LAN & NSW, ENG & AUS [35155] : 1830-1875 DRALOUGH, MOG, IRL [34022] : PRE 1850 WEX, IRL [34060] : WILLIAM JAMES PRE 1850 ARM, IRL [34310] : 1720+ DRUMHOLM, DON, IRL [34408] : ALL DON, IRL [34874] : 1827+ TYR, IRL [35101] : 1800-1850 NEWRY, DOW, IRL [35228] : ALEX 1800-1848 DON, IRL [35320] : 1800S GARVAGH & GLENDERMOTT, LDY, IRL [35395] : 1800-1950 BALLYMONEY, ANT, IRL [35395] : 1821-1872 KILLMURRAY, CLA, IRL [35763] : PRE 1880S MULLABRACK, ARM, IRL [35852] : PRE 1780 BANBRIDGE, DOW, IRL [35962] : 1810-1835 BALLYWALTER, WHITECHURCH, DOW, IRL [36264] : 1830-1860 KIRKISTOWN, DOW, IRL [36867] : PRE 1830 ANT, IRL [37146] : 1860 DUBLIN, IRL [37791] : HUGH PRE 1913 ENNISKILLEN AREA, FER, IRL [37992] : C1817 COR, IRL [38485] : 1840-50 SEAGOE, ARM, IRL [38583] : 1840S DON, IRL & NZ [36809] : PETER 1770-1850 IRL & USA [37806] : 1840+ LYTTELTON, CHCH, NZ [33926] : 1830+ CANTERBURY, NZ

546

[36858] : JOSEPH PRE 1839 LISBOA, LISBON, PT & ENG [37143] : PRE 1820 BEW, SCT [33999] : 1800+ SCT [33999] : 1800S FORGUE, ABD, SCT [34336] : PRE 1803 COLDINGHAM PARISH, BEW, SCT [34491] : ALL EDINBURGH, SCT [34674] : PRE 1840 EDINBURGH, SCT [34816] : ALEX 1800-1848 PAISLEY, RFW, SCT [35320] : 1600-1700 ST ANDREWS, FIF, SCT [35627] : PRE 1840 DFS, SCT [35719] : 1750+ WEISDALE, SHI, SCT [35719] : PRE 1850 PETERCULTER, ABD, SCT [35819] : 1750-1850 SCT [36261] : PRE 1825 LEITH, SCT [36451] : 1850+ PETERHEAD, ABD, SCT [36971] : PRE 1855 PER, SCT [37946] : 1800-1900 ESSEX, OH, USA [35316] : THOMAS 1785-1846 HILLSBORO, NC, USA [36319] : LESTER 1853+ TRUMBULL CO., OH & MI, USA [36319] : JAMES PRE 1870 TRUMBULL CO., OH, USA [36319] : PRE 1760 CHESTER CO., PA & DE, USA [36319] : JAMES 1860+ HOLLY, OAKLAND CO., MI, USA [36319] : 1800+ GALLATIN CO., IL, USA [36565] : 1900+ CAMDEN, NJ, USA [36578] : 1780-1810 DUTCHESS CO., NY, USA [36710] : WILLIAM 1830-1836 ALLEGHENY, PA, USA [36908] : SAMUEL 1792-1871+ FRYEBURG, ME, USA [36948] : JOHN 1860-1900S GRANT CO., WI, USA [37001] : C1830-1840 OGDENSBURG, NY, USA [37474] : JOHN 1639+ STRATFORD, FAIRFIELD, CT, USA [37540] : ALBERT 1812+ TICONDEROGA, ESSEX, NY, USA [37540] : 1845-1850 KENNEBEC CO., ME, USA [37571] : 1820-1850S OH, USA [37600] : 1800-1855 HENRY CO., KY, USA [37740] : JOSEPH 1800-1880 WOODSTOCK, IL, USA [37806] : 1800-1900 STE GENIVIEVE, MO, USA [37822] : 1800-1900 KY, USA [37822] : 1825-1900 PERRY CO., IL, USA [37822] : 1800 TOMPKINS, NY, USA [38022] : WILLIAM 1720-1750 ORANGE CO., NY, USA [38130] : 1700-1750 LITCHFIELD CO., CT, USA [38130] : 1800 CHESTER, VT, USA [38131] : HENRY 1864 WOODFORD CO., IL, USA [38132] : J. HUGH 1813+ SC, USA [38141] : JOSEPH C1783 HARTSVILLE, STEUBEN CO., NY, USA [38172] : 1720-1970+ CAPE NEWAGEN, MA, USA [38308] : LEONARD 1850-1900 SONOMA, CA, USA [38320] : C1800 RANDOLPH CO., IN, USA [38367] : JOS. 1800+ CLEVELAND, OH, USA [38369] : JAMES 1880+ MI & ONT, USA & CAN [35648] : ALL WORLDWIDE [35268]

THOMPSON-HOOPER 1820+ MARGATE, ENG [33867]

THOMS 1700+ NORTHWICH, CHS, ENG [36818] : PRE 1850 OPR, GER [38648]

THOMSEN C1820 DEN [33809] : ALL ODSTED, DEN [34308] : PRE 1864 CARLOW, SHO, DEN [37978] : MADS C1860 HORSENS, VEJLE, DEN [37982] : C1760 WESSELBUREN, SHO, GER [38671]

THOMSOM PRE 1825 INNERLITHAN, PEE, SCT [34489]

THOMSON 1885-1910 COLLINGWOOD & CARLTON, VIC, AUS [36268] : 1866+ MANNING RIVER, NSW, AUS [36293] : 1800S CHATHAM, ONT, CAN [37443] : C1700-1800 FANSBURG, DEN [37977] : 1840S KINGSTEIGNTON, DEV, ENG [33870] : JOHN 1800 DEPTFORD, KEN, ENG [35899] : 1860S BOW, MDX, ENG [36041] : PRE 1870 FER, IRL [34569] : 1850S LDY, IRL & AUS [36268] : 1800+ AUCKLAND, NZ [38273] : BARBARA PRE 1829 EDINBURGH, MLN, SCT [33807] : C1780-1920 STEWARTON, AYR & MLN, SCT [34040] : 1881+ GLASGOW, SCT [34100] : C1630 DUNFERMLINE, FIF, SCT [34118] : C1786 PAISLEY, RFW, SCT [34122] : PRE 1800 STONEHOUSE, LKS, SCT [34197] : CHARLES 1750-1850 EDINBURGH, SCT [34274] :

1780-1810S OLD MONKLAND, LKS, SCT [34359] : 1800S GLASGOW, SCT [34483] : PRE 1788 CERES, FIF, SCT [34622] : 1800+ CERES, FIF, SCT [34637] : ALL ABD & LKS, SCT [34861] : PRE 1850 KENNOWAY, FIF, SCT [35045] : C1830 DALRYMPLE, LKS, SCT [35152] : PRE 1850 GOVAN, LKS, SCT [35229] : WILLIAM 1875+ MOTHERWELL, LKS, SCT [35411] : 1700+ BUNCLE, BEW, SCT [35475] : PRE 1855 ARNGASK & ST ANDREWS, FIF, SCT [35496] : 1800+ TAIN, ROC, SCT [35644] : JOHN 1788+ STEVENSTON, AYR, SCT [35780] : 1800-1850 DNB, SCT [35813] : 1776 CROMARTY, ROC, SCT [35905] : PRE 1798 CARLUKE, LKS, SCT [35929] : 1820+ CUPAR, FIF, SCT [35959] : 1840+ DUNOON, ARL, SCT [35959] : PRE 1840 KILFINAN, ARL, SCT [35959] : 1850+ BOTHKENNAR, STI, SCT [35979] : 1800+ GLASGOW, LKS, SCT [36195] : MARY PRE 1850 DUMFRIES, DFS, SCT [36388] : 1800+ LERWICK & WALLS, SHI, SCT [36869] : DUNCAN 1821 LOCHGILPHEAD, ARL, SCT [37123] : PRE 1830 ARL, SCT [37423] : 1780-1820 HUTNLY, ABD, SCT [37442] : 1840+ EDINBURGH, MLN, SCT [37483] : C1800 EDINBURGH, MLN, SCT [37552] : 1780+ CANONBIE, DFS, SCT [37628] : PRE 1900 MARKINCH, FIF, SCT [37631] : 1890+ BONNYBRIDGE, STI, SCT [37631] : PRE 1770 PRESTONPANS, ELN, SCT [37852] : 1820S DALSERF PARISH, LKS, SCT [37879] : 1830S EDINBURGH, MLN, SCT [38206] : 1750+ WESTERKIRK, DFS, SCT [38388] : 1800+ STORNOWAY, INV, SCT [38481] : PRE 1870 EDINBURGH & GLASGOW, MLN, SCT & AUS [34845] : ALL DUNDEE, ANS, SCT & NZ [34617] : 1780+ BRADDAN & ONCHAN, IOM, UK [36768]

THOMTER 1900+ AUS [33878]

THONGER 1700+ OXF & NTH, ENG [34236]

THORBURN 1700+ AYR, SCT [35407] : C1845 GLASGOW, LKS, SCT [36262] : 1780S JOHNSTONEBRIDGE, DFS, SCT [37751] : 1830-1900 PEE, SCT & AUS [37134]

THORGOOD 1840+ LONDON, ENG & AUS [38204]

THORLEY 1791+ SYDNEY, NSW, AUS [35759] : 1880+ ARMIDALE & URALLA, NSW, AUS [37966] : PRE 1800 CHEADLE & CAVERSWALL, STS, ENG [36196]

THORMAHLEN 1800+ BRUNSBUTTEL, SHO, GER [37949]

THORN 1781 FORDINGTON, DOR, ENG [33967] : PRE 1855 BARNSTAPLE, DEV, ENG [34582] : PRE 1853 SALISBURY, WIL, ENG [34816] : 1840-1880 EAST LONDON, ENG [35975] : 1800S WESTMINSTER, LND, ENG [36868] : PRE 1880 BISHOPS LYDEARD, SOM, ENG [37322] : 1788+ DEVON, DEV, ENG & AUS [36642] : 1800 WARREN CO., OH, USA [37028] : C1820 NELSON CO., KY, USA [37527] : ALL ORANGE CO. & STUBEN, NY, USA [38522]

THORNBER PRE 1800 GISBURN, WRY, ENG [37246]

THORNBORROW 1600 ORTON, WES, ENG [36151]

THORNBURN 1700-1730 JOHNSTONE, DFS, SCT [38516]

THORNBURY 1860+ TAS, AUS [34283] : 1800+ STROUD, GLS, ENG [34283]

THORNDIKE 1750-1850 KEN, ENG [37137]

THORNE 1860+ SYDNEY, NSW, AUS [37128] : PRE 1908 COPMANHURST, NSW, AUS [37315] : PRE 1844 SCONE, NSW, AUS [37899] : RICHARD 1800+ AUS & NZ [35217] : 1540+ BARNSTAPLE, DEV, ENG [34747] : PRE 1846 SOM, ENG [34979] : 1840S LONDON, ENG [35011] : 1800+ ENFIELD, MDX, ENG [35214] : C1790 SOM, ENG [35951] : C1850

SOM, ENG **[35974]** : RICHARD 1800+ ESS, ENG **[35975]** : PRE 1842 NEW FOREST, HAM, ENG **[36079]** : PRE 1900 EXETER, DEV, ENG **[37214]** : 1800-1900 STOGUMBER, SOM, ENG **[38247]** : C1880 AUCKLAND, NZ **[35974]** : ELIZA 1903 HIGHLAND MILLS, NY, USA **[38233]**

THORNETT PRE 1840 PAWLETT, SOM, ENG **[36204]**

THORNEYCROFT ALL NTH, ENG **[36179]**

THORNHILL 1750-1830 YKS, ENG **[34178]** : PRE 1910 LONDON, ENG **[37062]** : PRE 1800 LONDON, ENG **[37670]** : PRE 1900 HULL, ERY, ENG **[37774]** : 1700-1800 IRL **[33856]** : PRE 1882 STRATFORD, TARANAKI, NZ **[34270]**

THORNICROFT PRE 1850 NAPTON ON HILL, WAR, ENG **[34562]**

THORNLEY PRE 1820 SPITALFIELDS, LND, ENG **[38075]**

THORNTHWAITE 1800+ FLIMBY, CUL, ENG **[38067]**

THORNTON 1750+ LND, ENG **[33963]** : PRE 1873 NEWCASTLE, NBL, ENG **[34021]** : 1807 DUFFIELD, DBY, ENG **[34120]** : 1900 HORTON, WRY, ENG **[34957]** : 1813 HUNTON, NRY, ENG **[34957]** : PRE 1770 CHETWODE & TINGEWICK, BKM, ENG **[35030]** : PRE 1819 PERCY MAIN, NBL, ENG **[35236]** : 1894 RADFORD, NTT, ENG **[35529]** : MARGARET PRE 1894 LIVERPOOL, LAN, ENG **[36164]** : 1800-1871 LEI, ENG **[37207]** : PRE 1500 YKS, ENG **[37570]** : ALL CATON SKERTON & WHITTINGTON, LAN, ENG **[37673]** : PRE 1810 LINTHWAITE, YKS, ENG **[38690]** : PRE 1860 ARBROATH, ANS, SCT **[37200]** : 1780+ SHOTTS, LKS, SCT **[37767]** : PRE 1880 FRANKLIN CO., MS, USA **[36543]** : 1800-1830 BALTIMORE CITY, MD, USA **[36911]** : 1700S BUCKS CO., PA, USA **[36926]** : C1778 LONDONDERRY TWP LANCASTER CO., PA, USA **[37516]** : WILLIAM 1790+ WASHINGTON, DC, USA **[37673]** : WILLIAM 1785+ WILMINGTON, DE, USA **[37673]** : WILLIAM 1785+ PHILADELPHIA, NJ, USA **[37673]** : 1820-1880 CHENOA, EUREKA & MCLEAN, IL, USA **[38043]** : 1820-1880 WOODFORD, IL, USA **[38043]** : 1740+ BRIDGETOWN & ST MICHAEL, BARBADOS, W.INDIES **[37673]** : EDMUND C1760-C1860 ST GEORGES, GRENADA, W.INDIES **[37673]**

THORNWELL 1800-1850 ASTON, WAR, ENG **[36057]**

THOROGOOD 1800S WHITECHAPEL, MDX, ENG **[34887]** : PRE 1850 HITCHIN, HRT, ENG **[35776]**

THOROLD SARAH 1840+ SKIRBECK, LIN, ENG **[34916]**

THOROUGHGOOD PRE 1900 SYDNEY, NSW, AUS **[34025]** : PRE 1890 GOULBURN, NSW, AUS **[34417]** : 1840+ SYDNEY, NSW, AUS **[34979]**

THORP 1825+ LAUNCESTON, TAS, AUS **[33880]** : 1819-1825 SYDNEY, NSW, AUS **[33880]** : 1862+ DAYLESFORD, VIC, AUS **[34289]** : C1800-1855 BRUCEFIELD, ONT, CAN & ENG **[37790]** : C1790 DENTON, BDF, ENG **[33880]** : 1800 CHEAM, SRY, ENG **[34204]** : PRE 1848 YEOVIL, SOM, ENG **[35578]** : 1850+ ASHTON UNDER LYNE, LAN, ENG **[37073]** : 1880+ LANCASTER, LAN, ENG **[37073]** : 1860 MARION CO., IN, USA **[36446]** : 1700-1800 HENRICO CO., VA, USA **[36554]**

THORPE 1880+ WIMMERA, VIC, AUS **[35223]** : 1700S UPPINGHAM, RUT, ENG **[33916]** : 1790+ BAKEWELL, DBY, ENG **[34790]** : 1800 HUDDERSFIELD, YKS, ENG **[35061]** : SARAH 1751 MANCHESTER, LAN, ENG **[35369]** : C1750 BKM, ENG **[35476]** : 1700-1900 GLEADLESS, YKS, ENG **[35600]** : 1800+ CHELMSFORD, ESS & HRT, ENG **[36123]** : ALL LEIGH, LAN, ENG **[36743]** : 1800-1867 SHOREDITCH, LND, ENG **[36874]** : ADLARD

C1630-1740 SIBSEY, LIN, ENG **[36880]** : 1800+ KNOTTINGLY, YKS, ENG **[37112]** : C1825 MANCHESTER, ENG **[37158]** : 1655-1750 STEVENTON, HAM, ENG **[38003]** : 1790-1850 LINCOLN, LIN, ENG **[38511]** : 1800+ VA & SC, USA **[37795]**

THORPE (SEE THORP) **[36554]**

THORRINGTON 1750+ LONDON, MDX, ENG **[36987]**

THORROLD 1700-1800 BOUGHTON, NFK, ENG **[36410]**

THORSON ALL MADISON & NANSTAD, MN, USA & NOR **[37440]**

THORUP C1700-1850 COPENHAGEN, DEN **[37642]**

THOULESS ALL NFK, ENG **[33849]**

THOULISS 1850+ VIC, AUS **[33849]**

THRAPP ALL JACKSON CO., OH & IA, USA **[34116]**

THRASHER 1800+ HASTINGS, ONT, CAN **[34107]**

THRAVES ALL BINGHAM, NTT, ENG **[36532]**

THRELFALL PRE 1850 CHURCHTOWN, LAN, ENG **[34696]** : ANN 1800-1850 WIGAN, LAN, ENG **[35006]**

THRESH ALL HORBURY, WRY, ENG **[33916]**

THRESHER PRE 1850 TAUNTON, SOM, ENG **[37325]**

THRIPPLETON PRE 1900 LEEDS, WRY, ENG **[36034]**

THRISCUTT C1700+ GORRAN, CON, ENG **[35851]**

THROOP KAZIA 1840-1926 ENG **[34219]**

THROP PRE 1865 WAKEFIELD, YKS, ENG **[34384]**

THROPE 1777 DEPTFORD, LND, ENG **[35560]**

THROSBY PRE 1870 BILLESDON, LEI, ENG **[34241]**

THROUP 1830-1855 SILSDEN, YKS, ENG **[35196]** : 1800 SILSDEN, WRY, ENG **[35809]**

THROWER 1700+ HEMPNALL, NFK, ENG **[34420]**

THRUN 1830 BUETOW, POM, GER **[34388]**

THRUSH PRE 1780 LONG DITTON, SRY, ENG **[33905]**

THULIN OLA 1839 ELJAROD, KRISTIAMSTADT, SWE **[38193]**

THUMBLERT PRE 1800 PA, MD & NY, USA **[38049]**

THUMM JOHANN FRED. 1806-1865 SHORNHOUSEN, WUE, GER & USA **[37813]**

THURBANE 1750-1850 BARBADOS **[38355]**

THURBER 1800+ RENSSELAER CO., NY, USA **[36577]**

THURGATE 1800+ BECCLES, SFK, ENG **[35824]**

THURLBY PRE 1900 BRANSTON, NTT, ENG **[36387]** : 1800-1880 CARRINGTON, LIN, ENG **[37342]**

THURLOW PRE 1900 LONDON, ENG **[33859]** : 1820S PALGRAVE, NFK, ENG **[35151]** : 1700+ GRAVESEND & MILTON, LND, ENG **[36818]** : PRE 1806 SUDBURY, SFK, ENG **[37082]**

THURLOWAY 1890+ GLENPATRICK, VIC, AUS **[35482]** : 1856+ AUS **[35482]** : 1839-56 DUR, ENG **[35482]** : 1851-57 WINGATE, DUR, ENG **[35482]**

THURLWELL PRE 1855 THORP ARCH, WRY, ENG **[38577]**

THURMAN 1850+ PORTLAND, VIC, AUS **[35205]** : PRE 1800 LEI & WAR, ENG **[35205]** : 1800+ SHOREDITCH, LND, ENG **[35205]** : C1780 WOODHOUSE, LEI, ENG **[37053]** : 1800-1900 BUCHANAN CO., MO, USA **[37798]**

THURNELL PRE 1845 RATCLIFFE, LND, ENG **[34612]**

THUROW PRE 1813 POM, GER **[38630]**

THURSFIELD ALL ENG **[33776]** : ALL ENG **[36045]**

THURSTIN 1830S CROYDON, SRY, ENG **[34518]**

THWAITES 1858+ QUEENSCLIFF, VIC, AUS **[38205]** : C1850 TUDOR, ONT, CAN **[34133]** : PRE 1830 PUTNEY, SRY, ENG **[35360]** : 1800+ LND, ENG **[37861]** : PRE 1900 BETHNAL GREEN, LND, ENG **[38205]** : PRE 1850 HASTINGS, SSX, ENG **[38746]**

THWEATT PRE 1750 BRUNSWICK CO., VA, USA **[38783]**

THYNNE PRE 1860 CLA, IRL [35032] : 1800+ CLA, IRL [35499] : PRE 1850 EDINBURGH, SCT [34433]

TIBATTS MARY 1773 LONDON, ENG [34091]

TIBBETS 1811 OH, USA [38121]

TIBBEY ALL SRY, ENG [37133]

TIBBITS 1800+ BARTON SEAGRAVE, NTH, ENG [35970]

TIBBLES ALL RICKMANSWORTH, HRT, ENG [36981]

TIBBOEL ALL USA [38707]

TIBBS PENELOPE 1825-1861 DALLAS CO., MO & TN, USA [34481] : ANDERSON PRE 1860 DALLAS CO., MO & TN, USA [34481] : DANIEL 1739 WESTMORELAND CO., VA, USA [38152]

TIBEAUDO C1893 MILDURA, VIC, AUS [35708]

TIBERIO PRE 1830 CASALBORDINO, CHIETI, ITL [34127]

TIBULLS PRE 1713 COLCHESTER, ESS, ENG [34142]

TIBURSKI 1800-1900 JONKENDORF, OSTPREUβEN, GER [38603]

TICE 1800-1850 AMELIASBURGH, ONT, CAN [37011] : PRE 1850 PA, USA [37587]

TICEHURST 1796 BISHOPSTONE, SSX, ENG [34708] : 1700+ STORRINGTON, SSX, ENG [35824] : PRE 1870 BRIGHTLING, SSX, ENG [36612]

TICHBORN 1500-1800 ENG & IRL [38754]

TICHBORNE C1827 ENNISKILLEN, FER, IRL [34371]

TICKELL 1890+ HAWTHORN, VIC, AUS [34871] : ALL DEV, ENG [34550] : PRE 1870 TAVISTOCK, DEV, ENG [34871] : 1700S DEVONPORT, DEV, ENG [35830] : C1824 TAVISTOCK, DEV, ENG [37302]

TICKLE 1870+ GLEN INNES, NSW, AUS [35740] : 1860+ WALCHA, NSW, AUS [35740] : 1870+ LISMORE, NSW, AUS [35740] : 1850+ DUNGOG, NSW, AUS [35740] : 1870+ MURRURUNDI, NSW, AUS [35740] : 1890+ QUIRINDI, NSW, AUS [35740] : JOHN 1824+ TAVISTOCK, DEV, ENG [35471] : PRE 1850 MARYSTOW, DEV, ENG [35740] : 1800-1870 APPLETON & KINGSLEY, CHS, ENG [36740] : C1860 PLYMOUTH, DEV, ENG [38290] : PRE 1800 BRIDESTOWE, DEV, ENG [38290] : ALL NC & VA, USA [38060]

TICKNER 1839+ CAMDEN, NSW, AUS [34426] : 1800+ CAMBER, SSX, ENG [34426] : 1800+ WITTERSHAM, KEN, ENG [34426] : 1700+ TICEHURST, SSX, ENG [34426] : 1800-1880 ORDINGTON, KEN, ENG [37339] : ROXEY 1846-1902 CHILLICOTHE, IL & MN, USA [38124]

TIDCOMBE PRE 1820 WIL, ENG [34848]

TIDD 1795+ LND, ENG [35414] : ALL ENG [35901] : 1740-1840 TIP, IRL [34514]

TIDDY ALL WORLDWIDE [36199]

TIDEMANN PRE 1870 GRAM, HADERSLEV, DEN [38111]

TIDFORD ALL WORLDWIDE [36172]

TIDMAN 1850+ TAS, AUS [35853] : PRE 1850 KEN, ENG [35853]

TIDMARSH PRE 1800 GLOUCESTER & PADLESTROP, GLS & WOR, ENG [34727]

TIDMAS ALL WORLDWIDE [35177]

TIDSER PRE 1900 MANCHESTER, LAN, ENG [36578] : 1900+ CAMDEN, NJ, USA [36578]

TIDSWELL JAMES 1800-1880 MANCHESTER, CHS, ENG [34143] : 1800-1900 BRADFORD, YKS, ENG [36150]

TIDY PRE 1845 ENG [34719] : 1800-1900 SHOREDITCH, MDX, ENG [37747] : PRE 1840 TOOTING, SRY, ENG [37986] : 1700-1800 RUDGEWICK, SSX, ENG [38287]

TIEDE 1850-1920 ZHITDMIR, SU [34223]

TIEDEMANN 1858+ YOUNG, NSW, AUS [33763] : PRE 1858 OEREL, HBG, GER [33763]

TIERNAN 1850+ LESMAHAGAN, LKS, SCT [36826]

TIERNEY PRE 1861 MELBOURNE, VIC, AUS [35419] : 1840S MAITLAND, NSW, AUS [35516] : 1870+ MANCHESTER, LAN, ENG [35107] : C1836 WESTMINSTER ST JAMES, MDX, ENG [35133] : C1815-30 IRL [33828] : C1840-55 KER, IRL [33828] : 1840+ BAGENALSTOWN, CAR, IRL [34237] : 1850+ OFF, IRL [34956] : 1800+ ROS & MEA, IRL [38079] : 1850+ LESMAHAGAN, LKS, SCT [36826] : 1900-1960 DENVER, CO, USA [35107]

TIETZ 1600-1700 WELSOW, UCKERMARK, BRA [38603] : 1863+ KOKOTZKO, W PRE [35266]

TIFFEN ALL ASPATRIA, CUL, ENG [34835] : 1780 WIGGENHALL, NFK, ENG [34844]

TIFFORD ALL WORLDWIDE [36172]

TIGHE 1850-1900 SYDNEY, NSW, AUS [34682] : 1800+ AUS [37970] : 1830-1990 CALEDON, ONT, CAN [35833] : C1830 WEM, IRL [34682] : ALL WORLDWIDE [36083]

TILBROOK PRE 1950 NEWMARKET, CAM, ENG [36489]

TILBURY PRE 1740 WEST WYCOMBE, BKM, ENG [33796] : 1800-1900 BRENTFORD & HAMMERSMITH, MDX, ENG [34187] : PRE 1824 STEVENTON, HAM, ENG [36650] : PRE 1909 OVERTON, HAM, ENG & WORLDWIDE [36650]

TILDEN-RICHARDS 1895-1940+ CHICAGO, IL, USA [38401]

TILEY 1820S BRISTOL, SOM, ENG [35612] : PRE 1890 SHOREDITCH, LND, ENG [36249] : 1833-1873 MARYLEBONE, LND, ENG [37445] : 1830-1850 CHELSEA, LND, ENG [38777]

TILG ALL WORLDWIDE [37529]

TILING C1610 BREMEN, BRM, GER [38750]

TILKENS 1753-1989 VELM, LBG, BEL [38158] : 1865-1989 NAMEN & UMSTREKEN, NMR, BEL [38158]

TILKER PRE 1850 GER [34383]

TILL PRE 1849 COBHAM, KEN, ENG [35956] : 1800 STOKE ON TRENT, STS, ENG [37215] : PRE 1800 SSX & HAM, ENG [37882] : PRE 1800 ORANGEBERG, SC, USA [38536]

TILLACK C1873 RADNITZ CROSSEN ON ODER, BRA, GER [34195] : PRE 1890 POM, GER [34837]

TILLCOCK C1889 CHISWICK, MDX, ENG [37992]

TILLEARD ALL LND, ENG [35628]

TILLER 1600-1850 SRY, ENG [35069] : PRE 1800 TREGONY, CON, ENG [35736] : 1840S PENRYN, CON, ENG [35882] : PRE 1800 FAWLEY, SOTON, HAM, ENG [36155] : 1790-1850 MILLBROOK, HAM, ENG [37129]

TILLETT C1850-1870 COLCHESTER, ESS, ENG [35726] : 1875-1885 CHELMSFORD, ESS, ENG [35726] : 1880S COBHOLM ISLAND (YARMOUTH), NFK, ENG [35726]

TILLEY 1880+ MOSS VALE, NSW, AUS [35567] : 1855+ PETERSHAM, NSW, AUS [35567] : 1902+ ESSENDON, VIC, AUS [36279] : 1800S CHRISTCHURCH, HAM, ENG [35567] : 1700+ BEECHINGSTOKE, WIL, ENG [35874] : 1700-1800 SOM, ENG [36242] : 1800+ LONDON, ENG & AUS [34864] : 1800+ OTSEGO CO., NY, USA [36577] : 1675-1761 BOSTON, MA, USA [36577]

TILLFORD PRE 1811 WAKEFIELD, WRY, ENG [37856]

TILLIS ALL WORLDWIDE [38536]

TILLMAN 1878+ SYDNEY, NSW, AUS [35410] : 1800+ SOUTHWICK, DUR, ENG [35410]

TILLSON PRE 1900 BIRMINGHAM, WAR & LND, ENG [36899]

TILLY ALL FARNHAM, SRY, ENG [36232] : 1800+ LONDON, ENG & AUS [34864] : HILDA 1881+ BROOKLYN, USA [38560] : ELIANA C1901 USA [38560]

TILNEY ALL LONDON &, SFK, ENG [34033]

TILSON 1800S BELTURBET, CAV, IRL [33767]

TILSTON 1800-1900 WLS [35954]

TILTON 1750-80 HAMPDEN, MA, USA [38054]

TILY ALL ALDERSHOT, HAM, ENG [36232]

TIMAN 1650+ BELLERSEN, WEF, GER [35460]

TIMBERLAKE 1700+ BKM, ENG [35880]

TIMBLICK 1700+ BKM, ENG [35880] : 1800+ BURNHAM, BRK, ENG [35947]

TIMBREL 1750+ KINGSBURY, TAMWORTH, WKS, STS & LEI, ENG [36329]

TIMBRELL 1790+ ENG [35573] : 1700+ WIL, ENG [36568] : C1823 WEXFORD, WEX, IRL [35573]

TIMEWELL 1860S CARAMUT, VIC, AUS [34279]

TIMINS C1860 ADELAIDE & PT AUGUSTA, SA, AUS [35401]

TIMMERMAN 1770 RECHTEREN DALFSEN, OIJ, NL [34398] : PRE 1900 GLANERBRUG, OIJ, NL [36283]

TIMMERMANN 1700+ SCT [34624]

TIMMINS PRE 1800 TIPTON, STS, ENG [34822] : PRE 1880 TIPTON, STS, ENG [36424] : 1790+ SEIGHFORD, STS, ENG [36997] : PRE 1837 DUDLEY, STS, ENG [37726] : JAMES PRE 1798 CAV, IRL [35852]

TIMMIS 1880+ KIDDERMINSTER, WOR, ENG [34113]

TIMMONS PRE 1842 WEX, IRL [34693]

TIMMS ROBERT 1860S WALLSEND, NSW, AUS [34764] : LUCY 1850-1916 NEWCASTLE, NSW, AUS [34783] : 1820+ LEIGHTON BUZZARD, BDF, ENG [34764]

TIMPE ALL ASCHENDORF, HAN, GER [36571]

TIMSON 1700-1990 UK & AUS [35421]

TINDALE 1930 NSW, AUS [34456] : 1800+ NSW, AUS [35465] : C1850 HOBART, TAS, AUS [37159] : 1850+ NRY, ENG [34456]

TINDALL 1810+ SYDNEY, NSW, AUS [34901] : PRE 1830 PENRITH, NSW, AUS [35211] : 1890+ SYDNEY, NSW, AUS [35374] : 1860+ MUDGEE, NSW, AUS [35374] : 1887-1906 SETTRINGTON, YKS, ENG [33779] : 1800S LONDON, ENG [34908] : C1851 HALTON, CHS, ENG [35374] : C1815 MANCHESTER, LAN, ENG [35374] : PRE 1880 SCALBY, NRY, ENG [36757] : 1400-1900S CHATTON, NBL, ENG [36776] : 1900+ CHRISTCHURCH, CANT, NZ [36757] : ALL CROMARTY, ROC, SCT [36552]

TINDELL 1780-1880 SCAMPSTON & LEEDS, YKS, ENG [34352]

TINDLE ALL EDINBURGH, MLN, SCT [34619]

TINDLEY ALL WORLDWIDE [36090]

TING ALL LONDON, ENG [37133]

TINGATE 1800 PETWORTH, SSX, ENG [37952] : 1800 PETWORTH, SSX, ENG [37952]

TINGAY 1862+ CASTLEMAINE, VIC, AUS [35349] : C1800 ESS, ENG [35349] : PRE 1900 WISBECH, CAM & NFK, ENG [38280]

TINGLEY 1750-1850 LONDON, ENG [35285]

TINGUE 1750+ KINDERHOOK, NY, USA [34408]

TINIAN PRE 1827 WHITEHAVEN, CUL, ENG [33806]

TINKER ALL RASEN, LIN, ENG [36382] : 1800S SHEPLEY, WRY, ENG [36842] : ALL KIRKBURTON & HOLME VALLEY, WRY, ENG [37372] : ALL UK [37421]

TINKLER PRE 1630 ENG [34162] : ALL WALTHAM ON THE WOLDS, LEI, ENG [35899] : PRE 1835

ENG [37034] : 1800S STAMFORD, LIN, ENG [38272] : 1600-1700 DOCKING, NFK, ENG [38453]

TINLIN 1852+ AUS [34005] : PRE 1852 NBL, ENG [34005]

TINLINE C1772 ANCRUM, ROX, SCT [34239]

TINLING 1600-1900 BORDERS, SCT & ENG [38278]

TINNEY 1830-1943 MONTREAL, QUE, CAN [35316] : ALL FONTMELL MAGNA, DOR, ENG [35297]

TINSLEY 1857+ NSW, AUS [37911] : PRE 1816 ARNOLD, NTT, ENG [37911] : WILLIAM PRE 1900 STONEYFORD & LISBURN, ANT, IRL [37755] : ANN 1772-1847 BALLYMACWARD & LISBURN, ANT, IRL [37755] : 1850-1990 COOSA, AL, USA [36735] : 1860-1880 TALLADEGA, AL, USA [36735] : 1798-1850 ABBEVILLE, SC, USA [36735] : PRE 1750 ORANGE CO., VA, USA [36927]

TINSON ALL AUS [34685] : PRE 1838 BATH, WIL, ENG [34685] : PRE 1800 LECHLADE, GLS, ENG [37253]

TINTI C1500-C1780 CASTELLEONE DI SUASA, ITL [36139]

TIP 1820S-1870S LINCOLN CO., ONT, CAN [34094]

TIPLADY 1800+ HENDON, MDX & HRT, ENG [36123] : ALL WHARFEDALE, WRY, ENG [36144] : 1800-1900 NEWCASTLE, NBL, ENG [36397] : 1800-1900 YORK, NRY, ENG [36397] : C1800 YKS, ENG [37259]

TIPP C1844 TORONTO, ONT, CAN [34133]

TIPPER ALL SUSSEX, HAM, ENG [37044] : C1790 CH. BROUGHTON, DBY, ENG [37661] : ALL DBY & STS, ENG [37661]

TIPPETT 1910+ MELBOURNE, VIC, AUS [36077] : PRE 1719 ST COLUMB MAJOR, CON, ENG [34573] : PRE 1800 ST COLUMB, CON, ENG [34684] : PRE 1840 TOTNES, DEV, ENG [35229] : ALL NEWLYN EAST, CON, ENG [35235] : 1700-1800 ST NEWLYN EAST, CON, ENG [36205] : 1800S PLYMOUTH, DEV, ENG [37560] : 1800S SOUTHWARK, SRY, ENG [37560] : 1740 MD, USA [38143]

TIPPIN 1800+ RETFORD, NTT, ENG [37241]

TIPPING 1870+ BLACKHEATH, KEN, ENG [35726] : 1800+ RETFORD, NTT, ENG [37241] : JANET PRE 1840 DUNGANNON & MOY, TYR, IRL [33816] : WILLIAM PRE 1840 DUNGANNON & MOY, TYR, IRL [33816] : 1800S TYR, IRL [35424] : PRE 1863 DUNDALK, LOU & LOG, IRL [35883]

TIPTAFT ALL ENG [37283]

TIPTON 1800+ SAL, ENG [33855] : PRE 1800 SAL, ENG [37681] : PRE 1820 JEFFERSON CO., OH, USA [36709]

TIRI 1700-1800 BEL [38170]

TIRMENSTEIN 1838+ ST LOUIS, MO, USA [36912]

TIRY 1700-1800 ATW, BEL [38170]

TISBURY 1800-1865 SHOREDITCH & MILE END, LND & MDX, ENG [36017] : 1880-1872 HACKEY & STEPNEY, MDX, ENG [36017]

TISCH 1800+ DARMSTADT, HES, BRD [36869]

TISCHMANN PRE 1875 HAGEN, NRW, BRD [35021]

TISDALL 1800S PANCRAS, LND, ENG [36055] : 1795+ ST GILES, MDX, ENG [38375]

TISKEN ALL SOLINGEN, WEF, GER [34861]

TISLEY 1800 BETHNAL GREEN, MDX, ENG [34204]

TISSHAW 1880-1870 BETHNAL GREEN, LND, ENG [36111]

TISSMER PRE 1875 BISMARK, WPR, GER [36839]

TISSOT 1852 GE, CH [38348]

TISSOTT ALL VIC, AUS [35082]

TITCHEN ALL WORLDWIDE [35893]

TITCHENER PRE 1850 BISHOPSTONE, WIL, ENG [37101]

TITCHMARSH PRE 1830 CAM, NFK & SFK, ENG [37646]

TITFORD ALL WORLDWIDE [36172]

TITIUS 1661 MAGDEBURG, GER [38750]

TITLEY 1800-1900 NSW & VIC, AUS [33836] : 1700+ COTTESMORE CUM BARROW, RUT, ENG [34455] : 1800S LIVERPOOL, LAN, ENG [38285]

TITMAN 1885+ ROCKHAMPTON, QLD, AUS [33920] : PRE 1789 TITCHMARSH, NTH, ENG [35864]

TITMARSH ALL CROYDON, CAM, ENG [34838]

TITMUS 1740S BENNINGTON, HRT, ENG [34563]

TITMYS 1800S PIRTON, HRT, ENG [37423]

TITTERELL PRE 1800 ESS, ENG [36379]

TITTERTON C1800-1850 DERBY, DBY, ENG [36053] : 1650-1850 SAL, ENG [36988]

TITTLEY 1800-1900 NSW & VIC, AUS [33836]

TITUS PRE 1900 NB, CAN [36933] : 1630-1790 NASSAU CO., NY, USA [37477]

TIZZARD PRE 1900 SOUTHAMPTON, HAM, ENG [36021] : 1750-1875 NEWINGTON, SRY, ENG [36879]

TJERNBERG OLOF 1825-1900 VANNAS, VASTERBOTTEN, SWE [38104] : CAJSA LOVISA 1852-1940 VANNAS, VASTERBOTTEN, SWE [38104]

TOASE 1750+ HINDERWELL & RUNSWICK BAY, NRY, ENG [34375]

TOBECK PRE 1870 HANOVER, HAN, GER [36766]

TOBERT 1800-1900 GER [37464] : 1800-1900 RUSSIA [37464]

TOBIAN 1800S BRD [38281] : 1800S DDR [38281]

TOBIN THOMAS 1910+ GRETA & MAITLAND, NSW, AUS [33839] : 1800-1850 SAINT JOHN, NB, CAN [36390] : 1780-1800 DIGBY, NS, CAN [36390] : THOMAS C1800 COR, IRL [33928] : WILLIAM 1815 JOHNSWELL, KIK, IRL [34176] : 1800-1860S ARDFINNAN, TIP, IRL [35589] : PRE 1860S CLONMEL, TIP, IRL [35589] : 1830+ BANSHA, TIP, IRL [35847] : JAMES PRE 1850 BANTRY, COR, IRL & AUS [33839] : 1830-1990 WAT, IRL & AUS [35718] : THOMAS 1860+ BANTRY, COR, IRL & ITL [33839] : CATHERINE 1860+ BANTRY, COR, IRL & ITL [33839] : MARTHA 1860+ BANTRY, COR, IRL & ITL [33839] : BRIDGET 1860+ BANTRY, COR, IRL & ITL [33839]

TOBITT 1750-1850 HAWKHURST, KEN, ENG [38287]

TOBRIDGE 1800-1820 MUSKINGUM CO., OH, USA [38180] : PRE 1820 VA, USA [38180]

TOBY PRE 1830 NEW ENGLAND, USA [37764] : ALL NY, USA [37764]

TOCHER ALEXANDER 1852+ OCHILTREE, AYR, SCT [37444]

TOCKNELL PRE 1850 CHELTENHAM, GLS, ENG [34750]

TOD C1700 CARMICHAEL, LKS, SCT [34118] : PRE 1852 CARNBEE, FIF, SCT [35347] : 1857+ ST MONANCE, FIF, SCT [35347] : PAT PRE 1835 DUNDEE, ANS, SCT [37228]

TODD 1900+ BALLARAT, VIC, AUS [38729] : 1800S CAVAN & DURHAM, ONT, CAN [36727] : 1854 GREAT MARLOW, BKM, ENG [34305] : 1820 SHOTTON, DUR, ENG [35912] : PRE 1800 BURNLEY, LAN, ENG [36159] : EDWARD C1842 EIGHTON BANKS, DUR, ENG [36270] : 1800-1950 ANT & DRY, IRL [35395] : 1800+ HAMILTON, LKS, SCT [33800] : ALL FORGAN, FIF, SCT [34074] : PRE 1805 LARBERT, STI, SCT [36431] : C1909 LANCASTER, PA, USA [37022] : PRE 1800 SC, USA [38576] : C1845 NEWPORT, MON, WLS [35708]

TODDIE 1650+ PITTENWEEM, FIF, SCT [35627]

TODE 1835+ STURRY, KEN, ENG [35054]

TODMAN ALL UK [37674] : ALL SRY & ALL, UK [37674]

TODT 1700+ LOHBARBEK, SHO, GER [37542]

TODY 1875+ CA, USA [35000]

TOENNES CARL 1893+ SWE [38564]

TOEPFNER 1677-1746 LANDSBERG, WPR, GER [38626]

TOFANI 1928+ ANCONA, ITL [38758]

TOFFTS PRE 1800 WHITECHAPEL, MDX, ENG [36099]

TOFT PRE 1900 SHO, DEN & GER [34419]

TOGNOLINI 1800+ TIRANO, MILANO, ITL [36284]

TOHILL 1878+ ELMORE, VIC, AUS [34174]

TOLAN 1880+ TERANG, VIC, AUS [35869]

TOLAND 1880+ KIRKSTALL, VIC, AUS [35869]

TOLANO PRE 1850 LND & MDX, ENG [34791] : ALL WORLDWIDE [34791]

TOLBART 1700+ BKM, ENG [36026]

TOLBERT 1858-1862 WOLLONGONG, NSW, AUS & USA [35075]

TOLBORT PRE 1800 SHERBORNE, DOR, ENG [35758] : 1800S WOOLHOPE, HEF, ENG [36633]

TOLDERBY PRE 1650 LECHLADE, GLS, ENG [38746]

TOLE ALL WORLDWIDE [35176]

TOLEFFSON PRE 1890 HURSTVILLE, NSW, AUS [36369]

TOLEMAN PRE 1800 LYDEARD ST LAWRENCE, SOM, ENG [34201] : ALL SOUTH BRENT, SOM, ENG [36664] : ALL EXETER, DEV, ENG [36664]

TOLENTINO PRE 1873 CALUMPIT, BULACAN, PHILIPPINE [34891]

TOLERTON PRE 1800 MONRAVERTY, ARM, IRL [35897]

TOLHURST C1868 ORANGE, NSW, AUS [36312] : 1850+ MELBOURNE, VIC, AUS [36462] : PRE 1838 KEN, ENG [34696] : PRE 1841 ROMNEY MARSH, KEN, ENG [37313] : C1880 MAIDSTONE, KEN, ENG [37359]

TOLL 1817+ SOUTH CREAKE, NFK, ENG [37314] : PRE 1700 ST KEVERNE, CON, ENG [37913] : ALL WORLDWIDE [35176]

TOLLARD PRE 1831 ST MARY BOURNE, HAM, ENG [34785]

TOLLE ALL ENG [35176]

TOLLEFSEN DALEN OLAF 1860-1937 VINJE, TELEMARK & ALB, NOR & CAN [34481]

TOLLEMACHE 1700-1800 SFK, ENG [34740]

TOLLEMAN 1700S HEINKENSZAND, ZEL, NL [38350]

TOLLENEERS ALL NL [38169]

TOLLERTON PRE 1855 CABRAGH, DOW, IRL [37925]

TOLLEY PRE 1890 BERMONDSEY, LND, ENG [34612] : 1840S WRIBBENHALL, WOR, ENG [36086] : ALL NTT, ENG [36105]

TOLLEYFIELD 1770-1810 WEYMOUTH, DOR, ENG [37095] : 1770-1855 LKS, SCT [37095]

TOLLIS 1800S SYDNEY, NSW, AUS [34977] : C1797 NSW, AUS [36856] : 1700S KEN, ENG [34977] : C1797 MAIDSTONE, KEN, ENG [36856]

TOLLIVER 1750-1850 ASHE CO., NC, USA [38044]

TOLMAN THOMAS 1678 DORCHESTER, MA, USA [35273]

TOLMIE 1800+ LONDON, ENG [34232] : C1835 DUBLIN, IRL & SCT [37263] : PRE 1880 ARDERSIER, INV, SCT [33993] : 1800+ EDINBURGH, MLN, SCT [34232] : 1800+ ABERLOUR, BAN, SCT [34232] : C1790 INV & NAI, SCT [37263]

TOLONEN ALL WORLDWIDE [38547]

TOLPEE 1780+ SOBERTON, HAM, ENG [36871]

TOLSON 1900+ BRADFORD, YKS, ENG [34512] : 1800+ DEWSBURY, WRY, ENG [34512] : PRE 1750 COCKERMOUTH, CUL, ENG [38708]

TOM 1870 AUS [36250] : 1860 CAMBORNE, CON, ENG [36250]

TOMAN 1700-1800 SANCREED, CON, ENG [35712]

TOMBLISON REBECCA PRE 1783 SEDGLEY, STS, ENG [36374]

TOMBROEK PRE 1775 ZUH, NL [34180]

TOMBS 1900+ FREMANTLE, WA, AUS [35800] : PRE 1800 CHURCHDOWN & NORTON, GLS, ENG [35542] : 1866 WALWORTH, SRY, ENG [35800] : 1790-1820 CUMBERLAND CO., ME & NY, USA [36546]

TOMELTY C1820 PORTAFERRY, DOW, IRL & SCT [37143]

TOMES 1500S ENG [37803]

TOMEY ALL UK [36530]

TOMKIES C1920 HACKNEY, LND, ENG [35489]

TOMKIN 1800+ BIRMINGHAM, WAR, ENG [34640]

TOMKINS 1820+ BLENRY, BKM, ENG [34029] : PRE 1780 CHESHAM, BKM, ENG [34041] : ALL NTH, ENG [35177] : PRE 1900 ESS, ENG [37668] : PRE 1860 WIC, IRL [35488] : PRE 1860 DUBLIN, IRL [35488]

TOMKINSON PRE 1850 NANTWICH, CHS, ENG [33796] : 1680+ CHEDDLETON, STS, ENG [36701]

TOMLIENS PRE 1800 SOUTHWARK, SRY, ENG [36752]

TOMLIN 1900S BIRMINGHAM, WAR, ENG [34909] : 1800+ FRAMPTON, LIN, ENG [35992] : 1780+ CORBY, LIN, ENG [37328] : 1770-1850 SHORNE NEWINGTON, KEN, ENG [38354]

TOMLINS PRE 1800 DORRINGTON, SAL, ENG [37722]

TOMLINSON C1835 HARPURS HILL, NSW, AUS [36520] : 1857+ HEXHAM, VIC, AUS [36623] : 1850+ FRANKTOWN, ONT, CAN [35627] : 1820-1900 DUFFIELD, DBY, ENG [34729] : 1800S CALDER, LAN, ENG [34857] : BENHAM C1861 MARYLEBONE, MDX, ENG [34893] : C1879-1889 PADDINGTON & SHEPHERDS BUSH, MDX, ENG [34893] : 1660-1840 HATFIELD & BARNBY DUN, WRY, ENG [36147] : ALL CASTLE DONINGTON, LEI, ENG [36163] : 1830+ WHITE WALTHAM, BRK, ENG [36163] : 1800+ DERBY, DBY, ENG [36241] : PRE 1835 SOUTH WEST, LAN, ENG [36520] : 1700-1850 SANDON, STS, ENG [36623] : 1800+ IDLESTOP, LIN, ENG [37050] : 1800+ DONCASTER, ERY, ENG [37050] : PRE 1810 YKS, ENG [37477] : 1740-1990 STOKE ON TRENT, STS, ENG [37608] : PRE 1790 BREEDON ON THE HILL, LEI, ENG [37754] : C1850 FORT WILLIAM, CALCUTTA, INDIA [36520] : PRE 1815 AGHADE & MILLPARK, CAR, IRL [33812] : PRE 1690 DERBY, CT, USA [37510] : PRE 1870 WINDHAM CO., CT, USA [38116]

TOMME 1750-1800 LANCASTER CO., PA, USA [38088]

TOMPKINS 1880+ SHEPPARTON, VIC, AUS [34919] : 1820+ CAN [37427] : PRE 1780 CHESHAM, BKM, ENG [34041] : PRE 1900 LEICESTER, LEI, ENG [36113] : C1860 WELLINGTON, NZ [35357] : PRE 1780 WESTCHESTER CO., NY, USA [37460]

TOMPKINSON 1750+ STAFFORD, STS, ENG [35737]

TOMPSON 1600+ DOWNHAM, CAM, ENG [34221] : C1670 GRIMSBURY, OXF, ENG [35030]

TOMS 1850+ YARRAWONGA, VIC, AUS [35437] : 1879 ST THOMAS, DEV, ENG [33810] : 1800S WINIFRITH, DOR, ENG [35437] : PRE 1850 CON & DEV, ENG [38735]

TOMSETT 1700-1760 MAIDSTONE, KEN, ENG [34623] : C1770-C1870 SSX, ENG [36024]

TOMSON 1700+ WARTON & WHITTINGTON, LAN, ENG [36227]

TONAGH 1877-1912 GLASGOW, LKS, SCT [33811]

TONE 1800S+ CAPHEATON, NBL, ENG [38436] : 1880+ JESMOND, NBL, ENG [38436]

TONER 1880 ORVILLE, VIC, AUS [35350] : C1850 SYDNEY, NSW, AUS [35859] : 1840+ NSW, AUS [35862] : C1800 BALLYMORE, ARM, IRL [35859] : PRE 1840 MARLACOO, ARM, IRL [35862]

TONES ALL WORLDWIDE [37615]

TONG 1800S WYMESWOULD, LEI, ENG [36531] : 1700+ MYLOR, CON, ENG [37224]

TONGE C1875 MANCHESTER, LAN, ENG [34360] : EDWARD 1780-1990 LIVERPOOL, LAN, ENG [36832] : 1840-1880 YORK, YKS, ENG [37757] : 1858-1990 AUCKLAND, NZ [36832]

TONGUE C1880-1900 BIRMINGHAM, WAR, ENG [35791]

TONKEN 1700-1850 MULLION, CON, ENG [34697] : 1650-1700 RUAN MAJOR, CON, ENG [34697]

TONKIN THOMAS 1800+ NEWQUAY, ST. COLUMB, CON, ENG [34078] : PRE 1890 TYWERDREATH, CON, ENG [34603] : ALL PENZANCE & NEWLYN, CON, ENG [34724] : 1700+ LOSTWITHIEL, CON, ENG [34742] : C1797 GRADE, CON, ENG [34752] : 1800 REDRUTH, CON, ENG [35023] : 1750+ CON, ENG [35060] : PRE 1820 ST AGNES, CON, ENG [35441] : 1800S ST AGNES, CON, ENG [35500] : PRE 1800 PENZANCE, CON, ENG [36469] : PRE 1900 PAUL, CON, ENG [37680] : ALL KENWYN & TREGONY, CON, ENG & AUS [35712]

TONKS C1845 WOLVERHAMPTON, STS, ENG [34239]

TONNELIER PRE 1750 NRY, ENG [38768]

TONNER PRE 1850 GIRVAN, AYR, SCT & IRL [34835]

TONNESDATTER PRE 1875 VAMDRUP, RIBE, DEN [37034]

TOOBY 1700-1870 CASTLE GRESLEY, DBY, ENG [38251]

TOOEKTJE FOEKTE C1850 NL [35607]

TOOGOOD AMELIA PRE 1881 VIC, AUS [35137] : PRE 1850 SOM, ENG [36025] : ALL CHELMSFORD, ESS, ENG [36154] : 1770+ LKS, SCT [37095]

TOOHEY PRE 1886 BENALLA, VIC, AUS [34452] : PRE 1913 NSW, AUS [34978] : 1858 MELBOURNE, VIC, AUS [37163] : PRE 1856 NENAGH, TIP, IRL [34452] : 1826-1860 CAHERCONLISH, LIM, IRL [35763]

TOOHILL PRE 1835 PALLASKENRY, LIM, IRL [33939]

TOOK PRE 1850 NFK, ENG [34317]

TOOLE PRE 1850 STEPNEY, LND, ENG [34776] : 1800+ BRIERLEY HILL, STS, ENG [37367] : PRE 1841 FORKHILL, ARM, IRL [36629]

TOOLEY ALL BYWELL, NBL, ENG [34074] : C1810 ISLINGTON, MDX, ENG [37885]

TOOLSON PRE 1895 HUNSLET & FEATHERSTONE, WRY, ENG [34382]

TOOMER 1750-1900 ROMSEY, HAM, ENG [37211]

TOOMEY 1829-1897 WINDSOR AREA, NSW, AUS [35092] : 1811-1829 CORK CITY, COR, IRL [35092] : PRE 1880 KER, IRL [35406] : PRE 1850 COR, IRL [38447]

TOON PRE 1810 ENG [37515] : 1700-1900 WAR & LEI, ENG [37858]

TOONE PRE 1860 LONDON, ENG [37515]

TOOP 1759 SHERFORD, DEV, ENG [37418] : ALL WORLDWIDE [34994]

TOOTELL C1810 HOLBORN, LND, ENG [35726] : 1857+ SEVENOAKS, KEN, ENG [35726]

TOOTH PRE 1860 DRAYTON, SAL, ENG [33766] : 1700+ RUGELEY, STS, ENG [34639] : 1830-1874 CHELTENHAM, GLS, ENG [34649] : 1840S BELPER, DBY, ENG [37230]

TOOVEY 1800+ WA, AUS [34846] : 1800+ BKM & HRT, ENG [36123] : C1650 SHIRBURN, OXF, ENG [36431] : ALL LONDON, MDX, ENG [38376] : ALL WORLDWIDE [34471]

TOPCLIFFE 1600-1750 NFK, ENG [38035]

TOPEN 1700-1760 BRIGHTON, SSX, ENG [36534]

TOPHAM 1850+ YKS, ENG [35169] : 1806 WOODKIRK, YKS, ENG [35369] : PRE 1800 PENTRICH, DBY, ENG [37381] : PRE 1810 ERY, ENG [37913]

TOPLEY ALL ARMAGH & BELFAST, IRL [37518]

TOPLIFF C1850 KINGSTON, ONT, CAN [37518] : ALL ARMAGH & BELFAST, IRL [37518]

TOPLISS PRE 1880 DBY, ENG [37353] : 1780+ HORNCASTLE, LIN, ENG [37692] : PRE 1800 DBY, ENG [37692] : ALL ARMAGH & BELFAST, IRL [37518] : ALL WORLDWIDE [37692]

TOPPEN 1500-1600 NEWHAVEN, SSX, ENG [36534]

TOPPING 1830+ WIGAN, LAN, ENG [37732]

TORBETT ROBERT 1770+ DUNDEE, ANS, SCT [37153]

TORCK 1600 MUNSTER, WESTFALEN, GER [38641] : 1200+ HERRINGEN, WESTFALEN, GER [38641] : 1600 GOCH, NIEDERRHEIN, GER [38641] : 1300 OESEL, LIEVLAND, OST [38641]

TORGERSON 1850+ DANE CO., WI, USA [36326]

TORGESDATTER 1800+ NOR & SWE [34568]

TORKA 1700 STOBERAU, SCHLESIEN, GER [38641]

TORKE 1700 MILITSCH (KREIS), SCHLESIEN, GER [38641] : 1885 GROβ WARTENBERG, SCHLESIEN, GER [38641] : 1850 KASWE, SCHLESIEN, GER [38641] : 1800 LEIPZIG, SACHSEN, GER [38641] : 1778 KL. UJOSCHUTZ, SCHLESIEN, GER [38641] : 1873 SULAU, SCHLESIEN, GER [38641] : 1800 BRESLAU, SCHLESIEN, GER [38641]

TORKINGTON 1795-1875 OLDHAM & CHADDERTON, LAN, ENG [38370]

TORLEY 1852+ TAS, AUS [34853] : 1840S LIVERPOOL, ENG & AUS [34845] : ALL WORLDWIDE [34853]

TORPEY 1800+ BALLINAKILL, GAL, IRL [35054]

TORPY PRE 1874 TIP, IRL [35895]

TORR PRE 1800 SHEFFIELD, YKS & LAN, ENG [34743] : 1630+ GRINDON, STS, ENG [36701]

TORRANCE PRE 1890 GLASGOW & CAMBUSLANG, LKS & AYR, SCT [34706] : 1800+ EDINBURGH, MLN, SCT [34922] : 1800S EDINBURGH, MLN, SCT [35468] : 1750+ LESMAHAGOW, LKS, SCT [38388] : C1750+ CARLUKE, LKS, SCT [38492] : JANE 1830-1860 EDINBURGH, SCT & NZ [35999]

TORRIE 1700S ANS, SCT [34053]

TORSTENSSON BJORN 1600+ UDDHEDEN & GRASMARK, VARMLAND, SWE [38551]

TORVILLE C1868 NEW SLEAFORD, LIN, ENG [36668]

TORWELLE PRE 1886 HAN, GER [37504]

TOSCHINI PRE 1850 LEONTICA, TI, CH [35718]

TOSDEVINE PRE 1876 CHRISTCHURCH, HAM & CAE, ENG & WLS [38437]

TOSE 1750+ HINDERWELL & RUNSWICK BAY, NRY, ENG [34375] : 1800+ WHITBY & SNEATON THORPE, NRY, ENG [34375] : ALL WORLDWIDE [34375]

TOSH ALL NBL, ENG [33974]

TOSHAK PRE 1792 SALINE, FIF, SCT [35525]

TOSPELL 1850 LONDON, ENG [34793]

TOSTEVIN 1860+ ST HELIER, JERSEY, CHI, ENG [33920]

TOTHAM 1850-1930 HOBART, TAS, AUS [34551] : PRE 1820 COLCHESTER, ESS, ENG [34551] : C1814 COLCHESTER, ESS, ENG [36803]

TOTHILL PRE 1800 MEMBURY & AXMINSTER, DEV, ENG [35701]

TOTMAN PRE 1850 HRT, ENG [36361]

TOTORN 1684 MIDDLESEX, MA, USA [38022]

TOTTERDALE PRE 1794 COMBE FLOREY, SOM, ENG [34840]

TOTTLE PRE 1800 MEMBURY & AXMINSTER, DEV, ENG [35701]

TOTTON 1900-1950 LONDON, ENG [37608]

TOUCHARD 1700-1800 BETHNAL GREEN, LND, ENG [38516] : PRE 1730 FRA [38516]

TOUCHELL 1700+ ABERDEEN, ABD, SCT [35445] : 1700+ GREENOCK, RFW, SCT [35445]

TOUCHET ALL WORLDWIDE [34742]

TOUCHOR 1700-1800 BETHNAL GREEN, LND, ENG [38516]

TOUGAS 1695-1946 MONTREAL, QUE, CAN [34217] : 1800+ ORMSTOWN, QUE, CAN [36686]

TOUGH PRE 1750 ENG [37851]

TOULMIN 1600-1700 BOLTON LE SANDS, LAN, ENG [34872]

TOULOUSE 1700-1900 WORCESTER, WOR, ENG [38244]

TOUPIN PIERRE 1850+ MASKINONGE, QUE, CAN [36678]

TOURELLE PRE 1855 LONDON, ENG [34652]

TOURNAY C1880 BBT, BEL [34521]

TOURTELOTT 1850+ SCOTIA, NY, USA [34465]

TOUSSAINT PRE 1615 METZ, LOR, FRA [38659]

TOUT 1840+ WLS, ENG [35287] : 1875+ CLINTON CO., MI, USA [35287] : 1865+ ONTARIO CO., NY, USA [35287]

TOVEE PRE 1880 ESS, ENG [34261]

TOVERY 1704 BISHOPS WALTHAM, HAM, ENG [36263]

TOVEY PRE 1900 LONDON, ENG [34772] : 1900+ NZ [37115]

TOWARD ALL ENG & SCT [36119]

TOWART ALL ENG & SCT [36119] : PRE 1850 DUMBARTON, DNB, SCT [34598] : PRE 1850S PERTH, PER, SCT [35702]

TOWE 1700-1900 IRL [34081]

TOWEL ALL CHITTLEHAMPTON, DEV, ENG [35001]

TOWELL 1750+ KETTERING, NTH, ENG & AUS [38204] : C1750 YORK CO., PA, USA [37536]

TOWERD ALL ENG & SCT [36119]

TOWERS 1880S MELBOURNE, VIC, AUS [35877] : 1880+ LEICESTER, LEI, ENG [34260] : HENRY 1700S YKS, ENG [36291] : THOMAS 1800S BENTHAM, YKS, ENG [36291] : 1800S LIN, ENG [36851]

TOWERSEY ALL LONG CRENDON, BKM, ENG [36866]

TOWEY 1800-1842 MAY, IRL [38180]

TOWLE 1866+ MAITLAND, NS, CAN [38766] : ALL STAPLEFORD, NTT, ENG [34734]

TOWLER PRE 1833 CORNHOLME, YKS & LAN, ENG [35490] : PRE 1833 COLNE, LAN, ENG [35490] : WILLIAM 1700-1786 BLADEN CO., NC, USA [35315]

TOWN 1850+ MELBOURNE, VIC, AUS [35982] : PRE 1800 YKS, ENG [34383] : 1830+ WESTMINSTER, LND, ENG [35982] : 1850+ LAMBETH, SRY, ENG [35982] : PRE 1750 WRY, ENG [36380] : 1860S LONG DITTON, SRY, ENG [36788] : C1800 GRAVESEND, KEN, ENG [37652] : PRE 1880 CALDER VALLEY, WRY, ENG [37754] : 1860+ DENBY PAR & HUDDERSFIELD, WRY, ENG [37754]

TOWNDROW 1800-1870 DBY, ENG [37829]

TOWNELEY 900-1800 BURNLEY, LAN, ENG [36560]

TOWNEND PRE 1837 ENG [35713] : PRE 1840 BACUP, LAN, ENG [37414]

TOWNER C1800 EAST GULDEFORD, SSX, ENG [34426]

TOWNESEND 1580-1650 ALVESTON, WAR, ENG [36595]

TOWNLEY ELIZABETH 1680-1750 PRESTBURY, CHS, ENG [34143] : ALL LAN, ENG [35063] : PRE 1811 TEWKESBURY, GLS, ENG [36177]

TOWNROW PRE 1704 NOTTINGHAM, NTT, ENG [36532]

TOWNSEND 1820+ PARRAMATTA, NSW, AUS [34758] : 1850+ FRYERS CREEK & COLLINGWOOD, VIC, AUS [35214] : JOSEPH 1863-1888 ADELAIDE, SA, AUS [35223] : 1840S CIRCULAR HEAD, TAS, AUS [35422] : 1750+ ARGENTEUIL CO., QUE, CAN [34199] : 1800-1875 BROME, QUE, CAN [36938] : MOSES 1800+ TAUNTON, SOM, ENG [33923] : 1840+ NORTHAMPTON, NTH, ENG [33945] : 1800+ OXFORD, OXF, ENG [34455] : 1640+ PAINSWICK, GLS, ENG [34747] : PRE 1780 LND, ENG [34804] : C1823 PUTNEY, SRY, ENG [35223] : 1580+ TYSOE, WAR, ENG [36516] : ANN PRE 1789 ST MARYS, NOTTINGHAM, NTT, ENG [36532] : 1758-1790 NORWICH, NFK, ENG [36864] : 1796-1818 GRAVESEND, KEN, ENG [36864] : 1800 NORTHAMPTON, NTH, ENG [36887] : PRE 1860 DEV, ENG [36923] : GEORGE C1819 CHARLTON, WIL, ENG [37002] : ALL CASTLE EATON, LIN, ENG [37115] : ALL WIL, ENG [37115] : ALL GLS, ENG [37115] : ALL LATTON, LIN, ENG [37115] : 1880S FALMOUTH, CON, ENG [37151] : P. LIMBURGH 1856-1927 SOHO & MAIDENHEAD, LND & BRK, ENG [37227] : 1700 WITNEY, OXF, ENG [37277] : ALL NORWICH, NFK, ENG [37689] : 1400+ LND, ENG [38016] : PRE 1650 NFK & MA, ENG & USA [38746] : 1800S ANT, IRL [35968] : 1750+ ST ALBANS, VT, USA [34199] : PRE 1850 KNOX CO., OH, USA [35312] : 17898-1850 FREEPORT, ME, USA [35314] : 1790+ NANTUCKET, MA, USA [35314] : 1690-1748 HINGHAM, MA, USA [35314] : 1780+ HENNIKER, NH, USA [35314] : 1650-1800 READING, MA, USA [35314] : 1750-1825 TYRINGHAM, MA, USA [35314] : 1700-1800 NEW SALEM, MA, USA [36938] : 1630+ MA & ME, USA [38016] : 1760-1770 TAUNTON, MA, USA [38099] : 1750-87 BERKELEY, MA, USA [38151] : 1800S CUYAHOGA CO., OH, USA [38369]

TOWNSHEND 1758+ ENG [34387] : 1500-1700 BRADLEY BY STAFFORD, STS, ENG [36062] : ALL NORWICH, NFK, ENG [37689]

TOWNSLEY C1770 BROTHERTON, WRY, ENG [36111] : C1854 BALLYCASTLE, ANT, IRL [34474]

TOWNSON 1700-1850 ULVERSTON, LAN, ENG [36065] : 1889+ CARNFORTH, LAN, ENG [36227] : PRE 1800 CONISTON & ULVERSTON, LAN, ENG [37710] : 1900+ NZ [37710]

TOWSE C1830 COOKVILLE, NB, CAN [34358]

TOWSEY 1750-1900 TREGONY, CON, ENG [35736]

TOY PRE 1830 WENDRON & BREAGE, CON, ENG [34865] : PRE 1827 ST JUST IN R & GERRANS, CON, ENG [36039] : ALL CON, ENG [37818] : 1840+ HENDERSON CO., KY, USA [38091] : ALL WORLDWIDE [36083]

TOYE ALL WORLDWIDE [36083]

TOYNE 1890 SYDNEY, NSW, AUS [35508] : 1800+ KIRTON, LIN, ENG [35992] : 1700+ CRIPPLEGATE, LND, ENG [35992]

TOZER 1800S+ GOULBURN, NSW, AUS [35537] : 1800+ CRANTOCK, CON, ENG [35993] : PRE 1880 DEV, ENG [37500]

TOZZI 1855 FLORENCE, ITL [35405]

TRACE C1800 EAST OGWILL, DEV, ENG [35938] : 1850-1920 BARGOED, GLA, WLS [34842]

TRACEY PRE 1850 TIP, IRL [34025] : PRE 1840 OFF, IRL [35246] : PRE 1830 MAY, IRL [36325] : PRE 1860 DUBLIN, IRL [36906] : C1880 CHATTANOOGA, TN, USA [36906]

TRACHSEL 1800-1900 FRUTIGEN, BE, CH [35283] : PRE 1850 RUEGGISBERG, BE, CH [38747]

TRACY 1850+ MELBOURNE, VIC, AUS [34969] : PRE 1850 GAL, IRL [35042] : C1838 BALLINASLOE, GAL, IRL [35249] : 1596-1650 LEIDEN, HOLLAND, NL [36560] : PRE 1890 CLEVELAND, OH, USA [36679]

TRAHAN GUILLAUME 1600+ FRA [37429]

TRAHER 1700-1920 TRURO, CON, ENG [34257] : 1870-1950 HALIFAX, YKS, ENG [34257] : 1600-1900 TRIER, BRD & RPF, GER [34257] : 1860-1960 MANTICOKE, PA, USA [34257] : 1890-1980 DETROIT, MI, USA [34257] : 1898-1950 CLEVELAND, OH, USA [34257] : 1870-1960 WILKES BARRE, PA, USA [34257] : 1860-1950 DENVER, CO, USA [34257]

TRAIL ALL ONT, CAN [34465] : ALL FRASERBURGH, ABD, SCT [36061]

TRAILL 1890 WILLIAMSTOWN, VIC, AUS [35204] : 1817-1820 MILE END, LND, ENG [35402]

TRAILLE ALL WORLDWIDE [34660]

TRAIN 1800+ DUR, ENG [35364] : 1750-1850 COTTINGHAM & BEVERLY, YKS, ENG [36688] : PRE 1870 CLARKSTON NEWMONKLAND, LKS, SCT [33978] : PRE 1813 CAMPBELTOWN, ARL, SCT [35807]

TRAINER PRE 1835 IRL [35493] : PRE 1830 ARM, IRL [36664] : 1835+ IRL & AUS [33926]

TRAINOR 1850-1900 BRANXHOLME & HAMILTON, VIC, AUS [33834] : 1850-1900 REDRUTH, VIC, AUS [33834] : 1850-1917 MELBOURNE & COLERAINE, VIC, AUS [33834] : PRE 1866 WALHALLA, VIC, AUS [34421] : ALL CHILTERN & RUTHERGLEN, VIC, AUS [35538] : ALL BEAUFORT, VIC, AUS [35538] : ALL PEI, CAN [34356] : PRE 1857 WIC, IRL [35399] : 1820-1900 STATEN ISLAND, NY, USA [33834]

TRALKA 1800 KONICE, POL [35000] : 1875+ USA [35000]

TRAMPEDACH PRE 1750 KASSEL, GER [38642] : PRE 1750 HES, GER [38642] : PRE 1800 GER [38642]

TRAND 1830-1900 IRL & AUS [37153]

TRANMER 1800S THIXENDALE, ERY, ENG [37357]

TRANTER ALL STOKENCHURCH, OXF & BKM, ENG [33995] : 1800+ SHIFNAL, MADELEY, SAL, ENG [34315] : 1870-1900 WILLENHALL, STS, ENG [36495]

TRAPNELL ALL WORLDWIDE [36012]

TRAPP 1851 SYDNEY, NSW, AUS [35855] : ALL GLS, ENG [34210] : ALL PER, SCT [34938]

TRAPPIT 1700S GRAVESEND, KEN, ENG [34937]

TRAPSKI PRE 1900 TUSEWARK, GD, POL [36893]

TRASHER SARAH 1849 KEWANEE, IL, USA [38124]

TRASK 1790S MONTACUTE & ODCOMBE, SOM, ENG [37533] : 1830S PRESTON, SOM, ENG [37533] : CUYLER 1810+ ONTARIO CO., NY, USA [36575] : DANIEL 1810+ ONTARIO CO., NY, USA [36575] : DANIEL PRE 1810 MA, USA [36575]

TRATHEN 1700-1800 BEER FERRIS, DEV, ENG [35712] : PRE 1850 REDRUTH, CON, ENG [38735]

TRATT PRE 1800 MEMBURY, DEV, ENG [35701] : C1800 SOM, ENG [38052]

TRATTEN PRE 1800 CON, ENG [38735]

TRAUB PRE 1750 RAPPACH, WUE, GER [35242]

TRAUNTER 1500S BANBURY, OXF, ENG [35030]

TRAUTMAN PRE 1910 ODESSA, UKRAINIAN, RUSSIA [36929] : 1738-1800 NORTHUMBERLAND, PA, USA [37011]

TRAUTMANN 1656-1710 LAMBSBORN, RPF, BRD [37011] : 1900-1925 ST LOUIS, MO, USA [37605]

TRAUTWEIN 1850-1900 HUDSON, NJ, USA [38061]

TRAVAS C1846 NORTHAMPTON, NTH, ENG [34898]

TRAVERS C1840-1850 ONT, CAN [34153] : 1800S RINGWOOD, HAM, ENG [34080] : C1846 NORTHAMPTON, NTH, ENG [34898] : PRE 1780 BRIDPORT, DOR, ENG [36478] : 1870+ POOLE, DOR, ENG [37360] : 1700-1900 DUBLIN, IRL [37844] : 1870S CLAREMORRIS, MAY, IRL [38267] : 1826-1867 GORTENAGREENANE & TIMOLEAGUE, COR, IRL &, JAMAICA [33847]

TRAVILLA ALL WORLDWIDE [37808]

TRAVIS 1855+ NORTH MELBOURNE, VIC, AUS [35526] : PRE 1830 MANCHESTER, LAN, ENG [33771] : PRE 1771 KELFIELD, LIN, ENG [33992] : 1896 SALE, CHS, ENG [38267] : 1790-1885 + DUBLIN, IRL & USA [36960] : JOHN OR JAMES 1828 LIVINGSTON CO., KY, USA [37590]

TRAXLER ALL USA [36540]

TRAYNOR C1830 ARMAGH, ARM, IRL [35859]

TRAYNOR (SEE TRAINOR [35399]

TRAYTON ALL SSX, ENG [34505]

TREACEY 1839+ GEELONG, VIC, AUS [34173]

TREACY PRE 1860 TIPPERARY, TIP, IRL [34037]

TREADAWAY PRE 1830 LND, ENG [37655]

TREADGOLD C1795+ BINTON, WAR, ENG [37265] : 1735+ DUNCHURCH, WAR, ENG [37265]

TREADWELL 1830-1900 LND, ENG [35402] : ALL ENG [35933] : PRE 1820 BECKLEY, SSX, ENG [37137] : C1820 OXFORD, OXF, ENG [37847] : 1840+ MARYLEBONE, MDX, ENG [37847]

TREASURE 1801+ SYDNEY & BATHURST, NSW, AUS [34698] : ALL LONDON, ENG [34669] : C1798 HOLCOMBE, SOM, ENG [36949]

TREAT 1500-1650 PITMINSTER, SOM, ENG [37783] : ALL CT, USA [37803]

TREBILCOCK 1860-1880 KEWEENAW CO., MI, USA [38009]

TREBING 1709-1731 GROSSALMERODE, GHE, GER [38750]

TREBLE 1550-1850 EXETER, DEV, ENG [34191]

TREBY PRE 1850 TIVERTON, DEV, ENG [33935] : 1850S MARYLEBONE, MDX, ENG [36741]

TRECARTIN GEORGE 1828-1909 DEER ISLAND, NB, CAN [38785] : GEORGE 1862-1909 HICKORY, WI, USA [38785]

TREDENICK 1800-1846 KELLS, MEA, IRL [34022]

TREDGETT 1880+ SASKATOON, SAS & BC, CAN & USA [37322] : ALL CAM, ENG [33764]

TREDREA 1760-1860 LUDGVAN, CON, ENG [35102] : 1850 CLIFTON, WI, USA [35102]

TREE C1835 EXETER, DEV, ENG [35158] : PRE 1760 ENG [36002] : PRE 1750 DEV, ENG [36064] : 1860-1912 WAPPING, LND, ENG [36064]

TREEBY PRE 1808 AVETON GIFFORD, DEV, ENG [35895]

TREEVE 1740+ PAUL, CON, ENG [36833]

TREFRY 1700-1850 CALSTOCK, CON, ENG [37761] : 1600-1800 EAST, CON, ENG [37761]

TREGARTHON 1820 MELBOURNE, VIC, AUS [35089]

TREGEMBA 1660+ BREAGE, CON, ENG [35587]

TREGILGAS PRE 1800 MEVAGISSEY, CON, ENG [37319]

TREGLOAN PRE 1810 ILLOGAN, CON, ENG [37343] : 1912-1949 HELSTON, CON, ENG [37975]

TREGLOHAN ALL ENG [37158]

TREGONING 1750+ CON, ENG [36058]

TREGONNING 1700-1750 GWENNAP, CON, ENG [34793] : 1600-1800 GWENNAP, CON, ENG [36806]

TREGOWETH PRE 1864 TRURO, CON, ENG [36888]

TREGUNNA 1750+ GWENNAP, CON, ENG [35847]

TREHY 1853+ NSW, AUS [35406] : PRE 1853 TIPPERARY, TIP, IRL [35406]

TREIBER 1450-1650 MUEHLHAUSEN, BAW, BRD [38654]

TREIPE ALL WORLDWIDE [37240]

TRELEAVEN PRE 1800 LANLIVERY, CON, ENG [35621]

TRELEGGAN PRE 1850 CON, ENG [34615] : 1700-1750 CONSTANTINE, CON, ENG [34793]

TRELFA 1750 MIDDLEWICH, CHS, ENG [37039]

TRELIVING ALL CON, ENG [34550]

TRELOAR C1872 REDRUTH, CON, ENG [34193] : ALL HELSTON, CON, ENG & NZ [33981]

TRELOUR GRACE PRE 1848 SA & VIC, AUS & ENG [33840]

TREMAIN 1871+ HOBART, TAS, AUS [36622] : ALL ST COLUMB MAJOR, CON, ENG [36748] : 1782+ ALTARNUM, CON, ENG [38151] : 1845-93 MARSHALL CO., IL, USA [38151]

TREMAINE 1690S CONSTANTINE, CON, ENG [34793] : 1750+ ALTARNUM, CON, ENG [38151]

TREMAYNE 1700+ HELSTON, CON, ENG [34742]

TREMBATH PRE 1860 MORVAH, CON, ENG [34929] : 1840+ TRURO, CON, ENG [36909] : PRE 1850 UK [38363] : 1865-1885 KEWEENAW CO., MI, USA [38009]

TREMBLAY 1820+ WINNEPEG, MAN, CAN [37432]

TREMBLE 1800 ASPATRIA, CUL, ENG [34940] : PRE 1790 STRATTON, CON, ENG [37320]

TREMBLEY 1600-1700 NL & FRA [38216]

TREMEDICK PRE 1836 ST HILARY, CON, ENG [35425]

TREMELLING 1700S CROWAN, CON, ENG [34920]

TREMLIN C1886 BOURNEMOUTH, HAM, ENG [37886]

TREMMEL 1700+ BERLIN, PA, USA [37010] : ALL WORLDWIDE [38733]

TRENAMAN PRE 1841 ST IVE (NEAR LISKEARD), CON, ENG [35428]

TRENCH PRE 1840 DUNBAR & LEITH, SCT [37491]

TRENCHARD PRE 1850 SOUTH PETHERTON, SOM, ENG [33876] : ALL YARCOMBE, SOM, ENG [33884] : THOMAS 1866 PLYMOUTH, DEV, ENG [38193] : ALL WORLDWIDE [33884]

TRENDE ALL DANZIG, POM, GER [37164] : ALL WORLDWIDE [37164]

TRENEMAN 1700-1850 REDRUTH, CON, ENG [35395]

TRENGOVE 1750-1830 GWENNAP & PERRANARWORTHAL, CON, ENG [34274]

TRENGROVE ALL WORLDWIDE [34245]

TRENHOLM PRE 1815 POINT DE BUTE, NB, CAN [34519]

TRENHOLME 1100-1900 NORTHALLERTON, NRY, ENG [36141] : PRE 1680 NORTHALLERTON, YKS, ENG [36619]

TRENNUM 1780+ ENG [34130]

TRENOWYTH 1800+ CON, ENG [35776]

TRENT 1835 OKMULGEE, OK, USA [38012]

TRENTHAM 1790-1810 SC, USA [35307]

TREPESS PRE 1800 WARWICK, WAR, ENG [37247]

TREPTAU PRE 1850 OPR, GER [38648]

TRESIDDER 1700-1850 HELSTON & WENDRON, CON, ENG [34687] : PRE 1840 WENDRON, CON, ENG [35151] : PRE 1860 PERRANWHARF, CON, ENG [36310]

TRESIDER 1860-1885 KEWEENAW CO., MI, USA [38009]

TRESTINOWITCZ ALL POL **[38481]**

TRESTRAIL C1855-1920 CLARE, SA, AUS **[35550]** : PRE 1727 CON, ENG **[33777]**

TRETFORD C1500 ENG **[34395]**

TRETHEWEY 1860-1880 KEWEENAW CO., MI, USA **[38009]**

TRETT PRE 1870 LND, ENG **[35709]** : 1922+ USA **[35709]**

TREVAIN ALL WORLDWIDE **[37060]**

TREVAN ALL WORLDWIDE **[37060]**

TREVANION 1700+ WORLDWIDE **[35080]**

TREVANNION 1898+ QLD, AUS **[35392]** : PRE 1898 PENRYN, CON, ENG **[35392]**

TREVARTHAN PRE 1813 ST ERTH, CON, ENG **[34010]** : PRE 1880 CON, ENG & USA **[37018]**

TREVARTHEN PRE 1860 ENG **[35255]**

TREVASKIS 1910+ LOCKHART, NSW, AUS **[36622]** : ALL WORLDWIDE **[36339]**

TREVEAL 1780+ GWENNAP, CON, ENG **[35847]** : PRE 1860 KEA, CON, ENG **[37729]**

TREVEHEN PRE 1800 CON, ENG **[37060]**

TREVEIGHAN PRE 1800 WORLDWIDE **[37060]**

TREVELLIAN ALL CLARE, SA, AUS **[35520]**

TREVENA PRE 1800 TREFULA & REDRUTH, CON, ENG **[34881]**

TREVETHAN ALL ST ISSEY, CON, ENG & AUS **[33799]**

TREVETT 1700+ UPMARDEN & BOSHAM, SSX, ENG **[34747]**

TREVILLE ALL WORLDWIDE **[37808]**

TREVILLER ALL WORLDWIDE **[37808]**

TREVILLIAN ALL WORLDWIDE **[33768]**

TREVIS C1800 WORCESTER, WOR, ENG **[37918]**

TREVOR C1750 GREAT NESS, SAL, ENG **[37508]** : 1700+ DUBLIN, IRL **[34303]**

TREVORROW ALL WORLDWIDE **[36506]**

TREW PRE 1840 WICKET, SOM, ENG **[33874]** : 1800+ CHELTENHAM, GLS, ENG **[36434]**

TREWARTHA PRE 1812 CON, ENG **[33821]** : 1700+ ST AGNES, CON, ENG **[35391]** : 1855-1870 KEWEENAW CO., MI, USA **[38009]**

TREWAVAS PRE 1800 MOUSEHOLE, CON, ENG **[37832]**

TREWEEK 1650-1720 GWENNAP, CON, ENG **[34793]** : 1800+ REDRUTH, CON, ENG **[35355]** : 1850S KENWYN, CON, ENG **[37178]** : ALL CON, ENG & NZ **[34617]**

TREWENACK PRE 1800 MAWGAN, CON, ENG **[38290]**

TREWHELLA 1890-1940 BRUNSWICK, VIC, AUS **[34767]**

TREWIN PRE 1700 CON, ENG **[35255]**

TREWOLLA ALL WORLDWIDE **[36945]**

TREWREN C1860 PLYMOUTH, DEV, ENG **[38290]**

TREYFOOT PRE 1875 PETERBOROUGH, NTH, ENG **[37753]**

TREZISE 1850-1880 KEWEENAW CO., MI, USA **[38009]**

TRIBBANCE 1800+ WIL, ENG **[35975]**

TRIBBLE 1820-1900 ERITH, KEN, ENG **[34069]**

TRIBBLESAY PRE 1840 ENG **[37948]**

TRIBE 1860-1889 MOREE AREA, NSW, AUS **[35092]** : PRE 1842 APPLEDORE, KEN, ENG **[38389]** : ALL WORLDWIDE **[37043]**

TRIBOULET 1700-1800 PFALZBURG, ZABREM RHINE, FRA **[36328]**

TRICE PRE 1880 VA, USA **[35270]**

TRICK C1810 BARNSTAPLE, DEV, ENG **[35848]** : PRE 1750 DEV, ENG **[37807]**

TRICKETT ALL NEWARK, NTT, ENG **[36174]** : PRE 1900 CREWE, CHS, ENG **[37237]**

TRICKEY 1892 EUPHRASIA, ONT, CAN **[34224]** : C1807 LONDON, ENG **[35714]**

TRICKS PRE 1830 EXETER, DEV, ENG **[37687]**

TRIEBE 1823-1875 SACHS, ALTENBURG, SAB **[36317]**

TRIEM 1700+ KRAHENBERG PFALZ, BAV, GER **[37516]** : PRE 1798 GROSSBUNDENBACH PFALZ, BAV, GER **[37516]** : PRE 1700 KRAHENBERG PFALZ, BAV, GER **[37516]** : C1821 NEIDERBEXBACH PFALZ, BAV, GER **[37516]** : 1830-1877 CANTON STARK CO., OH, USA **[37516]** : ALL WORLDWIDE **[37516]**

TRIFFITT 1808-1900 TAS, AUS **[34928]** : 1790-1810 NSW, AUS **[34928]** : 1700-1850 LIN, ENG **[34928]** : 1700-1850 YKS, ENG **[34928]** : JAMES 1769 WHIXLEY, YKS, ENG **[37106]**

TRIFTS 1951+ CHARLOTTETOWN, PEI, CAN **[34111]**

TRIFTSHALL 1970+ CHARLOTTETOWN, PEI, CAN **[34111]** : 1970+ USA **[34111]**

TRIGG 1700-1950 NORTON & HIGHNAM, GLS, ENG **[36556]** : ALL ESS, ENG **[37741]** : 1860 WI, USA **[37449]**

TRIGGER PRE 1850 PLYMOUTH, DEV, ENG **[35451]** : PRE 1850S ENG **[36146]** : 1700S DEV, ENG **[36289]**

TRIGGS 1844 SYDNEY, NSW, AUS **[38282]** : 1800S REDRUTH, CON, ENG **[37343]** : PRE 1850 TIP, IRL **[38777]**

TRIGORI PRE 1775 FRA **[38386]**

TRIHY 1832+ NEWCASTLE, TIP, IRL **[34781]** : PRE 1832 NEWCASTLE, TIP, IRL **[34781]** : ALL WORLDWIDE **[34781]**

TRILL C1815 BATLEY, SSX, ENG **[34685]** : C1760 WESTHAM, SSX, ENG **[34806]**

TRILOCK PRE 1590 BRK, ENG **[37420]**

TRIM PRE 1780 HAM, ENG **[34660]** : 1800S HAM, ENG **[35243]** : 1800+ DOR, ENG **[35998]**

TRIMBLE SARAH JANE 1859-1927 ONT, CAN **[38451]** : ROBERT 1790+ ENNISKILLEN, FER, IRL **[38595]** : PRE 1860 JACKSON CO., AR, KY & OH, USA **[38570]**

TRIMBY PRE 1920 SOUTH FULHAM, LND, ENG **[35493]** : PRE 1885 WORLDWIDE **[37512]**

TRIMEN 1889+ VICTORIA, BC, CAN **[37890]**

TRIMMER 1860+ SYDNEY, NSW, AUS **[34425]**

TRINDER 1855+ TAS, AUS **[34853]** : 1855+ NEWNHAM, TAS, AUS **[35127]** : PRE 1852 GSY, CHI **[34039]** : PRE 1890S BIDDULPH, STS, ENG **[34605]** : PRE 1855 CHARLTON KINGS, GLS, ENG **[35127]** : 1860-1883 OXFORD, OXF, ENG **[35455]** : 1750+ OXF, ENG **[36872]** : PRE 1890 OXF, LND & SRY, ENG **[37321]**

TRINER PRE 1890S BIDDULPH, STS, ENG **[34605]**

TRINNERY PRE 1866 HERTFORD, HRT, ENG **[35335]**

TRIP ALL WORLDWIDE **[37240]**

TRIPE PRE 1850 ST MARY CHURCH, DEV, ENG **[34809]** : ALL WORLDWIDE **[37240]**

TRIPHOOK ALL WORLDWIDE **[35181]**

TRIPLETT PRE 1850 POUNDSTOCK, CON, ENG **[35255]**

TRIPP 1800+ ONT, CAN **[33909]** : ALL BKM, ENG **[34744]** : ALL HRT, ENG **[34744]** : CATHERINE PRE 1835 ENG **[36634]** : C1796 WANTAGE, BRK, ENG **[37144]** : 1600-1817 GER & USA **[33909]** : C1830 BROOME CO., NY, USA **[36356]** : 1800S+ BOSTON, MA, USA & AUS **[37153]** : ALL WORLDWIDE **[37240]**

TRIPPICK PRE 1800 HAM, ENG **[36400]**

TRIPPIOCK PRE 1800 HAM, ENG **[36400]**

TRIPPIT PRE 1802 WOMERSLEY & BARLBY, WRY, ENG **[37710]**

TRISTRAM 1750-1850 TIPTON, STS, ENG [37339] :
1800+ TIRUPUTTY (TIRUPATI), MADRAS,
INDIA [37400]

TRITTON 1880+ TOWNSVILLE, QLD, AUS [35548] :
ALL SEVENOAKS, KEN, ENG [35548] : ALL
WOOLWICH, KEN, ENG [35548]

TRIVILE ALL WORLDWIDE [37808]

TRIZISE ALL ST AGNES, CON, ENG [35500]

TROASE 1680+ WHITSTONE, CON, ENG [34804]

TROCHMANN 1840-1870 NSW, AUS & DEN [38082]

TRODD C1810 HURSLEY, HAM, ENG [34839] :
1841+ COMPTON, HAM, ENG [34839] : PRE 1800
GOSPORT, HAM, ENG [36079] : PRE 1841
GOSPORT, HAM, ENG [36079] : PRE 1811
WILMINGTON, KEN, ENG [36866]

TRODDEN 1800+ LEADGATE, DUR & ARM, ENG
& IRL [36503]

TROGE 1860 TEMPLEBURG, GER [37531]

TROHMEL 1700+ PETERSBURG LPZ, SAX, DDR
[37010]

TROLIP C1800 TROWBRIDGE, WIL, ENG [34999]

TROLLOP PRE 1850 ENG [37957]

TROMPF ALL WORLDWIDE [35747]

TRONCHET 1840+ FRA [36848]

TRONCK ALL NL [38350]

TRONSON HUMPHREY 1870-1890 ILFRACOMBE,
DEV, ENG [38409]

TROON 1780+ MANACCAN, CON, ENG [35959]

TROPAZZI 1890 CALABRIA, ITL [36679]

TROSCHITZ 1800+ ROSSAU, KSA, GER [38651]

TROST C1698 NUSSLOCH, BAD, GER [34239] : 1800S
IMSBACH, RPR, GER [37814] : PRE 1780 BODDIN,
MSW, GER [38125]

TROTIER ALL TROIS RIVIERES, QUE, CAN [37537]

TROTMAN 1800 BATH, SOM, ENG [35186] : 1817
BAMPTON, OXF, ENG [35493]

TROTT 1850+ LAMBTON CO., ONT, CAN [34375] :
PRE 1850 STAINTONDALE & FYLINGDALE,
NRY, ENG [34375] : 1850-1895 SNEATONTHORPE
& FYLINGDALES, NRY, ENG [34375] : PRE 1800
MEMBURY & GITTISHAM, DEV, ENG [35701] :
PRE 1590 PITMINSTER, SOM, ENG [38135] : 1789+
WINDHAM, CUMBERLAND, ME, USA [38571]

TROTTER 1850-1960 DAYLESFORD, VIC, AUS
[44462] : 1860+ DAYLESFORD, VIC, AUS [34919] :
1870 QUAMBATOOK & DAYLESFORD, VIC, AUS
[34919] : WILLIAM 1886-1942 LINDSAY, ONT, CAN
[36677] : C1800 NBL, ENG [35646] : 1800-1850
LALEHAM, SRY, ENG [36474] : 1600-1750 SRY,
ENG [38041] : 1800S TANDRAGEE &
PORTADOWN, ARM, IRL [34919] : PRE 1850
LARNE & GLENARM, ANT, TYR & FER, IRL
[37246] : JANE C1800-1854 FER & QUE, IRL & CAN
[36904] : 1850+ NZ [34919] : PRE 1853 EDROM,
BEW, SCT [44462] : MARGARET 1880-1885 SCT
[37444] : 1600-1750 MD, USA [38041]

TROTTIAN 1868+ BALLARAT & SCOTCHMANS
LEAD, VIC, AUS [36622]

TROUGHOTT PRE 1850 KUNITZ, PRE, GER [38768]

TROUGHTON 1810 PRESBURY, GLS, ENG [34236] :
PRE 1850 KENDAL, WES, ENG [36159] : PRE 1890
RICHHILL, ARM, IRL [36877]

TROUNCE 1700-1950 CON, ENG [36007]

TROUP WILLIAM 1820-1870 BALLATER, SCT [36316]
: ALL FYVIE, ABD, SCT [37972]

TROUPE PRE 1900 WRAGLEY, HORNCASTLE, LIN,
ENG [33863]

TROUSE PRE 1850 OXFORD, ONT, CAN [36726]

TROUT 1770S KINGSBRIDGE, DEV, ENG [37169] :
1841 HARDINGTON MANDEVILLE, SOM, ENG
[37378] : 1740-1820 CHARD, SOM, ENG [38028] :

1811+ ARKSEY, WRY, ENG [38469] : 1800-1910
BLAIR CO., PA, USA [38106]

TROUTMAN 1870-1890S USA [37600]

TROVERO 1900+ LES AMENIERS, RHA, FRA
[35448]

TROVILLO ALL WORLDWIDE [37808]

TROW PRE 1880 STROUD, GLS, ENG [37851]

TROWBRIDGE PRE 1900 ANSTY & TISBURY, WIL,
ENG [34836] : 1800+ TOLLARD ROYAL, WIL,
ENG [34899] : 1500-1600 TAUNTON, SOM, ENG
[37783] : PRE 1800 NY, USA [36702]

TROWELL PRE 1780 NTH, ENG [37706]

TROWER C1860+ CLUNES, VIC, AUS [35834] : 1787
CARLTON COLVILLE, SFK, ENG [33762] : 1700+
STORRINGTON, SSX, ENG [35824] : C1800+
CAMBRIDGE, CAM, ENG [35834]

TROY ALL NSW, AUS [33799] : 1854+
COLLINGWOOD, VIC, AUS [35218] : ALL CAR,
IRL [33799] : PRE 1850 TIP, IRL [35013] : 1825+
WATERGRAPE HILL, COR, IRL [35218]

TRUAN ELIZABETH 1874 CON, ENG [35471]

TRUAX 1690-1750 NJ, USA [38061]

TRUCHON PRE 1750 BRT, FRA [35649]

TRUCKLE C1800 AMESBURY, WIL, ENG [38288]

TRUDDEN 1800+ LEADGATE, DUR & ARM, ENG
& IRL [36503]

TRUDGEN PRE 1900 MELBOURNE, VIC & CON,
AUS & ENG [34439]

TRUDGEON ALL TORONTO, ONT, MAN & BC,
CAN [34348] : PRE 1850 ST AUSTELL, CON, ENG
[38288]

TRUDGETT ALL CAM, ENG [33764] : 1811 INGHAM,
SFK, ENG [37106]

TRUDGIAN ALL TORONTO, ONT, MAN & BC, CAN
[34348]

TRUE C1850+ WOOLLAND, DOR, ENG [33922] :
1800-1850 STEUBEN CO., NY, USA [36334]

TRUELOVE PRE 1850 SHEFFIELD, WRY, ENG
[36403] : C1800 STUKELEY, HUN, ENG [37420]

TRUEMAN ELIZABETH 1835 LONDON, ENG [34091]
: 1820+ LND, ENG [36068] : 1820-1890 BEDFORD,
BDF, ENG [38004] : 1700-1800 BILSDALE, NRY,
ENG [38269] : 1700-1899 KILLYMAN,
DUNGANNON, TYR, IRL [36080] : PRE 1860
CONNAUGHT, IRL [37521]

TRUESDALE 1855+ LEWISTON, NY, USA [34129]

TRUHOL 1750-1800 DRESDEN, KSA, GER [38628]

TRULL C1790 KEMPSFORD, GLS, ENG [36975]

TRULOCK 1600S MARSH GIBBON, BKM, ENG
[35030] : PRE 1590 BRK, ENG [37420]

TRUMAN 1870+ INVERELL, NSW, AUS [33836] :
1700-1800 LONDON AREA, ENG [33836] : PRE 1860
YAXLEY, HUN, ENG [33836] : C1650-1800 NY CO.,
NY, USA [38767] : C1650-1800 FISHKILL, NY, USA
[38767] : ALL WORLDWIDE [33836]

TRUMANE 1700-1800 LONDON AREA, ENG [33836]

TRUMBLE AUGUSTUS PRE 1850 MONTGOMERY
CO., NY, USA [36950]

TRUMP 1800S BAV, GER [38153] : PRE 1900
WORLDWIDE [38196]

TRUMPER C1840 HAREFIELD, MDX, ENG [37552]

TRUNZ 1814-1895 NIEDERHELFENSCHWIL, SG,
CH [33754]

TRURAN 1700-1880 TRURO AREA, CON, ENG
[38224]

TRUSCOTT 1880 ZEEHAN, TAS, AUS [35800] : 1700-
1850 STOKE CLIMSLAND, CON, ENG [34920] :
PRE 1832 ST AUSTELLS, CON, ENG [35091] :
1750+ MEVAGISSEY & ST AUSTELL, CON, ENG
[35306] : 1800+ REDRUTH, CON, ENG [35355] :
PRE 1800 CAL, CON, ENG [35494] : PRE 1880 CON,
ENG [35800] : C1700+ GORRAN, CON, ENG

[35851] : JOHN & PETER PRE 1880 ST EWE & TREGONY, CON, ENG [36575] : 1750+ CREED & PHILLEIGH, CON, ENG [37224]

TRUSLOVE PRE 1830 BURBAGE, LEI, ENG [35246]

TRUSSELL 1800+ ESS, ENG [34818] : PRE 1900 LONDON, MDX, ENG [37561] : ALL WORLDWIDE [36548]

TRUST PRE 1820 TORQUAY, DEV, ENG [38292]

TRUSWELL 1740-1770 NORTH COLLINGHAM, NTT, ENG [37929]

TRUTTER 1600-1750 JEDBURGH, ROX, SCT [38041]

TRYGSTAD MITTE 1890-1905 KEEWANAW CO., MI, USA [38573]

TRYK 1700+ WORLDWIDE [34419]

TRYON 1600-1800 ENG [36346] : 1750-1880 GREENE, NY, USA [36346] : 1700-1850 NY, USA [36346] : 1700-1850 CT, USA [36346] : 1800-1860 TIOGA, NY, USA [36346]

TRZONSKI ALL PRZELAJKA, SIL, GER [38678]

TUAR ALL ENG & SCT [36119]

TUARD ALL ENG & SCT [36119]

TUART ALL ENG & SCT [36119]

TUBB 1700+ WAR, ENG [35060] : 1800-1840 BRAMLEY, HAM, ENG [35375] : 1700+ OXFORD, OXF, ENG [36685] : PRE 1850 HAM, ENG [37061]

TUBBS 1876+ ST GILES SOUTH, MDX, ENG [36519] : 1790-1810 ALBANY, NY, USA [37576]

TUBMAN ALL NBL & DUR, ENG [38754] : THOMAS 1822+ SWANLINBAR, CAV, IRL [35615] : C1830S CAV, IRL [37498]

TUCK ALL KERANG, VIC, AUS [37497] : 1700S WOOTTON BASSETT, WIL, ENG [35899] : 1800S BKM, ENG [35899] : PRE 1730 NEEDINGWORTH, HUN, ENG [36425] : PRE 1835 ENG [37497] : C1800 HODDESDON, HRT, ENG [37770] : 1800S MDX, ENG [37868] : 1848+ MDX, ENG [38212] : ALL ORPINGTON & LONDON, KEN & LND, ENG & AUS [33919] : 1620-1730 BEVERLY, MA, USA [37432] : 1630 SALEM, MA, USA [37531] : 1750-1900 LLANBEDR PAINSCASTLE, RAD, WLS [36109]

TUCKER 1876+ IPSWICH, QLD, AUS [33782] : ALL MORPETH, NSW, AUS [34044] : ALL MACKAY, QLD, AUS [34044] : GEORGE 1800-1880 VIC & NSW, AUS [35103] : 1800-1880 VIC, AUS [35103] : 1866 NEWPORT, VIC, AUS [37963] : 1800S CARBONEAR, NFD, CAN [38406] : WILLIAM 1700-1850 DEV, ENG [33814] : 1780-1790 MORCHARD BISHOP, DEV, ENG [34448] : PRE 1850 ST MEWAN & WENDRON, CON, ENG [34783] : PRE 1600 KILKHAMPTON, CON, ENG [35255] : PRE 1810 TIVERTON, DEV, ENG [35496] : ELIZABETH C1810 SHAFTESBURY, DOR, ENG [35955] : PRE 1660 SANDFORD, DEV, ENG [36389] : ELIZABETH 1800S SRY, ENG [36633] : 1840+ BRISTOL, ENG [36995] : 1823+ SOUTH MOLTON, DEV, ENG [36995] : PRE 1800 SOUTH MOLTON, DEV, ENG [37725] : PRE 1860 WESTON ZOYLAND, SOM, ENG [38577] : PRE 1850 SOM, ENG [38746] : C1800 SAL, ENG [38777] : DRURY 1780-1825 CLAIBORNE CO., MS, USA [35267] : 1700-1990 WV, USA [35313] : 1820-1860 VA & IL, USA [36334] : 1800-1840 BOURBON CO., KY, OH & IL, USA [36901] : 1830+ MASON CO., KY, IL & ND, USA [38050] : 1810-1850 MADISON CO., IN, USA [38108] : 1840-1860 IN & IL, USA [38367]

TUCKETT 1700S CHUDLEIGH, DEV, ENG [36865] : 1800S LYDFORD, DEV, ENG [36865] : 1740+ LOOE, CON, ENG [37088]

TUCKEY 1833+ MAITLAND, NSW, AUS [37316] : 1650 BRISTOL, ENG [34321] : PRE 1729 RODBOURN, WIL, ENG [35016] : PRE 1729 LYDIARD TREGOZE, WIL, ENG [35016] : 1800-50 LYDIARD MILLICENT, WIL, ENG [36880] : PRE 1799 HAM, ENG [37316]

TUCKFIELD 1749-1791+ BREAGE, CON, ENG [37108]

TUCKLEY PRE 1900 ENG [37739]

TUCKNOTT PRE 1800 SSX, ENG [37321]

TUDOR PRE 1850 TAS, AUS [35865] : 1800+ WEDNESBURY, STS, ENG [36821] : ALL STS, SAL & WAR, ENG [38754] : 1500-1800 SAL, ENG & WLS [36062] : 1810-1820 HIGHLAND CO., OH, USA [38334]

TUDWAY ALL WELLS, SOM & GLS, ENG [35723]

TUEART ALL ENG & SCT [36119]

TUELL 1700+ YORK, ME, USA [36931]

TUER ALL ENG & SCT [36119]

TUERD ALL ENG & SCT [36119]

TUERSLEY PRE 1851 ALTON, HAM, ENG [35113]

TUERT ALL ENG & SCT [36119]

TUFE PRE 1750 ENG [37851]

TUFF C1800 SAS, CAN [37851] : 1700+ WOOTTON BASSETT, WIL, ENG [33918] : 1750-1900 POPLAR, MDX, ENG [37651] : PRE 1750 ENG [37851] : PRE 1750 WOOTTON BASSETT AREA, WIL, ENG [37851]

TUFFE PRE 1750 ENG [37851]

TUFFERY PRE 1749 WESTERN ON THE GREEN, OXF, ENG [36281] : 1820-1840 WESTMINSTER, MDX, ENG [36803]

TUFFIN C1910 SHERBORNE, DOR, ENG [34393] : 1900 TOLLARD ROYAL, WIL, ENG [36825]

TUFFNELL PRE 1900 WORLDWIDE [37339]

TUFFS 1800S ENG [33840] : 1700-1730 IRL [37740]

TUGGEY 1700S HAM, ENG [37228]

TUGWELL 1850+ NEEDLES, IOW, ENG [35152]

TUINMAN C1900 YLST, FRG, NL [38713]

TULETT 1750+ LINGFIELD, SRY, ENG [36088]

TULEY PRE 1825 YKS, ENG [34383]

TULIP 1850+ MORPETH, NSW, AUS [35348] : C1796 TYNEMOUTH, NBL, ENG [35348] : PRE 1800 DURHAM, DUR, ENG [35348] : 1780+ HAM & SSX, ENG [35760]

TULK ALL WORLDWIDE [35356]

TULL 1750+ CHS, ENG [34408] : 1500+ MCNAIRY CO., TN, DE & AR, USA & ENG [36970]

TULLEKEN PRE 1750 WALCHEREN, ZEL, NL [38702]

TULLETT 1780+ HAM & SSX, ENG [35760]

TULLIS ALL WORLDWIDE [38536]

TULLIUS 1700-1800 GER [36579]

TULLOCH 1850+ MELBOURNE, VIC, AUS [34424] : 1700-1830 PARKSTONE, DOR, ENG [37709] : PRE 1800 HADDINGTON, ELN, SCT [33821] : 1750+ HUNTLY, ABD, SCT [34606]

TULLY PRE 1900 AUS [34196] : 1840 MELBOURNE, VIC, AUS [37163] : 1800+ LONDON, ENG [33979] : 1870+ SHIPLEY, SSX, ENG [36212] : 1800S LONDON, ENG [38502] : 1800+ CLONMEL, TIP, IRL [33861] : 1830 COR, IRL [35295] : PRE 1836 BELFAST, ANT, IRL [35597] : PRE 1815 IRL [38056] : PRE 1799 IRL [38340] : ALL CORK, COR, IRL [38502] : 1900+ NJ, USA [36320] : 1812 OH, USA [38121]

TUMBER 1870S KEN, ENG [37751]

TUMELTY C1820 PORTAFERRY, DOW, IRL & SCT [37143]

TUMEY 1800S LAWRENCE CO., IN, USA [37028]

TUMITH PRE 1840 DRUMKERRAN, FER, IRL [38214]

TUMMY 1790+ WALFORD, HEF, ENG [35886]

TUNBRIDGE 1800+ PLYMOUTH, DEV, ENG [36758]

TUNEN VAN ALL NOH, NL & CAN [38707]

TUNICLIF 1500-1700 WHALLEY, LAN, ENG [34004]

TUNICLIFF 1600-1900 ASHBOURNE, DBY, ENG [34004]

TUNIS JACKSON 1850-1860 PEORIA CO., IL, USA [38132]

TUNKS 1850+ LAUNCESTON, TAS, AUS [34541] : C1792 WOR, ENG [34296] : PRE 1850 WORCESTER, WOR, ENG [37067]

TUNMORE 1800+ COLTISHALL, NFK, ENG [37276]

TUNN 1880S ANDERSONS CREEK, VIC, AUS [37999] : 1801+ SHARNBROOK, BDF, ENG [34039]

TUNNAH ALL OLDHAMSTOCKS, ELN, SCT [33959]

TUNNECLIFF PRE 1900 DBY, ENG [37377]

TUNNEL 1700-1750 NRY, ENG [38768]

TUNNEY LAWRENCE C1762 IRL [38724] : 1800+ MAY, IRL [38725]

TUNNICLIFF 1750-1900 COVENTRY, WAR, ENG [34004]

TUNNY PRE 1820 DONOUGHMORE, DON, IRL [35157]

TUOHY C1800 CLONLEA, CLA, IRL [35203]

TUPEN 1600-1700 BRIGHTON, SSX, ENG [36534]

TUPENNY MARY 1700 TICEHURST, SSX, ENG [35361]

TUPP C1840 CANTERBURY, KEN, ENG [36860]

TUPPACK 1850S GER [35123]

TUPPEN 1500-1600 ROTTINGDEAN, SSX, ENG [36534] : GEORGE 1800-1860 BRIGHTON, SSX, ENG [36534]

TUPPEN-LASHMER 1800+ BRIGHTON, SSX, ENG [36534]

TUPPENN 1600-1630 BRIGHTON, SSX, ENG [36534]

TUPPEN-SCRASE 1600+ BRIGHTON, SSX, ENG [36534]

TUPPER 1850-1900 BRIGHTON, SSX, ENG [36534] : PRE 1500 ESS, ENG [38745]

TUPPYN 1500-1600 NEWHAVEN, SSX, ENG [36534]

TUPYN 1500-1600 BRIGHTON, SSX, ENG [36534]

TURBERFIELD 1650S NEW HAVEN, CT, USA [38066]

TURBERT MARGARET 1880+ ATTIMANUS, LET, IRL [38233]

TURBERVILLE WILLIAM C1770-1800 BOSBURY, HEF, ENG [36633] : PRE 1780 WAR, ENG [37085]

TURBETT 1780+ LOUDOUN, AYR, SCT [35799]

TURBITT PRE 1800 LIMAVADY, LDY, IRL [36437]

TURCAN 1700+ SALINE, FIF, SCT [34420]

TURK CAROLINE 1831-1908 WARKWORTH, ONT, CAN & USA [36677] : PRE 1880 WIL & LND, ENG [37057]

TURLEY 1826+ MAITLAND, NSW, AUS [34019] : 1815-1830 TAS & NSW, AUS [34422] : PRE 1850 HANDSWORTH, STS, ENG [33958] : PRE 1850 BIRMINGHAM, WAR, ENG [33958] : 1750-1850 LAN, ENG [34422] : 1884 NEWRY, DOW, IRL [35405]

TURNBELL 1882 MARYSVILLE, YUBA CO., CA, USA [33754]

TURNBILL (SEE TURNBU [34552]

TURNBULL JOHN 1856+ ARMIDALE, NSW, AUS [35084] : 1840+ HORSHAM & MELBOURNE, VIC, NSW & NBL, AUS & ENG [35383] : 1833+ KIRKWALL, ONT, CAN [34507] : 1800-1850 STELLARTON, NS, CAN [34525] : PRE 1850 ENG [34046] : 1700-1770 KEMPSEY, WOR, ENG [34552] : 1815+ SKIPTON, WRY, ENG [34675] : PRE 1845 ALNWICK, NBL, ENG [35383] : 1850+ LONDON, ENG [35414] : ALL ILFORD, ESS, ENG [35936] : 1700S HEWORTH, DUR, ENG [36364] : PRE 1820 SIMONBURN, NBL, ENG [37663] : 1820+ EBCHESTER, NBL, ENG [37663] : 1870+ AUCKLAND, NZ [35414] : PRE 1789 GALASHIELS & SELKIRK, SEL, SCT [33806] : PRE 1850 SCT [34046] : ALL DUMFRIES, SCT [34140] : 1700+ GLASGOW, LKS, SCT [34229] : C1847 GLASGOW, LKS, SCT [34474] : PRE 1772 WILTON, ROX, SCT [34501] : PRE 1833 DARNICK, SEL, SCT [34507] : JOHN PRE 1837 GLASGOW, LKS, SCT [35084] : C1740 ANNAN, DFS, SCT [35225] : PRE 1743 ANNAN, DFS, SCT [35578] : 1767+ HADDINGTON, ELN, SCT [35921] : 1700-1850 BORDERS, SCT [36463] : 1700+ EDINBURGH, MLN, SCT [37572] : 1850-1872 COLCHESTER & MCDONOUGH, IL & IA, USA [33754] : 1850-1950 WARREN CO., IL, USA [38154] : ALL WORLDWIDE [36295]

TURNER MARK 1863+ BOGGABRI, NSW, AUS [33939] : MARK PRE 1863 LOCHINVAR, NSW, AUS [33939] : CATHERINE 1884+ NARRABRI, NSW, AUS [33939] : 1870+ ROCKHAMPTON, QLD, AUS [34021] : WILLIAM 1860+ GOLDEN GROVE & CRYSTAL BROOK, SA, AUS [34279] : JAMES 1860+ GOLDEN GROVE & CRYSTAL BROOK, SA, AUS [34279] : PRE 1890 NSW, AUS [34902] : PRE 1900 NSW, AUS [34968] : JANE PRE 1850 SYDNEY, NSW, AUS [35077] : C1850 PICTON, NSW, AUS [35203] : 1910+ BRISBANE, QLD, AUS [35808] : C1870 MORPETH, NSW, AUS [35826] : C1820 SYDNEY, NSW, AUS [35826] : WILLIAM JOHN ALL NSW, AUS [35831] : 1870-80S EMERALD HILL, VIC, AUS [36301] : 1871+ IRONMINE & COPPERHOUSE, SA, AUS [36597] : MARTHA 1860+ WINDSOR & MUDGEE, NSW, AUS [36600] : C1857 COLLINGWOOD, VIC, AUS [37302] : GEORGE 1850+ SYDNEY, NSW, AUS [37831] : EBENEZER T. 1881+ ADELAIDE, SA, AUS [37960] : 1850+ SURRY HILLS, NSW, AUS [38204] : 1849+ MELBOURNE, VIC, AUS [38753] : WILLIAM 1791+ LA & KENT CO., ONT, CAN [34154] : PRE 1752+ HALIFAX, NS, CAN [35585] : PRE 1769 CUMBERLAND, NS, CAN [36700] : WILLIAM 1890+ GREENWOOD, MAN, CAN [37444] : 1800S PORT PERRY, ONT, CAN [38418] : PRE 1820 ST PETER PORT, GSY, CHI [36696] : 1800-1850 HUDDERSFIELD, WRY, ENG [33778] : 1700-1800 BRIGHTLING, SSX & KEN, ENG [33785] : 1830+ BIRMINGHAM, WAR, ENG [33960] : PRE 1840 NEWBANK, NORTHOWRAM, WRY, ENG [34003] : 1840+ YARNSCOMBE, DEV, ENG [34075] : 1813-1900 NEWTON IN MAKERFIELD, LAN, ENG [34238] : PRE 1800 MITCHELDEAN, GLS, ENG [34258] : C1840 DENSTON, SFK, ENG [34358] : 1845 TEDDINGTON, MDX, ENG [34388] : 1700-1750 OTTERY ST MARY, DEV, ENG [34552] : PRE 1800 CHAPEL EN-LE FRITH, DBY, ENG [34588] : 1870+ BETHNAL GREEN, MDX, ENG [34710] : 1760 KIRKLAND, WES, ENG [34731] : SELINA 1840-1850S STS, ENG [34764] : C1885 CROYDON, SRY, ENG [34812] : ALL BUCKINGHAM, ENG [34838] : 1700+ LAVENHAM, SFK, ENG [34943] : 1700-1850 HOLLINGTON, SSX, ENG [34975] : C1850+ PETERBOROUGH, NTH, ENG [35163] : ALL ALFRISTON, SSX, ENG [35177] : PRE 1850 ST PANCRAS, LND, ENG [35181] : PRE 1800 WELLINGTON, SAL, ENG [35181] : 1750-1800 LONDON, ENG [35285] : 1650-1750 NUTHURST, SSX, ENG [35288] : ALFRED HENRY 1850+ HAM, LND & SRY, ENG [35362] : PRE 1855 LIVERPOOL, ENG [35384] : C1830 OXF, ENG [35414] : JAMES PRE 1880 READING, BRK, ENG [35462] : C1814 WOOLDALE, WRY, ENG [35478] : 1800S LEIGH, LAN, ENG [35505] : PRE 1750 GARBOLDISHAM, NFK, ENG [35571] : ALL SANDFORD, ESS, ENG [35577] : PRE 1800 PEASMARSH, SSX, ENG [35587] : 1750+ DEV, ENG [35603] : ALL NFK, ENG [35628] : CHARLES 1822+ WHEATHAMPSTEAD, HRT,

ENG [35634] : PRE 1550 ESS, ENG [35642] : JANE 1821 + SELMESTON, SSX, ENG [35716] : 1840S KENTISH TOWN, LND, ENG [35728] : C1832 BROMWICH, STS, ENG [35748] : ABRAHAM 1802 + ROCHDALE, LAN, ENG [35815] : 1816 HARBORNE, STS, ENG [35824] : 1816 HARBORNE, WAR, ENG [35824] : 1830 + WOLVERHAMPTON, STS, ENG [35847] : 1770 + ROTHWELL, NTH, ENG [35921] : PRE 1900 LIVERPOOL, ENG [36052] : PRE 1885 ULVERSTON, LAN, ENG [36074] : PRE 1820 BRIERLEY HILL & KINGSWINFORD, STS, ENG [36110] : PRE 1720 WALSALL & WILLENHALL, STS, ENG [36110] : 1830S WINTERBOURNE, GLS, ENG [36138] : PRE 1800 WALSALL, STS, ENG [36188] : PRE 1900 WOLVERHAMPTON, STS, ENG [36188] : 1860 BOW, MDX, ENG [36253] : C1870 BROOKENDE, ESS, ENG [36265] : 1750-1790 PERSHORE, WOR, ENG [36293] : PRE 1725 BRADFIELD, WIX & IPSWICH, ESS & SFK, ENG [36384] : C1850 NORTHOWRAM, WRY, ENG [36391] : PRE 1850 SHEFFIELD, WRY, ENG [36403] : 1600-1700 NUNEATON, WAR, ENG [36410] : 1500-1650 COLESHILL AREA, WAR, ENG [36410] : 1700-1800 HINCKLEY AREA, LEI, ENG [36410] : 1790 + HAVERHILL, SFK, ENG [36558] : PRE 1730 ST BART GREAT, MDX, ENG [36701] : 1780 KEN, ENG [36860] : JOHN 1789 ILCHESTER, SOM, ENG [36872] : C1770 WETHERDON, SFK, ENG [36945] : 1800 + LONDON, MDX, ENG [36997] : C1770 PATTISWICK, ESS, ENG [37053] : C1770 COGGESHALL, ESS, ENG [37053] : JOHN C1689 PRESTON, LAN, ENG [37103] : 1800-1850 TWICKENHAM, MDX, ENG [37166] : PRE 1820 SANDFORD & CREDITON, DEV, ENG [37195] : 1850-1900 MANSFIELD, NTT, ENG [37208] : CLARK C1820 + IPSWICH, SFK, ENG [37311] : WILLIAM CLARK C1840 + IPSWICH, SFK, ENG [37311] : JOSEPH 1837-1904 IPSWICH, SFK, ENG [37311] : 1890 + ESS, ENG [37347] : ALL LONDON &, BKM, ENG [37366] : 1795 + WALLSEND, NBL, ENG [37395] : PRE 1870 NTT, ENG [37412] : 1820 + CASTLEACRE, NFK, ENG [37483] : 1800 + SWAFFHAM, NFK, ENG [37483] : 1825 + LIVERPOOL, LAN, ENG [37500] : PRE 1785 GREAT HENNY, ESS, ENG [37568] : PRE 1800 GRAVESEND, KEN, ENG [37652] : PRE 1760 CANTERBURY AREA, KEN, ENG [37720] : PRE 1830 BILLINGSHURST, SSX, ENG [37729] : 1700 EAST DEVON, DEV, ENG [37733] : 1860S NEWINGTON, SRY, ENG [37778] : THOMAS 1800S ROTHERHAM, WRY, ENG [37831] : EDWARD 1890 + MANCHESTER, LAN, ENG [37831] : BENJAMIN 1852 PITSMOOR, WRY, ENG [37831] : 1900 + HORNCASTLE, LIN, ENG [37850] : 1700-1800 SPILSBY, LIN, ENG [37850] : C1870 HULL, ERY, ENG [37856] : PRE 1835 THURLSTONE, WRY, ENG [37893] : C1800 HEREFORD, HEF, ENG [37918] : 1827 ISLINGTON, LND, ENG [37920] : 1800 THEBERTON, SFK, ENG [37928] : 1750-1820 TAUNTON, SOM, ENG [38028] : PRE 1850 GILBERDYKE, YKS, ENG [38091] : 1850-1900 GRINTON, NRY, ENG [38244] : 1750 + BRADWORTHY, DEV, ENG [38446] : PRE 1700 ESS & DEV, ENG [38746] : ALL STS, SAL & WAR, ENG [38754] : 1770 + HOUGHTON ON THE GREEN, BKM, ENG & AUS [36642] : 1860S WESTPORT, ROSS & HOKITIKA, NZ [34680] : 1860 + WEST COAST, SI, NZ [35704] : 1860S WELLINGTON, NZ & AUS [34680] : ALL GLASGOW, LKS, SCT [34093] : PRE 1850 RATHVEN, CAI & SUT, SCT [36963] : 1790 + KILMUN & STRACHUR, ARL, SCT [37881] : 1790 + GLENFINART, ARL, SCT [37881] : 1635 ON

BOARD SHIP HOPEWELL, UK & USA [37683] : PRE 1856 NEW YORK CITY, NY, USA [35704] : 1700-1850 NEWPORT, RI, USA [36335] : ALL PERQUIMANS CO., NC, USA [36557] : FIELDING 1713 + FAIRFAX CO., VA, USA [36572] : 1900 + SAN FRANCISCO, CA, USA [37394] : CHARLES 1800-1850 SUMNER CO., TN, USA [37786] : CHARLES 1825-1850 SIMPSON CO., KY, USA [37786] : JOHN 1800-1815 LOGAN CO., KY, USA [37786] : 1810-1850 STEUBEN CO., NY, USA [38129] : AMOS 1775 + BERTIE, NC, USA [38185] : REUBIN 1780 + SUMPT, SC, USA [38185] : AMOS 1775 + G-TWN, SC, USA [38185] : 1700S SHOREHAM, VT, USA [38336] : 1630 + MA & CT, USA [38746]

TURNESS PRE 1830 LEWES & BARCOMBE, SSX & KEN, ENG [38254]

TURNEY PRE 1800 SEDGEBROOK, LIN, ENG [35548] : 1800 + LONDON, ENG [35896] : 1700-1840 IVINGHOE, BKM, ENG [37845] : 1700-1900 ANT & DOW, IRL & CAN [35630]

TURNOCK 1725 + RUGELEY, STS, ENG [34639]

TURPIE 1750 WEMYSS, FIF, SCT [33767]

TURPIGN PRE 1500 + BRIGHTON, SSX, ENG [36534]

TURPIN ALL AVOCA, VIC, AUS [35480] : 1750-1812 UPMINSTER, ESS, ENG [33787] : 1850-1875 SOUTHWARK & BERMONDSEY, SRY, ENG [34719] : ALL LEIGHTON BUZZARD, BDF, ENG [35480] : 1750-1800 LEWES, SSX, ENG [36534] : 1830 + BRIGHTON, SSX, ENG [37280] : PRE 1900 UPMINSTER, ESS, ENG [37280] : 1830 + THURROCK, ESS, ENG [37445] : ALL FRA [35617] : ALL USA [38325]

TURR ANNA 1653 HAXEY, LIN, ENG [34091] : ALL HAXEY, LIN, ENG [36635]

TURTLE ALL RYDE, NSW, AUS [33799] : ALL HAM & LND, ENG [33799] : 1700S HENLEY, OXF, ENG [36981] : PRE 1760 ANT, ARM & DOW, IRL [35897]

TURTON 1660 + ST MICHAELS, BARBADOS [38235] : PRE 1790 ABERFORD & ROTHWELL, WRY, ENG [34382] : PRE 1900 MANCHESTER, LAN, ENG [37353] : PRE 1830 YKS, ENG [37923]

TURVEY 1850 + GEELONG, VIC, AUS [38289] : PRE 1840 HAUGHTON REGIS, ENG [34633] : 1700-1823 EATON BRAY, HRT, ENG [37845]

TUSCH PRE 1860 KARLSBAD AREA, BOHEMIA, CS [36963]

TUSHAW 1760-1860 BETHNAL GREEN, LND, ENG [38516]

TUSTEN PRE 1900 WINCHCOMBE, GLS, ENG [36998]

TUSTIN 1850S ALVECHURCH, WOR, ENG [37230]

TUTCHEN 1700 + SOUTH PETHERTON, SOM, ENG [36868]

TUTFORD ALL WORLDWIDE [36172]

TUTT HERBERT C. ALL NSW, AUS [35831] : ELIZ 1861 + BRIGHTON, SSX, ENG [34247]

TUTTELL PRE 1800 POSTWICK, NFK, ENG [36037]

TUTTEN PRE 1740 IOW, ENG [36478]

TUTTLE 1830-1892 OAKLAND CO., MI, USA [37810]

TUTTY PRE 1800 ULCEBY & ALFORD, LIN, ENG [34745]

TUVE MANSSON PRE 1550 DEN [38544]

TWADDLE PRE 1770 DON, IRL [37040] : PRE 1870 STRATHAVEN, LKS, SCT [35347]

TWAITS PRE 1800 BRADENHAM, NFK, ENG [37726]

TWAMLEY 1820-1900 ONT, CAN [36935] : 1600 + BIRMINGHAM, ENG [37422] : PRE 1850 IRL [36935] : 1700 + SHILLELAGH, WIC, IRL [38385] : 1850 + CANANDAIGUA, NV, USA [36935]

TWATT PRE 1808 HARRAY, OKI, SCT [35021]

TWEEDAL 1770 + CARLISLE, CUL, ENG [37258]

TWEEDALE 1600-1750 ALMONDBURY, WRY, ENG [36635] : 1710-1764 WEST BRETTON, WRY, ENG [36635] : C1700 THORNTON IN CRAVEN, WRY, ENG [36635]

TWEEDIE 1830+ DAPTO, NSW, AUS [35358] : 1800+ JAIPUR, INDIA [36637]

TWEEDY 1795-1816 DOW, IRL [35266] : 1750-1776 CAMPBELL CO., VA, USA [36354]

TWEMLOW WILLIAM PRE 1848 YKS, ENG [34447]

TWENTYMAN 1700-1800 WORKINGTON & ALLONBY, CUL, ENG [34762] : 1650+ CARLISLE, CUL, ENG [37258] : 1750-1800 CUL, ENG [37613]

TWIBLE ALL DEN [34894] : ALL CON, ENG [34894] : ALL YKS, ENG [34894] : ALL ENG [34894] : 1700+ IRL [34894] : ALL HOLLAND, NL [34894] : ALL USA [34894] : ALL WLS & ENG [34894] : ALL WORLDWIDE [34894]

TWIDLE ALL ENG [34951]

TWIDNEY ALL ELSING, NFK, ENG [36846]

TWIGG 1890S SYDNEY, NSW, AUS [35855] : PRE 1856 BRADFIELD, WRY, ENG [34358] : 1906 HARBORNE, STS, ENG [35855] : 1874 ASTON, WAR, ENG [35855]

TWIGGER 1870+ MEADOWS, NTT, ENG [37829]

TWIGLEY 1840+ BATHURST, NSW, AUS [36305] : 1830S WAKEFIELD, WRY, ENG [36867]

TWILLEY 1785-1815 WORCESTER CO., MD & OH, USA [36546]

TWIN ALL WORLDWIDE [36500]

TWINBERROW 1790+ WOR, ENG [38020]

TWINE PRE 1850 GREAT SOMERFORD, WIL, ENG [36424] : MARY 1800+ BRIGHTON, SSX, ENG [37055]

TWINING PRE 1838 PAINSWICK, GLS, ENG [37913]

TWISS 1860+ INDIA [35377]

TWIST PRE 1890 MORPETH, NBL, ENG [34696] : THOMAS 1823+ PARR, LAN, ENG [35634]

TWITCHELL ALL CHESHAM, BKM, ENG & USA [35289]

TWOHILL 1856+ ILLAWARRA, NSW, AUS [36597] : PRE 1856 BALLINGLANNAH, COR, IRL [36597]

TWYMAN PRE 1850 KEN, ENG [36480]

TYACK 1650-1850 ST AGNES, CON, ENG [34697] : 1860+ BALDHU & TRURO, CON, ENG [34854] : 1600-1900S ST AGNES, CON, ENG [35776]

TYCE 1900S MOSS VALE, NSW, AUS [35567]

TYDEMAN 1893+ GLEBE & PADDINGTON, NSW, AUS [38277] : 1700-1850 BROCKFORD AREA, SFK, ENG [37042]

TYE 1820+ SYDNEY, NSW, AUS [34860] : PRE 1900 BIRMINGHAM, WAR, ENG [36998] : ALL WORLDWIDE [36083]

TYERMAN C1850 HARTLEPOOL, DUR, ENG [35860] : 1732-1800 FLINTHAM, NTT, ENG [38401] : PRE 1770+ SHELTON & NEWARK, NTT, ENG [38401]

TYERS C1890 AUS [36616]

TYLDESLEY C1840 LAN, ENG [34654] : ALS PHILLIPS 1700-1810 WIGAN, LAN, ENG [36587]

TYLEE 1650-1750 BATH, SOM, ENG [37233]

TYLER 1863-1865 GEELONG, VIC, AUS [34284] : 1866-1918 MELBOURNE, VIC, AUS [34284] : 1825-1858 STEPNEY, LND, ENG [34284] : C1500 ENG [34395] : WILLIAM PRE 1839 GLS, ENG [34557] : PRE 1840 BARKING, ESS, ENG [34576] : PRE 1842 WALFORD, HEF, ENG [35440] : ALL BATH & BRISTOL, SOM, ENG [35924] : PRE 1860 NEWINGTON, SRY, ENG [36019] : PRE 1860 LEI, ENG [36054] : 1750+ ESS & HRT, ENG [36123] : PRE 1890 SFK & ESS, ENG [36479] : 1800-1875 NEWINGTON, SRY, ENG [36879] : 1784 PRINCE GEORGE'S CO., MD, USA [36358]

TYLOR 1860-1990 WA, AUS [34846] : PRE 1900 PA, USA [34846]

TYMAN C1800-1900 ORSTON, NTT, ENG [38401] : 1650+ BELLERSEN, WEF, GER [35460]

TYMMS PRE 1852 LONDON, ENG [34177] : 1820S LAMBETH, LND, ENG [35728]

TYNTE C1650 IRL [34521]

TYRELL THOMAS 1807-1877 REDRUTH, CON, ENG [33892] : 1700+ LAN, ENG [34522]

TYRER 1880+ LIVERPOOL, LAN, ENG [34341] : ALL LAN, ENG [37761] : PRE 1850 RAINFORD & KIRKBY, LAN, ENG [38586]

TYRRELL 1850S RICHMOND, VIC, AUS [33934] : 1860+ BALDHU & TRURO, CON, ENG [34854] : 1800+ WATERFORD, WAT, IRL [33924] : C1885 ATHLONE, ROS, IRL [36307]

TYSOE 1850+ DUNOLLY, VIC, AUS [35448]

TYSON 1855+ LAUNCESTON, TAS, AUS [36644] : 1700S HAWKSHEAD, LAN, ENG [34053] : 1840+ LEICESTER, LEI, ENG [34241] : 1800+ GLOUCESTER & TEWEKSBURY, GLS, ENG [34241] : 1700-1800S ENNERDALE, CUL, ENG [34241] : C1800 LIVERPOOL, LAN, ENG [34274] : C1750 ESKDALE, CUL, ENG [35085] : 1560+ WHITGIFT & SHEFFIELD, YKS, ENG [35257] : 1781-1827+ WHITEHAVEN, CUL, ENG [35497] : 1840S-1860 ASHTON UNDER LYME, LAN, ENG [36319] : C1779 SHEFFIELD, YKS, ENG [36644] : PRE 1800 TEALBY, LIN, ENG [37692] : 1850-1880 DENTON CO., TX, USA [38367]

TYTHERLEIGH 1700+ DEV & SOM, ENG [35836]

TYTLER ALL PAISLEY, RFW, SCT [34263] : 1600-1800 MIDMAR, ABD, SCT [36951] : 1600+ ALFORD, ABD, SCT [36951]

TYZACK 1750-1800 S YKS, ENG [36084]

UBEL 1830-1850 PRE, GER [38150] : 1850-1910 FLORIDA, OH, USA [38150]

UBYCH PRE 1900 SIERADZ, SI, POL [38164]

UDALE ALL DFS & CUL, SCT & ENG [37396]

UDALL C1800 WIRKSWORTH, DBY, ENG [34345] : 1800S HAM & KEN, ENG [38258]

UDELL PRE 1800 WIL & SOM, ENG [37695]

UDNY 1800 CRUDEN, ABD, SCT [35369]

UERKFITZ PRE 1865 POM, GER [38235]

UFF PRE 1940 PADDINGTON & HENDON, LND, ENG [37096]

UFFINDELL 1800-1860 NEWINGTON, SRY, ENG [35285] : 1850-1900 CLERKENWELL, MDX, ENG [35285]

UGLOW 1874 ENG [35906]

UHL 1850+ MILWAUKEE CO., WI, USA [36962]

UHLHORN 1800+ OLDENBURG, OLD, GER [37116]

UHLRICH 1870+ GALENA, IL, USA [38343]

UHR PRE 1650 SWE [38561]

UIL 1786+ VEENDAM, GRO, NL [38685]

UITDENBOGERD 1800+ WORLDWIDE [34180]

UITTENBOGAARD 1700+ ZUH, NL [34180]

ULBERT PRE 1880 OES [38033]

ULENHAUT PRE 1800 BRAUNSCHWEIG, HAN, GER [36968]

ULLEY 1700-1820 ECCLESFIELD, WRY, ENG [35550]

ULM 1750S FRA & BRD [36964]

ULMER PRE 1728 PLEDELSHEIM, BAW, BRD [38509] : 1780+ GER [35190]

ULOTH ALL ALS, FRA [38677]

ULRICH ALL WEYERSHEIM, ALS, FRA [38416] : 1700-1800 ALMKE, NEINDORF, BSW, GER [36340]

ULRICI PRE 1600 REMDA WEIMAR, THU, GER [38663] : PRE 1700 LEGELSHURST, BAW, GER [38663]

UMBACK 1855+ BOMBALA, NSW, AUS [34977] : PRE 1855 FEUDENHEIM, BAD, GER [34977]

UMBERS ALL STRATFORD UPON AVON, WAR, ENG [35721]

UMNEY ALFRED 1700+ SHERRINGTON, WIL, ENG [34511]

UMPHERSTON PRE 1850 CAMBUSLANG, LKS, SCT [35810]

UMPLEBY PRE 1850 RIPLEY, YKS, ENG [35470] : ALL COLLINGHAM, WRY, ENG [35588]

UNCLE PRE 1848 MDX, ENG [33886]

UND 1830-60 WORLDWIDE [38533]

UNDERDOWN C1700-1900 UPNOR & QUEENBOROUGH, KEN, ENG [34718] : 1700+ DEV, ENG & AUS [37970]

UNDERHILL C1810 WEST BROMWICH, STS, ENG [37298] : 1600-1750 NY, USA [34123] : NAOMI 1750+ NC, USA [38374] : JOHN PRE 1815 MIAMI CO., OH, USA [38374] : JOHN 1790+ NC, USA [38374] : JOHN 1750+ WORLDWIDE [38374]

UNDERWOOD 1791 SYDNEY, NSW, AUS [33970] : 1850 MELBOURNE, VIC, AUS [34594] : 1840+ IPPOLLITTS, HRT, ENG [33920] : ALL SOM, ENG [34299] : PRE 1826 DEVIZES, WIL, ENG [34584] : PRE 1818 MELTON MOWBRAY, LEI, ENG [35572] : PRE 1860 HRT & BDF, ENG [35701] : 1821 ST IVES, HUN, ENG [35922] : 1800S ST MARGARETS, LEI, ENG [36511] : 1800-1850 ESS, ENG [37166] : 1800S LONDON, ENG [37898] : 1820+ WOODFORD, ESS, ENG & AUS [36238] : PRE 1850 GLASGOW, LKS, SCT [36583] : 1700-1900 MI, USA [38278]

UNDY PRE 1851 TAS, AUS [33786]

UNGER PRE 1860 DANZIG, PRE & HAN, GER [35205]

UNGERER PRE 1855 WUE, GER [34886]

UNICUME 1800+ CRANBROOK, KEN, ENG [37088] : ALL WORLDWIDE [37088]

UNSWORTH PRE 1857 CHORLTON ON MEDLOCK, LAN, ENG [36230] : 1800+ MANCHESTER, LAN, ENG [36257] : 1814+ MARY TAVY, DEV, ENG [36376]

UNTHANK C1800 MONKWEARMOUTH, DUR, ENG [35564] : 1800-1846 FRA [36010]

UNWIN PRE 1801 SAL, ENG [35021] : PRE 1870 STOW-CUM-QUY, CAM, ENG [36489] : PRE 1800 YOULGREAVE, DBY, ENG [37643]

UPCHURCH 1770+ ESS, ENG [36871]

UPDEGRAFF 1865-1880 KEWEENAW CO., MI, USA [38009]

UPDIKE 1640+ USA [38015]

UPFIELD ALL WORLDWIDE [35643]

UPFOLD PRE 1900 LONDON, ENG [34948]

UPHAM 1700-1990 BRIXHAM, DEV, ENG [36398] : ALL WELLINGTON, SOM, ENG & WLS [35588] : ALL WORLDWIDE [37264]

UPHAVERING 1650-1750 DAGENHAM, ESS, ENG [37670]

UPHILL 1780 BURCOMBE, WIL, ENG [34204]

UPRICHARD 1850+ BELFAST, ANT, DOW & ARM, IRL [35636]

UPRIGHT 1789 SAMPFORD COURTNEY, DEV, ENG [35282]

UPSAL 1550+ LANEHAM, NTT, ENG [34408]

UPSHALL 1830+ DOR, ENG [35631]

UPSON ALL ENG [35933]

UPSTILL 1855+ MELBOURNE, VIC, AUS [34019] : C1826 BROADWAY, SOM, ENG [34019]

UPSTONE 1700S GLS, ENG [38745]

UPTON 1853+ DONNYBROOK, VIC, AUS [35427] : 1830+ ONT, CAN [33909] : 1600-1830 PETWORTH, SSX, ENG [33909] : PRE 1875 LONDON, ENG [34948] : 1750+ BECKLEY, SSX, ENG [35157] : PRE 1828 KEN, ENG [35575] : 1800-1900 RATCLIFFE ON

WREAKE, LEI, ENG [36496] : 1740-1800S OAKTHORPE, DBY, ENG [36980] : 1740-1800S NETHERSEAL, LEI, ENG [36980] : PRE 1800 IRL [38399] : 1650 CHARLES CITY CO., VA, USA [34991]

UPWOOD ALL WORLDWIDE [37720]

URAN ALL WORLDWIDE [37408]

URBAN PRE 1760 SCHEIDT, LAHNKREIS, GER [38690]

URBANSKI ALL LIDZIANKA, VOL, SU [37041]

URCH GEORGE 1854+ MORUYA & COONAMBLE, NSW, AUS [35250] : 1894+ PERTH, WA, AUS [36645] : PRE 1880 BATTERSEA, LND, ENG [36645] : 1800+ WORLDWIDE [34724]

URCH-WILLIAMS C1880 REDFERN, NSW, AUS [34857]

URE 1830-1870S KIRKINTILLOCH, DNB, SCT [34359] : C1770 PORT MENTEITH, PER, SCT [35764] : 1720S DUNDEE, ANS, SCT [37129]

UREN 1851 ADELAIDE, SA, AUS [34595] : 1869+ ORANGE, NSW, AUS [34595] : 1883+ CLUNES, VIC, AUS [36622] : PRE 1900 MELBOURNE, VIC, AUS [38082] : PRE 1800 CON, ENG [33972] : PRE 1802 UNY LELANT, CON, ENG [34816] : RICHAD 1800+ CAMBORNE, CON, ENG [34916] : 1740+ ST HILARY, CON, ENG [35349] : 1600+ WENDRON, CON, ENG [35587] : 1840+ REDRUTH, CON, ENG [35959] : PRE 1840 WENDRON, CON, ENG [35959] : 1820 KENWYN, CON, ENG [38317] : 1800-1860 ENNIS, CLA, IRL [34769] : 1865-1880 KEWEENAW CO., MI, USA [38009] : ALL WORLDWIDE [37408]

URI PRE 1650 UR, CH [38561]

URIN ALL WORLDWIDE [37408]

URMSON 1820+ RUSHALL, STS, ENG [35584] : ALL OLDHAM & ASHTON, LAN, ENG [37732]

URNE ALL WORLDWIDE [37408]

URON ALL WORLDWIDE [37408]

URQUARDT 1700+ ISLE OF WIGHT, VA, USA [38195]

URQUEHART 1720 MD, USA [37570]

URQUHART PRE 1879 KILLARNEY, QLD, AUS [34978] : 1870+ BC, CAN [34639] : 1770-1890 KINGSTON & NORTH HATLEY, ONT & QUE, CAN & SCT [34249] : ALL GREAT YARMOUTH, NFK, ENG [37164] : PRE 1803 ARBROATH, ANS, SCT [34053] : PRE 1806 EDINBURGH, MLN, SCT [34275] : 1700-1850 KILTARLITY, INV, SCT [34639] : TOM C1770-1800 ROC, SCT [34646] : TOM C1770-1860 BAN, SCT [34646] : 1820-1840 ROSEMARKIE, ROC, SCT [34930] : PRE 1900 INV, SCT [35077] : 1780+ RESOLIS, ROC, SCT [35905] : 1870+ INV, SCT & NZ [34639]

URREN ALL WORLDWIDE [37408]

URRY PRE 1854 BRADING, IOW, ENG [35650]

URTON 1840-1860 GARRARD CO., KY, USA [36901]

URWICK ALL WORLDWIDE [37361]

URWIN 1920-1990 ENG [34249] : 1700-1990 NEWCASTLE, NBL, ENG [34249] : PRE 1900 BRUNTON, NBL, ENG [37744] : PRE 1900 WORLDWIDE [36932]

USBORNE 1770-1850 MARDEN, KEN, ENG [37880]

USCOCOAVITCH C1870 SA, AUS [37944]

USHAW PRE 1865 DRIFFIELD, ERY, ENG [34617]

USHER 1883+ SLACKS CREEK, QLD, AUS [34802] : 1820 SHEERNESS, KEN, ENG [34565] : PRE 1882 NORWICH, NFK, ENG [34802] : 1800 USWORTH, DUR, ENG [37975] : 1705 BARNBY UPON DON, WRY, ENG [38469] : 1800+ TEMPLEMORE, TIP, IRL [35951] : PRE 1850 IRL [36299] : 1800-1900 GALWAY CITY, GAL, IRL [38301] : 1860+ PATEA, TAR, NZ [35951]

USLER PRE 1795 KENWALL, CON, ENG [35441]

USSHER 1800+ TEMPLEMORE, TIP, IRL [35951] :
PRE 1850 IRL [36299] : 1800-1900 GALWAY CITY,
GAL, IRL [38301] : 1860+ PATEA, TAR, NZ [35951]

USTERWALDER ALL WORLDWIDE [38633]

UTGENANNT 1793-1805 RELLINGHAUSEN, RPR,
GER [38750]

UTT 1836-60 JERSEYVILLE, IL, USA [38151] : 1818-35
PA, USA [38151]

UTTERIDGE 1786 LANDBEACH, CAM, ENG [38209]

UTTING 1850+ CASTLEACRE, NFK, ENG [37483] :
ALL NFK, ENG [37612] : ALL KINGS LYNN, NFK,
ENG [38753] : ALL NFK, ENG [38753] : PRE 1860
LONDON & ENVIRONS, ENG [38753] : ALL
MOOLTAN, INDIA [38753] : 1859+ CAPETOWN,
CAPE, RSA [38753] : ALL WORLDWIDE [38753]

UTTON 1808+ TRIPASSOE, INDIA [34609]

UTZ 1500S GEDDELSBACH & UNTERHEIMBACH,
WUE, GER [33901] : 1800-1860 FRANKLIN CO., PA,
USA [38139]

UYTENBOGAERT 1600+ NL [34180]

UZWISZYN PRE 1900 GALICIA, POL & SU [34146]

UZZELL ALL GLS, ENG [36975] : ALL WIL, ENG
[36975] : 1790+ KEMPSFORD, GLS, ENG [36975] :
1831+ CHADDLEWORTH, BRK, ENG [36975] :
ALL WORLDWIDE [36975]

VACHER PRE 1795 MILTON ABBAS, DOR, ENG
[35252]

VACHON 1600-1700 COPECHAMIERE & VENDEE,
PCH, FRA [35649]

VAELE ALL WORLDWIDE [38159]

VAGG PRE 1887 BOOLIGAL, NSW, AUS [34968] :
PRE 1856 ENG [34968]

VAIL 1820+ HEREFORD, HEF, ENG [35998] : 1620+
SOUTHWOLD, SFK, ENG [37564] : 1618+ ENG
[37802]

VAINE C1812 SPARSHOLT, HAM, ENG [34839]

VALBRECHT ALL LONDON, ENG [38512]

VALE 1806+ RICHMOND, NSW, AUS [35759] : PRE
1850 EAST END, LND, ENG [33847] : 1800S
HOLBROOK, SFK, ENG [35377] : C1850
SHOREDITCH, LND, ENG [35708] : 1820+
HEREFORD, HEF, ENG [35998] : PRE 1900 LEEDS,
WRY, ENG [36034] : 1772 WEST STOW, SFK, ENG
[38209] : 1800-1900 IA, USA [35305] : ALL
WORLDWIDE [38159]

VALENCE 1600-1800 WIRKSWORTH, DBY, ENG
[34739] : PRE 1845 CUMNOCK, AYR, SCT [34494]

VALENDER 1755 SNOWSHILL, GLS, ENG [37827]

VALENTINE 1770-1830 FOURDOUN, KCD, SCT
[35798]

VALKS 1745-1826 SEDGEFIELD, DUR, ENG [34706] :
PRE 1705 SEDGEFIELD, DUR, ENG [35779]

VALLACK C1750 MAKER, CON, ENG [35512]

VALLANCE 1700+ OLD CUMNOCK, AYR, SCT
[36749]

VALLE C1823 GENOA, ITL [37318]

VALLEAU 1780-1820 ITHACA, NY, USA [38151]

VALLEE 1800+ MOOSE CREEK, ONT, CAN [36686]

VALLELY 1880S BRISBANE, QLD, AUS [37500]

VALLENDER ALL STOKE PRIOR & LICKEY HILLS,
WOR, ENG [37937]

VALLER ALL ENG [36221]

VALLINGS ALL ENG [34671]

VALLIS 1840-1850 MARSTON, SOM, ENG [35102] :
ALL WINCANTON, SOM, ENG [37833]

VALLOR ALL ENG [36221]

VALPY 1650+ ENG [37216]

VAN ACK 1600-1680 HAMBURG, HBG, BRD [34514]

VANADA PRE 1872 WEINGARTEN, GER [38605] :
PRE 1852 KY, USA [38605]

VAN AKKEREN PRE 1820 HARLINGEN, FRI, NL
[38694]

VAN AMBURG 1780 VA, USA [35325]

VAN APELDORN ALL NL [34478]

VAN ASSCHE 1600-1990 ONDORP BUGGENHOUT,
OVL, BEL [38165]

VAN ATTA 1790-1840 BEAVER CO., PA, USA [34882]

VANATTA JOHN 1805-32 BEAVER CO., PA, USA
[38086] : ALL WORLDWIDE [38605]

VAN AVERY MARTIN 1791-1880 SARATOGA CO.,
NJ, USA [38140]

VAN BEETHOVEN 1485-1990 GENT MECHELEN,
OVL, BEL [38165] : PRE 1725 OVL, BEL [38697]

VAN BENSCHOTEN ALL WORLDWIDE [37572]

VAN BILJON 1600+ WORLDWIDE [38378]

VAN BLOOIS 1700S DREISCHOR, ZEL, NL [38350]

VAN BOMMEL PRE 1850 DELFSHAVEN &
ROTTERD, ZUH, NL [38646]

VAN BRUCKE 1592+ HANAU, HEN, GER [38667]

VAN BRUEGGE 1592+ HANAU, HEN, GER [38667]

VAN BUREN 1700-1800 KINDERHOOK, NY, USA
[37783] : 1790-1820 OSWEGO CO., NY, USA [37783] :
O.J. 1770S KINDERHOOK, NY, USA [38038]

VAN BUSKIRK ABRAHAM 1700S HUNTERDON
CO., NJ, USA [36322]

VAN CAMP 1825 NJ, USA [37531]

VAN-CASHE C1590 MECHELEN, BBT, BEL [37706]

VANCE C1845+ HUNGERFORD & BELLEVILLE,
ONT, CAN [35466] : ALL ENG & IRL [36052] : PRE
1859 ENNISKILLEN, FER, IRL [34365] : 1800+
DUNGANNON, TYR, IRL [34970] : C1860 IRL
[37131] : 1800-1850 OGHILL, FER, IRL [37943] : PRE
1823 PAISLEY, LKS, SCT [34115] : 1884+
HELENSBURGH, DNB, SCT [37131] : 1880+ IA,
USA [35287] : 1800+ OH, USA [35287] : 1865-1875 IN,
USA [35287] : PRE 1850 FAYETTE CO., PA, USA
[38335] : CHARLES H. C1903 WACO, MCLENNAN
CO., TX, USA [38724] : ALL MILLICAN, BRAZOS
CO., TX, USA [38724] : CHARLES H. C1875
FAIRVIEW ALPHA, LA, USA [38724] : CHARLES
H. C1875 ALPHA, LA, USA [38724]

VAN CLEVE ALL WORLDWIDE [37028]

VAN CLEYNENBREUGEL 1775-1850 HOLSBEEK,
BBT, BEL [38405]

VAN COEHOORN 1550-1950 GRO, FRI & BRA, NL
[38704]

VAN CORLER 1800-1900 PUTTEN & NYKERK, GEL,
NL [34069]

VAN DAALEN PRE 1900 NL [34478]

VANDAL ANTOINE C1771 SAS, CAN [36678] :
ANTIONE C1819 SAS, CAN [36678]

VAN DAM 1840+ ZWOLLE, OIJ, NL [35338]

VAN DE AKKER ALL UTR, NL [38716]

VAN DE HORST 1835 UTR, NL [38716]

VAN DE KERKHOVE C1874 HOUSTON, TX, USA
[38166]

VAN DE MOER ALL WORLDWIDE [38350]

VAN DEN BERGE ALL NIEUWERKERK, ZEL, NL
[38694]

VAN DENBERGH ALL NY, USA [37803]

VANDENBOGAERT 1600+ NL [34180]

VAN DEN BOGAERT ALL NL & BEL [37385]

VAN DEN HEEVER 1600+ WORLDWIDE [38378]

VAN DEN HELM 1700S WERKHOVEN, UTR, NL
[38350]

VAN DE PAEREL 1700S ZUID BEVELAND, ZEL, NL
[38350]

VANDEPUT PRE 1568 ANTWERP, ATW, BEL [36880]
: HENRY 1568+ LONDON, ENG [36880]

VAN DE PUTT 1600S MILLINGEN A/D RIJN, GEL,
NL [38350]

VAN DER AVERT ALL WORLDWIDE [38170]

VAN DER AVOIRT ALL WORLDWIDE [38170]

VAN DER AVOORT ALL WORLDWIDE [38170]

VAN DER BEN 1920+ GATESHEAD, DUR, ENG [37704] : 1850-1920 MARYLEBONE, LND, ENG [37704] : PRE 1850 GOUDA, NL [37704]

VANDERBOOR PRE 1890 GRO, NL [34390]

VAN DER DAF 1600S SINT ANNALAND, ZEL, NL [38350]

VANDER EECKEN PRE 1800 OORDEGEM, FLANDERS, BEL [35173]

VAN DER FEEN 1850S SEA LAKE, VIC, AUS [35721]

VAN DER GEEST ALL WORLDWIDE [34095]

VAN DER GOES 1500-1600 NMR, MECHELIN, BEL [36943]

VAN DER GOOR 1870S STRYP, NBT, NL [35557]

VANDERGRIFF 1770+ KNOX CO., TN, USA [37004]

VANDER GROEF 1800-1850S NL [35298] : 1860-1890S KALAMAZOO, MI, USA [35298]

VAN DER HEIDE 1900+ STEDUM, GRO, NL [35753]

VANDERHEYDEN 1650-1840 ALBANY, NY, USA [34115]

VAN DER HILST 1800+ AMSTERDAM, NOH, NL [35338]

VANDERHULST ALL NL [38162]

VAN DER HULST ALL WORLDWIDE [38162]

VAN DER LINDE ALL DREISCHOR, ZEL, NL [38350]

VANDERLIP PRE 1770 PA, USA [35620]

VAN DER LOO 1870S SON, NBT, NL [35557]

VAN DER LUSDONK 1800-1850 HARDINXVELD & ROTTERDAM, ZUH, NL [37187]

VAN DER MADE 1850S AMSTERDAM, NL [33802]

VAN DER MEER 1840-1880 PIERSHIL, ZUH, NL [37187]

VAN DER MEULEN 1624+ NEW AMSTERDAM, NY, USA [36335]

VAN DER MOER ALL WORLDWIDE [38350]

VANDER MUELIN 1700-1800S LND, ENG [34887]

VAN DER NOOT PRE 1543 BBT, BEL & FRA [37623] : PRE 1543 NL [37623]

VANDERNOT 1552+ LND, ENG [37623] : 1576+ BOSTON, LIN, CAM & HUN, ENG [37623]

VAN DER PIET ALL WVL, BEL [38170]

VAN DER PIJCK 1600S COLIJNSPLAAT, ZEL, NL [38350] : 1600S GOUDA, ZUH, NL [38350]

VAN DER SAAL 1760-1800 LANCASTER CO., PA, USA [38114]

VANDERSALL 1810-1900 STARK, OH, USA [38114] : 1810-1900 WAYNE, OH, USA [38114]

VANDER SAY 1700-1800+ GER [37814]

VAN DER SCHOUTEN ALL ZUTPHEN, OIJ, NL [38694]

VANDERSLICE 1650+ BURLINGTON, NJ & PA, USA [37826]

VAN DER STELLE 1600S COLIJNSPLAAT, ZEL, NL [38350]

VAN DER VOORT 1670+ NEW YORK CITY, NY, USA & NL [37581]

VAN DER WAERT ALL ST MAARTENSDIJK, ZEL, NL [38694]

VANDERWAL SJOUKE C1850 NL [35607]

VAN DER WEELE 1700S SCHOUWEN DUIVELAND, ZEL, NL [38350]

VAN DER WERTH ALL WORLDWIDE [35310]

VAN DER WESTHUISEN ALL RSA [36456]

VAN DER WESTHUIZEN 1650S BEL [36456] : 1900S MEXICO [36456] : 1650S NL [36456] : ALL RSA [36456]

VAN DER WESTHUYSEN ALL RSA [36456]

VAN DER WESTHUYZEN ALL RSA [36456]

VANDERWOLF JAMES ALL TIARO & BUNDABERG, QLD, AUS [35122]

VAN DER ZANDT PRE 1854 MIDDELBURG, TVL, RSA [36459]

VAN DE STEEN 1730-1815 OORDEGEM, OVL, BEL [38405]

VAN DE VELDE 1487-1990 LOKEREN, OVL, BEL [38165]

VAN DE VLAG 1800-1900 PUTTEN, GEL, NL [34069]

VAN DE VOORDE 1595-1990 POEKE, OVL, BEL [38165]

VAN DE VREDE 1700S YERSEKE, ZEL, NL [38350]

VAN DE WEERD PRE 1925 GEL, NL [38351]

VAN DIEST 1760-1818 ZUH, NL [38698]

VANDIKE 1810-1990 BUCK CO., PA, USA [38308]

VAN DINGEMANS ALL NEDERL KEMPEN, NBT, NL [38170]

VAN DOLAH 1790S-1870S FAYETTE CO., PA & IL, USA [38532]

VAN DONGE 1667 KEN, ENG [35444] : 1667 CRANBROOK, KEN, ENG [35444] : 1600+ DONGEN, NL [35444]

VAN DUIJME 1600S ZIERIKZEE, ZEL, NL [38350]

VAN DUIN C1810 SASSENHEIM, ZUH, NL [38698]

VAN DUREN PRE 1900 ALKEMADE, ZUH, NL [34613]

VAN DUSEN 1845-50 NY, USA [36722]

VANDY PRE 1854 LND, ENG [36968]

VANDYBECK 1700 PINCHBECK, LIN, ENG [35369]

VAN DYKE 1790-1900S PA, USA [38308]

VANE 1825+ KELSO, NSW, AUS [35504]

VAN ELST ALL HEILOO, NOH, NL [34801]

VAN ETTEN JACOB 1821-1897 PIKE CO., PA, USA [37596]

VAN EYK 1762+ CAPE TOWN, CAPE, RSA [34947]

VANGEFFEN 1800 MAASEIK, LBG, BEL [38167]

VAN GELDEREN PRE 1750 NASSAU USINGEN, GER [38690]

VAN GENECHTEN ALL MECHELEN, ATW, BEL [36230]

VAN GINKEL 1700S AMERONGEN, UTR, NL [38350]

VANHAGEN ALL LND, ENG [37617]

VAN HAMEREN PRE 1890 ALKEMADE, ZUH, NL [34613]

VAN HET KLOOSTER 1806 SOEST, UTR, NL [38716]

VAN HOEVEN 1700-C1740S DRIEWEGEN, ZEL, NL [38350]

VAN HOLTEN 1800+ AMSTERDAM, NOH, NL [35338]

VANHOVE C1920 ARGENTINIE [38159]

VAN IDERSTINE C1753 PA, NY & NJ, USA [34096]

VAN INTHOUT C1740-1800 WEZEMAAL, BBT, BEL [38405]

VAN KOEVERINGE ALL ZUID BEVELAND, ZEL, NL [38350]

VAN KOOIJ 1750 LEERSUM, UTR, NL [38716]

VAN LEER 1750 OVERLANGBROEK, UTR, NL [38716]

VAN LEUKEN ALL DE PEEL, NBT, NL [38703]

VAN LEUSEN PRE 1790 NYEVEEN, OIJ, NL [36283]

VAN LIEROP ALL EMMERICH, REES, GER [37569] : PRE 1730 HAARLEM, NOH, NL [37569] : 1880-1900 PARAMARIBO, SURINAM [37569]

VAN LIEWEN C1660 LONG ISLAND, NY, USA [34573]

VAN LIJNDEN 1300-1800 GEL, NL [36682]

VAN LOAN 1650-1850 NY, USA [38113]

VAN MATRE 1790-1850 HIGHLAND CO., OH, USA [38108]

VAN MEURS PRE 1830 ALKEMADE, ZUH, NL [34613]

VAN MOURIK 1852 UTR, NL [38716]

VAN MUIJLAERTS PRE 1725 OVL, BEL [38697]

VANN 1900+ BIRMINGHAM, WAR, ENG [36521] : 1900+ NOTTINGHAM, NTT, ENG [36521] : PRE 1830 ASTON & BIRMINGHAM, WAR, ENG [37325]

VAN NESS 1839 FLORENCE, AL, USA [37799]
VAN NIEKERK 1600+ WORLDWIDE [38378]
VAN NIEUWENHUISEN PRE 1700 NL [34478]
VAN NIMWEGEN PRE 1820 ZEIST, UTR, NL [38694]
VAN NOORT 1703-1987 SASSENHEIM, ZUH, NL [38711]
VAN NUFFEL 1400-1990 AALST, OVL, BEL [38165]
VAN OEIJ 1700S KEKERDOM, GEL, NL [38350]
VAN OGTEN 1700S UTRECHT, UTR, NL [38350]
VAN OOSTEN 1775+ LEER, NDS, BRD [38685] : 1774 MAASSLUIS, ZUH, NL [38163]
VAN OOSTERDIJK ALL WORLDWIDE [38350]
VAN OTTERLOO PRE 1900 NL [34478]
VAN OVERVELD 1708 RUCPHEN, NBT, NL [38715]
VAN PATTEN ALL NY, USA [37787]
VAN PEE ALL BRA, BEL [38169]
VAN PUYENBROECK 1580-1990 ST NIKLAAS, OVL, BEL [38165]
VANQUELIN (SEE VAUGE [37654]
VAN REEDE 1450-1550 DEVENTER, OIJ, NL [36682] : 1540-1650 UTRECHT, UTR, NL [36682] : 1550-1750 AMERONGEN, UTR, NL [36682] : 1350-1550 SAESFELD, OIJ, NL [36682]
VAN RESPAILLE ALL WORLDWIDE [38162]
VAN RHIJNBERK 1750-1850 ZOELMOND, GEL, NL [36682] : 1830-1880 BEUSICHEM, GEL, NL [36682] : PRE 1770 BUREN, GEL, NL [36682]
VAN RIJNSOEVER 1802 UTR, NL [38716]
VAN ROOIJ C1774 APELDOORN, GEL, NL [38698]
VANROOSE 1600-1990 OOSTENDE, WVL, BEL [38165]
VAN RYSSEGHEM C1910 DETROIT, MI, USA [38166]
VANSAC 1879-1953 FARRELL & MERCER, PA, USA & CZEC [38063]
VAN SCHAFTEN 1786-1816 ZWARTSLUIS, OIJ, NL [34398]
VAN SCHAICK 1680 NY, USA [38143]
VANSLYKE 1850+ ELGIN CO., ONT, CAN [34480]
VAN SLYKE 1810+ EAST, ONT, CAN [34480] : C1800 HUDSON MOHAWK, NY, USA [34480]
VAN SON PRE 1900 NL [38159]
VAN SPANJE ALL WORLDWIDE [37461]
VAN STEENIS 1750-1820 ERICHEM, GEL, NL [36682] : PRE 1730 METEREN, GEL, NL [36682] : 1770-1800 ASCH, GEL, NL [36682] : 1700-1750 GELDERMALSEN, GEL, NL [36682] : 1800-1850 BUREN, GEL, NL [36682]
VANSTON C1870 LANCEFIELD, VIC, AUS [35434] : C1820 MONTREATH, LEX, IRL [35434] : PRE 1959 DUBLIN, IRL [35521]
VANSWERINGEN 1667-1736 ST MARY'S CO., MD, USA [37029]
VANT ALL YKS, ENG [35176] : PRE 1830 KEN, ENG [36255] : 1600-1681 PARIS, RPA, FRA [34514]
VAN TEXEL 1600 ISLE OF TEXEL, HOLLAND, NL [37501]
VAN THIL PRE 1850 BERGSCHENHOEK, ZUH, NL [38646]
VAN TRICHT 1800+ HAAFTEN, NL [33769]
VAN TRUMP ALL WORLDWIDE [38196]
VAN'T SPIJKER 1700+ HASSELT, OIJ, NL [35338]
VAN UTTERBEEK ALL ATW, BEL [38169]
VAN VALKENBUGH 1770+ KINDERHOOK, NY, USA [34408]
VAN VALKENBURG 1700-1850 KINDERHOOK, NY, USA [37783]
VAN VECHELEN ALL THOLEN, ZEL, NL [38694]
VAN VECHTEN ALL NL [37803] : ALL NY, USA [37803]
VAN VELZOR PRE 1800 NL [35165]
VAN VLEET ALL WORLDWIDE [35289]

VAN VLIET ALL AMSTERDAM, NL [36894] : ALL UTR, NL [38716]
VAN VOLKENBURG 1750-1850 ERIE, NY, USA [38194]
VAN WAES C1920 ARGENTINIE [38159]
VAN WART ALL WORLDWIDE [35924]
VAN WEEREN ALL LEIDEN, ZUH, NL [38705]
VAN WIEREN 1768 RECHTEREN DALFSEN, OIJ, NL [34398]
VAN WINKLE ALL BENTON, NY & NJ, USA [38522]
VAN WINSEN C1805 MAARSSEN, UTR, NL [38698]
VAN WOERT 1830-1850 SARATOGA CO., NY, USA [36444] : 1870 BUTTE CO., CA, USA [36444]
VANWOLLEGHEM ALL MOORSELE, WVL, BEL [38164]
VAN WORMER 1780-1880 ALBANY & ADAMS, NY, USA [38537]
VAN WORTH PRE 1863 USA [37787]
VAN WOUDENBERG ALL NL [38701] : ALL UTR, NL [38716]
VAN WYCK 1860+ TORONTO, ONT, CAN [34474]
VANZA 1800+ BIASCO, TI, CH [37116]
VANZANDT 1800-1870 ALBANY CO., NY, USA [37591]
VAN ZANT 1800S METCALFE CO., KY, USA [38108]
VAN ZEE PRE 1850 NL [38769]
VAN ZEGUE 1600-1680 HAMBURG, HBG, BRD [34514]
VAN ZELDEN 1700S AMERONGEN, UTR, NL [38350]
VAN ZIJP C1710 VALKENBURG, ZUH, NL [38698]
VAN ZIJTVELD ALL NL [34478]
VARDAMAN 1750-1800 NEWBERRY CO., SC, USA [38088]
VARDON PRE 1845 JSY, CHI [37760]
VARDY PRE 1881 STOKE NEWINGTON, MDX, ENG [34031] : 1800-1870 HEXHAM, NBL, ENG [37419]
VARE 1700S SOUTH STONEHAM, HAM, ENG [34709]
VARGA PRE 1800 SZENDROLAD, BORSOD, HU [37547]
VARLEY PRE 1772 SELBY & KIRKBY WHARFE, WRY, ENG [36039] : 1930-1952 ACTON, MDX, ENG [37657] : 1952-1980 BRENTFORD, MDX, ENG [37657] : MOSES C1770-1850 ENG [37679] : ALL HALIFAX & BRADFORD, WRY, ENG [37679] : WILLIAM 1836-1899 SOUTH LEEDS, WRY, ENG [37887] : GEORGE 1869-1933 SOUTH LEEDS, WRY, ENG [37887] : WILLIAM 1759-1845 MOORALLERTON, LEEDS, WRY, ENG [37887] : ALL WORLDWIDE [36789]
VARLOW C1800 GLS, ENG [37698]
VARNADO AGNES 1849 PIKE, MS, USA [37801] : RACHEAL C1812 MS, USA [37801]
VARNDALL PRE 1837 LURGASHALL, SSX, ENG [37771]
VARNELL 1700+ BRIXHAM, DEV, ENG [36000]
VARNER 1700-1800 IRL [38065] : 1800-1880 TN, USA [38576]
VARNEY 1700-1900 ST ALBANS, HRT, ENG [38073] : PRE 1812 NY, USA [37795]
VARNHAGEN ALL WORLDWIDE [38638]
VARNUM C1776 VA, USA [36319]
VARTH PRE 1850 PITTSBURG, PA, USA [34410]
VARTY 1800S CUL, ENG [34509]
VARVILL ALL ERY, ENG [34728] : ALL LND, ENG [34728] : ALL NFK, ENG [34728] : ALL WORLDWIDE [34728]
VASHON ALL MIDLANDS, ENG [35649]
VASS 1900+ AUS [37500] : PRE 1800 NIGG, ROC, SCT [34192] : 1800+ INVERESK & EDINBURGH, SCT [35015] : 1730+ MOR, SCT [37794] : PRE 1700 UK [34327] : PRE 1700 WORLDWIDE [34327]

VASSALL ALL WORLDWIDE [37378]

VASSELL 1760 QUEEN ANNE CO., MD, USA [38143]

VASSIE PRE 1841 KENSINGTON, MDX, ENG [34043]

VASTBINDER PRE 1744 BENDORF, RPR, GER [37811]

VASTIERS ALL WORLDWIDE [38681]

VATCHER 1800S CROCKERS COVE NR CARBENEER, NFD, CAN [37818] : 1855 BLANDFORD, DOR, ENG [35252] : 1800S LND, ENG [37497]

VATT 1800+ BATH, SOM, ENG [35566]

VAUDIN ALL CHI [36890]

VAUGELIN 1700-1800 NORMANDIE, FRA [37654] : 1700-1830 CALCUTTA, BENGAL, INDIA [37654]

VAUGEOIS ALL HN, FRA [34061]

VAUGHAN 1850S MORPETH, NSW, AUS [35123] : 1828+ AUS [35241] : 1884+ RIVERSTONE, NSW, AUS [35569] : 1841+ GEELONG, VIC, AUS [36296] : 1854+ NSW, AUS [36299] : 1800-1840 BROAD COVE, NFD, CAN [33852] : 1820-1990 BEAUHARNOIS DIST, QUE, CAN [34377] : 1800-1850 BRIDGNORTH, SAL, ENG [33767] : 1835-1849 BARNSTAPLE, DEV, ENG [33795] : PRE 1849 TIVERTON, DEV, ENG [33795] : PRE 1849 APELDORE, DEV, ENG [33795] : 1700+ NEWENT, GLS, ENG [35138] : 1750+ WOR, ENG [35241] : PRE 1860 YKS, ENG [35331] : 1815-1838 ASHTON UNDER LYNE, LAN, ENG [35569] : C1830-1860 LEWISHAM, KEN, ENG [35726] : 1857+ SEVENOAKS, KEN, ENG [35726] : PRE 1790 RUSPER, SSX, ENG [35764] : PRE 1815 SLAUGHAM, SSX, ENG [35764] : 1800+ RUYTON, SAL, ENG [36135] : PRE 1850 WHITTINGTON, SAL, ENG [36385] : PRE 1839 SOUTHAMPTON, HAM, ENG [36993] : PRE 1850 TIPTON, STS, ENG [37357] : ALL MDX, ENG [37682] : 1750-1840 SOHO, MDX, ENG [37765] : PRE 1850 NENAGH, TIP, IRL [34025] : PRE 1835 KILKENNY, KIK, IRL [34368] : 1814 CLONDERMOT, LDY, IRL [35123] : 1818+ CASL, COR, IRL [36296] : PRE 1854 CLA & MAY, IRL [36299] : 1790S NENAGH, TIP, IRL [37106] : PRE 1880 DUNSFORT & KILLOUGH, DOW, IRL [37405] : 1840+ PITTSBURGH, PA, USA [34827] : 1800S SCHOHARIE CO., NY, USA [37490] : ALL PENRHIWCEIBER, GLA, WLS [35391] : 1760+ ALBERBURY, MGY, WLS [35719] : PRE 1760 ALBERBURY, MGY, WLS [35719] : 1750+ LLANGATTOCH, MON, WLS [35886] : PRE 1880 MON, WLS [35895] : ALL WORLDWIDE [35875]

VAUGHAN-BROOKMAN PRE 1919 SWINDON, WIL, ENG [35141]

VAUGHN 1828+ AUS [35241] : 1750+ WOR, ENG [35241] : PRE 1820 WOLVERHAMPTON, STS, ENG [36270] : ALL COLEFORD, GLS, ENG [36359] : 1680-1850 LANCASTER, PA, USA [35300] : C1850 CALOWELL CO., KY, USA [37527] : ALL TN, USA [37593] : 1851-1870 KEWEENAW CO., MI, USA [38009]

VAUGHT ALL VA & WV, USA [37036]

VAUPEL PRE 1841 WUPPERTAL, RPR, GER [38647]

VAUQUELIN PRE 1665 CAEN-FLERS, BN, FRA [36972]

VAUSTON PRE 1822 CAR, IRL [35557]

VAUX 1705-1850S SEDGEFIELD, DUR, ENG [34706] : PRE 1757 SOUTH PETHERTON, SOM, ENG [35252]

VAUX (SEE VALKS) [35779]

VAVASOR ALL WORLDWIDE [37084]

VAVASOUR ALL WORLDWIDE [37084]

VAYL 1820+ HEREFORD, HEF, ENG [35998]

VEAL PRE 1820S ALWINGTON, DEV, ENG [33780] : PRE 1608 ST JUST, CON, ENG [34043] : PRE 1850

CON, ENG [34615] : 1800+ BRISTOL, GLS, ENG [35715]

VEALE PRE 1874 DARTMOUTH, CON, ENG [35441] : PRE 1600 IRON ACTON, GLS, ENG [37154] : ALL ENG [37827] : PRE 1860 INWARDLEIGH, DEV, ENG [38418] : PRE 1928 TE AROHA, NZ [34663]

VEALS PRE 1850 WOR, ENG [34383]

VEAR 1850+ SOUTHAMPTON, HAM, ENG [33857] : 1700S SOUTH STONEHAM, HAM, ENG [34709]

VEASEY 1800+ DUNCHURCH, WAR, ENG [34315]

VEAZY 1830 WARREN, GA, USA [36946]

VEEDER ADELIA 1818-1847 IL, USA [38124]

VEENSTRA HENDRIK ANNES C1850 NL [35607] : LIEPPE 1880 WIERINGEN, NOH, NL [35607]

VEFFUER 1625-1700 TAARNBORG, SORO, DEN [37547]

VEICHARD C1700-1870 COPENHAGEN, DEN [37642]

VEICKERT C1700-1870 COPENHAGEN, DEN [37642]

VEIT ALL MAGDEBURG DRESDEN, GER [35767]

VEITCH 1833+ GEELONG, VIC, AUS [36271] : 1800S LONDON, ENG & SCT [37539] : C1810 KIRKURD, PEE, SCT [34515] : C1837 GOREBRIDGE, MLN, SCT [35057] : 1800+ EDINBURGH, SCT [36271] : PRE 1833 EDINBURGH, SCT & AUS [35381] : 1850-1990 KY & OH, USA [37539]

VEKEY ALL TOKAJ, HU & AUS [37287]

VELACOTT ALL WEST BUCKLAND, DEV, ENG [35222]

VELDEN VAN DE 1817-1916 BOUCHAUTE & ROTTERDAM, NH, BEL & NL [38712]

VELENSKI PRE 1900 STANSLAW, GER & POL [33966]

VELINDER 1755 WINCHCOMBE, GLS, ENG [37827]

VELLENOWETH 1790+ GULVAL & MADRON, CON, ENG [35208]

VELT ALL WORLDWIDE [38329]

VENABLES 1800-1860 WAMBROOK, NSW, AUS [36315] : 1800-1900 ADAMINABY, NSW, AUS [36315] : 1785+ BIRMINGHAM, WAR, ENG [37762] : 1300-1500 BOLLIN, CHS, ENG [38216] : PRE 1800 RAD, PEM & STS, WLS & ENG [38461]

VENES ELEANOR 1813-1889 BRIGHTLING, SSX, ENG [38397]

VENESS PRE 1850 BRIGHTLING, SSX, ENG [36612]

VENIN 1650S THORNEY ABBEY, CAM, ENG [34204]

VENIS PRE 1800 DANBY, YKS, ENG [36481]

VENN 1880+ LONDON, ENG [33960] : C1800 EXETER, DEV, ENG [34151]

VENNAL PRE 1800 SSX, ENG [37875]

VENNARD PRE 1830 ANT, IRL [34090] : PRE 1830 ARM, IRL [34090]

VENNELL PRE 1853 BATH, WIL, ENG [34191]

VENNELS ALL KEN, ENG [36041]

VENNESS 1880S STRATFORD ON AVON, WAR, ENG [35066]

VENTER PRE 1900 ROTH, RPF, BRD [35311]

VENTERS PRE 1837 BURNTISLAND, FIF, SCT [35223]

VENTOM 1700-1800 LONDON, ENG [36081]

VENTRESS 1730-1835 LOFTUS, YKS, ENG [37011]

VENUS C1600 NAUNDORF, ERF, DDR [38677]

VERALDI 1800S TAVERNA, CATANZARO, ITL [34371]

VERBICKUS PRE 1900 PIJAVONIS, LITHUANIA [37496]

VERBIST 1860-1875 ANTWERP, BEL [36116] : C1890 LONDON, ENG [36116]

VERBRUEGGEN 1592+ HANAU, HEN, GER [38667]

VERCOE 1841 ROCHE, CON, ENG [34120] : PRE 1841 ST MAWES, CON, ENG [35898] : PRE 1860 MERTHER, CON, ENG [36272]

VERDINE 1845-1855 KEWEENAW CO., MI, USA [38009]

VERDON ALL CLA & GAL, IRL [38084] : ALL WORLDWIDE [37688]

VERDUN 1845-1855 KEWEENAW CO., MI, USA [38009]

VERE C1635 KEN, ENG [34568] : 1700-1785 MARY TAVY, DEV, ENG [38459] : 1700-1785 TAVISTOCK, DEV, ENG [38459] : 1730-1780 ABERDEEN, SCT [38459]

VERGE ALL ENGLISH HARBOUR TRINITY, NFD, CAN [34093]

VERHAEF 1700-1990 MAARSSEVEEN, UTR, NL [38713]

VER HAEGEN 1600-1990 OUDEGEM, OVL, BEL [38165]

VERHOEVEN PRE 1661 BAARLE HERTOG, ATW, BEL [35008] : 1800-1900 BIENGEMEBEN, NL [38337]

VERHOOSEL ALL NL [38159]

VERHOOSELE ALL WORLDWIDE [38159]

VERIOD ALL WORLDWIDE [34712]

VERIOTT ALL WORLDWIDE [34712]

VERITY 1850 DUKINFIELD, CHS, ENG [37299]

VERMAZEN C1700 HEEREWAARDEN, GEL, NL [38705]

VERMEER ALL NL [33751] : ALL NL [38692] : ALL WORLDWIDE [33751] : ALL WORLDWIDE [38692]

VERMEESCH 1850+ NEWTOWN, NSW, AUS [38582] : JEAN LOUIS 1825-1840 FRA [38724]

VERMESH JEAN LOUIS 1825-1840 FRA [38724]

VERMEULEN 1830-1900 HERENTHOUT, ATW, BEL [38405]

VERNDELL C1774 ALVERSTOKE, HAM, ENG [37168]

VERNEY PRE 1800 FRITHLESTOCK, DEV, ENG [35032]

VERNIER 1600-1680 VITRY LE FRANCOIS, CHA, FRA [34514]

VERNON 1865-1900 WILLIAMSTOWN, VIC, AUS [34191] : ALL VIC, AUS [35707] : 1880-1900 NSW, AUS [36663] : 1600 CHS, ENG [33910] : WILLIAM PRE 1850 BRISTOL, GLS, ENG [34963] : JOHN C1858 STARCROSS, DEV, ENG [34963] : HENRY PRE 1820 SOUTH MOLTON, DEV, ENG [34963] : ARTHUR C1854 BRISTOL, GLS, ENG [34963] : HENRHYNN 1850+ LONDON & SOUTHERN COUNTIES, ENG [35106] : ANN PRE 1817 AUDLEM, CHS, ENG [35778] : THOMAS 1840-1860 CHELSEA, LND, ENG [36018] : PRE 1830 WOLVERHAMPTON & BILSTON, STS, ENG [36110] : 1750-1800 TIBBERTON, GLS, ENG [36663] : 1800+ GNOSALL, STS, ENG [37608]

VERRALL JANE PRE 1870 BRIGHTON, SSX, ENG [34247] : PRE 1844 EASTBOURNE & HAILSHAM, SSX, ENG [34706]

VERRAN 1800+ VERYAN & ST BLAZEY, CON, ENG [37905]

VERRELL PRE 1800 LEWES, SSX, ENG [36589]

VERRET PRE 1850 QUE, CAN [34106]

VERRIER 1856+ ALBERTON, SA, AUS [34595] : ALL PAULTON, SOM, ENG [34595] : PRE 1612 LITTLEBOURNE & SUTTON, KEN, ENG [36532]

VERRY 1800S BRK, ENG & NZ [36607]

VERSCHOYLE 1770-1840 DUBLIN, IRL [38054]

VERSTEEGEN 1782+ ELDRIK, GEL, NL [38350]

VERSTREPEN PRE 1700 BORGERHOUT, OVL, BEL [38697]

VERTY 1600+ OUSBY & LANGWATHBY, CUL, ENG [36701]

VESEBACKER C1775 NUSSLOCH, BAD, GER [34239]

VESEY 1800-1842 MAY, IRL [38180] : 1870 DALLES, IN & OR, USA [36899]

VESSEY 1800-1880 OWMBY & PANTON, LIN, ENG [34329]

VESSHOFF ALL HUESTEN & LETMATHE, WEF, GER [34861]

VESTER PRE 1800 SCT & ENG [38356]

VETCH 1880-1950 LONDON & NEWCASTLE, NBL, ENG [34249]

VETCHER 1855+ BLANDFORD, DOR, ENG [35252]

VETT PRE 1857 ANGELTHURN, BAD, GER [37819]

VETTER 1850S AUS [36289] : ALL AURICH, VAIHINGEN, WUE, BRD [37045] : ALL BAD, GER [36532] : ALL NEUDORF, GALACIA, OES [37045]

VEVERS 1800-1900 CASTLETON, ROX, SCT [37396]

V.EWYK ALL WESTBROEK, LITR, NL [33751]

V. EWYK ALL WESTBROEK, UTR, NL [38692]

VEYLL MARIA PRE 1823 PLUDERHAUSEN, GER [36453]

VEYSEY PRE 1780 RACKENFORD, DEV, ENG [35866] : PRE 1780 CREACOMBE & WITHERIDGE, DEV, ENG [35866]

VIAL 1800+ KENWYN, CON, ENG [38292]

VIALL PRE 1850 CRAMBOURNE, CON, ENG [36766]

VIBEY ALL WORLDWIDE [35489]

VICARS 1830-1900 BISHOP AUCKLAND, DUR, ENG [33991] : 1793 LITTLEOVER, DBY, ENG [34120]

VICARY 1820-1870S WINDSOR, NSW, AUS [35785] : 1775-1900 BLACK DOG, DEV, ENG [34232] : 1700-1800S BROAD CLYST, DEV, ENG [35785] : PRE 1860 OTTERY ST MARY, DEV, ENG [36113] : 1800-1900 BLACK DOG, DEV, ENG [38456]

VICCARS ALL ENG [37738]

VICKARS PRE 1700 BASLOW, DBY, ENG [37875]

VICKERAGE 1800S SOM, ENG [34298]

VICKERMAN PRE 1860 BRIDLINGTON, NRY, ENG [36759] : 1700+ BRIDLINGTON, ERY, ENG [37443]

VICKERS PRE 1700 MUGGINTON, DBY, ENG [34311] : GEORGE 1813 WARDLE & BUNBURY, CHS, ENG [35120] : 1800-1860 NEWINGTON, SRY, ENG [35285] : 1800S PENRITH, CUL, ENG [35377] : PRE 1860 CHS & LAN, ENG [36363] : PRE 1800 MANCHESTER, LAN, ENG [37913] : 1700+ BOLTON, LAN, ENG [38034] : 1700S BUCKS CO., PA, USA [36926] : PRE 1850 COPIAH CO., MS, USA [38783]

VICKERY 1900S CHARTERS TOWERS, QLD, AUS [37178] : PRE 1630 ENG [34162] : 1847 WELLINGTON, SOM, ENG [34224] : PRE 1900 MDX, ENG [36893] : 1850+ MARWOOD, DEV, ENG [37178] : PRE 1800 BIRMINGHAM, WAR, ENG [37736] : PRE 1830 BRISTOL, ENG [38289] : 1800-1900 BLACK DOG, DEV, ENG [38456] : 1630-1700 PLYMOUTH, MA, USA [34162] : 1640-1700 HULL, MA, USA [34162]

VICKLEY JANE 1810+ MANCHESTER, LAN, ENG [37748]

VIDAL 1846+ DENHAM COURT, NSW, AUS [35141] : PRE 1860 JAMAICA [34519] : 1760+ KINGSTON, JAMAICA, W.INDIES [35141]

VIDETTO PRE 1720S MA, CT & NY, USA [37522]

VIDLER JAMES &SYLVIA C1830 TICEHURST, SSX, ENG [34810] : 1700-1850 TICEHURST, SSX & KEN, ENG [35394]

VIECK PRE 1850 BRA & MST, GER [38648]

VIELEMEYER 1800-1900 GER [36589]

VIETCH PRE 1930 SHEETRIM, IRL [38226] : 1800+ PEEBLES, PEE, SCT [38288]

VIETH ALL KOBLENZ, RPR, GER [38637] : ALL AACHEN, WEF, GER [38637] : ALL RECKLINGHAUSEN, WEF, GER [38637] : PRE 1780 SOLINGEN, RPR, GER [38647]

VIGARS 1800S TAVISTOCK, DEV, ENG [34871] :
ARTHUR 1780+ LAMBERTON, DEV, ENG [35471]
: C1831 TAVISTOCK, DEV, ENG [37302]

VIGERS 1800+ DEV, ENG [38540]

VIGGERS ALL BARNET, HRT, ENG [35901]

VIGNERON PRE 1594 GENEVA, GE, CH [38348]

VIGNOLA 1756 WORLDWIDE [38364]

VIGOR PRE 1800 BURWASH, SSX, ENG [34655] :
1600-1750 HEMINGTON, SOM, ENG [35288] : ALL
KEN & E SSX, ENG [37714]

VIKERY 1800-1900 BLACK DOG, DEV, ENG [38456]

VILLANEUVA PRE 1868 CANDABA, PAMPANGA,
PHILIPPINE [34891]

VILLANOVA 1750-1850 HUESCA, ESP [36937]

VILLARREAL FRANCISCO 1820S MALAGA,
ANDALUSIA, ESP [35471]

VILLERAY ROUER DE 1500S TOURAINE, FRA
[35617]

VILLEROY DUKES OF 1600+ VILLEROY, FRA
[36756]

VILLERS ALL WAR, ENG [38514] : PRE 1840 ARM,
IRL [33954]

VILLIERS PRE 1830 FRA [34090] : 1800+ WLS [34568]

VILLIS PRE 1780 IOW, ENG [36478] : C1750 IOW,
ENG [38700]

VILLMAN 1822+ LOVIISA, UUSIMAA, FIN [38758]

VINCE 1800S ELLINGHAM, NFK, ENG [35046] : 1810
NFK & WA, ENG & AUS [37888]

VINCENT 1876+ ROEBOURNE, WA, AUS [34530] :
1849-1937 FREMANTLE & ADELAIDE, WA & SA,
AUS [34530] : 1796+ FREMANTLE, WA, AUS
[34530] : 1860S BALLARAT, VIC, AUS [34793] :
1845+ THE ROCK, NSW, AUS [35203] : C1857
SANDHURST, VIC, AUS [35885] : C1870 WAGGA
WAGGA, NSW, AUS [37500] : 1865+ ADELAIDE,
SA, AUS [38209] : H.E. 1850S SOUTHALL, LND,
ENG [33949] : PRE 1850 SOM, ENG [34131] : 1796+
DOR, ENG [34530] : 1730-1830 GWENNAP, CON,
ENG [34793] : 1711 STITHIANS, CON, ENG [34793] :
PRE 1855 TRURO, CON, ENG [34875] : PRE 1750
NORTH LOPHAM, NFK, ENG [35157] : PRE 1838
DEWLISH, DOR, ENG [35203] : PRE 1801
CHATHAM, KEN, ENG [35561] : 1790S
WANSTROW, SOM, ENG [35815] : C1650-1730 ENG
[36289] : 1750-1800 ENG [36688] : ALL NORWICH,
NFK, ENG [37612] : PRE 1900 WILLINGTON,
DUR, ENG [37899] : 1700-1800 GLASTONBURY,
SOM, ENG [37924] : C1840 BROADWINDSOR,
DOR, ENG [37983] : 1885+ SKEFFINGTON, LEI,
ENG [37983] : 1750+ FLETCHING & BRIGHTON,
SSX, ENG [38209] : 1776 EDMONTON, MDX, ENG
[38469] : ALL CON & DEV, ENG [38735] : 1800+
BATH, SOM, ENG & AUS [36835] : 1846+
HAMILTON & CAMBRIDGE, WAIKATO, NZ
[36835] : 1850S GLASGOW, LKS, SCT [37983] : 1890S
DENHAM SPRINGS, LA, USA [36543] : C1822
HARTSVILLE, STEUBEN CO., NY, USA [38172]

VINCZE PRE 1772 RUDABANYA, BORSOD, HU
[37547]

VINE 1700+ ST ERTH & NEWLYN EAST, CON,
ENG [35235] : C1800 ST JUST, CON, ENG [35375] :
PRE 1760 NJ, USA [34205]

VINES 1855+ GEELONG, VIC, AUS [37300] : PRE
1860 ENG [34958] : 1799-1850 LITTLETON DREW,
WIL, ENG [35839] : 1730S-1800 BRINKWORTH,
WIL, ENG [35839] : PRE 1850 BRINKWORTH, WIL,
ENG [37300] : 1790+ READING, BRK, ENG [37300]
: 1700-1900 BRINKWORTH, WIL, ENG [37403] :
1800-1850 LITTLETON DREWW, WIL, ENG [37403]
: ALL NFK, ENG [37612] : PRE 1860 MAURITIUS
[34958]

VINEY 1820+ PEEL, YORK, ONT, CAN [34982] : ALL
ENG [37705]

VINICOMBE 1600+ NEWTON ST CYRE &
SHOBROOKE, DEV, ENG [34747]

VINING 1880+ SPRING FARM, GOODNA, QLD,
AUS [33782] : 1870+ BATH, SOM, ENG [35461] :
1643-1743 MIDDLESEX CO., MA, USA [38088]

VINK ALL NOORDWYK, ZUH, NL [38703]

VINNECOMBE 1900+ LONDON, ENG [35783]

VINNICOMBE PRE 1900 CON, ENG [35783]

VINSON 1860+ BRISBANE & TOOWOOMBA, QLD,
AUS [35442] : 1700-1850 NEWPORT, RI, USA [36335]

VINSONHALER 1825 BERKELEY CO., WV, USA
[35266]

VINTON CAROLINE 1800S ROCHESTER, KEN,
ENG [34499] : 1800S DON, IRL [37818] : JOHN 1656
LYNN, MA, USA [35273]

VINZANT 1700-1800 FRA [38324] : 1780-1820 NC, USA
[38324] : 1790-1830 OH, USA [38324] : 1700-1800 MD,
USA [38324] : 1700-1800 GA, USA [38324] : ALL
WORLDWIDE [38324]

VINZEL ALL WORLDWIDE [38613]

VIOBLET PRE 1840 VAUFFELIN, BE, CH [36405]

VIOLETT 1700 PRINCE WILLIAM CO., VA, USA
[37582]

VIPOND PRE 1830 COLNE, LAN, ENG [35490] : PRE
1830 KENDAL, WES, ENG [35490]

VIRCOE 1840S ROSS, TAS, AUS [35501]

VIRET 1920+ MONTREAL, QUE, CAN [37623] : PRE
1773 WHEATFIELD & TETSWORTH, OXF & LND,
ENG [37623]

VIRGO ALL ONT, CAN [33909] : 1780-1884
WESTBURY ON SEVERN, GLS, ENG [37118] : PRE
1800 CHIDDINGSTONE, KEN, ENG [38700]

VIRR 1700-1800 BEL [37779] : 1750-1800 YORK, YKS,
ENG [37779] : 1700-1800 NL [37779]

VIRTUE 1840+ MARYBOROUGH, VIC, AUS [35868]

VISSCHER ALL VOLLENHOVE, OIJ, NL [38705]

VISSER JOHANNESZ C1715 GRAAUW, ZEL, NL
[38706]

VITLER PRE 1860 HOVE, SSX, ENG [37325]

VITTY C1800 CAMBRIDGE, CAM, ENG [35032]

VITULI PRE 1900 JANINA, CAIRO, GREECE [36455]

VIVA PRE 1910 SALO, ITL [37510]

VIVASH PRE 1900 SALFORD, LAN, ENG [34604]

VIVERS 1870-1950 BEDFORD, BDF, ENG [37396] :
ALL CANONBIE & LANGHOLM, DFS & ROX,
SCT [37396] : 1800-1900 CASTLETON, ROX, SCT
[37396]

VIVIAN 1871 STRATHALBYN, SA, AUS [34446] :
1855+ CLUNES, STAWELL & CALLAWADDA,
VIC, AUS [36622] : 1780-1820 CAMBORNE, CON,
ENG [35192] : PRE 1812+ CON, ENG [35759] : 1780
RUAN LANIHORN, CON, ENG [37224] : 1855-1915
KEWEENAW CO., MI, USA [38009]

VIVIKIN 1550-1600 NMR, BEL [36943]

VIVION JOHN PRE 1690 MIDDLESEX, VA, USA
[33757]

VIX ALL WORLDWIDE [38680]

VIZARD C1785 BRINKWORTH, WIL, ENG [33918] :
C1700 BRINKWORTH, WIL, ENG [37002]

VIZE 1810 BRK, ENG [34731] : 1800+ LONDON,
ENG [35194] : PRE 1840 SHOREDITCH, MDX, ENG
[37362] : PRE 1850 CLA, IRL [33928]

V.KOMMER ALL LITR, NL [33751]

V. KOMMER ALL UTR, NL [38692]

VLACK 1680 UTRECHT, UTR, NL [38706]

VLAM 1600S NIEUWERKERK, ZEL, NL [38350]

VLIMMENS 1725-1815 GELRODE, BBT, BEL [38405]

VOADEN 1723+ BRATTON CLOVELLY, DEV, ENG
[37092]

VOB 1800+ LENSAHN, SHO, GER [33996]

VOCE 1600+ LIVERPOOL & WARRINGTON, LAN, ENG [37625] : PRE 1800 ROLLESTONE, NTT, ENG [37893]

VOEGELI PRE 1800 GRAFENREID, BE, CH [36405]

VOETELINK 1800+ GENEMUIDEN, ZWOLLE, OIJ, NL [35338]

VOGAN PRE 1816 CAV, IRL [37478]

VOGEL PRE 1810 AG, CH [38029] : PRE 1800 NEEWILLER PRES LAUTERBOURG, ALS, FRA [36964] : 1800+ EIDINGHAUSEN, WEF, GER [38023]

VOGELE PRE 1820 CRIESBRAC, WUE, GER [34031]

VOGELGESANG ALL WORLDWIDE [36548]

VOGELGESANGER 1500-1700 RHINELAND, GER [38224]

VOGL C1692 SCHORNDORF, BAV, GER [38322]

VOGLER PRE 1900 WORLDWIDE [36930]

VOGT 1920+ NEWCASTLE, NSW, AUS [33800] : 1804-1844 KUELLSTEDT, PRE, GER [38626] : ALL HAMMELBURG, BAV, GER [38644] : ALL BORSCH (RHOEN), THU, GER [38644] : 1872-1881 NEW YORK CITY, NY & NJ, USA [37591] : ALL LYONS & BURLINGTON, WI, USA [38644]

VOIGHTS PRE 1860 HANSTEDT EBSTORF, UELZEN, HAN, GER [37804]

VOIGT ALL SA, AUS [35380] : PRE 1880 'BUCKAU', KSA, GER [35380]

VOISINE FRANCOIS 1700-1770 FRA [37479]

VOKES PRE 1790 GODALMING & CHIDDINGFORD, SRY, ENG [34382]

VOLD 1600+ FLAA, HALLINGDAL, NOR [36905]

VOLKE 1861 MONK TWP., ONT, CAN [37439]

VOLKMAR PRE 1800 GER [37823]

VOLKSTAEDT ALL MEK, GER [36694]

VOLLMER PRE 1830 ALS, FRA [36965] : PRE 1800 GER [37823] : ALL WORLDWIDE [36965]

VOLLPRECHT ALL CLAUSTHAL AND ZELLERFIELD, HAN, GER [38211]

VOLMER PRE 1830 ALS, FRA [36965] : ALL WORLDWIDE [36965]

VOLTZ PRE 1800 HERSCHBERG, RPF, GER [38681]

VON AESCH 1850+ USA [38686]

VONARB 1665-1700 CH [37504] : PRE 1870 ALS, FRA [37504]

VON ARB PRE 1870 FRA & CH [37504]

VON BERENS MARY PRE 1850 HASELUNNE, NSA, BRD [34481]

VON BEUCK ALL GER [35884]

VON BORIS C1820 BRA, GER [36520]

VON BREE PRE 1500 LBG, BEL [38658]

VON BROICH PRE 1820 NRW & RPF, BRD [38616]

VON BRUCKHE 1592+ HANAU, HEN, GER [38667]

VON CRONHOLM PRE 1900 MALMS, SWE [35451] : 1800+ NY, USA [35451] : ALL WORLDWIDE [35451]

VON DER CHAMEN PRE 1425 DINANT, BEL [38658]

VON DER LINDE 1600+ BRA & BLN, GER [38622]

VON DER SCHMIDT PRE 1710 PFUNGSTADT, HES, GER [36972]

VON DER TRUPE PRE 1500 BREMEN, BRM, GER [37819]

VONDERVILLE C1850S LONDON, ENG [34238]

VON DER WERTH ALL WORLDWIDE [35310]

VON DOEHREN 1696-1763 WESSELN, SHO, GER [38671]

VON ENSE PRE 1600 WEF, WAL & RPR, GER [38638]

VON EROLZHEIM ALL WORLDWIDE [38675]

VONESCHEN PRE 1906 ZURICH, ZH, CH [36215]

VON FORIS ALL WORLDWIDE [38682]

VON FORISCH ALL WORLDWIDE [38682]

VON FORISCHHIDVAR ALL WORLDWIDE [38682]

VON FORYSZ ALL WORLDWIDE [38682]

VON FRAGSTEIN UM NIENSDORFF ALL WORLDWIDE [37728] : ALL WORLDWIDE [37728]

VON GLAHN ALL WORLDWIDE [36922]

VON GOSTOMSKI ALL WORLDWIDE [38687] : BABKA ALL WORLDWIDE [38687]

VON GRUENHAGEN ALL WORLDWIDE [38688]

VON HAANEL 1840+ BRESLAU, SIL, GER [34367]

VON HARTEN 1600+ HOLTE, HAN, GER [34421] : 1800+ USA [34421]

VON HEGI ALL WORLDWIDE [38693]

VON HERDIBERG PRE 1400 ZURICH, ZH, CH [38665] : PRE 1400 HERRLIBERG, ZH, CH [38665]

VON HERRLIBERG PRE 1850 HERRLIBERG, ZH, CH [38665] : PRE 1850 ZURICH, ZH, CH [38665]

VON KASANOWSKI ALL WORLDWIDE [38687]

VON KOPP C1830 FRANKFURT AM ODER, PRE, GER [38711]

VON KRAFFZIG ALL WORLDWIDE [38687]

VON LAHER C1695 BREMEN, BRM, GER [37819]

VON LANCKEN PRE 1750 SHO, GER [38669]

VON MLOT TRZEBIATOWSKI ALL POM & WPR, GER [38687]

VON MUES ALL WORLDWIDE [38631]

VON MUNSTER 1789 BAMBERG, GER [34793]

VON NIDA PRE 1800 WEINGARTEN, GER [38605]

VON OEHSEN ALL AHRENSFELDE, NSA, BRD [38634] : ALL RITTERHUDE, NSA, BRD [38634]

VON OSTERWALD ALL WORLDWIDE [38633]

VON PALMOWSKI ALL POL [38687]

VON PEIN 1680+ RENZEL, SHO, GER [37542]

VON PODGURSKI 1775-1820 RAHMEL, GER [35315]

VON REINDE 1300S ESCHWEGE, GHE, GER [38635] : 1300S MUEHLHAUSEN, THU, GER [38635]

VON REYNDE 1300S ESCHWEGE, GHE, GER [38635] : 1300S THU, GER [38635]

VON RONNE C1664 WEDDERWARDEN, BRAKE, GER [35828] : 1234+ WESERMARSCH, BRM, GER [35828]

VON RONNEN C1664 WEDDERWARDEN, BRAKE, GER [35828]

VON SCHAUSSENBURG C1800 MEK, DDR [38452]

VON SIEDBRUECKBURG ALL WORLDWIDE [38682]

VON SPRECHEN PRE 1882 WESSELBUREN, SHO, GER [35616] : 1882 JONES CO., IA, USA [35616]

VON SPRENCKEL ALL WORLDWIDE [37604]

VON TRZEBIATOWSKI 1850 STOLP, POM, GER [34388]

VON USEDOM ALL WORLDWIDE [38675]

VON VARSFELDE 1400-1500 WOLFSBURG, BSW, GER [36420]

VON VOLTZHORN C1702 LIP, GER [37819]

VON VORSFELDE 1400-1500 HEHLINGEN, BSW, GER [36420]

VON VULZHORN C1702 LIP, GER [37819]

VON WALHORN PRE 1500 LBG, BEL [38658]

VON WERDEN ALL VEJLE, DEN [34308]

VON WERNER PRE 1860 BADEN BADEN, BAW, BRD [35649]

VON WNUK LIPINSKI ALL WORLDWIDE [38687]

VON WOLLMERSHAUSEN ALL WORLDWIDE [38657]

VON ZUREK ALL POL [38678]

VON ZUREK-EICHENAU ALL POL [38678]

VOORHIES C1851 MO, USA [38184]

VORE PRE 1900 FREDERICKTOWN, OH, USA [35312] : ALL WORLDWIDE [37570]

VORHOOP 1650+ BREMEN, BRM, GER [35460]

VORST 1750+ GUNTZENHAUSEN, BAY, BRD [36987]

VORT ALL WORLDWIDE [35771]

VORT-RONALD ALL WORLDWIDE [35771]

VOSE 1890S ATHERTON, LAN, ENG [36867] : 1800-1900 KRAMPENDACK, PRE, GER [36898] : SARAH 1684+ SWANSEA, MA, USA [35271]

VOSS 1850S+ SYDNEY, NSW, AUS [38211] : 1800+ ZIELBECK, LUE, GER [37170] : 1800 BARKAU, GER [37170] : PRE 1820 FRANKFURT & MAIN, GER [37703] : REBEKA 1830+ HAN, GER & USA [38186] : PRE 1850 SWANSEA, GLA, WLS [38211]

VOSSELIER PRE 1850 NJ, USA [37034]

VOSSEN 1735+ BORGHOLZ, SHO, GER [37542]

VOST 1880+ AUS [37917] : PRE 1880 MDX, ENG [37917]

VOUT 1550-1830 NFK, ENG [34219] : 1840S ROCKLAND ST MARY, NFK, ENG [36843] : 1860S LOWESTOFT, SFK, ENG [36843]

VOUTIER 1851+ BALLARAT, VIC, AUS [35425] : PRE 1851 ST MARYS PARISH, JSY, CHI [35425]

VOYLE ALL LEEDS, YKS & LEI, ENG [35954]

VOYSEY 1883+ NSW, AUS [35569] : 1900 RIVERSTONE, NSW, AUS [35569] : C1880 SRY, ENG [35569] : C1841 KINGSKERSWELL, DEV, ENG [35569]

VREDENBURG ALL ROTTERDAM, NL [35390]

VRIES DE REIJNIER PRE 1738 GREETSIEL, OST & FRI, FRG [38706]

VROLIJK 1786-1816 ZWARTSLUIS, OIJ, NL [34398]

V.STAVEREN 1700 DEVENTER, NL [33751]

V. STAVEREN 1700 DEVENTER, NL [38692]

VULKIS 1860 MDX, ENG [34540]

VULPIONI PRE 1910 MARCHE, ITL [37510]

VYE PRE 1860 WEYMOUTH, DUR, ENG [38263] : ALL WORLDWIDE [38215]

VYLE C1800 STOKE SUB HAMDON, SOM, ENG [36247]

VYSE PRE 1915 ARARAT, VIC, AUS [35233]

WAAGE-PETERSEN ALL DEN [35063]

WAARA 1865-1880 KEWEENAW CO., MI, USA [38009]

WABEKE 1660-1690S KAPELLE, ZEL, NL [38350]

WACKER 1800S TARMSTEDT, BRM, BRD [38019]

WACKERBARTH PRE 1805 WEHREN & GUDENSBERG, HES, GER [38642]

WADDE PRE 1750 ZONNEMAIRE, ZEL, NL [38350]

WADDEL 1750-1800 METHVEN, PER, SCT [38407]

WADDELL JOHN 1890+ WOORAGEE, VIC, AUS [35541] : 1800S OTTERBURN, NBL, ENG [35774] : 1823 ENG [37897] : 1850+ BELFAST, ANT, DOW & ARM, IRL [35636] : 1867 DUNEDIN, OTAGO, NZ [35774] : 1867+ OAMARU, NZ [35774] : PRE 1870 EDINBURGH, SCT [35541] : 1800+ AVONSIDE, STI, SCT [37480] : 1700+ LESMAHAGOW, LKS, SCT [37480] : 1750-1800 METHVEN, PER, SCT [38407] : C1700-1820 VA & KY, USA [38242] : 1200-1990 WORLDWIDE [36114]

WADDELOW ALL NFK, ENG [34259]

WADDILOW 1800S RATCLIFFE, LAN, ENG [36642]

WADDINGTON PRE 1827 BARNSLEY, YKS, ENG [34959] : C1700-1850 BRACEWELL, YKS, ENG [35490] : 1850+ PADIHAM, LAN, ENG [38288]

WADDY 1700-1800 NRY, ENG [37858]

WADE ALL TAS, AUS [33791] : 1860S CRESWICK, VIC, AUS [35136] : 1860+ OBERON, NSW, AUS [35586] : 1800-1849 COGGESHALL, ESS, ENG [33791] : 1854+ DITCHEAT, SOM, ENG [33852] : 1836 KENNINGTON, LND, ENG [34193] : 1833+ IOW, ENG [35136] : PRE 1820 ALDEBURGH, SFK, ENG [35406] : PRE 1829 OLDHAM, LAN, ENG [35459] : 1830+ WEDMORE & WELLS, SOM, ENG [35982] : 1800S WARE, HRT, ENG [35987] : 1700S GREAT & LITTLE ABINGTON, CAM, ENG [35987] : C1840+ BILLESDON, LEI, ENG [36258] : C1822 PHILLEIGH, CON, ENG [36276] : 1812-1871+ PRITTLEWELL, ESS, ENG [37108] : PRE 1720

ESHTON, YKS, ENG [37671] : 1800+ LEEDS, WRY, ENG [37907] : JOHN 1845-1849 COTTON, SFK, ENG [38307] : SARAH 1849 EYE, SFK, ENG [38307] : PRE 1850 TIP, IRL [35722] : 1800+ FERNHILL, DUB, IRL [38279] : 1790-1860 PERSON, NC, USA [38576]

WADEL 1850S ADELAIDE, SA, AUS [35377]

WADESON 1800 LANCASTER, LAN, ENG [36151] : 1900 SOUTHPORT, LAN, ENG [36151] : 1700 HOLME, LAN, ENG [36151] : ALL LAN & VIC, ENG & AUS [35345]

WADHAM 1800+ LAMBETH, SRY, ENG [36868] : 1600-1900 POOLE, DOR, ENG [37709] : C1810 KILKENNY, KIK, IRL [35865] : ALL WORLDWIDE [37505]

WADHAMS 1780+ NETHER HEYFORD, NTH, ENG [37357] : ALL WORLDWIDE [37505]

WADILL C1700 PRINCE EDWARD'S CO., VA, USA [36354]

WADKINSON PRE 1793 PLEASLEY, DBY, ENG [35029]

WADLAND 1800-1850 TAVISTOCK, DEV, ENG [35602]

WADLEIGH MARY 1807+ BRATTLEBORO, VT, USA [36322]

WADLEY PRE 1808 WOR, ENG [37316]

WADLING PRE 1750 ESS, ENG [35642]

WADROP ALL LKS, SCT [33980]

WADSWORTH 1750+ GREAT BARFORD, BDF, ENG [34416] : PRE 1870 WAKEFIELD, YKS, ENG [34442] : PRE 1758 HEPTONSTALL & HAWORTH, YKS, ENG [35459] : 1697+ LITTLE BOWDEN, NTH, ENG [35921] : PRE 1850 HOLME ON THE WOLDS, YKS, ENG [37094] : 1800+ DRUMRALLA, FER, IRL [35915] : 1850-60 WORLDWIDE [36845]

WAECHTER C1860 BAW, BRD [34581]

WAFER 1750-1850 LAN, ENG [34422]

WAGENBLAST PRE 1700 TIEFENBACH, GER [38681]

WAGENMAKERS PRE 1800 SNEEK, FRI, NL [38646]

WAGGETT PRE 1854 KEEPER GRANGE, DUR, ENG [35236]

WAGGRELL C1750 DUNDEE, ANS, SCT [35938]

WAGHORN 1860+ SYDNEY, NSW, AUS [34670] : PRE 1868 COLLINGWOOD, VIC, AUS [35578] : 1830+ DARTFORD, KEN, ENG [34670] : C1770 SALEHURST, SSX, ENG [35203] : 1774-1839 TICEHURST, SSX, ENG [36071] : 1794-1821 CHATHAM, KEN, ENG [37921]

WAGHORNE 1750-1850 BRENCHLEY, KEN, ENG [37340]

WAGLIN 1700+ KILSHANNIG BY MALLOW, COR, IRL [35364] : 1747 NEWBERRY, COR, IRL [35560]

WAGNER GEORGE 1900+ PROVOST, ALB, CAN [37440] : PRE 1859 LIVERPOOL, LAN, ENG [35344] : PRE 1700 OEHRINGEN, WUE, GER [33901] : 1700S DARMSTADT, HES, GER [33901] : 1850S BERLIN, PRE, GER [35050] : PRE 1850 SCG, GER [35344] : EVA PRE 1752 RHINE RiVER, WUE, GER [37574] : 1830-39 HIGHLANDS, GER [38151] : 1800-20 BUCHENBACH, PRE, GER [38202] : FRED PRE 1860 MEK, GER [38222] : PRE 1800 ENZWEIHINGEN, WUE, GER [38333] : 1800+ GELENAU, KSA, GER [38651] : 1790-1850S LUX [37548] : 1860-1890 DEKALB, IL, USA [36561] : ALL MO, USA [36919] : 1855-1875 KEWEENAW CO., MI, USA [38009] : 1850-1930 DES MOINES CO., IA, USA [38154]

WAGNOR 1850-1860 OH, USA [37815]

WAGON 1820+ BOULOGNE SUR MER, FRA [36239]

WAGONSCHUTZ 1870-1900 FARMINGTON, MI, USA [36551]

WAGSCHAL 1650+ ROCKWINKEL, BRM, GER [35460]

WAGSTAFF PRE 1872 MARYLEBONE, MDX, ENG [34463] : PRE 1795 NORTHILL, BDF, ENG [35728] : C1831 MIDDLECLIFF, WRY, ENG [35729] : 1700-1900 LONDON, ENG [36261] : PRE 1800 STORRINGTON, SSX, ENG [37069] : PRE 1800 DRUMBESS, CAV, IRL [38292]

WAGSTAFFE PRE 1831 MIDDLECLIFF, WRY, ENG [35729]

WAHL 1634 RHODEN, WAL, GER [34912]

WAHLERS ALL SCHMALKALDEN, THU, GER [38606]

WAHLSTROM C1800 STOCKHOLM, SWE [38064]

WAILES 1856 DEWSBURY, YKS, ENG [36319]

WAIN PRE 1780 KNIVETON, DBY, ENG [34311] : PRE 1900 CHISLEHURST, KEN, ENG [34314] : PRE 1803 CHESTERFIELD, DBY, ENG [35090] : C1860 MARKET BOSWORTH, LEI, ENG [35807]

WAINE 1700 WITNEY, OXF, ENG [37277]

WAINWRIGHT 1800S SYDNEY, NSW, AUS [35513] : 1800+ ST MARYS, NSW, AUS [37839] : 1800+ MUDGEE, NSW, AUS [37839] : PRE 1840 ENG [33937] : PRE 1820 CLAINES, WOR, ENG [34198] : 1781 WOODKIRK, YKS, ENG [35369] : C1742 ROTHWELL, WRY, ENG [36459] : 1700-1820 BARNSLEY, YKS, ENG [37372] : 1700+ NTT, ENG [37839] : 1700+ LITTLEPORT, CAM, ENG [37839] : PRE 1890 ENG [38286] : 1700-1900 PECKFIELD, WRY, ENG [38381]

WAIRE 1800-1841 SOM, ENG [35903]

WAIT PRE 1850 CORNWALL, ONT, CAN & USA [38386] : 1750S WORFIELD, SAL, ENG [35794] : 1883-1940 AUSTIN, MN, USA [38133]

WAITE PRE 1860 LANARK CO., ONT, CAN [34376] : ALBERT 1849+ HORSLEY, GLS, ENG [34475] : JOHN C1803 AVENING, GLS, ENG [34475] : PRE 1870 GRANTHAM, LIN, ENG [34797] : 1700+ SSX, ENG [35555] : 1800+ WHITBY, YKS, ENG [35908] : PRE 1835 EASTON, WIL, ENG [36636] : PRE 1835 BURBAGE, WIL, ENG [36636] : PRE 1760 HOLBORN, LND, ENG [36752] : 1800+ HULL, ERY, ENG [37626] : 1800+ LIN, ENG [37626] : 1800-1835 BOLTON, LAN, ENG [38007] : PRE 1890 GRAYTOWN, NZ [34797] : 1700+ NY, USA [34486] : 1700-1800S VA, USA [36579] : 1750-1800 EXETER, RI, USA [37013] : PRE 1900 NY, USA [37787]

WAITES 1850+ HARTLEPOOL, DUR, ENG [35908]

WAITS 1800-1900 CAMBRIDGE, CAM, ENG [37807]

WAITT PRE 1879 GREAT AMWELL, HRT, ENG [34584]

WAKE PRE 1875 MACCLESFIELD, SA, AUS [35528] : 1700-1880 NORTH BARROW & BRUTON, SOM, ENG [36816] : PRE 1850 KEW, SRY, ENG [37753]

WAKEFER ALL WORLDWIDE [35877]

WAKEFIELD 1790+ NOTTINGHAM, NTT, ENG [34238] : 1750S HAZLETON, GLS, ENG [35261] : PRE 1820 SITTINGBOURNE, KEN, ENG [36673] : C1745 DERBY, DBY, ENG [37661]

WAKEFORD 1764+ FITTLEWORTH, SSX, ENG [34693]

WAKEHAM 1860+ BIGBURY, DEV, ENG [35989]

WAKELAM WILLIAM PRE 1810 DUDLEY, WOR, ENG [36374] : JOSEPH PRE 1783 SEDGLEY, STS, ENG [36374] : ALL WORLDWIDE [37739]

WAKELIN 1840+ BATHURST, NSW, AUS [35412] : PRE 1840+ NEWCASTLE, STS, ENG [35412] : 1750+ WETHERDEN, SFK, ENG [37262]

WAKELING 1852+ NSW, AUS [33781] : 1800S BAIRNSDALE, VIC, AUS [37167] : ROBERT 1812+ LINTON, CAM, ENG [33764] : 1800+ LINTON,

CAM, ENG [33781] : ALL ENG [35987] : ALL GREAT THURLOW, SFK, ENG [37167]

WAKELY 1800+ DEV, ENG [35951] : 1600+ CHARDSTOCK, DOR, ENG [38745] : 1840-1918 ATWORTH, WIL, ENG & AUS [34942]

WAKEMAN 1800-1850 BIRMINGHAM, WAR, ENG [38091]

WAKFER ALL WORLDWIDE [35877]

WALBANCHE PRE 1800 SC, USA [38237]

WALBRIDGE (SEE WALLB [37658]

WALBRUHL 1815-1865 MEHLEM AREA, RPR, GER [38528]

WALBY 1850+ WANDSWORTH, SRY, ENG [35078] : ALL NBL, ENG [35579]

WALCH PRE 1900 TAS, AUS [34590] : PRE 1800 CHORLEY, LAN, ENG [37939] : PRE 1860 RUABON, DEN, WLS [36061]

WALDACK 1850-1880 BENDIGO, VIC, AUS [38166] : ALL EEKLO & WAARSCHOOT, OVL, BEL [38166] : 1600-1700 VEURNE & OOSTENDE, WVL, BEL [38166] : ALL GENT, EVERGEM & SLEIDINGE, OVL, BEL [38166] : 1680-1740 KORTRIJK & MENEN, WVL, BEL [38166] : 1810 LERIDA, ESP [38166] : 1933 PARIS, RPA, FRA [38166] : 1813 METZ, LOR, FRA [38166] : 1500-1570 BERGUES, NOR, FRA [38166] : 1870-1900 ROUBAIX, NOR, FRA [38166] : 1892 MARCQ EN BAROEUL, NOR, FRA [38166] : 1917 EVRY, RPA, FRA [38166] : 1922 MARSEILLE, PCA, FRA [38166] : C1900 NANTERRE, RPA, FRA [38166] : C1710 AARDENBURG, ZEL, NL [38166] : C1860 CINCINNATI, OH, USA [38166]

WALDE PRE 1900 DIERSBURG, BAW, BRD [37565] : 1900S OH, USA [37565]

WALDECK 1800S BRD [35024]

WALDEGRAVE 1600-1660 STANNINGHALL, NFK, ENG [36880]

WALDEN 1820+ WILBERFORCE & BELMONT, NSW, AUS [33996] : 1870+ CLARE, SA, AUS [38209] : JOB 1826-1850 SOM, ENG [33933] : PRE 1870 YARMOUTH, NFK, ENG [36178] : PRE 1870 BARKING & SAFFRON WALDEN, ESS, ENG [36178] : ALL LONG BUCKBY, NTH, ENG [37730] : ALL CANEWDON, ESS, ENG [37730] : C1800 SHOTESWELL, WAR, ENG [38209] : PRE 1823 KILLESHANDRA, CAV, IRL [34380] : ALL GSY, CHI, UK [37730] : 1712-1843 HARRISON CO., KY, USA [33761] : 1760-1770 CAROLINE CO., VA, USA [33761] : C1670 WENHAM, MA, USA [34395] : ALL WORLDWIDE [33913]

WALDENSIAN PRE 1740 CH [34253]

WALDER 1870+ WATCHEM, VIC, AUS [34962] : ALL ALB, CAN [36384] : PRE 1870 POPLAR, LND, ENG [34962] : PRE 1752 BOLNEY, BRIGHTON & CROYDON, SSX & SRY, ENG [36384]

WALDIE PRE 1860+ ARARAT, VIC, AUS [34877] : 1850+ GEELONG & BALLARAT, VIC, AUS [34877] : 1858+ DUNEDIN, OTAGO, NZ [36877] : 1760+ MOREBATTLE, ROX, SCT [34474] : 1800-1850 ASHKIRK, ROX, SCT [35595] : PRE 1860 BLACKHALL & EDINBURGH, MLN, SCT [36877]

WALDIN 1800+ NTH, ENG [35951] : SUSAN C1807+ USA [37951]

WALDMANN ALL BRECKERFELD & VOERDE, WEF, GER [34861]

WALDNER JOHN ADAM 1801-1862 KIRCHHEIM U/TECK, WUE, GER [38127]

WALDOCK 1640-1900 HUN, ENG [35451] : 1640-1900 BDF, ENG [35451] : C1600-1700S HUN, ENG [36289] : C1500-1700S BDF, ENG [36289]

WALDON 1860S ASHFIELD, NSW, AUS [35509] : 1750 LANGDON HILLS, ESS, ENG [34204] : C1780 ESS, ENG [36978]

WALDRON SAMUEL 1750+ MORWENSTOW, CON, ENG [34078] : 1600-17002 PORTSMOUTH, HAM, ENG [34504] : 1826 STOWBRIDGE, WOR, ENG [35251] : 1800S+ GUNNISLAKE, CON, ENG [35489] : PRE 1710 DEV & CON, ENG [36594] : PRE 1850 CHAGFORD, DEV, ENG [37060] : 1750-1850 LAMBOURNE, BRK, ENG [37188] : PRE 1827 ROS, IRL [35088] : PRE 1900 IRL & GER [35604] : 1800+ BOTAINE, NY, USA [34140]

WALDRUP 1720-1750 CAROLINE CO., VA, USA [36737] : 1750-1820 SPARTENBURG, SC, USA [36737]

WALDSECK 1750-1850 ASCH, OES [38194]

WALDUCK THOMAS 1650-1750 BARBADOS [36103]

WALE ALL COVENTRY, WAR, ENG [34730] : ALL LITTLE BARDFIELD HALL, ESS, ENG [34778] : PRE 1800 NEWPORT, IOW, ENG [36021]

WALES PRE 1800 DEV, ENG [33948] : 1830 WILBARSTON, NTH, ENG [35024] : PRE 1750 GARBOLDISHAM, NFK, ENG [35571] : 1600-1700 ENG [36898] : 1850+ NFK, ENG [37347] : 1600-1650 LEIGH, LAN, ENG [37783] : ALL ANS, SCT [38100] : RACHEL 1725 BRAINTREE, MA, USA [35273]

WALESBY 1795 WASHINGBOROUGH, LIN, ENG [34176]

WALFORD 1540-1700S FINCHINGFIELD & BIRDBROOK, ESS, ENG [35096] : 1800S ISLINGTON, LND, ENG [36055] : PRE 1850 PADDINGTON, MDX, ENG [37718] : 1824 MD, USA [38121]

WALINSKI (SEE VELENS [33966]

WALKDEN 1800+ MOBBERLEY, CHS, ENG [37598]

WALKEDEN ALL WORLDWIDE [35476]

WALKER WILLIAM 1864 BUENOS AIRES, ARGENTINA [34539] : 1800+ MONARO, NSW, AUS [33769] : SARAH PRE 1870 FITZROY, VIC, AUS [33890] : 1840-1890 GEELONG, VIC, AUS [33991] : 1849-1937 FREMANTLE & ADELAIDE, WA & SA, AUS [34530] : PRE 1927 SYDNEY, NSW, AUS [34860] : 1880+ PARRAMATTA, NSW, AUS [34979] : C1856 GEELONG, VIC, AUS [35233] : PRE 1800+ CORNWALLIS, NSW, AUS [35237] : PRE 1860+ WINDSOR, NSW, AUS [35237] : JAMES 1840 LONGFORD & LAUNCESTON, TAS, AUS [35336] : JAMES PRE 1843 BATHURST, NSW, AUS [35344] : 1894+ COOTAMUNDRA, NSW, AUS [35536] : 1800S BUNGAY & WINGHAM, NSW, AUS [35546] : ELLEN C1840 BEAUFORT, VIC, AUS [35747] : C1860 WICKLIFFE, VIC, AUS [35841] : GEORGE 1880 CAVENDISH, VIC, AUS [35877] : 1870+ GOULBURN, NSW, AUS [36600] : 1852+ BENDIGO, VIC, AUS [37303] : 1840S MT KEMBLA, NSW, AUS [37971] : C1860+ SYDNEY, NSW, AUS [37987] : WILLIAM C1855 PARRAMATTA & O'CONNELL, NSW, AUS [37988] : EVELYN 1903+ DEVONPORT, TAS, AUS [37999] : EVELYN 1922+ MELBOURNE, VIC, AUS [37999] : HENRY 1861+ LAUNCESTON, TAS, AUS [37999] : ALL CAVAN & VICTORIA, ONT, CAN [33854] : 1800-1900 BC, CAN [34135] : ROBERT 1825-1850S LEEDS, ONT, CAN [34200] : C1790 NB, CAN [34521] : C1840 ONT, CAN [34521] : HESTER 1800+ TONBRIDGE, KEN, ENG [33785] : PRE 1830 KIMBOLTON, NTH, ENG [33860] : PRE 1858 WOLLESTON, NTH, ENG [33860] : SARAH PRE 1870 YKS, ENG [33890] : C1820 ASTON UNDER LYNNE, LAN, ENG [33917] : 1650+ KESWICK, CUL, ENG [33973] : 1830S ECCLESHILL, YKS, ENG [34335] : 1750-1800 MANFIELD, NRY, ENG [34552] : 1800+ SOUTHSEA & PORTSMOUTH, HAM, ENG [34639] :

C1808 CHESTERFIELD, DBY, ENG [34661] : SAMUEL PRE 1860 BRADFORD, WRY, ENG [34701] : PRE 1820 HORSENDEN, BKM, ENG [34716] : 1787-1990 DERBY, DBY, ENG [34729] : HENRIETTA C1850-1900 BRADFORD, YKS, ENG [34745] : 1866 LUTON, BDF, ENG [34878] : PRE 1840 HOLBEACH, LIN, ENG [34931] : PRE 1823 FLIXTON, LAN, ENG [35097] : PRE 1785 NEWARK ON TRENT, NTT, ENG [35238] : PRE 1840 CHS, ENG [35344] : HENRY PRE 1840 ENG [35382] : SARAH 1797-1840 HULL, YKS, ENG [35412] : PRE 1870 KETTLEWELL, YKS, ENG [35546] : PRE 1860 HOLBORN, MDX & LND, ENG [35701] : PRE 1860 HALIFAX, WRY, ENG [35744] : PRE 1820 ROTHERHITHE, SRY, ENG [35758] : WILLIAM PRE 1850 PIDLEY, HUN, ENG [35877] : PRE 1859 BINGHAM, NTT, ENG [35904] : SARAH PRE 1861 LINTHWAITE, WRY, ENG [35955] : PRE 1840 BAKEWELL, DBY, ENG [35974] : 1748-1860 HALIFAX, WRY & LND, ENG [36049] : PRE 1740 KEELBY, LIN, ENG [36059] : BIGLAND 1817-1899 AMBLESIDE, CUL & LAN, ENG [36082] : PRE 1813 SPALDING, LIN, ENG [36102] : 1800-1840 DBY, ENG [36189] : 1800+ BARTON, ENG [36236] : PRE 1880 GLOSSOP, DBY, ENG [36242] : 1810+ BILSTON, STS, ENG [36254] : THOMAS 1750+ SELBY, NRY, ENG [36294] : THOMAS C1750 THORPE WILLOUGHBY, NRY, ENG [36294] : DAVID 1823+ HOLME UPON SPALDING MOOR, NRY, ENG [36294] : PRE 1800 YKS, ENG [36399] : WILLIAM PRE 1859 READING, BRK, ENG [36475] : ELIZABETH C1810 CHATHAM, KEN, ENG [36479] : 1800S NOTTINGHAM, NTT, ENG [36506] : 1800S SNEINTON & SUTTON IN ASHFIELD, NTT, ENG [36511] : 1890-1930 GRIMSBY, LIN, ENG [36511] : PRE 1850 LETCHMORE HEATH, HRT, ENG [36514] : 1880-1920 WIGAN, LAN, ENG [36587] : ALL SOUTH WINGFIELD, DBY, ENG [36587] : 1800+ SHREWSBURY & MUCH WENLOCK, SAL, ENG [36587] : KATE 1884+ TOTTENHAM, LND, ENG [36598] : C1840 BRISTOL, SOM, ENG [36610] : 1850 WINDSOR, BRK, ENG [36851] : ALL CUL, ENG [36861] : PRE 1780 RADFORD, NTT, ENG [37000] : RICHARD PRE 1833 MANCHESTER, LAN, ENG [37002] : 1800+ LEAKE, YKS, ENG [37048] : C1850 WITNEY, OXF, ENG [37053] : HUMPHREY 1840S BIGGLESWADE, BDF, ENG [37151] : C1860 WOLVERHAMPTON, STS, ENG [37233] : 1800-1850 HEATON NORRIS, LAN, ENG [37255] : 1750-1850 MIDDLEWICH, CHS, ENG [37255] : 1750-1837 BROMYARD, HEF, ENG [37278] : 1837-1900 TEWKESBURY, GLS, ENG [37278] : 1800+ LONDON, ENG [37306] : ISAAC 1700-1800 LAN, ENG [37330] : ISAAC 1800S YKS, ENG [37330] : HENRY 1815 LAN, ENG [37330] : ALL FURNESS, CUL, ENG [37379] : PRE 1840 CHORLEY, LAN, ENG [37414] : 1800S PIRTON, HRT, ENG [37423] : PRE 1850 ROLLESTON, STS, ENG [37671] : 1890 LAMBETH, MDX, ENG [37690] : PRE 1837 FLAXTON & HARTON, ERY, ENG [37710] : 1700-1920 HUDDERSFIELD, WRY, ENG [37736] : 1750-1850 ORLETON, HEF, ENG [37833] : PRE 1717 MAUNBY, KIRBY WISKE, NRY, ENG [37852] : 1700-1870 CUL, ENG [37858] : C1914 ISLINGTON, LND, ENG [37865] : PRE 1850 ASKRIGG, YKS, ENG [38039] : JAMES PRE 1848 QUERNMORE & CLAUGHTON, LAN, ENG [38248] : 1700+ WINKFIELD, BRK, ENG [38498] : C1806-1835 SCARBOROUGH, YKS, ENG [38499] : 1800-1850 STONEGRAVE, NRY, ENG [38516] : 1830 HAWKHURST, KEN, ENG [38719] : HENRY 1849+ NEWCASTLE, STS & NSW, ENG & AUS [35155] :

PRE 1883 ENG & IRL [37701] : ROBERT PRE 1890 LND, ENG & NZ [37987] : GRACE C1820S INDIA [38744] : ROBERT 1780-1825 SLI, IRL [34200] : 1750-1900 DOW, IRL [34229] : PRE 1876 BALLYMENA, ANT, IRL [34277] : PRE 1880 CANONERY, TRY, IRL [34442] : 1700-1800 DONNAGHMORE, TYR, IRL [35006] : ELIZA 1830-1880 BELFAST, ANT, IRL [35006] : ALL GAL, IRL [35139] : 1840-1868 BARNA, GAL, IRL [35865] : PRE 1850 PORTADOWN, ARM, IRL [35866] : PRE 1850 ARM, IRL [37961] : PRE 1864 KISH, FER, IRL [37971] : 1849-1901 CLA, IRL [38102] : C1890 DUNEDIN, OTAGO, NZ [35826] : 1860+ NZ [36761] : 1820-1912 GLASGOW, LKS, SCT [33811] : JAMES C1840-1900 CLARKSTON NEWMONKLAND, LKS, SCT [33978] : 1871-1971 EDINBURGH, MLN, SCT [33978] : PRE 1850 SCT [33999] : PRE 1880 ST ANDREWS, FIF, SCT [34018] : C1750+ PER, SCT [34040] : 1800S NEWBURGH, FIF, SCT [34053] : C1780 BIGGAR, LKS, SCT [34118] : 1600+ LEITH, ELN, SCT [34303] : WILLIAM C1819 GLASGOW, LKS, SCT [34539] : PRE 1780 GALSTON, AYR, SCT [34993] : 1834+ FALKIRK, STI, SCT [35194] : PRE 1800 FALKIRK, STI, SCT [35261] : 1810+ WIGTOWN & KNIGHTSWOOD, WIG & DNB, SCT [35579] : ELIZ. MCA. K. 1850 AYR, SCT [35717] : PRE 1850 NORTH BERWICK, SCT [35866] : PRE 1850 ROX, SCT [35934] : MARGARET PRE 1880 DUNFERMLINE, FIF, SCT [35962] : ANN 1832-1872 DUNDEE, ANS, SCT [36320] : JEAN 1830S DUMFRIES, DFS, SCT [36633] : PRE 1810 ABERDOUR, FIF, SCT [36704] : 1820-1850 BATHGATE, WLN, SCT [36762] : 1800+ CUMBERNAULD, DNB, SCT [36875] : 1750+ BEITH, AYR, SCT [37110] : PRE 1830 MAYBOLE, AYR, SCT [37169] : 1765+ DREGHORN, AYR, SCT [37205] : 1780-1930 BEITH, AYR, SCT [37205] : ALL CAMPBELTOWN, ARL, SCT [37303] : 1800S TILLICOULTRY, CLK, SCT [37329] : PRE 1800 GARVALD & BARRA, ELN, SCT [37353] : 1800S NIGG, KCD, SCT [37476] : ELIZA 1830+ PAISLEY, RFW, SCT [37666] : PRE 1850 ABERDEEN, ABD, SCT [37832] : 1901 MOSSGREEN, FIF, SCT [38470] : 1830+ JEDBURGH, ROX, SCT [38539] : ROBERT 1873 GLASGOW, SCT & USA [34539] : 1912 NJ, USA [33811] : ROBERT 1800S BUCKS CO., PA, USA [34309] : 1800 ADAIR, KY, USA [34388] : 1840-1850S MI, USA [34521] : 1770-1931 BOSTON, MA, USA [36915] : 1793-1848 HAMPDEN, ME, USA [36944] : 1620-1790 EASTHAM, MA, USA [36944] : 1875+ SACRAMENTO CO., CA, USA [37048] : C1830 CHRISTIAN CO., KY, USA [37527] : PRE 1835 PA, USA [37528] : CHARLES 1700S-1800S WASHINGTON CO., VA, USA [37794] : 1650+ JAMES CITY CO., VA, USA [38120] : MORGAN 1828-1880 JACKSON CO., MO, USA [38187] : 1820+ SCHUYLER, IL, USA [38517] : PRE 1850 KY, USA [38527] : PRE 1820 NC, USA [38576] : WILLIAM HENRY 1849-1888 IL, USA [38732]

WALKER-GARRATT C1892-1970 BINGHAM, NTT, ENG [38401]

WALKER JONES 1850-1930 NSW, AUS [37943] : C1750-1900 CORWEN, MER, WLS [37943]

WALKEY PRE 1700 DEV, ENG [36986]

WALKING CHIEF ALL CAN [33903]

WALKINGTON ALL KIRKBY MOORSIDE & MALTON, NRY, ENG [35460]

WALL PRE 1880 WOR, ENG [34615] : 1872 WIRKSWORTH, DBY, ENG [34957] : NATHANIEL PRE 1820 CHATHAM, KEN, ENG [35371] : 1700-1800 SAL & HFD, ENG [36003] : PRE 1700 DBY, ENG [36084] : 1586+ STOTTESDON, SAL, ENG [36488] : 1750+ FAIRFORD, GLS, ENG [37686] :

THOMAS 1870+ ABBEY DORE, HEF, ENG [37827] : 1800-1900 NFK, ENG [37884] : PRE 1800 SOM, ENG [38746] : PRE 1834 WATERFORD, WAT, IRL [33924] : 1818+ NEWTOWN, COR, IRL [34288] : C1800 TINTERN, WEX, IRL [35744] : C1874 NTH DUBLIN, IRL [36802] : PRE 1900 KILKENNY, KIK, IRL [37521] : C1840 BALLINGARRY, LIM, IRL & AUS [35365] : C1900 WISHAW, LKS, SCT [36802] : PRE 1850 HIERSCHAU, TAURIEN, SU [36543] : PRE 1900 CLA, IRL &, USA, AUS & [38305]

WALLACE ROBERT PRE 1864 WOODSIDE, SA, AUS [33943] : ABORIGINE PRE 1824 HAWKESBURY RIVER, NSW, AUS [34273] : MICHAEL 1840+ WINCHELSEA, VIC, AUS [34541] : EMILY J. 1885-1950 SYDNEY, NSW, AUS [34699] : 1800+ BALLARAT WALLACE, VIC, AUS [37995] : JOHN PRE 1856 MELBOURNE, VIC, AUS & SCT [35958] : DAVID PRE 1900 TORONTO, ONT, CAN [33808] : 1890-1962 WENTWORTH, ONT, CAN [37469] : 1824 LIVERPOOL, LAN, ENG [34529] : ALL HARTLEPOOL, DUR, ENG [34619] : PRE 1850 KETTERING, NTH, ENG [35365] : PRE 1857 SOM, ENG [35393] : 1900+ SOUTHEND, ESS, ENG [35783] : 1880+ LONDON, ENG [35783] : 1800-1900 HUNTINGDON, HUN, ENG [35923] : 1926 GREENWICH, ESS, ENG [36606] : 1650-1750 CHATTON, NBL, ENG [36776] : ALL BRK, ENG [37638] : 1830+ CALVERLEY, CHS, ENG [37734] : 1870+ EAST HEDLEY HOPE, DUR, ENG [37911] : PRE 1900 ENG & SCT [37739] : 1875+ PARIS, FRA [35783] : 1800S BALLYMENA, ANT, IRL [34336] : MICHAEL 1800+ GAL, IRL [34541] : 1900+ BELFAST, ANT, DOW & ARM, IRL [35636] : 1606+ ANT, IRL [36782] : JOHN 1800+ BRANIEL, DOW, IRL [36813] : 1900+ BELFAST, ANT, IRL [36853] : 1860+ CARRICKFERGUS, ANT, IRL [36853] : PRE 1850 DOW, IRL [37180] : PRE 1900 KILMARNOCH & MAUCHLINE, AYR, SCT [33808] : 1861-1913 GLASGOW, LKS, SCT [33811] : PRE 1900 PAISLEY, RFW, SCT [34060] : PRE 1800 IRVINE, AYR, SCT [34112] : 1835+ LKS & AYR, SCT [34373] : 1858 BEITH, AYR, SCT [34529] : PRE 1840 EDINBURGH, MLN, SCT [34689] : 1860-1880S ARISAIG, INV, SCT [35081] : DONALD M. 1890S GLASGOW, LKS, SCT [35081] : JAMES 1859 EDINBURGH, MLN, SCT [35081] : 1800+ KENNOWAY, FIF, SCT [35524] : 1850-1940 GLASGOW, LKS, SCT [35783] : PRE 1830 NEILSTON, RFW, SCT [36583] : PRE 1606 CRAIGIE, SCT [36782] : 1870S ARBROATH, ANS, SCT [37200] : 1800+ NEW DEER & PETERHEAD, ABD, SCT [37628] : PRE 1861 KILSYTH, STI, SCT [37925] : 1800+ PETERHEAD, ABD, SCT [38213] : 1860-1880 LEVIN, FIF, SCT [38475] : JEAN C1798+ KETTINS, PER, SCT [38567] : 1789-1990 TN, USA [35313] : 1845-1920 ROCHESTER, NY, USA [36935] : 1830-1900 INYO, CA, USA [37038] : 1800-1900 NY, USA [37464] : 1850-1870 SAN FRANCISCO, CA, USA [38045] : 1865-1910 PORTLAND, OR, USA [38045] : 1820-1850 HALIFAX, VA, USA [38342]

WALLADGE C1850S NSW, AUS [33794]

WALLBRIDGE ALL DOR & HAM, ENG [37658]

WALLDER 1890-1930S KILMORE, VIC, AUS [35777]

WALLE PRE 1900 CLA, IRL &, USA, AUS & [38305]

WALLEN 1764 WILTON, SOM, ENG [35815]

WALLER 1906+ BRISBANE, QLD, AUS [35455] : 1800S GREAT YARMOUTH, NFK, ENG [34086] : PRE 1800 ROGATE, SSX, ENG [34112] : 1750S KIRKOSWALD, CUL, ENG [34688] : PRE 1750 CLEY NEXT THE SEA, NFK, ENG [34828] : 1851+ LONDON, MDX, ENG [35455] : 1790+ SFK & ESS, ENG [35632] : 1750-1900 STS & DBY, ENG [36007] :

PRE 1850 WAINFLEET, LIN, ENG [36168] : PRE
1750 BEARSTEAD, KEN, ENG [36326] : PRE 1800
LUTON, BDF & LND, ENG [36396] : ALL
KINGSLANGLEY, HRT, ENG [36744] : ALL
STOTFOLD, BDF, ENG [36744] : 1800-1850 KY, USA
[36346] : 1800+ OH, USA [38735] : 1800+
BURLINGTON, IA & IN, USA [38735]

WALLETT 1800S BILSTON, STS, ENG [36253]

WALLEY ALL DERBY, DBY, ENG [34822] : PRE 1870
GREAT NESTON, CHS, ENG [37989]

WALLING SAMPSON PRE 1861 TOPSHAM, DEV,
ENG [37986] : 1790-1850 MENDON, MA & CT, USA
[38025]

WALLINGFORD PRE 1900 LONDON, ENG [34562] :
1800-1900 WIMBORNE MINSTER, DOR, ENG
[36820] : 1845-1900 WINCHESTER, HAM, ENG
[36820]

WALLIS PRE 1870 SYDNEY, NSW, AUS [34978] : PRE
1740 TEVERSHAM, CAM, ENG [34445] : C1810
THURLASTON, LEI, ENG [34548] : 1820+
COMBERTON, CAM, ENG [35214] : ALL MDX,
ENG [35707] : PRE 1860 LND, ENG [35949] : 1700-
1900 WESTMINSTER, LND, ENG [36176] : PRE
1863 SPILSBY, LIN, ENG [36748] : C1820 GLS, ENG
[37180] : 1800-1900 CAMBRIDGE, CAM, ENG
[37807] : C1838 GRAFTON REGIS, NTH, ENG
[37915] : 1700 FEERING, ESS, ENG [37928] : ALL
STROUD, GLS, ENG [38215] : 1840-1865 CORK,
COR, IRL [38117]

WALLISS 1800-1860 ADELAIDE, SA, AUS [34815]

WALLOF 1900+ HAMILTON, ONT, CAN [36203]

WALLS PRE 1850 LAN, ENG [34730] : 1700S
BENNINGTON, HRT, ENG [34776] : C1844
WORKINGTON, CUL, ENG [35384] : PRE 1800 FIF,
SCT [34861]

WALLWORK 1800+ BURY, LAN, ENG [37626]

WALMESLEY 1750-1900 CHORLEY, LAN, ENG
[35614]

WALMSLEY 1880 GAWLER, SA, AUS [34844] : 1923+
REGINA, SAS, CAN [37072] : 1750+ DARWEN,
LAN, ENG [36991]

WALNE ALL WORLDWIDE [35169]

WALRAVE 1750 VEERE, ZEL, NL [38696]

WALROND 1900+ RSA [34760]

WALSH EDMUND 1870+ CHARTERS TOWERS,
QLD, AUS [33797] : MATTHEW 1850+ BATHURST,
NSW, AUS [33933] : 1850S BALLARAT, VIC, AUS
[34175] : 1863+ ROMA, QLD, AUS [34276] : JAMES
PRE 1860+ HARTLEY, NSW, AUS [35105] : JAMES
PRE 1860+ MUDGEE, NSW, AUS [35105] : PRE
1845 LAUNCESTON, TAS, AUS [35336] : 1898+
ROCKHAMPTON, QLD, AUS [35452] : 1850+
NEWCASTLE, NSW, AUS [36293] : 1850+
MAITLAND, NSW, AUS [37133] : 1841 VIC, AUS
[37986] : 1800-1860 SYDNEY, NSW, AUS [38070] :
1820S NS, CAN [34175] : 1900+ BROCKVILLE,
ONT, CAN [34402] : 1800+ FORTUNE BAY, NFD,
CAN [36684] : 1800+ HERMITAGE BAY, NFD,
CAN [36684] : 1844-1936 KINGSTON, ONT, CAN
[38102] : PRE 1750 MORPETH, NBL, ENG [33905] :
JAMES PRE 1864 ACCRINGTON, LAN, ENG
[34929] : PHILIP 1790S LIVERPOOL, LAN, ENG
[35815] : 1750+ DARWEN, LAN, ENG [36991] : PRE
1800 CHORLEY, LAN, ENG [37939] : 1928+
BIRMINGHAM, WAR, ENG & IRL [34351] : PRE
1827 IRL [33777] : EDMUND PRE 1840
BALLYPOREEN, TIP, IRL [33797] : 1800+ OOLA,
LIM, IRL [33829] : PRE 1860 BALLYLONGFORD,
KER, IRL [33871] : 1820 KIK, IRL [34015] : C1863
HEADFORD, GAL, IRL [34276] : PRE 1841
CLOGHERMORE & CLAREMORRIS, MAY, IRL
[34305] : 1800+ RUAN, CLA, IRL [34453] : ALL

CASTLECOMER, KIK, IRL [34593] : JOHANNA
PRE 1858 DUNNAMRY, KIK, IRL [34781] :
MARTHA KNOX C1840 WEXFORD TOWN, WEX,
IRL [34810] : PRE 1840 WEX, IRL [34984] : SHEILA
1790-1860 SKIBBEREEN, COR, IRL [35003] : 1869
KID, IRL [35452] : C1840 DUBLIN, IRL [35560] :
JANE PRE 1817 DUBLIN, IRL [36270] : MICHAEL
1842-1919 TIP, IRL [36293] : EDMUND 1759-1832
TEMPLEORUM, KIK, IRL [36293] : PRE 1850
CAPPAWHITE, TIP, IRL [36468] : PRE 1840 KIK,
IRL [36518] : 1750-1818 KER, IRL [36618] : 1800-1860
LIM, IRL [36780] : ALL LIMERICK, IRL [36834] :
PRE 1840 KIK, IRL [37027] : C1840 THREE
CASTLES, KIK, IRL [37083] : 1800+ THREE
CASTLES, KIK, IRL [37534] : PRE 1900 WEX, IRL
[37750] : 1770-1870 WALSH PARK, TIP, IRL [37844] :
THOMAS C1830 WAT, IRL [37960] : 1830+
KILKENNY, IRL [37986] : PRE 1860 CASHEL, TIP,
IRL [38299] : ALL STEVENSON, AYR, SCT [38067] :
1850+ SUSQUEHANNA CO., PA & NY, USA
[35299] : MICHAEL J. PRE 1900 WHITEHALL, NY,
USA [36563] : 1850S PEORIA, IL, USA [37027] : 1808-
1890 HEMLOCK, MI, USA [38102] : 1850+ WI, USA
[38324] : PHILIP 1814+ HOLYHEAD, AGY, WLS
[35815] : PRE 1860 RUABON, DEN, WLS [36061]

WALSHAW 1875 SUNDERLAND, DUR, ENG [33929]
: 1800+ LEEDS, YKS, ENG [38395]

WALSHE 1800-1990 EDGEWATER, NJ, USA [35421]

WALSTRUM C1900 NEW ORLEANS, LA, USA [38064]
: 1935+ COOK CO., IL, USA [38064]

WALTE 1700+ DIERSBURG, BAD, GER [38529]

WALTER PRE 1710 RANTON, STS, ENG [36701] :
1750-1890 SSX & KEN, ENG [37338] : PRE 1880
COULSDEN, SRY, ENG [37901] : C1821
PFEDELBACH, WUE, GER [35733] : ALL BAD,
GER [36532] : 1800-1900 SARATOV, SAMARA, SU
[34081] : ALL ACCOMACK CO., VA, USA [36557] :
1650+ SUSSEX CO., DE, USA [36914] : 1700S
BRONANT, CGN, WLS [37250]

WALTERS 1800+ TENTERFIELD, NSW, AUS [34421]
: 1850-1900 ADELONG, NSW, AUS [34436] : C1930
UNDERCLIFFE, NSW, AUS [34694] : 1750+
CHAMPNEYS, NFD, CAN [33852] : 1920S
SASKATOON, SAS, CAN [36158] : 1800S
UXBRIDGE, ONT, CAN [36727] : C1835-45 WOR,
ENG [33828] : 1700+ CORWEN, CON, ENG [33963]
: PRE 1840 WALMER, KEN, ENG [34138] : PRE
1818 SOM, ENG [34421] : PRE 1860 ELMDON, ESS,
ENG [34869] : 1800 ENG [35023] : 1800+
WELLINGTON, SOM, ENG [36158] : 1800+
YEOVIL, SOM, ENG [36158] : 1800+ HELSTON,
CON, ENG [36785] : 1840S+ WALSALL, ENG
[36809] : PRE 1800 STS, ENG [37098] : 1750-1900 SSX
& KEN, ENG [37338] : 1800+ SHIFNAL, SAL, ENG
[37705] : 1800+ WOLVERHAMPTON, STS, ENG
[38046] : C1900 GLOVERSVILLE, NY, USA [36158] :
PRE 1850 HERKIMER CO., NY, USA [36319] : 1635-
1785 PITTSYLVANIA CO., VA, USA [38107] : PRE
1850 DEWITT CO., IL, USA [38196] : JACOB PRE
1820 TIONESTA, PA, USA [38394] : 1800-1850
GOWER PENINSULA, GLA, WLS [35153] :
MARGARET 1830S+ PEMBROKE, PEM, WLS
[35876]

WALTERSDORF PRE 1883 LUNEBURG, HAN, GER
[35863]

WALTH ALL WORLDWIDE [37600]

WALTHALL 1700S HORSLEY, DBY, ENG [38478]

WALTHER PRE 1861 GERSDORF, PSA, GER [35065]

WALTHO PRE 1826 WAR & STS, ENG [33762]

WALTON 1850+ RICHMOND, VIC, AUS [35043] :
1800S WOLLOMBI, NSW, AUS [35159] : C1925
VANCOUVER, BC, CAN [34372] : ELIZABETH 1790

PETROLIA, ONT, CAN & ENG **[34164]** : 1782
WEARSDALE, DUR, ENG **[33754]** : PRE 1834
ALSTON, CUL, ENG **[33775]** : C1800-1895
GOSFORTH & NEWCASTLE, NBL, ENG **[34372]** :
ANN 1834 MANCHESTER, LAN, ENG **[34539]** :
1650-1750 SEDGEFIELD, DUR, ENG **[34552]** : PRE
1839 IPSWICH, SFK, ENG **[34616]** : PRE 1850
BARNSTAPLE, DEV, ENG **[34741]** : 1800-1900
BISHOPWORTH, DUR, ENG **[34748]** : 1750 +
SCULCOATES HULL, YKS, ENG **[35370]** : 1860
LND, ENG **[35870]** : PRE 1860 THURLSTONE,
WRY, ENG **[35946]** : PRE 1810 ECCLESFIELD,
WRY, ENG **[36102]** : PRE 1855 SUNDERLAND,
DUR, ENG **[36202]** : 1830-1850S SYSTON, LEI, ENG
[36285] : PRE 1850 RIPON, YKS, ENG **[36679]** :
C1750 WEARDALE, DUR, ENG **[36961]** : PRE 1857
NORTHALLERTON, YKS, ENG **[37148]** : 1600-1900
ALSTON, CUL, ENG **[37290]** : 1700S DONCASTER,
WRY, ENG **[37570]** : 1840 + SHOREDITCH, LND,
ENG **[37775]** : THOMAS 1840 + ISLINGTON, LND,
ENG **[37775]** : 1840 + CROMER, NFK, ENG **[37775]** :
1700-1800 LIN, ENG **[37924]** : 1780-1850
BASCHURCH, SAL, ENG **[38453]** : PRE 1750 MUCH
WENLOCK, SAL, ENG **[38461]** : PRE 1850
ABERNETHY, PER, SCT **[34587]** : 1800-1820
DAIRSIE & ST ANDREWS, FIF, SCT **[35494]** : 1802-
1839 WYTHE CO., VA, USA **[37029]** : 1860-1889
ADAMS CO., IL, USA **[38101]** : PRE 1860 PA, USA
[38303] : 1800 + TUSCAWARWAS, OH, USA **[38769]**
WALTZ PRE 1700 GOEPPINGEN, WUE, GER **[38683]**
: ALL PA & OH, USA & GER **[38180]**
WALUDA ALL TUCZNABABA, KRAKOW, POL
[38678]
WALZ PRE 1898 REUTLINGEN, WUE, GER **[34175]**
WAMSLEY PRE 1875 FER, IRL **[38413]**
WAND ALL BOURNE, LIN, ENG **[34421]**
WANDHAUSE ALL BRD **[33836]** : 1700-1900
HANNOVER, GER **[33836]**
WANLASS C1725-1775 FIF, SCT **[36327]** : 1700-1900
WORLDWIDE **[36977]**
WANLASSE C1725-1775 FIF, SCT **[36327]**
WANLESS 1780-1850 LONGBENTON, NBL & DUR,
ENG **[37129]**
WANN 1800-1923 HAMILTON, LKS, SCT **[33800]** :
1800-1923 DUNDEE, FORFAR, ANS, SCT **[33800]** :
1600-1900 GUARDBRIDGE, FIF, SCT **[34004]**
WANNAMAKER 1850 PRINCE EDWARD CO., ONT,
CAN **[36655]** : 1800 NL **[36655]**
WANNER C1780 ROTTERDAM, ZUH, NL **[38698]** :
1750-1900 BERKS CO., PA, USA **[35318]**
WANSBANE ALL BKM, ENG **[35909]**
WANSBONE ALL BKM, ENG **[35909]**
WANSBOURN ALL BKM, ENG **[35909]**
WANSBROUGH 1860 + KAPUNDA, SA, AUS **[37179]** :
PRE 1840 SHREWTON, WIL, ENG **[37179]**
WANSTALL PRE 1852 GOODNESTONE, KEN, ENG
[36804]
WANT PRE 1860 ENG **[36511]**
WAPLES 1830 + WOLLONGONG, NSW, AUS **[34273]**
: C1807 NTH, ENG **[34273]** : 1750-1850 NORTH
CRAWLEY, BKM, ENG **[34552]**
WAPSHORE ALL ENG **[34671]**
WARBRICK 1800 + GUNDAGAI & SYDNEY, NSW,
AUS **[34538]** : 1700 + LYTHAM, LAN, ENG **[34538]** :
1857 + MANCHESTER & WIGAN, LAN, ENG
[34609] : 1800 + NZ **[34538]**
WARBROOKE 1848 PRESCOT, LAN, ENG **[36860]** :
1824 KILCUMMIN, WIC, IRL **[36860]**
WARBURTON PRE 1800 LYMM, CHS, ENG **[35945]** :
WILLIAM D 1820-1913 MANCHESTER, LAN, ENG
[38259]

WARBY JOHN 1770 COTTERED, HRT, ENG **[34539]** :
JOHN PRE 1764 BARLEY, HRT, ENG **[34539]**

WARD 1845 + BERRIMA, NSW, AUS **[34534]** : JOHN
1839 + NEW ENGLAND, NSW, AUS **[34539]** :
1854 + BALMAIN, NSW, AUS **[34542]** : C1833
SINGLETON, NSW, AUS **[34913]** : 1875 +
BUNDABERG, QLD, AUS **[35034]** : 1840-1905
WESTBURY, TAS, AUS **[35195]** : 1860 +
PARRAMATTA, NSW, AUS **[35405]** : 1889
MELBOURNE, VIC, AUS **[35405]** : 1860S
BENDIGO, VIC, AUS **[35509]** : C1830 SYDNEY,
NSW, AUS **[35826]** : RICHARD 1873 + SYDNEY,
NSW, AUS **[36192]** : JOHN 1877 + SYDNEY, NSW,
AUS **[36192]** : FRED 1840 + NEW ENGLAND,
NSW, AUS **[36629]** : 1828 + PADDYS RIVER, NSW,
AUS **[37131]** : PRE 1854 GOULBURN, NSW, AUS
[37899] : JOHN 1880 + BURNIE, TAS, AUS **[38729]** :
PRE 1900 LAUNCESTON & HOBART, TAS, AUS &
ENG **[34604]** : 1820-60 PERTH, ONT, CAN **[35638]** :
1900 + CAN **[38261]** : C1800-1900 ONT, CAN & IRL
[38242] : 1820 + ST PETER PORT, GSY, CHI **[35847]** :
PRE 1787 CARLTON COLVILLE, SFK, ENG **[33762]**
: C1838 DEPTFORD, KEN, ENG **[33796]** : C1850
LEEDS, WRY, ENG **[33796]** : 1800 +
NOTTINGHAM, NTT, ENG **[33855]** : 1711
SOUTHWARK, MDX, ENG **[34142]** : JUSTINAH
1720-1793 WILMSLOW, CHS, ENG **[34143]** : 1700 +
LONDON, ENG **[34258]** : PRE 1800 SOUTHWARK,
LND, ENG **[34316]** : PRE 1850 LONDON, ENG
[34317] : 1803 + STAFFORD, STS, ENG **[34334]** :
CHRISTINA L. C1847-1870 ENG **[34391]** : 1820-1880
LEWISHAM, KEN, ENG **[34399]** : PRE 1823
CROWLE, LIN, ENG **[34494]** : ANN 1850 +
DEWSBURY AREA, WRY, ENG **[34512]** : PRE 1850
CROXTON KEYRIAL, LEI, ENG **[34621]** : 1700-1900
LAN, ENG **[34624]** : 1800 + GLS, ENG **[34684]** :
ALFRED ALL NORMANTON, WRY, ENG **[34701]** :
1800-1900 BERMONDSEY & DEPTFORD, LND,
ENG **[34749]** : 1750-1820 DARFIELD, YKS, ENG
[34762] : PRE 1850 CHATHAM, KEN, ENG **[34814]** :
1800 COLCLEUGH, NBL, ENG **[34890]** : PRE 1900
DERBY, DBY, ENG **[34909]** : THOMAS 1696
MORTON MORRELL & WARWICK, WAR, ENG
[35013] : PRE 1913 LEEDS, WRY, ENG **[35031]** : 1844
GOSPORT, HAM, ENG **[35041]** : 1850 +
WILMSLOW, CHS, ENG **[35123]** : PRE 1800
BOURNE & CROWLAND, LIN, ENG **[35181]** :
1800 + WALSOKEN, NFK & CAM, ENG **[35342]** :
1879 + LND, ENG **[35528]** : C1826 + ICKLETON,
CAM, ENG **[35537]** : SARAH PRE 1820 HOLBORN,
LND, ENG **[35574]** : MARK 1840 + SFK, ENG
[35583] : 1870 AMWELL, MDX, ENG **[35705]** : 1837
WOOLWICH, ESS, ENG **[35770]** : C1860 GRIMSBY,
LIN, ENG **[35807]** : PRE 1850 ISLINGTON &
CLERKENWELL, MDX, ENG **[35914]** : PRE 1860
MILDENHALL, SFK, ENG **[35915]** : 1750 +
CHEDDAR, SOM, ENG **[35918]** : 1800 + PORTSEA,
HAM, ENG **[35977]** : 1830 + WEDMORE & WELLS,
SOM, ENG **[35982]** : 1800S LIN, ENG **[36038]** : PRE
1841 DANBY, NRY, ENG **[36046]** : PRE 1850
WOODBRIDGE, SFK, ENG **[36086]** : 1860-1920
BETHNAL GREEN & WEST HAM, MDX & ESS,
ENG **[36101]** : 1870 + CODDINGTON & NEWARK,
NTT, ENG **[36105]** : 1845 + OLDBURY, WOR, ENG
[36110] : PRE 1880 BRIERLEY HILL & BILSTON,
STS, ENG **[36110]** : ALL NEWARK, NTT, ENG
[36174] : JOHN PRE 1733 KENDAL, WES, ENG
[36192] : C1800 + HOUGHTON ON THE HILL, LEI,
ENG **[36258]** : PRE 1850 STEPNEY, MDX, ENG
[36270] : 1792 GREAT YARMOUTH, NFK, ENG
[36301] : PRE 1800 FEWSTON, WAR, ENG **[36380]** :
C1730 WORKSOP, NTT, ENG **[36426]** : 1700-1850

NRY, ENG [36472] : 1700-1800 SHEPSHED, LEI, ENG [36531] : ALL HAXEY, LIN, ENG [36635] : PRE 1850 COVENTRY, WAR, ENG [36635] : PRE 1794 TURTON, LAN, ENG [36742] : PRE 1850 YKS, ENG [36840] : PRE 1880 HENDON, MDX, ENG [36891] : 1800+ WOLVERHAMPTON, STS, ENG [36971] : 1800+ LAMBETH, SRY, ENG [36978] : 1500S-1638 NRY, ENG [37028] : C1770+ BOLDRE, HAM, ENG [37063] : PRE 1780 BOCKING, ESS, ENG [37063] : C1855+ SOUTHAMPTON, HAM, ENG [37063] : C1845+ PORTSEA, HAM, ENG [37063] : C1780+ KELVEDON, ESS, ENG [37063] : PRE 1920 CHELSEA, LND, ENG [37102] : 1800+ LEIGH, LAN, ENG [37258] : ALL EXBOURNE, DEV, ENG [37269] : 1750+ TODDINGTON, BDF, ENG [37306] : C1800 LAN, ENG [37309] : C1750 ALDBOURNE, WIL & HAM, ENG [37335] : 1800S BLACKBURN, LAN, ENG [37442] : PRE 1800 BAINTON, NTH, ENG [37463] : PRE 1733 HOLBETON, DEV, ENG [37610] : PRE 1860 SHOTLEY, NBL, ENG [37663] : 1827-99 MYERSCOUGH & GT ECCLESTON, LAN, ENG [37710] : 1790+ SOUTHWARK & NEWINGTON, SRY, ENG [37721] : C1790+ SAL, ENG [37762] : 1800-1900 LEICESTER, LEI, ENG [37858] : AUSTIN WM. PRE 1872 ENG [37897] : 1700-1800 BIRMINGHAM, WAR, ENG [37924] : 1810-1840 NTT, ENG [37999] : 1800-1900 CAMBRIDGE, ENG [38070] : 1750+ HOLBEACH, LIN, ENG [38280] : 1810 SHARPLES, LAN, ENG [38283] : 1700-1750 HOLBETON, DEV, ENG [38516] : BENJAMIN 1850+ BRIGHTON, SSX, ENG [38549] : CHARLES 1800+ BRIGHTON, SSX, ENG [38549] : 1795+ BAGENALS TOWN, CAR, IRL [34237] : 1780-1880 CARRICKMACROSS, MOG, IRL [34346] : PRE 1850 WIC, IRL [34429] : PRE 1850 TANNAGHMORE, ANT, IRL [35064] : 1800+ DUBLIN, IRL [35352] : PRE 1845 MEA & WEM, IRL [35824] : 1600-1900 GAL, IRL [35944] : MARY PRE 1860 ENNISCORTHY, WEX, IRL [36619] : PRE 1866 AUCKLAND, NZ [36748] : ANN PRE 1850 LANARK, LKS, SCT [36192] : 1880-1920 ADDIWELL, MLN, SCT [38526] : 1900+ PHILADELPHIA, PA, USA [34237] : 1900+ NEW YORK, NY, USA [34237] : 1650 CT, USA [36730] : W.A. 1829-1910 COFFEY CO., KS, USA [37014] : WILLIS 1860-1934 GREENE CO., MO, USA [37014] : 1700S GLOUCESTER CO., NJ, USA [37028] : PRE 1800 LINCOLN CO., NC, USA [38017] : MARY ANN 1809-1852 USA [38124] : ALL VA, KY & CA, USA [38363] : 1750-1850 MORRIS, NJ, USA [38366] : 1700-1800 ESSEX, NJ, USA [38366] : 1800-1900 SHELBYVILLE, IL, USA [38531] : 1790+ DUPLIN, NC, USA [38576]

WARDEL 1700+ HOUGHTON LE SPRING, DUR, ENG [36609]

WARDELL 1800+ HALDIMAND, ONT, CAN [34497] : DEBBIE C1780-1850 SMITHVILLE, LINCOLN CO., ONT, CAN [36712] : 1786+ CAN [38448] : 1700+ HEBBURN & HEBRON, NBL, ENG [36609] : PRE 1795 NORTON, YKS, ENG [36673] : ALL WOR, ENG [36998] : PRE 1800 MONMOUTH CO., NJ, USA [38448]

WARDEN ALL YASS, NSW, AUS [35518] : 1700+ BIRMINGHAM, WAR, ENG [37924] : 1830+ DUNDEE, ANS, SCT [34637] : C1830+ LKS, SCT & AUS [37287]

WARDER PRE 1800 NEWPORT, IOW, ENG [36021]

WARDLAW 1800S DOWNSVIEW, ONT, CAN [37458]

WARDLE C1850 BOWNESS ON SOLWAY, CUL, ENG [35470] : 1820 BRADFORD, WRY, ENG [36263] : 1700S HARTINGTON, DBY, ENG [36670] : 1770+ LEEK, STS, ENG [37666]

WARDMAN ALL SNAILBEACH, SAL, ENG [36866]

WARDROBBER PRE 1767 KINNAIRD, PER, SCT [34389]

WARDROBE ALL DUR, ENG [36639]

WARDROP 1850+ MELBOURNE, VIC, AUS [36761] : PRE 1927 STONEHOUSE, LKS, SCT [35007]

WARDSWORTH 1770-1830 PENISTONE, WRY, ENG [33767]

WARE JOHANNA 1780-1840 BOVINGDON, MDX, ENG [33961] : 1872 SHOREDITCH, LND, ENG [34224] : 1750+ CHESHAM & AMERSHAM, BKM, ENG [34416] : C1850 OKEHAMPTON, DEV, ENG [35057] : 1850+ WINKLEIGH, DEV, ENG [35057] : 1800+ IDDESLEIGH, DEV, ENG [35057] : 1740 PETER TAVY, DEV, ENG [35332] : 1810+ HONITON, DEV, ENG [35438] : PRE 1800 MINEHEAD, SOM, ENG [36069] : 1800+ SAMPFORD PEVERELL, DEV, ENG [36069] : 1773+ MARY TAVY & PETER TAVY, DEV, ENG [36376] : PRE 1550 PICKERING, YKS, ENG [37094] : PRE 1874 STEPNEY, MDX, ENG [37259] : 1850 WOKINGHAM, BRK, ENG [37690] : PRE 1880 HAMILTON CO. & GLOUCESTER CO., NJ & OH, USA [35270] : ALL MI & MS, USA [36540]

WAREHAM 1800+ BASINGSTOKE, HAM, ENG [34299] : PRE 1820 VERNHAM, HAM & WIL, ENG [34343] : C1877 WARRINGTON, LAN, ENG [34893]

WAREHIME 1800S BUTLER, PA, USA [34353]

WARF PRE 1850 VA & TN, USA [38217]

WARFIELD 1860S FULTON CO., IL, USA [38223]

WARFORD 1675-1775 ENG [36898]

WARGULA PRE 1900 PO, POL [36355]

WARHURST 1835+ ADELAIDE, SA, AUS [36297] : 1855-1930 BALLAN & MELBOURNE, VIC, AUS [36297] : PRE 1860 MANCHESTER & STOCKPORT, LAN, ENG [36297]

WARING 1850+ PRESTON, LAN, ENG [33894] : 1700-1800S BUGBROOK & FROI WORTH, NTH & LEI, ENG [36665] : 1750+ KIRKHAM, LAN, ENG [38034] : 1750+ BLACKBURN, LAN, ENG [38034] : 1700+ LONDON, ENG [38215]

WARK 1850S CHILTERN, VIC, AUS [35136] : 1800S MUDGEE, NSW, AUS [35359] : 1832+ DONEGAL, DON, IRL [34509] : HENRY PRE 1851 IRL [34993] : PRE 1850 SCT [34222]

WARKE 1900S CAN [35395] : 1800-1950 STRABANE, LDY, IRL [35395] : 1800S BUSHMILLS, ANT, IRL [35395]

WARLICH 1750-1850 ZELLERFELD, NSA, GER [38643]

WARLOW 1800S WLS [35744]

WARLTIRE ALL AUS [34745] : PRE 1880 BUCKHALL & WALSALL, STS, NTH & WOR, ENG [34745] : ALL GR [34745]

WARMAN 1820+ MELBOURNE, VIC & NSW, AUS [34177] : PRE 1820 HACKNEY, MDX & LND, ENG [34177] : 1700-1800S KEN, ENG [34483] : PRE 1780 FOLKESTONE, KEN, ENG [38389]

WARMINGER 1780-1800 NORWICH, NFK, ENG [34088]

WARMOLL 1700-1850 NFK, ENG [37207]

WARMOTH 1800-1900 POWELL CO., KY, USA [38089]

WARMOUTH 1800-1900 POWELL CO., KY, USA [38089] : 1820-1900 WA, USA [38089]

WARMSLEY 1800 BLACKPOOL, LAN, ENG [37262]

WARNE 1750+ CON, ENG [35060] : PRE 1840 WINGFIELD, SFK, ENG [35212] : 1854+ CUBERT, CON, ENG [35536] : PRE 1855 NFK, ENG [36050]

WARNEFORD ALL YKS, ENG [35950]

WARNER 1780-1990 OSNABRUCK, ONT, CAN [34077] : 1700S CATARAQUI, ONT, CAN [38072] : C1830 EVERSLEIGH, HAM, ENG [33772] : PRE 1864

CHATHAM, KEN, ENG [33914] : PRE 1900
LONDON, ENG [33972] : 1800-1960 ISLINGTON,
LND, ENG [34135] : 1800S LONDON, ENG [34205] :
1600-99 STOCKTON, WAR, ENG [34315] : 1823 +
GREENWICH, LND, ENG [34810] : ALL YKS, ENG
[35359] : PRE 1900 ST JOHNS WOOD, LND & MDX,
ENG [35950] : 1830 + KEN, ENG [35998] : 1700S
MEDWAY, KEN, ENG [37228] : PRE 1783
SHOREDITCH, LND, ENG [37228] : PRE 1850 ENG
[37595] : 1600-1800S FARNHAM, SRY, ENG [37898] :
1870 + EAST HEDLEY HOPE, DUR, ENG [37911] :
1850 + RUGBY, WAR, ENG [38047] : 1800 +
BRAUNSTON, NTH, ENG [38047] : C1750-1900
LND & SRY, ENG [38242] : 1750-1760
ALVECHURCH, WOR, ENG [38465] : 1700-1832
HANOVER, GER [36440] : 1800-1888 LAMLASH,
ARRAN IS., SCT [36960] : C1770 BROOKFIELD,
MA, USA [33905] : C1800 WASHINGTON CO., NY,
USA [36319] : 1870S NEW YORK, NY, USA [38369] :
1500 + BEDFORD CO., PA, USA & ENG [36970] :
PRE 1700 BOXTED, MA & SFK, USA & ENG [38746]
: ALL ANTIGUA, W.INDIES [35359]

WARNES PRE 1860 NFK, ENG [35488]

WARNOCK 1700-1899 MONAGHAN &
COOKSTOWN, MOG & TYR, IRL [36080] : PRE
1840 TULLYLISH, DOW, IRL [36273] : PRE 1850
PORTAVOGIE, DOW, IRL [37035] : 1700 +
WORLDWIDE [35580]

WARR 1850 + MYRTLEFORD, VIC, AUS [38071]

WARRACK PRE 1854 W.INDIES [33777]

WARRE ALL NL [38350]

WARREN THOMAS 1850-1875 FRANKLIN, TAS,
AUS [33933] : ELIZA 1842 KELSO, NSW, AUS
[34302] : ELIZA 1841 + BATHURST, NSW, AUS
[34302] : 1864 + VIC, AUS [34412] : 1850
GOULBURN, NSW, AUS [34421] : 1860-1930
NORTH, NSW, AUS [34438] : 1835-1870 ADELAIDE,
SA, AUS [34438] : RICHARD 1903 + BREDBO,
NSW, AUS [34885] : 1800S MUDGEE, NSW, AUS
[35567] : PETER 1860S + DAYLESFORD, VIC, AUS
[35876] : 1931 WELSHPOOL, WA, AUS [36606] :
CATH 1872 BALLARAT, VIC, AUS [37123] : 1850S
ANTICOSTI ILD, QUE, CAN [34349] : ALL
HERRING NECK, NFD, CAN [35264] : JANE C1850
ONT, CAN [36677] : 1830 + OTTAWA VALLEY,
ONT, CAN [37443] : 1780 + PEI, CAN [38460] :
1800 + NORTHUMBERLAND CO., NB, CAN
[38460] : PRE 1900 LONDON, ENG [33883] : DAVID
C1830-1850 WATERSIDE, CAM, ENG [34007] : PRE
1730 ILMINSTER, SOM, ENG [34270] : PRE 1864
BOURNE END, HRT, ENG [34412] : 1800 BATH,
SOM, ENG [34421] : 1750-1850 ST JUST IN
PENWITH, CON, ENG [34535] : 1750-1875
SENNEN, CON, ENG [34535] : 1750-1890 LONDON,
ENG [34615] : 1800 + OLD NEWTON, SFK, ENG
[34640] : ALL MACCLESFIELD, CHS, ENG [34674] :
1700-1750 WINSHAM, SOM, ENG [35098] : JOHN R
1890-1915 CHISWICK, MDX, ENG [35124] : EMILY
1870-1915 DORMANS PARK, SRY, ENG [35124] :
JONATHAN 1860-1900 CHISWICK, MDX, ENG
[35124] : 1850S SRY, ENG [35156] : 1800S HITCHIN,
HRT, ENG [35650] : PRE 1800 HARLINGTON, BDF,
ENG [35701] : 1700S MILDENHALL, SFK, ENG
[35858] : PRE 1850 POLSTEAD, SFK, ENG [36215] :
1700-1900 LOUGHBOROUGH & ASHBY, LEI, ENG
[36531] : 1800-1900 NTT, ENG [36531] : 1851 GREAT
MARYLEBONE, LND, ENG [36606] : PRE 1800
WITHAM, ESS, ENG [37006] : 1820-1930
BIRMINGHAM, WAR, ENG [37074] : C1700-1750
WIL, ENG [37086] : PRE 1880 PENSAX, WOR &
DEV, ENG [37096] : PRE 1857 BRIXTON, WIL,
ENG [37131] : PRE 1860 IPSWICH, SFK, ENG

[37768] : PRE 1800 BOTESDALE, SFK, ENG [38420] :
PRE 1832 WEST HALLAM, DBY, ENG [38449] :
1863 + MARLPOOL, DBY, ENG [38449] : JOHN
1800-1880 WEX, IRL [34143] : 1805 + DOW, IRL
[34993] : C1835 BELFAST, ANT, IRL [35391] : 1840S
WATERFORD, WAT, IRL [35464] : C1821
KINGUSSIE, INV, SCT [34058] : PRE 1775 CEDAR
CREEK, SSX CO., DE, USA [34992] : 1800-1860
OTSEGO CO., NY & MN, USA [36334] : MOSES
1850 NY, USA [37596] : 1780-1850 MADISON CO.,
NY, USA [38009] : 1840-1900 MARSHALL, MI, USA
[38010] : 1850S PASSAIC CO., NJ, USA [38035] :
1620 + PLYMOUTH, MA, USA [38195] : C1880
MARION CO., AL, USA [38590] : ALL
WORLDWIDE [35268]

WARRENDER 1700-1900 BOSTON, LIN, ENG [37342]

WARRENER PRE 1840 GLOSSOP, DBY, ENG [33940] :
PRE 1840 ATTENBOROUGH, NTT, ENG [35898] :
1820-1850 DARLTON, NTT, ENG [36112] : PRE 1650
COLYTON, DEV, ENG [38746]

WARRICK 1600-1800 ENG [37015] : 1780-1820
WASHINGTON CO., PA, USA [37015] : 1800-1820
RICHLAND CO., OH, USA [37015]

WARRICKER PRE 1895 + ESS, ENG [35928]

WARRIE 1700-1750 LONDON, ENG [36081]

WARRINER ALL TAS, AUS [35806]

WARRING C1750-1820 LIN, ENG [35238]

WARRINGTON C1840 DAPTO, NSW, AUS [34426] :
1862 + SYDNEY, NSW, AUS [38597] : ALL LEI,
ENG [36005] : 1840 + BRAMPTON, HUN, ENG
[38572] : 1820-1830S INCHAGUIRE, KID, IRL
[34359]

WARRY ALL SOM, ENG [36531]

WARTMAN C1700 OSMARSLEBEN, HAL, DDR
[37918]

WARTON 1873 + GRENFELL, NSW, AUS [34030] :
PRE 1860 SAL, ENG [37273] : PRE 1800 STEPNEY,
LND, ENG [37361]

WARWICK 1830 + WINDSOR, NSW, AUS [33933] :
ALL DIDCOT & SOUTH MORETON, BRK, ENG
[35181] : PRE 1880 HARTLEY, NBL, ENG [36793] :
1850 + LIVERPOOL, LAN, ENG [37865] : PRE 1850
IRL [37865] : ALL NZ [34647] : C1809 PT [37865] :
1780-1820 FRANKLIN CO., VA, USA [38144] : ALL
WORLDWIDE [37922]

WASBOROUGH PRE 1850 STROUD, GLS, ENG
[37454]

WASER PRE 1860 KAPAUITZ, GER [35818]

WASH 1805 NOTTINGHAM, NTT, ENG [34540] :
1880-1920 EDMONTON, MDX, ENG [37859] : 1750-
1870 WETHERSFIELD, ESS, ENG [37859]

WASHBURN 1600-1800 ONT, CAN [38128] : 1785 +
LENNOX & ADDINGTON, ONT, CAN [38517] :
1700-1920 NATICK, MA, USA [34004] : PRE 1880
CATTARAUGUS CO. & TOLLAND CO., CT & NY,
USA [35270] : C1800 MIDDLESEX, CT, USA [38173] :
C1840 SUMMIT CO., OH, USA [38173] : 1800-1827
KEENE, NY, USA [38741]

WASHER 1880 + COOTAMUNDRA, NSW, AUS
[34899] : 1545-1660 ENG [38040]

WASHINGTON 1840 + TAS, AUS [35043] : C1860
WOODEND, VIC, AUS [35203] : C1885 +
KEMPSEY, NSW, AUS [35527] : 1830 LEIGHTON
BUZZARD, BDF, ENG [34633] : C1850 KINVARA,
GAL, IRL [35203] : 1883 LYTTELTON, NZ [35527]

WASLEY PRE 1820 BLACKWATER, CON, ENG
[34031] : 1830 + CHACEWATER & TRURO, CON,
ENG [34881] : 1800-1900 GLOUCESTER, GLS, ENG
[36262] : 1800-1900 TEWKESBURY, GLS, ENG
[36262]

WASNER 1600S PANGAU, SIL, GER [33901]

WASON PRE 1840 GIRVAN, AYR, SCT **[34713]** :
C1800 AYR, AYR, SCT **[34713]**

WASS PRE 1900 WA, AUS **[34562]** : 1700+ STOKE BY
NAYLAND, SFK, ENG **[33938]** : ALL NTT & DBY,
ENG **[37412]**

WASSALL 1700+ WINDSOR, BRK, ENG **[34664]**

WASSELL 1700+ WINDSOR, BRK, ENG **[34664]**

WASSINK 1700S DOETINCHEM, GEL, NL **[38350]** :
ALL UTRECHT, UTR, NL **[38350]**

WASSON C1850 NEWTON STEWART, TYR, IRL
[34494]

WASTELL PRE 1900 HACKNEY, MDX, ENG **[36108]**

WASTENEDGE PRE 1850 SHEFFIELD, YKS, ENG
[37442]

WASTREN PRE 1800 SWE **[35500]**

WATERBURY 1670-1780 STAMFORD, CT, USA
[36310]

WATERFALL ELIZABETH 1783 ENG **[35607]**

WATERFIELD 1750S BULWICK, NTH, ENG **[33967]** :
1700-1900 LONDON, MDX, ENG **[38115]**

WATERHOUSE 1900+ VICTORIA, BC, CAN **[36716]** :
ALL ALLERTON MAULEVERER, WRY, ENG
[35588] : ALL SSX & KEN, ENG **[36584]** : 1700+
KINGSLEY, STS, ENG **[36701]** : 1800-1810
SOUTHAMPTON, HAM, ENG **[37869]** : PRE 1800
ENG **[38754]** : 1710+ USA **[37592]**

WATERLOW 1600+ CANTERBURY, KEN, ENG
[37659] : 1700+ LONDON, ENG **[37659]** : 1800+
REIGATE, SRY, ENG **[37659]**

WATERMAN 1800+ UPPER CLATFORD, HAM,
ENG **[34405]** : C1792 MDX, ENG **[35560]** : 1830S
SPITALFIELDS, LND, ENG **[37080]** : ALL TEST
VALLEY, HAM, ENG **[38350]** : PRE 1840 BAW, GER
[38029] : 1760-1800 JOHNSTON, RI, USA **[38131]** :
C1940-1960S FREDDY MAGICIAN, USA **[38350]**

WATERS 1860-1870S WESTBURY, TAS, AUS **[34452]** :
1884+ MOSS VALE, NSW, AUS **[35567]** : 1860-1915
ST ARNAUD, VIC, AUS **[35717]** : 1850+
INVERELL, NSW, AUS **[36628]** : PRE 1841
GOLDEN SQUARE, LND, ENG **[34043]** : PRE 1822
BOUGHTON MONCHELSEA, KEN, ENG **[34325]** :
PRE 1810 EAST GRINSTEAD, SSX, ENG **[34325]** :
PRE 1850 REDRUTH, CON, ENG **[34783]** : 1830-
1900 LONDON, ENG **[34850]** : C1820 DEVIZES,
WIL, ENG **[34974]** : PRE 1807 MDX, ENG **[34977]** :
PRE 1760 BENENDEN, KEN, ENG **[35227]** : C1840
NUNTAN, WIL, ENG **[35349]** : PRE 1848 SSX, ENG
[35407] : 1820-1850 KEN, ENG **[35717]** : 1840S
PENZANCE, CON, ENG **[35730]** : 1800 KEN, ENG
[36480] : C1850 CROWAN & ST KEW, CON & DEV,
ENG **[37556]** : PRE 1800 TEALBY, LIN, ENG **[37692]**
: PRE 1850 SFK, ENG **[38390]** : SARAH 1848+
SALFORD, LAN, ENG **[38410]** : PRE 1800 FOXLEY,
NFK, ENG & AUS **[35535]** : ALL CLIFFORD, WRY,
ENG & IRL **[36159]** : PRE 1820 CORK, COR, IRL
[34452] : 1829+ DUNMORE, KIK, IRL **[34781]** :
1800-1850S BALLYVAUGHAN, CLA, IRL **[35206]** :
EZEKEIL PRE 1838 AUGHALOO, TYR, IRL **[35541]**
: PRE 1900 WEX, IRL **[37750]** : HUGH ALEX. 1800-
1850 GLASGOW AREA, LKS, SCT **[38006]** : PRE
1850 YELL CO., AR, USA **[36939]**

WATERSON 1841+ DALEFIELD, WAIRARAPA, NZ
[33950] : 1800S DUNFERMLINE, FIF, SCT **[34809]**

WATERSTON PRE 1800 PAISLEY, RFW, SCT **[35871]**

WATERTON 1884+ BIRMINGHAM, WAR, ENG
[35033]

WATES PRE 1775 RAMPTON, NTT, ENG **[36434]**

WATFORD ALL LINDFIELD, SSX, ENG **[34308]**

WATHEN 1880+ BRISBANE, QLD, AUS **[34868]** :
PRE 1880 LONDON, ENG **[34868]**

WATHERSTON C1860-1920 PORT LINCOLN, SA,
AUS **[35550]**

WATHEW 1700-1800 LIN, ENG **[37924]**

WATHY C1830 KEGWORTH, LEI, ENG **[33912]**

WATKIN 1700-1800 PREES, SAL, ENG **[38474]**

WATKINS 1836-1850 BATHURST, NSW, AUS **[35187]** :
PRE 1917 FOREST LODGE, NSW, AUS **[36632]** :
WILLIAM 1850+ LAUNCESTON, TAS & VIC, AUS
[37134] : 1850+ DUDLEY, WOR, ENG **[34782]** : PRE
1799 KEN, ENG **[34858]** : 1822+ STANLOKE, OXF,
ENG **[35436]** : 1822+ STANLOKE, OXF, ENG
[35436] : PRE 1793 PETERCHURCH, HEF, ENG
[35713] : SARAH 1780S GLOUCESTER, GLS, ENG
[35815] : ALL WHITE WALTHAM, BRK, ENG
[36163] : 1773-1793 LAMBETH & BERMONDSEY,
SRY, ENG **[36184]** : 1700-1775 EAST CHINNOCK,
SOM, ENG **[36184]** : 1760-1775 GREENWICH, KEN,
ENG **[36184]** : 1780-1880 EMPINGHAM &
UPPINGHAM, RUT, ENG **[36184]** : 1750-1900
HORSHAM, SSX, ENG **[36184]** : 1800-1845 SFK,
ENG **[36184]** : 1773-1796 SOUTHWARK, SRY, ENG
[36184] : 1500-1775 SOM & DOR, ENG **[36184]** : 1780-
1880 EASTON, NTH, ENG **[36184]** : 1800-1900
WORCESTER & CLAINS, WOR, ENG **[36184]** :
ELIZABETH PRE 1840 BISHOPS FROME, HEF,
ENG **[36889]** : PRE 1820 LEEDS, YKS, ENG **[38690]** :
C1860 LONDON, SCT **[34814]** : PRE 1796 WAYNE
CO., NC, USA **[36570]** : C1858 MECKLENBURG
CO., VA, USA **[36903]** : 1810-1830 JESSIAMINE CO.,
KY, USA **[38334]** : C1870 LLANFYLLIN, MGY, WLS
[34395] : JAMES C1801 GLYNFACH, BRE, WLS
[35391] : PRE 1820 ST MARYS, PEM, WLS **[35457]** :
1750+ PEMBROKE, PEM, WLS **[36209]** : 1870-1910
WELSHPOOL, MGY, WLS **[36990]**

WATKINSON PRE 1793 PLEASLEY, DBY, ENG
[35029] : PRE 1800 ADEL & COOKRIDGE, WRY,
ENG **[36034]** : ALL BRAINTREE & BOCKING, ESS,
ENG **[37321]**

WATKINS-WILSON PHILLIP 1875+ HEF, ENG
[36600]

WATKISS ALL WORLDWIDE **[37857]**

WATLEN C1830 PADDINGTON, MDX, ENG **[35990]**

WATLING 1849+ TOWRANG, NSW, AUS **[34009]** :
C1829 CHATHAM, KEN, ENG **[36888]** : 1700S CAM,
ENG **[38478]**

WATMOUGH 1753 BLACKROD, LAN, ENG **[35560]** :
PETER 1806+ DEANE BY BOLTON, LAN, ENG
[36314] : 1808+ BURY, LAN, ENG **[37175]**

WATMOUTH PRE 1850 MANCHESTER, LAN &
WRY, ENG **[35354]**

WATROUS 1710+ CT, USA **[37592]**

WATSON C1860 BENDIGO, VIC, AUS **[33881]** : 1816+
SYDNEY, NSW, AUS **[34177]** : 1844+ VIC, AUS
[34412] : ALL DOUTTA GALLA, VIC, AUS **[34877]** :
ELIZABETH 1871-1948 BRUSHY HILL, NSW, AUS
[34942] : 1858+ MELBOURNE, VIC, AUS **[35136]** :
1860+ PENSHURST & MELBOURNE, VIC, AUS
[35137] : 1800S FERN GULLY, VIC, AUS **[35159]** :
1890+ PERTH, WA, AUS **[35347]** : 1840+
WARRNAMBOOL, VIC, AUS **[35347]** : 1860+
NEWCASTLE, NSW, AUS **[35356]** : 1814-1846 PORT
DALRYMPLE, TAS, AUS **[35384]** : C1890+
GALAQUIL, VIC, AUS **[35527]** : 1820+ SYDNEY,
NSW, AUS **[35814]** : 1874 BALLARAT, VIC, AUS
[35855] : J.A. 1810+ DRESDEN, ONT, CAN **[34154]** :
1845+ PRINCE EDWARD CO., ONT, CAN **[34365]** :
JOSEPH 1830-1900 STRATFORD, ONT, CAN **[34515]**
: JOSEPH C1856+ ONT & MAN, CAN **[35778]** :
1800+ BEDFORD TWP, FRONTENAC CO., ONT,
CAN **[36664]** : PRE 1797 WHITEHAVEN, CUL, ENG
[33806] : PRE 1810 GIRTON, CAM, ENG **[33998]** :
1800-1860 HEMINGFORD, HUN, ENG **[34003]** :
PRE 1818 YKS, ENG **[34177]** : C1800 SRY, ENG
[34258] : C1808 WEYBRIDGE, SRY, ENG **[34319]** :

PRE 1870 WINSTER, DBY, ENG [34329] : PRE 1845 ENG [34365] : 1800S YKS, ENG [34377] : PRE 1844 LIVERPOOL, LAN, ENG [34412] : PRE 1790 KEN, ENG [34445] : PRE 1725 MARSKE BY THE SEA, YKS, ENG [34519] : 1800+ MANCHESTER, LAN, ENG [34684] : C1800 NOKE, OXF, ENG [34814] : ALL LINCOLN, ENG [34877] : PRE 1850 DEDHAM, ESS, ENG [35113] : 1800S NEWCASTLE UPON TYNE, NBL, ENG [35347] : PRE 1834 LANGHAM, SFK, ENG [35441] : CAROLINE C1820+ LONDON, ENG [35447] : JAMES C1820-1870 LONDON, ENG [35447] : SARAH 1860 MANCHESTER, LAN, ENG [35529] : 1800+ ROLVENDEN, KEN, ENG [35543] : WILLIAM C1820 WICKEN, ESS, ENG [35726] : C1829 ENG [35910] : 1850+ DISTINGTON, CUL, ENG [35979] : EDWARD 1820-1860 HOXTON, MDX, ENG [36064] : PRE 1820 TANFIELD, DUR, ENG [36102] : GRACE ANN PRE 1845 LEEDS, WRY, ENG [36192] : MARY PRE 1810 NAFFERTON, ERY, ENG [36192] : PRE 1755 STANHOPE, DUR, ENG [36202] : ANN 1776-1810 BEVERLEY, ERY, ENG [36391] : 1800-1990 WEST DEREHAM, NFK, ENG [36394] : C1814 YORK, YKS, ENG [36426] : JOHN C1811 BROOME & DITCHENHAM, NFK, ENG [36590] : 1750-1850 HARROGATE, YKS, ENG [36724] : ABRAHAM PRE 1687 BURTON ON THE HILL, GLS, ENG [36817] : C1770 LANCHESTER, DUR, ENG [36961] : PRE 1691 ENG [36972] : 1750+ DARWEN, LAN, ENG [36991] : 1750-1900 NEWCASTLE, NBL, ENG [37064] : PRE 1790 COCKFIELD, DUR, ENG [37103] : PRE 1864+ DEPTFORD, LND, ENG [37108] : PRE 1850 ST CLEMENT, OXF, ENG [37150] : PRE 1760 HOLME UPON SPALDING MOOR, YKS, ENG [37288] : 1750-1816 ORPINGTON, KEN, ENG [37340] : 1800-1900 YKS, ENG [37495] : PRE 1857 STOCKTON ON TEES, DUR, ENG [37635] : PRE 1756 MIDDLETON TYAS, NRY, ENG [37635] : 1700+ WHITTLESEY & MARCH, CAM, ENG [37686] : 1860+ MIDDLETON, LAN, ENG [37828] : 1870 WESTERHAM, KEN, ENG [37841] : PRE 1800 SEPLESCOMBE & MOUNTFIELD, SSX, ENG [37875] : 1750 METFIELD, SFK, ENG [37928] : THOMAS PRE 1825 WHITWICK, LEI, ENG [37961] : 1734+ ST BEES, CUL, ENG [38067] : PRE 1850 DUR, ENG [38217] : 1800+ FRAMPTON, LIN, ENG [38280] : 1800+ TENDRING & COLCHESTER, ESS & SFK, ENG [38395] : WILLIAM 1821-1880 HUNTINGDON, NTH, ENG & AUS [34942] : 1848 POONAMALLEE, INDIA [34609] : ALL COOTEHILL, CAV, IRL [33823] : 1700+ COOKSTOWN, TYR, IRL [34271] : 1800+ TYR, IRL [35137] : 1800-1860 CRAIGS, ANT, IRL [35243] : C1836 RATHDRUM, WIC, IRL [35365] : 1800-1900 DRUMAVADDY, ANT, IRL [35480] : 1800+ BELFAST, ANT, DOW & ARM, IRL [35636] : 1700+ DUBLIN &, LEX, IRL [36087] : PRE 1900 BALLYMENA & CARNLOUGH, ANT, IRL [36529] : C1842 AVOCA, WIC, IRL [36772] : PRE 1900 BELFAST, ANT, IRL [36801] : PRE 1900 CAV, IRL [36801] : PRE 1920 DROMORE, DOW, IRL [37807] : WILLIAM C1895 BELFAST, IRL [38072] : 1828-1898 TEMPLETON, CANT, NZ [34622] : 1840S PAISLEY, RFW, SCT [33934] : AGNES C1850 GLASGOW, SCT [34222] : THOMAS 1700+ PAISLEY, RFW, SCT [34263] : C1830 BIGGAR, LKS, SCT [34556] : 1700+ ARBUTHNOTT, KCD, SCT [34560] : JANET PRE 1800 DRUMMOND PARK, PER, SCT [34610] : PRE 1900 ARL, SCT [34647] : 1800+ SCT [34647] : 1853 FIFE KILRENEY, RFW, SCT [34761] : WHISKY C1840+ DUNDEE, PER, SCT [35053] : 1800-1830S FALKIRK, STI, SCT [35136] : JAMES 1806

ABERDEEN, ABD, SCT [35377] : 1800+ LOUDOUN, AYR, SCT [35527] : 1700+ CARNBEE, FIF, SCT [35627] : 1700+ AUCHTERHOUSE, ANS, SCT [35644] : 1800+ MONIFIETH, ANS, SCT [35644] : 1821 ROX, SCT [35855] : 1700-1900 SKELMORLIE, AYR, SCT [35923] : PRE 1858 GLASGOW, LKS, SCT [35985] : 1750-1850 CURRIE, MLN, SCT [36098] : C1750 ANS, SCT [36327] : JAMES C1800 GLASGOW, LKS, SCT [37143] : C1847 SCT [37474] : C1900 DUNDEE, ANS, SCT [37474] : 1700+ LESMAHAGOW, LKS, SCT [37480] : 1770-1800 FORDOUN, KCD, SCT [37485] : PRE 1880 HAMILTON, LKS, SCT [37630] : PRE 1850 DUNDEE, ANS, SCT [37727] : PRE 1850 IRVINE & MAYBOLE, AYR, SCT [37736] : PRE 1841 FIF, SCT [37828] : C1830 LEITH, MLN, SCT [37982] : 1830+ DUNDEE, ANS, SCT [38274] : PRE 1900 ABERDEEN, ABD, SCT [38412] : 1900+ CA, USA [34647] : JACOB C1808-1861 PICKAWAY CO., OH, USA [35284] : EDMONDSON 1800+ KY, USA [35328] : EDMONDSON PRE 1800 DANDRIDGE, VA, USA [35328] : C1809 NH, USA [36544] : PRE 1800 VA & NC, USA [36570] : 1800-1860 KY, USA [36908] : C1800 FORT ANN, NY, USA [37017] : 1810-1860 MADISON CO., OH, USA [37576] : PRESCOTT 1850S IN, USA [37585] : EDMISTON 1770S ABINGDON, VA, USA [37585] : ALL CAPE COD, MA, USA [37627] : 1850-1900 BROWN, OH, USA [38054] : ALL CO, USA [38067] : 1800+ KANSAS CITY, MO, USA [38067] : 1790-1825 LOUDOUN CO., VA, USA [38088] : 1780+ MERCER, IL, USA & IRL [36931] : ALL WORLDWIDE [35875]

WATT 1860+ KANGAROO FLAT, VIC, AUS [35391] : 1850+ CAMPBELLFIELD, VIC, AUS [35526] : 1880+ MELBOURNE, VIC, AUS [36077] : 1850+ SOUTH COAST, NSW, AUS [36637] : 1800-1900 BRIXTON, DEV, ENG [34069] : JAMES 1900+ RIEGATE, SRY, ENG [34916] : ALL LIVERPOOL, LAN, ENG [36822] : PRE 1900 BARROWFORD, LAN, ENG [38464] : 1700+ DRUMIGNY, DON, IRL [33986] : 1800+ ADDINGTON, DON, IRL [34785] : PRE 1800 COLERAINE, LDY, IRL [35773] : PRE 1863 BALLYMONEY, ANT, IRL [36888] : 1820+ SPITTAL, SCT [33795] : PRE 1850 MAUCHLINE, AYR, SCT [33808] : 1790S MONTROSE, ANS, SCT [33811] : PRE 1850 ABD, SCT [34053] : 1800+ BOHARM, BAN, SCT [34075] : PRE 1830 GAMRIE, BAN, SCT [34192] : PRE 1840 GIRVAN, AYR, SCT [34197] : 1700+ ST MONANCE, FIF, SCT [34637] : PRE 1823 GAMRIE, BAN, SCT [34840] : SARAH ALL LKS, SCT [35122] : ANDREW 1808+ HADDINGTON, ELN, SCT [35391] : 1600+ GAMRIE, BAN, SCT [35627] : PRE 1730 FIF, SCT [35745] : PRE 1857 AYR, SCT [35799] : 1880+ GLASGOW, RFW, SCT [35825] : 1750-1875 KEMNAY & INVERUERIE, ABD, SCT [35981] : PRE 1880 KCD, SCT [36077] : 1900 ABERDEEN, ABD, SCT [37703] : 1800-1870 EAST KILBRIDE, LKS, SCT [37783] : PRE 1832 ABERLADY, MLN, SCT [37978] : 1800-1850 ABERDEEN, ABD, SCT [38355] : PRE 1880 ABERDEEN, SCT [38464] : C1790 ROCKINGHAM CO., NC, USA [36354]

WATTAM PRE 1800 SOUTH WILLINGHAM, LIN, ENG [37692]

WATTE PRE 1820 WESTMINSTER & HOLBORN, MDX, ENG [38258]

WATTERS 1800 CROWAN, CON, ENG [35023] : PRE 1896 YELVERTON, DEV, ENG [35587] : 1800+ CROWAN, CON, ENG [36785]

WATTERSON PRE 1700 STS, WAR & WOR, ENG [36140] : PRE 1610 WORCESTER, WOR, ENG [36976] : PRE 1610 KINGS NORTON, WAR, ENG

[36976] : 1805-1840 PERTH, PER, SCT [33950] :
MARTHA C1850-1900 NY, USA [35324]
WATTIS 1790+ POWICK, WOR, ENG [38020]
WATTLES PRE 1750 CT, USA [37018]
WATTLETON C1650-1800 GUILDFORD, SRY, ENG [37618]

WATTON PRE 1600 NTH, ENG [38023]
WATTS 1849-1906+ SYDNEY, NSW, AUS [34651] :
1881 PORT ESPERANCE, TAS, AUS [34761] : 1859+
BRISBANE, QLD, AUS [34860] : 1884+ NSW, AUS
[34860] : C1850 GEELONG, VIC, AUS [34903] :
1840+ HOBART, TAS, AUS [36749] : 1870+ ROSS
CREEK, VIC, AUS [38205] : 1850+ ELTHAM, VIC,
AUS [38213] : PRE 1900 NB, CAN [36933] :
ANTHONY 1700+ ENG [33827] : 1700-1900
TOLPUDDLE, DOR, ENG [33875] : 1760S
RAMSBURY, WIL, ENG [34205] : ROBERT 1896+
LONDON, ENG [34259] : HARRIET 1809-1869 NTH
& LEI, ENG [34314] : PRE 1813 HUCKNALL, NTT,
ENG [34329] : C1810 SHERBORNE, DOR, ENG
[34393] : C1830-1850 SPARKFORD, SOM, ENG
[34393] : SARAH 1810 AVENING, GLS, ENG [34475]
: 1600+ UPLOWMAN, DEV, ENG [34747] : PRE
1859 CAMBERWELL, SRY, ENG [34860] : 1900+
LONDON, ENG [35939] : C1840 TITCHFIELD,
HAM, ENG [36154] : PRE 1750 CHICHESTER, SSX,
ENG [36154] : SAMUEL 1830 CHEWSTOKE, SOM,
ENG [36274] : ELIZABETH 1833 CHEWSTOKE,
SOM, ENG [36274] : EDWIN 1837 CHEWSTOKE,
SOM, ENG [36274] : C1840 MIDDLETON CHENEY,
NTH, ENG [36370] : 1700+ BRISTOL, SOM, ENG
[36743] : C1740 WHITFIELD, NTH, ENG [36945] :
1830 KEN, ENG [37006] : 1800 YARMOUTH, NFK,
ENG [37125] : 1800+ BARKINGSIDE, ESS, ENG
[37223] : 1850+ MANCHESTER, LAN, ENG [37225] :
PRE 1900 COVENTRY, WAR, ENG [37225] : ALL
SOM & SSX, ENG [37269] : PRE 1870 LANGPORT,
SOM, ENG [37322] : 1770+ CAM, GLS, ENG [37343]
: 1841 HARDINGTON MANDEVILLE, SOM, ENG
[37378] : 1800S ENG [37391] : ALL NORWICH, NFK,
ENG [37689] : 1850S BRACKNELL, BRK, ENG
[37751] : ALL ESS, ENG [37884] : PRE 1900
BRAUNTON, DEV, ENG [38205] : 1700+
ADSTOCK, BKM, ENG [38213] : WILLIAM C1840-
1920 ENG & WLS [37813] : 1750+ CUMBERLAND
CO., PA, USA [36895] : 1800+ THOMAS CO., GA,
USA [37010] : SARA PRE 1800 CHRISTIAN CO.,
KY, USA [38536] : 1650-1800 HEMPSTEAD, NY,
USA [38767]

WAUCHOPE 1900 PAKENHAM, VIC, AUS [38213]
WAUD PRE 1823 CROWLE, LIN, ENG [34494]
WAUER PRE 1858 MST, GER [35310]
WAUGH 1850+ DANDENONG, VIC, AUS [34541] :
PRE 1800 LONDON, ENG [34117] : PRE 1850
ROCHDALE, LAN, ENG [34541] : 1770+ WILTON
ON REDCAR, YKS, ENG [35908] : 1850-1880
SOUTH SHIELDS, DUR, ENG [34867] : C1730-1840
NEWCASTLE ON TYNE, NBL, ENG [36877] :
1820+ LIVERPOOL, LAN, ENG [37986] : 1870-1920
TIMARU, CANTY, NZ [38272] : 1800+ AIRDRIE,
LKS, SCT [35244] : 1840-1880 ARDCHONICH, INV,
SCT [36877] : ALL SCT & AUS [38356] : 1720-1800
LITCHFIELD, CT, USA [37783]

WAVELL PRE 1800 NEWPORT, IOW, ENG [36021]
WAY 1850-1900 VIC, AUS [34641] : C1813 TAUNTON,
SOM, ENG [33936] : PRE 1830 LONDON, ENG
[34343] : PRE 1850 GREAT TORRINGTON, DEV,
ENG [37670] : 1800-1850 IOW, ENG [38007] : 1700-
1880 NETHERBURY, DUR, ENG [38250] : PRE 1850
WESTON SUPER MARE, SOM, ENG [38783] : 1850-
1900 NELSON, NZ [34641]

WAYLAND ALL WORLDWIDE [36030]

WAYLETT PRE 1900 CLAVERING, ESS, ENG [35443]
WAYMAN PRE 1835 ETON, BKM, ENG [34445]
WAYPER JOSH C1850-1900 WATERLOO CO., ONT,
CAN [34215]
WAZE PRE 1600 ROTHERBY, LEI, ENG [35572]
WEADON C1850 LAMBETH, MDX, ENG [38078]
WEAFER 1860+ HAMILTON, ONT, CAN [34466] :
1840+ KEMPTVILLE, ONT, CAN [34466]
WEAKLEY 1840-1918 ATWORTH, WIL, ENG & AUS
[34942]
WEAKLIM 1790+ KILLYNANGLE, DON, IRL
[38171]
WEAL 1750+ LONDON, ENG [34768] : C1800
BIRMINGHAM, WAR, ENG [35456]
WEALLENS 1825+ NEWBURN, NBL, ENG [38436]
WEARE ALL WELSH BICKNOR ENGLISH
BICKNOR, GLS, ENG [37746]
WEARMOUTH 1860-1980 ORANGE, CA, USA [38768]
WEARNE ALL CAMBORNE, CON, ENG [35517]
WEART 1780-1990 OSNABRUCK, ONT, CAN [34077]
WEATHERALL 1804-1900 PARRAMATTA, NSW, AUS
[36595] : PRE 1870 ENG [35546] : C1850 NEWTON
LIMAVADY, LDY, IRL [36806]
WEATHERLEY 1855-1914 ILFORD, NSW, AUS [35864]
: PRE 1855 RUISLIP & PINNER, MDX, ENG [35864]
: PRE 1873 HILLINGDON, MDX, ENG [35895] :
ALL RUISLIP, MDX, ENG [35984] : ALL
HILLINGTON, MDX, ENG [35984] : 1873-1881 NZ
[35895]
WEATHERLY PRE 1850 CHOLLERTON &
KIRKWHELPINGTON, NBL, ENG [36110]
WEATHERS 1828 GA, USA [36358]
WEAVER 1900+ NORTH PERTH, WA, AUS [35526] :
1820 KIDDERMINSTER, WOR, ENG [35041] :
C1800 DILTON, WIL, ENG [35076] : 1800-1900 ENG
[35884] : 1500-1900 HOLLEY BUSH, WOR, ENG
[36689] : PRE 1800 WORCESTER, WOR, ENG
[36789] : 1790-1865 HESKETH & WHITEHAVEN,
LAN, ENG [36798] : ALL SOM, ENG [37268] : PRE
1830 ACTON, CHS, ENG [37722] : 1530-1650
RUSHBURY, SAL, ENG [38315] : 1600-1900
GEMMENGEN, BAD, GER [38574] : FRANCIS
WM. 1796 STROMBERG, PRE, GER [38780] :
HERCULES PRE 1833 RENSSELAER, NYS, USA
[36447] : PRE 1830 NC & SC, USA [37587] :
CATHERINE 1799+ WYTHE CO., VA, USA [37604]
: JOHN PRE 1800 FREDERICK CO., VA, USA
[37781] : JOHN 1805-1840 RICHLAND CO., OH,
USA [37781] : 1850-1880 WILLIAMSON CO., IL,
USA [37822] : 1820-1875 MS, USA [37822] : 1650+ RI,
USA [38015] : ERHART 1754-1795 UPPER SAUCON
TWP., PA, USA [38127] : ADAM 1850-80 SUMMIT
CO., OH, USA [38138] : ADAM 1820-50 STARK CO.,
OH, USA [38138] : 1820 OH, USA [38143] : 1650-1800S
YORK & NEW KENT CO., VA, USA [38315] : PRE
1900 CULPEPER, VA, USA [38574] : 1820-1860
BEDFORD CO., PA, USA [38742] : WM. HENRY
1750-1760 ABBOTTSTOWN, ADAMS, PA, USA
[38780]
WEAVER-HAYTER SARAH 1700-1800 DILTON
MARSH, WIL, ENG [35361]
WEAVERS 1800S TWINSTEAD, ESS, ENG [36776]
WEAVIN 1650-1720 LITTLE HINTON, WIL, ENG
[36595]
WEAVING PRE 1860 ST JUST, CON, ENG [33884]
WEBB 1814+ PARRAMATTA, NSW, AUS [34967] :
SARAH 1800S TAS & VIC, AUS [35127] : CHARLES
1850+ SYDNEY, NSW, AUS [35240] : JOSEPH
1900+ HORNSBY, NSW, AUS [35409] : JAMES 1790
WINDSOR, NSW, AUS [35756] : 1850-1950
NEWCASTLE, NSW, AUS [36293] : ALL ERIN,
ONT, CAN [35618] : 1820+ ONT, CAN [36687] :

1838+ ROSENEATH, ONT, CAN [38450] : 1750+
BINFIELD & READING, BRK, ENG [34008] : ALL
FAREHAM, HAM, ENG [34160] : PRE 1860 BISHOP
SUTTON, SOM, ENG [34269] : 1750 RAMSBURY,
WIL, ENG [34321] : 1700+ ABBOTS ANN, HAM,
ENG [34405] : PRE 1850 PRIORS MARSTON, WAR,
ENG [34562] : ALL TOWCESTER, NTH, ENG
[34597] : 1700-1900 ENG [34624] : NEHEMIAH PRE
1714 NEAR BRISTOL, GLS, ENG [34908] : C1820
GRAYS, ESS, ENG [35203] : 1900+ CAMBERWELL
& KIDBROOKE, LND & SRY, ENG [35495] : PRE
1900 CAMBERWELL, SRY & LND, ENG [35495] :
1915+ CAMBERWELL & STANMORE, LND &
SRY, ENG [35495] : C1750 HAWKESBURY, GLS,
ENG [35563] : PRE 1876 TAVISTOCK, DEV, ENG
[35709] : 1700S FORDHAM, CAM, ENG [35858] :
1820-1900 LEWISHAM, KEN, ENG [36101] : 1770S-
1806 ST BLAZEY, CON, ENG [36190] : 1700S HAM,
ENG [36289] : PRE 1880 LUTON, BDF, ENG [36293]
: JOHN 1840-1900 LND, ENG [36316] : PRE 1720
WHITCHURCH, OXF, ENG [36326] : 1750+
TAMWORTH, STS & WAR, ENG [36329] : C1800
DEPTFORD, KEN & LND, ENG [36478] : ALL
WEST, SFK, ENG [36479] : C1800 BIRMINGHAM,
WAR, ENG [36779] : 1700+ DUDLEY, WOR, ENG
[36794] : 1700+ LEXDEN, ESS, ENG [36794] : 1800S
COLCHESTER, ESS, ENG [36876] : WILLIAM
C1832 HADLEIGH, SFK, ENG [36876] : WILLIAM
1850-1900 COLCHESTER, ESS, ENG [36876] : PRE
1775+ MILDENHALL, SFK, ENG [36955] : 1800
ATON, WIL, ENG [36956] : 1870-1940 FULHAM,
LND, ENG [36990] : PRE 1800 CAM, COALEY, GLS,
ENG [37101] : 1800-1839 BRIGHTON, SSX, ENG
[37207] : 1800+ HACKNEY, MDX, ENG [37251] :
1700-1850 EAST PECKHAM, KEN, ENG [37365] :
1800S NFK, ENG [37733] : 1700-1800 KENCOT,
OXF, ENG [37763] : 1840-1900 BRERETON, STS,
ENG [37850] : 1800-1900 ABINGDON, BRK, ENG
[37877] : PRE 1890 ISLINGTON, MDX, ENG [37885]
: PRE 1850 STOWMARKET, SFK, ENG [38483] :
ALL ST CLEER, CON & DEV, ENG [38522] :
C1797+ KINGSTON, SRY & NSW, ENG & AUS
[35547] : 1830 BIRR, OFF, IRL [35903] : 1780S
DONAGHADEE, DOW, IRL [36862] : 1875-1892
RUSSELL, NZ [35709] : 1800+ MONROE CO., TN,
USA [36351] : 1790-1825 JEFFERSON & LAURENS,
GA, USA [36911] : 1850+ BROOKE CO., WV, USA
[36956] : 1820S WAYNE CO., TN, USA [37027] : 1769-
1820 STOKES CO., NC, USA [37027] : 1820S PERRY
CO., TN, USA [37027] : 1800+ PERSON CO., NC,
USA [37583] : PRE 1894 PROVIDENCE, RI, USA
[37662] : MARTIN H. 1850-1860 OH, USA [37815] :
1853-1920 WA, USA [38100] : MATTHEW C1883 NY,
USA [38450] : PRE 1700 MA, USA & ENG [38745] :
PRE 1725 MONSERRAT, W.INDIES [36180] : C1800
NASH, MON, WLS [36247] : 1800+ MON, WLS
[36956] : CHARLES 1784+ WORLDWIDE [38450]

WEBBER 1800+ AUS [34005] : PRE 1914 AUS [36214] :
PRE 1910 FAIRHOLME, ONT, CAN [34055] : 1860-
1940S HARBOR GRACE, NFD, CAN [34208] : PRE
1900 NFD, CAN [37761] : PRE 1850 PHILLACK,
CON, ENG [33972] : PRE 1800 LND, ENG [34005] :
PRE 1846 PLYMOUTH, DEV, ENG [36079] : 1800-
1900 PLYMOUTH, DEV, ENG [36214] : 1800+
LIFTON & LAUNCESTON, DEV, ENG [38213] :
PRE 1800 PROBUS, CON, ENG [38263] : 1870
VESPREY, INDIA [34609] : 1780-1870 LDY, IRL
[34687] : PRE 1800 NOH, NL [34005] : PRE 1914 RSA
[36214] : 1700+ LONDON, ENG & MA, USA [38025]

WEBB WILLIAMS 1837+ LICHFIELD, WAR, ENG
[36296]

WEBER PRE 1850 WATERLOO CO., ONT, CAN
[34159] : 1500+ RAPPERSWIL, BE, CH & USA
[36970] : PRE 1825 BADEN, BAD, GER [34238] : PRE
1750 WALDBACH, WUE, GER [35242] : 1800+ SHO,
GER [36662] : 1750-1900 ESCHNAU, BAV, GER
[36962] : 1815+ BAD, GER [37532] : ALL
FALKENBURG & DARMBURG, POM, GER [37607]
: PRE 1850 BERLIN, BLN, GER [37820] : PRE 1800
WATTENHEIM, RPF, GER [38681] : GERD 1770-
1900 GER [38781] : MENNEN 1770-1900 GER [38781]
: MENA JURGENS 1770-1900 GER [38781] : 1850+
MILWAUKEE CO., WI, USA [36962] : FREDERICK
1850+ FRANKLIN CO., OH, USA [37565]

WEBSTER EDMUND 1840+ VIC, AUS [33764] :
1880+ BRIGHTON, VIC, AUS [35527] : C1830
HEATHER, LEI, ENG [33912] : 1830-1870 ABBOTS
RODING, ESS, ENG [34556] : C1830 LONDON,
ENG [34556] : 1835 NORWICH, NFK, ENG [34594] :
1829+ BERWICK UPON TWEED, NBL, ENG
[34702] : 1700S NFK, ENG [34937] : PRE 1800
STOCKWELL & LAMBETH, SRY, ENG [35198] :
C1800-1810 SOUTHWARK, SRY, ENG [35198] :
C1720 HOLBORN, LND, ENG [35261] : 1860S
PICCADILLY, LND, ENG [35261] : JOHN 1800
CON, ENG [35343] : 1820+ BODMIN, CON, ENG
[35343] : 1600+ BUNGAY, ENG [35824] : 1800S LEI,
ENG [36005] : PRE 1900 RETFORD, NTT, ENG
[36040] : 1750-1800 S YKS, ENG [36084] : PRE 1880
HUYTON, LAN, ENG [36522] : PRE 1750
AYLSHAM, NFK, ENG [36593] : 1800S
CAMBERWELL, LND, ENG [36799] : EDWARD
1822-1850S DERBY, DBY, ENG [36876] : EDWARD
1850-1900 BROMLEY, MDX, ENG [36876] : C1851-
1900 BOW & BROMLEY, MDX, ENG [36876] :
C1822-1851 DERBY, DBY, ENG [36876] : EDWARD
1850-1900 BOW, MDX, ENG [36876] : JOS. C1850-
1930S ECKINGTON, DBY, ENG [37486] : PRE 1800
RADBOURNE, DBY, ENG [37675] : PRE 1810
DRIGHLINGTON & BIRSTALL, WRY, ENG
[37754] : 1859 BEIGHTON, DBY, ENG [37986] :
C1790 WHEATHAMPSTEAD, HRT, ENG [38489] :
C1790 SANDRIDGE, HRT, ENG [38489] : PRE 1900
DUBLIN, IRL [34626] : ALL IRL [34938] : ALL
ENNISCORTHY, WEX, IRL [35063] : 1850+
NELSON, NZ [37552] : 1773-1870 ABERDEEN, ABD,
SCT [33811] : 1773-1870 MONTROSE, ANS, SCT
[33811] : 1820S FIF, SCT [33934] : C1788 INCHTURE,
PER, SCT [34389] : 1870+ GLASGOW, LKS, SCT
[34713] : C1790 DUN, ANS, SCT [34713] : 1760+
EDZELL, ANS, SCT [34713] : JAMES & JOHN
C1748-C1788 ELIE, FIF, SCT [35072] : PRE 1808
SCOONIE, FIF, SCT [35229] : CATHERINE 1830
KINTORE, ABD, SCT [35369] : 1750+
KINGOODIE, PER, SCT [35644] : 1700+ OLD
MACHAR, KCD, SCT [36824] : C1800 PETERHEAD,
ABD, SCT [37245] : PRE 1780 ABERDEEN, ABD,
SCT [37513] : 1790+ EDINBURGH & LEITH, MLN,
SCT [37552] : C1700-1859 PITGAIR, GAMRIE, BAN,
SCT [37977] : 1600-1900S VA, IA & IN, USA [37812] :
1810-1840 COFFEE CO., TN, USA [38092] : 1840-1850
MS, USA [38092] : 1860-1900 BASTROP CO., TX,
USA [38092] : 1870-1940 MCLENNAN CO., TX, USA
[38092] : 1850-1860 CRAWFORD CO., AR, USA
[38092] : 1870-1900 LIMESTONE CO., TX, USA
[38092] : 1700S USA [38184]

WECK 1800-1900 COLOGNE, PRE, GER [36898]

WEDD 1870+ SA, AUS [35222] : PRE 1850 LIN, ENG
[34335]

WEDDELL 1200-1990 WORLDWIDE [36114]

WEDDERSPOON PRE 1870 PER, SCT [34603]

WEDEKIND C1815 WOLFENBUETTEL, NSA, FRG
[38660]

WEDER PRE 1776 SSX, ENG [35512]

WEDGE PRE 1850 HADLEY & WELLINGTON, SAL, ENG [36104] : PRE 1800 CT, USA & ENG [38746]

WEDLOCK WILLIAM 185+ MACLEAY RV DIST., NSW, AUS [35816] : 1700-1800S ARKESDEN, ESS, ENG [35816] : 1800+ CON, ENG [36785]

WEEBER PRE 1800 LONDON, ENG [36790] : PRE 1790 WURTEMBERG, WUE, GER & ENG [35542]

WEED 1750-1820 SIMSBURY, CT, USA [38054] : 1770S HARTFORD, CT, USA [38054]

WEEDE ALL WORLDWIDE [35418]

WEEDEN PRE 1835 SAFFRON WALDEN, ESS, ENG [35253] : ALL MAIDSTONE, KEN, ENG [36801] : 1775-1845 ST LUKES, MDX, ENG [37336] : 1880-1940 FINSBURY, MDX, ENG [37336] : 1880-1905 ILFORD, ESS, ENG [37336] : 1910-1915 CHELMSFORD, ESS, ENG [37336] : 1845-1880 LIMEHOUSE, MDX, ENG [37336] : CHARLES 1827-1861 MAIDSTONE, KEN, ENG & AUS [34447]

WEEDON PRE 1600 HUGHENDEN, BKM, ENG [33796] : 1800+ BERKHAMSTED, HRT, ENG [36071] : PRE 1826 UXBRIDGE, MDX, ENG [36290] : ALL MAIDSTONE, KEN, ENG [36801]

WEEDOW ALL LAN, ENG [37127]

WEEDRIGHT 1830-39 HIGHLANDS, GER [38151] : 1840-1848 CINCINATTI, OH, USA [38151]

WEEDS 1797 BECCLES, SFK, ENG [37250]

WEEKES PRE 1840 TENTERDEN AREA, KEN, ENG [35862] : 1700-1800 WOODCHURCH, KEN, ENG [36106] : 1850+ RODNEY STOKE, SOM, ENG [36195] : 1860 TORQUAY, DEV, ENG [37418] : 1600-1870 SOUTHPOOL & SHERFORD, DEV, ENG [37418] : PRE 1650 COLYTON, DEV, ENG [38746]

WEEKS C1857-1900+ SYDNEY, NSW, AUS [34651] : 1800+ ADOLPHUSTOWN, ONT, CAN [34109] : PRE 1800 IDDLESLEIGH & BROADWOOD KELLY, DEV, ENG [34214] : 1600+ STAVERTON, DEV, ENG [34747] : PRE 1850 RYE, SSX, ENG [35232] : 1800-1810 WHITSTABLE, KEN, ENG [36264] : PRE 1838 HANDLEY, DOR, ENG [36629] : C1800 DEV, ENG [37180] : ALL ST BEES, CUL, ENG [37484] : ALL HAWKHURST, KEN & SSX, ENG [38230] : 1750+ BELFAST, ANT, IRL [35475] : CYRUS 1800S OH, USA [36321]

WEELINK 1890+ ZWOLLE, OIJ, NL [35338]

WEEMS 1700-1900 GREENE CO., TN, USA [37539]

WEERD-DE ALL NL [38707] : ALL USA [38707]

WEETMAN C1750 KENILWORTH, WAR, ENG [37846] : C1750 TAMWORTH, STS, ENG [37846]

WEFERS PRE 1820 NRW & RPF, BRD [38616]

WEGE 1835-1842 MAHDEL HERZBERG, KSA, GER [38750]

WEGENER PRE 1860 BREDELEM, HAN, GER [34801] : FRED PRE 1860 MEK, GER [38222]

WEGGENSTAPEL 1700+ HOLTEN, OIJ, NL [34398]

WEGG-HORNE 1880+ COLLINGWOOD, VIC, AUS [36295]

WEGHMANS 1700S MILLINGEN A/D RIJN, GEL, NL [38350]

WEGNER ALL MSW, GER [34488]

WEHLING PRE 1800 WINGERODE, PSA, GER [38048]

WEHNAU ALL KRS. GUMBINNEN, OPR, GER [38649]

WEHR 1787+ KUELLSTEDT, PRE, GER [38626] : ALL GER & USA [37805]

WEHRLE C1760 SCHWAERZENBACH, BAD, GER [33772]

WEIBEL 1700-1900 PA & MD, USA [37517]

WEIBLE WILLIAM 1788-1850 WESTMORELAND CO., PA, USA [38150] : 1850-1858 LUCAS CO., OH, USA [38150]

WEIBLER ALL STOLZ ENFELL, KAPELLEN, BRD [34308]

WEIBYE ALL WORLDWIDE [35489]

WEICKER 1859-1870 MISSISSIPPI CO., MO, USA [38187]

WEIDE PRE 1804 WETTER, GHE, GER [38647]

WEIDENBORNER 1800 HERBSTEIN, HES, BRD [37028]

WEIDMAN ALL NY & CT, USA [37787]

WEIDMER 1914 REICHELSDORF, BAY, GER [38750]

WEIDNER 1855+ TOLEDO, OH, USA [37572]

WEIDTMAN 1431+ JUELICHERLAND, RPR, GER [38644]

WEIDTMANN 1647+ RATINGEN, RPR, GER [38644]

WEIGAND 1750 REUCHELHEIM, STADT-ARNSTEIN, BRD [38327] : 1800 MARBACH, STADT-ARNSTEIN, BRD [38327]

WEIGANDT 1408 WURZBURG, STADT-ARNSTEIN, BRD [38327] : PRE 1811 FEITSHOF, BAV, GER [36358]

WEIGEL 1650-1850 LAUTER, KSA, GER [38628]

WEIGHELL PRE 1804 WEST HARLSEY, YKS, ENG [34487]

WEIGHTMAN PRE 1840 EMBLETON, NBL, ENG [34198] : PRE 1850 ALLERTON, NTT, ENG [34611] : PRE 1800 NTT, ENG [36411]

WEIGHTON C1740+ PER, SCT [34040] : ALL SCT [38735]

WEIGOLD PRE 1910 AUERBACH, HES, BRD [35311]

WEIJTJES ALL HERWEN, GEL, NL [38350]

WEIKERT C1700-1870 COPENHAGEN, DEN [37642]

WEIL PRE 1850 LANG-GONS, HES, BRD [34753]

WEILAND 1700-1810 KEDRICH, LUX [38024]

WEILER 1855-1910 LORAIN CO., OH, USA [38106]

WEIN JOHN 1822-1850 DARMSTADT, HES, GER [38127]

WEINAND PRE 1850 TRECHTINGSHAUSEN, RPF, GER [35147] : PRE 1800 TRASSEM, RPF, GER [38681]

WEINBEER PRE 1800 WOERSBACH, RPF, GER [38681]

WEINBRENNER ALL GER [38610]

WEINERT PRE 1795 GRUENBERG, SIL, GER [36954]

WEINGARTZ 1750 DUSSELDORF, GER [38379]

WEINIG PRE 1900 WESTHEIM, BAY, BRD [35311]

WEINMANN PRE 1820 ALTENRIET, GER [37587]

WEINRAUCH 1929 LAMPMAN, SAS, CAN [37493]

WEINSTEIN ALL WORLDWIDE [34318]

WEIR JOHN PRE 1865 EUROA, VIC, AUS [34433] : 1840-1940 TENTERFIELD, NSW, AUS [36315] : 1880S GOULBURN, NSW, AUS [36599] : ALL ONT, CAN [34465] : 1800+ CON, ENG [38846] : 1843 SECUNDERABAD, MADRAS, IND & SCT [33812] : 1800-1850 ARM, IRL [36315] : ALL CAV, IRL [37584] : PRE 1900 WESTPORT, NZ [34431] : ALL NZ [35994] : JOHN PRE 1831 EDINBURGH, SCT [34433] : PRE 1762 CARLUKE, LKS, SCT [34501] : 1810 AIRDRIE, LKS, SCT [34618] : JOHN PRE 1850 INNERLEITHEN, PEE, SCT [34935] : 1800+ KIRKINTILLOCH, DNB, SCT [35051] : ALL GLASGOW, SCT [36094] : 1850S GLASGOW, SCT [36659] : SUSAN 1780S LESMAHAGOW & AVONDALE, LKS, SCT [36678] : 1800-1900 EDINBURGH, MLN, SCT [36884] : PRE 1800 DALKEITH, MLN, SCT [37127] : 1820S AYR, SCT [37263] : 1750+ LESMAHAGOW, LKS, SCT [38388] : 1750-1850 ROCKBRIDGE CO., VA, USA [38154]

WEISCHEDEL PRE 1855 FEUERBACH, WUE, GER [35393]

WEISGERBER 1750-1850 HEN, BRD [38342]

WEISINGER ALL WORLDWIDE [38576]

WEISKOPF PRE 1950 BOHEMIA, CS [34634]

WEISS 1700+ EICHACH, BAW, GER [35355] : 1800+
LANGENLONSHEIM, RPR, GER [37042] : 1700+
STAUDERNHEIM, RPR, GER [37042] : 1850-1920
ZHITDMIR, SU [34223] : JOHANN 1883-1894 ST
LOUIS, MO, USA [38655] : THERESIA 1894+ USA
[38655] : JOHN 1883-1894 ST LOUIS, MO, USA
[38655]

WEISSEL 1880+ SA, AUS [38539] : 1880+ VIC, AUS
[38539]

WEISSFLOG 1630-1830 LAUTER, KSA, GER [38628]

WEISSKOPF PRE 1950 BOHEMIA, CS [34634]

WEISSMANN PRE 1700 TRIPPSTADT, RPF, GER
[38681]

WEIST ALL WORLDWIDE [38648]

WEKEY ALL TOKAJ, HU & AUS [37287]

WELBOURNE 1775-1880 BINGHAM, NTT, ENG
[38401]

WELBURN PRE 1917 HORSFORTH, YKS, ENG
[35985]

WELBY PRE 1845 LIMERICK CITY, LIM & GAL,
IRL [37368] : 1870+ RSA [37368] : ALL
WORLDWIDE [37368]

WELCH PRE 1825 PARISH OF ELDON, NSW, AUS
[34265] : 1835+ PORT ARTHUR, TAS, AUS [34455] :
1840+ GOULBURN, NSW, AUS [35510] : 1858+
PATERSON, NSW, AUS [35536] : PRE 1760 HRT,
ENG [34041] : 1800-1840 NITON, IOW, ENG [34658] :
ALL ISLINGTON, LND, ENG [34723] : PRE 1900
LAMBETH, LND, ENG [34723] : PRE 1820
LITTLEBURY, ESS, ENG [34739] : PRE 1820 BKM,
ENG [35030] : PRE 1843 ILFORD, ESS, ENG [35536]
: C1800 STANDON, HRT, ENG [35582] : PRE 1810
SUNDERLAND, DUR, ENG [36202] : PRE 1850
CAM & HUN, ENG [36216] : ALL STOWMARKET,
LIN, ENG [36382] : 1800+ HOLBORN, LND, ENG
[36510] : 1600-1900 DUR, ENG [36689] : ALL ENG
[36839] : 1769+ STEEP, HAM, ENG [36959] : 1550-
1990 SOUTHWARK, LND, ENG [37670] : PRE 1800
MAIDSTONE, KEN, ENG [37773] : PRE 1800
CHORLEY, LAN, ENG [37939] : C1700-1800 IRL
[34214] : ALL WAIRARAPA, NZ [34647] : ALL NZ
[36839] : PRE 1834 STRANRAER, WIG, SCT [34214] :
ABNER 1814-1870 TUSCARAWAS CO., OH, USA
[37014] : HIRAM 1863-1886 LIVINGSTON CO., IL,
USA [38132] : FRANK 1896-1930 COOK CO., IL,
USA [38132] : 1830 PENOBSCOT, ME, USA [38143]

WELCOME ALL CAN & USA [35640]

WELDE 1900S OH, USA [37565]

WELDERT 1830-1910 HEN, GER [36913] : 1850-1880
MCLEAN CO., IL, USA [36913]

WELDON 1852+ VIC, AUS [35482] : C1700-1900
SHAFTESBURY, DOR, ENG [36478] : C1840
DUBLIN, IRL [35131] : 1800-90 DUBLIN, DUB, IRL
[35482] : C1826-1908 RATHGAR, DUB, IRL [35482] :
1800-90 CORK, COR, IRL [35482] : 1831-52 CLA, IRL
[35482] : 1920 WAITARERE BCH, WGTN, NZ
[36250] : 1920 MIRAMAR, WGTN, NZ [36250]

WELEFELD C1800 ARNHEM, GEL, NL [38698]

WELFARE 1680-1740 HORSTED KEYNES, SSX, ENG
[34697] : MARY E. 1841+ ISLINGTON, DEV, ENG
[35583]

WELFORD 1850+ HARTLEPOOL, DUR, ENG [35908]
: 1800+ ELWICK, DUR, ENG [35908]

WELGE 1850+ QLD, AUS [35561]

WELK ALL WORLDWIDE [38613]

WELKE PRE 1816 PRITTISCH, POS, GER [35351]

WELL 1840+ ONT, CAN [35297] : PRE 1840 WUE,
GER [35297]

WELLAND 1700+ ADELAIDE, SA, AUS & ENG
[36303]

WELLARD JOHN TREVANIO 1774-1844 DOVER,
KEN, ENG [34181] : THOMAS C1725 KEN, ENG

[34181] : PRE 1715 GRAVESEND, KEN, ENG [37142]
: PRE 1900 ALL HALLOWS, HOO, KEN, ENG
[38027] : PRE 1827 FOLKESTONE, KEN, ENG &
AUS [34845]

WELLBY ALL AUS [34462] : 1859+ AUS [37143] : PRE
1850 ENG [34462] : C1800 WISBECH, LIN, ENG
[37143]

WELLER 1800S TORONTO, ONT, CAN [36670] :
1700+ HANDBOROUGH, OXF, ENG [34121] : PRE
1840 HIGH WYCOMBE, BKM, ENG [35215] : C1750-
1850 SEVENOAKS, KEN & SRY, ENG [35238] :
1727-1758 HIGH WYCOMBE, BKM, ENG [35966] :
1790-1840 CHATHAM, KEN, ENG [35966] : 1758-
1800 AMERSHAM, BKM, ENG [35966] : PRE 1750
LEWES, SSX, ENG [36589] : 1770+ STONE IN
OXNEY, KEN, ENG [37132] : 1700+ TUNSTALL
AREA, KEN, ENG [37411] : PRE 1850 LONDON,
ENG [37743] : 1810 WOOLWICH, KEN, ENG [38270]
: 1800-1830 STUTTGART, WUE, GER [36921] :
C1840 DARMSTADT, HES, GER [37022] : C1850
WASHINGTON CO., IN, USA [34395] : C1650 MA,
USA [34395] : 1830-1880 BALTIMORE, MD, USA
[36921]

WELLER (COASTGUARD) CHARLES 1870-1900
ANNALONG & KILHORNE, DOW, IRL [36398]

WELLER-WILLIAMS 1860-1870S BRISTOL, GLS,
ENG [35966] : 1876+ DUNEDIN, OTAGO, NZ
[35966]

WELLES PRE 1640 WHICHFORD, WAR, ENG [38135]

WELLESLEY C1770 DUBLIN, IRL [38769]

WELLFORD 1700S WADDESON, BKM, ENG [35256]

WELLING 1824-1850 CALHOUN CO., MI, USA [38139]

WELLINGTON C1855 BALLARAT, VIC, AUS [35564] :
PRE 1900 HAYTOR VALE, DEV, ENG [37949] :
DUKE OF C1770 DUBLIN, IRL [38769]

WELLMAN ALL HAMPSTEAD, BRK, ENG [35566] :
1840-1846 VT, USA [38099]

WELLS WILLIAM PRE 1843 SUTTON FOREST &
BERRIMA, NSW, AUS [33812] : PRE 1870
FITZROY, VIC, AUS [33890] : JOHN 1850+
ADELAIDE, SA, AUS [34298] : 1895+
COLLINGWOOD, VIC, AUS [34549] : 1870+
ADELAIDE, SA, AUS [35116] : C1906+
DONNYBROOK, WA, AUS [35249] : JOHN 1827+
WOLLOMBI, NSW, AUS [35420] : PRE 1856
MARYBOROUGH, VIC, AUS [35751] : 1791+
PARRAMATTA, NSW, AUS [36600] : 1820 NEW
NORFOLK, TAS, AUS [37989] : 1768+ ENGLISH
HARBOUR, NFD, CAN [33852] : ALL ENGLISH
HARBOUR TRINITY, NFD, CAN [34093] : 1816+
NEW BRUNSWICK, NS, CAN [36960] :
CATHERINE PRE 1770 CON, ENG [33757] : PRE
1870 KEN, ENG [33890] : JOHN C1790
CAVERSHAM, OXF, ENG [33928] : PRE 1900
LONDON, ENG [33987] : ALL GLS, ENG [34151] :
ALL WAR, ENG [34151] : ALL POOLE, DOR, ENG
[34298] : PRE 1800 BERKHAMSTED &
NORTHCHURCH, HRT, ENG [34316] : C1840-1850
LONDON, ENG [34393] : C1840 SOM, ENG [34393] :
1700+ STOW UPLAND, SFK, ENG [34640] : ALL
NFK, ENG [34758] : PRE 1841 LASHAM, HAM,
ENG [34911] : PRE 1800 WHEPSTEAD, SFK, ENG
[35391] : 1846+ AYLESBURY, BKM, ENG [35393] :
C1800 NOTTINGHAM, NTT, ENG [35595] : PRE
1840 TOTTERNOE & HOUGHTON REGIS, BDF,
ENG [35701] : 1820-1860 BUSHEY & WATFORD,
HRT, ENG [36044] : 1830+ ARNOLD, NTT, ENG
[36105] : 1700-1850 REDBOURN, HRT, ENG [36108] :
1800+ LEWES, SSX, ENG [36434] : PRE 1980
WILBRAHAM, CAM, ENG [36489] : PRE 1870
MAIDSTONE & CHATHAM, KEN, ENG [36765] :
PRE 1850 HUDDERSFIELD, YKS, ENG [36765] :

JOSEPH PRE 1910 LISS, HAM, ENG [36880] :
EDWARD CHAS C1860S MINSTERWORTH, GLS,
ENG [36880] : 1700+ LUTON, BDF, ENG [36922] :
1750+ BROAD BLUNSDON, WIL, ENG [36975] :
C1860 STEPLE ASTON, OXF, ENG [37200] : 1900+
HEATHFIELD, SSX, ENG [37206] : PRE 1850 YKS,
ENG [37379] : RICHARD 1850S HULL, YKS, ENG
[37383] : 1800S MACCLESFIELD, CHS, ENG [37413]
: 1850+ CAMBERWELL, LND, ENG [37718] : PRE
1815 WINDSOR, BRK, ENG [37726] : PRE 1800
GILLINGHAM, KEN, ENG [37773] : 1800S
STEDHAM, SSX, ENG [37833] : C1700-1800 LEI,
ENG [38512] : ALETHEA 1800+ LIVERPOOL, LAN,
ENG [38540] : PRE 1839 LOCHMABEN, DFS, SCT
[35061] : C1822 MIDDLEBIE, DFS, SCT [35249] :
1800 MONONGALIA CO., VA, USA [36446] : 1784
MD, USA [36446] : 1715-85 MD, USA [37533] : 1830-
1900 CHEROKEE & BARTOW CO., GA, USA
[37587] : 1859-1890 BLOUNT & ST CLAIR CO., AL,
USA [37587] : PRE 1830 BUNCOMBE & ROWAN
CO., NC, USA [37587] : PRE 1830 NEW YORK
CITY, NY, USA [37804] : PRE 1660 VA, USA [38311] :
FREEMAN 1780-1840 HALIFAX CO., VA, USA
[38315] : WILLIAM 1830-1860S HENRY CO. &
BRINSWICK CO., VA, USA [38315] : 1840S DE
KALB CO., IN, USA [38339] : 1800-1870S MENAI,
AGY, WLS [36522]

WELLSPRING NATHANAEL PRE 1707
PUDDLETOWN, DOR, ENG [33929] : BARNABAS
1790 DEAL, KEN, ENG [33929]

WELLSTEED C1740 WHITEPARISH, WIL, ENG
[35349]

WELS 1788-1836 AMERSFOORT, UTR, NL [38711]

WELSCH PRE 1830 BAV, GER [38191]

WELSH 1800+ AUS [33769] : 1891 CARCOAR, NSW,
AUS [34965] : 1800+ HERMITAGE BAY, NFD,
CAN [36684] : PRE 1760 HRT, ENG [34041] : PRE
1900 LIVERPOOL, LAN, ENG [35199] : 1830
CHALE, IOW, ENG [36253] : PRE 1850 LND & SRY,
ENG [37091] : 1800-99 FULHAM, MDX, ENG [37756]
: C1860-1930 TUNBRIDGE WELLS, ERITH, KEN,
ENG [37756] : WILLIAM C1820-1840 MONKEN
HADLEY, HRT, ENG [37756] : WILLIAM C1850-
1870 PIMLICO, WESTMINSTER, MDX, ENG
[37756] : C1770 IRL [34367] : 1840S WATERFORD,
WAT, IRL [35464] : 1840-1860 COR, IRL [38134] :
THOMAS PRE 1800 LISBURN, ANT, IRL [38731] :
PRE 1850 DALMELLINGTON, AYR, SCT [35406] :
ELIZABETH 1864-1914 + GRANITEVILLE, MA,
USA [34432] : 1800-1820S PA, USA [38180] : ALL
MCCONNELLSVILLE, OH, USA [38180] : PRE 1860
RUABON, DEN, WLS [36061]

WELSH (SEE WELCH) [36689]

WELSHMAN ALL WORLDWIDE [37772]

WELTON 1700-1800 SFK, ENG [36081] : 1600-1750
KENTON, SFK, ENG [36213] : PRE 1740 CT, USA
[38017] : 1750 VA, USA [38017]

WELZ 1800-1850 BLAUBEUREN, WUE, GER [38528]

WEMBRIDGE 1830-1920 BROADWAY & ASHILL,
SOM, ENG [36373]

WENAU ALL KRS. GUMBINNEN, OPR, GER [38649]

WENDELKEN C1850 STEPNEY & ST GEORGE IN
EAST, LND, ENG [35411] : PRE 1850
SCHARMBECK, HAN, GER [35411]

WENDELL PETER 1718-85 AHUS, SKANE, SWE
[38550]

WENDEROTH 1600S OSTHEIM, GER [38374]

WENDON PRE 1850 ESS, ENG [37832]

WENDT 1870S MARYBOROUGH, QLD, AUS [35144] :
1900+ BEECHWORTH, VIC, AUS [35466] : PRE
1873 STOLP, POM, GER [35144] : 1768-1815

BRUCHHAUSEN, WEF, GER [38750] : 1707-1890
SIERAKOWICE, GDANSK, POL [38148]

WENGEL 1700-1820 HARMSDORF, POM, GER
[38372]

WENGER 1900+ KALAMAZOO, MI, USA [34148]

WENHAM 1800S GRAFTON, NSW, AUS [37910] :
1750-1850 STOKE JOXTA GUILDFORD, SRY, ENG
[34687] : PRE 1735 SSX, ENG [37875]

WENIG C1769 KOENIGSHOFEN, BAW, GER [38626]

WENK PRE 1850 RACHLAU, UPPER LUSATIA, GER
[34766]

WENKE PRE 1850 RACHLAU, UPPER LUSATIA,
GER [34766]

WENLOCK 1750+ ELLESMERE, SAL, ENG [34405] :
1700+ SHERIFHALES, STS, ENG [34964] : 1700+
ELLESMERE, SAL, ENG [34964] : 1655+ SHIFNAL,
SAL, ENG [34964] : PRE 1843 BARKING, ESS, ENG
[35536]

WENMAN 1850-1900 REDFERN, NSW, AUS [37904] :
1800-1860 SOUTHWARK, SRY, ENG [37904]

WENN PRE 1870 CHATHAM, KEN, ENG [37067] :
PRE 1800 MATTISHALL & EAST DEREHAM,
NFK, ENG [37712]

WENSLEY 1700-1800 BAMPTON, DEV, ENG [36389]

WENT 1852+ NSW, AUS [33781] : ALL HEF, ENG
[36375]

WENTWORTH JANE PRE 1886 GIPPSLAND, VIC,
AUS [35729] : PRE 1800 SHOREDITCH, LND, ENG
[34117] : ALL HONOLULU, HI, USA [33756]

WENZ PRE 1839 HATTENHEIM, HEN, GER [34886]

WENZEL 1800S FFO, DDR [37910] : 1900+
PLYMOUTH, DEV, ENG [36376] : PRE 1855
BIBERACH, WUE, GER [34886]

WENZLAFF 1800S GROSS JANNEWITZ, POM, GER
[35340]

WEPENER 1730-1865 GRAAF REINETT, CAPE, RSA
[34947]

WEPPNER 1860-1880 ELMORE, VIC, AUS [35726] :
1820-1860 SEEBURG, HAN, GER [35726]

WERA ALL WORLDWIDE [38159]

WERBISKI ALL GALICIA, POL & SU [34146]

WERE 1700+ WELLINGTON, SOM, ENG [37088] :
1600+ SAMPFORD ARUNDEL, DEV, ENG [37088]

WERENKE ALL RECKE, WEF & MD, GER & USA
[35299]

WERFELE 1400-1500 KEN, ENG [36420]

WERLING PRE 1900 HATZENBIEHL,
RHEINPFALTS, GER [34061]

WERLY PRE 1838 CANTON, GR, CH [37820] : PRE
1850 CANTON, MO, USA [37820]

WERMUTH ALL WORLDWIDE [37600]

WERNER LOUIS 1900-1920 EMMAVILLE &
TENTERFIELD, NSW, AUS [33807] : C1866
BORBECK, NRW, FRG [38717] : C1857 BONN,
NRW, FRG [38717] : PRE 1850 BONN, NRW, FRG
[38717] : 1700-1800S STEINBERG, MEK, GER
[35874] : PRE 1900 VENLO, LMB, NL [38717] : C1909
LANCASTER, PA, USA [37022]

WERNHAM 1800-1850 LONDON, ENG [34735] : PRE
1750 CHIEVELEY, BRK, ENG [35866]

WERRETT 1550-1700 WICKWAR, GLS, ENG [37222]

WERRING PRE 1854 MILTON ABBOT, DEV, ENG
[35428]

WERTHEIM 1800-1870 EAST END, LONDON, ENG
& GER [37194]

WERTHEIMS 1900S HAMPSTEAD, MDX, ENG
[37931]

WESCOMBE ALL SHEPTON MALLET, SOM, ENG
[34046] : 1812 SOM, ENG [34446] : ALL NTH
CURRY, SOM, ENG [36242]

WESCOTT PRE 1620 YEOVIL, SOM, ENG [38135] :
1700+ OTSEGO & ERIE, NY, USA [36341] : ALL

BERKSHIRE CO., MA & NY, USA **[38522]** : 1810+
GORHAM, CUMBERLAND, ME, USA **[38571]**
WESEMANN 1905-1972 ELBRINXEN, LIP, GER
[38750]
WESLAKE 1700S EXETER, DEV, ENG **[35131]**
WESLAND C1810-1860 HAMPRESTON, DOR & SOM,
ENG **[37287]**
WESLEY 1858+ AYLESBURY, BKM, ENG **[35393]**
WESMAN PRE 1850 SCHIEDAM & ROTTERDAM,
ZUH, NL **[38646]**
WESNEDGE PRE 1850 SHEFFIELD, YKS, ENG
[37442]
WESNER 1770+ LW, POL **[38650]**
WESSEL 1600+ KREMPE, SHO, GER **[38651]**
WESSELEUS JAN C1850 (SOLDIER IN HOLLAND),
FRA **[35607]**
WESSELL 1750+ VT & ONT, USA & CAN **[38241]**
WESSELS 1850+ NL **[34303]**
WESSON 1750+ LONDON, ENG **[34846]** : 1895+
BUTTE, MT, USA **[36909]**
WEST 1870+ LAUNCESTON, TAS, AUS **[34770]** :
JOHN C1854 FALBROOK, NSW, AUS **[34913]** :
WILLIAM 1882+ SYDNEY, NSW, AUS **[35099]** :
FREDERICK 1895+ BRISBANE, QLD, AUS **[35099]**
: GEORGE 1879+ SYDNEY, NSW, AUS **[35099]** :
ALBERT 1888+ SYDNEY, NSW, AUS **[35099]** :
MARTHA 1875+ BRISBANE, QLD, AUS **[35099]** :
BERTIE 1884+ SYDNEY, NSW, AUS **[35099]** :
HARRIET 1873+ BRISBANE, QLD, AUS **[35099]** :
AGNES 1878+ BRISBANE, QLD, AUS **[35099]** :
THOMAS 1886+ SYDNEY, NSW, AUS **[35099]** :
ANTHONY 1844+ FULLERTON COVE, NSW,
AUS **[35462]** : 1880+ CLUNES, VIC, AUS **[36622]** :
1836+ NIAGARA, ONT, CAN **[33908]** : 1800+
HAMBLEDON, HAM, ENG **[33893]** : MAJOR PRE
1850 N.IRL & ENG **[34013]** : 1850+ ISLINGTON,
MDX, ENG **[34238]** : SARAH 1750+ ALLESLEY &
CORLEY, WAR, ENG **[34363]** : THOMAS 1793+
MARSTON & LEAMINGTON, WAR, ENG **[34363]** :
JOHN 1854+ SANDWICH & WINGHAM, KEN,
ENG **[34545]** : C1800 CAMBORNE, CON, ENG
[34644] : WILLIAM 1820-1880 BIRMINGHAM,
WAR, ENG **[34751]** : 1789 FOULMERE, CAM, ENG
[34761] : 1750-1830 POTTERHANWORTH, LIN,
ENG **[34769]** : PRE 1859 SALFORD, LAN, ENG
[35061] : 1750+ WESTMINSTER, LND, ENG **[35125]**
: PRE 1780 BREDE, SSX, ENG **[35128]** : PRE 1844
SHENLEY, BKM, ENG **[35462]** : PRE 1870S
BROUGHTON, OXF, ENG **[35544]** : 1800+
WORCESTER, WOR, ENG **[35554]** : 1800+
HENLEY, SSX & HAM, ENG **[35760]** : PRE 1860
COLEFORD, SOM, ENG **[35764]** : 1760+
CHOLSEY, OXF, ENG **[35822]** : 1850-1890 MILE
END, MDX, ENG **[36017]** : 1850-1880 STEPNEY &
BETHNAL GREEN, MDX, ENG **[36017]** : 1870+
NOTTINGHAM, NTT, ENG **[36105]** : WILLIAM
1820S BIRMINGHAM, WAR, ENG **[36239]** : C1860
MILTON, OXF, ENG **[36253]** : 1750-1850
FARNHAM, SRY, ENG **[36256]** : MICHAEL PRE
1778 NORTH AYLESFORD, KEN, ENG **[36309]** :
JOHN PRE 1851 PLYMOUTH, DEV, ENG **[36310]** :
AMY PRISCILLA 1860-1920+ SRY & MDX, ENG
[36594] : 1800+ GOSPORT, HAM, ENG **[36662]** :
HENRY C1827+ 62 NORTHGATE,
CANTERBURY, KEN, ENG **[36767]** : HENRY
1804+ ASH & WROTHAM, KEN, ENG **[36767]** :
WILLIAM C1780 ASH & WROTHAM, KEN, ENG
[36767] : ALL HIGH WYCOMBE & HUGHENDON,
BKM, ENG **[36922]** : CHRISTOPHER C1815
ORCHESTON ST MARY, WIL, ENG **[37002]** :
1780+ EAST FARNDON, NTH, ENG **[37070]** :
1850+ KEN & MDX, ENG **[37128]** : 1906+ YKS,
ENG **[37318]** : PRE 1710 METHERINGHAM, LIN,
ENG **[37318]** : 1700-1950 ESS, ENG **[37344]** : PRE
1800 LANGPORT & CURRY RIVEL, SOM, ENG
[37410] : PRE 1800 BKM, ENG **[37498]** : SUSANNA
1860-1944 LONDON, ENG **[37637]** : PRE 1860
LAMBETH & FINSBURY, SRY, ENG **[38258]** : 1870-
1920 ASHFORD, KEN, ENG **[38513]** : PRE 1850
LIMAVADY, DRY, IRL **[34013]** : 1850S BELFAST,
ANT, IRL **[35925]** : 1700-1860 CLOONE, LET, IRL
[38054] : 1800 DRUMBORE, LET, IRL **[38054]** : 1800-
1810 CARRICK ON SHANNON, LET, IRL **[38054]** :
1700-1860 DRUMDARKIN, LET, IRL **[38054]** : PRE
1900 N.IRL **[34013]** : 1900+ TE KOPURU, NZ **[37206]**
: PRE 1800 PENNAN, ABD, SCT **[34192]** : PRE 1833
LINLITHGOW, SCT **[34489]** : PRE 1800 PENNAN,
ABD, SCT **[34840]** : 1700+ MACDUFF, BAN, SCT
[34840] : 1600+ GAMRIE, BAN, SCT **[35627]** :
MARTHA 1871 WESTMORELAND CO., PA, USA
[36448] : PRE 1940 BAKER, OR, USA **[36899]** : C1830-
80 CUYAHOGA CO., OH, USA **[38173]** : 1790 KING
WILLIAM, VA, USA **[38198]** : 1890-1934 WISE CO.,
TX, USA **[38505]** : 1780-1830 CHEROKEE LORDS,
SC, USA **[38737]** : PRE 1880 BARRY, GLA, WLS
[35745] : LEWIS PRE 1860 MACHEN & ALL, MON,
WLS **[36082]**
WESTACOT 1750+ COBBATON, SWYMBRIDGE,
DEV, ENG **[34188]**
WESTACOTT GEORGE 1828-1843 BARNSTAPLE &
ILFRACOMBE, DEV, ENG **[38127]**
WESTAWAY 1800+ ALB, CAN **[34485]** : 1800+ SAS,
CAN **[34485]** : 1880+ VICTORIA CO., ONT, CAN
[34485] : ALL WORLDWIDE **[37264]**
WESTBROOK PRE 1840 ENG **[33937]** : 1800-1900 LND
& SRY, ENG **[34749]** : 1650-1870 ALTON, HAM,
ENG **[37615]** : 1860+ HANCOCK CO., IL, USA
[35629] : 1800+ VA, KY & IL, USA **[35629]** : 1850-
1875 MO, USA **[36732]** : 1800-1830 NY, USA **[36732]** :
1830-1875 CA, USA **[36732]** : 1800-1850 OH, USA
[36732]
WESTBROOM 1750 KIRBY LE SOKEN, ESS, ENG
[37928]
WESTBURY 1875+ ECHUCA, VIC, AUS **[34702]** : ALL
WOR & WIL, ENG **[33975]** : 1770+ FAIRFORD,
GLS, ENG **[34591]** : ALL MANCHESTER, LAN,
ENG **[35115]** : 1750+ WAR, ENG **[37462]** : 1760+
WOR, ENG **[37462]**
WESTBY 1840+ ONT, CAN **[34153]**
WESTCOTT PRE 1845 CAMBERWELL, LND, ENG
[34584] : PRE 1860 TOPSHAM, DEV, ENG **[35496]** :
1784 ST BRIDE, DEV, ENG **[38699]** : 1820
SALTASH, DEV, ENG **[38699]**
WESTENDORP 1710 ZWOLLE, OIJ, NL **[34390]**
WESTENHAVER PRE 1856 OH, USA **[36965]**
WESTER C1780 USA **[38340]**
WESTERBEEK PRE 1860 STEENWYKERWOLD, OIJ,
NL **[36283]**
WESTERDALE PRE 1820 GREAT EATON, LEI, ENG
[37379]
WESTERMAN MARY 1853+ MANARO, NSW, AUS
[34885]
WESTERN 1888+ EAST TRENTHAM & ECHUCA,
VIC, AUS **[36622]** : 1888+ CASTLEMAINE, VIC,
AUS **[36622]** : C1700 WITHERIDGE, DEV, ENG
[35038] : 1750-1850 CROWCOMBE, SOM, ENG
[36130] : 1800+ LONDON, ENG **[37306]**
WESTERVELT 1800-1880 BERGEN CO., NJ, USA
[38337]
WESTERWOUT C1780 LEIDERDORP, ZUH, NL
[38698]
WESTFALL ALL WORLDWIDE **[36548]**
WESTGATE 1790S LEWES, SSX, ENG **[36425]** : ALL
NFK, ENG **[37409]**

WESTLAKE PRE 1755 COMPTON DUNDON, SOM, ENG [34270] : ALL NORTON ST PHILIP, SOM, ENG [34284] : C1800S CON, ENG [35381] : 1818-1848 MARK, SOM, ENG [35565] : PRE 1900 CHATHAM, KEN, ENG [35853] : 1800+ ST GILES IN THE HEATH, DEV & CON, ENG [37224]

WESTLEY 1786 HAVERSHAM, BKM, ENG [35256] : PRE 1700 LONDON, ENG [35285]

WESTLING PRE 1895 VISBY, GOTLAND, SWE [34780]

WESTMAN 1850+ SYDNEY, NSW, AUS [34977] : 1800S ROSENALLIS, LEX, IRL [38498]

WESTMORLAND ALL MILBURN, WES, ENG [36180]

WESTNEDGE PRE 1850 SHEFFIELD, YKS, ENG [37442]

WESTNEY ALL SHEFFIELD, YKS, ENG & NZ [34604]

WESTON 1860+ VIC, AUS [33887] : 1800+ DAPTO & MONARO, NSW, AUS [35159] : ALL LONDON, ENG [33887] : ALL SRY, ENG [33887] : ALL HRT, ENG [33887] : ALL LEAMINGTON, WAR, ENG [33887] : 1800+ SHREWSBURY, SAL, ENG [33887] : 1700+ BRK, ENG [33998] : 1700+ OXF, ENG [33998] : ALL ENG [34131] : PRE 1856 SSX, ENG [34652] : ALL BALDEN MARSH, OXF, ENG [35231] : PRE 1748 SOUTH CROXTON, LEI, ENG [35572] : PRE 1920 SHEFFIELD, YKS, ENG [36181] : 1845 CALNE, WIL, ENG [36367] : 1800-1900 SHRAWARDINE, SAL, ENG [36587] : 1800+ SRY, ENG [36858] : C1800 CALNE, WIL, ENG [37082] : PRE 1891 MDX, ENG [37358] : PRE 1850 DOVER, KEN, ENG [37371] : 1800+ LONDON, MDX, ENG [37483] : 1800-50 TENTERDEN, KEN, ENG [37541] : PRE 1780 SHALBOURNE, WIL, ENG [37687] : 1700S-1800S LONDON, MDX & SRY, ENG [38034] : 1800-1870 LAN, ENG [38299] : 1825-1845 MEXICO [37630] : 1840-1850 KEENE, NY, USA [38741] : PRE 1832 CRIGGION, MGY, WLS [37899]

WESTON (SEE WESTERN) [36622]

WESTOVER 1780+ CAN [38235] : ALL CAN & USA [37043] : ALL WORLDWIDE [38218]

WESTPHALEN C1770 HUSUM, SHO, GER [38671]

WESTRAY PRE 1839 WHITEHAVEN, WLS & CUL, ENG [37840]

WESTROP 1850+ MT GAMBIER, SA, AUS [36622]

WEST-SPENCER 1825+ CONNELLS BUSH, NSW, AUS [38204]

WESTSTRATE 1700S ZUID BEVELAND, ZEL, NL [38350]

WESTWATER C1790 FIF, SCT [35223]

WESTWOOD 1870+ DAYLESFORD, VIC, AUS [35204] : 1895+ ROSEDALE, VIC, AUS [35835] : PRE 1822 STOCKTON ON TEES, DUR, ENG [34487] : 1800+ WEATHERSFIELD, ESS, ENG [35204] : 1815+ WEDNESBURY, STS, ENG [36254] : 1800S LYE, WOR, ENG [36670] : 1820+ LND, ENG & AUS [35828] : C1800 DUNFERMLINE, FIF, SCT [34345]

WETENHALL C1816 RATTLESDEN, SFK, ENG [36820]

WETHERBY PRE 1697 MDX, ENG [35895] : PRE 1750 LYDIATE, LAN, ENG [37072]

WETHEREL PRE 1850 CHOLLERTON & KIRKWHELPINGTON, NBL, ENG [36110]

WETHERELL PRE 1800 NEWBURY & THATCHAM, BRK, ENG [34669] : PRE 1840 DINNINGTON, SOM, ENG [36581]

WETHERELT C1812 GRASMERE, WES, ENG [34392] : PRE 1852 CUL, ENG [34392]

WETHERILT 1840S LAMBETH, SRY, ENG [33899] : ALL DUR & WAR, ENG [37750]

WETHERLEY PRE 1861 MDX, ENG [35895]

WETHERLY PRE 1833 HILLINGDON, MDX, ENG [35895]

WETLAND PRE 1880 GDANSK, GD, POL [36941]

WETMUR 1900 MORGAN HILL, CA, USA [37024] : 1830S ORANGE CO., NY, USA [37024]

WETTENGEL 1758-1804 GUNZENHAUSEN, BAW, GER [38626]

WETZEL PRE 1875 WALDORFT & KNITTLINGEN, WUE, GER [37587] : 1870-1891 PHILADELPHIA, PA, USA [37587] : DANIEL 1800+ MAHANTOGO TWP., PA, USA [38127]

WETZLER 1800-1950 CS [36962] : 1850+ USA [36962]

WEYERS PRE 1900 TVL, RSA [36459]

WEYGOLD 1650-1780 AUERBACH, HES, BRD [35311]

WEYMOUTH PRE 1850 DUBLIN, IRL [35360]

WEYMUELLER CATHERINE 1741+ YORK CO., PA, USA [37604]

WEYRAUCH PRE 1700 WUERZBURG, BAV, GER [38681]

WEYRELIJKHUYSEN PRE 1750 ANTWERP, ATW, BEL [38708]

WHALE ALL WIL, ENG [34733] : 1830-1880 ROMSEY, HAM, ENG [36536] : PRE 1850 WOR, ENG [37739] : PRE 1840 CON, ENG [38075] : PRE 1840 DEV, ENG [38075]

WHALEBELLY ALL NFK & SFK, ENG [37712]

WHALEN 1850+ DURROW, LEX, IRL [38189] : 1710+ DUTCHESS CO., NY, USA [37591]

WHALES 1600+ HASTINGS, SSX, ENG [34747]

WHALEY 1800+ LIVERPOOL, NSW, AUS [34533] : 1820-1990 BEAUHARNOIS DIST, QUE, CAN [34377] : 1800S ONT, CAN [38468] : PRE 1765 NC, USA [38340]

WHALLAN PRE 1860 IRL [37416]

WHALLEY 1700+ NORTHWICH, CHS, ENG [36818]

WHAPLES 1650 GREAT WALTHAM, ESS, ENG [37928]

WHARAM 1600-1800 YORK, ERY, ENG [35010] : 1600-1800 KINGSTON UPON HULL, ERY, ENG [35010] : 1600-1800 BEVERLEY, ERY, ENG [35010] : 1829+ DONCASTER, WRY, ENG [38469]

WHARE SARAH PRE 1844 ENG [35615]

WHAREKIRI PRE 1860 WAIROA, NZ [33954]

WHARFF ALL BANGOR & GUILFORD, ME, USA [36915]

WHARLEY PRE 1857 TIP, IRL [34797]

WHARMBY PRE 1859 NEWTON HEATH, MANCHESTER, LAN, ENG [33860] : 1800S BOLTON, LAN, ENG [36066]

WHARRIE C1800-1900 LESMAHAGOW, LKS, SCT [33971]

WHARTON 1800S OXF, ENG [35017] : PRE 1800 RADNAGE, BKM & OXF, ENG [36175] : MARGARET PRE 1800 KENDAL, WES, ENG [36192] : C1820-1890 LONDON, SRY, ENG [37236] : ALL OXF, ENG [37236] : PRE 1860 SAL, ENG [37273] : PRE 1830 HOLMES CHAPEL & DAVENHAM, CHS, ENG [38248] : 1700-1800S VA, USA [36579]

WHATLEY 1750-1825 LEICESTER, LEI, ENG [35320] : 1800+ WILTON, WIL, ENG [35358] : 1800-1900 WILTON, WIL, ENG [36438] : 1700-1800 WARMINSTER, WIL, ENG [37038] : ALL GLS, ENG [37281] : ALL HEF, ENG [37281]

WHATLING 1700S LAXFIELD, SFK, ENG [37250]

WHATMORE PRE 1840 MORTLAKE, SRY, ENG [35544]

WHATSON ALL NSW, AUS [34974] : C1800 SRY, ENG [34258] : PRE 1839 GUESTLING & TAREE, SSX, ENG [35189]

WHAYMAN ROBERT PRE 1887 BRUNY ISLAND, TAS, AUS [36634]

WHEALY (SEE WHALEY) [34377]

WHEAR 1850S GUILDFORD, VIC, AUS [35721] : ALL GERMOE, CON, ENG [35721] : 1785 ST ERTH, CON, ENG [36640]

WHEARE PRE 1816 PILL, GLS, ENG [37878] : 1927+ ABBOTS LEIGH, GLS, ENG [37878] : PRE 1870 CHURCHILL, SOM, ENG [37878]

WHEATER PRE 1830 LEEDS, WRY, ENG [35470]

WHEATLAND PRE 1840 NEWBURY, BRK, ENG [35384] : PRE 1875 ST MARY PADDINGTON, MDX, ENG [36597]

WHEATLEY 1800+ TAS & VIC, AUS [35836] : C1842 URCHFONT, WIL, ENG [34239] : PRE 1652 WHITEHAVEN, NTH, ENG [34992] : PRE 1736 WELDON, NTH, ENG [35597] : 1750+ ELSTED & PAGHAM, SSX, ENG [35891] : PRE 1760 WOKINGHAM, BRK, ENG [36425] : 1830+ OCKBROOK, DBY, ENG [37051] : 1920+ LEEDS, WRY, ENG [37202] : 1656+ LONGPARISH, HAM, ENG [37321] : PRE 1790 BARROW ON SOAR, LEI, ENG [37706] : 1750-1800 NEWPORT, SAL, ENG [38474] : PRE 1850 HATFIELD, HRT, ENG [38722] : PRE 1838 SSX, ENG & AUS [34463]

WHEATTON MEHITABLE 1680-1716 REHOBOTH, MA, USA [35271]

WHEELDON PRE 1800 WAR, ENG [36411] : PRE 1800 DBY, ENG [36411] : PRE 1800 STS, ENG [36411] : PRE 1850 NTT, ENG [36411] : PRE 1800 LEI, ENG [36411] : PRE 1800 CHS, ENG [36411]

WHEELER ALL NSW & QLD, AUS [33799] : 1840+ PERTH & AUBURN, TAS & NSW, AUS [35189] : 1891+ ROCKHAMPTON, QLD, AUS [35507] : 1820+ SYDNEY, NSW, AUS [35735] : 1890+ WIMMERA, VIC, AUS [36622] : 1850+ SYDNEY, NSW, AUS [38490] : 1800-1900 DUNDAS, ONT, CAN [34402] : 1750-1850 MISSISQUOI, QUE, CAN [37486] : ALL LONGBRIDGE, WIL, ENG [33799] : PRE 1789 SHIRBURN & PYRTON, OXF, ENG [33866] : PRE 1800 WORCESTER, WOR, DBY & LEI, ENG [33890] : PRE 1818 SOMERTON, DOR, ENG [34696] : C1582 FARMINGTON, GLS, ENG [35261] : C1800S CHELSEA, MDX, ENG [35342] : PRE 1800 CALCOTT, SOM, ENG [35462] : C1848 BERMONDSEY, SRY, ENG [35507] : PRE 1850 FROME, SOM, ENG [35764] : 1780S WORFIELD, SAL, ENG [35794] : PRE 1840 SHRIVENHAM, BRK, ENG [35866] : PRE 1840 CHRISTIAN MALFORD, WIL, ENG [35866] : 1831+ SHERMANBURY, SSX, ENG [36212] : PRE 1650 MDX, ENG [36972] : PRE 1830 NEWBURY, BRK, ENG [37687] : 1760-1880 GLS, ENG [37870] : 1800+ HULL, ENG [37907] : 1800 BROMLEY, KEN, ENG [38288] : PRE 1834 LONDON, ENG [38490] : ALL WAR, ENG [38514] : 1798 ENG [38756] : PRE 1840 COR, IRL [37249] : HUGH 1840-1890 SULLIVAN CO., IN, USA [35329] : WILLIAM 1870-1875 CAMDEN CO., MO, USA [35329] : C1851 NEW YORK, NY, USA [35585] : 1650+ CAVENDISH, VT, NH & MA, USA [36931] : HENRY 1850+ MCHENRY CO., IL & WI, USA [37001] : HENRY 1800-1840S SCHOHARIE CO., NY, USA [37001] : 1821-1873 WAYNE CO., TN, USA [37029] : PRE 1860 BROWN CO., OH, USA [37037] : ALL WILLIAMSBURG CO., SC, USA [37789] : ALL JOHNSTON CO., NC, USA [37789] : OBADIAH 1608-1671 CONCORD, MIDDLESEX, MA, USA [38183] : 1816+ GA, USA [38360] : 1855+ CHICKASAW CO., MS, USA [38360] : 1847+ AL, USA [38360] : 1849+ MONROE CO., MS, USA [38360] : 1700+ MARION CO., OH, USA [38745] : ALL WORLDWIDE [35832]

WHEELHOUSE PRE 1750 COLLINGHAM & LINTON, WRY, ENG [36159] : PRE 1916

SHEFFIELD, YKS, ENG [36181] : PRE 1700 HAMPSTHWAITE, YKS, ENG [36447] : 1810+ USA [36447]

WHEELTON 1800S MACCLESFIELD, CHS, ENG [36032]

WHEELWRIGHT 1800 LEEDS, WRY, ENG [38381]

WHELAN 1858-1914 MELBOURNE & BAIRNSDALE, VIC, AUS [34971] : ALL TAS & VIC, AUS [35063] : ALL GLANWORTH, COR, IRL [34460] : ALL FERMOY, COR, IRL [34460] : ALL BALLYHOOLY, COR, IRL [34460] : PRE 1835 TIP, IRL [34959] : 1880 CALLAN, KIK, IRL [35350] : C1770 WEX & KIK, IRL [36028] : 1800-1850 WAT, IRL [36297] : 1800-1950 BALLYMACARBERRY & CLONMEL, WAT, IRL [36565] : 1700-1800S KID, IRL [36796] : 1827-1847 KILMEADEN, WAT, IRL [38117] : 1800-1900S HOKITIKA, WESTLAND, NZ [36796]

WHELDALE 1700-1800 LUDBOROUGH, LIN, ENG [37487]

WHELDON 1891+ TAS, AUS [33786] : PRE 1891 FRANKLIN, TAS, AUS [33786] : C1895 HULL, ERY, ENG [34752] : PRE 1790 NORTHALLERTON, NRY, ENG [35212]

WHELPTON 1900+ ONT, CAN [38323]

WHEREAT 1861+ TENTERFIELD, NSW, AUS [37830] : C1765 TROWBRIDGE, WIL, ENG [37830]

WHERRITT THEODOSIA PRE 1794 LONDON, ENG [34247]

WHETHERSTONE PRE 1870 HANBOROUGH, OXF, ENG [36883]

WHETNALL PRE 1800 AUDLEY, STS, ENG [37389]

WHETNELL PRE 1900 STS, ENG [37389]

WHETTER C1727 ST STEPHEN IN BRANNEL, CON, ENG [34573] : 1600-1800 ST STEPHEN IN BRANNEL, CON, ENG [37457]

WHETZEL ALL WORLDWIDE [37785]

WHEWALL PRE 1750 CHEDDLETON, STS, ENG [36701]

WHIBBERLEY 1800-1870 ASHFORD & BAKEWELL, DBY, ENG [36189]

WHIBLEY C1862 ENG & NZ [36840]

WHICHELO 1700+ OXFORD, OXF, ENG [36685]

WHICKER C1790-1850 FUGGLESTONE & WILTON, WIL, ENG [37287]

WHIDDETT ALL KEN, ENG [33925]

WHIDDON 1650+ STAVERTON & BROADHEMPSTON, DEV, ENG [34747] : 1800-1900 DEV, ENG [35621] : ALL USA [38340]

WHIFFEN 1700S KEN, ENG [37019]

WHIFFIN PRE 1800 NORTH, KEN, ENG [34720]

WHIMSETT PRE 1880 TEYNHAM, KEN, ENG [36082]

WHINFELL 1500+ CLIBURN, WES, ENG [36256]

WHINNA 1775-1825 WHITEHAVEN, CUL, ENG [37740] : 1825-1875 PHILADELPHIA, PA, USA [37740]

WHINNELL PRE 1800 DOR, ENG [36380]

WHIPP ROBERT C1824 BURNLEY, LAN, ENG [37992]

WHIPPLE 1560-1637 ENG [35287] : 1637+ MA, USA [35287] : 1774-1826 PROVIDENCE, RI, USA [35287] : 1826+ OH, USA [35287] : 1865-1877 KEWEENAW CO., MI, USA [38009] : SARAH JANE 1750-1800 SMITHFIELD PROVIDENCE, RI, USA [38130] : 1770-1850 SARATOGA CO., NY, USA [38153] : 1617+ WLS & ENG [37592]

WHISH 1750+ CAM, ENG [35824]

WHISKER PRE 1820 YORK, YKS, ENG [34588]

WHISKIN ALL ESS, ENG [35840]

WHISLER 1920 GAGE, NE, USA [38095]

WHISTLER PRE 1885 BIRMINGHAM, ENG [33890] : 1700-1850 BASINGSTOKE, HAM, ENG [35375] :

1600S FACOMB, HAM, ENG [35375] : 1600-1800 MAGHERAFELT, LDY, IRL [35375]

WHISTON 1800-1840 BIRMINGHAM, STS, ENG [34448] : C1740 IPSTONES, STS, ENG [35920]

WHITACRE ALFRED PRE 1830 VA & OH, USA [38181]

WHITAKER ALL MANCHESTER, LAN, ENG [33771] : 1850+ DORCHESTER, DOR, ENG [35701] : 1860+ LAMBETH, SRY & LND, ENG [35701] : 1750-1900 BATH & MONKTON COMBE, SOM, ENG [35701] : TABITHA 1750+ STOURTON, WIL, ENG [35815] : PRE 1860 HAWORTH, WRY, ENG [36022] : ALL BAILDON & GUISELEY, WRY, ENG [36159] : PRE 1850 ADDINGHAM, WRY, ENG [36159] : 1600-1900 OTLEY, WRY, ENG [37854] : 1600-1800 KEIGHLEY, WRY, ENG [37854]

WHITAKER (SEE WHITTA [36270]

WHITALL PRE 1675 WOLSTANTON, STS, ENG [36701]

WHITBECK 1646-1800 ALBANY CO., NY, USA [37591]

WHITBROTH 1740S BRIGHTON, SSX, ENG [35261]

WHITBURNE 1690S ST ENODER, CON, ENG [34793]

WHITBY PRE 1700 NOTTINGHAM, NTT, ENG [36532] : PRE 1780 YEOVIL, SOM, ENG [37361] : 1700-1800 CULLOMPTON, DEV, ENG [37943]

WHITCHER 1800S ENG [37857] : 1800-1850 VT, USA [33753]

WHITCHURCH PRE 1850 DEV & CON, ENG [36594]

WHITCHURCH-BENNETT ALL WORLDWIDE [36594]

WHITCOMB 1600-1720 GROTON & LACASTER, MA, USA [36944] : 1700+ BOLTON, MA, USA [38015]

WHITCROFT ALL MOG, IRL [36702]

WHITE GEORGE 1900+ FREMANTLE, WA, AUS [33842] : DENIS 1840+ HAMILTON, TAS, AUS [33933] : MICHAEL 1890-1923 RICHMOND, VIC, AUS [33933] : 1845 MOUNT GAMBIER, SA, AUS [34446] : ALL CALLINGTON, SA, AUS [34561] : 1853+ GEELONG, VIC, AUS [34685] : 1880+ MINYIP, VIC, AUS [34685] : FELIX P. 1870-1900 MONARO AREA, NSW, AUS [34842] : FELIX P. 1860-1872 MT GAMBIER, SA, AUS [34842] : ROBERT 1855+ MAJORS CREEK, NSW, AUS [35084] : LABAN 1824+ NSW, AUS [35086] : C1800+ BATHURST, NSW, AUS [35099] : C1832+ SYDNEY, NSW, AUS [35099] : JAMES 1860+ HAWKESBURY RIVER, NSW, AUS [35099] : C1845+ NARRAWONG, VIC, AUS [35223] : HENRY 1866+ SYDNEY OR LISMORE, NSW, AUS [35330] : PRE 1857+ ST ARNAUD, VIC, AUS [35453] : 1880+ PINJARRA, WA, AUS [35533] : 1880 EAGLEHAWK, VIC, AUS [35755] : HENRY C1860+ ROKEWOOD, VIC, AUS [35834] : FANNY C1870+ ECHUCA, VIC, AUS [35834] : HENRY 1850+ GEELONG, VIC, AUS [35834] : HUNTER K. 1843 HOBARTVILLE RICHMOND & MUDGEE, NSW, AUS [36311] : 1826+ LIVERPOOL & GUNDAGAI, NSW, AUS [36597] : BENJAMIN 1840-1860 AUS [37617] : C1853 GEELONG, VIC, AUS [37894] : PRE 1853 WINDELIMA, NSW, AUS [37901] : GEORGE ALEX 1860+ COONAMBLE, NSW, AUS [38500] : 1860+ CARCOAR, NSW, AUS [38582] : 1820-1850 RED CLIFF, NFD, CAN [33852] : 1860+ LISTOWEL, ONT, CAN [34379] : 1860+ FARNHAM, QUE, CAN [34379] : GEORGE HENRY 1800+ ORILLIA, ONT, CAN [34511] : PRE 1866 ST THOMAS, ONT, CAN [34588] : 1850+ GREY CO., ONT, CAN [36690] : ROBERT 1840+ BRUCE CO., ONT, CAN [36697] : 1800S GUELPH & WELLINGTON, ONT, CAN [36727] : 1775+ NFD, CAN [37479] : WILLIAM HENRY 1827 SMITH CREEK, ONT, CAN [37788] : 1800S ELIZABETHVILLE, ONT, CAN [38418] :

DORCAS 1890+ LEEDS CO., ONT, CAN [38431] : 1800S OTTAWA, ONT, CAN [38468] : 1700-1860 HAZELMERE, SRY, ENG [33842] : C1842 NORTH BURTON, BRIDLINGTON, NRY, ENG [33863] : ANNIE C1850+ WOOLLAND, DOR, ENG [33922] : 1835 SOUTHWARK, SRY, ENG [33967] : 1840 ENG [33999] : JAMES C1800-1850 LONDON, ENG [34007] : 1880S FINCHAMPSTEAD, BRK, ENG [34027] : PRE 1835 WROTHAM, KEN, ENG [34115] : RICHARD 1600S SOUTH EAST, KEN, ENG [34181] : 1790S WALPOLE, SFK, ENG [34205] : 1830+ STEPNEY, MDX, ENG [34237] : 1880+ LAMBETH, SRY, ENG [34313] : PRE 1750 SOHAM, CAM, ENG [34316] : JIM C1910 TYNEMOUTH, NBL, ENG [34372] : 1700+ STRETTON, WAR, ENG [34414] : ALICE 1855-1870 LANGLEY, SSX, ENG [34505] : PRE 1820 SALISBURY, WIL, ENG [34588] : C1800 REDRUTH, CON, ENG [34644] : PRE 1850 ISLEWORTH, PADDINGTON, LND, ENG [34669] : PRE 1853 HUTTON, SOM, ENG [34685] : 1825+ MORNINGTHORPE, NFK, ENG [34710] : 1600+ HASTINGS, SSX, ENG [34747] : FELIX P. 1830-1865 NEWBURY, BRK, ENG [34842] : MARTHA PRE 1815 BRISTOL, GLS, ENG [34862] : 1800 CAMBORNE, CON, ENG [34890] : C1838 GREAT TORRINGTON, DEV, ENG [34898] : 1700S ST ERTH, CON, ENG [34920] : ARTHUR PRE 1652 WHITEHAVEN, NTH, ENG [34992] : PRE 1910 GILDERSOME, WRY, ENG [35031] : ROBERT PRE 1855 LND, ENG [35084] : PRE 1801+ KIDDERMINSTER, WOR, ENG [35109] : PRE 1851 ALTON, HAM, ENG [35113] : PRE 1840 EXETER, DEV, ENG [35229] : JULIA C1850 SRY, ENG [35255] : SARAH 1823 WAKEFIELD, YKS, ENG [35369] : C1830 BIRMINGHAM, WAR, ENG [35377] : 1860S ROCHDALE, LAN, ENG [35406] : PRE 1875 CARLISLE, CUL, ENG [35406] : 1860S NETHERTON, WRY, ENG [35406] : ALEX 1800S BRISTOL, SOM, ENG [35408] : 1840S CLERKENWELL, LND, ENG [35408] : JOSEPH THOMAS C1829 ENG [35447] : C1832 HURSLEY, HAM, ENG [35457] : PRE 1900 BRIDLINGTON, ERY & WAR, ENG [35495] : PRE 1880 BEDWORTH, WAR, ENG [35533] : C1850 SOUTHWARK, SRY, ENG [35576] : C1828 MAIDSTONE, KEN, ENG [35576] : 1880-1960 SHOREDITCH & ISLINGTON, LND, ENG [35576] : SAMUEL 1820-1840 HOLBEACH, LIN, ENG [35726] : SAMUEL 1840+ LITTLEPORT, CAM, ENG [35726] : LOVE 1770S DRAYTON, SOM, ENG [35798] : C1800+ HATTON ON THAMES, LND, ENG [35834] : ALL DEAL, KEN, ENG [35896] : PRE 1884 IOW, ENG [35934] : 1850-1900 WINDSOR, BRK, ENG [36007] : THOMAS PRE 1880 SUDBURY, SFK, ENG [36050] : GEORGE 1760S WIL & SOM, ENG [36100] : C1800 ORDSALL & E.RETFORD, NTT, ENG [36112] : PRE 1860S BRISTOL & SOM, ENG [36146] : 1740+ NEWINGTON, KEN, ENG [36236] : 1770+ OXF, ENG [36239] : PRE 1715 BECKLEY & UDIMORE, SSX, ENG [36272] : PRE 1850 BRIDGEWATER, SOM, ENG [36275] : 1750-1850 COLLINGBOURNE KINGSTON, WIL, ENG [36286] : C1800S WIL, ENG [36289] : ALL CAVERSHAM, OXF, ENG [36326] : PRE 1750 CITY, LND, ENG [36396] : PRE 1830 ASKERSWELL & BRIDPORT, DOR, ENG [36424] : 1900+ CONSETT, DUR & YKS, ENG [36503] : RICHARD 1800+ IDLE & THACKLEY, WRY, ENG [36617] : 1860 KEA, CON, ENG [36640] : PRE 1710 DEVON, DEV, ENG [36679] : C1810 WEST KEAL, LIN, ENG [36820] : 1780 KEN, ENG [36860] : C1734+ HARTING, SSX, ENG [36875] : 1808 ALFRETON, DBY, ENG [36907] : CHARLES 1880+

SALTBURN, YKS, ENG [36967] : 1800-1900
STUTTON, SFK, ENG [37042] : C1720-1800 WYLYE
& STOCKTON, WIL, ENG [37086] : SARAH PRE
1850 CHILD OKEFORD, DOR, ENG [37105] : PRE
1900 BATTERSEA, SRY, ENG.[37171] : PRE 1900
WANDSWORTH, SRY, ENG [37171] : ALL YEOVIL,
SOM, ENG [37269] : 1800+ LONDON, ENG [37294] :
ANNIE 1800S TWYNING, GLS & WOR, ENG
[37299] : C1820 WITLEY, SRY, ENG [37309] : C1750
HILPERTON, WIL, HAM & DOR, ENG [37335] :
1700-1900 TWYFORD, DBY, ENG [37487] : JOHN
C1800 CHARLTON MACKEREL, SOM, ENG
[37508] : 1830+ HASTINGS, SSX, ENG [37560] : ALL
WARMINSTER, WIL, ENG [37617] : C1800
BROTHERTON, WRY, ENG [37665] : 1850+
SITTINGBOURNE, KEN, ENG [37677] : 1600-1900
ST JUST & MORVAH, CON, ENG [37680] : PRE
1850 MID, NFK, ENG [37718] : PRE 1900 AUDLEY,
STS, ENG [37722] : WILLIAM 1685-1750 ENG [37722]
: 1800-1860 WHISSONSETT, NFK, ENG [37845] :
WILLIAM PRE 1870 KINGSBRIDGE, DEV, ENG
[37948] : 1800+ DURHAM, DUR, ENG [37984] : PRE
1820 TORQUAY, DEV, ENG [38292] : C1830
WINCHESTER, HAM, ENG [38292] : 1700-C1740S
THORNBOROUGH, BKM, ENG [38350] : HARRIET
C1860-1887 LOWESTOFT, SFK, ENG [38402] :
JAMES PRE 1870 SOUTH PETHERTON, SOM,
ENG [38431] : CHARLES 1800S HYDERBAD,
INDIA [35177] : PRE 1900 POONA,
MAHARASHTRA, INDIA [37101] : ALL INDIA
[37920] : PRE 1830 ARM, IRL [34090] : PRE 1830
ANT, IRL [34090] : PRE 1840 MAGHERALOUGH,
TYR, IRL [34137] : WILLIAM 1800-1880 COR, IRL
[34476] : 1770+ OMAGH, TYR, IRL [34649] : PETER
1844+ GRAIGUE, WIC & DUB, IRL [35013] : PRE
1864 BAUNREIGH, KIK, IRL [35197] : PATRICK
1811+ COR, IRL [35223] : JAMES PRE 1860 WIC,
IRL [35382] : PRE 1835+ GAL, IRL [35453] :
WILLIAM C1827 ANACARTY, TIP, IRL [35772] :
1865+ GREYABBEY, DOW, IRL [36264] : ALL
BAILIEBOROUGH, CAV, IRL [36608] : MARY 1825-
45 BORRISNAFARNEY, TIP, IRL [37171] : 1870-90
CURRAGH CAMP, KID, IRL [37171] : MARY 1825-
45 KILMOYLAN, LIM, IRL [37171] : MARY 1825-45
TOEM, TIP, IRL [37171] : MARY 1825-45
WHITEVILLE, TIP, IRL [37171] : MARY 1825-45
LISOWEN, LIM, IRL [37171] : 1840S TYR, IRL
[37577] : 1700+ BROUGHSHANE & BALLYMENA,
ANT, IRL [37625] : JOHN 1840-1890 DERRY, DON,
IRL [38045] : JOHN 1760S OMAGH, TYR, IRL
[38537] : 1866+ VICTORIA VALLEY, NZ [34588] :
C1767 ANCRUM, ROX, SCT [34239] : RICHARD
1700+ FIF, SCT [34419] : PRE 1900 DUNDEE, ANS,
SCT [34758] : 1700+ AIRTH, STI, SCT [34977] :
1700+ ST MONANCE, FIF, SCT [35627] : 1750+
STEWARTON, AYR, SCT [35909] : C1800
SHETLAND, SHI, SCT [36585] : ANNE 1863+
GLASGOW, SCT [37135] : NEIL PRE 1850 ISLAY,
ARL, SCT [38403] : ALL USA [35896] : PLEASANT
1796-1810 ELBERT CO., GA, USA [36330] :
PLEASANT SR. 1800-1810 ELBERT CO., GA, USA
[36330] : 1700-1760 ORANGE CO., VA, USA [36566] :
ABNER 1790-1900 RUTLAND CO. & FRANKLIN
CO., VT, USA [37586] : ROBERT 1800-1840 BEAVER
CO., PA, USA [37590] : 1750-1813 WASHINGTON
CO., MD, USA [38026] : 1810-1891 CLEVELAND,
OH, USA [38102] : 1850-1860 SAINT CLAIR TWP.,
PA, USA [38105] : PRE 1759 FREDERICK CO., MD,
USA [38120] : 1770 ALONG TAR RIVER, NC, USA
[38188] : HANNAH 1770+ NC, USA [38374] :
HANNAH 1770+ PA, USA [38374] : 1800S
WARREN CO., OH, USA [38531] : PRE 1800 MD,

USA [38576] : NORMAN 1847-1900 BRADFORD
CO., PA, USA [38732] : ALL WORLDWIDE [38766]
WHITEAR 1830+ TAS, AUS [34904] : PRE 1831 ENG
[36754]
WHITECHURCH 1600-1900 CAM, ENG [35178] : 1800-
1900 LND, ENG [35178] : 1600-1750 HUN, ENG
[35178] : 1860+ BOURN, CAM, ENG [36772] : 1800+
HARLTON, CAM, ENG [36772] : 1800+ BISHOPS
STORTFORD, HEF, ENG [36772]
WHITECROSS 1846+ VIC, AUS [34412] : PRE 1846
SCT [34412] : PRE 1850 CRUDEN, ABD, SCT [34784]
WHITEFIELD 1850+ DEV, ENG [35362]
WHITEFORD 1820S ANT, IRL [36292] : 1750+ BEITH,
AYR, SCT [37110] : HUGH 1796-1880 POTSDAM, ST
LAWRENCE CO., NY, USA & IRL [38140]
WHITEHEAD 1800+ TAS, AUS [34590] : 1890+
COONAMBLE, NSW, AUS [35567] : 1800S
LONDON, ENG [34178] : MARY ANN 1816+
HOLLINWOOD & NEWTON, LAN, ENG [34181] :
ABEL 1825 YKS, ENG [35120] : 1750-1875 ENG
[35136] : 1800-1838 BIRMINGHAM, WAR, ENG
[35377] : C1840 WEST BARMING, KEN, ENG
[35456] : 1700+ TROWELL, NTT, ENG [35847] :
1800+ OLDHAM, LAN, ENG [35847] : 1750+
KINGSBURY, WATER EATON, WAR & OXF,
ENG [36329] : GEORGE PRE 1830 KEN, ENG
[36469] : SARAH 1830-1871+ DENTON, LAN, ENG
[37546] : PRE 1900 UPWELL & KINGS LYNN, NFK,
ENG [37617] : ANNE PRE 1840 BRISTOL, YKS,
ENG [38049] : PRE 1860 ENG [38184] : PRE 1950+
OLD LEAKE, LIN, ENG [38401] : 1912+
PIETERMARITZBURG & DURBAN, NATAL, RSA
[37202] : 1776 LECROPT, STI, SCT [34635] : PRE 1810
SWINTON, BEW, SCT [36497]
WHITEHILL 1870+ WHATCOM, WA, USA [37781]
WHITEHORNE 1865+ LONDON, ENG [36237] :
1830+ BRK, ENG [36237]
WHITEHOUSE 1872 TROWBRIDGE, WIL, ENG
[34120] : ALL BIRMINGHAM, WAR, ENG [34351] :
1820-1950 BIRMINGHAM, WAR, ENG [34458] :
1880S WHITEHEATH, STS, ENG [34782] : PRE 1870
BIRMINGHAM, WAR, ENG [35523] : C1840
BIRMINGHAM, WAR, ENG [35744] : PRE 1800
SEDGLEY, STS, ENG [36110] : PRE 1816
BIRMINGHAM, WAR, ENG [36177] : PRE 1850
HANDSWORTH, STS, ENG [36424] : 1810-1870
WARREN CO., KY, USA [36734]
WHITEHURST 1650+ CHESTER, CHS, DBY & STS,
ENG [35445]
WHITELAW 1855+ VIC, AUS [34412] : 1650-1850
BOTHWELL SHIELS, LKS, SCT [33978] : PRE 1855
ROX, SCT [34412] : 1700+ STI, SCT [35627] : C1880
GLASGOW, LKS, SCT [37106]
WHITELEGG 1623 NORTHENDEN, CHS, ENG
[35097]
WHITELEY 1820+ NSW & VIC, AUS [35841] : PRE
1805 YKS, ENG [38080]
WHITELOCK 1730-1830 SKELTON, CUL, ENG
[36098]
WHITELY ALL HURON CO., ONT, CAN [38419] :
ALL IRL [38419]
WHITEMAN 1840+ SYDNEY, NSW, AUS [36607] :
1859+ YOUNG, NSW, AUS [37919] : PRE 1880
HENLEY ON THAMES, OXF, ENG [34245] : PRE
1810 LEWES, SSX, ENG [35354] : PRE 1800
HOLBORN, LND, ENG [35354] : PRE 1840
UDIMORE, SSX, ENG [36607] : 1800+ UDIMORE,
SSX, ENG [36843] : 1880+ WOOBURN GREEN,
BKM, ENG [36975] : C1600-1800 LEWES, SSX, ENG
[37642] : C1600-1800 CLERKENWELL &
SHOREDITCH, MDX, ENG [37642] : C1825

FORFAR, CAI, SCT & AUS [35079] : RICHARD PRE 1830 HAMPSHIRE CO., WV, USA [37580]

WHITEOAK 1850+ BINGLEY, YKS, ENG [35734] : MARTHA P. 1880 ENG OR SCT [37411]

WHITER 1810+ BETHNAL GREEN & SHOREDITCH, LND, ENG [34063] : 1850S WHITECHAPEL, LND, ENG [35815]

WHITEROW PRE 1860 WAREHAM & CORFE, DOR, ENG [38483]

WHITESELL 1650+ SALEM, NJ & PA, USA [37826]

WHITESIDE ALL AUS [33907] : ALL CAN [33907] : ALL ENG [33907] : ALL IRL [33907] : 1788-1830S TYR, IRL [33924] : 1700+ COLTRIM, LDY, IRL [34271] : PRE 1880 BELFAST, ANT, IRL [37636] : PRE 1830 STONEYFORD, ANT, IRL [37927] : ALL NZ [33907] : ALL SCT [33907] : 1820S GLASGOW, LKS, SCT [33924] : ALL USA [33907]

WHITEWAY PRE 1900 NFD, CAN [33904] : PRE 1740 SHRIVENHAM, BRK, ENG [35866] : PRE 1830 KINGSTON, SRY, ENG [37107]

WHITEWOOD 1771-1865 KEN, ENG [36836] : 1865+ WELLINGTON, NZ [36836]

WHITFIELD 1850S PORTSEA, HAM, ENG [34435] : ALL BRK, ENG [36076] : 1826 IDLE, YKS, ENG [37174] : PRE 1820 TYR, IRL & AUS [35079] : 1920+ PORTLAND, OR, USA [36076] : 1675-1685 NANSEMOND CO., VA, USA [38119] : ALL WORLDWIDE [36155]

WHITFOOT PRE 1663 RADCLIFFE ON TRENT, NTT, ENG [36532]

WHITFORD 1700+ COX HILL & CHACEWATER, CON, ENG [34650] : 1800+ KENWYN, CON, ENG [35776] : ALL YKS, ENG [36656] : ALL LAN, ENG [36656] : ALL REDRUTH, CON, ENG & CAN [36656] : PRE 1850 JACKSON CO., MI, USA [38231] : PRE 1850 VT, USA [38231]

WHITHAM PRE 1850 ADDINGHAM, WRY, ENG [36159]

WHITING 1850+ SALE, VIC, AUS [35726] : PRE 1900 SYDNEY, NSW, AUS [38585] : 1809+ HAVERHILL, SFK, ENG [34334] : PRE 1878 LONDON, ENG [34463] : 1700+ SOHAM, CAM, ENG [34650] : PRE 1900 DISS, NFK, ENG [35470] : C1820-1850 KINGSLEY, HAM, ENG [35726] : 1800+ EAST END, LND, ENG [35942] : PRE 1890 HAVERHILL, SFK, ENG [36020] : PRE 1840 ESS, ENG [37280] : PRE 1840 LND, ENG [37280] : PRE 1840 MDX, ENG [37280] : PRE 1810 ORPINGTON, KEN, ENG [37989] : 1500-1700 DESFORD, LEI, ENG [38229] : ALL COR, IRL [36801] : PRE 1900 MAURICEVILLE, NZ & ENG [34604] : PRE 1900 BLAENAVON, MON, WLS [36801]

WHITLA C1850 NEWTOWNARDS, DOW, IRL [35722]

WHITLARK 1700-1800 WAVENDON & BOW BRICKHILL, BKM, ENG [35701]

WHITLAW 1855+ VIC, AUS [34412] : C1850 NEWTOWNARDS, DOW, IRL [35722] : PRE 1855 ROX, SCT [34412]

WHITLEY 1750+ HODDERSTON, HRT, ENG [36088] : 1700-1900 CHS & LAN, ENG [37880] : 1760S LINCOLN CO., NC, USA [37027] : 1760-98 TYRON OC., NC, USA [37027]

WHITLOCK 1850-1862 TULBOT, VIC, AUS [34693] : 1800-1850 EALING, MDX, ENG [34693] : 1700-1800 WAVENDON & BOW BRICKHILL, BKM, ENG [35701] : ALL EDINBURGH, SCT [35936]

WHITLOW C1870 WALHALLA, VIC, AUS [35127] : PRE 1800 MANCHESTER, LAN, ENG [35127]

WHITMAN 1700-1800 PROVIDENCE, RI, USA [38025]

WHITMARSH 1860+ BREWARRINA, NSW, AUS [34806] : PRE 1850 CATSFIELD, SSX, ENG [34806] : ALL WILTON, DEVIZES & CHIPPENHAM, WIL,

ENG & NZ [33981] : 1661-1718 WEYMOUTH, MA, USA [38518]

WHITMEE ALL LONDON, NSW & QLD, AUS & ENG [34955]

WHITMORE 1846+ MELBOURNE, VIC, AUS [35797] : PRE 1600 ENG [34395] : 1700+ FINDERN, DBY, ENG [35183] : 1870S PANCRAS, LND, ENG [35188] : C1828 ISLINGTON, MDX, ENG [35391] : 1750+ HORLEY, SRY, ENG [36088] : 1800-1900 LONDON, ENG [37166] : C1800 LONDON, ENG [37898] : 1800+ RSA [35032] : 1750+ ME & MA, USA [38739]

WHITMORE (SEE WITMER [36972]

WHITNEY 1860+ CAMPBELL TOWN, TAS, AUS [34910] : C1870 LIVERPOOL, NSW, AUS [35401] : 1800+ ONT, CAN [34119] : 1797+ PRESCOTT, ONT, CAN [35626] : 1892+ LANGDON, ALB, CAN [35626] : C1800 SIDNEY, NS, CAN [35626] : PRE 1826 BKM, ENG [34041] : PRE 1817 HEREFORD, HEF, ENG [34696] : 1790-1840 WATERLOO, LND, ENG [34834] : 1732+ HIGH EASTER, ESS, ENG [34910] : 1630S LONDON, ENG [35626] : 1500-1630 WHITNEY ON WYE, HEF, ENG [35626] : ALL EDMONTON, MDX, ENG [37667] : 1915+ NZ [37661] : JOHN PRE 1791 NY, USA [34064] : PETER PRE 1791 NY, USA [34064] : 1635-1797 WATERTOWN, MA, USA [35626]

WHITSETT 1830-1860 IL, USA [36908]

WHITSEY ALL HUN, ENG [35069]

WHITSITT ALL AUS [33907] : ALL CAN [33907] : ALL ENG [33907] : ALL IRL [33907] : ALL USA [33907]

WHITTAKER 1878+ QUIRINDI, NSW, AUS [36270] : 1850+ MAITLAND, NSW, AUS [36270] : LAWRENCE 1805+ SYDNEY, NSW, AUS [36638] : SAMUEL 1801+ SOUTH COAST & SYDNEY, NSW, AUS [36638] : PRE 1800 HALIFAX, NS, CAN [36270] : 1830-1900 BRADFORD, WRY, ENG [35402] : PRE 1801 HALIFAX, WRY, ENG [36270] : 1825+ CHATHAM, KEN, ENG [37310] : PRE 1800 STS, ENG [37389] : JOHN 1827+ WINCHAM & NORTHWICH, CHS, ENG [37546] : 1750-1800 DARWEN, LAN, ENG [37613] : 1792+ FISHLAKE, WRY, ENG [38469] : ALL LAN, ENG [38514]

WHITTAM PRE 1880 OLDHAM, LAN, ENG [36028] : 1800-1906 AMBLESIDE, WES, ENG [37437]

WHITTEL 1670-1730 BOLTON, LAN, ENG [36635]

WHITTEM PRE 1819 PLYMOUTH, DEV, ENG [38416] : 1819-1875 MOBILE, AL, USA [38416]

WHITTEMORE 1750+ ME & MA, USA [38739]

WHITTEN PRE 1835 ST EBBS, OXF, ENG [34043] : PRE 1730 DRAYTON, ENG [35118] : 1800S TANDERAGEE, ARM, IRL [36800]

WHITTER PRE 1874 TIVERTON, DEV, ENG [34847]

WHITTET 1835 PER, SCT [38282]

WHITTICK ALL WORLDWIDE [37233]

WHITTINGHAM PRE 1750 ADDINGHAM & DRAUGHTON, WRY, ENG [36159] : 1860-1900 SOLIHULL, WAR, ENG [36530]

WHITTINGTON 1850+ BALLARAT, VIC, AUS & NZ [36257] : ALL CARISBROOKE, ISLE OF WIGHT, HAM, ENG [33802]

WHITTLE PRE 1860 TOW LAW, DUR, ENG [35255] : C1769 BARKBY, LEI, ENG [35773] : 1820+ UPWAY, DOR, ENG [36296] : PRE 1812 BOLTON LE MOORS, LAN, ENG [36742] : PRE 1850 PRESTON, LAN, ENG [36998] : 1846+ WESTHOUGHTON & WIGAN, LAN, ENG [37131] : 1600-1800 THURNING, NTH, ENG [38003] : 1880+ OR, USA [35505] : JOHN PRE 1800 JEFFERSON CO., GA, USA [38536]

WHITTMORE 1750+ ME & MA, USA [38739]

WHITTOCK ALL SOM, ENG [37233] : ALL WORLDWIDE [37233]

WHITTOME 1790S HILGAY, NFK, ENG [36966]
WHITTON PRE 1890 TRYPHINIA, QLD, AUS [35118]
: EDWARD PRE 1788 GREENWICH, KEN, ENG
[35530] : 1800+ WILTON, WIL, ENG [36885] : 1700+
GOSFORTH & DRIGG, CUL, ENG [37073] : 1810+
DUNDEE, ANS, SCT [34637]
WHITTY C1790 BROADWAY, DOR, ENG [37378]
WHITWELL 1853+ ADELAIDE, SA, AUS [38209] :
1840-1910 ROCHDALE, LAN, ENG [34175] : PRE
1860 YKS, ENG [34175] : 1770+ SUTTON, CAM,
ENG [38209] : 1700-1900 WORLDWIDE [36977] :
1800-1900 WORLDWIDE [36977]
WHITWILL 1700-178 HAXBY, NRY, ENG [36147]
WHITWORTH PRE 1900 AMHERST, VIC, AUS
[35404] : 1840 THRAPSTON, NTH, ENG [35376] :
1860 NORTHAMPTON, NTH, ENG [35376] : 1880
MANCHESTER, LAN, ENG [37690]
WHOLAHAN C1800 CLONMEL, TIP, IRL [35203]
WHOLEY 1700+ ENG [34572] : 1800+
SCULCOATES, ERY & KEN, ENG [36093]
WHOLLY 1810-1850 NY, USA [35317]
WHOLOHAN 1840-1900 BOBS RANGE, NSW, AUS
[33766] : PRE 1840 THURLES, TIP, IRL [33766]
WHOMES PRE 1875 LAMBETH, SRY, ENG [34105]
WHORROD 1800+ DRAYTON, SOM, ENG [37905]
WHYATT ALL LEI, ENG [37487]
WHYBROW 1850-1900 WHITECHAPEL, LND, ENG
[34469]
WHYMAN PRE 1830 DARLASTON, STS, ENG [36424]
WHYMARK PRE 1900 SFK, ENG [35577]
WHYMER 1830+ CORTON, SFK, ENG [35726]
WHYTE PRE 1850 SYDNEY, NSW, AUS [34287] : ALL
ENG [35913] : 1750-1850 CLONMEL, TIP, IRL
[34346] : ALL NZ [35913] : 1750 BLACKBORD, PER,
SCT [34098] : JOHN C1803 PORTMOAK, KRS, SCT
[34447] : PRE 1900 KILSYTH, STI, SCT [35111] :
1750+ LESLIE, FIF, SCT [35558] : 1800+ GOVAN,
LKS, SCT [35977] : ALL FRASERBURG, ABD, SCT
[36743] : 1780+ NEW DEER, ABD, SCT [36833] :
C1800 MUTHILL, PER, SCT [37512] : 1760S OLD
DEER, ABD, SCT [38422] : 1750-1790 FYVIE, ABD,
SCT [38422] : 1800S MAINS FO BYNDALIE, ABD,
SCT [38422]
WIBBERLEY 1640-1900 OSMASTON &
ASHBOURNE, DBY, ENG [35937]
WIBERG PRE 1880 TRONDHEIM, NOR [36750] :
1880+ CANTERBURY, NZ [36750]
WICH PRE 1883 NEUFANG, BAY, BRD [36338] :
1881+ ROCK ISLAND, IL, USA [36338]
WICHMANN PRE 1890 GER [37009] : 1700-1850
RAWA-MAZ, WA, POL [38652]
WICKEM C1670 WARMINSTER, WIL, ENG [35076]
WICKENDEN 1808-1834 SHOREDITCH, LND, ENG
[36836] : 1700-1850 TONBRIDGE, KEN, ENG [37365]
WICKENS ALL AUS [34961] : 1882 SUNDERLAND,
DUR, ENG [35416] : PRE 1820 SSX, ENG [37646] :
1300-1400+ SSX, ENG [37648] : 1800S LKS, SCT
[36642]
WICKERS PRE 1821 LIMEHOUSE, LND, ENG [37610]
WICKERSHAM PRE 190 NY & SC, USA [35312]
WICKES ALL LUTTERWORTH, LEI, ENG [36162]
WICKETT 1800+ ONT, CAN [37478]
WICKEY ALL WORLDWIDE [38653]
WICKHAM C1852+ FLEMINGTON & HEATHCOTE,
VIC, AUS [35525] : 1830-40S LONGSUTTON &
SUTTONBRIDGE, LIN, ENG [35525]
WICKI ALL WORLDWIDE [38653]
WICKLIFFE 1692+ NORTHUMBERLAND CO., VA,
USA [38120]
WICKS 1855+ COLLINGWOOD, VIC, AUS [35134] :
1853+ SYDNEY, NSW, AUS [37987] : ALL
BUCKLAND, SRY, ENG [34351] : PRE 1830

WORTHING, SSX, ENG [34909] : 1850S SOMERS
TOWN, LND, ENG [35134] : PRE 1854 LEWES, SSX,
ENG [35232] : PRE 1700 CHESTERTON, CAM, ENG
[35238] : ALL LEI & NTT, ENG [37078] : 1800-1880
SWINDON & LIDIARD MILLICENT, WIL, ENG
[37877] : PRE 1880 CARSHALTON & MITCHAM,
SRY, ENG [37987]
WICKSTEAD PRE 1800 WEYMOUTH, DOR, ENG
[35261]
WICKY ALL WORLDWIDE [38653]
WIDDER 1750-1800 CARTMEL IN FURNESS, LAN,
ENG [37379]
WIDDERS 1800S PORTSEA, HAM, ENG [37898] :
1800S ROMSEY, HAM, ENG [37898]
WIDDINSON C1810 RUDDINGTON, NTT, ENG
[34319]
WIDDOWS 1680-1750 MARLBOROUGH, WIL, ENG
[37233] : 1680-1750 ENBORNE, BRK, ENG [37233] :
1670-1750 WOODHAY, HAM, ENG [37233] : 1700-
1820 NC, USA [38366] : PRE 1770S PA, USA [38366] :
1800+ IN, USA [38366] : 1840S+ MAHASKA CO.,
IA, USA [38366]
WIDDOWSON PRE 1858 SHOREDITCH, LND, ENG
[37647]
WIDDRINGTON PRE 1650 KIRKWHELPINGTON,
NBL, ENG [36502]
WIDDUP ALL BARROWFORD & SALTERFORTH,
LAN, ENG [34564] : 1800+ LAN, ENG [36042] :
1850+ NZ [34564] : ALL WORLDWIDE [34564]
WIDEMAN PRE 1850 JACKSON CO., AR, USA
[38570]
WIDGER PRE 1810 DEV, ENG [37180]
WIDMER PRE 1850 FISCHENGEN, TG, CH [37554]
WIDNER 1865-1875 IA, USA [38133]
WIEBKIN ALL WORLDWIDE [37637]
WIECHMANN PRE 1720 DASSOW, MSW, GER
[35157]
WIECHMANS 1670+ QUICKBORN, SHO, GER
[37542]
WIECZOREK PRE 1826 WOJNOWICE, SIL, GER
[38618]
WIEDELMANN PRE 1730 DINGELSTADT, PSA,
GER [38048]
WIEDERECHT 1830-39 HIGHLANDS, GER [38151]
WIEDERKEHR ALL DIETIKON, ZH, CH [38609]
WIEDERMANN 1500-1800 THOMASWALDAU, SIL,
GER [38654]
WIEDMANN PRE 1750 DRACKENSTEIN, WUE,
GER [38679]
WIELAND PRE 1850 PRENZLAU, PRE, GER [34931]
WIENKEMEIER 1968-1975 BAD PYRMONT, PYR,
BRD [38750] : 1948 ELBRINXEN, LIP, GER [38750]
WIENMAN DANIEL 1868 ALS, FRA [38062]
WIER PRE 1885 WOR & STS, ENG [36613]
WIERBIKEN ALL GER [34861]
WIESNER PRE 1840 PRE, GER [34766] : 1819
ORDERAND, KSA, GER [35369]
WIETING PRE 1860 RUGEN, MEK, GER [34840]
WIETSMA ALL NL [38707] : ALL USA [38707]
WIFFEN 1853+ BELLARINE, VIC, AUS [38205] :
1800+ ST PANCRAS, MDX, ENG [34882] : PRE
1900 FINCHINGFIELD, ESS, ENG [38205]
WIGBY ALL NFK & SFK, ENG [36760]
WIGENT ALL USA [38287]
WIGG C1811+ BROMPTON & FAVERSHAM, KEN,
ENG [34374]
WIGGENS T.BRACY 1750+ ENG [33963]
WIGGIN 1850+ PLEASINGTON, CA, USA [38454]
WIGGINGTON PRE 1765 NUNEHAM COURTNAY,
OXF, ENG [34370]
WIGGINS C1800+ AUS [34444] : T.BRACY 1750+
ENG [33963] : C1803 EASTBOURNE, SSX, ENG

[36185] : 1500+ ENG **[37099]** : ALL IRL **[37930]** : PRE 1896 PALMERSTON NORTH, MWT, NZ **[33964]** : 1775 NC, USA **[37570]**

WIGGINTON 1740-1850 BEDFORD & HANOVER CO., VA, USA **[38315]**

WIGHT 1800+ GUILDFORD, SRY, ENG **[34243]** : 1600 TEWKESBURY, GLS, ENG **[34466]** : 1600-1700 WOR, ENG **[34930]** : 1700-1780 LEITH, MLN, SCT **[34623]** : 1820+ GIFFORD, ELN, SCT **[36871]** : PRE 1740 COLDINGHAM, BEW, SCT **[37463]**

WIGHTON PRE 1845 SINGLETON, NSW, AUS **[37142]** : 1854 MONEYDIE & PITLANDIE, PER, SCT **[37769]** : 1790+ BLAIRGOWRIE & RATTRAY, PER, SCT **[38349]** : ALL SCT **[38735]**

WIGLAND ALL WUSTEROT NECKAR, BAW, BRD **[35264]**

WIGLE 1784-1804 FREDERICK, MD, USA **[38348]**

WIGLEY PRE 1700 BONSALL, DBY, ENG **[38321]**

WIGMORE 1800+ BROMLEY, KEN, ENG **[38288]**

WIGNEY ALL WORLDWIDE **[36028]**

WIGZELL 1910-1920 RAVENSTHORPE, WA, AUS **[35438]**

WIJMER PRE 1730 ZUTPHEN, GEL, NL **[36630]**

WIJTSMA ALL NL **[38707]** : ALL USA **[38707]**

WIKI ALL WORLDWIDE **[38653]**

WIKSTROM MARTA 1873+ ARE, JAMTLAND, SWE **[38566]**

WILBARGER 1800-1830 BOURBON CO., KY, USA **[36349]** : 1830+ PIKE CO., MO, USA **[36349]**

WILBEE 1800+ FOLESHILL, WAR, ENG **[35737]** : PRE 1827 NTH, ENG **[37899]**

WILBER 1700+ YKS, ENG **[37620]**

WILBERT (SEE WILBER) **[37620]**

WILBIE 1800-1850 MAITLAND & ARMIDALE, NSW, AUS **[34307]**

WILBRAHAM 1740-1820 MALPAS, CHS, ENG **[37975]**

WILBRECHT 1839 ROGASLEN, ERF, DDR **[36900]**

WILBUR PRE 1700 MA, USA **[38746]**

WILBURN 1763-1780 AMHERST CO., VA, USA **[38107]**

WILBY JOHN C1700+ FRISKNEY, LIN, ENG **[36880]** : ALL WORLDWIDE **[35331]**

WILCH 1650-1775 AUERBACH, HES, BRD **[35311]**

WILCHON 1650-1775 AUERBACH, HES, BRD **[35311]**

WILCOCK PRE 1830 HALIFAX, YKS, ENG **[36360]** : PRE 1860 LEEDS, YKS, ENG **[36793]** : PRE 1829 IRL **[38393]**

WILCOCKS 1750+ NORTH PETHERWIN, CON, ENG **[37224]** : 1829 PHILADELPHIA, PA, USA **[36572]**

WILCOCKSON PRE 1830 EDALE, DBY, ENG **[34588]**

WILCOX 1800S ONT, CAN **[38393]** : C1700 LONDON, ENG **[34296]** : 1700S TYSOE, WAR, ENG **[34435]** : 1800S LIVERPOOL, LAN, ENG **[34688]** : PRE 1850 LND, ENG **[35055]** : EDITH 1830-1860 BATH, SOM, ENG **[35798]** : PRE 1880 LONG HOPE, HEF, ENG **[36277]** : PRE 1900 STS, ENG **[37098]** : 1800+ CAV, IRL **[34568]** : PRE 1829 IRL **[38393]** : ALL GARDNER, ND, USA **[34220]** : 1852 WAYNE CO., PA, USA **[37531]** : 1881 WAUPACA, WI, USA **[37531]** : 1821 HARTFORD CO., CT, USA **[37531]** : 1800-1900 OH & IL, USA **[37539]** : 1800-1850 NY & IL, USA **[38039]** : 1885-1900 GUTHRIE CO., IA, USA **[38318]** : 1920-42 WRIGHT CO., MO, USA **[38318]** : 1860-80 STEUBEN CO., IN, USA **[38318]** : 1818-1819 OH, USA **[38318]** : 1905-13 MEADE CO., SD, USA **[38318]** : 1900-01 LOS ANGELES, CA, USA **[38318]** : 1830-50 MONROE CO., MI, USA **[38318]** : 1650-1800 OXFORD, CT, USA **[38588]**

WILCOXSON ALL ST ALBANS, DBY, ENG **[34342]**

WILD 1850-1900 ALBURY, NSW, AUS **[36618]** : 1700+ WISBOROUGH GREEN, SSX, ENG **[34747]** : 1864 WIGAN, LAN, ENG **[36253]** : 1800 SHEFFIELD,

WRY, ENG **[36480]** : 1700-1800 DBY, ENG **[36480]** : ALL DISLEY & WHALEY BRIDGE, CHS, ENG **[36587]** : PRE 1860 LEATHERHEAD, SRY, ENG **[37062]** : ALL TOLLERTON, NTT, ENG **[37774]** : ALL OLDHAM, ASHTON UNDER LYNE, LAN, ENG **[38580]** : 1713-1764 NEIDERBEXBACH PFALZ, BAV, GER **[37516]** : PRE 1833 ANGELTHURN, BAD, GER **[37819]** : ALL BUKOVINA, RO **[34488]**

WILDBER 1800+ HUN, ENG **[37409]**

WILDBLOOD ALL WORLDWIDE **[35778]**

WILDBORE PRE 1690 MELTON MOWBRAY, LEI, ENG **[36160]**

WILDE C1750-1830 WAKEFIELD, WRY, ENG **[33862]**

WILDEBOER PRE 1785 ONNA, OIJ, NL **[36283]**

WILDEN ALL STOWMARKET, SFK, ENG **[36382]** : ALL WOR, ENG **[37950]** : 1770+ BETHNAL GREEN & SUDBURY, SFK & LND, ENG **[38046]**

WILDER C1860 NEWBURY, BRK, ENG **[36975]** : 1800+ WASHINGTON CO., ME, USA **[38050]** : TRUMAN HARIS 1840-1849 BYRON, IL, USA **[38784]** : HIRAM 1809 ROCHESTER, NY, USA **[38784]** : HIRAM 1890 CRESWELL, CO, USA **[38784]** : LORENZO 1840-1847 BYRON, IL, USA **[38784]** : RANSOM 1840-1853 BYRON, IL, USA **[38784]** : RANSOM 1853-1860 CARROLL CO., IL, USA **[38784]** : RANSOM 1860 SAVANNA, IL, USA **[38784]** : RANSOM 1865 ELDORA, IA, USA **[38784]** : ELIAS 1795 NY, USA **[38784]** : ELIAS 1775 ONTARIO CO., NY, USA **[38784]** : ELIAS 1842 STEPHENSON CO., IL, USA **[38784]** : ORIN 1820 ONTARIO CO., NY, USA **[38784]** : ORIN 1840 OGLE, IL, USA **[38784]**

WILDES ALL LONDON & BRIGHTON, LND & SSX, ENG **[34317]**

WILDEY 1780S GLOUCESTER, GLS, ENG **[35815]**

WILDGOOSE PRE 1900 DBY, ENG **[36216]**

WILDI PRE 1830 AARAU, AG, CH **[37103]**

WILDING 1880+ MONTREAL, QUE, CAN **[36654]** : 1700S HEF & SAL, ENG **[37331]** : PRE 1860 RAD, WLS **[37332]**

WILDISH 1860S LND, ENG **[36803]** : C1840 CANTERBURY, KEN, ENG **[36860]**

WILDMAN 1840+ MAITLAND, NSW, AUS **[35756]** : PRE 1725 CHEAPSIDE, LND, ENG **[34243]** : 1700+ TAMWORTH, STS, ENG **[34243]** : 1815 EAST BARNET, HRT, ENG **[35756]** : PRE 1850 BENTHAM, WRY, ENG **[36040]** : 1820+ BRADFORD, YKS, ENG **[36769]**

WILDSMITH PRE 1830 BROMSGROVE, WOR, ENG **[34548]**

WILER ALL WORLDWIDE **[37600]**

WILES 1893+ BOMBALA, NSW, AUS **[34977]** : PRE 1679 GREAT BROMLEY, ESS, ENG **[34142]** : 1800-1900 BRIDLINGTON, ERY, ENG **[35495]** : 1850+ CAM, ENG **[37347]** : 1800 KER, IRL **[35970]** : JOHN 1808-1883 CHENANGO & OTSEGO CO., NY, USA **[35271]** : ALL WORLDWIDE **[37404]**

WILEY PRE 1850 NRY & ERY, ENG **[36048]** : 1800+ KILLANEY, DOW, IRL **[33977]** : PRE 1840 BALLINAKILL, LEX, IRL **[38420]** : 1800+ PINE MEADOWS, CT, USA **[33977]** : PRE 1820 JOHNSTOWN, NY, USA **[37510]** : 1850-1900 NAVARRO CO., TX, USA **[38092]**

WILFORD PRE 1930 MELTON MOWBRAY & WOLVERHAMPTON, LEI & STS, ENG **[34314]** : PRE 1857 BEESTON, NTT, ENG **[36148]** : PRE 1850 ENG **[37515]** : PRE 1750 LEI, ENG **[38080]**

WILHELM MICHAEL 1800S WILMOT TWP., ONT, CAN **[34378]** : 1850 ESPENSHEID, HEN, GER **[33929]** : ANDREAS PRE 1800 BREITENBACH, HES, GER **[34378]** : 1800+ GER & USA **[38065]** :

ELEANOR 1767-1850 STEUBEN CO., NY, USA **[35271]**

WILHELMS 1800+ LIVERPOOL, LAN, ENG **[35979]**

WILHITE 1865-1985 SCHWAIGERN, WUE, GER **[38574]** : PRE 1900 CULPEPER, VA & IL, USA **[38574]**

WILKEN PRE 1880 ZARPEN, SHO, GER **[37563]**

WILKENS PRE 1860 CANNINGTON, SOM, ENG **[38577]**

WILKERSON 1750-1880 ROYSTON, HRT, ENG **[36485]** : PRE 1850 NEWARK, NTT, ENG **[37892]** : PRE 1850 NFK, ENG **[37892]** : 1834-1875 CLARK CO., IL, USA **[35316]**

WILKES C1903 MULLUMBIMBY, NSW, AUS **[34694]** : 1850 STAFFORD, STS, ENG **[35019]** : 1810S BIRMINGHAM, ENG **[37024]**

WILKIE PRE 1860 SKIPTON & BALLARAT, VIC, AUS **[35087]** : C1800+ BREMEN, BRM, GER **[33792]** : 1819+ INVER, DON, IRL **[38291]** : 1780S-1840 PERTH, PER, SCT **[33950]** : 1800+ ABERDOUR & DUNFERMLINE, FIF, SCT **[33970]** : PRE 1860 ARBROATH, ANS, SCT **[37200]** : PRE 1820 AIRLIE, ANS, SCT **[37727]** : ALL AIRDRIE, LKS, SCT **[37767]** : PRE 1864 EDINBURGH, MLN, SCT **[37852]** : PRE 1800 CRAIL & DYSART, FIF, SCT **[37913]**

WILKIN ROBT. & JESSE 1880+ NSW & QLD, AUS **[35854]** : PRE 1850 CAMBRIDGE, CAM, ENG **[35835]** : ALL BURSTALL, SFK, ENG **[35835]** : C1700-1900 STIFFKEY & RAINHAM, NFK, ENG **[36128]** : 1650-1750 TOSTOCK, SFK, ENG **[36213]** : C1835 PORTSMOUTH & SOUTHAMPTON, HAM, ENG **[37214]** : C1800-1900 PA & IL, USA **[35305]**

WILKINS 1820+ PORT MACQUARIE, NSW, AUS **[34860]** : 1840S HOBART, TAS, AUS **[35509]** : PRE 1900 SPARSHOLT, HAM, ENG **[33966]** : C1800 WICKWAR, GLS, ENG **[34475]** : PRE 1790 DORKING, SRY, ENG **[35016]** : HENRY 1720 SPALDING, LIN, ENG **[35369]** : ALL WEDNESBURY, STS, ENG **[35854]** : 1600-1870 APPLEBY MAGNA, LEI, ENG **[35955]** : 1760+ BREMHILL, WIL, ENG **[36323]** : PRE 1850 YKS, ENG **[36840]** : PRE 1850 MALMSBURY, WIL, ENG **[37034]** : 1800 ALDWORTH, BRK, ENG **[37170]** : PRE 1815 THORPE ACRE, LEI, ENG **[37207]** : 1750-1820 WRY, ENG **[37589]** : 1800+ BIRMINGHAM, WAR, ENG **[38481]** : 1700+ BINTON, WAR, ENG **[38498]** : C1790-1870 LAMBETH & BATTERSEA, LND, ENG **[38541]** : PRE 1842 GLS, ENG & AUS **[34845]** : 1800 WELLESLEY, MA, USA **[35276]** : 1840+ PA, USA **[36393]** : 1780+ IL, USA **[38058]** : ALL BERRYVILLE, AR, USA **[38605]** : PRE 1700 BRE, WLS **[38311]**

WILKINSON 1866+ ST KILDA, VIC, AUS **[34184]** : 1850-1990 GOULBURN & SYDNEY, NSW & QLD, AUS **[34294]** : 1882+ SYDNEY, NSW, AUS **[34786]** : 1799+ PARRAMATTA, NSW, AUS **[34967]** : JOHN 1832+ GREENDALE, NSW, AUS **[35066]** : JOHN 1800-1818 PARRAMATTA, NSW, AUS **[35066]** : 1850+ PENNANT HILLS, NSW, AUS **[35511]** : 1850+ ILFORD & BATHURST, NSW, AUS **[35736]** : 1860+ FASSIFERN, QLD, AUS **[36286]** : ALL IPSWICH, QLD, AUS **[36616]** : 1820+ LANARK & RENFREW, ONT, CAN **[36695]** : PRE 1870S BARTON, NTT, ENG **[33780]** : PRE 1800 KEN & WOR, ENG **[33812]** : ALL LAN, ENG **[33953]** : 1800-1860 FELTHORPE, NFK, ENG **[34003]** : ALL KNARESBOROUGH, YKS, ENG **[34155]** : ALL BLACKBURN, YKS, ENG **[34155]** : GEORGE 1700+ MARKSE IN CLEVELAND, NRY, ENG **[34181]** : PRE 1815 MORTON IN THE MARSH, GLS, ENG **[34184]** : JANE PRE 1850 OVINGHAM, NBL, ENG **[34583]** : 1750-1800 WIL, ENG **[34664]** :

PRE 1850 SKIPTON, WRY, ENG **[34675]** : JAMES & DINAH 1820+ HABERGHAM EAVES & BURNLEY, YKS, ENG **[34810]** : C1838 NORTH SHIELDS, NBL, ENG **[34852]** : JOHN 1799 SALFORD, LAN, ENG **[35066]** : ALL CUL, ENG **[35293]** : C1800 FINSTHWAITE, LAN, ENG **[35349]** : 1805 KIRKHEATON, YKS, ENG **[35535]** : PRE 1800 LEI, ENG **[35573]** : 1800S ENG **[35743]** : 1850+ DISTINGTON, CUL, ENG **[35979]** : C1760 WOODBRIDGE, SFK, ENG **[36076]** : PRE 1840 GATESHEAD, DUR, ENG **[36102]** : PRE 1720 NEWCASTLE UPON TYNE, NBL, ENG **[36110]** : PRE 1900 NEWCASTLE UPON TYNE, NBL & DUR, ENG **[36176]** : JANE C1790 LONDON CITY, ENG **[36225]** : 1750+ STURTON LE STEEPLE, NTT, ENG **[36426]** : PRE 1690 LITTLEBOROUGH, NTT, ENG **[36426]** : PRE 1849 PORTSEA, HAM, ENG **[36475]** : GEORGE C1818 LITTLE BERKHAMSTEAD, HRT, ENG **[36616]** : PRE 1858 SCALBY, NRY, ENG **[36757]** : 1700+ SEDBERGH, WRY, ENG **[36821]** : 1850+ WARTER, ERY, ENG **[36846]** : 1780+ YKS, ENG **[36887]** : 1700S WELBOURN, LIN, ENG **[37039]** : 1770S WIMBISH, ESS, ENG **[37080]** : C1800+ WESTMINSTER, LND, ENG **[37351]** : C1850S RICKMANSWORTH, HRT, ENG **[37351]** : PRE 1900 WHITBY & CLOUGHTON, NRY, ENG **[37616]** : PRE 1819 HOUGHTON LE SPRING, DUR, ENG **[37635]** : PRE 1760 THURLSTONE & PENISTONE, WRY, ENG **[37754]** : ALL WADDINGTON & CLITHEROE, LAN, ENG **[37774]** : PRE 1884 GRIMSBY, LIN, ENG **[37830]** : 1850-1800 ST BEES, CUL, ENG **[37858]** : 1800+ DUR, ENG **[38454]** : PRE 1830 CORK HARBOUR, COR, IRL **[36695]** : PRE 1830 ARM, IRL **[36695]** : 1800S ANT, IRL **[36858]** : ALL NZ **[34155]** : PRE 1830 SCT **[36858]** : ALL TWYNHOLM & KIRKCUDBRIGHT, KKD, SCT **[37972]** : SHADARACK 1845 RANDOLPH CO., AL, USA **[38155]** : JAMES HENRY 1843 RANDOLPH CO., AL, USA **[38155]** : JOHN 1654-1708 PROVIDENCE, RI, USA **[38172]** : 1800-1900 IN, USA **[38328]**

WILKS 1840+ LAUNCESTON, TAS, AUS **[34579]** : 1930+ SYDNEY, NSW, AUS **[34579]** : ALL STAWELL, VIC, AUS **[35480]** : PRE 1800 SKIPTON, WRY, ENG **[34675]** : ALL BLAKESLEY, NTH, ENG **[35334]** : ALL BLAKESLEY, NTH, ENG **[35480]** : 1790+ BUSHLEY, WOR, ENG **[35886]** : 1750+ WALTON CARDIFF, GLS, ENG **[35886]** : 1750-1790 WOR, ENG **[36293]** : PRE 1830 CASTLEBAR, MAY, IRL **[35530]** : 1830+ MONMOUTH, MON, WLS **[34650]** : 1849-1930 SWANSEA, GLA, WLS **[34844]**

WILLAN PRE 1700 YKS, ENG **[34579]** : ALL TUNSTALL, LAN, ENG **[36144]** : 1700-1750 DENT, WRY, ENG **[36635]** : PRE 1850 CROYDON, SRY, ENG **[37067]** : C1695 TAGMON, WEX, IRL **[34579]** : 1700+ PORTMARNOCK, DUB, IRL **[34579]**

WILLARD 1840+ COOMBING CREEK, NSW, AUS **[36316]** : 1820+ DUNDAS CO., ONT, CAN **[34051]** : 1820+ MONTREAL, QUE, CAN **[34051]** : 1783+ HASTINGS & WINCHELSEA, SSX, ENG **[35013]** : PRE 1700 KEN & MA, ENG & USA **[38746]** : 1800 BARRE, VT, USA **[34051]** : 1868+ COLUMBIA CO., WI, USA **[38751]**

WILLBERG 1880+ SYDNEY, NSW, AUS **[35915]** : PRE 1900 REVAL, SU **[35915]**

WILLCOCKS 1850+ SYDNEY, NSW, AUS **[37119]** : PRE 1790 DARTMOUTH, DEV, ENG **[34389]**

WILLCOX 1890+ TRUNDLE, NSW, AUS **[34421]** : 1700+ BERE REGIS & WEYMOUTH, DOR, ENG **[34714]**

WILLE PRE 1800 HES, GER **[38669]**

WILLENS ALL ANTRIM, ANT, IRL **[35474]**

WILLERS ALL WORLDWIDE [36794]
WILLERTON 1800S GREAT CARLTON & LOUTH, LIN, ENG [34380]
WILLETT 1800+ NORTHAMPTON, NTH, ENG [34315] : JOHN 1869 MADELEY, STS, ENG [34499] : 1800+ GOUDHURST, KEN, ENG [35829]
WILLETTE 1800+ FOURNIER, ONT, CAN [38462]
WILLETTS C1837 BRISTOL, GLS, ENG [35990]
WILLEY ALL DRAYTON, SOM, ENG [34298] : 1680-1750 LANDEWEDNACK, CON, ENG [34697] : PRE 1704 GRADE & RUAN MINOR, CON, ENG [34752] : PRE 1770 ROTHERHAM, WRY, ENG [34974] : PRE 1800 SHEFFIELD, YKS, ENG [36403]
WILLFORD PRE 1930 MELTON MOWBRAY& WOLVERHAMPTON, LEI & STS, ENG [34314]
WILLGOOSE PRE 1850 SHEFFIELD, YKS, ENG [34809] : C1750 ALFRETON, DBY, ENG [35079]
WILLIAM 1800+ WASHINGTON CO., NY, USA [38572] : 1800+ CADOXTON, JUXTA & NEATH, GLA, WLS [36209]
WILLIAMS THOMAS 1869+ MOONTA, SA, AUS [34035] : PRE 1900 EVANDALE, TAS, AUS [34170] : PRE 1900 BEACONSFIELD, TAS, AUS [34301] : 1847+ VIC, AUS [34412] : 1854+ KAPUNDA, SA, AUS [34440] : C1860 MELBOURNE, VIC, AUS [34456] : 1850-1900 ADELAIDE, SA, AUS [34462] : 1853+ GEELONG, VIC, AUS [34542] : JOHN 1815 SYDNEY, NSW, AUS [34581] : JOHN 1860+ ECHUCA, VIC, AUS [34702] : PRE 1860 RICHMOND, NSW, AUS [34758] : 1900+ DELORAINE, TAS, AUS [34770] : GEORGE 1860+ SA, AUS [34775] : RONALD S.M. 1908+ BRUNSWICK, VIC, AUS [34896] : 1850+ ASHFIELD & HOMEBUSH, NSW, AUS [34899] : 1870+ MUNGINDI, NSW, AUS [35073] : C1845 SYDNEY, NSW, AUS [35089] : AVEAN C1845 SYDNEY, NSW, AUS [35089] : 1840S BRIDGEMAN, NSW, AUS [35156] : JOHN PRE 1870 BEECHWORTH, VIC, AUS [35200] : 1840+ COWRA & YOUNG, NSW, AUS [35241] : JOHN PRE 1856 WESTBURY, TAS, AUS [35258] : 1850+ QUEANBEYAN, NSW, AUS [35410] : PRE 1846 GOORANGOOLA, NSW, AUS [35425] : MORTIMER C1835 HOBART, TAS, AUS [35434] : HUGH 1874+ FORBES, NSW, AUS [35557] : HUGH 1860+ ORANGE, NSW, AUS [35557] : C1907 FITZROY, VIC, AUS [35708] : 1870+ NORTH MELBOURNE, VIC, AUS [35708] : 1870+ CHEWTON, VIC, AUS [35708] : ALBERT C1886 SALE & GIPPSLAND, VIC, AUS [35729] : ALBERT PRE 1886 GLENGARRY & GIPPSLAND, VIC, AUS [35729] : C1850 COLLINGWOOD, VIC, AUS [35764] : MARGARET 1863+ BOWNING, NSW, AUS [35787] : 1855+ CRESWICK, VIC, AUS [35814] : C1860 MITTAGONG, NSW, AUS [35872] : 1870+ NORTH FITZROY, VIC, AUS [36278] : 1850+ LOCHINVAR, NSW, AUS [36632] : 1855+ SOUTH YARRA, VIC, AUS [37158] : STEPHEN 1842+ BURROWA, NSW, AUS [38288] : WILLIAM 1870+ BENDIGO, VIC, AUS & ENG [35432] : EMMA PRE 1860 ADELAIDE, SA, AUS & ENG [35592] : 1841+ TAPLEYTOWN, ONT, CAN [34357] : 1800+ LANARK CO., ONT, CAN [37427] : 1785+ LENNOX & ADDINGTON, ONT, CAN [38517] : JOSEPH 1790S EAST RETFORD, NTT, ENG [33917] : 1720+ ST TUDY, CON, ENG [33963] : 1400+ ST MERRYN, CON, ENG [33989] : JOHN 1811-1850 TORRINGTON, DEV, ENG [34078] : 1850+ ISLINGTON, MDX, ENG [34092] : PRE 1800 LANCING, SSX, ENG [34112] : PRE 1780 FOWEY, CON, ENG [34139] : PRE 1800 FEOCK, CON, ENG [34214] : PRE 1750 FALMOUTH, CON, ENG [34258] : ALL ENG [34301]

: EDWARD PRE 1840 WOOLWICH, KEN, ENG [34384] : 1840-1880 CLON, SAL, ENG [34399] : PRE 1833 LIVERPOOL, LAN, ENG [34412] : 1700 WHITEPARISH, WIL, ENG [34466] : 1700 OLD SODBURY, SOM, ENG [34466] : 1650-1700 BROMYARD, HEF, ENG [34552] : 1800-1850 ABINGDON, BRK, ENG [34552] : 1841 WELLINGTON, ENG [34636] : 1650-1900 REDRUTH, CON, ENG [34697] : 1650+ BREAGE, CON, ENG [34747] : 1650+ NORTH MOLTON, DEV, ENG [34747] : PRE 1800 GWINEAR, CON, ENG [34753] : 1850+ MUCH WENLOCK, SAL, ENG [34782] : 1775 GWENNAP, CON, ENG [34793] : JOSEPH PRE 1830 REDRUTH, CON, ENG [34881] : THOMAS PRE 1854 ST JAMES, LND, ENG [34901] : C1841 BIRMINGHAM, WAR, ENG [34972] : PRE 1908 WEST BROMWICH, STS, ENG [34982] : HARVEY GIBSON 1930+ SEAFORTH, LAN, ENG [35025] : PRE 1600 GRANDBOROUGH, BKM, ENG [35030] : C1830 HELSTON, CON, ENG [35045] : 1750+ CON, ENG [35060] : 1750-1850 CAMBRIDGE, CAM, ENG [35070] : 1800-1850 TAVISTOCK, DEV, ENG [35076] : 1850-75 HOVE, SSX, ENG [35130] : 1800-1850 ST DAY, CON, ENG [35151] : PRE 1780 GWENNAP, CON, ENG [35153] : 1800+ LND, ENG [35156] : SARAH C1800-1860 BRISTOL, GLS, ENG [35271] : PRE 1845 CON, ENG [35425] : PRE 1870 ST ERTH, CON, ENG [35432] : PRE 1870 ST JUST, CON, ENG [35432] : PRE 1797 KENWALL, CON, ENG [35441] : PRE 1850 REDRUTH, CON, ENG [35540] : PRE 1844 ROSCROWGEY, CON, ENG [35576] : PRE 1720 WENDRON, CON, ENG [35587] : 1830-1850 GNOSALL, STS, ENG [35708] : PRE 1800 PAUL, CON, ENG [35736] : STEPHENS 1700S CON, ENG [35768] : PRE 1850 LIVERPOOL, ENG [35818] : 1830+ GWENNAP, CON, ENG [35847] : JOHN PRE 1830 ST ERVE, CON, ENG [35867] : PRE 1804 STOGUMBER, SOM, ENG [35872] : PRE 1863 CLAPHAM, LND, ENG [35885] : ESTHER 1800+ ASTON, BIRMINGHAM, WAR, ENG [35911] : C1870 BIRMINGHAM, WAR, ENG [35956] : 1840-1870S BRISTOL, GLS, ENG [35966] : 1800+ LIVERPOOL, LAN, ENG [35979] : 1840+ HEREFORD, HEF, ENG [35998] : 1840+ ISLINGTON, MDX, ENG [36061] : PRE 1830 STS, ENG [36062] : THOMAS 1840S (JOINER) SALFORD, LAN, ENG [36066] : PRE 1850 SOUTHWARK, LND, ENG [36076] : C1815 ASTON, WAR, ENG [36102] : 1780-1840 HENLEY ON THAMES, OXF, ENG [36150] : ALL LONDON, ENG [36174] : 1810-20S GILLINGHAM, KEN, ENG [36190] : PRE 1841 BIRKENHEAD, CHS, ENG [36278] : THOMAS C1800 CROWAN, CON, ENG [36294] : PETER 1818+ PRAZE, CON, ENG [36294] : WEBB 1810+ SAL, ENG [36296] : PRE 1800 ESS, ENG [36379] : PRE 1900 LIVERPOOL, LAN, ENG [36387] : PRE 1750 TALLATON, DEV, ENG [36389] : 1790-1830 LONDON, ENG [36484] : 1750-1800 WADEBRIDGE, CON, ENG [36536] : 1850+ KEN, ENG [36574] : WILLIAM R. 1843-1915 BIRKENHEAD, CHS, ENG [36590] : 1850 KIDDERMINSTER, WOR, ENG [36649] : PRE 1850 EDGBASTON & SELDON, WAR, ENG [36652] : PRE 1840 LIVERPOOL, LAN, ENG [36849] : ALL DEV, ENG [36861] : ALL NTT, ENG [36861] : 1826+ BRISTOL, ENG [36995] : 1781+ TETBURY, GLS, ENG [36997] : PRE 1900 SHOREHAM, SSX & KEN, ENG [37089] : PRE 1800 SAL, ENG [37098] : JOHN F. C1812 LONDON, ENG [37106] : THOMAS PRE 1830 STAFFORD, STS, ENG [37124] : 1823 CLAPHAM, SRY, ENG [37158] : 1815 ECCLESHALL, STS, ENG

[37209] : PRE 1850 EXETER, DEV & WES, ENG
[37246] : PRE 1800 REDRUTH, CON, ENG [37264] :
1775-1875 HEF & GLS, ENG [37269] : 1750 +
WANTAGE, BRK, ENG [37328] : RICHARD C1830
SIDMOUTH, DEV, ENG [37356] : PRE 1860
LONDON, ENG [37392] : 1886 OLD ST PANCRAS,
MDX, ENG [37418] : JOHN 1824-1849 ST AUSTELL,
CON, ENG [37443] : JOHN 1849-1870S LUXULYAN,
CON, ENG [37443] : PRE 1850 FERSFIELD, NFK,
ENG [37512] : BENJAMIN PRE 1836
MANCHESTER, LAN, ENG [37726] : 1750 +
WIGAN, LAN, ENG [37735] : ALL POTTERSPURY,
NTH, ENG [37857] : 1800-1900 LIVERPOOL, LAN,
ENG [37870] : 1750-1840 GLS, ENG [37870] : 1850-
1900 SHOREHAM, SSX, ENG [37914] : 1750
SHOBDEN, HEF, ENG [37928] : 1800
KENSINGTON, LND, ENG [37928] : WILLIAM
1860-1878 BIRKENHEAD, CHS, ENG [37929] : PRE
1863 LONDON, ENG [37948] : PRE 1850
BERMONDSEY, LND, ENG [37989] : 1770-1820
WHITCHURCH, HAM, ENG [38003] : 1450-1608
MARTHAM, NFK, ENG [38051] : 1450-1608 REPPS,
NFK, ENG [38051] : 1450-1608 WEST SOMERTON,
NFK, ENG [38051] : ANNE 1858 + NEWARK, NTT,
ENG [38083] : 1842 + ENG [38212] : 1840
WESLEIGH, DEV, ENG [38270] : STEPHEN PRE
1810 BRK, ENG [38288] : EMMA PRE 1849 KEN,
ENG [38298] : JOHN C1800 KEN, ENG [38298] : ALL
BEDMINSTER, SOM, ENG [38357] : 1900 +
BARNSTAPLE, DEV, ENG [38473] : PRE 1800
GOODLEIGH, DEV, ENG [38473] : PRE 1805
APPLEDORE & NORTHAM, DEV, ENG [38580] :
JANE C1766 BRISTOL, ENG [38724] : MARY ANN
1811-1856 LND, ENG & AUS [35498] : JOSHUA PRE
1850 FIJI [35189] : 1740 + KUMARKHALI,
BENGAL, INDIA [37673] : 1800 + CLA & GAL, IRL
[34526] : HENRY PRE 1840 LONGFORDS, LIM,
IRL [34610] : 1800 + DUNGIVEN, LDY, IRL [35194] :
1840 + DUBLIN, IRL [35971] : C1854
TARTARINGHAM & PORTADOWN, ARM, IRL
[37556] : 1850 + DUNEDIN, NZ [33758] : 1870 +
DUNEDIN, OTAGO, NZ [35966] : 1820 + LISBON,
PT [35814] : PRE 1863 DUNDEE, ANS, SCT [37442] :
PRE 1870 USA [34245] : ISHAM 1796 + TOLLAND,
CT, USA [35272] : DANIEL 1820-1870S PIKE CO.,
PA, USA [35298] : DANIEL 1800-1820 NJ, USA
[35298] : ALL PIKE CO., PA, USA [35298] : ELIJAH
JOHN 1834 + PROSPECT, CT, USA [35391] : JAMES
1806 + NORWICH, USA [35391] : PRE 1720
WESTFIELD, MA, USA [36319] : 1860-1880 MEIGS,
OH, USA [36346] : 1850-1900 KNOX, IL, USA [36346]
: 1765 LOUDON CO., VA, USA [36446] : 1800-1900
GRANT PARISH, LA, USA [36449] : JOHN C. 1787-
1872 PHILADELPHIA & LAKE WINOLA, PA, USA
[36948] : STEPHEN PRE 1800 NEWBERRY CO., SC,
USA [36969] : PRE 1770 RI, USA [37018] : PRE 1776
ST MARY'S CO., MD, USA [37029] : 1835-1860 AL,
USA [37029] : ISHAM 1796 WINDHAM, CT, USA
[37030] : 1700-1850 CT, USA [37538] : 1850 + NEW
ORLEANS, LA, USA [37583] : 1843-1880
KEWEENAW CO., MI, USA [38009] : 1780-1850
RUSSELL, VA, USA [38061] : 1826 NY, USA [38098] :
1775-1900 POLK CO., GA, USA [38107] : 1836-93
TAUNTON, MA, USA [38151] : ABNER 1824 +
TALLADEGA CO., AL, USA [38187] : 1720 +
HANOVER CO., VA, USA [38190] : 1806 +
HENDERSON CO., KY, USA [38190] : 1746 +
GRANVILLE CO., NC, USA [38190] : 1821 +
HICKMAN CO., KY, USA [38190] : 1880S
HAMILTON CO., OH, USA [38331] : 1830 +
MONROE, MI, USA [38517] : C1840 +
PONTYPOOL, MON, WLS [33922] : JOHN 1810 +

LLANDDEW, BRE, WLS [34134] : WILLIAM 1820 +
BRECON, BRE, WLS [34134] : WILLIAM 1770 +
TALACHDDU, BRE, WLS [34134] : PRE 1818
LLANASA, FLN, WLS [34370] : ELEANOR C1806
WLS [34389] : 1840-1910 LLANDUDNO, CAE, WLS
[34399] : 1750-1850 NANTMEL, RAD, WLS [34552] :
SARAH PRE 1851 WLS [34553] : PRE 1850 LLAN
FAIR AR-Y-BRYN, CMN, WLS [34569] : 1800-1900
CARDIFF, WLS [34641] : 1850-1900 CARMARTHEN
TOWN, CMN, WLS [34729] : RACHEL 1800S
SWANSEA, GLA, WLS [34889] : PRE 1850
NEWPORT, GLA & MON, WLS [35199] : JOHN 1800
MONMOUTH, WLS [35361] : 1750 + CAE, WLS
[35377] : 1800 + ABERSYCHAN, MON, WLS [35436]
: 1850S LLANWENARTH, MON, WLS [35516] :
JOHN PRE 1860 AGY, WLS [35557] : 1800 + DEN,
WLS [35566] : 1810 LLANTWIT MAJOR, GLA, WLS
[35966] : 1840-1850 MERTHYR TYDFIL, GLA, WLS
[35966] : 1800-1850 CRICKARDARN, BRE, WLS
[36047] : PRE 1860 RUABON, DEN, WLS [36061] :
1834 + ST CLEAR, CMN, WLS [36117] : C1829
BASSALLEG, MON, WLS [36185] : ELLEN 1806 +
MERTHYR TYDFIL, GLA, WLS [36296] :
CATHERINE 1771 + COLWINSTON, GLA, WLS
[36296] : 1800-1880 GLA, WLS [36346] : RICHARD
1870-1944 NEFYN, CAE, WLS [36590] : JOHN 1838-
1926 ROWEN & LLITHFAEN, CAE, WLS [36590] :
HENRY 1800 + LLANGOGH & ROWEN, AGY &
CAE, WLS [36590] : PRE 1844 BODWROG &
LLANFAIR, AGY, WLS [36650] : 1844 +
LLANGEFNI, AGY, WLS [36650] : THOMAS PRE
1830 MONMOUTH, MON, WLS [37124] : C1900
PONTYPRIDD, CMN & GLA, WLS [37285] : PRE
1851 LLANEDWEN, AGY, WLS [37318] :
ELIZABETH C1871 TREHERBERT, GLA, WLS
[37399] : HARRY C1720 DOLGELLEY, MER, WLS
[37649] : ESTHER 1736 RUABON, DEN, WLS [37649]
: ALL TREFNANT, DEN, WLS [37667] : JOHN PRE
1880 DOLWYDDELAN, CAE, WLS [37671] : ISAAC
C1837 FLN, WLS [37697] : PRE 1851 BARDSEY,
CAE, WLS [37858] : ALL MON, WLS [37885] :
WILLIAM 1830-1890 DENBIGH, DEN, WLS [37929]
: PRE 1900 COYCHURCH, GLA, WLS [38027] : 1840
LLANGERDEIRNE, CMN, WLS [38282] : 1850-1900
SWANSEA, GLA, WLS [38331] : PRE 1857 CAE,
WLS [38437] : SARAH JANE 1850-1900 GLA, WLS
[38740] : WILLIAM PRE 1840 FLINT &
BIRKENHEAD, FLN & CHS, WLS & ENG [36590]

WILLIAMSON 1900 + HOBART, TAS, AUS [33960] :
JAMES 1841 + GLEN INNES, NSW, AUS [34539] :
1856-1858 BRISBANE WATER, NSW, AUS [35226] :
1856 + WOODSIDE, VIC, AUS [35708] : ALL
MAIDSTONE, VIC, AUS [35731] : PETER 1850S
HAMILTON, VIC, AUS [35877] : 1822 + HOBART,
TAS, AUS [36622] : 1857 + COLAC, ROKEWOOD &
TARNAGULLA, VIC, AUS [36622] : 1857 + ONDIT,
VIC, AUS [36622] : 1840 + PARRAMATTA &
MOLONG, NSW, AUS [37307] : 1880 + SYDNEY,
NSW, AUS [37554] : 1800S PENNANT HILLS &
BELL RIVER, NSW, AUS [37988] : 1930 +
GOSFORD, NSW, AUS & SCT [33881] : 1790-1850
EAST WITTON, YKS, ENG [33861] : C1854
MONMOUTH, DEV, ENG [34653] : 1850S
PADDINGTON, LND, ENG [35226] : PRE 1817 +
FOLESHILL, WAR, ENG [35453] : PRE 1860
LADHILL GILL, YKS, ENG [35932] : 1870 +
ARNOLD, NTT, ENG [36105] : JOHN PRE 1860
BAGTHORPE, NTT & DBY, ENG [36148] : PRE 1890
DBY, ENG [36387] : JAMES C1800 ECCLES, LAN,
ENG [36585] : 1840 + HOLMFIRTH, WRY, ENG
[37241] : PRE 1850 YKS, ENG [37379] : PRE 1681
BOLTON LE SANDS, LAN, ENG [37524] : C1700

YORK, YKS, ENG [37735] : SAMUEL 1820+ WAR & LEI, ENG [38031] : ALICE 1850-1936 WAR & LEI, ENG [38031] : PRE 1850 THORMANBY, YKS, ENG [38135] : PRE 1850 COXWOLD, YKS, ENG [38135] : 1700-1900 SWALE MEDWAY, KEN, ENG [38249] : 1800+ DUNGIVEN, LDY, IRL [35194] : JAMES C1811 AUGHALOO, TYR, IRL [35541] : 1870+ ANT, IRL [37260] : 1863-1990 POKENO, AUCK, NZ [36832] : PRE 1835 KIRKCALDY, FIF, SCT [34758] : PRE 1850 INVERESK & FISHERROW, MLN, SCT [34849] : CHARLES 1800-1860 PER, SCT [35094] : DAVID R. 1750-1850 FIF, SCT [35094] : PRE 1852 FORRES & ELGIN, MOR, SCT [35226] : DAVID PRE 1837 DYSART, FIF, SCT [35250] : PRE 1736 CADDER, LKS, SCT [35252] : 1800+ TAIN, ROC, SCT [35644] : 1800+ AUCHTERMUCHTY, FIF, SCT [35644] : 1750+ WHALSAY, SHI, SCT [35824] : ARCHIBALD PRE 1850 ANNAN, BAN, SCT [35877] : 1780+ ABBOTSHALL, FIF, SCT [35977] : PRE 1850 KILCHRENZIE, ARL, SCT [36583] : ALL FRASERBURGH, ABD, SCT [36743] : 1780+ LOANHEAD, MLN, SCT [36871] : 1800+ MONTROSE, ANS, SCT [36971] : PRE 1880 RFW & LKS, SCT [37554] : JOHN & MARTHA PRE 1839 DUNFERMLINE, FIF, SCT [37906] : ALL UK [37674] : ALL WORLDWIDE [33868]

WILLIAMSON (SEE WILL [37556]

WILLIDEN ALL ENG [34621]

WILLIE C1800 DURHAM, DUR, ENG [35348]

WILLING 1700-1800 MODBURY, DEV, ENG [34928] : 1600-1800 GER [34928]

WILLINGALE C1710 MALDON, ESS, ENG [35552]

WILLINGHAM PRE 1810 BDF, ENG [35701]

WILLINGTON PRE 1856 NEWPORT, GLS, ENG [35564] : 1800+ WOLVERHAMPTON, STS, ENG [36971]

WILLINS 1800-1900 BRIGHTON & PORTSLADE, SSX, ENG [34749]

WILLIS EMMA 1851+ CANTERBURY, NSW, AUS [34841] : FALCONER 1800+ CANTERBURY, NSW, AUS [34841] : HERBERT 1880-1960S PARRAMATTA, NSW, AUS [34841] : SAMUEL 1871-1940S SYDNEY, NSW, AUS [34841] : HENRY 1864-1940S NORTH SYDNEY, NSW, AUS [34841] : ALFRED 1830-1900 PARRAMATTA, NSW, AUS [34841] : 1880+ BOX HILL, VIC, AUS [35204] : C1885+ JUNEE, NSW, AUS [35230] : PRE 1860 MAITLAND, NSW, AUS [35400] : 1823+ CAMPBELL TOWN, TAS, AUS [35929] : 1904+ MELBOURNE, VIC, AUS [36628] : 1920-1939 ALB, CAN [36047] : 1850 BENTINCK, ONT, CAN [38422] : 1700+ WESTBURY, WIL, ENG [34121] : 1800 SHOREDITCH, MDX, ENG [34204] : REBECCA PRE 1829 OVERSTONE, NTH, ENG [34310] : PRE 1850 HAM & DOR, ENG [34317] : 1750+ BELBROUGHTON, WOR, ENG [34420] : C1856 STRATFORD ON AVON, WAR, ENG [34806] : BOORMAN 1700+ WOODCHURCH & TENTERDEN, KEN, ENG [34841] : HENRY 1827+ LONDON, MDX, ENG [35059] : 1800S SHERBORNE, DOR, ENG [35187] : 1850 NEWPORT, IOW, HAM, ENG [35204] : C1847 MARYLEBONE, LND & MDX, ENG [35460] : PRE 1690 SHRIVENHAM, BRK, ENG [35866] : PRE 1800 KIRKOSWALD, CUL, ENG [35929] : 1800+ LONDON, ENG [35929] : 1700-1750 ELVETHAM, HAM, ENG [36047] : 1814-1900 BASINGSTOKE, HAM, ENG [36047] : PRE 1720 TIPTON, STS, ENG [36110] : 1770+ WHITBY, NRY, ENG [36238] : C1832 WHITCHURCH, BKM, ENG [36253] : 1800+ WHITCHURCH, BKM, ENG [36257] : WILLIAM PRE 1830 WIL, ENG [36270] : WILLIAM 1860

POPLAR, MDX, ENG [36270] : 1800+ LONDON, ENG [36749] : 1800+ WOLVERHAMPTON, STS, ENG [36971] : DANIEL C1830 ENG [37024] : 1859+ ESS, ENG [37656] : ALL CLIFTON, BRS, ENG [37950] : 1800-1850S SOM, ENG [38422] : BETSY PRE 1820+ WOODCHURCH, KEN, ENG [38567] : C1850 ENG & USA [35532] : 1809-1821 ARM, IRL [34200] : 1852 CHRISTCHURCH, NZ [35187] : 1870+ ASHBURTON, NZ [35929] : 1850+ ALCORN CO., MS, USA [35262] : 1870+ CLEVELAND, OH, USA [36971] : JOHN 1900S SUPERIOR, WI, USA [37024] : 1820-1835 LINCOLN CO., TN, USA [37029] : PRE 1810 GALLIA & WASHINGTON CO., OH, USA [37604] : 1870 LEXINGTON, MI, USA [38422] : ALL MERTHYR TYDFIL, GLA, WLS [37950] : WALPOLE ALL WORLDWIDE [34841]

WILLISON 1840S HOBART TOWN, TAS, AUS [35342] : PRE 1850 SCT [35806]

WILLITS ALL USA [37808]

WILLMORE PRE 1740 SEDGLEY, STS, ENG [36110] : ALL DEWITT, IL, KY & OK, USA [38230]

WILLMOTH 1750-1850 OK, USA [38287]

WILLMOTT 1870S BRISBANE, QLD, AUS [33870] : 1870+ MUDGEE & GULGONG, NSW, AUS [34969] : 1859+ HOLBORN, MDX, ENG [34452] : 1736 BEER HACKETT, DOR, ENG [34777] : 1830+ LONDON, ENG [34969] : PRE 1859 DARLEY DALE, DBY, ENG [35061] : PRE 1800 BIRMINGHAM, WAR & MDX, ENG [37251] : 1800+ HACKNEY, MDX, ENG [37251] : 1500-1920 WOR, ENG [38420]

WILLOTT 1790+ HANLEY, STS, ENG [37908]

WILLOUGBY-MARSHALL WILLIAM C1804+ LUTON, BDF, ENG [36767]

WILLOUGHBY 1840 BRAIDWOOD, NSW, AUS [34940] : SARAH 1800-1880 SMITHS FALLS, ONT, CAN [34143] : 1860S MONTAGUE, ONT, CAN [37568] : ALL WALTON ON THE HILL, SRY, ENG [34366] : 1700-50 SLEAFORD, LIN, ENG [36827] : PRE 1870 ANT, IRL [33964] : PRE 1870 WIC, IRL [33964] : PRE 1835 KIK, IRL [37568] : PRE 1890 IRL & AUS [34003] : PRE 1895 NORTH WAIROA, NZ [33964]

WILLOWS ALL LIN, ENG [34054] : 1750+ CAM, ENG [36470]

WILLOX WILLIAM 1799 TYRIE, ABD, SCT [34499]

WILLRICH 1875 DEMMIN, POM, GER [34388]

WILLS JOHN 1830+ SYDNEY, NSW, AUS [35574] : 1877+ NSW, AUS [37556] : PRE 1842 BERE FERRERS, DEV, ENG [33781] : PRE 1810 TALLAND, CON, ENG [34445] : PRE 1860 KELLY, DEV, ENG [34652] : 1700+ TOTNES, DEV, ENG [34970] : 1802 WARWICK, WAR, ENG [34995] : C1830 ST TRUO, CON, ENG [35152] : JOHN PRE 1830 LONDON, ENG [35574] : 1650+ DARTMOUTH, DEV, ENG [36000] : PRE 1920 DOR, ENG [36201] : JOHN C1805+ KINGSBRIDGE, DEV, ENG [37146] : PRE 1877 CAMBORNE & CROWAN, CON, ENG [37556] : PRE 1900 PLYMOUTH, DEV, ENG [37771] : PRE 1800 RAINHAM, KEN, ENG [37773] : PRE 1825 ST ERME & WITHIEL, CON, ENG [37814] : PRE 1825 BODMIN, GLENWYN & ROCHE, CON, ENG [37814] : PRE 1880 COULSDEN, SRY, ENG [37901] : 1760-1790S SOUTHAMPTON, HAM, ENG [38350] : ELIZABETH 1784-1836 LONDON, ENG & AUS [34447] : PRE 1840 BALLINAKILL, LEX, IRL [38420] : PRE 1840 FORRES DYKE, MOR, SCT [35862] : 1776+ CHARLES & PRINCE GEORGES COS., MD, USA [37583]

WILLSEA 1870S EVERTON, LAN, ENG [35390]

WILLSHAW PRE 1830 CHEDDLETON & CAVERSWALL, STS, ENG **[37650]**

WILLSON 1830-1860S TORONTO, ONT, CAN **[34248]** : 1800+ YORK, ONT, CAN **[34982]** : 1800-1900 YORK CO., ONT, CAN **[37477]** : PRE 1839 EXETER, DEV, ENG **[36761]** : PRE 1910 LONDON, ENG **[37062]** : 1700+ BDF, ENG **[37304]** : 1680-1768 CARRICKFERGUS, ANT, IRL **[37477]** : 1800+ LARNE, ANT, IRL **[38726]**

WILMANS C1510 BIEFELDT, PRE, GER **[37819]**

WILMER (SEE WILMORE) **[34424]**

WILMERDING 1550-1700 BRAUNSCHWEIG, NSA, BRD **[35283]**

WILMERSON 1700S HINDOLVESTON, NFK, ENG **[35322]**

WILMORE PRE 1900 BKM, ENG **[34424]** : 1750+ BKM & HRT, ENG **[36042]**

WILMOT 1830S MONTREAL, QUE, CAN **[38442]** : 1700S DEV, ENG **[34188]** : 1750S EXETER, DEV, ENG **[35261]** : 1758 TEWKESBURY, GLS, ENG **[35261]** : C1742 YATTON, SOM, ENG **[36185]** : 1728 WENDRON, CON, ENG **[37975]** : 1600S ENG **[38478]**

WILMOTT 1800-1835 GLS, ENG **[34022]**

WILNER 1700-1900 GHE & HEN, GER **[35630]** : PRE 1890 WAYNE CO., MI, USA **[38135]**

WILPE (VAN) 1750-1990 SWOLLE, OY, NL **[38713]**

WILSDON 1700-1850 HRT, ENG **[36165]**

WILSHAW 1500-1750 STS, ENG **[36062]**

WILSON 1850+ WALHALLA, VIC, AUS **[34421]** : ALL EUROA, VIC, AUS **[34674]** : 1870S ALEXANDRA, VIC, AUS **[34961]** : 1800-1900 TAMWORTH, NSW, AUS **[35103]** : PRE 1831+ HOBART, TAS, AUS **[35109]** : C1860 WARWICK, QLD, AUS **[35158]** : 1860+ MURRUMBURRAH, NSW, AUS **[35347]** : 1860+ MALDON & GOWAR, VIC, AUS **[35379]** : 1850-1900 MELBOURNE, VIC, AUS **[35379]** : ALL MORNINGTON, VIC, AUS **[35389]** : C1830 CAMBRIDGE, TAS, AUS **[35389]** : PRE 1855 GLEBE, NSW, AUS **[35400]** : 1857-1875 CASTLEMAINE, VIC, AUS **[35436]** : 1837+ PITTWATER, NSW, AUS **[35464]** : 1854+ BENDIGO, VIC, AUS **[35468]** : 1856+ BATHURST, NSW, AUS **[35504]** : 1870+ CORROWA, NSW, AUS **[35524]** : 1800S TAS, AUS **[35531]** : SOPHIA 1830S-1900 SYDNEY, NSW, AUS **[35735]** : CHARLES 1833+ NSW, AUS **[35743]** : THOMAS 1870-1905 RICHMOND, VIC, AUS **[35841]** : EDMUND 1830-1880 TAS & VIC, AUS **[35841]** : FRED WILLIAM 1916 (SAILOR) BRISTOL, ENG & ACT, AUS **[36311]** : MATILDA 1853+ BROADMEADOWS, VIC, AUS **[36621]** : ANN 1806+ LANCASTER & SYDNEY, NSW, AUS **[36638]** : 1840+ CLARENDON & SYDNEY, NSW, AUS **[37139]** : 1844+ OBERON & JENOLAN CAVES, NSW, AUS **[37556]** : ALEXANDER C1880S CRESWICK, VIC, AUS **[37906]** : 1880-1960 GARDENVALE, VIC, AUS **[38465]** : 1840+ NSW, AUS **[38485]** : ALFRED 1900+ BURNIE, TAS, AUS **[38729]** : J.C. C1879 RYERSON, ONT, CAN **[34058]** : JOSEPH C1835 MANVERS TWP., ONT, CAN **[34064]** : MARY 1850-1852 FREDERICKSBURG TWP., ONT, CAN **[34365]** : 1820+ MONTREAL, QUE, CAN **[34368]** : 1870-1890 NB, CAN **[34409]** : C1865 ONT, CAN **[34521]** : 1800-1900 RENFREW CO., ONT, CAN **[34996]** : FRED 1861-1885 LONGUEUIL, QUE, CAN **[35615]** : CATHERINE C1835+ KINGSTON, NB, CAN **[36244]** : 1830+ INVERNESS, QUE, CAN **[36704]** : DAVID 1850S MIDDLESEX CO., ONT, CAN **[36729]** : VIOLET 1921+ CAN **[37147]** : THOMAS 1800S+ BENTINCK TWP., ONT, CAN **[37458]** : 1830-1900 THOMASBURGH, ONT, CAN **[37487]** : JOHN 1845+ EGREMONT, GREY CO., ONT, CAN **[38396]**

: MARGARET C1833 ONT, CAN **[38584]** : C1855+ SAINT JOHN, NB, CAN & SCT **[34339]** : PETER C. PRE 1853 FREDERICKSHAVEN & SAEBY, HJORRING, DEN **[35724]** : 1850-1900 EASTBOURNE, SSX, ENG **[33787]** : ANN PRE 1840 LENHAM, KEN, ENG **[33943]** : 1750+ WES, ENG **[33986]** : 1650-1850 BREEDON, LEI, ENG **[34054]** : JOHN 1800S CUL, ENG **[34102]** : PRE 1834 BERKHAMSTED & NORTHCHURCH, HRT, ENG **[34316]** : C1860 SOUTH SHIELDS, DUR, ENG **[34329]** : PRE 1850 LAN, ENG **[34343]** : PRE 1750 YKS, ENG **[34364]** : C1780 BARAM, SSX, ENG **[34426]** : ANN PRE 1807 ORSMKIRK, LAN, ENG **[34461]** : ROBERT PRE 1869 LIVERPOOL, LAN, ENG **[34545]** : JOHN PRE 1850 OVINGHAM, NBL, ENG **[34583]** : 1800+ ST PANCRAS, LND, ENG **[34637]** : PRE 1850 BOOTLE, LAN, ENG **[34769]** : 1818 STEPNEY, LND, ENG **[34777]** : PRE 1770 WORKINGTON, CUL, ENG **[34795]** : 1750-1850 HUCKLOW, DBY, ENG **[34822]** : PRE 1800 ELLOUGHTON, ERY, ENG **[34866]** : PRE 1855 ATHERSTONE, WAR, ENG **[34875]** : 1730 PETWORTH, SSX, ENG **[34909]** : MATTHEW PRE 1835 BRADFORD, WRY, ENG **[35023]** : 1800+ YKS, ENG **[35060]** : PRE 1828 SCULCOATES, YKS, ENG **[35061]** : ELIZABETH PRE 1808 HUN, ENG **[35164]** : PRE 1750 NEWARK ON TRENT, NTT, ENG **[35238]** : C1819 BERMONDSEY, SRY, ENG **[35251]** : PRE 1855 LEEDS, YKS, ENG **[35379]** : 1882 SUNDERLAND, DUR, ENG **[35416]** : 1800+ BIRMINGHAM, WAR, ENG **[35436]** : PRE 1837 MAIDSTONE, KEN, ENG **[35464]** : 1711-1789 COLNE, LAN, NFK & YKS, ENG **[35490]** : C1810 COLNE, LAN, ENG **[35490]** : PRE 1850 LONDON, ENG **[35503]** : 1790-1850 FOWLMERE, CAM, ENG **[35554]** : C1854 CLEATOR MOOR, CUL, ENG **[35585]** : 1835+ STAVELEY, WRY, ENG **[35706]** : PRE 1832 SSX, ENG **[35748]** : 1850+ WOLVERHAMPTON, STS, ENG **[35847]** : 1800S MARKET HARBOROUGH, LEI, ENG **[35858]** : 1800S YKS, ENG **[35899]** : 1780-1850 LAN, ENG **[35916]** : 1785+ WHITEHAVEN, CUL, ENG **[35921]** : PRE 1850 BKM, ENG **[35930]** : 1850+ LONDON, ENG **[35939]** : 1800+ THETFORD, NFK, ENG **[35939]** : ARCHIBALD PRE 1890 FALMOUTH, CON, ENG **[35962]** : ARCHIBALD PRE 1890 PENRYN, CON, ENG **[35962]** : 1800+ FAVERSHAM, KEN, ENG **[36118]** : 1750-1860 RAMSBURY, WIL, ENG **[36130]** : PRE 1810 HULL, YKS, ENG **[36168]** : 1780-1810 ROWLAND, DBY, ENG **[36189]** : 1800S BURTON ON TRENT, DBY, ENG **[36253]** : CHARLES C1866 ATTERCLIFFE, NRY, ENG **[36294]** : C1850 BRISTOL, SOM, ENG **[36386]** : 1800+ CARLISLE, CUL, ENG **[36386]** : PRE 1850 WALTON LE DALE, LAN, ENG **[36386]** : ALFRED PRE 1900 LND, ENG **[36399]** : PRE 1800 ALDERMASTON & SWALLOWFIELD, BRK, ENG **[36401]** : PRE 1800 KINGSCLERE, HAM, ENG **[36401]** : PRE 1980 WILBRAHAM, CAM, ENG **[36489]** : ALEXANDER 1850+ ENG **[36601]** : 1846 CLERKENWELL, MDX, ENG **[36640]** : 1740-1800 BRADFORD, WRY, ENG **[36682]** : PRE 1839 EXETER, DEV, ENG **[36761]** : JAMES 1780+ NEWINGTON, SRY, ENG **[36871]** : WALTER PRE 1900 LND, ENG **[36899]** : 1790+ RICKMANSWORTH, HRT, ENG **[36975]** : 1800+ WADWORTH, ERY, ENG **[37050]** : PRE 1928 BATTERSEA, LND, ENG **[37102]** : PRE 1780 LONDON, ENG **[37133]** : 1800+ COCKERMOUTH, CUL, ENG **[37147]** : C1820-1850 GREASLEY, NTT, ENG **[37148]** : C1847-1864 OLD LENTON, NTT, ENG **[37148]** : 1800-1880 WESTMINSTER, MDX,

ENG [37211] : THOMAS PRE 1850 HULL, ERY, ENG [37299] : JAMES 1830S SWINESHEAD, LIN, ENG [37352] : 1800-1900 STOCKPORT, CHS, ENG [37389] : PRE 1888 NORWICH, NFK, ENG [37442] : ALL NORWICH, NFK, ENG [37629] : 1800-1900 POPLAR, MDX, ENG [37651] : 1650-1850 ASPATRIA, CUL, ENG [37654] : 1850 MIDDLETHORPE, WRY, ENG [37694] : PRE 1850 NTH, ENG [37741] : PRE 1850 EAST HAGBOURNE, BRK, ENG [37743] : BENJAMIN C1850-1900 BERMONDSEY, SRY, ENG [37752] : 1739-1837 KINGSTON, STS, ENG [37762] : C1850 KEMERTON, WOR, ENG [37827] : 1800S GRANGE, CUL, ENG [37834] : 1850+ NEWCASTLE, CUL & NBL, ENG [37853] : C1880 MARYLEBONE, LND, ENG [37865] : 1800S+ BIRMINGHAM, WAR, ENG [37868] : 1750-1830 HELMSLEY, NRY, ENG [37872] : C1830 NEWTON ON OUSE, YKS, ENG [37883] : ROBERT C1806 CARLISLE, CUL, ENG [37960] : ROBERT 1829 EVERTON, LAN, ENG [37960] : ROBERT 1837-1842 OXTON, CHS, ENG [37960] : 1560-1800 CASTLE BYTHAM, LIN, ENG [38265] : 1830+ LINCOLN CITY, LIN, ENG [38272] : C1800 WAKEFIELD, WRY, ENG [38272] : ALL FROME & BEDMINSTER, SOM, ENG [38357] : PRE 1870 FOLKESTONE, KEN, ENG [38389] : C1790 LONDON, ENG [38485] : 1650-1750 STENSON, DBY, ENG [38524] : C1817 MUTTRA, INDIA [38485] : C1910 MAGHERAFELT, DRY, IRL [33902] : 1850+ BELFAST, IRL [34098] : PRE 1830 BELFAST, ANT, IRL [34137] : 1800-1850 KID, IRL [34183] : C1871 BELFAST, ANT, IRL [34385] : C1806 DERRYINVER, ARM, IRL [34385] : C1600 IRL [34395] : 1840+ ARMAGH, IRL [34421] : WILLIAM 1905-1908 CULLYBECKIE, ANT, IRL [34487] : HUGH 1901-1905 BALLYMENA, ANT, IRL [34487] : HUGH 1860-1900 BELFAST, ANT, IRL [34487] : JOHN PRE 1860 DUBLIN, IRL [34557] : 1840+ PORTADOWN, ARM, IRL [34665] : 1800-1900 BALIEBORO, CAV, IRL [34748] : ALL ANT, IRL [34877] : DR THOMAS PRE 1845 BLESSINGTON & ELVERSTOWN, KID, IRL [35217] : C1853 LARONE, TYR, IRL [35336] : 1800S KINGS, OFF, IRL [35342] : ALEXANDER PRE 1856 MOIRA, DOW, IRL [35344] : 1800S DERRYHILLAUGH, FER, IRL [35395] : JAMES 1800+ PORTERDOWN, ARM, IRL [35468] : PRE 1880 TYR, IRL [35913] : 1800S MAY, IRL [36205] : 1800-1853 TYR, IRL [36312] : ALL BANBRIDGE, DOW, IRL [36428] : REBECCA 1800+ TYR, IRL [36697] : 1700+ LEX, IRL [36857] : 1800S BELFAST AREA, DOW & ANT, IRL [37496] : JOHN 1807-1827 ENNISKILLEN, FER, IRL [38396] : 1840-50 ARM, IRL [38583] : WILLIAM PRE 1844 TEMPO & BALLINAMALLRD, FER & TYR, IRL & AUS [37556] : C1834 HOLLAND, NL [36289] : JANE PRE 1790 EDINBURGH, MLN, SCT [33774] : 1860 BONNYBRIDGE & DENNY, STI, SCT [33936] : PRE 1850 CURRIE, EDINBURGH, ELN & MLN, SCT [33959] : GEORGE 1880-1960 HAMILTON, LKS, SCT [33978] : 1800+ JEDBURGH, ROX, SCT [34109] : PRE 1800 IRVINE, AYR, SCT [34112] : JANET C1825 RAW YARDS, AIRDRIE, LKS, SCT [34369] : 1840+ LKS & AYR, SCT [34373] : 1813+ BARR HEAD, RFW, SCT [34421] : HUGH PRE 1861 GOVAN, GLASGOW, LKS, SCT [34487] : JAMES 1700+ COLLESSIE, FIF, SCT [34571] : ALL AVOCH, ROC, SCT [34674] : C1830-1850 GOVAN, LKS, SCT [34748] : C1822 OLD DEER, ABD, SCT [34840] : 1820 PAISLEY, SCT [34843] : ELEANOR 1806+ DNB, SCT [34954] : C1816 PARTICK, GLASGOW, SCT [34993] : MARGARET PRE 1715 ELIE, FIF, SCT [35072] : SUSANNA ALL NEW

CUMNOCK, AYR, SCT [35234] : 1712 CAMPSIE, STI, SCT [35252] : PRE 1860 MOFFAT, DFS, SCT [35337] : JANET 1753 KEITH, BAN, SCT [35369] : 1800+ LEITH, MLN, SCT [35370] : PRE 1865 CRIEFF, PER, SCT [35379] : 1800S RFW & LKS, SCT [35395] : ANDREW C1808+ KINROSS, KRS, SCT [35427] : PRE 1856 POOLE OF MUCKHART, PER, SCT [35504] : 1750+ PRESTWICK, AYR, SCT [35558] : 1600+ ST MONANCE, FIF, SCT [35627] : 1860 JOHNSTONE, RFW, SCT [35820] : PRE 1896 GLASGOW, LKS, SCT [35820] : ARCHIBALD C1842 KIRRIEMUIR, ANS, SCT [35827] : W.J. C1940 PAISLEY, RFW, SCT [35848] : ISABELLA C1782 FOCHABERS, MOR, SCT [35848] : PRE 1800 LARBERT, STI, SCT [35865] : 1838 ABERDEEN, ABD, SCT [35922] : TOM & MARY 1850+ GLASGOW, LKS, SCT [35952] : ALL EAGLESHAM, RFW, SCT [35984] : ALL RUTHERGLEN, LKS, SCT [35984] : 1830+ GLASGOW, LKS, SCT [36195] : C1824 MEARNS, RFW, SCT [36302] : ALL PER, SCT [36429] : 1600-1800 DYSART, FIF, SCT [36556] : PRE 1850 AYR, AYR, SCT [36664] : 1800S SELKIRK, SEL, SCT [36874] : 1800+ ELGIN, MOR, SCT [36885] : 1600-1900 ALFORD, ABD, SCT [36951] : 1770-1855 CATHCART & EASTWOOD, RFW, SCT [37095] : 1770-1855 STRATHAVEN, LKS, SCT [37095] : PRE 1870 AYR, AYR & LKS, SCT [37238] : 1820S LIBERTON, MLN, SCT [37329] : 1790-1880 EDINBURGH, MLN, SCT [37338] : THOMAS 1800+ GLASGOW, LKS, SCT [37437] : 1800-1860 KIRKOSWALD & DUNDONALD, AYR, SCT [37456] : 1840+ EDINBURGH, MLN, SCT [37483] : JOSEPH 1780-1820 MONTROSE, ANS, SCT [37485] : WILLIAM 1800-1830 ABERDEEN, ABD, SCT [37485] : WILLIAM GIBBS 1847+ GLASGOW, LKS, SCT [37713] : GEORGE 1803+ GLASGOW & BEITH, AYR, SCT [37713] : ROBERT 1770+ BEITH, AYR, SCT [37713] : JAMES FORBES 1840+ GLASGOW, LKS, SCT [37713] : JOHN 1775-1830 GLASGOW & BEITH, AYR, SCT [37713] : ROBERT 1845+ GLASGOW, LKS, SCT [37713] : ROBERT 1830-1860 BOTHWELL, LKS, SCT [37713] : PRE 1836 PAISLEY & GLASGOW, LKS, SCT [37852] : PRE 1828 CRAIGHALL & NEWTON, MLN, SCT [37852] : PRE 1860 RFW, SCT [37923] : PRE 1860 LKS, SCT [37923] : C1770 GLENGARRY, INV & PER, SCT [38079] : MARGARET C1836-1878 GLASGOW, SCT & AUS [33847] : 1800+ SELKIRK, SLK, SCT & AUS [34008] : JULIA PRE 1900 PAISLEY, RFW, SCT & ENG [36639] : 1800+ KILMARNOCK, AYR, SCT & NZ [36869] : ALL UK [37421] : 1730-1800 SUSSEX CO., NJ, USA [34364] : 1750-1950 MIDDLESEX CO., VA, USA [35318] : 1820-1860 FLOYD CO., VA & IL, USA [36334] : 1700-1850 NEWPORT, RI, USA [36335] : 1800S IA, USA [36709] : 1880+ ALLEGHENY CO., PA, USA [37549] : 1850+ BALTIMORE, MD, USA [37549] : 1795 WESTMORELAND CO., PA, USA [37795] : 1808 DAUPHIN CO., PA, USA [37795] : 1845-1870 KEWEENAW CO., MI, USA [38009] : 1809 ROWAN CO., NC, USA [38103] : 1840+ IA, USA [38197] : 1790-1810 PA, USA [38201] : SAM 1900+ DALLAS, TX, USA [38312] : LAWSON 1800S IN, USA [38312] : JERRY 1850+ IL & IN, USA [38312] : 1800-1900 KY, VA & IN, USA [38328] : 1791-1830 SARATOGA, NY, USA [38347] : PRE 1678 ANDOVER, MA, USA [38348] : 1700-1800 BEDFORD CO., VA, USA [38524] : GEORGE 1840-1868 CHAMPAIGN CO., OH, USA [38573] : ISAAC 1783-1800 NORTHUMBERLAND CO., PA, USA [38573] : 1815-1868 CHAMPAIGN CO., OH, USA [38573] : WILLIAM 1847-1880S OR, USA [38573] : WILLIAM 1847-1880S CA, USA [38573] : ISAAC

1758-1778 MORRIS CO., NJ, USA **[38573]** : ANGUS C1850 CINCINNATI, OH, USA & SCT **[36969]**

WILTON 1800+ NSW, AUS **[35080]** : PRE 1871 NEWTOWN, NSW, AUS **[35781]** : 1856+ GEELONG, VIC, AUS **[36276]** : ALL TELLISFORD, SOM, ENG **[34429]** : PRE 1850 BRISTOL, ENG **[35404]** : PRE 1800 ST COLUMB, CON, ENG **[35500]** : 1802+ WARMINSTER & BRADFORD ON AVON, WIL, ENG **[36276]** : 1600-1900 MONACUTE, SOM, ENG **[38278]**

WILTSE 1780-1840 WILTSETOWN & BROCKVILLE, ONT, CAN **[36938]**

WILTSEY PRE 1890 MOOSELAKE, MN, USA **[38746]**

WILTSHIRE 1890+ MELBOURNE, VIC, AUS **[36295]** : PRE 1800 BREMHILL, WIL, ENG **[34588]** : 1873 WINCHCOMBE, GLS, ENG **[35761]** : 1820S RAYLEIGH & THUNDERSLEY, ESS, ENG **[35793]** : ALL CHIPPENHAM, WIL, ENG **[35842]** : 1700+ STERT, WIL, ENG **[37843]** : 1700-1800 WICKWAR, GLS, ENG **[37870]**

WIMBECK ALL WORLDWIDE **[38616]**

WIMBELEY PRE 1750 JONES CO., GA, USA **[38783]**

WIMBERLEY 1500+ LIN, ENG **[35723]**

WIMBISH SARA 1700S NC & VA, USA **[38536]**

WIMBLE 1750-1850 WARTLING & HASTINGS, SSX, ENG **[36786]**

WIMER BENJAMIN 1850-1857 PICKAWAY CO., OH, USA **[35329]** : CHRISTOPHER 1857-1875 KNOX CO., IN, USA **[35329]** : ADAM 1830-1845 MERCER & LAWRENCE CO., PA, USA **[37590]** : ISAAC 1830 BUTLER CO., PA, USA **[37590]**

WIMMER C1698 NUSSLOCH, BAD, GER **[34239]**

WINANS GEORGE 1910-1925 LOS ANGELES, CA, USA **[38132]**

WINBANKS 1819 LIVERPOOL, LAN, ENG **[35377]**

WINBOLT 1700-1800 SOM, ENG **[35968]**

WINBURN 1800 NC, USA **[38143]**

WINCEY 1700+ GSY, CHI **[34425]** : 1700+ HAM, ENG **[34425]**

WINCH C1870 BENDIGO, VIC, AUS **[33796]** : PRE 1850 RIVER THAMES PARISHES, ENG **[33796]** : ALL QUEENBOROUGH, KEN, ENG **[34718]** : GEORGE 1743+ KINGS WALDEN & HITCHIN, HRT, ENG **[36068]** : 1800S POPLAR, MDX, ENG **[36070]** : 1860+ SITTINGBOURNE, KEN, ENG **[37213]** : C1837+ KEN, ENG & AUS **[36313]** : ALL WORLDWIDE **[33796]**

WINCHESTER 1831+ BLACKHEATH, NSW, AUS **[35394]** : PRE 1880 ST EBBS, CON, ENG **[34750]** : C1810 HEATHFIELD, SSX, ENG **[36271]** : PRE 1832 HAILSHAM, SSX, ENG **[36281]** : ALL NEW CALEDO **[37340]** : ALL SHI, SCT **[37340]**

WINCKELS ALL GER **[34861]**

WINCOTE MARY 1841 LEAMINGTON PRIORS, WAR, ENG **[36782]** : CHARLES 1815 LEAMINGTON PRIORS, WAR, ENG **[36782]**

WINDALL C1780 COGGESHALL, ESS, ENG **[37053]**

WINDELL 1900 HEMINGTON, SOM, ENG **[35288]**

WINDER PRE 1800 OVER WYERSDALE, LAN, ENG **[36198]** : 1800+ BOLTON, LAN, ENG **[36198]** : PRE 1800 CUL & WES, ENG **[36198]** : PRE 1710 LND, ENG **[37603]** : PRE 1760 BRAY & WINKFIELD, BRK, ENG **[37603]** : 1787+ WES, ENG & AUS **[36238]** : 1743-1850 WASHINGTON CO., MD, USA **[37603]** : 1760-1830 WASHINGTON CO., PA, USA **[37603]** : 1732+ BUCKS CO., PA, USA **[37603]** : 1704+ NJ, USA **[37603]** : 1798-1850 SOMERSET CO., PA, USA **[37603]**

WINDLE 1700+ DOWNEND, GLS, ENG **[34908]** : PRE 1800+ LAN, ENG **[35505]** : PRE 1883 KNOCKFINISK, LIM, IRL **[36631]** : 1849-1990 PHILADELPHIA, PA, USA **[38139]**

WINDLER 1700-1950 LIVERPOOL, LAN, ENG **[36983]**

WINDLINGER C1900 HECHINGEN, BAW, GER **[38604]**

WINDOVER 1790-1900 ONT, CAN & USA **[34520]**

WINDRIDGE ALL ENG **[36045]**

WINDROSS PRE 1840 YKS, ENG **[35533]**

WINDSOR 1880S BALA, ONT, CAN **[34103]** : FREDERICK 1868-1880S BARRIE, ONT, CAN **[34103]** : MARY ROBERTA 1940+ CARBERRY, MAN, CAN **[36678]** : RICHARD 1700+ QUEEN CAMEL, SOM, ENG **[35361]** : JANE 1833 QUEEN CAMEL, SOM, ENG **[35361]** : ALEXANDER 1700-1800 QUEEN CAMEL, SOM, ENG **[35361]** : JOHN JONES 1800 QUEEN CAMEL, SOM, ENG **[35361]** : 1802 ALDERBURY, WIL, ENG **[35369]** : PRE 1850 QUEEN CAMEL, SOM, ENG **[35821]** : 1800S BURNARDSLEY, CHS, ENG **[36018]** : 1700-99 BROADWAY, YEOVIL, SOM, ENG **[37756]** : 1650-1750 BOURNE, LIN, ENG **[38287]** : THOMAS PRE 1855 LONDON, ENG **[38289]**

WINDUSS ALL WORLDWIDE **[35797]**

WINEBRENNER ALL USA **[38610]**

WINEKSDORF 1832-1854 PA, USA **[38101]**

WINEMILLER JOHN 1866 SACRAMENTO, CA, USA **[38122]**

WINES PRE 1850 SOM, ENG **[34865]**

WINFIELD ALL WEAVERHAM, CHS, ENG **[33916]** : PRE 1823 SPONDON, DBY, ENG **[34661]** : C1830 BURTON JOYCE, NTT, ENG **[34734]** : PRE 1800 EWELME, OXF, ENG **[35838]** : 1770+ LANCASTER, LAN, ENG **[36768]**

WINFREY C1800 TEALBY, LIN, ENG **[37039]** : CHARLES PRE 1800 NEW KENT, VA, USA **[33757]**

WING 1780-1900 ELIZABETH TOWN, ONT, CAN **[36938]** : PRE 1800 WHITTLESEY, CAM, ENG **[34884]** : PRE 1826 GRANTHAM, LIN, ENG **[35724]** : 1750-1840 LONDON, ENG **[36484]** : 1700+ ALLINGTON, LIN, ENG **[37248]** : PRE 1660 BANBURY, WAR, ENG **[38226]** : 1782-1801 OBLONG & PAWLING, NY, USA **[36938]** : 1890+ NE, USA **[36962]** : 1660+ USA **[38226]**

WINGATE C1850-1870 GOVAN, LKS, SCT **[34748]**

WINGER C1800+ FRANKLIN CO., PA & IN, USA **[36540]**

WINGETT ALL PLYMOUTH, DEV, ENG **[36999]**

WINGFIELD 1800+ NORTON, DBY, ENG **[34243]** : 1800+ BRANTHAM & LETHERINGHAM, SFK, ENG **[34243]** : 1834-1850 FINSBURY, LND, ENG **[34284]** : 1800S HASTINGS, SSX, ENG **[34292]** : 1830+ LONDON, ENG **[34292]** : PRE 1866 NOTTINGHILL, LND, ENG **[36632]**

WINGHAM ALL BRIGHTON, SSX, ENG **[37373]**

WINGROVE THOS 1770-1828 MOULTON, NTH, ENG **[36712]**

WINK C1750 KELLAS, MOR, SCT **[36431]**

WINKELMANN 1800+ BARMSTADT, MEK, GER **[34556]**

WINKLER PRE 1777 SCHWEDT, BRA, GER **[34083]** : 1700+ GER **[35566]** : 1750-1850 KNAUTTKLEEBURG & LEIPZIG, SAX, GER **[36953]** : C1840 SU **[38618]** : 1500+ ROWANCO, NC, KY & IL, USA & GER **[36970]**

WINKLEY PRE 1870 LND, ENG **[35135]**

WINLOW PRE 1800 ISLINGTON, MDX, ENG **[34311]**

WINN 1850+ AUS **[36395]** : C1743 ALFORD, LIN, ENG **[35746]** : 1800-1900 ISLINGTON, DEV, ENG **[36395]** : PRE 1900 KENDAL, CUL, ENG **[37237]** : ALL WESTMINSTER, LND, ENG **[37453]** : PRE 1864 YKS, ENG **[37760]** : 1780+ VT, USA **[38116]**

WINNALL 1700-1750 OMBERSLEY, WOR, ENG **[34552]**

WINNE 1850S COLUMBIA CO., NY, USA **[37568]**

WINNETT 1810S BALTINGLASS, WIC, IRL & AUS [35075] : ALL WORLDWIDE [36298]

WINNEY PRE 1820 ASSINGTON, SFK, ENG [36388]

WINNICKI 1920-1930 FRA [38164] : ALL LWOW, LW, POL [38164]

WINNICOTT C1800 ST BUDEAUX & E. STONEHOUSE, DEV, ENG [37770]

WINQVIST GUSTAV 1887+ MN, USA [38557] : NELLIE MAY 1883+ MN, USA [38557] : CARLALBIN 1875+ SAINT PAUL, MN, USA [38557] : EMMA KRISTINA 1885+ MN, USA [38557] : HULDA HILMA 1887+ MN, USA [38557]

WINROW PRE 1872 LONDON, ENG [34278] : PRE 1880 ORMSKIRK, LAN, ENG [37708] : C1872-1889 TIMARU, NZ [34278]

WINSBY 1800+ LONDON, ENG [35905]

WINSCOMBE SUSAN C1849 BARROW GURNEY, SOM, ENG [36332] : CHARLES JOS. C1849 BARROW GURNEY, SOM, ENG [36332] : ADELAIDE 1869+ SOM, ENG [36332]

WINSER 1850 CASTLEMAINE, VIC, AUS [37163]

WINSKILL 1800-1850 LONDON, ENG [35285]

WINSLADE ALL FARNHAM, SRY, ENG [36179]

WINSLET 1760+ RICHMOND, SRY, ENG [36179]

WINSLEY 1700-1800 BAMPTON, DEV, ENG [36389]

WINSLOW PRE 1700 WOR, ENG [38746]

WINSOR ALL DENMAN, NSW, AUS [35541] : 1700+ HARBERTON & IVYBRIDGE, DEV, ENG [34970]

WINSTANLAW 1780 DALTON, DFS, SCT [35350]

WINSTANLEY PRE 1860 MANCHESTER, LAN, ENG [36604]

WINSTER JOSEPH 1700-1800 KILLINGTON, WES, ENG [35006]

WINSTONE PRE 1850 HATHEROP, GLS, ENG [35515]

WINTCOAT PRE 1775 LEICESTER, LEI, ENG [34370]

WINTER 1850+ WATERLOO CO., ONT, CAN [34075] : PRE 1800 SOM, ENG [34099] : 1620 BROMPTON RALPH, SOM, ENG [34204] : C1800 WIL, ENG [34296] : C1800 HRT, ENG [34550] : 1600-1900 NEWTIMBER, SSX, ENG [34749] : PRE 1800 TAUNTON, SOM, ENG [34780] : C1774 LONG SUTTON, HAM, ENG [35247] : PRE 1808 WIL, ENG [35252] : PRE 1810 DEPTFORD, KEN, ENG [35544] : PRE 1800 ENG [36639] : 1775 BRAUNCEWELL, LIN, ENG [37039] : PRE 1900 ANDOVER, HAM, ENG [37226] : ALL NORWICH, NFK, ENG [37612] : ALL LONDON, MDX, ENG [37884] : C1698 NUSSLOCH, BAD, GER [34239] : C1749 STEINEN, BAD, GER [37504] : 1800 OSTFRIESLAND, PRE, GER [38039] : 1750-1840 ALBERSWEILER, RPF, GER [38374] : ALL GER [38664] : PRE 1855 KILMEEDY, LIM, IRL [34039] : 1750-1850 LET, IRL [38575] : C1740 VOLLENHOVE, OIJ, NL [38705] : 1770-1850 GDANSK AREA, POL [35153] : 1800+ NEW KINGSTON, NY, USA [37572]

WINTERBOTTOM PRE 1840 HOBART, TAS, AUS [34698] : 1850+ CARCOAR, NSW, AUS [35238] : C1900+ PERTH, WA, AUS [38510] : PRE 1832 MOTTRAM, CHS, ENG [35238]

WINTERBOURNE PRE 1750 IRL [34312]

WINTERBURN 1800+ LONDON, ENG [34670] : C1800 YEADON, WRY, ENG & AUS [35079]

WINTERBURNE PRE 1750 IRL [34312]

WINTERHAGEN ALL WEI, GER [38607]

WINTERMUTE PRE 1800 GER [38235]

WINTERS C1700-1860 NC & MO, USA [38242]

WINTERTON 1837+ WAR, ENG [36296]

WINTLE ALL WESTBURY ON SEVERN, GLS, ENG [34837] : C1800+ BREAM, GLS, ENG [37494]

WINTON 1750+ EDDERTON, ROC, SCT [33986] : 1800 DUNDEE, ANS, SCT [34098] : ALL UK [36382]

WINTRODE 1600-1732 BAMMENTAL & MECKESHEIM, GER [38374]

WINTROP PRE 1840 WOOLER, NBL, ENG [34201]

WINUP PRE 1885 SRY, ENG [37358]

WINWICK PRE 1825 UNST, SHI, SCT [34814] : ELIZ ALL SHI, SCT [36697]

WINWOOD 1790+ LACKFORD, SFK, ENG [34179] : 1650-1750 CHELMARSH & OMBERSLEY, SAL & WOR, ENG [34552]

WINZELHAEUSER C1460 STUTTGART, BAW, FRG [38660]

WINZENBERG 1800-1900 AUS [34928] : 1700-1900 GER [34928]

WIRE 1827+ HOBART, TAS, AUS [35394]

WIRTH ALL NIEMEGK, DDR, GER [34938] : 1800S MALLMITZ, SIL, GER [38623]

WIRTNER ALL ST LOUIS, MO & IA, USA [33756]

WISBEY PRE 1800 DUXFORD, CAM, ENG [35440] : 1794 FEN DITTON, CAM, ENG [35835] : 1700+ DUXFORD, CAM, ENG [35846]

WISBY 1820S THUNDERSLEY & RAYLEIGH, ESS, ENG [35793]

WISCHER 1798 RUSSEE, SHO, BRD [35809]

WISDOM 1880+ SCOTT & NEW MADRID CO., MO, USA [35286] : 1812+ HICKMAN CO., TN, USA [35286] : 1700-1760 KING & QUEEN CO., VA, USA [36566]

WISE MARY ANN 1840S SYDNEY, NSW, AUS [37906] : 1700+ ANDOVER, HAM, ENG [34405] : 1700+ SOUTHAMPTON, HAM, ENG [34405] : 1800+ ABBOTS ANN, HAM, ENG [34405] : FLORENCE 1940S HOXTON, LND, ENG [36430] : 1850-1900 ASHTON UNDER LYNE, LAN, ENG [37373] : 1700S BALLYHAY, COR, IRL [37906] : SUSAN 1800S ROCKINGHAM CO., VA, USA [36322] : 1800-1900 LINCOLN, NE, USA [36951] : 1700S WASHINGTON CO., PA, USA [37004] : ELIZABETH 1818-1826 KY, USA [38145] : 1818 WASHINGTON, MD, USA [38348]

WISEHEART PRE 1790 KILRENNY, FIF, SCT [35525]

WISELY C1850S NSW, AUS & USA [37130] : 1700-1800S INSCH, ABD, SCT [34032]

WISEMAN C1830 NSW, AUS [34286] : 1850+ SYDNEY, NSW, AUS [34969] : 1842-60 BLAND PLAINS, NSW, AUS [37919] : C1900 TUBBUL & YOUNG, NSW, AUS [37919] : PRE 1785 NFK, ENG [34139] : C1777 ESS, ENG [34286] : PRE 1860 WIDFORD, HRT, ENG [34571] : PRE 1840 BLACKBURN, LAN, ENG [35546] : PRE 1850 NFK, ENG [36067] : ALL ST ALBANS, HRT, ENG [37082] : ALL BARKING, ESS, ENG [37125] : PRE 1740 STEPNEY, LND, ENG [37420] : PRE 1850 SIBLE HEDINGHAM, ESS, ENG [37693] : ALL NZ [34286] : PRE 1800 GARDENSTOWN, BAN, SCT [34192] : PRE 1860 RENFREW, RFW, SCT [34571] : PRE 1861 GARDENSTOWN, BAN, SCT [34840] : 1773+ DUNNICHEN, ANS, SCT [35560] : 1600+ GAMRIE, BAN, SCT [35627] : 1750-1870 BLYTHSWOOD, GLASGOW, SCT [35790] : 1820+ MOR, SCT [35943] : PRE 1850 MOR, SCT [36792] : ALL STRATHAVEN, LKS, SCT [37480]

WISH PRE 1860 DEV, ENG [35757]

WISHART PRE 1848 WESTMINSTER, MDX, ENG [36079] : PRE 1880 FIF, SCT [33966] : 1770S ABERFELDY, PER, SCT [34991] : PRE 1800 ELIE, FIF, SCT [37179] : 1800+ DUNFERMLINE, FIF, SCT [37376] : 1850+ ABERDEEN, ABD, SCT [37376]

WISHERT 1700-1820 SCT [37599]

WISKEN ALL ESS, ENG [35840]

WISLER 1700-1850 BASINGSTOKE, HAM, ENG [35375]

WISNER JOHN 1700-1800 ORANGE CO., NY, USA [38130]

WISSMAN 1770S PHILADELPHIA, PA, USA [38066]

WISSMANN 1600-1700 PFEFFINGEN, WUE, GER [38599]

WISWELL 1830+ CHENANGO CO., NY, USA [36356]

WITCHER 1750-1800 PITTSYLVANIA CO., VA, USA [36737] : 1730-1750 GLOUCESTER CO., VA, USA [36737] : 1750-1800 SURRY CO., NC, USA [36737]

WITCOMBE PRE 1850 COMPTON DUNDUN, SOM, ENG [36676]

WITHALL C1750+ ENG [37292]

WITHAM 1870+ TOWNSVILLE & BRISBANE, QLD, AUS [35111] : 1700-1900 NTT, ENG [36531] : 1800+ NTT, ENG [37839] : 1600 ST CHALMFORD, ESS, ENG [38240] : 1885 WILSON CO., KS, USA [38240]

WITHERELL 1800-1840 IRL [36331]

WITHERINGTON PRE 1837 GLENORCHY, TAS, AUS [35074]

WITHERS C1868+ ADELAIDE, SA, AUS [34035] : 1820+ NSW, AUS [37900] : 1850+ CHILTERN, VIC, AUS [38213] : PRE 1820 BRISTOL, GLS, ENG [33771] : 1700 LEICESTER, LEI, ENG [34321] : 1780 FARRINGTON, HAM, ENG [34909] : ALL BISHOPSTEIGNTON, DEV, ENG [36163] : PRE 1830 BOLTONSBOROUGH, SOM, ENG [37169] : PRE 1900 ALTON & BENTWORTH, HAM, ENG [37371] : ALL CARTMEL IN FURNESS, LAN, ENG [37379] : 1800S PORTSEA, HAM, ENG [37898] : 1800S ROMSEY, HAM, ENG [37898] : PRE 1820 NEWBURY, BRK, ENG [37900] : 1750S GREAT COXWELL, BRK, ENG [38206] : 1800+ BAYDON, WIL, ENG [38213] : PRE 1846 RADFORD, NTT, ENG [38568] : 1800+ SOM, ENG & AUS [36266] : DANIEL C1817 DUBLIN, IRL [37106] : 1800-1930 POWELL CO., KY, USA [38089] : 1650+ WOODBRIDGE, NJ, USA [38235]

WITHERSPOON 1800S VINTON CO., OH, USA [35278]

WITHERWAX 1733 DUTCHESS, NY, USA [38022]

WITHEY 1750+ EAST COKER, SOM, ENG [35760] : 1850+ ENG [35760] : PRE 1850 DOR, SOM & WIL, ENG [36166] : GEORGE PRE 1580 WEST COKER, SOM, ENG [38483]

WITHNALL WILLIAM 1830-1860 LAUNCESTON, TAS, AUS [33900]

WITHNELL 1850 WAPPING, MDX, ENG [35255]

WITMER PRE 1733 PALATINATE, GER [36972]

WITNEY 1800+ WALSEA ISLAND, ESS, ENG [35129]

WITT 1828+ MARYBOROUGH, QLD, AUS [35463] : 1860+ SUTTON FOREST, NSW, AUS [35567] : 1750+ SOUTHAMPTON, HAM, ENG [35830] : 1800 DAMEROW, POM, GER [37170] : 1650+ BEIDENFLETH, SHO, GER [38651] : ALL UK [37674] : PRE 1770 VA, USA [37587]

WITTE PRE 1828 GRANOW, BERNSTEIN, GER [35463] : C1812 KIEL, SHO, GER [37819]

WITTEMER PRE 1800 ROCKENHAUSEN, RPF, GER [38681]

WITTEN PRE 1858 MT VINCENT, NSW, AUS [37963]

WITTERS 1700S BERKS CO., PA, USA [37028] : 1749+ BERKS CO., PA, USA [38330]

WITTICH PRE 1875 ASBACH, HES, BRD [35635]

WITTIG 1880+ KEMPSEY, NSW, AUS [35425] : PRE 1880 CHERUN, GER [35425]

WITTKOWSKI 1900-1850 LINDENORT, KRIES, OPR [38427]

WITTLOCK SVEN 1750 KARLSKRONA, BLEKINGE, SWE [38550]

WITTMAN 1876+ ELLIS CO., KS, USA [38057]

WITTON 1600-1700 CASTERTON, WMD, ENG [36635] : 1825+ LONDON, MDX & SRY, ENG [36997] : C1750 GAYTON LE MARSH, LIN, ENG [37039]

WITTS THOMAS A. 1840-1929 STAUNTON COLFORD, GLS, ENG [38394] : ARTHUR JOHN 1878-1970 STANLEY ROAD, GLS, ENG [38394] : ANTHONY BRIAN 1936+ MAIDSTONE, KEN, ENG [38394] : DEREK E. 1939+ HASTINGS, ENG [38394] : ARTHUR CYRIL 1900-1990 MAIDSTONE, KEN, ENG [38394]

WIVANS ALL WIVERLIPSCOMBE, SOM, ENG [37950]

WIVELL 1700-1900 PA & MD, USA [37517]

WIX 1750+ LAYSTON, HRT, ENG [36978]

WIXTED KATHLEEN ALL MECHANICVILLE, NY, USA [36563]

WIZNIAK ALL GALICIA, SU & POL [34146]

WOARE ALL WELSH BEICKNOR GOODRICH, HEF, ENG [37746] : ALL FOREST OF DEAN, GLS, ENG [37746] : ALL MONMOUTH, MON, WLS [37746]

WOART C1784 FARNINGHAM & BEXLEY, KEN, ENG [38485]

WODAMS 1750+ NETHER HEYFORD, NTH, ENG [37357]

WODE PRE 1860 ALTONA, DEN [35144] : PRE 1858 ALTONA, DEN [37104]

WOFFINDEN ALL HUTTONS AMBO, YKS, ENG [37383]

WOGAN 1870+ HUNDLETON, PEM, WLS [35338]

WOHLERS ALL HOYERHAGEN, BRM, GER [34959] : 1830-1880 DOLLERN, HAN, GER [36952] : 1894-1912 MANNING, CARROLL CO., IA, USA [36952] : 1914-1924 SCOBEY, DANIELS CO., MT, USA [36952] : 1880-1890 LYONS, CLINTON CO., IA, USA [36952]

WOHLGEHAGEN PRE 1880 SCHONBERG, SHO, GER [35425]

WOHLLENBEN 1800 REICHMANSDORF, BAY, BRD [37028]

WOIDIG PRE 1860 KARLSBAD AREA, BOHEMIA, CS [36963]

WOIZEKOWSKI ALL WORLDWIDE [35291]

WOJCIECHOWSKA ALL WORLDWIDE [35291]

WOJCIK 1953+ LIVERPOOL, CHS, ENG [35626]

WOLCUTT C1800 VA, USA [38323]

WOLD 1600+ FLAA, HALLINGDAL, NOR [36905]

WOLF 1777-1871+ PRITTLEWELL, ESS, ENG [37108] : PRE 1830 STAENALTZ, ALS, FRA [34488] : ALL GER [34861] : ALL WIE, OES [37268] : ALL WORLDWIDE [37785]

WOLFE 1842-1905 BOMBALA, NSW, AUS [34966] : PRE 1846 VIC, AUS [35148] : PETER 1774-1846 TORONTO & DEREHAM TWP., ONT, CAN [34524] : JAMES C1810+ DEREHAM TWP, OXFORD CO., ONT, CAN [34524] : 1800+ SOM, ENG [35370] : PRE 1885 ALBINCK, WPR, GER [34567] : 1780+ SKIBBEREEN, COR, IRL [35971]

WOLFENDEN 1700-1850 ROYTON & OLDHAM, LAN, ENG [37508] : 1793-1900 OLDHAM & ROCHDALE, LAN, ENG [38370]

WOLFERS ALL NBT, NL [38170]

WOLFERSTAN ALL DEV & STS, ENG [34671]

WOLFF ALL GUSTROW, MEK, DDR [34812] : 1750-1850 REIMERSWILLER, ALS, FRA [36898] : C1843 SOMMERFELD, BRA, GER [35391] : PRE 1892 MOCKER, LEOBSCHUTZ, GER [36458] : PRE 1720 HARDENBURG, RPF, GER [38681]

WOLFRUM 1830+ WEST BEND, WI, USA [36935]

WOLFRUN PRE 1850 BAV, GER [36935]

WOLGROVE 1800S CON, ENG [35337]

WOLKISER 1600-1900 POL [38128]

WOLLAND 1650+ HALBERTON, DEV, ENG **[34747]** : PRE 1860 MINEHEAD, SOM, ENG **[35889]**

WOLLENWEBER 1800-1925 HAMILTON CO., OH, USA **[36973]**

WOLOWIC PRE 1920 COOK CO., IL, USA **[38538]**

WOLRIDGE PRE 1700 DOR, ENG **[36679]**

WOLSKI 1700-1850 MICHELSDORF, LUBLIN, POL **[38652]**

WOLSTENHOLME C1880 YKS, ENG **[34195]** : C1850 NEWTON LE WILLOWS, LAN, ENG **[34467]**

WOLTER 1700S GRAMNITZ & HAGENOW, MSW, GER **[38745]**

WOLTON PRE 1810 WOODBRIDGE, SFK, ENG **[33992]**

WOLVERS (SEE WOLFERS [38170]

WOLZ PRE 1850 LINDELBACH, GER **[38676]**

WOMBELL ALL GILLINGHAM, KEN, ENG & NZ **[36840]**

WOMBOUGH ALL OH & NJ, USA **[34301]** : ALL WORLDWIDE **[34301]**

WOMELSDORF 1889-1910 TILLAMOOK CO., OR, USA **[38101]** : 1854-1898 ADAMS CO., IL, USA **[38101]**

WONHILL PRE 1850 DEV, ENG **[37393]**

WONNACOTT PRE 1820 CHITTLEHAMPTON, DEV, ENG **[36514]**

WOOD C1860S REDBANK, SA, AUS **[33849]** : 1886+ TAMWORTH, NSW, AUS **[34277]** : 1863+ SCONE, NSW, AUS **[34277]** : CHAS JOSEPH 1860-1879 GREAT WESTERN, VIC, AUS **[34308]** : CHAS JOSEPH 1879+ HOBART TOWN, TAS, AUS **[34308]** : 1871-1927 BUNBURY & ADELAIDE, WA & SA, AUS **[34530]** : 1850+ COOKTOWN, QLD, AUS **[34883]** : ALBERT 1855+ SYDNEY, NSW, AUS **[34978]** : 1840+ BALLINA, NSW, AUS **[35117]** : JOHN 1861+ WARATAH, NSW, AUS **[35239]** : PRE 1880 SYDNEY, NSW, AUS **[35339]** : 1888 WAVERLEY, NSW, AUS **[35414]** : WILLIAM C1880 CASTLEMAINE, VIC, AUS **[35427]** : MARY 1850+ RANDWICK, NSW, AUS **[35703]** : GERTRUDE 1900S WA, AUS **[35706]** : 1802-1841 SYDNEY, NSW, AUS **[36293]** : 1818-1854 BRUNDAH & CASTLEREAGH, NSW, AUS **[36618]** : THOMAS C1859 GULGONG, NSW, AUS **[37553]** : ALL ADELAIDE & FREMANTLE, SA & WA, AUS & ENG **[34561]** : 1840 MOIRA, ONT, CAN **[34084]** : 1850-1950 CAN **[34135]** : JOHN PRE 1830 LOUGHBORO TWP., ONT, CAN **[34365]** : 1820+ MERRICKVILLE, ONT, CAN **[34466]** : 1860+ MOUNT FOREST, ONT, CAN **[34466]** : GEORGE PRE 1890 NORWICH, ONT, CAN **[36652]** : 1800-1950 HASTINGS & PRINCE EDWARD CO., ONT, CAN **[36688]** : JOHN 1800+ CUMBERLAND CO., NS, CAN **[38421]** : 1770+ JSY, CHI **[33982]** : ALL POYNTON & WORTH, CHS, ENG **[33765]** : PRE 1850 GLS, ENG **[33799]** : 1800S LONDON, ENG **[33982]** : MARY 1800-1880 CAPESHORNE, CHS, ENG **[34143]** : 1700S WAKEFIELD, WRY, ENG **[34228]** : 1835+ TORQUAY, DEV, ENG **[34238]** : JAMES C1800 ISLINGTON, LND, ENG **[34274]** : PRE 1806 OFFHAM, KEN, ENG **[34277]** : PRE 1750 ETWALL, DBY, ENG **[34311]** : ABRAHAM 1779-1855 CRANBROOK, KEN, ENG **[34325]** : SYDNEY 1867-1946 TOWER HAMLETS & MAIDSTONE, LND & KEN, ENG **[34325]** : ALL SOUTH THORESBY, LIN, ENG **[34505]** : 1800+ CAMPSALL, WRY, ENG **[34505]** : CECIL 1880-1897 LONDON, ENG **[34505]** : PRE 1859 CROYDON, SRY, ENG **[34548]** : JOSEPH 1700+ NOTTINGHAM, NTT, ENG **[34571]** : 1739 EASTBOURNE, SSX, ENG **[34708]** : 1870+ POPLAR, MDX, ENG **[34710]** : PRE 1850 LORTON, CUL, ENG **[34755]** : 1830-1840 STEPNEY, MDX, ENG **[34832]** : 1700-1800 PAINSWICK, GLS, ENG **[34872]** : 1800-1900 FINSBURY, LND, ENG **[34872]** : PRE 1856 PITSFORD, NTH, ENG **[35070]** : PRE 1789 EALING, MDX, ENG **[35095]** : PRE 1820 WORCESTER, WOR, ENG **[35117]** : JOHN 1790S NOTGROVE, GLS, ENG **[35261]** : PRE 1870 LND, ENG **[35339]** : 1750+ DEPTFORD, KEN, ENG **[35370]** : C1866 STS, ENG **[35414]** : WILLIAM C1866 GREENWICH, LND, ENG **[35427]** : PRE 1766+ KENILWORTH, WAR, ENG **[35453]** : GEORGE PRE 1838 CANTERBURY, KEN, ENG **[35553]** : SELBY 1770+ CHISLEHURST, KEN, ENG **[35560]** : PRE 1629 SOUTH CROXTON, LEI, ENG **[35572]** : 1850-1950 BOULTON & SHARPLES, ENG **[35581]** : PRE 1810 ST ALKMUND, DBY, ENG **[35745]** : PRE 1830 OXTON, NTT, ENG **[35898]** : 1800 CHS, ENG **[35970]** : PRE 1800 BDF, BKM & HRT, ENG **[36042]** : PRE 1775 WORLABY, LIN, ENG **[36059]** : PRE 1820 WHITECHAPEL, MDX, ENG **[36099]** : 1700-1770 LONDON, ENG **[36107]** : ROBERT C1747 ENG **[36107]** : ALL FINNINGLEY, WRY, ENG **[36126]** : 1797-1850 BASWICH, STS, ENG **[36304]** : 1825-50 RUGELEY, STS, ENG **[36304]** : PRE 1850 COGGESHALL, ESS, ENG **[36379]** : 1700-1800 KEN, ENG **[36480]** : 1855-1875 TORQUAY, DEV, ENG **[36530]** : 1700-1900 HYKEHAM, LIN, ENG **[36531]** : PRE 1800 ST MARYS, NOTTINGHAM, NTT, ENG **[36532]** : GEORGE PRE 1830S LEICESTER, LEI, ENG **[36652]** : PRE 1800 BOOTLE, CUL, ENG **[36701]** : PRE 1765 DILHORNE, STS, ENG **[36701]** : C1750+ BADDESLEY ENSOR, WAR, ENG **[36753]** : WILLIAM 1816 OLD SWINFORD, WAR, ENG **[36860]** : 1766 HARWICH, ESS, ENG **[37250]** : PETER 1860+ LAUGHTON, SSX, ENG **[37293]** : ELLEN 1800S BIRMINGHAM, STS, ENG **[37299]** : 1800+ MILTON, KEN, ENG **[37328]** : HARRY 1850+ WOOLWICH ARSENAL, KEN, ENG **[37444]** : ALL CLOPTON, SFK, ENG **[37487]** : THOMAS C1834-1856 SOUTH HAMPTON, HAM, ENG **[37553]** : 1700S DONCASTER, WRY, ENG **[37570]** : 1700-1850 WOLVERHAMPTON, STS, ENG **[37609]** : PRE 1900 TRYSULL, STS, ENG **[37722]** : 1700-1800 LINCOLN CITY, LIN, ENG **[37843]** : 1720S BECKENHAM, KEN, ENG **[37869]** : ROBERT PRE 1790 BREASTON, DBY, ENG **[38248]** : PRE 1900 NORTHAMPTON, NTH, ENG **[38280]** : ALL HALIFAX, YKS, ENG **[38332]** : JOHN H. 1858-1885 SHREWSBURY, SAL, ENG **[38417]** : 1798-1842 FISHLAKE, WRY, ENG **[38469]** : 1759+ ARKSEY, WRY, ENG **[38469]** : 1816+ DONCASTER, WRY, ENG **[38469]** : 1705-1791 BARNBY UPON DON, WRY, ENG **[38469]** : 1820 BURNAGE, LAN, ENG **[38719]** : 1869 ESTON, NRY, ENG **[38719]** : PRE 1900 MCHENAGHE KILLEGAR, LET, IRL **[34466]** : 1800+ LOU, IRL **[34918]** : MARY 1837+ IRL **[35703]** : C1806 FER, IRL **[35824]** : 1839+ AUCKLAND, NZ **[34277]** : CECIL 1910-1943 SWATOW, S.CHINA **[34505]** : PRE 1760 WICK, CAI, SCT **[33873]** : 1650-1750 GLADSMUIR, MLN, SCT **[33908]** : C1750 CRAILING, ROX, SCT **[34239]** : C1792 AUCHEN CRAW, BEW, SCT **[34491]** : 1830 KINGHORN, FIF, SCT **[34914]** : PRE 1854 TWEEDLE, FIF, SCT **[34914]** : 1800+ MONKLAND & HUTCHESON TOWN, LKS, SCT **[35051]** : 1850+ EDINBURGH, MLN, SCT **[35112]** : PRE 1837 LARGS, RFW, SCT **[35407]** : PRE 1800 COLDINGHAM, BEW, SCT **[36497]** : 1700+ PAISLEY, RFW, SCT **[36794]** : PRE 1830 CARLUKE, LKS, SCT **[36955]** : HELEN JANE 1885-1909 BAN, SCT **[37023]** : 1770+ EDINBURGH, MLN, SCT **[37333]** : C1720+ NY, USA **[34084]** : 1780-1821 CAMDEN, NY & MA, USA **[36354]** : PRE 1810 SC,

USA [36570] : CALVIN 1840-1900 PUTNAM CO., IN, USA [36901] : HELEN JANE 1909-1936 CHICAGO, IL, USA [37023] : C1750 UNION CO., SC, USA [37032] : ALL ULSTER CO., NY, USA [37584] : 1830 DANDRIDGE, TN, USA [38198] : PRE 1776 BENNINGTON, VT, USA [38231] : PRE 1800 LOUP CO., NE, USA [38745] : 1700S CT, USA [38745] : PRE 1840 ROCKLAND CO., NY, USA [38783] : PRE 1730 NJ, USA & ENG [38746] : HORTENSIA 1770-1840 CARDIFF, GLA, WLS [38409] : LITTLETON ALL WORLDWIDE [36998]

WOODAGE 1760+ LONDON, ENG [35066]

WOODALL PRE 1800 SHREWSBURY, SAL, ENG [37273] : PRE 1800 WOR, ENG [37739] : 1800-1900 DUDLEY, WOR, ENG [37884] : 1850-1920 NASHVILLE, HOWARD CO., AR, USA [36449]

WOODARD PRE 1873 ORFORD, SFK, ENG [36230] : 1600-1750 GREAT FARINGDON, BRK, ENG [36595]

WOODARDS ELIZABETH 1700S ABBOTS LANGLEY, HRT, ENG [35634] : 1800+ ENG [36662]

WOODBRIDGE 1750+ BRISTOL, GLS, ENG [35627] : PRE 1800 KINGSEY, BKM, ENG [36204] : C1492 STANTON FITZWARREN, WIL, ENG [37564] : 1800S ABINGDON, BRK, ENG [38206]

WOODBURN PRE 1902 VIC, AUS [33777] : PRE 1742 KIRKBY IRELETH, CUL, ENG [36204] : PRE 1902 LKS, SCT [33777]

WOODBURY 1790-1870 WALLACER, NS, CAN [34162] : PRE 1849 HOLCOMBE BURNELL, DEV, ENG [33795] : PRE 1820 TAUNTON, SOM, ENG [35798] : C1830 SOM & DEV, ENG [36753] : 1800+ AYR, SCT [35951]

WOODCOCK PRE 1861 HASTINGS CO., CAN [34090] : PRE 1840 HOLBEACH, LIN, ENG [34931] : 1830+ CORTON, SFK, ENG [35726] : 1700+ BDF, ENG [37304] : PRE 1860 LONDON, ENG [37308] : ALL ST FAITHS, NFK, ENG [37689] : PRE 1750 ENG & IRL [34068] : C1860 PER, SCT [35863]

WOODCRAFT C1790-1840 MILLBROOK, BDF, ENG [33845]

WOODCROFT C1869 SHEFFORD, BDF, ENG [35585]

WOODD 1830+ NSW, AUS [33768]

WOODED PRE 1780 SCALFORD, LEI, ENG [35745]

WOODEND 1878+ CUL, ENG [35293]

WOODERSON 1800-1833 CARLISLE, NBL, ENG [34274]

WOODFIN ALL USA [34981] : 1700+ HENRICO CO., VA, USA [38032] : 1700+ POWHATAN CO., VA, USA [38032] : 1800+ CUMBERLAND CO., VA, USA [38032] : ALL BUCKINGHAM CO., VA, USA [38032] : 1700+ RICHMOND CITY, VA, USA [38032]

WOODFINE PRE 1867 FINSBURY, MDX, ENG [34665]

WOODFORD 1800+ AUS [34538] : 1800+ RYDE, NSW, AUS [34538] : ALL HERRING NECK, NFD, CAN [35264] : 1600+ TAUNTON, SOM, ENG [34538] : PRE 1850 IOW, ENG [34879] : 1600-1800 BRIGHSTONE, IOW, ENG [38420] : C1850-1855 CHRISTCHURCH, NZ [34879]

WOODGATE 1900+ WA, AUS [37401] : 1825+ NSW, AUS [37401] : 1600-1800 HAWKHURST, KEN, ENG [34623] : 1700S BEER, DEV, ENG [34715] : 1700+ WATTISHAM & THORINGTON, SFK, ENG [37401] : PRE 1799 ACTON & LAVENHAM, SFK, ENG [37655] : 1900+ NZ [37401]

WOODGER 1800-1840 CHATHAM, KEN, ENG [34016]

WOODHAM PRE 1820 GAMLINGAY & SPALDWICK, CAM & HUN, ENG [35866]

WOODHAMS ALL SPELDHURST, KEN, ENG [34110] : 1800S HASTINGS, SSX, ENG [35046] : 1840+ BRISTOL, ENG [37357] : ALL ENG [37357] : 1800S CHARTWELL, KEN, ENG [38289] : PRE 1850 GUESTLING, SSX, ENG [38746]

WOODHEAD C1863 HALIFAX, YKS, ENG [34133] : ALL YKS, ENG [34981] : 1800+ SHELF & HALIFAX, WRY, ENG [36391] : 1874-1918 INGLEWOOD, TARANAKI, NZ [35895] : PRE 1874 LKS, SCT [35895]

WOODHOUSE 1800-1920 AUS [37348] : PRE 1850 HUDDERSFIELD, WRY, ENG [35151] : ALL BISHOPS FROME, HEF & WOR, ENG [35417] : ALL POPLAR, MDX, ENG [36571] : PRE 1821 ST PANCRAS OLD CHURCH, LND, ENG [37192] : 1700-1920 BRK, ENG [37348] : PRE 1850 TUNSTEAD, NFK, ENG [37512] : PRE 1850 CASTLE HEDINGHAM, ESS, ENG [37753] : PRE 1900 CLERKENWELL, MDX, ENG [37753] : PRE 1700 BASLOW, DBY, ENG [37875] : ALL PORTADOWN, ARM, IRL [37154]

WOODHURST PRE 1900 LONDON, MDX, ENG [38263]

WOODING PRE 1840 YARDLEY HASTINGS, NTH, ENG [35129] : 1700-1800 MDX, ENG [36081] : 1850+ CRANFIELD & MARSTON, BDF, ENG [36414] : 1800-1900 YARDLEY HASTINGS, NTH, ENG [37495]

WOODINGTON 1800+ WARWICK & BUDBROOKE, WAR, ENG [34243]

WOODIWIS ALL WORLDWIDE [37059]

WOODIWISS ALL WORLDWIDE [37059]

WOODLAND ALL CREDITON, DEV & SOM, ENG [37717] : ALL WORLDWIDE [34944]

WOODLANDS 1842-1900 PORT MACQUARIE, NSW, AUS [38761] : 1800-1841 SELLINGE & MONKS HORTON, KEN, ENG [38761]

WOODLEY 1800S CARSHALTON, SRY, ENG [36275] : PRE 1565 HARWELL, BRK, ENG [37420] : PRE 1800 BRK, ENG [37715]

WOODLING 1800+ ENG [35905]

WOOD LYSAGHT ALL YKS, ENG [34847]

WOODMAN 1750-1810 MORCHARD BISHOP, DEV, ENG [34448] : C1785-1846 AYLESBURY, BKM, ENG [36425] : 1750-1850 CERNE ABBAS, DOR, ENG [36484] : PRE 1800 HAM, ENG [37693]

WOODMANCY PRE 1800 THORNGUMBALD, ERY, ENG [33940]

WOODMASS 1700-1800 ALSTON, CUL, ENG [37290]

WOODMORE ALL WORLDWIDE [37214]

WOODROW 1750-1810 CORTON DENHAM, SOM, ENG [34448] : 1600-1800 NFK, ENG [36462] : 1800+ WYMONDHAM, NFK, ENG [37411] : 1700-1850 KILBARCHAN, RFW, SCT [35395] : PRE 1800 PAISLEY, RFW, SCT [35871]

WOODRUFF PRE 1860 DEAL, KEN, ENG [37169]

WOODRUP PRE 1852 BINGLEY, YKS, ENG [38085]

WOODS 1830+ HOBART, TAS, AUS [34795] : 1850S DUNGOG, NSW, AUS [35156] : PRE 1853+ CLARENCE TOWN, NSW, AUS [35412] : PRE 1860 NEWTOWN & BUNGENDORE, NSW, AUS [36369] : C1850 WILLIAMSTOWN, VIC, AUS [37302] : 1700-1990 BRICKFIELD HILL, NSW, AUS & UK [35421] : 1840+ HURON CO., ONT, CAN [34502] : PRE 1860 RICHIBUCTO, NB, CAN [37473] : ANN PRE 1787 LAN, ENG [34487] : PRE 1800 DUNCTON, SSX, ENG [34725] : MARIA PRE 1845 RISELEY, BDF, ENG [34855] : PRE 1780S CHERTSEY, SRY, ENG [34873] : PRE 1820 LEAKE, LIN, ENG [35029] : PRE 1870 BOSTON, LIN, ENG [35029] : C1823 COLLYWESIN, NTH, ENG [35091] : PRE 1830 SUTTON, SRY, ENG [35126] : C1833 NFK, ENG [35458] : ROBERT PRE 1886 IPSWICH, SFK, ENG [35757] : PRE 1890 GORLESTON, NFK, ENG [36067] : C1800 NFK, ENG [36478] : WILLIAM 1850-70

DOWNHAM, NBL, CAM & ESS, ENG [36696] :
GEORGE 1780-1880 PRESTON, LAN, ENG [36998] :
C1760 WITLEY, SRY, ENG [37309] : 1822 +
DOWNHAM, CAM, ENG [37314] : PRE 1840
WELLS, NFK, ENG [37964] : 1760 CHRISHALL,
CAM, ENG [38209] : 1820S PEMBERTON, LAN,
ENG [38281] : SUSANNAH 1800S
OSWALDTWISTLE, LAN, ENG [38284] : 1800-1875
CARRICKMACROSS, MOG, IRL [34346] : PRE 1840
ARM, IRL [34502] : PRE 1840 GAL, IRL [34804] :
1800S TEMPLEMORE, TIP, IRL [35331] : PRE 1900
DRY, IRL [36893] : ALL IRL [37884] : 1800-1880
WESTPORT, MAY, IRL [38201] : ALL
MAWILLIAN, LDY, IRL [38275] : ALL MAURITIUS
[34170] : ALL WELLINGTON, NZ [38275] : ALL
KUMARA, NZ [38275] : 1873 DEN DALRY, AYR,
SCT [36599] : 1855-1930 MS, USA [36324] : PRE 1861
MONROE CO., TN, USA [36351] : WILSON PRE
1850 WORLDWIDE [36930]

WOODSIDE 1830-1850 ANT, IRL [33835]

WOODSTOCK 1860 + BRUCE CO., CAN [34090] :
1700S AYLESBURY, BKM, ENG [36981]

WOODTHORPE C1700-1850 LND, ENG [35997]

WOODVINE PRE 1870 SHREWSBURY, SAL, ENG
[37414]

WOODWARD ALL SURRY HILLS, NSW, AUS [35234]
: 1900 + LAVENHAM, MAN, CAN [36704] : C1780
NEWPORT PAGNELL, BKM, ENG [34041] : 1800S
CAMBERWELL, SRY, ENG [34309] : ALL LIN,
ENG [34361] : 1750 + LEAMINGTON, WAR, ENG
[34363] : 1850 TEDDINGTON, MDX, ENG [34388] :
1600 + COLDRIDGE, DEV, ENG [34747] : 1815
BIRMINGHAM, WAR, ENG [35041] : 1750-1800
EAST NEWLYN, CON, ENG [35076] : FRANCIS
PRE 1835 LONDON, ENG [35234] : C1860
HANSLOPE & HAVERSHAM, BKM, ENG [35387] :
1790 + SHREWSBURY, SAL, ENG [35554] : ALL
LIVERPOOL, ENG [35707] : C1600 + CALKE &
TICKNALL, DBY, ENG [35851] : ALL
BIRMINGHAM, WAR, ENG [35868] : 1864 + LEE,
KEN, ENG [36171] : C1839 DATCHETT, BKM, ENG
[36265] : ROBERT 1821 + MARYLEBONE, MDX,
ENG [36294] : PRE 1850 GLS, ENG [36508] : 1600-
1750 GREAT FARINGDON, BRK, ENG [36595] :
1830 + PECKHAM, SRY, ENG [36704] : 1890 +
PLYMOUTH, DEV, ENG [36704] : ALL
ARKENGARTHDALE, YKS, ENG [36704] : ALL
GRINTON, YKS, ENG [36704] : 1780 + BARNARD
CASTLE, DUR, ENG [36704] : ALL SWALEDALE,
YKS, ENG [36704] : ALL GUNNERSIDE, YKS,
ENG [36704] : 1810 + HULL, YKS, ENG [36704] :
1800 + STOCKTON ON TEES, DUR, ENG [36704] :
PRE 1780 EASTON, SFK, ENG [37420] : 1800-80
WHITCHURCH, SAL, ENG [37946] : C1811
HORNSEY, MDX, ENG [38441] : C1850 GOULDS
GREEN, KEN, ENG [38441] : C1825 HANWELL,
MDX, ENG [38441] : 1920 + CAPETOWN, RSA
[36704] : 1780-1870 PETERSHAM & DANA, MA,
USA [36335] : 1700-1800 NH, USA [37538] :
ABRAHAM PRE 1800 QUEEN ANN, MD, USA
[38049]

WOODWARDS PRE 1720 BRK, ENG [35866]

WOODWORTH PRE 1830 ALBERT CO., NB, CAN
[38447] : WILLIAM 1760-1820 BARTHOMLEY, CHS,
ENG [34143] : RICHARD 1758-1843 DUBLIN, DUB,
IRL [37014]

WOODY 1725 SIBTON, ESS, ENG [37928] : 1740-1844
GOOCHLAND & FRANKLIN CO., VA, USA [38315]
: PRE 1850 NC, USA [38576]

WOODYATT ALL ASHPERTON, HEF, ENG [36633]

WOODYEAR 1725-1800 CAMBERWELL, SRY &
KEN, ENG [37087] : 1725-1800 ST KITTS, W.INDIES
[37087]

WOODZELL ALL KEN & SSX, ENG [38570]

WOOF PRE 1851 MELKINTHORPE & LOWTHER,
WES, ENG [34584]

WOOKEY ALL ENG [34415] : ALL CLUTTON, SOM,
ENG [36152] : 1790-1850 SOM, ENG [38742]

WOOL 1880 + BRISBANE, QLD, AUS [33782] : 1830 +
LONDON, MDX, ENG [35112]

WOOLAGE C1870S COONABARABRAN &
GUNNEDAH, NSW, AUS [33794] : 1750-1850 NH,
USA [36733]

WOOLASTON PRE 1830 BIRMINGHAM, WAR, ENG
[35523]

WOOLCOCK 1823 + PENZANCE, CON, ENG [34627]
: PRE 1800 GWINEAR, CON, ENG [34616] : 1800 +
CROWAN, CON, ENG [37149] : PRE 1900 CON,
ENG [37749] : 1840 + BLYTH, NBL, ENG [38324]

WOOLCOTT PRE 1850 EXETER, DEV, ENG [34268] :
1849 + SHEPPY, KEN, ENG [35704] : 1700-1800
CHARD & THORNCOMBE, SOM & DOR, ENG
[37838] : 1827 + GIBRALTAR [35704] : 1800-1900
BARBADOS, W.INDIES [34641]

WOOLDRIDGE 1860 + FORBES, NSW, AUS [35497] :
C1814 ST HELIER, JSY, CHI [35478] : PRE 1814
PLAISTOW, SSX, ENG [34057] : PRE 1900 OLD
SWINFORD & WOLVERHAMPTON, WOR & STS,
ENG [34314] : 1700S SEIGHFORD, STS, ENG [35256]
: ALL DEV, ENG [37092] : 1650 + SILEBY, LEI,
ENG [37266]

WOOLEN THOMAS 1812 LEXINGTON, KY, USA
[38086]

WOOLER PRE 1910 LONDON, ENG [37062]

WOOLERTON 1600 + LEI, ENG [37266]

WOOLES PRE 1830 BRISTOL, GLS, ENG [34197]

WOOLET ALL WORLDWIDE [37417]

WOOLETT ALL WORLDWIDE [37417]

WOOLF 1800 + EXETER, DEV & WAR, ENG [38261] :
1830 + NEW YORK & NEW ORLEANS, LA, USA
[35342] : 1700-1800 FAUQUIER CO., VA, USA [38524]

WOOLFORD 1700-1800 RAMSBURY, WIL, ENG
[34623] : PRE 1838 WOTTON BASSETT, WIL, ENG
[34816] : 1750 + WEDMORE, SOM, ENG [35112] :
C1800 LONDON, ENG [35563] : PRE 1850
MANCHESTER, LAN, ENG [37913]

WOOLGER PRE 1855 KEN, ENG [34979] : PRE 1800
LONDON, SRY, ENG [37773]

WOOLHOUSE 1800S BERWICK PRIOR, OXF, ENG
[35024] : PRE 1840 MANCHESTER, LAN, ENG
[36840] : 1732-1791 CONISBOROUGH, WRY, ENG
[38469]

WOOLL 1550 UPWELL, NFK, ENG [34321] : JAMES
1825 + CORK, IRL [35583]

WOOLLACOTT PRE 1820 + KINGSKERSWELL,
DEV, ENG [37912]

WOOLLAM 1800 + ENG [36470]

WOOLLAMS 1700S LONDON, MDX, ENG [35542]

WOOLLARD PRE 1900 FEN DITTON.&
CHESTERTON, CAM, ENG [33883] : 1790 + SFK &
ESS, ENG [35632] : 1800 + ENG [36470]

WOOLLAS ALL HESSLE, YKS, ENG [35814]

WOOLLATT ALL DUFFIELD, DBY, ENG [36532]

WOOLLEN LEAVEN 1770 TAYLOR'S ISLAND, MD,
USA [35328] : LEVIN 1770S DORCHESTER CO.,
MD, USA [37585]

WOOLLET ALL WORLDWIDE [37417]

WOOLLETT PRE 1860 ROCHESTER, KEN, ENG
[36517] : PRE 1872 STAPLEHURST, KEN, ENG
[37890] : ALL WORLDWIDE [37417]

WOOLLEY 1848 + HOBART & FRANKLIN, TAS,
AUS [34853] : 1800 + COWDEN, KEN, ENG [34711] :

WOUDSTRA PRE 1880 APPELSCHA, FRI, NL [36283]

WOULFE PRE 1896 ATHEA, LIM, IRL [36631]

WRAGG C1840 HASLAND, DBY, ENG [33870] : 1850+ YKS, ENG [33925]

WRAIGHT 1898+ MELBOURNE, VIC, AUS [35221]

WRATHER 1800+ BRAFFERTON & HARROGATE, NRY, ENG [36791]

WRATT C1856 SPRING GROVE, NELSON, NZ [35885]

WRAY C1855 WILLIAMSTOWN, VIC, AUS [37302] : 1840+ MONTREAL, QUE, CAN [34144] : 1850-1900 DARLINGTON, DUR, ENG [34211] : PRE 1850 GRANTHAM, LIN, ENG [36380] : 1700S WRY, ENG [38577] : PRE 1840 MOUNT CHARLES, DON, IRL [34144] : 1780+ DON, IRL [38221] : 1783-1891 HUNTINGDON CO., PA, USA [38094] : 1815-1891 ALEXANDRIA, PA, USA [38094] : MARY J. 1812-1891 HUNTINGDON CO., PA, USA [38371]

WRAY (ROY) SEE ROY-W [34985]

WREBEL PRE 1790 SZAMOTULY, POS, GER [38618] : PRE 1750 WROMBLEWO, POS, GER [38618] : ALL WORLDWIDE [38618]

WREFORD PRE 1750 COLEBROOKE & CREDITON, DEV, ENG [37195] : PRE 1860 CREDITON & EXETER, DEV, ENG [37393]

WREN ALL VIC, AUS [37176] : C1845-1901 NARELLAN, NSW, AUS [37553] : 1800-1900 ENG [33998] : 1750+ CARLISLE, CUL, ENG [34243] : ALL ENG [37176] : 1600+ HAM, ENG [37448] : 1575-1650 KESWICK, CUL, ENG [37460] : ALL CAPETOWN, RSA [37176]

WRENCH ALL BASLOW, DBY & LND, ENG [36477] : ALL LIN, ENG [37407]

WRESTLER 1732 TITCHFIELD, HAM, ENG [35903]

WRIGG C1790 ENG & WLS [35381] : C1800 WLS [36271]

WRIGG-LEE C1805 TONGE, LAN, ENG [38284]

WRIGGLESWORTH 1800+ BRADFORD, YKS, ENG [35891] : 1800S LONDON, ENG [37167]

WRIGGLEY THOMAS C1815 TONGE, LAN, ENG [38284]

WRIGHT 1860S+ JAMBEROO, NSW, AUS [33930] : 1873-1990 MUDGEE & GLEN INNES, NSW, AUS [34294] : JOHN 1819+ BATHURST & ORANGE, NSW, AUS [34545] : WILLIAM 1837-1893 ORANGE & BOURKE, NSW, AUS [34545] : C1909 MARRICKVILLE, NSW, AUS [34694] : WILLIAM C1837 BATHURST, NSW, AUS [34806] : MARY JANE 1873+ BOURKE, NSW, AUS [34806] : JOHN 1884 CONOBLAS, NSW, AUS [34806] : 1856+ MELBOURNE, VIC, AUS [34962] : JOSEPH 1858 BATHURST, NSW, AUS [35066] : 1870S BALLARAT, VIC, AUS [35136] : 1850-1900 WENTWORTH, NSW, AUS [35146] : 1840+ MAITLAND, NSW, AUS [35543] : 1830+ MUSWELLBROOK, NSW, AUS [35740] : 1855+ GOULBURN, NSW, AUS [35741] : 1870+ CASTERTON, VIC, AUS [35943] : C1860S NSW, AUS & USA [37130] : LEMUEL 1800 STANSTEAD CO., QUE, CAN [34129] : 1830+ CAMLACHIE, ONT & QUE, CAN [34375] : 1850+ WESTMINSTER TWP., ONT, CAN [34480] : PRE 1899 ST MARYS, ONT, CAN [38480] : PRE 1826 GREAT YARMOUTH, NFK, ENG [33762] : C1800+ SSX, ENG [33812] : 1778 BARROWDEN, RUT, ENG [33967] : 1800+ BRISTOL, GLS, ENG [34082] : SHEDRACK 1900 SAL, ENG [34132] : WILLIAM 1792 WADDINGTON, LIN, ENG [34176] : 1800S LONDON, ENG [34178] : 1730+ FLEET, LIN, ENG [34221] : PRE 1870 HELIONS BUMPSTEAD, ESS, ENG [34294] : 1750-1900 AYOT ST PETER & PIRTON, HRT, ENG [34411] : 1700-1800 SHILLINGTON & MEPPERSHALL, BDF, ENG

[34411] : PRE 1850 BEDALE, NRY, ENG [34617] : 1830+ NORWICH, NFK, ENG [34710] : PRE 1812 MDX, ENG [34758] : WALTER 1840+ NOTTINGHAM, NTT, ENG [34788] : PRE 1837 BECKENHAM, KEN, ENG [34797] : JOHN C1800 POPLAR, LND, ENG [34806] : JOHN ARMSTRON C1839 HUDDERSFIELD & LOCKWOOD, YKS, ENG [34881] : PRE 1825 IOW, ENG [34909] : 1830 LINCOLN, LIN, ENG [34940] : PRE 1850 FOXTON, CAM, ENG [34962] : PRE 1890 STOKE ON TRENT, STS, ENG [35018] : PRE 1816 PRITTLEWELL, ESS, ENG [35157] : 1700-1860 EDGBASTON, WAR, ENG [35228] : JAMES 1856+ MANCHESTER, LAN, ENG [35357] : WILLIAM 1880+ MANCHESTER, LAN, ENG [35357] : PRE 1800 OLNEY, BKM, ENG [35397] : PRE 1865 NFK, ENG [35488] : PRE 1870 LEYTONSTONE, ESS, ENG [35540] : PRE 1700 ESS, ENG [35642] : PRE 1780 NFK, ENG [35642] : 1850+ REIGATE, SRY, ENG [35644] : 1800-1830 BISLEY, GLS, ENG [35741] : 1830-1853 BUSSAGE, GLS, ENG [35741] : 1730-1830 STROUD, GLS, ENG [35741] : 1850+ ORDSALL, NTT, ENG [35847] : C1829 LIVERPOOL, LAN, ENG [35910] : 1900+ GRANTHAM, LIN, ENG [35943] : PRE 1900 SOUTHPORT, LAN, ENG [36040] : C1805 LITTLE DUNHAM, NFK, ENG [36086] : JOHN PRE 1898 HEDDON ON-THE-WALL, NBL, ENG [36149] : PRE 1800 COLLINGHAM, WRY, ENG [36159] : 1850+ BOXFORD, SFK, ENG [36215] : PRE 1850 POLSTEAD, SFK, ENG [36215] : C1800 EXETER, DEV, ENG [36271] : PRE 1820 ASTLEY, WAR, ENG [36429] : 1800+ LEI, ENG [36429] : 1800-1900 CHS, ENG [36482] : 1800-1900 STS, ENG [36482] : PRE 1868 LIVERPOOL, LAN, ENG [36522] : 1750+ NTH & BKM, ENG [36574] : THOMAS 1690-1753 NEW BRENTFORD, MDX, ENG [36700] : 1600-1700 ALDINGTON, KEN, ENG [36700] : WILLIAM 1800+ BERMONDSEY, LND, ENG [36818] : PRE 1850 FRAMLINGHAM, SFK, ENG [36829] : 1900S BECCLES, SFK, ENG [36829] : 1700+ PAUL, CON, ENG [36833] : PRE 1874 SFK, ENG [36888] : 1700-1900 NFK, ENG [36977] : PRE 1850 LAN, ENG [37061] : PRE 1850 CHATHAM, KEN, ENG [37067] : PRE 1825 WHITECHAPEL, LND, ENG [37067] : PRE 1810 PERSHORE, WOR, ENG [37097] : 1780-1850 BIRSTALL, LEI, ENG [37129] : SUSANNA C1800 WISBECH, LIN, ENG [37143] : 1600-1650 BARKWAY, HRT, ENG [37166] : 1750-1910 DEEPING ST NICHOLAS, LIN, ENG [37194] : 1765+ BROAD CHALK & BISHOPSTONE, WIL, ENG [37226] : PRE 1900 HASTINGS & TICEHURST, SSX, ENG [37339] : ISAAC 1800+ LND, ENG [37345] : CHARLES 1860-1920 ISLINGTON, LND, ENG [37345] : 1780-1850 LITTLE LEIGHS, ESS, ENG [37477] : PRE 1800 SAXLINGHAM, NFK, ENG [37725] : PRE 1850 MOUSEHOLE, CON, ENG [37832] : C1810 LOUTH, LIN, ENG [37834] : FRANCES 1835-1841 DODCOTT, CHS, ENG [37934] : 1750+ WRENBURY, CHS, ENG [37934] : 1750-1850 NORBURY, CHS, ENG [37934] : 1800-1850 MARBURY CUM QUOISLEY, CHS, ENG [37934] : 1700-1780 BARNINGHAM, SFK, ENG [38003] : PRE 1820 STS, ENG [38056] : 1700+ STOCKPORT, CHS, ENG [38215] : ELIZABETH PRE 1813 SHEFFIELD, YKS, ENG [38248] : PRE 1860 MAIDENHEAD, BRK, ENG [38276] : PRE 1850 YKS, ENG [38299] : ALL LANGHAM, SFK, ENG & AUS [33919] : MARY 1775+ YORK & SYDNEY, YKS & NSW, ENG & AUS [35155] : PRE 1835 BRD, GER [37048] : C1820 DOUGLAS, IOM [37169] : THOMAS 1800+ CAV, IRL [34161] : JAMES C1850S

BALLYMURPHY, DOW, IRL [34788] : JOHN C1850S GREY ABBEY, DOW, IRL [34788] : JOSEPH PRE 1850 TULLYCORBETT, MOG, IRL [35066] : ALL STRABANE, FER, IRL [36784] : PRE 1764 SKIBBEREEN, COR, IRL [37623] : PRE 1900 DONEGORE, ANT, IRL [37636] : PRE 1851 DOAGH, ANT, IRL [37636] : 1862 + NZ [33988] : 1862 + DUNEDIN, OTAGO, NZ [33988] : 1840 + SCT [33930] : JAMES 1841-1865 BATHGATE, STI, SCT [33951] : 1880-1950 AIRDRIE, LKS, SCT [33978] : PRE 1850 DURRIS, KCD & ABD, SCT [34360] : PRE 1840 STIRLING, STI, SCT [34428] : 1770S-1840S OCHILTREE & TARBOLTON, AYR, SCT [34635] : PRE 1830 AYR, AYR, SCT [34835] : 1800-1860 MLN, SCT [36239] : 1700-1935 EDINBURGH & COLINTON, MLN, SCT [36652] : 1700+ CRIEFF, PER, SCT [36652] : RACHEL 1759-C1852 EDINBURGH, SCT [36880] : WILLIAM 1820-1841 DALKEITH, MLN, SCT [37444] : SARAH C1800+ PAISLEY, RFW, SCT [38593] : PRE 1854 BEDFORD, MI, USA [34252] : SIMEON 1720+ NY & VT, USA [34486] : RICHARD 1730-1880 RANDOLPH CO., NC & IN, USA [36901] : 1800-1840 KY, USA [36908] : 1800-1887 ST JOHNSBURG & BARTON, VT, USA [36915] : WILLIAM P. 1844+ FRANKLIN CO., VA, USA [37443] : PRE 1760 VA, USA [37587] : 1780-1842 COLUMBIA CO., NY, USA [37591] : 1750-1910 ROANOKE CO., VA, USA [37798] : 1845-1900 KEWEENAW CO., MI, USA [38009] : 1822 RUSSELL CO., VA, USA [38151] : PRE 1750 RICHMOND & NORTHUMBERLAND, VA, USA [38311] : 1820-1850 GREENSBORO, VT, USA [38465] : SETH C1700-1800 TOLLAND CO., CT, USA & GER [37813] : 1750-1800 WELSHPOOL, MGY, WLS [36081]

WRIGHTSON PRE 1800 LONDON, ENG [33912] : 1700+ LIN & YKS, ENG [37827]

WRIGLEY 1855+ BUNINGYONG, VIC, AUS [33837] : 1864-1900 PORT MACQUARIE, NSW, AUS [38761] : THOMAS 1842 MIDDLETON, LAN, ENG [38284] : THOMAS 1815 TONGE, LAN, ENG [38284] : DANIEL 1800-1850 ENG [38337] : 1835-1863 BURY, LAN, ENG [38761]

WROBLEWSKY PRE 1950 ISTANBUL, TURKEY [36030]

WROE 1865-1904+ MARYBOROUGH, QLD, AUS [35737]

WROOT PRE 1720 ISLE OF AXHOLME, LIN, ENG [37371]

WROTH 1550-1700 ENFIELD, MDX, ENG [37077]

WROUT ALL WORLDWIDE [37371]

WRUCK 1870+ GROSSCATZENBERG, POM, GER [34768]

WRYCROFT 1750+ KETTERING, NTH, ENG [38204]

WTENBOGAERT 1400+ NL [34180]

WUERZ PRE 1600 NRW & NSA, BRD [38616]

WULF PRE 1800 OLDENBURG, SHO, GER [38648]

WULFRATH ALL GUSTROW, MEK, DDR [34812]

WULLIN 1831+ MULLHEIM, BAD, GER [37504]

WUNDER PRE 1800 AUGSBURG, BAY, BRD [36963]

WUNDERLICH 1600-1700 BERKHOLZ, BRA, GER [35968] : JOHANN PRE 1846 KRS. ASCH, SUDETENLAND, OES, CSR &, GER [38649]

WUNDERLICHT 1849 SELB, BAV, GER [37531]

WUNDERLIN 1870+ CAMDEN, NJ, USA [36578]

WUNSCHE ALL WORLDWIDE [38666]

WURM 1759-1823 WEISSENFELS, KSA, GER [38750]

WURTH PRE 1836 CRIESBRAC, WUE, GER [34031]

WURZ 1800+ ST ILGEN (LIEGE), HEIDLEBURG, BEL [35856]

WYANTON 1800S DON, IRL [37818]

WYATT 1880-1900 BRISBANE, QLD, AUS [33782] : 1848+ STROUD, NSW, AUS [35147] : 1836 KENNINGTON, LND, ENG [34193] : 1700-1800 OXFORD, OXF, ENG [34552] : PRE 1803 NEMPNETT, SOM, ENG [34978] : 1750+ BUCKLAND ST MARY, SOM, ENG [35112] : PRE 1848 ASHBURTON, DEV, ENG [35147] : PRE 1803 MENPRETT, SOM, ENG [35368] : PRE 1850 DEV, ENG [35491] : 1800+ TAUNTON, SOM, ENG [35632] : PRE 1600 ESS, ENG [35642] : C1818 PORTSMOUTH, HAM, ENG [35990] : PRE 1816 ST BREOCK, CON, ENG [36039] : 1862-1900 WORCESTER, WOR, ENG [36109] : 1817-1862 OLDSWINFORD, WOR, ENG [36109] : PRE 1863 PORTSMOUTH, HAM, ENG [36255] : 1800+ WIX, ESS, ENG [36287] : C1800 PORTSEA, HAM, ENG [36859] : PRE 1807 BURWELL, CAM, ENG [37131] : 1859-1889 WALTHAMSTOW, ESS, ENG [37418] : PRE 1697 NTH, ENG [37706] : ROBERT 1845-1900 BATHFORD, SOM, ENG [37800] : CHARLES 1800S BATHFORD, SOM, ENG [37800] : 1700-1850 TAUNTON, SOM, ENG [37843] : PRE 1796 MARTIN, NC, USA [36570] : WILLIAM 1850+ BUNCOMBE CO., NC, USA [37527] : 1850-60 HEMPSTEAD CO. & PULASKI CO., AR, USA [37533]

WYBER 1750-1900 EDINBURGH, MLN, SCT [34632]

WYBERGH PRE 1690 WARCOP, WES, ENG [36180]

WYBORN PRE 1870S ENG [36146] : 1600-1800 KEN, ENG [36480]

WYBOROUGH ALL CAMBRIDGE, CAM, ENG [37884]

WYBURN 1858+ ST KILDA, VIC, AUS [34579]

WYCHE 1600-1700 SUTTON, SRY, ENG [36556] : 1400-1600 DAVENHAM, CHS, ENG [36556]

WYCLIFFE 1800S ST ALBANS, VT, USA [34199]

WYDOODT 1500+ WORLDWIDE [38161]

WYE 1890+ CAM, ENG [37347]

WYER PRE 1850 HINDON, WIL, ENG [36474]

WYETH LESLIE 1953+ BOTSWANA [37055] : 1840-1850S PRESTON & CANDOVER, HAM, ENG [36285] : WILLIAM 1787-1840 ENG [37055] : WILLIAM 1787-1840 BRIGHTON, SSX, ENG [37055] : LESLIE 1953+ MOZAMBIQUE [37055] : LESLIE 1953+ S.AFRICA [37055] : LESLIE 1953+ ZAMBIA [37055] : LESLIE 1948+ UMTALI, ZIMBABWE [37055]

WYFFELS PRE 1800 ROLLEGEM, WVL, BEL [38164]

WYGENT (SEE WIGENT) [38287]

WYGLINSKI ALL WORLDWIDE [38481]

WYKERT ALL WORLDWIDE [37453]

WYLAM 1827-55 KIBBLESWORTH, DUR, ENG [36412]

WYLD PRE 1800 CHAPEL EN-LE FRITH, DBY, ENG [34588]

WYLDER ALL USA [38013]

WYLD-STARK C1840 SCT [35025]

WYLER PRE 1850 INNERBIRRMOOS, BE, CH [38747]

WYLES ALL FAVERSHAM, KEN, ENG [34131] : 1800S DUDDINGTON, NTH, ENG [35531]

WYLEY PRE 1630 WALSALL & WOLVERHAMPTON, STS, ENG [36110] : PRE 1830 EXETER, DEV & KEN, ENG [36396]

WYLIE 1860 KANDY, CEYLON [33932] : 1800+ KILLANEY, DOW, IRL [33977] : PRE 1860 FER, IRL [34840] : 1870 COOKSTOWN, TYR, IRL [37952] : 1840 BELFAST, ANT, IRL [37952] : C1760 DREGHORN, AYR, SCT [34118] : 1834 CANONBIE, DFS, SCT [34195] : MARY PRE 1819 GLASGOW, LKS, SCT [34539] : 1800-1900 GLASGOW, LKS, SCT [34557] : ALEXANDER 1830S GLASGOW, LKS, SCT [35794] : 1750+ STEWARTON, AYR, SCT [35909] :

1800-1840 GLASGOW, LKS, SCT [37650] : 1600-1750 ABERDEEN, SCT [38115] : C1890 DETROIT, MI, USA [33902] : 1800+ PINE MEADOWS, CT, USA [33977]

WYLLIE C1840 MOTHERWELL, LKS, SCT [35089] : 1750-1850 KILMARNOCK, AYR, SCT [35151] : C1830 MUIRKIRK, AYR, SCT [35866] : ALL AYR, SCT [35927] : JAMES 1830+ GALSTON, AYR, SCT [36749] : DAVID 1820+ KILMARNOCK, AYR, SCT [36749] : WILLIAM 1770+ OCHILTREE, AYR, SCT [36749]

WYLY PRE 1750 ST BEES, CUL, ENG [36490] : C1700 THOMASTOWN, KID, IRL [36490] : C1700 LEX, IRL [36490]

WYMAN 1856+ IPSWICH AREA, QLD, AUS [37896] : WALLACE J. 1832-1895 SEATTLE, WA, AUS [37951] : FRANCIS L. 1866+ SEATTLE, WA, AUS [37951] : 1770-1850+ WILDEN & RAVENSDEN, BDF, ENG [34738] : 1890 ISLINGTON, MDX, ENG [37677] : PRE 1856 BRAUGHING, HRT, ENG [37896] : JOSEPH C1807+ USA [37951] : JOHN C1782+ USA & ENG [37951]

WYMER PRE 1839 TRINITY NEWINGTON, SRY, ENG [34166]

WYND ALL ANS, SCT [35950]

WYNDHAM ALL WORLDWIDE [38237]

WYNES PRE 1900 WORLDWIDE [37874]

WYNN 1887 ELLESMERE, SAL, ENG [35720] : 1800S PAINSWICK, GLS & SRY, ENG [37972] : THOMAS PRE 1850 GA, USA [38536] : 1790+ USA & UK [36357]

WYNNE 1700-1800 HEF, ENG [37457] : PRE 1800 KEN, ENG [38235] : PRE 1821 CAR, IRL [35223] : ALL MOSTYN, FLN, WLS [37667]

WYNTER 1786+ TAREE, NSW, AUS & ENG [37130] : PRE 1720 LONDON, ENG [34033] : PRE 1720 PLYMOUTH & ALDEBURGH, DEV, ENG [34033]

WYRILL 1800S WORLDWIDE [35964]

WYSE C1818+ NEWCASTLE, NB, CAN & SCT [34339]

WYSE (SEE WISE) [37906]

WYSS JOHN 1883-1894 ST LOUIS, MO, USA [38655] : THERESIA 1894+ USA [38655] : JOHANN 1883-1894 ST LOUIS, MO, USA [38655]

WYTSMA ALL NL [38707] : ALL USA [38707]

YABSLEY C1815 MODBURY, DEV, ENG [34880]

YAEGER 1845-1900 BALTIMORE, MD, USA [38321]

YAGER 1750+ PA, USA [34497] : 1820-1830 MADISON CO., VA, USA [36731] : 1830-1850 HIGLAND CO., OH, USA [36731] : 1850+ ANGOLA, IN, USA [37572] : 1700+ COLUMBIA CO., NY, USA [37572]

YAHNE ALL STARK CO., OH & IN, USA [38230]

YALE LUCY 1865+ GUILFORD, NY, USA [36356]

YANCEY 1700-40 HANOVER CO., VA, USA [37533] : 1642-1700S LYNCHBURG, VA, USA [37533] : 1760-90 MECKLENBURG CO., VA, USA [37533]

YANKOP 1855-1865 KEWEENAW CO., MI, USA [38009]

YANZER 1850 YORK TWP., IL, USA [38327]

YAP 1740+ BROMYARD, HEF, ENG [37833]

YAPP PRE 1800 KINGTON, HEF, ENG [37816] : PRE 1830 EAST HARPTREE, SOM, ENG [38376]

YARBER 1850-1930 AL, USA [36449]

YARBROUGH PRE 1850 AK, USA [38576]

YARD C1828 LONGLOAD, SOM, ENG [35760]

YARDLEY C1850 GREENWICH, KEN, ENG [35418] : 1820-1850 THORLEY, HRT, ENG [36017] : 1700-1800 FORTON, SAL, ENG [38453] : 1800S NEW MONKLAND, LKS, SCT [36032] : 1800S CARLUKE, LKS, SCT [36032]

YARDY 1880+ NSW, AUS [34421]

YARGUS ALL WORLDWIDE [38527]

YARNOLD 1830+ NSW, AUS [35520]

YARNTON ALL WORLDWIDE [34048]

YARROW ALL GUILDEN MORDEN, CAM, ENG [34838]

YARWOOD 1700-1900S LIVERPOOL, LAN, ENG [37221]

YATES WILLIAM 1830+ LAUNCESTON & LONGFORD, TAS, AUS [34910] : C1500-1700 MORLAND, WES, ENG [34296] : 1792+ MANCHESTER & WIGAN, LAN, ENG [34609] : C1900 PECKHAM, LND, ENG [34792] : 1800+ REDDITCH, WAR, ENG [35015] : C1865-1914 BANK TOP, LAN, ENG [35052] : 1813+ PLYMPTON, DEV, ENG [35706] : PRE 1811 ARKSEY, WRY, ENG [36011] : 1700+ LAN, ENG [36603] : 1800+ ECCLES, LAN, ENG [36603] : 1800+ BLACKBURN, LAN, ENG [36603] : PRE 1750 RANTON, STS, ENG [36701] : C1780-1820 SHIFNAL, SAL, ENG [36877] : 1740-1880 STAFFORD, STS, ENG [37118] : C1785 SAWDON, YKS, ENG [37536] : PRE 1800 YKS, ENG [37776] : 1700+ NTT, ENG [37839] : 1800S+ MDX, ENG [37868] : 1700-1900 SWALE MEDWAY, KEN, ENG [38249] : 1900+ RSA [34760] : 1400+ BOTHWELL, LKS, SCT [33989] : PRE 1820 LKS, SCT [36754] : 1700-1850 NEWPORT, RI, USA [36335] : 1700-1710 DUXBURY, MA, USA [38099] : PRE 1840 RAPPAHANNOCK CO., VA, USA [38311] : 1760-1835 CULPEPER CO., VA, USA [38311] : 1720-80 CAROLINE CO., VA, USA [38311]

YATES (SEE YEATES) [37658]

YAW PRE 1850 NY, USA [35295]

YAWKINS ALL WORLDWIDE [35924]

YAXLEY 1880S PENGUIN, TAS, AUS [35800] : 1800-1850 SYDERSTONE, NFK, ENG [35151]

YEA PRE 1800 DEV, ENG [34576]

YEAGER 1750+ PA, USA [34497] : 1739 MASONTOWN, PA, USA [37008]

YEALDING (SEE YIELDI [33918]

YEAMAN PRE 1850 EDINBURGH, SCT [37105]

YEAMON PRE 1820 EDINBURGH, MLN, SCT [35932]

YEANDLE ALL TIMBERSCOMBE, SOM, ENG [37378]

YEARDLEY C1856 HOLBROCK, WRY, ENG [34358] : PRE 1885 SHEFFIELD, WRY, ENG [37318]

YEARGIN ALL WORLDWIDE [38439]

YEARSLEY 1700+ LIVERPOOL, LAN, ENG [36769]

YEAST ALL ENG [37199]

YEATES 1700S TOLLER PORCORUM, DOR, ENG [35964] : ALL TUNSTALL, LAN, ENG [36587] : PRE 1685 SUTTON COURTNEY, BRK, ENG [37420] : ALL HAM, ENG [37658] : JOSEPH C. C1880 HANDSWORTH, STS, ENG [38452] : ALL DUTCHESS CO., NY, USA [37658]

YEATMAN 1951+ WA, AUS [34045] : 1785+ GILLINGHAM, DOR, SOM & WIL, ENG [34045] : PRE 1805 LEWISHAM, KEN, ENG [34105]

YEATS 1800+ FORGUE & NEW DEER, ABD, SCT [34326] : 1830+ GAMRIE, BAN, SCT [34515]

YEELEAS C1815 BERMONDSEY, LND, ENG [34972]

YEELES C1815 BERMONDSEY, LND, ENG [34972]

YEHLING 1800-1950 SYRACUSE, NY, USA [35318]

YELDON 1800S SPITALFIELDS, MDX & IOW, ENG [34887]

YELDS ALL WORLDWIDE [38329]

YELL C1805 LITTLE DUNHAM, NFK, ENG [34518] : PRE 1750 ESS, ENG [35642]

YELLAND 1800+ PLYMOUTH, DEV & CON, ENG [34718] : 1650-1750 ST STEPHENS IN BRANNEL, CON, ENG [35267] : 1700-1800 ST STEPHEN IN BRANNEL, CON, ENG [37457] : 1915-1935 SAN ANTONIO, TX, USA [35267]

YEMM 1760-1890 WESTBURY ON SEVERN, GLS, ENG [37118]

YENDRICK 1882-1945 FARRELL & MERCER, PA, USA &, SLOVAKIA [38063]

YENSCH C1870-1900 GIN GIN DISTRICT, QLD, AUS [35158] : C1851 STENDLE & STETTIN, PRE, GER [35158]

YENTOM ALL ENG [37670]

YEO 1900+ CAMBERWELL, SRY & LND, ENG [35495] : ALL TORRINGTON, DEV, ENG [37922] : PRE 1850 STOKE RIVERS, DEV, ENG [38205]

YEOLAND 1500+ DEV, ENG & AUS [33790]

YEOMANS C1730 AMHERST, NS, CAN [33910] : 1750-1800 PENSCOMBE, HEF, ENG [34552] : 1770+ MDX, ENG [36179] : PRE 1870 MANCHESTER, LAN, ENG [38428] : PRE 1900 UK [34944] : ALL WORLDWIDE [34944]

YESS PRE 1860 KROTOSHIN, POS, GER [38052]

YETTER PRE 1747 ROTTERDAM, NL [36958]

YETTS PRE 1820 EDINBURGH, MLN, SCT [35932]

YIBERNAS ALL ESP [38730] : ALL PHILIPPINE [38730] : ALL PT [38730]

YIELDING C1840 BATTLE, SSX, ENG [33918]

YOHO ALL WORLDWIDE [37036]

YONGE PHILIP 1770 SAVANNAH, GA, USA [35328] : FRANCIS 1740S SAVANNAH, GA, USA [37585]

YONKER DAVID P. 1819 OH, USA [37788]

YONTZ 1800-1850 FRANKLIN CO., PA, USA [38139]

YORCUM ALL PA & OH, USA [38043]

YORK 1806+ NSW, AUS [38771] : ANN 1761 BURTON STATHER, LIN, ENG [34091] : PRE 1855 SOM, ENG [35389] : 1600-1800 DALLINGTON & EWHURST, SSX, ENG [36485] : ALL SSX, ENG [37285] : PRE 1800 SOM, ENG [38771] : EDWARD 1812-1881 FINEDON, NTH, ENG [38776]

YORKE ALL SIMCOE CO., ONT, CAN [34465] : 1500-1800 NTH, ENG [34746] : ALL LEEDS, YKS, ENG [34765] : PRE 1830 MOULTON, NTH, ENG [34765] : 1800S MOULTON, NTH, ENG [35024] : PRE 1828 CLEVELAND, YKS, ENG [36039] : PRE 1900 LIVERPOOL, LAN, ENG [37776] : EDWARD 1812-1881 FINEDON, NTH, ENG [38776] : LUKE 1775-1855 OUNDLE, NTH, ENG [38776] : PRE 1900 IRL [37776] : PRE 1650 UK [34746]

YORKSTON PRE 1850 LINLITHGOW, STI, SCT [34097] : PRE 1860 EDINBURGH, MLN, SCT [34713] : PRE 1740 ELN, SCT [36679]

YOST PRE 1848 NORKA, SU [36721] : 1800+ PHILADELPHIA, PA, USA [36347]

YOUD 1720+ LIVERPOOL, LAN, ENG [36875]

YOUDEL PRE 1850 OLDHAM, LAN, ENG [36380]

YOUDLE PRE 1800 WIL & SON, ENG [37695]

YOUENS 1880+ BALLARAT, VIC, AUS [33915]

YOUKER JACOB 1790+ FULTON CO., NY, USA [36950] : PHILIP 1830+ FULTON CO., NY, USA [36950]

YOUNG JAMES 1863+ SANDHURST, VIC, AUS [33917] : 1852+ ADELAIDE, SA, AUS [33950] : 1850S MELBOURNE & GEELONG, VIC, AUS [34177] : 1860+ MAFFRA, VIC, AUS [34412] : 1848+ NSW, AUS [34534] : 1890-1990 MERRIWA, NSW, AUS [34534] : JAMES 1855-1874 BANDON, NSW, AUS [34698] : 1800S HOBART, TAS & SA, AUS [34971] : 1880S COSTERFIELD, VIC, AUS [35039] : 1803+ TAS, AUS [35062] : 1860+ BRISBANE, QLD, AUS [35442] : HARRIET 1846-1896 NSW & QLD, AUS [35501] : 1880+ MINMI, NSW, AUS [35573] : PRE 1871 LOCHINVAR, NSW, AUS [35573] : WILLIAM P. 1886 MELBOURNE, VIC, AUS [35593] : C1850+ NEWCASTLE, NSW, AUS [35598] : 1880S HEATHCOTE, VIC, AUS [35777] : 1850+ BUNBARTHA, VIC, AUS [35856] : 1884+

NEWCASTLE, NSW, AUS [36293] : 1860+ GEELONG, VIC, AUS [36612] : 1880-1940 TOWNSVILLE, QLD, AUS [37171] : 1880+ MARYBOROUGH, QLD, AUS [37171] : 1870+ FORDWICH, ONT, CAN [34080] : JAMES C1850 MONTREAL, QUE, CAN [36356] : 1821+ LANARK CO., ONT, CAN [36955] : ADAM 1833-1917 ALMONTE, ONT, CAN [37458] : 1780-1840 YORK CO., ONT, CAN [37477] : LEVEN PRE 1832 CAN [37837] : 1800S WELLAND CO., ONT, CAN [38440] : PRE 1848 LONGSHAWS MILL, NBL, ENG [33863] : JOSEPH 1800S CARLISLE, CUL, ENG [33950] : PRE 1850 MDX, ENG [33953] : HENRY PRE 1850 WOR, ENG [34222] : PRE 1880 WEST BROMWICH, STS, ENG [34615] : JOHN 1700-1900 BERMONDSEY, LND, ENG [34749] : 1800+ HARLOW, ESS, ENG [34818] : 1850 NORWICH, NFK, ENG [34890] : RICHARD PRE 1710 LONG COMPTON, WAR, ENG [34908] : 1700+ GRITTLETON, WIL, ENG [34970] : JOHN C1853-1917 PADDINGTON, LND, ENG [34997] : PRE 1891 LONDON, ENG [35048] : C1822 TONBRIDGE, KEN, ENG [35261] : C1770 CHITTINGFOLD, SRY, ENG [35261] : PRE 1760 GREAT BEDWYN, WIL, ENG [35346] : ALL LONDON, ENG [35346] : 1750+ YKS, ENG [35370] : PRE 1850 SWAFFHAM, NFK, ENG [35462] : HANNAH C1803 STROUD, GLS, ENG [35560] : MARIA 1813-1888 KIMPTON, HRT, ENG [35634] : PRE 1650 ESS, ENG [35642] : 1840S BRIGHTSON, IOW, ENG [35728] : ALL BUTTERWICK, LIN, ENG [36144] : C1800 BRISTOL, GLS, ENG [36161] : 1848-1884 ALVINGTON, GLS, ENG [36293] : JAMES 1850S BRIGHTON, ENG [36316] : PRE 1680 LENHAM, KEN, ENG [36326] : 1850+ LIVERPOOL, ENG [36368] : 1700-1800 GREAT LANGTON, NRY, ENG [36472] : PRE 1800 DOR, ENG [36479] : 1800-1820 ST BRIDES, LND, ENG [36586] : PRE 1860 SOUTHWARK, LND & SRY, ENG [36612] : 1820 RUGELEY, STS, ENG [36649] : C1720+ BOCKING, ESS, ENG [37063] : PRE 1880 BIRKENHEAD, CHS, ENG [37171] : 1700+ CAMPTON, BDF, ENG [37304] : 1700S WITLEY, SRY, ENG [37309] : ALL EAST CHINNOCK, SOM, ENG [37378] : PRE 1850 KIRTLINGTON, OXF, ENG [37832] : LEVEN 1832+ LONDON, ENG [37837] : 1700+ NTT, ENG [37839] : C1830 GATESHEAD, DUR, ENG [37859] : 1700-1850 BRAYTON, WRY, ENG [38381] : JOHN PRE 1840 BALLYMONEY, ANT, IRL [33940] : CATHERINE 1740-1844 TIP, WAT & LEX, IRL [34514] : MARIA 1740-1844 TIP, WAT & LEX, IRL [34514] : PRE 1850 IRL [35414] : ALL BELFAST, ANT, IRL [35474] : WILLIAM 1800S LONDONDERRY, IRL [35593] : WILLIAM P. 1860S LONDONDERRY, IRL [35593] : PRE 1884 BELFAST, ANT, IRL [35601] : PRE 1850 TIP, IRL [35750] : ALL SLI, IRL [35824] : 1700-1899 DRUMNABOLESS & KILLYMADDY, TYR, IRL [36080] : 1700-1800 IRL [36679] : 1800+ NIBLOCH, ANT, IRL [36827] : MARY 1830 MANORHAMILTON, LET, IRL [36860] : 1700-1800 WEX, IRL [37844] : OSBORNE PRE 1850S OMAGH, TYR, IRL [37906] : ALEXANDER PRE 1850S EDENFOGARY (OMAGH), TYR, IRL [37906] : 1700+ ANNYGINNY, TYR, IRL [38001] : 1858+ DUNEDIN, NZ [34673] : ALL TIMARU, NZ [36870] : 1862+ HOKITIKA, NZ [36870] : 1880+ WINTON, SOUTH IS., NZ [38288] : PRE 1851 DUMFERMLINE, FIF, SCT [33866] : 1800+ CELLERDYKE, FIF, SCT [33955] : PRE 1838 INVERNESS, INV, SCT [34080] : ALL EDINBURGH, MLN, SCT [34093] : C1790 INVERKEITHING, FIF, SCT [34118] : 1750+

CRAILING, ROX, SCT [34239] : JOHN PRE 1850
COLDSTREAM, BEW, SCT [34282] : ADAM PRE
1850 COLDSTREAM, BEW, SCT [34282] : 1800-1830S
LOCHWINNOCH, RFW, SCT [34359] : PRE 1805
WILTON, ROX, SCT [34501] : CATHARINE PRE
1850 SCT [34553] : PRE 1805 ANS, SCT [34617] : PRE
1858 MLN, SCT [34673] : C1820 BRECHIN, ANS,
SCT [34713] : C1840 FARNELL, ANS, SCT [34713] :
1770S LANGHOLM, DFS, SCT [34991] : PRE 1800
DUNDEE, ANS, SCT [35007] : ALEXANDER PRE
1840 INVERNESS, INV, SCT [35250] : 1736-74
CADDER, LKS, SCT [35252] : PRE 1900
CLYDEBANK, DNB, SCT [35378] : JANE PRE
1870S LOGIE, FIF, SCT [35433] : PRE 1800
KINCLAVEN, PER, SCT [35448] : WILLIAM 1750+
DUNDEE, ANS, SCT [35911] : JAMES ALL EAST
KILBRIDE, LKS, SCT [35957] : MATTHEW 1836+
EAST KILBRIDE, LKS, SCT [35957] : PRE 1750
OKI, SCT [36436] : PRE 1850 RENFREW, RFW, SCT
[36765] : ALL TILLICOULTRY, CLK, SCT [36870] :
1700-1921 DUNFERMLINE, FIF, SCT [36894] : PRE
1850 CARMUNNOCK & EAST KILBRIDE, LKS,
SCT [36955] : ANDREW 1813+ LKS, SCT [36955] :
ISABEL C1760S DUNNING, PER, SCT [37106] :
HELEN C1836 GARVALD, ELN, SCT [37168] :
HELEN C1836 PATHHEAD, ELN, SCT [37168] :
JAMES C1830 SPOTT, ELN, SCT [37168] : JAMES
C1830 GARVALD, ELN, SCT [37168] : HELEN
C1836 SPOTT, ELN, SCT [37168] : JAMES C1830
PATHHEAD, ELN, SCT [37168] : 1700+ AYR, SCT
[37434] : 1740-1920 EAGLESHAM, RFW, SCT [37783]
: 1880S GORE BRIDGE, MLN, SCT [38475] :
THOMAS 1820+ SYMINGTON, LKS, SCT [38492] :
ROBERT PRE 1888 DALMELLINGTON, AYR, SCT
& CAN [36677] : 1900-1950 NEW YORK, NY, USA
[34242] : 1860-1900 SPENCER CO., IN, USA [35307] :
1615-1745 EATHAM, MA, USA [36944] : PRE 1800
GREENVILLE, SC, USA [38027] : 1759-80
MONTGOMERY, NY, USA [38151] : 1700S SUSSEX
CO., NJ, USA [38440] : 1700-1800 NEWARK, NJ,
USA [38524] : 1820S MON, WLS [35156] : ALL
WORLDWIDE [35875]

YOUNG, JOHN PRE 1922 REGENTS PARK ZOO,
LND, ENG [35551]

YOUNGBERRY 1856+ TENTERFIELD, NSW, AUS
[34775] : PRE 1856 SWE [34775]

YOUNGBLOOD 1820S SC, USA [37792]

YOUNGER PRE 1867 ALLOA, CLK, SCT [37975]

YOUNGHUSBAND 1860 SOUTH SHIELDS, NBL,
ENG [35756] : 1695-1750 HENRICO CO., VA, USA
[36337]

YOUNGMAN PRE 1858 LONDON, ENG [34648] :
1750-1890 SUDBURY, SFK, ENG [35775]

YOUNGS 1800+ KENNINGHALL, NFK, ENG
[34639] : PRE 1900 MANNINGTREE, ESS, ENG
[36477] : 1894 PA, USA [38450]

YOUNGSON ALL EDINBURGH, MLN, SCT [34093]

YOUNKINS 1800-1900 VANDERGRIFT, PA, USA
[36958]

YOUREN ALL WORLDWIDE [37408]

YOURIN ALL WORLDWIDE [37408]

YOURN ALL WORLDWIDE [37408]

YOURNE ALL WORLDWIDE [37408]

YOUSON PRE 1850 LEICESTER, LEI, ENG [34311]

YOUST 1770 BAV, GER [36446]

YOXALL 1803 FINSBURY, MDX, ENG [34726]

YOXON ALL WORLDWIDE [34433]

YUCHACKA 1892 CRACOW, KR, POL [38537]

YUGERE C1814 QUE, CAN [37030]

YUILE ANDREW 1800S RENFREW, RFW, SCT
[36633]

YUILL 1841+ BATHURST & YOUNG, NSW, AUS
[33763] : PRE 1841 BALFRON, STI, SCT [33763] :
PRE 1859 SCT [33777] : 1700-1850 EAST KILBRIDE,
LKS, SCT [37783]

YUILLE 1800-1850 EDINBURGH & GLASGOW, VIC,
AUS [33836] : ALL DARLEITH, DNB, SCT [34173]

YULE 1840-1900 VIC, AUS [33836] : 1876+ IPSWICH
& RICHMOND, QLD, AUS [34189] : 1919
PARRAMATTA, NSW, AUS [35409] : 1800-1850
EDINBURGH & GLASGOW, SCT [33836] : 1800-
1850 DUNFERMLINE & KIRKALDY, FIF, SCT
[36268]

YUTZE 1870-1900 OR, USA [36934]

YVANCSAK 1870S ZDIAR, SLOVAKIA, CS [38223]

ZABEL C1800-190! GRAUDENZ, WPR, GER & USA
[38309] : 1825-1901 VALLEY CO., NE & WI, USA &
GER [38309]

ZABELL PRE 1900 LND, ENG [38777]

ZABINSKI ALL LIBIAZ, KRAKAU, POL [38678]

ZACHARIAH 1800+ BRIDGEND, GLA, WLS [37985]

ZACHARY PRE 1850 MDX & ESS, ENG [37320]

ZACKRISEN 1865-1900 STOCKHOLM, SWE [37822]

ZACKRISON 1865-1900 STOCKHOLM, SWE [37822]

ZAHM 1700+ ALS, FRA [34405] : 1800+ NY, USA
[34405]

ZAHN ALL LUBBUN, GER [36571] : 1848-1888
GRAND RIDGE, IL, USA [37810]

ZAHNER PRE 1858 WUE, GER [34886]

ZAININGER PRE 1855 GER [34886]

ZAK PRE 1880 KRALOVIC, PLZEN, CS [35290]

ZALAC 1873-1929 DETROIT & WAYNE, MI, USA &
YU [38063]

ZAMBURG 1700-1990 EUROPE [38096] : 1700-1990
NEW YORK, NY, USA [38096]

ZANETTI 1800-1900 BELLUNO, ITL [38337]

ZANKER 1880+ MELBOURNE, VIC, AUS [34904]

ZAPATA 1500-1630 MEXICO CITY, MEXICO [36340]

ZAPLE 1837-1860 TORQUAY, DEV, ENG [37418]

ZASTROW ALL STOLP, POM, GER [37349] : 1900-
1925 NEW PLYMOUTH, NZ [37349]

ZAWADZKI ALL WORLDWIDE [35257]

ZEBIERE C1880 BBT, BEL [34521] : C1860-1920
CHARLEROI, HNT, BEL [34521] : C1905 OAK
LAKE, MAN, CAN [34521] : 1900-1930 PIPESTONE,
MAN, CAN [34521] : 1925-1930 DUMAS, SAS, CAN
[34521]

ZECHNULA PRE 1914 CS [37519] : PRE 1914 HU
[37519] : PRE 1914 VIENNA, OES [37519] : PRE 1914
YU [37519]

ZECKER PRE 1880 TEMPLIN, PREUSZEN, GER
[36918]

ZEEB PRE 1880 BRD [38238]

ZEIMER PRE 1875 SAAFELD, MOHRUNGEN, GER
[35463] : 1870+ BUFFALO, NY, USA [35463]

ZEINCKS 1700-C1740S GEL, NL [38350]

ZEISBERG ALL SIL, GER [38607]

ZEITLER 1600-1675 WESTHEIM, BAY, BRD [35311]

ZEITLINGER JOHN 1824-1844 BAV, GER [38150]

ZELDER 1880+ ALLEGENY, PA, USA [38185]

ZELKOVITZ 1900-30 VONAJ, HU [38236]

ZELL PRE 1810 BALTIMORE, MD, USA [38321]

ZELLEN C1800+ FRANKFURT, FFO, DDR [33792]

ZELLER PRE 1866 FRANKFORT MAIN, GER [38222]

ZELLMER 1800+ GER & SU [34087]

ZELTNER PRE 1880 ENG [35757] : PRE 1880
LITHUANIA [35757]

ZEMBRYZKI ALL WORLDWIDE [35257]

ZENOR 1765-1900 PA, OH & KY, USA [36901]

ZERBE PRE 1700 KETTENBACH, GER [37587] : PRE
1712 PA, USA [37587]

ZERHER BARB 1843-1860 SPEYER, BAV, GER [33752]

ZERON 1780+ STORMONT CO., ONT, CAN [38411]

ZETTEL 1831 WATERLOO TWP.& CULROSS TWP, ONT, CAN [34503]
ZEVEN ALL WORLDWIDE [35389]
ZEVENBERGEN 1800+ HARDERWIJK, OIJ, NL [35338]
ZEVENBOOM PRE 1900 NL [34478]
ZIEGLER PRE 1850 HEIDELBURG, ONT, CAN [34159] : ALL STETTEN, SH, CH [35334] : PRE 1840 GER [34159] : PERRY 1815-1902 UNITY, COLUMBIANA CO., OH, USA [38127]
ZIELINSKI ALL LIDZIANKA, VOL, SU [37041]
ZIELMINSKI 1853+ HERRON, POS, GER [37503] : 1853+ IL, USA [37503]
ZIEMANN 1825+ DRAMBURG, PREUBEN, POM, GER [34238]
ZIGARLOVICOVA ALL WORLDWIDE [38733]
ZIGLER ADAM 1800+ BOWERS, BERKS CO., PA, USA [38127]
ZIJTVELD PRE 1900 NL [34478]
ZILLMANN 1780-1850 REHDEN, WPR, GER [38599]
ZILM 1700-1800 BRA, GER [38490]
ZIMERMAN ALL NABURN, WUE, GER [38176]
ZIMMERDAHL ALL WORLDWIDE [36320]
ZIMMERMAN ALL DAUPHIN CO., PA, USA [35304] : 1700-1850 BUTLER CO., PA, USA [36924] : GEORGE 1850 SENECA CO., NY, USA [38142]
ZIMMERMANN 1800 BINSWANGER, GER [36596] : 1700+ DELLANBURG, GER & OES [38735]
ZINK 1885+ BURWOOD, NSW, AUS [34588] : 1800+ NUREMBERG, BAV, BRD [34922] : 1860+ SOUTHSEA, HAM & LND, ENG [34922] : ALL GOTHA, GER [34588]
ZINSS C1891 BALTIMORE, MD, USA [38650]
ZIPF ALL KIPPENHEIMWEILER, BAD, GER [36532]
ZIPFIN PRE 1831 MOSBACH, BAD, GER [37819]
ZIPPEL PRE 1852 NECKEN, PRUSSIA [35438]
ZIPPRICH C1800 EISLEBEN, HAL, DDR [38677]
ZIRBEL PRE 1836 POTSDAM, GER [35465]
ZIRCKEL C1700 WORMS, RPF, GER [38348]
ZIV 1900+ POL [38481]
ZIZL 1700+ ZNOJMO, MORAVIA, CS [37088]
ZOCK ALL WORLDWIDE [38189]
ZOELDER 1880+ GER [38185]
ZOLLER PRE 1855 DORFPROZOLTERN, BAV, GER [34886] : PRE 1896 LODZ, POL [37574]
ZONDAGH PRE 1900 CAPE, RSA [36432]
ZORICHAK 1870S ZDIAR, SLOVAKIA, CS [38223]
ZORN 1925-1955 VANDERGRIFT, PA, USA [37597]
ZOSOBNEKE PRE 1900 LUBNA GONEZ, GER [35339]
ZOUVER 1800S OH, USA [36338]
ZSCHORN PRE 1850 LE, POL [35208]
ZUANE 1800+ CTE VAUDREUIL, QUE, CAN [36657]
ZUBLER ALL GER & USA [38043]
ZUCZNIK PRE 1900 LWOW, LW, POL [38164]
ZUFELD PRE 1800 RHINEBECK, NY, USA & GER [38386]
ZUFTEN 1800S ZARPEN, SHO, GER [34688]
ZUG 1725+ LANCASTER CO., PA & VA, USA [36540]
ZUGEL ALL WORLDWIDE [37808]
ZUIDWEG 1700S ZUID BEVELAND, ZEL, NL [38350]
ZUKERMAN PRE 1899 ENG & POL [35757]
ZUR BRUCKEN 1592+ HANAU, HEN, GER [38667]
ZURBRUGG 1700-1850 FRUTIGEN, BE, CH [35283]
ZURCHER PRE 1870 LANGNON, LU, CH [38125] : ALL WORLDWIDE [36078]
ZUREK ALL MYSLOWITZ, SIL, GER [38678]
ZUR GATHEN 1750+ METTMAN, GER [35370]
ZUVER 1800S OH, USA [36338]
ZWEIFEL 1800S SONOMA CO., CA, USA [37048]
ZWEIGBERGK EVA MAR L. 1868 SKARA, SWE [38564]

ZWEMER (SEE SWEMER) [38350]
ZWIETEREN VAN 1760+ RAASVELD & ROTTERDAM, PRE & ZH, FRG & NL [38712]
ZWIETON (VAN) C1900 ALPHEN & RUYN, ZUH, NL [38713]
ZYMUTTA 1732-1874 DREISSIGHUFEN & DOEHLAU, OPR, GER [34083]

SUBJECTS

The following subject entries, submitted by contributors, have been divided into eight categories listed below. Within each category the items have been listed alphabetically according to the main entry but not necessarily alphabetically within an identical main entry.

Future entry forms will enable contributors to indicate under which category they require their entry to appear. It is suggested that the article following the Introduction be read for further particulars.

Categories:

G:	General	O:	Occupations
I:	Individuals	P:	Places
M:	Migration	R:	Religion
MY:	Military	S:	Shipping & Ships.

The items listed in this section are in no way linked to the main Surname section of this Directory.

The I: (Individuals) category of this section allows the contributor to record more biographical data than what is normally allowed in the main Surname section of the Directory. Some of the other categories will be of assistance in seeking out a particular person by association with a place, occupation, military service etc. Other entries in this section of the Directory indicate that the contributor has a specialist interest in that subject and is interested in corresponding with others with the same interest.

G: **ABORIGINES** QLD, AUS. 1850+ **[37350]**
G: **ADAMS CARS, TAXI SERVICE** ROSEBUD & DROMANA, VIC, AUS. PRE 1960 **[36621]**
G: **AFRICAN AMERICANS** BRISTOL, MA, USA. PRE 1880 **[37807]**
G: **ALIASES, USE OF** MACKISON & MAXWELL, PER, SCT. PRE 1830 **[36125]**
G: **AMALGAMATED WORKDERS ASSN** KALGOORLIE. WA, AUS. 1897-1903 **[35570]**
G: **ANCIENT KLEVE AM RHINE** VAN KLEVE, ORIGINS OF CLIVE. 600-1400 **[36169]**
G: **ANTI-RENT WARS** NEW YORK. ALL **[38369]**
G: **ARMIGERS MIGRATING TO** CAN. ALL **[38439]**
G: **ASYLUMS & HOSPITALS** SSX, ENG. 1600S **[36679]**
G: **AUSTRALIAN ABORIGINES** JENOLAN CAVES, OBERON & COWRA, NSW, AUS. 1800S **[37556]**
G: **AUSTRALIAN FLAG** WINNERS COMPETITION DESIGN OF. 1901 **[35375]**
G: **AYDON VETCH** OFFICER, RN. 1914-1918. 1880-1945 **[34249]**
G: **BC SHUSWAP INDIANS,** CAN KAMLOOPS & SAVONA TRIBES. PRE 1895 **[36729]**
G: **BELTON AS A FORENAME.** ALL **[37241]**
G: **BISHOPS CLOSE METHODIST SCHOOL** IN TUDHOE GRANGE, DUR, ENG. C1900 **[38269]**
G: **BLUE COAT SCHOOL** LIVERPOOL, LAN, ENG. 1841+ **[34624]**
G: **BONDS AND SHARES** WITH ORIGINAL SIGNATURE. PRE 1850 **[38616]**
G: **BOUND BOYS APPRENTICES** – ENG TO CAN. 1820+ **[34140]**
G: **BREWERY** PENKETH BREWERIES, LAN, ENG. 1850+ **[36815]**
G: **BRITISH EAST INDIA COMPANY** LOGANS, IN ANY CAPACITY. ANY **[36001]**
G: **BRITISH OCCUPATION OF BERMUDA** . 1770-1780 **[37821]**
G: **BROWN FAMILY** BROWN QUERY QUEST. 1600-1900 **[36321]**
G: **BRUCE FAMILY** BRUCE QUERY QUEST. 1600+ **[36321]**
G: **BUTCHER** PHILIP HAFFNER, KINGSTON, ONT, CAN. 1830+ **[37047]**
G: **CALLIGRAPHY** . ALL **[34949]**
G: **CAMBODIA** PHNOM PENH FAMILIES. 1863+ **[38005]**
G: **CAMBODIA** ROYAL FAMILY. 1773+ **[38005]**
G: **CANALS** – ROCHDALE, LAN, ENG COGSWELL FAMILY 1790-1860. **[38259]**
G: **CAR ACCIDENTS,** LND, ENG INVOLVING WOMEN. PRE 1920 **[35362]**
G: **CARGO COMPANY** CALEB MAULIN OF BECKINHAM, NTT, ENG. 1760+ **[35092]**
G: **CARNEGIE MEDAL FOR BRAVERY** TOM HASSELL. 1800+ **[35403]**
G: **CARTOLOGY** PROVINCIAL MAPS. ALL **[34949]**
G: **CEMETERY** BALMAIN "CATHOLIC", NSW, AUS. **[35843]**
G: **CERTIFICATES (AUSTRALIAN)** UNWANTED, COLLECTION AND INDEX OF. **[35198]**
G: **CHANGE OF NAME** WALLACE-HARKISON, SCT-MELBOURNE. PRE 1850S **[35958]**
G: **CHANGE OF NAME** WANTED FOR ALFRED LEAHY ARELETT. 1872+ **[35754]**
G: **CHILD WELFARE RECORDS** FOSTER CHILDREN – NSW, AUS. 1880+ **[36272]**
G: **CINEMAS** SCT. C1915 **[37330]**
G: **COLBY ON SAMS ISLAND** RASMUSEN – BIRTHS. 1735-1760 **[36340]**
G: **COMPUTER INDEXING** IBM COMPATIBLE SHAREWARE. ALL **[36551]**
G: **COMPUTERS** GENEALOGICAL USES. ALL **[38377]**
G: **COMPUTER USING** ARCHIMEDES SOFTWARE. **[37698]**
G: **CONVICTS** FEMALE MORETON BAY, AUS. 1826-1839 **[33783]**
G: **CONVICTS** BLACKBURN, LAN, ENG, TO AUS. ALL **[35362]**
G: **CONVICTS FROM** MON, WLS & GLS, ENG TO AUS. 1841+ **[37040]**
G: **CONVICTS** SOUTH WEST OF WESTERN AUSTRALIA. 1850+ **[35139]**
G: **CONVICT JOHN WARD,** LONGFORD & BURNIE, TAS, AUS. 1850-60 **[38729]**
G: **CRAWFORD PEERAGE** IRISH LINDSAY-CRAWFORD CLAIMANTS. 1810-48 **[38054]**
G: **CRAWFORD PEERAGE** IRISH CRAWFORD CLAIMANTS. 1810-48 **[38054]**
G: **CURACAO (SLAVE) TRADERS.** 1750-1830 **[36340]**
G: **CURACAO JEWS.** 1750-1830 **[36340]**
G: **CURLING** WORLDWIDE. 1700-1950 **[38388]**
G: **CURRITUCK CO.,** NC, USA JURY LISTS. 1700-1760 **[38326]**
G: **CUSTOMS, PECULIAR** SCT. 1600-1900 **[38388]**
G: **CYCLE CLUBS** LONDON, ENG. 1870-1900 **[36794]**
G: **DARTFORD FOOTBALL CLUB** INDEX OF PLAYERS AND OFFICIALS. 1880+ **[37213]**
G: **DESERTERS** POLAND WAR. 1885-1915 **[38369]**
G: **DESMOND REVENUE CRUISER** WOOLNER, DAVID, CON, ENG. 1825-1880 **[36398]**
G: **DISAPPEARED** – HOUDE (AIME) DETROIT, MI, USA AREA BORN 1906. 1925-1932 **[38525]**
G: **DISORDERS OF THE NERVOUS SYSTEM** OF POSSIBLE HEREDITARY NATURE. 1800+ **[37754]**
G: **DOMESDAY BOOK** SPURR, SPUR, SPURRE REFERENCES. 1086 **[36463]**
G: **DRUMMOND ISLAND** VOYAGEURS. 1700-1825 **[36703]**
G: **DYING TECHNOLOGY** RIVER IRK, LAN, ENG. PRE 1850 **[36635]**
G: **EARLY CLOSING (8 HRS)** BALLARAT, VIC, AUS. 1850+ **[36240]**
G: **ENGLISH ESTATES** OWNERS, STAFF, TENANTS. PRE 1930 **[35362]**
G: **FAMILIES** BEL. 1600-1900 **[38676]**
G: **FAMILIES** GER. 1600-1800 **[38676]**
G: **FARNHAM ESTATE** CAV, IRL. 1760-1830S **[34088]**
G: **FARRARS ISLAND,** VA, USA A HISTORY. 1600+ **[38326]**
G: **FARRARS ISLAND,** VA, USA SOME DESCENDANTS. 1600+ **[38326]**
G: **FREDRICH WILHELM II, KING OF PRUSSIA** ILLEGITIMATE CHILDREN OF. **[38495]**

G: **FREEMAN OF CITY OF LONDON** ROBERT WINTER FORREST, LONDON, ENG. 1813 **[37341]**
G: **FRENCH ARISTOCRATIC FAMILIES** MONTREAUX MUSEUM, CH. 1700+ **[36624]**
G: **FRENCH ORIGIN** JOLIN & ARAULT. PRE 1732 **[36418]**
G: **GAMBLING, POKER** DUBBO & PROSPECT, NSW, AUS. C1840+ **[33930]**
G: **GAS** HISTORY OF PROVISION OF GAS IN QLD, AUS. 1860+ **[35853]**
G: **GENEALOGIES** EUROPEAN ROYALTY. ANY **[34416]**
G: **GENEALOGIES** EUROPEAN NOBILITY. ANY **[34416]**
G: **GENEALOGIES** GERMAN ROYALTY. ANY **[34416]**
G: **GENEALOGY & COMPUTERS** COMPUTER PROGRAMS. ALL **[36713]**
G: **GOLDEN CROSS MINE** WAITEKAURI, NZ — HISTORY OF. 1900S **[36611]**
G: **GRENADA, WEST INDIES** DEATHS. 1840S **[35813]**
G: **GUARDIAN SOCIETY FOR PROTECTION OF YOUNG LADIES** WHITECHAPEL, LND, ENG. 1815-1825 **[38731]**
G: **GYPSIES** NEW FOREST (WIL & HAM), ENG. 1700 **[34121]**
G: **GYPSY LEE** SOUTHERN ENGLAND. **[36978]**
G: **GYPSY QUEEN** URANIA BOSWELL. **[36978]**
G: **HANDWRITING** . ALL **[34949]**
G: **HAWKSHEAD GRAMMAR SCHOOL, CUL, ENG** PUPILS. 1790-1810 **[34241]**
G: **HERALDRY** MEMORIALS AND ARMS OF CLIVE & CLIFFE. 1100-1800 **[36169]**
G: **HERALDRY** SURNAME INDEX WORLDWIDE. ALL **[35783]**
G: **HIGHLAND CLEARANCES** KILMUIR, ISLE OF SKYE. C1780 **[38391]**
G: **HOMOSEXUALS** CONVICTS IN AUS. PRE 1900 **[35697]**
G: **HOUSING, RURAL** SCT. 1700-1850 **[38388]**
G: **HUDSONS BAY COMPANY** ORKNEY EMPLOYEES. 1700-1850 **[37426]**
G: **HUDSONS BAY COMPANY** CREE INDIAN MARRIAGES. 1700-1850 **[37426]**
G: **HUGUENOTS** MOWE, MOE FAMILY. 1580-1640 **[38054]**
G: **HUNTERS OF NORTHUMBERLAND** ALPHABETIC DIRECTORY. ALL **[37835]**
G: **ILLEGITIMATE CHILD** WHAT BECAME OF ALFRED LEAHY ARELETT. 1872+ **[35754]**
G: **INDEXES IN AUSTRALIA** ON SPECIALISED TOPICS, REGISTER OF. **[35198]**
G: **INDIAN EMPIRE** CLIVE SEVERALLY IN INDIA AND ARMIES. 1600-1800 **[36169]**
G: **INDIANS** USA. ALL **[38023]**
G: **INN AT "SIGN OF THE STILL"** BOSTON, LIN, ENG, PASS FAM. 1800S **[34335]**
G: **ISOLATED GRAVES, AUS** IN UNCONSECRATED GROUND. **[34534]**
G: **JACOBITE ACTIVITY** IN IRELAND. 1689-1715 **[38054]**
G: **KILKENNY JAILS** . 1770-1938 **[38299]**
G: **KILLINGWORTH COLLIERY** . 1900-1930 **[35570]**
G: **KING JOHN** ILLEGITIMATE CHILDREN. ALL **[35901]**
G: **KINGSTON ESTATE RECORDS** TENANTS OF. 1800-1850 **[38299]**
G: **KKD, SCT** RESEARCH HELP WITH YOUR NAMES IN THIS CO.. 1700+ **[37644]**
G: **KNIGHTS OF ENGLAND** COMPLETE LIST FROM EARLIEST TIMES. **[36619]**
G: **KNIGHTS OF HASTINGS** THOSE WHO FOUGHT IN THE BATTLE. 1066 **[36619]**
G: **LADY SHENTON GOLD MINE** MENZIES, WA, AUS — HISTORY OF. 1900S **[36611]**
G: **LALOR, LAWLOR & LAWLER** IN AUS & NZ. PRE 1900 **[35697]**
G: **LANDHOLDERS INDEX** ALL NSW, AUS. 1885 **[37561]**
G: **LATIN COGNOMA** BERBER ORIGINS OF SOME LATIN NAMES. ALL **[37742]**
G: **LATIN SCHOOL** D-7312 KIRCHHEIM, GER. 1250-1950 **[38673]**
G: **LITERATURE AND GENEALOGY** GERMAN LITERATURE. 1500-1850 **[38667]**
G: **LIVERPOOL INSTITUTE, ENG** STUDENTS. 1922-1928 **[35025]**
G: **LONGEVITY** AGE 90+, ALL ENG & AUS. ANY **[35117]**
G: **LOYALISTS UE** SCT — NY — SHELBURNE, NS, CAN. 1783+ **[36713]**
G: **LOYALISTS** CAN & USA. C1765 **[37180]**
G: **LUMBIS** FAMILY NAME DERIVATIONS. ALL **[36473]**
G: **MANORIAL RECORDS** SFK, ENG. ALL **[37473]**
G: **MARIONETTENSPIELER** ALL. PRE 1990 **[38664]**
G: **MARIONETTENSPIELER** GER. PRE 1990 **[38664]**
G: **MARRIAGES** MANCHESTER CATHEDRAL, ENG. 1825+ **[37259]**
G: **MASONIC ORDER** DIVER DR GORDON R.. C1870-90 **[38466]**
G: **MAYOR & MAGISTRATE** BARROW IN FURNESS, LAN, ENG. 1903-1906 **[37120]**
G: **METROPOLITAN — VICERS CO LTD** REGISTER OF EX-APPRENTICES. 1902-1957 **[37759]**
G: **MICROFICHE PUBLICATIONS** SASE FOR LIST. ALL **[36551]**
G: **MIDVALE STEEL** PHILADELPHIA, PA, USA, DESCENDANTS OF FORMER EMPLOYEES. 1880-1920 **[37793]**
G: **MISSING - HOUDE (AIME)** DETROIT, MI, USA AREA BORN 1906. 1925-1932 **[38525]**
G: **MOSS END IRON WORKS** LKS, SCT. 1850S **[35565]**
G: **MOWAT** SURNAME HISTORY. ALL **[34381]**
G: **NANCOLLAS** ANY CAN & USA. 1800-99 **[36404]**
G: **NEWMAN** ALIAS & NAME CHANGE. ALL **[34079]**
G: **NEWSPAPER INDEXES IN AUSTRALIA** REGISTER OF. **[35198]**
G: **NORFOLK ISLAND** CONVICTS. 1836+ **[37497]**
G: **NORMAN POWS** SURNAMES OF INTERNEES AT NORMAN CROSS PETERBOROUGH, CAM, ENG. 1785-1820 **[37347]**
G: **NSW, AUS** LANDHOLDERS INDEX HELD. 1885 **[37561]**

G: **OLD BAILEY, LND, ENG, CONVICTIONS** COX, FRANCES. 25 FEB 1789 **[33864]**
G: **OPERA "WILLIAM DERRINCOURT" BY ROBERT SMALLEY. [37976]**
G: **ORANGE LODGE** HOLYTOWN, LKS, SCT. 1850S **[35565]**
G: **ORPHANAGE, CHERTSEY, SRY, ENG** RECORDS, ORPHANS. ALL **[35362]**
G: **PACKARD FAMILY** PACKARD QUERY QUEST. 1600-1900 **[36321]**
G: **PEARLY KINGS & QUEENS** . 1900+ **[36978]**
G: **PELLY (EX. IRL) TO USA, CAN & AUS.** 1800+ **[38301]**
G: **PERSONAL COATS OF ARMS** OWNERS TO DESCENDANTS, AUS, NZ. TO 1991 **[38754]**
G: **PHILLIPS FAMILY** PHILLIPS QUERY QUEST. 1600-1900 **[36321]**
G: **PHOTOGRAPHS** DATING & IDENTIFYING OLD PHOTOS. 1849-1950 **[36551]**
G: **PIERROT & PIERRETTE SHOWS** SCOTTISH HOLIDAY RESORTS. 1910-1920S **[34229]**
G: **PIONEER REGISTERS IN AUSTRALIA** LISTING OF. **[35198]**
G: **POOR LAW SETTLEMENT ROLL** ENG. 1600-1900 **[34236]**
G: **POOR LAW UNION WORKHOUSES** ENG. 1600-1900 **[34236]**
G: **POORHOUSES** RESIDENTS OF GOODMANHAM, YKS, ENG. 1800-1850 **[34143]**
G: **POSTCARDS & STAMPS** EXCHANGED WORLDWIDE. **[35291]**
G: **POW (PRISONER OF WAR)** RUSSIA/POLAND. 1885-1915 **[38369]**
G: **PRIVATE BOYS COLLEGE** NELSON, NZ. 1876+ **[36624]**
G: **PUBLIC WATER SUPPLY TO CITY** GLASGOW, SCT. 1790-1830 **[36985]**
G: **QUARTER SESSIONS RECORDS** WRY, ENG. 1640-1840 **[37754]**
G: **R CANADIAN MOUNTED POLICE** AMOS & JENNY WELLER, CAN. 1890-1930 **[36398]**
G: **RAC ACU** MOTOR CYCLING. ALFRED JAMES DIXON. 1900+ **[35403]**
G: **RAGGED SCHOOLS** DOWN, IRL. 1880-1920 **[35219]**
G: **RAILWAY ACCIDENTS** NAVIGATORS. 1860-1870 **[34828]**
G: **RAILWAY HISTORY** GREAT WESTERN RAILWAY, ENG. 1840+ **[36462]**
G: **RAYMENT** ONE NAME STUDY. ANY **[35174]**
G: **RECORDS, MILL HOUSE ACADEMY** RUNCORN, CHS, ENG. 1860-1868 **[35341]**
G: **ROBERTSONS IN LKS, SCT** WIVES AND FAMILIES. ALL **[35415]**
G: **ROBERTSONS IN MLN, SCT** WIVES AND FAMILIES. ALL **[35415]**
G: **ROSS CIRCUS** USA. 1900+ **[34790]**
G: **ROYAL DESCENT** OF ENG, SCT, IRL, EUROPE. ALL **[36619]**
G: **ROYAL PRUSSIAN ORDER** . 1873 **[35018]**
G: **RUSSIAN DYNASTIC FAMILIES** RURICK PRINCES OF. PRE 1820 **[37742]**
G: **RUTHIN GRAMMAR SCHOOL, WLS** STUDENTS. 1920-1922 **[35025]**
G: **SANDERSON** SCT. ANY CONNECTION WITH LUSK AND LINDSEY. 1800-99 **[37756]**
G: **SCHAUSPIELER** GER. PRE 1990 **[38664]**
G: **SCHAUSTELLER** GER. PRE 1990 **[38664]**
G: **SEDORE** UEL'S BAY OF QUINTE. 1700+ **[34485]**
G: **SEPHARDIC JEWS** TO AMSTERDAM, NL. 1600+ **[36630]**
G: **SEPHARDIC JEWS** TO BAYONNE. 1600+ **[36630]**
G: **SEPHARDIC JEWS** TO BORDEAUX & ROUEN, FRA. 1600+ **[36630]**
G: **SEPHARDIC JEWS** TO LONDON, ENG. 1600+ **[36630]**
G: **SHEEP RANCHING** WESTERN AUSTRALIA. 1920+ **[34230]**
G: **SHILLINGFORD** ORIGIN OF NAME IN WEST INDIES. ALL **[38002]**
G: **SHIPS** TRADING FROM NSW TO TAS, AUS. 1850-1870 **[38585]**
G: **SINGLE TAX LEAGUE** MELBOURNE, VIC, AUS. 1920S **[34019]**
G: **SKREGG & ROSS ESTATE** IRL. 1800S **[35865]**
G: **SNOWDROP** ICE CREAM COMPANY. 1900S **[35059]**
G: **SPENNYMOOR IRONOPOLIS F.C.** A COUNTY DURHAM SOCCER TEAM, ENG. 1904-1930 **[38269]**
G: **SPENNYMOOR WEDNESDAY F.C.** A COUNTY DURHAM SOCCER TEAM, ENG. 1910-1950S **[38269]**
G: **SPRINGSTEEL** TWIN HOUSE GRANGER. PRE 1870 **[34409]**
G: **ST ENOCHS SCHOOL, GLASGOW, IRL** . PRE 1900 **[38298]**
G: **ST MARY MAGDALENE, SOUTH CREEK** ST MARYS, NSW, AUS PARISH REGISTERS. 1840+ **[37500]**
G: **ST THOMAS HOSPITAL, SOUTHWARD, LND, ENG** STAFF OF. 1790-1830 **[34452]**
G: **STARR BOWKETT BUILDING SOC** SYDNEY, AUS. 1920S **[35111]**
G: **STEREO PHOTOGRAPHERS** BURKE, WALTER, AUS & NZ. 1890+ **[35494]**
G: **STEREO PHOTOGRAPHERS** ZIMMERMAN, AUS & NZ. 1890+ **[35494]**
G: **SUN TOUR, MOTOR CYCLE TOUR** GENERAL INFORMATION. 1939 **[36621]**
G: **THE OUSLEY GENEALOGICAL SOCIETY** SOCIETY MEMBERSHIPS — FAMILY DESCENDANTS. **[36114]**
G: **THE OUSLEY NEWSLETTER** NEWSLETTER PUBLICATION. ALL **[36114]**
G: **THEATRE** BRITISH. 1860-1880 **[35018]**
G: **THEATRE** GERMAN. 1860-1890 **[35018]**
G: **THEATRE** LENINGRAD, SU. 1850-1920 **[37670]**
G: **TOUTES INFORMATIONS** PILET, FRA. 1600-1750 **[36699]**
G: **TRANSYLVANIAN SAXONS** . **[38519]**
G: **UNITED EMPIRE LOYALIST, CAN** WHITE. **[36690]**
G: **UNITED EMPIRE LOYALIST, CAN** DUNCAN. **[36690]**
G: **UNIVERSITIES, PRIVATE ADDRESSES** OF IN UK, IRL, CAN & USA. **[38501]**
G: **VAN DIEMENS LAND CO.** OPERATIONS IN LANCS, YORKS, ENG. 1820+ **[36635]**
G: **WATERMILLS** BRK, ENG. ALL **[36401]**
G: **WATERMILLS** HAM, ENG. ALL **[36401]**

G: **WEEKS FAMILY** WEEKS QUERY QUEST. 1600-1900 **[36321]**
G: **WESTON-SUPER-MARE, SOM, ENG** HISTORY OF AREA. ALL **[36012]**
G: **WILLIAM PERRY & CO** WAREHOUSEMEN, SYDNEY, AUS. 1870S **[35111]**
G: **WILLIAMSON AS A FORENAME.** ALL **[37241]**
G: **WINDMILL CHURCH HILL,** SYDNEY, AUS. 1810-1838 **[33841]**
G: **WINE MERCHANT, INNKEEPER** HEATH, LAN, ENG. 1871+ **[37120]**
G: **WOONACHTIG BRUSSEL** GOUDSMID. 1800+ **[38162]**
G: **WORKHOUSE TENTERDEN,** KEN, ENG. C1863 **[35980]**
G: **WORLD WAR 2 EVACUEES TO AUS** HAMILTON FAMILY LIVED WEST EALING, LND, ENG. 1939+ **[37638]**
G: **WRY, ENG** PEOPLE, HISTORY, LIVING CONDITIONS. 1860-1880S **[36837]**
G: **YOUNG AUSTRALIA LEAGUE** IMMIGRANTS FROM UK JUNIOR FARM WORKERS. LATE 1920S **[35025]**
G: **ZOON CASSIMIR** . 1800-1865 **[38162]**
I: **'BOY GREY'** A SPENNYMOOR, DUR, ENG ATHLETE. 1904-1912 **[38269]**
I: **50TH REGT, WEST KENT** PRIVATE MICHAEL STAFFORD. PRE 1864 **[35729]**
I: **ABBOTT, ARTHUR** BUILDER OF BALLARAT, VIC, AUS. PRE 1900 **[35435]**
I: **ABBOTT, ARTHUR** BUILDIER, SOUTHERN ENG. 1800-1860 **[35435]**
I: **ABERNETHY, JOHN** PRINTERS APPRENTICE, DUB, IRL. 1840-50 **[37518]**
I: **ABRAMS, WILLIAM** PASSENGERS ON TO VIC, AUS. 1841 **[37964]**
I: **ACREE, MARTHA** TN, USA, MAY BE WIFE TO PITTS BEASLEY SR. 1801+ **[38743]**
I: **ADDISON, REV. ROBERT** SPGFP MISSIONARY, NIAGARA, CAN. 1792-1829 **[37461]**
I: **ADIE, JAMES** MARINER. C1800-1870 **[37752]**
I: **ADLAM, CHRISTIANA** SWINDON, WIL, ENG. 1870+ **[36739]**
I: **ADLER, CHAIM & JOACHIM** BROTHERS, JEWS, RUDAWA, KR, POL. C1860 **[35717]**
I: **AISHE** ONE NAME STUDY. **[38252]**
I: **ALDERTON FAMILY** EAST ANGLIA, ENG. ALL **[36223]**
I: **ALLAN, PETER** FARMER, STIRLING AREA, SCT. ALL **[38477]**
I: **ALLAN, SOPHIA** STIRLING AREA, SCT. ALL **[38477]**
I: **ALLEN, AMBROSE** CARPENTER, READING, BRK, ENG. 1830+ **[37153]**
I: **ALLEN, ARTHUR** PROFESSEUR, CO.WICKLOW, IRL. 1790+ **[34168]**
I: **ALLEN, L.C. – HIGGS** MARRIAGE IN NZ LIVED AT TE KARAKA, NORTH IS. IN 1912. **[37498]**
I: **ALLEN, URSULA** PARENTS, MARSHALL CO., TN, USA. PRE 1850 **[38743]**
I: **ALLEN, WILLIAM** CAPTAIN, MERCHANT NAVY. 1840-50S **[37707]**
I: **ALSOP, THOMAS** ARMY OFFICER, LUTON, ENG. C1780 **[37903]**
I: **AMOS, ARTHUR JESSE** NAVAL WIRELESS STATION, ST JOHNS, NFD, CAN. C1915 **[37777]**
I: **AMOS, ROBERD DAVID (ANDY)** VICKERS, WEYBRIDGE, SRY, ENG. 1935-1984 **[37777]**
I: **ANDERSON, CHARLES** LAKE TO AUS. 1880+ **[37231]**
I: **ANDERSON, ROBERT** BATTLE OF PRESTON PANS. PRE 1745+ **[35585]**
I: **ANDREW, WILLIAM** YARN MANUFACTURER, RAWTENSTALL, ENG. 1795-1870 **[34448]**
I: **ANKIEWICZ, JOHANN MALTHEUS** PRUSSIAN ARMY, PRE, GER. 1860-70S **[36452]**
I: **ANKWICZ, JOSEPH** CONFED. OF TARGOWICA, WA, POL. 1793 **[36452]**
I: **ARELETT, ALFRED LEAHY** CHANGE OF NAME WANTED. 1872+ **[35754]**
I: **ARELETT, ALFRED LEAHY** WAS HE ADOPTED AND NAME CHANGED. 1872+ **[35754]**
I: **ARGYLL, 9TH EARL OF** FEMALE OR ILLEGITIMATE DESCENDANTS. 1685+ **[35624]**
I: **ARTHUR, CAPT. JOHN OF WISBECH,** CAM, ENG MERCH SERV & ANY RELATIONS. ALL **[36363]**
I: **ARTHUR, FELIX** TN & NC, USA. PRE 1836 **[38768]**
I: **ARTHUR, JOHN** STONE MASON OF MACOSQUIN, LDY, IRL. 1823-1851 **[34244]**
I: **ARTHUR, JOHN** TAILOR OF STREET, BUTLEIGH, SOM, ENG. 1770-1900 **[34855]**
I: **ARTHURS, JAMES,** WM USA & CAN. 1900S+ **[37930]**
I: **ASCOUGH, EMILY & INEZ** NSW, AUS. C1890-1910 **[37498]**
I: **ASHBRIDGE, JOHN** KILNWORKER & RESIDENT AT CROOK, DUR, ENG. 1900-25 **[35696]**
I: **ASHENDEN, EDWARD JENNINGS** ORIGINS, SITTINGBOURNE, KEN, ENG. 1830S **[35754]**
I: **ASHENDEN, EDWARD JENNINGS** DID HE RETURN TO ENG. 1859+ **[35754]**
I: **ASHENDEN, EDWARD JENNINGS** SURVEYOR, VIC, AUS. 1859+ **[35754]**
I: **ASHE** ONE NAME STUDY. **[38252]**
I: **ASKER, NOR** FAMILIES. 1600-1750 **[36335]**
I: **ATHERTON, 'GEORGE' (SEPTIMUS)** PHILANDERER OF LONDON, ENG. 1862-1937 **[36998]**
I: **AULD, CHRISTINA** MARRIED JAMES JACKSON, LKS, SCT. PRE 1880 **[36282]**
I: **AUSTIN, ISABEL** OF LND OR MDX, ENG. 1862 **[34363]**
I: **AUSTIN, JAMES EDWARD** BUTLER IN LND, ENG. 1860+ **[36378]**
I: **AVORTIUS** BENELUX. ALL **[38170]**
I: **AYLWIN, GUILIELMUS G.** COOPER, CAMBERWELL, SRY, ENG. 1880-1918 **[35074]**
I: **AYTON, SAMUEL** BAKER, LND, ENG. C1840 **[35662]**
I: **BACKENS** FAMILIENVERBAND. ALL **[38669]**
I: **BACK** FAILIENVERBAND. ALL **[38669]**
I: **BACON, WILLIAM** LND, ENG. **[35939]**
I: **BAERUM, NOR** FAMILIES. 1600-1750 **[36335]**
I: **BAGIER, THOMAS** CAB DRIVER, LONDON, ENG. 1900 **[36525]**
I: **BAGIER, THOMAS** RAILWAY PORTER, EDINBURGH, SCT. PRE WWI **[36525]**
I: **BAGSHAW, SARAH ANN** DBY, ENG. 1818 **[36386]**
I: **BAILEY, RICHARD,** M. ANNIE M.WEBBER FIJI. 1872 **[34005]**

I: **BAILEY, RICHARD** SOMPTING & WORTHING, SSX, ENG. 1840 + **[34005]**
I: **BAIN, PETER & JANET MORISON** YASS, NSW, AUS. 1856 + **[35230]**
I: **BAKER, EDWARD WILLIAM & LOTTIE** DESCENDANTS OF, NZ. 1900S **[35230]**
I: **BALAM ONE NAME STUDY** ALSO BELAM. ALL **[37882]**
I: **BALDWIN, STANLEY** PRIME MINISTER ENG. 1923-39 **[36614]**
I: **BALLARD, RICHARD ALFRED SAMUEL** CINEMA OWNER OF CARDIFF, WLS. 1894-1970S **[36230]**
I: **BALTIKUM FAMILIE.** BIS 1632 **[38641]**
I: **BANKS, ROBERT** PUBLICAN OF LND, ENG. 1842 **[36076]**
I: **BANNING, CHARLES ERNEST** AND RELATIVES OF. PRE 1905 **[36468]**
I: **BANNISTER, HENRY** CLERK TO LORD DUDLEY, STS, ENG. PRE 1840S **[36808]**
I: **BANNISTER, HENRY** YOUNG WIDOWER TO NZ VIA AUS. 1840S-50S **[36808]**
I: **BAPTISTE-NOCKER, JOHN** BRISTOL, ENG. 1800S **[36290]**
I: **BARBER, LUKE** WINE MERCHANT, CARTMEL, ENG. PRE 1817 **[37696]**
I: **BAREFIELD, JOHN FRANCIS** ENG. PRE 1755 **[37505]**
I: **BARNES, ELEANOR** BRISTOL, GLS, ENG. 1820-1840 **[36739]**
I: **BARON DE CAMIN (TITLE)** ORIGIN, NATIONALITY, ALL TITLE-HOLDERS. ALL **[34391]**
I: **BARRY, PATRICK** ARGENTINIAN NAVY. 1881 + **[37686]**
I: **BARTLEY, ROBERT** BORN 1776, NC, USA. **[37933]**
I: **BATCHELOR, WILLIAM** GROCER OF WIGGINGTON, HRT, ENG. 1710-1720S **[36068]**
I: **BATES, ANN & LIPSCOMBE, RICHARD** MARRIAGE AT SAUNDERTON, BKM, ENG. 1761 **[37498]**
I: **BATES, FAIRHALL** YEOMAN OF RYE, E.SSX, ENG. 1736-1818 **[36413]**
I: **BATES, JULIA** MOTHER OF CHILD, STEWART. 1867-1870 **[36330]**
I: **BATES, JULIA** WIFE OF JOHN HARWELL. 1867-1875 **[36330]**
I: **BATES, NATHAN JOHN** FARMER OF KENT & E.SSX, ENG. 1830-96 **[36413]**
I: **BATES, RICHARD** FATHER OF, SC, USA. 1810-1848 **[36330]**
I: **BATES, SAMUEL** YEOMAN OF SANDHURST, KEN, ENG. C1700 **[36413]**
I: **BATHURST, EDWARD** BRITISH VICE-CONSUL AT COPENHAGEN, DEN. 1844-1846 **[35810]**
I: **BAWDEN, JOHN** SHIP DESERTER, FREMANTLE, WA, AUS. C1880 **[37111]**
I: **BAYHA EMIGRANTS TO AUS.** 1930 + **[38660]**
I: **BAYHA EMIGRANTS TO USA & CAN.** 1600-1900 **[38660]**
I: **BEAL, JAMES** SKIRPENBECK, ERY, ENG. C1650-1715 **[35996]**
I: **BEARD FAMILY** STONEMASONS OF DEV AND LONDON, ENG. 1800-1950 **[36998]**
I: **BEARDSELL, THOMAS** GLUEMAKER OF LND, ENG. 1800-1840S **[34385]**
I: **BEASLEY BROTHERS** IRL TO TN, USA, COBBLER, DISTILLER & INNKEEPER. 1700 + **[38743]**
I: **BEASLEY, PITTS SR** PARENTS, WIFE RUTHERFORD CO., TN, USA. 1775 + **[38743]**
I: **BEASLEY WHO BEASLEY, WIFE 1 TO WM BURNETT.** 1830 + **[38743]**
I: **BEATTIE, WILLIAM WILSON** AND FAMILY — BULLENBALONG/COOMA, NSW, AUS. 1830-1870 **[37965]**
I: **BEATTY, JAMES** BLACKSMITH OF CO. SLIGO, IRL. PRE 1860 **[36417]**
I: **BEATTY, JOHN** BLACKSMITH, IRL, DEATH OF. 1870+ **[36417]**
I: **BEATTY, LETITIA** WIFE OF JOHN, IRL, DEATH OF. 1863 + **[36417]**
I: **BEAULIEU, MATHILDE** MENAGERE. 1850-1900 **[36657]**
I: **BECHTEL OF GERMAN ORIGIN.** ALL **[38469]**
I: **BECKER** . ALL **[38748]**
I: **BECKETT, MARY** BORN WES. HOLME, AGE 5 WHERE? UK. 1851 CENSUS **[36467]**
I: **BECKETT, MARY** BORN WES. HOLME, AGE 15 WHERE? UK. 1861 CENSUS **[36467]**
I: **BEEBY, BRUCE** ACTOR OF SYDNEY, AUS. 1950S **[35111]**
I: **BEEBY, DORIS ISABEL** COMMUNIST PARTY, AUS. 1930S **[35111]**
I: **BEEBY, MARJORIE** SINGER OF SYDNEY, AUS. 1930S **[35111]**
I: **BEEBY, SIR GEORGE STEPHENSON** JUDGE OF SYDNEY, AUS. 1930S **[35111]**
I: **BELL, ALEXANDER GRAHAM** FAMILY HISTORY. ALL **[34140]**
I: **BENNETT FAMILIES** SOUTH AFRICA. 1850 + **[35975]**
I: **BENNETT, JAMES** SHOEMAKER OF WORFIELD, STS, ENG. C1820-36 **[37406]**
I: **BENNETT, JOHN** MERCER OF TAVISTOCK & PLYMOUTH, DEV, ENG. 1786-1832 **[36594]**
I: **BENSLEY, ELIZABETH & HENRY,** TWINS BORN TO HENRY & FISHER, MARY AT GATELY, NFK, ENG. 1790 **[37498]**
I: **BENSLEY, HENRY & NUNN, ELIZABETH** BANNS AT FRANSHAM, NFK, ENG. 1811 **[37498]**
I: **BERGMAN EMIGRATON.** 1900 + **[38668]**
I: **BIBB, THOMAS** CARPET-WEAVER, KIDDERMINSTER, ENG. PRE 1906 **[36525]**
I: **BIFFIN, THOMAS** WEST LAVINGTON, WIL, ENG. 1794-1838 **[34791]**
I: **BILENS, ROBERT** LONDON, ENG. PRE 1818 **[35542]**
I: **BIRKBY ONE NAME STUDY.** WORLDWIDE **[36763]**
I: **BISHOP, WILLIAM I** EAST BRANTFORD TWP. ONT, CAN. 1861 **[34251]**
I: **BISHOP** GLOUCESTER, ENG. ALL **[36248]**
I: **BLACK, GEORGE & ELIZABETH** OF BLAYNEY, NSW, AUS FAMILIES OF. 1864 + **[36641]**
I: **BLACK, WILLIAM** MARINE ENGINES — SOUTH SHIELDS, DUR, ENG. 1800-1880 **[37419]**
I: **BLACKET OR SADLER, ISAAC** NBL, ENG. 1750 + **[36609]**
I: **BLAKE, WALTER (EDWD)** SOUTHWARK, SRY, ENG. 1800S **[34335]**
I: **BLANCHFIELD, LOUISA** WIDOW NORTHWICH, ENG. 1877 + **[36410]**
I: **BLEVINGS, MARTHA GRAY** D.13 APR 1938, NEWTOWNARDS, IRL. C1870-1938 **[34215]**
I: **BLEVINGS, ROBERT** WOODVALE RD. BELFAST, IRL. C1870-1890S **[34215]**
I: **BLOMFIELD, DANIEL STEPHEN** NFK, ENG. 1840 + **[37737]**

I: **BLYTH, JAMES** WEAVER-GARDENER, FIF & GLASGOW, SCT. 1800S **[33966]**
I: **BOLTON, JOHN** AUCTIONEER OF BIRMINGHAM, ENG. C1870 **[36116]**
I: **BOND, FRANK** COAL PORTER, LND, ENG. 1880-1890S **[35074]**
I: **BOND, JAMES** THATCHER, LND, ENG. 1850-1890S **[35074]**
I: **BONIFACE, JAMES** FLY PROPRIETOR OF BRIGHTON, ENG. 1800-90 **[33858]**
I: **BOSTOCK, JOHN** PRIVATE 15TH HUSSARS. C1825 **[35456]**
I: **BOULTER, ROBERT** FARMHAND, CHIPPENHAM, WLS & ENG. 1818+ **[35939]**
I: **BOULTER, THOMAS** YKS EX LND, ENG. 1920+ **[35939]**
I: **BOULTON, LOUISA** 1903. **[35122]**
I: **BOULTON, MILLICENT GERTRUDE ELIZA** . PRE 1903 **[35122]**
I: **BOULTON ROBERT CHARLES HENRY.** 1903 **[35122]**
I: **BOWERS, WILLIAM** MIDSHIPMAN ON M.V.TAUNTON CASTLE. 1801-1870 **[36010]**
I: **BOX, JANE, HOWE, WILLIAM FAMILY** SOUTHGATE AREA, LONDON, MDX, ENG. 1750+ **[35668]**
I: **BOYD CLAN HISTORY & FAMILY TREES.** 1200+ **[38597]**
I: **BOYD, ROBERT KILGOUR** DYSART, FIF, SCT. 1830-1911 **[34006]**
I: **BOYD DESCENDANTS OF JOHN KNOX.** ALL **[36982]**
I: **BOYD IN AUS.** 1788+ **[38597]**
I: **BRABNER, ANDREW** JOINER OF EDINBURGH, SCT. PRE 1834 **[35542]**
I: **BRACEGIRDLE-HALL MARRIAGE** LAN OR CHS, ENG. PRE 1876 **[35137]**
I: **BRADFIELD, JAMES** IN MAITLAND, NSW, AUS. 1853 **[36300]**
I: **BRADLEY, JAMES** OF VIRGINIA, USA. 1780-1805 **[38535]**
I: **BRADLEY, WILLIAM** GAMEKEEPER, CHS, ENG. 1810+ **[34435]**
I: **BRADSHAW, MINNIE C.** 54 EGLINTON ST, BELFAST, IRL. PRE 1899 **[34385]**
I: **BRANDON, HENRY** MERCHANT OF ST HELENS & ST LEONARDS, SHOREDITCH, MDX, ENG. PRE
    1848 **[35997]**
I: **BRANDT, OSCAR** BILL BROKER, GER & CHINA. C1820-1890 **[35568]**
I: **BREUX, CLAUDE & MADELEINE LECOMPTE** BN FRA HISTOIRE FAMILLE. C1760 **[38467]**
I: **BRIGGS, ALFRED ERNEST** FOOTBALLER, HEARTS, EDINBURGH, SCT. 1912-1920 **[34326]**
I: **BRIGHT** DAUGHTER OF LEILA/LILLAH, PECKHAM, LND, ENG. 1890-1914 **[36378]**
I: **BRIMS, DANIEL & CATHERINE JONES** DESCENDANTS OF, LIVERPOOL, LAN, ENG. 1800+ **[34699]**
I: **BRIMS, WILLIAM & ELLEN SULLIVAN** DESCENDANTS OF, MANNING RV, NSW, AUS. 1846+ **[34699]**
I: **BRIMS, WILLIAM** BROTHERS OF, LIVERPOOL, LAN, ENG TO USA & CAN. 1830+ **[34699]**
I: **BROAD, WILLIAM & ROBERT** (WATCHMAKERS) LONDON, ENG & NSW, AUS. 1770-1881 **[37554]**
I: **BROCKWELL, WILLIAM** LND, ENG. 1772-1820S **[34385]**
I: **BRODIE, DAVID MCGREGOR** OLRIG CAITHNESS, SCT. PRE 1940 **[36290]**
I: **BROOKS, CHARLES** DOB 7TH DECEMBER. 1884 **[37241]**
I: **BROOKS, JOSHUA** WEAVER, HEYSIDE, LAN, ENG. 1800-1840 **[36898]**
I: **BROOKS, MAY** DOB 19TH NOVEMBER. 1906 **[37241]**
I: **BROOKS, SARAH MAY** DOB 19TH NOVEMBER. 1906 **[37241]**
I: **BROS** ALL CONNECTING BRANCHES, POLAND. 1800-1900 **[37544]**
I: **BROWN, THOMAS NOBLE** FRENCH POLISHER, NSW, AUS. 1890S **[36749]**
I: **BROWN, ANNIE OF WEARDALE, TEACHER** HER PRIVATE DAY SCHOOL IN WATERHOUSES, DUR,
    ENG. 1890S **[38269]**
I: **BROWN, JOHN HENRY & ALICE TOWERS** DESCENDANTS OF LEICESTER, LEI, ENG. 1887-1990
    [34260]
I: **BROWN, MALCOLM** SCOT, DROWNED NZ. 1856 **[36864]**
I: **BROWNE, WILLIAM ALEXANDER F.** DOCTOR, DUMFRIES, SCT. 1805-85 **[36999]**
I: **BROWNE, WILLIAM** (MERCHANT) INDIA & NSW, AUS. 1762-1833 **[37554]**
I: **BROWNE, WILLIAM** LIEUTENENT, ROYAL ARTIFICERS. 1748-1833 **[36999]**
I: **BRUCE KING ROBERT I.** 1200-1800 **[33986]**
I: **BRUNS EMIGRATION.** 1773+ **[38668]**
I: **BRYAN, GUY** ANY, ENG. PRE 1800 **[36986]**
I: **BRYANT, AMBROSE** CONVICT STONEMASON. 1800S **[34842]**
I: **BRYDEN, THOMAS** COALMINER, IRVINE, AYR, SCT. 1820S **[36749]**
I: **BRYENTON** ALL REFERENCES — ENG. ALL **[38282]**
I: **BUCHANAN, HUGH** PUBLICAN OF GLASGOW, SCT. 1870-1900 **[36705]**
I: **BULL, KNUD** CONVICT ARTIST, AUS. **[38212]**
I: **BULLOCK, BENJAMIN (CONVICT)** SHIP "SUSAN" TO AUS. 1834 **[34019]**
I: **BULLOCK, JOSEPH (CONVICT)** SHIP "HIVE" TO AUS. 1834 **[34019]**
I: **BULMER, THOMAS** YEOMAN & WATER CARTMAN. ORIGINS(BOOMER/BOWMER) LIVING IN ST
    OSWALDS, DUR, ENG. 1764-1815 **[38269]**
I: **BULMER, THOMAS** YEOMAN & WATER CARTMAN, ORIGINS. MARRIED TO JANE & THE
    MARTHA (FITZGERALD). 1740?-1815 **[38269]**
I: **BULMER, THOMAS** YEOMAN & WATER CARTMAN. FREEMAN OF ELVETTMOOR. SON OF JOHN.
    MARRIED TO JANE. 1740?-1815 **[38269]**
I: **BUNN, JOHN** INNKEEPER 'KINGS HEAD' FILBY, NFK, ENG. 1800-1850 **[35173]**
I: **BURBRIDGE, CHARLES** WESLEYAN MINISTER OF ENG. 1855+ **[36167]**
I: **BURBRIDGE, JOHN** MUSICIAN OF KEW, ENG. PRE 1828 **[36167]**
I: **BURDETT** JAMES EDWARD. LND, ENG. 1908+ **[35939]**
I: **BURGES, GEORGE (CLASSICAL SCHOLAR)** TRINITY COLLEGE, CAMBRIDGE, ENG. 1810-1864
    [34006]
I: **BURGES, JANE NEE ISAACS** WIFE OF GEORGE, ST PANCRAS, LND, ENG. 1820-1882 **[34006]**

I: **BURGESS, EMMA** SWINDON, WIL, ENG. 1889+ **[36739]**
I: **BURNE, GARY** BALLET DANCER – LONDON & GER. 1950-1975 **[36463]**
I: **BURNETT, WILLIAM** TN, USA, FAMILY OF, 2 BEASLEY WIVES. PRE 1855 **[38743]**
I: **BURNS, ARCHIBALD** ARTILLERYMAN, CEYLON. 1830S **[34887]**
I: **BURR, CAPT** USA REVOLUTIONARY WAR. 1789 **[38537]**
I: **BURTON CHRONICLES** ONE NAME GENEALOGY. 1600-1800 **[38326]**
I: **BUTLER, WILLIAM** SADDLE MAKER, LND, ENG. 1800-50 **[35662]**
I: **BUTT, DAME CLARA** PROGRAMME PHOTOGRAPHS. ALL **[37973]**
I: **BUTTONSHAW** ONE NAME STUDY INC VARIATIONS OF NAME. **[37715]**
I: **BYARD,CAPT SIR THOMAS** RN . 1743-1798 **[34550]**
I: **BYERS, WILLIAM** FARMER OF WES, YKS, ENG. 1780-1880 **[34855]**
I: **CADDY FAMILY** VIC, AUS COMPILING SOCIAL HISTORY. 1854+ **[37972]**
I: **CAESAR, AUGUSTUS SHERIDAN** ENGINEER OF ADELAIDE, SA, AUS. 1872+ **[35105]**
I: **CAHILL, JOHN** ASSIZE PROSECUTOR, CO. TIP, IRL. C1825+ **[37415]**
I: **CALDWELL, WILLIAM JOHN** SEATTLE, WA, USA. 1900-1958 **[35610]**
I: **CALHOUN, JOHN C.** LIVED FAYETTE CO., PA, USA. 1846-1890 **[36908]**
I: **CALLANAN, JOHN** SCHOOL MASTER, CORK CITY, IRL. PRE 1835 **[37696]**
I: **CAMBORN FAMILY** OF WINTERBOURNE, GLS, ENG. PRE 1700 **[34908]**
I: **CAMPBELL, EDWARD ELLIOTT** LT HM 18TH FOOT, DIED JAMAICA. C1780-1813 **[37339]**
I: **CAMPBELL, JOHN** COUPER, CAI, SCT. 1770-1850 **[34646]**
I: **CAMPTON, MOSES** SERGEANT, SURREY MILITIA, WKS, ENG. 1775-1825 **[36429]**
I: **CARBIS, RICHARD** ROOK, PEN, COR, ENG, DESCENDANTS. 1800+ **[36885]**
I: **CARLSON(DOTTER), LOUISA** BEXHEDA JONKOPING, SWEDEN. 1856 **[38543]**
I: **CARMICHAEL, MARTHA** SCT, WIFE OF WILLIAM HARVEY. C1800+ **[34330]**
I: **CARR, EDWARD JAMES** ANCESTRY IN ENG. PRE 1870 **[38585]**
I: **CARRADICE, JOHN** BORN MIDDLETON IN LONSDALE, WES, ENG. C1746 **[37196]**
I: **CARRAHER, JOSEPH** COASTGUARD/LIGHTHOUSE, KINSALE, IRL. 1865+ **[37079]**
I: **CARTER, JOHN** SMUGGLER, CON, ENG. 1750-1800 **[36145]**
I: **CARYSFORTH, HENRY RICHARD** FOSTERED, BERLIN. 1863+ **[34323]**
I: **CARYSFORTH, HENRY** ENGINEER, AMERICA. 1860S **[34323]**
I: **CASE, THOMAS** STOCKBROKER OF LIVERPOOL, ENG. 1840+ **[34591]**
I: **CASE** MAYOR OF LIVERPOOL, ENG. C1780 **[34591]**
I: **CASH** ONE NAME STUDY, WILL EXCHANGE INFO. ALL **[37972]**
I: **CATES, ANDREW JACKSON** MAINE, USA TO NC & BC, CAN. 1832-1904 **[37048]**
I: **CATES, ASA** RESIDENT OF MACHIASPORT, ME, USA. 1799-1872 **[37048]**
I: **CAVALLO, GAETANO** ITL TO USA, BOY ORPHAN, ELLIS ISLAND. 1895+ **[38743]**
I: **CAWLEY, HENRY** GENTLEMAN OF ISLINGTON, MDX, ENG. 1810-1830 **[37885]**
I: **CESAR, JULES (OR JULIUS)** MAURITIUS, INDIAN OCEAN ISLAND. 1807-1833 **[37867]**
I: **CHAMBERLAIN, JAMES** WATCHMAKER, ENG, CAN, AUS, USA. 1850-1930 **[34855]**
I: **CHAMBERLAIN, WILLIAM** FISH CURER, LAN, ENG. PRE 1900 **[34855]**
I: **CHANGE OF NAME** FROM ALFRED LEADY ARELETT TO ?. 1872+ **[35754]**
I: **CHAPMAN, JOHN** MASON, IOM. 1830-1915 **[36476]**
I: **CHAPMAN, ROBERT** SOLDIER, IOM & ENG. 1799-1816 **[36476]**
I: **CHAPMAN, ROBERT** TAILOR, IOM. 1816-1850 **[36476]**
I: **CHARLES II** ESCAPE TO FRANCE. 1651 **[35261]**
I: **CHARTERS** CEYLON. 1840-1870 **[37220]**
I: **CHARTER** CEYLON. 1850-1870 **[37220]**
I: **CHILE** NITRATE MINES ROBERT JEFFERY. 1860-1900 **[38391]**
I: **CHRISTIAN, JOHN** NAVAL RECORDS, ENG. C1720 **[38725]**
I: **CHRISTIE, CHARLES THOMAS** ENGINEER OF LND, ENG, DIED HONG KONG?. 1825-95 **[37339]**
I: **CHURCH, THOMAS** CHINA & GLASS DEALER, OF DEVISES, WIL, ENG. 1850-1880 **[37070]**
I: **CHUTER** ENG & AUS. 1800S **[35865]**
I: **CLAPHAM, GEORGE** WHALER LOST IN PACIFIC. 1830-40S **[36856]**
I: **CLARK FAMILY** ULSTER, IRL TO PA & KY, USA. 1770-1790 **[37533]**
I: **CLARK, CAPT WILLIAM** 94TH REGT, ENG. C1800 **[35257]**
I: **CLARKE, REV JAMES** . C1858-1942 **[33768]**
I: **CLASEN & CLAUSSEN** GER (SHO). PRE 1800 **[38748]**
I: **CLASING** . ALL **[38748]**
I: **CLAYTON, JOHN** COTTON MILL OWNER, BOLTON, ENG. 1898-1902 **[36984]**
I: **CLAYTON, JOHN** MASONIC KNIGHT TEMPLAR, USA. 1902+ **[36984]**
I: **CLEIFE, HENRY HOLDITCH THOMAS** RECTOR OF HARDINGTON MANDEVILLE, SOM, ENG. 1883-1914 **[37378]**
I: **CLEMENTS, JAMES** SILVERSMITH OF LND, ENG. 1815-1840S **[34385]**
I: **CLEMENTS, WILLIAM** LND, ENG. 1720-1770 **[34385]**
I: **CLEMSON, WILLIAM & VAUGHAN, SARAH** ALBERBURY, SHROPSHIRE & WALES – DESCENDANTS. 1760+ **[35719]**
I: **CLEVERLEY, CHARLES ST.GEORGE** SURVEYOR GENERAL, HONG KONG. 1850S **[35568]**
I: **CLIFTON, HENRY WILL** GENTLEMAN OF BRUFIELD (BEL & ENG). C1850 **[36802]**
I: **CLIFTON, ROBERT** BR CHAPLAIN BRUGES (BEL). C1790-1840 **[36802]**
I: **CLINE, KLEIN, KLINE** USA. 1600-1900 **[36943]**
I: **CLUGSTON, JOHN & THOMPSON, MARY** MARRIAGE IN ARM, IRL. C1830S **[37498]**
I: **COFFEY, EPHRAIM JAMES** SEALING & WHALING SHIPS, SYDNEY, AUS. **[34659]**

I: **COFFEY, JOHN** TEACHER, COR, IRL. 1800+ **[34764]**
I: **COKER ONE NAME STUDY** ALSO COAKER. ALL **[37882]**
I: **COLE, ANDREW** SOLDIER, GRENADIER GUARDS, ENG. 1826-1845 **[36873]**
I: **COLE, HARRY** RESIDENT OF EVERTON, LIVERPOOL, ENG. 1834+ **[34330]**
I: **COLE, POLLY** RESIDENT OF EVERTON, LIVERPOOL, ENG. 1834+ **[34330]**
I: **COLEMAN, JOHN** FATHER OF, BORN VA, USA. 1765 **[36330]**
I: **COLLARD, JOHN** BOATSWAIN OR COOK IN NAVY, ENG. C1805 **[35560]**
I: **COLLIER, MARTIN** FARMER, SMITHSTOWN, KIK, IRL. C.1830 **[33775]**
I: **COLSON, THOMAS** WEAVER, SFK, ENG. 1720-1800 **[34716]**
I: **COMPTON, MOSES** SERGEANT, SURREY MILITIA, WKS, ENG. 1775-1825 **[36429]**
I: **CONN, ROBERT & LOUDON, MARGARET** MARRIED AT NEWTONWHAMILTON, ARM, IRL. C1880 **[37498]**
I: **CONNELL, DOROTHY** NEE MILES, LIVERPOOL, ENG. 1931+ **[36052]**
I: **CONNOLLY, CHRISTINA & KATE** DERRY CONVENT, IRL. 1800S **[35865]**
I: **COOK, DANIEL** CHILDREN JAMES, ROSA, SETH, HAM, ENG. C1860+ **[35565]**
I: **COOK, JAMES** SA RAILWAYS. AUS. 1880S+ **[35565]**
I: **COOMBES, ROBERT LEWIS** VANISHED, VIC, AUS. 1893+ **[35472]**
I: **COPPERTHWAIGHT, ALFRED FLINT** BOOKBINDER, STOKER & SHIPS STEWARD, SOUTHAMPTON, ENG. **[33802]**
I: **CORBOULD FAMILY** PEDIGREE. 1393-1930 **[37759]**
I: **CORRIGAN, JAMES** DECORATION: MEDAL OF TOULOUSE. C1813-1830 **[33812]**
I: **COSGROVE, JAMES** R.C.SCHOOL TEACHER, SYD, AUS. 1850 **[35560]**
I: **COSTIGAN, JAMES & CATHARINE DUNN** LEX, IRL FAMILY HISTORY. C1825 **[38467]**
I: **COTHER ONE NAME STUDY** WORLDWIDE. **[37715]**
I: **COTTERELL** 2 LT. E. WWI 124 LABOUR CO. FRA. 1914+ **[37756]**
I: **COUANE, ANTOINE** JOURNALIER. 1850-1900 **[36657]**
I: **COULSON, DOUGLASES** OF SUNDERLAND, DUR, ENG. PRE 1900 **[37693]**
I: **COUNT RAYMOND DE TOULOUSE** FAMILY HISTORY, TOULOUSE, FRANCE. ALL **[34140]**
I: **COX, CATHERINE MARY** NURSE & MIDWIFE OF WHITE CLIFFS, NSW, AUS. C1901 **[35810]**
I: **COX, MATTHEW DILLON THOMAS** HORSEDEALER OF BATAVIA, JAVA. 1860S **[35810]**
I: **CRABBE, EMANUEL** SYDNEY, NSW, AUS. 1833 **[34791]**
I: **CRAIGIE, GIBBS GAIL** HASLETT, MI, USA - CONTACT REQUIRED. **[36004]**
I: **CRAIK, ALEX C.** S.S.EMPRESS OF IRELAND. C1875-1914 **[34215]**
I: **CREIGHTONS IN DON, IRL & CUMBRIA, ENG** CHARLES BORN 1786 WENT TO GOSFORTH. 1700-1899 **[38567]**
I: **CREW, ABRAHAM** INNKEEPER, WOR, ENG. **[34764]**
I: **CREW, WILLIAM** COWKEEPER OF ST MARYLEBONE, MDX, ENG. C1868 **[35683]**
I: **CRITCHLEY, WILLIAM** ROYAL VETERANS, NSW, AUS. 1800+ **[34596]**
I: **CROCKER, WILLIAM JOHN** VERGER, GRACE CHURCH, BROOKLYN, NY, USA. 1890-1895 **[34469]**
I: **CUBBON, RICHARD & JANE QUAYLE** DESCENDANTS OF MARRIAGE, IOM. 1806+ **[34125]**
I: **CULP FAMILY IN CANADA** CONNECTING THE BRANCHES. 1786+ **[38448]**
I: **CURRIE, JAMES & TERRENCE** BELTURBET, FER, IRL. 1820-1830 **[35372]**
I: **CURRY, JOSEPH** MAP PUBLISHER, BRADFORD, ENG. 1860S **[35996]**
I: **CURTIS FAMILY HISTORY (STEPHEN)** STOREKEEPER, FORDINGBRIDGE, HAM, ENG. 1700+ **[35668]**
I: **CURTIS, JAMES WEBB** MASTER MARINER, MYLOR, CON, ENG. 1817-53 **[36190]**
I: **CUTLER STONES** CORNER, BRISBANE. PRE 1900 **[35122]**
I: **DALY, JOHN** OF THE ROPE WALK, BALLYSHANNON, IRL. PRE 1860 **[38239]**
I: **DALY, MARY ANNE** MRS WILLIAM MCSHEA OF CO. DON, IRL. C1841-1877 **[38239]**
I: **DALY, PATRICK** BORN OFF, IRL. 1844+ **[34767]**
I: **DARG FAMILY HISTORY** HADDINGTON, DIRELTON, EDINBURGH, SCT. 1700-1900 **[35668]**
I: **DARKE, LILLIAN M.** BORN SAN FRANCISCO, CA, USA. C1870 **[38239]**
I: **DARKE, LILLIAN M.** MARRIED ERLE EVERETT JACKSON, NYC, USA. 1893 **[38239]**
I: **DAVEY, GRACE LOUISA** MY GODMOTHER, BRISTOL, ENG. 1898+ **[36995]**
I: **DAVIDSON, HANNAH** MARRIED JAMES NOBLE, SCT. PRE 1845 **[36496]**
I: **DAVIES, EDWARD** MALTSTER, LLANDRE, CGN, WLS. C1826 **[37649]**
I: **DAVIES, ISAAC** FARMER OF DENBIGH, WLS. PRE 1865 **[36052]**
I: **DAVIES, LEWIS** LEAD MINER, LLANBRYNMAIR, WLS. 1850-1891 **[37649]**
I: **DAVIES, THOMASINA ANNE** ENG, AUS, NZ. 1915+ **[37696]**
I: **DAVIS & DAVIES FAMILY** FENDERMAKERS OF HEATH MILL LN, B'HAM, ENG. 1800-1900 **[36998]**
I: **DAVIS, THOMAS & CHARLOTTE** OF BLAYNEY, NSW, AUS FAMILIES OF. 1854+ **[36641]**
I: **DAVISON RAILWAYMEN** TANFIELD, WHICKHAM, HEWORTH, HOUGHTON & SEAHAM, DUR. CHURTON, NBL. 1805-1929 **[38269]**
I: **DAVISON, JOHN — ORIGINS** MARRIED RYTON 1771 LIVED TANFIELD TO 1817. 1730S-1817 **[38269]**
I: **DAWN, ILMA & VERNA** A PHOTOGRAPH NZ. C1900 **[37498]**
I: **DAWSON, ABNER BECK** GRIMESCAR, SCRUTON, NRY, ENG. 1852+ **[35996]**
I: **DAWSON, ALFRED** MINSKIP GRANGE, WRY, ENG. 1866+ **[35996]**
I: **DE COURCY** FRENCH BARONESS. 1790-1830 **[38007]**
I: **DE HORA, MANDEL HERRERA** BOER WAR SERVICE. 1894-1906 **[37653]**
I: **DE LA PITTE (FAMILY)** LEFT NORMANDIE, FRA FOR ENG. C1066 **[35453]**
I: **DE LA WARR** ENGLISH LORD. PRE 1610 **[36969]**
I: **DEES FAMILY** ONE NAME STUDY GT BRITAIN. ALL **[37859]**

I: **DEIDERT** . ALL **[38748]**
I: **DELANEY, CONSTABLE THOMAS** PARRAMATTA & WINDSOR, NSW, AUS. PRE 1859 **[36600]**
I: **DELL, JAMES** E.W. BUFFS REGIMENT. 1860S-1950S **[34284]**
I: **DEMPSEY, TENIS** DUDDESTON, WAR, ENG, DESCENDANTS. 1850 + **[36885]**
I: **DENMAN, JAMES & CATHERINE BAIN** DESCENDANTS OF, BATLOW, NSW, AUS. 1890 + **[35230]**
I: **DENOVAN, TIMOTHY FRANCIS DE COURCY** BORN 31 AUG 1834, CORK CITY, IRL. 1834 + **[35554]**
I: **DERRINCURT (DAY), WILLIAM** CONVICT. 1830-1897 **[37976]**
I: **DESC SEPARATIST PASTOR RICHARD CLYFTONS** FAMILY (ENG & NL). 1500-1990 **[36802]**
I: **DEWAR** WHISKY MERCHANTS, PER, SCT. C1840 + **[35053]**
I: **DEWLEY, JAMES** TRANSPORTED TO AUS. 1829 **[35598]**
I: **DIBLEY** ONE NAME STUDY WORLDWIDE. **[38258]**
I: **DICK** FAMILY LANARK CO, ONT, CAN. 1822 + **[34052]**
I: **DICK, ALEXANDER LINDSAY** MASON OF DUNDEE, SCT. 1818-1855 **[34922]**
I: **DICKINSON, MATTHEW** FARMER, URSWICK IN FURNESS, CUL, ENG. C1800 **[35722]**
I: **DICKSON, JOHN** PRISON WARDER, MANCHESTER, ENG; THEN HOTELIER. C1876-1912 **[36024]**
I: **DIEHL, JOHANNA KATHARINA** COURT SINGER IN MANNHEIM, GER. 1819 + **[34519]**
I: **DIGBY, ROBERT** ADMIRAL OF DORSET, ENG. 1732-1814 **[37979]**
I: **DISMORE, BATEMAN** WHEREABOUTS AFTER LONDON, ENG. 1785 **[37077]**
I: **DIXON, RALPH & A.M.S. DORIS** ATWEEDSIDERS R.N. CAREER. 1805-1820 **[38269]**
I: **DIXON, WILLIAM** R.N. RESCUE OF WM JONES AT MARSKE-IN-CLEVELAND. 10.8.1847 **[38269]**
I: **DIXON, WILLIAM** ROYAL NAVY & COASTGUARD CAREER. 1840S **[38269]**
I: **DIXON, WILLIAM** CAREER ON HMS VESTAL. 1840S **[38269]**
I: **DODSON, JEREMIAH** BIRTHPLACE PLEASE. 1770-1780 **[37077]**
I: **DODWELL** BIRTH OF THOMAS. PRE 1667 **[34079]**
I: **DOLLING, JAMES** BREWER OF MDX, ENG. 1708-1773 **[34743]**
I: **DOLLING** ONE NAME STUDY WORLDWIDE. **[38258]**
I: **DONDE, PETER** CAPTAIN 7TH FUSILIERS. 1756 + **[35456]**
I: **DORRINGTON, DOUGLAS** LND, ENG. 1830-1870 **[34385]**
I: **DORRINGTON, STEPHEN** DOR, ENG. 1760-1820 **[34385]**
I: **DORRINGTON, THOMAS** DOR, ENG. 1800-1850 **[34385]**
I: **DOUCHE DE CAESBECQUE** PEPERSTAFT, BLAESVELD. C1500 **[38167]**
I: **DOUGLAS RESEARCH** FAMILY. ALL **[38675]**
I: **DOWNES, WILLIAM** GARDENER, OF BAUGHTON FIELDS, WORCESTER, ENG. 1813-1856 **[37181]**
I: **DRAKE, C.A.** DARLINGHURST RD, DARLINGHURST, NSW, AUS. 1930S **[37498]**
I: **DRAKE, RICHARD BAKER** BLACKSMITH OF NFK, ENG. 1798 + **[37737]**
I: **DRESSER, JOSEPH** RESIDENT OF LEAKE, YKS, ENG. 1815 + **[37048]**
I: **DROUGHT, REV ROBERT** IRL TO ENG & AUS. 1774-1836 **[36095]**
I: **DUCK, JONATHAN** TAILOR, WHITBY, ENG. 1800-1840 **[37435]**
I: **DUKE OF KENT** NATURAL CHILDREN. 1780-1815 **[35375]**
I: **DUKES OF BURGUNDY** HISTORY. 1200-1600 **[36943]**
I: **DULANTY, JOHN WHELAN** C.B., C.B.E., ACADEMIC, CIVIL SERVANT, DIPLOMAT. 1881-1955 **[37883]**
I: **DUNCAN, GEORGE C,** MD BIOG. DETAILS, LND, ENG & MILAN, ITL. C1885-1936 **[34479]**
I: **DUNNE, PETER FINLEY** AMERICAN WRITER, CHICAGO, USA — ANCESTORS. PRE 1910 **[38042]**
I: **DURRANT, SUSANNA** HOUSEMAID, HOLKHAM HALL, NFK, ENG. 1866 **[37719]**
I: **EAGLE** FAMILY MEMBERS OF CROMWELLS ARMY WHO WENT TO IRL. 1650-1660 **[34531]**
I: **EDWARDS, JAMES** BUTCHER, LONDON, ENG. C1820-1848 **[35447]**
I: **EDWARDS, JOHN** BARBER OF MACHYNLLETH, WLS. 1771-1825 **[37649]**
I: **EDWARDS, NORA ESTELLE** WHITEHALL, IL, USA. 1870S **[34997]**
I: **EDWARDS, REES** COUNTY GAOLER, DOLGELLEY, WLS. 1750S **[37649]**
I: **ELDER, JOHN & JANE** ROSEMARKE, ROC, SCT, DESCENDANTS. 1800 + **[36885]**
I: **ELLIOTT, ROBERT** CLERGYMAN IN AUS. 1890-1920 **[35485]**
I: **ELLIOTT** FROM IOM. 1820 + **[34125]**
I: **ELLIS, CHARLES HUBERT** BRADFORD, ENG. 1849-1931 **[36570]**
I: **ELLIS, DEMAS** BRADFORD, ENG. 1823-1899 **[36570]**
I: **ELSTON, GEORGE** BOOTMAKER, DEV, ENG. C1850 **[35662]**
I: **ELY 4TH MARQUESS AND MARCHIONESS** OF. C1850-1890 **[36469]**
I: **EMANUEL ALFRED** FARMER IN PEEL CO., ONT, CAN. PRE 1861 + **[35618]**
I: **EMPSOM, SAMUEL** PORT BUTCHER, NTT, ENG. C1860 **[34342]**
I: **EMTAGE, JOHN** CHURCH WARDEN, MAIDSTONE, KEN, ENG. 1650-1750 **[37386]**
I: **ENGLISH, STODDARD** PAPERMAKER, NBL, ENG. 1790 **[34827]**
I: **ENTWISLE (JAMES)** HAND LOOM WEAVER OF DARWEN, ENG. 1800-1830S **[35052]**
I: **ERNST, GEORGE** FIREWORK ARTIST OF LONDON, ENG & SWITZERLAND. C1797-1842 **[37279]**
I: **ETHERINGTON, JOSHUA** OF WRY, ENG. C1700-1768 **[37076]**
I: **EU, THE COUNTS OF** FROM NORMANDY TO ENG. 1054-1300 **[36015]**
I: **EVANS, HARRIET** SELBORNE, HAM, ENG. 1800S **[37778]**
I: **EVEREST** FAMILY TREES ALL. **[35468]**
I: **EVEREST, HENRY & ELIZABETH** VOYAGE OF ENG TO AUS. 1851 **[35468]**
I: **FARAGHER, DANIEL** FARMER, IOM, UK. PRE 1866 **[35231]**
I: **FARROW, JOHN** POLICEMAN — UXBRIDGE, MDX, ENG. C1826 **[36290]**
I: **FELLS, JAMES** PLATERS COTTAGES, SUDBURY, HARROW, MDX, ENG. 1860-1870 **[37079]**
I: **FERGUSON, ROBERT** COMMERCIAL TRAVELLER, SCT. 1800S **[35691]**
I: **FIELDHOUSE, RICHARD** AGE 4 WHERE? UK. 1851 CENSUS **[36467]**

I: **FIELDHOUSE, RICHARD** AGE 14 WHERE? UK. 1861 CENSUS **[36467]**
I: **FIELDS, RICHARD** ENGLISH TRADER TN & NC, USA. 1700-1835 **[38768]**
I: **FINCH, FREDERIC** BLACKSMITH, KEN, ENG. PRE 1874 **[38752]**
I: **FINN, JAMES & SUSAN** MIGRANTS AUS TO WELLINGTON, NZ. C1897 **[38752]**
I: **FISHER, JOHN** NOTTINGHAM, ENG. 1800+ **[36386]**
I: **FISHER, MARY & BENSLEY, HENRY** MARRIAGE AT ELSING, NFK, ENG. 1777 **[37498]**
I: **FITZSIMMONS, LAWRENCE JOSEPH** JOURNEYMAN TAILOR, IRL. PRE 1856 **[37696]**
I: **FLANAGAN, ROBERT & THOMPSON, AGNES** MARRIED ARM/MOG, IRL. C1848 **[37498]**
I: **FLANAGAN, ROBERT** SON OF ROBERT & CATHERINE BORN NEWTONHAMILTON, ARM, IRL.
     C1820 **[37498]**
I: **FLINN** VIC, AUS. **[35865]**
I: **FLOYD, HENRY ROWE** . 1840+ **[36508]**
I: **FLYNN** VIC, AUS. **[35865]**
I: **FOEHN, CATHARINA THERESIA** DESCENDANTS USA. 1883+ **[38655]**
I: **FOEHN, THERESIA** DESCENDANTS USA. 1883+ **[38655]**
I: **FOGARTY-FEGEN, CAPTAIN** VICTORIA CROSS RECIPIENT. 1939 **[37415]**
I: **FOGGON, JOHN** PMC MINISTER, DURHAM, TAS & NSW, AUS. 1800-1905 **[37988]**
I: **FOORD, JAMES** CONVICT - ARR. NSW, AUS 'CLAUDINE'. 1829 **[35501]**
I: **FOORD, JOHN** (COACHBUILDER & SETTLER) NSW & VIC, AUS. 1819-1883 **[37554]**
I: **FORD, JOHN & ELIZA** ARR. NSW, AUS FROM SSX, ENG. ALL DESCENDS.. 1839+ **[35501]**
I: **FORDE, MARY ANNE** DERRINRAW, ARM, IRL. 1866 **[34385]**
I: **FORSTER FAMILY** CONNECTING THE BRANCHES. ALL **[35341]**
I: **FORSYTH, JOHN** CLACKMANNAN & ALLOA, SCT. PRE 1870 **[38477]**
I: **FORSYTH, WILLIAM** LANDAGENT OF ADELAIDE, SA, AUS. 1882-1883 **[35810]**
I: **FOULGER TAILORS**, MARYLEBONE, LONDON, ENG. 1830-1880 **[37232]**
I: **FRANCIS, HENRY JAMES** WINDOW CLEANER, LONDON, ENG. 1920-40S **[36252]**
I: **FRANCIS, JACK** TAXI DRIVER, LONDON, ENG. 1920-40S **[36252]**
I: **FRANCIS, JOHN** OF STAVELEY, ENG. 1888-90S **[37267]**
I: **FRASER, ROBERT** MASON OF GLASGOW & KINTYRE, SCT. 1855-1907 **[34156]**
I: **FRAZIER, JAMES J.** UNDERTAKER, PHILADELPHIA, PA, USA. 1835-1906 **[36580]**
I: **FRENCH (NEE GIBSON), EVA** DESCENDANTS OF BC, SAS & ONT, CAN. 1910+ **[34260]**
I: **FREW** WORLDWIDE. 1800 **[34112]**
I: **FRY FAMILY, ALL TREES** SUTTON BENGER, WIL, ENG. 1627+ **[36767]**
I: **FRY, PETER & BALL, SELINA** MARR AUCKLAND, NZ 1884. DETAILS OF ALL CHILDREN DESIRED.
     [37498]
I: **FUNKHOUSER, CHRISTINA** MARRIAGE TO NIDEVER. 1770-1850 **[38768]**
I: **GAETHJE & GOETJE** GER (SHO). ALL **[38748]**
I: **GAETJE & GOEDEKE** GER (SHO). ALL **[38748]**
I: **GAGE, SIMON** LOCATION WTO EX NZ. 1830S **[36840]**
I: **GALLOWAY, ANNE MCFARLANE** RELICT OF WILLIAM HARVEY. 1830+ **[34330]**
I: **GALLOWAY, ANNE MCFARLANE** BORN IN GORBALS, SCT. 1830+ **[34330]**
I: **GAREY & TERRY** STAGE ARTISTS, TOURING CONTINENT. 1855-1890 **[33821]**
I: **GATES, THOMAS ADKISSON** MASTER BUILDER, MIDHURST, SSX, ENG. PRE 1830 **[35446]**
I: **GATES. THOMAS** CLOTHIER & WEAVER, MIDHURST, SSX, ENG. PRE 1750 **[35446]**
I: **GAUDRY, G. AND LESLIE** NSW, AUS. C1900 **[37498]**
I: **GAUNT, JOSHUA** HATMAKER, PENISTONE, YKS, ENG. 1750-1850 **[36898]**
I: **GEE, WILLIAM** BOOT FINISHER, LONDON, ENG. 1860-1900 **[35175]**
I: **GENTLEMAN** WORLDWIDE. ANY **[34182]**
I: **GERAGHTY, PATRICK** FARMER OF VIC, AUS. 1842-1899 **[35443]**
I: **GIBB, HENRY** NAVAL OFFICER, PER, SCT. PRE 1845 **[37903]**
I: **GIBBON, JANE SARAH HOWARD** ESTATE, HASTINGS, E SSX, ENG. 1874+ **[36967]**
I: **GIBSON, BARNABIE (C1525-1596)** LITTLE STONHAM, SFK, ENG, DESCENDANTS OF. **[37874]**
I: **GILCHRIST, FREDERICK CHARLES** LIMEHOUSE MANAGER, LND, ENG. C1800 **[34034]**
I: **GILES, ELIZABETH** 5 PETER LANE, YORK CITY, ENG. 1879+ **[35996]**
I: **GILES, GEORGE** LIGHTERMAN, LIMEHOUSE DOCKS, LND, ENG. 1881 **[38417]**
I: **GILKES, HENRY & WEST, ELIZABETH** MARR AT PRINCES RISBOROUGH, BKM, ENG. 1796 **[37498]**
I: **GILLINGHAM, JULIAN** ORGAN BUILDER, ENG. 1860-1900 **[37877]**
I: **GISBORN, JOHN ALBERT** DESCENDANTS, LEI, ENG. 1910+ **[34260]**
I: **GLASHUETTEN** EUROPE (BRD, GER, DEN, NOR, SWE). 1400-1900 **[38748]**
I: **GLENDINNING, WILLIAM AND ANN (NEE WALLACE)** MISSIONARIES (URFA, SYRIA). C1890+
     [36853]
I: **GOODE, HETTY, NORMAN & OTHERS** NSW, AUS & NZ. C1900 **[37498]**
I: **GOODILL, MARK** SHEPHERD, YKS, ENG. PRE 1900 **[34855]**
I: **GOODMAN, PATRICK** POST MILL HILL ORPHANAGE, ENG. 1935+ **[36889]**
I: **GORDON, ARTHUR** OF SALFORD, LAN, ENG. C1897 **[38072]**
I: **GORDON, COLIN** SOLDIER, FARMER & WEAVER, SUT, SCT. 1780-1850 **[36559]**
I: **GOVE, REVEREND SAMUEL F.** STATE REPRESENTATIVE, GEORGIA, USA, 1868. 1835-1903 **[34004]**
I: **GRAHAM, THOMAS** METROPOLITAN POLICE, NSW, AUS. 1850-1900 **[36040]**
I: **GRANT, EDWARD** TEXTILE WORKER, LAN, ENG – POSSIBLE SCOTTISH ORIGINS. PRE 1894 **[36024]**
I: **GRANT, LT JAMES** 1772-1833 EXPLORER, AUST COASTAL. 1800-02 **[35223]**
I: **GRANT, ROBERT** RAILWAY BRIDGE BUILDER, GLASGOW, SCT. 1810-1850 **[38007]**
I: **GRAY, CHARLES** EARWAKER SSX, ENG. C1828+ **[36024]**

I: GRAY, LAWRENCE BLACKSMITH OF SUNDERLAND, ENG. 1600+ [35802]
I: GRAY, LAWRENCE PILOT OF SUNDERLAND, ENG. 1700+ [35802]
I: GRAY, WILLIAM SADDLER, ENG. 1800S [37453]
I: GREEN, JANE A. BEDLINGTON, NBL, ENG. 1855+ [36609]
I: GREEN, ROBERT GOLDMINER, NBL, ENG, SHIPWRECKED LIVERPOOL. 1880+ [36609]
I: GREEN, SUSANNAH USA. 1900S + [37930]
I: GREENING GLOUCESTER, ENG. ALL [36248]
I: GREGORY STONEMASONS, OXF, ENG. PRE 1670 [35030]
I: GRIFFITHS, WILLIAM BORN WEDNESBURY, STS, ENG. C1843 [35942]
I: GRIGGS, WILLIAM & FISHER, ANN MARRIED AT GATELY, NFK, ENG. 1769 [37498]
I: GROMMEN, ANNA HANN KERZ, TRANSYLVANIA, RO. 1839-1932 [38519]
I: GROMMEN, PETER KERZ, TRANSYLVANIA, RO. 1839-1918 [38519]
I: GROO — RESIDENTS SARATOV, SAMARA SSFR, SU. 1800-1900 [34081]
I: GROSS, MARIA MARKSCHELKEN, TRANSYLVANIA, RO. 1847-1914 [38519]
I: GUNCKEL & KUNKEL . ALL [38748]
I: GUNDELACH . ALL [38748]
I: HAGEN, CHARLES NOR. 1850+ [38059]
I: HALDANE, RICHARD PLYMOUTH, DEV, ENG. 1840S [36862]
I: HALL, AMBROSE JOHN BDF, ENG. PRE 1845 [34855]
I: HALL, AMOS SHOEMAKER, SOM, ENG. 1840 [36253]
I: HALL, HENRY WILLIAM AUSTRALIA. 1856-1900 [38171]
I: HALL, T. LONDON TAXIDERMIST. 1780-1820 [38171]
I: HALLIDAY, JAMES PLANTATION, ISLAND OF NEVIS, WEST INDIES. 1790-1853 [35739]
I: HALTON, LAWRENCE FARMER OF CO. CAV, IRL. PRE 1860 [38239]
I: HALTON, THOMAS FARMER OF DRUMHOWNA, CO. CAV, IRL. C1832-1908 [38239]
I: HAMMOND BREECHESMAKERS, LONDON, ENG. C1850 [37232]
I: HAMMOND STATIONERS, ISLINGTON, LONDON, ENG. 1860-1890 [37232]
I: HANCOCK, JOSEPH MINER, KIDSGROVE, STS, ENG. 1840-1850S [35074]
I: HANCOCK, MOSES MINER, KIDSGROVE, STS, ENG. 1840-1850S [35074]
I: HANCOCK, THOMAS COLLIER, KIDSGROVE, STS, ENG. 1820-1860S [35074]
I: HANCOCK, WILLIAM COLLIER, KIDSGROVE, STS, ENG. 1840-1850S [35074]
I: HANCOCK, WILLIAM VICTUALLER, NEWCASTLE, STS, ENG. 1858-1860S [35074]
I: HANLON, DANIEL FARMER OF CO. LOG, IRL. PRE 1865 [38239]
I: HANRAHAN, PATRICK JOHN JOCKEY, IRL & GER. C1845-1865 [37111]
I: HANSORD, FRANCIS DRAPER OF HARWICH, ENG. 1772-1846 [37653]
I: HARDING, JOHN CHEMIST IN LONDON. 1810+ [35053]
I: HARGRAVE, JOHN ROLLINSON SHOEMAKER, LEEDS, YKS, ENG. 1840+ [35017]
I: HARGRAVE, OWEN RIVETTER, LEEDS, YKS, ENG. 1860S [35017]
I: HARGRAVES, JOHN DROVER & SOLDIER. 1911-1945 [36303]
I: HARRIS, MOSES EMIGRATED FROM WEX, IRL TO CAN. 1822 [38404]
I: HARRIS, REV GEORGE GRAVESEND, KEN, ENG. 1787-1866 [34019]
I: HARRIS, REV WILLIAM GRAVESEND, KEN, ENG. 1777-1830 [34019]
I: HARRIS, WALTER EDWARD SHIPS STEWARD P&O, UK TO SYDNEY, AUS. C1920-30S [36252]
I: HARRISON, JOSHUA BUILDER OF LEICESTER, ENG. 1770-1832 [36827]
I: HARRISON, MARY & PEACOCK, JONATHAN MARRIED COVERHAM PARISH, NRY, ENG. 1785
        [37498]
I: HARVEST, GEORGE EXCISE OFFICER, MDX, ENG. 1810-42 [35662]
I: HARVEY, AGNES BORN IN GLASGOW, SCT. 1853+ [34330]
I: HARVEY, ANN BORN IN GLASGOW, SCT. 1856+ [34330]
I: HARVEY, JOHN BORN IN GLASGOW, SCT. 1852+ [34330]
I: HARVEY, JOHN W/WIFE MARGARET, ORANGE CO., VA, USA. 1700S [38768]
I: HARVEY, MARY BORN IN GLASGOW, SCT. 1860+ [34330]
I: HARVEY, WILLIAM GALLOWAY SCT, EMIGRANT TO PIPESTONE, MAN, CAN. 1882+ [34330]
I: HARVEY, WILLIAM GALLOWAY BORN IN GLASGOW, SCT. 1857+ [34330]
I: HARVEY, WILLIAM RAG MERCHANT OF GLASGOW, SCT. C1826+ [34330]
I: HARVEY, WILLIAM SCT, FARMER, HUSBAND OF MARTHA CARMICHAEL. C1800+ [34330]
I: HARWELL, JESSIE FATHER OF, VA, USA. 1800-1810 [36330]
I: HARWELL, LOUDEN FAMILY OF IN & SC, USA. 1810 [36330]
I: HARZ NSA & PSA FAMILIES. 1700-1900 [38643]
I: HASLACH (PLZ 7033) ORTSSIPPENBUCH. ALL [38669]
I: HAWES, MARY ARRIVAL IN AUS FROM IRL. C1881 [34971]
I: HAWKES, WILLIAM I EAST BRANTFORD TWP. ONT, CAN. 1861 [34251]
I: HAWKINS, ALFRED PAINTER, MARYLEBONE, LND, ENG. 1880-1890S [35074]
I: HAWKINS, JAMES AND SAVAGE, ELIZABETH TO NZ. 1864 [36253]
I: HAWKINS, JOHN MASTER MARINER OF WHITBY, YKS, ENG. 1800+ [36609]
I: HAYNES DYERS, ENG. ALL [37453]
I: HAYWARD, MICHAEL FARMER OF CASTLE HILL, NSW, AUS. PRE 1844 [34887]
I: HEATLEY, EMMA MRS JOHN PHILLIPS OF ENG & NYC, USA. C1865-1924 [38239]
I: HEATLY, EMMA MRS JOHN PHILLIPS OF ENG & NYC, USA. C1865-1924 [38239]
I: HELD . PRE 1800 [38748]
I: HELSTROP ORIGINS OF NAME AND ORIGINS OF JOHN AND JANE HELSTROP LIVING BIRKBY,
        NRY, ENG. 1738 [38269]

I: **HENDERSON, HENRY** SHIPWRIGHT OF SUNDERLAND, DUR, ENG. 1830+ **[36609]**
I: **HENDERSON, JAMES** MASTER MARINER OF SUNDERLAND, DUR, ENG. 1800+ **[36609]**
I: **HENDRIKSZ, JAN** DR ON BARBESTYN, DUTCH EAST INDIES, NL. 1719 **[36453]**
I: **HENNIGHAUSEN** FAMILY RESEARCH. **[38601]**
I: **HENSEL & HAENSEL** . ALL **[38748]**
I: **HEPPLE, MARY** EMIGRATED FROM CHOLLERTON, NBL, ENG. C1871 **[34827]**
I: **HEROD, ANN** GT YARMOUTH, NFK, ENG. 1820+ **[35939]**
I: **HERTZUM, MARTIN** DANISH SOLDIER — GERMAN SCHLESWIG HOLSTEIN WAR. 1850-1900S
    [36706]
I: **HESSEN** FAMILIEN. PRE 1900 **[38606]**
I: **HESTER, CHARLES** BAKER OF LND, ENG. 1820-1840S **[34385]**
I: **HETHERINGTON, CATHERINE** WIDOWED AT ALBANY, NY, USA. 1846 **[36129]**
I: **HETHERINGTON, JOHN** ST LOUIS, USA. 1850+ **[36129]**
I: **HETHERINGTON, JOSHUA** OF WRY, ENG. C1700-1768 **[37076]**
I: **HETHERINGTON, WILLIAM** ST LOUIS, USA. 1850+ **[36129]**
I: **HEWETT, EDITH ROBINA** BOSTON, USA. 1906+ **[37626]**
I: **HEWITSON, WALTER** BC, CAN. 1900-1990 **[37670]**
I: **HICKIN, CHARLES** SADDLER OF BIRMINGHAM, ENG. 1840-50S **[35136]**
I: **HICKS, HARVEY** BORN GA, TX, USA, 1850-60, MARGARET MCDONALD. 1814+ **[38743]**
I: **HIGGS, ANN** WIFE OF JAMES DIED AT TE KARAKA, NZ 1912. ANY DESCENDANTS PLEASE
    CONTACT. **[37498]**
I: **HIGGS, JAMES & LIPSCOMBE, ANN** MARR AT MDX, ENG — TO NZ WITH SARAH, JAMES &
    HENRY. 1867/73 **[37498]**
I: **HILDEBRAND** ALL CONNECTING BRANCHES, SWEDEN. 1800-1950 **[37544]**
I: **HIND, JOHN RUSSELL** MATHEMATICIAN AND ASTRONOMER, LND, ENG. 1840+ **[36386]**
I: **HOBBS** MILLIONS LEGACY TO ROBERT HOBBS OF PITT TOWN, NSW, AUS. **[33939]**
I: **HOBSON, GEORGE** LONDON TAILOR. B1822-? **[38171]**
I: **HOLLAND, JAMES CHARLES** DROVER. 1880-1930S **[35373]**
I: **HOLLAND, JOHN JAMES THOMAS** LAWYER'S CLERK, COLCHESTER, ENG. 1780-1820 **[35370]**
I: **HOLLAND, WILLIAM** EMIGRATED FROM KIK, IRL TO CAN. 1830S **[38404]**
I: **HOLT, JOSEPH MARION** ORANGE CO., NC & TN, USA, FAMILY, PARENTS. 1787+ **[38743]**
I: **HOLT** TN, USA, MAY BE WIFE TO PITTS BEASLEY SR. 1800+ **[38743]**
I: **HOLYOAK, GEORGE** CARPENTER, NEWPORT PAGNALL, BKM, ENG. 1788+ **[35939]**
I: **HOMES, JAMES EDMUND** ACCOMMODATION — HOUSE KEEPER. C1875 **[35527]**
I: **HOOD, MARGARET** TO USA. 1920S **[34300]**
I: **HOOLEY, JOHN** JOINER IN AUS & ENG. 1834-1904 **[34034]**
I: **HOOLEY, WILLIAM** JOINER & CARPENTER, ENG. C1800 **[34034]**
I: **HOPKINS, THOMAS & HANNAH** WELLES KEN, ENG. C1820 **[34435]**
I: **HORA, JAMES** SURGEON OF LONDON, ENG. 1795-1843 **[37653]**
I: **HORA, TUDOR TRAVERS** CHEMIST OF LONDON, ENG. 1872-1937 **[37653]**
I: **HORA, WILLIAM** SILK MERCHANT OF LONDON, ENG. C1790-1841 **[37653]**
I: **HORNER, JANE & LOUDON, WILLIAM** MARRIED ULSTER, IRL. C1800-15 **[37498]**
I: **HOUDE, AIME** MISSING DETROIT AREA, MI, USA — BORN CAN 1906. 1925-1932 **[38525]**
I: **HOULD, RICHARD ARTHUR, BORN DUNEDIN, NZ** ACTOR (HOLLYWOOD) 1930-40S. 1924+ **[37498]**
I: **HOUSTON, GENERAL SAM. (TX, USA)** ANCESTRAL CONNECTIONS TO ANT, IRL. 1600-1700 **[37425]**
I: **HOW, THOMAS** DEANS, ELIZABETH, SPOUSE, ENG. 1820-1870 **[34248]**
I: **HOWARTH, ISAAC** CONVICT 'INDIAN' NSW. 1810 **[36856]**
I: **HOWE, HENRY** LABOURER AT THE DOCKS, ST GEORGE IN THE EAST, MDX, ENG. C1800-1861
    [35997]
I: **HOWELL, GEORGE** MILLS OF PARRAMATTA, NSW, AUS. 1802+ **[36269]**
I: **HUCKS, ROBERT** BREWER OF MDX, ENG. 1700-1750 **[34743]**
I: **HUGGINS** ONE NAME SOCIETY. 1600+ **[38326]**
I: **HUGHES, ALBERT THOMAS** MECHANICAL ENGINEER & INVENTOR, ENG. 1885-1940 **[36193]**
I: **HUGHES, DAVID & MARYANN** CHURCH HOUSE LLANIGON, BRE,WLS. 1880-1949 **[35942]**
I: **HUGHES, MARYANNE** POST OFFICE, LLANIGON, BRE, WLS. 1920-1949 **[35942]**
I: **HUGHES, THOMAS** SHOEMAKER OF HOBART, TAS, AUS. C1829 **[35137]**
I: **HUGHES, THOMAS** SURGEON AND GENTLEMANS OUTFITTER, LONDON, ENG. 1798-1867 **[37246]**
I: **HUGUENOTS** OF FRANCE INC. DEPARTURE TO AMERICA. ALL **[38369]**
I: **HUMBY, JOHN THOMAS** REGISTRAR, WIL, ENG. 1870+ **[35418]**
I: **HUMBY, MISS** SCHOOLTEACHER, WIL, ENG. 1870+ **[35418]**
I: **HUMPHREY, HENRY** SPANISH CONNECTION, SSX, ENG. 1800S **[36786]**
I: **HUNT, SARAH** LND, ENG. 1800-1840S **[34385]**
I: **HUNTER, ANDREW** FARMER OF DOAGH, ANT, IRL. C1869 **[34385]**
I: **HUNTER, JANE** DOAGH, ANT, IRL. 1869 **[34385]**
I: **HUNTER, OLLO** TINGWELL, SHETLAND ISLANDS — DESCENDANTS. C1785 **[35719]**
I: **HURRY** FAMILY PEDIGREE. 1690-1912 **[37759]**
I: **HUTCHISON, HENRY** SPIRIT MERCHANT, EDINBURGH, SCT. 1800-1870 **[37727]**
I: **INGWERSEN, NICHOLAS** RESIDENT OF CLINTON, IA, USA. 1852+ **[35616]**
I: **INGWERSEN, PETER** RESIDENT OF CLINTON, IA, USA. 1852+ **[35616]**
I: **JACKLIN, WILLIAM** SHIPS MASTER, LINCOLN, ENG. 1770-1790 **[35092]**
I: **JACKMAN (ANY)** BOOTMAKER, DEV, ENG. 1820 **[36253]**
I: **JACKSON, EDWIN** SCT OR ENG. C1870S **[38239]**

I: JACKSON, ERLE EVERETT TOBACCO SALESMAN OF BUFFALO, NY, USA. PRE 1937 [38239]
I: JACKSON, HENRY LABOURER, KENSINGTON, MDX, ENG. 1800S [36817]
I: JACKSON, ROBERT, CHEMIST ST GEORGES HOSPITAL, ENG. C1854 [35554]
I: JAMES, NICHOLAS SHOEMAKER, HELSTON, CON, ENG. 1820-1880 [35017]
I: JAMES, WILLIAM OWEN LND, ENG. 1895+ [35939]
I: JARRETT, JAMES A. CABINETMAKER, PIMLICO, LND, ENG. 1835-1860S [37634]
I: JARRETT, JOSEPH CHERINGTON, WAR, ENG. C1770 [36014]
I: JARVIS, SAPPER A. (BERT?) ESS & LND, ENG. 1817+ [37756]
I: JEFFERY, WILLIAM FAMILIES & RESIDENT, LISKEARD, CON, ENG. 1850-90+ [35696]
I: JEFFERYS, WM LAMPLIGHTER, BATH, ENG. C1900-1905 [34400]
I: JEFFRIES RECORDS, FAUQUIER CO., VA, USA. 1759+ [37527]
I: JEFFRIES RECORDS, HARDIN CO., KY, USA. 1810+ [37527]
I: JENNINGS, GEORGE SLANEY PLACE, ISLINGTON, ENG. 1700+ [36864]
I: JESSE, WILLIAM HENRY DISAPPEARED — LONDON, ENG. 1900S [36456]
I: JESSE, WILLIAM HENRY IMMIGRANT TO USA. 1900S [36456]
I: JIMMY THE WHISPERER BUSHRANGER?, LIGHTNING RIDGE REGION. 1850-1930 [33846]
I: JOERG, MICHAEL II, 1569+ ANCESTRY. PRE 1569 [38608]
I: JOERGENSEN ANCESTRY. PRE 1500 [38608]
I: JOHN HENRY CLIVE 1787-1851 TRANSCRIPTION OF HIS PAPERS. 800-1840 [36169]
I: JOHN TAYLOR & SONS CARTAGE CONTRACTOR, LIVERPOOL, ENG. 1800-1870 [36522]
I: JOHNSON, ALPHONSO LADIES MANTLE CUTTER OF KINGSTON, ONT, CAN. 1850-1950 [36990]
I: JOHNSON, BRAGANZA WALLER THEACHER SCT & RSA. 1847-1932 [36452]
I: JOHNSON, JACK GOLD MINER, QLD, AUS. 1890-1920 [35434]
I: JOHNSON, STEPHEN WILLIAM REVOLUTIONARY WAR VETERAN, USA. 1749-1834 [38537]
I: JOHNSTON, ELIZABETH DRUMKEERAN, FER, IRL. PRE 1854 [34965]
I: JOHNSTON, GEORGE & SUSAN ARMSTRONG DRUMKEERAN, FER, IRL. PRE 1854 [34965]
I: JOHNSTON, JAMES NURSERYMAN OF EDMONTON, ENG. PRE 1897 [36167]
I: JONES, ARCHIE WILLIAM GENERAL SEC'Y, TYPOGRAPHICAL ASSO.. 1862-1901 [36171]
I: JONES, EDWARD HAVARD BORN BRIDGE ST., ABERYSTWYTH, WLS. 1867 [38239]
I: JONES, ELIZABETH MRS HAMILTON LEWIS OF CO. CGN, WLS. C1810-1861+ [38239]
I: JONES, HAMILTON LEWIS OF ABERYSTWYTH, WLS & NYC, USA. 1870-1924 [38239]
I: JONES, HUGH OWEN WLS TO AUS, DESCENDANTS. 1856+ [36885]
I: JONES, JAMES ISAACS WEAVER OF LONDON, MDX, ENG. C1866 [35683]
I: JONES, REV WM. NEFYN, CAE, WLS, DESCENDANTS. 1832+ [36885]
I: JONES, WILLIAM LORANDO SCULPTOR FROM MERTHYR TYDFIL, WLS. 1820-1893 [35784]
I: JOY, AUGUSTUS SYDNEY, NSW, AUS. C1883 [37173]
I: JOYNES, COL. LEVIN PLANTER OF ACCOMACK CO., VA, USA. ALL [36557]
I: KAPPIE, JOHANNA NEE KAZY GRAVE & DATE OF DEATH. 1900S [35468]
I: KASCHUBISCHER ADEL EMIGRATION. 1700-1945 [38687]
I: KEEN, GEORGE SHOEMAKER OF CHARLTON HORETHORNE, SOM, ENG. C1886 [37721]
I: KEEN, HENRY BOOTMAKER OF KENSINGTON & HAMMERSMITH, MDX, ENG. C1860 [37721]
I: KEEN, RICHARD BAPTISM AND PARENTAGE. C1773 [37721]
I: KEEN, RICHARD BOOTMAKER OF NEWINGTON & KENT RD, SRY, ENG. 1795-1842 [37721]
I: KELLY, JAMES A., D.C.M. ROYAL INNISKILLING FUSILIERS, IRL. C1870-1920 [34215]
I: KEMP, JOHN OF WORKINGTON, ENG. 1887-89 [37267]
I: KENT, ALFRED RICHES BORN TAS, AUS. 1842+ [37300]
I: KENT, JOHN RICHES VIC, AUS. 1840S-50S [37300]
I: KERR FAMILY ULSTER, IRL TO PA & KY, USA. 1720-1790 [37533]
I: KERR, ROBERT & ELLEN SMAIL AUSTRALIAN DESCENDANTS, 1838+ [37349]
I: KIDD, JANE BORN PER. SCONE, AGE 5 WHERE? UK. 1881 CENSUS [36467]
I: KIDWELL, SARAH & THOMPSON, JOHN MARRIAGE AT LONGHAM(?), NFK, ENG. C1790 [37498]
I: KIMBRO, KATHERINE ORANGE CO., NC & TN, USA, FAMILY, PARENTS. 1797+ [38743]
I: KIMPTON & KEMPTON IMMIGRANTS, ENG TO NZ. 1800-1990+ [33961]
I: KING EDWARD OF ENG DESCENDANTS OF. ALL [35655]
I: KING JOHN ILLEGITIMATE CHILDREN. ALL [35901]
I: KING, DAVID GUILDFORD ROYAL GRAMMAR SCHOOL, ENG. PRE 1960 [35551]
I: KING, DUNCAN WATCHMAKER OF FORE ST, PORT GLASGOW, SCT. 1820S [35229]
I: KING, JOHN WIFE ELIZABETH WADE, SOM, ENG. 1855 [36253]
I: KINNEY, HENRY PLOUGHMAN OF IRL. C1804+ [38067]
I: KINVIG, JOHN & JONEY, IOM DESCENDANTS OF MARRIAGE. 1730+ [34125]
I: KIRWAN OF DALGIN DALGAN, IRL. C1500+ [34005]
I: KIRWAN, MARIA A. M.COUSIN WALTER PATK 29/5/1846 DUB, IRL. 1846 [34005]
I: KIRWAN, MARTIN EDWARD BORN DUB, IRL. 1800+ [34005]
I: KLAY . ALL [38748]
I: KLEINGARTNER, CHRISTIAN BLACKSMITH OF MECKLENBURG. C1700-1788 [37036]
I: KNIGHT, JAMES BRUSHMAKER, KENSINGTON, MDX, ENG. 1800S [36817]
I: KNIGHT, STEPHEN TAILOR OF SHEEN, HOLBORN & RAMSGATE. 1776-1867 [37339]
I: KNIGHT, THOMAS SOLDIER OF NOTTINGHAM, ENG. 1806 [34371]
I: KNIGHT, WILLIAM WIFE ANN OF WEST BRIDGFORD, NTT, ENG. C1785 [34371]
I: KNOWLES, JOHN MARRIAGE TO ELIZABETH YEATES SOUGHT. C1790 [36587]
I: KNOWLES, PTE B.G. 2/23RD LND REGT. 1917+ [37756]
I: KOCHER, FERDINAND HORSE-DRAWN CARRIAGE DRIVER, VIENNA, ORS. PRE 1900 [37268]

I: **KUCHENMEISTER, HEINRICH** GABENDORF, MEK, GER TO AUS. 1852 **[35810]**
I: **KUMMER MULLERFRAM** . ALL **[38628]**
I: **KUNDE, EILEEN** SINGER, DELORAINE, TAS, AUS. 1900+ **[34770]**
I: **KURZ, KURZA, KURTZ (EFRAIM)** JEW, BOLECHOWICE, KR, POL. 1860-1900 **[35717]**
I: **KYLE, ANN** BORN IN GLASGOW, SCT. 1864+ **[34330]**
I: **KYLE, SETH** DETECTIVE OFFICER OF GLASGOW, SCT. C1820+ **[34330]**
I: **KYMPTON & KIMPTON** RESIDENTS OF MDX, ENG. 1600-1800 **[33961]**
I: **LAMAR CO., TX,** USA ALL CEMETERIES AND GRAVES. ALL **[36947]**
I: **LAMBE, ALFRED BOYDELL** WINEMERCHANT, LONDON, ENG. 1817-1881 **[36967]**
I: **LAMBERT FAMILY** HUNTERDON CO, NJ, USA. PRE 1802 **[34052]**
I: **LAMBERT FAMILY** NIAGARA CO, ONT, CAN. 1784+ **[34052]**
I: **LAMBERT FAMILY** PRINCE EDWARD CO, ONT, CAN. 1802+ **[34052]**
I: **LANE, COUNCILLOR JOSIAH** J.P., GLASS MANUFACTURER, DUDLEY, WORCS, ENG. 1860-1932 **[37883]**
I: **LANE, HENRY** B 1834, 29 VITTORIA ST, ISLINGTON, ENG, DESCENDANTS. 1850+ **[36864]**
I: **LANE, JOSEPH** B 1835, 29 VITTORIA ST, ISLINGTON, ENG, DESCENDANTS. 1850+ **[36864]**
I: **LANE, LYDIA** B 1840, 29 VITTORIA ST, ISLINGTON, ENG, DESCENDANTS. 1840+ **[36864]**
I: **LANE, SAMUEL & ELIZABETH** 29 VITTORIA ST, ISLINGTON, ENG. 1820-1860 **[36864]**
I: **LANE, SAMUEL** B 1824, SHOREDITCH, ENG, DESCENDANTS. 1840+ **[36864]**
I: **LARKUM** CEYLON. 1850-1890 **[37220]**
I: **LARSEN, CHRISTEN** ENGINEER, BUNDABERG, QLD, AUS. 1885-1914 **[35662]**
I: **LARSSEN, SVEN** OF SWEDEN. 1845-69 **[38535]**
I: **LATIMER** DESCENDANTS OF MARTYRED BISHOP. 1555+ **[35624]**
I: **LATTA, EPHRAIM** S HUNTINGDON TWP, WESTMORELAND CO., PA, USA. 1783-1804 **[36908]**
I: **LAWRANCE, JAMES** DESCENDANTS OF AUS. 1910+ **[34260]**
I: **LAYT WORLDWIDE** ONE NAME STUDY. ALL **[35160]**
I: **LEAKER, HENRY** MASTER SHIP SMITH OF BRISTOL, ENG. 1850+ **[37406]**
I: **LEDGER (LEGER) FAMILY HISTORY** ABBOTSKERSWELL AREA, DEV, ENG. 1600+ **[35668]**
I: **LEDWARD, THOMAS DENMAN** HMS BOUNTY. 1787+ **[36983]**
I: **LEE, MARY ANN** VIC, AUS. 1840+ **[34907]**
I: **LEEDHAM** WATER COLOUR ARTIST. 1830+ **[34338]**
I: **LEES, JOHN** SURGEON OF ASHTON UNDER LYNE, ENG. 1750-1850 **[37255]**
I: **LEEVES FAMILY CONNECTIONS** SOM, DOR, SSX, KEN, MDX & OTHER PARTS OF ENG. 1500+ **[37206]**
I: **LESLIE, ELIZABETH HARRIETT** TOURIST HOME – BRIGHT, VIC, AUS. 1835-1923 **[34006]**
I: **LEVER, ROBERT JAMES** YACHT SAILOR, FATHER DANIEL. PRE 1897 **[36496]**
I: **LEWIS FAMILY HISTORY** LITTLE FARINGTON, OXF, & LECHLADE, GLS, ENG. 1600+ **[35668]**
I: **LEWIS, HAMILTON** TAILOR OF ABERYSTWYTH, WLS. C1810-1871+ **[38239]**
I: **LEWIS, WILLIAM** MASTER MARINER, WLS. C1818 **[35447]**
I: **LICKISS, WILLIAM** BAKER OF PETERGATE, ENG. 1800+ **[36557]**
I: **LIDSTER, BERTHA** DAU OF RALPH & ELIZABETH (LANG). PHOTOGRAPH. NSW, AUS. C1920 **[37498]**
I: **LIMPERANI, JOSEPH** PROFESSOR OF LANGUAGES. C1800 **[36928]**
I: **LINDALL, JOHAN** SHIPS CREW. 1876-1956 **[34432]**
I: **LINGLEY, CHARLES** WEAVER OF NORWICH, NFK, ENG. 1820-1880S **[37689]**
I: **LIPHARD & LIPHARDT** . ALL **[38748]**
I: **LIPSCOMBE, JOSEPH & GILKES, MARY** MARR AT MONKS RISBOROUGH, BKM, ENG 1827. DETAILS OF DEATHS BY 1872 DESIRED. **[37498]**
I: **LIST** FAMILY TREE. 1400+ **[38624]**
I: **LITTLE, GEORGE BARTHOLOMEW** CARPENTER - RICHMOND, VIC, AUS. 1852-1885 **[37120]**
I: **LITTLE, JAMES KEEN** OF NELSON, NZ. 1890S **[37721]**
I: **LIVINGSTON, ROBERT** FIREMAN & ENGINEER OF AYR, SCT. 1840-1850 **[35354]**
I: **LLOYD, EDWARD** IRON WORKER, STS, ENG. 1882 **[35074]**
I: **LLOYD, MARIE** ANCESTRY OF MUSIC HALL ARTIST, ENG. PRE 1870 **[36107]**
I: **LOCHEARN** FAMILY HISTORY WANTED. **[34373]**
I: **LOGAN, JAMES** ROPEMAKER OF BANBRIDGE, IRL. 1860-1872 **[36001]**
I: **LOGANS (ANY)** MAKERS OF ROPE & TWINE IN ULSTER, IRL. ANY **[36001]**
I: **LOUDON (LOWDEN ETC)** ALL IN ULSTER, IRL ESPECIALY CONNECTED WITH SCT. PRE 1850 **[37498]**
I: **LOWDEN, MARY & SPRATT, HANS** WIDOWER OF DOW, IRL MARRIAGE AT NEWTOWNHAMILTON, ARM, IRL. 1845 **[37498]**
I: **LUNN, HENRY** FATHER PERCY LUNN, ANY RELATIVES. 1900-1958 **[36430]**
I: **LUTHER, JACOB** BROTHER OF MARTIN, GER. 1490-1571 **[37683]**
I: **LYDIARD & ENMORE, BISHOP** OF DESC & LINEAGE, SOM & ESS, ENG. PRE 1750 **[38768]**
I: **LYNEHAM** FAMILIES IN AUS. 1860+ **[33887]**
I: **MACAULAY** CLAN HISTORY. ALL **[36240]**
I: **MACGREGOR** CLAN HISTORY & GENEALOGY, ALIASES, INDEX. **[36635]**
I: **MACK** NAVY COOK, UK. 1930S **[36164]**
I: **MACMILLAN, HELEN** METIS/FUR TRADE. C1813 **[38466]**
I: **MAGEE, THOMAS (STN MASTER)** TO PA, USA FROM CAV, IRL. 1880-1940 **[38302]**
I: **MAGILL, JOHN** GENTRY, CO.DOWN, IRL. 1800-1847 **[34244]**
I: **MALLEY, LEONARD** ROPEMAKER OF IRL. PRE 1804 **[36052]**
I: **MANNINGS – CARVER MARRIAGE** POSS BATH OR HOLLOWAY, SOM, ENG. PRE 1828 **[37972]**

I: **MARCIEA, HENRY PIERRE** SEAMAN OF SALEM, MA, USA. 1807-12 **[37019]**
I: **MARKS, HANNAH** MCPHAIL, NSW, AUS. 1880+ **[36129]**
I: **MARRIAGE RECORDS** ALL MADDOX PLUS VARIANT SURNAMES. PRE 1870 **[36947]**
I: **MARRINER, FRANCIS** BOOTMAKER OF CHATHAM, ENG. 1737+ **[37595]**
I: **MARRINER, JOHN** OF KEN, ENG. 1710-1770 **[37595]**
I: **MARSDEN FAMILY** SMITHYBROOK, STANHILL, OSWALDTWISTLE, LAN, ENG. 1900+ **[35942]**
I: **MARSH (MAISH) FAMILY HISTORY** BAYCLIFFE FARM, MAIDEN BRADLEY, WIL, ENG. 1600+ **[35668]**
I: **MARTIN, EDWARD** CHURCH ORGANIST, DEPTFORD & LEWISHAM, LND, ENG. 1850-70 **[37670]**
I: **MARTIN, JAMES** CARPENTER, SCT, MARRIED ISABELLA BAIRD. 1800+ **[33784]**
I: **MARTIN, NORTH WALL, DUB** TO AUS. C1890 **[38302]**
I: **MARTIN, THOMAS** COLLIER OF LONGDON, STS, ENG. 1700-1750S **[34385]**
I: **MARTIN, WILLIAM** USA. 1900S+ **[37930]**
I: **MASON, KITTY** DANCER OF LONDON, ENG. PRE 1930 **[37750]**
I: **MASON DAVID CHARLES**, ENGINEER. 1880-1890 **[37232]**
I: **MATHER, ELLIS** JUSTICE OF PEACE, LIVERPOOL, ENG & WLS. 1880+ **[36815]**
I: **MATHER, WILLIAM** PENKETH BREWERY, LAN, ENG. 1870+ **[36815]**
I: **MAY, ALBERT H.** INDIANA, USA. 1836-1855 **[38768]**
I: **MAY, WILLIAM** JAMESTOWN, VA, USA. 1607-1680 **[38768]**
I: **MAYER, ARTHUR** ENGINEER, PANAMA CANAL CONST'N. 1904-14 **[38002]**
I: **MAYO, DANIEL** CABINETMAKER, ISLINGTON, LND, ENG. 1800+ **[35939]**
I: **MCANULTY, THOMAS** ROYAL ENNISKILLEN FUSILIERS WWI. **[34373]**
I: **MCCALLUM, MALCOLM** JOINER, BARONY, LKS, SCT. 1830+ **[36749]**
I: **MCCORMICK, DUNCAN & CATHERINE CAMPBELL** ISLE OF MULL, SCT – DESCENDANTS WORLDWIDE. 1830+ **[35952]**
I: **MCDONALD, FLORA** DESCENDANTS. ALL **[34937]**
I: **MCDONALD, MARGARET** HALF CHEROKEE, TRAIL OF TEARS, GA, TX, AR, USA. PRE 1860 **[38743]**
I: **MCDONALD, W.G. AND FAMILY** – BULLENBALONG/COOMA, NSW, AUS. 1838-1870 **[37965]**
I: **MCGEE, THOMAS (STN MASTER)** TO PA, USA FROM CAV, IRL. 1880-1940 **[38302]**
I: **MCGILL, JOHN** TULLYCARN, CO.DOWN, IRL. 1800+ **[34244]**
I: **MCGOWAN, ELIZA** QUAKER RUNAWAY SCT TO LIVERPOOL, ENG. 1810-1838 **[37671]**
I: **MCGUIRE, JANE** IRL. 1800-1827 **[36739]**
I: **MCGUIRK, ISABELLA** COOKSTOWN, TYR, IRL. C1846-1870 **[37436]**
I: **MCHAFFIE, WILLIAM** B WIG 1820, SHEEP FARMER AUS. 1850+ **[36864]**
I: **MCHAFFIE, WILLIAM** RESIDENT OF OLD KILPATRICK, SCT. 1800-1850 **[38521]**
I: **MCILMENE ROLAND & JONET** GALLOWAY RAMIST. PRE 1600 **[37644]**
I: **MCINNES, JOHN** PUBLICAN OF BIRMINGHAM, ENG. 1885-1920 **[36592]**
I: **MCINTYRE, JOHN** DROWNED IN LAKE MICHIGAN. 1850+ **[37424]**
I: **MCIVOR, WILLIAM** FARMER OF MINNESOTA, USA. PRE 1880 **[33858]**
I: **MCKENZIE, DUNCAN** SHIPS JOINER, GOVAN, LKS, SCT. 1860S **[36749]**
I: **MCKINNON, ANGUS JOHN** FARMER OF HANTS CO, NS, CAN. 1864-1891 **[34251]**
I: **MCLAURIN, JAMES & MCGIBBON, MARY** AUSTRALIA – DESCENDANTS. 1807+ **[35719]**
I: **MCLEAN, JOHN** MAGISTRATE, JAMAICA, WEST INDIES. 1830+ **[33921]**
I: **MCLEAN, KEN** CARPENTER, CAI, SCT. 1770-1850 **[34646]**
I: **MCLEOD, ANNIE** MARRIAGE, PROBABLY IN SASK OR ALB, CAN. C1930-1940 **[34260]**
I: **MCMAHON, M.** PHOTOGRAPHER NEAR GISBORNE NZ. C1913 **[37498]**
I: **MCMILLAN, ARTHUR** SURGEON, UK & BURMA. PRE 1931 **[35551]**
I: **MCMILLAN, DANIEL** MERCHANT, LEOMINSTER, ENG. PRE 1920 **[35551]**
I: **MCMILLAN, DANIEL** TEA PLANTER, CEYLON. PRE 1920 **[35551]**
I: **MCNAMARA, BRIDGET** NUN, CLA, IRL. 1860-1890 **[33947]**
I: **MCNAMARA, THOMAS** KILFENORA, CLA, IRL. 1800+ **[35105]**
I: **MCNAMARA, THOMAS** PUBLICAN, CLA, IRL. 1830-1870 **[33947]**
I: **MCNAMARA, WILLIAM** MERCHANT, CLA, IRL. 1860-1890 **[33947]**
I: **MCPHAN** ONE NAME STUDY, WORLDWIDE. **[33931]**
I: **MCSHEA, WILLIAM** IRL. C1800-1860+ **[38239]**
I: **MCSHEA, WILLIAM** WHITESMITH OF BALLYSHANNON, IRL. C1825-1888 **[38239]**
I: **MCSHEE, WILLIAM** IRL. C1800-1860+ **[38239]**
I: **MCSHEE, WILLIAM** WHITESMITH OF BALLYSHANNON, IRL. C1825-1888 **[38239]**
I: **MELLOR, JAMES** BRASSFOUNDER OF MANCHESTER, ENG. 1800-1860 **[35354]**
I: **MERCER, REDMOND** FARMER, BRUNSWICK CO., NC, USA. 1790-1858 **[37789]**
I: **MEREWEATHER, JOHN DAVIES** BRITISH CLERGYMAN IN AUS & ITL. 1850-1896 **[37289]**
I: **MERKEL** . PRE 1900 **[38748]**
I: **MERVILL, MARY** BATHEASTON, SOM, ENG. 1800S **[36739]**
I: **METCALF, GEORGE** SON OF ANTHONY & ELIZABETH (WINTERSGILL) BORN MASHAN, NRY, ENG. 1825 **[37498]**
I: **METIER PROFESSION** PILET, FRA. 1600-1750 **[36699]**
I: **MEYER, HENRI** NAPOLEONIC WAR, NEHWEILER, ALS, FRA. 1750-1850 **[36898]**
I: **MIELL, HERBERT** SADDLE & HARNESS MAKER, ENG & NSW, AUS. 1850-1870 **[35400]**
I: **MIERS** WORLDWIDE. ALL **[38627]**
I: **MILDNER** NAMESTRAGER . ALL **[38628]**
I: **MILLS, PETER** OF CT, USA, DESC. OF. 1660+ **[36335]**
I: **MILLWARD, JOHN** MUTINEER ON HMS *BOUNTY*. 1766-92 **[36230]**

I: **MILNER, JAMES** CHAPLAIN TO DUKE OF KENT, HALIFAX, ENG. 1770-1820 **[36217]**
I: **MITCHELL, EDWARD JAMES** WIMBLEDON, SRY, ENG. 1890+ **[36300]**
I: **MITCHELL, EDWARD JAMES** INDIAN CIVIL SERVICE, ENGINEER, INDIA. 1859+ **[36300]**
I: **MITCHELL, HENRY EDWARD** INDIAN CIVIL SERVICE, ENGINEER, INDIA. 1850 & 1883 **[36300]**
I: **MITCHELL, JOHN** ENG. 1730+ **[38059]**
I: **MOFFAT, WILLIAM** FARMER OF IRL. C1745+ **[38067]**
I: **MONGAN, EDWARD** WI, USA. 1858 **[34582]**
I: **MOON** NEW ENGLAND ORIGIN, USA. 1600-1900 **[36943]**
I: **MOORE, HENRY** 23 DANUBE ST, BELFAST, IRL. 1899 **[34385]**
I: **MOORE, HENRY** 4 ALLOA ST, BELFAST, IRL. C1898 **[34385]**
I: **MOORE, JAMES** BOATSWAIN, DEV, ENG. 1800-1850 **[34716]**
I: **MOORE, JAMES** FARMER, LARNE, ANT, IRL. C1870 **[34385]**
I: **MOORE, WILLIAM** BORN BANHAM, NFK, ENG TO JOHN & WALLACE, MARY. 1799 **[37498]**
I: **MOORE, WILLIAM** BORN TO WILLIAM & THOMPSON, SUSAN AT GREAT FRANSHAM, NFK, ENG. 1823 **[37498]**
I: **MORAN & SEFTON** FAMILIES PICTURED WITH T-MODEL FORD CAR, NORTH IS., NZ. C1910 **[37498]**
I: **MORGAN — BEARD** MARRIAGE POSS BATH, SOM, ENG, EXCHANGE INFO. PRE 1830 **[37972]**
I: **MORRISON, KITTY** DEATH AT LIVERPOOL, ENG. 01 APR 1865 **[36712]**
I: **MORTLOCK BRUSH OR CHINA CO** LONDON, LAVENHAM, SFK, ENG. 1600+ **[35668]**
I: **MUES** EMIGRATION POS & USA. 1700-1933 **[38631]**
I: **MULDOON, THOMAS** LABOURER, OFF, IRL. PRE 1819 **[37903]**
I: **MUNDY RENATUS.** SHOEMAKER, HELSTON, CON, ENG. 1820-1880 **[35017]**
I: **MUNN** ROYAL NAVY, GLASGOW, SCT. C1815 **[34615]**
I: **MURDOCH, JAMES** LAWYER OF NEWMILNS & GLASGOW, SCT. 1820-1880 **[35354]**
I: **MURPHY, FRANCES** BORN SAN FRANCISCO, USA. 1889 **[35405]**
I: **MURRAY, ANNIE** USA. 1900S+ **[37930]**
I: **MURRAY, MARGARET** USA. 1900S+ **[37930]**
I: **MURRAY, WILLIAM RUSSELL** SCT TO NZ. 1856 **[38282]**
I: **MUTIMER, CHRISTOPHER** SHOTESHAM, NFK, ENG. 1700-1780 **[34716]**
I: **MYRES, WILLIAM** GREEN COURT, ST ANDREWS, NEWCASTLE, NBL, ENG. 1851 **[36609]**
I: **NAISSANCE MARIAGE, DECES.** C1500-1650 **[34516]**
I: **NANCOLLAS** GRAVES. ALL **[36404]**
I: **NAPIER ROBT. & DAVID** FAMILIES SHIPBUILDING, CLYDE, SCT. ALL **[35999]**
I: **NAPOLEON I** ILLEGITIMATE SONS OF. 1785+ **[34519]**
I: **NEEDHAM, ELIZABETH** FIRST FLEET, ENG TO AUS. 1787-1788 **[35721]**
I: **NEIGER, JACOB & KLARA** JEWS, BRONX, NY, USA. 1920-1965 **[35717]**
I: **NELLIST** FAMILY TO USA, CAN & AUS. ALL **[36481]**
I: **NEWBOLD, HENRY** CYCLE MANUFACTURER, DERBY, ENG. **[34659]**
I: **NEWGATE PRISON,** ENG ROGER STEVENS, WLS. 1700-1725 **[36669]**
I: **NEWLAND, WILLIAM** WIRE WORKER OF LND, ENG. 1800S **[34887]**
I: **NEWMAN** ALL NAMED SEBASTIAN. 1700+ **[34079]**
I: **NEWMAN** BIRTH OF EDWARD. C1708 **[34079]**
I: **NEYNOE, JOSEPH** DUBLIN, IRL. ALL **[35377]**
I: **NICHOLAS, WILLIAM HENRY** SALVATIONIST, EASTBOURNE, ENG. 1850-1930 **[37351]**
I: **NICHOLLS, CHARLES** JOCKEY. C1850 **[37340]**
I: **NICHOLLS, G.M.C.** DARLINGHURST RD, DARLINGHURST, NSW, AUS. 1930S **[37498]**
I: **NOBLE, HENRY, QUARRYMAN** CAREER WITH ORD & MADDISON OF CRAWLEYSIDE & AYCLIFFE, DUR, ENG. 1860-1917 **[38269]**
I: **NOBLE, HENRY, QUARRYMAN** CAREER WITH ORD & MADDISON OF HULANDS, NRY, ENG. 1860-1917 **[38269]**
I: **NOBLE, WILLIAM** BLACKSMITH, RANGIORA, NZ. C1878 **[38752]**
I: **NOCKER, JOHN BAPTISTE** BRISTOL, ENG. PRE 1832 **[36290]**
I: **NORMAN, FLETCHER** MILLER OF CAMERTON, CUL, ENG. 1840+ **[37073]**
I: **NORMAN, JOSHUA** MILLER OF SEATON, CUL, ENG. 1850+ **[37073]**
I: **NORMAN, PETER** MILLER OF GREAT BROUGHTON, ENG. 1850-60 **[37073]**
I: **NORMAN, PETER** MILLER OF SEATON, CUL, ENG. 1840-50 **[37073]**
I: **NORRIS, GEORGE HENRY** PIG KEEPER, MITCHAM, SRY, ENG. 1920S **[37778]**
I: **NORRIS, GEORGE** GARDENER, CHELSEA, MDX, ENG. 1800S **[37778]**
I: **NUNN, ELIZABETH & BENSLEY, HENRY** MARRIAGE, NFK, ENG. 1812 **[37498]**
I: **O'CONNOR** ALL CONNECTING BRANCHES, USA. 1700-1800S **[37544]**
I: **O'DWYER, JEREMIAH** IRISH REGT, FRENCH ARMY. 1650-1800 **[33916]**
I: **O'HARA, PETER** 5 PA. CALVARY, PHILADELPHIA, PA, USA. 1861-1865 **[36580]**
I: **O'MEAGHER, RICHARD** SCHOOLTEACHER, WOODFORD, VIC, AUS. 1845-1870 **[35017]**
I: **O'ROURKE, FLORENCE** BROTHERS OF, TRALEE, KER, IRL, TO CAN & USA. 1870+ **[34699]**
I: **O'ROURKE, MAURICE & ELLEN** O'SULLIVAN DESCENDANTS OF, KERRY, IRL. 1800+ **[34699]**
I: **ODDY, JOSHUA JEPSON** MERCHANT OF LONDON & ST PETERSBURG. 1769-1814 **[37339]**
I: **ODGERS, MARY JANE** AGE 10 WHERE? UK. 1861 CENSUS. **[36467]**
I: **OGDEN, JOHN** SEA CAPTAIN. PRE 1850 **[36066]**
I: **OHROGGE** GER (NSA). PRE 1900 **[38748]**
I: **OLIVER** FAMILY TAILORS LIVING IN MERRINGTON, DUR, ENG 1729+. 1700-1900 **[38269]**
I: **OLIVER, FANNY OR FRANCES** BOTLEY NR SOUTHAMPTON, ENG. 1840S **[33802]**
I: **ORMEROD, SUTCLIFFE** HALIFAX & BIRMINGHAM, ENG. 1835-1907 **[36998]**

I: **ORTLEY, MARY** LONGDON, STS, ENG. 1700-1750S **[34385]**
I: **OTWAY, WILLIAM BEAUCLERE** OF ENG, IRL, USA & INDIA. 1818+ **[35137]**
I: **OULTRE-MEER D'DOCHEZ ESQUIRE** EDWARD III. PRE 1400 **[38167]**
I: **OWEN, OWEN** LABOURER OF MEOPHAM, ENG. PRE 1815 **[37325]**
I: **PAGE SURNAME HISTORY & ORIGIN** IN ENG. PRE 1675 **[35321]**
I: **PALATINE GERMANS** NEW YORK STATE, USA. 1700+ **[34377]**
I: **PALMER, MARY BETT** WESTGATE ON SEA, KEN, ENG. 1880S **[36967]**
I: **PAMMENT, CHARLES EDWIN** CAM AND SFK, ENG. 1820-60 **[37606]**
I: **PAMMENT, EDWARD** LABORER OF ISLEHAM, ENG. 1824-81 **[37606]**
I: **PARDY, CAPT. THOMAS** OF GSY, CHI. 1800+ **[35137]**
I: **PARDY, HENRY** YEOMAN OF SOPLEY, HAM, ENG. C1750 **[37173]**
I: **PARDY, JOHN** BLACKSMITH OF CHRISTCHURCH, HAM, ENG. 1760-1800 **[37173]**
I: **PARKER, JOHN COWHAM** BARRISTER OF HULL, COAT OF ARMS. C1800 **[35009]**
I: **PARKER, JOHN** TRAVELLING SALESMAN, AUS. C1850-1890 **[35828]**
I: **PARKER, ROBERT AUGUSTUS** COPPER SMITHS LABORER, BATTERSEA, LONDON, ENG. 1900+
     [37778]
I: **PARRY, THOMAS** COTTON BROKER OF YKS, ENG. PRE 1888 **[36052]**
I: **PARRY** FROM LLANERFYL, MGY, WLS. 1870+ **[34125]**
I: **PATERSON, JAMES** ENGINEER OF PORT PHILLIP, AUS. 1840S+ **[34922]**
I: **PATEY, WILL** LONDON, ENG & SPAIN. ALL **[36501]**
I: **PATMOS** AS A CHRISTIAN NAME. ANY **[35560]**
I: **PATTERSON, ELIZABETH** MUDGEE, NSW, AUS. PRE 1860+ **[35105]**
I: **PATTERSON, ELIZABETH HARTLEY,** NSW, AUS. PRE 1860+ **[35105]**
I: **PATULLO, CREIGHTON & ANDERSON** FAMILIES IN AUS. 1850+ **[38567]**
I: **PAYNE, MARY** OF STAVELEY, ENG. 1884-90S **[37267]**
I: **PEACOCK, GEORGE & SARAH** AT 43 EARL ST, MANCHESTER RD, BRADFORD, YKS, ENG. C1861
     [37498]
I: **PEACOCK, HANNAH NEE WINTERSGILL** DEATH AT WHETLEY FOLD, BRADFORD, YKS, ENG. 1844
     [37498]
I: **PEACOCK, JONATHAN & HACKNESS, JANE** MARRIED AT WENSLEY, NRY, ENG. C1840 **[37498]**
I: **PEACOCK, JONATHAN & PICKERING, JANE** MARRIAGE AT COVERHAM, NRY, ENG. 1760 **[37498]**
I: **PEACOCK, JONATHAN & JANE** TEN CHILDREN, SHEPHERD, AT JONDARYAN, QLD, AUS. 1863
     [37498]
I: **PEACOCK, JONATHAN** OF 'TEMPLE', PARISH OF WEST WITTON, NRY, ENG. C1760-80 **[37498]**
I: **PEACOCK, PICKERING** DEATH AT HEALEY, NRY, ENG. 1840 **[37498]**
I: **PEARCE, WILLIAM CHARLES** ENG & SCT. 1870-1930S **[36290]**
I: **PEATTIE, JOHN & HELEN NESS** LARGO, FIF, SCT, DESCENDANTS OF. 1796+ **[36776]**
I: **PECHTEL** OF GERMAN ORIGIN. ALL **[38469]**
I: **PENROSE, RICHARD** A FARMER NEAR BATHURST, NSW, AUS. C1849 **[37498]**
I: **PENSTONE, CAPT. GILES** WHEN, WHO, WHERE DID HE MARRY. 1830+ **[35180]**
I: **PERCHARD, PETER** LORD MAYOR OF LONDON. 1700-1800 **[34550]**
I: **PERCIVAL, SIR WILLIAM** DBY, ENG. 1700S **[35009]**
I: **PERHAM, GEORGE** COASTGUARD, ENG. 1800+ **[37351]**
I: **PERHAM, RICHARD FRANCIS BURDEN** ROYAL NAVAL ENGINEER, CHATHAM, ENG. 1800-1890
     [37351]
I: **PERHAM JEWELLERS,** TORONTO, CAN. 1800-1900 **[37351]**
I: **PERKIN, MATILDA** LND, ENG. 1850+ **[35939]**
I: **PERRAULT, LEON JEAN BASILE** FRENCH PAINTER. PRE 1908 **[35180]**
I: **PERRIAM FAMILIES** RESIDENT HIGHBRIDGE, HAMMERSMITH, LND, ENG. 1820+ **[35975]**
I: **PETERS, JOHN** RESIDENT OF IA, USA. 1852+ **[35616]**
I: **PETHICK, JANE** HOUSEWIFE, CARBONDALE, PA, USA. 1880S **[35074]**
I: **PETTEY, WILLIAM** SHOEMAKER OF EAST HORRINGTON, SOM, ENG. 1850-70S **[37406]**
I: **PHILLIPS, FRANK** - FORMERLY PERCY FIELD OF ROCKHAMPTON, QLD, AUS. 1920S **[34738]**
I: **PHILLIPS, JAMES** CARPENTER OF WLS OR ENG. C1840S **[38239]**
I: **PHILLIPS, JOHN** MARINER OF WLS OR ENG & NYC, USA. C1840-1897 **[38239]**
I: **PHILLIPS, MARY MARGARET** RC, IRL TO PUEBLO CO, USA. 1899 **[34342]**
I: **PHILLIPS, MAY LOUISA** BORN MAY 20, 317 WEST 36 ST, NYC, USA. 1897 **[38239]**
I: **PHILLIPS, MOSES** WATCHMAKER OF LND, ENG. 1800-1880 **[34791]**
I: **PHILLIPS, WILLIAM** ELECTRICIAN, BORN JULY 2, NYC, USA. 1895 **[38239]**
I: **PHILLIPS TN,** USA. MAY BE WIFE TO PITTS BEASLEY SR. 1800+ **[38743]**
I: **PHIPPS, IDA E.** MARRIED ALBERT H.STENNING. 1888 **[34906]**
I: **PHIPPS, JAMES BIRD** VACCINATED BY DR EDWARD JENNER. 1780-1800 **[34241]**
I: **PICKERDEN** ONE NAME STUDY. **[38252]**
I: **PICKERING, GABRIEL & TAYLOR, ELIZABETH** MARRIAGE AT COVERHAM, NRY, ENG. PRE 1750
     [37498]
I: **PICKLE** OF GERMAN ORIGIN. ALL **[38469]**
I: **PIDGEON FAMILY** WINCHCOMBE, SHROPSHIRE & BIRMINGHAM, ENG. 1700-1900 **[36998]**
I: **PIERCE, THOMAS W.** VETERINARY SURGEON OF ESS, ENG. C1860 **[36116]**
I: **PIKE, HARWIN** COACHBUILDER, NFK, ENG. C1900 **[36580]**
I: **PILSON, WILLIAM** SCHOOLTEACHER OF WIC, IRL. 1840-1850 **[38455]**
I: **PINNELL** ENG TO AUS. 1860-1880 **[36282]**
I: **PINNELL** ENG TO NZ. 1860-1880 **[36282]**

I: **PLYTER, CAPT GEORGE** UNITED EMPIRE LOYALIST. 1736-1830S **[36707]**
I: **POLIT, LOUIS** CARVER OF LND, ENG. 1830-1840S **[34385]**
I: **POLLARD, WILLIAM** RESIDING BERMUDA. 1616-1630 **[35130]**
I: **POLLARD, WILLIAM** RESIDING BARBADOS. 1630+ **[35130]**
I: **POLLARD, WILLIAM** WIFE & CHILDREN, BERMUDA. 1616+ **[35130]**
I: **POOK, ELI** FARM SHEPHERD. 1885-1930 **[36501]**
I: **POOK, FANNY** FARM SHEPHERDS WIFE. 1885-1930 **[36501]**
I: **POOK, SIDNEY** MILLWRIGHT. 1885-1930 **[36501]**
I: **POPE, LILLIAN** MRS EDWIN JACKSON OF SCT OR ENG. C1870S **[38239]**
I: **POTTER, FRANCIS** CABINET MAKER, EDINBURGH, SCT. 1818-1850S **[35074]**
I: **POWER, JAMES & FRAHER, CATHERINE** TRAMORE & DUNGARVAN, EIRE — DESCENDANTS. C1890 **[35719]**
I: **PRESTON, LAN, ENG** WILLIAM HARRISON. PRE 1870 **[35473]**
I: **PRICE, FRANCIS SWAIN** RET. COMMANDER, ROYAL NAVY. 1785-1855 **[34448]**
I: **PRICE, JOHN FOUNTAIN** FREE MERCHANT, ENG & INDIA. 1700S **[36786]**
I: **PRICE, THOMAS** MASTER, ROYAL NAVY. 1750-1820 **[34448]**
I: **PRICE, WILLIAM ANDREW** CHIEF OF SURAT, INDIA. 1700S **[36786]**
I: **PRIOR FAMILY (MILLERS & VICTUALLERS)** SODBURY, NIBLEY, GLS, ENG. 1600+ **[35668]**
I: **PROVAN (MARY)** GLASGOW SCT. C1876 **[35051]**
I: **PROVAN (TOM)** GLASGOW SCT. C1869 **[35051]**
I: **PROWD & PROUD** NAME CHANGE STUDY. ALL **[34925]**
I: **PROWD, ALICE & THOMAS CHEEVERS** DESCENDANTS, VIC, AUS. 1916+ **[34925]**
I: **PROWD, ESTER & JAMES LOTHION** DESCENDANTS, VIC, AUS. 1905+ **[34925]**
I: **PROWD, ETHEL & HAROLD GALE** DESCENDANTS, VIC, AUS. 1926+ **[34925]**
I: **PROWD, JAMES & CAROLINE WOODBRIDGE** DESCENDANTS, VIC, AUS. 1876+ **[34925]**
I: **PROWD, JANE & NICHOLAS DOOLAN** DESCENDANTS, VIC, AUS. 1851+ **[34925]**
I: **PROWD, MARY & JOHN FORSTER** DESCENDANTS, VIC, AUS. 1854+ **[34925]**
I: **PROWD, MYRTLE & JOHN SMART** DESCENDANTS, VIC, AUS. 1915+ **[34925]**
I: **PROWD, THELMA & SIMPSON** DESCENDANTS, NZ. 1920+ **[34925]**
I: **PROWD, VIOLET & JAMES ASHLEY** DESCENDANTS, VIC, AUS. 1919+ **[34925]**
I: **PROWD, WILLIAM & MARY DOOLAN** DESCENDANTS, VIC, AUS. 1851+ **[34925]**
I: **PUBLICANS** JOHN MOON, LONDON OR WILTS ENG. C1850 **[38391]**
I: **PUCK, CHARLES** MINER, VIC, AUS. 1840-1909 **[34907]**
I: **PUDDY, ISAAC** SA RAILWAYS, AUS. 1865+ **[35565]**
I: **PUTNAM, GEN. ISRAEL** SEEKING FAMILY INFO — USA. 1700+ **[35137]**
I: **QUAIL, WILLIAM** AYR, SCT. 1847+ **[35105]**
I: **RANDALL, ROBERT & CURRELL, MARY** MARR AT PRINCES RISBOROUGH, BKM, ENG. 1769 **[37498]**
I: **RANSOM, THOMAS** CONVICT, NORWICH, NFK, ENG. PRE 1790 **[35662]**
I: **RATCLIFFE, MARY** DERWENTWATER FAMILY. 1700-1745 **[34743]**
I: **RAWLINSON, MARY** LND, ENG. 1770-1800 **[34385]**
I: **RAYMENT** ONE NAME STUDY. ANY **[35174]**
I: **READ, JAMES** HORTICULTURIST OF MDX, ENG. 1835-1915 **[37958]**
I: **READ, SEPTER JAMES** GARDENER OF MELBOURNE, VIC, AUS. 1911+ **[37958]**
I: **READ, SEPTER JAMES** GARDENER OF MDX, ENG. 1871-1911 **[37958]**
I: **READFORD, THOMAS (CONVICT)** SHIP "MARQUIS OF WELLINGTON" TO AUS. 1815 **[34019]**
I: **REED, JAMES** PRINTER, BATH, SOM, ENG. 1800S **[36739]**
I: **REED, SOPHIA** BATH, SOM, ENG. 1800S **[36739]**
I: **REED, WILLIAM** COUNCILLOR, WEYBRIDGE, SRY, ENG. 1875-1918 **[37777]**
I: **REED, WILLIAM** NEWSAGENT, WEYBRIDGE, SRY, ENG. 1875-1918 **[37777]**
I: **REED, WILLIAM** STONEDRESSER, WEYBRIDGE, SRY, ENG. 1875-1885 **[37777]**
I: **REID, WILLIAM** GAS WORKS MANAGER, WEST IRL. 1800S **[36794]**
I: **REILLY, CATHERINE** MRS DANIEL HANLON OF CO. LOG, IRL. C1820S-1865+ **[38239]**
I: **RENDALL, GEORGE LANGMAN** GROOM OF ST JAMES WESTMINSTER, ENG. 1813 **[37701]**
I: **REVERE, PAUL** NEED INFORMATION ON FAMOUS RELATIVE. 1735-1818 **[36463]**
I: **RICHARDS, BARON JOHN** JUDGE, MADRAS, INDIA, AND DUBLIN, IRL. 1790-1872 **[35738]**
I: **RICHARDS, JOHN** GILDER, ST PANCRAS, LND, ENG. 1835+ **[35939]**
I: **RICHARDS, THOMAS** CARPENTER, SYDNEY, NSW, AUS. C1830 **[37903]**
I: **RICHARDS, WILLIAM** INNKEEPER OF TAVISTOCK, DEV, ENG. 1736+ **[36594]**
I: **RICHARDSON, ELIZABETH** TN, USA, MAY BE WIFE TO WILLIAM BURNETT. 1801+ **[38743]**
I: **RICHARDSON, JOSHUA** FATHER OF ELIZABETH RICHARDSON BURNETT. PRE 1800 **[38743]**
I: **RICKSON, JOHN (JESSIE)** ARMY OFFICER, ENG & CAN. 1880S **[36840]**
I: **RILEY, DISTRICT CONSTABLE JOHN** PROSPECT & PARRAMATTA, NSW, AUS. 1820-1832 **[36600]**
I: **RILEY, JOHN** SAILED ON HMS DUNCAN. PRE 1900 **[37436]**
I: **ROB ROY MACGREGOR** HISTORY & DESCENDANTS OF. **[36635]**
I: **ROBINSON** — CHANCERY COURT CASES, EARL OF RIPON. 1920-1930 **[37207]**
I: **ROE, JAMES** COALMINER OF IRL. C1770+ **[38067]**
I: **ROHWEDDER, JURGEN** RESIDENT OF MO, USA. 1852+ **[35616]**
I: **ROLLESTON, ISAAC KING** ACCOUNTANT & BOOKKEEPER OF BELFAST, IRL. 1860+ **[35997]**
I: **ROSS, DAVID** WEAVER OF KESWICK, CROSTHWAITE, CUL, ENG. C1800+ **[35997]**
I: **ROSSETTI, INEZ MAUDE** KENNINGTON RD, LONDON, ENG. 1890S **[38002]**
I: **ROTH, STEPHEN LUDWIG** MEDIASH, TRANSYLVANIA, RO. 1796-1849 **[38519]**
I: **ROWE** — SOAP BOILERS ACTON & BRENTFORD, ENG. 1780-1934 **[37657]**

I: **RUDKIN, HARRY** OXFORD, OXF, ENG. 1800S **[36739]**
I: **RUDKIN, IDA FRANCES** SWINDON, WIL, ENG. 1800S **[36739]**
I: **RUMMERY, ALFRED EDWARD** BATTLE & MOUNTFIELD, SSX, ENG. 1875+ **[37436]**
I: **RUSSELL FAMILY** SUMMERS LANE, ABERDEEN, SCT. 1850-1900 **[36559]**
I: **RUSSELL, ELIZABETH MCPHAIL** LANARKSHIRE, SCT. **[35122]**
I: **RUSSELL, GEORGE LOVELL** BUILDER OF ISLINGTON, ENG. 1850-1910 **[35532]**
I: **RUSSELL, GEORGE** INDEPENDENT INVENTOR OF ENG. PRE 1835 **[35532]**
I: **RUSSELL, JAMES** MEDICAL DOCTOR, EDINBURGH, SCT. 1830+ **[37153]**
I: **RUSSELL, JOHN** TOLLKEEPER & ROAD CONTRACTOR, MOR, SCT. 1810-60 **[36559]**
I: **RUSSELL, WILLIAM, A.G.** SHIPSURGEON, ELLERMAN SHIPLINE. 1890S **[36559]**
I: **RUTHERFORD, JANE** CHATTON, NBL, ENG, ANCESTRY OF. 1842+ **[36776]**
I: **RUTHERFORD, ROBERT** PARISH CLERK, CHATTON, NBL, ENG. C1860+ **[36776]**
I: **RUTHERFURD, HENRY CHARLES** PHYSICIAN OF CAEN, FRA. C1830-1840 **[38072]**
I: **RUTHERFURD, HENRY** MELBOURNE LEATHER MERCHANT, VIC, AUS. PRE 1900 **[38072]**
I: **RYAN, PATRICK** EMIGRATED FROM WAT, IRL TO CAN. 1830S **[38404]**
I: **SACHSEN FAMILIEN.** PRE 1800 **[38606]**
I: **SADDLER, WILLIAM** FARMER, CARMICHAEL, LKS, SCT. 1820S **[36749]**
I: **SANDERSON/SAUNDERSON, JOHN** SOLDIER, NTT, ENG. PRE 1823 **[37903]**
I: **SANDERSON MARY ANN,** BORN C1839 SCT. C1839-1860 **[37756]**
I: **SARGEANT, JOHN THOMAS** DOCTOR OR MINER, VIC, AUS. 1850-1910 **[35724]**
I: **SARGENT, JOHN THOMAS** CHEMIST OF SPITTLEGATE, GRANTHAM, ENG. 1825-1850 **[35724]**
I: **SAUNDERS, JAMES** WRITER, DUNDEE, SCT. 1800+ **[36999]**
I: **SCARR, ELIZABETH** THORLBY, NR SKIPTON, YKS, ENG. 1878+ **[35996]**
I: **SCHLESIEN FAMILIEN.** PRE 1945 **[38606]**
I: **SCHMIDT - RESIDENTS** TAGNAROG, KUBAN, SU. 1800-1900 **[34081]**
I: **SCHMIDTS — RESIDENTS** UKRAINE - LOWER DNIEPER RV, SU. 1800-1925 **[34081]**
I: **SCHMIDT ESSEN,** RPR, GER. ALL **[38748]**
I: **SCHMIST - RESIDENTS** ALEXANDRODAR, KUBAN, SU. 1800-1900 **[34081]**
I: **SCHWERIN, FRANZ JACOB** LANDSMAN. 1850S **[34932]**
I: **SCOBIE, JAMES** HORSE TRAINER OF VIC, AUS. 1880-1940 **[36193]**
I: **SCOLLARD, BARRY & JULIA KEEFE** KER, IRL, DESCENDANTS OF. C1800+ **[36776]**
I: **SCOTLAND, ROBERT** ARTIFICIAL LIMB MAKER, GLASGOW, SCT. PRE 1887-1970 **[37138]**
I: **SCOTT, JOSEPH** INDENTURED SERVANT, SC & TN, USA. 1720-1740 **[36940]**
I: **SEDDON, RICHARD** BLACKSMITH OF LIVERPOOL, ENG. C1800 **[34887]**
I: **SEFTON, P.J. — HIGGS MARRIAGE IN NZ** LIVED AT TE KARAKA, NORTH IS. IN 1912. **[37498]**
I: **SEHL** ALL CONNECTING BRANCHES, GERMANY. 1800-1900 **[37544]**
I: **SELBY WALTER.** CONNECTION WITH AMIEL. C1770-1830 **[37756]**
I: **SELL, WILLIAM AND LYDIA** ROCHESTER DESCENDANTS. 1850-1950 **[36864]**
I: **SHAND, JAMES FORBES LEITH** MONTREAL, QUE, CAN. 1855 **[33784]**
I: **SHAND, JAMES** FARMER, SCT, MARRIED MARGARET BREMNER. 1820+ **[33784]**
I: **SHAND, WILLIAM** ENGINEER, MONTREAL & VANCOUVER, CAN. 1900+ **[33784]**
I: **SHARP, MARY (NEE PROVAN)** GLASGOW SCT. 1874 **[35051]**
I: **SHARP, ROBERT** FARMER OF PRESTON, LAN, ENG. 1800-20 **[37701]**
I: **SHAW, ANNIE EMMA** DOMESTIC SERVANT IN ENG & AUS. 1842 **[34034]**
I: **SHAW, BERNARD** WRITER OF DUBLIN, IRL. ALL **[36428]**
I: **SHEFFORD** ENG TO NZ. PRE 1900 **[36282]**
I: **SHEPHERD, ALEXANDER LOWE** BORN MANCHESTER, ENG. 1845 **[37196]**
I: **SHEPHERD, HENRY ARTHUR** BONCHURCH RD, NOTTINGHAM, LND, ENG. 1915-1925 **[37079]**
I: **SHEPHERD, SYDNEY CHARLES** 3 & 18 APPLEFORD RD, NO. KENSINGTON, LND, ENG. 1915-1925 **[37079]**
I: **SHEPHERD, WILLIAM BISSETT** COFFEE PLANTER OF CEYLON. 1870-1885 **[34420]**
I: **SHEPPARD, GEORGE** MILL OWNER, FROME, SOM, ENG. 1730-1810 **[34550]**
I: **SHILLINGFORD, CHARLES** PANAMA CANAL CONSTRUCTION. 1904-14 **[38002]**
I: **SHIP BUILDING** APPRENTICES, COLLINS. 1800-1820 **[38774]**
I: **SHIRLEY, GEORGE** DESCENDANTS, NTT, ENG. 1864 **[37375]**
I: **SHIRLEY, LAWRENCE 4TH EARL FERRERS** ILLEGITIMATE CHILDREN OF. C1745+ **[34577]**
I: **SHOWALTER, JACOB** DESCENDANTS OF. ALL **[36540]**
I: **SHUTTLEWORTH, MARGARET** WORKINGTON, ENG. 1887-89 **[37267]**
I: **SIEVERS, NICHOLAS EDWIN** OF BELLARINE, VIC, AUS — DESCENDANTS. 1884+ **[38307]**
I: **SILLENCE, JAMES** FARMER, NEW FOREST, ENG. 1775+ **[37926]**
I: **SIMMONS, CAPT & EMMA COBBLEDICK** PLYMOUTH, DEV, ENG. 1800S **[35230]**
I: **SIMPSON, ALFRED** IPSWICH, SFK, ENG. BORN 1850 **[36739]**
I: **SIMPSON, JOHN** CARRIER — IVER, BKM, ENG. C1826 **[36290]**
I: **SIMPSON, ROBERT** FARMER, WES, YKS, ENG. 1780-1900 **[34855]**
I: **SINGLETON, JOSEPH** MANUFACTURING CHEMIST, BIRMIGHAM, ENG. PRE 1865 **[37725]**
I: **SMILY, WILLIAM** CITIZEN & GOLDSMITH OF LONDON, ENG. 1840S **[36430]**
I: **SMITH, ADAM** EXCISE OFFICER, LND, ENG. 1790-1840 **[36019]**
I: **SMITH, ALEXANDER** MARRIED ELIZABETH MCINTOSH, SCT. PRE 1845 **[36496]**
I: **SMITH, ELIZABETH** 2 BARNSDALE RD, PADDINGTON, LND, ENG. 1907 **[37079]**
I: **SMITH, GEORGE** OF COX GREEN, DUR & HIS MIGRATION TO MON, WLS & RETURN HOME. 1803-1856 **[38269]**
I: **SMITH, JOHN GEORGE** SCHOOL SPORTING & BUSINESS CAREER IN SPENNYMOOR, DUR, ENG.

1890-1943 **[38269]**
I: **SMITH, JOHN** STONEMASON, BUSCO BECK, GLAISDALE, ENG. C1840+ **[35447]**
I: **SMITH, ROBERT FULLER** BRICKLAYER, SFK, ENG. PRE 1856 **[35231]**
I: **SMITH, SARAH ANN** MILLINER OF NOTTINGHAM, ENG. 1830-1905 **[35688]**
I: **SMITH, THOMAS** ENGRAVER OF BIRMINGHAM, ENG. 1798-1830S **[34385]**
I: **SMITHE, EDWARD** CAPTAIN 2ND FRENCH CHASSEURS. C1840+ **[37415]**
I: **SMITHS IN MONMOUTHSHIRE** PHILIS & GEORGE OF PANTEG, CMNOY, PONTYPOOL, WLS. 1803-1856 **[38269]**
I: **SMITHSON, ELIZABETH** LND, ENG. 1772-1820S **[34385]**
I: **SMITHSON, JANE** DOCTOR, ENG. 1860S **[35913]**
I: **SOULIE** ORIGIN AS GIVEN NAME, SCT. 1850-1900 **[34373]**
I: **SPEARS, ALEXANDER** BLACKSMITH, ENG. PRE 1849 **[35435]**
I: **SPEARS, ALEXANDER** FARMER, SCT. PRE 1870 **[35435]**
I: **SPEERS, ALEXANDER** BLACKSMITH, SCT. PRE 1849 **[35435]**
I: **SPENCE** COACHMEN, ABERDEEN, SCT. 1849-1907 **[34615]**
I: **SPICER, JOHN** JOCKEY, SHROPSHIRE, ENG. 1800-1820 **[35434]**
I: **SPILLER, EDWIN JAMES** MINER, TREHERBERT, WLS. 1900-1912 **[37268]**
I: **SPODE, JOSIAH** FOUNDER OF POTTERY BUSINESS & FAMILY. 1733+ **[37846]**
I: **SPURR, ROBERT, BORN ENG** LEFT ENG 3 APR 1635 ON 'PAUL'. 1610-1660 **[36463]**
I: **SQUIRE, J.C.** CELESTE OCTET, LONDON, ENG. 1900-1930 **[37670]**
I: **STAFFORD, DANIEL** COTTON MFG NEW MILLS, DBY, ENG. 1760-1810 **[34474]**
I: **STAFFORD, PRIVATE MICHAEL** 50TH REGT, WEST KENT. PRE 1864 **[35729]**
I: **STANTON, EDWARD** KEMPSEY, WOR, ENG. 1800+ **[35542]**
I: **STANTON, JAMES LEIGH** GLS, ENG. 1820+ **[35542]**
I: **STARLING, ALICE LOUISA** SOMERSTOWN, LND, ENG. 1908+ **[35939]**
I: **STARLING, AMY GERTRUDE** LND, ENG. 1908+ **[35939]**
I: **STARLING, FLORENCE MAUDE** LND, ENG. 1895+ **[35939]**
I: **STARLING, LILLIAN ROSETTA** SOMERSTOWN, LND, ENG. 1888+ **[35939]**
I: **STARLING, WILLIAM** BUILDER, SOMERSTOWN, LND & NFK, ENG. 1860+ **[35939]**
I: **STARLING, WILLIAM** MARINER OF SOUTHTOWN, GT YARMOUTH, NFK, ENG. 1840+ **[35939]**
I: **STEEL, LOUISA** BORN STOKE, STS, ENG, MARRIED C. CHRISTIE. 1832-75 **[37339]**
I: **STENNING, ALBERT HENRY** PLASTERER OF MOONEE PONDS, VIC, AUS. 1888+ **[34906]**
I: **STEPHENS, FRANCES BEATRICE SOPHIA** TIVERTON & PLYMOUTH, ENG. 1860+ **[34650]**
I: **STEPHENS, GEORGINA CHARLOTTE** TIVERTON & PLYMOUTH, ENG. 1865+ **[34650]**
I: **STEPHENSON, EDWARD** GOVERNOR OF BENGAL. 1691-1768 **[34717]**
I: **STEVENS, RUSSELL** GREATER LONDON — EXCISE. 1790-1842 **[38171]**
I: **STEWART, SARAH** NFK & LND, ENG & SCT. 1884-1940 **[37737]**
I: **STICKNEY, RICHARD EDWIN** VANCOUVER, BC, CAN. 1890+ **[35610]**
I: **STOTT, JAMES** DAKOTA CITY, NE, USA. 1851+ **[37626]**
I: **STOTT, JOHN** CHICAGO, IL, USA. 1851+ **[37626]**
I: **STOTT, MATTHEW** GRINDROD AUS. 1862+ **[37626]**
I: **STOTT, PHEBE** DAKOTA CITY, NE, USA. 1851+ **[37626]**
I: **STUART, RICHARD V., B** 1920-30S (MOTHER MARIE GRACE) DIED 1950 SUTHERLAND, NSW, AUS. 1920-1991 **[36311]**
I: **STUDEMAN, ERNEST** RESIDENT OF IA, USA. 1852+ **[35616]**
I: **STURGEON, GEORGE** CONVICT OF OATLANDS, TAS, AUS. 1822-1868 **[35443]**
I: **SUTTON** SAMUEL & MARY OF WEX, IRL. C1821-1850 **[37436]**
I: **SWANSON, JOHN COLUMBUS** PRIEST, RAMSGATE COLLEGE. C1900 **[36390]**
I: **TACEY, JAMES WARD** MASTER MARINER, ENG. C1800+ **[35254]**
I: **TAYLOR, REBECCA** DAU OF ROBERT & CHARLOTTE BORN MOUNTMELLICK, LEX, IRL. C1810 **[37498]**
I: **TAYLOR, REV JAMES** LOST IN VA, USA OR CAPUTH, PER, SCT. 1786+ **[37972]**
I: **TAYLOR, ROBERT** BORN EDINBURGH, SCT, BOMBAY CIVIL SERVICE. 1751-1800S **[37339]**
I: **TAYLOR, ROBERT** SON OF WILLIAM & HANNAH BORN MOUNTMELLICK, LEX, IRL. C1775 **[37498]**
I: **TAYLOR, WILLIAM** WORCESTERSHIRE, ENG TO MICHIGAN, USA. C1919 **[35417]**
I: **TELTOW (SIEDLUNG SIGRIDSHORST)** FAMILIEN. 1920-1950 **[38649]**
I: **TEMPERANCE MOVEMENT** JOSEPH LIVESEY. 1800+ **[34522]**
I: **TERRY & GAREY** STAGE ARTISTS, TOURING CONTINENT. 1855-1890 **[33821]**
I: **TERRY, HENRY B.** PARENTS, MARSHALL CO., TN, USA. C1801 **[38743]**
I: **THICTHENER, WILLIAM** WATCHMAKER OF GOSWELL RD, LND, ENG. 1805 **[35229]**
I: **THOMAS, C. — HIGGS** MARRIAGE IN NZ LIVED AT TARUHERU, NORTH IS. IN 1912. **[37498]**
I: **THOMAS, MARY** MRS JAMES PHILLIPS OF WLS OR ENG. C1840S **[38239]**
I: **THOMASWALDAU (SIL, GER)** FAMILIEN. 1500-1800 **[38654]**
I: **THOMPSON, EDWARD JAMES** BORN PLYMPTON, DEV, ENG. 1876 **[36376]**
I: **THOMPSON, EDWARD VICTOR** COOPER OF SYDNEY, AUS. 1850S **[35111]**
I: **THOMPSON, HANS** ANY OF THIS NAME IN ARM, IRL. PRE 1860 **[37498]**
I: **THOMPSON, JAMES & THOMPSON, JANE** MARRIAGE ARM, IRL. C1820S **[37498]**
I: **THOMPSON, JAMES** SON OF ROBERT & JANE BORN AT NEWTOWNHAMILTON, ARM, IRL. C1803 **[37498]**
I: **THOMPSON, JANE** DAU OF ROBERT & AGNES (GARMONEY) BORN NEWTOWNHAMILTON, ARM, IRL. C1804 **[37498]**
I: **THOMPSON, MARY & LOUDON, SAMUEL** MARRIED NEWTOWNHAMILTON, ARM, IRL. 1841

[37498]

I: **THOMPSON, SUSAN** BORN LONGHAM, NFK, ENG TO JOHN & KIDWELL, SARAH. 1797 [37498]
I: **THOMPSON, WILLIAM & CHARTERS, JANE** DFS, SCT — DESCENDANTS. C1830 [35719]
I: **THOMSON** DAY COLLIS FROM SCT. ALL [36982]
I: **THOROGOOD, JOHN** CABINET MAKER OF LND, ENG. 1800S [34887]
I: **THUERINGEN** FAMILIEN. PRE 1800 [38606]
I: **TILLEY, GEORGE** INNKEEPER OF BOSTON, MA, USA. 1700-1761 [36577]
I: **TIMMS, DANIEL** BLACKSMITH, BDF, ENG. 1840 + [34764]
I: **TIMMS, ROBERT** BLACKSMITH, WALLSEND, NSW, AUS. 1860 + [34764]
I: **TINDALL** FAMILY BROOMHOUSE, CHATTON, NBL, ENG. 1400-1925 [36776]
I: **TOLANO, RAPHAEL** CONVICT, NSW, AUS. 1837 [34791]
I: **TOLLIEFIELD, ANN** WIDOW OF WEYMOUTH, ENG. 1790S + [37095]
I: **TOMEY, JOSEPH & SONS** GLASS MAKERS, ASTON, BIRMINGHAM, ENG. 1850-1950 [36530]
I: **TOMPKINS** ENG TO USA. PRE 1770 [37460]
I: **TONNELIER, GUILLAUM(E)** PHELAN LEGRAND, IEVI, FRA. 1675-1705 [38768]
I: **TOOZE, MARK** WEBBER, ELIZABETH, SPOUSE, ENG. 1820-1870 [34248]
I: **TOULOUSE-LAUTREC, HENRI DE** FAMILY HISTORY, TOULOUSE, FRANCE. 1864 + [34140]
I: **TOWNSEND, JOSEPH** CHEMIST OF QUE, CAN. 1850-1875 [34199]
I: **TOWNSEND, JOSEPH** COACHMAN, LND, ENG. 1800-1860S [35074]
I: **TOWNSEND, THOMAS JOHN** COACHPAINTER, SOUTHWARK, LND, ENG. 1800S [36817]
I: **TOZER, JOHN & ANN PERRYMAN** BUILDER, DEV, ENG. 1822 + [34435]
I: **TRAILL, ELIZABETH ROSE** LADY, CAI, SCT. 1800 [34028]
I: **TREMBLAY, CECIL** FRA TO CAN. 1885-1900 [37432]
I: **TREVENA** FAMILIES OF REDRUTH, CON, ENG, & DESCENDANTS. ANY [34881]
I: **TREVISA, JOHNATHAN** MARRIAGE TO ANN?, LONDON, ENG. 1730-1740 [36619]
I: **TROTTER, JOHN** COACHMAN, COBB & CO., DAYLESFORD, AUS. 1860S + [34919]
I: **TRUMAN, JONATHON** LABOURER OF YAXLEY, HUN, ENG. 1800-1849 [33836]
I: **TRUMAN, SIR BENJAMIN** BREWER OF LONDON, ENG. 1700-1750S [33836]
I: **TUCK, ROBERT** CONVICT IN TAS, AUS & NORFOLK IS.. 1836 + [37497]
I: **TUCKER, JAMES** SEA CAPTAIN IN AUS. 1800-1880 [35103]
I: **TUNNEL, WILLIAM** MARRIAGE TO ANN HOWARD, NRY, ENG. 1730-1736 [38768]
I: **TURNER (ANY)** SOLICITORS, BOW, MDX, ENG. 1860 [36253]
I: **TURNER, EDWARD** HAIRDRESSER OF MARYLEBONE, ENG. 1772-1848 [36491]
I: **TURNER, HENRY WILLIAM** PAINT & PAPERHANGER, BERMONDSEY & LAMBETH, SRY, ENG.
      C1800-1870 [35997]
I: **TURNER, RICHARD** HAIRDRESSER OF MARYLEBONE, ENG. 1809-1845 [36491]
I: **TURNER, RICHARD** PIG DEALER, NEWINGTON, SRY, ENG. 1900S [37778]
I: **TYLEE** QUAKERS, ENG. 1670-1760 [37232]
I: **TYSON, WILLIAM** ANY FROM ENNERDALE, CUL, ENG. B.1780-1783 [34241]
I: **UNDERHILL, SAMUEL** GAMEKEEPER OF BICKENHILL, ENG. 1840-50S [35136]
I: **VAN DER MEULEN** OF NY & CT, USA. 1624 + [36335]
I: **VAN DER WESTHUYSEN, PETER** EARLY SETTLER CAPE GOOD HOPE. 1650S [36456]
I: **VANHAGEN** DESCENDANT. 1500 + [38638]
I: **VARDY** SOUTH AVE, DOUBLE BAY, NSW, AUS. 1930S [37498]
I: **VASSALL, WILLIAM** RECTOR OF HARDINGTON MANDEVILLE, SOM, ENG. 1857-1883 [37378]
I: **VEDIN, ELVIN** UMEA, SWE. 1920 + [38059]
I: **VENTOM, HEZEKIAH** MATHMATICAL INST. MAKER, MILE END, LND, ENG. 1780S-1810 [37670]
I: **VERALDI, ANTONIO** RESIDENT OF TAVERNA, ITL. 1860S [34371]
I: **VERE, ROGER** ENG & SCT ALL MARRIAGES. 1750-1795 [38459]
I: **VERE, ROGER** ENG & SCT ALL BIRTHS. 1730-1770 [38459]
I: **VETERAN'S CORP** INVALID ALEXANDER ARTHUR. 1800-1810 [35583]
I: **VICARY, THOMAS** FROM DEV, ENG TO USA. 1850-1870 [36113]
I: **VIDAL, CHARLES LOUIS** "VIDALS PROSPECT" PLANTATION, JAMAICA. PRE 1815 [34519]
I: **VINCENT, FRANCIS HENRY** ROTTNEST ISLAND. 1830 + [34530]
I: **VINCENT, JOHN** EDITOR OF KINGSTON, CAN. 1830 + [38072]
I: **VINDON** LONDON, ENG. PRE 1890 [37926]
I: **VON GOSTOMSKI** EMIGRATION. ALL [38687]
I: **VON USEDOM** RESEARCH FAMILY INSEL RUGEN. [38675]
I: **VOS JENNEKE** EMIGRATION TO USA. 1879-1975 [38646]
I: **WAGSTAFF** ONE NAME SOCIETY. [38290]
I: **WALKER, CHARLES** WHITESMITH. PRE 1883 [37701]
I: **WALKER, JOHN** ENGINEER, YKS, DUR & WANDSWORTH, ENG. 1835-1884 [34335]
I: **WALKER, JOSEPH** RAILWAYMAN, SALOP & LAN, ENG. 1860-1915 [36587]
I: **WALLACE, JOHN** MERCHANT, REMITTANCE MAN. PRE 1856 [35958]
I: **WALLACE, MARY & MOORE, JOHN** MARRIAGE, NFK, ENG. C1770 [37498]
I: **WALLACE, MARY ANN** DAU OF THOMAS POSS BORN SYDNEY, NSW, AUS. C1838 [37972]
I: **WALTER — RESIDENTS** SARATOV, SAMARA SSFR, SU. 1800-1900 [34081]
I: **WARD, BRYAN(T)** IRL OR ENG TO COLONIES (USA). 1700S [38768]
I: **WARREN, JAMES & REBECCA MORGAN** DESCENDANTS, AUS & NZ. 1877 + [34925]
I: **WASH** FAMILY ONE NAME STUDY GT BRITAIN. ALL [37859]
I: **WATMOUGH, GUY** TAILOR & DRAPER OF MANCHESTER, ENG. 1800-1860 [35354]
I: **WATSON & HUNTER** COMPANY ACTIVITIES. 1839-1850 [37964]

I: **WATSON, JAMES** SHOEMAKER, LONDON, ENG. C1820-1870 **[35447]**
I: **WATSON** WHISKY MAKERS, PERTH, SCT. C1840+ **[35053]**
I: **WATT, SARAH** NEW MONKLANDS, SCT. PRE 1912 **[35122]**
I: **WATTS, AGNES MAY** CASTLE ACRE, NFK, ENG. 1893+ **[35939]**
I: **WATTS, ALBERT SIDNEY** LND, ENG. 1900+ **[35939]**
I: **WATTS, CONSTANCE CAROLINE** LND, ENG. 1900+ **[35939]**
I: **WATTS, FLORENCE MATILDA** LND, ENG. 1900+ **[35939]**
I: **WATTS, FRANCIS WILLIAM** LND, ENG. 1900+ **[35939]**
I: **WATTS, FREDERICK JAMES W.S.** LND, ENG. 1908+ **[35939]**
I: **WATTS, HERBERT HENRY** LND, ENG. 1900+ **[35939]**
I: **WAYNE, ERNEST ALEXANDER** SWINDON, WIL, ENG. 1873+ **[36739]**
I: **WAYNE, SYDNEY GRANVILLE** SWINDON, WIL, ENG. 1871+ **[36739]**
I: **WEALANDS, THOMAS** PILOT & LIGHTHOUSE KEEPER, NSW, AUS. 1823+ **[35691]**
I: **WEAVER, PER, SCT** DEACON ALEXANDER FERRIER. C1790 **[35729]**
I: **WEBB, JAMES** SECOND FLEET TO AUS. 1790 **[35756]**
I: **WEBBER, WILLIAM** SHOEMAKER, CON, ENG. 1840-1850S **[35074]**
I: **WECK, JOHN & WILLIAM** INSTRUCTOR, HEIDELBERG, WUE, GER. 1775-1875 **[36898]**
I: **WEEBER, JACOB** WURTEMBERG, GERMANY & LONDON, ENG. PRE 1790 **[35542]**
I: **WEEDON, WILLIAM** CONVICT — UXBRIDGE, MDX, ENG. C1826 **[36290]**
I: **WEIR, ROBERT DUNDAS** SERVICE IN INDIA. C1800-1860 **[33812]**
I: **WEISS CHILDREN** ADOPTIONS USA. 1886+ **[38655]**
I: **WEISS, JOHN (1859-1894)** DESCENDANTS MO, USA. 1886-1895 **[38655]**
I: **WEISS, THERESIA** DESCENDANTS MO, USA. 1886+ **[38655]**
I: **WEISS** BAPTISMS ST LOUIS, MO, USA. 1886-1895 **[38655]**
I: **WELLER, AMOS** RN WEST MOUNTED POLICE, CAN. 1890-1930 **[36398]**
I: **WELLER-WILLIAMS, GEORGE** GROCER, DUNEDIN, NZ. 1880+ **[35966]**
I: **WELLSTEAD, PTE F. (FRANK?)** 2/23RD LND REGT. 1917+ **[37756]**
I: **WEST, AMY PRISCILLA** WIFE OF THOMAS GEORGE BENNETT. 1860-1920+ **[36594]**
I: **WEST, FRANCES** NEE BLOMFIELD, NFK, ENG. 1853+ **[37737]**
I: **WEST, THOMAS & HELEN** WORCESTER, WOR, ENG. 1860+ **[35554]**
I: **WESTON FAMILIES** MIGRATION FROM SAL, ENG. 1820-1840 **[33887]**
I: **WESTON, JOHN** SURGEON, LONDON, ENG. C1802 **[35257]**
I: **WESTON, WILLIAM PRICHARD** POLITICIAN & PREMIER, TAS, AUS. 1804-1888 **[35257]**
I: **WESTON-SUPER-MARE, SOM, ENG** HISTORY OF FAMILIES OF. ALL **[36012]**
I: **WHEELER FAMILY** EMIGRATION FROM CORK, IRL TO USA. ALL **[37249]**
I: **WHEELER, HENRY E.** OF AUBURN, NY, USA. C1855-1900+ **[38239]**
I: **WHITE, ELIZABETH** LND, ENG. 1720-1770 **[34385]**
I: **WHITE, JOSEPH THOMAS** CARPENTER, ENG. C1829 **[35447]**
I: **WHITEHEAD, HARRY** PACKING CASE MAKER, LND, ENG. 1835-1900 **[37696]**
I: **WHITEMAN, JOHN** HOLBORN, LND, ENG. 1740-1800 **[35354]**
I: **WHITING, JOSEPH WILLIAM** BORN EAST END OF LND, ENG. C1842 **[35942]**
I: **WILCOXSON, WILLIAM** WEAVER, ST ALBANS, DBY, ENG. 1600 **[34342]**
I: **WILD** HOCKERLEY HALL, WHALEY BRIDGE, CHS, ENG. ALL **[36587]**
I: **WILKINS, MARY ANNE** ENG. 1830S **[36840]**
I: **WILKINSON, ISAAC** SURVEYOR, LONDON, ENG. 1800-1860S **[37351]**
I: **WILLIAM RILEY** COBB & CO. 1883-1895 **[36600]**
I: **WILLIAM TATUM** CAPT, OF LND, ENG. 1830S **[34627]**
I: **WILLIAMS, CLIFFOD** GROCER, DUNEDIN, NZ. 1880-1926 **[35966]**
I: **WILLIAMS, RICHARD** MERCHANT, MERTHYR TYDFIL, WLS. 1840+ **[35966]**
I: **WILLIAMS, RICHARD** MERCHANT, DUNEDIN, NZ. 1870-1898 **[35966]**
I: **WILLIAMS, WILLIAM** COOPER OF SOUTHWARK, LND, ENG. C1840 **[36076]**
I: **WILLIAMSON HISTORY (JOHN & MARGARET)** GULLANE, EDINBURGH, SCT. 1800+ **[35668]**
I: **WILLIS, ISABELLA** DAU OF GEORGE & JANE (TUBMAN) BORN BELTURBET, CAV, IRL. C1835
   [37498]
I: **WILSON, CHRISTOPHER THOMAS** WATCHMAKER, LEICESTER, ENG. C1900 **[35416]**
I: **WILSON, FRED WM.,B** BRISTOL, AVON, ENG JUMPED SHIP (MOTHER MARY FUSSELL) HE LIVED
   ACT, AUS. 1894-1950S **[36311]**
I: **WILSON, HANNAH MARIA** THETFORD, NFK, ENG. 1850+ **[35939]**
I: **WILSON, HANNAH RICHARDSON HIND** DRESSMAKER. 1854 **[36386]**
I: **WILSON, JAMES** BOILER MAKER OF PAISLEY, SCT. 1800-1890 **[36639]**
I: **WILSON, JOHN** 35 GLENALLEN ST, BELFAST, IRL. 1894 **[34385]**
I: **WILSON, JOSEPH** GENTLEMAN OF PRESTON, ENG. 1795+ **[36386]**
I: **WILSON, PETER CHRISTIAN** SAILOR OF FREDERICKSHAVEN, DEN. 1825-1852 **[35724]**
I: **WILSON, ROBERT** BLACKSMITH, THETFORD, NFK, ENG. 1840+ **[35939]**
I: **WILSON, ROBERT** BLACKSMITH, LND, ENG. 1870+ **[35939]**
I: **WINCH, HENRY THOMAS** BARGEMASTER OF QUEENBOROUGH, ENG. 1849-1899 **[34718]**
I: **WINTERSGILL, GEORGE & RIPLEY, ELIZABETH** MARRIED MASHAM PARISH, NRY, ENG. C1770
   [37498]
I: **WINTERSGILL, HANNAH & ELIZABETH, TWINS** BORN MASHAM, NRY, ENG. C1780 **[37498]**
I: **WITTON, REV JOSEPH** LND, ENG. 1780-1800 **[35662]**
I: **WOOD, JOHN** STONEMASON, LIN, ENG. 1840-1850S **[35074]**
I: **WOODS, ELIZABETH** MIDWIFE, ENG & QLD, AUS. PRE 1885 **[35662]**

I: **WOODS, JAMES C.** PLANTER OF LOUISIANA, USA. 1850-1900 **[36324]**
I: **WOOLCOCK, RICHARD TREVITHICK** MARINER OF PENZANCE, ENG. 1853 **[34627]**
I: **WORRALL, WILLIAM** SOLDIER, SERGEANT 2ND EAST YORKSHIRE REGT. 1850-90 **[37707]**
I: **WORTHINGTON** FROM NEWTOWN, MGY, WLS. 1870+ **[34125]**
I: **WREN, SIR CHRISTOPHER** DESCENDANTS OF. 1650+ **[37448]**
I: **WRIGHT, DESCENDANTS** VISITATION OF KEN, ENG. 1619+ **[36700]**
I: **WRIGHT, SAMUEL** GALLOW, NFK, ENG. PRE 1787 **[37737]**
I: **WYATT, ISHAM W.** SHIP CAPTAIN ALONG ATLANTIC COAST. 1845-1855 **[37533]**
I: **WYSS CHILDREN** ADOPTIONS USA. 1886+ **[38655]**
I: **WYSS, JOHANN (1859-1894)** DESCENDANTS MO, USA. 1886-1895 **[38655]**
I: **WYSS, THERESIA** DESCENDANTS MO, USA. 1886+ **[38655]**
I: **WYSS BAPTISMS** ST LOUIS, MO, USA. 1886-1895 **[38655]**
I: **YATES (THOMAS)** OVERLOOKER OF BANK TOP, ENG. 1900-1914 **[35052]**
I: **YELDON, WILLIAM** BUTLER OF LND, ENG. C1800S **[34887]**
I: **YOUNG, JOHN** GARDENER, REGENTS PARK ZOO, LND, ENG. PRE 1922 **[35551]**
I: **ZINK, GEORGE FREDERICK** PAINTER OF MINIATURE PORTRAITS, LND, ENG. 1860S+ **[34922]**
I: **ZINK, LOUIS** DIAMOND CUTTER & SETTER, LND, ENG. 1860S+ **[34922]**
M: **ACTON, WILLIAM** FROM NOTTINGHAM, ENG. 1820-70 **[37412]**
M: **AG, CH TO USA** . 1800-1930 **[38609]**
M: **ARISTOCRATS** EUROPE TO AUS, NZ. TO 1991 **[38754]**
M: **ARMIGERS** MIGRATING TO CAN. ALL **[38439]**
M: **ARRAN ISLAND** MIGRATION TO AYR, SCT. 1800S **[33966]**
M: **ASSISTED MIGRANTS** TO AUS ON SHIP NAMED WILLIAM NICOL. 1837 **[35143]**
M: **ASSISTED MIGRANTS** TO AUS ON SHIP NAMED NEPTUNE. 1839 **[35143]**
M: **ASSISTED MIGRATION** SOMERSET TO VICTORIA, AUS. 1839-72 **[35210]**
M: **ASSISTED MIGRATION** BRISTOL TO VICTORIA, AUS. 1839-72 **[35210]**
M: **AUSTRALIA** CABBAN FAMILY, EX LONDON, ENG. 1800-1840 **[36383]**
M: **AUSTRALIA** CHARLES BLANCHFIELD. 1870+ **[36410]**
M: **AYR TO GLASGOW, SCT.** 1770-1850 **[38388]**
M: **BAMBER, LEONARD** LIVERPOOL TO CAN. 1920S **[36052]**
M: **BARTLEY** IMMIGRATION FROM UK TO USA. PRE 1800 **[37933]**
M: **BEXHEDA** JONKOPING, SWEDEN NEW YORK, USA. 1884 **[38543]**
M: **BIRBECK, MAVIS** TO SOUTH AFRICA. 1945-1950 **[34834]**
M: **BOHEMIA & MORAVIA** TO TEXAS, USA. 1860-85 **[38314]**
M: **BOHEMIA** TO CHICAGO, USA. PRE 1900 **[37440]**
M: **BRAZIL** TO NEW YORK, USA. 1654 **[38035]**
M: **BRIEN** FERMANAGH, IRL, TO USA. 1845-1865 **[34965]**
M: **BRISTOL** MIGRATION TO VICTORIA, AUS. 1839-72 **[35210]**
M: **CAN, SOUTHERN ONT** TO WESTERN CAN. 1860-1900 **[38388]**
M: **CANADIAN PASSENGER LISTS** FROM ENG. C1900S **[35980]**
M: **CARIBBEAN** TO USA. 1600-1900 **[36324]**
M: **CHALMERS, JOHN** DUMBARTON, DNB, SCT, TO ALB, CAN. C1920 **[34260]**
M: **CHANNEL ISLANDS** GUERNSEY TO ONT, CAN. 1850-1900 **[36671]**
M: **CLA, IRL** TO LEEDS, ENG. 1870+ **[37202]**
M: **COLONISTS** NEUDORF, GALACIA FROM WUERTTEMBURG, BRD. **[37045]**
M: **CON, ENG** TO VIC, AUS. 1850+ **[35489]**
M: **CORNISH MINERS** TO MICHIGAN, USA. 1843-1873 **[38179]**
M: **CORNWALL, ENG** TO CARBONDALE, PA, USA. 1850-1880 **[35074]**
M: **CZECHOSLOVAKIA** EMIGRATION. 1875-1920 **[38618]**
M: **DANIELLS, WM** WESTCOTT TO SIDBURY, RSA. 1790-1830 **[34834]**
M: **DENMARK** TO ADELAIDE, SA, AUS. 1840-1850 **[37488]**
M: **DENMARK** TO AUS. 1880-1890 **[35115]**
M: **DENMARK** TO USA. 1850+ **[35489]**
M: **DIGGLE** FROM LAN, ENG TO USA & AUS. ALL **[36419]**
M: **DON, IRL** TO NZ . 1870+ **[35975]**
M: **DONEGAL, IRL** FROM SCT. PRE 1700 **[34537]**
M: **DOWN, IRL** TO PITTSBURGH, PA, USA. 1843-1860 **[37514]**
M: **DUTCH IMMIGRATION** TO UK. 1500+ **[37448]**
M: **DUTCH** TO NEW YORK CITY, USA. 1700-25 **[37764]**
M: **EAST PRUSSIA** DANZIG NOVA SCOTIA, CAN. 1850-90 **[36404]**
M: **EMIGRANTS** TO NZ PROVINCIAL GOVERNMENT. 1850+ **[36026]**
M: **EMIGRATION** MY-S DE FRANCE AU CANADA. 1690-1698 **[38430]**
M: **EMIGRATION** DE QUEBEC AU MICHIGAN. 1870-1950 **[38430]**
M: **EMTAGE, JOHN** TO BARBADOES, WEST INDIES. ALL **[37386]**
M: **ENG SOUTHWEST** TO IRL. 1600-1760 **[37244]**
M: **ENG TO AMERICA** . 1683 **[37698]**
M: **ENG TO CAN** . PRE 1850 **[37698]**
M: **ENGLAND EMIGRATION** TRYON TO CT, USA. 1600-1700 **[36346]**
M: **ENGLAND TO AMERICA** SHIPS DOCTORS & PASSENGERS. 1820-1821 **[38258]**
M: **ENGLAND** JESSEE, TO NC, USA. PRE 1750 **[37794]**
M: **ENGLAND** LEA, TO VA, USA. 1600S+ **[37794]**
M: **ENGLAND** TO AUS. 1883-1885 **[35115]**

M: **ENGLAND** TO AUS. 1921-1924 [35115]
M: **ENGLISH EMIGRATION** TO JAVA. PRE 1850 [38708]
M: **ENGLISH** MIGRATION FROM CON & SOM TO DEV, ENG. 1775-1875 [37020]
M: **ENGLISH** TO DARTMOUTH, NOVA SCOTIA, CAN. 1750 [35299]
M: **ENG** TO CAN. C1906 [37173]
M: **ENG** TO USA. 1600-1800 [36133]
M: **ETHERINGTON** MIGRATION WITHIN YKS, ENG. 1500-1900 [37076]
M: **ETHERINGTON** MIGRATION TO LEEDS, WRY, ENG. 1500-1900 [37076]
M: **EUROPEAN EMIGRANTS** IN SOUTH AMERICA . ALL [38697]
M: **FAMILY COLONIZATION LOAN SOC** MARCHIONESS OF LONDONDERRY. 1854 [35111]
M: **FAMINE IMMIGRANTS** COR, IRL, TO LND, ENG. 1845-1860 [35003]
M: **FARM LABOURERS,** CAM, ENG MIGRATION TO NSW, AUS. 1850-1860 [35770]
M: **FARMERS** IN USA FROM CH. 1800 + [36982]
M: **FEMALE EMIGRATION SCHEME** BY "STATELY" TO AUCKLAND, NZ. 1851 [36247]
M: **FIDLER, VALENTINE** OVERSEER OF CONVICTS, TAS, AUS. 1843-1853 [33879]
M: **FRA TO ENG** BONTEM(P)S. PRE 1811 [37760]
M: **FRANCE** TO ENG. 1500-1600 [36133]
M: **FREE CHURCH** SCT TO NZ. ANY [35909]
M: **FRENCH EMIGRATION** FROM NOR TO JSY. 1870-1892 [38178]
M: **FRENCH-CANADIAN** MISSISSIPPI VALLEY. 1650-1820 [38312]
M: **FRENCH** TO QUE, CAN. 1693 + [38417]
M: **FROM BRETAGNE, FRA** TO ENGLISH MIDLANDS. 1650-1750 [35649]
M: **GER & PRE** TO RUSSIA VOLGA RIVER COLONIES. 1764-1859 [36958]
M: **GER TO ANYWHERE** . PRE 1945 [38618]
M: **GERMAN AUSTRIANS** BUKOVINA TO CAN. 1903 [37045]
M: **GERMAN BOUNTY** "SHIP KINNEAR" LND TO AUS. 1837-38 [34418]
M: **GERMAN BOUNTY** IMMIGRANTS NSW, AUS. 1847-1855 [36267]
M: **GERMAN EMIGRATION** TO SWE . 1775-1825 [37821]
M: **GERMAN EMIGRATION** ANYWHERE. ALL [38678]
M: **GERMANS** FROM RUSSIA VOLHYNIA, USSR TO MICHIGAN, USA. 1860-1912 [37545]
M: **GERMANS** IN RUSSIA TO DAKOTAS, USA. 1800S [37805]
M: **GERMANS** TO NSW, AUS. 1840-1860 [38585]
M: **GERMANY** TO ANYWHERE LIST FAMILY. 1400 + [38624]
M: **GERMANY** TO UK . 1700-1920 [37639]
M: **GERMAN** IMMIGRATION TO NB AND NS, CAN. 1700S [38447]
M: **GERMAN** MIGRATION TO LIVERPOOL, ENG. 1860-1925 [37020]
M: **GER** TO NY & MD, USA. 1860-1880 [36920]
M: **GER** TO OHIO PORT OF ENTRY. C1850 [38369]
M: **GISBORN, MARY ELIZABETH** LEICESTER, LEI, ENG, TO MONTREAL, QUE, CAN. C1924 [34260]
M: **GLASGOW, SCT** TO AUSTRALIA. 1800-1850 [34824]
M: **GOVE, JOHN** IN NEW HAMPSHIRE, USA. 1625-1640 [34004]
M: **GREECE, METAXAS** TO LONDON, ENG. 1850-1910 [37219]
M: **GREECE, METAXAS** TO PARIS, FRA. 1850-1900 [37219]
M: **HAITI (SANTA DOMINGO)** FRENCH EVACUATION TO BALTIMORE, MD, USA. 1793 [36911]
M: **HARTKOPF** PRE TO USA. 1835-1880 [37822]
M: **HESSIANS** TO USA . 1800-1850 [35630]
M: **HETHERINGTON** MIGRATION TO LEEDS, WRY, ENG. 1500-1900 [37076]
M: **HETHERINGTON** MIGRATION WITHIN YKS, ENG. 1500-1900 [37076]
M: **HOLLAND** TO ANYWHERE . 1600 + [38605]
M: **HOLLAND,** NL TO OHIO, USA. 1790S [36328]
M: **HUGUENOTS** FRENCH SETTLERS, THORNEY ABBEY, CAM, ENG. 1650 [34204]
M: **HUGUENOTS** TO USA. 1650-1750 [36324]
M: **IMMIGRATION (ITALIAN)** FROM APRIGLIANO, COSENZA, ITALY. 1900 + [34047]
M: **IN, USA** TO IA, USA. 1840-1860 [36940]
M: **INDIA** TO TRINIDAD, W INDIES. 1850-90 [36955]
M: **IRELAND** TO AUS. 1850-1880S [33825]
M: **IRELAND** TO JAMAICA, WEST INDIES. ANY [33921]
M: **IRISH EMIGRATION** FROM SLI, IRL TO CAN. 1840-1855 [38178]
M: **IRISH EMIGRATION** TO SLI, IRL. PRE 1821 [38178]
M: **IRISH IMMIGRANTS** TO VIC PER "EBBA BRAHE" OR "GENGHIS KHAN". 1850S [36268]
M: **IRISH** IN LANCASHIRE, ENG . 1840S-1910 [37821]
M: **IRISH** IN QUEBEC GATINEAU VALLEY. 1800-1900 [35630]
M: **IRISH** MIGRATION TO SOUTH AFRICA. 1840S [34431]
M: **IRISH PROTESTANTS** TO NZ. TO 1991 [38754]
M: **IRISH** TO AUS & USA EX KIK, IRL COLLIER (SMITHSON) COMERFORD (CRUCKAWN). 1830-1865
      [33775]
M: **IRISH** TO CAN FAMINE. 1840-1865 [35630]
M: **IRISH** MIGRATION TO LIVERPOOL, ENG. 1840-1900 [37020]
M: **IRISH** TO ENG & USA. 1800 + [38015]
M: **IRISH** TO LONDON DOCKS. 1847 + [38417]
M: **IRISH** TO NEW YORK CITY, USA. 1875-90 [37764]
M: **IRISH** TO SUSQUEHANNA CO., PA, USA. 1830 + [35299]

M: **IRL TO AUS. 1858+** [35372]
M: **IRL TO GLASGOW, SCT. 1870S** [36417]
M: **IRL TO JAPAN. PRE 1900** [36417]
M: **IRL TO LND, ENG. C1800-1820S** [34518]
M: **ITALIAN IMMIGRATION** TO NORTH BAY, ONT, CAN. 1900+ [34047]
M: **ITALY TO ENG. 1830+** [37390]
M: **JACOB NOLL, GER TO USA** . [38619]
M: **JOERG BAY, GER TO SHO, GER. 1400+** [38608]
M: **JOHNS FAMILIES IN AUS FOR DATA BASE. PRE 1900** [35585]
M: **JOSEFSBERG, GALICIA, OES** TO JOSEPHSBURG, ALB, CAN. C1800 [34356]
M: **KIDSGROVE, STS, ENG** TO BALLARAT, VIC, AUS. 1850S [35074]
M: **LATIN AMERICA** IRISH IN. ALL [37750]
M: **LEGARE, GILLES** PARIS AU QUEBEC, CAN. 1665+ [34168]
M: **LEGARE, NICOLAS** PARIS AU QUEBEC, CAN. 1665+ [34168]
M: **LEI, ENG TO USA. 1800S** [38369]
M: **LINCONSHIRE** TO LAN, ENG. 1800-1830 [36635]
M: **LLOYD, SARAH JANE** ENG TO CAN. C1900-1905 [34997]
M: **LOYALISTS** WYOMING VALLEY, USA. 1769-1778 [37811]
M: **LUSATIA** TO SOUTH AUSTRALIA. ANY [34801]
M: **MACHYNLLETH** TO BALLARAT, AUS. ALL [37649]
M: **MANCHESTER TO SA, AUS** . 1900+ [35565]
M: **MCDOUGALL, HENRY** TO CAN. 1875+ [37926]
M: **MCLEOD, ANNIE** GLASGOW, LKS, SCT, TO SAS OR ALB, CAN. C1930 [34260]
M: **MECKLENBURG** TO STOCKHOLM, SWE. 1730S [37036]
M: **MENNONITES** TO PA, USA. 1700-1750 [34741]
M: **MURPHY, FRANCES** SAN FRANCISCO TO AUS. 1889+ [35405]
M: **MUSSELYVILLE** CANADA. ALL [36982]
M: **NBL, ENG TO AUS, NAMED EMERY. 1800-1900** [36461]
M: **NBL, ENG TO CAN, NAMED EMERY. 1600-1900** [36461]
M: **NBL, ENG TO USA, NAMED EMERY. 1600-1900** [36461]
M: **NBL, ENG TO W INDIES, NAMED EMERY. 1600-1900** [36461]
M: **NEIL ANNIE & WILLIE JAMIESON** DUMBARTON, DNB, SCT, TO DETROIT, MI, USA. C1930 [34260]
M: **NIZHNY NOVGAROD SU** TO LONDON, ENG (JEWISH). 1890-1900 [36889]
M: **NORMANDIE, FRA** QUEBEC, CAN. 1650-1670 [37429]
M: **NORTHERN IRL** TO NSW, AUS. 1820-1860 [34537]
M: **NORWAY IMMIGRATION** TO QLD, AUS. 1880-1900 [35548]
M: **NORWEGIANS** TO AUS ALL ENTRIES AND DESCENDANTS. 1788-1900 [38567]
M: **NZ, NELSON AREA** FROM GERMANY. 1800-1890 [34634]
M: **OLDHAM HERBERT** TO AUS. 1870+ [36980]
M: **ONEIDA CO., NY, USA** WELSH SETTLERS BEFORE 1820. [37510]
M: **ORPHAN GIRLS** IRL TO TAS, AUS. 1840S [38073]
M: **PALATINATES** GER TO IRL. 1600-1700 [33905]
M: **PALATINE MIGRATION** FROM GER TO IRL & AMERICA. 1709+ [35874]
M: **PALATINES** RHEINLAND-PFALZ TO IRELAND. 1600-1715 [33862]
M: **PARIS, FRA, METAXAS** TO LONDON, ENG. 1890-1902 [37219]
M: **PASSENGER LISTS** GER TO ENG. 1830-1850 [36522]
M: **PEARSON/GRAND RAPIDS** TO PETERBOROUGH, CAN. C1870 [38466]
M: **POLISH MIGRATION** VIA HAMBURG TO NZ. 1870-1890 [33966]
M: **PORTSMOUTH, ENG** TO RUSSELL CO. CAN. 1818-20S [35605]
M: **PORTUGAL** IRISH IN. ALL [37750]
M: **PRINCE, LLEWELLYN** TO PERTH, AUS. C1900-1910 [36229]
M: **PRUSSIA, GER** TO MANCHESTER, ENG. 1830-1850 [36522]
M: **PRUSSIA** TO BERLIN, ONT, CAN. 1870S [34468]
M: **PRUSSIA** TO OHIO, USA. 1790S [36328]
M: **REDSHAW REUBEN** TO AUS. 1845+ [36980]
M: **RHEINLAND-PFALTZ** TO PA, USA. 1700S [37785]
M: **ROBINSON, HERBERT** TO MEXICO. 1905-1915 [35935]
M: **ROX, SCT** TO CAN. 1820-1825 [34489]
M: **RUSSIAN EMIGRATION** TO ENG. C1800-1930S [37742]
M: **SALTERS COMPANY** COLONIZATION, LOUGH NEAGH, IRL. 1600S [35375]
M: **SAXONY, GER** TO AUSTRALIA. 1880-1890S [34803]
M: **SCOTLAND** TO JAMAICA, WEST INDIES. ANY [33921]
M: **SCOTLAND** TO LAN, ENG. 1800-1850 [36635]
M: **SCOTLAND** TO NOVA SCOTIA, CAN. 1830-1864 [34251]
M: **SCOTTISH MIGRANTS** TO AUS ON SHIP NAMED WILLIAM NICOL. 1837 [35143]
M: **SCT** TO CAN. 1750-1950 [38388]
M: **SCT** TO NSW, AUS. 1820-1860 [34537]
M: **SHARP, MARY ELIZABETH & HENRY** LEICESTER, LEI, ENG, TO MONTREAL, QUE, CAN. C1924 [34260]
M: **SICKOLD MIGRATION** BEL & NL TO GER. 1700-1770 [34418]
M: **SIMON FROM FRA** TO GSY. PRE 1600 [37229]
M: **SNAPE, FRANK & ANN** TO BOSTON, USA. 1870-1880 [35935]

M: **SOM, ENG** TO CHANNEL ISLANDS. 1820-1850 **[36671]**
M: **SOMERSET MIGRATION** TO VICTORIA, AUS. 1839-72 **[35210]**
M: **SOMERSET** SYDNEY, NSW, AUS. 1850-1860S **[35360]**
M: **SPAIN** IRISH IN. ALL **[37750]**
M: **SWE TO GER (SIL)** . 1800-1900 **[38607]**
M: **SWEDEN** TO KANSAS, USA. 1845-69 **[38535]**
M: **SWEDISH** TO WISCONSIN VIA NEW YORK, USA. 1880S **[34473]**
M: **SWISS** ERNST FAMIY TO LONDON, ENG. PRE 1825 **[37279]**
M: **SWITZERLAND TO ANYWHERE** LIST FAMILY. 1200+ **[38624]**
M: **SWITZERLAND** TO NZ. 1910S **[35954]**
M: **TERJARV**, FINLAND TO NEW YORK, USA. 1850-1930 **[38757]**
M: **TIP, IRL** TO ONT, CAN. 1830-1840S **[38593]**
M: **TN, USA** TO IN, USA. 1820-1850 **[36940]**
M: **TO USA, CAN & AUS** OF NELLIST'S. ALL **[36481]**
M: **TORONTO AREA** TO SOUTHWEST ONT, CAN. 1840-1880 **[38388]**
M: **UNITED EMPIRE LOYALISTS** MIGRATONS TO CAN. 1776+ **[34377]**
M: **UNITED EMPIRE LOYALISTS** USA TO ONT, CAN. 1780+ **[33905]**
M: **USA** FROM BOLTON, ENG, JOHN CLAYTON. 1902-3 **[36984]**
M: **VASSY, BN, FRA** VASSIE FAMILY TO ENG. 1700S **[34043]**
M: **VIRGINIA** TO KENTUCKY, USA. 1780-1805 **[38535]**
M: **WATERLOO — BATTLE OF** HILL, MAJOR HUGH. 1815 **[38004]**
M: **WELSH COAL MINERS** TO NZ & AUS. TO 1900 **[38754]**
M: **WELSH MINERS** TO USA. 1700S **[38026]**
M: **WELSH** ANY. EMIGRATED TUNBRIDGE WELLS, KEN TO CAN & AUS. C1890-1930 **[37756]**
M: **WEST PRUSSIA** TO AUS. 1880S **[34932]**
M: **WICKLOW, IRL** TO ONT, CAN. 1820-1850 **[38455]**
M: **WILLINGORE, LIN, ENG** TO MELBOURNE, VIC, AUS. 1847-1850S **[35074]**
M: **WILTS, ENG** TO ARGENTINA & URUGUAY. 1868+ **[38261]**
M: **WURTTEMBERG, GER** TO YKS, ENG. 1830-1870 **[37609]**
M: **YORKSHIRE, ENG** TO AUS. 1788-1990 **[35470]**
M: **YORKSHIRE, ENG** TO ONT, CAN, VIA QUEBEC CITY. 1840S **[34216]**
M: **YORKSHIRE, ENG** TO USA. 1800+ **[36557]**
M: **ZACHRISEN** SWE TO USA. 1865-1890 **[37822]**
M: **ZACHRISON** SWE TO USA. 1865-1890 **[37822]**
M: **ZACKRISEN** SWE TO USA. 1865-1880 **[37822]**
M: **ZACKRISON** SWE TO USA. 1865-1890 **[37822]**
M: **CONVICTS** FROM MON, WLS & GLS, ENG TO AUS. 1841+ **[37040]**
MY: **(MAC)CARRAGHER** FRANCE, IRISH BRIGADES. **[37079]**
MY: **101 SQUADRON** BOMBER COM. AIR CREW. 1939-44 **[36420]**
MY: **11TH REGT OF FOOT** BRITISH ARMY. 1820-1840 **[34827]**
MY: **11TH REGT.** SYDNEY, AUS. 1845-1850 **[35573]**
MY: **12TH REGIMENT — SUFFOLK** AUSTRALASIA. 1854-1865 **[35688]**
MY: **12TH REGIMENT — SUFFOLK** ENG & IRL. 1866-1876 **[35688]**
MY: **12TH REGT OF FOOT** JOHN NORRIS PTE. PRE 1860 **[37876]**
MY: **12TH REGT OF FOOT** GIBRALTAR. 1824 **[37876]**
MY: **12TH REGT OF FOOT** MCKONE FAMILY. 1834 **[37876]**
MY: **12TH REGT OF FOOT** POSTINGS. 1824-54 **[37876]**
MY: **12TH REGT. LIGHT DRAGOONS** SERVICE & INFORMATION. 1760-1806 **[35813]**
MY: **13TH LIGHT DRAGOONS** E.V.GOAD. **[36028]**
MY: **17TH LANCERS** CRIMEA. 1854-5 **[35693]**
MY: **17TH REGT (LEICESTER)** MEMBERS: EDWARDS & CAMPBELL. C1830 **[35009]**
MY: **1ST REGT. OF FOOT, ROYAL SCOTS** SOLDIERS DIARIES. 1811-1834 **[37263]**
MY: **2/14 AIF WW2 FIELD ENGINEERS** MEMBERS FROM QLD & NSW. 1942-1945 **[35025]**
MY: **27TH FOOT** JOHN MACLEOD. PRE 1800 **[37459]**
MY: **2ND EUROPEAN MADRAS LIGHT** INDIA. 1841+ **[34667]**
MY: **2ND FLYING CORP** MEMBERS OF. 1914 **[34757]**
MY: **2ND FRENCH CHASSEURS** CAPTAIN EDWARD SMITHE. C1840+ **[37415]**
MY: **3RD REGT (BUFFS)** SYD, AUS. 1820 **[35361]**
MY: **40TH REGT FOOT (2ND SOMERSETSHIRE)** SERVICE IN AFGHANISTAN AND INDIA. 1841-1845
   [36625]
MY: **40TH REGT FOOT (2ND SOMERSETSHIRE)** . ALL **[36625]**
MY: **48TH NORTHAMPTONSHIRE MILITIA** JAMES SPENCE, COLOUR SGT, GIBRALTAR. **[34615]**
MY: **48TH REGIMENT OF FOOT** HISTORY OF. 1800-1840 **[35151]**
MY: **48TH REGIMENT** AUS IMMIGRANTS. 1824 **[33841]**
MY: **49TH REGIMENT** IN GARRISON OF MONTREAL, QUE, CAN. 1808-1811 **[35527]**
MY: **50TH REGT** GEORGE RAMSAY, NORFOLK IS. C1834-40 **[35442]**
MY: **51ST INFANTRY "C" COMPANY** LILYDALE. 1914 **[34568]**
MY: **56 REGT, SRY, ENG** . C1810 **[36256]**
MY: **56TH LIGHT FOOT REGIMENT** MAJOR JOHN MEREDITH. 1800+ **[34602]**
MY: **57TH REGT. OF FOOT** JOSEPH ANDERSON. 1790+ **[34063]**
MY: **5TH PIONEER BATTALION** WWI, AUS. **[35565]**

MY: **61ST REGT OF FOOT** CAMPAIGNS IN SPAIN. 1810-1815 **[38597]**
MY: **6TH LIGHT HORSE** MIDDLE EAST. 1914-1918 **[36600]**
MY: **74TH REGT** SCT & NB, CAN. 1770-1783 **[34124]**
MY: **77 IRISH FUSILIERS** INDIAN MUTINY. 1800+ **[36303]**
MY: **77 IRISH FUSILIERS** CRIMEAN WAR. 1800+ **[36303]**
MY: **7TH FUSILIER REGT** MOVEMENT BY SHIP. 1790-1791 **[38459]**
MY: **7TH FUSILIER REGT** MOVEMENT TO ABERDEEN, SCT. 1785-1786 **[38459]**
MY: **81ST REGT. OF FOOT** TIMOTHY LOUGHLIN. PRE 1900 **[35934]**
MY: **93RD HIGHLAND REGT** AREAS OF SERVICE. 1800S **[38433]**
MY: **94TH REGT** ALEXANDER SPENCE IN TRANSVAAL. 1880S **[34615]**
MY: **95TH REGT. OF FOOT** DERBYSHIRES. ANY **[36138]**
MY: **99TH FOOT REGT** BRITISH ARMY, CAN. 1815-1830 **[37461]**
MY: **9TH REGT OF LANCERS** INDIA. 1850S **[37080]**
MY: **A.A.N.C.** LAURA JOYCE LOWRY. PRE 1947 **[35122]**
MY: **A.S.C.** POOK SIDNEY. 1900-1930 **[36501]**
MY: **AFGHAN WAR (2ND)** EVENTS IN. 1878-1880 **[36122]**
MY: **AMERICAN CIVIL WAR** VETERANS GRAVES. ALL **[36557]**
MY: **AMERICAN CIVIL WAR** 22 VA CAVALRY. 1861-1865 **[34350]**
MY: **AMERICAN CIVIL WAR** VETERAN'S GRAVES. **[37095]**
MY: **AMERICAN CIVIL WAR** NAMES OF FRENCH ENLISTED. 1861-65 **[36304]**
MY: **AMERICAN CIVIL WAR** BATTLE OF PERRYVILLE, KY, USA. **[36946]**
MY: **AMERICAN CIVIL WAR** VETERANS GRAVES (PARKER) USA. ALL **[38477]**
MY: **AMERICAN CIVIL WAR** UNION VETERANS GRAVES. ALL **[37535]**
MY: **AMERICAN CIVIL WAR** 95TH OVI REGIMENT, CO. B & CO. K. 1861-1865 **[37580]**
MY: **AMERICAN CIVIL WAR** 8TH LA INF. 1861-1862 **[35267]**
MY: **AMERICAN CIVIL WAR** MD TROOPS, SOUTHERN CAMPAIGN. 1777-1782 **[36973]**
MY: **AMERICAN CIVIL WAR** 8TH KY CAVALRY (UNION). 1862-1865 **[36973]**
MY: **AMERICAN CIVIL WAR** MILITIA, SOUTHERN CAMPAIGN. 1777-1781 **[36973]**
MY: **AMERICAN CIVIL WAR** FRANKLIN SHARP SHOOTERS LA. 1861-1862 **[35267]**
MY: **AMERICAN CIVIL WAR** MISSISSIPPI CONFEDERATE SOLDIERS. ALL **[37796]**
MY: **AMERICAN REVOLUTION** JAMES SNEDDEN, BRITISH 82ND REGT. ANY **[34259]**
MY: **AMERICAN REVOLUTIONARY WAR** FRONTIER FORTS & MILITIA. 1770-1795 **[38177]**
MY: **AMERICAN WAR OF INDEPENDENCE** JOHN & MARTIN CARLOW, NB, CAN. 1770+ **[37717]**
MY: **ARAB UPRISING** MIDDLE EAST, ROYAL ENGINEERS. PRE 1939 **[36609]**
MY: **ARMOURED CORPS** OLIVER THOMAS LUMBIS. 1920-50 **[36473]**
MY: **ARMY — AUS** CORPORAL SHIRLEY. C1940 **[37375]**
MY: **ARMY 2ND EAST YORKSHIRE REGT** WILLIAM WORRALL, SERGEANT. 1850-90 **[37707]**
MY: **ARMY DISCHARGE OVERSEAS** HERBERT KEDGE, RSA. 1944+ **[36026]**
MY: **ARMY IN INDIA** GROVE FAMILY. 1800-1900 **[37844]**
MY: **ARMY PERSONNEL RECORDS** PAID WORK UNDERTAKEN. 1800-1900 **[37095]**
MY: **ARMY REGTS, 12TH AUST LIGHT HORSE** SERVICE IN WWI. 1915-1919 **[35874]**
MY: **ARMY REGTS, 99TH FOOT** IRL, AUS & NZ. 1838-1856 **[35874]**
MY: **ARMY** ALL RANKS NAMED NELLIST. ALL **[36481]**
MY: **ARMY** MDX REGT. 2ND VOL. 1887-1928 **[36117]**
MY: **ARMY** MDX REGT. 44TH VOL. 1860-1887 **[36117]**
MY: **ARMY** OXFORD MILITIA. 1804-1812 **[36117]**
MY: **ARMY** PERCY LOWRY. PRE 1924 **[35122]**
MY: **ARTILLERYMAN** ARCHIBALD BURNS, CEYLON. 1830S **[34887]**
MY: **ARTILLERYMAN** MA, USA. 1700+ **[37049]**
MY: **ASHANTI WAR** GOLD COAST REGT. 1800S **[38381]**
MY: **AYR MILITIA** LOGANS ON MUSTER ROLLS. 1640-1840 **[36001]**
MY: **BALTZAR PETERSEN** MARINER, DEN. 1800-1850 **[36248]**
MY: **BANGALORE CANTONMENT** MYSORE, INDIA. 1900-1945 **[34667]**
MY: **BARRACK MASTER, INDIA** KILPATRICK, WILLIAM SAMUEL. 1800-1840 **[35472]**
MY: **BATTLE OF AUSTERLITZ** GERMANS IN NAPOLEONS ARMY, STORY. 1804-1806 **[38616]**
MY: **BATTLE OF PLAINS OF ABRAHAM** QUE, CAN. 1759 **[37049]**
MY: **BATTLE OF WATERLOO** VETERANS IN AUS MILITARY & SETTLERS. **[35467]**
MY: **BATTLE OF WATERLOO** DUKE OF WELLINGTON. 1815 **[35573]**
MY: **BATTLESHIP MISSOURI,** USA ROBERT DAVISON, NAVY TRAINING OFFICER. 1949 **[36412]**
MY: **BAVARIAN ARMY** PETER PELLY. 1720-1770 **[38301]**
MY: **BE(E)CHER** BENGAL ARMY. 1700+ **[34109]**
MY: **BENNIS, MICHAEL** SOLDIER. C1820 **[34827]**
MY: **BOER WAR — HONOURS MEDALS** WILLIAM BECKETT, GREAT YARMOUTH, ENG. **[38255]**
MY: **BOER WAR** CHESHIRE YEOMANRY 1900-1902. **[38259]**
MY: **BOER WAR** SOUTH AFRICA. 1900+ **[33825]**
MY: **BRITISH AIRBORNE FORCES (NZ)** INC 'AIRBORNE SPECTACULAR NZ 1990'. **[38586]**
MY: **BRITISH ARMY IN INDIA** LOGANS, ALL RANKS. ANY **[36001]**
MY: **BRITISH ARMY PERSONNEL** BELTURBET, IRL. 1800+ **[37459]**
MY: **BRITISH ARMY REGTS** IN NL. 1680-1700 **[37764]**
MY: **BRITISH ARMY REGT** 1ST & 12TH EAST SUFFOLK REGT OF FOOT (INF). ALL **[34584]**
MY: **BRITISH ARMY** ARMY SERVICE CORPS. 1902-1920 **[37407]**
MY: **BRITISH ARMY** BARTHOLOMEW LYNCH, COR, IRL. C1850 **[35519]**

MY: **BRITISH ARMY** INDIA. 1800-1838 **[35573]**
MY: **BRITISH ARMY** JOHN BAREFIELD, ENG. PRE 1755 **[37505]**
MY: **BRITISH ARMY** LANCASHIRE FUSILIERS. 1890-1930 **[37407]**
MY: **BRITISH ARMY** LEGATION GUARDS PEKING. 1900-1920 **[37407]**
MY: **BRITISH ARMY** SERVING IN CEYLON. C1830S **[34913]**
MY: **BRITISH ARMY** TO WEST INDIES. 1740+ **[37386]**
MY: **BRITISH ARMY** TO WEST INDIES. PRE 1850 **[36324]**
MY: **BRITISH DESERTERS** IN SOUTH AFRICA. PRE 1898 **[36466]**
MY: **BRITISH REGIMENT** IN PIEDMONT, ITALY. 1696 **[37293]**
MY: **BRITISH REGT OF FOOT IN AUSTRALASIA** DESCENDANTS. 1810-1870 **[35467]**
MY: **BRITISH** IN TRINIDAD. 1810-1870 **[38388]**
MY: **BRITISH MEDICAL OFFICER.** 1830-1870 **[38388]**
MY: **BROCKVILLE DRAGOONS** CAPT ROBERT HERVEY. 1838-1840 **[34365]**
MY: **BUFFS, THE** 2ND & 1ST VOLUNTEER BATTALIONS. 1876-1906 **[37701]**
MY: **BURMA** 82ND (WEST AFRICAN) DIVISION. C1940-1945 **[37356]**
MY: **CAMPAIGNS IN SOUTH AFRICA** CAPTAIN JAMES SAMUEL SEARLE. PRE 1900 **[38772]**
MY: **CAMPERDOWN** NAVAL BATTLE OF. 1797 **[34550]**
MY: **CAN-USA WAR 1812** NICHOLAS URQUHART, WINDSOR, ENG. 1780-1850 **[34249]**
MY: **CANADIAN AIR FORCE** . 1918 **[34496]**
MY: **CANADIAN FORCES BOER WAR** MOUNTED CONTINGENT STH AFRICA. 1898-1904 **[36463]**
MY: **CANADIAN SOLDIERS GRAVES IN FRA** SHARPE NAMES. 1914-18 **[37878]**
MY: **CAN VETERANS BATTALION.** 1805-1817 **[37515]**
MY: **CARRAGHER, TIMOTHY ALOYSIUS** PERSONAL AIDE, PRES. F.D. ROOSEVELT. 1929-1941 **[37079]**
MY: **CARRAHER, PATRICK** CIVIL WAR, USA, UNION SERVICE RECORD. 1860+ **[37079]**
MY: **CHELSEA PENSIONERS** INVERNESS, INV, SCT. 1800-1855 **[38476]**
MY: **CHINESE ARTILLERY CONTINGENT** WOOLNER, JOHN OLIVER, CON, ENG. 1800-1850 **[36398]**
MY: **COL JOHN BYS SAPPERS & MINORS** JOHN MCDONALD, SCT, IRL & ONT, CAN. 1790-1835 **[36669]**
MY: **CRIMEAN WAR** 6TH INNISKILLINGS. 1853 **[35261]**
MY: **CRIMEAN WAR** TIMOTHY FRANCIS DE COURCY DENOVAN. 1854+ **[35554]**
MY: **CRIMEAN WAR** VETERANS FROM QUE, CAN. **[35649]**
MY: **CRIMEAN WAR** WILLIAM LEACH, H.M. SOLDIER. 1854-56 **[34363]**
MY: **CRITCHLEY, WILLIAM** ROYAL VETERANS, NSW, AUS. 1800+ **[34596]**
MY: **DUNDEE FAMILY** DESCENDANTS OF. ALL **[35456]**
MY: **DUNN, MICHAEL** 75TH REGT, ENG CHELSEA OUT-PENSIONER WINDSOR, PARRAMATTA, SYDNEY, NSW, AUS. 1791-1829 **[36311]**
MY: **EAST INDIA COMPANY** REGTS IN MADRAS & HYDERABAD. PRE 1860 **[33812]**
MY: **EAST KENT YEOMANRY HORSE REGT,** ENG. 1914-1918 **[35980]**
MY: **EAST LANCASHIRE** 2ND REGT. 1899-1942 **[37701]**
MY: **EAST YORK MILITIA** CAR, IRL. 1810-1813 **[33812]**
MY: **EASTER UPRISING,** DUBLIN BRITISH UNITS SENT FROM FRANCE. 1916 **[35252]**
MY: **EMBARQUEMENT** PILET, FRA. 1675-1725 **[36699]**
MY: **ENGLISH NAVY RECORDS** . 1870-90 **[36624]**
MY: **EUREKA STOCKADE** 12TH REGT OF FOOT. 1854 **[37876]**
MY: **FAIREY FANTOME-FEROCE** IN REPUBLICAN AIR FORCE. 1936+ **[34079]**
MY: **FENIAN WAR, CAN** JAMES WALLER, WAGON DRIVER. 1860-70S **[35632]**
MY: **FENIANS** IN CAN, USA & IRL. 1800-1880 **[35630]**
MY: **FLEMING, PVT.WM.** 7TH CO RSM, ENG & CAN. PRE 1831 **[36652]**
MY: **FRANCE REGIMENT** CARIGNAN & SALIERES. 1600-1670 **[37429]**
MY: **FRANCO-PRUSSEN WAR** ENLISTMENT NAMES. 1870+ **[34932]**
MY: **FRANCO-PRUSSEN WAR** VETERANS GRAVES. 1870+ **[34932]**
MY: **GERMAN ARMY** IN POLAND NEAR WARSAW. 1860S **[36683]**
MY: **GOAD, E.V.** 13TH LIGHT DRAGOONS. **[36028]**
MY: **GOGGINS** KILLED IN ACTION. ALL **[38296]**
MY: **GORDON HIGHLANDERS** TIMOTHY CONNELL, ABD, SCT. 1895-1946 **[34243]**
MY: **GREAVES FAMILY** ENGLISHMEN IN OES NAVY & ARMY. 1800-1900 **[37289]**
MY: **GURKHA RIFLES** NICOLAY FAMILY. 1835-1938 **[33795]**
MY: **HAILE, JOEL** REVOLUTIONARY WAR, NC, USA. 1775-1781 **[37794]**
MY: **HAMPSHIRE REGT** 15TH BATTALION. 1917-1919 **[34711]**
MY: **HANNOVARIAN ARMY** COMMISSIONS. 1800S **[35009]**
MY: **HAZAR & MIRANZAE 1891 CAMPAIGN** INDIA NORTH WEST FRONTIER. **[36398]**
MY: **HESSIAN SOLDIERS** FIGHTING FOR GEORGE III. 1776 **[34377]**
MY: **HIGHLAND REGIMENT** 79TH FOOT CAMERONS. 1810-1825 **[34283]**
MY: **HM 14TH LIGHT DRAGOONS** . 1810+ **[34568]**
MY: **HM 84TH OF FOOT** INDIA & CHATHAM. 1840-60 **[35697]**
MY: **INDEPENDANT COMPANIES OF THE AMERICAN REVOLUTION** MAJOR HIERLIHY. 1777+ **[38460]**
MY: **INDIAN ARMY** 3 MADRAS NATIVE INFANTRY. 1860+ **[35930]**
MY: **INDIAN ARMY** 7TH BENGAL NATIVE INFANTRY. 1800S **[35956]**
MY: **INDIAN ARMY** ROBERT CLAYTON. ALL **[36984]**
MY: **INDIAN ARMY** VETERANS GRAVES, BURMA. 1885+ **[35930]**
MY: **INDIAN ARMY** VETERANS GRAVES, INDIA. 1885+ **[35930]**
MY: **INDIAN MUTINY** LIEUT GEORGE WILLOUGHBY. 1857-59 **[34366]**

MY: **IRISH IN FRENCH ARMY** JEREMIE O'DWYER OF TIPPERARY. 1650-1800 **[33916]**
MY: **IRISH REBELLION** PATRICK HANRAHAN. 1798 **[35205]**
MY: **IRISH SOLDIERS IN FRANCE** ENGLISH OR FRENCH MILITARY. 1700-1850 **[34937]**
MY: **KAFFIR WARS** RSA. 1799+ **[35009]**
MY: **KINGS 64TH REGT OF FOOT** OTHER RANKS VITAL RECORDS. 1826-1848 **[37816]**
MY: **KINGS ROYAL REGT** PERCIVAL JAMES GROVE BROMLEY, ENG. 1870-1900 **[36398]**
MY: **KNIGHTS OF THE GOLDEN CIRCLE** IN SHELBY & JOHNSON CO.S, IN, USA. 1861-1865 **[36336]**
MY: **LACE** INDIANA — CIVIL WAR. 1861-1865 **[37794]**
MY: **LAKEMANS RIFLES** BRITISH ARMY TIMOTHY FRANCIS DE COURCY DENOVAN. 1852+ **[35554]**
MY: **LOYAL CHESHIRE REGT** CAPT JAMES STEWART. 1790S **[35196]**
MY: **MAGEE, ROBERT HERBERTSON** ARMY BARRACKS, LONGFORD TOWN, IRL. C1898 **[38302]**
MY: **MAORI WARS** JAMES SAMUEL SEARLE. PRE 1870 **[38772]**
MY: **MARINE CORPS** EDGE, FANE, STRANGE. C1790 **[33864]**
MY: **MAURITIUS, BRIT. ARMY** OFFICERS OR RANKS. 1840+ **[35975]**
MY: **MCGEE, ROBERT HERBERTSON** ARMY BARRACKS, LONGFORD TOWN, IRL. C1898 **[38302]**
MY: **MILITARY VOLUNTEER FORCE** WESTERN AUS. 1861-1903 **[36645]**
MY: **MILITIA ARTILLERY** CORK CITY, IRL. ALL **[37696]**
MY: **MILITIA MA**, USA. 1750+ **[37049]**
MY: **MONTGOMERIES HIGHLANDERS** PERSONNEL PAPERS. 1757-70 **[38391]**
MY: **NAPOLEON'S GENERAL** COUNT JEAN RAPP. 1771-1821 **[35079]**
MY: **NAPOLEONIC WARS** CASUALTIES & SURVIVORS. 1800+ **[34377]**
MY: **NAPOLEONIC WAR** HENRI MEYER, NEHWEILER, ALS, FRA. 1750-1850 **[36898]**
MY: **NAVAL COLLEGE, ENG** JOSEPH IGNATIUS RICHARDS. PRE 1860 **[33964]**
MY: **NAVAL ORPHANAGE** DEVONPORT, DEV, ENG. 1800-1900 **[36398]**
MY: **NAVAL RECORDS** JOHN CHRISTIAN, ENG. C1720 **[38725]**
MY: **NAVAL RECORDS** ROBERT PRIESTWOOD, ENG. C1700 **[38725]**
MY: **NB REGT (FENCIBLES)** NB, CAN. 1790-1830 **[34124]**
MY: **NEW ZEALAND DISCHARGE DEPOT** TORQUAY, DEV, ENG. 1917-1919 **[34711]**
MY: **NEWMAN, CAPT RICHARD** AT BATTLE OF WORCESTER. 1651 **[34079]**
MY: **NORFOLK REGT** CAMBRIDGE FAMILY. ALL **[36473]**
MY: **NORFOLK YEOMANRY** CAMBRIDGE FAMILY. ALL **[36473]**
MY: **NORTH AFRICAN PROVINCES OF ROMAN EMPIRE** AUXILLIARY LEGIONS & INDIVIDUALS
      SERVING IN FORMER NUMIDIA & MAURETANIA. **[37742]**
MY: **NSW CORPS** BIOGRAPHICAL INDEX. 1789-1809 **[36364]**
MY: **NSW STAFF CORPS** SOLDIER DETAILS. ALL **[34696]**
MY: **NZ ARMY HISTORY** AUCKLAND, NORTH HEAD. PRE 1950 **[33949]**
MY: **OLD WARS**, USA US 1ST CAVALRY. 1852+ **[38190]**
MY: **ORLANDO NEWTON** BRITISH ARMY 39TH REGIMENT. 1800-1900 **[36794]**
MY: **ORPHANAGE, NAVAL** DEVONPORT, DEV, ENG. 1800-1900 **[36398]**
MY: **PASSENGERS LISTS** LIVERPOOL TO QUE, CAN. 1792-1795 **[38459]**
MY: **PENINSULAR (SPANISH) WARS** 74TH HIGHLAND REGT. 1813-1832 **[33812]**
MY: **PENINSULAR WAR** SOLDIERS DIARIES. ALL **[37263]**
MY: **PHOTOGRAPHIC RECCONAISANCE** WORLD WAR 2 — NO 2 P.R.U.. 1939-1945 **[36463]**
MY: **PORTER, JAMES** SOLDIER, DOW, IRL. 1810-1830S **[34229]**
MY: **PRISONERS OF WAR** TAKEN AT TALAVERA, ESP. 1809+ **[37675]**
MY: **PRUSSIAN ARMY** ANKIEWICZ JOHANN MALTHEUS, PRE, GER. 1860-70S **[36452]**
MY: **PRUSSIAN ARMY** GENERAL FROHWIRT, MSW, GER. 1780-1840 **[35205]**
MY: **QLD IRISH VOLUNTEER CORPS** SGT THOMAS HURLEY. PRE 1899 **[36621]**
MY: **RAF #1 CANADIAN WING**. 1919-1920 **[34496]**
MY: **RANCE** INDIAN MUTINY. ALL **[34831]**
MY: **REBELLION OF 1848** SHO VS DENMARK. 1848 **[35630]**
MY: **REBELS OF MAYO, IRL** NAMES OF. 1798 **[36191]**
MY: **RED COATS, SYDNEY, AUS** LISTINGS OF. 1845-1849 **[35573]**
MY: **REGT 40TH OF FOOT** AUS — HISTORY & NAMES. 1820S **[38760]**
MY: **REGT. 58TH OF FOOT** SYDNEY & TAS, AUS. 1845+ **[35573]**
MY: **REVOLUTIONARY WAR CAPTAIN**, USA FATHER OF MARIETTA BURR. 1789 **[38537]**
MY: **REVOLUTIONARY WAR** 1776+ VETERANS GRAVES. ALL **[37470]**
MY: **REVOLUTIONARY WAR** BRITISH REGIMENTS IN HALIFAX, NS, CAN. 1776-1783 **[37580]**
MY: **REVOLUTIONARY WAR** BRITISH REGIMENTS DEPARTING ENG. 1776 **[37580]**
MY: **REVOLUTIONARY WAR** BRITISH REGIMENTS IN QUEBEC, QUE, CAN. 1776-1777 **[37580]**
MY: **RINGGOLD CAVALRY** WASHINGTON CO., PA, USA. 1861 **[38235]**
MY: **ROYAL ARMY HOSPITAL CORPS** SHARP, JAMES. 1870-1890 **[34131]**
MY: **ROYAL ARMY HOSPITAL CORPS** PERRY, CHARLES. 1870-1890 **[34131]**
MY: **ROYAL ARTILLERY** CAPE COLONY EDWARD EVANS BOMBADIER. 1834+ **[36451]**
MY: **ROYAL ARTILLERY** 5TH BATTALION. 1812-1814 **[37485]**
MY: **ROYAL ARTILLERY** EDWARD EVANS BOMBADIER. 1825+ **[36451]**
MY: **ROYAL CUMBERLAND MILITIA** MUSTER. 1800-1810 **[34241]**
MY: **ROYAL ENGINEERS** PORTON, ENG, PALESTINE. 1935 **[36609]**
MY: **ROYAL IRISH FUSILIERS** INDIA. 1880S-90S **[37080]**
MY: **ROYAL MARINE LIGHT INFANTRY** 18 COY, PORTSMOUTH DIVISION. 1861-1883 **[34711]**
MY: **ROYAL MARINES** PERKINS, J.F.. PRE 1800+ **[36423]**
MY: **ROYAL MARINES** PORTSMOUTH, HAM, ENG. 1820-1850 **[34881]**

MY: **ROYAL MARINES** WILLIAM REECE & WILLIAM BOYT. 1820-47 **[36828]**
MY: **ROYAL NAVY AIR SERVICE** #3 WING. 1915-1918 **[34496]**
MY: **ROYAL NAVY CENSUS RETURNS.** 1860+ **[37862]**
MY: **ROYAL NAVY LIEUT** WILLIAM STORIE. 1770+ **[34602]**
MY: **ROYAL NAVY** WILLIAM STEVENS. C1810 **[37223]**
MY: **ROYAL NEW SOUTH WALES VETERAN COMPANIES** . 1825+ **[35359]**
MY: **ROYAL SAPPERS & MINERS** ENG & RIDEAU CANAL, CAN. 1820-30 **[36652]**
MY: **ROYAL STAFF CORPS** UK & QUE, CAN. 1825-1832 **[34365]**
MY: **ROYAL VETERAN CORP** THOMAS RODWELL, NSW, AUS. 1826-31 **[38729]**
MY: **ROYAL VETERANS, NSW, AUS** WILLIAM CRITCHLEY. 1800+ **[34596]**
MY: **SC ROYALIST REGT. USA** LIEUT COL JOSEPH ROBINSON. PRE 1783 **[37460]**
MY: **SCOTTISH REGIMENTS, AMERICAN REVOLUTION** . 1770-1780 **[37821]**
MY: **SEVENTEENTH LANCERS** WHEREABOUTS & BATTLES. 1870-1880 **[34158]**
MY: **SEVERS, FREDERICK** CAPT CREEK MOUNTED VOLS. 1861-63 **[38012]**
MY: **SGT, BRITISH ARMY** JOHN BAREFIELD, USA. 1754+ **[37505]**
MY: **SHETLANDERS** IN ROYAL NAVY. PRE 1820 **[37340]**
MY: **SIR FRANCIS DRAKE** CREWS OF. **[34476]**
MY: **SMITH, THOMAS** INDIA & SOUTH AFRICA. 1800S+ **[37210]**
MY: **SOLDIERS** NORTHUMBERLAND FUSILIERS, ENG. PRE 1918 **[37979]**
MY: **SONS OF LIBERTY** IN SHELBY & JOHNSON CO.S, IN, USA. 1861-1865 **[36336]**
MY: **SOUTH WALES BORDERERS** ANY RECORDS OF ENLISTMENTS. 1918-1920 **[34182]**
MY: **SPANISH CIVIL WAR** DOCTORS FROM UK. 1930+ **[35783]**
MY: **ST HELENA ARTILLERY** MEMBERS OF. 1831-1836 **[35132]**
MY: **SWORDS** KILLED IN ACTION. ALL **[38296]**
MY: **USS MONITOR** STARBOARD WATCH SOCIETY. CIVIL WAR **[35328]**
MY: **VETERAN (OR INVALID) COMPANY OF NSW** BIOGRAPHICAL INDEX. 1810-1823 **[36364]**
MY: **VETERAN'S CORP** WILLIAM HEATH. 1788-1828 **[35583]**
MY: **VICTORIA CROSS RECIPIENT** CAPTAIN FOGARTY-FEGAN. 1939 **[37415]**
MY: **VICTORIA CROSS RECIPIENTS.** 1856-1904 **[35172]**
MY: **VOLUNTEER MILITARY FORCE** WESTERN AUS. 1861-1903 **[36645]**
MY: **VOLUNTEERS BOER WAR** LADYSMITH SIEGE BOER WAR. 1899+ **[36471]**
MY: **W PRUSSIAN ARMY** SCHMIDT, MICHAEL, STRASBURG. 1800+ **[35266]**
MY: **WAR OF 1812-1814** VETERANS GRAVES. ALL **[37470]**
MY: **WAR OF 1812** STEPHAN O'GUIN. 1810S **[37507]**
MY: **WARREN'S ACTION** NAVAL ENGAGEMENT. 1798 **[34550]**
MY: **WARWICK MILITIA** LT COL E.W.DICKENSON, STS, ENG. 1800+ **[34243]**
MY: **WELSH REGT** MEMBERS OF. PRE 1919 **[34757]**
MY: **WEST MIDDX MILITIA** NCO'S AND OFFICERS. 1798-1800 **[36410]**
MY: **WESTERN AUS DEFENCE FORCES.** 1826-1903 **[36645]**
MY: **WESTERN AUS VOLUNTEER MILITARY FORCE.** 1861-1903 **[36645]**
MY: **WHITNEY REVOLVERS** CIVIL WAR PRODUCTION. 1847-1865 **[35626]**
MY: **WORCESTER MILITIA** . C1860 **[34711]**
MY: **WORLD WAR 1** 11TH HUSSARS. 1914-18 **[38549]**
MY: **WORLD WAR 1** 301 INF. 76 DIV.. 1918 **[37041]**
MY: **WORLD WAR I** INTERNMENT IN ENG — JOHANNES STEINMANN. 1914-1918 **[37020]**
MY: **WORLD WAR I** PRISONERS OF WAR IN BELGIUM. 1914-1918 **[34293]**
MY: **WORLD WAR ONE** AIF, JUNEE & DISTRICT, NSW, AUS, SOLDIERS & NURSES. 1914-1919 **[34446]**
MY: **WWI SOLDIERS** ST MARYS ENLISTEES (NSW). 1914-1918 **[35101]**
MY: **YORK LIGHT INFANTRY** . 1800-1818 **[35359]**
MY: **ZULU WAR** BATTLES. 1879 **[34158]**
O: **'BENGER BABY FOODS'** BENGER, GEORGE (MANUFACT), DORSET, ENG. 1800-70+ **[35696]**
O: **'HOPE & ANCHOR'** INNKEEPERS, KEIGHLEY, YKS, ENG. 1850+ **[35734]**
O: **ACROBATS** LONDON THEATRE HALLS. 1830-1850 **[38073]**
O: **ALDERMAN, ERSKINEVILLE, NSW, AUS** JOHN WILLIAM PECK. 1920S **[35583]**
O: **ANTRIM IRON ORE COMPANY** ROBERT LAW COMPANY CASHIER/SECRETARY. 1870-1920 **[37425]**
O: **APOTHECARY** JAMES STREET. 1700S **[36381]**
O: **APPRENTICE MASONS** KKD, SCT. 1700S **[36705]**
O: **ARCHITECT** ALBERT ALEXANDER WILLIAMS, DUBLIN, IRL. 1840+ **[35971]**
O: **ARTIFICIAL LIMB MAKER** ROBERT SCOTLAND, GLASGOW, SCT. PRE 1887-1970 **[37138]**
O: **ARTISTIC PHOTOGRAPHER** E.T.KENNEDY, HUNTLEY, NZ. 1890+ **[35567]**
O: **ARTIST** DORE EDWARD, ISLE OF WIGHT, ENG. 1800S **[33802]**
O: **ARTIST** JOSEPH F.GILBERT, ENG. 1813-1855 **[35720]**
O: **ARTIST** KNUD BULL, NOR. **[38212]**
O: **ASHTON, GEORGE** HATTER & FURRIER, MONTREAL, QUE, CAN. 1842-1850 **[38384]**
O: **ASHTON, JOHN PEACOCK** HATTER & FURRIER, MONTREAL, QUE, CAN. 1842-1865 **[38384]**
O: **ASHTON, JOSEPH** HATTER, MANCHESTER, ENG. 1811+ **[38384]**
O: **ASHTON, JOSEPH** HATTER, DENTON, LAN, ENG. 1806+ **[38384]**
O: **ASHTON, THOMAS P.** HATTER, MONTREAL, QUE, CAN. 1844+ **[38384]**
O: **AUCTIONEERS** DUBLIN, IRL. **[37407]**
O: **AUSTRIAN SERVICE** JOHN PELLY. 1716-1755 **[38301]**
O: **BAILLIES** PEMBROKE TRIBE, BERMUDA. 1616 **[35130]**
O: **BAKERS** EARLY SYDNEY, NSW, AUS. 1788-1830 **[35585]**

O: **CARPENTER** JOHN GOULD, BIRMINGHAM, ENG. 1830-1880 **[34736]**
O: **CARPENTER** RICHARD WILLIAM PATMORE. 1860S-C1877 **[37634]**
O: **CARPENTER** URIAH BAKER, W YKS, ENG. 1820-1855 **[34369]**
O: **CARPET MANUFACTURERS** WILLIAM MILLWARD & SONS, MANCHESTER, ENG. 1874-1960S **[36230]**
O: **CARPET MANUFACTURER** JAMES NOBLE, STOWAWAY TO USA. 1880-1950 **[36129]**
O: **CARRIERS TO LONDON** ALFRED JOHN DIXON. 1750+ **[35403]**
O: **CARRIERS** SCT. 1700-1850 **[38388]**
O: **CARTER** JOHN BAXTER, GLASGOW, SCT. 1850+ **[34369]**
O: **CARVERS & GILDERS** BOX & CLEETS FAMILIES. 1790+ **[37834]**
O: **CASTLEFIELD MILLS** ELLIS FAMILY, BRADFORD & BINGLEY, ENG. 1803-1930 **[36570]**
O: **CHAIRMAKERS** BRISTOL & SWANSEA, ENG, WLS. 1700-1840 **[35232]**
O: **CHAUFFEURS** EMPLOYERS & TYPE OF WORK, ENG. PRE 1920 **[35362]**
O: **CHEMICAL MANUFACTURERS** SALTLEY CREOSOTE & NAPTHA CO., B'HAM, ENG. ALL **[37883]**
O: **CHEMISTS & DRUGGISTS OF LUDLOW AND LND, ENG** . 1700-1900 **[36256]**
O: **CHEMIST** JOHN THOMAS SARGENT, GRANTHAM, ENG. 1825-1850 **[35724]**
O: **CHEMIST** JOSEPH TOWNSEND, QUE, CAN. 1850-1875 **[34199]**
O: **CHEMIST** ROBERT BATTEN, BRISTOL, GLS, ENG. 1825-1850 **[35215]**
O: **CHINA & GLASS DEALER** THOMAS CHURCH, DEVISES, WIL, ENG. 1850-1880 **[37070]**
O: **CHORISTERS** TEWKESBURY ABBEY, GLS, ENG. 1830-1860 **[34241]**
O: **CHRISTIAN AUTHORS** AFRICA. ALL **[36458]**
O: **CINEMATOGRAPH OPERATORS** LAN, ENG. PRE 1940 **[35362]**
O: **CIRCUS & MUSIC HALL PERFORMERS** WORLDWIDE. 1890-1920 **[37330]**
O: **CIRCUS FAMILIES** BRITAIN. 1900+ **[34790]**
O: **CIRCUS PERFORMERS** AUS. 1842+ **[38073]**
O: **CIVIL ENGINEER & SURVEYOR** GLASGOW AREA, SCT. 1800-1850 **[36985]**
O: **CLERGY** EARLY CHURCH OF ENG CLERICS. PRE 1675 **[38229]**
O: **CLOCK & WATCHMAKERS** IN & TO AUS. 1788-1901 **[38000]**
O: **CLOCKMAKERS** GLASGOW, EBENEZER ROBERTSON. 1780+ **[37834]**
O: **CLOCKMAKER** BETTERIDGE, ENG. C1730-1800 **[36210]**
O: **CLOCKMAKER** JOHN DAVIDGE, LONDON, ENG. 1800-1820 **[37433]**
O: **CLOCKMAKER** ROBERT MCGEAGH, TORONTO, CAN. 1860+ **[37462]**
O: **CLOCKMAKER** SIDERY HAMPSTEAD NORRIS, BRK, ENG. PRE 1850 **[36401]**
O: **CLOCKMAKER** WILLIAM KEDGE, POLSTEAD, SFK, ENG. 1820+ **[36026]**
O: **CLOTHIER** BRADFORD, WRY, ENG. 1700-1800 **[36682]**
O: **CLOTHIER** JAMES TEMPLETON, GLASGOW, SCT. 1870-1880S **[35767]**
O: **COACH TRIMMER** ROBERT REW, STAINES, MDX, ENG. 1828+ **[37168]**
O: **COACHBUILDERS** FROM ENG TO NSW, AUS. 1860+ **[38760]**
O: **COACHBUILDING, FARNHAM, SRY, ENG** . PRE 1900 **[36256]**
O: **COACHMAN** THOMAS CHARLWOOD, PADDINGTON, ENG. 1860-1870S **[35727]**
O: **COACHMAN** . PRE 1800 **[34104]**
O: **COAL MINERS** NORTHERN DURHAM, ENG. PRE 1914 **[34293]**
O: **COAL MINERS** SOUTH MAITLAND COALFIELDS, NSW, AUS. 1890+ **[35539]**
O: **COAL MINING** MOON RUN, PA, USA. 1900-1910 **[34839]**
O: **COAL MINING** S WLS. 1750-1850 **[36682]**
O: **COALFIELD PERSONNEL & ASSOCIATES** WARATAH/RASPBERRY GULLY, NSW, AUS. TO 1900 **[38754]**
O: **COALFIELD PERSONNEL & ASSOCIATES** REDBANK/GOODNA, QLD, AUS. TO 1900 **[38754]**
O: **COALFIELD PERSONNEL & ASSOCIATES** AUCKLAND PROVINCE, NZ. TO 1900 **[38754]**
O: **COALMINERS OF OLD MONKLAND** LKS, SCT. 1850+ **[35341]**
O: **COALMINERS OF DUR, ENG. PRE 1860 **[37693]**
O: **COALMINERS** SCT. 1700-1900 **[38388]**
O: **COALMINER** MCKNIGHTS, CUMNOCK, SCT. 1700-1880 **[37805]**
O: **COALMINING** DURHAM CO., ENG. 1870-99 **[35696]**
O: **COALMINING** HEMMINGS OF MON, WLS. 1870+ **[37885]**
O: **COASTGUARD** WILLIAM SHEPHERD, ISLE OF SHEPPEY. 1840-1860 **[34824]**
O: **COBB & CO. DRIVER** JOHN TROTTER, DAYLESFORD, AUS. 1860S+ **[34919]**
O: **COLLIERY MGR** DAVID PENMAN, ARBUCKLE, NEW MONKLAND, SCT. 1845-1870 **[34369]**
O: **COLLIERY MGR** JAS BROWN, RAW YARDS, LKS, SCT. 1845+ **[34369]**
O: **COMBER, RICHARD** CLOCKMAKER, LEWES, SUSSEX, ENG. 1780-1824 **[37867]**
O: **COMBER, THOMAS** CHURCHWARDEN, RINGMER, SUSSEX, ENG. 1670-1680 **[37867]**
O: **COMBMAKERS** ANY REFERENCE TO. ANY **[36010]**
O: **COMEDIANS** JOHNNY COWAN, AUS. 1880-1910 **[33795]**
O: **COMMERCIAL TRAVELLER** SHOE TRADE IN LEICESTER, ENG. 1870-1930 **[36006]**
O: **COMMISSION AGENTS** SYDNEY MARKETS, NSW, AUS. 1840+ **[34428]**
O: **COMPOSITOR** JAMES TOLMIE, LONDON, ENG. ALL **[34232]**
O: **COMPOSITOR** M.V.BLIGH OF BRIGHTON, ENG. 1891+ **[34057]**
O: **COOPERS** ISLINGTON, LND, ENG. 1800 **[36072]**
O: **COOPER** JACOB JAUCH, SCHWENNINGEN, GER. 1825+ **[36920]**
O: **COOPER** MALCOLM MCCALLUM, GLASGOW, SCT. 1830+ **[38515]**
O: **COOPER** MICHAEL MORIARTY, HALIFAX, CAN. PRE 1923 **[34206]**
O: **COOPER** WILLIAM WILLIAMS, SOUTHWARK, LND, ENG. C1840 **[36076]**
O: **COPPER MINERS** MICHIGAN UPPER PENINSULA, USA. 1840-1880 **[38179]**

O: **COPPER MINERS** WILLIAM HENRY HICKS, CON, ENG TO USA. C1900 [35980]
O: **COPPER MINING** WISEMANS CK NEAR O'CONNELL, BATHURST, NSW, AUS. 1820 + [35361]
O: **CORDWAINERS** COLCHESTER, ENG. 1800-1860 [35756]
O: **CORDWAINERS** NEWCASTLE UPON TYNE, ENG. 1750-1850 [36220]
O: **CORDWAINERS** VIPOND OF COLNE, ENG. 1800-90 [35490]
O: **CORDWAINERS** WILSON OF COLNE, ENG. 1800-60 [35490]
O: **CORN MILLERS** LAN, YKS, ENG. 1700-1900 [37330]
O: **CORNISH MINERS** LAKE SUPERIOR, MICHIGAN, USA. 1840-1880 [38179]
O: **COTTON MERCHANTS** SWISS FAMILIES IN EGYPT. ALL [36982]
O: **COTTON MILL OWNER** JOHN CLAYTON, BOLTON, LAN, ENG. 1898-1902 [36984]
O: **COTTON OVERLOOKER** JOHN CLAYTON, BOLTON, LAN, ENG. 1890-1898 [36984]
O: **COTTON OVERLOOKER** JOHN CLAYTON, ASHTON UNDER LYNE, ENG. 1880-1890 [36984]
O: **COUNCIL WORKERS** SSX, ENG. 1900 + [33998]
O: **COWKEEPERS** ISAAC DIXON. 1700 + [35403]
O: **CRAFTSMEN** GUILDS OF TYNESIDE, ENG. 1645-1800 [37419]
O: **CUSTOM BOATMAN** JOHN FOLEY, EDEN, NSW, AUS. 1857-1872 [36600]
O: **CUSTOMS OFFICERS** DEV, ENG. 1800-1850 [34809]
O: **DAIRY FARMING** FARMS, HERD WORKERS, ENG. PRE 1935 [35362]
O: **DECORATOR** OLIVER HEGGS, BLACKPOOL, LAN, ENG. 1800S [38284]
O: **DECORATOR** WALTER HEGGS, BLACKPOOL, LAN, ENG. 1800S [38284]
O: **DENTIST** ANY, WORLDWIDE. 1700-1900 [36143]
O: **DENTIST** ROBERT E.R.SAWYER, CALGARY, ALB, CAN. C1917-1958 [34997]
O: **DOCTORS & SURGEONS** DOLLING, ENG & AMERICA. 1700 + [38258]
O: **DOCTORS** SCT. 1750-1900 [38388]
O: **DOCTOR** GEORGE N.RIDLEY, KIMBOLTON, HUN, ENG. 1794-1824 [34133]
O: **DOCTOR** JANE SMITHSON, ENG. 1860S [35913]
O: **DOCTOR** JOHN THOMAS SARGENT, AUS, ENG & USA. 1850-1910 [35724]
O: **DOCTOR** MARSEILLES, ONT, CAN. 1800S [34133]
O: **DOMESTIC** FRANCES MURPHY, ROCKHAMPTON, AUS. 1909 + [35405]
O: **DOWDEN** COACHMAN, OSBORNE HOUSE, IOW, ENG. 1800-1860 [35173]
O: **DRAPERS** COMPANY CHIPPERFIELD, LND, ENG. 1700S-1800S [34278]
O: **DRAPERS** BIRMINGHAM, WAR, ENG. 1800-1900 [34269]
O: **DRAPERS** STRAND, LONDON, ENG. 1600 + [36434]
O: **DRESS DESIGNER — QUEEN VICTORIA** JESSE, WILLIAM HENRY. 1890-1901 [36456]
O: **DRESSMAKERS** APPRENTICES LONDON, ENG. 1880 + [35418]
O: **DRESSMAKER** BLYTH OF GLASGOW, SCT. 1800S [33966]
O: **DROVER** JAMES CHARLES HOLLAND. 1880-1930S [35373]
O: **EARTHENWARE** MANUFACTURING IN CHURCH GRESLEY, DBY, ENG. 1830-1900 [36008]
O: **ELECTRICIAN** BUCKINGHAM PALACE, LND, ENG. C1890 [34007]
O: **ENGINE DRIVER** IN GLA, WLS. 1880S [33930]
O: **ENGINEER** CHARTER(S), CEYLON. 1840-1870 [37220]
O: **ENGINEER** JAMES HART, KYNETON, VIC, AUS. 1860S + [35876]
O: **ENGINEER** JAMES MUSGROVE, TRURO, CON, ENG. 1830-1840 [34036]
O: **ENGINEER** LARKUM, CEYLON. 1850-1891 [37220]
O: **ENGINEER** WILLIAM HASLAM, BOSTON, LIN, ENG. 1840S [35876]
O: **ENGINEKEEPER & GROCER** DAVID BROWN, GLASGOW, SCT. 1870-1885 [34369]
O: **ENTERTAINERS** MINSTRALS, AUS. 1880 + [33795]
O: **EXCISE OFFICER** ADAM SMITH, LND, ENG. 1790-1840 [36019]
O: **EXCISE OFFICER** WILLIAM SUTTON, LONDON, ENG. 1780S [36595]
O: **EXPLORER** SIR DOUGLAS MAWSON, AUS. 1800S-1900S [34133]
O: **FAIRGROUND** BRITAIN. 1850 + [34790]
O: **FARMER** IN ENG LOWTHER. 1700-1970 [36227]
O: **FARMERS** SCT. 1700-1850 [38388]
O: **FARMER** EMANUEL ALFRED, PEEL CO., ONT, CAN. 1861 [35618]
O: **FARMER** JOHN DUNN. PRE 1829 [35236]
O: **FARMER** ROBERT SIMPSON, WES, YKS, ENG. 1780-1900 [34855]
O: **FARMER** THOMAS MAGUIRE. PRE 1877 [35236]
O: **FARMER** WILLIAM BYERS, WES, YKS, ENG. 1780-1880 [34855]
O: **FARRIERS**, SUTHERLAND FAMILY KEN, ENG-NARACOORTE, SA, AUS. C1876 + [35025]
O: **FELLMONGERS** ROBERT CURRIE AND SONS, SCT. 1845-1920 [35486]
O: **FELLS NAPTHA CORP.**, USA FOUNDER, FELLS — HIS HISTORY. 1865 + [37079]
O: **FEUARS** LEGERWOOD, BEW, SCT. C1800 [34126]
O: **FIREMAN** JAMES MARSH, ECHUCA, VIC, AUS. 1870S [35876]
O: **FIREWORK ARTIST** GEORGE ERNST OF LONDON, ENG & SWITZERLAND. C1797-1842 [37279]
O: **FISHCURER** WILLIAM CHAMBERLAIN, LAN, ENG. PRE 1900 [34855]
O: **FISHERMAN** HURR. ALL [34813]
O: **FISHERMAN** POPE OF FOLKESTONE, ENG. 1850-1930 [38513]
O: **FLAX TRADE** PER, SCT. 1700-1900 [36220]
O: **FRAMEWORK KNITTERS** HINCKLEY DISTRICT, ENG. 1700-1850 [36410]
O: **FREEDOM OF CITY OF LONDON, ENG** CARPENTRY CERT FOR JOHN SIBLEY FINCH. 1804 [33889]
O: **FRUIT FARMER** ERNEST BOOKER, HAVELOCK NORTH, NZ. 1919 + [37990]
O: **FUR TRADE IN CANADA** ORKNEY EMPLOYEES. 1700-1850 [34362]

O: **FUR TRADE, WEBER** LONDON & GERMANY. 1800+ **[34274]**
O: **FUR TRADER** PIERRE GODIN. 1800-1820 **[38312]**
O: **GAMBLING, POKER** DUBBO & PROSPECT, NSW, AUS. C1840+ **[33930]**
O: **GAMEKEEPER** CHARLES VALLENDER, OF WOR, ENG. 1890+ **[37937]**
O: **GAMEKEEPER** SAMUEL UNDERHILL, BICKENHILL, ENG. 1840-50S **[35136]**
O: **GARDENERS** ALBERT HOWES, SYDNEY, NSW, AUS. 1900+ **[34533]**
O: **GARDENERS** ENGLISH GARDENS & NURSERIES. PRE 1940 **[35362]**
O: **GARDENERS** GLASGOW AREA, SCT. 1780-1830 **[36985]**
O: **GARDENER** JOSEPH BISHOP, TAUNTON, SOM, ENG. 1890+ **[37719]**
O: **GAS INSTALLATIONS** WESTERN IRL. 1800S **[36794]**
O: **GERMAN BUTCHERS IN UK** . 1800+ **[37639]**
O: **GERMAN CLERGY IN UK** . 1800+ **[37639]**
O: **GILDERS & CARVERS BRISTOL CITY,** ENG HENESS FAMILIES. 1790-1899 **[38567]**
O: **GLASS BLOWERS** BIRMINGHAM, ENG. 1800-1900 **[36530]**
O: **GLASS MANUFACTURERS** JOSIAH LANE & SONS LTD., B'HAM/DUDLEY, ENG. ALL **[37883]**
O: **GLASSBLOWERS** BRISTOL, GLS, SOM & DEV, ENG. PRE 1756 **[37289]**
O: **GLASSBLOWERS** NOR, MIGRANTS FROM ENG. 1750+ **[37289]**
O: **GLASSMAKERS** IN BOHEMIA AND SILESIA. **[38495]**
O: **GLASSMAKERS** STOURBRIDGE, B'HAM AND LEEDS, ENG. ALL **[37883]**
O: **GLAZIERS** BRK, ENG. 1770 **[36072]**
O: **GOLD MINING** PRESTON HILL, CARNGHAM, VIC, AUS. 1860S **[35709]**
O: **GOLD MINING** ROBERT BROWN, BLUE SPUR, NZ. ALL **[37162]**
O: **GOLD MINING** YUKON TERRITORY, CAN. 1890-1900S **[33825]**
O: **GOLDMINERS** DANISH, HEATHCOTE, VIC, AUS. 1850-1870 **[37488]**
O: **GOLDSMITH** ROBERT DAVID FORREST, LONDON, ENG. 1845-1875 **[37341]**
O: **GRAVEDIGGER** UNDERTAKER, SAXON, GER, EAST. 1850+ **[35641]**
O: **GROCERY STORE** HAYHOE IN DERBY, ENG. 1900+ **[34338]**
O: **GROOM** LIST OF EMPLOYEES — COBB & CO, VIC, AUS. C1864 **[35453]**
O: **GUNMAKERS, UK** NAMES & FAMILIES IN GUN TRADE. 1600-1880 **[36169]**
O: **GUNSMITHS** AUS. 1788-1900 **[36310]**
O: **HAND LOOM WEAVERS** CADDER LKS SCT. C1850 **[35051]**
O: **HAND LOOM WEAVER** JAMES ENTWISLE, OVER DARWEN, ENG. 1806-1841 **[35052]**
O: **HARBOUR MASTER** WILLIAM TOSE, WHITBY, NRY, ENG. 1850-1876 **[34375]**
O: **HARNESS MAKERS** ORANGE, NSW, AUS. PRE 1900 **[35232]**
O: **HATMAKER,** PENISTONE, YKS, ENG JOSHUA GAUNT. 1750-1850 **[36898]**
O: **HATTER (GENTLEMAN'S)** WEBB. 1900-1950 **[36990]**
O: **HATTERS** RETAILERS, STRAND, LND, ENG. 1880-1910 **[34007]**
O: **HORSE TRAINER** JAMES SCOBIE, VIC, AUS. 1880-1940 **[36193]**
O: **HOSIER** HALL — LONDON, ENG. 1800+ **[33889]**
O: **HOSIER** JAMES PURCHALL, BRAMLEY, SRY, ENG. 1800-1860 **[37259]**
O: **HOT-PRESSERS** . PRE 1850 **[38068]**
O: **INDIGO PLANTER** IVIE ALEXANDER GREGG, INDIA. 1820-30S **[35261]**
O: **INN KEEPERS** ENG. **[35573]**
O: **INNKEEPERS & PUBLICANS** PURCHASE TERRITORY, LA, USA. PRE 1830 **[36353]**
O: **INNKEEPERS** 'HOPE & ANCHOR' KEIGHLEY, YKS, ENG. 1850+ **[35734]**
O: **INNKEEPER** INNS IN EDGEWARE, MDX, ENG. 1700+ **[36165]**
O: **INNKEEPER** ISAAC MOORE, ARGYLE ST, SYDNEY, NSW, AUS. C1860 **[35237]**
O: **INNKEEPER** REGISTRY LICENCES. PRE 1881 **[36674]**
O: **INNKEEPER** WALTER GOWANS, HAMILTON, SCT. 1821-1860S **[34088]**
O: **INSTRUCTOR** JOHN & WILLIAM WECK, HEIDELBERG, WUE, GER. 1775-1875 **[36898]**
O: **IRON MOULDERS** DE BOARD. ALL **[36508]**
O: **IRON TURNER** GLASGOW, LKS, SCT. 1800-1850 **[36682]**
O: **ITALY** PLASTER FIGURE MAKERS, GENOA. ALL **[37390]**
O: **IVORY MANUFACTURERS** LONDON, ENG. 1800-1840S **[34028]**
O: **JAPANNERS** JOHN RYTON, WOLVERHAMPTON, ENG. 1750-1790 **[37609]**
O: **JEWELLERS, BANKERS** — BERLIN NEUMANN, CARLE OR SIGISMUND. PRE 1830 **[33864]**
O: **JEWELLERS** MAYO, IRL. 1850-1950 **[36794]**
O: **JEWELLERS** PITTSBURGH, PA, USA. 1800+ **[37462]**
O: **JEWELLERS** PUTNEY, SRY, ENG. 1850+ **[36026]**
O: **JEWELLER** CHARLES SYKES, SHEFFIELD, WRY, ENG. 1800S **[36678]**
O: **JEWELLER** PETER GRAHAM, EDINBURGH, SCT. 1800+ **[34232]**
O: **JOCKEY** PATRICK HANRAHAN, CLARE, IRL. C1845-1865 **[37111]**
O: **JONES, JAMES GOULD** STOREKEEPER, STANLEY, AUS. 1850-1880 **[33900]**
O: **JONES, JAMES GOULD** CARPENTER, LONDON, ENG. PRE 1850 **[33900]**
O: **JOURNALISTS** NZ TIMES & DOMINION. 1880-1900 **[35357]**
O: **JUDGE** RT. HON. BARON JOHN RICHARDS, MADRAS, INDIA & DUBLIN, IRL. 1811-1859 **[35738]**
O: **KEELMEN** OF SUNDERLAND, DUR, ENG. PRE 1850 **[37693]**
O: **LACEMAKERS** OF CALAIS, FRA & NOTTINGHAM LACEMAKERS, ENG. 1830-1850 **[36365]**
O: **LAND SURVEYING** APPRENTICESHIP RECORDS. 1700-1850 **[38753]**
O: **LANDLORDS** ROYAL EXCHANGE HOTEL, NEWCASTLE, NSW, AUS. 1880-1900 **[35598]**
O: **LATH RENDERS & WOODWORKERS** . 1850+ **[33998]**
O: **LAVENDER STILLS** GROWERS, SFK, ENG. 1750-1890 **[35775]**

O: **LAW** CARTER MOORE, SFK, ENG. 1840-60 **[36717]**
O: **LIBRARY** TUPPENS ROYAL MARINE, BRIGHTON, ENG. C1820 **[36534]**
O: **LICENCED VICTUALLER** SAMUEL WHARAM, KINGSTON UPON HULL, ERY, ENG. 1803 **[35010]**
O: **LICENCED VICTUALLERS** ROBERT WHARAM, KINGSTON UPON HULL, ERY, ENG. 1848-1850S
    [35010]
O: **LIGHTERMEN, EDWARD CROSS** 1812+ **[37834]**
O: **LIGHTERMEN** RIVERS THAMES & MEDWAY, ENG. 1800-1900 **[34738]**
O: **LIVING-IN BARMAIDS** MANCHESTER, LAN, ENG. 1851 **[36635]**
O: **LOCKHARTS BOAT BUILDERS**, BRENTFORD, ENG. 1934-1952 **[37657]**
O: **LONDONDERRY RAILWAY** SUNDERLAND TO SEAHAM, DUR, ENG. 1837-1891 **[38269]**
O: **LUMBERING** MURRAY, MN, USA. 1880+ **[36934]**
O: **MAGISTRATES** CAVAN, IRL. 1790+ **[37459]**
O: **MANUFACTURING CHEMIST** JOSEPH SINGLETON, BIRMINGHAM, ENG. PRE 1865 **[37725]**
O: **MAP PUBLISHER** JOSEPH CURRY, BRADFORD, ENG. 1860S **[35996]**
O: **MARINE ENGINEER** HUGH BUCHANAN OF PER, SCT. 1850-1870 **[36705]**
O: **MARINERS** ALBANY, WA, AUS. 1830-1900 **[35845]**
O: **MARINERS** BARBADOS. 1660+ **[38235]**
O: **MARINERS** DANIEL WHARAM, KINGSTON UPON HULL, ERY, ENG. 1831 **[35010]**
O: **MARINERS** ROBERT WHARAM, KINGSTON UPON HULL, ERY, ENG. 1838 **[35010]**
O: **MARINER** ALFRED JAMES PEARCE, CON, ENG. 1870 **[35235]**
O: **MARINER** OLIVER KING. 1867-1900 **[37311]**
O: **MARSDEN, WILLIAM** MUSIC TEACHER OF BRADFORD, ENG. 1850-1876 **[36228]**
O: **MASON** CORNELIUS, DEVONPORT, ENG. 1700-1825 **[37740]**
O: **MASON** ROBERT FRASER OF GLASGOW & KINTYRE, SCT. 1855-1907 **[34156]**
O: **MASTER BUILDER** ALEXANDER ARCHER, ENG. 1800S **[34133]**
O: **MASTER BUTCHERS** COTTERILL, LONDON, ENG. 1750-1850 **[35434]**
O: **MASTER MARINERS OF SOUTH SHIELDS** DUR, ENG. 19TH CENTURY **[36364]**
O: **MASTER MARINERS** AUS. 1840S-1870S **[34431]**
O: **MASTER MARINERS** CORNWALL, ENG. 1800S **[34634]**
O: **MASTER MARINERS** PLYMOUTH, DEV, ENG. 1830-1865 **[35955]**
O: **MASTER MARINER** DAVID COWAN, PORT GLASGOW SCT. C1856-1878 **[35625]**
O: **MASTER MARINER** GEORGE SNAD, SHIREHAMPTON & BRISTOL, ENG. 1790+ **[37990]**
O: **MASTER MARINER** JOSEPH ROYER THOMPSON, SYDNEY, NSW, AUS. 1850-1900 **[36647]**
O: **MASTER MARINER** NORMAN THOMAS, HOBART, TAS, AUS. 1915+ **[34904]**
O: **MASTER MARINER** ROBERT MITCHELL, LEITH, FIF, SCT. 1840S+ **[35876]**
O: **MECHANIC** THOMAS THOMAS, ENG. 1880-1890S **[34904]**
O: **MECHANIC** THOMAS THOMAS, LAUNCESTON, TAS, AUS. 1880-1890S **[34904]**
O: **MEDICAL PRACTITIONERS** SPANISH CIVIL WAR. 1930+ **[35783]**
O: **MERCHANTS − DUBLIN, IRL** BURKE. 1750-1850 **[35494]**
O: **MERCHANTS** BARBADOS. **[38235]**
O: **METROPOLITAN POLICE** CHARLES WALL, PLYMOUTH, DEV, ENG. 1867-99 **[37686]**
O: **MIDVALE STEEL** PHILADELPHIA, PA, USA, DESCENDANTS OF FORMER EMPLOYEES. 1880-1920
    [37793]
O: **MIDWIVES** SWANSEA, GLA, WLS. 1881 **[37330]**
O: **MILITARY TAILOR** MACH OF BOHEMIA, CS. C1875 **[37440]**
O: **MILITIA COMMANDER** BARON DE ROTTENBURG, BELL, ONT, CAN. C1839 **[34133]**
O: **MILLERS & BAKERS** BRADFORD-ON-AVON, WIL, ENG. PRE 1770 **[34908]**
O: **MILLERS & MILLWRIGHTS** ROCHESTER, KEN, ENG. MEDWAY TOWNS & MEDWAY VALLEY.
    1750-1900 **[34738]**
O: **MILLERS & MILLWRIGHTS** KEN & SSX, ENG: FIELD, STEDMAN, FRIDAY, BOYER. 1750-1900
    [34738]
O: **MILLERS OF AVERNISH** KYLE OF LOCHALSH, ROC, SCT. 1800-50 **[37518]**
O: **MILLERS** HALL FAMILY, NBL, ENG. PRE 1800 **[34827]**
O: **MILLER** GIBBS FAMILY, KINGSBRIDGE, ENG. 1775-1820S **[34088]**
O: **MILLER** WILLIAM JONES OF BROADWAY & HARVINGTON, WOR, ENG. 1829+ **[36171]**
O: **MILLER** WILLIAM MYERS, YORKSHIRE, ENG. 1800+ **[36609]**
O: **MILLINER** SMITH, GEORGE, NOTTINGHAM, ENG. 1800+ **[35688]**
O: **MINER** ISAAC STINGERS, ALSTON, CUL, ENG. C1834 **[33775]**
O: **MINER** WILLIAM MENZIES, KILSYTH, SCT. C1880 **[35111]**
O: **MINER** WM & JAMES SEARLE, DEV, ENG. PRE 1800 **[38772]**
O: **MINIATURE PAINTER** EASTON, REGINALD, LND, ENG. 1807-1893 **[34627]**
O: **MINING** OPERATIONAL MINES IN NW LANCS, ENG. 1800+ **[35514]**
O: **MINISTERS** GERMANY. PRE 1650 **[38035]**
O: **MISSIONARIES (URFA, SYRIA)** WILLIAM GLENDINNING, ANN GLENDINNING (NEE WALLACE).
    C1890+ **[36853]**
O: **MISSIONARIES** AFRICA. ALL **[36458]**
O: **MISSIONARY** EDGAR, TIBET. 1900+ **[37109]**
O: **MOUNTED POLICE** EUREKA STOCKADE, VIC, AUS. C1850-1860 **[34533]**
O: **MUSIC SHOP, HARP MAKER** ALEX BLAIZDELL, OXFORD ST, LONDON, ENG. 1800-1840 **[33821]**
O: **MUSICIAN** JOHN BURBRIDGE OF KEW, ENG. PRE 1828 **[36167]**
O: **NAVAL OFFICER** WILLIAM KING, ENG. 1830 **[36600]**
O: **NEEDLEMAKERS** REDDITCH, WOR, ENG. 1800+ **[35650]**

O: **NEEDLEMAKERS** WILLIAM HALL & CO, STUDLEY, ENG. 1820+ **[34582]**
O: **NEEDLEWOMAN** . PRE 1800 **[34104]**
O: **NEWHAVEN FISHERFOLK** THE RAMSAY FAMILY. 1600-1990 **[34718]**
O: **NEWSPAPER INDUSTRY** WRY, ENG, HERBALISTS. 1750-1890S **[36837]**
O: **NEWSPAPER** RICHARD ELIAS ROBINSON, IL, USA. 1860-90 **[36717]**
O: **NORTH WEST SUBURBAN, LICENCED VICTUALLERS ASSOCIATION** ALFRED ARCHER DIXON. 1850+ **[35403]**
O: **NURSERYMAN** JOHNSTON, ALEXANDER, SCT & EDMONTON, ENG. 1808-1875 **[36167]**
O: **O'BRIEN, JOHN OR THOMAS** FIREMAN OF FORTH WORTH, TX, USA. 1880-1930 **[35003]**
O: **OIL MERCHANTS** LONDON, ENG. **[35573]**
O: **OPTICIAN** ROBERT TIERNEY, GLOSSOP, ENG. 1920 **[35107]**
O: **ORCHID GROWING** LONDON, ENG. 1800 **[34112]**
O: **ORD & MADDISON QUARRIES** QUARRIES IN CRAWLEYSIDE, DUR, HULAND, NRY & AYCLIFFE, DUR, ENG. 1860-1917 **[38269]**
O: **ORGAN BUILDERS** JULIAN MOSES, GILLINGHAM, ENG. 1860-1900 **[37877]**
O: **ORGANISTS** GEORGE GROSS, LONDON, ENG. PRE 1800 **[37080]**
O: **OSTLER, WILLIAM GIBBS, LND, ENG** C1840. **[36076]**
O: **PAINTER** WILLIAM EDWARD EFEMEY. 1868+ **[36496]**
O: **PAPERHANGERS** WESTMINSTER, MDX, ENG. 1851-1909 **[36117]**
O: **PAPERMAKERS** JAMES MAYGER, KEN, ENG. C1800 **[35532]**
O: **PAPIER MACHER** GER. PRE 1900 **[38748]**
O: **PARKER LORD LTD** MANCHESTER TEXTILE FIRM, ENG. 1860-1935 **[36635]**
O: **PATTERN MAKER** LAN & GLS, ENG. ALL **[36508]**
O: **PAVIOUR** J. COWLEY, ENG. 1850-1900 **[35292]**
O: **PERFUMIERS** PIESSE AND LUBIN, LND, ENG. 1804-1940 **[36378]**
O: **PHOTOGRAPHERS** JAMES ARMSTRONG, CHATHAM, KEN, ENG. C1850+ **[36767]**
O: **PHOTOGRAPHERS** OF NORTH WEST KEN, ENG. 1870+ **[37213]**
O: **PHOTOGRAPHS** OF HERSTMONCEUX, SSX, ENG. 1860+ **[37293]**
O: **PIANO FORTE MAKERS** CLEMENT TATE. 1825+ **[37834]**
O: **PIANO-FORTE MAKERS** JARRETT, HACKNEY, LND, ENG. 1860S-1900 **[37634]**
O: **PILOTS & CAPTAINS** STEAMBOATS, OHIO RIVER. 1810-1880 **[36897]**
O: **PILOTS & LIGHTHOUSE KEEPERS** ALBANY, WA, AUS. 1830-1900 **[35845]**
O: **PILOTS** NORTH SEA, SUNDERLAND, ENG. 1600+ **[35802]**
O: **PILOT** EDWARD COULSON OF WHITBY, YKS, ENG. 1800+ **[36609]**
O: **PIPE MAKERS** ALL ENG. 1600-1920 **[37232]**
O: **PLASTERERS** WILLIAM DUNN, EDINBURGH, SCT. C1897 **[34913]**
O: **PLASTERER** THOMAS PADLEY, LONDON, ENG. 1840S **[35876]**
O: **PLUMBERS, BRK, ENG** 1770. **[36072]**
O: **POLICE FORCE** DURHAM, ENG. PRE 1930 **[38594]**
O: **POLICEMAN, NSW, AUS** THOMAS GRAHAM. 1850-1900 **[36040]**
O: **POLICEMAN** MOORE OF NORTHALLERTON, ENG. 1820-1857 **[38513]**
O: **POLICEMEM** DEPTFORD, KEN, ENG. 1830+ **[37560]**
O: **POLICE** ALBERT JOHN GRIMES, BRIGHTON, ENG. 1876-1901 **[38549]**
O: **POLICE** BIRMINGHAM RECORDS INDIVIDUALS, ENG. 1830-50 **[36224]**
O: **POLICE** BOMBALA, NSW, AUS. 1850-1910 **[35843]**
O: **POLICE** CITY OF LONDON, ENG. 1834-1837 **[37297]**
O: **POLITICAL SPEAKER** MOORE OF KIRKSTALL, LEEDS, ENG. 1880-1920 **[38513]**
O: **POLITICIAN** JOHN FITZGERALD BURNS, MAITLAND, NSW, AUS. C1850 **[35237]**
O: **PORK BUTCHERS** WURTTEMBERG, GER. 1800-1850 **[37609]**
O: **PORT BUTCHER** SAMUEL EMPSOM, NTT, ENG. C1860 **[34342]**
O: **PORTER** WILLIAM NORTH, WAPPING, LND DOCKS, ENG. PRE 1830 **[38731]**
O: **POSTAL WORKERS** OFFICES & SYSTEM, LAN, ENG. PRE 1940 **[35362]**
O: **POTTER** JOSIAH SPODE AND FAMILY. ALL **[37846]**
O: **PRINTER, LONDON, ENG** DAVID WILLIAM THOMAS. 1851+ **[35252]**
O: **PRINTER-ENGRAVER** JOHN BOYDELL, LONDON, ENG. 1719-1804 **[36967]**
O: **PRINTERS APPRENTICE** JOHN ABERNETHY OF DUB, IRL. 1840-50 **[37518]**
O: **PRINTERS, BIRMINGHAM, ENG** DRAKE. PRE 1850 **[34274]**
O: **PRINTERS, LND, ENG** . 1840+ **[36256]**
O: **PRINTERS** JOHN PURCHALL'S, ENG. 1780-1910 **[37259]**
O: **PRINTER** ALBERT HILDESHEIMER, MANCHESTER, ENG. 1830 **[37931]**
O: **PRINTER** JOHN COLLARD, SALISBURY, ENG. 1790-1850 **[34610]**
O: **PRINTER** WILLIAM COLLARD, BRISTOL, ENG. 1750-1860 **[34610]**
O: **PRINTING INDUSTRY** IN LND, ENG. 1840-1890 **[36462]**
O: **PRINTING** FARLEY AND BONNER, BRISTOL, ENG. ALL **[38718]**
O: **PRISON MATRONS** CORK & DUBLIN, IRL. 1850-1875 **[37415]**
O: **PRISON WARDERS** MANCHESTER, ENG. C1876-1900S **[36024]**
O: **PRIVATE SCHOOL** ANN HICKEY, BENT ST, SYDNEY. 1821 **[35583]**
O: **PROCTORS OF THE ARCHES** . ALL **[36172]**
O: **PROCTORS** DOCTORS COMMONS, LND, ENG. 1750-1850 **[37293]**
O: **PROFESSEUR** ARTHUR ALLEN, CO.WICKLOW, IRL. 1790+ **[34168]**
O: **PROFESSOR OF LANGUAGES** LIMPERANI, JOSEPH. C1800 **[36928]**
O: **PROFESSOR OF MUSIC (PIANO)** ISIDOR COHN, LONDON & MANCHESTER, ENG. 1850-1930 **[35591]**

O: **PROSPECTOR** JOHN CANOL HANRAHAN, MEEKATHARRA, WA, AUS. C1930 **[37111]**
O: **PROTECTOR OF SLAVES** EDWARD HOWARD GIBBON, BRITISH GUIANA. 1832-33 **[36967]**
O: **PUBLICAN** ALFRED HOCKEY. 1860-1930 **[35236]**
O: **PUBLICAN** FARMERS HOME HOTEL, DUNGOG, NSW, AUS. 1880+ **[38729]**
O: **PUBLICAN** ROBERT BANKS, LND, ENG. 1842 **[36076]**
O: **PUBLICAN** . PRE 1800 **[34104]**
O: **PUBLISHERS, PRINTERS, LONDON** DEAN & BAILEY. 1700+ **[34274]**
O: **QUARRIER** JAMES BROWN OF STEWARTON (SCT). C1800 **[36802]**
O: **RAILWAY STAFF RECORDS** HUYTON, LAN, ENG. 1859 **[37560]**
O: **RAILWAY STATION MASTERS** VIC, AUS. 1850S-1940 **[34431]**
O: **RAILWAY SURVEYORS** LIMA TO OROYA RAILWAY, PERU. 1870+ **[37415]**
O: **RAILWAY WORKERS** ACCIDENTS AT WORK, LAN, ENG. PRE 1925 **[35362]**
O: **RAILWAY WORKERS** WILLIAM & JOSEPH WALKER, SAL, DBY, YKS & LAN, ENG. 1830-1915 **[36587]**
O: **RAILWAYS, SA, AUS** COOK, JAMES. 1880S+ **[35565]**
O: **RAILWAYS, SA, AUS** PUDDY, ISAAC. 1865+ **[35565]**
O: **RANSLEY GANG** ROMNEY MARSH SMUGGLERS. 1800-1827 **[35394]**
O: **RECTOR, C OF E** ARTHUR HIBBIT, MALTON, YKS, ENG. 1880-1890 **[34243]**
O: **REGISTRAR, WIL, ENG** HUMBY, JOHN THOMAS. 1870+ **[35418]**
O: **RELIGIOUS SPEAKER** MOORE OF KIRKSTALL, LEEDS, ENG. 1880-1920 **[38513]**
O: **REVENUE OFFICERS, IRL** DALTON & KEIGHTLY. 1710-1785 **[38731]**
O: **RIBBON MANUFACTURERS** COVENTRY, WAR, ENG. 1750-1860 **[36635]**
O: **ROAD SURVEYORS** BKM, WAR & STS, ENG. 1790-1890 **[35232]**
O: **ROBINSON,** JOHN CARPENTER PETROLIA, ONT, CAN. 1890-1901 **[37518]**
O: **ROOF THATCHERS** WEBBER FAMILY, SOM, ENG. ALL **[35353]**
O: **ROPE & TWINE MANUFACTURER** JOHNSON. 1750-1837 **[36990]**
O: **ROPE MAKING** GLASGOW, LKS, SCT. 1800+ **[34624]**
O: **ROPE MAKING** TOPSHAM & BRIDPORT, DEV, ENG. 1700-1900 **[37757]**
O: **SADDLER & HARNESS MAKER** HERBERT MIELL, ENG & NSW, AUS. 1850-1870 **[35400]**
O: **SADDLER** CHARLES HICKIN, BIRMINGHAM, ENG. 1840-50S **[35136]**
O: **SAIL MAKERS** LAWRENCE - GRIMSBY, LIN, ENG. 1850+ **[35125]**
O: **SAIL MAKERS** LAWRENCE - HULL, YKS, ENG. 1850+ **[35125]**
O: **SAILMAKERS** ADELAIDE, SA, AUS. 1845-1850 **[37488]**
O: **SAILMAKERS** COPENHAGEN, DEN. 1820-1850 **[37488]**
O: **SAILMAKERS** MELBOURNE, VIC, AUS. 1850-1870 **[37488]**
O: **SAILMAKER** JAMES ARTHUR FURLONG, WAT & WEX, IRL. 1800+ **[36043]**
O: **SAILMAKER** MICHAEL FURLONG, WAT & WEX, IRL. 1700+ **[36043]**
O: **SAILMAKER** ROBERT BELL, SUNDERLAND, NBL, ENG. 1830-60 **[36717]**
O: **SAILOR (MERCHANT)** HURR. ALL **[34813]**
O: **SAILOR (RN)** LIDDIARD. 1900S **[34813]**
O: **SANDYS CLERGY,** CHURCH IRL, LDY, ARM, WAT, IRL. ALL **[34109]**
O: **SAWYER** ELI SIMS, NEW FOREST, HAM, ENG. 1852+ **[37259]**
O: **SAWYER** JAMES SMITH, LONDON, ENG. 1820-1840 **[34036]**
O: **SCHOOL TEACHER** JOHN FOLEY, ENG. 1830 **[36600]**
O: **SCHOOL TEACHER** SAMUEL SMITH, DUNGOG, NSW, AUS. 1840+ **[36647]**
O: **SCHOOL TEACHER** WILLIAM PILSON, TORONTO, CAN. 1840-1880 **[38455]**
O: **SCHOOLMASTERS – CARTLEDGE** MANCHESTER, ENG. C1836 **[36294]**
O: **SCHOOLTEACHER, WIL, ENG** HUMBY, MISS. 1870+ **[35418]**
O: **SCHOOLTEACHERS & PARISH CLERKS** DON, IRL. 1840+ **[35975]**
O: **SCHOOLTEACHER** JOHN MCKENZIE, BALLYCASTLE & BELFAST, IRL. 1860+ **[33921]**
O: **SCT** LOWER TO MIDDLE CLASS. 1700-1900 **[38388]**
O: **SCULPTOR:** WATKIN JONES FROM MERTHYR TYDFIL, WLS, & LONDON, ENG. 1823+ **[35784]**
O: **SCULPTOR:** WILLIAM LORANDO JONES MELBOURNE & SYDNEY, AUS. 1856-1893 **[35784]**
O: **SCULPTOR:** WILLIAM LORANDO JONES FROM MERTHYR TYDFIL, WLS & LONDON, ENG. 1843-1855 **[35784]**
O: **SEA CAPTAIN** ANDRE POTHIER OF WEDGEPORT, NS, CAN. 1870-1899 **[34251]**
O: **SEA CAPTAIN** JOSEPH PINKHAM, BOOTHBAY, ME, USA. 1700 **[37576]**
O: **SEA CAPTAIN** WILLIAM BREMNER, CAI & GLASGOW, SCT. 1800S **[34028]**
O: **SEAMAN** HENRY PIERRE MARCIEA, SALEM, MA, USA. 1807-12 **[37019]**
O: **SEAMAN** WILLIAM T.CHARLWOOD, LND, ENG. 1880-1890S **[35727]**
O: **SEAMEN** NAMED NELLIST . ALL **[36481]**
O: **SHEARING** NSW & QLD, AUS. 1880-1890S **[33825]**
O: **SHEPHERD** MARK GOODILL, EYR, ENG. PRE 1900 **[34855]**
O: **SHERIFF** BAINBRIDGE WAR ASSIZES, ENG. 1790+ **[35232]**
O: **SHIP BUILDERS** WILLIAMS, HOBART, TAS, AUS. 1830-1850 **[35434]**
O: **SHIP CAPTAINS** BROOKLYN, NY, USA. 1840+ **[38235]**
O: **SHIP CONSTRUCTION** PLYMOUTH DOCK, ENG. 1780-1820 **[38499]**
O: **SHIP CONSTRUCTION** ROTHERHITHE, ENG. 1770-1800 **[38499]**
O: **SHIPBUILDERS** ROTHERHITHE, LND, ENG. 1705 **[37293]**
O: **SHIPBUILDING, CLYDE, SCT** NAPIER FAMILIES OF ROBT. & DAVID. 1800-1860 **[35999]**
O: **SHIPOWNER** MACMILLAN, RONALD JAMAICA, W INDIES. C1807 **[38466]**
O: **SHIPS CAPTAIN** LEMUEL H.SABEAN, NOVA SCOTIA, CAN. 1904+ **[34206]**
O: **SHIPS CREW** JOHAN LINDALL. 1876-1956 **[34432]**

O: **SHIPS ENGINEER** JOHN TURNBULL. 1839-1842 **[35084]**
O: **SHIPS FIREMAN** O'GRADY, JOHN, SOUTHAMPTON, ENG. **[33802]**
O: **SHIPS MASTER** WILLIAM JACKLIN. 1770-1790 **[35092]**
O: **SHIPSMITH** LORRENS GRAY, SUNDERLAND, ENG. 1600+ **[35802]**
O: **SHIPWRIGHTS** LIVERPOOL, ENG. 1800S **[36164]**
O: **SHIPWRIGHTS** LND, ENG. 1750-1900 **[36006]**
O: **SHIPWRIGHT** RICHARDSON, NORTH SHIELDS, ENG. 1830-1890 **[36934]**
O: **SHIPWRIGHT** THOMPSON ERNEST, PORTSMOUTH, ENG. 1874+ **[38255]**
O: **SHIPWRIGHT** WILLIAM ANDERSON, BELFAST, ANT, IRL. 1800-1850S **[34028]**
O: **SHOE & BOOTMAKER** WOOD (ABRAHAM, SYDNEY & STEPHEN). 1780-1946 **[34325]**
O: **SHOEMAKERS, CON, ENG** POTTER. 1820+ **[34274]**
O: **SHOEMAKERS** BLAY. PRE 1860 **[37984]**
O: **SHOEMAKERS** MAYBOLE, AYR, SCT. 1840-1911 **[34345]**
O: **SHOEMAKERS** PETERHEAD, ABD, SCT. PRE 1900 **[35917]**
O: **SHOEMAKERS** STREATS, BRK, ENG. 1700-1900 **[35591]**
O: **SHOEMAKER** BACON, ESS, ENG. 1718-1892 **[34142]**
O: **SHOEMAKER** BERWICK, NBL, ENG. C1850 **[34007]**
O: **SHOEMAKER** CHARLES MARTIN, ST PANCRAS, LND, ENG. 1871-1912 **[37719]**
O: **SHOEMAKER** DENNIS RYAN CORK CITY, IRL. 1820-1850 **[36647]**
O: **SHOEMAKER** JAMES BENNETT, WORFIELD, STS, ENG. C1820-36 **[37406]**
O: **SHOEMAKER** PRASSE, SAXON, GER, EAST. 1870+ **[35641]**
O: **SHOEMAKER** ROBERT WATTS, EASTWINCH, NFK, ENG. 1820S+ **[34259]**
O: **SHOEMAKER** THOMAS FROST, WALWORTH, LND, ENG. 1840-1900 **[37259]**
O: **SHOEMAKER** WILLIAM DAVIES, OF MARYLEBONE, LND, ENG. C1840 **[37937]**
O: **SHOEMAKER** WILLIAM MYRES, NBL & YKS, ENG. 1835+ **[36609]**
O: **SHOPKEEPER** JOHN SHEEHAN, WAT, IRL. 1700+ **[36043]**
O: **SHUTTLE MAKER** JAMES LEIPER GLASGOW, SCT. 1850-1900 **[36647]**
O: **SILK FACTORY OVERLOOKER** CHARLES WILLIAM LINGLEY. C1870S **[37689]**
O: **SILK WEAVING** NORWICH, NFK, ENG. ALL **[37629]**
O: **SILKWEAVERS** OF ANDOVER, HAM, ENG. ALL **[37693]**
O: **SILVERSMITHS – CARTLEDGE** LONDON, ENG. C1800 **[36294]**
O: **SILVERSMITHS** LEIPZIG, GER. 1790-1795 **[38499]**
O: **SINGING TEACHER** WILLIAMS, EILEEN DELORAINE, TAS, AUS. 1900+ **[34770]**
O: **SKINNERS** GLASGOW AREA, SCT. PRE 1830 **[36140]**
O: **SMITH (MASTER SHIP)** HENRY LEAKER, BRISTOL, ENG. 1850+ **[37406]**
O: **SMUGGLING** PEVENSEY, SSX, ENG. 1700-1830 **[37293]**
O: **SNOOK, WILLIAM** RAILWYAMAN, ENG. 1870+ **[37201]**
O: **SOAP BOILERS** ROWE, ACTON & BRENTFORD, ENG. 1780-1934 **[37657]**
O: **SOLICITORS CLERK** HENRY BATES, STAINES, MDX, ENG. C1878-96 **[37168]**
O: **SOLICITOR** CHARLES BURNS, SYDNEY, NSW, AUS. C1852 **[35237]**
O: **SPRITSAIL BARGEMASTER** HENRY WINCH, QUEENBOROUGH, ENG. 1849-1899 **[34718]**
O: **ST THOMAS HOSPITAL, SOUTHWARK, LND, ENG** STAFF OF. 1790-1830 **[34452]**
O: **STAGECOACH OPERATOR** WILLIAM HUDSON, MDX, ENG. C1820 **[35079]**
O: **STEAMBOAT PILOTS & CAPTAINS** OHIO RIVER, USA. 1810-1880 **[36897]**
O: **STEVEDORE** LIDDIARD. 1900S **[34813]**
O: **STONE MASON** THOMAS HOSKINS, AUS & NZ. 1877+ **[35092]**
O: **STONEMASONS NAMED GREGORY** OXF, ENG. PRE 1670 **[35030]**
O: **STONEMASONS NAMED BRINE**, HAM, ENG. 1850+ **[35650]**
O: **STONEMASONS** SYDNEY, NSW, AUS. 1800-1900 **[35843]**
O: **SUGAR REFINER** DANIEL DODDRELL, GLASGOW, SCT. 1800+ **[37990]**
O: **SULKY RACING** GREY DRIVER, ONT, CAN. 1880-95 **[37518]**
O: **SURGEON** JOHN LATHAM, LIVERPOOL, ENG. C1800 **[35971]**
O: **SURVEYING** THOMAS FLORANCE, UPPER CANADA. 1803-1816 **[34849]**
O: **SURVEYORS, AUS** PARKINSON & DRAKE. 1840+ **[34274]**
O: **TAILOR & UNDERTAKER** SHOPS OWNED BY BRUTON IN WATFORD ENG. 1800+ **[36165]**
O: **TAILOR – BEITH** MELBOURNE OR VIC, AUS. 1840S **[33930]**
O: **TAILOR JOURNEYMAN** RICHARD PARKINSON, GLASGOW, SCT. 1860-1880 **[34824]**
O: **TAILOR, LONDON, ENG** WILLIAM FRANCIS THOMAS. 1820+ **[35252]**
O: **TAILORS** BILLINGHAM, DUR, ENG. PRE 1800 **[34908]**
O: **TAILOR** CORNWALL FAMILY OF DUB, IRL. PRE 1850 **[38772]**
O: **TAILOR** EDWARD TYLER, STEPNEY, LND, ENG. C1818-1858 **[34284]**
O: **TAILOR** JOHN ARTHUR, SOM, ENG. 1800-1900 **[34855]**
O: **TAILOR** JONATHAN DUCK, WHITBY, ENG. 1800-1840 **[37435]**
O: **TAILOR** PATRICK MADDEN, TIP & WAT, IRL. 1700+ **[36043]**
O: **TAILOR** ROBERT CARTER, SOUTHAMPTON, HAM, ENG. 1800+ **[34065]**
O: **TAILOR** SMITH, NTH & WAR, ENG. 1750-1820 **[37650]**
O: **TALLOW CHANDLER** WILLIAM SLY, WESTMINSTER, LND, ENG. 1800-40S **[36688]**
O: **TALLOW CHANDLER** WILLIAM TERREY, NOT SUSSEX, ENG. 1810-1830 **[37857]**
O: **TANNING INDUSTRY** SOUTHERN CUL, ENG. 1700S **[34241]**
O: **TANNING** IN W. HERTS & E. BUCKS, ENG. 1550-1750 **[36042]**
O: **TAYLOR** JAMES MACKEN, ST JAMES, LND, ENG. 1870S **[35720]**
O: **TAYLOR** WILLIAM FLETCHER, OXF, ENG. PRE 1900 **[36145]**

O: **TEA & SILK MERCHANTS** BARRY FAMILY, IRL. 1700-1950 **[35308]**
O: **TEAMAKER** JOHN BROOKS, MANCHESTER, LAN, ENG. 1800S **[35567]**
O: **TEAMAKER** JOHN BROOKS, CHS, ENG. 1800S **[35567]**
O: **TEXTILES** MA, USA. 1800 + **[38015]**
O: **TEXTILES** STROUD, GLS, ENG. 1700 + **[34119]**
O: **TOBACCO PIPE MAKERS** ALL SWINYARDS. ALL **[37857]**
O: **TOBACCO PIPE MAKERS** ALL ENG. 1600-1920 **[37232]**
O: **TOBACCO PLANTATION** JAMES CARLISLE, LOUDOUN CO., VA, USA. 1700-1800 **[35266]**
O: **TOBACCO** JOHN LLOYD, DUNGOG, NSW, AUS. 1860 + **[38729]**
O: **TORKSEY CASTLE HOTEL** TORKSEY, LIN, ENG, LISTER. 1750-1850 **[34501]**
O: **TOWN CLERKS** NEWCASTLE ON TYNE, NBL, ENG. 1800 + **[35862]**
O: **TOWN CRIER** WORLDWIDE, PAST AND PRESENT. ALL **[37397]**
O: **TURNER – IVORY, BONE, HARDWOOD** HASTILOW, LND, ENG. C1815-1915 **[34213]**
O: **TURNKEYS** NEWGATE PRISON, LND, ENG. ALL **[37297]**
O: **TUTOR TO EMPEROR OF CHINA** ERRINGTON. C1850-80 **[35624]**
O: **TUTOR TO EMPEROR OF CHINA** DUNLOP. C1850-80 **[35624]**
O: **TYPOGRAPHICAL ASSO.** ARCHIE WILLIAM JONES – GENERAL SECRETARY. ALL **[36171]**
O: **UMBRELLA MAKER** THOMAS SMITH, SSX, ENG. 1830 + **[37259]**
O: **UNDERTAKER** CHARLES MILLS, LND, ENG. 1822 + **[35958]**
O: **UNDERTAKER** GEORGE EDWARDS, LND, ENG. 1852 + **[35958]**
O: **UNIVERSITIES, PRIVATE ADDRESSES OF** IN UK, IRL, CAN & USA. **[38501]**
O: **URDON CHEMICALS** AYDON & URWIN. 1790-1990 **[34249]**
O: **VARLEY PUMPS** ACTON & BRENTFORD, ENG. 1930-1980 **[37657]**
O: **VAUDEVILLE** JOHNNY COWAN, AUS. 1880-1910 **[33795]**
O: **VETERINARIAN** EDWARDS, BRINKWORTH, WIL, ENG. 1900 + **[37468]**
O: **VICE-REGAL STAFF** DESCENDANTS, AUS, NZ. TO 1991 **[38754]**
O: **VICTUALLER** WILLIAM BRADY, HURLEY, BRK, ENG. ALL **[36407]**
O: **VINEDRESSERS – GERMAN** HUNTER VALLEY, NSW, AUS. 1847-1860 **[36267]**
O: **VITICULTURISTS** LOWER HUNTER VINEYARDS, NSW, AUS. 1820 + **[35539]**
O: **WAGON MAKER** JOHN PERRY, ORLEANS CO., NY, USA. 1815-1830 **[37576]**
O: **WAGONMAKER & WHEELWRIGHT** JOSEPH ROCK, VT & KS, USA. 1820-1880 **[35284]**
O: **WAREHOUSE PACKER** JOHN CLAYTON, STOCKPORT, ENG. 1880 **[36984]**
O: **WAREHOUSEMAN** JOHN TATE, LND, ENG. 1780-1800 **[34088]**
O: **WATCH MAKER** PAVEY'S ENG. 1850-1880 **[35638]**
O: **WATCHMAKER & JEWELLER** SPERRIN. 1875-1925 **[36990]**
O: **WATCHMAKER-JEWELLER** THOMAS CLAYTON SMITH, TORQUAY, ENG. C1895 **[34238]**
O: **WATCHMAKER-JEWELLER** WILLIAM SMITH, NOTT, ENG. 1845-1880 **[34238]**
O: **WATCHMAKERS** GILBERT & HELMSLEY, CHICHESTER, SSX, ENG. 1800 **[35720]**
O: **WATCHMAKERS** LANG, EDINBURGH, SCT. 1800-1850 **[34971]**
O: **WATCHMAKER** CONDON, LIMERICK, IRL. 1800-1860 **[36642]**
O: **WATCHMAKER** HARSTROM, NY, USA. 1870 + **[38552]**
O: **WATCHMAKER** JAMES CHAMBERLAIN, ENG, CAN, AUS, USA. 1850-1930 **[34855]**
O: **WATCHMAKER** JAMES TIERNEY, STOCKPORT, ENG. 1900S **[35107]**
O: **WATCHMAKER** JOHN MARTYN, GSY, CHI. 1830-1880 **[33984]**
O: **WATCHMAKER** JOHN MARTIN, LOOE BAY, ENG. 1790-1830 **[33984]**
O: **WATCHMAKER** JOHN MILLWARD, KENDAL, ENG. 1832-95 **[36230]**
O: **WATCHMAKER** ROBERT BROWNE, ISLINGTON, ENG. 1800-75 **[35532]**
O: **WATER COLOUR ARTIST** LEEDHAM. 1830 + **[34338]**
O: **WATER MILLING** EAST SSX, ENG. PRE 1865 **[34847]**
O: **WATERMAN (JOURNEYMAN)** SAMUEL HEATH, MDX, ENG. PRE 1886 **[37120]**
O: **WATERMAN** WARD, ST OLAVES, ENG. 1711-1846 **[34142]**
O: **WATERMEN & LIGHTERMEN** ON THE THAMES, LND, ENG. 1800-1860S **[34431]**
O: **WATERMEN & LIGHTERMEN** THAMES, LND, ENG. PRE 1880 **[34733]**
O: **WEAVER, HEYSIDE, LAN, ENG** JOSHUA BROOKS. 1800-1840 **[36898]**
O: **WEAVER, SCOTTISH** JOHN COWAN, GREY CO., ONT, CAN. 1850-1900 **[36712]**
O: **WEAVERS (CARPET)** KIDDERMINSTER, ENG. 1700-1990 **[34711]**
O: **WEAVERS** IN CUMBRIA, ENG. 1850S **[38399]**
O: **WEAVERS** BUCHANANS OF KIRKINTILLOCH, SCT. ALL **[36282]**
O: **WEAVERS** IMMIGRATION TO ENG FROM FRA & BEL. PRE 1600 **[36140]**
O: **WEAVERS** ULSTER, IRL. PRE 1870 **[34733]**
O: **WEAVERS** WEAVERS OF GLASGOW, SCT. ALL **[36695]**
O: **WEAVER** DILTON MARSH, WESTBURY, WIL, ENG. 1700-1900 **[34994]**
O: **WEAVER** MARRIOT, FRA. PRE 1600 **[37277]**
O: **WEAVER** MARRIOTT, ENG. PRE 1600 **[37277]**
O: **WEAVER** MARRIOTT, OXF, ENG. PRE 1600 **[37277]**
O: **WEAVER** PETER MURRAY NUT, NBL, ENG. 1890 + **[34243]**
O: **WEAVER** SAXON, GER, EAST. 1870 + **[35641]**
O: **WEAVER** THOMAS NAIRN, HOXTON, ENG. 1860 **[36600]**
O: **WEAVING** UK. 1650-1850 **[36682]**
O: **WEED INSPECTORS** WESTERN CAN. 1900-1920 **[34525]**
O: **WELSH MINING** COAL MINER, WLS. PRE 1901 **[34757]**
O: **WESLEYAN MINISTER** CHARLES BURBRIDGE OF RICHMOND, SRY, ENG. 1855 + **[36167]**

O: **WHALERS** LONG ISLAND & NJ, USA. 1650-1750 [36897]
O: **WHALER** GEORGE CLAPHAM. 1830-40S [36856]
O: **WHALING** CAPT JAMES WILLIAMS, NZ. 1830-1850S [34849]
O: **WHEELWRIGHT & BUILDER** EMANUEL SMITH OF PERSHORE, WOR, ENG. 1822-71 [36190]
O: **WHEELWRIGHTS** IN SOM, ENG. 1880S [38399]
O: **WHITAWER** LEI, ENG. 1700S [37515]
O: **WILLOW SQUARE MNFR** LACEY, LONDON, ENG. 1820-1870 [37716]
O: **WINE MERCHANT** RICHARD SYMONDS & CO, LONDON, ENG. 1800-1912 [33875]
O: **WIRE WORKER (JOURNEYMAN)** WILLIAM NEWLAND, LND, ENG. 1800S [34887]
O: **WOODMAN** . PRE 1800 [34104]
O: **WOOL MERCHANTS** BRADFORD, WRY, ENG. 1820-1880S [37236]
O: **WRITER** BERNARD SHAW, DUBLIN, IRL. ALL [36428]
P: **ALABAMA, USA** ADOPTEE/BIRTH PARENT. 1818-1990 [38040]
P: **ALABAMA, USA** ESTATE SETTLEMENTS. 1818-1990 [38040]
P: **ALABAMA, USA** LAWRENCE CO.1818-1990. [38040]
P: **ALABAMA, USA** LEGAL. 1818-1990 [38040]
P: **ALABAMA, USA** MISSING PERSONS. 1818-1990 [38040]
P: **ALABAMA, USA** MORGAN CO.. 1818-1990 [38040]
P: **ALABAMA, USA** RESIDENTS OF. 1818-1990 [38040]
P: **ALBANIA** PETRA SPIRO ANGJO OF POGRADEC. PRE 1950 [36646]
P: **ALBANIA** STAVRE NIKOLA JOTTA OF SHIPSKE. PRE 1950 [36646]
P: **ALDENHAM, HERTS, ENG** PEOPLE & PLACES OF. ALL [37413]
P: **ALDERTON VILLAGE** SFK, ENG. ALL [36223]
P: **ALTENBACH, BAV, GER** RESIDENTS OF. PRE 1870 [35878]
P: **ALTHEIM, RPF, BRD** RESIDENTS OF. PRE 1800 [36964]
P: **ANNANDALE LORDSHIP** DESCENDANTS OF. 1300-1990 [33986]
P: **ARDNAMURCHAN, SCT** MCPHERSON, HENDERSON & MCCALL FAMILIES. PRE 1839 [37972]
P: **ARLINGTON ST, SALFORD, MAN, ENG** RESIDENTS OF. [35565]
P: **ARMIDALE WEST, NSW, AUS** RESIDENTS. ALL [36632]
P: **ATHERINGTON, DEV, ENG** HISTORY & PEOPLE. ALL [35362]
P: **ATHERSTONE, WAR, ENG** RESIDENTS OF UNION WORKHOUSE. 1860S [37698]
P: **AUBURN, QLD, AUS** DJAKUNDA TRIBE. PRE 1900 [35111]
P: **AYR** SCT. 1650-1900 [38388]
P: **AYTON, SCT** HISTORY OF. 1760 + [35341]
P: **BALLENY, DROMORE, DOW, IRL** MUSSEN FAMILY. PRE 1850 [38084]
P: **BALLYMORE, ARM, IRL** RESIDENTS. C1800 [35859]
P: **BALMAIN "CATHOLIC" CEMETERY** LOCATION & HISTORY OF. [35843]
P: **BALNEARN (BAILE NA FHEARNA)** FEARNAN, P FORTINGALL, SCT. [36635]
P: **BANK TOP, LAN, ENG** RESIDENTS OF. 1802-1900 [35052]
P: **BARBADOS** PARLIAMENT, GOVERNMENT, SOCIAL HISTORY. 1750-1950 [38355]
P: **BARBADOS** ST MICHAELS. 1660 + [38235]
P: **BATESFORD, VIC, AUS** RESIDENTS OF. 1835-1900 [37156]
P: **BATHURST AREA, NSW, AUS** NAMES INDEX. ALL [34778]
P: **BAYONNE, FRANCE** DUTCH COMMUNITY. 1650-1750 [34948]
P: **BELFAST, IRL** REV THOMAS DREW RECTOR CHRISTCHURCH. 1830-1870 [38084]
P: **BELMULLET, MAY, IRL** RESIDENTS OF. ALL [35548]
P: **BENGALLA, NSW, AUS** RESIDENTS OF. ANY [35740]
P: **BERMUDA** PEMBROKE TRIBE. 1616-30 [35130]
P: **BESIEDLUNG RAUM** NEUSTADT SACHSEN. [38628]
P: **BIRMINGHAM, ENG** BULLOCKS CUTLERY MANUFACTURERS. 1800 + [34586]
P: **BLACKALL, QLD, AUS** RESIDENTS OF. 1850 + [35878]
P: **BLACKBURN, LAN, ENG** HISTORY & PEOPLE. ALL [35362]
P: **BLUE MTS, NSW, AUS** HEATHER BRAE HOMESTEAD. ANY [35111]
P: **BOMBALA, NSW, AUS** FAMILIES. 1830 + [36295]
P: **BOMBAY, INDIA** DIVER FOUNDED MASONS. C1870-90 [38466]
P: **BONNIE DOON & DISTRICT, VIC, AUS** LANDHOLDERS & RESIDENTS. 1860 + [34925]
P: **BONNIE DOON & MAINDAPLE** STATE SCHOOL ROLLS HISTORY, VIC, AUS. C1860-1920 [34925]
P: **BORSCH (RHOEN)** ALL FAMILIES. 1600 + [38644]
P: **BOWEN MOUNTAIN, NSW, AUS** FAMILIES OF, PLUS ANY HISTORICAL INFORMATION,
PHOTOGRAPHS. 1794-1991 [37121]
P: **BRANDENBURG STATE, GER** ALL MIERS. 1400-1990 [38627]
P: **BRANDENBURG STATE, GER** IMMIGRATION MIERS. 1700-1850 [38627]
P: **BRICKSTONE SQUARE** STREETS IN BRADFORD & LONDON, ENG. PRE 1850 [35164]
P: **BRIGHTONS BARRACKS** ENG. 1800S [34126]
P: **BRITISH COLUMBIA, CAN** CENSUS, PARTIAL INDEX. 1891 [34237]
P: **BRITISH GUIANA** RESIDENTS OF. 1840-50S [36509]
P: **BROMHAM, WIL, ENG** MINTY & ATTWOOD FAMILIES, EXCHANGE INFO. ALL [37972]
P: **BROMPTON, CHELSEA** LONDON, ENG. PRE 1880 [37080]
P: **BROOKWOOD CEMETERY**, SRY, ENG HISTORY OF NOTABLE M.I. TO BE RECORDED. 1853 +
[37862]
P: **BULFORD, WIL, ENG** HISTORY. ALL [37063]
P: **BUNBURY/TIVERTON, CHS, ENG** DAVIES FAMILY. ANY [36066]

P: BUNGONIA, NSW, AUS EARLY RESIDENTS & HISTORY. 1820+ [36316]
P: BURYONG NSW, AUS, WHERE?. 1880-1889 [34971]
P: BYRNE PHOTO 'MOUNT VERNON' KEMPS CR & HOME 'OCEAN VIEW' NTH STEYNE, MANLY, NSW, AUS (WISE). 1880S [36311]
P: CABARRUS CO., NC, USA EUPHRAIN DRAKE HARRISS. 1800 [37585]
P: CABARRUS CO., NC, USA JOHN HENRY MILLER. 1790-1820 [37585]
P: CABRACH, BAN, SCT DEVERON VALLEY FAMILIES & LOCAL HIST. 1750-1850 [34479]
P: CALKE, DBY, ENG INHABITANTS OF. 1500-1900 [36233]
P: CAMDEN DISTRICT SC, USA RESIDENTS OF. PRE 1775 [37460]
P: CAMDEN, NSW, AUS & DISTRICT SURNAME INDEX HELD. PRE 1920 [37561]
P: CAMPBELLS RIVER, NSW, AUS RESIDENTS OF. 1830-80 [36648]
P: CANOONA GOLD RUSH. 1859 [34303]
P: CAN SCOTS IN. 1780-1950 [38388]
P: CARNOCK, SCT GRAHAM, ROBERTSON & ROSS FAMILIES. ALL [37972]
P: CASTLE DONINGTON, LEI, ENG RESIDENTS & HISTORY OF. ALL [36163]
P: CASTLEREAGH, NSW, AUS FAMILIES OF, PLUS ANY HISTORICAL INFORMATION, PHOTOGRAPHS. 1794-1991 [37121]
P: CASTLETHORPE, BKM, ENG RESIDENTS OF. 1800S [35256]
P: CASTLETOWN METH PARISH REC ISLE OF MAN. 1800+ [34485]
P: CATTAI, NSW, AUS FAMILIES OF, PLUS ANY HISTORICAL INFORMATION, PHOTOGRAPHS. 1794-1991 [37121]
P: CESSNOCK, NSW, AUS RESIDENTS OF. 1820+ [35539]
P: CEYLON SCOTTISH COFFEE PLANTERS. 1850-1890 [34420]
P: CHARNWOOD FOREST, LEI, ENG THE GRAZIERS OF. ALL [37295]
P: CHEDWORTH, GLS, ENG RESIDENTS OF. ANY [35256]
P: CHEETHAM, MANCHESTER, ENG HISTORY OF. ALL [36063]
P: CHERTSEY, SRY, ENG ORPHANAGE RECORDS & ORPHANS. ALL [35362]
P: CHICHESTER WORKHOUSE, SSX, ENG EDWARD A.GILBERT, MASTER. 1840S [35720]
P: CHURCH GRESLEY, DBY, ENG LOCAL HISTORY. 1800-1900 [36008]
P: CITY OF LONDON, ENG POLICE. 1834-1837 [37297]
P: CLERMONT, FL, USA HISTORY OF TOWN NAME. [34506]
P: CLERMONT, QUE, CAN HISTORY OF TOWN NAME. [34506]
P: CLIFF MINE, MICHIGAN, USA WANTED PHOTOGRAPHS AND RECORDS. 1840-1880 [38179]
P: CLIFF MINE, MICHIGAN, USA VILLAGERS AND WORKERS. 1840-1880 [38179]
P: CLOCK FACE PUBLIC HOUSE PUBLICAN — COOPER. PRE 1850 [36066]
P: COCKATOO ISLAND SYDNEY, AUS. 1845-1850 [35573]
P: COCOS ISLAND SHERLOCK HARE, PLANTER. 1850-1890 [37609]
P: COLBY ON SAMS ISLAND RASMUSEN — BIRTHS. 1735-1760 [36340]
P: COLLINGWOOD, VIC, AUS RESIDENTS. 1850-1870 [33928]
P: COLO COUNCIL, NSW, AUS MEMBERS & EMPLOYEES OF. 1900+ [37121]
P: COLO DISTRICT, NSW, AUS FAMILIES OF, PLUS ANY HISTORICAL INFORMATION, PHOTOGRAPHS. 1794-1991 [37121]
P: COOKTOWN, QLD, AUS HOSPITAL ADMISSIONS (INDEX). 1884-1920 [35198]
P: COOPERS PLAINS, QLD, AUS ROSE & CROWN HOTEL. 1890S [35111]
P: COPPID HALL STIFFORD, ESS, ENG. PRE 1835 [35781]
P: CORTACHY, ANS, SCT RESIDENTS OF. PRE 1800 [36401]
P: CRADELEY, STS, ENG LOCAL HISTORY. 1800-1837 [36008]
P: CRESWICK, VIC, AUS ITS PEOPLE. 1840+ [34890]
P: CROMDALE, MOR, SCT SOCIAL HISTORY. 1800-1950 [38355]
P: CROYDON, QLD, AUS HOSPITAL ADMISSIONS (INDEX). 1888-1919 [35198]
P: CRUDEN BAY, SCT INFORMATION ON. ALL [38412]
P: CUBBINGTON-RADFORD SEMELE, WAR, ENG FAMILIES OF. 1750-1880 [37556]
P: CUNNAMULLA, QLD, AUS PIONEERS, RESIDENTS, LOCAL HISTORY. ALL [35198]
P: CUPAR, SCT FORRETT, LARENCE, DEMPSTER & BARCLAY FAMILIES. ALL [37972]
P: CURACAO (SLAVE) TRADERS. 1750-1830 [36340]
P: CURACAO JEWS. 1750-1830 [36340]
P: CURIOSITY HOUSE FINSBURY SQ, LONDON, ENG. 1790-1840 [38171]
P: CZECHOSLOVAKIA EMIGRATION. 1875-1920 [38618]
P: DALBY, QLD, AUS RESIDENTS OF. 1800S [35878]
P: DAPTO, NSW, AUS RESIDENTS & LIFESTYLE. 1840S [34809]
P: DARJEELING, INDIA ENG RESIDENTS OF. 1800-1900 [36197]
P: DARRIWILL, VIC, AUS RESIDENTS OF. 1835-1900 [37156]
P: DARTFORD & DISTRICT PHOTOGRAPHS — GROUPS OF PEOPLE. 1870+ [37213]
P: DARTFORD & DISTRICT PHOTOGRAPHS OF FOOTBALL TEAMS. 1880+ [37213]
P: DARTFORD & DISTRICT PHOTOGRAPHS — TOPOGRAPHICAL. 1870+ [37213]
P: DARTMOOR, DEV, ENG LYDFORD, WIDECOMBE, HOLNE +. ALL [37882]
P: DARWEN, LAN, ENG MANOR OF OVER DARWEN. 1700+ [36991]
P: DEANSBIGGINS FARM KIRKBY LONSDALE, CUL, ENG. ALL [36890]
P: DELTING PARISH SHETLAND, SCT. ALL [37340]
P: DENISTONE, NSW, AUS RESIDENTS OF. 1792-1900 [34026]
P: DENMARK HILL, BATHURST, NSW, AUS EXACT LOCATION OF. 1840-1860 [34693]
P: DETROIT, MI, USA AIME HOUDE, MISSING - BORN CAN 1906. 1925-1932 [38525]

P: **DOMINICA ISLAND** GORDONS. ALL [34170]
P: **DONERAILE, COR, IRL** RESIDENTS OF. 1800-1900 [37156]
P: **DOWNHAM, CAM, ENG** FAMILIES OF. 1600+ [37494]
P: **DRAYTON PARSLOW PARISH** BKM, ENG. 1700+ [35874]
P: **DRUMLEMBLE, SCT** RESIDENTS OF. 1800S [34156]
P: **DRUMLICH** BALQUHIDDER, PER, SCT. 1650-1750 [36635]
P: **DRYMEN, SCT** RESIDENTS OF. 1840-1854 [34156]
P: **DUBLIN, IRL** EMIGRATION TO CAN. 1820-1850 [38455]
P: **DUBLIN, IRL** MERCHANTS — BURKE. 1750-1850 [35494]
P: **DUMPLINGTON** LAN, ENG. PRE 1800 [36635]
P: **DUNGOG, THALABA, NSW, AUS** EARLY HISTORY. 1800-1900 [35668]
P: **EARDSWICH HALL, CHS, ENG** DAVIES FAMILY. PRE 1820 [36066]
P: **EASTHAMPTON, MA, USA** TEXTILES. 1850+ [38015]
P: **EASTWOOD, NSW, AUS** RESIDENTS OF. 1792-1900 [34026]
P: **EBENEZER, NSW, AUS** FAMILIES OF, PLUS ANY HISTORICAL INFORMATION, PHOTOGRAPHS. 1794-1991 [37121]
P: **ECKINGTON, WOR, ENG** RESIDENTS OF. 1850+ [36171]
P: **EDENGLASSIE, NSW, AUS** RESIDENTS OF. ANY [35740]
P: **EIFEL** FAMILIES. 1600-1800 [38617]
P: **ELMTON, DBY, ENG** FAMILIES OF. ALL [38265]
P: **ENNERDALE BRIDGE, CUL, ENG** TYSON FAMILY. PRE 1800 [34241]
P: **ENNISKILLEN, FER, IRL** MIGRANT FEMALES TO AUS. 1850S [34043]
P: **ERF/DDR** . PRE 1750 [38620]
P: **ERLIGHEIM (WUE)** GER FAMILIES. 1700-1900 [38728]
P: **EST-/LIVLAND** HENNIG-/HUNNIGHAUSEN FAMILY. 1300+ [38601]
P: **EULO, QLD, AUS** RESIDENTS OF. ALL [35198]
P: **EUROA, VIC, AUS** RESIDENTS OF. 1850-1880 [34433]
P: **EVERCREECH, SOM, ENG** RESIDENTS OF. ALL [35878]
P: **EXETER, DEV, ENG** SCHOOLTEACHERS & PUPILS. 1750-1900 [34833]
P: **FAIRWATER ASYLUM, SOM, ENG** STAFF & LUNATICS. ALL [36131]
P: **FAKENHAM, NFK, ENG** PARISH RECORDS. 1844 [34182]
P: **FANGDALEBECK** SMITHY A FORGE IN BILSDALE, NRY, ENG. 1770-1860 [38269]
P: **FARM — MARSH HOUSE** FAWFIELD HEAD, STS, ENG. 1600+ [37375]
P: **FARM — REWLACH** FAWFIELD HEAD, STS, ENG. 1600+ [37375]
P: **FEHMARN ISLAND** OFFERING DATES OF FAMILIES. PRE 1870 [38632]
P: **FEHMARN ISLAND** SHIPPING & EMIGRATION. ALL [38632]
P: **FETLAR, SCT** COMPLETE RESIDENTS. 1730-1965 [34830]
P: **FIELD OF MARS CEMETERY, NSW, AUS** KNOWN BURIALS AT. 1890-1960 [34026]
P: **FIELD OF MARS, NSW, AUS** RESIDENTS OF. 1792-1850 [34026]
P: **FIJI** RABONE FEEZ & CO. 1850-1900 [34303]
P: **FINLAND** SIPPOLA & VEHKALAHTI. 1540-1860 [38562]
P: **FLINTSHIRE, NTH WALES (CLWYD)** LIST OF PARISH CHURCHES FOR STANFIELD NAME. 1808-1990S [36311]
P: **FOLIEJON PARK, BRK, ENG** LOCAL HISTORY. ALL [38498]
P: **FORT ROSALIE** NATCHEZ, MS, USA. 1700S [36964]
P: **FREEMANS REACH, NSW, AUS** FAMILIES OF, PLUS ANY HISTORICAL INFORMATION, PHOTOGRAPHS. 1794-1991 [37121]
P: **FROME, SOM, ENG** MANORIAL RECORDS. ALL [36172]
P: **FROME, SOM, ENG** MILL OWNERS OF. 1700-1900 [34550]
P: **FROME, SOM, ENG** WOOL MERCHANTS OF. 1700-1900 [34550]
P: **FURRACABAD** NSW, AUS, EARLY RESIDENTS. C1885 [34971]
P: **FYVIE, ABD, SCT** HILTON, TROUP, HATT & LAWRENCE FAMILIES. ALL [37972]
P: **GARRYHINCH ESTATE** OFF, IRL. PRE 1823 [38460]
P: **GASPE, QUE** ENGLISH SPEAKING FAMILIES OF. ALL [38406]
P: **GENERAL HOSPITAL** SYDNEY, NSW, AUS. 1800+ [35911]
P: **GERMAN VINE LABOURERS** HUNTER VALLEY, NSW, AUS. 1847-1860 [36267]
P: **GERMANY** GRELCK FAMILIES. ALL [38585]
P: **GHERINGHAP, VIC, AUS** RESIDENTS OF. 1835-1900 [37156]
P: **GLADESVILLE MENTAL HOSPITAL, NSW, AUS** WORKER IN, BURIALS AT. 1830-1920 [34026]
P: **GLADESVILLE, NSW, AUS** RESIDENTS OF. 1792-1900 [34026]
P: **GLANVILLE BLOCKS, SA, AUS** RESIDENTS OF. 1914 [35565]
P: **GLENLYON STATION** HISTORY. 1840+ [34303]
P: **GLESCH/PAFFENDORF — RHINELAND** RESIDENTS OF. PRE 1800 [37456]
P: **GLOSSODIA, NSW, AUS** FAMILIES OF, PLUS ANY HISTORICAL INFORMATION, PHOTOGRAPHS. 1794-1991 [37121]
P: **GOULBURN, NSW, AUS** COTTON VALLEY SETTLERS. 1850-60S [35111]
P: **GOURDON VILLAGE** KCD, SCT, HISTORY OF. [34381]
P: **GRABAN, EXTINCT MEDIEVAL SETTLEMENT** HISTORY & RESIDENTS OF. ALL [38768]
P: **GRANITE HILL, VIC, AUS** GOLDMINING TOWN. 1850S [33849]
P: **GREAT BOWDEN, LEI, ENG** LOCAL HISTORY. [35858]
P: **GREAVE FARM** LANGFIELD, P HALIFAX, WRY, ENG. 1750-1830 [36635]
P: **GREENSLOPES** AUS ARMY NURSING COR.. PRE 1947 [35122]

P: **GRESSE ST, LONDON, ENG** CHARLES MARTIN, SHOEMAKER. 1871-1912 **[37719]**
P: **GROOMBRIDGE, KEN, ENG** SOCIAL HISTORY. 1650-1850 **[38355]**
P: **GROSE VALE, NSW, AUS** FAMILIES OF, PLUS ANY HISTORICAL INFORMATION, PHOTOGRAPHS.
    1794-1991 **[37121]**
P: **GUMBINNEN (KREISGEBIET)** OSTPREUβEN. 1600-1945 **[38649]**
P: **GYORKONY TOLNA, HU, GERMANS** OF. 1700+ **[34335]**
P: **HABITAT RESIDENCE** PILET, FRA. 1600-1750 **[36699]**
P: **HADIKFALVA, BOKOVINA, OES** RESIDENTS OF. ALL **[37453]**
P: **HAMBURG, GERMANY** DUTCH COMMUNITY. 1650-1750 **[34948]**
P: **HAMILTON, ONT, CAN** EMIGRANTS FROM NE SCT. 1840-1880 **[34479]**
P: **HAMMELBURG** ALL FAMILIES. 1525+ **[38644]**
P: **HANSLOPE, BKM, ENG** RESIDENTS OF. 1800S **[35256]**
P: **HARDINGTON MANDEVILLE PARISH** SOM, ENG. 1750-1914 **[37378]**
P: **HARTINGTON, DBY, ENG** CENSUS. 1841-1881 **[36670]**
P: **HAWKESBURY DISTRICT, NSW, AUS** FAMILIES OF, PLUS ANY HISTORICAL INFORMATION,
    PHOTOGRAPHS. 1794-1991 **[37121]**
P: **HELLINGLY, SSX, ENG** RESIDENTS OF. 1740+ **[37560]**
P: **HERM (CHANNEL ISLAND)** RESIDENTS OF. ALL **[36671]**
P: **HERMANN, MO, USA** RESIDENTS OF. 1800-1860 **[38035]**
P: **HESSEN-NASSAU (STATE, GER)** FAMILIES. 1500+ **[38677]**
P: **HIKURANGI NORTHLAND, NZ.** TO 1930 **[38754]**
P: **HINDRINGHAM, NFK, ENG** RESIDENTS OF. 1700-1800 **[34828]**
P: **HOFEN (WUE) GER** FAMILIES. 1700-1900 **[38728]**
P: **HOLMES CO., MS, USA** JOSHUA JAMES FAMILY. 1830S **[37585]**
P: **HOLT, NORWAY** . PRE 1855 **[37510]**
P: **HORNCLIFFE MILL NORHAM PARISH, NBL, ENG.** 1790-1837 **[38269]**
P: **HORSENDON MANOR** BKM, ENG. 1500-1900 **[35781]**
P: **HORSHAM ST FAITHS** RESIDENTS OF. ALL **[37689]**
P: **HUNGERFORD, QLD, AUS** RESIDENTS OF. ALL **[35198]**
P: **HUNTLY, ABD, SCT** SOCIAL HISTORY. 1800-1950 **[38355]**
P: **HYTHE, KEN, ENG** ORDNANCE ARMS INN. 1881 **[35560]**
P: **INDIAN QUEENS INN** ST COLUMB MAJOR, CON, ENG. 1760-1960 **[37905]**
P: **INDIA (J. SPEAK)** POLICE INSPECTOR, E.I.R.. 1850-1890 **[36262]**
P: **IRL, MAYO & GALWAY** RESIDENTS, EMIGRANTS & RECORDS. 1600-1900 **[36551]**
P: **IRL FGS EXCHANGE – ALL SURNAMES.** ALL **[36551]**
P: **ISLAND OF NEVIS, WEST INDIES** RESIDENTS OF. 1700-1860 **[35739]**
P: **ISLE OF GIGHA, SCT** RESIDENTS OF. 1700-1800 **[34156]**
P: **ITALY** GENEALOGICAL INFORMATION. ALL **[37390]**
P: **JAMBEROO, STH COAST, NSW, AUS** RESIDENTS RICE & MAY FAMILIES. 1843+ **[35696]**
P: **JAVA** RESIDENT BRITISH MERCHANTS. 1850-1890 **[37236]**
P: **JOUY LES REIMS, CHA, FRA** RESIDENTS OF. PRE 1750 **[36964]**
P: **JURON CO, ONT, CAN** FRENCH SETTLEMENT. 1845-1990 **[34106]**
P: **KANDAHAR, INDIA** MAJOR SHOWELL, 92ND GORDON HIGHLANDERS. **[34373]**
P: **KAROW, SACHSEN, GER** RESIDENTS OF. ANY **[34801]**
P: **KAWAKAWA NORTHLAND, NZ.** TO 1930 **[38754]**
P: **KAYUGA, NSW, AUS** RESIDENTS OF. ANY **[35740]**
P: **KERMADEC ISLANDS, NZ** SHIP H.M.S.HERALD. 1854 **[33952]**
P: **KETTLESTON, NFK, ENG** PARISH RECORDS. 1881 **[34182]**
P: **KILBIRNIE PRESBYTERIAN CHURCH, AYR, SCT** THE CRAWFORD GALLERY. ALL **[36890]**
P: **KILCOOLY PARISH - PALATINE SETTLEMENT** TIP, IRL. 1760+ **[35874]**
P: **KILFINANE PARISH** LIM, IRL. 1740+ **[35874]**
P: **KILLIN, SCT** ROBERTSON, MCNAB & MCDIARMID FAMILIES. ALL **[37972]**
P: **KILMADOCK PARISH** PER, SCT. PRE 1855 **[36635]**
P: **KILSKERRY, FER, IRL** FAMILIES OF AND EMIGRATION. 1750-1900 **[37556]**
P: **KINAWLEY, FER, IRL** PARISH MIGRATION TO AMERICA. 1820-1870 **[34094]**
P: **KINGSCLERE, HAM, ENG** RESIDENTS OF. PRE 1800 **[36401]**
P: **KINGSTON ESTATE** TENANTS OF. 1810-1850 **[38299]**
P: **KINNEGAD, WEM, IRL** HISTORY. **[35494]**
P: **KIRCHHEIM (D-7312) GER** STUDENTS AT THE LATIN SCHOOL. 1250-1950 **[38673]**
P: **KIRKBY LONSDALE, CUL, ENG** ST MARY'S CHURCH. ALL **[36890]**
P: **KIRRIBILLI HOUSE, NSW, AUS** HISTORY. 1850+ **[34303]**
P: **KIRTON IN HOLLAND, LIN, ENG** RESIDENTS OF. ALL **[35878]**
P: **KISSING POINT, NSW, AUS** RESIDENTS OF. 1792-1850 **[34026]**
P: **KOELN** FAMILIES. 1600-1800 **[38617]**
P: **KURRAJONG, NSW, AUS** FAMILIES OF, PLUS ANY HISTORICAL INFORMATION, PHOTOGRAPHS.
    1794-1991 **[37121]**
P: **KURRI KURRI, NSW, AUS** RESIDENTS OF. 1900+ **[35539]**
P: **LANCASHIRE** BOATMEN NARROW BOATS. PRE 1900 **[34370]**
P: **LANCASHIRE, ENG** RESIDENTS OF. PRE 1900 **[34944]**
P: **LARRAS LAKE, NSW, AUS** RESIDENTS OF. 1840S-1860 **[33930]**
P: **LARVIK, NORWAY** RESIDENTS OF. ALL **[35548]**
P: **LAVENHAM, MAN, CAN** RESIDENTS & BUSINESSES. 1880-1980 **[36704]**

P: LAXFIELD, SFK, ENG RESIDENTS OF. PRE 1850 **[37874]**
P: LEI, ENG RESIDENTS OF. ALL **[38369]**
P: LENGNAU (AG, CH) FAMILIES. ALL **[38609]**
P: LESLIE HILLS LOCATED IN LAN, ENG. PRE 1860 **[37035]**
P: LIDNIE (SYDNEY?), AUS DEATH OF ALEXANDER IRVINE. 23 OCT 1863 **[36712]**
P: LISBURN, ANT, IRL MUSSEN FAMILY TALLOWCHANDLERS. 1780-1880 **[38084]**
P: LKS SCT. 1650-1900 **[38388]**
P: LLANIGON, BRE, WLS CHURCH HOUSE, RESIDENTS OF. 1865-1900 **[35942]**
P: LOECHGAU (WUE) GER FAMILIES. 1700-1900 **[38728]**
P: LOWER PORTLAND, NSW, AUS FAMILIES OF, PLUS ANY HISTORICAL INFORMATION,
    PHOTOGRAPHS. 1794-1991 **[37121]**
P: LUDHAM, NFK,ENG MIGRANTS TO AUS. 1840-1860 **[33928]**
P: MADEIRA ISLAND RESIDENTS OF. 1800-1900 **[33875]**
P: MADEIRA ISLAND ROBERT REID KALLEY'S CONVERTS. PRE 1850 **[36546]**
P: MAGHERACULMONEY, FER, IRL FAMILIES MIGRATING TO AUS. 1840-1842 **[38291]**
P: MAGHERAGALL, ANT, IRL RESIDENTS & LOCAL HISTORY. PRE 1900 **[38298]**
P: MAGHERAGALL, ANT, IRL GARRETT, MCNAUGHT & MUSSEN FAMILIES. PRE 1870 **[38084]**
P: MAINE, USA MACNIELL'S FROM PEI, CAN. 1850 **[35651]**
P: MALLOW, COR, IRL RESIDENTS OF. 1800-1900 **[37156]**
P: MALMO, SWE PRIESTS, MAYORS, COUNCILMEN. 1500-1800 **[36320]**
P: MARCH, CAM, ENG DURRANT FAMILY. 1840 + **[37719]**
P: MARSFIELD, NSW, AUS RESIDENTS OF. 1792-1900 **[34026]**
P: MASHOCKMILL HOUSE CARLUKE, LKS, SCT, PETTIGREW. 1600-1800 **[34501]**
P: MAYO, IRL POTATO FAMINE IN. 1840S **[36191]**
P: MCDONALD RIVER, NSW, AUS FAMILIES OF, PLUS ANY HISTORICAL INFORMATION,
    PHOTOGRAPHS. 1794-1991 **[37121]**
P: MCGRATHS HILL, NSW, AUS FAMILIES OF, PLUS ANY HISTORICAL INFORMATION,
    PHOTOGRAPHS. 1794-1991 **[37121]**
P: MDX, ENG, CEMETERIES LIST OF CEMETERIES OR AUSTIN GRAVES. 1800 + **[34363]**
P: MEATH & ARMAGH, IRL "THE COLLIER GANG". 1820S **[35599]**
P: MEDWAY TOWNS & MEDWAY VALLEY MILLERS & MILLWRIGHTS. 1750-1900 **[34738]**
P: MELBOURNE HOSPITAL, AUS SURGERY ON ALEXANDER IRVINE. OCT 1863 **[36712]**
P: MELBOURNE, VIC, AUS RESIDENTS OF. 1850S **[35958]**
P: MELROSE, ROX, SCT RESIDENTS OF. 1770-1776 **[36626]**
P: MERTON, NSW, AUS RESDIENTS OF. 1820S-1870S **[35740]**
P: METHLICK, SCT PARK & LAWRENCE FAMILIES, EXCHANGE INFO. ALL **[37972]**
P: MID & SOUTH YELL, SHETLAND IS, SCT COMPLETE RESIDENTS. 1720-1965 **[34830]**
P: MIDHURST, SSX, ENG . ALL **[35446]**
P: MILDENHALL, SFK, ENG LOCAL HISTORY. **[35858]**
P: MILFORD, AL, USA THOMAS MALONE. 1830-50S **[37585]**
P: MILL HILL ORPHANAGE RECORDS AND RESIDENTS. 1926-40 **[36889]**
P: MILLIE RUN BETWEEN NARRABRI & MOREE, NSW, AUS. 1834-1872 **[33939]**
P: MINING TOWNS WA, USA. 1875-1890 **[35267]**
P: MOLE CREEK, TAS, AUS . ALL **[34186]**
P: MONARO, NSW, AUS FAMILIES. 1820+ **[36295]**
P: MORA NORET, SWE ERICK LAWSON FAMILY. 1750-1850 **[37805]**
P: MOUNT MORGAN, QLD, AUS RESIDENTS OF. ALL **[38361]**
P: MT SPURR VOLCANIC MOUNTAIN ALASKA. 1895-1990 **[36463]**
P: MULGRAVE, NSW, AUS FAMILIES OF, PLUS ANY HISTORICAL INFORMATION, PHOTOGRAPHS.
    1794-1991 **[37121]**
P: MULL, ISLAND OF, SCT FAMILIES OF. 1700-1890 **[35961]**
P: MURGA, NSW, AUS TOWNSHIP. 1880 + **[33867]**
P: MUSWELLBROOK, NSW, AUS RESIDENTS OF. ANY **[35740]**
P: MYALL CREEK STATION EMPLOYEES, NSW, AUS. PRE 1870 **[35232]**
P: NATCHEZ, MS, USA FORT ROSALIE. 1700S **[36964]**
P: NB, CAN DUMMER FAMILY IN. 1876 + **[38782]**
P: NEGOA, NSW, AUS RESIDENTS OF. ANY **[35740]**
P: NEILLEY PARK PARIS, FRA. ALL **[34937]**
P: NEUDORF, GALACIA RESIDENTS OF. 1850 + **[37045]**
P: NEUDORF, HES, BRD EMIGRANT VINELABOURERS TO NSW. 1847-1855 **[36267]**
P: NEW ENGLAND, USA GOODWIN FAMILY IN. ALL **[38782]**
P: NEW ENGLAND, USA HUTCHINSON FAMILY IN. ALL **[38782]**
P: NEW FAIRFIELD, CT, USA RECONSTRUCTION OF VITAL RECORDS. 1700-1850 **[38051]**
P: NEW FAIRFIELD, CT, USA BEERS AND LEWIS FAMILIES. 1700-1850 **[38051]**
P: NEW FARM, QLD, AUS NEW FARM PARK KIOSK. 1920S **[35111]**
P: NEW FOREST, ENG WORKERS IN. 1800-80S **[37335]**
P: NEW QUAY NOW DERELICT PORT ON TAMAR RV, DEV, ENG. 1840-70 **[35471]**
P: NEWFOUNDLAND — CHAMPNEYS RESIDENTS OF. ALL **[33852]**
P: NEWFOUNDLAND — ENGLISH HARBOUR RESIDENTS OF. ALL **[33852]**
P: NEWGATE PRISON, LND, ENG OFFICERS (TURNKEYS). ALL **[37297]**
P: NEWLANDS, DRAINIE, MORAY, SCT THOM FAMILY. 1740-1805 **[36559]**
P: NFK, ENG FAMILY PEDIGREES. 1563-1618 **[37759]**

P: **NIEDER-WIESEL, HES, BRD** EMIGRANTS TO USA. 1780+ **[34183]**
P: **NIEDER-WIESEL, HES, BRD** EMIGRANTS TO LIVERPOOL, LAN, ENG. 1800+ **[34183]**
P: **NIEDER-WIESEL, HES, BRD** EMIGRANTS TO AUS. 1850S **[34183]**
P: **NORFOLK, ALB, CAN** RESIDENTS OF. PRE 1916 **[34153]**
P: **NORTH MAVINE PARISH, SHETLAND IS, SCT** COMPLETE BAPTISM/MARRIAGE/DEATH. 1758-1965 **[34830]**
P: **NORTH RYDE, NSW, AUS** RESIDENTS OF. 1792-1900 **[34026]**
P: **NORTH UIST, INV, SCT** RESIDENTS OF. 1700-1850 **[34876]**
P: **NORTH YELL, SCT** COMPLETE RESIDENTS. 1800-1965 **[34830]**
P: **NORWEGEN AUSWANDERER.** 1700-1989 **[38641]**
P: **NORWOOD JEWISH ORPHANAGE** RECORDS AND RESIDENTS. 1905-15 **[36889]**
P: **NOTTINGHAM, ENG** RESIDENTS OF. PRE 1850 **[34944]**
P: **NUNKIRCHEN, RPF** GENERAL INFORMATION. 1700-1800 **[36346]**
P: **OAKHAM, RUT, ENG** HISTORY & FAMILIES OF. PRE 1877 **[35180]**
P: **OAKLEY, STS, ENG** RESIDENTS OF. PRE 1830 **[36066]**
P: **OAKTHORPE PARISH** DBY, ENG. 1700+ **[35874]**
P: **OBERERHRENDINGEN (AG, CH)** FAMILIES. ALL **[38609]**
P: **OBERON, NSW, AUS** EARLY SETTLEMENT. 1820-1900 **[37556]**
P: **OHIO PICKAWAY AND ROSS COUNTIES, USA.** 1800-1830 **[36546]**
P: **OLD MEADOWS, BACUP LAN, ENG.** PRE 1800 **[36635]**
P: **OLDHAM, LAN, ENG** BOARDMAN, BROWN & KERSHAW FAMILIES. ALL **[37972]**
P: **OPUA NORTHLAND, NZ.** TO 1930 **[38754]**
P: **OSTPREUSSEN (OPR)** HENNIGHAUSEN FAMILY. 1700+ **[38601]**
P: **OSTPREUSSEN** FAMILIES. PRE 1945 **[38629]**
P: **OSWALDTWISTLE, LAN, ENG** MANGNOLLS BAR HOUSE, HISTORY & RESIDENTS OF. 1880-1900 **[35942]**
P: **OTTAWA, CAN. PARLIAMENT RE-BUILDING** PETER LYALL & SONS CONTRACTOR. 1916S **[38449]**
P: **OTTERY ST MARY, DEV, ENG** CARPENTERS & SHOEMAKERS OF. ALL **[36389]**
P: **OUNDLE, NTH, ENG** THE FAMILIES OF. 1750-1900 **[38279]**
P: **OVER DARWEN, LAN, ENG** RESIDENTS OF. 1750-1840 **[35052]**
P: **OVERTON, NSW, AUS** RESIDENTS OF. ANY **[35740]**
P: **PA, USA** GOODWIN FAMILY IN. ALL **[38782]**
P: **PA, USA** HALEY FAMILY IN. ALL **[38782]**
P: **PANTHEON BAZAAR & PICTURE GALLERY** PAINTINGS, EXHIBITIONS, LND, ENG. 1850S **[35720]**
P: **PARRAMATTA RIVER** FERRYMEN, FISHERMEN AND SPORTSMEN. 1792-1920 **[34026]**
P: **PHILADELPHIA, PA, USA** MIDVALE STEEL, DESCENDANTS OF EMPLOYEES. 1880-1920 **[37793]**
P: **PICKERING, NSW, AUS** RESIDENTS OF. ANY **[35740]**
P: **PICTON, NSW, AUS & DISTRICT** SURNAME INDEX HELD. PRE 1920 **[37561]**
P: **PIERCEFIELD, NSW, AUS** RESIDENTS OF. ANY **[35740]**
P: **PITT TOWN, NSW, AUS** FAMILIES OF, PLUS ANY HISTORICAL INFORMATION, PHOTOGRAPHS. 1794-1991 **[37121]**
P: **POORHOUSE** CRAIGLEITH, EDINBURGH, SCT. C1900 **[34515]**
P: **PORT ARTHUR, TAS, AUS** EVENING SCHOOL. 1835-1850 **[37113]**
P: **PORT NOLLOTH, RSA** RESIDENTS OF. 1800+ **[34944]**
P: **PORTLAND HEAD, NSW, AUS** FAMILIES OF, PLUS ANY HISTORICAL INFORMATION, PHOTOGRAPHS. 1794-1991 **[37121]**
P: **PORTSEA ISLAND, HAM, ENG** RESIDENTS OF. 1800-1889 **[34824]**
P: **PRISONS, RUSSIA** ESCAPEES/PRISONERS. 1885-1915 **[38369]**
P: **PUTNEY, NSW, AUS** RESIDENTS OF. 1792-1900 **[34026]**
P: **QUEENBOROUGH, KEN, ENG** PEOPLE & OCCUPATIONS. 1700-1900 **[34718]**
P: **RAASAY, INV, SCT** RESIDENTS OF. 1760-1860 **[37964]**
P: **RANDALSTOWN, ANT, IRL** RESIDENTS OF. **[35565]**
P: **RATHKEALE PARISH** LIM, IRL. 1709+ **[35874]**
P: **REDFERN, NSW, AUS** PICTURES OF, MAINLY, THE REDFER, PITT & GEORGE STREETS AREA. PRE 1950 **[37498]**
P: **RERRICK, KKD, SCT** RESIDENTS OF. ANY **[34345]**
P: **RHEINLAND-PFALZ** FAMILIES. 1600-1800 **[38617]**
P: **RICHMOND COUNCIL, NSW, AUS** MEMBERS & EMPLOYEES OF. 1870+ **[37121]**
P: **RICHMOND, NSW, AUS** FAMILIES OF, PLUS ANY HISTORICAL INFORMATION, PHOTOGRAPHS. 1794-1991 **[37121]**
P: **RIVER PLATE** SCOTTISH SETTLERS. 1800-1824 **[37759]**
P: **RIVERSTONE & DISTRICT, NSW, AUS** LOCAL HISTORY OF. 1810+ **[36641]**
P: **ROCHDALE, LAN, ENG** WILLIAM LEACH OR LEIGH FAMILY. 1800+ **[34363]**
P: **ROCKHAMPTON, QLD, AUS** RESIDENTS OF. ALL **[38361]**
P: **ROCKHAMPTON, QLD, AUS** HISTORY. 1850-1900 **[34303]**
P: **ROGATE** SSX, ENG. 1800 **[34112]**
P: **ROMNEY MARSH, KEN, ENG** LOCAL HISTORY. ALL **[36413]**
P: **ROWS OF GT YARMOUTH** NFK, ENG. ANY **[34086]**
P: **ROYAL HOTEL** MANCHESTER, LAN, ENG. 1851 **[36635]**
P: **RSA, ROODEPOORT CITY** CEMETERIES DATA CO-ORDINATED BY ME. 1850+ **[36467]**
P: **RUNSWICK BAY, NRY, ENG** HISTORY OF. ANY **[34375]**
P: **RUSSIA/POLAND** POW (PRISONER OF WAR). 1885-1915 **[38369]**

P: **RYDE, NSW, AUS** RESIDENTS OF. 1792-1900 **[34026]**
P: **RYPIN, BY, POL** RESIDENTS OF. PRE 1920 **[34246]**
P: **SAARLAND** FAMILIES. 1600-1800 **[38617]**
P: **SACKVILLE, NSW, AUS** FAMILIES OF, PLUS ANY HISTORICAL INFORMATION, PHOTOGRAPHS. 1794-1991 **[37121]**
P: **SALLE PARISH** NFK, ENG. 1650-1850 **[34007]**
P: **SAO SALVADOR, BRAZIL** LINCOLNSHIRE MEN WORKERS. 1840-1860S **[37445]**
P: **SCARBOROUGH, ONT** CAN. 1790-1950 **[38388]**
P: **SCHLIENGEN (BAW, GER)** FAMILIES. ALL **[38609]**
P: **SCHNEISINGEN (AG, CH)** FAMILIES. ALL **[38609]**
P: **SCONE OLD & NEW VILLAGES, PER, SCT** RESIDENTS. 1800+ **[36467]**
P: **SCONE OTHER PLACES** GEOGRAPHIC LOCATIONS PLEASE. ALL **[36467]**
P: **SCONE, NSW, AUS** RESIDENTS. 1820+ **[36467]**
P: **SERSHEIM (WUE) GER** FAMILIES. 1700-1900 **[38728]**
P: **SHANGHAI, CHINA** STANDARD OIL COMPANY. 1900+ **[34230]**
P: **SHARPHAM HOUSE, DEV, ENG** ANY INFORMATION. 1700+ **[36637]**
P: **SKELLATOR, NSW, AUS** RESIDENTS OF. ANY **[35740]**
P: **SLAVIC MACEDONIA** KICHEVO AND BITOLA. PRE 1900 **[36963]**
P: **SMISBY PARISH** DBY, ENG. 1800+ **[35874]**
P: **SMITHSTOWN, KIK, IRL** MARTIN COLLIER, FARMER. 1848-1858 **[33775]**
P: **SOHAM, CAM, ENG** HISTORY OF. PRE 1900 **[35168]**
P: **SOM, ENG** HARDINGTON MANDEVILLE PARISH. 1750-1914 **[37378]**
P: **SOUTH AFRICA** 1820 SETTLERS. 1818-1850 **[36988]**
P: **SOUTH CARLTON, LIN, ENG** MANOR, PARISH AND RESIDENTS. 1500-1900 **[37742]**
P: **SPENNYMOOR, DUR, ENG** ATHLETE 'BOY GREY'. 1904-1912 **[38269]**
P: **ST ALBANS, NSW, AUS** FAMILIES OF, PLUS ANY HISTORICAL INFORMATION, PHOTOGRAPHS. 1794-1991 **[37121]**
P: **ST BUDEAUX PARISH** DEV, ENG. 1750-1820 **[34550]**
P: **ST CHRISTOPHER — W INDIES** EARLY SETTLEMENT EX ENG. 1550-1675 **[36463]**
P: **ST HELENA ISLAND** RESIDENTS OF. 1800-1900 **[36468]**
P: **ST HELENA ISLAND** RESIDENT STAFF. 1815-1821 **[36410]**
P: **ST HELENA** ANY INFORMATION. PRE 1885 **[37715]**
P: **ST HELIERS, NSW, AUS** RESIDENTS OF. ANY **[35740]**
P: **ST KITTS, W INDIES** RESIDENTS OF. 1700-1800 **[37087]**
P: **ST KITTS, WEST INDIES** T.A.C. ARMBRISTER, RECTOR OF. 1875-80 **[36412]**
P: **ST MARK DALSTON, MDX** CEMETERY GEORGE AUSTIN. PRE 1886 **[34363]**
P: **ST MARTINS IN THE FIELD** LND, ENG. 1800S **[34126]**
P: **ST MARY MAGDALENE, SOUTH CREEK ST MARYS, NSW, AUS** PARISH REGISTERS. 1840+ **[37500]**
P: **ST NEOTS, HUN, ENG** THOS. HODGSON, RURAL DEAN OF. 1902-14 **[36412]**
P: **ST SAMPSONS, GSY, ENG** SURNAMES OF FRENCH DESCENT. ALL **[35433]**
P: **ST SYLVESTER, ONT, CAN** PROTESTANT IRISH IMMIGRANTS. 1840-70 **[37528]**
P: **STANFORD-IN-THE-VALE, BRK, ENG** HISTORY & FAMILIES OF. PRE 1900 **[35180]**
P: **STAPLEGROVE, SOM, ENG** ALL FAMILIES. ALL **[36131]**
P: **STOCKHOLM, SWE** CERTIFICATES. 1830S **[35709]**
P: **STOKE ABBEY, ENG** FAMILY MANSION. PRE 1840 **[35164]**
P: **SUDETENLAND** RESIDENTS OF. PRE 1950 **[34634]**
P: **SUNDAY ISLAND, NZ** CAPTAIN H.M.DENHAM. 1854 **[33952]**
P: **SUNDERLAND** DUR, ENG, HISTORY OF. 1600+ **[35802]**
P: **SUTHERLANDS CREEK, VIC, AUS** RESIDENTS OF. 1835-1900 **[37156]**
P: **SWANNINGTON, NFK, ENG** HISTORY OF. PRE 1800 **[36122]**
P: **SYDLING, DOR, ENG** INGRAM & KINGSTON ESTATES. C1823 **[34900]**
P: **SYDNEY MARKETS, NSW, AUS** COMMISSION AGENTS. 1840+ **[34428]**
P: **TARBERT, ARL, SCT** SOCIAL HISTORY. 1800-1950 **[38355]**
P: **TARBOCK, LAN, ENG** RESIDENTS OF. 1800+ **[37560]**
P: **TASMANIA** CONVICT SUPERVISORS. 1843-1853 **[33879]**
P: **TEMESVAR** HUNGARY. 1800+ **[34029]**
P: **THAMES SOAP WORKS** T.B.ROWE, BRENTFORD, ENG. 1799-1934 **[37657]**
P: **THARGOMINDAH, QLD, AUS** RESIDENTS OF. ALL **[35198]**
P: **THE COPPINS ESTATE** IVOR, KEN, ENG. 1800+ **[34485]**
P: **THOMASTOWN WESLEYAN CEMETERY, VIC, AUS** ALL BURIALS. 1855-1955 **[37962]**
P: **THORVERTON, DEV, ENG** EMIGRANTS. 1800S **[34833]**
P: **THORVERTON, DEV, ENG** PARISH HISTORY. ALL **[34833]**
P: **TICKNALL, DBY, ENG** INHABITANTS OF. 1500-1900 **[36233]**
P: **TIMISOARA** ROMANIA. 1800+ **[34029]**
P: **TOLLARD ROYAL, WIL, ENG** PRE 1900 FAMILIES. **[36825]**
P: **TONGE HALL TONGE, BOLTON, LAN, ENG.** 1800S **[38284]**
P: **TOULOUSE, FRANCE** FAMILY HISTORY OF TOULOUSE FAMILY. ALL **[34140]**
P: **TOWNSVILLE, QLD, AUS** WITHAM'S BAKERY. 1880+ **[35111]**
P: **TRAVEMUENDE** POSTCARDS. PRE 1960 **[38632]**
P: **TRAVEMUENDE** SHIPPING & EMIGRATION. ALL **[38632]**
P: **TREHERNA, MAN, CAN** RESIDENTS & BUSINESSES. 1875-1980 **[36704]**
P: **TUAM, GAL, IRL** RESIDENTS OF. 1800-1860 **[34433]**

P: **TUBBRID, TIP, IRL** LOCAL HISTORY. ALL **[36602]**
P: **TUCHEIM, SACHSEN, GER** RESIDENTS OF. ANY **[34801]**
P: **TWICKENHAM, MDX, ENG** RESIDENTS OF. **[35565]**
P: **ULVA, SCT** RESIDENTS OF & VISITORS TO. PRE 1900 **[36191]**
P: **UPPER CANADA** RESIDENTS OF. C1820-1860 **[35618]**
P: **URSWICK IN FURNESS, CUL, ENG** RESIDENTS OF. C1800 **[35722]**
P: **USA** EMIGRATION. 1700-1870 **[38606]**
P: **VALCARTIER** SETTLEMENT OF. 1818-1880 **[34489]**
P: **VENICE, ITL** BRITISH RESIDENTS IN. 1850-1900 **[37289]**
P: **VERNON & DIST, BC, CAN** BIRTH, MARRIAGES & DEATHS INDEX. 1891 + **[34237]**
P: **WA, USA** CORNISH MINERS. 1875-1890 **[35267]**
P: **WALES, BRECON** HISTORY & RESIDENTS OF. PRE 1700 **[38768]**
P: **WALHEIM (WUE) GER** FAMILIES. 1700-1900 **[38728]**
P: **WARATAH** NSW, AUS. TO 1880 **[38754]**
P: **WELLINGROVE, NSW, AUS** PAST RESIDENTS & CEMETERY. 1850 + **[34185]**
P: **WERNERSREUTH (SUDETENLD)** ASCH U. UMGEBUNG. 1600-1945 **[38649]**
P: **WEST RYDE, NSW, AUS** RESIDENTS OF. 1792-1900 **[34026]**
P: **WESTFALEN (NRW)** HENNIGHAUSEN FAMILY. 1200 + **[38601]**
P: **WESTON, NFK, ENG** RESIDENTS OF, HISTORY OF. PRE 1800 **[36122]**
P: **WESTON-SUPER-MARE, SOM, ENG** HISTORY, SOCIAL & GENERAL. ALL **[36012]**
P: **WHITE HEART INN** PADSTOW, CON, ENG. 1600 + **[34028]**
P: **WHITE HILL, SELBOURNE, HAM & SSX, ENG** RESIDENTS OF. C1889 **[35565]**
P: **WHITESHAW HOUSE** CARLUKE, LKS, SCT, MURE. 1700-1800 **[34501]**
P: **WHITNEYVILLE, CT, USA** HISTORY OF. 1830-1870 **[35626]**
P: **WICKLOW, IRL** EMIGRATION TO CAN. 1820-1850 **[38455]**
P: **WICKLOW, IRL** RESIDENTS OF. 1800-1850 **[38455]**
P: **WIGGATON, DEV, ENG** RESIDENTS OF. ALL **[36389]**
P: **WILBERFORCE, NSW, AUS** FAMILIES OF, PLUS ANY HISTORICAL INFORMATION,
       PHOTOGRAPHS. 1794-1991 **[37121]**
P: **WILMINGTON, NC, USA** JOSHUA JAMES. 1800-1890S **[37585]**
P: **WINDSOR COUNCIL, NSW, AUS** MEMBERS & EMPLOYEES OF. 1870 + **[37121]**
P: **WINDSOR, NSW, AUS** FAMILIES OF, PLUS ANY HISTORICAL INFORMATION, PHOTOGRAPHS.
       1794-1991 **[37121]**
P: **WISCONSIN, USA** AUSWANDERER. 1801-1990 **[38641]**
P: **WISCONSIN** SHAWANO CO., USA. 1870-1900 **[36546]**
P: **WISEMANS CK** NEAR O'CONNELL, BATHURST, NSW, AUS COPPER MINING. 1820 + **[35361]**
P: **WISEMANS FERRY, NSW, AUS** FAMILIES OF, PLUS ANY HISTORICAL INFORMATION,
       PHOTOGRAPHS. 1794-1991 **[37121]**
P: **WOLLOMBI, NSW, AUS** RESIDENTS OF. 1820 + **[35539]**
P: **WOOLVERTON** SOMERSET, ENG. 1600-1800 **[37232]**
P: **WOOTTON RIVERS** PARISH WIL, ENG. 1700 + **[35874]**
P: **WORMS (STOLON, GER)** EMIGRATION. 1720-1740 **[38662]**
P: **WROMBLEWO (POL)** FAMILIES. ALL **[38618]**
P: **WRY, ENG** NEWSPAPER INDUSTRY, HERBALISTS. 1750-1890S **[36837]**
P: **WRY, ENG** PEOPLE, HISTORY, LIVING CONDITIONS. 1860-1880S **[36837]**
P: **WURTTEMBERG, GER** INNKEEPERS. 1700-1850 **[37609]**
P: **WYALONG, NSW, AUS** PIONEER RESIDENTS OF. PRE 1920 **[34183]**
P: **WYNYARD PARK** SYDNEY, NSW, GARDENERS. 1900 + **[34533]**
P: **YAXLEY, HUN, ENG** RESIDENTS OF. 1750-1900 **[33836]**
P: **YORK, ONT, CAN** EARLY SETTLERS OF. PRE 1800 **[36707]**
P: **YORKSHIRE, ENG** RESIDENTS OF. PRE 1900 **[34944]**
R: **AMERICAN REVOLUTION** MENNONITE ACTIVITY. 1775-1800 **[34741]**
R: **ANGLICAN CHURCH OF AUST** . **[33768]**
R: **ANTI-PAPIST DEMONSTRATIONS** COLCHESTER, ESS, ENG. 1640-1642 **[34019]**
R: **ANTINOMIANS** MEMBERS IN BOSTON, MA, USA. 1630-40 **[37806]**
R: **AUXERRE, FRA** VINES SISTERS MISSION. 1800S **[35375]**
R: **BAPTIST CHURCH** BARTON IN THE BEANS, LEI, ENG. PRE 1800 **[37675]**
R: **BAPTISTS** CURTIS FAMILY OF MARYLEBONE AND HACKNEY, MDX, ENG. 1800-1860 **[37253]**
R: **BAPTISTS** PA, USA. 1700S **[34350]**
R: **BAPTISTS** ULSTER, IRL. 1600 + **[34350]**
R: **BRYAN CLERGY,** ALL DENOMINATIONS. 1800-1900 **[36986]**
R: **BURIAL GROUND** BALLAST HILLS, NEWCASTLE UPON TYNE, ENG. 1700 + **[36220]**
R: **CHAPLAIN TO DUKE OF KENT** JAMES MILNER, HALIFAX, ENG. 1770-1820 **[36217]**
R: **CHURCH MEMORIALS** LAUNCESTON, TAS, AUS. 1820 + **[33791]**
R: **CHURCH OF ENGLAND** MISSIONARIES IN AUS. 1850-1920 **[35485]**
R: **CHURCH OF SCOTLAND** MINISTERS . 1860-1900 **[35179]**
R: **CHURCH OF SCOTLAND** CLERGY SURNAME LISTON. ANY **[35999]**
R: **CHURCH OF THE BRETHREN** DESCENDANTS OF MICHAEL FRANTZ. ALL **[36540]**
R: **CHURCH ST MICHAELS** NY, NY, USA. 1900-1958 **[37375]**
R: **CLAPHAM SECT** . 1750-1850 **[36380]**
R: **CLARKE, REV JAMES** . C1858-1942 **[33768]**
R: **CONGREGATIONALISTS** MA, USA. 1620 + **[37049]**

R: **CONGREGATIONALISTS** SMITH GROUP. 1620+ **[37049]**
R: **DARWEN, LAN, ENG** NONCONFORMIST. 1750+ **[36991]**
R: **DESCENT FROM THE SAINTS** OF ENG, SCT, IRL, EUROPE. ALL **[36619]**
R: **EBENEEZER BAPTISTS** BACUP, ENG. 18TH CENT **[36635]**
R: **EDITH GROVE CHAPEL** LONDON BAPTIST CHURCH. 1900-1920 **[36802]**
R: **EMLY C OF I DIOCESE, IRL** REV THOMAS RYAN, CHANCELLOR. 1790-1807 **[38084]**
R: **EPISCOPALIAN CHURCHES** LONG ISLAND, NY, USA. 1700-1770 **[36624]**
R: **EPPING, NSW, AUS** HISTORY OF ST ALBAN'S ANGLICAN CHURCH. **[33768]**
R: **FETTER LANE INDEPENDENT CHURCH** OFF FLEET ST, LND. 1800+ **[34711]**
R: **FREE CHURCH OF ENGLAND** CLERGY LISTS. C1870 **[38409]**
R: **FREE CHURCH** SCT TO NZ. ANY **[35909]**
R: **GERMAN BAPTIST BRETHREN** DESCENDANTS OF MICHAEL FRANTZ. ALL **[36540]**
R: **GLASITES** DUNDEE, SCT. 1740+ **[36220]**
R: **GRACE CHURCH, BROOKLYN, NY, USA** RECORD OF EMPLOYEES. 1890-1895 **[34469]**
R: **HUGUENOT EMIGRATION** HARVEST FAMILY. ALL **[35662]**
R: **HUGUENOTS IN GUYENNE PROVINCE** . 1600S **[37821]**
R: **HUGUENOTS** CAR, IRL, NAME GERMAINE. 1700+ **[34602]**
R: **HUGUENOTS MIGRANTS** – ANGERS, FRA TO LEICESTERFIELDS, LND, ENG. 1600+ **[36123]**
R: **HUNTERS HILL, NSW, AUS** HISTORY OF ANGLICAN CHURCH. **[33768]**
R: **IRISH QUAKER FAMILIES** . 1650-1900 **[34717]**
R: **JEW, KURTZ, EFRAIM (JACOB)**, BOLECHOWICE, KR, POL. 1860-1900 **[35717]**
R: **JEWS NAMED ADLER** OF THE VILLAGES OF BOLECHOWICE, KARNIOWICE, RUDAWA &
      KURDWANOW, KR, POL. 1830+ **[35717]**
R: **KALLEY, ROBERT REID** FREE CHURCH, MADEIRA ISLAND. PRE 1850 **[36546]**
R: **KIRK ELDERS** PER, SCT. 1820-1830 **[36635]**
R: **KNOX CHURCH, DUNEDIN, NZ** DR D.M. STUART. 1860+ **[36669]**
R: **LONDON MISSIONARY SOCIETY** . 1775-1820 **[34387]**
R: **LUTHER, DR MARTIN** REFORMATOR, GER. 1483-1545 **[37683]**
R: **MCKENZIE-ROSS** PRESBYTERIAN MINISTER, SCT-AUS. 1820-1840 **[38007]**
R: **MENNONITE** DESCENDANTS OF HEINRICH FUNKE. ALL **[36540]**
R: **METHODISM BRITISH** CIRCUIT PLANS, CLASS TICKETS, POSTCARDS. 1800+ **[37766]**
R: **METHODIST CIRCUIT RIDER** JOSEPH WILSON, MANVERS TWP, ONT, CAN. 1835+ **[34064]**
R: **METHODIST CONVERSIONS** TEWKESBURY, GLS, ENG. 1840S **[34241]**
R: **METHODISTS** – EAST SSX & KEN, ENG EMIGRANTS TO AUS. 1830-1850 **[36272]**
R: **MISSIONARY (ALEX IRVINE)** DEATH AT LIDNIE (SYDNEY?), AUS. 23 OCT 1863 **[36712]**
R: **MISSIONARY, L.M.SOCY** BROCKWAY. 1840+ **[33937]**
R: **NEVERSWEATS** ROSE, WAYNE CO., NY, USA. PRE 1855 **[37510]**
R: **OLD MEETING HOUSE** BULL RING, KIDDERMINSTER, ENG. 1750-1990 **[34711]**
R: **OLD TESTAMENT** GENEALOGIES THEREIN. ALL **[37420]**
R: **ORDER OF EASTERN STAR** ROBERT MORRIS DESCENDANTS. 1800-1990 **[37804]**
R: **PLYMOUTH BRETHREN** RECORDS, STI & LKS, SCT. 1830S-1880S **[37354]**
R: **PRESBYTERIAN** SIMPSON, CO. DOWN, IRL. 1700-1838 **[35266]**
R: **PRIMITIVE BAPTISTS** NC & VA, USA. 1800S **[34350]**
R: **PRIMITIVE METHODISTS** ALSTON, CUL, ENG. 1834+ **[33775]**
R: **PROSPECT UNITED CHURCH** RECORDS PROSPECT, ONT, CAN. 1800+ **[37568]**
R: **QUAKER RESEARCH** ENG TO USA. C1678 **[38605]**
R: **QUAKERS** BKM, ENG. PRE 1818 **[36767]**
R: **QUAKERS** DOWNEND, GLS, ENG. 1600+ **[34908]**
R: **QUAKERS** HAVERFORDWEST, PLM, WLS. 1600-1700 **[36898]**
R: **QUAKERS** IRL. 1650-1850 **[36172]**
R: **QUAKERS** NTT, ENG. PRE 1750 **[36140]**
R: **QUAKERS** OF SIBLE HEDINGHAM, ESS, ENG. PRE 1900 **[37693]**
R: **QUAKERS** USA. ALL **[36347]**
R: **RABBIS** EASTERN EUROPE TO USA. **[33756]**
R: **REDFERN, NSW, AUS** HISTORY OF ST SAVIOURS CHURCH. **[33768]**
R: **REVEREND (CONGREGATIONAL)** JOHN OWEN, AGY, WLS. 1820-1900 **[35430]**
R: **ROMAN CATHOLICS IN ENG** WYNTER & TILNEY. PRE 1820 **[34033]**
R: **ROSS** PRESBYTERIAN MINISTER, SCT-AUS. 1820-1840 **[38007]**
R: **SALVATION ARMY** MISSIONARIES IN INDIA. 1887+ **[36683]**
R: **SANDEMANIANS** SCT & ENG. 1740+ **[36220]**
R: **SCOTTISH COVENANTER** JOHN WHITELAW. 1650-1750 **[33978]**
R: **SHELDON, ARCHBISHOP GILBERT** DESCENDANTS OF. 1598-1800 **[33841]**
R: **SHORTWOOD MEETING HOUSE** EMIGRATION FROM GLS, ENG TO NSW & SA, AUS. 1830S-1850S
      [37988]
R: **ST ANNES C OF E, RYDE, NSW, AUS** CHRISTENINGS, MARRIAGES, FUNERALS, BURIALS. 1826-
      1900 **[34026]**
R: **ST AUGUSTINE'S MORELAND, VIC, AUS** PARISHIONERS OF. 1891-1991 **[35597]**
R: **ST CHARLES RC CHURCH, RYDE, NSW, AUS** CHRISTENINGS, MARRIAGES, FUNERALS,
      BURIALS. 1840-1920 **[34026]**
R: **ST GEORGES PRES CHURCH, WELLINGTON ST, COLLINGWOOD, VIC, AUS** CONGREGATION
      MEMBERS PHOTOGRAPHS. 1854+ **[35051]**
R: **ST KITTS, WEST INDIES** T.A.C. ARMBRISTER, RECTOR OF. 1875-80 **[36412]**

R: **ST MARY'S CATHOLIC BAPTISMS** IPSWICH, QLD, AUS. 1849-1867 **[34449]**
R: **ST MARY'S CATHOLIC CHURCH MARRIAGES** IPSWICH, QLD, AUS: TRANSCRIBED TO
    COMPUTER. 1849-1909 **[34449]**
R: **ST NEOTS, HUN, ENG** THOS. HODGSON, RURAL DEAN OF. 1902-14 **[36412]**
R: **STRATON, REV GEORGE** MINISTER BRECHIN, ANS, SCT. 1790S **[36749]**
R: **UNITARIAN CHAPEL, GEE CROSS, LAN ENG.** NEWTONS & KELLETTS WITHIN CONGREGATION.
    1750-1900 **[35591]**
R: **UNITED BRETHREN** THE 'DUNKERS'. 1800S **[37823]**
R: **VALDENSIANS** . ALL **[36464]**
R: **WESLEYAN CHURCH** ASHBURTON, DEV, ENG. **[37014]**
R: **WESLEYAN MINISTER** GEORGE MCDONALD FROM IRL. 1800+ **[36614]**
R: **WESLEYAN MINISTER** GEORGE MCDONALD TO MANCHESTER, ENG. 1800+ **[36614]**
R: **WILSON QUAKERS.** PRE 1850 **[36929]**
R: **YAXLEY PARISH, HUN, ENG** CHURCH RECORDS. 1750-1900 **[33836]**
S: **'ACHILLES' (HMS)** IRON SCREW SHIP, 20 GUNS. 1869-1870 **[34711]**
S: **'ADIE' SEAMEN,** ANY REFERENCES. 1850-1950 **[34831]**
S: **'AGNUS MUIR'** VOYAGE TO NZ. 1872 **[35960]**
S: **'ALBERT WILLIAM'** VOYAGE TO NZ. 1864 **[35960]**
S: **'ANN WILSON'** LIVERPOOL, ENG, TO WELLINGTON, NZ. 1856-57 **[34667]**
S: **'ANNE I'** CRIMES OF CONVICTS. 1801 **[35155]**
S: **'ARAMINTA'** LIST OF PASSENGERS TO SYDNEY, AUS. 29 JULY 1854 **[35164]**
S: **'ASIA' (HMS)** 2ND RATE, 84 GUNS. 1864 **[34711]**
S: **'ATHLETAE'** VOYAGE BIRKENHEAD, ENG TO PORTLAND, AUS. 1854-55 **[35223]**
S: **'ATLANTA'** PLYMOUTH TO VIC, AUS. 1858 **[36862]**
S: **'BARBESTYN'** DR JAN HENDRIKSZ, DUTCH EAST INDIES, NL. 1719 **[36453]**
S: **'BARGE' (SCHOONER)** WILLIAM B.FANCHER. 1922-1923 **[34206]**
S: **'BEAUTY & PLENTY'** ALL. 1860-90 **[37114]**
S: **'BEDFORD'** HMS . 1797 **[34550]**
S: **'BEEJAPORE'** BUILT IN ST JOHNS, CANADA. HISTORY OF. C1750-1900 **[35164]**
S: **'BERCINI'** SYDNEY, NSW, AUS TO LOMBARDY, ITL. 1890+ **[35519]**
S: **'BOUNTY' (HMS)** THOMAS DENMAN LEDWARD. 1787+ **[36983]**
S: **'BOURNEUF'** REGISTER OF DESCENDANTS, MELBOURNE, VIC, AUS. 1852 **[35380]**
S: **'BRILLIANT' PASSENGER LIST** TOBERMORY, MULL TO SYDNEY, AUS. 1837-1838 **[33874]**
S: **'BRITISH QUEEN'** CAPTAIN OFFICER & CREW. 1791 **[35149]**
S: **'CALCUTTA'** FAMILIES OF PASSENGERS. 1835 **[35589]**
S: **'CALEDONIA'** SCT TO AUS. 1830S **[34809]**
S: **'CALPHURNIA'** PASSENGERS ON. 1848 **[34600]**
S: **'CAMEO'** IMMIGRANT SHIP – CREW, PASSENGERS. 1859 **[35360]**
S: **'CASTLE ROCK'** PETER JOHNSON OF SHETLAND, SCT. 1894 **[34627]**
S: **'CHALLENGER' (HMS)** ANY INFORMATION. 1858-1921 **[37715]**
S: **'CHARLES DICKENS'** . 1800+ **[35465]**
S: **'CHARMING MOLLY'** BOSTON TO ANNAPOLIS NS. 1760 **[36463]**
S: **'CHINA'** ARR SYDNEY, NSW, AUS. 1854 **[35843]**
S: **'CHRISTINA'** VOYAGE SCT TO AUS. 1838-39 **[36606]**
S: **'CLONTARF'** ENG TO NZ. 1858-9 **[36790]**
S: **'CLYDE'** LIVERPOOL TO SYDNEY, AUS VIA HOBART, AUS. 1834 **[36244]**
S: **'COMMODORE PERRY'** LIVERPOOL, ENG TO AUCKLAND, NZ. SEP 1860 **[36864]**
S: **'COMMODORE PERRY'** PASSENGERS ON. 1855 **[34886]**
S: **'CONSTANTINOPLE'** LONDON, ENG TO AUCKLAND, NZ. 1850 **[36864]**
S: **'CORBIN' (STEAM YACHT)** LND TO MARGATE, KEN, ENG. 1820S **[34602]**
S: **'COROMANDEL I'** CONVICT TRANSPORT, ENG TO AUS. C1802 **[36638]**
S: **'COROMANDEL'** HMS PASSENGER & CONVICT LISTS. 1802+ **[33867]**
S: **'COROMANDEL'** ENG TO VIC, AUS. 1840 **[36862]**
S: **'CREOLE' & 'PALME'** SLAVE SHIPS. PRE 1850 **[34170]**
S: **'CRESSY'** VOYAGE TO NZ. 1849 **[35960]**
S: **'DAVERGNE'** CRAWFORD FAMILY TO SOUTH AUS. 1839 **[35444]**
S: **'DAVID MALCOLM' (SS)** ARR SYDNEY, AUS. 1845 **[35573]**
S: **'DAWESTON'** MADRAS TO SYDNEY, AUS. 1854 **[35697]**
S: **'DONALD MACKAY'** LIVERPOOL, ENG TO MELBOURNE, AUS AND RETURN. 1858-9 **[36390]**
S: **'DUCHESS OF NORTHUMBERLAND'** CORK, IRL TO SYDNEY, AUS. 1836 **[35357]**
S: **'DUCHESS OF RICHMOND'** SCOTTISH IMMIGRANTS TO CAN. C1830 **[34126]**
S: **'DUKE OF MANCHESTER'** ENG TO AUS – PICTURES & LOG. 1842 **[34896]**
S: **'DUNBAR CASTLE'** VOYAGES TO AUS. 1870-1890 **[37114]**
S: **'DUNCAN' (HMS)** JOHN RILEY. PRE 1900 **[37436]**
S: **'EARL OF BALCARRAS'** INDIAN MUTINY. 1857-1858 **[38007]**
S: **'EARL OF CHARLEMONT'** SHIPWRECK OFF VIC, AUS. 1853 **[37497]**
S: **'EARL OF EGLINTON'** GREENOCK, SCT TO AUS PASSENGERS. 1854 **[35051]**
S: **'EARL ST VINCENT'** CONVICT PASSENGERS TO TAS, AUS. 1826 **[36290]**
S: **'EMERALD'** ENG TO VDL (TAS), AUS. 1820-21 **[36626]**
S: **'EMMA COLVIN'** ENG TO NZ. 1856 **[36790]**
S: **'EMU' (SCHOONER)** CAPTAIN ADAMS, SINGAPORE. C1847 **[36621]**
S: **'FERRET' STEAMSHIP** DESCENDANTS 1880 CREW WLS, ENG, AUS. 1881+ **[34855]**

S: 'FIERY CROSS' . 1883 [36320]
S: 'FORFARSHIRE' AUST CONVICT TRANSPORT. 1842-43 [38073]
S: 'FOUDROYANT' HMS . 1798 [34550]
S: 'FRANCIS' (SLAVER) IN JAMAICA 1744, ANY INFO. [36522]
S: 'GANGES' (HMS) ANY INFORMATION. 1821-1861 [36535]
S: 'GENERAL BOYD' CAPTAIN. 1800 [35149]
S: 'GIRVAN' ENG TO AUS. 1870S [34809]
S: 'GLATTON' HMS PASSENGER & CONVICT LISTS. 1803 + [33867]
S: 'GRACE HARWAR' LIST OF CREW - AUS TO ENG - LAST GRAIN RACE. 1929 [35401]
S: 'GRAHAM' NEWFOUNDLAND SHIPWRECK. 1820-1830 [36718]
S: 'GREENWICH' CAPTAIN OFFICER & CREW. 1796 [35149]
S: 'HECTOR AND MARTHA' ENG TO BOSTON, USA. ARRIVED JULY 1637 [37584]
S: 'HERALD OF THE MORNING' IRL & AUS. 1865 [38007]
S: 'HERCULES' CAPTAIN OFFICER & CREW. 1797 [35149]
S: 'HERCULES' PASSENGERS, ABERDEEN-QUE, CAN. 1834 [34479]
S: 'HESPERUS', SCHOONER WRECKED OFF BOSTON, USA. [35254]
S: 'HOPE' (HMSS) 400 TON BARQUE, LND TO MELB, AUS. MARCH 1853 [34906]
S: 'HYDASPUS' VOYAGE TO NZ. 1873 [35960]
S: 'IRENE' ANY DATA RE THIS SHIP. 1845-1860 [38004]
S: 'JAMES NICHOL FLEMING' VOYAGE TO NZ. 1869 [34615]
S: 'JAVA' TO SYDNEY, AUS. 1853 [35261]
S: 'JOHN BARRY' VOYAGE, ENG TO SYDNEY, AUS. 1825-1826 [38597]
S: 'JOHN KNOX' PASSENGER LIST, PLYMOUTH TO AUS. 1851 + [34925]
S: 'JOHNSTONE' AUS TO ENG - PICTURES & LOG. 1848 [34896]
S: 'JUMNA' (HMS) IRON SCREW TROOPSHIP. 1876-1879 [34711]
S: 'KINNEAR' BUILT LONDON, HISTORY OF. 1834 + [34418]
S: 'KINNEAR' LND TO AUS (GER BOUNTY EMIGRANTS). 1837-38 [34418]
S: 'KITTY' ENG TO AUS VOYAGE. 1792 [36600]
S: 'LA BRETAGNE' (SS) LE HAVRE TO NY, USA. 1892 [36405]
S: 'LA ESCOCESA' LONDON & FRENCH TO NZ. 1870 + [36624]
S: 'LADY MCNAGHTEN' ARRIV AUS 1837 - IMMIGRANTS. 1837 [38000]
S: 'LADY NUGENT' VOYAGE TO NELSON, NZ. 1850 [36862]
S: 'LARKINS' MANCHESTER, ENG, TO INDIA. 1841 [34667]
S: 'LIGHT OF THE AGE' ENG TO AUS - PICTURES & LOG. 1859 [34896]
S: 'LIZZIE CORY' (SEVILLA). 1900 [34381]
S: 'LOCH AWE' . 1869-1896 [37713]
S: 'LOCH ECH' . 1874-1894 [37713]
S: 'LOCH LINE' . 1867 + [37713]
S: 'LOCH LINNHE' . 1876-1898 [37713]
S: 'LOCH RANZA' . 1875-1897 [37713]
S: 'MARCHIONESS OF LONDONDERRY' ENG - SYDNEY, AUS. 1854 [35111]
S: 'MARIA' WILLIAM ALLEN, COMMANDER. 1840-50S [37707]
S: 'MARINER' CONVICT TRANSPORT. 1816 [35511]
S: 'MARNHULL' VOYAGES & FATE. 1855-1865 [34079]
S: 'MARTIN LUTHER' LIVERPOOL TO MELB, VIC, AUS. 1852 [33928]
S: 'MAYFLOWER' CARVER, JOHN, FIRST GOVERNOR. 1620 [33952]
S: 'MAYFLOWER' PASSENGER WILLIAM BRADFORD. 1620 [37804]
S: 'MONITOR' (USS) PLANS SENT TO RUSSIAN NAVY. CIVIL WAR [35328]
S: 'NATIVE LASS' NFD, CAN. C1850-1900 [38778]
S: 'NELEUS' LONDON TO MELB, VIC, AUS. 1854 [33928]
S: 'NEPTUNE' GRAVESEND, ENG TO SYDNEY, AUS. 1839 [35143]
S: 'NESBIT' SCOTTISH IMMIGRANTS TO CAN. C1830 [34126]
S: 'NORA(H) CRIENA' IRL & NFD, CAN. C1790-1840 [38778]
S: 'NOURMAHAL' EMIGRANT SHIP TO NZ. 1857-1858 [34711]
S: 'OMEGA' FAMILIES OF PASSENGERS. 1853-1854 [35589]
S: 'OUR HOPE' ST JOHN NB, CAN TO INVERCARGILL, NZ. 1863 [36244]
S: 'PARMELIA' 1834 CONVICTS CONVICTED MAYO, IRL 24 JULY 1833 & TRANSPORTED ON THIS
    SHIP. [38075]
S: 'PATRICIA' PASSENGER LISTS FROM OES TO AUS. 1912-1914 [37519]
S: 'PAUL' OF LONDON, ENG SAILED GRAVESEND 3 APR 1635. 1600-1700 [36463]
S: 'PEERLESS' PASSENGERS. C1850 [35859]
S: 'PEMBROKE' (HMS) INVOLVEMENT IN BOER WAR. 1899-1901 [37353]
S: 'PITT' EDGE, SARAH. 1791-2 [33864]
S: 'POICTIERS' VOYAGE TO SOUTH AUSTRALIA. 1848 [34194]
S: 'PONCE' (SS) MERCHANT NAVY. WWII [38412]
S: 'RED ROVER' PASSENGERS. 1830S [38760]
S: 'REPULSE' (HMS) INVOLVEMENT IN BOER WAR. 1899-1901 [37353]
S: 'ROSEANNE' SHIP'S LIST. 1847 [34244]
S: 'ROYAL ADMIRAL' EMIGRANT SHIP. C1835-1840 [38068]
S: 'SAN DOMINGO' FROM WEX, IRL TO PEI, CAN. 1822 [38404]
S: 'SARAH PILE', SCHOONER, ENG . 1880S [35235]
S: 'SHENANDOAH' CSS HISTORY OF. 1861-1865 [34550]

S: **MERCHANT NAVY SHOREHAM, SSX, ENG. PRE 1840 [36486]**
S: **MERCHANT SEAMAN WILLIAM LEE, IPSWICH, ENG. PRE 1800 [37700]**
S: **MERCHANT SHIPS SWE TO LND, ENG. 1850-1900 [36006]**
S: **MIDLOTHIAN MIGRANTS FROM THE ISLE OF SKYE TO NSW, AUS. 1837 [37349]**
S: **NORTH ATLANTIC CABLES SHIP 'DACIA'. 1900-1905 [38483]**
S: **NORTH-WEST TASMANIA, AUS COASTAL TRADE. 1855-1890 [38072]**
S: **ORLANDO TO HULL, ENG FROM HULL TO NEW YORK, USA. 1884 [38543]**
S: **P AND O SHIPYARDS HONG KONG. 1855-1865 [38007]**
S: **P AND O SHIPYARDS NAGASAKI, JAPAN. 1855-1865 [38007]**
S: **PALMYRA EURASIAN EXPERIMENT IMMIGRANTS. 1854 [35697]**
S: **PASSENGER LISTS - ARMY FROM GIBRALTAR TO QUE, CAN. 1791 [38459]**
S: **PASSENGER LISTS FROM HOLLAND, NL. 1853-5 [36240]**
S: **PASSENGER LIST SHIP TO DORCHESTER, MA, USA. 1633 [36550]**
S: **PROVIDENCE COMPANY TO USA & BARBADOS. 1600S [35558]**
S: **SEALING & WHALING SHIPS EPHRAM JAMES COFFEY, SYDNEY, AUS. [34659]**
S: **SEAMAN OFFICER MARTIN V.BLIGH. 1840 + [34057]**
S: **SEAMAN WILLIAM T.CHARLWOOD, LND, ENG. 1880-1890S [35727]**
S: **SHAND, I SAILOR, EASTERN CANADA. 1820-1870 [34222]**
S: **SHIP-BUILDING BIDEFORD, DEV, ENG. PRE 1818 [38460]**
S: **SHIPBUILDERS HADFIELD FAMILY, MANCHESTER, LAN, ENG. C1850 [35079]**
S: **SHIPS & SHIPPING JAMAICA TO NEW ORLEANS, USA. 1830-1860 [36324]**
S: **SHIPS ENGINEERS COASTAL – GREYMOUTH TO LYTTELTON, NZ. 1870-1920 [36778]**
S: **SHIPS NAME REQUIRED FOR A CAPTAIN MARTIN. 1854 [37459]**
S: **SHIPS STEWARD P&O UK TO SYDNEY, AUS (WALTER EDWARD HARRIS). C1920-30S [36252]**
S: **SHIPYARDS LEITH, SCT. 1845-1857 [38007]**
S: **SINCLAIRS SLIEVES JUTE BARQUES, LIVERPOOL, ENG TO RANGOON. 1860-1890 [37779]**
S: **SIR WILLIAM EYRE DIARIES OF VOYAGE ENG TO AUS. 1859 [35468]**
S: **SOUTH AFRICA 1820 SETTLERS. 1818-1850 [36988]**
S: **SPRITSAIL BARGES OF THE SWALE, MEDWAY & THAMES. 1800-1899 [34718]**
S: **ST JEAN DE LA ROCHELLE, FRA L'ACADIE, CAN. 1630 [37429]**
S: **STEAM DREDGE NSW, AUS. 1872-1892 [36600]**
S: **STEAM YACHT CORBIN LND TO MARGATE, KEN, ENG. 1820S [34602]**
S: **STEAMBOATS CAPTAINS & PILOTS, OHIO RIVER, USA. 1810-1880 [36897]**
S: **TIMBER TRADE AGENTS IN LIVERPOOL, ENG. 1800-1820 [38407]**
S: **TIMBER TRADE HAMILTON BROS. HAWKESBURY, CAN. 1800-1820 [38407]**
S: **TIMBER TRADE QUEBEC CITY TO LIVERPOOL, ENG. C1800 [38407]**
S: **TRADE BETWEEN UK & SPAIN HARRISON – SEA CAPTAIN. PRE 1850 [35473]**
S: **TYNESIDE DOCKYARDS BLACKSMITHS & CARPENTERS. 1860-1914 [35756]**
S: **UK TO WELLINGTON, NZ. 1903 [35954]**
S: **UNITED FRUIT COMPANY CAPTAIN WILLIAM CARSON LAW. 1900-1924 [37425]**
S: **WHALERS LONG ISLAND & NJ, USA. 1650-1750 [36897]**
S: **WHITBY, ENG SHIPS & SHIPOWNERS. 1700 + [34375]**
S: **WILLIAM PROWSE EURASIAN EXPERIMENT IMMIGRANTS. 1852 [35697]**
S: **WYATT, ISHAM W. SHIP CAPTAIN ALONG ATLANTIC COAST. 1845-1855 [37533]**
S: **YORKSHIRE, ENG TO QUEBEC CITY, CAN. 1840S [34216]**

CONTRIBUTORS

The following list of people have recorded entries in this edition of the Directory. They expect to be written to about their specific entry and not to be pestered by people selling other goods and services.

Care should be taken to write to a contributor only when the specific details recorded indicate that you may be of assistance to one another. It is suggested that the INTRODUCTION of this book be read before writing to a contributor.

The Editors recommend to readers, that as a courtesy when making contact for the FIRST time with a contributor, you enclose a self addressed stamped envelope for reply within your own country and 2 International postal coupons if writing to another country.

People receiving letters are requested to reply even if not able to assist. It should be remembered that even if two correspondents find that they are not related they at least become aware of one another's field of research and can keep this in mind when researching in the future. A number of contributors have reported that some of their best clues came from people who were not directly related to them but who had kept notes in the past, on unrelated persons sharing the same surname in the same region.

If all else fails you may make a new friend !
Remember — if you want assistance, try to assist others.

CONTACTING CONTRIBUTORS

Thought and care should be exercised when a reader of this *Directory* wishes to contact one of the contributors listed.

Points to Note:—

1. When addressing the envelope, spell the country of destination out in full if writing to another country. Write the full address as shown; even if it does not make sense to you, the post office of destination will understand. Be particularly clear in writing out postal codes.

2. Do not make your initial contact with contributors by telephone, you may be intruding on their privacy and valuable time.

3. We suggest you send a postage stamp for local reply

4. Send all international mail by AIR.

5. Enclose a simple family tree chart if possible as it can be understood far more easily than pages of explanations.

6. Do not write to every person researching a particular name unless you are interested in that name worldwide. It can be irritating for contributors to receive queries which obviously do not in any way relate to their entries in the *Directory*. e.g. If a contributor is searching the name MULLER in Stuttgart, Germany 1700-1750, do not write to them about your MULLER ancestor, who arrived in New York USA in 1875 or Brisbane AUS in 1880 unless you believe that he came from Stuttgart.

7. If you expect help try to help others. If the family names of your ancestors are not listed in this *Directory*, then you obviously have not entered particulars of them.

33751 VERMEER, S., ACHILLESSTR 10I., AMSTERDAM, 1076 RB NETHERLANDS
33752 HELM, MR D., 4505 S.E.17., DES MOINES, IA 50320 USA
33753 STEWART, MR L., 2688 WRIGHT AVE., PINOLE, CA 94564 USA
33754 BROWN, B., 16472 SW BONAIRE AVE., LAKE OSWEGO, OR 97035 USA
33755 ALBRIGHT, SHANNON, 4430 CHEYENNE RD., RICHMOND, VA 23235 USA
33756 GARNITZ, DAN, 3077 HOLMES RUN RD., FALLS CHURCH, VA 22042 USA
33757 SPENCER, THELMA, 11036 CHARLESTON ST., RANCHO CUCAMONGA, CA 91701 USA
33758 AMIEL, MR L., 3906 FOREST ST., BURNABY, BC V5G 1W8 CAN
33759 DWYER, BEVERLEY, 735 COLBORNE ST., BRANTFORD, ONT N3S 3R9 CAN
33760 LUTHER, KEM, 18 MAYFIELD AVE., TORONTO, ONT M6S 1K3 CAN
33761 JOHNSTON, MRS D., 658 ALBERT ST., NANAIMO, BC V9R 2W4 CAN
33762 MARSHALL, MARJORIE, RR1 PART LOT 110 CON C., PALMERSTON, ONT N0G 2P0 CAN
33763 TIEDEMANN, JANETTE, "SUMMER HILL" BOOROWA RD., YOUNG, NSW 2594 AUS
33764 MACKEN, SUSAN, GPO BOX 707., SYDNEY, NSW 2001 AUS
33765 BANN, BOB, 3 PRINCE ALFRED ST., BERRY, NSW 2535 AUS
33766 RALPH, DAVID, 18 GAHANS LANE., WOONONA, NSW 2517 AUS
33767 GARRETT, WILLIAM, 28 GOODHOPE ST., PADDINGTON, NSW 2021 AUS
33768 HUBBARD, NIGEL, 10 ELSTON AVE., DENISTONE, NSW 2114 AUS
33769 BLOM, PETER, PO BOX W296., WEST TAMWORTH, NSW 2340 AUS
33770 MURPHY, JEAN, 8 MCINNES ST., GRIFFITH, NSW 2680 AUS
33771 STONE, SHIRLEY, "BONNIE BANKS" RSD., EASTVILLE, VIC 3463 AUS
33772 HERBSTREIT, ROBERT, 19 VIOLA AVE., MOUNT DANDENONG, VIC 3767 AUS
33773 COUCH, MRS M., RMB 4420., TIMBOON, VIC 3268 AUS
33774 CURNICK, MRS G., PO BOX 1114., TRARALGON, VIC 3844 AUS
33775 COLLIER, LYNDON, 107 KENT ST., RICHMOND, VIC 3121 AUS
33776 CLARKE, IAN, 63 TALBOT AVE., BALWYN, VIC 3103 AUS
33777 PITTS, JOY, 57 SUNNYSIDE CRES., WATTLE GLEN, VIC 3096 AUS
33778 DEE, R., PO BOX 112., SEYMOUR, VIC 3660 AUS
33779 GIBSON, JENNIFER, 18 ROBSON ST., KILCOY, QLD 4515 AUS
33780 MCKELL, JENNIFER, 100 JOHNSTON ST., SOUTHPORT, QLD 4215 AUS
33781 MITCHELL, MRS H., 27 CROXLEY ST., MT GRAVATT, QLD 4122 AUS
33782 KRUGER, PETER, PO BOX 580., INDOOROOPILLY, QLD 4068 AUS
33783 HARRISON, JENNIFER, 6 MARSTON AVE., INDOOROOPILLY, QLD 4068 AUS
33784 SHAND, ROBERT, 8 PHOTINIA PL., BELLBOWRIE, QLD 4070 AUS
33785 BOTTING, IRENE, 31 FURNIVAL ST., NARROGIN, WA 6312 AUS
33786 GADD, MRS S., 11 TURNER ST., KALGOORLIE, WA 6430 AUS
33787 GREEN, VERA, 3 PINNOCK PL., BUSSELTON, WA 6280 AUS
33788 HICKS, BONNIE, 72 FRANCIS ST., LOWER KING, WA 6330 AUS
33789 STORER, JOHN, PO BOX 258., STRATHALBYN, SA 5255 AUS
33790 YEOLAND, ROSEMARY, 27 ALEXANDER ST., SANDY BAY, TAS 7005 AUS
33791 GILL, MISS J., 120 ELPHIN RD., LAUNCESTON, TAS 7250 AUS
33792 WILKIE, MRS M., 23 HAIG ST., ASHGROVE, QLD 4060 AUS
33793 JORDAN, SUSAN, 94B THE BOULEVARD., SHEPPARTON, VIC 3630 AUS
33794 BLACKA, JUDY, 43 GEORGE ST., WARILLA, NSW 2528 AUS
33795 BYFIELD, JEANETTE, 113 DENISON ST., MUDGEE, NSW 2850 AUS
33796 NAPIER-WINCH, LORD JOHN, 9 WOODFORD CRT., KOONDOOLA, WA 6064 AUS
33797 BURROWS, BRIAN, 62 LARSEN RD., BYFORD, WA 6201 AUS
33798 LUCK, MARGARET, 19 HAYWARD ST., MACGREGOR, ACT 2615 AUS
33799 TURTLE, LAURENCE, 39 ROBERTSON ST., KURRAJONG, NSW 2758 AUS
33800 WANN, JACK, 1/18 ALEXANDRIA AVE., EASTWOOD, NSW 2122 AUS
33801 MCLAUGHLIN, ALISON, 95 WARRAWEE CIR., FRANKSTON, VIC 3199 AUS
33802 DOORNEKAMP, YVONNE, PO BOX 446., GREENSBOROUGH, VIC 3088 AUS
33803 KIDGELL, BRUCE, 49 BARTLEY RD., BELGRAVE HEIGHTS, VIC 3160 AUS
33804 BIRCH, DONALD, 6 WELLESLEY RD., RINGWOOD NORTH, VIC 3134 AUS
33805 CANTY, PAT, 6 CITY RD., RINGWOOD, VIC 3134 AUS
33806 BOX, MRS V., 39 CARLINGA DR., VERMONT, VIC 3133 AUS
33807 TABER, ALAN, 12 THE GRANGE., NERANG, QLD 4211 AUS
33808 PALMER-GARD, SUZANNE, 185 TOOLOOA ST., GLADSTONE, QLD 4680 AUS
33809 BERTHELSEN, ROSLYN, "COORANGA" M/S 322., GAYNDAH, QLD 4625 AUS
33810 ANDERSON, KAREN, C/O 34 HORNBY ST., EVERTON PARK, QLD 4053 AUS
33811 BELCHER, MARGARET, 118 BUENA VISTA AVE., COORPAROO, QLD 4151 AUS
33812 CORRIGAN, BARBARA, 17 ANSTEY ST., PEARCE, ACT 2607 AUS
33813 SMITH, PHIL, 4 FARNCOMBE PL., GOWRIE, ACT 2904 AUS
33814 FREI, PATRICIA, 2 EUCUMBENE DR., DUFFY, ACT 2611 AUS
33815 WOOLLCOTT, ROBYN, PO BOX 181., BELCONNEN, ACT 2616 AUS
33816 BATTERHAM, MARJORIE, RMB 2088., COWES, PHILLIP ISLAND, VIC 3922 AUS
33817 COLE, THOMAS, 99 FOWLER RD., ILLAWONG, NSW 2234 AUS
33818 CONNORS, DESMOND, 2 MOORAMIE AVE., KENSINGTON, NSW 2033 AUS
33819 FLANAGAN, L. & E., 30 HIGHLAND ST., GORDON PARK, QLD 4031 AUS
33820 GAUCI, JOAN, 5 BARRINE CL., WESTLAKE, QLD 4074 AUS
33821 TULLOCH, BETTY, 47 GLENHOLM ST., MITCHELTON, QLD 4053 AUS
33822 GRINLY, MERLE, 4 CLUNE ST., OXLEY, QLD 4075 AUS

33823 MURPHY, JAN, 29 ELGATA ST., THE GAP, QLD 4061 AUS
33824 POMMER, MARY, 51 PANORAMA PDE., PANANIA, NSW 2213 AUS
33825 PERKINS, DAVID, PO BOX 421., MUSWELLBROOK, NSW 2333 AUS
33826 JOHNSTON, ARTHUR, 15/8 CASUARINA DR., CHERRYBROOK, NSW 2126 AUS
33827 MCKENZIE, FAY, 3 FREEMAN AVE., CASTLE HILL, NSW 2154 AUS
33828 WALTERS, STEPHEN, 49 KIRKDALE RD., CHAPEL HILL, QLD 4069 AUS
33829 DINEEN, DESMOND, 10 HARLAND SQ., WANTIRNA, VIC 3152 AUS
33830 HALLOWS, PETER, 10 SHERWOOD RD., MOUNT WAVERLEY, VIC 3149 AUS
33831 FENTON, HERBERT, 11 DEANSWOOD CL., STH WANTIRNA, VIC 3152 AUS
33832 GEE, GORDON, PO BOX 1131., ROXBY DOWNS, SA 5725 AUS
33833 TUCKER, MAGGIE, GPO BOX 2242., ADELAIDE, SA 5001 AUS
33834 TRAINOR, JULIA, 2 HILL CORNER., YARRALUMLA, ACT 2600 AUS
33835 MCAULIFFE, PETER, 26 TURNER ST., WONTHAGGI, VIC 3995 AUS
33836 QUARTERMAN, DUNCAN, 36 FEAKES PL., CAMPBELL, ACT 2601 AUS
33837 RAY, ENDREE, PO BOX 3., MACEDON, VIC 3440 AUS
33838 EVELYN, MS J., PO BOX 970., BATEMANS BAY, NSW 2536 AUS
33839 TOBIN, MICHAEL, 9 WILLIAM ST., FAIRLIGHT, NSW 2094 AUS
33840 DUKE, CHRISTINE, 4 FRENCHAM ST., GOLDEN SQUARE, VIC 3555 AUS
33841 SHELDON, PAMELA, 44 TOWNSON ST., BLAKEHURST, NSW 2221 AUS
33842 NOT IDENTIFIED, C/O EDITORS, PO BOX 795., NORTH SYDNEY, NSW 2059 AUS
33843 POULTON, DR G., 1961 KINGS RD., VICTORIA, BC V8R 2P4 CAN
33844 FITZHENRY, JUDITH, 8 COWDROY AVE., CAMMERAY, NSW 2062 AUS
33845 GOUDIE, DONALD, PO BOX 203., GLEBE, NSW 2037 AUS
33846 HERITAGE, CHERYL, "ROSEHILL" PO BOX 164., BREWARRINA, NSW 2839 AUS
33847 KERR, RODNEY, LOT 3 UTSCHINK RD., KLEINTON, QLD 4352 AUS
33848 MURRELL, CAMPBELL, 2 AUSTIN ST., RYE, VIC 3941 AUS
33849 MULLER, ROBYN, FT MUDDLY RSD FOSTERVILLE RD., BAGSHOT, VIC 3551 AUS
33850 GREGAN, GWEN, 1 COLUMBIA CL., BANNOCKBURN, VIC 3331 AUS
33851 CROTHERS, DR I., 2275 LEICH SQ., PORT COQUITLAM, BC V3L 3B9 CAN
33852 PIKE, DAVID, 391 PHILLIP MURRAY AVE., OSHAWA, ONT L1J 1H1 CAN
33853 NOEL, WINNIFRED, 9548-63 AVE., EDMONTON, ALB T6E 0G4 CAN
33854 MORIARTY, JO-ANNE, GENERAL DELIVERY., PORT ELGIN, ONT N0H 2C0 CAN
33855 LEWIS, FRANCES, 5110 SHERBROOKE ST W APT 10., MONTREAL, QUE H4A 1T1 CAN
33856 HENSMAN, RICHARD, BOX 831., STOUFFVILLE, ONT L4A 7Z9 CAN
33857 VEAR, DR H., 631 STONEBRIDGE LN., PICKERING, ONT L1W 3A6 CAN
33858 EVERITT, STEVE, BOX 472., KITIMAT, BC V8C 2R9 CAN
33859 BARRETT, DAVID, PO BOX 128., BEXLEY, NSW 2207 AUS
33860 RICHARDSON, MRS M., 33 BORONIA CRES MS 1102., MARCOOLA BCH, QLD 4564 AUS
33861 PLACE, MR G., 73 KARINGAL DR., GREENSBOROUGH, VIC 3088 AUS
33862 CONNAGHAN, SHIRLEY, 29 FAIRWAY DR., YALLOURN HEIGHTS, VIC 3825 AUS
33863 NOWLAND, MARLENE, GREGORY ST., BURKETOWN, QLD 4830 AUS
33864 DELLAR, ILA, 10 IRWIN ST., LEEMING, WA 6155 AUS
33865 MCBRIDE, WAYNE, 19 DUDLEY RD., GUILDFORD, NSW 2161 AUS
33866 COLLINS, ARNOLD, 2/110 WOODLAND ST., BALGOWLAH HEIGHTS, NSW 2093 AUS
33867 HILL, JANET, 117 WELLINGTON ST., BONDI BEACH, NSW 2026 AUS
33868 CANFIELD, CAROL, RMB 235., INGLEWOOD, VIC 3517 AUS
33869 JENSEN, JOANNE, "CARINYA"., BISHOPSBOURNE,TAS 7301 AUS
33870 WORT, HEATHER, 34 BAMBARRA ST., SOUTHPORT, QLD 4215 AUS
33871 DONNELLY, MRS S., 31 KING ARTHUR TCE., TENNYSON, QLD 4105 AUS
33872 MCNAMARA, BRUCE, 22 LILLEY RD., BARDON, QLD 4065 AUS
33873 HAMILTON, ISOBEL, 48 MASSON ST., TURNER, ACT 2601 AUS
33874 MCEACHERN, BETTY, PO BOX 696., ARMIDALE, NSW 2350 AUS
33875 SYMONDS, MR R., 42 FOREST AVE., BLACK FOREST, SA 5035 AUS
33876 MACKINNON, ALEX, 20 FIRST ST., BLACK ROCK, VIC 3193 AUS
33877 ROBERTS, ROBYN, RMB 6808., WODONGA, VIC 3691 AUS
33878 OLDAKER, TRUDY, PO BOX 45., LILYDALE, VIC 3140 AUS
33879 FIDLER, BRIAN, 6 CLONARD AVE., ELSTERNWICK, VIC 3145 AUS
33880 BABAUTA, MRS H., 18 CULCAIRN DR., FRANKSTON, VIC 3199 AUS
33881 ROWBOTTOM, ANN, 21 HELLER ST., BRUNSWICK, VIC 3056 AUS
33882 BALLINGER, L., 1 TAMALA AVE., NORTH CLAYTON, VIC 3168 AUS
33883 PAXMAN, RICHARD, 53 KINGS ROW., MILLENDON, WA 6056 AUS
33884 PRIDDLE, JOHN, 16 NEVILLE AVE., CLARENCE GDNS, SA 5039 AUS
33885 LILLEY, ROY, 10 WOODCHESTER CL., NAMBOUR, QLD 4560 AUS
33886 GERRARD, HEATHER, 27 STRATHAIRD ST., STRATHMORE, VIC 3041 AUS
33887 WESTON, DAVID, 17 CHARDONNAY ST., MUSWELLBROOK, NSW 2333 AUS
33888 LINTON, ALICE, 16 GUERIN ST., BUSSELTON, WA 6280 AUS
33889 FINCH, MERYL, 20 GLENDA AVE., MORPHETT VALE, SA 5162 AUS
33890 TUNE, MRS M., 13 MARTLESHAM CRES., DAW PARK, SA 5041 AUS
33891 PLATT, ANNE, 9 CUTHBERT CIR., WANNIASSA, ACT 2903 AUS
33892 SNOWDEN, JANICE, 56 MARINE PDE., SEACLIFF, SA 5049 AUS
33893 MEARING, MRS N., 18 GOOYONG ST., KEIRAVILLE, NSW 2500 AUS
33894 WILLCOX, MARGARET, 19 TUGGERAWONG RD., WYONGAH, NSW 2259 AUS

33895 STREET, GWEN, PO BOX 5061 SCMC., NAMBOUR, QLD 4560 AUS
33896 DUNCAN, MARIE, PO BOX 9., KOJONUP, WA 6395 AUS
33897 MCNAMARA, MR W., 65 BEATRICE ST., BALGOWLAH, NSW 2093 AUS
33898 CAMPBELL, MRS E., 2 VIOLA PL., QUEANBEYAN, NSW 2620 AUS
33899 LINDSAY, MRS J., 8 SCADDEN PL., CURTIN, ACT 2605 AUS
33900 JONES, ALAN, 23 JETTY RD., LARGS BAY, SA 5016 AUS
33901 SCHOCH, GUNTER, 635 BARDAL BAY., WINNIPEG, MAN R2G 0J1 CAN
33902 MCBRIDE, TERRY, 218 ASSINIBOINE DR., SASKATOON, SAS S7K 4A2 CAN
33903 LEIPPY, JEAN, BOX 1682., VALLEYVIEW, ALB T0H 3N0 CAN
33904 WEST, DONALD, 40 COURTNEY DR., MONTREAL WEST, QUE H4X 1M5 CAN
33905 MAIN, GORDON, 103-70 BAIF BLVD., RICHMOND HILL, ONT L4C 5L2 CAN
33906 BURT, HEATHER, 35 CHURCH ST APT.807., TORONTO, ONT M5E 1T3 CAN
33907 WHITESIDE, DON, 4 NEWGALE ST., NEPEAN, ONT K2H 5R2 CAN
33908 MACDOUGALL, JEAN, 30 IDAHO DR., SAULT STE MARIE, ONT P6A 4X7 CAN
33909 TRIPP, PAT, 336 PICCADILLY ST., LONDON, ONT N6A 1S7 CAN
33910 VERNON, RALPH, 109 LAKEVIEW CRES., NANAIMO, BC V9S 5N7 CAN
33911 OESTRIKE, IRENE, 5857 BROCKTON DR #3., INDIANAPOLIS, IN 46220 USA
33912 DAVEY, NORMAN, 41 COCKLE ST., O'CONNOR, ACT 2601 AUS
33913 COULSON, VICKI, PO BOX 43., YANDINA, QLD 4561 AUS
33914 RICHARDSON, MRS J., 9 OVENS CT., DANDENONG NTH, VIC 3175 AUS
33915 DAWBER, GAYLE, 8 TABULAM CRT., GROVEDALE, VIC 3216 AUS
33916 SOUTHWELL, MARY, 50 DEUTSCHER ST., AVONDALE HEIGHTS, VIC 3034 AUS
33917 REED, CHRISTINE, 6 TABULAM CRT., GROVEDALE, VIC 3216 AUS
33918 STEVENS, MRS M., PO BOX 66., EAST BENTLEIGH, VIC 3165 AUS
33919 TUCK, CAROLYN, 3 FREEMAN AVE., TRANMERE, SA 5073 AUS
33920 GENT, ELAINE, BOX 68., TRAYNING, WA 6488 AUS
33921 MCKENZIE, JAMES, 56 GLADSTONE AVE., SOUTH PERTH, WA 6151 AUS
33922 MERREY, NORMA, 72 BUCKTIN ST., COLLIE, WA 6225 AUS
33923 BOYCE, KAY, 8 DELL PDE., MORUYA, NSW 2537 AUS
33924 RAWLINGS, MRS B., 31 WOODVILLE AVE., WAHROONGA, NSW 2076 AUS
33925 HARRINGTON, PHILIP, "MERTON PARK" COOMA RD., VIA BRAIDWOOD, NSW 2622 AUS
33926 THOMPSON, MRS R., 593 PROGRESS., YANCO, NSW 2703 AUS
33927 PHILLIPS, JOHN, 44 GLEN ORME AVE., ORMOND, VIC 3204 AUS
33928 BROWN, ANN, 51 LEE ANN ST., FOREST HILL, VIC 3131 AUS
33929 HARDIE, MRS D., 152 TROUTS RD., EVERTON PARK, QLD 4053 AUS
33930 BAKEWELL, SHARON, PO BOX 30., WOY WOY, NSW 2256 AUS
33931 RICKARD, MRS B., 20 DEWDNEY RD., EMU PLAINS, NSW 2750 AUS
33932 MARTYR, JOAN, MAYNESIDE STATION., WINTON, QLD 4825 AUS
33933 BURKE, BRENDA, PO BOX 542., LIVERPOOL, NSW 2170 AUS
33934 ANDERSON, BARBARA, PO BOX W85., WEST PENNANT HILLS, NSW 2125 AUS
33935 BRAZIER, ALEC, 3 HEAL ST., HAMILTON HILL, WA 6163 AUS
33936 WAY, LESLEY, 1 HOLYROOD DR., VERMONT, VIC 3133 AUS
33937 JOHNSON, MRS I., PO BOX 215., BURLEIGH HEADS, QLD 4220 AUS
33938 COOK, SHELAGH, 395 BUNNERONG RD., MAROUBRA, NSW 2035 AUS
33939 TATTAM, MARIE, "TUNCOOEY" MSF 2284., MOREE, NSW 2400 AUS
33940 BESTFORD, MR J., 140 FLETCHER ST., WOOLLAHRA, NSW 2025 AUS
33941 CROSS, MRS D., 424 BOWNDS ST., LAVINGTON, NSW 2641 AUS
33942 TOCHER, MRS L., 11 CORANTO ST., ABBOTSFORD, NSW 2046 AUS
33943 HARPER, RENA, PO BOX 136., LEIGH, NTH AUCKLAND NZ
33944 HAY, LAURENCE, PO BOX 40-542., UPPER HUTT, NZ
33945 FORREST, JOHN, 5 RIMU ST., NEW LYNN, AUCK 1207 NZ
33946 BUCKINGHAM, LOUISE, 17 GROVE RD., KELBURN, WLTN 6005 NZ
33947 MCCOOL, PAULA, PO BOX 5893, WELLESLEY ST., AUCKLAND, NZ
33948 HARVEY, HEATHER, C/O POST OFFICE., MOORINE ROCK, WA 6425 AUS
33949 DOUGHTY, ALLAN, PO BOX 68-147., NEWTON, AUCK NZ
33950 CURSON, IRIS, 10 PLUNKET RD., MT EDEN, AUCK 4 NZ
33951 GARSCADDEN, WILLIAM, 1 WAIPARA ST., CHRISTCHURCH, 8002 NZ
33952 FLETCHER, PETER, 354 MUTU ST., TE AWAMUTU, NZ
33953 WATTS, HARVEY, 104 KAMAHI ST., STOKES VALLEY, LOWER HUTT NZ
33954 ANGELINI, HENRY, RD2., PAHIATUA, NZ
33955 NAYLOR, ROSS, "SPENNYMOORE" 1RD., OMAKAU, CENTRAL OTAGO NZ
33956 MOOR, JUDITH, 12 SYDNEY ST., KAIKOHE, NLAND NZ
33957 MCCARTHY, PATRICIA, 3 TAINUI TCE., TAWA, WGTN NZ
33958 TURLEY, MARJORIE, 59 KONTIKI RD., WHIRITOA, 2990 NZ
33959 HANSEN, RAEWYN, 122 LEWIS ST., INVERCARGILL, NZ
33960 PRICE, MARION, 79A NAYLOR ST., HAMILTON, NZ
33961 KEMPTON, MARGARET, "ELM GROVE" KEMPTON'S LINE., GREYTOWN, WAIRARAPA NZ
33962 PETRICEVICH, COLLEEN, 28 CASSINO ST., BAYSWATER, NORTH SHORE NZ
33963 ROBERSON, MRS M., 21 TRINIDAD RD., SUNNYNOOK, AUCK 10 NZ
33964 PITTAMS, VICKI, ECHOLANDS RD4., TAUMARUNUI, NZ
33965 CHERITON, IRIS, 62 RANGINUI ST., NGONGOTAHA, ROTORUA NZ
33966 SWITALLA, NOELINE, PDC BOX 12., MAKIKIHI, STH CNTBY 8790 NZ

33967 GALLIVAN, BRIAN, 33 BEACH ST., ST CLAIR, DUNEDIN OTAGO NZ
33968 MONAHAN, MRS E., 11 DAGMAR ST., DANNEVIRKE, NZ
33969 HUGGARD, DENNIS, 71 TIRIMOANA RD., GLENDENE, AUCK 1208 NZ
33970 KIRKBY, GAYNOR, 5 LESNEY ST., MARY HILL, DUNEDIN NZ
33971 ALCOCK, JULIANNE, 327 RUAHINE ST., PALMERSTON NORTH, NZ
33972 WARNER, MARIE, 10 MALLARD DR., ROTORUA, NZ
33973 PATTERSON, BEVERLEY, 22 WINDSOR ST., PALMERSTON NORTH, NZ
33974 BIRCHLER, DAVID, 56 KING EDWARD ST., ELTHAM, TARANAKI 4751 NZ
33975 GODFREY, MARGARET, 34 MORNINGTON RD., DUNEDIN, NZ
33976 MCKINSTRY, NEWTON, 13 MCCURDY ST., UPPER HUTT, NZ
33977 DAVIES, HAZEL, 2/21 TRENTHAM RD., PAPAKURA, NZ
33978 LESLIE, MAY, 13 TE PAKA CRES., KAMO, WHANGAREI NZ
33979 LAMB, JOY, 81 MARTIN ST., ROTORUA, NZ
33980 GIDDY, LEONIE, 9 MITCHELL ST., TAURANGA, NZ
33981 WHITMARSH, ROGER, 51 HOROEKA ST., STOKES VALLEY, LOWER HUTT NZ
33982 DAVIES, JACKIE, 74 LINTON ST., PALMERSTON NORTH, NZ
33983 BARON VON KOHORN, RALPH, PO BOX 2837., WELLINGTON, NZ
33984 PETERSON, NOLA, 2 RANELAGH TCE., CHRISTCHURCH, 2 NZ
33985 HUDSON, DOREEN, MAIN SOUTH RD NO 4 RD., GORE, SOUTHLAND NZ
33986 HARWOOD, MAC, RD1 TAKAKA., NELSON, NZ
33987 TURNER, MR W., 31 AOTAKI ST., OTAKI, NZ
33988 BOTTLE, JOAN, O'BRIEN RD 2 RD., WINTON, SOUTHLAND NZ
33989 WILLIAMS, GEOFFREY, 2 MORAY PL., WHIRITOA, 2991 NZ
33990 PULLAR, GRAEME, 11 WAINONE PL., WARKWORTH, 1492 NZ
33991 MCLEOD, JAMES, 22 BOWEN ST., CHRISTCHURCH, 4 NZ
33992 WILLIAMS, SHARRON, 188 STUDHOLME ST., MORRINSVILLE, NZ
33993 DREAVER, ISOBEL, RD2., OWAKA, SOUTH OTAGO NZ
33994 MORRIS, MR L., 676 SANDRINGHAM RD., MT ALBERT, AUCK 10 NZ
33995 BINSTED, AUDREY, PO BOX 79., MATAKANA, NZ
33996 BULL, MAUREEN, 36 WYNYARD CRES., TAMATEA, NAPIER NZ
33997 CLOUGH, HELEN, 58B PATESON ST., MT MAUNGANUI, NZ
33998 LYNG, DIANE, 34 MCINNES RD., WEYMOUTH, AUCK NZ
33999 HENRIKSON, CORINNE, C/O POST OFFICE TATUANUI., MORRINSVILLE, WTN NZ
34000 MIDDLETON, KAREN, BOAT HARBOUR RD RD1., WHITIANGA, 2856 NZ
34001 MORGAN, PATRICIA, 19 EASTONS RD., WESTPORT, NZ
34002 RIVERS, LORNA, PO BOX 42., HAPPY VALLEY, SA 5159 AUS
34003 CHRISTIANSEN, ANTHONY, 3 KOWHAI ST., HAWERA, NZ
34004 LUCAS, LORAINE, WEST RIVERBANK FARM., RD1 MOTUEKA, NELSON NZ
34005 MALCOLM, ELIZABETH, 3/5 MAIDA RD., EPPING, NSW 2121 AUS
34006 BURGES, PATRICIA, 1 PENINSULA CT., THURGOONA, NSW 2640 AUS
34007 SPRINGALL, RICHARD, PO BOX 92., MT ELIZA, VIC 3930 AUS
34008 MORRISON, BRUCE, 4 MALBA PL., ESPERANCE, WA 6450 AUS
34009 SHEPHERD, JOY, 22 GROSE AVE., BARRACK HEIGHTS, NSW 2528 AUS
34010 STORCK, JOHN, 117 HIGH ST., DONCASTER, VIC 3108 AUS
34011 GARDNER, NORMA, 145 GRAHAM RD., ROSANNA, VIC 3084 AUS
34012 REYNOLDS, HUNTLEY, PO BOX 1., BRAIDWOOD, NSW 2622 AUS
34013 SHERMAN, ANNE, 42 NORTH ARM RD., MIDDLE COVE, NSW 2068 AUS
34014 COLLYER, DAVID, 40 PRINCES ST NORTH., BALLARAT, VIC 3350 AUS
34015 HAMMOND, JEAN, 6 SCHOOL RD., ELIMBAH, QLD 4516 AUS
34016 PHILBEY, MARILYN, PO BOX 308., KADINA, SA 5554 AUS
34017 KNOLLE, WENDY, 4/1 BATTERY SQUARE., BATTERY POINT, TAS 7004 AUS
34018 BRANNIGAN, EDWARD, 15 THE GARDENS, 22 JANE ST., ARANA HILLS, QLD 4054 AUS
34019 BULLOCK, MISS E., 15 CRESFIELD ST., ZILLMERE, QLD 4034 AUS
34020 DOSSETTO, DAVID, PO BOX 145., KEDRON, QLD 4031 AUS
34021 HOLDING, MARGARET, 24 COLLINGS ST., GEEBUNG, QLD 4034 AUS
34022 DAWSON, BRIAN, 1 BAYVIEW TCE., CLAYFIELD, QLD 4011 AUS
34023 CROWLEY, RICHARD, 5 DAY ST., LEICHHARDT, NSW 2040 AUS
34024 ROBERSON, DARYL, 37 LAGOON ST., MORUYA, NSW 2537 AUS
34025 VELLA, JAN, 6 WHYALLA CL., ST JOHNS PARK, NSW 2176 AUS
34026 RYDE DIST HISTORICAL SOC INC, 770 VICTORIA RD., RYDE, NSW 2112 AUS
34027 CASSIDY, JENNIFER, 4/577 WEBB ST., LAVINGTON, NSW 2641 AUS
34028 MALONE, ENID, 298 SYLVANIA RD., GYMEA, NSW 2227 AUS
34029 CLEMENTS, PAUL, 46 MORTON RD., BURWOOD, VIC 3125 AUS
34030 MCGRODER, MRS J., 39 HOBSON ST., STRATFORD, VIC 3862 AUS
34031 VARDY, JUDITH, 18 KENTUCKY AVE., NORLANE, VIC 3214 AUS
34032 CHRISTIE, MRS K., 10 BISCAY CT., DINGLEY, VIC 3172 AUS
34033 MCDONELL, IAN, PO BOX 272., GISBORNE, VIC 3437 AUS
34034 BRIGGS, MRS N., 6 DALTON CRT., WANGARATTA, VIC 3677 AUS
34035 ELLIS, ROBYN, 1/112 NORTH RD., RESERVOIR, VIC 3073 AUS
34036 RANIERI, PATRICIA, 13 ELSIE GVE., MT EVELYN, VIC 3796 AUS
34037 MILLER MRS M., 6 VIEWHILL CRES., ELTHAM, VIC 3095 AUS
34038 PETERS, MARLENE, 35 LANDERS RD., LANE COVE, NSW 2066 AUS

34039 NEILL, MRS S., 9 NEWTON ST., STAWELL, VIC 3380 AUS
34040 MINTER, MRS M., 237 MCCAFFREY DR., RANKIN PARK, NSW 2287 AUS
34041 EARL, MAVIS, 6 DEAKIN ST., SUNBURY, VIC 3429 AUS
34042 SMITH, EDNA, 19 ST JAMES ST., WHITTINGTON, VIC 3219 AUS
34043 VASSIE, IAN, 34 CANBERRA GVE., EAST BRIGHTON, VIC 3187 AUS
34044 ABEL, LORRAINE, 4 BUNTING CRT., MUNDINGBURRA, QLD 4812 AUS
34045 SHOOTER, EDWINA, PO BOX 292., NARROGIN, WA 6312 AUS
34046 WESCOMBE, GARY, 9 SAUNDRIDGE RD., COOEE, TAS 7320 AUS
34047 RICHER, M. L, 429-840 SPRINGLAND., OTTAWA, ONT K1V 6L6 CAN
34048 KRISTIANSEN, ELAINE, 12576 103 AVE., SURREY, BC V3V 3G4 CAN
34049 SCOTT, MAUREEN, 14 PRINCES ST., CAMBRIDGE, WKT NZ
34050 MOGINIE, MRS J, 30 HARBOURVIEW RD., LOWER HUTT, NZ
34051 BARLOW, CHERYL, 353A COLLEGE ST., COBOURG, ONT K9A 3V5 CAN
34052 LAMBERT, RONALD, 11 ELLEN ST W., KITCHENER, ONT N2H 4K1 CAN
34053 WALKER, MRS L., 138 KENNINGTON BAY., WINNIPEG, MAN R2N 2L3 CAN
34054 SIMMONS, MARJORIE, 280 REGENT ST., KINGSTON, ONT K7L 4K6 CAN
34055 PURDY, MONICA, 17173-75 AVENUE., EDMONTON, ALB T5T 2R3 CAN
34056 PURDY, JUDITH, 2041 FLEETWOOD AVE., KAMLOOPS, BC V2B 4S3 CAN
34057 BUCKRELL, RITA, RR2., BURGESSVILLE, ONT N0J 1C0 CAN
34058 WILSON, MR J., 304-460 WESTVIEW ST., COQUITLAM, BC V3K 6C9 CAN
34059 OPPERTSHAUSER, JOAN, 3886 CEDAR HILL RD., VICTORIA, BC V8P 3Z6 CAN
34060 WALLACE, MARY, RR2., MOUNT HOPE, ONT L0R 1W0 CAN
34061 VAUGEOIS, P.-M., 17 MADONNA DR., ST-ALBERT, ALB T8N 1G9 CAN
34062 PEARSON, ALMA, BOX 888., WHITEWOOD, SAS S0G 5C0 CAN
34063 OSTROWSKI, MAE, 306-36 EAST 14TH AVE., VANCOUVER, BC V5T 4C9 CAN
34064 WILSON, MR S., 703, 321-10 ST NW., CALGARY, ALB T2N 1V7 CAN
34065 BULLOCK, NELDA, 3310 KEHO PL., LETHBRIDGE, ALB T1K 3P9 CAN
34066 SMITH, DAVID, RR#3 SITE 42., SUMMERLAND, BC V0H 1Z0 CAN
34067 COTTON, ROSS, 673 GEORGE ST., BURLINGTON, ONT L7R 2V8 CAN
34068 RASHOTTE, DEBORAH, 24 LIBERTY ST NO., BOWMANVILLE, ONT L1C 2L6 CAN
34069 GALE, ANNA, 1827 HURRICANE RD., RR2 WELLAND, ONT L3B 5N5 CAN
34070 SPALL, BONITA, 19 CALEDONIA ST., GUELPH, ONT N1G 2C4 CAN
34071 LEGAULT, LOLA, 519 ANDERSON DR., CORNWALL, ONT K6H 5N4 CAN
34072 MCCAMUS, GLADYS, 640 MONTROSE ST., PETERBOROUGH, ONT K9J 3C4 CAN
34073 BEDELL, JOHN, 140 LOTHIAN AVE., TORONTO, ONT M8Z 4L4 CAN
34074 STERRITT, NEIL, 1407 CHARTRAND AVE., ORLEANS, ONT K1E 1H9 CAN
34075 VIRKUTIS, DEBRA, 1033 VALETTA ST., LONDON, ONT N6H 2Z9 CAN
34076 GENN, DAVID, 10251 ALGONQUIN DR., RICHMOND, BC V7A 3A5 CAN
34077 WARNER, STERLING, VARTY RD RR#3., TWEED, ONT K0K 3J0 CAN
34078 JACKSON, WESLEY, 4 BLAIRWOOD TCE., SCARBOROUGH, ONT M1W 1W8 CAN
34079 NEWMAN, TONY, 155 LAVEROCK AVE., RICHMOND HILL, ONT L4C 4K1 CAN
34080 MONTGOMERY, NELLIE, #305-1437 MARTIN ST., WHITE ROCK, BC V4B 3W8 CAN
34081 BARDWELL, MR H., 1040 CONNAUGHT CRES., SARNIA, ONT N7S 1C6 CAN
34082 GODIN, JOHN, 19 MILTON AVE W., CAMBRIDGE, ONT N3C 2Y3 CAN
34083 PETERSEN, THOMAS, 1003-900 DYNES RD., OTTAWA, ONT K2C 3L6 CAN
34084 ASSAILLY, MARY ANN, BOX 1306., BIGGAR, SAS S0K 0M0 CAN
34085 COLLIER, MRS A., BOX 1228., VIRDEN, MAN R0M 2C0 CAN
34086 SUMMERER, MARION, 411 ROCKLAND RD., CAMPBELL RIVER, BC V9W 1N7 CAN
34087 FRISKE, MARLENE, RR5 SITE 6 COMP 8., PRINCE GEORGE, BC V2N 2J3 CAN
34088 BROWN, MR D., 6 INGLEWOOD DR., TORONTO, ONT M4T 1G8 CAN
34089 MEGOW, DEE, 23 AYRE PT RD., SCARBOROUGH, ONT M1M 1G4 CAN
34090 SMITH, BONITA, 55 WILSONVIEW AVE., GUELPH, ONT N1G 2W5 CAN
34091 NORRISH, MIRIAM, 32229 14TH AVE., MISSION, BC V2V 2N6 CAN
34092 COOK, MRS S., RR#2 (DENNISS DR)., BRACEBRIDGE, ONT P0B 1C0 CAN
34093 YOUNG, SUSAN, 75 GRASS AVE., ST CATHARINES, ONT L2R 1T2 CAN
34094 COMFORT, MAURICE, RR#2., THORNDALE, ONT N0M 2P0 CAN
34095 DEN OUDEN, OLAV, 64 CENTENNIAL CR., NEW HAMBURG, ONT N03 2G0 CAN
34096 HARPER, RUTH, 2 CAROL PL., PORT HOPE, ONT L1A 3Y5 CAN
34097 DUROCHER, MR C., 76 BELL ST., DELHI, ONT N4B 1X1 CAN
34098 WILSON, LILLIAN, 334 CHARLTON AVE WEST., HAMILTON, ONT L8P 2E7 CAN
34099 BIRD, CHARLES, BOX 165., MIRROR, ALB T0B 3C0 CAN
34100 THOMPSON, EDNA, 1124 EDGEWOOD RD., NORTH VANCOUVER, BC V7R 1Y9 CAN
34101 MCCONNELL, MS B., #306-615-6TH NW., PORTAGE LA PRAIRIE, MAN R1N 2K3 CAN
34102 BAILEY, MRS P., PO BOX 479., ENGLEHART, ONT P0J 1H0 CAN
34103 ELLIOTT, JOHNSTON, 667 LAKESHORE DR., NORTH BAY, ONT P1A 2G1 CAN
34104 MARTIN, FRANK, 1117 MUNRO ST., VICTORIA, BC V9A 5P2 CAN
34105 SHONE, DAVID, 966 PARKHILL AVE., BURLINGTON, ONT L7T 1T8 CAN
34106 COXON, ELAINE, RR#2., LUCAN, ONT N0M 2J0 CAN
34107 ANDERSON, ROBERT, 101 CHIPPEWA CRES W., LETHBRIDGE, ALB T1K 5B4 CAN
34108 OLDE, EVELYN, PO BOX 297., CLINTON, ONT N0M 1L0 CAN
34109 WILSON, ELENORA, 5004 BRISEBOIS DR NW., CALGARY, ALB T2L 2G5 CAN
34110 SIMPSON, HARVEY, COMP 45 SITE 20 RR1., ENDERBY, BC V0E 1V0 CAN

34111 HALL, BILL, 256 ATHABASCA AVE., FORT MCMURRAY, ALB T9J 1G6 CAN
34112 FREW, NORMA, RR1., NESTLETON, ONT L0B 1L0 CAN
34113 EDEY, JOHN, 9254-74 ST., EDMONTON, ALB T6B 2B4 CAN
34114 MCBRIDE, CHARLES, 10 OLD ORCHARD AVE., GRIMSBY, ONT L3M 3H7 CAN
34115 MARSHALL, STEVE, 434 TALLWOOD DR., ORILLIA, ONT L3V 2G9 CAN
34116 THRAPP, SHIRLEY, 303-5926 TISDALL ST., VANCOUVER, BC V5Z 3N2 CAN
34117 ANDERSON, JOAN, 501 BOLIVAR ST., PETERBOROUGH, ONT K9J 4R5 CAN
34118 STEELE, THOMAS, 4550 VENABLES ST., BURNABY, BC V5C 3A7 CAN
34119 MATHIESON, MR H., 676 BOREBANK ST., WINNIPEG, MAN R3N 1G2 CAN
34120 GUEST, MARGARET, 24 WESLEY RD., REGINA, SAS S4S 5P4 CAN
34121 CORSON, LILY, PO BOX 41., PLENTY, SAS S0L 2R0 CAN
34122 NAGY, WILMA, 2820 SHAKESPEARE ST., VICTORIA, BC V8R 4H1 CAN
34123 FOSKETT, MRS H., 712 BROOKRIDGE PL., VICTORIA, VC V8Z 3B9 CAN
34124 DAHLING, ROBERT, 401 MCFONLAN CRT. 510 COMOX RD., NANAIMO, BC V9R 3J1 CAN
34125 KINVIG, ELLEN, JONES FLAT RD RR3., SUMMERLAND, BC V0H 1Z0 CAN
34126 FOX, MRS L., RR 4 BOX 18 SHAVER RD., QUESNEL, BC V2J 3H8 CAN
34127 BERMAN, GAYE, 25 PAYNTER DR., WILLOWDALE, ONT M2H 2G4 CAN
34128 MINHINNICK, JOYCE, 4 LORNE AVE., LEAMINGTON, ONT N8H 2H7 CAN
34129 YOUNG, BRENDA, 14 NASSAU RD., ST CATHARINES, ONT L2M 4B1 CAN
34130 JACKSON, MRS M., 60 LORAINE DR., ST CATHARINES, ONT L2P 3N8 CAN
34131 PERRY, FRANK, 1297 AMESBROOKE DR., OTTAWA, ONT K2C 2E8 CAN
34132 SWEET, MR H., PO BOX 29., LOWBANKS, ONT N0A 1K0 CAN
34133 MCCARTNEY, SHEILA, 513 BOND ST E., OSHAWA, ONT L1G 1C2 CAN
34134 WILLIAMS, HESBA, 96 HOWARD AVE., HAMILTON, ONT L9A 2W5 CAN
34135 MAIDES, KAREN, 14 BURNHAM RD., OTTAWA, ONT K1S 0J8 CAN
34136 THOMAS, PHILIPPE, BUREAU OUTREMONT CP 72., MONTREAL, QUE H2V 4M6 CAN
34137 CAIN, JOYCE, 26 NORTHWOOD DR., WILLOWDALE, ONT M2M 2J8 CAN
34138 LYONS, MRS M., 5 SHADY GOLFWAY APT 1219., DON MILLS, ONT M3C 3A5 CAN
34139 DUINKER, PAULINE, 266 DONNELLY DR., MISSISSAUGA, ONT L5G 2M5 CAN
34140 GREEN, MRS C., 21 RAVINA PL., BROCKVILLE, ONT K6V 4S8 CAN
34141 PHILLIPS, RUTH, BOX 267., RAPID CITY, MAN R0K 1W0 CAN
34142 BROWNING, PEARL, 27 CHEROVAN DR SW., CALGARY, ALB T2V 2P3 CAN
34143 ROOK, GORDON, BOX 494., LASHBURN, SAS S0M 1H0 CAN
34144 ROGERS, BERNICE, 17 MONTCALM AVE., CAMROSE, ALB T4V 2K9 CAN
34145 SAYERS, JAMES, 12 NORWICH RD., STONEY CREEK, ONT L8E 1Z6 CAN
34146 MOSIUK, BRENDA, #425-1630 HENDERSON HWY., WINNIPEG, MAN R2G 2B9 CAN
34147 MURPHY, WILLIAM, 60 INVERLOCHY BLVD APT 702., THORNHILL, ONT L3T 4T7 CAN
34148 HODGSON, ROD, PO BOX 134., HUDSON, QUE J0P 1H0 CAN
34149 HODSOLL, DOREEN, 66 THE KINGSWAY., TORONTO, ONT M8X 2T4 CAN
34150 LEWIS, OLGA, 190 MASSEY CRES., RENFREW, ONT K7V 4C1 CAN
34151 WELLS, MARIAN, BOX 2112., SWAN RIVER, MAN R0L 1Z0 CAN
34152 MAVINS, JACK, BOX 6 GRP 70., RR1 ANOLA, MAN R0E 0A0 CAN
34153 TANNER, FRANCES, 512-36 ST SW., CALGARY, ALB T3C 1P7 CAN
34154 REAUME, HELEN, 204-10 TRILLIUM VILLAGE., CHATHAM, ONT N7L 4A1 CAN
34155 FISHER, JOAN, 131 SWANWICK AVE., TORONTO, ONT M4E 2A2 CAN
34156 BEARSS, CATHERINE, PO BOX 13., SPRINGFIELD, ONT N0L 2J0 CAN
34157 RILEY, CATHY, #604-705 NORTH RD., COQUITLAM, BC V3J 1P7 CAN
34158 NEUFELD, MISS D., 4½ 8 AVE SOUTH., KENORA, ONT P9N 2G8 CAN
34159 MICHAELS, LOIS, 905 RANKIN RD., VICTORIA, BC V9A 6V7 CAN
34160 MITCHELL, DIANE, 124 DIVADALE DR., TORONTO, ONT M4G 2P4 CAN
34161 GUILBAULT, JEAN, SITE 6 BOX 11 RR1., CARVEL, ALB T0E 0H0 CAN
34162 VICKERY, VERNON, 102 SOUVENIR DR., PINCOURT, QUE J7V 3N8 CAN
34163 COBURN, KENNETH, BOX 1266., VANDERHOOF, BC V0J 3A0 CAN
34164 MANSUS, ROXY, 1051 BATTLE ST., KAMLOOPS, BC V2C 2N2 CAN
34165 O'BYRNE, RITA, 57 OTTAWA ST., SOUTHAMPTON, ONT N0H 2L0 CAN
34166 HAMBLETON, GRETA, BLACKWATER RD RR#4., SUNDERLAND, ONT L0C 1H0 CAN
34167 MCLEOD, MARGARET, BOX 385., COBDEN, ONT K0J 1K0 CAN
34168 LEGARE, BLANCHE, 310 ST-GEORGES O #202., LEVIS, QUE G6V 7E6 CAN
34169 GRAHAM, DOROTHY, 1107-1590 HENDERSON HWY., WINNIPEG, MAN R2G 2B8 CAN
34170 CLAUSING, JAMES, 23 GORDON ST., CLIFTON HILL, VIC 3068 AUS
34171 HELLWEGE, THOMAS, 17 PIPER ST., KILMORE, VIC 3764 AUS
34172 POPE, JOANNE, 915 BELLERINE HWY., LEOPOLD, VIC 3224 AUS
34173 MARTIN, ANTHONY, 3 FARMER ST., EAST BRIGHTON, VIC 3187 AUS
34174 DRUMMOND, GERARD, 15 MYRTLE ST., GLEN WAVERLEY, VIC 3150 AUS
34175 WHITWELL, MICHAEL, 37 DUFF PDE., VIEWBANK, VIC 3084 AUS
34176 TOBIN, JUNE, 6 BEDDOE AVE., EAST BRIGHTON, VIC 3187 AUS
34177 TYMMS, MS S., 1 LUCERNE ST., ASHBURTON, VIC 3147 AUS
34178 JAMES, MARILYN, PO BOX 403., HORSHAM, VIC 3402 AUS
34179 RIVETT, MISS S., BOX 431., UNLEY, SA 5061 AUS
34180 UITDENBOGERD, JOHN, 24 CRANWELL ST., THORNLIE, WA 6108 AUS
34181 MCPHAIL, MRS D., PO BOX 343., WILLETTON, WA 6155 AUS
34182 GENTLEMAN, STEPHEN, 20 ROSE ST., BLACKALLS PARK, NSW 2283 AUS

34183 WILSON, UNA, PO BOX 194., ROSE BAY, NSW 2029 AUS
34184 MILLHOUSE, MAXWELL, PO BOX 106., PADSTOW, NSW 2211 AUS
34185 NEWSOME, CAROL, "SPRINGFIELD" WELLINGROVE., VIA GLEN INNES, NSW 2370 AUS
34186 DANE, GEOFF, PO BOX 492., BELCONNEN, ACT 2616 AUS
34187 COGHLAN, ROBYN, 92 ERLDUNDA CIRCUIT., HAWKER, ACT 2614 AUS
34188 PEARSON, ALISON, "BROOKLANDS" CORDELIA., INGHAM, QLD 4850 AUS
34189 REES, MRS V., 164 JESMOND RD., INDOOROOPILLY, QLD 4068 AUS
34190 RICHARDSON, SHIRLEY, 228 MALLAWA DR., PALM BEACH, QLD 4221 AUS
34191 KELLY, JACKIE, 3 IRENE CRT., CHELTENHAM, VIC 3192 AUS
34192 SHAND, MISS M., 52 RIO VISTA BLVD., FLORIDA GARDENS, QLD 4218 AUS
34193 TRELOAR, TRISHA, 29 DEVON AVE., NEWTON, SA 5074 AUS
34194 BUNDEY, DAVID, 57 SYDNEY ST., GLENSIDE, SA 5065 AUS
34195 MULLER, JANET, PO BOX 76., MOUNT GAMBIER, SA 5290 AUS
34196 KINKEAD, GRANT, BOX 4083MM GPO., MELBOURNE, VIC 3001 AUS
34197 PATTISON, JOHN, 12 TOOWONG AVE., KENSINGTON PARK, SA 5068 AUS
34198 KING, MRS A., 67 LINKSVIEW RD., SPRINGWOOD, NSW 2777 AUS
34199 MONETTE, JEAN, PO BOX 478., GRACEFIELD, QUE J0X 1W0 CAN
34200 LEWIS, URSULA, 216 HAYSBORO CRES SW., CALGARY, ALB T2V 3G3 CAN
34201 HEIGHES, PEGGY, 16A STONEHILL CT., KANATA, ONT K2M 1E5 CAN
34202 O'MALLEY, ARNOLD, 1709-641 BATHGATE DR., OTTAWA, ONT K1K 3Y3 CAN
34203 SCHUMACHER, VIRGINIA, 401-8TH ST EAST., DRUMHELLER, ALB T0J 0Y5 CAN
34204 CORNWALL, FRANK, RR3 UPPER GANGES RD., GANGES, BC V05 1E0 CAN
34205 PHILIP, CONNIE, BOX 2D-9., KNUTSFORD, BC V0E 2A0 CAN
34206 DOHERTY, PATRICIA, PO BOX 579., HANTSPORT, NS B0P 1P0 CAN
34207 SCHWARTZ, MARILYN, PO BOX 333., LR SACKVILLE, NS B4C 2T2 CAN
34208 PRETTY, HAROLD, 1974 MICHIGAN AVE., OTTAWA, ONT K1H 6Y2 CAN
34209 CHAPLIN, PHILIP, 263 FLORA ST APT 1., OTTAWA, ONT K1R 5R8 CAN
34210 COX, FLORENCE, 76 MARSHALL CRES., WINNIPEG, MAN R3T 0R4 CAN
34211 HYSLOP, JAYNE, 86 KENSINGTON AVE S., HAMILTON, ONT L8M 3H2 CAN
34212 STEHR, JENS, 1926 DANNISTON CRES., ORLEANS, ONT K1E 3R6 CAN
34213 KEATES, MARJORIE, PO BOX 78., ELGIN, ONT K0G 1E0 CAN
34214 LANCASTER, ELIZABETH, 67 SALEM GVE., LONDON, ONT M6K 1T9 CAN
34215 HANNA, WILLIAM, 605 UNION ST W., FERGUS, ONT N1G 2W1 CAN
34216 RULLER, MEL, PO BOX 749., ELORA, ONT N0B 1S0 CAN
34217 TETREAULT, ROLAND, 71 HILLTOP ST., SPRINGFIELD, MA 01128 USA
34218 WILSON, MRS D., 4660 VANTREIGHT DR., VICTORIA, BC V8N 3X1 CAN
34219 VOUT, GORDON, 14 PARKWOOD DR., COBOURG, ONT K9A 4J2 CAN
34220 WATSON, DONA, PO BOX 92., NEW SAREPTA, ALB T0B 3M0 CAN
34221 OSTROWSKI, JEAN, 115-1718 NEWTON ST., VICTORIA, BC V8R 2R2 CAN
34222 MORE, ROSEMARIE, 5730-9 AVENUE., EDSON, ALB T7E 1J4 CAN
34223 OBEE, DAVID, 4124 55TH ST N E., CALGARY, ALB T1Y 4B6 CAN
34224 KENNEDY, DARA, 85 MURRAY DR., AURORA, ONT L4G 2C4 CAN
34225 MAYNARD, CATHERINE, #309-1948 MCCALLUM RD., ABBOTSFORD, BC V2S 3M9 CAN
34226 MCCONNELL, MARGARET, BOX 161., DODSLAND, SAS S0L 0V0 CAN
34227 DURNING, MS C., 2130 SCOTT APT 12., ST LAURENT, QUE H4M 1T2 CAN
34228 DUNNILL, MARY, 405-165 N COURT ST., THUNDER BAY, ONT P7A 7V1 CAN
34229 PETERS, DOROTHY, 110-999 BERKLEY RD., VANCOUVER, BC V7H 1Y3 CAN
34230 SANDERSON, MRS E., 3017 LARKDOWNE RD., VICTORIA, BC V8R 5N3 CAN
34231 ROBERTS, MARY, 198 LOCKHART DR., ST CATHARINES, ONT L2T 1W4 CAN
34232 JOHNSON, DONALDA, BOX 165A., CENTRAL BUTTE, SAS S0H 0T0 CAN
34233 BRYANS, JERRY, 324 PRESTON DR., OSHAWA, ONT L1J 6Y7 CAN
34234 CLARKE, MARION, BOX 461 ELM AVE., HUDSON HEIGHTS, QUE J0P 1J0 CAN
34235 GRANT, JACK, 9227-168 ST., EDMONTON, ALB T5R 2V8 CAN
34236 BAYLISS, GEORGE, SITE 6A COMP 13 RR5., VERNON, BC V1T 6L8 CAN
34237 BAYLISS, PATRICIA, SITE 6A COMP 13 RR5., VERNON, BC V1T 6L8 CAN
34238 TURNER, DOROTHY, RR1., ROCKWOOD, ONT N0B 2K0 CAN
34239 ROACH, MARY LOUISE, 190 SOUTH KENOGAMI AVE., THUNDER BAY, ONT P7B 4R9 CAN
34240 HAYES, MS C., BOX 138., MEOTA, SAS S0M 1X0 CAN
34241 PHIPPS, SHEILA, RR3., AILSA CRAIG, ONT N0M 1A0 CAN
34242 DE LEEUW, CLAIRE, RR3., COLBORNE, ONT K0K 1S0 CAN
34243 CONNELL, MARY, 329 ROSEDALE DR., WHITBY, ONT L1N 1Z2 CAN
34244 MCGILL, JEAN, 501-190 COLIN AVE., TORONTO, ONT M5P 2C6 CAN
34245 BELLEMARE, LAVERNE, 905-52 STREET., EDSON, ALB T7E 1K4 CAN
34246 SCHULTZ, EARL, 1358 MOUNTAINSIDE CRES., ORLEANS, ONT K1E 3G4 CAN
34247 MOWAT, WILLIAM, PO BOX 1334., STOUFFVILLE, ONT L4A 8A3 CAN
34248 HILL, DOUGLAS, 1939 MULBERRY CRES., GLOUCESTER, ONT K1J 8J8 CAN
34249 STAPLETON, MRS D., 330 CENTRUM BLVD APT 407., ORLEANS, ONT K1E 3W2 CAN
34250 HALFYARD, ROBERT, 9 FRONTENAC DR., ST CATHARINES, ONT L2M 2E1 CAN
34251 BISHOP, FRANCES, 50-1750 FRESHFIELD RD., KAMLOOPS, BC V2E 1R6 CAN
34252 KEELY, CAROL, 8848 ROSLIN PL., SURREY, BC V3V 6L8 CAN
34253 MACVICAR, WAYNE, 527 HAY ST., GLACE BAY, NS B1A 5L8 CAN
34254 DE CAEN, ROLAND, 3822-6TH STREET SW., CALGARY, ALB T3S 2M8 CAN

34255 MELLEN, FRED, PO BOX 374., BOW ISLAND, ALB T0K 0G0 CAN
34256 GLADISH, DOROTHY, PO BOX 1887., HIGH RIVER, ALB T0L 1B0 CAN
34257 TRAHER, JOSEPH, 928 WELLINGTON ST N., LONDON, ONT N6A 3S9 CAN
34258 LUKEY, PAULINE, 404-562 RITHET ST., VICTORIA, BC V8V 1E2 CAN
34259 BYRNE, CAROL, 93 BINSWOOD AVE., TORONTO, ONT M4C 3P1 CAN
34260 BROWN, SHEILA, 2204-650 PARLIAMENT ST., TORONTO, ONT M4X 1R3 CAN
34261 BEESON, IVY, UNIT 11 BOX 117., GOSNELLS, WA 6110 AUS
34262 CHARLTON, MRS C., PO BOX 25., STANLEY, TAS 7331 AUS
34263 MACALPINE, MRS L., 79 BEACONSFIELD RD., CHATSWOOD, NSW 2067 AUS
34264 BUTTERFIELD, HEATHER, 30 CYPRESS AVE., WENDOUREE, VIC 3355 AUS
34265 OSCARI, DEIRDRE, 3 VICTORIA ST., BULLEEN, VIC 3105 AUS
34266 STOOKE, BRIAN, 12 YORK AVE., IVANHOE EAST, VIC 3079 AUS
34267 BURDEU, PERCIVAL, 335 JELLS RD., MULGRAVE, VIC 3170 AUS
34268 GRANT, RODERICK, C/O CRA LTD., GPO BOX 384D., MELBOURNE, VIC 3001 AUS
34269 BROOKES, AVERIL, 5 LUTZ CRT., BUNDABERG, QLD 4670 AUS
34270 BELCHER, HARRY, 17 MILLCAN ST., WAVELL HEIGHTS, QLD 4012 AUS
34271 CROCE, JULIE, 212 VICTORIA ST., ST GEORGE, QLD 4487 AUS
34272 HUTCHIN, ERIC, 2 MCMULLEN AVE., CARLINGFORD, NSW 2118 AUS
34273 HEDGES, ANNETTE, 14 CARRINGTON AVE., STRATHFIELD, NSW 2135 AUS
34274 SNOW, GINETTE, 6 VANCOUVER ST., RED HILL, ACT 2603 AUS
34275 TOWNS, BEVERLEY, 34 GELLIBRAND ST., CAMPBELL, ACT 2601 AUS
34276 DE BOARD, MARGARET, LOT 108 ROSEHILL DR., BURPENGARY, QLD 4505 AUS
34277 LEGGE, DENISE, 58 CHAPMAN ST., PROSERPINE, QLD 4800 AUS
34278 FLESSER, DEBORAH, 6 BALOO CRES., NERANG, QLD 4211 AUS
34279 MEMBREY, DIANNE, 15 DIMBOOLA RD., HORSHAM, VIC 3400 AUS
34280 HARRISON, BETTY, 35 HAVERFIELD ST., ECHUCA, VIC 3564 AUS
34281 GLOVER, JOHN, 6 IVY ST., HORSHAM, VIC 3400 AUS
34282 YOUNG, PETER, 4 KERIN ST., MOE, VIC 3825 AUS
34283 STIRLING, BARBARA, 13 TREVELYAN ST., ELSTERNWICK, VIC 3185 AUS
34284 JOHNSON, HEATHER, LOT 18 DANDENONG-HASTINGS RD., LANGWARRIN, VIC 3910 AUS
34285 BAKER, WENDY, 103 RATTRAY RD., MONTMORENCY, VIC 3094 AUS
34286 MOTT, MR P., 5 FORREST AVE., VALLEY VIEW, SA 5093 AUS
34287 MCLEARY, MRS S., 7 KADINA ST., THE GAP, QLD 4061 AUS
34288 TAITE, CAVELL, 50 PARADISE ISLAND., SURFERS PARADISE, QLD 4217 AUS
34289 LEWIS, JUNE, 59 WILLIAMS RD., NORTH COBURG, VIC 3058 AUS
34290 GROVE, JEAN, C/O A.NORRIS, PO BOX 162., ECHUCA, VIC 3564 AUS
34291 ROBERTS, MISS N., 56 UNION ST., EAST BRIGHTON, VIC 3187 AUS
34292 LEE, ADRIENNE, 16 BROMLEY ST., BECKENHAM, WA 6107 AUS
34293 JOHNSON, TERRY, 79 THE ESCARPMENT., WILLETTON, WA 6155 AUS
34294 WILKINSON, VIC, PO BOX 35., KOORINGAL, NSW 2650 AUS
34295 COSIER, MRS J., 4 STANLEY ST., MERRYLANDS, NSW 2160 AUS
34296 NOKES, MRS J., 42 JOHNSTON ST., ANNANDALE, NSW 2038 AUS
34297 MADDERN, MRS A., BOX 36., KANIUA, VIC 3419 AUS
34298 BRAY, ROBIN, 37 SMITH ST., MACEDON, VIC 3440 AUS
34299 MORRISON, MR V, HAROLD RD., SKYE, VIC 3977 AUS
34300 HOOD, ROBERT, 2 OVENS COURT., CROYDON, VIC 3136 AUS
34301 LLOYD, LEANNE, 19 DEAN ST LONG GULLY., BENDIGO, VIC 3550 AUS
34302 PRIOR, JOHN, 107 WEE WAA ST., BOGGABRI, NSW 2382 AUS
34303 WESSELS, PIETER, PO BOX 219., POTTS POINT, NSW 2011 AUS
34304 HOWES, BERNICE, 66 HARE ST., CASINO, NSW 2470 AUS
34305 EDWARDS, YVONNE, 59 DEBENHAM AVE., LEUMEAH, NSW 2560 AUS
34306 THOMAS, CAROLE, 10 EDITH AVE., CONCORD, NSW 2137 AUS
34307 BUSCALL, BETTY, C/O POST OFFICE., UKI, NSW 2484 AUS
34308 WOOD, EDNA, 46 HALL ST., SHERWOOD, QLD 4075 AUS
34309 BINNS, ELIZABETH, 3A CHAMBERLAIN ST., TOOWOOMBA, QLD 4350 AUS
34310 SIMPSON, LACHLAN, PO BOX 161., NEDLANDS, WA 6009 AUS
34311 HOWELL-JONES, MADELINE, THE LODGE., NASEBY, NTH NN6 7DP ENG
34312 ARNOPP, MR R., 6/69B STATION RD., LONDON, E7 0EU ENG
34313 CRITTELL, ANNETTE, 6 LINNET CL., SELSDON, SRY CR2 8PZ ENG
34314 CUTTEN, DAVID, 26 CORNEL, AMINGTON., TAMWORTH, STS B77 4EF ENG
34315 JENSON, VALERIE, 18 PEMBROKE GDNS., RAINHAM, KEN ME8 8TD ENG
34316 DAWSON, DENISE, 109 CROFTON RD., ORPINGTON, KEN BR6 8HX ENG
34317 PERRY, JAMES, 7 HOLMESDALE, BRIDGEWATER RD., WEYBRIDGE, SRY KT13 0EG ENG
34318 JOSEPH, ANTHONY, 25 WESTBOURNE RD., EDGBASTON, B15 3TX ENG
34319 EASTLAKE, MISS S., 9 CRACKWELL ST., TENBY, PEM SA70 7HA WLS
34320 WHITE, MISS D., RUPERT LODGE, LYNDHURST RD., LANDFORD, WIL SP5 2AF ENG
34321 MOORE, RICHARD, 1 CAMBRIDGE CL., SWINDON, SN3 1JG ENG
34322 PALLETT, MR C., 55 WEST VIEW., PARBOLD, LAN WN8 7NT ENG
34323 CARYSFORTH, ROBERT, 70 PRIORY LANE., PENWORTHAM, LAN PR1 04S ENG
34324 BROWN, AUBREY, 9 WYNDHAM RD., TAUNTON, SOM TA6 6DX ENG
34325 SINCLAIR, BELINDA, 26 DORRINGTON CRT., S. NORWOOD HILL, LND SE24 6BE ENG
34326 BRIGGS, SUSAN, 9 KINGFISHER RISE, POPLARS., STEVENAGE, HRT SG2 9PF ENG

34327 FITZGERALD, T., 39 OAKGROVE RD., BISHOPSTOKE EASTLEIGH, HAM S05 6LN ENG
34328 WALKER, RITA, 9 DYSON HILL., HONLEY, YKS HD7 2JJ ENG
34329 VESSEY, MARIAN, 6 OAKDALE RD., BROADMEADOWS, DBY DE55 3PA ENG
34330 COLE, DARRELL, 15-1680 ST MARY'S RD., WINNIPEG, MAN R2N 1C9 CAN
34331 BRUTON, ROSE, 4390 GRAND BLVD #201., MONTREAL, QUE H4B 2X8 CAN
34332 ROOCROFT, JANIS, 291 MAPLE ST., NEWMARKET, ONT L3Y 3K3 CAN
34333 COATES, MAX, 123 WATHAMAN TCE., SASKATOON, SAS S7K 4P5 CAN
34334 MARSH, SHEILA, COMP 1 SITE #5 RR#6., VERNON, BC V1T 6Y5 CAN
34335 SHEEN, GLORIA, 76 GARDEN AVE., RICHMOND HILL, ONT L4C 6M1 CAN
34336 MILLER, CATHERINE, 40 COPPERFIELD DR., CAMBRIDGE, ONT N1R 7V4 CAN
34337 BROWN, LORNA, 1596 CHAMPLAIN DR., PETERBOROUGH, ONT K9L 1N6 CAN
34338 HAYHOE, MISS E., 126 KING ST WEST., HAMILTON, ONT L8S 1M4 CAN
34339 WYSE, JUDITH, 7 EDGEHILL RD., ETOBICOKE, ONT M9A 4N1 CAN
34340 MOORE, JOHN, 2971 EAST 3RD AVE., VANCOUVER, BC V5M 1H7 CAN
34341 LONGBOURNE, JAMES, 1961 SOUTHMERE CRES., SURREY, BC V4A 7B9 CAN
34342 MCGEE, MARJORIE, #5-5484 OK LND RD., VERNON, BC V1T 7A8 CAN
34343 MASLENKI, DOROTHY, RR3 SPIERS RD., KELOWNA, BC V1Y 7R2 CAN
34344 RIOUX, PIERRE, 44 8EME RUE EST., RIMOUSKI, QUE G5L 2H8 CAN
34345 MCDOWALL, MR W., 22 VICTORIA AVE., PARRY SOUND, ONT P2A 2C1 CAN
34346 WHYTE, ISABEL, 7811 YONGE ST #310., THORNHILL, ONT L3T 4S3 CAN
34347 ROBBINS, MARJORIE, RR#1., HARLEY, ONT N0E 1E0 CAN
34348 MCDONALD, MR I., 33 KEEWATIN CRES., NEPEAN, ONT K2E 5S2 CAN
34349 ATKINSON, RETA, 7 PROMENADE DR., GUELPH, ONT N1E 5Y6 CAN
34350 BOYD, CARL, PO BOX 795., MCBRIDE, BC V0J 2E0 CAN
34351 SHEARD, BERYL, 4030 BRAEFOOT RD., VICTORIA, BC V8X 2B7 CAN
34352 MANN, MARGARET, BOX 479., VICKING, ALB T0B 4N0 CAN
34353 SPETZ, TROY, 630 GRACELAND AVE., KINGSTON, ONT K7M 7P7 CAN
34354 HUNTER, KAREN, KENNEDY RD RR#1., CHELTENHAM, ONT L0P 1C0 CAN
34355 BAYLISS, CHARLES, 98 CHESTNUST CRES., SCARBOROUGH, ONT M1L 1Y5 CAN
34356 CROKEN, MRS C., 351 HAMILTON CRES., CHATHAM, NB E1N 2M2 CAN
34357 WILLIAMS, MRS G., SITE 400 BOX 36 RR NO 4., WASAGA BEACH, ONT L0L 2P0 CAN
34358 CLAYTON, MARILYN, BOX 525., FISHER BRANCH, MAN R0C 0Z0 CAN
34359 CONDON, JANICE, 434-19 ST NE., MEDICINE HAT, ALB T1C 1B3 CAN
34360 SHIN, JOYCE, 120 PORTSDOWN RD., SCARBOROUGH, ONT M1P 1V5 CAN
34361 FRISKNEY, MS E.J., 29 MOULTREY CRES., GEORGETOWN, ONT L7G 4N4 CAN
34362 NORBERG, ELLEN, 2203 CAMERON ST., REGINA, SAS S4T 2V9 CAN
34363 MACNEIL, PATRICIA, 14 SHANA PL., DOLLARD DES ORMEAUX, QUE H9B 1V3 CAN
34364 WILSON, MARGARET, BOX 686., ROSEBUD, ALB T0J 2T0 CAN
34365 WOOD, WILMA, BOX 99 HOLTON ST., FLINTON, ONT K0H 1P0 CAN
34366 GRANT, MS T., 305-55 PARK AVE., OTTAWA, ONT K2P 1B1 CAN
34367 MARTIN, PETER, 2422 MAGNUS AVE., OTTAWA, ONT K1G 1J8 CAN
34368 KERR, JAMES, 338 PALACE RD., KINGSTON, ONT K7L 4T3 CAN
34369 BROWN, IRIS, 12121 JASPER AVE #1407E., EDMONTON, ALB T5N 3X7 CAN
34370 JONES, MURIEL, 1468 WESTVIEW VILLAGE., WINTERBURN, ALB T0E 2N0 CAN
34371 VERALDI, MYRTLE, 74-437 JOHN ST., COBOURG, ONT K9A 3T6 CAN
34372 SWAIN, GORDON, 51 ST VITAL RD., WINNIPEG, MAN R2M 1Z4 CAN
34373 SHOTTON, AILEEN, 219-80 BAYLOR AVE., WINNIPEG, MAN R3T 3K1 CAN
34374 SMITH, MARION, 80 BEXLEY CRES., TORONTO, ONT M6N 2P7 CAN
34375 TOSE, MS B., 225 MACLAREN ST APT 30., OTTAWA, ONT K2P 0L4 CAN
34376 STREMES, GRAHAM, 502 BEVAN AVE., OTTAWA, ONT K1Z 5S7 CAN
34377 FITZSIMONDS, ENID, 11535-141 STREET., EDMONTON, ALB T5M 1T7 CAN
34378 BARON, MARILYN, 104-55 GREENVALLEY DR., KITCHENER, ONT N2P 1Z6 CAN
34379 ARMSTRONG, MARY, 100 DEVON ST., STRATFORD, ONT N5A 2Z3 CAN
34380 WILSON, MARJORIE, RR#4., STRATFORD, ONT N5A 6S5 CAN
34381 MOWATT, ALEX, RR#1., FERGUS, ONT N1M 2W3 CAN
34382 COLLINS, GAIL, 508½ NIAGARA ST., ST CATHARINES, ONT L2M 3P5 CAN
34383 MOORHOUSE, BRUCE, 153 FAIRVIEW AVE., ST THOMAS, ONT N5R 4X8 CAN
34384 PEAT, CYNTHIA, 36 DEEPWOOD CRES., DON MILLS, ONT M3C 1N8 CAN
34385 MOORE, HERBERT, 587 LANSDOWNE AVE., WESTMOUNT, QUE H3Y 2V7 CAN
34386 JUTRA, CORA, PO BOX 77., MORRIS, MAN R0G 1K0 CAN
34387 GIBB, MRS H., PH1 2167 BELLEVUE AVE., WEST VANCOUVER, BC V7V 1C2 CAN
34388 NUTHACK, JOACHIM, 11418-70 STREET., EDMONTON, ALB T5B 1T4 CAN
34389 JEATT, MRS J., 6456 GORDON AVE., BURNABY, BC V5E 3M1 CAN
34390 BERKHUIZEN, JOHN, 240 HORSHAM AE., WILLOWDALE, ONT M2N 2A6 CAN
34391 MASSENA, ADELE, C/O 36 AMBERJACK BLVD., SCARBOROUGH, ONT M1H 2J3 CAN
34392 ABRAM, DORIS, 103 CHESLEY AVE., LONDON, ONT N5Z 2C3 CAN
34393 WATTS, ARCHIE, 217 HOLMES AVE., WILLOWDALE, ONT M2N 4M9 CAN
34394 DETLOR, HETTY, BOX 296., BLACK DIAMOND, ALB T0L 0H0 CAN
34395 WATKIN, ELEANOR, 1635 ST ANDREWS PL NW., CALGARY, ALB T2N 3Y4 CAN
34396 LOWING, MR R., 1916-2 STREET SW., CALGARY, ALB T2S 1SE CAN
34397 DUNNILL, JOHN, 409-335 ADELAIDE ST., THUNDER BAY, ONT P7A 7T1 CAN
34398 KUIPERS, GERHARD, 10839-147 STREET., EDMONTON, ALB T5N 3E1 CAN

34399 DIGNEY, ERNEST, COMP.24 SITE 12A, RR7., VERNON, BC V1T 7Z3 CAN
34400 MATTHEWS, VIOLET, BOX 174., WILBERFORCE, ONT K0L 3C0 CAN
34401 ARISS, MARLENE, 1109 SIMPSON AVE., MOOSE JAW, SAS S6H 4M7 CAN
34402 WOOD, HELEN, 2 COLBORNE STREET APT 404B., LINDSAY, ONT K9S 5B5 CAN
34403 MACAULAY, MURIEL, 57 GATES LANE., HAMILTON, ONT L9B 1T8 CAN
34404 AITKEN, KENNETH, 2426E DEWDNEY AVE., REGINA, SAS S4N 4V5 CAN
34405 WISE, GEORGE, 2205 MCINTYRE ST., REGINA, SAS S4P 2S1 CAN
34406 SPRIGGS, JEAN, 779 LEAHEY ST., PEMBROKE, ONT K8A 1B5 CAN
34407 ORR, MS K., 2911 BAYVIEW AVE STE K110., WILLOWDALE, ONT M2K 1E8 CAN
34408 CLAUS, WILLIAM, RR#2., KENT BRIDGE, ONT N0P 1V0 CAN
34409 SPRINGSTEEL, LOUISE, BOX 13 SITE 3 RR1., THORSBY, ALB T0C 2P0 CAN
34410 HOLLOWAY, STEVEN, BOX 38 ST FXU., ANTIGONISH, NS B2G 1C0 CAN
34411 LEWIS, MARGARET, 121 MOSS AVE., MT HELEN, VIC 3350 AUS
34412 PRENDERGAST, JOAN, 7 BIRCHWAY CT., BAIRNSDALE, VIC 3875 AUS
34413 GROVE, DONALD, 50 ROSTREVOR PDE., MONT ALBERT NORTH, VIC 3129 AUS
34414 NORTH, MR W., 29 ANDERSON ST., TORQUAY, VIC 3228 AUS
34415 PAWSEY, MARIDA, SOUTHAM DR., TAGGERTY, VIC 3714 AUS
34416 HASHIM-JONES, ALLEN, 25 VERRAN ST., BELLBIRD PARK, QLD 4300 AUS
34417 ARGUS, WENDY, 10 DROUYN ST., DEAGAN, QLD 4017 AUS
34418 SECKOLD, ROY, PO BOX 346., GOSFORD, NSW 2250 AUS
34419 TRYK, MRS S., 69 FRANK ST., ELTHAM, VIC 3095 AUS
34420 BELLAMY, JEAN, 22 STONEY CREEK RD., BEVERLY HILLS, NSW 2209 AUS
34421 VON HARTEN, JOY, 54 DALE ST., NARRABRI, NSW 2390 AUS
34422 GARVIN, JOSEPH, 6 MURDOCH CRES., CONNELS POINT, NSW 2221 AUS
34423 ADAMS, MRS B., 52 WHEELERS LANE., EAST DUBBO, NSW 2830 AUS
34424 DEELEY, MR W., PO BOX 726., BATHURST, NSW 2795 AUS
34425 GILLIS, MR J., 1 OAK ST., NORMANHURST, NSW 2076 AUS
34426 LAIDLEY, MAX, 11 MARTIN ST., RYDE, NSW 2112 AUS
34427 POLLARD, ROBERT, 19 YIMBALA ST., DUNDAS, NSW 2116 AUS
34428 HOWE, HAROLD, 50 MCINTOSH ST., GORDON, NSW 2072 AUS
34429 STURGESS, NANCY, 6 YENDON RD., CARNEGIE, VIC 3163 AUS
34430 BEHAN, MARGARET, 87 LISBETH AVE., MITCHAM, VIC 3132 AUS
34431 MOSS, MRS C., 37 GREENOCK CRES., WANTIRNA, VIC 3152 AUS
34432 HOLLAND, MRS A., 163A WATTLE VALLEY RD., CAMBERWELL, VIC 3124 AUS
34433 MCKAY, PATRICIA, PO BOX 35., TARADALE, VIC 3447 AUS
34434 JAMIESON, BETTY, 24 ROSSHIRE RD., WEST NEWPORT, VIC 3015 AUS
34435 IRVINE, MRS J., 1 NAPIER CRT., MT WAVERLEY, VIC 3149 AUS
34436 BUTTON, MARION, PO BOX 28., GISBORNE, VIC 3437 AUS
34437 POTTER, CAROL, 3 WILLIAM ST., CLARENCE PARK, SA 5034 AUS
34438 CLARKE, MRS L., 10 FULLWOOD ST., WESTON, ACT 2611 AUS
34439 BLACKABY, MRS N., 6 WYLES PL., FLYNN, ACT 2615 AUS
34440 STRICKLAND, MARGARET, 33 WILLIAM ST., MACKAY, QLD 4740 AUS
34441 STEELE, BRIAN, PO BOX 14., INDOOROOPILLY, QLD 4068 AUS
34442 HARRIS, RHONDA, M/S 368., GIN GIN, QLD 4671 AUS
34443 MCLEISH, ANN, 156 GIBBS ST., CANNINGTON, WA 6107 AUS
34444 ROBERTS, JUNE, 69 MALUKA ST., BELLERIVE, TAS 7018 AUS
34445 PITHOUSE, REX, 23 BAYFIELD ST., BELLERIVE, TAS 7018 AUS
34446 GAMBLE, DIANNE, 20 ELIZABETH ST., JUNEE, NSW 2663 AUS
34447 DICKSON, JOHN, 45 HUDSON ST., HURSTVILLE, NSW 2220 AUS
34448 ANDREW, BRIAN, 19 COVERDALE ST., CARLINGFORD, NSW 2118 AUS
34449 THOMPSON, LAURELLE, 26 TANJENONG PL., BURLEIGH HEADS, QLD 4220 AUS
34450 WILMOT, SANDRA, 23 DIAMOND AVE., ST ALBANS, VIC 3021 AUS
34451 PIGRUM, DENNIS, 99 HINKLER RD EAST., GLEN WAVERLEY, VIC 3150 AUS
34452 HEALEY, NEIL, 16 GAINSBOROUGH RD., MENTONE, VIC 3194 AUS
34453 LIVY, MR M., 6 EVON AVE., EAST RINGWOOD, VIC 3135 AUS
34454 HOGAN, CARMEL, PO BOX 494., MENTONE, VIC 3194 AUS
34455 MEWKILL, MARY, 4/311 DANDENONG RD., ARMADALE, VIC 3143 AUS
34456 BOWDEN, MR G., 10 BELMONT AVE., BALWYN, VIC 3103 AUS
34457 WEST, MRS J., 9 PRINCESS ST., CALLALA BEACH, NSW 2540 AUS
34458 FOX, JOHN, 31 MEREDITH ST., BLAXLAND, NSW 2774 AUS
34459 MURPHY, DOROTHY, 7 BLAKE CRT., DENILIQUIN, NSW 2710 AUS
34460 DUGGER, PATRICK, 245 RIDING RD., BALMORAL, QLD 4171 AUS
34461 WADDINGTON, HEATHER, 19 SUNDANCE WAY., RUNAWAY BAY, QLD 4216 AUS
34462 GRANT, MARGARET, 6 WEEMALA ST., FLINDERS PARK, SA 5025 AUS
34463 HARPER, JOY, 8 ANTILL ST., BLAXLAND, NSW 2774 AUS
34464 HOWARTH, WALTER, 2 LAWRENNY, ALTON LN., FOUR MARKS, GU34 5AL ENG
34465 RICHARDSON, WALTER, RR#1., BARRIE, ONT L4M 4Y8 CAN
34466 RICHARDSON, CYNTHIA, RR#1., BARRIE, ONT L4M 4Y8 CAN
34467 MANN, GAYLE, 1602-200 RONALD ST., WINNIPEG, MAN R3J 3J3 CAN
34468 STEWART, JUANITA, 630 EBERT AVE., COQUITLAM, BC V3J 2L2 CAN
34469 BULLER, MARIAN, C1 RR2 MALASPINA RD., POWELL RIVER, BC V8A 4Z3 CAN
34470 GRAFF, MARGARET, RR1., OSGOODE, ONT K0A 2W0 CAN

34471 REIMER, AUDREY, 1056 DUDLEY AVE., WINNIPEG, MAN R3M 1S7 CAN
34472 FELTMATE, PEGGY, 44 NORMANDY BLVD., TORONTO, ONT M4L 3K2 CAN
34473 MOODIE, EILEEN, 44 BRANTFORD DR., AGINCOURT, ONT M1W 1E6 CAN
34474 GORDON, EILEEN, 116 RIVER RD., KAMLOOPS, BC V2C 4P9 CAN
34475 O'FALLON, ROCHELLE, 11057 84A AVE., DELTA, BC V4C 3A9 CAN
34476 GUSCOTT, WARREN, BOX 286., KLEINBURG, ONT L0J 1C0 CAN
34477 MATHERS, BARBARA, RR2 SITE 15 COMP. 4., LUMBY, BC V0E 2G0 CAN
34478 ZYTVELD, MR E., 85 COTE DES NEIGES RD., NEPEAN, ONT K2G 2C7 CAN
34479 RAMP, WILLIAM, PRC, TRENT UNIVERSITY., PETERBOROUGH, ONT K9J 7B8 CAN
34480 VANSLYKE, REV J., 16 PEGGY AVE., MT ELGIN, ONT N0J 1N0 CAN
34481 RAWE, MR T., 420 BUTCHART DR., EDMONTON, ALB T6R 1R1 CAN
34482 MILLS, MRS S., BOX 912., BEAVERLODGE, ALB T0H 0C0 CAN
34483 HANSON, MRS T., 524 TAYLOR RD RR1., VICTORIA, BC V8X 3W9 CAN
34484 WARD, JO-ANNE, RR3., ORO STATION, ONT L0L 2E0 CAN
34485 DRAPER, JEANETTE, BOX 208., MACTIER, ONT P0C 1H0 CAN
34486 LUCAS, JOAN, 1469 WINDERMERE AVE., PETERBOROUGH, ONT K9J 6T1 CAN
34487 BERRY, MRS E., 13019-15TH AVE., WHITE ROCK, BC V4A 1K6 CAN
34488 WOLF, COLLEEN, #201-2167 ANGUS ST., REGINA, SAS S4T 2A1 CAN
34489 GOODFELLOW, MARJORIE, PO BOX 1135., SHERBROOKE, QUE J1H 5L5 CAN
34490 BUFFETT, MR C., 1226 AIRPORT RD RR1-BOX 8., NORTH BAY, ONT P1B 8G2 CAN
34491 MCIVER, JANET, 411 WELLINGTON CRES., DAUPHIN, MAN R7N 0M4 CAN
34492 TURNER, MEL, 2638 EHMAN BAY., REGINA, SAS S4V 0L6 CAN
34493 LITTLE, MARY LOU, BOX 866., BLENHEIM, ONT N0P 1A0 CAN
34494 ELLIOTT, JOHN, RR #5., PETITCODIAC, NB E0A 2H0 CAN
34495 BROWN, MR G., 1473 NORMAN AVE., LONDON, ONT N6K 2A6 CAN
34496 GLEN, FLORENCE, 108-111 ST WEST., SASKATOON, SAS S7N 1S7 CAN
34497 FAIR, CLOAH, 714 FIDDLER'S GR RR #2., ANCASTER, ONT L9G 3L1 CAN
34498 FIRTH, JEAN, 144 ST CLAIR AVE., HAMILTON, ONT L8M 2N7 CAN
34499 BLACKBURN, MS C., 25 ALGONQUIN AVE., KIRKLAND LAKE, ONT P2N 1C1 CAN
34500 CROMIE, ANNE, RR #3., HAVELOCK, ONT K0L 1Z0 CAN
34501 LITTLE, ELIZABETH, RR1 SITE 138 C-6., QUALICUM BEACH, BC V0R 2T0 CAN
34502 MONTGOMERY, ARLYN, RR #1., BELGRAVE, ONT N0G 1E0 CAN
34503 STROME, LAURIE, 510 E SUNNYDALE PL., WATERLOO, ONT N2L 4T1 CAN
34504 GILDAY, JOAN, 274 TURKEY HILL RD., RR2 BROME, QUE J0E 1K0 CAN
34505 WOOD, LEILAH, BOX 126., PLEASANTDALE, SAS S0K 3H0 CAN
34506 CLERMONT, ALFRED, BOX 4 MCMORIN MANOR., ASSINIBOIA, SAS S0H 0B0 CAN
34507 JOHANNESEN, CHERRIE, 1258 MOFFAT AVE., QUESNEL, BC V2J 3A7 CAN
34508 MANNESS-SMITH, ADELE, 708, 1712 PORTAGE AVE., WINNIPEG, MAN R3J 0E3 CAN
34509 WARK, MARY, RR #2., BLACKIE, ALB T0L 0J0 CAN
34510 JONES, PAT, 15 STIKINE ST., KITIMAT, BC V8C 1W6 CAN
34511 WHITTINGTON, ANNE, 98 ANGLE ST., KITIMAT, BC V8C 2N3 CAN
34512 LANGTON, JUDY, 1077 CLEARVIEW AVE., BURLINGTON, ONT L7T 2J2 CAN
34513 SMALL, CAPT D., 1263 WILLOWDALE AVE., OTTAWA, ONT K1H 7S7 CAN
34514 MARTIN, GAIL, 2368 RIDGECREST PL., OTTAWA, ONT K1H 7V7 CAN
34515 HAMILTON, JONNETTE, BOX 400., PONOKA, ALB T0C 2H0 CAN
34516 LANGELIER, PAUL-ANDRE, 4114 AVENUE MARLOWE., MONTREAL, QUE H4A 3M2 CAN
34517 OUELLET-BOUCHER, JEANNINE, CP 1653., R-DU-LOUP, QUE G5R 4M2 CAN
34518 STANTON, EDWARD, 6670 LAUREL ST., VANCOUVER, BC V6P 3T5 CAN
34519 SMAHA, SALLY, RR3 MERKLEY RD., TERRACE, BC V8G 4R6 CAN
34520 CORUPE, LINDA, 210 ALLAN DR., BOLTON, ONT L7E 1Y7 CAN
34521 PADLEY, LISA, 332 HOLLYBURN DR., KAMLOOPS, BC V2E 1W5 CAN
34522 WIKSTROM, RACHEL, 692 FANSHAWE PARK RD., LONDON, ONT N5X 2B9 CAN
34523 MCKELVIE, NELSON, 2594 BUCKINGHAM DR., WINDSOR, ONT N8T 2B6 CAN
34524 MCKINNEY, LOIS, 318 QUEEN ST SOUTH., MISSISSAUGA, ONT L5M 1M2 CAN
34525 DOUBT, JANE-ELLEN, 29-931 GLENEAGLES DR., KAMLOOPS, BC V2E 1KY CAN
34526 ROBB, DAVID, 555 QUEEN ST., GANANOQUE, ONT K7G 2A9 CAN
34527 STAINTON, MARCI, 51 CADILLAC AVE NORTH., OSHAWA, ONT L1G 6B8 CAN
34528 DRAPER, LYNDA, PO BOX 1707., VIRDEN, MAN R0M 2C0 CAN
34529 WALLACE, MRS E., 186 SALISBURY AVE., CAMBRIDGE, ONT N1S 1K4 CAN
34530 PEZY, RENE, 6 LIPSON AVE., KADINA, SA 5554 AUS
34531 EAGLE, MICHAEL, 10 WELD ST., SOUTH HOBART, TAS 7004 AUS
34532 COLLINS, OLIVE, 160 AUGUSTA RD., LENAH VALLEY, TAS 7008 AUS
34533 COURT, MISS J., 52 LOWER MOUNT ST., WENTWORTHVILLE, NSW 2145 AUS
34534 YOUNG, MRS M., 45/29 DENMAN PDE., NORMANHURST, NSW 2076 AUS
34535 WARREN, BESSIE, 44/3 KANDY AVE., EPPING, NSW 2121 AUS
34536 SUMNER, SUSAN, LOT 3 FARRANTS RD., CONDONG, NSW 2484 AUS
34537 MUNRO, ALLAN, 3 MARS ST., PADSTOW, NSW 2211 AUS
34538 WARBRICK, SYD, 1/34 LALAGULI DR., TOORMINA, NSW 2452 AUS
34539 FREEMAN, DAVID, PO BOX 694., TAREE, NSW 2430 AUS
34540 HILLS, LYNETTE, 6 GAILES ST., SUTHERLAND, NSW 2232 AUS
34541 ALLISON, MRS R., 59 MEREDITH ST., KOTARA, NSW 2289 AUS
34542 TANKARD, MR J., 41 WOOLWICH RD., HUNTERS HILL, NSW 2110 AUS

34543 RENTON, JACK, 150 PENNANT PDE., EPPING, NSW 2121 AUS
34544 KEENE, BOB, 25 DAY ST., HENTY, NSW 2658 AUS
34545 MORGAN, KENNETH, 23 CHATEAU CRES., ST CLAIR, NSW 2759 AUS
34546 DUNBAR, MARGARET, 14 BLACKWOOD ST., MURRUMBEENA, VIC 3163 AUS
34547 PINCH, MRS M., 60 BURWOOD HWY., EAST BURWOOD, VIC 3151 AUS
34548 BERESFORD, NIGEL, 218 CENTRE DANDENONG RD., DINGLEY, VIC 3172 AUS
34549 FITZGERALD, GARY, PO BOX 185., WOORI YALLOCK, VIC 3139 AUS
34550 SHEPPARD, BYARD, 107 YALLAMBIE RD., MACLEOD, VIC 3085 AUS
34551 STREET, MR D., 8 DIANNE CT., VERMONT SOUTH, VIC 3133 AUS
34552 SCOTT, RAY, PO BOX 642., FRANKSTON, VIC 3199 AUS
34553 BRAND, MRS G., 172 MAROONDAH HWY., CROYDON, VIC 3136 AUS
34554 RIDER, HOWARD, 232 CUMBERLAND RD., PASCOE VALE, VIC 3044 AUS
34555 FLYNN, WILLIAM, 9 HUMBER RD., CROYDON, VIC 3136 AUS
34556 ISLES, JANENE, 10 BRIGHT ST., CAMPBELLFIELD, VIC 3061 AUS
34557 GLASSON, ANN, 17 MARINA ST., VERMONT, VIC 3133 AUS
34558 KIDGELL, MERNA, 5 JAMES ST., PAKENHAM, VIC 3810 AUS
34559 BAKER, 26 DROVERS LN., SOMERVILLE, VIC 3912 AUS
34560 GREEN, HEATHER, 18 EAST VIEW CRES., EAST BENTLEIGH, VIC 3165 AUS
34561 JENNER, ELVIE, 71 SHEARN CRES., DOUBLEVIEW, WA 6018 AUS
34562 STORER, MRS H., PO BOX 42., PINGELLY, WA 6308 AUS
34563 FUNNELL, PATRICIA, PO BOX 102., BALINGUP, WA 6253 AUS
34564 CLAYTON, JEAN, 12 WEST ST., BUSSELTON, WA 6280 AUS
34565 SMITH, MRS I., 8 ESTUARY PL., WANNANUP, WA 6210 AUS
34566 ENGLISH, LORRAINE, 225 YANGEBUP RD., YANGEBUP, WA 6164 AUS
34567 COOK, GLORIA, 37 CHURCH ST., BOONAH, QLD 4310 AUS
34568 REILLY, ENA, 69 RODERICK ST., IPSWICH, QLD 4305 AUS
34569 SAWDEN, DELPHINE, 64 PLEYSTOWE CRES., HENDRA, QLD 4011 AUS
34570 WALLACE, JUDY, 31 ANNIE WOOD AVE., NORTH MACKAY, QLD 4740 AUS
34571 BERRY, MRS J., 97 SMITH ST., CLEVELAND, QLD 4163 AUS
34572 ROBINSON, PETER, 15 HUTTON CRT., BLACKWATER, QLD 4717 AUS
34573 LAFFERTY, MR M., 33 GREGORY ST., TOOWONG, QLD 4066 AUS
34574 SCOTT, MYRIAM, 6 MAGDALA CRT., STAWELL, VIC 3380 AUS
34575 HOLMES, RONALD, 11 HURLEY ST., BALLARAT, VIC 3350 AUS
34576 KELLY, MR P., 16 ROBERTS ST., EAST BRUNSWICK, VIC 3057 AUS
34577 LEWELLIN, KATHLEEN, 2/12 ALBENCA ST., MENTONE, VIC 3194 AUS
34578 HAMILTON, LEANNE, 21 AKOONAH DR., GOLDEN SQUARE, VIC 3555 AUS
34579 HEATHCOTE, JILL, 136 HARRINGTON RD., WARRNAMBOOL, VIC 3280 AUS
34580 FOSTER, MARJORY, 36 SUNRAY AVE., CHELTENHAM, VIC 3192 AUS
34581 KOPP, MR T., 50 QUAYS DR., BALLINA, NSW 2478 AUS
34582 PROUD, JOAN, 65 EDGECUMBE ST., COMO, WA 6152 AUS
34583 CAMERON, ROY, PO BOX 305., CURTIN, ACT 2605 AUS
34584 KRUGER, VALMA, C/O PO BOX 1083., ROCKHAMPTON, QLD 4701 AUS
34585 STURTON, GRETA, 62 FARRELL ST., ASHGROVE, QLD 4060 AUS
34586 PATRICK, MRS V., 38 ISLAND DR., CANNONVALE, QLD 4802 AUS
34587 ASHWIN, PATTI, PO BOX 5906., BUNDALL, QLD 4217 AUS
34588 QUINN, SANDRA, C/O POST OFFICE., COEN, QLD 4871 AUS
34589 LEWIS-HUGHES, MR J., 2 NORFOLK ST., KILLARA, NSW 2071 AUS
34590 STEWART, ROBYNNE, 11 NAOMI ST NTH., BAULKHAM HILLS, NSW 2153 AUS
34591 STEAD, SANDRA, C/O POST OFFICE., GLENROWAN, VIC 3675 AUS
34592 BURNELL, BEVERLY, 97 MCINTOSH RD., ALTONA NORTH, VIC 3025 AUS
34593 LONGWOOD, ANN, 159 GREENWOOD DR., BUNDOORA, VIC 3083 AUS
34594 SUTTON, SUSAN, 21 ERVINE CL., SUNBURY, VIC 3429 AUS
34595 ORGAN, MRS S., 8 CAULFIELD DR., NORTH HAVEN, SA 5018 AUS
34596 ANTARAKIS, JOAN, 9 CRAMER CRES., CHATSWOOD, NSW 2067 AUS
34597 HOLDER, MR V., 18 KADINA RD., GOOSEBERRY HILL, WA 6076 AUS
34598 BREMNER, JESSIE, PO BOX 2190., WHYALLA, SA 5608 AUS
34599 ELSEY, MARGARET, 221 BURROWYE CRES., KEILOR, VIC 3036 AUS
34600 WOODS, MRS S., 50 BETHANGA ST., MT ELIZA, VIC 3930 AUS
34601 FINCHER, MRS B., 55 MOLESWORTH ST., KEW, VIC 3101 AUS
34602 COLE, KAYE, 15 HOWITT ST., NORTHCOTE, VIC 3070 AUS
34603 GRAY, MARYANNE, 20 WADSWORTH ST., TAKAKA, NZ
34604 VIVASH, CLAIRE, 52 CLAYBURN RD., GLEN EDEN, AUCK NZ
34605 COX, MR J., 123 STANLEY RD., GLENFIELD, AUCK 10 NZ
34606 GLENDENNING, FRANCES, 189 WELCOME BAY RD., TAURANGA, 3001 NZ
34607 FORDE, JUNE, 38 VERNON ST., INVERCARGILL, NZ
34608 SIMPSON, PHYLLIS, 49 RUSSLEIGH DR., HAMILTON, NZ
34609 WARBRICK, IRENE, 63 ALLENBY RD., PAPATOETOE, AUCK NZ
34610 COLLARD, ERIC, 96 RIDDELL RD., GLENDOWIE, AUCK NZ
34611 BATHE, GLENICE, 22 EPPING PL., TAUPO, 3300 NZ
34612 TOLLEY, IRIS, 24 OAKLEY AVE., AUCKLAND, 7 NZ
34613 VAN AMSTERDAM, MARLENE, 18 GREAT COLLINS ST., OHAUPO, WAIKATO NZ
34614 COXON, VALERIE, 17 ROLLIN ST., CHRISTCHURCH, 2 NZ

34615 SPENCE, DAWN, 186A MASSEY ST., HAMILTON, 2001 NZ
34616 DOOLE, MR & MRS T. & B., 57 HINEWAI ST., OTOROHANGA, KING COUNTRY NZ
34617 THOMSON, SHIRLEY, ASHDOWN PARK, WELD RD, RD4., NEW PLYMOUTH, 4621 NZ
34618 CAMPBELL, ALLAN, 48 ORARI ST., CHRISTCHURCH, 8007 NZ
34619 SCOTT, MR L.W., PO BOX 4062., HASTINGS, HB 4200 NZ
34620 HOLT, MARY, 10B GREENDALE SPUR., AUCKLAND, 10 NZ
34621 AINGE, NANETTE, 35 BISHOP ST., CHRISTCHURCH, 1 NZ
34622 SMITH, ANDREA, 39 NEALE AVE., STOKE, NELSON NZ
34623 SHAW, JANET, 6 GRANADA PL., GLENDOWIE, AUCK 5 NZ
34624 GORE, MISS D., GORE RD, RD1., TIRAU, NZ
34625 DIETSCH, DORIS, 3 HARDING AVE., TE ATATU STH, AUCK 8 NZ
34626 DAVIES, DESMOND, 5 CRANLEY ST., TAINUI, DUNEDIN NZ
34627 JOHNSON, MRS C., 2 CASPER ST., HAMILTON, NZ
34628 ROSS, BETTY, 408 SANDES ST., THAMES, NZ
34629 KERR, JACQUI, RD3., TE AWAMUTU, NZ
34630 BURGE, RUSSELL, 6 TIFFEN PL., NAPIER, NZ
34631 BARNES, JOAN, 1 ANGLESEY PL., PALMERSTON NORTH, NZ
34632 LETHAM, KAY, 16 HUIA ST., PICTON, MARLBOROUGH NZ
34633 SMITH, GAIL, 111 WELD ST., HOKITIKA, WESTLAND NZ
34634 JURAN, LOIS, 59 COCKLE BAY RD., HOWICK, AUCK NZ
34635 MCKIRDY, MS P., 53 BLEDISLOE CRES., WAINUIOMATA, NZ
34636 JARDEN, LLOYD, 1 GRAFTON RD., ROSENEATH, WGTN NZ
34637 MORETON, MADELINE, 6 ROSEVALE PL., RICHMOND, NELSON NZ
34638 SINNOTT, REX, 4 ELY GVE., WAINUIOMATA, NZ
34639 GORDON, LOMA, 18D ALMA ST., DANNEVIRKE, HB NZ
34640 GRANGER, EILEEN, 35 BRIGGS RD., CHRISTCHURCH, CANT 8005 NZ
34641 KING, SYLVIA, 1 DORIS ST., RICHMOND, NELSON NZ
34642 SKYNNER, FRANCIS & JOAN, UNIT 2, 1 HART ST., TAKAPUNA, AUCK 9 NZ
34643 BYRON, FRAN, 3 ALDERTON PL., PAPAKURA, AUCK NZ
34644 MOORE, MR W., BLAKES RD, NO 6 RD., CHRISTCHURCH, NZ
34645 MCGUTCHEON, AVIS, 130 VOGEL ST., PALMERSTON NORTH, 5301 NZ
34646 CAMPBELL, JOHN, 2 RATHLIN ST., REDWOOD, CHCH 5 NZ
34647 MACE, MR H., SCOTT RD, 4 RD., WHANGAREI, NORTHLAND NZ
34648 DITTMER, SHIRLEY, TAONUI RD, NO 5 RD., FEILDING, NZ
34649 WHITE, MISS P., 36B ROBERTSON ST., GORE, SOUTHLAND 9700 NZ
34650 STICHBURY, JUDITH, PO BOX 262., MANUREWA, AUCK NZ
34651 RUSSELL, RAY, 4 GERRAND PL., CHARTWELL, HAMILTON NZ
34652 TOURELLE, JOHN, 129 LORN ST., INVERCARGILL, SLD 9501 NZ
34653 AKROYD, ROWENA, 70 DAFFODIL ST., TITIRANGI, AUCK 8 NZ
34654 SMITH, RAEANNE, PO BOX 255., HASTINGS, HB NZ
34655 GOOD, MRS J., 477 RIDDELL RD., GLENDOWIE, AUCK 5 NZ
34656 SAKKERS, NEVILLE, 6 ANNAN ST., NIGHTCAPS, SOUTHLAND NZ
34657 HEWITT, MRS V., 26 GLASGOW ST., PALMERSTON NORTH, NZ
34658 NEALE, PHYLLIS, 227 TRIG RD WHITFORD RD1., HOWICK, AUCK NZ
34659 COOK, TONI, R.D.44 MAIN NTH RD., URENUI, TARANAKI NZ
34660 LELO, MRS W., 14A PANAMA RD., MT WELLINGTON, AUCK 6 NZ
34661 SIMPSON, MR P., 49 ANZAC ST., TAKAPUNA, AUCK 9 NZ
34662 CLAUSON, LORNA, 14 GILLS AVE., PAPAKURA, NZ
34663 YOUNG, ELIZABETH, 478 RIVER RD., HAMILTON, 2001 NZ
34664 WILLIAMS, LYNN, 33B KIMBERLEY ST., CHRISTCHURCH, 5 NZ
34665 BLOOMBERG, JUDITH, 24 SELWYN ST., BLENHEIM, 7301 NZ
34666 ROUSE, TRISH, 4 REDWOOD AVE., TAWA, WGTN NZ
34667 KEARSE, MR P., 73 IKITARA RD., WANGANUI, 5001 NZ
34668 BARRETT, MAVIS, 19 RAVENSWOOD DR., FORREST HILL, AUCK 10 NZ
34669 EDRIDGE, MR E., PUKEARUHE RD, R.D.44., URENUI, TARANAKI NZ
34670 WINTERBURN, JOAN, CHORLTON RD., AKAROA, BANKS PENINSULA NZ
34671 VALLINGS, ROSAMUND, 101 WALLER AVE., BUCKLANDS BEACH, AUCK NZ
34672 HYNDMAN, DOMINICK, 42 BRITTAN TCE., LYTTELTON, CHCH NZ
34673 FOWLER-DANENBERG, PETINA, PO BOX 7471., SYDENHAM, CHCH NZ
34674 CLARK, KAY, 22 PUKEKO ST., TAIHAPE, NZ
34675 WILKINSON, MRS D., 4 LAUD AVE., ELLERSLIE, AUCK NZ
34676 GAITT, MISS A., 431 SOMME PDE., WANGANUI, NZ
34677 SHANKS, JUDY, PENCARROW RD, R.D.3., HAMILTON, NZ
34678 MICHEL, ALLEN, 24 QUEBEC RD., NELSON, NZ
34679 MALLETT, ESTHER, GODFREY RD, R.D.2., BLENHEIM, MARLB NZ
34680 PATTERSON, SHIRLEY, 17 PINEWOOD AVE., NTH NEW BRIGHTON, CHCH 9 NZ
34681 FRENCH, NORMA, 93 JACARANDA ST., RED CLIFFS, VIC 3496 AUS
34682 GOOLEY, BRUCE, 11 PARSLOW ST., MALVERN, VIC 3144 AUS
34683 LOWSBY, LOIS, 163 GLENHUNTLY RD., ELWOOD, VIC 3184 AUS
34684 JOSEPH, BETTE, 4 STRATHNAVER AVE., STRATHMORE, VIC 3041 AUS
34685 TINSON, MARGARET, 107 BIRMINGHAM RD., MT EVELYN, VIC 3796 AUS
34686 HOLLOWAY, DAVID, 1 SHIBOR DR., VERMONT, VIC 3133 AUS

34687 GRAHAM, MRS P., 42 PURDOM RD., WEMBLEY DOWNS, WA 6019 AUS
34688 ARMSTRONG, DAVID, PO BOX 136., MAYLANDS, WA 6051 AUS
34689 HEAD, DAVID, 106 HEWLETT ST., BRONTE, NSW 2024 AUS
34690 HERIVEL, JAN, 59 SECOND ST., BOOLAROO, NSW 2324 AUS
34691 NUTZ, BARBARA, PO BOX 167., WILLOUGHBY, NSW 2068 AUS
34692 MORGAN, MRS M., 27 PATRICK ST., BELMONT, NSW 2280 AUS
34693 MARSTON, MRS L., 11 ELECTRA ST., HEATHCOTE, NSW 2233 AUS
34694 CAWLEY, JACK, 13 BERRICO PL., BANGOR, NSW 2234 AUS
34695 CAMERON, ROBERT, 101 ADELAIDE PDE., WOOLLAHRA, NSW 2025 AUS
34696 HUNT, GARY, 160B TERRY ST., CONNELLS POINT, NSW 2221 AUS
34697 GOODWIN, JAMES, 3 ZEALANDER ST., SANS SOUCI, NSW 2219 AUS
34698 BROWN, LYNDAL, 63 VISCOUNT ST., BRAY PARK, QLD 4500 AUS
34699 BRIMS, ALAN, 55 GLADSTONE RD., SADDLERS CROSSING, QLD 4305 AUS
34700 BATZE, T., 5 LOTUS PL., CAIRNS, QLD 4870 AUS
34701 SKINNER, BRONWYN, 15/3 MITCHELL AVE., JANNALI, NSW 2226 AUS
34702 DRYSDALE, MR & MRS D. & J., 100 SMITH ST., MACEDON, VIC 3440 AUS
34703 CROSTON, RACHEL, RMB 9105B NTH TENESSEE RD., BORNHOLM, WA 6330 AUS
34704 GOAD, DOROTHY, 9/45 SHOLL ST., MANDURAH, WA 6210 AUS
34705 DENT, ROBERT, "MAGHEALLA" CASUARINA CRES., FITZROY FALLS, NSW 2577 AUS
34706 CAMERON, DR S., 4 YULE ST., DULWICH HILL, NSW 2203 AUS
34707 JAMES, ALFRED, 65 BILLYARD AVE., WAHROONGA, NSW 2076 AUS
34708 KINNISON BOURKE, MRS J., ROSECOT., CHAPEL ROW, HERSTMONCEUX, SSX BN27 1RB ENG
34709 CLEMENTS, JOAN, 3 ORCHARD RISE., GROOMBRIDGE, KEN TN3 9RU ENG
34710 HIPPERSON, MARTIN, 104 WARREN DR., HORNCHURCH, ESS RM12 4QX ENG
34711 BURDEN, CYRIL, 4 BLYTHSWOOD CRES., TORQUAY, DEV TQ1 3HJ ENG
34712 BLACKBURN, HERMAN, 38 HAWTHORN DR., NORTH HARROW, MDX HA2 7NX ENG
34713 WEBSTER, MR D., 30 HATHAWAY DR., GIFFNOCK, LKS G46 7AD SCT
34714 BROWN, DAVID, 25 RICHARDS CL., WELLINGTON, SOM TA21 0BD ENG
34715 MORLEY, JUNE, 8 FAIRFIELD RD., HAVANT, HANTS PO9 1BA ENG
34716 COLSON, ROBIN, UPPER THROUGHAM, THE CAMP., NR STROUD, GLS GL6 7HG ENG
34717 GOODBODY, MICHAEL, OLD RECTORY, WICKHAM ST PAULS., HALSTEAD, ESS C09 2PJ ENG
34718 WINCH, JACK, 23 ARKLESTON RD., PAISLEY, RFW PA1 3TE SCT
34719 HOBBS, GRAHAM, 1 BURCOMBE VILLAS, CHALFORD HILL., STROUD, GLS GL6 8BN ENG
34720 BALLANGER, WILLIAM, HASELEY READING RD., WOODCOTE, RG8 0QY ENG
34721 HOLDEN, SAMUEL, 23 BARDSLEY GATE AVE., STALYBRIDGE, CHS SK15 2TA ENG
34722 STILL, MICHAEL, 15A KENWAY RD., LONDON, SW5 0RP ENG
34723 CAREY, JENNIFER, 69 MELBOURNE RD., LONDON, E6 2RU ENG
34724 AIKEN, MS E., 45 FURNIVAL AVE., SLOUGH, BERKS SL2 1DH ENG
34725 JACK, MRS E., 11 OLD CHELTENHAM RD., GLOUCESTER, GLS GL2 0AS ENG
34726 STRUDWICK, ANITA, 48 BRUCE AVE., WORTHING, SSX BN11 5JU ENG
34727 FLETCHER, GERALD, 40 TRENT RD., WORTHING, SSX BN12 4EL ENG
34728 VARVILL, MICHAEL, 6 BOWERDEAN ST., LONDON, SW6 3TW ENG
34729 PRESBURY, MRS H., 64 DUPONT GDNS., LEICESTER, LEICS LE3 8LD ENG
34730 MARSDEN, JANE, 70C CAUSEWAY END RD., LISBURN, ANT BT28 2ED N IRELAND
34731 RUSHTON, JENNIFER, 162 MARLOW BOTTOM RD., MARLOW, BUCKS SL7 3PP ENG
34732 MOSQUERA, DAMIEN, 11A KNIGHTSBRIDGE RD., OLTON, WAR B92 8RF ENG
34733 STRATFORD, DR M., 10 ASHFORD RD., FULSHAW PARK, CHS SK9 1QE ENG
34734 SMITH, DAVID, 124 STEPHENSON WAY., BOURNE, LIN PE10 9DD ENG
34735 HAYES, ROY, WYCHES FARM, NETHER ALDERLEY., MACCLESFIELD, CHS SK10 4TU ENG
34736 GOULD, STANLEY, 146 NORRINGTON RD., NORTHFIELD, WAR B31 5PA ENG
34737 BLANN-FRY, MRS L., 4 CORONATION COT., ROUTS WAY, ROWNHAMS, HAM SO1 8JG ENG
34738 HOWARD EDWARDS, JOHN, 81 NORTHWOOD AVE., PURLEY, SRY CR8 2ES ENG
34739 BOURTON, MR C., 19 MYTTEN CL., CUCKFIELD, SSX RH17 5LN ENG
34740 FAIRCLOUGH, CHRIS, 2 SPRINGCLOUGH DR., WORSLEY, M28 5HS ENG
34741 OVERHOLT, JOHN, 17 THETFORD RD., NEW MALDEN, SRY KT3 5DN ENG
34742 HIGMAN, J., 42 ALDWORTH AVE., WANTAGE, OXON OX12 7EJ ENG
34743 BROWN, MICHAEL, THE OLD BAKERY., TILMANSTONE, KEN CT14 0JQ ENG
34744 BEATTY, G., 186 MAYORS WALK., PETERBOROUGH, CAMS PE3 6HQ ENG
34745 FROST, COLIN, 12 HIGHGATE DR., WEST KNIGHTON, LEI LE2 6HH ENG
34746 CRAWFORD, JOHN, 368 ABERGELE RD., OLD COLWYN, CLWYD LL29 9LV WLS
34747 BEADEN, JOHN, ABBOTTS MEAD, EARLS DOWN., DALLINGTON, SSX TN21 9LU ENG
34748 SHEEDY, GLENYS, PO BOX 233., NEW GISBORNE, VIC 3438 AUS
34749 EAMES, EUNICE, PO BOX 198., BOX HILL, VIC 3128 AUS
34750 PARKER, WILMA, 68 GEOFFREY DR., KILSYTH, VIC 3137 AUS
34751 GHERARDIN, MRS C., PO BOX 550., MT WAVERLEY, VIC 3149 AUS
34752 BAUER, MARGARET, 15 HORTON ST., BUNDABERG, QLD 4670 AUS
34753 LANGDON, KENNETH, 30 LOVELL DR., WARRAGUL, VIC 3820 AUS
34754 MCKEON, CORAL, 7 JOHN ST., DALBY, QLD 4405 AUS
34755 GIRDLER, MAREE, 13 CREEK ST., GLEBE, NSW 2037 AUS
34756 SENN, ROBYN, PO BOX 202., EDMONTON, QLD 4869 AUS
34757 NORRIS, WENDY, 83 LAWSON ST., MUDGEE, NSW 2850 AUS
34758 CONNELLY, SANDRA, 10 APPLEBY ST., GRAFTON, NSW 2460 AUS

34759 EGAN, ELAINE, 37 BRADYS GULLY RD., NORTH GOSFORD, NSW 2250 AUS
34760 RODDA, MRS G., 145 KILBY RD., EAST KEW, VIC 3102 AUS
34761 WATTS, JOY, 6 OAK ST., DROUIN, VIC 3818 AUS
34762 QUINN, CAROL, 1 LLOYD CRT., BROWNS PLAINS, QLD 4118 AUS
34763 WAGSTAFF, HELEN, 143 KERRIGAN ST., FRENCHVILLE, QLD 4701 AUS
34764 DYTLEWSKI, MARGARET, 12 FLINDERS ST., MT HAWTHORN, WA 6016 AUS
34765 PEPPER, ALWYN, 65 BRIGHTON RD., SCARBOROUGH, WA 6019 AUS
34766 WENKE, STEPHEN, 18 STUART TCE., PORT AUGUSTA, SA 5700 AUS
34767 CORCORAN, MARY, 34 GRAMMAR ST., WENDOUREE, VIC 3355 AUS
34768 FARMER, JOYCE, 123 BARTON ST., EVERTON PARK, QLD 4053 AUS
34769 SMITH, GWENDA, 15 BENECIA ST., WAVELL HEIGHTS, QLD 4012 AUS
34770 SMITHURST, LEONA, PO BOX 1050., CARINDALE, QLD 4152 AUS
34771 CRUICKSHANK, MRS E., "KIRKLAND"., MOREE, NSW 2400 AUS
34772 MURPHY, ANNETTE, RMB 555 MIDDLE ARM RD., GOULBURN, NSW 2580 AUS
34773 BARRETT, LILLA, 468 PRESIDENT AVE., KIRRAWEE, NSW 2232 AUS
34774 BRERETON, MR D., 10 DREW ST., WESTMEAD, NSW 2145 AUS
34775 YOUNGBERRY, MARGARET, 79 GEORGE ST., KADINA, SA 5554 AUS
34776 ROBINSON, RON, 12 RIDGEFIELD AVE., SEAVIEW DOWNS, SA 5049 AUS
34777 COLMAN, TAMARA, 12 RICHARDSON CRES., PT AUGUSTA, SA 5700 AUS
34778 JEUKEN, MRS H., PO BOX 591., BATHURST, NSW 2795 AUS
34779 CONDRICK, MAUREEN, 37 HIGH ST., TENTERFIELD, NSW 2372 AUS
34780 HENRY, MARGARET, 4/15 WELLS ST., EAST GOSFORD, NSW 2250 AUS
34781 ARDILL, JOHN, 13 MONTAUBAN AVE., SEAFORTH, NSW 2092 AUS
34782 FORGE, JACQUELINE, 66 BRUDENELL DR., JERRABOMBERRA, NSW 2619 AUS
34783 CUMMINGS, MRS F., 6 MOLONG RD., GYMEA BAY, NSW 2227 AUS
34784 SHEARER, MRS J., 15 ORANA AVE., SEVEN HILLS, NSW 2147 AUS
34785 TOLLARD, JULIE, 58 MARLIN AVE., FLORAVILLE, NSW 2280 AUS
34786 BAXTER, MR L., 13 JACANA GVE., HEATHCOTE, NSW 2233 AUS
34787 JONES, CLARE, 1 GRAND VIEW RD., MT VICTORIA, NSW 2786 AUS
34788 SZALAY, MRS P., 10 EMU RD., GLENBROOK, NSW 2773 AUS
34789 PAYNE, GORDON, 126 FARMBOROUGH RD., UNANDERRA, NSW 2526 AUS
34790 ROSS, IRENE, MULLUMBURRA BINGI., VIA MORUYA, NSW 2537 AUS
34791 HILL, KIM, 6 ZOLA AVE., RYDE, NSW 2112 AUS
34792 BRACKEN, TASMAN, PO BOX 81., RAILTON, TAS 7305 AUS
34793 PARKINSON, BARRY, PO BOX 200., CROYDON, VIC 3136 AUS
34794 CHERRETT-JONES, KAREN, 68 FRANCIS ST., BAIRNSDALE, VIC 3875 AUS
34795 MCLENNAN, WENDY, "BURRA" RMB 2750., COBDEN, VIC 3266 AUS
34796 HORSBURGH, MALCOLM, "GLAMORGAN" YANNATHAN RD., NYORA, VIC 3987 AUS
34797 MENZIES, PAM, 13 STANLEY ST., TOORA, VIC 3962 AUS
34798 GREGORY, GENNI, 22 MEADOW AVE., TOOTGAROOK, VIC 3941 AUS
34799 STOKES, REX, 11/26 ROTHERWOOD ST., RICHMOND, VIC 3121 AUS
34800 MURPHY, BEATRICE, 2 KEMSLEY CT., HAWTHORN, VIC 3123 AUS
34801 VAN ELST, BARBARA, PO BOX 42., GAYNDAH, QLD 4625 AUS
34802 SHAILER, NICHOLAS, 153 HAROLD ST., TOWNSVILLE, QLD 4810 AUS
34803 MENGEL, PATRICIA, PO BOX 678., PROSERPINE, QLD 4800 AUS
34804 SINCLAIR, MARY, 11 JACANA ST., ROCHEDALE, QLD 4123 AUS
34805 HAGAN, MRS J., 9 HALL ST., DALBY, QLD 4405 AUS
34806 LOCKE, ROSS, C/O COMMONWEALTH BANK., MACKAY, QLD 4740 AUS
34807 CARTER, KAREN, 190 ROYAL PDE., ALDERLEY, QLD 4051 AUS
34808 MARKWELL, PAULINE, 8 LOMATTA ST., THE GAP, QLD 4061 AUS
34809 HENDERSON, ALASTAIR, 125 ANNIE ST., TORWOOD, QLD 4066 AUS
34810 SOMERS, STANLEY, 7 COLWORTH ST., SUNNYBANK HILLS, QLD 4109 AUS
34811 BRENNAN, MRS N., PO BOX 278., GARBUTT, QLD 4814 AUS
34812 MACKAY, CHRISTINE, PO BOX 627., HERMIT PARK, QLD 4812 AUS
34813 LIDDIARD, ROBERT, 14 GIFFORD WAY., DIANELLA, WA 6062 AUS
34814 HUKIN, ROBYN, 7 JADE ST., ARMADALE, WA 6112 AUS
34815 SCARLETT, JOY, 9 BELVEDERE CRES., EATON, WA 6230 AUS
34816 RUSSELL, MR W., 48 BEDELIA WAY., HAMMERSLEY, WA 6022 AUS
34817 FRENCH, PETER, THE MOORINGS, MAIN ST., CHILTHORNE DOMER, SOM BA22 8RD ENG
34818 BREWER, JENNIFER, 50 DORVILLE RD., LEE, LND SE12 8EB ENG
34819 PEARMAN, DEREK, 8 DANEBURY FIELDWAY., NEW ADDINGTON, LND CR0 9EU ENG
34820 INMAN, TERENCE, 8 LATYMER RD., LOWER EDMONTON, LND N9 ENG
34821 STAFFORD-HILL, PETER, 80A REDDOWN RD., COULSDON, SRY CR5 1AL ENG
34822 JONES, MYRA, 34 POYNDERS CRT., LONDON, SW4 8NL ENG
34823 TAYLOR, MAUREEN, 143 TUFFLEY AVE., GLOUCESTER, GLS GL1 5NP ENG
34824 PARKINSON, RAYMOND, 128A DOYLE GDNS., WILLESDEN, NW10 3SR ENG
34825 BIRD, MRS P., 49 OAKHURST GR., EAST DULWICH, LND SE22 9AH ENG
34826 HEYBOURN, MAJOR A.S., 15 SPELDHURST RD., CHISWICK, LND W4 1BX ENG
34827 VAUGHAN, MR F., 11 HILLSIDE GDNS., HARROW, MDX HA3 9UW ENG
34828 DEW, ELIZABETH, 52 ABBISS HSE., HAZELWOOD CL., HITCHIN, HERTS SG5 1PR ENG
34829 CLARKE, BRUCE, 7 WARWICK SQ., WESTMINSTER, LND SW1V 2AA ENG
34830 JOHNSON, ROBERT, SETTER., MID YELL, SHETLAND ZE2 9BJ SCT

34831 ADIE, NICHOLAS, 9 ALEXANDRA RD., ST LEONARDS-ON-SEA, SSX TN37 6LD ENG
34832 FENWICK, GRANT, 13 PADDOCK CT., 142 GRAND DR., LONDON, SW20 9EA ENG
34833 STOYLE, IAN, "FAIRFIELD"., THORVERTON, DEV EX5 5NG ENG
34834 ASHFORD, ANNA, 25 BEECHFIELD RD., BROMLEY, KEN BR1 3BT ENG
34835 ALLISON, MRS E., HIGH TOR, GREY RD., ALTRINCHAM, CHS WA14 4BT ENG
34836 BENNETT, CHRISTINE, 8 WELLINGTON GR., PORTCHESTER, HAM PO16 9RX ENG
34837 ROBB, HEATHER, 244 QUEENS ESP., THORNESIDE, QLD 4158 AUS
34838 YARROW, MR C. & MRS J., 12 DRAPER LN., D'AGUILAR, QLD 4514 AUS
34839 BEST, VALERIE, 5 JILBARD DR., SLACKS CREEK, QLD 4127 AUS
34840 SHAW, MRS P., 52 ARTHUR ST., GRACEMERE, QLD 4702 AUS
34841 WILLIS, JOHN, 113 COX'S RD., NORTH RYDE, NSW 2113 AUS
34842 BRYANT, TOM, 31 LISGAR ST., GOULBURN, NSW 2580 AUS
34843 PRIMMER, LORRAINE, LOT 16 MURRAY RD., WINGHAM, NSW 2429 AUS
34844 BH FAMILY HIST GP, PO BOX 779., BROKEN HILL, NSW 2880 AUS
34845 MOORE, PETER, 12 ELLIOTT PL., BAULKHAM HILLS, NSW 2153 AUS
34846 ROWBOTTOM, JENNIFER, 5 LETHBRIDGE CT., PORT AUGUSTA, SA 5700 AUS
34847 PETERS, JACK, 11 DENMAN RD., ALBANY, WA 6330 AUS
34848 SMITH, ALISON, 53 CAMBRIDGE CRES., ROCKINGHAM, WA 6168 AUS
34849 PITCHER, MR H., PO BOX 424., NORFOLK ISLAND, 2899 AUS
34850 DE GRUSSA, MR A. & MRS P., PO BOX 458., ESPERANCE, WA 6450 AUS
34851 COLEMAN, LINDA, 3 COOPER ST., MULLALOO, WA 6025 AUS
34852 GODFREY, MRS B., VELLUM DOWNS PMB 43., HUGHENDEN, QLD 4821 AUS
34853 POLLITT, MRS V., PO BOX 56., SOUTH MACKAY, QLD 4740 AUS
34854 LAMB, REBECCA, 37 MICHIE ST., WANNIASSA, ACT 2903 AUS
34855 CHAMBERLAIN, MRS D., 14 REIBEY PL., CURTIN, ACT 2605 AUS
34856 DOWNES, SUSAN, 10 SEGERS AVE., PADSTOW, NSW 2211 AUS
34857 RUTTLEY, HELEN, 62 WHELAN AVE., CHIPPING NORTON, NSW 2170 AUS
34858 BORWICK, MAUREEN, 16 WINSFORD AVE., HEBERSHAM, NSW 2770 AUS
34859 LUKE, MRS M., 45 KIRKHAM CRES., TAMWORTH, NSW 2340 AUS
34860 MCTAGGART, GRAEME, 32 CLINTON CL., BEROWRA HEIGHTS, NSW 2082 AUS
34861 SCHIEREN, HEATHER, 26 CURRY RD., PARK ORCHARDS, VIC 3114 AUS
34862 EMBLIN, LYNNE, 9 LOWE ST., MT ELIZA, VIC 3930 AUS
34863 BATTLEY, MRS L., 62 SEVENOAKS AVE., CROYDON, VIC 3136 AUS
34864 BERGIN, PETER, 15 NAVIGATOR ST., MCCRAE, VIC 3938 AUS
34865 EVANS, ALLEN, LOT 3 WELLINGTON RD., LYSTERFIELD, VIC 3156 AUS
34866 STENNETT, MARGARET, 60 VORES RD., WHITESIDE, QLD 4503 AUS
34867 MORIARTY, MR R., "YANDOOYA" FLYING FOX CREEK., CANUNGRA, QLD 4275 AUS
34868 ROBINSON, BARBARA, 20/104 DORNOCH TCE., HIGHGATE HILL, QLD 4101 AUS
34869 SALTER, LEISA, 66 HALY ST., KINGAROY, QLD 4610 AUS
34870 GLASSICK, LINDA, 6 CLINTON AVE., BURLEIGH HEADS, QLD 4220 AUS
34871 SOWTER, BARBARA, MS 1536 BAHDILLI CRES., DIDDILLIBAH, QLD 4560 AUS
34872 EASTGATE, MARIANNE, 6/226 MORAY ST., NEW FARM, QLD 4005 AUS
34873 JOHNSTON, MISS M., 106 DERWENT AVE., LINDISFARNE, TAS 7015 AUS
34874 THOMPSON, ALAN, 81 CASTLETON CRES., GOWRIE, ACT 2904 AUS
34875 REID, HUGH, 82 YERRIN ST., BALWYN, VIC 3103 AUS
34876 MCPHERSON, HOWARD, PO BOX 440., HEALESVILLE, VIC 3777 AUS
34877 STRINGER, VALERIE, 31 BORVA DR., EAST KEILOR, VIC 3033 AUS
34878 WALKER, JOAN, 56 HAWTHORY RD., KILSYTH, VIC 3137 AUS
34879 STEVENS, DENISE, RMB E 900., BALLARAT, VIC 3352 AUS
34880 MCCOOL, ROSS, 51 GRACE ST., FERNDALE, WA 6155 AUS
34881 BALDWINSON, MRS M., 16 NOONGAH PL., NOLLAMARA, WA 6061 AUS
34882 HARRISON, MR R., 9 TRALEE RD., FLOREAT PARK, WA 6014 AUS
34883 MCRAE, COLIN, RMB 3006., MURRAY BRIDGE, SA 5253 AUS
34884 FLETT, STANLEY, 14 WADE ST., LISMORE, NSW 2480 AUS
34885 RITCHIE, ENID, 39 OSGATHORPE RD., GLADESVILLE, NSW 2111 AUS
34886 ZAHNER, BRIAN, PO BOX 515., STRATHFIELD, NSW 2135 AUS
34887 MARTIN, MR L., PO BOX 143., CASINO, NSW 2470 AUS
34888 GREGORY, IAN, 50 WAIRAKEI RD., WAMBERAL, NSW 2260 AUS
34889 JOBLING, DAREN, 5 MONT ALBERT RD., GEELONG WEST, VIC 3220 AUS
34890 LAWRENCE, VALERIE, 1 YORKSHIRE ST., BLACKBURN NTH, VIC 3130 AUS
34891 ONA, JUAN, GPO BOX 232., SYDNEY, NSW 2001 AUS
34892 BELLAMY, PATRICIA, 73 WATTLE RD., JANNALI, NSW 2226 AUS
34893 CLARRY, SHIRLEY, 4/20 ROSEMOUNT TCE., WINDSOR, QLD 4030 AUS
34894 TWIBLE, PATRICIA, 54 ALLAMBIE ST., CAMP HILL, QLD 4152 AUS
34895 MCGIFFERT, JOHN, 23 RINGDUFFERIN RD., TOYE, DOWN BT30 9PH N. IRELAND
34896 FORD, MR C., 4 CAMIRA ST., PYMBLE, NSW 2073 AUS
34897 MCALISTER, DAVID, 32 WALKER ST., COWRA, NSW 2794 AUS
34898 MALTBY, JOHN, 84 SUFFOLK AVE., COLLAROY, NSW 2097 AUS
34899 HANNAH, MRS E., 53 HECTOR ST., SEFTON, NSW 2162 AUS
34900 MCCORMICK, MARY, 13 OXFORD ST., MERRYLANDS, NSW 2160 AUS
34901 GEDDES, MRS N., 402 WAGGA RD., LAVINGTON, NSW 2641 AUS
34902 QUINN, SANDRA, 27 MERNAGH ST., ASHCROFT, NSW 2168 AUS

34903 FLETCHER, MRS C., TYRILLY, CANYONLEIGH RD., BRAYTON, NSW 2579 AUS
34904 DEARING, GEOFFREY, 38 JACANA GVE., HEATHCOTE, NSW 2233 AUS
34905 PACEY, MRS S., 1 HAZELWOOD PL., EPPING, NSW 2121 AUS
34906 STENNING, IVY, 69 BUSBY RD., BUSBY, NSW 2168 AUS
34907 CROSTON, RACHAEL, RMB 9105B., BORNHOLM, WA 6330 AUS
34908 PHILLIPS, YVONNE, SEVILLA, BLACKWALL RD., BLACKWALL, TAS 7275 AUS
34909 DENNIS, PHILIP, 4 NEVIN ST., ROSSARDEN, TAS 7213 AUS
34910 REES, MRS H., 4 QUANDONE AVE., MOUNT GAMBIER, SA 5290 AUS
34911 CARR, DAVID, PO BOX 368., PLYMPTON, SA 5038 AUS
34912 EBBINGHAUS, HEINZ, 5 RICHMOND ST., KENSINGTON, SA 5068 AUS
34913 PIPER, DEBBIE, 79 HENRY MELVILLE CRES., GILMORE, ACT 2905 AUS
34914 SIEDE, BETTY, PO BOX 159., EUROA, VIC 3666 AUS
34915 BUNCE, MRS L., PO BOX 48., YARRAM, VIC 3971 AUS
34916 COWIE, MARJ, THIRTEEN MILE RD., GARFIELD, VIC 3814 AUS
34917 HALL, LAWRIE, 9 LENNOX ST., NORTHCOTE, VIC 3070 AUS
34918 MCKENNA, MRS H., 33/26 RUTHERFORD RD., VIEW BANK, VIC 3084 AUS
34919 TROTTER, JOHN, 122 STIRLING RD., METUNG, VIC 3904 AUS
34920 MORLEY, KENNETH, 13-14 DIRLTON CRES., PARK ORCHARDS, VIC 3114 AUS
34921 LOWE, MRS E., 54 QUEEN ST., FRANKSTON, VIC 3199 AUS
34922 MILNE, MISS J., 19 MARION AVE., MOOROOLBARK, VIC 3138 AUS
34923 HAMMOND, MR K., 15 KERRI CT., SUNBURY, VIC 3429 AUS
34924 CAMPBELL, KATHLEEN, 4 CULVERLANDS RD., HEATHMONT, VIC 3135 AUS
34925 PROWD, ERIC, 21 DAHLIA ST., DROMANA, VIC 3936 AUS
34926 BECKETT, SANDRA, PO BOX 381., HASTINGS, VIC 3915 AUS
34927 GREAVES, SHIRLEY, 8 JURA AVE., PARK ORCHARDS, VIC 3114 AUS
34928 TRIFFETT, ALFRED, 4 HALWYN CRES., PRESTON, VIC 3072 AUS
34929 WRIGHT, MRS C., MS 368., GIN GIN, QLD 4671 AUS
34930 ROSS, MARGARET, 61 TRUDGIAN ST., SUNNYBANK, QLD 4109 AUS
34931 HORWOOD, TED & LOLA, 3 BERNBOROUGH CRT., KELSO, QLD 4815 AUS
34932 SCHWERIN, VICKI, 306 MACKENZIE ST., TOOWOOMBA, QLD 4350 AUS
34933 STILLS, NOELEEN, 12 JODEN PL., SOUTHPORT, QLD 4215 AUS
34934 LEGGATE, JOHN, PO BOX 712., KENMORE, QLD 4069 AUS
34935 HIGGINS, M., 199 MUSGRAVE ST., ROCKHAMPTON, QLD 4701 AUS
34936 COLLITT, ANNE, 62 MANLY DR., ROBINA WATERS, QLD 4226 AUS
34937 NEILLEY, MRS D., "GLENELG", MOURA, QLD 4718 AUS
34938 ANDERSEN, MERLE, RIVERDALE., GOONDIWINDI, QLD 4390 AUS
34939 DWYER, BEVERLEY, PO BOX 34., MIAMI, QLD 4220 AUS
34940 DRURY, NITA, 34 JARRAH ST., NORTH MACKAY, QLD 4740 AUS
34941 LOGUE, FAYE, PO BOX 482., TULLY, QLD 4854 AUS
34942 GROSSI, FAYE, PO BOX 287., INGHAM, QLD 4850 AUS
34943 TURNER, MR H., 76 WITSTINKHOUT AVE., SAFARI GARDENS, TVL 0300 RSA
34944 MACALISTER, HEATHER, 9 MISTEAL CL., LAKESIDE, CP 7951 RSA
34945 LAUTRE, GRAHAM, PO BOX 419 CRAMERVIEW., SANDTON, 2060 RSA
34946 RAIMONDO, DAWN, 26 BISHOPS COURT DR., BISHOPSCOURT, CAPE 7700 RSA
34947 STAPLETON, ROY, BOX 6219., JOHANNESBURG, TVL 2000 RSA
34948 SCOGINGS, MICHAEL, 41 MAUD AVE., PIETERMARITZBURG, NATAL 3201 RSA
34949 ROELOFFZE, MR C., 55 SECOND AVE., LAMBTON, GERMISTON, 1401 RSA
34950 BLAIR, BEVERLEY, 38 PRINCE CHARLES RD., WESTVILLE, NATAL 3630 RSA
34951 SPRIGHTON, CHARLES, 56 WINCHELSEA AVE., WENTWORTH, NATAL 4052 RSA
34952 GALL, SHIRLEY, 106 KIRBY RD., ASPLEY, QLD 4034 AUS
34953 DIXON, JEANNE, 43 RIAWEENA ST., THE GAP, QLD 4061 AUS
34954 BOOTH, GWENDA, 18 KERRABEE ST., NERANG, QLD 4211 AUS
34955 BURBIDGE, LORRAINE, 2 BUSHWICK ST., THE GAP, QLD 4061 AUS
34956 KEMP, IRENE, 18 EILEEN AVE., SOUTHPORT, QLD 4215 AUS
34957 CRISAFULLI, JOY, 5 CHURCH ST., VICTORIA POINT, QLD 4165 AUS
34958 HAMILTON, JOHN, 7 FRANCIS ST., RICHMOND, VIC 3121 AUS
34959 SUMBLER, EDWARD, 22 BAYVIEW ST., ALTONA, VIC 3018 AUS
34960 COCKRAM, PEGGY, 1/46 OAKLAND ST., MORNINGTON, VIC 3931 AUS
34961 LEE, ELAINE, 39 HERBERT ST., PARKDALE, VIC 3195 AUS
34962 PICKERING, JOAN, RMB 736., NHILL, VIC 3418 AUS
34963 VERNON, MR N., 27 NIXON ST., ROSEBUD, VIC 3939 AUS
34964 LAMING, WALLACE, 24 TEMPLESTOWE RD., BULLEEN, VIC 3105 AUS
34965 BRIEN, HARRY, 9 WINDSOR AVE., ROLEYSTONE, WA 6111 AUS
34966 CAMPBELL, MR G.L., 12 PARK ST., TAHMOOR, NSW 2573 AUS
34967 AHERN, SUSAN, 38 CLEVELAND ST., WAHROONGA, NSW 2076 AUS
34968 SAMUELS, MRS D., 59 ROBERTA ST., TUMBI UMBI, NSW 2261 AUS
34969 ASHBY, ANN, 7 NEW FARM RD., WEST PENNANT HILLS, NSW 2125 AUS
34970 GRIFFIN, GWEN, 163 LAKE RD., PORT MACQUARIE, NSW 2444 AUS
34971 CARDIFF, FRANK, 123 VICTORIA ST., EAST GOSFORD, NSW 2250 AUS
34972 HAILS, VICKI, 8/18 BRETT ST., KINGS LANGLEY, NSW 2147 AUS
34973 FEARBY, JANET, 46 CARROLL ST., GUNNEDAH, NSW 2380 AUS
34974 OWEN, MRS H., 31 COPPERLEAF WAY., CASTLE HILL, NSW 2154 AUS

34975 PARKER, GEOFFREY, 77 DUNALBAN AVE., WOY WOY, NSW 2256 AUS
34976 DOUCH, CAROLE, ADELAIDE ST., GREENWELL POINT, NSW 2540 AUS
34977 LAING, MISS H., 101 HILLCREST AVE., GREENACRE, NSW 2190 AUS
34978 LAING, MISS H., 101 HILLCREST AVE., GREENACRE, NSW 2190 AUS
34979 LAING, MISS H., 101 HILLCREST AVE., GREENACRE, NSW 2190 AUS
34980 JONES, MR R.H., 1096 FOSTER AVE., COQUITLAM, BC V3J 2M7 CAN
34981 ROSIE, RUTH, 14239 MELROSE DR., SURREY, BC V3R 5R3 CAN
34982 PEARSON, MARION, PO BOX 107., GLEN MORRIS, ONT N0B 1W0 CAN
34983 BRUDER, DONNA, 2929 DEMODE RD., HOLLY, MI 48442 USA
34984 FRAGASSO, MICHEL, 12235 GOURDEAU., QUEBEC, QUE G2A 3E3 CAN
34985 BRULE-GERMAIN, LOUISE, 3650 DES CHENAUX., TROIS-RIVIERES, QUE G8Y 1A4 CAN
34986 BHAR, JILL, 8 HOBBS AVE., NEPEAN, ONT K2H 6W9 CAN
34987 BAGLOLE, KEVIN, 193 MARGARET AVE., KITCHENER, ONT N2H 4J1 CAN
34988 HILL, MARY LOU, 4707-35 AVE SW., CALGARY, ALB T3E 1B5 CAN
34989 SHAW, BERYL, BOX 364., CARDSTON, ALB T0K 0K0 CAN
34990 HAASDYK, ULRICH, 64 STRATHCONA RD SW., CALGARY, ALB T3H 1X5 CAN
34991 MASON, PHYLLIS, 4581 JOHN ST., VANCOUVER, BC V5V 3X3 CAN
34992 LUSCHER, DOROTHY, 37-1916 8TH ST NORTH., CRANBROOK, BC V1C 3N3 CAN
34993 CROFT, MARY, 1127 BOUNDARY RD., PEMBROKE, ONT K8A 7T9 CAN
34994 TOOP, DARREN, 192 ANNA AVE., OTTAWA, ONT K1Z 7V2 CAN
34995 SAULT, PENNY, 7604 CUNLIFFE RD., VERNON, BC V1B 1T3 CAN
34996 BUTLER, ROBERT, 240 SUNRISE CRES., OAKVILLE, ONT L6L 3L3 CAN
34997 LYLE, ANDREA, B12-2820 HARRIET RD., VICTORIA, BC V9A 1T1 CAN
34998 PAFFORD, FRED, PO BOX 108., WESLEYVILLE, NFD A0G 4R0 CAN
34999 SHAW, MARC, 144 JAMES ST., KINGSTON, ONT K7K 1Z4 CAN
35000 KOCUR, MITCHELL, 84 LOCKWOOD RD., REGINA, SAS S4S 2C6 CAN
35001 LIMEBEER, WILLIAM, 51 ALLAN AVE., GUELPH, ONT N1H 3G3 CAN
35002 GOFFARD, MARTIN, 121 GABLES CT., WINNIPEG, MAN R2C 4H2 CAN
35003 RUSHTON, PATRICK, PO BOX 904., ALMONTE, ONT K0A 1A0 CAN
35004 HAVELANGE, SHELLEY, #707-3 DONALD ST., WINNIPEG, MAN R3L 2P6 CAN
35005 SLINN, CONNIE, 9 ANCONA CRT., NEPEAN, ONT K2G 0N4 CAN
35006 SCHENKEL, PHYLLIS, 65 KING GEORGE'S RD., ETOBICOKE, ONT M8X 1L8 CAN
35007 BENNETT, ARTHUR, 16 OSMAND ST., WANNIASSA, ACT 2903 AUS
35008 VERHOEVEN, GERARD, 7 TANNABAR PL., ISABELLA PLAINS, ACT 2905 AUS
35009 SHEPHERD, PETA, 52 PEARSON ST., HOLDER, ACT 2611 AUS
35010 WHARAM, BERYL, 2 BARLOW PL, NARROWS., DARWIN, NT 0820 AUS
35011 REES, MISS K., GPO BOX 1271., HOBART, TAS 7001 AUS
35012 BENNETTS, ROSLYN, PO BOX 1701., ALBANY, WA 6330 AUS
35013 BAGLEY, JUNE, 18 BRODRICK ST., KARRINYUP, WA 6018 AUS
35014 ARCHIBALD, MR T., 116 CORDELIA AVE., COOLBELLUP, WA 6163 AUS
35015 YATES, MARGARET, RMB 305., WITCHCLIFFE, WA 6286 AUS
35016 WEBB, GILLIAN, 197 SELBY ST., FLOREAT, WA 6014 AUS
35017 MEAGHER, MARGRET, PO BOX 252., WAGIN, WA 6315 AUS
35018 HACKETT, NOREEN, 56 VICTORIA PDE., AUGUSTA, WA 6290 AUS
35019 FELTHOUSE, MARGARET, 3/64 FIFTH RD., ARMADALE, WA 6112 AUS
35020 BEE, DIANNE, C/O PO BOX 60., BRUNSWICK JUNCTION, WA 6224 AUS
35021 LUDECKE, GRAHAM, NAT AUST BANK, 50 ST GEORGES TCE., PERTH, WA 6000 AUS
35022 BIRKS, GREG, PO BOX 718., SOUTH PERTH, WA 6151 AUS
35023 HINNRICHSEN, KAY, 15 BRIGADOON CL., MANDURAH, WA 6210 AUS
35024 MILENTIS, MRS S., 14 SMALLMAN CRES., GREENWOOD, WA 6024 AUS
35025 LAWRIE, MR V., 4 KING ST., GERALDTON, WA 6530 AUS
35026 APEL, MRS G., MOUNT TOM., MIRIAM VALE, QLD 4677 AUS
35027 CLARK, MRS B., 60 WHITE PATCH ESP., BRIBIE ISLAND, QLD 4507 AUS
35028 FREEMAN, JOHN, 23 TOSTI ST., SORRENTO, QLD 4217 AUS
35029 WILLIAMS, MRS B., 1 TORTUGA ST., DECEPTION BAY, QLD 4508 AUS
35030 HRABANEK, MRS A., LOT 38 TARATA RD., GUANABA, QLD 4210 AUS
35031 WILKINSON, MRS G., 11 GLEN RD., THE GAP, QLD 4061 AUS
35032 SULLIVAN, DR M., BUNYIP ST., BURBANK, QLD 4156 AUS
35033 SAMIEC, CHARLOTTE, 3 CANMAROO ST., NAMBOUR, QLD 4560 AUS
35034 REDCLIFFE GENEAL SOC, PO BOX 249., REDCLIFFE, QLD 4020 AUS
35035 BEAVIS, CORALIE, 15 GARDEN GROVE CRES., KIRWAN, QLD 4817 AUS
35036 DEAN, MRS E., 50 MORIALTA ST., MANSFIELD, QLD 4122 AUS
35037 MONTEY, KAREN, 384 TOR ST., TOOWOOMBA, QLD 4350 AUS
35038 BANKS, MARGARET, 48 BELCLARE ST., THE GAP, QLD 4061 AUS
35039 RICE, YVONNE, 19 EVANDALE AVE., NUNAWADING, VIC 3131 AUS
35040 MILLER, MR J., 23 SCARLET ASH DR., LOWER TEMPLESTOWE, VIC 3107 AUS
35041 SKINNER, EDNA, 43 LYTTON ST., GLENROY, VIC 3046 AUS
35042 CHANDLER, EDNA, RMB 1018., PICOLA, VIC 3639 AUS
35043 HOUGHTON, STANLEY, 35 SUNBEAM AVE., EAST RINGWOOD, VIC 3135 AUS
35044 MONAGHAN, JOHN, C/O POST OFFICE., CALLINGTON, SA 5254 AUS
35045 MCLEAN, STEVE, 26 ELLIOTT AVE., BALWYN, VIC 3103 AUS
35046 SAVAGE, DENNIS, 6 LARA CL., PAYNESVILLE, VIC 3880 AUS

35047 LEMON, MRS J., 5 DAVIES ST., WARRAGUL, VIC 3820 AUS
35048 DE LA HAYE, PHILLIP, 2/26 SPRING ST., HASTINGS, VIC 3915 AUS
35049 SARTORI, MRS D., RMB 2575., YANDOIT, VIA DAYLESFORD, VIC 3461 AUS
35050 MEARS, MARY, 5 SUTHERLAND AVE., MELTON SOUTH, VIC 3338 AUS
35051 NAPOLITANO, MRS S, 44 LANTANA ST., IVANHOE, VIC 3079 AUS
35052 ENTWISTLE, ROY, 56 DRYSDALE AVE., NORTH GEELONG, VIC 3215 AUS
35053 SMITH, ROMA, PO BOX 80., ORBOST, VIC 3888 AUS
35054 BROWN, MARY, 134 BAILLIE ST., HORSHAM, VIC 3400 AUS
35055 SHINE, SALLY, PO BOX 276., MOE, VIC 3825 AUS
35056 JOYCE, CHERYL, RMB 8348., SOUTH WANGARATTA, VIC 3678 AUS
35057 IRWIN, LILIAN, 4 MALMSBURY ST., HAWTHORN, VIC 3122 AUS
35058 COOMBS, REV. RICHARD, 7 COLES CT., BEAUMARIS, VIC 3193 AUS
35059 HARTMAN , PAULINE, 9 COLIN AVE., PARK ORCHARDS, VIC 3114 AUS
35060 WARNE, GWEN, 46 MURLONG ST., SWAN HILL, VIC 3585 AUS
35061 BROWN, LINDA, 36 ALLENBY AVE., RESERVOIR, VIC 3073 AUS
35062 LUDEKE, BERNHARD, 157 BINNEY ST EAST., EUROA, VIC 3666 AUS
35063 NETHERTON, SHERYLE, 49 ROSS ST., HUNTINGDALE, VIC 3166 AUS
35064 MARSH, MILLICENT, 57 FIRST ST., BLACK ROCK, VIC 3193 AUS
35065 JOHNSON, MRS I, 9 BOULTON CRES., TYERS, VIC 3844 AUS
35066 MARTIN, MRS L, 3/60 CONDELL ST., FITZROY, VIC 3065 AUS
35067 CRADDOCK, DOROTHY, 8 VALENCIA ST., ESSENDON, VIC 3040 AUS
35068 HANSLOW, MR J, 20 DUNCAN ST., HUSKISSON, NSW 2540 AUS
35069 KILFORD, JOHN, 19 NELSON ST., ANNANDALE, NSW 2038 AUS
35070 NEWMAN, RAYMOND, 14 CHRISTOPHER CRES., BATEHAVEN, NSW 2536 AUS
35071 DUNN, ROBERT, 13 BRETT ST., KINGS LANGLEY, NSW 2147 AUS
35072 TAYLOR, ESMA, 2 JASPRIZZA AVE., YOUNG, NSW 2594 AUS
35073 KIPP, MR K, 14 WELLESLEY ST., PITT TOWN, NSW 2756 AUS
35074 HANCOCK, FAY, 28 EDNA DR., TATHRA, NSW 2550 AUS
35075 PHEE, MRS M, 205 HUDSON PDE., CLAREVILLE BEACH, NSW 2107 AUS
35076 MARSHMAN, ERIC, 13 GOVERNMENT RD., NORDS WHARF, NSW 2301 AUS
35077 BAKER, MR E, PO BOX 13., KINGSWOOD, NSW 2747 AUS
35078 LEACH, WILLIAM, 20 BAYSWATER AVE., HURSTVILLE, NSW 2220 AUS
35079 HODGSON, MRS R, 50 MALTON RD., BEECROFT, NSW 2119 AUS
35080 FLORANCE, MRS S, 'TILLY' SNOWY MT HWY., NUMBUGGA, NSW 2550 AUS
35081 WALLACE, BRUCE, 9 NAYLOR PL., INGLEBURN, NSW 2565 AUS
35082 ROY, JEAN, PO BOX 10E., EAST CORRIMAL, NSW 2518 AUS
35083 HOPE, CAROLE, 7 NUTHALL CRES., YOUNG, NSW 2594 AUS
35084 WOOD, GALINDA, 4/41 ATKINSON ST., QUEANBEYAN, NSW 2620 AUS
35085 HARTLEY, LAUREEN, 19 JAMIESON ST., CARDWELL, QLD 4816 AUS
35086 CAPPLE, MRS L, 525 ARGENT ST., BROKEN HILL, NSW 2880 AUS
35087 GOLDSMTIH, ELIZABETH, 7 DUKE ST., JUNEE, NSW 2663 AUS
35088 ROOS, LYNETTE, 18 FARRER PL., FRENCHS FOREST, NSW 2086 AUS
35089 CATHRO, ADELE, 164 DENISON ST., W TAMWORTH, NSW 2340 AUS
35090 DODD, MRS J, PO BOX 155., COONAMBLE, NSW 2829 AUS
35091 HAWKINS, DAWN, 45 HILDA RD., BAULKHAM HILLS, NSW 2153 AUS
35092 HOGGARD, CHRISTINE, 125 WESTMORELAND RD., LEUMEAH, NSW 2560 AUS
35093 GOERING, TRACI, 1 BARLINGS DR, BURRI HEIGHTS., TOMAKIN, NSW 2537 AUS
35094 HARDY, RONALD, 90 SEAHAM ST., HOLMESVILLE, NSW 2286 AUS
35095 COX, DARRELL, PO BOX 26., CAMBRIDGE PARK, NSW 2747 AUS
35096 DRODGE, GERELLE, 21 SALADIN AVE., GLEN WAVERLEY, VIC 3150 AUS
35097 BRECKELL, PATRICIA, PO BOX 47., KEMPSEY, NSW 2440 AUS
35098 GRIFFITH, WILLIAM, 67 KALAKAU AVE., FORRESTERS BEACH, NSW 2260 AUS
35099 WEST, MR K, RMB 3230., CENTRAL MANGROVE, NSW 2250 AUS
35100 COYNE, LES, 40 OAKLEIGH AVE., THORNLEIGH, NSW 2120 AUS
35101 NORCOTT, LYN, PO BOX 23., WERRINGTON, NSW 2747 AUS
35102 OLUFSON, MRS J, 231 BOX RD., SYLVANIA, NSW 2224 AUS
35103 TUCKER, LOUISE, RMB 1015 SHOWGROUND RD., BUNGENDORE, NSW 2621 AUS
35104 ZAMMIT, BARBARA, PO BOX 7., KOGARAH, NSW 2217 AUS
35105 DALEY, BARBARA, 26 GLENAIR AVE., NOWRA, NSW 2541 AUS
35106 DUNN, ELIZABETH, 1/426 BEVAN ST., LAVINGTON, NSW 2641 AUS
35107 COOK, MRS N, PO BOX 135., AUGUSTA, WA 6290 AUS
35108 ROGERS, MARK, 58 DALEY CRES., FRASER, ACT 2615 AUS
35109 LEWIS, MR M, C.M.B., JUDBURY, TAS 7109 AUS
35110 GLASS, MRS S, PO BOX 40., GEORGE TOWN, TAS 7253 AUS
35111 TATTON, TERRI, PO BOX 380., DARRA, QLD 4076 AUS
35112 GUPPY, AMY, PO BOX 93., CHILDERS, QLD 4660 AUS
35113 LAWLOR, NOELINDA, 53 JUDE ST., BRACKENRIDGE, QLD 4017 AUS
35114 PRESCOTT, RICHARD, 6 HASSALL ST., CORINDA, QLD 4075 AUS
35115 KILLIP, CAROLYN, 10 HARVEY ST., BUNDABERG, QLD 4670 AUS
35116 WILSON, MRS J, 45 SEAGULL AVE., CALOUNDRA, QLD 4551 AUS
35117 MANWARING, GLENDA, 11 ORANA ST., KINGSTON, QLD 4114 AUS
35118 PACEY, MARGARET, 19 ARRAS ST., YERONGA, QLD 4104 AUS

35119 FREEMAN, MRS M, 8 PUMICESTONE RD., TOORBUL, QLD 4510 AUS
35120 PALMER, MR A, PO BOX 1., PENTLAND, QLD 4816 AUS
35121 PORTER, WENDY, 6 BLACKALL COURT., NORTH MACKAY, QLD 4740 AUS
35122 VANDERWOLF, MAXINE, PO BOX 62., MOUNT LARCOM, QLD 4695 AUS
35123 AICKIN, CARMEL, 107 EDWARD ST., DALBY, QLD 4405 AUS
35124 SCOWN, MARJORIE, 8 HIGH VIEW CRT., BALNARRING, VIC 3926 AUS
35125 LAWRENCE, NOELA, 11 CHURCHILL ST., DONCASTER EAST, VIC 3109 AUS
35126 BOWMAN, ROBIN, EDGAR RD., LONGWARRY, VIC 3816 AUS
35127 PARKER, ANN, 11 MARRIOTT ST., PARKDALE, VIC 3195 AUS
35128 BINGHAM, MRS S, 36 MONT VUE., LILYDALE, VIC 3140 AUS
35129 COBRAM GENEALOGICAL GROUP,, PO BOX 75., COBRAM, VIC 3643 AUS
35130 MCINTYRE, BEATRICE, 4 KOLORA CRES., MT ELIZA, VIC 3930 AUS
35131 PEARSE, CAROLYN, 5 SELOLA CRT., NORTH FAWKNER, VIC 3060 AUS
35132 PARKER, LEO, 14 MORVEN ST., MORNINGTON, VIC 3931 AUS
35133 BREEZE, MRS B, 4 CONE ST., BULLEEN, VIC 3105 AUS
35134 COSTELLO, EDWARD, 20 ESSEX RD., MT MARTHA, VIC 3934 AUS
35135 MCLENNAN, MARGARET, PO BOX 114., COHUNA, VIC 3568 AUS
35136 KELSO, MARION, GPO BOX 1148K., MELBOURNE, VIC 3001 AUS
35137 TOWERS, MRS L, 28A GLENMORGAN ST., EAST BRUNSWICK, VIC 3057 AUS
35138 KUHN, MRS L, 54 TWYNAM ST., BELMONT, QLD 4153 AUS
35139 RODGERS, PATRICIA, 'SPRINGHILL' SPRINGHILL RD., AUSTRALIND, WA 6230 AUS
35140 HIGGINS, RAYMOND, 46 KILLARNEY RD., LOWER TEMPLESTOWE, VIC 3107 AUS
35141 LAMMEREE, LEONIE, 7 PALM GROVE., NORMANHURST, NSW 2076 AUS
35142 WARNER, SUSAN, 1/14 BROSA AVE., EAST BENTLEIGH, VIC 3165 AUS
35143 FINN, MR E, PO BOX 282., PUNCHBOWL, NSW 2196 AUS
35144 WODE, CAROLE, 22 MERRIMAN CRES., MACARTHUR, ACT 2904 AUS
35145 MARLAND, RAYMOND, 16 HERBERT ST., MT WAVERLEY, VIC 3149 AUS
35146 BERIMAN, VINCENT, 10 HOME ST., RESERVOIR, VIC 3073 AUS
35147 KNAUTH, MRS C, 37 ARCHDALE RD., FERNY GROVE, QLD 4055 AUS
35148 CANTWELL, LEON, 11 TANGMERE ST., CHAPEL HILL, VIC 4069 AUS
35149 MCGUIRK, MR W, 12 FINNEY ST., OLD TOONGABBIE, NSW 2146 AUS
35150 STEVENSON, ALAN, PO BOX 908., MORPHETT VALE, SA 5162 AUS
35151 BUTLER, GEOFF, PO BOX 292., TAMWORTH, NSW 2340 AUS
35152 BENSON, NORMAN, 90 TAMARIND DR, COACHWOOD PK., UNANDERRA, NSW 2526 AUS
35153 FUNNELL, INEZ, 44 STEWART ST., BATHURST, NSW 2795 AUS
35154 KEALY, MOYA, 40 MIRIAM RD., DENISTONE, NSW 2114 AUS
35155 MINNICAN, DIANNE, 18 BERSHIRE AVE., MEREWETHER HEIGHTS, NSW 2291 AUS
35156 ALLAN, MRS K, 4 QUEEN ST., WARATAH, NSW 2298 AUS
35157 BLACK, PATRICIA, 19 TARO ST., BLAKEHURST, NSW 2221 AUS
35158 FLEMING, MR P, 9 COORELI CL., RAYMOND TERRACE, NSW 2324 AUS
35159 POWER, LEONY, PO BOX 837., COOMA, NSW 2630 AUS
35160 BLACKBURN, JUNE, 44 NAPOLI ST., PADSTOW, NSW 2211 AUS
35161 ARKEY, PETER, 16 LEETON CRES., PANANIA, NSW 2213 AUS
35162 AUBUSSON, MR K, PO BOX 25., CROYDON, NSW 2132 AUS
35163 MARLOW, JUDITH, 4 DAVID ST EAST., SPRINGWOOD, NSW 2777 AUS
35164 GOODMAN, MAURICE, 58 LEURA RD., ORANGE, NSW 2800 AUS
35165 BANKS, BETH, 124 GREENACRES., WETHERAL, CUL CA4 8LD ENG
35166 COLLINGBOURNE, PETER, 26 WEBB LANE, HALL GREEN., BIRMINGHAM, B28 0EA ENG
35167 BOON, JOHN, 12 BLACKHORSE LANE., NORTH WEALD, ESS CM16 6EP ENG
35168 TEBBIT, ARTHUR, 'BIRDS HILL', CHALK LANE., EAST HORSLEY, SRY KT24 6TJ ENG
35169 GARNETT, LESLEY, 10 DERBY RD., DRAYCOTT, DBY DE7 3NJ ENG
35170 POTTS, MICHAEL, BROOKE HOUSE, THE PARADE., PARKGATE, CHES L64 6RN ENG
35171 HORNELL, KATHLEEN, 6 RIDGWAY RD., FARNHAM, SRY GU9 8NW ENG
35172 TAMBLING, VICTOR, 8 CEDARWOOD CROFT., GREAT BARR, W MIDS B42 1HS ENG
35173 LEACH, DENNIS, 'MEADOW COT.'., TREBURLEY, LAUNCESTON, CORN PL15 9PU ENG
35174 RAYMENT, DAVID, 20 LEASWAY., WICKFORD, ESS SS12 0HF ENG
35175 PARISH, JOY, 25 KEATS CL., NEWPORT PAGNELL, MK16 8DW ENG
35176 TOLL, KEN, 20 NORTH RD, THREE BRIDGES., CRAWLEY, SSX RH10 1JX ENG
35177 HUNT, PAUL, 7A CHURCH HILL., WOODHOUSE EAVES, LEICS LE12 8RT ENG
35178 COUSINS, BRIAN, WAGTAILS, HILLBOROUGH AVE., SEVENOAKS, KENT TN13 3SG ENG
35179 COVENTRY, CHARLES, 27/1 JAMAICA MEWS., EDINBURGH, EH3 6HL SCOTLAND
35180 WILLIAMSON, MRS B, 5 PERCY CL, BEAUMONT PK., HEXHAM, NBL NE46 2JD ENG
35181 TURNER, ROBERT, 19 HORNBEAM CL., THEYDON BOIS, EPPING, ESS CM16 7JT ENG
35182 RIRIE, CHRISTIAN, 19 SHELSMORE., GIFFARD PARK, BKM MK14 5HU ENG
35183 MARSHALL, MRS M, 9 BROADFIELD CL., DENTON, M34 1BN ENG
35184 BEER, PAULINE, 4 CLEVELAND CL., CHANDLERS FORD, HAM SO5 1PX ENG
35185 LACE, DALLAS, 31 WINDARRA ST., NARWEE, NSW 2209 AUS
35186 SCHENK, ALISON, 23 LINSLEY ST., GLADESVILLE, NSW 2111 AUS
35187 FULLER, LYN, 100 BLAXLAND RD., WENTWORTH FALLS, NSW 2782 AUS
35188 FRANKLIN, MR R, PO BOX 800., NORTH SYDNEY, NSW 2059 AUS
35189 WHATSON, BERYL, 23 CATHY ST., BLAXLAND, NSW 2774 AUS
35190 ROCHE, BARBIE, LOT 4, MILL POINT RD., TOORLOO ARM, VIC 3909 AUS

35191 PEARSON, LAURIE, 13 CYPRUS ST., LALOR, VIC 3075 AUS
35192 ROWLEY, MR L, 31 STANHOPE GROVE., CAMBERWELL, VIC 3124 AUS
35193 CORFMAT, TOM, PO BOX 752., RINGWOOD, VIC 3134 AUS
35194 COFFEY, BILL, PO BOX 135., SOUTH MELBOURNE, VIC 3161 AUS
35195 JONES, GAIL, 12/63 CAVILL AVE., SURFERS PARADISE, QLD 4217 AUS
35196 PATEN, MR R, PO BOX 407., ASHGROVE, QLD 4060 AUS
35197 QUINN, DENISE, 12 TRUSCOTT ST., TOOWOOMBA, QLD 4350 AUS
35198 HISTORY PROJECT GP,, C/O 77 CHALFONT ST., SALISBURY, QLD 4107 AUS
35199 COMMON, DR BRENT, 37 PIMELANDS ST., LOGANLEA, QLD 4131 AUS
35200 THATCHER, KEN, 16 ACACIA ST., DOVETON, VIC 3177 AUS
35201 STRAUSS, VALDA, PO BOX 30., KALLISTA, VIC 3791 AUS
35202 RICHARDSON, MRS P, 5 MURRAY CT., VERMONT SOUTH, VIC 3133 AUS
35203 WASHINGTON, JOAN, 3 BAY RD., EAGLE POINT, VIC 3878 AUS
35204 VAUGHAN, MRS Y, 7 SYCAMORE RD., FRANKSTON, VIC 3199 AUS
35205 BALGOWAN, JAN, 145 BONDS RD., LOWER PLENTY, VIC 3093 AUS
35206 KIERCE, MICHAEL, 18 MCGHEE AVE., MITCHAM, VIC 3132 AUS
35207 LATHAM, MARION, 57 HILLSIDE GROVE., AIRPORT WEST, VIC 3042 AUS
35208 BEDELLA, WAYNE, 95 CHAPPLE ST., WODONGA, VIC 3690 AUS
35209 BATES, MARGARET, 5 BLACKHILL RD., GISBORNE STH, VIC 3437 AUS
35210 CHUK, FLORENCE, 8B SWEENEY ST., BALLARAT, VIC 3350 AUS
35211 MARRIOTT, TRACEY, 15 REGENCY CRT., TRARALGON, VIC 3844 AUS
35212 YOUNG, VICKI, 20 KALMIA ST., FRANKSTON, VIC 3199 AUS
35213 JONES, FAYE, 2 ASCOT ST STH., BALLARAT, VIC 3350 AUS
35214 RASO, SUSAN, 11 MERIBIL CL., MT ELIZA, VIC 3930 AUS
35215 HOLDING, MRS M, 9 MOURILYAN ST., LAKES ENTRANCE, VIC 3909 AUS
35216 CATLING, MS M, 4/179 BEACH RD., SANDRINGHAM, VIC 3191 AUS
35217 SPITTALL, MARY, PO BOX 9., NOBLE PARK, VIC 3174 AUS
35218 BLACKMORE, DONNA, 58 MARRIOTT ST., PARKDALE, VIC 3195 AUS
35219 DEVONSHIRE, MRS M, 10 COLIN AVE., PARK ORCHARDS, VIC 3114 AUS
35220 BURGESS, LORRAINE, 16 BULLEN ST., EAST DONCASTER, VIC 3109 AUS
35221 BOOTH, MR K, 3 HILL CT., MACLEOD, VIC 3085 AUS
35222 SMITH, EUGENIE, 38 LANGRIGG AVE., EDITHVALE, VIC 3196 AUS
35223 GRANT, MRS J, PO BOX 58., TALLANGATTA, VIC 3700 AUS
35224 O'CALLAGHAN, MRS G, RMB 3390., YARRAM, VIC 3971 AUS
35225 YATES, LEANNE, C/-BROADRIBB BROOKERS RD., SHANNONBROOK, NSW 2470 AUS
35226 GLOVER, HONORAH, 74A ALT ST., ASHFIELD, NSW 2131 AUS
35227 COLLINS, GEOFFREY, 31 ROSS CRES., BLAXLAND, NSW 2774 AUS
35228 MORGAN, JUNE, 6/154 HOMER ST., EARLWOOD, NSW 2206 AUS
35229 FEGENT, JOYCE, 3/140 BURNS BAY RD., LANE COVE, NSW 2066 AUS
35230 HILLARD, MISS D, RMB 109 MIMOSA RD., TEMORA, NSW 2666 AUS
35231 PITSON, BEVERLEY, 'CARINYA'., CULCAIRN, NSW 2660 AUS
35232 ALLUM, MRS E, 28 WARRINGTON AVE., KILLARA, NSW 2071 AUS
35233 CROWE, LESLEY, 49 WOODWARD ST., PARKES, NSW 2870 AUS
35234 LEE, LORELLE, 113 VEGA ST., REVESBY HEIGHTS, NSW 2212 AUS
35235 TIPPETT, DIANNE, 21 ALLARD ST., REDHEAD, NSW 2290 AUS
35236 ROESE, GREG, PO BOX 299., LEETON, NSW 2705 AUS
35237 ROESE, KATHERINE, PO BOX 299., LEETON, NSW 2705 AUS
35238 STROUD, BARBARA, PO BOX 4., SOUTH WAGGA WAGGA, NSW 2650 AUS
35239 RIETH, KATHLEEN, 40 BROMBOROUGH RD., ROSEVILLE, NSW 2069 AUS
35240 WEBB, NORMA, 2 HITTER AVE., BASS HILL, NSW 2197 AUS
35241 PICKERING, MR W, 39 ANDREWS RD., CROWS NEST, QLD 4355 AUS
35242 DARVENIZA, MRS G, PO BOX 85., SOUTH JOHNSTONE, QLD 4859 AUS
35243 PETERSEN, MRS E, 31 STRATHDALE ST., ASPLEY, QLD 4034 AUS
35244 RAYNER, JEANNE, 225 TUFNELL RD., BANYO, QLD 4014 AUS
35245 CHANDLER, JENNIFER, 24 IDRIESS ST., OXLEY, QLD 4075 AUS
35246 EITE, NINA, 10 VERNON ST., CLONTARF, QLD 4019 AUS
35247 CHIVERTON, KENNETH, 3 BAMBAROO CL., NAMBOUR, QLD 4560 AUS
35248 MCKEON-PICKING, VALERIE, 9 OLIVIA AVE., SALISBURY, QLD 4107 AUS
35249 LANE, MAUREEN, 10 TREVELLOE ST., ROCHEDALE, QLD 4123 AUS
35250 WOODS, MONA, SUGARLOAF RD., MUTDAPILLY, QLD 4307 AUS
35251 BURKHARDT, MERLYN, 10 FERGUSON ST., GYMPIE, QLD 4570 AUS
35252 KING, LOUISE, 33 MAYFIELD ST., BUDERIM, QLD 4556 AUS
35253 DALBY FAMILY HIST SOC,, PO BOX 962., DALBY, QLD 4405 AUS
35254 HANSON, MORRELL, 48 FERGUSON ST., SUNSHINE BEACH, QLD 4567 AUS
35255 GREEN, ELAINE, 10 ALBERT ST., BUSSELTON, WA 6280 AUS
35256 KIRBY, SANDY, 7 MALBARU AVE., INGE FARM, SA 5098 AUS
35257 MILEWICZ, MS E., DEPT OF SOCLGY, GPO BOX 252C., HOBART, TAS 7001 AUS
35258 GIBSON, JUDY, 9 WARWICK PL., KINGS MEADOWS, TAS 7249 AUS
35259 MORRISON, DOUG, PO BOX 575., LANE COVE, NSW 2066 AUS
35260 MORRISON, DOUG, PO BOX 575., LANE COVE, NSW 2066 AUS
35261 MORRISON, DOUG, PO BOX 575., LANE COVE, NSW 2066 AUS
35262 DIEMERT, MS L., 3810 SOUTH 312TH., AUBURN, WA 98001 USA

35263 RUDA, CAROLINE, 283 AVENUE C APT 4-H., NEW YORK, NY 10009 USA
35264 STEINER, JOHN, 22 ESTABROOK RD., LEXINGTON, MA 02173 USA
35265 SHAN SELLERS, LUCY, 3354 BANKHEAD AVE., MONTGOMERY, AL 36106 USA
35266 CARLISLE, GERRY, 1210 ORANGEWOOD DR., ESCONDIDO, CA 92025 USA
35267 DRUM, WINIFRED, 1315 BLACK MT RD., HILLSBOROUGH, CA 94010 USA
35268 CARTER, BEVERLEY, RR #1 BOX 1830., BINGHAM, ME 04920 USA
35269 STEWART, GRAECHEN, 1083 CANTERBURY RD., GROSSE POINTE, MI 48236 USA
35270 BOUIS, CHARLES, 1093 DAWN VIEW LANE, NW., ATLANTA, GA 30327 USA
35271 WYKSTRA, LEORA, 455 BRANNON PIKE., NICHOLASVILLE, KY 40356 USA
35272 IRWIN, GLEN, 6830 ELMRICH CT., ANCHORAGE, AK 99504 USA
35273 CLARK, RUTH, 875 STONY HILL RD., WILBRAHAM, MA 01095 USA
35274 MAINS, ROBERT, 5149 MARLOWE DRIVE, SE., KENTWOOD, MI 49548 USA
35275 CULP, MARY, 5581 SIERRA PARK DR., PARADISE, CA 95969 USA
35276 CARLSON, HELEN, 3901 E PINNACLE PEAK #47., PHOENIX, AZ 85024 USA
35277 VERRILL, DOUGLAS, BOX 1032., INTERNATIONAL FALLS, MN 56649 USA
35278 FERGUSON, MRS C., 2436 BRUNSWICK LANE., HUDSON, OH 44236 USA
35279 MCCREARY, CHARLOTTE, 2025 E STATE AVE., PHOENIX, AZ 85020 USA
35280 RICE, ROSALIE, 10675 SW 135 AVE., BEAVERTON, OR 97005 USA
35281 HUCKINS, WILLIAM, 1320 LAIRD AVE., SALT LAKE CITY, UT 84105 USA
35282 COOKSON, ALAN, 3441 EDGEWOOD RD., EUREKA, CA 95501 USA
35283 BURR, WILLIAM, 4735 BROOKWOOD ST., EUGENE, OR 97405 USA
35284 CHURCHILL, HAZEL, 98 APPLEWOOD DR., FAIRFIELD, OH 45014 USA
35285 PANNELL, JAMES, PO BOX 2061., DUNNELLON, FL 32630 USA
35286 SUNDBERG, PAUL, 4700 W 115TH PLACE., ALSIP, IL 60658 USA
35287 NORRIS, DWANE, 4540 HENDEE RD., JACKSON, MI 49201 USA
35288 STRASSER, ALBERTA, 208 S PRAIRIE., CRESTON, IL 60113 USA
35289 HENRY, LEON, S.V.L. BOX 8849., VICTORVILLE, CA 92392 USA
35290 GILLILAND, MARION, 5849 SE 45TH., TECUMSEH, KS 66542 USA
35291 LORENTI, DOROTHY, 2877 JASPER ST., PHILADELPHIA, PA 19134 USA
35292 JACKSON, TOM & BARBARA, 135 NAUTILUS DR., MANAHAWKIN, NJ 08050 USA
35293 MILLER, BRENDA, 21640 CHALON., ST CLAIR SHORES, MI 48080 USA
35294 VIERA, JUDITH, 18 BONAD RD., STONEHAM, MA 02180 USA
35295 MARLING, BETTY JO, 3 PEPPER TREE LANE., TOPEKA, KS 66611 USA
35296 OLD, GRACE, 1865 STEARNLEE AVE., LONG BEACH, CA 90815 USA
35297 LITTON, MRS P, 2864 MCFARLAN PARK DR., CINCINNATI, OH 45211 USA
35298 WILLIAMS, SIGRID, 9921 WARNER AVE., FREMONT, MI 49412 USA
35299 MANTHORNE, JEAN, 1 HERITAGE HILL RD., WINDHAM, NH 03087 USA
35300 BARON, MR R, 6969 W YALE AVE., DENVER, CO 80227 USA
35301 MUCKEY, CHARLOTTE, 1709 TENNESSEE ST., LAWRENCE, KS 66044 USA
35302 REDMOND, SUE, 603 ASH ST., AUBURNDALE, FL 33823 USA
35303 BRALEY, MARJORIE, 4339 SASSE RD., HEMLOCK, MI 48626 USA
35304 MALLORY, CAROL, 2339 SE JEFFERSON., TOPEKA I, KS 66605 USA
35305 SCHNELL, ANN, 26 BEVERLY DR., BROCKPORT, NY 14420 USA
35306 CRICHTON-HARRIS, ANN, PO BOX 218., COLUMBIA FALLS, ME 04623 USA
35307 BARBER, KEITH, 9708 LAMAR AVE., OVERLAND PARK, KS 66207 USA
35308 SULLIVAN, BARRY, 15322 WEST FAIR LANE., LIBERTYVILLE, IL 60048 USA
35309 BARROWS, EMMA M., 124 ELDREDGE DR., VESTAL, NY 13850 USA
35310 CIZMAR, MRS G., 331 OYSTER COVE., MISSOURI CITY, TX 77459 USA
35311 VENTER, ROBERT, 2799 IONE DR., SAN JOSE, CA 95132 USA
35312 HOLT, MARY-ANN, 437 DEL ORO AVE., DAVIS, CA 95616 USA
35313 LEONHARDT, AUDREY, 197 KEHO CT., SAN JOSE, CA 95136 USA
35314 TOWNSEND, CHARLES, 5721 ANTIETAM DR., SARASOTA, FL 34231 USA
35315 TOWLER, MARY, 1421 SE 20TH ST., CAPE CORAL, FL 33990 USA
35316 HOLLINGSWORTH, DOROTHY, 3108 WINDSOR TCE., OKLAHOMA CITY, OK 73122 USA
35317 SAMPSON, MRS S., PO BOX 206., HOFFMAN, MN 56339 USA
35318 GOULD, KENNETH, 10409 MEDINA RD., RICHMOND, VA 23235 USA
35319 RAIFORD, WILLIAM, 12011 OLD BRIDGE RD., ROCKVILLE, MD 20852 USA
35320 CAMPBELL, ALYCE, 24 VICTORY DR., BELLMAWR, NJ 08031 USA
35321 PAGE, GEORGE, RT 2 BOX 148., BRYANS RD, MD 20616 USA
35322 HEATH, WINIFRED, 1433 SHAFFER DR., SAN JOSE, CA 95132 USA
35323 STOCK, LISA, 5019 8TH AVE NE., SEATTLE, WA 98105 USA
35324 HOLT, RUSSELL, PO BOX 53., CANDIA, NH 03034 USA
35325 BEADLE, TERRY, BOX 153., AVALON, CA 90704 USA
35326 HALBROOKS, J.C., 357 SNAKE MEADOW HILL RD., STERLING, CT 06377 USA
35327 HOWATT, ALIX, 2527-70 AVE SOUTH., ST PETERSBURG, FL 33712 USA
35328 MILLER JR., J.A., 2810-K CARRIAGE DR., WINSTON-SALEM, NC 27106 USA
35329 JENSEN, CAROL, 4009 ORME ST., PALO ALTO, CA 94306 USA
35330 HUMBLEY, DEBRA, 10 CEDUNA ST., LOGANHOLME, QLD 4129 AUS
35331 JOHNSTON, LEIGH, 12 WYNFLO ST., LABRADOR, QLD 4215 AUS
35332 WARE, LOUISE, 14 ARDEN CRT., YAMANTO, QLD 4305 AUS
35333 MANZ, FRANCES, CLARENDON RD, MS 454., LOWOOD, QLD 4311 AUS
35334 EVANS, DAVID, 27 SPITFIRE AVE., STRATHPINE, QLD 4500 AUS

35335 GRANT, KATHY, 488 ZILLMERE RD., ZILLMERE, QLD 4034 AUS
35336 WALKER, MRS F., PO BOX 72., CLERMONT, QLD 4721 AUS
35337 STENNING, ROBYN, 106 MOOLOOLAH RD., MOOLOOLAH, QLD 4553 AUS
35338 MORRIS, MRS C., 18 HAWKINS DR., BLACKWATER, QLD 4717 AUS
35339 MOORE, BARBARA, PO BOX 1004., MT ISA, QLD 4825 AUS
35340 KENNY, ANTONIA, 1/2 ANDREA AVE, SOUTHSIDE., GYMPIE, QLD 4570 AUS
35341 NUNN, JOAN, 16 PARSONS ST., NAMBOUR, QLD 4560 AUS
35342 COLLEY, HELEN, 1 ST JOHN'S CRT., KINGSLEY, WA 6026 AUS
35343 EMERY, ANN, 6 TROJAN CL., BUSSELTON, WA 6280 AUS
35344 BUCKINGHAM, MRS J., 16 THE RIDGE., WOODVALE, WA 6026 AUS
35345 MCCAMEY, MERLE, 103 ROCHDALE RD., MT CLAREMONT, WA 6010 AUS
35346 STRONACH, DAVID, 8 GRENADIER DR., THORNLIE, WA 6108 AUS
35347 TODD, JEAN, 5 HASELMERE CIRCUS., ROCKINGHAM, WA 6168 AUS
35348 TULIP, MR R., 25 MARANON CRES., BEECHBORO, WA 6063 AUS
35349 CAMPBELL, VICTOR, 18 PETHER RD., COMO, WA 6152 AUS
35350 MCLERNON, ROMA, 72 GUPPY ST., PEMBERTON, WA 6260 AUS
35351 SALTMARSH, ROSEMARY, 31 MT BARKER ST., MT BARKER, WA 6324 AUS
35352 NEWTON, GAIL, C/O ELDERS, PO BOX 534., KATHERINE, NT 0850 AUS
35353 MCARTHUR, EDITH, RSD 204 WEST MOOREVILLE RD., BURNIE, TAS 7320 AUS
35354 BAILEY, WENDY, 20 OSBORNE ESP., KINGSTON BEACH, TAS 7050 AUS
35355 MCCANN, MRS D., 17 JOSEPHINE ST., RIVERWOOD, NSW 2210 AUS
35356 LATTA, JEANETTE, 16 EINSTEIN ST., WINSTON HILLS, NSW 2153 AUS
35357 TOOTH, MRS S., 108 JERSEY RD., WOOLLAHRA, NSW 2025 AUS
35358 WHITE, MRS R., 118 MAUD ST., GOULBURN, NSW 2580 AUS
35359 BROWN, MRS D., PO BOX 254., WEST RYDE, NSW 2114 AUS
35360 LEMON, ALAN, 36 JACANA GVE., HEATHCOTE, NSW 2233 AUS
35361 TOOHEY, NOELENE, "GLENCOE" PO BOX 36., EUGOWRA, NSW 2806 AUS
35362 TURNER, GWEN, 55 DIGILAH ST., DUNEDOO, NSW 2844 AUS
35363 MELTON, SUZANNE, 3 AVALON ST., BATEMANS BAY, NSW 2536 AUS
35364 SCHWARZE, FRANCES, 158 KINGSWOOD RD., ENGADINE, NSW 2233 AUS
35365 PIPER, MRS K., 19 MATTHEW FLINDERS DR., PORT MACQUAIRE, NSW 2444 AUS
35366 GAINSFORD, MS V., 9 CASINO RD., GREYSTANES, NSW 2145 AUS
35367 COX, MRS S., PO BOX 251., RICHMOND, NSW 2753 AUS
35368 HODGSON, MARIE, 569 ARGYLE ST., MOSS VALE, NSW 2577 AUS
35369 RIDINGS, REV. CHRISTOPHER, 13 TASMAN PL., NORTH RYDE, NSW 2113 AUS
35370 WOOD, BETTY, 15 BLAXLAND ST., FRENCHS FOREST, NSW 2086 AUS
35371 WORCHURST, SUE, 7 MIMULUS PL., CARINGBAH, NSW 2229 AUS
35372 CURRIE, NOELA, 48 EDENHOLME RD., FIVE DOCK, NSW 2046 AUS
35373 BALES, MRS S., PO BOX 63., GOSFORD, NSW 2250 AUS
35374 SUMMERS, VALERIE, 86 BURNET ST., BALLINA, NSW 2478 AUS
35375 COOPER, DOROTHY, RSD 143 MAIN RD., GILDEROY, VIC 3797 AUS
35376 OLSSON, NARELLE, PO BOX 231., RED CLIFFS, VIC 3496 AUS
35377 LILYDALE & CROYDON FHC, PO BOX 200., CROYDON, VIC 3136 AUS
35378 ANDERSON, SUSAN, 21 AUGUSTA RD., THE BASIN, VIC 3154 AUS
35379 HEALY, KARENE, PO BOX 622., MOE, VIC 3825 AUS
35380 MUIR, OSCAR, 94 MARLBOROUGH ST., EAST BENTLEIGH, VIC 3165 AUS
35381 ELLIOTT, HILMAIE, 37 MARKET ST., YARRAGON, VIC 3823 AUS
35382 GOUGH, BARBARA, 7 DUDLEY RD., WONGA PARK, VIC 3115 AUS
35383 LEYH, MR K., 14 RAGLAN ST., BACCHUS MARSH, VIC 3340 AUS
35384 DARE, GEOFF, 19 OLEANDER ST., GLEN WAVERLEY, VIC 3150 AUS
35385 GILPIN, JUDITH, 11 NAUGHTON GR., BLACKBURN, VIC 3130 AUS
35386 ALLAN, COLLEEN, PO BOX 16., AVOCA, VIC 3467 AUS
35387 CROOK, NORMA, 16 YOUNG ST., ALBERT PARK, VIC 3206 AUS
35388 HOGARTH, VALERIE, RMB 1568C., COBRAM, VIC 3644 AUS
35389 POTTS, BETTY, 45 O'GRADYS RD., KILMORE EAST, VIC 3764 AUS
35390 BRUNSDON, KERRY, PO BOX 162., SEBASTOPOL, VIC 3356 AUS
35391 EMERALD GENEALOGY GP, 62 MONBULK RD., EMERALD, VIC 3782 AUS
35392 SCARBOROUGH, ENID, BOX 196., REDCLIFFE, QLD 4020 AUS
35393 ROBINSON, MRS G., 21 BAYVIEW TCE., GEEBUNG, QLD 4034 AUS
35394 RANSLEY, JOHN, 18 ROSARY CRES., HIGHGATE HILL, QLD 4101 AUS
35395 STEVENSON, MARION, 61/98 BAYVIEW ST., RUNAWAY BAY, QLD 4216 AUS
35396 REECE, DR I., BOX 7051 MAIL CENTRE., TOOWOOMBA, QLD 4352 AUS
35397 CUNNINGHAM, COLIN, 142 IRONWOOD ST., ASPLEY, QLD 4034 AUS
35398 FOLEY, MRS M., 28 CROWLEY DR., MACKAY, QLD 4740 AUS
35399 CANAVAN, MS M., 26 GOBLE ST., HENDRA, QLD 4011 AUS
35400 AITCHISON, DAVID, 16 ROBB ST., OAKEY, QLD 4401 AUS
35401 GALPIN, PATRICIA, 88 THE LAKE TCE EAST., MT GAMBIER, SA 5290 AUS
35402 BOND, GREGORY, BRAESIDE RD., FRANKLIN, TAS 7113 AUS
35403 DIXON, CHRISTOPHER, 18 CLARKE CRES., KATHERINE, NT 0850 AUS
35404 JAMES, DONELLE, 23 WHITWORTH ST, SUNSET BCH., GERALDTON, WA 6530 AUS
35405 TURLEY, GLORIA, 76 VENN ST., COLLIE, WA 6225 AUS
35406 MORLING, MRS L, 37 WESTON DR., SWAN VIEW, WA 6056 AUS

35407 HAWKINS, MS L, 60 WONGAROO RD., GULGONG, NSW 2852 AUS
35408 PAY, MS M, 19 CUNNINGHAM PL., STH WINDSOR, NSW 2756 AUS
35409 YULE, SUSAN, 53 TRAMWAY RD., NTH AVOCA, NSW 2260 AUS
35410 MULDOON, VALERIE, 27 CHARLES ST., CARLINGFORD, NSW 2118 AUS
35411 LEHRLE, ANGELA, 47 NORTH ROCKS RD., NORTH ROCKS, NSW 2151 AUS
35412 ARNOLD, ELEANOR, LOT 167 WAVERLEY ST., GUNDY, NSW 2337 AUS
35413 PEARSON, MR R, 25 BURLING AVE., FAIRY MEADOW, NSW 2519 AUS
35414 WOOD, LYNNETTE, 188 GRAYS POINT RD., GRAYS POINT, NSW 2232 AUS
35415 ROBERTSON, ROBERT, 36 WYONG ST., CANLEY VALE, NSW 2166 AUS
35416 HERRING, MRS M, 6 TURNER ST., BUNBURY, WA 6230 AUS
35417 DAWSON, SUSAN, C/-24 BROOME TCE., NORTHAM, WA 6401 AUS
35418 PARR, MR M, 24 KURRAJONG RD., SAFETY BAY, WA 6169 AUS
35419 BOWDEN, EILEEN, 178 PRESIDENT AVE., MIRANDA, NSW 2228 AUS
35420 SMITH, HAZEL, 12 CANBERRA RD., SYLVANIA, NSW 2224 AUS
35421 COOMBES, MRS M, 12 KENNETH ST., LONGUEVILLE, NSW 2066 AUS
35422 LOVEGROVE, MR G, 'VALLAGROVE' EAST WEST RD., VALLA, NSW 2448 AUS
35423 MOSCROP, BARRY, 157 EWOS PDE., CRONULLA, NSW 2230 AUS
35424 DONNELLY, JAYNE, 82 EASTERN RD., TURRAMURRA, NSW 2074 AUS
35425 WOHLGEHAGEN, THELMA, 30 OLINDA RD., MT EVELYN, VIC 3796 AUS
35426 THOMPSON, GLORIA, 32 MCEWEN CRES., WODONGA, VIC 3690 AUS
35427 RUMNEY, MAVIS, MARGUERITE ST., RANELAGH, TAS 7109 AUS
35428 COLLETT, LINDA, 8 BATTUNGA ST., WISHART, QLD 4122 AUS
35429 SUNDSTRUP, DR B, 116 FRANKLAND ST., LAUNCESTON, TAS 7250 AUS
35430 LUNN, MS ʿ, 2 DUNOON ST., BEROWRA HEIGHTS, NSW 2082 AUS
35431 DOWNEY, MICHAEL, 4/1 WOOD ST., MANLY, NSW 2095 AUS
35432 TABONE, NOELENE, 14 REVELL CRES., ST ALBANS, VIC 3021 AUS
35433 HOLBROOK, MR A, 8 MCINTYRE ST., EAST-GEELONG, VIC 3219 AUS
35434 JOHNSON, MERVYN, KENNAS LANE., GLENORMISTON SOUTH, VIC 3265 AUS
35435 ABBOTT, MR N, ALEXANDER RD., WARRANDYTE, VIC 3113 AUS
35436 GUY, WINIFRED, 10/276 DORSET RD., CROYDON, VIC 3136 AUS
35437 WELTON, JANINE, 48 DUNCAN ST., BIRCHIP, VIC 3483 AUS
35438 EDWARDS, MRS D, BOX 488., MILLICENT, SA 5280 AUS
35439 SMYTHE, MR G, 3 BETULA RD., MOUNT GAMBIER, SA 5290 AUS
35440 SHORING, PETER, 31 DELAVAN ST., WISHART, QLD 4122 AUS
35441 GIBSON, JUDITH, PO BOX 209., PALM BEACH, QLD 4221 AUS
35442 RENTON, PETER, 4 ST JOHN ST., BELGIAN GDNS, QLD 4810 AUS
35443 GOULD, COLLEEN, MS 435, SCHULZ RD., LOWOOD, QLD 4311 AUS
35444 SMITH, MISS C, 3A OLIVER CT., KARDINYA, WA 6163 AUS
35445 WHITEHURST, THELMA, 27 WALLER ST., LATHLAIN, WA 6100 AUS
35446 BLACKLEY, MRS G, 17 AMETHYST CRES., ARMADALE, WA 6112 AUS
35447 QUIRK, MARILYN, 2 LINTON AVE., RSD PENGUIN, TAS 7316 AUS
35448 HANSEN, MILDRED, 36 FAIRFIELD RD., LINDISFARNE, TAS 7015 AUS
35449 BLAZELY, CHRISTINE, 31 MAIN RD., GRAVELLY BEACH, TAS 7276 AUS
35450 MCKENDRICK, IAN, 73 BROADWALK., WILMSLOW, CHS SK9 5PN ENG
35451 CHRISTENSEN, DULCIE, 9 TEAK ST, RACEVIEW., IPSWICH, QLD 4305 AUS
35452 IRVING, LEXIE, 123 DEE ST., NORTH ROCKHAMPTON, QLD 4701 AUS
35453 BOSANKO, JUDITH, 68 WICKHAM ST., BRIGHTON, QLD 4017 AUS
35454 ROBINS, LINDA, PO BOX 452., INNISFAIL, QLD 4860 AUS
35455 MILNER, SANDRA, 19 BRIDGE ST., CHELMER, QLD 4068 AUS
35456 FASANO, DEBRA, 22-24 NORRIS ST., CAIRNS, QLD 4870 AUS
35457 COOK, WILLIAM, 81 POINT CARTWRIGHT DR., BUDDINA, QLD 4575 AUS
35458 REINKE, SYLVIA, 24 EASTON ST., BOOVAL, QLD 4304 AUS
35459 SMITH, DIAN, 7 CORMORANT CRES., JACOBS WELL, QLD 4208 AUS
35460 MCARTHUR, DOROTHY, 33 REDGRAVE ST., STAFFORD HEIGHTS, QLD 4053 AUS
35461 MACINTOSH, MRS E, 351 UPPER BROOKFIELD RD., BROOKFIELD, QLD 4069 AUS
35462 DUNCAN, MARGARET, 2 CROWNDALE ST., WAVELL HEIGHTS, QLD 4012 AUS
35463 MCLELLAN, DOT, MS 299 NORTH BUCCA RD., BUNDABERG, QLD 4670 AUS
35464 MAHONY, PEARL, 18 ELLIOTT RD., BANYO, QLD 4014 AUS
35465 ZIRBEL, PHYLLIS, 42 WINTON ST., GOONDIWINDI, QLD 4390 AUS
35466 KIDSTON, RODERICK, 13 LEVIEN ST., SCULLIN, ACT 2614 AUS
35467 MCKERNAN, CHRISTINE, 14 BUCKLAND CRES., EPPING, VIC 3076 AUS
35468 BARNES, SHARON, 20 ROBYN AVE., ST ALBANS, VIC 3021 AUS
35469 LUCAS, ALICE, C/O 5 NEW ST., MORWELL, VIC 3840 AUS
35470 MIDDLETON, SHEILA, 24 WILLANA AVE., HAMLYN HEIGHTS, VIC 3215 AUS
35471 COOK, THOMAS, 10 PICCADILLY PL., BULLEEN, VIC 3105 AUS
35472 POCKNALL, HEATHER, 83 KNIGHT ST., MAFFRA, VIC 3860 AUS
35473 BROWNE, FAYE, 104 WILSON ST., BRUNSWICK, VIC 3056 AUS
35474 ROMERIL, MISS J, 12 DUDLEY PDE., CANTERBURY, VIC 3126 AUS
35475 HITCHINS, BETTY, PO BOX 397., MAFFRA, VIC 3860 AUS
35476 FABRE, LEONE, 239 GREENWOOD DR., BUNDOORA, VIC 3083 AUS
35477 CHRISTIE, JOAN, LOT 1, PURVES RD., MAIN RIDGE, VIC 3928 AUS
35478 HEMPHILL, JOYCELYN, PO BOX 91., MAFFRA, VIC 3860 AUS

35479 RICKARDS, SANDRA, RMB 5735 COAST RD., MIRBOO NORTH, VIC 3871 AUS
35480 HOLMES, MR D, 5 CLIFTON ST., WARRNAMBOOL, VIC 3280 AUS
35481 JARMAN, MARGOT, 42 COOK ST, NEWTOWN., GEELONG, VIC 3220 AUS
35482 CHEESMAN, LINDSAY, C/O EULALIE DRISCOLL, RMB 5122., BARKLY, VIC 3381 AUS
35483 MOYLE, MRS B, 6 JULIS ST., SOUTH OAKLEIGH, VIC 3167 AUS
35484 HARPER, MR W, 1 KANANOOK AVE., SEAFORD, VIC 3198 AUS
35485 LAMBOURNE, MRS M, 2/25 CHESTNUT ST., CARNEGIE, VIC 3163 AUS
35486 CURRIE, RONALD, 11 EDWARD COURT., HASTINGS, VIC 3915 AUS
35487 O'TOOLE, LOIS, 12 CYPRESS AVE., WENDOUREE, VIC 3355 AUS
35488 CLARK, JOHN, 30 ROBERT ST., BULLEEN, VIC 3105 AUS
35489 NEWTON, MRS M, 12 BARILLA RD., MOORABBIN, VIC 3189 AUS
35490 STEVENSON, KATHLEEN, 29 SELWYN ST., TRIABUNNA, TAS 7190 AUS
35491 MARSHALL, MRS R, RSD 598., LATROBE, TAS 7307 AUS
35492 PRATT, MISS E, 37 AVENUE RD., HIGHGATE, SA 5063 AUS
35493 KILPATRICK, JACQUELINE, 3 HAKEA ST., MOUNT GAMBIER, SA 5290 AUS
35494 PIGOTT, MRS S, 39 SUMMERHAYES DR., KARRINYUP, WA 6018 AUS
35495 WHITE, JULIA, 4 BAYLISS RD., KARDINYA, WA 6163 AUS
35496 BARNETT, MS J, 3 KAVANAGH ST., WEMBLEY, WA 6014 AUS
35497 CHILDS, BERNARD, 135 BALLINA ST., LISMORE, NSW 2480 AUS
35498 HUGHES, MARGARET, 28 PARMAL AVE., PADSTOW, NSW 2211 AUS
35499 HOLT, MRS B, 8/156 RUSSELL AVE., DOLLS POINT, NSW 2219 AUS
35500 JAMES, MAVIS, 22 ADELAIDE ST., LAWSON, NSW 2783 AUS
35501 TAMSITT, MIGNON, 1 INVERNESS PL., KAREELA, NSW 2232 AUS
35502 MCGREEHAN, MRS M, PO BOX 522., BROKEN HILL, NSW 2880 AUS
35503 PEIRCE, MRS E, 32 MOALA ST., CONCORD WEST, NSW 2138 AUS
35504 CHURCHES, CAROL, 6/150 KEPPEL ST., BATHURST, NSW 2795 AUS
35505 WINDLE, AUDREY, PO BOX 27., BEGA, NSW 2550 AUS
35506 BARRETT, DENIS, 15 BRUCEDALE AVE., EPPING, NSW 2121 AUS
35507 STEVENSON, PATRICIA, 15 NORTHCOTT AVE., KINGSGROVE, NSW 2208 AUS
35508 BAKER, LORRAINE, 46 STUART ST., BLAKEHURST, NSW 2221 AUS
35509 PLOWES, JENNIFER, 44 ILLILIWA ST., CREMORNE, NSW 2090 AUS
35510 STURGISS, NEVILLE, 86 EAST ST., NOWRA, NSW 2541 AUS
35511 SHAW, MR A, 74 LAKESHORE DR., NTH AVOCA, NSW 2251 AUS
35512 GOODWIN, MRS C, PO BOX 58., WALCHA, NSW 2354 AUS
35513 MEREDITH, MR R, PO BOX 614., CHARLESTOWN, NSW 2290 AUS
35514 BANNON, IAN, 2 LIDDELL AVE., RUTHERFORD, NSW 2320 AUS
35515 HICKS, MR I, 6 TYGH ST., LAPSTONE, NSW 2773 AUS
35516 MANTLE, JANET, 2 GEORGE BOOTH DR., BUCHANAN, NSW 2323 AUS
35517 HEWITT, MRS S, 3 HUMBERSTONE AVE., GYMEA, NSW 2227 AUS
35518 FLEMING, MRS M, 22/2 REST POINT PDE., TUNCURRY, NSW 2428 AUS
35519 DALITZ, HELEN, JOHN ST., THE OAKS, NSW 2570 AUS
35520 O'CONNELL, MARGARET, 16 BONVILLE ST., COFFS HARBOUR, NSW 2450 AUS
35521 FREEMAN, MRS M, 178 SUTTON ST., COOTAMUNDRA, NSW 2590 AUS
35522 MCDONNELL, JUDY, 61 SILVER ST., MARRICKVILLE, NSW 2204 AUS
35523 WOOLASTON, MRS J, RMB 491A DARUKA RD., TAMWORTH, NSW 2340 AUS
35524 CLOUGH, EILEEN, 35 EPWORTH ST., OCEAN GROVE, VIC 3226 AUS
35525 WICKHAM, MRS J, 2 COOK RD., MELTON SOUTH, VIC 3338 AUS
35526 RIDDELL, MRS L, 107 WINIFRED ST., OAK PARK, VIC 3046 AUS
35527 BARNES, FAY, 54 DURHAM RD., SURREY HILLS, VIC 3127 AUS
35528 TOMLINSON, SUE, 45 CAMPBELL PDE., CRANBOURNE, VIC 3977 AUS
35529 PAYNE, SHIRLEY, 9 WELSHPOOL RD., TOORA, VIC 3962 AUS
35530 MARTIN, DR J, 1 LEICESTER ST., NORTH BALWYN, VIC 3104 AUS
35531 CLARKE, AILEEN, 8 SIMON CRT., ROSANNA, VIC 3084 AUS
35532 EDWARDS, SUE, 43 THORNHILL WAY., GREENWOOD, WA 6024 AUS
35533 WELLINGTON, MRS G, 3 MCKENNA MEWS., LESCHENAULT, WA 6230 AUS
35534 FALLON, MISS J, 5/774 BROWNS PLAINS RD., MARSDEN, QLD 4132 AUS
35535 MCLEAN, KAYE, 34 STUART ST., EASTERN HEIGHTS, QLD 4305 AUS
35536 TAYLOR, IRENE, 12 WARRAMBEEN PL., BONOGIN, QLD 4213 AUS
35537 SNOW, SANDRA, R15 BOSCOBEL RD., LONDONDERRY, NSW 2753 AUS
35538 DOYLE, MARION, PO BOX 755., ALBURY, NSW 2640 AUS
35539 CESSNOCK F. H. GROUP,, PO BOX 225., CESSNOCK, NSW 2325 AUS
35540 WILLIAMS, PETER, 8 BLAIR CRES., KURRI KURRI, NSW 2327 AUS
35541 CAMPBELL, ANN, 76 BOWDEN ST., HEDDON GRETA, NSW 2321 AUS
35542 BROWN, MRS J, 64 EDINBURGH RD., WILLOUGHBY, NSW 2068 AUS
35543 JUPP, MRS F, 61 CURTIN ST., EAST MAITLAND, NSW 2323 AUS
35544 BALFOUR, MRS C, 56 GILMORE ST., GOULBURN, NSW 2580 AUS
35545 FULTON, THOMAS, 9 CAMPBELL ST., KINGSTON, TAS 7050 AUS
35546 RYAN, MRS A, 47 COCKLE ST., O'CONNOR, ACT 2601 AUS
35547 MCINTOSH, MARIE, 1B PARNELL RD RMC., DUNTROON, ACT 2600 AUS
35548 RAY, MRS L, PO BOX 710., WODEN, ACT 2606 AUS
35549 BAKER, JULIA, 16 BONIWELL ST., HIGGINS, ACT 2615 AUS
35550 DAVIS, MR C, 6 TRALEE RD., FLOREAT PARK, WA 6014 AUS

CONTRIBUTOR ADDRESSES

35551 MCMILLAN, MR D., 138 BROOME ST., COTTESLOE, WA 6011 AUS
35552 ALLPORT, MR D., 218 LENAH VALLEY RD., LENAH VALLEY, TAS 7008 AUS
35553 TANNER, MRS R., 75 MAYNE ST., INVERMAY, TAS 7248 AUS
35554 LUKER, MRS L., 9 DYSON ST., GLENELG EAST, SA 5045 AUS
35555 KERNICK, LORRAINE, 1 RICHMAN AVE., PROSPECT, SA 5082 AUS
35556 ROTH, SHIRLEY, PO BOX 86., MUDGEE, NSW 2850 AUS
35557 VAN DER LOO, GLORIA, 163 RUSDEN RD., BLAXLAND, NSW 2774 AUS
35558 GODDARD, MRS L., 712 PORT HACKING RD., CARINGBAH, NSW 2229 AUS
35559 STEWART, ERIC, 32 FRIENDSHIP KEY., FORSTER KEYS, NSW 2428 AUS
35560 PURNELL, KAYE, 6 CARYSFORT ST., HURSTVILLE, NSW 2220 AUS
35561 BECKINGHAM, MRS F., 28 ESROM ST., BATHURST, NSW 2795 AUS
35562 BLAKE, ZANDRA, "SERENITY" WARROO., VIA FORBES, NSW 2871 AUS
35563 SHARPE, DONALD, 21 CULLODEN RD., EASTWOOD, NSW 2122 AUS
35564 MASON, ANNE, 69 CUTLER AVE., COOTAMUNDRA, NSW 2590 AUS
35565 EDGAR, BARBARA, ROSEWOOD, WOLLOMOMBI., ARMIDALE, NSW 2350 AUS
35566 LITTLE, MARGARET, 80 UNDOLA RD., HELENSBURGH, NSW 2508 AUS
35567 BROOKS, MRS G., 16 HUGH AVE., PEAKHURST, NSW 2210 AUS
35568 CLOSE, DASHA, 22B WATERS RD., NEUTRAL BAY, NSW 2089 AUS
35569 PHILLIS, ROSEMARY, 67 RIVERSTONE RD., RIVERSTONE, NSW 2765 AUS
35570 GILBERT, JOHN, 9 VIRTUE ST., CONDELL PARK, NSW 2200 AUS
35571 COOKE, CECIL, 1 NEALE AVE., FORESTVILLE, NSW 2087 AUS
35572 ALLEN, DONALD, 1 NEALE AVE., FORESTVILLE, NSW 2087 AUS
35573 CURWEN, MRS G., 6 SANRAY CRES., MUSWELLBROOK, NSW 2333 AUS
35574 SMITH, MRS J., 6 HARPER PL., FRENCHS FOREST, NSW 2086 AUS
35575 LE ROY, DAVID, 62 PALOMINO RD., EMU PLAINS, NSW 2750 AUS
35576 WHITE, ELIZABETH, 35 DODSON CRES., WINSTON HILLS, NSW 2153 AUS
35577 LEET, VALERIE, 7 GIRRA CL., TAMWORTH, NSW 2340 AUS
35578 HUXLEY, MR K., 152 KENNEDY DR., PORT MACQUARIE, NSW 2444 AUS
35579 NORTHCOTE, VIVIENNE, 17 BOURKE ST., CARRINGTON, NSW 2294 AUS
35580 MARSH, DR J., PO BOX 20., MITTAGONG, NSW 2575 AUS
35581 ISRAEL, JANICE, PO BOX 50., EASTWOOD, NSW 2122 AUS
35582 JOHNSTON, PETER, 4 WARRINA ST., BEROWRA HEIGHTS, NSW 2082 AUS
35583 BRIERLEY, MRS L., 20 BEATTIE ST., JAMBEROO, NSW 2533 AUS
35584 SCOTT, LEILA, 8/75 GLASSOP ST., BALMAIN, NSW 2041 AUS
35585 HAEUSLER, CORAL, 31 FIFTH AVE., BLACKTOWN, NSW 2148 AUS
35586 PARKER, MRS B., 32 BEASLEY CRES., RANKIN PARK, NSW 2287 AUS
35587 HUTCHINS, MISS K., 78 HERBERT ST., MORNINGTON, VIC 3931 AUS
35588 TAYLOR, EDNA, 7 KERRY CL., BERWICK, VIC 3806 AUS
35589 RAY, IAN, 35 GRAY ST., DONCASTER, VIC 3108 AUS
35590 PHILLIPS-OSBORNE, MRS S., 48 MALE ST., BRIGHTON, VIC 3186 AUS
35591 STREAT, GABRIELLE, 1/26 HIGHETT RD., HAMPTON, VIC 3188 AUS
35592 CRETTENDEN, MRS K., 12 FINTONA CRT., COLDSTREAM, VIC 3770 AUS
35593 VINEN, SUSAN, 5 PLUNKETT AVE., ORMOND, VIC 3163 AUS
35594 GIBB, JILL, 108 CHUTE ST., MORDIALLOC, VIC 3195 AUS
35595 THOMAS, MRS B., 36 FARADAY RD., CROYDON SOUTH, VIC 3136 AUS
35596 TAYLOR, ELIZABETH, 5 THE CREST., BULLEEN, VIC 3105 AUS
35597 SHERLOCK, PETER, 2 MCKENZIE ST., BRUNSWICK, VIC 3056 AUS
35598 GILLESPIE, MARILYN, 34 FARADAY RD., SOUTH CROYDON, VIC 3136 AUS
35599 PATTERSON, JUNE, 18 ORCHARD GVE., BLACKBURN SOUTH, VIC 3130 AUS
35600 MCCLINTOCK, HEATHER, 1 MOORBELL ST., TARRAGINDI, QLD 4121 AUS
35601 LAZZAROTTO, JEAN, 1801 – 3 AVE SE., SALMON ARM, BC V1E 1V1 CAN
35602 HAYCOCK, KENNETH, 11913 – 77A AVE., DELTA, BC V4C 7K2 CAN
35603 LILLIE, ALAN, 3768 REVELSTOKE DR., OTTAWA, ONT K1V 7C4 CAN
35604 MILES, CAROL, BOX 531., MINDEN, ONT K0M 2K0 CAN
35605 SURTEES, RUSSELL, RR#1 BOX 94., NORTH LANCASTER, ONT K0C 1Z0 CAN
35606 STETNER, NORMAN, 433 – 17TH AVE E., REGINA, SAS S4N 0Y4 CAN
35607 VEENSTRA, ALFREDA, 25 SINCLAIR CRES., AYLMER, ONT N5H 3B6 CAN
35608 SMITH, GEORGE, 208 STANLEY ST., SIMCOE, ONT N3Y 1N1 CAN
35609 GULLEN, MALCOLM, 21 KAYMAR DR., GLOUCESTER, ONT K1J 7C8 CAN
35610 CALDWELL, MR R, 4466 ELAINE DR., GLOUCESTER, ONT K1J 8S3 CAN
35611 MORRISON, KAIREEN, BOX 1065, 20 MAIN ST., WAWA, ONT P0S 1K0 CAN
35612 PEPPIN, RUTH, 55 CALEDONIA ST., GUELPH, ONT N1G 2C8 CAN
35613 SHELDRICK, BOYD, 33 CLEADON DR., NEPEAN, ONT K2H 5P4 CAN
35614 KELLY, PATRICK, 4190 BLENKINSOP RD., VICTORIA, BC V8X 2C4 CAN
35615 TUBMAN, DAISLEY, BOX 351., WOLSELEY, SASK S0G 5H0 CAN
35616 SENTES, ETHEL, 1341C GRACE ST., REGINA, SAS S4T 5M9 CAN
35617 ROBERGE, JOHN, 550 LANGS RD, APT 105., OTTAWA, ONT K1K 4C2 CAN
35618 DREHER, EVELYN, BOX 144., OXBOW, SAS S0C 2B0 CAN
35619 DENNEY, NORMAN, S19 C40 RR1., SORRENTO, BC V0E 2W0 CAN
35620 MONLEZUN, MARJORIE, 11108 – 13A ST., DAWSON CREEK, BC V1G 3X5 CAN
35621 HARRIS, ARTHUR, 1103 – 510 5TH AVE N., SASKATOON, SAS S7K 2R2 CAN
35622 PICKARD, CATHERINE, BOX 58, 133 WILMOT TRAIL, GROUP 1, RR#1., NEWCASTLE, ONT L0A 1H0 CAN

35623 DOBSON, EARLE, 26 KENNINGHALL BLVD., MISSISSAUGA, ONT L5N 1J4 CAN
35624 BOND, ANTHONY, BOX 85, STATION A., TORONTO, ONT M5W 1A2 CAN
35625 MACMILLAN, SHIRLEY, 3556 JOYCE AVE., POWELL RIVER, BC V8A 2Y5 CAN
35626 WHITNEY, WILLIAM, 185 BECKER CRES., FT MCMURRAY, ALB T9K 1M6 CAN
35627 O'CONNOR, HELEN, 6027 SOUTHBOINE DR., WINNIPEG, MAN R3R 0B5 CAN
35628 FERGUSON, MRS V, 1225 WEST 20TH ST., NORTH VANCOUVER, BC V7P 2B8 CAN
35629 STUBBERFIELD, NEIL, 7046 ABBOTSFORD ST., POWELL RIVER, BC V8A 2G1 CAN
35630 CLELAND, JAMES, BOX 284., ST BASILLE, NB E0L 1H0 CAN
35631 ADKINS, GRACE, BOX 458., EXETER, ONT N0M 1S6 CAN
35632 WALLER, RUSS, 114 ROBERT WALLACE DR., KINGSTON, ONT K7M 1Y2 CAN
35633 AUGUSTEIJN, ELEANOR, BOX 308., CALEDON EAST, ONT L0N 1E0 CAN
35634 HERMANN, GAIL, 426 BROCK ST., WINNIPEG, MAN R3N 0Z1 CAN
35635 TAYLOR, ALVIN, 814 – 73 WIDDIPOMBE HL BD., ETOBICOKE, ONT M9R 4B3 CAN
35636 BLACK, ALAN, 24 SUMMERFIELD., HUDSON, QUE J0P 1H0 CAN
35637 JONES, DARLENE, BOX 895., VERNON, BC V1T 6M8 CAN
35638 BOTEL, RUTH, VICTORIA AVE, GEN DELIVERY., WINTER HARBOUR, BC V0N 3L0 CAN
35639 LEFEBVRE, LESLIE, 110 HILLSIDE GARDEN., FORT MCMURRAY, ALB T9H 3V2 CAN
35640 FONTAINE, DANIEL, 4412 DELORIMIER., MONTREAL, QUE H2H 2H2 CAN
35641 BENJAMIN, BEVERLEY, RR#1., SMITHERS, BC V0J 2N0 CAN
35642 POOLE, ALAN, 14 MILLBANK AVE., TORONTO, ONT M5P 1S3 CAN
35643 SAYERS, JOHN, 2157 FILLMORE CRES., GLOUCESTER, ONT K1J 6A1 CAN
35644 PEEBLES, MR G, #2702 311 – 6TH AVE NORTH., SASKATOON, SAS S7K 7A9 CAN
35645 HAYES, ADRIAN, PO BOX 849., WINCHESTER, ONT K0C 2K0 CAN
35646 EVEREST, LOUISE, RR2, C15, HULLCAR RD., ARMSTRONG, BC V0E 1B0 CAN
35647 KELLY, BETTY, 1964 LENARTHUR DR., MISSISSAUGA, ONT L5J 2J2 CAN
35648 THOMPSON, JAMES, 4 REGENCY CRES., WHITBY, ONT L1N 7G1 CAN
35649 VACHON, PIERRE, 1025 MANAWAGONISH RD., SAINT JOHN, NB E2M 3X4 CAN
35650 FREDEEN, A JOAN, BOX 1810., LACOMBE, ALB T0C 1S0 CAN
35651 JENSEN, WENDY, 23 W NICOWA ST., KAMLOOPS, BC V2C 1J5 CAN
35652 FREDERICKSON, LORI, BOX 1596., STRATHMORE, ALB T0J 3H0 CAN
35653 STRIKE, DOROTHY, #201-1145 FORESTWOOD DR., MISSISSAUGA, ONT L5C 1H5 CAN
35654 LE CLERE, RENE, PO BOX 329, VICTORIA STATION., WESTMOUNT, QUE H3Z 2V8 CAN
35655 FLETCHER, DIANE, 13 BATY ST., ST LUCIA, QLD 4067 AUS
35656 LUSH, JEAN, 42 MEE ST., CARINA, QLD 4152 AUS
35657 ROBOTHAM, MRS S, 2 TUNNEY ST., WISHART, QLD 4122 AUS
35658 RITTMEIR, MARGARET, PO BOX 920., AITKENVALE, QLD 4814 AUS
35659 VANDERKRUK, MRS R, 72 ENGLEFIELD RD., OXLEY, QLD 4075 AUS
35660 ZORNIG, PATRICIA, 29 TAROOKO ST., MANLY WEST, QLD 4179 AUS
35661 WARREN, MAUREEN, 61 SHETLAND DR., WANTIRNA, VIC 3152 AUS
35662 PRENDERGAST, JOAN, 33 INDRA RD., BLACKBURN SOUTH, VIC 3130 AUS
35663 BURTON, KAREN, 88 AVOCA ST., BUNDABERG, QLD 4670 AUS
35664 CHANDLER, GARY, 111 MCCAUL ST., TARINGA, QLD 4068 AUS
35665 KIDD, PHYLLIS, 261 HOLMES RD., FORRESTFIELD, WA 6058 AUS
35666 MORTON, CHRISTOPHER, 10 COILA ST., TURRAMURRA, NSW 2074 AUS
35667 RYAN, MRS M, 32 BAKER ST., BUNDEENA, NSW 2230 AUS
35668 GRANGER, JOY, 19 MARKS PDE., MARKS POINT, NSW 2280 AUS
35669 CROSS, PAM, 4 WILSON PDE., HEATHCOTE, NSW 2233 AUS
35670 DYBALL, MRS C, PO BOX 383., PADSTOW, NSW 2211 AUS
35671 KIRKUP, MAUREEN, 6 MOSS ST., COOK, ACT 2614 AUS
35672 COFFEY, PAULINE, 118 REGENCY DR., THORNLIE, WA 6108 AUS
35673 HAWKSWORTH, DON, 7 CANDY ST., MORLEY, WA 6062 AUS
35674 RICKETTS, PATRICIA, MARLOW RD., DENMARK, WA 6333 AUS
35675 MEDHURST, MRS B, CNR CRUTCHETT RD & MUDDY LN., NORTH MOONTA, SA 5558 AUS
35676 BELL, VONDA, 27 WILKINS ST., GLENGOWRIE, SA 5044 AUS
35677 PHILLIPS, DR GAEL, 27 MELVILLE ST., SOUTH PLYMPTON, SA 5038 AUS
35678 QUATERMASS, JOHN, PO BOX 21., KINGAROY, QLD 4610 AUS
35679 BARTLETT, CHERYL, 19 CHARLES HODGE AVE., NORTH MACKAY, QLD 4740 AUS
35680 FULWOOD, MS N, PO BOX 261., SPRING HILL, QLD 4004 AUS
35681 NAUMANN, GLENDA, 4 LISLANE ST., FERNY GROVE, QLD 4055 AUS
35682 HORN, ROSS, 3/40 VICTOR ST., HOLLAND PARK, QLD 4121 AUS
35683 EDWARDS, MERLE, 35 11TH AVE., HOME HILL, QLD 4806 AUS
35684 CALLAGHAN, NOELINE, 338 SCARBOROUGH RD., SCARBOROUGH, QLD 4020 AUS
35685 ROOKS, MRS E, PO BOX 1222., SOUTHPORT, QLD 4215 AUS
35686 EMMERSON, MISS W, 4 SHIEL ST., TOOWOOMBA, QLD 4350 AUS
35687 MILLER, MS W, 26 OSPREY ST., INALA, QLD 4077 AUS
35688 HUNTER, MERLE, 119 TOWNSON AVE., PALM BEACH, QLD 4221 AUS
35689 TAYLOR, WENDY, 'HALIWELL' C/-POST OFFICE., MAPLETON, QLD 4560 AUS
35690 PRICE, ALISON, 42 EASTCOTE RD., EPPING, NSW 2121 AUS
35691 FERGUSON, MR K, 169 LAWES ST., EAST MAITLAND, NSW 2323 AUS
35692 HUME, PAULA, 12 SERPENTINE CRES., BALGOWLAH NTH, NSW 2093 AUS
35693 BERCKELMAN, MARGARET, 11 UPPER SPIT RD., MOSMAN, NSW 2088 AUS

35694 PALMER, MRS J, 16 FOX ST., WAGGA WAGGA, NSW 2650 AUS
35695 MCDONALD, EMILE, 22 SHANNON PDE., BERKELEY VALE, NSW 2259 AUS
35696 ASHBRIDGE, KAYE, 65 BURWOOD RD., WHITEBRIDGE, NSW 2290 AUS
35697 HAY, BOB, PO BOX 108., NEWTOWN, NSW 2042 AUS
35698 ARGALL, MRS B, 49 BOUNDARY ST., FORSTER, NSW 2428 AUS
35699 BURLISON, JOHN, 23 KETHEL RD., CHELTENHAM, NSW 2119 AUS
35700 STEWART, ROBERT, 30 VIEW ST., WAVERLEY, NSW 2024 AUS
35701 WHITAKER, PETER, 30 NALYA RD., BEROWRA HEIGHTS, NSW 2082 AUS
35702 CAMPBELL-WRIGHT, MRS S., PO BOX 82., GLENBROOK, NSW 2773 AUS
35703 PUNTON, HAZEL, 99 PRINCE EDWARD ST., MALABAR, NSW 2036 AUS
35704 BUTLER, MRS J., 8 BENNETT ST., BASS HILL, NSW 2197 AUS
35705 REED, JANINE, "JILDERIE" TAYLORS ARM RD., MACKSVILLE, NSW 2447 UAS
35706 FOX, DIANNE, 53 SOUTHERN RD., HEIDELBERG HEIGHTS, VIC 3081 AUS
35707 WALLIS, CAROLINE, PO BOX 172., MT EVELYN, VIC 3796 AUS
35708 PETERS, MR R., 15 GORDON GVE., PRESTON, VIC 3072 AUS
35709 WEBB, NOEL, 41 JENNER ST., SOUTH BLACKBURN, VIC 3130 AUS
35710 FRASER, MR R., BOX 1245., GLEN WAVERLEY, VIC 3150 AUS
35711 JENKINS, JOAN, RMB 310, CRAIG RD., NANNEELLA, VIC 3561 AUS
35712 ANNEAR, LINDA, PO BOX 1271., SWAN HILL, VIC 3585 AUS
35713 DUNCAN, JANET, 3/202 BEACH RD., MORDIALLOC, VIC 3195 AUS
35714 KLOEDEN, SUE, 14 O'CONNOR ST., HORSHAM, VIC 3400 AUS
35715 XANTHOUDAKIS, LEE, 26 GOODRICH ST., STH OAKLEIGH, VIC 3167 AUS
35716 RODGERS, PAULA, PO BOX 55., TERANG, VIC 3264 AUS
35717 MORTON, MRS D., 20 COBDEN ST., BRIGHT, VIC 3741 AUS
35718 CLARKE, MRS J., 21 MORSHEAD AVE., MT WAVERLEY, VIC 3149 AUS
35719 KENNEDY, MARGARET, PO BOX 718., SHEPPARTON, VIC 3630 AUS
35720 GILBERT, MR G., 16 THE CRESCENT., WESBURN, VIC 3799 AUS
35721 O'HAGAN, GARY, 32 WILLIAM ST., ST ALBANS, VIC 3021 AUS
35722 LEWIS, ALAN, 14 CARAVELLE CRES., STRATHMORE, VIC 3041 AUS
35723 CRUMPLER, DIANA, RSD., TENNYSON, VIC 3572 AUS
35724 SARGEANT, VIC, 353 RICHARDSON ST., MIDDLE PARK, VIC 3206 AUS
35725 PALMER, DAVID, 14 GLENBROOK CL., FRANKSTON, VIC 3199 AUS
35726 PALMER, DAVID, 14 GLENBROOK CL., FRANKSTON, VIC 3199 AUS
35727 CHARLWOOD, RICHARD, 20 PROSSER ST., BUNBURY, WA 6230 AUS
35728 BAKER, SUE, 201 ERINDALE RD., HAMERSLEY, WA 6022 AUS
35729 NORMAN, MRS T., 4 CROWCOMBE WAY., KARRINYUP, WA 6018 AUS
35730 SHORT, MAUREEN, 14 WHITTAKER CRES., BULLCREEK, WA 6155 AUS
35731 LOVE, DAVID, 12 BUNBURRA ST., PARA HILLS WEST, SA 5096 AUS
35732 MAHADY, MATTHEW, 508 MAIN RD., WELLINGTON POINT, QLD 4160 AUS
35733 BARRON, PETER, 61 NELSON ST., CORINDA, QLD 4075 AUS
35734 HAMMOND, MRS J., 29A CURZON ST., TOOWOOMBA, QLD 4350 AUS
35735 BELL, MEG, 28 NULLAGINE ST., FISHER, ACT 2611 AUS
35736 ROSEWARNE, MARIE, C/O 6 HACK ST., O'CONNOR, ACT 2601 AUS
35737 CARTER, NANCY, SPRINGDALE., BARRABA, NSW 2347 AUS
35738 BASKIN, MISS M., 2 BUNDANOON RD., ENGADINE, NSW 2233 AUS
35739 SHIPP, THOMAS, 20 ROSEBERY ST., PENSHURST, NSW 2222 AUS
35740 TICKLE, ROBERT, PO BOX 554., MUSWELLBROOK, NSW 2333 AUS
35741 WRIGHT, GRAHAME, 134 CLIFFORD ST., GOULBURN, NSW 2580 AUS
35742 BURKE, MRS D., 14 TWEED ST., BRUNSWICK HEADS, NSW 2483 AUS
35743 STACEY, BARBARA, 18 RICHMOUNT ST., CRONULLA, NSW 2230 AUS
35744 WALKER, MRS D., 53 WASSELL ST., CHIFLEY, NSW 2036 AUS
35745 WATSON, ANNETTE, 103 URALBA ST., LISMORE, NSW 2480 AUS
35746 IRETON, TANIA, PO BOX 371., CHELSEA, VIC 3196 AUS
35747 CHELLEW, DARYL, 1/17 HARRISON ST., MITCHAM, VIC 3132 AUS
35748 FREEMAN, MICHELLE, 15 SAUNDERS CRES., TRARALGON, VIC 3844 AUS
35749 BAILEY, SHIRLEY, 48 JACKSONS RD., CHELSEA, VIC 3196 AUS
35750 BEASLEY, ANNETTE, 6 THOMPSONS CRT., NORTH BALWYN, VIC 3104 AUS
35751 FORMAN, MRS B., PO BOX 215., HUNTLY, VIC 3551 AUS
35752 HEARNE, VICTOR, 54 MARSHALL ST., WODONGA, VIC 3690 AUS
35753 SCANLAN, FRIEDA, 6 WRENSWOOD DR., DEVONPORT, TAS 7310 AUS
35754 PERRY, NANCYE, 32 OUTLOOK DR., EAGLEMONT, VIC 3084 AUS
35755 SCULLY, MRS J., 154 FERNLEIGH RD., WAGGA WAGGA, NSW 2650 AUS
35756 CARTER, MR M., PO BOX 1048., BANKSTOWN, NSW 2200 AUS
35757 SMITH, MRS E., 5 CAMBRIAN MALL., ALEXANDER HTS, WA 6064 AUS
35758 KNIGHT, FRANK, 665 HODGE ST., ALBURY, NSW 2640 AUS
35759 STIFF, MRS D., 71 BANFF ST., COROWA, NSW 2646 AUS
35760 COX, MARGARET, 49 PRINCE EDWARD ST., CARLTON, NSW 2218 AUS
35761 FINDLAY, NOEL, 15 LOMBARD ST., CARINA, QLD 4152 AUS
35762 MAGNANI, MRS L., PO BOX 1459., INGHAM, QLD 4850 AUS
35763 PEERS, MARION, 37 GORDON ST., LABRADOR, QLD 4215 AUS
35764 WEST, DEANNE, 29 MCLEAN ST., REDBANK PLAINS, QLD 4301 AUS
35765 LANG, ELLEN, 14 DUNDONALD ST., EVERTON PK, QLD 4053 AUS

35766 OLIVER, SYBIL, LOT 7 OLD GYMPIE RD., BEERWAH, QLD 4519 AUS
35767 TEMPLETON, JACKIE, BEAVER ROCK RD MS 781., MARYBOROUGH, QLD 4650 AUS
35768 BLEAKLEY, BERYL, LOT NO 27 GLEN CIRCUIT., CLAGIRABA, QLD 4211 AUS
35769 VELLA, MARGARET, M/S 2042., WALKERSTON, QLD 4751 AUS
35770 MARSH, WILLIAM, 34 BENTHAM ST., YARRALUMLA, ACT 2600 AUS
35771 VORT-RONALD, MICHAEL, 3 GRAVES ST., KADINA, SA 5554 AUS
35772 FRANCIS, LYNETTE, 109 GRADIENT WAY., BELDON, WA 6025 AUS
35773 SWAN, JANICE, BLOOMFIELD RD RMB 5610., WARRAGUL, VIC 3820 AUS
35774 HEDLEY, BARBARA, KORUMBURRA RD., DROUIN SOUTH, VIC 3818 AUS
35775 HOLLINGSWORTH, MR K., PO BOX 81., RINGWOOD EAST, VIC 3135 AUS
35776 CASBOLT, ADELE, 3 MATTHEWS CRT., MILL PARK, VIC 3082 AUS
35777 DONELLY, RODNEY, 19 STAMFORD ST., MOE, VIC 3825 AUS
35778 STUBBS, SHARLIE, 68 TIMMS AVE., KILSYTH, VIC 3137 AUS
35779 VAUX, MR L., 74 VICTORIA CRES., MONT ALBERT, VIC 3127 AUS
35780 DUNSTAN, ANN, "SWANDALE" RMB 828., DONALD, VIC 3480 AUS
35781 CRAWFORD, DAN, 9 NAREEN PDE., NARRABEEN, NSW 2101 AUS
35782 USSHER, MRS G., 122 WELLS ST., SPRINGFIELD, NSW 2250 AUS
35783 WALLACE, BILL, PO BOX 38., EAST GOSFORD, NSW 2250 AUS
35784 PARKINS, JUNE, 12 DOUGLAS ST., PANANIA, NSW 2213 AUS
35785 SHEARER, MRS C., 180 MADAGASCAR DR., KINGS PARK, NSW 2148 AUS
35786 THOMPSON, MR & MRS F., PO BOX 577., COOTAMUNDRA, NSW 2590 AUS
35787 HARDY, MARGARET, 50 LETHBRIDGE ST., PENRITH, NSW 2750 AUS
35788 SETTER, KEVIN, 130 HANNANS RD., NARWEE, NSW 2209 AUS
35789 SPAIN, BRIAN, 5 MINAWA ST., COOMA, NSW 2630 AUS
35790 MENZIES, COLIN, 1 LESLEY AVE., REVESBY, NSW 2212 AUS
35791 HOY, SAMANTHA, 2/53 LOCKSLEY RD., IVANHOE, VIC 3079 AUS
35792 BURNSIDE, MARIE, 10 LOCKSLEY ST., WENDOUREE, VIC 3355 AUS
35793 BEAUMONT, MARY, 7 BULGA ST., MOOROOLBARK, VIC 3138 AUS
35794 ROWLEY, ROSS, 2 DROVERS CL., MAIDEN GULLY, VIC 3551 AUS
35795 ONLEY, DAVID, 32 HUTTON ST., THORNBURY, VIC 3071 AUS
35796 CHAPMAN, VALERIE 33 EPSTEIN ST., RESERVOIR, VIC 3073 AUS
35797 NORMAN, PAMELA, 28 OLYMPIC AVE., FRANKSTON, VIC 3199 AUS
35798 BOYER, MRS J., PO BOX 280., DOVETON, VIC 3177 AUS
35799 GOW, BRUCE, 21 DUNLOP ST., SHEPPARTON, VIC 3630 AUS
35800 MOWAT, MRS D., 1 MONICA CL., MT WAVERLEY, VIC 3149 AUS
35801 CHITTY, JENEFER, 41 BROWN ST., LEONGATHA, VIC 3953 AUS
35802 GRAY, NORMAN, 7 RENWICK RD., FERNTREE GULLY, VIC 3156 AUS
35803 FORRESTER, ROBYN, PO BOX 12., BRIGHT, VIC 3741 AUS
35804 MAPSTONE, MARILYN, 41 GREENHILL RD., NTH BAYSWATER, VIC 3153 AUS
35805 BARFOOT, MAVIS, PO BOX 50., NOBBY BEACH, QLD 4218 AUS
35806 PURVIS, HEATHER, 11 ESSEX CRT., BUDERIM, QLD 4556 AUS
35807 PICKERING, JUNE, 25 TODDS RD., LAWNTON, QLD 4501 AUS
35808 CANE, DENISE, MS 396., NANANGO, QLD 4615 AUS
35809 ANDERSEN, MRS V., PO BOX 21., YANGAN, QLD 4371 AUS
35810 FORSYTH, DOROTHY, 3 MACLACHLAN ST., HOLDER, ACT 2611 AUS
35811 FLAVEL, RONDA, 129 ESSINGTON LEWIS AVE., WHYALLA, SA 5600 AUS
35812 SHARPLES, MEL, PO BOX 46D., DON, TAS 7310 AUS
35813 HARLAND, MOYNA, 87 MARMION ST., FREMANTLE, WA 6160 AUS
35814 KINGSTON, ROBYN, "TORWOOD" MS 411., MARYBOROUGH, QLD 4650 AUS
35815 DAY, CATHY, 3 ILLINGWORTH ST., WANNIASSA, ACT 2903 AUS
35816 AULMANN, ROBYN, RMB 6540., WODONGA, VIC 3691 AUS
35817 STURZAKER, RUSSELL, PO BOX 175., VERMONT, VIC 3133 AUS
35818 WARD, YVONNE, 41 SPRING ST., TULLAMARINE, VIC 3043 AUS
35819 COWLEY, DAWN, 26 SHANAHAN PDE., NEWBOROUGH, VIC 3825 AUS
35820 STEWART, MR K., 575 WARRIGAL RD., ASHWOOD, VIC 3147 AUS
35821 WINDSOR, ANN, 20 JAMES ST., SHEPPARTON, VIC 3630 AUS
35822 CARSTAIRS, MS J., 127 POWER ST., ST ALBANS, VIC 3021 AUS
35823 ROY, DOROTHY, 72 SHARPS RD., TULLAMARINE, VIC 3043 AUS
35824 HENRY, MARY, SYMBISTER PK., RSD MCDONALDS LN., RIDDELLS CK, VIC 3431 AUS
35825 MACDOUGALL, MRS C.A., PO BOX 1067., FRANKSTON, VIC 3199 AUS
35826 GOLDSTONE, LOIS, 18 FLETCHER AVE., MIRANDA, NSW 2228 AUS
35827 WILSON, JUNE, 1 SALISBURY PL., GYMEA, NSW 2227 AUS
35828 REYNOLDS, MRS M., 24 ZIONS AVE., MALABAR HEIGHTS, NSW 2036 AUS
35829 BLACKWOOD, MRS P., 14/74 WARDELL RD., EARLWOOD, NSW 2206 AUS
35830 ANNABELL, WENDY, 35 CAPRICORN CRES., JUNCTION HILL, NSW 2460 AUS
35831 HUNT, ANNETTE, KYDARA MS-2., DUBBO, NSW 2830 AUS
35832 DEMAS, MARCEL, PO BOX 858., RAYMOND, ALB T0K 2S0 CAN
35833 MAURICE, TERRY, 39 CARFRAE ST., LONDON, ONT N6C 1G1 CAN
35834 MENSFORTH, ESTHER, BOX 666., SWAN HILL, VIC 3585 AUS
35835 HORSBURGH, JOAN, "RIVERHAVEN" RSD SPEEWA., VIA SWAN HILL, VIC 3585 AUS
35836 JENNINGS, MRS J., PO BOX 2., BALLARAT, VIC 3350 AUS
35837 STEVENS, ELAINE, 18 GREEN ST., CARLSBROOK, VIC 3464 AUS

35838 PHILLIPS, MRS A., 28 COUNTRY CLUB DR., CHIRNSIDE PARK, VIC 3116 AUS
35839 HORWOOD, LYELL, 13 KALKEE RD., HORSHAM, VIC 3400 AUS
35840 WISKEN, MRS G., 21 HALLEY ST., BLACKBURN, VIC 3130 AUS
35841 BERRY, MARC, 10 KANOWNA ST., HAMPTON, VIC 3188 AUS
35842 WILTSHIRE, ANNE, 127 UPPER ST., TAMWORTH, NSW 2340 AUS
35843 ELLIOTT, RICHARD, 3 BELL ST., MINMI, NSW 2287 AUS
35844 LANCASTER, RICHARD, 11 AVONA CRES., SEAFORTH, NSW 2092 AUS
35845 HERBERT, EUGENE, 29A WHARF RD., BIRCHGROVE, NSW 2041 AUS
35846 HOLLAND, AUDREY, 19 DUDLEY ST., MIDLAND, WA 6056 AUS
35847 WHITEHEAD, JOAN, 77 WOOD ST., SWANBOURNE, WA 6010 AUS
35848 MCKENZIE, JEAN, 4 GOODHART PL., SANDY BAY, TAS 7005 AUS
35849 CLARK, SYLVA, PO BOX 583., TABUBIL, WESTERN PROVINCE PNG
35850 BAKER, GWYNETH, 3 DANIELS RD., PANORAMA, SA 5041 AUS
35851 MCMAHON, DAPHNE, 42 ROMEA ST., THE GAP, QLD 4061 AUS
35852 LAWLESS, JENNIFER, 'WATERFORD'., GOONDIWINDI, QLD 4390 AUS
35853 FLEMING, MARTIN, 14 KUNDEEN ST., THORNESIDE, QLD 4158 AUS
35854 LONG, ERICA, 33 LAWRENCE RD., WEST CHERMSIDE, QLD 4032 AUS
35855 LOWRIE, MRS V, PO BOX 1465., ROCKHAMPTON, QLD 4700 AUS
35856 KEDZLIE, ROBIN, PADDYS PLAIN RD., NORTH DORRIGO, NSW 2453 AUS
35857 HAYMET, CORAL, 15 BORAMBIL PL., LONGUEVILLE, NSW 2066 AUS
35858 KANG, DR G, 26 EGLINTON RD., GLEBE, NSW 2037 AUS
35859 TONER, GARY, PO BOX 1283., GOSFORD SOUTH, NSW 2250 AUS
35860 FELLOWES, DOROTHY, PO BOX 417., WAGGA WAGGA, NSW 2650 AUS
35861 DAVIS, LOLA, 24 MEEKS CRES., FAULCONBRIDGE, NSW 2776 AUS
35862 BRADFORD, ROSLYN, 25 LAKE RD., BALCOLYN, NSW 2264 AUS
35863 MCKINNON, MRS R, 107 NATIONAL AVE., LOFTUS, NSW 2232 AUS
35864 ISAACS, CAROL, 15 HIGHLAND CL., CHARLESTOWN, NSW 2290 AUS
35865 SEARS, MALCOLM, 4 OSTEN PL., LANGFORD, WA 6155 AUS
35866 TERRETT, DR A, PHILLIP INST. OF TECH., BUNDOORA, VIC 3083 AUS
35867 ALLEN, FLORENCE, 14 ALBANY CRES., ASPENDALE, VIC 3195 AUS
35868 JACKEL, LINDSAY, 11 LYRIC CRT., GLEN WAVERLEY, VIC 3150 AUS
35869 MCCARTIN, MARGARET, 6/132A LEAMINGTON ST., RESERVOIR, VIC 3073 AUS
35870 HOLMES, ROBERT, 2 HONEYSUCKLE ST., JANNALI, NSW 2226 AUS
35871 WOODROW, PAMELA, 45 WOODROW DR., COORPAROO, QLD 4151 AUS
35872 TRANTER, MR P, 23 VERA ST., REDLAND BAY, QLD 4165 AUS
35873 PARK, JANICE, BOX 4., DURANILLIN, WA 6393 AUS
35874 ASTLE-STEEP, DOROTHY, 21 MACLEAY ST., GLOUCESTER, NSW 2422 AUS
35875 CONDON, DOROTHY, 53 KARS ST., FRANKSTON, VIC 3199 AUS
35876 HART, DEVON, 23 THIRD ST., BLACK ROCK, VIC 3193 AUS
35877 TOWERS, SUE, 21 MOOMBA AVE., SEAFORD, VIC 3198 AUS
35878 GILL, ELIZABETH, 2/15 MITCHELL ST., DONCASTER EAST, VIC 3109 AUS
35879 TRAVERS, MURIEL, 14 COOLABAH ST., MENTONE, VIC 3194 AUS
35880 CLOW, MARGARET, ROTO-O-RANGI, RD3., CAMBRIDGE, NZ
35881 GREENE, SUE, 31 FREEMANS RD., OTAKI, NZ
35882 RUSH, JULIE, 312 HAVELOCK ST., ASHBURTON, NZ
35883 WALKER, BRIAN, 81 TOSSWILL RD., TAHUNANUI, 7001 NZ
35884 CORKILL, JENNY, PO BOX 566., TEPUKE, BOP 3071 NZ
35885 HENDERSON, STEPHEN, 80 LAUDERDALE RD., BIRKDALE, AUCK NZ
35886 HAMBLYN, MARIAN, 5 LONG MELFORD RD., PALMERSTON NORTH, NZ
35887 KERN, MRS I, 201 ONEWA RD., BIRKENHEAD, AUCK 10 NZ
35888 MACKENZIE, MRS V, 15 STEPHEN ST, HALFWAY BUSH., DUNEDIN, OTG NZ
35889 MOULDEY, LOIS, PO BOX 320., WHANGAREI, NZ
35890 MAASS, MR A, 7 LONGVIEW CRES., OTOROHANGA, NZ
35891 MOREY, ELIZABETH, 2/9 FAIRLEIGH AVE., MT ALBERT, AUCK NZ
35892 WEHIPEIHANA, THELMA, 65 KIWI RD., RAUMATI BEACH, PARAPARAUMU NZ
35893 TITCHEN, MONICA, PO BOX 220., NAPIER, NZ
35894 RADFORD, NOELENE, 37 ALMA ST., RENWICK, MARL NZ
35895 STOCKS, PETER, PO BOX 25., RANGIORA, NORTH CANT NZ
35896 BURGESS, BEVERLEY, PO BOX 97., DARGAVILLE, NZ
35897 WESLEY-SMITH, ROBERT, 22 STEYNE AVE., PLIMMERTON, NZ
35898 ISTED, BRUCE, 30 NIBLETT ST., WANGANUI, NZ
35899 BLINCOE, PAM, 19 MARNANE TCE., HAMILTON, NZ
35900 HUNT, JOHN, 1RD, WAIRIO., OTAUTAU, SOUTHLAND NZ
35901 COOMBE, WAYNE, 15 WHITCOMBE RD., OPUNAKE, TARANAKI NZ
35902 BUSHELL, VALERIE, 67 SMYTHE RD., HENDERSON, AUCK NZ
35903 HILTON, CHRISTINE, 20 CHEQUERS AVE., HAMILTON, NZ
35904 BANKS, MARIAN, PO BOX 38-118., HOWICK, AKLD NZ
35905 BAKER, JANET, 33 NERI CRES., ROTORUA, 3201 NZ
35906 ENRIGHT, JENNIFER, 85 ARGYLE ST., MOSGIEL, OTAGO NZ
35907 COURTNEY, MRS P., HARRIS RD, NO 5 RURAL DEL., WHANGAREI, NZ
35908 BARROW, MRS L.C., 29 LOCKHART AVE., PALMERSTON NORTH, NZ
35909 POOL, MARGARET, 6 BONITA AVE., WHANGAPARAOA, AUCK NZ

35910 CAMERON, MRS J., 48 BRINKBURN ST., OAMARU, NZ
35911 RUSSELL, JOAN, 4 BERNARD ST., PAPATOETOE, AUCK NZ
35912 SUTTON, EDWARD, 27 LUNE ST., OAMARU, OTAGO 8901 NZ
35913 PONT, MRS S., 19 CLUTHA ST., ALEXANDRA, OTAGO NZ
35914 MAJOR, JOYCE, PO BOX 5413 WELLESLEY ST., AUCKLAND, NZ
35915 WADSWORTH, MRS D., 7 ALPHA ST., CAMBRIDGE, NZ
35916 BALL, JOHN, PO BOX 1430., WHANGAREI, 0100 NZ
35917 MCGREGOR, WINIFRED, 8 PRINCE ST., WINTON, 9662 NZ
35918 PRESTON, JOYCE, 13 TITOKI AVE., MANGERE BRIDGE, AUCK NZ
35919 MCROBBIE, JANET, PO BOX 48., POKENO, 1872 NZ
35920 ANDREWS, MICHAEL, PO BOX 38., BAYLYS BEACH, 0300 NZ
35921 GERSLOV, MARION, 56 SELWYN CRES., MILFORD, AUCK 9 NZ
35922 WHITTFIELD, MISS K., PO BOX 1483., ROTORUA, NZ
35923 ATKINSON, PAMELA, 156 STOBO ST., INVERCARGILL, NZ
35924 LAMONT, ALLEN, 11 CROFTON RD., NGAIO, WLGTN NZ
35925 EDWARDS, ALAN, 8A HART ST., DUNEDIN, NZ
35926 BAXTER, CHRISTINE, 6 BARRIE AVE., PAPATOETOE, AUCK NZ
35927 KEARTON, BASIL, 40 HOSPITAL RD., TE KUITI, 2500 NZ
35928 CLEVERLEY, MARION, 31 NGATITIOA ST., TAWA, NZ
35929 CULLEN, ZENDA, 6 HAMILL RD., EAST TAMAKI, AUCK 1701 NZ
35930 MOOAR, TONY, 20 MANUKA ST., CHRISTCHURCH, 1 NZ
35931 SINGLETON, RITA, 54 SHOREHAM ST., BLOCKHOUSE BAY, AUCK 7 NZ
35932 BRANT, JEANNETTE, 41 REGENT ST., PAPATOETOE, AUCK NZ
35933 MCCONACHIE, MRS B., 48 BUICK CRES., PALMERSTON NORTH, NZ
35934 FOUNTAINE, EVELYN, 56 MARSTON RD., TIMARU, NZ
35935 BAUCKE, ANITA, RURAL DELIVERY 1., HAVELOCK, SI NZ
35936 TURNBULL, RUTH C., 16 MOANA RD., PARAPARAMU, 6152 NZ
35937 GIBB, JUNE, 1/10 FLORANCE PL., CHRISTCHURCH, 9 NZ
35938 CURTIS, MR I., PO BOX 1222., GISBORNE, NZ
35939 STARLING, JOAN, BOX 125., WAITATI, OTAGO 9160 NZ
35940 PROUT, LOIS, 3 AUCKLAND TCE., WELLINGTON, 3 NZ
35941 HERBERT, JUDY, 17 PRINCES ST., HAWERA, TARANAKI NZ
35942 HUGHES, MRS V., 1405 WARWICK PL., HASTINGS, NZ
35943 HOWAT, ESTHER, 86 MCALISTER ST., WHAKATANE, NZ
35944 DUNSTALL, THELMA, 32A BOLLARD AVE., AUCKLAND, 7 NZ
35945 LOMAX, MAUREEN, 138 DEEP CREEK RD., TORBAY, AUCK 10 NZ
35946 NICHOLLS, DR G., 469 RIDDELL RD., GLENDOWIE, AUCK 5 NZ
35947 MILLER, BARBARA, 41 ALEXANDRA ST., MARTON, 5151 NZ
35948 GEORGE, IRIS, 85 WEST END RD., AUCKLAND, NZ
35949 STEDMOND, JOAN, 252 CENTAURUS RD., CHRISTCHURCH, 8002 NZ
35950 WARNER, DONNA, 18B TINIRAU ST., WANGANUI, NZ
35951 THIELE, JOHN, 46 ACHERON RD., PARAMATA, AUCK NZ
35952 FARR, BARBARA, RUNDLES RD, NO 6 RD., ASHBURTON, 8300 NZ
35953 CLEGHORN, VAL, RD3., WOODVILLE, NZ
35954 VOYLE, MARY, 41 CLARE ST., CAMBRIDGE, NZ
35955 PRICE, NEVILLE, 15 MCENROE GVE., LOWER HUTT, NZ
35956 SMITH, MRS C., 41 QUEEN VICTORIA ST., MOTUEKA, NELSON NZ
35957 YOUNG, MR G.C., 3 HUXLEY ST., PAHIATUA, 5471 NZ
35958 MCCLUNIE, MRS P., 161 STAFFORD ST., HOKITIKA, NZ
35959 EDGAR, CLAIRE, 74 ORIEL AVE., TAWA, WLGTN NZ
35960 FRENCH, MR M., 326B OCEAN RD., WHANGAMATA, 2992 NZ
35961 DUNBAR, MR G., 19 HADLOW PL., CHRISTCHURCH, NZ
35962 RAIT, BARRY, LONGWOOD NO 1 RD., RIVERTON, NZ
35963 MULLIGAN, BRYAN, 3 MOA ST., LOWER HUTT, NZ
35964 WYRILL, PATRICIA, 1/1567 GREAT NORTH RD., AVONDALE, AUCK 7 NZ
35965 RYAN, IRENE, 47 LEMINGTON RD., WESTMERE, AUCK 2 NZ
35966 WILLIAMS, MARTYN, 196 TAITA DR., LOWER HUTT, NZ
35967 GREENLEES, CHRISTINE, 269 RICHARDSON RD., MT ROSKILL, AUCK 4 NZ
35968 HARDING, MRS L., 90 WILLIAMS ST., CAMBRIDGE, WKTO 2351 NZ
35969 NORTHCOTT, MARGARET, BOX 5308 WELLESLEY ST., AUCKLAND, NZ
35970 CROOK, RICHARD, 192/1 MUTU ST., TE AWAMUTU, 2400 NZ
35971 DUNN, MR D., THE GRANGE, ROSLYN RD., LEVIN, NZ
35972 SHERWIN, OLWYN, 39 WM SOUTER ST., FORREST HILL, AUCK 10 NZ
35973 WEVELL, NOELENE, 5 TERRACE ST., PALMERSTON NORTH, NZ
35974 MCNAUGHTON, MOERA, 11 HEATH ST., MOUNT MAUNGANUI, 3002 NZ
35975 KENT-JOHNSTON, LOMA, 84 GILLIES AVE., TAUPO, NZ
35976 STRAWBRIDGE, MARGARET, 17 EDEN TCE., WHANGAREI, NZ
35977 RIENKS, ALLISON, 2 REID GVE., TAUPO, 3300 NZ
35978 EDMUNDS, AILEEN, 5A TERRACE AVE., MOUNT MAUNGANUI, 3002 NZ
35979 WILLIAMS, DOROTHY, 3/132 ROBERTS ST., TAUPO, 3300 NZ
35980 PELLETT, MRS K., 24 GORDON ST., WESTON, OAMARU NZ
35981 KERR, BARBARA, "KERR DOWNS" HEDGEHOPE RD2., INVERCARGILL, STHLAND NZ

35982 DUDER, NOELINE, NORTH RD., CLEVEDON RD2., PAPAKURA, AUCK NZ
35983 GRANT-TAYLOR, SHONA, 95 WATERLOO RD., LOWER HUTT, NZ
35984 WILSON, LOIS, 49S CAREY ST., HAMILTON, NZ
35985 AUSTIN, SANDRA, PO BOX 69078., GLENDENE, AUCK 8 NZ
35986 KEARNS, HUGH, 37 AURORA ST., CHRISTCHURCH, 8004 NZ
35987 WADE, DIANA, 12 BRIDGE AVE., TE ATATU SOUTH, AUCK 1208 NZ
35988 MACQUIBBAN, ANGELA, 2/78 IRELAND RD., PANMURE, AUCK 1106 NZ
35989 CHIRNSIDE, MARGARET, 127 EASTHER CRES., DUNEDIN, OTAGO 9001 NZ
35990 ALLCOTT, MR G., 6 FRATLEY AVE., PAKURANGA, AUCK 1706 NZ
35991 HARVIE, FIONA, C/O 32 SOUTH RD, RD12., HAWERA, TARANAKI NZ
35992 JEFFRIES, MARY, 15 LEMON ST., OTAKI, NZ
35993 HELEM, GEORGE, 151 IKITARA RD., WANGANUI EAST, NZ
35994 WEIR, MARGARET, 17 COPPELL PL., CHRISTCHURCH, 8002 NZ
35995 CRAWFORD, MRS E., 59 FRANKLYN RD., TAWA, WLGTN 6203 NZ
35996 CURRY, JANE, 3 ALLEYNE CT., UPPER HUTT, 6401 NZ
35997 LANDER, MRS S., 424 WORCESTER ST., CHRISTCHURCH, 1 NZ
35998 TAYLOR, HARRIET, 29 RIMU ST., HELENSVILLE, NZ
35999 NEVILLE, ALISON, BERWICK NO 1 RD., OUTRAM, OTAGO NZ
36000 HOOPER, TREVOR, 42 HARRIS CRES., CHRISTCHURCH, 5 NZ
36001 LOGAN, JOAN, PO BOX 218., WELLINGTON, 6000 NZ
36002 BERRY, LESLIE, 3 BRYCE AVE., EDINBURGH, MLN EH7 6TX SCT
36003 DERRISCOTT, ALAN, 17 BROOKWAY., WALLASEY, L45 4SD ENG
36004 GILLARD, DOREEN, 4 AINTREE RD., FURNACE GREEN, CRAWLEY, SSX ENG
36005 COOKE, VALERIE, 13 GRANARY CL., KIBWORTH BEAUCHAMP, LEI LE8 0HZ ENG
36006 ROSE, ANN, 275 KINGS RD., KINGSTON UPON THAMES, SRY KT2 5JJ ENG
36007 HEARLE, ANN, THE OLD VICARAGE., MELLOR, STOCKPORT, CHS SK6 5LX ENG
36008 SANKEY, TIMOTHY, 16 CHURCH RD., OWLSMOOR, CAMBERLEY, SRY GU15 4TJ ENG
36009 CHURCHWARD, BRIAN, 38 LONGHOUSE BARN., PENPERLLENI, GWENT NP4 0BD WALES
36010 BOWERS, RONALD, ROAD END COTTAGE., STOCKLAND, DEV EX14 9LJ ENG
36011 FRYER, BETTY, 9 GLENHEADON RISE., LEATHERHEAD, SRY KT22 8QT ENG
36012 AUSTIN, BRIAN, 11 ALMA ST., WESTON-SUPER-MARE, SOM BS23 1RB ENG
36013 ATTWOOLL, MS H., PUCKPOOL HOUSE, HIGH ST., ARLINGHAM, GLS SL2 7JN ENG
36014 JARRETT, MR P., WINTERS COT., WINTERS CROSS, HUISH CHAMPFLOWER, SOM TA4 2HD
       ENG
36015 BRIMSON, DAVID, 84 DENE RD., HEADINGTON, OXF OX3 7EG ENG
36016 DERBY, MATTHEW, 42 EDINBURGH RD., DUMFRIES, DFS DG1 1JQ SCOTLAND
36017 GILBERT, CYRIL, 1B/5 ST MATTHEWS GDNS., ST LEONARDS ON SEA, E. SSX TN38 0TS ENG
36018 VERNON, ESTHER, 31 INTAKE AVE., MANSFIELD, NOTTS NG18 5EJ ENG
36019 SANDERSON, JAMES, 16 FOUNTAINS CRES., SOUTHGATE, LONDON, MDX N14 6BE ENG
36020 CASPER, MRS G., 8 ROSEVALE TCE., SCARBOROUGH, N YKS YO12 5EW ENG
36021 WALE, DIANA, 6 LANDGUARD MANOR RD., SHANKLIN, IOW PO37 7HZ ENG
36022 SWINDLEHURST, JOAN, 10A SOUTHFIELD RD., BINGLEY, WRY BD16 1EA ENG
36023 BATTS, GEOFFREY, OLD COTT, NO.6 SPAREACRE LN., EYNSHAM, OXF OX8 1NH ENG
36024 MORRIS, MS K., 3 MORAVIAN CL., DUKINFIELD, CHS SK16 4EW ENG
36025 HASSALL, MARK, INST OF ARCHAEOL, 31-34 GORDON SQ., LONDON, WC1H 0PY ENG
36026 KEDGE, THOMAS, 2 YORK RD., BRENTFORD, MDX TW8 0QP ENG
36027 HOTTEN, ELIZABETH, 37 ACACIA AVE., HAYES, MDX UB3 2ND ENG
36028 HORNBY, ANTHONY, GLEBE HOUSE., SHUDY CAMPS, CAMBS CB1 6RB ENG
36029 CLAXSON, ROBERT, 60 DONCASTER WAY., UPMINSTER, ESS RM14 2PL ENG
36030 AUSTIN-COOPER, RICHARD, BUTTERHILL HOUSE., WANSFORD, CAMBS PE8 6LB ENG
36031 BOYD, NINA, 91 TINSHILL RD., LEEDS, WRY LS16 7DN ENG
36032 BROWN, JOHN, 15 DORSET AVE., DIGGLE, NR OLDHAM, LAN OL3 5PS ENG
36033 CLAYBURN, MR R., 4 WINNHAM DR., FAREHAM, HAM PO16 8QE ENG
36034 HOGG, MR M., 18 GREEN HILL RD., LEEDS, W YKS LS12 3QA ENG
36035 HOWLETT, PETER, 3 MORLAND CL., LUTON, BEDS LU6 3QB ENG
36036 MARYON, ALAN, 37 PICKARDS WAY., WISBECH, CAMBS PE13 1SD ENG
36037 JOHNSON, LINDA, 47 BURLEIGH AVE., WALLINGTON, SRY SM6 7JG ENG
36038 GOODMAN, BETTY, 8 GWENBROOK AVE., CHILWELL, NOTTS NG9 4BA ENG
36039 ANDREW, JAMES, 44 BROOKSIDE WALK., TADLEY, HAM RG26 6RW ENG
36040 GRAHAM, ROBERT, 34 PARK LN., KIDDERMINSTER, WOR DY11 6TG ENG
36041 DONALD, ALASTAIR, ROSE COTTAGE, HIGH ST., WIDDINGTON, ESS CB11 3PG ENG
36042 HILTON, MRS M., 3 THE LEYS LANGFORD., BIGGLESWADE, BDF SG18 9RS ENG
36043 FURLONG, MISS J., 73 ST JAMES CRES., BEXHILL-ON-SEA, E. SSX TN40 2DL ENG
36044 SUTTON, MS J., 26 WELLINGTON RD., OLD COLWYN, CLWYD LL29 9NE WLS
36045 THURSFIELD, MARK, 2/32 MOAT LN., BIRMINGHAM, WAR B26 1TJ ENG
36046 PINKNEY, RICHARD, 11 PINE RD., ORMESBY, C'LAND TS7 9DH ENG
36047 KELLY, BERYL, 65 OAKLANDS., SOUTH GODSTONE, SRY RH9 8HX ENG
36048 KERRIDGE, ANDREW, 93 NEVILLE RD., LIMBURY, LUTON, BEDS ENG
36049 FORSYTHE, JUDITH, 27 CORNSLAND., BRENTWOOD, ESS CM14 4HP ENG
36050 RAMSEY, COLIN, 121 UPPER BRISTOL RD., WESTON SUPER MARE, SOM BS22 9AW ENG
36051 SULLIVAN, PHYLLIS, 53 HIGH ST., GATEHOUSE-OF-FLEET, KKD DG7 2HR SCOTLAND
36052 CLUGSTON, MRS P., TY-NEWYDD GELL., TROFARTH, CLWYD LL22 8RE WALES

36053 BLACKLOCK MISS A., 1 BELL VIEW CL., WINDSOR, BRK SL4 4EX ENG
36054 POMEROY, MR A., 182 KINGS HALL RD., BECKENHAM, KENT BR3 1LJ ENG
36055 OLIVER, BARRY, 32 BEDALE RD., ENFIELD, MDX EN2 0NP ENG
36056 BRAMFITT, GUY, 4 NEWALL RD., ANDOVER, HANTS SP11 8HP ENG
36057 HARRIS, HUGH, 33 EDEN RD., NEWTON AYCLIFFE, DUR DL5 5RL ENG
36058 HAWKES, GORDON, 24 KIDDERMINSTER RD., BEWDLEY, WORCS DY12 1AG ENG
36059 PADDISON, MR P., 69 WYATTS DR., SOUTHEND ON SEA, ESS SS1 3DG ENG
36060 LOVEGROVE, ROGER, 11 MARLBOROUGH RD., BOWES PARK, LND N22 4NB ENG
36061 LANGRIDGE, MR L., 2 ROWANTREE RD., ENFIELD, MDX EN2 8QA ENG
36062 JAMES, MR W., ASKEW GREEN., WITHERSLACK, CUM LA11 6SA ENG
36063 LEGGETT, MR L., 102 SYLVAN AVE., TIMPERLEY ALTRINCHAM, CHS WA15 6AB ENG
36064 HERBERT, CYRIL, 12 NEW PLACE SQ, DRUMMOND RD., LONDON, SE16 2HW ENG
36065 HANDS, MR S., 99 LANSDOWNE AVE., LEIGH-ON-SEA, ESS SS9 1LJ ENG
36066 BLADEN, GILLIAN, 44 BODDENS HILL RD., STOCKPORT, CHS SK4 2DG ENG
36067 WOODS, JOHN, 23 KNIGHTS AVE., CLAPHAM, BEDS MK41 6DF ENG
36068 BATCHELOR, KENNETH, 3 ELVEN LN., EAST DEAN, SSX BN20 0LG ENG
36069 FOX, MR J., 44 MANOR LN., LEWISHAM, LND SE13 5QP ENG
36070 GILBERT, JACQUELINE, 67 CONNAUGHT AVE., CHINGFORD, LND E4 7AP ENG
36071 JONES, LYNDA, 63 DEEPDENE VALE., DORKING, SRY RH4 1NJ ENG
36072 LUKER, PETER, 17 ROSSLYN CRES., WEMBLEY, MDX HA9 7NZ ENG
36073 LAGRUE, REV B., ST EDMUND'S COLLEGE., WARE, HRT SG11 1DS ENG
36074 HILEY, MR A., 5 THE PINGLE., SPONDON, DBY DE2 7RD ENG
36075 HURST, MR N.G., 10 AGHNAHOE RD., DUNGANNON, TYR BT70 1TN N IRELAND
36076 WHITFIELD, JOHN, 263 DUNKERY RD., MOTTINGHAM, LND SE9 4HW ENG
36077 EWEN, GRAHAM, 84 DONBANK TCE., ABERDEEN, AB2 2SD SCOTLAND
36078 CLAOUE, CHARLES, 2 ROCQUE LN, POND RD., BLACKHEATH, LND SE3 9JN ENG
36079 PUSEY, WILLIAM, 57 REYNARDS CL, WINNERSH., WOKINGHAM, BRK RG11 5NU ENG
36080 HAZELTON, MAY, 114 ERINVALE AVE., BELFAST, BT10 0FP N IRELAND
36081 HALL, PHILIP, MAYFIELD VICARAGE., ASHBOURNE, DBY DE6 2JR ENG
36082 BAMKIN, ROGER, 14 FORRESTER AVE., WESTON ON TRENT, DBY DE7 2HX ENG
36083 CURTIS, KAY, BALTANA, LONDON RD., BARKWAY., ROYSTON, HERTS SE8 8EY ENG
36084 HAWKSWORTH, MR K., 48 HIGHER BLANDFORD RD., BROADSTONE, DOR BH18 9AQ ENG
36085 FAIRLEY, GEORGE, 28 ST JOHN'S RD., ALTRINCHAM, CHS WA14 2NA ENG
36086 JONES, ANTONY, 1 OAKLANDS, OAKHILL RD., HORSHAM, SSX RH13 5LG ENG
36087 STOREY, HAROLD, 2 ORCHARD CL., CHEADLE HULME, CHS SK8 7ET ENG
36088 FREEMAN, JAMES, 56 CULVERDEN DOWN., TUNBRIDGE WELLS, KEN TN4 9SG ENG
36089 CANT, ROBERT, 3 LONDON RD., BALDOCK, HRT SG7 6LE ENG
36090 DUNN, LOIS, 6 BEVERLEY CL., MARLOW, BKM SL7 2RD ENG
36091 BARBER, WILLIAM, 29 HIGHLANDS WAY., WHITEPARISH, WIL SP5 2SZ ENG
36092 BELLINGER, BARRY, 20 MERSEY WAY., THATCHAM, BRK RG13 3DL ENG
36093 HARE, GEOFF, 12 COLBURN AVE., CATERHAM, SRY CR3 6HU ENG
36094 PARKINSON, RAYMOND, 128A DOYLE GDNS., WILLESDEN, LND NW10 3SR ENG
36095 PIPER, WILLIAM, SUTTON HSE., SCHOOL LN., SUTTON VALENCE, KENT ME17 3HH ENG
36096 ELWORTHY, SIMON, LT FRITH FARM, NEWNHAM., SITTINGBOURNE, KENT ME9 0NG ENG
36097 CARDEN, ARTHUR, 20 WODEHOUSE TCE., FALMOUTH, CON TR11 3EN ENG
36098 SWINBURN, LINDA, 10 SOUTHGATE RD., BURY, LAN BL9 8DZ ENG
36099 DULLEY, THELMA, 46 HILLVIEW RD., CHISLEHURST, KEN BR7 6DS ENG
36100 HASELGROVE, MRS S., 14 DAFFORDS BLDGS., BATH, AVON BA1 6SG ENG
36101 ROBINSON, S.F., 35B HANLEY RD., HORNSEY, LND N4 3DU ENG
36102 GREEN, MISS H., 12 THORNTON DR, UPTON PK., CHESTER, CHS ENG
36103 BARNWELL, JOHN, BEECHEN CL., HOME LN., SPARSHOLT, HANTS SO21 2NN ENG
36104 ATKINSON, JOHN, 7 FLEET AVE., DARTFORD, KENT DA2 6NL ENG
36105 MELLORS, JOHN, C/O OIC, CSOS., , BFPO 1
36106 PROWSE, MICHAEL, 13 GUILDFORD RD., FLEET, HAM GU13 9EN ENG
36107 WOOD, TOM, 4 GEORGIAN HSES., NORTH THORESBY, LIN DN36 5RF ENG
36108 BIRKMIRE, DAVID, 6 PICKERING CL., URMSTON, M31 3DB ENG
36109 EVANS, MR M., 51 LEYFIELDS CRES., WARWICK, WAR CV34 6BA ENG
36110 ROWLEY, JANET, 21A GROSVENOR RD., BIRMINGHAM, B20 3NW ENG
36111 MOODY, GILLIAN, 106 GRANNY HALL LN., BRIGHOUSE, WRY HD6 2JJ ENG
36112 BUTT, MRS B., THE OLD BAKERY, CHORLTON., MALPAS, CHS SY14 7ER ENG
36113 CLARK, IAN, 10 ST HELENS CL., GRANTHAM, LIN NG31 7EE ENG
36114 WEDDELL, MONTY, 725 BLUEGRASS., DALLAS, TX 75211 USA
36115 DALLAT, CAHAL, 9 ATLANTIC AVE., BALLYCASTLE, ANT BT54 6AL IRELAND
36116 BOLTON, COLIN, 30 COURT MOOR AVE., FLEET, HANTS GU13 9UF ENG
36117 LANE, ALAN, 21 ST PETERS AVE., TELSCOMBE CLIFFS, SSX BN10 7DU ENG
36118 BOVIS, PETER, 92 LARKFIELD RD., BELFAST, ANT BT4 1QF IRELAND
36119 TUEART, PETER, HIGHWAY HSE., DEDSWELL DR., WEST CLANDON, SRY GU4 7TQ ENG
36120 DOXON, ANTOINETTE, 19 THE VALE, OVERBROOK., HYTHE, HAM SO4 5ET ENG
36121 RAINBIRD, ROSEMARY, 2 BEACH RD., WEST MERSEA, ESS CO5 8AA ENG
36122 CASE, DR DAVID, 7 EDEN CL., WILMSLOW, CHES ENG
36123 BOYLES, RICHARD, 9 NARVIK RD., CORBY, NTH NN18 9DW ENG
36124 MOORE, MISS P., 28 LE STRANGE CL., NORWICH, NFK NR2 3PW ENG

36125 MACKISON, JAMES, 179 ROTHBURY TCE., HEATON, NE6 5DB ENG
36126 BINNS, JUDI, 3 SHRUBBERY GVE., ROYSTON, HRT SG8 9LJ ENG
36127 HYATT, ROBERT, 13 ALBERT RD., HENDON, LND NW4 2SH ENG
36128 PURDY, NORMA, 25 LANGMERE RD., WATTON, NFK IP25 6LG ENG
36129 HETHERINGTON, DAVID, 104 CLABBY RD., LURGANCLABBY, TYR BT75 0QY N.IRELAND
36130 SMITH, JOHN, 12A BELLE VUE RD, ROUNDHAM., PAIGNTON, DEV TQ4 6ER ENG
36131 HALL, DAVID, THE OLD VICARAGE, ELM GVE., TAUNTON, SOM TA1 1EH ENG
36132 BESWICK, DAVID, "HILLSIDE", BARTON LN., BARTON, LAN PR3 5AU ENG
36133 MAXIM, PHILIP, 21 WYNDHAM AVE., HIGH WYCOMBE, BUCKS HP13 5ER ENG
36134 HALLAM, PAUL, TANGLEWOOD, THE WARREN., EAST HORSLEY, SRY KT24 5RH ENG
36135 BUNYAN, TERRY, 10 KENTON CL., BRACKNELL, BERKS RG12 3AZ ENG
36136 PRINCE, BARBARA, 35 SOPERS LN., POOLE, DOR BH17 7EW ENG
36137 STEED, DAVID, SPRATLING COURT FARM, MANSTON., RAMSGATE, KENT CT12 5AN ENG
36138 MONTGOMERY, MRS H., 32 PADDOCK WOOD., MIDDLESBROUGH, CLV TS8 0SA ENG
36139 SIGNORACCI, SILVERIO, VIA F.LLI ROSSELLI 21., S.LORENZO IN CAMPO, PS 61047 ITALY
36140 HUNTER, ALBERT, 88 MAIN ST., BURTON JOYCE, NTT NG14 5EP ENG
36141 TRENHOLME, BASIL, STRETCHGATE, ROOKES LN., NORWOOD GREEN, W.YKS HX3 8PU ENG
36142 DYKE, MISS S., 29 WESTBY RD., BOSCOMBE, DOR BH5 1HA ENG
36143 HILLAM, MR D., 6 BRANCOTE RD., OXTON, BIRKENHEAD, L43 6TJ ENG
36144 PETYT, ANTHONY, 10 STATION ST., SANDAL, WRY WF1 5AF ENG
36145 BOASE, MISS H., 40 ROSEHILL., ST BLAZEY, CON PL24 2LG ENG
36146 NEWBOLD, MICHAEL, 124 HILLCROSS AVE., MORDEN, SRY SM4 4EG ENG
36147 JAGGER, DENIS, "LEAWAY" SOUTHWELL RD., KIRKLINGTON, NOTTS NG22 8NF ENG
36148 BOND, MISS M., 566 RICHMOND RD., SHEFFIELD, S YKS S13 8NB ENG
36149 STEELE, SHEILA, 10 BACK ST., BIGGLESWADE, BDF SG18 8JA ENG
36150 WILLIAMS, MR D., 5 EASTCLIFFE., WINCHESTER, HAM SO23 8JB ENG
36151 MCINTOSH, MRS L, 'CARTREF MELYS' DRURY LANE., DRURY, CH7 3DY WALES
36152 HERRING, PETER, 212 STORTFORD HALL PARK., BISHOPS STORTFORD, HERTS CM23 5AS
        ENG
36153 CASEY, MR R, 24 PERSHORE RD., BASINGSTOKE, HAM RG24 9BQ ENG
36154 PEARCE, FRANK, 16 SCRATTON FIELDS., SOLE STREET, KEN DA12 3AS ENG
36155 POPPLESTONE, JOAN, 119B PORTSWOOD RD., PORTSWOOD, HAM S02 1FX ENG
36156 HADLER, STUART, 9 BLAKE END., KEWSTOKE, AVON BS22 9LS ENG
36157 CHEESMAN, BRIAN, 5 WINIFREDE PAUL HSE, 1 YORK RISE., LONDON, NW5 1DX ENG
36158 TASKER, BRIAN, 29 MANOR RD., PAWLETT, SOM TA6 4SN ENG
36159 CLAYTON, BRIAN, 26 ST PHILIPS WAY., BURLEY IN WHARFEDALE, WRY LS29 7EW ENG
36160 LUCAS, CHARLES, OLD OAST PL., ICKLESHAM, SSX TN36 4AP ENG
36161 PESTER, LYNN, 14 FRANCIS RD., STOCKTON HEATH, CHES WA4 6EB ENG
36162 ELTON, GEORGE, 35 INNESCOURT O.P.E., HULL, ERY HU6 9SS ENG
36163 TOMLINSON, MRS K, 37 NORTH ROCKS RD., PAIGNTON, DEV TQ4 6LF ENG
36164 KELLY, PAUL, 61 LLOYD DR., GREASBY, WIRRAL, MSY L49 1RH ENG
36165 BRUTON, ROGER, 29 RABOURNMEAD DR., NORTHOLT, MDX UB5 6YH ENG
36166 SWEET, JACK, 15 WINSTON DR., YEOVIL, SOM BA21 3BH ENG
36167 ROBINSON, MARION, 133 RODMELL AVE., SALTDEAN, SSX BN2 8PH ENG
36168 O'NEILL, CHRISTINE, 36 GLOSSOP RD., SOUTH CROYDON, CR2 0PU ENG
36169 CLIVES, STANLEY, 42 FRITH VIEW., CHAPEL EN LE FRITH, DBY SK12 6TT ENG
36170 GOODDEN, MICHAEL, KEEPERS COTTAGE., NETHER COMPTON, DOR DT9 4QT ENG
36171 MORTER, IAN, 60 BUXTON RD., CHADDESDEN, DBY DE2 4JL ENG
36172 TITFORD, JOHN, YEW TREE FM, HALLFIELDGATE., HIGHAM, DBY DE5 6AA ENG
36173 MIMMS, PETER, 20 LONSDALE RD., BOURNEMOUTH, DOR BH3 7LX ENG
36174 TANN-WATSON, LYNNE, 2 ABTHORPE AVE., KINGSTHORPE, NTH NN2 8NS ENG
36175 FOSTER, ANTHONY, MANSION VIEW, GWYSTRE., LLANDRINDOD WELLS, LD1 6RN WALES
36176 LEDGER, MR F, 1 SHENTON CL., SWINDON, WIL SN3 4NG ENG
36177 MOLE, EDNA, 24 CHANTREY CRES., GREAT BARR, B43 7PA ENG
36178 HUBBARD, KENNETH, 691 NEWPORT RD., RUMNEY, GLA CF3 8DB WALES
36179 OWAIN-JONES, MISS P, 85 CHELVERTON RD., PUTNEY, LND SW15 1RW ENG
36180 WESTMORLAND, DICKON, 190 HUISH., YEOVIL, SOM BA20 1BJ ENG
36181 FRANCIS, SHEILA, 14 BRYNGWASTAD RD., GORSEINON, GLA SA4 2XG WALES
36182 BOOKER, KATHLEEN, 104 BROAD RD., LOWER WILLINGDON, E SSX BN20 9RD ENG
36183 HOLMES, MRS S, 191 SUTTON RD., WALSALL, W MIDS WS5 3AW ENG
36184 BLACKWOOD, ANGELA, 7 COLLEGE HILL, BARGATE WOOD, GODALMING, SRY GU7 1YA
        ENG
36185 HEDLEY-JONES, MR R, 18 DRYHILL RD., TONBRIDGE, KEN TN9 1LX ENG
36186 PLIM, PAUL, 5 PELHAM CRES., LONDON, SW7 2ND ENG
36187 STARKEY, ALAN, 28 BISHOPS WAY., MELTHAM, WRY HD7 3BW ENG
36188 BARGERY, AVIS, 45 ASHFIELD RD., COMPTON, W MIDS WV3 9DP ENG
36189 MORSE, JOHN, 72 ROLAND AVE., HOLBROOKS, WAR CV6 4HR ENG
36190 JONES, MISS M, 17 DUNSTER GDNS., CHELTENHAM, GLS GL51 0QT ENG
36191 MCANNA, JAMES, 32 ST JAMES CRT, 17 WESTERN PDE., SOUTHSEA, HANTS P05 3RL ENG
36192 KENDAL-WARD, CLIFFORD, 3 MARCHFIELD TCE., EDINBURGH, MLN EH4 7AE SCOTLAND
36193 BOWE, CAROL, STATION FM., SOUTH OTTERINGTON, N. YKS DL7 9JB ENG
36194 SWINNERTON, COL. I, YEW TREE COT., BLACKFORD., STOKE ST MILBOROUGH, SAL SY8 2ET
        ENG

36195 BOURTON, MR J, FLAT D, 44 WESTBOURNE GDNS., LONDON, W2 5NS ENG
36196 WHITE, JOSEPHINE, 4 HAZEL CL., LEAMINGTON SPA, WAR CV32 5XL ENG
36197 PUGH, RICHARD, 2 LODGE DR., MALVERN, WORCS WR14 4LS ENG
36198 WINDER, STEWART, 16 THORN ST., BOLTON, LAN ENG
36199 POWELL, LOIS, 36 TOWER HILL., UPHOLLAND, WN8 0DU ENG
36200 LE QUESNE, WALTER, CICADELLA, ROUTE DE NOIRMONT, ST BRELADE, JSY JE3 8AJ UK
36201 CARE, IAN, 8 KINGS DR., LITTLEOVER, DBY DE3 6EU ENG
36202 STEWARD, MRS A, 6 BERESFORD DR., SUTTON COLDFIELD, WEST MID B73 SQZ ENG
36203 ARTIS, CHARLES, 12 YEW TREE RD., MADELEY, TF7 5TE ENG
36204 COLLIER, JAMES, 29 STATION RD., GROTTON, LAN 0L4 5SF ENG
36205 MATTHEWS, CRAUFURD, 58 DURFORD RD., PETERSFIELD, HAM GU31 4HA ENG
36206 WILLIAMS, MICHAEL, 75 BALDWIN AVE., EASTBOURNE, SSX BN21 1UL ENG
36207 NOONEY, MURIEL, 1 HIGHFIELD CL., CHANDLERS FORD, HAM SO5 2JU ENG
36208 POLKEY, ANDREW, 12 ROYAL AVE., LONG EATON, NTT NG10 1NU ENG
36209 NICHOLAS, PHILIP, 25 SARNFAN, BAGLAN., PORT TALBOT, W. GLAM SA12 8DY WALES
36210 BETTERIDGE, HAROLD, 29 SOUTH ST., ELIE, FIFE KY9 1DN SCT
36211 COX, BRENDA, 52 PENN HILL AVE, LWR PARKSTONE., POOLE, DOR BH14 9NA ENG
36212 STEVENS, CONNIE, 115 BEVENDEAN CRES., BRIGHTON, SSX BN2 4RE ENG
36213 COMPTON, JOHN, 14 CLARKFIELD., RICKMANSWORTH, HRT WD3 2FH ENG
36214 MORRISON, MRS P, 15 SANDHURST DR., BUCKINGHAM, BKM MK18 1DT ENG
36215 VONESHEN, SUSAN, 113 STATION RD., WEST BYFLEET, SRY KT14 6DT ENG
36216 FENNER, MR C, 10 SINGLETON WAY., PRESTON, LAN PR2 4PX ENG
36217 SMITH, ANN, 1 WOODHOUSE AVE., PERIVALE, MIDDX UB6 8LE ENG
36218 STERRY, MRS C, WATERGATE HSE, BETHESDA ST., UP. BASILDON, BRK RG8 8NT ENG
36219 LUDLAM, MISS H, 38 SUN RD., SWANSCOMBE, KENT DA10 0BH ENG
36220 PROCTOR, DR H, 7 TUDOR GVE., STREETLY, WAR B74 2LL ENG
36221 GURDIN, GEOFFREY, 36 ARBUTUS RD., MEADVALE, SRY RH1 6LH ENG
36222 CRUTTENDEN, IAN, 43 EASTCOTE DR., HARPENDEN, AL5 1SE ENG
36223 ALDERTON, HUGH, 16 WOODFIELD DR., ROMFORD, ESS RM2 5DH ENG
36224 HALFPENNY, CYRIL, 182 TEAN RD., CHEADLE, STS ST10 1NQ ENG
36225 BASSINGTON, GEOFFREY, THE BREEZES, LYDNEY RD., BREAM, GLS GL15 6EW ENG
36226 DANIELL, PETER, 58 EAST LODGE PARK., FARLINGTON, HAM PO6 1AG ENG
36227 LOWTHER, LEVI, HIGH ASH FM, ALLERTON RD., BRADFORD, YORKS BD15 8AB ENG
36228 MARSDEN, JOHN, 3 HESKETH RD., SALE, CHS M33 5AA ENG
36229 SMITH, JOHN, 22 JASMINE RD., MALVERN WELLS, WOR WR14 4XD ENG
36230 BALLARD, VIVIENNE, TANGLEWOOD, QUEENS ST., BLOXHAM, OXF OX15 4QQ ENG
36231 HOLWAY, MRS S, 1 CHOBHAM CL., STREATLEY, WILTS SN3 4UL ENG
36232 FLETCHER, DIANA, WESTBROOK RHINEFD. RD., BROCKENHURST, HANTS SO42 7SR ENG
36233 BROWN, SUE, 25 HOMECROFT DR., PACKINGTON, LEICS LE6 2WG ENG
36234 IRELAND, MRS K, HEYTHROP COTTAGE., CHURCH ENSTONE, OXON OX7 4NN ENG
36235 WALL, NICOLA, 44 HULBERT END, BEDGROVE., AYLESBURY, BKM ENG
36236 WOOLLEY, MS B, 198 FRANKSTON-FLINDERS RD., BALNARRING, VIC 3926 AUS
36237 NIELSEN, MRS J, 99 SYDNEY PARKINSON AVE., ENDEAVOUR HILLS, VIC 3802 AUS
36238 PRENTICE, RONALD, 6 BURRAN AVE., MOSMAN, NSW 2088 AUS
36239 LOVEGROVE, VICKI, LOT 577 BATTUNGA RD., MEADOWS, SA 5201 AUS
36240 MACAULAY, ROBERT, C/-7 PARKWOOD ST., ALFREDTON, VIC 3350 AUS
36241 CORY, PAM, 9 COLO ST., ARANA HILLS, QLD 4054 AUS
36242 BIRCH, MRS C, 8 SUNNYVIEW DR., UPPER HUTT, 6401 NZ
36243 HAY, ERIC, 177 RIVERBEND RD., NAPIER, NZ
36244 SCHOLLUM, STEPHEN, 96 SHAKESPEARE RD., MILFORD, AUCK 1309 NZ
36245 SMITH, JEAN, MAHOENUI VY RD., COATESVILLE RD3 ALBANY, AUCK NZ
36246 ROBERTSON, MRS A, 76 EMMETT ST., TAURANGA, 3001 NZ
36247 ALISON, JOAN, BOX 4114 KAMO., WHANGAREI, NZ
36248 COLE, KATHLEEN, 16 HOGAN ST., HAMILTON, 2001 NZ
36249 BRAY, CYRIL & JEANETTE, 19 SUNHAVEN DR., NEWLANDS, WTN 4 NZ
36250 KING, ELDA, 14 FREYBERG ST., LEVIN, NZ
36251 SCRAGG, LEATHA, RD 1, TUCKER RD., GISBORNE, NZ
36252 FRANCIS, LEN, 17/119 LUMSDEN RD., HASTINGS, NZ
36253 SUTTON, MRS N, 36 TRELAWN PL., HOWICK, AUCK NZ
36254 MATTHEWS, ROBERT, 25 JASON ST., DUNEDIN, OTAGO NZ
36255 MILLER, HEATHER, 8 RODNEY ST., OTAHUHU, AUCK NZ
36256 COULSTON, ISOBEL, 21 EMILY ST., MANGAPAPA, GISBORNE 3801 NZ
36257 BREWER, ADRIENNE, 4 LINWOOD AVE., FORREST HILL, AUCK 10 NZ
36258 WARD, RUTH, 18 JOHN SIMS DR., BROADMEADOWS, WGTN 6003 NZ
36259 MATHERS, BRUCE, PARAGON HEIGHTS, PO BOX 212., WAIHI, BOP 2991 NZ
36260 FRASER, MR A, 15 RANGITIKI CRES., LYNFIELD, AUCK 1004 NZ
36261 REES, KEVYN, 44 ISLAND TCE., PORT CHALMERS, OTG 9005 NZ
36262 STACEY, BERYL, 2 MATUHI RISE., HENDERSON, AKD 8 NZ
36263 PACE, MAL, 181 VICTORIA ST., CAMBRIDGE, NZ
36264 HARWOOD, MRS B, 136A BATH ST., LEVIN, NZ
36265 SMITH, MRS L, 40 HOBBY AVE., BIRKENHEAD, AUCK NZ
36266 SCOLLAY, RUTH, 1 TRIPOLI ST., ONEKAWA, NAPIER NZ

36267 SZACSVAY, MRS S, 23 LOCKINVAR PL., HORNSBY, NSW 2077 AUS
36268 SMITH, JILL, SCHOOL RES., THOMPSON ST., COOTAMUNDRA, NSW 2590 AUS
36269 HARDY, MRS A, 31 CANNON ST., DAPTO, NSW 2530 AUS
36270 MIERENDORFF, WILLIAM, PO BOX 7., NEWCASTLE, NSW 2300 AUS
36271 WATKINS, RICHARD, 26 BROOKLANDS RD., GLENBROOK, NSW 2773 AUS
36272 LIGHTFOOT, MR D, G.F.H.S., PO BOX 574., TORONTO, NSW 2283 AUS
36273 CURRY, MRS P, LOT 12 TENNYSON RD., TENNYSON, NSW 2754 AUS
36274 O'KEEFE, THERESA, 4 GREENHILL CRES., WERRIBEE, VIC 3030 AUS
36275 REID, ELIZABETH, 36 MULKARRA DR., CHELSEA, VIC 3196 AUS
36276 CHAMP, PETER, 45 PLENTY RIVER DR., GREENSBOROUGH, VIC 3088 AUS
36277 MORTON, LESLEY, 51 PAXTON ST., EAST MALVERN, VIC 3145 AUS
36278 MCNALLY, JEAN, 7 CORONATION CRT., TRARALGON, VIC 3844 AUS
36279 FOLEY, SHIRLEY, 18 BOWMAN ST., MORDIALLOC, VIC 3195 AUS
36280 CRIPPS, DAVID, 28 DRISCOLL ST., ROSETTA, TAS 7010 AUS
36281 GRANLAND, MARGARET, 9 NYRAN PL., ARMADALE, WA 6112 AUS
36282 PINNELL, DONNA, 2 NEWMAN PL., KENWICK, WA 6107 AUS
36283 CORTIS, MRS M, 32 WALLACE ST., CABOOLTURE, QLD 4510 AUS
36284 TOGNOLINI, ENID, 2 MAYLEEN ST., CLONTARF HEIGHTS, QLD 4019 AUS
36285 CHARLES, LYN, 'KOOLGUNYAH', PO BOX 134., TEXAS, QLD 4385 AUS
36286 NUTLEY, CAROL, 4 LANGRIDGE ST., RACEVIEW, QLD 4305 AUS
36287 SOUTHGATE, GLENDA, 22 EDWARD ST., BOYNE ISLAND, QLD 4680 AUS
36288 MARTIN, JILL, 26 FARRAR ST., ACACIA RIDGE, QLD 4110 AUS
36289 CROSSWELL, MR L, LOT 19 COVERTY RD., ROCKDALE MS 660, PROSTON QLD 4613 AUS
36290 FERGUSON, MRS L, 5/30 LEIPER ST., STAFFORD, QLD 4053 AUS
36291 MCCORD, ELAINE, 100 MACQUARIE AVE., CAMPBELLTOWN, NSW 2560 AUS
36292 SMITH, MATTHEW, 119 MISSISSIPPI RD., SEVEN HILLS, NSW 2147 AUS
36293 YOUNG, PHIL, PO BOX 114., GLEBE, NSW 2037 AUS
36294 WALKER, MRS M, 112 STAFFORD ST., GERROA, NSW 2534 AUS
36295 TURNBULL, MR S, PO BOX 375., ST MARYS, NSW 2760 AUS
36296 GARTON, VALERIE, PO BOX 364., ROSE BAY, NSW 2029 AUS
36297 WARHURST, KEVIN, C/O CCD-OCSS, PO BOX A226., SYDNEY SOUTH, NSW 2000 AUS
36298 MALTBY, MRS M, 4/3 GLADSWOOD GDNS., DOUBLE BAY, NSW 2028 AUS
36299 USSHER, JEMMA, 12 PEBBLE BEACH DR., RUNAWAY ISLANDS, QLD 4216 AUS
36300 KING, MRS C, C/O CHAPLAINS OFFICE, RAAF BASE., AMBERLEY, QLD 4306 AUS
36301 DICKSON, MRS M, 239 MANNING RD., WATERFORD, WA 6152 AUS
36302 JOLLY, MR I, PO BOX 2057., SHEPPARTON, VIC 3632 AUS
36303 HABRES, MARGARET, FARM 254 CASSIA RD., LEETON, NSW 2705 AUS
36304 HAZELMAN, MRS H, 13 WHARF RD., BLI BLI, QLD 4560 AUS
36305 COURT, LYNNE, 88 LIVINGSTONE ST., BOWEN, QLD 4805 AUS
36306 BLUMKE, FRANK, 21 COULDREY ST., RAINWORTH, QLD 4065 AUS
36307 MCMAHON, MRS R, 24 MARRAGAL ST., KIRWAN, QLD 4817 AUS
36308 EDWARDS, RUTH, PO BOX 85., WARRNAMBOOL, VIC 3280 AUS
36309 YOUNG, PATRICIA, 5 DOON CRT., BRIAR HILL, VIC 3088 AUS
36310 BIENVENU, F & D, PO BOX 382., MYRTLEFORD, VIC 3737 AUS
36311 HARRISON, MRS R, 28 BAYSWATER RD., LINDFIELD, NSW 2070 AUS
36312 SHEPHERD, JOY, 184 LAKE ALBERT RD., WAGGA WAGGA, NSW 2650 AUS
36313 ANDERSON, ROBYN, 21 MORSE AVE., DAPTO, NSW 2530 AUS
36314 COOTE, VERONICA, 22 MAUDE ST., BARRABA, NSW 2347 AUS
36315 CLIFFORD, MARGARET, 90 FARNELL ST., MERRYLANDS, NSW 2160 AUS
36316 SMITH, ANN, 24 WHITWORTH ST., WESTMEAD, NSW 2145 AUS
36317 SCHIRMER, MR R, 8978 EAST ANNA PL., TUCSON, AZ 85710 USA
36318 O'CONNELL, JOSEPH, 501 N PROVIDENCE RD (610)., MEDIA, PA 19063 USA
36319 MILLER, MARVIN, 1507 45TH AVE SW., SEATTLE, WA 98116 USA
36320 BROWN, SUSANNE, 6081 DANA CIRCLE., MAGALIA, CA 95954 USA
36321 PACKARD-SCHLERF, JERI, 2855 MONTEREY ST., TORRANCE, CA 90503 USA
36322 STADTMAN, MARY, 2992 LA PAZ AVE., HEMET, CA 92343 USA
36323 MCCURDY, ROSS, 1 FOREST VIEW DR., CUMBERLAND, RI 02864 USA
36324 SNYDER, DOROTHY, 610 S TANGLEWOOD DR., SPRINGFIELD, OH 45504 USA
36325 KANE, MS M, 137 E SELBY BLVD., WORTHINGTON, OH 43085 USA
36326 PRINCE, JACOB, 1053 MILLBRANCH CRT., COLUMBUS, GA 31907 USA
36327 GRINTON, PHILIP, 828 BEAVER ST., SANTA ROSA, CA 95404 USA
36328 HERTRICH, MAXINE, 2417 18TH ST., SANTA MONICA, CA 90405 USA
36329 STANLEY, CONSTANCE, 93 MACKTOWN RD., SYLVA, NC 28779 USA
36330 HARWELL, HAROLD, 2100 MOCKING BIRD., MCALESTER, OK 74501 USA
36331 JOHNSON, KENNETH, 16132 ANSTELL CT., MT CLEMENS, MI 48044 USA
36332 THORNTON, ELSIE, 4113 FOGEL LN., SILVER SPRING, MD 20906 USA
36333 SMYTH, ELLEN, 15 VILLAGE LN., ARLINGTON, MA 02174 USA
36334 CURTIS, DAWN, 6915 LOGAN AVE NO., BROOKLYN CENTER, MN 55430 USA
36335 ULLMANN, HELEN, 713 MAIN., ACTON, MA 01720 USA
36336 GERMAN, JOHN, 2631 KITLEY RD., WANAMAKER, IN 46239 USA
36337 PLEASANT, MS M, 5702 SCRIPPS ST., SAN DIEGO, CA 92122 USA
36338 INGOLDSBY, BETH, 220 EAST 20TH ST., GRAND ISLAND, NEB 68801 USA

36339 CURNOW, WILLIAM, 18 SMOKE RISE RD., BEDMINSTER, NJ 07921 USA
36340 ACOSTA, URSULA, PO BOX 8., HORMIGUEROS, PR 00660 USA
36341 HILL, ROBERT, 4417 EDINBROOK TCE., BROOKLYN PARK, MN 55443 USA
36342 LANE, MARILYN, 201 FLYNN AVE #3., MOUNTAIN VIEW, CA 94043 USA
36343 GRIFFIN, JOAN, 45541 DENISE DR., PLYMOUTH, MI 48170 USA
36344 HUTCHINSON, HARRY, 26209 JOHNSON DR., DAMASCUS, MD 20872 USA
36345 HOWARTH, HARRY, 35 CROWN RD., TRENTON, NJ 08638 USA
36346 JACKSON, CLARA, 614 NORTH DARWOOD., SAN DIMAS, CA 91773 USA
36347 STACKHOUSE, EUGENE, 508 E LOCUST AVE., PHILADELPHIA, PA 19144 USA
36348 GRIFFITH, HOWARD, 40 HILLSDALE DR., COUNCIL BLUFFS, IA 51503 USA
36349 CLIFTON, BETTY, 900 WARD CREEK RD., TAYLORSVILLE, CA 95983 USA
36350 STRAUSS, LAURA, 3554 SECOND ST., HADLEY, MI 48440 USA
36351 WOODS, BETTY, 16126 LINSEY LN., LOCKPORT, IL 60441 USA
36352 BOYD, RICHARD, PO BOX 539., MT MORRIS, MI 48458 USA
36353 BOLING, YVETTE, 4724 ASHBURY DR., JEFFERSON, LA 70121 USA
36354 METTS, COL. ALBERT, 4019 SYLVAN OAKS DR., SAN ANTONIO, TX 78229 USA
36355 GRALEY, JAMES, 727 STOLLE RD., ELMA, NY 14059 USA
36356 SEABRIDGE, ROBERT, PO BOX 10785., RENO, NV 89510 USA
36357 DEAN, LLOYD, 6770 U S 60 EAST., MOREHEAD, KY 40351 USA
36358 ADAMS, JOEDY, 4065 PADUCAH DR., SAN DIEGO, CA 92117 USA
36359 BROWN, JOHN, 1408 GILPIN AVE., WILMINGTON, DE 19806 USA
36360 TIMBURY, MRS C, 5 CRUICKSHANK AVE., OCEAN GROVE, VIC 3226 AUS
36361 MYLES, MRS K, 18 VICTORIA ST., PARKDALE, VIC 3195 AUS
36362 HILDRETH, MRS A, 14 PEATEY ST., MACKAY, QLD 4740 AUS
36363 EDDISFORD, MR A, 4 EWELL ST., BONDI, NSW 2026 AUS
36364 ROBINSON, JANET, 34 HAMPDEN AVE., WAHROONGA, NSW 2076 AUS
36365 GIFFORD, JUDITH, 12 GLOSTER CL., EAST GOSFORD, NSW 2250 AUS
36366 WRIGHT, CHRISTINE, 31 ELRINGTON ST., BRAIDWOOD, NSW 2622 AUS
36367 ROBERTS, SHIRLEY, 61 WELFARE AVE., BEVERLY HILLS, NSW 2209 AUS
36368 LINDSAY, IAN, 5/38 MEACHER ST., MT DRUITT, NSW 2770 AUS
36369 HOSKING, BARBARA, 72 BARNARDS AVE., HURSTVILLE, NSW 2220 AUS
36370 PEGG, ROBERT, 35 CUTTLEFISH PDE., ST HUBERTS ISLAND, NSW 2257 AUS
36371 BERRIMAN, DON & NELL, 30 WOODLANDS AVE., NEW LAMBTON, NSW 2305 AUS
36372 SHANNON, MARGARET, 13 FRASER ST., WESTMEAD, NSW 2145 AUS
36373 SHACKELL, FAITH, BARRINGTON HSE, CARY RD., NTH CADBURY, SOM BA22 7DB ENG
36374 WAKELAM, WILLIAM, HILL CREST EWYAS HAROLD., ABBEYDORE, HEF HR2 0JF ENG
36375 WENT, DERRICK, WOODSIDE COTTAGE, CAMP RD., ROSS ON WYE, HEF HR9 5NJ ENG
36376 THOMPSON, MR A, 21 OLD PARK RIDINGS., WINCHMORE HILL, LND N21 2EX ENG
36377 CODLIN, MRS E, 88 THE FAIRWAY., DYMCHURCH, KEN TN29 0QP ENG
36378 DOMMINNEY, MISS H, 9 CEDAR CL., ST LEONARDS ON SEA, SSX TN37 7HR ENG
36379 PARKES, A, SCHOOL HSE, CHURCH CL., DONINGTON ON BAIN, LINCS LN11 9TL ENG
36380 SCOTT, JOHN, BEMERTON, LINGFIELD RD., EAST GRINSTEAD, SSX RH19 2EJ ENG
36381 ROGERSON, BETTY, R. FELIZARDO DE LIMA 149., PORTO, 4100 PORTUGAL
36382 PEET, JOHN, 24 BRITTENS CL., GUILDFORD, SRY GU2 6RJ ENG
36383 CABBAN, PAUL, 23 DOWNS RD., HASTINGS, SSX TN34 2DX ENG
36384 CHITTENDEN, BERYL, 18 CONIFER CL., CHURCH CROOKHAM, HANTS GU13 0LS ENG
36385 VAUGHAN, EDGAR, 109 WHITECREST., GREAT BARR, B43 6EX ENG
36386 HOWE, JOAN, 2 COTTESMORE DR., HESWALL, L60 1YG ENG
36387 HOLLINGSWORTH, FRED, 115 WOLVERHAMPTON RD., PELSALL, W.MID WS3 4AD ENG
36388 ASHCROFT, BRENDA, 12 DOWNSIDE CL., SHOREHAM BY SEA, W SSX BN43 6AF ENG
36389 BENDING, ARTHUR, 51 PARKERS RD., STARCROSS, DEV EX6 8QN ENG
36390 TOBIN, JOHN, THE OLD HOUSE., STANFORD IN THE VALE, OXON SN7 8HY ENG
36391 MEGSON, JOHN, 11/6 SOUTH OSWALD RD., EDINBURGH, MLN EH9 2HQ SCT
36392 CUNNINGHAM, M, 26 PEARCE AVE., EDINBURGH, EH12 8SW SCT
36393 CHAPMAN, DR S, HOPE HOUSE., WINTERBOURNE ZELSTONE, DOR DT11 9EU ENG
36394 FORRESTER, JEAN, 199 KINGSWAY., OSSETT, YKS WF5 8ED ENG
36395 MORROTT, MR G, 17 VANBRUGH GATE., SWINDON, WIL SN3 1NQ ENG
36396 LEMON, ROSEMARY, 4 APPLETON RD., UPTON BY CHESTER, CHES CH2 1JJ ENG
36397 MOODY, JOHN, 21 ELM PARK VIEW., YORK, NRY Y03 0DY ENG
36398 WOOLNER, GEORGE, 34 DOLPHIN SQ., PLYMSTOCK, DEVON PL9 8RW ENG
36399 COHEN, PATRICIA, THE ANCHORAGE., PORTSCATHO, CON TR2 5HE ENG
36400 PARSONS, IAIN, 'FAR HILLS', CAPON TREE RD., BRAMPTON, CUL CA8 1NG ENG
36401 FALCONER, MR B, WEDGEWOOD HOLLOWAY HILL., GODALMING, SRY GU7 1RZ ENG
36402 ROWLAND, DAVID, 99 FITZSTEPHEN RD., DAGENHAM, ESSEX RM8 2YH ENG
36403 SMITH, MARTIN, 10 HOLMLEA ROAD., GORING, RG8 9EX ENG
36404 NANCOLLAS, MICHAEL, 73 EDWIN RD., GILLINGHAM, KEN ME8 0AB ENG
36405 HUME-VOEGELI, ANDREW, 35 SPOTTISWOODE ST., EDINBURGH, EH9 1DQ SCT
36406 MYLAM, CYRIL, 87 WANSUNT RD., BEXLEY, KEN DA5 2DJ ENG
36407 KIMBLE, FAY, 52 BRIDGE ST., LEOMINSTER, HEF ENG
36408 FLINT, EDWARD, 24 SOUTH BEECHWOOD., EDINBURGH, MLN EH12 5YR SCOTLAND
36409 BLANDFORD, PAT, 13 PETWORTH RD., PORTSMOUTH, HANTS PO3 6DH ENG
36410 TURNER, MR C, 1 NEWHAM RD., STAMFORD, LINCS PE9 1BZ ENG

36411 WHEELDON, HOWARD, 17 RUSSELL AVE., SPROWSTON, NFK NR7 8XE ENG
36412 HODGSON, JOSEPH, 4/155 SOUTHFIELD RD., MIDDLESBROUGH, CLEV TS1 3HE ENG
36413 BATES, MR N, 9 CECIL PL., SOUTHSEA, HANTS PO5 3BU ENG
36414 FARNSWORTH, MISS J, 96 MOUNT PLEASANT., KEYWORTH, NTT NG12 5EH ENG
36415 CLITHERO, JAMES, HIGHACRES HARTFORD., NORTHWICH, CHS CW8 1PP ENG
36416 LLOYD, PHILIP, 268 UPPER CHORLTON RD., MANCHESTER, M16 0BN ENG
36417 BEATTIE, PETER, 1 POPE RD., BROMLEY, KENT BR2 9QA ENG
36418 JOLIN, MR G, 18 OAKLEIGH AVE., BOLTON, LAN BL3 2ES ENG
36419 DIGGLE, IAN, 7 BROADFIELD TCE. FIELDING LN., OSWALDTWISTLE, LAN BB5 ENG
36420 WORSFOLD, ALAN, 29 MADEIRA GVE., WOODFORD GREEN, ESSEX 1G8 7QH ENG
36421 MANN, MRS A, 5 OFFORD RD., GODMANCHESTER, CAMBS PE18 8LD ENG
36422 NEIGHBOUR, MICHAEL, 27 KNUTSFORD AVE., WATFORD, HRT WD2 4EQ ENG
36423 COPPINS, PHYLLIS, 12 FROGNAL GDNS., TEYNHAM, KENT ME9 9SB ENG
36424 HARRIS, GARETH, 32 CARSHALTON WAY., EARLEY, BRK RG6 4EP ENG
36425 WESTON, ROGER, 4 HASLAM CL., ICKENHAM, MDX UB10 8TJ ENG
36426 JOHNSON, CATHERINE, 37 BINGHAM RD., COTGRAVE, NTT NG12 3JS ENG
36427 STICKLAND, MICHAEL, C/O LLOYDS BANK, 80 HIGH ST., BATTLE, SSX TN33 0AG ENG
36428 CHAMBERS, DAVID, 238 DONAGHADEE RD., NEWTOWNARDS, DOW BT23 3QD IRL
36429 MOFFAT, MRS K, 91 SHACKERDALE RD., LEICESTER, LEI LE2 6HT ENG
36430 MONK, MRS S, 12 JOHNSTON WALK., GUILDFORD, SRY GU2 6XP ENG
36431 WINK, MARY, LITTLE BROOM, WOOD DR., SEVENOAKS, KENT TN13 2NL ENG
36432 STEPHENS, MRS J, 115 HASLEMERE RD., LIPHOOK, HAM GU30 7BU ENG
36433 GIBB, JEAN, 88A GRAHAMS RD., FALKIRK, STI FK2 7DL SCOTLAND
36434 HASTINGS, MRS J, VALLEY COTTAGE, HIGH ST., COMBE MARTIN, DEV EX34 0HR ENG
36435 RONAN, MS S., 16 HOLLY HSE, 53 PEMBERLEY RD., ACOCKS GREEN, W MIDS B27 7TB ENG
36436 RUSSELL, JOHN, DRUMWALLS., GATEHOUSE OF FLEET, KIRKCUDBRIGHT, DG7 2DE SCT
36437 MOORE, CHRISTOPHER, 6 LONSDALE TCE., EDINBURGH, EH3 9HN SCOTLAND
36438 CANNINGS, HILARY, THE SUMMIT DUCK LN., BARFORD ST MARTIN, WIL SP3 4AN ENG
36439 DIXON, MR P, 10 MACRINA ST., OAKLEIGH, VIC 3166 AUS
36440 LDS FAMILY HISTORY CENTRE,, BOX 115., BAYSWATER, WA 6053 AUS
36441 GAINER, MISS P, 8 ST TROPEZ TCE., SORRENTO, QLD 4217 AUS
36442 HOLLMEYER, ROBERT, 1 NCNB PLAZA T-39., CHARLOTTE, NC USA
36443 BIGLIN, LORNA, 23 CHURCHILL ST., PUKE KOHE, STH AUCK 1800 NZ
36444 CALLAHAN, MS K, 5405 NE 29TH ST., TACOMA, WA 98422 USA
36445 PEITSMEYER, MRS J, PO BOX 65., GRANDRONDE, OR 97347 USA
36446 FOSTER, MRS V, 7906 OAK KNOLL LN., PALOS HEIGHTS, IL 60463 USA
36447 HILKE, MRS C, 15107 INTERLACHEN DR #926., SILVER SPRING, MD 20906 USA
36448 LAMBETH, LEE & JO, 13319 BELFIELD., FARMERS BRANCH, TX 75234 USA
36449 DEAN, MRS D, 829 HOLBROOK CIRCLE., FORT WALTON BCH, FL 32547 USA
36450 HANNAMAN, KENNETH, 3527 FEDERAL WAY #11., BOISE, ID 83705 USA
36451 PALMER, CORAL, BOX 955, HOUGHTON., JOHANNESBURG, 2198 RSA
36452 ANKIEWICZ, MR L, PO BOX 30., GROOTVLEI, 2420 RSA
36453 MCCULLAGH, RUTH, 4 SAVOY, HIGH LEVEL/ARTHURS RD., SEA POINT, CP 8001 RSA
36454 SLABBERT, GLENN, PO BOX 216., PIETERSBURG, 0700 RSA
36455 RUBIN, MR L, PO BOX 30, 661 BRAAMFONTEIN., JOHANNESBURG, TVL 2017 RSA
36456 VAN DER WESTHUIZEN, PIETER, 14 WESTON ST., MOSSEL BAY, CAPE 6500 RSA
36457 PUTTER, PHILLIPUS, PRIVATE BAG X308., PRETORIA, TVL 0001 RSA
36458 LE ROUX, REV H., PO BOX 3130., RANDGATE, 1763 RSA
36459 BELDON, MR W, 44 MERCUTIO ST, BEDELIA., WELKOM, OFS 9459 RSA
36460 ODENDAAL, RIAAN, PO BOX 990., STRAND, 7140 RSA
36461 EMERY, DR ASHTON, PO BOX 55322., NORTHLANDS, 2116 RSA
36462 WOODROW, PAMELA, 3 OAKLEIGH DR., HOWICK, NATAL 3290 RSA
36463 SPURR, MR B, 70 HUNTERS WAY, UMGENI PARK., DURBAN NTH, NATAL 4051 RSA
36464 MALAN, DR H, PO BOX 7128., BLYVOORUITSIG, 2504 RSA
36465 REY, PAUL, PO BOX 925, HIGHLANDS NTH., JOHANNESBURG, TVL 2037 RSA
36466 FAMILY HISTORY CENTRE,, PO BOX 10702 STRUBENVALE., SPRINGS, TVL 1572 RSA
36467 SMITH, COLIN, BOX 6178., ANSFRERE, 1711 RSA
36468 ROY, MRS J, 13 COLONIAL MEWS, VAUSEDALE RD., QUEENSBURGH, NATAL 4093 RSA
36469 CAITHNESS, MRS A, 110 BRABAZON AVE., MONDEOR, TVL 2091 RSA
36470 WILLIAMS, LESLIE, 36 ERITH ST, MOUNT CROIX., PT ELIZABETH, CAPE 6001 RSA
36471 CLARK, BARBARA, 3B HATON NICHOLLS RD., KLOOF, NATAL 3610 RSA
36472 BOWE, KATHLEEN, CARTREF, CLIFF LANE., CURBAR, S30 1XD ENG
36473 LUMBIS, KEVIN, 49 NORWOOD ST., SCARBOROUGH, NRY YO12 7EG ENG
36474 LORRAIN, MRS P, 19 THE CROFT., BISHOPSTONE, WIL SP5 4DF ENG
36475 SMITH, BETTY, 8 GROVE CL., WOKINGHAM, BRK RG11 3NA ENG
36476 SMITH, STELLA, 72 BLACKBOROUGH RD., REIGATE, SRY RH2 7DF ENG
36477 HOBSON, DR J, FIELD HEAD, NETHERTON FOLD., NETHERTON, W YORKS HD4 7HB ENG
36478 WEBB, STANLEY, 11 HAREFIELD RD., RICKMANSWORTH, HRT WD3 1LY ENG
36479 COOK, STAN, 20 CAUTLEY CL., QUAINTON, BKM HP22 4BN ENG
36480 WILD, JUNE, 66 GOLF RD., DEAL, KENT CT14 6QB ENG
36481 NELLIST, MICHAEL, 210 ALBERT RD., JARROW ON TYNE, NE32 5JA ENG
36482 PLANT, WM KEITH, 22 CHAPEL CROFT., CHELFORD, CHS SK11 9SU ENG

36483 DAY, BASIL, WOODLAND COURT, GREEN LANE., BEETLEY, NFK NR20 4DL ENG
36484 GUPTA, MRS P, 19 COURTS HILL RD., HASLEMERE, SRY GU27 2PN ENG
36485 BAKER, BERNARD, 12 PEARSONS CL., ROTHERHAM, YORKS S65 3BU ENG
36486 STIDOLPH, NORMAN, 27 WORTHING RD., SOUTHSEA, HAM PO5 2RJ ENG
36487 SEPHTON, ROBERT, 2 OSWESTRY RD., OXFORD, OXON OX1 4TL ENG
36488 ANGELL, LORD GRANVILLE, 34 MANOR AVE., CANNOCK, STS WS11 1AA ENG
36489 SETCHELL, JOHN, 85 ALL SAINTS RD., NEWMARKET, SFK CB8 8ES ENG
36490 WYLY, PETER, 8 BURNHAM CL., CULCHETH, CHS WA3 4LJ ENG
36491 TURNER, DR J, 1 CALDER GDNS., LINSLADE, BEDS LU7 7XE ENG
36492 DUKE, ELISABETH, AXHOLME HSE, THE NOOKING., HAXEY, S YORKS DN9 2JQ ENG
36493 NOON, MARY, 44 STERNDALE RD., MILLHOUSES, YKS S7 2LD ENG
36494 BABER, VERA, 14 BRANKSOME CL., HEMEL HEMPSTEAD, HERTS HP2 7AG ENG
36495 HARRISON, DAVID, 120 KESTREL WAY., CHESLYN HAY, STS WS6 7LQ ENG
36496 PICKERING, MS S, 26 HOE LANE., NORTH BADDESLEY, HAM SO52 9NH ENG
36497 MIDONA, ALAN, 1 OLD MALTHOUSE, NOTTINGTON., WEYMOUTH, DOR DT3 4BH ENG
36498 PICKETT, JEAN, 84 RIDGE LANGLEY., SANDERSTEAD, SRY CR2 0AR ENG
36499 BOWES, SHIRLEY, 50 FIRST AVE., CANVEY ISLAND, ESSEX SS8 9LP ENG
36500 SMITH, JOHN, 37 CORNER AVE., EASTWOOD, ESS SS9 5EN ENG
36501 POOK, SIMON, 203 COOMBFIELD DR., DARENTH, KEN DA2 7LF ENG
36502 HEDGES, FIONA, 51 HILLVIEW RD., OXFORD, OXON OX2 0DA ENG
36503 THOMPSON, JOHN, 10 ALLENDALE TCE., ANNFIELD PLAIN, DURHAM DH9 8JT ENG
36504 POWELL, EVELYN, 48 HEATHEND RD., ALSAGER, STS ST7 2SH ENG
36505 RYMELL, JOHN, 5 BIRCHWOOD RD., WOLLATON, NOTTS NG8 2ES ENG
36506 WOODS, MARY, 15 GLOUCESTER RD., GRANTHAM, LIN NG31 8RJ ENG
36507 STREETER, MR P., WATERMANS END COT., MATCHING GN., HARLOW, ESS CM17 0RQ ENG
36508 FAIRHURST, KEITH, 6 DELAMERE AVE., BUCKLEY, CLWYD CH7 3BU WALES
36509 HEBENTON, GEORGE, 13 SHEEPBURN RD., UDDINGSTON, LKS G71 7DT SCOTLAND
36510 MILLER, MRS V, 208 LATIMER RD., EASTBOURNE, SSX BN22 7IF ENG
36511 PERRY, JEAN, 48 BLACKBROOK CLOSE., SHEPSHED, LEICS LE12 9LD ENG
36512 ROUSE, JUDITH, 18 SARSEN CL., SWINDON, WILTS SW1 4LA ENG
36513 ADDISON, DOREEN, 7 BANKSIDE CL., WORCESTER, WR3 7BG ENG
36514 CLARK, DORIS, 33 WALESBY LANE., NEW OLLERTON, NOTTS NG22 9RB ENG
36515 STARK, BILL, 34 PORTCHESTER RD., BINGHAM, NTT NG13 8ES ENG
36516 BLIGHT, RAYMOND, 74 HAYWARDS RD., HAYWARDS HEATH, W SSX RH16 4JB ENG
36517 KIDWELL, MR A, 21 OAKHILL RD., ASHTEAD, SRY KT21 2JG ENG
36518 POOLE, KEITH, SMESTOW GATE FARM, SWINDON., NR DUDLEY, W MIDS DY3 4PJ ENG
36519 TYSOME, PATRICIA, 8 FROGMORE GDNS., NORTH CHEAM, SURREY SM3 9RZ ENG
36520 FITTON, BRIAN, HOOFDSTRAAT 157., SASSENHEIM, ZUH 2171 BB NETHERLANDS
36521 BLETSO, DAVID, 27 ARUNDEL RD., BATH, AVON BA1 6EF ENG
36522 HURST, PETER, 18 CHESTERTON ST., GARSTON, LAN L19 8LB ENG
36523 BAGUETTE, SYLVIA, 81 MARLAND FOLD., ROCHDALE, LAN 0L11 4RF ENG
36524 HARRISON, STUART, 6 FELLOWES PL., PLYMOUTH, DEV PL1 5NB ENG
36525 BIBB, ERIC, 65 ENDCLIFFE AVE., BOTTESFORD, S HUMBS DN17 2RB ENG
36526 HORN, IRENE, 17 KINGSWOOD CL., SWANAGE, DORSET ENG
36527 SEARLE, ANN, 4 CROSS ST., LETCHWORTH, HRT SG6 4UD ENG
36528 SHERWIN, MR D, 46 HEBDEN CL., E.M.E., LEI LE2 9RG ENG
36529 HAMILTON, MRS L, 30 MULLAGHBOY HGTS., MAGHERAFELT, LDY BT45 5NU IRELAND
36530 BOWEN, JANE, 79 PRIORY RD., ALCESTER, WAR B49 5EA ENG
36531 NOBLE, KEVIN, 11 AUGUSTUS RD., COVENTRY, CV1 5BZ ENG
36532 ZIPF, PATRICIA, 12 OAKLAND RD., JAMESBURG, NJ 08831 USA
36533 ROWLAND, MORRIS, 13 CHURCH CL, STUDHAM., DUNSTABLE, BEDS LU6 2QE ENG
36534 TUPPEN, ALBERT, 64 CHESIL ST., WINCHESTER, HAM ENG
36535 HAILEY, JOHN, 1A ASHURST WALK., CROYDON, SRY CR0 7JX ENG
36536 WILLIAMS, GEOFFREY, MANOR WOOD., COLTISHALL, NFK NR12 7DU ENG
36537 PRUCHA, PATRICIA, 5711 BARKLEY CT., FAIRFIELD, OH 45014 USA
36538 CRAWFORD, JILL, 3854 HIGUERA RD., SAN JOSE, CA 95148 USA
36539 LEDOUX, THOMAS, RD#1 BOX 1375., SWANTON, VT 05488 USA
36540 FRANTZ EDWARDS, LORRAINE, PO BOX 2076., LANCASTER, CA 93539 USA
36541 SIMONS, SUSAN, 887 SONOMA AVE, APT 3., SANTA ROSA, CA 95404 USA
36542 KLINK, BARB, W1494 POND RD., RUBICON, WI 53078 USA
36543 GOERTZEN, JERRY, BOX 160., O'NEALS, CA 93645 USA
36544 MCCLURE, RHONDA, 516 MASSACHUSETTS AVE., ST CLOUD, FL 34769 USA
36545 CRITTENBERGER-NALL, MS J., 47 EVERGREEN DR., WILLINGBORO, NJ 08046 USA
36546 BRITTENHAM, WILLIAM, 84 HILLIS TCE., POUGHKEEPSIE, NY 12603 USA
36547 MATTHEWS, EDWIN, 22 SLATER DR., SCOTIA, NY 12302 USA
36548 OLDHAM, DOROTHY, 8330 CLEVELAND COVE., KANSAS CITY, KS 66109 USA
36549 SOWERBY, MAXINE, 4392 SHERIDAN RD., SHERIDAN, MI 48884 USA
36550 ALLAN, MR W, 230 SANTA MARIA ST E-432., VENICE, FL 34285 USA
36551 MORRIS, ANDREW, PO BOX 535., FARMINGTON, MI 48332 USA
36552 BUMANN, FRANCES, 9540 ORION AVE., SEPULVEDA, CA 91343 USA
36553 TENBARGE, ELEANOR, 621 E IOWA ST., EVANSVILLE, IN 47711 USA
36554 ALBRIGHT, ANNIE, 23 MEADOWLARK LN., RICHMOND, VA 23228 USA

36555 HECKEL, JEANNE, 432 PARTRIDGE CIRCLE., SARASOTA, FL 34236 USA
36556 CURTIS, JOANNA, 1156 RED PINE CT., SAN JOSE, CA 95125 USA
36557 JOYNES, DENSELL, 226 W MCGINNIS CIR., NORFOLK, VA 23502 USA
36558 DAUGHERTY, CAROL, 358 CHESTERFIELD RD., WINCHESTER, NH 03470 USA
36559 WALLUM, JENNIFER, PO BOX 789 (ADB)., MANILA, 1099 PHILIPPINES
36560 JACKSON, JANE, 1880 CUTLASS COVE DR., VERO BEACH, FL 32963 USA
36561 CAMERON, BETTE, 3020 NORTH SHORE DR., DELAVAN, WI 53115 USA
36562 PROCTER, LELAND, PO BOX 134, 1 SOUTH RD., HAMPDEN, MA 04036 USA
36563 PREBLE, CHARLES, 8027 GARLOT DR., ANNANDALE, VA 22003 USA
36564 DORSEY, MRS M, 730 WILDCAT CANYON RD., BERKELEY, CA 94708 USA
36565 LANDIS, MARY ELLEN, 21346 SARAHILLS DR., SARATOGA, CA 95070 USA
36566 BRENNAN, RONALD, 65 MOOCK RD., WILDER, KY 41071 USA
36567 OSBORNE, WILLIAM, 507 MUELLER CT., ST LOUIS, MO 63125 USA
36568 DUMONT, SHARON, 20 OLYMPIA., NORTON, MA 02766 USA
36569 MCWOOD, MARGARET, 410 ELLESMERE DR #75., DIXON, CA 95620 USA
36570 WATKINS, S. RAYBURN, 2704 POPLAR HILL CRT., LOUISVILLE, KY 40207 USA
36571 MARTZKE, RUTH, 2429 MURRAY DR., TOLEDO, OH 43613 USA
36572 DENNIS, PHANIA, 10615 PIPING ROCK LN., HOUSTON, TX 77042 USA
36573 KING, DR M, 103 MONTCLAIR CT., E PEORIA, IL 61611 USA
36574 LEBUTT, MARIANNE, 6204 TAYWOOD RD, APT G., ENGLEWOOD, OH 45322 USA
36575 KACENAK, CAROL, 5026 GRIZZARD RD., HUNTSVILLE, AL 35810 USA
36576 HOWE, ROBERT, 250 N ARCADIA AVE, APT 1013., TUCSON, AZ 85711 USA
36577 TILLEY, MERRITT, 109 JAYSON RD., WILMINGTON, DE 19803 USA
36578 COOK, WENDY, 425 BIRCH AVE., BENSALEM, PA 19020 USA
36579 MANNIX, LORRAINE, 16C WATER WHEEL DR., MONTGOMERY, NY 12549 USA
36580 O'HARA, SHAUN, PO BOX #555., BURTONSVILLE, MD 20866 USA
36581 POWERS, JANET, 2421 BALTUSROL DR., ALHAMBRA, CA 91803 USA
36582 BARTON, ELYNORE, 1601 NORTH LINWOOD AVE., SANTA ANA, CA 92701 USA
36583 MILLER, SUSAN, 36 BRANZIERT RD NORTH., KILLEARN, STI G63 9RF SCOTLAND
36584 CULLEN, MICHAEL, 9 DECOY DR., EASTBOURNE, E SSX BN22 0AB ENG
36585 COOKSON, ELIZABETH, 72 MALMESBURY RD., CHIPPENHAM, WILTS SN15 1QD ENG
36586 COLTMAN, NIGEL, GREENACRES, MARSHFOOT LN., HAILSHAM, SSX BN27 2RA ENG
36587 WALKER, MR C, 11 OAKFIELD CRES., ASPULL, LAN WN2 1XJ ENG
36588 FINCH, MR J, 72 POYNES RD., HORLEY, SURREY RH6 8LT ENG
36589 HOOPER, PETER, 16 QUEEN ELEANORS RD., ONSLOW, SRY GU2 5SL ENG
36590 COOPER, NIGEL, 13 WROXHAM DR., UPTON, WIRRAL L49 0TS ENG
36591 SCAMELL, VICTOR, 58 HOMESTEAD RD., DAGENHAM, ESS RM8 3DR ENG
36592 JENNINGS, JEAN, 12 LEOFRIC CT, ELVETHAM RD., BIRMINGHAM, WAR B15 2LY ENG
36593 KEYMER, IAN, THE OLD SMITHY, THE GREEN., EDGEFIELD, NFK NR24 2AL ENG
36594 WHITCHURCH-BENNETT, RICHARD, 22 MAYFLOWER DR., YATELEY, SRY GU17 7RR ENG
36595 TANCRED, PAMALA, 6/65 RAILWAY PDE., LAKEMBA, NSW 2195 AUS
36596 DALY, YVONNE, 146 RICHMOND RD., KINGSWOOD, NSW 2747 AUS
36597 MCDONELL, JOYCE, 21 ROBERTSON ST., CONISTON, NSW 2500 AUS
36598 EDWARDS, CAMPBELL, 15 CRINOLINE ST., QUEANBEYAN, NSW 2620 AUS
36599 MCKINLEY, MAREE, 27 GEOFFREY CRES., LOFTUS, NSW 2232 AUS
36600 RILEY, R, PO BOX 7., CANLEY HEIGHTS, NSW 2166 AUS
36601 WILSON, MR M, 32 PARK RD., MT WAVERLEY, VIC 3149 AUS
36602 DOWLING, MICK, 47 PATTERSON ST., COBURG, VIC 3058 AUS
36603 MOLLOY, DENISE, 4 ERRARD ST SOUTH., BALLARAT, VIC 3350 AUS
36604 WINSTANLEY, MRS H, 699 PARK RD., PARK ORCHARDS, VIC 3114 AUS
36605 SPINNER, MYRA, 2 CORNWALL RD., PASCOE VALE, VIC 3044 AUS
36606 MCKELLAR, IAN, 9 HOMEBUSH CRT., HEATHMONT, VIC 3135 AUS
36607 CAMERON, KAYE, PO BOX 187., DALBY, QLD 4405 AUS
36608 SINGH, ROBYN, 16 PITTARDS RD., BUDERIM, QLD 4556 AUS
36609 MCKINNA, NANCY, PO BOX 336., COOKTOWN, QLD 4871 AUS
36610 TARRANT, MRS P, 11 WRIXON ST., LATHAM, ACT 2615 AUS
36611 ADAMS, JILL, PO BOX 3632., DARWIN, NT 0801 AUS
36612 REBETT, MICHAEL, 13 DARCY CRES., GOULBURN, NSW 2580 AUS
36613 ATTWOOD, ROSEMARY, 8 WOODSTOCK ST., MAYFIELD, NSW 2304 AUS
36614 RAE, GWENYTH, 1 MCMULLEN AVE., CARLINGFORD, NSW 2118 AUS
36615 BLEAKLEY, MR R, 3 LALOR ST., AINSLIE, ACT 2602 AUS
36616 ANDERSON, KAYE, 8 TOPAZ ST., HOLLAND PARK, QLD 4121 AUS
36617 AVERN, JOCELYN, 5/201 GLADSTONE RD., HIGHGATE HILL, QLD 4101 AUS
36618 FITZPATRICK, STAN, 18 FROST ST., MT GRAVATT, QLD 4122 AUS
36619 HART, KENNETH, 264 DUNBAR ST., ROCKHAMPTON, QLD 4701 AUS
36620 FLEMING, MRS J, 5 HORNE ST., ECHUCA, VIC 3564 AUS
36621 CHITTENDEN, MRS J, 6 WATSON ST., AVENEL, VIC 3664 AUS
36622 HARRIS, CAROLYN, PO BOX 412., LAVERTON, VIC 3028 AUS
36623 WADE, HEATHER, 9 STEPHENS ST., WARRNAMBOOL, VIC 3280 AUS
36624 KILLIAN, JOHN, LOT 58 FRANKSTON RD., CARRUM DOWNS, VIC 3201 AUS
36625 YOUNG, TERENCE, 37 LEE AVE., NORTH SPRINGVALE, VIC 3171 AUS
36626 AMOS, J, ., ST ARNAUD, VIC 3478 AUS

36627 COOMBER, COLIN, 133 STAWELL ST., SALE, VIC 3850 AUS
36628 GIRLE, MARGOT, 9 MCELHONE CT., BELCONNEN, ACT 2617 AUS
36629 MCKENZIE, MRS J, 36 DE GRAAFF ST., HOLDER, ACT 2611 AUS
36630 MENDES DA COSTA, ARMAND, PO BOX 400., KYOGLE, NSW 2474 AUS
36631 WOULFE, KATHRYN, 121 GALSTON RD., HORNSBY HTS, NSW 2077 AUS
36632 ARMIDALE FAMILY HIST GP,, PO BOX 1378., ARMIDALE, NSW 2350 AUS
36633 SMITH, DIANE, 8 RUSSELL CT., TAMWORTH, NSW 2340 AUS
36634 DAWKING, KIM, 72 RENWAY AVE., LUGARNO, NSW 2210 AUS
36635 WARD, DR JOHN, 2 RUSSELL ST., EASTWOOD, NSW 2122 AUS
36636 WARD, MRS M., 2 RUSSELL ST., EASTWOOD, NSW 2122 AUS
36637 CARTER, ANNE, 71A BAYVIEW AVE., EARLWOOD, NSW 2206 AUS
36638 PROCTOR, MRS J, PO BOX 311., LEICHHARDT, NSW 2040 AUS
36639 DUNCOMBE, MARGARET, 27 MCRAE ST., TAMWORTH, NSW 2340 AUS
36640 SHAW, MAXINE, 2 CLIFF AVE., PEAKHURST, NSW 2210 AUS
36641 DAVIS, MERVYN, 1 HUNT ST., SCHOFIELDS, NSW 2762 AUS
36642 SHEPHERD, ELIZABETH, 28 FLANDERS AVE., MILPERRA, NSW 2214 AUS
36643 BENNETT, SUSAN, 27 CAMBRIDGE AVE., WINDSOR, NSW 2756 AUS
36644 BISSETT, MURIEL, PO BOX 1407., LAUNCESTON, TAS 7250 AUS
36645 PEET, LINDSAY, 39 BEATRICE RD., DALKEITH, WA 6009 AUS
36646 SPIRO, MRS A, PO BOX 156., APPLECROSS, WA 6153 AUS
36647 DEAN, ROSS, 93 MARINE DR., TEA GARDENS, NSW 2324 AUS
36648 HERRING, KEVIN, 'CAMWOOD' OSBORNE RD., BURRADOO, NSW 2576 AUS
36649 BLACKWELL, BRIAN, BOX 364., SECHELT, BC V0N 3A0 CAN
36650 WALKER, ROBERTA, BOX 614., MELITA, MAN R0M 1L0 CAN
36651 EGELAND-EADY, C, 9083 PEMBERTON PL., DELTA, BC V4C 3J6 CAN
36652 SHAW, PAUL, 663 CHESTNUT ST., NANAIMO, BC V9S 2L1 CAN
36653 GRANT, VIOLET, 11404 75A AVENUE., NORTH DELTA, BC V4C 1H7 CAN
36654 MCCORMICK, MS J, R R #5., PETERBOROUGH, ONT K9J 6X6 CAN
36655 SWICHENIUK, CHERYL, BOX 2885., MELFORT, SASK S0E 1A0 CAN
36656 AMANN, NINA, 2422 DELKUS CRES., MISSISSAUGA, ONT L5A 1KY CAN
36657 TREMBLAY, SIMON PIERRE, 12 RUE JOLY, B.M.A1., RIGAUD, QUE J0P 1P0 CAN
36658 NEUFELD, EUNICE, 438 AINSLIE ST., WINNIPEG, MAN R3J 2Z9 CAN
36659 DAVIS, DIANE, 48 SLEEMAN AVE., GUELPH, ONT N1H 6E9 CAN
36660 PORTER, LISE, 13 EASTBROOK AVE., DARTMOUTH, NS B3A 1R6 CAN
36661 STRUEBY, MARILYNNE, 231 WAYNE RD., CAMPBELL RIVER, BC V9W 1T5 CAN
36662 HALL, BEVERLY, BOX 117., SIOUX LOOKOUT, ONT P0V 2T0 CAN
36663 IRVING, LORRAINE, 1131 E 23RD AVE., VANCOUVER, BC V5V 1Y8 CAN
36664 BONNER, BARBARA, 1398 MONTREAL ST., KINGSTON, ONT K7K 3L6 CAN
36665 WRIGHT, MARY ANNE, 246 BICKNELL CRES., KINGSTON, ONT K7M 4T6 CAN
36666 MACKEY, ALAN, RR2., CARLETON PLACE, ONT K7C 3P2 CAN
36667 FARQUHAR, JOAN, BOX 669., STIRLING, ONT K0K 3E0 CAN
36668 RUFFETT, BRENDA, 165 7TH AVE EAST., OWEN SOUND, ONT N4K 2W8 CAN
36669 STUART, ELIZABETH, RR2., OSGOODE, ONT K0A 2W0 CAN
36670 WARDELL, FRED, 101 CHRISTIE ST., TORONTO, ONT M6G 3B1 CAN
36671 BULFORD, DAVID, RR #1., WAWA, ONT P0S 1K0 CAN
36672 COLTER, MR G, 8707 ANCOURT ROAD SE., CALGARY, ALB T2H 1V3 CAN
36673 MAUGHAN, MR R, 18 THAMES AVE., ETOBICOKE, ONT M8W 2N6 CAN
36674 BLAY, ELIZABETH, 965 BAY ST #2705., TORONTO, ONT M5S 2A3 CAN
36675 REMPEL, IOLA, 32894 10TH AVE., MISSION, BC V2V 2K1 CAN
36676 PATMORE, GLADYS, GENERAL DELIVERY., PIPESTONE, MAN R0M 1T0 CAN
36677 CUNNINGHAM, EDITH, 5521 39 ST., LLOYDMINSTER, ALB T9V 1J8 CAN
36678 REVELSTOKE GENEALOGY SOC,, BOX 2613., REVELSTOKE, BC V0E 2S0 CAN
36679 GENEALOGY SOC,, BOX 2613., REVELSTOKE, BC V0E 2S0 CAN
36680 CLARK, BRUCE, 182 AMBER AVE., OSHAWA, ONT L1J 7V8 CAN
36681 LAZURE, LAURENT-GILLES, 570 AVE CASTELNEAU., ST HYACINTHE, QUE J2S 6S2 CAN
36682 ROBINSON, MRS N, 32559 WILLINGDON CRES., CLEARBROOK, BC V2T 1S1 CAN
36683 BIRD, SHAWN, 6945 GLENVIEW DR., PRINCE GEORGE, BC V2K 2N9 CAN
36684 LEE, GEORGE, BOX 116., MILLTOWN, NFD A0H 1W0 CAN
36685 ROWE, CECIL, BOX 481., MINDEN, ONT K0M 2K0 CAN
36686 CZUBOKA, WILLIAM, 5 WHITEHILL AVE., NEPEAN, ONT K2G 3A9 CAN
36687 CAMPBELL, MRS D, BOX 101., SOVEREIGN, SASK S0L 3A0 CAN
36688 CARTER, JANICE, B4-15, 280 PHILLIP ST., WATERLOO, ONT N2L 3X1 CAN
36689 TANNER, MILDRED, 300 30TH AVE SOUTH., CRANBROOK, BC V1C 5M9 CAN
36690 PURCHES, ROBERT, 64 MARION CR., MARKHAM, ONT L3P 6E4 CAN
36691 ELVIN, PHYLLIS, 12302 95 ST., EDMONTON, ALTA T5G 1N3 CAN
36692 GRANT, JESSIE, 89 GRENVIEW BLVD S., ETOBICOKE, ONT M8Y 3S7 CAN
36693 SURRIDGE, CAROL, BOX 255., STIRLING, ONT K0K 3E0 CAN
36694 BARKHAUSEN, CHARLEEN, BOX 45053, OCEAN PK R.P.O., S. SURREY, BC V4A 9L1 CAN
36695 GRAHAM, JOHN, 1331 GROVER AVE., COQUITLAM, BC V3J 3G3 CAN
36696 LE SAUVAGE, JULIE, PO BOX 173., NEUSTADT, ONT N0G 2M0 CAN
36697 ROBB, ALAN, #302 2335 W 3RD AVE., VANCOUVER, BC V6K 1L6 CAN
36698 HIBBERT, DOROTHY, APT 412, 1201 RICHMOND ST., LONDON, ONT N6A 3L6 CAN

36699 VOLICOEUR, RENE, 150 PLACE BEAUMONT., LA PRAIRIE, QUEBEC J5R 4L8 CAN
36700 WRIGHT, GEORGE, 205 MT EDWARD RD., SHERWOOD, PEI C1A 5T1 CAN
36701 BOWERS, MR K, 3 SELBY ST., TORONTO, ONT M4Y 1W3 CAN
36702 MCCALLUM, MR J, PO BOX 71., MONKTON, ONT N0K 1P0 CAN
36703 BELANGER, MARION, 9 ROSETTA ST., PARRY SOUND, ONT P2A 1G2 CAN
36704 WOODWARD, GARTH, BOX 67., TREHERNE, MAN R0G 2V0 CAN
36705 ST JOHN, CATHERINE, 966 INVERHOUSE DR. #401., MISSISSAUGA, ONT L5J 4B6 CAN
36706 BURNS, HELEN, R R #1., WAUBAUSHENE, ONT L0K 2C0 CAN
36707 PLAYTER, STEVE, 43 BALMORAL DR., BRAMPTON, ONT L6T 1V2 CAN
36708 HOGAN, KATHLEEN, 5840 BRIER AVE., DUNCAN, BC V9L 3E2 CAN
36709 SILLJER, KEITH, 1117 ROBINSON ST., REGINA, SK S4T 2N1 CAN
36710 GARNER, JOHN, 980 GEORGINA BAY., THUNDER BAY, ONT P7E 3H7 CAN
36711 CLOGSTON, MARIE, 741 MILL ST., WATERTOWN, NY 13601 USA
36712 DUNCAN, FLORA, BOX 2627., LACOMBE, AB T0C 1S0 CAN
36713 CAMPBELL, MR I, 6101 JUBILEE RD., HALIFAX, NS B3H 2E6 CAN
36714 SACHS TAIT, MARLENE, 150 HERBERT ST W., LISTOWEL, ONT N4W 1X4 CAN
36715 MOODY, MARIE, 1280 DOGWOOD CRES., NORTH VANCOUVER, BC V7P 1H3 CAN
36716 MOSER, BLANCHE, R R #3., WELLESLEY, ONT N0B 2T0 CAN
36717 OAKDEN, GWENDOLYN, 65 DANE AVE., TORONTO, ONT M6A 1G4 CAN
36718 GRAHAM, DONALD, 2026 EAST HILL., SASKATOON, SASK S0M 2C0 CAN
36719 GROSSKLEG, TERRY, 323 WOODBINE AVE., TORONTO, ONT M4L 3P3 CAN
36720 CARON, ELAINE, BOX 127., KAPUSKASING, ONT P5N 2Y3 CAN
36721 KENNY, ELIZABETH, 5115 126TH ST., EDMONTON, ALB T6H 3W1 CAN
36722 KIRKLAND, JOHN, 5 TIBBITS RD., REGINA, SAS S4S 1N5 CAN
36723 PAULHUS, YVONNE, BOX 1240., WEYBURN, SASK S4H 2L5 CAN
36724 MCLENNAN, GORDON, 21 RUTTAN BAY., WINNIPEG, MB R3T 0H5 CAN
36725 CURRIE, ROY, 2842 ARGYLE ST., REGINA, SASK S4S 2A7 CAN
36726 HALLMAN, JEANANNE, 478 GREENBROOK DR., KITCHENER, ONT N2M 4K6 CAN
36727 HAWKINS, THOMAS, 660 BAY ST., MIDLAND, ONT L4R 1L9 CAN
36728 HARRIS, WILFRID, 23060 117TH AVE., MAPLE RIDGE, BC V2X 2K4 CAN
36729 CORNWALLIS-BATE, LILLIE, 7199 SKYLINE CRES., RR3, SAANICHTON BC V0S 1M0 CAN
36730 GULLBORG, MRS R, 2 LAMBERTIN LN., ST LOUIS, MO 63122 USA
36731 EDWARDS, MRS B, R R 2, BOX 54., CLARION, IA 50525 USA
36732 DOUD, COL. H, 1306 EAST UNION ST., FULLERTON, CA 92631 USA
36733 OSGOOD, MR D, 4464 ELMSHAVEN DR., DAYTON, OH 45424 USA
36734 BEST, MR J, 10761 BERRY PLAZA., OMAHA, NE 68127 USA
36735 CATCHINGS, MR R, 1314 7TH ST., ALEXANDER CITY, AL 35010 USA
36736 FLEMING, MRS D, 42 RICHARD RD., GALES FERRY, CT 06335 USA
36737 DAUGHERTY, MS F, 598 CHARLTON CT., MARIETTA, GA 30064 USA
36738 PHILLIPS, MRS I, 6256 FOREST LANE., PARADISE, CA 95969 USA
36739 KIVI, BERTA, 67 TARAWERA TCE., AUCKLAND, 5 NZ
36740 PERCIVAL, ROBERT, 1 COOKS LN., CHRISTCHURCH, 2 NZ
36741 FERABEND, JUDY, 64 OMANA RD., PAPATOETOE, AUCK NZ
36742 NATHAN, MRS M, PO BOX 24., RUAWAI, NLAND NZ
36743 COOPER, BARBARA, MCALPINE ROAD RD 12., HAWERA, NZ
36744 READ, DAWN, PRIVATE BAG PIRONGIA STORE., PIROGIA, WKT NZ
36745 BRONLUND, JOYCE, PO BOX 21., COROMANDEL, 2851 NZ
36746 BIRCH, RAEWYN, 68 ORION ST., ROTORUA, BOP NZ
36747 CRAMOND, CHARLES, 18 ASHBOURNE PL., GLENDENE, WAITAKARA CITY AUCK 1208 NZ
36748 HOLDEN, CLARE, R D 7., OTOROHANGA, NZ
36749 WYLLIE, ELAINE, CLAREMONT R D 2., TIMARU, NZ
36750 ROBINSON, JOHN, 33 MAIRE ST., NELSON, 7001 NZ
36751 COLWELL, MISS E, 42A HOPEFARM AVE., PAKURANGA, NZ
36752 CLAPHAM, MR I, 7 TAUPO TCE., FEILDING, 5600 NZ
36753 MILLER, JEANETTE, BOX 121., WAIPAWA, NZ
36754 SPURR, JOYCE, 4 SAVAGE ST., KAINGA, CHCH 9 NZ
36755 RINCKES, JON, 467 WAIRAKEI RD., CHRISTCHURCH, 8005 NZ
36756 LUCAS, BERT, 65 ST MARYS RD., ST MARYS BAY, AUCK 1 NZ
36757 PEMBERTON, EILEEN, 52 TAHAPA CRES., MEADOWBANK, AUCK 5 NZ
36758 GRANT, ROSS, 35 SEYMOUR AVE., PAPATOETOE, NZ
36759 HAFFENDEN, NANCY, 19 BREEZES RD., CHRISTCHURCH, NZ
36760 WIGBY, MRS J, 20 CASSINO ST., AUCKLAND, 9 NZ
36761 LOUDON, MRS V, 2 GLENCARRON ST., ALEXANDRA, OTAGO 9181 NZ
36762 COBELDICK, TREVOR, PORT BOX 13-320., JOHNSONVILLE, WLGN NZ
36763 CANNON, MRS B, 15 ANZAC RD., WHANGAREI, NZ
36764 STONE, HELEN, PO BOX 83., MORRINSVILLE, 2251 NZ
36765 LAYCOCK, DAVID, 5 MCDOUGALL ST., MANUREWA, 1702 NZ
36766 MCNAE, LORRAINE, 24 WESTVIEW CRES., ONERAHI, WHANGAREI NZ
36767 HEWITT, FREDA, 6 WAITATI PL., AVONDALE, AUCK 7 NZ
36768 LINKHORN, LOIS, 100 PRINCES ST., OTAHUHU, AUCK NZ
36769 ALDERSON, BEVERLY, 22 DEANE AVE., TITIRANGI, AUCK 7 NZ
36770 TAYLOR, ANTHONY, 5 RANFURLY RD., FEILDING, NZ

36771 WILKIN, LOIS, 94 GLANDOVEY RD., FENDALTON, CHCH NZ
36772 MARTIN, MRS J, 1 ATHLONE CRES., LOWER HUTT, NZ
36773 BEDGGOOD, LEONIE, WAIMATE NORTH RD 2., KAIKOHE, NTHLD 0454 NZ
36774 CUNNINGHAM, MRS M, 14 TUAKAU RD., PUKEKOHE, STH AUCK 1800 NZ
36775 ROWE, MARY, 5 REGENT ST., WAIHI, 2991 NZ
36776 PEATTIE, JOAN, SOUTHBURN, NO 2 RD., TIMARU, NZ
36777 HAYES, MARGARET, 39 CLARKE ST., TAURANGA, BOP NZ
36778 MCCARTHY, NGAIRE, 28 STANDEN AVE., REMUERA, AUCK NZ
36779 BROWNE, HELEN, PO BOX 128., TE PUKE, 3071 NZ
36780 MANU, TERRI, 44 MANAWA AVE., PARAPARAUMU, NZ
36781 LEE, KATHLEEN, 21 PHILLIP ST., ROTORUA, NZ
36782 YOUNG, R, PO BOX 110., PIOPIO, NZ
36783 LEWIS, ROSEMARY, 23 WILLIAMS AVE., KAIKOHE, NORTH IS NZ
36784 CAREY, NOELINE, 2/28 HAMBLYN ST., NEW PLYMOUTH, NZ
36785 SHRAMKA, ELSIE, 103 RICHMOND ST., PETONE, NZ
36786 FITCHETT, PAULINE, 3 ARAPIKO ST., JOHNSONVILLE, WLTN NZ
36787 MCCORMICK, MRS P, RUNDLES ROAD NO 6 RD., ASHBURTON, NZ
36788 DUSTIN, SUSAN, 34 WHITE HERON DR., MASSEY EAST, AUCK 8 NZ
36789 JAMIESON, MR D, 43 DRIVERS RD., DUNEDIN, NZ
36790 STEER, MICHAEL, 50 MIDDLETON RD., JOHNSONVILLE, WLTN NZ
36791 SPENCER, MRS M, 47 PARKER AVE., LEVIN, NZ
36792 WISEMAN, MRS S, PO BOX 54., MATAMATA, NZ
36793 HURST, CAROL, 4 HUATA PL., PALMERSTON NORTH, NZ
36794 MAY, YVONNE, 88 KINGS RD., PANMURE, AUCK 6 NZ
36795 LAWSON, MRS P, 6B ELMSLIE RD., PINEHAVEN, UPPER HUTT NZ
36796 SOLWAY, ELISABETH, 226 DOBSON ST., ASHBURTON, 8300 NZ
36797 BRIGHTING, LESLEY, 71 KAURI ST., TOKOROA, NZ
36798 LARK, B, 1 AMBURY PL, MERRILANDS., NEW PLYMOUTH, TARANAKI NZ
36799 REED, DOREEN, 38 JERVIS ST., ROTORUA, NZ
36800 FORSYTH, JULIA, 261 BLEAKHOUSE RD., HOWICK, AUCK 1705 NZ
36801 WEEDON, SHEILA, LOWER SHOTOVER RD, RD1., QUEENSTOWN, NZ
36802 GRIMWOOD, HEATHER, 29 TINDALLS BAY RD., WHANGAPARAOA, AUCK NZ
36803 NZSG TE PUKE GP, C/0 D MUTTON, NO 1 RD RD2., TE PUKE, NZ
36804 WARNER, MRS R, 22 SIMPSON RD., PAPAMOA BEACH, BOP NZ
36805 TURNBULL, PAT, TUSSOCK CREEK NO 1 RD., WINTON, SOUTHLAND NZ
36806 TREGONNING, MARGARET, 140 PACIFIC PDE., ARMY BAY, WHANGAPARAOA NZ
36807 HIRST, MRS V, 24 BELLFIELD PL., TAURANGA, NZ
36808 BANNISTER, IAN, 15 THYNNE ST., FOXTON, NI 5551 NZ
36809 SMITH, ROSALIE, 19 KIPLING ST., PALMERSTON NORTH, 5301 NZ
36810 WILKINS, NORMA, 20 BAILEY AVE., HAMILTON, NZ
36811 REID, ANN, GREENS RD RD 4 1., PALMERSTON NORTH, NZ
36812 GUNDESEN, YVONNE, 25 FALKIRK AVE., WELLINGTON, 6003 NZ
36813 MOWAT, MARGARET, 329 COBHAM DR., HAMILTON, 2001 NZ
36814 TERRY, PAMELA, 14 ILES RD, LYNMORE., ROTORUA, NZ
36815 MACKINTOSH, MRS P, WHITE ROCK MAINS, PRIVATE BAG., RANGIORA, NZ
36816 WAKE, MRS E, 125 DITTMER DR., PALMERSTON NORTH, NZ
36817 WATSON, MRS H, 60 GORDON ST., DARGAVILLE, NTHLAND NZ
36818 HARROP, MARGARET, 8 WAINGARO RD., NGARUAWAHIA, NZ
36819 RICKARD, DONALD, 252 TANCRED ST., ASHBURTON, NZ
36820 MACFARLANE, PAT, FOREST HILL RD, RD 1., PALMERSTON NTH, NZ
36821 O'SULLIVAN, MRS J, 2 HARWOOD ST., SANDRINGHAM, AUCK 3 NZ
36822 WATT, MR C, 48 CLIFF VIEW DR., GREEN BAY, AUCK 7 NZ
36823 HARRISON, LESLEY, 46 OREGON DR., UPPER HUTT, 6401 NZ
36824 GRANT, RON & NOELINE, 44 RUTHERFORD TCE., AUCKLAND, 5 NZ
36825 WILLIAMS, ROBYN, 9 BOORALEE AVE., HOWICK, AUCK NZ
36826 BOTT, LENISE, 18 COLWILL RD., ROYAL HEIGHTS, AUCK 8 NZ
36827 MARSHALL, LUCY, 10 ESPLANADE., CAMPBELLS BAY, AUCK 10 NZ
36828 MUNFORD, PAULA, 75 LA ROSA ST., GREEN BAY, AUCK NZ
36829 PERKINS, GEOFF, PO BOX 37 640., PARNELL, AUCK 1 NZ
36830 HONISS, ENID, KAPIRO RD, RD 1., KERIKERI, NZ
36831 VERCOE, GAYE, NO 2 RD., TE PUKE, BOP NZ
36832 SULLIVAN, COLLEEN, 46 MATENE ST., OTAKI, WELL NZ
36833 REID, PATRICIA, 19A DUDDING AVE., NORTHCOTE, AUCK 9 NZ
36834 KING, MR A, 16 HIKURANGI ST., TRENTHAM, 6402 NZ
36835 VINCENT, KEITH, 27 LEE ST., BLENHEIM, NZ
36836 MCNAULL, MRS J, 65 WARATAH ST., TAURANGA, NZ
36837 CALVERLEY, RICHARD, PO BOX 54 033., BUCKLANDS BEACH, AUCK NZ
36838 JONES, PAMELA, JONES RD, RD 2., PUTARURU, NZ
36839 THESSMAN, MR M, 61 MAIRANGI RD., WELLINGTON, NZ
36840 WOOLHOUSE, BRENT, 41 POWER RD., GREYMOUTH, 7801 NZ
36841 THESSMAN, MRS E, 61 MAIRANGI RD., WELLINGTON, NZ
36842 CATHRO, BARBARA, 9 BOMBAY ST, ARAMOHO., WANGANUI, NZ

36843 BAXTER, BEVERLEY, 11 EDEN TCE., KAMO, WHANGAREI NZ
36844 DENNISTON, MARGIE, 92 DARRAGHS RD., OTUMOETAY, TAURANGA NZ
36845 MARSHALL, ELIZABETH, 56 OLD TE KUITI RD., OTOROHANGA, NZ
36846 DORSEY, LILLIAN, 41 DRIVERS RD, MAORI HILL, DUNEDIN, OTAGO NZ
36847 BIRCH, AUDREY, 18 KERERU ST, MAUNU., WHANGAREI, NLD NZ
36848 KERR, HELEN, 18 BURNETT ST., TIMARU, SC NZ
36849 RANDLES, MAY, 22 GRASSMERE RD., HENDERSON, AUCK NZ
36850 DAVIDSON, DAWN, 61 HINEWAI ST., OTOROHANGA, NZ
36851 TOWERS, MARION, 3 LEYS CRES., AUCKLAND, 1105 NZ
36852 GUTHRIE, MARIE, 54 ARUN ST., OAMARU, NORTH OTAGO NZ
36853 COOPER, JUNE, POMONA RD, WEST MAKAREWA, NO 6 RD., INVERCARGILL, SLD NZ
36854 STOCKS, JOHN, 139 INNES RD., CHRISTCHURCH, CANT 5 NZ
36855 MONTGOMERY, MRS D, 34 MILBURN ST, KEW., DUNEDIN, OTAGO NZ
36856 LEGARTH, MARY, PO BOX 327., LEVIN, NZ
36857 MCDONALD, AVIS, PO BOX 42., GORE, STH'LD NZ
36858 PEARCE, VIVIENNE, 5 WALTER MACDONALD ST., HOWICK, AUCK 1705 NZ
36859 WYATT, WALTER, 130 FORREST HILL RD., TAKAPUNA, AUCK 10 NZ
36860 WARBROOKE, IREEN, 5 GERWYN PL., PAKURANGA, AUCK 1706 NZ
36861 CARPENTER, JOHN, 7 ANNE ST., TOKOROA, 2392 NZ
36862 BELL, MRS J, 44 JADE AVE., PAKURANGA, NZ
36863 LOOSE, MRS A, 18 WOODGLEN RD., GLEN EDEN, AUCK 7 NZ
36864 COWAN, ERICA, 12 KORAHA ST., REMUERA, AUCK 5 NZ
36865 TUCKETT, ROBYN, 58 BRENTWOOD ST., TRENTHAM, 6402 NZ
36866 STRETTON, RONALD, 15 TASMAN ST., OPUNAKE, TARANAKI NZ
36867 RAMSHAW, HILARY, 59 WHITBY CRES., HASTINGS, 4201 NZ
36868 TAYLOR, AVIS, 3 JAEMONT AVE., TE ATATU SOUTH, AUCK 8 NZ
36869 LONGSTAFFE, ESTELLE, 3 EPSILON ST., BELLEKNOWES, DUNEDIN NZ
36870 GOODGER, MRS J, 98 BRISTOL ST., CHRISTCHURCH, 8001 NZ
36871 CHISHOLM, YVONNE, 67B HOROKIWI RD WEST., NEWLANDS, WLGN 6004 NZ
36872 TURNER, IRIS, 25 MCVAY ST., NAPIER, HB NZ
36873 BROWN, MR R, C/0 5 EMILY ST., GISBORNE, NZ
36874 TURK, STEPHANIE, 43 PURCELL ST., FOXTON, 5551 NZ
36875 MANNING, GLENNIS, 6 DISCOVERY DR., WHITBY, WLTN NZ
36876 DOWNES, ADRIENNE, 22 YORK AVE., HERETAUNGA, WGTN NZ
36877 POINTON, MRS S, 348 RUAHINE ST., PALMERSTON NORTH, 5301 NZ
36878 ROWE, MRS L, 116 TANGAROA RD., WHANGAMATA, NI NZ
36879 TYLER, IAN, 977 FERGUSSON DR., UPPER HUTT, WGTN NZ
36880 DAVIS, MYK, 27 MAIRE ST., HAWERA, TAR NZ
36881 SORENSER, JEANNETTE, 21 LORNE CRES, FLAX., HASTINGS, HB NZ
36882 MCINTYRE, RODERICK, 12 OTAIKA RD., WHANGAREI, NZ
36883 SOUTHEN, HELEN, 6 BRACO PL., CHRISTCHURCH, 4 NZ
36884 DALES, JEAN, 9 KARE KARE RD., RAUMATI SOUTH, PARAPARAUMU NZ
36885 JONES, ESME, 39 ALLNATT ST., TEMUKA, NZ
36886 ADAMS, JUDITH, RURAL DELIVERY., DARFIELD, CANTY NZ
36887 BENNETT, MRS J, 4 GRAHAM ST., ELTHAM, NZ
36888 TREGOWETH, SUE, PO BOX 374., TE KUITI, NI NZ
36889 MILLS, RUTH, 262 CAMBRIDGE AVE., ASHHURST, NZ
36890 LE GROS, JEAN, 57 TANE RD., LAINGHOLM, AUCK 7 NZ
36891 BRIGHT, PETER, 112A PAPANUI ST., TOKOROA, NZ
36892 NORGROVE-PAICE, H, PO BOX 9419., NEWMARKET, AUCKLAND NZ
36893 WOODS, BETTY, 9 MCWILLIAM AVE., WINTON, SOUTHLAND 9662 NZ
36894 BLOM, CYNTHIA, 124A GLENDALE RD., GLEN EDEN, AUCK 7 NZ
36895 DUNCAN, DOLORES, 16 COLLEGE CIR., STAUNTON, VA 24401 USA
36896 DEIS, DR F, 111 S 4TH AVE., HIGHLAND PARK, NJ 08904 USA
36897 SAYRE, CLIFFORD, 1415 LADD ST., SILVER SPRING, MD 20902 USA
36898 JONES, LESTER, 24716 AVENUE 95., TERRA BELLA, CA 93270 USA
36899 BURKS, LERONA, 596 HERMITAGE DR., SAN JOSE, CA 95134 USA
36900 HARTMAN, VALERIA, 1156 KAMELA DR S., SALEM, OR 97306 USA
36901 MATKINS, ROBERT, 3120 QUINCY ST., BUTTE, MT 59701 USA
36902 MCCALL, SARAH, 11409 BRIGHT STAR TRAIL., MORENO VALLEY, CA 92387 USA
36903 WATKINS, DEWEY, 1811 IRVING ST NW., WASHINGTON, DC 20010 USA
36904 SAMSON, GORDON, 2636 HADDAM RD., CLEVELAND, OH 44120 USA
36905 GREGERSON, MR W, US 53-35, N5995., ONALASKA, WI 54650 USA
36906 REIDY, ELINOR, 65 MADISON AVE., BERGENFIELD, NJ 07621 USA
36907 PECK, BARBARA, 216 MADISON ST., MONTGOMERY, IL 60538 USA
36908 CALHOUN, PAUL, 129 LINCOLN DR., PORT CLINTON, OH 43452 USA
36909 BENNETT, WILLIAM, 2044 W 235TH PL., TORRANCE, CA 90501 USA
36910 JAMESON, JUNE, 1938 SHERLYNN., BRIGHTON, MI 48116 USA
36911 HUDSON, FRANK, 7 IVY CHASE., ATLANTA, GA 30342 USA
36912 NORTH, MR J, 806 BROOKRIDGE DR., ST LOUIS, MO 63119 USA
36913 BROWN, NORVIL, 42733 KEYSTONE., CANTON, MI 48187 USA
36914 GRAY, PATRICIA, 718 SOUTH BLVD., TAMPA, FL 33606 USA

36915 HARTMAN, KATHERINE, 1044 SO IRONWOOD RD., STERLING, VA 22170 USA
36916 JEZEK, DELORES, 7620 S SHERIDAN CT., LITTLETON, CO 80123 USA
36917 DASINGER, NANCY, 509 4TH ST SE., SIDNEY, MT 59270 USA
36918 SIMECKA, KAREN, 1529 SW PLASS., TOPEKA, KS 66604 USA
36919 MASON, BETTY, 106 SO IRVING., FREMONT, NE 68025 USA
36920 JAUCH, JOHN, 131 GALE AVE., PUEBLO, CO 81004 USA
36921 STEELE, VIRGINIA, 1505 ECHO DR., WHITE CLOUD, MI 49349 USA
36922 DIEZEMANN, MR G, 63 BRADLEY HILL RD., HINGHAM, MA 02043 USA
36923 SANFORD, MR W, 7031 VIA VALVERDE., SAN JOSE, CA 95135 USA
36924 BABBITT, BERNARD, 9564 BELLEVUE RD., BATTLE CREEK, MI 49017 USA
36925 KLAPP, ESTHER, 201 LAKE AVE., PLYMOUTH, IN 46563 USA
36926 NULISCH, NANCY, 9646 NORTHCLIFF DR., DALLAS, TX 75218 USA
36927 SCHAFFER, BETTY, 1745 BUTTERFIELD LN., FLOSSMOOR, IL 60422 USA
36928 THOMPSON, MARION, 18135 MARTIN APT 1SE., HOMEWOOD, IL 60430 USA
36929 STRAIN, CARL, 9301 FOLIAGE LN., MUNSTER, IN 46321 USA
36930 VOGLER, CYNTHIA, RR2 BOX 241., NEW ATHENS, IL 62264 USA
36931 ELLER, SYLVIA, 2056 SE GRANDVIEW CT., MILWAUKIE, OR 97267 USA
36932 IRWIN, HARRY, 3707 ACOSTA RD., FAIRFAX, VA 22031 USA
36933 HAINES, JOHN, 53 JAMES ST., BELLINGHAM, MA 02019 USA
36934 PASTORINO, BONNIE, 22219 S LINDSAY RD., CHANDLER, AZ 85249 USA
36935 LATZ, EDWARD, 155 HOWELL ST., CANANDAIGUA, NY 14424 USA
36936 STANTON, MR H, 104 NORTH MCLANE RD., PAYSON, AZ 85541 USA
36937 SOLIVAN DE ACOSTA, JAIME, CALLE SEGOVIA 12-10, URB TORRIMAR, PR 00657 USA
36938 LAWRENCE, LORRAINE, 1569 E 88TH ST., BLOOMINGTON, MN 55425 USA
36939 LITTLE, HELEN, 4452 E CORNELL., FRESNO, CA 93703 USA
36940 MATUSIK, ROBERT, 349 PLEASANT ST, C-15., MALDEN, MA 02148 USA
36941 GRABOWSKI, MARY ANN, 341 FOURTH ST., MANISTEE, MI 49660 USA
36942 COULTER, VONDA, 10704 VANCIL RD SE #2., YELM, WA 98597 USA
36943 BRZOSKA, ELLEN, 402 W NOB HILL BLVD., YAKIMA, WA 98902 USA
36944 WHITNEY, LYNN, 95 OAKWOOD AVE., WEST HARTFORD, CT 06119 USA
36945 SAVOR, JOAN, 1099 88TH AVE W #233., DULUTH, MN 55808 USA
36946 DEAS, THOMAS, 421 WISTER RD., WYNNEWOOD, PA 19096 USA
36947 BROTHERS, RON, 3301 FM 1417, APT 1222., SHERMAN, TX 75090 USA
36948 CLAXTON, LORRAINE, 32 LINDBERGH AVE., NEEDHAM HEIGHTS, MA 02194 USA
36949 HODSON, MR A, 12970 BROOKPARK RD., OAKLAND, CA 94619 USA
36950 MOYER, ROBERT, 2679 E WAYWARD CT., BREA, CA 92621 USA
36951 AKERS, LILLIAN, 13611 YUKON AVE #316., HAWTHORNE, CA 90250 USA
36952 WOHLERS, LYNNE, 710 WEST 37TH STREET #7., SAN PEDRO, CA 90731 USA
36953 ERDAHL, MRS R, 6808 BAKER NE., ALBUQUERQUE, NM 87109 USA
36954 MARTIN, DR D, PO BOX 1211., LIBERAL, KS 67905 USA
36955 BAKAR, LOIS, 2490 PICO AVE., CLOVIS, CA 93612 USA
36956 CRAFT, BOYD, PO BOX 602., LAJUNTA, CO 81050 USA
36957 FRANK, CAROL, 1512 LOMBARD DR., FULLERTON, CA 92632 USA
36958 HAMBURG, SARAH, 1905 LINWOOD ST., SAN DIEGO, CA 92110 USA
36959 STETSON, MARJORIE, 812 MAIN ST., CONCORD, MA 01742 USA
36960 IVERSON, HELEN, 14362 PENNOCK AVE., APPLE VALLEY, MN 55124 USA
36961 FERRON, GENE, 1642 SUZANNE DR., WEST CHESTER, PA 19380 USA
36962 LAND, JAY, 2701 REVERE ST, APT 241., HOUSTON, TX 77098 USA
36963 CHAPMAN, WILLIAM, 9062 ANGELL ST., DOWNEY, CA 90242 USA
36964 BARRAS, STANLEY, 4313 CLEVELAND PL., METAIRIE, LA 70003 USA
36965 WORTMAN, NORMA, 195 MOOR RD., SHREVEPORT, LA 71106 USA
36966 KISHPAUGH, KELLEY, 524 N OCOTILLO ST., COTTONWOOD, AZ 86326 USA
36967 REYNOLDS, SHARRY, PO BOX 369., ORANGE GROVE, TX 78372 USA
36968 MARBLE, DUANE, 1310 LANGSTON DR., UPPER ARLINGTON, OH 43220 USA
36969 WILSON, NANNETTE, 6731 W FENNER RD., LUDLOW FALLS, OH 45339 USA
36970 RATHBUN, FRED, 4672 S FOUNTAIN CIR., LITTLETON, CO 80127 USA
36971 ALLEN, KAREN, 136 CARMIA RD., MUNROE FALLS, OH 44262 USA
36972 MILIKIN, PAUL, 2536 CANTERBURY RD., COLUMBUS, OH 43221 USA
36973 MUELLER, THOMASINE, 3348 STONECREST CT., ATLANTA, GA 30341 USA
36974 MILLER, DOROTHY, 540 SOLANO NE., ALBUQUERQUE, NM 87108 USA
36975 LILLEY, MARGARET, HAZELCOT HIBBERT RD., BRAYWICK, BRK SL6 1UT ENG
36976 WATTERSON, A, 7 GRESHAM GARDENS., WOODTHORPE, NTT NG5 4LU ENG
36977 CRANSTON-CALLAGHAN, MS V., 46 EDINBURGH AVE., GORLESTON, NFK NR31 7OZ ENG
36978 AYRES, LEIGH, 67 MANCHESTER DR., LEIGH ON SEA, ESS SS9 3EZ ENG
36979 WOOLVIN, RICHARD, 2/17 PERCY RD., LONDON, W12 9PX ENG
36980 UPTON, MISS S, 6 MAIN ST., STONESBY, LEI LE14 4QX ENG
36981 HEATH, KAREN, 41B LAWN LN., HEMEL HEMPSTEAD, HRT HP3 9HL ENG
36982 PENNY, ALEXANDRINE, 1 EGERTON RD., BIRKENHEAD, WIRRAL L43 1UL ENG
36983 LEDWARD, MR K, 71 ELLERBROOK DR., BURSCOUGH, LAN L40 5SY ENG
36984 LOMAS, HELEN, 26 BERROW CRT, GARDENS WALK., UPTON UP SEVERN, WOR WR8 0JP ENG
36985 MACQUISTEN, MR F., 15 THE OAKS, COMON MEAD LN., GILLINGHAM, DOR SP8 4SW ENG
36986 BRYAN, EARDLEY, 3 CHURCHFIELD CRES., POOLE, DOR BH15 2QS ENG

36987 FOSTER, DR ROY, 2A BELMONT PARK RD., MAIDENHEAD, BRK SL6 6HT ENG
36988 SLEE, MR D, 147 QUEENS RD., TEDDINGTON, TW11 0LZ ENG
36989 JEFFRIES, DOROTHY, 20 SEELEY CRES., STREET, SOM BA16 0RN ENG
36990 JOHNSON, DAVID, 19 UPPER PARK., HARLOW, ESS CM20 1TN ENG
36991 FOSTER, MR G, 142 COTSWOLD CRES., BURY, LAN BL8 1QP ENG
36992 COTTON, MICHAEL, WILLOW GREEN, THE WARREN., ASHTEAD, SRY KT21 2SG ENG
36993 BARTON, RICHARD, MULBERRIES, BADINGHAM RD., FRAMLINGHAM, SFK 1P13 9HS ENG
36994 ASLETT, DENNIS, 48 CHATSWORTH RD., FARNBOROUGH, HANTS GU14 7DZ ENG
36995 SOLOMONS, RONI, 15 MANOR AVE., KIDDERMINSTER, DY11 6EA ENG
36996 JONES, MARTYN, 4 SCHOOL TCE, CHAPEL LN, EBLEY., STROUD, GLS GL5 4TE ENG
36997 OLLIER, PATRICIA, 288 CREWE RD, GRESTY., CREWE, CHES CW2 5AQ ENG
36998 ATHERTON, RALPH, 10 TURNCLIFF CRES., MARPLE, CHS SK6 6JP ENG
36999 HEARDER, IAN, FLORENCE HALL, SHOPFORD., BEWCASTLE, CUL CA6 6PS ENG
37000 HUBBARD, BETTY, 160 WOLLATON VALE., WOLLATON, NOTTS NG8 2PL ENG
37001 WHEELER, CINDRA, 10136 NANTUCKET DR., SAN RAMON, CA 94583 USA
37002 CABLE, JULIE, 615 CUMBERLAND AVE., TULLAHOMA, TN 37388 USA
37003 ALLEN, BOBBIE, 2832 CAMINO DEL REY., SAN JOSE, CA 95132 USA
37004 GENTRY, JEANNE, 16385 SE 232 DR., BORING, OR 97009 USA
37005 ERIKSON, VERNA, RR 1 BOX 389., MONTICELLO, IN 47960 USA
37006 MEYERS, CAROL, PO BOX 766., CAYUCOS, CA 93430 USA
37007 NEFSTEAD, MARJORIE, 1250 VISCAINO RD., SANTA BARBARA, CA 93103 USA
37008 KILE, EDWIN, PO BOX 1352., PALISADE, CO 81526 USA
37009 GUSTAFSON, LEONA, 425 DAYTON TOWERS DR #10M., DAYTON, OH 45410 USA
37010 KEMP, EDWARD, PO BOX 1172., BRANDON, FL 33509 USA
37011 DICKEY, GARY, 22167 BRYANT ST., WEST HILLS, CA 91304 USA
37012 KROEHLER, MARJORIE, 6910 N ROCKVALE., PEORIA, IL 61614 USA
37013 JOSLYN, JEAN, 848 S LORAINE., SPRINGFIELD, IL 62704 USA
37014 MURDOCK, ANN, 9707 CARRIAGE RD., KENSINGTON, MD 20895 USA
37015 SWENSON, MR S, 9731 BELLDER DR., DOWNEY, CA 90240 USA
37016 FLORY, BARBARA, 2550 SE PECK RD., TOPEKA, KS 66605 USA
37017 WHIPPLE, CAROLYN, 1379 WOODSIDE DR., MCLEAN, VA 22102 USA
37018 DAVIS, NANCY, 725 CAMP WOODS RD., VILLANOVA, PA 19085 USA
37019 CONARY, ELEANOR, PO BOX 896., BETHEL, ME 04217 USA
37020 LUNN, MS J, 4270 KLING ST., BURBANK, CA 91505 USA
37021 BORNHOLDT, JOHN, BOX 1191E RD1., MT HOLLY, NJ 08060 USA
37022 LUTZ, RICHARD, 1248B DIAMOND BAR BLVD., DIAMOND BAR, CA 91765 USA
37023 KINDNESS, JUNE, 8360 STRUB AVE., WHITTIER, CA 90605 USA
37024 SCHROEDER, KATHY, PO BOX 304., WASECA, MN 56093 USA
37025 SHAWVER, JEAN, 1830 OPALINE DR., LANSING, MI 48917 USA
37026 SPENCER, JACK, 1303 AZALEA LN., DEKALB, IL 60115 USA
37027 BEASLEY, CHARLES, 330 W SANTA INEZ AVE., HILLSBOROUGH, CA 94010 USA
37028 CORBIN, ADELE, 4119 GLENHAVEN RD., CINCINNATI, OH 45238 USA
37029 RANDOLPH, ELIZABETH, 1148 HOYT DR., ST LOUIS, MO 63137 USA
37030 IRWIN, GLEN, 6830 ELMRICH CT., ANCHORAGE, AK 99504 USA
37031 SKEFFINGTON, MARILYN, 515 JACKSON AVE., RIVER FOREST, IL 60305 USA
37032 LINN, PAMELA, BOX 337., SACO, MT 59261 USA
37033 WEBBER, EDITH, 404 W PAWNEE APT 221., WICHITA, KS 67213 USA
37034 NEATE, KEN, 240 WEST SEVENTH ST., MARYSVILLE, OH 43040 USA
37035 PARKER, MARTHA, 3366 LA MESA #10., SAN CARLOS, CA 94070 USA
37036 JACOBS, MARGARETA, 1600 S EADS ST #311-S., ARLINGTON, VA 22202 USA
37037 GARDNER, GLENN, 6091 PEACHVIEW DR., CINCINNATI, OH 45247 USA
37038 DAVIS, LARUE, 75 WELBY ST., HELPER, UT 84526 USA
37039 STRANG, CORA, 3256 DURHAM PL W., HOLLAND, PA 18966 USA
37040 SHOUP, MRS L, 4126 LUPINE ST., COLORADO SPRINGS, CO 80918 USA
37041 BAKER, JO, 1399 INDIAN ROCKS RD., LARGO, FL 34640 USA
37042 WYANT, PETER, 116 MIKKELSON DR., REGINA, SAS S4T 6R5 CAN
37043 TRIBE, MR S, 2233 6TH ST E., COURTENAY, BC V9N 7T8 CAN
37044 HAGGART, MARILYN, 379 HURTEAU., DOLLARD DES ORMEAUX, QUE H9G 2L7 CAN
37045 DALEY, JEAN, 412 MOODY AVE., SELKIRK, MAN R1A 0E8 CAN
37046 EARTHY, DOUGLAS, 149 ELLIOTT ST., LONDON, ONT N5Y 2G1 CAN
37047 HAFFNER, PHILIP, 926 MULHOLLAND DR., PARKSVILLE, BC V9P 1Z4 CAN
37048 CHICKITE, CANDY-LEA, 1451-A N ISLAND HWY., CAMPBELL RIVER, BC V9W 2E4 CAN
37049 KEMPTON, RICHARD, BOX 483., KITSCOTY, ALB T0B 2P0 CAN
37050 TWOMEY, MRS A, 313 CADDY ST., PETERBOROUGH, ONT K9H 1M2 CAN
37051 HOARE, MISS J, 54 SPIELPLATZ, LYNE LN., BRICKET WOOD, HRT AL2 3TO ENG
37052 CLEGG, ISABEL, 25 KENWYN CL., HOLT, NFK NR25 6RS ENG
37053 HANKINS, IRIS, 51 ELMS AVE., PARKSTONE, DOR BH14 8EE ENG
37054 JUPP, DAVID, 12 MOUNTWOOD, HURST PARK., EAST MOLESEY, SRY KT8 9RP ENG
37055 BOYCE, MARY, THE OLD PARSONAGE., STEEPLE ASHTON, WIL BA14 6HH ENG
37056 PEARSON, MR R, 1 STONEY PATH., SHAFTESBURY, DOR SP7 8HR ENG
37057 GIDDINGS, KIM, 343A BEXLEY RD., ERITH, KEN DA8 3EZ ENG
37058 GRACE, MARK, 39 HASTED CL., GREENHITHE, KNT DA9 2HS ENG

37059 WOODIWISS, FRANK, 4 BARRATT CL., BEESTON, NG9 6AE ENG
37060 TREVAN, MARY, THE OLD FORGE, HORSINGTON., TEMPLECOMBE, SOM BA8 0DN ENG
37061 POLLARD, ROBERT, 28 LAYLAND RD., NORTH SKELTON, CLEVELAND TS12 2AQ ENG
37062 DONOVAN, JOHN, 92 HOLLY PARK RD., FRIERN BARNET, LND N11 3HB ENG
37063 WARD, MICHAEL, 21 WENLOCK WAY., THATCHAM, BRK RG13 4SQ ENG
37064 STOCKWELL, ROBERT, 22 PALMER AVE., CHEAM, SUTTON, SRY SM3 8EG ENG
37065 SULLIVAN, LINDA, 5A ZANGWILL RD., LONDON, SE3 8EH ENG
37066 PURCELL, MARGARET, 128 RED BANK RD., BISPHAM BLACKPOOL, LAN FY2 9DZ ENG
37067 PACKHAM, JOHN, 16 WESTBURY RD., NEW MALDEN, SRY KT3 5BE ENG
37068 CLARKE, MRS B, 45 'OLD' CHESTER RD., CASTLE BROMWICH, B36 9DP ENG
37069 DENNIS, FREDERICK, 62 ARCHERS COURT RD., WHITFIELD, KEN CT16 3HU ENG
37070 SMEETON, BRIAN, 15 ST JOHN'S WAY., PIDDINGTON, NTH NN7 2DL ENG
37071 CAMPBELL, MRS J, 7 VICTORIA RD., FELIXSTOWE, SFK IP11 8BZ ENG
37072 EMMERSON, JOAN, 55 MOSS LN., HESKETH BANK, LAN PR4 6AA ENG
37073 THORP, MARY, 9 KENTMERE CRES., BARROW IN FURNESS, CUL LA14 4NL ENG
37074 LLOYD, ANDREW, 21 QUEENS RD., FLEET, HAM GU13 9LE ENG
37075 DENMAN, BARRY, 8A CHOBHAM RD., LONDON, E15 1LU ENG
37076 HETHERINGTON, FLORENCE, 19 CHANDOS AVE., ROUND HAY, W YORKS L58 1QU ENG
37077 SHERBORN, DEREK, 161 MARINE PDE., BRIGHTON, SSX BN2 1EJ ENG
37078 DAY, ANGELA, 37 THE STREET, MANUDEN, HERTS CM23 1DF ENG
37079 CARAHER-MANNING, DOREEN, C/O 643 FLEMING RD., HINESVILLE, GA 31313 USA
37080 HAINES, MR C, 17 BROOMHILL RD., GOODMAYES, ESS IG3 9SH ENG
37081 SALKELD, MR R, 124 COOMBE RD., SALISBURY, WIL SP2 8BL ENG
37082 THURLOW, BARBARA, 2 LUCASTES LN., HAYWARDS HEATH, WEST SSX RH16 1LD ENG
37083 ROBERTS, TIM, 61 FALMOUTH RD., CHELMSFORD, ESS CM1 5JA ENG
37084 BEAUFONT-BISHOP, MR D, MYRTLE HSE, OXFORD ST., EVERCREECH, SOM BA4 6HT ENG
37085 MILLER, MISS K, 210C WALMERSLEY RD., BURY, LAN BL9 6LL ENG
37086 BROOK, MRS D, 7 WERFA ST., ROATH PARK, GLA CF2 5EW WALES
37087 HOSKYNS, MR H, 16 CHATHAM PK, CLEVELAND WALK., BATH, AVON BA2 6JR ENG
37088 SMITH, SARAH, PENHILL FARM, PENDOMER., YEOVIL, SOM BA22 9PA ENG
37089 OLIVER, HELEN, 143 NORFOLK AVE., SOUTH CROYDON, SRY CR2 8BY ENG
37090 SERMON, JOHN, HILL RISE HOOSE, HETHE., BICESTER, OXF OX6 9HD ENG
37091 CURTIS, PETER, BROCKHURST FARM., ALFOLD, SRY GU6 8JB ENG
37092 JANES, MR A, 14 COURT HILL., HOVELANDS PARK, SOM TA1 4SX ENG
37093 BENTOTE, MALCOLM, 25 CHESTNUT DR., PINNER, MDX HA5 1LX ENG
37094 ATKINSON, DAVID, 23 DELABERE RD., CHELTENHAM, GLOS GL52 4AN ENG
37095 MARTIN, PATRICIA, 6 UNDERHILL CL., MAIDENHEAD, BERKS SL6 4DS ENG
37096 MYTTON, JONATHAN, 99 HILL HOOD RD., SUTTON COLDFIELD, W. MIDS B74 4ED ENG
37097 LANGFORD, PETER, 7 WILLIAM BURT CL., WESTON TURVILLE, BKM HP22 5QX ENG
37098 WILCOX, RICHARD, 2 SOUTH DR., JIMPERLEY, CHS WA15 6QJ ENG
37099 AIKEN, ARTHUR, 6 BURLEIGH WAY., CUFFLEY, HRT ENG
37100 MACKMAN, JAMES, 35 SITWELL GVE., ACOMB, NRY Y02 5JG ENG
37101 GABB, ALFRED, CHURCH FARM BUNGALOW., OVERTON, NRY Y03 6YL ENG
37102 GRANEA, DORIS, 3 WOODLANDS CL., UCKFIELD, SSX TN22 1TS ENG
37103 RENOLD, RICHARD, 18 WORDSWORTH CL., LICHFIELD, STS WS14 9BY ENG
37104 LAWSON, MRS J, PO BOX 2090., TOOWOOMBA, QLD 4350 AUS
37105 OSBORNE, RON, PO BOX 345., NERANG, QLD 4211 AUS
37106 GREGORY, MARGARET, 106 LOGAN ST., BEENLEIGH, QLD 4207 AUS
37107 BLOM, JOHN, 4 NYE AVE., BUDERIM, QLD 4556 AUS
37108 ENNOR, MRS J., 28 LANDSCAPE DR., BORONIA, VIC 3155 AUS
37109 EDGAR, NOLA, 22 BAGGOTT DR., HOPPERS CROSSING, VIC 3029 AUS
37110 EADE, PATRICIA, 30 OWEN AVE., GLEN WAVERLEY, VIC 3150 AUS
37111 HANRAHAN, PETER, 5 PARSON CT., GERALDTON, WA 6530 AUS
37112 HARDY, MICHAEL, 53/299 BURNS BAY RD., LANE COVE, NSW 2066 AUS
37113 MCDONALD, MAUREEN, 96 BOGALARA RD., TOONGABBIE, NSW 2146 AUS
37114 BONOMINI, MRS P, PO BOX 994., MURWILLUMBAH, NSW 2484 AUS
37115 ATKINSON, DENISE, 7 SHORT ST., EAST BALLINA, NSW 2478 AUS
37116 BOND, ADELAIDE, 521 GREAT WESTERN HGWY., FAULCONBRIDGE, NSW 2776 AUS
37117 HINCHLIFFE, JOHN, 5 ROSS CRES., BLAXLAND, NSW 2774 AUS
37118 PEARSON, BETTY, 2/4 MOIRA CRES., RANDWICK, NSW 2031 AUS
37119 WILLCOCKS, MARLENE, 6 FINCH AVE., RYDALMERE, NSW 2116 AUS
37120 MCANDREW, MRS S, PO BOX 466., ENFIELD, NSW 2136 AUS
37121 LOCAL STUDIES,, HAWKESBURY CITY LIBY, DIGHT ST., WINDSOR, NSW 2756 AUS
37122 RING, MAREE, 14 OAKBANK AVE., MONTROSE, TAS 7010 AUS
37123 DAWSON, VALERIE, 455 SANDGATE RD., SHORTLAND, NSW 2307 AUS
37124 WILLIAMS, GEORGE, NO 1 VENA AVE., GOROKAN, NSW 2263 AUS
37125 SMITH, ELWYN, 2 FLETCHER AVE., MIRANDA, NSW 2228 AUS
37126 LAURIE, CHRISTINE, 20 MORUYA ST., MORUYA, NSW 2537 AUS
37127 RUMBLE, YVONNE, WYANDA., DENILIQUIN, NSW 2710 AUS
37128 MILES, KEN, 15 KEATS ST., CARLINGFORD, NSW 2118 AUS
37129 ELLIOTT, MAVIS, PO BOX 230., MATRAVILLE, NSW 2036 AUS
37130 CALVERT, ANNE, PO BOX 596., TAREE, NSW 2430 AUS

37131 EARNSHAW, MARY, KUNDLE KUNDLE RD., CUNDLETOWN, NSW 2430 AUS
37132 SMITH, MS J, 33 BARRALIER AVE., WOODBERRY, NSW 2322 AUS
37133 KENNY, SUE, 13 CASCADE DR., CASINO, NSW 2470 AUS
37134 ELLERY, JOAN, PO BOX 5., KINGSGROVE, NSW 2208 AUS
37135 HOGAN, ROBYN, 2 BLAXLAND ST., HUNTERS HILL, NSW 2110 AUS
37136 KELSO, MRS J, 49 TOWNSON AVE., LEUMEAH, NSW 2560 AUS
37137 SINCLAIR, MRS C, 7 PEPPERINA PL., CARLINGFORD, NSW 2118 AUS
37138 SCOTLAND, MOYNA, 77 CAMPBELL HILL RD., CHESTER HILL, NSW 2162 AUS
37139 RAMAGE, PAULINE, MAIN ST., COWRA, NSW 2794 AUS
37140 REDHEAD, PETER, PO BOX 228., MILSONS POINT, NSW 2061 AUS
37141 TAYLOR, MAVIS, 9 DAVID ST EAST., SPRINGWOOD, NSW 2777 AUS
37142 FARRELL, MICHAEL, PO BOX 1043., CASINO, NSW 2470 AUS
37143 BRIEN, JEAN, 31 HANNA ST., COWRA, NSW 2794 AUS
37144 SHIPP, BRIAN, 21 NAROOMA PL., GYMEA BAY, NSW 2227 AUS
37145 DUNN, CATHLEEN, 33 KALANG AVE., ULLADULLA, NSW 2539 AUS
37146 SCOTT, WILLIAM, RMB 124., TAMWORTH, NSW 3084 AUS
37147 JONES, LINDA, 8 CHERANA PL., KAREELA, NSW 2232 AUS
37148 JOHNSON, BETTY, 20 TRAYNOR AVE., KOGARAH, NSW 2217 AUS
37149 DALLY, LINDSAY, 45 HILTON ST., MT WAVERLEY, VIC 3149 AUS
37150 SWIFT, GRAHAM, 2 LANE ST., BLACKBURN, VIC 3130 AUS
37151 BUTCHER, FLORENCE, 1 MIRBOO ST., NEWBOROUGH, VIC 3825 AUS
37152 BOTT, WILLIAM, PO BOX 204., MAFFRA, VIC 3860 AUS
37153 HOYSTED, MRS K, 15 THE BOULEVARD., MONTROSE, VIC 3765 AUS
37154 BLUME, MALCOLM, 2 CAMPBELL ST., CASTLEMAINE, VIC 3450 AUS
37155 HERBERT, MRS M, PO BOX 131., ROSANNA, VIC 3084 AUS
37156 BLACKALL, DR B, 2 TRAVELLYN CRT., BLACKBURN SOUTH, VIC 3130 AUS
37157 HUTCHINSON, DOUGLAS, 429 SPRINGFIELD RD., MITCHAM, VIC 3132 AUS
37158 KAAN, MARGARET, 3 CORRONG CRT., ELTHAM, VIC 3095 AUS
37159 WERE, DIANNE, 41 RUTHERFORD RD., ROSANNA, VIC 3084 AUS
37160 JACOBSEN, MRS E, 23 GRAMMAR ST., STRATHMORE, VIC 3041 AUS
37161 HEYDON, MARY, 10 ROYCROFT AVE., MILL PARK, VIC 3082 AUS
37162 CUNNINGHAM, MR J, 51 TRACEY ST., EAST DONCASTER, VIC 3109 AUS
37163 MCDONALD, JUDY, 44 BELMONT RD., IVANHOE, VIC 3079 AUS
37164 PARKER, KAREN, C/O PARKER BROS. RSD, BENALLA RD., SHEPPARTON, VIC 3630 AUS
37165 COOPER, VICKI, 15 FALCON ST., NARROGIN, WA 6312 AUS
37166 MORLEY, DAPHNE, 5 IRELAND AVE., DONCASTER EAST, VIC 3109 AUS
37167 DOWNES, MRS V, PO BOX 771., SALE, VIC 3850 AUS
37168 BATES, JAMES, 3 PIONEER AVE., UPWEY, VIC 3158 AUS
37169 WOODRUFF, MR G, PO BOX 344., MT PLEASANT, QLD 4740 AUS
37170 BUNNING, WAYNE, 128 SUSSEX ST., MARYBOROUGH, QLD 4650 AUS
37171 LEES, EVELYN, 59 ROBERTS ST., HERMIT PARK, QLD 4812 AUS
37172 BENNETT, MRS J, 3 KOKODA AVE, MS 1536., NAMBOUR, QLD 4560 AUS
37173 PARDEY, PETER, 33 NOTT ST., MOURA, QLD 4718 AUS
37174 TOMKINS, GLORIA, 50 BROOKE AVE., SOUTHPORT, QLD 4215 AUS
37175 JOHNSON, ALBERT, 32 PAVO ST., CAMP HILL, QLD 4152 AUS
37176 WREN, MRS L, PO BOX 433., IPSWICH, QLD 4305 AUS
37177 BROWN, WENDY, 27 LANGDON ST., TANNUM SANDS, QLD 4680 AUS
37178 KELLY, IAN, 16 SHEEHAN AVE., ROCKHAMPTON, QLD 4700 AUS
37179 PERRY, MR R, 34 CHIPPING DR., CITY BEACH, WA 6015 AUS
37180 BARNES, EDWARD, 454 HECTOR ST., MOUNT YOKINE, WA 6060 AUS
37181 DOWNES, JOAN, 89 CARSON TCE., GERALDTON, WA 6530 AUS
37182 BURNSIDE, IAN, 50 AMAROO ST., REID, ACT 2601 AUS
37183 NUM, MRS C, 17 PENDRED ST., PEARCE, ACT 2607 AUS
37184 FENNELL, MRS L, 1 SCHARENBERG CRT., PORT AUGUSTA, SA 5700 AUS
37185 GOODEVE-BALLARD, COL M., 5 BRODERICK CRT., GAWLER EAST, SA 5118 AUS
37186 SPENCER, JOHN, 12 VALLEY VIEW DR., NARACOORTE, SA 5271 AUS
37187 SCHELLEN, B, RMB 7401., MANNUM, SA 5238 AUS
37188 AYRES, NEIL, 15 GLENGARRY ST., WOODVILLE, SA 5011 AUS
37189 GOULD, MRS B, 11 MILTON ST., OAKLANDS PARK, SA 5046 AUS
37190 HURD, MR P, 8 SMITHURST AVE., SOUTH HOBART, TAS 7004 AUS
37191 FELGATE, TONY, 56 WONGA RD., LIVERPOOL, NSW 2170 AUS
37192 LIVERPOOL F.H.SOC,, PO BOX 830., LIVERPOOL, NSW 2170 AUS
37193 BARROW, MR G, 52 LYTTON AVE., ENFIELD LOCK, MDX EN3 6EN ENG
37194 HUTT, BRYAN, 158 PINNER RD., OXHEY, HERTS WD1 4EW ENG
37195 CORNISH, ROGER, 216 OUTLAND RD., PLYMOUTH, DEV PL2 3PE ENG
37196 CARRODUS, FRANCIS, 5 WIBBERSLEY PK., FLIXTON, MANCHESTER ENG
37197 HIGGS, MICHAEL, 20 WARWICK WAY., RICKMANSWORTH, HERTS WD3 3SA ENG
37198 KILMISTER, MICHAEL, 45 LONG EIGHTS., NORTHWAY, GLS GL20 8QZ ENG
37199 EAST, ANDREE, BAINTON FARMHOUSE., BAINTON, OXON OX6 9RL ENG
37200 BOWEN, JOHN, 3B PARKLANDS AVE., BOGNOR REGIS, W SSX PO21 2BA ENG
37201 SNOOK, MRS H, 33 MILLERS GROVE, FORDS FARM., CALCOT, BERKS RG5 5PH ENG
37202 STEELE, MRS D, 2 BLETCHINGDON RD., ISLIP, OXF OX5 2TQ ENG

37203 SANNE, MR K, 6 RUE DE HOLLENFELS., TUNTANGE, L-7481 LUXEMBOURG
37204 DAKIN, PAULINE, 6 HAZELBANK RD., COUNTESTHORPE, LEI LE8 3RR ENG
37205 MCCULLOCH, JANET, 13 CAEREX, LLANBLETHIAN., COWBRIDGE, GLA CF7 7JS WALES
37206 MARTIN, ANTHONY, 5 OTLINGE CL., ST MARY CRAY, KENT BR5 3SH ENG
37207 WILKINS, PETER, 21 PINE TREES., WESTON FAVELL, NTH NN3 3ET ENG
37208 EASINGWOOD, NEVILLE, 30 DOWNHAM AVE, OFF ABBEY LN., LEICESTER, LE4 0DH ENG
37209 MURPHY, JEAN, 34 KINGSLEIGH DR., CASTLE BROMWICH, WAR B36 9DQ ENG
37210 SMITH, MR J, 21 THE GROVE., CATERHAM, SRY CR3 5QD ENG
37211 MOLE, MRS S, 2 SECOND AVE., WORTHING, W SSX BN14 9NX ENG
37212 HUMPHRIES, ERIC, 19 ADDINGTON RD., WOODFORD, NTH NN14 4ES ENG
37213 BROWN, ANTHONY, 52 WEARDALE AVE., DARTFORD, KEN DA2 6LE ENG
37214 BRIDGER, MRS T, 25 CLIVE RD., FRATTON, HANTS P01 5JB ENG
37215 NORMAN, JEAN, 31 WALLFIELDS CL., FINDERN, DBY DE6 6QL ENG
37216 CHANEY, MR C, 48 BEAN OAK RD., WOKINGHAM, BRK RG11 1RN ENG
37217 MANTON, DOUGLAS, 85 BURMAN RD, SHIRLEY., SOLIHULL, WAR 2BQ ENG
37218 FENNESSY, EDWARD, NORTHBROOK LITTLEFD. LN., SHAMLEY GREEN, SRY GU5 0RH ENG
37219 ROOTS, PAUL, HILLCOT HOUSE, BITTERLEY., LUDLOW, SALOP SY8 3HR ENG
37220 LARKUM, MR M, 27 PARK RD., CHEAM, SRY SM3 8PY ENG
37221 TUCKER, MRS B, LITTLE COTTAGE, PORTLOE., TRURO, CON TR2 5QU ENG
37222 BISHOP, IAN, 32 HENFIELD CRES., OLDLAND COMMON, BRISTOL BS15 6SF ENG
37223 KINGSTON, DON, 21 ST JAMES GDNS., WESTCLIFF ON SEA, ESS SS0 0BU ENG
37224 BLUETT, VALERIE, 63 OLD LAIRA RD., LAIRA, DEV PL3 6BL ENG
37225 DOWNS, KATE, 45 THE PASTURES., WESTWOOD, WILTS BA15 2BH ENG
37226 WRIGHT, MR M, 284 RINGWOOD RD., TOTTON, HAM SO4 3EN ENG
37227 CHARLES, MISS P, 4 MEADOW CL., MOULSFORD, OXF OX10 9JL ENG
37228 SPASHETT, JEAN, 23 HAMPTON PIER AVE., HERNE BAY, KENT CT6 8EW ENG
37229 SIMON, JANET, WHITE ODGE, RUETTE DES FRIES., CATEL, GUERNSEY CHANNEL ISL.
37230 TAYLOR, PATRICIA, 15 WARREN DR., DORRIDGE, SOLIHULL B93 8JY ENG
37231 ANDERSON, SHIRLEY, 35 LANGDON RD., CHELTENHAM, GLS GL53 7NZ ENG
37232 LEWCUN, MAREK, 13 CANTERBURY RD., BATH, AVON BA2 3LG ENG
37233 LEWCUN, MAREK, 13 CANTERBURY RD., BATH, BA2 3LG ENG
37234 GIRDLESTONE, MR K, 14 EASTERN CRES., THORPE ST ANDREW, NFK NR7 0UE ENG
37235 MUNDY, MRS P, 14 MEDLOCK ST., DROYLSDEN, LAN M35 7AT ENG
37236 MARTEN, RODNEY, 3A WARWICK RD., LONDON, W5 3XH ENG
37237 EDWARDS, LORNA, 31 CUMBERLAND AVE., SOUTH BENFLEET, ESS SS7 5NU ENG
37238 JOLLY, ELIZABETH, 153 OKUS RD., SWINDON, WILTS SN1 4JY ENG
37239 MARTIN, ERNEST, 23 ROGERON CL., HUNDON, SUDBURY, SFK CO10 8SB ENG
37240 DE RUSETT, JOHN, 6 ST PETERS CURT., BYKER, NE6 2XH ENG
37241 PRICE, SARAH, 43 PERRYFIELDS., BURGESS HILL, SSX RH15 8TU ENG
37242 THOMPSON, SYLVIA, 45 POLLOCK WALK., DUNFERMLINE, FIF KY12 9DA SCT
37243 LORD, ROLAND, 22 ELIZABETH CRES., EAST GRINSTEAD, SSX RH19 3JA ENG
37244 HODGE, JOHN, 21 HIGHVIEW RD., EALING, W13 0HA ENG
37245 MITCHELL, DURNO, 17 ST MARYS CL., SOUTHAM, WAR CV33 0EW ENG
37246 BAIRD, ALAN, 28A KENNYLANDS RD., SONNING COMMON, OXF RG4 9JT ENG
37247 TREPESS, MR P, WP51, INST OF DRILLG, LEOBEN MINING UNI., A 8700 AUSTRIA
37248 PINCHIN, AUDREY, SWEET OAKS, KENNION RD., WELLS, SOM BA5 2NP ENG
37249 SALISBURY, MRS J, HILLVIEW NEWGROUND., WIGGINTON, HRT HP23 6DN ENG
37250 RUSSILL, JUDITH, WYE BARN, THE QUAY., TINTERN, GWENT NP6 6SZ WALES
37251 JENKINS, JOAN, MEADOWSIDE, BOTTLESFORD., PEWSEY, WIL SN9 6LW ENG
37252 HOMES, ALAN, 3 CRESWICK WALK, ADDINGTON RD., BOW, LND E3 2AQ ENG
37253 WAKEFORD, DAVID, CARPALLA VILLA, FOXHOLE., ST AUSTELL, CON PL26 7TY ENG
37254 BURFOOT, ROBERT, 419 CANTERBURY RD., DENSOLE, FOLKESTONE, KEN CT18 7BH ENG
37255 BLACKBURNE, PATRICIA, 43 HOLLINS RD., HINDLEY, LAN WN2 4JZ ENG
37256 CHEVALIER, JOHN, KARDON RUE DE CAUSIE PONTAC., ST CLEMENT, JSY JE2 6SQ CHI. UK
37257 HOBBIS, ARTHUR, BROOKMEDE, WORCESTER RD., SHRAWLEY, WOR WR6 6TD ENG
37258 PEGG, RICHARD, 19 RIDGWAY RD., KETTERING, NTH NN15 5AQ ENG
37259 SIMS, MARION, OWL COTTAGE BROOM WAY., OATLANDS PARK, SRY KT13 9TG ENG
37260 MILNE, MRS J, 21 ROSEBERRY RD., BRISTOL, BS5 9QD ENG
37261 BOWMAN, DOROTHY, 43 THE SCARR., NEWENT, GL18 1DQ ENG
37262 BARKER, BRENDA, CAMB. VICT. HOMES, VICTORIA RD., CAMBRIDGE, CB4 3DX ENG
37263 LLEWELLYN, MRS J, 34 WINDLEHURST RD., HIGH LANE, CHS SK6 8AB ENG
37264 UPHAM, MR R, 'KWAI LO', WINTERHAY GREEN., ILMINSTER, SOM TA19 9PL ENG
37265 TANNER, TINA, 153 SPRINGTHORPE RD., ERDINGTON, WAR B24 0SN ENG
37266 LEWIS, WENDY, 95 RUSKIN AVE., LONG EATON, NTT NG10 3HX ENG
37267 KEMP, MICHAEL, 38 BANCROFT ST., NOTTINGHAM, NTT NG6 9HF ENG
37268 SMITH, MR M, 16 WILSON AVE., HENLEY ON THAMES, OXF RG9 1ET ENG
37269 WHITE, MS S, 6 WINSLOW WAY., WALTON ON THAMES, SRY KT12 3DH ENG
37270 KENNEY, JOHN, 16 BRAYWICK RD., MAIDENHEAD, BERKS SL6 1DA ENG
37271 ENSTONE, BERNARD, 43 WINCHESTER RD., NORTHAMPTON, NN4 9AZ ENG
37272 CHARLETON, PAUL, 4 KEYNSHAM WAY., OWLSMOOR, SRY GU15 4SB ENG
37273 JOBSON, PETER, 78 THE DRIVE., TOTTON, HAM SO4 4EN ENG
37274 JARVIS, MRS D., 278 VALENCE AVE., DAGENHAM, ESSEX RH8 3QX ENG

37275 AMPHLETT, RONALD, THE GEORGE HOUSE, HIGH ST., AYLESFORD, KEN ME20 7AX ENG
37276 COLMAN, MR M., 85 CROSTWICK LN., SPIXWORTH, NFK NR10 3NT ENG
37277 MARRIOTT, JOHN, SWAREBROOK., GREAT MILTON, OXF OX9 7NJ ENG
37278 WALKER, MR R, PROSPECT HOUSE, SANDBEDS., QUEENSBURY, WRY BD13 1AP ENG
37279 DANIEL, JEREMY, 23 GILDA CRES., POLEGATE, SSX BN26 6AW ENG
37280 TURPIN, MRS O, PRIMROSE FM., BLACKBOROUGH END., KINGS LYNN, NFK PE32 1SG ENG
37281 TAYLOR, JOHN, 113 BEACH AVE., LEIGH ON SEA, ESS SS9 1HD ENG
37282 HAWKES, MR R., 26 RAVENS WAY., BURTON ON TRENT, STS DE14 2JS ENG
37283 HUGHES, SHIRLEY, 14 CRISS GVE., CHALFONT ST PETER, BUCKS SL9 9HG ENG
37284 KINSELLA, JOAN, 141 CAVENDISH RD., LONDON, E4 9NG ENG
37285 HAYNES, MRS K., 5 ALFRISTON RD., SEAFORD, E SSX BN25 3QD ENG
37286 SHERLOCK, GRAHAM, 81 HIGH ST., OFFORD D'ARCY, CAMBS PE18 9RH ENG
37287 DEVEKEY, MISS M., 215 HEMPSTEAD RD., WATFORD, HRT WD1 3HH ENG
37288 BARKER, MRS M, RIVERDALE, MEADOWFIELD TCE., STOCKSFIELD, NBL NE43 7LJ ENG
37289 PEIN, OLE, BP 8., SANT JULIA, ANDORRA
37290 HANWELL, ADRIAN, 59 WESTERN RD., BRENTWOOD, ESSEX CM14 4SU ENG
37291 DAVIS, HILDA, 21 WARREN RD., NARBOROUGH, LEI LE9 5DR ENG
37292 SHEW, MR B, 18A QUEENS AVE., WHETSTONE, LND N20 0JE ENG
37293 BURCHETT, MR R, 25 MOUNT RD., NEWHAVEN, SSX BN9 0LT ENG
37294 MARTIN-TAYLOR, MICHELE, 6 DINGLE RD., ASHFORD, MDX TW15 1HE ENG
37295 MERRIMAN, RICHARD, VICARAGE FLAT, HIGH ST., KIMBOLTON, CAMBS PE18 0HB ENG
37296 HEMMER, ALBERT, 68 YORK AVE., JARROW, T & W NE32 ENG
37297 FENN, RICHARD, 31 UFFINGTON RD., WEST NORWOOD, LND SE27 0RW ENG
37298 SOAR, LEONARD, WITS END, PARK LN., PRESTBURY, GLOS GL52 3BN ENG
37299 WILSON, JAYNE, 19 DICKINSON ST., DERBY, DBY DE2 8WJ ENG
37300 KENT, GARY, 4 BERKELEY GDNS., HOLT, ACT 2615 AUS
37301 LANSDELL, MORRIS, 7 NIXON ST., SANDY BAY, TAS 7005 AUS
37302 THOMSON, LAUREN, 11 WINTON ST., BURWOOD, VIC 3125 AUS
37303 MARTIN, MISS J, 76 COOLOONGATTA RD., CAMBERWELL, VIC 3124 AUS
37304 FINESTONE, MRS L, 1/74 KING WILLIAM ST., RESERVOIR, VIC 3073 AUS
37305 GILLESPIE, BARBARA, 3 CULLIVER ST., HORSHAM, VIC 3400 AUS
37306 HAYWARD, VALERIE, 35 JUNE RD., SAFETY BAY, WA 6169 AUS
37307 HEANY, FAYE, PO BOX 996., MACKAY, QLD 4740 AUS
37308 CHARLES, HAZEL, 'RAMAH' TENTERDEN., GUYRA, NSW 2365 AUS
37309 BARNES, MRS G, 13 ULTIMO ST., CARINGBAH, NSW 2229 AUS
37310 SAWYERS, MAXWELL, 8 COOINDA ST., ST MARYS, NSW 2760 AUS
37311 TURNER, JENNIFER, 46 DOVER RD., ROSE BAY, NSW 2029 AUS
37312 MCMILES, LAUREL, 1 ZARLEE ST (C/O POST OF)., FAIRFIELD WEST, NSW 2165 AUS
37313 FORD, DENISE, 21 HARRISON ST., OLD TOONGABBIE, NSW 2146 AUS
37314 MASSURIT, COLLEEN, 90 HIGH ST., PARKES, NSW 2870 AUS
37315 RAE, DOUGLAS, 91 CLIFF RD., EPPING, NSW 2121 AUS
37316 POSTANS, MRS K, 57 RUSDEN ST., KELVIN GROVE, QLD 4059 AUS
37317 NIXON, JOY, 52 NIXON RD, TAUPAKI., HENDERSON RD3, AUCK NZ
37318 WEST, ALAN, 19 CLEVEDON GDNS., CRANFORD, MDX TW5 9TT ENG
37319 ADAMS, JOAN, 16 KELMSCOTT RD., HARBORNE, B17 8QN ENG
37320 ROBERTS, ANDY, 9 CONNAUGHT RD., NEW MALDEN, SRY KT3 3PZ ENG
37321 MASON, MRS J, 34 HILLCREST., BAR HILL, CMB CB3 8TG ENG
37322 DYER, MR M, 81 PADIHAM RD., SABDEN, LAN BB6 9EX ENG
37323 STRATTON, JOHN, 'CHADDESLEY' BROADWAY., LLANDRINDAD WELLS, POWYS LD1 5HT UK
37324 DUN, MICHAEL, 59 DALHOUSIE RD., BROUGHTY FERRY, DUNDEE DD5 2SU SCOTLAND
37325 VANN, PETE, 1 MENDIP HSE, LABURNUM GVE., GRAVESEND, KEN DA11 9QS ENG
37326 LONGHORN, VICTOR, 53 THEYDON AVE., WOBURN SANDS, MK17 8PN ENG
37327 BOCKETT, MABEL, 6 CAMPBELL MANS, CAMPBELL RD., SOUTHSEA, HANTS P05 1RP ENG
37328 PERROTT, PETER, 5 SHEPHERDS RISE., VERNHAM DEAN, HAM SP11 0HD ENG
37329 MACDONALD, MARY, 'MAORIHA' BRUMLEY BRAE RD., ELGIN, MOR IV30 2PP SCOTLAND
37330 HUGHES, GEOFFREY, 217 STOKE LN., WESTBURY ON TRYM, AVON BS9 3RX ENG
37331 DANGERFIELD, JEAN, 69 SHENSTONE RD., BIRMINGHAM, B43 5LW ENG
37332 KENNETT, JOSIE, WHITE HSE., HEADCORN RD., SUTTON VALENCE, KEN ME17 3EH ENG
37333 PATTERSON, JOHN, 1 WOODSTOCK RD., ABERDEEN, ABD AB2 4ET SCOTLAND
37334 FELTON, ROGER, 9 KINGSLEY PARK., WHITCHURCH, HAM RG28 7HA ENG
37335 DEACON, ANDREW, 78 NORTHCROFT., SLOUGH, BRK SL2 1HP ENG
37336 WEEDEN, JOHN, SYRA, SOUTHVIEW DR., WALTON ON NAZE, ESS CO14 8EP ENG
37337 ALSOP, PAMELA, 74 BRANDISH CRES., CLIFTON, NOTTS NG11 9JX ENG
37338 KERR, IAIN, 51 CLEWER PARK., WINDSOR, BERKS SL4 5HD ENG
37339 SPEAR, PETER, 58 GALLY HILL RD., FLEET, HANTS GU13 0RU ENG
37340 BEATTIE, ALAN, 9 BURNTWICK DR., LOWER HALSTOW, KEN ME9 7DX ENG
37341 BAXTER, MARY, 86 APSLEY WAY., PETERBOROUGH, CAM PE3 6PF ENG
37342 THACKER, NORMAN, 49 LAMBS LN., COTTENHAM, CAM CB4 4TB ENG
37343 WOOLWARD, MARY, 20 SOUTH VALE., UPPER NORWOOD, LND SE19 3BA ENG
37344 PYE, PATRICIA, 10 BRIGHTLAND RD., EASTBOURNE, E SSX BN20 8BG ENG
37345 WRIGHT, PETER, 5 THE PERRINGS., NAILSEA, AVON BS19 2YD ENG
37346 MARCH, JOHN, 1 BEECHFIELD CL., GREAT GLEN, LEICS LE8 0EU ENG

37347 SHAWL, HAROLD, 2 ELM CL., NEWARK, NOTTS NG24 1SG ENG
37348 RENDELL, MAUREEN, 17 WESTERN AVE., THORPE-EGHAM, TW20 8QB ENG
37349 SMITH, EVELYN, 11 TALLGUMS AVE., WEST PENNANT HILLS, NSW 2125 AUS
37350 ACKERLY, MISS S, M/S 361., MURGON, QLD 4605 AUS
37351 PERHAM, HEATHER, 60 MIMMS HALL RD., POTTERS BAR, HERTS EN6 3DU ENG
37352 FENBY,, PEACEHAVEN COTTAGE., BOLTON NR WILBERFOSS, YKS Y04 5QS ENG
37353 BOWES, MR G, WOODBURNE STABLES, CERES., CUPAR, FIF KY15 5PY SCOTLAND
37354 COSSAR, A, 49 HENDHAM RD., LONDON, SW17 7DH ENG
37355 LIVERMORE, ALAN, 75 RICHMOND PARK RD., KINGSTON ON THAMES, SRY 6AF ENG
37356 SPRY, MR W, 5 ST TEILO'S WAY., WATFORD FARM EST, MID GLAM CF8 1FA WALES
37357 CARR, MR A, 30 WISHAW CL, GREENLANDS., REDDITCH, WOR B98 7RE ENG
37358 BENTON, EDWARD, 99 LITTLE PYNCHONS., HARLOW, ESS CM18 7DF ENG
37359 DOWN, DENISE, 46 ROCK AVE., GILLINGHAM, KENT ME7 5PT ENG
37360 GOLDING, MRS P, 48 ST MICHAELS AVE., YEOVIL, SOM BA21 4LH ENG
37361 SHERLOCK, CAROLINE, 24 CHAMPION GVE., LONDON, SE5 8BW ENG
37362 BURR, MRS J, 26 BIRKDALE CRT., FORNHAM ST MARTIN, SFK IP28 6XF ENG
37363 SHAAK, BRUCE, 2 GRAYSHOTT CL., SITTINGBOURNE, ME10 4PU ENG
37364 SWAIN, CLAUDE, 29 SPRINGHEAD., TUNBRIDGE WELLS, KENT TN2 3NY ENG
37365 FARMER, ALICE, 2 MOLYNEUX PARK RD., TUNBRIDGE WELLS, KENT TN4 8DN ENG
37366 PADRAZOLLA, JANET, 41 ASHLEY DR., BOREHAMWOOD, HERTS WD6 2JT ENG
37367 GITTINS, SHEILA, 85 TOWER HILL., GREAT BARR, WAR B42 1LQ ENG
37368 WELBY, D., BOTSCHAFT RIAD, POSTFACH 1500., 5300 BONN 1, VERSANDWEG LF GER
37369 NOCK, TERRY, 64 NAPIER RD., GILLINGHAM, KENT ME7 4HD ENG
37370 ROUGHTON-SKELTON, HENRY, 32 SOUTHVIEW RD., MARLOW, BKM SL7 3JP ENG
37371 NIGHTINGALE, JOHN, 60 CROMWELL RD., BECKENHAM, KEN BR3 4LN ENG
37372 HOLLAS, CYNTHIA, 176 SCAR LN., MILNSBRIDGE, WRY HD3 4PY ENG
37373 WINGHAM, GAYNOR, 17 GREENHOLM RD., ELTHAM, LND SE9 1UQ ENG
37374 DONALD, GRANT, 134 BALGREEN RD., EDINBURGH, EH12 5XF SCOTLAND
37375 BELLAMY, DAVID, 45 CROSSDALE DR., KEYWORTH, NTT NG12 5HP ENG
37376 KNIGHTS, PHILIP, 6 RUSKIN CL, POUND HILL., CRAWLEY, SSX RH10 3TP ENG
37377 HOWCROFT, WILLIAM, 189 WARWICK AVE., DERBY, DBY DE3 6HN ENG
37378 DANES, DESMOND, 1 HILL END., HARDINGTON MANDEVILLE, SOM BA22 9PW ENG
37379 BINNS, ALAN, 518 COLNE RD., REEDLEY, LAN BB10 2LD ENG
37380 JONES, MISS B, 1 NORTHFIELD GDNS., TAUNTON, SOM TA1 1XN ENG
37381 ARMSTRONG, GILES, 35 CEDARS RD., LONDON, W4 3JP ENG
37382 FRYER, JOHN, 6 MEADOWLANDS., HAVANT, HAM PO9 2RP ENG
37383 WELLS, PETER, HIGH TREES, DARK LN., HENBURY, CHES SK11 9PE ENG
37384 SHORE, MRS S, 2 ELIZABETH CRT., HEATON NORRIS, CHS SK4 2HY ENG
37385 TRESCOTT, DR A, 19 DELVES WOOD RD., HUDDERSFIELD, W YORKS HD4 7AS ENG
37386 EMTAGE, LOUISA, HILLSIDE COTTAGE., CHESTERTON, WAR CV33 9LD ENG
37387 PALMER, MS D., 40 PARK CT., GROSVENOR PARK RD., WALTHAMSTOW, LND E17 9PE ENG
37388 HUDSON, BRYAN, 10 SCHOOL CL., MARSKE BY SEA, CLEV TS11 7AS ENG
37389 LESTER, DAPHNE, 17 HARMONY HILL., MILNTHORPE, CUMBRIA LA7 7QA ENG
37390 GIBIRDI, MR D, 19 LULWORTH RD., FULWOOD, LANCS PR2 4EY ENG
37391 RYAN, CAROLYN, 1 FAIRVIEW AVE., WHETSTONE, LEI LE1 8JQ ENG
37392 BEALL, RONALD, THE JAYS BRUNDALL RD., BLOFIELD, NFK NR13 4LB ENG
37393 HOOKWAY, ALEXANDRA, 2A FAIRWAY AVE., BOREHAMWOOD, HERTS WD6 1PR ENG
37394 MINERS, MR W, 44 ABERNETHY QUAY., SWANSEA, SA1 1UF WALES
37395 ROBSON, VALERIE, HARLOW KEEP, CATTON., HEXHAM, NBL NE47 9LN ENG
37396 ROGERS, PHILIP, 31 WHEATLANDS RD EAST., HARROGATE, NRY HG2 8QS ENG
37397 CRADDOCK, BEVAN, 44 HALING RD., PENKRIDGE, STS ST19 5DA ENG
37398 MARSHALL, MS S., HILL HSE., WEST RD., FORNCETT ST PETER, NFK NR16 1LF ENG
37399 PRITCHARD, MARGARET, 8 CHEMIN DU PONT., 69570 DARDILLY, FRANCE
37400 LYON, CARON, 30 MORTIMER RD, BUNTINGSDALE., TERN HILL, SAL TF9 2EP ENG
37401 WOODGATE, JOHN, 6 CRISPIN FIELD., PITSTONE, BEDS LU7 9BG ENG
37402 DORE, EDMUND, 28A WOODSETTS RD., NORTH ANSTON, YKS S31 7EQ ENG
37403 HAND, MICHAEL, PEG TILE COTTAGE., LADDINGFORD, KEN ME18 6BX ENG
37404 BARNES, GRACE, 14 WELLESBOURNE RD., COVENTRY, WAR CV5 7HG ENG
37405 ARNOLD, PHILIP, 4 BRIARWOOD DR., BANGOR, DOW BT19 2UW N IRELAND
37406 ROBINSON, JOHN, 34 GREATFIELD RD., KIDDERMINSTER, WOR DY11 6PH ENG
37407 GANLY, SGT MICHAEL, UFA, QUEENS GURKHA ENGINEERS., BFPO 1,
37408 BARRETT, CHRIS, 15 LIMES RD., FOLKESTONE, KEN CT19 4AU ENG
37409 SMITH, MARTYN, 63 MILL LN., RAMSEY, CAM PE17 1EF ENG
37410 OSTAFEW, MRS D, 20 WALROND RD., SWANAGE, DOR BH19 1PB ENG
37411 HEATON, DOREEN, 4 SOUTH CRES., GARLIESTON, WIG DG8 8BQ SCOTLAND
37412 ACTON, JOHN, BARN CLOSE COT., THE BARTON., CORSTON, BA2 9AJ ENG
37413 ANNAL, DAVID, 35A MEAD WAY., BUSHEY, HRT WD2 2DH ENG
37414 HARTLEY, DAVID, 677 BACUP RD., WATERFOOT, LANCS BB4 7HB ENG
37415 SHORTALL, MYLES, 'LAUREL LODGE', DOWNSHIRE RD., NEWRY, DOW BT34 1EE IRELAND
37416 HERRIDGE, KEVIN, TREETOPS UPP, HIGHLAND RD., RYDE, IOW PO33 1EA ENG
37417 WOOLLETT, DAVID, CTGE. HOW GREEN FM., HEVER EDENBRIDGE, KEN TN8 7NN ENG
37418 WEEKES, MAUREEN, 29 MAXWELL RD, HULLBRIDGE., HOCKLEY, ESSEX SS5 6HF ENG

37419 BULL, MRS R, 11 TORBAY RD., URMSTON, MANCHESTER M31 1LH ENG
37420 DENYER, RON, 20 LAKE DR., MIDDLETON, M24 1WB ENG
37421 FARNATH, MR A, 5 LAURENCE GVE., TETTENHALL, W MIDS WV6 9QN ENG
37422 JOHNSTONE, MYRTLE, 215 BAYFIELD RD., GODERICH, ONT N7A 3G4 CAN
37423 WALKER, MS J., 1780 BALDY MTN RD RR#1, SHAWNIGAN LK., BC V0R 2W0 CAN
37424 REID, GEORGE, BOX 1807., ST MARYS, ONT N0M 2V0 CAN
37425 MCCLEAN, ROBERT, 26 GREENE DR., BRAMPTON, ONT L6V 2R6 CAN
37426 JOHNSON, ADELE, 218 MUIR CRES NW., MEDICINE HAT, ALB T1A 6W5 CAN
37427 BERTRAND, FAY, 3094 E 43 AVE., VANCOUVER, BC V5R 2Z6 CAN
37428 LEMIRE, MICHEL, 6384 AVE DE CHATEAUBRIAND., MONTREAL, QUE H2S 2N4 CAN
37429 POWER FINLAY, MME A, 107 BOUL HENRI BOURASSA Q., MONTREAL, QUE H3L 1M9 CAN
37430 GILISSEN, LEON, 1485 RTE 138., HUNTINGDON, QUE J0S 1H0 CAN
37431 CARMODY, TOM, 9TH LINE RD., CARLSBAD SPRINGS, ONT K0A 1K0 CAN
37432 TREMBLAY, JEAN, 5242 CINDY LN., BURLINGTON, ONT L7L 3Y2 CAN
37433 PACILLI, MRS D, 20 SHALLMAR BLVD, APT 411., TORONTO, ONT M5N 1J5 CAN
37434 DAVEY, MYRA, 72 BROOMFIELD DR., SCARBOROUGH, ONT M1S 2W1 CAN
37435 DUCK, WILLIAM, 82 DIVADALE DR., TORONTO, ONT M4G 2P2 CAN
37436 SUTTON, ROD, 845 BEATRICE CRES., SUDBURY, ONT P3A 3E6 CAN
37437 HEADLAND, RONALD, 76 FIFTH AVE., POINTE CLAIRE, QUE H9S 5E1 CAN
37438 CARLSON, PHYLLIS, BOX 99., DARLINGFORD, MAN R0G 0L0 CAN
37439 MCAULEY-SMITH, KAREN, RR#1., HUNTSVILLE, ONT P0A 1K0 CAN
37440 WAGNER, JUDY, #1 MERRYWOOD CRES., SHERWOOD PARK, ALB T8A 0M8 CAN
37441 WILCOX, DOROTHY, 2544 SANDRA AVE., NORTH BAY, ONT P1B 7W8 CAN
37442 MCMILLAN, J., 3927 CHINA CREEK RD., PORT ALBERNI, BC V9Y 1R6 CAN
37443 MCMILLAN, J., 3927 CHINA CREEK RD,, PORT ALBERNI, BC V9Y 1R6 CAN
37444 BAIRD, GAYLE, 3846 SAANICH RD., VICTORIA, BC V8X 3Y9 CAN
37445 JENKINSON, JEAN, 3099 DEPARTURE BAY RD., NANAIMO, BC V9T 1B6 CAN
37446 LOUDEN, JANET, 7916-145 STREET., EDMONTON, ALB T5R 0S6 CAN
37447 DALGLISH, MISS B, 501-420 LINDEN AVE., VICTORIA, BC V8V 4G3 CAN
37448 CLINKER, ERNEST, 18 WILSON ST – BOX 1107., UXBRIDGE, ONT L0C 1K0 CAN
37449 BROWN, DAVID, 42 CAYLEY ST., DUNDAS, ONT L9H 2E7 CAN
37450 HALE, GEORGE, RR#2., WATERVILLE, NS B0P 1V0 CAN
37451 MACDONALD, MR J, 1099 CHECKERS RD., OTTAWA, ONT K2C 2S5 CAN
37452 OSACHOFF, LESLEY, BOX 461., REVELSTOKE, BC V0E 2S0 CAN
37453 CHIBI, DIANE, 4025 NOOTKA ST., VANCOUVER, BC V5R 2E1 CAN
37454 GABINIEWICZ, BEAU, 426 ALBERTA ST., NEW WESTMINSTER, BC V3L 3J7 CAN
37455 RIEDSTRA, LUTZEN, 24 ST ANDREW ST., STRATFORD, ONT N5A 1A3 CAN
37456 PORTER, BRIAN, #211 – 1435 NELSON ST., VANCOUVER, BC V6G 2Z3 CAN
37457 BURNS, BARRIE, 12 CARR CRES., KANATA, ONT K2K 1K4 CAN
37458 WILSON, DONNA, 18 RUTLEY ST., REGINA, SASK S4R 5Y6 CAN
37459 MACLEOD, JAMES, 4148 PRINCESS ST., REGINA, SAS S4S 3N3 CAN
37460 HODGSON, WILLIAM, 54 FOLKESTONE CT., FREDERICTON, NB E3B 4V1 CAN
37461 STEVENSON, ADRIENNE, 238 FAIRCREST RD., OTTAWA, ONT K1H 5E1 CAN
37462 WESTBURY, ROBERT, 4012 COMANCHE RD NW., CALGARY, ALTA T2L 0N8 CAN
37463 MCKINNON, D, 812 SILVERSTONE AVE., WINNIPEG, MB R3T 2W6 CAN
37464 KLOHN, JEAN, 15816 – 106 AVE., EDMONTON, ALB T5P 0W5 CAN
37465 GLEN, WILLIAM, RURAL ROUTE NO 1., BONSHAW, PEI C0A 1C0 CAN
37466 COOK, CHARLES, 46 KING STREET., TILLSONBURG, ONT N4G 3G7 CAN
37467 ROMULD, MRS M, 35 EASTBROOK WAY., BROOKS, ALB T1R 0H7 CAN
37468 FRIE, DAWN, 667 BRIGHTSAND CRES., SASKATOON, SK S7J 4Y7 CAN
37469 DONALD, GARY, 404 MCNEILLY RD., FRUITLAND, ONT L0R 1L0 CAN
37470 JAMIESON, JAMIE, 2876 S 46TH ST., MILWAUKEE, WI 53219 USA
37471 HOLMES, JAMES, 90 JUNE DR., ORILLIA, ONT L3V 3R1 CAN
37472 URBATSCH, HARLEY, 736 S CENTRAL ST., FOREST CITY, IA 50436 USA
37473 MOODY, JOHN, 644 WESTON DR., OTTAWA, ONT K1G 1V8 CAN
37474 LIVINGSTONE, DAWN, 49 HEWSON CRES., GEORGETOWN, ONT L7G 2P1 CAN
37475 MONTAMBAULT, ERIC, 1335 MONTARVILLE., ST BRUNO, QUE J3V 3T3 CAN
37476 HUDSON, HEATHER, BOX 135., LEFROY, ONT L0L 1W0 CAN
37477 EVERINGHAM, ERNEST, BOX 19, RR4., ROSENEATH, ONT K0K 2X0 CAN
37478 SAUNDERSON, MS L, 602 – 270 MOHAWK RD E., HAMILTON, ONT L9A 2H9 CAN
37479 DURAND, MRS J, 39 CHESTNUT ST., MARLBOROUGH, MA 01752 USA
37480 STEELE, JOHN, 61 AGASSIZ DR., WINNIPEG, MAN R3T 2K9 CAN
37481 RIEBERGER, KATHY, SS#1 SITE 19-63., CRANBROOK, BC V1C 4H4 CAN
37482 KELLY, DENNIS, 488 WOODLAND AVE., OTTAWA, ONT K2B 5E5 CAN
37483 WESTON, BEV, BOX 306., LUMSDEN, SAS S0G 3C0 CAN
37484 SMITH, GLADYS, 207 TWILLINGATE RD., CAMPBELL RIVER, BC V9W 1V1 CAN
37485 DEMPSEY, RON, A506 – 715 DON MILLS RD., DON MILLS, ONT M3C 1S4 CAN
37486 WEBSTER, BRUCE, 12270 WOOD AVE., MONTREAL, QUE H4K 2B9 CAN
37487 BROWN, EVELYN, 3024 – 14TH AVE SW., CALGARY, ALB T3C 0X1 CAN
37488 KIRBY, MR R, 396 DARALEA HEIGHTS., MISSISSAUGA, ONT L5A 3H6 CAN
37489 JAMIESON, MARY, BOX 351., PUGWASH, NS B0K 1L0 CAN
37490 BROWN, NANCY, 311 ELGIN ST., SARNIA, ONT N7T 5B5 CAN

37491 RAMSAY, DOUGLAS, 3314 WESTMINSTER RD., REGINA, SAS S4V 0S4 CAN
37492 RUDDELL, MS J, 60 MAIN ST NORTH., GEORGETOWN, ONT L7G 3H3 CAN
37493 BERG, AUDREY, 6979 JASPER ST., POWELL RIVER, BC V8A 1N4 CAN
37494 WINTLE, MRS R, 425 PARKVIEW DR., KINGSTON, ONT K7M 4B4 CAN
37495 CORBY, DENIS, 1782 ADANAC ST., VICTORIA, BC V8R 2C5 CAN
37496 WILSON, LENNINE, RR#2., PUSLINCH, ONT N0B 2J0 CAN
37497 ST CLAIR, MAREE, PO BOX 115., STRATHFIELDSAYE, VIC 3551 AUS
37498 LOUDON, MR R, 77 OLINDA GVE., MOUNT NELSON, TAS 7007 AUS
37499 LOGAN, BARBARA, 5038 MANSON AVE., POWELL RIVER, BC V8A 3N9 CAN
37500 THOMPSON, LYNETTE, PO BOX 38., WOODFORD, NSW 2778 AUS
37501 FREITAS, CAROLE, 15600 CANON DR., LOS GATOS, CA 95030 USA
37502 FISHER-APONTE, HELEN, 1901 CHERRY ST., DENVER, CO 80220 USA
37503 SMITH, PATRICIA, 1224 ELFORD CT., GROSSE POINTE WOODS, MI 48236 USA
37504 PELLING, DONALD, 6723 LANDERWOOD LN., SAN JOSE, CA 95120 USA
37505 WADHAM, AMBROSE, 618 N PASADENA AVE., GLENDORA, CA 91740 USA
37506 CHARLSON, SHARON, 21602 S LANCE CT., BEAVER CREEK, OR 97004 USA
37507 O'GUIN-RUSH, RANDY, 401 CATTELL ST., EASTON, PA 18042 USA
37508 JOSEPH, JOAN, 116 PEMBERTON ST #1., PHILADELPHIA, PA 19147 USA
37509 FORSYTHE, W, BOX 1299., ELLENSBURG, WA 98926 USA
37510 ANDERSON, PAMELA, 6530 OFFSHORE DR., MADISON, WI 53705 USA
37511 HAYES, ELIZABETH, 3109 N DOUGLAS AVE., LOVELAND, CO 80538 USA
37512 MONTEATH, PATRICIA, 15 FAIRWAY LN., PLEASANTON, CA 94566 USA
37513 ROHLOFF, HOWARD, 2324 RIDGE RD., NORTH HAVEN, CT 06473 USA
37514 YOUNG, EVELYN, 2840 PIONEERS BLV., LINCOLN, NE 68502 USA
37515 FORTIER, ALBERT, 90 CRAFTSLAND RD., CHESTNUT HILL, MA 02167 USA
37516 RYAN, MRS J, 1018 — 172 AVE NE., BELLEVUE, WA 98008 USA
37517 STOBIE, DAVID, 8821 CEDAR., PRAIRIE VILLAGE, KS 66207 USA
37518 TOPLIFF, MRS F, 5963 HELM RD., DULUTH, MN 55811 USA
37519 DI IORIO, ELLEN, 521 CUMBERLAND ST., WESTFIELD, NJ 07090 USA
37520 HART, HERBERT, 5248 N LECLAIRE AVE., CHICAGO, IL 60630 USA
37521 DERWIN, DAVID, 95 IDYLWOOD AVE., WATERBURY, CT 06705 USA
37522 CORCORAN, SANDRA, PO BOX 492., AURORA, OR 97002 USA
37523 LAUDERDALE, JILL, 405 NESTLE AVE., RESEDA, CA 91335 USA
37524 WENGER, MARJORIE, 3178 MEADOWBROOK DR., CONCORD, CA 94519 USA
37525 GRUNDY, RICHARD, 8905 LINTON LN., ALEXANDRIA, VA 22308 USA
37526 GLEESON, VINCENT, 812D HARDY SPRINGS CIR., MCALESTER, OK 74501 USA
37527 JEFFRIES, STEVEN, 4800 ERIE ST., COLLEGE PARK, MD 20740 USA
37528 HARPER, WILLIAM, 3770 E CLARENCE RD — ROUTE 5., HARRISON, MI 48625 USA
37529 CAVANAUH, MICHAEL, 1851 W 11TH PL., LOS ANGELES, CA 90006 USA
37530 KILDUFF, CHRISTI, 3416 ECHO SPRINGS RD., LAFAYETTE, CA 94549 USA
37531 BATTEN, GORDON, N10435 2ND AVE., CAMP DOUGLAS, WI 54618 USA
37532 SCHAEFER, JEAN, 3913 WOODTHRUSH DR., CINCINNATI, OH 45251 USA
37533 CLARK, AUBREY, PO BOX 284., HALLETTSVILLE, TX 77964 USA
37534 BAKEWELL, DAVID, 4728 N 15TH ST, APT 109., PHOENIX, AZ 85014 USA
37535 SCHOENEMAN, MARCELLE, 3174 SOUTH 57TH ST., MILWAUKEE, WI 53219 USA
37536 PAGE, MARY LEE, 2534 CAMPCREEK CIR SE., HUNTSVILLE, AL 35803 USA
37537 GALLEN, JAMES, 2312 MAYBROOK LN., ST LOUIS, MO 63122 USA
37538 LUDLOW, CAROL, 995 E 1050 N., BOUNTIFUL, UT 84010 USA
37539 FARRIS, EDITH, 3745 WOODHURST DR., COVINA, CA 91724 USA
37540 BUCKLEY, WILLIAM, 9 FOX HOLLOW., DERRY, NH 03038 USA
37541 FRISBIE, DOROTHY, 2315 PATTERSON RD., ESCONDIDO, CA 92027 USA
37542 BENTZ, JOHN, 13139 OLD WEST AVE., SAN DIEGO, CA 92129 USA
37543 SAVAGE, MR A, 1770 CAROL CT., DEERFIELD, IL 60015 USA
37544 HALE, MRS C, 309 SUMMIT AVE., SYRACUSE, NY 13207 USA
37545 GREENLEE, JANET, 2514 EAST HAYES., DAVENPORT, IA 52803 USA
37546 MILLINGTON, ELIZABETH, 66 MAIDSTONE PL., VINCENTOWN, NJ 08088 USA
37547 NIELSEN, FRANK, 5228 WEST VIRGINIA AVE., PHOENIX, AZ 85035 USA
37548 DICKEN, LILLIAN, 1553 W 222ND ST., TORRANCE, CA 90501 USA
37549 GARLAND, ANN, 17322 GLASGOW CIR., YORBA LINDA, CA 92686 USA
37550 FRASE, ROSALIE, RT 2 BOX 285., PRESTON, MD 21655 USA
37551 GIBSON, ELINOR, PO BOX 387., ELDORADO, CA 95623 USA
37552 STORER, MRS C, 45 GREENWOOD AVE., NARRAWEENA, NSW 2099 AUS
37553 JOHNSON, GRAHAM, 14 ADRIAN PL., GREYSTANES, NSW 2145 AUS
37554 BROWNE, CAROL, 19 TOORAK PARK AVE., MERMAID WATERS, QLD 4218 AUS
37555 CHAMBERS, MRS G, 'GLENORIA'., GULARGAMBONE, NSW 2828 AUS
37556 BEATTIE, ROSS, 21 HONITON AVE EAST., CARLINGFORD, NSW 2118 AUS
37557 DURDEN, MR J, RSD TYNTYNDER., VIA SWAN HILL, VIC 3585 AUS
37558 BURSTALL, MYRA, PO BOX 36., UNDERBOOL, VIC 3509 AUS
37559 MITCHELL, FRANK, 102 GOODWIN ST., LYNEHAM, ACT 2602 AUS
37560 ARTHUR, PATRICIA, 45 FISHER RD., THORNESIDE, QLD 4158 AUS
37561 VINCENT, MRS E, PO BOX 111., PICTON, NSW 2571 AUS
37562 FORTUNE, MRS L, 9800 BOLSA AVE #26., WESTMINSTER, CA 92683 USA

37563 WILKEN, MICHAEL, 4615 CUMING ST., OMAHA, NE 68132 USA
37564 PENROSE, CHARLES, RT #5 BOX #409., POTSDAM, NY 13676 USA
37565 SANDOVAL, CAROL, 233 PRENTICE DR., NEW CARLISLE, OH 45344 USA
37566 WILKEY, DUNCAN, 108 MIDDLE RD., PORTSMOUTH, RI 02871 USA
37567 DILELLO, ELEANORE, 4 TOD RD., NORWALIK, CT 06851 USA
37568 BARNES, ROBERT, 68 COVINGTON RD., ROCHESTER, NY 14617 USA
37569 SEVREN, MARION, 1119 VILLAGE ONE., CAMARILLO, CA 93012 USA
37570 VORE, JEAN, 1524 N 7TH ST., GRAND JUNCTION, CO 81501 USA
37571 THOMPSON, WILLIAM, 37 WHITEWATER DR., CORONA DEL MAR, CA 92625 USA
37572 BOEGEHOLD, JOHN, 4940 WOODMAN AVE #6., SHERMAN OAKS, CA 91423 USA
37573 MITCHEL, FRANK, 5808 N 81ST ST., SCOTTSDALE, AZ 85250 USA
37574 SWEENEY, NEIL, 20248 LABRADOR ST., CHATSWORTH, CA 91311 USA
37575 HARRISON, JOHN, 25115 KIRBY ST #551., HEMET, CA 92343 USA
37576 PERRY, SUSIE, PO BOX 7294., LAGUNA NIGUEL, CA 92677 USA
37577 SHONK, CLARA, 128 MAPLE HILL., HARTFORD, MI 49057 USA
37578 JOHNSEN, MS TERRY, 2088 IDA DR., TROY, MI 48083 USA
37579 KIRKHAM, DONALD, 75 MORNING DEW LN., STRATFORD, CT 06497 USA
37580 MARTIN, MR J, 61 EAST FIFTH ST., LONDON, OH 43140 USA
37581 HATCH, ROBERT, 125 N LAYTON DR., LOS ANGELES, CA 90049 USA
37582 SCHNEIDER, KAREN, 3306 EAST MENLO AVE., FRESNO, CA 93710 USA
37583 WILLS-HENRY, KAREN., 14 'T' STREET N.E. #1., WASHINGTON, DC 20002 USA
37584 GUNNELL, JOAN, RT 2 BOX 144., MONETA, VA 24121 USA
37585 MILLER, LOCKE, 2810-K CARRIAGE DR., WINSTON-SALEM, NC 27106 USA
37586 ELVEY, HAZEL, 415 LA FONDA AVE., SANTA CRUZ, CA 95065 USA
37587 MONTOYA, LEIGH, BOX 26748., PRESCOTT VALLEY, AZ 86312 USA
37588 BIDWELL, FRANK, 1755 TRINITY AVE, APT 1., WALNUT CREEK, CA 94596 USA
37589 BIER, NANCY, 4021 VIA PICAPOSTE., PALOS VERDES EST, CA 90274 USA
37590 MARSH, ELIZABETH, 8625 PINECLIFF DR., FREDERICK, MD 21701 USA
37591 WHITBECK, ALICE, 2456 BAYVIEW HTS DR., LOS OSOS, CA 93402 USA
37592 DIXON, WINIFRED, 1350 WALENTA DR., MOSCOW, ID 83843 USA
37593 BEYER, EDWARD, 255 KEEL WAY., OSPREY, FL 34229 USA
37594 LOWNDS, ROSEMARIE, 65 HILL ST., SUFFIELD, CT 06078 USA
37595 MARRINER, HARRY, AA 100510., BOGOTA, COLOMBIA
37596 SEIDELMAN, JAMES, 1203 N SWEETZER AVE #107., W HOLLYWOOD, CA 90069 USA
37597 DEBOK, ELENE, 41 BLACKHAWK DR., THORNTON, IL 60476 USA
37598 ROYSTON, BASIL, 750 SEQUOIA DR., MILPITAS, CA 95035 USA
37599 NEELAND, JOHN, 2 NW 41 TERRACE., KANSAS CITY, MO 64116 USA
37600 GOTTIER, LEO, 2301 WEST 59TH PL., DENVER, CO 80221 USA
37601 GRAESER, HELEN, 54 N OCEAN AVE., CENTER MORICHES, NY 11934 USA
37602 BROMLEY, MICHAEL, 1030 E MANHATTON DR., TEMPE, AZ 85282 USA
37603 WINDER, ROBERT, PO BOX 21., EAST WATERFORD, PA 17021 USA
37604 TAYLOR, JULIA, 9481 CHADBURN PL., GAITHERSBURG, MD 20879 USA
37605 PORTER, JUNE, 14704 CAYO CT., RANCHO MURICTA, CA 95683 USA
37606 NOVAK, STEVEN, 1834 TAYLOR AVE., FT WASHINGTON, MD 20744 USA
37607 MARQUARDT, STEVEN, 200 E 10 STREET., JULESBURG, CO 80737 USA
37608 TILLEY, MOLLIE, 67 CHURCH ST., CHURCH GRESLEY, STS DE11 9NP ENG
37609 ANDREWS, JOHN, UNIVERSITY LIBRARY, STOCKER RD., EXETER, DEV EX4 4PT ENG
37610 STEDMAN, JOHN, 5 MIDDLE ST, BROCKHAM GREEN., BETCHWORTH, SRY RH3 7JT ENG
37611 DEAN, JEAN, 15 ELMSWOOD CL, KINGSDOWN., SWINDON, WIL ENG
37612 LAMBERT, MR & MRS, 47 CHESTERFIELD RD., CAMBRIDGE, CAMBS CB4 1LN ENG
37613 GREGSON, BARBARA, 5 ULLSWATER RD., CONGLETON, CHS CW12 4LX ENG
37614 BROTHERWOOD, BETTY, 1 SEYMOUR RD., CHIPPENHAM, WILTS SN15 3NH ENG
37615 WESTBROOK, TONY, 5 NEWLANDS., NORTHALLERTON, NRY DL6 1SJ ENG
37616 MITCHELL, SUSAN, 7 PARK GATE, MOUNT AVE., EALING, LND W5 1PX ENG
37617 TAMES, KENNETH, 21 HOWARD RD., REIGATE, SRY RH2 7JE ENG
37618 BARKER, DAVID, 47 SAYES CRT., ADDLESTONE, SRY KT15 1NA ENG
37619 MACKENZIE, MRS G, 78 STEADE RD., SHEFFIELD, YKS S7 1DU ENG
37620 HEWISON, MRS J, 148 LYMINGTON AVE., LEIGH ON SEA, ESS S59 2AN ENG
37621 DAWSON, JEAN, 273 QUEENS RD., HALIFAX, WRY HX1 4NS ENG
37622 JOHNSON, MR D, 18 MOFFAT RD., CHRISTCHURCH, DOR BH23 1HQ ENG
37623 WRIGHT-NOOTH, MR P, 7 NORMAN DR., HATFIELD, YKS DN7 6AQ ENG
37624 LASHBROOK, GEORGE, 32 WINCHESTER ST., TAUNTON, SOM TA1 1Q6 ENG
37625 VOCE, ALAN, 5 CHURCH PATH., HALBERTON, TIVERTON, DEV EX16 7AT ENG
37626 STOTT, NEVILLE, 32 LANDSWOOD PARK, HARTFORD., NORTHWICH, CHS CW8 1NF ENG
37627 SNELLING, MANDY, 2 ROSELEIGH COTTAGES, HOLLAND LN., OXTED, SRY RH8 9AR ENG
37628 DICKEY, MARGARET, DOVE COTTAGE, OUTWOODS LN., ANSLOW, STS DE13 0AB ENG
37629 SENDALL, ANTONY, 2 CROWN OFFICE ROW., TEMPLE, LND EC4Y 7HJ ENG
37630 BALLANTYNE, ROBERT, 61 COPSE AVE., FARNHAM, SRY GU9 9DZ ENG
37631 THOMSON, IAN, 143 POTTINGFIELD RD., RYE, SSX TN31 7BW ENG
37632 SANDERS, JEAN, 59 HEATHER RD., WEST MIDLANDS, WS3 2QA ENG
37633 WHYMAN, MARK, 7 ROCKWOOD CL., GUISBOROUGH, TS14 7BG ENG
37634 SAUNDERS, PAT, 24 WESTGATE., CHICHESTER, W. SSX PO19 3EU ENG

37635 BRACK, MARY, MOSS HOUSE, RICHMOND RD., SHERBORNE, DOR DT9 3HL ENG
37636 FORSYTHE, IAN, 7 WYNCHURCH RD., BELFAST, BT6 0JH N IRELAND
37637 FEAKES, GERALD, CHURCH VIEW CHAPEL LN., HOUGHTON, HUNT, CAM PE17 2AY ENG
37638 HAMILTON, DENIS, 13A GRANGE MEWS, GRANGE RD., EASTBOURNE, SSX BN21 4EU ENG
37639 LONGBOTTOM, JOHN, 75 CHATSWORTH RD., PUPSEY, WRY LS28 8JX ENG
37640 COWLING, JAMES, 38 BROAD ST., SYSTON, LEICS LE7 8GH ENG
37641 SWIGGS, JOHN, PINEHAVEN DRIVING LN., PAR, CON PL24 2RH ENG
37642 WHITEMAN, MR N, 1 BEACON HILL HSE, COURT RD., NEWTON FERRERS, DEV PL8 1DB ENG
37643 BOOTH, J, 22 NEWLANDS RD., ST HELENS, WA11 9AU ENG
37644 WICKHAM, MR K, 30 MANOR WAY., PETTS WOOD, KEN BR5 1NW ENG
37645 LUDLOW, MR D., THE ORCHARD, PEMBURY RD., TUNBRIDGE WELLS, KEN TN2 4ND ENG
37646 STOWELL, JOHN, 'BELMONT' THE STREET., GODMERSHAM, KENT CT4 7DU ENG
37647 THOMAS, JOAN, 10 DELL RISE, PARK ST., ST ALBANS, HERTS AL2 2QJ ENG
37648 LAVENDER, CHARLES, 24 FAIRLANDS RD., GUILDFORD, SRY GU3 3JB ENG
37649 GLOVER, D.R., 34 GLEBELANDS RD., KNUTSFORD, CHS WA16 9DZ ENG
37650 HOLDEN, JOHN, 14 GOODWOOD CL., BURGHFIELD COMMON, BERKS RG7 3EZ ENG
37651 PRISMALL, PETER, 23 HILLCREST RD., PURLEY, SURREY CR8 2JF ENG
37652 GUTTERIDGE, JOAN, 9 QUEENS COTTAGES., READING, BRK RG1 4BE ENG
37653 HORA, SUSAN, 51 EASTERN AVE., READING, BRK RG1 5SQ ENG
37654 LONG, BERYL, HIGHLANDS, KINGS RD., BERKHAMSTED, HERTS HP4 3BP ENG
37655 FORNO, JUDY, 92 CROCKFORD PARK RD., ADDLESTONE, SRY KT15 2LR ENG
37656 LEFLEY, AUDREY, 7 RAMSHOLT CL., NORTH WALTHAM, HANTS RG25 2DG ENG
37657 CROUCHMAN, TED, 95 ALLENBY RD., SOUTHALL, MDX UB1 2EZ ENG
37658 DURHAM, JOHN, 11 BRAESIDE PK., BALLOCH., INVERNESS, INV IV1 2HL SCOTLAND
37659 CHRISTIE, JEAN, SEAHAVEN, ALBERT ST., NAIRN, IV12 4HF SCOTLAND
37660 UPEX, MRS D, 'HIGHTIME', PIGHTLE WAY., WALTON ON NAZE, ESS CO14 8UJ ENG
37661 JACKSON, MARTIN, 7 LLYS-Y-BERLLAN., HOLYWELL, CWD CH8 7QZ WALES
37662 TOWNSEND, JOYCE, 25 RUSSELL DR., MALVERN, WOR WR14 2LE ENG
37663 BOORMAN, ELIZABETH, 59 POPLAR WAY., BARKINGSIDE, ESS IG6 1EN ENG
37664 CROSS, WILLIAM, 6 KING HENRYS DR., ROCHFORD, ESS SS4 1HY ENG
37665 SCOLES, COLIN, 99 NEW DOVER RD., CANTERBURY, KENT CT1 3ED ENG
37666 GOULD, ALLAN, PLACE FARM, GLEMSFORD., SUDBURY, SFK CO10 7QF ENG
37667 METCALFE, PETER, 27 BRUSHWOOD AVE., FLINT, CLWYD CH6 5TY WALES
37668 CHESTER, BRENDA, 110 SWISS AVE., CHELMSFORD, ESS CM1 2AF ENG
37669 SHERWOOD, RUTH, 92 BROADWAY., LLANBLETHIAN, S. GLAM CF7 7EY WALES
37670 MOORE, NORAH, 7 WEALD WAY., CATERHAM, SRY CR3 6EL ENG
37671 GWILLIM, DAVID, PO 345., LAE, PAPUA NEW GUINEA
37672 NETCOTT, MRS D, ADDINGTON HOUSE, THE VILLAGE., BURRINGTON, BS18 7AD ENG
37673 THORNTON, ROY, 2 ELEANOR PL, HALL PK., GT BARTON, SFK IP31 2TQ ENG
37674 CASSEY, MICHAEL, 69 CEDAR WALK., HEMEL HEMPSTEAD, HERTS HP3 9ED ENG
37675 MURFIN, SUE, 114 DERBY RD., MELBOURNE, DBY DE7 1FL ENG
37676 GRANNUM, GUY, TASMA, OLD SEAVIEW LN., SEAVIEW, IOW PO34 5BJ ENG
37677 BONN, DAVID, 15 DUMARESQ ST., DICKSON, ACT 2602 AUS
37678 MCCAULEY, MALACHY, 55 MANORDENE RD., THAMESMEAD, LND SE28 8ET ENG
37679 VARLEY, SUSAN, 12 SILVER BIRCH AVE., WYKE, WRY BD12 9EP ENG
37680 TONKIN, MISS N, 27 HIGHERTOWN., TRURO, CON TR1 3QE ENG
37681 BUTLER, NORA, 9 HIGH ST., KIMBOLTON, PE18 0HB ENG
37682 LLOYD, VIVIEN, POOL GRANGE, POOL QUAY., WELSHPOOL, POWYS SY21 9JU WALES
37683 KAUDELA OSORIO, BARBARA, 67 HEYSHAM DR., WATFORD, HERTS WD1 6YH ENG
37684 SMITH, FRANK, 21 LADY EDITHS PARK., SCARBOROUGH, YKS YO12 5PB ENG
37685 POSTLE, MRS H, 18 WESTMORELAND AVE., WELLING, KENT DA16 2QD ENG
37686 BARRY, ANTHONY, 1 HAWKWOOD LN., CHISLEHURST, KEN BR7 5PW ENG
37687 STEVENS, MS M, 11 KINGSHILL CL., MALVERN, WOR WR14 2BP ENG
37688 MORGAN, ERIC, 38 MEADWAY DR., HORSELL, WOKING GU21 4TD ENG
37689 LINGLEY, ADAM, 21 BECK LN, ST FAITHS., NORWICH, NFK NR10 3LD ENG
37690 LAUDER, MRS J, 20 SUTHERLAND CL., BARNET, HRT EN5 2JL ENG
37691 HIGHAM, ANNE, 21 LINDSEY ST., EPPING, ESS CM16 6RB ENG
37692 RUSSELL, ALAN, 139 WESTWICK RD., BILBOROUGH, NTT NG8 4HB ENG
37693 HAMMOND, BRIAN, 7 PORTHMEOR RD., HOLMBUSH, ST AUSTELL, CON PL25 3LT ENG
37694 PHILLIPS, MR L, 11 HENFIELD CL., GORING BY SEA, W SSX BN12 6BE ENG
37695 EVANS, ROGER, CHEZ NOUS, SOUTH VIEW RD., LONG LAWFORD, WAR CV23 9BP ENG
37696 BINYON, JAMES, 15 COVERT RD, NORTHCHURCH., BERKHAMPSTED, HRT HP4 3RR ENG
37697 JOHNSON, BRIAN, 3 LINKSWAY CL., STOCKPORT, CHS SK4 4AR ENG
37698 BUCKWELL, PAUL, 9 THE CRESCENT., SOUTHWICK, SSX BN42 4LB ENG
37699 MERRICK, JOANNA, 23 RAVEN LN., BILLERICAY, CM12 0JB ENG
37700 CARR, ROY, 11 NETTLEFOLD HSE, 367 BETHNAL GREEN RD., LONDON, MDX E2 0AZ ENG
37701 RANDALL, BARRIE, 43 BIRCH RD., BURGHFIELD COMMON, BRK RG7 3LU ENG
37702 NEAVE, DAVID, 'CROPTHORNE' 1E VERNON DR., HAREFIELD, MDX UB9 6EG ENG
37703 BENNETT, MR R, 16 GRAYSHOTT LAURELS., LINDFORD, HANTS GU35 0QB ENG
37704 GALLOWAY, RON, 15 TORVER CL., NEWCASTLE UPON TYNE, NE13 7HJ ENG
37705 MORGAN-SMITH, DENISE, 3 COAST RD., PEVENSEY BAY, SSX BN24 6AG ENG
37706 LEE, MONICA, CAMELOT CARAVAN PARK., LONGTOWN, CUL CA6 5SZ ENG

37707 FISHPOOL, JOHN, 19 DERING RD., HERNE BAY, KENT CT6 5RD ENG
37708 BEDFORD, MR J, 14 CASTLE PARK., BELFAST, ANT BT15 5FF N IRELAND
37709 BENNETT, JONE, 106 BISHOPS MANS, BISHOPS PK RD., LONDON, SW6 6DY ENG
37710 DAVIES, ANNE, 11 LOWTHER DR., GARFORTH, YORKS LS25 1EW ENG
37711 MITCHELL, RAYMOND, 6 ANSCOMB GDNS., NEWCASTLE ON TYNE, NBL NE7 7BB ENG
37712 PORRETT, MISS S, 4 EMANUEL HSE, 18 ROCHESTER ROW., LONDON, SW1P 1BS ENG
37713 WILSON, RICHARD, HUCKHAM LODGE SHROPHAM., ATTLEBOROUGH, NFK NR17 1ED ENG
37714 PAINE, MR D, 5 FRESHNEY WAY., BOSTON, LINCS PE21 7PZ ENG
37715 WAGER, MRS B, 38 LOOSEN DR., MAIDENHEAD, BERKS SL6 3UT ENG
37716 GREEN, ELIZABETH, 31 CASTLETHORPE RD., HANSLOPE, BKM MK19 7HQ ENG
37717 CARLOW, DR JOHN, 19 ELMSLEIGH GDNS., BASSETT, HAM SO2 3GE ENG
37718 FISHER, MR M, 208 STOUGHTON RD., GUILDFORD, SRY GU2 6PN ENG
37719 WALSH, MRS H, 51 WHITE COTTAGE CL., FARNHAM, SURREY GU9 0NL ENG
37720 TURNER, ALAN, BANC-Y-FELIN, ABERBECHAN., NEWTOWN, SY16 3AW ENG
37721 FRENCH, OLIVIA, 15 LAVENDER RD, LAVENDER QUAY., ROTHERHITHE, LND SE16 1DZ ENG
37722 WHITE, MR D, HIGH ONN FARM., CHURCH EATON, STS ST20 0AX ENG
37723 WATKINS, BRENDA, 67 TOWNLEY RD., BEXLEYHEATH, KEN DA6 7HW ENG
37724 SLEMMINGS, BARRY, 34 PRETORIA RD., ROMFORD, RM7 7AS ENG
37725 COOMBER, JOHN, 12 HOLLINGWORTH WAY., WESTERHAM, KEN TN16 1BS ENG
37726 WILLIAMS, CELIA, 36 NAPIER RD., HAMWORTHY, DOR BH15 4NA ENG
37727 NICHOLSON, MR D, 10 THORNFIELD RD., LINTHORPE, CLE TS5 5LA ENG
37728 BILLINGS, INGRID, 85 THE STREET., LATCHINGDON, ESS CM3 6JP ENG
37729 HUDSON, VALDA, 6 INGLE DELL., CAMBERLEY, SRY GU15 2LP ENG
37730 WALDEN, D., 2 MAISON DE BAS COT., MAISON DE BAS RD., VALE GUERNSEY, CHI. UK
37731 CHATTERTON, MEREDITH, MARYVALE CATHERINE RD., BENFLEET, ESSEX SS7 1HY ENG
37732 URMS, MRS N, 4 BRISCOE ST., OLDHAM, LAN OL1 3RW ENG
37733 BURKINSHAW, MRS M, 2 FARLEY HSE, PORTLAND AVE., EXMOUTH, DEV EX8 2BS ENG
37734 SANDERSON, LOIS, 84 STRATHEARN RD., EDINBURGH, MLN EH9 2AF SCOTLAND
37735 GILLBERRY, GEORGE, 20 OLD ANCOTT RD, AMBROSDEN., BICESTER, OXF OX6 0LT ENG
37736 QUARMBY, RAYMOND, 12 ASHER REEDS., LANGTON GREEN, KEN TN3 0AL ENG
37737 STEWART, MS F, 90 MIDDLETON RD., LONDON, E8 4LN ENG
37738 NELDER, MARY, 33 CROWN ST., REDBOURN, HRT AL3 7JX ENG
37739 WAKELAM, MRS J, 5 MORESBY CL., WESTLEA, SWINDON, WIL SN5 7BX ENG
37740 CORNELIUS, JAMES, PSC BOX 3602/48 TFW HOSPITAL., APO, NY 09179 USA
37741 MURPHY, DEREK, ELGSTIEN 34., 4637 KRISTIANSAND, NORWAY
37742 HEMPSALL, JOHN, 114 BURRINGHAM RD., SCUNTHORPE, HUMBERSIDE DN17 2DE ENG
37743 MORRIS, GEOFFREY, 12 ST MICHAELS RD., BROXBOURNE, HRT EN10 7JL ENG
37744 RUSSELL, JIM, 11 RAILWAY COTS, REDESMOUTH., HEXHAM, NBL NE48 2ET ENG
37745 LEE-MAGEE, MR T, 17 LANGMANS, GOLDSWORTH PL., WOKING, SRY GU21 3QY ENG
37746 SMITH, JENNIFER, AVALON SWAN LN., EDENBRIDGE, KEN TN8 6BA ENG
37747 MEADEN, MARY, SPRINGFIELD COT, MORLEYS RD., WEALD, KEN TN14 6QY ENG
37748 BEESTON, MARION, 53 SUNNINGDALE DR., IRLAM, LAN M30 6NJ ENG
37749 CLEAVE, MARK, 11 CHANTRELL RD., WEST KIRBY, WIRRAL, CHS L48 9XR ENG
37750 MESTEL, LOUISE, 13 PRINCE EDWARDS RD., LEWES, SSX BN7 1BJ ENG
37751 RUSSELL, JOHN, 16 FIRWOOD GVE., ASHTON IN MAKERFIELD, GTR MAN WN4 9ND ENG
37752 DRURY, MS S, 19A OLD PARK RD., PALMERS GREEN, N13 4RG ENG
37753 READ, JOHN, 16 THORNCROFT., SAFFRON WALDEN, ESSEX CB10 2AZ ENG
37754 TOWN, AUDREY, 33 NEW LN., SKELMANTHORPE, WEST YORKS HD8 9EY ENG
37755 HARBINSON, ISOBEL, 7 RUSHYHILL RD., BALLYMACWARD, ANT BT28 3TA IRELAND
37756 MERRYWEATHER, ALAN, FRITHWOOD COTTAGE., BUSSAGE, GLS GL6 8AE ENG
37757 HOWELL, MR D, 28 MINCINGLAKE RD., STOKEHILL, DEV EX4 7EA ENG
37758 SKEPPER, DEREK, 87 KILN LN., ST HELENS, LAN WA10 6AZ ENG
37759 BARFIELD, RONALD, 14 BRUNSWICK ST., WALTHAMSTOW, LND E17 9NB ENG
37760 NIELD, MRS B, 41 MIDHURST GDNS., HILLINGDON, MDX UB10 9DN ENG
37761 JANES, RONALD, 85 WIGAN RD, WESTHEAD., LATHOM, LANCS L40 6HY ENG
37762 MOUNSEY, MS S, 57 ROMSEY RD., WINCHESTER, HAM SO22 5DE ENG
37763 WEBB, GERALD, 100 QUEENS CRES., CHIPPENHAM, WILTS SN14 0NP ENG
37764 SMITH, EARLE, 2 HAZEL DR., HORRINGER, SFK IP29 5ST ENG
37765 FEAKES, DAPHNE, 24 FORD GVE., LONDON, N21 3DN ENG
37766 HAMBLY, ALLEN, 645 NEWPORT RD., CARDIFF, CF3 8DB WALES
37767 BURGESS, ANNE, 21 WOODSIDE PL., FOCHABERS, MOR IV32 7HE SCOTLAND
37768 DIXON, DR R, DEPT OF BIOMEDL SCIENCES., UNIV OF BRADFORD, WRY BD7 1DP ENG
37769 DUNCAN, ROBERT, 13 LEYLAND RD., RAINFORD, LAN WA11 8HF ENG
37770 BROWN, MRS Y, 43 ELMWOOD RD., CHATTENDEN, KENT ENG
37771 PARSONS, D., WILLOWBK., BRICKYARD LN., DRAKES BROUGHTON, WORC WR10 2AH ENG
37772 HARDY, MRS J, 2 MAPLE AVE., MILTON OF CAMPSIE, G65 8BB SCOTLAND
37773 WILLS, ALAN, 8 LANERCOST RD., LONDON, SW2 3DN ENG
37774 STEGEMAN, MARGARET, 17 QUARRY RD., RICHMOND, N YKS DL10 4BP ENG
37775 KNIGHTS, MS G., 3 EYSHAM CT, STATION RD., NEW BARNET, HERTS EN5 1PS ENG
37776 FRYATT, ELIZABETH, 42 MANOR GDNS., BUCKDEN, HUNT, CAM PE18 9TN ENG
37777 AMOS, DUNCAN, EWE COT, PRESTWICK MANOR FM., CHIDDINGFOLD, SRY GU8 4XS ENG
37778 WESTON, ROSE, THESLUM, TOWPATH., SHEPPERTON, MDX TW17 9LL ENG

37779 MCNICOL, PETER, 43 GRANGE PARK AVE., WILMSLOW, CHS SK9 4AL ENG
37780 BOWCHER, HEATHER, 15 ASHLEY WAY., SAWSTON, CAM CB2 4DY ENG
37781 MCCULLEY, BONNIE, 9809 N 56TH ST., SCOTTSDALE, AZ 85253 USA
37782 DECHANT, MS S, 3960 E GERMAN RD., KETTLE FALLS, WA 99141 USA
37783 ADAMS, MR W, 127 GREENBERRY DR., ELKVIEW, WV 25071 USA
37784 MOORE, DON, RR3 BOX 19., DELPHI, IN 46923 USA
37785 DOVE, GLENDA, 92 BLACKBERRY SCHOOL RD., YORK SPRINGS, PA 17372 USA
37786 GANT, CLIFFORD, 55441 FIRESTONE., LA QUINTA, CA 92253 USA
37787 SPRINGER, MILDRED, 256 PROSPECT VALLEY RD., WILLSEYVILLE, NY 13864 USA
37788 WHITE, BARBARA, 205 SOUTH OVID ST., ELSIE, MI 48831 USA
37789 MERCER, CHARLES, RT 2, BOX 150-A., ELLERBE, NC 28338 USA
37790 FUNSTON, ZELMA, 1808 W 21ST TERRACE., LAWRENCE, KS 66046 USA
37791 O'LOUGHLIN, GRACE, 191 OLEANDER WAY., INDIAN RIVER SHORES, FLA 32963 USA
37792 CALAMETTI, BARBARA, 19030 RIO VISTA DR., FAIRHOPE, AL 36532 USA
37793 WREGE, CHARLES, 23 WORTHINGTON ST., SPRING LAKE, NJ 07762 USA
37794 HALE, MARY, PO BOX 2823., DURHAM, NC 27705 USA
37795 RATLIFF, LUCY, 755 GREENVILLE AVE., GLENDALE, OHIO 45246 USA
37796 LOWERY, RICHARD, 4140 SO OAK., GASPER, WY 82601 USA
37797 KREHBIEL, BARBARA, 27 CIRCLE DR., CHARLESTON, IL 61920 USA
37798 REYNOLDS, JAMES, 4611 SO T CIRCLE., FORT SMITH, AR 72903 USA
37799 ERLICK, RALPH, 3830 SUPERIOR AVE., CINCINNATI, OH 45236 USA
37800 MCCOURT, DONALD, 7927 PRATHER RD., CENTRALIA, WA 98531 USA
37801 GRAHAM, STANLEY, 4518 FRANKLIN DR., VERNON, TX 76384 USA
37802 NIELSEN, H. EUGENE, 795 E 900 N., BOUNTIFUL, UT 84010 USA
37803 MELVILLE, MARTHA, PO BOX 343., ANNAPOLIS JCT, MD 20701 USA
37804 HILLMER, BONITA, 1606 WILLIAM AND MARY CMN., SOMERVILLE, NJ 08876 USA
37805 WEHR, DORIS, PO BOX 12., FARGO, ND 58107 USA
37806 BRIGGS, GEORGE, RD #1, BOX 401M., GREENWICH, NY 12834 USA
37807 WATSON, DR C, 98 CONSTITUTION ST., BRISTOL, RI 02809 USA
37808 BARTLETT, TED, 2922 N TROY ST., CHICAGO, IL 60618 USA
37809 WATKINS, AVIS, 8 GARDNER ST, APT 1., EXETER, NH 03833 USA
37810 TAGGETT, PAUL, 1616 S IVY TRAIL., BALDWINSVILLE, NY 13027 USA
37811 FIELD, CHARLES, 1763 ROGERS AVE., DOUGLAS, AZ 85607 USA
37812 MORROW, BETTY, RT 2, BOX 96 — BUTLER RD., TEAGUE, TX 75860 USA
37813 COOLEY, GEORGE, 920 ARLINGTON., LA GRANGE, IL 60525 USA
37814 QUANDT, WESLEY, STAR ROUTE BOX 23., BOURBON, MO 65441 USA
37815 CAYOU, ALVIN, 1804 AXIAL DR., LOVELAND, CO 80538 USA
37816 QUIRKE, TERENCE, 2310 JUNIPER CRT., GOLDEN, CO 80401 USA
37817 GREESON, DORIS, 7101 MALTA ST., SAN DIEGO, CA 92111 USA
37818 WEBB, CAROL, 91 BOW BOG RD., BOW, NH 03304 USA
37819 JACKSON, GEORGE, ROMANACH 306., RIO PIEDRAS, PR 00926 USA
37820 YOUNG, RONALD, 11415 MORNINGSIDE., MABELVALE, AR 72103 USA
37821 LABEREE, JANE, 11 LITTLEHALE RD., DURHAM, NH 03824 USA
37822 LIMON, BARBARA, 2123 RESERVOIR ST., LOS ANGELES, CA 90026 USA
37823 FULMER, BARBARA, 1 ASPEN TREE., IRVINE, CA 92715 USA
37824 LEE, VALORIE, 2500 N VAN DORN #227., ALEXANDRIA, VA 22302 USA
37825 FARLEY, LORIMER, 7990 SO HWY A1A., MELBOURNE BEACH, FL 32951 USA
37826 RICHARDSON, PATRICIA, 5022 TIERRA ANTIGUA DR., WHITTIER, CA 90601 USA
37827 MARLBOROUGH, MRS F, 31 GLENWOOD RD., WESTMOORS, DOR BH22 0EN ENG
37828 HAINSWORTH, FREDA, 68 MILTON AVE., WHISTON, MERSEY L35 2YB ENG
37829 SMART, MR R, 18 SOMERSET CL, GRANGE PK., LONG EATON, NTT NG10 2ET ENG
37830 STENNETT, MRS K, 17 BEMBRIDGE GDNS., LUTON, BED LU3 3SH ENG
37831 TURNER, MR R, 99 BRIDGE LN., BRAMHALL, CHS SK7 3AS ENG
37832 MANN, GEOFFREY, BAYTREES, BURNHAMS RD., BOOKHAM, SRY KT23 3AU ENG
37833 DOVEY, MRS J, 61 MALMAINS WAY., BECKENHAM, KENT BR3 2SB ENG
37834 MAYBURY, SARA, 18 CROFTERS GN., EUXTON, LANCS PR7 6LQ ENG
37835 HUNTER, MELVYN, 39 FIRST AVE., WELLINGBOROUGH, NTH NN8 3PT ENG
37836 ELMER, ROBERT, 93 CLIFTON RD., WOKINGHAM, BRK RG11 1NJ ENG
37837 QUARTERMAN, ALEC, 5 COTTESMORE., BRACKNELL, BERKS RG12 4YL ENG
37838 REYNOLDS, EDNA, 54 PARKHILL RD., BEXLEY, KEN DA5 1HY ENG
37839 BRAZIER, MRS I, 'DINLLEYN', VILLA RD., KEYWORTH, NTT NG12 5HD ENG
37840 BELL, ANGUS, 29 ELM RD NORTH., PRENTON, L42 9PB ENG
37841 RAY, MRS W, 228 HILLBURY RD., WARLINGHAM, SRY CR3 9TF ENG
37842 BOWYER, ROSEMARY, MOORFIELD, CAUSEY HILL., HEXHAM, NBL NE46 2DW ENG
37843 SIMS, FRANCIS, ROSENBORG GATE 14., 0356 OSLO 3, NORWAY
37844 DISNEY, HUGH, 121 CUMNOR HILL., OXFORD, OXON OX2 9JA ENG
37845 TURVEY, ALAN, CALLE SAN PEDRO 14., ELSAUZAL, TENERIFE SPAIN
37846 RODEN, PETER, 6 YEW TREE AVE., BRADFORD, YKS BD8 0AD ENG
37847 GALE, TERENCE, 3 WELBY CRES, WINNERSH., WOKINGHAM, BRK RG11 5SW ENG
37848 GUISELEY, EDEN, 17 GRESHAM CL., WEST BRIDGFORD, NTT NG2 7RQ ENG
37849 ELLISON, MR K., 11 GLENMORE HSE, RICHMOND HILL., RICHMOND, SRY TW10 6BQ ENG
37850 MORTER, JANET, 2 CASTLE CROFT., OLDBURY, W MID B68 9BQ ENG

37851 TUFF, WALFORD, GREENBANK HOUSE., OTHERY BRIDGWATER, SOM TA7 0PX ENG
37852 DEIGHTON, EDGAR, 34 SPOTTISWOODE RD., EDINBURGH, LOTHIAN EH9 1BL SCOTLAND
37853 HIGGINS, MRS J, SOMERVILLE HSE, ALLENDALE RD., HEXHAM, NBL NE46 2NB ENG
37854 DOUBLE, NOEL, 78 COLNE RD, GLUSBURN., KEIGHLEY, WRY BD20 8PJ ENG
37855 BUNGEY, GRACIE, 2 GREEN CL., HEADBOURNE WORTHY, HAM SO23 7J2 ENG
37856 MASON, SALLY, 9 CHATSWORTH DR., LITTLE EATON, DBY DE2 5AP ENG
37857 JELLEY, SHEILA, 37 COPPERKINS LN., AMERSHAM, BKM HP6 5QF ENG
37858 COULTHARD, JILL, MILLBROOK, STATION RD, VERWOOD., WIMBORNE, DOR 6PU ENG
37859 PARKER, KEITH, 5 KILVINTON DR., ENFIELD, MDX EN2 0BD ENG
37860 BODFISH, MISS M, 47 TALBOT RD., SMETHWICK, W MIDS B66 4DX ENG
37861 ARGYLE, HEATHER, 17 FAIRLIGHT DR, HAREFIELD RD., UXBRIDGE, MDX UB8 1XP ENG
37862 SHAMBROOK, BERNARD, 2 HILLSBOROUGH PARK., CAMBERLEY, SRY GU15 1HG ENG
37863 NARRACOTT, JOHN, 89 THE GREENWAY., ICKENHAM, MIDDX UB10 8LX ENG
37864 IVES, CHRISTINE, 4 GUNHILL PL., BASILDON, ESSEX SS16 5UX ENG
37865 WILSON, MRS P, HILLSIDE, STATION RD., GEDNEY HILL, LIN PE12 0NP ENG
37866 LLEWELLYN, ELIZABETH, 3A COOPERS LN., GROVE PARK, SE12 0QA ENG
37867 CESAR, NOEL, 25 DAVIDSON RD., ADDISCOMBE, SRY CR0 6DL ENG
37868 CULLEY, CAROLE, 46 BROOK RD., SOUTH BENFLEET, ESS SS7 5JF ENG
37869 LAKE, MRS M, 16 WESTERN AVE., FELIXSTOWE, SFK IP11 9SB ENG
37870 JONES, GERALDINE, 1 OVERLORD CL., CAMBERLEY, SURREY GU15 4LX ENG
37871 THOMPSON, GEORGE, 1 RIVERSIDE CT., KISLINGBURY, NTH NN7 4AF ENG
37872 COOK, ALEXANDER, 21 OVER LINKS DR., POOLE, DOR BH14 9QU ENG
37873 JACKSON, MR R, 20 AYCLIFFE DR., GROVEHILL, HERTS HP2 6DE ENG
37874 GIBSON-WYNES, KIM, 9 ARLINGTON RD., EASTBOURNE, SSX BN21 1DJ ENG
37875 LANDROCK, BETTY, 1 HINDOVER CRES., SEAFORD, SSX BN25 3NP ENG
37876 SOUTHEY, VALERIE, 6 CAMBRIDGE RD., SALISBURY, WILTS SP1 3BW ENG
37877 CLEMENT, MRS D, 29 KINGS RD., BENFLEET, ESS SS7 1JP ENG
37878 TEMPLE, DAISY, 14 CASTLE RISE., BELMESTHORPE, LINCS PE9 4JL ENG
37879 KILLICOAT, GORDON, 1 KYLE CRES, LOANS., TROON, AYR KA10 7EZ SCOTLAND
37880 BEECHING, NICHOLAS, 37 ESHE RD NORTH., BLUNDELLSANDS, L23 8UE ENG
37881 NAISMITH, MARY, 13 WARDLAW RD., BEARSDEN, G61 1AL SCOTLAND
37882 BELAM, CAROLINE, FORE STOKE FARM, HOLNE., NEWTON ABBOT, DEV TQ13 7SS ENG
37883 LANE, MARGARET, 32 CHEVIOT WAY., UPPER HOPTON, W. YKS WF14 8HW ENG
37884 FINCH, RICHARD, 14 HILARY AVE, LOWTON., WARRINGTON, CHS WA3 2ET ENG
37885 COX, HELEN, 11 QUEENS RD., ENFIELD, MDX EN1 1NE ENG
37886 DUNNICO, MRS R, 69 DANESCROFT DR., LEIGH ON SEA, ESSEX SS9 4NN ENG
37887 THOMPSON, JEAN, 62 RINGWAY., GARFORTH, YORKS LS25 1BZ ENG
37888 HADDEN, FLORENCE, 60 MOPSA WAY., COOLBELLUP, WA 6163 AUS
37889 HARRISON, ALLAN, 1 ARCADIA AVE., DRUMMOYNE, NSW 2047 AUS
37890 NATHAN, ANNE, 14 HOLLAND ST., GLADSTONE, QLD 4680 AUS
37891 BEST, HUGH, 59 DENNY ST., LATHAM, ACT 2615 AUS
37892 HAWORTH, RITA, 15 SMULLIN ST., HAMILTON HILL, WA 6163 AUS
37893 ROGERS, MARY, 5 PITTWATER CL., KALLAROO, WA 6025 AUS
37894 PLATZ, DIANA, 5 NIMRUD ST., SOUTHPORT, QLD 4215 AUS
37895 DOWLING, BRUCE, BOX 390., ATHERTON, QLD 4883 AUS
37896 TAYLOR, PENELOPA, 6 CHURCH ST., KIPPARING, QLD 4020 AUS
37897 WARD, HELEN, 2/4 BRIXTON ST., BONBEACH, VIC 3197 AUS
37898 GRANT, WILLIAM, PO BOX 607., FRANKSTON, VIC 3199 AUS
37899 WESTON, DONALD, 15 BROUGHAM AVE., WERRIBEE, VIC 3030 AUS
37900 KNIGHT, MARGARET, 'BARINGAMA' PO BOX 141., LEETON, NSW 2705 AUS
37901 WILLS, RICHARD, 17 CHICO ST., COPACABANA, NSW 2251 AUS
37902 CALLINAN, CHRISTINE, 1 MARY ST., HOLMESVILLE, NSW 2286 AUS
37903 CHAPMAN, MARGARET, 3 ARNETT ST., WENTWORTHVILLE, NSW 2145 AUS
37904 GLASBY, MRS J, 3 LANG AVE., PAGEWOOD, NSW 2019 AUS
37905 SYMONDS, DR JOHN, 14 TALOOMBI ST., CRONULLA, NSW 2230 AUS
37906 WISE, JUDITH, 25 PHEASANT POINT DR., KIAMA, NSW 2533 AUS
37907 APPLEBY, MR B, 99 PIONER PDE., BANORA PT, NSW 2486 AUS
37908 LEE, JUDITH, PO BOX 572., TWEED HEADS, NSW 2485 AUS
37909 WINDON, HELEN, 12 MAITLAND RD., MAYFIELD, NSW 2304 AUS
37910 EDWARDS, TRACIE, 36 WOLLOMBI RD., MUSWELLBROOK, NSW 2333 AUS
37911 MCCULLOCH, MARGARET, 9 MARY ST., SPEERS POINT, NSW 2284 AUS
37912 MURRAY, CORAL, 51 COONONG RD., GYMEA BAY, NSW 2227 AUS
37913 TWINING, SANDRA, C/O 41 KINGSTON AVE., SEACOMBE GARDENS, SA 5047 AUS
37914 FORSHEY, ROBERT, 2 SOMERSET ST., KIPPA-RING, QLD 4021 AUS
37915 PALMER, PATRICIA, 47 HUNTER ST., MALVERN, VIC 3144 AUS
37916 REDDAN, CLIVE, PO BOX 155., CAMMERAY, NSW 2062 AUS
37917 VOST, MR W, PO BOX 515., NOWRA, NSW 2541 AUS
37918 WARMERDAM, SUZANNE, PO BOX 431., ALSTONVILLE, NSW 2477 AUS
37919 WILLIAMS, THELMA, 32 ESROM ST., BATHURST, NSW 2795 AUS
37920 PARSONS, MARGARET, 233 GRANDVIEW RD., WALLSEND STH, NSW 2287 AUS
37921 HANDLEY, ROBIN, 84 GUNDAGAI RD., JUNEE, NSW 2663 AUS
37922 SAYERS, ALAN, 61 ABSHOT RD., TITCHFIELD COMMON, HANTS PO14 4NB ENG

37923 CRESSWELL, STUART, 28 MONREITH RD., GLASGOW, G43 2NY SCOTLAND
37924 PENN, MONICA, 28 PETVIN CL., STREET, SOM BA16 0SX ENG
37925 CHRISTIE, JEAN, THE GABLES, BELLEVUE AVE., KIRKINTILLOCH, G66 1AJ SCOTLAND
37926 PARLETT, MR G, 11 UPPER MOORFIELD RD., WOODBRIDGE, IP12 4JW ENG
37927 MCCALL, IVAN, APT 28, TYRONE HSE, ADELAIDE ST., BELFAST, BT2 8HR IRELAND
37928 TURNER, ANN, 1 ROBIN CL., GREAT BENTLEY, ESS C07 8QH ENG
37929 EMPTAGE, EILEEN, 48 LICHFIELD RD., GRIMSBY, LIN DN32 8JZ ENG
37930 MURRAY, JOHN, 143 SNUGVILLE ST., BELFAST, ANT BT13 1NF N IRELAND
37931 HILDESLEY, JAMES, 13 TREES RD., HUGHENDEN VY, BUCKS HP14 4PN ENG
37932 FROSTICK, RAYMOND, 425 UNTHANK RD., NORWICH, NFK NR4 7QB ENG
37933 BARTLEY, MR H, RT 2, BOX 244., COOPER, TX 75432 USA
37934 STRAITON, JULIA, CULVER FM., OLD COMPTON LN., FARNHAM, SURREY GU9 8EJ ENG
37935 GOODSTEIN, MRS K, IBSGAARDEN 196., ROSKILDE, 4000 DENMARK
37936 ELLSON, CHARLES, 27 HUNTERS GVE., KENTON, MDX HA3 9AB ENG
37937 BUCKINGHAM, LYNDA, 124 HAYHURST RD., LUTON, BDF LU4 0DB ENG
37938 LACY, ALBERT, 1 THE MOUNT., SNYDALE RD, YKS WF6 1NU ENG
37939 SMITH, EVA, 64 THE HEYS., COPPULL-CHORLEY, LAN PR7 4NX ENG
37940 GEGG, MR M, 19 FULLERTON WAY., BYFLEET, SRY KT14 7TD ENG
37941 JEWELL, RONALD, 82 ELMSHOTT LN., SLOUGH, BRK SL1 5QZ ENG
37942 ADAMS, MISS L, PO BOX 48., CREMORNE, NSW 2090 AUS
37943 DEANE, MRS J, 9 CLIVE RD., EASTWOOD, NSW 2122 AUS
37944 PASSFIELD, COLLEEN, 141 LOWER WASHINGTON DR., BONNET BAY, NSW 2226 AUS
37945 MCGRATH, LYNETTE, PO BOX 231., MILLER, NSW 2168 AUS
37946 SHARP, MRS J, 41 RYAN ST., INNISFAIL, QLD 4860 AUS
37947 ROWE, BAILEY, 272 EKIBIN RD EAST., TARRAGINDI, QLD 4121 AUS
37948 APSEY, LEONIE, 5 VICTORIA ST., INGLEWOOD, QLD 4387 AUS
37949 BUTT, ANN, MAIL SERVICE 509., SARINA, QLD 4737 AUS
37950 PAYNE, EVELYN, 6 PETERSEN ST., SARINA, QLD 4737 AUS
37951 WYMAN, CRAIG, 53 ASHGROVE AVE., BIGGERA WATERS, QLD 4215 AUS
37952 CROSS, JACK, 363 HALIFAX ST., ADELAIDE, SA 5000 AUS
37953 LOVIBOND, ANDREW, 9 DILLON ST., BELLERIVE, TAS 7018 AUS
37954 AHEIMER, ROSEMARY, 47 SUNSHINE RD., AUSTINS FERRY, TAS 7011 AUS
37955 TEARLE, PETA, 58 BUSSELL HWY., BUSSELTON, WA 6280 AUS
37956 NUTTALL, MARGARET, 18 WATSON ST., CHARLTON, VIC 3525 AUS
37957 WALKER, MARGARET, PO BOX 1129., THORNBURY, VIC 3071 AUS
37958 READ, GEOFFREY, 3 NORRIS RD., ROWVILLE, VIC 3178 AUS
37959 BAGGALLAY, KIM, 1 RIVERVIEW CRES., DOVETON, VIC 3177 AUS
37960 MOORE, OLIVE, 30 KARINGAL ST., CROYDON NORTH, VIC 3136 AUS
37961 SEEBECK, JOHN, 113 ARUNDEL AVE., PARK ORCHARDS, VIC 3114 AUS
37962 PATULLO, BERYL, 30 ARNDELL ST., THOMASTOWN, VIC 3074 AUS
37963 SHELTON, MAUREEN, PO BOX 694., JAMISON CENTRE, ACT 2614 AUS
37964 COCHRAN, MR I, 43 CURLEWIS CRES., GARRAN, ACT 2605 AUS
37965 ABBEY, MRS J, 37 BLUETT CRES., WAGGA WAGGA, NSW 2650 AUS
37966 POST, VERONICA, 1 EMILY ST., THE ROCK, NSW 2655 AUS
37967 EASTBURN, MR J, 'LYNWOOD'., BARADINE, NSW 2396 AUS
37968 ALLEN, JULIE, 55 EVANS ST., COWRA, NSW 2794 AUS
37969 STOKES, NORMA, 18 BROCKLESBY RD., MEDOWIE, NSW 2301 AUS
37970 ALLAN, PETRIE, REAR 19 REDLEAF AVE., WAHROONGA, NSW 2076 AUS
37971 WILLS, SHIRLEY, BRAESIDE., GREENETHORPE, NSW 2809 AUS
37972 ROBERTSON, BETH, 12 POATE PL., DAVIDSON, NSW 2085 AUS
37973 POOLE, ROBIN, 19 MERRELL ST., NORTH BOOVAL, QLD 4304 AUS
37974 GOUGH, DON, PO BOX 331., MOOROOKA, QLD 4105 AUS
37975 USHER, IRIS, 9 KENILWORTH RD., BROOLOO, QLD 4570 AUS
37976 CARSON, JUNE, 23 AGATE ST., BAYVIEW HEIGHTS, QLD 4868 AUS
37977 GRENDON, ADELAIDE, M/S 283., MACKAY, QLD 4740 AUS
37978 ANTCLIFF, MRS S, 9 ANNA ST., BEAUDESERT, QLD 4285 AUS
37979 BROWN, DAWN, 46 GREGORY ST., ACACIA RIDGE, QLD 4110 AUS
37980 OSBORNE, DR MARSHALL, 67 GUY ST., WARWICK, QLD 4370 AUS
37981 MERCER, PENNY, C/O 50 ST PHILLIP ST., BRUNSWICK EAST, VIC 3057 AUS
37982 CHAPMAN, MR A, PO BOX 729., SALE, VIC 3850 AUS
37983 CHARLES, MRS W, 4 DONNELLY CRT., KEALBA, VIC 3021 AUS
37984 MARTIN, MRS S, LOT 4 EAST RD., HUNTLY, VIC 3551 AUS
37985 CALDWELL, JOYCE, 7 WHITE ST., HENLEY BEACH, SA 5022 AUS
37986 BOLLENHAGEN, MRS M, BOX 2 PO., LYRUP, SA 5343 AUS
37987 WALKER, HEATHER, 12 ROSSALL RD., SOMERTON PARK, SA 5044 AUS
37988 PROCTOR, PETER, 55 KALLARA CL., DUFFY, ACT 2611 AUS
37989 ALCOCK, PAMELA, 10 BERRELL ST., CHISHOLM, ACT 2905 AUS
37990 PALMER, IRIS, 6 STOKES ST., PARAP, NT 0820 AUS
37991 ATKINSON, MRS N, 495 CHAPMAN RD., GERALDTON, WA 6530 AUS
37992 STOW, SANDRA, 18 ALICE ST., CLONTARF, QLD 4019 AUS
37993 GOSS, DOREEN, 6 DANCER ST, COLLINGWOOD PARK., IPSWICH, QLD 4301 AUS
37994 NOLAN, GREGORY, 177 BELL ST., COBURG, VIC 3058 AUS

37995 HARROWFIELD, MS D, 5/22 HOWSON ST., WEST BRUNSWICK, VIC 3055 AUS
37996 KELLY, JOHN, 19 TRAWALLA CRT., CROYDON, VIC 3136 AUS
37997 HANSON, MARJORIE, 2 ELEVENTH AVE., ANGLESEA, VIC 3230 AUS
37998 CROUCH, KATH, 13 BREEN ST., MURTOA, VIC 3390 AUS
37999 MCALPINE, WENDY, PO BOX 202., YARRAM, VIC 3971 AUS
38000 MCINTYRE, PERRY, 12 BELMONT RD., MOSMAN, NSW 2088 AUS
38001 LINSLEY, JOY, 63 BUNBERRA ST., BOMADERRY, NSW 2541 AUS
38002 SHILLINGFORD, SUSAN, DOCKYARD RD., MILLERS FOREST, NSW 2324 AUS
38003 GARSIDE, MS E, 43 ARLINGTON ST., GOROKAN, NSW 2263 AUS
38004 HILL, SUSAN, 578 WYSE ST., ALBURY, NSW 2640 AUS
38005 CORFIELD, JUSTIN, 37 MIRIAM ST., ROSANNA, VIC 3084 AUS
38006 CARRINGTON, LOIS, 70 DRYANDRA ST., O'CONNOR, ACT 2601 AUS
38007 GRANT, IAN, 19 DORLTON ST., KINGS LANGLEY, NSW 2147 AUS
38008 DUPREZ, GLADYS, LYNELLA., NEMINGHA, NSW 2340 AUS
38009 ZDUNIC, M, 6450 NEWBERRY RD., DURAND, MI 48429 USA
38010 ZDUNIC, M, 6450 NEWBERRY RD., DURAND, MI 48439 USA
38011 CRESSWELL, GRACE, 48 COLLEGE AVE., NORTH TARRYTOWN, NY 10591 USA
38012 SWANSON, GORDON, 2832 DUNLEER PL., LOS ANGELES, CA 90064 USA
38013 MCLAUCHLAN, JAMES, 4212 HWY 159 S., EDWARDSVILLE, IL 62025 USA
38014 CARLSON, AMERICA, 7052 FALLBROOK CT., NEW PORT RICHEY, FL 34655 USA
38015 BOWEN, JOHN, 613 CHICHESTER LN., SILVER SPRING, MO 20904 USA
38016 DUTTON, ELIZABETH, 447 NIMITZ AVE., STATE COLLEGE, PA 16801 USA
38017 NOBLE, CAROL, 492 MARIETTA PL., PITTSBURGH, PA 15228 USA
38018 GRAHAM, MURIEL, 2018 COOLIDGE CT., MIDDLETON, WI 53562 USA
38019 GREGG, DR WILLIAM, RR1, 38 PEEPSOCK CL., HOUGHTON, MI 49931 USA
38020 BURRUP, JAY, 6602 W KING VALLEY RD., WEST VALLEY, UT 84120 USA
38021 BOBALJIK, MR J., LINGUISTICS, RM 20D-219 MIT., CAMBRIDGE, MA 02139 USA
38022 BURT, MS J, 5510 SOUTH 3910 WEST #21., KEARNS, UT 84118 USA
38023 SELMER, SUSAN, 6062 LAKE NADINE PL., AGOURA, CA 91301 USA
38024 MCILWEE, PATRICK, 4644E LE MARCHE AVE., PHOENIX, AZ 85032 USA
38025 LAUERMAN, YOLANDA, 407 WEST FLOWER ST., PHOENIX, AZ 85013 USA
38026 STARMAN, WANDA, 13210 FRAME CRT., POWAY, CA 92064 USA
38027 OWEN, MARILYN, PO BOX 2613., SANTA BARBARA, CA 93120 USA
38028 CRIDDLE, MARLIN, 4566 WOOD DUCK LN., SALT LAKE CITY, UT 84117 USA
38029 NOLTE, MARLENE, 24000 ARCHWOOD ST., WEST HILLS, CA 91307 USA
38030 PEARCE, FRANCES, 1804 BIRCH RD., MCLEAN, VA 22101 USA
38031 FERRIS, CHUCK, 2002 S HIGHLAND., LAS VEGAS, NV 89102 USA
38032 TOWNSEND, PATRICIA, 6100 FLORENCE LN., ALEXANDRIA, VA 22310 USA
38033 BEDELL, LINDA, PO BOX 487., GREEN COVE SPRINGS, FL 32043 USA
38034 WADE, ANNE, 2915 DARTMOUTH DR., ANCHORAGE, AK 99508 USA
38035 POLHEMUS, JOHN, 19 BRIDLE PATH LN., MANCHESTER, CT 06040 USA
38036 LINGENFELTER, ROBERT, 5295 ROLLING AVE., LORAIN, OH 44055 USA
38037 POMEROY, LORAINE, 22070 33 MILE RD., ARMADA, MI 48005 USA
38038 WHEELER, IVAJEAN, 9 OLD OAK DR., SIMSBURY, CT 06070 USA
38039 KENT, ROBERT, 903 S HARRIET., ALGONA, IA 50511 USA
38040 BLAXTON, PEGGY, 3327 DANVILLE RD SW., DECATUR, AL 35603 USA
38041 HIGGINS, MARY, 9144 LAKEWOOD DR., WINDSOR, CA 95492 USA
38042 PATTERSON, CARL, 9444 DRAKE AVE., EVANSTON, IL 60203 USA
38043 EDMONDS, JUDY, 1205 HICKORY TER., ROUND LAKE BEACH, IL 60073 USA
38044 TOLLIVER, KATHLYN, 1255 – 14 AMETHYST ST., MENTONE, CA 92359 USA
38045 RUSSELL, MARY, 3383 WELLESLY AVE., SAN DIEGO, CA 92122 USA
38046 SNYDER, BARBARA, 1366 W 243RD ST., HARBOR CITY, CA 90710 USA
38047 BRUSO, SHIRLEY, PO BOX 73789., PUYALLUP, WA 98373 USA
38048 BREITENSTEIN, JOSEPH, 2012 SW 30TH ST., TOPEKA, KS 66611 USA
38049 MARTIN, MR M, PO BOX 2011., SONOMA, CA 95476 USA
38050 ROBERTS, MRS J, 12347 SE MADISON ST., PORTLAND, OR 97233 USA
38051 WILLIAMS, REV E, 11A ROUTE US 4 WEST., WOODSTOCK, VT 05091 USA
38052 GESS, MINNIE, W3862 LOWER HEBRON RD., FORT ATKINSON, WI 53538 USA
38053 MEARNS, SHIRLEY, 79 DUNNEMANN AVE., KINGSTON, NY 12401 USA
38054 SMITH, MRS R, 10897 NE SEABORN RD., BAINBRIDGE ISLAND, WA 98110 USA
38055 SECRIST, DR ROBERT, 264 MADISON AVE., YOUNGSTOWN, OH 44504 USA
38056 HOLMES, JAMES, 244 FLANDERS RD., WESTBOROUGH, MA 01581 USA
38057 WITTMAN, JEAN, 238 BREVARD AVE., VENTURA, CA 93003 USA
38058 WILKINS, JAMES, 427 HONEY LOCUST., WILLOWBROOK, IL 60514 USA
38059 MITCHELL, LANNE, 1015 SUNSET BLVD., ARCADIA, CA 91007 USA
38060 KNEWSTEP, SHIRLEY, 505 ROLAND DR., NORFOLK, VA 23509 USA
38061 ERLENKOTTER, DONALD, PO BOX 3474., SANTA MONICA, CA 90408 USA
38062 SMITH, MRS L, 6190 EAST HOLLY RD., HOLLY, MI 48442 USA
38063 BEYRAND, SHIRLEY, 5 FAIRLANE HARBOUR, 235 ARBOR LN., VERO BEACH, FL 32960 USA
38064 WINTER, PATRICIA, 227 ANDERSON BLVD., GENEVA, IL 60134 USA
38065 LINSTROT, PAULA, 2689 W 63RD AVE., MERRILLVILLE, IN 46410 USA
38066 AMUNDSEN, MRS R, 338 OTTAWA ST., PARK FOREST, IL 60466 USA

38067 MAVAR, JOYCE, 24720 PRESIDENT AVE., HARBOR CITY, CA 90710 USA
38068 KERVILLE, PETER, 12 DEHAVILLAND AVE., BENOWA WATERS, QLD 4217 AUS
38069 HANSON, MAUREEN, INNISPLAIN M/S 576., BEAUDESERT, QLD 4285 AUS
38070 MILLARD, DARYL, 100 ALBION RD., BOX HILL, VIC 3128 AUS
38071 CARLYLE, MRS C, RMB 1048., CORRYONG, VIC 3707 AUS
38072 WATSON, DR E, 36 MYEE CRES., LANE COVE, NSW 2066 AUS
38073 ST LEON, MARK, PO BOX 315., GLEBE, NSW 2037 AUS
38074 SNELSON, JOHN, 40 TENNYSON AVE., TURRAMURRA, NSW 2074 AUS
38075 STEMP, PATRICIA, 55 RIVERVIEW AVE., KYLE BAY, NSW 2221 AUS
38076 KIRKLAND, RAY, 5 SIESTA CRT., ALSTONVILLE, NSW 2477 AUS
38077 HEFFERNAN, MRS L, 122 OLD PITT TOWN RD., BOX HILL, NSW 2765 AUS
38078 DAY, MARJORIE, 10/1A QUEEN ST., MOSMAN, NSW 2088 AUS
38079 TRINDER, AILEEN, 5 GARBALA RD., GYMEA, NSW 2227 AUS
38080 WATSON, ANNETTE, 103 URALBA ST., LISMORE, NSW 2480 AUS
38081 BADE, GEORGINA, 8/77 KIRKLAND AVE., COORPAROO, QLD 4151 AUS
38082 ANDERTON, MR C, 6 CHIFLEY CT., SUNBURY, VIC 3429 AUS
38083 SMITH, MAXWELL, 10 LANGLEY PL., KAMBAH, ACT 2902 AUS
38084 JOHNSON, KEITH, PO BOX 795., NORTH SYDNEY, NSW 2059 AUS
38085 GAUTIER, MME V, MJC CHAT. DES TERRASSES., CONFLANS STE HONORINE, 178700 FRA
38086 BATTERSHELL, MRS D, 319 BIRCH WAY., HUTCHINSON, KS 67502 USA
38087 MCLAUGHLIN, MR D, 23614 DUNSMORE LN., VALENCIA, CA 91354 USA
38088 GORDON, DR R, 2122 EAST REDFIELD RD., PHOENIX, AZ 85022 USA
38089 WITHERS, E, PO BOX 3726., MERCED, CA 95344 USA
38090 DEGRAFF, MRS M, 8763 WEST CENTER AVE., LAKEWOOD, CO 80226 USA
38091 SELLERY, MRS M, 5735 ROOSEVELT ST., MIDDLETON, WI 53562 USA
38092 SOMOZA, MS A, 1412 RIVER CREEK CIRCLE., MODESTO, CA 95351 USA
38093 MUTSCHLER, MR P, 151 REMSEN ST., BROOKLYN, NY 11201 USA
38094 EGGLESTON, MR W, 20 CLINTON DRIVE E., BATTLE CREEK, MI 49017 USA
38095 WHITE-ROSE, RAE, 241 CENTER AVE., APTOS, CA 95003 USA
38096 SEGAL GOLOS, MRS V, 5830 EAST 8TH STREET., TUCSON, AZ 85711 USA
38097 WUNDER, MRS S, PO BOX 2807., CHEYENNE, WY 82003 USA
38098 MILLER, MRS J, 337 ORCHARD ST., STANDISH, MI 48658 USA
38099 ROSENBAUM, MR E, PO BOX 1224., PINECREST, CA 95364 USA
38100 SCHOONOVER, MRS H, 2 EL VERTA CIRCLE., CHICO, CA 95926 USA
38101 HAWLEY, MRS L, 1301 E LAKESHORE DR., LAKE STEVENS, WA 98258 USA
38102 MURPHY, J, 4842 NORTHERLY ST., OCEANSIDE, CA 92056 USA
38103 WILSON, MR J, 6216 MICHAEL LN., LAKELAND, FL 33811 USA
38104 SPRINGER, MISS C, 7228 TURKEY RUN DR., FT WAYNE, IN 46815 USA
38105 ALLINGTON, MS M, 8501 KENDOR DR., BUENA PARK, CA 90620 USA
38106 WEILER, MR T, 1132 BRANDON RD., CLEVELAND HEIGHTS, OH 44112 USA
38107 SORRELLS, MR R, RT 2, 238 HAPPY VALLEY RD., BELL BUCKLE, TN 37020 USA
38108 HODSON, MR G, 962 EVA LANE., UPLAND, IN 46989 USA
38109 SEAMONE, MRS P, 270 WEST MAIN ST., SALEM, WV 26426 USA
38110 CORBETT, REV G, 2220 BOSTON CRT., INDIANAPOLIS, IN 46208 USA
38111 PETERSON, MS P, 3704 UTAH NE., ALBUQUERQUE, NM 87110 USA
38112 BOTHMANN, MS K, 16947 SHADY MEADOW DR., HACIENDA HEIGHTS, CA 91745 USA
38113 WEIR, BERNICE, 6 SCHOOL LN., HUNTINGTON, NY 11743 USA
38114 VANDERSALL, MR L, 1448 S KOHLER RD., ORRVILLE, OH 44667 USA
38115 WATERFIELD, MARJORIE, PO BOX 7007., BOWLING GREEN, OH 43402 USA
38116 STEWARD, MR D, 157 2ND ST, APT 214., FRAMINGHAM, MA 01701 USA
38117 CALLANAN, ELIZABETH, 397 HAYWARD MILL RD., CONCORD, MA 01742 USA
38118 MATZ, MRS S, 5843 COSTELLO AVE., VAN NUYS, CA 91401 USA
38119 GUNN, MRS J, RT 4, BOX 842., REIDSVILLE, NC 27320 USA
38120 BARNETT, MR E, 1001 CARPENTERS WAY, APT F-415., LAKELAND, FL 33809 USA
38121 STAHL, MS F, 2614 S GOYER RD., KOKOMO, IN 46902 USA
38122 AVERY, MRS E, 741 DONNER AVE., SOMOMA, CA USA
38123 BETHUNE, MR L, 125 COOLIDGE AVE #403., WATERTOWN, MA 02172 USA
38124 BENDER, ILLENE, 4610 FREEMAN RD., MANHATTAN, KS 66502 USA
38125 STAMBAZZE, MISS D, 287 MILLARD., CRYSTAL LAKE, IL 60014 USA
38126 WALKER, MR L, 1813 CARSON DR., NORRISTOWN, PA 19403 USA
38127 LIPPINCOTT, MRS D, 88C3 MORGAN RAIDERS LN., CINCINNATI, OH 45236 USA
38128 ENRICK, MR N, PO BOX 264., TALLMADGE, OH 44278 USA
38129 RAWLS, MR R, 36 FOREST DR., MOUNTAINTOP, PA 18707 USA
38130 CONKLIN, MRS E, ONE SPANKTOWN RD., WARWICK, NY 10990 USA
38131 NEUMANN, MS L, 3963 DRINKWATER ST., FORT IRWIN, CA 92310 USA
38132 DAUM, HAROLD, RT 1, BOX 125., SEDALIA, MO 65301 USA
38133 STADLER, MRS W, 4431 SE 69TH ST., BERRYTON, KS 66409 USA
38134 STAHL, J, 13 SOUTH INLET DR., OCEAN CITY, NJ 08226 USA
38135 WILLIAMSON, DR R, 107 WILLEFORD DR., SAVANNAH, GA 31411 USA
38136 CAINE, MRS M, 10454 GOLF COURSE RD., OCEAN CITY, MD 21842 USA
38137 LANDERS, MRS J, RT 2, BOX 4170., BERRYVILLE, VA 22611 USA
38138 WOODRING, MRS J, 2387 BRADY LAKE RD., RAVENNA, OH 44266 USA

38139 HUGHES, MRS J, 3024 MAPLE SHADE LN., WILMINGTON, DE 19810 USA
38140 O'BRIEN, MRS P, 54 PLANT RD., CLIFTON PARK, NY 12065 USA
38141 COATES, MRS C, 423 MACEDONIA RD., ASHEVILLE, NC 28804 USA
38142 MERWIN, MRS L, 8900 E JEFFERSON, APT 1420., DETROIT, MI 48214 USA
38143 EIKE, R, RT 1, BOX 1138., AMANA, IA 52203 USA
38144 CAIL, MRS J, #2916, 6110 PLEASANT RIDGE RD., ARLINGTON, TX 76016 USA
38145 WALKER, MS J, 4201 SE 4TH ST., RENTON, WA 98059 USA
38146 FARR, MRS R, 15776 CAMERON., SOUTHGATE, MI 48195 USA
38147 NICHOLS, MRS S, ONE CLUBHOUSE DR., REHOBOTH, DE 19971 USA
38148 DRYVER, REV A, E 16414 MAIN AVE., VERADALE, WA 99037 USA
38149 BRAWN, MRS I, 3012 HEGRY CIR., CINCINNATI, OH 45238 USA
38150 FOSTER, MRS V, PO BOX 271., HASTINGS, NE 68902 USA
38151 ADAY, MRS E, 5805 SE WESTFORK., PORTLAND, OR 97206 USA
38152 SPAHR, MRS V, 12850 WEST RD., ZIONSVILLE, IN 46077 USA
38153 ROHDE, MRS M, 25 FLINT ST., MARBLEHEAD, MA 01945 USA
38154 KUNKLE, MR J, PO BOX #3047., DENVER, CO 80201 USA
38155 MCLELLAN, MRS H, 13537 TERRA VISTA DR., SUN CITY WEST, AZ 85375 USA
38156 BILLINGS, MRS J, R#1, BOX 88., ORCHARD, NE 68764 USA
38157 WEST, DR TOMMY, 1688 N ACADEMY., GALESBURG, IL 61401 USA
38158 GREGOIRE, L.M.G., LEUVENSE STRAAT 110A., SINT JURIS WEERT, 3051 BELGIUM
38159 VERHOOSELE, F.J.C., ROLLEBAAN 101., OOSTERZELE, B 9860 BELGIUM
38160 SCHATS, AL, LIEVEN GEVAERTSTRAAT 78., MORTSEL, B 2640 BELGIUM
38161 MERLEVEDE, DANIEL, BRUGSEWEG 32., IEPER, 8900 BELGIUM
38162 VERSPAILLE, JEAN MARIE, KEIZERLYKE PLAATS 61., AALST, 9300 BELGIUM
38163 DENGLER, FREDERIC, ARGENTINIELAAN 67 BUS 5., ANTWERPEN, 2030 BELGIUM
38164 DEPAEPE, POL, OLIEBERGSTRAAT 3., OLSENE, 9870 BELGIUM
38165 OOST VLAANDEREN, MARC MACYENS, OUDE WEG 48., HOLEGEM, B 9991 BELGIUM
38166 WALDACK, FELIX, JOZEF VAN DE VELDESTRAAT 7., LAARNE, B 9270 BELGIUM
38167 DOCHEZ, CH L.J., FRUITHOFLAAN 33-5E., BERCHEM, ATW 2600 BELGIUM
38168 GRANT, WILLY, FR COECKELBERGSSTRAAT 12., HEIST-OP-DEN-BERG, 2220 BELGIUM
38169 LE PAGE, H, ROOILAAN 4., ANTWERPEN, 2600 BELGIUM
38170 AVORT, DR LUC VANDER, 17 KERKSTRAAT., DAMME, B 8340 BELGIUM
38171 ENGELMART, MARGARET, 72 BRINKERHOFF ST., PLATTSBURGH, NY 12901 USA
38172 CARSCALLEN, MURIEL, 1623 EL VERANO., THOUSAND OAKS, CA 91362 USA
38173 DIEDRICHS, MRS T, 2804 WALNUT., CEDAR FALLS, IA 50613 USA
38174 KELLY, ROBERTA, PO BOX 9102., WARWICK, RI 02889 USA
38175 SCARLETT, CAROL, 12830 MOUNT ROYAL LN., FAIRFAX, VA 22033 USA
38176 WILSON, G, 3310 APPLEGATE CT., ANNANDALE, VA 22003 USA
38177 EDKIN, BARBARA, 105 WOODRIDGE PL., OAKLEY, CA 94561 USA
38178 CIROU, JOSEPH, 13145 S HOUSTON AVE., CHICAGO, IL 60633 USA
38179 ZDUNIC, MARGARET, 6450 NEWBERRY RD., DURAND, MI 48429 USA
38180 STEPHENS, JOHN, 11628 RAVENNA RD., TWINSBURG, OH 44087 USA
38181 HEIL, ROBERT, 33536 CALLE MIRAMAR., SAN JUAN CAPISTRANO, CA 92675 USA
38182 DANIELSEN, KIM, PO BOX 1656., YUMA, AZ 85366 USA
38183 REED, ALICE, 2221 N 81ST WAY., SCOTTSDALE, AZ 85257 USA
38184 NASH, DORIS, 17422 GEMINI ST., LA PUENTE, CA 91744 USA
38185 TURNER, ALTON, 475 44 AVE NE., ST PETERSBURG, FL 33703 USA
38186 OEHLSCHLAEGER, FRED, 8383 CHEVIOT RD., CINCINNATI, OH 45247 USA
38187 BUNT, LA DORNA, 4611 DUNSMORE AVE., LA CRESCENTA, CA 91214 USA
38188 SEXTON, BARBARA, 3824 58TH AVE N., MINNEAPOLIS, MN 55429 USA
38189 MCCARTHY, MRS L, 1920 N INDIAN HILL., CLAREMONT, CA 91711 USA
38190 WALLACE, EVELYN, 28306 REY DE COPAS LN., MALIBU, CA 90265 USA
38191 LA BOMASCUS, JULIE, 242 WISCONSIN ST., MAYVILLE, WI 53050 USA
38192 ANDERSON, FREDERICK, 621 MONTCLAIRE., OHATHE, KS 66061 USA
38193 PETERSEN, RUTH, 16966 LAKE KNOLL LN., YORBA LINDA, CA 92686 USA
38194 ROHRER, RONALD, 317 RUBY AVE., BALBOA ISLAND, CA 92662 USA
38195 LEWELLEN, IMOGENE, PO BOX 1082., LAKE ELSINORE, CA 92331 USA
38196 VAN TRUMP, GEORGE, PO BOX 260170., LAKEWOOD, CO 80226 USA
38197 WILSON, LORENA, 1200 COLORADO., ELK CITY, OK 73644 USA
38198 AUSTIN, MRS B, 25 PARK RD., DAYTON, OH 45419 USA
38199 NEUENDORF, MS B, 59 WASHINGTON ST., PORT CHESTER, NY 10573 USA
38200 HUBBARD, MRS J, PO BOX 34., JEFFERSONVILLE, VT 05464 USA
38201 STONER, MRS A, 6330 BLACKFOOT DR., HELENA, MT 59601 USA
38202 WAGNER, MR P, 7206 WOOLRICH RD., LOUISVILLE, KY 40222 USA
38203 GUNDERSON, BERNICE, 3753 E 15TH STREET., LONG BEACH, CA 90804 USA
38204 BROWNE, TERRY, 14 BRUNTON ST., WANNIASSA, ACT 2903 AUS
38205 THWAITES, IAN, 3 LODDON CL., ROWVILLE, VIC 3178 AUS
38206 HILES, LUCY, 5/1B MELVILLE RD., WEST BRUNSWICK, VIC 3055 AUS
38207 GRESLEY, STUART, 34 DOLLY AVE., SPRINGFIELD, NSW 2250 AUS
38208 KAVANAGH, MERLE, 6 SUMNER ST., SUTHERLAND, NSW 2232 AUS
38209 SEARS, MR H, 6 ST HELENA ST., FLAGSTAFF HILL, SA 5159 AUS
38210 COZENS, MARGARET, PO BOX 149., ATHERTON, QLD 4883 AUS

38211 PEARCE, MARK, 61 MALONGA AVE., KELLYVILLE, NSW 2153 AUS
38212 MOSELEY, VALMA, 40 MELDRUM AVE., MIRANDA, NSW 2229 AUS
38213 WATTS, HENRY, 134 FRYARS RD., BEENLEIGH, QLD 4207 AUS
38214 BALL, RONALD, 55 PARKLANDS RD., NORTH RYDE, NSW 2113 AUS
38215 GOW, JAN, 18 MODENA CRES., AUCKLAND, 5 NZ
38216 CLARK, BARBARA, 5705 NW LANDING DR., PORTLAND, OR 97229 USA
38217 HEIN, JACKIE, 2129 NO 6TH STREET., CONCORD, CA 94519 USA
38218 MASCO, JEAN, 967 PINE HILL RD., PALM HARBOR, PA 34683 USA
38219 KURTZ, MAURICE, 285 TEMPLE ST., SATELLITE BEACH, FL 32937 USA
38220 FOX, JOANN, SUITE 102-101, 1840 41ST AVE., CAPITOLA, CA 95010 USA
38221 KARPF, ELIZABETH, 1817 INDIANA., ALBUQUERQUE, NM 87110 USA
38222 WEGENER, MARY EDITH, 3181 MAPLE RD., NEWFANE, NY 14108 USA
38223 SCOLES, GLORIA, 3209 ALMA., MANHATTAN BEACH, CA 90266 USA
38224 TRURAN, SUZANNE, 42 CENTER ST., BREWSTER, NY 10509 USA
38225 MCAULIFFE, EDWARD, 15161 MYSTIC ST., WHITTIER, CA 90604 USA
38226 HANNA, WILLIAM, 145 KENWOOD AVE., SYRACUSE, NY 13208 USA
38227 FORRESTER, SUSAN, 29 KING LN., CONCORD, MA 01742 USA
38228 FORSBERG, SHIRLEY, 14673 SW SCARLETT DR., TIGARD, OR 97224 USA
38229 BUNNING, LESTER, 19101 SIERRA MAJORCA RD., IRVINE, CA 92715 USA
38230 SMEED, JOHN, 3655 GLEN OAK DR., EUGENE, OR 97405 USA
38231 BRENGEL, MARY HELEN, 1307 WOODLAWN AVE., DALLAS, TX 75208 USA
38232 GODZIEMBA-MALISZEWSKI, WACLAW, 73 PLUMTREES RD., BETHEL, CT 06801 USA
38233 KANE, THOMAS, 24 S CRESTVIEW DR., N SCITUATE, RI 02857 USA
38234 BECKETT, EUGENE, PO BOX 502., CAMBRIA, IL 62915 USA
38235 ERKFRITZ, DONALD, 7905 ESTON SO., CLARKSTON, MI 48348 USA
38236 ROSENBAUM, MR P, 19 PINE NEEDLE RD., WAYLAND, MA 01778 USA
38237 BALLENTINE, MELISSA, 472 WIMBLEDON DR., CHARLESTON, SC 29412 USA
38238 CONYERS, JANIE, 12500 MONTANA., EL PASO, TX 79936 USA
38239 JACKSON, RONALD, PO BOX 39145., FORT LAUDERDALE, FL 33339 USA
38240 MCBRIDE, TOM, 1221 MAYBERRY LN., STATE COLLEGE, PA 16801 USA
38241 CARLTON, CHESTER & MARGERY, 32512 BERTRAM DR., WESTLAND, MI 48185 USA
38242 REESE, JUNE, 6302 SOUTHWIND DR., WHITTIER, CA 90601 USA
38243 GRAY, EILEEN, 1913 WEST PARK DR., FLORENCE, OR 97439 USA
38244 BIRKBECK, JOSEPHINE, 19 KINGLAKE RD., WALLASEY, CHS L44 8BS ENG
38245 CORBETT, JOHN, 36 SUMMERFIELDS WAY., ILKESTON, DBY DE7 9HF ENG
38246 BLAND, RICHARD, 33 PARK AVE., HAWARDEN, CLWYD CH5 3HY ENG
38247 THORNE, RITA, 20 DARNFORD MOORS., LICHFIELD, STS WS14 9RL ENG
38248 HOLLAND, JOAN, 115 MANOR RD., DROYLSDEN, LAN M35 6QD ENG
38249 SAVAGE, KEN, 53 LINDEN DR., SHEERNESS, KEN ME12 1LG ENG
38250 WAY, DEREK, 59 IVY LANE., MACCLESFIELD, CHS SK11 6NU ENG
38251 SPENCER, CHRISTOPHER, 17 BLACK BULL LN., FULWOOD, LAN PR2 3PT ENG
38252 ASH, MR H J, 39 CHURCH RD., NEWICK, EAST SSX BN8 4JX ENG
38253 MCMEEKIN, JOHN, 18 GRIEVE CROFT., BOTHWELL, LKS G71 8LU SCOTLAND
38254 CLARK, IAN, 4 THE CREST., SURBITON, SRY KT5 8JZ ENG
38255 THOMPSON, PATRICIA, 10 WESTON RISE., CAISTER ON SEA, NFK NR30 5AT ENG
38256 CALZADA, JUAN, 1326 SO PARK AVE., POMONA, CA 91766 USA
38257 ROGERS, TIM, 27 STONEACRE AVE., SHEFFIELD, S12 4NT ENG
38258 ANSELL, DOREEN, 189 WESTWOOD LN., WELLING, KEN DA16 2HR ENG
38259 COGSWELL, MR A, 6 ARRAN AVE., SALE, CHES M33 3NQ ENG
38260 KING, MR B, 17 ROMNEY RD., BOLTON, LAN BL1 5TT ENG
38261 HENLY, MR R, 99 MOREDON RD., SWINDON, WIL SN2 2JG ENG
38262 JONES, REV. WILLIAM, ST PAULS, RAYNEL DR., LEEDS, W YORKS LS16 6BS ENG
38263 ANDREWS, JAMES, 5 HOE COURT, THE HOE., PLYMOUTH, PL1 2QG ENG
38264 SKINNER, JOHN, 52 ARUNDEL DRIVE EAST., SALTDEAN, SSX BN2 8SL ENG
38265 ARCHER, STEPHEN, 90 ST ALBANS RD., DARTFORD, KEN DA1 1TY ENG
38266 MORRIS, MARJORIE, 6 LYNDALE CL., WILPSHIRE, LAN BB1 9LX ENG
38267 TRAVIS, CHRISTOPHER, 97 PARTRIDGE WAY., CHADDERTON, OL9 0NT ENG
38268 WEBB, SHEILA, 29 MANOR DR., EWELL, SRY KT19 0EX ENG
38269 DAVISON, PETER, 27 FRYUP CRES., GUISBOROUGH, CLEVE TS14 8LG ENG
38270 TAUNTON, PATRICIA, 41 WYNYARD CRES., TAMATEA, NAPIER NZ
38271 MCDONALD, JEAN, 'BRAESIDE', CHARLTON NO 4 RD., GORE, STHLAND NZ
38272 BOYD, JACK, 187 BALMACEWEN RD., DUNEDIN, OTO NZ
38273 HOSKING, SHIRLEY, STANLEY ROAD RD 24., STRATFORD, 4700 NZ
38274 POPE, MRS D, 3 VERA RD., TE ATATU, AUCK 8 NZ
38275 GARDNER-BROWN, ANN, 34 AVIEMORE DR., HOWICK, AUCK NZ
38276 DILLON, BRIAN & SONIA, 4 LANGANA DR., BROWNS BAY, AUCK 1310 NZ
38277 TURNER, DOROTHY, 80 BLANKNEY ST., CHRISTCHURCH, 4 NZ
38278 HORNE, MISS L, PO BOX 2836., WELLINGTON, NZ
38279 ASHTON, ANNA, 11 SPEY PL., PAPAKOWHAI, WLTN NZ
38280 PARKER, ANDREW, 8 KAURI CRES., HAWERA, NZ
38281 WATSON, JILL, PO BOX 50., REEFTON, WESTLAND NZ
38282 GREGORY, VAL, 26 STANLEY RD., GLENFIELD, AUCK 10 NZ

38283 ANDERTON, ERIC, 87 WOOLFIELD RD., PAPATOETOE, AUCK 1701 NZ
38284 NABNEY, LYDIA, 3/114 VODANOVICH RD., TE ATATU SOUTH, AUCK 8 NZ
38285 SANDHAM, MURIEL, 14 PARK RISE., CAMPBELLS BAY, AUCK 10 NZ
38286 DONNELL, ANNE, 6 PLUNKET ST., KELBURN, WLTN NZ
38287 JENNINGS, RHODA, 7721 118TH ST E., PUYALLUP, WA 98373 USA
38288 MCLAREN, MRS H, 152 RAMSGATE RD., RAMSGATE, NSW 2217 AUS
38289 LOVETT, STEVE, PO BOX 144., DENILIQUIN, NSW 2710 AUS
38290 KING, ARTHUR, 19 MACQUARIE TCE., BALMAIN, NSW 2041 AUS
38291 BELLAMY, HOWARD, 111 CREEK RD., MT GRAVATT, QLD 4122 AUS
38292 FLACK, MRS M, 15 BARNSBURY RD., BALWYN, VIC 3103 AUS
38293 PRATT, MRS Y, 8 BUSANA WAY., NUNAWADING, VIC 3131 AUS
38294 DENNEEN, ROSS, 71 PARK ST., ERSKINEVILLE, NSW 2043 AUS
38295 CALLINAN, WILLIAM, ., KILFENORA, CO. CLARE IRELAND
38296 GOGGINS, JOHN, ST MARTINS RD., ROSSLARE HBR, CO. WEXFORD IRELAND
38297 COYLE, JAMES, 13 CARRICK CT., PORTMARNOCK, DUBLIN IRELAND
38298 MAYRS, ENID, 1 NEWTOWN PARK AVE., BLACKROCK, CO. DUBLIN IRELAND
38299 NOLAN, PATRICK, IRISH ORIGINS RESEARCH AGENCY., KILKENNY, IRELAND
38300 SHORTALL, DR PATRICK, LAYTOWN RD., JULIANSTOWN, MEA IRELAND
38301 PELLY, FRANK, 116 ENNAFORT RD., RAHENY, DUBLIN 5 IRELAND
38302 MAGEE, EILEEN, PARCNASILLA., SHANKILL, CO. DUBLIN IRELAND
38303 DOUGLASS, HEATHER, 28 PINE COURT., BLACKROCK, CO. DUBLIN IRELAND
38304 RYAN-HACKETT, DR R, 17 CHERRY COURT., KILLINEY, CO. DUBLIN IRELAND
38305 LACY, MS D, BALLYMILISH, DUNGRIFFIN RD., HOWTH, CO. DUBLIN IRELAND
38306 JEFFRESON, MRS E, 61 STARKEY ST., FORESTVILLE, NSW 2087 AUS
38307 FORSYTH, MR W, 3 MACLACHLAN ST., HOLDER, ACT 2611 AUS
38308 IODER, ALBERTA, RFD 2., BRADFORD, IL 61421 USA
38309 PUTMAN, GLORIA, 219 LOMA DEL ESCOLAR., LOS ALAMOS, NM 87544 USA
38310 BETHEL, ROY, 211 WEST ST., GROVEPORT, OH 43125 USA
38311 MINNIS, MR M, 6275 OLD CENTREVILLE RD., CENTREVILLE, VA 22020 USA
38312 EDDLEMON, AMELIA, 5445 GLENBRIER., MEMPHIS, TN 38119 USA
38313 LEE, ROBERT, 66689 DESERT VIEW., DESERT HOT SPRINGS, CA 92240 USA
38314 MOZISEK, BETTY, 4332 SAN PABLO CIR., YORBA LINDA, CA 92686 USA
38315 WELLS, BETTY, 423 MARC AVE., STOCKTON, CA 95207 USA
38316 MAAS, RAY, 16989 HINTON CT., CASTRO VALLEY, CA 94546 USA
38317 WEBSTER, MS L, 6841 GLENDALE AVE., BOARDMAN, OH 44512 USA
38318 WILCOX, BRENT, 9271 RIDGE POST., SAN ANTONIO, TX 78250 USA
38319 KOMP, NANCY, 2072 NW WOODLAND DR., CORVALLIS, OR 97330 USA
38320 BOURNER, LINDA, 22019 PORT GAMBLE RD., POULSBO, WA 98370 USA
38321 FORSYTH, BETTY, 1207 CLINTON AVE., IRVINGTON, NJ 07111 USA
38322 GIORDANI, L, 4449 N STEWART AVE., BALDWIN PARK, CA 91706 USA
38323 COURTNAGE, CAMERON, 26355 ADRIAN AVE., HAYWARD, CA 94545 USA
38324 CRAIG, MR J, 4751 MT LA PALMA DR., SAN DIEGO, CA 92117 USA
38325 TURPIN, JOAN, 38563 151ST STREET EAST., LAKE LOS ANGELES, CA 93550 USA
38326 PAUL, LEE, 108 B TIMBER LANE., BAY ST LOUIS, MS 39520 USA
38327 WEIGAND, ROY, 313 N CHARLOTTE ST., LOMBARD, IL 60148 USA
38328 MOUNTS, HENRY, 8622 LYNX RD., SAN DIEGO, CA 92126 USA
38329 DE BERNARDO, BARBARA, PO BOX 595., SAN DIMAS, CA 91773 USA
38330 STEWART, ELLEN, 20323 SE 281ST STREET., KENT, WA 98042 USA
38331 WILLIAMS, MARY, 1051 OVERLOOK RD., BERKELEY, CA 94708 USA
38332 LEAMON, LESLEY, 2023 HULDY, #4., HOUSTON, TX 77019 USA
38333 KLENK, JANET, 6467 DALY RD., CINCINNATI, OH 45224 USA
38334 JAMES, PEARL, 519 SOUTH 20TH., BETHANY, MO 64424 USA
38335 MCLEOD-CEASAR, BRUCE, 1102 CLAREMONT PL., POMONA, CA 91767 USA
38336 HAYDOCK, THOMAS, 1937 GREGORY LANE., CINCINNATI, OH 45206 USA
38337 BYLE, BARNEY, 1465 KOOSER RD., SAN JOSE, CA 95118 USA
38338 AUNGER, KARA, 300 RIDGE RD., NOVATO, CA 94947 USA
38339 COPPES, JOHN, 5440 BEN ALDER., WHITTIER, CA 90601 USA
38340 TULLY, LAURA, 2722 SUNNYBROOK RD., JACKSONVILLE, FL 32216 USA
38341 HUBBELL, HAROLD, 16 ROTON AVE., ROWAYTON, CT 06853 USA
38342 SMITH, EDWIN, 2850 RHONDA WAY., SACRAMENTO, CA 95821 USA
38343 HENIFIN, SHARON, 6046 46TH SW., SEATTLE, WA 98136 USA
38344 SEATON, SCOTT, PO BOX 4338., BALBOA, CA 92661 USA
38345 RICKARDS, RUSS, 4427 DOWNING CT., PLEASANTON, CA 94566 USA
38346 OLTRA, MICHELE, 785 NAUGATUCK AVE., MILFORD, CT 06460 USA
38347 DUNWOODY, WILLIAM, 2906 SCOTT RD., BURBANK, CA 91504 USA
38348 DAKE, MR B, 1267 MANZANITA WAY NE., KEIZER, OR 97303 USA
38349 MCARTHUR, CLAUDIA, 239 LILLIAN CRES., BARRIE, ONT L4N 5Y6 CAN
38350 SCOTT, MR R, PO BOX 4232 STN 'A'., VICTORIA, BC V8X 3X8 CAN
38351 SCHOONDERBEEK, MR W, 3408-102 AVE., EDMONTON, ALB T5W 0A3 CAN
38352 SPRACKLIN, GORDON, 31 BIRCHARD ST., AGINCOURT, ONT M1T 1Z3 CAN
38353 DARLINGTON, ROBERT, 1820 MERIDA PL., VICTORIA, BC V8N 5C9 CAN
38354 PLETSCH, KATHLEEN, BOX 598., SEAFORTH, ONT N0K 1W0 CAN

38355 DONALD, JOHN, 18B LAWLEY CRES., PYMBLE, NSW 2073 AUS
38356 GADEN, CAROLINE, 37 GARIBALDI ST., ARMIDALE, NSW 2350 AUS
38357 WATTS, VALERIE, 97 GREENWICH RD., GREENWICH, NSW 2065 AUS
38358 SCOTT, MR R, PO BOX 4232 STN 'A'., VICTORIA, BC V8X 3X8 CAN
38359 DERY, DOROTHY, 109 NO ADAMS #1., GLENDALE, CA 91206 USA
38360 WILLIAMS, DOROTHY, 6417 DALLAS WAY., SACRAMENTO, CA 95823 USA
38361 BRIGHT, SUSAN, 22 MARILYN CIRCLE., SACRAMENTO, CA 95838 USA
38362 BADGETT, AUDREY, 2103 HARRISON NW STE 2 #373., OLYMPIA, WA 98502 USA
38363 PADILLA, BETTY, 1836 NO KIBBY RD., MERCED, CA 95340 USA
38364 BANKS, LES & CLAIRE, 87 OHIO AVE., PROVIDENCE, RI 02905 USA
38365 CULLEN, MR R, 101 N GEORGE MASON DR #2., ARLINGTON, VA 22203 USA
38366 COLE, DIANE, 7385 ROXBURY AVE., MANASSAS, VA 22110 USA
38367 RICE, W SCOTT, 912 OXFORD CT., PALATINE, IL 60067 USA
38368 JAFFE, MARCIA, 4624 FAYETTE CT., DAYTON, OH 45415 USA
38369 SIRSE, GAIL, 45569 RUSSIA RD., OBERLIN, OH 44074 USA
38370 RICHARD, DIANE, 720 PULITZER LN., ALLEN, TX 75002 USA
38371 OTTOSON, WILLIAM, RT 7 BOX 587., AMARILLO, TX 79118 USA
38372 SAUER, RUTH V., 10821 PT VASHON DR SW., VASHON, WA 98070 USA
38373 GLOVER, CLIFTON, 29177 SE HWY 224., EAGLE CREEK, OR 97022 USA
38374 GRIMMER, YVONNE, 1468 WHITEFIELD RD., PASADENA, CA 91104 USA
38375 DE VILLIERS, WILLIAM, 1 RYE RD., MOWBRAY, 7700 RSA
38376 BANKS, MR D, 28 MELROSE PL., DURBAN NORTH, NATAL 4051 RSA
38377 HAYES, STEPHEN, PO BOX 7648., PRETORIA, 0001 RSA
38378 VAN BILJON, AUBREY, 18 ALBERT RD., TAMOERSKLOOF, CAPE 8001 RSA
38379 MITCHELL, DAVE, 38 RIVERTON RD., RONDEBOSCH, CAPE 7700 RSA
38380 LINDSAY, BERYL, 8 RENFREW RD, EASTLEA., HARARE, ZIMBABWE
38381 DELPLANQUE, GWEN, BOX 64168 HIGHLANS NORTH., JOHANNESBURG, TVL 2037 RSA
38382 DE SILVA, NATALI, 23 ERLSWOLD WAY., SAXONWOLD, JHB 2196 RSA
38383 REIM, MR C, 71 MANOR DR., DURBAN, 4001 RSA
38384 ROGERS, RUTH, 864 – 52ND AVE., LACHINE, QUE H8T 2X8 CAN
38385 JACKSON, EILEEN, 303 - 90 DUKE ST., HAMILTON, ONT L8P 1X6 CAN
38386 LONGEWAY, BRIAN, BOX 820., CARSTAIRS, ALB T0M 0N0 CAN
38387 LAKE, JEAN, RR #3., PETERBOROUGH, ONT K9J 6X4 CAN
38388 MCCOWAN, NANCY, RR #1., PICKERING, ONT L1V 2P8 CAN
38389 LINK, KATRINA, BOX 1301, RR #1., CLEARWATER, BC V0E 1N0 CAN
38390 NELSON, JOYCE, 22 HOSKING PL., GUELPH, ONT N1G 3R9 CAN
38391 SMYTH, PATRICIA, 45 FRANCIS ST., LINDSAY, ONT K9V 3S3 CAN
38392 SCHRYVER, MRS C, 301 ALLEN DR., SWIFT CURRENT, SASK S9H 3A4 CAN
38393 MACDONALD, MERLE, 416 GORE ST., NELSON, BC V1L 5B9 CAN
38394 WALTERS, MURIEL, 2305 – 23 AVE SOUTH., LETHBRIDGE, ALB T1K 1K8 CAN
38395 BIRT, NEIL, 55 GLENGARRY RD., ST CATHARINES, ONT L2T 2V4 CAN
38396 LE MASURIER, MURRAY, 77 CRANBROOKE AVE., TORONTO, ONT M5M 1M3 CAN
38397 MCKINNON, LILLIAN, BOX 48 PEBBLE BEACH RD., POWELL RIVER, BC V8A 4Z2 CAN
38398 KING, RITA, 18 ROSEDALE AVE., HALIFAX, NX B3N 2J3 CAN
38399 HAMILTON, MAY, BOX 3165., OLDS, ALB T0M 1P0 CAN
38400 PATERSON, DOREEN, BOX 1000., SORRENTO, BC V0E 2W0 CAN
38401 RICHARDS, KATHLEEN, 44 STUBBS DR, APT 410., WILLOWDALE, ONT M2L 2R3 CAN
38402 SMITH, DAVID, 39 SHIRLEY AVE., BARRIE, ONT L4N 1M8 CAN
38403 PLEASANCE, ALLAN, 1294 GREENOAKS DR., MISSISSAUGA, ONT L5J 3A5 CAN
38404 FRASER, MARIE, 4221 PASCHAL PL., PRINCE GEORGE, BC V2N 3J7 CAN
38405 AERTS, PIERRE, 261 STRASBOURG., DOLLARD DES ORMEAUX, QUE H9G 1R9 CAN
38406 PATTERSON, CURTIS, 54 CUTTING ST., COATICOOK, QUE J1A 2G3 CAN
38407 GILLIE, MARION, 35 AMBLESIDE AVE., TORONTO, ONT M8Z 2H8 CAN
38408 ROUSSEAU, MONTIQUE, 85 RENAUD., LAVAL, QUE H7M 1W6 CAN
38409 RIMMER, JEWEL, 267 MORTLAKE AVE., ST LAMBERT, QUE J4P 3C4 CAN
38410 STIBBARD, JOCELYN, RR #1 THORNTON., ONT, ONT L0L 2N0 CAN
38411 SCHMIDT, ALICE, 72 PATTANDON AVE., KITCHENER, ONT N2M 3S5 CAN
38412 CRUDEN, MISS S, 181 WELBORNE AVE., KINGSTON, ONT K7M 4G2 CAN
38413 MCKERCHAR, GORDON, 903 DAWN LN., VICTORIA, BC V9B 5A6 CAN
38414 LAWSON, JEAN, BOX 4244 STATION D., HAMILTON, ONT L8V 4L6 CAN
38415 COLLISON, EDITH, 955 KING RD, UNIT 9., BURLINGTON, ONT L7T 4J6 CAN
38416 HOLTZ, MRS R, RR #1 SOUTH MARY LAKE RD., PORT SYDNEY, ONT P0B 1L0 CAN
38417 GILES, PETER, 26 BLAKE AVE., SAULT STE MARIE, ONT P6B 4X4 CAN
38418 HILL, SHARON, 357 HICKLING TRAIL., BARRIE, ONT L4M 6A4 CAN
38419 JUDD, ANNE, R 1., PORT ELGIN, ONT N0H 2C5 CAN
38420 MARION, MR R, 1703 BUCKINGHAM DR., WINDSOR, ONT N8T 2A5 CAN
38421 COLCHESTER HIST SOC GENEALOGY GP,, 29 YOUNG ST., TRURO, NS B2N 5C5 CAN
38422 LEGGOTT, LOIS, 4206 – 71 STREET., CAMROSE, ALTA T4V 3Z4 CAN
38423 GALE, JOYCE, 312 ISABELLA ST EAST., SASKATOON, SASK S7J 0B4 CAN
38424 CARSON, MRS J, 6 KIRBY AVE., GREENSVILLE, ONT L9H 5K9 CAN
38425 JOYCE, ELAINE, 320 LINDEN AVE., WINNIPEG, MAN R2K 0N4 CAN
38426 GENT, ALAN, 51 CRANBROOK CRES., WELLAND, ONT L3C 3P5 CAN

38427 DORIN, EMIL, RR #1., INNISFAIL, ALTA T0M 1A0 CAN
38428 HOLMES, MRS F, 982 ROYAL YORK RD., TORONTO, ONT M8X 2E9 CAN
38429 BEATSON, BRIAN, 441 BEECHCROFT PL., PORT PERRY, ONT L9L 1N5 CAN
38430 MONTPAS, YVES, 601 RUE NICOLET., MONTREAL, QUE H1W 3K2 CAN
38431 SHIRE, DAN, 22 – 1235 RADOM ST., PICKERING, ONT L1W 1J3 CAN
38432 SWAINE, PAM, BOX 90 RR1., CHURCHILL, ONT L0L 1K0 CAN
38433 NEWALL, ELSPETH, 37 CRICKLEWOOD CR., THORNHILL, ONT L3T 4T8 CAN
38434 CENTRAL BUTTE GENEAL SOC,, BOX 429., CENTRAL BUTTE, SASK S0H 0T0 CAN
38435 FOLKERS, PATRICIA E., #503 – 365 KENNEDY RD., BRAMPTON, ONT L6W 3H3 CAN
38436 MCKINLAY, FRANCES, 11 JAMES LN., ST JOHNS, NFLD A1E 3H3 CAN
38437 ROBERTS, MRS K, 1775 SOLITAIRE CT., MISSISSAUGA, ONT L5L 2P2 CAN
38438 MAITLAND, SHANE, 912 GLADMER PARK., REGINA, SAS S4P 2XB CAN
38439 EDWARDS, PETER, 117 AIRDRIE RD., TORONTO, ONT M4G 1M6 CAN
38440 LIGHTBURN, REETA, 7958 TAULBUT ST., MISSION, BC V2V 3W7 CAN
38441 YEO, ADRIENNE, 15490 - 98 AVENUE., SURREY, BC V3R 7G4 CAN
38442 GOWERS, MRS T, 107 MCELROY RD E., HAMILTON, ONT L9A 1Z1 CAN
38443 LEVERTON, DAVID, 302 - 1040 W 8TH AVE., VANCOUVER, BC V6H 1C4 CAN
38444 SWARBRICK, ALAN, BOX 1504., LACOMBE, ALTA T0C 1S0 CAN
38445 FERRELL, NORMA, 2539 SANDALWOOD DR., KAMLOOPS, BC V2B 6V3 CAN
38446 GANNON, BESSIE, 468 SIMCOE ST N., OSHAWA, ONT L1G 4T6 CAN
38447 EASLER, TIMOTHY, 206 W SAINT ANDREWS RD., MIDLAND, MI 48640 USA
38448 CULP, GARY, 7589 WILSON CRES., NIAGARA FALLS, ONT L2G 4S3 CAN
38449 MARSHALL, PAT, BOX 855., TILBURY, ONT N0P 2L0 CAN
38450 CROXALL, CAROL, 2852 BRITTON RD., QUESNEL, BC V2J 4X5 CAN
38451 KINDERSLEY GENEALOGY SOCIETY,, BOX 842., KINDERSLEY, SAS S0L 1S0 CAN
38452 HURST, SHARON, LOT 16 HUGHES DR., GILFORD, ONT L0L 1R0 CAN
38453 WESTBURY, JUNE, 227 MONTGOMERY AVE., WINNIPEG, MB R3L 1T1 CAN
38454 HAHN, MARION, PO BOX 88., BENTLEY, ALB T0C 0J0 CAN
38455 PILSON, MRS J, 151 ALBERT ST., BOLTON, ONT L7E 3G5 CAN
38456 MACK, SHIRLEY, 24 EAST PARK DR., GLOUCESTER, ONT K1B 3Z8 CAN
38457 SMALL, CAROL, RR 1., DENFIELD, ONT N0M 1P0 CAN
38458 VAN KESTEREN, MR A, 6 LANSDOWNE PL., ST JOHNS, NFLD A1A 2V9 CAN
38459 VEER, GUY, 714 DE STRASBOURG., STE-FOY, QUE G1X 3A7 CAN
38460 COUGHLIN, GLENDA, 745 FLAMINGO DR., SUMMERSIDE, PEI C1N 4S1 CAN
38461 KUCHINKA, BARNEY T., BOX 130., MACOUN, SAS S0C 1P0 CAN
38462 MICKLEBOROUGH, WARREN, BOX 22, RR #2., REGINA, SAS S4P 2Z2 CAN
38463 ELDER, CATHERINE, 46 DUNVEGAN DR., CHATHAM, ONT N7M 4Z8 CAN
38464 HOLMES, VERA, 9412 TUBA CT., VIENNA, VA 22182 USA
38465 KERR, JOHN, 128 CRAIG DR., KITCHENER, ONT N2B 2J3 CAN
38466 MACMILLAN, HUGH, 21 SUFFOLK ST W., GUELPH, ONT N1H 2H9 CAN
38467 LEBREUX, MME A., CP 198., GRANDE RIVIERE OUEST, GASPE QUE G0C 1W0 CAN
38468 PARKER, JUDY, PO BOX 99., KITSCOTY, ALB T0B 2P0 CAN
38469 WOOD, STEPHEN, 225 EUCLID ST., WHITBY, ONT L1N 5B4 CAN
38470 MYLES, PHILIP, BOX 1795., PINCHER CREEK, ALTA T0K 1W0 CAN
38471 HOPKINS, DEREK, 6640 BIARRITZ., BROSSARD, QUE J4Z 2A2 CAN
38472 CLEVETTE, CHRIS, 55 RACE ST, APT 12., CORNWALL, ONT K6H 1G7 CAN
38473 MARTIN, ROBERT W., 116 CLEARSPRING RD., WHITBY, ONT L1N 5R5 CAN
38474 MURRAY, TOM, BOX 132., OWEN SOUND, ONT N4K 5P1 CAN
38475 YOUNG, KEN, 1096 – 11TH AVE EAST., OWEN SOUND, ONT N4K 5Y8 CAN
38476 AITKEN, BARABARA, 4242 BATH RD., KINGSTON, ONT K7M 4Y7 CAN
38477 FORSYTH, JESSIE, 15 WELLINGTON AVE., VICTORIA, BC V8V 4H5 CAN
38478 BARBER, NELLIE, BOX 272., CARNDUFF, SASK S0C 0S0 CAN
38479 FORRESTER, JIM, RR #1., WESTPORT, ONT K0G 1X0 CAN
38480 MELLOR, JAMES, 21 LARKFIELD DR., DON MILLS, ONT M3B 2H2 CAN
38481 WAGAR SCHOOL GENE. CLUB,, 5785 PARKHAVEN., COTE ST LUC, QUE H4W 1X8 CAN
38482 SCHAMPEL, GRETCHEN, 2191 CARTER AVE., ST PAUL, MN 55108 USA
38483 ROBINSON, H, LOT 26 CHIFLEY DR., DARGAN, NSW 2786 AUS
38484 WRIGHT, ELAINE, 31 RAYMOND ST., SHORNCLIFFE, QLD 4017 AUS
38485 MACKENZIE, PATRICIA, 16 YOWANI ST., ROBINA, QLD 4226 AUS
38486 MAYNARD, JOHN, 7 ISABEL AVE., RINGWOOD EAST, VIC 3135 AUS
38487 JOHNSTON, GLENYS, 1 SHAW ST., SPRINGVALE SOUTH, VIC 3172 AUS
38488 ANDREWS, MALCOLM, 100 ELIZABETH ST., ROSALIE, QLD 4064 AUS
38489 DRAPER, ROMA, 2/6 VISTA ST., GREENWICH, NSW 2065 AUS
38490 CARTER, MRS S, PO BOX 25., BERMAGUI SOUTH, NSW 2546 AUS
38491 DRURY, KATHLEEN, WOODBURN RD., MILTON, NSW 2538 AUS
38492 CANNON, JOHN, RSD 687B., GAWLER, TAS 7315 AUS
38493 THERRIEN, LEO, 761 ST ANTOINE., BON CONSEIL, QUE J0C 1A0 CAN
38494 VOSS, PAMELA, C/-ROBINSON 16/12 WARATAH ST., CRONULLA, NSW 2230 AUS
38495 TOWARZYSTWO GENEALOGICZNO-HERALDYCZNE,, WODNA 27., PALAC GORKOW, POZNAN 61-781 POLAND
38496 POOLE, MR H, LES CANEBIERES 487., LE MUY, 83490 FRANCE
38497 WELSH, GRAHAM, 522 PINE TREE DR., LONDON, ONT N6H 3N1 CAN

38498 LOVEJOY, GERALD, 3112 50 ST SW., CALGARY, ALTA T3E 6P6 CAN
38499 BOOKER, MR R, 42 LAKESHORE BLVD, RR1., ENNISMORE, ONT K0L 1T0 CAN
38500 SMITH, FRANK, PO BOX E27., WEST MARRICKVILLE, NSW 2204 AUS
38501 SIGNORACCI, COUNT D.S., VIA F.LLI ROSSELLI, 21., S. LORENZO, PS 61047 ITALY
38502 TULLY, MRS L, 74 BLENHEIM WAY., YAXLEY, CAM PE7 3WF ENG
38503 ELLIOTT, MRS M, 24 CALVERT RD., DORKING, SRY RH4 1LS ENG
38504 CAMPBELL, MRS B, 21 PETRIE ST., ROTORUA, NZ
38505 WHEELIS, MRS J, 1012 WESTERFIELD DR NE., ALBUQUERQUE, NM 87112 USA
38506 PLUNKETT, B, 36 DAGLISH ST., WEMBLEY, WA 6014 AUS
38507 COLE, MR R, 26 ASQUITH ST., OATLEY, NSW 2223 AUS
38508 HUNTER, MISS J, 15 QUEEN ST., MARYBOROUGH, QLD 4650 AUS
38509 MACQUEEN, MISS L, 6 ILLAWARRA CRES., NORTH DANDENONG, VIC 3175 AUS
38510 WINTERBOTTOM, JANET, PO BOX 240., WAGGA WAGGA, NSW 2650 AUS
38511 BECKETT, JAMES D, 34 EASTWOOD AVE., DROYLSDEN, LANCS M35 6BJ ENG
38512 UNWIN, JEANETTE, 191 ROLLESTON RD., BURTON-ON-TRENT, STAFFS DE13 0LD ENG
38513 MOORE, DONALD, 28 CLEVELAND RD., SOUTH WOODFORD, LND E18 2AL ENG
38514 GILLBANKS, BRIAN, 102 HORNDEAN RD., EMSWORTH, HAM PO10 7TL ENG
38515 MCCALLUM, MR & MRS D., 14 PALM CLOSE., LITTLEOVER, DBY ENG
38516 YOUNG, MRS O, 3 OAK DENE., EALING, LND W13 8AW ENG
38517 BURNETT, LARRY, PO BOX 6394., SAN FRANCISCO, CA 94101 USA
38518 FAIRFIELD, CARL, 2164 FICKLE HILL RD., ARCATA, CA 95521 USA
38519 ROTH, LAWRENCE, 4844 VESCA WAY., SAN JOSE, CA 95129 USA
38520 ARBON, BEVERLY, 915 E 1600 S., MAPLETON, UT 84664 USA
38521 MACHAFFIE, BRUCE, 5014 BROADMOOR BLUFFS DR., COLORADO SPRINGS, CO 80906 USA
38522 MACDONALD, ELIZABETH, 1100 CODY., HAYS, KS 67601 USA
38523 CARRINGTON, MARGARET, 612 HERMOSA ST., SOUTH PASADENA, CA 91030 USA
38524 STEFFEN, RUTH, 3033 JORDAN LN., STEVENS POINT, WI 54481 USA
38525 HOUDE, JOHN, PO BOX 82., GLENCOE, IL 60022 USA
38526 GODIN, GERALDINE, PO BOX 520848., BIG LAKE, AK 99652 USA
38527 MEDINA, MARY KAY, 3855 LESSER DR., NEWBURY PARK, CA 91320 USA
38528 SCHLESIER, ROBERT, PO BOX 219., EL CAJON, CA 92022 USA
38529 ROWLES, JAMES, 408 GARFIELD ST, PO BOX 5., BLOOMDALE, OH 44817 USA
38530 FALCK, MYRON, 707 S 7 STREET., ST PETER, MN 56802 USA
38531 BUTLER, JOANN, RT 1 BOX 140 (421 POPLAR)., BURDEN, KS 67019 USA
38532 HIGHMAN, CLIFTON, 1056 COLUMBIA PL., BOULDER, CO 80303 USA
38533 STOUT, FLORENCE, 150 N MAIN., LOMBARD, IL 60148 USA
38534 RODEN, JOAN, 118 W CHANDLER DR., MUNDELEIN, IL 60060 USA
38535 BRADLEY, JAMES, 1406 EVERGREEN LN., DERBY, KS 67037 USA
38536 TILLIS, MARSHALL, 110 VALENCIA DR., SANFORD, FL 32771 USA
38537 HUNGERFORD, RICHARD, 13810 FREDERICK AVE., OMAHA, NE 68138 USA
38538 PRICE, EMMA LEE, 104 PRENTISS ST., THOUSAND OAKS, CA 91360 USA
38539 BARBER, HELEN, 1229 NORTH RD., OAKLEIGH SOUTH, VIC 3167 AUS
38540 HAWORTH, ESME, 64 WHITEHEAD GR W., WEST ROSEBUD, VIC 3940 AUS
38541 WILKINS, MRS A, 9 KERR ST., HORNSBY, NSW 2077 AUS
38542 LAINE, MARIANNE, YLIKYLANTIE 43 AS 11., PORI, 28220 FINLAND
38543 DAHL, BITTEN, BOSTALLSGATAN 98., LINKOPING, S 58331 SWEDEN
38544 KANTELE, OLAVI, LAHNATIE 14., ESPOO, 02170 FINLAND
38545 KARLSSON, INGVAR, CARL BERGSTENS GATA 108., NORRKOPING, 603 78 SWEDEN
38546 JORSELL, KERSTIN, ROSENVAGEN 3 D., VAROBACKA, N 430 22 SWEDEN
38547 METHER, LEIF, ALLEGATAN 6AA15., ABO, 20140 FINLAND
38548 RYD, ULLA, BOX 53 VILLA GRANKULLEN., TENHULT, 560 27 SWEDEN
38549 WARD, KEVIN, KNAPPSTADSV 8., KARLSTAD, 653 42 SWEDEN
38550 KOHLER, CHRISTER, TRADGARDSGATAN 26A., LULEA, S-951 35 SWEDEN
38551 LUNDGREN, BERTIL, SKRADDAREV 3., KUNGSBACKA, S-434 40 SWEDEN
38552 MODIG, OLOF, MELLANVAGSGATAN 13., VASTRA FROLUNDA, S-421 33 SWEDEN
38553 STENFELT, GORAN, HAGELAKRAVAGEN 10., MALILLA, S-570 82 SWEDEN
38554 IDOFSSON, SVEN-INGE, BOLMARYD, NOTTJA., HAMNEDA, S-340 13 SWEDEN
38555 JENSEN, LARS OLOF, HEDVAGEN 35., ULLARED, 310 60 SWEDEN
38556 ANDERSSON, KERSTIN, LYNAS PL 1531., BERGVIK, 820 23 SWEDEN
38557 NILSSON, INGER, BJALOSAGATAN 25., LJUNGSBRO, 590 60 SWEDEN
38558 RYBERG, BENGT, STUREST 33., BORAS, S-502 31 SWEDEN
38559 ROBERTSSON, SVEN, GUBBANGSV 31., ENSKEDE, STOCKHOLM 122 45 SWEDEN
38560 PAULSSON, BODIL, KRONBORGSVAGEN 18 D., MALMO, 217 42 SWEDEN
38561 SKOLD, H., ARDENNERGATAN 36 G., YSTAD, S-271 37 SWEDEN
38562 SIPPU, SEPPO, METSAAHONTIE 10., INKEROINEN, SF-46900 FINLAND
38563 ROSENBAHR, CHRISTER, APELGATAN 21 B., UPPSALA, C 754 35 SWEDEN
38564 KREY, JAN, VALASENS HERRGARD., KARLSKOGA, S-691 94 SWEDEN
38565 BILKENROTH, OLOF, GENVAGEN 8., HUDDINGE, S141 37 SWEDEN
38566 EDELSVARD, CURT, LINNEGATAN 13., SODERTALJE, S-151 44 SWEDEN
38567 ANDERSON, PATRICIA, LILLE STRANDGATE 7., LARVIK, N-3250 NORWAY
38568 BASHFORD, PETER, 22 AVANDINA CRES., GREENSBOROUGH, VIC 3088 AUS
38569 JAMES, JO DEAN, RT 1 BOX 13AC., TYRONE, OK 73951 USA

38570 WOODZELL, PATTY, PO BOX 278., WARM SPRINGS, VA 24484 USA
38571 MEALER, NATALIE, BOX 202., WALNUT GROVE, CA 95690 USA
38572 WARRINGTON, EVELYN, 1108 7TH AVE N., HUMBOLDT, IA 50548 USA
38573 WILSON, LELAND, PO BOX 893., LINDALE, TX 75771 USA
38574 KILPATRICK, MARGARET, 1854 INDIANA DR., GALESBURG, IL 61401 USA
38575 HALPIN, FRANK, 9048 N 107TH PLACE., SCOTTSDALE, AZ 85258 USA
38576 HARGRAVE, MRS G, PO BOX 2681., LUBBOCK, TX 79408 USA
38577 KNIGGE, CAROL, 8206 PENNY LN., RICHMOND, IL 60071 USA
38578 HIRSH, ALLAN, 11 SLADE AVE, APT 710., BALTIMORE, MD 21208 USA
38579 NEWELL, PETER, 4 PEPPERCOMBE CL., URCHFONT, WIL SN10 4QS ENG
38580 MOSS, MRS V, BEECHWOOD, BOX LN., BOVINGDON, HERTS HP3 0DS ENG
38581 DORRINGTON, IRENE, 404 BATH RD., HOUNSLOW, MDX TW4 7RP ENG
38582 MACKAY, MARION, 19 STYLES PL., MERRYLANDS, NSW 2160 AUS
38583 DUQUETTE, JOAN, 480 HARVEY ST., NORTH BAY, ONT P1B 4G9 CAN
38584 TYSON, MRS J, 94 BINSWOOD AVE., TORONTO, ONT M4C 3N9 CAN
38585 DIFFEY, KAREN, 10/6 GORDON ST., PORT MACQUARIE, NSW 2444 AUS
38586 PROFFITT, JOHN, 19 TIVERTON CRES., NEW PLYMOUTH, NZ
38587 BRYSON, WILLIAM, PO BOX 16321., HOUSTON, TX 77222 USA
38588 ETHIER, L, 10515 NE 122 STREET., KIRKLAND, WA 98034 USA
38589 HILTON, JOHN, 2226 COMMONWEALTH AVE., NEWTON, MA 02166 USA
38590 SMALL, JANET, 94 BALDRIDGE RD., GREERS FERRY, AR 72067 USA
38591 TAYLOR, MARY, PO BOX 68., BURSON, CA 95225 USA
38592 SITTON, VERONICA, 3105 NW GARFIELD AVE., CORVALLIS, OR 97330 USA
38593 MCDONALD, RITA, 2108 W 32ND ST., PUEBLO, CO 81008 USA
38594 BLAKIE, MISS L, 1/92 BEACH RD., BUNBURY, WA 6230 AUS
38595 TRIMBLE, DOROTHY, 26 KENNEDY STREET WEST., AURORA, ONT L4G 2L5 CAN
38596 ELLIS, MARGARET, 49 BORONIA ST., WENTWORTHVILLE, NSW 2145 AUS
38597 BOYD, MIKE, 42 ROSMAN CIRCUIT., GILMORE, ACT 2905 AUS
38598 HERDA, BRIGITTE, KIRCHWEG 42., PLUEDERHAUSEN, BRD D-7067 GERMANY
38599 HERTER, HERR GERO, TRAUTENAUER STR 6., BERLIN, BRD 1157 GERMANY
38600 HERZOG, BRUNO HEINZ, IM GEERIG 39., MELLINGEN, CH 5507 SWITZERLAND
38601 HENNIGHAUSEN, DR HELMUT, BAHNHOFSTR 52., WABERN, BRD 3583 GERMANY
38602 HINTERTHUR, KLAUS, SOPHIENSTR 115., KARLSRUHE 1, BRD 7500 GERMANY
38603 HOFFMEISTER, ARNOLD, ALTER GRENZWEG 28., LEVERKUSEN, NRW 5090 GERMANY
38604 HOFMEISTER, DR KARL HEINZ, VOLTASTR 144., BREMEN 33, BRD 2800 GERMANY
38605 HOLENSTEIN, OPAL MISAE, SCHUETZENSTRASSE 7., SCHWYZ, CH 6430 SWITZERLAND
38606 JERICHO, HORST, LORTZINGSTR 3., LEBACH, BRD 6610 GERMANY
38607 JOHNSON, GERHARD, IM WINKEL 1., NETPHEN, BRD 5902 GERMANY
38608 JUERGENS, WOLF D., ROSTOCKER STR 2., KOBLENZ, BRD D-5400 GERMANY
38609 KAUL, BERNHARD, ABTEI HAUTERIVE., POSIEUX, CH L725 SWITZERLAND
38610 KLASSEN, HORST A., HELLENTHALER WEG 11., ERFTSTADT, GER D-5042 GERMANY
38611 KLAUSER, WERNER, TANNENBACHSTR 19., OBERRIEDEN, CH 8942 SWITZERLAND
38612 KLEINSCHROTH, WERNER, MARTIN-LUTHER-STRASSE 1., GOSLAR, D-3380 GERMANY
38613 KNEIP, HANS-DIETER, HAUPTSTR 118., ST SEBASTIAN, D-5401 GERMANY
38614 KNOPF, HELGE, RUEDESHEIMER STRASSE 18., WIESBADEN, BRD D-6200 GERMANY
38615 KOSTER, AXEL, EBER HARDSTRASSE 27., LAUFFEN AM NECKAR, BRD 7128 GERMANY
38616 KRAEMER, JOHANNES, LERCHENWEG 49., KOELN 30, BRD D-5000 GERMANY
38617 KRAEMER, H.J., SCHREBERSTRASSE 7., TROISDORF, D-5210 GERMANY
38618 KREJCIK, KLAS-DIETER, LINDENSTRASSE 36., SCHAAFHEIM 1, D-6117 GERMANY
38619 LAUX, RENATE, RHEINSTRASSE 24., NENTERSHAUSEN, 5431 GERMANY
38620 LESSER, ANDREAS, LUITPOLDSTR 1., GAUTING, BRD 8035 GERMANY
38621 LIEBEZEIT, FALK, HINDENBURGSTR 31., DIEPHOLZ, W-2840 GERMANY
38622 LINDE, ROLAND, PFUHLSTR 10., HORN-B.M.1, BRD W-4934 GERMANY
38623 LINDNER, HERBERT, STARENWEG 5., WEILHEIM/TECK, BAD/WUE W 7315 GERMANY
38624 LIST, DR BRUNO, IM LEE 19., ARLESHEIM, CH-4144 SWITZERLAND
38625 MAEGLI, PETER, RATHAUSSTRASSE 21., LIESTAL, CH 4410 SWITZERLAND
38626 MENKE, HARTMUT LUDWIG, KONSUL-LIEDER-ALLEE 32., HEIKENDORF, W-2305 GERMANY
38627 MIERS, HORST E., P.O.B. 70 1211., HAMBURG 70, D-2000 GERMANY
38628 MILDNER, DR SIEGFRIED, 54 SONDERSHAUSEN, FRANZ-LISZT-STR. 8, O-5400 AUSTRIA
38629 MOROFKE, JENS MICHAEL, ENZSTRASSE 6., LUDWIGSBURG, 7140 GERMANY
38630 MUELLER, MATTHIAS, STUCKBERGSTR 19., BAYREUTH, 8580 GERMANY
38631 MUES, KLAUS, ZU MEYERS FOEHR 1., SOLTAU, BRD D-3040 GERMANY
38632 MULL-EHLER, MELITTA, WIESENWEG 2., WESTFEHMARN, D-2448 GERMANY
38633 OSTERWALD-LENUM, KURT., SKIPPINGEVEJ 14, KOPENHAGEN, 2700 DENMARK
38634 PETERSEN-ROIL, ALMUTH, PO BOX 440101., MUNICH 44, BRD 8000 GERMANY
38635 RENDA, DR ERNST-GEORG, AM DAMSBERG 12., MAINZ 43, BRD D-6500 GERMANY
38636 RETHAGEN, ANDREAS, ADLERWEG 17., KASSEL, D-3500 GERMANY
38637 RINGLEB, ADOLF, PAPENHORSTER STR 44., NIENHAGEN, 3101 GERMANY
38638 SCHOLZ-BEHLAU, ARMIN, MORGENGRABEN 2., KOLN 80, 5000 GERMANY
38639 SEELAENDER, JOHANNES, KOENIGSBERGERSTR 35., BAD DUERRHEIM 1, D-7737 GERMANY
38640 SWINNE, DR AXEL HILMAR, POSTF. 1160., BAD RAPPENAU, D-W 6927 GERMANY
38641 TORKE, GUNTER, HEIDESTR 28., ALPEN, BRD 4234 GERMANY

38642 TRAMPEDACH, HENNING, ROENNE ALLE 3, BOX 57., VIBY SJAELLAND, DK-4130 DENMARK
38643 VAN AALST, HANS ERIK, FALKENWEG 7., BAD GANDERSHEIM, D-3353 GERMANY
38644 VOGT, HELMUT, BARIGAUER WEG LL PF 13., MELLENBACH, DDR 6428 GERMANY
38645 SCHNITZLEIN, WALTER, WILLINGER STR 14., BAD AIBLING, 8202 GERMANY
38646 WAGENMAKERS, JOHANNES PIETER, BERGSTRASSE 18., HINWIL, CH 8340 SWITZERLAND
38647 WEIDE, BERNOL, PETER-OTTEN STR 11., BERGHEIM, BRD 5010 GERMANY
38648 WEIST, ARMIN, JACQUES-DUCLOS-STR 64., BERLIN, O-1156 GERMANY
38649 WENAU, LUTZ, AM KONIGSDAMM 10., LILIENTHAL, 2804 GERMANY
38650 WESNER, DORIS, RIESWEILERHOHL., SIMMERN, 6540 GERMANY
38651 WESSEL, HANS-PETER, JAGDGRUND 14., HAMBURG 61, 2000 GERMANY
38652 WICHMANN, ARNOLD, ADALBERTSTR 31., KIEL 1, D-2300 GERMANY
38653 WICKI-DERUNGS, WALTER, NIDERBERGSTR 20, PO BOX., STANS, CH 6370 SWITZERLAND
38654 WIEDERMANN, DR ROLF, WIESEN STR 18., ODENTHAL, 5068 GERMANY
38655 WYSS, WALTER, KRUMMACKERWEG 31., OLTEN, CH 4600 SWITZERLAND
38656 SPRIET, J., SNEPPESTRAAT 10., LENDELEDE, 8860 BELGIUM
38657 AICHER, HERR M., NEUMUEHLE., KEMPTTHAL, CH 8310 SWITZERLAND
38658 BALTUS, KURT, PFR LEGEMANN STR 16., NORVENICH, 5164 GERMANY
38659 BARTH, HEINO, OBERE WAIBLINGERSTRASSE 158., STUTTGART, D-7000 GERMANY
38660 BAYHA, HORST, HAUBLICKSTRASSE 20., LE-MUSBERG, BRD 7022 GERMANY
38661 BENDEL, HELMUT, SAARLANDSTR 14., MEMMINGEN, 8940 GERMANY
38662 BERGSTRASSER, ERWIN, ROMERSTRASSE 4., WORTH 2, 6729 GERMANY
38663 BERTGES, WILLY, KLOSTERSTRASSE 1 B., SCHWEICH, BRD 5502 GERMANY
38664 BILLE, KURT, HILDESHEIMER STR. 16., HAMELN, 3252 GERMANY
38665 BINDSCHEDLER, HANS-MARTIN, IM NAF 959., HORGENBERG, CH 8815 SWITZERLAND
38666 BOLLENHAGEN-AMMERMANN, HELGA, WEINBRENNERSTR 14., KARLSRUHE, 7500 GER
38667 BREYMAYER, REINHARD, STARENWEG 5., OFTERDINGEN, BRD W-7404 GERMANY
38668 BRUNS, GUENTER A., ALSTERWEG 41., HAMBURG 63, BRD 2000 GERMANY
38669 BRUNS, HORST, FUSISTRASSE 34., HERRENBERG-HASLACH, 7033 GERMANY
38670 DABEKAUSSEN, HENRI A., DE MERODELAAN 72/1., LANAKEN, 3620 BELGIUM
38671 DEDERT, HANS, LOHERWEG 165., LOHE-RICKELSHOF, BRD 2240 GERMANY
38672 DE PRINS, PAUL, WALDSTRASSE 8., MUENCHEN 82, 8000 GERMANY
38673 DINKEL, THILO, IN DER WARTH 60., KIRCHHEIM/TECK, 7312 GERMANY
38674 DIX, OLIVER, MYRTENWEG 1., BRAUNSCHWEIG, D-3300 GERMANY
38675 DOUGLAS, GUNTHER, MITTELGASSE 30., EROLZHEIM, 7951 GERMANY
38676 DRIES, WINFRIED PETER, MORTAGNEWEG 8., AUMUEHLE, BRD D-2055 GERMANY
38677 EICHBAUM, GUSTAF, EIFELWEG 5., BERGSHAUSEN, BRD W-3501 GERMANY
38678 FREIH VON ZUREK-EICHENAU, W., AM DIETRICHSBERG 45., VOLKLINGEN, D-6620 GER
38679 FAIST, WILHELM, RINGSTR 13., OBERNDORF, 7238 GERMANY
38680 FIX, PETER, ROERMONDER STR 404., AACHEN, D-5100 GERMANY
38681 FOERSTER, HERR W.L., MANNHEIMER STRASSE 60., OFTERSHEIM, D-6836 GERMANY
38682 FORISCH, KARL ERNST, DEUTSCHER RING 2., HUERTH, D-5030 GERMANY
38683 FRIEDERICH, DR KARL-ERNST, NEUMATTENSTR 29., FREIBURG, D-7800 GERMANY
38684 FUHRMANN, CRAIG, PLITTERSDORFER STRASSE 135., BONN 2, RFA 5300 GERMANY
38685 FUNK, GOTTFRIED, TULPENWEG 5., WESTERSTEDE, 2910 GERMANY
38686 GAMMA, MARIE-LOUISE, KILCHGRUNDSTRASSE 35., RIEHEN, CH 4125 SWITZERLAND
38687 VON GOSTOMSKI, JULIUS ANTON, KULMERSTR. 57., BREMEN, 2128 BRD GERMANY
38688 GRUENHAGEN, RUTH, KAISERSWERTHERSTR. 129, DUESSELDORF 30, D-4000 GERMANY
38689 GUGGENBERGER, SIGRID, SEEWEG 52., DIETZENBACH, D-6057 GERMANY
38690 HARDCASTLE, MICHAEL, DUESSELDORFER STR. 27, MOENCHENGLADBACH 2, D-4050 GER
38691 ONNEWEER-BAJETTO, BJ, TOLHUIS 2040., NYMEGEN, 6537LX NEDERLAND
38692 VERMEER, S., ACHILLESSTR 10 I., AMSDERDAM, 1076RB NEDERLAND
38693 HEGIE, B.S., NOORDERWERF 31., GOUDA, 2804 LN NEDERLAND
38694 DE RIJKE, A.J., BAARNSEWEG 64., DEN DOLDER, 3734 LL NEDERLAND
38695 SEUNTJENS, WILLEMS, JULIANAPLEIN 4., BLADEL, 5531 HP NEDERLAND
38696 FRANCOIS, W., MEDOCGAARD 4., SPIJKENISSE, 3206 PG NEDERLAND
38697 GOEDEMONDT, F.M.P., GEN VAN HEUTSZLN 13., APELDOORN, 7316 CD NEDERLAND
38698 LUT, W.J.F., EIKENLAAN 16., LEIDERDORP, 2351 NT NEDERLAND
38699 FERGUSON, H.M., K.HASSELAARSTRAAT 89., VLISSINGEN, 4382 AH NEDERLAND
38700 RANDALL, S.V., FLORALAAN 11., HILVERSUM, 1211 JT NEDERLAND
38701 VAN WOUDENBERG, G, PROF DR HESSELAAM STRAAT 7., NIEUWEGEIN, 3431 CD NL
38702 KENGEN, J, K DOOR MANSTR 75., DINTELOORD, 4671 AC NL
38703 VAN LEUKEN, A, WORMERVEERSTRAAT 257., THE HAGUE, 2547 XR NL
38704 VON KOHORN, BARON R, PO BOX 2837., WELLINGTON, 6000 NZ
38705 JAGER, J, LICHTENBERG 37., EINDHOVEN, 5655 BD NL
38706 VISSER, J, L DE KEIJSTRAAT 14., ALMERE-BUITEN, 1333 NP NL
38707 WIETSMA, B, J-LIGTHARTSTR 144., HEEMSKERK, 1964 HX NL
38708 KIRK, R, MOZARTLAAN 1., VELP, 6881 PJ NL
38709 HARWIG, F, H. VAN VIANDERSTRAAT 7., HASSELT, 8061 CV NL
38710 EHRHARDT,, DE BIRD STRAAT 104., LEEUWARDEN, 8918 GA NL
38711 ONNEWEER-BAJETTO, B, TOLHUIS 2040., NYMEGEN, 6537 LX NL
38712 DE HEK, R, DONKERSINGEL 226., ROTTERDAM, 3052 PP NL
38713 BAALBERGEN, J, MEANDER STRAAT 49., ANDYK, 1619 XR NL

38714 OOSTHOEK, J, BERGSTRAAT 13., KAPELLE, 4421 EP NL
38715 ARNOLD, M, KALSDONKSESTR 113., ROOSENDAAL, 4702 ZC NL
38716 VAN WOUDENBERG, G, PROF HESSELAAN STRAAT 7., NIEUWEGEIN, 3431 CD NL
38717 WERNER, H, ORLEANSHOF 3., EINDHOVEN, 5627 LM NL
38718 SNOWMAN, MRS B, RUSHALL PARK, RUSHALL CRES., NORTH FITZROY, VIC 3068 AUS
38719 JAMES, MELVA, 58 CHURCH RD., YARRAM, VIC 3971 AUS
38720 MACARTNEY, MR J, 4 THE OAKS, GRANSHA RD., BANGOR, DOWN BT19 2RY N IRELAND
38721 ADAMS, MRS J, 60A (BASEMENT) MILDMAY PARK., ISLINGTON, LND N1 4PR ENG
38722 DORE, DOROTHY, 79 CHAWORTH RD., WEST BRIDGFORD, NOTTS NG2 7AE ENG
38723 SIMPSON, ELIZABETH, 2 STELLA GROVE., TOLLERTON, NTT NG12 4EY ENG
38724 VANCE, LEON, 25 – 19TH ST., WARRAGAMBA, NSW 2752 AUS
38725 HAILL, GRAEME, 9 SONNECK SQ., SCARBOROUGH, ONT M1E 1A8 CAN
38726 MCCLOY, TERRENCE, 3023 – 7 ST S.W.., CALGARY, ALTA T2T 2X6 CAN
38727 ST GERMAIN, ANGE-ANNETTE, 52 MAPLE LN., OTTAWA, ONT K1M 1G7 CAN
38728 HEMMINGER, HORST, KELTERSTRASSE 70., REMSECK 2, D-7148 GERMANY
38729 SENGOS, PATRICK, 4/23 ANN ST., ARNCLIFFE, NSW 2205 AUS
38730 CLIFT, RUSS, 6 KARRATHA CT., MERMAID WATERS, QLD 4218 AUS
38731 JOHNSON, KEITH, PO BOX 795., NORTH SYDNEY, NSW 2059 AUS
38732 FORD, MRS P, 6516 N 111 E., WICHITA, KS 67226 USA
38733 BALBACH, MARYANN, 214 ATHENS ST., HARTWELL, GA 30643 USA
38734 MCGREGORY, LORAINE, 5852 MONTGOMERY ST., JUNEAU, AK 99801 USA
38735 MORRISH, ADRIENNE, 11229 GOLDEN WAY., NEVADA CITY, CA 95959 USA
38736 MCINTYRE, STUART, 3848 CRESTA WAY., SACRAMENTO, CA 95864 USA
38737 MARSHALL, JANICE, 840 8TH AVE., REDWOOD CITY, CA 94063 USA
38738 JENSEN, MARY ANNE, PO BOX 943., EAST HELENA, MT 59635 USA
38739 KNEBEL, MARVEEN, 3101 BUTTERCUP., BILLINGS, MT 59102 USA
38740 SMITH, ELWOOD, 10402 CAMPANA DR., SUN CITY, AZ 85351 USA
38741 POSTON, SHIRLEY, 6010 HWY 12 WEST., HELENA, MT 59601 USA
38742 SCHEER, LILA, PO BOX 336., OCEAN PARK, WA 98640 USA
38743 CAVALLO, LINDA, 5234 SELMARAINE DR., CULVER CITY, CA 90230 USA
38744 SAINTY, MALCOLM, PO BOX 795., NORTH SYDNEY, NSW 2059 AUS
38745 LYBBERT, DONNA M., 422 BUENA VISTA ST., CHENEY, WA 99004 USA
38746 LYBBERT, DONNA M., 422 BUENA VISTA ST., CHENEY, WA 99004 USA
38747 BLOESCH, PAUL, LOGENGASSE 8., BIEL, CH-2502 SWITZERLAND
38748 BECKER, DIRK, WEIDENKAMP 5., LINDEN/D, BRD 2241 GERMANY
38749 BECKER, DIRK, WEIDENKAMP 5., LINDEN/D, BRD 2241 GERMANY
38750 BECKER, DIRK, WEIDENKAMP 5., LINDEN/D, BRD D-2241 GERMANY
38751 MILLER, JEAN, 1603 PINE HILL RD., ASHTON, IL 61006 USA
38752 CARROLL, MRS J, 45 PERRY ST., UPPER HUTT, NZ
38753 OWEN, LESLEY, BOX 40-113., GLENFIELD, AUCK 10 NZ
38754 MADDEN, IAN, 15 BELVEDERE ST., EPSOM, AUCK 3 NZ
38755 HARDY-CRUMP, MRS V, 3 MATHIS PL., INGLEBURN, NSW 2565 AUS
38756 PHILLIPS, JUNE, 5 GIRVAN CRES., CORRIMAL, NSW 2518 AUS
38757 ANDTBACKA, HANS-ERIK, KRONOBYVAGEN 255., KRONOBY, SF-68500 FINLAND
38758 FLINCK, JARI, NEITSYTPOLKU 4 B 14., HELSINKI, SF-00140 FINLAND
38759 SODERBERG-OLSSON, MRS L, HARBERGAGRAND 8., 21230 MALMO, SWEDEN
38760 ABOUCHAR, MRS B, 65 CARLYLE RD., EAST LINDFIELD, NSW 2070 AUS
38761 HILL, MRS B, 1 CARCOOLA CRES., NORMANHURST, NSW 2076 AUS
38762 OVERSON, RAYMOND, 48 HANDCOCK CRES., MACGREGOR, ACT 2615 AUS
38763 DUNCAN, PATRICK, PO BOX 4283., HELENA, MT 59604 USA
38764 LEWIS & CLARK CO. GENEAL. SOC.,, PO BOX 5313., HELENA, MT 59604 USA
38765 HOFF, GEORGE, PO BOX 1206., HELENA, MT 59624 USA
38766 MERRITT, LINDA, 37 WEST ST., COLUMBIA, CT 06237 USA
38767 CHAMBERLAIN, MARJORIE, PO BOX 25., EAST POLAND, ME 04230 USA
38768 GRABHAM, GEORGANNE, PO BOX 595., WICHITA, KS 67201 USA
38769 WALTON, NANCY, 1589 SOUVENIR DR., EL CAJON, CA 92021 USA
38770 HARRIS, DR B., 11323 GLENARM RD., GLENARM, MD 21057 USA
38771 RYALL, CHARLES, 1109 PACIFIC HWY., COWAN, NSW 2081 AUS
38772 SEARLE, MICHAEL, 1056 NEPEAN HWY., MORNINGTON, VIC 3931 AUS
38773 MCPHERSON, LEO, PO BOX 906., PORT MACQUARIE, NSW 2444 AUS
38774 COLLINS, RAY, 32 MANORWOOD RD., SCARBOROUGH, ONT M1P 4G7 CAN
38775 MERRITT, DAVID, 12 EDGAR CT., EDGAR CL., SWANLEY, KENT BR8 7JJ ENG
38776 YORKE, BERNARD, 24 MULGOWIE ST., SUNNYBANK, QLD 4109 AUS
38777 RADFORD, FRANCES, PO BOX 62., THE BASIN, VIC 3154 AUS
38778 DOYLE, ARTHUR, 574 BARNETT PLACE., RIDGEWOOD, NJ 07450 USA
38779 MARTIN, GAIL, 2368 RIDGECREST PL., OTTAWA, ONT K1H 7V7 CAN
38780 NORTON, MARY, LOT 418, 10005 BAY PINES BLVD., ST PETERSBURG, FL 33708 USA
38781 GOOSMAN, CHARLES, 2424 S CHOCTAW., EL RENO, OK 73036 USA
38782 DUMMER, DAVID, 10900 ROCKVILLE PIKE., ROCKVILLE, MD 20852 USA
38783 BEATTIE, LINDA, 19759 REEDVIEW DR., ROWLAND HEIGHTS, CA 91748 USA
38784 DAVIS, DR D, 12131 GODDARD., OVERLAND PARK, KS 66213 USA
38785 GILLESPIE, LOIS, 1680 SOUTH GARFIELD ST., DENVER, CO 80210 USA

ONE NAME STUDIES & ORGANISATIONS
AUX FAMILLES SOUCHES

This section is much expanded from its beginnings last year. It gives organisations or persons wishing to receive all references to a particular surname, the opportunity of recording this fact here. It is difficult to ascertain in the main Surname listing if a person recording their interest in "ALL" Brown's "Worldwide" has lost their senses or is in fact a person building up a useful database.

We regret that we must charge for entries in this section. However, the charges can be incorporated in the basic cost of purchasing a copy of the book in which the entry is to appear. Alternatively, an entry in this section can be placed as part of the basic 15 surname entries and replaces 5 of them.

Thus an entry may be placed in this section by:

    1. Payment of the flat fee (which for 1992 will be US$4.00 Stg. £2 or the local equivalent.

OR

    2. Payment in ADVANCE for the Directory in which the entry will appear. (Thus obtaining the book and the entry at the book-only price).

OR

    3. Paying the entry fee set for 15 Surname entries but submitting only 10 Surname entries plus the One Name listing.

The One Name listings will be restricted to three lines: The name of the Society (or 'One Name'), the name and address of the contact person plus telephone number if required, and an additional line of information eg. "Reunion being held at.... on...." OR "Book recording all the "Smiths of Devon, England available at Stg £35.00 write for details".

During the year we will be mailing "One Name" entry forms to as many such organisations of this nature as we can locate. If you wish to place an entry and wish to receive an entry form, please write to one of our agents listed on page 4.

ENTRIES CLOSE 30 NOVEMBER

- **ACRES:** First Fleeter — Thomas Acres Society. *Contact:* Miss A. Akers. *Address:* PO Box 484, Dee Why 2099, Australia.* *Tel.:* (02) 971 7474. *Area of interest:* Cornwall, Eng & Australia.

- **ADAMS:** Adams Addenda. *Contact:* Dorothy A. Griffith. *Address:* Adams Addenda, 6611 Clayton Road, #104, St Louis MO 63117, USA. *Tel.:* 314 428 7048. *Area of interest:* North America. Periodical for researchers of Adams families. Over 100 indexed pages. 20 vols. available, send SASE for brochure.

- **ALLGOOD:** *Contact:* Linda J. Curtis. *Address:* 3709 S. Mission Pkwy, Aurora, CO 80013, USA. *Tel.:* 303 693 0175. *Area of interest:* USA. Collects and publishes data in *ALLGOOD ANCESTRY.*

- *AMSDEN:* *Contact:* Peter C. Amsden. *Address:* Oakbank, Southwaite, Cumbria CA4 0EW, Eng. *Area of interest:* Worldwide. History published, updated edition in progress.

- *ANGEL:* Angel-Angell Family History Group. *Contact:* Granville Angell. *Address:* Lord of Cannock, 34 Manor Avenue, Cannock, Staffordshire, Eng.* *Tel.:* 0543 503764. *Area of interest:* Worldwide. Newly formed. Collecting data.

- *ANSTIS:* *Contact:* Ray Anstis. *Address:* Little Basing, Vicarage Walk, Bray, Berks SL6 2AE, Eng. *Tel.:* 0628 27127. *Area of interest:* Worldwide. A collection of all references to Anstis and its variants.

- *APPLEBY:* Appleby Research Organisation. *Address:* 32 Palleg Road, Lower Cwmtwrch, Swansea, SA9 2QE, Wales. *Area of interest:* Worldwide. One-name study in progress - free information from databank.

- *ARCHER:* The Archer Assocation. *President:* George W. Archer. *Address:* PO Box 6233, McLean, VA 22106, USA. *Tel.:* 703 264 1372. *Area of interest:* USA & Canada. Surname clearinghouse for Archer and variants; publishes the *ARCHER QUARTERLY.*

- *ARNDELL:* Thomas Arndell Family Association. *Secretary:* Mr R. Davis. *Address:* 31 Clarinda Street, Hornsby 2077, Australia. *Tel.:* (02) 477 1138. *Area of interest:* Australia. Reunion at Caddie 9 June 1991. The *ARNDELL FRIEND-SHIP* published 3 times per year.

- *ASHE:* *Contact:* Richard Ashe. *Address:* 5 Adcocks Yard, High Street, Measham, Burton-on-Trent, DE12 7JA, Eng.* *Tel.:* 0530 71173. *Area of interest:* Worldwide.

- *ATTRILL:* (Atril/Atterill/Atral). *Contact:* Christine Mackay. *Address:* PO Box 627, Hermit Park 4872, Australia.

- *AUSTERBERRY:* The Austerberry Family. *Contact:* David Austerberry. *Address:* The Rectory, Kinnerley, Oswestry, Shropshire, SY10 3DE, Eng. *Area of interest:* Worldwide.

- *BABER:* Baber Family Worldwide. *Contact:* Mrs Vera Baber. *Address:* 14 Branksome Close, High Street Green, Hemel Hempstead, Herts, HP2 7AG, Eng.* *Tel.:* 0442 64649. *Area of interest:* All information gratefully received. Queries answered. Return envelope only required.

- *BACKENS:* Familienverband. *Kontaktperson:* Horst Bruns, Schriftfuhrer. *Anschrift:* Jusistr 34, 7033 Herrenberg, Haslach, Germany. *Tel.:* 07032 21561. Familientreffen Ostern 1992.

- *BALAM:* *Contact:* C. Belam. *Address:* Fore Stoke Farm, Holne, Newton Abbot, Dev TQ13 7SS, Eng. *Area of interest:* Worldwide. Also Belam/Belem & variants.

- *BALCHIN:* Balchin One Name Society. *Contact:* Mrs Pat Green. *Address:* Balchins, White Lackington, Ilminster, Somerset TA19 9EF, Eng.* *Tel.:* (0460) 54838. *Area of interest:* Worldwide. Any details relating to Balchins wanted. Comprehensive birth, death and marriage indexes, copies of wills, plus much more. Possible newsletter 1991.

- *BASTER:* The Baster Study Group. *Sec./Editor:* Miss M.P. Hooper. *Address:* 35 Goodwin Drive, Sidcup, Kent DA14 4NX, Eng.* *Tel.:* 081 300 6543. *Area of interest:* Worldwide. Australian Rep. Harold M. Basterallen, 3 Dallas Avenue, Hughesdale 3166, Australia.

- *BEART:* *Contact:* Mr G.D. Allcott. *Address:* 6 Fratley Avenue, Pakuranga,

Auckland, NZ. *Tel.:* (09) 567 764. *Area of interest:* Worldwide.

- *BEATSON:* Beatson Family History Society. *Contact:* Brian L. Beatson. *Address:* 441 Beechcroft Place, Port Perry, Ontario, L9L 1N5, Can. *Tel.:* (416) 985 0727. *Area of interest:* Worldwide. Data sought from all sources for family information repository.

- *BELAM: Contact:* C. Belam. *Address:* Fore Stoke Farm, Holne, Newton Abot, Dev TQ13 7SS, Eng. *Area of interest:* Worldwide. Also Balam/Belem & variants.

- *BELCHER: Contact:* Harry Belcher. *Address:* 17 Millcan Street, Wavell Heights 4012, Australia.* *Tel.:* (07) 266 8175. *Area of interest:* Worldwide. Card Index 20,000, contributions welcome, pre 1900.

- *BELGROVE: Contact:* Lily Corson. *Address:* Box 41, Plenty, Sask, S0L 2R0, Can. *Tel.:* 1 306 932 2119. *Area of interest:* OXF, Eng. Personal search.

- *BELL:* The Bell Clan. *Contact:* Bill Claus. *Address:* RR #2 Kent Bridge, Ontario, N0P 1V0, Can. *Tel.:* (519) 676 2838. *Area of interest:* Worldwide. Quarterly Newsletter beginning 1991. Next reunion Napanee, Ontario, Can. August 1992.

- *BETHANIEN:* Association des Descendants de 'Mirjam of Bethania'. *Kontaktperson:* Buro F. Deutschland: Johannes T. Schmidt. *Anschrift:* Mittelweg 16, 6300 Giessen, Germany. *Tel.:* 0641 29915.

- *BEYNON:* Beynon Family Association. *Secretary:* Mrs Doris Patrick. *Address:* Suite 605, 170 Yonge Street South, Aurora, Ontario L4G 6H7, Can. Family history developing. Irish family, descended from John Beynon, formerly Bannon, of King's Co. (now Offaly), Ireland.

- *BIRKBECK:* Birkbeck Information Bank. *Contact:* Jo Birkbeck. *Address:* 19 Kinglake Road, Wallasey, Cheshire, L44 8BS, Eng. *Area of interest:* Worldwide. One name study to include all spellings i.e. Birbeck — Burkbeck and Birchbeck.

- *BISHOPRICK: Contact:* D. Hopkins. *Address:* 6640 Biarritz, Brossard, Que, J4Z 2A2, Can. Or Lois Pearson, Busby Road, Katikati, NZ. Reunion of descendants (NZ) of Charles/Maria of YKS/DOR, ENG in Te Puke NZ Jan/Feb 1992.

- *BLOMFIELD: Contact:* F. Stewart. *Address:* 90 Middleton Road, London, E8 4LN, Eng. *Area of interest:* England. Data collection point: Blomfield/Bloomfield.

- *BLUNDEN:* The Blunden Family History Society. *Contact:* Mrs America M. Carlson. *Address:* 7052 Fallbrook Court, New Port Richey, Florida, 34655, USA.* *Tel.:* (813) 376 4619. *Area of interest:* Worldwide.

- *BLUNTISH:* Bluntach. *Contact:* Michael Cotton. *Address:* Willow Green, The Warren, Ashtead, Surrey KT21 2SG, Eng. *Tel.:* (0372) 275 553. *Area of interest:* Worldwide.

- *BOFF: Contact:* K.J. Boff. *Address:* 21 St Johns Court, Beaumont Avenue, St Albans, Herts, AL1 4TS, Eng.* *Area of interest:* Worldwide.

- *BONSER:* Bonser Register. *Contact:* Peter B. Edwards. *Address:* 117 Airdrie Road, Toronto, Ont M4G 1M6, Can. *Tel.:* 416 423 9979. *Area of interest:* Worldwide. Database in preparation.

- *BORROR:* Borror's Corners. *Contact:* Lillian M. Kennedy, ed. *Address:* 12150 Peach Road, Plymouth, IN 46563, USA. *Tel.:* 219 936 7628. *Area of interest:* Worldwide.

- *BOURKE: Contact:* Peggy Cockram. *Address:* 1.46 Oakland Street, Mornington 3931, Australia. *Tel.:* 059 755 361. *Area of interest:* Worldwide. Data collection point only. A family reunion GAL, IRL in June 1991.

- *BOWYER:* Bowyer Study Group. *Contact:* Denis A. Bowyer. *Address:* Conkers, Hurst Green, Etchingham, Sussex TN19 7QD, Eng. * *Area of interest:* Worldwide. Newsletter, Worksheet, Indexes, Help-wanted, Queries.

- *BOYD:* House of Boyd Society. *Contact:* Henry F. Boyd. *Address:* 5200 Brittany Drive South #1301, St Petersburg, FL 33175, USA. *Area of interest:* Worldwide. Newsletter *THE DEAN ROAD* published four times yearly. 1991 annual meetings — Stone Mountain, GA — July 11 and 14, Oct 17-20.

- *BRASHEAR:* Br(e)ashe(a)r(s) Family Branches. *Editor:* Arzella Brashear Spear. *Address:* Box 603, Bedford, TX 76095, USA. *Tel.:* 817 268 1581. *Area of interest:* Worldwide. Family reunion normally held first weekend of August, Palestine, IL. USA.

- *BRIDGE:* Joseph Bridge Family History Society. *Contact:* Secretary, Alfred Bridge Watts. *Address:* 52 Samantha Cres., Kincumber, NSW 2251, Australia. *Tel:* (043) 69 4894. *Area of interest:* Lan, ENG & Australia. Descendants of Joseph Bridge and Elizabeth Buffey who arrived in Australia in 1806.

- *BRIMSON:* Brimson Family History Research. *Contact:* David P. Brimson. *Address:* 84 Dene Road, Headington, Oxford OX3 7EG, Eng.* *Tel.:* 0865 64026. *Area of interest:* Worldwide. Collecting all data on the Brimson's and registered with the 'Guild of One Name Studies'.

- *BRINKE:* Brinke/Prinke. *Contact:* Towarzystwo Genealogiczno Heraldyczne. *Address:* Wodna 27, Palac Gorkow, 61-781 Poznan, Poland. *Area of interest:* Worldwide. All families from Bohemia and Silesia.

- *BROTHERHOOD:* *Contact:* Mrs Beryl Brotherhood. *Address:* 219 Humberston Road, Cleethorpes, DN35 0PH, South Humberside, Eng. *Area of interest:* Worldwide.

- *BROUGHAM:* Brougham One-Name Group. *Contact:* P.B. Wyly. *Address:* 8 Burnham Close, Culcheth, Cheshire, WA3 4LJ, Eng.* *Tel.:* 0925 763485. *Area of interest:* Worldwide.

- *BURDICK:* The Burdick International Ancestry Library. *Executive Director:* Frank P. Mueller. *Address:* 2317 Riverbluff Parkway # 249, Sarasota, FL 34231, USA. *Area of interest:* Worldwide.

- *BURKE:* *Contact:* Peggy Cockram. *Address:* 1.46 Oakland Street, Mornington 3931, Australia. *Tel.:* 059 755 361. *Area of interest:* Worldwide. Data collection point only. A family reunion GAL, IRL in June 1991.

- *BURNETT:* Burnett Society. *Secretary:* Mary Dunklee. *Address:* 1232 N. Harrison Avenue, Fresno, CA 93728, USA. *Tel.:* (209) 266 2306. *Area of interest:* Worldwide. Publishes quarterly newsletter, which includes free query section, promotes the Burnett family's Scottish heritage.

- *BURSZTYNOWICZ:* Bursztynowicz/Worsztynowicz. *Contact:* Towarzystwo Genealogiczno Heraldyczne. *Address:* Wodna 27, Palac Gorkow, 61-781 Poznan, Poland.

- *BUSHONG:* *Contact:* Carol Willsey Bell, C.G. *Address:* 4649 Yarmouth Lane, Youngstown, OH 44512, USA. *Tel:* (216) 782 8380. *Area of interest:* USA. *Publication:* Bushong Bulletin, quarterly; $10.00 per year.

- *BYARD:* *Contact:* Mrs E.M. James. *Address:* 20 Wray Park Road, Reigate, Surrey RH2 0DD, Eng.* *Tel.:* 0737 245486. *Area of interest:* Worldwide.

- *CAESAR:* 'Caesar/Cesar Researches'. *Co-ordinator:* Mr N.J.I Cesar. *Address:* 25 Davidson Road, Croydon, Surrey CR0 6DL, Eng. *Tel.:* 081 654 2649. *Area of interest:* Worldwide.

- *CALBERSON:* Fam. Vereeniging Calberson. *Contactpersoon:* Marcel Calberson. *Contactadres:* Gewad 48 B-9000, Gent, Belgie.* *Tel.:* 091 234510. *Zone van belangstelling:* US-Europa, GB, Frankryk, Belgie.

- *CANFIELD:* Canfield Family Association. *Editor:* Genevieve (Canfield) Martinson. *Address:* 1144 North Gordon, Wichita, Kansas 67203, USA. *Tel.:* 316 942 7120. *Area of interest:* Worldwide. Repository for Canfield, Camfield and Campfield information. Publication, quarterly — 10th year.

- *CAREW:* *Contact:* Mrs J.A. Carew Richardson. *Address:* 127 Marvels Lane, Grove Park, London SE12 9PP, Eng. *Area of interest:* Worldwide.

- *CHARLEMAGNE:* The International Society of the Descendants of Charlemagne. *Address:* Office of the Governor General, P.O. Box 76, Sylvester, WV 25193, USA.

- *CHOUINARD:* Association des Chouinard d'Amérique du Nord. *Président:* Jean Chouinard. *Adresse:* C.P. 425 St Hyacinthe, P. Quebec, J25 7B8, Can. *Tel.:* (514)

779 0961. *Région de l'interérêt:* Amérique du Nord. Un dictionnaire dénéalogique sera mis en vente en 1992.

- *CHRISTMAS: Contact:* Brian W. Christmas. *Address:* 74 Oakwood Road, Maidstone, Kent, ME16 8AL, Eng. *Tel.:* 0622 674647. *Area of interest:* Worldwide.

- *CLIVE:* Clive Family Society. *President:* Stanley W. Clives. *Address:* 42 Frith View, Chapel en le Frith, Derbys, SK12 6TT, Eng. *Area of interest:* Worldwide. Associates overseas by invitation (Clive or Collaterals).

- *CLOUD:* Cloud Family Association. *Secretary:* Betty Ferguson. *Address:* 1617 Bradley, Bossier City, LA 71112, USA. *Area of interest:* USA. Quarterly: *CLOUD FAMILY JOURNAL.* Dues $20.00 per year.

- *COAKER: Contact:* C. Belam. *Address:* Fore Stoke Farm, Holne, Newton Abbot, Dev, TQ13 7SS, Eng. *Area of interest:* Worldwide.

- *COBBLEDICK:* Cobbledick, Cobeldick, Cuppleditch Names Study Association. *Contact:* Trevor M. Cobbledick. *Address:* PO Box 13-320, Johnsonville, Wellington, New Zealand. *Area of interest:* Worldwide. Publishes *COBELDICK COBBLEDICK NOTES.*

- *COBBETT:* The Cobbett Study Group. *Contact:* Mr P.M. Cobbett. *Address:* 13 St Andrew's Road, Earlsdon, Coventry, CV5 6FP, Eng. *Tel.:* 0203 674900. *Area of interest:* Worldwide.

- *COBBING: Contact:* Bob Cobbing. *Address:* 89a Petherton Road, London, N5 2QT, Eng. *Tel.:* 071 226 2657. *Area of interest:* Worldwide.

- *COKER: Contact:* C. Belam. *Address:* Fore Stoke Farm, Holne, Newton Abbot, Dev, TQ13 7SS, Eng. *Area of interest:* Worldwide. Also Coaker.

- *COLFER: Contact:* N.J. Colfer. *Address:* Christian Lodge, Church Road, Rudgeway, Bristol, BS12 2SH, Eng.* *Tel.:* 0454 418025. *Area of interest:* Worldwide.

- *COOK:* Andrew Cook Genealogical Society Inc. *Contact:* GAO — Fred Pres Charlie. *Address:* 46 King Street, Tillsonburg, Ont, N4G 3E7, Can. *Tel.:* 519 842 9433 or 416 628 8747. *Area of interest:* Canada. Clearing-House for 'Cook' in Canada. Second international Cook reunion — Marshfield, Wis, USA 1991.

- *COOLE: Contact:* Mrs Beryl Brotherhood. *Address:* 219 Humberston Road, Cleethorpes, DN35 0PH, South Humberside, Eng.* *Area of interest:* Worldwide.

- *CORBIN:* Corbin Family Research. *Contact:* Kenneth C. Corbin. *Address:* 10315 Lagrange Road, Louisville, KY 40223, USA. *Tel.:* 1 502 245 7317. *Area of interest:* Worldwide.

- *COROUGH: Contact:* Keith Johnson. *Address:* PO Box 795, North Sydney 2059, Australia. *Area of interest:* Down, Ireland. *Area of interest:* Worldwide.

- *CORSON:* Corson/Colson Family History Association. *Address:* Secretary, 9311-P Golden Way Court, Richmond, VA 23294, USA. *Tel.:* (804) 747 8180. *Area of interest:* Worldwide. Quarterly Newsletter *CORSON COUSINS.*

- *CORYELL:* Coryell Newsletter. *Editor:* N.B. Coryell. *Address:* PO Box 662, Santa Barbara, CA 93102, USA.* *Tel.:* (805) 965 3749. *Area of interest:* USA. 690 Coryell family group sheets and 29 back issues of newsletter available.

- *COTTON: Contact:* Ross G.H. Cotton. *Address:* 673 George Street, Burlington, Ont, L7R 2V8, Can.* *Tel.:* (416) 747 4084. *Area of interest:* Worldwide. Contact member for 'Guild of One-Name Studies'.

- *COULLIER: Contact:* Norbert Coullier. *Adresse:* 20 Rue du Casino, 9100 Saint-Nicolas, Belgique.* *Région interessé:* France.

- *CRAWFORD: CRAWFORD EXCHANGE. Editor:* Wilton M. Whisler. *Address:* 121 South 168, Seattle, WA 98148, USA. Published quarterly, family lineages, queries, $12.50 per year. *Area of interest:* Worldwide.

- *CREED:* Creed Family Association. *Contact:* Nyla Creed DePauk. *Address:* 2832 Andiron Ln, Vienna, Virginia 22180, USA. *Tel.:* (703) 560 8006. *Area of interest:* USA. Newsletter queries, exchange.

- *CRUTTENDEN:* Cruttenden Connections. *Contact:* Ian Cruttenden. *Address:* 43 Eastcote Drive, Harpenden, Herts, AL5 1SE, Eng. *Area of interest:* Worldwide. All information relating to Cruttenden and Crittenden.

- *CRUXTON: Contact:* Mr P. Cruxton. *Address:* 73 Brown Avenue, Church Lawton, Stoke on Trent, ST7 3ER, Eng.* *Area of interest:* England & Wales.

- *CUTTEN: Contact:* David Cutten. *Address:* 26 Cornel, Amington, Tamworth, Staffs, B77 4EF, Eng. *Tel.:* 0827 58202. *Area of interest:* Worldwide.

- *CUZNER: Contact:* Roger J. Evans. *Address:* Chez Nous, South View Road, Long Lawford, Rugby, War, CV23 9BP, Eng. *Tel.:* 0788 571529. *Area of interest:* Worldwide.

- *DACRE: Contact:* Mrs B. Prince. *Address:* 35 Sopers Lane, Poole, Dorset, BH17 7EW, Eng. *Area of interest:* Worldwide.

- *DAKER: Contact:* Mrs B. Prince. *Address:* 35 Sopers Lane, Poole, Dorset, BH17 7EW,Eng. *Area of interest:* Worldwide.

- *DALLISON: Contact:* Malcolm Dallison. *Address:* 45 Leigh Close, Walsall, West Midlands, W54 2DU, Eng. *Tel.:* 0922 35551. *Area of interest:* Worldwide. Publication *HISTORY IN THE TREES* 60 pages A5. Price £5.00 inc. p & p.

- *DALRYMPLE: Contact:* R.A. Dalrymple. *Address:* Hornby Castle, 7 Blacksmiths Lane, Hockley Heath, Solihull, West Midlands, B94 6QP, Eng. *Tel.:* 0564 783736. *Area of interest:* Worldwide.

- *DENNISTON:* Member of Guild One Name Studies. *Contact:* Margie Denniston. *Address:* 92 Darraghs Road, Otumoe Tai, Tauranga, New Zealand.* *Tel.:* 075 63796. *Area of interest:* Worldwide.

- *DEVONISH: Contact:* Lionel Devonish. *Address:* 118 Dugdale Hill Lane, Potters Bar, Herts, EN6 2DJ, Eng. *Area of interest:* Worldwide. Index kept, mainly Essex & London Eng. data welcomed reciprocal all derivations earliest to modern unwanted copies B.M.D. Certs sought.

- *DOANE:* Doane Family Association of America, Inc. *Contact:* Mrs Frank E. Barrows — historian.* *Tel.:* 607 785 7172.

- *DOBSON:* Dobson Family Society. *Contact:* Earle Dobson. *Address:* 26 Kenninghall Blvd, Mississauga, Ont, L5N 1J4, Can. *Tel.:* 416 276 7954. *Area of interest:* CAN, USA, UK, AUS & NZ. Dobson, Dopson, Dotson & Dobston.

- *DOPP:* Dopp Family Newsletter. *Contact:* Mrs Marie F. Forehan. *Address:* 503 Welty Street, Greensburg, PA 15601, USA. *Area of interest:* USA, Canada, Germany. Quarterly published. Annual Reunion in Wisconsin.

- *DORRELL:* The Dorrill-Dorrell-Darrell Society. *Contact:* (UK) E. Henry Dorrell, (USA) James S. Dorrill. *Address:* (UK) 2 Ainslie Close, Hereford, HR1 1JH, Eng. (USA) 156 Lewiston Road, Grovetown, Georgia 30813, USA. *Area of interest:* Worldwide.

- *DOUBT:* Doubt One Name Study. *Contact:* Jane-Ellen Doubt. *Address:* 29-931 Gleneagles Dr, Kamloops, BC V2E 1K4, Can. *Tel.:* 604 374 7941. *Area of interest:* Worldwide. *Newsletter: DIGGING UP DOUBTS* annually.

- *DOUGHTIE:* Researchers, DOWTY. *Contact:* A.R. Doughty. *Address:* PO Box 68-147, Newton, Auckland, New Zealand. *Area of interest:* Yorkshire, Eng.

- *DOUGHTY:* Researchers, DOWTY. *Contact:* A.R. Doughty. *Address:* PO Box 68-147, Newton, Auckland, New Zealand. *Area of interest:* Yorkshire, Eng.

- *DOUGHWAITE:* Researchers, DOWTY. *Contact:* A.R. Doughty. *Address:* PO Box 68-147, Newton, Auckland, New Zealand. *Area of interest:* Yorkshire, Eng.

- *DOUTHWAITE:* Researchers, DOWTY. *Contact:* A.R. Doughty. *Address:* PO Box 68-147, Newton, Auckland, New Zealand. *Area of interest:* Yorkshire, Eng.

- *DOUTY:* Researchers, DOWTY. *Contact:* A.R. Doughty. *Address:* PO Box 68-147, Newton, Auckland, New Zealand. *Area of interest:* Yorkshire, Eng.

- *DOWTY:* Researchers, DOWTY. *Contact:* A.R. Doughty. *Address:* PO Box 68-147, Newton, Auckland, New Zealand. *Area of interest:* Yorkshire, Eng.

- *DREW: Contact:* Keith Johnson. *Address:* PO Box 795, North Sydney 2059,

Australia. *Area of interest:* LIM, CLA, COR, WAT & KIK, IRL. Anglo Irish Protestant families.

- *DUCKETT:* The Duckett One Name Study. *Custodian:* R.S. Duckett. *Address:* Outwood Hills Farm, Lower Outwoods Road, Burton-on-Trent, DE13 0QX, Eng.* *Tel.:* 0283 61557. *Area of interest:* Worldwide. Newsletters sent on receiving a 9"x6" SAE or I.R.C.'s.

- *DUNBAR:* Clan Dunbar of House of Gospatric. *Genealogist:* Ann T. Chaplin. *Address:* Snackerty Enterprises, RFD 2 Box 668, Center Barnstead, NH 03225, USA. *Area of interest:* Worldwide. Annual meetings, 10th ozark Scottish Festival. April 5-7, 1991 Batesville Arkansas.

- *DUNN:* Dun Trust. *Address:* The Secretary, 59 Dalhousie Road, Broughty Ferry, Dundee, Scotland.* *Tel.:* 0382 78249. *Area of interest:* Scotland. The Trust promotes research into Dunn & Dun families who have Scottish origins.

- *DUNNICLIFFE: Contact:* Roy R. Dunnicliffe. *Address:* 15 Hillsway, Chellaston, Derby, Eng.* *Tel.:* 0332 701521. *Area of interest:* Worldwide.

- *DURKEE:* Society of Genealogy of Durkee. *Editor:* Bernice B. Gunderson. *Address:* 3753 E. 15th Street, Long Beach, CA 90804, USA. *Tel.:* (213) 494 2836. *Area of interest:* USA, Canada, British Isles. *Publication: DURKEE FAMILY NEWSLETTER* quarterly, $7.50 per year. Solicit information and/or queries.

- *EAST: Contact:* Mrs A.L. East. *Address:* Bainton Farmhouse, Bainton, Bicester, Oxon, OX6 9RL, Eng. *Area of interest:* Worldwide.

- *EDGAR:* Edgar Clearing House. *Contact:* Mrs Gay McNamara. *Address:* 4116 Kingscrest Cove, Memphis, Tenn. 38115, USA. *Area of interest:* Worldwide.

- *EDKINS: Contact:* Mrs Jean Tooke. *Address:* Woodside Close, Caterham, Surrey, CR3 6AU, Eng.* *Tel.:* (0883) 344569. *Area of interest:* Worldwide.

- *EGAN:* Clan Egan Association. *Contact:* Mrs Elaine Egan. *Address:* 37 Bradys Gully Road, North Gosford 2250, Australia. *Area of interest:* Worldwide. Australian clan gathering October 1991.

- *EMERY:* Emery One-Name Study Group. *President:* Dr Ashton Emery. *Address:* PO Box 55322, Northlands, 2116, South Africa. *Tel.:* 27 11 884 5427. *Area of interest:* Worldwide. Particular research in 1991 in Border Country Emerys, Imries and Imbrys living 1600-1800, England and Scotland.

- *ENSTONE: Contact:* B.W. Enstone. *Address:* 43 Winchester Road, Northampton, Eng. *Tel.:* 0604 761739. *Area of interest:* Worldwide. Including variants (H)Enston(e).

- *ENTWISTLE:* One-Name Study. *Contact:* Julia Straiton. *Address:* Culver Farm, Old Compton Lane, Farnham, SRY GU9 8EJ, Eng. *Tel.:* 0252 724924. *Area of interest:* Worldwide. Data collection and exchange including variants.

- *FAIRFAX: Contact:* J.E. Fairfax. *Address:* No. 9 The Ball, Bratton, Wiltshire, BA13 4SB, Eng.* *Area of interest:* Worldwide.

- *FALLOW(E)S: Contact:* Mrs Ruth Sherwood. *Address:* 92 Broadway, Llanblethian, Cowbridge, S. Glamorgan, CF7 7EY, Wales. *Tel.:* 0446 772119. *Area of interest:* England, USA, Australia.

- *FEAKES: Contact:* Gerald Feakes. *Address:* Church View, Chapel Lane, Houghton, Huntingdon, Cambs PE17 2AY, Eng. *Tel.:* 0480 69376. *Area of interest:* Worldwide. Data available on Fake, Feakes and Feek families.

- *FENN: Contact:* R.E. Fenn. *Address:* 31 Uffington Road, West Norwood, London, SE27 0RW, Eng. *Area of interest:* Worldwide.

- *FORISCH:* Familien Archiv 'Forisch'. *Kontaktperson:* Dipl.-Vww. Karl Ernst Forisch. *Anschrift:* Deutscher Ring 2, D-5030 Huerth, Germany. *Tel.:* 02233 75491. *Interessengebiet:* Weltweit.

- *FORRESTER:* Forrester Family Association. *Contact:* Jim Forrester. *Address:* RR #1, Westport, Ontario, K0G 1X0, Can. *Tel.:* (613) 273 3596. *Area of interest:* NY, USA & Durham, Eng. Annual reunion, Foley Mtn. Park, Westport, 2nd Sunday in July. *Publication: DESCENDANTS OF OLIVER C. FORRESTER* by Susan Forrester, Concord, MA 01742, USA.

- *GAGNON-BELZILE:* Familles Gagnon & Belzile Inc. *Président:* J. Paul Gagnon. *L'adresse:* 228 Ave Hickson, St Lambers (MTL), Que, J4R 2N8, Can. *Tel.:* (514) 671 6390. *Région:* Mondial. En preparation, Dictionnaire Généalogique des Familles Gagnon et Belzile, over 250,000 files.

- *GARRUD: Contact:* Derek Hopkins. *Address:* 6640 Biarritz, Brossard, Que, J4Z 2A2, Can. *Area of interest:* All birth, marriage & death 1837-1984 recorded plus Suffolk Parish Registers.

- *GAYLORD:* Gaylord Family Organization. *Contact:* Barry C. Wood. *Address:* 3275 Blue Ridge Cir, Stockton, CA 95219, USA.* *Area of interest:* USA.

- *GEER:* Geer Family Association. *Historian:* Ginger August. *Address:* 32 Stetson Way, Princeton, NJ 08540, USA. *Tel.:* (609) 924 6391. *Area of interest:* USA & Canada. Publishing "Additions and Corrections to 1923 *GEER GENEALOGY* (by Walter Geer)" due out 1991.

- *GILBERT:* Gilbert Gallery. *Contact:* Donna Potter Phillips. *Address:* 2204 W. Houston, Spokane, WA 99208, USA. *Tel.:* 509 326 2089. *Area of interest:* Worldwide.

- *GILLON: Contact:* Dr G. Kang. *Address:* 26 Eglinton Road, Glebe 2037, Australia. *Tel.:* (02) 660 1250. *Area of interest:* Scotland. Index of 350 Scottish families.

- *GODSON: Contact:* Mrs Celia J. Dodd. *Address:* 19 Godmans Lane, Marks Tey, Colchester, Essex, CO6 1LU, Eng. *Area of interest:* Worldwide.

- *GOSSELIN:* Associations des Familles Gosselin. *Présidente:* Denise Gosselin. *Adresse:* 1647 chemin Royal, St-Laurent, Ile d'Orléans, Qué, G0A 3Z0, Can. *Tel.:* 418 829-2847, 418 828-2896.

- *GRAVES:* The Graves Family Association. *Contact:* Kenneth V. Graves. *Address:* 261 South St, Wrentham, MA 02093, USA. *Tel.:* (508) 384 8084. *Area of interest:* Worldwide. Other spellings Grave, Greaves. Newsletter and books.

- *GRIER: Contact:* Mr J.C. Grier. *Address:* 10a Cairneyhill Road, Crossford, FIF, KY12 8NZ, Sct.* *Area of interest:* Worldwide.

- *GROSE: Contact:* William J. Grose. *Address:* 120 Foxcote, Wokingham, Berkshire, RG11 3PE, Eng.* *Tel.:* 0734 734209. *Area of interest:* Worldwide. One name study mainly centred on ancestry from Cornwall, Eng.

- *HACKWOOD: Contact:* Dr Patricia Kelvin. *Address:* Orchard House, 66 Ladder Hill, Wheatley, Oxford, OX9 1HY, Eng. *Area of interest:* Worldwide.

- *HAILEY: Contact:* Mr John Hailey. *Address:* 1a Ashurst Walk, Croydon, Surrey, CR0 7JX, Eng. *Area of interest:* Eng.

- *HALFYARD: Contact:* Robert R. Halfyard. *Address:* 9 Frontenac Dr., St Catharines, Ont, L2M 2E1, Can. *Tel.:* (416) 934 3651. *Area of interest:* Worldwide. *Publication: HALFYARD HERITAGE* 4 issues per year, subscription $8.00 US.

- *(H)ALLMARK:* Allmark and Hallmark. *Contact:* Mrs Olwen Allmark Taylor. *Address:* White Cottage, Townside, Haddenham, Aylesbury, Bucks, HP17 8BG, Eng. *Tel.:* 0844 292305. *Area of interest:* Worldwide with origins in Cheshire, Eng.

- *HAMBROOK:* Hambrook Family History Society. *Contact:* Kenneth G. Aitken. *Address:* 2426E Dewdney Avenue, Regina, SK S4N 4V5, Can. *Tel.:* (306) 789 8215. *Area of interest:* Worldwide.

- *HAMMOND:* Hammond Association. *Contact:* Joseph C. Hammond. *Address:* 1702 N. Delaware St., Roswell, NM 88201, USA.* *Tel.:* (505) 622 7053. *Area of interest:* Continental USA. (Starting 1991) The *HAMMOND SENTINEL* a quarterly publication. Assistance with Hammond family research.

- *HARDWICK:* Hardwick Family. *Contact:* Joyce Jones-Hardwick. *Address:* 1 Stencills Rd., Walsall, WS4 2HJ, Eng.* *Tel.:* 0922 276320. *Area of interest:* Worldwide. Data collection. Reunion date — contact above for information.

- *HARMAN: Contact:* David L.N. Harman. *Address:* 30 Audley Rise, Tunbridge, Kent, TN9 1TU, Eng.* *Tel.:* 0732 770176. *Area of interest:* UK.

- *HARMER:* Harmer Family Association. *Research Secretary:* Mrs Cora Num. *Address:* 17 Pendred St., Pearce 2607, Australia.

- *HARNEY:* Harney Family Association. *Contact:* Linda Harney MacDonald. *Address:* 6696 Hollow Dale Drive, Salt Lake City, UT 84121, USA. *Area of interest:* Worldwide. Quarterly publication — *HARNEY UPDATE.*

- *HARRINGTON:* Harrington Family Miscellany. *Contact:* Duncan Harrington. *Address:* Ashton Lodge, Church Road, Lyminge, Folkestone, Kent, CT18 8JA, Eng.*

- *HEGI:* Wezzelo de Hegy Familienarchiv. *Kontaktperson:* Johannes T. Schmidt. *Anschrift:* Mittelweg 16, 6300 Giessen, Germany. *Tel.:* 0641 29915. *Interessengebiet:* alle Schreibweisen.

- *HOFFMEISTER:* Familienverband Hoffmeister. *Kontaktperson:* Arnold Otto Hoffmeister. *Anschrift:* Alter Grenzweg 28, 5090 Leverkusen 1, Germany. *Tel.:* 0214 76555. *Interessengebeit:* Ost-und Westpreußen.

- *HOLLICK:* Hollick Archive. *Contact:* David A. Hollick. *Address:* 10 Rushford Close, Solihull, W. Mid, B90 4UF, Eng.* *Area of interest:* Worldwide.

- *HOLT:* The Holt Association of America. *President:* Russel E. Holt. *Address:* PO Box 53, Candia, NH 03034, USA. *Tel.:* (603) 483 8293. *Area of interest:* USA & Canada. Annual meeting and reunion in July.

- *HOVENDEN:* One Name Study. *Contact:* Zenda Cullen. *Address:* 6 Hamill Road, East Tamaki, Auckland, New Zealand. *Tel.:* (09) 274 8436. *Area of interest:* Worldwide.

- *HUBBELL:* Hubbell Family Historical Society. *Corr. Secretary:* Claire Hubbel Pierce. *Address:* North Ridge, Sutton, VT 05867, USA. *Tel.:* 802 467 3470. *Area of interest:* USA & Canada. Members ($15.00 dues) receive 2 issues of *FAMILY NOTES* and one *ANNUAL* each year, special prices on books *HISTORY & GENEALOGY OF HUBBELL FAMILY, HUBBELL PIONEERS* and *FAMILY FARE.*

- *HULLEY: Contact:* Ray Hulley. *Address:* Longview, Felden Lane, Hemel Hempstead, Herts, HP3 0BB, Eng.* *Tel.:* 0442 68395. *Area of interest:* Worldwide. All enquiries and/or information on Hulley families welcomed.

- *HUNGERFORD:* The Hungerford & Associated Families Society. *Secretary:* Mr R.H. Prentice. *Address:* 6 Burran Avenue, Mosman 2088, Australia. *Tel.:* (02) 969 2168. *Area of interest:* Worldwide. Membership invited, family reunion planned, and publications proposed.

- *HUNTLEY:* Huntley National Association. *Treasurer:* Virgil W. Huntley. *Address:* 27 Pearl St., Mystic, CT 06355, USA.* *Tel.:* 203 536 8702. *Area of interest:* USA & Canada. 45th annual reunion in August, 1991, Seattle, WA, USA. Reprint book I, John Huntley of Lyme, CT $27.95 postpaid.

- *HYATT: Contact:* Robert Hyatt. *Address:* 13 Albert Road, Hendon, London, NW4 2SH, Eng. Wishes to act as the data collection point. Worldwide data appreciated.

- *ILES:* La Maison des Iles. *Secretary:* Ronald Arthur Iles. *Address:* 18 Woodland View, Lanivet, Bodmin, Cornwall, PL30 5HQ, Eng.* *Tel.:* 0208 831 688. *Area of interest:* Worldwide.

- *IRELAND: Contact:* Mr W.E. James. *Address:* Askew Green, Witherslack, Cumbria, LA11 6SA, Eng. *Tel.:* Witherslack 274. *Area of interest:* Worldwide. Hibernia, DeIrlond, DeIreland, Hirlond, Hirlaund.

- *JENNINGS:* The *JENNINGS NEWSLETTER. Contact:* Janet E. Thomas. *Address:* 8534 W. Indianola, Phoenix, AZ 85037, USA. *Tel.:* (602) 873 6747. *Area of interest:* Worldwide. A genealogical publication on various spellings of Jennings. Three issues a year for $10.00.

- *JOSSELIN:* Josselin Society. *Contact:* Peter Josling. *Address:* 61 Golden Dell, Welwyn Garden City, Herts, AL7 4EE, Eng.* *Area of interest:* Worldwide. Now compiling a database list of name and its variations. All mentions of name welcome.

- *JUNIPER:* One Name Study. *Contact:* Mr M.G. Juniper. *Address:* 83 Thornhill, North Weald, Essex, CM16 6DP, Eng. *Area of interest:* Worldwide.
- *KILDUFF:* Kilduff One-Name Study. *Contact:* Mrs Christi Kilduff. *Address:* 3416 Echo Springs Road, Lafayette, CA 94549, USA. *Area of interest:* Worldwide. Please share your family tree, all are welcome! Will gladly exchange info, or answer queries with enclosed SASE (USA only), or 2 IRC's elsewhere.
- *KINVIG: Contact:* Mrs Ellen B. Kinvig. *Address:* Jones Flat Rd., R.R.3, Summerland, BC V0H 1Z0, Can.* *Tel.:* 604 494 8119. *Area of interest:* Worldwide. Data collection on Kinvigs from Isle of Man.
- *KNEESHAW:* Kneeshaw Family Association. *Secretary:* Mrs Josephine Boos. *Address:* 38 Springhome Rd., Barrie, Ontario, L4N 2W8, Can. *Tel.:* (705) 728 7147. *Area of interest:* Worldwide. Biennial reunions in Ontario. Newsletter. Members descended from Kneeshaws originating in Yorkshire, Eng.
- *KNOBLOCH (KNOBLAUCH):* Towarzystwo Genealogiczno Heraldyczne. *Address:* Wodna 27, Palac Gorkow, 61-781 Poznan, Poland.
- *KRAJKOWSKI (KRAYKOWSKI):* Towarzystwo Genealogiczno Heraldyczne. *Address:* Wodna 27, Palac Gorkow, 61-781 Poznan, Poland.
- *LACKEN: Contact:* Keith A. Johnson. *Address:* PO Box 795, North Sydney 2059, Australia. *Area of interest:* Worldwide.
- *LACOMBE:* Association des Lacombe Inc. *Archiviste:* Normand Lacombe. *L'adresse:* 2266 De Mexico, Laval, Que, H7M 3C9, Can. *Tel.:* 514 667 9546. *R/e' gion de l'intérêt:* Amerique du Nord. Bulletin Bilingue Trimestriel *LA VOIX DES LACOMBE.*
- *LAKER: Contact:* Mrs Patsy Laker. *Address:* 13 College Road, Southwater, Horsham, Sussex, Eng. *Tel.:* 0403 730143. *Area of interest:* Worldwide.
- *LARCHER: Contact:* Mrs D. Upex. *Address:* 'Hightime' Pightle Way, Walton on Naze, Essex, CO14 8UJ, Eng. *Area of interest:* England.
- *LASHBROOK: Contact:* George W.D. Lashbrook. *Address:* 32 Winchester St, Taunton, Som, TA1 1QG, Eng. *Tel.:* 0823 337233. *Area of interest:* Worldwide.
- *LEGGETT:* The Leggett (and variants) F.H.S. *Contact:* Mr L. Leggett. *Address:* 102 Sylvan Ave, Timperley, Altrincham, Cheshire, WA15 6AB, Eng. *Area of interest:* Worldwide. Journal published quarterly.
- *LEMON:* Lemon Genealogical Society Australia & NZ. *Contact:* Alan C. Lemon. *Address:* 36 Jacana Grove, Heathcote 2233, Australia. *Tel.:* (02) 520 8733. *Area of interest:* Australia & NZ. Connecting all the branches for data collection and distribution.
- *LIDSTONE:* Lidstone Family History Society. *Secretary:* Hugh R.G. Lidstone. *Address:* 11 Furzehatt Avenue, Plymstock, Plymouth, PL9 8LJ, Eng.* *Area of interest:* Worldwide. *Publication: LIDSTONE OF THE SOUTH HAMS OF DEVON* £15.00 incl. pp.
- *LITTLECHILD: Contact:* S.C. Littlechild. *Address:* White House, The Green, Tanworth-in-Arden, W.Mids, B94 5AL, Eng.* *Area of interest:* Worldwide.
- *LITTLEFORD: Contact:* Mrs S. Foot. *Address:* 28 Augustine Road, St Pauls Cray, Orpington, Kent, BR5 3JZ, Eng.*
- *LOBDELL:* Lobdell Family Reunion. *Secretary:* Helen Chadderdon. *Address:* RD1, Box 153, 1a Vernon Center, NY 13477, USA.* *Tel.:* 315 829 2261. *Area of interest:* Worldwide. Aug 11, 1991 Oquaga Creek State Park, Rt 8 — 15 miles from Deposit NY.
- *LONGDEN/LONGDON:* Longden/Longdon Surname Registry. *Contact:* Mr Garth Woodward. *Address:* Box 67, Treherne, Man, R0G 2V0, Can.
- *LOVE:* Love Family History Society. *Contact:* David R. Love. *Address:* 12 Bunburra St., Para Hills West 5096, Australia.
- *LOVEGROVE: Contact:* Roger Lovegrove. *Address:* 11 Marlborough Rd., Bowes Park, London, N22 4NB, Eng. *Tel.:* 081 888 5609. *Area of interest:* Worldwide.
- *LOWTHER: Contact:* Mrs Betty Lowther. *Address:* High Ash Farm, Allerton,

Bradford, West Yorks, BD15 8AB, Eng. *Tel.:* 0274 546074. *Area of interest:* Lancs., England.

- *LUMLEY: Contact:* Nigel M. Lumley. *Address:* 16 Warnington Drive, Doncaster, DN4 6SS, Eng.* *Tel.:* 0302 868479. *Area of interest:* Worldwide.

- *LUTHER:* Luther Family Association. *Secretary:* George A. Luther. *Address:* 2531 Lakeview St., Lakeland, FL 33801, USA. *Tel.:* 813 665 5788. *Area of interest:* USA. Fourth National Luther family reunion, Swansea, Mass., August 10, 11, 1991.

- *LUTKIN: Contact:* Mrs T. Daglish. *Address:* B Flight, 26 Su(t), RAF Gatow, BFPO 45, UK.* *Area of interest:* Worldwide.

- *LYFORD: Contact:* Mrs Anne Higham. *Address:* 21 Lindsey Street, Epping, Essex, CM16 6RB, Eng. *Tel.:* 0378 74943. *Area of interest:* Worldwide.

- *McBRATNEY: Contact:* Mrs J.R. Shanks. *Address:* Pencarrow Road, RD3, Hamilton, New Zealand. *Tel.:* 071 562640. *Area of interest:* Worldwide.

- *McLINTOCK: Contact:* Doris K. Dietsch. *Address:* 3 Harding Ave, Te Atatu South, Auckland 8, New Zealand. *Area of interest:* Glasgow, Scotland.

- *MA(E)YENS:* Family Association. *President:* Marc Maeyen. *Address:* Oude Weg 48, B-9991 Adegem, Belgium. *Tel.:* 50 713646. Request for informations and documents. Origin - Knesselare, Belgium 1545.

- *MANLEY: Contact:* Mrs Trudi Manley, 171 Nathan Drive, Bohemia, NY 11716-1319. Editor of *Manley Family Newsletter. Area of interest:* mostly USA, some Worldwide.

- *MARENGO: Contact:* Mr Brian Meringo. *Address:* 6 Rue Windsor; 92200 Neuilly-Sur-Seine, France. *Tel.:* (1) 46 24 72 61. *Area of interest:* Worldwide.

- *MARTIN:* The Family History Society of Martin. *Membership Secretary:* David Martin. *Address:* 14 Sevenoaks Ave, Croydon 3136, Australia.* *Tel.:* (03) 723 5082. *Area of interest:* Worldwide. *Journal: DELICHON URBICA* 4 per year. Members' Interests Directory. *Membership:* $A8.00, $NZ10.50, Canada $13.00, UK 7.00, USA $11.50, personal cheque OK.

- *MATKINS:* Matkins Information Center. *Contact:* Bob Matkins. *Address:* 3120 Quincy St., Butte, MT 59701, USA. *Tel.:* (406) 494 4126. *Area of interest:* USA & England. Matkins Information Center members receive Matkins Journal each quarter. Low cost $10.00 per year US membership.

- *MEADEN: Contact:* Mrs M.L. Meaden. *Address:* Springfield Cottage, Morleys Rd., Sevenoaks Weald, TN14 6QY, Eng. *Area of interest:* Worldwide. All enquiries welcome.

- *MEGSON: Contact:* John R. Megson. *Address:* 11/6 South Oswald Road, Edinburgh, EH9 2HQ, Eng. *Tel.:* 031 667 0479. *Area of interest:* Worldwide.

- *MERLEVEDE: Contact:* Daniel Merlevede. *Address:* Brugseweg 32, 8900 Ieper, Belgium. *Tel.:* 057 202353. *Zone van belangstelling:* Wereldwijd.

- *MERRITT:* Merritt International Family History Society. *Editor:* David C. Merritt. *Address:* 12 Edgar Court, Edgar Close, Swanley, Kent, BR8 7JJ, Eng.* *Tel.:* 0322 65974. *Area of interest:* Worldwide. Journal published in April & October (80 pages plus each edition) Family queries welcome.

- *MERRY: Contact:* Jill Bhar. *Address:* 8 Hobbs Ave., Nepean, Ontario, K2H 6W9, Canada. *Tel.:* 613 828 8569. *Area of interest:* Worldwide. *Newsletter: MERRY TIMES* published quarterly. Computerised database.

- *MERWIN:* Miles (1623-1697) Merwin Association, Inc. *President:* Charles L. Merwin. *Address:* 4113-49th Street NW, Washington, DC 20016, USA. *Tel.:* 202 363 1340. *Area of interest:* USA, Canada & Berkshire, Eng. Published *THE MERWIN FAMILY IN NORTH AMERICA* 1978, 83 & 90.

- *METCALFE:* The Metcalfe Society. *Secretary:* Mrs Nina Benson. *Address:* 29 Skelton Rd., Langthorpe, Boroughbridge, North Yorkshire, Y05 9GD, Eng. *Tel.:* 0423 324018. *Area of interest:* Worldwide. AGM & Muster on 2nd Saturday in October annually.

- *MIGNEAULT:* L'Association des descendants de Jean Mignaux de Châtillon. *President:* Père Yvon Migneault o.p. *Adresse:* 8811 rue Centrale, La Salle, Qué, H8P 1P1, Can. *Tel.:* Rés 1 514 365 9503, Bur. 1 514 365 4000. 350e anniversaire célébré à Beauport, près de Québec, en 1993.

- *MILDRED: Contact:* Jeremy W. Daniel. *Address:* 23 Gilda Crescent, Polegate, East Sussex, BN26 6AW, Eng. *Tel.:* 03212 6460. *Area of interest:* Worldwide.

- *MIMMS: Contact:* Peter Mimms. *Address:* 20 Lonsdale Road, Bournemouth, BH3 7LX, Eng. *Tel.:* 0202 557069. *Area of interest:* UK. All Mims/Mimms events in UK collected.

- *MINNEY: Contact:* Mr B. Minney. *Address:* 2 Stanley Cottages, Sheffield Park, East Sussex, TN22 3QG, Eng. *Area of interest:* Worldwide. Newsletter twice a year. Large index.

- *MIRUS:* Mirusbund c.v. *Vorsiternder:* Hellmut Mirus. *Anschrift:* Haus Rosemarie, D-8602 Gleissenberg, Germany. *Tel.:* 09552 1502. The 17 Intern. Mirus reunion, 28th Sep. 1991, Bavaria.

- *MOORE: Contact:* Donald Moore. *Address:* 28 Cleveland Road, South Woodford, London, E18 2AL, Eng. *Tel.:* 081 530 4934. *Area of interest:* N. Yorks, Eng. Variations of Moore Moor More sought.

- *MORIARTY: THE MORIARTY CLAN. Editor:* Dan Moriarty. *Address:* 1410 2nd Ave., Newport, MN 55055, USA. Worldwide family name newsletter — $5.00 per year.

- *MORIER: Contact:* Mr S.J. Turnbull. *Address:* PO Box 375, St Marys 2760, Australia. *Tel.:* 61 2 834 2832. *Area of interest:* UK, CH & Aus.

- *MORRILL:* Morrell, Morrill Families Association. *Contact:* Mrs Ann Lisa Pearson. *Address:* 3312 E. Costilla Ave., Littleton, CO 80122, USA.* *Tel.:* 303 770 7164. *Area of interest:* Worldwide. Newsletter, repository for all with the surname variations.

- *MORRIS:* Morris Families Archives. *Contact:* Andrew J. Morris. *Address:* PO Box 535, Farmington, MI 48332, USA. *Area of interest:* Worldwide. Morris journal and data exchange — send info & SASE.

- *MORSE:* The Morse Society. *President:* Lola L. Morse. *Address:* RFD # 2, Box 379, Tilton, NH 03276, USA.* *Tel.:* 603 286 4690. *Area of interest:* USA. New England region reunion — October 12, 1991. *MORSE FAMILY HISTORY*, Volume 1 (incl. first 6 generations in US).

- *MORTIBOYS:* One Name Study. *Contact:* Philip Mortiboy. *Address:* 72 Uplands, Stevenage, Hertfordshire, SG2 7DW, Eng.* *Area of interest:* Worldwide. All queries and information welcome on this surname and its variants.

- *MURPHY: Contact:* Mr W. Murphy. *Address:* Apt 702 — 60 Inverlochy Blvd., Thornhill, Ont., L3T 4T7, Can. *Area of interest:* Worldwide.

- *MURRELL(S):* Murrell(s) Family History Society. *Organiser:* D.J. Murrells. *Address:* 428 Bedonwell Road, Abbey Wood, London, SE2 0SE, Eng.* *Tel.:* 081 310 6773. *Area of interest:* Worldwide.

- *MUSSEN: Contact:* Keith Johnson. *Address:* PO Box 795, North Sydney 2059, Australia. *Area of interest:* Worldwide. Especially ANT & DOW, IRL since 1660 & LUX & FRA pre 1665.

- *NADIN:* Naden/Nadin Family History Society. *Contact:* Revd Dennis Nadin. *Address:* 79 Bishopsfield, Harlow, Essex, CM18 6UN, Eng. *Tel.:* 0279 430176. *Area of interest:* Worldwide. All variants of name included.

- *NEIGHBOUR:* The Neighbour Family. *Contact:* Mike Neighbour. *Address:* 27 Knutsford Ave, Watford, Herts., WD2 4EQ, Eng. *Tel.:* (0923) 224907. *Area of interest:* Worldwide. Data exchange; quarterly newsletter; GRO index 1837-1900.

- *NEVILL(E):* The Nevill(e)s of Shenstone and S. Staffordshire. *Contact:* Mr G.N. Hawkes. *Address:* 24 Kidderminster Road, Bewdley, Worcs, DY12 1AG, Eng. Data collection — several correspondents.

- *NEWMAN:* Newman Genealogical Circle. *Contact:* Tony Newman. *Address:* 155

Laverock Avenue, Richmond Hill, Ont. L4C 4K1, Can. *Tel.:* 416 883 5269. *Area of interest:* Worldwide. Bi-annual journal & annual register of Newman studies.

● *NORTHMORE: Contact:* Mrs Doreen M. Heaton. *Address:* 4 South Crescent, Garlieston Newton Stewart, Wigtownshire, DG8 8BQ, Scotland. *Area of interest:* Worldwide. For free *NORTHMORE NEWSLETTER* please send SAE or 3 IRC's.

● *NYE:* Nye Family of America Association. *Newsletter Editor:* A. Leonard. *Address:* PO Box 134, East Sandwich, MA 02537, USA. *Tel.:* 508 888 2368 or 508 888 4213. *Area of interest:* Worldwide. Nye family reunion, August 1991; write or call for specifics.

● *ONION(S): Contact:* Miss C.M. Onion. *Address:* 224 Penn Road, Wolverhampton, West Midlands, WV4 4AA, Eng.* *Area of interest:* Worldwide. Data collection point.

● *ORM(E)ROD:* One Name Study. *Contact:* Julia Straiton. *Address:* Culver Farm, Old Compton Lane, Farnham, Surrey, GU9 8EJ, Eng. *Tel.:* 0252 724924. *Area of interest:* Worldwide. Data collection and exchange including variants.

● *OSTRANDER:* Ostrander Family Association, Inc. *Genealogist:* Emmett Ostrander. *Address:* 115 Lincoln Ave. E., Cranford, NJ 07016, USA. *Area of interest:* USA & Canada. National membership, reunions, publications.

● *OSWALD:* Oswald-t Outlines. *Contact:* Donna Potter Phillips. *Address:* 2204 W. Houston, Spokane, WA 99208, USA. *Tel.:* 509 326 2089. *Area of interest:* Worldwide.

● *OUELLET-TE:* Association des Familles Ouellet-te Inc. (L'Afoi). *Dir.-Général:* Alphonse Ouellet. *L'adresse:* 13 reu Garant, Levis, Qué, Can. *Tel.:* (418) 835 1254. *Région de l'intérêt:* L'Amérique du Nord. 25th Meeting, 1st September 1991. 3200, West, King Street, Sherbrooke, Qc, Can. G1L 1C9.

● *PACKARD:* Packard and Allied Families Association. *Contact:* Brigadier J.J. Packard. *Address:* 143 Thomas More House, Barbican, London, EC24 8BU, Eng. *Tel.:* 071 628 6904. *Area of interest:* Worldwide.

● *PADRAZOLLA: Contact:* Mrs J.A. Padrazolla. *Address:* 41 Ashley Drive, Borehamwood, Herts, WD6 2JT, Eng. *Tel.:* 081 953 5402. *Area of interest:* Worldwide.

● *PAGOWSKI: Contact:* Towarzystwo Genealogiczno Heraldyczne. *Address:* Wodna 27, Palac Gorkow, 61-781 Poznan, Poland.

● *PAINE: Contact:* Derek J. Paine. *Address:* 'Ebbanea' 5 Freshney Way, Boston, Lincolnshire, PE21 7PZ, Eng. *Area of interest:* Kent, Eng.

● *PARK/E/S:* Parke Society, Inc. *Registrar:* Theodore E. Parks. *Address:* PO Box 590, Milwaukee, WI 53201, USA. *Area of interest:* British Isles & USA. 28th Couvocation, Philadelphia PA, July 11-14, 1991. 16 page Newsletter issued 3 per year.

● *PEAPELL: Contact:* Mrs Beryl Hurley. *Address:* 21 Elizabeth Drive, Jump Farm, Devizes, Wilts, SN10 3SB, Eng. *Tel.:* 0380 722893. *Area of interest:* Worldwide. All variants collected of over 60 different spellings.

● *PENNYMAN: Contact:* Mark Whyman. *Address:* 7 Rockwood Close, Guisborough, TS14 7BG, Eng. *Area of interest:* Worldwide except USA.

● *PERIMAN:* Periman Pathways Family Association. *Coordinator:* Ida Periman Miller. *Address:* 1314 West Glenn, Springfield, IL 62704, USA.* *Tel.:* (217) 546 4591. Quarterly newsletter, $8.00 per year, a research tool.

● *PERRETT:* The P(a/e/i/o/u)rr(a/e/i/o/u)tt Society. *Secretary:* P.J. Perrott. *Address:* 5 Shepherds Rise, Vernham Dean, Andover, Hants, SP11 0HD, Eng. *Area of interest:* Worldwide. The society for those bearing one of the 25 variations of the name. Quarterly 28pp journal to members worldwide.

● *PHELPS:* Phelps Connections. *Contact:* Nancy J. Pennington/Margaret Swanson. *Address:* 6204 S Halifax Ave., Edina, MN 55424, USA and 3290 Cebada Canyon Rd., Lompoc, CA, USA. *Tel.:* (612) 927 9365. *Area of interest:* USA. Collecting all Phelps data; purpose to update the Phelps Genealogy.

- *PHELPS:* Phelps Family Association of America. *President:* Dallas L. Phelps. *Address:* 1002 Queen St., Camden, SC 29020, USA. *Tel.:* (803) 432 8432. *Area of interest:* Worldwide. Phelps Veterans of the Revolutionary War Index, 1990, 25pp. *PHELPS FAMILY NEWS* – monthly newsletter.

- *PINARD:* Les Descendants de Louis Pinard, Inc. *Siège Social:* Lucien Florent. *L'adresse:* 3155 Chambois, Brois-Rivieres-Ouest, Québec, G8Y 3M7, Can. *Tel.:* (819) 375 7520. *Région de l'intérêt:* Amerique du Nord. *Revue:* La Pinardière (parution 2 fois par année): $15.00. *Livre:* Louis Pinard et ses descendants: $40.00.

- *PLANT:* Contact: William Keith Plant. *Address:* 22 Chapel Croft, Chelford, Cheshire, Eng. *Tel.:* 0625 860074. *Area of interest:* Worldwide. Regular journal.

- *POOK: Contact:* Mrs M.J. Spiller. *Address:* 29 Gainsborough Court, Station Ave., Walton-on-Thames, Surrey, KT12 1NH, Eng.* *Tel.:* 071 269 7377. *Area of interest:* Worldwide.

- *POTTER:* Potter Profiles. *Contact:* Donna Potter Phillips. *Address:* 2204 W. Houston, Spokane, WA 99208, USA. *Tel.:* 509 326 2089. *Area of interest:* Worldwide.

- *POWLING: Contact:* Mr R.D. Powling. *Address:* 35 Limes Ave, Chigwell, Essex, IG7 5NX, Eng.* *Tel.:* 081 500 9615. *Area of interest:* Worldwide.

- *QUARTERMASS: Contact:* John J.G. Quartermass, *Address:* PO Box 21, Kingaroy 4610, Australia. *Tel.:* (071) 621543. *Area of interest:* Worldwide.

- *RADCLIFFE:* One-Name Study. *Contact:* Julia Straiton. *Address:* Culver Farm, Old Compton Lane, Farnham, Surrey, GU9 8EJ, Eng. *Tel.:* 0252 724924. *Area of interest:* Worldwide. Data collection and exchange including variants.

- *RAINES: Contact:* Jemma Ussher. *Address:* 12 Pebble Beach Dve., Runaway Islands 4216, Australia. *Area of interest:* Worldwide.

- *RATHBUN/RATHBONE/RATHBURN:* Family Association. *President:* Frank H. Rathbun. *Address:* 11308 Popes Head Road, Fairfax, VA 22030, USA. *Tel.:* 703 278 8512. Quarterly publication. Dues $15.00. Bi-annual reunion, July 1991, Springfield, Illinois, USA.

- *RAWES: Contact:* J.A. Rawes. *Address:* 11 Trowscoed Ave., Cheltenham, Eng. *Tel.:* (0242) 245259. *Area of interest:* Worldwide. Also interested in Raws and Rawse.

- *RAWDON: Contact:* Stanley C. Rawdon. *Address:* 98a Main Road, Hursley, Winchester, Hampshire, SO21 2JY, Eng.* *Tel.:* 0962 75258. *Area of interest:* Worldwide.

- *RAYTON: Contact:* Clare N. White. *Address:* The Fightingclose Cottage, Southam Street, Kineton, Warks, CU35 0LN, Eng.

- *RAZEY:* The Razey Connection. *Secretary:* Brian Johnson. *Address:* Farthings, The Copse, Alderbury, Salisbury, Wilts, SP5 3BL, Eng.* *Area of interest:* Worldwide.

- *RICHARDS: Contact:* J.C. Kennett. *Address:* The White House, Headcorn Road, Sutton Valence, Kent, ME17 3EH, Eng. *Area of interest:* Rad, Wales. One-Name Study.

- *RICKETTS: Contact:* Mrs S.A. Dyson. *Address:* 8 Water Lane, Richmond, Surrey, TW9 1TJ, Eng.* *Area of interest:* Worldwide. All variations also of interest.

- *RODEN: Contact:* Peter F.C. Roden. *Address:* 6 Yew Tree Ave., Bradford, BD8 0AD, Eng. *Area of interest:* West Midlands, Eng.

- *ROWORTH (and variants): Contact:* Miss Audrey Town. *Address:* 33 New Lane, Skelmanthorpe, Huddersfield, West Yorks, HD8 9EY, Eng. *Area of interest:* Worldwide, especially East Midlands area, Eng. Compilation of Census/Will/PR data – contributions/enquiries welcome.

- *RUSH:* Ruth Family Association. *Contact:* Susan Selmer. *Address:* 6062 Lake Nadine Place, Agoura Hills, CA 91301, USA. *Tel.:* (818) 991 7691. *Area of interest:* Worldwide. Rush database and newsletter.

- *SAINTY: Contact:* Malcolm Sainty. *Address:* PO Box 795, North Sydney 2059, Australia. *Area of interest:* NFK, ENG & AUS. Collecting all references to this family.

- *SANKEY: Contact:* Malcolm Sainty. *Address:* PO Box 795, North Sydney 2059, Australia. *Area of interest:* ENG & Worldwide. Collecting all references. Also contact Tim Sankey, 16 Church Rd., Owlsmoor, Surrey, GU15 4TJ, Eng.

- *SCHMIECHEN:* Familienverein Schmiechen e.v. *Kontaktperson:* Gert Schmiechen. *Anschrift:* Kirchfeldstr 38, D-4300 Essen 18, Germany. *Tel.:* 020541 5543. *Area of interest:* Worldwide.

- *SCOLTOCK: Contact:* Mr J.K. Scoltock. *Address:* 43 Peacroft Lane, Hilton, Derby, DE6 5GH, Eng.* *Tel.:* (0283) 733441. *Area of interest:* Worldwide. Scoltock family bulletin published occasionally.

- *SHAMBROOK: Contact:* Bernard J. Shambrook. *Address:* 2 Hillsborough Park, Camberley, Surrey, GU15 1HG, Eng.* *Tel.:* (0)276 65839. *Area of interest:* Worldwide. 1991/2 — wish to contact families in USA & Canada.

- *SHERRARD: Contact:* Mr S.T.C. Sharred. *Address:* 30 Upton Road, South Yardley, Birmingham, B33 8SY, Eng.* *Tel.:* 021 784 0024. *Area of interest:* Great Britain.

- *SHOLL: Contact:* Mr Philip E. Lloyd. *Address:* 268 Upper Chorlton Road, Manchester, M16 0BN, Eng. *Area of interest:* Worldwide.

- *SHRIMPTON: Contact:* Valda Shrimpton. *Address:* 143a Grosvenor Road, Langley Vale, Epsom Downs, Surrey, KT18 6JF, Eng. *Area of interest:* Worldwide.

- *SILK: Contact:* A.P. Silk. *Address:* 20 Sandhill, Shrivenham, Swindon, Wilts, SN6 8BQ, Eng. *Tel.:* Swindon (0793) 783647. *Area of interest:* Worldwide.

- *SONKEY: Contact:* Malcolm Sainty. *Address:* PO Box 795, North Sydney 2059, Australia. *Area of interest:* ENG. Pre 1700. Collecting any references.

- *SOUTHALL: Contact:* Keith A. Johnson. *Address:* PO Box 795, North Sydney 2059, Australia. *Area of interest:* Birmingham, Eng & NSW, Aus.

- *SOWTER: Contact:* Richard Sowter. *Address:* 2 Hill House Road, Downend, Bristol, BS16 5RR, Eng.* *Tel.:* 0272 560106. *Area of interest:* Worldwide. 30,000 references indexed.

- *SPEAKE:* The Speake Family History Society. *Founder:* John D. Speake. *Address:* 21 Highfield Ave., Cambridge, CB4 2AJ, Eng. *Tel.:* 0223 312827. *Area of interest:* Worldwide. For all Speake etc. families with Shropshire origins or Shropshire descendants.

- *SPODE: Contact:* Peter F.C. Roden. *Address:* 6 Yew Tree Ave., Bradford, BD8 0AD, Eng. *Area of interest:* Worldwide.

- *SPOTTISWOODE:* Spottiswoode Family History Society. *Contact:* Mrs D. Dore. *Address:* 79 Chaworth Road, West Bridgford, Nott, NG2 7AE, Eng. *Area of interest:* Worldwide. Spottiswoode — Spotswood Family Reunion, England, June 1991.

- *STARKEY: Contact:* Alan Starkey. *Address:* 28 Bishops Way, Meltham, Huddersfield, W Yorkshire, HD7 3BW, Eng. *Tel.:* 0484 852420. *Area of interest:* Worldwide. Also include variants - Starkie, Starky, Starkye, etc. Still collecting data. Extracted all Starkey's etc from 1984 IGI, LAN & CHS.

- *STE-MARIE:* Association des Ste-Marie D'Amerique Inc. *Président:* Richard Ste-Marie. *L'adresse:* C.P. 151 La Prairie, Québec, J5R 3Y2, Can. *Tel.:* 514 632 0354. *Région de l'intérêt:* L'Amerique du Nord. Voyage de Retour aux sources en France des Ste-Marie D'Amérique du 11 Av 26 Septembre 1991.

- *STEWART: THE STEWART NEWSLETTER. Contact:* Janet E. Thomas. *Address:* 8534 W. Indianola, Phoenix, AZ 85037, USA. *Tel.:* (602) 873 6747. *Area of interest:* Worldwide. A genealogical publication on various spellings of Stewart. Three issues a year for $10.00.

- *STICKLEY: Contact:* Mildred West. *Address:* 40 Courtney Dr., Montreal West,

Qué, H4X 1M5, Can. *Tel.:* (514) 482 7665. *Area of interest:* North America. All Stickleys from Newfoundland or Dorset (England) families.

- *STOWELL: Contact:* J.A. Stowell. *Address:* Belmont, The Street, Godmersham, Canterbury, Kent, Eng. *Area of interest:* Worldwide. Data collection point.

- *STRAITON:* One-Name Study. *Contact:* Julia Straiton. *Address:* Culver Farm, Old Compton Lane, Farnham, Surrey, GU9 8EJ, Eng. *Tel.:* 0252 724924. *Area of interest:* Worldwide. Data collection and exchange including variants.

- *STRAWSON:* Strawson Surname Registry. *Contact:* Mr Garth Woodward. *Address:* Box 67, Treherne, Man., R0G 2V0, Can.

- *STRUDLING: Contact:* Keith Johnson. *Address:* PO Box 795, North Sydney 2059, Australia. *Area of interest:* London, Eng.

- *SWAIN:* Walter Joseph Swain. *Contact:* J.W.(Jack) Grant. *Address:* 9227 – 168 St., Edmonton, Alberta, T5R 2V8, Can. *Tel.:* 1 403 489 8271. Born 30th Sept 1865 – 21 Duke St., Southwark, Surrey, Eng.

- *SWAIN: Contact:* Claude Swain. *Address:* 29 Springhead, Tunbridge Wells, Kent, TN2 3NY, Eng. *Tel.:* 0892 34699. *Area of interest:* Worldwide.

- *SWINNE: Kontaktperson:* Dr Axel Swinne. *Anschrift:* D-W 6927 Bad Rappenau, Postfach 1160, Germany. *Tel.:* 0764 7871. *Interessengebiet:* Baltikum, Deutschland, Groß Britannien, Belgien, Niederlande, USA und Australien.

- *SWINNERTON:* The Swinnerton Society. *Contact:* Col. I.S. Swinnerton. *Address:* Yew Tree Cottage, Blackford, Stoke St Milborough, near Ludlow, SY8 2ET, Eng. *Tel.:* 058475 301. *Area of interest:* Worldwide. Triennial reunion 1992 at Swynnerton, Staffs.

- *SWINTON:* Swinton One Name Study. *Contact:* A.J. Swinton. *Address:* 47 Ellerslie Road, Loganlea 4131, Australia. *Tel.:* 07 2005634. *Area of interest:* Worldwide, from Scotland and England.

- *TATCHELL: Contact:* J.A. Tatchell. *Address:* Via Principe Eugenio 60, Rome 00185, Italy.* *Tel.:* Rome 446 5048. *Area of interest:* Worldwide. Member 1528 – Guild One Name Studies.

- *THERRIEN:* Ralliement des famillies Therrien. *Président:* Léo Therrien. *Adresse:* 761 St-Antoine, Bon-Conseil, Qué, J0C 1A0, Can. *Tel.:* 819 336 2807. *Région de l'intérêt:* l'Amerique du Nord, France. 1 dictionnaire (15000 mariages). 1 réunion Windsor 17 Oout 1991.

- *TIFAULT:* Les Tifault d'Amérique Inc. *Président:* Paul E. Thiffault. *Adresse:* 145 de Boucherville, Trois-Rivières, Qué, G8Y 4L5, Can. *Tel.:* 819 373 6521. *R[e' gion de l'intérêt:* Amérique du Nord.

- *TIMPERLEY: Contact:* Dave Timperley. *Address:* 11 Chester Road, Hazel Grove, Stockport, Cheshire, SK7 6HG, Eng. *Tel.:* 061 487 2868. *Area of interest:* Worldwide.

- *TOLL: Contact:* Ken Toll. *Address:* 20 North Road, Three Bridges, Crawley, W. Sussex, RH10 1JX, Eng. *Area of interest:* Data exchanged on British Toll Families and their worldwide descendants.

- *TORKE:* Verband der Familien Torke und verwandter. *Kontaktperson:* Familien e.v. *Anscvhrift:* 1 Vorsitzender: Günter Torke. Heidestr 28, 4234 Alpen.*(H) *Tel.:* 02802 2677. *Interessengebiet:* Schlesien, Posen, Westfalen, Lievland.

- *TRAPNELL: Contact:* Brian Austin. *Address:* 11 Alma St., Weston-Super-Mare, Avon, BS23 1RB, Eng. *Area of interest:* Worldwide. Comprehensive data collected over 30 years.

- *TREAT:* Treat Family Association. *Contact:* Nell Johnson. *Address:* 357 South Main St., Deep River, CT 06417, USA.* *Tel.:* 203 526 2326. *Area of interest:* USA. Reunion, June 22, 23, 1991, Marshall, Arkansas.

- *TRIBE:* Guild of One Name Studies. *Contact:* Mr S.E. Tribe. *Address:* 2233 – 6th St. E., Courtenay, BC, V9N 7T8, Can. *Tel.:* (604) 334 3145. *Area of interest:* Worldwide. Objectives – collect data, promote data exchange among researchers.

- *TRITT:* Tritt Family Research. *Contact:* Donald Tritt. *Address:* 4072 Goose

Lane, Granville, OH 43023, USA. *Tel.:* (614) 587 0213. *Area of interest:* World-wide.

- *TUDWAY:* Tudway Society. *President:* S. Tudway. *Address:* 7 Heath Lawns, Fareham, Hants, PO15 5QB, Eng. *Tel.:* 0329 289416. *Area of interest:* Worldwide. Collecting entries for "Register of Private Sources for Family History". Please write for details — registration free.

- *TURNBULL: Contact:* Mr S.J. Turnbull. *Address:* PO Box 375, St Marys 2760, Australia. *Tel.:* 61 2 8342832. *Area of interest:* Worldwide. Includes variations Tremblay, Trimble, Trumble & Trumbull.

- *TWYFORD: Contact:* Mr A. Twyford. *Address:* 2 Weedon Cl., Peterborough, Cam, PO4 6XE, Eng. *Area of interest:* Worldwide.

- *TYE: Contact:* E.C. Curtis. *Address:* Baltana, London Road, Barkway, Royston, Herts, SE8 8EY, Eng. *Area of interest:* Worldwide.

- *UPCHURCH:* Michael Enterprises. *Editor:* R.P. Upchurch. *Address:* PO Box 35804, Tucson, AZ 85740, USA. *Tel.:* (602) 742 2669. *Area of interest:* Worldwide. *UPCHURCH BULLETIN* Quarterly, $15.00 per year.

- *UPWOOD:* One Name Study. *Contact:* Alan Turner. *Address:* Banc-Y-Felin, Aberbechan, Newtown, Powys, SY16 3AW, Wales. *Area of interest:* Worldwide. Also researching Upward variant.

- *UREN: Contact:* Chris Barrett. *Address:* 15 Limes Rd., Folkestone, Kent, CT19 4AU, Eng. *Area of interest:* Worldwide. Data collection point and research en-quiries.

- *VENABLES: Contact:* Michael K. Venables. *Address:* "Arrow Lawn", Kington, Herefordshire, HR5 3AL, Eng. *Tel.:* (0544) 230431. *Area of interest:* England.

- *VERNIERS:* Familievereniging. *Contactperson:* Marc Verniers. *Contactadres:* Liersesteenweg, 193, 2860 St-Kat-Waver, Belgium.* *Tel.:* 015 20 62 46. *Area of interest:* Wereldwud (Worldwide). Alles over Narmgenoten — Familiearchief en Driemarndelijks Familieblad.

- *VINDEN: Contact:* Alan McGowan. *Address:* 105 High Street, Aldershot, Hampshire, GU11 1BY, Eng. *Area of interest:* Worldwide.

- *VON ROY:* Association of the Family of Peter von Roy. *Chairman:* Joachim von Roy. *Address:* D-5309 Meckenheim, Weissdornstr 5, Germany.* *Area of interest:* The Association researches family members who emigrated to the USA.

- *VON SCHLICHTING:* Association of the noble von Schlichting family (founded in Silesia in 1575). *Representative:* Joachim von Roy. *Address:* D-5309 Meckenheim, Weissdornstr 5.

- *VON ZUREK:* Ordo Equestris Baronum Liberorum. *Anschrift:* Am Dietrichsberg 45, D-6620 Volklingen, Germany. *Tel.:* 06898 79467. *Interessengebiet:* Schlesien, Polen, Russland. Interessengemeinschaft des in Deutschland nicht im-matrikulierten polnishen Adels, Ritterorden, Genealogische Hilfe, Adelsforschung.

- *WAGSTAFF: Contact:* Mrs Barbara Kent. *Address:* 17 Red Hill, Stourbridge, West Midlands, DY8 1NA, Eng. *Area of interest:* Also variants. Information from computer index, include SSAE.

- *WALISZEWSKI: Contact:* Towarzystwo Genealogiczno Heraldyczne. *Address:* Wodna 27, Palac Gorkow, 61-781, Poznan, Poland.

- *WATERLAND: Contact:* Rosemary Oliver. *Address:* 11 Gravel Road, Bromley, Kent, BR2 8PE, Eng.* *Tel.:* 081 462 6508. *Area of interest:* Worldwide.

- *WATTAM: Contact:* Mrs J.A. Foster. *Address:* 172 Grimsby Road, Humberston, Grimsby, S. Humbs, DN36 4AG, Eng. *Area of interest:* Worldwide.

- *WEBB: Contact:* Evelyn Campbell. *Address:* Box 101, Sovereign, Sask, S0L 3A0, Can. *Area of interest:* Worldwide. Data collection for those with Webb ancestors from all parts of Ireland.

- *WELBY: Contact:* Daniel A.F. Welby. *Address:* Botschaft Riad, Postfach 1500, 5300 Bonnl, W. Germany. *Area of interest:* Worldwide. Collection and exchange of data.

- **WELLS:** Wells Family Association, Midwest. *Secretary:* Charles Chauncey Wells. *Address:* 735 N Grove Ave., Oak Park, IL 60302, USA.* *Tel.:* (708) 524 0695. *Area of interest:* USA & England. Descendants of Jonathan and Sylvia Phelps Wells (1791-1866) of Niles MI. Reunion: Sun of Labor Day Weekend at Dowagiac, MI.

- **WESSEL:** *Anschrift:* Jagdgrund 14, 2000 Hamburg 61, Germany. *Tel.:* 040 583862. *Interessengebiet:* Holstein und Hamburg, Ger.

- **WEYCHAN:** *Contact:* Towarzystwo Genealogiczno Heraldyczne. *Address:* Wodna 27, Palac Gorkow, 61-781 Poznan, Poland.

- **WHITEHOUSE:** Whitehouse Information Centre. *Contact:* Mr K. Percy. *Address:* 63 The Ridgway, Sutton, Surrey, SM2 5JX, Eng. *Tel.:* (081) 642 9151. *Area of interest:* Free searches made in extensive private records pre 1880 Eng.

- **WINDER:** *Contact:* R.G. Winder. *Address:* 'Overdale End', Ashtead, Surrey, KT21 1PZ, Eng.* *Tel.:* 0372 277277 or 0306 880088. *Area of interest:* Worldwide.

- **WOODEN:** *Founder:* Terry Wooden. *Address:* 6 Heath Rise, Westcott, Surrey, RH4 3NN, Eng. *Tel.:* 0306 882624. *Area of interest:* Worldwide. Initial newsletter (*CHIPS OFF THE OLD BLOCK*) published Dec. 1990.

- **WOODIWISS:** One Name Study. *Contact:* Frank Woodiwiss. *Address:* 4 Barratt Close, Attenborough, Beeston, Nottingham, NG9 6AE, Eng. *Area of interest:* Worldwide.

- **YEARGIN:** Yeargin Register. *Secretary:* Peter B. Edwards. *Address:* 117 Airdrie Rd., Toronto, Ont, M4G 1M6, Can. *Tel.:* (416) 423 9979. *Area of interest:* Worldwide. Database in preparation.

- **YOUNG:** *BORN YOUNG* newsletter. *Contact:* Vicki Young Albu. *Address:* 347 – 12th Ave. N., South St Paul, MN 55075, USA. *Area of interest:* Worldwide. Subscription rate $10.00 per year; free queries accepted.

- **YULE:** Yule-Yuille-Yool Connection. *Contact:* Estella Yule Pryor. *Address:* 1267 Tucker Road #7, Hood River, OR 97031, USA. *Tel.:* 503 386 9166. *Area of interest:* Worldwide. Data exchange all 100 spellings.

- **ZOLTOWSKI:** *Contact:* Towarzystwo Genealogiczno Heraldyczne. *Address:* Wodna 27, Palac Gorkow, 61-781 Posnan, Poland.

PLEASE REPLY TO LETTERS & SEND POSTAGE

When writing to a contributor who has entries listed in this *Directory* the Editors recommend that as a courtesy you enclose a self addressed stamped envelope or 2 International postal coupons if writing outside your own country. Please do not bother contributors if the geographical location you are searching is remote from that listed in the *Directory*.

People receiving letters are requested to reply even if not able to assist. It should be remembered that even if two correspondents find that they are not related they at least become aware of one another's field of research and can keep this in mind when researching in the future. A number of contributors have reported that some of their best clues came from people who were not directly related to them.

DIRECTORY OF GENEALOGICAL SOCIETIES

AUSTRALIA

FEDERATION

- **AUSTRALASIAN FEDERATION OF FAMILY HISTORY ORGANISATIONS (AFFHO)**
  C/o Richmond Villa, 120 Kent St, SYDNEY, NSW 2000.
  The Federation covers Australia and New Zealand. Full membership (A$30.00) is only available to genealogical organisations within AUS & NZ. Others may join as Associate members ($10). Membership is not available to individuals. The Federation does not answer personal research queries. For Conferences see the Calendar of Genealogical Events section in this *Directory. President:* Malcolm Sainty. *Secretary:* Perry McIntyre. *Treasurer:* Dr Ken Knight.

NEW SOUTH WALES (NSW)

- **SOCIETY OF AUSTRALIAN GENEALOGISTS**
  Richmond Villa, 120 Kent St., SYDNEY, NSW 2000.
  Library: As above. *Hours:* Tues., Wed., Thurs., Sat. 11am-4pm. Open to non members for a daily fee of $12.00. *Journal: DESCENT* 4 per year. *Research Enquiries:* Free to members. *Membership:* $30.00 ($40.00 couples). *Joining Fee:* $10.00. The Society was founded in 1932, its principal objective is to provide research facilities for family historians. It has an extensive library of genealogical reference books for Australia and overseas countries, a general index of over half a million cards, 20,000 primary record files containing family papers plus a large collection of newspaper clippings and similar documents. The Society instituted a Diploma in Family Historical Studies (Dip.F.H.S.) in 1974 to accredit genealogists. Candidacy for the examination is restricted to members of the Society. *President:* Evan C. Best, M.A., Dip.F.H.S., F.S.A.G. *Exec. Officer:* Heather Garnsey, Dip.F.H.S.

- **FELLOWSHIP OF FIRST FLEETERS ***
  105 Cathedral St., EAST SYDNEY, 2000.
  "First Fleet House", Tel. 360 3988 or 360 3788. *President:* James Hugh Donohoe.

- **THE 1788-1820 PIONEER ASSOCIATION**
  P.O. Box 57, CROYDON, NSW 2132.
  Library: 6/8 Meta St., Croydon. *Hours:* Tues., Wed. 10am-3pm. Open to non members. *Newsletter:* 6 per year, available to non members at 50c plus postage. *Research Enquiries:* are welcome, relating to families within the 1788-1820 timespan; $10.00 per hour or part thereof. *Membership:* Initial joining fee $10.00. Annual Sub. $20.00. *Other Particulars:* General Meetings on 2nd Saturday, Feb. to Nov. 6/8 Meta St., Croydon at 2pm. *President:* Mr W. Bayliss.

NSW REGIONAL GROUPS

- **ARMIDALE FAMILY HISTORY GROUP**
  P.O. Box 1378, ARMIDALE 2350.

- **FAMILY HISTORY GROUP OF BATHURST INC.**
  P.O. Box 1058, BATHURST 2795.
  Journal: CARILLION CHIMES 6 per year, free to members, $1.50 plus postage to non members. *Membership:* $15.00 per year plus $10.00 joining fee plus $3.00 if Journal posted. *Meetings & Research Nights:* 3rd Tues. each month (except Dec. & Jan.) in Bathurst City Library at 7.30pm. *Research Enquiries:* on application. *President:* Mr John Williams. *Secretary:* Mrs Helen Jeuken.

- **BEGA VALLEY GENEALOGY SOCIETY**
  P.O. Box 19, PAMBULA 2549.
  Newsletter: 3 per year. $3.00 + post. *Research Enquiries:* Small charge for non mem-

bers. *Membership:* $15.00. *Meetings:* 4th Tues of each month except Dec. & Jan. *President:* Mr P. Rice. *Secretary:* Mrs J. Hellstrom.

- **BLUE MOUNTAINS FAMILY HISTORY SOCIETY**
  P.O. Box 97, SPRINGWOOD 2776.
  Quarterly Journal: THE EXPLORERS' TREE available to non members $3.00.
  Meetings: 2nd Mon. of the month, 8pm. Springwood Library, Macquarie Rd, Springwood. *Membership:* $25.00 single, $30.00 family. *Society Project:* Transcribe and publish local cemeteries — volumes 1, 2 & 3 now available. *President:* John Hinchliffe.
  Secretary: Colin Slade. Tel. 047-82-1648.

- **BOTANY BAY FAMILY HISTORY SOCIETY**
  P.O. Box 600, SUTHERLAND, NSW 2232.
  Journal: THE ENDEAVOUR. Available to non members at $2.00. *Membership:* $15.00 ($20.00 family). *Meetings:* 1st Wednesday each month at 7.30pm at Multi Purpose Centre, Flora St., Sutherland. *President:* Mrs Maree McKinley. *Secretary:* Mrs Merle Kavanagh.

- **BOURKE FAMILY HISTORY GROUP ***
  P.O. Box 565, BOURKE 2840.

- **BROKEN HILL FAMILY HISTORY GROUP**
  P.O. Box 779, BROKEN HILL, NSW 2880.
  Meetings: monthly 1st Wed. *Membership:* $10.00. *Newsletter:* 2 per year. *Corres Secretary:* Jenny Camilleri.

- **BURWOOD DRUMMOYNE & DISTRICTS FAMILY HISTORY GROUP**
  C/o Burwood Central Library, 4 Marmaduke St., BURWOOD, NSW 2134

- **CAMPBELLTOWN DISTRICT FAMILY HISTORY SOCIETY ***
  P.O. Box 57, CAMPBELLTOWN 2560.

- **CAPE BANKS FAMILY HISTORY SOCIETY**
  P.O. Box 67, MAROUBRA, NSW 2035.
  Library: 47 Portland Cres., Maroubra. *Hours:* Mon. 11am to 2pm. Wed. 1pm to 4pm. Sat. 1pm to 4pm. *Journal: KITH AND KIN* postage $5.00. *Membership:* Single $17.00, family $25.00. *Meetings:* 2nd Fri. each month, Maroubra Senior Citizen's Centre 7.30pm. *President:* Mrs S. Harper. *Secretary:* Mrs J. Bakewell Tel. (02) 661 4911.

- **CASINO & DISTRICT FAMILY HISTORY GROUP INC.**
  P.O. Box 586, CASINO, NSW 2470.
  Newsletter: THE CROSSING PLACE, 4 per year $1.00 for non members; *Membership:* $15.00 single; $20.00 family; $8.00 pensioner. *Meetings:* 2nd Wed., each month (except Jan.) in Casino School of Arts at 10am. *Research Nights:* 4th Thurs. each month from 7pm. *Research Enquiries:* $10.00 per enquiry to non members. *President:* Mrs Bronwyn Sims. *Secretary:* Mrs Janet Caban.

- **CENTRAL COAST FAMILY HISTORY GROUP ***
  P.O. Box 1257, GOSFORD SOUTH 2250.

- **CESSNOCK FAMILY HISTORY GROUP ***
  P.O. Box 225, CESSNOCK, NSW 2325.

- **COFFS HARBOUR DISTRICT FAMILY HISTORY SOCIETY INC.**
  P.O. Box J42, COFFS HARBOUR JETTY, NSW 2450.
  President: Rosemary Doherty. *Secretary:* Mrs Margaret Heffernan.

- **COONAMBLE GENEALOGY GROUP ***
  'Glenoria', GULARGAMBONE, NSW 2828.

- **COROWA AND DISTRICT FAMILY HISTORY SOCIETY**
  P.O. Box 104, COROWA, NSW 2646.

Meetings: 2nd Tues. except January. 7.30 pm at Milpara, Guy St. *Newsletter: PAST LINKS. President:* Robert Dickins. *Secretary:* Mrs Roslyn Bock.

● **COWRA FAMILY HISTORY GROUP**
P.O. Box 495, COWRA, NSW 2794.

● **DENILIQUIN & DISTRICT FAMILY HISTORY GROUP**
P.O. Box 144, DENILIQUIN 2710.

● **DUBBO MACQUARIE FAMILY HISTORY SOCIETY INC. ***
C/o The Dubbo Museum, 232-234 Macquarie St., DUBBO, NSW 2830. (Tel. (068) 818 635).
Postal Address: P.O. Box 868, DUBBO, NSW 2830. *Library:* As above. *Hours:* Thurs. 2pm-4.30pm. Fri. 9.30-12.30pm. Sat. 1.30-4.30pm. Open to non members for a fee of $5.00. *Journal: WESTERN CONNECTIONS* 4 per year. Avail. to non-members $4.00 incl. post. each. *Research Enquiries:* on application. *Membership:* $25.00 single. $30.00 joint $2.00 joining fee. *President:* Cynthia Foley. *Secretary:* Pam Harvey.

● **EUROBODALLA FAMILY HISTORY SOCIETY**
PO Box 440, MORUYA 2537.
President: Faye Clulee (044) 742 146.

● **FORBES FAMILY HISTORY GROUP INC**
P.O. Box 574, FORBES 2871.

● **GOULBURN & DISTRICT FAMILY HISTORY SOCIETY ***
P.O. Box 611, GOULBURN 2580.

● **GRIFFITH GENEALOGICAL & HISTORICAL SOCIETY**
P.O. Box 270, GRIFFITH, NSW 2680.
Library: Tranter Place (behind CWA Hall) Griffith. *Hours:* Sat 1pm-5pm and the 2nd & 4th Thurs. of the month 2-5pm. *Newsletter:* for members — up to 12 per year. *Journal: IBIS LINKS* 4 per year. $4.00. *Research Enquiries:* 2 free per member per year. *Membership:* Single $20.00, Family $25.00. *Meetings:* 1st Tues. of the month at Tranter Place, 7.30pm. *President:* Mrs Margaret Hare. *Secretary:* Mrs Vicki Moran.

● **GUNDAGAI FAMILY HISTORY GROUP ***
C/o Library, Sheridan St., GUNDAGAI, NSW 2722.

● **GWYDIR FAMILY HISTORY SOCIETY**
PO Box 61, EAST MOREE, NSW 2400.

● **HASTINGS VALLEY FAMILY HISTORY GROUP INC.**
P.O. Box 1359, PORT MACQUARIE 2444.

● **HAWKESBURY FAMILY HISTORY GROUP**
C/o Hawkesbury City Council Library, Dight St., WINDSOR, NSW 2756.
Library: As above. *Hours:* Mon. to Fri. 10am-5.30pm. Sat 9am-1pm. Sun. 2pm-5pm. Open to public — no charge. *Newsletter:* 4 per year. $12.00 pa. *Research Enquiries:* Contact Library for current position. *Membership:* No charge. *Other Particulars:* Meetings held at Windsor Library every 2nd Wed. of month except Jan. 10am-12noon. (045 77 3357) Michelle Nichols, Co-ordinator.

● **HORNSBY KURING-GAI FAMILY HISTORY SOCIETY**
P.O. Box 500, TURRAMURRA 2074.

● **HURSTVILLE FAMILY RESEARCH GROUP**
C/o Hurstville Municipal Library, MacMahon St., HURSTVILLE, NSW 2220.

● **ILLAWARRA FAMILY HISTORY GROUP INC.**
P.O. Box 1652, WOLLONGONG, NSW 2500.
Library: Reference Section, Wollongong City Library. *Hours:* Mon. to Sat. Library hours. Open to non members. *Journal:* 4 per year. Available to non members at $3.00. *Research Enquiries:* Information on request. *Membership:* $20.00 single, $25.00 fam-

ily, $15.00 pensioner. *Meetings:* 3rd Wed. of each month. *President:* Mr David Coates. *Secretary:* Mrs Wendy Nunan.

- **INVERELL DISTRICT FAMILY HISTORY GROUP INC.** *
  P.O. Box 367, INVERELL, NSW 2360.

- **LEETON FAMILY HISTORY SOCIETY**
  Room 2 Centrepoint Arcade, LEETON. (PO Box 475, LEETON 2705).

- **LITHGOW & DISTRICT FAMILY HISTORY SOCIETY INC.**
  P.O. Box 516, LITHGOW 2790.
  Meetings: 1st Mon. each month 5.30-9.30 and each Fri. 12n-5.30pm at Lithgow Information and Neighbourhood Centre. Corner Padley St. and Railway Pde. *Secretary:* Mrs Y.G. Jenkins (063) 556 207.

- **LIVERPOOL & DISTRICT FAMILY HISTORY SOCIETY** *
  PO Box 830, LIVERPOOL, NSW 2170.
  Newsletter: LINKS 'N' CHAINS 6 per year. *Meetings:* 1st Wed. evening of each month 7.30pm. *Membership:* Joining Fee $10.00 + annual $5.00. *Workshops:* Liverpool City Library 3rd Sat. of each month. Beginners 11am, others 1pm. *President:* John Briggs. *Secretary:* Stephanie Champion.

- **MANNING WALLAMBA FAMILY HISTORY SOCIETY**
  P.O. Box 48, TAREE 2430.

- **MILTON ULLADULLA GENEALOGICAL SOCIETY**
  Woodburn Rd., via MILTON 2538.
  Meetings: 2nd Sun. each month. at "Kendall Cottage" Princes Hwy., Ulladulla at 2pm. *Membership:* $10.00 *Newsletters:* 4 per yr. $1 each. *Secretary:* Mrs K. Drury.

- **MORUYA & DISTRICT HISTORICAL SOCIETY INC. Genealogy Group**
  P.O. Box 259, MOYUYA 2537.
  The Museum: 85 Campbell St. Genealogy Research room. *Genie's Journal:* 4 per year. *Membership:* $20.00 single, $25.00 family, $17.00 pensioners. *Research:* $5 per name, $5 per day. *Secretary Genealogy:* Denice Collis.

- **NEPEAN FAMILY HISTORY SOCIETY INC.** *
  P.O. Box 81, EMU PLAINS, NSW 2750. (Tel. (047) 353 798).
  Library Hours: Mon. to Thurs. 10am-2pm. Thurs. 7pm-9pm. Sat 2-5pm. Open to non members, Daily fees. *Membership:* $5.00 joining fee, $24.00 single, $29.00 family. *Newsletter:* 6 per year. *Journal: TIMESPAN* 4 per year $16.00. *Research Enquiries:* free to members. *Meetings:* 1st Tues. each month, Tindale St., Penrith. *President:* Mrs Heather Lighezzolo. *Secretary:* Mrs Lesley Whitford.

- **NEWCASTLE FAMILY HISTORY SOCIETY**
  P.O. Box 189, ADAMSTOWN, NSW 2289.
  Meetings: 1st Tues. each month (except Jan.) at Community Arts Centre, Parry St, Newcastle West 2302. *Research Enquiries:* $15.00 non members. *Hon. Secretary:* Ian J. Lyons.

- **ORANGE FAMILY HISTORY GROUP**
  P.O. Box 930, ORANGE, NSW 2800.
  Meetings: 3rd Tues. monthly at Orange Museum, MacNamara St. *Membership:* $15.00 (July to June). *Newsletter:* 4 per yr. *President:* Mrs P. Lawry. *Secretary:* Mrs Sue Griffin.

- **PARKES & DISTRICT HISTORICAL SOCIETY INC.** *
  316 Clarinda St., PARKES, NSW 2870.

- **PICTON & DISTRICT HISTORICAL & FAMILY HISTORY SOCIETY.**
  P.O. Box 64, PICTON, NSW 2571.
  Hon. Secretary: J. Ross.

- **RICHMOND RIVER HISTORICAL SOCIETY INC. ***
  P.O. 467, LISMORE, NSW 2480.
  Secretary: Mrs K.J. Day.

- **RICHMOND-TWEED FAMILY HISTORY SOCIETY INC.**
  P.O. Box 817, BALLINA, NSW 2478.
  Research Room: The Pilot's Cottage, Ballina. *Hours:* Mon. 10am-1pm. Wed. and Sat. (except 1st Sat. of month) 2-4pm. *Newsletter:* 4 per year. $2.50 per copy to non members. *Research Enquiries:* Small charge for non members. *Membership:* $10.00 single $15.00 double. *Meetings:* 1st Sat. of the month (except Jan.) at 2pm in Ballina Players Theatre, Swift St., Ballina. *President:* Mrs J. Blakey. *Secretary:* Mrs Audrey Chappell (066) 863 495.

- **SHOALHAVEN GENEALOGICAL SOCIETY INC.**
  P.O. Box 591, NOWRA, NSW 2541.
  Secretary: Marie Boyd.

- **FAMILY HISTORY SOCIETY — SINGLETON INC.**
  P.O. Box 422, SINGLETON, NSW 2330.
  Newsletter: 4 per year. Available to non members at $1.50 plus 60c postage. *Membership:* $15.00. *Meetings:* 4th Mon. of each month (Dec./Jan. excluded). *Research Enquiries:* Financial Members, limit of 5 enquiries per year. Non members $10.00 per Enquiry. *President:* Mr John Tindale. *Secretary:* Mrs Carol Garvie.

- **TAMWORTH & DISTRICT FAMILY HISTORY GROUP INC.**
  P.O. Box 1188, TAMWORTH 2340.

- **TUMUT FAMILY HISTORY GROUP ***
  P.O. Box 162, TUMUT 2720.

- **WAGGA WAGGA & DISTRICT FAMILY HISTORY SOCIETY, INC.**
  P.O. Box 307, WAGGA WAGGA, NSW 2650.
  Meetings: 3rd Wed. of month. *Membership:* $15.00. *Journal:* 4 per year. *Corres. Secretary:* Dorothy Fellowes.

- **WARIALDA FAMILY HISTORY SOCIETY ***
  105 High St., WARIALDA, NSW 2402.

- **WINGHAM FAMILY HISTORY SOCIETY ***
  C/o Mrs D. Brooker, 139 Bugary Rd., WINGHAM 2429.

- **WYONG FAMILY HISTORY GROUP**
  P.O. Box 103, TOUKLEY 2263.
  Secretary: Mrs Margaret Long.

- **YOUNG & DISTRICT FAMILY HISTORY GROUP, INC.**
  P.O. Box 586, YOUNG 2594.

QUEENSLAND (QLD)

- **GENEALOGICAL SOCIETY OF QUEENSLAND, INC.**
  1st Floor Woolloongabba P.O. Stanley St., WOOLLOONGABBA, Qld 4102.
  Postal Address: P.O. Box 423, Woolloongabba, Qld 4102. *Library:* As above. *Hours:* Tues., Thurs. & Fri. 10am-3pm, Wed. 10am-12.30pm, Sat. 1pm-4pm, 2nd & 4th Wed. evening 7pm-9pm. Open to non members for a daily fee of $10.00 Tues., Thurs. & Fri. $6.00 Wed. & Sat. *Journal: GENERATION* 4 per year. *Research Enquiries:* Free to members, $20.00 per hour to non members. *Membership:* $30.00 single, $40.00 family,plus Joining Fee $10.00 *Other Particulars:* G.S.Q. has branches throughout Qld. Reciprocal use of Library with other Societies. *President:* Mrs Margaret Verran. *Secretary:* Mrs Annette Budd. *Resource Centre Supervisor:* Ms Beryl Young.

- **QUEENSLAND FAMILY HISTORY SOCIETY, INC.**
  P.O. Box 171, INDOOROOPILLY, QLD 4068.
  Library: 50 Campbell St., Bowen Hills. *Hours:* Tues. & Thurs. 10am-12.30pm. Wed.
  10am-3pm, Sat. & Sun. 1pm-4pm (subject to change). Open to non members, daily
  fee of $5.00. *Journal: QUEENSLAND FAMILY HISTORIAN* 6 per year. $2.00 each.
  Research Enquiries: Free to members. Non members fee on application. *Membership:*
  $30.00. Family $35.00 additional joining fee $8.00. *Other Particulars:* Please provide
  s.a.e. when making enquiries to ensure prompt reply. *President:* Mrs D. Grice. *Secretary:* Mrs P. Mahony.

- **BAYSIDE**
  Contact: Mrs Pat Zornig, 29 Tarooka St., Manly West, 4179. (07) 396 4703. *Meetings:*
  1st Thurs., 7.30pm, Wynnum Central State School.

- **BEAUDESERT**
  Contact: Mrs Maureen Hanson, Oaky Creek Rd., Innisplain, Beaudesert, 4285. (075)
  441 105. *Meetings:* 4th Wed., 10am, (venue is movable — please contact Mrs Hanson).

- **CABOOLTURE ANCESTRAL RESEARCH GROUP, INC.**
  P.O. Box 837, CABOOLTURE, 4510.
  Meetings: 2nd Fri., 7.30pm, 20 George St., Caboolture. *Library Hours:* Wed. and Sat.
  9am-12n. *Library Phone:* (074) 951 072.

- **CAIRNS & DISTRICT FAMILY HISTORY SOCIETY INC**
  P.O. Box 5069MSO, CAIRNS, QLD 4871.
  Library: 30 Cominos Place, Manunda. *Hours:* Tues. Wed. Thurs. 10am-2pm, (2nd &
  3rd Wed. 5.30pm-9.30pm. 2nd & 3rd Thurs. 7.30pm-9.30pm, 3rd Sat. every month
  10am-4pm. *Journal: ORIGINS* 4 per year. $3.00. *Research Enquiries:* $5.00 non members. *Membership:* Single $25.00, Family $30.00, $5.00 joining fee. *Meetings:* 4th Wed.
  of the month at 30 Cominos Pl. Manunda 7.30pm. *President:* Joan Dennis. *Secretary:*
  Dorothy Candlish.

- **CHARTERS TOWERS & DALRYMPLE FAMILY HISTORY ASSO., INC.**
  P.O. Box 783, CHARTERS TOWERS 4820.
  Secretary: Glenda Carr.

- **DARLING DOWNS FAMILY HISTORY SOCIETY ***
  C/o Mrs Mary Hollis, 30 Smithfield St., TOOWOOMBA 4350.
  Meetings: 2nd Tues. 7.30pm Teachers' Education Centre, Baker St., Toowoomba.
  Phone (076) 361 283.

- **GLADSTONE**
  Contact: C/o Kin Kora P.O., Gladstone 4680. (079) 77 2355.

- **GOLD COAST & ALBERT GENEALOGICAL SOCIETY, INC. : 1 P.O. Box 2763,
  SOUTHPORT 4215.**
  Meetings: 1st Fri. 7.30pm. *Library Hours:* Tues. & Wed. 9.30am-2.30pm. Thus.
  4.30pm.-8pm. Sat. 1.30pm-4.30. *Secretary:* Betty D'Arcy.

- **GOODNA**
  Contact: Mrs Elaine Walters, 4 View St., Goodna, 4300. (07) 288 1171. *Meetings:* 2nd
  Tues., 7.30pm, 4 View St., Goodna.

- **GYMPIE ANCESTRAL RESEARCH SOCIETY INC**
  Contact: The Secretary, P.O. Box 767, GYMPIE Qld, 4570.
  Meetings: 3rd Wed. each month 7.30pm. Society Library. *Library Address:* Old Railway Station, Gympie. *Workshops:* Every Wed. 7.00pm-9.30pm. Every 1st and 3rd
  Sat., 1.00pm-4.00pm. *Library Hours:* Every Tues. and Wed. 9.30am-2.00pm. Open to
  non members for a daily fee of $10.00. *Membership:* $30.00 single, $40.00 family,
  $5.00 joining fee. *Journal: RESEARCHER* 4 per year.

- **IPSWICH GENEALOGICAL SOCIETY, INC.**
  Room 2w, TAFE College Workshop, Ellenborough St., IPSWICH, Qld 4305. (P.O. Box 323).
  Meetings: 1st Wed. of month 7.30pm. *Research:* Every Mon. & Thurs. 9.30am-2.30pm., 2nd, 3rd & 4th Tues. of month 7-9pm. *President:* Mrs D. Hayward. *Secretary:* Mrs C. Robinson. P.O. Box 323, Ipswich, Qld 4305.

- **MACKAY**
  Contact: P.O. Box 882, MACKAY, QLD 4740.
  Meetings: 1st Wed., 7.30pm, Mackay High School, Milton St., Mackay. *Phone:* J. Turvey (079) 57 7764 (A.H. only).

- **MARYBOROUGH DISTRICT FAMILY HISTORY SOCIETY, INC.**
  P.O. Box 408, MARYBOROUGH Qld 4650.
  Library & Viewing Rooms: 254 Kent St., Maryborough, above the Medical Centre. *Hours:* Sat. 1.30pm-4.30pm, Wed. 7pm-9.30pm. Small fee to non members. *Journal:* 4 per year. Non members $2.00 each + postage. *Research Enquiries:* Information on request. *Membership:* $20.00 single, $25.00 family. *Meetings:* 3rd Sat. each month. *President:* Miss K. Gassan. *Secretary:* Mrs M. Deacon.

- **MOUNT ISA FAMILY HISTORY SOCIETY, INC**
  P.O. Box 1832, MOUNT ISA, QLD 4825.
  Meetings: 2nd & 4th Tues. of month 10am-2pm & 7.30-10pm at the Irish Club. *Membership:* $20.00 — family $25.00, students & pensioners $10.50. ½ year also available Jan.-June. Quarterly Journal. Research enquiries welcomed, donation on application & S.A.E.

- **MOURA FAMILY HISTORY GROUP ***
  P.O. Box 145, MOURA Qld 4718.
  Meetings: Last Sat. each month (except Dec.) at Lions Den, Lions Park, Moura, at 2pm. *Research Enquiries:* Send S.S.A.E.

- **REDCLIFFE & DISTRICT FAMILY HISTORY GROUP**
  P.O. Box 196, REDCLIFFE Qld 4020.
  Meetings: 1st Thurs. of each month (except Jan.), 7.30pm. Redcliffe Education Centre, Henzell St. *Membership:* $25.00 single, $30.00 family. *Newsletter:* Monthly. *Secretary:* Julie Crowley. (07) 284 3347.

- **REDCLIFFE BRANCH, GENEALOGICAL SOCIETY OF QLD, INC.**
  Contact: President: P.O. Box 249, REDCLIFFE 4020. Tel. (07) 284 3842. *Secretary:* Val Colledge.

- **REDLANDS BRANCH, GENALOGICAL SOCIETY OF QLD, INC.:1** *Contact:* Mrs Julie Adamson, 11 Weymouth St, Alexandra Hills. (07) 824 4932. *Meetings:* 2nd Wed., 7.30pm, Cleveland Primary School.

- **ROCKHAMPTON**
  Contact: Mrs Greta Brady. P.O. Box 992, Rockhampton, 4700. (079) 284 770. *Meetings:* 2nd Tues., 7.30pm, Capricorn Education Centre, Cnr. North & Murray Sts.

- **ROCKHAMPTON — CENTRAL QUEENSLAND FAMILY HISTORY ASSOC., INC.**
  PO Box 6000, ROCKHAMPTON Mail Centre, QLD 4702.
  Library: 62 McKelligett St. *Meetings:* 7pm, 2nd Wed. of every month (except Jan) at Capricorn Education Centre, North St., Rockhampton. *Journal:* Quarterly, $3.00 each to non members. *Research Enquiries:* Free to members, and non members prepared to reciprocate in their area. *Membership:* Yearly $20.00 single, $25.00 family. Overseas A$30.00. Half-yearly membership also available Jan.-June or July-Dec. *President:* Mr Noel Woodhouse. *Secretary:* Mrs Rosemary Barnes. *Projects:* Index to Immigrant arrivals QLD 1848-1900 and Pioneer Register of Central QLD — residents living in the area pre 1900. All enquiries to include SAE.

- **SOUTHERN SUBURBS BRANCH, GENEALOGICAL SOCIETY QLD, INC.**
  Contact: Mrs Bronwen Thompson, 16 Arura St., Mansfield, 4122. (07) 343 1700.
  Meetings: 3rd Mon., 7.30pm Cavendish Road High School.

- **SUNSHINE COAST ***
  Contact: Mrs Barbara Sowter, P.O. Box 61, Nambour 4560, (071) 485 619. *Meetings:*
  2nd Sat., 1pm.

- **TOWNSVILLE — FAMILY HISTORY ASSOCIATION OF NORTH QLD, INC.**
  P.O. Box 577, HERMIT PARK Qld 4812.
  Library: 83 Flinders St. East, Townsville Qld 4810. *Hours:* Tues. 10am-1pm. Wed. &
  Thurs. 10am-12noon. Fri. 7.30-10pm. Sat 10am-2pm. *Membership:* $5.00 joining fee
  plus $20.00 p.a. plus $10.00 optional extra for *Journal: RELATIVELY SPEAKING.*
  Meetings: 2nd Wed. of month, (except Dec. & Jan.) 7.30pm at library address. Tel.
  (077) 725 945. Please address all correspondence to PO Box.

SOUTH AUSTRALIA (SA)

- **SOUTH AUSTRALIAN GENEALOGY AND HERALDRY SOCIETY, INC.**
  G.P.O. Box 592, ADELAIDE, SA 5001.
  Library: 201 Unley Rd., Unley. *Hours:* Tues., Thurs. 10.30-2.30pm, Tues. evening
  (2ND & 4TH OF MONTH) 7-9.30pm, Sat. 1-4.30pm. Wed. (2nd & 4th of month)
  10.30-2.30pm. Sun. (2nd & 4th of month) 1-4.30pm. Open to non members at a daily
  fee of $6.00. *Journal: THE SOUTH AUSTRALIAN GENEALOGIST* 4 per year at
  $3.00 per copy. *Research Enquiries:* $10.00 per hour to members. $20.00 per hour for
  non members. *Membership:* $30.00, $21.00 students and pensioners, $12.00 associates.
  Other Particulars: South Australians 1836-1885 — 2 volumes, $120.00 plus postage.
  President: Dean Boundy. *Secretary:* M. Dale Johns. *BRANCHES:*
  Yorke Peninsula Family History Group, P.O. Box 260, Kadina, SA 5554.
  South-East Family History Group, P.O. Box 758, Millicent, SA 5280.
  Riverland Family History Group, P.O. Box 234, Loxton, SA 5333.

- **PORT PIRIE FAMILY HISTORY LIBRARY ***
  Dunn St., PORT PIRIE, SA 5540.
  Library: As above. *Hours:* Tue. 7pm-10pm,Thurs. 10am-4pm. Sat. 1pm-4pm. Open to
  non members at no charge. *President:* Denis J. Kemp, 22 Warren st., Port Pirie (086)
  321 904. *Secretary:* Maxine Lucas, 45 Grey Tce., Port Pirie (086) 324 349.

- **SOUTHERN EYRE PENINSULA FAMILY HISTORY GROUP**
  Contact: Mrs B. Duns, 1/11 El Alamein St., PORT LINCOLN 5606.

- **SOUTH EAST FAMILY HISTORY GROUP**
  P.O. Box 758, MILLICENT SA 5280.
  Newsletter: 4 per year. Available to non members at $7.00 per year. *Membership:* In-
  cludes The South Australian Genealogy and Heraldry Society Inc. as per their Subscription Fees plus Newsletter Fee of South East Family History Group as we are a
  branch of the above Society. *Meetings:* 4th Thurs. of each month (Dec. & Jan. excluded) at 14 Stuckey st., Millicent. *Research Enquiries:* Financial Members of
  SAGHS $10.00, Non members $20.00 per query. *President:* Mrs Rosemary McCourt.
  Tel. (087) 352 080. *Secretary:* Mrs Eileen Brooks. Tel. (087) 354 253.

TASMANIA (TAS)

- **GENEALOGICAL SOCIETY OF TASMANIA INC.**
  P.O. Box 60, PROSPECT, Tas 7250.
  Journal: TASMANIAN ANCESTRY 4 per year. *Research Enquiries:* Handled by all
  branches for fee. *Membership:* $29.00 Joint, $22.00 single, $14.00 pensioner/student
  (Social Security no needed), $29.00 Corporate. *BRANCHES:*
  Burnie: P.O. Box 748, Burnie 7320. *Library:* 1st Floor, 62 Bass Hwy, Cooee.
  Hobart: G.P.O. Box 640G, Hobart 7001. *Library:* 19 Cambridge Rd, Bellerive.

Huon: P.O. Box 117, Huonville 7109. *Library:* Ranelagh Hall.

Devonport: P.O. Box 587, Devonport 7310. *Library:* 3rd Floor, Days Bldgs, Cnr Best & Rooke Sts.

Launceston: P.O. Box 1290, Launceston 7250. *Library:* 1st Floor, 72 Elizabeth St.

All branches have extensive library holdings. Access for non members at a small fee.

VICTORIA (VIC)

● **THE GENEALOGICAL SOCIETY OF VICTORIA**
5th Floor, Curtin House, 252 Swanston St., MELBOURNE, VIC 3000.
Library: 6th floor as above. *Hours:* Tues. Wed. Thurs. & Sat. 11am-3.30pm. Fri. 11am-8pm. Open to non members, for a daily fee of $7.50. *Journal: ANCESTOR* 4 per year. $5.00 plus postage for non members. *Research Enquiries:* handled. *Membership:* $30.00 single, $45.00 joint, $10.00 joining fee. *President:* Mr G.A. Reynolds. *Secretary:* Mrs D.J. Roy. *Branch Groups:* 31 Regional Groups. Descendants of Convicts Group, 1850's Group, Port Phillip Pioneers, International Settlers, VIC GUM (Genealogists using micro, mini & mainframe computers), Irish Ancestory Group, Scottish Group, Heraldry Group.

● **AUSTRALIAN INSTITUTE OF GENEALOGICAL STUDIES**
P.O. Box 339, SOUTH BLACKBURN, VIC 3130.
Library: 6 Lavelle St., Nunawading 3131. *Hours:* Mon., Tue., Wed. 10am-2pm, Sat. 2pm-5pm. 1st, 3rd, 4th & 5th Tues. monthly 7pm-10pm. Open to non members for a daily fee of $7.50. Not open public holidays. *Journal: THE GENEALOGIST* 4 per year $20.00 per annum. *Journal Research Enquiries:* $5.00 members, $10.00 non members *Membership:* $27.50 ($35.00 household) $20.00 concess. pensioner/student. *Other Particulars:* Library Tel.: (03) 877 3789. *Meetings:* write for particulars.

● **AUSTRALIAN FAMILY RESEARCHERS**
PO Box 52, WEST ROSEBUD 3940.
Membership: $10.00, married couples $16.00. *Meetings:* Twice monthly. SAE for details.

● **AUSTRALIAN JEWISH HISTORICAL SOCIETY — VICTORIA, INC.**
PO Box 255, CAMBERWELL 3124. Tel.: (03) 882 2600.
President: Dr Howard Freeman. *Hon. Secretary:* Mrs Beverley Davis.

● **FIRST FLEET FELLOWSHIP**
Cnr Phayer St. and Normanby Rd., STH MELBOURNE 3205.
Secretary: Mrs Cheryl Timbury, 5 Cruickshank Ave. Ocean Grove 3226. Tel. (052) 55 2477. *Enquiries:* C/o Polly Woodside, Cnr Phayer St. & Normanby Rd, Sth Melbourne 3205.

● **COBRAM GENEALOGICAL GROUP**
P.O. Box 75, COBRAM 3643.
Chairman: Mrs G. Primmer. *Secretary:* Mrs R. Thomas. Tel. (058) 73 2481.

● **MORNINGTON PENINSULA GROUP, G.S.V.**
Contact: 11 Meribil Cl., MOUNT ELIZA 3930.
Research Room: Ballam Park Homestead Resource Centre, Frankston. *Chairman:* Sue Towers. *Secretary:* Marj Knight.

● **SALE AND DISTRICT FAMILY HISTORY GROUP, INC.**
P.O. Box 773, SALE, VIC 3850.

● **SWAN HILL GENEALOGICAL & HISTORICAL SOCIETY, INC.**
P.O. Box 1232, SWANHILL, Vic 3585.
Chairman: V. Plumridge. *Secretary:* Helen Howley.

● **YARRAM GENEALOGY GROUP ***
PO Box 42, YARRAM 3971

WESTERN AUSTRALIA (WA)

- **WESTERN AUSTRALIAN GENEALOGICAL SOCIETY, INC.**
  Unit 5, 48 May St., BAYSWATER, WA 6053.
  Library: 5/48 May St., Bayswater, 6053. *Hours:* Mon. 9.30am-9.00pm. tues.-Fri.
  9.30am-2.30pm, Sat. 1-5.00pm. Open to non members at a daily fee of $6.00. *Journal:*
  WESTERN ANCESTOR 4 per year $3.00 each. *Membership:* Single $30.00, joint
  $40.00 plus joining fee $10.00. *Meetings:* 1st Tues. 8pm 3rd floor, 150 Adelaide Tce.,
  Perth. *President:* Raema Gooch. All correspondence to be addressed to Unit 5, 48
  May St., Bayswater. Tel. (09) 271 4311.

- **GERALDTON FAMILY HISTORY SOCIETY**
  C/o Mrs J. Downes, 89 Carson Terrace, GERALDTON, WA 6530.
  Meetings: 2nd Thurs. of each month 7.30pm at 'The Residency' 321 Marine Terrace,
  Geraldton. *Library:* 'The Residency' 10am-12noon Fridays & 1st Sat. each month.
  Small fee to non members. *Secretary:* Mrs D.J. Downes.

AUSTRALIAN CAPITAL TERRITORY (ACT)

- **THE HERALDRY AND GENEALOGY SOCIETY OF CANBERRA**
  G.P.O. Box 585, CANBERRA, ACT 2601.
  Library: Iluka St., Narrabundah, ACT. *Hours:* Tues. 12.30-3.30pm 7-10pm. Thurs.
  11.00am-2.00pm. Sat. and Sun. 2-5pm. Open to non members, fee $5.00 per 3 hr.
  session. *Journal: THE ANCESTRAL SEARCHER* 4 per annum, $3.00 per issue. *Research Enquiries:* Members no charge for first half hour, non members minimum
  charge $12.00 per hour. *Membership:* Single $25.00, family $35.00, student $13.00,
  pensioner — single $13.00, pensioner — couple $17.00, corporate body $35.00. *Other
  Particulars:* Meetings held 1st Wed. each month except Jan. Griffin Centre, Civic,
  8pm. *President:* June Penny. *Secretary:* Barbara Moore.

NORTHERN TERRITORY (NT)

- **GENEALOGICAL SOCIETY OF THE NORTHERN TERRITORY**
  P.O. Box 37212, WINNELLIE, NT 0821.
  Library: 2nd Floor, State Reference Library Bldg., Cavenagh St., DARWIN, NT
  0801. *Hours:* Tue. 11am-5pm., Wed. 5pm-7pm., Sat. 1pm-530pm. Tel. during library
  hours 817 363. *Journal: PROGENITOR* 4 per year. *Research Enquiries:* Free to members. Non members $10.00 per hour. Minimum Deposit $10.00. *Membership:* Joining
  fee $5.00 Ordinary $30.00, Joint family $40.00, Pensioner $20.00, Country $20.00,
  Corp. $20.00. *Meetings:* 2nd Sat. of each month in Society Rooms at 1pm. *Presient &
  Secretary:* Mrs June Tomlinson (A.H. 32 1716).

AUSTRALIA AND NEW ZEALAND

FEDERATION

- **AUSTRALASIAN FEDERATION OF FAMILY HISTORY
  ORGANISATIONS (AFFHO)**
  C/o Richmond Villa, 120 Kent St, SYDNEY, NSW 2000.
  For details see above at beginning of Australia.

AUSTRIA — AUTRICHE — OESTERREICH

- **HERALDISCH-GENEALOGISCHE GESELLSCHAFT "ADLER"** *
  Haarhof 4a, A-1014 WIEN (Vienna).
  Oeffnungszeiten: Mittwoch 17-19 h. (ausgenommen Juli/ Aug.). Auch fuer
  Nichtmitglieder zugaenglich. *Mitgliedsbeitrag:* HATS. 450. DEM 65. *Zeitschrift:*
  ADLER, ZEITSCHRIFT FUER GENEALOGIE u. HERALDIK.
  Erscheinungsweise: Vierteljaehrlich. *Preis von Einzelheften:* HATS. 120. *Suchanzeigen:* Pro Druckzeile DEM 3.20 *Beantwortung der Anfragen:* Brieflich

(Rueckporto beilegen). *Weitere Angaben:* Jahrbuch durchschnittlich alle 2 bis 3 jahre. *Praesident:* Hofrat Dr. Berthold (Graf) Waldstein-Wartenberg. *Schriftfuehrer:* Count Hartig, Dr. phil. Dr. iur.
Office Hours: Wed. 5-7pm (except July & Aug.). Open also to non members. *Membership Sub.:* 450 Austrian Schillings or 65 German Marks. *Journal:* (named above) published quarterly. *Price:* HATS. 120. *Journal Enquiry Cost:* DEM 3.20 per printed line. *Mail Enquiries:* Enclose return postage. *Extra Details:* Yearbook published about every 2 to 3 years. *Secretary:* Count Hartig, Dr. Phil. Dr. iur. (address above).

- **BÖHMEN – MÄHREN – ÖSTERREICHISCH-SCHLESIEN (vor 1918).** *
  Siehe Ausland (Eastern Europe) Vereinigung Sudetendeutscher Familienforscher.

BELGIUM – BELGIQUE – BELGIEN

- **ARCHIVES VERVIETOISES**
  Secretary: rue Jardon 42, B-4800 VERVIERS. Ph: 087 33 17 59.

- **ASSOCIATION OF THE FRIENDS OF THE ROYAL LIBRARY**
  Secretary: Koninklijke Biliotheek Albert I, Keizerslaan 4, B-1000 BRUSSELS. Ph: 02 519 58 49.
  Royal Library Hours: Week: 09-20 hrs, Sat.: 09-17 hrs. *Fee:* 100 Bfr a week & 400 Bfr a year. *Phone:* 02 519 53 11. *Fax:* 02 519 56 79.

- **ASSOCIATION DES DESCENDANTS DES LIGNAGES DE BRUXELLES**
  Rue Landrain 9, B-1070 WEZEMBEEK, Belgium.

- **ASSOCIATION DE LA NOBLESSE DE BELGIQUE, COMMISSION HISTORIQUE ET HERALDIQUE DE L'A.N.R.B.**
  Rue Souveraine 96, B-1000 BRUSSELS. Ph: 02 647 79 89.

- **ASSOCIATION ROYALE DES DEMEURES HISTORIQUES DE BELGIQUE**
  Rue Vergote 24, B-1200 BRUSSELS, Belgium. Ph. 02-735 09 65.

- **LES DESCENDANTS DES MEMBRES DU CONGRES NATIONAL DE BELGIQUE**
  Avenue des Hortensias 11, B-1640 RHODE ST GENESE, Belgium.

- **FEDERATION GENEALOGIQUE ET HERALDIQUE DE BELGIQUE**
  BELGISCHE FEDERATIE VOOR GENEALOGIE EN HERALDIEK
  rue de la Procession 4, B-1460 ITTRE, Belgique.
  Création: 11 mai 1970. *Buts:* créer et entretenir des liens de collaboration entre diverses associations membres et les représenter sur le plan national et international. *Publications: Cahier* (parution irrégulière) et *Circulaire* d'informations fédérales (semestrielle). *Prix* Prince Alexandre de Merode (créé le 23 mars 1984) récompense (en Belgique) un travail de généalogie et/ou d'héraldique considéré comme un ouvrage de référence, tous les trois ans.

- **FEDERATION DES ASSOCIATIONS DE FAMILLE**
  Ten Bosstraat 5, B-1050 BRUSSELS, Belgium.

- **VLAAMSE VERENIGING voor FAMILIEKUNDE, v.z.w. (V.V.F.)**
  Van Heybeeckstraat 3, B-2060 ANTWERPEN-Merksem, Belgium.
  Library: As above. *Hours:* Wed. 14-19h., Sat. 14-18h. Open to non members. No fee. *Journal: VLAAMSE STAM* 11 per year. Available to non members at 75 B.Fr. *Research Enquiries:* Cost of entries 3 coupon-response internat. (or I.R.C.). *Membership:* Benelux 700 BF; Other 1000 BF. *Secretary:* E.A. Van Haverbeke. *Other Particulars:* Has special sections for computer genealogy (with periodical), one family Society, International genealogical periodicals, USA/Canada, Great Britain/Australia, Netherland, France, Germany, etc., sections in nearly every Belgian city, 3,000 members (same address as society).
  Section: ANTWERP. *Secretary:* Liliane van Dijck, Quarteerstraat 6, B-2621

SCHELLE (ph. 03 887 70 55). *Journal: NIEUWSBRIEF* 4 editions per year.

Section: BRABANT. *Secretary:* Carine Dehertog, Vergoeienveld 5, B-1900 OVERIJSSE. *Journal: V.V.F.* info bimountly. *Reunions:* Trefcentrum Elzenhof, Kroonlaan 12-14, B-1050 ELSENE, Brussels, 3rd Thurs. at 20hrs.

Section: LIMBURG. *Secretary:* Piet Severijns, Maastrichter steenweg 115, B-3700 TONGEREN (ph. 012 23 78 05). *Journal: THE RED LION* montly. *Reunions:* Cultureel Centrum, B-3500 HASSELT, 2nd Tues. 20hrs.

Section: WEST-VLAANDEREN. *Secretary:* Karel de Lille, Cartonstraat 40, B-8900 IEPER (ph. 057 20 22 96). *Library:* Kan L. Coolestraat 6, B-8400 OOSTEND. *Hours:* Wed. 14-18hrs, Fri. 20-23hrs, Sun. 11-12hrs., Sat. 14-18hrs. Several regional Journals and Reunions.

Section: GENT. *Secretary:* Florimond van Beethoven, Zalmstraat 43, B-9000 GENT (ph. 091 25 94 83). *Library:* Brusselse steenweg 395, B-9230 Melle (Belgium) (ph. 091 52 26 47). *Hours:* Wed. 09-16h., Sat. 09-12h. or appointment. *Journal: INFORMATIEBLAD V.V.F. GENT* Available to non members at 300 B.Fr. when member V.V.F. at 250 B.Fr yearly (Bank: 001-138983-63). *Reunions:* Salon Napoleon, Coupure 497, B-9000 GENT, 4th Monday at 20h. Several genealogical books to buy in Dutch.

● **OFFICE GENEALOGIQUE ET HERALDIQUE DE BELGIQUE, a.s.b.l. (O.G.H.B.)**
Parc du Cinquantenaire 10, B-1040 BRUSSELS, Belgium.
Library: As above. *Hours:* 14-17h. No fee. *Journal: LE PARCHEMIN* 6 per year and *RECUEIL GENEALOGIQUE ET HERALDIQUE DE BELGIQUE* 1 per annum. *Membership:* 1050 FB. *Président:* Prince Alexandre de Merode. *Secrétaire:* C. de Fossa.

● **SERVICE DE CENTRALISATION DES ETUDES GENEALGIQUES ET DEMOGRAPHIQUES DE BELGIQUE (S.C.G.D.), a.s.b.l.**
Maison des Arts — Chaussée de Haecht 147, B-1030 BRUSSELS, Belgium.
Library: As above. *Hours:* Mon. 16-19h. No fee. *Journal: L'INTERMEDIAIRE DES GENEALOGISTES* 6 per year. *Membership:* 1000 BF. Local sections in French Belgium: Liège, Luxembourg (Arlon), Hainaut (Mons), Namur. *Research & Enquiry Service:* Mailing — write to the President, G. Waltenier (address as above).

● **SOCIETE ROYALE DES BIBLIOPHILES LIEGEOIS**
Rue de Fragnee 129, B-4000 LIEGE, Belgium.
Secretary: Réne Wattiez (Même adresse).

BRITISH ISLES

(see also under England, Ireland, Scotland and Wales)

NATIONAL

● **SOCIETY OF GENEALOGISTS**
14 Charterhouse Buildings, Goswell Rd., LONDON, EC1M 7BA, England.
Library: As above. *Hours:* Tues., Fri., Sat. 10am-6pm; Wed. & Thurs. 10am-8pm. Open to non members. Daily fee £2.50 hour, £6.00 for 3½, £8.00 full day. *Journal: GENEALOGISTS' MAGAZINE* also *COMPUTERS IN GENEALOGY* 4 per year. *Membership:* £25.00 Town, £16.00 Country & Overseas. Joining fee £7.50. *Other Particulars:* Journals may be subscribed to separately by non members — Genealogists' Magazine at £12.00 p.a. and Computers in Genealogy at £6.00 (or £7.00 for non members) p.a. *President:* H.R.H. Prince Michael of Kent. *Chairman:* S.G. Hale, M.A. *Director:* Anthony J. Camp, B.A., F.S.G. (Hon).

● **FEDERATION OF FAMILY HISTORY SOCIETIES**
The Benson Room, Birmingham & Midland Institute, Margaret St., BIRMINGHAM, B3 3BS, England.

Correspondence to: Administrator: Mrs Pauline Saul, FSG., above address. *Membership:* This is an International Federation and membership is open to genealogical societies, worldwide. *President:* Col. I.S. Swinnerton TD, DL, JP, FSG. *Chairman:* George Pelling, FSG.

- **BRITISH ASSOCIATION FOR CEMETERIES IN SOUTH ASIA (BACSA)**
  76½ Chartfield Ave., LONDON SW15 6HQ, England.
  Newsletter: CHOWKIDAR 2 per year. 50p + SAE to non members. *Research Enquiries:* Mrs. H.M. Stokes, Research Co-ordinator, (C/o Hon. Sec.). *Membership:* £2.00. Additional joining fee £8.00. *President:* Sir John Cotton, KCMG, OBE. *Secretary:* T.C. Wilkinson MBE. *Other Particulars:* Specialist Officer on Family History matters, Miss E. de Bourbel (C/o Hon. Secretary).

- **GUILD OF ONE-NAME STUDIES**
  Box G, C/o 14 Charterhouse Building, Goswell Rd., LONDON, EC1M 7BA.
  Journal: THE JOURNAL OF ONE-NAME STUDIES 4 per year. *Membership:* £6.00. Plus registration fee £4.00. *Chair:* Peter Towey. *Sec.:* Jessica Freeman.

- **HUGUENOT SOCIETY OF GREAT BRITAIN & IRELAND ***
  Huguenot Library, University College, Gower St., LONDON WC1E 6BT, England.
  Library: As above. *Hours:* Open only to members by appointment. *Journal: PROCEEDINGS OF THE HUGUENOT SOCIETY OF GREAT BRITAIN & IRELAND* Available to non members at £8.00 per part plus postage. *Membership:* £7.50 (Fellows), £10.00 (Libraries). Additional joining fee £5.00. *President:* T.L.G. Landon. *Hon. Secretary:* Mrs Mary Bayliss, M.A. *Editor:* J.R. Vigne, M.A. F.S.A. *Other Particulars:* Quarto series, issued at irregular intervals, comprising edited transcripts of MSS, catalogues and other material.

- **THE INSTITUTE OF HERALDIC AND GENEALOGICAL STUDIES**
  79-82 Northgate, CANTERBURY, Kent CT1 1BA, England.
  Library: As above. *Hours:* Mon., Wed., Fri. 10-4.30pm. Open to non members at a daily fee of £7.50. *Journal: FAMILY HISTORY* available to non members at £8 per year. *Membership:* £15, Joining fee £5.00. *Other Particulars:* The Institute is an incorporated educational trust running regular, full-time, residential and correspondence courses and providing for post-graduate studies. Syllabus for teachers and students and lecture programme available on request. *Patron:* The Duke of Norfolk, K.G. *President:* The Viscount Monckton of Brenchley. *Secretary:* C.H. Schofield. *Principal:* C.R. Humphery-Smith. *Director:* G.M. Swinfield.

- **ANGLO-GERMAN FAMILY HISTORY SOCIETY**
  Secretary: Mrs J. Rushton, 162 Marlow Bottom Rd, Marlow, Bucks, SL7 3PP, England.
  Membership: £5.00 single, £6.00 joint, £7.50 o.s. *Journal:* "Mitteilungsblatt" (quarterly newsletter available to non-members).

CHANNEL ISLANDS (CHI) — ILES ANGLO-NORMANDES

- **CHANNEL ISLANDS FAMILY HISTORY SOCIETY**
  P.O. Box 507, St. Helier, JERSEY, JE4 8XZ, Channel Islands.
  Journal: THE CHANNEL ISLANDS FAMILY HISTORY SOCIETY JOURNAL 4 per year. *Research Enquiries:* £5.00 per hr. for members £7.00 non members. *Membership:* £6.00 Channel Islands. £7.00 Overseas. *President:* Mr. M.J. Vautier. *Secretary:* Mrs. S. Payn.

ISLE OF MAN (IOM)

- **ISLE OF MAN FAMILY HISTORY SOCIETY ***
  C/o Treasurer, Roger J. Christian, Croit-Y-Keeil, PORT GRENAUGH, Santon, Douglas, Isle of Man, British Isles.
  Application for membership to the Treasurer. *membership:* £6.00 Isle of Man & UK, £7.50 family, £8.00 o.s. Membership runs from 01 Jan to 31 Dec. *Journal: FRAUEYN AS BANGLANEYN* 4 per year. *Other Particulars:* Meetings held at the Loch Promen-

ade Church, Douglas, on the 3rd Friday of each month, including July & August commencing at 7.30pm. You don't have to be a member to attend.

CANADA

NATIONAL

- **CANADIAN FEDERATION OF GENEALOGICAL & FAMILY HISTORY SOCIETIES, INC.**
  40 Celtic Bay, WINNIPEG, MAN. R3T 2W9.
  Membership: $25.00 Full, $10.00 others. *Newsletter: CANFED* 2 per yr. $3.00 each to non members. *President:* Dolores Christie. *Secretary:* Ruth M. Breckman.

- **UNITED EMPIRE LOYALISTS' ASSOCIATION OF CANADA**
  The George Brown House, 50 Baldwin St., TORONTO, ONT, M5T 1L4.
  Library: As above. *Hours:* Mon.-Fri. 10-3pm. Open to non members, no fee. *Journal: LOYALIST GAZETTE* 2 issues per year. Cost — in Canada $12.50, in the USA $12.50 US, per year. In other countries $15.00 US per year. Available to non members. *Research Enquiries:* For subscribers. *Membership:* initial joining fee $20.00. Branch membership dues — between $20.00 and $30.00 annually (includes *Loyalist Gazette*). *Office Administrator:* D. Chisholm. *Editor:* D.K. Dorward. *Other Particulars:* Has 30 branches across Canada — write for a list.

- **CANADIAN SOCIETY OF MAYFLOWER DESCENDANTS**
  Historians Address: East: Arthur S. Harris, #45, 3665 Flamewood Dr., Mississauga, ONT. L4Y 3P5. West: Phillip P. Thorpe, 2220 Paliswood Pl. S.W., Calgary, ALB, T2V 3R2.
  Library: Housed at the North York Library, Toronto. *Entrance Fee:* $42.00. *Membership Fees:* $20.00 yr. *Newsletter: CANADIAN PILGRIM* 2 per year; members also receive the *MAYFLOWER QUARTERLY* 4 per year. *Meetings:* Annually, Apr. and Nov.; executive meetings quarterly. *Other Particulars:* A branch of the General Society of Mayflower Descendants in Plymouth, Mass., this is a hereditary society with membership open to descendants of passengers on the ship *Mayflower* which landed at Plymouth, Mass. in 1620.

- **THE FAMILY HISTORY ASSOCIATION OF CANADA ***
  L'ASSOCIATION CANADIENNE DE L'HISTOIRE DES FAMILLES
  P.O. Box 91398, West Vancouver, BC V7V 3P1, Canada.
  Our Association maintains a research library for the use of scholars, University faculty, genealogists and family historians. *President:* Dr Thomas M. Warren. *Secretary:* Judith Gwynn Koren.

- **HUGUENOT SOCIETY OF CANADA**
  10 Adelaide E., Toronto, ONTARIO, M5C 1J3, Canada. Tel (416) 361 1685.
  Library: As above. *Hours:* By appointment. *Journal: HUGUENOT TRAILS* 4 per year $4.00 each. *Membership:* $25.00. *President:* Peter Douglas DuPuy. *Meetings:* 2 per year, April and the end of October.

- **SOCIETE GENEALOGIQUE CANADIENNE-FRANCAISE ***
  Case Postale 335, Place d'Armes, MONTREAL, QUE H2Y 2H1.
  Bibliothèque: 3300 Boul. Rosemont, Suite 110, Montréal, Qué. *Heures:* lundi-mardi 19-22. jeudi-samedi 10-16. Eté: lundi 19-22 et sam. 10-16. ouverte aux membres en règle. *Revue: MEMOIRES DE LA SOCIETE GENEALOGIQUE CANADIENNE-FRANCAISE* 4 par année. *Coût des inscriptions:* Gratuit. Pour les membres en règle seulement. 5.50$ le numéro. *Cotisation annuelle:* $25 Can. pour le Canada, $28.00 U.S. pour autres pays $30 Can. pour institutions canadiennes, $30 U.S. autres pays. *Présidente:* Mme Marthe Faribault-Beauregard. *Secrétaire:* Mme Yvonne Lambert-Tardif. *Réunions:* Deuxième mercredi de chaque mois de septembre à mai inclusivement. Congrès quinquennal prochain en 1993. Cours de généalogie.

● **UKRAINIAN GENEALOGICAL & HISTORICAL SOCIETY OF CANADA ***
PO Box 902, Stn G, CALGARY, ALB T3A 3G2.
Library: Travelling mobile − used at Ukrainian events and genealogical seminars.
Open to non members, $3.00 per surname. *Journal: OUR PEOPLE* to begin soon.
Research Enquiries: $3.00/surname. *Membership:* $10.00 per year. *President:* Walter
Rusel. *Secretary:* Murial Pierson. *Meetings:* Feb., May, Sept., Dec. *Other Particulars:*
We encourage local areas to form their own branches to enhance genealogical work.
We are collecting Ukrainian surnames prepatory for the 1991 Centennial honouring
our pioneers who came to Canada. This collection will be the basis of a Resource
Centre. Planning a Canadian Western regional genealogical seminar in the fall 1991.

ALBERTA (ALB)

● **ALBERTA GENEALOGICAL SOCIETY**
P.O. Box 12015, EDMONTON, ALB T5J 3L2.
Library: Red Deer, Alberta. *Newsletter/Journal: RELATIVELY SPEAKING* 4 per
year. Available to non members at $5.50. *Research Enquiries:* Free to members. *Mem-
bership:* $20.00 (under review). Additional membership fee for joining the Branches.
Subscription $22.00. *Other Particulars:* We have been recording and have published
many cemetery records, now being compiled on a Master Data Bank. Available for
purchase. Have published "Ancestor Index" annually for 13 years. Available for purchase. Publications list available on request. *President:* Dolores Christie. *Secretary:*
Mrs Muriel Jones. *Meetings:* 5-6 per year. Conference and annual meeting in April.

● **BROOKS & DISTRICT BRANCH, ALBERTA GENEALOGICAL SOCIETY**
PO Box 1538, BROOKS, AB, T0J 0J0.
Library: Brooks Public Library, Mon.-Fri. 10am-4pm, L.D.S. Church, Tue., Thurs. 7-
9pm, Sat. 8-10am. *Journal: B&D HEIRLINES* 2 per year, $2.50 each. *Research En-
quiries:* Free. *Membership:* $7.00 + $20.00 A.G.S. *President:* Clara Iwaasa. *Secretary:*
Kay McKay. *Meetings:* 2nd Thurs. of month except July & August at Southern Computers Services Ltd. 107 1st Street W. Brooks.

● **EDMONTON BRANCH, ALBERTA GENEALOGICAL SOCIETY**
P.O. Box 754, EDMONTON, ALB, T5J 2L4.
Library: 916, 10136 100 Street, Edmonton. *Hours:* Tues., Wed. & Fri. 10am-3pm.
Open to non members. Newsletter, 4 per yr. *Journal: CLANDIGGER* $1.50 to non
members. reserach enquiries included. *Membership:* $7.00 *Meetings:* 4th Thurs.
Monthly except July, Aug. & Dec. *President:* Mrs Georgina Smith. *Secretary:* Sue
Philips.

● **FORT MCMURRAY BRANCH, ALBERTA GENEALOGICAL SOCIETY**
PO Box 6253, FT. MCMURRAY, AB, T9H 4W1.
Library: open Wed. 1-3pm, evenings by appointment. *Journal: LINES OF DE-
SCENT* 4 per year, $2.50 each. *Membership:* $7.00 + $15.00 A.G.S. *President:* Bill
Pacey. *Secretary:* Leslie Lefebve. *Meetings:* 3rd Tues. of month except July & Aug.
Hosting A.G.S. Conference April 1990.

● **GRANDE PRAIRIE & DISTRICT BRANCH, ALBERTA GENE. SOCIETY ***
PO Box 1257, GRANDE PRAIRIE, AB, T8V 4Z1.
Library: Grande Prairie Public Library, Mon.-Fri. 10am-9pm, Sat. 10am-5pm, Sun. 2-
5pm. *Journal: THE HERITAGE SEEKERS* 4 per year, $2.50 each. *Research Enquir-
ies:* $2.50, receive issue free query is in. *Membership:* $6.00 + $15.00 A.G.S. *President:*
Paulette Hrychiw. *Secretary:* Rev. Mina Pool. *Meetings:* 3rd Tues. of month, Grande
Prairie Public Library.

● **LETHBRIDGE & DISTRICT BRANCH ALBERTA GENEALOGICAL SOCIETY**
PO Box 1001, LETHBRIDGE, AB, T1K 4A2.
(located Rm 1:28 − 909 3rd Ave N., Lethbridge).
Library: As above, Tues., Wed., Fri. 1.30-4.30pm Free. *Journal: YESTERDAYS
FOOTPRINTS* 3 per year. *Membership:* $7.00 + $20.00 A.G.S. *President:* Gordon
Bruins. *Secretary:* Colleen Wright. *Meetings:* 3rd Thurs. Sept.-Nov.; Jan.-June. Elec-

tions Feb 1990.

- **MEDICINE HAT & DISTRICT BRANCH, ALBERTA GENE. SOC. ***
  PO Box 971, MEDICINE HAT, AB, T1A 7G8.
  Library: Meeting Room, open Meeting nights 7-10pm, not open to non members.
  Journal: SAAMIS SEEKER 4 per year. $6.00 year. *Research Enquiries:* Free. *Membership:* $22.00. *President:* John Dowler. *Secretary:* Patti Forbes. *Meetings:* First Wed.
  each month except July & Aug. at Westminster Church, Allan Hall.

- **THE ALBERTA FAMILY HISTORIES SOCIETY ***
  P.O. Box 30270, Station B, CALGARY, AB T2M 4P1.
  Library: 2323 Osborne Cres. S.W., Calgary. *Hours:* During Society meetings. 7-
  9.30pm. Open to non members. *Newsletter:* 12 per year. *Journal: ALBERTA FAMILY HISTORIES SOCIETY QUARTERLY* . Available to non members at $3.00.
  Membership: $20.00. *Meetings:* 1st Mon. of month all year at 2323 Osborne Cres.
  President: Barb Thorpe. *Secretary:* Wanda Pedersen.

BRITISH COLUMBIA (BC)

- **THE BRITISH COLUMBIA GENEALOGICAL SOCIETY**
  P.O. Box 94371, RICHMOND, BC V6Y 2A8.
  Library: Aberthau Cultural Centre. *Hours:* Tues., Thurs., 11am-3pm & 7-9pm; Sat. 1-
  3pm. Open to non members by arrangement. *Newsletter:* 6 per year. *Journal: B.C.
  GENEALOGIST* 4 Per year. Back issues available to non members at $2.00. *Research
  Enquiries:* Free to members. Advertising rates variable. *Membership:* $20.00. ($15.00
  for seniors) *Other Particulars:* Meetings: 2nd Wednesday each month. *President:* Mrs
  Margaret (Dolly) Hannay. *Secretary:* Betty Allen.

- **ABBOTSFORD GENEALOGICAL GROUP**
  P.O. Box 672, ABBOTSFORD, BC, V2S 6R7.
  Library: 32383 South Fraser Way, Clearbrook, BC. *Hours:* 2-4pm + 7-9pm Tues. +
  Thurs., 7-9pm Wed. Open to non members. *Newsletter: ABBOTSFORD GENEALOGICAL GROUP NEWSLETTER* 6 per year. $1.00 + post to non members. *Research Enquiries:* free. *Membership:* $10.00. *President:* Mrs Patricia Cline Confrey.
  Secretary: Mrs Dolores MacBeth Grant. *Meetings:* 3rd Wed. of each month, except
  July + Aug.

- **CAMPBELL RIVER GENEALOGY CLUB**
  Box 884, CAMPBELL RIVER, BC, V9W 6Y4.
  Membership: $10.00 *Journal: TREEHOUSE* 4 per yr. $2.50 to non members. *Meetings:* 1st Wed of month except July & Aug. at School Library at 7.30pm. *President:*
  Marion Summerer. *Secretary:* Donna Cox.

- **CHASE & DISTRICT FAMILY HISTORY ASSOCIATION**
  Box 254, SORRENTO, BC, V0E 2W0.
  Membership: $10.00. *Secretary:* Mrs. Dene Pierce. *Meetings:* 3rd Tuesday each month
  except July + Aug. in members homes. For information re research and meetings
  write association.

- **KAMLOOPS FAMILY HISTORY SOCIETY**
  Box 1162, KAMLOOPS, BC, V2G 6H3.
  Library: North Kamloops Library. *Hours:* 4th Wed. of month 7-9.00pm. members
  only. *Newsletter:* 2 per year. *Journal: FAMILY FOOTSTEPS* $2.50 to non members.
  Research Enquiries: $3.00. *Membership:* $15.00. *President:* Betty Harmsworth. *Secretary:* Joan Nethery. *Meetings:* 4th Wed. of the month, 7.30pm. North Kamloops Library.

- **KELOWNA & DISTRICT GENEALOGICAL SOCIETY ***
  Box 501, Station A, KELOWNA, BC, V1Y 7P1.
  Area of Interest: Central Okanagan Valley. *Library:* as above, open 1st and 3rd Mondays 7-9pm. Open to non members but no borrowing privileges. *Newsletter:* 4 per
  year. *Journal: THE OKANAGAN RESEARCHER* $2.50 per issue to non members.

Research Enquiries: Members Free, $1.00 non members. *Membership:* $15.00 ($20.00 family). *Meetings:* 1st Mon. each month. (except July & Aug.). *President:* Marie Ablett. *Secretary:* Susan Fitzgerald.

● **KITIMAT FAMILY HISTORY GROUP**
83 Swallow St., KITIMAT, BC, V8C 1K6.
President: Mary Sheil. *Secretary:* Lorraine McLean. *Meetings:* 1st Monday each month, Sept.-June at Northwest Community College, Kitimat, Wheelchair accessible. *Membership:* $10.00. Records of Kitimat Municipal Cemetery available.

● **NANAIMO FAMILY HISTORY SOCIETY**
P.O. Box 1027, NANAIMO, BC V9R 5Z2.
Newsletter: 4 per year. *Journal: ANCESTREE* $10.00 Year. postage. *Queries:* $2.00 each non members. *Membership:* $15.00, Seniors $13.00. *Meetings:* 3rd Thurs. monthly except Aug & Dec. 7.30pm Public Library Auditorium, Lower Rear, 580 Fitzwilliam St., Nanaimo. Wheelchair accessible. *President:* Kay Warn. *Secretary:* Ralph Vernon.

● **POWELL RIVER GENEALOGY GROUP**
Box 446, POWELL RIVER, BC V8A 5C2.
Library: Public Library. *Hours:* Daily except on Sun. & Thurs. 10am-5pm. *Membership:* $15.00. *Meetings:* Last Sun. of month 7pm. *Other Particulars:* Will answer simple enquiries particularly on local history and local sources etc. *President:* Moyra Palm. *Secretary:* Marian Buller.

● **PRINCE GEORGE FAMILY HISTORY SOCIETY**
P.O. BOX 1056, PRINCE GEORGE, BC V2L 4V2.
Meetings: 2nd Thurs. every month at 7.30pm at the Multi Cultural Folkfest Office, 1188 6th Ave., Prince George BC. *Newsletter: TREE TRACER* 4 per year. Will accept research enquiries. *Membership:* $15.00. *President:* Elayne Brielsman. *Secretary:* Jean Gordon. *Treasurer:* Leslie Ball.

● **QUESNEL BRANCH OF BC GENEALOGICAL SOCIETY**
PO Box 4454, QUESNEL, BC, V2J 3J4.
Library: Held in Public Library. *Hours:* Daily except Sunday and Monday. *Meetings:* 3rd Tues. every month in Public Library. *Membership:* $20.00. *Newsletter:* 3 per year. *President:* Gord Lester. *Secretary:* Linda Sarabyn.

● **REVELSTOKE GENEALOGY GROUP**
PO Box 2613, REVELSTOKE, BC, V0E 2S0.
President: Jewelle Lewis. *Secretary:* Brenda Cooper. *Meetings:* 2nd Tues. of the month — Public Library.

● **VERNON & DISTRICT FAMILY HISTORY SOCIETY** *
P.O. Box 1447, VERNON, BC, V1T 6N7.
Library: Small collection housed at Vernon Museum, Vernon, B.C. *Hours:* Mon.-Sat. 10am to 5pm. *Journal: SPLITTING HEIRS* 4 per year, free to members, non-members write for details. *Membership:* CAN$15.00 per year single, CAN$20.00 per year couple. *Co-Chairpersons:* Gail Mackay & Margaret Bayliss. *Secretary:* Mrs Dolores Butler. *Secretary:* Margie McGee. *Meetings:* 2nd Wed. each month except July & Aug. *Other Particulars:* Monument inscriptions books for 37 cemeteries in the area. These can be purchased. Write for list & prices. Currently indexing 1891 BC Census.

● **VICTORIA GENEALOGICAL SOCIETY** *
P.O. Box 4171, Station A, VICTORIA, BC, V8X 3X8.
Library: 545 Superior St., Victoria (upstairs). *Hours:* Tues. 9.30-11am, Wed. 6.30-8pm, Thurs. 1-3pm. *Newsletter:* 6 per year. *Membership fees:* $18.00 ($24.00 family). *Research Enquiries:* free. *President:* Jean Martyn. *Secretary:* Donna Hamill. *Meetings:* 2nd Tues. of each month. Victoria Genealogical Society wish to exchange Journals/Newsletters with other Societies. Fun Fair held with Annual Meeting June 1990.

MANITOBA (MAN)

- **MANITOBA GENEALOGICAL SOCIETY**
  420-167 Lombard Ave., WINNIPEG, MAN, R3B 0T6.
  Library: As above. *Hours:* Mon. & Fri. 9.00-11.30am & 12.15-4.30pm. Tues., Wed., Thurs. 12.15-4.30pm, Sun. 1-4pm. Open to non members. *Journal: GENERATIONS* Available to non members at $5.00. *Research Enquiries:* Cost of entries $2.50. *Membership:* $25.00. Branch fees $5.00; Dauphin, Winnipeg, South-West, Swan River Valley. *Other Particulars:* Non members may use the library materials but they are not allowed to borrow them. *Meetings:* Winnipeg branch; 3rd Thurs. of month, Museum of Man & Nature, 7.30pm. South-West branch; 1st Wed. of month, Ag. Ex. Centre, 7.30pm. Dauphin branch; last Thurs. of the month, RM of Dauphin Office, 7.30pm. Swan River Valley branch; 2nd Mon. of month, Town Office Meeting Room, 7.30pm. Inawendiwin branch, $5.00. East European branch, $10.00. *President:* Thelma Findlay. *Administrator:* Mavis Menzies. *Project:* Indexing of Manitoba Cemeteries and indexing of vital statistics from local newspapers.

- **LA SOCIÉTÉ HISTORIQUE DE SAINT-BONIFACE ***
  200 Ave de la Cathédrale, SAINT-BONIFACE, MAN. R2B 0H7.
  Bibliothèque: 200 Ave de la Cathédrale, Saint-Boniface, MANITOBA, R2B 3B4. *Heures:* lundi au vendredi, 13h30à16h30. *Bulletin:* par année 4. *Cotisation annuelle:* $10.00 étudiants et personnes d'âge d'or (student + senior citizen), $18.00 membre régulier (regular member), $25.00 membre de soutien (sustaining member), $30.00 institutions, $200.00 membres à vie (life members). *Président:* Jacqueline Blay. *Directeur général:* Gilles Lesage. *Secretary:* Michel Forest.

NEW BRUNSWICK (NB)

- **NEW BRUNSWICK GENEALOGICAL SOCIETY**
  Box 3235, Station B, FREDERICTON, NB, E3A 5G9.
  Library: NB Prov. Archives, University of NB Campus, Fredericton, NB. *Hours:* Mon.-Sat. 8.30-5.00pm. *Newsletter: GENERATIONS* 4 per year. Available to non members at $5.00. *Research Enquiries:* Cost of entries $1.00, $2.00 non members. *Membership:* $20.00. *President:* Ken Kanner. *Secretary:* Dorothy Wiggs. *Meetings:* Annual in May, executive meetings bi-monthly.

- **LA SOCIETE HISTORIQUE NICOLAS DENYS. ***
  Centre Universitaire de Shippagan, SHIPPAGAN, NB, E0B 2P0.
  Bibliothèque: Centre de Documentation SHND, Centre Universitaire, Shippagan, NB. *Heures:* Mercredi, 1-4, 7-9pm. *Bulletin: LA REVUE d'HISTOIRE* par année 3. $15.00. *Président:* Mgr. Donat Robichaud. *Secrétaire:* Céline Pinet.

- **CENTRE d'ETUDES ACADIENNES**
  Université de Moncton, MONCTON, NB, E1A 3E9.
  Bulletin: CONTACT-ACADIE . Heures: lun-ven 8h45 à 17h et mardi 19h à 22h (été: lun-ven 8h45 à 16h30. *Directeur:* Ronald Labelle. *Généalogiste:* Stephen A. White.

NEWFOUNDLAND (NFD)

- **NEWFOUNDLAND & LABRADOR GENEALOGICAL SOCIETY INC.**
  Colonial Building, Military Rd., ST. JOHN'S, NFD, A1C 2C9.
  Library: Harvey Rd., Government Bldg. *Library Hours:* 8.30am – 5pm daily. *Newsletter: THE NEWFOUNDLAND ANCESTOR* 4 per year. *Research Enquiries:* Free. Non members can purchase newletters at $3.00 per issue plus $1.00 post. *Membership:* $20.00. *Meetings:* 4th Tues. of each month except Dec., June, July & Aug. *President:* Mr Kevin Reddigan. *Secretary:* Calvin Best. *Meetings:* 4th Tues. of the month.

NOVA SCOTIA (NS)

● **GENEALOGICAL ASSOCIATION OF NOVA SCOTIA ***
P.O. Box 641, Station M, HALIFAX, NS, B3J 2T3.
Journal: THE NOVA SCOTIA GENEALOGIST 3 per year. Available to non members at $5.00 per issue. *Research Enquiries:* Cost of entries − $1.00 members/$5.00 non members. *Membership:* $15.00. *Meetings:* Lecture Series − monthly. *Chairperson:* Julie Morris. *Correspondence Secretary:* Freda Withrow.

● **AMHERST TOWNSHIP HISTORICAL SOCIETY**
150 Church St., AMHERST, NS, B4H 3C3.
Archives Hours: June 1 to Labour Day:-Mon. to Sat. 9am-5pm. Sun. 2-5pm. Labour Day to Nov. 30:-Tues. to Sat. 10am-4pm. Dec. 1 to Feb. 29:-Wed. to Sat. 10am-4pm. Mar. 1 to May 31:-Tues. to Sat. 10am-4pm. *Newsletter: THE CUMBERLAND REFLECTOR* 6 per year. *Research Enquiries:* free to members. *Membership:* $10.00. *President:* Bruce Baxter. *Secretary:* Vicki Randall. *Meetings:* From Sept.-Nov. and Jan.-May last Tues. of the month 7.30pm at the County Court House, Victoria St., Amherst.

● **CAPE BRETON GENEALOGICAL SOCIETY**
P.O. Box 53, SYDNEY, NS, B1P 6G9.
Newsletter: 2 per year. *Research Enquiries:* in Newsletter, $1 ($2 non-members). *Journal:* $4.00 per issue to non members. *Membership:* $8.00. *Chairperson:* Mildred Howard, GRS(C).

● **COLCHESTER HISTORICAL SOCIETY, GENEALOGY GROUP**
P.O. Box 412, TRURO, NS, B2N 5C5.
Library: 29 Young St., Truro. *Hours:* Tues. to Fri. 10-12am. & 2-5pm. Open to non members, daily fee $2.00. *Newsletter:* 11 per year. *Meetings:* monthly except July & Aug. *Membership:* $15.00 *Research fee:* $20 per family. *Genealogy Co-ordinator:* Marjorie Bulmer.

● **QUEENS COUNTY HISTORICAL SOCIETY**
P.O. Box 1078, LIVERPOOL, NS, B0T 1K0.
Library: As above. *Hours:* Winter − Tues. to Fri. 1.00-5.00pm. Sat. 9-5. Summer − daily 9.30-5.30 Sun. 1-5.30pm. Open to non members. *Membership:* $5.00 person, $10.00 family. *President:* Arlyene Barrett Corkum. *Secretary:* Mrs Marjorie Horner. *Meetings:* Sept. to June held on 3rd Wed. of each month. *Other Particulars:* Research Library is known as the Thomas H. Raddall Research Centre.

● **SHELBURNE COUNTY GENEALOGICAL SOCIETY**
Box 248, SHELBURNE, NS, B0T 1W0. (Coyle House, Dock Street).
Membership: $8.00 ($12.00 per family). Life $125.00 ($175 per couple). *Hours:* Tues., Thurs. & Sat. 1-4pm. Summer Hours, Mon. to Sat. 9am-5pm. *Phone:* 1-902-875-4299. *Newsletter:* 4 per year.

● **SOUTH SHORE GENEALOGICAL SOCIETY**
Townsend St., P.O. Box 901, LUNENBURG, NS, B0J 2C0.
Library: Townsend Street, Lunenburg. *Hours:* Wed. & Thurs. 2pm-9pm. Open to non members daily − fee of $2.00. *Newsletter:* 6 per year. *Research Enquiries:* Cost of entries 50c per entry. *Membership:* CAN$8.00 single, $12.00 family. *President:* Paul Jodrey. *Secretary:* Barbara B. Spindler. *Meetings:* Second Monday of every second month. Jan., Mar., May, July, Sept., Nov.

● **YARMOUTH COUNTY HISTORICAL SOCIETY GENEALOGY GROUP**
22 Collins St., YARMOUTH, NS, B5A 4B1.
Library: As above. *Hours:* When Museum is open or by appointment. Open to non members for daily fee of $1.00. *Newsletter: HISTORIGRAM* 12 per year. *Membership:* $12.00. *Chairman of Genealogy Group:* Ron Oxner. *Secretary:* Betty Newell. *Meetings:* 7.30pm 3rd Thurs. (except Dec.). We answer written queries − $5.00 minimum fee.

ONTARIO

- **ONTARIO GENEALOGICAL SOCIETY**
  40 Orchard View Blvd., Suite 251, TORONTO, ONT M4R 1B9.
  Library: 5120 Yonge St., NORTH YORK, ONT M2N 5N9. (6th Floor). *Hours:*
  Mon.-Thurs. 9am-8pm; Fri. 9am-6pm.; Sat. 9am-5pm. Open to non members. *News-
  letter: NEWSLEAF* 4 per year. *Journal: FAMILIES* 4 per year. *Research Enquiries:*
  Cost of entries on application. *Membership:* $30.00 individual, $5.00 per associate
  Founded in 1961. The Society has 5,000 members plus 27 branches operating in 11 re-
  gions of the Province. *President:* Alison Lobb. *Secretary:* Ann Rowe.

- **SOCIETE FRANCO-ONTARIENNE D'HISTOIRE ET DE GENEALOGIE**
  C.P. 720, succursale B, OTTAWA, ONT K1P 5P8.
  Bibliothèque: 50 rue Vaughan, Ottawa. ouverte-dim., lundi, jeudi 13h00 à 16h00, mer-
  credi 10h00 à 16h00 et 19h00 àa● 2200. *Bulletin: LE CHAINON* 2 par année.
  Président: Maurice Berthiaume. *Secrétaire:* Patricia Leduc. R un io ns : mensuelles.
  Cotisation annuelle: $15.00 par année.
  LES REGIONALES
  WINDSOR-ESSEX *
  C.P. 1021, Belle-Rivière, ONT N0R 1A0.
  Prés: Cecile Beneteau.
  OTTAWA-CARLETON *
  C.P. 7291 — Succ. Vanier, VANIER, ONT K1L 5A0.
  Prés: Guy-Yves Pelletier.
  SUDBURY-LAURENTIENNE *
  C.P. 1363 — Succ. B, SUDBURY, ONT P3E 5K4.
  Prés: Jacques Brault.
  DU NIAGARA *
  670 rue Tanguay, WELLAND, ONT L3B 4G2.
  Prés: Lorraine Talbot. S ec : Margaret Tilburt.
  LA SEIGNEURIE *
  449, chemin Laflèche, HAWKESBURY, ONT K6A 1M8.
  Prés: Jean-Roch Vachon.
  LA BOREALE *
  C.P. 362, KAPUSKASING, ONT P5N 2Y5.
  Prés: Claudetta Parent.
  SAINT-LAURENT
  C.P. 1894, CORNWALL, ONT K6H 6N6.
  Pré' s: Mme Marcelle Paquette. *Secrétaire:* Sr Rachel Lavoie C.S.C. *Bibliothèque:*
  300 chemin Montréal, Cornwall — ouverte aux membres, mercredi, samedi,
  dimanche — 14h00 à 16h00. *Bulletin: A LA RECHERCHE DE NOS ANCESTRES* 3
  par année, $2.00 par année. *Cotisation annuelle:* $15.00. *Réunions:* le 2 mercredi du
  mois de 16h00 á 17h00.

- **BRANT COUNTY BRANCH, ONTARIO GENEALOGICAL SOCIETY**
  P.O. Box 2181, BRANTFORD, ONT N3T 5Y6.
  Library: 34 Market St. *Hours:* Wed. & Sat. 1-4pm. Open to non-members $2.00 daily.
  Newsletter: 4 per year. $1.00 per issue non-members. *Research Enquiries:* in newslet-
  ter $2.00. *Membership:* $10.00 single, $12.00 family plus a Branch Associate Fee of
  $5.00. *Meetings:* 4th Sun. each month except June, July, Aug. & Dec. *Chairman:* Jim
  Files. *Secretary:* Charles MacKenzie.

- **BRUCE & GREY BRANCH, ONTARIO GENEALOGICAL SOCIETY**
  P.O. Box 66, OWEN SOUND, ONT, N4K 5P1.
  Library: Owen Sound Public Library. 1st Ave. West, Owen Sound. *Newsletter:* 4 per
  year, can be purchased for 25c each. *Research Enquiries:* Free. *Membership:* $10.00.
  Meetings: 4th Tues. of month except Dec. *President:* Audrey Clarke.

- **BRUCE COUNTY GENEALOGICAL SOCIETY**
  General Delivery, PORT ELGIN, ONT. N0H 2C0.
  Newsletter: 4 per yr. *Membership:* $8.00 plus $5.00 joining fee. *Meetings:* 3rd Mon.
  each month. *President:* Ms Sharon Marshman. *Secretary:* Ms Jo-Anne Moriarty.

- **ELGIN COUNTY BRANCH, ONTARIO GENEALOGICAL SOCIETY ***
  P.O. Box 416, ST. THOMAS, ONT, N5P 3U2.
  Library: St Thomas Public Library, 153 Curtis St., St Thomas. *Hours:* Mon.-Fri.
  9.30am-8.30pm, Sat. 9.30am-5pm. *Newsletter: TALBOT TIMES* 4 per year, non
  members may purchase newsletter after 1 year $2.00 per issue. *Research Enquiries:*
  Free to members. $3.00 for non-members. *Membership:* Branch — CAN$8.00.
  Chairperson: Mrs Jean Bircham, 43 Anne St., Aylmer, ONT N5H 3A1. *Secretary:* Mr
  Frank Clarke. *Meetings:* Second Wednesday each month, except July & August.
  8.00pm, in Carnegie Room, Public Library, St. Thomas. *Other Particulars:* Visitors
  and inquiries welcome. Publications upon request.

- **ESSEX COUNTY BRANCH, ONTARIO GENEALOGICAL SOCIETY ***
  Box 2 Station "A", WINDSOR, ONT, N9A 6J5.
  Library: Currently at Bishop Cody Sep. School, 1213 EC Row, Windsor. Open to
  members 3rd Mon. of month, 7.30-9pm, check newsletter for summer hours. open to
  non members. *Newsletter:* 4 per year. *Journal: TRAILS* Available to non members
  $1.00 each. 2 per member per issue free. *Research Enquiries:* $3.00 for non members.
  Membership: $10.00 individual. *President:* Sally O'Rourke. *Secretary:* Cheryl Gay.
  Meetings: 4th Mon. of month (except July, Aug.) at 754 California Ave, Windsor.

- **THE GLENGARRY GENEALOGICAL SOCIETY (HIGHLAND HERITAGE)**
  R.R. # 1, LANCASTER, ONT, K0C 1N0.
  Library: C/o Rhoda Ross, Curry Hill, R.R.1, Bainsville, ONT, K0C 1E0. (Tel. 613-
  347-3180) open by appointment, fees for all users $10.00 minimum first hour, $6.00
  each additional hour or $30 per day. *Journal: BRIDGING THE GAP* 6 per year,
  $3.00 per issue. *Research Enquiries:* 3 per yr. free to members otherwise $3.00 each.
  Membership: Canada $15.00CAN; USA $14.00US; International $16.00US. *Pres-
  ident:* Alex W. Fraser. *Other Particulars:* Book lists of publications for sale available.
  Write for particulars.

- **HALTON-PEEL BRANCH, ONTARIO GENEALOGICAL SOCIETY**
  Box 373, OAKVILLE, ONT, L6J 5A8.
  Library: Chinguacousy Public Library, 150 Central Park Dr., Bramalea, ONT. *Hours:*
  Mon.-Thurs. 10am-9pm, Fri. 10am-6pm, Sat. 10am-5pm, Sun. 1pm-5pm (Sept.-May
  only on Sun.). *Newsletter:* 5 per year. *Research Enquiries:* free to members, $3.00 non
  members. *Membership:* $8.00. *Chairman:* Lawrence Nicoll. *Secretary:* Mrs. Jane
  Watt. *Meetings:* 9 per year (except July, Aug. + Dec.) 4th Sun. each month at library.

- **HAMILTON BRANCH, ONTARIO GENEALOGICAL SOCIETY**
  P.O. Box 904, STA 'A', HAMILTON, ONT, L8N 3P6.
  Library: Room 215 Hamilton Public Library, 55 York Blvd., Hamilton. *Hours:* 3rd
  Wed. monthly except Dec. Open to public. *Journal: THE HAMILTON BRANCH
  BULLETIN* 4 per year. Entries to non members $6.00. *Research Enquiries:* $6.00 to
  non members. *Membership:* $10.00 individual, $14.00 family. There is an OGS $5 sur-
  charge to Branch only members. *Other Particulars:* We cover Wentworth &
  Haldimand Cos as well as the city of Hamilton. We have a queries committee who
  will do some research for a fee. Our surname file holds over 500,000 names indexed
  from our publications and published genealogies. *Meetings:* Usually 3rd Sun. each
  month except July & Aug., 2pm at Auditorium A, Hamilton Library. *Chairman:* Mr
  Kenneth Bird.

- **HURON COUNTY BRANCH, ONTARIO GENEALOGICAL SOCIETY ***
  Box 469, GODERICH, ONT, N7A 4C7.
  Library: R.R. # 4, Goderich,Ont N7A 3Y1,519 524 4219. *Hours:* By appointment
  only, Mon.-Fri. 9am-5pm. *Newsletter:* 3 per year. *Journal: ROOTING AROUND
  HURON* Non members $2.00 plus postage. *Research Membership:* $7.00. *Chairper-*

son: Mrs Yvonne Porter. *Secretary:* Mrs Grace Adkins. *Meetings:* Monthly from March to November, 1st Wed., 7.30pm. Annual beginners seminar in April.

- **JEWISH GENEALOGICAL SOCIETY OF TORONTO**
  PO Box 446, Station 'A', WILLOWDALE, ONT, M2N 5T1.
  Library: C/o Canadiana Room, North York Central Library. *Newsletter: SHEMTOV* 4 per year, back issues $4.00. *Research Enquiries:* 25 words $5.00. *Membership:* $25.00. *President:* Dr Rolf Lederer. *Secretary:* Mrs Selma Sacrob. *Meetings:* Sept.-June, usually last Wed. of month. – See also: Can. Jewish News "Miriam Herman Column".

- **KAWARTHA BRANCH, ONTARIO GENEALOGICAL SOCIETY**
  Box 162, PETERBOROUGH, ONT, K9J 6Y8.
  Library: Public Library. *Hours:* Regular. *Newsletter:* 4 per year. Non-members $2.00 + postage. *Research Enquiries:* printed free, donation welcome. *Membership:* $8.00. *Meetings:* 3rd Wed. evening except July & Aug. *Chairperson:* Mrs Alvina Seawright. *Secretary:* Mrs Susanne Tanney. *Other Particulars:* Publications of area interest for sale – available on request.

- **KENT COUNTY BRANCH, ONTARIO GENEALOGICAL SOCIETY**
  Box 964, CHATHAM, ONT, N7M 5L3.
  Library: 120 Queen St., Chatham, N7M 2G6. *Hours:* Mon.-Sat. library hours. Open to non members. *Newsletter:* 4 per year. *Journal: ROOTS, BRANCHES + TWIGS* Available to non members $2.00 plus postage. *Membership:* $10.00. *President:* Mary Lou Little. *Secretary:* Mr Bert Wees. *Meetings:* 2nd Friday each month, except July + Aug. Meeting place – Thamesview Lodge, Grand Ave.W. Chatham. *Other Particulars:* Many publications – send for list.

- **KINGSTON BRANCH, ONTARIO GENEALOGICAL SOCIETY** *
  P.O. Box 1394, KINGSTON, ONT, K7L 5C6.
  Library: Kingston Public Library, 130 Johnson St., Kingston. *Hours:* Mon.-Fri. 9am-9pm; Sat. 9am-5pm; Sun. 1pm-5pm (closed summer). *Newsletter: KINGSTON BRANCH NEWSLETTER* 5 per year. Cost on application. *Membership:* $8.00. *Meetings:* 3rd Sat. each month (except July, Aug., Dec.) 10am, Wilson Room, Kingston Public Library, 130 Johnson St. *President:* Mrs. Mary Ann Wright. *Secretary:* Mrs Rosalie Wintle. *Other Particulars:* Hosting O.G.S. Seminar 1991, May 24-26, "Kingston: Gateway to Upper Canada". Write for details.

- **LAMBTON COUNTY BRANCH, ONTARIO GENEALOGICAL SOCIETY**
  P.O. Box 2857, SARNIA, ONT, N7T 7W1.
  Library: L.D.S. Church, 1400 Murphy Rd., Sarnia. *Hours:* Tues., 7.00-9.00pm except July & Aug. *Newsletter: LAMBTON LIFELINE* 4 per year, available to non members $1.50. *Research Enquiries:* 2 free to members, $1.00 each for non members. *Membership:* $9.00. *Meetings:* 2nd Tues. each month at 7.30pm. except Dec. 1st Tues. *President:* Mrs Helen Clark. *Secretary:* Mrs Isabel Racher. *Other Particulars:* No meetings July & Aug.

- **LANARK COUNTY GENEALOGICAL SOCIETY** *
  C/o Robert C.M. Allan, Secretary, R.R. #3, PERTH, ONT K7H 2C5.
  Library: Smiths Falls Public Library, 81 Beckwith St. N., Smiths Falls, ONT. *Hours:* Mon., Tues., Thurs. 1-5.30pm, 7-9pm, Thurs. 9-11.30am, Wed. 12-5pm, Fri. 10-5pm, Sat. 10-4.30pm. *Newsletter:* 11 per year. Available to non members $6.00/year. *Research Enquiries:* Free (subject to change). *Membership:* $6.00. *Meetings:* 1st Wed. every month except Jan. *President:* Marilyn Snedden. *Secretary:* Robert C.M. Allan.

- **LEEDS & GRENVILLE GENEALOGICAL SOCIETY** *
  P.O. Box 536, BROCKVILLE, ONT K6V 5V7.
  Library: Brockville Public Library, 21 George St., Brockville, ONT. *Hours:* Weekdays 10am-12.30pm, 1.30pm-6pm. Thurs. & Tues. nights 6pm-8pm. Sun. 1pm-5pm. *Newsletter:* 10 per year. *Membership:* $10.00 Canadians, $12.00 USA members. *Meetings:* 2nd Mon. every month except July & Aug. *President:* Duncan MacDonald. *Secretary:* Alice Hughes.

● LONDON BRANCH, ONTARIO GENEALOGICAL SOCIETY *

P.O. Box 871, Station 'B', LONDON, ONT, N6A 4Z3.
Library: 1017 Western Rd., London, Ont. *Hours:* June-1 Sept. — Fri. 12noon-4pm; Sat. 12n-5pm. 1 Sept.-1 June — Sat. 12n-5pm. *Queries:* non members $3.00 per query to 60 words. *Newsletter: LONDONLEAF* 4 per year. *Research Enquiries:* 2 per year for members, free. *Membership:* CAN$12.00 family; CAN $9.00 individual. *Meetings:* 2nd Mon. Sept.-May except 3rd Mon. in Oct. at First St. Andrews United Church, Waterloo & Queens. *Pres.:* William M. Campbell. *Sec.:* Mrs Gerry Tordiff.

● MUSKOKA-PARRY SOUND GENEALOGY GROUP *

PO Box 2857, HUNTSVILLE, ONT, P0A 1K0.
Library: Contact Muskoka Pioneer Village, Huntsville, 705 789 7576. *Hours:* Mon.-Fri. by appointment. *Newsletter:* 2 per year, $2.00 each. *Research Enquiries:* $3.00. *Membership:* $7.00. *President:* Mrs Caroline Wood. *Secretary:* Mrs Ruth Holtz. *Meetings:* 4th Tuesday; April, June, August, October.

● NIAGARA PENINSULA BRANCH, ONTARIO GENEALOGICAL SOCIETY *

Box 2224, Station B, ST. CATHARINES, ONT, L2M 6P6.
Library: Pelham Public Library. *Hours:* Library hours. *Newsletter: NOTES FROM NIAGARA* 4 per year, $2.00 non-members. *Research Enquiries:* $4.00 each. *Membership:* $10.00. *Chairman:* Corleen Taylor. *Secretary:* Marjorie Sherk. *Meetings:* 2nd Thurs. every month. E.L. Crosley Secondary School, or Pelham Library, Fonthill.

● NIPISSING DISTRICT BRANCH, ONTARIO GENEALOGICAL SOCIETY

Box 93, NORTH BAY, ONT, P1B 8G8.
Library: North Bay Public Library, 271 Worthington E., North Bay. Open to non members. *Hours:* Mon. to Sat. 9am-9pm. *Newsletter:* 4 per year. *Journal: THE NIPISSING VOYAGEUR* $2.00 for non members. *Research Enquiries:* Members free, non members $2.50 per query. *Membership:* $7.00. *Meetings:* 2nd Thurs. each month Sept-June. *President:* Donald E. Carney. *Secretary:* Mrs Pat Coles.

● NORFOLK COUNTY BRANCH, ONTARIO GENEALOGICAL SOCIETY

P.O. Box 145, DELHI, ONT N4B 2W9.
Library: 51 Church St. E., Delhi N4B 2W9. *Hours:* By appointment, non-members $3.50. *Journal: NORFOLKS* 4 per year. *Research Enquiries:* 2 free for members, non-members $3.00 each. *Membership:* $8.00 single, $10.00 family. *Meetings:* 3rd Tues. each month except July & Aug. *Chairman:* Ken Waite. *Secretary:* Shirley Godfree.

● NORWICH & DISTRICT HISTORICAL SOCIETY

C/o Archives, R.R. #3, NORWICH, ONT. N0J 1P0.
Archives Reading Room: 91 Stover St. North, Norwich. *Hours:* Tues.-Sat. 10am-4pm. Material relating to Oxford County. Free research assistance for those visiting in person. Research by mail, free consultation then hourly fee. *Archives Newsletter* 4 per yr. for $4.00. Research queries published free. *Correspondence:* Betty Jo Moore, Assistant Archivist.

● OTTAWA BRANCH, ONTARIO GENEALOGICAL SOCIETY

P.O. Box 8346, OTTAWA, ONT K1G 3H8.
Newsletter: 6 yearly. *Research Enquiries:* Free in Branch News. Charges for research undertaken. *Membership:* $10.00 ($13.00 family). *Meetings:* 3rd Tues., Sept.-June, 20:00 at auditorium of National Library of Canada, Wellington St., Ottawa, ONT. *Library:* City of Ottawa Archives, Stanley Ave., Ottawa, ONT. Tel. 613 564 1348 for times. *Chairman:* Mr Brian O'Regan. *Editor:* Mr Brian O'Regan. *Secretary:* Heather Oakley. *Other Particulars:* Gene-O-Rama held each year in March — attendance about 250.

● OXFORD COUNTY BRANCH, ONTARIO GENEALOGICAL SOCIETY *

Box 1092, WOODSTOCK, ONT, N4S 8P6.
Library: County Library, 93 Graham St., Woodstock. *Hours:* Mon.-Fri. 9-5pm. *Newsletter:* 4 per year. *Journal: OXFORD TRACER Membership:* $8.00. *President:* Mrs Mary Evans. *Secretary:* Mrs. Margaret Phillips, RR4 Ingersoll, ONT, N5C 3J7. *Meetings:* 2nd Thurs. of the month except July & Aug.

- **PERTH COUNTY BRANCH, ONTARIO GENEALOGICAL SOCIETY** *
  Box 9, STRATFORD, ONT, N5A 6S8.
  Library: at Perth Co. Archives, 24 St Andrew St., Stratford, N5A 1A3. Tel. 1-519-273-0399. *Hours:* Mon.-Sat. 9-5. Open to non members. *Newsletter: PERTH COUNTY PROFILES* 4 per year. *Research Enquiries:* free to members, $1.00 for non members. Back issues $2.50 each. *Membership:* $9.00. *Meetings:* 3rd Tues. each month except June, July & Aug. 7.30pm. Kiwanis Centre, Lakeshore Drive. *President:* Beryl Morningstar. *Secretary:* Mr Les Wilker.

- **QUINTE BRANCH, ONTARIO GENEALOGICAL SOCIETY**
  Box 301, BLOOMFIELD, ONT. K0K 1G0.
  Library: Basement Educentre. *Hours:* Tues. 1-4pm. Open to non members. *Journal: THE SEARCHLIGHT* 4 per yr. *Research queries:* 2 per yr for members, others $1.00 each. *Membership:* $13.00 *Meetings:* 2nd Tues each month except July & Aug. *President:* Rodney Green. *Corres. Secretary:* Betty Bruce.

- **RAINY RIVER VALLEY GENEALOGICAL SOCIETY** *
  Route One, FORT FRANCES, ONT, P9A 3M2.
  Newsletter: 4 per year. *Journal: RAINY RIVER VALLEY ROOTS* . *Research Enquiries:* First two $2.50 each, rest free in one year period. *Membership:* $5.00. *President:* Carole Cress. *Secretary:* Keith W.D. Watson. *Meetings:* 1st Fri. monthly except July & August at L.D.S. F.H.L., Faries Ave., Fort Frances, 7pm. *Other Particulars:* Will research names in Rainy River Valley district Ont. & Koochiching Co., Minn. USA, for modest fee. send S.A.S.E.

- **SIMCOE COUNTY BRANCH, ONTARIO GENEALOGICAL SOCIETY**
  P.O. Box 892, BARRIE, ONT L4M 4Y6.
  Library: in Barrie Public Library, 37 Mulcaster St., Barrie. *Hours:* Library hours, Mon. to Sat. *Journal: SIMCOE COUNTY ANCESTOR NEWS* $1.20 an issue non members. *Research Enquiries:* free members, $3.00 non members. *Membership:* $10.00. *Meetings:* 10 a year: Sept.-June — speakers, workshops etc. *Chairman:* Mrs Mary Garbutt. *Secretary:* Mrs Claudia McArthur. *Other Particulars:* Members and non members may send queries to our Queries Director for personal attention.

- **STORMONT, DUNDAS & GLENGARRY GENEALOGICAL SOCIETY**
  P.O. Box 1522, CORNWALL, ONT, K6H 5V5.
  Newsletter: 6 per year. *Research Enquiries:* Free for members only. *Membership:* $15.00. *Meetings:* 4th Tues. month at Trinity Anglican Church Hall, Choir Rm. 105 Second St. W., Cornwall. *President:* Sandra MacMillan. *Secretary:* Lois Pearson.

- **SUDBURY & DISTRICT BRANCH, ONTARIO GENEALOGICAL SOCIETY** *
  C/o Sudbury Public Library, 200 Brady St., SUDBURY, ONT, P3E 5K3.
  Library: As above. *Hours:* Mon.-Sat. 9.00-5.00pm. Open to non members. *Newsletter:* 4 per year. *Journal: ANCESTOR HUNTING* $2.00 for non-members. *Research Enquiries:* Free. *Membership:* $7.00. *President:* Zona Sauve. *Secretary:* Betty Boyce. *Meetings:* 2nd Monday of month except July + Aug.

- **THUNDER BAY DIST. BRANCH, ONTARIO GENEALOGICAL SOCIETY** *
  P.O. Box 373, THUNDER BAY, ONT, P7C 4V9.
  Library: Brodie Resource Library, 216 South Brodie St., Thunder Bay. *Hours:* Mon.-Fri. 9am-9pm; Sat 9am-5pm; Sun. 1pm-5pm (except summer). Open to non members free of charge. *Newsletter: PAST TENTS* 4 per year. *Research Enquiries:* Will be undertaken — minimum charge of $5.00. *Membership:* CAN$10.00 family; CAN$8.00 individual. *Meetings:* 7.30pm 2nd Thurs. each month except June, July & Aug. at University's Teacher's College. *President:* Mr Jack Parr.

- **TORONTO BRANCH, ONTARIO GENEALOGICAL SOCIETY**
  Box 147, Station Z, TORONTO, ONT, M5N 2Z3.
  Library: Incorporated into Canadiana Collection, Central Library, 5120 Yonge St., North York, M2N 5N7. *Hours:* Mon-Thurs. 9-8.30pm, Fri. 9-6pm, Sat 9-5pm, Sun. 1-5pm (late Sep. to mid May). *Newsletter: TORONTO TREE* 7 per year. *Research Enquiries:* free to members, $2.00 per query for non members. *Membership:* $10.00,

$30.00 O.G.S. *Meetings:* 4th Mon. monthly except Dec. & June – Aug. at Toronto Educational Centre, 155 College St., Toronto. Visitors welcome. *Chairperson:* Frank T. Hankins. *Membership:* Cliff Collier. *Editor – Toronto Tree:* Jane MacNamara.

- **UPPER OTTAWA VALLEY GENEALOGICAL GROUP**
  Box 972, PEMBROKE, ONT. K8A 7M5.
  Library: LDS, Perawawa. *Hours:* 3rd Wed. each month 1-3pm. open to non members and 7pm before meetings. *Meetings:* 3rd Thurs. each month. *Newsletter:* *TIMBERLINE* 6 per year. Avail to non members at $2.12 each posted. *Membership:* $10.00 plus $3.00 for family. *Chairperson:* Norah H. Cousins-La Rocque. *Secretary:* Mrs May Prange.

- **WATERDOWN-EAST FLAMBOROUGH HERITAGE SOCIETY**
  PO Box 1044, WATERDOWN, ONT, L0R 2H0.
  Journal: HERITAGE HAPPENINGS 8 per year, $1.00 per copy. *Research Enquiries:* Free. *Membership:* $12.00. *Meetings:* 4th Fri. each month except May, Aug. & Dec. *President:* Robert E. Wray. *Secretary:* Mrs Donna Terry. *Other Particulars:* Small Flamborough Archives in process of being prepared for Public use 1991.

- **WATERLOO-WELLINGTON BRANCH, ONTARIO GENEALOGICAL SOC.**
  Box 603, KITCHENER, ONT N2G 4A2.
  Library: Kitchener Public Library, Queen St. *Hours:* 10am-9pm Mon.-Thurs., 10am-5pm Fri.-Sat. *Newsletter: BRANCH NOTES* 4 per year. *Membership:* $9.00. *Meetings:* 2nd Mon. of month, except Oct. – 3rd Mon. No meeting June to Aug., 7.30pm at Kitchener Public Library; also bi-monthly, 4th Mon. starting Sept. 1990, 7.30pm. at Orange Hall, Guelph. *President:* Ronald D. Lambert.

- **WHITBY-OSHAWA BRANCH, ONTARIO GENEALOGICAL SOCIETY**
  Box 174, WHITBY, ONT, L1N 5S1.
  Library: 405 Dundas St.W., Whitby, ONT. *Hours:* Mon.-Fri. 9.30-9.00pm. Sat. 9.00-5.00pm. *Newsletter:* 4 per year. *Journal: KINDRED SPIRITS* 75c for non members. *Research Enquiries:* $2.00 for non members. *Membership:* $9.00. *Meetings:* 1st Tues. every month at Whitby Public Library, 405 Dundas St.W., Whitby, L1N 6A1. 7.15pm-10.00pm. *President:* Mrs Marion Lapp. *Secretary:* Mrs Catherine Pickard.

PRINCE EDWARD ISLAND (PEI)

- **PRINCE EDWARD ISLAND GENEALOGICAL SOCIETY, INC.**
  P.O. Box 2744, CHARLOTTETOWN, PEI, C1A 8C4.
  Library: Books and records stored courtesy PEI Museum & Heritage Foundation 2 Kent St., Charlottetown. Newsletter: 4 per year. *Membership:* $10.00 ($12.00 family or inst.) other US$12.00. *Meetings:* 3rd Thurs. Feb., Apr., Sept., Nov. *President:* Ann Coles. *Membership Secretary:* Nelda Murray.

- **PRINCE EDWARD ISLAND MUSEUM AND HERITAGE FOUNDATION**
  2 Kent St., CHARLOTTETOWN, PEI, C1A 1M6.
  Library: As above. *Hours:* Summer hours - Mon.-Fri. 9.00am-noon., 1.15-4.00pm; winter hours – Mon. to Fri. 10am-noon, 1.15-5.00pm. Wednesday evening by appointment. Open to non members for a daily fee of $3.00. *Newsletter:* 4 per year. *Membership:* CAN$15.00. *Director:* Mr David Webber. *Secretary:* Ms. Barbara MacEachern. *Genealogists:* Mr Douglas Fraser & Ms. Charlotte Stewart.

QUEBEC (QUE)

- **FEDERATION QUEBECOISE DES SOCIETES DE GENEALOGIE**
  C.P. 9454, SAINTE-FOY, QUE, G1V 4B8.
  Bulletin: INFO-GENEALOGIE par année 3, nouvelles des sociétés membres et développement de la généalogie québécoise. *Cotisation annuelle:* $10.00 abonnement au bulletin pour organismes. *Réunions:* août – oct – février – avril - juin. *D'autres renseignements:* Regroupe les sociétés de généalogie du Québec. *Présidente:* Jacqueline Faucher-Asselin. *Secrétaire:* Léo-Paul Landry.

• SOCIETE DE GENEALOGIE DE QUEBEC
C.P. 9066, SAINTE-FOY, QC, G1V 4A8.
Bibliothèque: Local 1246, Pavillon Casault, 1210 av. du Séminaire, Cité universitaire, STE-FOY, Québec, Canada. *Bulletin: L'ANCETRE* 10 numéros par an. $2.00 le numéro. (plus frais de poste). *Coût des inscriptions:* (Research Enquiries) Réservé aux membres. *Cotisation annuelle:* (Membership) $25.00. *Président:* Guy W. Richard. *Secrétaire:* Jacques Tardif. *Réunions:* le 3è mercredi de chaque mois. *Autres renseignements:* Editeur de publications généalogiques.

• SOCIETE DE GENEALOGIE DE L'OUTAOUAIS, INC.
C.P. 2025, Succ. "B", HULL, QUE, J8X 3Z2.
Bibliothèque: 170 rue Hôtel-de-Ville,Salle S-120, Hull, Québec. *Heures:* (Hours) lundi á vendredi 8h30 á 16h30, mardi et mercredi, le soir 19h á 22h. ouverte au public. *Bulletin: L'OUTAOUAIS GENEALOGIQUE* par année 5. Anciens numéro 5 (back issues) $2.00 l'unité 1985-88 $3.00 l'unité, 1988-90 $3.60 l'unité. *Coût des Inscriptions:* (Research Enquiries) Membres — gratuit; non membres — $2.00 la question. *Cotisation annuelle:* $20.00 ($27.00 par couple). *Prés.:* Jean de Chantal. *Secrétaire:* Luc Girard. *Réunions:* Tous les 3e jeudi du mois (3rd Thurs. per month). *D'autres renseignements:* Nous publions aussi des répertoires des paroisses de l'Outaouais.

• QUEBEC FAMILY HISTORY SOCIETY
P.O. Box 1026, POINTE CLAIRE, QUE, H9S 4H9.
Library: 173a Cartier ave, suite 3, Pointe Claire. *Hours:* Mon.-Thus. 10am-3pm & Wed. 7pm-9pm., Sun. 1pm-4pm. *Newsletter: CONNECTIONS* 4 per year. Non-members $2.00 + $1.00 post. *Research Enquiries:* $2.00 per entry. *Publication: MEMBERS INTEREST & SURNAME CATALOGUE* 1 per year. Cemetery Index of Quebec & adjoining areas. Research by mail is not done. However a list of professional researchers will be provided — send S.A.S.E. *Membership:* Can. $30.00. *President:* Hugh M. Banfill. *Secretary:* Joan Benoit. *Meetings:* 2nd Tues. at La Maison de Brasseur, 2901, St. Joseph St., Lachine.

• MISSISQUOI HISTORICAL SOCIETY
P.O. Box 186, STANBRIDGE EAST, QUE, J0J 2H0.
Newsletter: 4 p/a. *Membership:* $5.00. *Pres.:* Stuart Bird. *Sec.:* Mrs Pamela Realffe.

• LA SOCIETE DE GENEALOGIE DES CANTONS DE L'EST, INC. *
C.P. 635, SHERBROOKE, QUE, J1H 5K5.
Bibliothèque: 1215 rue Kitchener, local 301, Sherbrooke, Que. *Heures:* lundi au vendredi, 13h30 à 16h30, 19h00 à 22h00. *Revue: L'ENTRAIDE GENEALOGIQUE* par année 4. $1.50. *Cotisation annuelle:* (Membership) $20.00 individuelle, $25.00 couple. *Réunions:* 9 réunions mensuelles — 1 voyage en juin. *Présidente:* Madame Micheline Gilbert. *Secrétaire:* Réjean Roy.

• SOCIETE DE GENEALOGIE DE LA COTE-NORD INC. *
649 Boulevard Laure, SEPT-ILES, QUE, G4R 1X8.
Heures: Mercredi 7h a 10h. *Cotisation annuelle:* $20.00. *Présidente:* Pierrette Thibeault. *Secrétaire:* Rejeanne Delarosbil.

• SOCIETE D'HISTOIRE ET DE GENEALOGIE DE DOLBEAU, INC.
C.P. 201, DOLBEAU, QUE, G8L 2P9.
Bibliothèque: 1150 boul. Wallberg. *Houres:* tous les jours. *Bulletin: LA SOUVENANCE* 4 par année. $10.00 avec revue. *Réunions:* mensuelle. *Président:* Marie Brossard. *Secrétaire:* Marline Potuin.

• SOCIETE GENEALOGIQUE DE L'EST DU QUEBEC
C.P. 253, RIMOUSKI, QUE, G5L 7C1.
Biblioth• que: 337 Moreault, Rimouski. (Archives Nationales). *Heures:* Du lundi au vendredi, 8h30 à 12h00, 13h00 à 16h30, de plus le mercredi de 19h00 à 22h00. *Bulletin: L'ESTUAIRE GENEALOGIQUE* par année 4. $2.50 + Frais de poste. *Cotisation annuelle:* (Membership) $15.00 (Canada), $17.00 (ext'rieur du Canada), membre à vie $15.00. *Réunions:* 1er et 3ième mardis du mois. *Président:* Rodolphe Tremblay. *Secrétaire-Trésorier:* Pierre Rioux.

- **SOCIETE GENEALOGIQUE DE LA REGION DE L'AMIANTE**
  671 boul. Smith Sud, THETFORD MINES, QUE, local 1114, G6G 1N1.
  Bibliothèque: comme ci-dessus. *Heures:* horaire de la bibliothèque du Collége de la
  région de l'Amiante. *Cotisation annuelle:* \$10.00. *Autres renseignements:* éditeur de
  publications généalogiques. *Président:* Paul Vachon. *Secrétaire:* Jocelyne Vallières.

- **SOCIETE DE GENEALOGIE DE LANAUDIERE, INC. ***
  C.P. 221, JOLIETTE, QUE, J6E 3Z6.
  Bibliothèque: 20 St Charles Borroméé, Sud, Joliette. *Heures:* lun. mar. merc. jeudi-
  vend - 9à17hre. *Bulletin: NOS SOURCES* par année 4. *Cotisation annuelle:* (Membership) \$18.00 Canada (\$18.00 Autres). *Réunions:* 2e mardi de chaque mois (pas
  juillet, août). *Président:* Claude Amyot. *Secrétaire:* Cecile P. Webster.

- **SOCIETE D'HISTOIRE ET DE GENEALOGIE DE MATANE**
  C.P. 608, 145 Soucy, MATANE, QUE, G4W 3P6.
  Heures: Lundi au vendredi. 13.30h à 16.30h. *Bulletin: AU PAYS DE MATANE* 2 par
  année. \$3.00 le numéro. *Cotisation annuelle:* \$10.00. *Réunions:* à chaque mois au be-
  soin. *Président:* Robert Tournier. *Secrétaire: Jeannette Bernier.*

- **SOCIETE D'HISTOIRE ET DE GENEALOGIE DE LA MATAPEDIA**
  C.P. 1737, AMQUI, QUE, G0J 1B0.
  Bibliothèque: 123 Desbiens, Amqui, local 324. *Heures:* mardi, mercredi et samedi de
  14h à 17h. *Cotisation annuelle:* \$20.00 *Président:* Jean-Francois Bouchard. *Secrétaire:*
  Sylvie Tremblay.

- **SOCIETE DE GENE. DE LA MAURICIE ET DES BOIS-FRANCS, INC. ***
  C.P. 901, TROIS-RIVIERES, QUE, G9A 5K2.
  Bibliothèque: 1800 rue St. Paul, Trois-Rivières. *Heures:* (Hours) lundi et mercredi
  19h00 à 22h00, jeudi 9h30 à 11h30 and 13h30 à 16h00, samedi (1er et 3ième) 13h30 à
  16h30. *Bulletin: HERITAGE* 10 par année, \$2.00/l'unité. *Coût des Inscriptions:* (Re-
  search Enquiries) pour les membres seulement. *Cotisation annuelle:* (Membership)
  \$20.00. *Réunions:* 3ieme mardi du mois à 20h00. Bibliothèque, possédons une copie
  des microfilms des actes d'éstats civils, greffes de notaires et d'arpenteurs dont les
  originaux sont conservés au Archives Nationales de Trois-Riviè● res. *Président:*
  Jean-Paul Boisvert. *Secrétaire:* Jeannine Turcotte.

- **SOCIETE D'HISTOIRE ET DE GENEALOGIE DE RIVIERE-DU-LOUP**
  65 rue Hôtel-de-Ville, RIVIERE-DU-LOUP, QUE, G5R 1L4.
  Bibliothèque: la même que ci-haut. Heures: tous les jrs 9 à 4. *Réunions:* 6 par année.
  Cotisation annuelle: \$5.00. *Président: Marcelle Savard. Secrétaire:* Céline Lévesque.

- **SOCIETE PATRIMOINE & GENEALOGIE ROUYN-NORANDA**
  541 Laliberté, ROUYN-NORANDA, QUE, J9X 3X7.
  Archives Nationales: Rue du Terminus, Rouyn-Noranda. *Heures:* 5 jrs. 9 à 12, 13.30 à
  16.30. *Citisation annuelle:* \$5.00 particulier. \$6.00 famille. *Réunions:* sur demande
  mais au moins 4 par année. *Président:* J.A. Sylva Cloutier. *Secrétaire:* Rita Deschenes
  Cloutier.

- **SOCIETE GENEALOGIQUE DU SAGUENAY, INC. ***
  930 Jacques Cartier Est, C.P. 814 CHICOUTIMI, QUE, G7H 5E8.
  Bibliothèque: 930 Jacques Cartier Est, Chicoutimi Local A-004 et B-410. *Heures:*
  mardi 19.30-22.00pm; mercredi 13.30-16.30pm. *Cotisation annuelle:* (Membership)
  \$15.00. *Président:* Marcel Thivierge. *Secrétaire:* Reine-Marie Côté. *Réunions:* Pas
  régulièrement.

- **SOCIETE D'HISTOIRE ET D'ARCHEOLOGIE DES MONTS ***
  675 Chemin Du Roy, C.P. 1192, SAINTE-ANNE-DES-MONTS, QUE.
  Bibliothèque Heures: du lundi au vendredi 9-17h. *Cotisation annuelle:* \$10.00.
  Présidente: Marcienne Pelletier. *Secrétaire:* Jean-Yves Gagnon. *Réunions:* 1 Fois le
  mois et selon les besoins. *D'autres renseignements:* Bienvenue aux correspondants.

SASKATCHEWAN (SAS)

- **SASKATCHEWAN GENEALOGICAL SOCIETY**
  P.O. 1894, REGINA, SAS, S4P 3E1.
  Library: #201 — 1870 Lorne St., Regina. *Hours:* Mon.-Fri. 9.30am-5pm. Open 3 Sat.
  of month then closed following Mon. Open to non members. *Journal: THE BUL-
  LETIN* 4 per year. Available to non members — $3.00. *Research Enquiries:* Free to
  members; $5.00 non members. *Membership:* $25.00. *Other Particulars:* Library Collection includes St. Catherine House Index, IGI, Large Ontario collection, Griffith
  Valuation, 15 000 reference articles. *Meetings:* Seminar Oct. and AGM April. *President:* Celeste Rider. *Executive Director:* Marge Thomas. *Phone:* (306) 780 9207.

- **BATTLEFORD'S BRANCH, SASKATCHEWAN GENEALOGICAL SOCIETY**
  Box 32, NORTH BATTLEFORD, SAS, S9A 2X6.
  Meetings: 3rd Wed, each month except July & Aug. *Membership:* $10.00 + S.G.S. fee.
  Newsletter: THROUGH THE BRANCHES Local research available for $10.00 fee.
  President: Carolyn Hayes (306) 892 4314.

- **BIGGAR BRANCH, SASKATCHEWAN GENEALOGICAL SOCIETY**
  PO Box 1424, BIGGAR, SAS, S0K 0M0.
  Membership: $5.00 + S.G.S. Fee. *Meetings:* 2nd Wed. each month except July & Aug.
  Contact person: Mr C.P. Poitras. (306) 948 5110.

- **CENTRAL BUTTE BRANCH, SASKATCHEWAN GENE. SOCIETY** *
  CENTRAL BUTTE, SAS, S0H 0T0.
  Membership: $5.00 + S.G.S. Fee. *Meetings:* 4th Thurs. of month except July & Aug.
  President: Joanne Berg. *Secretary:* Frances Pollock. *Other Particulars:* Local history
  book "Our Heritage, A View From the Butte". Local research available.

- **CRAIK BRANCH, SASKATCHEWAN GENEALOGICAL SOCIETY** *
  Box 337, CRAIK, SAS, S0G 0V0.
  Library: Open on request, no fee. *Membership:* $5.00 + S.G.S. Fee. *Meetings:* 3rd
  Mon. of every month. *President:* June Exelby. *Secretary:* Dorothy Brown.

- **GRASSLANDS BRANCH, SASKATCHEWAN GENEALOGICAL SOCIETY** *
  HAZENMORE, SAS, S0N 1C0.
  Library: As above. Open to non members. Contact Alice 264 5149. *Newsletter:* 3 per
  year. *Journal: GRASSROOTS* Non members $1.00 per copy. *Research Entries:* in
  Journal: $2.00 for non-members. *Research Enquiries:* $5.00 per hour + $1.00 fee +
  SASE. *Membership:* CAN$6.00. *President:* Mrs Beverly Switzer. *Secretary:* Miss
  Linda Calvin. *Meetings:* Second Wed. each month except July & August, 7.30pm.

- **GRENFELL BRANCH, SASKATCHEWAN GENEALOGICAL SOCIETY** *
  GRENFELL, SAS, S0G 2B0.
  Library: Open 8pm-10pm 3rd Tues. of each month, not open to non-members. *News-
  letter: KITH ●N KIN* 3 per year. *Research Enquiries:* Free. *Membership:* $25.00 per
  family. *Meetings:* 3rd Tues. of each month except July & Aug. *President:* Edna S.
  Laidlaw. *Secretary:* M. Agnes Reeve.

- **KINDERSLEY GENEALOGICAL SOCIETY**
  Box 842, KINDERSLEY, SAS, S0L I50.
  Journal: THE ROOT CELLAR. Membership: $7.00. *Meetings:* 4th Tues. each month.
  President: Joan Hppner. *Secretary:* Betty Francis.

- **RADVILLE BRANCH, SASKATCHEWAN GENEALOGICAL SOCIETY.** *
  Box 1082, WEYBURN, SAS, S4H 2L3.
  LIBRARY: Open to non-members, $1.00 per use. *Meetings:* 3rd Wed. *President:* Mrs
  Ruth Henheffer. *Secretary:* Mrs Eileen Bouchard. *Other Particulars:* Weekly column
  in newspaper "Radville Roots".

● **SASKATOON BRANCH, SASK. GENEALOGICAL SOCIETY**
Box 8651, SASKATOON, SASK., S7K 6K8.
Library: Albert Community Centre. *Hours:* During meetings, 6.30-9.00pm. Members only. *Newsletter: ARMCHAIR GENEALOGIST* 10 per year. Members only. *Membership:* $6.00 Branch plus $25.00 Sask. Gen. Soc. (Senior $22.00). *President:* James (Jay) Dynes. *Secretary:* Evelyn Ballard. *Meetings:* 2nd Wed. evening 7-9pm, Except July + Aug. Albert Community Centre, Clarence Ave. + 12th St.

● **SWIFT CURRENT GENEALOGICAL SOCIETY**
Box 307, SWIFT CURRENT, SAS, S9H 3V8.
Meetings: 4th Mon. each month. *President:* Anne Knowlton. *Secretary:* Pat Cammer.

● **WEST CENTRAL BRANCH, SASKATCHEWAN GENEALOGICAL SOCIETY**
Box 36, ESTON, SAS, S0L 1A0.
Journal: ROOT TOOTIN. Membership: $7.00. *Meetings:* 3rd Tues. every month, 9.30am. at Regional Library in Eston. This Library open Mon.-Sat. 2-5pm. *President:* Gail Milton (306) 962 3382. *Secretary:* Eileen Martsch (306) 962 4577.

● **WEYBURN BRANCH, SASKATCHEWAN GENEALOGICAL SOCIETY**
Box 1422, WEYBURN, SAS, S4H 2J8.
Library: 23 6th Street N.E., open Mon.-Fri., 9am-12n, 1-5pm, not open to non members. *Newsletter: HERITAGE ECHO'S* about 4 per year. *Research Entries:* Free. *Membership:* $8.00. *President:* Hannah Bell. *Secretary:* Charmane Johnson. *Meetings:* 4th Mon. of month.

YUKON (YUK)

● **DAWSON CITY MUSEUM & HISTORICAL SOCIETY ***
Box 303, DAWSON CITY, YUK Y0B 1G0, Canada.
Library Hours: Summer; Mon.-Fri. 1-5pm. Winter; by appointment only. Free with admission to Museum. *Journal: DAWSON CITY MUSEUM NEWSLETTER* 4 per year. *Membership:* $10.00. *Director:* Valerie Baggaley. *Other Particulars:* Researching done at $15/hr, the first ½ hour is free of charge.

CZECHOSLOVAKIA

● **BÖHMEN – MÄHREN – ÖSTERREICHISCH-SCHLESIEN (vor 1918). ***
Siehe Ausland (Eastern Europe) Vereinigung Sudetendeutscher Familienforscher.

● **CZECHOSLOVAK GENEALOGICAL SOCIETY**
PO Box 16225, ST PAUL, MN 55116, USA.
Membership: $10.00 ($15.00 family). *Meetings:* Quarterly. *Newsletter: SLOVO* 10 per year.

DENMARK – DANMARK

● **SAMFUNDET FOR DANSK GENEALOGI OG PERSONALHISTORIE ***
Bulgariensgade 5 St., DK-2300, KOBENHAVN S., Denmark.
Journal: PERSONAL HISTORISK TIDSSKRIFT. Available to non members at 111 Dkr. *Membership:* 110 Dkr. *Other Particulars:* We collaborate with Sammenslutningen af slaegtshistoriske Foreninger (SSF) in all matters, including *Hvem fosker Hvad, our research directory. President:* Hans H. Worsoe. *Secretary:* Finn Andersen.

● **SLAEGTS – OG LIKALHISTORISK FORENING i BORDING ***
Vestervang 12, DK-7441 BORDING, Denmark.
President: Svend Skyum.

● **SLAEGTS – OG LOKALHISTORISK FORENING for BOLLING-NORRE HORNE HERRED ***
Kongevej 56, DK-6900 SKJERN, Denmark. *President:* Bent Pedersen.

- **SYDVESTJYSK EGNS – OG SLAEGTSHISTORISKE FORENING ***
  Byhistorisk Arkiv, Teglvaerksgade 1 B, DK-6700 ESBJERG, Denmark.
  President: Jorgen Dieckmann Rasmussen.

- **SLAEGTS – OG LOKALHISTORISK FORENING i FREDERIKSHAVN ***
  Holmbovej 41, DK-9900 FREDERIKSHAVN, Denmark.
  President: Verner Melchiorsen.

- **GRINDSTED OG OMEGNS SLAEGTS – OG LOKALHISTORISKE FORENING**
  Ravlundvej 9, Filskov, DK-7200 GRINDSTED, Denmark. *
  President: Judith Sorensen.

- **SLAEGTSHISTORISK FORENING i HERNING ***
  Rugvaenget 41, DK-7400 HERNING, Denmark.
  President: Jorgen Ostergaard.

- **SLAEGTSHISTORISK FORENING for HJORRING OG OMEGN ***
  Christiansgade 24, DK-9800 HJORRING, Denmark.
  President: Per Maack Andersen.

- **EGNS – OG SLAEGTSHISTORISK FORENING i HOLSTEBRO ***
  Saerkaerparken 76, DK-7500 HOLSTEBRO, Denmark.
  President: Ejner G. Petersen.

- **SLAEGTSHISTORISK FORENING i IKAST ***
  Sobjergvej 44, DK-7430 IKAST, Denmark.
  President: Gunnar Joakobsen.

- **KORSOR SLAEGTSHISTORISK FORENING ***
  Humlevaenget 1, DK-4220 KORSOR, Denmark.
  President: Jens Hojgaard Sorensen.

- **SLAEGTSHISTORISK FORENING for STORKOBENHAVN ***
  MacDonald Allé 15, DK-2750 BALLERUP, Denmark.
  President: Jorgen Aasberg.

- **SLAEGTSHISTORISK FORENING for MORS ***
  Rorsangervej 37, DK-7900 NYKOBING M, Denmark.
  President: Jakob Albrektsen.

- **SLAEGTSHISTORISK FORENING i ODENSE ***
  Filosofgangen 23, 2, DK-5000, ODENSE C, Denmark.
  President: Lise Lund.

- **SLAEGTS – OG EGNSHISTORISK FORENING for RANDERS ***
  Vindingholmsvej 12, Kousted, DK-8900 RANDERS, Denmark.
  President: Ruth Pedersen.

- **ROSKILDEEGNENS SELSKAB FOR GENE. OG PERSONALHISTORIE ***
  Bankholmvej 5, Veddelev, DK-4000 ROSKILDE, Denmark.
  President: Jens V. Olsen.

- **LOKAL – OG SLAEGTSHISTORISK FORENING for SAEBY OG OMEGN ***
  Algade 3, lejl nr 5, DK-9300 SAEBY, Denmark.
  President: Villy Them Hansen.

- **SLAEGTSHISTORISK FORENING i SONDERJYLLAND ***
  Mosevang 29, Ulkebol, DK-6400 SONDERBORG, Denmark.
  President: Jorgen Wangel.

- **TREKANTOMRADETS SLAEGTSHISTORISKE FORENING ***
  Limskov Vestergaard, DK-7183 RANDBOL, Denmark. 2 *President:* Else Udsen.

- **SLAEGTSHISTORISK FORENING i VESTSJAELLAND ***
  Lundforlundvej 8, DK-4200 SLAGELSE, Denmark.
  President: Ole G. Nielsen.

- **SLAEGTSHISTORISK FORENING for VIBORG OG OMEGN ***
  Skovstien 22, Birgittelyst, DK-8800 VIBORG, Denmark.
  President: Ingvar Musaeus.

- **SLAEGTSHISTORISK FORENING i AARHUS ***
  Peter Fabers Vej 9, DK-8210 AARHUS V, Denmark.
  President: S.E. Sorensen.

- **SAMMENSLUTNINGEN AF SLAEGTSHISTORISKE FORENINGER ***
  DK-8210 AARHUS V, Denmark.
  Journal: HVEM FORSKER HVAD Available to non members at 30 Dkr. 1 per year.
  President: S. Sorensen.

DEUTSCHLAND (siehe GERMANY)

ENGLAND (see also British Isles)

NATIONAL

- **SOCIETY OF GENEALOGISTS**
  14 Charterhouse Buildings, Goswell Rd., LONDON, EC1M 7BA, England.
  Library: As above. *Hours:* Tues., Fri., Sat. 10am-6pm; Wed. & Thurs. 10am-8pm.
  Open to non members. Daily fee £2.50 hour, £6.00 for 3½, £8.00 full day. *Journal:*
  GENEALOGISTS' MAGAZINE also *COMPUTERS IN GENEALOGY* 4 per year.
  Membership: £25.00 Town, £16.00 Country & Overseas. Joining fee £7.50. *Other Particulars:* Journals may be subscribed to separately by non members — Genealogists'
  Magazine at £12.00 p.a. and Computers in Genealogy at £6.00 (or £7.00 for non
  members) p.a. *President:* H.R.H. Prince Michael of Kent. *Chairman:* S.G. Hale, M.A.
  Director: Anthony J. Camp, B.A., F.S.G. (Hon).

- **CATHOLIC RECORD SOCIETY**
  C/o 114 Mount St., LONDON, W2Y 6AH, England.
  Journal: RECUSANT HISTORY 2 per year. *Research Enquiries:* Source information
  supplied, no research undertaken. *Membership:* £15.00; US$30.00 overseas. *President:* Rt. Rev. Bishop Mullins. *Secretary:* Ms. Rosemary Rendel.

- **CATHOLIC FAMILY HISTORY SOCIETY ***
  C/o 2 Winscombe Crescent, Ealing W5 1AZ, LONDON, England.
  Journal: CATHOLIC ANCESTOR 4 per year. *Research Enquiries:* Available to
  members through journal. *Membership:* £6 (U.K.); £8 (overseas). *President:* Hon.
  Georgina Stonor. *Secretary:* Mrs Barbara Murray.

- **FEDERATION OF FAMILY HISTORY SOCIETIES**
  The Benson Room, Birmingham & Midland Institute, Margaret St., BIRMINGHAM, B3 3BS, England.
  Correspondence to: Administrator: Mrs Pauline Saul, FSG., above address. *Membership:* This is an International Federation and membership is open to genealogical societies, worldwide. *President:* Col. I.S. Swinnerton TD, DL, JP, FSG. *Chairman:*
  George Pelling, FSG.

- **GUILD OF ONE-NAME STUDIES**
  Box G, C/o 14 Charterhouse Buildings, Goswell Rd., LONDON, EC1M 7BA.
  Journal: THE JOURNAL OF ONE-NAME STUDIES 4 per year. *Membership:*
  £6.00. Plus registration fee £4.00. *Chair:* Peter Towey. *Secretary:* Jessica Freeman.

- **HUGUENOT SOCIETY OF GREAT BRITAIN & IRELAND ***
  Huguenot Library, University College, Gower St., LONDON WC1E 6BT, England.

Library: As above. *Hours:* Open only to members by appointment. *Journal: PRO-CEEDINGS OF THE HUGUENOT SOCIETY OF GREAT BRITAIN & IRELAND* Available to non members at £8.00 per part plus postage. *Membership:* £7.50 (Fellows), £10.00 (Libraries). Additional joining fee £5.00. *President:* T.L.G. Landon. *Hon. Secretary:* Mrs Mary Bayliss, M.A. *Editor:* J.R. Vigne, M.A. F.S.A. *Other Particulars:* Quarto series, issued at irregular intervals, comprising edited transcripts of MSS, catalogues and other material.

- **HUGUENOT & WALLOON GAZETTE ASSOCIATION ***
  Secretary: Mrs J. Tsushima, 'Malmaison', Church St., Great Bedwyn, Wilts, SN8 3PE, England.

- **THE INSTITUTE OF HERALDIC AND GENEALOGICAL STUDIES ***
  79-82 Northgate, CANTERBURY, Kent, CT1 1BA, England. Tel: 0227 768664.
  Library: As above. *Hours:* Mon., Wed., Fri. 10-4.30pm. Open to non members at a daily fee of £7.50; £5.00 for half day. *Journal: FAMILY HISTORY* Available to non members at £8.00. *Membership:* £15.00. Joining fee £15.00. *Other Particulars:* The Institute is an incorporated educational trust running regular, full-time, residential and correspondence courses and providing for post-graduate studies. Syllabus for teachers and students and full range of qualifications, both academic and vocational, available on request. *Patron:* The Duke of Norfolk, K.G. *President:* The Viscount Monckton of Brenchley. *Principal:* C.R. Humphery-Smith; *Director:* G.M. Swinfield; *Registrar:* Janet Carter.

AVON (AVN)

- **BRISTOL & AVON FAMILY HISTORY SOCIETY**
  C/o 12 Cadbury Road, Keynsham, BRISTOL, BS18 1JW, England.
  Library: At meetings only. *Hours:* Days of meetings, 7-10pm. *Journal: JOURNAL OF THE BRISTOL & AVON FAMILY HISTORY SOCIETY* 4 per year. Available to non member. Price on application. *Research Enquiries:* apply to Sec. *Membership:* £6.00 local. £7.00 overseas. *Other Particulars:* Meetings on 3rd Mon. most months between Sept. & June at Lecture Theatre One, School of Chemistry, Bristol University, 7.30-9.30pm. *Chairman:* Bob Brown. *Secretary:* Bob Grace, Address as above.

- **WESTON-SUPER-MARE FAMILY HISTORY SOCIETY**
  Secretary: Mrs M. Knox, 8 Woodland Glade, Clevedon, Avon, BS21 6AL, England.

BEDFORDSHIRE (BDF)

- **BEDFORDSHIRE FAMILY HISTORY SOCIETY**
  C/o 7 Braeside, BEDFORD MK41 9BL, England.
  Journal: BEDFORDSHIRE F.H.S. JOURNAL 4 per year, free with membership. *Publications:* Index to 1851 Census of Bedfordshire published in 25 books £2 per book plus postage. Bedfordshire Strays Index £9.00 plus postage. *Membership:* £7.00 (Jan. 1991). *Chairperson:* Mrs Mary Owen. *Honorary Secretary:* Mrs Pamela E. Ormerod, 7 Braeside, Bedford, MK41 9BL. Membership details and other information from address above. Please enclose S.S.A.E. at least 220mm x 110mm or 3 IRCs.

BERKSHIRE (BRK)

- **BERKSHIRE FAMILY HISTORY SOCIETY**
  C/o 87 Finchampstead Road, WOKINGHAM, Berks RG11 2PE, England.
  Library: As above, open at meeting. *Journal: BERKSHIRE FAMILY HISTORIAN* 4 per year. Available to non members at 50p plus postage. (Back nos. only). *Membership:* £6.00; additional joining fee 50p. £7.00 family. £8.00 overseas airmail. *Hon, Secretary:* Meg Goswell.

BIRMINGHAM

- **BIRMINGHAM & MIDLAND SOCIETY FOR GENEALOGY AND HERALDRY**
  92 Dimmingsdale Bank, Birmingham, West Midlands, B32 1ST, England.
  Library: The Reference Library is now in the Kingsley Norris Room at The Birmingham & Midland Institute, Margaret St., Birmingham. *Hours:* Mon.-Fri. 10am-4pm. Open to non members. *Journal: THE MIDLAND ANCESTOR* 4 per year. Back issues available to non members. Price on application. *Research Enquiries:* Members only. *Membership:* £8.00. *President:* Col. I.S. Swinnerton, T.D., J.P., D.L., F.S.G. *Secretary:* Mrs. J. Watkins.

BUCKINGHAMSHIRE (BKM)

- **BUCKINGHAMSHIRE FAMILY HISTORY SOCIETY** *
  Varneys, Rudds Lane, Haddenham, nr. AYLESBURY, Bucks., HP17 8JP England.
  Library: As above. Open by appointment. *Journal: ORIGINS* 4 per year. Available to non members at £1.80 (overseas £1.95. *Research Enquiries:* Members only. *Membership:* £6.00 UK; £7.50 family UK. overseas mail US, CAN £7.50; AUS, NZ £7.75. *Other Particulars:* 3rd Sat. afternoon Aylesbury. Information about additional meetings on request. *Chairman:* F.S.M. Clarke. *Secretary:* Mrs. Eve McLaughlin.

CAMBRIDGESHIRE (CAM)

- **CAMBRIDGESHIRE FAMILY HISTORY SOCIETY**
  1 Ascham Lane, Whittlesford, CAMBRIDGE, CB2 4NT, England.
  Journal: CAMBS F.H.S. JOURNAL 4 per year. Available to non members at £1.00 + p.p. *Research Enquiries:* Available to members and non members. Donations requested from non members. *Membership:* £5.00, £7.50 overseas. *Chairman:* Michael Farrar. *Secretary:* Mrs B. Ward.

- **PETERBOROUGH & DISTRICT FAMILY HISTORY SOCIETY**
  44 The Steynings, Werrington, PETERBOROUGH PE4 6QL, England.
  Journal: P.& D. F.H.S. Journal 4 per year. *Membership:* £6.00, family £8.00, overseas £5.00. *President:* Mr. Hugh Cave. *Secretary:* Ron Sharp.

CHANNEL ISLANDS (CHI) See BRITISH ISLES.

CHESHIRE (CHS)

- **FAMILY HISTORY SOCIETY OF CHESHIRE** *
  C/o 5 Henbury Rise, Henbury, MACCLESFIELD, CHS SK11 9NW, England.
  Journal: FAMILY HISTORY SOCIETY OF CHESHIRE 4 per year. *Local Groups:* Altrincham, Birkenhead, Chester, Congleton, Macclesfield, Nantwich, Northwich, Runcorn and Daresbury, Wirral. *Membership:* £6.00 UK. £8.50 overseas. *Chairman:* David S. Lambert. *Secretary:* Peter D. Dewdney.

- **NORTH CHESHIRE FAMILY HISTORY SOCIETY**
  2 Denham Dr., Bramhall, STOCKPORT, SK7 2AT, England.
  Library: Park House, Sale, & Civic Hall, Hazel Grove, Cheshire. *Hours:* at meetings, Park House, Sale, 1st Fri. in month. Civic Hall, Hazelgrove 3rd Tues., Wilmslow Library 4th Wed., all 7.30-10pm. *Journal: FAMILY HISTORIAN* 4 per year. Available to non members. *Research Enquiries:* On request. *Membership:* £5.00 full members (£7.00 overseas); £4.50 country members. *President:* Colonel Day. *Secretary:* Rhoda Clarke.

CLEVELAND (CLV)

- **CLEVELAND FAMILY HISTORY SOCIETY** *
  1 Oxgang Close, REDCAR, Cleveland TS10 4ND, England.
  Journal: CLEVELAND F.H.S. JOURNAL 4 per year. Available to non members at £1.00. *Research Enquiries:* Free to members. *Membership:* £8.00 overseas airmail;

£5.50 overseas surface; £4.50 UK. *President:* Mr. P.R. Joiner. *Secretary:* Mr. A. Sampson. *Branches:* Redcar, Whitby, Hartlepool, Darlington.

CORNWALL (CON)

● **CORNWALL FAMILY HISTORY SOCIETY**
11 Penrose Rd., FALMOUTH, Cornwall TR11 2DU, England.
Library: For callers at Headquarters, 3 Calenick St., Truro, Cornwall. *Journal: CORNWALL HISTORY SOCIETY JOURNAL* 4 per year. *Research Enquiries:* Material held in our own Library searched in return for a small donation. *Membership:* £10.00 UK. £14.00 overseas airmail. *Other Particulars:* Major meetings in Cornwall in mid-May and mid-November, with local meetings around the county at other times. Overseas groups also meet in USA, Canada and Australia. *Chairperson:* Mrs K. Arundel. *Secretary:* Mrs Gillian Thompson.

CUMBRIA (CMA)

● **CUMBRIA FAMILY HISTORY SOCIETY** *
32 Granada Road, DENTON, Manchester, M34 2LJ, England.
Newsletter: 4 per year. *Membership:* £4.50 U.K., £5.50 Surface, £7.50 Airmail. *President:* C. Roy Huddleston, M.A., F.S.A., F.S.A.(Scot.). *Secretary:* Mrs. M.M. Russell.

DERBYSHIRE (DBY)

● **DERBYSHIRE FAMILY HISTORY SOCIETY** *
Secretary: Mrs P. Marples, 15 Elmhurst Rd, FOREST TOWN, Mansfield, Notts, NG19 0EV, England.

● **CHESTERFIELD & DISTRICT FAMILY HISTORY SOCIETY**
Secretary: Mrs Mavreen Pearce, 10 Burgess Close, HASLAND, Chesterfield, Dby, S41 0NP, England.

DEVON (DEV)

● **DEVON FAMILY HISTORY SOCIETY**
12 Whitehall Close, South Molton, DEVON, EX36 4EQ, England.
Journal: THE DEVON FAMILY HISTORIAN Feb., May, Aug., Nov. Available to non members at £1.00 plus p+p. *Membership:* £6.00 U.K., £8.00 Overseas. *Chairman:* Maurice Pike. *Secretary:* John Parsons.

DORSET (DOR)

● **DORSET FAMILY HISTORY SOCIETY**
311 Herbert Ave., Parkstone, Poole, DORSET BH12 4HT, England.
Library: 361 Sopwith Cres., Merley, Dorset, BH21 1XQ. By appointment. *Journal: JOURNAL OF THE DORSET FAMILY HISTORY SOCIETY* 4 per year. *Membership:* £5.00. *Chairperson:* Mrs Anne Lhoas. *Secretary:* Mrs June Clist.

SOMERSET & DORSET FAMILY HISTORY SOCIETY See SOMERSET.

DURHAM (DUR) See NORTHUMBERLAND and also CLEVELAND

ESSEX (ESS)

● **ESSEX SOCIETY FOR FAMILY HISTORY**
C/o The Old Granary, Justice Wood, POLSTEAD, Suffolk, CO6 5DH, England.
Journal: ESSEX FAMILY HISTORIAN published quarterly to members. *Member-*

ship: Joining fee £2 and annual subscription of £8 or £10 for two adults of the same family. *President:* John Rayment F.S.G. *Chairman:* Geoff Howlett. *Secretary:* Peter J. Moore, (above address). *Other Particulars:* Library and bookstall open on days of meetings. Enquiries to Secretary.

● **WALTHAM FOREST FAMILY HISTORY SOCIETY** *
1 Gelsthorpe Road, Romford, ESSEX RM5 2NB, England.
Journal: Roots in the Forest. 4 per year. Available to non members at 50p plus post.
Membership: Individual £5, family £7.50, senior citizen £2.75, overseas £7.50 *Chairman:* Ron Ambrose. *Secretary:* John F. Bowen.

GLOUCESTERSHIRE (GLS)

● **GLOUCESTERSHIRE FAMILY HISTORY SOCIETY**
21 Lancaster Drive, LYDNEY, Glos. GL15 5SJ, England.
Journal: GLOUCESTERSHIRE F.H.S. JOURNAL 4 per year. Available to non members at £1.50 inc. P & P overseas, £1 inland. *Membership:* £6.00, £8.00 family, £10.00 overseas airmail. *Secretary:* Mr N.C. Phillips (as above) *Tel.:* 0594 841028.

HAMPSHIRE (HAM)

● **THE HAMPSHIRE GENEALOGICAL SOCIETY**
C/o Secretary, 77 Athelstan Rd., BITTERNE, Hants, SO2 4DE, England.
Journal: THE HAMPSHIRE FAMILY HISTORIAN Available to non members, £1.25 incl. p.p. *Membership:* Year begins 1 April. £6.00, overseas £9.00 (payable in Sterling only) (includes Air Mail postage). *Secretary:* Mrs S.A. Naish.

HEREFORDSHIRE (HEF)

● **HEREFORDSHIRE FAMILY HISTORY SOCIETY**
C/o Mrs M. Cave, 14a Tillington Rd., HEREFORD, HR4 9QJ, England.
Journal: HEREFORDSHIRE FAMILY HISTORY SOCIETY JOURNAL 4 per year. Available to non members at £1.50 incl. post. *Research Enquiries:* Limited research for members only, £1 per hour up to 3 hrs. *Membership:* £6.00 single, £8.00 family. *Chairperson:* Mr J. Harnden. *Secretary:* Mrs M. Cave.

HERTFORDSHIRE (HRT)

● **HERTFORDSHIRE FAMILY AND POPULATION HISTORY SOCIETY**
6 The Crest, WARE, Herts., SG12 0RR England.
Journal: HERTFORDSHIRE PEOPLE 3 per year. Available to non members at £1.00 + postage. *Membership:* £4.00 UK individual; £5.00 UK family; £7.50 overseas airmail; £5.50 overseas surface. Remittances in Sterling only. *President:* Mr Anthony Camp. *Secretary:* Mrs Patricia Betty.

HUNTINGDONSHIRE (HUN)

● **HUNTINGDONSHIRE FAMILY HISTORY SOCIETY**
11 Longholme Road, UPWOOD, Huntingdon, Cambs, PE17 1QD, England.
Journal: THE HUNTSMAN at present 2 per year to all members plus 2 newsletters to UK members. Available to non members for £1.50 + p.p. *Membership:* £5.00 UK. £7.50 overseas airmail. *Other Particulars:* Meetings take place once a month at Huntingdonshire College. 7.30pm on the 3rd Wed. of the month Sep.-June inclusive. *Secretary:* Mrs Joan Whitwell.

ISLE OF WIGHT (IOW)

● **ISLE OF WIGHT FAMILY HISTORY SOCIETY**
All enquiries to the Hon. Sec., Miss S.J. McConkey, 37 James Ave., Lake, Sandown, IOW PO36 9NH.
Library: Available at meetings only. *Journal: IOWFHS* Journal 4 per year. *Research Enquiries:* Details from the secretary on request. *Other Particulars:* Meetings 1st Mon.

and additional meetings at Athena House, John Street, Ryde, IOW. *Membership:* £6.00 UK, £8.00 overseas. *Chairman:* Mrs B. James.

KENT (KEN)

- **KENT FAMILY HISTORY SOCIETY**
  8 Malvern Rd., Ashford, KENT TN24 8HP, England.
  Library: 212 Tonbridge Rd., Wateringbury, Maidstone, Kent ME18 5NU. *Hours:* By appointment. *Journal: KENT F.H.S. JOURNAL* 4 per year. Available to non members at £1.00 per copy. *Research Enquiries:* Free to members. £1.00 to non members. *Membership:* £6.00 single; £7.00 family membership. Secretary: Mr Michael Davis.

- **FOLKESTONE & DISTRICT FAMILY HISTORY SOCIETY** *
  69 Cudworth Road, ASHFORD, Kent, TN24 0BE, England.
  Library: Ted Friend. *Journal: FOLKESTONE & DISTRICT F.H.S. JOURNAL* 4 per year. Available to non members on request. *Membership:* £7.00 a year single, £8.50 joint membership. Overseas extra according to postal rates. *Chairperson:* Mrs Maureen Criddle. *Secretary:* Anita P. Gavin. *Other Particulars:* One-day Conference held usually every 18 months.

- **NORTH WEST KENT FAMILY HISTORY SOCIETY**
  190 Beckenham Rd., BECKENHAM, Kent, BR3 4RJ, England.
  Journal: NORTHWEST KENT FAMILY HISTORY 4 per year. Available to non members at £1.30. *Research Enquiries:* donation appreciated. *Membership:* £5.50 single, £7.50 family. *President:* Mr. C.L. Bourton, C.B. *Chairperson:* Mrs Jean Stirk. *Secretary:* Mrs. H.F. Norris.

- **WOOLWICH & DISTRICT FAMILY HISTORY SOCIETY**
  C/o 4 Church Road, BEXLEYHEATH, Kent, England.
  Journal: WOOLWICH & DISTRICT F.H.S. JOURNAL 3-4 per year. Previous years available to non members at 50p plus post. *Membership:* £5.00. (pensioner UK £2.50), overseas £6.00. *Chairperson:* Fred Reynolds. *Secretary:* Sue Highley.

LANCASHIRE (LAN) (see also LIVERPOOL)

- **LANCASHIRE FAMILY HISTORY AND HERALDRY SOCIETY**
  183 Bolton St., Ramsbottom, Lancs. BL0 9JD, England.
  Journal: LANCASHIRE 4 per year. Photocopies of articles in back numbers available. Facility for copying frames from microfiche at a reasonable charge. *Research Enquiries:* Members only. No charge. *Membership:* £6.00; £8.00 overseas/airmail. *Secretary:* Mrs Dorothy Frankcom.

- **MANCHESTER & LANCASHIRE FAMILY HISTORY SOCIETY**
  Clayton House, 59 Piccadilly, MANCHESTER M1 2AQ, England.
  Tel.: 061 236 9750. *Library:* As above. *Hours:* 9.30am-noon weekdays (exc. Wed.) *Journal: MANCHESTER GENEALOGIST* 4 per year. *Research Enquiries:* No research is undertaken for non members. *Membership:* £7.00 & £10.00 family in the UK. £10.00 overseas. *Meetings:* 2nd Thurs. monthly. Manchester Town Hall. *Groups:* Bolton & District – Friends Meeting House, Silverwell St., Bolton. Anglo/Scottish section – 3rd Sun. at Clayton House. *Secretary:* Mrs. E. Smith.

LEICESTERSHIRE (LEI)

- **LEICESTERSHIRE FAMILY HISTORY SOCIETY**
  25 Home Croft Drive, Packington, ASHBY DE LA ZOUCH, Leics. LE6 5WG, England.
  Newsletter: 4 per year. Available to non members at £1.00 each. *Research Enquiries:* 10p per word. *Membership:* £6.00 UK. £7.00 overseas surface, £8.00 airmail. *Chairman:* Mick Billings. *Secretary:* Sue Brown.

LINCOLNSHIRE (LIN)

- ## LINCOLNSHIRE FAMILY HISTORY SOCIETY
  Secretary, 135 Balderton Gate, NEWARK, Notts, NG24 1RY, England.
  Newsletter: 4 per year. *Membership:* £7.00; £8.00 family membership; £10.00 overseas. *Chairman:* Mrs A. Cole *Secretary:* Mrs. E.B. Robson.

- ## BOSTON FAMILY HISTORY GROUP
  C/o Mrs K. Hancock, Members Interests, 4 Almond Close, BOSTON, Lincolnshire, PE21 8HL, England.
  This group is a branch of the Lincolnshire Family History Society. *Meetings:* 1st Friday each month at 7.30pm at the Mormon Church, Woodthorpe Avenue, Boston. All are welcome. *Chairperson:* Mrs C. Harley, 129 Spilsby Rd, Boston.

- ## ISLE OF AXHOLME F.H.S. *
  Secretary: Mrs A. Turner, 294 Melton Rd, Sprotborough, Doncaster, DN5 7NX, England.

LIVERPOOL

- ## LIVERPOOL & SW LANCASHIRE FAMILY HISTORY SOCIETY
  'Ashlea', Station Rd., LYDIATE, Mersyside L31 4EY, England.
  Library: Liverpool Record Office. *Hours:* Mon.-Sat. 9am-9pm. *Journal: LIVERPOOL FAMILY HISTORIAN* 4 per year. Available to non members at £1.00. *Research Enquiries:* This service available by arrangement. *Membership:* £6.00 UK. *President:* Janet Smith, B.A., D.A.A. *Secretary:* Mrs Sheila Powell.

LONDON (LND) & MIDDLESEX (MDX)

- ## EAST OF LONDON FAMILY HISTORY SOCIETY
  C/o 50 Grange Park Rd., LONDON, E10 5ES, England.
  Journal: COCKNEY ANCESTOR 4 per year. Back issues available to non members. Prices on application. *Research Enquiries:* None. *Membership:* £4.00 individual. *Other Particulars:* Meetings once a month from Sept. to June, inclusive. Barking & Dagenham Branch have regular meetings, Havering Branch have regular meetings. *Chairman:* Mr David Webb, Bishopsgate Institute. *General Secretary:* Mrs J. Vagg. *President:* Mr Frederick Filby F.S.G.

- ## CENTRAL MIDDLESEX FAMILY HISTORY SOCIETY *
  155 Harrow View, Harrow, MDX HA1 4SX England.
  Journal: GREENTREES 4 per year. Available to non members at 75p each. *Research Enquiries:* Free to members. Non-members 5 lines = 50p. *Membership:* £4.00 individual; £6.00 overseas. *Secretary:* Mr Michael Fountain. *Other Particulars:* Meetings held at Friends Meeting House, 456 Rayners Lane, Pinner, Middlesex, at 8pm on second Friday each month except August.

- ## NORTH MIDDLESEX FAMILY HISTORY SOCIETY *
  6 Milton Court, 83 Hoe Street, WALTHAMSTOW, London, E17 4SA, England.
  Journal: THE NORTH MIDDLESEX 4 per year. Available to members at 75p. *Research Enquiries:* Free to members. 50p per 5 lines or £1.00 for quarter page. *Membership:* £3.00 Journal only; £4.00 individual; £5.00 family. *Chairman:* Mr. Michael Gandy. *Secretary:* Miss Janet Lewis.

- ## WEST MIDDLESEX FAMILY HISTORY SOCIETY
  53 Osterley Rd., ISLEWORTH, MDX, TW7 4PN, England.
  Journal: WEST MIDDLESEX F.H.S. JOURNAL 4 per year. Available to non members at £1.40 incl p.p. *Research Enquiries:* cost of entries £2.00. *Membership:* Individual £6.00, overseas £7.00, family £8.50. *Meetings:* Every 2nd Fri. each month, Montague Hall, Hounslow. *Members Scretary:* Mrs D. Bradley.

- **HILLINGDON F.H.S. ***
  Secretary: Ms Jane Pain, 8 Hillside Road, Northwood, Middlesex, HA6 1QA, England.

MANCHESTER See LANCASHIRE.

MIDDLESEX (MDX) See LONDON.

NORFOLK (NFK)

- **NORFOLK & NORWICH GENEALOGICAL SOCIETY**
  Kirby House, 38 St. Giles St., NORWICH, NR2 1LL, England.
  Library: Kirby House, 38 St Giles St., Norwich. For members only, Wed. 10am-1pm, 2.30-5.30pm and 7-9pm, last Sat. in each month 9am-noon. *Journal: NORFOLK ANCESTOR* 4 per year. Available to non members at 50p. *Membership:* £8.00. (£10.00 overseas). *Other particulars: Horfolk Genealogy* an annual hardback vol. is supplied free to members. *Branches:* West Norfolk & London. *President:* Sir Charles Mott-Radclyff. *Chairman:* Mr P.M. Green. *Librarian:* Miss C. Hood, B.A.

NORTHAMPTONSHIRE (NTH)

- **NORTHAMPTONSHIRE FAMILY HISTORY SOCIETY**
  19 Ridgway Rd., Kettering, NORTHAMPTON NN15 5AQ, England.
  Journal: FOOTPRINTS 4 per year. *Membership:* £6.00 individual; £7.00 family; £8.00 (Sterling only) overseas. *Chairperson:* Mrs J. Meads. *Secretary:* Mrs. A. Pegg.

NORTHUMBERLAND (NBL)

- **NORTHUMBERLAND & DURHAM FAMILY HISTORY SOCIETY**
  10 Melrose Grove, Jarrow, TYNE & WEAR, NE32 4HP, England.
  Journal: Quarterly Journal available to non members £1.50. *Membership:* £6.00 UK plus £3 joining fee, £10.00 plus £5.00 joining fee, overseas. *Secretary:* John Ashburner. *Chairman:* Mr G. Nicholson.

NOTTINGHAMSHIRE (NTT)

- **NOTTINGHAMSHIRE FAMILY HISTORY SOCIETY**
  C/o 10 Lyme Park, WEST BRIDGFORD, Nottingham, NG2 7TR, England.
  Journal: NOTTINGHAMSHIRE FAMILY HISTORY SOCIETY JOURNAL 4 per year. *Research Enquiries:* Research scheme for members only. *Membership:* £6.00; £9.00 overseas members. *Publications:* Record series, indexes to sources for Notts. details from Miss E. deVille, 275 Dysart Rd., Grantham, Links, NG31 7LP. *Secretary:* Miss S.M. Leeds.

- **MANSFIELD AND DISTRICT FAMILY HISTORY SOCIETY ***
  2 Millersdale Ave., MANSFIELD, Nottinghamshire, NG18 5HS, England.
  Journal: ROOTS 4 per year. Available to non members at 30p. *Research Enquiries:* Free to members, non members: first two hours free, then £2.00 per hour. *Membership:* Individual members, £4.00 plus £1.00 enrolment fee, family membership, £6.00 plus £1.00 enrolment fee. *Library:* Local Studies Section, Central Library, West Gate, Mansfield, Notts, NG18 1NH. *Hours:* Mon., Tue., Thurs., Fri.: 9am-7pm; Wed.: 9am-5pm; Sat.: 9am-1pm. *Chairman:* Dennis Hill. *Secretary:* Hazel Hargate.

OXFORDSHIRE (OXF)

- **THE OXFORDSHIRE FAMILY HISTORY SOCIETY**
  C/o 10 Bellamy Close, Southmoor, ABINGDON, Oxon, OX13 5AB, England.
  Journal: THE OXFORDSHIRE FAMILY HISTORIAN 3 per year plus (free booklet in lieu of 4th Journal). Available to non members at £1.25 + 70p. postand + £1.75 (overseas airmail). *Membership:* £6.00 UK individual; £8.00 UK family; £8.00 Institutional; £10.00 overseas airmail, sterling cheques only please. *Other particulars:* A

number of publications and research services are available, write for particulars. *President:* Mr. Peter Lawrence, M.A. *Chairman:* Mrs Joan Howard-Drake. *Secretary:* Mrs Jill Muir.

SHROPSHIRE (SAL)

● **SHROPSHIRE FAMILY HISTORY SOCIETY**
8 Sefron Dr., Bomere Heath,Shrewsbury, Shrop, SY4 3NL, England.
Journal: SHROPSHIRE F.H.S. JOURNAL 4 per year. Available to non members at £1.20. *Research Enquiries:* Cost of entries on request. *Membership:* £6.00. *President:* Mr. John Dugdale, H.M.'s Lord Lieutenant for Shropshire. *Secretary:* Mr S.C Clifford.

SOMERSETSHIRE (SOM)

● **SOMERSET & DORSET FAMILY HISTORY SOCIETY ***
P.O. Box 170, TAUNTON, Somerset, TA1 1HF, England.
Journal: THE GREENWOOD TREE published quarterly. *Local Group Meetings:* Held regularly throughout the two counties.

STAFFORDSHIRE (STS) See BIRMINGHAM & MIDLAND.

SUFFOLK (SFK)

● **SUFFOLK FAMILY HISTORY SOCIETY**
30 Gowers End, Glemsford, SUFFOLK C010 7UF, England.
Journal: SUFFOLK ROOTS 4 per year. *Membership:* Full membership £6.00; family membership £8.00; OAP & under 16 £4.50. Overseas: £8.00 *Chairman:* Mr D. Palgrave. *Secretary:* Dr. Monica Barnett. Groups meet at Bury St. Edmunds, Haverhill, Ipswich & Lowestoft.

● **FELIXSTOWE FAMILY HISTORY SOCIETY**
C/o Mrs M. Lake, Orwell High School, Maidstone Rd., FELIXSTOWE, Suffolk, England.
Journal: ROOTS & BRANCHES 4 per year. Price available on request. Issued to all members. *Membership:* £6.00, family £9.00, overseas £9.00. *President:* Rev. K. Francis. *Chairman:* M.T.H. Durrant Esq. *Secretary:* Mrs M. Lake. *Meetings:* Held monthly at the Central Library, Crescent Rd., Felixstowe. Reading. *Research Room:* Orwell School as above.

SURREY (SRY)

● **EAST SURREY FAMILY HISTORY SOCIETY**
C/o Mrs J. Sinclair, 15 Apeldoorn Drive, WALLINGTON, Surrey, SM6 9LF, England.
Journal: EAST SURREY FAMILY HISTORY SOCIETY JOURNAL 4 per year. Available to non members on request. *Research Enquiries:* Members only. *Membership:* £5.00 single; £6.00 family. *Other Particulars:* Meetings held 3rd Monday each month at Civic Offices, St. Nicholas Way, Sutton, Surrey. Meetings held every other month at St. Marys Church Hall, Caterham on the Hill and United Reformed Church Hall, Addiscombe Grove, Croydon. Also at Balham and Southwark. *Chairman:* Mrs S. Gallagher. *Secretary:* Mrs. J. Sinclair.

● **WEST SURREY FAMILY HISTORY SOCIETY**
Bradstone Garden Cottage, Christmas Hill, Shalford, GUILDFORD, Surrey GU4 8HR, England.
Library: Open during meetings or by post. *Journal: ROOT AND BRANCH* 4 per year. Available to non members at 80p plus postage. *Research Enquiries:* Members free. £1.00 to non members. *Membership:* £6.00; £9.00 family; £5.00 s.c., £7.00 o.s. *Other Particulars:* Meetings monthly at Camberley, Dorking, Farnham, Guildford, Walton-on-Thames & Woking. *Publications for Surrey:* More than 60 available. For

free descriptive leaflet, send SAE (or 37p british stamps) to Mrs R. Cleaver, 17 Lan End Dr., Knaphill, Surrey, GU21 2QQ, UK. *Indexes:* All Surrey Records inc. Surrey Marriage Index — specific searches free to members. *President:* Mr R. Anstis. *Secretary:* Mrs J.E.Downham.

SUSSEX (SSX)

- **SUSSEX FAMILY HISTORY GROUP**
  45 Park Terrace East, HORSHAM, W. SSX, RH13 5DJ, England.
  Journal: SUSSEX FAMILY HISTORIAN 4 per year. *Membership:* £7.00 single; £8.50 joint. *Other Particulars:* Meetings second Wednesday of every month at Ventnor Hall, Ventnor Villas, Hove, at 7.30pm. Conference & AGM in March. *President:* Rt. Hon. Lord Teviot, F.S.G. *Secretary:* Brian Tayler.

- **FAMILY ROOTS FAMILY HISTORY SOCIETY (EASTBOURNE & DISTRICT)**
  22 Abbey Rd., EASTBOURNE, Sussex. BN20 8TE.
  Journal: FAMILY ROOTS 4 per year. Free to members - available to non-members £1.00 including postage UK. *Research Enquiries:* £1.00 for non-members. *Membership:* £6.00, joint (husband/wife) £8.00, overseas £7.00 includes 4 journals airmail. *Meetings:* 2nd Thurs. of each month at 7.30pm. *Chairman:* Mr Ken Alderton. *Secretary:* Mrs Phyl Webb.

- **HASTINGS AND ROTHER FAMILY HISTORY SOCIETY**
  C/o 30A Church Rd., ST. LEONARDS, E. SSX, TN37 6HA, Eng.
  Library: Available at monthly meetings. *Journal:* 4 per year. *Meetings:* 2nd Wed. each month at 7.30pm. *Subscription:* £5.00, £7.50 family, £10.00 overseas. *Chairperson:* Mr Don Beney. *Secretary:* Mrs Sonia Hillier.

WARWICKSHIRE (WAR) See BIRMINGHAM & MIDLANDS.

WEST MIDLANDS See BIRMINGHAM.

WILTSHIRE (WIL)

- **WILTSHIRE FAMILY HISTORY SOCIETY ***
  C/o 65 New Park St., DEVIZES, Wiltshire, SN10 1DR, England.
  Journal: WILTSHIRE FAMILY HISTORY SOCIETY 4 per year. Available to non members at £1.00 plus p.p. *Research Enquiries:* Leaflet available. *Membership:* £5.00 UK; £6.00 family; £7.00 overseas. *Other Particulars:* Meetings at six branches: request leaflet. *Chairman:* Richard Moore. *General Secretary:* Mrs Barbara Fuller.

WORCESTERSHIRE (WOR), SEE BIRMINGHAM & MIDLAND

YORKSHIRE (YKS)

- **BRADFORD FAMILY HISTORY SOCIETY ***
  C/o 8 Coates Terrace, West Bowling, BRADFORD, BD5 7AB, England.
  Journal: THE BODKIN 4 per year. *Membership:* £5.00 individual, £7.00 family. *Chairperson:* K. Kenzie. *Secretary:* Mrs Josie Walsh.

- **CALDERDALE FAMILY HISTORY SOCIETY**
  Secretary: Mrs I.M. Walker, 61 Gleanings Ave., Norton Tower, Halifax, W Yorks, HX2 0NU, England.

- **DONCASTER SOCIETY FOR FAMILY HISTORY**
  5 The Brow, Brecks, ROTHERHAM, S65 3HP, England.
  Library: Available at all meetings. *Journal: THE DONCASTER ANCESTOR* 2 per year. Available to non members at 50p each plus 25p p+p. *Membership:* £6.00. *Other Particulars:* Meetings eleven times a year on the third Thursday of each month, excluding Aug. *President:* Mr. D.A. Palgrave. *Secretary:* Mrs J.E. Grundy. *Chairman:* Mrs G.M. Briscoe.

- **EAST YORKSHIRE FAMILY HISTORY SOCIETY ***
  C/o 367 Main Road, BILTON, Hull, HU11 4DS, England.
  Library: C/o Mrs E. Tarlton, above address. *Journal: THE BANYAN TREE* 4 per year. Available to non members at 75p. *Membership:* £4.00 single; £5.50 family. *Meetings:* 1st Tues. each month, Montgomery centre, Museum of Army Transport, Flemingate, Beverley & last Tues. at friends meeting house, York Place, Scarborough — 7.30pm. *Chairman:* Mr P. Butler. *Membership Secretary:* Mrs L. Scaife.

- **HUDDERSFIELD & DISTRICT FAMILY HISTORY SOCIETY**
  Secretary: Mrs M. Bowers, 31 Kingshead Road, Mirfield, W. Yorkshire, WF14 9SJ, England.

- **RIPON & DISTRICT FAMILY HISTORY GROUP**
  Secretary: Mrs P. Litton, The White Cottage, 2 Florence Road, Harrogate, N Yorks, HG2 0LD, England.

- **SHEFFIELD AND DISTRICT FAMILY HISTORY SOCIETY ***
  359 Baslow Road, SHEFFIELD, S17 3BH, England.
  Journal: THE FLOWING STREAM 4 per year. Available to non members at 75p plus postage. *Research Enquiries:* Open to members only. *Membership:* £6.00, £8.00 overseas.

- **CITY OF YORK AND DISTRICT FAMILY HISTORY SOCIETY**
  C/o Mrs M. Varley, Ascot House, Cherry Tree Ave., Newton on Ouse, YORK, Y06 3EN, England.
  Newsletter: 3 per year. *Research Enquiries:* (in newsletter): Free to members. £2.00 to non members. *Membership:* £4.00. *Chairperson:* Mrs I. Slater. *Editor:* Mrs J. Simpson.

- **YORKSHIRE ARCHAEOLOGICAL SOC., THE FAMILY HISTORY SECTION**
  Claremont, 23 Clarendon Road, LEEDS, LS2 9NZ, England.
  Library: As above. *Hours:* Tues. & Wed. 2pm-8.30pm. Thus.-Sat. 9.30am-5pm. Open to non members. *Newsletter: THE YORKSHIRE FAMILY HISTORIAN* 6 per year. Available to non members on request. *Research Enquiries:* Members only. *Membership:* Various. Available on request. *Chairman:* Mrs M. Morton. *Secretary:* Mrs S. Skelton, Meadowbrow, Harewood Rd., Collingham.

ESPAGNE (see SPAIN)

FINLAND

- **GENEALOGISKA SAMFUNDET i FINLAND**
  Snellmansgatan 9-11, HELSINKI, Finland.

- **HELSINGFORS SLAKTFORSKARE R.F.**
  C/o N. Nock, Kentelevagen 42, SF-00320 HELSINGFORS, Finland.
  Library: Elisabetsgatan 27. *Hours:* 18-20 Every 1st & 3rd Thurs. in month. *Newsletter:* Info. letter to members only. *Research Enquiries:* Included in the publication series *Uppsatser.* One published almost every year. *President:* Nils Nock. *Secretary:* G. Busck-Nielsen.

FRANCE

FEDERATION

- **FEDERATION DES SOCIETES FRANCAISES DE GENEALOGIE.
  D'HERALDIQUE ET DE SIGILLOGRAPHIE**
  B.P. 63, F-75261 PARIS CEDEX 06, France.

NATIONAL

● CENTRE D'ENTRAIDE GENEALOGIQUE DE FRANCE

B.P. 101, 75862 PARIS, Cedex 18, France.

Bibliothèque: adresse ci-dessus, membres seulement, les 1er, 3ème et, éventuellement, 5ème samedi du mois, 14-17 h. *Bulletin: LA FRANCE GENEALOGIQUE* trimestriel, abmt 95 F. + frais de poste. *Demandes Recherches:* membres seulement. *Cotisation:* droit d'entreée 10 F. + 35 F par an. *Autres Renseignements:* bourse d'echange de recherches généalogiques et fichiers divers à la disposition des membres, conditions dans le Bulletin. *Président:* M. Rene Allard. *Secrétaire:* M. Jacques Bergounhoux. *Library:* address as above, members only, the 1st, 3rd and, if required, 5th Saturday of the month, 14-17h. *Journal:* as above, 4 per year, *Subs.:* 95 F. + postage. *Research Enquiries:* members only. *Membership:* entry fee 10 F. + 35 F. annually. *Other Particulars:* genealogical research exchange service and various indexes available to members on the terms given in the journal.

● CERCLE DE GENEALOGIE JUIVE (FRANCE)

15 ave du 8 Mai 1945, F-95200 SARCELLES, France.

Bibliothèque: adresse ci-dessus, membres seulement, lundi à jeudi 14-19 h. *Bulletin: CERCLE DE GENEALOGIE JUIVE* trimestriel, abmt 200 F. *Demandes Recherches:* questions et réponses – membres seulement. *Cotisation:* 200 F. France. *Autres Renseignements:* réunions 1er lundi du mois 18 h.30. Tout courrier à l'adresse audessus. *Président:* M. Michel Mayer-Cremieux. *Secrétaire:* Mme. Madeleine King.

    Library: address as above, members only, Monday to Thursday 14-19 h. *Journal:* as above, 4 per year. *Subs.:* 200 F. *Research Enquiries:* questions and replies – members only. *Membership:* 200 F. France. *Other Particulars:* meetings 1st Monday of month 18.30 h. All mail to: 38 rue du Père-Corentin, 75014 PARIS.

● CERCLE D'ETUDES DES DYNASTIES ROYALES EUROPEENNES (C.E.D.R.E.)

3 rue des Ternes, F-75017 PARIS, France.

Bulletin: BULLETIN DU C.E.D.R.E. trimestiel, abmt 130 F, vente aux non membres. *Demandes Recherches:* ouvertes à tous, gratuites. *Cotisation:* 130 F. *Autres Renseignements:* association crèèe en 1980 dont 50% des membres sont français et les autres repartis à L'étranger. *Président:* M. Jean-Fréd Tourtchine. *Secrétaire:* Mme. Florence Lefebvre.

    Journal: as above, 4 per year. *Subs.:* 130 F. sale to non members same price. *Research Enquiries:* open to all, free. *Membership:* 130 F. *Other Particulars:* association created in 1980, membership 50% France, 50% abroad.

● CERCLE GENEALOGIQUE ET HERALDIQUE DE L'EDUCATION NATIONALE

37, rue Jacob, F-75006, PARIS, France.

Cotisation: 160F. *Bulletin: DU PASSE AU PRESENT* 4 par an. *Président:* M. Jacques Dupaquier. *Secrétaire:* Mme M.M. Hyppolite.

● CERCLE GENEALOGIQUE DES P.T.T.

B.P. 33, F-75721 PARIS Cedex 15, FRANCE.

Bibliothèque: membres seulement, au cours des réunions. *Bulletin: BULLETIN du CERCLE GENEALOGIQUE DES PTT* trimestriel. *Demandes Recherches:* ouvertes a³ tous. *Cotisation:* 65 F. *Autres Renseignements:* réunions à Paris, Bordeaux, Châteauroux, Clermont-Ferrand, Lyon, Montpellier, Nancy, Narbonne, Nimes, Orléans, Rennes, St. Lô, Strasbourg et Toulouse – pour plus de précisions consulter le Bulletin. *Président:* M. Gaston Sagot. *Secrétaire:* Jean-Claude Pericard.

    Library: members only, during meetings. *Journal:* as above, 4 per year. *Research Enquiries:* open to all. *Membership:* 65 F. including journal. *Other Particulars:* meetings in Paris, Bordeaux, Châteauroux, Clermont-Ferrand, Lyon, Montpellier, Nancy, Narbonne, Nimes, Orléans, Rennes, St. Lô, Strasbourg and Toulouse – for more details refer to the Journal.

- **ASSOCIATION GENEALOGIQUE D'ECHANGE**
  38 allée des Hirondelles, F-77380 COMBS LA VILLE, France.
  Bibliothèque: municipale tous les jours sauf dimanche 14-19 h. Ouverte à tous. *Bulletin: NOUVELLES RACINES* trimestriel, abmt 30 F, vente aux non membres 10 F le numéro. *Demandes Recherches:* pour tous conte rmbt frais. *Cotisation:* 50 F. *Autres Renseignements:* réunions le 2è mardi du mois au centre social rue Pablo Picasso à partir de 20 h.30. *Président:* M. Marc Hairabedian. *Secrétaire:* Mme. Marie Cecile Formaux.
  Library: open to all, municipal library every day but Sunday 14-19 h. *Journal:* as above, 4 per year. *Subs.:* 10 F, sale to non members 10 F. each. *Research Enquiries:* open to all on payment of expenses. *Membership:* 50 F. *Other Particulars:* meetings 2nd Tuesday of the month at the social centre, rue Pablo Picasso starting 20.30 h.

- **SOCIETE D'EMULATION GENEALOGIQUE**
  abs. Pascal CEDAN, 8 rue Volta, F-75003 PARIS, France.
  Bibliothèque: sur rendez-vous, ouverte à tous, gratuite. *Cotisation:* 0. *Autres Renseignements:* Réunions sur rendez-vous. *Président:* Francois Barbier. *Secrétaire:* M. Pascal Cedan.
  Library: by appointment, open to all free. *Journal:* as above, 4 per year. *Subs.:* 100 F. sale to non members 25 or 50 F. *Membership:* 100 F. *Other Particulars:* meetings by appointment.

- **SOCIETE FRANCAISE D'ONOMASTIQUE**
  60 rue des Francs-Bourgeois, F-75003 PARIS, France.
  Bibliothèque: ouverte à tous, lundi à samedi 10-17 h. *Bulletin: NOUVELLE REVUE D'ONOMASTIQUE* annuel, en dècembre, abmt 240 F, vente aux non membres 200 F. *Cotisation:* comprise dans l'abonnement. *Autres Renseignements:* réunions tous les 2 mois, le 3ème jeudi à 17 h. *Président:* M. Jacques Chaurand. *Secrétaire:* M. Pierre-Henri Billy.
  Library: open to all, Monday to Saturday 10-17 h. *Journal:* as above, annual, in December. *Subs.:* 240 F, sale to non members 200 F. *Membership:* included in the subscription. *Other Particulars:* meetings every other month, the 3rd Thursday at 17 h.

- **SOCIETE HISTOIRE DU PROTESTANTISME FRANCAIS**
  54 rue des Saints-Pères, F-75007 PARIS, France.
  Bibliothèque: adresse ci-dessus, ouverte à tous, mardi à samedi inclus 14-18 h. *Bulletin: CAHIERS du CENTRE DE GENEALOGIE PROTESTANTE* trimestriel, 170 F. vente aux non membres 40 F. le numéro. *Demandes Recherches:* membres seulement. *Cotisation:* 60 F. *Autres Renseignements:* réunions (voir Bulletin ou affiches sur place). *Président:* M. Jacques Evesque. *Secrétaire:* Mme. Elisabeth Escalle.
  Library: address as above, open to all, Tuesday-Saturday 14-18 h. *Journal:* as above, 4 per year. 170 F, sale to non members 40 F each. *Research Enquiries:* members only. *Membership:* 60 F. *Other Particulars:* meetings (see Journal or notice board).

- **UNION SPORTIVE ET CULTURELLE PEUGEOT, Section généalogique.**
  75 avenue de la Grande Armée, F-75116 PARIS, France.
  Bibliothèque: adresse ci-dessus, membres seulement lundi 12-13 h.30. *Cotisation:* 70 F. *Autres Renseignements:* réunions une fois par semaine. *Demandes Recherches:* ouvertes à tous. *Président:* M. Ruddy Broussard. *Secrétaire:* M. Thierry Lemaitre.
  Library: address as above, members only, Monday 12-13.30 h. *Research Enquiries:* open to all. *Membership:* 70 F. *Other Particulars:* meetings once each week.

REGIONAL

ALSACE (Bas-Rhin, Haut-Rhin)

- **BERGHA**
  B.P. 18, 68790 MORSCHWILLER LE BAS, France.
  Bulletin: BERGHA, coût de l'abonnement 100F. *Président:* André Ganter. Mise à disposition des abonnés de renseignements généalogiques inédits concernant la Haute-Alsace, rubrique de paléographie allemande et francaise.

- **INSTITUT DE RECHERCHE SUR L'HISTOIRE DES FAMILLES EN HAUT ALSACE (IRHFA)**
  B.P. 18, 68790 MORSCHWILLER LE BAS, France.
  Demandes de recherches: ouvertes à tous, tarif sur demande (Research requests open to all, rates on request). *Président:* Gérard Flesch & André Ganter.

- **CERCLE GENEALOGIQUE D'ALSACE**
  Archives du Bas-Rhin, 5 rue Fischart, F-67000 STRASBOURG, France.
  Président: M. André Ganter.

AQUITAINE (Dordogne, Gironde, Landes, Lot-et-Garonne, Pyrénées-Atlantiques)

- **CERCLE GENEALOGIQUE DU PAYS BASQUE ET BAS ADOUR**
  9, rue Louise Darracq, F-64100 BAYONNE, France.
  Cotisation: 110 F. *Réunions:* 1st Sat. of each month 15-19h. Château de Sainsontan, Bayonne. *Bulletin: DE LIAISON DU C.G. DU PAYS BASQUE ET BAS ADOUR* 1 par an. Sale to non members 40 francs plus postage. *Research Enquiries:* Open to all, cost variable. *Other Particulars:* Covers the Basque provinces of Labourd, Soule, Basse Navarre and the Gascon speaking areas of Orx and Orthe on the right bank of the Adour. *Président:* Marcel Douyrou. *Secrétaire:* Mme F. Cervera Marzal.

- **AMITIES GENEALOGIQUES BORDELAISES**
  2 rue Paul Bert, F-33000 BORDEAUX, France.
  Cotisation: 130F. *Bulletin: INFORMATIONS* A.G.B. bimestriel. *Président:* M. Pierre Dupouy. *Secrétaire:* Andree Charrier. *Travaux en cours:* Relevé systématique des actes d'Etat-civil antérieurs à la Révolution en Gironde, relevé des embarquements (1714-1787), relevé des actes notariés (mariages, testaments, partages, inventaires, donations) antérieurs à 1700.

- **CERCLE HERALDIQUE, GENEALOGIQUE ET HISTORIQUE DE LOT ET GARONNE**
  Chez M. Ehasseriaud, Lionel "Mirepoix" Bias, 47300 VILLENEUVE SUR LOT, France.
  Cotisation annuelle: 120F, comprenant le bulletin (bulletin included). *Bibliothèque:* Bibliothè municipale, horaires voir Centre culturel de Villeneuve sur Lot. *Réunions:* 2 & 4 samedi de chaque mois sauf août, Centre culturel de Villeneuve sur Lot de 16 à 18h. *Bulletin:* Bulletin du C.H.G.H.47, trimestriel ou semestriel, mais toujours quatre n annuel (quarterly or twice a year, but always four issues per year). Vente aux non-membres: 40F. *Demandes de recherches:* ouvertes à tous, coût 300F. *Président:* Jean Delaneuville. *Secrétaire:* Lionel Echasseriaud.

- **CENTRE GENEALOGIQUE DU SUD-OUEST**
  1 place Bardineau, F-33000 BORDEAUX, France.
  Cotisation annuelle: 150F. *Bulletin: GENEALOGIES DU SUD-OUEST* semestriel, 50F non membres. *Président:* Professeur Claude Masse. *Secrétaire:* Mme. Marie-Thérèse Couffin.

- **CERCLE D'HISTOIRE DES FAMILLES PERIGOURDINES**
  St. Sernin de Beaupouyet, F-24400 MUSSIDAN, France.
  Président: M. Xaxier Pazat. *Secrétaire:* M. Michel Rateau.

- **CERCLE DE GENEALOGIE DU PERIGORD**
  Pavillon 25, La Barriere Mauzac 24150 LALINDE, France.
  Cotisation: 130 F. Student 60 F. Benefactor 150 F. *Meetings:* Variable. *Bulletin: GENEALOGIES PERIGOURDINES* 4 par an. Sale to non members de 40F du 60F. *Research Enquiries:* Members, and non members belonging to societies with which reciprocity agreements exist. The society publishes other documents besides the journal. In the journal, absolute priority is given to the question & answer column. *Président:* Michel Rateau. *Secrétaire:* Eiko Rateau.

- **CERCLE D'HISTOIRE ET DE GENEALOGIE DES HUGUENOTS D'AFRIQUE AUSTRALE**
  Pavillon 25, la Barrière, Mauzac, 24150 LALINDE, France.
  Droit d'entrée: 10F. *Cotisation annuelle:* 130F. *Bibliothèque:* ouverte à tous, à la demande. *Bulletin:* prochainement, probablement trimestriel, en 1989 *GENEALOGIES HUGUENOTES. Abonnement:* 40F prix de vente aux non-membres: 40F. (Bulletin: to appear in 1989, probably quarterly) *Président:* Michel Rateu. *Secrétaire:* Eiko Rateau. *Other Particulars:* Nous parlons huit langues, dont le Français, l'Anglais, l'Afrikaans, et l'Allemand. Nous pratiquons des réunions et e⁵changes d'études. L'association est au stade de la création. (We speak eight languages, including French, English, Afrikaans, and German. We have meetings and exchanges of studies. The association is in the formation stage).

- **REVUE D'ETUDES BASQUES EKAINA**
  Route d'Arbonne, 64210 BIDART, France.
  Bulletin: Revue *EKAINA*, trimestrielle (quarterly). *Abonnement:* 120F, prix de vente aux non-menbres 30F le n. Demandes de recherches ouvertes à tous, gratuites. *Président:* H. Lamant-Duhart. *Secrétaire:* Marianne Joly.

AUVERGNE (Allier, Cantal, Haute-Loire, Puy-de-Dôme)

- **CERCLE GENEALOGIQUE ET HERALDIQUE DU BOURBONNAIS**
  93 rue de Paris 03000 MOULINS, France.
  Président: M. Pierre Durye. *Secrétaire:* Mme. Delode.

- **ASSOCIATION DE RECHERCHES GENEALOGIQUES ET HISTORIQUES D'AUVERGNE**
  Maison des Consuls, Place Poly, F-63100 CLERMONT-FERRAND, France.
  Cotisation: 30F. *Bulletin: LE GONFANON* trimestriel. *Cout de l'abonnement:* 160F. *Président:* Mme. Marie Sauvadet. *Secrétaire:* M. Raymond Bogros.

- **CERCLE GENEALOGIQUE ET HERALDIQUE DE L'AUVERGNE ET DU VELAY (C.G.H.A.V.)**
  45 Quai Carnot, F-92210 SAINT-CLOUD, France.
  Président: M. Michel Teillard d'Eyry. *Secrétaire:* Mme. Brigitte Alizard.

- **CENTRE GENEALOGIQUE DE TOURAINE**
  43 Boulevard Beranger, F-37000 TOURS, France.
  Bibliothèque: 11 rue des Tanneurs, TOURS, the 1st & 3rd Mon., 2nd, 3rd & 4th Sat. of each month, 14-17h & 3 lectures per year (Mar., June, Oct.). *Bulletin: INFORMATIONS GENEALOGIQUES* 4 per year, sale to non members 35 F. *Research Enquiries:* Members only, free. *Cotisation:* 150 F. including journal. *Other Particulars:* All genealogical contacts to M. Pierre Robert, Vice-President, 7 rue James-Pradier, 37300 Joue-Les-Tours, France. *Président:* M. Raymond Renault. *Secrétaire:* M. Jean Simon.

- **SALON GENEALOGIQUE DE VICHY ET DU CENTRE**
  48 Boulevard de Sichon, 03200 VICHY, France.
  Cotisation: 145 F. *Library:* Members only, Mon., Wed. 15h-18h or by appointment. *Réunions:* 1 Mercredi du Mois a Vichy 17h30. Dernier Samedi du Mois A Gannat – 15h. *Bulletin: VICHY GENEALOGIE 03* 4 par an., price included in membership dues. *Research Enquiries:* 1,50 par Fiche & Timbres. *Président:* Raymond Boudry. *Secrétaire:* Jean Michel.

BRITANNY (Côtes-du-Nord, Finistère, Ille-et-Vilaine, Morbihan)

- **CENTRE GENEALOGIQUE DES COTES DU NORD**
  4, rue Saint Vincent de Paul 22000 SAINT BRIEUC, France.
  Cotisation: 100F. *Bibliothèque:* ouverte à tous les jours de réunions, de 14h15-17h00
  (Library open to all on meeting days, 2.15 to 5.00pm). *R*unions: premier samedi du
  mois sauf en juillet et août (Meetings first Saturday of each month except July and
  August). *Bulletin: GENEALOGIQUE 22* trimestriel. Prix de vente aux non-membres:
  20F. *Président:* Jean Bourel. *Secrétaire:* Marc Leleux. *Other Particulars:* Nous avons
  un service d'entraide qui effectue bénévolement des recherches aux A.D. des Côtes du
  Nord pour nos adhérents éloignés (We have an aid service which does research on a
  volunteer basis in the departmental archives of the Côtes du Nord for members at a
  distance).

- **CERCLE GENEALOGIQUE DU RENNAIS**
  6 rue Frédéric Mistral, F-35100 RENNES, France.
  Président: M. Celestin Denis. *Secrétaire:* Mme. Andrée Marquet.

BURGUNDY (Côte-d'Or, Nièvre, Saône-et-Loire, Yonne)

- **CRECLE GENEALOGIQUE DE SAONE ET LOIRE**
  115 rue des Cordiers, F-71000 MACON, France.
  Cotisation annuelle: 50F. *Bibliotheque:* Mercredi et 1er samedi dumois 14h-17h. *Re-unions:* 1er samedi du mois 14h-17h. *Bulletin: NOS ANCETRES ET NOUS* tri-mestriel. *Cout de l'abonnement:* 140F. *President:* Dr Notel.

- **RECHERCHES ET ETUDES GENEALOGIQUES DES PAYS DE L'AIN (REGAIN)**
  Maison des Sociétes, Boulevard Irène Joliot-Curie, F-01000 BOURG-EN-BRESSE,
  France.
  Cotisation annuelle: 180F. *Bulletin: NOS ANCETRES ET NOUS* trimestriel.
  Président: M. Pierre-Henri Chaix.

- **SOCIETE GENEALOGIQUE DE L'YONNE**
  Dixmont, 89500 VILLENEUVE SUR YONNE, France.
  Cotisation annuelle: 150F. *Bibliothèque:* chez le secrétaire Piane Bonicel, 60, quai
  Fosses Riviеères 89100 Sens (Library at the home of the secretary, Piane Bonicel, 60,
  quai Fosses Rivières, 89100 Sens). *Bulletin:* de liaison de la SGY, trimestriel. Ecrire
  pour l'état de publications pour les prix (Write for list of publications and their
  prices). *Demandes de recherches:* ouvertes à tous et gratuites. *Président:* Alain Noel.
  Secrétaire: Piane Bonicel.

CENTRE (Cher, Eure-et-Loir, Indre, Indre-et-Loire, Loir-et-Cher, Loiret)

- **ASSOCIATION GENEALOGIQUE DE LA LOIRE**
  Rue Barrouin, F-42000 SAINT-ETIENNE, France.
  Cotisation annuelle: 60F. *Bibliotheque:* 1 et 3 samedis de chaque mois 14h-17h. *Re-unions:* 1 et 3 samedis de chaque mois au Centre Coligny, 19 Rue Elisée Reclus,
  42000 SAINT-ETIENNE. *Bulletin: GENEALOGIE ET HISTOIRE* fin de trimestre.
  non-membres 100F. *President:* Henry Jean Paul. *Secretaire:* Pauze Anare.

- **CERCLE GENEALOGIQUE DU HAUT-BERRY**
  43 Boulevard Beranger, F-37000 TOURS, France.
  Président: M. Raymond Renault. *Secrétaire:* M. Jean Simon.

- **CERCLE GENEALOGIQUE DE LOIR-ET-CHER**
  45 quai du Foix, 41000 BLOIS, France.
  Cotisation annuelle: 40F. *Reunions:* Trimestriel. *Bulletin: INFORMATIONS
  GENEALOGIQUES* 4 par an. 35F le numero non-membres. *Président:* Michel de
  Sachy. *Secrétaire:* Mme. Rabier-Leroux.

- **LE LOIRET GENEALOGIQUE**
  B.P. 9, 45016, ORLEANS, Cedex, France.
  Président: M. Michel Riviere. *Secrétaire:* M. Jean Muzeau.

- **CENTRE GENEALOGIQUE DE L'OUEST**
  26 Rue Léon-Jamin, F-44000 NANTES, France.
  Cotisation Annuelle: 40F. *Bibliotheque:* Mon 14h45-16h30, Sat 10-12. The library is open to the public, but only members can borrow books. *Reunions:* 1st Wed of the month. *Bulletin: BULLETIN DU C.G.O.* trimestrial. Non-membres 35F le numéro. *Président:* Jacques Pecquenard. *Secretaire:* Jacqueline Nicolle.

- **ASSOCIATION CEUX DU ROANNAIS**
  Bibliotheque Municipale, 4 place Clemenceau, F-42328 ROANNE CEDEX, France.
  Cotisation Annuelle: 60F. *Bibliotheque:* 2me marcredi, chaque mois 14h-17h. *Reunions:* 2 samedi chaque mois 14h-17h, 2 mercredi chaque mois 14h-17h. *Bulletin: LETTRE A CEUX DU ROANNAIS* 1 ou 2 par an. *President:* J.A. Forges. *Secretaire:* Philippe Boisselot.

CHAMPAGNE-ARDENNE (Ardennes, Aube, Marne, Haute-Marne)

- **CERCLE DE GENEALOGIE ET D'HERALDIQUE DES ARDENNES**
  Hôtel de Ville, F-08000 CHARLEVILLE MEZIERES, France.
  Cotisation: 125F. *Président:* Colonel Jean Paul Jaquemin. *Secrétaire:* M. Alain Moreau. *Bulletin: ARDENNES, TIENS FERME* trimestrielle. Le Cercle est affilié à la Fédération Francaise des Sociétés de Généalogie.

- **CENTRE GENEALOGIQUE DE CHAMPAGNE**
  3E rue des 16e et 22e Dragons, F-51100 REIMS, France. (courrier seulement).
  Président: Paul F. Cabanis. *Secrétaire:* M. Jean-Yves Sureau.

- **CENTRE GENEALOGIQUE DE LA MARNE**
  Boite Postale 20, F-51005 CHALONS-EN-CHAMPAGNE CEDEX, France.
  Cotisation annuelle: 30F. *Bibliotheque:* L, M, M, J, V et 1er Samedi chaque mois. 8½h-12h & 14h-17h, 9h-12h le samedi. *Reunions:* 1er Samedi de chaque mois de 9h-12h. *Bulletin: BULLETIN DE LIAISON DU CENTRE GENEALOGIQUE DE CHAMPAGNE* trimestriel. non-membres 40F le numéro. *President:* Jean-Paul Denise. *Secretaire:* Joelle Monwit.

FRANCHE-COMTE (Doubs, Jura, Haute-Saone, Territoire-de-Belfort)

- **CENTRE D'ENTRAIDE GENEALOGIQUE DE FRANCHE-COMTE**
  3 rue Beauregard, F-25000 BESANCON, France.
  Président: M. Daniel Foltete.

- **CERCLE GENEALOGIQUE HAUT-SAONOIS (S.A.L.S.A.)**
  1 rue des Ursulines, F-70000 VESOUL, France.
  Président: André Thevenin. *Secrétaire:* Jacques Bringout.

ILE-DE-FRANCE (Essonne, Hauts-de-Seine, Paris, Seine-et-Marne, Seine-Saint-Denis, Val-de-Marne, Val-d'Oise, Yvelines).

- **CERCLE GENEALOGIQUE DES CHEMINOTS**
  1 bis, rue d'Athènes, 75009 PARIS, France.
  Cotisation annuelle: 40F. *Bibliothèque:* ouverte à tous, 1er samedi de chaque mois, 14h-17h. *Réunions:* 1er samedi du mois. Tel. (President) 69 24 43 45. *Bulletin:* trimestriel, abonnement 80F. *Président:* Serge Esnard. *Secrétaire:* Pascal Le Ster. Tel. 64 90 64 76 apres 18h30.

- **CERCLE GENEALOGIQUE DE LA BRIE**
  Hôtel de Ville, 77100 MEAUX, France.
  Bibliothèque: ouverte les jours des réunions (Library open meeting days). *Runions:* 2e

samedi des mois impairs, 14h30, Hôtel de Ville de Meaux (Meetings 2nd Sat. odd-numbered months, Hôtel de Ville, Meaux). *Bulletin: GENEALOGIE BRIARDE* 4 par an, abonnement 100F, prix de vente aux non-membres, 100F. *Président:* Daniel Troublé, 5, allée de Multien, 77165 Saint Soupplets. *Secrétaire:* Claude Roussin.

- **ASSOCIATION GENEALOGIQUE D'ECHANGE A.G.E.**
  4, avenue Galliéni 91800 BRUNOY, France.
  Droit d'entrée: 50 F. *Cotisation:* 100 F. *Bibliothèque:* ouverte aux membres seulement (Library open to members only). *Demandes de recherches:* ouvertes à tous. *Réunions:* 2ème samedi du mois à 14h30 à Fontainebleau (Meetings second Saturday of each month, 2:30pm, Fontainebleau). *Bulletin:* inclus dans cotisation, trimestriel (Bulletin included in the dues, quarterly). *Président:* Marc Hairabedian. *Secrétaire:* Michelle Palazzolo.

- **CERCLE DE GENEALOGIE ET D'HERALDIQUE DE SEINE ET MARNE**
  Boîte Postale 113, F-77002 MELUN CEDEX, France.
  Entry: 30 F. *Cotisation:* 110 F. in 1987. *Réunions:* 1st Sat. of the month at Melun, 2nd Sat. Lagny Sur Marne-Fontaiebleau, 3rd Sat. Provins, 4th Sat. Coulommiers. 14h30. *Research Enquiries:* Members, and non members belonging to an association affiliated with the Fédération des Sociétés Françaises de Généalogie, d'Héraldique et de Sigillographie, or a national federation accepting exchanges of research requests. *Other Particulars:* Cercle created in 1984. *Président:* Pierre Jacques Castaing. *Secrétaire:* Christian Vecten.

- **CERCLE D'ETUDES GENEALOGIQUES ET HERALDIQUES DE L'ILE-DE-FRANCE**
  46 route de Croissy, F-78110 LE VESINET, France.
  Cotisation & abonnement: France 165F, etranger 175F. *Bulletin: STEMMA* au numero: France 45F, etranger 50F. *Research Enquiries:* 10F la ligne non-membres. *Président:* M. Philippe Jost. *Secrétaire:* M. Paul Degobert.

- **CENTRE GENEALOGIQUE DE L'ESSONNE**
  Le Coudreau, F-91498 MILLY LA FORET, France.
  Président: M. Foulques Josseaume. *Secrétaire:* M. Herve Girard.

- **RENAISSANCE ET CULTURE**
  Mairie d'Epinay, en face Dauchez, 21 grande rue, F-91360 EPINAY, France.
  Président: M. Hardel. *Secrétaire:* M. Neau.

- **RENAISSANCE ET CULTURE**
  Mairie d'Epinay, en face Dauchez, 21 grande rue, F-91360 EPINAY, France.
  Cotisation: 70 F. *Bibliothèque:* ouverte à tous. (Library open to all). *Demandes de recherches:* ouvertes à tous, pour l'Essone. Coût: timbres pour réponses. (Research requests open to all, for the department of Essone, send stamps for the reply). No Bulletin. *Réunions:* trois fois par an sur convocations (Meetings called three times a year). *Président:* M. Hardel. *Secrétaire:* M. Neau.

- **CENTRE GENEALOGIQUE DE PARIS**
  11 boulevard Pershing, F-78000 VERSAILLES, France.
  Cotisation annuelle: 120F. *Bulletin: HERALDIQUE & GENEALOGIE* 4 per year. *Président:* M. Gérard de Villeneuve. *Secrétaire:* M. Dan Cernovodeanu.

- **CERCLE GENEALOGIQUE DU C.E. DE LA CAISSE D'EPARGNE DE PARIS**
  19, rue du Louvre, F-75001 PARIS, France.
  Secrétaire: M. Alain Muntener.

- **ASSOCIATION HISTORIQUE, GENEALOGIQUE ET HERALDIQUE DU VAL D'OISE**
  46, rue de St. Prix, F-95320 ST. LEU LA FORET, France.
  Président: M. Jean Pierre Lange. *Secrétaire:* Mme. Denise Delsaux.

- **CERCLE GENEALOGIQUE DE VERSAILLES ET DES YVELINES**
  26 avenue des Combattants, F-78220 VIROFLAY, France.
  Cotisation: 130F. *Bulletin: GENEALOGIE EN YVELINES. Président:* Mme. Nicole Dreneau. *Secrétaire:* Mme. Nicole Bourrée.

- **CERCLE GENEALOGIQUE DU PERSONNEL DE LA R.A.T.P.**
  B.P. 82 F-78110 LE VESINET, France.
  Cotisation: 110 FF. *Library:* Address as above, every other Tuesday, 13:30-18h. Meetings every two months, in the afternoon. *Bulletin: NOS ANCESTRES* 3 par an. Price included in membership, not sold to non members. *Research Enquiries:* Members only, free. *Pre' sident:* Pinck. *Secrétaire:* Delarue. *Particulars:* Has a patronymic directory for the Cercle (Possède annuaire patronymique du Cercle).

LANGUEDOC-ROUSSILLON (Aude, Gard, Hérault, Lozère, Pyrénées-Orientales)

- **CERCLE GENEALOGIQUE DE LANGUEDOC**
  18 rue de la Tannerie, F-31400 TOULOUSE, France.
  Cotisation annuelle: 165F. *Bulletin: REVUE DU CERCLE GEN. DE LANGUEDOC* 4 annually. *Président:* M. Patrice de Viguerie. *Secrétaire:* Jean-Pierre Uguen.

LIMOUSIN (Corrèze, Creuse, Haute-Vienne)

- **ATELIER DE RECHERCHES GENEALOGIQUES ET ONOMASTIQUES**
  31 av. Jean Javrès, F-19100 BRIVE, LA GAILLARDE, France.
  Cotisation: 200F. *Bulletin: ECHOS ET NOUVELLES DE L'ARGO* 4 par an. *Président:* M. Christian Mazenc, Tujac — Le Nivernais, F-19100 BRIVE.

- **INSTITUT EUROPEEN FORMATION GENEALOGIQUE ZUP de TUJAC — le Nivernois**
  19100 BRIVE, France.
  Cotisation annuelle: 350F. *Bibliothèque:* gratuite pour tous (Free library open to all). *Président:* Ch. Mazenc. *Other particulars:* L'I.F.E.G. est le seul centre permanent de formation généalogique en Europe. (The I.F.E.G. is the only permanent genealogical training center in Europe).

- **ASSOCIATION NATIONALE DES GENEALOGISTES FAMILIAUX ZUP de TUJAC — Le Nivernois**
  19100 BRIVE, France.
  Cotisation annuelle: 200F. *Bibliothèque:* ouverte à tous sur rendez-vous (Library free to all, by appointment). *Président:* Christian Mazenc. *Other particulars:* L'ANGF ne regroupe que des professionnels et joue le role du consultant et de conseil (The ANGF groups only professionals and plays the role of consultant and advisor).

- **CERCLE GENEALOGIQUE ET HERALDIQUE DE LA MARCHE ET DU LIMOUSIN**
  26 rue de Nexon, F-87000 LIMOGES, France.
  Bulletin: D'ONTE SES? trimestrielle. *Cotisation annuelle:* 130F (France), 135F (Europe), 140F (outremer DOM/TOM). *Président:* M. Michel Sementery. *Secrétaire:* M. Joël Aubailly.

LORRAINE (Meurthe-et-Moselle, Meuse, Moselle, Vosges)

- **CERCLE GENEALOGIQUE DE LORRAINE**
  Archives de Meurthe et Moselle, 1 rue de la Monnaie, F-54000 NANCY, France.
  Président: M. Georges Marande. *Secrétaire:* M. Pierre Colin.

- **UNION DES CERCLES GENEALOGIQUES DE LORRAINE**
  B.P. 8, 54130 SAINT-MAX, France.
  Cotisation annuelle: 50 F. *Bibliothèque:* ouverte à tous mercredi-vendredi 14h à 17h30 (Library open to all Mon.-Fri. 2-5.30pm). *Bulletin: CENEALOGIE LORRAINE* trimestrielle. *Coût de l'abonnement:* 100F, prix de vente aux non-members: 120F

l'Exemplaire. *Demandes de recherches:* ouvertes à tous, gratuites sauf participation aux frais. (Research requests open to all, free except for costs). *Président:* François Meyer. *Secretaire:* Pierre Colin.

MIDI-PYRENEES (Ariège, Aveyron, Haute-Garonne, Gers, Lot, Hautes-Pyrénées, Tarn, Tarn-et-Garonne)

- **GROUPE GENEALOGIQUE DE LA VALLEE DE GISTAIN**
  B.P. No 2, F-65240 ARREAU, France.
  Président: M. Henri Mir. *Secrétaire:* M. Henri Noguero.

- **CERCLE GENEALOGIQUE DE LANGUEDOC**
  18 rue de la Tannerie, F-31400 TOULOUSE, France.
  Cotisation annuelle: 165F. *Bulletin: REVUE DU CERCLE GEN. DE LANGUEDOC*
  4 annually. *Président:* M. Patrice de Viguerie. *Secrétaire:* Jean-Pierre Uguen.

NORD-PAS-DE-CALAIS (Nord, Pas-de-Calais)

- **GROUPE DE GENEALOGISTES AMATEURS DU CAMBRESIS**
  Centre Social Saint Roch, rue du 4è Cuirassiers, F-59400 CAMBRAI, France.
  Cotisation: 100F. *Président:* Mr. Gérard Domise. *Secrétaire:* M. Didier Laurent.

- **ASSOCIATION GENEALOGIQUE FLANDRE-HAINAUT**
  159 rue du Quesnoy, F-59321 VALENCIENNES, France.
  Président: M. Jean-Jacques Tailliez. *Secrétaire:* Mme. Maryse Boudard.

- **ASSOCIATION GENEALOGIQUE DU PAS-DE-CALAIS**
  Maison des Scoiétés, 16 rue Aristide Briand, F-62000 ARRAS, France.
  Cotisation: 35F. *Bulletin: GENEALOGIE 62.* Le Congress National de Genealogie –
  Arras 4-7 Mai 1989. *Président:* M. Patrick Warin. *Secrétaire:* M. Henri Desmaret.

NORMANDY (LOW) (Calvados, Manche, Orne)

- **CERCLE CAENNAIS de GENEALOGIE**
  9 residence l'Orée d' Hastings, F-14000 CAEN, France.
  Président: M. François Boismard. *Secrétaire:* M. Daveux.

- **CERCLE GENEALOGIQUE DU PAYS BAS NORMAND**
  Château Duhazé, rue du Collège, B.P. 232, F-61100 FLERS, France.
  Cotisation: 90F. *Reunions:* 1 samedi chaque mois de 14 a 18h. *Président:* M. Guy Peschet. *Secretaire:* Mr Gerard Villeroy.

NORMANDY (HIGH) (Eure, Seine-Maritime)

- **CERCLE GENEALOGIQUE ET HERALDIQUE DE NORMANDIE**
  17 rue Louis Malliot, F-76000 ROUEN, France.
  Président: Comte d'Arundel de Conde. *Secrétaire:* Comte de Gennes.

PAYS DE LA LOIRE (Loire-Atlantique, Maine-et-Loire, Mayenne, Sarthe, Vendée)

- **CERCLE GENEALOGIQUE DE MAINE ET PERCHE**
  3, av. Olivier Heuzé, F-72000 LE MANS, France.
  Cotisation: 40 F & 80 F for the bulletin. *Library:* Address as above, members only, Mercredi-Ocutredi 14h-17h30 and by appointment. Free. *Réunions:* At the Maison des Associations second Saturday of each month, 14-17h. *Bulletin: LE BORDAGER* 4 par an. Non-membres 100F par an. *Research Enquiries:* Free to members only. *Reunions:* 2 samedi de chaque mois a le Mans, 3 mercredi de chaque mois a Laval. *Président:* André Leschot. *Secrétaire:* Y. Beutherault.

- **C.R.G.PERCHE-GOUET**
  6, Porte de l'Hortiau F-72570 MONTMIRAIL, France.
  Cotisation: 100 FF, includes bulletin. *Library:* Address as above, members only. *Réunions:* June and Sept., Sun. 9:30-18h. *Bulletin: C.R.G. PERCHE-GOUET* quarterly. Price to non members 100 FF. *Research Enquiries:* Members only, free for questions, price of research depends on its nature and length. *Président:* M. Gérard Cruchet. *Secrétaire:* Mme Monique Menard. *Particulars:* Computerization of research information in progress. (Relevés systematiques par T.U.C. — Etablissement Tables mariages en cours. Informatisation progressive des actes.)

- **ASSOCIATION GENEALOGIQUE DE L'ANJOU**
  18 rue de Bretagne, F-49100 ANGERS, France.
  Cotisation: 130F. *Bibliothéque:* 4 rue Paul Bert, 49000 Angers. (Tel.) 41-86 8765. *Président:* M. Jacques Chopin. *Secrétaire:* Jacqueline Passelande.

POITOU CHARENTES (Charente, Charente Maritime, Deux-Sèvres, Vienne)

- **ASSOCIATION GENEALOGIQUE DE LA CHARENTE**
  24 avenue Gambetta, F-16000 ANGOULEME, France.
  Président: M. Gabriel Delage. *Secrétaire:* M. Henry Le Diraison.

- **CERCLE GENEALOGIQUE D'AUNIS ET SAINTONGE**
  83 avenue R. Poincar' , F-17000 LA ROCHELLE, France.
  Président: M. André Boussaton. *Secrétaire:* M. Henri Menudier.

PROVENCE-ALPES-COTE-D'AZUR (Alpes-de-Haute-Provence, Hautes Alpes, Alpes-Maritimes, Bouches-du-Rhône, Var, Vaucluse)

- **A.S.C.C.H.C. CENACLE GENEALOGIQUE**
  Centre Hospitalier, 18 avenue des Broussailles 06401 CANNES, France.
  Cotisation: 90F, 110F, 130F. *Bibliothèque:* ouverte à tous, 2ème et 4ème jeudi par mois, 17h à 20h (Library open to all, second and fourth Thursdays, 5-8pm). *Runions:* 2ème et 4ème jeudi par mois (Meetings 2nd & 4th Thurs.). *Bulletin: ASCCHC CENACLE GENEALOGIQUE*, trimestriel. Prix de vente aux non-membres 20 francs + port. *Demandes de recherches:* ouvertes à tous, gratuit. *Président:* Dr J.P. Boulogne et Mr B. Babolat. *Secrétaire:* Mme. Baracani et Mme. Guien. *Particulars:* Premier Cenacle genealogical hospitalier. En cours de creation un reseau inter-hospitalier (First hospital genealogical group. In the process of creating an inter-hospital network).

- **ASSOCIATION GENELOGIQUE DU VAC**
  Maison pour tous, rue Francois Paul, F-83160 LA VALETTE DU VAR, France.
  Cotisation annuelle: 140F. *Bibliotheque:* 1st & 3rd Monday, 14h-16h. *Reunions:* 1st Monday 16h-18h. *Bulletin: PROVENCE GENEALOGIE* twice a month. *President:* Henri Mauzin. *Secretaire:* Ginette Delayes.

- **ASSOCIATION GENEALOGIQUE DES HAUTES ALPES**
  Archives Départementales, Route de Rambaud 05000 GAP, France.
  Entry fee: 30 francs. *Cotisation annuelle:* 140F. *Réunions:* dernier vendredi de chaque mois (last Fri.) à 17h30 au siège (5:30pm at headquarters). *Bibliothèque:* open to members Friday 14-18h. *Research requests:* small research requests accepted (recherches sommaires). *President:* François Collin. *Secrétaire:* Marcelle Orcier. *Particulars:* as of October 1, 1988, the Association had 60 members. It is a member of the Centre Généalogique Midi-Provence at Port de Bouc, which publishes a bi-monthly bulletin, *PROVENCE GÉNÉALOGIE.*

- **CERCLE DE GENEALOGIE DE NICE**
  7 avenue de Fabron, F-06200 NICE, France.
  Président: M. Gé' rard Beltrutti. *Secrétaire:* Mme. Anne-Marie Grimoult.

● **CERCLE GENEALOGIQUE ET HERALDIQUE CANNOIS**
258 avenue Michel-Jourdan, F-06150 CANNES-LA BOCCA, France.
Président: M. Pierre Ipert. *Secrétaire:* Mme. Christine Rostagni.

● **ASSOCIATION GENEALOGIQUE DES BOUCHES-DU-RHONE, Section Marseille**
Archives Communales, Place A. Carli, F-13001 MARSEILLE, France.
Président: M. Georges Reynaud. *Secrétaire:* Mme. Geneviève Stefani.

● **CERCLE GENEALOGIQUE DE VAUCLUSE**
Ecole Sixte Isnand, 31 Ten Avenue de la Trillode, F-84000, AVIGNON, France.
Cotisation annuelle: 160F. *Bibliotheque:* Mercredi 14h-18h. *Reunions:* Mercredi 14h-18h. *Bulletin: BULLETIN C.G.V.* semestriel. Non-membres 50F. *Président:* Mme de Cockborne. *Secrétaire:* Mme. Fraysse.

● **ASSOCIATION GENEALGIQUE ET HERALDIQUE DES ALPES MARITIMES ET MONACO**
Archives départementales des Alpes Maritimes, Route de Grenoble, F-06036 NICE CEDEX, France.
Président: M. Roger Viout. *Secrétaire:* Mme Louise Ferment.

RHONE-ALPES (Ain, Ardèche, Drôme, Isère, Loire, Rhône, Savoie, Haute-Savoie)

● **CENTRE GENEALOGIQUE DU DAUPHINE**
Bibliothèque Municipale d'Etude Lyautey, B.P. 1095 R.P., F-38021 GRENOBLE CEDEX, France.
Président: M. Robert Allier. *Secrétaire:* M. J. Brun.

● **SOCIETE GENEALOGIQUE DU LYONNAIS**
7 rue Major Martin, F-69006, LYON, France.
Président: M. Philippe Castagnary. *Secrétaire:* Mme. Micheline Lhopital.

● **CENTRE GENEALOGIQUE DE SAVOIE**
Romblaz d'en Haut, F-74250 SAINT-JEAN-DE-THOLOME, France.
Président: Mme. Anne Druart. *Secrétaire:* Mme. Michèle Metral.

OVERSEAS

ISLAND OF REUNION

● **CERCLE GENEALOGIQUE DE BOURBON**
Archives Départementales de la Réunion, Le Chaudron, 97490 STE CLOTHIDE, REUNION.
Cotisation: 100F. *Bulletin:* Trimestriel. *Président:* Mme Hèléne Thazard. *Secrétaire:* M. Louis De Lavergne.

● **CHANNEL ISLANDS FAMILY HISTORY SOCIETY**
P.O. Box 507, ST HELIER, JERSEY, Channel Islands, JE4 8XZ.
Journal: THE CHANNEL ISLANDS FAMILY HISTORY SOCIETY JOURNAL 4 per year. *Research Enquiries:* £5.00 per hr. for members, £7.00 non members. *Membership:* £6.00 Channel Islands, £7.00 overseas. *Président:* Mr. M.J. Vautier *Secrétaire:* Mrs S. Payn.

GERMANY – DEUTSCHLAND

INLAND (NATIONAL) & GENERAL

- **ARBEITSKREIS GENEALOGIE**
  Gutenbergstr. 12b, D-3300 BRAUNSCHWEIG, W. Germany.
  Telefon: 0531/321308. *Mitgliedsbeitrag:* DM 20.-*Zeitschrift: GENEALOGISCHE MITTEILUNGEN DES ARBEITSKREISES GENEALOGIE. Erscheinungsweise:* viertelj. *Nichtmitglieder:* DM 10.-*Beantwortung der Anfragen:* Brieflich (Bedingung: Rückporto), wobei unser Arbeitsgebiet Ost – und Mittel-Deutschland, Polen und das Baltikum (Litauen, Lettland, Estland) ist. *Weitere Angaben:* Mitarbeiter des Arbeitskreises Genealogie treffen sich an jedem 1. Dienstag im Monat in der Geschäftsstelle des Bundes der Vertriebenen, Kreisverband Braunschweig e.V. Gutenbergstr. 12b, D-3300 Braunschweig um 18.30 Uhr. Interessenten und Gäste können Auskünfte dort bekommen. *Vorsitzender:* Kurt Fünfeich. *Gründungsvorsitzender:* Oliver Dix.

- **DEUTSCHE ARBEITSCGEMEINSCHAFT GENEALOGISCHER VERBANDE (D.A.G.V.)**
  C/o NW Personenstandsarchiv Rheinland, Schloss-Str. 12, D-5040 BRUHL, (Telefon: 02232-42948).
  Die von der DAGV veranstalteten Deutschen Genealogentage sind auch Nichtmitgliedern zugänglich. *Mitgliedsbeitrag:* DM 0,30 pro Mitglied des Mitgliedsvereins. *Zeitschrift:* Die von Gerhard GeBner herausgegebene Zeitschrift *GENEALOGIE* ist das Organ der DAGV. *Erscheinungsweise:* vierteljährlich. *Preis von Einzelheften für Nichtmitglieder:* DM 12,50. Genealogische Anfragen werden entweder hier bearbeitet oder an den zuständigen Mitgliedsverein weitergeleitet. Die von hier aus erteilten Auskünfte sind kostenlos – es wird aber um die Erstattung der Portokosten gebeten – , müssen sich aber in der Regel auf den Nachweis von Forschungsmöglichkeiten beschränken. *Vorsitzender:* Dr. Jörg Füchtner.

- **HEROLD**
  Gebaeude des Geh. Staatsarchivs.
  Archiv Str. 12-14, D-1000 BERLIN 33. Zimmer 45-47, W. Germany.
  Telefon: (030) 832031. *OEFFNUNGSZEITEN:* Dienstags 15.00-19.30 Uhr. Auch fuer Nichtmitglieder zugaenglich. *Mitgliedsbeitrag:* DM 45.-Allgemein. DM 50.-fuer Mitglieder in Berlin. *Zeitschrift: DER HEROLD. Erscheinungsweise:* Vierteljaehrlich. Kein Abornnement der Vierteljahrschrift möglich. *Suchanzeigen:* werden nicht angenommen. *Beantwortung der Anfragen:* Unentgeltlich, muendlich in der Geschaeftsstelle. Bei schriftlichen Anfragen wird Rueckporto erwartet. *Weitere Angaben:* Herolds-Ausschuss der Deutschen Wappenrolle; Buchreihe "Deutsche Wappenrolle", bisher 52 Baende; Heraldischer Auskunftsdienst. Gelegentlich Sonderhefte des Vierteljahrschrift *DER HEROLD. Forschungsgebiet:* Heraldik, Genealogie, Sphragistik, Numismatik, Ortsgeschichte, u. verwandte Gebiete (Militaergeschichte). *Vorsitzender:* Dr Phil Knut Schulz (from 3 Feb 1990 onwards).
  Office: as above. *Hours:* Tues. 3-7.30pm. Open to non members. *Membership sub.:* DM 45.-& DM 50.-for members in Berlin. *Journal:* named above. *Published:* quarterly. Subscription of the quarterly only with membership. Journal enquiries are not accepted. *Mail enquiries:* We only give literature assistance for personal research. Return postage expected. Extra details: Herald Committee for German Heraldry; Series "Deutsche Wappenrolle" (52 volumes). Heraldic information service. Occasional special issues of *DER HEROLD. Area of interest:* Heraldry, Genealogy, Sphragistics, Numismatics, Local history and related subjects including Military history. *President:* (see above.).

- **ZENTRALSTELLE FUER PERSONEN-UND FAMILIENGESCHICHTE, Institut für Genealogie.**
  Geschaeftsstelle: Birkenweg 13, D-6382 FRIEDRICHSDORF 4, W. Germany.
  Archiv und Bibliothek: in 6230 Frankfurt – Höchst (Benutzung nach Vereinbarung

mit dem Geschäftsführer). Es werden Anfragen beantwortet und Ratschläge für weitere Forschungsmöglichkeiten gegeben (bitte 2 Internationale Antwortscheine beifügen). Herausgabe des *GENEALOGISCHES JAHRBUCH* (jährlich) und der *AHNENLISTENKARTEI* (in unregelmässiger Zeitfolge). Federführung bei den Ortssippenbüchern Reihen A und B. Zur Unterstützung der Stiftung besteht Verein zur Förderung der Zentralstelle für Personen-und Familiengeschichte e.V. Berlin, Archivstr. 12-14 (Staatsarchiv), D-1000 Berlin 33 (Dahlem). *Vorsitzender:* Senatspräsident i.R. Jürgen Arndt, Berlin. *Mitgliedsbeitrag:* DM 40.-p.a. Mitglieder erhalten das Genealogische Jahrbuch kostenlos. *Telefon:* 06172-78263. *Geschaeftsfuehrer:* Dr Ludwig Becker, Friedrichsdorf 4.

● **GRUPPE FAMILIEN-UND WAPPENKUNDE IM BUNDESBAHN-SOZIALWERK**
Gueterstrasse 9, D-6000 FRANKFURT (Main), Germany.
Telefon: (069) 265 3124. *Mitgliedsbeitrag:* DM 24.-jaehrlich. *Zeitschrift: DER EISENBAHNER-GENEALOGE. Erscheinungsweise:* halbjaehrlich. *Preis von Einzelheften fuer Nichtmitglieder:* DM 5.-. *Beantwortung der Anfragen:* in beschraenktem Umfang. *Weitere Angaben:* Eisenbahner-Archiv. *Vorsitzender:* Eberhard Loeflund.
Membership sub.: DM 24.-. *Journal:* named above. *Published:* half yearly. *Non members price:* DM 5.-. *Mail enquiries:* limited replies only. Railway employees archives.

GERMAN RESEARCH IN OTHER COUNTRIES

AUSLAND — USA — (siehe USA — National)

● **GERMAN GENEALOGICAL SOCIETY OF AMERICA**

OSTEUROPE (EAST EUROPE) & DDR (EAST GERMANY)

● **ARBEITSGEMEINSCHAFT FUER MITTELDEUTSCHE FAMILIENFORSCHUNG E.V.**
Anschrift des Vorsitzenden Goldbergstr. 23, D-3550 MARBURG, W. Germany, (Dr. Anderson).
Telefon: 06421 44249 (des Vorsitzenden). *Mitgliedsbeitrag:* DM 50.-in den U.S.A. $35.00. *Zeitschrift: MITTELDEUTSCHE FAMILIENKUNDE. Erscheinungsweise:* vierteljaehrlich. *Preis von Einzelheften fuer Nichtmitglieder:* DM 15.-ueber den Verlag Degener & Co. D-8530 Neustadt/Aisch zu beziehen. *Suchanzeigen:* bei dem Verlag zu erfragen. *Beantwortung der Anfragen:* durch den Vorsitzenden. 7 doppeltes Ruckporto exforelerick. *Forschungsgebiet:* Sachsen, Thueringen, Anhalt, Brandenburg, Berlin, Mecklenburg. *Vorsitzender:* Dr. Hans-Joachim Anderson.
Membership cost: DM 50.-, $35.00 in USA. *Journal:* named above. *Published:* quarterly. *Non members price:* DM 15.-available through the publisher Degener & Co. (address above). *Cost of journal enquiries:* ask publisher. *Mail enquiries:* answered by President. 2 international answer coupons required. *President:* Dr. Hans-Joachim Anderson.

● **ARBEITSKREIS DONAUSCHWAEB, FAMILIENFORSCHER (AKdFF)**
Weinbergsweg 2, D-6905 SCHRIESHEIM, W. Germany (Herr Kniesel).
Telefon: 06203/61706. *Oeffnungszeiten:* Archiv im Haus der Donauschwaben, Goldmuehlestr. 30, D-7032 Sindelfingen ganztaegig geoffnet. *Mitgliedsbeitrag:* DM 30.-. *Zeitschrift: DONAUSCHWAEBISCHE FAMILIENKUNDLICHE FORSCHUNGSBLAETTER. Erscheinungsweise:* vierteljaehrlich. *Preis von Einzelheften fuer Nichtmitglieder:* DM 3.-. *Suchanzeigen:* fuer Mitglieder kostenlos. *Beantwortung der Anfragen:* Durch forschungskundige Mitarbeiter. *Forschungsgebiet:* Donauschwaebischer Raum (Volksdeutsche aus Jugoslawien Ungarn und Rumaenien.) *Vorsitzender:* Wilfried Kniesel.
Archives: Open daily, second address above. *Membership sub.:* DM 30.50. *Journal:* named above. *Published:* quarterly. *Non members price:* DM 3.-. *Journal enquiries:* free to members. *Mail enquiries:* answered by competent colleagues. *Area of inter-*

est: Danube — Schwaben (foreign Germans from Yugoslavia, Hungary and Romania.)

● **ARBEITSGEMEINSCHAFT OSTDEUTSCHER FAMILIENFORSCHER E.V.**
(Detlef Kuehn) Fuhrweg 29, D-5300 BONN 3, W. Germany.
Telefon: (Vorsitzender) 0228-482804. *Mitgliedsbeitrag:* DM 53.-jaehrlich, Ausland:
DM 60.-. *Zeitschrift: ARCHIV OSTDEUTSCHER FAMILIENFORSCHER
(AOFF). Erscheinungsweise:* 6 Lieferungen im Jahr und *OSTDEUTSCHE
FAMILIEN KUNDE (OFK)* 4 x jährlich. *Preis von Einzelheften fuer Nichtmitglieder:*
ca. DM 10.-. *Beantwortung der Anfragen:* durch unsere Forschungstellen. *Weitere
Angaben:* AGoFF — Wegweiser, Genealogical Guide. *Forschungsgebiet:* Ostdeutsche
Gebiete oestlich der OderNeisse, sudeten deutsche Gebiete sowie deutsche
Siedlungsgebiete in Ost-und Suedosteuropa. *Vorsitzender:* Detlef Kuehn.
Phone: President. *Membership sub.:* DM 40.-annually. *Journal:* named above.
Published: 6 issues per year. *Non members price:* DM 3,50 to 4.-. *Mail enquiries:*
answered by our search offices, write for conditions. *Extra details:* AGoFF-Guide
and a Genealogical Guide for sale. *Area of interest:* East German areas east of the
Oder-Neisse, Sudeten German areas and German settlement areas in eastern and
southeastern Europe. *President:* Detlef Kuehen.

● **VEREINIGUNG SUDETENDEUTSCHER FAMILIENFORSCHER. (VSFF)**
SUDETENDEUTSCEHS GENEALOGISCHES ARCHIV (SGA)
Erikaweg 58, D-84000 REGENSBURG, W. Germany.
Telefon: (0941) 709102. *Oeffnungszeiten:* nach Vereinbarung. Auch fuer
Nichtmitglieder zugaenglich nach Vereinbarung. *Mitgliedsbeitrag:* DM 25.-.
Zeitschrift: SUDETENDEUTSCHE FAMILIENFORSCHUNG. Erscheinungsweise:
Jahreshefte. Preis von Einzelheften fuer Nichtmitglieder DM 25.-. *Suchanzeigen:*
nach Vereinbarung. *Beantwortung der Anfragen:* nur gegen ein Unkostenpauschale
DM 15.-. *Vorsitzender:* Prof. Richard W. Eichler, SteinkirchnerstraBe 15, D-8000
München 71.
Office Hours: by appointment. Open to non members. *Membership:* DM 25.-.
Journal: named above. *Published:* yearly. *Non members price:* DM 25.-. *Cost of
Journal enquiries:* on application. *Mail enquiries:* expenses cost of DM 15.-. *President:* Prof. Richard W. Eichler (see above).

BADEN-WUERTTEMBERG

● **VEREIN FUER FAMILIEN — U. WAPPENKUNDE IN WUERTTEMBERG UND
BADEN E.V.**
Konrad — Adenauer — Str. 8, D-7000 STUTTGART, W. Germany.
Telefon: 0711/212-5404. *Oeffnungszeiten:* jeweils Donnerstags v.14.30-18 h. Auch
fuer Nichtmitglieder zugaenglich. *Mitgliedsbeitrag:* jaehrlich DM 33.-. *Zeitschrift:
BLAETTER FUER SUEDWESTDEUTSCHE FAMILIEN — UND
WAPPENKUNDE. Erscheinungsweise:* 4 x jaehrlich. *Preis von Einzelheften fuer
Nichtmitglieder:* DM 10.-. *Suchanzeigen:* Zeilenpreis DM 1.50 Mitglieder haben 5
Zeilen frei. *Beantwortung der Anfragen:* Entweder durch Auswertung der in Vereinsbuecherei oder Vereinsarchiv vorhandenen Unterlagen (ehrenamtlich) oder
durch Mitarbeiter aus dem Mitgliederkreis im Lande gegen Honorar. Anfragen ohne
beigelegtes ausreichendes Rückporto (intern. Antwortscheine) können nicht mehr
beantwortet werden. Mitgliedschaft von ausländischen Personen hat nur Sinn, wenn
diese über ausreichende Deutschkenntnisse verfügen. *Weitere Angaben:* Allmonatliche Versammlungen (mit Ausnahme der Monate Juni-August und Dez.) mit
Vortraegen und Aussprachen. Sonderveroeffentlichungen ueber erarbeitete
Forschungsergebnisse. *Vorsitzender:* Dr. Hans Ulrich Frhr.v. Ruepprecht.
Geschaeftsfuehrer: Ursula Strohbucker.
Office hours: Thurs. 2.30pm-6pm. *Membership:* DM 33.-. *Journal:* named above.
Published: quarterly. *Non members price:* DM 10.-. *Journal enquiry cost:* DM 1.50
per line. Members receive 5 lines free. *Mail enquiries:* answered by honorary
members only from research in the Society's own records. Additional research

carried out for a fee. Inquiries without sufficient return postage will not be answered. Membership of foreigners only makes sense if they have a sufficient command of the German language. *Extra details:* Monthly meetings (except June, Jly. Aug. & Dec.) with lectures. Special publications with research results. *President & Director:* named above.

BAYERN (BAVARIA)

● **GESELLSCHAFT FUER FAMILIENFORSCHUNG IN FRANKEN E.V.**
Archivstr. 17, D-8500 NUERNBERG 10, W. Germany.
Telefon: 0911-358939. *Oeffnungszeiten:* Mittwochs von 14.00 Uhr bis 17.00 Uhr. Auch fuer Nichtmitglieder zugaenglich. *Mitgliedsbeitrag:* zur Zeit DM 25.-jaehrlich, Aenderungen vorbehalten. *Zeitschrift: BLAETTER FUER FRAENKISCHE FAMILIENKUNDE. Erscheinungsweise:* halbjaehrlich. *Preis von Einzelheften:* zur Zeit fur Mitglieder DM 12,50 p.Stück, füu" r Nichtmitglieder DM 16.-p.Stück, Aenderungen vorbehalten. *Suchanzeigen:* DM 3.-pro Zeile. *Beantwortung der Anfragen:* je nach Moeglichkeit der Bearbeitung, so schnell wie moglich. *Forschungsgebiet:* Ober – Mittel – und Unterfranken.
Office hours: Wed. 2pm-5pm. *Membership sub.:* DM 25.-. *Journal:* named above. *Published:* half yearly. *Members price:* DM 12.50, *Non members Price:* DM 16.- each. *Journal enquiry cost:* DM 3.-per line. *Mail enquiries:* Answered as soon as possible. *Area of interest:* Upper, middle and lower Francony. *President:* Eberhard Krauss (see above).

● **BAYERISCHER LANDESVEREIN FUER FAMILIENKUNDE E.V.**
Ludwigstrasse 14/1, 8000 München 22, W. Germany.
Telefon: 089 21 98-398. *Oeffnungszeiten:* Mittwoch von 13-16 Uhr, zusätzlich an jedem ersten Mittwoch im Monat bis 18.30 Uhr ja zur Beratung. *Mitgliedsbeitrag:* DM 60,00 für Bez.Gr. Augsburg, Neuburg und Regensburg, DM 62,00 für Bez.Gr. München. Blätter des Bayerischen Landesverein für Familienkunde und Informationsblatt (für Mitglieder) 3 x jährlich. Preis von Einzelheften für Nichtmitglieder DM 36,00 Inland, DM 39,00 Ausland inclus. Versandkosten. Wir u₁bernehmen keine Recherchen; Anfragen werden mit Standardbrief und allgem. Hinweisen beantwortet. Rückporto erfoderlich, aus Übersee mind. 2 Internationale Antwortscheine. *Archivdirektor:* Dr Ludwig Morenz.

BREMEN

● **DIE MAUS, GESELLSCHAFT FUER FAMILIENFORSCHUNG E.V., BREMEN.**
Am Staatsarchiv 1 Fedelhören, D-2800 BREMEN 1, W. Germany.
Telefon: 0421/361621 (Staatsarchiv). *Oeffnungszeiten:* Oeffentliche Sprechstunden im Gebaeude des Staatsarchivs Donnerstags 16-20 Uhr (ausser Juli). *Mitgliedsbeitrag:* DM 35.-fuer Einzelmitglieder. DM 50.-fuer Ehepaare. *Zeitschrift: NORDDEUTSCHE FAMILIENKUNDE. Erscheinungsweise:* vierteljaehrlich (mit 4 anderen Vereinen). *Weitere Angaben:* Fachbuecherei zur freien Benutzung fuer jedermann, ebenso umfangreiche Sammlungen genealogischen Inhalts. *Forschungsgebiet:* Familienkunde und im Zusammenhang damit Wappenkunde und andere verwandte Gebiete, Bremen und nahe Umgebung. *Vorsitzender:* Dr Wolfgang Bonorden, Staustr. 6, D-2800 Bremen 61, (Tel. 831 310).
Office hours: Public enquiries in State Archives building, Thursdays 4pm-8pm (except July). *Memberships subs.:* DM 35.-for individuals. DM 50.-married couples. *Journal:* named above. *Published:* quarterly with 4 other Societies. *Mail enquiries:* will be answered. *Extra details:* Specialist library free to all, also extensive collection on genealogical subjects. *Area of interest:* Genealogy and Heraldry in Bremen and immediate area. *President:* Dr Bonorden (see above).

HAMBURG

● **GENEALOGISCHE GESELLSCHAFT, SITZ HAMBURG, E.V.**
Postfach 302042, D-2000 HAMBURG 36, W. Germany.
Mitgliedsbeitrag: DM 50.-fuer korp. Mitgl. DM 50.-*Zeitschrift: ZEITSCHRIFT*

FUER NORDDEUTSCHE FAMILIENKUNDE in Verbindung mit *NIEDEUTSCHER FAMILIENKUNDE. Erscheinungsweise:* Vierteljährlich. *Beantwortung der Anfragen:* schriftlich. *Weitere Angaben:* gelegentlich Sonderveroeffentlichungen. *Forschungsgebiet:* Hamburg, Nord-Niedersachsen, Schleswig-Holstein, Mecklenburg. *Vorsitzender:* Rolf Hillmer.

> *Membership sub.:* DM 50.-corporate DM 50.-. *Journal:* named above. *Published:* three monthly. *Mail enquiries:* answered. *Area of interest:* Hamburg, Nord-Niedersachsen, Schleswig-Holstein, Mecklenburg.

HESSEN (HESSE)

● **HESSISCHE FAMILIENGESCHICHTLICHE VEREINIGUNG**
Schloss, D-6100 DARMSTADT, W. Germany.
Telefon: (06151) 125760. *Oeffnungszeiten:* Dienstag, Donnerstag, Samstag 9-11.30 Uhr. Auch fuer Nichtmitgleder zugaenglich. *Mitgliedsbeitrag:* Jahresbeitrag DM 36.- . *Zeitschrift: HESSISCHE FAMILIENKUNDE. Erscheinungsweise:* vierteljaehrlich. *Preis von Einzelheften fuer Nichtmitglieder:* DM 8.-zuzuegl. Porto. *Suchanzeigen:* es werden keine Anzeigen aufgenommen. *Beantwortung der Anfragen:* Soweit aus unseren umfrangreichen Karteien zu ermitteln, werden Anfragen beantwortet, aber keine Forschung vorgenommen. Nur bei Beilage des Rueckporto! *Forschungsgebiet:* Das Gebiet des ehemaligen Grossherzogtums Hessen. *Vorsitzender:* Dr Manfred Knodt, Pfarrer I.R. D-6100 Darmstadt, Heinrich-Fuhr-Str. 13A.

> *Office hours:* Tues. Thurs. Sat. 9.00-11.30am. Open to non members. *Membership sub.:* DM 36.-. *Journal:* named above. *Published:* quarterly by the cooperative of genealogical societies in Hessen. *Non members price:* DM 8.-plus postage. Journal enquiries not accapted. *Mail enquiries:* Answered as far as possible from our extensive files but no research undertaken. Enquiries answered only if return postage paid. *Area of interest:* The former Grand Duchy of Hesse. *President:* Dr Manfred Knodt (see above).

NIEDERSACHSEN (LOWER SAXONY)

● **NIEDERSAECHSISCHER LANDESVEREIN FUER FAMILIENKUNDE E.V.**
Koebelingerstr. 59 (Stadtarchiv), D-3000 HANNOVER 1, W. Germany.
Auch fuer Nichtmitglieder zugaenglich. *Mitgliedsbeitrag:* DM 48.-fuer Auswaertige. DM 54.-fuer Hannoveraner jaehrlich. *Zeitschrift: NORDDEUTSCHE FAMILIENKUNDE. Erscheinungsweise:* vierteljaehrlich. *Suchanzeigen:* Familienkundliche Nachrichten. *Beantwortung der Anfragen:* kostenlos - Portoerstattung. *Weitere Angaben:* Sonderveroeffentlichungen kostenlos an Mit glieder im Erscheinungsjahr. *Vorsitzender:* Juergen Ritter.

> *Membership sub.:* DM 54.-for Hannover, DM 48.-elsewhere. *Journal:* named above. *Published:* quarterly. *Journal entry cost: FAMILIENKUNDLICHE NACHRICHTEN. Mail enquiries:* Free of charge – refund postage. *Extra details:* Special publications free to members in year of publication. *President and Secretary:* named above.

● **GENEALOGISCH-HERALDISCHE GESELLSCHAFT MIT DEM SITZ IN GÖTTINGEN.**
Postfach 2062, D-3400, GÖTTINGEN, W. Germany.
Oeffnungszeiten: Freitags 15-18 Uhr. Stadtbibliothek, Gotmar Str. 8, Göttingen. Auch fuer Nichtmitglieder zugaenglich. *Mitgliedsbeitrag:* DM 40.-. *Zeitschrift: NORDDEUTSCHE FAMILIENKUNDE. Erscheinungsweise:* Viertelj. *Preis von Einzelheften fuer Nichtmitglieder:* DM 8,50. *Anfragen:* Aus zeittichen Gruenden nur in Sonderfaellen moeglich. *Weitere Angaben:* Registerwerk "Der Schlussel". *Vorsitzender:* Franz Schubert. *Geschaeftsfuehrer:* Hans-Heinrich Hillegeist.

NORDRHEIN WESTFALEN (NORTH RHINE WESTPHALIA)

● **WESTDEUTSCHE GESELLSCHAFT FUER FAMILIENKUNDE E.V. SITZ KOLN.**
Postfach 100 822, D-5270 GUMMERSBACH, W. Germany.

Mitgliedsbeitrag: DM 45.-fuer Koerperschaften DM 50.-. *Zeitschrift:* *MITTEILUNGEN DER WESTDEUTSCHEN GESELLSCHAFT FUER FAMILIENKUNDE.* *Erscheinungsweise:* vierteljaehrlich. *Preis von Einzelheften fuer Nichtmitglieder:* DM 12.-. *Suchanzeigen:* Mindestens DM 5.-. *Beantwortung der Anfragen:* Bei Rueckporto und DM 3.-Mindestgebuehr. *Vorsitzender:* Bernhard F. Lesaar. *Geschaeftsfuehrer:* Henning Schröder.

Membership sub.: DM 45.-corporate DM 50.-. *Journal:* named above. *Published:* quarterly. *Non members price:* DM 12.-. *Journal enquiry cost:* DM 5.-minimum. *Mail entries:* Return post requested and a minimum fee of DM 3.00. *President and Secretary:* named above.

- **ROLAND ZU DORTMUND e.V. GENEALOGISCHE-HERALDISCHE ARBEITSGEMEINSCHAFT**
Postfach 103326, D-4600 DORTMUND 1, W. Germany.
Telefon: 0231/732 616. Auch fuer Nichtmitglieder zugaenglich. *Mitgliedsbeitrag:* DM 40.-. *Zeitschrift:* *ROLAND ZU DORTMUND.* *Erscheinungsweise:* 4xjahrlich. *Beantwortung der Anfragen:* schriftlich. *Weitere Angaben:* genealogische Bibliothek im Stadtarchiv Dortmund, monatliche Arbeitssitzungen. *Vorsitzender:* Erich W. Rickenbrauck.

Phone: above. Open to non members. *Membership sub.:* DM 40.-. *Journal:* named above. 4 per year. *President:* named above.

- **WESTFAELISCHE GESELLSCHAFT FUER GENEALOGIE U. FAMILIENFORSCHUNG**
Warendorfer Str. 24, Postfad 6125, D-4400 MUENSTER. W. Germany.
Oeffnungszeiten: Montags 8.30 h. — 12.30 h. *Mitgliedsbeitrag:* persoenl. Mitglieder DM 30.-korporative DM 45.-. *Zeitschrift:* *BEITRAEGE ZUR WESTFAELISCHEN FAMILIENFORSCHUNG.* *Erscheinungsweise:* jaehrlich. *Preis von Einzelheften fuer Nichtmitglieder:* Buchhandelspreis ca. 40.-/58.-. *Beantwortung der Anfragen:* Schriftlich durch die Geschaeftsstelle gegen Gebuehr von DM 7,00, ggf. Vermittlung eines Genealogen, mit dem ein Honorar zu vereinbaren ist. *Weitere Angaben:* Alle 2 Jahre wird ein Mitgliederverzeichnis herausgegeben, das auch die von den Mitgliedern bearbeiteten Familien mit ihren Herkunftsorten resp. — raeumen auffuehrt und durch mehrere Indizes erschlossen wird. Im Winter monatliche Treffen mit Vortrag. *Vorsitzender:* Clemens Steinbicker. *Geschaeftsfuehrer:* Dr. Werner Frese.

Office hours: Mondays 8.30am-12.30pm open to non members. *Membership sub.:* personal DM 30.-, institutionald DM 45.p *Journal:* named above. *Published:* annually. Non members price ca. 40,58.-, *Mail enquiries:* Answered in writing by the inquiry office for a fee of DM 7,00, in some cases by nomination of a genealogist, with whom a fee must be arranged. *Extra details:* every 2 years a list of members is issued, which also gives the families researched and their places of origin, and is indexed. *President and Secretary:* named above.

NIEDERSACHSEN (LOWER SAXONY)

- **OLDENBURGISCHE GESELLSCHAFT FUER FAMILIENKUNDE**
29 OLDENBURG, Lerigauweg 14, W. Germany (Buesing).
Telefon: 0441-503622 (Buesing) (nur abends). *Mitgliedsbeitrag:* DM 20.-. *Zeitschrift:* *OLDENBURGISCHE FAMILIENKUNDE.* *Erscheinungsweise:* vierteljaehrlich. *Preis von Einzelheften fuer Nichtmitglieder:* nach Umfang verschieden. *Beantwortung der Anfragen:* Nur bei Rueckporto; Genealogische Forschungen koennen von uns nicht uebernommen werden. *Weitere Angaben:* Regelmässiges Vortragswesen (jl. 6 Vortraege). *Forschungsgebiet:* ehemaliges Land Oldenburg. *Vorsitzender:* Wolfgang Buesing.

Phone: as above (only evenings). *Membership sub.:* DM 20.-. *Journal:* named above. *Published:* quarterly. *Non members price:* varies according to size. *Mail enquiries:* only with return post. Genealogical research cannot be undertaken by us. *Extra details:* Regular meetings (6 lectures per year). *Area of interest:* Former state of Oldenburg. *President:* W. Buesing.

RHEINLAND-PFALZ

● **ARBEITSGEMEINSCHAFT PFAELZISCH-RHEINISCHE FAMILIENKUNDE**
Rottstr. 17, D-6700 LUDWIGSHAFEN, W. Germany.
Oeffnungszeiten: Donnerstags 14-18 Uhr, Mittwochs 14-16 Uhr. *Mitgliedsbeitrag:*
DM 30.-. *Zeitschrift: PFAELZISCH-RHEINISCHE FAMILIENKUNDE.*
Erscheinungsweise: 3 x im Jahr. *Preis von Einzelheften fuer Nichtmitglieder:* Werden
nicht abgegeben. *Suchanzeigen:* Frei (nur fuer Mitglieder). *Beantwortung der
Anfragen:* Aus den Unterlagen des Vereinsarchivs. Keine Forschungsauftraege!
Weitere Angaben: 3 x jaehrlich Informationsdienst mit Spitzenahnen der Mitglieder.
Forschungsgebiet: Rheinland-Pfalz, Rheinhessen u. ehem. Kurpfalz. *Vorsitzender:*
Oskar Poller. *Geschaeftsfuehrer:* Peter Ruf.
Office Hours: Thurs. 3pm-6pm open to non members. *Membership sub.:* US
$20.00. *Journal:* named above. *Published:* three times per year. *Journal enquiry
cost:* free (for members only). *Mail enquiries:* answered from the Society's ar-
chives. Research requests not undertaken. *Extra details:* Three times a year infor-
mation service with leading forbears of members. *Area of interest:* Rheinland-
Pfalz, Rheinhessen. *President & Director:* named above.

SAARLAND

● **ARBEITSGEMEINSCHAFT FUER SAARLAENDISCHE FAMILIENKUNDE E.V.**
Hebbelstr. 3, D-6625 PUETTLINGEN, W. Germany. (Norbert Emanuel)
Mitgliedsbeitrag: DM 36.-jaehrlich. *Zeitschrift:* a) *SAARLAENDISCHE
FAMILIENKUNDE* (88 Hefte), b) *INFORMATIONSDIENST* (92 Hefte).
Erscheinungsweise: vierteljaehrlich. *Preis von Einzelheften fuer Nichtmitglieder:* DM
4.-. *Suchanzeigen:* (nach Vereinbarung). *Beantwortung der Anfragen:* Im Rahmen des
Moeglichen von den Mitgliedern des Vorstandes, anderfalls Verweis an
auskunftsfaehige Vereinsmitglieder. Anfragen ohne Rueckporto werden nicht in
jedem Fall beruecksichtigt. Antwort geht direkt an Anfrager. *Weitere Angaben:* a)
Reihe:-Saarlaendische Ahnen − u. Stammreihen (38 Nummern), b) Reihe:-
Sonderbaende (zumeist Orts-Familienbuecher) (26 Titel. Nur a) im Mitgliedsbeitrag
enthalten. Erscheinungsweise unregelmaessig. *Forschungsgebiet:* Genealogie der
Saargegend. *Vorsitzender:* Dr. Werner Habicht. *Geschaeftsfuehrer:* Norbert Emanuel.
Membership sub.: DM 36.-. *Journal:* named above. *Published:* quarterly a) 88
issues, b) 92 issues. *Non members price:* DM 4.-. *Journal enquiry cost:* by arrangement. *Mail enquiries:* As far as possible by members of the executive, otherwise an
appropriate Society member is indicated. Inquiries without return postage *not*
answered in all cases. *Extra details:* a) Series "Saarlaendische Ahnenu.
Stammreihen" (38 Nos.) b) Series "Sonderbaende" (mostly local family books)
(26 titles). Only a) included in subscription. *Published:* irregularly. *Areas of interest:* Genealogy of the Saar area. *President & Director:* named above.

SCHLESWIG-HOLSTEIN

● **SCHLESWIG-HOLSTEINISCHE GESELLSCHAFT FUER
FAMILIENFORSCHUNG UND WAPPENKUNDE E.V. KIEL**
Gartenstr. 12, D-2300 KIEL 1, W. Germany.
Mitgliedsbeitrag: DM 40.-jaehrlich; fuer Schueler und Studenten DM 10.-.
Zeitschrift: FAMILIENKUNDLICHES JAHRBUCH SCHLESWIG-HOLSTEIN
(seit 1962). *Erscheinungsweise:* jaehrlich. *Preis von Einzelheften fuer Nichtmitglieder:*
unverkaeuflich. *Beantwortung der Anfragen:* schriftlich in deutscher und englischer
Sprache. *Forschungsgebiet:* Schleswig-Holstein. *Vorsitzender:* Irmgard Khuen,
Esmarchstr 28, D-2300 Kiel 1.
Membership sub.: DM 40.-Students DM 10.-. *Journal:* named above. *Published:*
annually. Not for sale to non members. *Mail enquiries:* Answered in writing in
German or English. Please enclose international coupons with your inquiries. *Re-
search area:* Schleswig-Holstein. *President:* named above.

● **AMERICAN/SCHLESWIG-HOLSTEIN HERITAGE SOCIETY (ASHHS)**
PO Box 21, LECLAIRE, IA, 52753, USA.
President: Glenn Sievers. *Secretary:* Jean Mumm.

GREECE – HELLAS

● **HERALDIC & GENEALOGICAL SOCIETY** *
56 Patriarchou Ioakim St., GR-10676, ATHENS, Greece.
Tel.: 30.1.7235792. *Office hours:* every Thurs. 6-9pm. Open also to non members.
Membership: $20 yearly. *Journal: DELTION ERALDIKIS KAI GENEALOGIKIS ETERIAS* (Bulletin of Hellenic Heraldic and Genealogical Society). Published yearly, free for members, for non members price $13.00. 8 issues have been published (every article on heraldry, Genealogy and sigilography is covered by a summary in English). The Society organises lectures and symposiums. *President:* Anthony Delenda.

HUNGARY

● **HISTORICAL SOCIETY OF HUNGARY (GENEALOGY SECTION)** *
C/o Faculty of Letters, University Eoetveos Lorand, Pesti Barnabas utca 1, H-1052, BUDAPEST V, Hungary.
Tel.: 180 966. *Vice President:* Dr. Ivan Bertenyi.

● **MAGYAR HERALDIKAI ES GENEALOGIAI TARSASAG** *
Ungarische Heraldische und Genealogische Gesellschaft
Budapest V. Pesti Barnabas u.l., Elte BTK, 1364 Budapest Pf. 107, H-1364, Hungary.
Präsident: Dr Prof Kállay István. *Vizepräsident:* Dr Prof Bertényi Iván. *Sekretär:* Dr Pandula Attila. *Forschungsgebiet:* Heraldik, Genealogie, Faleristik, Siegelkunde unsw.

ICELAND

● **AETTFRAEDIFELAGID (THE GENEALOGICAL SOCIETY)** *
Postholf 829, IS-121 REYKJAVICK, Island (Iceland).
Newsletter: 3 per year. *Research Enquiries:* Cost of entries on application. *Membership:* $4.00. *Other Particulars:* Most of our research takes place at libraries and The National Archives facilities in Reykjavik. Our Society has published censuses of 1703, 1801, 1816 and 1845 comprising the entire population of the country. We are now planning the publication of the 1910 census (publ. year probably 1986). Everybody is welcome to visit the National Archives at no cost. Since the National Archives offer no service to genealogists through post, genealogical inquiries are referred to individual membes of our Society. All inquiries must be very specific. *Chairperson:* Mr. John Gislason. *Secretary:* Mr. Arngrimur Sigurdsson, B.A.

INTERNATIONAL

● **ASSOCIATION OF PROFESSIONAL GENEALOGISTS**
Box 11601, SALT LAKE CITY, Utah 84147, USA.
Publication: APG QUARTERLY 4 per year. Available to non members at $10.00 per issue. APG members get 15% discount on publications, back issues, newsletter issues, ads., etc. *Membership:* US $35.00; Canada US$35.00; overseas US$45.00. *President:* Shirley Langdon Wilcox.

● **CONFEDERATION INTERNATIONALE DE GENEALOGIE ET D'HERALDIQUE** *
Secrétariatgénéral: 24 rue Saint-Louis-en-i'Ile, F-75004 PARIS, France.
President: Mr. Cecil R. Humphery Smith. *Secretary:* M. Francois-Louis a'Weng.

- **INTERNATIONAL GENEALOGY FELLOWSHIP OF ROTARIANS**
  5721 Antietam Drive, SARASOTA, Florida 33581, USA.
  Library: As above. Open by appointment. Open to non members, daily fee of $5.00
  hr. *Journal: ROTA-GENE* 6 per year. Available to non members at $15.00 yr. *Research Enquiries:* Free to members. *Membership:* $15.00. *Worldwide Membership:*
  Non-Rotarians urged to subscribe to *ROTA-GENE* . *President:* James E. Bellarts.
  Secretary: Charles D. Townsend.

- **INTERNATIONAL SOCIETY FOR BRITISH GENEALOGY AND FAMILY
  HISTORY**
  PO Box 20425, CLEVELAND, OH, 44120, USA.
  Newsletter: 4 per year, included with individual membership US$10.00. Reserved enquiries of 60 words or less free for members only. Subscriptions for Societies & Institutions US$10.00. British Genealogical Publications for sale (US$). *President:* Joy
  Wade Moulton. *Secretary:* Gracelouise Moore. *Editor:* Joy Wade Moulton.

- **FAMILY HISTORY LIBRARY OF THE CHURCH OF JESUS CHRIST OF
  LATTER-DAY SAINTS.**
  35 N. West Temple Street, SALT LAKE CITY, Utah, 84150 USA.
  Library: As above. *Hours:* Mon. 7.30am-6.00pm; Tues.-Fri. 7.30am-10.00pm; Sat.
  7.30am-5.00pm. The microfilm holdings of the library are available through over
  1500 family history centres. A list of local centres is available by writing to the above
  address. The library is open to non members. *Director:* David M. Mayfield.

IRELAND-EIRE

ALL IRELAND (see also below BASED OUTSIDE IRELAND)

- **IRISH FAMILY HISTORY SOCIETY**
  PO Box 36, NAAS, Co. Kildare, Rep. of Ireland.
  Journal: IRISH FAMILY HISTORY annually. *Membership:* IR£10.00 (US$20.00)
  which includes the journal and two newsletters. Society formed in 1984, the objects of
  the society include the promotion of Irish family history through the indexing of
  parish records and census returns, the collection of old wills, estate rentals, the compilation of tombstone records and other genealogical sources. The Society is keen to
  'repatriate' information from overseas on Irish emigrants to fill in the gaps in Irish
  genealogical material. *Chairman:* Mr Noel Reid, Clane, Co. Kildare.

REPUBLIC

(Note: some of the following are government repositories, see also list of repositories in front of this Directory)

CLARE (CLA)

- **CLARE HERITAGE CENTRE**
  Corofin, Co. CLARE, Ireland.
  i Tel.: 065-27955 . Centre open Weekdays 9-5pm. plus weekends by appointment.
  Large collection of indexes to church registers.

CORK (COR)

- **CORK HERITAGE CENTRE ***
  P.O. Box 17, Bandon, CORK, Ireland.
  Indexing of parish records of RC dioceses of Cork & Ross, Church of Ireland, and
  West Cork Methodist Graveyard surveys. *Research Fees:* A fee of £20 ($25) covers a
  preliminary report and administrative cost and includes an initial search of source
  material. A fee of up to £75 ($100) may be required to complete a full search and
  cover all expenses and time expended by the Centre up to eight hours. *Secretary:*
  John Hurley.

DONEGAL (DON)

- **RAMELTON HERITAGE PROJECT**
  Parochial Centre, Tank Road, Pamelton, Co. DONEGAL, Ireland.
  Indexes of most of the Presbyterian, Church of Ireland and Methodist records for the
  County, and also Ramelton Roman Catholic parish. A fee of £20.00 covers a prelimi-
  nary report and initial search of source material. A fee of up to £75.00 may be re-
  quired for a full 8 hour search. *Co-ordinator:* Derek McDermott.

GALWAY (GAL)

- **GALWAY COUNTY FAMILY HISTORY SOCIETY**
  (Galway Genealogical Research Society)
  Postal Address: 46 Maunsells Park, GALWAY CITY, IRL.
  Personal Callers: Research Centre, 4 New Docks, Galway City, Ireland. Continuing a
  project of indexing parish records and the sources for genealogical research in the
  Galway region. *Project Co-Ordinator* Mrs N. Silke. The following RC parishes in-
  dexed: Athenry: Castlegar: Claregalway: Clifden: Headford: Rahoon: all Galway
  City 3 Parishes. All County Galway Trade Directories indexed. Registration fee of
  £20 (sterling), US$40.00 for initial evaluation of your research problem or origin &
  history of family Surname. Many publications for sale. List & prices on request.
  Please enclose 2 I.R.C. with inquiries.

- **GALWAY EAST**
  Woodford Heritage Centre. Woodview House, WOODFORD, Co. Galway, Ireland.

LEITRIM (LET)

- **LEITRIM HERITAGE CENTRE**
  Cc. Library, BALLINAMORE, Co. Leitrim, Ireland.
  Tel.: (078) 44012. *Other particulars:* All church records of baptism, marriage and
  death for all churches are indexed up to 1900. All graveyard inscriptions are collected
  and indexed. Other records, including newspapers are indexed. *Research:* Short
  search £45 (US$80) and full report £60 (US$100). Write for particulars.

LIMERICK (LIM)

- **LIMERICK REGIONAL ARCHIVES**
  The Granary, Michael St., Limerick City, Ireland.
  Hours: 10am-4.30pm. *Contact:* Dr. Chris O'Mahony, Tel. 061-319101.

LOUTH (LOU) (see ARMAGH under Northern Ireland)

MAYO (MAY)

- **MAYO FAMILY RESEARCH SOCIETY**
  Bushfield House, HOLLYMOUNT, Co. MAYO, Ireland.
  Formed in 1985. *Membership:* £10. *Recording Secretary:* Brigid Clesham.

- **NORTH MAYO FAMILY HISTORY RESEARCH CENTRE**
  Enniscoe, Crossmolina, Co. Mayo, Ireland.
  Partial research service.

- **SOUTH MAYO FAMILY RESEARCH CENTRE**
  Town Hall, BALLINROBE, Co. Mayo, Ireland.
  Research contact: Gerard M. Delaney.

MEATH (MEA)

- **MEATH HERITAHE CENTRE**
  High Street, TRIM, Co. Meath, Ireland.
  Founded 1987. Indexing parish records and collecting family history material for the

County including monumental inscriptions. *Project co-ordinator:* Noel E. French. *Research:* fee of £10.00 is charged for initial evaluation of your research problem.

OFFALY (OFF)

● **OFFALY FAMILY HISTORY SOCIETY**
Charleville Road, Tullamore, Co. OFFALY, Ireland.
Most church records in Co. Offaly indexed plus some for Counties Laois and Westmeath. Write for further details to John Kearney including two international reply coupons.

ROSCOMMON (ROS)

● **COUNTY ROSCOMMON HERITAGE & GENEALOGY CENTRE**
Church Street, STROKESTOWN, Ireland.
Genealogical information pertaining to all parishers of the County and many other sources available. *Research:* A fee of IR£30 covers a preliminary report and includes an initial search of source material. Write for costs of a more extensive search.

SLIGO (SLI)

● **SLIGO FAMILY RESEARCH SOCIETY**
Columban Centre, Castle Street, SLIGO, Ireland.
Tele.: (071) 43728.

● **SLIGO HERITAGE & GENEALOGICAL CENTRE**
Stephen's Street, SLIGO, Ireland.

TIPPERARY (TIP)

● **NENAGH DISTRICT HERITAGE SOCIETY**
The Heritage Centre, NENAGH, Co. Tipperary, Ireland.
Has gravestone inscriptions and indexed transcripts of parish Registers, all denominations, for north-west Tipperary. Contact the administrator for research fees.

● **THURLES PARISH RECORDS**
Thurles Teachers Centre, Ursuline Convent, THURLES, Co. Tipperary, Ireland.
Hours: 3.30-7.30pm Mon. to Thurs. Tel. (0504) 23365. Have baptismal and matrimonial records for 21 parishes in the Diocese of Cashel & Emly (covering a good portion of Tipperary County).

● **TIPPERARY HERITAGE UNIT**
Marian Hall, St Michael's St., Tipperary. Ireland.
Tel.: (062) 52725. Indexing of parish records of Archdiocese of Cashel & Emily. *Research fees:* £10.00 (US$17.60) for an initial search, £25.00 (US$44.00) for a more detailed search. *Project Co-ordinator:* Mrs Anne P. Moloney.

WATERFORD (WAT)

● **WATERFORD HERITAGE SURVEY**
Jenkins Lane, WATERFORD, Ireland.
Parish register indexing centre for county Waterford.

WEXFORD (WEX)

● **WEXFORD FAMILY HISTORY SOCIETY**
C/o Mrs Eithne Scallan, Hon. Sec., Saint Magdalen's House, WEXFORD, Ireland.
Organises monthly lectures. *Meetings:* In Wexford town, 2nd Mon. each month. *President:* Mr Hilary Murphy.

NORTHERN IRELAND

- **NORTH OF IRELAND FAMILY HISTORY SOCIETY**
  Queens University, Dept of Education, 69 University St, BELFAST, BT7 1HL N.Irl.
  Journal: NORTH IRISH ROOTS 2 per year. Available to associate members. *Fees:*
  £4.50 stg UK, £5.50 stg Republic of Ireland, £6.50 stg Continental Europe, £7.50 stg
  Residents in other parts of the world. *President:* Randal D. Gill. *Correspondence Secretary:* (Associate Membership) Charles McClatchey. The Society fosters interest in
  the study of family history, with special reference to families with roots in this part of
  Ireland. At present the Society has seven branches in the North of Ireland.

- **ULSTER HISTORICAL FOUNDATION**
  68 Balmoral Ave., BELFAST, BT9 6NY, Northern Ireland.
  Tel.: (0232) 681365. *Interest List:* 1 per year. *Familia:* 1 per year; journal of the Ulster
  Genealogical and Historical Guild. Available to non members £4.00 each (add £2.00
  for airmail). Research enquiries invited, prompt search assessment service. *Membership:* £12. *Secretary:* Mr J.A. Walsh.

ARMAGH (ARM)

- **ARMAGH RECORDS CENTRE**
  Archdiocese of Armagh, Ara Coeli, ARMAGH, BT61 7QY, N. Ireland.
  Research: Searches in computerised indexes of Catholic parish registers for most of
  Co. Armagh, a large part of Co. Tyrone and all of Co. Louth. A deposit of £10.00.

CAVAN (CAV)

- **CAVAN HERITAGE & GENEALOGY CENTRE**
  C/o Cavan County Library, CAVAN, Ireland.

LONDONDERRY (LDY)

- **DERRY GENEALOGY CENTRE**
  Heritage Library, 14 Bishop St., DERRY, BT48 6PW, N. Ireland.
  Indexes of 1831 census, tithe & Griffiths records. Have begun to computerise pre-1900 B.M.D's of RC Diocese of Derry. *Co-odrinator:* Brian Mitchell, *Assistant:* Ms
  Christine McDaid. Write for details of publications and research services.

BASED OUTSIDE IRELAND

- **IRISH GENEALOGICAL RESEARCH SOCIETY**
  Library: at the Challoner Club, 61 Pont St., LONDON, SW1X 0BG.
  Hours: Sat. 1430-1730. (ex. Christmas & Easter). *Librarian:* T.G. Chartres. *Membership:* £12.00 Stg. *Journal: THE IRISH GENEALOGIST* issued annually to members.
  The Society is a learned registered charity composed of several hundred members. It
  does not offer a research service. Visitors fee to Library £3.00 per afternoon. (Society
  founded in 1936.) *Hon. Secretary:* Miss R. McCutcheon. Branch for members resident in Norhtern Ireland and Irish Republic *Hon. Secretary:* Dermot Blunden, 6
  Eaton Brae, Orwell Rd., Dublin 14, Ireland.

- **THE IRISH FAMILY NAMES SOCIETY**
  P.O. Box 2095, LA MESA, CA 92043-2095, USA.
  Newsletter: 3 per year. Available to members at $12.00. *Book: A GUIDE TO IRISH
  ROOTS* $19.95 in U.S., outside U.S. $24.95. Post Paid surface mail. *Other Particulars:*
  We collect and publish the traditional origin of Irish families. Our findings are published in book form. *Director:* William P. Durning.

- **IRISH GENEALOGICAL SOCIETY**
  PO Box 16585, SAINT PAUL, MN 55116, USA.
  Library: Located at Minnesota Genealogical Society (see under USA) Tel. (612) 222-6929. Irish day at Library, 2nd Sat each month. *Membership:* $10.00 *President:* Dan
  Moriarty. *Library Chair:* Beth Mullinax, Tel. (612) 574-1436.

ITALY

- **ACCADEMIA INTERNAZIONALE DI ARALDICA AIA ***
  Consulta Internazionale Araldica CIA
  Via Vivaldi, 13, 00199, ROMA, Italy.

- **ASSOCIAZIONE 'HISTORIAE FIDES' ***
  Via Francesco Petrarca, 4, 20123, MILANO, Italy.

- **COLLEGIO ARALDICO**
  Conte Raoul Bertini Frassoni, Via S. Maria dell'Anima, 16, 00186, ROMA, Italy.
  Tel: 06 656 13 95.

- **ISTITUTO COCCIA ***
  Borgo Santa Croce, 6, 50122, FIRENZE, Italy.
  Tel: 055 24 29 14.

- **ISTITUTO GENEALOGICO ITALIANO ***
  Palazzo Gondi, via Torta, 14, 50122, FIRENZE, Italy.

- **ISTITUTO GENEALOGICO ***
  Conti Guelfi Camajani, Palazzo Manetti, Via Santo Spirito, 27, 50125, FIRENZE,
  Italy.
  Tel: 055 21 30 90 — 26 31 38.

- **SOCIETA ITALIANA DI STUDI ARALDICI**
  Via Regis 26, 10064 PINEROLO, (TO), Italy.

- **STUDIO GENEALOGICO ***
  Via Topino, 24, 00122, ROMA, Italy.
  Tel: 06 85 06 10.

LUXEMBURG

- **CONSEIL HERALDIQUE DU LUXEMBOURG ***
  Monsieur R. Matagne, 3 rue Bellevue, LUXEMBOURG.

- **ARCHIVES DE L'ETAT DU GRAND DUCHE DE LUXEMBOURG ***
  Plateau du Saint-Esprit, LUXEMBOURG.

- **ARCHIVES DE LA VILLE DE LUXEMBOURG ***
  Hotel de Ville, Place Guillaume, LUXEMBOURG

- **GRAND DUCHE DE LUXEMBOURG ***
  Association Luxembourgeoise de généalogie
  12 Saandgaass, L-5404 BECH-KLEIRMACHER, Luxembourg.

NETHERLANDS — NEDERLAND

- **NEDERLANDSE GENEALOGISCHE VERENIGING**
  Postbus 976, NL-1000 AZ, AMSTERDAM, Netherlands.
  Library: Adr. Dortsmanplein 3a, NL-1411 RC, Naarden. *Hours:* 20-22h. Thursday,
  11-16h. Saturday. *Journal: GENS NOSTRA* 12 per year. *Membership:* Hfl. 55. *President:* Mr. J.W.M. Rademaker. *Secretary:* M. Ijzerman. *Other particulars:* The NGV
  consists of about 7000 members all over the country. It is a completely voluntary association with 29 departments.

- **CENTRAAL BUREAU VOOR GENEALOGIE**
  Postanschrift: P.O. Box 11755, NL-2502 AT 'S-GRAVENHAGE, Netherlands.
  Office & Reading rooms: Prins Willem-Alexanderhof 22, NL-2595 BE 'S-GRAVENHAGE. *Tel.:* 070-81 46 51 international: 0031-70 81 46 51. *Reading room
  hours:* Mo-Fr 9.30-16.00; Tues. 19.00-21.30, Sat. 9.00-13.00. *Reading room Heraldry:*

Mo and Tuesday evening closed. Visitors fee for a non member $3.50 a day. *Membership:* ('Friend'): $34.00. *Journal: MEDEDELINGEN* (quarterly). *Annual: JAARBOEK* . Charges for advertisement in our journal per mm of a column: $1.75. *Research rates:* $34.00 per hour and 'Friends' $20.00. Mentioned amounts are minimun rates. Registration of coat-of-arms: $430.00. *President:* Mr A. Snethlage. *Director:* Drs. A.D. de Jonge. *Sub-directors:* C.W. Delforterie and N. Plomp.

- **STICHTING "GENEALOGISCH CENTRUM ZEELAND"**
  Wyngaatdstraat 3, 4461DA GOES, Netherlands.
  Hours: Thurs. 9.30-15.00 and 19.00-21.00. Every first Saturday of the month 9.30-16.00. Donation Hfl 20,-/year or Hfl 3,-/day. *Other Particulars:* Collection with biographical index of more than 20,000 surnames, over 2 million genealogical data, mainly from 1585-1810. The society has published several books.

- **KONINKLIJK NEDERLANDSCH GENOOTSCHAP VOOR GESLACHT – EN WAPENKUNDE.**
  Prins Willem Alexanderhof 24, 2595 BE 'S-GRAVENHAGE, Netherlands.
  Journal: DE NEDERLANDSCHE LEEUW , 12 per year. *Membership:* $43.00.

- **ZUIDHOLLANDSE VERENIGING VOOR GENEALOGIE**
  Postbox 404, 3000 AK ROTTERDAM, Netherlands.
  Bibliotheek: (gratis boekuitlening aan leden) Jacob Marisplein 9 te Rotterdam (Hillegersberg). *Geopend:* iedere 2e zaterdagmiddag van de maand (uitgezonderd juli en augustus) van 13.00 tot 16.00 uur en iedere 4e dinsdagavond van de mmand (uitgezonderd juli, augustus en december) van 19.30 tot 22.00 uur. *Lidmaatschap:* f.50.-per jaar, voor leden in het buitenland f.60.-per jaar (wijzeigingen voorbehouden) Aanmelden als lid d.m.v. een briefkaart aan het secretariaat. Men ontvangt hierna een acceptgirokaart. Het maandblad *ONS VOORGESLACHT* verschijnt 11 maal per jaar (1 dubbelnummer) en biedt een gervarieerd aanbod van genealogische, heraldische, historische en bronnenpublikaties. Leden kunnen gratis gebruik maken van de Vraag en Antwoord rubriek. Met ingang van 1988 worden er eigen lezingen en contactavonden gehouden die vrij toegankelijk zijn voor leden en niet-leden.

- **CHARLES MIX COUNTY GENEALOGICAL SOCIETY**
  Kardoenhof 57, 3193 JD HOOGVLIET, RT, Netherlands.
  U.S.A. Address: P.O. Box 488, Platte, SD 57369. De verening stelt zich tot doel het bevorderen van de beoefening van Genealogie in Charles Mix County, Zuid Dakota en het verzamelen van genealogisch en historisch materiaal m.b.t. Charles Mix County. In noordelijk Charles Mix County vestigden zich, in de tweede helft van de 19e eeuw, met name veel Nederlandse en Scandinavische emigraten.

- **CALEDONIAN SOCIETY**
  Dutch-Scottish Genealogical and Culturel Society
  Secretary: Mrs A.A.M. Sutherland, Grote Spie 53, 4819 CN, BREDA, Netherlands.
  Genealogical divission: Mrs G. Grevers, Leith, Carel Fabritiuslaan 27, 2343 SE, OEGSTGEEST, Netherlands. *Membership:* Hfl. 35.-p.a. *Journal: MEDEEDELINGENBLAD* .

- **PRAE-1600 CLUB**
  De Komme 3, 4421ES KAPELLE, Netherlands.

- **ZEEUWS DOCUMENTATIECENTRUM (ZEALAND DOCUMENTATION CENTRE)**
  Kousteensedijk 7, 4331 JE, MIDDELBURG, Netherlands.
  Post-address: P.O. Box 8004, 4330 EA, MIDDELBURG, Nederland. *Opening hours:* mo. 5.30pm-9.00pm, tu.-fr. 10.00am-9.00pm, sa. 10.00am-1.00pm, su. closed. We can offer the genealogist and other interested people documentation about every town and city in the province of Zealand and on almost every item of daily life in this century and sometimes before. For instance, there are maps, postcards and photographs to illustrate your family history as far as it is part of the Zealand history.

NEW ZEALAND

- **NEW ZEALAND SOCIETY OF GENEALOGISTS, INC.**
  P.O. Box 8795, AUCKLAND 3, New Zealand.
  Journal: THE NEW ZEALAND GENEALOGIST 6 per year plus index. *Research Enquiries:* Overseas enquirers are offered limited free research on receipt of $NZ2.00 donation. *Membership:* New Members joining fee $7.00. annual subscription $31.00. Meetings held at over 50 locations throughout New Zealand. *President:* Mr Bruce Ralston. *Secretary:* Mrs Kay Guthrie.

- **THE NEW ZEALAND FAMILY HISTORY SOCIETY, INC.**
  P.O. Box 13,301 ARMAGH, CHRISTCHURCH, New Zealand.
  Library: 399 Papanui Road, Christchurch. *Hours:* 1st Tues. of month (evening). *Morning Learners Group:* Alternate Wed. mornings 10am-12n, 399 Papanui Rd. *Journal: THE FAMILY TREE* 4 per year $4.00 each. *Research Enquiries Notices:* $2.00 per entry to non members. *Membership:* $20.00, badge $5.00. *Meetings:* at Library, 1st Tues. each month at 7.45pm. *President:* Mr W. Greenwood. *Secretary:* Mrs J. Lord.

- **N.Z. FENCIBLE SOCIETY, INC**
  PO Box 8415, Symonds St., AUCKLAND, 3, NZ.
  Journal: FENCIBLE BUGLE 6 per year. *Research Enquiries:* Enquirers are offered limited free research. *Membership:* $2.00 joining fee, $15.00 per annum. *President:* Mr K.J. McAnulty. *Secretary:* Mrs R. Singleton.

NORWAY

- **NORSK SLEKTSHISTORISK FORENING ***
  PO Box 9562, Egertorget, 0128 OSLO 2, Norway.
  Library: As above. *Hours:* Thurs. 6-8pm. *Journal: NORSK SLEKTSHISTORISK TIDSSKRIFT* Available to non members on request. *Research Enquiries:* Members free. *Membership:* US $30.00. *President:* Per Seland.

- **VESTERHEIM GENEALOGICAL CENTER**
  Norwegian-American Museum.
  Library: (by appointment) 4909 Sherwood Road, Madison, WI 53711, USA. *Journal: NORWEGIAN TRACKS . Editor:* Gerhard B. Naeseth (C/o library). *Subscription:* $16.00 including Membership: in Norwegian-American Museum, 502 W. Water St., Decorah, IA 52101, USA.

- **NORWEGIAN AMERICAN HISTORICAL ASSOCIATION**
  St. Olaf College, NORTHFIELD, MN 55057, USA.
  Newsletter Editor: Lloyd Hustvedt.

OESTERREICH (siehe AUSTRIA)

POLAND

- **TOWARZYSTWO GENEALOGICZNO-HERALDYCZNE**
  Wodna 27, Palac Gorkow, 61-781 POZNAN, Poland.
  Membership cost: US$15.00 (or equivalent) paid with bank draft or International Money Order. *Journal:* GENS, available to members only (annual subscription US$10.00 *Published:* quarterly, with summaries of articles in English. *Library & Archives:* open daily 9.00-15.00 above address. *Enquiries:* answered by the President only on general matters. Specific enquiries or requests for research are made available to members for individual contacts. The Genealogical Heraldic Society was founded in Sept. 1987 as the first one of this kind in Poland. *Available to members are:* lists of surnames researched by members, booklet on genealogical research for beginners, bimonthly information sheet in Polish and English. *Special Projects:* compilation of bibliography on Polish genealogy & heraldry. *Pres:* Rafal T. Prinke.

- **NACZELNA ARCHIWOW DYREKCJA (POLISH NATIONAL ARCHIVES)**
  Ul Dluga 6 Skr. POCZT. 1005 00-950, WARSZAWA, Polska (Poland)

- **POLISH GENEALOGICAL SOCIETY, INC. ***
  984 N. Milwaukee Ave., CHICAGO, IL 60622, USA.

- **POLISH NOBILITY ASSOCIATION**
  Villa Anneslie, 529 Dunkirk Road, ANNESLIE, MD 21212, USA.
  Library: As above. Open by appointment. *Newsletter:* 1 per year. *Research Enquiries:* Cost of entry $25.00. *Membership:* $25.00. *President:* Prince Roger Chylinski-Polubinski. *Secretary:* Leonard Suligowski, USA. Count Leonard v. Leszcynski, Europe.

PORTUGAL

- **INSTITUTO PORTUGUES DE HERALDICA ***
  Monsieur Jose Bernard Guedes, rue Cidade Quelimane, 21, 1, 1800 LISBOA, Portugal.

SCOTLAND

NATIONAL

- **SCOTTISH GENEALOGY SOCIETY**
  21 Howard Place, EDINBURGH, EH3 5JY, Scotland.
  Library: 15 Victoria Terrace, Edinburgh, EH1 2JL. *Journal: SCOTTISH GENEALOGIST* 4 per year. Available to non members at £3.25. *Research Enquiries in Journal:* Not more than 150 words. Free to members. £2.00 to non members. *Membership:* £12.00 (US $24.00). *Chairperson:* D.R. Torrance, B.Sc. *Secretary:* Miss Joan P.S. Ferguson, M.A., A.L.A.

- **SCOTS ANCESTRY RESEARCH SOCIETY**
  3 Albany St., EDINBURGH, EH1 3PY, Scotland.
  Set up in 1946 as a non-profit making organisation to assist persons of Scottish descent to trace their ancestry. Please send s.a.e. for leaflet.

- **SCOTTISH ASSOCIATION OF FAMILY HISTORY SOCIETIES**
  Chairman: Mrs M. Johnston, 12 Glamis Tce., DUNDEE, DD2 1NA, Scotland.

ABERDEEN

- **ABERDEEN & N.E. SCOTLAND FAMILY HISTORY SOCIETY**
  152 King St., ABERDEEN, AB2 3BD, Scotland.
  Research facilities: available by post for-out-of-town members, and at our Centre and Shop for personal callers. *Journal:* 4 per year. *Membership:* ordinary £8, family £7, overseas £12. *Chairman:* Bill Diack. *Secretary:* Violet Murray. *Membership Secretary:* Ronald Leith.

BORDERS

- **BORDERS FAMILY HISTORY SOCIETY**
  Secretary: Mrs C. Trotter, 15 Edinbugh Road, GREENLAW, Berwickshire, TD10 6XF, Scotland.

DUMFRIES & GALLOWAY

- **DUMFRIES & GALLOWAY FAMILY HISTORY SOCIETY**
  C/o Membership Secretary (see below).
  Membership: £6.00, family £7.50, students & seniors £5.00. *Chairman:* Mr Sandy Hall. *Editor:* Mrs Moira Aitken. *Membership Secretary:* Mrs Doreen Morgan. Corsewell Mill Cottage, Kirkcolm, WIG, DG9 0NZ, Scotland. *Secretary:* Mrs Betty

Watson, Kylelea, Corsock, Castle Douglas, DG7 3DN. *Exchange Publications Sec.:* Mrs Margaret Robinson, Dykenook, Colvend, Kirk., DG5 4QA, Scot.

GLASGOW

- **GLASGOW & WEST OF SCOTLAND FAMILY HISTORY SOCIETY**
  3 Fleming Road, BISHOPTON, PA7 5HW, Scotland.
  Newsletter: 2 per year. *Research Enquiries:* For members only in Newsletter. *Membership:* £6.00 (£10 airmail post). *Membership Sec.:* Mrs Mary Buchanan, 75 Antonine Road, Bearsden, G61 4DS, Sct. *Secretary:* Frank Inglis, (top address).

INVERNESS

- **HIGHLAND FAMILY HISTORY SOCIETY**
  Library: C/o Reference Room, Inverness Public Library, Farraline Park, Inverness, IV1 1NH, Sct.
  Hours: Mon.-Sat. Public Library Hours. Available to non members. *Journal: HIGHLAND F.H.S. JOURNAL* 4 per year. Members only. *Research Enquiries:* Members free, non members £1.00 per query. *Membership:* ordinary £6.00, pensioner £4.00. Overseas £8.00 & £6.00. *Other Particulars:* The Society does not act as a research agency. The material in the Society's library is a private collection to which the general public may have access but no borrowing facilities. *Chairman:* Neil Murray. *Secretary:* Mrs Maclean of Dochgarroch.

- **LARGS & DISTRICT FAMILY HISTORY GROUP**
  Secretary: Mrs J. Gillan, 28 Walkerston Ave., LARGS, KA30 8ER, Scotland.

TAY VALLEY

- **TAY VALLEY FAMILY HISTORY SOCIETY**
  C/o Carlton Gilruth, Solicitors, 30 Whitehall St., DUNDEE DD1 4AL, Scotland.
  Newsletter: 3 per year published. *Research Enquiries:* Free to members. *Membership:* £6.00 plus £2.00 overseas airmail. *Chairman:* Mr Euan K. Collins. *Secretary:* Mrs Alison Lawson.

SOUTH AFRICA

- **GENEALOGICAL SOCIETY OF SOUTH AFRICA**
  P.O. Box 1344, KELVIN, 2054, South Africa.
  Journal: FAMILIA 4 per year. *Newsletter:* 4 per year. *Membership:* R30.00. *Chairman:* Robert Laing. *Secretary:* A.J. Smith.

- **SOUTHERN TRANSVAAL BRANCH, G.S.S.A.**
  P.O. Box 57081, SPRINGFIELD, 2137.
  Membership: R40.00 which includes membership of the G.S.S.A. *Presidnet:* Conrad Mercer. *Secretary:* Mrs Natalie Da Silva.

- **HERALDRY SOCIETY OF SOUTHERN AFRICA (Est. 1953)**
  P.O. Box 4839, CAPE TOWN, 8000.
  Journal: ARMA 4 per year. *Membership:* R20.00. *Chairman:* Dr. C. Pama. *Secretary:* M.L. Purcell.

- **HUMAN SCIENCES RESEARCH COUNCIL**
  Genealogical Research Centre, Private Bag X41, PRETORIA, 0001.
  Library Hours: Mon.-Fri. 7.30am-4.00pm. Open to non members, membership and/or specific services available at a charge.

- **SWISS SOCIETIES IN SOUTHERN AFRICA**
  P.O. Box 3626, JOHANNESBURG, 2000.

- **HUGUENOT MEMORIAL MUSEUM**
  P.O. Box 37, FRANSCHHOEK, Cape 7690. (Tel. 02212 2532.)
  Research into Huguenot families who came to the Cape c.1680-1730.

- **SOUTH EAST WITWATERSRAND FAMILY HISTORY SOCIETY**
  Chairman: Mrs E. Harrison, 76 Holzgen St., Brackenhurst, Alberton 1450.
  Journal and members interest list. Starter Pack to beginners.

- **WEST RAND FAMILY HISTORY SOCIETY**
  P.O. Box 760, FLORIDA, 1710, South Africa.
  Membership: R15.00 per calendar year per individual or family unit. *Chairman:* Mark
  Tapping. *Meetings:* 1st Thurs. montly at 19h00 in the Community Room, Westgate
  Shopping Centre, Roodepoort.

- **1820 SETTLERS ASSOCIATION AT THE ALBANY MUSEUM**
  Somerset St., GRAHAMSTOWN, 6140. (Tel. 0461 22397.)
  Information available on 1820 Settler families and their descendants.

- **KAFFRARIAN MUSEUM**
  P.O. Box 1434, KING WILLIAM'S TOWN, Cape 5600. (Tel. 0433 24506.)
  Research into German settlers who came to British Kaffraria in 1857 and 1858-1859.

SPAIN — ESPAGNE

- **ARCHIVO HISTORICO NACIONAL**
  Serrano, 115., 28006, MADRID, Espagne.
  Tel: 2618003, 2618004, 2618005, 5635923. *Heures d'ouverture:* 8-18 heures (juillet et
  août: 8-15 heures). Prix d'entrée et d'emprunt d'un livre: On demande seulement une
  lettre d'introduction (d'un professeur, institution culturelle ou ambassade) et deux
  photographies. Il n'y a pas — d'emprunt des livres.

- **SOCIEDAD TOLEDANA DE ESTUDIOS HERALDICOS y GENEALOGICOS**
  Apartado de Correos No. 373, TOLEDO, Espagñe (Spain).

SWEDEN — SVERIGE

- Member organisations of The Federation of Swedish Genealogical Societies:
  The organisations are listed in geographical order. All welcomes inquiries, but do not
  forget to enclose 2 IRCs for your reply.

- **SVERIGES SLÄKTFORSKARFÖRBUND (The Federation of Swedish Genealogical
  Societies)**
  P.O.Box 15222, S-161 15 BROMMA, SWEDEN
  Chairman: Allan Grund. *Secretary:* Elisabeth Thorsell. *Journal:* Släkthistoriskt For-
  um (5 issues/year), queries accepted, subscription SEK 175 for foreign subscribers.
  The Federation also publishes a Yearbook and 2 issues/year of Svenska Antavlor
  (Swedish Ancestral charts).

- **FÖRENINGEN FÖR DATORHJÄLP I SLÄKTFORSKNINGEN, (DIS) (Swedish
  Society for Computers in Genealogy)**
  Sandgatan 10, kv, S-582 35 LINKÖPING, SWEDEN
  Chairman: Sture Bjelkaker *Secretary:* Olof Cronberg *Journal:* Diskulogen (5/yr).
  Computer program DISGEN 5.O for IBM compatibles, Macintosh.

- **STORSTOCKHOLMS GENEALOGISKA FÖRENING**
  c/o Bergwall, Ringvägen 123, 3 tr, S-116 61 STOCKHOLM, SWEDEN
  Chairman: Leif Gidlöf. *Secretary:* Gunilla Bergwall *Journal:* Anropet (4/yr)

- **BOTVIDSBYGDENS SLÄKTFORSKARFÖRENING**
  c/o Nils Dahlström, Palettvägen 6, S-146 00 TULLINGE, SWEDEN
  Chairman: Carl-Gustaf Lilje

- **SÖDERTÄLJE SLÄKTFORSKARFÖRENING**
  c/o Anna-Stina Strandin-Freij, Rödsippstigen 21, S-153 00 JÄRNA, SWEDEN
  Chairman: Anna-Stina Strandin-Freij *Journal:* Södertäljeprobanden (6/yr)

- **IBM-KLUBBENS SLÄKTFORSKNINGSSEKTION**
  Att: Kent Wallenbro, S-163 92 STOCKHOLM, SWEDEN
  Chairman: Carl-Göran Backgard

- **SÖDRA ROSLAGENS SLÄKTFORSKARFÖRENING**
  c/o Karl-Evert Gustafsson, Söravägen 15, S-184 37 AKERSBERGA, SWEDEN
  Chairman: Karl-Evert Gustafsson

- **SOLLENTUNA SLÄKTFORSKARFÖRENING**
  c/o Rolf Brodin, Folkungavägen 23, S-191 50 SOLLENTUNA, SWEDEN
  Chairman: Rolf Brodin

- **SKANES GENEALOGISKA FÖRBUND**
  c/o Börje Gunnarsson, Goenisses väg 10, S-231 66 TRELLEBORG, SWEDEN
  Chairman: Guno Haska *Journal:* Skane Genealogen

- **MALMÖ SLÄKTFORSKARFÖRENING**
  Box 5160, S-200 71 MALMÖ, SWEDEN
  Chairman: Gösta Andersson

- **LUNDABYGDENS GENEALOGISKA FÖRENING**
  Sankt Laurentiigatan 18, S-222 39 LUND, SWEDEN
  Chairman: Lennart Strandberg *Journal:* Lundagenealogen

- **SÖDERSLÄTTS SLÄKT-OCH HEMBYGDSFORSKARFÖRENING**
  Box 196, S-231 23 TRELLEBORG, SWEDEN
  Chairman: Claes Lindahl *Journal:* Slättforskaren

- **LOMMA-BURLÖV SLÄKT-OCH FOLKLIVSFORSKARE**
  c/o B Nilsson, Kadettvägen 3, S-237 00 BJÄRRED, SWEDEN
  Chairman: Birgitta Nilsson *Journal:* Anskriften

- **ESLÖVSBYGDENS SLÄKT-OCH FOLKLIVSFORSKARE**
  c/o Meijer, Skogsvägen 8, S-241 31 ESLÖV, SWEDEN
  Chairman: Bertil Jahrö *Journal:* Trehäradsbladet

- **MELLANSKANES SLÄKT-& HEMBYGDSFORSKARFÖRENING**
  Magistergatan 4, S-242 32 HÖRBY, SWEDEN
  Chairman: Gösta Sjöholm

- **KÄVLINGEBYGDENS SLÄKT-OCH FOLKLIVSFORSKARFÖRENING**
  Irisgatan 4, S-244 02 FURULUND, SWEDEN
  Chairman: Anna-Stina BÖa" ckström Gustafsson *Journal:* Släktbron

- **STAFFANSTORPS SLÄKTFORSKARFÖRENING**
  Box 7, S-245 00 STAFFANSTORP, SWEDEN
  Chairman: Barbro Lunsjö *Journal:* Släkttavlan

- **HELSINGBORGS SLÄKTFORSKARE-OCH BYGDEFÖRENING**
  c/o Studieförbundet Vuxenskolan, Södergatan 10, S-252 25 HELSINGBORG, SWE-
  DEN
  Chairman: Vally Little-Smith

- **KULLABYGDENS SLÄKTFORSKARE**
  Nicandersgatan 5, S-252 39 HELSINGBORG, SWEDEN
  Chairman: Sven Ragnarsson

- **SVALÖVBYGDENS SLÄKT-OCH FOLKLIVSFORSKARFÖRENING**
  Gyegarden, S-260 23 KAGERÖD, SWEDEN
  Chairman: Harry W Ebelin

- **ASBO SLÄKT-OCH FOLKLIVSFORSKAREFÖRENING**
  c/o Denny Lindau, Hättorna 164, S-260 70 LJUNGBYHED, SWEDEN
  Chairman: Denny Lindau *Journal:* Asbo släktblad

- **BJÄRE SLÄKTRING**
  c/o Henry Johansson, Vejby 257, S-260 83 VEJBYSTRAND, SWEDEN
  Chairman: Henry Johansson

- **ÄNGELHOLMS SLÄKT-OCH FOLKLIVSFORSKARFÖRENING**
  c/o Karl-Erik Härse, Sigridsvägen 8, S-260 83 VEJBYSTRAND, SWEDEN
  Chairman: Malte Pahlsson

- **LANDSKRONABYGDENS SLÄKT-OCH FOLKLIVSFORSKARE**
  c/o Wallin, Ringvägen 13B, S-261 42 LANDSKRONA, SWEDEN
  Chairman: Nils Wallin

- **ÖSTERLENS SLÄKT OCH FOLKLIVSFORSKARE**
  Ingelstorp 10, S-270 21 GLEMMINGEBRO, SWEDEN
  Chairman: Nils-Henrik Salomonsson

- **GÖINGE SLÄKT-OCH HEMBYGDSFORSKARFÖRENING**
  c/o Cixthenson, Pl 9150, S-281 90 HÄSSLEHOLM, SWEDEN
  Chairman: Kjell Jönsson *Journal:* Gydhingen

- **KRISTIANSTADSBYGDENS SLÄKTFORSKARFÖRENING**
  c/o Sundius, Prästall§n 21, S-291 43 KRISTIANSTAD, SWEDEN
  Chairman: Bodil Persson *Journal:* C4häradsbladet

- **HALLANDS GENEALOGISKA FÖRENING**
  Kyrkogatan 12, S-302 42 HALMSTAD, SWEDEN
  Chairman: Sperling Bengtsson *Journal:* Hallandsfararares information

- **BLEKINGE SLÄKTFORSKARFÖRENING**
  c/o Hasselgren, Sommarvägen 7, S-374 30 KARLSHAMN, SWEDEN
  Chairman: Margareta Hasselgren *Journal:* BGF-nytt

- **KRONOBERGS GENEALOGISKA FÖRENING**
  Storgatan 1, S-342 00 ALVESTA, SWEDEN
  Chairman: Harry Hjertquist *Journal:* KGF-Nytt (4/yr)

- **VÄSTRA SVERIGES GENEALOGISKA FÖRENING**
  Postgatan 4, S-411 13 GÖTEBORG, SWEDEN
  Chairman: Johan von Sydow *Journal:* VSGF-bladet (4/yr)

- **FÖRENINGEN ORUSTS SLÄKTFORSKARE,**
  c/o Pär-Uno Appelgren, Slanbärsvägen 6, S-440 80 ELLÖS, SWEDEN
  Chairman: Pär-Uno Appelgren

- **ALINGSAS SLÄKTFORSKARFÖRENING**
  c/o Tor Cullberg, Högen 3802, S-441 63 ALINGSAS, SWEDEN
  Chairman: Tor Cullberg

- **UDDEVALLA SLÄKTFORSKARE**
  Box 117, S-451 16 UDDEVALLA, SWEDEN
  Chairman: Stig Rahm

- **MARKS HÄRADS SLÄKTFORSKARFÖRENING**
  c/o Britt Hagman, Box 3004 Örby, S-511 03 KINNA, SWEDEN
  Chairman: Britt Hagman *Journal:* Markrötter

- **VÄSTGÖTA GENEALOGISKA FÖRENING**
  Box 22, S-515 01 VISKAFORS *Chairman:* Per Ahl§n *Journal:* Västgötagenealogen
  (4/yr)

- **SKÖVDE GENEALOGISKA FÖRENING Box 96068, S-541 06 SKÖVDE, SWEDEN**
  Chairman: Eiler Karlsson

- **MULLSJÖ GENEALOGISKA FÖRENING**
  c/o Tage Andersson, Sjövägen 47, 565 00 MULLSJÖ, SWEDEN
  Chairman: Tage Andersson

- **SÄLLSKAPET ANE FINNVEDEN**
  c/o E Gradeen, Klevaliden 2, S-331 33 VÄRNAMO, SWEDEN
  Chairman: Ewert Apelmo *Journal:* Medlemsblad

- **WAGGERYDS GENEALOGISKA FÖRENING**
  c/o Barbro Lundgren, Badplatsvägen 16, S-567 00 VAGGERYD, SWEDEN
  Chairman: Barbro Lundgren *Journal:* Medlemsblad

- **NÄSSJÖBYGDENS GENEALOGISKA FÖRENING**
  c/o Sven Danielsson, Bäverstigen 29, S-571 42 NÄSSJÖ, SWEDEN
  Chairman: Carl Wilborn Agren *Journal:* Släktposten

- **TRANAS/YDRE SLÄKTFORSKARFÖRENING**
  Manstensvägen 25 A, S-573 36 TRANAS, SWEDEN
  Chairman: Olof Ludvigsson. *Secretary:* Göran Sparrlöf

- **NJUDUNGS GENEALOGISKA FÖRENING**
  Östersandsvägen 15, S-574 34 VETLANDA, SWEDEN
  Chairman: Birger Johansson

- **VIMMERBY-HULTSFREDS SLÄKTFORSKARFÖRENING**
  Humlestigen 16, S-598 00 VIMMERBY, SWEDEN
  Chairman: Gunnar Nilsson

- **KALMAR LÄNS GENEALOGISKA FÖRENING**
  c/o T Alriksson, Lagmansgatan 2 A, 3 tr, S-392 35 KALMAR, SWEDEN
  Chairman: Kerstin Jonmyren

- **PERSON-OCH LOKALHISTORISKT FORSKARCENTRUM (PLF)**
  Box 23, S-572 21 OSKARSHAMN, SWEDEN
  Chairman: Gunnar Källeius. *Secretary:* Sam Blixt *Journal:* PLR-Nytt This society is working on a computerized database of all church records for Kalmar county before 1895.

- **TJUST SLÄKTFORSKARFÖRENING**
  c/o Holger Kanth, Esplanaden 19 A, S-593 31 VÄSTERVIK, SWEDEN
  Chairman: Holger Kanth *Journal:* Wara rötter

- **ÖSTGÖTA GENEALOGISKA FÖRENING**
  c/o Göran Lindahl, Ödegardsgatan 10, S-582 57 LINKÖPING, SWEDEN
  Chairman: Göran Lindahl. *Secretary:* Lars Bäcklund *Journal:* ÖGF-lövet (4/yr)

- **GOTLANDS GENEALOGISKA FÖRENING**
  C/o öhman, Myrstigen 44, S-621 50 VISBY, SWEDEN.
  Chairman: Swen-Erik öhman *Journal:* Orä follk

- **NYKÖPING-OXELÖSUNDS SLAKTFORSKARKLUBB**
  C/o Stalbrand, Gruvvägen 30, S-611 65 NYKöPING, SWEDEN
  Chairman: Margareta Stalbrand *Journal:* Anknytningen

- **KATRINEHOLM-FLEN-VINGAKERS SLAKTFORSKARKLUBB**
  C/o Katrineholms Stadsbibliotek, Box 90, S-641 21 KATRINEHOLM, SWEDEN
  Chairman: Gunvar Christensson

- **ESKILSTUNA STRÄNGNÄS SLÄKTFORSKARKLUBB**
  C/o Lars Henning, Lektorsgatan 14, S-645 30 STRÄNGNÄS, SWEDEN
  Chairman: Lennart Eriksson/Arne Norman *Journal:* Anbudet

- **AMALS SLÄKTFORSKARE**
  C/o Kjell Josefson, Nolbygatan 57, S-662 00 AMAL, SWEDEN
  Chairman: Kjell Josefson

- **VÄRMLANDS SLÄKTFORSKARFORENING**
  C/o L-G Sander, Norra Berghaget, S-667 00 FORSHAGA, SWEDEN
  Chairman: Lars-Gunnar Sander *Journal:* Nytt fran Värmlands släktforskarförening

- **KARLSKOGA-DEGERFORS SLÄKTFORSKARKLUBB**
  C/o Olga Engström, Gösta Berlings väg 33, S-691 38 KARLSKOGA, SWEDEN
  Chairman: Olga Engström *Journal:* Strödda Annotationer (4/yr, in cooperation with
  other nearby societies)

- **HALLSBERGS SLÄKTFORSKARKLUBB**
  C/o Majken Kumlin, Stocksätersvägen 22, S-694 00 HALLSBERG, SWEDEN
  Chairman: Ake Ellbén *Journal:* Strödda Annotationer

- **KUMLA SLÄKTFORSKARKLUBB**
  Byrsta 6609, S-694 00 HALLSBERG, SWEDEN
  Chairman: Evert örnell *Journal:* Strödda Annotationer

- **ASKERSUNDS SLÄKTFORSKARKLUBB**
  C/o Hammervik, Tikanäs, S-696 00 ASKERSUND, SWEDEN
  Chairman: Arne Hammervik *Journal:* Strödda Annotationer

- **ÖREBRO SLÄKTFORSKARE**
  Box 266, S-701 45 öREBRO, SWEDEN
  Chairman: Sture Jacobsson *Journal:* Strödda Annotationer

- **NORA SLÄKTFORSKARKLUBB**
  C/o Dalhammar, Radstugugatan 13, S-713 31 NORA, SWEDEN
  Chairman: Sven Dalhammar. *Secretary:* Bertil Davidsson *Journal:* Anno Domini
  (2/yr)

- **LJUSNARSBERGS SLÄKT-OCH HEMBYGDSFORSKARFÖRENING**
  Björkäng 8080, S-714 00 KOPPARBERG, SWEDEN
  Chairman: Margareta Frykberg

- **VÄSTERAS SLÄKTFORSKARKLUBB**
  C/o Sköld, Orkangatan 4, S-723 48 VÄSTERAS, SWEDEN
  Chairman: Ulla Sköld

- **SALA SLÄKTFORSKARFÖRENING**
  C/o Mats Eriksson, Marsgatan 4, S-733 40 SALA, SWEDEN
  Chairman: Börje Olsson

- **BJÖRKLINGEBYGDENS SLÄKTFORSKARFÖRENING**
  C/o Torbjörn Norman, Puckvägen 16, S-740 30 BJÖRKLINGE, SWEDEN
  Chairman: Torbjörn Norman *Journal:* Gnealogica Betuliensis

- **FÖRENINGEN SLÄKTFORSKARE I UPPLAND**
  C/o Einar Eiserman, Kastanjegatan 7, S-754 34 UPPSALA, SWEDEN
  Chairman: Björn Hagelin *Journal:* Medlemsblad

- **NORRTÄLJE SLÄKTFORSKARFÖRENING**
  Box 280, S-761 28 NORRTÄLJE, SWEDEN
  Chairman: Urban Johansson *Journal:* Anbladet

- **VÄSTERBERGSLAGENS SLÄKTFORSKARE**
  C/o Maj-Britt Jansson, Rotorvägen 20, S-771 00 LUDVIKA, SWEDEN
  Chairman: Jörgen Fryxell *Journal:* Släktforskaren (4/yr)

- **SÄLLSKAPET SLAKTFORSKARNE FAGERSTA**
  C/o Christian Nielsen, Karlavägen 6, S-773 00 FAGERSTA, SWEDEN
  Chairman: Christian Nielsen

- **FOLKARE SLÄKSTFORSKARFÖRENING**
  C/o Birgitta Larhm, Almgatan 28, S-775 00 KRYLBO, SWEDEN
  Chairman: Stig Thorsberg *Journal:* Ansiktet (4/yr)

- **OVANSILJANS SLÄKTFORSKARE**
  C/o T Näs, Vasgatan 32 ö G, S-792 00 MORA, SWEDEN
  Chairman: Torbjörn Näs *Journal:* OS-nytt

- **GÄSTRIKLANDS GENEALOGISKA FÖRENING**
  C/o Elon Sandberg, Durovägen 101, S-803 28 GÄVLE, SWEDEN
  Chairman: Elon Sandberg *Journal:* GGF

- **SÄLLSKAPET SLÄKTFORSKARNA I SANDVIKEN**
  Box 107, S-811 22 SANDVIKEN, SWEDEN
  Chairman: Kristina Arvidsson *Journal:* Stamträdet

- **FORSKARFÖRENINGEN SLÄKT & BYGD**
  Box 277, S-821 02 BOLLNÄS, SWEDEN
  Chairman: Sune Bengtsson

- **FORSKARFÖRENINGEN ALIR**
  C/o Rune Kjellberg, Vretvägen 8, S-826 00, SÖDERHAMN, SWEDEN
  Chairman: Rune Kjellberg *Journal:* Alir anor

- **JÄMTLANDS LÄNS SLÄKTFORSKAREFÖRENING**
  Box 418, 831 26 ÖSTERSUND, SWEDEN
  Chairman: Irma Ridbäck *Journal:* Jls-Nytt

- **MIDÄLVA GENEALOGISKA FÖRENING**
  C/o Lennart Lindqvist, Lejdarevägen 13, S-865 00, ALNÖ, SWEDEN
  Chairman: Viktor Magnusson *Journal:* MGF-nytt

- **HÄRNÖSANDS SLÄKTFORSKARE**
  C/o Roland Ek, Finsvik 2327, S-870 10 ÄLANDSBRO, SWEDEN
  Chairman: Roland Ek

- **ADALENS SLÄKTFORSKARFÖRENING**
  Skarpakersvägen 15, S-872 00 KRAMFORS, SWEDEN
  Chairman: Per Melander *Journal:* Adalingen

- **RAMSELE/JUNSELE SLÄKTFORSKARFÖRENING**
  Ängsvägen 1, S-880 40 RAMSELE, SWEDEN
  Chairman: Göran Stenmark

- **HEMBYGDS-OCH SLÄTFORSKARE NOLASKOGS**
  C/O M Sidborn, Följvägen 7, S-891 00 ÖRNSKÖLDSVIK, SWEDEN
  Chairman: Edit Westman

- **SÖDRA VÄSTERBOTTENS SLÄKTFORSKARE**
  Storgatan 99, S-902 44 UMEA, SWEDEN
  Chairman: Holger Sjöstedt *Journal:* Släkten

SWITZERLAND – SCHWEIZ

- **SCHWEIZERISCHE GESELLSCHAFT fuer FAMILIENFORSCHUNG (SGFF) ***
  Egg str. 46, CH 8102 OBERENGSTRINGEN, Switzerland.
  Auch fuer Nichtmitglieder zugaenglich. *Mitgliedsbeitrag*: Fr. 35. *Zeitschrift*: (1)
  MITTEILUNGSBLATT (2 x Jaehrlich, Suchanz); (2) *JAHRBUCH der SGFF*
  (jaehrlich); (3) *ARBEITSHILFEN fuer FAMILIENFORSCHER in der SCHWEIZ*
  (unregelmaessig). *Suchanzeigen*: Fr. 10.-. *Beantwortung der Anfragen*: durch unten
  erwaehnte Auskunftsstelle – schriftlich – *Weitere Angaben*: die 3 ersten
  Publikationen im Mitgliederbeitrag eingeschlossen Bibliothek mit 4500 Einheiten in
  der Schweizerischen Landesbibliothek in Bern. *Vorsitzender*: Hans Peyer.
  SWISS GENEALOGICAL ASSOCIATION
  Membership sub.: Fr. 35.-. *Publications*: Named above are published (1) twice
  yearly (includes enquiries); (2) annually; (3) irregularly. *President*: Hans Peyer (as
  above). *Extra Details*: Publications 1 and 2 are included in membership. Library
  of 5000 volumes in the Schweizerische Landesbibliothek in Bern.

- **GENEALOGISCH-HERALDISCHE GESELLSCHAFT ZUERICH (GHGZ) ***
  Friedhofstrasse 10 B, CH-8104 WEININGEN, Switzerland.
  Auch fuer Nichtmitglieder zugaenglich. *Mitgliedsbeitrag*: Fr. 15. *Beantwortung der
  Anfragen*: durch den Praesidenten, schriftlich (Rueckporto). *Weitere Angaben*: (eine
  ausfuehrliche Bibliographie zu Geschlechtern und deren Quellen fuer den Kanton
  Zuerich ist vorhanden). *Forschungsgebiet*: Kanton Zuerich.
  GENEALOGICAL AND HERALDRY ASSOCIATION OF ZURICH
  Membership sub.: Fr. 15. *Mail Enquiries*: Answered by the President. (enclose re-
  turn postage). *Extra details*: A comprehensive biblio of families and their sources
  for Kanton Zuerich is available. *Area of interest*: Kanton Zuerich.

- **SCHWEIZERISCHE VEREINIGUNG FÜR JÜDISCHE GENEALOGIE (SVJG) ***
  ASSOCIATION SUISSE DE GENEALOGIE JUIVE (ASGJ)
  SWISS SOCIETY FOR JEWISH GENEALOGY (SSJG)
  P.O. Box 876, CH-8021 ZÜRICH.
  Mitteilungsblatt: Erscheinungsweise jährlich. Preis per Einzelnumer Sfr. 15.-.
  Mitgliedjahresbeitrag im Inland: Sfr. 100.-/*Ausland*: Sfr. 130.-(Mitteilungsblatt in-
  begriffen). Suchanzeigen für Mitglieder gratis. Für Nichtmitglieder nach Tarif. *Pres-
  ident*: René Leob, P.O. Box 876, CH-8021, ZÜRICH. *Sekretrin*: Frau Dr. Hilde
  Shmerling. *Kassier*: Herr Raymond M. Jung.

UNITED STATES of AMERICA (USA)

NATIONAL (see also under: IRELAND, POLAND, NORWAY etc.)

- **NATIONAL GENEALOGICAL SOCIETY**
  4527 17th Street, North, ARLINGTON, VA 22207, USA.
  Library: As above. *Hours*: Mon. & Wed. 10am-9pm, Fri. & Sat. 10am-4pm. Open to
  non members, daily fee of $5.00. *Newsletter*: 6 per year. *Journal*: *NATIONAL
  GENEALOGICAL SOCIETY QUARTERLY* 4 per year. *Co-Editors*: Elizabeth S.
  Mills & Gary B. Mills. *Queries*: Free to members. Research service available to mem-
  bers for a fee. *Membership*: $30.00. *President*: Ralph E. Jackson. *Secretary*: Mary
  McCampbell Bell. *Exec. Director*: Edward A. Bannon.

- **FEDERATION OF GENEALOGICAL SOCIETIES**
  2324 E. Nottingham, SPRINGFIELD, MO, 65804-7821, USA.
  Newsletter: 4 per year. *Membership*: Only open to organizations and institutions.
  Membership: Sponsors a conference each year.

- **THE AMERICAN COLLEGE OF HERALDRY INC.**
  Drawer C.G., Tuscaloosa, ALABAMA 35486, USA.
  Library: As above. *Hours*: Mon.-Fri. 8am-5pm. *Journal*: *THE ARMIGER'S NEWS* 4
  per year. Members only. *Membership*: $25.00. *President*: Dr. David P. Johnson. *Secre-

- **NATIONAL SOCIETY, DAUGHTERS OF THE AMERICAN REVOLUTION**
  1776 D Street, NW, Washington, D.C. 20006-5392, USA.
  Library: As above. *Hours:* Mon.-Fri. 9am-4pm. Sun. (except holiday weekends) 1-5pm. Closed to non members mid-April. *Library Director:* Eric G. Grundset.

- **FAMILY HISTORY LIBRARY OF THE CHURCH OF JESUS CHRIST OF LATTER-DAY SAINTS.**
  35 N. West Temple Street, SALT LAKE CITY, Utah, 84150 USA.
  Library: As above. *Hours:* Mon. 7.30am-6.00pm; Tues.-Fri. 7.30am-10.00pm; Sat. 7.30am-5.00pm. The microfilm holdings of the library are available through over 1500 family history centres. A list of local centres is available by writing to the above address. The library is open to non members. *Director:* David M. Mayfield.

- **AMERICAN-CANADIAN GENEALOGICAL SOCIETY ***
  P.O. Box 668, MANCHESTER, NH 03105, USA. 603-622-1554.
  Library: Cnr Amory & Notre Dame Ave., NH 03102. *Hours:* Wed. 1-9pm, and Sat. 9am-4pm; Fri. 10am-9pm. Open to non members. First two visits free; after, $2.00 per visit. *Journal: THE GENEALOGIST* 4 per year. Available to non members at $3.50 each. *Research Enquiries:* $15.00 per direct line; $30.00 for non-members. *Membership:* $15.00. *President:* Lucille Lagasse. *Vice President:* Roger Lawrence.

- **AMERICAN-FRENCH GENEALOGICAL SOCIETY**
  78 Earle St., WOONSOCKET, RI 02860, USA.
  Library: As above. *Hours:* Tues. 1-10pm. *Journal: JE ME SOUVIENS (I REMEMBER)* 2 per year. Available to non members at $3.50 each. *Research Enquiries:* Cost of entries $2.00 members; $4.00 non members. *Membership:* $20.00. *Other Particulars* We have in our Library the Loiselle Files which include over one million marriages which took place in Canada, and also the newly acquired Rivest Index which includes parish Records listed by the female of the union Research French-Canadian & Acadian not France. *President:* Janice Burkhart. *Secretary:* Mrs. Eveline Desplaines.

- **AMERICAN/SCHLESWIG-HOLSTEIN HERITAGE SOCIETY (ASHHS)**
  PO Box 21, LECLAIRE, IA, 52753, USA.
  President: Glenn Sievers. *Secretary:* Jean Mumm.

- **INTERNATIONAL SOCIETY FOR BRITISH GENEALOGY AND FAMILY HISTORY**
  PO Box 20425, CLEVELAND, OH, 44120, USA.
  Newsletter: 4 per year, included with individual membership US$10.00. Reserved enquiries of 60 words or less free for members only. Subscriptions for Societies & Institutions US$10.00. British Genealogical Publications for sale (US$). *President:* Joy Wade Moulton. *Secretary:* Gracelouise Moore. *Editor:* Joy Wade Moulton.

- **BRITISH ISLES FAMILY HISTORY SOCIETY OF LOS ANGELES**
  22941 Felbar Ave, TORRANCE, CA, 90505, USA.
  President: Donald L. Hirst.

- **CROATIAN-SERBIAN-SLOVENE GENEALOGICAL SOCIETY**
  2527 San Carlos Ave., SAN CARLOS, CA 94070, USA.
  Library: As above. *Hours:* Mon. to Fri. 10am-4pm. Open to non members. *Membership:* $25.00 One time fee. *Research Enquiries:* Open to members. *President:* Adam S. Eterovich. *Secretary:* Jakobina Guzitza.

- **CZECHOSLOVAK GENEALOGICAL SOCIETY**
  PO Box 16225, ST PAUL, MN, 55116, USA.

- **FLEMISH AMERICAN, GENEALOGICAL SOCIETY OF. ***
  18740 13 Mile Road, ROSEVILLE, MI 48066, USA.
  Membership: $10.00. semi annual magazine included.

● **GERMAN GENEALOGICAL SOCIETY OF AMERICA**
P.O. Box 291818, Los Angeles, CA 90029, USA.
Library: 1420 North Claremont Boulevard, #207E, Claremont, California 91711 (not a mailing address). *Hours:* Sat. 1-5pm. Wed. 1-5pm. Other times by appointment (call (714) 621-7399. Open to non members, small donation requested. *Newsletter:* BULLETIN 6 per year. The *BULLETIN* was awarded first place (Class 1) in the National Genealogical Society Genealogical Newsletter: Competition for 1986, and first place (Class 3) in the same competition for 1987. *Research Enquiries:* $8.00 per hour for members, $10.00 per hour for non-members, minimum 2 hours. (payable upon completion of research; please send a S.A.S.E. for a Research Request Form). *Membership:* $18.00 regular, $26.00 family (2 people), $28.00 contributing, $50.00 supporting, $28.00 foreign. *Board Meetings:* 2nd Sat. of each month at 10am at the society's library (address above). *Other Particulars* Fall Seminar (Sep./Oct.) and Winter Seminar (Feb./Mar.), as announced in the *BULLETIN*. Queries published in the *BULLETIN* free of charge. Computer databases of earliest German ancestors and of German emigrants to North America. *President:* Kevin Tvedt. *Secretary:* Esther Senff. *Treasurer:* Jane Griffith. *Librarian:* Beatrice Beck, FSAScot. *Research Director:* Michael P. Palmer.

● **(GERMAN) IMMIGRANT GENEALOGICAL SOCIETY** *
5043 Lankershim Blvd., NORTH HOLLYWOOD, CA 91601, USA.
Tel.: (818) 762-7595. *Membership:* $15.00 (Overseas $25.00). *Mailing Address*: PO Box 7369, Burbank, CA 91510-7369. *Library Address*: 1013 W. Magnolia Blvd, Burbank, CA 91506. Tel: 848 3122. *Newsletter:* monthly.

● **GERMAN RESEARCH ASSOCIATION** *
P.O. Box 11293, SAN DIEGO, CA 92111, USA.
Newsletter: The German Connection 4 per year. *Meetings:* 4 per year. *Membership:* $10.00 ($15.00 for 2 in family), USA, $15.00 outside USA (in US dollars). plus seminar.

● **GERMANS FROM RUSSIA HERITAGE SOCIETY**
1008 East Central Ave., BISMARCK, ND 58501, USA.

● **THE IRISH FAMILY NAMES SOCIETY**
P.O. Box 2095, LA MESA, CA 92043-2095, USA.
Newsletter: 3 per year. Available to members at $12.00. *Book: A GUIDE TO IRISH ROOTS* $19.95 in U.S., outside U.S. $24.95. Post Paid surface mail. *Other Particulars* We collect and publish the traditional origin of Irish families. Researchers are encouraged to visit Ireland to collect information directly. Our findings are published in book form. *Director:* William P. Durning.

● **IRISH GENEALOGICAL SOCIETY**
PO Box 16585, SAINT PAUL, MN 55116, USA.
Library: Located at Minnesota Genealogical Society (see under USA) Tel. (612) 222-6929. Irish day at Library, 2nd Sat each month. *Membership:* $10.00 *President:* Dan Moriarty. *Library Chair:* Beth Mullinax, Tel. (612) 574-1436.

● **MENNONITE HISTORICAL LIBRARY** *
Goshen College, GOSHEN, IN 46526, USA.
Library: As above. Contains over 3800 books of a genealogical nature. Also a 55,000 card index to obituary notices from *Herald of Truth* (1864-1908) and *Gospel Herald* (1908-present). Also 80,000 Amish names from 120 family histories. Specializes in Mennonites and Amish including some material in the Netherlands and Germany. *Director:* Dr. John D. Roth.

● **NORWEGIAN AMERICAN HISTORICAL ASSOCIATION**
St. Olaf College, NORTHFIELD, MN 55057, USA.
Newsletter: *Editor:* Lloyd Hustvedt.

- **NORWEGIAN AMERICAN MUSEUM**
  502 W. Water St., Decorah Iowa, 52101, USA.
  VESTERHEIM GENEALOGICAL CENTRE
  4909 Sherwood Rd., MADISON, WI 53711, USA.
  Editor: Norwegian Tracks (Madison Address).

ALABAMA (AL)

- **ALABAMA GENEALOGICAL SOCIETY**
  Depository — Samford University Library. 800 Lakeshore Dr., BIRMINGHAM, AL 35229-0001.
  Journal: ALA GENEALOGICAL SOC MAGAZINE. Membership: $20.00/$25.00.
  Library: Samford University Library.

- **MOBILE GENEALOGICAL SOCIETY**
  P.O. Box 6224, MOBILE, AL 36660, USA.
  Journal: DEEP SOUTH GENELOGICAL QUARTERLY 4 per year. *Research Enquiries:* Free to members. *Membership:* $18.00. *President:* Mary Ann Ingram. *Corres. Secretary:* Edith K. Brown. *Editor:* Marie Nichols. *Meetings:* 2nd. Sat. each month.

ARIZONA (AZ)

- **ARIZONA STATE GENEALOGICAL SOCIETY**
  P.O. Box 42075, TUCSON, AZ 85733, USA.
  Publications: Copper State Bulletins. *Editor:* Floyd Negle. *Secretary:* Hazel Gibson.

- **COCHISE GENEALOGICAL SOCIETY**
  P.O. Box 68, PIRTLEVILLE, AZ 85626, USA.
  Journal: THE TOMBSTONE Available to non members at $2.00 per issue. *Research Enquiries*: Free to members. $2.00 to non members. We will search our extensive collection of tombstone inscriptions and sexton's records of Cochise County for free if SASE is sent. *Membership:* $5.00.

- **GENEALOGICAL COMMITTEE OF THE ARIZONA JEWISH HISTORICAL SOCIETY ***
  Carlton Brooks; 720 W. Edgewood, MESA, AZ 85202, USA.

ARKANSAS (AR)

- **ARKANSAS GENEALOGICAL SOCIETY ***
  P.O. Box 908, HOT SPRINGS, AR 71902, USA.
  Library: Little Rock Public Library, Little Rock, AR. *Journal: THE ARKANSAS FAMILY HISTORIAN* 4 per year. *Research Enquiries:* Free to members. *Membership:* $15.00. *Editor:* Margaret Hubbard.

- **OUACHITA-CALHOUN GENEALOGICAL SOCIETY ***
  P.O. Box 2092, CAMDEN, AR 71701, USA.

CALIFORNIA (CA)

- **CALIFORNIA GENEALOGICAL SOCIETY**
  P.O. Box 77105, SAN FRANCISCO, CA 94107, USA. (Tel. (415) 777 9936).
  Library: 300 Brannan St., San Francisco. *Hours:* Wed., Thurs. and Sat. 9-4pm. Open to non-members for daily fee except free 1st Sat. each month. *Newsletter:* 6 per year. *Membership:* $29.00 ($40.00 family). *Meetings:* 2nd Sat. afternoon, Jan., Mar., May, July, Sep., Nov. *Executive Director:* Audrey K. Doughty. *Corres. Secretary:* Mrs. Mary Sweetman.

- **CALIFORNIA STATE GENEALOGICAL ALLIANCE ***
  Wendy Elliott, C.G. 4808 E. Garland St, ANAHEIM, CA 92807, USA.
  President: Nancy Keeler Kepley. *Secretary:* Deannie Fish.

- **CONEJO VALLEY GENEALAGICAL SOCIETY, INC ***
  PO Box 1228, THOUSAND OAKS, CA, 91358, USA.

- **EAST BAY GENEALOGICAL SOCIETY**
  P.O. Box 20417, OAKLAND, CA 94620-0417, USA. Tel. (415) 524 2004.
  Newsletter: THE LIVE OAK 6 per year, members only. *Membership:* $10.00. *Meetings:* 2nd Wed. of each month. *President:* Sally Stevens. *Secretary:* Margaret Van Eck.

- **INTERMOUNTAIN GENEALOGICAL SOCIETY ***
  P.O. Box 399, BURNEY, CA 96013, USA.

- **LIVERMORE-AMADOR GENEALOGICAL SOCIETY ***
  P.O. Box 901, LIVERMORE, CA 94551, USA.

- **JEWISH GENEALOGICAL SOCIETY OF LOS ANGELES. ***
  P.O. Box 25245, LOS ANGELES, CA 90025, USA.
  Publication: ROOTS-KEY Quarterly. *Editor:* Gladys Gould, 16427 Plummer St., Sepulveda, CA 91343. *Corres. Secretary:* Dee Shkolnik, 10551, Wellworth Ave., Los Angeles, CA 90024.

- **MERCED COUNTY GENEALOGICAL SOCIETY**
  P.O. Box 3061, MERCED, CA 95344, USA.

- **NAPA VALLEY GENEALOGICAL & BIOGRAPHICAL SOCIETY**
  P.O. Box 385, NAPA, CA 94559-0385, USA.

- **NORTH SAN DIEGO COUNTY GENEALOGICAL SOCIETY**
  PO Box 581, CARLSBAD, CA 92008, USA.
  Library: Carlsbad City Library (Genealogy Section: 26,000 volumes), 1250 Elm Ave., Carlsbad, CA 92008. *Hours:* Mon.-Thurs. 9am-9pm; Fri.-Sat. 9am-5pm. Open to the public. *Newsletter:* monthly. *Membership:* $15.00 annual (calendar), $20.00 (family). *Meetings:* 2nd & 4th Tues. of each month (Dec. 2nd only) at 10am in Council Chambers, City Hall, City of Carlsbad, 1200 Elm Ave. *President:* Milt Cooper. *Secretary:* Anna Mae Kidd.

- **JEWISH GENEALOGICAL SOCIETY OF ORANGE COUNTY ***
  P.O. Box 2034, CYPRESS, CA 90630, USA.
  Publication: AVI-AVOT/FOREFATHERS. *Editor:* Irv Wenger, P.O. Box 2034, Cypress, CA 90630.

- **POCAHONTAS TRAILS GENEALOGICAL SOCIETY**
  6015 Robin Hill Dr., LAKEPORT, CA 95453-6007, USA.
  Est. 1983, quarterly Newsletter:. *Membership:* $10.00. *Meetings:* 3rd Sat. in Feb., May, Aug. & Nov. in Modesto, CA. Annual meetings in July at Seal Beach, CA, in May at Oakland, OR. *Enquiries:* Free to members, $3.00 to non members up to 150 words.

- **QUESTING HEIRS GENEALOGICAL SOCIETY, INC. ***
  P.O. Box 15102, LONG BEACH, CA 90815, USA.
  Library: Long Beach Public Library (Genealogy Section),101 Pacific Ave., Long Beach 90802. *Hours:* Mon. 10am-8pm; Tues.-Sat. 10am-5.30pm; Sun. 1.30pm-5pm. Open to non members – no charge. *Newsletter:* 12 per year. *Membership:* $20.00 *President:* Douglas Waide. *Secretary:* Sioux Stoceckle (Recording), Marjorie Tarbell (Corresp.). *Meetings:* 3rd Sunday of month, 2800 Studebaker Rd., El Dorado Park, Long Beach. *Other Particulars* (Each Year) Frances Parker Award – A monetary award to be presented for valuable dissemination of genealogical research and information.

- **RIVERSIDE GENEALOGICAL SOCIETY**
  P.O. BOX 2557, RIVERSIDE, CA 92516, USA.
  Library: Riverside City Library (Genealogical Section). volunteers assist the public Mon., Wed. and Sat. 1-4pm. Open to non members. *Journal:* LIFELINER Available to non members at $10.00 per volume, $15.00 CAN and $15.00 o'seas. 4 per year. *Re-*

search Enquiries: Cost of entries $2.00 for 50 words. *Membership:* $10.00. *President:* Mrs. Lois Lippman. *Secretary:* Mrs. Jacque Williams.

● **SAN BERNARDINO VALLEY GENEALOGICAL SOCIETY**
P.O. Box 2220, SAN BERNARDINO, CA 92406, USA.
*Publication: VALLEY QUARTERLY*4 per year. Available to non members at $3.00 each. *Membership:* $10.00 single, $15.00 family per year. *Meetings:* 1st Sat 10am. *President:* Allene Muffley. *Secretary:* Katy Beimer.

● **SAN DIEGO JEWISH GENEALOGICAL SOCIETY**
Carol Baird, 255 South Rios Ave., SOLANA BEACH, CA 92075, USA.
Publication: DISCOVERY Quarterly.

● **SAN FRANCISCO BAY AREA JEWISH GENEALOGICAL SOCIETY** *
Armand S. Cohn, President, 92150 El Camino Real, SAN MATEO, CA 94402, USA.
Publication: SAN FRANCISCO BAY AREA JEWISH GENEALOGICAL SOCIETY Newsletter: Quarterly. *Editor:* Martha L. Wise.

● **SANTA BARBARA COUNTY GENEALOGICAL SOCIETY**
P.O. Box 1303, SANTA BARBARA, CA 93116, USA.
Library: Room 8, Goleta Community Centre, 5689 Hollister Ave., Goleta. *Hours:* Thurs. 10am-3pm., Sat. 12.30-3pm. Open to non members. *Newsletter:* Monthly to members. *Journal: ANCESTORS WEST*, quarterly, free to members. *Membership:* $15.00. Includes subscriptions to Newsletter: and Journal, Family memberships, $20.00. *Research Enquiries:* Free as space allows. *Meetings:* Second Sat., 10.30am-12.30pm., Room 1, Goleta Community Centre. *President:* Beatrice Mohr McGrath. *Editor of A.W.:* Sharon Doyle.

● **SANTA CLARA COUNTY HISTORICAL AND GENEALOGICAL SOCIETY**
2635 Homestead Road, City Library, SANTA CLARA, CA 95051, USA.
Library: As above. *Hours:* Mon.-Fri. 9am-9pm; Sat. 9am-6pm; Sun. 1pm-5pm. Consultant: Mon.-Sun. 1pm-3pm; Mon.-Fri. 7pm-9pm. *Journal: SANTA CLARA COUNTY CONNECTIONS*, semi annually. *Research Enquiries:* $10.00 per hour + S.A.S.E. *Membership:* $10.00 annual; $15.00 couple; $25.00 contributing. *Secretary:* C/o above address.

● **SANTA CRUZ COUNTY GENEALOGICAL SOCIETY** *
P.O. Box 72, SANTA CRUZ, CA 95063, USA.

● **SOLANO COUNTY GENEALOGICAL SOCIETY, INC.**
P.O. Box 2494, FAIRFIELD, CA 94533, USA.
Newsletter: each month except July + Aug. *Journal: ROOT DIGGER* 4 per year. $3.50 each for non members *Research Queries:* $2.50 for up to 25 words. *Membership:* $10.00 individual, $12.50 family. *Meetings:* 4th Thurs. each month except July, Aug. & Dec. *President:* Ann Cade Phelps. *Secretary:* Rebecca Mills. *Other Particulars* Research done Solano Co. indexes at our library, $15.00 per surname.

● **SOUTH BAY CITIES GENEALOGICAL SOCIETY** *
P.O. Box 6071, TORRANCE, CA 90504, USA. (Tel. (213) 533 8243.)
Newsletter: 6 per year. Exchanges with Societies. *Research Enquiries:* free to members. $1.00 + S.A.S.E. or 3 IRC's each for non members. *Membership:* $10.00 USA, $15.00 others. *Meetings:* 3rd Wednesdays. *Seminar:*: Sept. yearly. *Workshop:* April yearly. *President:* Chris Velline. *Secretary:* Betty Moran.

● **SOUTHERN CALIFORNIA GENEALOGICAL SOCIETY**
P.O. Box 4377, BURBANK, CA 91503, USA.
Library: 122 South San Ferdinand Blvd. (rear), Burbank. *Hours:* Mon., Wed.-Sat. 10am-4pm; Tues. 10am-9pm 1st & 2nd Sun. 10-4pm. Open to non members at no charge. *Newsletter: THE SEARCHER* 12 per year. Available to non members at $1.50. *Research Enquiries:* Free to members − $1.00 to non members. *Membership:* $18.00. *President:* Virginia Emrey. *Secretary:* Frances Bumann. *Meetings:* 4th Sunday each month at 2pm. The Society holds a major Genealogical Jamboree each year, late

April or early May. (see EVENTS list in front part of this Directory.

- **WHITTIER AREA GENEALOGICAL SOCIETY**
  P.O. Box 4367, WHITTIER, CA 90607, USA.

COLORADO (CO)

- **THE COLORADO GENEALOGICAL SOCIETY, INC.**
  P.O. Box 9218, DENVER, CO 80209, USA.
  Library: Denver Public Library (Genealogical Dept.). *Hours:* Mon.-Wed. 10am-9pm,
  Thurs., Fri., Sat. 10-5.30, Sun. 1-5. Open to non members. *Newsletter:* 10 per year.
  Journal: THE COLORADO GENEALOGIST 4 per year. Available to non members
  at US$4 (Foreign, postal surcharge). *Research Enquiries*: Cost of entries $3.00 mem-
  bers, $5.00 non members. *Membership:* $20.00 family, $15.00 single.

- **COLUMBINE GENEALOGICAL & HISTORICAL SOCIETY, INC. ***
  P.O. Box 2074, LITTLETON, CO 80161, USA.

- **FOOTHILLS GENEALOGICAL SOCIETY OF COLORADO**
  P.O. Box 15382, LAKEWOOD, CO 80215, USA.
  Journal: FOOTHILLS INQUIRER Quarterly. *Membership:* 2nd Wed. each month.
  1pm at the First Pres. Church of Lakewood, 8210 W. 10th Ave., Lakewood, CO.
  Membership: $10.00 indivdual, $12.50 family (one Newsletter: only).

- **SAN LUIS VALLEY GENEALOGICAL SOCIETY**
  P.O. Box 1541, ALAMOSA, CO 81101, USA.
  Serving: Alamosa, Conejos, Costilla, Rio Grande, Saguache and Mineral Counties.
  Library: Genealogy room of the Southern Peaks Library, 423 4th St., Alamosa, CO.
  Hours: Thurs. 10am-7pm, Tues., Wed., Fri. & Sat. 10am-5pm. *Newsletter:* 12 per year.
  Journal: Semi annual. *Other Particulars* The Society has started a surname file to be
  housed in the Genealogy Room.

- **WELD COUNTY GENEALOGICAL SOCIETY**
  P.O. Box 278, GREELEY, CO 80632, USA.
  Journal: GSWC Quarterly.The GSWC staffs the volunteer genealogy section of Weld
  County Library. *Meetings:* 1st Thurs. each month, 7.30pm, Weld County Library,
  2227 23rd Ave., Greeley, CO. Same night mini classes at 7.00pm. *Membership:* $12.50
  individual, $15.00 family.

CONNECTICUT (CT)

- **CONNECTICUT SOCIETY OF GENEALOGISTS, INC.**
  P.O. Box 435, GLASTONBURY, CT 06033, USA.
  Newsletter: bi monthly. *Journal: CONNECTICUT NUTMEGGER* 4 per an. *Membership:* $25.00 US, $27.00 Can., $33.00 Overseas; plus $3.00 registration fee for new
  members. *Research* Available to members for small fee. *Meetings:* Sept. to May.

- **NEW CANAAN HISTORICAL SOCIETY ***
  13 Oenoke Ridge, NEW CANAAN, CT 06840.

- **FRENCH-CANADIAN GENEALOGICAL SOCIETY OF CONNECTICUT, INC. ***
  P.O. Box 45, TOLLAND, CT 06084, USA.

- **STAMFORD GENEALOGICAL SOCIETY, INC. ***
  P.O. Box 249, STAMFORD, CT 06904-0249, USA.
  Library: Ferguson Public Library, 96 Broad St., Stamford. *Hours:* Mon.-Fri. 9am-
  9pm, Sat. 9am-5.30pm, Sun. (except July and August and holidays) 1pm-5pm. *Jour-
  nal: CONNECTICUT ANCESTRY* quarterly. *Research Enquiries:* free to members.
  Meetings: dates and places are published in journal. Annual meeting in May. All
  meetings are open to the public. *Membership:* Individual, Husband/wife, Library,
  Society $15, Supporting member $25, Patron $50.

DELAWARE (DE)

- **DELAWARE GENEALOGICAL SOCIETY ***
  505 Market St. Mall, WILMINGTON, DE 19801, USA.
  Library: As above. *Hours:* Mon. 11am-9pm, Tues.-Fri. 9am-5pm. Open to non members. *Newsletter:* 5 per year. Contains research enquiries. *Journal: DELAWARE GENEALOGICAL SOCIETY JOURNAL* 2 per year. Available to non members for $3.50 current, $3.00 vol. 1. *Membership:* $10.00. *Meetings:* 3rd Tues. 7.30pm — Historical Society of Delaware (except summer months).

FLORIDA (FL)

- **FLORIDA STATE GENEALOGICAL SOCIETY**
  P.O. Box 10249, TALLAHASSEE, FL 32302, USA.
  Journal: THE FLORIDA GENEALOGIST plus Newsletter:. *Membership:* $18.00 single, $22.00 family. *Secretary:* Joan Bond. *President:* Harriet S. Liles.

- **FLORIDA GENEALOGICAL SOCIETY, INC.**
  P.O. Box 18624, TAMPA, FL 33679-8624, USA.

- **ALACHUA COUNTY GENEALOGICAL SOCIETY**
  P.O. Box 12078, GAINESVILLE, FL 32604, USA.
  Membership: $13.00, $15.00 family. *Meetings:* Sept.-May on 3rd Mon. each month at Masonic Temple, 201 N. Main St., Gainesville, FL 32601.

- **GENEALOGICAL SOCIETY OF BAY COUNTY**
  P.O. Box 662, PANAMA CITY, FL 32402, USA.
  Publication: COUNTY LINE 4 per year. $10.00 per year for non members. *Research Enquiries:* members — free, non members $2.00. *Membership:* $10.00 single, $12.50 family. *Meetings:* 1st Sat. of month. *Beginners Seminar:* Spring. *President:* Linda P. Kleback. *Secretary:* Virginia McLain. *Phone:* 785 3457 (Bay Co. Public Library).

- **GENEALOGICAL SOCIETY OF BROWARD COUNTY INC. ***
  P.O. Box 485, FT. LAUDERDALE, FL 33302, USA.

- **GENEALOGICAL SOCIETY OF COLLIER COUNTY ***
  P.O. Box 7933, NAPLES, FL 33941, USA.
  President: Lisa Lezgus. *Treasurer:* Allan Hoppenstedt.

- **INDIAN RIVER GENEALOGICAL SOCIETY, INC.**
  P.O. Box 1850, VERO BEACH, FL 32961, USA.
  Membership: $12.00 ($15.00 family). *Newsletter:* 4 per year. *President:* Bruce Wetmore.

GEORGIA (GA)

- **AUGUSTA GENEALOGICAL SOCIETY ***
  P.O. Box 3743, AUGUSTA, GA 30904, USA.

- **GEORGIA GENEALOGICAL SOCIETY ***
  P.O. Box 38066, ATLANTA, GA 30334, USA.
  Library: Dept. of Archives & History. *Hours:* Mon.-Fri. 8am-4.15pm; Sat. 9.30am-3.15pm. Open to non members — no charge. *Newsletter:* 4 per year. *Journal: GEORGIA GENEALOGICAL SOCIETY QUARTERLY* 4 per year. Available back issues for sale, send s.a.s.e. for price. *Research Enquiries:* Free to members. *President:* Rita Worthy. *Secretary:* Leoda Sherry. *Membership:* 2nd Sat. of Mar., May, Sept. & Dec.

- **CENTRAL GEORGIA GENEALOGICAL SOCIETY, INC.**
  P.O. Box 2024, WARNER ROBINS, GA 31099-2024, USA.
  Newsletter: 12 per year. *Journal: CENTRAL GEORGIA GENEALOGICAL SOCIETY QUARTERLY* 4 per year. *Research Queries:* Free to members. *Membership:*

$15.00. *President:* Judy G. Marable. *Corres. Secretary:* Addie P. Howell. *Meetings:* 3rd Thurs. – Flint Electric Bldg., Warner Robins.

● **NORTHWEST GEORGIA HISTORICAL & GENEALOGICAL SOCIETY, INC.**
P.O. Box 5063, ROME, GA 30161, USA.
Library: 205 Riverside Parkway, N.E., Rome. *Hours:* Mon.-Thurs. 9am-9pm. Fri. 9am-6pm. Sat. 9am-5pm. Summer hours vary. Available to non members. *Journal: QUARTERLY* 4 per year. Available to non members at $5.00. *Research Enquiries:* Free to members. *Membership:* $15.00. *Other Particulars* Genealogical Room in the above library has over 5,000 volumes. We use the auditorium of the library for all meetings. All of our material is located here. *President:* Mary Jo Posey. *Secretary:* Jackie Kinzer. *Meetings:* 2nd Sat. in Feb., May, Aug. & Nov. at Library. Luncheon in May. Workshop in Aug.

IDAHO (ID)

● **THE IDAHO GENEALOGICAL SOCIETY, INC.** *
4620Overland Rd., RM 204, ID 83705, USA. (Tel. (208) 384 0542.)
Library: At Idaho Historical Society. *Journal: THE IDAHO GENEALOGICAL SOCIETY QUARTERLY* 4 per year. Available to non members at $2.00. *Research Enquiries:* Free to members. $1.50 to non members. *Membership:* $10.00. *Meetings:* 2nd Thurs. of each month, 7pm. *President:* Jane Walls Golden. *Vice President:* John F. Erdle.

● **LATAH COUNTY GENEALOGICAL SOCIETY**
110 South Adams, MOSCOW, ID 83843, USA.

ILLINOIS (IL)

● **CHICAGO GENEALOGICAL SOCIETY**
P.O. Box 1160, CHICAGO, IL 60690, USA.
Library: 120 Berteau Ave., Elmhurst, IL 60126. *Hours:* 1-5pm by appointment only. *Newsletter:* 11 per year. *Journal: CHICAGO GENEALOGIST* 4 per year. Available to non members at $2.75. *Research Enquiries:* Brief suggestions or directions free; a list of researchers in the area is provided. *Membership:* $16.00. *President:* Herbert Hart. *Corres. Secretary:* Marge Topps. *Meetings:* 1st Sat., Sept. throught June.

● **NORTH SUBURBAN GENEALOGICAL SOCIETY** *
C/o Winnetka Public Library, 768 Oak St., WINNETKA, IL 60093, USA.
Library: As above. *Hours:* Mon.-Thurs. 9am-9pm; Fri. & Sat. 9am-5pm; Sun. 1pm-5pm. (Closed Sun. June-Aug.) Open to non members. *Newsletter:* 6 per year. Available for purchase by non members. *Membership:* $6.00 individual, $7.00 family. *Meetings:* Monthly, Jan.-Nov.

● **NORTHWEST SUBURBAN COUNCIL OF GENEALOGISTS**
P.O. Box AC, MT. Prospect, IL 60056, USA.
Library: Mt. Prospect, IL. *Hours:* Every day. *Newsletter:* 5 per year plus index. *Research Enquiries:* $1.00 per entry for non members. Members free. *Membership:* Single $10.00, Family $12.00, per year. Life $100. *Meetings:* 3rd Thurs. except June, July Aug. & Dec.

● **SOUTH SUBURBAN GENEALOGICAL & HISTORICAL SOCIETY**
P.O. Box 96, SOUTH HOLLAND, IL 60473, USA.
Library: 161st Place & Louis Ave. *Hours:* Mon. 10-4pm, Tues. 1-9pm, Wed. 10-4pm, Fri. 10am-4pm and Sat. 11-4pm. Open to non members. *Newsletter:* 12 per year. *Journal: WHERE THE TRAILS CROSS* 4 per year. Available to non members at $5.50. *Research Enquiries:* $5.00 per hour plus cost of copies. *Membership:* $15.00. *Other Particulars* Publication covers the South Cook North Will Counties in Illinois; hold Beginners' & Advanced Classes yearly. *President:* Barbara Smith. *Corres. Secretary:* Paula G. Malak.

- **JEWISH GENEALOGICAL SOCIETY OF ILLINOIS** *
  1025 Antique Lane, NORTHBROOK, IL 60062, USA. (Tel. (312) 564 1025.)
  Journal: SEARCH 4 per year. US$15.00 for non members. *Research Enquiries:* $5.00
  1st 25 words, 25c each additional word. *Membership:* $21.00 US. *Meetings:* last Sun.
  aft. or eve. monthly except May & Dec. *President:* Judith R. Frazin. *Editor:* Alan
  Spencer. *Other Particulars* Also sell *A Translation Guide to 19th Century Polish Language Civil Registration Documents* (Birth, Mar. & Death Records) 2nd edition, at
  US$22.50 including post.

- **BLACKHAWK GENEALOGICAL SOCIETY**
  Box 3912, ROCK ISLAND, IL 61204-3913, USA.
  Library: Moline Public Library, 504 17th St., Moline, IL. *Hours:* Mon.-Sat. 9am-9pm.
  Open to non members. *Journal: BLACKHAWK GENEALOGICAL SOCIETY
  QUARTERLY* 4 per year. Available to non members at $2.00 per quarter plus $1.00
  postage. *Research Enquiries:* Free to members, 100 words or less. *Membership:* $6.00.
  Acting President: Grace Eastland. *Corres. Secretary:* Barbara S. Scott, C.C.R.S.

- **CHAMPAIGN COUNTY GENEALOGICAL SOCIETY** *
  C/o Urbana Free Library Archives, 201 S. Race St., URBANA, IL 61801, USA.
  Library: As above. *Hours:* Mon.-Sat. 9am-4pm, Sun. 1pm-5pm. Open to non mem-
  bers. *Newsletter:* 4 per year. *Journal: CHAMPAIGN COUNTY GENEALOGICAL
  SOCIETY QUARTERLY* 4 per year. Available to non members at $2.50. *Quarterly
  Queries:* Free to members. *Membership:* $10.00. *Other Particulars* Meetings 2nd. Tues.
  each month at Urbana Free Library, 7.30pm. No meetings in Jan. or Aug. *President:*
  Jean Gordon. *Secretary:* Jean Wilson. *Editor:* James Campbell.

- **DECATUR GENEALOGICAL SOCIETY** *
  PO Box 1548, DECATUR, IL 62525-1548, USA. (Tel. 429 0135)
  Journal: CENTRAL ILLINOIS GENEALOGICAL QUARTERLY $3.00 for non
  members. *Research Enquiries:* Minimum of $3 members, $5 non members. *Member-
  ship:* $10.00. *Meetings:* 4th Tues. of month. *President:* Mary Wilking. *Secretary:* Helen
  Wiseley.

- **DOUGLAS COUNTY GENEALOGICAL SOCIETY**
  P.O. Box 113, TUSCOLA, IL 61953, USA.

- **DuPAGE COUNTY GENEALOGICAL SOCIETY**
  P.O. Box 133, LOMBARD, IL 60148, USA.
  Library: Wheaton Public Library, 225 N. Cross St., Wheaton, IL 60187. *Hours:* Normal library hours. Open to non members. *Newsletter: REVIEW* 7 per year. *Research
  Enquiries:* Free to members. *Membership:* $10.00 individual; $1.00 addl. person (fam-
  ily). *Other Particulars* Five yearly meetings with guest speakers. An educational, full-
  day workshop held each February also including guest speakers. Research policy
  $7.00 per family unit for non members, $5.00 for members. *President:* Tom Fetters.
  Corres. Secretary: Laurie Coolidge. *Meetings:* 7.30pm., 3rd Wed. odd months except
  July — McCormick Room, Wheaton Library.

- **EFFINGHAM COUNTY GENEALOGICAL SOCIETY**
  P.O. Box 1166, EFFINGHAM, IL 62401, USA.

- **FULTON COUNTY HISTORICAL & GENEALOGICAL SOCIETY**
  45 North Park Drive, CANTON, IL 61520, USA. (Tel. 309 647 0771.)
  Newsletter: $10.00 annual to non members. *Membership:* $10.00. *Meetings:* 2nd Sun.
  afternoon, Mar., July, Sept., Nov. 1st Sun. May. *President:* Dr. Marjorie Rich
  Bordner. *Secretary:* Mrs Tom Tracey.

- **ILLIANA GENEALOGICAL & HISTORICAL SOCIETY** *
  P.O. Box 207, DANVILLE, IL 61834, USA.
  Library: Danville Public Library, 307 N. Vermilion St., Danville, IL 61834. *Hours:*
  Limited hours. Open to non members. *Journal: ILLIANA GENEALOGIST* 4 per
  year. Available to non members at $2.50. *Research Enquiries:* Limited enquiries avail-
  able. Free to members. *Membership:* $10.00 individual; 50c additional persons in

household. *President:* Joan Griffis. *Secretary:* Betti Meinart. *Other Particulars* Queries free to members. Monthly meetings (except Jan., July & August) with guest speakers. We have for sale a Vermilion County History reprint, census indexes, cemeteries, marriages etc. of Vermilion County, IL and surrounding counties in IL and Indiana. A 23-year index to *Illiana Genealogist* published 1988.

- **ILLINOIS STATE GENEALOGICAL SOCIETY** *
  Stratton Building, Box 10195, SPRINGFIELD, IL, 62791, USA.

- **KENDALL COUNTY GENEALOGICAL SOCIETY**
  P.O. Box 1086, OSWEGO, IL 60543, USA.
  Journal: KENDALL COUNTY GENEALOGICAL SOCIETY NEWS 12 per year. Members only. *Research Enquiries:* Free. *Membership:* $12.00 individual. *Meetings:* 1st Tues. each month, 7.00pm. *President:* Mickie Meegan. *Secretary:* Helen Seal.

- **KNOX COUNTY GENEALOGICAL SOCIETY** *
  Box 13, GALESBURG, IL 61402-0013.
  Corresponding Secretary: Marian Witherbie.

- **McHENRY COUNTY ILLINOIS GENEALOGICAL SOCIETY** *
  1011 N. Green St., McHENRY, IL 60050, USA.
  Newsletter: 12 per year. *Journal: McHENRY COUNTY CONNECTION* 4 per year. Available to non members at $3.00. *Research Enquiries:* Free to members. *Membership:* $12.00 (USA), $16.00 (Foreign). *Other Particulars* Reprint of 1885 History of McHenry Co. available, $40.00 post paid and 1872 Atlas, $20.75. Federal Census 1840 $5.00, & 1860 $20.50 pp.

- **McLEAN COUNTY GENEALOGICAL SOCIETY**
  P.O. Box 488, NORMAL, IL 61761, USA.
  Library: McBarnes Bldg., 201 E. Grove, Bloomington, IL 61701. *Hours:* Each day (except Sat. & Sun.) 1-5pm. Open to non members — no charge. *Newsletter:* 12 per year. *Journal: GLEANINGS* 4 per year. *Research Enquiries:* Information on request. *Membership:* $15.00. *Meetings:* 3rd Mon. of each month. *President:* Paul Benjamin (309) 662 4780. *Secretary:* Lyn McCarthy, (309) 452 5869.

- **RICHLAND COUNTY GENEALOGICAL AND HISTORICAL SOCIETY** *
  C/o Jan Doan, R#1 CLAREMONT, IL 62421, USA.

- **GENEALOGY SOCIETY OF SOUTHERN ILLINOIS** *
  C/o John Logan College, R2, CARTERVILLE, IL 62918. (Tel. 618 985 6213.)
  Journal: THE SAGA OF SOUTHERN ILLINOIS 4 per year. $5.00 each (incl. postage) for non members. *Newsletter:* 12 per year. *Membership:* $16.00 per household, $5.00 for out of USA. *Meetings:* 2.00pm. 2nd Sunday of each month except Aug. — no meeting, October — Conf. on Sat. before the second Sunday. *President:* Mrs Jean Gehlbach Hauffe. *Librarian:* Tullyne S. Oliver.

- **WARREN COUNTY GENEALOGICAL SOCIETY** *
  P.O. Box 240, MONMOUTH, IL 61462, USA. (Tel. 309 734 2937.)
  Journal: PRAIRIE PIONEER 4 per year. $2.50 per issue for non members. *Research Enquiries:* Free for members, non members $2.00. *Membership:* $7.00 individual, $8.00 family. *Meetings:* 4th Thurs. of month. *President:* Tim Denison. *Secretary:* Beverly Clark.

INDIANA (IN)

- **CLAY COUNTY GENEALOGICAL SOCIETY, INC.** *
  P.O. Box 56, CENTERPOINT, IN 47840, USA.

- **LA PORTE COUNTY GENEALOGICAL SOCIETY** *
  904 Indiana Ave., LA PORTE, IN 46350, USA.

- **MONROE COUNTY HISTORICAL, GENEALOGICAL SOCIETY** *
  202 E. 6th St., BLOOMINGTON, IN 47408, USA.

- **NORTHWEST TERRITORY GENEALOGICAL SOCIETY**
  Lewis Historical Library-LRC, University, VINCENNES, IN 47591, USA.
  Library: As above. *Hours:* Mon.-Fri. 8.30-4.30pm. Open to non members. *Journal:*
  NORTHWEST TRAIL TRACER 4 per year. *Research Enquiries:* Free to members.
  Membership: $8.00. *Editor:* Donna Beeson.

- **PULASKI COUNTY GENEALOGICAL SOCIETY** *
  RR2 Box 133, STAR CITY, IN 46985, USA.

- **RIPLEY COUNTY HISTORICAL SOCIETY** *
  P.O. Box 525, VERSAILLES, IN 47042, USA.

- **TIPPECANOE COUNTY AREA GENEALOGICAL SOCIETY** *
  909 South St., LAFAYETTE, IN 47901, USA.
  Library: As above. *Hours:* Tues.-Fri. & 3rd Sat. 1-5pm. Open to non members. *News-letter:* 4 per year. *Membership:* $5.00 single, $7.50 couple. *President:* Peggy
  Basenfelder. *Secretary:* Jo Sanders.

- **INDIANA HISTORICAL SOCIETY — FAMILY HISTORY SECTION** *
  315 W. Ohio St., INDIANAPOLIS, IN 46202, USA.
  Journal: THE HOOSIER GENEALOGIST. Editor: Ruth Dorrel.

IOWA (IA)

- **IOWA GENEALOGICAL SOCIETY**
  P.O. Box 7735, DES MOINES, IA 50322, USA.
  Library: 6000Douglas, Suite 145, Des Moines, IA. *Hours:* Mon. — Fri. 9.00am-
  4.00pm. Sat. 10am-4pm. evening hours are seasonal. Open to non members, daily fee
  of $2.00. *Newsletter:* 6 per year. *Journal: HAWKEYE HERITAGE* 4 per year. *Re-search Enquiries:* In journal only. Free to members. $1.50 to non members. *Member-ship:* $20.00 single, $24.00 family.

- **GATEWAY GENEALOGICAL SOCIETY, CLINTON COUNTY** *
  618 14th Ave., CAMANCHE, IA 52730, USA.

- **GRUNDY COUNTY GENEALOGICAL SOCIETY** *
  P.O. Box 2, REINBECK, IA 50669, USA.

- **IOWA LAKES GENEALOGICAL SOCIETY**
  C/o Spencer Public Library, 21 E. 3rd St., SPENCER, IA 51301, USA.
  *Journal: ILGS TEASER*4 per year. $1.00 per issue for non members. *Research En-quiries*: $1.00 each. *Membership:* $5.00. *Meetings:* 3rd Saturday each month. *Pres-ident:* Neila Rohon. *Secretary:* Esther Connell.

- **JEFFERSON COUNTY GENEALOGY SOCIETY**
  Rt 1 Box 50, FAIRFIELD, IA 52556, USA.

- **LINN COUNTY HERITAGE SOCIETY** *
  Box 175, CEDAR RAPIDS, IA 52406, USA.
  Library: 101-8th Ave. S.E., Cedar Raids. Open to non members. *Hours:* Tues. 4-8pm,
  Wed. & Sat. 10am-4pm. *Membership:* $7.50 single, $10.00 couple at same address.
  Other Particulars Research Committee will de research for $5.00 per hour. *President:*
  Marilyn Walsh. *Secretary:* Dorathy Hronek.

- **POWESHIEK COUNTY HISTORICAL AND GENEALOGICAL SOCIETY**
  206 North Mill St., Box 280, MONTEZUMA, IA 50171, USA.
  President: Leta Hollmann.

KANSAS (KS)

- **KANSAS GENEALOGICAL SOCIETY**
  P.O. Box 103, DODGE CITY, KS 67801, USA.
  Library: 700 AvenueG. at Vine St. *Hours:* Mon.-Fri. 1.30-5.00pm. Open to non members — $3.00 per day. *Journal: THE TREESEARCHER* 4 per year; back issues by mail, 3 vols. $22.00, single $12.00. *Queries:* Free to members only. *Membership:* $14.00 regular, $19.00 family, $11.00 Public Library. *Other Particulars*: Quarterly Seminars featuring top genealogical speakers 2nd Thurs. in Jan., Apr., July & Oct.

- **BARTON COUNTY GENEALOGICAL SOCIETY ***
  Box 425, GREAT BEND, KS 67530, USA.
  Newsletter: 4 per year. *Research Enquiries:* Available on request. *Membership:* $10.00 plus $2.00 postage. *President:* Kathy Grover. *Secretary:* Ruth Wise. *Meetings:* 1st Mon., 7.30pm — King Memorial Methodist Church.

- **CHANUTE GENEALOGY SOCIETY ***
  1000 South Allen, CHANUTE, KS 66720, USA.

- **LYON COUNTY HISTORICAL MUSEUM LIBRARY/ARCHIVES. ***
  118 E. 6th, EMPORIA, KS 66801, USA.

- **MIDWEST HISTORICAL & GENEALOGICAL SOCIETY, INC. ***
  P.O. Box 1121, WICHITA, KS 67201, USA.

- **RILEY COUNTY KANSAS GENEALOGICAL SOCIETY ***
  2005 Claflin Road, MANHATTAN, KS 66502, USA.
  Library: As above. *Hours:* Tues., Thurs., Sat. 10am-4pm; Wed. 1-4pm, 7-9pm; Sun. 2-5pm. Open to non members. *Journal: KANSAS KIN* 4 per year. Available to non members at $1.00 — $2.50. *Research Enquiries:* Free to members. *Membership:* $10.00 household. *Other Particulars* We have for sale census indexes, cemeteries, marriages, etc. of Riley and surrounding counties. *President:* Evelyn Brown. *Secretary:* Pauline Norby. *Editor:* Harvey J. Littrell. *Meetings:* 1st Mon. Sept. through May except Dec.

- **TOPEKA GENEALOGICAL SOCIETY**
  P.O. Box 4048, TOPEKA, KS 66604-0048, USA.
  Library: (Circulating tomembers) 2717 Indiana Ave., Topeka. *Hours:* Wed., Thurs., Sat. afternoon. *Newsletter:* 4 per year. *Journal: TOPEKA GENEALOGICAL SOCIETY QUARTERLY* 4 per year. Available to non members. Price on request. *Researchers List*: Available on Request. *Membership:* $12.00 individual, $15.00 family. *Other Particulars* Queries are free to anyone if there is a Kansas connection pre-1900. Members' queries are free and may cover any time period or place. *President:* Mrs Colleen Wilson. *Corres. Secretary:* Mr E. Gene Dixon.

KENTUCKY (KY)

- **KENTUCKY GENEALOGICAL SOCIETY ***
  P.O. Box 153, FRANKFORT, KY 40602, USA.
  Society's Holdings locatedin Research Room, Public Records Division, Kentucky Department for Libraries, 300 Coffee Tree Road, Frankfort, KY. *Hours:* 8.00am-4.15pm., Tues.-Sat. closed Mon. *Journal: BLUEGRASS ROOTS* Quarterly. Back issues are $3.00. Cumulative index and all back issues are available for $30.00 (1973-1984). *Membership:* $10.00 individual, $10.00 family, $25.00 contributing member. Please send long S.A.S.E. for free KGS Brochure or membership card. *Meetings:* 2nd Mon. each month, except Aug. *Annual Seminar:* 1st Sat. in August in Frankfort. *Corresponding Secretary:* Mrs Donna Stark Thompson.

- **EASTERN KENTUCKY GENEALOGICAL SOCIETY, INC. ***
  P.O. Box 1544, ASHLAND, KY 41105-1011, USA.

- **LOUISVILLE GENEALOGICAL SOCIETY**
  P.O. Box 5164, LOUISVILLE, KY 40205, USA.
  Meetings: 2nd & 4th Tues. of eachmonth 1.00-3.00pm. St Andrew United Church of Christ, 2608 Browns Lane, Louisville, KY. *Publication: LINES & BYLINES* quarterly. *SURNAME INDEX* annually. *Membership:* Individual $10.00, family $12.00. *President:* Eugene Goodbub. *Corres. Secretary:* Ms Annette Roberts. *Treasurer:* Philip A. Wagner, Jr.

- **MAGOFFIN COUNTY HISTORICAL SOCIETY** *
  Box 222, SALYERSVILLE, KY 41465, USA. (Tel. (606) 349 2527 or (606) 349 1607.) *Journal: JOURNAL OF MAGOFFIN CO. HIST. SOC.* 4 per year. $3.00 each copy for non members. *Research Enquiries:* Free. *Membership:* $10.00. *Meetings:* 3rd Sun. each month, 2pm. *Conference:* Founders Day Festival, Labour Day Weekend. *President:* Todd Preston. *Secretary:* Connie A. Wireman.

- **WEST CENTRAL KENTUCKY FAMILY RESEARCH ASSOCIATION** *
  P.O. Box 1932, OWENSBORO, KY 42302, USA.
  Editor − Book Reviews: Mrs. Henry C. Alford, Jr.

LOUISIANA (LA)

- **LOUISIANA GENEALOGICAL & HISTORICAL SOCIETY** *
  P.O. Box 3454, BATON ROUGE, LA 70821, USA.

- **BATON ROUGE GENEALOGICAL & HISTORICAL SOCIETY** *
  P.O. Box 80565, S.E. Sta., BATON ROUGE, LA 70898-0565, USA.

- **SOUTHWEST LOUISIANA GENEALOGICAL SOCIETY** *
  P.O. Box 5652, LAKE CHARLES, LA 70606-5652, USA.
  Journal: KINFOLKS 4 p/a. $3.50 each. *Membership:* $10.00 ($15.00 family & $20.00 patron). *President:* Mrs. Pat Huffaker.

MAINE (ME)

- **MAINE GENEALOGICAL SOCIETY**
  P.O. Box 221, FARMINGTON, ME 04938, USA.
  Journal: THE MAINE SEINE 4 per year. Publishers Book Reviews. Queries from members only. *Newsletter:* 4 per year. *Membership:* $15.00 (+ $5.00 joining fee). Write for a list of available publications (S.A.S.E. please).

- **CHERRYFIELD-NARRAGUAGUS HISTORICAL SOCIETY**
  P.O. Box 96, CHERRYFIELD, ME 04622, USA.

- **FRANCO-AMERICAN GENEALOGICAL SOCIETY OF YORK COUNTY, MAINE** *
  P.O. Box 180, BIDDEFORD, ME 04005, USA.
  Library: McArthur Library, 270 Main St., Biddeford, ME. *Hours:* Mon.-Fri. 9am-8pm; Sat. 9am-5pm. Open to non members. *Journal: MAINE & FRANCO-AMERICAN HERITAGE* 1 per year. Available to non members at $5.00.

MARYLAND (MD)

- **MARYLAND GENEALOGICAL SOCIETY**
  201 West Monument St., BALTIMORE, MD 21201, USA.
  Library: As above. Entry by appointment. Open to non members. *Newsletter:* 4 per year. *Journal: MARYLAND GENEALOGICAL SOCIETY BULLETIN* 4 per year. Available to non members. Price on request. *Research Enquiries:* Cost of entries $8.00. *Membership:* $12.00. *President:* Jean K. Brandau. *Secretary:* Ella Rowe.

- **ANNE ARUNDEL GENEALOGICAL SOCIETY** *
  P.O. Box 221, PASADENA, MD 21122, USA.

- **BALTIMORE COUNTY HISTORICAL SOCIETY** *
  Agriculture Bldg., 9811 Van Buren Lane, COCKEYSVILLE, MD 21030, USA.

- **MONTGOMERY CO. HISTORICAL SOCIETY GENEALOGICAL CLUB.** *
  103 W. Montgomery Ave., ROCKVILLE, MD 20850, USA.
  Newsletter: LINE UPON LINE 10 per year. *Library:* As above. *Hours:* Tues.-Sat. 12-4pm; 1st Sun. of each month 2-5pm. *Membership:* $10.00 ($15.00 as joint member with the Historical Society). *Chairman:* Philip M. Ordway. *Corres. Secretary:* Mr. and Mrs. Leon Yeckley. *Meetings:* 4th Wed., 7.30pm, Stella B. Werner Council Office Building Auditorium, 100 Maryland Ave., Rockville, MD.

- **PRINCE GEORGE'S COUNTY GENEALOGICAL SOCIETY**
  P.O. Box 819, BOWIE, MD 20715-0819, USA.
  Library: Belair Stable Museum, 2835 Belair Drive, Bowie, MD. *Hours:* Wed. except hols., 10am-1pm. *Newsletter: PGCGS BULLETIN* 10 per year. Free queries. *Membership:* $10.00 ($15.00 for couples). *President:* Maxie D. Phillips. *Corresponding Secretary:* Carole Begenwald. *Meetings:* 1st Wed., 7.00pm, Sept. to June. Greenbelt Library, 11 Crescent Road, Greenbelt, MD. Sponsors free seminars for beginners in co-operation with the Prince George's County Memorial Library System. Has published seven volumes of County records.

MASSACHUSETTS (MA)

- **NEW ENGLAND HISTORIC GENEALOGICAL SOCIETY** *
  101 Newbury St., BOSTON, MA 02116, USA.
  Membership: $40.00 (family $60.00, student $10.00). *Library:* As above. *Hours:* Tues., Fri. & Sat. 9am-5pm. Wed. & Thurs. 9am-9pm. *Newsletter:* 6 per year. *Journal: NEW ENGLAND HISTORICAL & GENEALOGICAL REGISTER* 4 per year. *President:* Theodore Chase. *Corres. Secretary:* Mr. Nicholas Benton. *Register Editor:* Jane Fletcher Fiske. *Director:* Ralph J. Crandall.

MICHIGAN (MI)

- **THE DETROIT SOCIETY FOR GENEALOGICAL RESEARCH** *
  5201 Woodward Ave., DETROIT, MI 48202, USA.
  Journal: DSGR MAGAZINE Quarterly. Available to non members for $4.00 per issue. Free to members. *Membership:* $15.00 USA, $18.00 elsewhere. *Meetings:* 2nd Sat., monthly Sept.-June.

- **FRENCH CANADIAN HERITAGE SOCIETY OF MICHIGAN, DETROIT CHAPTER** *
  C/o G. Ricard, 1056 Balfour Road, GROSSE POINTE PARK, MI 48230, USA.

- **MICHIGAN, JEWISH GENEALOGICAL SOCIETY OF,** *
  Publication: GENERATIONS 3 per year. *Editor:* Esther A. Tschirhart, 19764 Cranbrook, Apt #c., Detroit, MI. *Subscriptions:* B. Koltonow, 3958 Winterset Ct., West Bloomfield, MI 48033; non member year subscriptions $10.00 US.

- **BRANCH COUNTY GENEALOGICAL SOCIETY**
  P.O. Box 443, COLDWATER, MI 49036, USA.

- **DOWNRIVER GENEALOGICAL SOCIETY**
  1394 Cleophus, Box 476, LINCOLN PARK, MI 48146, USA.
  Newsletter: THE DOWNRIVER SEEKER. Publications: write for list and prices. *Membership:* $7.00. *Meetings:* 3rd Wed. each month, except July, Aug. & Dec., at 7.30pm, Wayne Co. Com. College, Northline Rd., Southgate, MI 48195.

- **LAPEER COUNTY GENEALOGICAL SOCIETY** *
  Marguerite de Angeli Branch Library, 921 W. Nepessing St., LAPEER, MI 48446, USA.

- **MACOMB COUNTY GENEALOGY GROUP** *
  C/o Mount Clemens Public Library, 150 Cass Ave., MOUNT CLEMENS, MI 48043, USA.

- **MUSKEGON COUNTY GENEALOGICAL SOCIETY** *
  316 W. Webster, MUSKEGON, MI 49440, USA.

- **OAKLAND COUNTY GENEALOGICAL SOCIETY**
  P.O. Box 1094, BIRMINGHAM, MI 48012, USA.
  Journal: OAKLAND COUNTY GENEALOGICAL QUARTERLY Membership: US$10.00 individual, US$12.00 family. *Meetings:* 1st Tues. Oct. to June at Baldwin Library, Birmingham.

- **SAGINAW GENEALOGICAL SOCIETY, INC.**
  505 James Ave., SAGINAW, MI 48607, USA.
  Library: Hoyt Public Library. Above address. Open Mon.-Sat. Open to non members. *Newsletter:* 10 per year. *Journal: TIMBERTOWN LOG* 4 per year. Available to non members. *Research Enquiries:* Members only. *Membership:* $12.00 single, $15.00 double; outside USA: $14.00 single, $17.00 family. *President:* Darlene A. Hudson. *Corres. Secretary:* Jeanne S. White.

- **SHIAWASSEE COUNTY GENEALOGICAL SOCIETY**
  P.O. Box 841, OWOSSO, MI 48867, USA.

- **STERLING HEIGHTS GENEALOGICAL & HISTORICAL SOCIETY**
  P.O. Box 1154, STERLING HEIGHTS, MI 48311-1154, USA.
  Journal: THE ANCESTRAL TREE Quarterly. *Membership:* $8.00 single, $10.00 double. *Meetings:* 2nd Wed. each month at 7.30pm in the Naomi Gibbing School, 11303 Greendale (corner of Travis) Sterling Heights MI 48311-1154. Room.

MINNESOTA (MN)

- **MINNESOTA GENEALOGICAL SOCIETY**
  P.O. Box 16069, ST. PAUL, MN 55116, USA.
  Library: 1011 Fort Rd., St Paul. *Hours:* 6.30-9.30pm Wed., Thurs., 10am-4pm Sat. *Journal: THE MINNESOTA GENEALOGIST* 4 per year, also 4 Newsletter:s. *Membership:* $12.00 single, $15.00 family. Send S.A.S.E. for foreign postage information. *Meetings:* Quarterly — Mar., June, Sept., Dec. Various locations.

- **FREEBORN COUNTY GENEALOGICAL SOCIETY**
  P.O. Box 403, ALBERT LEA, MN 56007, USA.

- **RENVILLE COUNTY GENEALOGICAL SOCIETY**
  Box 331, RENVILLE, MN 56284, USA.
  Limited research on avolunteer basis. *Newsletter:* 4 per year.

- **VERNDALE HISTORICAL SOCIETY** *
  Verndale, MN 56481, USA.
  Publications: Several of interest to family historians of the Verndale area. Write for particulars. *President:* Marylu McClure.

MISSISSIPPI (MS)

- **MISSISSIPPI GENEALOGICAL SOCIETY** *
  JACKSON, MS 39296-5301, USA.

- **TIPPAH COUNTY HISTORICAL & GENEALOGICAL SOCIETY**
  308 North Commerce, RIPLEY, MS 38663, USA.
  Library: Asabove. *Hours:* Mon.-Sat. 9am-5pm. Open to non members. *Journal: NEWS & JOURNAL* 4 per year. Available to non members at $2.00. *Research Enquiries:* Free to members. *Membership:* $10.00. *Librarian:* Tommy Covington. *Meetings:* 3rd Thurs. each month.

- **NORTH EAST MISSISSIPPI HISTORICAL & GENEALOGICAL SOCIETY** *
  P.O. Box 434, TUPELO, MS 38802, USA.

MISSOURI (MO)

- **ST. LOUIS GENEALOGICAL SOCIETY** *
  9011 Manchester Road, ST. LOUIS, MO 63144, USA.
  Library: University City Library, 6701 Delmar, U. City, MO 63130. Open daily. Non members welcome. *Newsletter:* 12 per year. *Journal: ST. LOUIS GENEALOGICAL SOCIETY QUARTERLY* 4 per year. Available to non members at $3.00 each. *Research Enquiries:* Free to members. *Membership:* $10.00. *Other Particulars*: We publish a number of books relative to Missouri Research, a handbook for researchers *anQUESTors*, a guidebook covering research in eastern US *Tracing Family Trees in 11 States*, and a number of charts and forms for recording genealogical data. List of publications with prices, and a sample form, may be obtained by sending the society a SAE. Annual seminar in June.

- **HEART OF AMERICA GENEALOGICAL SOCIETY & LIBRARY** *
  C/o KansasCity Public Library, 311 E. 12th St., KANSAS CITY, MO 64106, USA.
  Library: As above, *Hours:* Mon.-Sat. 10am to 3pm. *Journal: THE KANSAS CITY GENEALOGIST* 4 pa. subscription $12.00. *Newsletter:* bi-monthly, members only. *Membership:* $10.00 (Journal extra). *President:* Ivan S. Waite. *Corres. Secretary:* Mary Helen Doran.

- **ADAIR COUNTY, MISSOURI HISTORICAL SOCIETY.** *
  C/o Eliz. Laughlin, 1315 S. 1st, KIRKSVILLE, MO 63501, USA (Tel. 816 665 2166).
  Newsletter: 4 per year. *Membership:* $5.00 single, $10.00 family. *Meetings:* Bi-monthly, varies. *President:* Emil Green. *Treasurer:* J. Eaton.

- **CASS COUNTY HISTORICAL SOCIETY, INC.**
  P.O. Box 406, HARRISONVILLE, MO 64701-0406, USA.
  Tel: (816) 887 2393.

- **GENEALOGICAL SOCIETY OF CENTRAL MISSOURI**
  P.O. Box 26, COLUMBIA, MO 65205, USA.

- **HARRISON COUNTY GENEALOGICAL SOCIETY**
  P.O. Box 65, BETHANY, MO 64424, USA. (Tel. 425 8039.)
  Journal: HERITAGE SEEKER 4 per year, $5.00 to non members. *Research Enquiries*: Donations. *Membership:* $5.00. *Meetings:* 1st Monday night each month. *President:* Maudine Bennum. *Secretary:* Pearl James.

- **LEWIS COUNTY HISTORICAL SOCIETY** *
  614 Clark St., CANTON, MO 63435, USA. Tel. (314) 288 3861
  Newsletter: NEWS & NOTES 4 per year, no charge to members, SASE to non members. *Membership:* $5.00. *Meetings:* 1st Tue. of each month. *President:* S.H. Purvines. *Secretary:* Jean Purvines.

- **OZARKS GENEALOGICAL SOCIETY, INC.** *
  P.O. Box 3494, SPRINGFIELD, MO 65808, USA.

- **NORTHWEST MISSOURI GENEALOGY SOCIETY**
  P.O. Box 382, ST. JOSEPH, MO 64502, USA.
  Library: Open to the publicno charge. *Hours:* Posted on the door of the library. *Phone*: (816) 233 0524. *Membership:* $10.00 single, $15.00 family. *Meetings:* 4th Thurs. of each month.

- **ST. CHARLES COUNTY GENEALOGICAL SOCIETY**
  P.O. Box 715, ST. CHARLES, MO 63302, USA.
  Journal: TANGLED ROOTS $1.00 to non members. *Research Enquiries:* Free to members, $1.00 to non members. *Membership:* $8.00. *Meetings:* 2nd Monday. *President:* Howard Liley. *Secretary:* Dorothy Long.

● **TEXAS COUNTY GENEALOGICAL & HISTORICAL SOCIETY** *
P.O. Box 12, HOUSTON, MO 65483, USA. (Tel. (417) 967 2532.)
Journal: OZARK HAPPENINGS 4 per year. $5.00 to non members. *Membership:*
$5.00. *Meetings:* 4th Fri. each month. *President:* Mildred Fourt Melton. *Secretary:*
Velma Adams. *Other Particulars* Annual workshop.

MONTANA (MT)

● **BROKEN MOUNTAINS GENEALOGICAL SOCIETY**
Box 261, CHESTER, MT 59522, USA.
Library: As above. *Hours:* Mon., Wed., Fri. 8am-5pm; Tues. & Thurs. 1-9pm. Open to
non members. *Journal: THE TRI-COUNTY SEARCHER* 2 per year. Available to
non members at $8.00 per year. *Research Enquiries:* Welcome. *Membership:* $10.00.
President: Maxine Ward. *Corres. Secretary:* Anna Mae Hanson. *Meetings:* 1st Thurs.
each month except July & Aug.

● **FORT ASSINIBOINE GENEALOGY SOCIETY** *
Box 321, Havre, Montana 59501, USA
Library: Open during meetings, 4th Tuesday of each month, or by special arrange-
ments. *Journal: SMOKE SIGNALS* 4 per year. Available to non-members at $4.00
per year. *Research Enquiries:* will be carried out by members, cost copying fees and
postage. *Membership:* $8.00 per year. Surname file kept. *President:* Mrs Roberta
Lener. *Secretary:* Lynn Ophus. *Library:* Barbara Van De Pete. Marie Marden. Newsletter: *Editor:* Bonnie Whittemore.

● **GREAT FALLS GENEALOGY SOCIETY** *
1400 First Avenue North, Room 30, GREAT FALLS, MT 59401, USA.

● **PARK COUNTY GENEALOGY SOCIETY**
C/o Public Library, 228 West Callender, LIVINGSTON, MT 59047, USA.
Meetings: 1st Tues. each month except July and Aug. *Membership:* $5.00 per year. For
information call (406) 222-7015, (406) 222-2033 or (406) 222-0968.

● **YELLOWSTONE GENEALOGY FORUM**
C/o Parmley Billings Library, 510 North Broadway, BILLINGS, MT 59101, USA.
Library: Parmley Billings Public Library Genealogy Room. *Hours:* Tues.-Thurs.
10am-8pm, Fri.-Sat. 10am-5pm, closed Sun. and Mon. Open to non members. *Jour-
nal: THE GEN-BUG NEWS* 4 per year, members only. *Membership:* $5.00 per year.
President: Louise LaRue. *Secretary:* Judy Kenney.

NEBRASKA (NE)

● **NEBRASKA STATE GENEALOGICAL SOCIETY** *
PO Box 5608, LINCOLN, NE 68505, USA.
For membership information: Anna May Mossman, NSGS Membership Chairman,
1705 Dianne Avenue, Bellevue, NE 68005, Tel: (402) 291 1441.

● **GREATER OMAHA GENEALOGICAL SOCIETY** *
PO Box 4011, OMAHA, NE 68104, USA.
Corres. Secretary: Aleatha Thilliander.

● **SOUTHEAST NEBRASKA GENEALOGICAL SOCIETY** *
PO Box 562, BEATRICE, NE 68310, USA.

NEVADA (NV)

● **NEVADA STATE GENEALOGICAL SOCIETY**
PO Box 20666, RENO, NV 89515, USA.

NEW HAMPSHIRE (NH)

- **NEW HAMPSHIRE SOCIETY OF GENEALOGISTS**
  P.O. Box 633, EXETER, NH 03833, USA.
  Newsletter: Quarterly and *Journal: THE NEW HAMPSHIRE GENEALOGICAL RECORD* 4 per year, $10.00 per year. *Queries:* First query free to members then $1.00 for 50 words or less. *Membership:* $10.00 ($15.00 household). *President:* George F. Sanborn Jr. *Corres. Secretary:* Mrs Helen Merrill. *Meetings:* Normally last Sat. in March & Sept.

- **ROCKINGHAM SOCIETY OF GENEALOGISTS**
  PO Box 81, EXETER, NH 03833, USA.
  Newsletter:/ *Journal: KINSHIP KRONICLE* $5.50per year. *Research Enquiries:* free. *Membership:* $8.50 (includes Newsletter:). *President:* Mr John J. Dow, Jr. *Meetings:* 2nd Sat. of month, Sept. thru May.

NEW JERSEY (NJ)

- **GENEALOGY CLUB OF THE NEW JERSEY HISTORICAL SOCIETY LIBRARY**
  230 Broadway, NEWARK, NJ 07104, USA.
  Library: As above. *Hours:* Wed.-Fri. and 3rd Sat. each month, 10am-4pm; closed selected holidays. *Newsletter:* Published 4 times per year. *Membership:* Open to any NJHS member. Rates on application. *Club Founder*: Harriet Stryker-Rodda. *President:* Linnea Foster. *Library* .i Director: Rozalind Libbey.

- **CAPE MAY COUNTY HISTORICAL AND GENEALOGICAL SOCIETY** *
  Route 9, Cape May Court House, NJ 08210, USA.
  Library: As above. *Hours:* Tues., Wed. & Fri. 10am-4pm and by appointment. Available to non members at an hourly fee. *Newsletter:* 4 per year. *Journal: CAPE MAY COUNTY MAGAZINE OF HISTORY & GENEALOGY* 1 per year. Available to non members at $3.00 incl. postage. *Research Enquiries:* Members free $2.00 to non members. *Membership:* Rates on application. *President:* Mrs James Wilson. *Secretary:* Mrs James Waltz.

- **GLOUCESTER COUNTY HISTORICAL SOCIETY LIBRARY**
  17 Hunter St., (PO Box 407) WOODBURY, NJ 08096, USA.
  Library: As above. *Hours:* Mon.-Thurs. 1-4pm, Fri. 1-4pm & 7-9.30pm. Last Sun. of month 2-5pm. Open to non members. Specialises in Genealogical Research. *Newsletter:* 4 per year. *Research Enquiries:* $5.00 for members' entries. *Membership:* $5.00. *Librarian:* Mrs Edith Hoelle. *President:* Richard M. Burr. Tel.: (609) 845 4771. *Secretary:* Mrs Euretha Batten. Publications program includes 98 books on the history and genealogy of South Jersey.

- **GENEALOGICAL SOCIETY OF THE WEST FIELDS.**
  550 E. Broad Street, WESTFIELD, NJ 07090, USA.
  President: Florence Haller.

NEW MEXICO (NM)

- **NEW MEXICO GENEALOGICAL SOCIETY** *
  PO Box 8283, ALBUQUERQUE, NM 87198, USA.
  Library: 423 Central Avenue, N.E. Albuquerque, NM. *Hours:* Wed., Fri. & Sat. 9am-5.30pm; Tues. & Thurs. 12.30-8pm. *Journal: NEW MEXICO GENEALOGIST* 4 per year. *Membership:* $8.00. *President:* Andres J. Segura. *Secretary:* Mabel Vigil-Collins. *Meetings:* 3rd Tues., 7.30pm at Library.

- **SIERRA COUNTY GENEALOGICAL SOCIETY** *
  C/o Public Library, P.O. Box 311, TRUTH OR CONSEQUENCES, NM 87901, USA.
  Meetings: 3rd Wed. pm. at public library in T or C. *President:* Caron Morgan. *Secretary:* Gertrude Howell. *Treasurer:* Eleanor Peacock. *Historian*: Evelyn Pyles.

● **SOUTHEASTERN NEW MEXICO GENEALOGICAL SOCIETY** *
P.O. Box 5725, HOBBS, NM 88241, USA.
Research Library: Will Rogers Community Centre, 200 E. Park, Room 115, Hobbs.
Librarian: Veta Blackburn.

NEW YORK (NY)

● **NEW YORK GENEALOGICAL & BIOGRAPHICAL SOCIETY**
122 East 58th Street, NEW YORK, NY 10022-1939, USA. (Tel. 212-755-8532).
Library: As above. *Hours:* Mon.-Fri. 9.30am-5pm (June-Sept.); Mon.-Sat. 9.30am-
5pm (Oct.-May) closed August. Open to non members – donation $3.00. *Journal:*
THE NEW YORK GENEALOGICAL & BIOGRAPHICAL RECORD 4 per year.
Journal sub. $25.00 p.a. or $6.50 each. *Queries in Record:* Free to members and subscribers. Non members $5.00 per 50 words. *Membership:* $50.00. *President:* Henry S.
Middendorf Jr. *Exec. Director:* William P. Johns. *Other Particulars* Educational
lecture programs offered each fall, and as announced. Library contains some 68,000
volumes & manuscripts, microfilm & fiche.

● **CENTRAL NEW YORK GENEALOGICAL SOCIETY** *
Box 104, Colvin Station, SYRACUSE, NY 13205, USA.
Journal: TREE TALKS 4 per year. *Meetings:* 6 per year. *Membership:* $18.00.
Chairperson: Tom Murray. *Secretary:* Elizabeth McDonald. *Editor:* Marcia
Eisenberg. *Membership Sec.:* Harriett Hall.

● **JEWISH GENEALOGICAL SOCIETY, INC.**
P.O. Box 6398, NEW YORK, NY 10128, USA. Tel. (212) 722 8456.
Contact: Michael Brenner (as above). *Publication: DOROT* Quarterly. *Editor:* Alex
Friedlander. Subscription by Society membership only.

● **JEWISH GENEALOGY SOCIETY OF LONG ISLAND**
C/o 37 Westcliff Dr., DIX HILLS, NY 11746, USA.
Publication: JGSLI LINEAGE. Editor: Renee Steinig. *President:* Les Goldschmidt.

● **HERKIMER COUNTY HISTORICAL SOCIETY** *
400 N. Main St., HERKIMER, NY 13350, USA.(Tel. 315 866 6413.)
Research Enquiries: $15.00. *Membership:* $10.00 single, $15.00 family. *President:*
James R. Lenney. *Secretary:* Ruthe P. Short.

● **HOLLAND SOCIETY OF NEW YORK** *
122 E. 58 St., NEW YORK, NY 10022, USA.

● **NIAGARA COUNTY GENEALOGICAL SOCIETY**
215 Niagara St. LOCKPORT, NY 14094, USA.
Library: Contact above for details. *Hours:* Thus., Fri., Sat. 1-5pm. Open to non members. *Newsletter:* 4 per year. *Research Enquiries:* Free to members. *Membership:*
$10.00 annual fee. *President of Board:* Douglas V. Farley. *Corres. Secretary:* Nancy
Balling Smith, at above address (Tel. 716-433-1033).

● **NORTHERN NEW YORK AMERICAN-CANADIAN GENEALOGICAL
SOCIETY**
P.O. Box 1256, PLATTSBURGH, NY 12901, USA.
Library: Community Centre, Keeseville, NY. *Hours:* Open to non members. *Journal:*
LIFELINES 2 per year. Available to non members at $8.00 each. *Research Enquiries:*
Limited to 2 marriage at a time and to Clinton Co. NY or Quebec Prov. only. *Mem-
bership:* $20.00 single, $25.00 family (2 people), Libraries & Inst. f/t students $7.50.
Meetings: Spring Conference, 2nd weekend in May. Fall Conference, 3rd weekend in
Oct. *Other Particulars* Two free query per journal per member, $3.00 each additional
query. Non members $5.00 per query.

● **ORANGE COUNTY GENEALOGICAL SOCIETY** *
101 Main St., GOSHEN, NY 10924, USA.
Library: As above. *Hours:* 1st Wed. in month 8.30am-5pm; 3rd Sat. in month 9.30am-

12noon; every Monday 8.30-11.30am. Open to non members – no fee. *Journal: ORANGE COUNTY GENEALOGICAL SOCIETY* 4 per year. $1.00 per issue. Vol 15+ $2.00 per issue. *Research Enquiries:* Free to members only. *Membership:* $10.00. *President:* Howard Case. *Secretary:* Mrs Colleen Lofrese. *Meetings:* 1st Sat. of each month at 10.00am. *Other Particulars* Our main project is compiling cemetery records – the records of three towns have been published and we are working on the fourth; latest pub. the Whig Press Marriages 1851-1865 and St James Epis. Church records, Goshen, NY. Cemeteries of the town of Minisink now available.

- **ROCHESTER HISTORICAL SOCIETY** *
  485 East Ave., ROCHESTER, NY 14607, USA.
  Phone: (716) 271 2705. *Archivist Elizabeth Yonkers.*

- **SUFFOLK COUNTY HISTORICAL SOCIETY – RESEARCH LIBRARY** *
  300 W. Main St., RIVERHEAD, NY 11901, USA.

- **WESTERN NEW YORK GENEALOGICAL SOCIETY** *
  P.O. Box 338, HAMBURG, NY 14075, USA.
  Library: reference only, Hamburg Historical Museum, 5859 South Park Ave. *Journal: W.N.Y.G.S. JOURNAL* 4 pa. *Research Enquiries:* No research or answers to enquiries made by mail. *Membership:* $15.00 ($17.00 family) + $3.00 foreign. *Meetings:* Seven per year, Sept.-May at Hamburg High School, write for details. SSAE.

NORTH CAROLINA (NC)

- **NORTH CAROLINA GENEALOGICAL SOCIETY**
  P.O. Box 1492, RALEIGH, NC 27602, USA.
  Journal: Quarterly with queries, book reviews. Bi-monthly Newsletter:. Periodic Workshops. *Membership:* $25.00 ($22.00 inst.). *Journal Editor:* Raymond A. Winslow, Jr.

- **FORSYTH COUNTY GENEALOGICAL SOCIETY**
  P.O. Box 5715, WINSTON-SALEM, NC 27113, USA.

- **OLD BUNCOMBE COUNTY GENEALOGICAL SOCIETY, INC.**
  P.O. Box 2122, ASHEVILLE, NC 28802, USA.
  Library: 2 Wall Street., Asheville 28801. *Hours:* Mon.-Fri. 9am-5pm. Open to non members. *Newsletter: A LOT OF BUNKUM* 10 issues per year, plus members' directory and annual index. Available to non members at $1.50 per issue. *Research Queries:* Free to members. *Membership:* $18.00. *Other Particulars* We operate a small bookstore service including basic genealogical supplies. *President:* Walter Hall. *Corres. Secretary:* Nancy Schuldheis.

OHIO (OH)

- **OHIO GENEALOGICAL SOCIETY**
  P.O. Box 2625, MANSFIELD, OH 44906, USA.
  Library: 34 Sturges Ave., Mansfield. *Hours:* Tues. through Sat. 9am-5pm. Open to non members. *Newsletter:* 12 per year. *Journal: THE REPORT* 4 per year. Available to non members at $25.00 year. *Research Enquiries:* Free to members. *Membership:* $25.00, $30.00 joint, $10.00 extra for foreign (postage). *President:* Jeanne Pramaggiore. *Chairman:* Robert Cunning. *Corres. Secretary:* Diane Gagel.

- **SOUTHERN OHIO GENEALOGICAL SOCIETY** *
  P.O. Box 414, HILLSBORO, OH 45133, USA.
  Journal: ROOTS & SHOOTS 4 per year. $6.00 for non members. *Research Enquiries*: 50 words free. *Membership:* $5.00, with *R & S*, $10.00.

- **ASHTABULA COUNTY GENEALOGICAL SOCIETY**
  54 E. Jefferson St., JEFFERSON, OH 44047, USA.
  Journal: ANCESTOR HUNT 4 per year with index. Back issues or copies $2.50 plus $1.00 postage for non members. *Membership:* $10.00, ($12.00 family). *Meetings:* 4th

Wed. of month except July. *President:* Fran Metcalf. *Secretary:* Corinne Loyd.

- **THE BROWN CO. GENEALOGICAL SOCIETY (Chapter of OGS)**
  P.O. Box 83, GEORGETOWN, OH 45121, USA.
  Library: Cnr. Apple & Cherry Sts., Georgetown. *Hours:* Thurs. & Sat. 12noon-5pm.
  Open to non members. *Newsletter:* 4 per year. *Research Enquiries:* Free to members.
  Membership: $7.00 single, $9.00 family. *Meetings:* 3rd Thurs. at 7pm.

- **CARROLL COUNTY GENEALOGICAL SOCIETY**
  59 3rd St., NE CARROLLTON, OH 44615, USA. (Tel. 216 627 2094.)
  Journal: CARROLL COUSINS 6 per year. *Research Enquiries:* Free, $1.00 if non
  member. *Membership:* $5.00. *Meetings:* 3rd Tues. each month. *President:* Marguerite
  Finnicum. *Secretary:* Sara Finnicum.

- **CENTERVILLE HISTORICAL SOCIETY** *
  89 W. Franklin St., CENTERVILLE, OH 45459, USA.

- **DARKE COUNTY GENEALOGY SOCIETY** *
  P.O. Box 908, GREENVILLE, OH 45331, USA.

- **DAYTON JEWISH GENEALOGY SOCIETY** *
  2536 England Ave., DAYTON, OH 45406, USA.
  President: Leonard Spialter.

- **EAST CUYAHOGA COUNTY CHAPTER, O.G.S.** *
  P.O. Box 24182, LYNDHURST, OH 44124, USA.

- **FRANKLIN COUNTY GENEALOGICAL SOCIETY**
  P.O. Box 2503, COLUMBUS, OH 43216, USA.
  Library: 570 W. Broad Street, Columbus, OH 43215. *Hours:* Mon.-Wed.-Fri. 10am-
  3pm. Open to non members. *Newsletter: THE FRANKLINTONIAN* 10 per year.
  Available to non members at $14.00 – 10 issues. *Research Enquiries:* Donation re-
  quested for research completed. *Membership:* $14.00. *President:* William D. Havens.
  Secretary: Margaret Hiles Scott.

- **GALLIA COUNTY CHAPTER, O.G.S.** *
  P.O. Box 295, GALLIPOLIS, OH 45631, USA.

- **GERMANTOWN HISTORICAL SOCIETY** *
  P.O. Box 29, 47 West Center Street, GERMANTOWN, OH 45327, USA.
  President: S. Shafer.

- **GREAT LAKES HISTORICAL SOCIETY** *
  480 Main Street, VERMILION, OH 44089, USA.

- **LICKING COUNTY GENEALOGICAL SOCIETY** *
  P.O. Box 4037, NEWARK, OH 43055, USA.
  Library: 743 E. Main Street, Room # 107, Newark, OH. *Hours:* Tues., Wed., Thurs.
  & Sat. 1-4pm. Open to non members. (Donation.) *Journal: THE LICKING LAN-
  TERN* 4 per year + index. *Research Enquiries:* 2 free with annual membership paid.
  Membership: $10.00 single, $12.00 joint, $9.00 if sent before Jan. 1st. *Other Particulars*
  Back issues of *Lantern* available with index at $4.00 year for 1976, '77, '78. Price is
  $5.00 year for 1979, '80, '81; $6.00 year 1982; $7.00 year 1983; $8.00 year 1984, '85.
  Lantern issues 1986 – $8.00, 1987-88 – $10.00. A list of books reprints, census in-
  dexes, other published material avail. from us can be obtained by writing to the ab-
  ove address and including long SASE. *president:* Pat Hollingsworth *Correspondence
  Secretary:* Ronna Eagle. *Recording* i Secretary: Vera Close.

- **MUSKINGUM COUNTY GENEALOGICAL SOCIETY** *
  P.O. BOX 3066, ZANESVILLE, OH 43702, USA.

- **PENINSULA LIBRARY AND HISTORICAL SOCIETY** *
  P.O. Box 236, PENINSULA, OH 44264, USA.

- **ROSS COUNTY GENEALOGICAL SOCIETY**
  P.O. Box 6352, CHILLICOTHE, OH 45601, USA.
  Library: 172 East Main Street. *Hours:* Mon. Wed., Fri. 1-4pm. *Newsletter:* 4 per year. *President:* Helen Rhoten. *Secretary:* Beverly Gray. *Meetings:* 2nd Tues. at McKell Library, 39 W. Fifth Street.

- **SOUTHWEST CUYAHOGA CHAPTER, O.G.S.** *
  18631 Howe Road, STRONGSVILLE, OH 44136, USA. (Tel. 216 238 6370.)
  Newsletter: 3 per year. Available to non members for $5.00. *Research Enquiries*: Free to members. *Membership*: $5.00. *Meetings*: 2nd Thurs. Feb.-May, Sept.-Dec. *President:* Willis Braun. *Corres. Secretary:* Grace Williams.

- **VILLAGE HISTORICAL SOCIETY, INC.**
  C/o Eugene B. Woelfel, President, 6590 Kilby Road, HARRISON, OH 45030, USA.

- **WASHINGTON COUNTY CHAPTER, O.G.S.**
  P.O. Box 2174, MARIETTA, OH 45750, USA.

- **WESTERN RESERVE HISTORICAL SOCIETY LIBRARY**
  10825 E. Boulevard, CLEVELAND, OH 44106, USA.
  Hours: 9am-5pm, Tues.-Sat. *Admission*: Society members free, adults $4.00, students and seniors $2.00. Extensive genealogy collections cover the area from New England to Georgia and west to the Mississippi River. Send SASE for brochure listing library services, fees and available genealogy collections. *Research*: of Library records, $20.00 per hour. *Bulletin 4 per year, $4.00 per year.*

- **STATE LIBRARY OF OHIO (GENEALOGY SECTION)**
  65 S. Front Street, COLUMBUS, OH 43266-0334, USA.
  Library: As above. *Hours:* Mon.-Thurs. 8am-5pm; Fri. 9am-5pm. Open to non members. *Head of Department*: Petta Khouw. Send SASE for brochure listing Library services.

OKLAHOMA (OK)

- **OKLAHOMA GENEALOGICAL SOCIETY**
  P.O. Box 12986, OKLAHOMA CITY, OK 73157, USA.
  Library: Books housed at the Oklahoma Historical Society. *Journal: QUARTERLY.*
  Membership: $10.00 single, $12.00 family.

- **NORTHWEST OKLAHOMA GENEALOGICAL SOCIETY** *
  P.O. Box 834, WOODWARD, OK 73802, USA. (Tel. 405 256 4609)
  Journal: KEYFINDER 4 per year. $4.00 to non members. *Research Enquiries:* $2.00. *Membership:* $10.00. *Meetings:* 3rd Tues. each month. *Conference:* Spring & Fall seminar. *President:* Alice Lynne Boydston. *Secretary:* Verlaine Clark.

- **SOUTHWEST OKLAHOMA GENEALOGICAL SOCIETY**
  P.O. 148, LAWTON, OK 73502, USA.
  Library: Jennie L. McCutcheon Research Room, Lawton Public Library. *Hours:* Mon.-Thus. 10am-9pm.; Fri. 10am-6pm.; Sat. 10am-5pm; Sun. 1-5pm (except summer). Open to non members. *Journal: THE TREE TRACERS* 4 per year. Available to non members at $10.00 year. *Research Enquiries:* Free to members. *Membership:* $10.00. *Life Membership:* $125.00. *Other Particulars* Weekly Newspaper Column for S.W. OK Queries – send to same address, (Sat.) *Lawton Morning Press. President:* Jay Irwin. *Secretary:* Aulena Scearce Gibson. *Meetings:* 3rd Mon. at Lawton Public Library, 110 SW 4, Lawton, OK. Books for sale of S.W. OK records, OK Tract Books Indexes Available.

- **OTTAWA COUNTY GENEALOGY SOCIETY** *
  Box 1383, MIAMI, OK 74355, USA.

- **POTEAU VALLEY GENEALOGICAL SOCIETY** *
  P.O. Box 1031, POTEAU, OK 74953, USA.

- **POTTAWATOMIE COUNTY GENEALOGY CLUB ***
  P.O. Box 3526, SHAWNEE, OK 74802, USA.
  Library: Mini Mall, Main and Broadway. *Hours:* Mon., Thurs., Sat. 10am-4pm, or by appointment. *Membership:* $10.00 individual, $15.00 family. *Meetings:* 2nd Mon. each month at Mini Mall. *President:* Daunita Kanedy. *Corres. Secretary:* Gail Loula.

OREGON (OR)

- **GENEALOGICAL FORUM OF OREGON, INC. ***
  1410 S.W. Morrison Street, PORTLAND, OR 97205, USA.
  Library: As above. *Hours:* Mon. to Sat. 9.30am-3pm Thurs. to 8pm. Open to non members for a fee. *Newsletter:* Various number published yearly. *Journal: BULLETIN GENEALOGICAL FORUM OF OREGON, INC.* 4 per year. Back issues on microfiche. *Research Enquiries:* Free to members. 50 words per $1.00 to non members. *Membership:* $18.00. *President:* Vickie Weber. *Secretary:* Patricia S. Burling. *Meetings:* 2nd Mon. each month Sept. to Apr. & June.

- **OREGON GENEALOGICAL SOCIETY INC. ***
  P.O. Box 10306, EUGENE, OR 97440-2306, USA. (Tel. (503) 342-4122).
  Library: 1001 Washington Street, Eugene. *Hours:* Mon., Fri. & Sat. 10am-2pm. Wed. 10am-9pm. 4th Sat. 2.30-4.30pm. Open to non members. *Annual Bulletin: OREGON GENEALOGICAL SOCIETY QUARTERLY* 4 per year. Available to non members at $3.00 each for back issues. *Research Inquiries*: will be turned over to Research Committee, donations requested. *Membership:* $15.00. *Meetings:* 4th Sat. (except Dec.) at EWEB Meeting Room, 500 E. 4th Street, Eugene. *President:* Carole Kucera. *Corresponding Secretary:* Mary Stapleton Lawlor.

PENNSYLVANIA (PA)

- **GENEALOGICAL SOCIETY OF PENNSYLVANIA ***
  1300 Locust St., PHILADELPHIA, PA 19107, USA.

- **ADAMS COUNTY HISTORICAL SOCIETY ***
  Drawer A, GETTYSBURG, PA 17325, USA.

- **BLAIR COUNTY GENEALOGICAL SOCIETY**
  P.O. Box 855, ALTOONA, PA 16601, USA. (Tel. 814 942 3681.)
  Newsletter: 4 per year. *Research Enquiries:* 1 free per year, additional 1, $1.00 each. *Membership:* $15.00. *Meetings:* 3rd Thurs. each month, 7.30pm. *President:* Carol Bravin. *Secretary:* Jennie Amrhein.

- **BUCKS COUNTY GENEALOGICAL SOCIETY**
  P.O. Box 1092, DOYLESTOWN, PA 18901, USA.
  Newsletter: 4 per year. *Newsletter query*: entries cost $2.00. *Membership:* $12.00. *Meetings:* Sep.-May, 2nd Thurs. *Conference*: April 27, 1991. *Other Particulars*: 30 mins. free search. *President:* Laura M. Hager.

- **CORNERSTONE GENEALOGICAL SOCIETY**
  P.O. Box 547, WAYNESBURG, PA 15370, USA.
  Library: Bowlby Public Library, 311 N. West St., Waynesburg, PA 15370. *Hours:* Every day but Sunday, various times. Open to non members — no fee. *Journal: CORNERSTONE CLUES* 4 plus index. Available to non members at $3.00 each. *Editor:* Norma T. Bell. *Research Enquiries:* Free to members. *Membership:* $12.00 (joining fee). *Meetings:* 2nd Tues. each month except Dec. *President:* Malvine Zollars. *Secretary:* Joseph Piatt.

- **FULTON COUNTY HISTORICAL SOCIETY, INC. ***
  Box 115, MCCONNELLSBURG, PA 17233, USA.

- **JEWISH GENEALOGICAL SOCIETY OF PHILADELPHIA**
  Contact: Jon E. Stein, 332 Harrison Ave., ELKINS PARK, PA 19117-2662, USA.
  Newsletter: CHRONICLES 4 per year. Back issues $3.50. Research ads in newsletter,

$6.00 25 words. *Meetings:* Generally 2nd Mon. except Jan., Feb., July & Aug. at 7.45pm. National Museum of American Jewish History, 55 N. 5th St., Philadelphia. *Library:* Accessible at meetings. *Membership:* $20.00 (family $30.00). *President:* Jon E. Stein.

● **LACKAWANNA HISTORICAL SOCIETY ***
232 Monroe Ave., SCRANTON, PA 18510, USA.

● **LANCASTER MENNONITE HISTORICAL SOCIETY**
2215 Millstream Rd., LANCASTER, PA 17602-1499, USA.
Tel: (717) 393 9745 (days); (717) 733 2311 (evenings). *Library:* As above. *Hours:* Tues.-Sat. 8.30am-4.30pm. Open to non members at $2.00 daily fee. *Newsletter: THE MIRROR* 6 per year. *Journal: PENNSYLVANIA MENNONITE HERITAGE* 4 per year. Available to non members at $5.00 per issue. *Research Enquiries:* Disc. to members. *Membership:* $20.00. *Director:* Carolyn C. Wenger. *Secretary:* Genealogist — David J. Rempel Smucker. *Librarian:* Lloyd Zeager.

● **PITTSBURGH JEWISH GENEALOGICAL SOCIETY ***
Contact: Julian Falk, 2127-31 Fifth Ave., PITTSBURGH, PA 15219, USA.
Publication: Z'CHOR/REMEMBER.

● **GENEALOGICAL SOCIETY OF SOUTHWESTERN PENNSYLVANIA**
P.O. Box 894, WASHINGTON, PA 15301, USA.

● **VENANGO COUNTY GENEALOGICAL CLUB**
P.O. Box 811, OIL CITY, PA 16301, USA.
President: A.E. Morrison. *Vice President:* B.M. Harvey.

● **VENANGO COUNTY HISTORICAL SOCIETY**
315 S. Park St., Box 101, FRANKLIN, PA 16323, USA. (Tel. 814 437 2275.)
Journal: THE INTELLIGENCER 4 per year, free for members. *Research Enquiries:* $10.00. *Membership:* $5.00. *Meetings:* date varies. *President:* Ruth R. Heasley. *Exec. Secretary:* Mary Sanford. *Genealogical Chairman:* Sylvia Coast.

● **WESTERN PENNSYLVANIA GENEALOGICAL SOCIETY**
4338 Bigelow Boulevard, PITTSBURGH, PA 15213-2695, USA.
Library: As above. *Hours:* Tues.-Sat. 9.30am-4.30pm. Open to non members — fee. *Newsletter:* 10 per year. *Journal: WESTERN PENNSYLVANIA GENEALOGICAL SOCIETY QUARTERLY.* Available to non members at $5.00. Editor; Jean S. Morris. *Membership:* $20.00. *Meetings:* 2nd Thurs. Sept. to June at 8pm. All day workshops, Saturdays Jan., Feb., Mar. at 10.00am.

● **WYOMING COUNTY HISTORICAL SOCIETY ***
P.O. Box 309, TUNKHANNOCK, PA 18657, USA.

RHODE ISLAND (RI)

● **RHODE ISLAND HISTORICAL SOCIETY LIBRARY**
121 Hope St., PROVIDENCE, RI 02906, USA.
Library Director: Madeleine B. Telfeyan.

● **THE CHURCH OF JESUS CHRIST OF LATTER-DAY SAINTS, FAMILY HISTORY LIBRARY.**
1000 Narragansett Parkway, WARWICK, RI 02888, USA.
Contact: Claire V. Banks (Director) 87 Ohio Ave, Prov., RI 02905. Tel: 401 461 8033.

SOUTH CAROLINA (SC)

● **SOUTH CAROLINA GENEALOGICAL SOCIETY ***
P.O. Box 16355, GREENVILLE, SC 29606, USA.
Publishes: THE CAROLINA HERALD (twice a year) and the SCGS Newsletter: (4 times a year). Annual Workshop in July, and an Annual Meeting in October. *Membership:* Is through one of 16 local chapters, Anderson, Hartsville, Charleston, Aiken-

Barnwell, Catawba-Watereee, Columbia, Dutch Fork, Greenville, Fairfield, Laurens, Old Edgefield District, Old 96 District, Pee Dee, Pinckney District, Pendleton District & Sumter.

TENNESSEE (TN)

● **THE TENNESSEE GENEALOGICAL SOCIETY**
P.O. Box 111249, MEMPHIS, TN 38111-1249, USA.
Journal: ANSEARCHIN' NEWS. Editor: Gery B. Spence.

● **EAST TENNESSEE HISTORICAL SOCIETY**
500 W. Church Ave., KNOXVILLE, TN 37902, USA. (mail only).
Library: Cnr. Clinch Ave.and Market St. *Newsletter: NEWSLINE* Quarterly. *Tri-Annual Genealogical Publication: TENNESSEE ANCESTORS. Annual Journal: PUBLICATIONS. Research Enquiries:* Available. *Membership:* $25.00.

● **HAWKINS COUNTY GENEALOGICAL SOCIETY** *
P.O. Box 429, ROGERSVILLE, TN 37857, USA.

TEXAS (TX)

● **CENTRAL TEXAS GENEALOGICAL SOCIETY, INC.**
Waco-McLennan County Library, 1717 Austin Ave., WACO, TX 76701, USA.
Library: As above. *Hours:* Mon.-Thurs. 9am-8.30pm; Fri., Sat. 9am-5.30pm. Open to non members. *Journal: HEART OF TEXAS RECORDS* 4 per year. *Research Enquiries*: Free, as space permits. *Membership:* $10.00. *President:* Bob Wiese. *Secretary:* Carla Machate.

● **NORTH TEXAS GENEALOGICAL ASSOCIATION** *
P.O. Box 4602, WICHITA FALLS, TX 76308, USA.
Quarterly: NORTH TEXAS TRACERS — 50+ page publication. 4 per year. Serves counties of Archer, Baylor, Clay, Montague, Wichita & Wilbarger. *Membership:* $10.00 individual; $15.00 family. *Queries:* Free to members, no limit; non members $1.00. Queries also run in monthly newspaper column. *Meetings:* 1st Thurs. each month 7.30pm, meeting room of North Texas Federal Savings & Loan, 2733 Midwestern Parkway. Visitors welcome. All day Seminar each fall. Supports Genealogy Room in Kemp Public Library, 1300 Lamar, Wichita Falls, TX 76301.

● **DALLAS GENEALOGICAL SOCIETY** *
Box 12648, DALLAS, TX 75225, USA.
Newsletter: 9 per year. *Journal: DALLAS QUARTERLY* 4 per year. Available to non members. *Research Enquiries:* Free to members. $3.00 to non members. *Membership:* $12.00. *Meetings:* Monthly except June, July, Aug. and Dec.

● **HOUSTON GENEALOGICAL FORUM** *
P.O. Box 271466, HOUSTON, TX 77277-1466, USA.
Journal: THE GENEALOGICAL RECORD 4 per year. *Research Enquiries:* $2.00. Published in journal. *Membership:* $13.00 single, $15.00 family. *President:* Norris Dennard. *Secretary:* Mrs Lorena Gould. *Meetings:* 1st Sat. each month at Bayland Community Centre, 6400 Bissonnet, Houston.

● **FORT BELKNAP GENEALOGICAL ASSOCIATION** *
H.C. #60, Box #409, GRAHAM, TX 76046, USA.

● **HEMPHILL COUNTY GENEALOGICAL SOCIETY** *
C/o Mrs John Ramp, Route 2, Box 15a, CANADIAN, TX 79014, USA.

● **HUTCHINSON COUNTY GENEALOGICAL SOCIETY**
C/o Hutchinson County Library, 625 Weatherly, BORGER, TX 79007, USA.
Membership: $5.00. *Meetings:* 3rd Thurs. each month, except Dec. *President:* Luther Fruit. *Secretary:* Charlene Ferrell.

- **GENEALOGICAL SOCIETY OF KENDALL COUNTY** *
  P.O. Box 623, BOERNE, TX 78006, USA.

- **MESQUITE HISTORICAL AND GENEALOGICAL SOCIETY** *
  P.O. Box 850165, MESQUITE, TX 75185, USA.
  Newsletter: .t *THE MESQUITE TREE* 4 per year. *Research Service*: Researchers and fees on request. *Membership:* $10.00 single, $12.00 family. *Meetings:* 2nd Thurs. each month. *Conference*: Sept. Fall Workshop. *Other Particulars* June Beginners Workshop. *President:* Martha Hartley. *Secretary:* Sharon Gibson. *Librarian:* Marjorie Bays, tel. (214) 216 6229.

- **MID CITIES GENEALOGICAL SOCIETY** *
  P.O. Box 407, BEDFORD, TX 76095-0407, USA.

- **MONTGOMERY COUNTY GENEALOGICAL AND HISTORICAL SOCIETY**
  P.O. Box 751, CONROE, TX 77305-0751, USA.
  Repository: Montgomery County Library. *Journal: THE HERALD* 4 per year, included with membership. Available to non members at $4.00 mailed. *Research Enquiries*: Free to members. *Membership:* $10.00 single, $12.00 family. *President:* Mr Leon Kennedy. *Secretary:* Mrs. Eileen L. Behrman.

- **RED RIVER COUNTY TEXAS GENEALOGICAL SOCIETY** *
  P.O. Drawer D, CLARKSVILLE, TX 75426, USA.

- **SOUTHEAST TEXAS GENEALOGICAL AND HISTORICAL SOCIETY**
  C/o Tyrrell Historical Library, P.O. Box 3827, BEAUMONT, TX 77704, USA.
  Library: 895 Pearl St., Beaumont,TX. *Hours:* Tues.-Sat. 9am-6pm. Open to non members — no fee. *Newsletter: YELLOWED PAGE*S 4 per year. Serves southeast Texas and southwest Louisiana. *Research Enquiries:* Free to members only. *Membership:* $12.00. *President:* Mrs Ednita Lane. *Meetings:* 1st Wed. each month except April Conference.

- **TARRANT COUNTY BLACK HISTORICAL AND GENEALOGICAL SOCIETY** *
  1020 E. Humbolt St., FORT WORTH, TX 76104, USA.

UTAH (UT)

- **UTAH GENEALOGICAL ASSOCIATION**
  P.O. Box 1144, SALT LAKE CITY, UT 84110, USA.
  Newsletter: 4 per year. *Journal: GENEALOGICAL JOURNAL* 4 per year. Available to non members at $7.50 each. *Research Enquiries:* Free to members. *Membership:* $25.00. *Editor:* Gordon Remington.

- **GENEALOGICAL LIBRARY OF L.D.S. (see under NATIONAL)**

VERMONT (VT)

- **GENEALOGICAL SOCIETY OF VERMONT** *
  RFD #3 Box 986, PUTNEY, VT 05346, USA.
  Library: P.O. Box 422, Pittsford, VT 05763. Open by appointment. Open to non members. *Journal: BRANCHES AND TWIGS* 4 per year. Available to non members at $4.00. *Research Enquiries:* Free to members. *Membership:* $15.00. *Other Particulars*: Mrs Carol Church, Editor and Librarian. *President:* Mrs Joann H. Nichols. *Treasurer:* Mrs Linda Drummond.

VIRGINIA (VA)

- **VIRGINIA GENEALOGICAL SOCIETY** *
  P.O. Box 7469, RICHMOND, VA 23221, USA.
  Newsletter: 6 per year. *Journal: MAGAZINE OF VIRGINIA GENEALOGY* 4 per year. Available to non members at $8.00 per Vol. 1-21 and $16.00 Vols 22-26 $18.00 (Vol 26 being 1988). *Research Enquiries:* Members only. *Membership:* $18.00. *Pres-*

ident: Edgar MacDonald. *Secretary:* Laura Ashworth Crumpler. *Meetings:* Announced in Newsletter:.

● **FAIRFAX GENEALOGICAL SOCIETY**
P.O. Box 2344, MERRIFIELD, VA 22116-2344, USA.
Newsletter: FGS NEWSLETTER 5 per year. Free queries. *Membership:* $10.00 single, $15.00 family. *President:* Mrs Shirley L. Wilcox. *Secretary:* Ms Shirley Hyland. *Meetings:* Usually 4th Thurs., 7.30pm, Sept. to May. Henry Thoreau Intermediate School cafeteria, 2505 Cedar Lane, Vienna, VA. Sponsors an all-day seminar each spring at George Mason University, Fairfax, VA. *Book in progress*: Fairfax County cemetery records.

● **NELSON COUNTY HISTORICAL SOCIETY ***
P.O. Box 254, LOVINGSTON, VA 22949, USA.

● **NORFOLK GENEALOGICAL SOCIETY ***
P.O. Box 12813, Thomas Corner, NORFOLK, VA 23502, USA.

● **PITTSYLVANIA HISTORICAL SOCIETY**
P.O. Box 429, CHATHAM, VA 24531, USA.

● **PRINCE WILLIAM COUNTY GENEALOGICAL SOCIETY**
P.O. Box 2019, MANASSAS, VA 22110-0812, USA.
Newsletter: 12 per year. *Research Enquiries:* free for members, $1.00 per query for non members. *Editor:* Donald L. Wilson. *Membership:* $10.00 single, $12.00 family. *Meetings:* 3rd Wed. of each month. Central Library, 8601 Mathis Ave., Manassas, VA, 7.00pm. *President:* Denison Miner, Jr. *Corres. Secretary:* Diane Cole 3693634. *Book in progress*: Manassas Funeral Home Records.

● **SOUTHWESTERN VIRGINIA GENEALOGICAL SOCIETY ***
P.O. Box 12485, ROANOKE, VA 24026, USA.

WASHINGTON (WA)

● **SEATTLE GENEALOGICAL SOCIETY ***
P.O. Box 549, SEATTLE, WA 98111, USA.

● **CLARK COUNTY GENEALOGICAL SOCIETY**
P.O. Box 2728, VANCOUVER, WA 98668, USA.
Library: 1511 Main St. *Hours:* Tues.-Sat. 1-5pm. Open to non members. *Newsletter:* 10 per year. *Journal: TRAILBREAKERS* 4 per year. Back issues $3.00 per copy. *Membership:* $12.00, $14.00 dual, $200.00 life, $50.00 or more contributing. *President:* Peggy Winston. *Vice President*: Dorothy Person.

● **GRANT COUNTY GENEALOGICAL SOCIETY ***
C/o Ephrata Public Library, 45 Alder St., N.W. EPHRATA, WA 98823, USA.

● **GRAYS HARBOR GENEALOGY CLUB ***
308 W. 6th St., ABERDEEN, WA 98520, USA.

● **NORTH CENTRAL WASHINGTON GENEALOGICAL SOCIETY**
P.O. Box 613, WENATCHEE, WA 98807, USA.
Journal: THE APPELAND BULLETIN 4 per year. *Research Enquiries:* One free. *Membership:* $10.00. *Meetings:* 4th Mon. 7.30pm. *President:* Ed Steinmasel. *Secretary:* Doris Moser. *Society Library:* Tel. 664 5989 ext 20. Open 1-4pm Tues, Thurs. & Sat.

● **SOUTH KING COUNTY GENEALOGICAL SOCIETY ***
P.O. Box 3174, KENT, WA 98032, USA.
Secretary: Louise Manning.

● **YAKIMA VALLEY GENEALOGICAL SOCIETY ***
P.O. Box 445, YAKIMA, WA 98907, USA.

Library: 3rd and "B", Yakima 98901. *Hours:* Mon. to Fri. 10am-4pm. Available to non members at $1.00 donation. *Journal: YAKIMA VALLEY GENEALOGICAL SOCIETY BULLETIN* 4 per year. Available to non members at $2.50 each. *Research Enquiries:* Free to members. *Membership:* $11.00. *Meetings:* 1st Thurs., 7.30pm, Sept. to June. Basement 1st Christian Church. *Librarian:* E. Brzoska.

WEST VIRGINIA (WV)

- **WEST AUGUSTA HISTORICAL AND GENEALOGICAL SOCIETY ***
  RT. 1 Box 5, Wittman Ln., WASHINGTON, WV 26181, USA.

WISCONSIN (WI)

- **WISCONSIN STATE GENEALOGICAL SOCIETY, INC.**
  2109 Twentieth Ave., MONROE, WI 53566, USA.
  Newsletter: WSGS NEWSLETTER (60 pages) 4 per year. Available to non members at $4.00 per copy. *Research Enquiries:* Members only. *Membership:* $14.00 (US funds), $22.00 (Canada & Mexico). Others write for rate. *President:* Lois Stein. *Secretary:* Ruth Steffen. *Meetings:* 1st Sat. in May in Madison. 3rd Sat. in Oct. in Milwaukee. *Other Particulars* Certificates issued to descendants of pioneer settlers in Wisconsin (before 1850). Many other indexes offered to county histories. Beginners' Kit, Workbook.

- **THE STATE HISTORICAL SOCIETY OF WISCONSIN ***
  816 State St., MADISON, WI 53706, USA.

- **STEVENS POINT AREA GENEALOGICAL SOCIETY**
  1325 Church St., STEVENS POINT, WI 54481, USA.

WYOMING (WY)

- **PARK COUNTY GENEALOGY SOCIETY ***
  P.O. Box 3056, CODY, WY 82414, USA.

U.S.S.R.

MOSCOW

- **ARCHIVE-SERVICE ***
  Genealogical Bureau, 103050, MOSCOW, USSR.

WALES

CLWYD

- **CLWYD FAMILY HISTORY SOCIETY**
  C/o Sec.: Werna, Ruthin Road, DENBIGH, CLWYD, LL16 3ER, Wales, UK.
  Journal: HELACHAU 3 per year. £1.00 plus post to non members. *Research Enquiries:* Limited research for members free of charge. *Membership:* £6.00 membership UK; £8.00 surface mail overseas; £10.00 airmail overseas. *Chairperson:* Mr W. Wynn-Woodhouse. *Secretary:* Mr T.H. Aldrich.

DYFED

- **DYFED FAMILY HISTORY SOCIETY**
  C/o 117 Hill Top, Swiss Valley Park, Llanelli, DYFED, SA14 8DB, Wales.
  Library: Reference Library, Carmarthen. *Hours:* 9am-7pm weekdays. 9am-1pm Sat. *Journal: DYFED FAMILY HISTORY SOCIETY JOURNAL* 3 per year. Available to non members at £1.50. *Research Enquiries:* Cost on application. *Membership:* £6.00 (£8.50 overseas. *Other Particulars* The Society consists of 5 branches. Meetings are also held in Carmarthen, Haverfordwest, Llanelli, London and Aberystwyth. *Secretary:* Mrs A. Rhydderch.

GLAMORGAN

- **GLAMORGAN FAMILY HISTORY SOCIETY**
  The Orchard, PENMARK, S. Glamorgan, CF6 9BN, Wales.
  Journal: GLAMORGAN FAMILY HISTORY SOCIETY JOURNAL 3 issues per
  year. £1.00 to non members. *Research Enquiries:* Cost on application. *Membership:*
  £6.00 ordinary; £5.00 senior citizen/student; £8.00 husband/wife/same household;
  £10.00 sterling or US$18.00 for overseas. Subs due 1 Jan. – half yearly rate 1 July to
  31 Dec. Meetings held Bridgend, Cardiff, Merthy Tydfil, Swansea & London. : i
  Chairpeson: Dr Keith Warren. *Secretary:* Maureen Bullows.

GWENT

- **GWENT FAMILY HISTORY SOCIETY**
  39 The Highway, Panteg nr. Pontypool, GWENT NP4 0PW, Wales.
  Journal: GWENT FAMILY HISTORY SOCIETY JOURNAL 3 per year. Available
  to non members at £1.00. *Membership:* Ordinary £6.00; family £8.00; overseas £8.00.
  Other Particulars Meetings held at Newport, Chepstow, Abergavenny, Pontypool
  and Ebbw Vale. Gwent is the old County of Monmouthshire. *Chairman:* Mr Len
  Hough. *Secretary:* J. Freer.

GWYNEDD

- **GWYNEDD FAMILY HISTORY SOCIETY**
  Cwm Arian, Pensarn Fawr, PEN-Y-SARN, Anglesey, Gwynedd, LL69 9BX, Wales.
  Journal: GWREIDDIAU GWYNEDD ROOTS 2 per year. Available to non members
  at £1.50. *Research Enquiries:* Free to members. *Membership:* £5.00 UK. Family
  £8.00. Overseas £6.00. *Other Particulars* Meetings held at: Pwllheli, Caernarfon,
  Conwy (Caernarfonshire): Dolgellau (Meirioneth): and Llangefni (Anglesey). *President:* Mr R.R. Williams. *Secretary:* Mrs J. Hinde.

POWYS

- **POWYS FAMILY HISTORY SOCIETY**
  Llys Awel, 26 Bryn Meadows, NEWTON, Powys, SY16 2DS, Wales.
  Library: Available at meetings or by appointment. Also available to non members
  £2.00 per hr. *Journal: POWYS CRONICLE* 2 per year. Available to non members at
  £1.00 + p.p. *Research Enquiries:* Cost of entries: non members £1.00 (max. 5 lines).
  Membership: £5.00 UK; £7.50 family; £10.00 overseas airmail. *Chairman:* Mr W.A.
  Pugh. *Secretary:* Mr A. Breese.

YUGOSLAVIA

- **CROATIAN-SERBIAN-SLOVENE GENEALOGICAL SOCIETY**
  2527 San Carlos Ave., SAN CARLOS, CA 94070, USA.
  Library: As above. *Hours:* Mon. to Fri. 10am-4pm. Open to non members. *Membership:* $25.00 One time fee. *Research Enquiries:* Open to members. *President:* Adam S.
  Eterovich. *Secretary:* Jakobina Guziza.

ZIMBABWE

- **HERALDRY AND GENEALOGY SOCIETY OF ZIMBABWE**
  BULAWAYO BRANCH: P.O. Box 1290, BULAWAYO, Zimbabwe. *Chairman:*
  R.G.B. Wilson. *Secretary:* D. Du Chemin.
  HARARE BRANCH: 8 Renfrew Road, EASTLEA, Zimbabwe.
  Chairman: A. Harris. *Secretary:* Mrs B. Lindsay. Researching into families and
  obtaining documents.

NOTE

* after a Society name indicates that a proof copy of the entry was not received back from the Society since the last edition. The entry may therefore be corrct but could be outdated.

CAUTION

The information contained in the Directory of Societies above has been obtained form the Societies and should not be reproduced without first referring to the Society.

For the NEXT DIRECTORY we will distribute a proof copy of the entry to each Society listed. These, together with entries for any new or unlisted non-profit Societies should be sent to any of our Agents (listed on page 4) no later than 30 December.

Pour le prochain GRD, veuillez envoyez toute augmentation ou modification à un représentant quelonque (éncumérés à la page 4) avant le Décembre 30.

Fuer die NAECHSTE AUSGABE sind Neueintragungen Ergaenzungen und Berichtigungen noch vorm 30 Dezember an einen jeden unserer Repraesentanten (siehe Lists Seite 4) einzusenden.

NOTICES

The Editors and Publishers of the GENEALOGICAL RESEARCH DIRECTORY cannot take the responsibility for the quality of of any goods or services which are mentioned in the following pages or be responsible for the outcome of any contract that may be entered into with persons offering services.

FOR
IRISH GENEALOGY
CONTACT

PAUL GORRY

**16, Hume Street,
St. Stephen's Green,
Dublin 2, Ireland
Tel: 616601 / 616608
Fax: 761757**

For prompt reply enclose 2 International Reply Coupons.

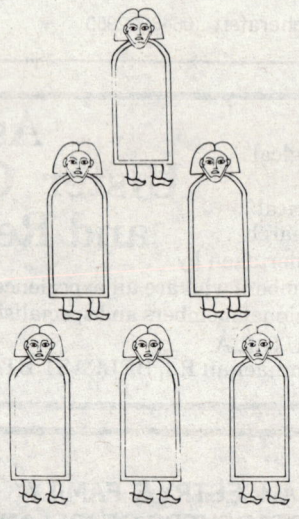

GORRY RESEARCH

**NOT METEORIC
- BUT METICULOUS**

Éireann Research

offers a professional service in tracing Irish Ancestry throughout all counties of Ireland

For more information, send 3 x IRCs to:

Éireann Research
64 Rathgar Road, DUBLIN 6 Ireland

TRACING YOUR RESEARCHING AN **IRISH** ANCESTORS PROJECT

For a Prompt and Efficient Research Service throughout Ireland contact

Joan Phillipson B.A.(Hons.) AUGRA — **Jennifer Irwin** B.A.(Hons.) AUGRA

Historical Research Associates

Glen Cottage, Glenmachan Road
BELFAST BT4 2NP

.For an initial
evaluation please enclose $5.00

or 7 Lancasterian Street
CARRICKFERGUS BT38 7AB

First Centre in **Ireland** to develop a complete index of all extant parish registers (R.C. and C. of I.) to 1900. Other sources available including the 1901 Census for Co. Clare and Griffiths Valuation. All enquiries on matters of Clare genealogy and family history welcome. Write for enquiry form:

IRELAND

Director. Clare Heritage Centre, Corofin
Co. Clare, Ireland Tel. (065) 2 7955

Clare Heritage Centre

Centre open   Nov.-March — Weekdays (only) 9 am-5 pm
April-Oct. — Daily 10 am-6 pm (at other times by appointment)

LIMERICK REGIONAL ARCHIVES

The Granary, Michael St, Limerick
☎ (061) 4 0777 FAX: (061) 31 5634

Director Dr S.C. O'Mahony   Research assistant: Mary Pyne M.A.

Specialists on Limerick & Tipperary

RESEARCH IRELAND

Trace your Ancestors anywhere in Ireland
Co Wicklow a speciality
Pamela Bradley A.P.G.I.
Fair View, Kindlestown Hill, DELGANY,
Co Wicklow   ☎ (01) 87 4034

DEBRETT ANCESTRY RESEARCH LIMITED

For over 200 years **Debrett** have chronicled
the families of the aristocracy. In modern times
Debrett's genealogists have helped thousands
of families of all walks of life to trace their ancestors,
in Britain and abroad.

Ancestry Research
A programme of research for a fixed budget,
employing skilled researchers throughout the world,
and always examining original sources
where available.

House Histories
**A study of a property and its occupants. For
pre-1900 properties in England, Scotland and Wales.**

Write for further details and a free assessment
of research prospects to:

**Debrett Ancestry Research Ltd, Dept.GD,
P.O. Box 7, Alresford, Hants., SO24 9EN
☎ (0962) 78 2676 *(24 hrs.)***

TRACING ANCESTORS IN LEITRIM
We deal with genealogical enquiries for Co Leitrim
Leitrim Heritage Centre
Co Library, Ballinamore, Co Leitrim, Ireland ☎ (078) 44012

Irish Genealogical Services

**111/113 South Parade
BELFAST BT7 2GN** Northern Ireland

All research undertaken by members of the Association
of Professional Genealogists in Ireland; and the
Association of Genealogists and Record Agents.

Please forward US$5.00 (£4.00) for an initial evaluation of your research
problem and we will forward our brochure and a 14-page booklet —
Tracing your Ancestors in Ireland   Phone/Fax: Belfast (0232) 64 6489

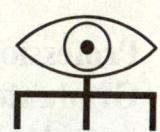

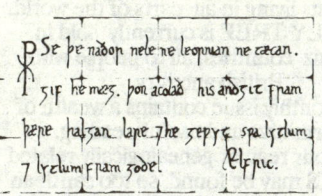

TRACE YOUR BRITISH ANCESTORS

---

through our expert, personal service.

You will receive:

- a bound report complete with all documents acquired during our search
- swift and reliable results
- thorough and accurate research
- all the convenience of a professional service.

Our network of trained researchers covers the whole of the United Kingdom and is ready to start working for you immediately.

Write today for a free brochure:

Windsor Ancestry Research

(GY/03) Queen's Road, Sunninghill
ASCOT, Berkshire SL5 9AF England

PLEASE MENTION 'GENEALOGICAL RESEARCH DIRECTORY' WHEN WRITING TO ADVERTISERS

887

FAMILY CREST

After having spent endless time tracing and drawing up your family tree, have you thought of doing justice to your Family Crest by having it hand woven in wool into a wall hanging unit. **The monetary exchange rate is in your favour.**

Write: **Pam Ricketts**, Design Expressions C.C., P.O. Box 39168 Bramley 2018, Johannesburg, South Africa.

Genealogical research in:

AFRICA (CENTRAL and SOUTHERN)

Mrs Valda Napier, P.O. Box 4882, RANDBURG, Transvaal 2125 Rep of South Africa

---

DESCENDANTS OF CONVICTS

THE DESCENDANTS of Convicts Group of the Genealogical Society of Victoria accepts membership from GSV members and affiliation from Genealogical Society members world wide.

Membership is available to all who claim descent from Convicts transported to Australian Colonies 1788 through 1868 and several hundred members already enjoy the fellowship and convict research assistance promoted by the Group.

Enquiries to the Secretary, Descendants of Convicts Group, Genealogical Society of Victoria, 252 Swanston Street, Melbourne 3000 AUS.

EASTGATE GENEALOGY

MARIANNE EASTGATE
M.A. (Hons.), Dip.Lib., Dip.F.H.S.
6/226, Moray St., New Farm, Q.4005, Aust.

Tracing lost ancestors in Queensland
Ph. (07) 358-1062

PHOTOGRAPHS COPIED

All work individually hand processed to your exact requirements
Damaged photos copied and restored

HENZO Acid-free Albums and ALBOX at discount prices

Enquiries welcome

Mrs KERRIN COOK
9a Gladstone Parade, Lindfield N.S.W. 2070
Phone: (02) 416 5113 (after 6pm)

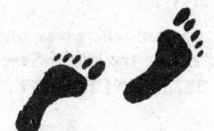

NOTICE: Re ship *WILLIAM NICOL*
Wanted any information on the name of any the immigrants, especially the wives, and children, that arrived on the *William Nicol* 27th October, 1837. From the Isle of Skye, Scotland. Will be greatly appreciated. **E. Finn, P.O. Box 282, PUNCHBOWL, NSW. 2196 AUS**

INFORMATION re HENRY EDWARD MITCHELL (Hon.
Captain & Engineer P.W.D., India) b. c.1825 d. 1883
Shahjahanpore, India; m. Margaret McGrath (née Wilkinson)
1858, India. Issue 6 sons, all engineers, India inc. Edward James
b. 1859, Gerald Wilkinson b. 1874, 1 dau, Nell **Mrs C. King, C/-
Chaplain's Office, RAAF Base, AMBERLEY, QLD. 4306** AUS

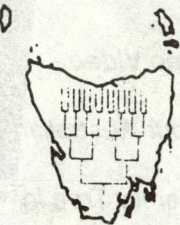

PLEASE MENTION 'GENEALOGICAL RESEARCH DIRECTORY' WHEN WRITING TO ADVERTISERS

Australian Genealogical Education Centre

incorporating

Kiama Family History Centre
Railway Parade, Kiama.
Tel: (042) 33 1122

This unique Family History Centre is located at Kiama, NSW, in the heart of the Leisure Coast, just 126 km south of Sydney. Easy access is provided by the F6 Freeway or via the excellent passenger rail service. The Family History Centre housing its search room, exhibition area and auditorium, complements the valuable work being carried out by family history societies and research groups everywhere.

Open Weekdays and First Weekend each Month
9.30 AM — 4.30 PM

Free Parking All Day

An exciting new centre for use by all with an in-house microform and data inventory both extensive and comprehensive.

The search room, with modern equipment, provides records and advice in a friendly atmosphere to all engaged in that exciting and sometimes elusive pastime — family and social history research.

Unrestricted Searching All Day

GENEALOGY — AN EDUCATIONAL TOOL

The Family History Centre has developed an exciting program of educational kits which will help in:—
- Creating a vivid, tangible picture of society in a historical context; and
- Revealing and highlighting a hidden history the text book barely skims.

This important educational component focuses on the use of genealogy as a society history tool.

With professionally compiled program kits for school children in years 4-6 (primary) and 7-12 (secondary), the pupils are led into an exciting investigative social history experience.

These programs now include kits on W.W.I and convicts.

Friendly Assistance Available at All Times

AUSTRALASIAN ASSOCIATION OF GENEALOGISTS & RECORD AGENTS

The Australasian Association of Genealogists & Record Agents was founded in 1977. It aims to offer the public the services of reliable & competent genealogists & record agents.

Membership is open only to well qualified persons of considerable practical experience in the fields of genealogy & record searching. On admission, each member is required to subscribe to a Code of Ethics which requires the highest standards of honesty & integrity in his dealings with the client & the preservation of complete confidentiality of the client's affairs.

Briefly, the Genealogist (G) compiles family histories & genealogies for clients & often is also responsible for effecting the publication of the finished project. The Record Agent (RA), on the other hand, specialises in the knowledge of records & sources, & the researching of these.

MEMBERSHIP LIST

NEW ZEALAND

Mrs V E MOSSONG, 1 Bruce Road, Glenfield, Auckland 10, New Zealand. (RA)

Mrs H J WEBBER, PO Box 30906, Lower Hutt, New Zealand. (RA)

AUSTRALIA

NEW SOUTH WALES
Dr Carol A LISTON, BA(Hons), PhD, Dip FHS, 85 Hull Road, Beecroft, NSW 2119. (RA)

Mrs F M YOUNG, Dip FHS, 84 Siandra Drive, Kareela, NSW 2232. (G) (RA)

Mrs T M WADDINGHAM, Dip FHS, 18 Waygrove Avenue, Earlwood NSW 2206 (RA)

Ms Jan WORTHINGTON, Dip FHS, PO Box 161, Lane Cove, NSW 2066. (G)

NORTHERN TERRITORY
Mrs June Tomlinson, PO Box 3988 Darwin Northern Territory 0801. (RA)

QUEENSLAND
Miss J REAKES, JP, Dip FHS, Accredited Genealogist (Aust) GSU, PO Box 937, Pialba, Queensland 4655. (RA)

Miss J WEBSTER, B App Sc (Med Tech), 77 Chalfont Street, Salisbury, Queensland 4107. (RA)

SOUTH AUSTRALIA

A G PEAKE, Esq, BA (Soc Wk), Dip FHS, FSAGHS, 14 Tudor Street, Dulwich, SA 5065. (G) (RA)

TASMANIA

Mrs Maree RING, 14 Oakbank Avenue, Montrose, Tasmania 7010. (RA)

Mrs T E SHARPLES, BA, ALAA, 330 Carella Street, Howrah, Tasmania 7018. (RA)

Mrs D SNOWDEN, BA(Hons) Dip Ed, Dip FHS, 473 Macqarie Street, South Hobart, Tasmania 7004. (RA)

VICTORIA

P E BROTCHIE, Esq, BA, Assoc Dip Pers Admin, Grad Dip Pers Admin, Dip FHS, IGCO, 130 Croydon Road, Croydon, Victoria 3136. (G) (RA)

D J BROWNING, Esq, BA (Leicester), MA(London), PO Box 1007, Ringwood, Victoria 3134. (G)

Ms H DOXFORD HARRIS, IGCO, 20 Abelia St, Nunawading, Victoria 3131. (RA)

Mrs M H HENRY, Symbister Park, RSD McDonalds Lane, Riddells Creek, Victoria 3431. (RA)

J F HOLT, Esq, 4/25 Shields Street, Flemington, Victoria 3031. (G) (RA)

Mrs A F JOHNSON, IGCO, 9 Murrumbeena Crescent, Murrumbeena, Victoria 3163. (RA)

Ms Sue E McBETH, BSc, APG, IGCO, PO Box 136, Hampton, Victoria 3188, telephone: (03) 598 0435; facsimile: (03) 598 0365. (RA)

Mrs I PEARCE, Dip FHS, RMB 1003, Picola, Victoria 3639, telephone: (058) 691 235. (G) (RA)

Mrs E E F PULLMAN, Dip FHS, IGCO 30 Silver Street, Cheltenham, Victoria 3192, telephone: Int'nl +613 584 6474. (G) (RA)

Mrs M R SHENNAN, 4 Albany Court, Noble Park, Victoria 3174. (RA)

Nick VINE HALL, AAIA (Dip), Dip FHS (Hons), FSAG, Fellow Utah Genealogical Association, 25 Mills Street, Middle Park, Victoria 3206. (G)

W A WELLSTED, Dip FHS, Esq, 13 Carcoola Road, East Ringwood, Victoria 3135. (RA)

WESTERN AUSTRALIA

B J CROKER, Esq, 1 Myera Street, Mount Claremont, WA 6010. (G) (RA)

Mrs L A MORLING, BA, ALAA, Dip FHS, 37 Weston Drive, Swan View WA 6056 (RA)

The following members of the Association are at present unavailable for private commissions:

Mrs E U BROWN, 66 Waimarie Drive, Mount Waverley, Victoria 3149. (RA)

Donald W M GRANT, FHG, FGSV, FAIGS (Registered Genealogist, Inst of Heraldic & Genealogical Studies, Kent, England), PO Box 66, South Oakleigh, Victoria 3167. (G) (RA)

A R JAMIESON, Esq, 56 Hurtle Square, Adelaide, SA 5000. (RA)

M C H KILLION, Esq , 5 Broula Avenue, Baulkham Hills, NSW 2153. (RA)

Abbreviations:
(G)	Genealogist
(RA)	Record Agent
Dip FHS	Diploma in Family Historical Studies awarded by the Society of Australian Genealogists (SAG)
GSU	Genealogical Society of Utah
IGCO	International Genealogy Consumer Organization
APG	Association of Professional Genealogists

Australasian Association of Genealogists & Record Agents
PO Box 268
Oakleigh Victoria 3166 Australia

The Founders of Australia

A BIOGRAPHICAL DICTIONARY
OF THE FIRST FLEET

The Book . . .

Mollie Gillen

On 13 May 1787 more than 1,500 people sailed with the eleven ships of the First Fleet to become the founders of the modern nation of Australia. After 20 years of research Mollie Gillen has produced the most comprehensive study to date of the people of the First Fleet. Based largely on original sources in Britain and Australia, it functions both as a detailed historical reference work with much new information and also as a very readable social history.

Every person who sailed with the Fleet or was born on board has been included whether a child, convict, sailor, marine or officer. The result is a fascinating series of pen-pictures in a total of 1,442 biographical entries. The background of each First Fleeter is examined (including the circumstances of the crime and trial of each convict) as well as their lives after 1788 as they spread through New South Wales, Norfolk Island, Van Diemen's Land and in some cases returned to England.

Mrs Gillen writes in a forthright and challenging introduction that the much mooted strategic reasons for colonizing Australia were no more than a smoke-screen for the British Government's real aim: the need to find a dumping ground for convicts no longer accepted by America. The establishment of a virtual slave colony was a "monstrous crime" which, as well as having a disastrous effect on the existing Aboriginal society, reaped a grim harvest of cruelty, suffering and premature death among its reluctant settlers. Yet, as the biographies show, many more First Fleeters survived the difficult early years to find an economic security in the new colony that completely transformed their lives as they formed the first generation of emancipists and free settlers. The progress of their lives reflects the growth of the embryonic Australian society and character.

The book includes extensive explanatory notes, is fully indexed with a number of maps, illustrations and the facsimile signatures and marks of hundreds of First Fleeters. Twelve appendices include abstracts of biographical information, descriptions of the First Fleet ships and their crews, a chronology of the First Fleet, miscellaneous facts of interest, statistics and the "Phantom Fleeters": persons inaccurately claimed in earlier publications to have been First Fleeters. Although mainly English, the First Fleeters were a remarkably diverse group. Appendix 3 shows that up to ten percent were Irish, while others were from Scotland, Wales, France, Sweden, Norway, Holland, Germany, Portugal, the West Indies, North America and Africa.

Brian Fletcher, Bicentennial Professor of Australian History at the University of Sydney describes the *Founders of Australia* as: *A work of wide-ranging scholarship... This is a very important reference book, but the word 'reference' fails to do justice to what is a lively, vivid, colourful piece of writing that in addition to being original and highly informative is enjoyable and readable.*

ENGLAND and WALES
Counties [Prior to 1974]

1 Worcestershire
2 Leicestershire
3 Rutland RUT
4 Northhamptonshire
5 Huntingdonshire
6 Cambridgeshire
7 Bedfordshire
8 Buckinghamshire
9 Hertfordshire
0 Middlesex

Northumberland NML

Cumberland CUL

Durham DUR

Westmorland — WES

Isle of Man IOM

Yks North Riding NRY

Yorkshire YKS

Yks West Riding WRY

Yks East Riding ERY

Anglesey AGY

Flintshire FLN

Denbighshire

Lancashire LAN

Lincolnshire LIN

Derbyshire DBY

Nottinghamshire NTT

CAE DEN

Cheshire CHS

Merioneth MER

Staffordshire STS

Norfolk NFK

Caernarvon

Shropshire SAL

LEI

Warwickshire WAR

Montgomeryshire

MGY

Cardiganshire

Radnor RAD

Herefordshire HEF

3

5

HUN

6

CAM

Suffolk SFK

NTH

4

BDF

BKM

Pembroke PEM

CGN

BRE

1 WOR

2

7

9

Carmarthen CMN

Brecknock

Glamorgan GLA

MON

Oxfordshire OXF

HRT

Essex ESS

MDX O

London LND

WALES (WLS)

Monmouthshire

Gloucestershire GLS

BRK Berkshire

8

Surrey SRY

Kent KEN

Wiltshire WIL

Hampshire HAM

Sussex SSX

Somerset SOM

Devon DEV

Dorset DOR

Isle of Wight IOW

Cornwall CON

ENGLAND (ENG)

Channel Islands CHI
Alderney ALD
Guernsey GSY
Jersey JSY

905

SCOTLAND

Counties [Prior to 1974]

Orkney Isles OKI

Shetland SHI

Caithness CAI

Sutherland SUT

1

Ross & Cromarty ROC

1

Nairn NAI

Moray MOR

Banff

BAN

Aberdeen ABD

2 Inverness INV

Kincardine KCD

Angus ANS

3

Perth PER

3 Argyll ARL

Kinross KRS

Fife FIF

Clackmannan CLK

Dunbarton

DNB

Stirling STI

West Lothian

East Lothian

WLN

Midlothian

ELN

RFW

MLN

Berwick BEW

Lanark LKS

Peebles PEE

Renfrew

Selkirk SEL

Roxburgh ROX

Ayr AYR

Dumfries DFS

SCOTLAND (SCT)

Kirkcudbright KKD

Wigtown WIG

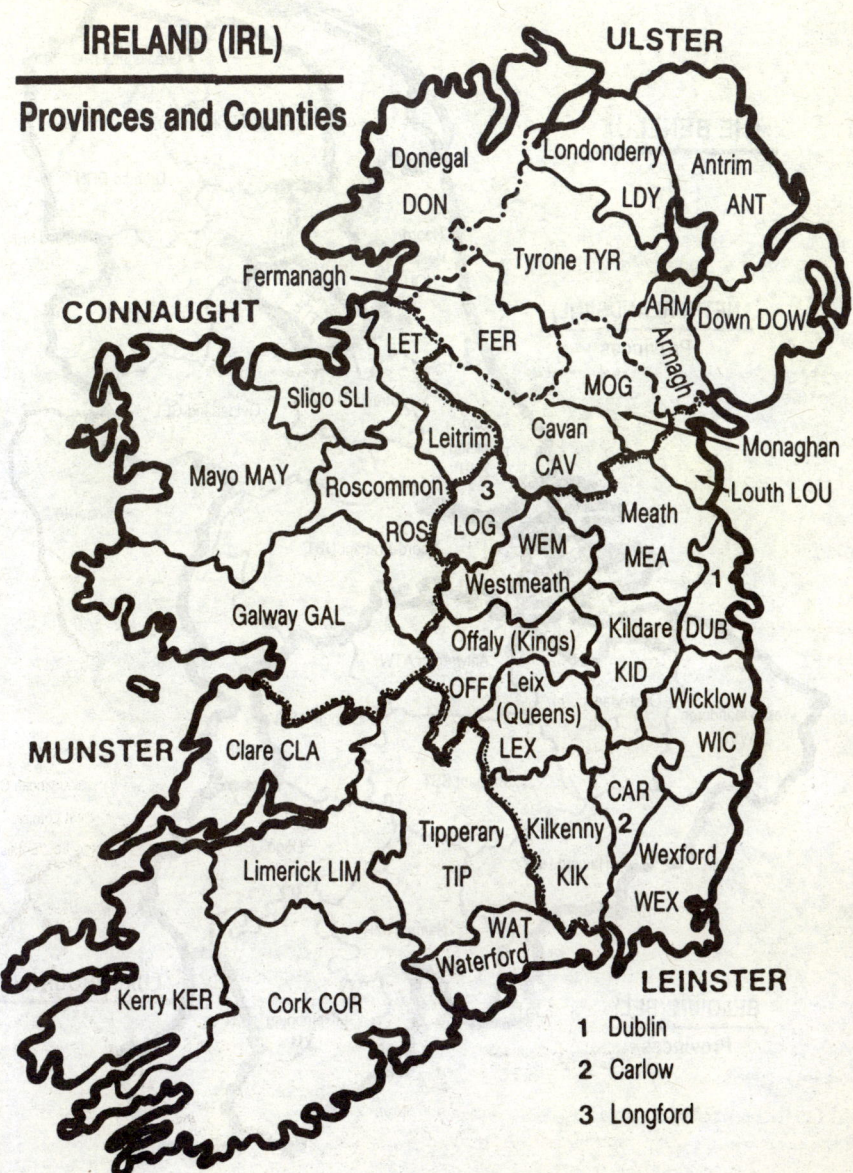

IRELAND (IRL)

Provinces and Counties

ULSTER

Donegal
DON

Londonderry

LDY

Antrim
ANT

Tyrone TYR

ARM

Down DOW

Fermanagh

CONNAUGHT

LET

FER

Armagh

Sligo SLI

MOG

Monaghan

Leitrim

Cavan
CAV

Mayo MAY

Roscommon

3

Louth LOU

Meath

ROS

LOG

MEA

WEM

Galway GAL

Westmeath

1

Offaly (Kings)

Kildare

DUB

OFF

KID

Leix
(Queens)

Wicklow

MUNSTER

Clare CLA

LEX

WIC

CAR

Tipperary

Kilkenny

2

Limerick LIM

TIP

KIK

Wexford

WEX

WAT

Waterford

LEINSTER

Kerry KER

Cork COR

1 Dublin

2 Carlow

3 Longford

THE BENELUX

NETHERLANDS (NL)
Provinces

Groningen GRO

Friesland FRI

Drenthe DRN

Noord-Holland NOH

Flevoland FLE

Overijssel OIJ

Utrecht UTR

Gelderland GEL

Zuid-Holland ZUH

Zeeland ZEL

Noord-Brabant NBT

Limburg

Antwerpen ATW

West-Vlaanderen WVL

Oost-Vlaanderen OVL

Limburg LBG

LMB

Brabant BBT

Liège LGE

Hainaut HNT

Namur NMR

BELGIUM (BEL)
Provinces

LUXEMBOURG (LUX

Luxembourg LXM

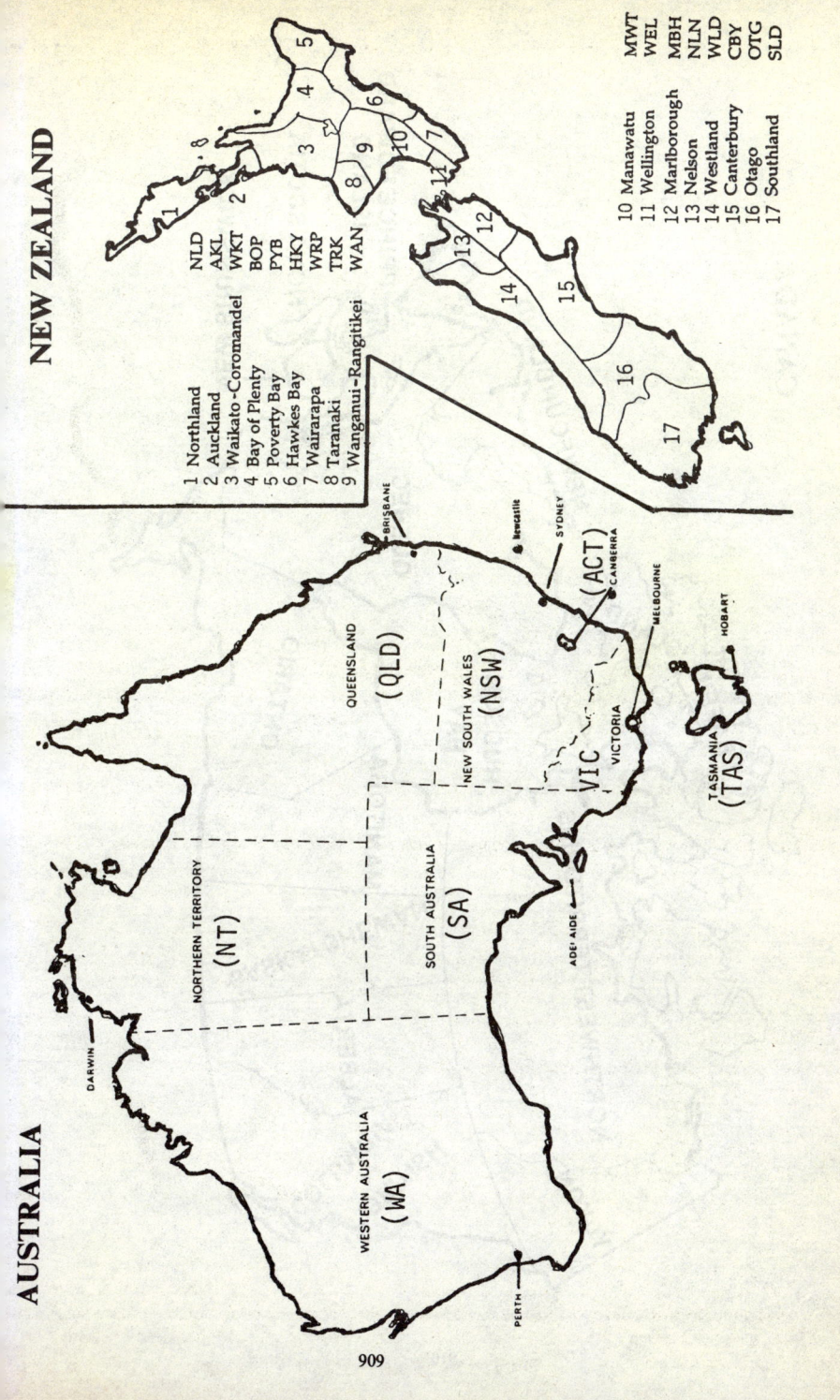

AUSTRALIA

NEW ZEALAND

1	Northland	NLD
2	Auckland	AKL
3	Waikato-Coromandel	WKT
4	Bay of Plenty	BOP
5	Poverty Bay	PYB
6	Hawkes Bay	HKY
7	Wairarapa	WRP
8	Taranaki	TRK
9	Wanganui–Rangitikei	WAN

10	Manawatu	MWT
11	Wellington	WEL
12	Marlborough	MBH
13	Nelson	NLN
14	Westland	WLD
15	Canterbury	CBY
16	Otago	OTG
17	Southland	SLD

909

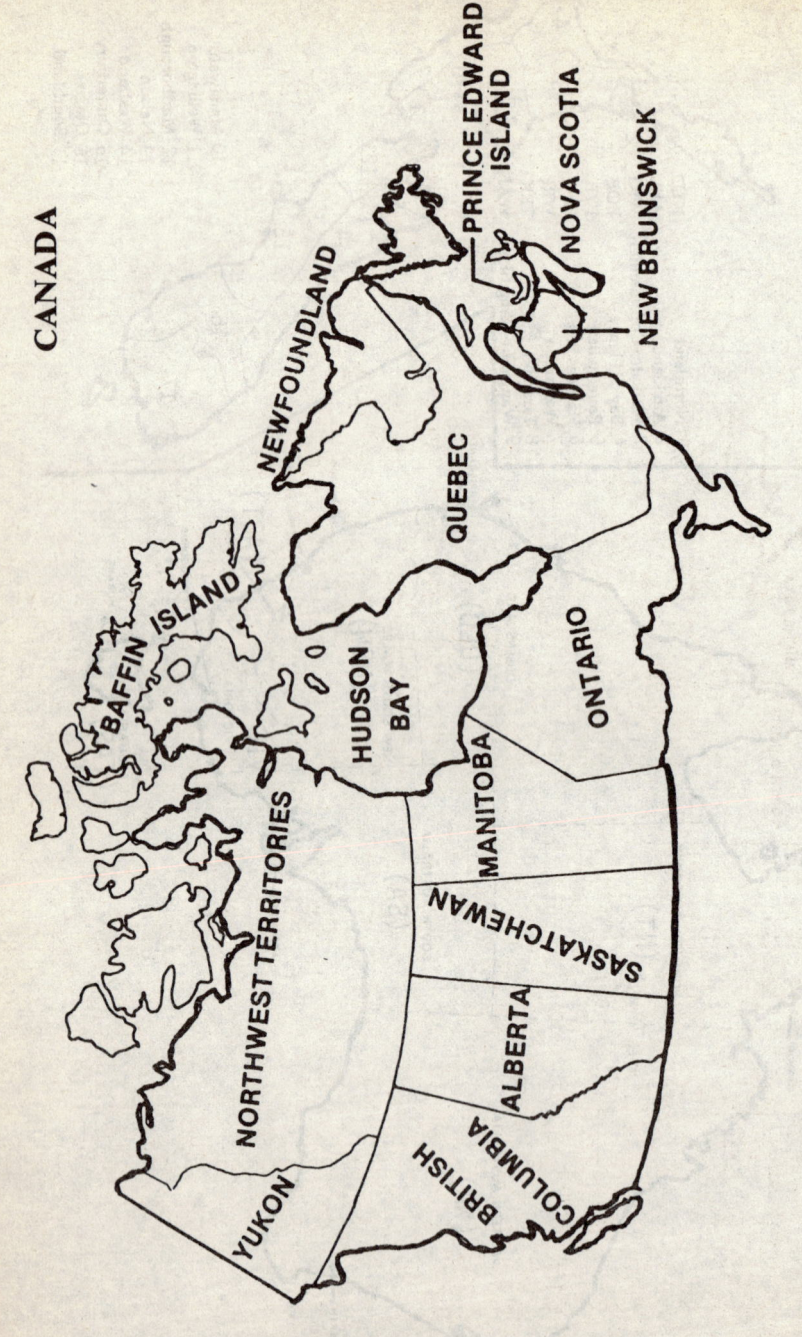

CANADA

UNITED STATES of AMERICA (USA)

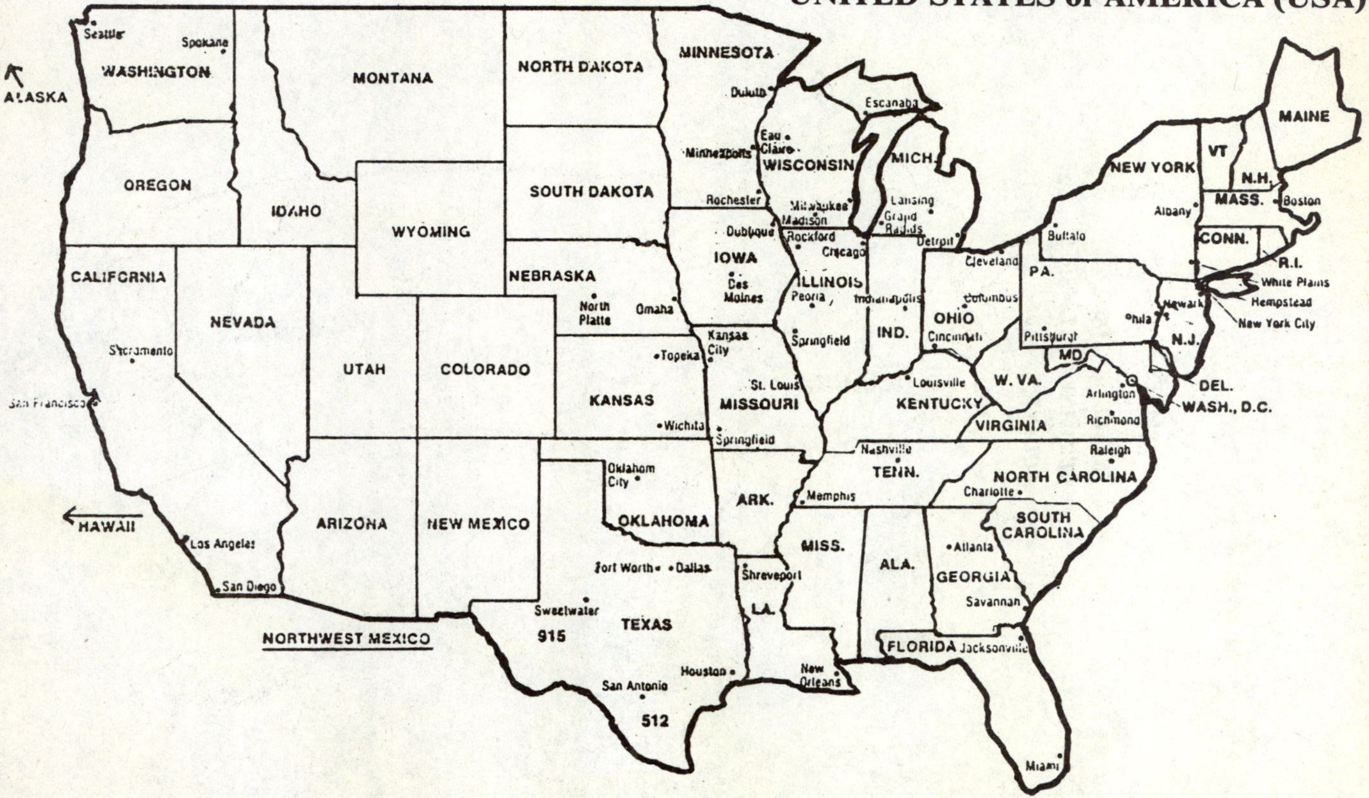

MAINE

N.H.

VT

MASS. • Boston

R.I.

CONN. • White Plains
• Hempstead
• New York City

NEW YORK

• Albany

N.J.

DEL.

WASH., D.C.

• Newark
• Phila.

Buffalo

PA.

MD.

• Pittsburgh

• Arlington
• Richmond

Raleigh

NORTH CAROLINA

SOUTH CAROLINA

W. VA.

VIRGINIA

• Cleveland
• Columbus

OHIO
• Cincinnati

KENTUCKY
• Louisville

TENN.
• Nashville

• Charlotte

Savannah

GEORGIA
• Atlanta

ALA.

• Miami

FLORIDA • Jacksonville

MICH.
• Lansing
• Grand Rapids
Detroit

Escanaba

WISCONSIN

IND.
• Indianapolis

ILLINOIS
Chicago

• Memphis

MISS.

MINNESOTA

• Duluth

Eau Claire
Minneapolis

• Milwaukee
• Madison • Rockford

• Peoria

• Springfield

• St. Louis

MISSOURI

• Springfield

ARK.

New Orleans

LA.

• Shreveport

Rochester

IOWA
• Des Moines

• Dubuque

• Kansas City

NORTH DAKOTA

SOUTH DAKOTA

NEBRASKA

• Omaha

• Topeka

KANSAS

• Wichita

• Kansas City

Oklahoma City

OKLAHOMA

• Dallas
• Fort Worth

Houston •

San Antonio •

TEXAS

512

North Platte

Sweetwater
915

MONTANA

WYOMING

COLORADO

NEW MEXICO

NORTHWEST MEXICO

UTAH

ARIZONA

IDAHO

NEVADA

• Los Angeles

• San Diego

WASHINGTON
• Spokane

• Seattle

OREGON

CALIFORNIA

• Sacramento

• San Francisco

HAWAII

ALASKA

911

MAPS